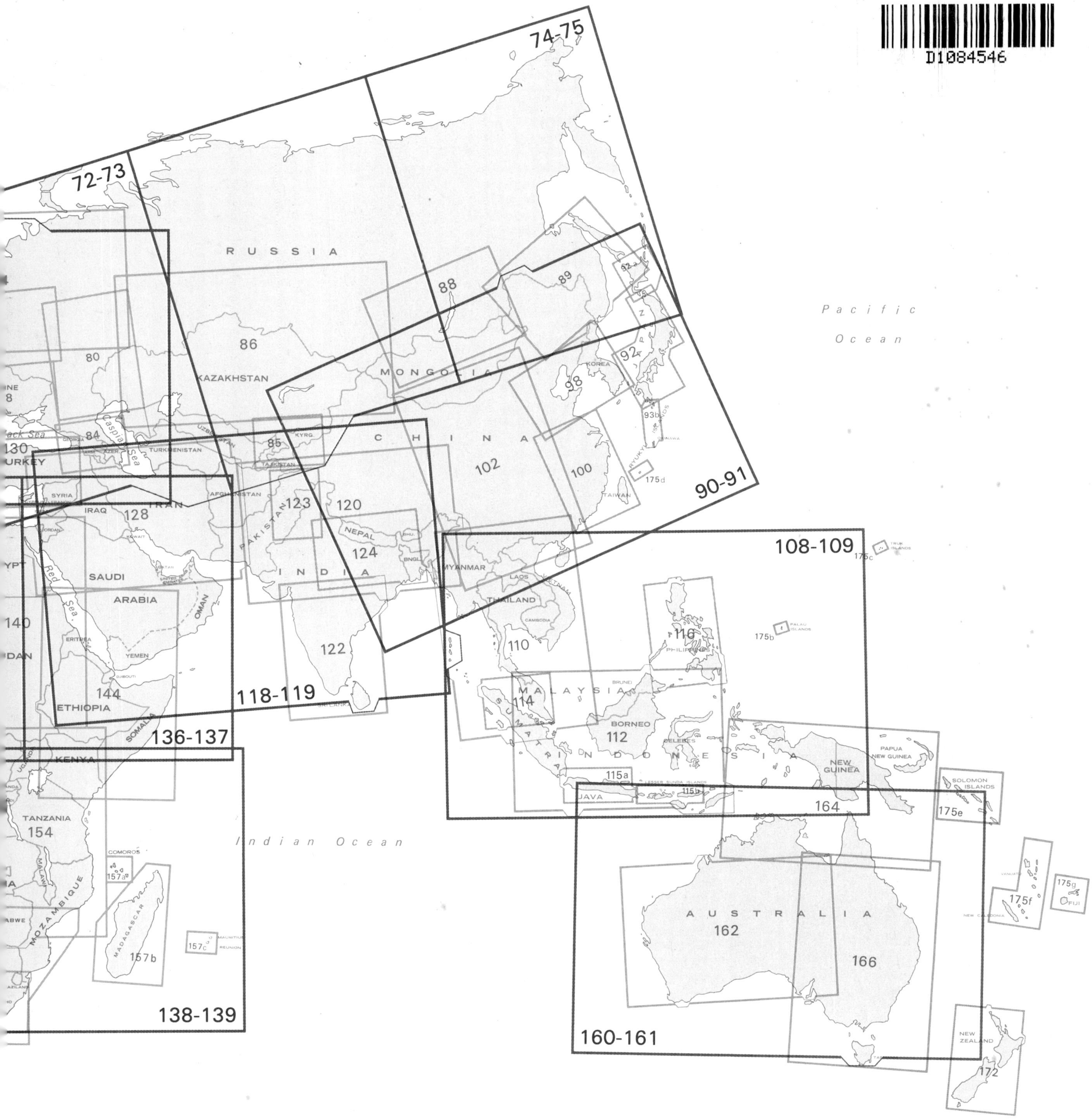

74-75
72-73
RUSSIA
88
89
92
Pacific Ocean
86
80
KAZAKHSTAN
MONGOLIA
98
93b
84
Caspian Sea
130
TURKEY
TURKMENISTAN
85
CHINA
102
100
175d
90-91
SYRIA
IRAQ
128
IRAN
AFGHANISTAN
123
120
PAKISTAN
NEPAL
124
TAIWAN
108-109
175c
SAUDI ARABIA
OMAN
INDIA
MYANMAR
LAOS
THAILAND
CAMBODIA
116
PHILIPPINES
175b
140
Red Sea
YEMEN
122
110
ETHIOPIA
144
118-119
MALAYSIA
BRUNEI
114
BORNEO
112
SOMALIA
136-137
KENYA
INDONESIA
115a
JAVA
115b
NEW GUINEA
164
PAPUA NEW GUINEA
SOLOMON ISLANDS
175e
TANZANIA
154
Indian Ocean
COMOROS
157a
MADAGASCAR
157b
157c
MOZAMBIQUE
138-139
AUSTRALIA
162
166
175f
175g
FIJI
160-161
NEW ZEALAND
172


A-510000-964 -4 -6 -3 -31

## Other features of the atlas


**Thematic maps of world geography, history, and economy**
(WORLD SCENE)

| | Pages | | Pages |
|---|---|---|---|
| Intergovernmental Organizations | xvii | Energy Production and Consumption | xxx-xxxi |
| Seaward Claims | xviii-xix | Gross National Product | xxxii-xxxiii |
| The World, 1914 | xx-xxi | International Trade | xxxii-xxxiii |
| The World, 1937 | xx-xxi | Climate | xxxiv |
| Population | xxii-xxiii | Time Zones | xxxv |
| Religions | xxiv-xxv | Surface Configuration | xxxvi-xxxvii |
| Languages | xxiv-xxv | Earth Structure and Tectonics | xxxvi-xxxvii |
| Agricultural Regions | xxvi-xxvii | Natural Vegetation | xxxviii-xxxix |
| Forests and Fisheries | xxvi-xxvii | Soils | xxxviii-xxxix |
| Minerals | xxviii-xxix | Drainage Regions and Ocean Currents | xl |

**Statistical data about countries and cities**

| | Pages |
|---|---|
| World Information Table | 296-299 |
| Metropolitan Areas Table | 300 |
| Population of Cities and Towns | 301-316 |

**Location of a specific place and the meaning of terms**

| | Pages |
|---|---|
| Index of all the places on the maps in the atlas | I•1-I•200 |
| Glossary and Abbreviations of Geographical Terms | 289-295 |

# List of Places

The following list gives the location, by page number, at which the best-scale depiction of an entire country or its chief administrative subdivisions (for Australia, Canada, United Kingdom, and United States) can be found.


**A**

Afghanistan 118-119
Africa 10-11
Alabama 195
Alaska 180-181
Albania 38-39
Alberta 184-185
Algeria 148-149
American Samoa 175a
Andorra 35
Angola 152-153
Anguilla 239
Antarctica 9
Antigua and Barbuda 239
Argentina 244-245
Arizona 201
Arkansas 194-195
Armenia 84
Aruba 241s
Asia 12-13
Asia Minor 23
Australia 160-161
Australian Capital Territory 171b
Austria 30-31
Azerbaijan 84

**B**

Bahamas, The 238-239
Bahrain 129
Bangladesh 121
Barbados 241g
Belarus 72
Belgium 30
Belize 233
Benin 151
Bermuda 240a
Bhutan 121
Bolivia 248-249
Bosnia and Herzegovina 36, 38
Botswana 156-157
Brazil 242-245
British Columbia 182-183
Britsh Virgin Islands 240m
Brunei 113
Bulgaria 38-39
Burkina Faso 150-151
Burma, see Myanmar
Burundi 154
Byelarus, see Belarus

**C**

California 204-205
Cambodia 110-111
Cameroon 135
Canada 176-177
Cape Verde 150a
Cayman Islands 238
Central African Republic 135
Central America 236-237
Chad 146-147
Chile 244
China 90-91
Colombia 246-247
Colorado 199-201
Comoros 157a
Congo 152
Connecticut 207
Cook Islands 15
Costa Rica 237
Cote d'Ivoire 150-151
Croatia 36, 38
Cuba 240p
Cyprus 130-131
Czech Republic 30-31

**D**

Delaware 208-209
Denmark 26
Djibouti 144
Dominica 240d
Dominican Republic 239

**E**

Ecuador 246
Egypt 140
El Salvador 236
England 28-29
Equatorial Guinea 152
Eritrea 144
Estonia 76
Ethiopia 144-145
Europe 22-23

**F**

Faeroe Islands 22
Falkland Islands 254
Fiji 175g
Finland 24-25
Florida 193
France 32-33
French Guiana 250
French Polynesia 15

**G**

Gabon 152
Gambia, The 150
Georgia (U.S.) 192-193
Georgia 84
Germany 30-31
Ghana 151
Gibraltar 34
Greece 39
Greenland 16
Grenada 241k
Guadeloupe 241o
Guam 174b
Guatemala 236
Guinea 150
Guinea-Bissau 150
Guyana 247

**H**

Haiti 238-239
Hawaii 229d
Honduras 236-237
Hong Kong 271d
Hungary 31

**I**

Iceland 24a
Idaho 202-203
Illinois 190, 194
India 119
Indiana 194
Indonesia 108-109
Iowa 190, 199
Iran 128-129
Iraq 128
Ireland 48-49
Israel 132-133
Italy 36-37
Ivory Coast, see Cote d'Ivoire

**J**

Jamaica 241q
Japan 92-93
Jersey 43b
Jordan 128

**K**

Kampuchea, see Cambodia
Kansas 199
Kazakhstan 72-73
Kentucky 192, 194
Kenya 154
Kiribati 15
Korea, North 99
Korea, South 99
Kuwait 128
Kyrgyzstan 72-73

**L**

Laos 110
Latvia 76
Lebanon 128
Lesotho 159
Liberia 150
Libya 146-147
Liechtenstein 59
Lithuania 76
Louisiana 195
Luxembourg 56

**M**

Macau 101
Macedonia 38-39
Madagascar 157b
Maine 186
Malawi 155
Malaysia 112-113
Maldives 13
Mali 134-135
Malta 37
Manitoba 184-185
Maritime Provinces 186-187
Marshall Islands 15
Martinique 240e
Maryland 188-189
Massachusetts 207
Mauritania 134
Mauritius 157c
Mayotte 157a
Melanesia 14-15
Mexico 232-233
Michigan 190-191
Micronesia, Federated States of 14-15
Middle East 128-129
Minnesota 190, 198
Mississippi 195
Missouri 194
Moldova 78
Monaco 63
Mongolia 90-91
Montana 198, 202-203
Montserrat 239
Morocco 148-149
Mozambique 138-139
Myanmar 110-111

**N**

Namibia 156
Nauru 174b
Nebraska 199
Nepal 124-125
Netherlands, The 52-53
Netherlands Antilles 241s
Nevada 204-205
New Brunswick 186
New Caledonia 175f
Newfoundland 187
New Hampshire 189
New Jersey 208, 211
New Mexico 196, 201
New South Wales 166-167
New York 188-189
New Zealand 172-173
Nicaragua 236-237
Niger 134-135
Nigeria 135
Niue 174v
North America 16-17
North Carolina 192
North Dakota 198
Northern Ireland 48-49
Northern Mariana Islands 14
Northern Territory 160-161
Northwest Territories 176-177
Norway 24-25
Nova Scotia 186-187

**O**

Ohio 188
Oklahoma 196
Oman 118
Ontario 176-177, 188-189
Oregon 202

**P**

Pakistan 120
Palau 14
Palestine 132-133
Panama 246
Papua New Guinea 165
Paraguay 249, 252-253
Pennsylvania 188-189
Peru 242
Philippines 116-117
Poland 31
Polynesia 15
Portugal 34
Prince Edward Island 186
Puerto Rico 240m

**Q**

Qatar 129
Quebec 177, 189
Queensland 161

**R**

Réunion 157c
Rhode Island 207
Romania 38
Russia 72-75
Rwanda 154

**S**

St. Christopher-Nevis 239
St. Helena 11
St. Kitts and Nevis 239
St. Lucia 241f
St. Pierre and Miquelon 187
St. Vincent and the Grenadines 241h
San Marino 66
São Tomé and Princípe 152
Saskatchewan 184-185
Saudi Arabia 118
Scandinavia 24
Scotland 46-47
Senegal 150
Seychelles 139
Siberia 74-75
Sierra Leone 150
Singapore 271c
Slovakia 31
Slovenia 36
Solomon Islands 175e
Somalia 144-145
South Africa 156-157
South America 18-19
South Australia 163
South Carolina 192
South Dakota 198-199
South Georgia and the South Sandwich Islands 19
South West Africa, see Namibia
Spain 34-35
Spanish Sahara, see Western Sahara
Sri Lanka 122
Sudan, The 140-141
Suriname 250
Swaziland 159
Sweden 24
Switzerland 58-59
Syria 128

**T**

Taiwan 101
Tajikistan 85
Tanzania 154-155
Tasmania 167
Tennessee 192, 194-195
Texas 196-197
Thailand 110-111
Tibet 90
Togo 151
Tokelau 15
Tonga 15
Trinidad and Tobago 241r
Tunisia 149
Turkey 130-131
Turkmenistan 129
Turks and Caicos Islands 239
Tuvalu 15

**U**

Uganda 154
Ukraine 78-79
United Arab Emirates 129
United Kingdom 28-29
United States 178-179
Uruguay 253
Utah 200-201
Uzbekistan 72

**V**

Vanuatu 175f
Vatican City 267a
Venezuela 246-247
Vermont 189
Victoria 167
Vietnam 110-111
Virginia 188, 192
Virgin Islands (U.S.) 240m

**W**

Wales 29
Wallis and Futuna 15
Washington 202
Western Australia 162
Western Sahara 148
Western Samoa 175a
West Indies 238-239
West Virginia 188, 192
Wisconsin 190
Wyoming 198-200, 202

**Y**

Yemen, Republic of 137, 144
Yugoslavia 38
Yukon 181

**Z**

Zaire 138
Zambia 138-139
Zimbabwe 155


For complete listing of places, including such physical features as seas, mountain ranges, lakes, and rivers, see the SELECTED MAP REFERENCES, p. *xvi*.

# Britannica Atlas

Encyclopædia Britannica, Inc.

CHICAGO

AUCKLAND • LONDON • MADRID • MANILA • PARIS

ROME • SEOUL • SYDNEY • TOKYO • TORONTO

**INTERNATIONAL PLANNING CONFERENCE**
**INTERNATIONALE BERATER-KONFERENZ**
**CONFERENCIA INTERNACIONAL DE CONSULTORES**
**CONFÉRENCE INTERNATIONALE DE CONSEILLERS**
**CONFERÊNCIA INTERNACIONAL DE CONSULTORES**

Dr. Manlio Castiglioni
Chief Editor, Touring Club Italiano, Milano

Dr. S. P. Chatterjee
Chairman (1970-1972), National Committee for Geography, India

Dr. Arch C. Gerlach
Chief Geographer, United States Geological Survey

Dr. Ir. Cornelis Koeman
Professor of Cartography, State University of Utrecht

Dr. André Libault
Department of Geography, Universidade de São Paulo

Brig. D. E. O. Thackwell
President (1964-1968), International Cartographic Association

Robert J. Voskuil
Adviser on Cartography,
United States Department of State

Dr. Akira Watanabe
Chairman, National Committee of Geography,
Science Council of Japan

**CARTOGRAPHIC FIRMS**
**KARTOGRAPHISCHE FIRMEN**
**FIRMAS CARTOGRÁFICAS**
**MAISONS D'ÉDITIONS CARTOGRAPHIQUES**
**CASA DE EDIÇÕES CARTOGRÁPHICAS**

RAND McNALLY & COMPANY, Chicago
Russell L. Voisin, Vice-President, Cartography
Jon M. Leverenz, Cartographic Editor

MONDADORI-McNALLY GmbH, Stuttgart
Helmut Schaub, Cartographic Editor

CARTOGRAPHIA, Budapest
Ervin Földi, Coordinator

ESSELTE MAP SERVICE, Stockholm
Gösta Lundqvist General Supervisor
Paul R. Kraske, Head of Editorial Staff

GEORGE PHILIP & SON LIMITED, London
Harold Fullard, Director and Cartographic Editor

TEIKOKU-SHOIN CO., LTD., Tokyo
Kimio Moriya, General Supervisor

**MAP ADVISERS**
**KARTOGRAPHISCHE BERATER**
**CONSEJEROS CARTOGRÁFICOS**
**CONSEILLERS CARTOGRAPHES**
**CONSELHEIROS CARTOGRÁFICOS**

Europe
Prof. Dr. Emil Meynen
Direktor des Instituts für Landeskunde, Bonn

Prof. Sándor Radó
Director, Department of Cartography, National Office of Lands and Mapping, Budapest

Dr. Hisashi Sato
Science Faculty, Geographical Institute, Tokyo University

Australia
Prof. R. O. Buchanan
Professor Emeritus, London School of Economics and Political Science, University of London

Anglo-America
Dr. Arch C. Gerlach
Chief Geographer,
United States Geological Survey

Latin America
Dr. André Libault
Department of Geography,
Universidade de São Paulo

Dra. Consuelo Soto Mora
Directora del Instituto de Geografía, Universidad Nacional Autónoma de México

Dr. Jorge A. Vivó Escoto
Centro de Investigaciones Geográficas, Facultad de Filosofía y Letras, Universidad Nacional de México

Metropolitan Area Maps
Prof. Harold M. Mayer
Department of Geography,
University of Wisconsin, Milwaukee

World Scene
Prof. Norton S. Ginsburg,
Prof. Chauncy D. Harris,
Prof. Marvin W. Mikesell
Department of Geography,
University of Chicago

**CONTRIBUTORS—WORLD SCENE**
**MITARBEITER—WELT-PANORAMA**
**COLABORADORES—PERSPECTIVA DEL MUNDO**
**COLLABORATEURS—LE MONDE AUJOURD'HUI**
**COLABORADORES—PERSPECTIVA DO MUNDO**

Robert C. Bergstrom
Department of Geology-Geography,
Morton College, Cicero, Illinois

Nathaniel B. Guyol
Consulting Economist on Energy, Interenergie,
San Rafael, California

Prof. Edwin H. Hammond
Department of Geography, University of Tennessee, Knoxville

Robert D. Hodgson
The Geographer (1970-1979),
United States Department of State

Prof. A. W. Küchler
Department of Geography-Meteorology,
The University of Kansas

Prof. G. Etzel Pearcy
Department of Geography,
California State College, Los Angeles

Prof. David E. Sopher
Department of Geography, Syracuse University

Prof. Richard S. Thoman
Department of Geography,
California State University, Hayward

Mrs. Evelyn Z. Thoman

Dr. William Van Royen
Director, Division of Environmental Sciences,
United States Army Research Office,
Durham, North Carolina

Prof. Philip L. Wagner
Department of Geography,
Simon Fraser University, British Columbia

Maps for the World Scene were designed especially for *Encyclopædia Britannica* by David L. Burke

---

**EDITORS**
**HERAUSGEBER**
**REDACTORES**
**ÉDITEURS**
**EDITORES**

William A. Cleveland
Editor

Staff:
Sujata Banerjee
Rosaline Jackson Keys
W. Peter Kindel
Stephen Neher
Marino P. PeBenito
Joseph R. Sturgis
Edward F. Vowell

ENCYCLOPÆDIA BRITANNICA, INC.
Joseph J. Esposito, *President and Chief Executive Officer*
Karen M. Barch, *Executive Vice President, Operations*


*Library of Congress Card Number: Map 69-1*
*International Standard Book Number: 0-85229-627-4*
*ISSN: 0068-1148*

Printed in U.S.A.

# Foreword

Throughout history, educators have pointed out that a deep gulf may separate knowledge of something from the understanding of it. The *Britannica Atlas* presents the latest facts about the present-day world at the same time that it attempts to add substantially to man's understanding of it. To produce a work that may give a reader this deeper insight, the editors have departed from traditional atlas-making in two important particulars: (1) greater internationalism of content and (2) complete comparability among the maps.

*Internationalism:* Too often an atlas will cater to local prejudices and tastes. To avoid this pitfall, the publishers of this atlas—Encyclopædia Britannica, Inc., and Rand McNally & Company—assured the truly international character of the content at the earliest planning stage by inviting a group of eminent scholars and cartographic houses from various parts of the world to participate in the work. The original planning group included members from France, Germany, India, Italy, Japan, the Netherlands, Sweden, the United Kingdom, and the United States. Actual compilation of the maps was carried out in six countries—Germany, Hungary, Japan, Sweden, the United Kingdom, and the United States.

In keeping with the international outlook of the atlas, the metric system of measurement has been used throughout the reference maps, rather than the British-U.S. system. Map scales and elevation and depth scales on the map pages are given in both systems of measurement. In the Legend to Maps meter-foot and kilometer-mile equivalents are given.

Most of the atlas carries parallel texts in English, German, Spanish, French, and Portuguese. Names of inhabited places and of physical features situated within the boundaries of one country appear on the maps in the local language; where space permits, the English alternate also is given if the local name is likely to be unfamiliar. The names of countries are in English, because some country names are extremely unfamiliar in the local language—Druk-Yul (Bhutan), Magyarország (Hungary), Nihon (Japan). On the larger-scale maps, however, the local form of a country name is shown also. The names of large bodies of water, mountain ranges, and other major physical features that extend across international boundaries are given in English on smaller-scale maps, but on large-scale maps both the English and local forms will be found. In transliterating place names into English from languages not written in the roman alphabet, every effort has been made to use internationally accepted systems of transliteration.

Geographical terms such as lake, mountain, island, etc., appear on the maps in the local language. Five-language glossaries of selected terms used on a map are printed in the margins of most pages, and a glossary of all terms appears on pages 289-295.

In the index, symbols are given with all entries except those naming cities or towns, to aid in identifying the features, e.g., ∧ for mountain, ≻ for cape, ≃ for river. The symbols represent graphically the broad categories of the features named. A five-language key at the bottom of the index pages associates each symbol with the class of terms it represents.

The World Scene is a separate section of topical maps. These maps summarize in cartographic form the patterns of man's physical environment and some of his more important economic activities, political alignments, and cultural distributions. Several maps are concerned with recent political history. In the maps that show climate, surface configurations, soils, natural vegetation, and drainage, the reader may identify the influence of the natural habitat on human settlement and activity.

Finally, the effort to ensure the international character of the atlas is manifest in the balanced coverage of the world's regions. The *Britannica Atlas* allots to each region of the world a map coverage that takes into account the region's economic and cultural significance, its population, and its surface area. Aproximately two-thirds of the map pages are devoted to Anglo-America, Asia, and Europe, and about one-third to Africa, Australia/Oceania, Latin America, and the former Soviet Union. A world map on pp. xiv-xv has blocked out on it the areas and page numbers of the various maps.

*Comparability.* All atlases have attempted, with varying degrees of success, to use uniform map scales wherever practical. This atlas has been prepared with a minimal number of map scales, selected to permit valid areal comparisons between all parts of the earth. At the beginning of the atlas there appear political and physical maps of the world at 1:75,000,000, maps of the oceans at 1:48,000,000, and relief maps of the continents at 1:24,000,000. Next, the major world regions are uniformly presented at 1:12,000,000 (190 miles to the inch).

Virtually the entire land area of the earth is portrayed again, in sections, at one of two larger scales. The less densely populated regions are at 1:6,000,000 (95 miles to the inch), and Europe, most of North America, and the most densely populated sections of South and East Asia are at 1:3,000,000 (47 miles to the inch). The 1:3,000,000 and 1:6,000,000 series are thoroughly comparable with one another. Both indicate the chief natural and man-made features of each region, showing elevations, rivers, major railroads and airports, two classes of highways, and even selected offshore water depths.

Finally, the scale of 1:1,000,000 (16 miles to the inch) has been used in presenting 50 key regions of the continents characterized by exceptional economic importance, high concentration of population, complexity of transportation development, or some combination of these. This scale is unusually large for a general atlas, and is ordinarily reserved for small inset maps dealing with special subjects. Its use in this atlas permits the inclusion of a multitude of place names and many other local details such as waterfalls, ruins, parks, bird and wildlife sanctuaries, shipyards, military installations, dams, and reservoirs.

At the back of the atlas is a 29-page section of 60 maps of the world's major urban centers, all at a scale of 1:300,000 (just under 5 miles to the inch). These maps display the land-use patterns and other local features of great metropolitan agglomerations. Nearly all of the most populous world metropolitan areas are shown, and a number of smaller but important areas are also included. Grouping these metropolitan maps in a separate section following the regional maps facilitates comparison between them and avoids interrupting continuity of the regional maps.

The arrangement of the maps is such that the reader gets a progressively more detailed, but always comparable, view of the earth's surface. There is first a global view of the world and of the oceans, then an overall survey of the continents, shown in hemispheres or quadrants of the earth. There follows a closer view of all regions within the continents, in maps that are primarily political. The regions are next shown in sections at a larger scale, with emphasis on the relationships between physical and cultural features. At a still larger scale, the cultural features of densely populated areas are shown in great detail. Finally, the close-up maps of cities and their environs include even more detail. A three-page Legend to Maps appears on pp. x-xii.

Collection and analysis of the map data have benefited from the recent accelerated progress in aerial and satellite surveying, radar and sonar technology, and electronic data processing. The shaded relief technique was used to give the maps the effect of a third dimension. All the resources of modern graphic arts were utilized to give form to the editorial plan.

# Vorwort

Pädagogen haben schon immer darauf hingewiesen, dass blosses Wissen und wahres Verstehen zwei ganz verschiedene Dinge sein können. Der *Britannica Atlas* nun versucht, nicht nur die letzten Errungenschaften der Wissenschaft darzulegen, sondern auch das Verständnis der Welt bedeutend zu vertiefen. Um dem Leser diesen tieferen Einblick zu gewähren, sind die Herausgeber von der beim Zusammenstellen von Atlanten üblichen Methode in zwei wichtigen Punkten abgegangen: sie haben erstens einen grösseren Internationalismus des Inhalts, zweitens eine vollkommene Vergleichbarkeit der einzelnen Karten untereinander angestrebt.

*Internationalismus.* Es geschieht allzu oft, dass ein Atlas national und provinziell anmutet. Um dies zu vermeiden, haben die Verleger des vorliegenden Atlasses—Encyclopædia Britannica, Inc., und Rand McNally & Company—den internationalen Charakter des Inhalts dadurch gewährleistet, dass sie eminente Wissenschaftler und kartographische Firmen aus aller Welt von Anfang an mit dem Unternehmen assoziiert haben. Die ursprüngliche Planungsgruppe zählte Mitglieder aus Frankreich, Deutschland, Indien, Italien, Japan, den Niederlanden, Schweden, Grossbritannien und den Vereinigten Staaten. Zusammengestellt wurden die Karten in sechs Ländern: in Deutschland, Ungarn, Japan, Schweden, Grossbritannien und in den Vereinigten Staaten.

Das metrische und nicht das angelsächsische Masssystem wird in den Karten benutzt. Die Massstäbe der Karten sowie die Farbskalen für Höhen und Tiefen am Rand jeder Karte werden in beiden Masssystemen angeführt. In die Zeichenerklärung wird die Gleichwertigkeit zwischen Metern und "feet" sowie zwischen Kilometern und Meilen gegeben.

Fast alle Texte des Atlasses sind zugleich in Englisch, Deutsch, Spanisch, Französisch und Portugiesisch gedruckt. Die Namen bewohnter Orte und physischer Gepräge, die innerhalb der Grenzen eines Staates liegen, erscheinen auf den Karten in der Landessprache; wo es der Platz erlaubte, ist der englische Name dann hinzugefügt, wenn der landessprachliche wahrscheinlich unbekannt ist. Die Namen der Länder werden in Englisch wiedergegeben, da manche Ländernamen in ihrer landessprachlichen Form überhaupt nicht geläufig sind—Druk-Yul (Bhutan), Magyarország (Ungarn), Nihon (Japan). Auf den Karten in grösserem Massstab findet sich jedoch auch die lokale Form eines Ländernamens. Die Namen grosser Gewässer, die Namen von Gebirgen und anderen grösseren physischen Geprägen, die sich über das Gebiet mehrerer Staaten erstrecken, sind auf den Karten in kleinerem Massstab nur auf Englisch eingezeichnet, auf den Karten in grösserem Massstab ist jedoch die landessprachliche Form hinzugefügt. Viel Mühe wurde darauf verwendet, international anerkannte Transliterationssysteme zu benutzen, um Ortsnamen aus Sprachen mit nichtlateinischen Schriftzeichen in Englisch wiederzugeben.

Geographische Begriffe wie See, Berg, Insel usw, sind auf den Karten in der Landessprache gedruckt. Am Rand der meisten Karten befinden sich fünfsprachige Glossare der wichtigsten Begriffe, die in den Karten vorkommen. Ein Verzeichnis aller Begriffe ist auf den Seiten 289-295.

Neben allen Namen, die im Register enthalten sind, ausgenommen Grossstädte und Städte, steht das entsprechende Symbol, das jeden Namen einer physischen Gegebenheit zuordnet: z.B. ∧ für Berg, ≻ für Kap, ≃ für Fluss. Die Symbole drücken in graphischer Form die Kategorien für die genannten physischen Gegebenheiten aus. Am Fuss der Registerseite befindet sich ein fünfsprachiges Verzeichnis, in dem jedes Symbol dem Begriff zugeordnet wird, den es darstellt.

Das World Scene (Welt-Panorama) ist eine besondere Reihe von thematischen Karten. Diese Karten stellen in kartographischer Weise die Gebilde der natürlichen Umgebung des Menschen dar. Sie zeigen ausserdem einige der bedeutenderen Wirtschaftsformen, politischen Verbände und Kulturgruppen. Die Reihe enthält einige Karten zur politischen Geschichte der jüngsten Vergangenheit. Mit Hilfe der Karten über Klima, Oberflächenformen, Bodenarten, natürliche Vegetation und Entwässerung kann der Leser den Einfluss der natürlichen Umbebung des Menschen auf menschliche Siedlungsformen und Tätigkeiten feststellen. Für diese Kartenreihe wurden die modernsten Informationen verwendet, die erhältlich waren.

Schliesslich zeigt die Auswahl der Karten das Bemühen um den internationalen Charakter des Atlasses. Der Kartenanteil, den der *Britannica Atlas* jeder Region einräumt, beachtet die ökonomische und kulturelle Bedeutung des Gebietes, seine Bevölkerungszahl und die Grösse des Territoriums. Ungefähr zwei Drittel der Kartenseiten stellen Anglo-Amerika, Asien und Europa dar, ungefähr ein Drittel Afrika, Australien/Ozeanien, Latein-Amerika und die ehemalige Sowjetunion. Auf den Seiten xiv-xv sind die Gebiete und Seitenzahlen der verschiedenen Karten auf einer Erdkarte skizziert.

*Vergleichsmöglichkeiten.* Mit unterschiedlichem Erfolg haben alle Atlanten versucht, wo es praktisch erschien, einheitliche Massstäbe für Karten zu verwenden. Dieser Atlas gebraucht eine sehr geringe Zahl von Massstäben, um fundierte Vergleiche zwischen Gebieten aus allen Teilen der Erde zu ermöglichen. Am Anfang des Atlasses stehen politische und physische Erdkarten im Massstab 1:75 000 000, Ozeankarten im Massstab 1:48 000 000 und Reliefkarten der Erdteile im Massstab 1:24 000 000. Als nächstes werden die Hauptgebiete der Erde alle im Massstab 1:12 000 000 (1 cm = 120 km) dargestellt.

Fast das gesamte Landgebiet der Erde wird in Ausschnitten in einem der beiden grösseren Massstäbe dargestellt. Die weniger dicht besiedelten Gebiete der Erde werden in 1:6 000 000 (1 cm = 60 km) abgebildet; Europa, der grösste Teil Nordamerikas und die am dichtesten besiedelten Regionen von Süd- und Ostasien werden in 1:3 000 000 (1 cm = 30 km) dargestellt. Diese beiden Kartenreihen sind miteinander vollständig vergleichbar. Beide Reihen stellen die wichtigsten natürlichen Gebilde und die von Menschenhand ausgeführten Konstruktionen jeder Region dar sowie Erhebungen, Flüsse, grössere Eisenbahnlinien und Flughäfen, zwei Klassen von Autostrassen und sogar manche Meerestiefen.

Der Massstab 1:1 000 000 (1 cm = 10 km) wird schliesslich verwendet, um 50 Schlüsselgebiete darzustellen, die eine oder mehrere der folgenden Besonderheiten zeigen: ausserordentliche wirtschaftliche Bedeutung, dichte Besiedlung und Komplexität des Verkehrsnetzes. Dieser Massstab ist für einen allgemeinen Atlas ungewöhnlich gross und ist normalerweise nur für kleine Nebenkarten reserviert, die spezielle Themen darstellen. Er wird jedoch in diesem Atlas verwendet, um viele Ortsnamen verzeichnen zu können sowie andere lokale Einzelheiten, z.B. Wasserfälle, Ruinen, Naturschutzgebiete, Werften, Militäranlagen, Talsperren und Wasserreservoirs.

Am Schluss des Kartenteils dieses Atlasses befindet sich eine Reihe von 60 Karten, die auf 29 Seiten im Massstab 1:300 000 (1 cm = 3 km) die grössten städtischen Siedlungsgebiete der Erde abbilden. Diese Karten zeigen die Bodennutzung und andere örtliche Gebilde innerhalb der Stadtregionen. Die meist besiedelten Stadtregionen der

Erde sind fast alle abgebildet sowie auch eine Anzahl kleinerer und dennoch wichtiger Stadtregionen. Die Zusammenfassung dieser Stadtregionen in einem besonderen Kartenteil erleichtert den Vergleich zwischen ihnen, ausserdem wird die Folge der Regionalkarten nicht unterbrochen.

Die Karten sind so angeordnet, dass der Leser eine fortschreitend detailliertere, aber immer vergleichbare Ansicht der Erdoberfläche bekommt, Zuerst findet er eine globale Darstellung der Welt und der Ozeane, dann eine allgemeine Übersicht der Erdteile, die in Hemisphären oder Quadranten der Erde gezeigt werden. Darauf folgt eine detailliertere Darstellung aller Regionen jedes Erdteils auf Karten, die vorwiegend politisch sind. In grösserem Massstab werden danach die Regionen in Ausschnitten abgebildet, wobei die Beziehungen zwischen physischen und kulturellen Gebieten betont werden. In noch grösserem Massstab wird sehr detailliert das kulturelle Gepräge dicht besiedelter Gebiete vorgeführt. Schliesslich gibt die Kartenreihe der Städte und ihrer Umgebungen eine noch mehr in Einzelheiten gehende Darstellung. Die Zeichenerklärung ist auf den Seiten x-xii zu finden.

Sammlung und Analyse der Karteninformation hat von dem rapiden Fortschritt in der Technik der Luft- und Satellitenaufnahmen, in der Radar-und Sonartechnik und in der elektronischen Datenverarbeitung profitiert. Die sogenannte Schummerungstechnik, die den Karten einen dreidimensionalen Effekt gibt, wurde verwand. Alle Mittel der modernen Graphik wurden gebraucht, um dem Plan der Herausgeber Gestalt zu verleihen.

## Prefacio

A través de la historia, los pedagogos han sabido muy bien, que el mero conocimiento y el legítimo entendimiento son conceptos que, pueden hallarse separados por un verdadero abismo. Una simple acumulación de datos muy bien puede resultar de escaso valor si el significado de los mismos y su interrelación no se comprenden plenamente.

Además de reflejar los últimos conocimientos que nos ofrece la ciencia, el *Britannica Atlas* tiene por meta el incrementar sustancialmente el grado de comprensión con que el hombre moderno mira a su mundo. Para lograr este fin, los editores se han apartado del curso tradicional en dos importantes sentidos: (1) más internacionalismo en cuanto al contenido y (2) una paridad metódica en el diseño de los mapas que permite su mejor comparación.

*Internacionalismo.* Frecuentemente, muchos atlas, tratan de satisfacer gustos y prejuicios locales. Para evitar esto, los responsables de la creación de esta obra—Encyclopædia Britannica, Inc., y Rand McNally & Company—desde un principio aseguraron el carácter verdaderamente internacional de su contenido al invitar a un grupo de eminentes geógrafos y firmas cartográficas de distintas partes del mundo a colaborar en su preparación. El grupo que participó en el proyecto original quedó constituido por representantes de Francia, Alemania, India, Italia, Japón, los Países Bajos, Suecia, el Reino Unido y los Estados Unidos de Norteamérica. La realización de los mapas en sí tuvo lugar en seis países—Alemania, Hungría, Japón, Suecia, el Reino Unido y los Estados Unidos de Norteamérica.

El sistema métrico ha sido usado en todos los mapas topográficos, en lugar del sistema anglo-norteamericano de medidas. Las escalas horizontales y las escalas verticales (alturas y profundidades) en las páginas de mapas se expresan en ambos sistemas, y en la Leyenda para los Mapas se ofrecen las equivalencias metro-pie y kilómetro-milla.

El inglés, el alemán, el español, el francés y el portugués se utilizan paralelamente en la mayor parte de la obra. Los nombres de los lugares habitados y de los accidentes geográficos situados dentro de los límites de un país dado se escriben en la lengua local; de permitirlo el espacio disponible, también se da el equivalente inglés si el nombre local no es fácilmente reconocible. Los nombres de los países se dan en inglés, puesto que algunos son muy difíciles de identificar si se expresan en el idioma local—Druk-Yul (Bhután), Magyarország (Hungría), Nihon (Japón). Ahora bien, en los mapas a mayor escala la forma local del nombre del país también se expresa. En cuanto a los nombres de grandes mares o lagos, cordilleras, u otros accidentes mayores que se extienden a través de las fronteras internacionales, éstos se dan en inglés en los mapas a escala reducida, y tanto en las formas locales como en inglés, en los mapas a mayor escala. A los efectos de "trasliterar" al inglés los nombres de lugares cuyas grafías originales no se escriben por medio del alfabeto latino, se ha puesto el mayor esfuerzo en seguir la guía de los sistemas de "trasliteración" más aceptados internacionalmente.

Términos geográficos tales como lago, monte, isla, etc., aparecen en los mapas en el idioma local. Sobre los márgenes de la mayor parte de las páginas se hallarán glosarios en cinco idiomas que incluyen la mayoría de las voces utilizadas en cada mapa, y en las páginas 289-295 se incluye un glosario completo.

Todas las entradas del índice, a excepción de las ciudades o poblaciones, van acompañadas de un símbolo gráfico que las identifica a primera vista como nombre de, v. gr., montaña ∧, cabo ≻, río ≏, etc. Y al pie de cada página del índice se hallará una clave en cinco idiomas en la que se equiparan los símbolos con las amplias categorías de accidentes geográficos que representan.

La World Scene (Perspectiva del Mundo) constituye una sección aparte dedicada a mapas especializados. Estos mapas compendian cartográficamente el medio físico en que habita la humanidad, y algunas de sus actividades económicas, alineamientos políticos y aspectos culturales más importantes. Varios de los mapas se ocupan de la historia política más reciente. En los mapas que se ocupan de aspectos de geografía física tales como la distribución de climas, las estructuras geológicas, los suelos, la flora, el régimen de vertientes, podrá el lector observar la influencia que sobre el asiento de las comunidades humanas y sus actividades ha tenido el medio físico.

Por último, *Britannica Atlas* pone de manifiesto el esfuerzo de asegurarle a la obra su carácter internacional cubriendo de forma equilibrada todas las regiones del mundo. Provee un mapa que abarca todas las regiones a nivel mundial, cuyo contenido toma en cuenta la importancia de su situación económica, demográfica y cultural además de sus dimensiones territoriales. La América Latina junto con África, Australia/Oceanía y la ex-Unión Soviética comprenden una tercera parte de los mapas; el resto es dedicado a la América anglosajona, Asia y Europa. Véase el mapamundi en las paginas *xiv-xv*, en el cual se han trazado las zonas, e indicado los folios a que corresponden los distintos mapas.

*Paridad de escalas.* Todos los atlas intentan, con mayor o menor éxito, y siempre que sea práctico, utilizar escalas uniformes. En este atlas se ha utilizado el mínimo posible de escalas, y éstas se han escogido de manera que permitan la comparación entre todas las porciones de la tierra en cuanto a su extensión superficial. En la sección inicial aparecen varios grandes mapas: mapamundis con información política y fisiográfica, a una escala de 1:75 000 000; mapas oceánicos, a 1:48 000 000; y mapas topográficos de los continentes, a 1:24 000 000. Seguidamente se agrupan las principales regiones del mundo, a una escala uniforme de 1:12 000 000 (o sea, cada centímetro corresponde a 120 kilómetros).

El resto de la superficie terrestre, en su casi totalidad, queda representado, por secciones, a base de una u otra de dos escales mayores. La de 1:6 000 000 (60 kms. por cm.) se aplica a las regiones menos pobladas, y la de 1:3 000 000 (30 kms. por cm.), a Europa, casi toda la América del Norte y las regiones más densamente pobladas del Asia meridional y del extremo Oriente. Las dos series son perfectamente comparables entre sí, pues ambas indican los principales rasgos de cada región, tanto naturales como artificales, tales como las cumbres más elevadas, las corrientes fluviales, los principales aeropuertos y vías ferroviarias, dos tipos de carreteras, y aun profundidades marinas representativas.

Por último, la escala de 1:1 000 000 (10 kms. por cm.) se ha destinado a la representación de 50 regiones estratégicas, escogidas atendiendo a su excepcional importancia económica, su gran densidad de población, la complejidad de sus redes de communicaciones, o alguna combinación de estos factores. Esta escala es mucho mayor de la que se acostumbra utilizar en atlas generales, y a lo sumo se reserva para pequeños recuadros especializados que se insertan dentro del marco de mapas mayores. Su uso en esta obra permite abundar en una verdadera riqueza de detalles—saltos de agua, restos arqueológicos, parques forestales y santuarios de flora y fauna, astilleros, instalaciones militares, presas y embalses, además de muchas poblaciones.

Al final de la obra hay una sección de 29 páginas que contiene 60 planos de los principales complejos urbanos, trazados todos a una escala de 1:300 000 (tres kms. por cm.). En estos mapas se muestran, entre otras, las características demográfico-territoriales de las grandes aglomeraciones urbanas. Casi todas las metrópolis más populosas de la Tierra están representadas, así como algunas menores pero realmente importantes. Estos mapas se han agrupado al final del atlas a fin de facilitar la comparación entre sí y para no interrumpir la continuidad de los mapas regionales.

Los mapas están ordenados de modo que el lector vaya obteniendo progresivamente imágenes cada vez más detalladas, si bien siempre comparables de la superficie terrestre. Primero, la visión global del mundo y sus océanos; seguidamente, una visión panorámica de los continentes, mostrados en sus respectivos hemisferios o cuadrantes terrestres. A continuación, la vista más cercana de todas las regiones dentro de los continentes, con énfasis principalmente político. Después, las subregiones, a mayor escala, con énfasis principalmente en las relaciones entre los rasgos físicos y los culturales. A escala aun mayor, se muestran en gran detalle los rasgos culturales de las zonas densamente pobladas. Y por último, los planos de las ciudades y sus alrededores, que incluyen aun más detalles. La sección denominada Leyenda para los Mapas ocupa las tres páginas x a xii.

La compilación y el análisis de datos cartográficos se han beneficiado con el reciente y aceleradísimo progreso logrado en las técnicas del reconocimiento aéreo, y del efectuado por medio de satélites, del radar o del sonar, así como del procesamiento de datos por medios electrónicos. Se ha aprovechado plenamente el sombreado al relieve, que produce un efecto tridimensional en el mapa forzosamente plano de un atlas. Todos los más modernos recursos de las artes gráficas se han puesto en juego al estructurar el plan editorial.

## Avant-propos

Tout au long de l'histoire, les éducateurs ont déploré le fossé profond qui sépare trop souvent le savoir accumulatif de la compréhension. Aussi *Britannica Atlas* ne se contente-t-il pas de rassembler les connaissances les plus récentes concernant la physionomie de la planète; il s'efforce d'élargir la compréhension qu'acquiert l'homme du monde au sein duquel il vit. Afin de dégager pour le lecteur le sens intime des faits, les éditeurs se sont écartés des méthodes traditionnelles: (1) par la présentation d'un contenu plus largement international; (2) en proposant une systématique complète de comparaison entre les cartes.

*Caractère international.* On constate souvent qu'en s'inspirant d'un certain esprit de clocher, tel atlas en arrive à ne plus guère refléter que les vues d'un nationalisme étriqué. Soucieux d'éviter cet écueil, c'est d'entrée de jeu que les éditeurs ont tenu à affirmer le caractère fondamentalement international du nouvel ouvrage. D'éminents spécialistes et plusieurs maisons d'éditions cartographiques du monde entier ont été invités à collaborer à cette œuvre. Des personnalités d'Allemagne, des États-Unis, de France, de Grande-Bretagne, de l'Inde, d'Italie, du Japon, des Pays-Bas et de Suède ont formé le groupe initial. Les documents cartographiques proviennent de six pays: l'Allemagne, les États-Unis, la Grande-Bretagne, la Hongrie, le Japon et la Suède.

On a utilisé dans l'ensemble des cartes les unités de mesure du système métrique de préférence à leurs équivalents anglo-américains. Toutefois, les échelles des cartes et les échelles altimétriques et bathymétriques sont indiquées dans les deux systèmes, métrique et anglo-américain. On trouvera, dans la légende des cartes, les rapports respectifs du mètre et du pied, du kilomètre et du mille.

La plupart des textes de l'Atlas sont présentés en cinq langues: anglais, allemand, espagnol, français et portugais. Les noms de lieux et de particularités géographiques sont, pour chaque pays, transcrits dans leur forme locale. Néanmoins, chaque fois que celle-ci risquait de paraître insolite, on l'a complétée par la variante anglaise pour autant que le permettait l'échelle de la carte. En ce qui concerne les noms de pays, on a eu recours à l'anglais, la version locale de certains d'entre eux risquant de demeurer hermétique au lecteur. Tel est le cas de Magyarország (Hongrie), Nihon (Japon) et Druk-Yul (Bhoutan). Cependant, les noms locaux apparaissent aussi sur les cartes à grande échelle. Dans le cas des océans, des chaînes de montagnes et des autres unités géographiques qui ignorent les frontières politiques, les cartes à petite échelle ne font état que de la seule appellation anglaise, tandis que les projections à grande échelle comportent les deux versions, locale et anglaise. La transcription correspondant à la graphie et à la phonétique anglaises de caractères étrangers à l'alphabet romain a été établie avec le souci de respecter au plus près les systèmes de translittération internationalement reconnus.

On a conservé leur forme locale aux termes génériques s'appliquant à des unités géographiques telles que lac, montagne, île. C'est pourquoi des glossaires succincts en cinq langues figurent en marge de la grande majorité des cartes. En outre, ces renseignements sont complétés aux pages 289-295 par un lexique exhaustif.

Exception faite pour les noms de villes, tous les mots figurant à l'index sont identifiés à l'aide de signes conventionnels représentant graphiquement les traits évocateurs des catégories considérées; c'est ainsi qu'on trouvera Λ pour montagne, ≻ pour cap, ≃ pour rivière. Une clé de cinq langues rappelle, en bas des pages d'index, la classe des termes associés à chaque signe conventionnel utilisé.

Une section séparée, intitulée World Scene (Le Monde Aujourd'hui), contient une série de cartes thématiques. Ces cartes présentent synthétiquement les différents types d'environnement physique auxquels l'homme se trouve associé et quelques-unes des activités économiques, dépendances politiques et aires culturelles les plus notables. Plusieurs cartes touchent à l'histoire politique récente. Dans les cartes consacrées aux climats, aux configurations de surface, aux sols, à la végétation naturelle et à l'hydrographie, le lecteur aura tout loisir de reconnaître les influences d'ordre écologique sur l'implantation et l'activité humaines.

Enfin, on retrouve ce caractère international de l'Atlas jusque dans l'équilibre respecté dans la représentation des différentes régions de la Terre. *Britannica Atlas* accorde à chaque région du monde une couverture cartographique tenant compte de son importance économique et culturelle, de sa densité démographique, de sa superficie. C'est ainsi qu'environ les deux tiers des pages de cartes portent sur le monde anglo-américain, l'Asie et l'Europe, tandis que le tiers restant se partage entre l'Afrique, l'Amérique latine, l'Australie et l'Océanie, et l'ancienne Unión soviétique. La repérage et l'identification des surfaces cartographiées dans l'Atlas sont assurés par une mappemonde avec renvoi aux pages où elles figurent (voir pages xiv et xv).

*Systématique de comparaison.* Avec un succès plus ou moins affirmé, tous les atlas ont jusqu'ici tendu à utiliser une gamme d'échelles uniformisées, dans la mesure où l'opération était techniquement possible. *Britannica Atlas* comporte un nombre restreint d'échelles soigneusement déterminées, propres à rendre vraiment significatives les comparaisons entre les différentes parties du monde. Les premières planches de l'Atlas permettent une vue d'ensemble sur le monde physique et politique grâce à des cartes au 1:75 000 000. Des projections au 1:48 000 000 sont consacrées aux océans, tandis que la figuration du relief des continents est reproduite au 1:24 000 000 (1 cm = 240 km). Ensuite, les vastes régions du globe sont toutes uniformément représentées au 1:12 000 000 (1 cm = 120 km).

Dans un découpage à plus grande échelle, la quasi-totalité des régions du monde est présentée de nouveau à l'échelle de 1:6 000 000 (1 cm = 60 km), pour les régions de moindre population, et à celle de 1:3 000 000 (1 cm = 30 km), pour l'Europe, la plus grande partie de l'Amérique du Nord et pour les régions les plus peuplées du Sud et de l'Est de l'Asie. Les séries au 1:6 000 000 et au 1:3 000 000 sont parfaitement comparables. L'une et l'autre indiquent les accidents naturels et les aspects proprement humains de chaque région: l'altitude, le système fluvial, les grands réseaux ferroviaires, les principaux aéroports, deux catégories de réseaux routiers et même les indications bathymétriques marquantes au large des côtes.

Enfin, on a fait appel à l'échelle de 1:1 000 000 (1 cm = 10 km) pour représenter 50 régions essentielles, choisies soit pour leur importance économique exceptionnelle, leur forte densité démographique, la complexité de leur réseau de transports, soit pour telle ou telle combinaison de ces facteurs. C'est une échelle inhabituellement grande dans les atlas généraux; on la réserve, d'ordinaire, aux cartons illustrant des études particulières. Elle a permis d'introduire quantité de noms de lieux ainsi que de multiples particularités locales: chutes d'eau, ruines, parcs, réserves ornithologiques et zoologiques, chantiers navals, installations militaires, barrages et réservoirs.

À la fin de l'Atlas, une section de 29 pages comprend 60 cartes au 1:300 000 (1 cm = 3 km) des centres urbains les plus importants. On y trouve l'aménagement et les traits caractéristiques des grandes agglomérations urbaines. Les principales concentrations urbaines y sont presque toutes comprises. Il s'y ajoute quelques agglomérations moins compactes mais non sans importance. Ce regroupement des zones citadines à la suite des cartes par régions offre l'avantage d'éviter toute rupture dans la succession de ces dernières.

La succession des cartes a été ordonnée de telle sorte que la surface de la Terre se dévoile progressivement du général au particulier, sans que le lecteur cesse de disposer de termes de comparaison. C'est d'abord une vue d'ensemble de la planète et de ses océans; puis, un survol général des continents présentés par hémisphère ou par quadrant terrestre. Suit l'examen plus poussé, sur des cartes principalement politiques, de toutes les régions qu'ils englobent. Celles-ci sont à leur tour projetées à grande échelle; l'accent est alors mis sur les relations de l'évolution culturelle et de l'environnement. Sous un verre plus grossissant apparaissent dans le détail les particularités culturelles des zones de forte densité démographique. Enfin, les gros plans des métropoles et de leurs agglomérations apportent au lecteur un faisceau d'informations plus détaillées. Les pages x à xii présentent la légende des cartes.

La collecte et l'analyse des données d'ordre physique destinées à la réalisation des cartes ont bénéficié des progrès de plus en plus rapides qui interviennent dans le domaine de l'observation aérienne et par satellites, de la technologie du radar et du sonar, enfin du traitement électronique de l'information. Le "relief ombré" a permis de conférer à nos cartes un aspect tridimensionnel. En un mot, toutes les ressources de l'art graphique contemporain ont été mises en œuvre afin d'atteindre le but que s'étaient fixé les éditeurs.

# Prefácio

Ao longo da história, sabem-no muito bem os pedagogos, o conhecimento das coisas e a sua compreensão são conceitos que podem estar separados por um verdadeiro abismo. Uma simples acumulação de dados pode valer muito pouco se o seu significado e sua inter-relação não forem plenamente compreendidos.

Além de refletir os mais recentes fatos em relação ao mundo de hoje, o *Britannica Atlas* tem por meta aumentar substancialmente o grau de compreensão que o homem moderno tem do mundo em que vive. Para atingir esse objetivo, os editores afastaram-se dos caminhos tradicionais em dois importantes aspectos: (1) maior internacionalismo de conteúdo, e (2) perfeita comparabilidade dos mapas.

*Internacionalismo.* Freqüentemente, muitos atlas procuram satisfazer gostos e preconceitos locais. Para evitar esse defeito, os responsáveis por esta obra—Encyclopaedia Britannica, Inc. e Rand McNally & Company—desde o princípio asseguraram o caráter verdadeiramente internacional de seu conteúdo convidando um grupo de eminentes geógrafos e firmas cartográficas de diversas partes do mundo para colaborar em seu preparo. O grupo que participou foi constituído por representantes do Brasil e Ibero-América, da França, Alemanha, Índia, Itália, Japão, Países Baixos, Suécia, Reino Unido, e os Estados Unidos.

O sistema métrico foi usado em todos os mapas topográficos em lugar do sistema anglo-americano de medidas. As escalas horizontais e verticais (altitudes e profundidades) são expressas, nas páginas dos mapas, em ambos os sistemas, e na *Legendas dos Mapas* figuram as equivalências metro-pé e quilômetro-milha.

O inglês, o alemão, o espanhol, o francês e o português são utilizados paralelamente na maior parte da obra. Os nomes dos lugares habitados e dos acidentes geográficos situados dentro dos limites de um dado país são escritos na língua local; se o espaço disponível o permitir, apresenta-se também o equivalente inglês, caso o nome local não seja facilmente reconhecível. Os nomes dos países são apresentados em inglês, uma vez que alguns são muito difíceis de identificar quando expressos na língua local: Druk-Yul (Butã), Magyarország (Hungria), Nihon (Japão). Contudo, nos mapas em escala maior figura também a forma local do nome do país. Os nomes dos grandes mares ou lagos, cordilheiras ou outros acidentes maiores, que se estendem através de fronteiras internacionais, são apresentados em inglês nos mapas em escala reduzida, e tanto nas formas locais como em inglês nos mapas em escala maior. Para fins de transliteração para o inglês dos topônimos em línguas que não utilizam o alfabeto latino, fez-se o maior esforço para seguir os sistemas de transliteração mais aceitos internacionalmente.

Termos geográficos tais como lago, monte, ilha etc., aparecem nos mapas na língua local. À margem da maior parte das páginas acham-se glossários, em cinco línguas, que incluem a maioria dos termos utilizados em cada mapa; um glossário completo figura às páginas 289-295.

Todas as entradas no índice, exceto as de cidades ou outros centros urbanos, são acompanhadas de um símbolo gráfico que os identifica, como, por exemplo, montanha Λ, cabo ≻, rio ≃ etc., e ao pé de cada página, encontra-se, em cinco línguas, a chave da equivalência dos símbolos às categorias maiores de acidentes geográficos que representam.

Esforço para assegurar à obra seu caráter internacional faz-se evidente no tratamento equilibrado dado às diversas regiões do mundo. O *Britannica Atlas* reparte entre as regiões do mundo o seu conteúdo cartográfico, levando em conta sua significação cultural, econômica, demográfica e territorial. A América Latina, juntamente com a África, Austrália/Oceania e a antiga União Soviética, compreendem, aproximadamente, a terça parte dos mapas, sendo os restantes dois terços dedicados à Anglo-América, Ásia e Europa. No mapa-múndi nas páginas xii-xv foram traçadas as zonas e indicadas as páginas em que correspondem os diversos mapas.

*Comparabilidade.* Todos os atlas, com êxito maior ou menor, e sempre que possível procuram utilizar escalas uniformes. No *Britannica Atlas* utilizou-se o menor número possível de escalas, e estas foram escolhidas de modo a permitir a comparabilidade de todas as partes da Terra no tocante à área. Na seção inicial do Atlas, aparecem vários mapas grandes: mapasmúndi, com informações políticas e fisiográficas, em escala de 1:75 000 000; mapas oceânicos, em escala de 1:48 000 000; e mapas dos continentes, em escala 1:24 000 000. A seguir, agrupam-se as principais regiões do mundo a uma escala uniforme de 1:12 000 000 (seja, cada centímetro corresponde a 120 quilômetros).

O restante da superfície terrestre, em sua quase totalidade, foi representada por seções, utilizando-se uma ou outra das duas escalas maiores. A de 1:6 000 000 (60 km por cm) aplica-se às regiões menos povoadas, e a de 1:3 000 000 (30 km por cm), à Europa, quase toda a América do Norte e às regiões mais densamente povoadas da Ásia Meridional e do Extremo Oriente. As duas séries são perfeitamente comparáveis entre si, pois ambas indicam os principais acidentes de cada região, tanto naturais como artificiais, tais como os picos mais elevados, os rios, os principais aeroportos a ferrovias, duas categorias de rodovias, e, ainda, as profundidades submarinas mais representativas.

Por último, a escala de 1:1 000 000 (10 km por cm) foi destinada à representação de 50 regiões estratégicas, escolhidas de acordo com a excepcional importância econômica, grande densidade demográfica, complexidade da rede de comunicações, ou alguma combinação desses fatores. Essa escala, muito maior que a habitualmente utilizada em atlas gerais, costuma ser reservada aos mapas que focalizam temas especiais insertos em mapas maiores. Seu uso nesta obra proporciona uma grande riqueza de detalhes, tais como quedas d'água, sítios arqueológicos, parques florestais, reservas naturais e biológicas, estaleiros, instalações militares, represas e barragens, além de muitos centros urbanos menores.

No final do Atlas figura uma seção de 29 páginas que contêm 60/mapas dos principais centros urbanos, traçados à escala única de 1:300 000 (3 km por cm). Esses mapas mostram a forma de uso do solo e outras características demográfico-territoriais das grandes aglomerações urbanas. Quase todas as áreas metropolitanas mais populosas do Mundo estão aí representadas, assim como algumas menores, mas igualmente importantes. Esses mapas foram agrupados em uma seção especial no final do Atlas para fins de comparabilidade, bem como para evitar a interrupção da continuidade dos mapas regionais.

Os mapas estão ordenados de modo a permitir ao leitor uma visão progressivamente mais detalhada, mas sempre comparável, da superfície terrestre. Primeiro, vem uma visão global do Mundo e dos oceanos; em seguida, uma visão panorâmica dos continentes, apresentados em seus respectivos hemisférios ou quadrantes terrestres. Segue-se uma visão mais próxima de todas as regiões dentro dos continentes, em mapas primordialmente políticos. Depois, as subregiões, em escala maior, com ênfase principalmente nas relações entre os acidentes físicos e os culturais. A escala ainda maior, apresentam-se, em grande detalhe, os acidentes culturais das zonas densamente povoadas. E por último, os mapas das cidades e seus arredores, que incluem ainda mais detalhes. A seção denominada *Legendas dos Mapas* ocupa a três páginas, de x a xii.

A compilação e a análise dos dados cartográficos beneficiaram-se com o recente e aceleradíssimo progresso alcançado pelas técnicas dos levantamentos aerofotogramétricos e por meio de satélites, pela tecnologia do radar e do sonar, e pelo processamento electrônico de dados. Utilizou-se a técnica do sombreado para o relevo, com o objetivo de dar aos mapas um efeito tridimensional. Todos os recursos das artes gráficas atuais foram empregados na execução do projeto editorial.

## SUMMARY OF CONTENTS


ADVISERS, CONTRIBUTORS, EDITORS AND STAFF ii
FOREWORD iii
SUMMARY OF CONTENTS vi
LIST OF MAPS vi–vii
LEGEND TO MAPS x–xii
WORLD AND REGIONAL INDEX MAPS xiii–xv
SELECTED MAP REFERENCES xvi
WORLD SCENE xvii–xl
MAPS (see *List of Maps,* vi–vii) 1–288
World, Ocean, and Continent Maps 1–19
Regional Maps 20–258
Metropolitan Area Maps 259–288
GLOSSARY AND ABBREVIATIONS OF GEOGRAPHICAL TERMS 289–295
WORLD INFORMATION TABLE 296–299
METROPOLITAN AREAS TABLE 300
POPULATIONS OF CITIES AND TOWNS 301–316
INDEX 317


## INHALTSVERZEICHNIS


BERATER, MITARBEITER, HERAUSGEBER UND REDAKTION ii
VORWORT iii–iv
INHALTSVERZEICHNIS vi
KARTENVERZEICHNIS vii
ZEICHENERKLÄRUNG x–xii
WELT- UND REGIONALE INDEXKARTEN xiii–xv
REGISTER WICHTIGER GEOGRAPHISCHER NAMEN xvi
WELT-PANORAMA xvii–xl
KARTEN (siehe *Kartenverzeichnis,* vii) 1–288
Weltkarten, Karten der Ozeane und Erdteile 1–19
Regionalkarten 20–258
Karten von Stadtregionen 259–288
VERZEICHNIS UND ABKÜRZUNGEN GEOGRAPHISCHER BEGRIFFE 289–295
WELT-INFORMATIONSTABELLE 296–299
TABELLE DER STADTREGIONEN 300
EINWOHNERZAHLEN VON GROSS-STÄDTEN 301–316
REGISTER 317


## SUMARIO DEL CONTENIDO


ASESORES, COLABORADORES, REDACTORES Y AYUDANTES ii
PREFACIO iv
SUMARIO DEL CONTENIDO vi
LISTA DE MAPAS vii–viii
LEYENDAS PARA MAPAS x–xii
INDICE DE LOS MAPAS DEL MUNDO Y REGIONALES xiii–xv
SELECCIONES DE REFERENCIAS DE LOS MAPAS xvi
PERSPECTIVA DEL MUNDO xvii–xl
MAPAS (véase *Lista de Mapas,* vii–viii) 1–288
Mapas del Mundo, Océanos y Continentes 1–19
Mapas Regionales 20–258
Mapas de las Áreas Metropolitanas 259–288
GLOSARIO Y ABREVIACIONES DE TÉRMINOS GEOGRÁFICOS 289–295
TABLA DE INFORMACIÓN MUNDIAL 296–299
TABLA DE LAS ÁREAS METROPOLITANAS 300
HABITANTES EN LAS CIUDADES Y POBLACIONES 301–316
INDICE 317


## TABLE DES MATIÈRES


CONSEILLERS, COLLABORATEURS, RÉDACTEURS ET PERSONNEL ii
AVANT-PROPOS iv–v
TABLE DES MATIÈRES vi
LISTE DES CARTES viii–ix
LÉGENDE DES CARTES x–xii
INDEX DES CARTES DU MONDE ET DES CARTES RÉGIONALES xiii–xv
INDEX CARTOGRAPHIQUE ABRÉGÉ xvi
LE MONDE AUJOURD'HUI xvii–xl
CARTES (voir *Liste des Cartes,* viii–ix) 1–288
Cartes du Monde, des Océans et des Continents 1–19
Cartes Régionales 20–258
Cartes des Zones Métropolitaines 259–288
GLOSSAIRE ET ABRÉVIATIONS DE TERMES GÉOGRAPHIQUES 289–295
TABLE D'INFORMATIONS MONDIALES 296–299
TABLE DES ZONES MÉTROPOLITAINES 300
POPULATION DES GRANDS CENTRES ET DES VILLES 301–316
INDEX 317


## SUMÁRIO


EDITORES, ASSESSORES E COLABORADORES ii
PREFÁCIO v
SUMÁRIO vi
LISTA DE MAPAS ix
LEGENDAS DOS MAPAS x–xii
ÍNDICE DES MAPAS DO MUNDO E REGIONAIS xiii–xv
REFERÊNCIAS A MAPAS SELECIONADAS xvi
PERSPECTIVA DO MUNDO xvii–xl
MAPAS (ver a *Lista de Mapas,* ix) 1–288
Mapas do mundo, dos oceanos e dos continentes 1–19
Mapas regionais 20–258
Mapas das áreas metropolitanas 259–288
GLOSSÁRIO E ABREVIAÇÕES DE TERMOS GEOGRÁFICOS 289–295
TABELA DE INFORMAÇÕES MUNDIAIS 296–299
TABELA DAS ÁREAS METROPOLITANAS 300
POPULAÇAÕ DOS CENTROS URBANOS 301–316
ÍNDICE 317


# List of Maps

## WORLD, OCEAN and CONTINENT MAPS


* Introduction 1
1:75 World: Political 2–3
1:75 World: Physical 4–5
1:48 Pacific and Indian Oceans 6–7
1:48 Atlantic Ocean 8
1:24 Antarctica 9
1:24 Europe and Africa 10–11
1:24 Asia 12–13
1:24 Australia and Oceania 14–15
1:24 North America 16–17
1:24 South America 18–19


## REGIONAL MAPS


Introduction 20–21


### Eurasia


1:12 Europe 22–23
1:6 Northern Europe 24–25
1:3 Southern Scandinavia 26–27
1:3 British Isles 28–29
1:3 Central Europe 30–31
1:3 France and the Alps 32–33
1:3 Spain and Portugal 34–35
1:3 Italy 36–37
1:3 Southeastern Europe 38–39
1:1 Stockholm - Karlstad 40
1:1 København - Malmö - Kiel 41
1:1 London - Birmingham - Cardiff 42–43
1:1 Dublin - Manchester - Newcastle upon Tyne 44–45
1:1 Glasgow - Edinburgh - Aberdeen 46–47
1:1 Dublin - Belfast - Cork 48–49
1:1 Paris - London - Bruxelles 50–51
1:1 Amsterdam - Düsseldorf - Hamburg 52–53
1:1 Berlin - Hamburg - Praha 54–55
1:1 Bruxelles - Frankfurt - Stuttgart 56–57
1:1 Zürich - Genève - Strasbourg 58–59
1:1 Nürnberg - München 60
1:3 Wien - Brno - Linz 61
1:1 Lyon - Marseille - Milano 62–63
1:1 München - Venezia - Firenze 64–65
1:1 Roma - Firenze - Napoli 66–67
1:1 Napoli - Messina - Bari 68–69
1:1 Palermo - Catania - Messina 70
1:1 Cagliari - Sassari 71
1:12 Northwest Asia 72–73
1:12 Northeast Asia 74–75
1:3 Baltic and Moscow Regions 76–77
1:3 Ukraine 78–79
1:3 Volga Region 80–81
1:1 Moskva - Tula - Tver' 82
1:1 Doneck - Lugansk - Rostov 83
1:3 Caucasus and Transcaucasia 84
1:3 Tashkent Region 85
1:6 Central Russia and Kazakhstan 86–87
1:3 Lake Baikal Region 88
1:6 Far Eastern Russia 89
1:12 China, Japan and Korea 90–91
1:3 Japan 92–93
1:1 Tōkyō - Nagoya - Kyōto 94–95
1:1 Ōsaka - Hiroshima - Fukuoka 96–97
1:3 Northeast China and Korea 98–99
1:3 East and Southeast China 100–101
1:6 Interior China 102–103
1:1 Shenyang -Fushun (Mukden - Fushun) 104
1:1 Beijing - Tianjin (Peking - Tientsin) 105
1:1 Shanghai - Nanjing (Shanghai - Nanking) 106
1:1 Chongqing - Chengdu (Chungking - Chengtu) 107
1:6 Southeast Asia 108–109
1:6 Myanmar, Thailand and Indochina 110–111
1:6 Malaysia and Western Indonesia 112–113
1:3 Malaya, Singapore and Northern Sumatra 114
1:3 Java • Lesser Sunda Islands 115
1:3 Philippines 116–117
1:12 India, Pakistan and Southwest Asia 118–119
1:6 Northern India and Pakistan 120–121
1:6 Southern India and Sri Lanka 122
1:3 Punjab and Kashmir 123
1:3 Ganges Lowland and Nepal 124–125
1:1 Calcutta - Dhaka - Jamshedpur 126–127
1:6 The Middle East 128–129
1:3 Turkey and Cyprus 130–131
1:1 Yerushalayim - Dimashq (Jerusalem - Damascus) 132–133


### Africa


1:12 Western North Africa 134–135
1:12 Eastern North Africa 136–137
1:12 Southern Africa 138–139
1:6 Egypt and Sudan 140–141
1:1 Al-Qāhirah - As-Suways (Cairo - Suez) 142–143
1:6 Ethiopia, Somalia and Yemen 144–145
1:6 Libya and Chad 146–147
1:6 Northwestern Africa 148–149
1:6 West Africa 150–151
1:6 Western Congo Basin 152–153
1:6 East Africa and Eastern Congo Basin 154–155
1:6 Southern Africa and Madagascar 156–157
1:3 South Africa 158–159


### Australia/Oceania


1:12 Australia 160–161
1:6 Western and Central Australia 162–163
1:6 Northern Australia and New Guinea 164–165
1:6 Eastern Australia 166–167
1:1 Perth • Adelaide 168
1:1 Melbourne - Geelong - Ballarat 169
1:1 Sydney - Newcastle 170
1:1 Brisbane • Canberra 171
1:3 New Zealand 172–173
*Various Scales*
Islands of the Pacific 174–175


### Anglo America


1:12 Canada 176–177
1:12 United States 178–179
1:6 Alaska and Yukon 180–181
1:6 Southwestern Canada 182–183
1:6 South-Central Canada 184–185
1:6 Southeastern Canada 186–187
1:3 Northeastern United States 188–189
1:6 Great Lakes Region 190–191
1:6 Southeastern United States 192–193
1:6 Mississippi Valley 194–195
1:6 Southern Great Plains 196–197
1:6 Northern Great Plains 198–199
1:6 Southern Rocky Mountains 200–201
1:6 Northwestern United States 202–203
1:6 California and Nevada 204–205
1:1 Montréal - Québec 206
1:1 Boston - New York - Albany 207
1:1 New York - Philadelphia - Washington - Norfolk 208–209
1:1 New York - Buffalo 210–211
1:1 Toronto - Ottawa 212–213
1:1 Pittsburgh - Cleveland - Detroit 214–215
1:1 Chicago - Detroit - Milwaukee 216–217
1:1 Indianapolis - Cincinnati - Louisville 218
1:1 St. Louis - Springfield 219
1:1 Miami - Tampa - Orlando 220–221
1:1 Houston - Dallas - Austin 222–223
1:1 Vancouver - Seattle - Portland 224–225
1:1 San Francisco - Reno - Bakersfield 226–227
1:1 Los Angeles - San Diego 228
*Various Scales*
Hawaii 229


### Latin America


1:12 Middle America 230–231
1:6 Mexico 232–233
1:3 Central Mexico 234–235
1:3 Central America 236–237
1:6 Caribbean Region 238–239
*Various Scales*
Islands of the West Indies 240–241
1:12 Northern South America 242–243
1:12 Southern South America 244–245
1:6 Colombia, Ecuador, Venezuela and Guyana 246–247
1:6 Peru, Bolivia and Western Brazil 248–249
1:6 Northeastern Brazil 250–251
1:6 Central Argentina and Chile 252–253
1:6 Southern Argentina and Chile 254
1:6 Southeastern Brazil 255
1:1 Rio de Janeiro - São Paulo 256–257
1:1 Buenos Aires - Montevideo 258


## METROPOLITAN AREA MAPS (1:300,000)


Introduction 259
London 260
Paris 261
Manchester - Liverpool 262
Ruhr Area 263
Berlin • Wien • Budapest 264
Sankt Peterburg • Moskva 265
Madrid • Milano • Lisboa • Barcelona 266
Roma • Athínai • İstanbul • Tehrān 267
Tōkyō - Yokohama 268


*Scale in millions

Krung Thep (Bangkok) • Thanh Pho Ho Chi Minh (Saigon) • Jakarta • Shanghai • T'aipei • Manila 269
Ōsaka - Kōbe - Kyōto 270
Beijing (Peking) • Sŏul • Singapore • Hong Kong 271
Delhi • Bombay • Calcutta 272
Lagos • Kinshasa - Brazzaville • Al-Qāhirah (Cairo) • Johannesburg 273
Sydney • Melbourne 274
Montréal • Toronto 275
New York 276–277
Chicago 278
Cleveland • Pittsburgh 279
Los Angeles 280
Detroit - Windsor 281
San Francisco - Oakland - San Jose 282
Boston 283
Buffalo - Niagara Falls • Baltimore • Washington 284
Philadelphia 285
Ciudad de México • La Habana • Caracas • Lima • Santiago 286
Rio de Janeiro • São Paulo 287
Buenos Aires 288

# Kartenverzeichnis

## WELTKARTEN, KARTEN DER OZEANE UND ERDTEILE

* Einleitung 1
1:75 Erde: Politisch 2–3
1:75 Erde: Physisch 4–5
1:48 Pazifischer und Indischer Ozean 6–7
1:48 Atlantischer Ozean 8
1:24 Antarktis 9
1:24 Europa und Afrika 10–11
1:24 Asien 12–13
1:24 Australien und Ozeanien 14–15
1:24 Nordamerika 16–17
1:24 Südamerika 18–19

## REGIONALKARTEN

Einleitung 20–21

### Eurasien

1:12 Europa 22–23
1:6 Nordeuropa 24–25
1:3 Südskandinavien 26–27
1:3 Britische Inseln 28–29
1:3 Mitteleuropa 30–31
1:3 Frankreich und die Alpen 32–33
1:3 Spanien und Portugal 34–35
1:3 Italien 36–37
1:3 Südosteuropa 38–39
1:1 Stockholm - Karlstad 40
1:1 København - Malmö - Kiel 41
1:1 London - Birmingham - Cardiff 42–43
1:1 Dublin - Manchester - Newcastle upon Tyne 44–45
1:1 Glasgow - Edinburgh - Aberdeen 46–47
1:1 Dublin - Belfast - Cork 48–49
1:1 Paris - London - Bruxelles 50–51
1:1 Amsterdam - Düsseldorf - Hamburg 52–53
1:1 Berlin - Hamburg - Praha 54–55
1:1 Bruxelles - Frankfurt - Stuttgart 56–57
1:1 Zürich - Genève - Strasbourg 58–59
1:1 Nürnberg - München 60
1:3 Wien - Brno - Linz 61
1:1 Lyon - Marseille - Milano 62–63
1:1 München - Venezia - Firenze 64–65
1:1 Roma - Firenze - Napoli 66–67
1:1 Napoli - Messina - Bari 68–69
1:1 Palermo - Catania - Messina 70
1:1 Cagliari - Sassari 71
1:12 Nordwestasien 72–73
1:12 Nordostasien 74–75
1:3 Baltenland und Mittelrussland 76–77
1:3 Ukraine 78–79
1:3 Wolgagebiet 80–81
1:1 Moskva - Tula - Tver' 82
1:1 Doneck - Lugansk - Rostov 83
1:3 Kaukasus und Transkaukasien 84
1:3 Taschkentgebiet 85
1:6 Mittelrussland und Kasachstan 86–87
1:6 Baikalseegebiet 88
1:6 Russlands Ferne Osten 89
1:12 China, Japan und Korea 90–91
1:3 Japan 92–93
1:1 Tōkyō - Nagoya - Kyōto 94–95
1:1 Ōsaka - Hiroshima - Fukuoka 96–97
1:3 Nordostchina und Korea 98–99
1:3 Ost- und Südostchina 100–101
1:6 Innerchina 102–103
1:1 Shenyang -Fushun (Mukden - Fushun) 104
1:1 Beijing - Tianjin (Peking - Tientsin) 105
1:1 Shanghai - Nanjing (Shanghai - Nanking) 106
1:1 Chongqing - Chengdu (Chungking - Chengtu) 107
1:6 Südostasien 108–109
1:6 Myanmar, Thailand und Indochina 110–111
1:6 Malaysia und westliches Indonesien 112–113
1:3 Malaya, Singapur und Nordsumatra 114
1:3 Java • Kleine Sundainseln 115
1:3 Philippinen 116–117
1:12 Indien, Pakistan und Südwestasien 118–119
1:6 Nordindien und Pakistan 120–121
1:6 Südindien und Sri Lanka 122
1:3 Pandschab und Kaschmir 123
1:3 Gangestiefland und Nepal 124–125
1:1 Calcutta - Dhaka - Jamshedpur 126–127
1:6 Vorderasien 128–129
1:3 Türkei und Zypern 130–131
1:1 Yerushalayim - Dimashq (Jerusalem - Damascus) 132–133

### Afrika

1:12 West Nordafrika 134–135
1:12 Ost Nordafrika 136–137
1:12 Südafrika 138–139
1:6 Ägypten und Sudan 140–141
1:1 Al-Qāhirah - As-Suways (Cairo - Suez) 142–143
1:6 Äthiopien, Somalia und Jemen 144–145
1:6 Libyen und Tschad 146–147
1:6 Nordwestafrika 148–149
1:6 Westafrika 150–151
1:6 Westliches Kongobecken 152–153
1:6 Ostafrika und Östliches Kongobecken 154–155
1:6 Südafrika und Madagaskar 156–157
1:3 Republik Südafrika 158–159

### Australien/Ozeanien

1:12 Australien 160–161
1:6 West-und Mittelaustralien 162–163
1:6 Nordaustralien und Neuguinea 164–165
1:6 Ostaustralien 166–167
1:1 Perth • Adelaide 168
1:1 Melbourne - Geelong - Ballarat 169
1:1 Sydney - Newcastle 170
1:1 Brisbane • Canberra 171
1:3 Neuseeland 172-173
*verschiedene Massstäbe*
Pazifische Inseln 174–175

### Anglo-Amerika

1:12 Kanada 176–177
1:12 Vereinigte Staaten 178–179
1:6 Alaska und Yukon 180–181
1:6 Südwestkanada 182–183
1:6 Südliches Mittelkanada 184–185
1:6 Südostkanada 186–187
1:3 Nordöstliche Vereinigte Staaten 188–189
1:6 Grosse Seen-Region 190–191
1:6 Südöstliche Vereinigte Staaten 192–193
1:6 Mississippi-Tiefland 194–195
1:6 Südliche Grosse Ebenen 196–197
1:6 Nördliche Grosse Ebenen 198–199
1:6 Südliches Felsengebirge 200–201
1:6 Nordwestliche Vereinigte Staaten 202–203
1:6 Kalifornien und Nevada 204–205
1:1 Montréal - Québec 206
1:1 Boston - New York - Albany 207
1:1 New York - Philadelphia - Washington - Norfolk 208–209
1:1 New York - Buffalo 210–211
1:1 Toronto - Ottawa 212–213
1:1 Pittsburgh - Cleveland - Detroit 214–215
1:1 Chicago - Detroit - Milwaukee 216–217
1:1 Indianapolis - Cincinnati - Louisville 218
1:1 St. Louis - Springfield 219
1:1 Miami - Tampa - Orlando 220–221
1:1 Houston - Dallas - Austin 222–223
1:1 Vancouver - Seattle - Portland 224–225
1:1 San Francisco - Reno - Bakersfield 226–227
1:1 Los Angeles - San Diego 228
*verschiedene Massstäbe*
Hawaii 229

### Latein-Amerika

1:12 Mittelamerika 230–231
1:6 Mexiko 232–233
1:3 Mittelmexiko 234–235
1:3 Zentralamerika 236–237
1:6 Mittelamerikanische Inselwelt 238–239
*verschiedene Massstäbe*
Westindische Inseln 240–241
1:12 Südamerika, nördlicher Teil 242–243
1:12 Südamerika, südlicher Teil 244–245
1:6 Kolumbien, Ecuador, Venezuela und Guayana 246–247
1:6 Peru, Bolivien und westliches Brasilien 248–249
1:6 Nordostbrasilien 250–251
1:6 Mittelargentinien und Mittelchile 252–253
1:6 Südliches Argentinien und südliches Chile 254
1:6 Südostbrasilien 255
1:1 Rio de Janeiro - São Paulo 256–257
1:1 Buenos Aires - Montevideo 258

## KARTEN VON STRADTREGIONEN (1:300 000)

Einleitung 259
London 260
Paris 261
Manchester - Liverpool 262
Ruhr Area 263
Berlin • Wien • Budapest 264
Sankt Peterburg • Moskva 265
Madrid • Milano • Lisboa • Barcelona 266
Roma • Athínai • İstanbul • Tehrān 267
Tōkyō - Yokohama 268
Krung Thep (Bangkok) • Thanh Pho Ho Chi Minh (Saigon) • Jakarta • Shanghai • T'aipei • Manila 269
Ōsaka - Kōbe - Kyōto 270
Beijing (Peking) • Sŏul • Singapore • Hong Kong 271
Delhi • Bombay • Calcutta 272
Lagos • Kinshasa - Brazzaville • Al-Qāhirah (Cairo) • Johannesburg 273
Sydney • Melbourne 274
Montréal • Toronto 275
New York 276–277
Chicago 278
Cleveland • Pittsburgh 279
Los Angeles 280
Detroit - Windsor 281
San Francisco - Oakland - San Jose 282
Boston 283
Buffalo - Niagara Falls • Baltimore • Washington 284
Philadelphia 285
Ciudad de México • La Habana • Caracas • Lima • Santiago 286
Rio de Janeiro • São Paulo 287
Buenos Aires 288

* Massstab in Millionen

# Lista de Mapas

## MAPAS DEL MUNDO, OCÉANOS Y CONTINENTES

* Introducción 1
1:75 Mundo: Político 2–3
1:75 Mundo: Físico 4–-5
1:48 Océanos Pacífico e Indico 6–7
1:48 Océano Atlántico 8
1:24 Antártida 9
1:24 Europa y África 10–11
1:24 Asia 12–13
1:24 Australia y Oceanía 14–15
1:24 América del Norte 16–17
1:24 América del Sur 18–19

*Escala en millones

## MAPAS REGIONALES

Introducción 20–21

### Eurasia

1:12 Europa 22–23
1:6 Europe Septentrional 24–25
1:3 Escandinavia Meridional 26–27
1:3 Islas Británicas 28–29
1:3 Europa Central 30–31
1:3 Francia y los Alpes 32–33
1:3 España y Portugal 34–35
1:3 Italia 36–37
1:3 Europa Sud-oriental 38–39
1:1 Stockholm - Karlstad 40
1:1 København - Malmö - Kiel 41
1:1 London - Birmingham - Cardiff 42–43
1:1 Dublin - Manchester - Newcastle upon Tyne 44–45
1:1 Glasgow - Edinburgh - Aberdeen 46–47
1:1 Dublin - Belfast - Cork 48–49
1:1 Paris - London - Bruxelles 50–51
1:1 Amsterdam - Düsseldorf - Hamburg 52–53
1:1 Berlin - Hamburg - Praha 54–55
1:1 Bruxelles - Frankfurt - Stuttgart 56–57
1:1 Zürich - Genève - Strasbourg 58–59
1:1 Nürnberg - München 60
1:3 Wien - Brno - Linz 61
1:1 Lyon - Marseille - Milano 62–63
1:1 München - Venezia - Firenze 64–65
1:1 Roma - Firenze - Napoli 66–67
1:1 Napoli - Messina - Bari 68–69
1:1 Palermo - Catania - Messina 70
1:1 Cagliari - Sassari 71
1:12 Asia Nor-occidental 72–73
1:12 Asia Nor-oriental 74–75
1:3 Regiones de Báltico y de Moscú 76–77
1:3 Ucrania 78–79
1:3 Región del Volga 80–81
1:1 Moskva - Tula - Tver' 82
1:1 Doneck - Lugansk - Rostov 83
1:3 Cáucaso y Transcaucasia 84
1:3 Región de Tachkent 85
1:6 Rusia Central e Kazajstan 86–87
1:6 Región del Lago Baikal 88

1:6 Extremo Oriente Ruso 89
1:12 China, Japón y Corea 90–91
1:3 Japón 92–93
1:1 Tōkyō - Nagoya - Kyōto 94–95
1:1 Ōsaka - Hiroshima - Fukuoka 96–97
1:3 China Nor-oriental y Corea 98–99
1:3 Este y Sudeste de la China 100–101
1:6 China Interior 102–103
1:1 Shenyang -Fushun (Mukden - Fushun) 104
1:1 Beijing - Tianjin (Peking - Tientsin) 105
1:1 Shanghai - Nanjing (Shanghai - Nanking) 106
1:1 Chongqing - Chengdu (Chungking - Chengtu) 107
1:6 Asia Sud-oriental 108–109
1:6 Myanmar, Siam e Indochina 110–111
1:6 Malasia e Indonesia Occidental 112–113
1:3 Malaya, Singapur y Sumatra Septentrional 114
1:3 Java • Islas Menores de la Sonda 115
1:3 Filipinas 116–117
1:12 India, Pakistán y Asia Sud-occidental 118–119
1:6 India Septentrional y Pakistán 120–121
1:6 India Meridional y Sri Lanka 122
1:3 Punjab y Cachemira 123
1:3 Llanuras del Ganges y Nepal 124–125
1:1 Calcutta - Dhaka - Jamshedpur 126–127
1:6 El Medio Oriente 128–129
1:3 Turquía y Chipre 130–131
1:1 Yerushalayim - Dimashq (Jerusalem - Damascus) 132–133

### África

1:12 Región Occidental de Africa Septentrional 134–135
1:12 Región Oriental de Africa Septentrional 136–137
1:12 África Meridional 138–139
1:6 Egipto y Sudán 140–141
1:1 Al-Qāhirah - As-Suways (Cairo - Suez) 142–143
1:6 Etiopía, Somalía y Yemen 144–145
1:6 Libia y el Chad 146–147
1:6 África Nor-occidental 148–149
1:6 África Occidental 150–151
1:6 Cuenca Occidental del Congo 152–153
1:6 África Oriental y Cuenca Oriental del Congo 154–155
1:6 África Meridional y Madagascar 156–157
1:3 Sudáfrica 158–159

### Australia/Oceanía

1:12 Australia 160–161
1:6 Australia Centro-occidental 162–163
1:6 Australia Septentrional y Nueva Guinea 164–165
1:6 Australia Oriental 166–167
1:1 Perth • Adelaide 168
1:1 Melbourne - Geelong - Ballarat 169
1:1 Sydney - Newcastle 170
1:1 Brisbane • Canberra 171
1:3 Nueva Zelanda 172-173
*Varias Escalas*
Islas del Pacífico 174–175

### América Anglosajona

1:12 Canadá 176–177
1:12 Estados Unidos 178–179
1:6 Alaska y Yukón 180–181
1:6 Canadá Sud-occidental 182–183
1:6 Centro Meridional del Canadá 184–185
1:6 Canadá Sud-oriental 186–187
1:3 Nor-este de los Estados Unidos 188–189
1:6 Región de los Grandes Lagos 190–191
1:6 Sud-este de los Estados Unidos 192–193
1:6 Valle del Misisipí 194–195
1:6 Grandes Llanos: zona meridional 196–197
1:6 Grandes Llanos: zona septentrional 198–199
1:6 Montañas Rocosas: zona meridional 200–201
1:6 Nor-oeste de los Estados Unidos 202–203
1:6 California y Nevada 204–205
1:1 Montréal - Québec 206
1:1 Boston - New York - Albany 207
1:1 New York - Philadelphia - Washington - Norfolk 208–209
1:1 New York - Buffalo 210–211
1:1 Toronto - Ottawa 212–213
1:1 Pittsburgh - Cleveland - Detroit 214–215
1:1 Chicago - Detroit - Milwaukee 216–217
1:1 Indianapolis - Cincinnati - Louisville 218
1:1 St. Louis - Springfield 219
1:1 Miami - Tampa - Orlando 220–221
1:1 Houston - Dallas - Austin 222–223
1:1 Vancouver - Seattle - Portland 224–225
1:1 San Francisco - Reno - Bakersfield 226–227
1:1 Los Angeles - San Diego 228
*Varias Escalas*
Hawaii 229

### América Latina

1:12 México, Centroamérica y Las Antillas 230–231
1:6 México 232–233
1:3 México Central 234–235
1:3 América Central 236–237
1:6 Región del Caribe 238–239
*Varias Escalas*
Islas de las Antillas 240–241
1:12 América del Sur: zona septentrional 242–243
1:12 América del Sur: zona meridional 244–245
1:6 Colombia, Ecuador, Venezuela y Guyana 246–247
1:6 Perú, Bolivia y Brasil Occidental 248–249
1:6 Brasil Nor-oriental 250–251
1:6 Argentina y Chile: zonas centrales 252–253
1:6 Argentina y Chile: zonas meridionales 254
1:6 Brazil Sud-oriental 255
1:1 Rio de Janeiro - São Paulo 256–257
1:1 Buenos Aires - Montevideo 258

### MAPAS DE LAS ÁREAS METROPOLITANAS (1:300 000)

Introducción 259
London 260
Paris 261
Manchester - Liverpool 262
Ruhr Area 263
Berlin • Wien • Budapest 264
Sankt Peterburg • Moskva 265
Madrid • Milano • Lisboa • Barcelona 266
Roma • Athínai • İstanbul • Tehrān 267
Tōkyō - Yokohama 268
Krung Thep (Bangkok) • Thanh Pho Ho Chi Minh (Saigon) • Jakarta • Shanghai • T'aipei • Manila 269
Ōsaka - Kōbe - Kyōto 270
Beijing (Peking) • Sŏul • Singapore • Hong Kong 271
Delhi • Bombay • Calcutta 272
Lagos • Kinshasa - Brazzaville • Al-Qāhirah (Cairo) • Johannesburg 273
Sydney • Melbourne 274
Montréal • Toronto 275
New York 276–277
Chicago 278
Cleveland • Pittsburgh 279
Los Angeles 280
Detroit - Windsor 281
San Francisco - Oakland - San Jose 282
Boston 283
Buffalo - Niagara Falls • Baltimore • Washington 284
Philadelphia 285
Ciudad de México • La Habana • Caracas • Lima • Santiago 286
Rio de Janeiro • São Paulo 287
Buenos Aires 288

*Escala en millones

---

# Liste des Cartes

## CARTES DU MONDE, DES OCÉANS ET DES CONTINENTS

* Introduction 1
1:75 Monde: Politique 2–3
1:75 Monde: Physique 4–5
1:48 Océans Pacifique et Indien 6–7
1:48 Océan Atlantique 8
1:24 Antarctique 9
1:24 Europe et Afrique 10–11
1:24 Asie 12–13
1:24 Australie et Océanie 14–15
1:24 Amérique du Nord 16–17
1:24 Amérique du Sud 18–19

## CARTES RÉGIONALES

Introduction 20–21

### Eurasie

1:12 Europe 22–23
1:6 Europe Septentrionale 24–25
1:3 Scandinavie Méridionale 26–27
1:3 Îles Britanniques 28–29
1:3 Europe Centrale 30–31
1:3 France et Alpes 32–33
1:3 Espagne et Portugal 34–35
1:3 Italie 36–37
1:3 Europe du Sud-Est 38–39
1:1 Stockholm Karlstad 40
1:1 København - Malmö - Kiel 41
1:1 London - Birmingham - Cardiff 42–43
1:1 Dublin - Manchester - Newcastle upon Tyne 44–45
1:1 Glasgow - Edinburgh - Aberdeen 46–47
1:1 Dublin - Belfast - Cork 48–49
1:1 Paris - London - Bruxelles 50–51
1:1 Amsterdam - Düsseldorf - Hamburg 52–53
1:1 Berlin - Hamburg - Praha 54–55
1:1 Bruxelles - Frankfurt - Stuttgart 56–57
1:1 Zürich - Genève - Strasbourg 58–59
1:1 Nürnberg - München 60
1:3 Wien - Brno - Linz 61
1:1 Lyon - Marseille - Milano 62–63
1:1 München - Venezia - Firenze 64–65
1:1 Roma - Firenze - Napoli 66–67
1:1 Napoli - Messina - Bari 68–69
1:1 Palermo - Catania - Messina 70
1:1 Cagliari - Sassari 71
1:12 Asie du Nord-Ouest 72–73
1:12 Asie du Nord-Est 74–75
1:3 Républiques Baltes et la Région de Moscou 76–77
1:3 Ukraine 78–79
1:3 Région de la Volga 80–81
1:1 Moskva - Tula - Tver' 82
1:1 Doneck - Lugansk - Rostov 83
1:3 Caucasie et Transcaucasie 84
1:3 Région de Tachkent 85
1:6 Russie Centrale et Kazakhstan 86–87
1:6 Région du Lac Baïkal 88
1:6 Extrême-Orient Russe 89
1:12 Chine, Japon et Corée 90–91
1:3 Japon 92–93
1:1 Tōkyō - Nagoya - Kyōto 94–95
1:1 Ōsaka - Hiroshima - Fukuoka 96–97
1:3 Nord-Est de la Chine et Corée 98–99
1:3 Chine de l'Est et du Sud-Est 100–101
1:6 Chine Intérieure 102–103
1:1 Shenyang -Fushun (Mukden - Fushun) 104
1:1 Beijing - Tianjin (Peking - Tientsin) 105
1:1 Shanghai - Nanjing (Shanghai - Nanking) 106
1:1 Chongqing - Chengdu (Chungking - Chengtu) 107
1:6 Asie du Sud-Est 108–109
1:6 Myanmar, Thaïlande et Indochine 110–111
1:6 Malaisie et Indonésie Occidentale 112–113
1:3 Malaya, Singapour et Sumatra Septentrional 114
1:3 Java • Petites Îles de la Sonde 115
1:3 Philippines 116–117
1:12 Inde, Pakistan et Asie du Sud-Ouest 118–119
1:6 Inde Septentrionale et Pakistan 120–121
1:6 Inde Méridionale et Sri Lanka 122
1:3 Punjab et Cachemire 123
1:3 Plaine du Gange et Népal 124–125
1:1 Calcutta - Dhaka - Jamshedpur 126–127
1:6 Le Moyen-Orient 128–129
1:3 Turquie et Chypre 130–131
1:1 Yerushalayim Dimashq (Jerusalem - Damascus) 132–133

### Afrique

1:12 Afrique du Nord Occidentale 134–135
1:12 Afrique du Nord Orientale 136–137
1:12 Afrique Méridionale 138–139
1:6 Égypte et Soudan 140–141
1:1 Al-Qāhirah - As-Suways (Cairo - Suez) 142–143
1:6 Ethiopie, Somalie et Yemen 144–145
1:6 Libye et Tchad 146–147
1:6 Afrique du Nord-Ouest 148–149
1:6 Afrique Occidentale 150–151
1:6 Bassin du Congo, partie Occidentale 152–153
1:6 Afrique Orientale et Bassin du Congo, partie Orientale 154–155
1:6 Afrique Méridionale et Madagascar 156–157
1:3 Afrique du Sud 158–159

### Australie/Océanie

1:12 Australie 160–161
1:6 Australie Occidentale et Centrale 162–163
1:6 Australie Septentrionale et Nouvelle Guinée 164–165
1:6 Australie Orientale 166–167
1:1 Perth • Adelaide 168
1:1 Melbourne - Geelong - Ballarat 169
1:1 Sydney - Newcastle 170
1:1 Brisbane • Canberra 171
1:3 Nouvelle Zélande 172–173
*Echelles Variées*
Îles du Pacifique 174–175

### Amérique Anglo-Saxonne

1:12 Canada 176–177
1:12 États-Unis 178–179
1:6 Alaska et Yukon 180–181
1:6 Sud-Ouest du Canada 182–183
1:6 Canada Central, partie Méridionale 184–185
1:6 Sud-Est du Canada 186–187
1:3 Nord-Est des États-Unis 188–189
1:6 Région des Grands Lacs 190–191
1:6 Sud-Est des États-Unis 192–193
1:6 Vallée du Mississippi 194–195
1:6 Grandes Plaines, partie Méridionale 196–197
1:6 Grandes Plaines, partie Septentrionale 198–199
1:6 Montagnes Rocheuses, partie Méridionale 200–201
1:6 Nord-Ouest des États-Unis 202–203
1:6 Californie et Névada 204–205
1:1 Montréal - Québec 206

*Echelle en millions

1:1 Boston - New York - Albany 207
1:1 New York - Philadelphia - Washington - Norfolk 208–209
1:1 New York - Buffalo 210–211
1:1 Toronto - Ottawa 212–213
1:1 Pittsburgh - Cleveland - Detroit 214–215
1:1 Chicago - Detroit - Milwaukee 216–217
1:1 Indianapolis - Cincinnati - Louisville 218
1:1 St. Louis - Springfield 219
1:1 Miami - Tampa - Orlando 220–221
1:1 Houston - Dallas - Austin 222–223
1:1 Vancouver - Seattle - Portland 224–225
1:1 San Francisco - Reno - Bakersfield 226–227
1:1 Los Angeles - San Diego 228
*Echelles Variées*
Hawaï 229

## Amérique Latine

1:12 Mexique, Amérique Centrale et Région des Caraïbes 230 –231
1:6 Mexique 232–233
1:3 Mexique Central 234–235
1:3 Amérique Centrale 236–237
1:6 Région des Caraïbes 238–239
*Echelles Variées*
Îles des Antilles 240–241
1:12 Amérique du Sud Septentrionale 242–243
1:12 Amérique du Sud Méridionale 244–245
1:6 Colombie, Équateur, Venezuela et Guyane 246–247
1:6 Pérou, Bolivie et Brésil Occidental 248–249
1:6 Nord-Est du Brésil 250–251
1:6 Argentine et Chili, parties Centrales 252–253
1:6 Argentine et Chili, parties Méridionales 254
1:6 Sud-Est du Brésil 255
1:1 Rio de Janeiro - São Paulo 256–257
1:1 Buenos Aires - Montevideo 258

## CARTES DES ZONES MÉTROPOLITAINES (1:300 000)

Introduction 259
London 260
Paris 261
Manchester - Liverpool 262
Ruhr Area 263
Berlin • Wien • Budapest 264
Sankt Peterburg • Moskva 265
Madrid • Milano • Lisboa • Barcelona 266
Roma • Athínai • İstanbul • Tehrān 267
Tōkyō - Yokohama 268
Krung Thep (Bangkok) • Thanh Pho Ho Chi Minh (Saigon) • Jakarta • Shanghai • T'aipei • Manila 269
Ōsaka - Kōbe - Kyōto 270
Beijing (Peking) • Sŏul • Singapore • Hong Kong 271
Delhi • Bombay • Calcutta 272
Lagos • Kinshasa - Brazzaville • Al-Qāhirah (Cairo) • Johannesburg 273
Sydney • Melbourne 274
Montréal • Toronto 275
New York 276–277
Chicago 278
Cleveland • Pittsburgh 279
Los Angeles 280
Detroit - Windsor 281
San Francisco - Oakland - San Jose 282
Boston 283
Buffalo - Niagara Falls • Baltimore • Washington 284
Philadelphia 285
Ciudad de México • La Habana • Caracas • Lima • Santiago 286
Rio de Janeiro • São Paulo 287
Buenos Aires 288

* Echelle en millions

# Lista de Mapas

## MAPAS DO MUNDO, DOS OCEANOS E DOS CONTINENTES

* Introdução 1
1:75 Mundo: Político 2–3
1:75 Mundo: Físico 4–5
1:48 Oceanos Pacífico e Indico 6–7
1:48 Oceano Atlântico 8
1:24 Antártida 9
1:24 Europa e África 10–11
1:24 Ásia 12–13
1:24 Austrália e Oceania 14–15
1:24 América do Norte 16–17
1:24 América do Sul 18–19

## MAPAS REGIONAIS

Introdução 20–21

### Eurásia

1:12 Europa 22–23
1:6 Europa Setentrional 24–25
1:3 Escandinávia Meridional 26–27
1:3 Ilhas Britânicas 28–29
1:3 Europa Central 30–31
1:3 França e os Alpes 32–33
1:3 Espanha e Portugal 34–35
1:3 Itália 36–37
1:3 Europa Sul-oriental 38–39
1:1 Stockholm - Karlstad 40
1:1 København - Malmö - Kiel 41
1:1 London - Birmingham - Cardiff 42–43
1:1 Dublin - Manchester - Newcastle upon Tyne 44–45
1:1 Glasgow - Edinburgh - Aberdeen 46–47
1:1 Dublin - Belfast - Cork 48–49
1:1 Paris - London - Bruxelles 50–51
1:1 Amsterdam - Düsseldorf - Hamburg 52–53
1:1 Berlin - Hamburg - Praha 54–55
1:1 Bruxelles - Frankfurt - Stuttgart 56–57
1:1 Zürich - Genève - Strasbourg 58–59
1:1 Nürnberg - München 60
1:3 Wien - Brno - Linz 61
1:1 Lyon - Marseille - Milano 62–63
1:1 München - Venezia - Firenze 64–65
1:1 Roma - Firenze - Napoli 66–67
1:1 Napoli - Messina - Bari 68–69
1:1 Palermo - Catania - Messina 70
1:1 Cagliari - Sassari 71
1:12 Ásia do Norte Ocidental 72–73
1:12 Ásia do Norte Oriental 74–75
1:3 Regiões do Báltico e de Moscou 76–77
1:3 Ucrânia 78–79
1:3 Região do Volga 80–81
1:1 Moskva - Tula - Tver' 82
1:1 Doneck - Lugansk - Rostov 83
1:3 Cáucaso e Transcaucásia 84
1:3 Região do Taschkent 85
1:6 Rússia Central e Casaquistão 86–87
1:6 Região do Lago Baikal 88
1:6 Extremo Oriente Russo 89
1:12 China, Japão e Coréia 90–91
1:3 Japão 92–93
1:1 Tōkyō - Nagoya - Kyōto 94–95
1:1 Ōsaka - Hiroshima - Fukuoka 96–97
1:3 Nordeste da China e Coréia 98–99
1:3 Leste e Sudeste da China 100–101
1:6 China Interior 102–103
1:1 Shenyang -Fushun (Mukden - Fushun) 104
1:1 Beijing - Tianjin (Peking - Tientsin) 105
1:1 Shanghai - Nanjing (Shanghai - Nanking) 106
1:1 Chongqing - Chengdu (Chungking - Chengtu) 107
1:6 Sudeste Asiático 108–109
1:6 Myanmar, Tailândia e Indochina 110–111
1:6 Malásia e Indonésia Ocidental 112–113
1:3 Malaia, Cingapura e Sumatra Setentrional 114
1:3 Java • Ilhas Menores da Sonda 115
1:3 Filipinas 116–117
1:12 Índia, Paquistão e Ásia do Sudoeste 118–119
1:6 Índia Setentrional e Paquistão 120–121
1:6 Índia Meridional e Sri Lanka 122
1:3 Punjab e Cachemira 123
1:3 Planície do Ganges e Nepal 124–125
1:1 Calcutta - Dhaka - Jamshedpur 126–127
1:6 Oriente Médio 128–129
1:3 Turquia e Chipre 130–131
1:1 Yerushalayim - Dimashq (Jerusalem - Damascus) 132–133

### África

1:12 África do Norte Ocidental 134–135
1:12 África do Norte Oriental 136–137
1:12 África Meridional 138–139
1:6 Egito e Sudão 140–141
1:1 Al-Qāhirah - As-Suways (Cairo - Suez) 142–143
1:6 Etiópia, Somália e Iêmen 144–145
1:6 Líbia e Tchad 146–147
1:6 África Norte-ocidental 148–149
1:6 África Ocidental 150–151
1:6 Bacia Ocidental do Congo 152–153
1:6 África Oriental e Bacia Oriental do Congo 154–155
1:6 África Meridional e Madagascar 156–157
1:3 África do Sul 158–159

### Austrália/Oceania

1:12 Austrália 160–161
1:6 Austrália Ocidental e Central 162–163
1:6 Austrália Setentrional e Nova Guiné 164–165
1:6 Austrália Oriental 166–167
1:1 Perth • Adelaide 168
1:1 Melbourne - Geelong - Ballarat 169
1:1 Sydney - Newcastle 170
1:1 Brisbane • Canberra 171
1:3 Nova Zelândia 172–173
*Várias Escalas*
Ilhas do Pacífico 174–175

### América Anglosaxônica

1:12 Canadá 176–177
1:12 Estados Unidos 178–179
1:6 Alasca e Yukon 180–181
1:6 Canadá: Sudoeste 182–183
1:6 Canadá Central, parte meridional 184–185
1:6 Canadá: Sudeste 186–187
1:3 Estados Unidos: Nordeste 188–189
1:6 Região dos Grandes Lagos 190–191
1:6 Estados Unidos: Sudeste 192–193
1:6 Vale do Mississippi 194–195
1:6 Grandes Planícies: zona meridional 196–197
1:6 Grandes Planícies: zona setentrional 198–199
1:6 Montanhas Rochosas: zona meridional 200–201
1:6 Noroeste dos Estados Unidos 202–203
1:6 Califórnia e Nevada 204–205
1:1 Montréal Québec 206
1:1 Boston - New York - Albany 207
1:1 New York - Philadelphia - Washington - Norfolk 208–209
1:1 New York - Buffalo 210–211
1:1 Toronto - Ottawa 212–213
1:1 Pittsburgh - Cleveland - Detroit 214–215
1:1 Chicago - Detroit - Milwaukee 216–217
1:1 Indianapolis - Cincinnati - Louisville 218
1:1 St. Louis - Springfield 219
1:1 Miami - Tampa - Orlando 220–221
1:1 Houston - Dallas - Austin 222–223
1:1 Vancouver - Seattle - Portland 224–225
1:1 San Francisco - Reno - Bakersfield 226–227
1:1 Los Angeles - San Diego 228
*Várias Escalas*
Havaí 229

### América Latina

1:12 México, América Central e Antilhas 230–231
1:6 México 232–233
1:3 México Central 234–235
1:3 América Central 236–237
1:6 Região do Caribe 238–239
*Várias Escalas*
Ilhas do Caribe (Índias Ocidentais) 240–241
1:12 América do Sul: zona setentrional 242–243
1:12 América do Sul: zona meridional 244–245
1:6 Colômbia, Equador, Venezuela e Guiana 246–247
1:6 Peru, Bolívia e Brasil Ocidental 248–249
1:6 Brasil: Nordeste 250–251
1:6 Argentina e Chile: zonas centrais 252–253
1:6 Argentina e Chile: zonas meridionais 254
1:6 Brasil: Sudeste 255
1:1 Rio de Janeiro - São Paulo 256–257
1:1 Buenos Aires - Montevideo 258

## MAPAS DAS ÁREAS METROPOLITANAS (1:300 000)

Introdução 259
London 260
Paris 261
Manchester - Liverpool 262
Ruhr Area 263
Berlin • Wien • Budapest 264
Sankt Peterburg • Moskva 265
Madrid • Milano • Lisboa • Barcelona 266
Roma • Athínai • İstanbul • Tehrān 267
Tōkyō - Yokohama 268
Krung Thep (Bangkok) • Thanh Pho Ho Chi Minh (Saigon) • Jakarta • Shanghai • T'aipei • Manila 69
Ōsaka - Kōbe - Kyōto 270
Beijing (Peking) • Sŏul • Singapore • Hong Kong 271
Delhi • Bombay • Calcutta 272
Lagos • Kinshasa - Brazzaville • Al-Qāhirah (Cairo) • Johannesburg 273
Sydney • Melbourne 274
Montréal • Toronto 275
New York 276–277
Chicago 278
Cleveland • Pittsburgh 279
Los Angeles 280
Detroit - Windsor 281
San Francisco - Oakland - San Jose 282
Boston 283
Buffalo - Niagara Falls • Baltimore • Washington 284
Philadelphia 285
Rio de Janeiro • São Paulo 287
Buenos Aires 288

*Escalas em milhões

# Legend to Maps/Zeichenerklärung
# Leyendas Para Mapas/Légende des Cartes/Legendas dos Mapas

The design and color of the map symbols are consistent throughout the Regional and Metropolitan Area maps, although the size of the symbol varies with scale. An asterisk marks those symbols which appear only on the 1:300,000 scale maps. Symbols for inhabited localities, boundaries, and capitals are given on page xi.

The symbol 80-81 in the margin of a map directs the reader to a map of the adjoining area.

A separate legend on page 1 identifies the land and submarine features which appear on the World, Ocean, and Continent maps.

Der Entwurf und die Farbe der Kartensymbole sind einheitlich für alle Regionalkarten und Karten von Stadtregionen, während die Grösse des Symbols sich mit dem Massstab ändert. Ein Stern kennzeichnet diejenigen Symbole, welche nur auf den Karten im Massstab 1:300 000 erscheinen. Symbole für bewohnte Orte, für Grenzen und Hauptstädte sind auf Seite xi angeführt.

Kennzeichen 80-81 am Rande einer Karte ist ein Hinweis für den Leser, die Karte eines angrenzenden Gebietes nachzuschlagen.

Eine andere Legende auf Seite 1 identifiziert die Land- und untermeerischen Phänomene, die auf den Weltkarten, Karten der Ozeane und Erdteile erscheinen.

El diseño y el color de los símbolos cartográficos son uniformes para todas los mapas regionales y de las áreas metropolitanas, aunque el tamaño del símbolo varía según la escala. Un asterisco distingue los símbolos que aparecen sólo en los mapas a 1:300 000. Los símbolos de lugares poblados, de límites y de capitales se hallan en la página xi.

El símbolo 80-81 al margen de un mapa dirige al lector a un mapa del área adyacente.

Otra leyenda, en la página 1, identifica la topografía terrestre y submarina que se encuentra en los mapas del Mundo, Océanos y Continentes.

La couleur et la forme des symboles cartographiques des cartes régionales et des cartes des zones métropolitaines sont identiques, bien que la grandeur des signes varie selon l'échelle. Un astérisque accompagne les symboles qui n'apparaissent que sur les cartes au 1:300 000. La légende des signes conventionnels pour les lieux habités, les frontières et les capitales se trouve à la page xi.

Le symbole 80-81 en marge d'une carte renvoie le lecteur à une carte de la région voisine.

Pour les cartes du monde, des océans et des continents une légende séparée, à la page 1, donne le sens des symboles représentant les paysages continentaux et les formes de relief sous-marin.

A cor e a forma dos símbolos cartográficos dos mapas regionais e das áreas metropolitanas são idênticos, ainda que a dimensão do símbolo varie segundo a escala. Um asterisco distingue os símbolos que só aparecem nos mapas da escala de 1:300 000. As legendas dos símbolos convencionais dos lugares povoados, fronteiras e capitais encontram-se à pág. xi.

O símbolo 80-81 à margem de um mapa, remete o leitor a um mapa da região vizinha.

Nos mapas do mundo, dos oceanos e dos continentes uma legenda separada, na pág. 1, indica o sentido dos símbolos representativos das paisagens continentais e das formas do relevo submarino.

## Hydrographic Features / Hydrographische Objekte / Elementos Hidrográficos
## Données Hydrographiques / Acidentes Hidrográficos

**Shoreline/Uferlinie**
Línea costanera/Trait de côte
Linha costeira

**Undefined or Fluctuating Shoreline**
Unbestimmte oder Veränderliche Uferlinie
Línea costanera indefinida o fluctuante
Trait de côte indéfini ou fluctuant
Linha costeira indefinida ou flutuante

Amur — **River, Stream/Fluss, Strom**
Río, Corriente/Rivière, Cours d'eau
Rio, curso d'água

**Intermittent Stream/Periodischer Fluss**
Corriente intermitente/Cours d'eau périodique
Rio, curso d'água intermitente

SALTO ANGEL — **Rapids, Falls/Stromschnellen, Wasserfälle**
Rápidos, Cascadas/Rapides, Chutes d'eau
Corredeiras, quedas d'água

764 ▽ — **Depth of Water/Wassertiefe**
Profundidad del aqua/Profondeur bathymétrique
Profundidade da água

9428 ▼ — **Greatest Depth** (Atlantic, Indian, Pacific oceans)
Grösste Tiefe (Atlantischer, Indischer, Pazifischer Ozean)
Profundidad más grande (Océanos Atlántico, Índico, Pacífico)
Profondeur maximum (océans Atlantique, Indien, Pacifique)
Profundidade máxima (oceanos Atlântico, Índico, Pacífico)

Canal du Midi — **Navigable Canal/Schiffbarer Kanal**
Canal navegable/Canal navigable
Canal navegável

**Irrigation or Drainage Canal**
Be- oder Entwässerungskanal
Canal de irrigación o desagüe
Canal d'irrigation ou de drainage
Canal de irrigação ou drenagem

Los Angeles Aqueduct — **Aqueduct/Aquädukt**
Acueducto/Aqueduc
Aqueduto

**Pier, Breakwater/Landungsbrücke, Wellenbrecher**
Embarcadero, Rompeolas/Jetée, Brise-lames
Cais, Quebra-mar

GREAT BARRIER REEF — **Reef/Riff**
Arrecife/Récif
Recife

Kumdah — **Uninhabited Oasis/Unbewohnte Oase**
Oasis deshabitado/Oasis inhabitée
Oásis desabitado

L. Victoria — **Lake, Reservoir/See, Stausee**
Lago, Embalse/Lac, Réservoir
Lago, reservatório (represa)

**Intermittent Lake, Reservoir**
Periodischer See, Stausee
Lago o Embalse intermitente
Lac ou Réservoir périodique
Lago, reservatório (represa) intermitente

Tuz Gölü — **Salt Lake/Salzsee**
Lago salado/Lac salé
Lago salgado

**Dry Lake Bed/Trockener Seeboden**
Lecho de lago seco/Fond de lac asséch
Leito de lago seco

The Everglades — **Swamp/Sumpf**
Pantano/Marais
Pântano

RIMO GLACIER — **Glacier/Gletscher**
Glaciar/Glacier
Geleira

(395) — **Lake Surface Elevation**
Seehöhe
Elevación del lago
Cote du niveau du lac
Altitude do nível do lago

## Topographic Features / Topographische Objekte / Elementos Topográficos
## Données Topographiques / Acidentes Topográficos

Matterhorn 4478 △ — **Elevation Above Sea Level**
Höhe über dem Meeresspiegel
Elevación sobre el nivel del mar
Cote au-dessus du niveau de la mer
Altitude acima do nível do mar

76 ▽ — **Elevation Below Sea Level**
Höhe unter dem Meeresspiegel
Elevación bajo del nivel del mar
Cote au-dessous du niveau de la mer
Altitude abaixo do nível do mar

Mount Cook 3764 ▲ — **Highest Elevation in Country**
Höchster Punkt des Landes
Elevación más alta en el país
Cote la plus élevée d'un pays
Altitude mais elevada de um país

133 ▼ — **Lowest Elevation in Country**
Tiefster Punkt des Landes
Elevación más baja en el país
Cote la plus basse d'un pays
Altitude mais baixa de um país

(106) — **Elevation of City**
Höhenangabe einer Stadt
Elevación de ciudad
Altitude d'une ville
Altitude de uma cidade

Khyber Pass 1067 — **Mountain Pass/Pass**
Paso/Col de montagne
Passo (de montanha)

* — **Rock/Fels**
Roca/Rocher
Rocha

**Lava/Lava**
Lava/Lave
Lava

**Sand Area/Sandgebiet**
Area de arena/Région sableuse, Erg
Região arenosa, Erg

**Salt Flat/Salzebene**
Salar/Dépression salée
Depressão salgada

A N D E S / KUNLUN SHAN — **Mountain Range, Plateau, Valley, etc.**
Gebirge, Hochebene, Tal, usw.
Sierra, Meseta, Valle, etc.
Chaîne de montagnes, Plateau, Vallée, etc.
Cadeia de montanhas. Planalto, Vale etc.

BAFFIN ISLAND / NUNIVAK ISLAND — **Island**
Insel
Isla
Île
Ilha

POLUOSTROV KAMČATKA / CABO DE HORNOS — **Peninsula, Cape, Point, etc.**
Halbinsel, Kap, Landspitze, usw.
Península, Cabo, Punta, etc.
Péninsule, Cap, Pointe, etc.
Península, Cabo, Ponta etc.

Highest Elevation and Lowest Elevation of a continent are underlined
Höchster und tiefster Punkt innerhalb eines Erdteils sind unterstrichen
Elevación más alta y más baja de un continente se subrayan
La cote la plus haute et la cote la plus basse d'un continent sont soulignées
As altitudes mais e menos elevadas de um continente são sublinhadas

Elevations and depths are given in meters
Höhen und Tiefen sind in Metern angegeben
Elevaciones y profundidades se dan en metros
Cotes et profondeurs sont indiquées en mètres
Altitudes e profundidades são apresentadas em metros

# Legend to Maps/Zeichenerklärung
# Leyendas Para Mapas/Légende des Cartes/Legendas dos Mapas

## Inhabited Localities / Bewohnte Orte / Lugares Poblados / Lieux Habités / Lugares Habitados

**The symbol represents the number of inhabitants within the locality/Die Signatur entspricht der Einwohnerzahl des Ortes**
**El símbolo representa el número de habitantes dentro del lugar/Le symbole représente le nombre d'habitants de la localité**
**O símbolo representa o número de habitantes do lugar**

| Scale | | Symbol | Population |
|---|---|---|---|
| 1:300,000 | 1:1,000,000 | • | 0—10,000 |
| 1:3,000,000 | 1:6,000,000 | ○ | 10,000—25,000 |
| | | ◉ | 25,000—100,000 |
| | | ▣ | 100,000—250,000 |
| | | ▣ | 250,000—1,000,000 |
| | | ■ | >1,000,000 |

| Scale | Symbol | Population |
|---|---|---|
| 1:12,000,000 | • | 0—50,000 |
| | ◉ | 50,000—100,000 |
| | ▣ | 100,000—250,000 |
| | ▣ | 250,000—1,000,000 |
| | ■ | >1,000,000 |

| Scale | Symbol | Population |
|---|---|---|
| 1:24,000,000 | • | 0—100,000 |
| 1:48,000,000 | ◉ | 100,000—1,500,000 |
| | ■ | >1,500,000 |

**The size of type indicates the relative economic and political importance of the locality**
**Die Schriftgrösse entspricht der relativen wirtschaftlichen und politischen Bedeutung des Ortes**
**El tamaño del tipo de imprenta indica la relativa importancia económica y política del lugar**
**La dimension des caractères indique l'importance économique et politique relative d'une localité**
**A dimensão dos caracteres tipográficos indica a importância econômica e política relativa do lugar**

Écommoy — Lisieux — **Rouen**
Trouville — **Orléans** — **PARIS**

*Hollywood* ▫ *Westminster* — **Section of a City, Neighborhood/Stadtteil, Nachbarschaft**
**Sección de una ciudad, Barrio/Arrondissement, Quartier**
**Seção de uma cidade, Bairro**

*Northland Center* ■ — * **Major Shopping Center/Haupteinkaufszentrum/Mercado principal**
**Centre commercial important/Centro comercial importante**

BYRD ▫ — **Scientific Station/Wissenschaftliche Station/Estación científica**
**Station scientifique/Estação científica**

*Bi'r Safājah* ○ — **Inhabited Oasis/Bewohnte Oase/Oasis habitado**
**Oasis habitée/Oásis habitado**

*Kumdah* ○ — **Uninhabited Oasis/Unbewohnte Oase/Oasis deshabitado**
**Oasis inhabitée/Oásis desabitado**

**Urban Area** (area of continuous industrial, commercial, and residential development)
**Stadtgebiet** (ausgedehntes industrie-, Geschäfts- und Wohngebiet)
**Zona urbanizada** (área de desarrollo industrial, comercial y residencial)
**Zone urbanisée** (zone d'occupation continue par des industries, des commerces, des habitations)
**Zona urbanizada** (área de ocupação contínua por indústrias, estabelecimentos comerciais e habitações)

* **Major Industrial Area/Hauptindustriegebiet/Zona principal industrial**
**Région industrielle importante/Zona industrial importante**

* **Wooded Area/Wald/Área de bosque**
**Région boisée/Área verde**

* **Local Park or Recreational Area/Park oder Erholungsgebiet**
**Parque municipal o área de recreo/Parc municipal ou zone de loisirs**
**Parque municipal ou área de lazer**

## Political Boundaries / Politische Grenzen / Límites Políticos / Frontières Politiques / Fronteiras e Limites

**International** (First-order political unit) **/Staatsgrenze** (Politische Einheit erster Ordnung)
**Internacionales** (Unidad política de primer orden) **/Internationales** (Entités politiques de premier ordre)
**Internacionais** (Unidade política de primeiro nível)

1:1,000,000 — 1:300,000 / 1:3,000,000 / 1:6,000,000 — 1:24,000,000 / 1:48,000,000 — 1:12,000,000

HUNGARY

**Demarcated, Undemarcated, and Administrative**
**Markiert, unmarkiert, verwaltungstechnisch**
**Demarcado, No demarcado, y Administrativo**
**Délimitées, Non-délimitées, Administratives**
**Delimitados, Não delimitados, Administrativos**

**Disputed de facto/Umstritten de facto**
**Disputado de hecho/Contestées de facto**
**Contestados de fato**

**Disputed de jure/Umstritten de jure**
**Disputado de derecho/Contestées de jure**
**Contestados de direito**

**Indefinite or Undefined/Unklar oder Unbestimmt**
**Indefinido o No determinado/Imprécises ou Non définies**
**Imprecisos ou Não definidos**

**Demarcation Line/Demarkationslinie**
**Línea de demarcación/Ligne de démarcation**
**Linha de demarcação**

### Capitals of Political Units
### Hauptstädte politischer Einheiten
### Capitales de Unidades Políticas
### Capitales d'Entités Politiques
### Capitais de Unidades Políticas

**BUDAPEST** — **Independent Nation**
**Unabhängiger Staat**
**Nación independiente**
**État indépendant**
**Estado independente**

**Cayenne** — **Dependency** (Colony, protectorate, etc.)
**Abhängiges Gebiet** (Kolonie, Protektorat, usw.)
**Dependencia** (Colonia, protectorado, etc.)
**Territoire dépendant** (Colonie, protectorat, etc.)
**Dependência** (Colônia, protetorado, etc.)

GALAPAGOS (Ecuador) — **Administering Country**
**Verwaltender Staat**
**País administrador**
**Pays administrateur**
**País administrador**

### Internal/Verwaltungsgrenze/Internos/Intérieures/Limites Internos

PERNAMBUCO

**State, Province, etc.** (Second-order political unit)
**Land, Provinz, usw.** (Politische Einheit zweiter Ordnung)
**Estado, Provincia, etc.** (Unidad política de segundo orden)
**État, Province, etc.** (Subdivision administrative de deuxième ordre)
**Estado, Província, etc.** (Unidade política de segundo nível)

**Recife** — **State, Province, etc./Land, Provinz, usw.**
**Estado, Provincia, etc./État, Province, etc.**
**Estado, Província, etc.**

SIENA — WESTCHESTER

**County, Oblast, etc.** (Third-order political unit)**/Grafschaft, Oblast, usw.** (Politische Einheit dritter Ordnung)
**Condado, Oblast, etc.** (Unidad política de tercer orden)
**Comté, Oblast, etc.** (Subdivision administrative de troisième ordre)
**Condado, Oblast, etc.** (Unidade política de terceiro nível)

**Ambāla** / **Johnstown** — **County, Oblast, etc./Grafschaft, Oblast, usw.**
**Condado, Oblast, etc./Comté, Oblast, etc.**
**Condado, Oblast, etc.**

*ISERLOHN*

**Okrug, Kreis, etc.** (Fourth-order political unit)**/Okrug, Kreis, usw.** (Politische Einheit vierter Ordnung)
**Okrug, Kreis, etc.** (Unidad política de cuarto orden)
**Okrug, Kreis, etc.** (Subdivision administrative de quatrième ordre)
**Okrug, Kreis, etc.** (Unidade política de quarto nível)

**Iserlohn** — **Okrug, Kreis, etc./Okrug, Kreis, usw.**
**Okrug, Kreis, etc./Okrug, Kreis, etc.**
**Okrug, Kreis, etc.**

**City or Municipality** (may appear in combination with another boundary symbol)
**Stadt oder Gemeinde** (kann zusammen mit einem anderen Begrenzungssymbol erscheinen)
**Ciudad o Municipio** (puede aparecer en combinación con otro símbolo de límite)
**Ville ou Municipalité** (peut paraître en combinaison avec un autre symbole de limites politiques)
**Cidade ou Municipalidade** (Pode aparecer em combinação com outro símbolo de limite político)

*NORMANDIE* — **Historical Region** (No boundaries indicated)
**Historische Landschaft** (Grenzen werden nicht gezeigt)
**Región Histórica** (Sin indicación de límites)
**Région Historique** (Sans indication de frontières)
**Região Histórica** (Sem indicação de fronteiras)

# Legend to Maps / Zeichenerklärung
# Leyendas Para Mapas / Légende des Cartes / Legendas dos Mapas

## Transportation / Verkehr / Transporte / Transports / Transporte

| Road / Strasse / Camino / Route / Rodovia | 1:300,000 | 1:1,000,000 | 1:3,000,000<br>1:6,000,000 | 1:12,000,000 |
|---|---|---|---|---|
| Primary / Erster Ordnung / Principal / de premier ordre / Principal | PASSAIC EXPWY. (I-80) | PENNSYLVANIA TURNPIKE | | |
| Secondary / Zweiter Ordnung / Secundario / de second ordre / Secundária | BERLINER RING | | | |
| Tertiary / Dritter Ordnung / Terciario / de troisième ordre / Terciária | | | | |
| Minor Road, Trail / Weg, Pfad<br>Rodera, Vereda / Route secondaire, Piste / Caminho, trilha | | | | |

| Railway / Eisenbahn / Ferrocarril / Voie ferrée / Ferrovia | | | | |
|---|---|---|---|---|
| Primary / Hauptbahn / Principal / Principale / Principal | CANADIAN NATIONAL | SANTA FE | | |
| Secondary / Sonstige Bahn / Secundario / Secondaire / Secundária | | | | |
| *Rapid Transit / Schnellverkehr / Tránsito rápido / Métro / Trânsito rápido (metrô) | | | | |
| Airport / Flughafen / Aeropuerto / Aéroport / Aeroporto | LONDON (HEATHROW) AIRPORT | DULLES INTERNATIONAL AIRPORT | | |
| *Rail or Air Terminal / Bahnhof oder Flughafengebäude<br>Terminal ferroviaria o aéro / Gare ou aérogare<br>Terminal ferroviário ou aéreo (estação) | SÜD-BAHNHOF | | | |

REICHS-BRÜCKE — Bridge / Brücke / Puente / Pont / Ponte

GREAT ST. BERNARD TUNNEL — Tunnel / Tunnel / Túnel / Tunnel / Túnel

Houston Ship Channel — Shipping Channel / Schiffahrtsrinne
Canal maritimo / Chenal maritime
Canal marítimo

Canal du Midi — Navigable Canal / Schiffbarer Kanal
Canal navegable / Canal navigable
Canal navegável

Intracoastal Waterway / Küstenschiffahrtsweg
Vía fluvial Intracostera / Canal côtier
Via costeira interna

TO MALMÖ — Ferry / Fähre
Balsadera / Bac
Balsa

## Miscellaneous Cultural Features / Sonstige Objekte / Elementos Culturales Misceláneos
## Éléments Culturels Divers / Acidentes Culturais Diversos

PARQUE NACIONAL LANÍN — National or State Park or Monument
National- oder Naturpark oder Denkmal
Parque o Monumento nacional o provincial
Parc ou Monument national ou régional
Parque ou Monumento nacional ou regional

EDISON NAT. HIST. SITE — National or State Historic(al) Site, Memorial
Historische Stätte, Gedenkstätte
Sitio histórico nacional o provincial, Monumento
Site historique national ou régional, Mémorial
Sitio histórico nacional ou regional, Monumento histórico

SEMINOLE IND. RES. — Indian Reservation / Indianerreservation
Reserva de indios / Réserve indienne
Reserva Indígena

FORT DIX — Military Installation / Militäranlage
Instalación militar / Installation militaire
Instalação militar

GREENWOOD CEMETERY — * Cemetery / Friedhof
Cementerio / Cimetière / Cemitério

SORBONNE — Point of Interest (Battlefield, museum, temple, university, etc.)
Sehenswürdigkeit (Schlachtfeld, Museum, Tempel, Universität, usw.)
Punto de interés (Campo de batalla, museo, templo, universidad, etc.)
Curiosité (Champ de bataille, musée, temple, université, etc.)
Pontos de interesse (Campo de batalha, museu, templo, universidade, etc.)

STEPHANSDOM — Church, Monastery / Kirche, Kloster
Iglesia, Monasterio / Église, Monastère
Igreja, Mosteiro

UXMAL — Ruins / Ruinen / Ruinas / Ruines / Ruínas

WINDSOR CASTLE — Castle / Burg, Schloss / Castillo / Château / Castelo

* Lighthouse / Leuchtturm
Faro / Phare / Farol

ASWĀN DAM — Dam / Damm / Presa / Barrage
Represa (barragem)

* Lock / Schleuse / Esclusa
Écluse / Eclusa

Crib — * Water Intake Crib / Wasseraufnahmestation
Toma de agua / Prise d'eau / Captação de água

Quarry or Surface Mine
Steinbruch oder Tagebau
Cantera o Mina de hoyo abierto
Carrière ou Mine à ciel ouvert
Pedreira ou mina a céu aberto

Subsurface Mine / Bergwerk
Mina subterránea / Mine souterraine
Mina subterrânea

* Oil Well / Ölbohrturm
Pozo de petróleo / Puits de pétrole
Poço de petróleo

## Metric-English Equivalents / Umrechnung metrischer Masse in englische Masse / Métrico-Equivalentes Ingleses
## Equivalences métriques des mesures anglaises / Equivalentes métricos das medidas inglesas

Areas represented by one square centimeter at various map scales
Flächen die einem cm² in den verschiedenen Kartenmassstäben entsprechen
Áreas representados por un centímetro cuadrado a varias escalas de mapas
Surface représentée par un cm² aux échelles indiquées
Áreas representadas por cm² nas escalas indicadas nos mapas

Meter = 3.28 feet
Kilometer = 0.62 mile
Meter² (m²) = 10.76 square feet
Kilometer² (km²) = 0.39 square mile

| | | |
|---|---|---|
| 1:300,000<br>9 km²<br>3.48 square miles | 1:6,000,000<br>3,600 km²<br>1,390 square miles | 1:48,000,000<br>230,400 km²<br>88,934 square miles |
| 1:1,000,000<br>100 km²<br>39 square miles | 1:12,000,000<br>14,400 km²<br>5,558 square miles | |
| 1:3,000,000<br>900 km²<br>348 square miles | 1:24,000,000<br>57,600 km²<br>22,234 square miles | |

Elevation tints shown only on 1:3,000,000 and 1:6,000,000 scale maps
Höhenschichten erscheinen nur auf Karten im Massstab 1:3 000 000 und 1:6 000 000
Se indica las tintas de elevación sólo en los mapas de escala 1:3 000 000 y 1:6 000 000
Teintes hypsométriques exprimées seulement sur cartes à 1:3 000 000 et 1:6 000 000
Indicaram-se as graduações de cor hipsométricas somente nos mapas de escalas 1:3 000 000 e 1:6 000 000

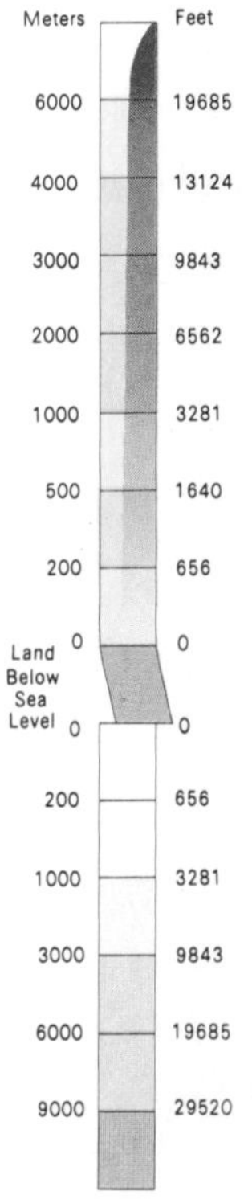
Meters
Feet
6000
19685
4000
13124
3000
9843
2000
6562
1000
3281
500
1640
200
656
Land 0
0
Below Sea Level 0
0
200
656
1000
3281
3000
9843
6000
19685
9000
29520

## Alternate Names / Alternative Namensformen / Nombres Alternativos
## Variantes Toponymiques / Variantes Toponímicas

**MOSKVA** MOSCOW
**Basel** Bâle

English or second official language names are shown in reduced size lettering
Englische Namen oder Namen in einer zweiten offiziellen Sprache erscheinen in kleineren Schriftgrössen
Los nombres en inglés o un segundo idioma oficial se muestran en tipo de imprenta mas pequeño
Les toponymes en anglais ou dans la seconde langue officielle sont indiqués en caractères plus petits
Os topônimos em inglês ou num segundo idioma oficial aparecem em tipologia menor

**VOLGOGRAD** (STALINGRAD)
**Ventura** (San Buenaventura)

Historical or other alternates in the local language are shown in parentheses
Historische oder alternative Namensformen einheimischen Sprache erscheinen in Klammern
Los nombres históricos y alternativos locales se muestran en paréntesis
Les noms historiques de lieux ou les variantes toponymiques locales sont mis entre parenthèses
Os topônimos históricos ou as variantes toponímicas locais aparecem entre parênteses

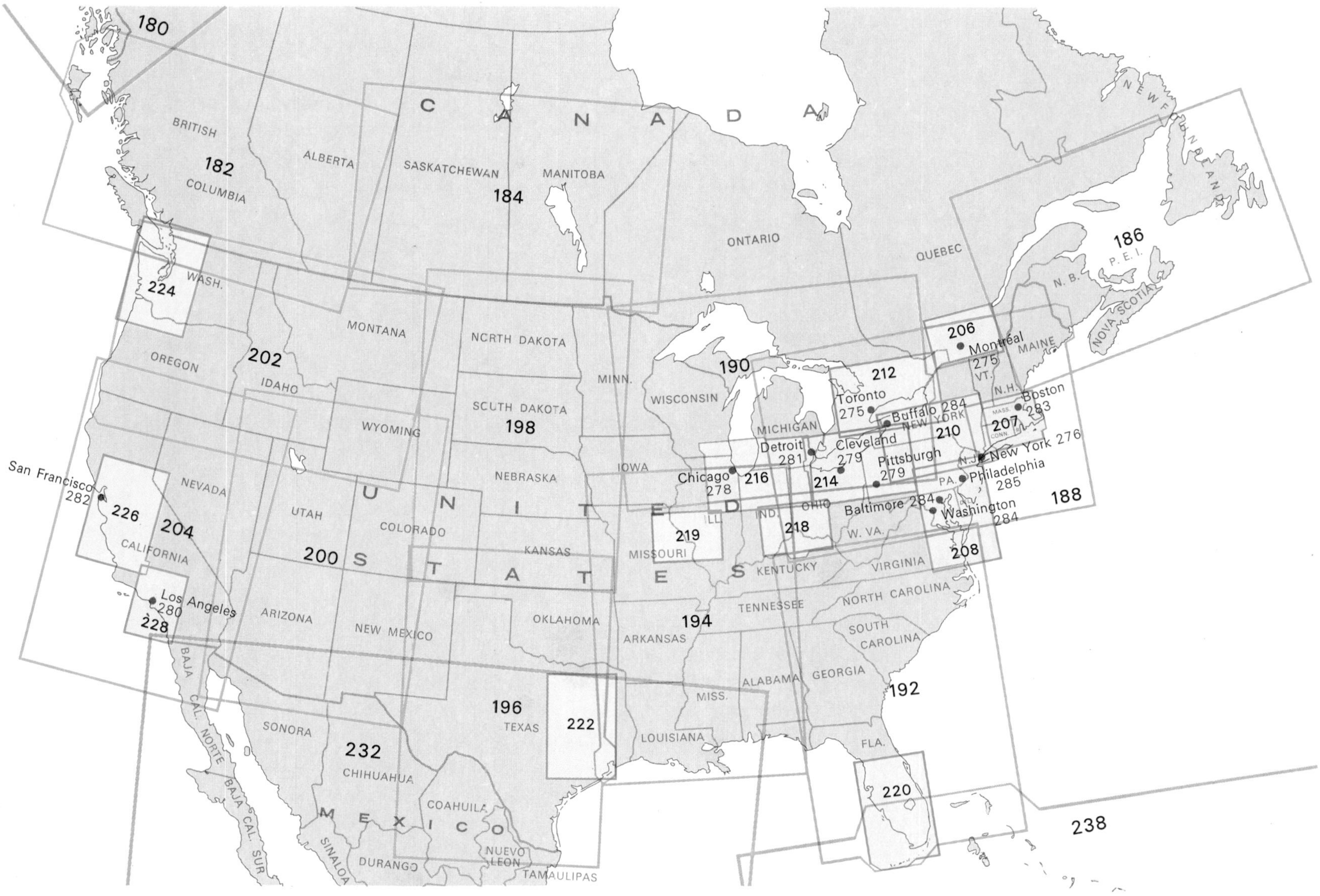
180
BRITISH COLUMBIA
182
ALBERTA
SASKATCHEWAN
MANITOBA
184
C A N A D A
ONTARIO
QUEBEC
NEWFOUNDLAND
186
P.E.I.
N.B.
NOVA SCOTIA
224
WASH.
MONTANA
NORTH DAKOTA
OREGON
202
IDAHO
MINN.
190
WISCONSIN
SOUTH DAKOTA
198
WYOMING
206
Montréal
275
VT.
MAINE
212
Toronto
275
N.H.
Boston
283
MICHIGAN
Buffalo 284
NEW YORK
210
207
MASS.
CONN.
R.I.
Detroit
281
Cleveland
279
Pittsburgh
279
N.J.
New York 276
Chicago
278
216
214
PA.
Philadelphia
285
IOWA
NEBRASKA
San Francisco
282
226
NEVADA
UTAH
204
U N I T E D
COLORADO
ILL.
IND.
218
OHIO
Baltimore 284
Washington
284
188
W. VA.
CALIFORNIA
200 S T A T E S
KANSAS
219
MISSOURI
KENTUCKY
VIRGINIA
208
Los Angeles
280
228
ARIZONA
NEW MEXICO
OKLAHOMA
194
ARKANSAS
TENNESSEE
NORTH CAROLINA
SOUTH CAROLINA
BAJA CAL. NORTE
ALABAMA
GEORGIA
MISS.
192
SONORA
196
TEXAS
222
232
CHIHUAHUA
LOUISIANA
FLA.
220
M E X I C O
COAHUILA
BAJA CAL. SUR
SINALOA
DURANGO
NUEVO LEON
TAMAULIPAS
238

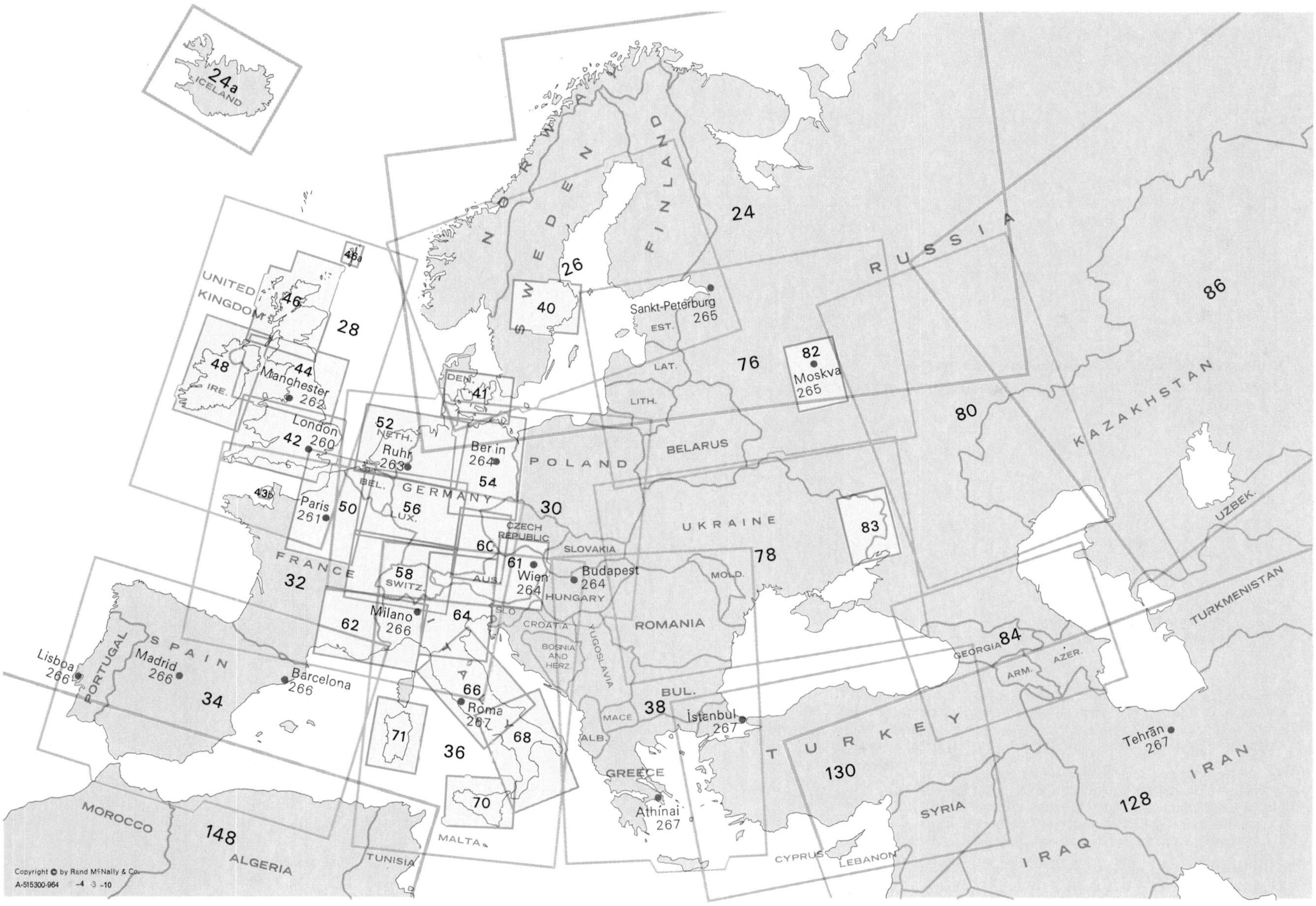
24a
ICELAND
46a
UNITED KINGDOM
46
28
48
IRE.
44
Manchester
262
London
260
42
43b
NORWAY
SWEDEN
FINLAND
26
40
24
Sankt-Peterburg
265
EST.
RUSSIA
86
82
Moskva
265
76
LAT.
LITH.
DEN.
41
52
NETH.
Ruhr
263
Berlin
264
POLAND
BELARUS
80
KAZAKHSTAN
BEL.
GERMANY
LUX.
56
54
30
Paris
261
50
CZECH REPUBLIC
SLOVAKIA
UKRAINE
83
UZBEK.
FRANCE
32
58
SWITZ.
60
61
AUS.
Wien
264
Budapest
264
HUNGARY
78
MOLD.
TURKMENISTAN
Milano
266
62
64
SLO.
CROATIA
ROMANIA
BOSNIA AND HERZ.
YUGOSLAVIA
GEORGIA
84
ARM.
AZER.
Lisboa
266
PORTUGAL
SPAIN
Madrid
266
34
Barcelona
266
ITALY
66
Roma
267
BUL.
38
MACE.
İstanbul
267
Tehrān
267
71
36
68
ALB.
T U R K E Y
130
IRAN
GREECE
70
Athínai
267
SYRIA
128
MOROCCO
148
ALGERIA
TUNISIA
MALTA
CYPRUS
LEBANON
IRAQ

ALEUTIAN ISLANDS
181a
ALASKA
180
GREENLAND
C A N A D A
182
184
186
202
190
188
198
U N I T E D
S T A T E S
204
200
194
192
196
BERMUDA
240a
229b 229c
229a
229d
HAWAII
232
M E X I C O
234
Ciudad de México
286
BAHAMAS
NEW PROVIDENCE
240b
CUBA
240p
HAITI
DOMINICAN REPUBLIC
PUERTO RICO
240m
SAINT CROIX
241n
JAMAICA
241q
238
ANTIGUA 240c
GUADELOUPE 241o
DOMINICA 240d
MARTINIQUE
240e
SAINT LUCIA 241f
BARBADOS 241g
SAINT VINCENT
241h
GRENADA
241k
TRINIDAD AND TOBAGO
241r
C a r i b b e a n S e a
NETH. ANTILLES 241s
BELIZE
GUAT.
HONDURAS
EL SALVADOR
NICARAGUA
236
COSTA RICA
Caracas
286
VENEZUELA
GUYANA
SURINAME
FRENCH GUIANA
P a c i f i c
O c e a n
246
COLOMBIA
GALAPAGOS ISLANDS
246a
ECUADOR
250
B R A Z I L
P E R U
Lima
286
248
BOLIVIA
255
SAMOA ISLANDS
175a
174y
MANUA ISLANDS
PARAGUAY
São Paulo
287
256
Rio de Janeiro
C H I L E
A R G E N T I N A
252
Santiago
286
Buenos Aires
288
URUGUAY
258
254
A t l a n t i c
O c e a n
ICELAND
24a
UNITED KINGDOM
IRE.
28
GERMANY
30
FRANCE
32
AZORES
148a
SPAIN
PORTUGAL
34
36
MOROCCO
148
ALGERIA
WESTERN SAHARA
CAPE VERDE
150a
MAURITANIA
MALI
NIGER
SENEGAL
GAMBIA
GUINEA-BISSAU
GUINEA
150
BURKINA FASO
NIGERIA
SIERRA LEONE
LIBERIA
COTE D'IVOIRE
GHANA
TOGO
BENIN
Lagos
273
CAMEROON
EQUAT. GUINEA
GABON

**MAP COVERAGE / KARTENAUSSCHNITTE**
**CONTENIDO DEL ATLAS / TABLEAU D'ASSEMBLAGE**
**ABRANGÊNCIA DO MAPA**

Map Scale

Manila 269 • 1:300,000

1:1,000,000 — 1:6,000,000

1:3,000,000 — 1:12,000,000

148 **Page Reference / Seitenangabe**
**Página de Referencia / Page de Référence / Página de Referência**

**Enlarged maps of Anglo-America and Europe on page xiii.**
**Vergrösserte Karten von Anglo-Amerika und Europa auf Seite xiii.**
**Mapas aumentados de América Anglosajona y Europa, página xiii.**
**Cartes à grande échelle de l'Amérique anglo-saxonne et de l'Europe à la page xiii.**
**Mapas ampliados da América Anglo-saxônica e da Europa, página xiii.**

**World, Ocean, and Continent maps on pages 2-19.**
**Weltkarten, Karten der Ozeane und Erdteile auf Seiten 2-19.**
**Mapas del Mundo, Océanos y Continentes, páginas 2-19.**
**Cartes du Monde, des Océans et des Continents aux pages 2-19.**
**Mapas do Mundo, dos Oceanos e dos Continentes, páginas 2-19.**

**Additional Pacific Ocean Island maps on pages 174-175.**
**Zusätzliche Karten der Inseln des Pazifischen Ozeans auf Seite 174-175.**
**Mapas adicionales de las Islas del Océano Pacífico, páginas174-175.**
**Cartes supplémentaires des Îles de l'Océan Pacifique aux pages 174-175.**
**Mapas suplementares das ilhas do Oceano Pacífico, páginas 174-175.**

RUSSIA
Pacific Ocean
Indian Ocean
24
76
80
86
88
89
KAZAKHSTAN
MONGOLIA
UKRAINE
78
Black Sea
Caspian Sea
TURKEY
130
84
85
UZBEKISTAN
TURKMENISTAN
KYRG.
TAJIKISTAN
CHINA
102
107
105
104
98
KOREA
92
94
96
93b
174m
175d
106
100
TAIWAN
IRAN
128
IRAQ
SYRIA
132
142
AFGHANISTAN
123
120
PAKISTAN
NEPAL
124
INDIA
126
EGYPT
SAUDI
ARABIA
OMAN
Red Sea
140
SUDAN
YEMEN
ERITREA
144
ETHIOPIA
SOMALIA
KENYA
TANZANIA
154
MOZAMBIQUE
COMOROS
157a
157b
157c
MADAGASCAR
MAURITIUS
REUNION
ZIMBABWE
MYANMAR
LAOS
THAILAND
VIETNAM
110
122
SRI LANKA
116
PHILIPPINES
175b
175c
MALAYSIA
114
BRUNEI
BORNEO
112
SUMATRA
INDONESIA
115a
115b
JAVA
CELEBES
PAPUA NEW GUINEA
NEW GUINEA
164
SOLOMON ISLANDS
175e
AUSTRALIA
162
166
168a
168b
169
170
171a
171b
TASMANIA
VANUATU
175f
175g
FIJI
NEW CALEDONIA
NEW ZEALAND
172
176
178
230
242
244
22
72
74
90
118
134
136
138
108
160

Selected Map References / Register Wichtiger Geographischer Namen / Selecciones de Referencias de los Mapas
Index Cartographique Abrégé / Referências a Mapas Selecionadas


Adriatic Sea 36-37
Aegean Sea 39
Afars and Issas, see Djibouti
Afghanistan 118-119
Africa 10-11
Alabama 195
Alaska 180-181
Albania 38-39
Alberta 184-185
Aleutian Islands 180-181
Algeria 148-149
Alps 33
American Samoa 175a
Andaman and Nicobar Islands 110-111
Andes 18-19
Andorra 35
Angola 152-153
Anguilla 239
Antarctica 9
Antigua and Barbuda 239
Appalachian Mountains 17
Arabian Peninsula 118
Arabian Sea 118-119
Aral Sea 86
Arctic Ocean 16
Argentina 244-245
Arizona 201
Arkansas 194-195
Armenia 84
Aruba 241s
Ascension 11
Asia 12-13
Asia Minor 23
Atlantic Ocean 8
Atlas Mountains 134-135
Australia 160-161
Australian Capital Territory 171b
Austria 30-31
Azerbaijan 84
Azores 148a
Bahamas 238-239
Bahrain 129
Baikal, Lake 88
Balearic Islands 35
Balkhash, Lake 87
Baltic Sea 24
Bangladesh 121
Barbados 241g
Belarus 76
Belgium 30
Belize 233
Bengal, Bay of 13
Benin 151
Bering Sea 16
Bermuda 240a
Bhutan 121
Bismarck Archipelago 165
Black Sea 23
Bolivia 248-249
Borneo 112-113
Bosnia and Herzegovina 36
Botswana 156-157
Brazil 242-245
British Columbia 182-183
British Honduras, see Belize
British Solomon Islands, see Solomon Islands
British Virgin Islands 240m
Brunei 113
Bulgaria 38-39
Burkina Faso 150-151
Burma see Myanmar
Burundi 154
California 204-205
Cambodia 110-111
Cameroon 135
Canada 176-177
Canary Islands 148
Cape Verde 150a
Caribbean Sea 238-239
Caroline Islands 14-15
Caspian Sea 72
Cayman Islands 238
Celebes 113
Central African Republic 135
Central America 236-237
Ceylon, see Sri Lanka
Chad 146-147
Channel Islands 43b
Chile 244
China 90-91
Cocos (Keeling) Islands 13
Colombia 246-247
Colorado 199-201
Comoros 157a
Congo 152
Connecticut 207
Cook Islands 15
Corsica 36-37
Costa Rica 237
Cote d'Ivoire 150-151
Crete 39
Croatia 36
Cuba 240p
Curacao 241s
Cyprus 130-131
Czech Republic 30-31
Dahomey, see Benin
Delaware 208-209
Denmark 26
Djibouti 144
Dominica 240d
Dominican Republic 239
Ecuador 246
Egypt 140
El Salvador 236
England 28-29
Equatorial Guinea 152
Erie, Lake 214-215
Eritrea 144
Estonia 76
Ethiopia 144-145
Europe 22-23
Faeroe Islands 22
Falkland Islands 254
Fiji 175g
Finland 24-25
Florida 193
France 32-33
French Guiana 250
French Polynesia 15
Gabon 152
Galapagos Islands 246a
Gambia 150
Georgia (U.S.) 192-193
Georgia 84
Germany 30-31
Ghana 151
Gibraltar 34
Gobi Desert 90-91
Great Britain, see United Kingdom
Great Lakes 190-191
Greece 39
Greenland 16
Grenada 241k
Guadeloupe 241o
Guam 174p
Guatemala 236
Guernsey 43b
Guinea 150
Guinea-Bissau 150
Guyana 247
Haiti 238-239
Hawaii 229d
Himalayas 120-121
Hispaniola 238-239
Holland, see Netherlands
Honduras 236-237
Hong Kong 271d
Hudson Bay 176-177
Hungary 31
Huron, Lake 191
Iceland 24a
Idaho 202-203
Illinois 190, 194
India 119
Indiana 194
Indian Ocean 6
Indonesia 108-109
Inner Mongolia 90-91
Iowa 190, 199
Iran 128-129
Iraq 128
Ireland 48-49
Isle of Man 44
Israel 132-133
Italy 36-37
Ivory Coast see Cote d'Ivoire
Jamaica 241q
Japan 92-93
Java 115a
Jersey 43b
Jordan 128
Kansas 199
Kazakhstan 72-73
Kentucky 192, 194
Kenya 154
Kiribati 15
Korea, North 99
Korea, South 99
Kuwait 128
Kyrgyzstan 85
Labrador 177
Laos 110
Latvia 76
Lebanon 128
Lesotho 159
Liberia 150
Libya 146-147
Liechtenstein 59
Lithuania 76
Louisiana 195
Luxembourg 56
Macau 101
Macedonia 38-39
Madagascar 157b
Madeira Islands 148
Maine 186
Malagasy Republic, see Madagascar
Malawi 155
Malaysia 112-113
Maldives 13
Mali 134-135
Malta 37
Manchuria 89
Manitoba 184-185
Maritime Provinces 186-187
Marshall Islands 15
Martinique 240e
Maryland 188-189
Massachusetts 207
Mauritania 134
Mauritius 157c
Mayotte 157a
Mediterranean Sea 10
Melanesia 14-15
Mexico 232-233
Mexico, Gulf of 231-232
Michigan 190-191
Michigan, Lake 190-191
Micronesia, Federated States of 14-15
Middle East 128-129
Midway Islands 174g
Minnesota 190, 198
Mississippi 195
Missouri 194
Moldova 78
Monaco 63
Mongolia 90-91
Montana 198, 202-203
Montserrat 239
Morocco 148-149
Mozambique 138-139
Myanmar 110-111
Namibia 156
Nauru 174b
Nebraska 199
Nepal 124-125
Netherlands 52-53
Netherlands Antilles 241s
Nevada 204-205
New Brunswick 186
New Caledonia 175f
Newfoundland 187
New Guinea 164-165
New Hampshire 189
New Hebrides, see Vanuatu
New Jersey 208, 211
New Mexico 196, 201
New South Wales 166-167
New York 188-189
New Zealand 172-173
Nicaragua 236-237
Niger 134-135
Nigeria 135
Niue 174v
Norfolk Island 174c
North America 16-17
North Carolina 192
North Dakota 198
Northern Ireland 48-49
Northern Mariana Islands 14
Northern Territory 160-161
North Sea 22
Northwest Territories 176-177
Norway 24-25
Nova Scotia 186-187
Nyasa, Lake 155
Ohio 188
Oklahoma 196
Oman 118
Ontario 176-177, 188-189
Ontario, Lake 212-213
Oregon 202
Orkney Islands 46
Pacific Ocean 6-7
Pakistan 120
Palau 14
Palestine 132-133
Panama 246
Papua New Guinea 165
Paraguay 249, 252-253
Pennsylvania 188-189
Persian Gulf 128-129
Peru 242
Philippines 116-117
Pitcairn 174e
Poland 31
Polynesia 15
Portugal 34
Portuguese Guinea, see Guinea-Bissau
Prince Edward Island 186
Puerto Rico 240m
Qatar 129
Quebec 177, 189
Queensland 161
Red Sea 137
Reunion 157c
Rhode Island 207
Rhodesia, see Zimbabwe
Rocky Mountains 16-17
Romania 38
Russia 72-75
Rwanda 154
Sahara Desert 134-135
St. Helena 11
St. Kitts and Nevis 239
St. Lucia 241f
St. Pierre and Miquelon 187
St. Vincent and the Grenadines 241h
San Marino 66
Sao Tome and Principe 152
Sardinia 71
Saskatchewan 184-185
Saudi Arabia 118
Scandinavia 24
Scotland 46-47
Senegal 150
Seychelles 139
Shetland Islands 46a
Siberia 74-75
Sicily 70
Sierra Leone 150
Singapore 271c
Sinkiang 90
Slovakia 31
Slovenia 36
Society Islands 15
Solomon Islands 175e
Somalia 144-145
South Africa 156-157
South America 18-19
South Australia 163
South Carolina 192
South China Sea 108
South Dakota 198-199
South Georgia 245
Southwest Africa, see Namibia
Spain 34-35
Spanish Sahara, see Western Sahara
Sri Lanka 122
Sudan 140-141
Sumatra 108
Superior, Lake 190-191
Suriname 250
Swaziland 159
Sweden 24
Switzerland 58-59
Syria 128
Taiwan 101
Tajikistan 72
Tanganyika, Lake 154-155
Tanzania 154-155
Tasmania 167
Tennessee 192, 194-195
Texas 196-197
Thailand 110-111
Tibet 90
Tierra del Fuego 254
Togo 151
Tokelau 15
Tonga 15
Transcaucasia 84
Transvaal 156-157
Trinidad and Tobago 241r
Tristan da Cunha 8
Tunisia 149
Turkey 130-131
Turkmenistan 72
Turks and Caicos Islands 239
Tuvalu 15
Uganda 154
Ukraine 78-79
United Arab Emirates 129
United Kingdom 28-29
United States 178-179
Ural Mountains 72-73
Uruguay 253
Utah 200-201
Uzbekistan 72
Vanuatu 175f
Vatican City 267a
Venezuela 246-247
Vermont 189
Victoria 167
Victoria, Lake 154
Vietnam 110-111
Virginia 188, 192
Virgin Islands 240m
Wake Island 174a
Wales 29
Wallis and Futuna 15
Washington 202
Western Australia 162
Western Sahara 148
Western Samoa 175a
West Indies 238-239
West Virginia 188, 192
White Russia, see Belarus
White Sea 25
Wisconsin 190
Wyoming 198-200, 202
Yellow Sea 91
Yemen 118
Yugoslavia 38-39
Yukon 181
Zaire 138
Zambia 138-139
Zanzibar 154
Zimbabwe 155

# World Scene

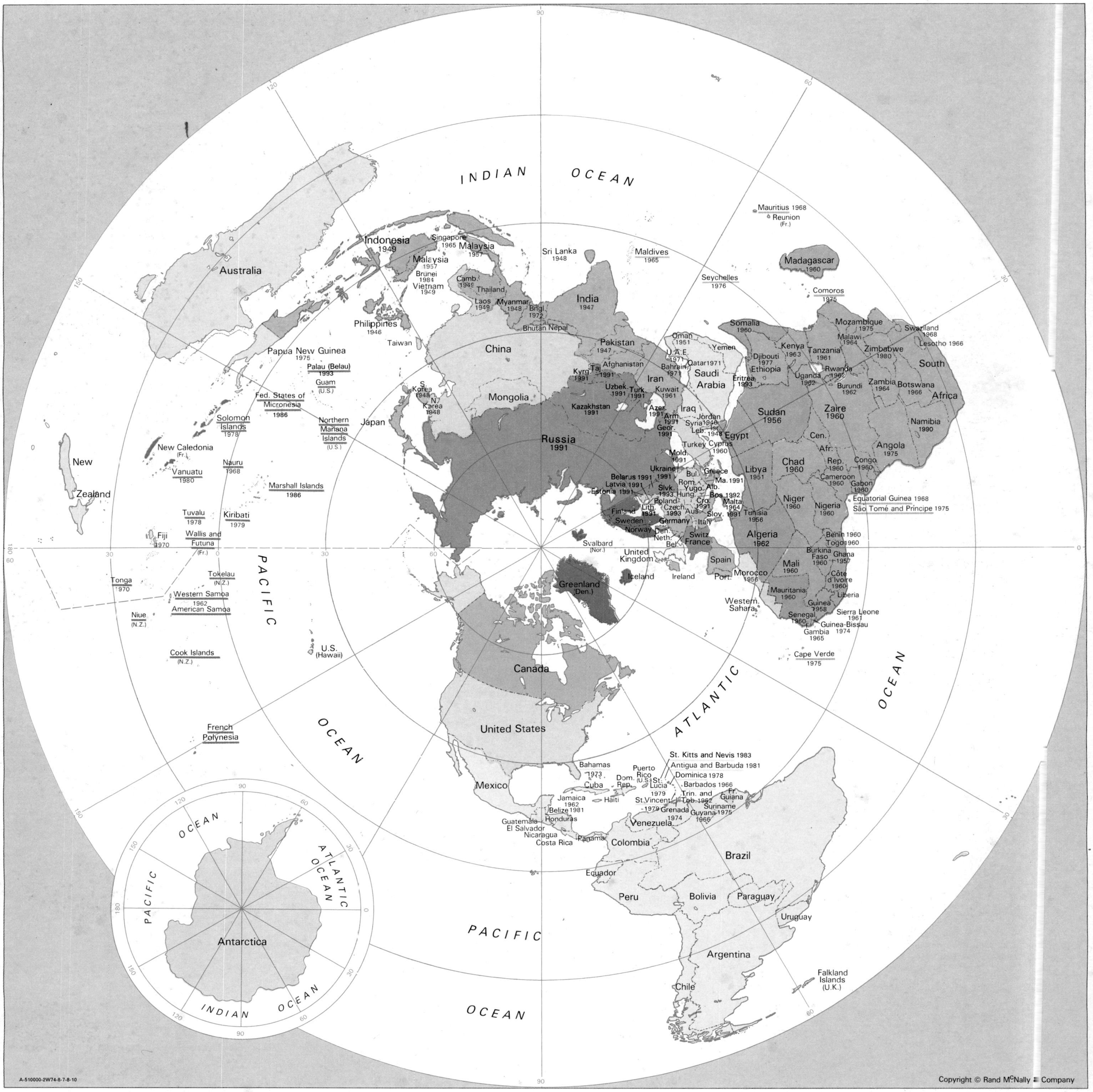
INDIAN OCEAN
PACIFIC OCEAN
ATLANTIC OCEAN
Australia
Indonesia 1949
Malaysia 1957
Singapore 1965
Brunei 1984
Vietnam 1949
Philippines 1946
Taiwan
Papua New Guinea 1975
Palau (Belau) 1993
Guam (U.S.)
Fed. States of Micronesia 1986
Northern Mariana Islands (U.S.)
Solomon Islands 1978
New Caledonia (Fr.)
Nauru 1968
Vanuatu 1980
Marshall Islands 1986
Tuvalu 1978
Kiribati 1979
Fiji 1970
Wallis and Futuna (Fr.)
Tonga 1970
Tokelau (N.Z.)
Western Samoa 1962
American Samoa
Niue (N.Z.)
Cook Islands (N.Z.)
French Polynesia
U.S. (Hawaii)
New Zealand
Japan
China
Mongolia
Russia 1991
Kazakhstan 1991
India 1947
Sri Lanka 1948
Maldives 1965
Pakistan 1947
Afghanistan
Iran
Saudi Arabia
Egypt
Sudan 1956
Libya 1951
Chad 1960
Niger 1960
Nigeria 1960
Algeria 1962
Mali 1960
Mauritania 1960
Morocco 1956
Western Sahara
Spain
Port.
Ireland
United Kingdom
Iceland
France
Greenland (Den.)
Svalbard (Nor.)
Madagascar 1960
Mauritius 1968
Reunion (Fr.)
Seychelles 1976
Comoros 1975
Somalia 1960
Kenya 1963
Tanzania 1961
Zaire 1960
Angola 1975
Namibia 1990
Botswana 1966
South Africa
Zimbabwe 1980
Mozambique 1975
Cape Verde 1975
Canada
United States
Mexico
St. Kitts and Nevis 1983
Antigua and Barbuda 1981
Dominica 1978
Barbados 1966
Venezuela
Colombia
Brazil
Ecuador
Peru
Bolivia
Paraguay
Uruguay
Argentina
Chile
Falkland Islands (U.K.)
Antarctica
A-510000-2W74-8-7-8-10
Copyright © Rand McNally & Company

## Intergovernmental Organizations: September 1, 1994

The admission of scores of new countries to the world community after World War II, indicated on the map above by the dates of their independence, created certain opportunities for these new countries that had formerly been the prerogative of a much smaller community of independent states. Until the 19th century, the countries to which international law was applicable was confined to the principal states of Europe and such others, like those of the Americas, as had asserted their independence and right to be treated as equals, or those older kingdoms and states like Siam and Ethiopia that had preserved their independence in an era of colonialism and had, perforce, to be treated as equals in treaty relationships. But equality as a matter of international law does not constitute equality of opportunity, identity of national interest, or safety from aggression. Consequently, despite the aims and achievements of the United Nations, there remains the need for intergovernmental organizations as a means for small *and* large countries to promote economic advancement, military security, or to assert their cultural identity with a stronger voice than a single country might possess. The organizations shown represent some of the principal regional and mutual-interest organizations created to advance those interests.

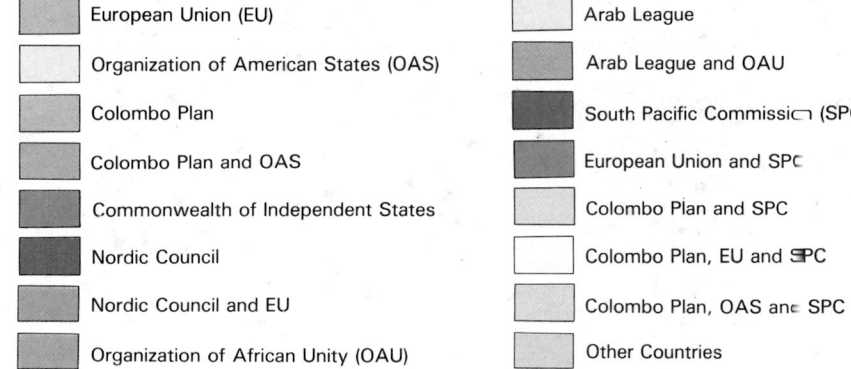

- European Union (EU)
- Organization of American States (OAS)
- Colombo Plan
- Colombo Plan and OAS
- Commonwealth of Independent States
- Nordic Council
- Nordic Council and EU
- Organization of African Unity (OAU)
- Arab League
- Arab League and OAU
- South Pacific Commission (SPC)
- European Union and SPC
- Colombo Plan and SPC
- Colombo Plan, EU and SPC
- Colombo Plan, OAS and SPC
- Other Countries

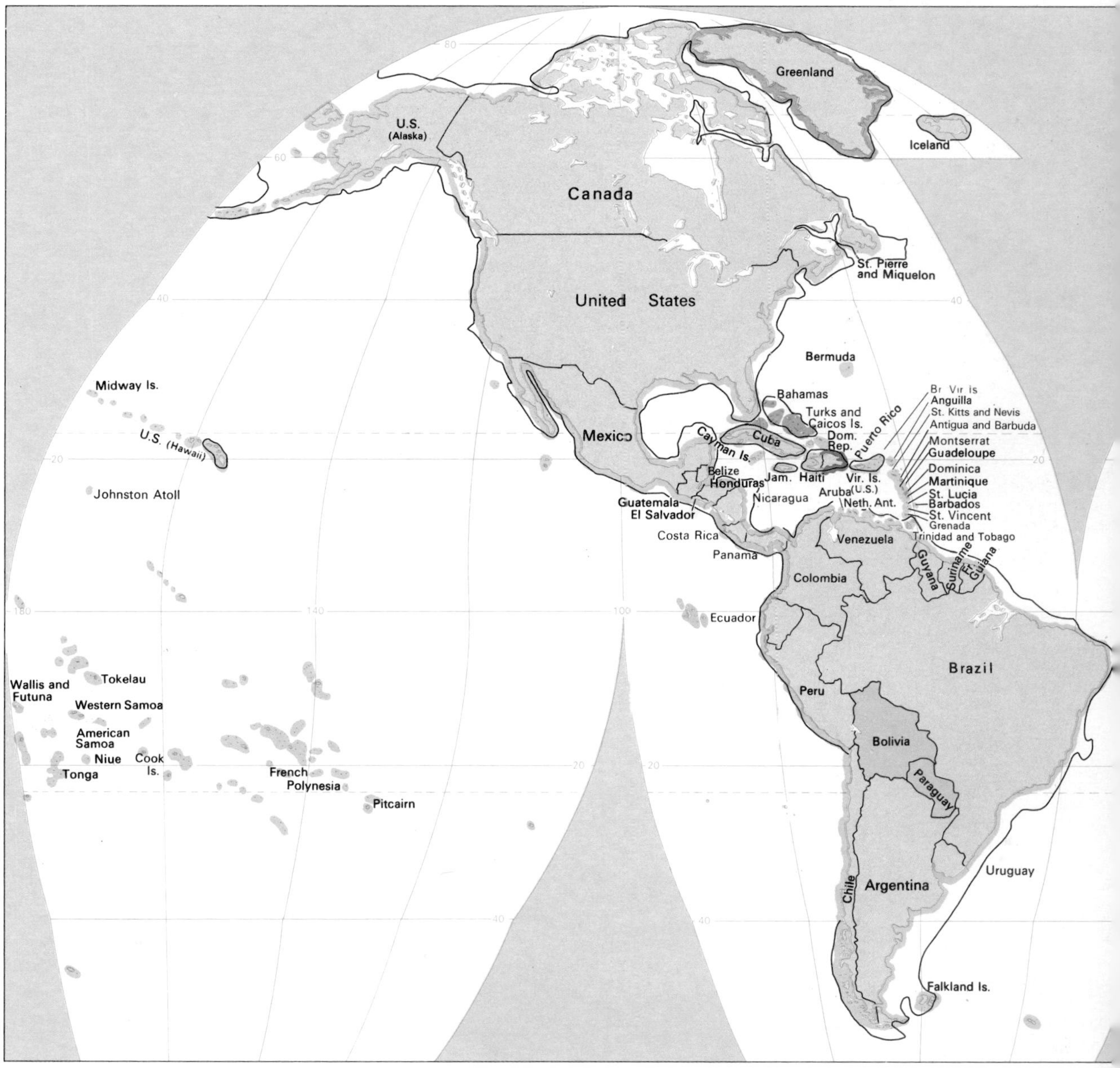
Greenland
Iceland
U.S.
(Alaska)
Canada
United States
St. Pierre
and Miquelon
Bermuda
Midway Is.
U.S. (Hawaii)
Johnston Atoll
Mexico
Bahamas
Turks and
Caicos Is.
Cuba
Cayman Is.
Dom.
Rep.
Puerto Rico
Jam.
Haiti
Belize
Honduras
Guatemala
El Salvador
Nicaragua
Costa Rica
Panama
Vir. Is.
(U.S.)
Aruba
Neth. Ant.
Br. Vir. Is.
Anguilla
St. Kitts and Nevis
Antigua and Barbuda
Montserrat
Guadeloupe
Dominica
Martinique
St. Lucia
Barbados
St. Vincent
Grenada
Trinidad and Tobago
Venezuela
Guyana
Suriname
Fr. Guiana
Colombia
Ecuador
Brazil
Peru
Bolivia
Paraguay
Chile
Argentina
Uruguay
Falkland Is.
Wallis and
Futuna
Tokelau
Western Samoa
American
Samoa
Niue
Cook
Is.
Tonga
French
Polynesia
Pitcairn

## Seaward Claims

### Common territorial sea claims

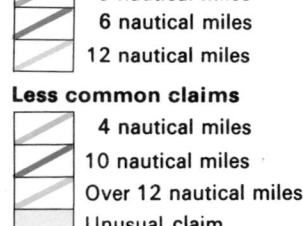

- 3 nautical miles
- 6 nautical miles
- 12 nautical miles

### Less common claims

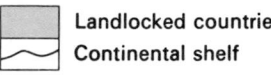

- 4 nautical miles
- 10 nautical miles
- Over 12 nautical miles
- Unusual claim

### Other features

- Landlocked countries
- Continental shelf

Note: Territorial claims of outlying islands to their offshore waters are the same as those of the administering country.

The growth of international law on the legal status of the portions of the seas claimed by coastal states probably began in the early 17th century, when conflicting claims to parts of the high seas by colonial and exploring European sea powers induced the Dutch jurist Hugo Grotius to write *Mare liberum* (1609), on the concept of the "free, or open, sea." His work was answered in 1617-18 by John Selden's *Mare clausum*, proposing that the seas were as subject to property rights and claims as land areas. The first successful synthesis of the two positions was Cornelis van Bynkershoek's *De dominio maris* (1702) in which he suggested that the seaward limit of a national claim should be that of its effective land-based control (the distance of a cannon-shot, three nautical miles). Though never universally accepted, that standard persisted well into the twentieth century.

After World War II, however, both traditional sea-based economic activity—fishing, commercial navigation—and activities made newly possible or intensified by technological change—exploitation of the seabed, pollution, scientific investigation—led coastal states to make increasingly wider claims to both territorial seas, those wholly subject to national law, and to zones in which some, but not all, sovereign rights were claimed, usually to protect economic, but especially fishing, interests. The first Law of the Sea Conference in 1958 attempted under UN auspices to codify international law in these areas. More than 14 years later at the final meeting of the Third Conference, a text representing the efforts of some 150 countries was opened for signature on Dec. 10, 1982 as the *United Nations Convention on the Law of the Sea*. Accessions were deposited that day by 119 states to a document providing definitions, guidelines, procedures, and institutions to govern a wide range of maritime law and activities.

Among the subjects relating to sovereignty delimited by the Convention were sections defining the rights, jurisdiction, and duties of coastal states in matters relating to the territorial sea, the right of innocent passage, international straits, archipelagic (island) states, exclusive economic zones (EEZ's), the continental shelf, the high seas, as well as access to, and use of, areas of the sea beyond the jurisdiction of a single national power.

Territorial sea may be claimed up to a distance of 12 nautical miles (n.m.) from either the shoreline of a coastal state (measured from low water on navigational charts), or from a straight baseline defined by the state when its shoreline is very irregular, as is that of Norway. Waters directly connected to the sea behind this baseline are called internal waters, and include bays (which may be closed at the mouth by a single baseline if they are less than 24 n.m. wide, and river mouths and estuaries. A zone contiguous to the territorial sea not wider than 24 n.m. beyond the baselines defining the territorial sea is defined in which states may exercise *limited* control for customs, immigration, fiscal, or sanitary reasons. Another zone, defined in relation to the continental shelf (the seaward prolongation of the coastal landmass beneath the sea) permits extension of the national sovereignty over the seabed and subsoil of the zone to the edge of the continental margin (the lower termination of the continental slope and rise) for purposes of exploration, scientific study, or economic exploitation of either biological or mineral resources.

In areas of the seas where coastal states lie in close proximity, the seaward extension of a national boundary may necessitate the drawing or negotiation of an international boundary in the sea. Where claims permissible under the Convention overlap, as in the Persian Gulf, median lines must be drawn so as to accommodate each state's maximum claim without disadvantaging bordering states.

The table opposite provides a description of the nature of current national claims to territorial seas and of the economic, usually fishing, zones that have been declared *within* the permissible 200-n.m. limits of the potential EEZ permitted by the Convention.

### Offshore zones

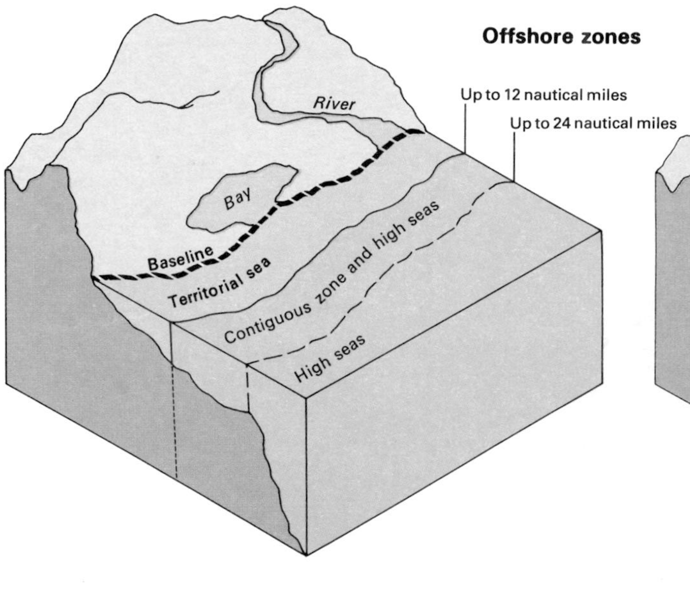
River
Bay
Baseline
Territorial sea
Contiguous zone and high seas
High seas
Up to 12 nautical miles
Up to 24 nautical miles

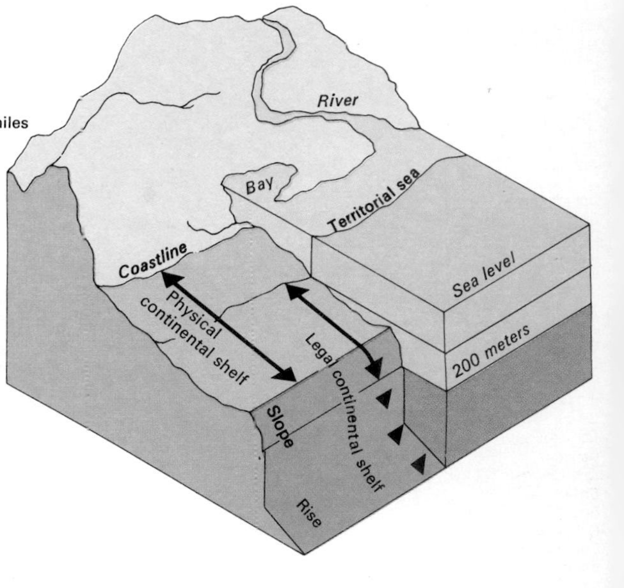
River
Bay
Territorial sea
Coastline
Sea level
200 meters
Physical continental shelf
Legal continental shelf
Slope
Rise

### Irregular coastline of Norway

**Norway measures its territorial sea from a straight baseline, which in general runs along the outer fringe of offshore islands and coastal promontories. The Law of the Sea Convention permits this type of claim in the case of highly irregular coastlines fringed with islands. In other cases the coastal features do not justify such claims to additional waters, and the claims may not be recognized.**

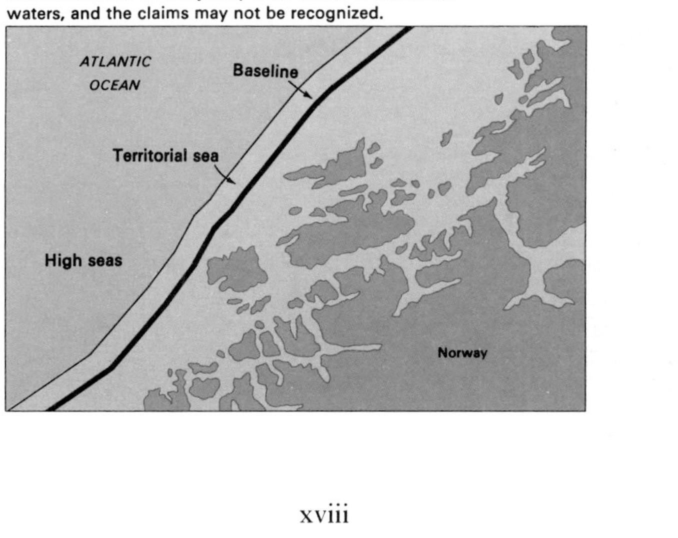
ATLANTIC
OCEAN
Baseline
Territorial sea
High seas
Norway

### Overlapping claims in the Persian Gulf

**The waters of the Persian Gulf are less than 200 meters in depth and the entire seabed is continental shelf. To determine the extent of jurisdiction that each state has over the resources of the seabed beyond its territorial sea, the Law of the Sea Convention provides for median lines, measured from the same baseline as the territorial sea. The median lines divide the continental shelf between opposite and adjacent states.**

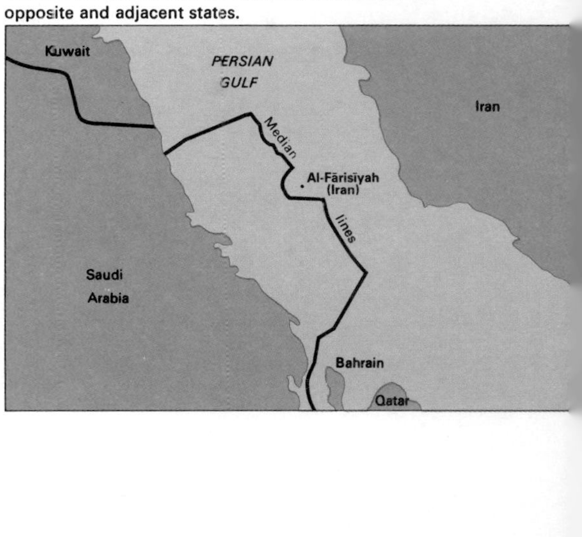
Kuwait
PERSIAN
GULF
Iran
Median lines
Al-Fārisīyah
(Iran)
Saudi
Arabia
Bahrain
Qatar

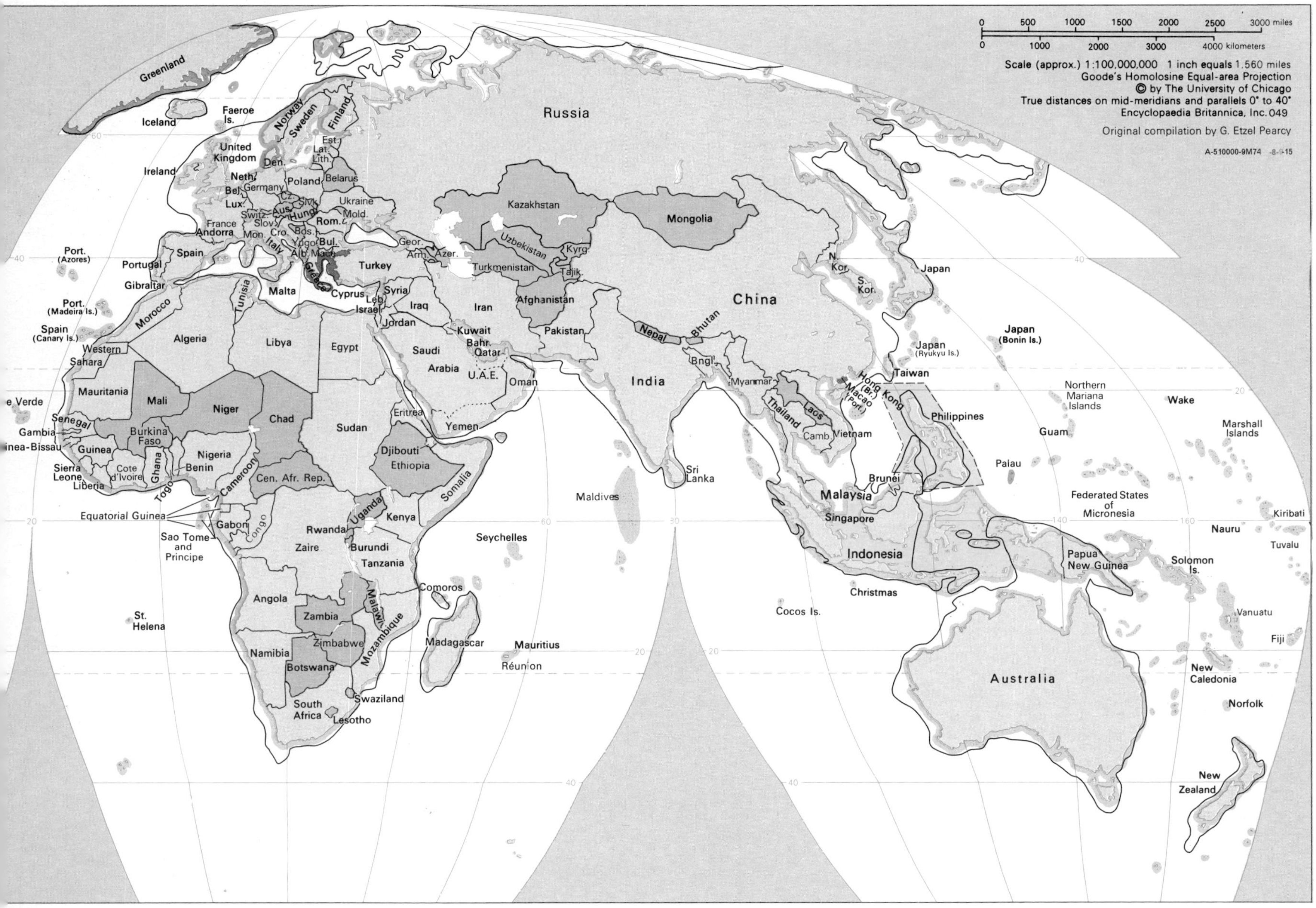

0 500 1000 1500 2000 2500 3000 miles
0 1000 2000 3000 4000 kilometers
Scale (approx.) 1:100,000,000 1 inch equals 1,560 miles
Goode's Homolosine Equal-area Projection
© by The University of Chicago
True distances on mid-meridians and parallels 0° to 40°
Encyclopaedia Britannica, Inc. 049
Original compilation by G. Etzel Pearcy
A-510000-9M74
Greenland
Iceland
Faeroe Is.
Norway
Sweden
Finland
Russia
Ireland
United Kingdom
Den.
Est.
Lat.
Lith.
Neth.
Bel.
Germany
Poland
Belarus
Lux.
Switz.
Aus.
Slvk.
Hung.
Ukraine
Mold.
Rom.
France
Andorra
Mon.
Slov.
Cro.
Bos.
Yugo.
Bul.
Italy
Alb.
Mace.
Port. (Azores)
Portugal
Spain
Gibraltar
Malta
Greece
Turkey
Geor.
Arm.
Azer.
Kazakhstan
Uzbekistan
Kyrg.
Turkmenistan
Tajik.
Mongolia
N. Kor.
S. Kor.
Japan
China
Cyprus
Leb.
Israel
Syria
Iraq
Iran
Afghanistan
Jordan
Kuwait
Bahr.
Qatar
Saudi Arabia
U.A.E.
Oman
Pakistan
Nepal
Bhutan
Bngl.
India
Myanmar
Thailand
Laos
Camb.
Vietnam
Hong Kong (Br.)
Macao (Port.)
Taiwan
Japan (Ryukyu Is.)
Japan (Bonin Is.)
Philippines
Northern Mariana Islands
Guam
Wake
Marshall Islands
Palau
Federated States of Micronesia
Kiribati
Nauru
Tuvalu
Brunei
Malaysia
Singapore
Indonesia
Papua New Guinea
Solomon Is.
Vanuatu
Fiji
Christmas
Cocos Is.
Australia
New Caledonia
Norfolk
New Zealand
Port. (Madeira Is.)
Spain (Canary Is.)
Morocco
Tunisia
Algeria
Libya
Egypt
Western Sahara
Mauritania
Mali
Niger
Chad
Sudan
Eritrea
Yemen
Djibouti
Ethiopia
Somalia
Senegal
Gambia
Burkina Faso
Guinea
Sierra Leone
Liberia
Cote d'Ivoire
Ghana
Togo
Benin
Nigeria
Cameroon
Cen. Afr. Rep.
Equatorial Guinea
Sao Tome and Principe
Gabon
Congo
Zaire
Uganda
Kenya
Rwanda
Burundi
Tanzania
Seychelles
Maldives
Sri Lanka
Comoros
Angola
Zambia
Malawi
Mozambique
Zimbabwe
Namibia
Botswana
Madagascar
Mauritius
Réunion
Swaziland
South Africa
Lesotho
St. Helena


| Political Unit | Territorial sea claim* | Exclusive economic zone*† |
|---|---|---|
| Albania | 12 A | |
| Algeria | 12 A | |
| Angola | 20 A | 200 D |
| Antigua and Barbuda | 12 C | 200 |
| Argentina | 12 A | 200 |
| Australia | 12 A | 200 |
| Bahamas | 3 | 200 D |
| Bahrain | 12 | |
| Bangladesh | 12 A | 200 |
| Barbados | 12 | 200 |
| Belgium | 12 | 200 D |
| Belize | 3-12 | 200 |
| Benin | 200 | |
| Bermuda | 12 B | 200 D |
| Brazil | 12 | 200 |
| Brunei | 12 | 200 |
| Bulgaria | 12 A | 200 |
| Cambodia | 12 A | 200 |
| Cameroon | 50 A | |
| Canada | 12 A | 200 D |
| Cape Verde | 12 C | 200 |
| Chile | 12 A | 200 |
| China | 12 A | |
| Colombia | 12 A | 200 |
| Comoros | 12 C | 200 |
| Congo | 200 | |
| Cook Islands | 12 B | 200 |
| Costa Rica | 12 | 200 |
| Cote d'Ivoire | 12 | 200 |
| Croatia | 12 | |
| Cuba | 12 A | 200 |
| Cyprus | 12 | |
| Denmark | 3 A | 200 D |
| Djibouti | 12 | 200 |
| Dominica | 12 | 200 |
| Dominican Republic | 6 A | 200 |
| Ecuador | 200 A | |
| Egypt | 12 A | 200 |
| El Salvador | 200 | |
| Equatorial Guinea | 12 | 200 |
| Eritrea | 12 A | |
| Estonia | 12 | 200 |
| Faeroe Islands | 3 B | 200 D |
| Falkland Islands | 12 B | 200 D |
| Fiji | 12 C | 200 |
| Finland | 4 A | 12 D |
| France | 12 A | 200 |
| French Guiana | 12 B | 200 |
| French Polynesia | 12 B | 200 |
| Gabon | 12 | 200 |
| Gambia | 12 | 200 D |
| Georgia | 12 | |
| Germany | 3-16 A | 200 D |
| Ghana | 12 | 200 |
| Greece | 6 | |
| Greenland | 3 B | 200 D |
| Grenada | 12 | 200 |
| Guatemala | 12 A | 200 |
| Guinea | 12 A | 200 |
| Guinea-Bissau | 12 A | 200 |
| Guyana | 12 | 200 D |
| Haiti | 12 A | 200 |
| Honduras | 12 | 200 |
| Iceland | 12 A | 200 |
| India | 12 | 200 |
| Indonesia | 12 C | 200 |
| Iran | 12 A | 200 |
| Iraq | 12 | |
| Ireland | 12 A | 200 D |
| Israel | 12 | |
| Italy | 12 | |
| Jamaica | 12 | 200 |
| Japan | 12 | 200 D |
| Jordan | 3 | |
| Kenya | 12 A | 200 |
| Kiribati | 12 C | 200 |
| Korea, North | 12 | 200 |
| Korea, South | 12 A | |
| Kuwait | 12 A | |
| Latvia | 12 | |
| Lebanon | 12 | |
| Liberia | 200 | |
| Libya | 12 A | |
| Lithuania | 12 | |
| Madagascar | 12 A | 200 |
| Malaysia | 12 A | 200 |
| Maldives | 12 | 35-310 |
| Malta | 12 A | 25 D |
| Marshall Islands | 12 C | 200 |
| Mauritania | 12 A | 200 |
| Mauritius | 12 A | 200 |
| Mexico | 12 A | 200 |
| Micronesia, Fed. States of | 12 | 200 |
| Morocco | 12 A | 200 |
| Mozambique | 12 A | 200 |
| Myanmar | 12 A | 200 |
| Namibia | 12 | 200 |
| Nauru | 12 | 200 D |
| Netherlands | 12 A | 200 D |
| New Caledonia | 12 B | 200 |
| New Zealand | 12 | 200 |
| Nicaragua | 200 | |
| Nigeria | 30 | 200 |
| Northern Mariana Islands | 12 B | 200 |
| Norway | 4 A | 200 |
| Oman | 12 A | 200 |
| Pakistan | 12 | 200 |
| Palau | 3 | 200 |
| Panama | 200 A | |
| Papua New Guinea | 12 C | 200 D |
| Peru | 200 | |
| Philippines | | 200 |
| Poland | 12 A | 200 |
| Portugal | 12 A | 200 |
| Puerto Rico | 12 B | 200 |
| Qatar | 12 | 200 |
| Romania | 12 | 200 |
| Russia | 12 A | 200 |
| St. Kitts and Nevis | 12 | 200 |
| Saint Lucia | 12 | 200 |
| St. Pierre and Miquelon | 12 B | 200 |
| St. Vincent and the Grenadines | 12 c | 200 |
| Sao Tome and Principe | 12 C | 200 |
| Saudi Arabia | 12 A | |
| Senegal | 12 A | 200 |
| Seychelles | 12 | 200 |
| Sierra Leone | 200 | |
| Singapore | 3 | 12 D |
| Slovenia | 12 | |
| Solomon Islands | 12 | 200 |
| Somalia | 200 A | |
| South Africa | 12 | 200 D |
| Spain | 12 A | 200 |
| Sri Lanka | 12 A | 200 |
| Sudan | 12 A | |
| Suriname | 12 | 200 |
| Sweden | 12 A | 200 |
| Syria | 35 A | |
| Taiwan | 12 | 200 |
| Tanzania | 12 A | 200 |
| Thailand | 12 A | 200 |
| Togo | 30 | 200 |
| Tonga | 12 A | 200 |
| Trinidad and Tobago | 12 C | 200 |
| Tunisia | 12 A | |
| Turkey | 6-12 A | 200 E |
| Tuvalu | 12 | 200 |
| Ukraine | 12 | 200 |
| United Arab Emirates | 12 | 200 |
| United Kingdom | 12 A | 200 D |
| United States | 12 | 200 |
| Uruguay | 200 | |
| Vanuatu | 12 | 200 |
| Venezuela | 12 A | 200 |
| Vietnam | 12 A | 200 |
| Western Samoa | 12 | 200 |
| Yemen | 12 | 200 |
| Yugoslavia | 12 A | |
| Zaire | 12 | 200 |

* Nautical miles
† When claim is beyond the territorial sea.
Data as of September 1, 1994.

A. Measured from a straight baseline.
B. Same as that of administering country.
C. Extends beyond a perimeter drawn around archipelago.
D. Fishing claim.
E. Black Sea only.

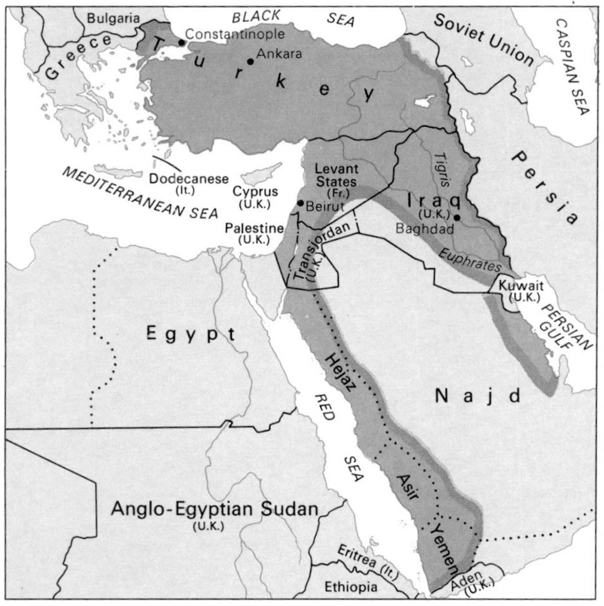
Bulgaria
BLACK SEA
Soviet Union
CASPIAN SEA
Greece
Constantinople
Ankara
Turkey
Persia
Dodecanese (It.)
MEDITERRANEAN SEA
Cyprus (U.K.)
Levant States (Fr.)
Beirut
Iraq (U.K.)
Baghdad
Tigris
Euphrates
Palestine (U.K.)
Transjordan (U.K.)
Kuwait (U.K.)
PERSIAN GULF
Egypt
Hejaz
Najd
RED SEA
Asir
Yemen
Anglo-Egyptian Sudan (U.K.)
Eritrea (It.)
Ethiopia
Aden (U.K.)

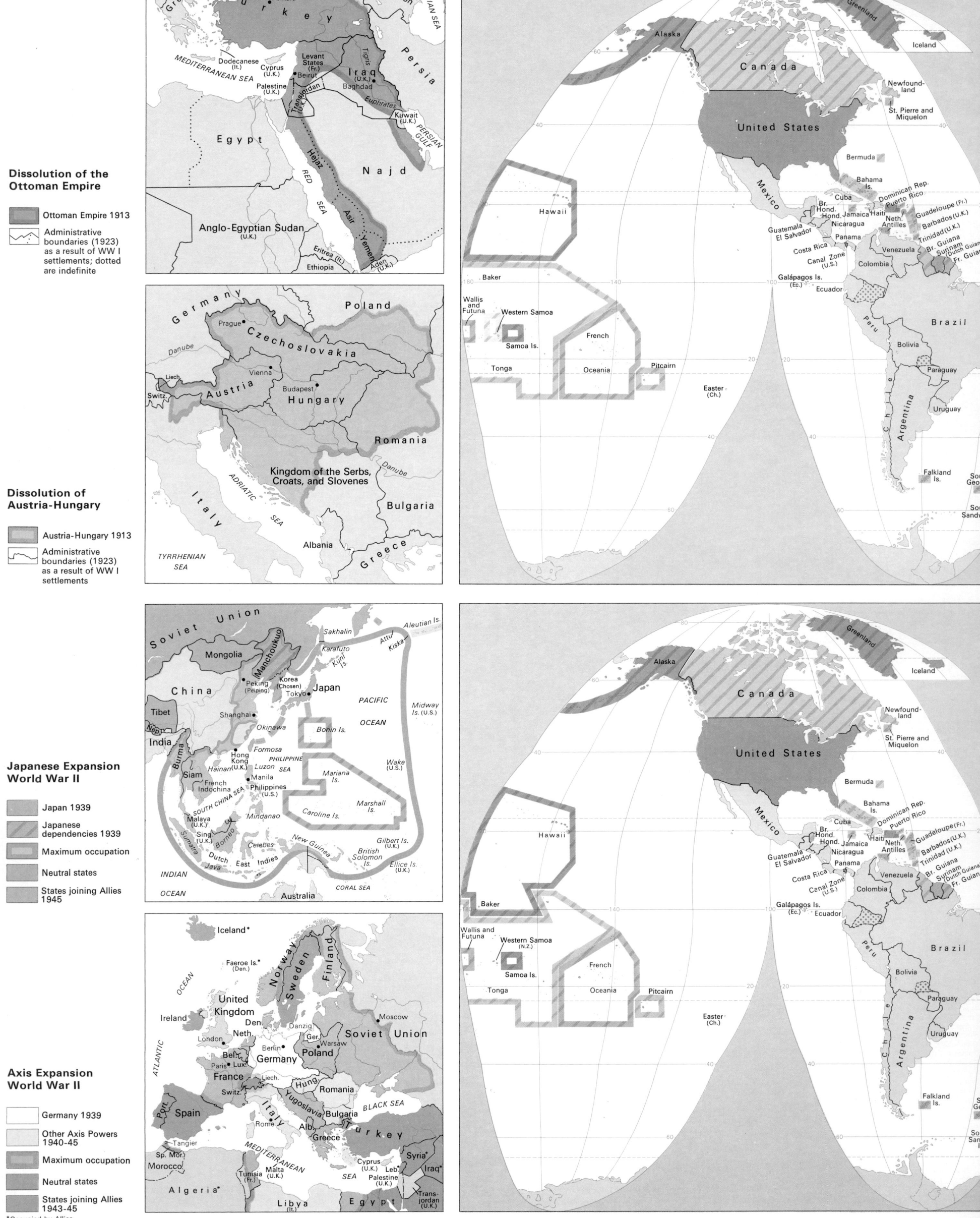

## Dissolution of the Ottoman Empire

- Ottoman Empire 1913
- Administrative boundaries (1923) as a result of WW I settlements; dotted are indefinite

Germany
Poland
Prague
Czechoslovakia
Danube
Vienna
Liech.
Switz.
Austria
Budapest
Hungary
Romania
Kingdom of the Serbs, Croats, and Slovenes
Danube
Italy
ADRIATIC SEA
Bulgaria
Albania
Greece
TYRRHENIAN SEA

## Dissolution of Austria-Hungary

- Austria-Hungary 1913
- Administrative boundaries (1923) as a result of WW I settlements

Soviet Union
Sakhalin
Aleutian Is.
Karafuto
Attu
Kiska
Mongolia
Manchoukuo
Kuril Is.
China
Peking (Peiping)
Korea (Chosen)
Tokyo
Japan
PACIFIC
OCEAN
Midway Is. (U.S.)
Tibet
Shanghai
Nepal
India
Okinawa
Bonin Is.
Burma
Formosa
Hong Kong (U.K.)
Hainan
PHILIPPINE SEA
Luzon
Wake (U.S.)
Siam
Manila
Mariana Is.
French Indochina
Philippines (U.S.)
SOUTH CHINA SEA
Marshall Is.
Malaya (U.K.)
Mindanao
Caroline Is.
Sumatra
Sing. (U.K.)
Borneo
Celebes
New Guinea
Gilbert Is. (U.K.)
Dutch East Indies
British Solomon Is.
Java
Ellice Is. (U.K.)
INDIAN OCEAN
Australia
CORAL SEA

## Japanese Expansion World War II

- Japan 1939
- Japanese dependencies 1939
- Maximum occupation
- Neutral states
- States joining Allies 1945

Iceland*
Faeroe Is.* (Den.)
OCEAN
Norway
Sweden
Finland
United Kingdom
Ireland
Den.
Moscow
Danzig
Neth.
Ger.
London
Warsaw
Soviet Union
Berlin
ATLANTIC
Bel.
Poland
Paris
Lux.
Germany
France
Liech.
Switz.
Hung.
Romania
Port.
Spain
Yugoslavia
Bulgaria
BLACK SEA
Italy
Rome
Alb.
Turkey
Greece
Tangier
Sp. Mor.
Morocco
MEDITERRANEAN SEA
Cyprus (U.K.)
Syria*
Leb.*
Iraq*
Malta (U.K.)
Tunisia (Fr.)
Palestine (U.K.)
Algeria*
Libya (It.)
Egypt
Trans-jordan (U.K.)

## Axis Expansion World War II

- Germany 1939
- Other Axis Powers 1940-45
- Maximum occupation
- Neutral states
- States joining Allies 1943-45

*Occupied by Allies

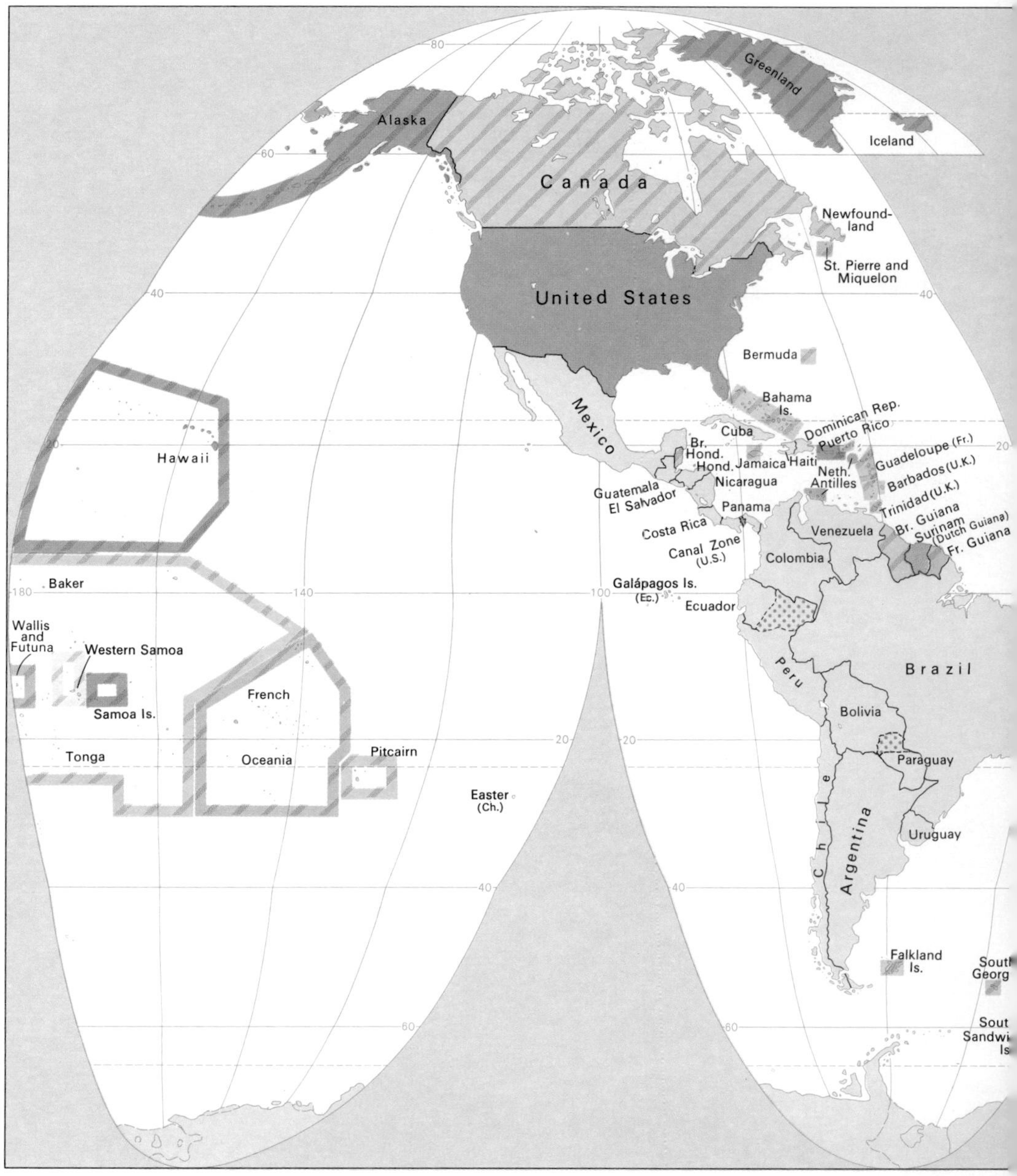
Greenland
Alaska
Iceland
Canada
Newfoundland
St. Pierre and Miquelon
United States
Bermuda
Hawaii
Bahama Is.
Mexico
Cuba
Dominican Rep.
Puerto Rico
Br. Hond.
Hond.
Jamaica
Haiti
Guadeloupe (Fr.)
Neth. Antilles
Barbados (U.K.)
Trinidad (U.K.)
Guatemala
El Salvador
Nicaragua
Costa Rica
Panama
Canal Zone (U.S.)
Venezuela
Br. Guiana
Surinam (Dutch Guiana)
Fr. Guiana
Colombia
Baker
Galápagos Is. (Ec.)
Ecuador
Wallis and Futuna
Western Samoa
Samoa Is.
French
Oceania
Tonga
Pitcairn
Peru
Brazil
Bolivia
Paraguay
Easter (Ch.)
Chile
Argentina
Uruguay
Falkland Is.

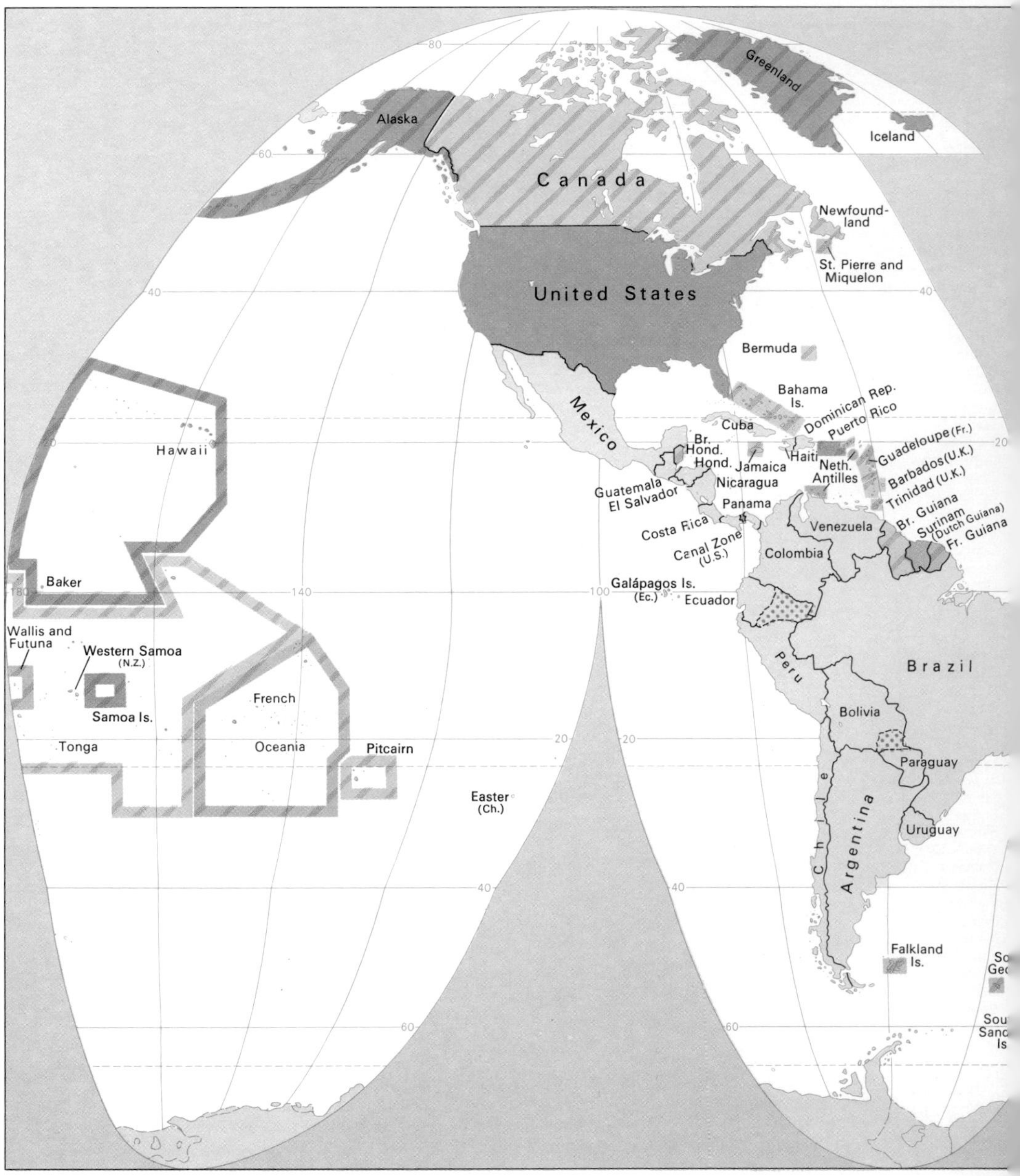
Greenland
Alaska
Iceland
Canada
Newfoundland
St. Pierre and Miquelon
United States
Bermuda
Hawaii
Bahama Is.
Mexico
Cuba
Dominican Rep.
Puerto Rico
Br. Hond.
Hond.
Jamaica
Haiti
Guadeloupe (Fr.)
Neth. Antilles
Barbados (U.K.)
Trinidad (U.K.)
Guatemala
El Salvador
Nicaragua
Costa Rica
Panama
Canal Zone (U.S.)
Venezuela
Br. Guiana
Surinam (Dutch Guiana)
Fr. Guiana
Colombia
Baker
Galápagos Is. (Ec.)
Ecuador
Wallis and Futuna
Western Samoa (N.Z.)
Samoa Is.
French
Oceania
Tonga
Pitcairn
Peru
Brazil
Bolivia
Paraguay
Easter (Ch.)
Chile
Argentina
Uruguay
Falkland Is.

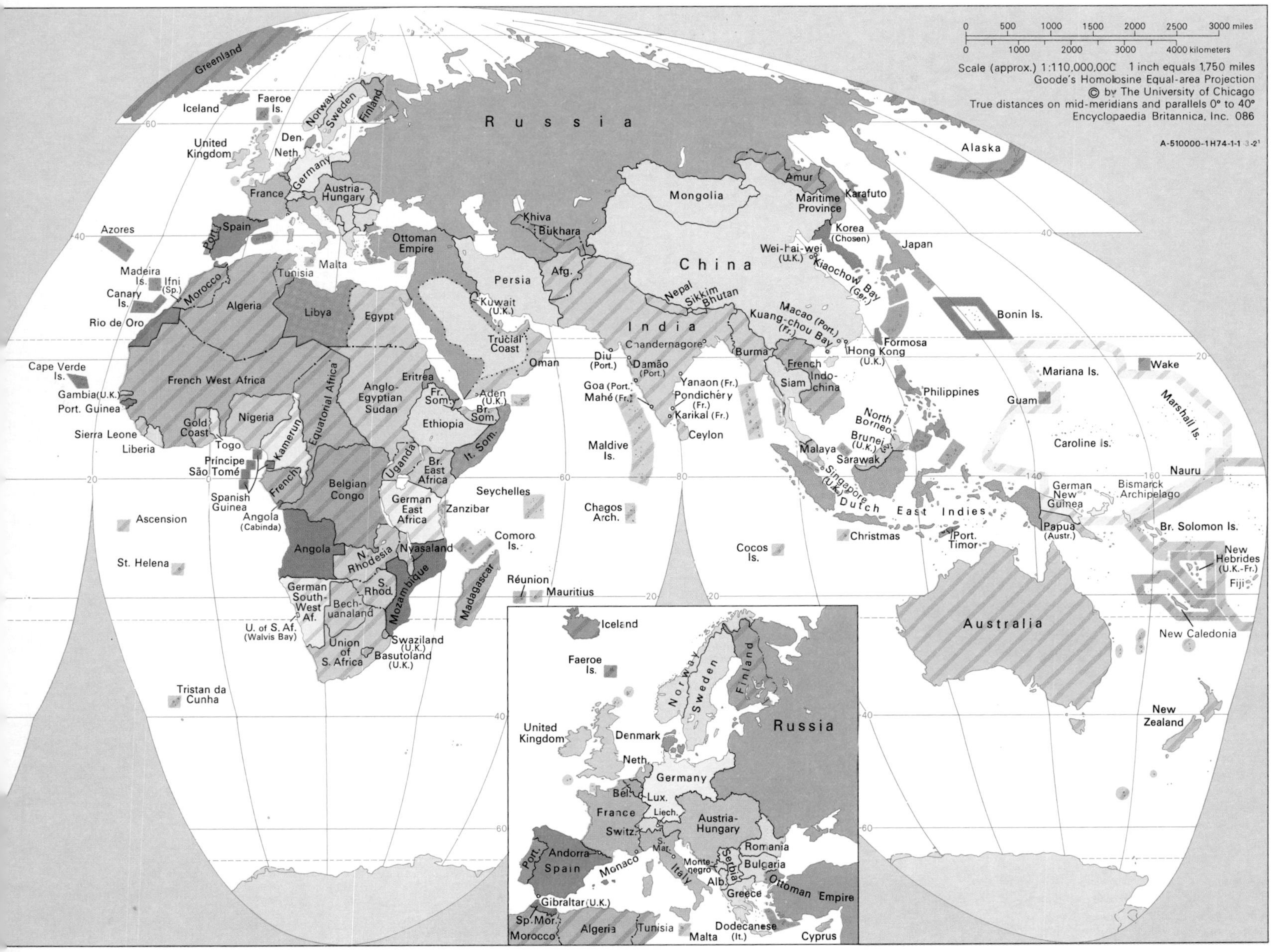

0 500 1000 1500 2000 2500 3000 miles
0 1000 2000 3000 4000 kilometers
Scale (approx.) 1:110,000,000 1 inch equals 1,750 miles
Goode's Homolosine Equal-area Projection
© by The University of Chicago
True distances on mid-meridians and parallels 0° to 40°
Encyclopaedia Britannica, Inc. 086
Greenland
Iceland
Faeroe Is.
United Kingdom
Den.
Neth.
Norway
Sweden
Finland
Germany
France
Austria-Hungary
Russia
Alaska
Amur
Karafuto
Maritime Province
Mongolia
Korea (Chosen)
Japan
Azores
Spain
Port.
Madeira Is.
Ifni (Sp.)
Canary Is.
Morocco
Tunisia
Malta
Ottoman Empire
Algeria
Libya
Egypt
Rio de Oro
Khiva
Bukhara
Persia
Afg.
China
Wei-hai-wei (U.K.)
Kiaochow Bay (Ger.)
Kuwait (U.K.)
Trucial Coast
Oman
Nepal
Sikkim
Bhutan
India
Chandernagore
Macao (Port.)
Kuang-chou Bay (Fr.)
Hong Kong (U.K.)
Formosa
Bonin Is.
Burma
Diu (Port.)
Damão (Port.)
Goa (Port.)
Mahé (Fr.)
Yanaon (Fr.)
Pondichéry (Fr.)
Karikal (Fr.)
Ceylon
French Indo-china
Siam
Philippines
Mariana Is.
Guam
Wake
Marshall Is.
Cape Verde Is.
Gambia (U.K.)
Port. Guinea
Sierra Leone
Liberia
Gold Coast
Togo
Nigeria
French West Africa
Equatorial Africa
Anglo-Egyptian Sudan
Eritrea
Fr. Som.
Aden (U.K.)
Br. Som.
Ethiopia
It. Som.
Kamerun
Principe
São Tomé
Spanish Guinea
Belgian Congo
Uganda
Br. East Africa
German East Africa
Zanzibar
Seychelles
Maldive Is.
Chagos Arch.
North Borneo
Brunei (U.K.)
Sarawak
Malaya
Singapore (U.K.)
Caroline Is.
Nauru
German New Guinea
Bismarck Archipelago
Dutch East Indies
Papua (Austr.)
Port. Timor
Christmas
Br. Solomon Is.
New Hebrides (U.K.-Fr.)
Fiji
New Caledonia
Ascension
Angola (Cabinda)
Angola
N. Rhodesia
Nyasaland
Comoro Is.
Cocos Is.
St. Helena
German South-West Af.
S. Rhod.
Bechuanaland
Mozambique
Madagascar
Réunion
Mauritius
Australia
U. of S. Af. (Walvis Bay)
Union of S. Africa
Swaziland (U.K.)
Basutoland (U.K.)
Tristan da Cunha
New Zealand
Iceland
Faeroe Is.
United Kingdom
Denmark
Norway
Sweden
Finland
Russia
Neth.
Germany
Bel.
Lux.
France
Liech.
Austria-Hungary
Switz.
Port.
Andorra
Spain
Monaco
Italy
Montenegro
Serbia
Romania
Bulgaria
Alb.
Greece
Ottoman Empire
Gibraltar (U.K.)
Sp. Mor.
Morocco
Algeria
Tunisia
Malta
Dodecanese (It.)
Cyprus


## The World January 1, 1914

- United Kingdom
  - Related areas
- France
  - Related areas
- Portugal
  - Related areas
- Spain
  - Related areas
- Netherlands
  - Related areas
- Belgium
  - Related areas
- Germany
  - Related areas
- Denmark
  - Related areas
- Japan
  - Related areas
- Italy
  - Related areas
- United States
  - Related areas
- Ottoman Empire
- Russia
  - Related areas
- Austria-Hungary
- Countries without related areas
- Disputed areas
- Intercolonial boundary

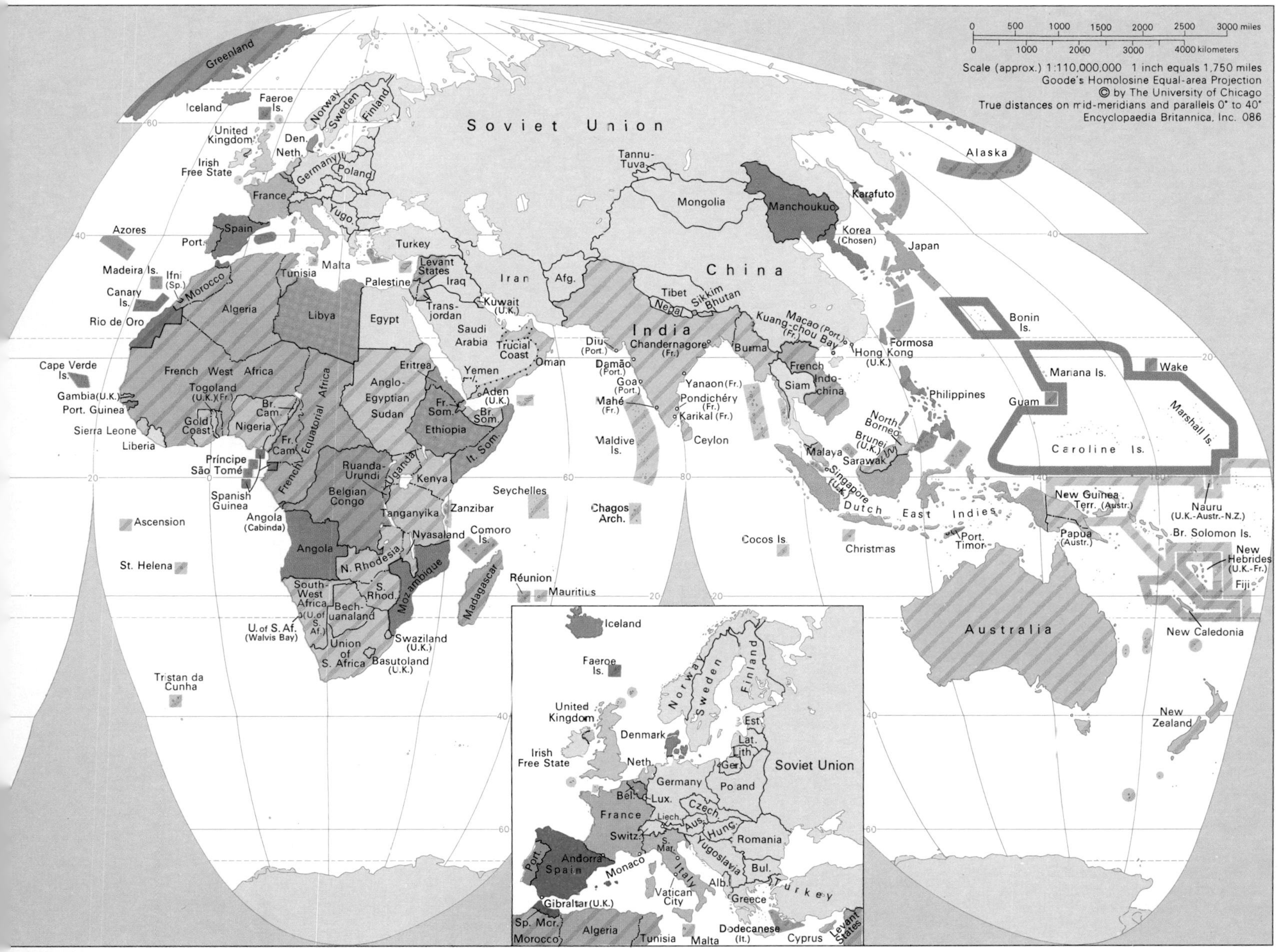

0 500 1000 1500 2000 2500 3000 miles
0 1000 2000 3000 4000 kilometers
Scale (approx.) 1:110,000,000 1 inch equals 1,750 miles
Goode's Homolosine Equal-area Projection
© by The University of Chicago
True distances on mid-meridians and parallels 0° to 40°
Encyclopaedia Britannica, Inc. 086
Greenland
Iceland
Faeroe Is.
United Kingdom
Irish Free State
Den.
Neth.
Norway
Sweden
Finland
Germany
Poland
France
Yugo.
Soviet Union
Alaska
Tannu-Tuva
Mongolia
Manchoukuo
Karafuto
Korea (Chosen)
Japan
Azores
Port.
Spain
Madeira Is.
Ifni (Sp.)
Canary Is.
Morocco
Tunisia
Malta
Turkey
Levant States
Palestine
Iraq
Trans-jordan
Saudi Arabia
Iran
Afg.
Tibet
Nepal
Sikkim
Bhutan
China
Kuwait (U.K.)
Trucial Coast
Oman
Yemen
Aden (U.K.)
Algeria
Libya
Egypt
Rio de Oro
India
Chandernagore (Fr.)
Macao (Port.)
Kuang-chou Bay
Hong Kong (U.K.)
Formosa
Bonin Is.
Burma
Diu (Port.)
Damão (Port.)
Goa (Port.)
Mahé (Fr.)
Yanaon (Fr.)
Pondichéry (Fr.)
Karikal (Fr.)
Ceylon
French Indo-china
Siam
Philippines
Mariana Is.
Guam
Wake
Marshall Is.
Caroline Is.
Cape Verde Is.
Gambia (U.K.)
Port. Guinea
Sierra Leone
Liberia
Gold Coast
Togoland (U.K.) (Fr.)
Nigeria
Br. Cam.
Fr. Cam.
French West Africa
Equatorial Africa
Anglo-Egyptian Sudan
Eritrea
Fr. Som.
Br. Som.
Ethiopia
It. Som.
Principe
São Tomé
Spanish Guinea
Ruanda-Urundi
Belgian Congo
Uganda
Kenya
Tanganyika
Zanzibar
Seychelles
Maldive Is.
Chagos Arch.
Malaya
Singapore (U.K.)
North Borneo
Brunei (U.K.)
Sarawak
Dutch East Indies
Port. Timor
New Guinea Terr. (Austr.)
Papua (Austr.)
Nauru (U.K.-Austr.-N.Z.)
Br. Solomon Is.
New Hebrides (U.K.-Fr.)
Fiji
New Caledonia
Ascension
Angola (Cabinda)
Angola
N. Rhodesia
Nyasaland
Comoro Is.
Cocos Is.
Christmas
St. Helena
South-West Africa
U. of S. Af.
S. Rhod.
Bechuanaland
Mozambique
Madagascar
Réunion
Mauritius
Australia
U. of S. Af. (Walvis Bay)
Union of S. Africa
Swaziland (U.K.)
Basutoland (U.K.)
Tristan da Cunha
New Zealand
Iceland
Faeroe Is.
United Kingdom
Irish Free State
Denmark
Norway
Sweden
Finland
Est.
Lat.
Lith.
Ger.
Soviet Union
Neth.
Germany
Poland
Bel.
Lux.
Czech.
France
Liech.
Aus.
Hung.
Switz.
Romania
Port.
Andorra
Spain
Monaco
S. Mar.
Yugoslavia
Italy
Bul.
Vatican City
Alb.
Greece
Turkey
Gibraltar (U.K.)
Sp. Mor.
Morocco
Algeria
Tunisia
Malta
Dodecanese (It.)
Cyprus
Levant States


## The World January 1, 1937

- United Kingdom
  - Related areas
- France
  - Related areas
- Portugal
  - Related areas
- Spain
  - Related areas
- Netherlands
  - Related areas
- Belgium
  - Related areas
- Denmark
  - Related areas
- Japan
  - Related areas
- Italy
  - Related areas
- United States
  - Related areas
- Countries without related areas
- Disputed areas
- Intercolonial boundary

# Population

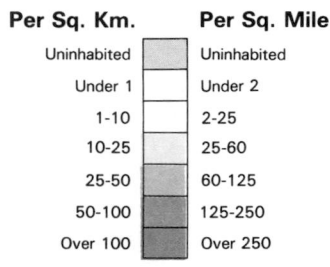

| Per Sq. Km. | | Per Sq. Mile |
|---|---|---|
| Uninhabited | | Uninhabited |
| Under 1 | | Under 2 |
| 1-10 | | 2-25 |
| 10-25 | | 25-60 |
| 25-50 | | 60-125 |
| 50-100 | | 125-250 |
| Over 100 | | Over 250 |

- ● Metropolitan areas over 2,000,000 population
- ○ Metropolitan areas 1,000,000 to 2,000,000 population

*Some cities are identified by initial letter only.*

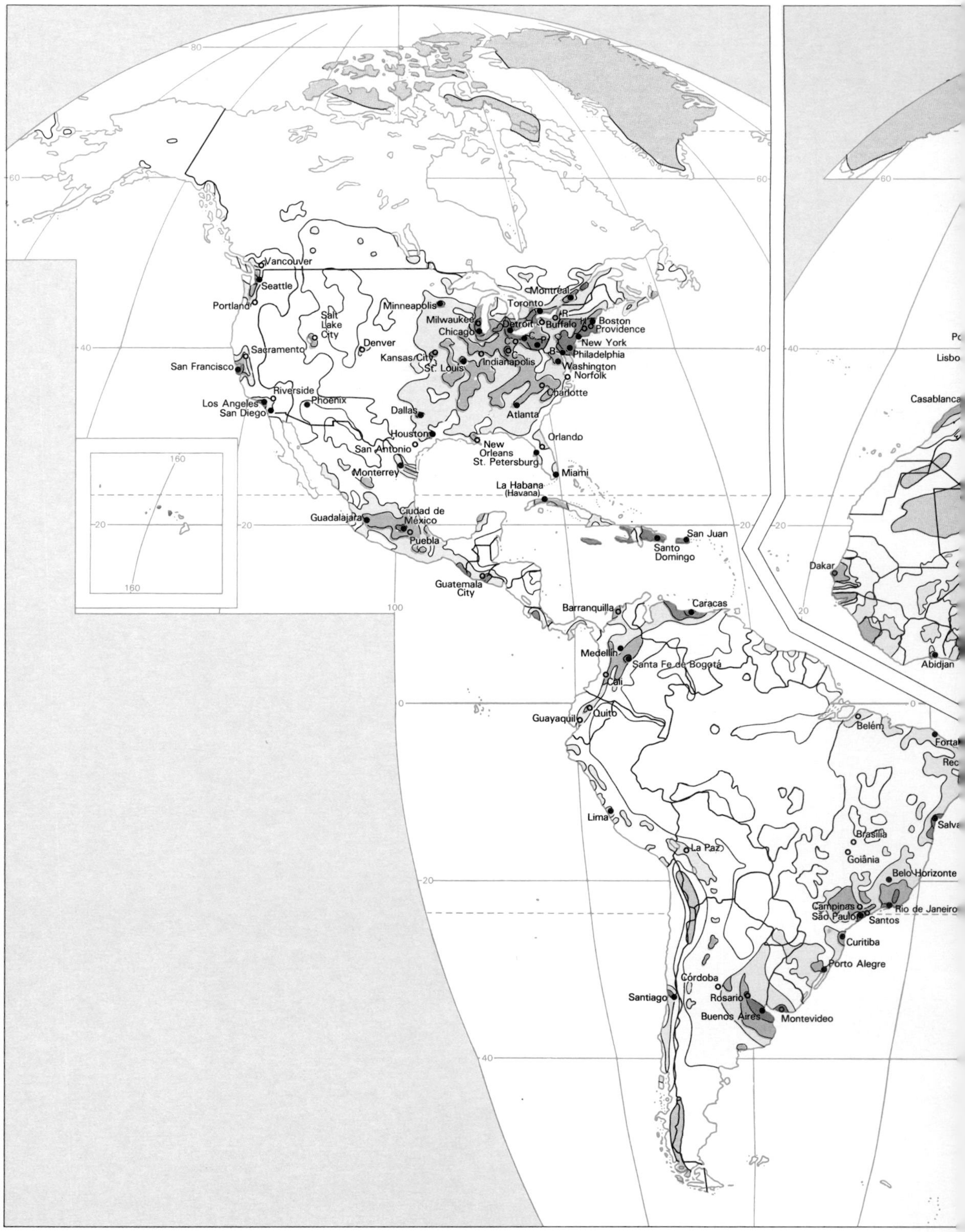
Vancouver
Seattle
Portland
Salt Lake City
Sacramento
San Francisco
Denver
Minneapolis
Milwaukee
Chicago
Detroit
Toronto
Montreal
Buffalo
Boston
Providence
New York
Philadelphia
Washington
Norfolk
Kansas City
St. Louis
Indianapolis
Charlotte
Atlanta
Riverside
Los Angeles
San Diego
Phoenix
Dallas
Houston
San Antonio
New Orleans
St. Petersburg
Orlando
Miami
Monterrey
La Habana (Havana)
Guadalajara
Ciudad de México
Puebla
San Juan
Santo Domingo
Guatemala City
Barranquilla
Caracas
Medellín
Santa Fe de Bogotá
Cali
Quito
Guayaquil
Belém
Lima
La Paz
Brasília
Goiânia
Belo Horizonte
Campinas
São Paulo
Rio de Janeiro
Santos
Curitiba
Porto Alegre
Córdoba
Rosario
Santiago
Buenos Aires
Montevideo
Dakar
Abidjan
Casablanca
Salvador
Recife
Fortaleza
Lisbon

The numbers and distribution of human beings on their planet and the forms that their occupance takes are controlled by a variety of factors. The main population map opposite focuses on identifying the location and density of the most populous regions and cities of the earth. The Urbanization inset highlights the propensity of man to congregate in cities and the group of "age pyramids" below illustrates some of the diversity that is concealed within apparently simple population totals.

**Population**

The patterns of distribution shown display certain characteristics worldwide: relative densities decline with altitude (and the capacity of the land to support higher densities); settlement patterns follow rivers, or focus on harbours opening on large bodies of water connecting populous, economically interrelated areas; populations tend to fill up contiguous areas of similar topographical and climatic opportunity, whether in coastal plains, intermontane basins, along railroad right-of-ways, or in biologically and climatically defined regions of similar soil, vegatative response, or access from more populous areas.

The main map also identifies the largest cities of the world, distinguishing between those of 1-2 million and more than 2 million population. The selection of cities is determined by the concept of "city proper," that is, usually the smallest contiguous civilly or adminstratively defined and named entity. The meaning of the concept in terms of local practice worldwide, however, is considerable. A city of 100,000 may in one country be a single social, economic, and administrative place, bound together fully by its transportation infrastructure and representing a single *urban* entity in its population's collective mind. A city of the same apparent size in another country, however, might represent something more nearly characterizable as 100 villages of 1,000 persons, pursuing separate economic activities in separate neighbourhoods, often poorly interconnected, sometimes still predominately rural in terms of economic activity, and perhaps not universally understood by its own people as the greater place seen by others.

**Urbanization**

The concept of "urban" exemplified on the inset map of urbanization is particularly elusive in international studies of population, as most countries have their own definition of the concept, appropriate to local conditions and discourse, but often unsuitable for international comparisons. It is that local concept which is mapped here. Size is a useful indicator as to whether a place is classifiable as "urban," but as indicated above, the "size" of a place, even in the presence of administrative requirements may be misleading. Japan defines a place as "urban" if it has 50,000 or more population and meets certain criteria for their location within the city. A smaller country with a less hospitable landscape, like Iceland or Norway, might, by the same token, define a place as small as 200 as "urban" if it had predominately non-rural employment patterns, administrative function, or its houses were closer together than some set distance. The concept of "metropolitan area," or urban areas contiguous with a central city that are economically dependent on it is also complex and interpreted differently thorughout the world. The inset map of urbanization extends the city proper concept of the main map by showing metropolitan areas of more than 2 million. As can be seen from comparison of the two maps, sometimes high urbanization may correlate with relatively low numbers or densities of population. This occurs when the majority of a population lives in large settlements, rather than distributed across an entire landscape and may happen either because of localized economic and employment opportunities in the city, or because the countryside is unsuitable for agricultural or other exploitation. The strong correlation, however, is still between highly populous areas and large cities.

**Age and sex composition**

Among the characteristics of a population having the greatest significance both in terms of current needs and future trends, the age and sex composition of a population is perhaps the most important. Several examples are presented at the right of a graphic called an "age pyramid," which summarizes the relative proportion of males and females in each age cohort of a population. These examples, drawn by five-year age groups, often illuminate the effects on the whole population of the recent history of the relative growth or diminution of smaller parts of the whole: war losses, emigration of the young for work abroad, natural causes like disasters.
The origins of the concern of many countries and organizations with uncontrolled population growth may be inferred from examples like Brazil, where the high proportion of young people means enormous numbers (both absolutely and relatively) in or near their childbearing years resulting in growth rates for the total population that can outrun the far more difficult-to-attain economic growth rates that determine the relative prosperity of a country. Japan, on the other hand, shows a pattern typical of a demographically mature population, that is, a population which is growing slowly or not at all, resulting in lower, more predictable, and more economically supportable demographic rates, but also foreshadowing the movement of large numbers of its people into the pensionable and financially dependent age groups without large numbers of younger workers to support them. The Japanese example also shows, in a somewhat smoothed form, the effects of some of the viscissitudes of Twentieth century history on the relative size of certain age groups.

### Age and Sex Composition

- Male
- Female

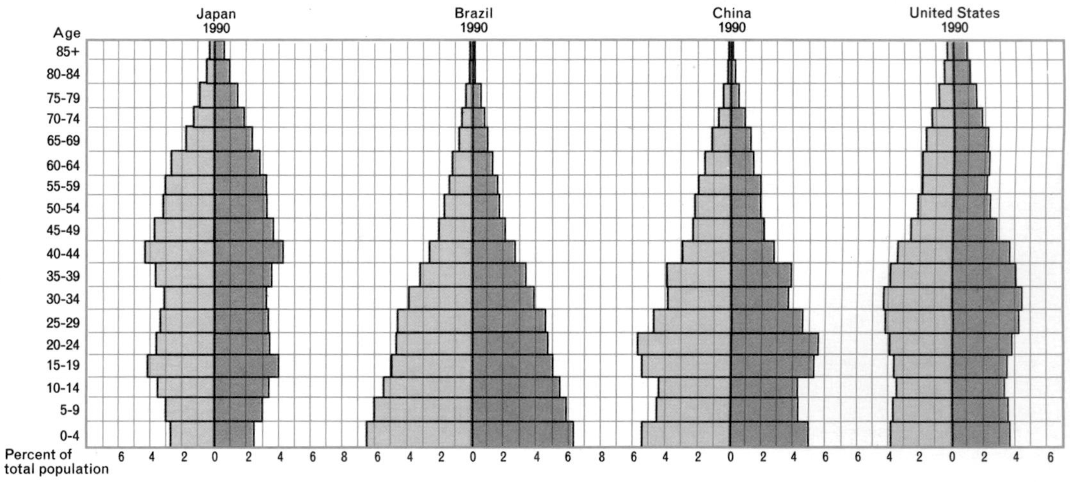
Japan 1990
Brazil 1990
China 1990
United States 1990
Age
85+
80-84
75-79
70-74
65-69
60-64
55-59
50-54
45-49
40-44
35-39
30-34
25-29
20-24
15-19
10-14
5-9
0-4
Percent of total population
6 4 2 0 2 4 6 8

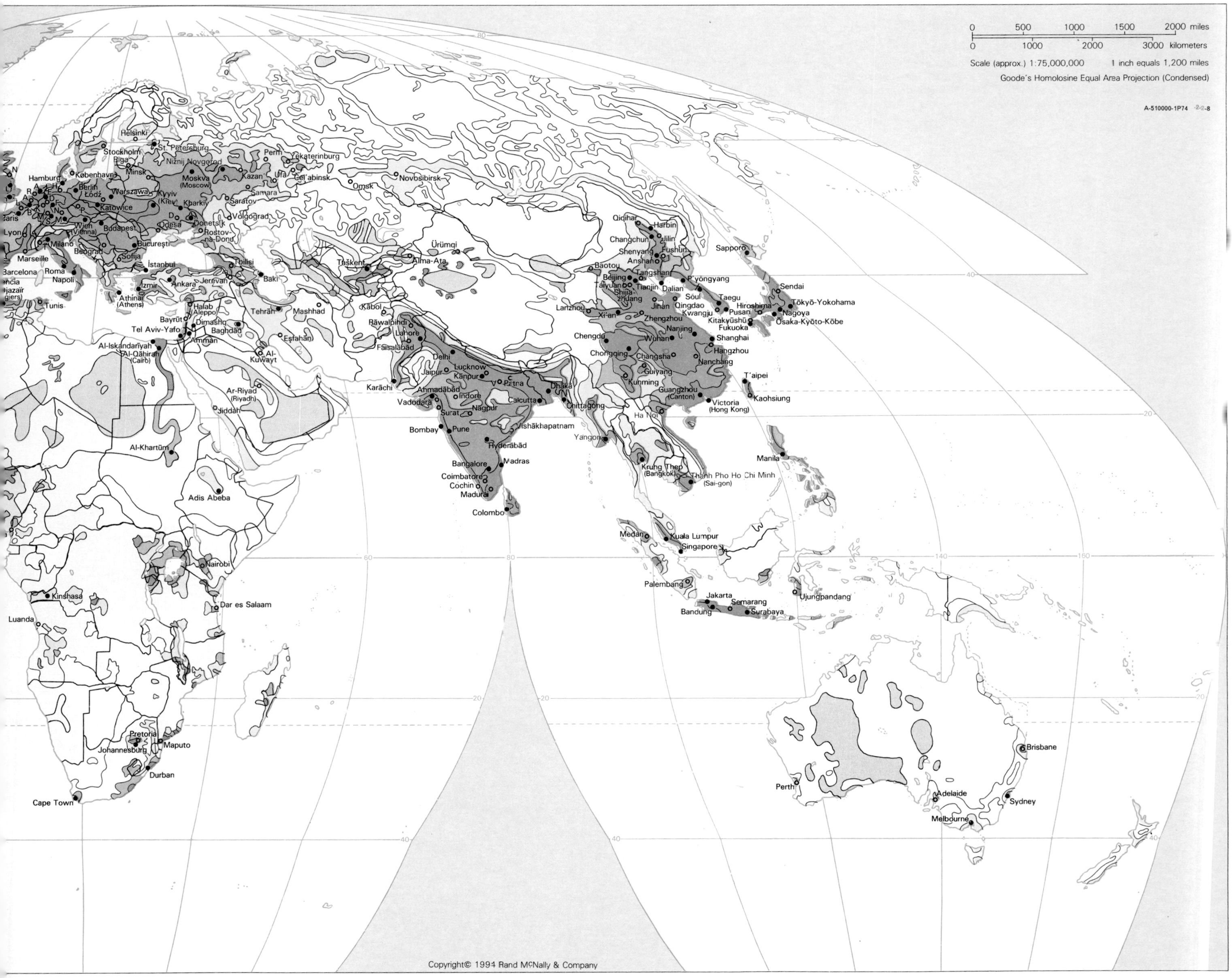
0 500 1000 1500 2000 miles
0 1000 2000 3000 kilometers
Scale (approx.) 1:75,000,000 1 inch equals 1,200 miles
Goode's Homolosine Equal Area Projection (Condensed)
Helsinki
St. Petersburg
Stockholm
Riga
Nizhnij Novgorod
Perm'
Yekaterinburg
København
Hamburg
Berlin
Minsk
Moskva (Moscow)
Kazan'
Ufa
Chel'abinsk
Omsk
Novosibirsk
Łódź
Warszawa
Kyyiv (Kiev)
Samara
Katowice
Khar'kiv
Saratov
Wien (Vienna)
Budapest
Odesa
Donets'k
Volgograd
Rostov-na-Donu
Milano
Lyon
Marseille
Beograd
București
Sofiya
Barcelona
Roma
Napoli
İstanbul
Tbilisi
Yerevan
Baki
Ankara
İzmir
Athinai (Athens)
Tunis
Halab (Aleppo)
Bayrūt
Dimashq
Tel Aviv-Yafo
'Ammān
Baghdād
Tehrān
Mashhad
Eşfahān
Al-Kuwayt
Al-Iskandarīyah
Al-Qāhirah (Cairo)
Ar-Riyāḑ (Riyadh)
Jiddah
Al-Kharṭūm
Adis Abeba
Nairobi
Dar es Salaam
Kinshasa
Luanda
Pretoria
Johannesburg
Maputo
Durban
Cape Town
Taškent
Alma-Ata
Ürümqi
Kābol
Rāwalpindi
Lahore
Faisalābād
Delhi
Jaipur
Lucknow
Kānpur
Patna
Karāchi
Ahmadābād
Indore
Vadodara
Surat
Nāgpur
Calcutta
Dhaka
Chittagong
Bombay
Pune
Vishākhapatnam
Hyderābād
Madras
Bangalore
Coimbatore
Cochin
Madurai
Colombo
Yangon
Ha Noi
Krung Thep (Bangkok)
Thanh Pho Ho Chi Minh (Sai-gon)
Manila
Medan
Kuala Lumpur
Singapore
Palembang
Jakarta
Bandung
Semarang
Surabaya
Ujungpandang
Qiqihar
Harbin
Changchun
Jilin
Shenyang
Fushun
Anshan
Baotou
Beijing
Tangshan
Taiyuan
Tianjin
Shijiazhuang
Dalian
P'yŏngyang
Sŏul
Taegu
Kwangju
Pusan
Jinan
Qingdao
Zhengzhou
Lanzhou
Xi'an
Nanjing
Shanghai
Hangzhou
Chengdu
Wuhan
Chongqing
Changsha
Nanchang
Guiyang
Kunming
Guangzhou (Canton)
Victoria (Hong Kong)
T'aipei
Kaohsiung
Sapporo
Sendai
Hiroshima
Kitakyūshū
Fukuoka
Nagoya
Tōkyō-Yokohama
Ōsaka-Kyōto-Kōbe
Brisbane
Perth
Adelaide
Sydney
Melbourne
Copyright© 1994 Rand McNally & Company

## Urbanization

Percentage of population living in urban areas

World Av. 43%

- >60%
- 45-60
- 30-45
- 15-30
- <15
- Uninhabited or sparsely populated

• Metropolitan areas over 5,000,000 population

○ Metropolitan areas 2,000,000 to 5,000,000 population

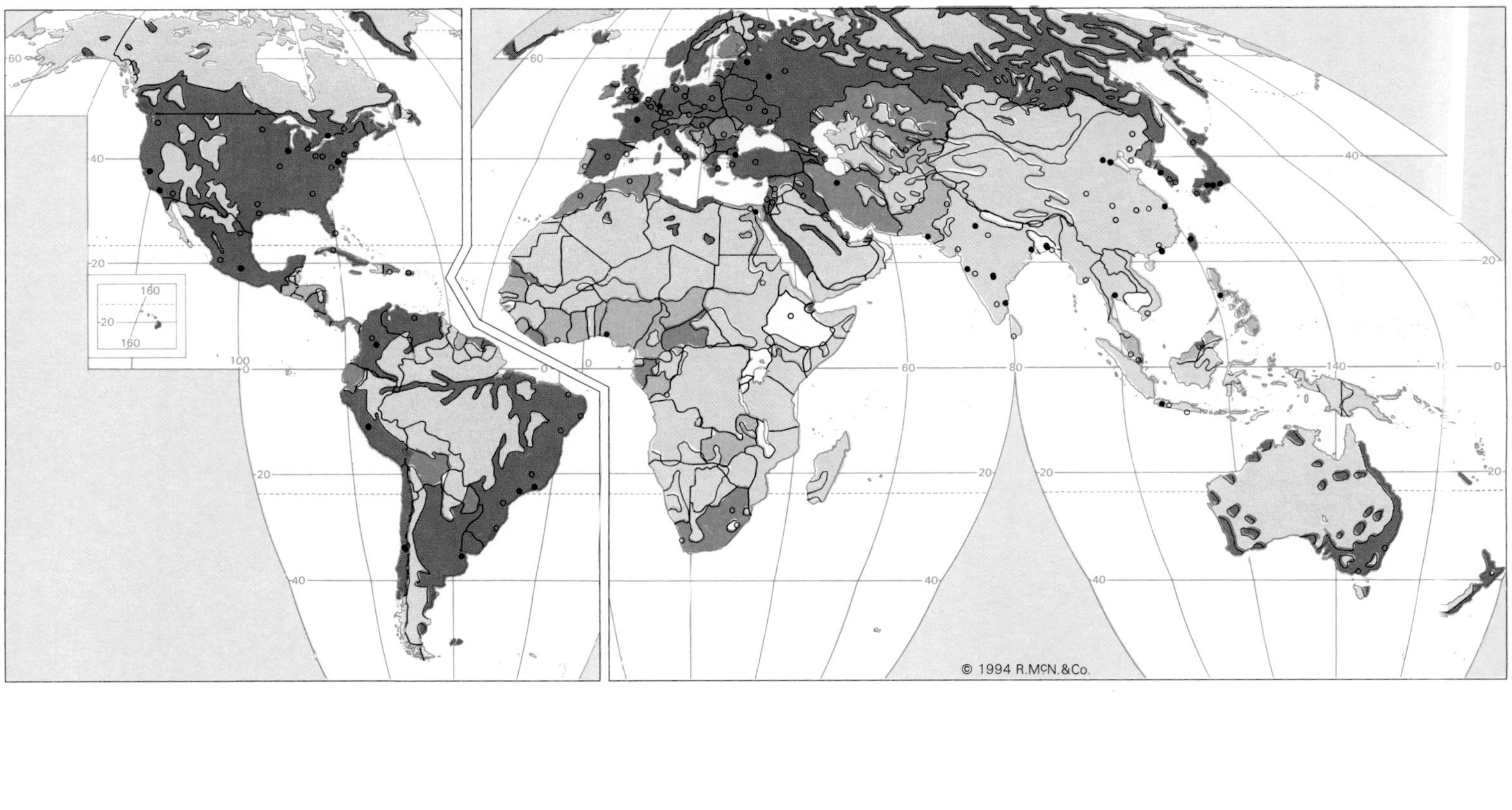
© 1994 R.McN.&Co.

## Religions

**The majority of the inhabitants in each of the areas colored on the map share the religious tradition indicated. Letter symbols show religious traditions shared by at least 25% of the inhabitants within areal units no smaller than one thousand square miles. Therefore minority religions of city-dwellers have generally not been represented.**

- R Roman Catholicism
- P Protestantism
- E Eastern Orthodox religions (including Armenian, Coptic, Ethiopian, Greek, and Russian Orthodox)
- M Mormonism
- C Christianity, undifferentiated by branch (chiefly mingled Protestantism and Roman Catholicism, neither predominant)
- I Islam, predominantly Sunni
- Sh Islam, predominantly Shia
- Theravada Buddhism
- L Lamaism
- H Hinduism
- J Judaism
- Ch Chinese religions*
- Ja Japanese religions*
- Korean religions*
- Vietnamese religions*
- T Simple ethnic (tribal) religions
- Sk Sikhism
- Areas long under Communist regimes; traditional religions often subject to official restraint
- Uninhabited

***In certain Eastern Asian areas, most of the people have plural religious affiliations. Chinese, Korean, and Vietnamese religions include Mahayana Buddhism, Taoism, Confucianism, and folk cults. The Japanese religions include Shinto and Mahayana Buddhism.**

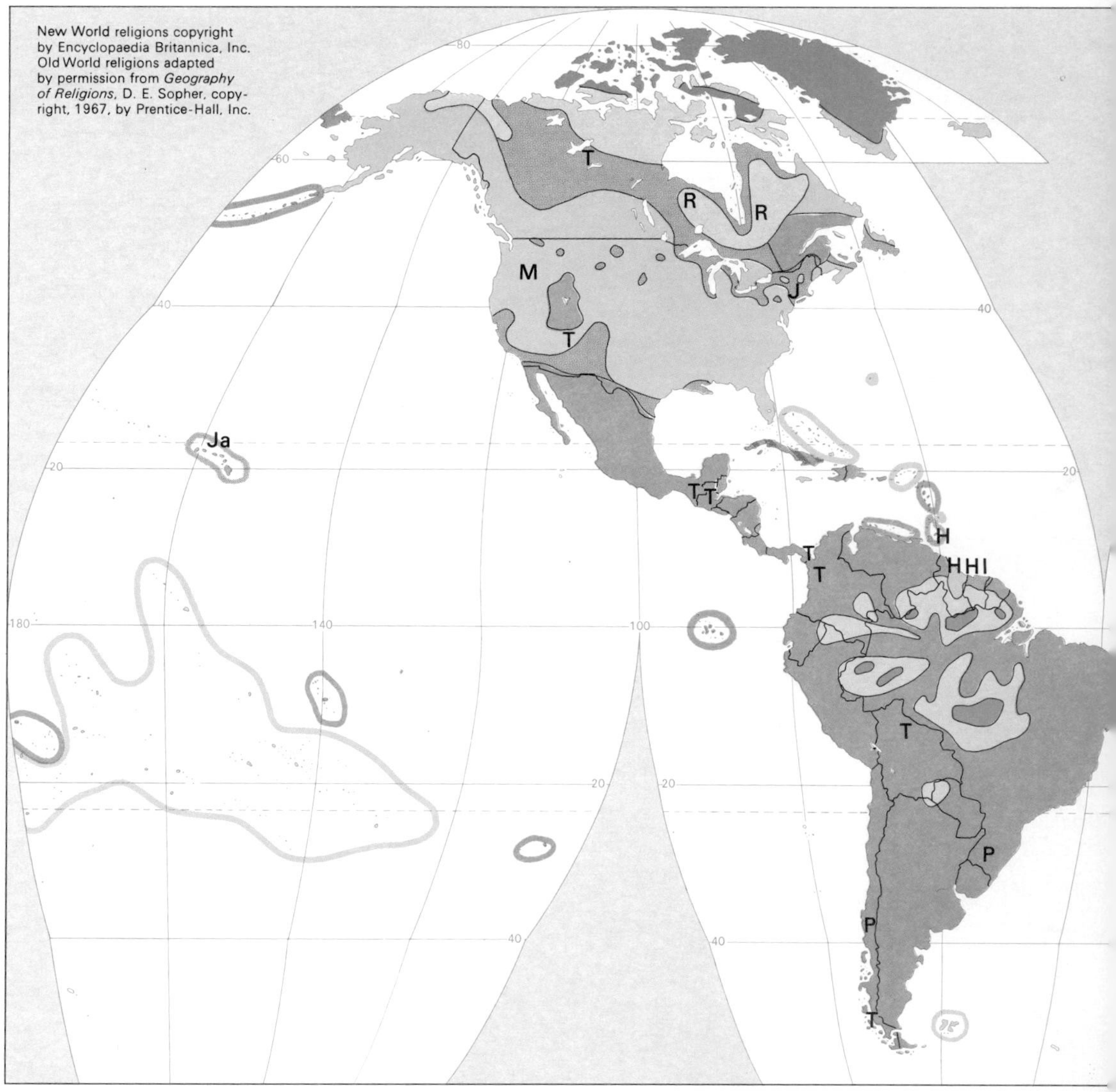
New World religions copyright by Encyclopaedia Britannica, Inc. Old World religions adapted by permission from *Geography of Religions*, D. E. Sopher, copyright, 1967, by Prentice-Hall, Inc.
T
R
R
M
T
J
Ja
TT
H
T
T
HHI
T
P
P
T

## Languages

### Languages of Europe

The following languages are ranked in descending order by number of speakers. Languages spoken by more than 4.5 million people are indicated by color. Others listed, spoken by fewer than 4.5 million persons, are named on the map.

Russian, German, Italian, English, French, Ukrainian, Polish, Spanish, Romanian, Serbo-Croatian, Dutch-Flemish, Hungarian, Portuguese, Czech, Belorussian, Greek, Bulgarian, Swedish, Catalan, Danish, Turkish, Slovak, Albanian, Finnish, All others

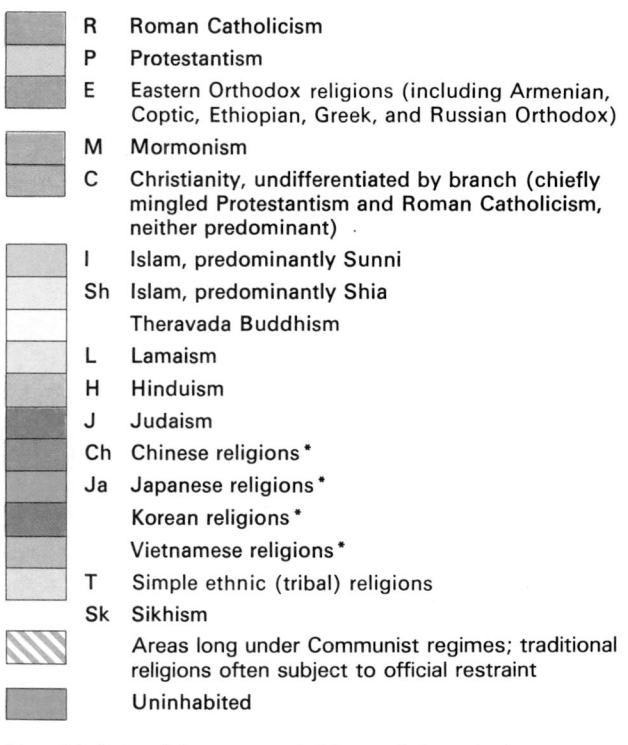

Norwegian, Lithuanian, Chuvash, Slovenian, Macedonian, Latvian, Mordvinian, Estonian, Breton

Basque, Irish-Gaelic, Mari, Welsh, Friulian, Komi, Frisian, Sardinian, Maltese

Karelian, Icelandic, Adyge, Scots-Gaelic, Romansh, Lappish, Lusatian, Ladin

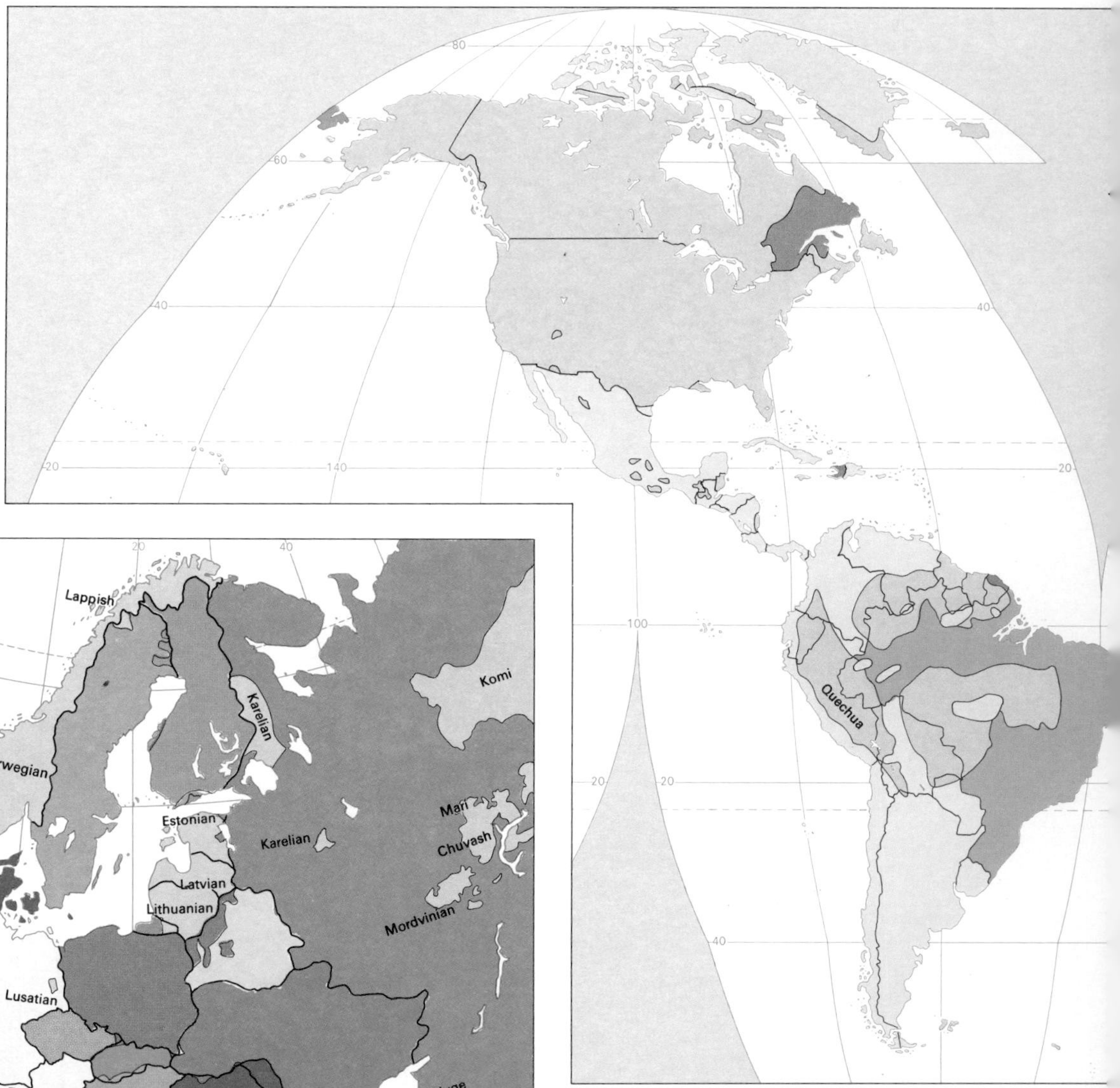
Quechua

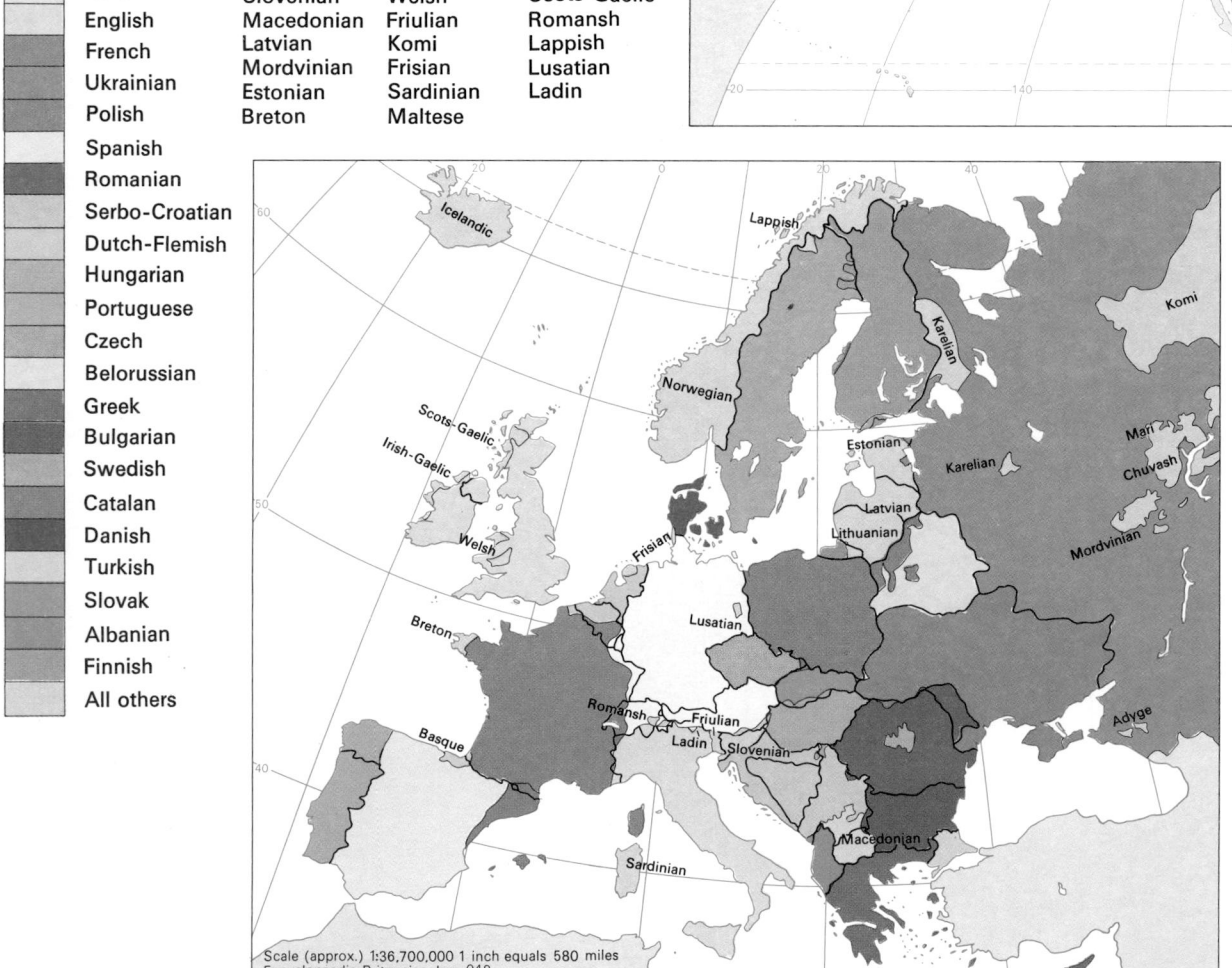

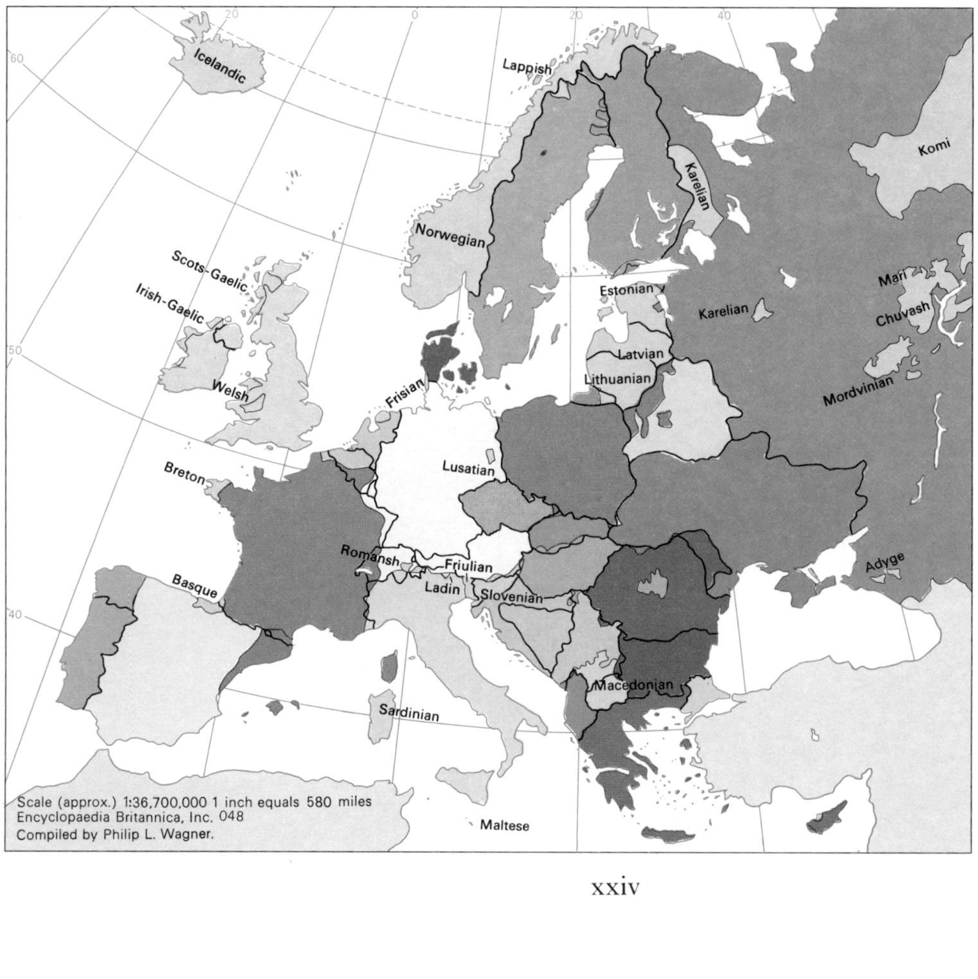
Icelandic
Lappish
Karelian
Komi
Norwegian
Scots-Gaelic
Irish-Gaelic
Estonian
Karelian
Mari
Chuvash
Latvian
Lithuanian
Welsh
Frisian
Mordvinian
Lusatian
Breton
Romansh
Friulian
Ladin
Slovenian
Basque
Adyge
Macedonian
Sardinian
Maltese
Scale (approx.) 1:36,700,000 1 inch equals 580 miles
Encyclopaedia Britannica, Inc. 048
Compiled by Philip L. Wagner.

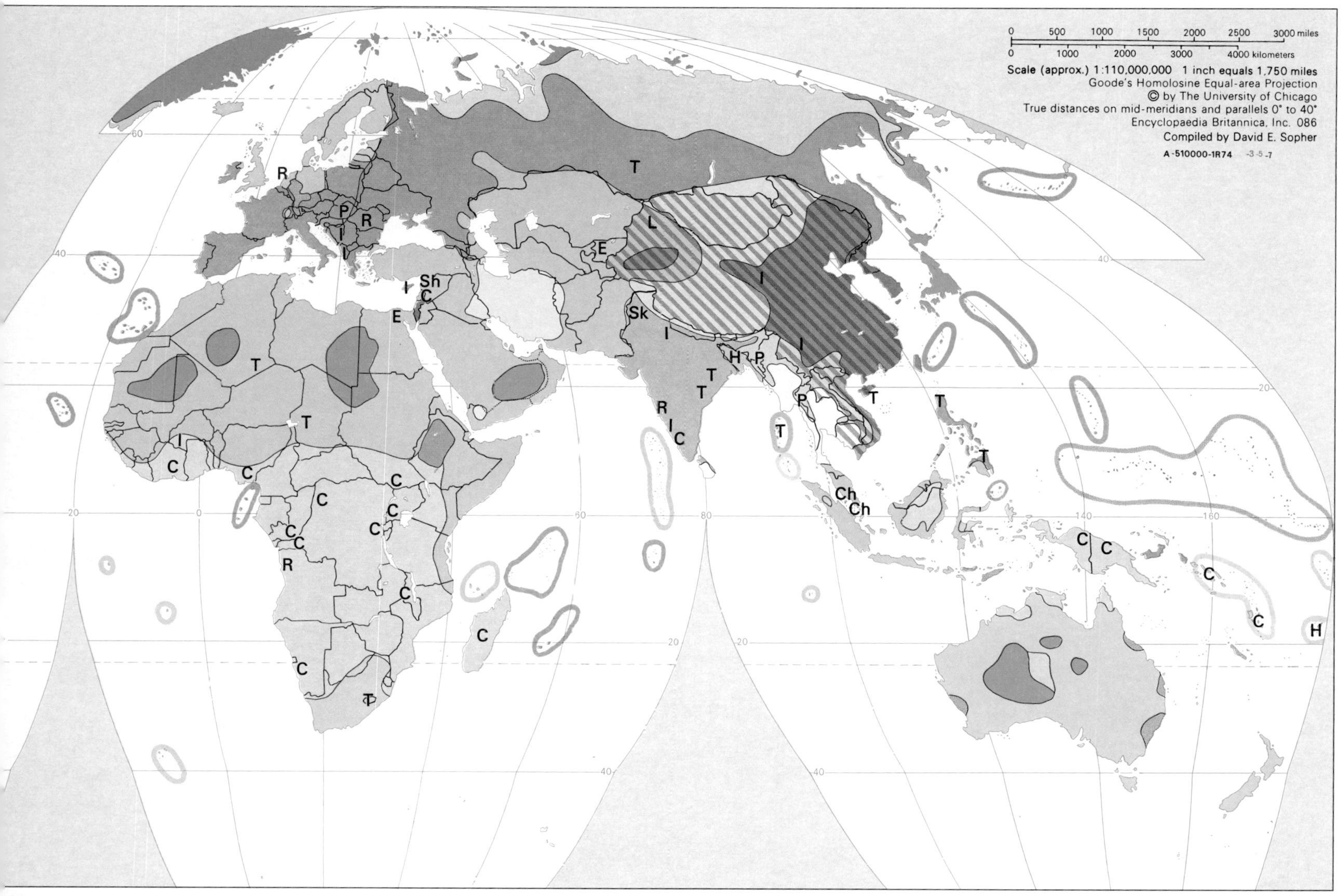
0 500 1000 1500 2000 2500 3000 miles
0 1000 2000 3000 4000 kilometers
Scale (approx.) 1:110,000,000 1 inch equals 1,750 miles
Goode's Homolosine Equal-area Projection
© by The University of Chicago
True distances on mid-meridians and parallels 0° to 40°
Encyclopaedia Britannica, Inc. 086
Compiled by David E. Sopher
A-510000-1R74
R
P
R
T
L
E
I
Sh
C
E
Sk
H
P
R
C
Ch
Ch
C
H

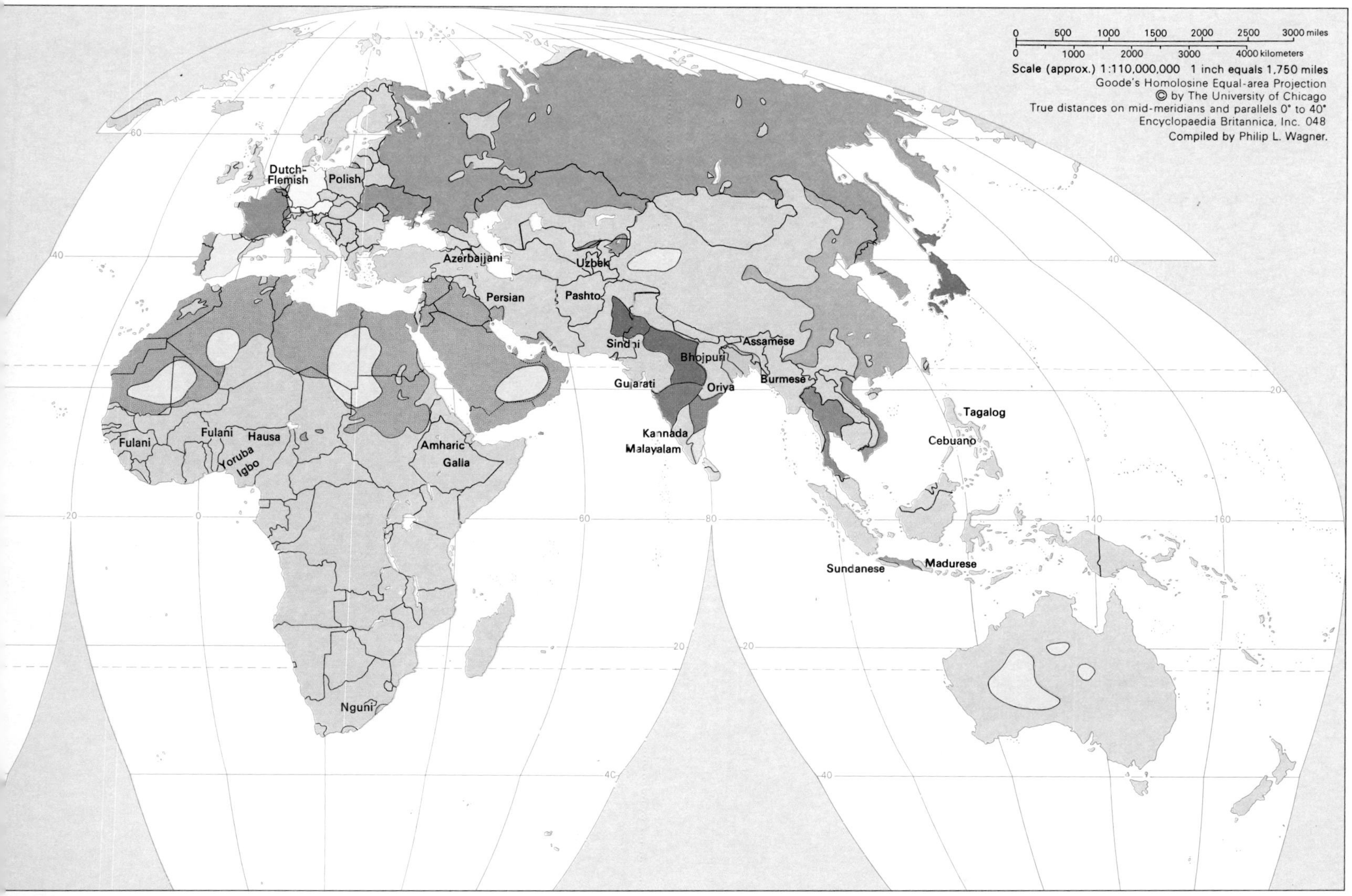
0 500 1000 1500 2000 2500 3000 miles
0 1000 2000 3000 4000 kilometers
Scale (approx.) 1:110,000,000 1 inch equals 1,750 miles
Goode's Homolosine Equal-area Projection
© by The University of Chicago
True distances on mid-meridians and parallels 0° to 40°
Encyclopaedia Britannica, Inc. 048
Compiled by Philip L. Wagner.
Dutch-Flemish
Polish
Azerbaijani
Uzbek
Persian
Pashto
Sindhi
Bhojpuri
Assamese
Gujarati
Oriya
Burmese
Tagalog
Cebuano
Kannada
Malayalam
Fulani
Fulani
Hausa
Yoruba
Igbo
Amharic
Galla
Sundanese
Madurese
Nguni

## Languages of the World

The following languages are ranked in descending order by number of speakers. Languages spoken by more than 40 million persons are indicated by color. Others listed, spoken by 10-40 million persons, are named on the map.

- Chinese
- Spanish
- English
- Hindi
- Bengali
- Arabic
- Russian
- Portuguese
- Japanese
- German
- Punjabi
- Javanese
- Korean
- Telugu
- Marathi
- French
- Italian
- Tamil
- Vietnamese
- Urdu
- Turkish
- Ukrainian
- Thai
- All others
- Uninhabited

Polish, Gujarati, Malayalam, Kannada, Oriya, Burmese, Persian, Hausa, Sundanese, Bhojpuri, Yoruba, Dutch-Flemish, Pashtu, Fulani, Igbo, Uzbek, Galla, Cebuano, Azerbaijani, Nguni, Tagalog, Assamese, Sindhi, Amharic, Madurese

## Agricultural Regions

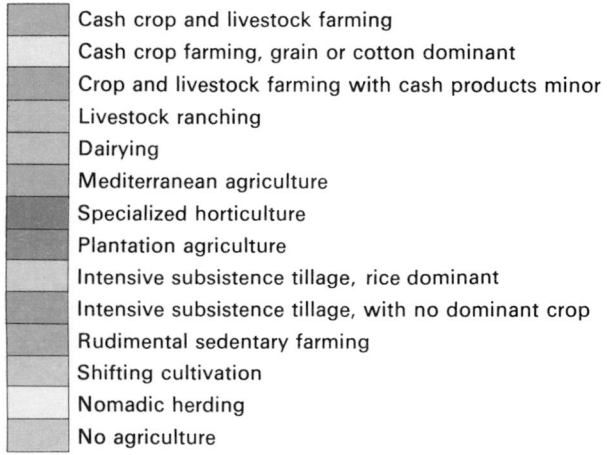

- Cash crop and livestock farming
- Cash crop farming, grain or cotton dominant
- Crop and livestock farming with cash products minor
- Livestock ranching
- Dairying
- Mediterranean agriculture
- Specialized horticulture
- Plantation agriculture
- Intensive subsistence tillage, rice dominant
- Intensive subsistence tillage, with no dominant crop
- Rudimental sedentary farming
- Shifting cultivation
- Nomadic herding
- No agriculture

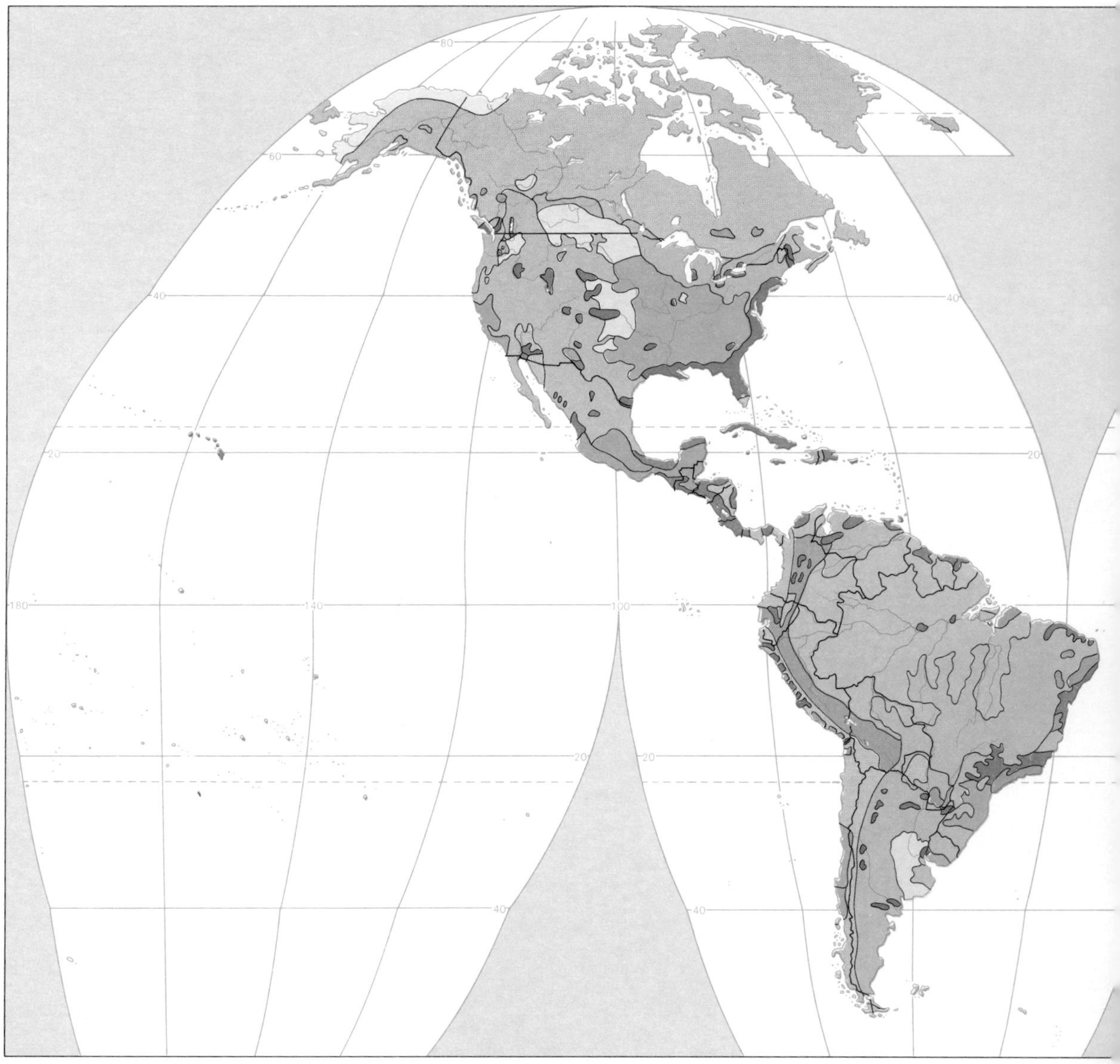

The agricultural systems classified and mapped here represent the primary *agricultural*, rather than economic, activity in the areas shown, since in many developed countries farm population may now constitute less than 5 percent of the total population.No particular level of technology is implied by the classification, as reindeer herding can be carried out with dogs or snowmobiles, crops be irrigated with bucket wheels or electric pumps, dairy cows milked by hand or by machine. Much of the activity shown is controlled, or more specifically, limited by topography and climate. Thus while it is easier to farm on flat land, terracing can create flat land where none exists; intermediate slopes can either be cropped by special techniques, as in Switzerland, or planted in a crop like tea or wine grapes for which slope, or attitude toward the sun and other climatic elements might determine the crop's success. Density of natural vegetation usually declines with altitude and rainfall and so livestock ranching can take place in the compass of a North American feedlot, an Australian cattle station, or a Papua New Guinean butterfly farm. Among the types of occupance listed, ''Mediterranean'' agriculture may be the least familiar to North Americans. It refers to a system developed in the Mediterranean basin's hot, dry summers that concentrates on hardy tree crops (olive, citrus) or vines (grape), interspersed with small plantings of vegetables or grain; few livestock are kept except in uplands, though small ruminants like goats may be kept lower down.

## Forests and Fisheries

### Forests

- Conifers: cedar, fir, hemlock, pine, redwood, spruce
- Regions of exploitation
- Tropical hardwoods: ebony, mahogany, rosewood, teak
- Regions of exploitation
- Temperate hardwoods: hickory, maple, oak, poplar, walnut, and some mixed hardwoods and conifers
- Regions of exploitation

### Fisheries

- Pelagic fishing regions: anchoveta, anchovy, herring, menhaden, pilchard, sardine, sprat, tuna
- Ground fishing regions: cod, haddock, hake, horse mackerel, mackerel, pollack, redfish
- Mixed ground and pelagic fishing regions
- Shellfish: clam, crab, lobster, mussel, oyster, scallop, shrimp, squid

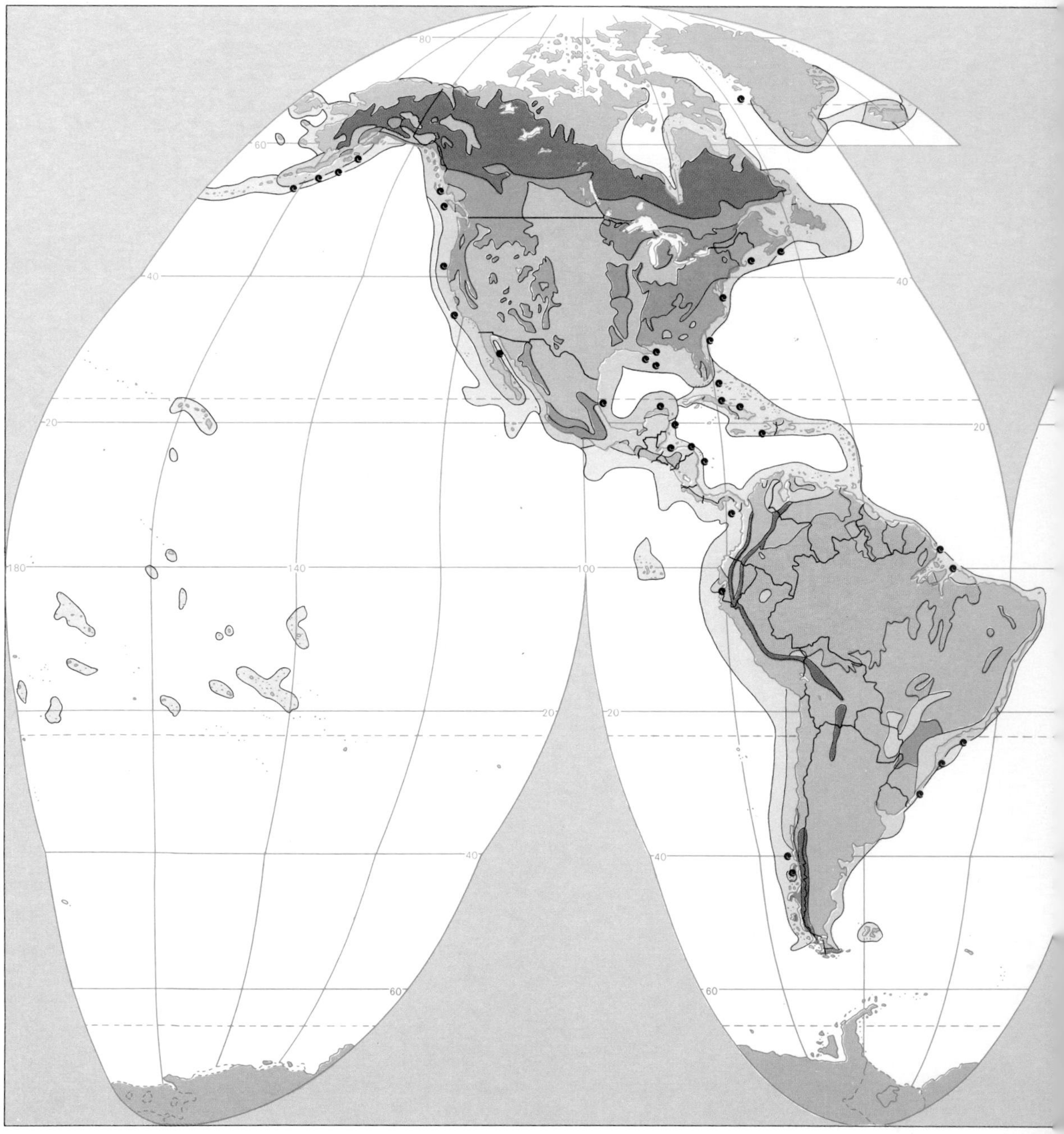

Two principal *commercial* activities are summarized on the map opposite: forestry, classified by type of forests exploited, and fisheries, classified by type of fishing grounds. Three forest types are shown, classified by the woods of chief economic interest within them, rather than by the predominant vegetation. For example, while the softwood conifers listed may actually predominate in many of the regions shown, there are very few areas where the temperate or tropical hardwoods listed will actually constitute the predominant or characteristic tree. Commercial exploitation concentrates on regions where the tree stock has reached economically significant size, is not diluted by other, uneconomical woods, and where transportation infrastructure permits economical removal.

Of the ocean fisheries shown, the term 'Pelagic' refers to near-surface fisheries, either near-shore or on the high seas. 'Ground' fisheries are those which exploit bottom-dwelling fish, or shellfish but should not be confused with the term 'fishing grounds,' which may be either pelagic or ground. The types of fish listed are the principal species exploited in terms of quantities landed. Ocean areas of greatest biological diversity may support both kinds of fish populations, such as those of the Grand Banks of Newfoundland. Commercial whaling is no longer significant although some traditional whaling from small boats still takes place.

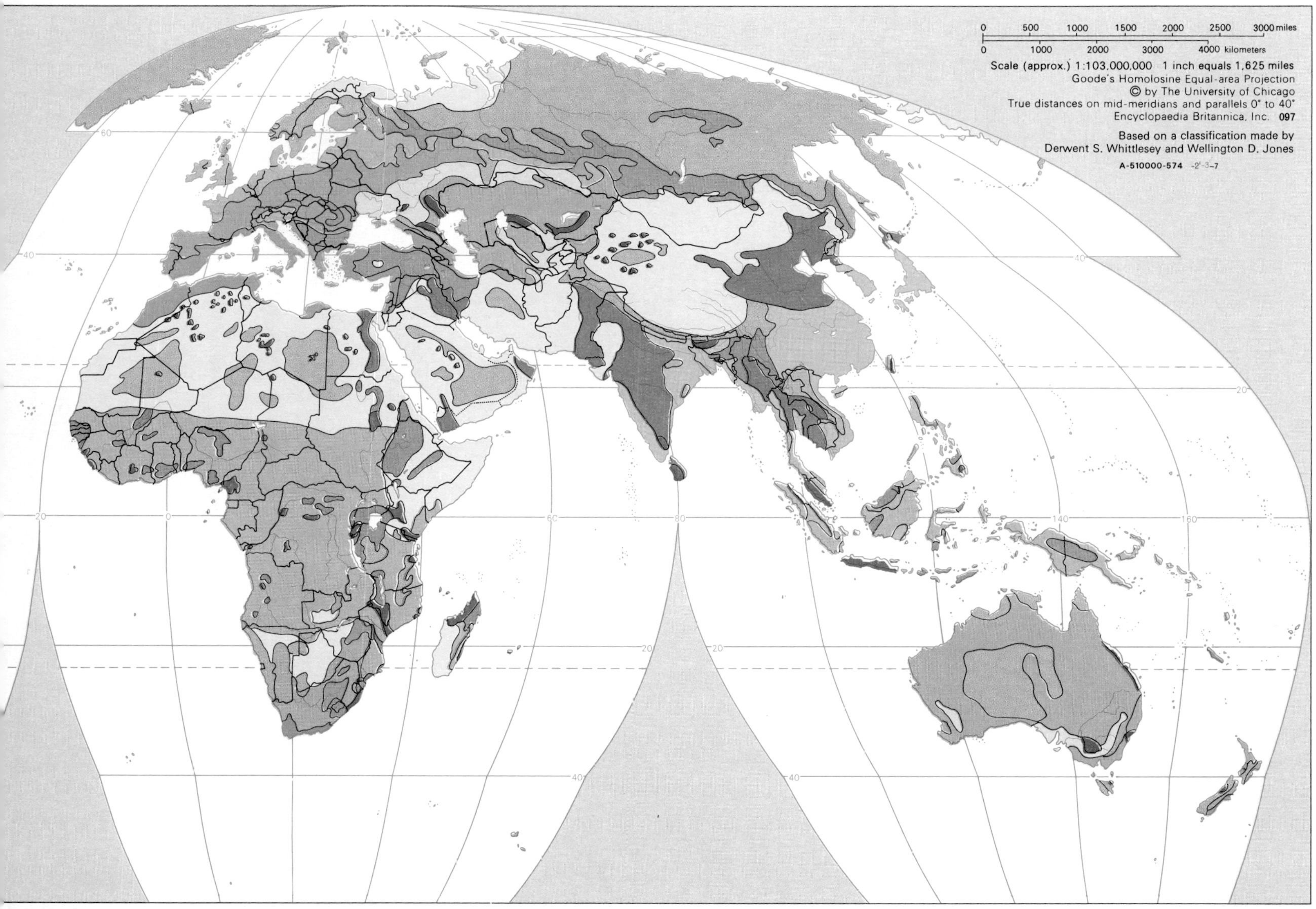
0 500 1000 1500 2000 2500 3000 miles
0 1000 2000 3000 4000 kilometers
Scale (approx.) 1:103,000,000 1 inch equals 1,625 miles
Goode's Homolosine Equal-area Projection
© by The University of Chicago
True distances on mid-meridians and parallels 0° to 40°
Encyclopaedia Britannica, Inc. 097
Based on a classification made by
Derwent S. Whittlesey and Wellington D. Jones
A-510000-574

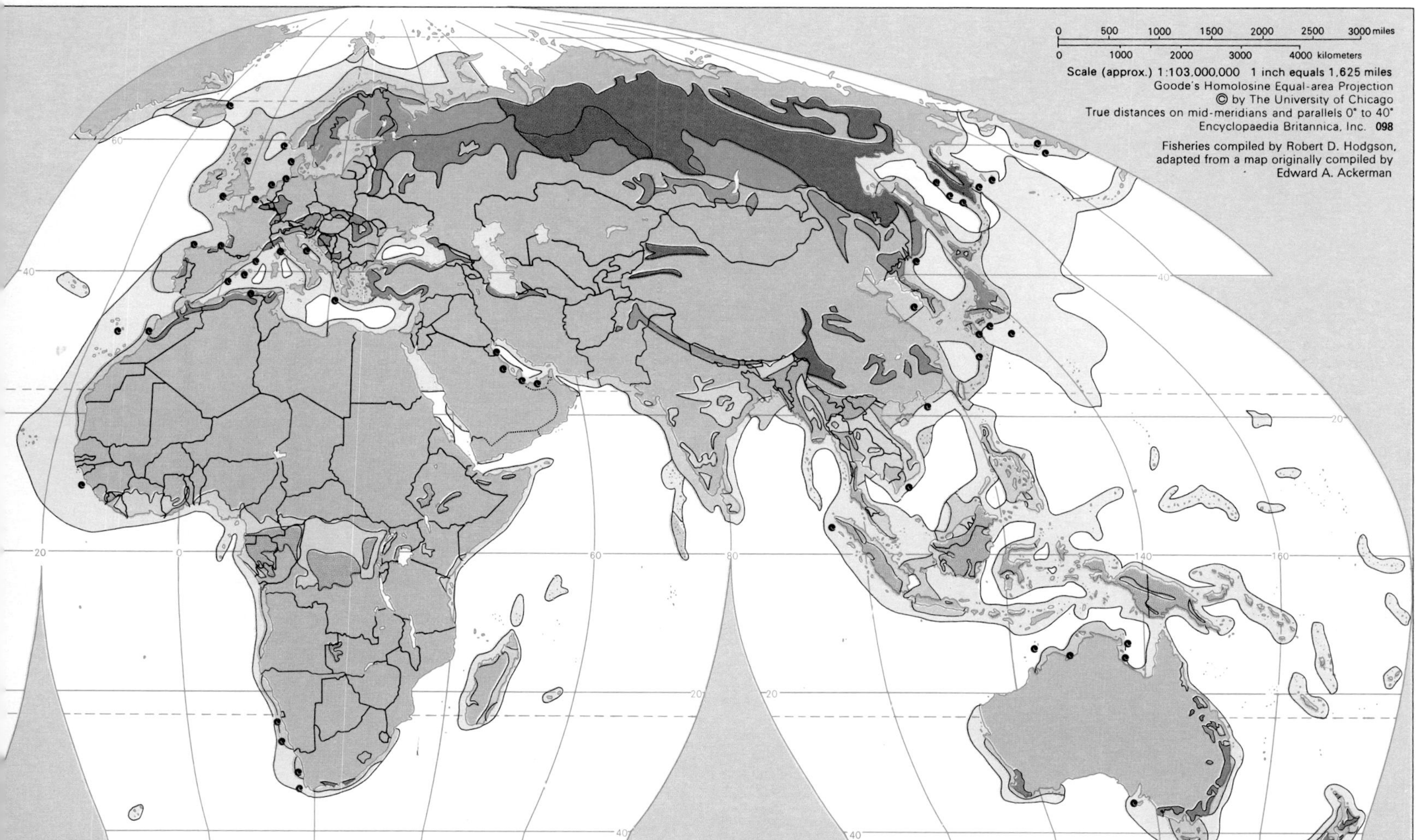
0 500 1000 1500 2000 2500 3000 miles
0 1000 2000 3000 4000 kilometers
Scale (approx.) 1:103,000,000 1 inch equals 1,625 miles
Goode's Homolosine Equal-area Projection
© by The University of Chicago
True distances on mid-meridians and parallels 0° to 40°
Encyclopaedia Britannica, Inc. 098
Fisheries compiled by Robert D. Hodgson,
adapted from a map originally compiled by
Edward A. Ackerman

## Minerals

4-year world average production shown in graphs. Producing areas shown on maps

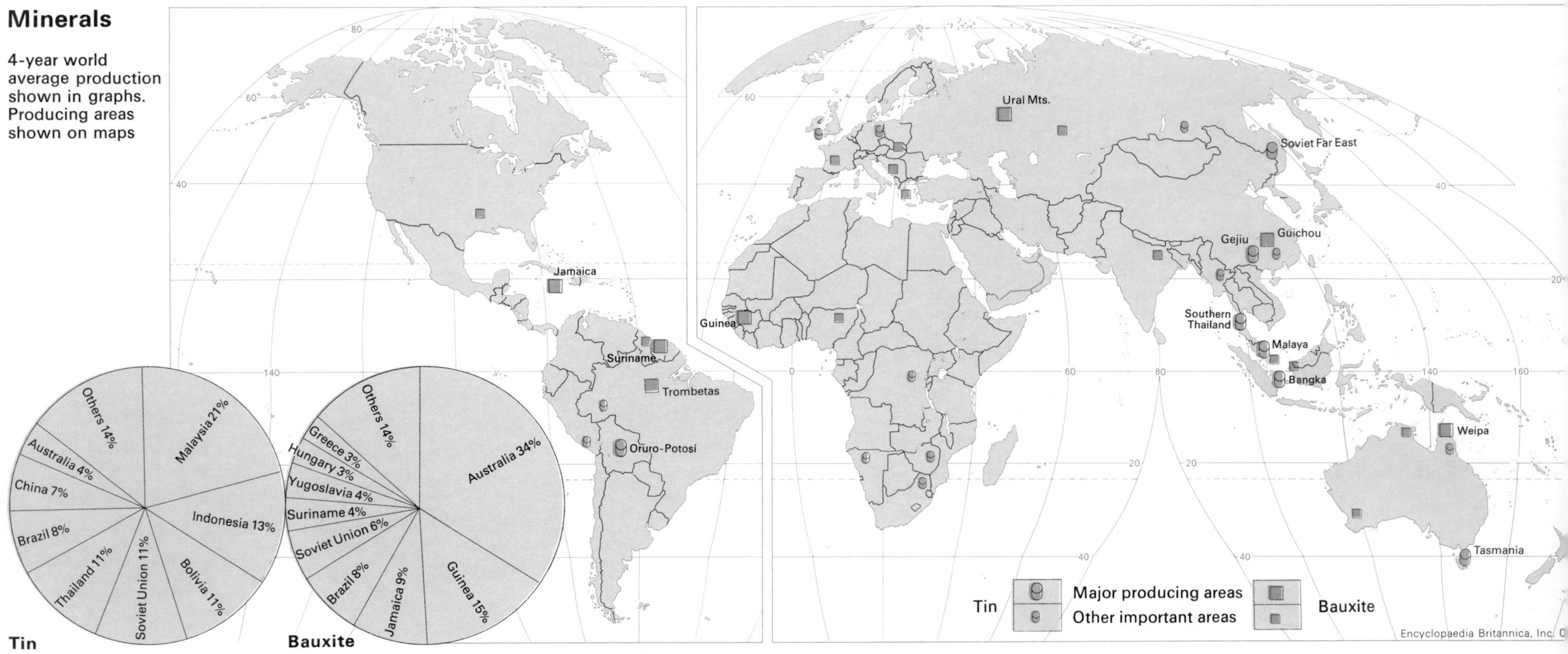
Others 14%
Malaysia 21%
Indonesia 13%
Bolivia 11%
Soviet Union 11%
Thailand 11%
Brazil 8%
China 7%
Australia 4%
Others 14%
Greece 3%
Hungary 3%
Yugoslavia 4%
Suriname 4%
Soviet Union 6%
Brazil 8%
Jamaica 9%
Guinea 15%
Australia 34%
Jamaica
Suriname
Trombetas
Oruro-Potosí
Guinea
Ural Mts.
Soviet Far East
Gejiu
Guichou
Southern Thailand
Malaya
Bangka
Weipa
Tasmania
Tin
Major producing areas
Other important areas
Bauxite
Encyclopaedia Britannica, Inc.

**Tin**
222,200 short tons
(201,600 metric tons)

**Bauxite**
91,290,000 short tons (82,817,000 metric tons)

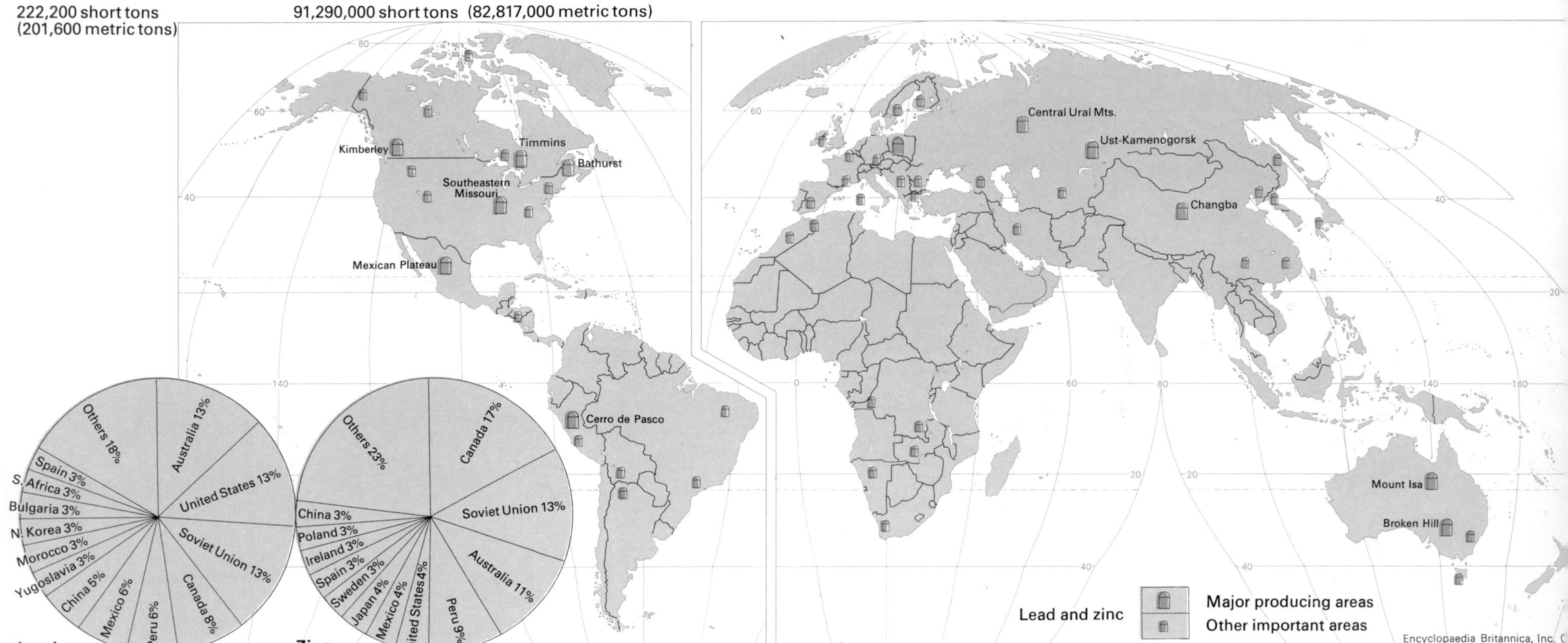
Others 18%
Australia 13%
United States 13%
Soviet Union 13%
Canada 8%
Peru 6%
Mexico 6%
China 5%
Yugoslavia 3%
Morocco 3%
N. Korea 3%
Bulgaria 3%
S. Africa 3%
Spain 3%
Others 23%
Canada 17%
Soviet Union 13%
Australia 11%
Peru 9%
United States 4%
Mexico 4%
Japan 4%
Sweden 3%
Spain 3%
Ireland 3%
Poland 3%
China 3%
Kimberley
Timmins
Bathurst
Southeastern Missouri
Mexican Plateau
Cerro de Pasco
Central Ural Mts.
Ust-Kamenogorsk
Changba
Mount Isa
Broken Hill
Lead and zinc
Major producing areas
Other important areas
Encyclopaedia Britannica, Inc.

**Lead**
3,700,600 short tons
(3,357,200 metric tons)

**Zinc**
7,081,300 short tons (6,424,100 metric tons)

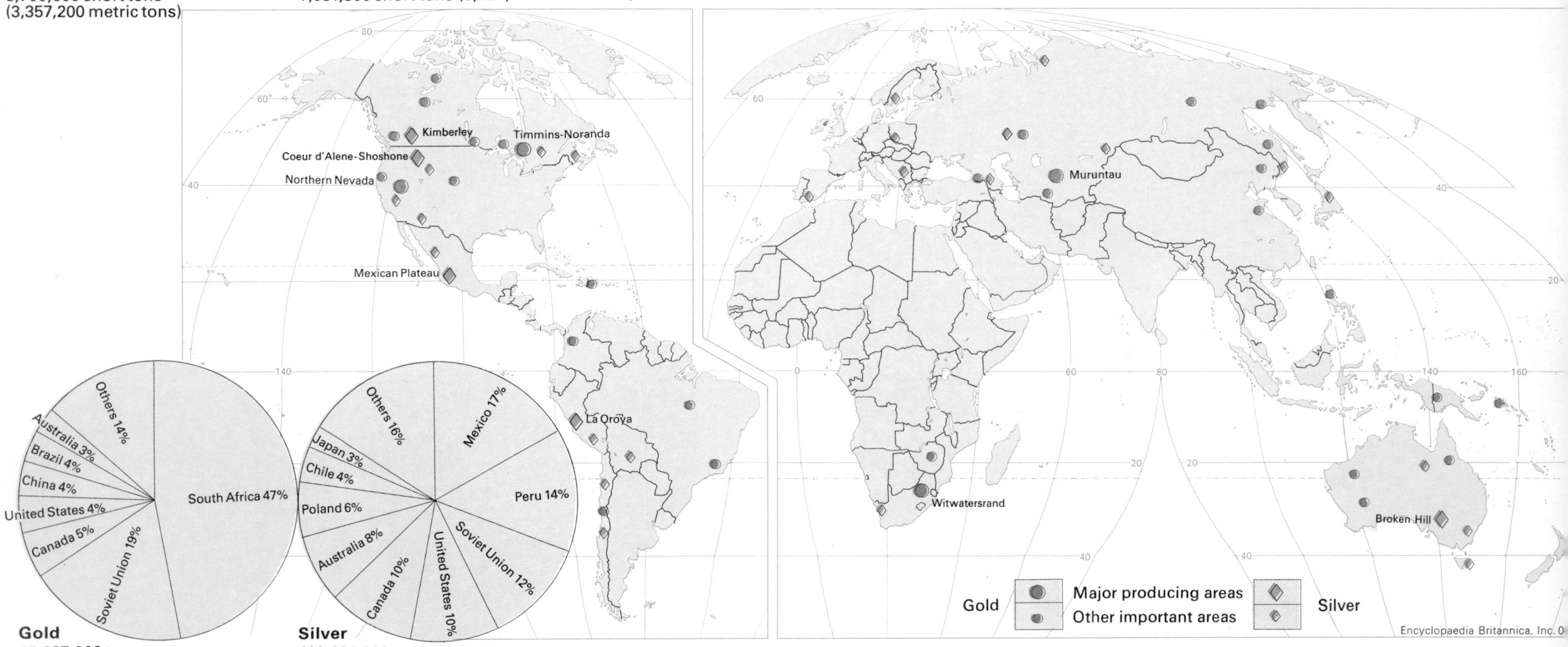
Others 14%
Australia 3%
Brazil 4%
China 4%
United States 4%
Canada 5%
Soviet Union 19%
South Africa 47%
Others 16%
Mexico 17%
Peru 14%
Soviet Union 12%
United States 10%
Canada 10%
Australia 8%
Poland 6%
Chile 4%
Japan 3%
Kimberley
Timmins-Noranda
Coeur d'Alene-Shoshone
Northern Nevada
Mexican Plateau
La Oroya
Muruntau
Witwatersrand
Broken Hill
Gold
Major producing areas
Other important areas
Silver
Encyclopaedia Britannica, Inc.

**Gold**
45,687,000 troy ounces
(1,421,000 kilograms)

**Silver**
400,634,000 troy ounces
(12,461,000 kilograms)

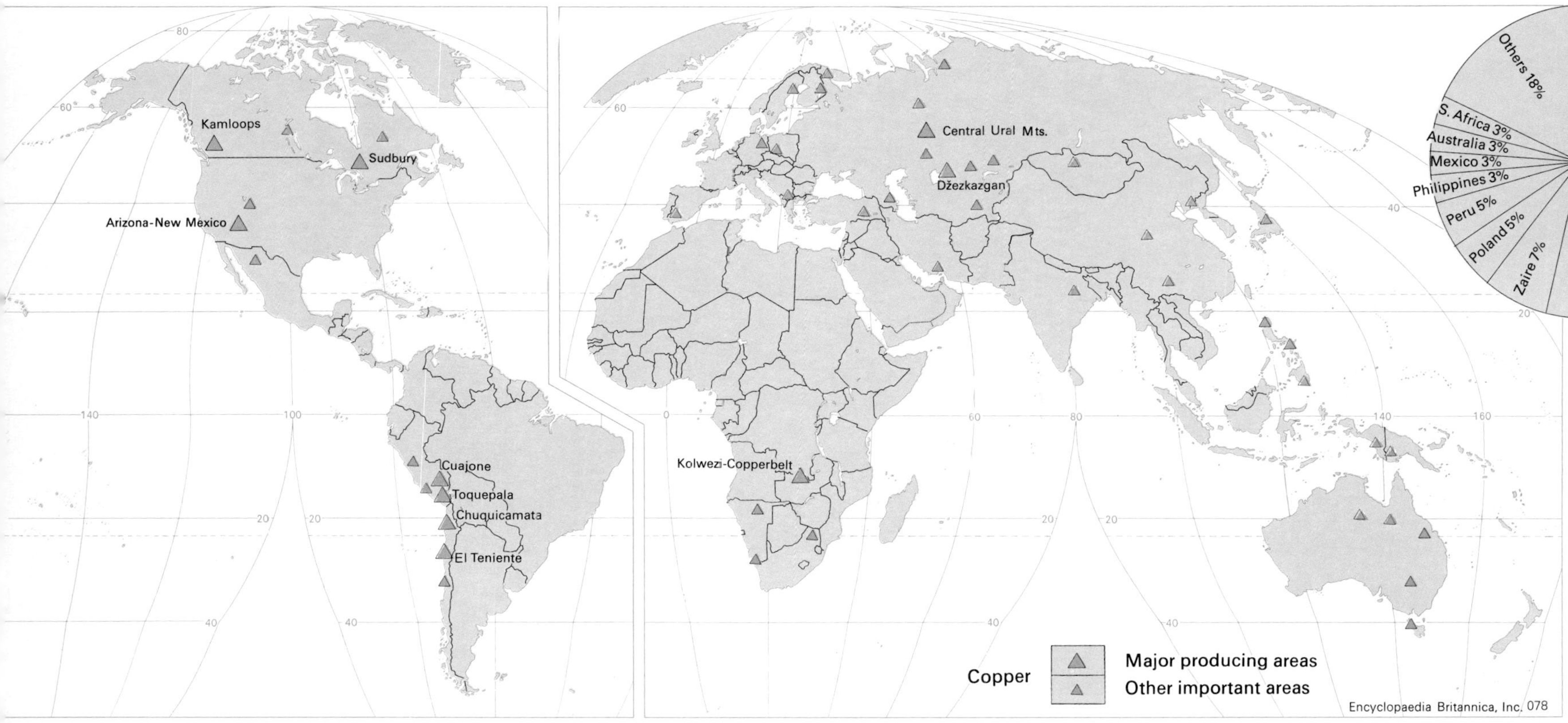
Kamloops
Sudbury
Arizona-New Mexico
Central Ural Mts.
Džezkazgan
Cuajone
Toquepala
Chuquicamata
El Teniente
Kolwezi-Copperbelt
Copper
Major producing areas
Other important areas
Encyclopaedia Britannica, Inc. 078

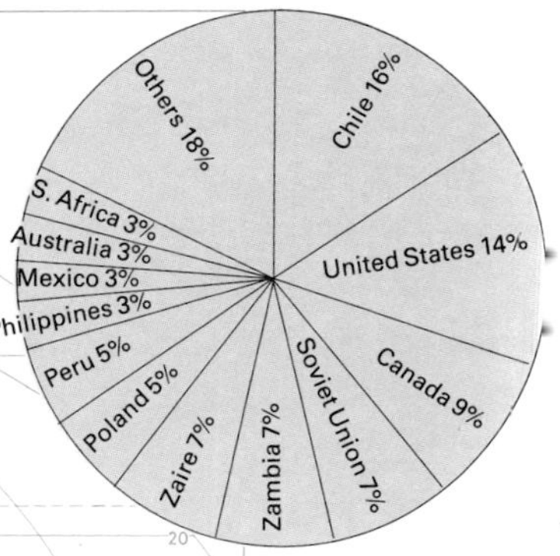
Others 18%
Chile 16%
United States 14%
Canada 9%
Soviet Union 7%
Zambia 7%
Zaire 7%
Poland 5%
Peru 5%
Philippines 3%
Mexico 3%
Australia 3%
S. Africa 3%

**Copper**
8,661,600
short tons
(7,857,700
metric tons)

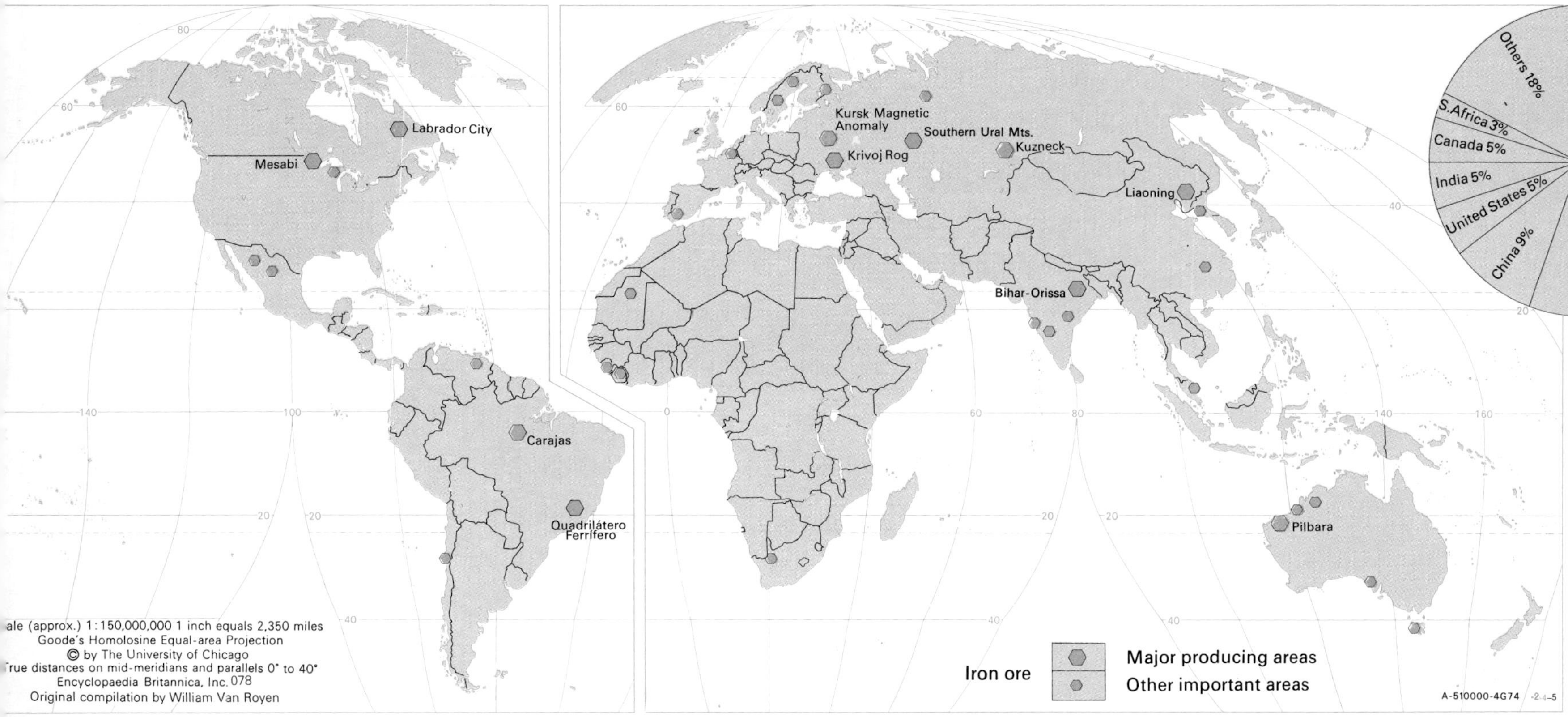
Labrador City
Mesabi
Kursk Magnetic Anomaly
Southern Ural Mts.
Kuzneck
Krivoj Rog
Liaoning
Bihar-Orissa
Carajas
Quadrilátero Ferrífero
Pilbara
ale (approx.) 1:150,000,000 1 inch equals 2,350 miles
Goode's Homolosine Equal-area Projection
© by The University of Chicago
True distances on mid-meridians and parallels 0° to 40°
Encyclopaedia Britannica, Inc. 078
Original compilation by William Van Royen
Iron ore
Major producing areas
Other important areas
A-510000-4G74

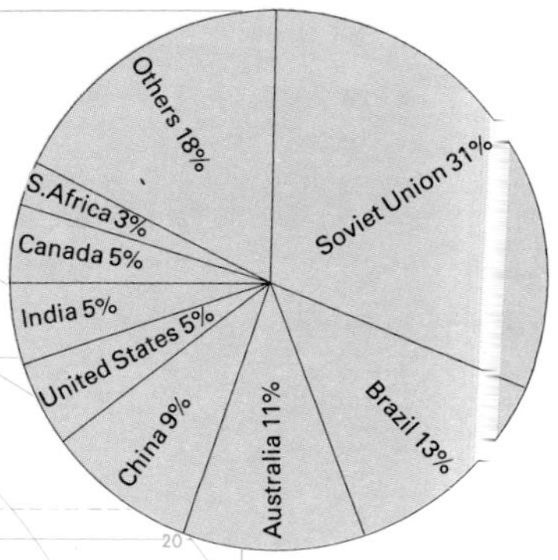
Others 18%
Soviet Union 31%
Brazil 13%
Australia 11%
China 9%
United States 5%
India 5%
Canada 5%
S.Africa 3%

**Iron ore**
883,984,900
short tons
(801,937,600
metric tons)

## Ferroalloying Minerals

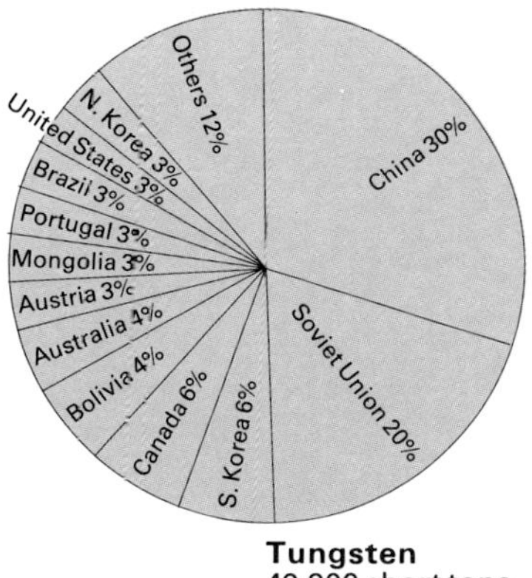
Others 12%
China 30%
Soviet Union 20%
S. Korea 8%
Canada 6%
Bolivia 4%
Australia 4%
Austria 3%
Mongolia 3%
Portugal 3%
Brazil 3%
United States 3%
N. Korea 3%

**Tungsten**
49,900 short tons
(45,300 metric tons)

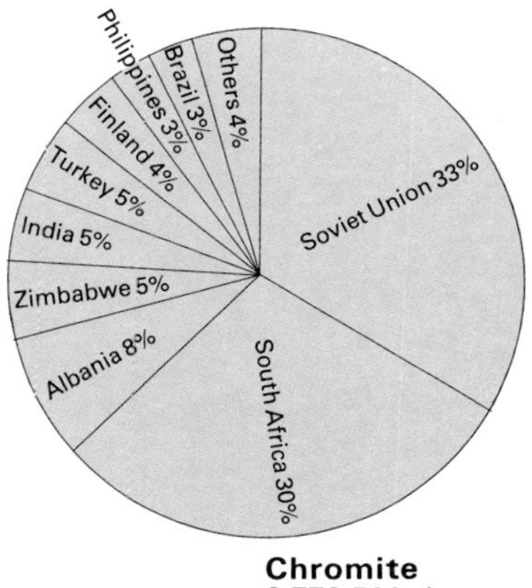
Others 4%
Soviet Union 33%
South Africa 30%
Albania 8%
Zimbabwe 5%
India 5%
Turkey 5%
Finland 4%
Philippines 3%
Brazil 3%

**Chromite**
9,779,500 short tons
(8,871,800 metric tons)

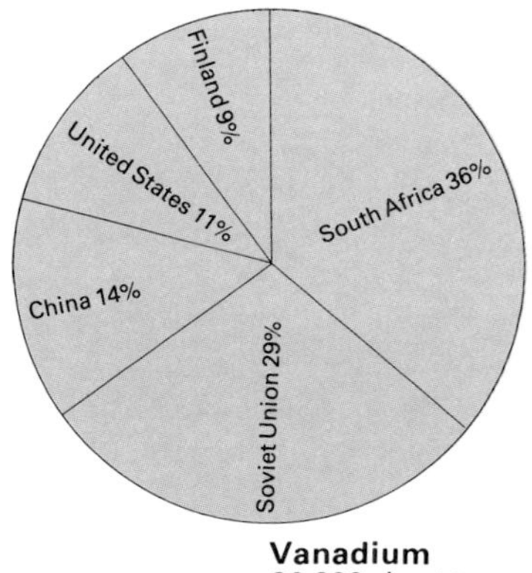
Finland 9%
South Africa 36%
Soviet Union 29%
China 14%
United States 11%

**Vanadium**
36,200 short tons
(32,900 metric tons)

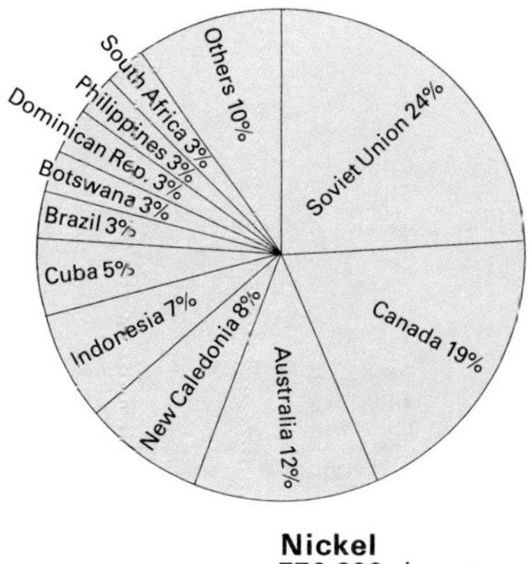
Others 10%
Soviet Union 24%
Canada 19%
Australia 12%
New Caledonia 8%
Indonesia 7%
Cuba 5%
Brazil 3%
Botswana 3%
Dominican Rep. 3%
Philippines 3%
South Africa 3%

**Nickel**
776,600 short tons
(704,500 metric tons)

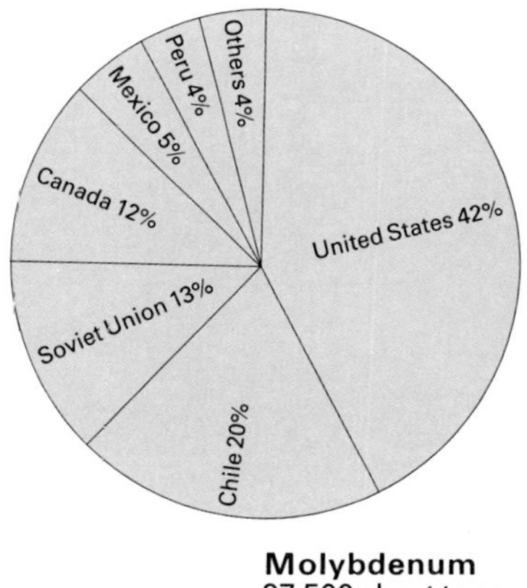
Others 4%
United States 42%
Chile 20%
Soviet Union 13%
Canada 12%
Mexico 5%
Peru 4%

**Molybdenum**
97,500 short tons
(88,400 metric tons)

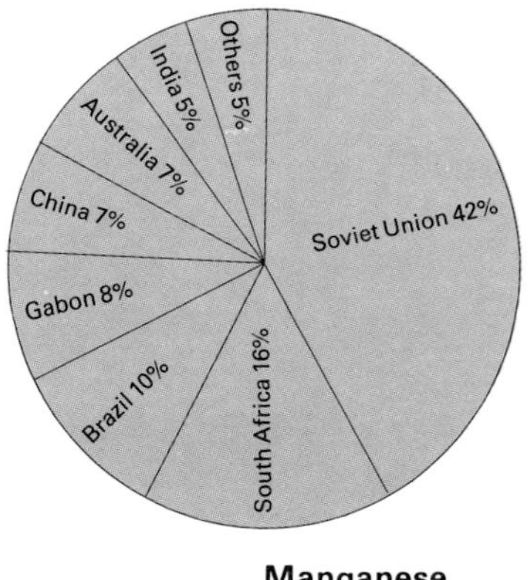
Others 5%
Soviet Union 42%
South Africa 16%
Brazil 10%
Gabon 8%
China 7%
Australia 7%
India 5%

**Manganese**
25,960,000 short tons
(23,550,500 metric tons)

# Energy Production and Consumption

Unit of measure is metric tons coal equivalent (m.t.c.e.)

## Production

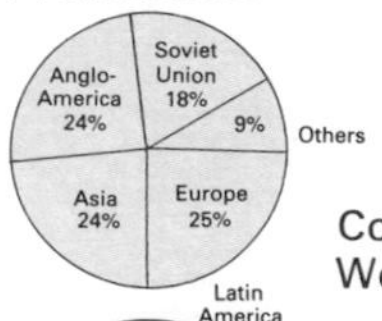
Anglo-America 24%
Soviet Union 18%
9%
Others
Asia 24%
Europe 25%

Coal and lignite
World total: **2,712,000,000**

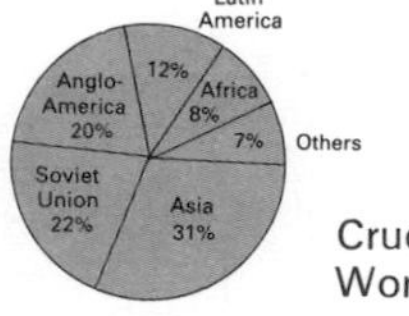
Latin America
Anglo-America 20%
12%
Africa 8%
7%
Others
Soviet Union 22%
Asia 31%

Crude petroleum
World total: **4,035,000,000**

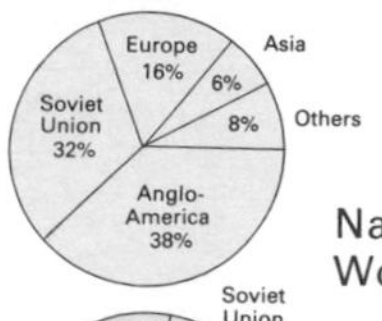
Europe 16%
Asia
6%
8%
Others
Soviet Union 32%
Anglo-America 38%

Natural gas
World total: **1,852,000,000**

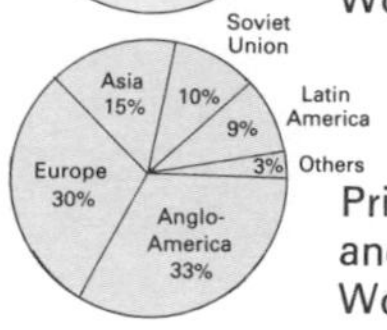
Soviet Union
Asia 15%
10%
Latin America
9%
3%
Others
Europe 30%
Anglo-America 33%

Primary electricity (hydro-, geothermal, and nuclear)
World total: **334,000,000**

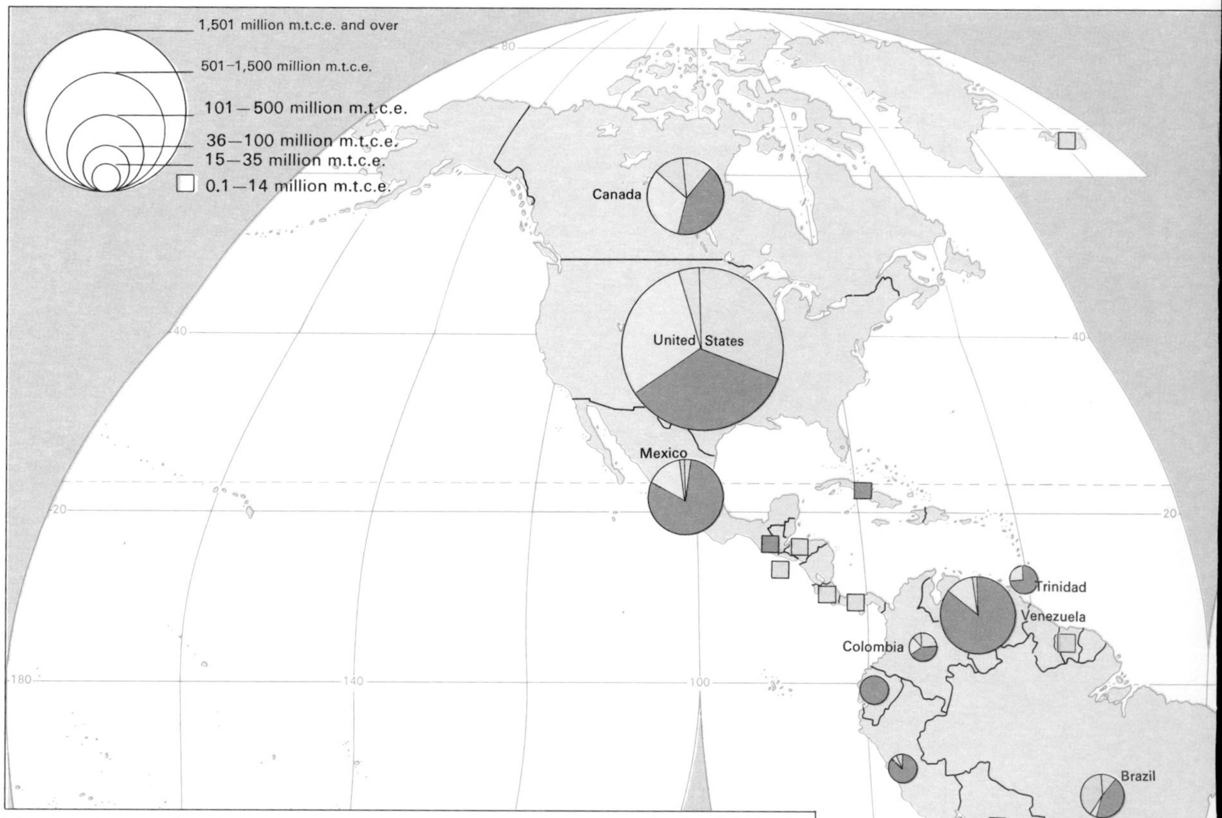
1,501 million m.t.c.e. and over
501–1,500 million m.t.c.e.
101—500 million m.t.c.e.
36—100 million m.t.c.e.
15—35 million m.t.c.e.
0.1—14 million m.t.c.e.
Canada
United States
Mexico
Trinidad
Venezuela
Colombia
Brazil
Argentina

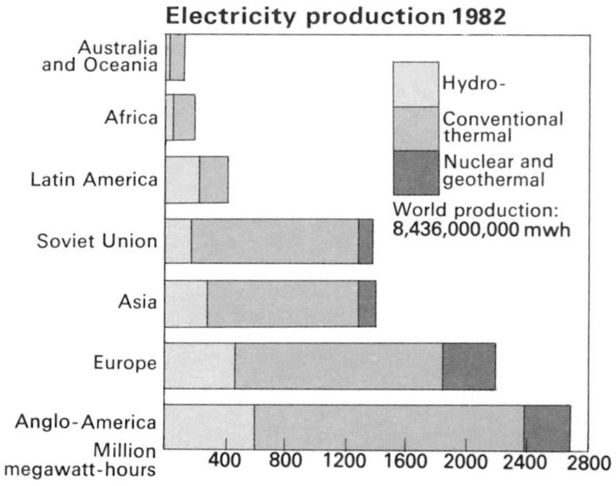
Electricity production 1982
Australia and Oceania
Africa
Latin America
Soviet Union
Asia
Europe
Anglo-America
Hydro-
Conventional thermal
Nuclear and geothermal
World production: 8,436,000,000 mwh
400
800
1200
1600
2000
2400
2800
Million megawatt-hours

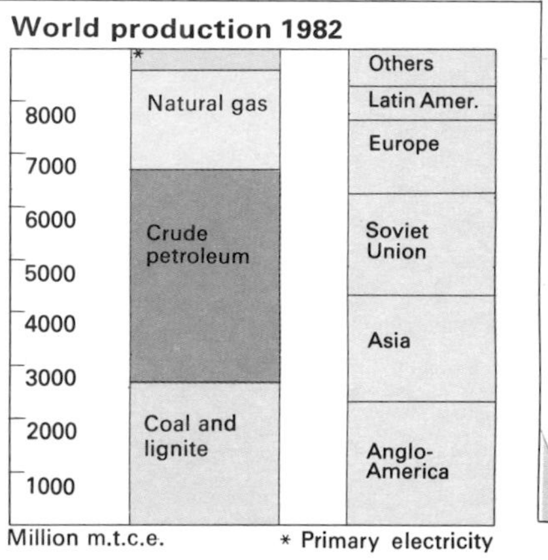
World production 1982
8000
7000
6000
5000
4000
3000
2000
1000
Million m.t.c.e.
Natural gas
Crude petroleum
Coal and lignite
Others
Latin Amer.
Europe
Soviet Union
Asia
Anglo-America
* Primary electricity

## Table of equivalents

| | |
|---|---|
| Coal, anthracite and bituminous | 1 metric ton = 1.0 m.t.c.e. |
| Lignite | 1 metric ton = 0.3 – 0.6 m.t.c.e. |
| Petroleum | 1 metric ton = 1.5 m.t.c.e. |
| Natural gas | 1,000 cubic meters = 1.33 m.t.c.e. |
| Hydro-, geothermal, and nuclear electricity | 1.0 megawatt-hour = 0.125 m.t.c.e. |

Potential energy of 1 metric ton of coal equals 28,000,000 B.T.U.

## Consumption

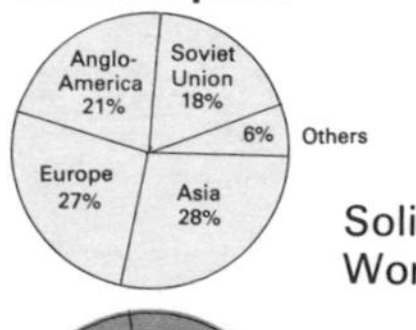
Anglo-America 21%
Soviet Union 18%
6%
Others
Europe 27%
Asia 28%

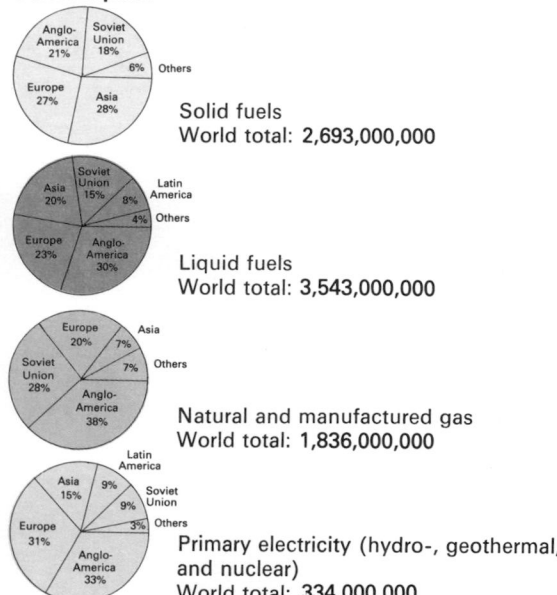

Solid fuels
World total: **2,693,000,000**

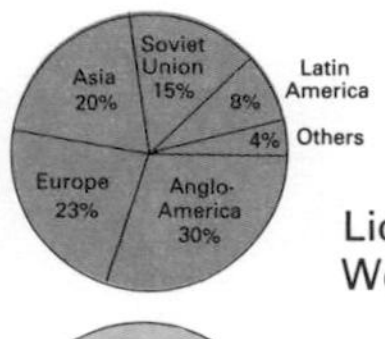
Soviet Union 15%
Latin America
Asia 20%
8%
4%
Others
Europe 23%
Anglo-America 30%

Liquid fuels
World total: **3,543,000,000**

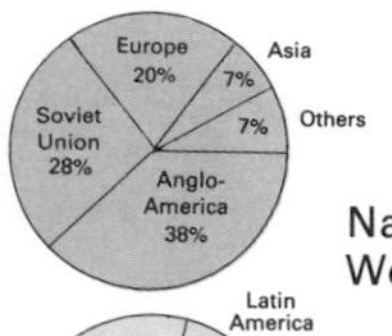
Europe 20%
Asia
7%
7%
Others
Soviet Union 28%
Anglo-America 38%

Natural and manufactured gas
World total: **1,836,000,000**

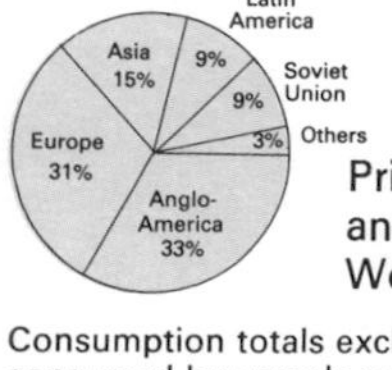
Latin America
Asia 15%
9%
Soviet Union
9%
3%
Others
Europe 31%
Anglo-America 33%

Primary electricity (hydro-, geothermal, and nuclear)
World total: **334,000,000**

Consumption totals exclude noncommercial fuels, fuels consumed by vessels engaged in international trade, and nonfuel petroleum products.

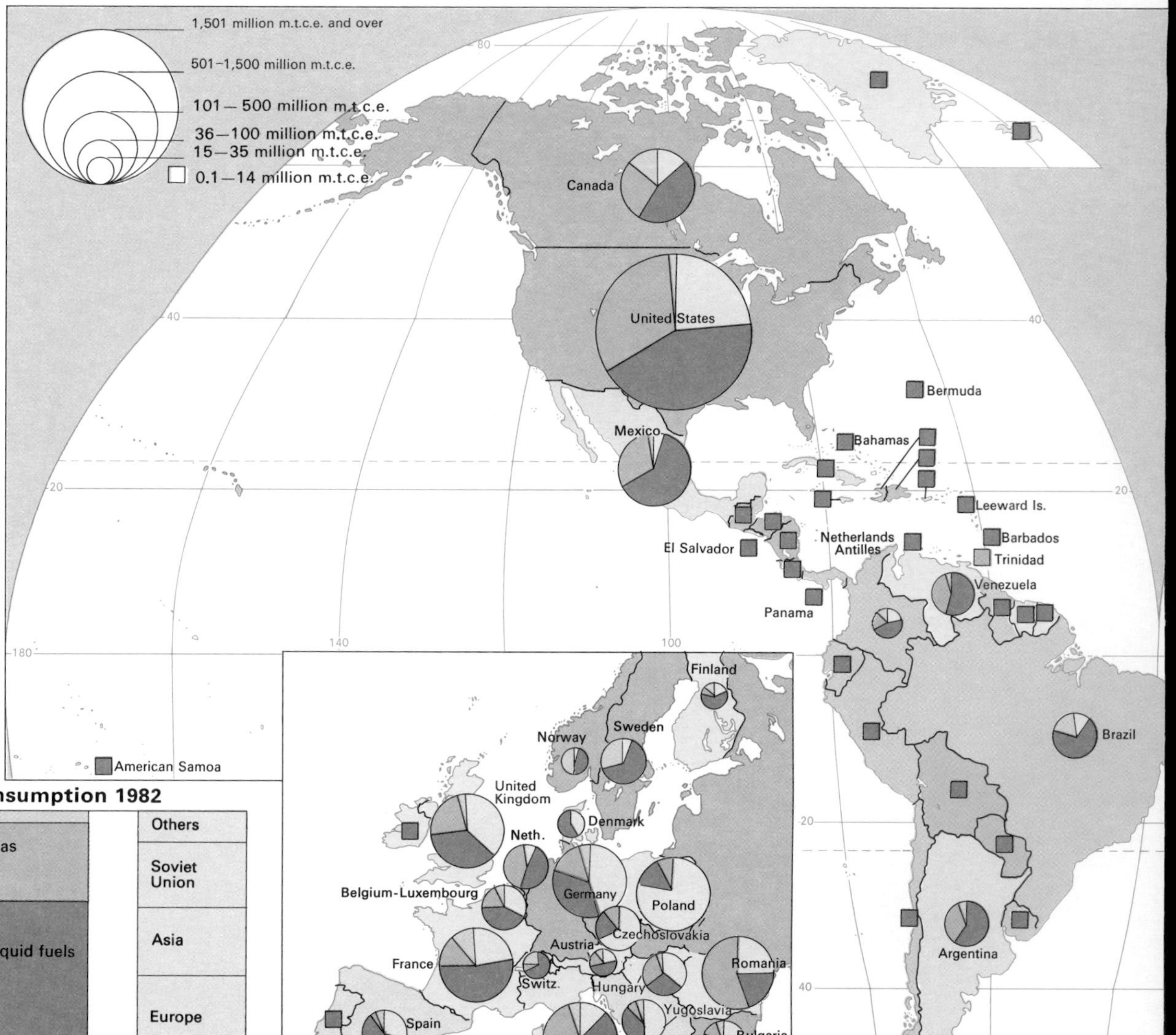
1,501 million m.t.c.e. and over
501–1,500 million m.t.c.e.
101— 500 million m.t.c.e.
36—100 million m.t.c.e.
15—35 million m.t.c.e.
0.1—14 million m.t.c.e.
Canada
United States
Mexico
Bermuda
Bahamas
Leeward Is.
Barbados
Trinidad
Netherlands Antilles
El Salvador
Venezuela
Panama
American Samoa
Brazil
Argentina
Finland
Norway
Sweden
United Kingdom
Denmark
Neth.
Belgium-Luxembourg
Germany
Poland
Czechoslovakia
Austria
France
Switz.
Hungary
Romania
Yugoslavia
Spain
Italy
Bulgaria
Malta

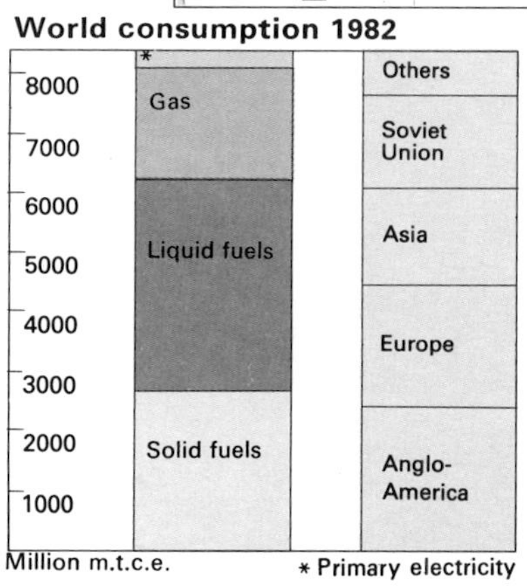
World consumption 1982
8000
7000
6000
5000
4000
3000
2000
1000
Million m.t.c.e.
Gas
Liquid fuels
Solid fuels
Others
Soviet Union
Asia
Europe
Anglo-America
* Primary electricity

## Per capita consumption

- 5.0 and more
- 2.5 – 4.9
- 1.0 – 2.4
- 0.5 – 0.9
- 0.2 – 0.4
- Less than 0.2

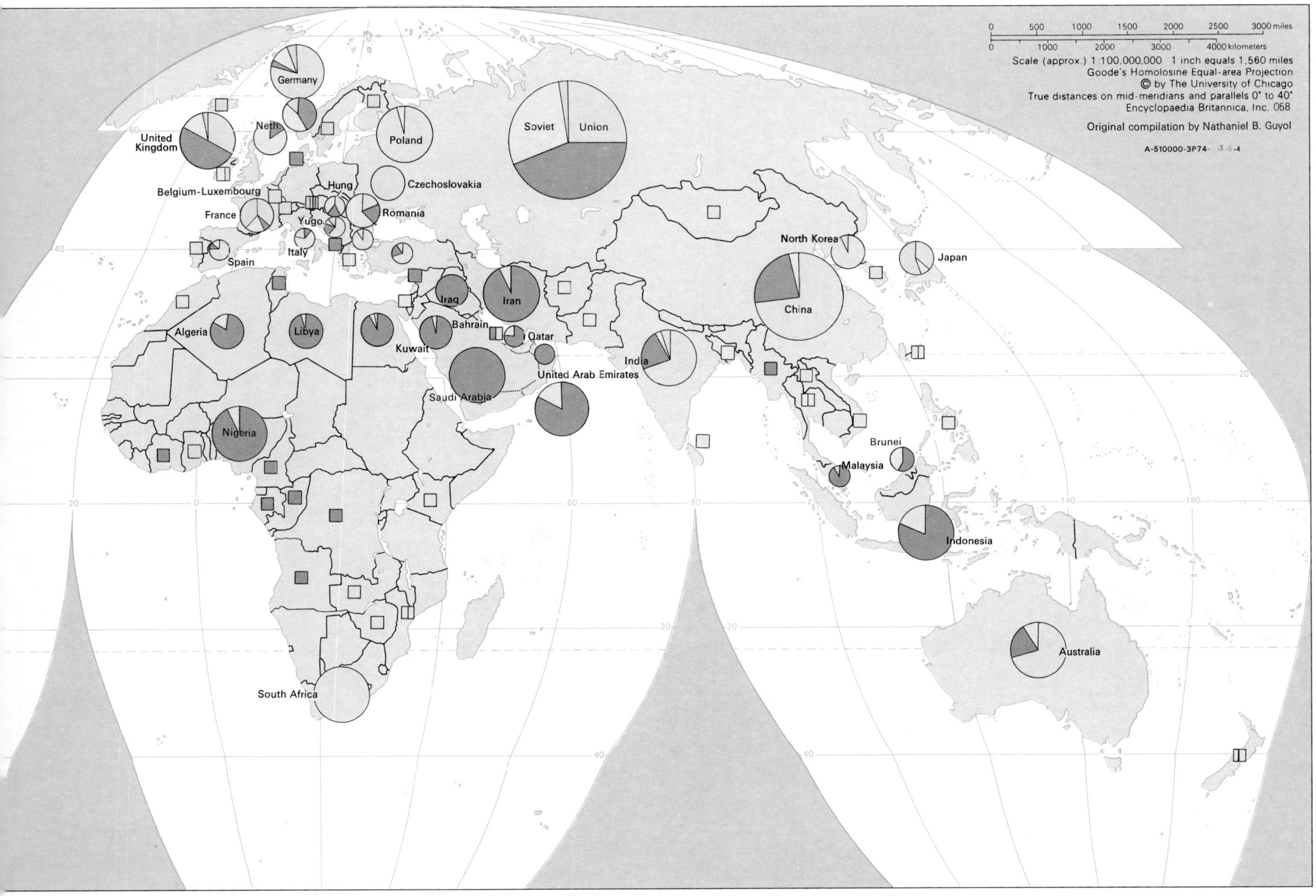

0 500 1000 1500 2000 2500 3000 miles
0 1000 2000 3000 4000 kilometers
Scale (approx.) 1:100,000,000 1 inch equals 1,560 miles
Goode's Homolosine Equal-area Projection
© by The University of Chicago
True distances on mid-meridians and parallels 0° to 40°
Encyclopaedia Britannica, Inc. 058
Original compilation by Nathaniel B. Guyol
A-510000-3P74-
Germany
United Kingdom
Neth.
Poland
Soviet
Union
Belgium-Luxembourg
Hung.
Czechoslovakia
France
Yugo.
Romania
Italy
Spain
North Korea
Japan
Iraq
Iran
China
Algeria
Libya
Kuwait
Bahrain
Qatar
India
United Arab Emirates
Saudi Arabia
Nigeria
Brunei
Malaysia
Indonesia
Australia
South Africa


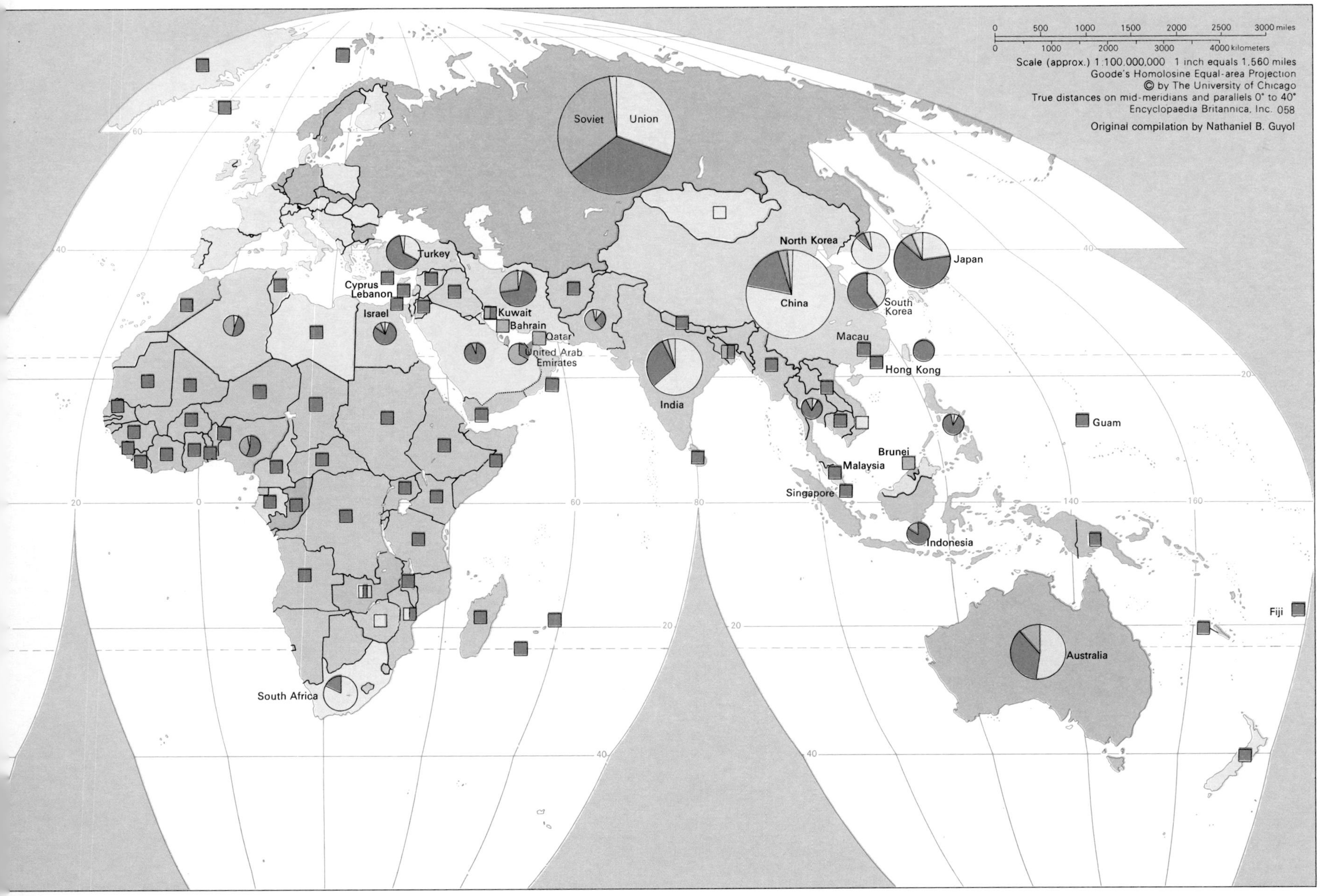

0 500 1000 1500 2000 2500 3000 miles
0 1000 2000 3000 4000 kilometers
Scale (approx.) 1:100,000,000 1 inch equals 1,560 miles
Goode's Homolosine Equal-area Projection
© by The University of Chicago
True distances on mid-meridians and parallels 0° to 40°
Encyclopaedia Britannica, Inc. 058
Original compilation by Nathaniel B. Guyol
Soviet
Union
North Korea
Japan
Turkey
China
South Korea
Cyprus
Lebanon
Israel
Kuwait
Bahrain
Qatar
United Arab Emirates
Macau
Hong Kong
India
Guam
Brunei
Malaysia
Singapore
Indonesia
Fiji
Australia
South Africa

## Gross National Product

| Total per country at market price<br>In billions of U.S. dollars | Number of countries |
|---|---|
| 300–3,670 | 9 |
| 50–300 | 26 |
| 10–50 | 28 |
| 3–10 | 34 |
| 1–3 | 32 |
| Less than 1 | 21 |
| No data available | |

| Per capita<br>In U.S. dollars | Number of countries |
|---|---|
| ■ 10,000–22,300 | 19 |
| ▮▮ 3,000–10,000 | 33 |
| ◗ 1,000–3,000 | 32 |
| ▲ 400–1,000 | 30 |
| ❤ 200–400 | 27 |
| ● Less than 200 | 15 |

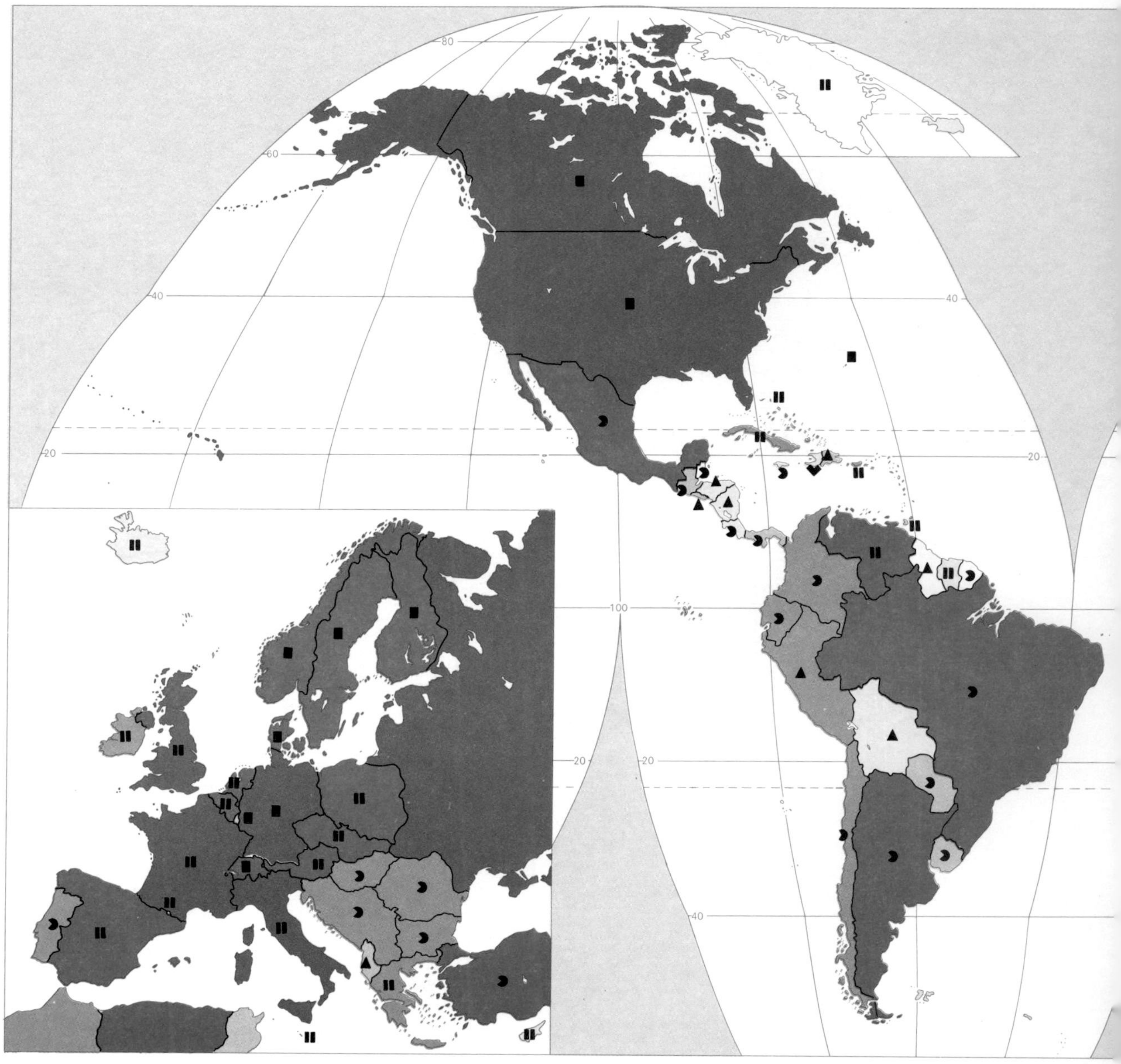

## International Trade

| Total per country<br>In billions of U.S. dollars | Number of countries |
|---|---|
| 100–560 | 10 |
| 30–100 | 18 |
| 10–30 | 25 |
| 3–10 | 19 |
| 1–3 | 33 |
| Less than 1 | 46 |
| No data available | |

| Per capita<br>In U.S. dollars | Number of countries |
|---|---|
| ■ 10,000–45,000 | 11 |
| ▮▮ 3,000–10,000 | 25 |
| ◗ 1,000–3,000 | 27 |
| ▲ 500–1,000 | 18 |
| ❤ 200–500 | 36 |
| ● Less than 200 | 39 |

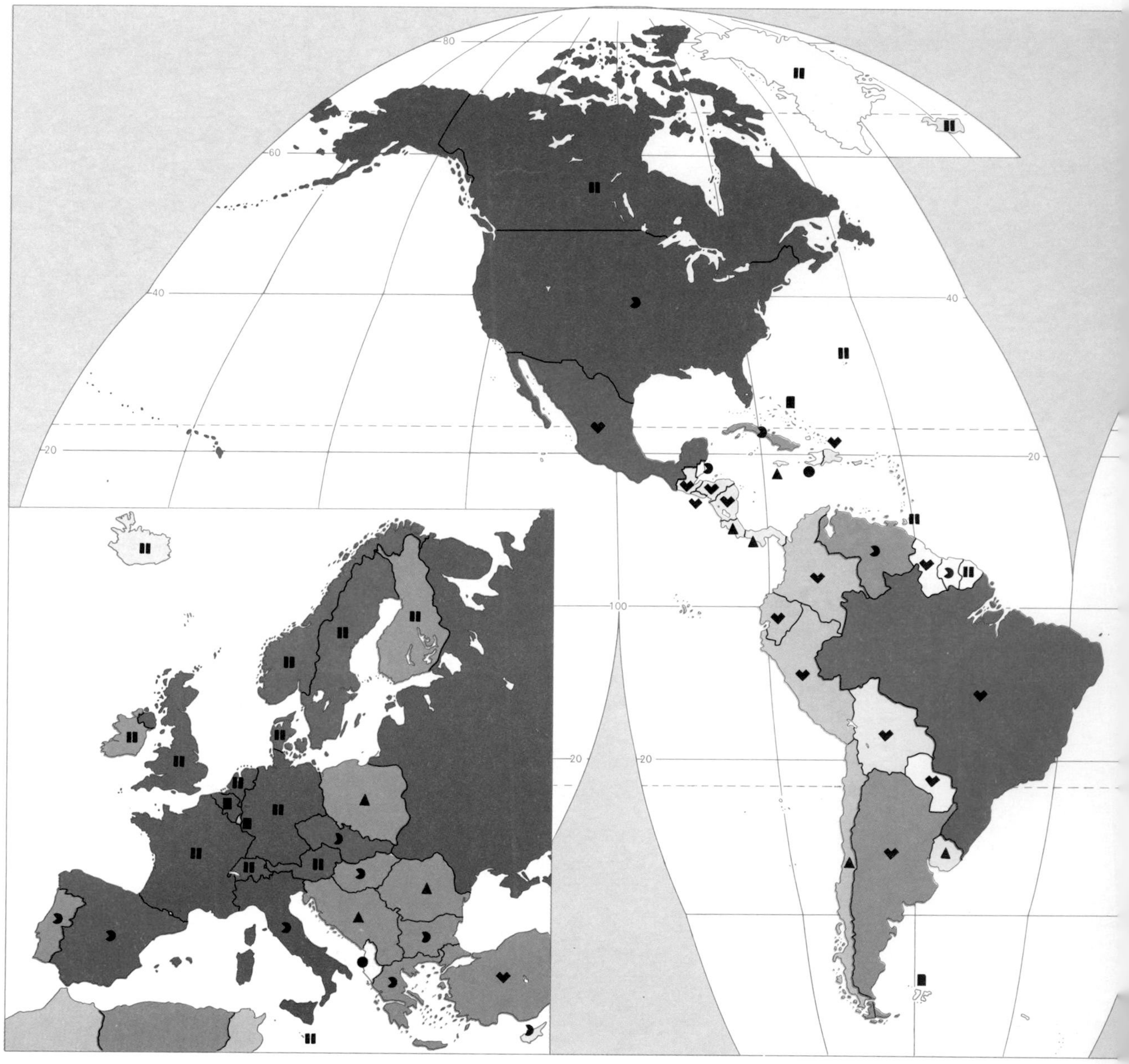

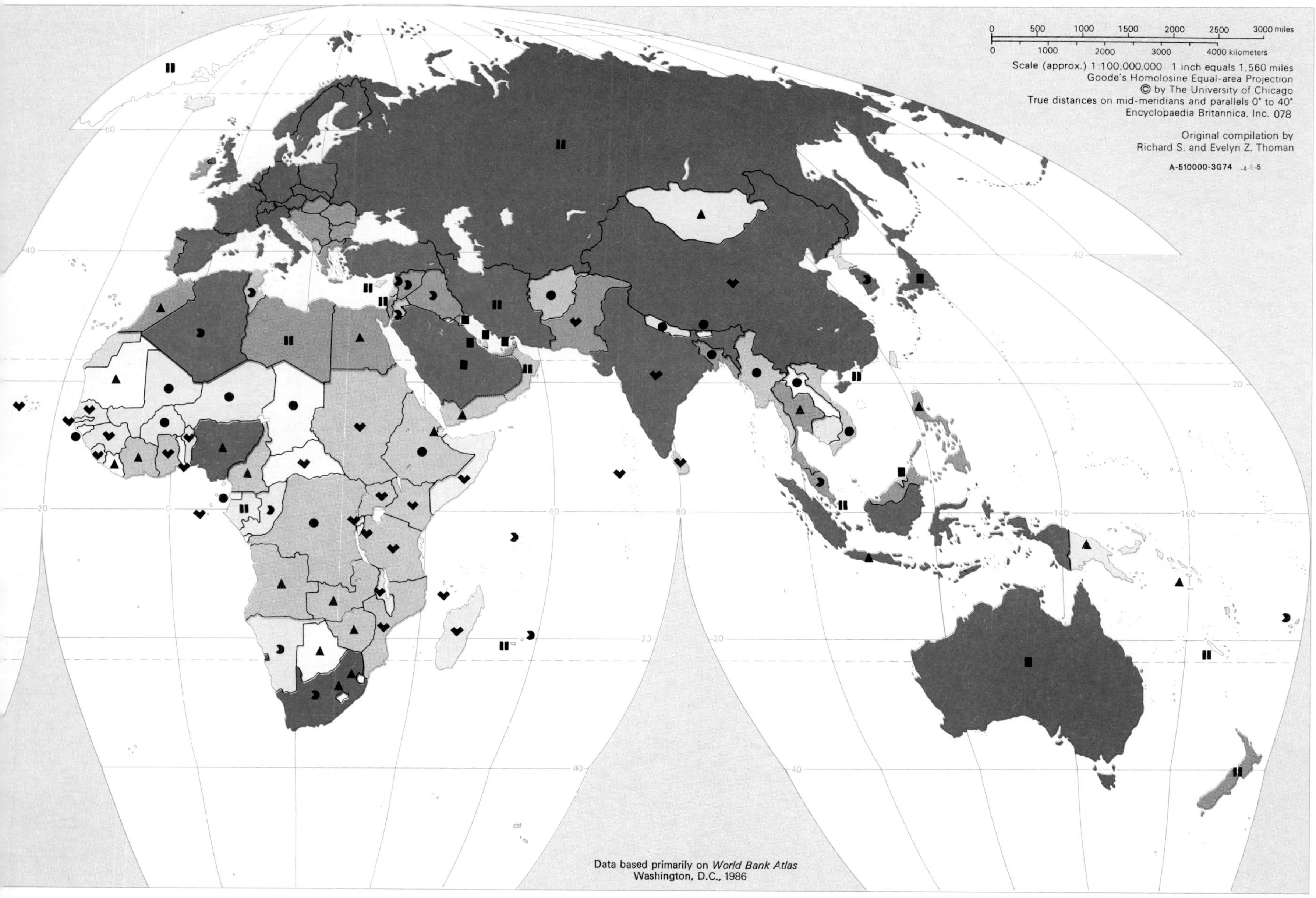
0 500 1000 1500 2000 2500 3000 miles
0 1000 2000 3000 4000 kilometers
Scale (approx.) 1:100,000,000 1 inch equals 1,560 miles
Goode's Homolosine Equal-area Projection
© by The University of Chicago
True distances on mid-meridians and parallels 0° to 40°
Encyclopaedia Britannica, Inc. 078
Original compilation by
Richard S. and Evelyn Z. Thoman
A-510000-3G74 -4-6-5
Data based primarily on *World Bank Atlas*
Washington, D.C., 1986

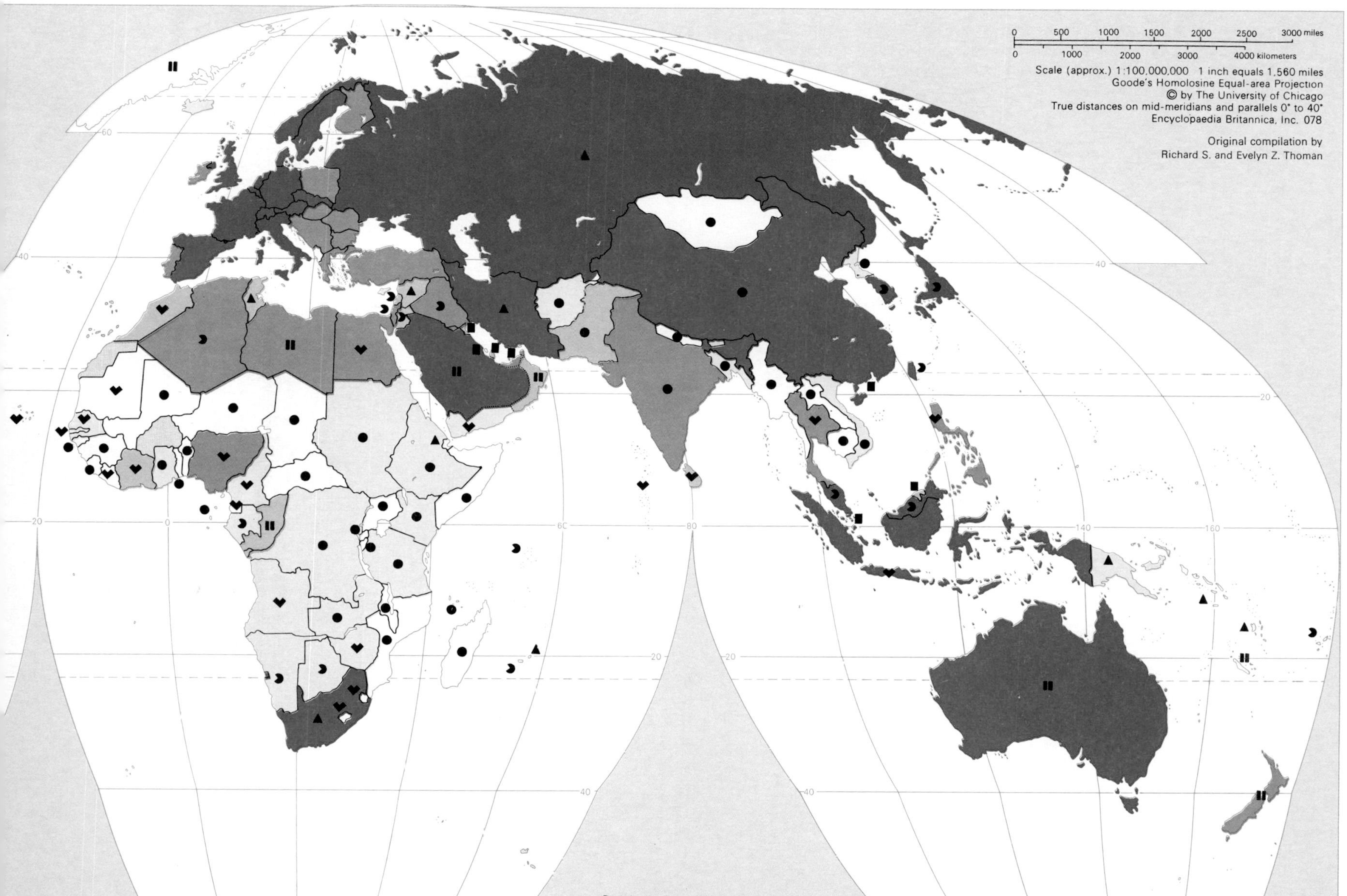
0 500 1000 1500 2000 2500 3000 miles
0 1000 2000 3000 4000 kilometers
Scale (approx.) 1:100,000,000 1 inch equals 1,560 miles
Goode's Homolosine Equal-area Projection
© by The University of Chicago
True distances on mid-meridians and parallels 0° to 40°
Encyclopaedia Britannica, Inc. 078
Original compilation by
Richard S. and Evelyn Z. Thoman
Based primarily on United Nations data, 1986

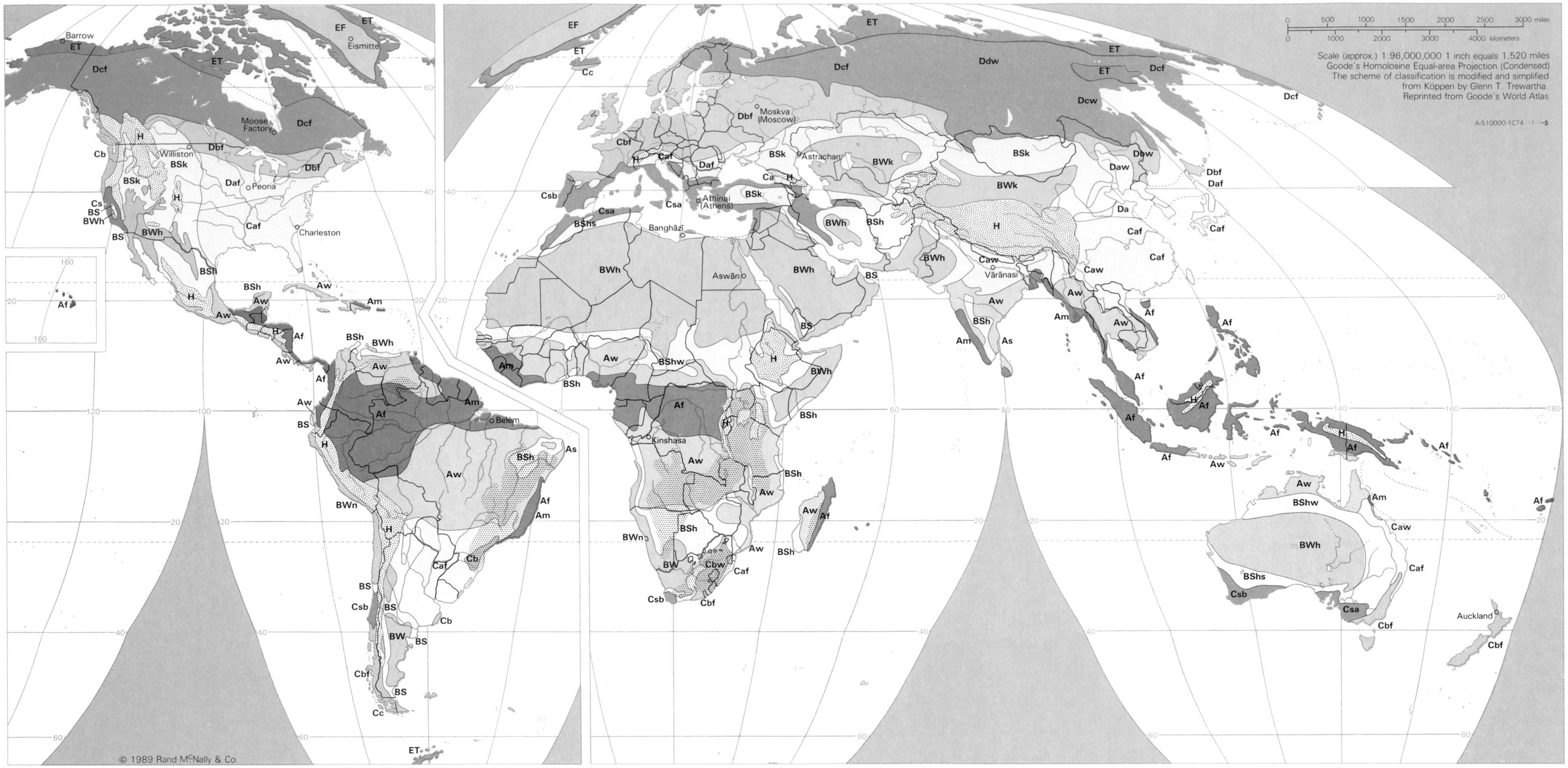
Scale (approx.) 1:96,000,000 1 inch equals 1,520 miles
Goode's Homolosine Equal-area Projection (Condensed)
The scheme of classification is modified and simplified from Köppen by Glenn T. Trewartha.
Reprinted from Goode's World Atlas
A-510000-1C74 -1 -1-5
© 1989 Rand McNally & Co.
Barrow
Eismitte
Moose Factory
Williston
Peoria
Charleston
Belém
Moskva (Moscow)
Astrachan'
Athínai (Athens)
Banghāzī
Aswān
Kinshasa
Vārānasi
Auckland

# Climate

**A. Tropical Rainy Climates**
- Tropical Rainforest (**Af**, **Am**)
- Tropical Savanna (**Aw**)
  - Cooler uplands stippled

**B. Dry Climates**
- Steppe (**BS**)
  - Tropical and Subtropical Steppe (**BSh**)
  - Middle latitude Steppe (**BSk**)
- Desert (**BW**)
  - Tropical and Subtropical Desert (**BWh**)
  - Middle latitude Desert (**BWk**)

**C. Humid Mesothermal Climates**
- Mediterranean or Dry Summer Subtropical (**Cs**)
- Humid Subtropical (**Ca**, warm summer)
- Marine West Coast (**Cb**, **Cc**, cool summer)

**D. Humid Microthermal Climates**
- Humid Continental, Warm Summer (**Da**)
- Humid Continental, Cool Summer (**Db**)
- Subarctic (**Dc**, **Dd**)

**E. Polar Climates**
- Tundra (**ET**)
- Ice Cap (**EF**)

**H. Extensive Uplands**

**Undifferentiated Highlands**

Two types of higher elevation climatic region are shown: (1) lower and flatter 'extensive uplands' areas above 2000 feet (600 meters), which, though cooler and wetter, contain no topographic barriers to climatic regions around them, and are thus classifiable with them; and (2) 'undifferentiated highlands,' mountainous regions of great elevation (forming barriers to regional atmospheric circulation) and great local relief, creating microclimates effectively unmappable at this scale.

## Type Regions and Subtypes

A – Tropical forest climates: coolest month above 64.4°F. (18°C.).

B – Dry climates

**BS** – Steppe or semiarid climate.

**BW** – Desert or arid climate.

*C – Mesothermal forest climates: coldest month above 32°F. (0°C.) but below 64.4°F. (18°C.); warmest month above 50°F. (10°C.).

*D – Microthermal, snow-forest climates: coldest month below 32°F. (0°C.); warmest month above 50°F. (10°C.).

E – Polar climates: warmest month below 50°F. (10°C.).

**ET** – Tundra climate: warmest month below 50°F. (10°C.) but above 32°F. (0°C.).

**EF** – Perpetual frost: all months below 32°F. (0°C.).

a – Warmest month above 71.6°F. (22°C.).

b – Warmest month below 71.6°F. (22°C.).

c – Less than four months over 50°F. (10°C.).

d – Same as "c", but coldest month below -36.4°F. (-38°C.).

f – Constantly moist; precipitation all through the year.

*h – Hot and dry; all months above 32°F. (0°C.).

*k – Cold and dry; at least one month below 32°F. (0°C.)

m – Monsoon rain; short dry season, but total rainfall sufficient to support rainforest.

n – Frequent fog.

s – Dry season in summer.

w – Dry season in winter.

* Modification of Köppen definition

Curves show Fahrenheit temperature; vertical bars show precipitation in inches.

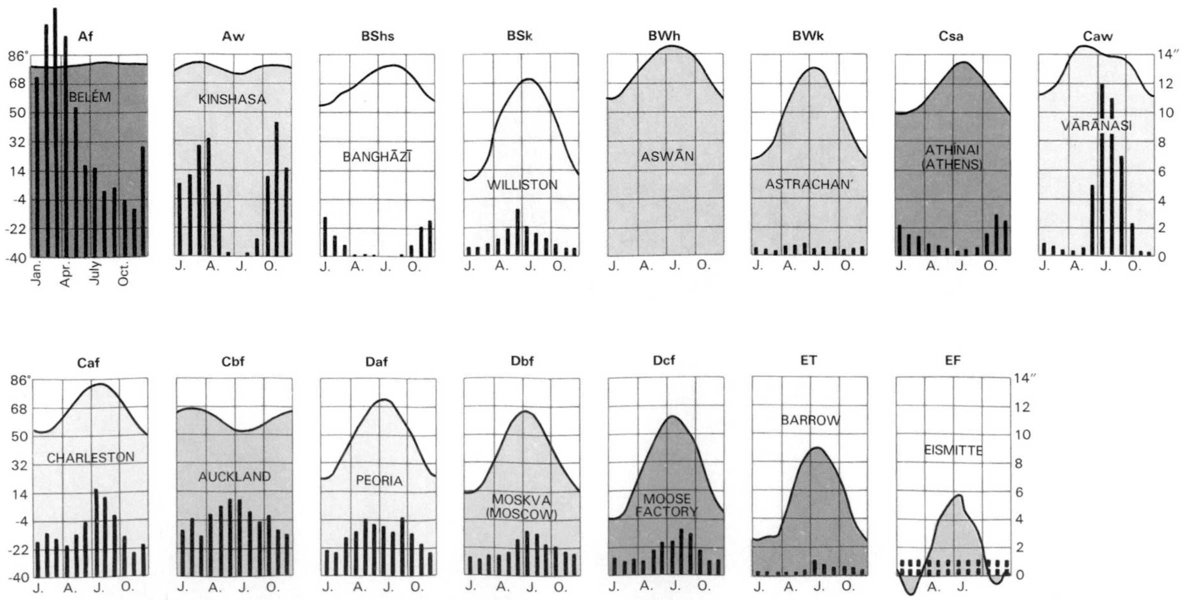
Af BELÉM
Aw KINSHASA
BShs BANGHĀZĪ
BSk WILLISTON
BWh ASWĀN
BWk ASTRACHAN'
Csa ATHÍNAI (ATHENS)
Caw VĀRĀNASI
Caf CHARLESTON
Cbf AUCKLAND
Daf PEORIA
Dbf MOSKVA (MOSCOW)
Dcf MOOSE FACTORY
ET BARROW
EF EISMITTE
86° 68 50 32 14 -4 -22 -40
14" 12 10 8 6 4 2 0
Jan. Apr. July Oct.
J. A. J. O.

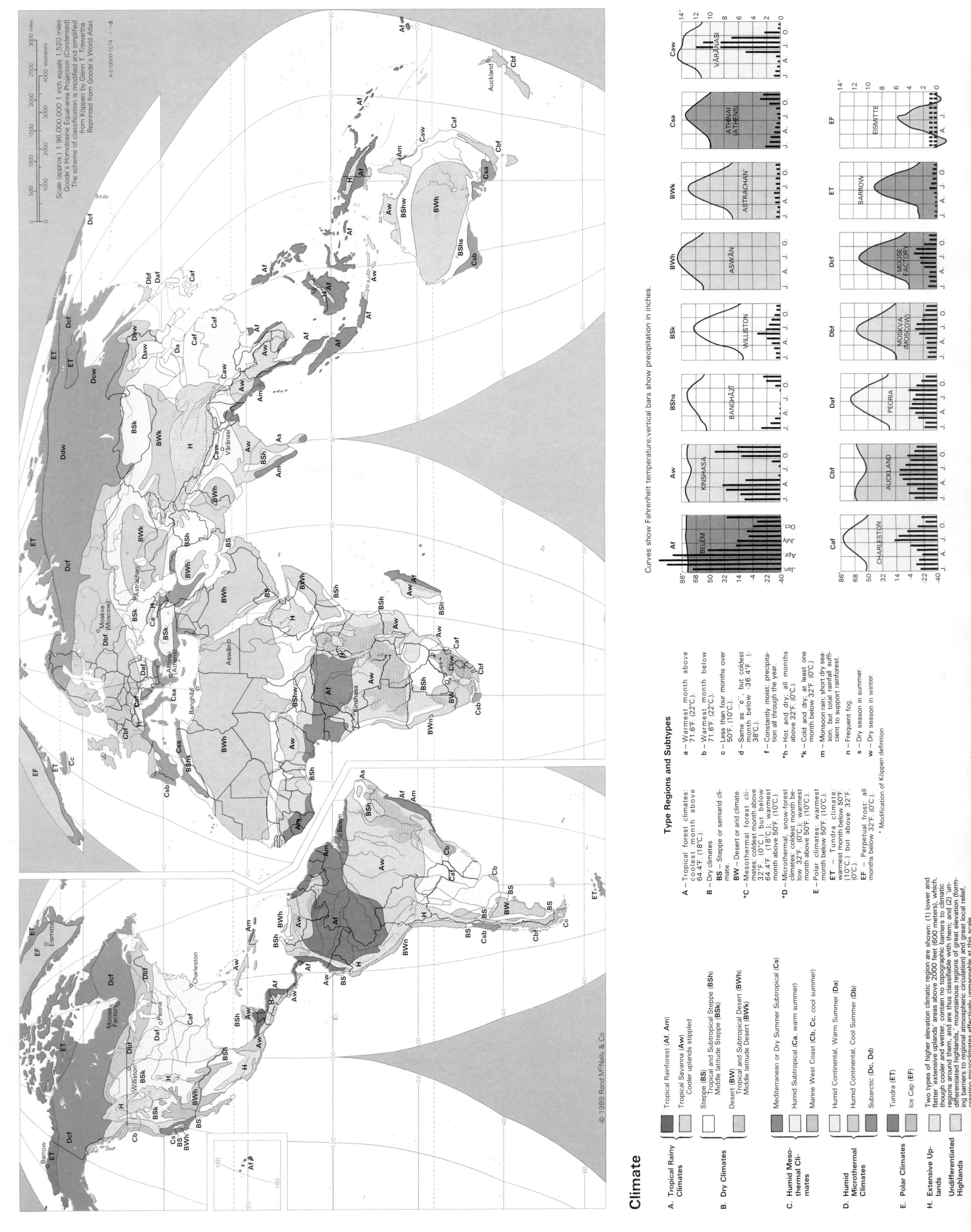

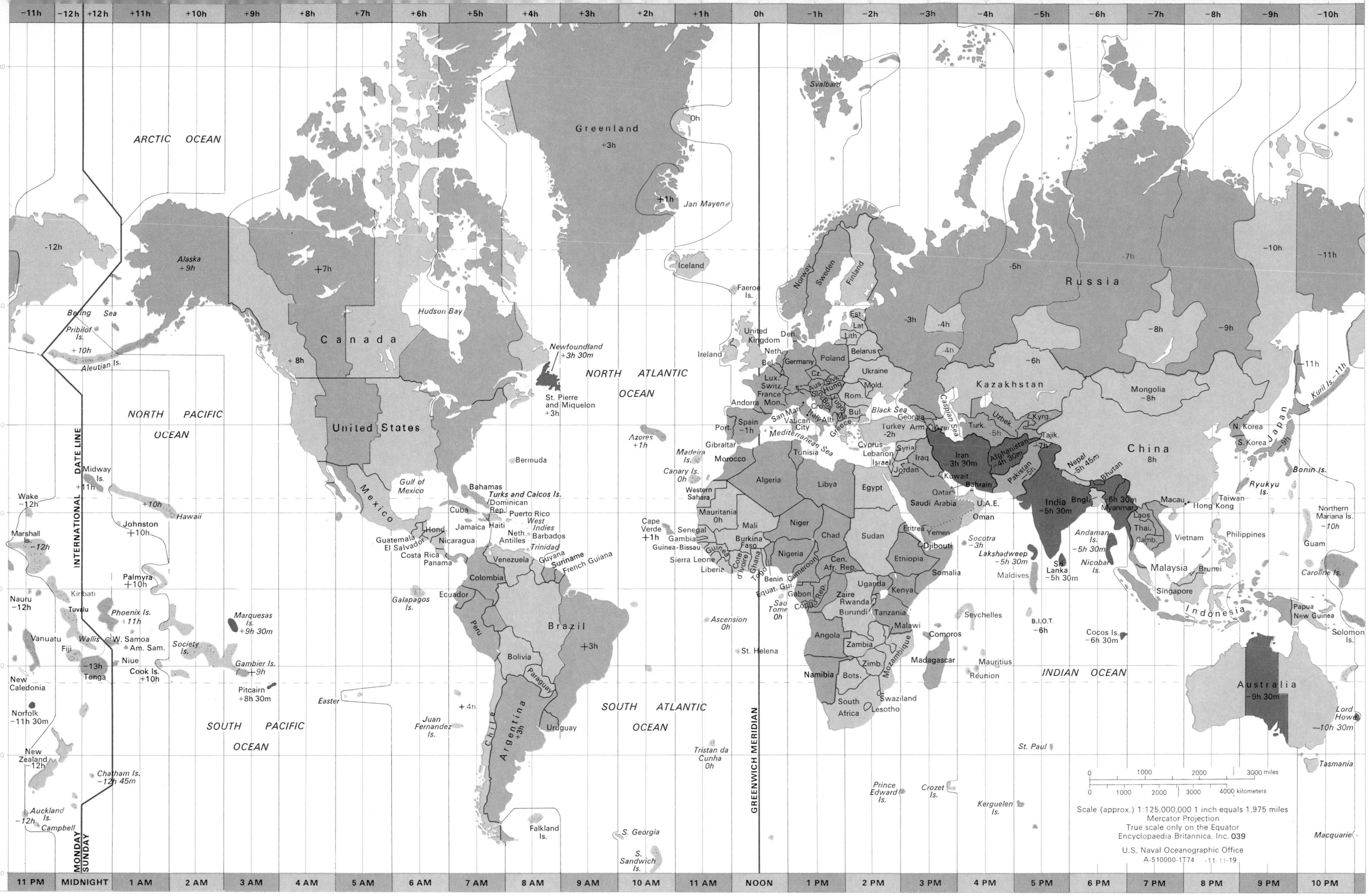
-11h -12h +12h +11h +10h +9h +8h +7h +6h +5h +4h +3h +2h +1h 0h -1h -2h -3h -4h -5h -6h -7h -8h -9h -10h
11 PM MIDNIGHT 1 AM 2 AM 3 AM 4 AM 5 AM 6 AM 7 AM 8 AM 9 AM 10 AM 11 AM NOON 1 PM 2 PM 3 PM 4 PM 5 PM 6 PM 7 PM 8 PM 9 PM 10 PM
INTERNATIONAL DATE LINE
MONDAY
SUNDAY
GREENWICH MERIDIAN
ARCTIC OCEAN
NORTH PACIFIC OCEAN
SOUTH PACIFIC OCEAN
NORTH ATLANTIC OCEAN
SOUTH ATLANTIC OCEAN
INDIAN OCEAN
Greenland +3h
Alaska +9h
Canada
United States
Mexico
Brazil +3h
Argentina +3h
Russia
China 8h
Kazakhstan
Mongolia -8h
India -5h 30m
Iran 3h 30m
Australia -9h 30m
Newfoundland +3h 30m
St. Pierre and Miquelon +3h
Chatham Is. -12h 45m
Marquesas Is. +9h 30m
Pitcairn +8h 30m
Norfolk -11h 30m
Lord Howe -10h 30m
Nepal 5h 45m
Cocos Is. -6h 30m
Scale (approx.) 1:125,000,000 1 inch equals 1,975 miles
Mercator Projection
True scale only on the Equator
Encyclopaedia Britannica, Inc. 039
U.S. Naval Oceanographic Office
A-510000-1T74 -11-11-19

## Time Zones

- Standard time zone of even-numbered hours from Greenwich time
- Standard time zone of odd-numbered hours from Greenwich time
- Time varies from the standard time zone by half an hour
- Time varies from the standard time zone by other than half an hour

h m hours, minutes

The standard time zone system, fixed by international agreement and by law in each country, is based on a theoretical division of the globe into 24 zones of 15° longitude each. The mid-meridian of each zone fixes the hour for the entire zone. The zero time zone extends 7½° east and 7½° west of the Greenwich meridian, 0° longitude. Since the earth rotates toward the east, time zones to the west of Greenwich are earlier, to the east, later.

Plus and minus hours at the top of the map are added to or subtracted from local time to find Greenwich time. Local standard time can be determined for any area in the world by adding one hour for each time zone counted in an easterly direction from one's own, or by subtracting one hour for each zone counted in a westerly direction. To separate one day from the next, the 180th meridian has been designated as the international date line. On both sides of the line the time of day is the same, but west of the line it is one day later than it is to the east.

Countries that adhere to the international zone system adopt the zone applicable to their location. Some countries, however, establish time zones based on political boundaries, or adopt the time zone of a neighboring unit. For all or part of the year some countries also advance their time by one hour, thereby utilizing more daylight hours each day.

## Surface Configuration

**Smooth lands**

- Level plains: nearly all slopes gentle; local relief less than 100 ft. (30 m.)
- Irregular plains: majority of slopes gentle; local relief 100-300 ft. (30-90 m.)

**Broken lands**

- Tablelands and plateaus: majority of slopes gentle, with the gentler slopes on the uplands; local relief more than 300 ft. (90 m.)
- Hill-studded plains: majority of slopes gentle, with the gentler slopes in the lowlands; local relief 300-1,000 ft. (90-300 m.)
- Mountain-studded plains: majority of slopes gentle, with the gentler slopes in the lowlands; local relief more than 1,000 ft. (300 m.)

**Rough lands**

- Hill lands: steeper slopes predominate; local relief less than 1,000 ft. (300 m.)
- Mountains: steeper slopes predominate; local relief 1,000-5,000 ft. (300-1,500 m.)
- Mountains of great relief: steeper slopes predominate; local relief more than 5,000 ft. (1,500 m.)

**Other surfaces**

- Ice caps: permanent ice
- Maximum extent of glaciation

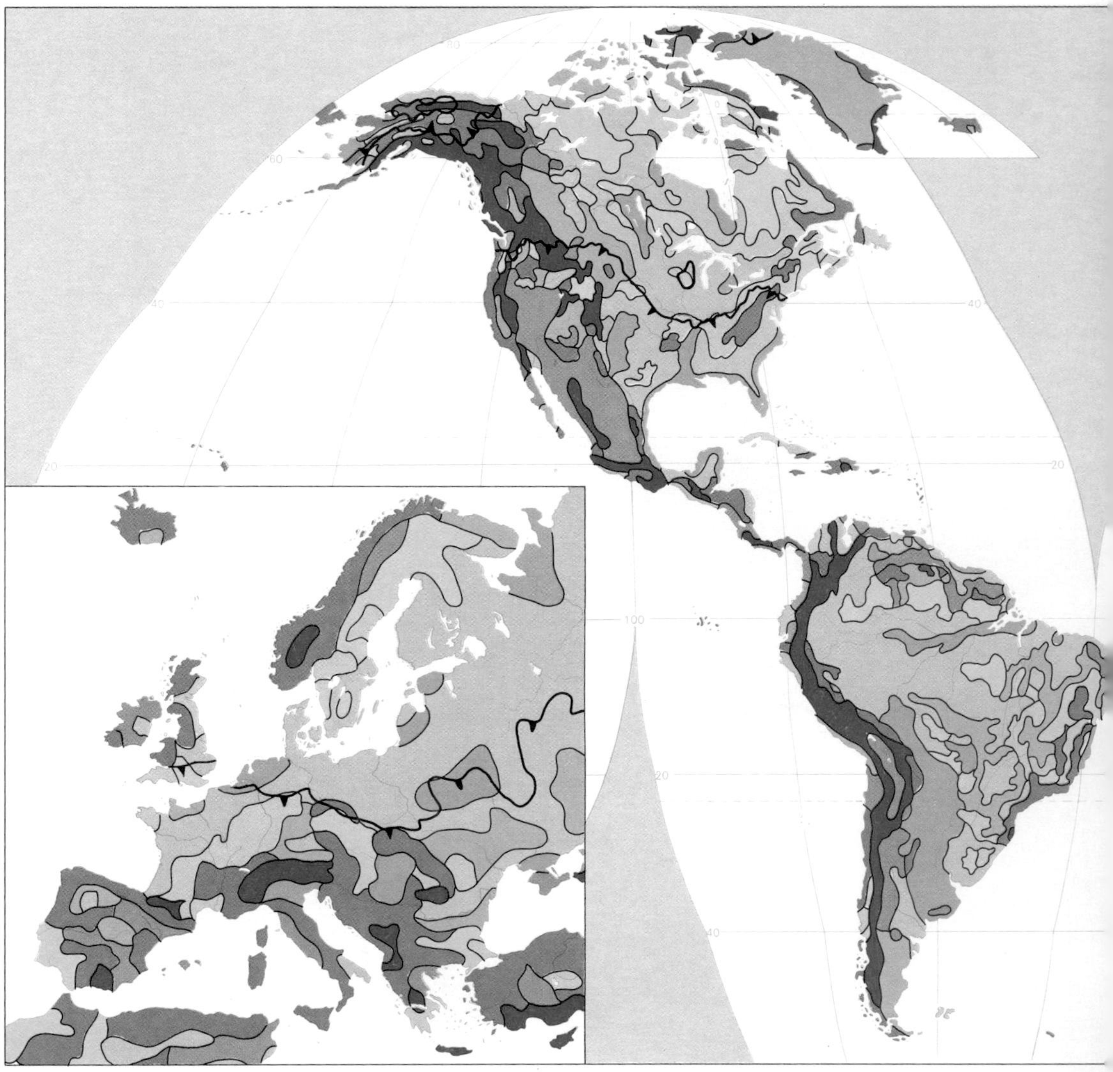

## Earth Structure and Tectonics

- Precambrian stable shield areas
- Exposed Precambrian rock
- Paleozoic and Mesozoic flat-lying sedimentary rocks
- Principal Paleozoic and Mesozoic folded areas
- Cenozoic sedimentary rocks
- Principal Cenozoic folded areas
- Lava plateaus
- Major trends of folding

**Geologic time chart**

Precambrian—from formation of the earth (at least 4 billion years ago) to 600 million years ago

Paleozoic—from 600 million to 200 million years ago

Mesozoic—from 200 million to 70 million years ago

Cenozoic—from 70 million years ago to present time

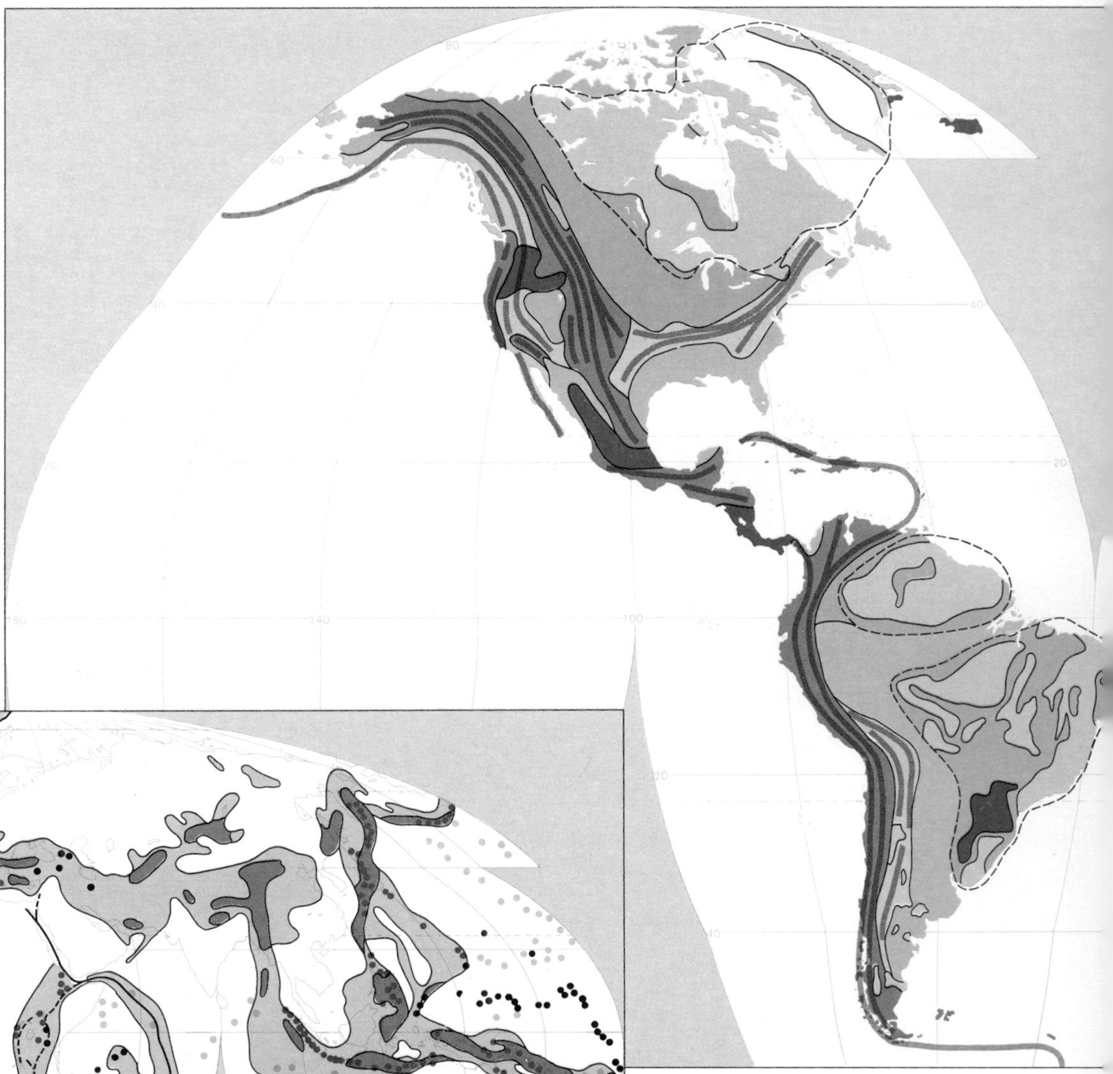

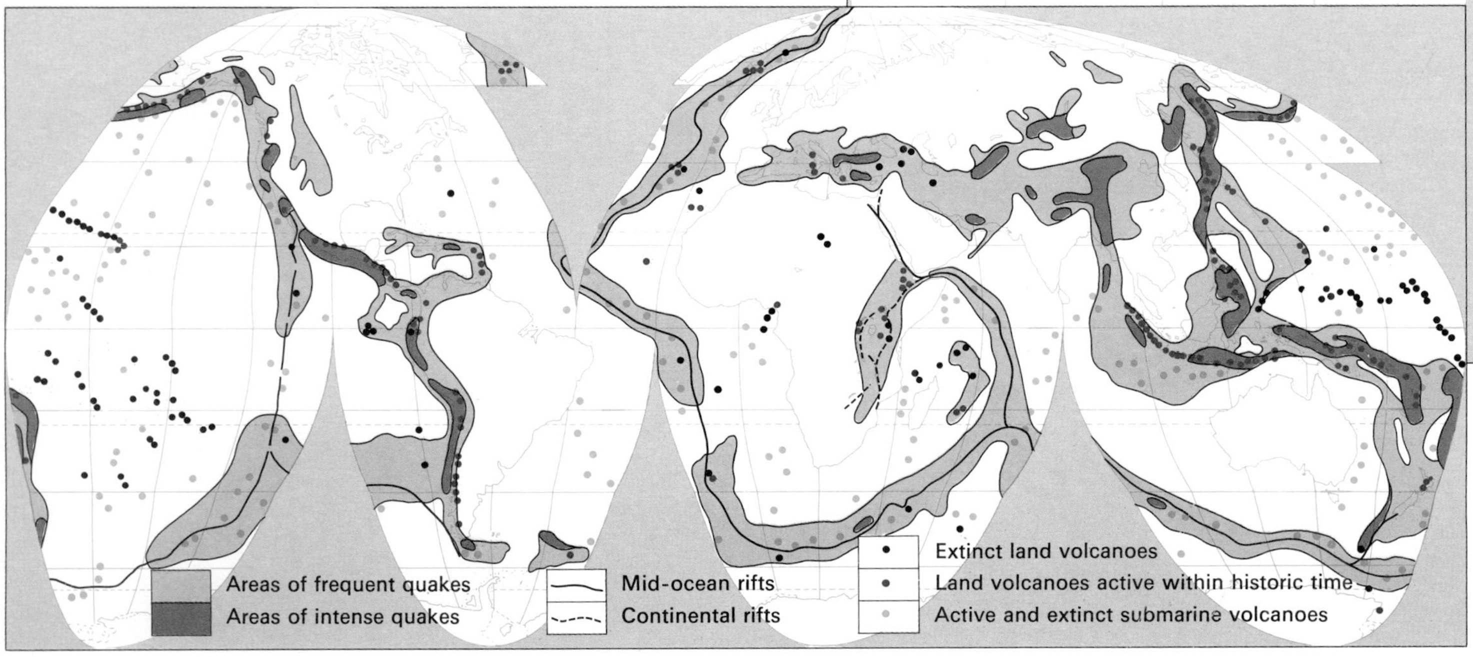
Areas of frequent quakes
Areas of intense quakes
Mid-ocean rifts
Continental rifts
Extinct land volcanoes
Land volcanoes active within historic time
Active and extinct submarine volcanoes

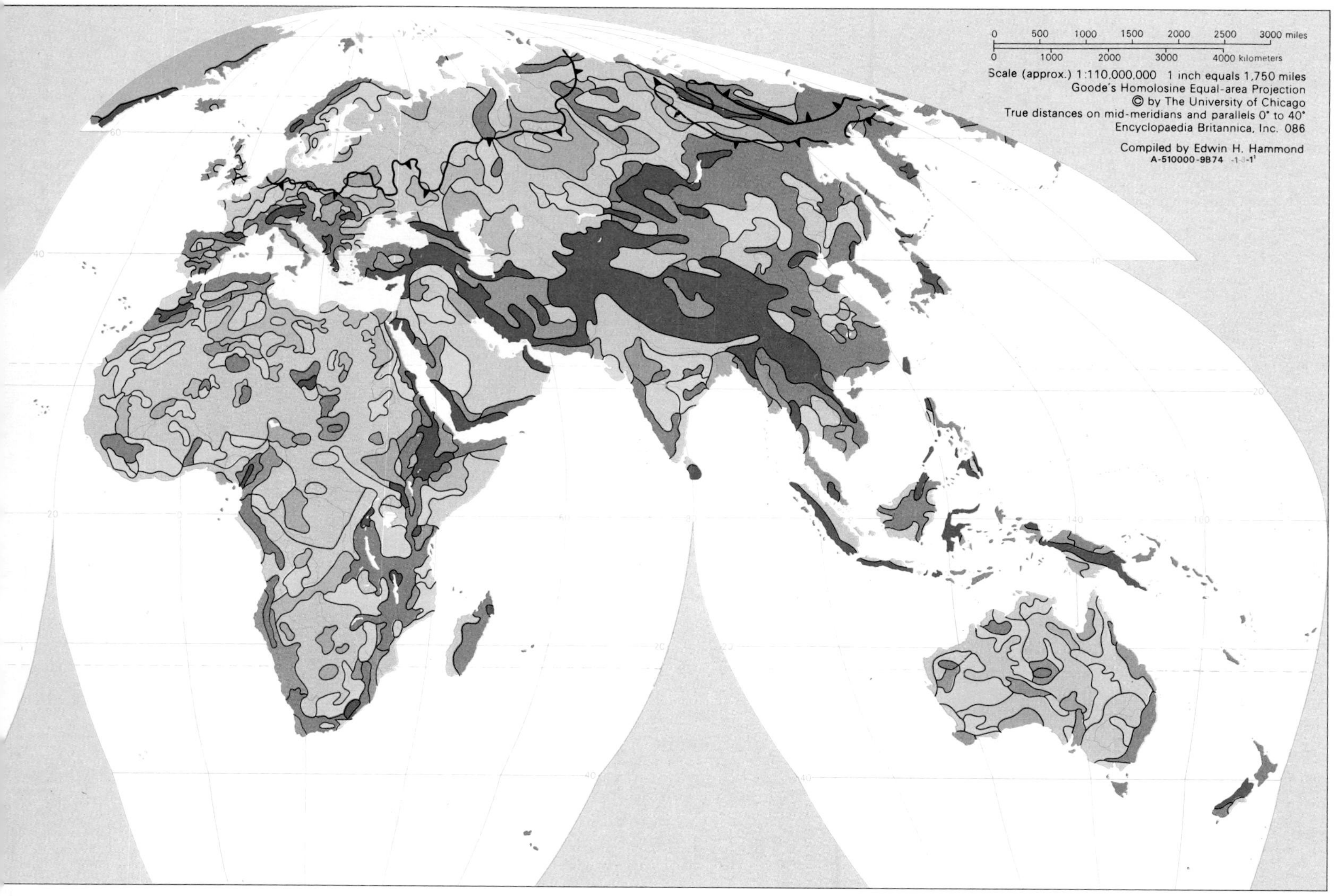
0 500 1000 1500 2000 2500 3000 miles
0 1000 2000 3000 4000 kilometers
Scale (approx.) 1:110,000,000 1 inch equals 1,750 miles
Goode's Homolosine Equal-area Projection
© by The University of Chicago
True distances on mid-meridians and parallels 0° to 40°
Encyclopaedia Britannica, Inc. 086
Compiled by Edwin H. Hammond

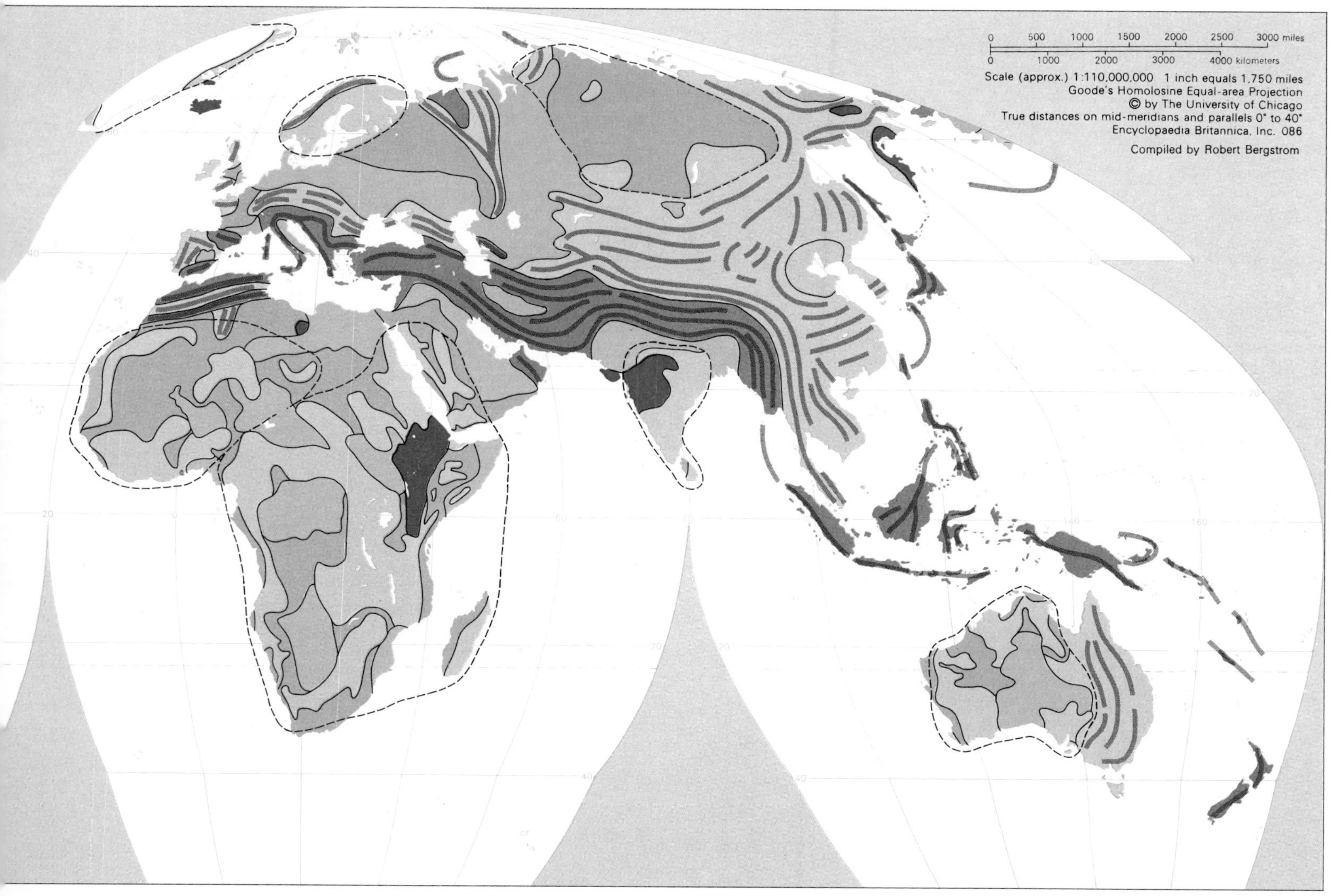
0 500 1000 1500 2000 2500 3000 miles
0 1000 2000 3000 4000 kilometers
Scale (approx.) 1:110,000,000 1 inch equals 1,750 miles
Goode's Homolosine Equal-area Projection
© by The University of Chicago
True distances on mid-meridians and parallels 0° to 40°
Encyclopaedia Britannica, Inc. 086
Compiled by Robert Bergstrom

## Development of the earth's structure

The earth is in process of constant transformation. Movements in the hot, dense interior of the earth result in folding and fracture of the crust and transfer of molten material to the surface. As a result, large structures such as mountain ranges, volcanoes, lava plateaus, and rift valleys are created. The forces that bring about these structural changes are called *tectonic forces*.

The present continents have developed from stable nuclei, or *shields*, of ancient (Precambrian) rock. Erosive forces such as water, wind, and ice have worn away particles of the rock, depositing them at the edges of the shields, where they have accumulated and ultimately become sedimentary rock. Subsequently, in places, these extensive areas of flat-lying rock have been elevated, folded, or warped, by the action of tectonic forces, to form mountains. The shape of these mountains has been altered by later erosion. Where the forces of erosion have been at work for a long time, the mountains tend to have a low relief and rounded contours, like the Appalachians. Mountains more recently formed are high and rugged, like the Himalayas.

The map above depicts some of the major geologic structures of the earth and identifies them according to the period of their formation. A geologic time chart is included in the legend. The inset map shows the most important areas of earthquakes, rifts, and volcanic activity. Comparison of all the maps will show the close correlation between present-day mountain systems, recent (Cenozoic) mountain-building, and the areas of frequent earthquakes and active volcanoes.

## Natural Vegetation

**Broad-leaved evergreen vegetation**
- Broad-leaved evergreen forest
- Broad-leaved evergreen shrub formation
- Scattered broad-leaved evergreen shrubs
- Scattered broad-leaved evergreen dwarf shrubs

**Broad-leaved deciduous vegetation**
- Broad-leaved deciduous forest
- Broad-leaved deciduous shrub formation
- Scattered broad-leaved deciduous shrubs
- Scattered broad-leaved deciduous dwarf shrubs

**Coniferous vegetation**
- Needle-leaved evergreen forest
- Scattered needle-leaved evergreen trees
- Needle-leaved deciduous forest

**Mixed vegetation without grass**
- Forest of broad-leaved evergreen and deciduous trees
- Forest of broad-leaved and needle-leaved evergreen trees
- Broad-leaved deciduous forests with broad-leaved evergreen shrubs
- Forest of broad-leaved deciduous and needle-leaved evergreen trees

**Mixed vegetation with grass**
- Grassland with scattered broad-leaved evergreen trees
- Grassland with broad-leaved evergreen shrubs
- Grassland with scattered broad-leaved deciduous trees
- Grassland with broad-leaved deciduous shrubs

**Grassland, tundra, barren**
- Grassland
- Patches of grass
- Lichens and grasses
- Lichens and mosses
- Barren

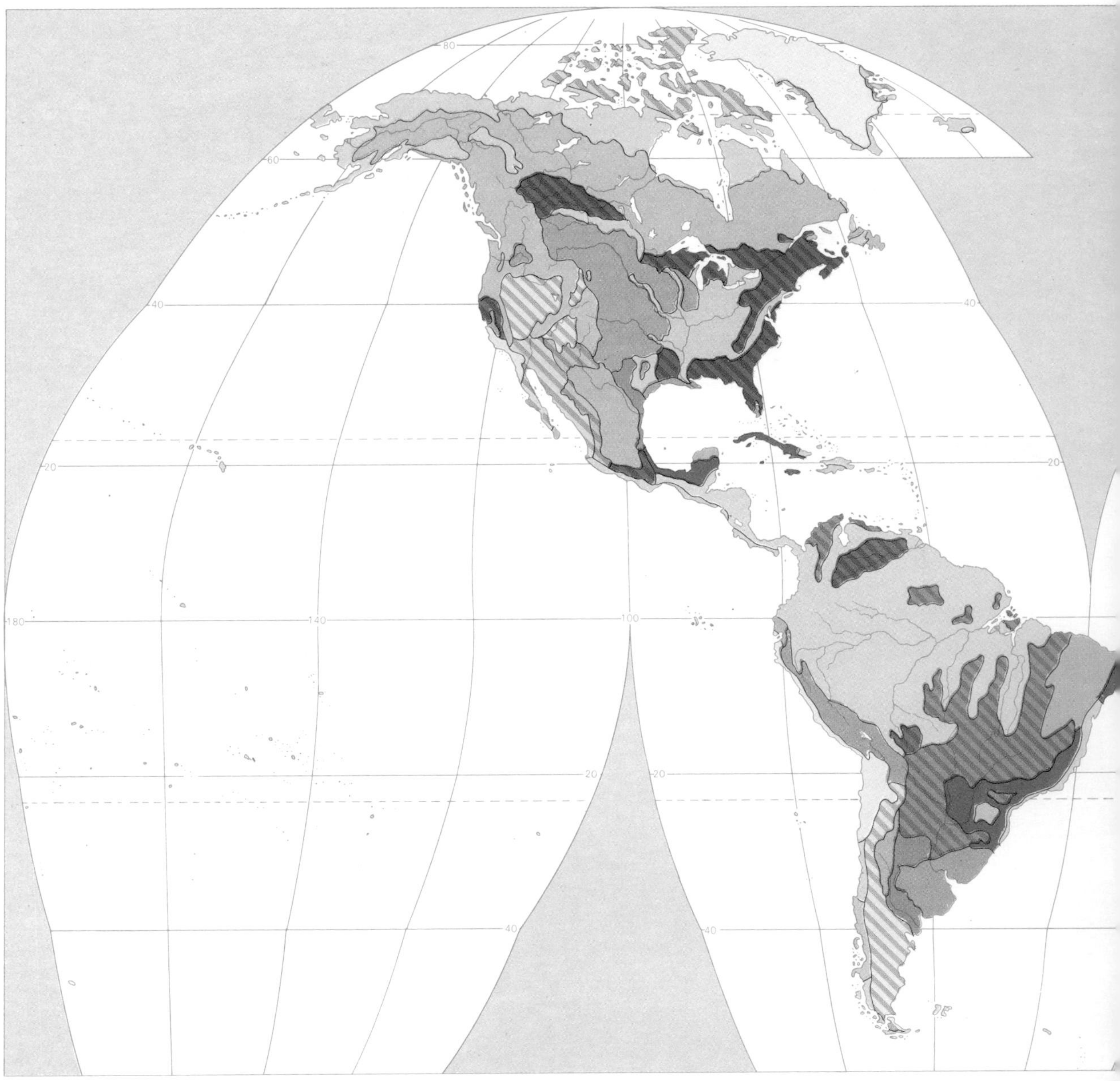

## Soils

- Tundra soils of frigid climates; commonly with permanently frozen subsoil; supports dwarf shrubs, mosses, and lichens; some used for reindeer pasture
- Podzolic soils of humid, cool climates; covered with predominantly coniferous forest; some farming, mainly subsistence
- Podzolic soils of humid, temperate climates; originally covered with predominantly deciduous forest, much of it removed to accommodate extensive general farming, industry, and cities
- Podzolic soils of humid, warm climates; covered with coniferous or mixed forest; general farming
- Chernozemic soils of subhumid and semiarid, cool to tropical climates; supports mainly grasslands; extensive grain and livestock farming
- Latosolic soils of humid or wet-dry tropical and subtropical climates; supports forest or savanna; shifting cultivation with some plantation agriculture
- Grumusolic soils of humid to semiarid and temperate to tropical climates, with distinct wet and dry seasons; mainly grass-covered; livestock and grain farming
- Desertic soils of arid climates; includes many areas of shallow, stony soils; sparse cover of shrubs and grass, some suitable for grazing; fertile if irrigated; dry farming possible in some areas
- Mountain soils of all climates; shallow, stony; barren, grass-covered, or forested, depending on climate; includes many areas of other soils
- Alluvial soils of all climates; deposited by water in flood plains and deltas of rivers; intensive farming in most temperate and some tropical regions (many smaller areas not shown)
- Ice cap of polar regions

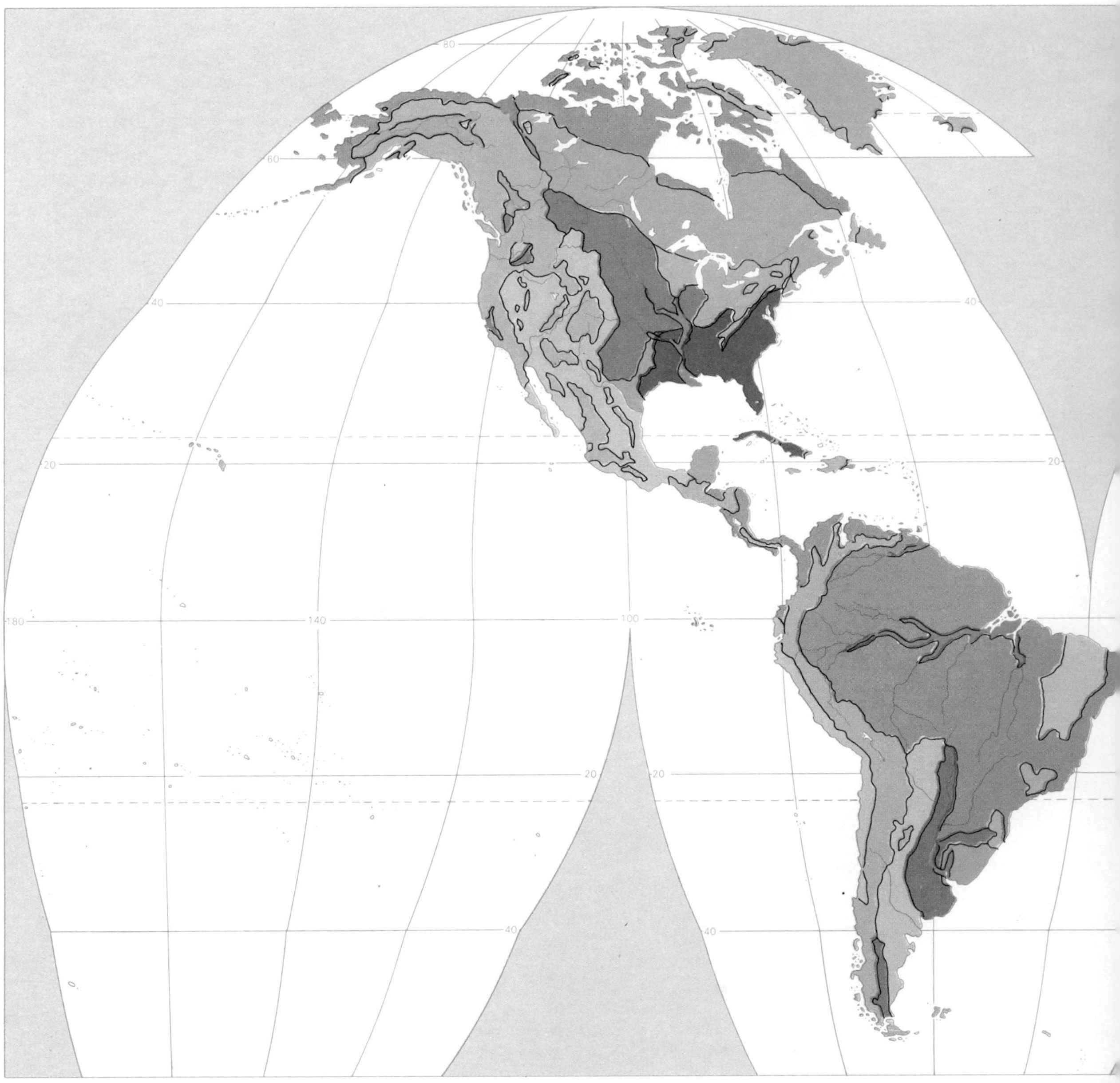

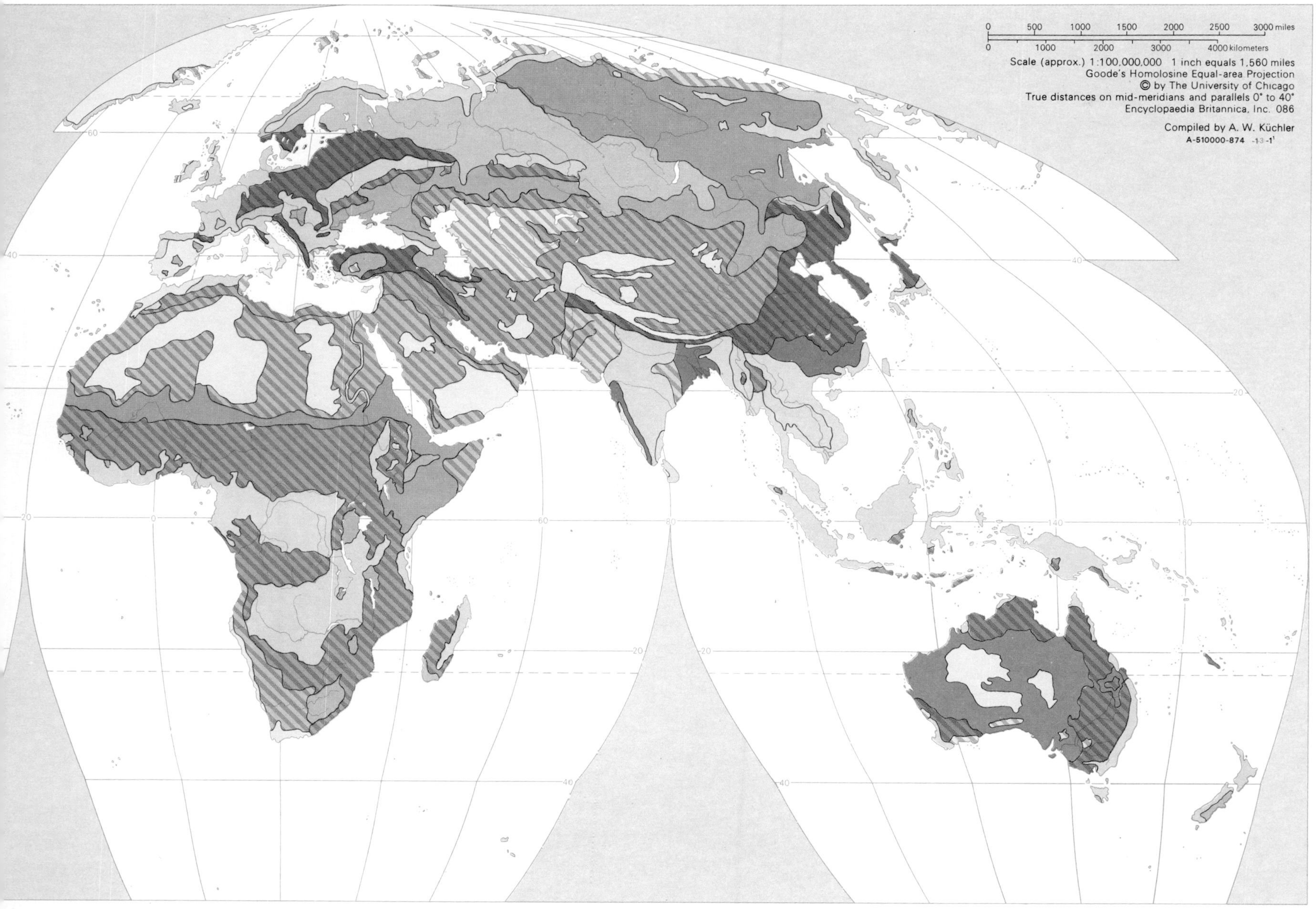
0 500 1000 1500 2000 2500 3000 miles
0 1000 2000 3000 4000 kilometers
Scale (approx.) 1:100,000,000 1 inch equals 1,560 miles
Goode's Homolosine Equal-area Projection
© by The University of Chicago
True distances on mid-meridians and parallels 0° to 40°
Encyclopaedia Britannica, Inc. 086
Compiled by A. W. Küchler
A-510000-874 -13-1'

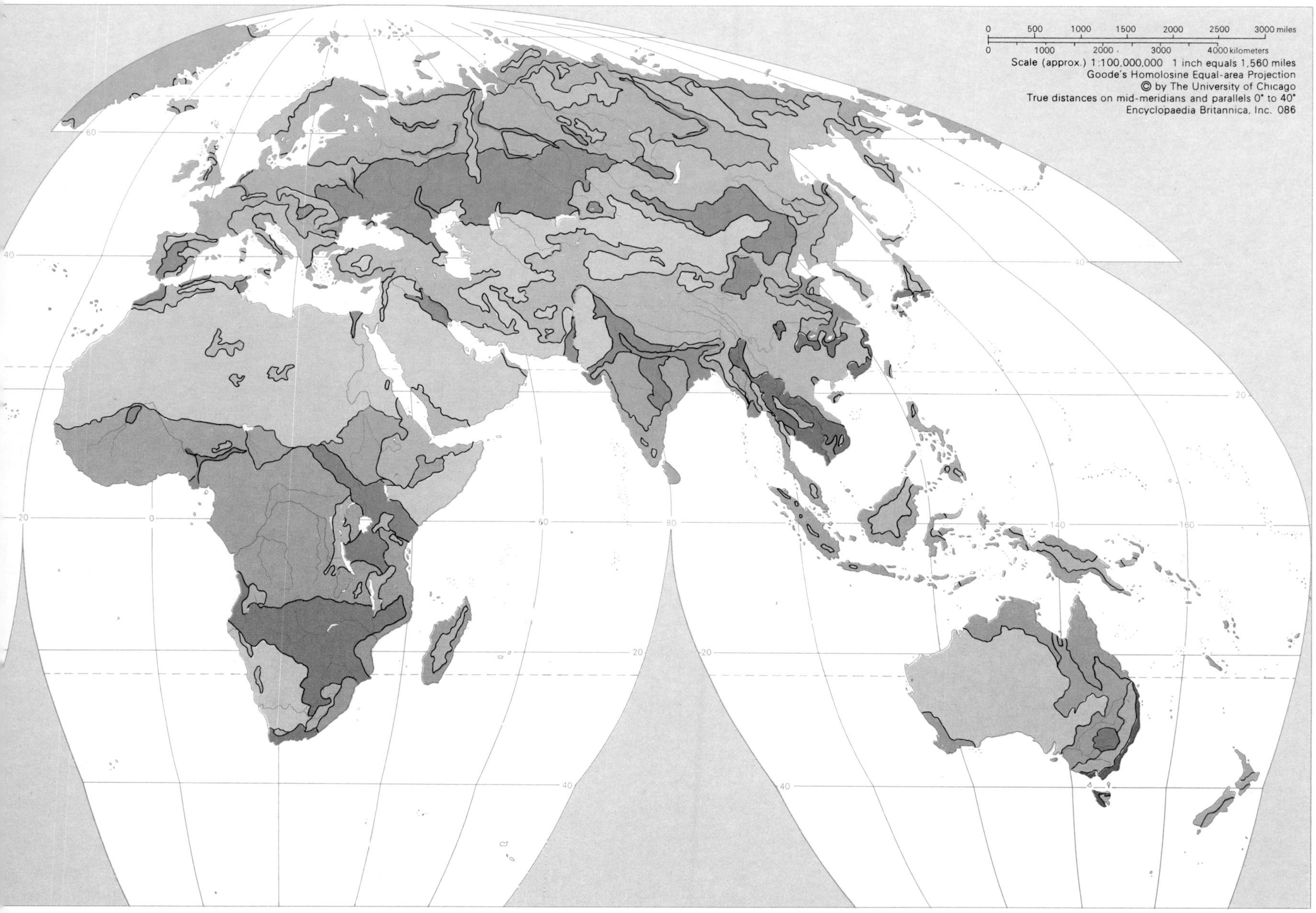
0 500 1000 1500 2000 2500 3000 miles
0 1000 2000 3000 4000 kilometers
Scale (approx.) 1:100,000,000 1 inch equals 1,560 miles
Goode's Homolosine Equal-area Projection
© by The University of Chicago
True distances on mid-meridians and parallels 0° to 40°
Encyclopaedia Britannica, Inc. 086

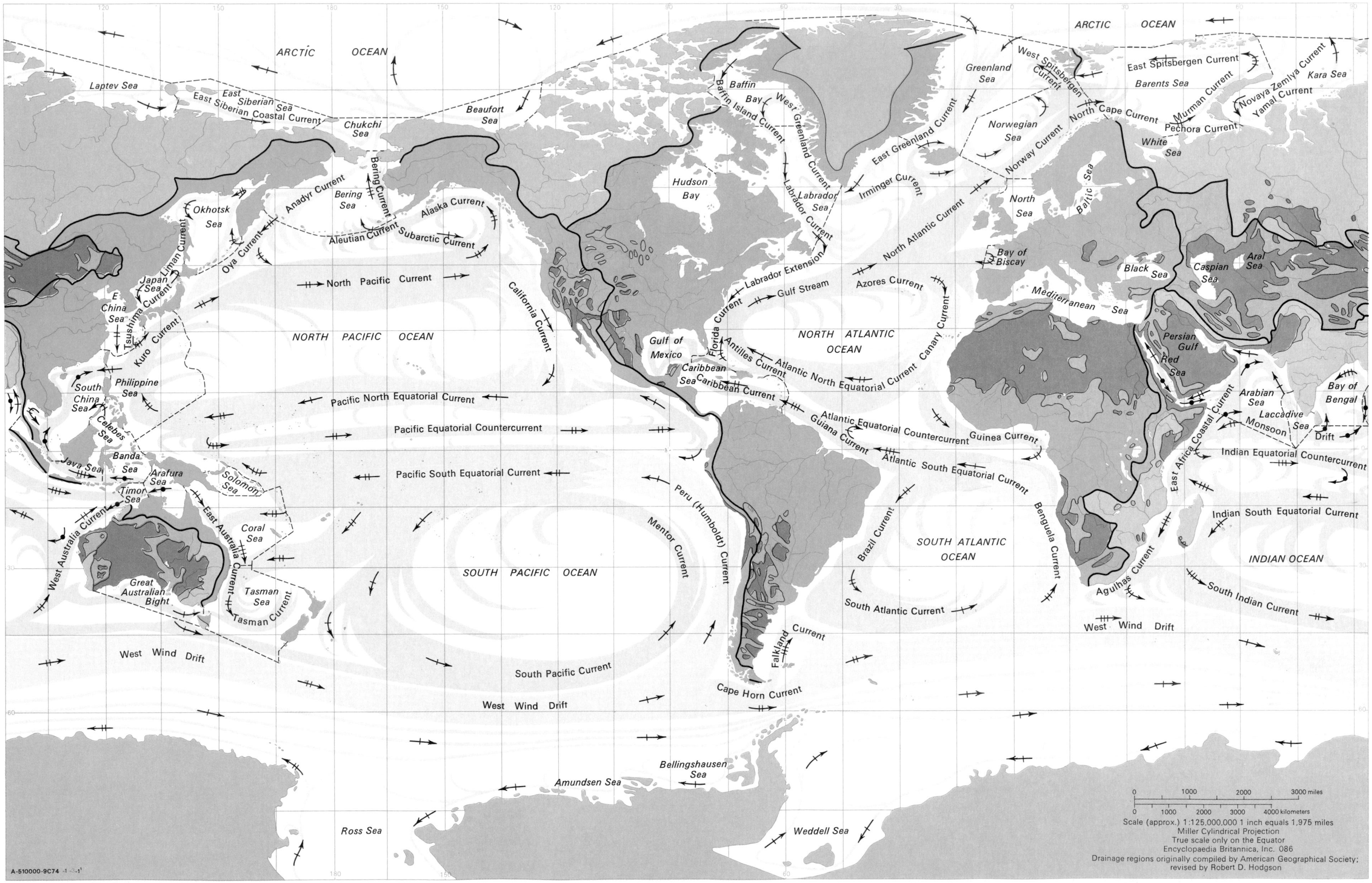
ARCTIC OCEAN
Laptev Sea
East Siberian Sea
East Siberian Coastal Current
Chukchi Sea
Beaufort Sea
Anadyr Current
Bering Sea
Bering Current
Okhotsk Sea
Alaska Current
Aleutian Current
Subarctic Current
Oya Current
Liman Current
Japan Sea
E China Sea
Tsushima Current
Kuro Current
North Pacific Current
California Current
NORTH PACIFIC OCEAN
Philippine Sea
South China Sea
Celebes Sea
Pacific North Equatorial Current
Pacific Equatorial Countercurrent
Pacific South Equatorial Current
Banda Sea
Java Sea
Arafura Sea
Timor Sea
Solomon Sea
Coral Sea
West Australia Current
East Australia Current
Great Australian Bight
Tasman Sea
Tasman Current
SOUTH PACIFIC OCEAN
Mentor Current
Peru (Humboldt) Current
West Wind Drift
South Pacific Current
West Wind Drift
Cape Horn Current
Falkland Current
Amundsen Sea
Bellingshausen Sea
Ross Sea
Weddell Sea
Hudson Bay
Baffin Bay
Baffin Island Current
West Greenland Current
Labrador Sea
Labrador Current
East Greenland Current
Irminger Current
Greenland Sea
West Spitsbergen Current
Norwegian Sea
Norway Current
North Cape Current
East Spitsbergen Current
Barents Sea
Murman Current
Pechora Current
White Sea
Novaya Zemlya Current
Yamal Current
Kara Sea
North Sea
Baltic Sea
Bay of Biscay
North Atlantic Current
Labrador Extension
Gulf Stream
Azores Current
Canary Current
NORTH ATLANTIC OCEAN
Gulf of Mexico
Florida Current
Antilles Current
Caribbean Sea
Caribbean Current
Atlantic North Equatorial Current
Atlantic Equatorial Countercurrent
Guiana Current
Guinea Current
Atlantic South Equatorial Current
Brazil Current
SOUTH ATLANTIC OCEAN
Benguela Current
South Atlantic Current
Mediterranean Sea
Black Sea
Caspian Sea
Aral Sea
Persian Gulf
Red Sea
Arabian Sea
Laccadive Sea
Monsoon Drift
Bay of Bengal
East Africa Coastal Current
Indian Equatorial Countercurrent
Indian South Equatorial Current
INDIAN OCEAN
Agulhas Current
South Indian Current
West Wind Drift
0 1000 2000 3000 miles
0 1000 2000 3000 4000 kilometers
Scale (approx.) 1:125,000,000 1 inch equals 1,975 miles
Miller Cylindrical Projection
True scale only on the Equator
Encyclopaedia Britannica, Inc. 086
Drainage regions originally compiled by American Geographical Society;
revised by Robert D. Hodgson
A-510000-9C74

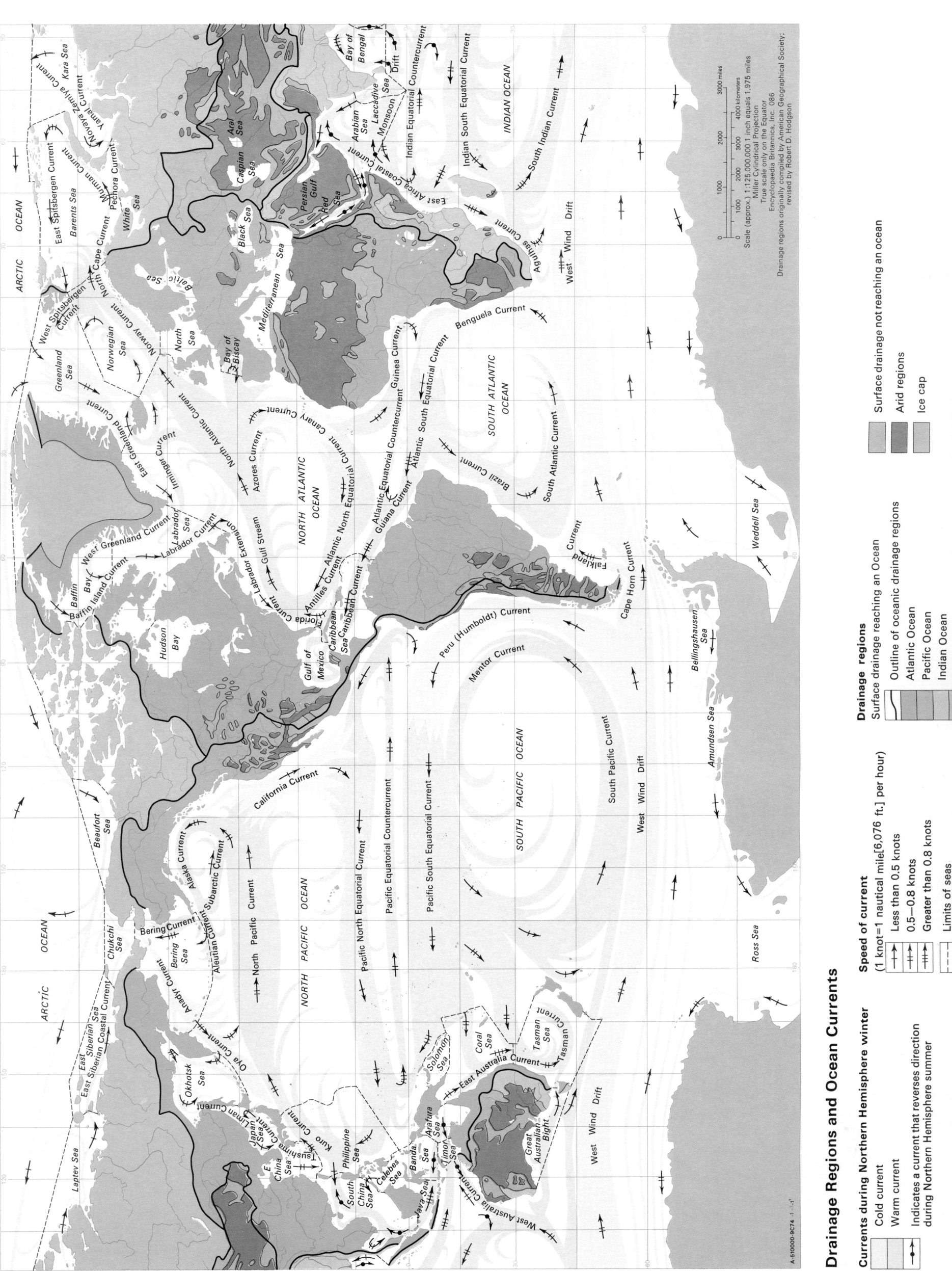

## Drainage Regions and Ocean Currents

**Currents during Northern Hemisphere winter**

- Cold current
- Warm current
- Indicates a current that reverses direction during Northern Hemisphere summer

**Speed of current**

(1 knot=1 nautical mile[6,076 ft.] per hour)

- Less than 0.5 knots
- 0.5–0.8 knots
- Greater than 0.8 knots
- Limits of seas

**Drainage regions**

Surface drainage reaching an Ocean

- Outline of oceanic drainage regions
- Atlantic Ocean
- Pacific Ocean
- Indian Ocean
- Arctic Ocean

- Surface drainage not reaching an ocean
- Arid regions
- Ice cap

THIS SECTION OPENS with World Political and World Physical maps at the scale of 1:75,000,000. There follow maps of the Pacific, Indian, and Atlantic oceans at the scale 1:48,000,000, the largest scale at which the total expanse of these bodies of water could be portrayed. Finally, a series of continent relief maps at the scale of 1:24,000,000 show a global view of the earth as it would appear from about 4,000 miles in space. The Azimuthal Equal-Area projection is used for the 1:24,000,000 maps, the scale being approximately that of a globe 20 inches in diameter.

The colors of the continent maps portray the land areas as if viewed from space during the growing season, without regard to the fact that the growing seasons are not concurrent in all areas. Underwater features and varying water depths are represented by shaded relief and different color tones. The result is a strong physical portrait of the earth's major land and submarine forms. The legend below shows how these different kinds of terrain and vegetation have been represented. The names of physical features—plateaus, basins, mountain ranges, seas, rivers, lakes, gulfs, trenches, bays, islands—predominate on these maps.

DIESER KARTENTEIL BEGINNT mit politischen und physischen Weltkarten im Massstab 1:75 Millionen. Dann folgen Karten des Pazifischen, Indischen und Atlantischen Ozeans in 1:48 Millionen, dem grössten Massstab, in dem diese Wasserflächen in ihrer ganzen Ausdehnung abgebildet werden konnten. Schliesslich folgt eine Reihe von Reliefkarten der Erdteile in 1:24 Millionen. Sie geben eine Übersicht der Erde, wie sie aus einer Entfernung von ungefähr 6 400 Kilometer aus dem Weltraum gewonnen würde. Den Karten im Massstab 1:24 Millionen liegt ein flächentreuer azimutaler Entwurf zugrunde, dieser Massstab entspricht ungefähr dem eines Globus von 50 cm Durchmesser.

Die Farben der Erdteilkarten bilden jedes Landgebiet so ab, wie es in der Vegetationsperiode aus der Vogelperspektive erschiene, ohne zu berücksichtigen, dass die Vegetationsperioden nicht in allen Gebieten gleichzeitig eintreten. Die Gliederung des Meeresbodens und die unterschiedlichen Meerestiefen werden durch Schummerung und verschiedene Farbstufen dargestellt. Das Ergebnis ist eine anschauliche physische Darstellung der wichtigsten terrestrischen und untermeerischen Formen der Erde. Die untenstehende Zeichenerklärung zeigt, wie diese verschiedenen Geländeformen und Vegetationsgebiete veranschaulicht werden. Namen physischer Objekte—Hochebenen, Becken, Gebirgszüge, Meere, Flüsse, Seen, Buchten, Gräben, Inseln—herrschen in diesen Karten vor.

ESTA SECCIÓN DA PRINCIPIO con los Mapas Políticos y Físicos del Mundo, a una escala de 1:75 000 000. A continuación están los mapas de los océanos Pacífico, Indico y Atlántico a una escala de 1:48 000 000, que es la mayor escala utilizable para la representación de esas masas de agua en toda su extensión. Por último, una serie de mapas del relieve de los continentes, a una escala de 1:24 000 000, proporcionan una vista global de la tierra tal como se apreciaría desde el espacio a una distancia aproximada de 6 400 kilómetros. La proyección azimutal equiárea se usa, para los mapas de 1:24 000 000, a una escala según la cual la tierra se reduciría a un globo de unos 50 cm de diámetro.

Los colores utilizados en los mapas de los continentes representan las diversas regiones de la tierra tal como se verían desde el espacio durante la estación en que la vegetación se desarrolla, sin tomar en cuenta que este fenómeno no se produce simultáneamente en todas las áreas. Las estructuras características del fondo marino y las variaciones de profundidad de los océanos se representan mediante relieve sombreado y distintos matices de color. El resultado es una imagen elocuente de las formas terrestres y submarinas más notables del planeta. La leyenda abajo explica cómo se representan estos diferentes tipos de terreno y vegetación. En estos mapas predomina la nomenclatura de elementos físicos: mesetas, cuencas, sierras, mares, ríos, lagos, golfos, bahías, trincheras, islas.

CETTE PARTIE comprend d'abord des cartes du monde politique et du monde physique à l'échelle de 1:75 000 000. Viennent ensuite les cartes des océans Pacifique, Indien et Atlantique à l'échelle de 1:48 000 000, la plus grande échelle qui a permis la reproduction complète de ces étendues d'eau. Pour terminer, une série de cartes en relief des continents à l'échelle de 1:24 000 000 donne une vue globale de la terre, telle qu'elle apparaîtrait vue de l'espace à une distance d'environ 6 400 kilomètres. La projection azimutale équivalente a été utilisée pour les cartes au 1:24 000 000ᵉ, dont l'échelle équivaut à celle d'un globe de 50 cm de diamètre environ.

Les couleurs des cartes font apparaître les continents tels qu'on les verrait de l'espace, pendant la saison de croissance végétale, mais sans tenir compte du fait que cette saison n'apparaît pas partout simultanément. Le relief sous-marin est représenté par un estompage et la profondeur des océans par une variation de la couleur. Il en résulte une reproduction vigoureuse des principaux paysages continentaux et des principales formes sous-marines. La légende ci-dessous indique de quelle façon ils sont cartographiés. Les noms d'éléments topographiques tels que plateaux, bassins, chaînes de montagnes, mers, cours d'eau, lacs, golfes, baies, crêtes, îles et fosses océaniques, prédominent dans ces cartes.

ESTA SEÇÃO PRINCIPIA com os mapas políticos e físicos do Mundo, em escala de 1:75 000 000. Seguem-se os mapas dos oceanos Pacífico, Índico e Atlântico na escala de 1:48 000 000, a maior escala que se pode utilizar para a representação dessas massas de água em toda a sua extensão. Finalmente, uma série de mapas de relevo dos continentes, na escala de 1:24 000 000, proporciona uma visão global da Terra tal como apareceria do espaço a uma distância aproximada de cerca de 6 400 km. A projeção azimutal equiárea foi usada para os mapas da escala de 1:24 000 000, segundo a qual a Terra se apresentaria como um globo de cerca de 50 cm de diâmetro.

As cores utilizadas nos mapas dos continentes representam as massas terrestres tal como apareceriam vistas do espaço durante a estação do crescimento vegetal, sem levar em conta que este fenômeno não se produz simultaneamente em todas as regiões. As características do fundo do mar e as variações de profundidade das águas são representadas por um relevo sombreado e por diferentes matizes de cor. O resultado proporciona uma imagem física eloqüente das principais formas terrestres e submarinas da Terra. As legendas abaixo explicam como foram representados os diversos tipos de terreno e de vegetação. Nestes mapas predomina a nomenclatura dos elementos físicos: planaltos, bacias, cadeias de montanhas, mares, rios, lagos, golfos, baías, fossas, ilhas.

Land Features / Land Phänomene / Elementos de la Tierra
Paysages Continentaux / Acidentes Continentais

Ice and Snow
Eis und Schnee
Hielo y nieve
Glace et neige
Gelo e neve

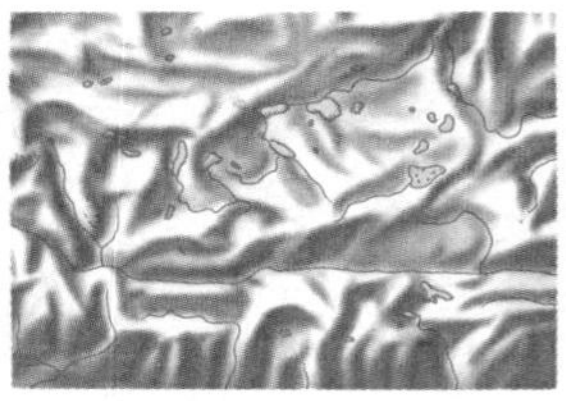

High Barren Area
Hochgebirgswüste
Alta zona árida
Région haute et aride
Alta zona árida

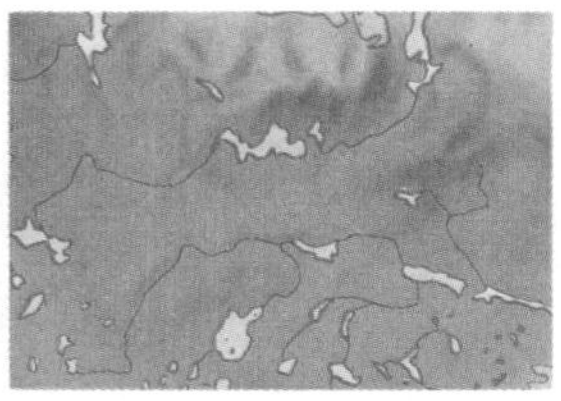

Tundra and Alpine
Tundra und Alpine Vegetation
Tundra y alpina
Toundra et végétation alpine
Tundra e vegetação alpina

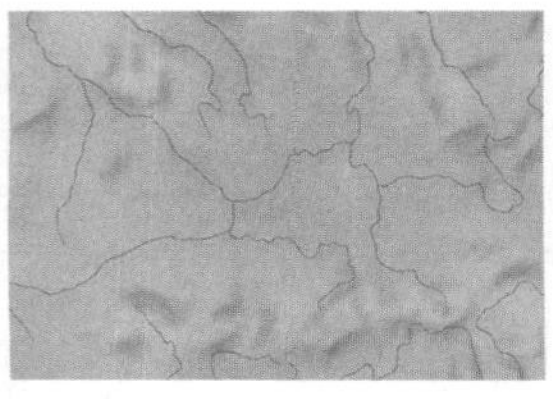

Needleleaf Trees
Nadelwälder
Coníferas
Forêt de conifères
Coníferas

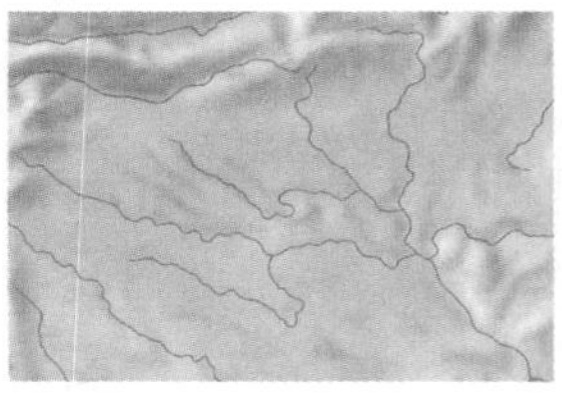

Broadleaf Trees
Laubwälder
Árboles de hojas anchas
Forêt à feuilles caduques
Árvores de folhas caducas

Tropical Rainforest
Tropischer Regenwald
Bosque tropical lluvioso
Forêt tropicale humide
Floresta tropical úmida

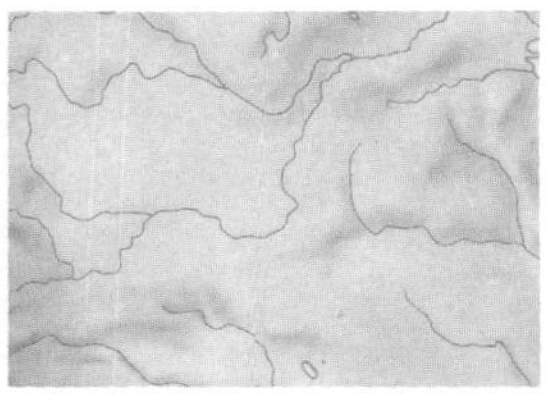

Grassland
Grasland
Pradera
Formations herbacées
Pradaria

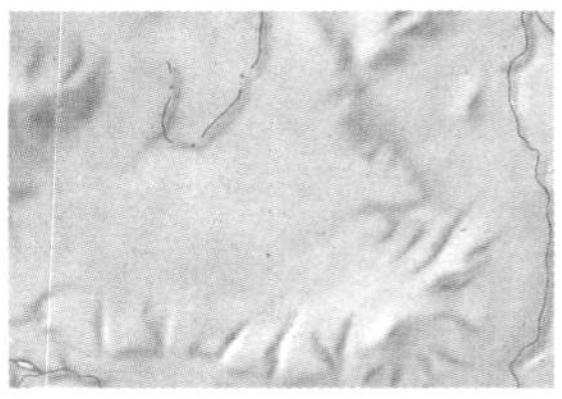

Dry Scrub
Trockenes Buschland
Matorral
Brousse sèche
Caatinga

Desert
Wüste
Desierto
Désert
Deserto

Submarine Features / Untermeerische Phänomene
Elementos Submarinos / Formes de Relief Sous-marin / Acidentes do Revelo Submarino

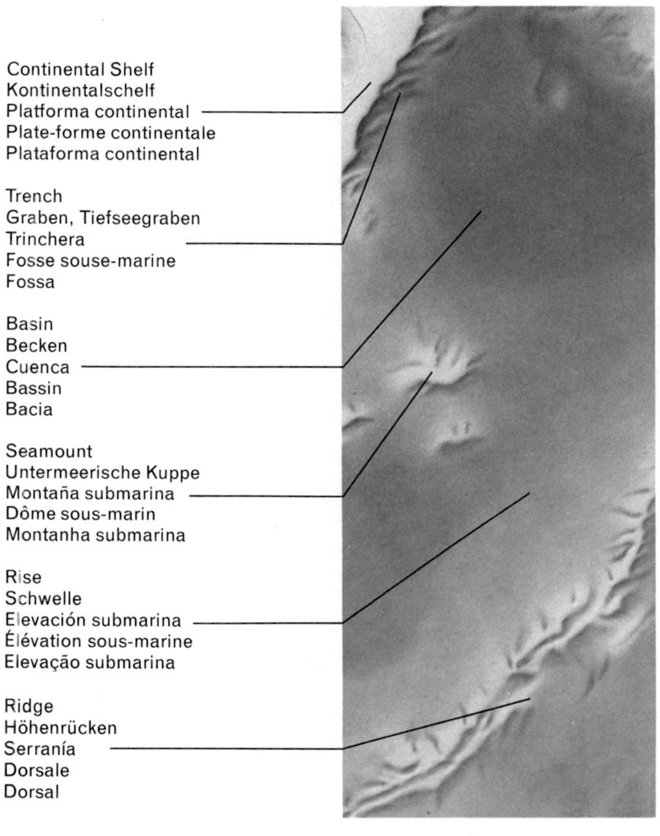
Continental Shelf
Kontinentalschelf
Platforma continental
Plate-forme continentale
Plataforma continental
Trench
Graben, Tiefseegraben
Trinchera
Fosse sousse-marine
Fossa
Basin
Becken
Cuenca
Bassin
Bacia
Seamount
Untermeerische Kuppe
Montaña submarina
Dôme sous-marin
Montanha submarina
Rise
Schwelle
Elevación submarina
Élévation sous-marine
Elevação submarina
Ridge
Höhenrücken
Serranía
Dorsale
Dorsal

ARCTIC OCEAN
Beaufort Sea
GREENLAND (Den.)
Greenland Sea
Thule
Baffin Bay
BAFFIN ISLAND
Godhavn
Godthåb
Angmagssalik
Reykjavík
ICELAND
VICTORIA ISLAND
UNITED STATES
RUSSIA
Nome
Fairbanks
Inuvik
Mount McKinley 6194
Anchorage
Yellowknife
Bering Sea
Gulf of Alaska
Juneau
Hudson Bay
Churchill
ROCKY MOUNTAINS
CANADA
Edmonton
ALEUTIAN ISLANDS
Calgary
Winnipeg
Lake Superior
Lake Huron
NEWFOUNDLAND
St. John's
Vancouver
Seattle
Portland
Minneapolis
Quebec
Ottawa
Montréal
Halifax
Toronto
Boston
NORTH AMERICA
CHICAGO
DETROIT
Lake Michigan
NEW YORK
PHILADELPHIA
WASHINGTON
Salt Lake City
Denver
St. Louis
APPALACHIAN MOUNTAINS
SAN FRANCISCO
UNITED STATES
ATLANTIC OCEAN
PACIFIC OCEAN
LOS ANGELES
San Diego
Phoenix
El Paso
Dallas
Atlanta
Houston
New Orleans
BERMUDA (U.K.)
MIDWAY ISLANDS (U.S.)
Gulf of Mexico
Miami
BAHAMAS
Monterrey
Tropic of Cancer
MEXICO
CABO SAN LUCAS
HAWAIIAN ISLANDS (U.S.)
Honolulu
LA HABANA
CUBA
Guadalajara
CIUDAD DE MÉXICO
MÉXICO CITY
DOMINICAN REPUBLIC
HAITI
PUERTO RICO (U.S.)
Port-au-Prince
SANTO DOMINGO
SAN JUAN
JAMAICA
Kingston
GUATEMALA
BELIZE
GUADELOUPE (Fr.)
JOHNSTON ATOLL (U.S.)
HONDURAS
Tegucigalpa
MARTINIQUE (Fr.)
San Salvador
EL SALVADOR
NICARAGUA
Caribbean Sea
BARBADOS
Managua
TRINIDAD AND TOBAGO
SAN JOSÉ
Panamá
Port of Spain
COSTA RICA
PANAMA
CARACAS
GUYANA
Georgetown
ÎLE CLIPPERTON (Fr.)
VENEZUELA
Paramaribo
FRENCH GUIANA
SURINAME
Medellín
SANTA FE DE BOGOTÁ
Cali
COLOMBIA
POLYNESIA
Equator
QUITO
ECUADOR
ARCHIPIÉLAGO DE COLÓN
GALAPAGOS ISLANDS (Ec.)
Guayaquil
Manaus
Belém
Amazon
Fortaleza
KIRIBATI
PHOENIX ISLANDS
Iquitos
CABO DE SÃO ROQUE
Natal
Recife
TOKELAU (N.Z.)
ÎLES MARQUISES
Trujillo
BRAZIL
PERU
ANDES
WALLIS AND FUTUNA (Fr.)
W. SAMOA
AM. SAMOA
Apia
LIMA
SOUTH AMERICA
Salvador
ÎLES TUAMOTU
Arequipa
LA PAZ
Goiânia
BRASÍLIA
FIJI
NIUE (N.Z.)
COOK ISLANDS (N.Z.)
FRENCH POLYNESIA
BOLIVIA
Sucre
Belo Horizonte
TONGA
PARAGUAY
Tropic of Capricorn
PITCAIRN (U.K.)
Antofagasta
SÃO PAULO
RIO DE JANEIRO
Santos
Curitiba
Asunción
ISLA DE PASCUA
EASTER ISLAND (Chile)
ISLA SAN AMBROSIO (Chile)
CHILE
International Date Line
Co. Aconcagua 6959
Córdoba
Porto Alegre
Valparaíso
SANTIAGO
Rosario
URUGUAY
ARCHIPIÉLAGO JUAN FERNÁNDEZ (Chile)
BUENOS AIRES
MONTEVIDEO
ARGENTINA
Concepción
Mar del Plata
Bahía Blanca
PACIFIC OCEAN
CHATHAM ISLANDS (N.Z.)
FALKLAND ISLANDS (U.K.)
Punta Arenas
SOUTH GEORGIA (U.K.)
CABO DE HORNOS
CAPE HORN
Drake Passage
SOUTH ORKNEY ISLANDS (U.K.)
Antarctic Circle
ANTARCTIC PENINSULA
Bellingshausen Sea
Weddell Sea
Ross Sea
Vinson Massif 4897
MARIE BYRD LAND
ROSS ICESHELF
ANTAR
IRELAND
DUBLIN
Glasgow
PORTUGAL
Porto
LISBOA
GIBRALTAR (U.K.)
RABAT
Casablanca
MOROCCO
AÇORES AZORES (Port.)
ARQUIPÉLAGO DA MADEIRA (Port.)
ISLAS CANARIAS
CANARY ISLANDS (Sp.)
WESTERN SAHARA
MAURITANIA
Nouakchott
CAPE VERDE
SENEGAL
DAKAR
GAMBIA
Banjul
GUINEA-BISSAU
GUINEA
Conakry
Bamako
SIERRA LEONE
Freetown
Monrovia
LIBERIA
ATLANTIC OCEAN
180°
165°
150°
135°
120°
105°
90°
75°
60°
45°
30°
15°
0°

ARCTIC OCEAN
ZEML'A FRANCA-IOSIFA
Barents Sea
NOVAJA ZEML'A
Karskoje more
NOVOSIBIRSKIJE OSTROVA
more Laptevych
Hammerfest
Murmansk
Dikson
Chatanga
Tiksi
Noril'sk
Igarka
Vorkuta
Salechard
Verchojansk
Arctic Circle
Anadyr'
Archangel'sk
SWEDEN
FINLAND
HELSINKI
STOCKHOLM
EST.
SANKT-PETERBURG (ST. PETERSBURG)
LAT.
LITH.
KØBENHAVN
BELARUS
MOSKVA
Nižnij Novgorod
Perm'
Jekaterinburg
Čel'abinsk
Samara
URAL'SKIJE GORY
RUSSIA
Lensk
Jakutsk
Magadan
Ochotsk
Sea of Okhotsk
Bering Sea
Petropavlovsk-Kamčatskij
ALEUTIAN IS. (U.S.)
Omsk
Novosibirsk
Krasnojarsk
Irkutsk
Čita
Nikolajevsk
OSTROV SACHALIN
POLAND
WARSZAWA
UKRAINE
KYIV
CZECH REP.
SLVK.
WIEN
AUS.
BUDAPEST
HUNG.
MOLD.
ROM.
CRO.
BOS.
YUGO.
BEOGRAD
BUCUREŞTI
BUL.
SOFIJA
Milano
ITALY
ROMA
Napoli
ALB.
MAC.
GREECE
ATHÍNAI
Black Sea
İstanbul
ANKARA
TURKEY
Volgograd
Astrachan'
gora El'brus 5642
GEOR.
ARM.
AZER.
BAKI
Caspian Sea
KAZAKHSTAN
Karaganda
Aral Sea
UZBEKISTAN
TURKMENISTAN
TAŠKENT
ALMATY
KYRG.
TADJ.
TIEN SHAN
Ürümqi
ALTAI
Ulaanbaatar
MONGOLIA
GOBI
Chabarovsk
Harbin
KURIL'SKIJE OSTROVA
Vladivostok
Sea of Japan
Sapporo
JAPAN
Sendai
TŌKYŌ
ŌSAKA
HONSHŪ
Fukuoka
Shenyang
N. KOREA
P'YŎNGYANG
S. KOREA
SŎUL
Pusan
Dalian
BEIJING (PEKING)
Tianjin
Hohhot
Qingdao
Yellow Sea
Lanzhou
Xi'an
Nanjing
Wuhan
SHANGHAI
Chengdu
Chongqing
Changsha
Fuzhou
T'AIPEI
TAIWAN
Kunming
Guangzhou
HONG KONG (U.K.)
HA NOI
LAOS
VIETNAM
THAILAND
KRUNG THEP (BANGKOK)
CAMB.
Phnum Penh
Thanh Pho Ho Chi Minh
South China Sea
MANILA
PHILIPPINES
Davao
ASIA
CHINA
Shache
Lhasa
HIMALAYAS
NEPAL
BHU.
Mount Everest 8848
Kātmāndu
BANGL.
DHAKA
CALCUTTA
MYANMAR
YANGON
Bay of Bengal
ANDAMAN ISLANDS (India)
NICOBAR ISLANDS (India)
INDIA
DELHI
New Delhi
Ahmadābād
BOMBAY
Hyderābād
Bangalore
Madras
Cochin
SRI LANKA
COLOMBO
MALDIVES
Tropic of Cancer
PAKISTAN
Islāmābād
Rawalpindi
Lahore
Karāchi
KĀBOL
AFGHANISTAN
TEHRĀN
IRAN
Eşfahān
Arabian Sea
OMAN
Masqat
QATAR
UNITED ARAB EMIRATES
AR-RIYĀḌ
SAUDI ARABIA
Makkah
KUWAIT
Ābādān
BAGHDĀD
IRAQ
SYRIA
LEB.
ISR.
JORDAN
San'a
YEMEN
Aden
SUQUTRĀ (Yem.)
GEES GWARDAFUY
Red Sea
TUNIS
MALTA
TARĀBULUS
TRIPOLI
Banghāzī
Al-Iskandarīyah (Alexandria)
AL-QĀHIRAH (CAIRO)
EGYPT
LIBYA
Aswān
Nile
AFRICA
NIGER
CHAD
N'Djamena
AL-KHARṬŪM
SUDAN
ERITREA
DJIBOUTI
Djibouti
ADIS ABEBA
ETHIOPIA
SOMALIA
Muqdisho
NIGERIA
Kano
Abuja
CAMEROON
CEN. AFR. REP.
Bangui
Yaoundé
GABON
CONGO
Brazzaville
KINSHASA
ZAIRE
UGANDA
KAMPALA
KENYA
NAIROBI
Kilimanjaro 5895
Mombasa
RWANDA
BURUNDI
Bujumbura
Lake Tanganyika
Dodoma
Zanzibar
DAR ES SALAAM
TANZANIA
SEYCHELLES
LUANDA
Lobito
ANGOLA
Lubumbashi
ZAMBIA
Lusaka
Lilongwe
MALAWI
HARARE
ZIMBABWE
MOZAMBIQUE
Mozambique Channel
ANTANANARIVO
MADAGASCAR
MAURITIUS
REUNION (Fr.)
Windhoek
Walvis Bay
NAMIBIA
BOTSWANA
Gaborone
PRETORIA
Johannesburg
MAPUTO
SWAZILAND
LESOTHO
Durban
SOUTH AFRICA
CAPE TOWN
Port Elizabeth
CAPE AGULHAS
Tropic of Capricorn
BRITISH INDIAN OCEAN TERRITORY
INDIAN OCEAN
Equator
MALAYSIA
Medan
KUALA LUMPUR
SINGAPORE
SUMATERA
BRUNEI
BORNEO
SULAWESI
INDONESIA
Palembang
Banjarmasin
Ujungpandang
JAKARTA
JAWA
Surabaya
TIMOR
CHRISTMAS ISLAND (Austl.)
COCOS ISLANDS (Austl.)
PALAU
FEDERATED STATES OF MICRONESIA
MICRONESIA
GUAM (U.S.)
NORTHERN MARIANA ISLANDS (U.S.)
WAKE ISLAND (U.S.)
MARSHALL ISLANDS
NAURU
KIRIBATI
TUVALU
PAPUA NEW GUINEA
Mount Wilhelm 4509
NEW GUINEA
Port Moresby
CAPE YORK
SOLOMON ISLANDS
MELANESIA
VANUATU
Fiji
Darwin
Gulf of Carpentaria
Cairns
Coral Sea
NEW CALEDONIA (Fr.)
Nouméa
Alice Springs
Rockhampton
AUSTRALIA
Brisbane
Perth
NORFOLK ISLAND (Austl.)
Darling
Adelaide
Canberra
Sydney
Melbourne
Mount Kosciusko 2228
Tasman Sea
TASMANIA
Hobart
NORTH ISLAND
Auckland
NEW ZEALAND
Wellington
SOUTH ISLAND
Christchurch
PACIFIC OCEAN
Philippine Sea
OGASAWARA-GUNTŌ (Japan)
NANSEI-SHOTŌ
International Date Line
ÎLES KERGUÉLEN (Fr.)
SOUTHERN OCEAN
Antarctic Circle
ENDERBY LAND
WILKES LAND
ANTARCTICA
Copyright © by Rand McNally & Co.
Map prepared by Rand McNally & Co.
A-510000-264
30°
45°
60°
75°
90°
105°
120°
135°
150°
165°
180°
15°
0°

Kilometers 0 1000 2000 3000 Km.
Statute Miles 0 1000 2000 3000 Mi.

One centimeter represents 750 kilometers.
One inch represents approximately 1200 miles.
Robinson Projection
Scale 1:75,000,000

ARCTIC OCEAN
ELLESMERE ISLAND
QUEEN ELIZABETH ISLANDS
Beaufort Sea
Baffin Bay
GRØNLAND
Greenland Sea
Chukchi Sea
UNITED STATES
Arctic Circle
BAFFIN ISLAND
Hudson Bay
ICELAND
Bering Sea
ALEUTIAN BASIN
ALEUTIAN TRENCH
Gulf of Alaska
Mount McKinley 6194
LABRADOR BASIN
Labrador Sea
CANADA
NORTH AMERICA
UNITED STATES
ROCKY MOUNTAINS
APPALACHIAN MOUNTAINS
NEW YORK
CHICAGO
Pikes Peak 4301
GREAT BASIN
LOS ANGELES
MENDOCINO FRACTURE ZONE
MURRAY FRACTURE ZONE
PACIFIC OCEAN
NORTH AMERICAN BASIN
ATLANTIC OCEAN
NEWFOUNDLAND BASIN
AZORES PLATEAU
WEST EUROPEAN BASIN
Sargasso Sea
Houston
Gulf of Mexico
MEXICO
CIUDAD DE MÉXICO
Tropic of Cancer
HAWAIIAN ISLANDS
HAWAIIAN RIDGE
CLARION FRACTURE ZONE
CLIPPERTON FRACTURE ZONE
CUBA
GREATER ANTILLES
Caribbean Sea
VENEZUELAN BASIN
CAPE VERDE BASIN
MAURITANIA
WESTERN SAHARA
CENTRAL PACIFIC BASIN
POLYNESIA
VENEZUELA
COLOMBIA
GUIANA BASIN
SIERRA LEONE BASIN
Equator
SOUTH AMERICA
BRAZIL
BOLIVIA
PARAGUAY
URUGUAY
Amazon
SELVAS
Recife
SÃO PAULO
RIO DE JANEIRO
BRAZIL BASIN
Tropic of Capricorn
PACIFIC OCEAN
EAST PACIFIC RISE
CHILE RISE
SANTIAGO
BUENOS AIRES
ARGENTINA
PATAGONIA
ARGENTINE BASIN
SOUTHWEST PACIFIC BASIN
SOUTHEAST PACIFIC BASIN
International Date Line
FALKLAND ISLANDS
TIERRA DEL FUEGO
Drake Passage
Scotia Sea
SOUTH SHETLAND ISLANDS
SOUTH ORKNEY ISLANDS
Antarctic Circle
Bellingshausen Sea
Amundsen Sea
Weddell Sea
Ross Sea
MARIE BYRD LAND
ROSS ICE SHELF
Vinson Massif 4897
RONNE ICE SHELF
FILCHNER ICE SHELF
ANT

World: Physical / Erde: Physisch / Mundo: Físico
Monde: Physique / Mundo: Físico

ARCTIC OCEAN
SEVERNAJA ZEML'A
ZEML'A FRANCA-IOSIFA
NOVOSIBIRSKIJE OSTROVA
more Laptevych
Karskoje more
Barents Sea
BARENTS TROUGH
Vostočno-Sibirskoje more
East Siberian Sea
OSTROV VRANGEL'A
Arctic Circle
SEVERO-SIBIRSKAJA NIZMENNOST'
SREDNES-SIBIRSKOJE
SIBERIA
PLOSKOGORJE
ZAPADNO-SIBIRSKAJA RAVNINA
SIBIR'
RUSSIA
VERCHOJANSKIJ CHREBET
CHREBET ČERSKOGO
Kolyma
Anadyr'
SWEDEN
FINLAND
Gulf of Bothnia
Baltic Sea
Beloje more
Onežskoje ozero
Ladožskoje ozero
SANKT-PETERBURG
MOSKVA
Volga
BELARUS
POLAND
BERLIN
UKRAINE
GERMANY
Danube
CARPATHIAN MTS.
ROMANIA
ALPS
ITALY
APENNINO
ROMA
Tyrrhenian Sea
Ionian Sea
Aegean Sea
Mediterranean Sea
Black Sea
Sea of Azov
Istanbul
TURKEY
Caspian Sea
KAZAKHSTAN
ASIA
Aral Sea
ozero Balchaš
PLATO UST'URT
KYZYLKUM
KARAKUMY
TURKMENISTAN
Amu Darya
SYRIA
IRAQ
TEHRAN
DASHT-E KAVĪR
IRAN
DASHT-E LŪT
CYPRUS
ISRAEL
AL-QĀHIRAH CAIRO
LIBYA
EGYPT
SAUDI
AN-NAFŪD
ARABIA
ARABIAN PENINSULA
Persian Gulf
Gulf of Oman
Jabal ash-Shām 3035
Red Sea
Nile
NUBIAN DESERT
SUDAN
TIBESTI
Emi Koussi 3415
CHAD
Lake Chad
NIGER
NIGERIA
Benue
ENNEDI
CENTRAL AFRICAN REPUBLIC
ETHIOPIA
ADIS ABEBA
Ras Dashen Terara 4620
Gulf of Aden
SOMALIA
Lake Rudolf
Kirinyaga 5199
Lake Victoria
Kilimanjaro 5895
TANZANIA
Lake Tanganyika
RIFT VALLEY
ZAIRE
KINSHASA
Congo
GABON
CONGO
ANGOLA
ZAMBIA
Lake Kariba
Zambezi
ZIMBABWE
Lake Nyasa
MOZAMBIQUE
Mozambique Channel
MADAGASCAR
Maromokotro 2876
NAMIBIA
BOTSWANA
KALAHARI DESERT
Limpopo
Johannesburg
Orange
SOUTH AFRICA
CAPE TOWN
CAPE AGULHAS
AGULHAS BASIN
CAPE BASIN
CAPE RISE
MOZAMBIQUE PLATEAU
MADAGASCAR BASIN
MASCARENE ISLANDS
MASCARENE PLATEAU
Tropic of Capricorn
SEYCHELLES
AMIRANTE ISLANDS
CHAGOS ARCHIPELAGO
SOMALI BASIN
ARABIAN BASIN
CARLSBERG RIDGE
Arabian Sea
LAKSHADWEEP
MALDIVE ISLANDS
CHAGOS-LACCADIVE PLATEAU
MID-INDIAN RIDGE
MID-INDIAN BASIN
INDIAN OCEAN
NINETYEAST RIDGE
WHARTON BASIN
SOUTHWEST INDIAN RIDGE
CROZET BASIN
ÎLE AMSTERDAM
ÎLE SAINT-PAUL
PRINCE EDWARD ISLANDS
ARCHIPEL CROZET
ATLANTIC-INDIAN RIDGE
ÎLES KERGUELEN
HEARD ISLAND
KERGUELEN PLATEAU
ATLANTIC-INDIAN BASIN
SOUTHEAST INDIAN RIDGE
SOUTH INDIAN BASIN
SOUTHERN OCEAN
Antarctic Circle
PAKISTAN
HINDU KUSH
PAMIR
pik Kommunizma 7495
K2 8611
TIEN SHAN
pik Pobedy 7439
TARIM PENDI
ALTUN SHAN
KUNLUN SHAN
QING ZANG GAOYUAN
HIMALAYAS
Mount Everest 8848
Indus
Sutlej
GREAT INDIAN DESERT
Ganges
INDIA
Brahmaputra
CALCUTTA
BOMBAY
Gulf of Khambhat
WESTERN GHATS
EASTERN GHATS
Godavari
Krishna
Bay of Bengal
SRI LANKA
Palk Strait
ANDAMAN ISLANDS
NICOBAR ISLANDS
Andaman Sea
MYANMAR
THAILAND
INDOCHINA
Gulf of Thailand
VIETNAM
CAMB.
MONGOLIA
GOBI
CHINA
BEIJING
Huang
Chang
SHANGHAI
Yellow Sea
East China Sea
Tropic of Cancer
Dongting Hu
HONG KONG
TAIWAN
Taiwan Strait
Luzon Strait
HAINAN DAO
South China Sea
SOUTH CHINA BASIN
PHILIPPINES
LUZON
Philippine Sea
PHILIPPINE BASIN
MINDANAO
Sulu Sea
MALAYSIA
SUNDA SHELF
Gunong Kinabalu 4101
Celebes Sea
CELEBES BASIN
BORNEO
SUMATERA
Strait of Malacca
Gunung Kerinci 3800
GREATER SUNDA ISLANDS
JAKARTA
JAWA
INDONESIA
Laut Jawa
SULAWESI
Laut Banda
MALUKU
HALMAHERA
NUSA TENGGARA
SUMBA
JAVA TRENCH
CHRISTMAS ISLAND
COCOS ISLANDS
TIMOR
Timor Sea
Arafura Sea
Joseph Bonaparte Gulf
Gulf of Carpentaria
Torres Strait
NEW GUINEA
PAPUA NEW GUINEA
Puncak Jaya 5030
Mount Wilhelm 4509
BISMARCK ARCHIPELAGO
Solomon Sea
SOLOMON ISLANDS
Coral Sea
CORAL SEA BASIN
MELANESIA
KIMBERLEY PLATEAU
GREAT SANDY DESERT
TANAMI DESERT
GIBSON DESERT
AUSTRALIA
Mount Woodroffe 1440
Lake Eyre North
GREAT VICTORIA DESERT
Shark Bay
Perth
DARLING RANGE
Darling
GREAT DIVIDING RANGE
GREAT BARRIER REEF
Sydney
Mount Kosciusko 2228
Great Australian Bight
Spencer Gulf
SOUTH AUSTRALIAN BASIN
Bass Strait
TASMANIA
Tasman Sea
TASMAN BASIN
NEW ZEALAND
NORTH ISLAND
SOUTH ISLAND
Mount Cook 3754
NEW CALEDONIA
NEW HEBRIDES
FIJI
LORD HOWE ISLAND
NORFOLK ISLAND
CAMPBELL PLATEAU
MACQUARIE ISLAND
Sea of Okhotsk
OKHOTSK BASIN
OSTROV SACHALIN
POLUOSTROV KAMČATKA
STANOVOJE NAGORJE
ozero Bajkal
Irkutsk
STANOVOJ CHREBET
Amur
SICHOTE-ALIN
Sea of Japan
JAPAN BASIN
HOKKAIDO
HONSHU
JAPAN
TOKYO
KYUSHU
SHIKOKU
KURIL TRENCH
Bering Sea
ALEUTIAN BASIN
ALEUTIAN TRENCH
ALEUTIAN ISLANDS
EMPEROR SEAMOUNTS
NORTHWEST PACIFIC BASIN
International Date Line
PACIFIC OCEAN
OGASAWARA-GUNTO
MINAMI-TORI-SHIMA
MARIANA ISLANDS
MARIANA TRENCH
MARIANA RIDGE
MICRONESIA
EAST MARIANA BASIN
WAKE ISLAND
MID-PACIFIC MOUNTAINS
CAROLINE ISLANDS
WEST CAROLINE BASIN
EAST CAROLINE BASIN
MARSHALL ISLANDS
KIRIBATI
TUVALU
SANTA CRUZ ISLANDS
Equator
WILKES LAND
AMERICAN HIGHLAND
AMERY ICE SHELF
ENDERBY LAND
MAC. ROBERTSON LAND
QUEEN MAUD LAND
ANTARCTICA
VICTORIA LAND
ROSS ICE SHELF
Ross Sea
Mount Kirkpatrick 4528
Mount Markham 4282
BALLENY ISLANDS
Copyright © by Rand McNally & Co.
Map prepared by Rand McNally & Co.

Kilometers 0 1000 2000 3000 Km.

Statute Miles 0 1000 2000 3000 Mi.

One centimeter represents 750 kilometers.
One inch represents approximately 1200 miles.
Robinson Projection
Scale 1:75,000,000

GREENLAND
ICELAND
Greenland Sea
Norwegian Sea
Arctic Circle
Barents Sea
NORWAY
SWEDEN
FINLAND
UNITED KINGDOM
IRELAND
North Sea
Baltic Sea
FRANCE
GERMANY
POLAND
UKRAINE
HUNGARY
ROMANIA
BULGARIA
Black Sea
Caspian Sea
TURKEY
MEDITERRANEAN SEA
SAHARA
Tropic of Cancer
LIBYA
EGYPT
SAUDI ARABIA
IRAN
IRAQ
AFGHANISTAN
PAKISTAN
INDIA
NEPAL
BHUTAN
KAZAKHSTAN
URAL'SKIJE GORY
URAL MOUNTAINS
ZAPADNO-SIBIRSKAJA RAVNINA
RUSSIA
SREDNESIBIRSKOJE PLOSKOGORJE
SIBERIA
MONGOLIA
GOBI
CHINA
TIEN SHAN
KUNLUN SHAN
QING ZANG GAOYUAN
HIMALAYAS
Sea of Okhotsk
Sea of Japan
JAPAN
N. KOREA
S. KOREA
Yellow Sea
East China Sea
South China Sea
TAIWAN
PHILIPPINES
Philippine Sea
MYANMAR
THAILAND
INDOCHINA
VIET-NAM
MALAYSIA
SINGAPORE
BORNEO
SUMATRA
INDONESIA
GREATER SUNDA ISLANDS
NEW GUINEA
PAPUA NEW GUINEA
Bay of Bengal
ARABIAN SEA
ARABIAN BASIN
SRI LANKA
MALDIVES
Gulf of Aden
AFRICA
SUDAN
ETHIOPIA
SOMALIA
KENYA
UGANDA
TANZANIA
ZAIRE
ZAMBIA
ZIMBABWE
MOZAMBIQUE
BOTSWANA
NAMIBIA
SOUTH AFRICA
MADAGASCAR
Mozambique Channel
SEYCHELLES
MAURITIUS
REUNION
Equator
SOMALI BASIN
MID-INDIAN RIDGE
CHAGOS-LACCADIVE PLATEAU
NINETY-EAST RIDGE
MID-INDIAN BASIN
INDIAN OCEAN
Tropic of Capricorn
WHARTON BASIN
JAVA TRENCH
NORTH AUSTRALIAN BASIN
AUSTRALIA
GREAT SANDY DESERT
GIBSON DESERT
GREAT VICTORIA DESERT
GREAT DIVIDING RANGE
GREAT BARRIER REEF
Gulf of Carpentaria
Great Australian Bight
PERTH BASIN
BROKEN RIDGE
MADAGASCAR BASIN
SOUTHWEST INDIAN RIDGE
CROZET BASIN
AGULHAS BASIN
SOUTH AUSTRALIAN BASIN
TASMANIA
SOUTHERN OCEAN
SOUTHEAST INDIAN RIDGE
SOUTH INDIAN BASIN
KERGUELEN PLATEAU
ATLANTIC-INDIAN RIDGE
ATLANTIC-INDIAN BASIN
Antarctic Circle
ENDERBY LAND
AMERY ICE SHELF
AMERICAN HIGHLAND
WILKES LAND
ANTARCTICA

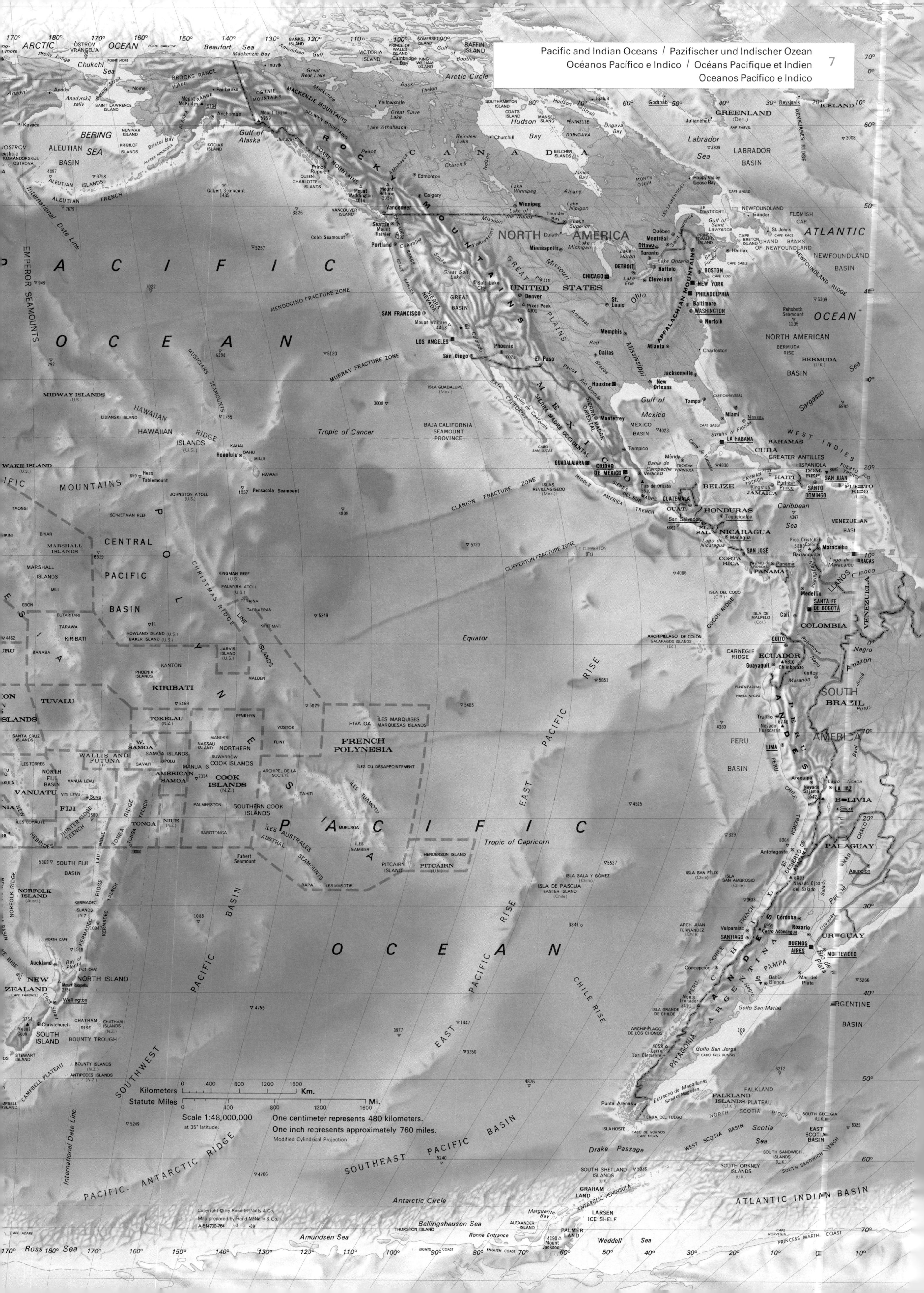
ARCTIC OCEAN
Beaufort Sea
Chukchi Sea
BERING SEA
ALEUTIAN BASIN
ALEUTIAN TRENCH
Gulf of Alaska
BROOKS RANGE
MACKENZIE MOUNTAINS
ROCKY MOUNTAINS
C A N A D A
Hudson Bay
Labrador Sea
LABRADOR BASIN
GREENLAND (Den.)
ICELAND
Arctic Circle
NORTH AMERICA
UNITED STATES
GREAT BASIN
GREAT PLAINS
APPALACHIAN MOUNTAINS
ATLANTIC OCEAN
NEWFOUNDLAND BASIN
NORTH AMERICAN BASIN
BERMUDA (U.K.)
Sargasso Sea
Gulf of Mexico
MEXICO BASIN
M E X I C O
WEST INDIES
CUBA
BAHAMAS
Caribbean Sea
BELIZE
HONDURAS
NICARAGUA
COSTA RICA
PANAMA
COLOMBIA
VENEZUELA
ECUADOR
PERU
BOLIVIA
PARAGUAY
URUGUAY
CHILE
ARGENTINA
SOUTH AMERICA
ARGENTINE BASIN
PATAGONIA
Drake Passage
Scotia Sea
SOUTH GEORGIA (U.K.)
FALKLAND ISLANDS (U.K.)
EAST SCOTIA BASIN
ATLANTIC-INDIAN BASIN
P A C I F I C
O C E A N
EMPEROR SEAMOUNTS
MENDOCINO FRACTURE ZONE
MURRAY FRACTURE ZONE
MIDWAY ISLANDS (U.S.)
HAWAIIAN ISLANDS (U.S.)
HAWAIIAN RIDGE
Tropic of Cancer
BAJA CALIFORNIA SEAMOUNT PROVINCE
CLARION FRACTURE ZONE
CLIPPERTON FRACTURE ZONE
MIDDLE AMERICA TRENCH
WAKE ISLAND (U.S.)
MOUNTAINS
CENTRAL PACIFIC BASIN
MARSHALL ISLANDS
KIRIBATI
TUVALU
CHRISTMAS RIDGE
LINE ISLANDS
Equator
ARCHIPIÉLAGO DE COLÓN GALAPAGOS ISLANDS (Ec.)
COCOS RIDGE
CARNEGIE RIDGE
PERU BASIN
TOKELAU (N.Z.)
W. SAMOA
AMERICAN SAMOA
WALLIS AND FUTUNA
FIJI
VANUATU
TONGA
NIUE (N.Z.)
COOK ISLANDS (N.Z.)
FRENCH POLYNESIA
ÎLES MARQUISES
ÎLES TUAMOTU
ÎLES AUSTRALES
PITCAIRN (U.K.)
POLYNESIA
P A C I F I C
Tropic of Capricorn
EAST PACIFIC RISE
ISLA DE PASCUA EASTER ISLAND (Chile)
CHILE RISE
SOUTH FIJI BASIN
NORFOLK ISLAND (Austl.)
KERMADEC TRENCH
NEW ZEALAND
NORTH ISLAND
SOUTH ISLAND
CHATHAM RISE
BOUNTY TROUGH
CAMPBELL PLATEAU
SOUTHWEST PACIFIC BASIN
PACIFIC-ANTARCTIC RIDGE
SOUTHEAST PACIFIC BASIN
International Date Line
Antarctic Circle
Bellingshausen Sea
Amundsen Sea
Ross Sea
Weddell Sea
LARSEN ICE SHELF
ANTARCTIC PENINSULA
GRAHAM LAND
PALMER LAND
Kilometers 0 400 800 1200 1600 Km.
Statute Miles 0 400 800 1200 1600 Mi.
Scale 1:48,000,000
at 35° latitude.
One centimeter represents 480 kilometers.
One inch represents approximately 760 miles.
Modified Cylindrical Projection
Copyright © by Rand McNally & Co.
Map prepared by Rand McNally & Co.

8
Atlantic Ocean / Atlantischer Ozean
Océano Atlántico / Océan Atlantique
Oceano Atlântico
GREENLAND
NORTH AMERICA
CANADA
UNITED STATES
ATLANTIC OCEAN
MID-ATLANTIC RIDGE
Sargasso Sea
Tropic of Cancer
Caribbean Sea
Gulf of Mexico
SOUTH AMERICA
BRAZIL
PACIFIC OCEAN
Tropic of Capricorn
ATLANTIC OCEAN
ANGOLA BASIN
BRAZIL BASIN
ARGENTINE BASIN
CAPE BASIN
AGULHAS BASIN
INDIAN OCEAN
AFRICA
SAHARA
EUROPE
Mediterranean Sea
Norwegian Sea
Barents Sea
Labrador Sea
Scotia Sea
Weddell Sea
Bellingshausen Sea
Amundsen Sea
ANTARCTICA
Antarctic Circle
Arctic Circle
Equator
Kilometers 0 400 800 1200 1600 Km.
Statute Miles 0 400 800 1200 1600 Mi.
Scale 1:48,000,000 at 35° latitude.
One centimeter represents 480 kilometers.
One inch represents approximately 760 miles.
Modified Cylindrical Projection
Copyright © by Rand McNally & Co.
Map prepared by Rand McNally & Co.

# Antarctica / Antarktis
# Antártida / Antarctique
# Antártida



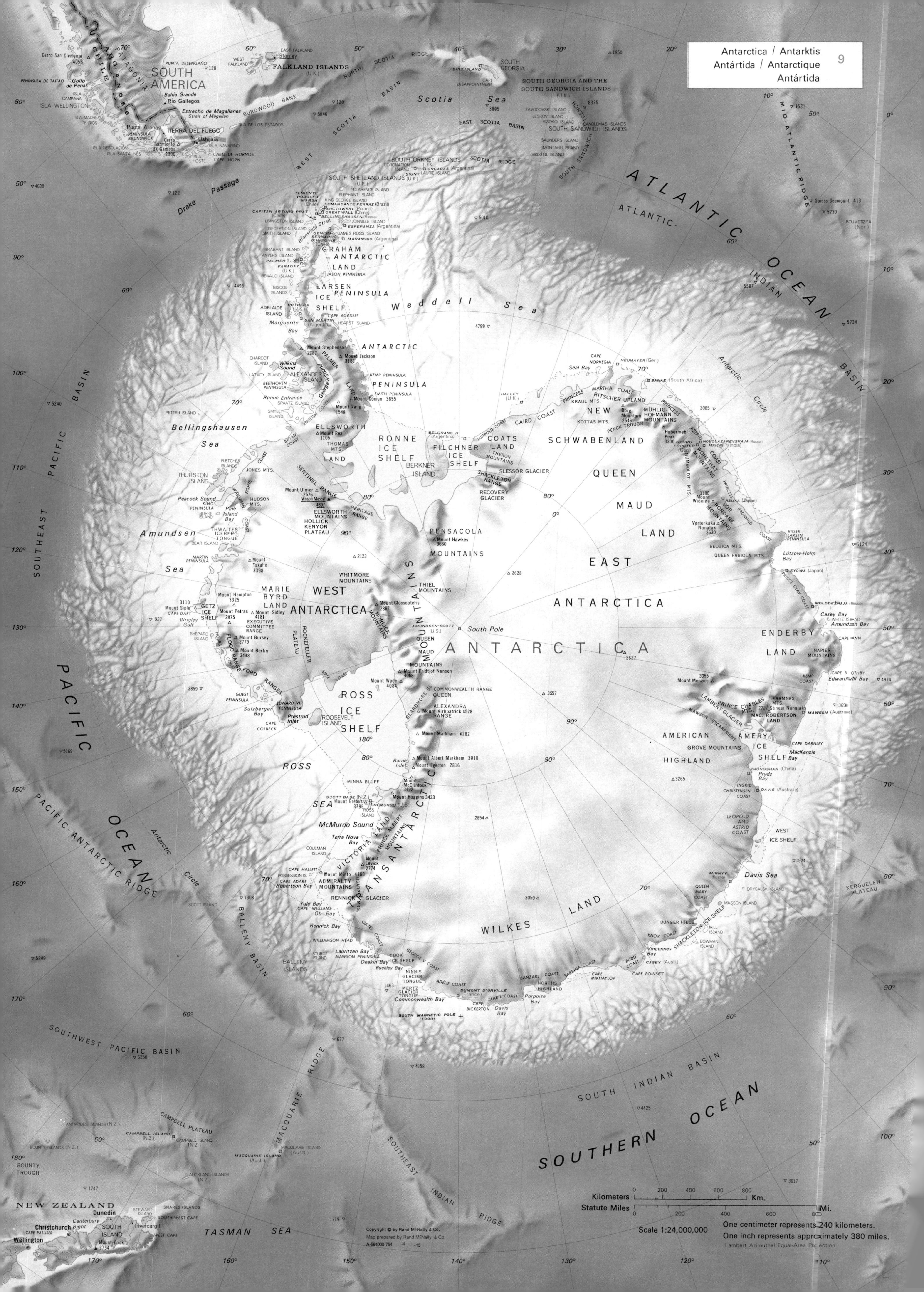
SOUTH AMERICA
PATAGONIA
ARGENTINA
CHILE
ANDES
FALKLAND ISLANDS (U.K.)
Stanley
Cerro San Clemente 4058
Golfo de Penas
ISLA WELLINGTON
Bahía Grande
Río Gallegos
Estrecho de Magallanes
Strait of Magellan
Punta Arenas
TIERRA DEL FUEGO
Ushuaia
CABO DE HORNOS
CAPE HORN
BURDWOOD BANK
NORTH SCOTIA RIDGE
SOUTH GEORGIA
SOUTH GEORGIA AND THE SOUTH SANDWICH ISLANDS (U.K.)
Scotia Sea
SCOTIA BASIN
EAST SCOTIA BASIN
SOUTH SANDWICH ISLANDS
SOUTH SANDWICH TRENCH
SOUTH ORKNEY ISLANDS (U.K.)
SCOTIA RIDGE
WEST SCOTIA BASIN
SOUTH SHETLAND ISLANDS (U.K.)
Drake Passage
MID-ATLANTIC RIDGE
Spiess Seamount 413
BOUVETØYA (Nor.)
ATLANTIC OCEAN
ATLANTIC-INDIAN OCEAN BASIN
Antarctic Circle
GRAHAM LAND
ANTARCTIC PENINSULA
LARSEN ICE SHELF
Weddell Sea
Marguerite Bay
Mount Stephenson 2587
Mount Jackson 3180
PALMER LAND
ALEXANDER ISLAND
KEMP PENINSULA
Mount Coman 3655
Ronne Entrance
Bellingshausen Sea
ELLSWORTH LAND
Mount Rex 1105
RONNE ICE SHELF
BERKNER ISLAND
FILCHNER ICE SHELF
COATS LAND
THERON MOUNTAINS
SHACKLETON RANGE
SLESSOR GLACIER
RECOVERY GLACIER
CAIRD COAST
PRINCESS MARTHA COAST
RITSCHER UPLAND
NEW SCHWABENLAND
MÜHLIG-HOFMANN MOUNTAINS
PRINCESS ASTRID COAST
WOHLTHAT MOUNTAINS
QUEEN MAUD LAND
SØR RONDANE MOUNTAINS
PRINCESS RAGNHILD COAST
BELGICA MTS.
QUEEN FABIOLA MTS.
Lützow-Holm Bay
PRINCE OLAV COAST
EAST ANTARCTICA
THURSTON ISLAND
JONES MTS.
HUDSON MTS.
Peacock Sound
Pine Island Bay
THWAITES ICEBERG TONGUE
Amundsen Sea
SENTINEL RANGE
Mount Ulmer 2576
Vinson Massif 4897
ELLSWORTH MOUNTAINS
HERITAGE RANGE
HOLLICK-KENYON PLATEAU
PENSACOLA MOUNTAINS
Mount Hawkes 3660
Mount Takahe 3398
WHITMORE MOUNTAINS
THIEL MOUNTAINS
MARIE BYRD LAND
WEST ANTARCTICA
GETZ ICE SHELF
Mount Hampton 3325
Mount Siple 3110
Mount Petras 2875
Mount Sidley 4181
EXECUTIVE COMMITTEE RANGE
Mount Bursey 2779
Mount Berlin 3498
FLOOD RANGE
FORD RANGES
ROCKEFELLER PLATEAU
HORLICK MOUNTAINS
Mount Glossopteris 2867
TRANSANTARCTIC MOUNTAINS
AMUNDSEN-SCOTT (U.S.)
South Pole
ANTARCTICA
QUEEN MAUD MOUNTAINS
Mount Fridtjof Nansen 4068
Mount Wade 4084
ROSS ICE SHELF
ROOSEVELT ISLAND
Sulzberger Bay
Prestrud Inlet
COMMONWEALTH RANGE
QUEEN ALEXANDRA RANGE
Mount Kirkpatrick 4528
BEARDMORE GL.
Mount Markham 4282
Mount Albert Markham 3010
Mount Egerton 2816
Barne Inlet
Ross Sea
MINNA BLUFF
Mount McClintock 3492
Mount Huggins 3433
SCOTT BASE (N.Z.)
Mount Erebus 3795
McMURDO (U.S.)
ROSS ISLAND
McMurdo Sound
Terra Nova Bay
VICTORIA LAND
PRINCE ALBERT MOUNTAINS
Mount Levick 2774
Mount Minto 4163
ADMIRALTY MOUNTAINS
CAPE HALLETT
Robertson Bay
RENNICK GLACIER
Yule Bay
Ob Bay
Rennick Bay
OATES COAST
Lauritzen Bay
Deakin Bay
Buckley Bay
GEORGE V COAST
NINNIS GLACIER TONGUE
MERTZ GLACIER TONGUE
Commonwealth Bay
ADÉLIE COAST
DUMONT D'URVILLE (France)
SOUTH MAGNETIC POLE (1990)
BALLENY ISLANDS
ENDERBY LAND
NAPIER MOUNTAINS
Mount Menzies 3355
PRINCE CHARLES MTS.
LAMBERT GLACIER
MAWSON ESCARPMENT
FRAMNES MTS.
MAWSON (Australia)
MAC. ROBERTSON LAND
AMERICAN HIGHLAND
GROVE MOUNTAINS
AMERY ICE SHELF
CAPE DARNLEY
MacKenzie Bay
Prydz Bay
DAVIS (Australia)
INGRID CHRISTENSEN COAST
LEOPOLD AND ASTRID COAST
WEST ICE SHELF
Davis Sea
QUEEN MARY COAST
MIRNYY (Russia)
BUNGER HILLS
SHACKLETON ICE SHELF
KNOX COAST
Vincennes Bay
BUDD COAST
CASEY (Austl.)
SABRINA COAST
BANZARE COAST
CAPE MIKHAYLOV
NORTHS HIGHLAND
Porpoise Bay
CLARIE COAST
Davis Bay
WILKES LAND
KERGUELEN PLATEAU
Casey Bay
Amundsen Bay
KEMP COAST
Edward VIII Bay
PACIFIC OCEAN
SOUTHEAST PACIFIC BASIN
PACIFIC-ANTARCTIC RIDGE
BALLENY BASIN
SOUTHWEST PACIFIC BASIN
MACQUARIE RIDGE
CAMPBELL PLATEAU
CAMPBELL ISLAND (N.Z.)
MACQUARIE ISLAND (Austl.)
BOUNTY TROUGH
NEW ZEALAND
Christchurch
Dunedin
Wellington
SOUTH ISLAND
STEWART ISLAND
Invercargill
Mount Cook 3754
TASMAN SEA
SOUTHEAST INDIAN RIDGE
SOUTH INDIAN BASIN
SOUTHERN OCEAN
Kilometers 0 200 400 600 800 Km.
Statute Miles 0 200 400 Mi.
Scale 1:24,000,000
One centimeter represents 240 kilometers.
One inch represents approximately 380 miles.
Lambert Azimuthal Equal-Area Projection
Copyright © by Rand McNally & Co.
Map prepared by Rand McNally & Co.
A-594000-764

ATLANTIC OCEAN
MID-ATLANTIC RIDGE
WEST EUROPEAN BASIN
GREENLAND
CANADA
ICELAND
Reykjavík
Labrador Sea
LABRADOR BASIN
IRMINGER BASIN
REYKJANES RIDGE
ICELAND BASIN
ROCKALL RISE
Denmark Strait
Norwegian Sea
NORWEGIAN BASIN
LOFOTEN BASIN
GREENLAND BASIN
Greenland Sea
Barents Sea
SPITSBERGEN SVALBARD (Nor.)
AZORES-GIBRALTAR RIDGE
CANARY BASIN
AZORES
Tropic of Cancer
Arctic Circle
E U R O P E
ASIA
RUSSIA
URAL'SKIJE GORY URAL MOUNTAINS
ZAPADNO-SIBIRSKAJA RAVNINA
KAZAKHSTAN
UZBEKISTAN
TURKMENISTAN
FINLAND
SWEDEN
NORWAY
DENMARK
UNITED KINGDOM
IRELAND
FRANCE
SPAIN
PORTUGAL
GERMANY
POLAND
BELARUS
UKRAINE
ITALY
ALPS
AUSTRIA
HUNGARY
ROMANIA
BULGARIA
GREECE
TURKEY
ASIA MINOR
CAUCASUS
SYRIA
IRAQ
IRAN
SAUDI ARABIA
ARABIAN PENINSULA
EGYPT
LIBYA
ALGERIA
TUNISIA
MOROCCO
WESTERN SAHARA
MAURITANIA
SAHARA
ATLAS MOUNTAINS
Mediterranean Sea
Black Sea
Caspian Sea
Aral Sea
Baltic Sea
North Sea
Adriatic Sea
Aegean Sea
Ionian Sea
Tyrrhenian Sea
Red Sea
Persian Gulf
Bay of Biscay
English Channel
Gulf of Bothnia
MOSKVA
SANKT-PETERBURG
LONDON
PARIS
BERLIN
ROMA
MADRID
LISBOA
WARSZAWA
WIEN
PRAHA
BUDAPEST
BUCURESTI
SOFIJA
BEOGRAD
ATHINAI
ISTANBUL
ANKARA
KYYIV
MINSK
HELSINKI
STOCKHOLM
KØBENHAVN
AMSTERDAM
BRUXELLES
DUBLIN
TEHRĀN
BAGHDĀD
DIMASHQ
AL-QĀHIRAH
TARĀBULUS
TUNIS
EL DJAZAÏR
RABAT
AR-RIYĀD
AL-KUWAYT

INDIAN OCEAN
ATLANTIC OCEAN
AFRICA
SOMALIA
ETHIOPIA
KENYA
UGANDA
RWANDA
BURUNDI
TANZANIA
ZAIRE
CONGO
GABON
EQUAT. GUI.
CAMEROON
CENTRAL AFRICAN REPUBLIC
NIGERIA
BENIN
TOGO
GHANA
COTE D'IVOIRE
LIBERIA
SIERRA LEONE
GUINEA
GUINEA-BISSAU
ANGOLA
ZAMBIA
MALAWI
MOZAMBIQUE
ZIMBABWE
BOTSWANA
NAMIBIA
SOUTH AFRICA
SWAZILAND
LESOTHO
MADAGASCAR
COMOROS
SAO TOME AND PRINCIPE
SEYCHELLES
MAURITIUS
REUNION (Fr.)
SAINT HELENA (U.K.)
Gulf of Guinea
Bight of Benin
Gulf of Aden
Mozambique Channel
Tropic of Capricorn
Equator
ADIS ABEBA
NAIROBI
KAMPALA
DAR ES SALAAM
KINSHASA
LUANDA
LUSAKA
HARARE
PRETORIA
MAPUTO
CAPE TOWN
ANTANANARIVO
LAGOS
ACCRA
ABIDJAN
Scale 1:24,000,000
One centimeter represents 240 kilometers.
One inch represents approximately 380 miles.
Lambert Azimuthal Equal-Area Projection
Kilometers
Statute Miles
Copyright © by Rand McNally & Co.
Map prepared by Rand McNally & Co.

ARCTIC
OCEAN
ATLANTIC
OCEAN
GREENLAND
UNITED STATES
North Pole
Greenland Sea
Norwegian Sea
Barents Sea
Kara Sea
Laptev Sea
East Siberian Sea
Chukchi Sea
Bering Sea
Sea of Okhotsk
Sea of Japan
Yellow Sea
EAST CHINA
North Sea
Baltic Sea
Black Sea
Caspian Sea
Aral Sea
Mediterranean Sea
SVALBARD
ZEML'A FRANCA-IOSIFA
FRANZ JOSEF LAND
SEVERNAJA ZEML'A
NOVOSIBIRSKIJE OSTROVA
OSTROV VRANGEL'A
ICELAND
Reykjavík
IRELAND
DUBLIN
UNITED KINGDOM
LONDON
NORWAY
SWEDEN
FINLAND
DENMARK
STOCKHOLM
HELSINKI
Oslo
KØBENHAVN
AMSTERDAM
BRUXELLES
BERLIN
WARSZAWA
PRAHA
WIEN
BUDAPEST
BEOGRAD
BUCUREŞTI
SOFIJA
ISTANBUL
ANKARA
RUSSIA
MOSKVA
MOSCOW
SANKT-PETERBURG
ST. PETERSBURG
KYIV
MINSK
RIGA
Tallinn
Vilnius
UKRAINE
BELARUS
POLAND
ROMANIA
BULGARIA
HUNGARY
TURKEY
ASIA MINOR
SYRIA
IRAQ
IRAN
TEHRĀN
BAGHDĀD
DIMASHQ
DAMASCUS
BAYRŪT
CAUCASUS
TBILISI
JEREVAN
BAKI
KAZAKHSTAN
UZBEKISTAN
TURKMENISTAN
KYRGYZSTAN
TAŠKENT
ALMATY
MONGOLIA
Ulaanbaatar
GOBI
ALTAI
TIEN SHAN
PAMIR
HINDU KUSH
TARIM PENDI
BEIJING
PEKING
TIANJIN
SHANGHAI
NANJING
XI'AN
P'YŎNGYANG
SŎUL
NORTH KOREA
SOUTH KOREA
JAPAN
TŌKYŌ
HONSHU
HOKKAIDO
OSTROV SACHALIN
SAKHALIN
KURIL'SKIJE OSTROVA
KURIL ISLANDS
POLUOSTROV KAMČATKA
URAL'SKIJE GORY
URAL MOUNTAINS
ZAPADNO-SIBIRSKAJA RAVNINA
SIBERIA
SREDNESIBIRSKOJE PLOSKOGORJE
CHREBET ČERSKOGO
DA HINGGAN LING
SICHOTE-ALIN'
ozero Bajkal
Lake Baikal
Irkutsk
Novosibirsk
Omsk
Jekaterinburg
Volgograd
Jakutsk
Magadan
Vladivostok
Chabarovsk
Noril'sk
Murmansk
Archangel'sk
Bering Strait
Arctic Circle

INDIAN OCEAN
ARABIAN SEA
Bay of Bengal
Andaman Sea
SOUTH CHINA SEA
Philippine Sea
Sulu Sea
Celebes Sea
Java Sea
Gulf of Aden
Red Sea
Gulf of Oman
Gulf of Thailand
Gulf of Tonkin
Gulf of Mannar
Lakshadweep Sea
INDIA
PAKISTAN
BANGLADESH
BHUTAN
NEPAL
MYANMAR (BURMA)
THAILAND
LAOS
VIETNAM
CAMBODIA
MALAYSIA
SINGAPORE
INDONESIA
PHILIPPINES
SRI LANKA
MALDIVES
OMAN
YEMEN
SOMALIA
ETHIOPIA
DJIBOUTI
UNITED ARAB EMIRATES
QATAR
SEYCHELLES
MAURITIUS
RÉUNION
MADAGASCAR
AUSTRALIA
GREATER SUNDA ISLANDS
BORNEO
SUMATERA
JAWA
ARABIAN PENINSULA
AR RUB' AL KHĀLĪ
DECCAN
HIMALAYA
DELHI
New Delhi
BOMBAY
CALCUTTA
MADRAS
BANGALORE
Hyderābād
KARĀCHI
COLOMBO
DHAKA
YANGON
KRUNG THEP (BANGKOK)
HA NOI
THANH PHO HO CHI MINH (SAIGON)
KUALA LUMPUR
JAKARTA
MANILA
HONG KONG
VICTORIA
ANTANANARIVO
Muqdisho
Perth
CARLSBERG RIDGE
MID-INDIAN RIDGE
NINETYEAST RIDGE
BROKEN RIDGE
SOUTHWEST INDIAN RIDGE
MID-INDIAN BASIN
WHARTON BASIN
SOMALI BASIN
MASCARENE BASIN
MASCARENE PLATEAU
MADAGASCAR BASIN
ARABIAN BASIN
PERTH BASIN
JAVA TRENCH
OWEN FRACTURE ZONE
CHAGOS-LACCADIVE PLATEAU
Tropic of Cancer
Tropic of Capricorn
Equator
Scale 1:24,000,000
One centimeter represents 240 kilometers.
One inch represents approximately 380 miles.
Lambert Azimuthal Equal-Area Projection
Copyright © by Rand McNally & Co.

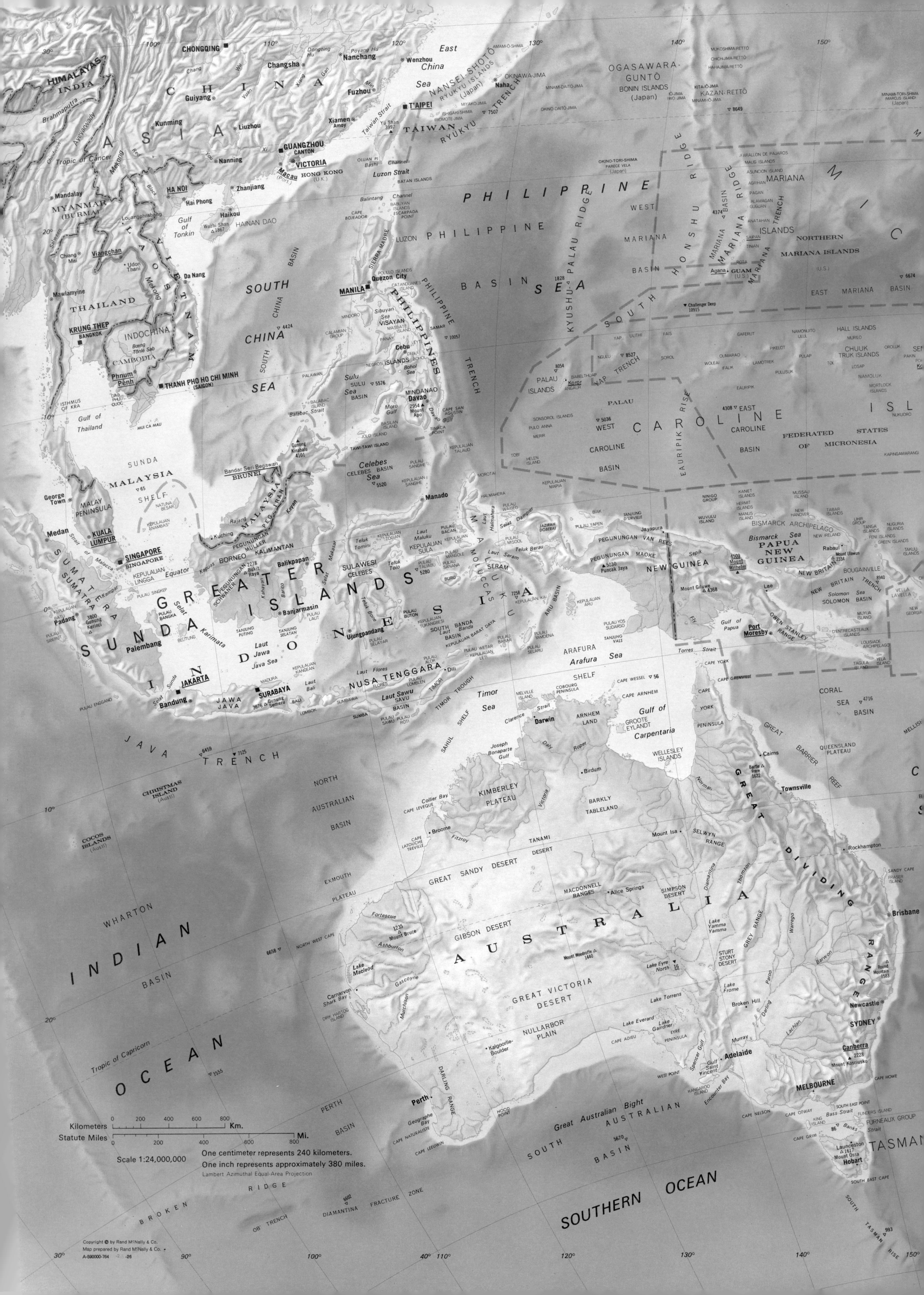
CHONGQING
Changsha
Nanchang
Wenzhou
East China Sea
Dongting Hu
Poyang Hu
HIMALAYAS
INDIA
C H I N A
A S I A
Guiyang
Kunming
Liuzhou
Fuzhou
Xiamen Amoy
T'AIPEI
TAIWAN
Taiwan Strait
Naha
OKINAWA-JIMA
NANSEI-SHOTO RYUKYU ISLANDS (Japan)
RYUKYU TRENCH
OGASAWARA-GUNTŌ BONIN ISLANDS (Japan)
KAZAN-RETTŌ
Brahmaputra
Ayeyarwady
Tropic of Cancer
Mekong
Nanning
GUANGZHOU CANTON
VICTORIA
HONG KONG (U.K.)
Macau (Port.)
Luzon Strait
Bashi Channel
BATAN ISLANDS
Mandalay
MYANMAR (BURMA)
HA NOI
Hai Phong
Zhanjiang
Haikou
HAINAN DAO
Gulf of Tonkin
Louangphrabang
LAOS
Viangchan
Udon Thani
Chiang Mai
Da Nang
VIETNAM
Mawlamyine
THAILAND
KRUNG THEP BANGKOK
INDOCHINA
CAMBODIA
Phnum Pénh
THANH PHO HO CHI MINH (SAIGON)
ISTHMUS OF KRA
Gulf of Thailand
MUI CA MAU
SOUTH CHINA SEA
SOUTH CHINA BASIN
PHILIPPINE SEA
WEST PHILIPPINE BASIN
LUZON
MANILA
Quezon City
PHILIPPINES
PHILIPPINE TRENCH
VISAYAN
Sibuyan Sea
Cebu
Bohol
Negros
PALAWAN
Sulu Sea
SULU BASIN
MINDANAO
Davao
Moro Gulf
Balabac Strait
Celebes Sea
CELEBES BASIN
Manado
SUNDA SHELF
MALAYSIA
Bandar Seri Begawan
BRUNEI
Gunung Kinabalu 4101
George Town
MALAY PENINSULA
KUALA LUMPUR
Medan
Strait of Malacca
SINGAPORE
Kuching
BORNEO
KALIMANTAN
Balikpapan
Equator
SUMATERA SUMATRA
Padang
Palembang
Banjarmasin
GREATER SUNDA ISLANDS
INDONESIA
SULAWESI CELEBES
Ujungpandang
Laut Jawa Java Sea
JAKARTA
Bandung
JAWA JAVA
SURABAYA
Laut Flores
NUSA TENGGARA
TIMOR
Dili
Laut Sawu
TIMOR TROUGH
Timor Sea
MALUKU MOLUCCAS
SERAM
Laut Banda
BANDA SEA
Laut Seram
Halmahera
Jayapura
PEGUNUNGAN MAOKE
Puncak Jaya 5030
NEW GUINEA
Mount Wilhelm 4509
PAPUA NEW GUINEA
Bismarck Sea
BISMARCK ARCHIPELAGO
NEW BRITAIN
BOUGAINVILLE
Rabaul
SOLOMON SEA
Lae
Gulf of Papua
Port Moresby
OWEN STANLEY RANGE
Torres Strait
ARAFURA SEA
Arafura Sea
ARU BASIN
PALAU ISLANDS
Koror
YAP TRENCH
KYUSHU-PALAU RIDGE
WEST MARIANA BASIN
MARIANA ISLANDS
NORTHERN MARIANA ISLANDS (U.S.)
MARIANA TRENCH
MARIANA RIDGE
GUAM (U.S.)
Agana
Challenger Deep 10915
EAST MARIANA BASIN
CAROLINE ISLANDS
WEST CAROLINE BASIN
EAST CAROLINE BASIN
EAURIPIK RISE
FEDERATED STATES OF MICRONESIA
CHUUK TRUK ISLANDS
HALL ISLANDS
CORAL SEA BASIN
QUEENSLAND PLATEAU
GREAT BARRIER REEF
CAPE YORK PENINSULA
Gulf of Carpentaria
GROOTE EYLANDT
ARNHEM LAND
CAPE ARNHEM
Darwin
JAVA TRENCH
CHRISTMAS ISLAND (Austl.)
COCOS ISLANDS (Austl.)
NORTH AUSTRALIAN BASIN
SAHUL SHELF
Joseph Bonaparte Gulf
KIMBERLEY PLATEAU
BARKLY TABLELAND
Birdum
WELLESLEY ISLANDS
Cairns
Townsville
Rockhampton
Broome
TANAMI DESERT
GREAT SANDY DESERT
EXMOUTH PLATEAU
Mount Isa
SELWYN RANGE
GREAT DIVIDING RANGE
MACDONNELL RANGES
Alice Springs
SIMPSON DESERT
AUSTRALIA
GIBSON DESERT
Mount Bruce 1235
Lake Eyre North
STURT STONY DESERT
GREY RANGE
Brisbane
Mount Woodroffe 1440
GREAT VICTORIA DESERT
Lake Torrens
Broken Hill
Darling
Lachlan
Newcastle
SYDNEY
Canberra
Mount Kosciusko 2228
NULLARBOR PLAIN
Kalgoorlie-Boulder
Lake Gairdner
Spencer Gulf
Adelaide
Murray
MELBOURNE
Bass Strait
Launceston
Hobart
TASMAN
Perth
DARLING RANGE
Great Australian Bight
SOUTH AUSTRALIAN BASIN
PERTH BASIN
WHARTON BASIN
INDIAN OCEAN
Tropic of Capricorn
SOUTHERN OCEAN
BROKEN RIDGE
DIAMANTINA FRACTURE ZONE
SOUTH TASMAN RISE
Kilometers 0 200 400 600 800 Km.
Statute Miles 0 200 400 600 800 Mi.
Scale 1:24,000,000
One centimeter represents 240 kilometers.
One inch represents approximately 380 miles.
Lambert Azimuthal Equal-Area Projection
Copyright © by Rand McNally & Co.
Map prepared by Rand McNally & Co.
A-590000-764 -26

MIDWAY ISLANDS (U.S.)
KURE ATOLL
PEARL AND HERMES ATOLL
LISIANSKI ISLAND
LAYSAN ISLAND
GARDNER PINNACLES
NECKER ISLAND
NIHOA
FRENCH FRIGATE SHOALS
NECKER RIDGE
HAWAIIAN RIDGE
HAWAIIAN ISLANDS (U.S.)
KAUAI
NIIHAU
OAHU
Honolulu
MOLOKAI
LANAI
MAUI
HAWAII
Hilo
Mauna Kea 4205
KA LAE
Loihi Seamount 969
Pensacola Seamount 1057
Swordfish Seamount
UNITED STATES
MOLOKAI FRACTURE ZONE
Tropic of Cancer
Guadalupe Seamount
International Date Line
Paul Seamount
Horizon Tablemount
Hess Tablemount 859
Karin Seamount
JOHNSTON ATOLL (U.S.)
Cape Johnson Tablemount
SCHJETMAN REEF
WAKE ISLAND (U.S.)
PACIFIC MOUNTAINS
MARSHALL ISLANDS
TAONGI
BIKAR
BIKINI
ENEWETAK
RONGELAP
UTIRIK
WOTHO
AILUK
WOTJE
MALOELAP
KWAJALEIN
UJAE
LAE
LIB
NAMU
RATAK CHAIN
RALIK CHAIN
AILINGLAPALAP
MAJURO
ARNO
NAMORIK
JALUIT
MILI
KILI
EBON
KOSRAE
PINGELAP
MARSHALL ISLANDS
CENTRAL PACIFIC BASIN
PACIFIC OCEAN
CHRISTMAS RIDGE
KINGMAN REEF (U.S.)
PALMYRA ATOLL (U.S.)
TERAINA
TABUAERAN
KIRITIMATI
LINE ISLANDS
JARVIS ISLAND (U.S.)
MALDEN
STARBUCK
POLYNESIA
MELANESIAN BASIN
BUTARITARI
TARAWA
ABEMAMA
KURIA
KIRIBATI
BANABA
NONOUTI
BERU
NIKUNAU
TABITEUEA
ONOTOA
TAMANA
ARORAE
NAURU
HOWLAND ISLAND (U.S.)
BAKER ISLAND (U.S.)
WINSLOW REEF
KIRIBATI
PHOENIX ISLANDS
KANTON
ENDERBURY
BIRNIE
RAWAKI
NIKUMARORO
ORONA
MANRA
Equator
SOLOMON ISLANDS
TUVALU
NANUMEA
NIUTAO
NANUMANGA
NUI
VAITUPU
NUKUFETAU
FUNAFUTI
NUKULAELAE
NIULAKITA
TOKELAU (N.Z.)
ATAFU
NUKUNONU
FAKAOFO
SWAINS ISLAND
AMERICAN SAMOA ISLANDS
SAMOA
WESTERN SAMOA
SAVAI'I
UPOLU
Apia
Pago Pago
TUTUILA
MANUA ISLANDS
ROSE ISLAND
SAMOA BASIN
WALLIS AND FUTUNA (Fr.)
ÎLES WALLIS
ÎLE FUTUNA
ÎLE ALOFI
Combe Bank
Home Seamount
ROTUMA
NORTH FIJI BASIN
FIJI ISLANDS
FIJI
VANUA LEVU
VITI LEVU
TAVEUNI
LAU GROUP
Suva
Koro Sea
KANDAVU ISLAND
TAFAHI
TOKU ISLAND
VAVA'U
VAVA'U GROUP
TONGA ISLANDS
TONGATAPU GROUP
TONGATAPU
Nuku'alofa
EUA
'ATA
TONGA
TONGA TRENCH
TONGA RIDGE
LAU BASIN
LAU RIDGE
NIUE (N.Z.)
NORTHERN COOK ISLANDS
NASSAU ISLAND
MANIHIKI
PENRHYN
SUWARROW
COOK ISLANDS (N.Z.)
PALMERSTON
AITUTAKI
MANUAE
TAKUTEA
MITIARO
ATIU
MAUKE
RAROTONGA
MANGAIA
SOUTHERN COOK ISLANDS
Merlin Seamount
VOSTOK
CAROLINE
FLINT
SANTA CRUZ ISLANDS
NENDO
UTUPUA
VANIKOLO
SANTA CRUZ BASIN
SAN CRISTOBAL
GUADALCANAL
MALAITA
ÎLES TORRES
ÎLES BANKS
VANUA LAVA
SANTA MARIA
ESPIRITU SANTO
MAEWO
PENTECÔTE
MALAKULA
AMBRYM
EPI
ÉFATÉ
Port Vila
ERROMANGO
TANNA
ANATOM
VANUATU
NEW HEBRIDES
NEW CALEDONIA (Fr.) NOUVELLE-CALÉDONIE
Nouméa
OUVÉA
LIFOU
MARÉ
ÎLES LOYAUTÉ
HEBRIDES TRENCH
ÎLE HUNTER
HUNTER RIDGE
HUNTER TRENCH
SOUTH FIJI BASIN
Osbourn Seamount
NORFOLK ISLAND (Austl.)
NORFOLK RIDGE
NEW CALEDONIA BASIN
LORD HOWE ISLAND (Austl.)
LORD HOWE RISE
Tasman Sea
RAOUL ISLAND
KERMADEC
CURTIS ISLAND
KERMADEC ISLANDS
KERMADEC RIDGE
KERMADEC TRENCH
LOUISVILLE RIDGE
Currituck Seamount
Seafox Seamount
Louisville Seamount
Burton Seamount
SOUTHWEST PACIFIC BASIN
THREE KINGS IS.
NORTH CAPE
TAURO POINT
GREAT BARRIER ISLAND
Auckland
Bay of Plenty
EAST CAPE
NEW ZEALAND
NORTH ISLAND
New Plymouth
CAPE EGMONT
Mount Ruapehu 2797
Napier
Hawke Bay
CAPE FAREWELL
Wellington
CAPE PALLISER
Cook Strait
Mount Cook 3754
Christchurch
SOUTH ISLAND
Canterbury Bight
CHATHAM RISE
CHATHAM ISLAND
CHATHAM ISLANDS (N.Z.)
BOUNTY TROUGH
Dunedin
WEST CAPE
Invercargill
SOUTH WEST CAPE
STEWART ISLAND
SNARES ISLANDS
CAMPBELL PLATEAU
ANTIPODES ISLANDS (N.Z.)
BOUNTY ISLANDS (N.Z.)
FRENCH POLYNESIA
SOCIETY ISLANDS
ARCHIPEL DE LA SOCIÉTÉ
SOCIETY RIDGE
MOTU ONE
MANUAE
MAUPIHAA
BORA-BORA
TAHAA
MOOREA
TAHITI
Papeete
MEHETIA
TETIAROA
MAKATEA
RAIATEA
KAUKURA
RANGIROA
TAKAROA
ÎLES TUAMOTU
TUAMOTU RIDGE
TUAMOTU ARCHIPELAGO
ANAA
HIKUERU
RAROIA
MAKEMO
HARAIKI
RAVAHERE
NENGONENGO
AMANU
HAO
MARUTEA
AHUNUI
VANAVANA
TEMATANGI
ÎLES DU DÉSAPPOINTEMENT
ÎLES DU ROI GEORGES
ÎLES MARIA
RIMATARA
RURUTU
TUBUAI
RAIVAVAE
ÎLES AUSTRALES
AUSTRAL SEAMOUNTS
RAPA
ÎLES MAROTIRI
Fabert Seamount
Tropic of Capricorn
160°
170°
180°
150°
140°
130°

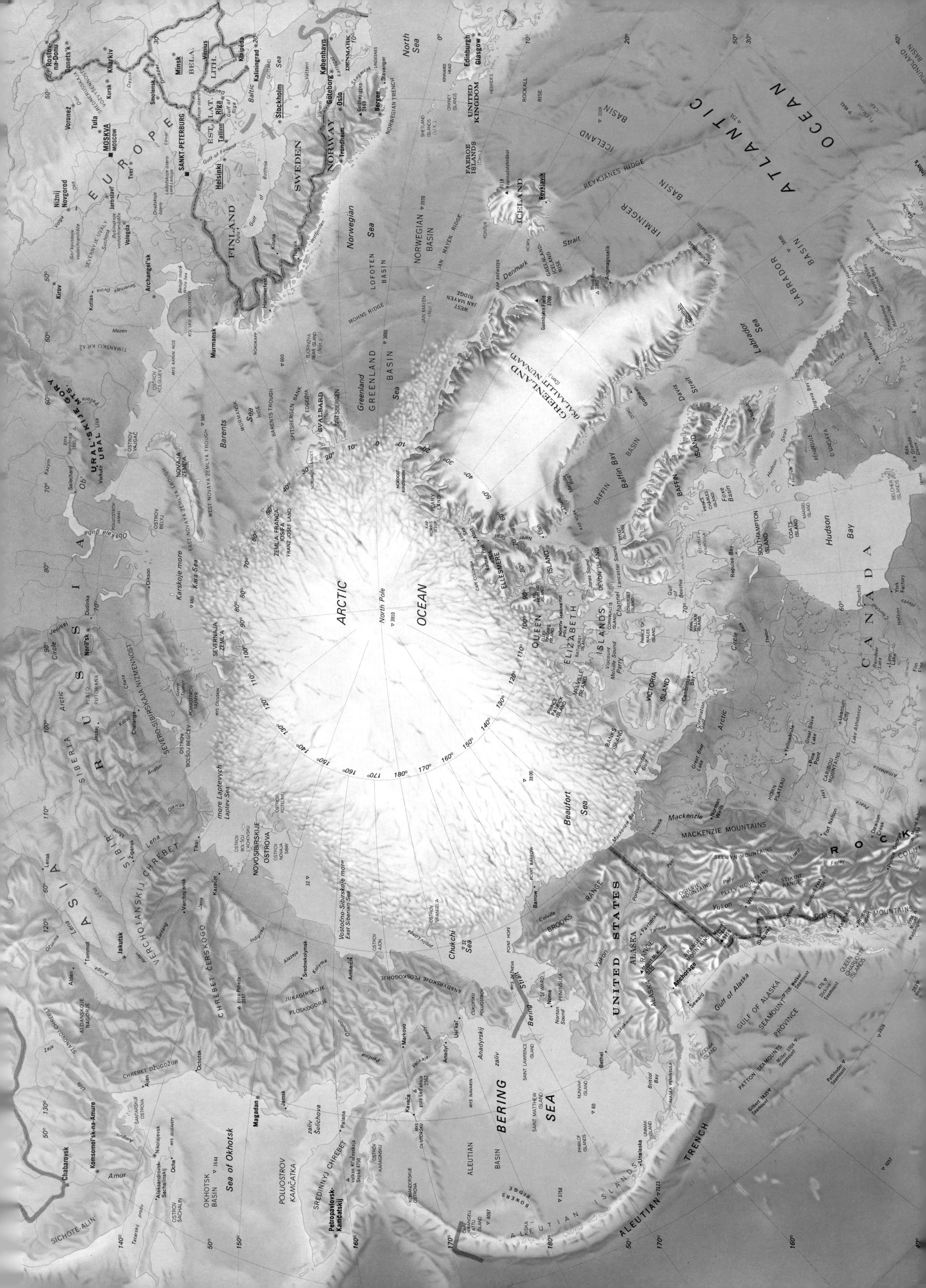
ARCTIC
OCEAN
North Pole
ATLANTIC
OCEAN
EUROPE
ASIA
RUSSIA
SIBERIA
CANADA
UNITED STATES
GREENLAND
(KALAALLIT NUNAAT)
ICELAND
NORWAY
SWEDEN
FINLAND
UNITED KINGDOM
FAEROE ISLANDS
SVALBARD
Norwegian Sea
Greenland Sea
Barents Sea
Kara Sea
Karskoje more
more Laptevych
Laptev Sea
Vostočno-Sibirskoje more
East Siberian Sea
Chukchi Sea
Beaufort Sea
BERING SEA
Sea of Okhotsk
Hudson Bay
Baffin Bay
Labrador Sea
Davis Strait
Denmark Strait
Bering Strait
Gulf of Alaska
North Sea
Baltic Sea
ALEUTIAN TRENCH
ALEUTIAN ISLANDS
QUEEN ELIZABETH ISLANDS
ELLESMERE
BAFFIN ISLAND
VICTORIA ISLAND
BANKS ISLAND
NOVAJA ZEML'A
SEVERNAJA ZEML'A
NOVOSIBIRSKIJE OSTROVA
ZEML'A FRANCA-IOSIFA
FRANZ JOSEF LAND
ROCKY MOUNTAINS
MACKENZIE MOUNTAINS
BROOKS RANGE
ALASKA RANGE
URAL'SKIJE GORY
URAL MTS.
VERCHOJANSKIJ CHREBET
CHREBET ČERSKOGO
MOSKVA
SANKT-PETERBURG
Helsinki
Stockholm
Oslo
København
Reykjavík
Murmansk
Archangel'sk
Norilsk
Jakutsk
Magadan
Anchorage
Nome
Barrow

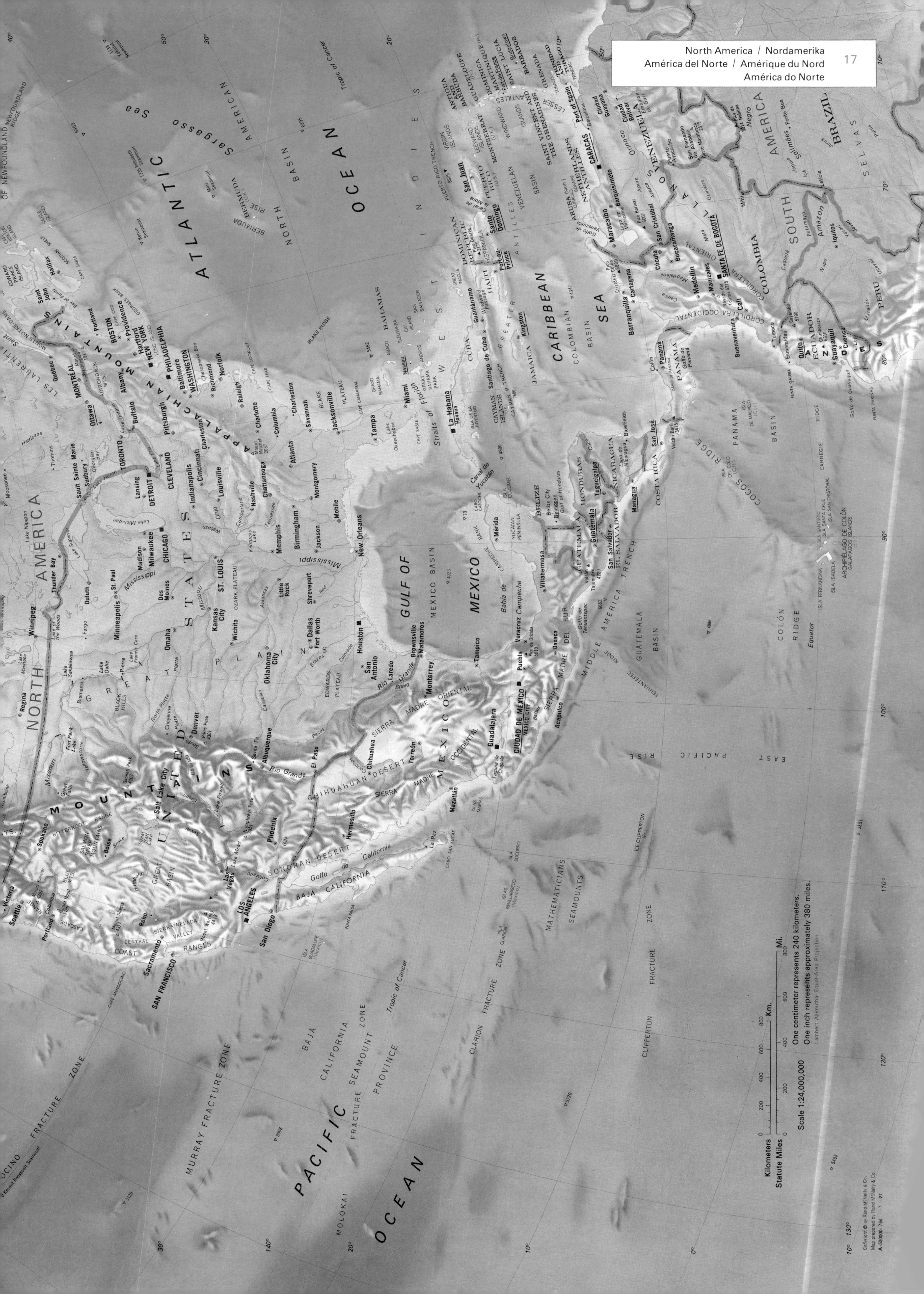
NORTH AMERICA
SOUTH AMERICA
ATLANTIC OCEAN
PACIFIC OCEAN
GULF OF MEXICO
CARIBBEAN SEA
Sargasso Sea
UNITED STATES
ROCKY MOUNTAINS
APPALACHIAN MOUNTAINS
GREAT PLAINS
MEXICO
CUBA
HAITI
DOMINICAN REPUBLIC
JAMAICA
BAHAMAS
BELIZE
GUATEMALA
HONDURAS
EL SALVADOR
NICARAGUA
COSTA RICA
PANAMA
COLOMBIA
VENEZUELA
ECUADOR
PERU
BRAZIL
WASHINGTON
NEW YORK
PHILADELPHIA
BOSTON
CHICAGO
DETROIT
CLEVELAND
TORONTO
MONTRÉAL
Ottawa
ST. LOUIS
LOS ANGELES
SAN FRANCISCO
CIUDAD DE MÉXICO
La Habana
CARACAS
SANTA FE DE BOGOTÁ
Tropic of Cancer
Equator
Kilometers
Statute Miles
Km.
Mi.
Scale 1:24,000,000
One centimeter represents 240 kilometers.
One inch represents approximately 380 miles.
Lambert Azimuthal Equal-Area Projection

NORTH AMERICA
UNITED STATES
ROCKY MTS.
APPALACHIAN MOUNTAINS
GREAT PLAINS
OZARK PLATEAU
EDWARDS PLATEAU
MEXICO
SIERRA MADRE ORIENTAL
SIERRA MADRE DEL SUR
Chicago
Des Moines
Omaha
Denver
Cheyenne
Kansas City
St. Louis
Wichita
Oklahoma City
Albuquerque
Santa Fe
El Paso
Cleveland
Pittsburgh
Indianapolis
Cincinnati
Louisville
Charleston
Nashville
Chattanooga
Memphis
Little Rock
Birmingham
Atlanta
Montgomery
Jackson
Dallas
Fort Worth
Shreveport
Houston
San Antonio
Laredo
Brownsville
New Orleans
Mobile
Savannah
Jacksonville
Tampa
Miami
Lake Okeechobee
Columbia
Charlotte
Raleigh
Richmond
Norfolk
WASHINGTON
Baltimore
PHILADELPHIA
NEW YORK
LONG ISLAND
GEORGES BANK
Chesapeake Bay
CAPE HATTERAS
CAPE LOOKOUT
CAPE FEAR
CAPE CANAVERAL
CAPE SABLE
BLAKE PLATEAU
BLAKE RIDGE
Mississippi
Missouri
Ohio
Wabash
Tennessee
Cumberland
Arkansas
Canadian
Red
Brazos
Colorado
Pecos
Rio Grande
Bravo
North Platte
South Platte
Platte
Monterrey
Matamoros
Torreón
Tampico
Guadalajara
Laguna de Chapala
CIUDAD DE MÉXICO
MEXICO CITY
Puebla
Veracruz
Pico de Orizaba 5610
Oaxaca
Villahermosa
Acapulco
Mérida
YUCATAN PENINSULA
ISLA COZUMEL
CABO CATOCHE
Canal de Yucatán
Bahía de Campeche
CAMPECHE BANK
GULF OF MEXICO
MEXICO BASIN
Straits of Florida
GRAND BAHAMA
GREAT BAHAMA BANK
ANDROS
Nassau
ELEUTHERA
CAT ISLAND
SAN SALVADOR
BAHAMAS
LA HABANA
HAVANA
CUBA
ISLA DE LA JUVENTUD
Santiago de Cuba
Guantánamo
CAYMAN ISLANDS (U.K.)
CAYMAN TRENCH
Windward Passage
GREATER ANTILLES
JAMAICA
Kingston
HAITI
Port-au-Prince
HISPANIOLA
Pico Duarte 3175
DOMINICAN REPUBLIC
SANTO DOMINGO
GREAT INAGUA
PUERTO RICO
SAN JUAN
PUERTO RICO TRENCH
Canal de la Mona
VIRGIN ISLANDS
WEST INDIES
ANTIGUA AND BARBUDA
MONTSERRAT
GUADELOUPE (Fr.)
DOMINICA
MARTINIQUE (Fr.)
Fort-de-France
SAINT LUCIA
BARBADOS
Bridgetown
SAINT VINCENT AND THE GRENADINES
GRENADA
TRINIDAD AND TOBAGO
Port of Spain
LEEWARD ISLANDS
WINDWARD ISLANDS
LESSER ANTILLES
ARUBA (Neth.)
CURAÇAO
BONAIRE
NETHERLANDS ANTILLES
VENEZUELAN BASIN
CARIBBEAN SEA
COLOMBIAN BASIN
BELIZE
Belize City
Belmopan
Gulf of Honduras
GUATEMALA
HONDURAS
Tegucigalpa
EL SALVADOR
San Salvador
NICARAGUA
Managua
Lago de Nicaragua
Bluefields
COSTA RICA
SAN JOSÉ
Volcán Barú 3475
PANAMA
Panamá
Colón
ISTMO DE PANAMÁ
Golfo de Panamá
Golfo de Tehuantepec
MIDDLE AMERICA TRENCH
TEHUANTEPEC RIDGE
GUATEMALA BASIN
COCOS RIDGE
PANAMA BASIN
ISLA DEL COCO (C.R.)
ISLA DE MALPELO (Col.)
CARNEGIE RIDGE
COLÓN RIDGE
ARCHIPIÉLAGO DE COLÓN
GALAPAGOS ISLANDS (Ec.)
ISLA ISABELA
ISLA FERNANDINA
ISLA SANTA CRUZ
ISLA SAN CRISTÓBAL
Equator
SOUTH AMERICA
VENEZUELA
CARACAS
Maracaibo
Lago de Maracaibo
Golfo de Venezuela
Barquisimeto
Barcelona
Ciudad Bolívar
Ciudad Guayana
Orinoco
Apure
Meta
Arauca
San Cristóbal
Pico Bolívar 5007
LLANOS
Puerto Ayacucho
San Fernando de Atabapo
Salto Ángel
ANGEL FALLS
Embalse de Guri
PAKARAIMA MTS.
Mount Roraima 2875
COLOMBIA
SANTA FE DE BOGOTÁ
Barranquilla
Cartagena
Medellín
Manizales
Cali
Bucaramanga
Cúcuta
Buenaventura
Nevado del Tolima 5215
CORDILLERA OCCIDENTAL
CORDILLERA ORIENTAL
Cauca
Magdalena
Guaviare
Mitú
Pico da Neblina 3014
GUYANA
Georgetown
Cuyuni
Essequibo
KAIETEUR FALL
SURINAME
Paramaribo
FRENCH GUIANA
Cayenne
Oiapoque
TUMUC-HUMAC MTS.
ECUADOR
QUITO
Guayaquil
Golfo de Guayaquil
Cuenca
Esmeraldas
Tumaco
Cayambe 5790
Chimborazo 6310
Loja
PERU
LIMA
Iquitos
Chiclayo
Trujillo
Cajamarca
Huaraz
Nevado Huascarán 6768
Nevado Yerupajá 6634
Cerro de Pasco
Huancayo
Pucallpa
Cusco
Ica
Puerto Maldonado
Marañón
Ucayali
Napo
Putumayo
PERU-CHILE TRENCH
ANDES
SELVAS
BRAZIL
Manaus
Amazon
Amazonas
Negro
Branco
Boa Vista
Japurá
Içá
Solimões
Fonte Boa
Leticia
Javari
Yavarí
Juruá
Purus
Madeira
Aripuanã
Juruena
Represa Balbina
Óbidos
Santarém
Tapajós
Xingu
Iriri
Jari
Porto de Moz
Macapá
Amapá
ILHA DE MARAJÓ
ILHA DE MARACÁ
ILHA CAVIANA DE FORA
CABO MAGUARI
CABO ORANGE
Pará
Belém
Tocantins
Araguaia
Marabá
São Luís
Parnaíba
Teresina
Fortaleza
Carolina
CHAPADA DAS MANGABEIRAS
Porto Nacional
ILHA DO BANANAL
Natal
João Pessoa
Campina Grande
Caruaru
Recife
Maceió
Aracaju
Penedo
Salvador
Juazeiro
São Francisco
Represa de Sobradinho
Paulistana
Barra
Pico das Almas 1836
Paraguaçu
SA. DO CACHIMBO
SA. FORMOSA
São Manuel
Porto Velho
Rio Branco
Riberalta
Guajará-Mirim
Cobija
Mamoré
Beni
Madre de Dios
Guaporé
Itenes
Trinidad
Mato Grosso
ATOL DAS ROCAS
ILHA FERNANDO DE NORONHA (Braz.)
CABO DE SÃO ROQUE
NORTH AMERICAN BASIN
BERMUDA (U.K.)
BERMUDA RISE
Muir Seamount
Kelvin Seamount
Rehoboth Seamount 1235
Yakutat Seamount 1133
Sargasso Sea
ATLANTIC OCEAN
MID-ATLANTIC RIDGE
Tropic of Cancer
CAPE VERDE BASIN
GUIANA BASIN
AZORES PLATEAU
AÇORES
AZORES (Port.)
FLORES
TERCEIRA
PICO
SÃO MIGUEL
SANTA MARIA
Great Meteor Tablemount 269

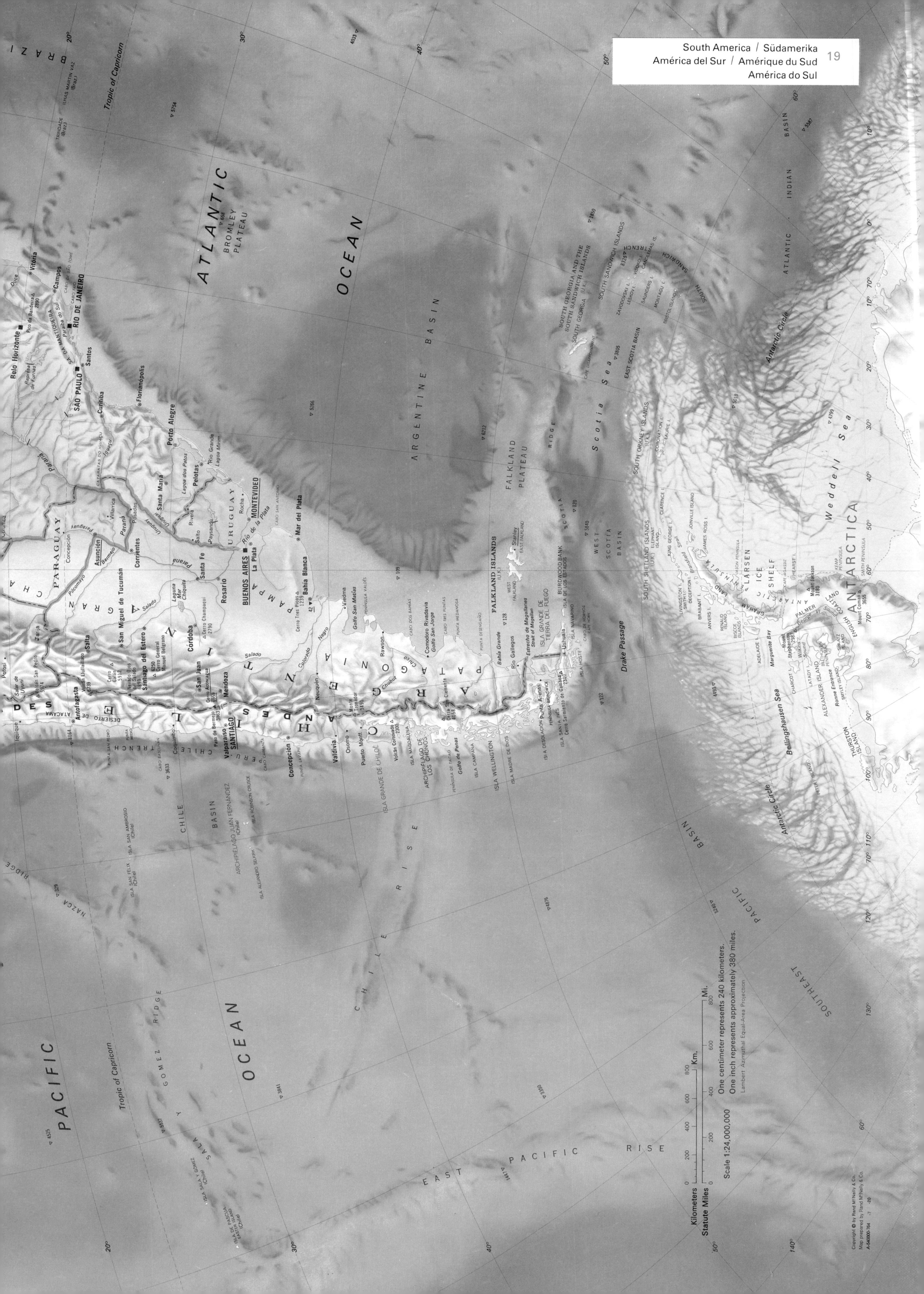
ATLANTIC
OCEAN
PACIFIC
OCEAN
BROMLEY PLATEAU
ARGENTINE BASIN
FALKLAND PLATEAU
Scotia Sea
WEST SCOTIA BASIN
EAST SCOTIA BASIN
SOUTH SANDWICH TRENCH
SOUTH GEORGIA AND THE SOUTH SANDWICH ISLANDS
SOUTH ORKNEY ISLANDS
SOUTH SHETLAND ISLANDS
Weddell Sea
ANTARCTICA
LARSEN ICE SHELF
Drake Passage
Bellingshausen Sea
ALEXANDER ISLAND
THURSTON ISLAND
Antarctic Circle
Tropic of Capricorn
CHILE BASIN
CHILE RISE
EAST PACIFIC RISE
SOUTHEAST PACIFIC BASIN
NAZCA RIDGE
SALA Y GOMEZ RIDGE
FALKLAND ISLANDS (U.K.)
BURDWOOD BANK
ISLA GRANDE DE TIERRA DEL FUEGO
PATAGONIA
PAMPA
GRAN CHACO
ANDES
PARAGUAY
URUGUAY
BUENOS AIRES
MONTEVIDEO
SANTIAGO
SÃO PAULO
RIO DE JANEIRO
Belo Horizonte
Porto Alegre
Asunción
Córdoba
Rosario
Mendoza
Mar del Plata
Bahía Blanca
Concepción
Valparaíso
Antofagasta
Puerto Montt
Punta Arenas
Ushuaia
Stanley
Scale 1:24,000,000
One centimeter represents 240 kilometers.
One inch represents approximately 380 miles.
Lambert Azimuthal Equal-Area Projection
Kilometers
Statute Miles
Copyright © by Rand McNally & Co.
Map prepared by Rand McNally & Co.

THE REGIONAL MAPS consist of three basic series, each distinctive in style, but using common symbols to ensure ease of understanding (see Legend to Maps, pages x-xii). Every major land region, continent or subcontinent, is introduced by one or more maps at the scale of 1:12,000,000. There follow maps at 1:6,000,000 and 1:3,000,000 which cover the region in sections, in greater detail. Except for scale, the 1:6,000,000 and 1:3,000,000 maps are alike. Finally, selected areas of special importance in the region are shown at 1:1,000,000. Each scale is identified by a color bar, and a locater map with the same color may be found in the margin of the map page. A sample area at each of the scales, including centimeter-kilometer and inch-mile equivalents, appears on page 21.

The three basic series differ in content and emphasis. The 1:12,000,000 maps, which are primarily political, present an overview of each region. They show national boundaries and, in some cases, subordinate administrative subdivisions as well. These introductory maps make it possible to compare location, areal extent, and shape among the nations of the world. The distribution of cities, towns and metropolitan areas is shown in the context of broad physical configurations. A selection of the most important railways and highways also appears.

The 1:6,000,000 and 1:3,000,000 maps together constitute about half of the map pages and provide the basic reference coverage of the Atlas. They show sections of regions in great detail—in some cases individual countries (Japan and New Zealand), in others, parts of countries (central Mexico), in still others, larger regions (the Middle East). The more densely settled areas appear at the larger 1:3,000,000 scale, the remaining areas at 1:6,000,000. Maps at these two scales present political and cultural information against the background of a detailed physical portrait of the terrain, which is depicted by both shaded relief and a spectrum of altitude tints. Bathymetric tints are used to show offshore water depths. The transportation pattern shown includes major railways, two classes of roads, and airports that offer either international or jet service. The names and boundaries of political subdivisions are given for selected countries.

In the 1:1,000,000 series, strategic areas that are of special interest because of economic importance, dense settlement, or both, appear in even greater detail. This series is designed to show the pattern of cities, towns, roads, railways, bridges, airports, dams, reservoirs, and other interrelated features reflecting man's dense occupancy in these areas. The most important parks, places of historical interest, and recreational facilities are indicated. Three classes of highways and two classes of railways are shown, and major roads are named. All features are portrayed against a topographic background of shaded relief.

Inhabited places on the regional maps are classified in two distinct ways. Cities and towns of different *population size* are distinguished by the *size and shape of the symbol* that locates the place. The symbol reflects the population within the municipal or corporate limits, exclusive of any suburbs. In countries where the limits of a municipality include rural areas, the symbol represents only the urban or agglomerated population. The *relative political and economic importance* of a place which may be independent of the number of its inhabitants, is indicated by the *size of type* in which its name appears.

DIE REGIONALKARTEN bestehen aus drei Serien, die im Stil verschieden sind, der besseren Lesbarkeit halber aber gemeinsame Kartensignaturen verwenden (siehe "Zeichenerklärung" S. x-xii). Jede Grossregion, jeder Kontinent oder Subkontinent werden durch eine oder mehrere Karten im Massstab 1:12 Millionen eingeleitet. Es folgen sodann Karten in den Massstäben 1:6 und 1:3 Millionen, welche die Region in Teilen und grösseren Einzelheiten darstellen. Die Karten in 1:6 Millionen und 1:3 Millionen unterscheiden sich nur im Massstab. Schliesslich werden ausgewählte Gebiete von besonderer Bedeutung innerhalb der Region in 1:1 Million dargestellt. Jede Massstabsangabe ist durch ein Farbfeld gekennzeichnet, und ein Lagekärtchen in derselben Farbe erscheint am Rand der Kartenseite. Kartenausschnitte als Beispiele für jeden dieser Massstäbe mit Angabe des Verhältnisses Zentimeter zu Kilometer und Zoll zu Meilen sind auf Seite 21 aufgeführt.

Die drei Kartenreihen unterscheiden sich in Inhalt und Betonung. Die Karten im Massstab 1:12 Millionen, die vor allem politische Karten sind, geben einen Überblick über jede Region. Sie zeigen die Staatsgrenzen und in manchen Fällen auch die Grenzen von nachgeordneten Verwaltungseinheiten. Diese einführenden Karten ermöglichen einen Vergleich der Lage, Ausdehnung und Gestalt der Staaten der Erde. Die Verteilung der städtischen Ballungsgebiete, Grossstädte und Städte wird in ihrem Zusammenhang mit dem grossräumigen Formenschatz des Reliefs dargestellt. Gezeigt wird auch eine Auswahl der wichtigsten Eisenbahnlinien und Fernverkehrsstrassen.

Die Karten 1:6 Millionen und 1:3 Millionen machen zusammen mehr als die Hälfte der Kartenseiten aus und bilden den grundlegenden Teil des Atlas. Sie zeigen sehr inhaltsreiche Ausschnitte von Regionen—in einigen Fällen einzeln Länder (Japan und Neuseeland), in anderen Landesteile (Zentralmexiko) und wieder anderen Grossräume (Mittlerer Osten).

Die dichter besiedelten Gebiete sind im Massstab 1:3 Millionen dargestellt, die übrigen Gebiete im Massstab 1:6 Millionen. Die Karten in diesen beiden Massstäben liefern politische und kulturgeographische Informationen vor dem Hintergrund einer detaillierten Geländedarstellung, gekennzeichnet durch Reliefschummerung und eine Skala von Höhenschichten. Tiefenstufen werden verwendet, um die Meerestiefen jenseits der Küsten zu gliedern. Das abgebildete Verkehrsnetz umfasst wichtige Eisenbahnlinien, zwei Klassen von Strassen und Flughäfen, die entweder im internationalen Verkehr oder von Düsenflugzeugen angeflogen werden. Die Verwaltungsgliederung wird für eine grosse Zahl von Staaten gezeigt.

In der Kartenserie 1:1 Million sind mit noch zahlreicheren Einzelheiten zentrale Räume dargestellt, denen infolge ihrer wirtschaftlichen Bedeutung, dichten Besiedlung oder durch beide Faktoren bedingt besonderes Interesse zukommt. Diese Kartenserie wurde entwikelt, um die Verteilung der Grossstädte, Städte, Strassen, Eisenbahnen, Brücken, Flughäfen, Dämme, Stauseen und anderer Objekte zu zeigen, die Ausdruck sind für die dichte Besiedlung. Verzeichnet sind auch die wichtigsten Parks, Örtlichkeiten von historischem Interesse und Erholungsstätten. Drei Strassenklassen und zwei Klassen von Eisenbahnlinien werden unterschieden. Die Darstellung ist mit einer Reliefschummerung unterlegt.

Die Siedlungen auf den Regionalkarten sind auf zwei bestimmte Arten klassifiziert. Grossstädte und Städte unterschiedlicher *Einwohnerzahl* sind durch *Grösse und Form der Signatur* unterschieden, die den Ort lokalisiert. Die Signatur entspricht der Zahl der Einwohner innerhalb der Stadtgrenzen, schliesst also nicht eingemeindete Vororte aus. In Staaten, in denen ländliche Gebiete in die Stadtgemeinden einbezogen sind, entsprechen die Signaturen nur der in den zentralen Siedlungen ansässigen Bevölkerung. Die *relative politische und wirtschaftliche Bedeutung* eines Ortes, die von der Zahl seiner Einwohner unabhängig sein kann, ist ausgedrückt durch die *Schriftgrösse*, in welcher der Ortsname erscheint.

LOS MAPAS REGIONALES integran tres series básicas, cada una con su estilo propio; pero los símbolos usados son en todas los mismos para facilitar su comprensión (véanse las Leyendas para Mapas, páginas x-xii). Cada una de las grandes regiones, continentes o subcontinentes, se presenta a través de uno o varios mapas a la escala de 1:12 000 000. A continuación hay mapas a escalas de 1:6 000 000 y 1:3 000 000 que presentan la región correspondiente en secciones, con mayores detalles. Con excepción de su escala, los mapas de 1:6 000 000 y 1:3 000 000 tienen las mismas características. Por ultimo, aparecen a la escala de 1:1 000 000 áreas de cada región seleccionadas por su importancia. Cada escala se identifica por una barra de color, y un mapa-guía con el mismo color se presenta en el margen de la página de cada mapa. La página 21 ofrece como ejemplo un área-muestra a cada una de las escalas, incluyendo equivalentes en centímetros-kilómetros y pulgadas-millas.

Las tres series básicas son diferentes en contenido y en énfasis. Los mapas a escala de 1:12 000 000, fundamentalmente políticos, ofrecen una vista general de cada región. Indican las fronteras nacionales y, en algunos casos, las subdivisiones administrativas secundarias. Son mapas introductivos que permiten comparar la ubicación, extensión territorial y forma de las distintas naciones. La distribución de ciudades, poblados y áreas metropolitanas se aprecia en un contexto físico esbozado a grandes rasgos. Los detalles incluyen una selección de las vías férras y las carreteras más importantes.

Las series de mapas a 1:6 000 000 y a 1:3 000 000 ocupan entre ambas cerca de la mitad de los mapas del atlas y en ellas se concentra el material de consulta básico de la obra. Los mapas muestran secciones de regiones en gran detalle: en algunos casos países enteros, como Japón y Nueva Zelandia; en otros, partes de países, como el centro de México; y en otros, regiones mas extensas, como el Medio Oriente. Las áreas con mayor densidad de establecimientos humanos se presentan a una escala mayor, la de 1:3 000 000, y las demás a la escala de 1:6 000 000. En estas dos escalas los mapas contienen información política y cultural, sobre un fondo que ilustra en detalle la configuración física del terreno, utilizando sombreado para el relieve y toda una gama de tintes para indicar las altitudes. Un colorido batimétrico señala las variaciones de profundidad en el suelo marino. El esquema de las vías de comunicación incluye las principales vías férreas, dos clases de caminos, y los aeropuertos que ofrecen servicio nacional o internacional de jets. Las subdivisiones políticas secundarias se dan para una selección de varios países.

En la serie de mapas de 1:1 000 000, las áreas estratégicas de especial interés por su importancia económica, su densidad de población, o ambos factores combinados, aparecen aún con mayor detalle. Esta serie se diseñó para mostrar la distribución de ciudades, poblados, caminos, vías férreas, puentes, aeropuertos, presas, embalses y otros elementos similares, que reflejan la densidad de la ocupación humana. También se consignan los parques más importantes, los sitios de interés histórico, los campos de recreo, tres clases de carreteras, y dos de ferrocarriles, se da los nombres de los caminos más importantes. Todos estos elementos aparecen sobre un fondo topográfico de relieve sombreado.

En los mapas regionales se hacen dos clasificaciones distintas de los lugares habitados. Las ciudades y las poblaciones *de diferente densidad de habitantes* se distinguen por la *forma y tamaño del símbolo* que las localiza en el mapa. Este símbolo refleja el tamaño de la poblacióin dentro de sus límites municipales, sin tomar en cuenta los suburbios. En los países donde los límites de una municipalidad incluyen áreas rurales, el símbolo se limita a representar el conglomerado urbano de habitantes. La *importancia económica y política de un lugar,* la cual puede ser independiente del número de sus habitantes, se indica mediante el *tamaño del tipo de imprenta* en que aparece su nombre.

Les cartes régionales sont de trois types principaux, chacun d'un style différent mais avec des symboles communs pour faciliter la compréhension (voir la légende des cartes pages x-xii). Chaque grande région, continent ou subcontinent, est représentée par une ou plusieurs cartes à l'échelle de 1:12 000 000ᵉ. Viennent ensuite des cartes au 1:6 000 000ᵉ et au 1:3 000 000ᵉ qui couvrent la région par sections plus détaillées; hormis la différence d'échelle, ces cartes sont semblables. Enfin, des secteurs particulièrement importants sont représentés au 1:1 000 000ᵉ. À chaque échelle correspond une bande colorée et une carte repère de même couleur, dans la marge de chaque page. Un échantillon de cartes aux diverses échelles est représenté à droite. Chaque carte est accompagnée d'une double échelle graphique donnant les rapports centimètre/kilomètre et inch/mille correspondants.

Les trois catégories de cartes diffèrent par le contenu et par ce qu'elles mettent en relief. Les cartes au 1:12 000 000ᵉ, qui sont essentiellement politiques, donnent un apercu général de chaque région. Elles indiquent les frontières nationales et, dans certains cas, les subdivisions administratives intérieures. Ces cartes d'introduction permettent de comparer la localisation, la superficie et la forme des pays du monde. La répartition des villes et des zones métropolitaines y apparaît dans le cadre des grandes régions naturelles. Les routes et les voies ferrées les plus importantes y figurent également.

Les cartes au 1:6 000 000ᵉ et au 1:3 000 000ᵉ forment la moitié de l'Atlas et en constituent la série cartographique essentielle. Elles représentent de façon plus détaillée une partie de pays (centre du Mexique), ou encore des régions plus vestes (Moyen-Orient) ou, parfois, des pays entiers (Japon, Nouvelle-Zélande). Les régions les plus peuplées sont représentées à plus grande échelle (1;3 000 000ᵉ) que les autres (1:6 000 000ᵉ). Ces cartes offrent des informations d'ordre politique et culturel sur un fond topographique précis où le relief est indiqué à la fois par un estompage et par des variations de couleur. Différentes teintes de bleu sont utilisées pour symboliser les profondeurs marines. Les réseaux de transport représentés comprennent les principales voies ferrées, deux catégories de routes et les aéroports internationaux ou desservis par des avions à réaction. Les subdivisions politiques d'un certain nombre de pays sont aussi tracées.

Dans la série de cartes au 1:1 000 000ᵉ, des régions très importantes, soit du fait de leur densité de population, soit du fait de leur rôle économique, sont représentées d'une manière encore plus détaillée. L'objectif de cette série de cartes est de montrer la répartition des villes, routes, voies ferrées, ponts, aéroports, barrages, lacs de barrages et autres données associées qui traduisent la densité de l'occupation humaine dans ces régions. Les parcs les plus importants, les sites historiques essentiels et les centres de loisirs sont indiqués. Toutes les informations se détachent sur un fond topographique où le relief apparaît en estompage.

Les centres urbains des cartes régionales sont classés de deux manières différentes. *L'importance de la population* des villes est indiquée par *la dimension et la forme du symbole* qui les situe sur la carte. Seule la population comprise dans les limites municipales est prise en considération; dans les pays où des espaces ruraux sont inclus dans les limites d'une municipalité, seule la population urbaine entre en ligne de compte. *L'importance politique et économique relative* d'une ville, qui n'est pas nécessairement liée au nombre d'habitants, est indiquée par la dimension des caractères qui composent son nom.

Os mapas regionais compreendem três séries básicas, cada uma em estilo diferente, mas que empregam os mesmos símbolos para facilitar sua compreensão (Ver as *Legendas dos mapas*, pág. x-xii). Os mapas de cada uma das principais regiões terrestres, continentes ou subcontinentes, são introduzidos por um ou mais mapas na escala 1:12 000 000. Em seguida, vêm mapas, nas escalas de 1:6 000 000 e 1:3 000 000, que apresentam, com maiores detalhes, seções da região considerada. Exceto quanto à escala, os mapas de 1:6 000 000 e 1:3 000 000 têm as mesmas características. Finalmente, aparecem, na escala de 1:1 000 000, os mapas das áreas mais importantes da região considerada. A cada escala corresponde uma barra colorida e um indicador da mesma cor, que se encontra à margem da página de cada mapa. À página 21, acha-se um exemplo de cada escala, bem como a equivalência das relações centímetro/quilômetro e polegada/milha.

As três séries básicas de mapas são diferentes quanto ao conteúdo e à apresentação. Os mapas em escala de 1:12 000 000, que são essencialmente políticos, oferecem uma visão geral de cada região. Indicam as fronteiras nacionais e, em alguns casos, as subdivisões administrativas internas. Esses mapas servem de introdução e permitem avaliar e comparar a posição, superfície e forma dos países do Mundo. Neles está claramente indicada a distribuição das cidades e outros centros urbanos, bem como as principais características da configuração do solo. Encontra-se neles também uma seleção das ferrovias e rodovias mais importantes.

A série de mapas das escalas de 1:6 000 000 e de 1:3 000 000 constituem o principal material de referência do Atlas e representa cerca de metade do conjunto de mapas. Entre eles há mapas detalhados de parte de um país (centro do México), de um país inteiro (Japão e a Nova Zelândia) ou de uma região mais extensa (Oriente Médio). As áreas de maior densidade demográfica são apresentadas em escala maior, a de 1:3 000 000, e as demais, na de 1:6 000 000. Nessas duas escalas, os mapas fornecem informações de ordem política e cultural sobre um fundo que indica a configuração detalhada das particularidades físicas do solo, cujo relevo se destaca por contrastes de sombras e cores. Diversos matizes do azul traduzem o mapa batimétrico da profundidade ao largo das costas. Indicam também os aeroportos internacionais, as principais ferrovias, duas categorias de rodovias. As subdivisões políticas internas de numerosos países estão igualmente assinalados.

Na série de mapas da escala de 1:1 000 000, certas áreas, de interesse estratégico conjugado à importância econômica, densidade demográfica, ou ambos os elementos combinados, aparecem em forma ainda mais detalhada. O objetivo dessa série é representar a distribuição dos grandes centros urbanos, cidades, rodovias, ferrovias, pontes, aeroportos, represas, reservatórios e outras características associadas às grandes densidades demográficas. Indicam-se, também, os parques mais importantes, os lugares de interesse histórico, as áreas de lazer, três categorias de rodovias, e duas de ferrovias; e a nomenclatura dos grandes itinerários rodoviários. Todos esses elementos destacam-se sobre um fundo topográfico do relevo, executado em matizes das diversas cores.

Nos mapas regionais, assinalam-se os centros urbanos de dois modos. A *grandeza da população* das grandes cidades e dos centros urbanos secundários é representada pela *dimensão e forma do símbolo* que as localiza no mapa. O símbolo só reflete a população situada dentro de limites administrativos, sem levar em conta os subúrbios. Nos países onde os limites de uma municipalidade incluem zonas rurais, o símbolo representa apenas a população. A *importância política e econômica* de uma cidade, que não se relaciona necessariamente com o número de seus habitantes, é indicada pela *dimensão* dos caracteres tipográficos com que se compõe o seu nome.

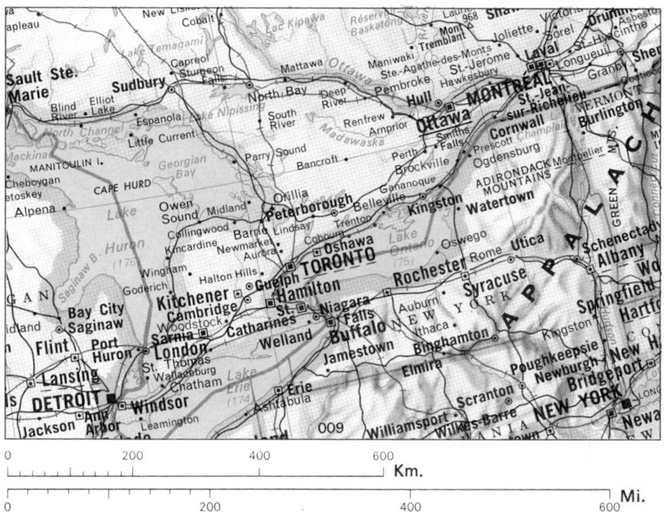
Sault Ste. Marie
Sudbury
North Bay
Ottawa
MONTRÉAL
TORONTO
Hamilton
Kitchener
London
DETROIT
Windsor
Buffalo
Rochester
Syracuse
Kingston
Peterborough
Saginaw
Flint
Lansing
Erie
Binghamton
Albany
0 200 400 600 Km.
0 200 400 600 Mi.

Scale 1:12,000,000
One centimeter represents 120 kilometers.
One inch represents approximately 190 miles.

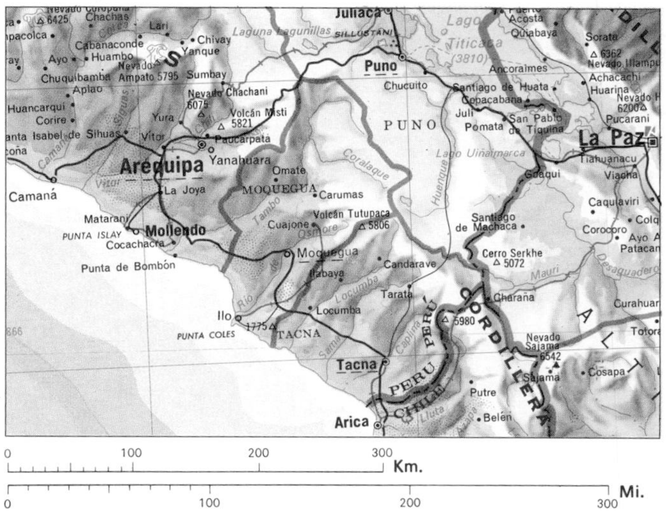
Juliaca
Puno
PUNO
Arequipa
Moquegua
Camaná
Mollendo
Ilo
Tacna
Arica
La Paz
0 100 200 300 Km.
0 100 200 300 Mi.

Scale 1:6,000,000
One centimeter represents 60 kilometers.
One inch represents approximately 95 miles.

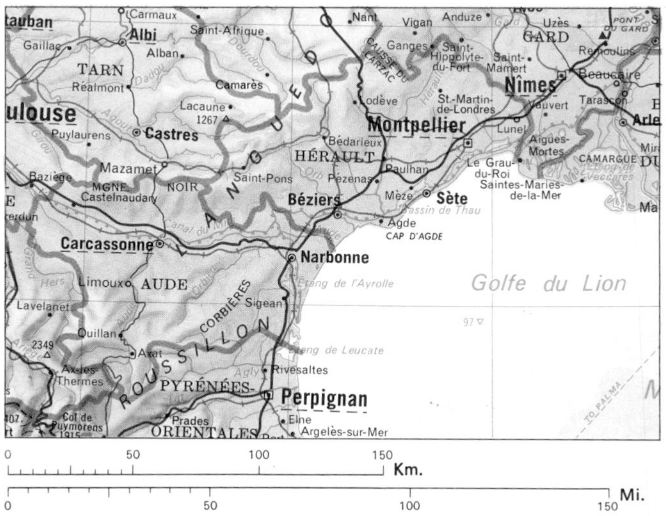
Albi
Castres
Montpellier
Nîmes
Béziers
Sète
Narbonne
Carcassonne
Perpignan
Golfe du Lion
HÉRAULT
AUDE
TARN
0 50 100 150 Km.
0 50 100 150 Mi.

Scale 1:3,000,000
One centimeter represents 30 kilometers.
One inch represents approximately 47 miles.

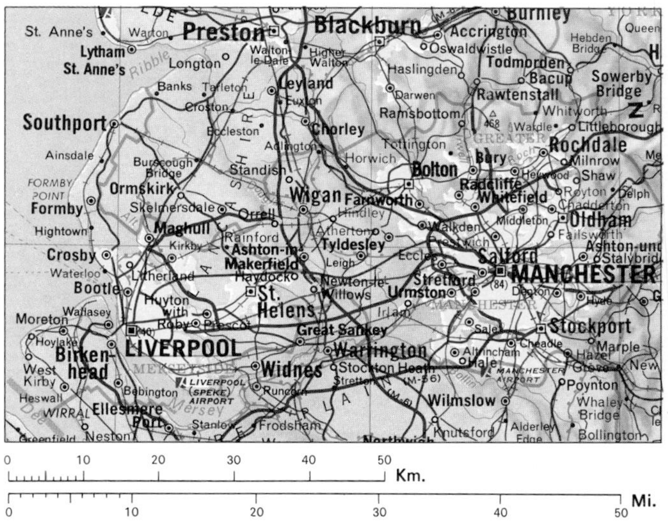
Preston
Blackburn
Southport
Bolton
Wigan
Oldham
Rochdale
Salford
MANCHESTER
St. Helens
LIVERPOOL
Birkenhead
Widnes
Warrington
Stockport
Wilmslow
0 10 20 30 40 50 Km.
0 10 20 30 40 50 Mi.

Scale 1:1,000,000
One centimeter represents 10 kilometers.
One inch represents approximately 16 miles.

ICELAND
Reykjavík
Akureyri
Arctic Circle
NORWEGIAN SEA
NORWAY
SWEDEN
FAEROE ISLANDS (Den.)
Tórshavn
SHETLAND ISLANDS
ORKNEY ISLANDS
ROCKALL (U.K.)
HEBRIDES
ATLANTIC OCEAN
IRELAND
DUBLIN
Cork
Limerick
Belfast
NORTHERN IRELAND
ISLE OF MAN
SCOTLAND
Glasgow
Edinburgh
Aberdeen
Dundee
Inverness
UNITED KINGDOM
GREAT BRITAIN
Newcastle
Sunderland
Middlesbrough
Leeds
Manchester
Liverpool
Sheffield
Kingston upon Hull
Nottingham
Leicester
Birmingham
WALES
Cardiff
Swansea
Bristol
Oxford
LONDON
Southampton
Portsmouth
Brighton
Bournemouth
Plymouth
Exeter
CELTIC SEA
English Channel
CHANNEL ISLANDS
GUERNSEY
JERSEY
NORTH SEA
Bergen
Stavanger
Oslo
Trondheim
Göteborg
Malmö
DENMARK
KØBENHAVN
COPENHAGEN
Århus
Odense
Kiel
Hamburg
Bremen
Lübeck
Rostock
Szczecin
Gdańsk
NETHERLANDS
AMSTERDAM
's-Gravenhage
The Hague
Rotterdam
Utrecht
Antwerpen
BRUXELLES
Lille
Liège
Köln
Düsseldorf
Essen
Dortmund
Hannover
BERLIN
Leipzig
Dresden
Magdeburg
Frankfurt
Bonn
LUXEMBOURG
GERMANY
PRAHA
PRAGUE
Nürnberg
Mannheim
Stuttgart
Strasbourg
München
WIEN
VIENNA
Bratislava
AUSTRIA
Zürich
Basel
Bern
Genève
SWITZERLAND
ALPS
FRANCE
PARIS
Le Havre
Rouen
Cherbourg
Brest
Rennes
Nantes
Le Mans
Tours
Orléans
Dijon
Lyon
Saint-Étienne
Grenoble
Clermont-Ferrand
Limoges
Bordeaux
Bay of Biscay
Toulouse
Montpellier
Marseille
Nice
Toulon
MONACO
Milano
Torino
Genova
Venezia
Bologna
Firenze
ITALY
ROMA
Napoli
Bari
Palermo
Catania
Messina
SICILIA
CORSE
CORSICA (Fr.)
SARDEGNA
SARDINIA (It.)
Cagliari
Tyrrhenian Sea
SPAIN
MADRID
Barcelona
Zaragoza
Valencia
Sevilla
Málaga
Granada
Córdoba
Murcia
Alacant
Bilbao
Oviedo
Gijón
La Coruña
Valladolid
Salamanca
Toledo
ILLES BALEARS
BALEARIC ISLANDS
Palma
MALLORCA
PORTUGAL
LISBOA
LISBON
Porto
Coimbra
Gibraltar (U.K.)
MEDITERRANEAN SEA
EL DJAZAÏR
ALGIERS
ALGERIA
ATLAS MOUNTAINS
Oran
RABAT
Casablanca
Fès
Meknès
Tanger
TUNIS
TUNISIA
Sfax
Sousse
Bizerte
MALTA
Valletta
Zagreb
Ljubljana
Rijeka
Trieste
Split
Beograd
HUNGARY
Katowice
Wrocław
Poznań
CZECH REP.
Brno
Ostrava
Ionian Sea
Copyright © by Rand McNally & Co.
Map prepared by Esselte Map Service AB, Stockholm

Map continues
pages 134-135

| MAP FORM | -älven | gora | île | islands | -øya | ozero | sea | vodochranilišče |
|---|---|---|---|---|---|---|---|---|
| ENGLISH | river | mountain | island | islands | island | lake | sea | reservoir |
| DEUTSCH | Fluss | Berg | Insel | Inseln | Insel | See | Meer | Stausee |
| ESPAÑOL | río | montaña | isla | islas | isla | lago | mar | embalse |
| FRANÇAIS | rivière | montagne | île | îles | île | lac | mer | réservoir |
| PORTUGUÊS | rio | montanha | ilha | ilhas | ilha | lago | mar | reservatório |

BARENTS SEA
White Sea
FINLAND
ESTONIA
LATVIA
LITHUANIA
BELARUS
UKRAINE
MOLDOVA
ROMANIA
BULGARIA
RUSSIA
KOMI
KAZAKHSTAN
TURKMENISTAN
UZBEK.
GEORGIA
ARMENIA
AZERBAIJAN
TURKEY
SYRIA
IRAQ
IRAN
CYPRUS
NORTH CYPRUS
BLACK SEA
CASPIAN SEA
Sea of Azov
Aral Sea
CAUCASUS
URAL'SKIJE GORY
URAL MOUNTAINS
ZAPADNO SIBIRSKAJA RAVNINA
MOSCOW MOSKVA
SANKT-PETERBURG
HELSINKI
Tallinn
RIGA
Vilnius
MINSK
KYYIV KIEV
Chişinău
BUCUREŞTI BUCHAREST
SOFIJA SOFIA
ANKARA
İstanbul
TBILISI
JEREVAN
BAKI BAKU
TEHRAN
BAGHDAD
Nicosia

Map continues pages 72-73

Map continues pages 118-119

Kilometers 0 200 400 600 Km.
Statute Miles 0 200 400 600 Mi.

Scale 1:12,000,000

One centimeter represents 120 kilometers.
One inch represents approximately 190 miles.
Miller Oblated Stereographic Projection

a
GREENLAND SEA
Denmark Strait
Arctic Circle
ICELAND
ISLAND
Reykjavík
Akureyri
ATLANTIC OCEAN
NORWEGIAN SEA
ATLANTIC OCEAN
NORTH SEA
Skagerrak
Kattegat
BALTIC SEA
Gulf of Bothnia
Bottenviken
Bottenhavet
Gulf of Finland
Gulf of Riga
Oslo
STOCKHOLM
HELSINKI
HELSINGFORS
KØBENHAVN
COPENHAGEN
RIGA
Tallinn
Vilnius
Göteborg
Gothenburg
Bergen
Trondheim
Tampere
Turku
Åbo
Gdańsk
(Danzig)
Kaliningrad (Königsberg)
HAMBURG
Bremen
Szczecin
(Stettin)
Luleå
Umeå
Oulu
Rovaniemi
Tromsø
Kiruna
Bodø
Stavanger
Kristiansand
Malmö
Ålborg
Århus

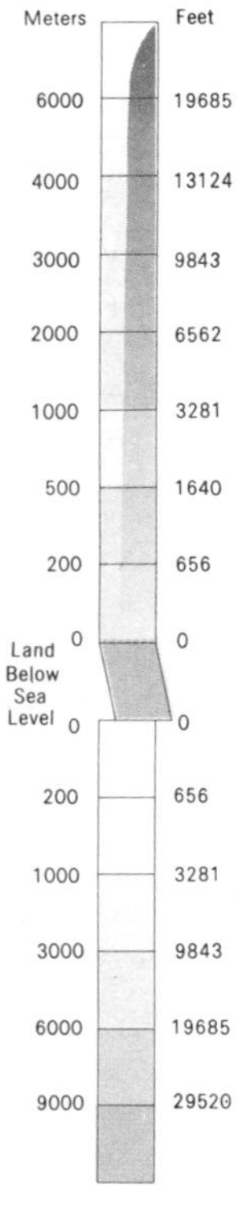
Meters
Feet
6000
19685
4000
13124
3000
9843
2000
6562
1000
3281
500
1640
200
656
0
0
Land Below Sea Level
0
0
200
656
1000
3281
3000
9843
6000
19685
9000
29520

| MAP FORM | -älven | -fjorden | guba | -joki | -jökull | lääni | -øya | ozero |
|---|---|---|---|---|---|---|---|---|
| ENGLISH | river | fjord, lake | bay | river | glacier | province | island | lake |
| DEUTSCH | Fluss | Fjord, See | Bucht | Fluss | Gletscher | Provinz | Insel | See |
| ESPAÑOL | río | fiordo, lago | bahía | río | glaciar | provincia | isla | lago |
| FRANÇAIS | rivière | fjord, lac | baie | rivière | glacier | province | île | lac |
| PORTUGUÊS | rio | fiorde, lago | baía | rio | geleira | província | ilha | lago |

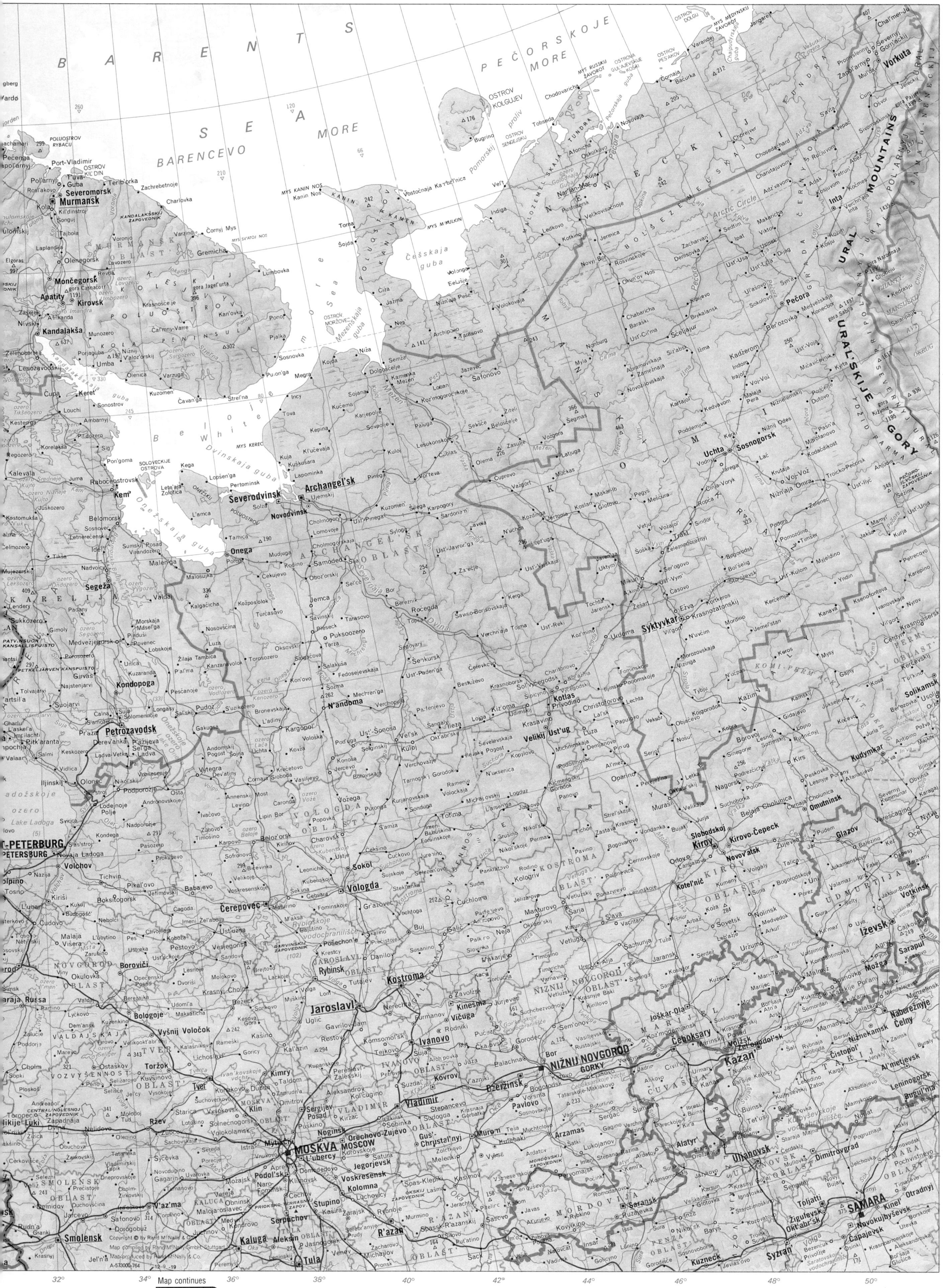
BARENTS SEA
BARENCEVO MORE
PEČORSKOJE MORE
White Sea
Beloje more
OSTROV KOLGUJEV
Murmansk
Severomorsk
Kandalakša
Kirovsk
Apatity
Kem'
Belomorsk
Segeža
Severodvinsk
Archangel'sk
Onega
Mezen'
Nar'jan-Mar
Pečora
Inta
Vorkuta
Uchta
Sosnogorsk
Syktyvkar
Kotlas
Velikij Ust'ug
Petrozavodsk
Kondopoga
ST.-PETERBURG
Volchov
Čerepovec
Vologda
Jaroslavl'
Kostroma
Ivanovo
Vladimir
Tver'
MOSKVA
MOSCOW
Kaluga
Tula
Smolensk
Rzev
Nižnij Novgorod
GORKY
Kirov
Kirovo-Čepeck
Glazov
Iževsk
Votkinsk
Sarapul
Kazan'
Čeboksary
Joškar-Ola
Uljanovsk
Syzran'
Tol'jatti
SAMARA
Novokujbyševsk
Dimitrovgrad
Naberežnyje Čelny
Al'metjevsk
Saransk
Arzamas
Murom
Rybinsk
Solikamsk
Kudymkar
Omutninsk
Arctic Circle
URAL MOUNTAINS
URAL'SKIJE GORY
Lake Ladoga
Ladožskoje ozero
Onežskoje ozero
Čėšskaja guba
Dvinskaja guba
Onežskaja guba
Mezenskaja guba
POLUOSTROV KANIN
KOL'SKIJ POLUOSTROV
BOL'ŠEZEMEL'SKAJA TUNDRA
ARCHANGEL'SKAJA OBLAST'
VOLOGODSKAJA OBLAST'
KOMI
KARELIJA
Copyright © by Rand McNally & Co.

Map continues
pages 86-87

Map continues
pages 76-77

Kilometers 0 100 200 300 Km.
Statute Miles 0 100 200 300 Mi.

Scale 1:6,000,000
One centimeter represents 60 kilometers.
One inch represents approximately 95 miles.
Lambert Conformal Conic Projection

NORWEGIAN SEA
NORTH SEA
Skagerrak
Kattegat
NORWAY NORGE
SWEDEN SVERIGE
DENMARK DANMARK
GERMANY DTSCH.
Bergen
Stavanger
Haugesund
Kristiansand
Ålesund
Trondheim
Oslo
Drammen
Skien
Porsgrunn
Fredrikstad
Sarpsborg
Halden
Moss
Lillehammer
Hamar
Karlstad
Örebro
Västerås
Uppsala
Eskilstuna
STOCKHOLM
Södertälje
Norrköping
Linköping
Nyköping
Jönköping
Borås
Göteborg
Gothenburg
Uddevalla
Trollhättan
Halmstad
Växjö
Kalmar
Karlskrona
Kristianstad
Helsingborg
Landskrona
Malmö
Lund
Trelleborg
KØBENHAVN
COPENHAGEN
Helsingør
Roskilde
Odense
Ålborg
Århus
Randers
Horsens
Vejle
Kolding
Fredericia
Esbjerg
Herning
Silkeborg
Viborg
Frederikshavn
Skagen
Flensburg
Schleswig
Kiel
Rendsburg
Neumünster
Visby
GOTLAND
ÖLAND
BORNHOLM
LOLLAND
FALSTER
SJÆLLAND
FYN
JÜTLAND
HORDALAND
ROGALAND
TELEMARK
BUSKERUD
OPPLAND
HEDMARK
MØRE OG ROMSDAL
SOGN OG FJORDANE
SØR-TRØNDELAG
JÄMTLAND
HÄRJEDALEN
DALARNA
VÄRMLAND
JOTUNHEIMEN
HARDANGERVIDDA
DOVREFJELL
Map compiled by Esselte Map Service AB, Stockholm.
Map produced by Rand McNally & Co.

| Meters | Feet |
|---|---|
| 6000 | 19685 |
| 4000 | 13124 |
| 3000 | 9843 |
| 2000 | 6562 |
| 1000 | 3281 |
| 500 | 1640 |
| 200 | 656 |
| 0 | 0 |
| Land Below Sea Level 0 | 0 |
| 200 | 656 |
| 1000 | 3281 |
| 3000 | 9843 |
| 6000 | 19685 |
| 9000 | 29520 |

Map continues pages 30-31

| MAP FORM | -älven | bugt | -fjället | -fjell | -fjorden | -järvi | -joki | -ö, -ön | -sjön | -vesi |
|---|---|---|---|---|---|---|---|---|---|---|
| ENGLISH | river | bay | mountain | mountain | fjord, lake | lake | river | island | lake | lake |
| DEUTSCH | Fluss | Bucht | Berg | Berg | Fjord, See | See | Fluss | Insel | See | See |
| ESPAÑOL | río | bahía | montaña | montaña | fiordo, lago | lago | río | isla | lago | lago |
| FRANÇAIS | rivière | baie | montagne | montagne | fjord, lac | lac | rivière | île | lac | lac |
| PORTUGUÊS | rio | baía | montanha | montanha | fiorde, lago | lago | rio | ilha | lago | lago |

Map continues pages 24-25

Gulf of Bothnia
Bottenviken
Perämeri
Bottenhavet
Selkämeri
Norra Kvarken
Merenkurkku
Gulf of Finland
Suomenlahti
Finskij zaliv
BALTIC SEA
Gulf of Riga
Riia laht
Rīgas jūras līcis
Irbenskij proliv
SWEDEN SVERIGE
FINLAND SUOMI
RUSSIA ROSSIJA
ESTONIA
LATVIA
LAPIN LÄÄNI
OULUN LÄÄNI
VAASAN LÄÄNI
KESKI-SUOMEN LÄÄNI
KUOPION LÄÄNI
POHJOIS-KARJALAN LÄÄNI
MIKKELIN LÄÄNI
HÄMEEN LÄÄNI
TURUN-PORIN LÄÄNI
UUDENMAAN LÄÄNI
KYMEN LÄÄNI
VÄSTERBOTTENS LÄN
VÄSTERNORRLANDS LÄN
NORRBOTTENS LÄN
ÅLAND AHVENANMAA
SUOMENSELKÄ
POHJANMAA
SATAKUNTA
KARELIJA
HIIUMAA
SAAREMAA
Luleå
Kemi
Oulu
Skellefteå
Umeå
Örnsköldsvik
Sundsvall
Hudiksvall
Vaasa
Kokkola
Seinäjoki
Kajaani
Kuopio
Joensuu
Jyväskylä
Tampere
Pori
Rauma
Turku
Hämeenlinna
Lahti
Kouvola
Lappeenranta
Mikkeli
Savonlinna
Imatra
Kotka
Hyvinkää
Espoo
HELSINKI HELSINGFORS
Vyborg
Sortavala
Tallinn
Narva
Tartu
Pärnu
SANKT-PETERBURG ST. PETERSBURG (LENINGRAD)
Kronštadt
Gatčina
Luga
Pskov
Novgorod
Ventspils
Liepāja
RĪGA
Jūrmala
Cudskoje ozero Peipsi järv
Ladožskoje ozero Lake Ladoga
ozero Il'men'

Map continues pages 76-77

Map continues pages 76-77

Kilometers 0 50 100 150 Km.
Statute Miles 0 50 100 150 Mi.

Scale 1:3,000,000

One centimeter represents 30 kilometers.
One inch represents approximately 47 miles.
Conic Projection, Two Standard Parallels

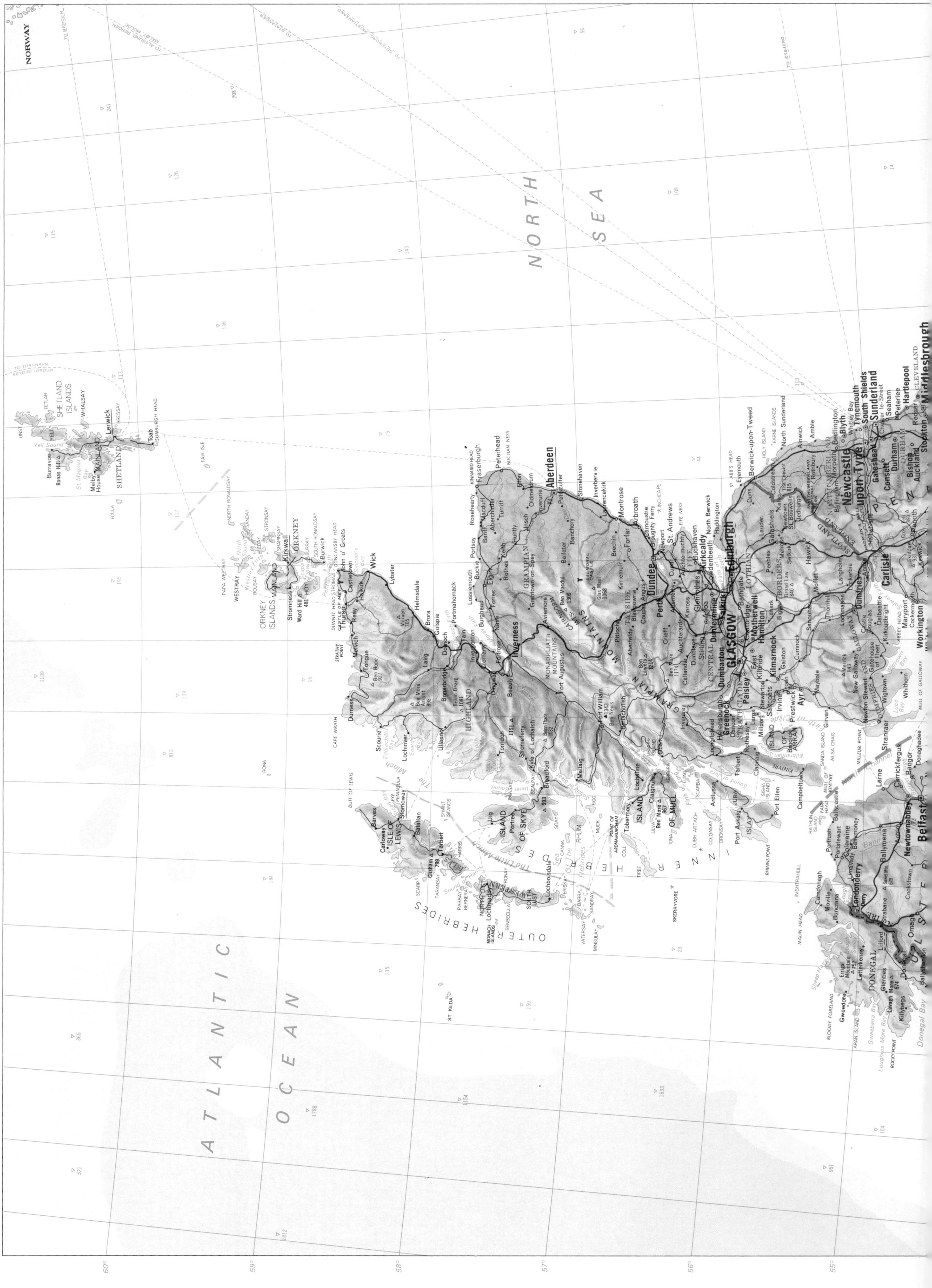
NORWAY
NORTH SEA
ATLANTIC OCEAN
SHETLAND ISLANDS
ORKNEY ISLANDS
OUTER HEBRIDES
Lerwick
Kirkwall
Wick
Inverness
Aberdeen
Dundee
Perth
Edinburgh
GLASGOW
Stornoway
ISLE OF LEWIS
ISLAND OF SKYE
Fort William
St. Andrews
Carlisle
Newcastle upon Tyne
Sunderland
Middlesbrough
Belfast
Londonderry
ST KILDA

Map continues pages 30-31

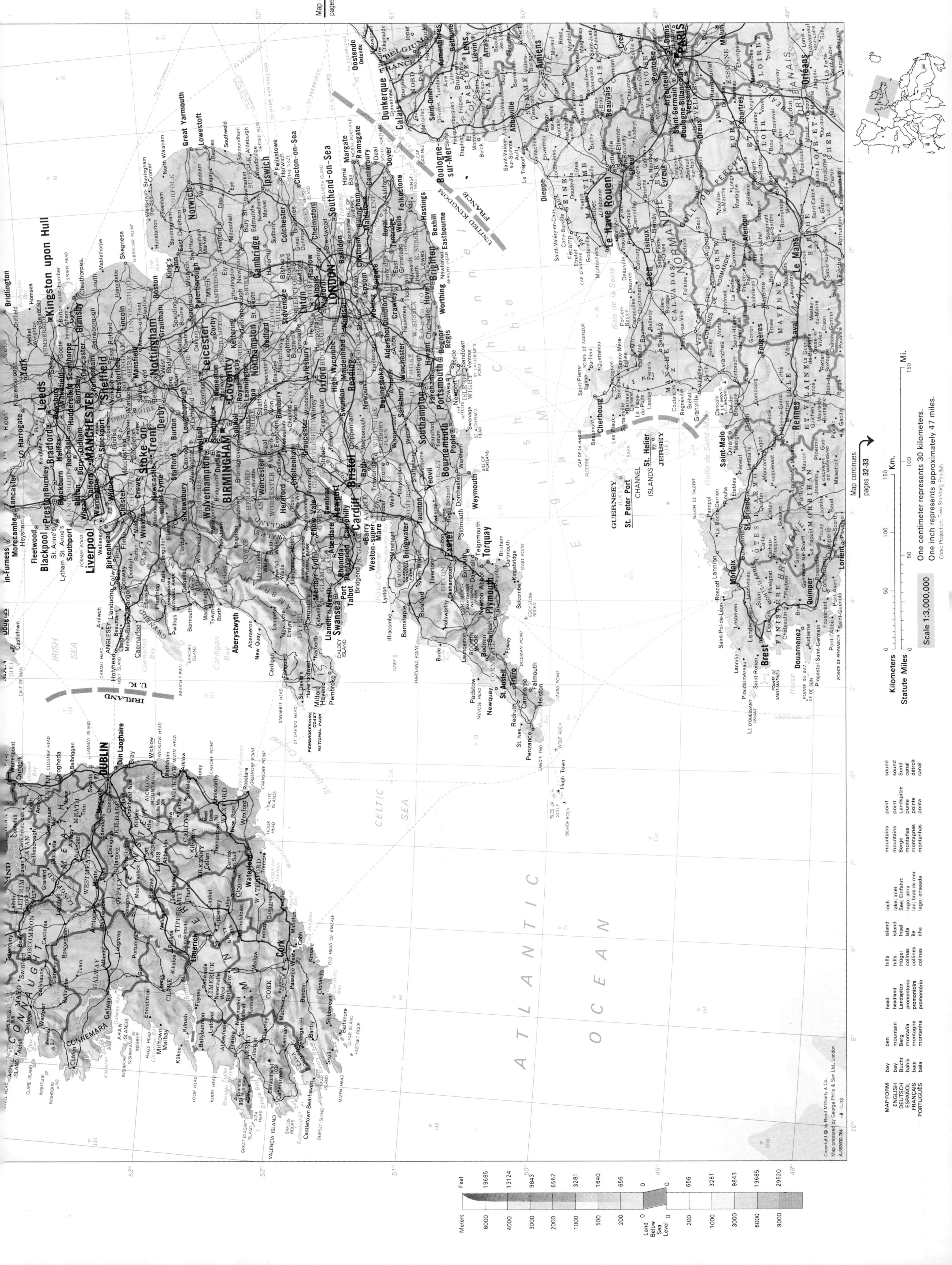
ATLANTIC OCEAN
CELTIC SEA
IRISH SEA
English Channel
La Manche
DUBLIN
LONDON
PARIS
BIRMINGHAM
MANCHESTER
Liverpool
Leeds
Sheffield
Nottingham
Leicester
Coventry
Bristol
Cardiff
Swansea
Plymouth
Southampton
Portsmouth
Brighton
Norwich
Ipswich
Cambridge
Oxford
Reading
Cork
Limerick
Waterford
Wexford
Le Havre
Rouen
Caen
Cherbourg
Brest
Rennes
Le Mans
Orléans
Amiens
Lille
Calais
Boulogne-sur-Mer
Dunkerque
Oostende
UNITED KINGDOM
FRANCE
IRELAND
U.K.
BELGIUM
Scale 1:3,000,000
One centimeter represents 30 kilometers.
One inch represents approximately 47 miles.
Conic Projection, Two Standard Parallels
Kilometers
Statute Miles
Map continues pages 32-33
MAP FORM / ENGLISH / DEUTSCH / ESPAÑOL / FRANÇAIS / PORTUGUÊS
bay / Bucht / bahía / baie / baía
ben / mountain / Berg / montaña / montagne / montanha
head / headland / Landspitze / promontorio / promontoire / promontório
hills / hills / Hügel / colinas / collines / colinas
island / island / Insel / isla / île / ilha
loch / lake; inlet / See; Einfahrt / lago; abra / lac; bras de mer / lago; enseada
mountains / mountains / Berge / montañas / montagnes / montanhas
point / point / Landspitze / punta / pointe / ponta
sound / sound / Sund / canal / détroit / canal
Copyright © by Rand McNally & Co.
Map prepared by George Philip & Son Ltd, London.
Feet
Meters
Land Below Sea Level

Map continues pages 26-27

NORTH SEA
FRISIAN ISLANDS
NORTH FRISIAN ISLANDS
Deutsche Bucht
DENMARK
GERMANY
NETHERLANDS
BELGIUM
LUXEMBOURG
FRANCE
SWITZERLAND
AMSTERDAM
HAMBURG
BRUXELLES
Bremen
Hannover
Köln
Düsseldorf
Frankfurt a. M.
Stuttgart
München
Nürnberg
Strasbourg
Basel
Zürich
Luxembourg
Rotterdam
Antwerpen
Kiel
Lübeck
Magdeburg
Rostock
Schwerin
Mannheim
Karlsruhe
Dijon
Besançon
Genève
Lausanne
Bern
Innsbruck
Metz
Nancy
Reims
Lille
Liège
Mainz
Wiesbaden
Kassel
Münster
Essen
Dortmund
Bonn
Koblenz
Würzburg
Augsburg
Regensburg
ARDENNES
ALPS
JURA

Map continues pages 28-29

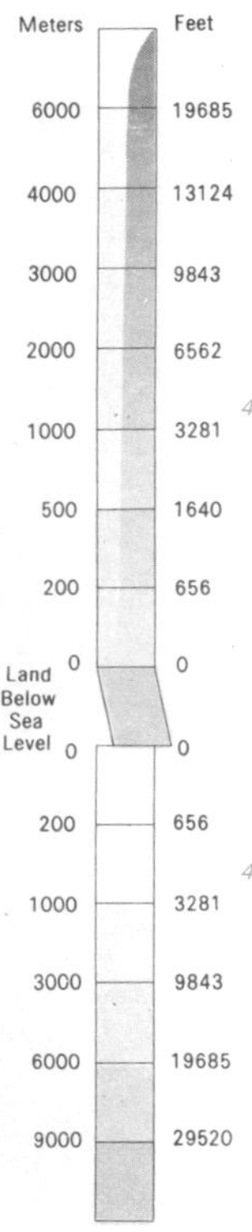
Meters
Feet
6000 19685
4000 13124
3000 9843
2000 6562
1000 3281
500 1640
200 656
0 0
Land Below Sea Level
200 656
1000 3281
3000 9843
6000 19685
9000 29520

| MAP FORM | Bucht | Gebirge | jezioro | Kanal | park narodowy | See | Wald |
|---|---|---|---|---|---|---|---|
| ENGLISH | bay | range | lake, lagoon | canal | national park | lake | forest, mountains |
| DEUTSCH | Bucht | Gebirge | See, Haff | Kanal | Nationalpark | See | Wald |
| ESPAÑOL | bahía | sierra | lago, laguna | canal | parque national | lago | bosque, montañas |
| FRANÇAIS | baie | chaîne | lac, lagune | canal | parc national | lac | forêt, montagnes |
| PORTUGUÊS | baía | serra | lago, laguna | canal | parque nacional | lago | floresta, montanhas |

Kilometers 0 50 100 150 Km.
Statute Miles 0 50 100 150 Mi.

Scale 1:3,000,000
One centimeter represents 30 kilometers.
One inch represents approximately 47 miles.
Conic Projection, Two Standard Parallels.

BALTIC SEA
Gulf of Gdansk
Kaliningrad (Königsberg)
Gdańsk (Danzig)
Gdynia
Szczecin (Stettin)
Bydgoszcz
Toruń
Olsztyn (Allenstein)
Białystok
Poznań
WARSZAWA WARSAW
Łódź
Wrocław (Breslau)
Lublin
Radom
Kielce
Częstochowa
Katowice
Kraków
Dresden
PRAHA PRAGUE
Brno
Ostrava
Olomouc
WIEN VIENNA
Bratislava
Győr
BUDAPEST
Debrecen
Miskolc
Košice
Szeged
Pécs
Graz
Linz
Brest
Hrodna
CARPATHIAN MOUNTAINS
Oradea
Arad
Subotica

Map continues pages 76-77

Map continues pages 78-79

continues 36-37

Map continues pages 28-29

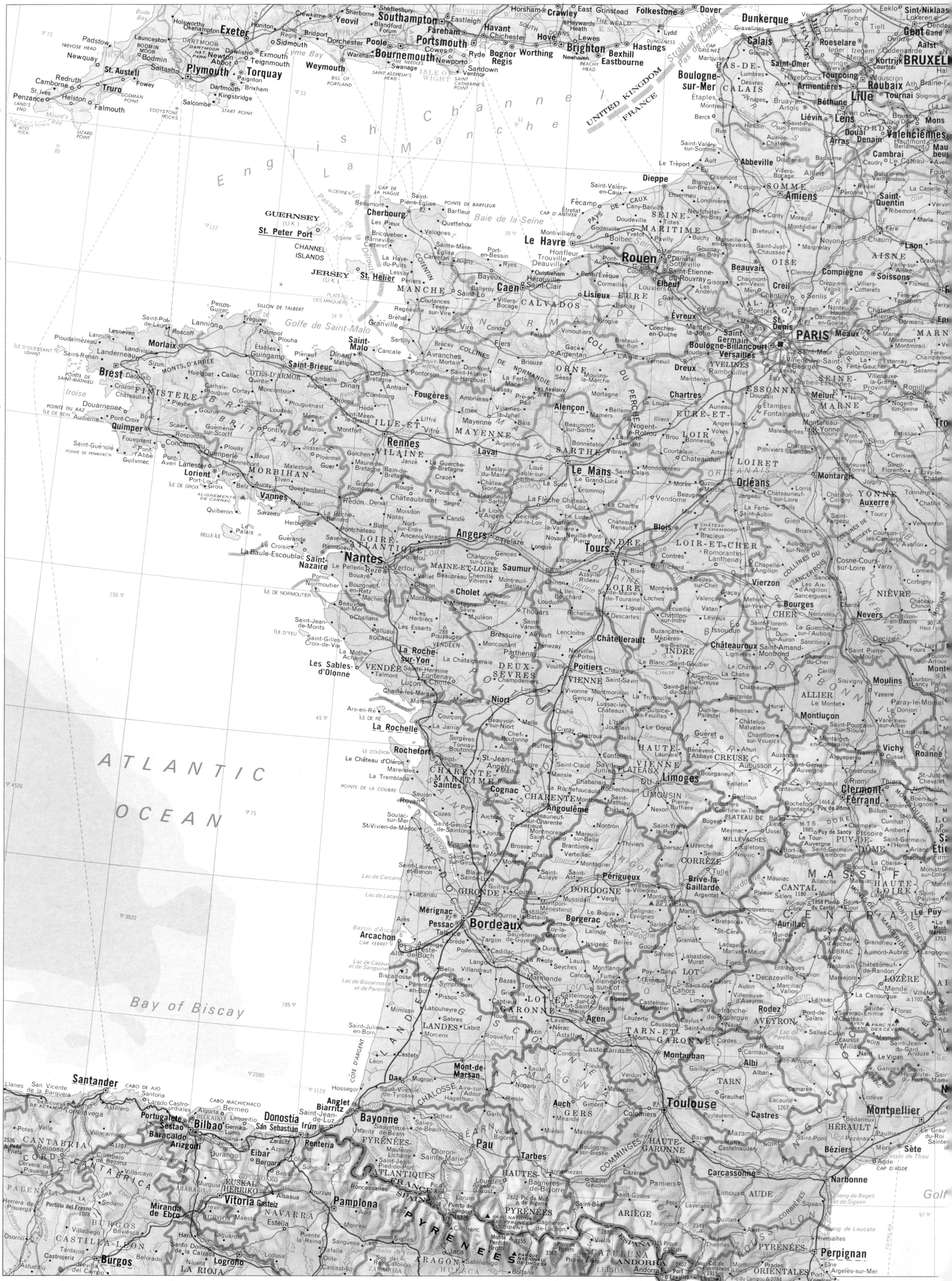
ATLANTIC OCEAN
Bay of Biscay
English Channel
La Manche
Golfe de Saint-Malo
CHANNEL ISLANDS
GUERNSEY (U.K.)
JERSEY (U.K.)
UNITED KINGDOM
FRANCE
Strait of Dover
Pas de Calais
PARIS
Bordeaux
Nantes
Toulouse
Rouen
Le Havre
Caen
Rennes
Brest
Lille
Amiens
Orléans
Tours
Le Mans
Angers
Limoges
Poitiers
La Rochelle
Montpellier
Perpignan
Clermont-Ferrand
Bilbao
Pamplona
Santander
Burgos
Vitoria Gasteiz
Donostia San Sebastián
Plymouth
Exeter
Southampton
Portsmouth
Bournemouth
Brighton
Dover
BRUXELLES
MASSIF CENTRAL
PYRÉNÉES
ANDORRA
ESPAÑA

Map continues pages 34-35

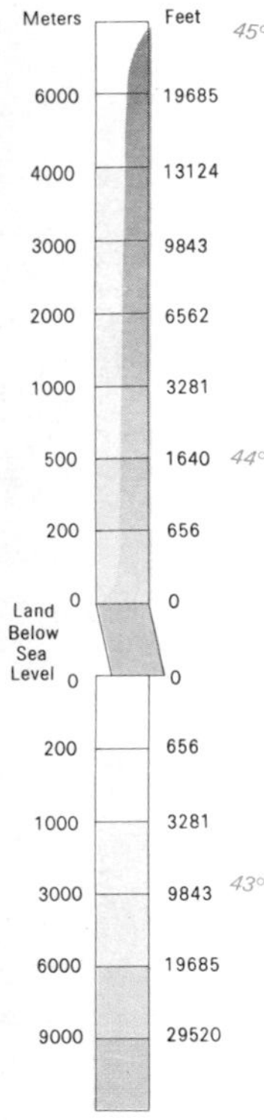
Meters
Feet
6000 19685
4000 13124
3000 9843
2000 6562
1000 3281
500 1640
200 656
0 0
Land Below Sea Level
200 656
1000 3281
3000 9843
6000 19685
9000 29520

| MAP FORM | canal | cap | île | lago | mont (e) | monts | pointe | See |
|---|---|---|---|---|---|---|---|---|
| ENGLISH | canal | cape | island | lake | mount | mountains | point | lake |
| DEUTSCH | Kanal | Kap | Insel | See | Berg | Berge | Landspitze | See |
| ESPAÑOL | canal | cabo | isla | lago | monte | montes | punta | lago |
| FRANÇAIS | canal | cap | île | lac | mont | monts | pointe | lac |
| PORTUGUÊS | canal | cabo | ilha | lago | monte | montes | ponta | lago |

Map continues
pages 30-31

Köln
Bonn
Koblenz
Frankfurt a. M.
Wiesbaden
Mainz
Darmstadt
Würzburg
Mannheim
Ludwigshafen
Heidelberg
Saarbrücken
Karlsruhe
Stuttgart
Nürnberg
Regensburg
Augsburg
MÜNCHEN
MUNICH
Salzburg
Innsbruck
Linz
Plzeň
PRAHA
PRAGUE
Chemnitz
Liège
Luxembourg
Metz
Nancy
Strasbourg
Mulhouse
Basel
Bâle
Zürich
Bern
Luzern
Lausanne
Genève
Geneva
Dijon
Besançon
Lyon
Grenoble
Torino
Turin
MILANO
MILAN
Genova
Genoa
Venezia
Venice
Verona
Padova
Trieste
Bologna
Firenze
Florence
Livorno
Leghorn
Nice
Cannes
Marseille
Toulon
Avignon
A L P S
APPENNINO
ADRIATIC SEA
Gulf of Venice
LIGURIAN SEA
MEDITERRANEAN SEA
CORSE
CORSICA
MONACO
SWITZERLAND
AUSTRIA
ITALY
FRANCE
GERMANY
CROATIA
SAN MARINO

Map continues
pages 36-37



Kilometers 0 50 100 150 Km.
Statute Miles 0 50 100 150 Mi.

Scale 1:3,000,000
One centimeter represents 30 kilometers.
One inch represents approximately 47 miles.
Lambert Conformal Conic Projection

# Spain and Portugal / Spanien und Portugal / España y Portugal
# Espagne et Portugal / Espanha e Portugal

Bay of Biscay
ATLANTIC OCEAN
ATLANTIC OCEAN
ALBORÁN SEA
SPAIN ESPAÑA
PORTUGAL
MOROCCO AL-MAGREB
MADRID
LISBOA LISBON
Porto
A Coruña
Santander
Bilbao
Valladolid
Salamanca
Sevilla Seville
Córdoba
Granada
Málaga
Cádiz
Gibraltar (U.K.)
Tanger Tangier
Ceuta (Sp.)
Melilla (Sp.)
Golfo de Cádiz
Strait of Gibraltar



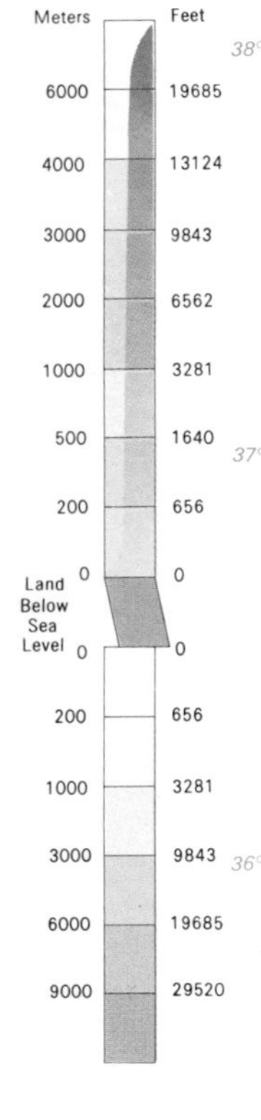
Meters
Feet
6000 19685
4000 13124
3000 9843
2000 6562
1000 3281
500 1640
200 656
0 0
Land Below Sea Level
200 656
1000 3281
3000 9843
6000 19685
9000 29520

| | | | | | | | | |
|---|---|---|---|---|---|---|---|---|
| ESPAÑOL | bahía | cabo | isla | embalse | puerto | punta | ría | sierra |
| ENGLISH | bay | cape | island | reservoir | port | point | estuary | mountains |
| DEUTSCH | Bucht | Kap | Insel | Stausee | Hafen | Landspitze | Trichtermündung | Berge |
| FRANÇAIS | baie | cap | île | réservoir | port | pointe | estuaire | montagnes |
| PORTUGUÊS | baía | cabo | ilha | reservatório | porto | ponta | estuário | serra |

Map continues
pages 32-33

Montauban
Toulouse
Albi
Nîmes
Avignon
Nice
Cannes
Antibes
Montpellier
Arles
Aix-en-Provence
Marseille
Toulon
Béziers
Sète
Carcassonne
Narbonne
Perpignan
Tarbes
Pau
Auch
Mont-de-Marsan
Dax
Golfe du Lion
PYRÉNÉES
ANDORRA
FRANCE
SPAIN
ESPAÑA
Huesca
Zaragoza
Lleida
Girona
Vic
Manresa
Sabadell
Terrassa
Mataró
Badalona
BARCELONA
L'Hospitalet de Llobregat
Vilanova i la Geltrú
Tarragona
Reus
CATALUNYA
DELTA DE L'EBRE
Vinaròs
Castelló de la Plana
Sagunt
València
Golf de València
Gandia
Alacant
Elx
Murcia
Cartagena
Benidorm
MENORCA
Maó
Ciutadella
MALLORCA
Palma
Manacor
EIVISSA
IBIZA
FORMENTERA
ILLES BALEARS
BALEARIC ISLANDS
MEDITERRANEAN SEA
EL DJAZAÏR
ALGIERS
Blida
Tizi-Ouzou
Bejaïa
Jijel
Wahran
Oran
Mestghanem
Ech Cheliff
ALGERIA
ALGÉRIE
ATLAS TELLIEN
Bou Saâda
Sidi bel Abbès

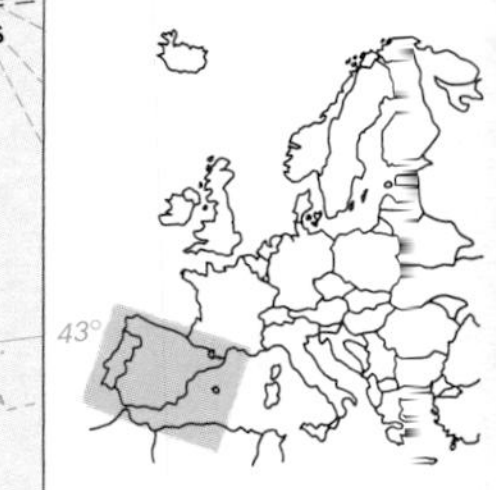

Map continues
pages 148-149

Kilometers 0 50 100 150 Km.
Statute Miles 0 50 100 150 Mi.

Scale 1:3,000,000
One centimeter represents 30 kilometers.
One inch represents approximately 47 miles.
Conic Projection, Two Standard Parallels

Map continues pages 38-39

Map continues pages 30-31

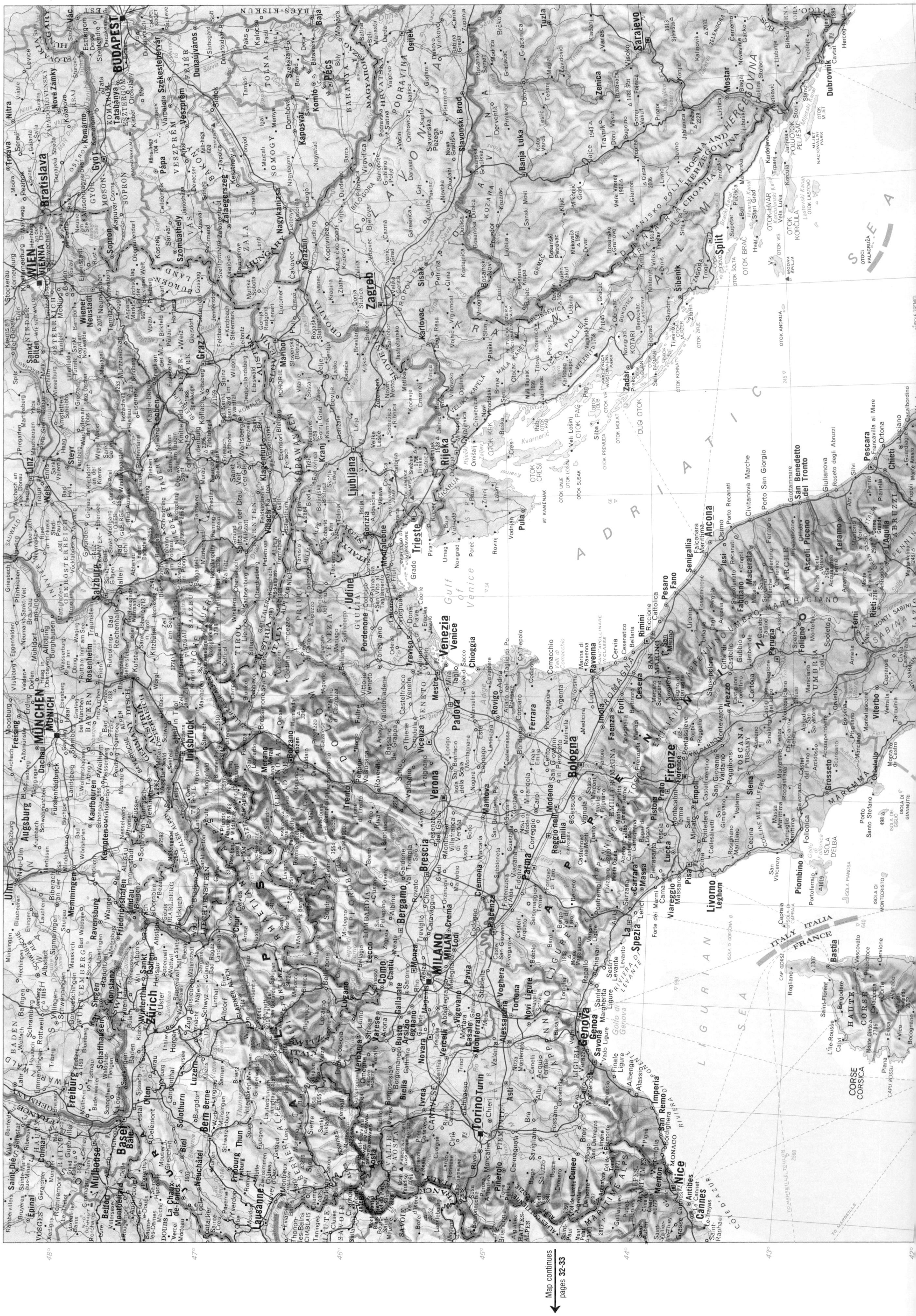
ADRIATIC SEA
LIGURIAN SEA
Gulf of Venice
MILANO
Torino
Venezia
Genova
Bologna
Firenze
Trieste
Ljubljana
Zagreb
WIEN
BUDAPEST
MÜNCHEN
Zürich
Bern
Innsbruck
Verona
Padova
Ravenna
Ancona
Pisa
Livorno
Nice
Monaco
Split
Sarajevo
Rijeka
Bratislava
Graz
Salzburg
CORSE CORSICA
Bastia
ISOLA D'ELBA

Map continues pages 32-33

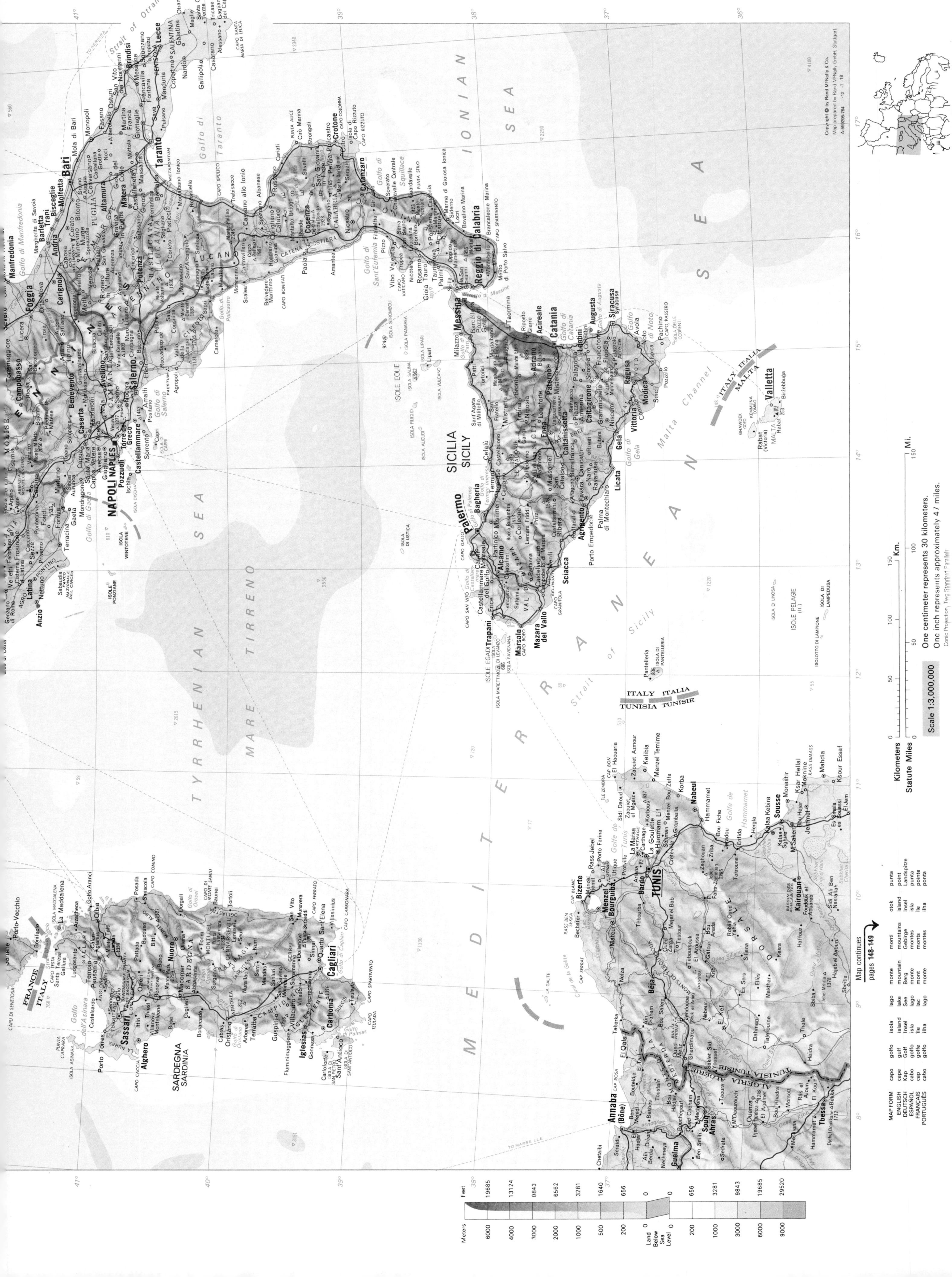
TYRRHENIAN SEA
MARE TIRRENO
IONIAN SEA
MEDITERRANEAN SEA
Strait of Sicily
Malta Channel
Strait of Otranto
Golfo di Taranto
SICILIA
SICILY
SARDEGNA
SARDINIA
FRANCE
ITALY
ITALY ITALIA
TUNISIA TUNISIE
ITALY ITALIA MALTA
ALGERIA ALGÉRIE TUNISIA TUNISIE
NAPOLI NAPLES
Palermo
Cagliari
TUNIS
Valletta
Bari
Taranto
Brindisi
Lecce
Foggia
Messina
Catania
Siracusa
Reggio di Calabria
Catanzaro
Cosenza
Salerno
Sassari
Annaba (Bône)
Bizerte
Sousse
Kairouan
ISOLE EOLIE
ISOLE EGADI
ISOLE PELAGIE
Pantelleria
Copyright © by Rand McNally & Co.
Map prepared by Rand McNally GmbH, Stuttgart.
Scale 1:3,000,000
Kilometers 0 50 100 150 Km.
Statute Miles 0 50 100 150 Mi.
One centimeter represents 30 kilometers.
One inch represents approximately 47 miles.
Conic Projection, Two Standard Parallels
Map continues pages 148-149
MAP FORM capo golfo isola lago monte monti otok punta
ENGLISH cape gulf island lake mountain mountains island point
DEUTSCH Kap Golf Insel See Berg Gebirge Insel Landspitze
ESPAÑOL cabo golfo isla lago monte montes isla punta
FRANÇAIS cap golfe île lac mont monts île pointe
PORTUGUÊS cabo golfo ilha lago monte montes ilha ponta
Meters 6000 4000 3000 2000 1000 500 200 0
Feet 19685 13124 9843 6562 3281 1640 656 0
Land Below Sea Level 0
200 1000 3000 6000 9000
656 3281 9843 19685 29520

Map continues pages 78-79

Kilometers 0 50 100 150 Km.
Statute Miles 0 50 100 150 Mi.

Scale 1:3,000,000

One centimeter represents 30 kilometers.
One inch represents approximately 47 miles.
Conic Projection, Two Standard Parallels

| MAP FORM | ákra | kólpos | lacul | límni | manastir | munţii | prohod | sea |
|---|---|---|---|---|---|---|---|---|
| ENGLISH | cape | bay | lake | lake | monastery | mountains | pass | sea |
| DEUTSCH | Kap | Bucht | See | See | Kloster | Berge | Pass | Meer |
| ESPAÑOL | cabo | bahía | lago | lago | monasterio | montañas | paso | mar |
| FRANÇAIS | cap | baie | lac | lac | monastére | montagnes | col | mer |
| PORTUGUÊS | cabo | baía | lago | lago | mosteiro | montanhas | passo | mar |

Map continues pages 30-31

BLACK SEA
Mouths of the Danube
CARPATHIAN MOUNTAINS
BUCUREŞTI
BUDAPEST
BEOGRAD
SOFIJA
Chişinău

Map continues pages 36-37

Map continues pages 130-131

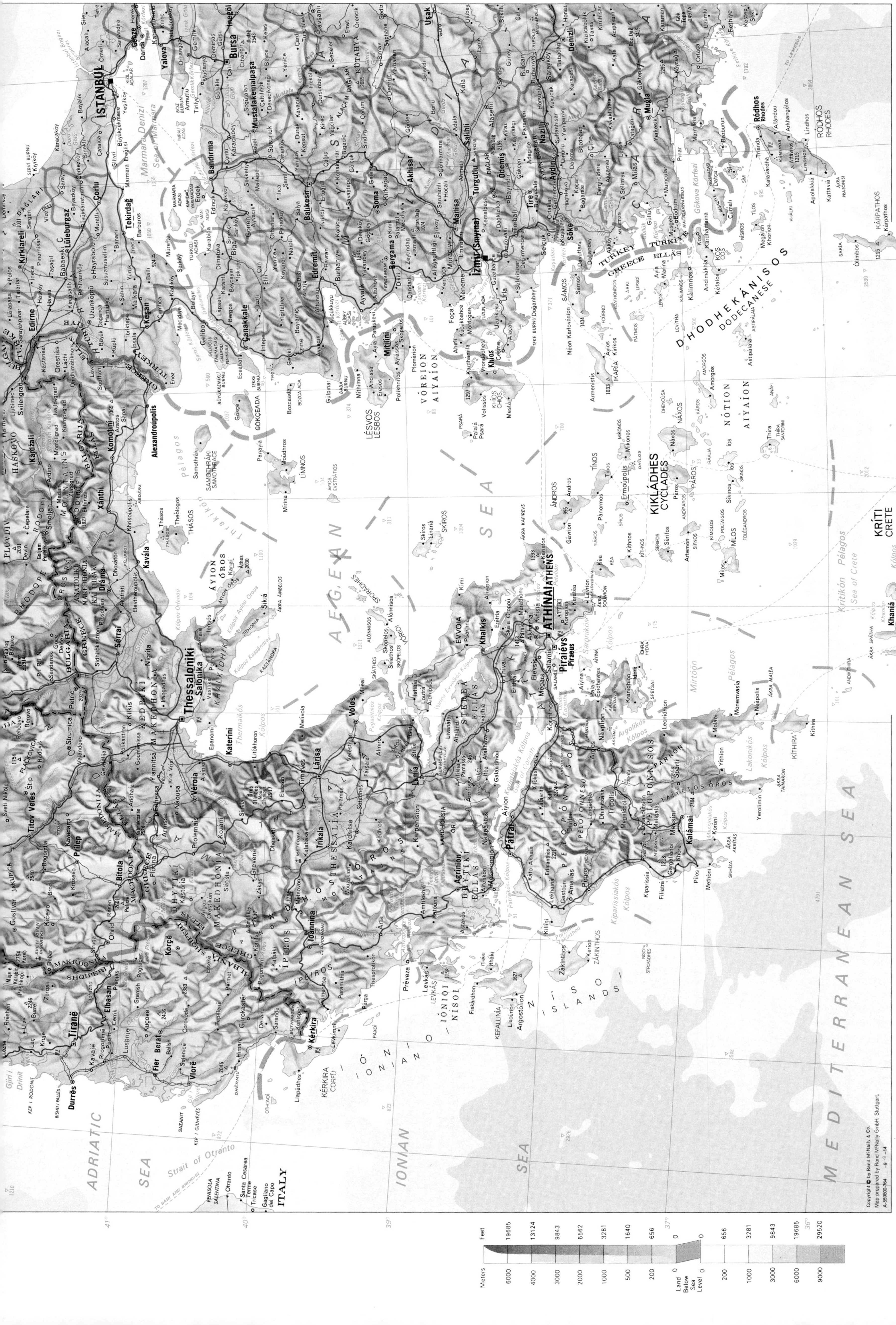
AEGEAN SEA
MEDITERRANEAN SEA
IONIAN SEA
ADRIATIC SEA
Strait of Otranto
ITALY
ATHÍNAI ATHENS
Thessaloníki Salonika
İSTANBUL
İzmir (Smyrna)
KRÍTI CRETE
KIKLÁDHES CYCLADES
DHODHEKÁNISOS DODECANESE
IÓNIOI NÍSOI
IONIAN ISLANDS
PELOPÓNNISOS
LÉSVOS LESBOS
RÓDHOS RHODES
Tiranë
Feet
19685
13124
9843
6562
3281
1640
656
0
0
656
3281
9843
19685
29520
Meters
6000
4000
3000
2000
1000
500
200
0
Land Below Sea Level 0
200
1000
3000
6000
9000
Copyright © by Rand McNally & Co.
Map prepared by Rand McNally GmbH, Stuttgart.

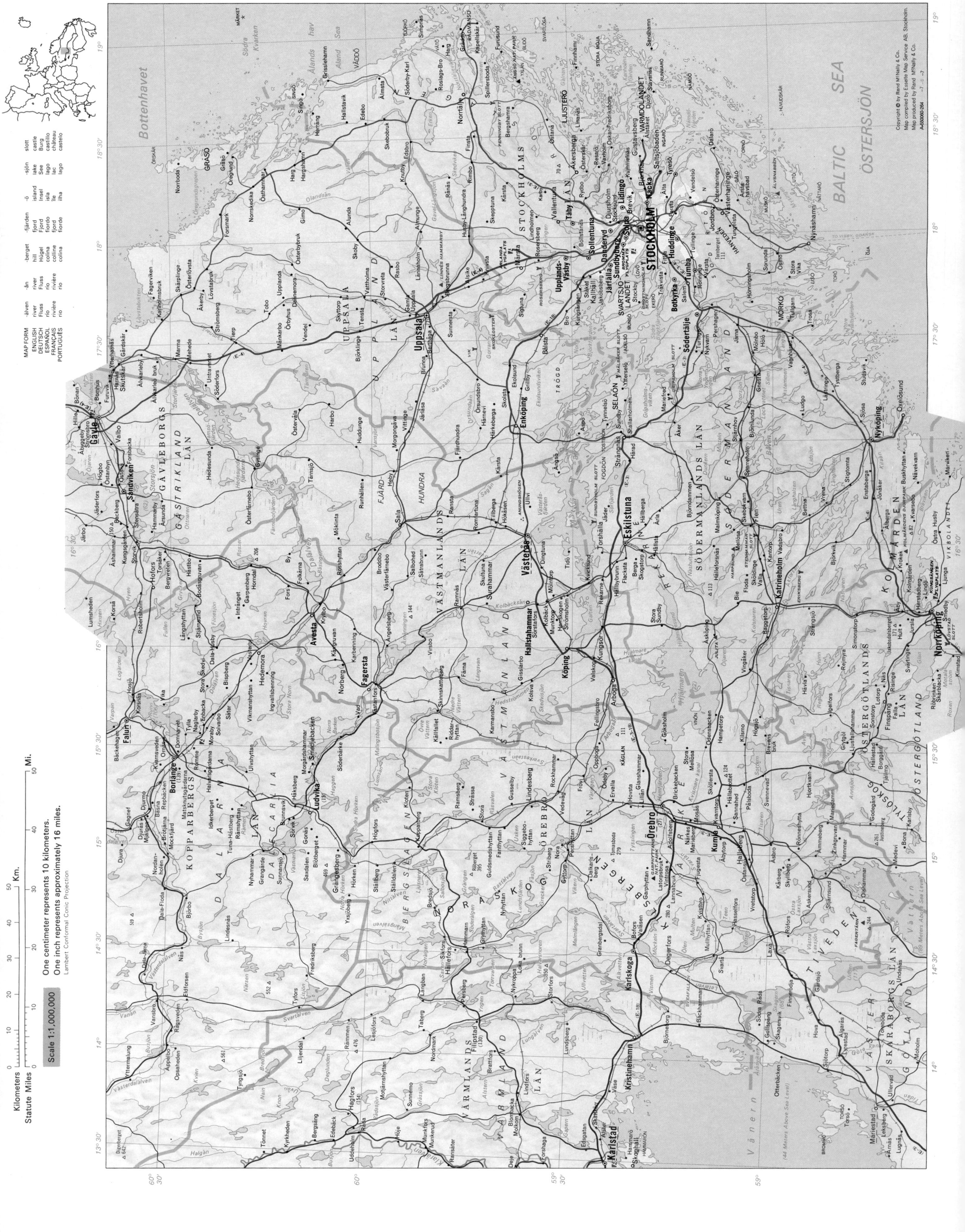

Kilometers 0 10 20 30 40 50 Km.
Statute Miles 0 10 20 30 40 50 Mi.
Scale 1:1,000,000
One centimeter represents 10 kilometers.
One inch represents approximately 16 miles.
Lambert Conformal Conic Projection
MAP FORM -älven -ån -berget -fjärden -ö -sjön slott
ENGLISH river river hill fjord island lake castle
DEUTSCH Fluss Fluss Hügel Fjord Insel See Burg
ESPAÑOL río río colina fiordo isla lago castillo
FRANÇAIS rivière rivière colline fjord île lac château
PORTUGUÊS rio rio colina fiorde ilha lago castelo
Copyright © by Rand McNally & Co.
Map compiled by Esselte Map Service AB, Stockholm.
Map produced by Rand McNally & Co.
Bottenhavet
BALTIC SEA
ÖSTERSJÖN
Ålands hav
STOCKHOLM
STOCKHOLMS LÄN
UPPSALA LÄN
VÄSTMANLANDS LÄN
SÖDERMANLANDS LÄN
ÖREBRO LÄN
KOPPARBERGS LÄN
GÄVLEBORGS LÄN
VÄRMLANDS LÄN
SKARABORGS LÄN
ÖSTERGÖTLANDS LÄN
Uppsala
Västerås
Örebro
Eskilstuna
Norrköping
Nyköping
Södertälje
Karlstad
Gävle
Sandviken
Falun
Borlänge
Ludvika
Avesta
Fagersta
Sala
Enköping
Köping
Arboga
Kumla
Karlskoga
Kristinehamn
Katrineholm
Hallstahammar
Norrtälje
Vänern
Vättern
Hjälmaren
Mälaren

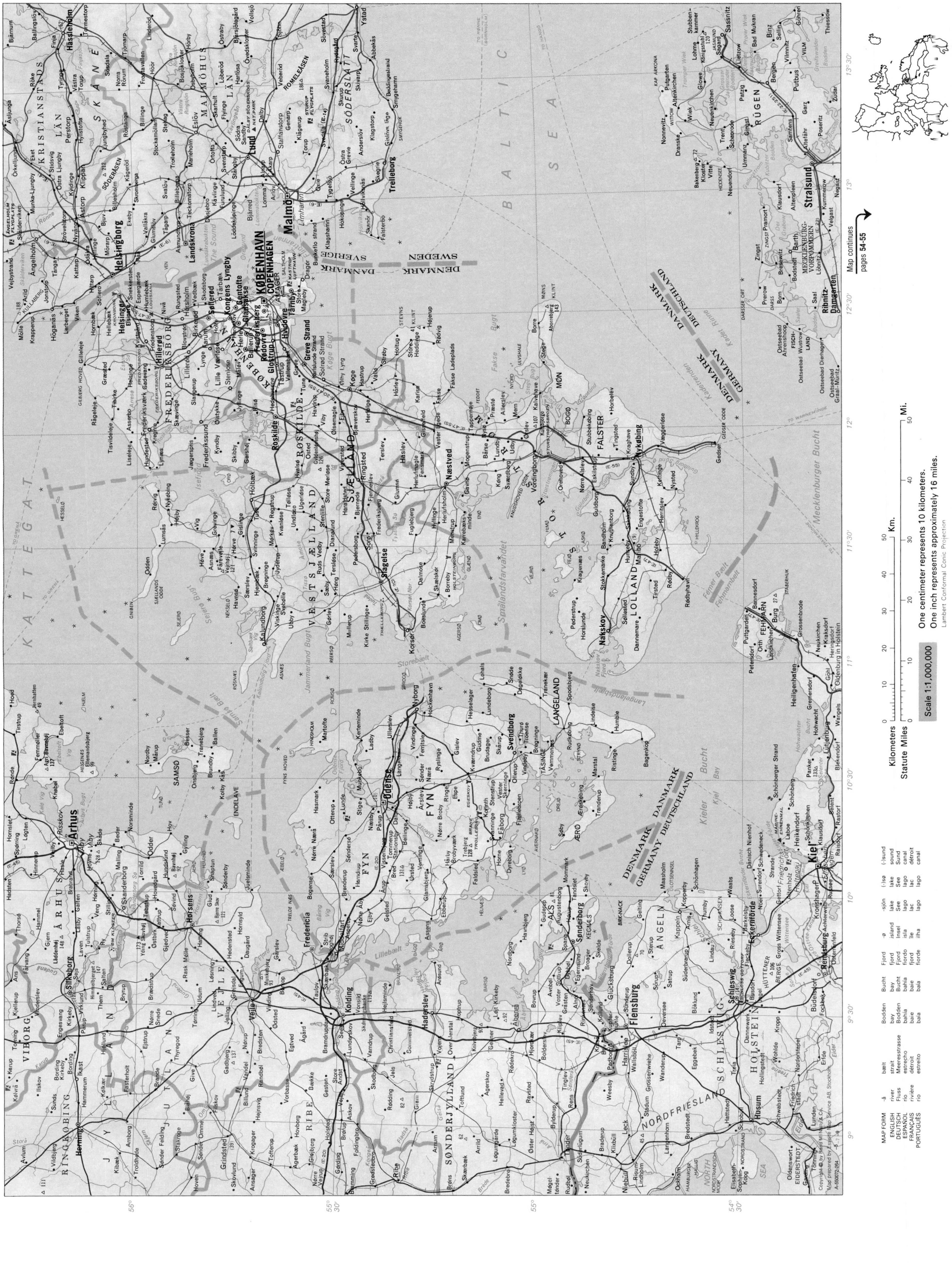
Scale 1:1,000,000
One centimeter represents 10 kilometers.
One inch represents approximately 16 miles.
Lambert Conformal Conic Projection
Map continues pages 54-55

Map continues pages 48-49

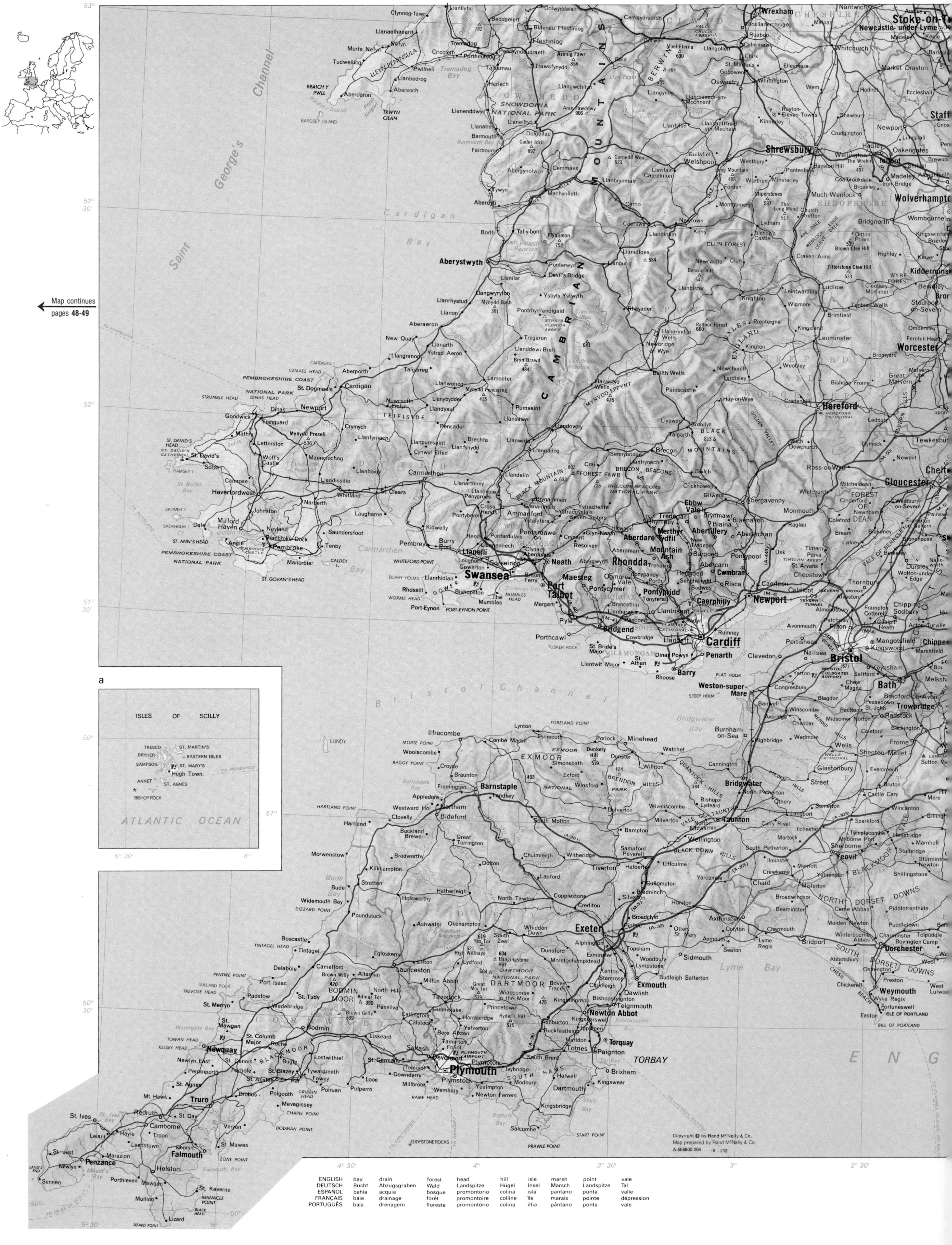
Saint George's Channel
Cardigan Bay
Bristol Channel
Carmarthen Bay
CAMBRIAN MOUNTAINS
SNOWDONIA NATIONAL PARK
PEMBROKESHIRE COAST NATIONAL PARK
BRECON BEACONS NATIONAL PARK
BLACK MOUNTAINS
EXMOOR
DARTMOOR
BODMIN MOOR
ISLES OF SCILLY
ATLANTIC OCEAN
Wrexham
Stoke-on-Trent
Newcastle-under-Lyme
Shrewsbury
Telford
Wolverhampton
Kidderminster
Worcester
Hereford
Gloucester
Aberystwyth
Cardigan
Carmarthen
Haverfordwest
Pembroke
Llanelli
Swansea
Neath
Port Talbot
Rhondda
Merthyr Tydfil
Caerphilly
Newport
Cardiff
Barry
Bristol
Bath
Weston-super-Mare
Bridgwater
Taunton
Yeovil
Dorchester
Weymouth
Exeter
Torquay
Plymouth
Barnstaple
Bodmin
Newquay
Truro
Falmouth
Penzance
Lyme Bay
TORBAY
Copyright © by Rand McNally & Co.
Map prepared by Rand McNally & Co.
A-556900-264

| ENGLISH | bay | drain | forest | head | hill | isle | marsh | point | vale |
|---|---|---|---|---|---|---|---|---|---|
| DEUTSCH | Bucht | Abzugsgraben | Wald | Landspitze | Hügel | Insel | Marsch | Landspitze | Tal |
| ESPAÑOL | bahía | acquia | bosque | promontorio | colina | isla | pantano | punta | valle |
| FRANÇAIS | baie | drainage | forêt | promontoire | colline | île | marais | pointe | dépression |
| PORTUGUÊS | baía | drenagem | floresta | promontório | colina | ilha | pântano | ponta | vale |

Map continues pages 44-45

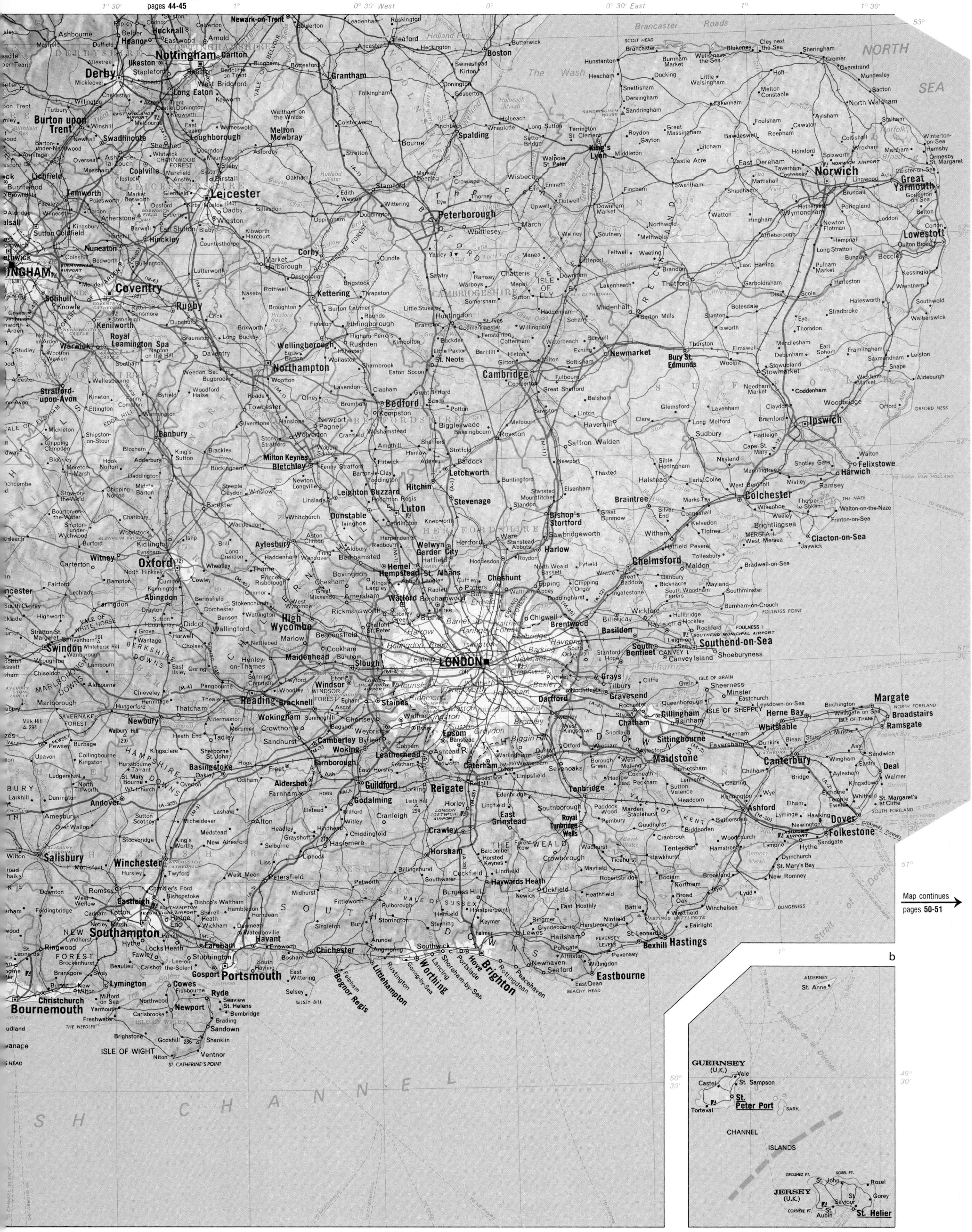
NORTH SEA
The Wash
Nottingham
Derby
Leicester
Coventry
Peterborough
Norwich
Great Yarmouth
Lowestoft
King's Lynn
Cambridge
Bedford
Northampton
Ipswich
Colchester
Chelmsford
Southend-on-Sea
LONDON
Oxford
Reading
Swindon
Salisbury
Winchester
Southampton
Bournemouth
Portsmouth
Brighton
Hastings
Eastbourne
Folkestone
Dover
Canterbury
Margate
Maidstone
Luton
Milton Keynes
Guildford
Reigate
ISLE OF WIGHT
CHANNEL
GUERNSEY (U.K.)
St. Peter Port
JERSEY (U.K.)
St. Helier
CHANNEL ISLANDS

Map continues pages 50-51

Kilometers 0 10 20 30 40 50 Km.

Statute Miles 0 10 20 30 40 50 Mi.

Scale 1:1,000,000

One centimeter represents 10 kilometers.
One inch represents approximately 16 miles.

Lambert Conformal Conic Projection

Map continues pages 46-47

Map continues pages 48-49

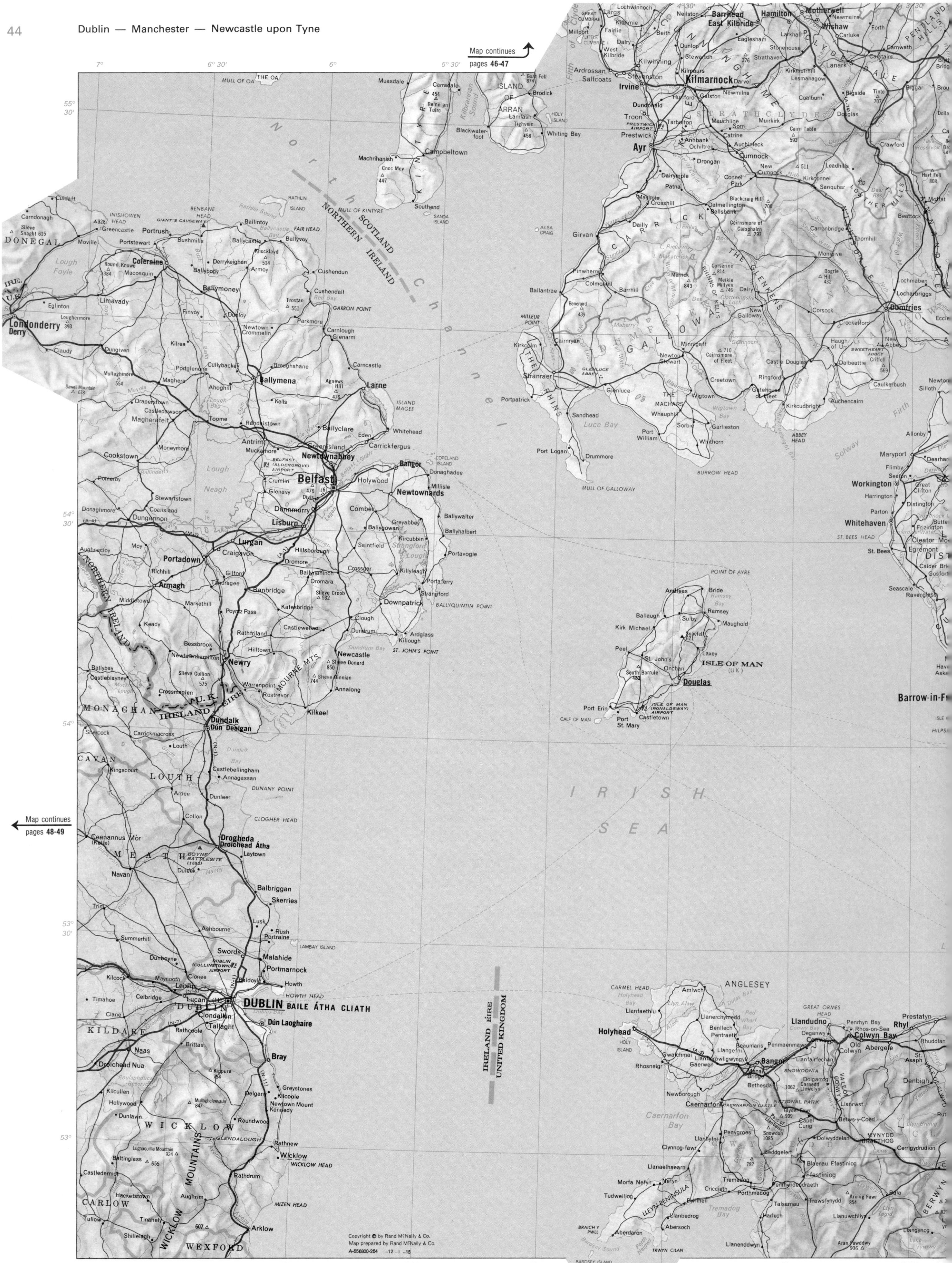

North Channel
IRISH SEA
NORTHERN IRELAND
SCOTLAND
ISLE OF MAN (U.K.)
ANGLESEY
IRELAND ÉIRE
UNITED KINGDOM
DUBLIN BAILE ÁTHA CLIATH
Belfast
Londonderry
Derry
Dundalk
Dún Dealgan
Drogheda
Droichead Átha
Dún Laoghaire
Bray
Wicklow
Arklow
Newry
Armagh
Portadown
Lurgan
Lisburn
Ballymena
Coleraine
Larne
Bangor
Newtownards
Downpatrick
Douglas
Kilmarnock
Ayr
Irvine
Stranraer
Girvan
Dumfries
Workington
Whitehaven
Barrow-in-F
Holyhead
Llandudno
Colwyn Bay
Rhyl
Caernarfon
DONEGAL
MONAGHAN
CAVAN
LOUTH
MEATH
KILDARE
WICKLOW
CARLOW
WEXFORD
MOURNE MTS.
WICKLOW MOUNTAINS
RHINNS OF GALLOWAY
Solway Firth
Caernarfon Bay
Tremadog Bay
Luce Bay



| MAP FORM | bay | dale | firth | forest | head | loch | moor | water |
|---|---|---|---|---|---|---|---|---|
| ENGLISH | bay | dale | estuary | forest | head | lake; inlet | moor | water (lake, river) |
| DEUTSCH | Bucht | Weites Tal | Trichtermündung | Wald | Landspitze | See; Einfahrt | Moor | See, Fluss |
| ESPAÑOL | bahía | valle | estuario | bosque | promontorio | lago; abra | páramo | lago, río |
| FRANÇAIS | baie | vallée | estuaire | forêt | promontoire | lac; bras de mer | lande | lac, rivière |
| PORTUGUÊS | baía | vale | estuário | floresta | promontório | lago; enseada | pântano | lago, rio |

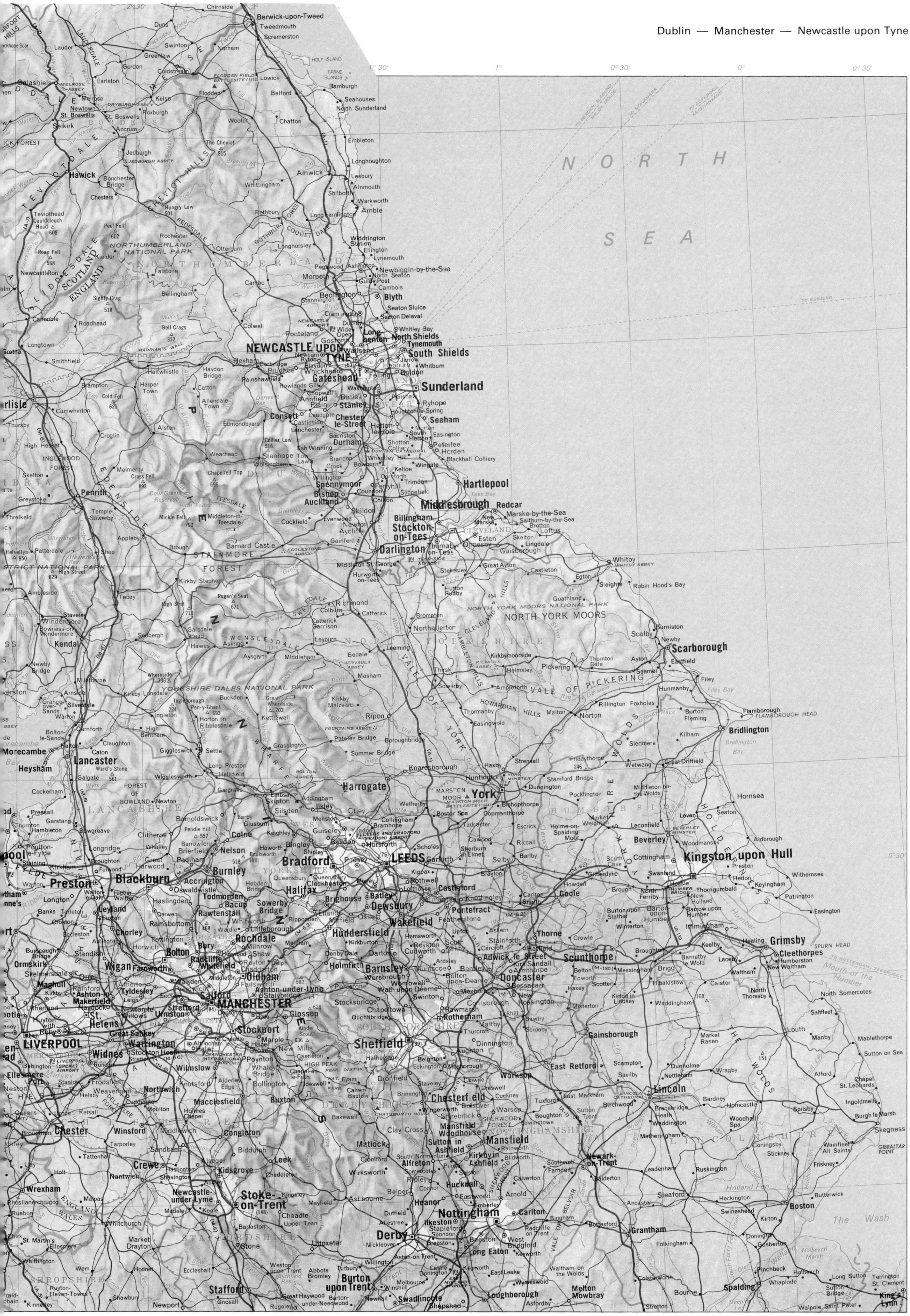
NORTH SEA
NEWCASTLE UPON TYNE
Gateshead
Sunderland
South Shields
Berwick-upon-Tweed
Hartlepool
Middlesbrough
Stockton-on-Tees
Darlington
Whitby
Scarborough
Bridlington
Harrogate
York
LEEDS
Bradford
Kingston upon Hull
Grimsby
Scunthorpe
Doncaster
Sheffield
Lincoln
Nottingham
Derby
Stoke-on-Trent
MANCHESTER
LIVERPOOL
Preston
Blackburn
Lancaster
Carlisle
Kendal
Chester
Wrexham
Stafford
Boston
The Wash
NORTHUMBERLAND NATIONAL PARK
NORTH YORK MOORS NATIONAL PARK
YORKSHIRE DALES NATIONAL PARK
VALE OF PICKERING
CHEVIOT HILLS
FLAMBOROUGH HEAD
SPURN HEAD
Mouth of the Humber

Map continues pages 42-43

Kilometers 0 10 20 30 40 50 Km.

Statute Miles 0 10 20 30 40 50 Mi.

Scale 1:1,000,000

One centimeter represents 10 kilometers.
One inch represents approximately 16 miles.

Lambert Conformal Conic Projection

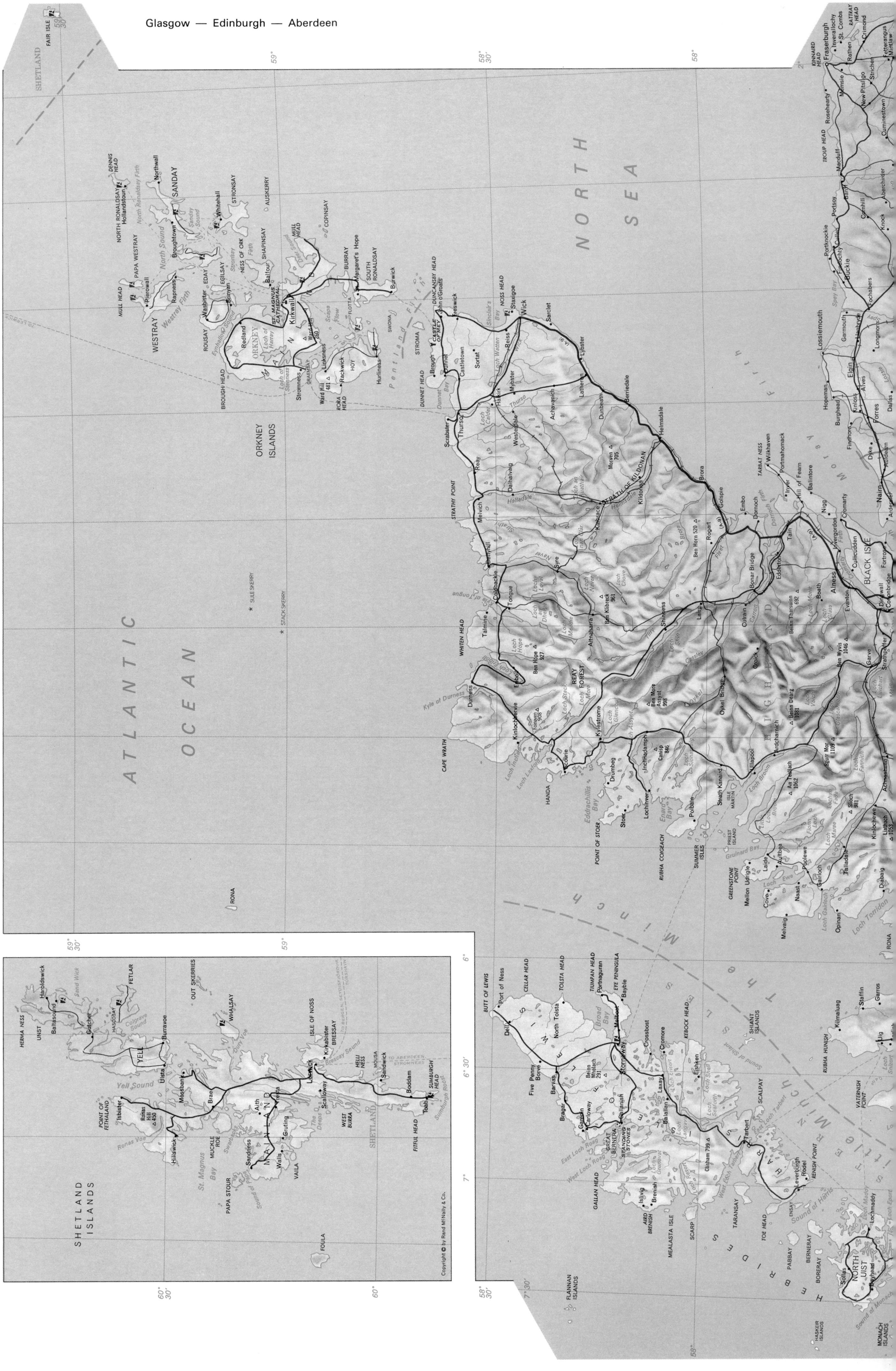
ATLANTIC OCEAN
NORTH SEA
ORKNEY ISLANDS
SHETLAND ISLANDS
Pentland Firth
The Minch
Little Minch
Moray Firth
OUTER HEBRIDES
LEWIS
HARRIS
NORTH UIST
BLACK ISLE
Kirkwall
Stromness
Thurso
Wick
Lerwick
Stornoway
Ullapool
CAPE WRATH
FAIR ISLE
FOULA
SULE SKERRY
STACK SKERRY
RONA
Copyright © by Rand McNally & Co.

NORTH SEA
Aberdeen
Dundee
Perth
Kirkcaldy
Dunfermline
EDINBURGH
GLASGOW
Stirling
Falkirk
Ayr
Oban
Fort William
Inverness
GRAMPIAN MOUNTAINS
CAIRNGORM MOUNTAINS
MONADHLIATH MOUNTAINS
LOCHABER
BADENOCH
FOREST OF ATHOLL
CUNNINGHAME
STRATHCLYDE
LAMMERMUIR
BORDERS
CHEVIOT HILLS
SCOTLAND
ENGLAND
NORTHUMBERLAND NATIONAL PARK
Firth of Forth
Firth of Lorn
Sea of the Hebrides
OUTER HEBRIDES
INNER HEBRIDES
SKYE
MULL
ISLAY
JURA
ISLAND OF ARRAN
KINTYRE
IRELAND
TIREE
COLL
SOUTH UIST
BARRA
Copyright © by Rand McNally & Co.
Map prepared by Rand McNally & Co.
A-553500-264 -8-8-10

Map continues pages 48-49

Map continues pages 44-45

| MAP FORM | bay | ben, beinn | firth | head | loch | sound | water |
|---|---|---|---|---|---|---|---|
| ENGLISH | bay | mountain | estuary | head | lake; inlet | sound | water (river) |
| DEUTSCH | Bucht | Berg | Trichtermündung | Landspitze | See; Einfahrt | Sund | Fluss |
| ESPAÑOL | bahía | montaña | estuario | promontorio | lago; abra | canal | río |
| FRANÇAIS | baie | montagne | estuaire | promontoire | lac; bras de mer | détroit | rivière |
| PORTUGUÊS | baía | montanha | estário | promontório | lago; enseada | canal | rio |

Kilometers 0 10 20 30 40 50 Km.
Statute Miles 0 10 20 30 40 50 Mi.

Scale 1:1,000,000

One centimeter represents 10 kilometers.
One inch represents approximately 16 miles.
Lambert Conformal Conic Projection

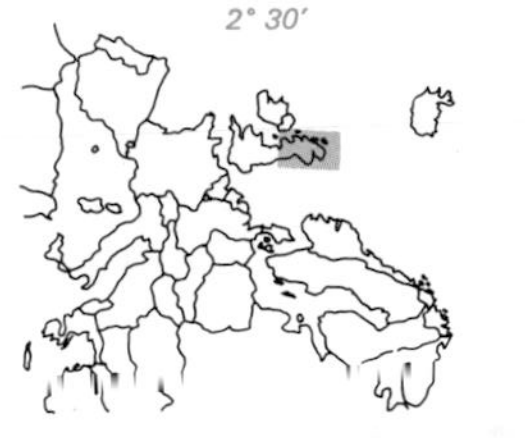

Map continues pages 44-45

Map continues pages 46-47

SCOTLAND
NORTHERN IRELAND
North Channel
ATLANTIC
OCEAN
IRISH
SEA
U.K.
IRELAND
ULSTER
DONEGAL
LEITRIM
SLIGO
MAYO
ROSCOMMON
CAVAN
MONAGHAN
LOUTH
MEATH
LONGFORD
CONNAUGHT
Belfast
Londonderry
Derry
Coleraine
Ballymena
Larne
Bangor
Newtownards
Lisburn
Lurgan
Portadown
Armagh
Newry
Dundalk
Dún Dealgan
Drogheda
Omagh
Strabane
Enniskillen
Donegal
Sligo
Sligeach
Ballina
Castlebar
Westport
Cavan
Monaghan
Navan
Letterkenny
Cookstown
Dungannon
Antrim
Newtownabbey
Carrickfergus
Downpatrick
Newcastle
Killybegs
Ballyshannon
Belmullet
Achill Island
Clare Island
SPERRIN MTS.
MOURNE MTS.
BLUE STACK MTS.
NEPHIN BEG RANGE
SLIEVE GAMPH
INISHOWEN
Lough Neagh
Lough Foyle
Lough Swilly
Donegal Bay
Sligo Bay
Clew Bay
Dundalk Bay
MALIN HEAD
RATHLIN ISLAND
TORY ISLAND
ARAN ISLAND
55°30'
55°
54°30'
54°
6°
6°30'
7°
7°30'
8°
8°30'
9°
9°30'
10°
10°30'

Map continues pages 42-43

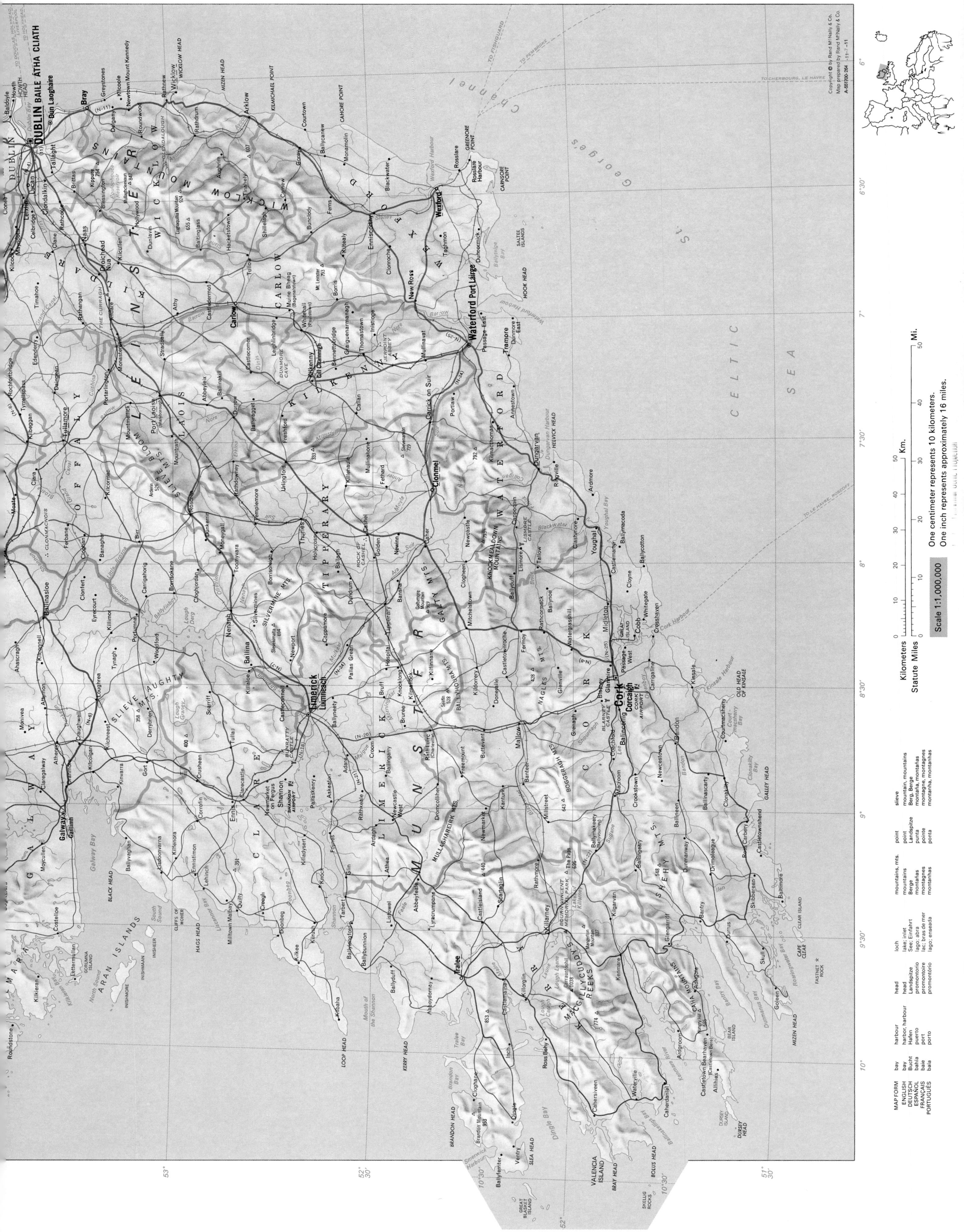
Scale 1:1,000,000
One centimeter represents 10 kilometers.
One inch represents approximately 16 miles.
Kilometers 0 10 20 30 40 50 Km.
Statute Miles 0 10 20 30 40 50 Mi.
MAP FORM bay harbour head loch mountains, mts. point sleeve
ENGLISH bay harbor, harbour head lake; inlet mountains point mountain, mountains
DEUTSCH Bucht Hafen Landspitze See; Einfahrt Berge Landspitze Berg, Berge
ESPAÑOL bahía puerto promontorio lago; abra montañas punta montaña, montañas
FRANÇAIS baie port promontoire lac; bras de mer montagnes pointe montagne, montagnes
PORTUGUÊS baía porto promontório lago; enseada montanhas ponta montanha, montanhas
Copyright © by Rand McNally & Co.
Map prepared by Rand McNally & Co.
CELTIC SEA
St. George's Channel
DUBLIN BAILE ÁTHA CLIATH
Belfast
Cork Corcaigh
Limerick Luimneach
Waterford Port Láirge
Galway Gaillimh

Map continues pages 56-57

Map continues pages 52-53

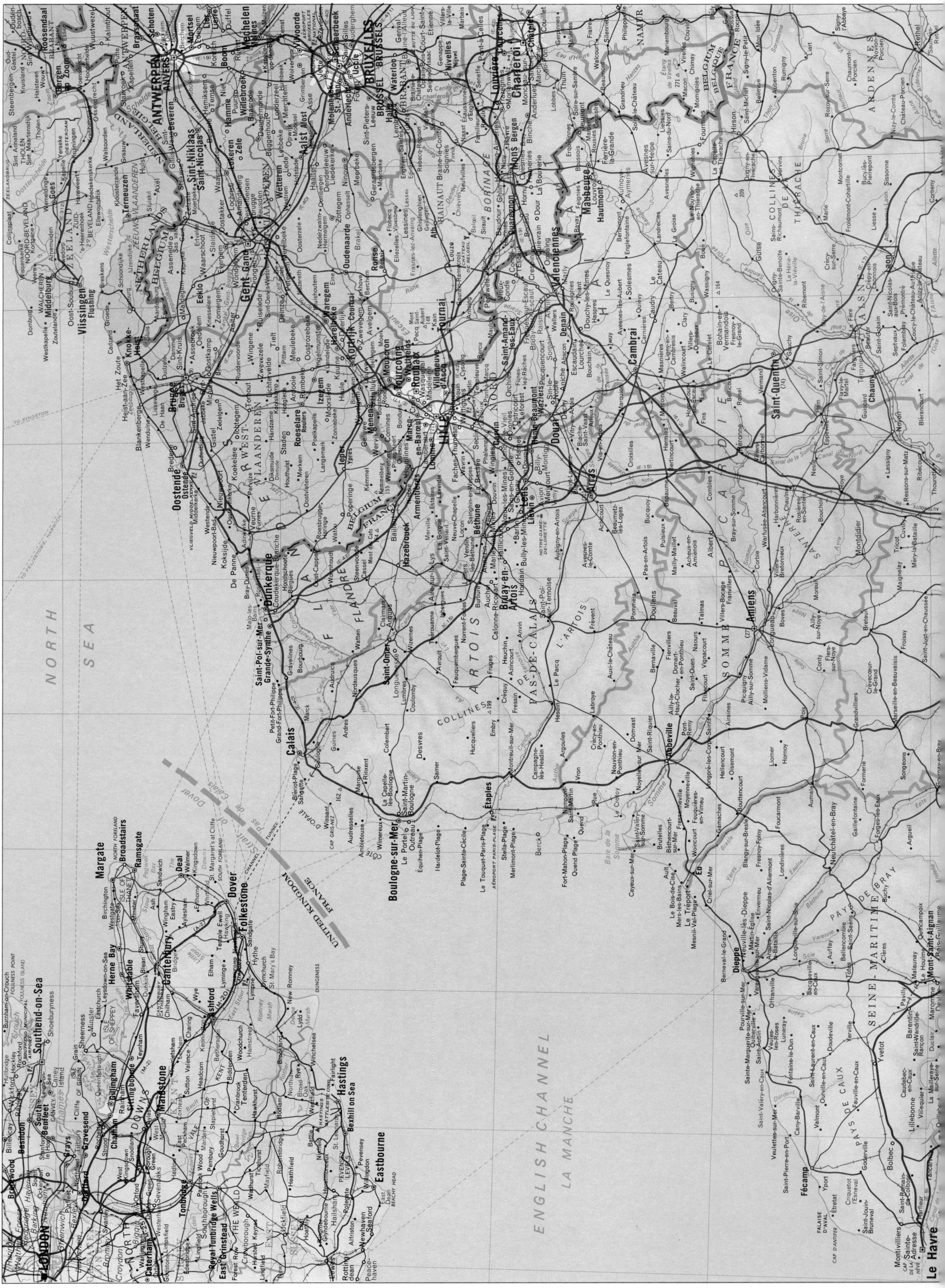
NORTH SEA
ENGLISH CHANNEL
LA MANCHE
LONDON
Dover
Folkestone
Calais
Dunkerque
Boulogne-sur-Mer
Oostende
Brugge
Gent
ANTWERPEN
BRUXELLES
Lille
Amiens
Dieppe
Le Havre
Abbeville
Arras
Cambrai
Valenciennes
Mons
Charleroi
Saint-Quentin
Canterbury
Maidstone
Hastings
Eastbourne
UNITED KINGDOM
FRANCE
BELGIUM

Map continues pages 42-43

Map continues pages 58-59

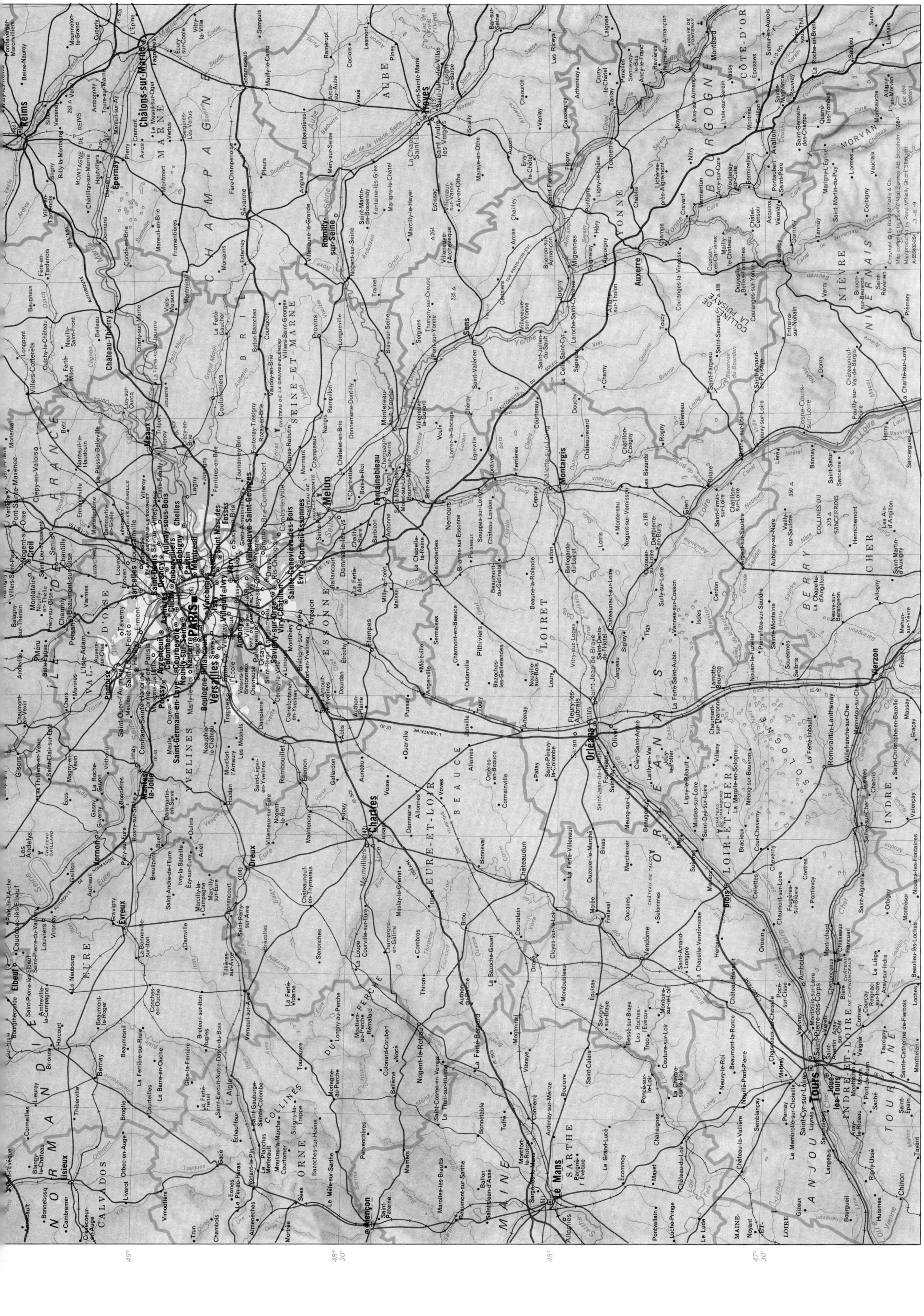
Reims
Châlons-sur-Marne
Épernay
Troyes
Auxerre
Meaux
PARIS
Versailles
Melun
Fontainebleau
Chartres
Orléans
Montargis
Sens
Évreux
Dreux
Le Mans
Tours
Blois
Vierzon
Alençon
Lisieux
Vernon
CHAMPAGNE
BEAUCE
LOIRET
ESSONNE
YVELINES
SARTHE
ORNE
EURE
BOURGOGNE
COTE-D'OR
YONNE
AUBE
MARNE
INDRE
CHER
ANJOU
TOURAINE
SOLOGNE

| FRANÇAIS | ENGLISH | DEUTSCH | ESPAÑOL | PORTUGUÊS |
|---|---|---|---|---|
| aéroport | airport | Flughafen | aeropuerto | aeroporto |
| canal | canal | Kanal | canal | canal |
| cap | cape | Kap | cabo | cabo |
| château | castle | Burg | castillo | castelo |
| collines | hills | Hügel | colinas | colinas |
| réservoir, rés. | reservoir | Stausee | embalse | reservatório |

Scale 1:1,000,000

One centimeter represents 10 kilometers.
One inch represents approximately 16 miles.

Kilometers 0 10 20 30 40 50 Km.
Statute Miles 0 10 20 30 40 50 Mi.

Lambert Conformal Conic Projection

3° 30'
4°
4° 30'
5°
5° 30'
6°
6° 30'
53° 30'
53°
52° 30'
52°
51° 30'
N O R T H
S E A
F R I S I A N
W A D D E N E I L A N D E N
Waddenzee
TEXEL
VLIELAND
TERSCHELLING
AMELAND
SCHIERMONNIKOOG
Den Helder
Harlingen
Leeuwarden
Groningen
FRIESLAND
GRONINGEN
DRENTHE
Assen
Sneek
Heerenveen
Drachten
Meppel
Hoogeveen
IJsselmeer (Zuiderzee)
Markermeer
NOORDOOSTPOLDER
FLEVOLAND
OOSTELIJK FLEVOLAND
ZUIDELIJK FLEVOLAND
Lelystad
Kampen
Zwolle
OVERIJSSEL
SALLAND
Deventer
Almelo
Hengelo
Enschede
Apeldoorn
GELDERLAND
Arnhem
Nijmegen
Harderwijk
Amersfoort
Ede
WEST FRIESLAND
NOORD-HOLLAND
Alkmaar
Hoorn
Enkhuizen
Medemblik
IJmuiden
Haarlem
Zaandam
AMSTERDAM
Hilversum
Bussum
Utrecht
Zeist
Veenendaal
Leiden
's-Gravenhage
The Hague
Delft
ZUID-HOLLAND
Gouda
ROTTERDAM
Schiedam
Vlaardingen
Dordrecht
Gorinchem
BETUWE
Tiel
BIESBOS
's-Hertogenbosch
Breda
Tilburg
Eindhoven
Helmond
NOORD-BRABANT
Roosendaal
Bergen op Zoom
ZEELAND
Middelburg
Vlissingen
Flushing
Goes
ZEEUWS-VLAANDEREN
Terneuzen
ANTWERPEN
ANVERS
Mechelen
Malines
Sint-Niklaas
Gent
Gand
Turnhout
Herentals
LIMBURG
Venlo
Krefeld
Mönchengladbach
Duisburg
Neuss
Kleve
Emmerich
Wesel
Goch
Geldern
BELGIUM
NETHERLANDS
NEDERLAND
BELGIË
GERMANY
DEUTSCHLAND
FLANDERS
DE GRAAFSCHAP
MEIERIJ
DE PEEL
TO HARWICH
TO HARWICH, KINGSTON

Map continues pages 50-51

Map continues pages 56-57

| DEUTSCH | Gebirge | Kanal | Moor | Naturpark | Stausee | Talsperre | Wald |
|---|---|---|---|---|---|---|---|
| ENGLISH | range | canal | moor | reserve | reservoir | dam | forest, mountains |
| ESPAÑOL | sierra | canal | páramo | reserva | embalse | presa | bosque, montañas |
| FRANÇAIS | chaîne | canal | lande | réserve | réservoir | barrage | forêt, montagnes |
| PORTUGUÊS | serra | canal | pântano | reserva natural | reservatório | represa | floresta, montanhas |

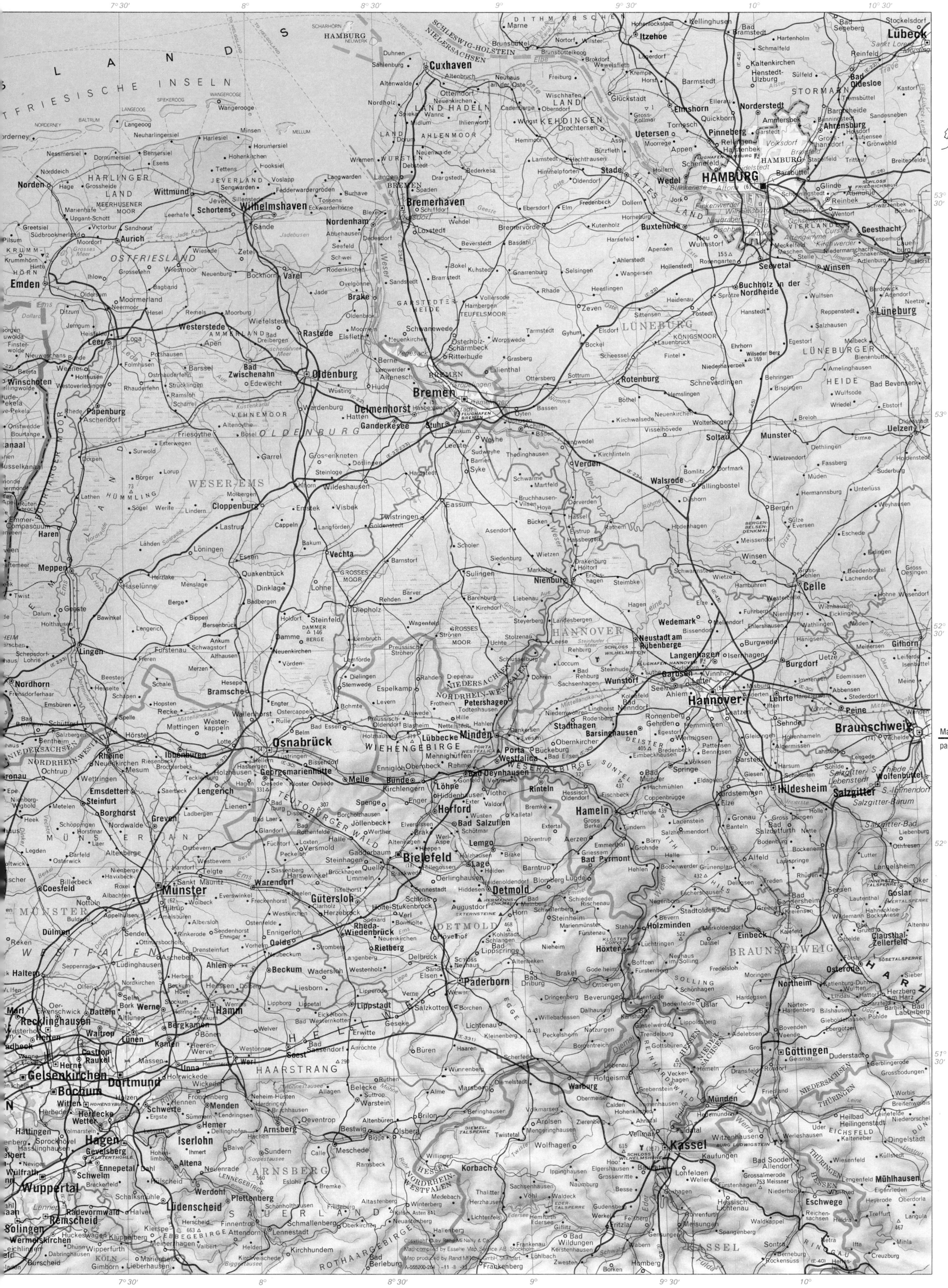
Hamburg
Bremen
Hannover
Lübeck
Cuxhaven
Bremerhaven
Wilhelmshaven
Emden
Oldenburg
Osnabrück
Bielefeld
Münster
Dortmund
Bochum
Gelsenkirchen
Wuppertal
Hagen
Kassel
Göttingen
Braunschweig
Hildesheim
Celle
Lüneburg
Uelzen
Minden
Hameln
Paderborn
Detmold
Herford
Salzgitter
Iserlohn
Lüdenscheid
Remscheid
Solingen
Recklinghausen
OSTFRIESISCHE INSELN
LÜNEBURGER HEIDE
TEUTOBURGER WALD
WESER-EMS
HAARSTRANG
SAUERLAND
SOLLING
HARZ
7° 30′
8°
8° 30′
9°
9° 30′
10°
10° 30′
53°
52° 30′
52°
51° 30′

Map continues pages 54-55

Kilometers 0 10 20 30 40 50 Km.

Statute Miles 0 10 20 30 40 50 Mi.

Scale 1:1,000,000

One centimeter represents 10 kilometers.
One inch represents approximately 16 miles.
Lambert Conformal Conic Projection

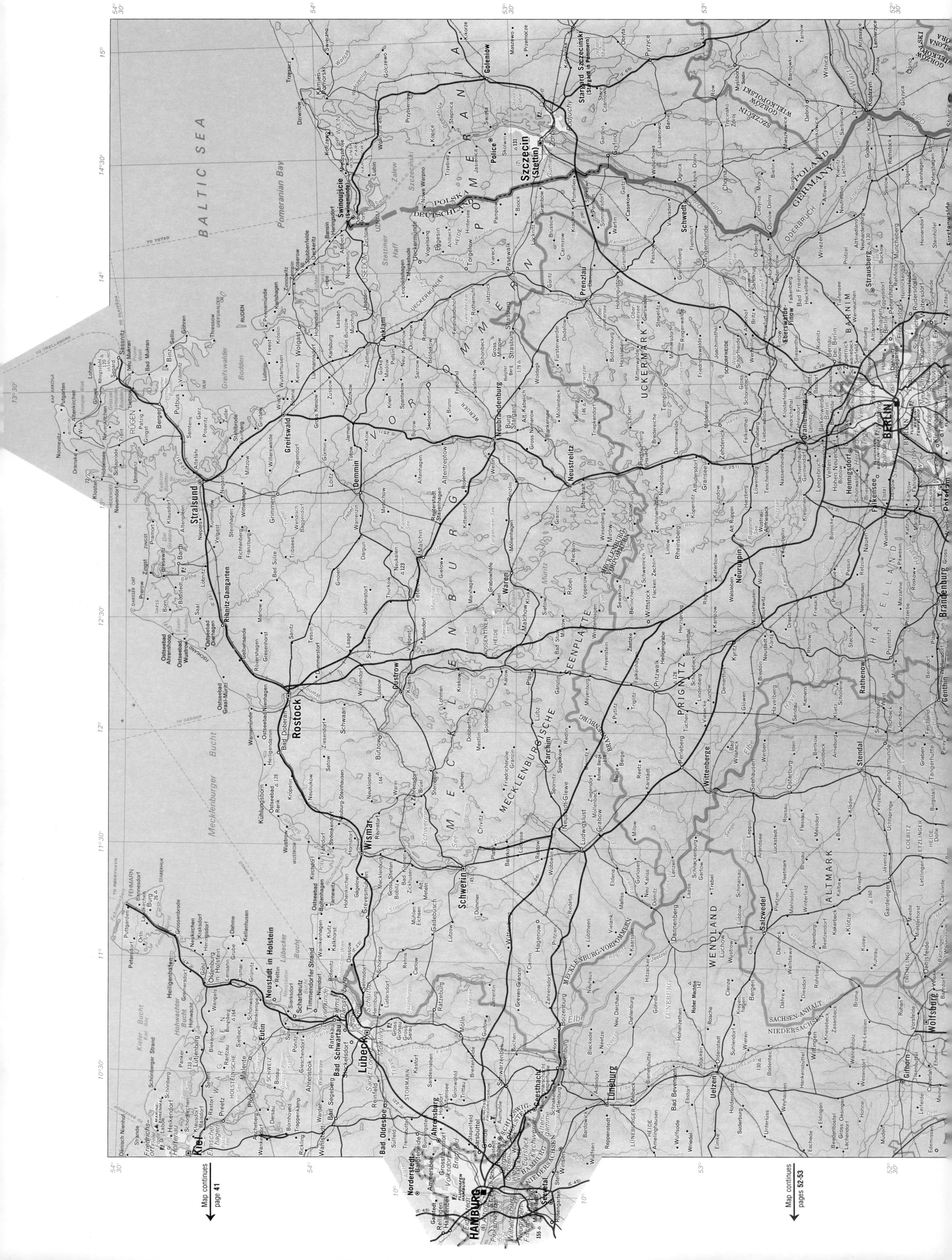
BALTIC SEA
Pomeranian Bay
Mecklenburger Bucht
Kieler Bucht
RÜGEN
FEHMARN
USEDOM
Stettiner Haff
POLSKA
DEUTSCHLAND
POLAND
GERMANY
VORPOMMERN
POMERANIA
MECKLENBURG
MECKLENBURGISCHE SEENPLATTE
UCKERMARK
PRIGNITZ
HAVELLAND
ALTMARK
WENDLAND
LÜNEBURGER HEIDE
BARNIM
SACHSEN-ANHALT
NIEDERSACHSEN
SCHLESWIG-HOLSTEIN
Elbe
Oder
Havel
Spree
Müritz
Kiel
Lübeck
Wismar
Rostock
Stralsund
Greifswald
Anklam
Demmin
Neubrandenburg
Neustrelitz
Prenzlau
Schwedt
Szczecin (Stettin)
Police
Świnoujście (Swinemünde)
Goleniów
Stargard Szczeciński (Stargard in Pommern)
Kostrzyn
Schwerin
Güstrow
Waren
Parchim
Ludwigslust
Wittenberge
Perleberg
Neuruppin
Oranienburg
Eberswalde-Finow
Bernau
Strausberg
Hennigsdorf
Falkensee
BERLIN
Potsdam
Brandenburg
Rathenow
Stendal
Salzwedel
Uelzen
Lüneburg
Geesthacht
Wolfsburg
Gifhorn
HAMBURG
Norderstedt
Ahrensburg
Bad Oldesloe
Bad Segeberg
Neustadt in Holstein
Eutin
Ribnitz-Damgarten
Sassnitz
Bergen
Barth
Pasewalk
Angermünde
Templin
Wolgast
Ratzeburg
Mölln
Ratzeburger See
Schweriner See
Dannenberg
Bad Doberan

Map continues page 41

Map continues pages 52-53

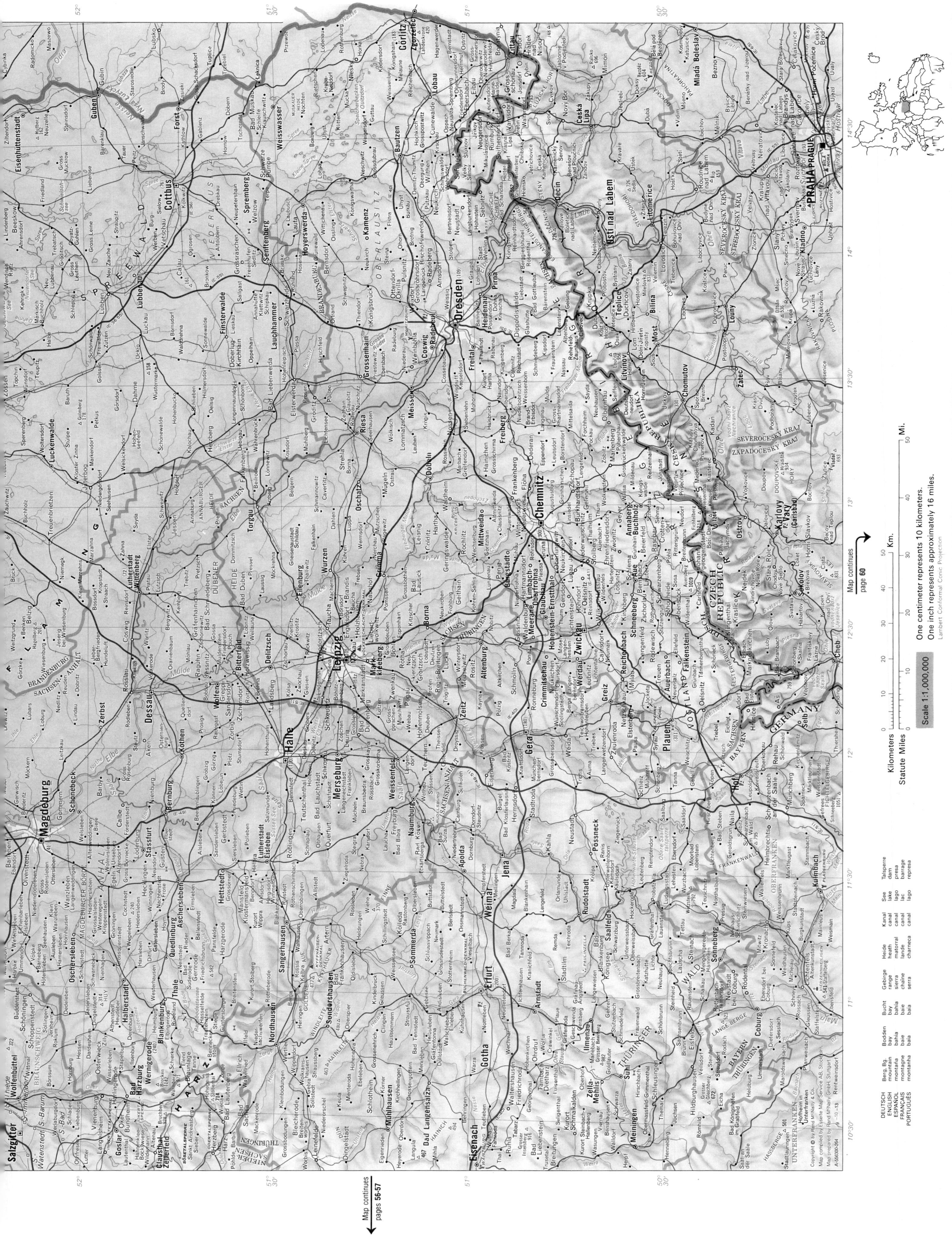
Scale 1:1,000,000
Kilometers
Statute Miles
One centimeter represents 10 kilometers.
One inch represents approximately 16 miles.
Lambert Conformal Conic Projection
Map continues page 60
Map continues pages 56-57

Map continues pages 52-53

Map continues pages 50-51

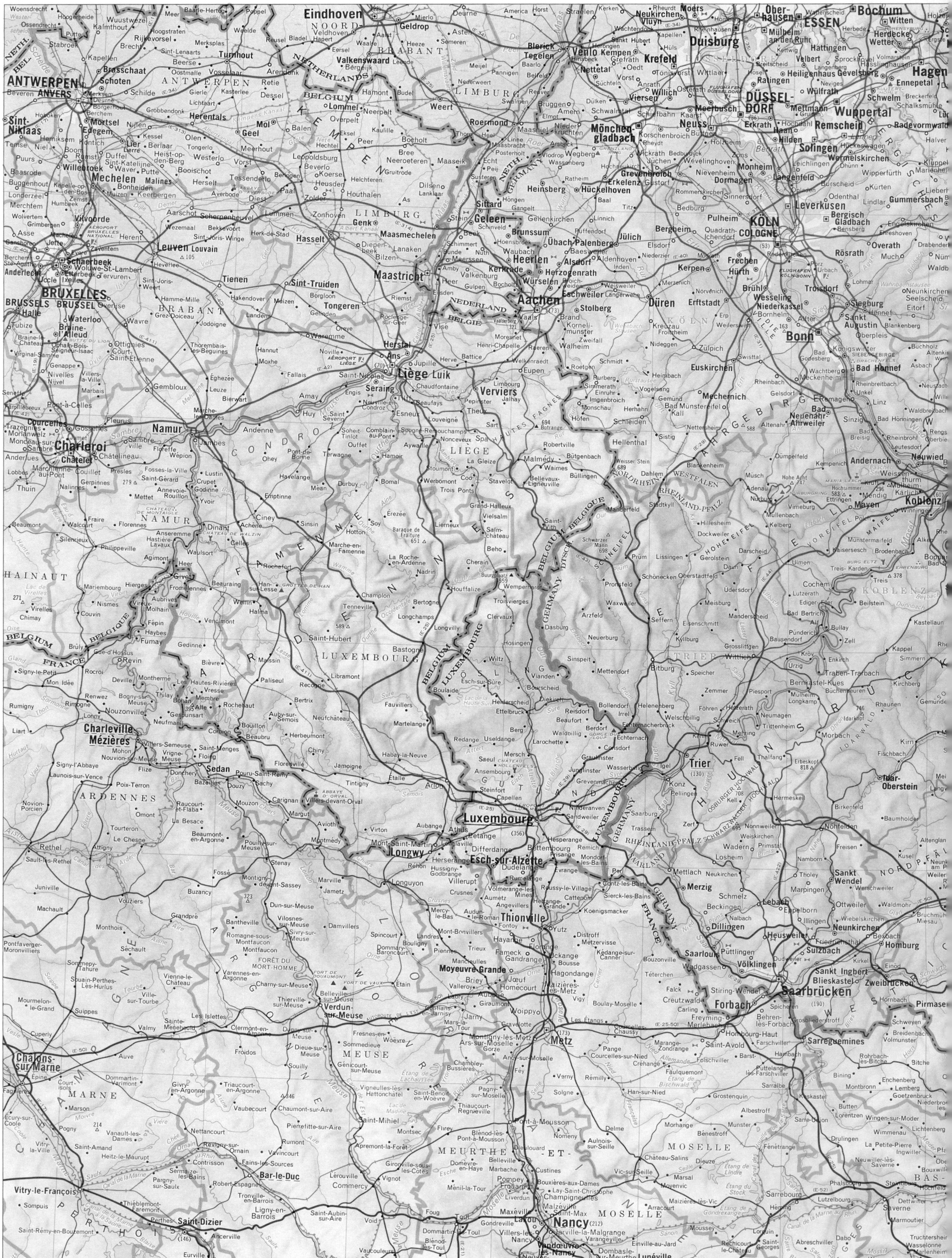
Eindhoven
ANTWERPEN ANVERS
BRUXELLES BRUSSEL
Mechelen Malines
Leuven Louvain
Sint-Niklaas
Charleroi
Namur
Liège Luik
Maastricht
Aachen
Hasselt
Verviers
Mönchengladbach
Venlo
Krefeld
Duisburg
ESSEN
Bochum
DÜSSELDORF
Neuss
Wuppertal
Remscheid
Solingen
KÖLN COLOGNE
Bonn
Düren
Koblenz
Trier
Luxembourg
Esch-sur-Alzette
Longwy
Thionville
Metz
Saarbrücken
Forbach
Nancy
Lunéville
Bar-le-Duc
Saint-Dizier
Vitry-le-François
Chalons-sur-Marne
Verdun-sur-Meuse
Sedan
Charleville Mézières
Idar-Oberstein
NETHERLANDS
BELGIUM
GERMANY
FRANCE
LUXEMBOURG
ARDENNES
MEUSE
MARNE
MOSELLE
HAINAUT
NAMUR
LIMBURG
BRABANT
ANTWERPEN
AUBE
HAUTE-MARNE
MEURTHE-ET-MOSELLE
4° 30′
5°
5° 30′
6°
6° 30′
7°
7° 30′
51°
50° 30′
50°
49° 30′
49°
48° 30′
Copyright © by Rand McNally & Co.
Map compiled by Esselte Map Service AB, Stockholm
Map produced by Rand McNally GmbH, Stuttgart

Map continues pages 58-59

| MAP FORM | aéroport | Berg | canal | chateau | étang | Gebirge | Naturpark | Stausee |
|---|---|---|---|---|---|---|---|---|
| ENGLISH | airport | mountain | canal | castle | pond | range | reserve | reservoir |
| DEUTSCH | Flughafen | Berg | Kanal | Burg | Teich | Gebirge | Naturpark | Stausee |
| ESPAÑOL | aeropuerto | montaña | canal | castillo | charca | cordillera | reserva | embalse |
| FRANÇAIS | aéroport | montagne | canal | château | étang | chaîne | réserve | réservoir |
| PORTUGUÊS | aeroporto | montanha | canal | castelo | lagoa | cordilheira | reserva | reservatório |

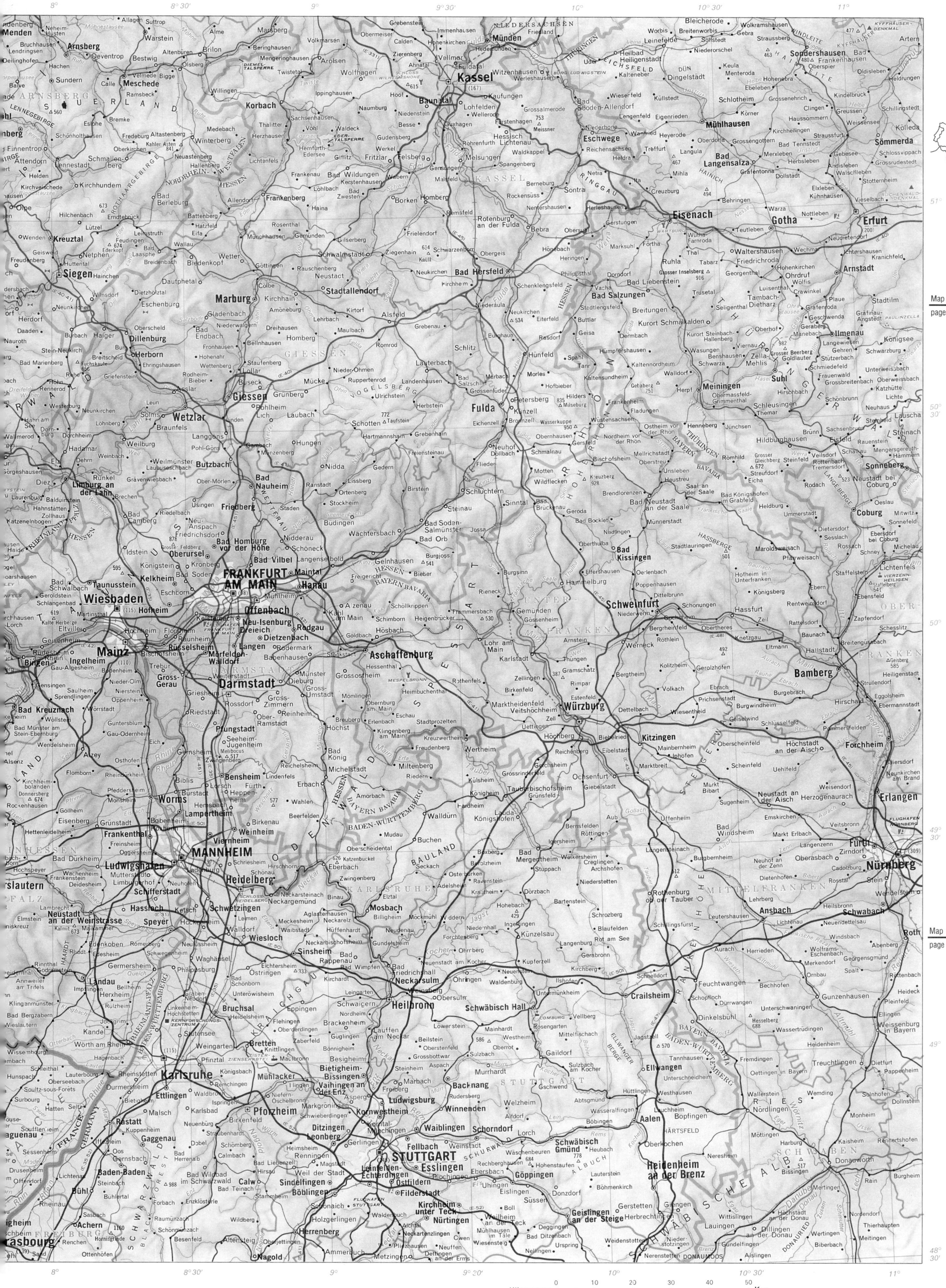
Kassel
Eisenach
Gotha
Erfurt
Marburg
Giessen
Fulda
Frankfurt am Main
Wiesbaden
Mainz
Darmstadt
Aschaffenburg
Würzburg
Schweinfurt
Bamberg
Erlangen
Nürnberg
Mannheim
Heidelberg
Heilbronn
Karlsruhe
Pforzheim
Stuttgart
Esslingen
Ansbach
Aalen

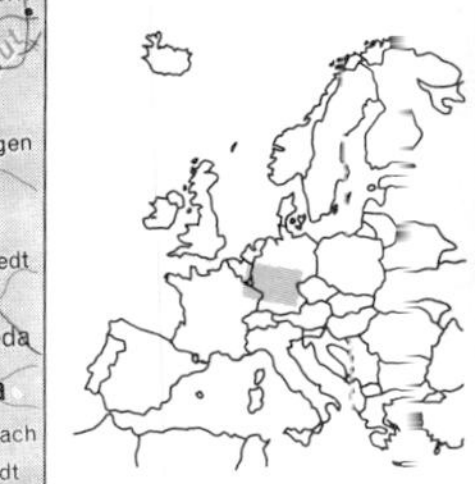

Map continues pages 54-55

Map continues page 60

Kilometers 0 10 20 30 40 50 Km.

Statute Miles 0 10 20 30 40 50 Mi.

Scale 1:1,000,000

One centimeter represents 10 kilometers.
One inch represents approximately 16 miles.
Lambert Conformal Conic Projection

Map continues pages 50-51

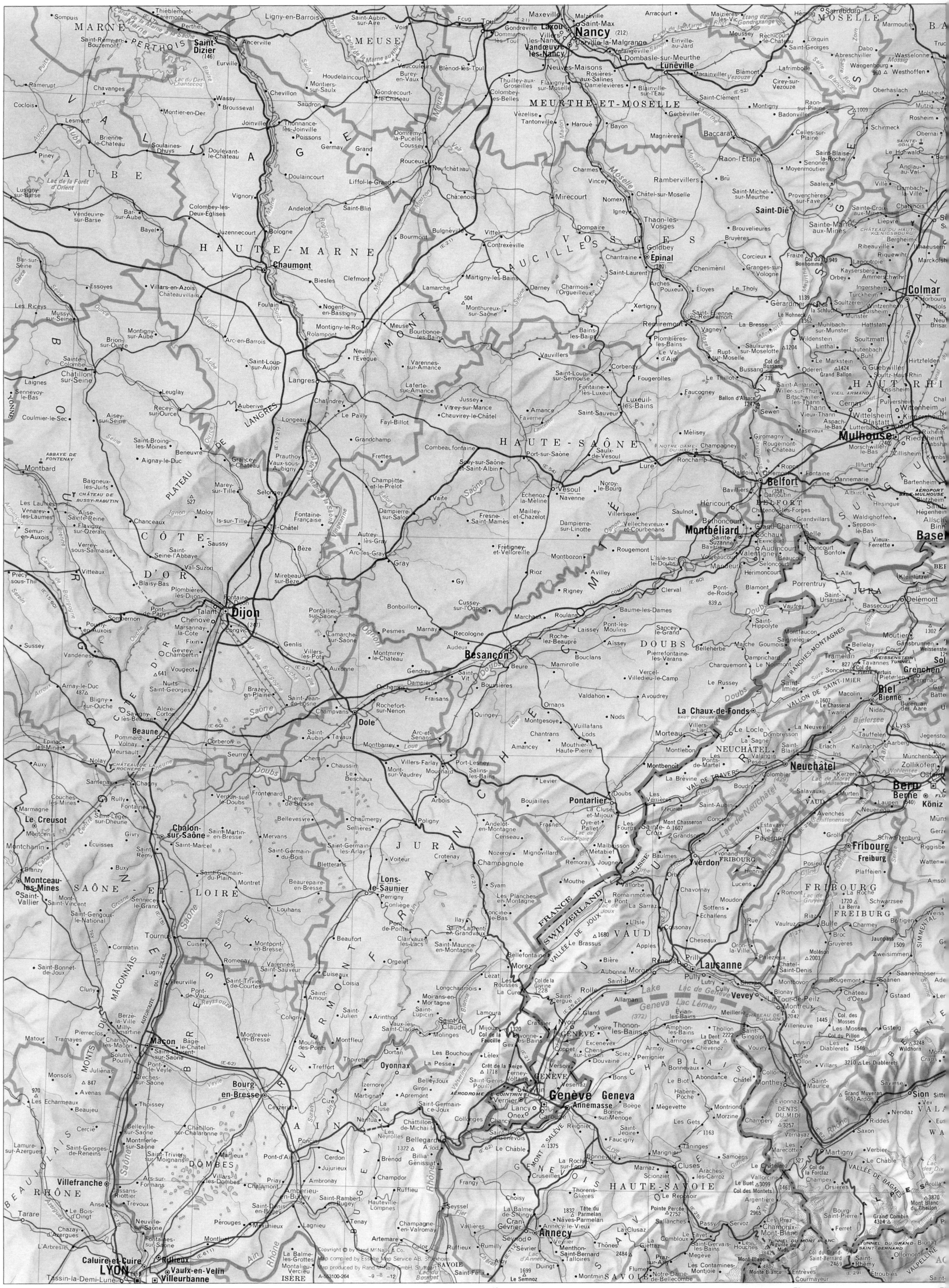

MARNE
HAUTE-MARNE
MEUSE
MEURTHE-ET-MOSELLE
MOSELLE
VOSGES
AUBE
HAUTE-SAÔNE
CÔTE-D'OR
DOUBS
JURA
SAÔNE-ET-LOIRE
AIN
HAUTE-SAVOIE
SAVOIE
RHÔNE
ISÈRE
VAUD
FRIBOURG
NEUCHÂTEL
FRANCE
SWITZERLAND
Saint-Dizier
Nancy
Lunéville
Épinal
Chaumont
Langres
Vesoul
Belfort
Mulhouse
Colmar
Montbéliard
Besançon
Dijon
Beaune
Dole
Pontarlier
Chalon-sur-Saône
Le Creusot
Montceau-les-Mines
Lons-le-Saunier
Mâcon
Bourg-en-Bresse
Villefranche
LYON
Villeurbanne
Annecy
Genève
Geneva
Lausanne
Neuchâtel
Fribourg
Bern
Biel
Sion
La Chaux-de-Fonds
Yverdon
Vevey
Lake Geneva
Lac Léman


| MAP FORM | col | Horn | lago | mont | passo | piz, -zo | See | Spitze | val |
|---|---|---|---|---|---|---|---|---|---|
| ENGLISH | pass | peak | lake | mount | pass | peak | lake | peak | valley |
| DEUTSCH | Pass | Horn | See | Berg | Pass | Gipfel | See | Spitze | Tal |
| ESPAÑOL | paso | pico | lago | monte | paso | pico | lago | pico | valle |
| FRANÇAIS | col | cime | lac | mont | col | cime | lac | cime | val |
| PORTUGUÊS | passo | pico | lago | monte | passo | pico | lago | pico | vale |

Map continues pages 56-57

8° 8°30′ 9° 9°30′ 10° 10°30′ 11°

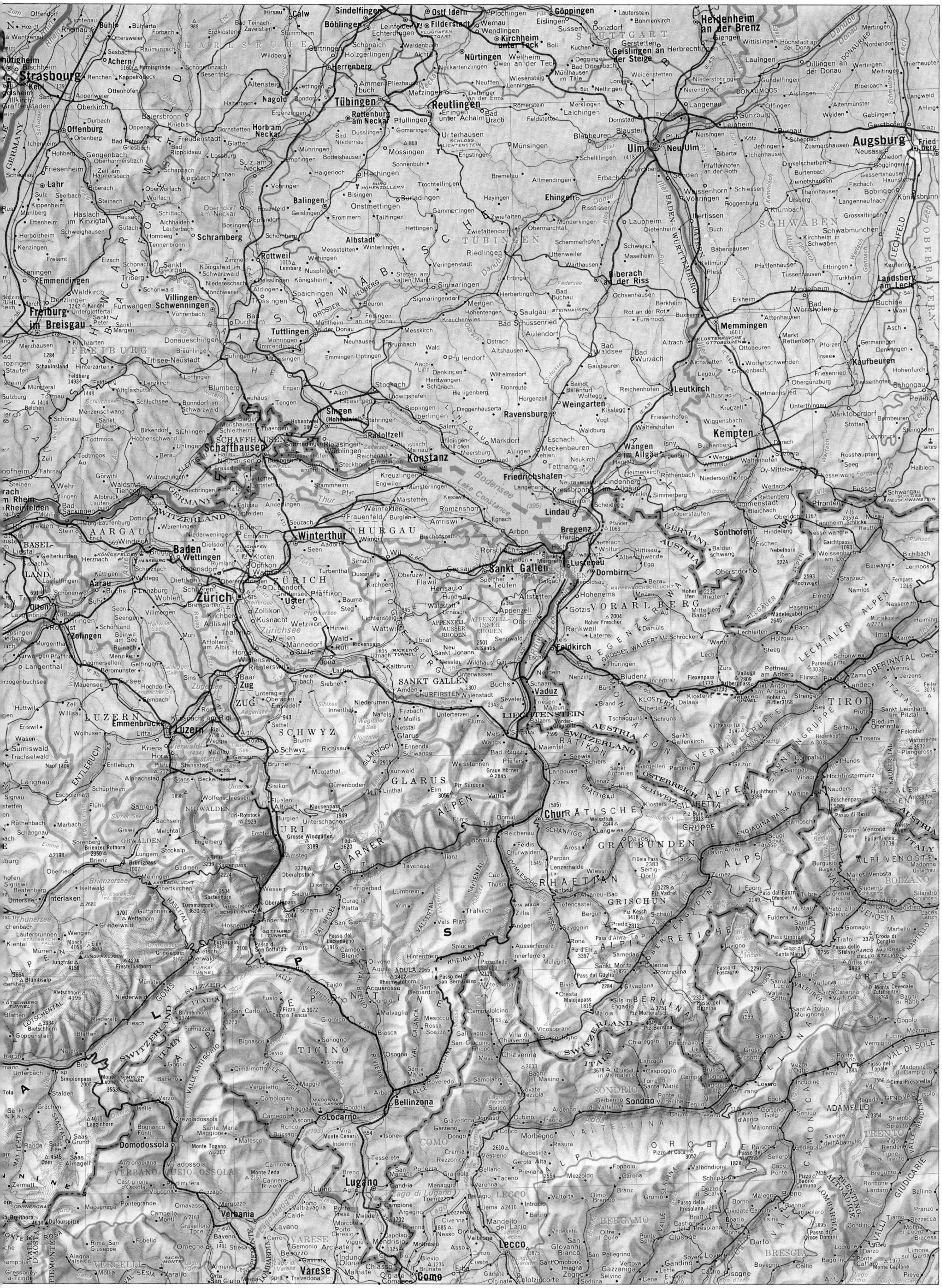
Strasbourg
Freiburg im Breisgau
Tübingen
Reutlingen
Ulm
Neu-Ulm
Augsburg
Schaffhausen
Konstanz
Winterthur
Zürich
Sankt Gallen
Luzern
Zug
Bregenz
Chur
Vaduz
LIECHTENSTEIN
Lugano
Locarno
Bellinzona
Domodossola
Varese
Como
Lecco
Sondrio
Bodensee
Lake Constance
GERMANY
SWITZERLAND
AUSTRIA
ITALY
TIROL
GRAUBÜNDEN
TICINO
RHAETIAN ALPS
SCHWABEN
OBERBAYERN
48° 30′
48°
47° 30′
47°
46° 30′
46°

Map continues page 60

Map continues pages 64-65

8° 8°30′ 9° 9°30′ 10° 10°30′

ontinues 62-63

Kilometers 0 10 20 30 40 50 Km.

Statute Miles 0 10 20 30 40 50 Mi.

Scale 1:1,000,000

One centimeter represents 10 kilometers.
One inch represents approximately 16 miles.
Lambert Conformal Conic Projection

Map continues pages 54-55

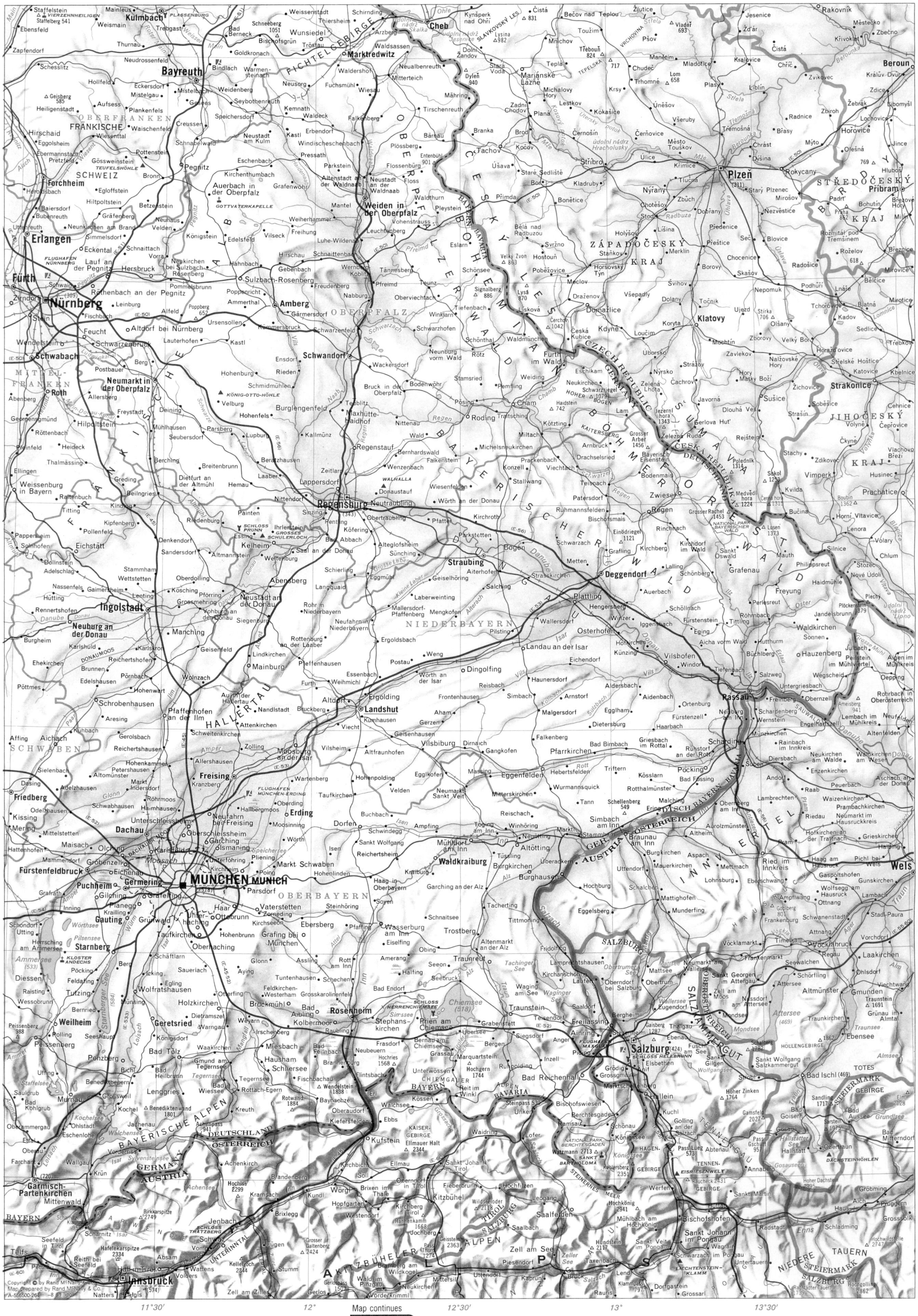

Kulmbach
Bayreuth
Cheb
Marktredwitz
Plzeň
Bamberg
Forchheim
Erlangen
Fürth
Nürnberg
Schwabach
Neumarkt in der Oberpfalz
Amberg
Weiden in der Oberpfalz
Schwandorf
Regensburg
Straubing
Deggendorf
Klatovy
Strakonice
Ingolstadt
Eichstätt
Landshut
Freising
Passau
MÜNCHEN MUNICH
Dachau
Fürstenfeldbruck
Rosenheim
Salzburg
Kufstein
Innsbruck
Garmisch-Partenkirchen
Bad Reichenhall
Wels
OBERPFALZ
NIEDERBAYERN
OBERBAYERN
FRÄNKISCHE SCHWEIZ
BÖHMERWALD
ŠUMAVA
ČESKÝ LES
CZECH REPUBLIC
GERMANY
AUSTRIA
DEUTSCHLAND
ÖSTERREICH
BAYERISCHE ALPEN
KITZBÜHELER ALPEN
SALZKAMMERGUT
FICHTELGEBIRGE


Map continues pages 56-57

Map continues pages 58-59

Map continues page 61

Map continues pages 64-65

| DEUTSCH | Berg | Gebirge | Pass | Schloss | See |
|---|---|---|---|---|---|
| ENGLISH | mountain | range | pass | castle | lake |
| ESPAÑOL | montaña | sierra | paso | castillo | lago |
| FRANÇAIS | montagne | chaîne | col | château | lac |
| PORTUGUÊS | montanha | serra | passo | castelo | lago |

Kilometers 0 10 20 30 40 50 Km.

Statute Miles 0 10 20 30 40 50 Mi.

Scale 1:1,000,000

One centimeter represents 10 kilometers.
One inch represents approximately 16 miles.

Modified Polyconic Projection

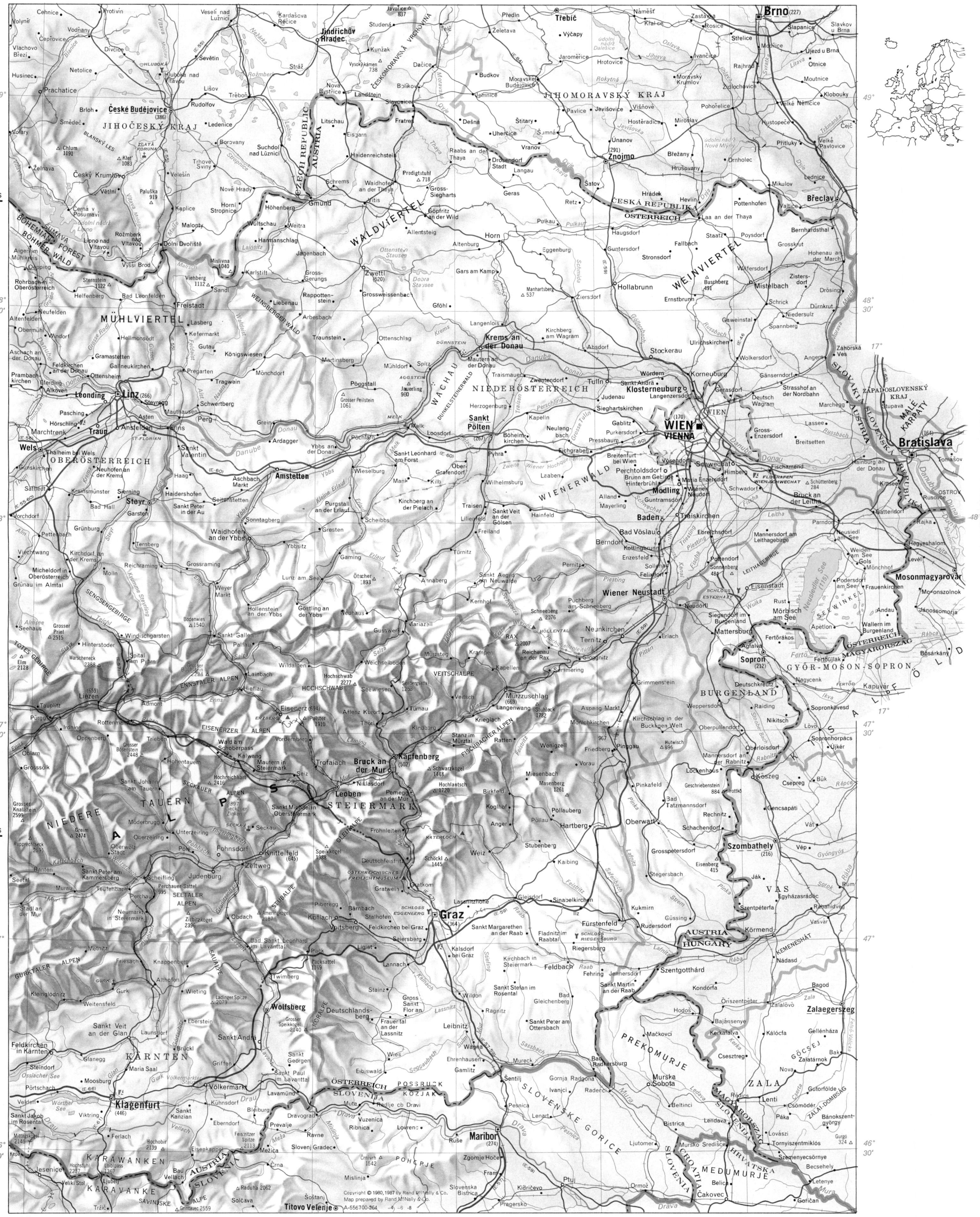
Brno
Třebíč
Znojmo
Břeclav
Jindřichův Hradec
České Budějovice
JIHOČESKÝ KRAJ
JIHOMORAVSKÝ KRAJ
CZECH REPUBLIC
AUSTRIA
ČESKÁ REPUBLIKA
ÖSTERREICH
WALDVIERTEL
WEINVIERTEL
MÜHLVIERTEL
BOHEMIAN FOREST
ŠUMAVA
BÖHMER WALD
Linz
Wels
Steyr
Enns
OBERÖSTERREICH
NIEDERÖSTERREICH
Krems an der Donau
Sankt Pölten
Amstetten
WIEN
VIENNA
Klosterneuburg
Mödling
Baden
WIENERWALD
Wiener Neustadt
Eisenstadt
Bratislava
SLOVAKIA
SLOVENSKÁ REPUBLIKA
ZÁPADOSLOVENSKÝ KRAJ
MALÉ KARPATY
Neusiedler See
Sopron
GYŐR-MOSON-SOPRON
Mosonmagyaróvár
BURGENLAND
Szombathely
VAS
AUSTRIA
HUNGARY
Zalaegerszeg
ZALA
Szentgotthárd
STEIERMARK
Graz
Bruck an der Mur
Leoben
Kapfenberg
NIEDERE TAUERN
ALPS
KÄRNTEN
Klagenfurt
Wolfsberg
KARAWANKEN
KARAVANKE
SLOVENIJA
Maribor
SLOVENSKE GORICE
PREKOMURJE
MEDJUMURJE
CROATIA
HRVATSKA
Titovo Velenje
Copyright © 1980, 1987 by Rand McNally & Co.
Map prepared by Rand McNally & Co.

| DEUTSCH | Alpe, -n | Berg | Gebirge | Sattel | Schloss | Wald |
|---|---|---|---|---|---|---|
| ENGLISH | mountains | mountain | range | saddle | castle | forest; mountains |
| ESPAÑOL | montañas | montaña | sierra | paso | castillo | bosque; montañas |
| FRANÇAIS | montagnes | montagne | chaîne | col | château | forêt; montagnes |
| PORTUGUÊS | montanhas | montanha | serra | passo | castelo | Floresta; montanhas |

Kilometers 0 10 20 30 40 50 Km.
Statute Miles 0 10 20 30 40 50 Mi.

Scale 1:1,000,000

One centimeter represents 10 kilometers.
One inch represents approximately 16 miles.
Lambert Conformal Conic Projection

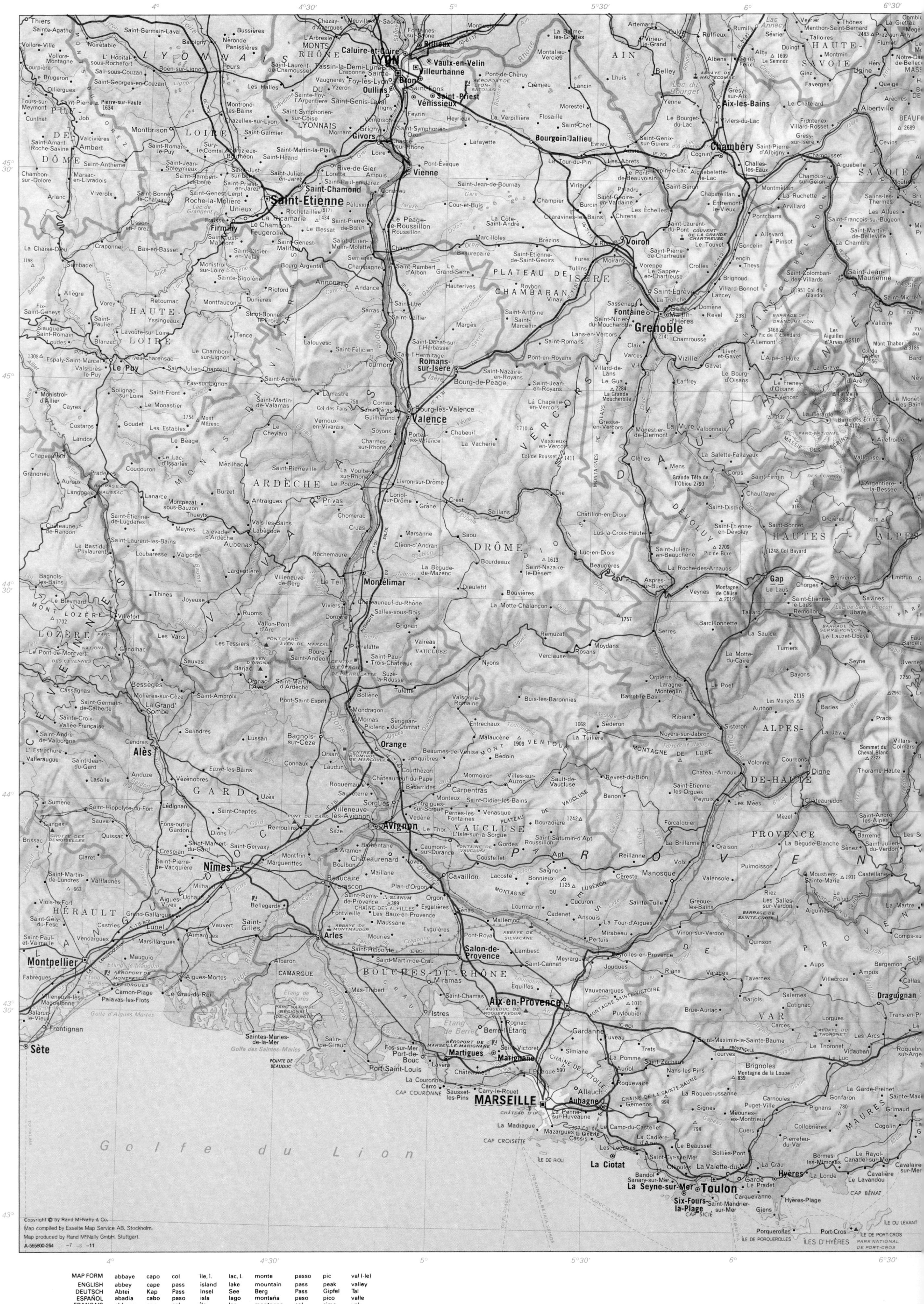

4°
4°30'
5°
5°30'
6°
6°30'
45° 30'
45°
44° 30'
44°
43° 30'
43°
LYON
Villeurbanne
Saint-Etienne
Grenoble
Valence
Montélimar
Avignon
Nîmes
Montpellier
Arles
Aix-en-Provence
MARSEILLE
Toulon
La Ciotat
Hyères
Sète
Alès
Orange
Chambéry
Voiron
Vienne
Le Puy
Gap
Digne
Draguignan
Salon-de-Provence
Martigues
Aubagne
Chambéry
Privas
Aubenas
Romans-sur-Isère
Bourgoin-Jallieu
ARDÈCHE
DRÔME
GARD
VAUCLUSE
HÉRAULT
LOZÈRE
BOUCHES-DU-RHÔNE
VAR
CAMARGUE
PROVENCE
Golfe du Lion
Copyright © by Rand McNally & Co.
Map compiled by Esselte Map Service AB, Stockholm.
Map produced by Rand McNally GmbH, Stuttgart.
A-555800-264


| MAP FORM | abbaye | capo | col | île, î. | lac, l. | monte | passo | pic | val (-le) |
|---|---|---|---|---|---|---|---|---|---|
| ENGLISH | abbey | cape | pass | island | lake | mountain | pass | peak | valley |
| DEUTSCH | Abtei | Kap | Pass | Insel | See | Berg | Pass | Gipfel | Tal |
| ESPAÑOL | abadia | cabo | paso | isla | lago | montaña | paso | pico | valle |
| FRANÇAIS | abbaye | cap | col | île | lac | montagne | col | cime | val |
| PORTUGUÊS | abadia | cabo | passo | ilha | lago | montanha | passo | pico | vale |

Map continues pages 58-59

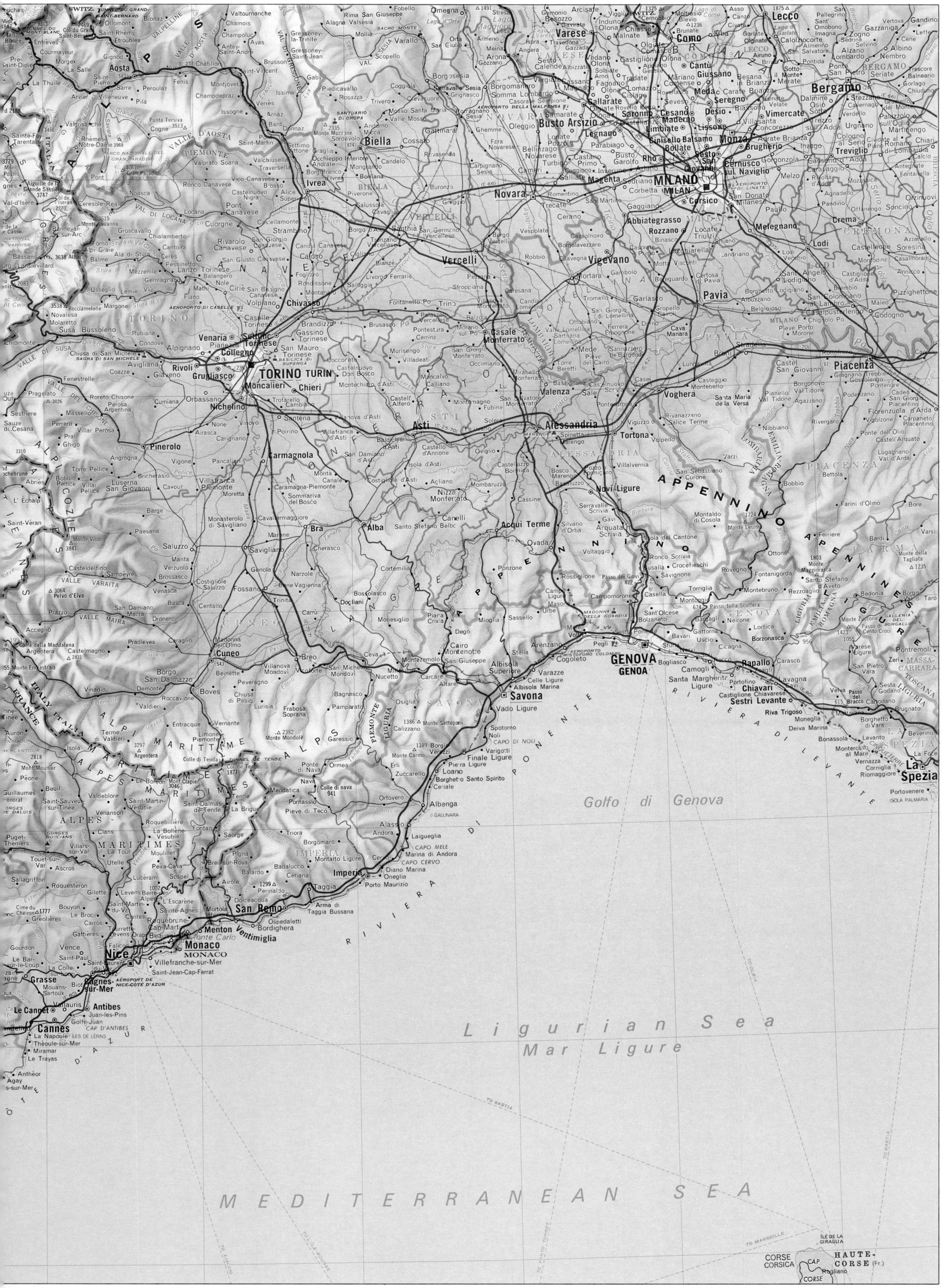
TORINO TURIN
MILANO
MILAN
GENOVA
GENOA
Golfo di Genova
Ligurian Sea
Mar Ligure
MEDITERRANEAN SEA
APPENNINO
APPENNINES
ALPI MARITTIME
ALPES MARITIMES
RIVIERA DI PONENTE
RIVIERA DI LEVANTE
Alessandria
Asti
Novara
Vercelli
Pavia
Piacenza
Bergamo
Como
Lecco
Varese
Savona
Cuneo
San Remo
Imperia
La Spezia
Nice
Monaco
MONACO
Cannes
Antibes
Grasse
Menton
Ventimiglia
Biella
Ivrea
Aosta
Pinerolo
Alba
Bra
Chiavari
Rapallo
Vigevano
Lodi
Monza
Voghera
Tortona
Novi Ligure
Acqui Terme
Casale Monferrato
HAUTE-CORSE (Fr.)
CORSE
CORSICA
7°
7°30'
8°
8°30'
9°
9°30'
45°
44°
43°

Map continues pages 64-65

Kilometers 0 10 20 30 40 50 Km.

Statute Miles 0 10 20 30 40 50 Mi.

Scale 1:1,000,000

One centimeter represents 10 kilometers.
One inch represents approximately 16 miles.
Lambert Conformal Conic Projection

Map continues page 61

Map continues page 60

MÜNCHEN
MUNICH
Salzburg
Innsbruck
Bolzano
Udine
Kempten
Rosenheim
Belluno
Merano
Villach
Sondrio

Map continues pages 58-59

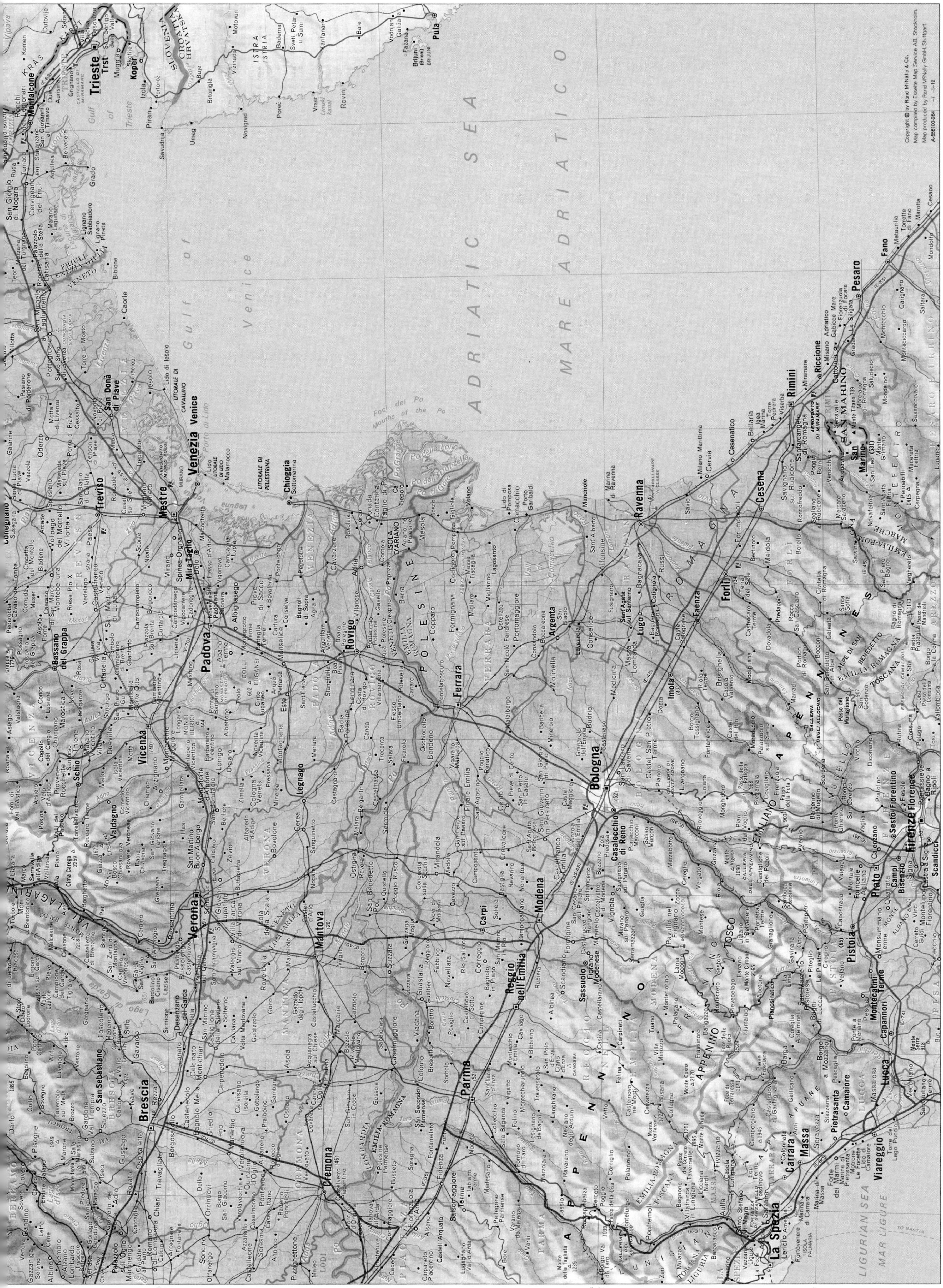

ADRIATIC SEA
MARE ADRIATICO
Gulf of Venice
LIGURIAN SEA
MAR LIGURE
Venezia Venice
Padova
Trieste Trst
Bologna
Firenze Florence
Ferrara
Ravenna
Rimini
Verona
Modena
Parma
La Spezia

Map continues pages 66-67

Map continues pages 62-63

| MAP FORM | Alpen | Berg | cima | Gebirge | monte | piz | Schloss | See | Spitze |
|---|---|---|---|---|---|---|---|---|---|
| ENGLISH | mountains | mountain | peak | range | mountain | peak | castle | lake | peak |
| DEUTSCH | Alpen | Berg | Gipfel | Gebirge | Berg | Gipfel | Schloss | See | Spitze |
| ESPAÑOL | montañas | montaña | pico | sierra | montaña | pico | castillo | lago | pico |
| FRANÇAIS | montagnes | montagne | cime | chaîne | montagne | cime | château | lac | cime |
| PORTUGUÊS | montanhas | montanha | pico | serra | montanha | pico | castelo | lago | pico |

Kilometers 0 10 20 30 40 50 Km.
Statute Miles 0 10 20 30 40 50 Mi.

Scale 1:1,000,000

One centimeter represents 10 kilometers.
One inch represents approximately 16 miles.
Lambert Conformal Conic Projection

Map continues pages 64-65

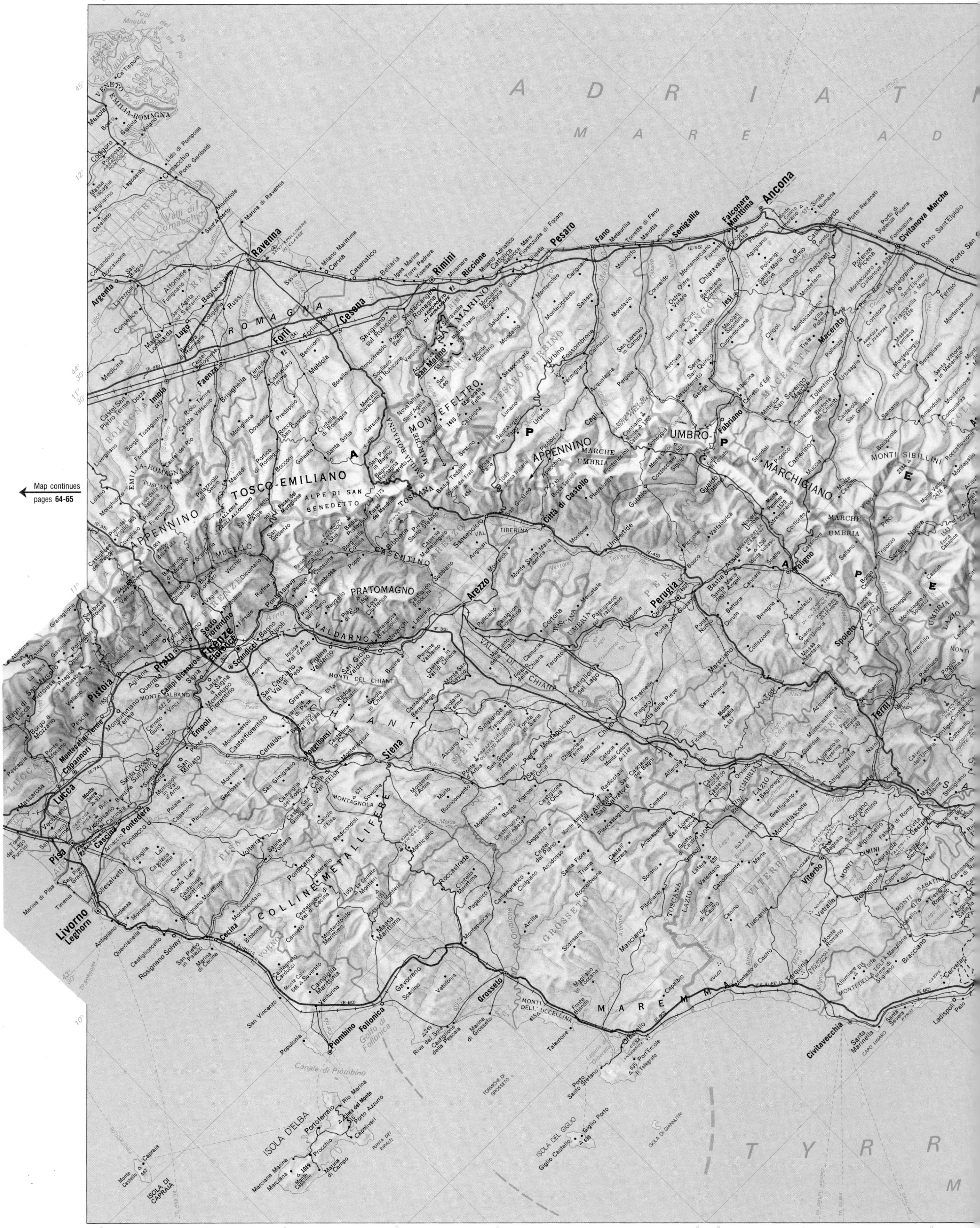
ADRIATIC
MARE ADRIATICO
TYRRHENIAN
APPENNINO TOSCO-EMILIANO
APPENNINO UMBRO-MARCHIGIANO
ROMAGNA
EMILIA-ROMAGNA
TOSCANA
UMBRIA
MARCHE
LAZIO
SAN MARINO
MONTEFELTRO
PRATOMAGNO
CASENTINO
MUGELLO
VALDARNO
CHIANTI
MONTI DEL CHIANTI
COLLINE METALLIFERE
MAREMMA
MONTI SIBILLINI
ISOLA D'ELBA
ISOLA DI CAPRAIA
ISOLA DEL GIGLIO
Canale di Piombino
Ravenna
Rimini
Cesena
Forlì
Pesaro
Fano
Senigallia
Ancona
Macerata
Civitanova Marche
Urbino
Faenza
Imola
Lugo
Firenze
Florence
Prato
Pistoia
Lucca
Pisa
Livorno
Leghorn
Empoli
Siena
Arezzo
Perugia
Assisi
Foligno
Spoleto
Terni
Orvieto
Viterbo
Grosseto
Piombino
Follonica
Civitavecchia
Città di Castello
Gubbio
Fabriano
Jesi
Cortona
Montepulciano
Chiusi
Poggibonsi
Volterra
Cecina
Portoferraio

| MAP FORM | golfo | isola | lago | monte | monti | passo | punta |
|---|---|---|---|---|---|---|---|
| ENGLISH | gulf | island | lake | mountain | mountains | pass | point |
| DEUTSCH | Golf | Insel | See | Berg | Berge | Pass | Landspitze |
| ESPAÑOL | golfo | isla | lago | montaña | montañas | paso | punta |
| FRANÇAIS | golfe | île | lac | montagne | montagnes | col | pointe |
| PORTUGUÊS | golfo | ilha | lago | montanha | montanhas | passo | ponta |

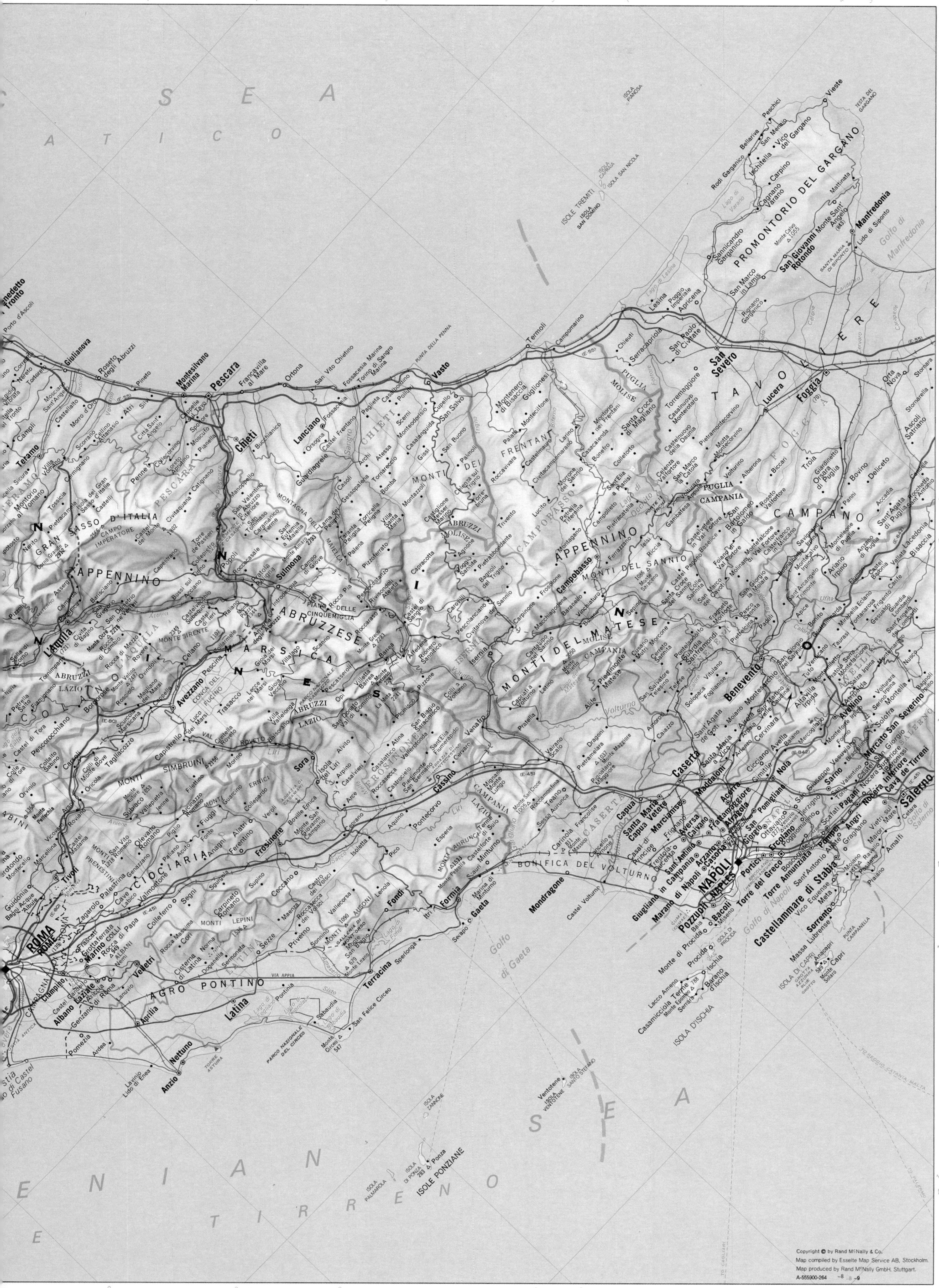
ROMA
NAPOLI
NAPLES
Pescara
Foggia
Benevento
Caserta
Salerno
Latina
Frosinone
Campobasso
Chieti
L'Aquila
Sulmona
Avezzano
Isernia
Gaeta
Terracina
Anzio
Nettuno
Vasto
Termoli
Lucera
San Severo
Manfredonia
Vieste
PROMONTORIO DEL GARGANO
TAVOLIERE
APPENNINO
MONTI DEL MATESE
ABRUZZESE
GRAN SASSO D'ITALIA
AGRO PONTINO
CIOCIARIA
ISOLE TREMITI
ISOLE PONZIANE
ISOLA D'ISCHIA
Golfo di Gaeta
Golfo di Manfredonia
BONIFICA DEL VOLTURNO

Map continues pages 68-69



Kilometers 0 10 20 30 40 50 Km.
Statute Miles 0 10 20 30 40 50 Mi.

Scale 1:1,000,000

One centimeter represents 10 kilometers.
One inch represents approximately 16 miles.
Lambert Conformal Conic Projection

A D R I A T I C
S E A
M A R E
A D R I A T I C O
CROATIA
ITALY
ISOLE TREMITI
PROMONTORIO DEL GARGANO
Golfo di Manfredonia
Vieste
Manfredonia
San Severo
Lucera
Foggia
Cerignola
Barletta
Trani
Bisceglie
Molfetta
Andria
Corato
Bari
Mola di Bari
Monopoli
Ostuni
Altamura
Gravina in Puglia
Matera
Taranto
Massafra
Martina Franca
PUGLIA
BASILICATA
CAMPANIA
MOLISE
Campobasso
Isernia
Benevento
Avellino
Potenza
Caserta
Cassino
NAPOLI
Pozzuoli
Torre del Greco
Torre Annunziata
Castellammare di Stabia
Sorrento
Salerno
Battipaglia
Eboli
Agropoli
Golfo di Salerno
Golfo di Gaeta
Gaeta
Formia
Fondi
Mondragone
Ischia
ISOLA DI CAPRI
VALLO DI DIANO
PIANA DEL SELE
BONIFICA DEL VOLTURNO
T Y R R H E

Map continues pages 66-67

| MAP FORM | capo | golfo | isola | lago | monte | monti | punta |
|---|---|---|---|---|---|---|---|
| ENGLISH | cape | gulf | island | lake | mountain | mountains | point |
| DEUTSCH | Kap | Golf | Insel | See | Berg | Berge | Landspitze |
| ESPAÑOL | cabo | golfo | isla | lago | montaña | montañas | punta |
| FRANÇAIS | cap | golfe | île | lac | montagne | montagnes | pointe |
| PORTUGUÊS | cabo | golfo | ilha | lago | montanha | montanhas | ponta |

Strait of Otranto
Golfo di Taranto
IONIAN SEA
MARE IONIO
MARE TIRRENO
Lecce
Galatina
Nardò
Copertino
Gallipoli
PENISOLA SALENTINA
Crotone
Cirò Marina
Catanzaro
Cosenza
Nicastro
Rossano
SILA
Golfo di Squillace
Golfo di Sant'Eufemia
Golfo di Gioia
Reggio di Calabria
Messina
SICILIA
CALABRIA
Stretto di Messina

Map continues page 70

Kilometers 0 10 20 30 40 50 Km.
Statute Miles 0 10 20 30 40 50 Mi.

Scale 1:1,000,000
One centimeter represents 10 kilometers.
One inch represents approximately 16 miles.
Lambert Conformal Conic Projection

Map continues pages 68-69

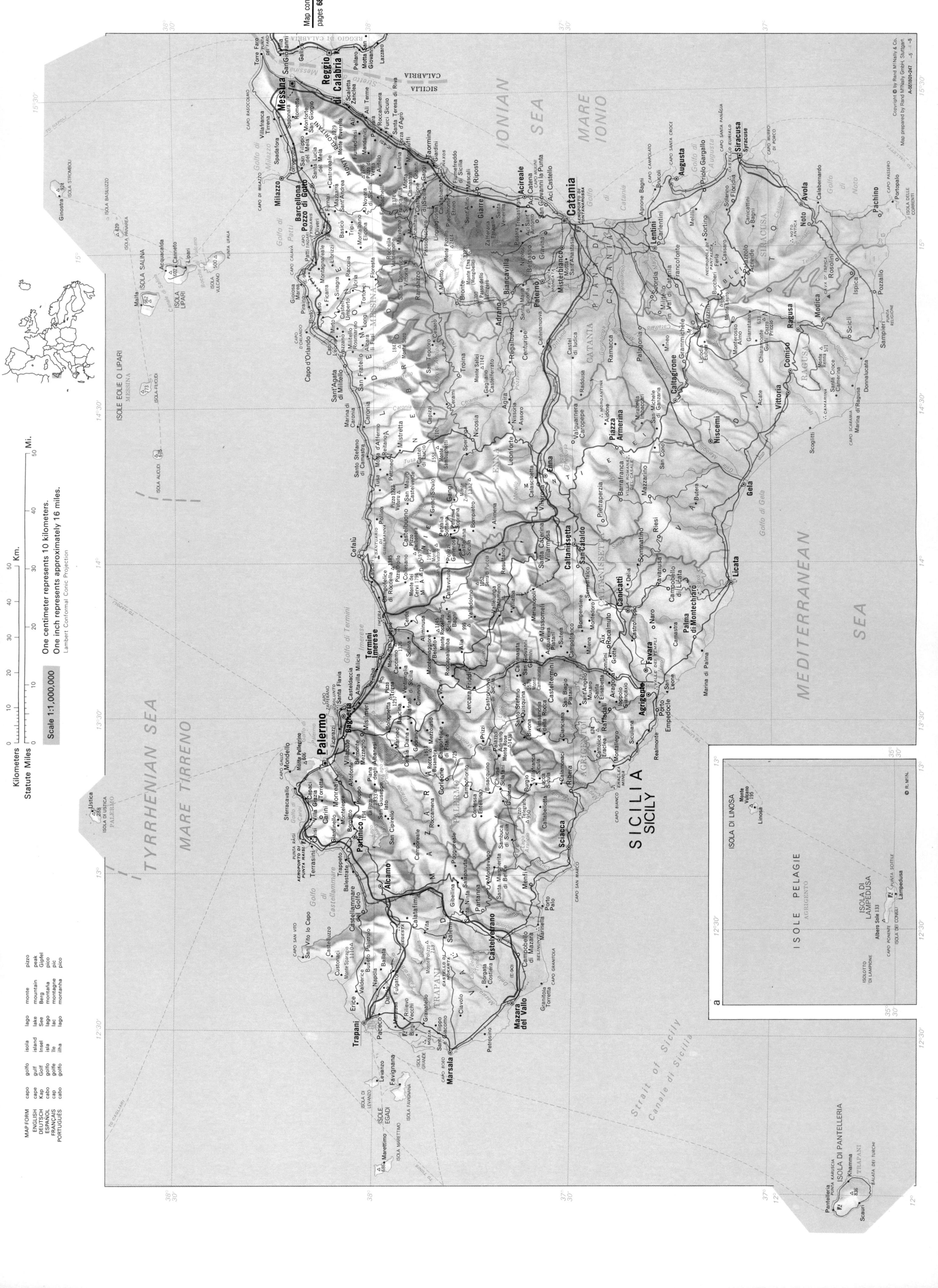
Kilometers
Statute Miles
Scale 1:1,000,000
One centimeter represents 10 kilometers.
One inch represents approximately 16 miles.
Lambert Conformal Conic Projection
MAP FORM capo golfo isola lago monte pizzo
ENGLISH cape gulf island lake mountain peak
DEUTSCH Kap Golf Insel See Berg Gipfel
ESPAÑOL cabo golfo isla lago montaña pico
FRANÇAIS cap golfe île lac montagne pic
PORTUGUÊS cabo golfo ilha lago montanha pico
TYRRHENIAN SEA
MARE TIRRENO
IONIAN SEA
MARE IONIO
MEDITERRANEAN SEA
Strait of Sicily
Canale di Sicilia
SICILIA
SICILY
CALABRIA
ISOLE EOLIE O LIPARI
ISOLE EGADI
ISOLE PELAGIE
ISOLA DI LAMPEDUSA
ISOLA DI LINOSA
ISOLA DI PANTELLERIA
Palermo
Catania
Messina
Reggio di Calabria
Siracusa
Agrigento
Trapani
Marsala
Caltanissetta
Enna
Ragusa
Copyright © by Rand McNally & Co.
Map prepared by Rand McNally GmbH, Stuttgart

CORSE
CORSICA
FRANCE
ITALY
ITALIA
CORSE-DU-SUD
SARDEGNA
Strait of Bonifacio
Bonifacio
ISOLA MADDALENA
La Maddalena
ISOLA CAPRERA
Palau
Santa Teresa Gallura
ISOLA ASINARA
Golfo dell'Asinara
Stintino
Porto Torres
Castelsardo
ANGLONA
GALLURA
Tempio Pausania
Olbia
Golfo Aranci
ISOLA TAVOLARA
San Teodoro
Sassari
NURRA
Alghero
LOGUDORO
Ozieri
Siniscola
Nuoro
Orosei
Golfo di Orosei
Dorgali
Cala Gonone
Bosa
Macomer
SARDEGNA
SARDINIA
Oristano
Golfo di Oristano
ARBOREA
BARBAGIA
GENNARGENTU
Tortolì
Arbatax
OGLIASTRA
Lanusei
TYRRHENIAN SEA
MARE TIRRENO
CAMPIDANO
Iglesias
Carbonia
Sant'Antioco
ISOLA DI SANT'ANTIOCO
ISOLA DI SAN PIETRO
Carloforte
Cagliari
Golfo di Cagliari
Quartu Sant'Elena
Villasimius
SARRABUS
Pula
Teulada
MEDITERRANEAN SEA
Copyright © by Rand McNally & Co.
Map prepared by Rand McNally GmbH, Stuttgart.

| MAP FORM | capo | golfo | isola | lago, l. | monte |
|---|---|---|---|---|---|
| ENGLISH | cape | gulf | island | lake | mountain |
| DEUTSCH | Kap | Golf | Insel | See | Berg |
| ESPAÑOL | cabo | golfo | isla | lago | montaña |
| FRANÇAIS | cap | golfe | île | lac | montagne |
| PORTUGUÊS | cabo | golfo | ilha | lago | montanha |

Kilometers 0 10 20 30 40 50 Km.

Statute Miles 0 10 20 30 40 50 Mi.

Scale 1:1,000,000

One centimeter represents 10 kilometers.
One inch represents approximately 16 miles.
Lambert Conformal Conic Projection

Map continues pages 22-23

Map continues pages 118-119

FINLAND
ESTONIA
LATVIA
LITHUANIA
POLAND
BELARUS
UKRAINE
HUNGARY
ROMANIA
MOLDOVA
GEORGIA
CAUCASUS
TURKEY
IRAN
AFGHANISTAN
TURKMENISTAN
UZBEKISTAN
KAZAKHSTAN
KYRGYZSTAN
TAJIKISTAN
BLACK SEA
Sea of Azov
CASPIAN SEA
Aral Sea
White Sea
HELSINKI
Tallinn
RIGA
Vilnius
MINSK
KYYIV
BUDAPEST
BUCUREȘTI
Chișinău
Odesa
TBILISI
JEREVAN
BAKI
TEHRAN
SANKT-PETERBURG (LENINGRAD)
MOSKVA
Volgograd (Stalingrad)
Astrachan'
Rostov-na-Donu
Saratov
Samara (Kujbyšev)
Kazan'
Perm'
Jekaterinburg
Čel'abinsk
Orenburg
Ufa
Murmansk
Archangel'sk
TAŠKENT
ALMATY
Biškek
Dušanbe
Ašchabad
Mashhad
KARAKUMY
KYZYL KUM


| MAP FORM | chrebet | gora | guba | mys | ostrov | ozero | poluostrov | proliv | vodochranilišče |
|---|---|---|---|---|---|---|---|---|---|
| ENGLISH | range | mountain | bay | cape | island | lake | peninsula | strait | reservoir |
| DEUTSCH | Gebirge | Berg | Bucht | Kap | Insel | See | Halbinsel | Meeresstrasse | Stausee |
| ESPAÑOL | sierra | montaña | bahia | cabo | isla | lago | península | estrecho | embalse |
| FRANÇAIS | chaîne | montagne | baie | cap | île | lac | péninsule | détroit | réservoir |
| PORTUGUÊS | serra | montanha | baía | cabo | ilha | lago | península | estreito | reservatório |

KARSKOJE MORE
KARA SEA
MORE LAPTEVYCH
LAPTEV SEA
NOVAJA ZEML'A
SEVERNAJA ZEML'A
OSTROV KOMSOMOLEC
OSTROV OKT'ABR'SKOJ REVOL'UCII
OSTROV BOL'ŠEVIK
TAJMYR
POLUOSTROV
GORY BYRRANGA
POLUOSTROV JAMAL
GYDANSKIJ POLUOSTROV
SEVERO - SIBIRSKAJA NIZMENNOST'
PLATO PUTORANA
SREDNE-SIBIRSKOJE PLOSKOGORJE
ZAPADNO-SIBIRSKAJA RAVNINA
RUSSIA
JAKUTIJA
BURJATIJA
STANOVOJE NAGORJE
STANOVOY MOUNTAINS
JABLONOVYJ CHREBET
ZAPADNYJ SAJAN
SAJAN MOUNTAINS
VOSTOČNYJ SAJAN
SAJANY
ALTAJ
TUVA
MONGOLIA
CHINA
XINJIANG UYGUR ZIZHIQU
SINKIANG
MONGOL ALTAJN NURUU
CHANGAJN NURUU
Vorkuta
Noril'sk
Dudinka
Igarka
Dikson
Chatanga
Surgut
Tomsk
Novosibirsk
Kemerovo
Novokuzneck
Barnaul
Bijsk
Krasnojarsk
Abakan
Bratsk
Irkutsk
Angarsk
Ulan-Ude
Čita
Pavlodar
Semipalatinsk
Ust'-Kamenogorsk
Rubcovsk
Ulaanbaatar
Darchan
Mirnyj
Lensk
Ozero Bajkal
Lake Baikal
Arctic Circle
Copyright © by Rand McNally & Co.
Map prepared by Esselte Map Service AB, Stockholm.

Map continues pages 74-75

Map continues pages 90-91

Kilometers 0 200 400 600 Km.
Statute Miles 0 200 400 600 Mi.

Scale 1:12,000,000

One centimeter represents 120 kilometers.
One inch represents approximately 190 miles.
Lambert Conformal Conic Projection

BARENTS SEA
NOVAJA ZEML'A
KARSKOJE MORE
KARA SEA
SEVERNAJA ZEML'A
MORE LAPTEVYH
LAPTEV SEA
POLUOSTROV TAJMYR
GORY BYRRANGA
POLUOSTROV JAMAL
GYDANSKIJ POLUOSTROV
SEVERO-SIBIRSKAJA NIZMENNOST'
PLATO PUTORANA
SREDNE-SIBIRSKOJE PLOSKOGORJE
ZAPADNO-SIBIRSKAJA RAVNINA
SIBERIA
RUSSIA
KAZAKHSTAN
MONGOLIA
CHINA
URAL'SKIJE GORY
STANOVOJE NAGORJE
STANOVOY MOUNTAINS
SAJAN MOUNTAINS
ZAPADNYJ SAJAN
VOSTOČNYJ SAJAN
ALTAJ
TUVA
BURJATIJA
JABLONOVYJ CHREBET
Noril'sk
Dudinka
Dikson
Vorkuta
Surgut
Omsk
Tomsk
Novosibirsk
Barnaul
Kemerovo
Novokuzneck
Krasnojarsk
Bratsk
Irkutsk
Angarsk
Ulan-Ude
Čita
Ulaanbaatar
Semipalatinsk
Ust'-Kamenogorsk
Pavlodar
Rubcovsk
Abakan
Copyright © by Rand McNally & Co.
Map prepared by Esselte Map Service AB, Stockholm.
A-579395-264 -8 12

Map continues pages 72-73

Map continues pages 90-91

| MAP FORM | chrebet | gora | guba | mys | ostrov | ozero | poluostrov | proliv | vodochranilišče |
|---|---|---|---|---|---|---|---|---|---|
| ENGLISH | range | mountain | bay | cape | island | lake | peninsula | strait | reservoir |
| DEUTSCH | Gebirge | Berg | Bucht | Kap | Insel | See | Halbinsel | Meeresstrasse | Stausee |
| ESPAÑOL | sierra | montaña | bahia | cabo | isla | lago | peninsula | estrecho | embalse |
| FRANÇAIS | chaîne | montagne | baie | cap | île | lac | péninsule | détroit | réservoir |
| PORTUGUÊS | serra | montanha | baía | cabo | ilha | lago | península | estreito | reservatório |

Kilometers 0 200 400 600 Km.
Statute Miles 0 200 400 600 Mi.

Scale 1:12,000,000

One centimeter represents 120 kilometers.
One inch represents approximately 190 miles.
Lambert Conformal Conic Projection

ALASKA
UNITED STATES
Chukchi Sea
Bering Sea
VOSTOČNO-SIBIRSKOJE MORE
EAST SIBERIAN SEA
SEA OF OKHOTSK
OCHOTSKOJE MORE
SEA OF JAPAN
PACIFIC OCEAN
POLUOSTROV KAMČATKA
KAMCHATKA
KURIL'SKIJE OSTROVA
KURIL ISLANDS
OSTROV SACHALIN
SAKHALIN
HOKKAIDŌ
HONSHŪ
JAPAN
MANCHURIA
HEILONGJIANG
NEI MONGGOL ZIZHIQU
JAKUTIJA
SIBERIA
CHREBET ČERSKOGO
CHREBET SUNTAR-CHAJATA
CHREBET DŽUGDŽUR
STANOVOJ CHREBET
ALDANSKOJE NAGORJE
KOLYMSKAJA NIZMENNOST'
JUKAGIRSKOJE PLOSKOGORJE
ANADYRSKOJE PLOSKOGORJE
KORJAKSKOJE NAGORJE
SREDINNYJ CHREBET
PENŽINSKIJ CHREBET
MOMSKIJ CHREBET
AN'UJSKIJ CHREBET
BUREINSKIJ CHREBET
SICHOTE-ALIN'
KOMANDORSKIJE OSTROVA
ŠANTARSKIJE OSTROVA
OSTROV VRANGEL'A
NUNIVAK ISLAND
SAINT LAWRENCE ISLAND
SAINT MATTHEW ISLAND
OSTROV KOTEL'NYJ
Habomai, Shikotan, Kunashiri, and Etorofu, occupied since 1945, are claimed by Japan pending a final peace treaty.
Jakutsk
Magadan
Petropavlovsk-Kamčatskij
Chabarovsk
Komsomol'sk-na-Amure
Južno-Sachalinsk
Blagoveščensk
Vladivostok
Nachodka
Ussurijsk
Harbin
Qiqihar Tsitsihar
Sapporo
Asahikawa
Hakodate
Aomori
Ochotsk
Anadyr'
La Perouse Strait
120°
125°
135°
145°
150°
160°
170°
175°
180°

Map continues pages 26-27

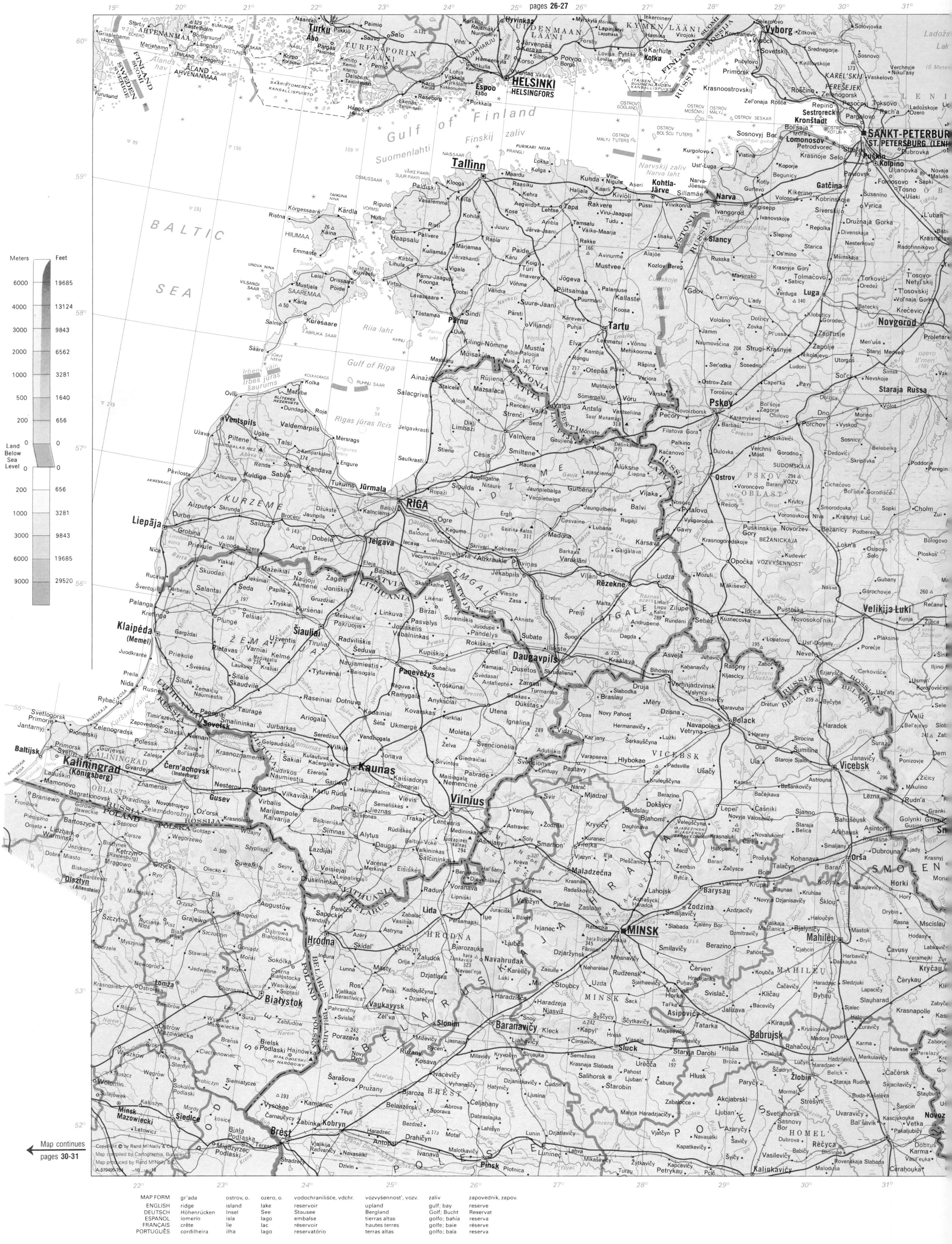
Gulf of Finland
Suomenlahti
Finskij zaliv
BALTIC SEA
Gulf of Riga
Riia laht
Rigas jūras līcis
HELSINKI
HELSINGFORS
SANKT-PETERBURG
ST. PETERSBURG
Tallinn
RIGA
Vilnius
MINSK
Kaliningrad
(Königsberg)
Novgorod
Pskov
Tartu
Daugavpils
Kaunas
Klaipėda
(Memel)
Liepāja
Hrodna
Brest
Vicebsk
Mahilëu
Meters
Feet
6000
19685
4000
13124
3000
9843
2000
6562
1000
3281
500
1640
200
656
0
Land Below Sea Level
9000
29520

Map continues pages 30-31

| MAP FORM | gr'ada | ostrov, o. | ozero, o. | vodochranilišče, vdchr. | vozvyšennost', vozv. | zaliv | zapovednik, zapov. |
|---|---|---|---|---|---|---|---|
| ENGLISH | ridge | island | lake | reservoir | upland | gulf; bay | reserve |
| DEUTSCH | Höhenrücken | Insel | See | Stausee | Bergland | Golf; Bucht | Reservat |
| ESPAÑOL | lomerío | isla | lago | embalse | tierras altas | golfo; bahía | reserva |
| FRANÇAIS | crête | île | lac | réservoir | hautes terres | golfe; baie | réserve |
| PORTUGUÊS | cordilheira | ilha | lago | reservatório | terras altas | golfo; baía | reserva |

Map continues pages 24-25

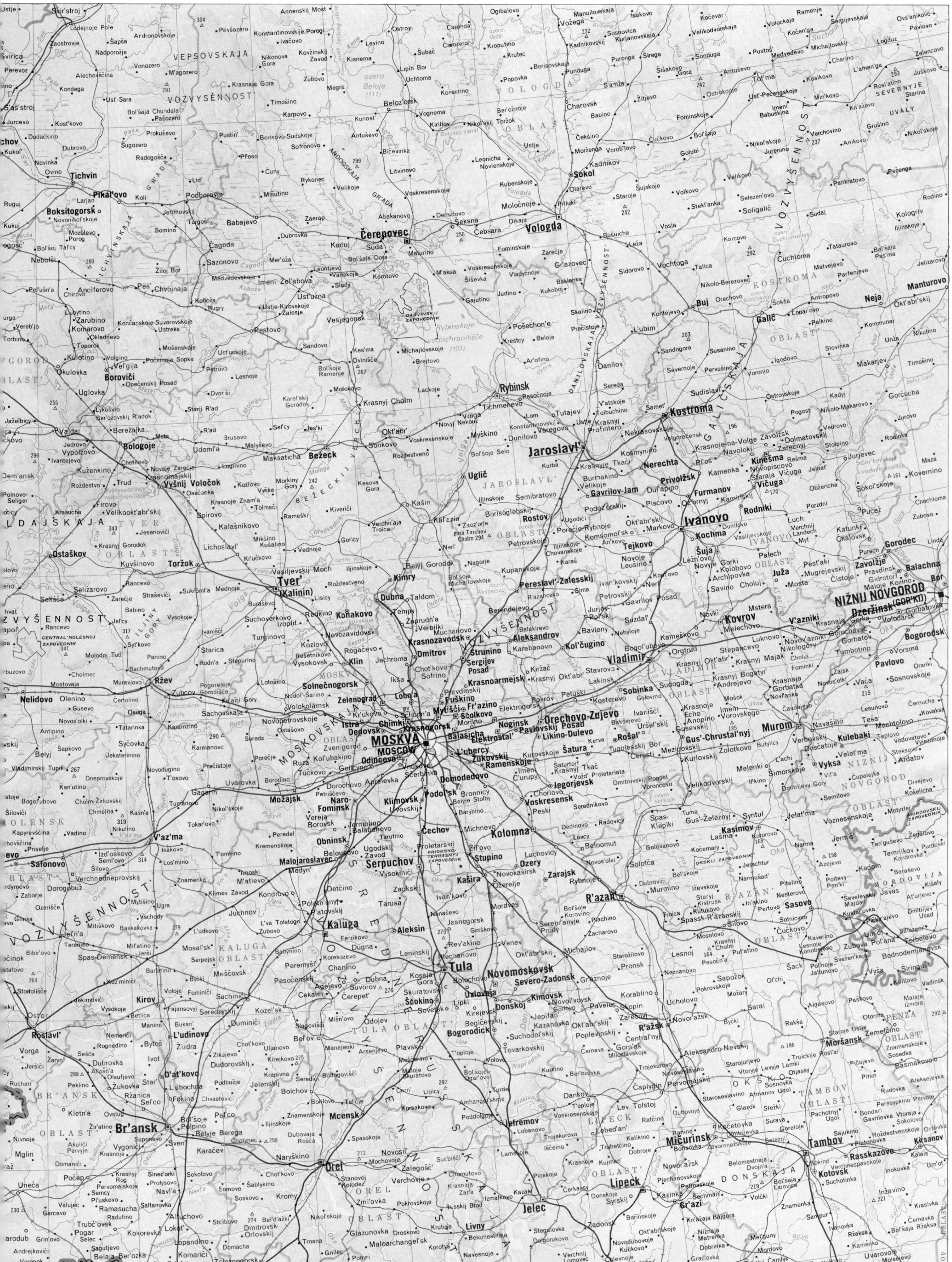
MOSKVA
MOSCOW
Tver' (Kalinin)
Jaroslavl'
Kostroma
Ivanovo
Vladimir
Rybinsk
Vologda
Čerepovec
Tula
Kaluga
Br'ansk
Orel
R'azan'
Lipeck
Tambov
Jelec
Mičurinsk
Nižnij Novgorod (Gor'kij)
Dzeržinsk
Smolensk
Tichvin
Boksitogorsk
Bologoje
Vyšnij Voloček
Toržok
Rževs
Kolomna
Serpuchov
Podol'sk
Kovrov
Murom
Novomoskovsk
Orechovo-Zujevo
Sergijev Posad
Dmitrov
Klin
Pereslavl'-Zalesskij
Rostov
Uglič
Galič
Buj
Manturovo
Neja
Kinešma
Sokol
Vjaz'ma
Roslavl'
Lodejnoje Pole
VEPSOVSKAJA VOZVYŠENNOST'
VOZVYŠENNOST'
JAROSLAVL' OBLAST'
KOSTROMA OBLAST'
VLADIMIR OBLAST'
MOSKOVSKAJA OBLAST'
TULA OBLAST'
KALUGA OBLAST'
BR'ANSK OBLAST'
OREL OBLAST'
LIPECK OBLAST'
TAMBOV OBLAST'
R'AZAN' OBLAST'
SREDNERUSSKAJA VOZVYŠENNOST'
OKSKO-DONSKAJA RAVNINA
Oka
Volga
Rybinskoje vodochranilišče
RUSSIA
UKRAINE

Map continues pages 80-81

Map continues pages 78-79

Kilometers 0 50 100 150 Km.
Statute Miles 0 50 100 150 Mi.

Scale 1:3,000,000

One centimeter represents 30 kilometers.
One inch represents approximately 47 miles.
Lambert Conformal Conic Projection

Map continues
pages 30-31

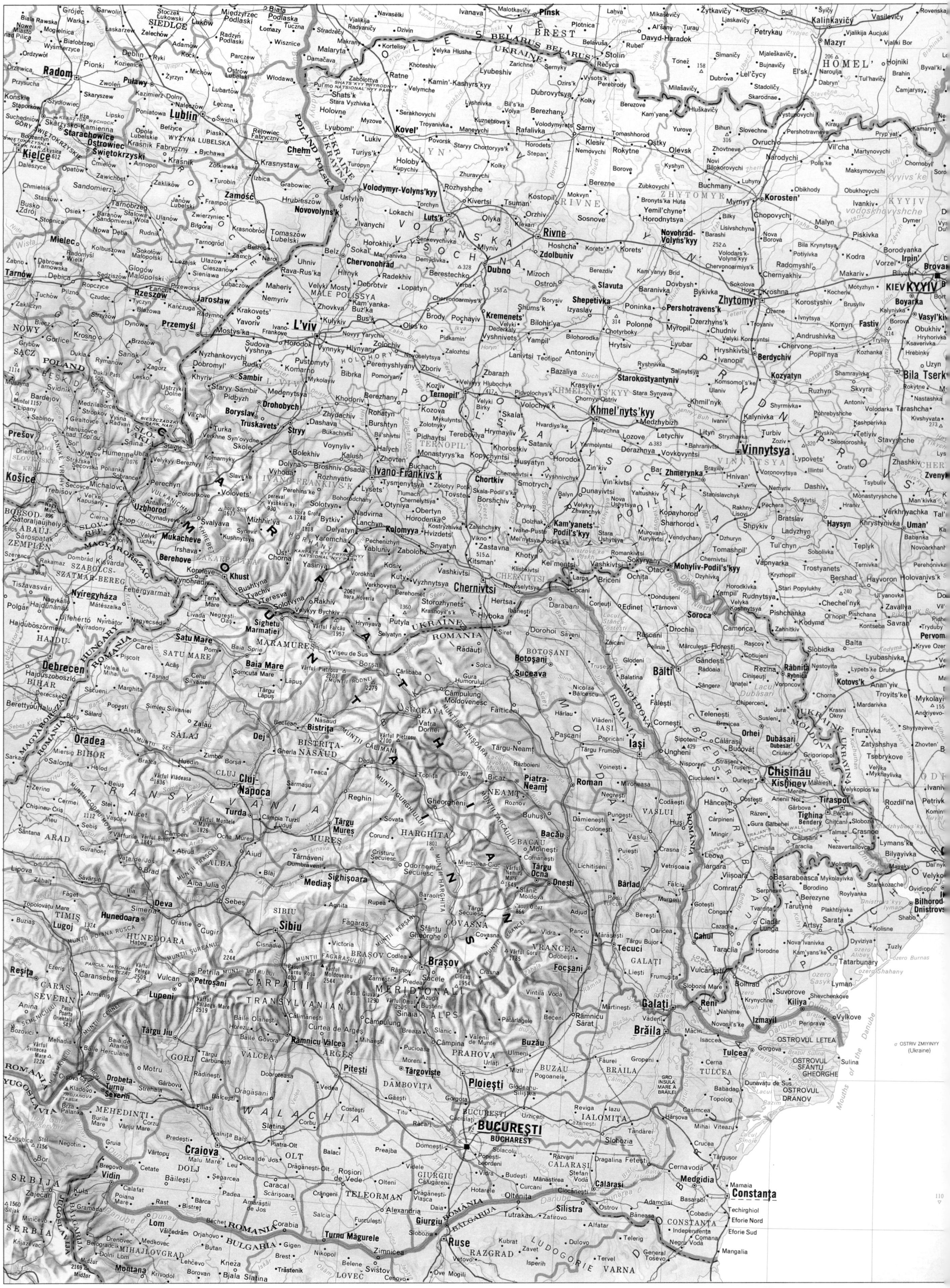
BELARUS
UKRAINE
POLAND
POLSKA
ROMANIA
MOLDOVA
HUNGARY
MAGYARORSZÁG
YUGOSLAVIA
BULGARIA
SLOVAKIA
CARPATHIANS
CARPAŢII MERIDIONALI
TRANSYLVANIAN ALPS
TRANSYLVANIA
WALACHIA
MOLDAVIA
VOLYN'
PODILLIA
Kiev KYYIV
L'viv
Rivne
Zhytomyr
Vinnytsya
Khmel'nyts'kyy
Ternopil'
Ivano-Frankivs'k
Chernivtsi
Lutsk
Uzhhorod
Chişinău
Iaşi
Cluj-Napoca
Braşov
Ploieşti
BUCUREŞTI
BUCHAREST
Constanţa
Craiova
Galaţi
Brăila
Lublin
Rzeszów
Kielce
Radom
Debrecen
Košice
Mouths of the Danube

Map continues
pages 38-39

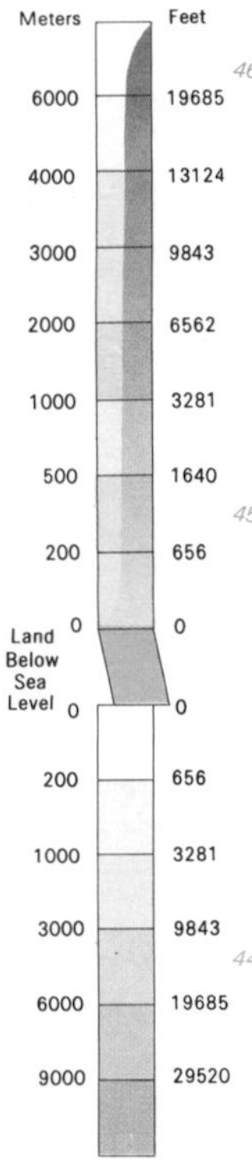
Meters
Feet
6000
19685
4000
13124
3000
9843
2000
6562
1000
3281
500
1640
200
656
0
0
Land Below Sea Level
0
0
200
656
1000
3281
3000
9843
6000
19685
9000
29520

| MAP FORM | hora | liman | lyman | mys | nyzovyna | ozero | vysochyna | zaliv | zatoka |
|---|---|---|---|---|---|---|---|---|---|
| ENGLISH | mountain | bay | bay | cape | plain | lake | upland | bay | bay |
| DEUTSCH | Berg | Bucht | Bucht | Kap | Ebene | See | Bergland | Bucht | Bucht |
| ESPAÑOL | montaña | bahía | bahía | cabo | llanno | lago | tierras altas | bahía | bahía |
| FRANÇAIS | montagne | baie | baie | cap | plaine | lac | hautes terres | baie | baie |
| PORTUGUÊS | montanha | baía | baía | cabo | planicie | lago | terras altas | baía | baía |

Map continues pages 76-77

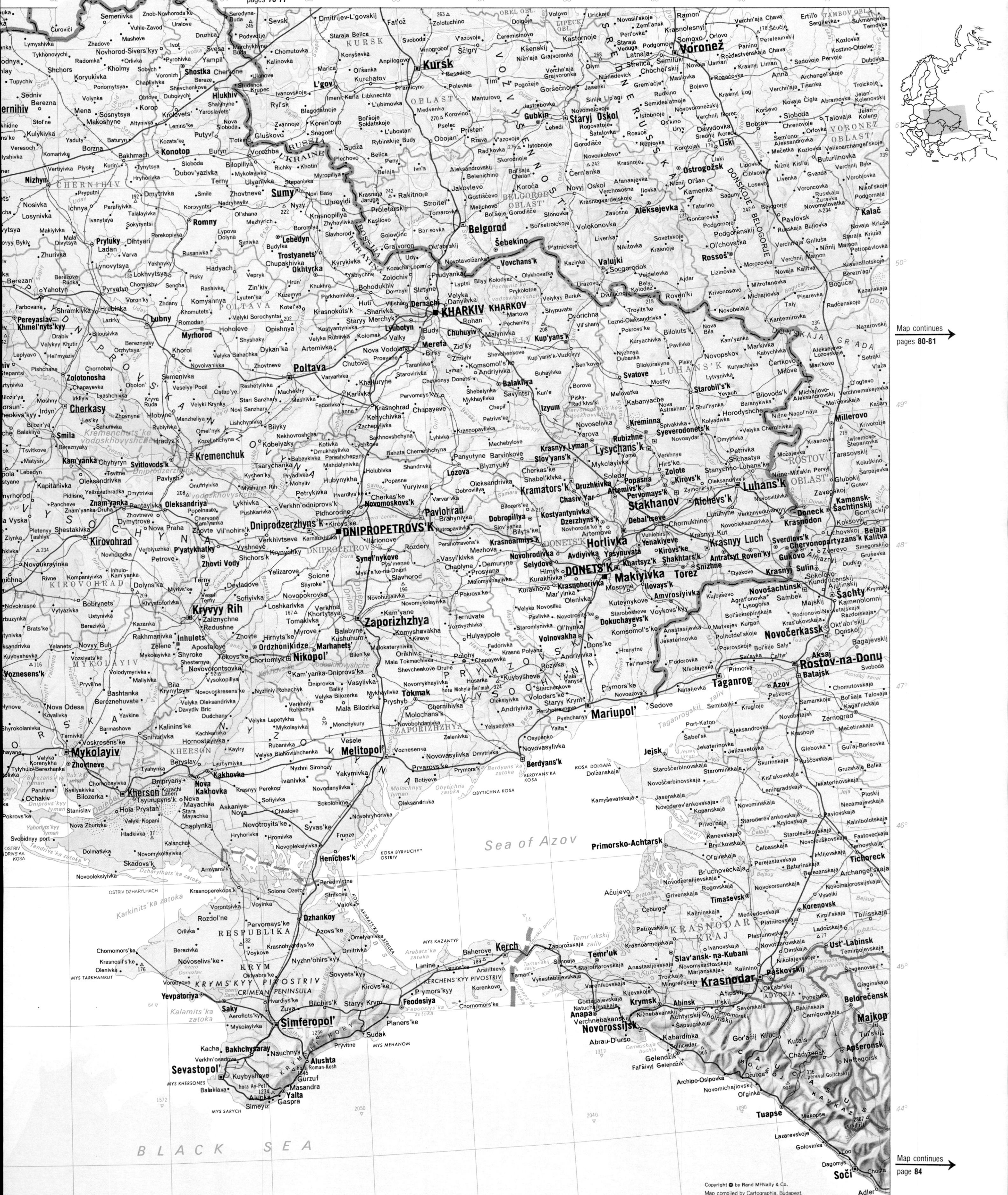
BLACK SEA
Sea of Azov
KHARKIV
DNIPROPETROVS'K
DONETS'K
Zaporizhzhya
Kryvyy Rih
Mykolayiv
Kherson
Simferopol'
Sevastopol'
Kerch
Poltava
Sumy
Kursk
Voronež
Belgorod
Luhans'k
Rostov-na-Donu
Krasnodar
Novorossijsk
Soči
Mariupol'
Taganrog
Melitopol'
Kremenchuk
Kirovohrad
Cherkasy
Konotop
KRYMS'KYY PIVOSTRIV
CRIMEAN PENINSULA
RESPUBLIKA KRYM
KRASNODAR KRAJ
ROSTOV OBLAST'
BELGOROD OBLAST'
KURSK
VORONEZ OBLAST'
Copyright © by Rand McNally & Co.
Map compiled by Cartographia, Budapest.
Map produced by Rand McNally & Co.
A-571900-764

Map continues pages 80-81

Map continues page 84

Kilometers 0 50 100 150 Km.
Statute Miles 0 50 100 150 Mi.

Scale 1:3,000,000
One centimeter represents 30 kilometers.
One inch represents approximately 47 miles.
Lambert Conformal Conic Projection

Map continues pages 24-25

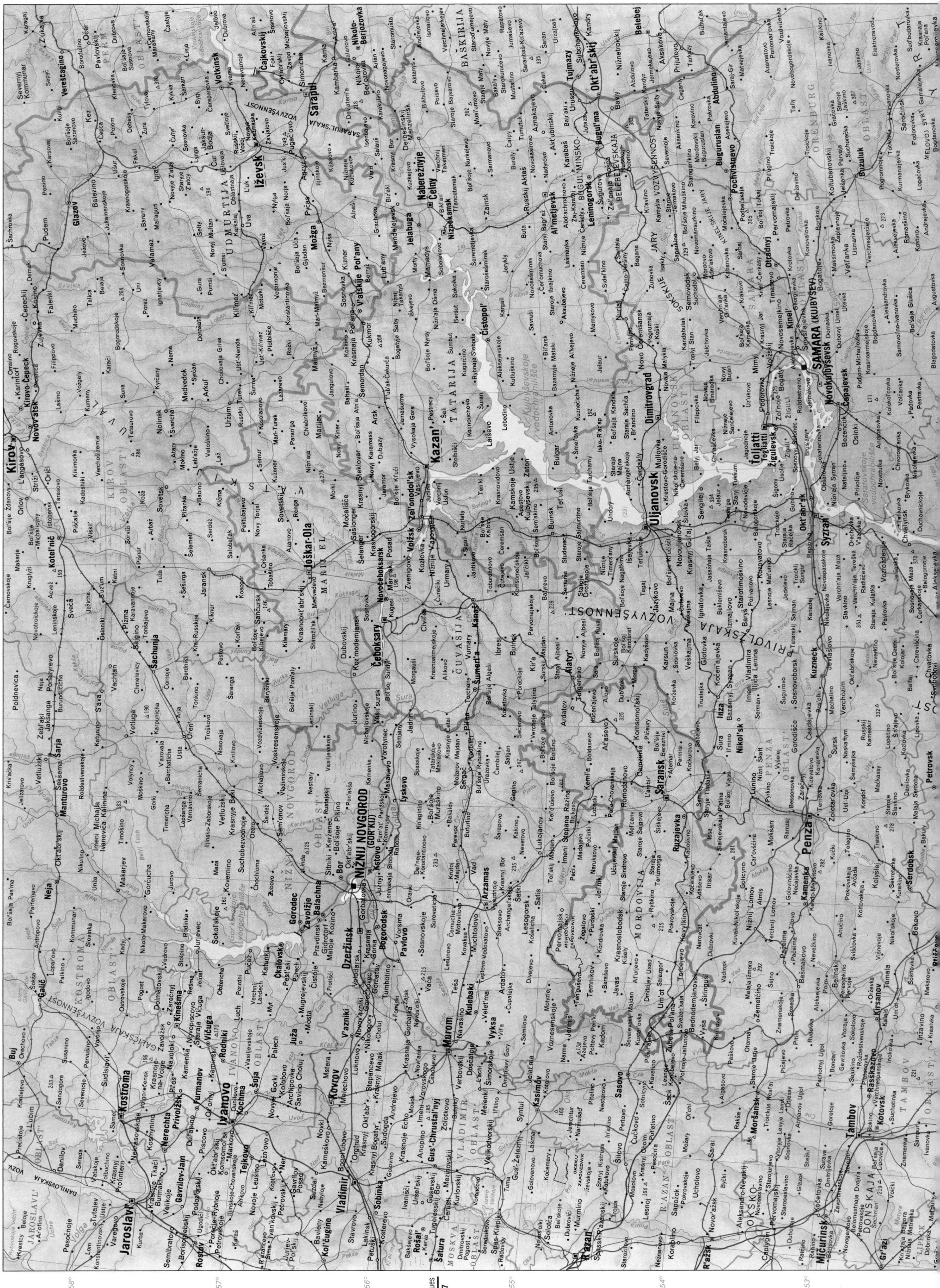
Kirov
Iževsk
Kazan'
Nižnij Novgorod (Gor'kij)
Jaroslavl'
Kostroma
Ivanovo
Vladimir
Čeboksary
Joškar-Ola
Uljanovsk
Samara (Kujbyšev)
Toljatti
Syzran'
Penza
Saransk
Tambov
Rjazan'
Dzeržinsk
Murom
Arzamas
Dimitrovgrad
Naberežnyje Čelny
Nižnekamsk
Al'metjevsk
Bugul'ma
Čistopol'
Sarapul
Votkinsk
Glazov
Mičurinsk
Tatarija
Udmurtija
Čuvašija
Mordovija

Map continues pages 76-77

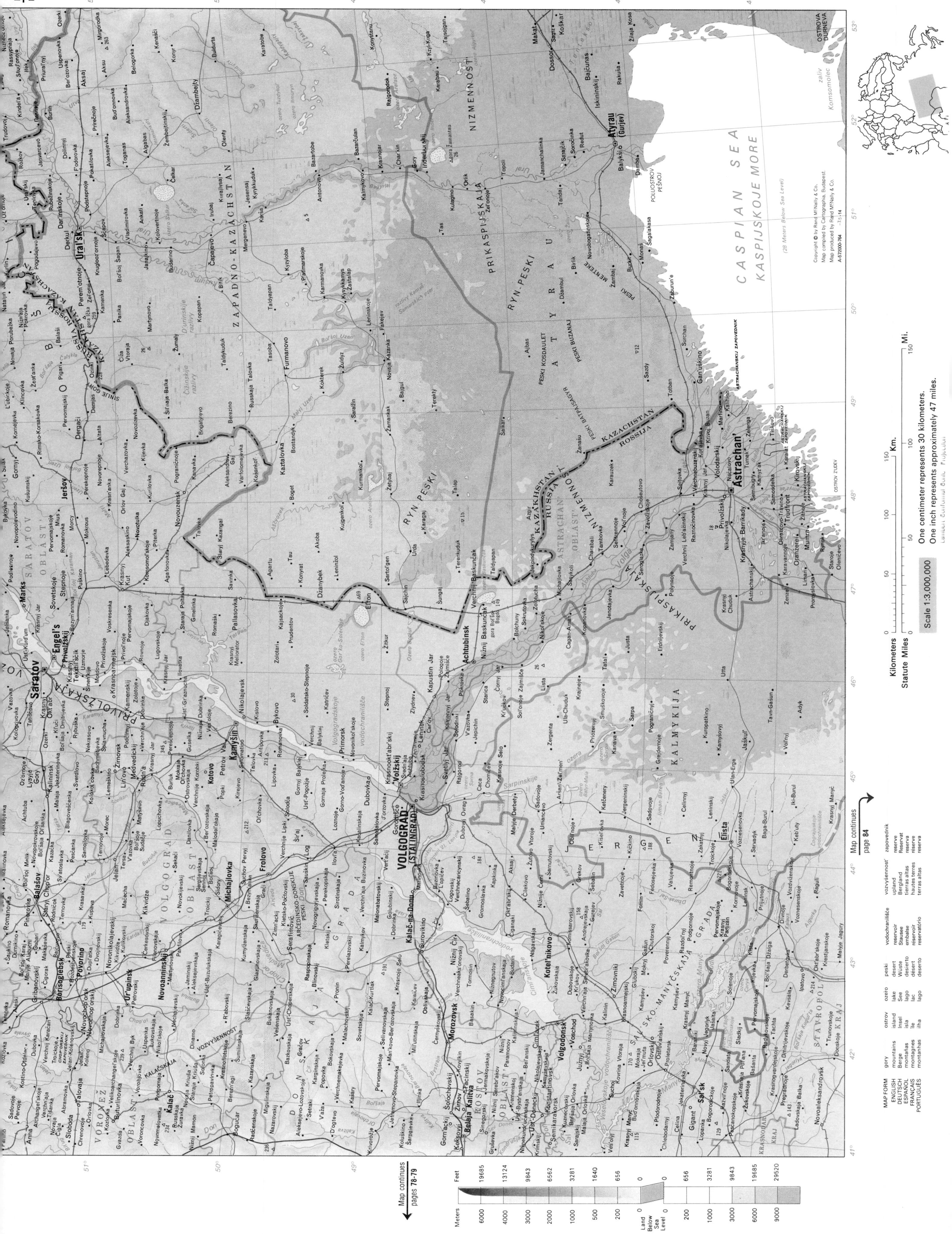
Map continues pages 86-87
Map continues page 84
Map continues pages 78-79
CASPIAN SEA
KASPIJSKOJE MORE
PRIKASPIJSKAJA NIZMENNOST'
ZAPADNO-KAZACHSTAN
SARATOV OBLAST'
VOLGOGRAD OBLAST'
ASTRACHAN' OBLAST'
KALMYKIJA
ROSTOV OBLAST'
VORONEŽ OBLAST'
STAVROPOL' KRAJ
KRASNODAR KRAJ
RYN-PESKI
PRIVOLŽSKAJA VOZVYŠENNOST'
KAZACHSTAN
ROSSIJA
Saratov
Engel's
Volgograd (Stalingrad)
Astrachan'
Atyrau (Gurjev)
Ural'sk
Elista
Kamyšin
Volžskij
Balašov
Michajlovka
Kalač
Volgodonsk
Sal'sk
Copyright © by Rand McNally & Co.
Map compiled by Cartographia, Budapest.
Map produced by Rand McNally & Co.
A-572000-764 -T3-14
Scale 1:3,000,000
One centimeter represents 30 kilometers.
One inch represents approximately 47 miles.
Kilometers
Statute Miles
MAP FORM
ENGLISH
DEUTSCH
ESPAÑOL
FRANÇAIS
PORTUGUÊS
Meters
Feet
Land Below Sea Level

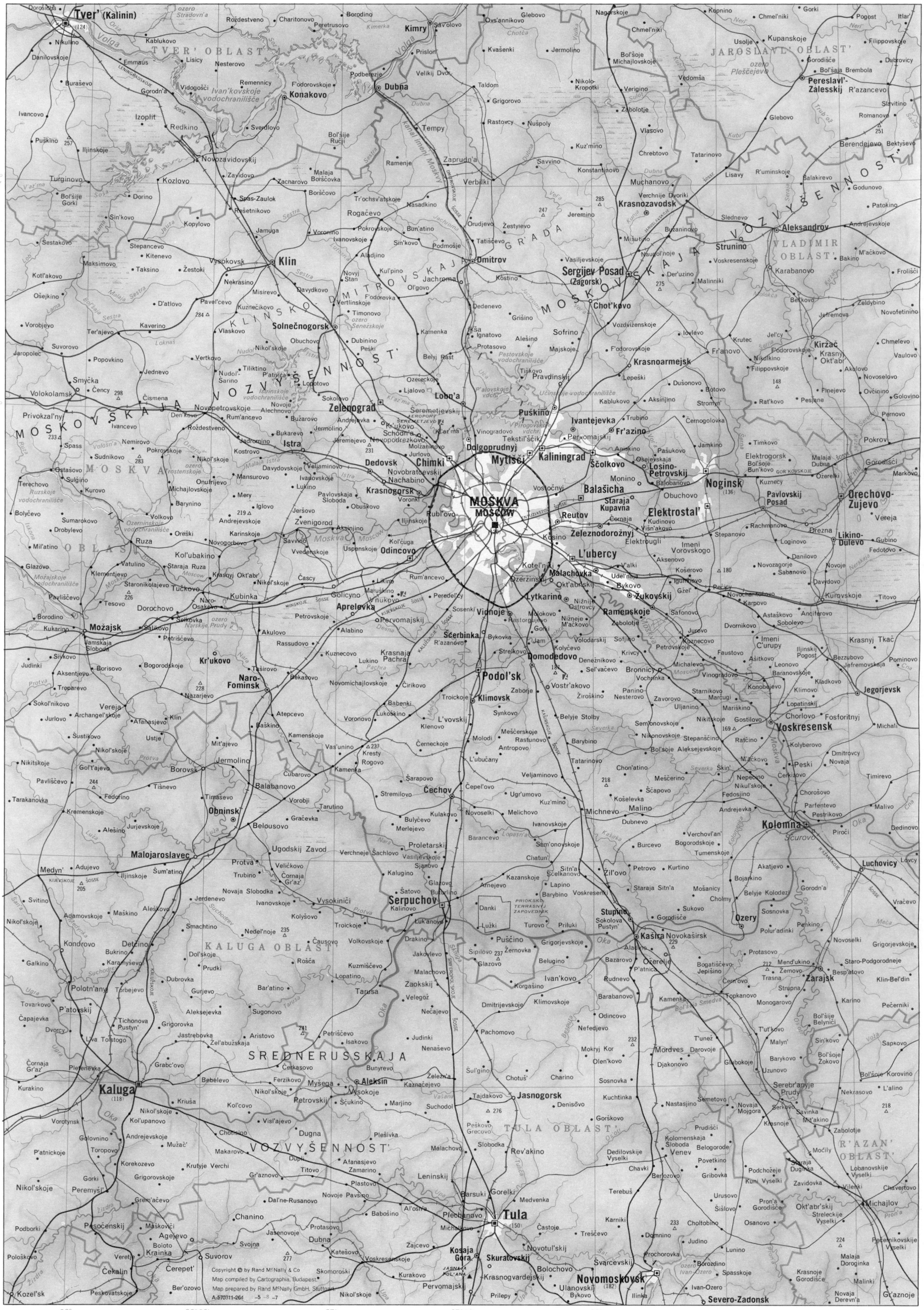
Tver' (Kalinin)
TVER' OBLAST'
JAROSLAVL' OBLAST'
Kimry
Dubna
Konakovo
Pereslavl'-Zalesskij
Aleksandrov
VLADIMIR OBLAST'
Klin
Dmitrov
Sergijev Posad (Zagorsk)
Solnečnogorsk
Zelenograd
Istra
Puškino
Mytišči
Kaliningrad
Fr'azino
Ščolkovo
Noginsk
Orechovo-Zujevo
Elektrostal'
Balašicha
Reutov
Železnodorožnyj
L'ubercy
MOSKVA
MOSCOW
Chimki
Krasnogorsk
Odincovo
Zvenigorod
Volokolamsk
Ruza
Možajsk
Naro-Fominsk
Podol'sk
Domodedovo
Vidnoje
Ramenskoje
Žukovskij
Voskresensk
Kolomna
Jegorjevsk
Serpuchov
Protvino
Obninsk
Malojaroslavec
KALUGA OBLAST'
Kaluga
Aleksin
SREDNERUSSKAJA VOZVYŠENNOST'
TULA OBLAST'
Tula
Novomoskovsk
Kašira
Stupino
Zarajsk
Luchovicy
Ozery
R'AZAN' OBLAST'
Čechov
MOSKOVSKAJA VOZVYŠENNOST'
KLINSKO-DMITROVSKAJA GR'ADA
MOSKVA OBLAST'
36°
36°30'
37°
37°30'
38°
38°30'
39°
56° 30'
56°
55° 30'
55°
54° 30'
Copyright © by Rand McNally & Co.
Map compiled by Cartographia, Budapest
Map prepared by Rand McNally GmbH, Stuttgart
A-570311-264 -5 -8 -7

| MAP FORM | gr'ada | ozero | vodochranilišče, vdchr. | vozvyšennost' | zapovednik |
|---|---|---|---|---|---|
| ENGLISH | ridge | lake | reservoir | upland | reserve |
| DEUTSCH | Höhenrücken | See | Stausee | Bergland | Reservat |
| ESPAÑOL | lomerío | lago | embalse | tierras altas | reserva |
| FRANÇAIS | crête | lac | réservoir | hautes terres | réserve |
| PORTUGUÊS | cordilheira | lago | reservatório | terras altas | reserva |

Kilometers 0 10 20 30 40 50 Km.
Statute Miles 0 10 20 30 40 50 Mi.

Scale 1:1,000,000

One centimeter represents 10 kilometers.
One inch represents approximately 16 miles.
Lambert Conformal Conic Projection

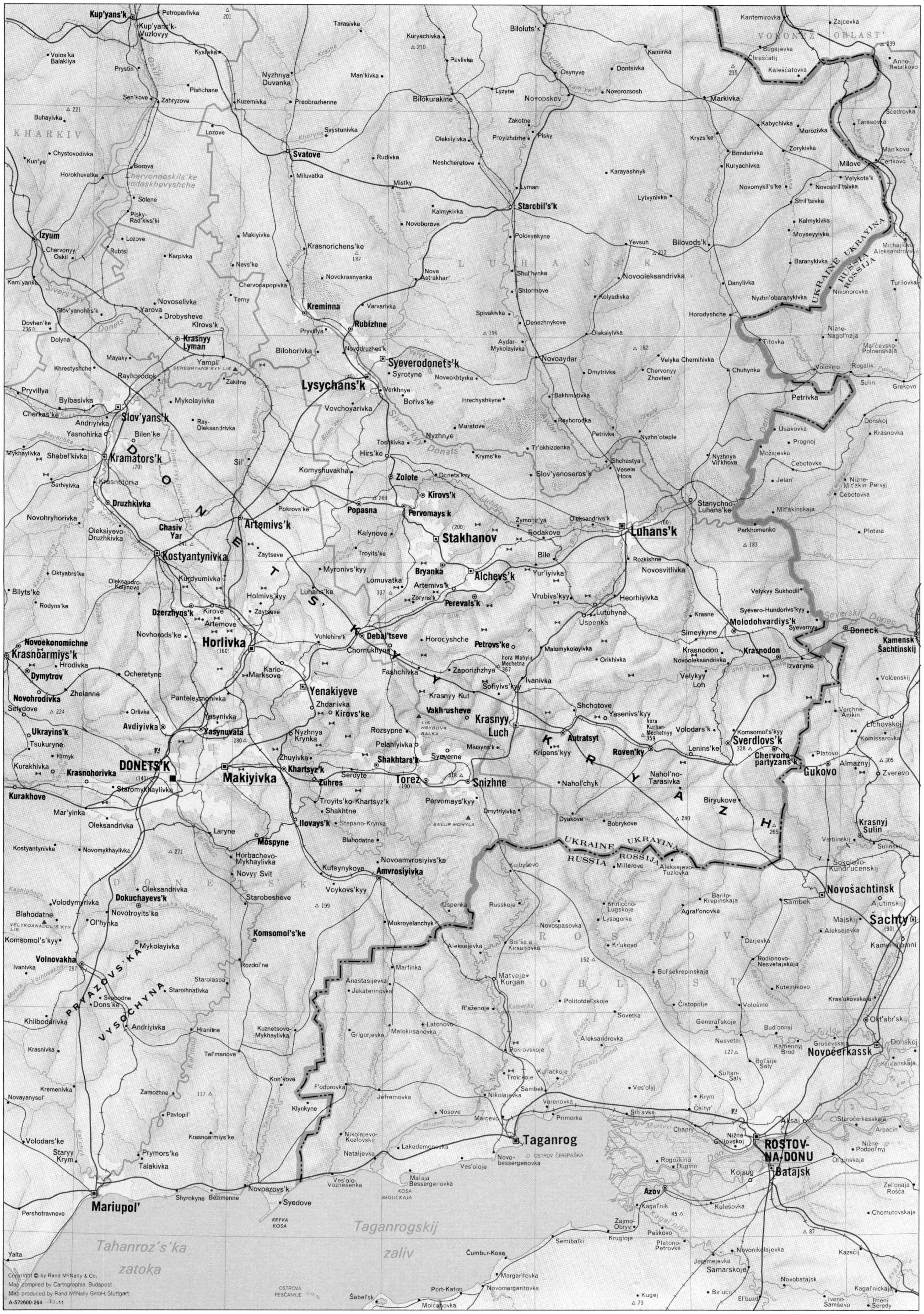
37° 30'
38°
38° 30'
39°
39° 30'
40°
49° 30'
49°
48° 30'
48°
47° 30'
47°
KHARKIV
LUHANSK
DONETSK
DONETS'KYY KRYAZH
VORONEZ' OBLAST'
ROSTOV OBLAST'
UKRAINE UKRAYINA RUSSIA ROSSIJA
PRYAZOVS'KA VYSOCHYNA
Sivers'kyy Donets'
Taganrogskij zaliv
Tahanroz's'ka zatoka
Kup'yans'k
Svatove
Starobil's'k
Izyum
Kreminna
Rubizhne
Syeverodonets'k
Lysychans'k
Slov'yans'k
Kramators'k
Druzhkivka
Kostyantynivka
Artemivs'k
Horlivka
Yenakiyeve
Makiyivka
DONETS'K
Krasnoarmiys'k
Kurakhove
Volnovakha
Mariupol'
Alchevs'k
Stakhanov
Luhans'k
Krasnyy Luch
Antratsyt
Sverdlovs'k
Krasnodon
Torez
Snizhne
Shakhtars'k
Khartsyz'k
Ilovays'k
Amvrosiyivka
Taganrog
ROSTOV-NA-DONU
Batajsk
Azov
Novočerkassk
Šachty
Novošachtinsk
Gukovo
Doneck
Kamensk Šachtinskij
Millerovo
Kantemirovka
Rossoš'
Bilovods'k
Markivka
Novopskov
Bilokurakine
Chervonopartyzans'k
Molodohvardiys'k
Rovenky
Debal'tseve
Dzerzhyns'k
Dymytrov
Dokuchayevs'k
Novoazovs'k
Matveyev Kurgan

| MAP FORM | kosa | ostrov, o. | vodoskhovyshche, vdskhv. | vysochyna, vys. | zaliv | zatoka |
|---|---|---|---|---|---|---|
| ENGLISH | spit | island | reservoir | upland | bay | bay |
| DEUTSCH | Landzunge | Insel | Stausee | Bergland | Bucht | Bucht |
| ESPAÑOL | lengua de tierra | isla | embalse | tierras altas | bahía | bahía |
| FRANÇAIS | flèche | île | réservoir | hautes terres | baie | baie |
| PORTUGUÊS | ponta de terra | ilha | reservatório | terras altas | baía | baía |

Kilometers 0 10 20 30 40 50 Km.
Statute Miles 0 10 20 30 40 50 M

Scale 1:1,000,000

One centimeter represents 10 kilometers.
One inch represents approximately 16 miles.
Lambert Conformal Conic Projection

# Caucasus and Transcaucasia / Kaukasus und Transkaukasien / Cáucaso y Transcaucasia
# Caucasie et Transcaucasie / Cáucaso e Transcaucásia

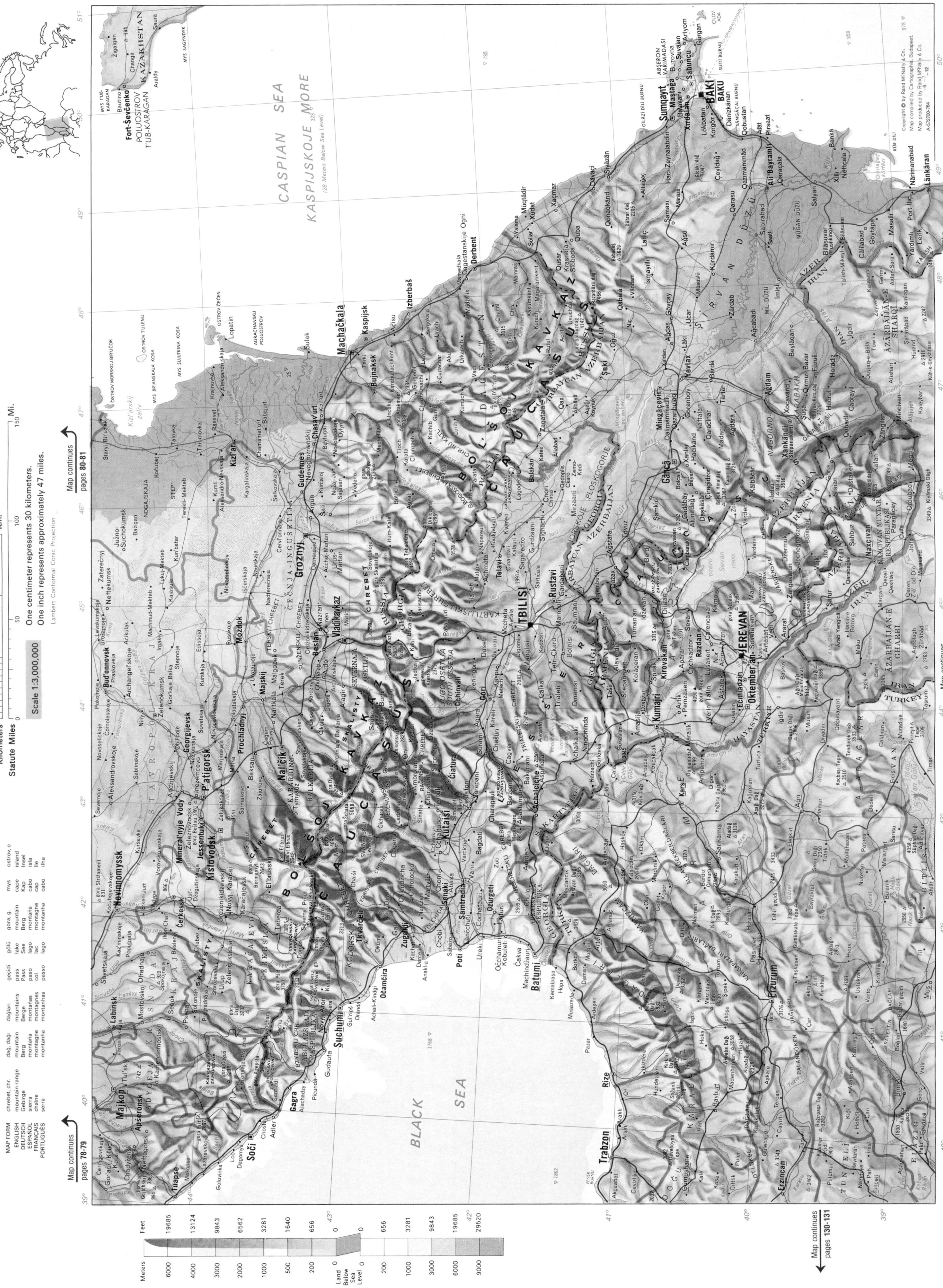

CASPIAN SEA
KASPIJSKOJE MORE
(28 Meters Below Sea Level)
BLACK SEA
BOL'ŠOJ KAVKAZ
CAUCASUS
KAZAKHSTAN
TBILISI
JEREVAN
BAKI
Groznyj
Machačkala
Vladikavkaz
Nal'čik
Suchumi
Batumi
Trabzon
Erzurum
Kilometers 0 50 100 150 Km.
Statute Miles 0 50 100 150 Mi.
Scale 1:3,000,000
One centimeter represents 30 kilometers.
One inch represents approximately 47 miles.
Lambert Conformal Conic Projection
Map continues pages 78-79
Map continues pages 80-81
Map continues pages 128-129
Map continues pages 130-131
MAP FORM / ENGLISH / DEUTSCH / ESPAÑOL / FRANÇAIS / PORTUGUÊS
chrebet, chr. / mountain range / Gebirge / sierra / chaîne / serra
dag, dagi / mountain / Berg / montaña / montagne / montanha
dağları / mountains / Berge / montañas / montagnes / montanhas
geçidi / pass / Pass / paso / col / passo
gölü / lake / See / lago / lac / lago
gora, g. / mountain / Berg / montaña / montagne / montanha
mys / cape / Kap / cabo / cap / cabo
ostrov, o / island / Insel / isla / île / ilha
Meters / Feet
6000 19685
4000 13124
3000 9843
2000 6562
1000 3281
500 1640
200 656
0 0
Land Below Sea Level
Copyright © by Rand McNally & Co.
Map compiled by Cartographia, Budapest.
Map produced by Rand McNally & Co.

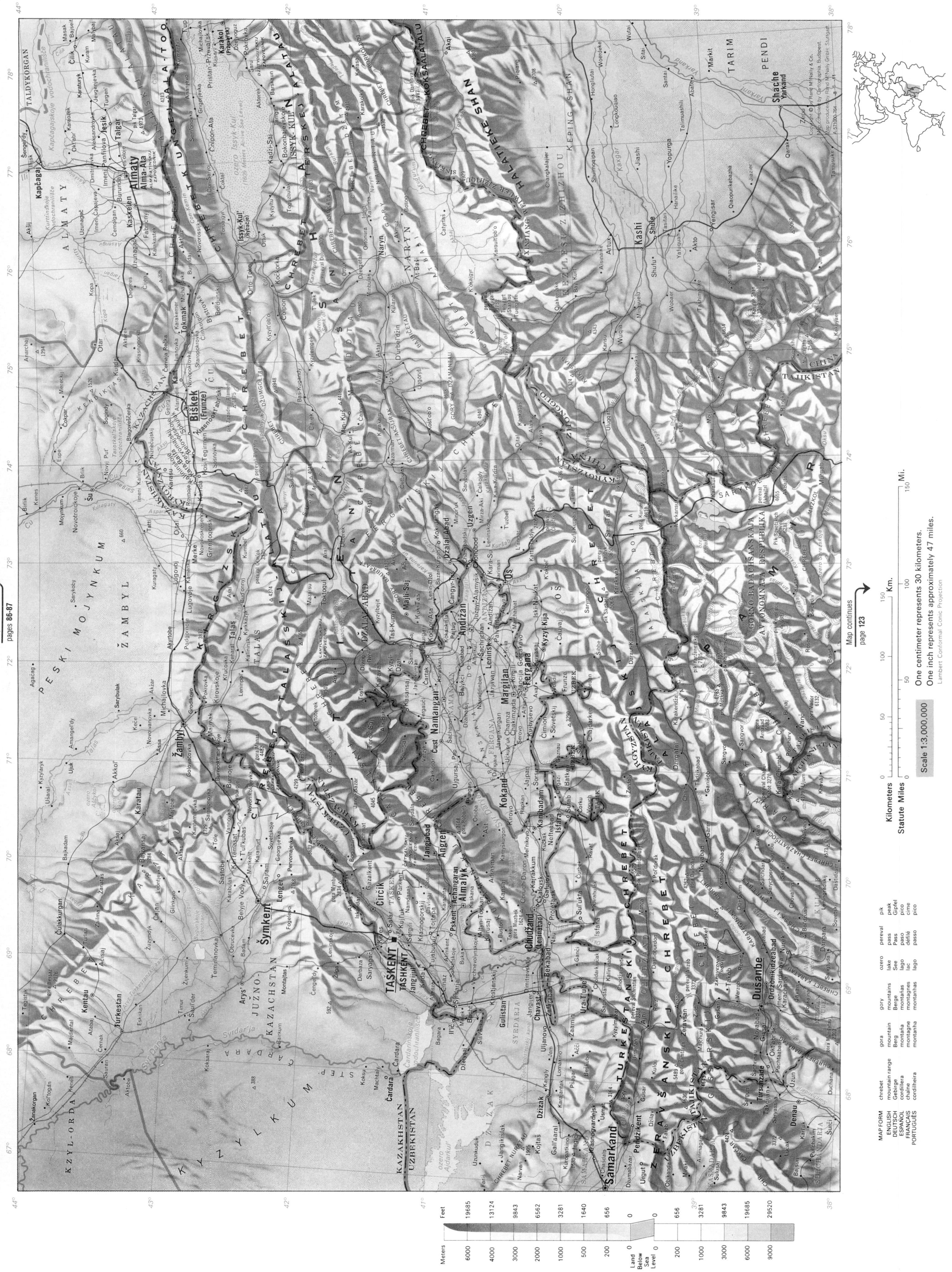
Map continues pages 86-87
Map continues page 123
Scale 1:3,000,000
One centimeter represents 30 kilometers.
One inch represents approximately 47 miles.
Lambert Conformal Conic Projection
Kilometers
Statute Miles
Km.
Mi.
MAP FORM
ENGLISH
DEUTSCH
ESPAÑOL
FRANÇAIS
PORTUGUÊS
chrebet
mountain range
Gebirge
cordillera
chaîne
cordilheira
gora
mountain
Berg
montaña
montagne
montanha
gory
mountains
Berge
montañas
montagnes
montanhas
ozero
lake
See
lago
lac
lago
pereval
pass
Pass
paso
défilé
passo
pik
peak
Gipfel
pico
cime
pico
Feet
Meters
Land Below Sea Level
TAŠKENT
Biškek
Almaty
Dušanbe
Samarkand
Kashi
Šymkent
Žambyl
Andižan
Namangan
Kokand
Fergana
Oš
KAZAKHSTAN
UZBEKISTAN
TAJIKISTAN
CHINA

Map continues pages 72-73

Map continues pages 24-25

Map continues pages 80-81

Kirov
Perm'
Iževsk
Kazan'
Ufa
Nižnij Tagil
JEKATERINBURG (SVERDLOVSK)
T'umen'
Kurgan
ČEL'ABINSK
Magnitogorsk
Orenburg
SAMARA
Ural'sk
Orsk
Akt'ubinsk
Kustanaj
Petropavlovsk
Kokčetav
Arkalyk
Aral'sk
Kzyl-Orda
Turkestan
Žezkazgan
Berezniki
Sterlitamak
Zlatoust
Miass
Novotroick
Naberežnyje Čelny
URAL'SKIJE GORY
KAZAKHSTAN KAZACHSTAN
UZBEKISTAN
RUSSIA ROSSIJA
KAZACHSTAN
KARAKALPAK RESPUBLIKA
Aral Sea
Caspian Sea
Copyright © by Rand McNally & Co.
Map compiled by Cartographia, Budapest.
Map produced by Rand McNally & Co.
A-579500-764

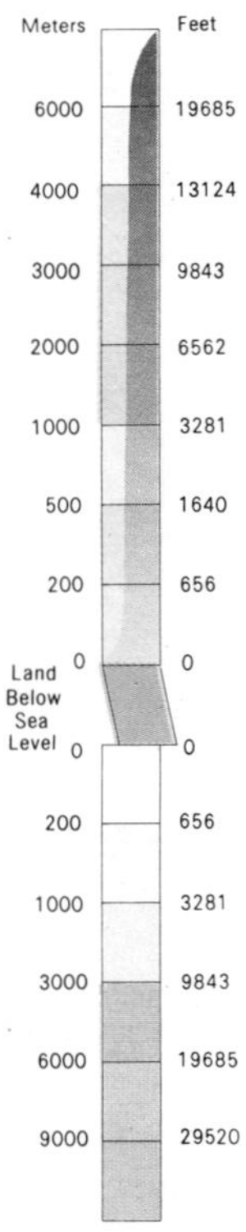
Meters
Feet
6000
19685
4000
13124
3000
9843
2000
6562
1000
3281
500
1640
200
656
0
0
Land Below Sea Level
0
0
200
656
1000
3281
3000
9843
6000
19685
9000
29520

Map continues page 85

| MAP FORM | chrebet | gora | hu | ozero | plato | porog |
|---|---|---|---|---|---|---|
| ENGLISH | mountain range | mountain | lake | lake | plateau | waterfall |
| DEUTSCH | Gebirge | Berg | See | See | Hochebene | Wasserfall |
| ESPAÑOL | cordillera | montaña | lago | lago | meseta | cascada |
| FRANÇAIS | chaîne | montagne | lac | lac | plateau | chute d'eau |
| PORTUGUÊS | cordilheira | montanha | lago | lago | planalto | queda d'água |

NOVOSIBIRSK
OMSK
Tomsk
Kemerovo
Novokuzneck
Barnaul
Pavlodar
Semipalatinsk
Ust'-Kamenogorsk
Karaganda
Krasnojarsk
Abakan
Bijsk
Almaty
Balchaš
T O M S K O B L A S T'
K R A S N O J A R S K I J K R A J
A L T A J
X I N J I A N G
U Y G U R
Z I Z H I Q U
T I E N S H A N
J U N G G A R P E N D I
TUVA
MONGOLIA
CHINA
KAZAKHSTAN
RUSSIA

Map continues page 88

Kilometers 0 100 200 300 Km.
Statute Miles 0 100 200 300 Mi.

Scale 1:6,000,000

One centimeter represents 60 kilometers.
One inch represents approximately 95 miles.
Lambert Conformal Conic Projection

Map continues page 89

Krasnojarsk
Irkutsk
Ulan-Ude
Čita
Bratsk
Ulaanbaatar
Kyzyl
Abakan
Angarsk
Ust'-Ilimsk
Baikal
RUSSIA
MONGOLIA
CHINA
STANOVOJE NAGORJE
SEVERO-BAJKAL'SKOJE NAGORJE
VITIMSKOJE PLOSKOGORJE
SAJANY SAJAN MOUNTAINS
JABLONOVYJ CHREBET
BURJATIJA
IRKUTSK OBLAST'
KRASNOJARSK KRAJ
TUVA
Copyright © by Rand McNally & Co.
Map compiled by Cartographia, Budapest.
Map produced by Rand McNally & Co.
A-572800-764 -5 -1-10

| MAP FORM | chrebet | gora | nuruu | nuur | ozero, o. | porog | uul |
|---|---|---|---|---|---|---|---|
| ENGLISH | mountain range | mountain | mountain range | lake | lake | waterfall | mountains |
| DEUTSCH | Gebirge | Berg | Gebirge | See | See | Wasserfall | Berge |
| ESPAÑOL | cordillera | montaña | cordillera | lago | lago | cascada | montañas |
| FRANÇAIS | chaîne | montagne | chaîne | lac | lac | chute d'eau | montagnes |
| PORTUGUÊS | cordilheira | montanha | cordilheira | lago | lago | queda d'água | montanhas |

Kilometers 0 100 200 300 Km.
Statute Miles 0 100 200 300 Mi.

Scale 1:6,000,000

One centimeter represents 60 kilometers.
One inch represents approximately 95 miles.
Lambert Conformal Conic Projection

Map continues pages 74-75

Map continues pages 86-87

Map continues pages 102-103

| Meters | Feet |
|---|---|
| 6000 | 19685 |
| 4000 | 13124 |
| 3000 | 9843 |
| 2000 | 6562 |
| 1000 | 3281 |
| 500 | 1640 |
| 200 | 656 |
| 0 | 0 |
| Land Below Sea Level 0 | 0 |
| 200 | 656 |
| 1000 | 3281 |
| 3000 | 9843 |
| 6000 | 19685 |
| 9000 | 29520 |

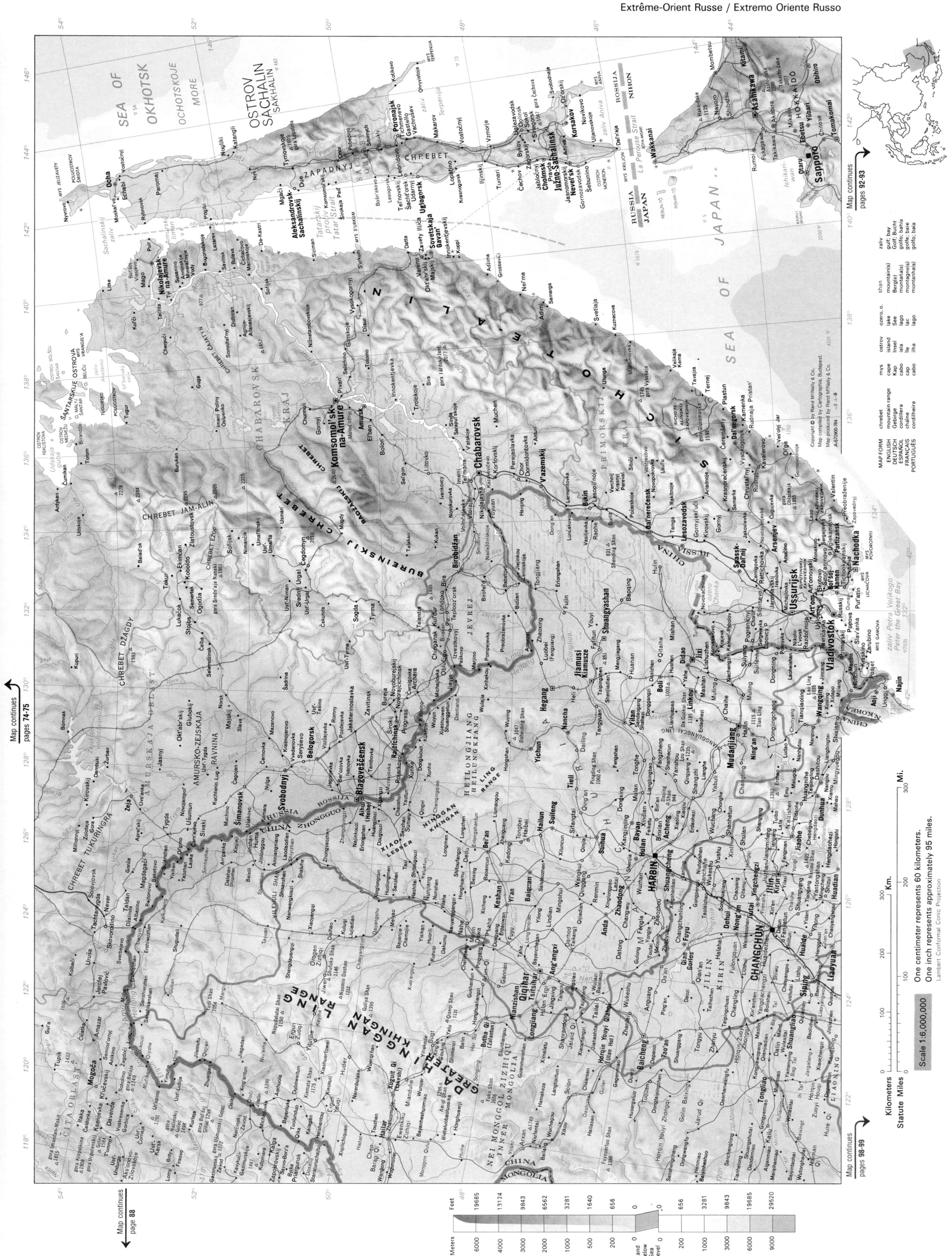

SEA OF OKHOTSK
OCHOTSKOJE MORE
OSTROV SACHALIN
SAKHALIN
SEA OF JAPAN
HOKKAIDO
Sapporo
Južno-Sachalinsk
Chabarovsk
Komsomol'sk-na-Amure
Vladivostok
Blagoveščensk
HARBIN
CHANGCHUN
Qiqihar
HEILONGJIANG
JILIN
NEI MONGOL ZIZHIQU
INNER MONGOLIA
CHINA
MONGOLIA
RUSSIA
JAPAN
ROSSIJA
NIHON
CHABAROVSKIJ KRAJ
PRIMORSKIJ KRAJ
AMURSKAJA OBLAST'
ČITINSKAJA OBLAST'
GREATER KHINGAN RANGE
LESSER KHINGAN RANGE
BUREINSKIJ CHREBET
SICHOTE-ALIN'
Nikolajevsk-na-Amure
Sovetskaja Gavan'
Ussurijsk
Nachodka
Birobidžan
Svobodnyj
Jiamusi
Mudanjiang
Jilin
Ocha
La Pérouse Strait
Tatar Strait
Peter the Great Bay

Map continues pages 74-75
Map continues page 88
Map continues pages 92-93
Map continues pages 98-99

Copyright © by Rand McNally & Co.
Map compiled by Cartographia, Budapest.
Map produced by Rand McNally & Co.
A-572000-764 -3 -4 -9

| MAP FORM | chrebet | mys | ostrov | ozero, o. | shan | zaliv |
|---|---|---|---|---|---|---|
| ENGLISH | mountain range | cape | island | lake | mountain(s) | gulf; bay |
| DEUTSCH | Gebirge | Kap | Insel | See | Berg(e) | Golf; Bucht |
| ESPAÑOL | cordillera | cabo | isla | lago | montaña(s) | golfo; bahía |
| FRANÇAIS | chaîne | cap | île | lac | montagne(s) | golfe; baie |
| PORTUGUÊS | cordilheira | cabo | ilha | lago | montanha(s) | golfo; baía |

Scale 1:6,000,000

One centimeter represents 60 kilometers.
One inch represents approximately 95 miles.
Lambert Conformal Conic Projection

Kilometers 0 100 200 300 Km.
Statute Miles 0 100 200 300 Mi.

| Meters | 6000 | 4000 | 3000 | 2000 | 1000 | 500 | 200 | 0 | Land Below Sea Level 0 | 0 | 200 | 1000 | 3000 | 6000 | 9000 |
|---|---|---|---|---|---|---|---|---|---|---|---|---|---|---|---|
| Feet | 19685 | 13124 | 9843 | 6562 | 3281 | 1640 | 656 | 0 | 0 | 656 | 3281 | 9843 | 19685 | 29520 | |

Map continues pages 74-75

KAZAKHSTAN
RUSSIA
TUVA
BURJATIJA
MONGOLIA
KYRGYZSTAN
TIEN SHAN
XINJIANG UYGUR ZIZHIQU
SINKIANG
TARIM PENDI
TAKLIMAKAN SHAMO
JUNGGAR PENDI
KURUKTAG
ALTUN SHAN
KUNLUN SHAN
QAIDAM PENDI
QINGHAI
TSINGHAI
XIZANG ZIZHIQU
TIBET
TANGGULA SHAN
GANGDISE SHAN
NYAINQENTANGLHA SHAN
HIMALAYAS
NEPAL
BHUTAN
BANGLADESH
INDIA
MYANMAR (BURMA)
THAILAND
LAOS
VIETNAM
BAY OF BENGAL
SICHUAN
SZECHWAN
YUNNAN
GANSU
KANSU
NINGXIA HUIZU ZIZHIQU
GUIZHOU
KWEICHOW
Irkutsk
Ust'-Kamenogorsk
Balchaš
ALMATY
ALMA-ATA
Biškek
(Frunze)
Ürümqi
Yining
Kashi
Shache
Hami
Lanzhou
Xining
Chengdu
Lhasa
Kathmandu
DHAKA
DACCA
CALCUTTA
Kunming
Mandalay
Chittagong
HA NOI
Vientiane
Luang Prabang
Chiang Mai
Lucknow
Kanpur
Allahabad
Varanasi
(Benares)
Patna
Cuttack
Vishakhapatnam
Jamshedpur
Raipur
Jabalpur
Dehra Dun
Meerut
Moradabad
Bareilly
Aligarh
Gorakhpur
Asansol
Khulna
Sittwe
(Akyab)
Henzada
Bago
Prome
Yumen
Golmud
Chongqing
Guiyang
Zunyi
Yinchuan
Baoji
Tianshui
Neijiang
Zigong
Yibin
Luzhou
Gejiu
Dali
Baoshan
Myitkyina
Shillong
Gauhati
Imphal
Silchar
Darjeeling
Muztag
7723
Chogori Feng (K2)
8611
Qomolangma Feng
(Mount Everest)
8848
Kangchenjunga
8598
Dhaulagiri
8172
Gongga Shan
7556
Namjagbarwa Feng
7756
Hkakabo Razi
5881
Pik Pobedy
7439
Fan Si Pan
3143
Mount Victoria
3053
MAP FORM

Map continues pages 118-119

| MAP FORM | bandao | dao | hu | -jima | pendi | shan | -shima |
|---|---|---|---|---|---|---|---|
| ENGLISH | peninsula | island | lake | island | basin | mountain(s) | island |
| DEUTSCH | Halbinsel | Insel | See | Insel | Becken | Berg(e) | Insel |
| ESPAÑOL | peninsula | isla | lago | isla | cuenca | montaña(s) | isla |
| FRANÇAIS | péninsule | île | lac | île | bassin | montagne(s) | île |
| PORTUGUÊS | península | ilha | lago | ilha | bacia | montanha(s) | ilha |

NORTH KOREA
SOUTH KOREA
JAPAN
RUSSIA
TAIWAN
PHILIPPINES
SEA OF JAPAN
YELLOW SEA
EAST CHINA SEA
SOUTH CHINA SEA
PHILIPPINE SEA
PACIFIC OCEAN
SEA OF OKHOTSK
HONSHŪ
HOKKAIDŌ
SHIKOKU
KYŪSHŪ
BEIJING
PEKING
TIANJIN
SHANGHAI
P'YŎNGYANG
SŎUL
TŌKYŌ
ŌSAKA
Tropic of Cancer
Copyright © by Rand McNally & Co.
Map prepared by Esselte Map Service AB, Stockholm.

Map continues pages 108-109

Kilometers 0 200 400 600 Km.
Statute Miles 0 200 400 600 Mi.

Scale 1:12,000,000
One centimeter represents 120 kilometers.
One inch represents approximately 190 miles.
Lambert Conformal Conic Projection

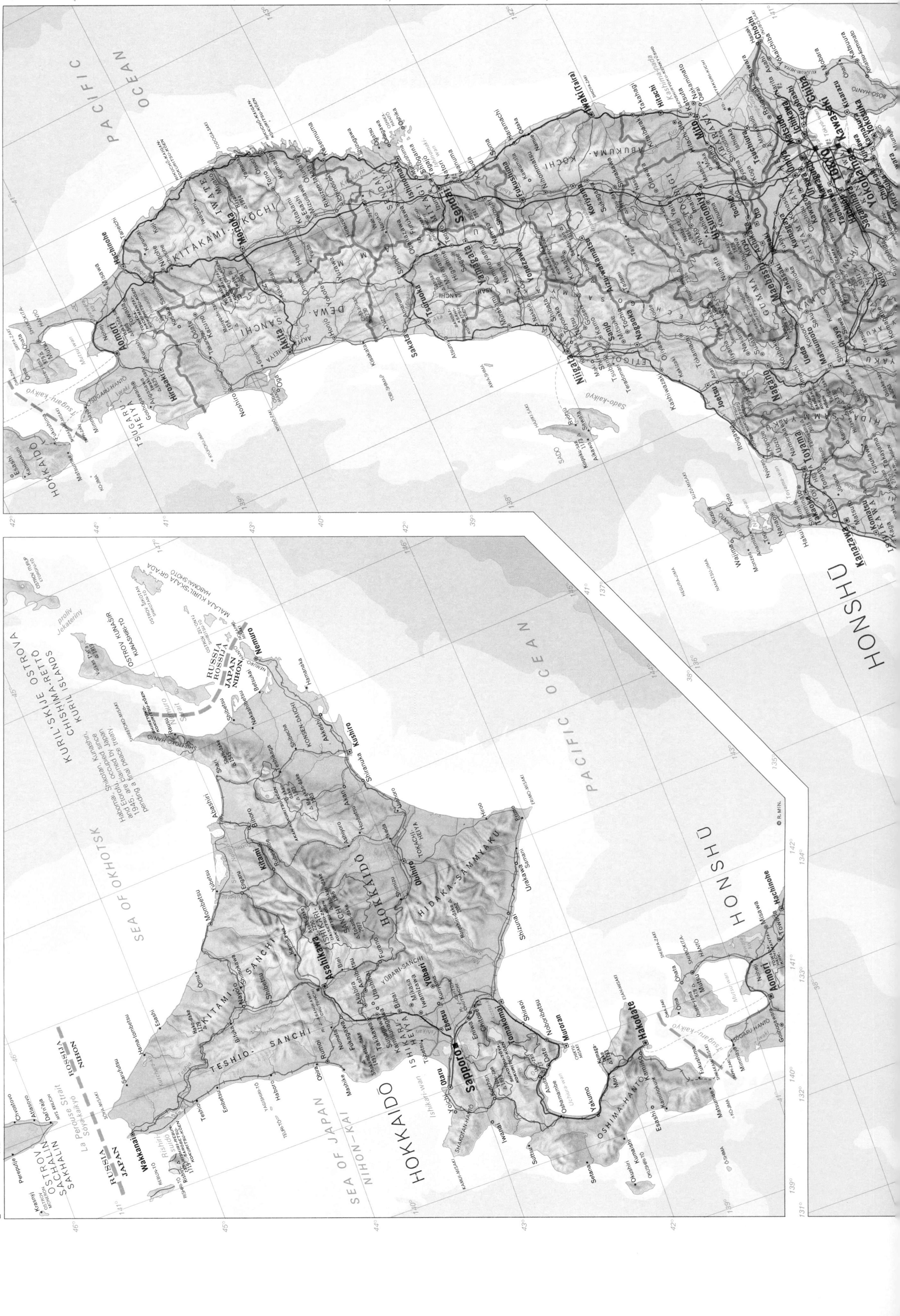
a
PACIFIC OCEAN
SEA OF OKHOTSK
SEA OF JAPAN
NIHON-KAI
HOKKAIDŌ
HONSHŪ
KURIL'SKIJE OSTROVA
CHISHIMA-RETTO
KURIL ISLANDS
OSTROV SACHALIN
SAKHALIN
RUSSIA
ROSSIJA
JAPAN
NIHON
La Perouse Strait
Sōya-kaikyō
Tsugaru-kaikyō
Sado-kaikyō
TESHIO-SANCHI
KITAMI-SANCHI
HIDAKA-SAMMYAKU
KITAKAMI-KŌCHI
DEWA-SANCHI
ABUKUMA-KŌCHI
Wakkanai
Asahikawa
Kitami
Sapporo
Otaru
Ebetsu
Tomakomai
Muroran
Hakodate
Obihiro
Kushiro
Nemuro
Aomori
Hachinohe
Hirosaki
Morioka
Akita
Sakata
Yamagata
Sendai
Fukushima
Niigata
Kōriyama
Iwaki (Taira)
Hitachi
Mito
Utsunomiya
Maebashi
Nagano
Jōetsu
Toyama
Kanazawa
Chōshi
Chiba
Tokyo
Kawasaki
Yokohama
SADO
© R.MTN.

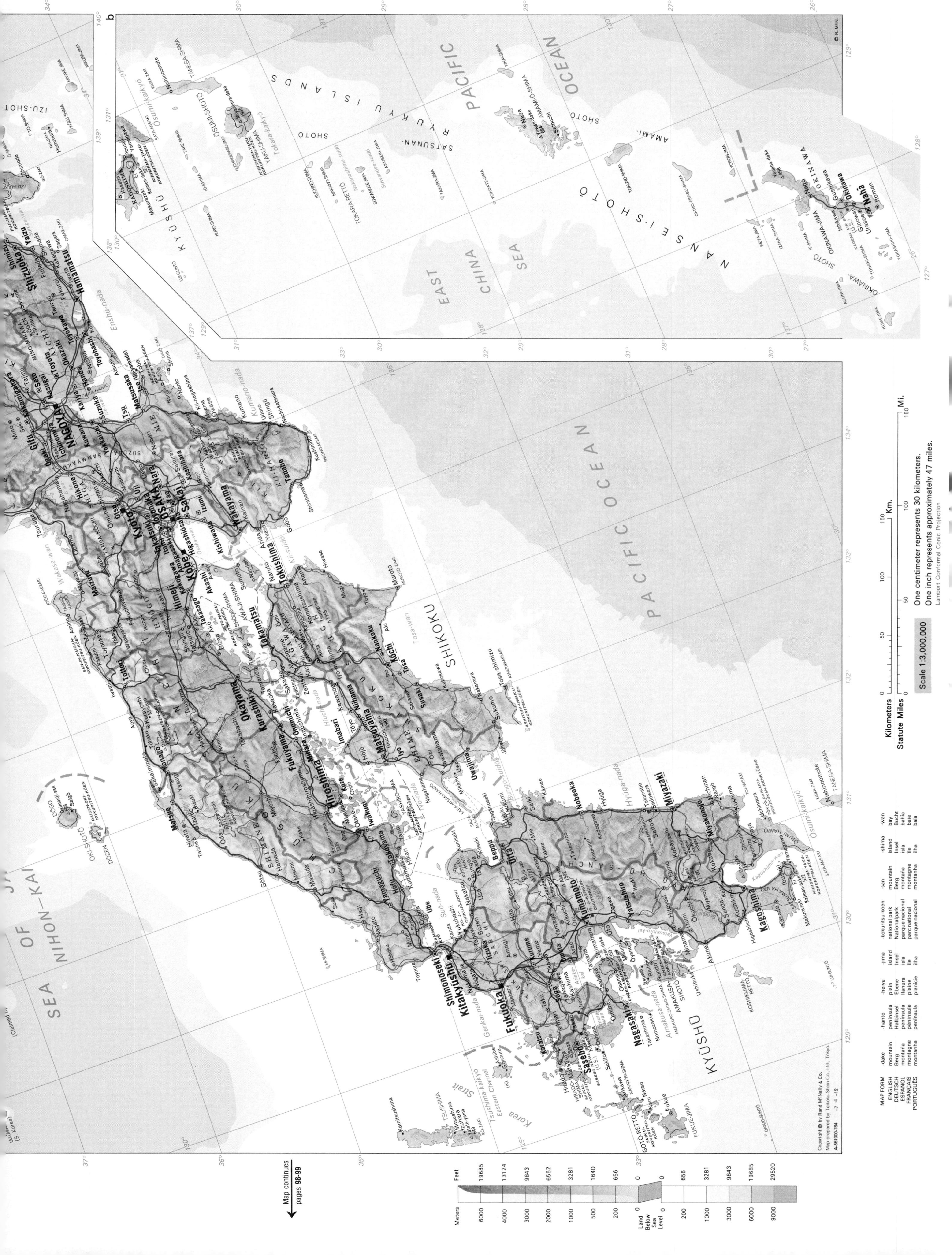
SEA OF JAPAN
NIHON-KAI
PACIFIC OCEAN
EAST CHINA SEA
SHIKOKU
KYŪSHŪ
NANSEI-SHOTŌ
RYUKYU ISLANDS
SATSUNAN-SHOTŌ
AMAMI-SHOTŌ
OKINAWA-SHOTŌ
OSUMI-SHOTŌ
OKI-SHOTŌ
Korea Strait
Tsushima-kaikyō
Eastern Channel
Osaka
Kyōto
Kōbe
Nagoya
Hiroshima
Fukuoka
Kitakyūshū
Kagoshima
Nagasaki
Kumamoto
Ōita
Miyazaki
Matsuyama
Takamatsu
Kōchi
Tokushima
Okayama
Wakayama
Shizuoka
Hamamatsu
Naha
b
Map continues pages 98-99
Meters
Feet
Land Below Sea Level
Kilometers
Statute Miles
Scale 1:3,000,000
One centimeter represents 30 kilometers.
One inch represents approximately 47 miles.
Lambert Conformal Conic Projection
MAP FORM
ENGLISH
DEUTSCH
ESPAÑOL
FRANÇAIS
PORTUGUÊS
-dake mountain Berg montaña montagne montanha
-hantō peninsula Halbinsel península péninsule península
-heiya plain Ebene llanura plaine planície
-jima island Insel isla île ilha
-kokuritsu-kōen national park Nationalpark parque nacional parc national parque nacional
-san mountain Berg montaña montagne montanha
-shima island Insel isla île ilha
-wan bay Bucht bahía baie baía
Copyright © by Rand McNally & Co.
Map prepared by Teikoku-Shoin Co., Ltd. Tokyo.
© R.M.N.

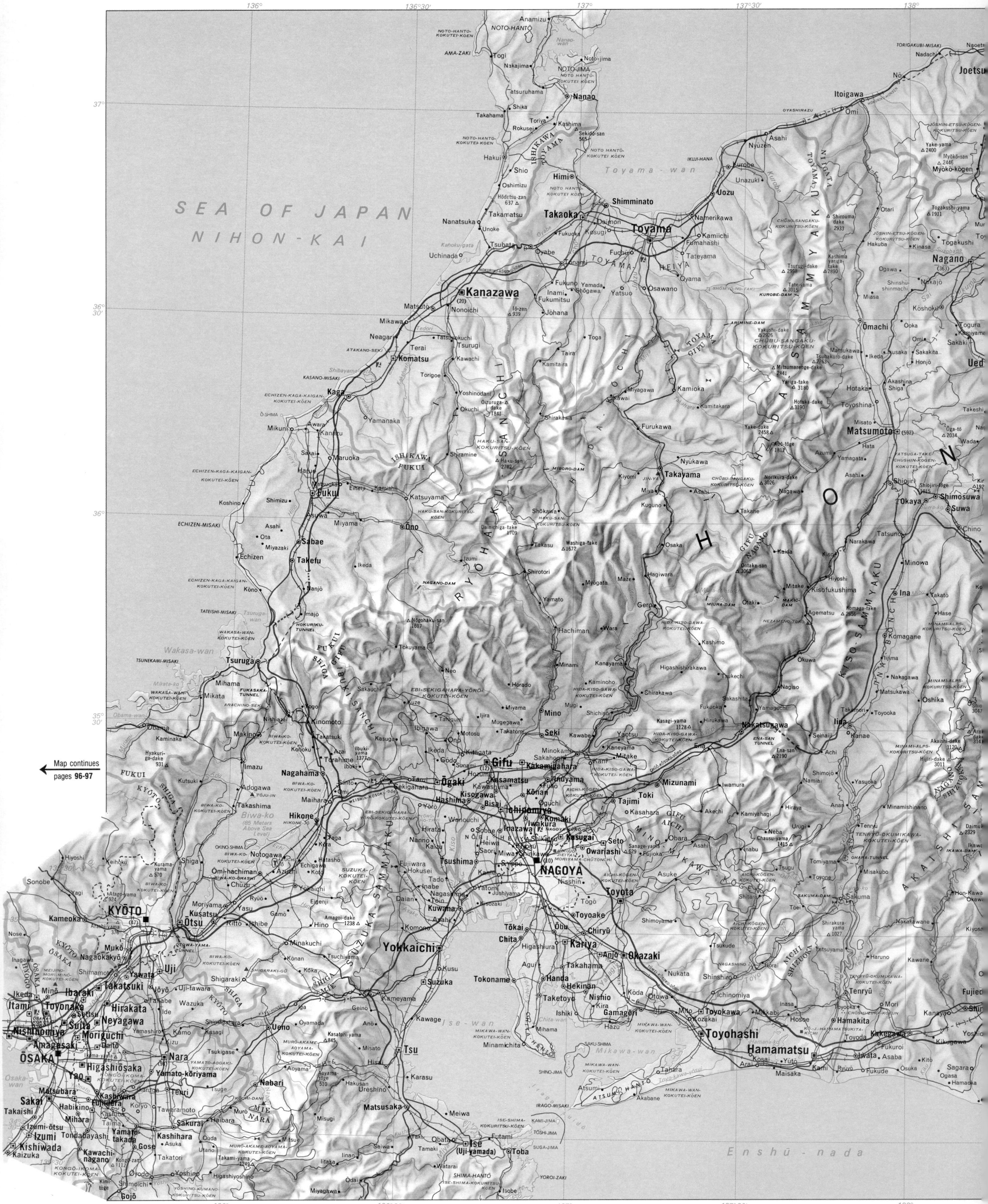
SEA OF JAPAN
NIHON-KAI
Toyama-wan
Wakasa-wan
Ise-wan
Mikawa-wan
Enshū-nada
Biwa-ko
NOTO-HANTŌ
Kanazawa
Toyama
Takaoka
Fukui
Gifu
NAGOYA
KYŌTO
ŌSAKA
Yokkaichi
Toyohashi
Hamamatsu
Matsumoto
Nagano
Tsu
Nara
Ōtsu
Takayama
HONSHU

Map continues pages 96-97

| MAP FORM | -dake | -hantō | -kokutei-kōen | -misaki | -san | -tōge | -wan | -yama | -zaki |
|---|---|---|---|---|---|---|---|---|---|
| ENGLISH | mountain | peninsula | national park | cape | mountain | pass | bay | mountain | point |
| DEUTSCH | Berg | Halbinsel | Nationalpark | Kap | Berg | Pass | Bucht | Berg | Landspitze |
| ESPAÑOL | montaña | península | parque nacional | cabo | montaña | paso | bahía | montaña | punta |
| FRANÇAIS | montagne | péninsule | parc national | cap | montagne | col | baie | montagne | pointe |
| PORTUGUÊS | montanha | península | parque nacional | cabo | montanha | passo | baía | montanha | ponta |

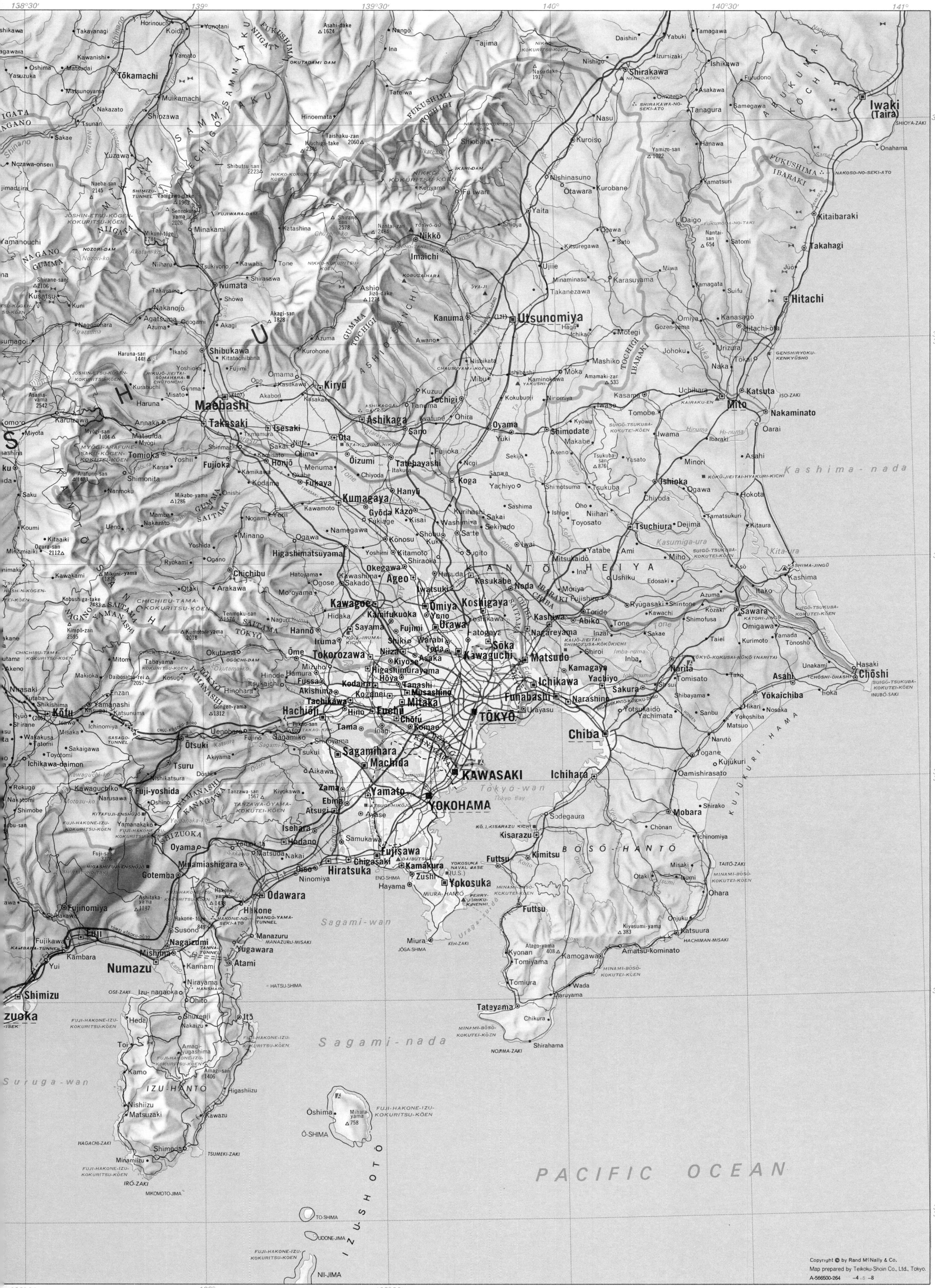
Tōkyō
Yokohama
Kawasaki
Chiba
Ōmiya
Urawa
Kawaguchi
Funabashi
Ichikawa
Matsudo
Hachiōji
Tachikawa
Musashino
Mitaka
Fuchū
Chōfu
Sagamihara
Machida
Yamato
Fujisawa
Kamakura
Yokosuka
Hiratsuka
Odawara
Atami
Numazu
Mishima
Fuji
Fujinomiya
Shimizu
Kōfu
Maebashi
Takasaki
Isesaki
Kiryū
Ashikaga
Ōta
Kumagaya
Kawagoe
Tokorozawa
Utsunomiya
Nikkō
Imaichi
Oyama
Koga
Mito
Katsuta
Hitachi
Takahagi
Kitaibaraki
Iwaki (Taira)
Shirakawa
Tsuchiura
Narita
Sawara
Chōshi
Kisarazu
Mobara
Tōkamachi
Numata
Chichibu
Ōtsuki
Gotemba
Tōkyō-wan
Tokyo Bay
Sagami-wan
Sagami-nada
Suruga-wan
Kashima-nada
Kasumiga-ura
KANTŌ HEIYA
BŌSŌ-HANTŌ
IZU-HANTŌ
IZU-SHOTŌ
Ō-SHIMA
TO-SHIMA
NII-JIMA
PACIFIC OCEAN
138°30′
139°
139°30′
140°
140°30′
141°
37°
36°30′
36°
35°30′
35°
34°30′

Kilometers 0 10 20 30 40 50 Km.
Statute Miles 0 10 20 30 40 50 Mi.

Scale 1:1,000,000

One centimeter represents 10 kilometers.
One inch represents approximately 16 miles.
Lambert Conformal Conic Projection

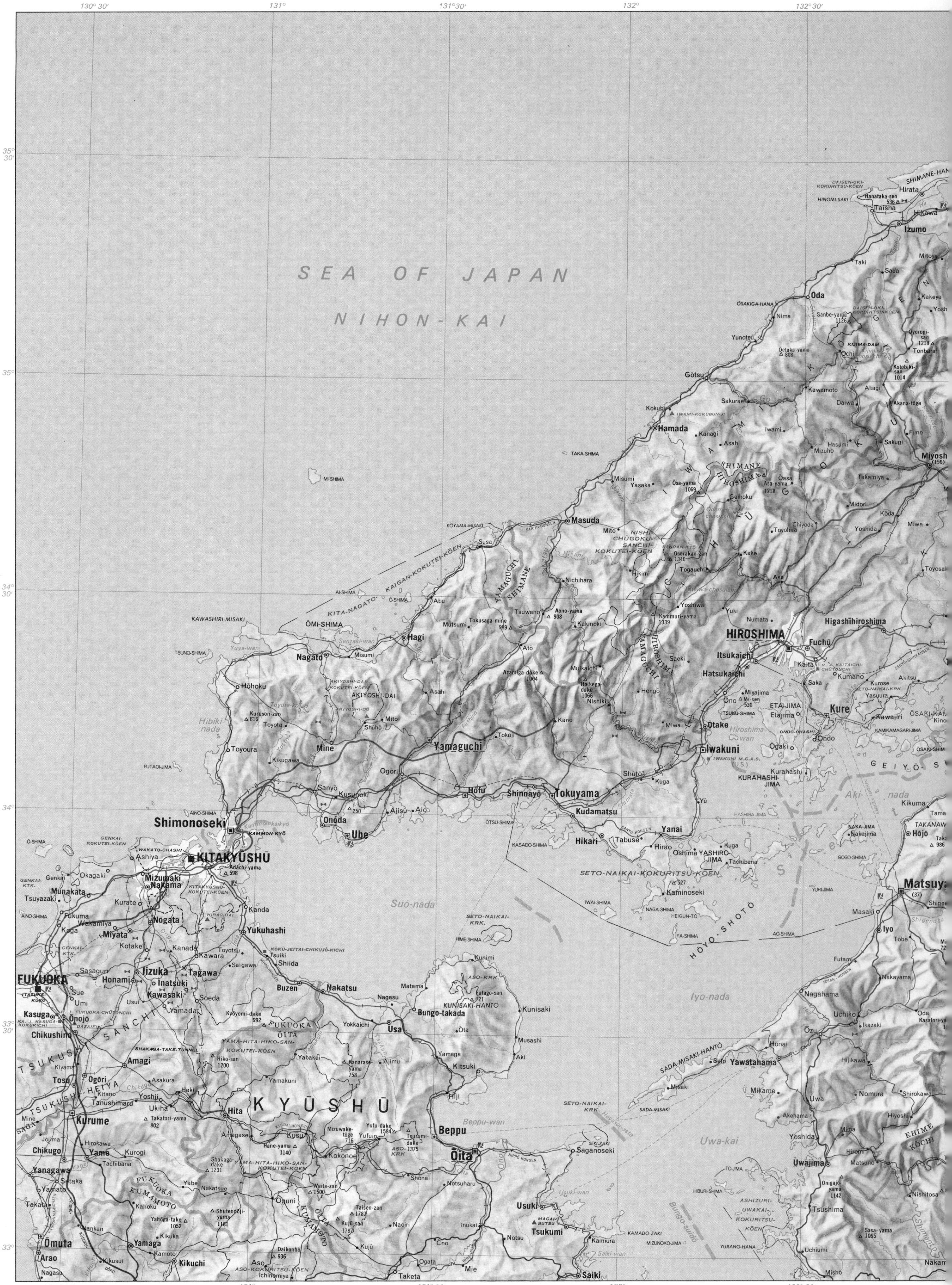

SEA OF JAPAN
NIHON-KAI
KYŪSHŪ
HIROSHIMA
KITAKYŪSHŪ
FUKUOKA
Shimonoseki
Yamaguchi
Hagi
Masuda
Hamada
Gōtsu
Oda
Izumo
Iwakuni
Kure
Tokuyama
Hōfu
Ube
Onoda
Nagato
Otake
Yanai
Hikari
Kudamatsu
Beppu
Ōita
Usa
Nakatsu
Buzen
Yukuhashi
Iizuka
Nōgata
Kurume
Ōmuta
Saiki
Usuki
Tsukumi
Uwajima
Yawatahama
Matsuyama
Suō-nada
Iyo-nada
Uwa-kai
Hibiki-nada
Beppu-wan
Hiroshima-wan
SETO-NAIKAI-KOKURITSU-KŌEN
Chikugo
Yame
Saganoseki
Kunisaki
Bungo-takada
KUNISAKI-HANTŌ
SADA-MISAKI-HANTŌ
HŌYO-SHOTŌ
130° 30′
131°
131° 30′
132°
132° 30′
35° 30′
35°
34° 30′
34°
33° 30′
33°


| MAP FORM | -jima | -misaki | -san | -sen | -shima | -tōge | -yama | -zen |
|---|---|---|---|---|---|---|---|---|
| ENGLISH | island | cape | mountain | mountain | island | pass | mountain | mountain |
| DEUTSCH | Insel | Kap | Berg | Berg | Insel | Pass | Berg | Berg |
| ESPAÑOL | isla | cabo | montaña | montaña | isla | paso | montaña | montaña |
| FRANÇAIS | île | cap | montagne | montagne | île | col | montagne | montagne |
| PORTUGUÊS | ilha | cabo | montanha | montanha | ilha | passo | montanha | montanha |

133° 30'
134°
134° 30'
135°
135° 30'
35° 30'
35°
34° 30'
34°
33° 30'
33°
Map continues pages 94-95
HONSHU
SHIKOKU
PACIFIC OCEAN
Tosa-wan
Kii-suidō
Harima-nada
Ōsaka-wan
Wakasa-wan
Miho-wan
Hiuchi-nada
Mizushima-nada
Inland Sea
BISAN-SHOTO
IESHIMA-SHOTO
SHIWAKU-SHOTO
AWAJI-SHIMA
KII-HANTŌ
TANGO-HANTŌ
SAN'IN-KAIGAN-KOKURITSU-KŌEN
DAISEN-OKI-KOKURITSU-KŌEN
SETO-NAIKAI-KOKURITSU-KŌEN
WAKASA-WAN-KOKUTEI-KŌEN
MUROTO-ANAN-KAIGAN-KOKUTEI-KŌEN
KYŌGA-MISAKI
MUROTO-ZAKI
OKITSU-ZAKI
INO-MISAKI
HANE-ZAKI
SHIONO-MISAKI
KYOTO
ŌSAKA
KOBE
Nara
Ōtsu
Wakayama
Tokushima
Takamatsu
Okayama
Kōchi
Himeji
Tottori
Yonago
Kurashiki
Fukuyama
Onomichi
Maizuru
Fukuchiyama
Ayabe
Toyooka
Miyazu
Akashi
Kakogawa
Sakai
Kishiwada
Nishinomiya
Amagasaki
Takatsuki
Naruto
Anan
Muroto
Susaki
Niihama
Marugame
Sakaide
Kurayoshi
Tsuyama
Sakaiminato
Tanabe
Gobō
Sumoto
Copyright © by Rand McNally & Co.
Map prepared by Teikoku-Shoin Co., Ltd., Tokyo.
A-566600-264 -4 -5 -6

Kilometers 0 10 20 30 40 50 Km.

Statute Miles 0 10 20 30 40 50 Mi.

Scale 1:1,000,000

One centimeter represents 10 kilometers.
One inch represents approximately 16 miles.
Lambert Conformal Conic Projection

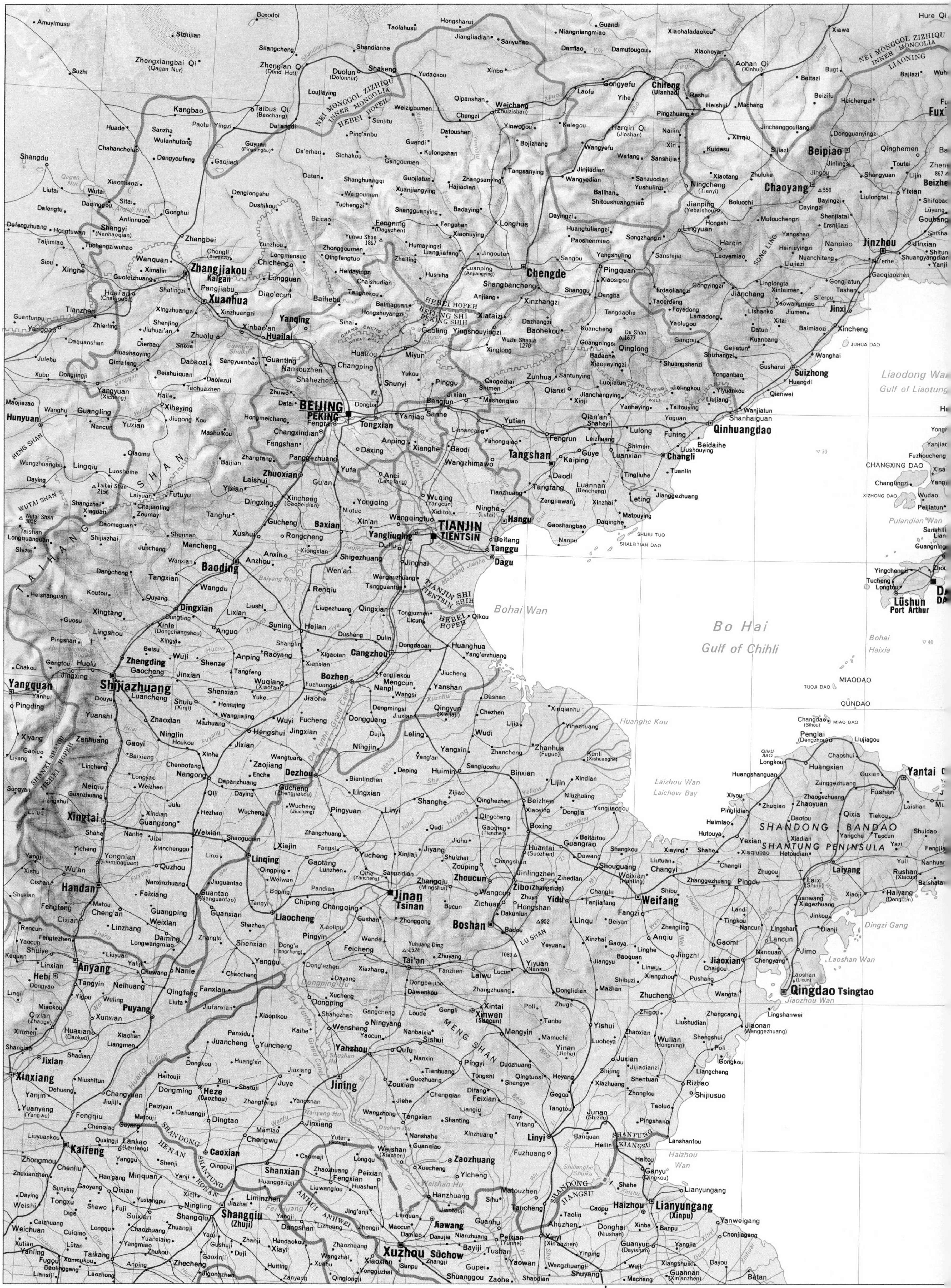
114°
115°
116°
117°
118°
119°
120°
121°
42°
41°
40°
39°
38°
37°
36°
35°
34°
NEI MONGGOL ZIZHIQU
INNER MONGOLIA
LIAONING
HEBEI HOPEH
BEIJING SHI PEKING SHIH
TIANJIN SHI TIENTSIN SHIH
SHANXI SHANSI
HEBEI HOPEH
SHANDONG
HENAN HONAN
ANHUI ANHWEI
JIANGSU KIANGSU
SHANDONG BANDAO
SHANTUNG PENINSULA
Liaodong Wan
Gulf of Liaotung
Bo Hai
Gulf of Chihli
Bohai Wan
Laizhou Wan
Laichow Bay
Huanghe Kou
Bohai Haixia
Haizhou Wan
Jiaozhou Wan
Dingzi Gang
Laoshan Wan
Pulandian Wan
TAIHANG SHAN
HENG SHAN
WUTAI SHAN
MENG SHAN
LU SHAN
SONG LING
BEIJING
PEKING
TIANJIN
TIENTSIN
Chengde
Zhangjiakou
Kalgan
Xuanhua
Qinhuangdao
Tangshan
Baoding
Shijiazhuang
Cangzhou
Dezhou
Jinan
Tsinan
Zibo
Weifang
Yantai
Qingdao Tsingtao
Xingtai
Handan
Anyang
Xinxiang
Kaifeng
Shangqiu
Xuzhou Süchow
Lianyungang
Linyi
Jining
Yanzhou
Tai'an
Boshan
Liaocheng
Dingxian
Hengshui
Chaoyang
Beipiao
Jinzhou
Lüshun
Port Arthur
Yangquan
Puyang
Heze
Zaozhuang
Chifeng
Map continues
pages 102-103

Meters | Feet
6000 | 19685
4000 | 13124
3000 | 9843
2000 | 6562
1000 | 3281
500 | 1640
200 | 656
0 | 0
Land Below Sea Level
0 | 0
200 | 656
1000 | 3281
3000 | 9843
6000 | 19685
9000 | 29520

Map continues pages 100-101

| MAP FORM | dao | -do | -gang | hu | kukrip kongwŏn | -san | shan | wan |
|---|---|---|---|---|---|---|---|---|
| ENGLISH | island | island | river | lake | national park | mountain | mountain(s) | bay |
| DEUTSCH | Insel | Insel | Fluss | See | Nationalpark | Berg | Berg(e) | Bucht |
| ESPAÑOL | isla | isla | río | lago | parque nacional | montaña | montaña(s) | bahía |
| FRANÇAIS | île | île | rivière | lac | parc national | montagne | montagne(s) | baie |
| PORTUGUÊS | ilha | ilha | rio | lago | parque nacional | montanha | montanha(s) | baía |

Map continues page 89

MANCHURIA
CHINA
RUSSIA
NORTH KOREA
SOUTH KOREA
JAPAN NIHON
SEA OF JAPAN
Korea Bay
YELLOW SEA
Korea Strait
Western Channel
Eastern Channel
Tsushima-kaikyō
LIAODONG BANDAO
LIAOTUNG PENINSULA
CHANGBAI SHAN
HAMGYŎNG SANMAEK
KANGNAM SANMAEK
MYOHYANG SANMAEK
NANGNIM SANMAEK
T'AEBAEK SANMAEK
SOBAEK SANMAEK
HAMGYŎNG PUKDO
HAMGYŎNG NAMDO
YANGGANG DO
CHAGANG DO
P'YŎNGAN PUKDO
P'YŎNGAN NAMDO
HWANGHAE PUKDO
HWANGHAE NAMDO
KANGWŎN DO
KYŎNGGI DO
CH'UNGCH'ŎNG PUKDO
CH'UNGCH'ŎNG NAMDO
KYŎNGSANG PUKDO
KYŎNGSANG NAMDO
CHŎLLA PUKDO
CHŎLLA NAMDO
Sŏjosŏn-man
Tongjosŏn-man
Kyŏnggi-man
Asan-man
Yanji
Tumen
Hunchun
Posjet
FUSHUN
SHENYANG
MUKDEN
Anshan
Liaoyang
Benxi
Dandong
Tonghua
Linjiang
Hyesan
Kanggye
Sinŭiju
P'YONGYANG
Namp'o
Haeju
Kaesŏng
Wŏnsan
Hamhŭng
Hŭngnam
Ch'ŏngjin
Kimch'aek
Najin
Musan
SŎUL
SEOUL
Inch'ŏn
Suwŏn
Sŏngnam-si
Ch'unch'ŏn
Kangnŭng
Wŏnju
Ch'ŏngju
Taejŏn
Chŏnju
Kunsan
Kwangju
Mokp'o
Yŏsu
Chinju
Masan
Pusan
Ulsan
P'ohang
Taegu
Andong
KOJE-DO
NAMHAE-DO
TSUSHIMA
Izuhara
Paektu-san 2744
Copyright © by Rand McNally & Co.
Map compiled by Cartographia, Budapest.
Map produced by Rand McNally & Co.
A-564400-764

Map continues pages 92-93

Kilometers 0 50 100 150 Km.

Statute Miles 0 50 100 150 Mi.

Scale 1:3,000,000

One centimeter represents 30 kilometers.

One inch represents approximately 47 miles.

Lambert Conformal Conic Projection

Map continues pages 98-99

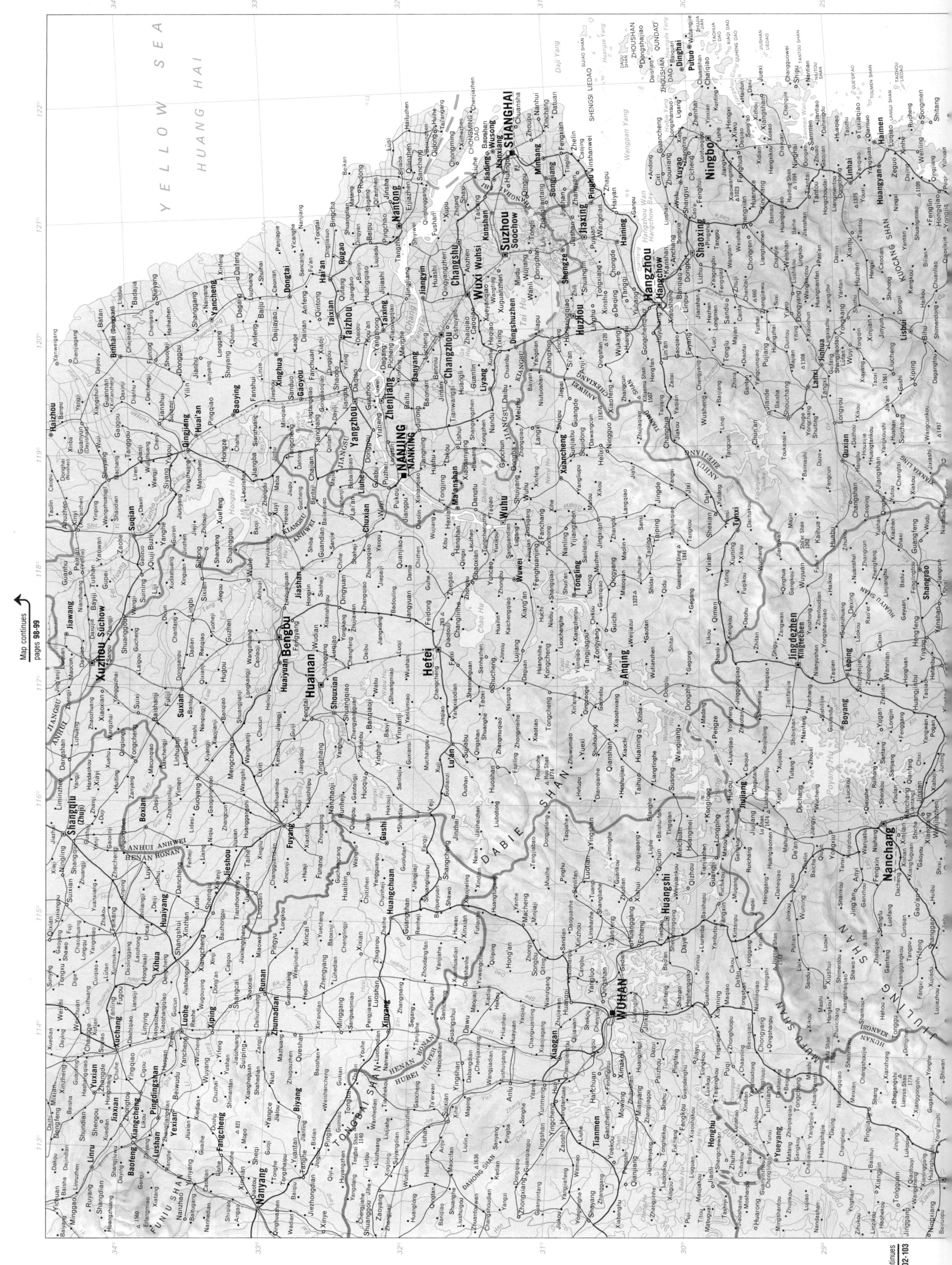
YELLOW SEA
HUANG HAI
SHANGHAI
NANJING
NANKING
WUHAN
Hangzhou
Suzhou
Soochow
Ningbo
Hefei
Nanchang
Bengbu
Huainan
Xuzhou
Nantong
Wuxi
Changzhou
Zhenjiang
Yangzhou
Anqing
Wuhu
Jingdezhen
Huangshi
Shaoxing
Huzhou
Jiaxing
Xinyang
Luoyang
Zhumadian
Nanyang
Yueyang
Xiaogan
DABIE SHAN
TONGBAI SHAN
FUNIU SHAN
MUFU SHAN
JIULING SHAN
JIANGSU
ANHWEI
ANHUI
HENAN
HONAN
HUBEI
HUPEH
KIANGSI
ZHEJIANG
CHEKIANG

Map continues pages 102-103

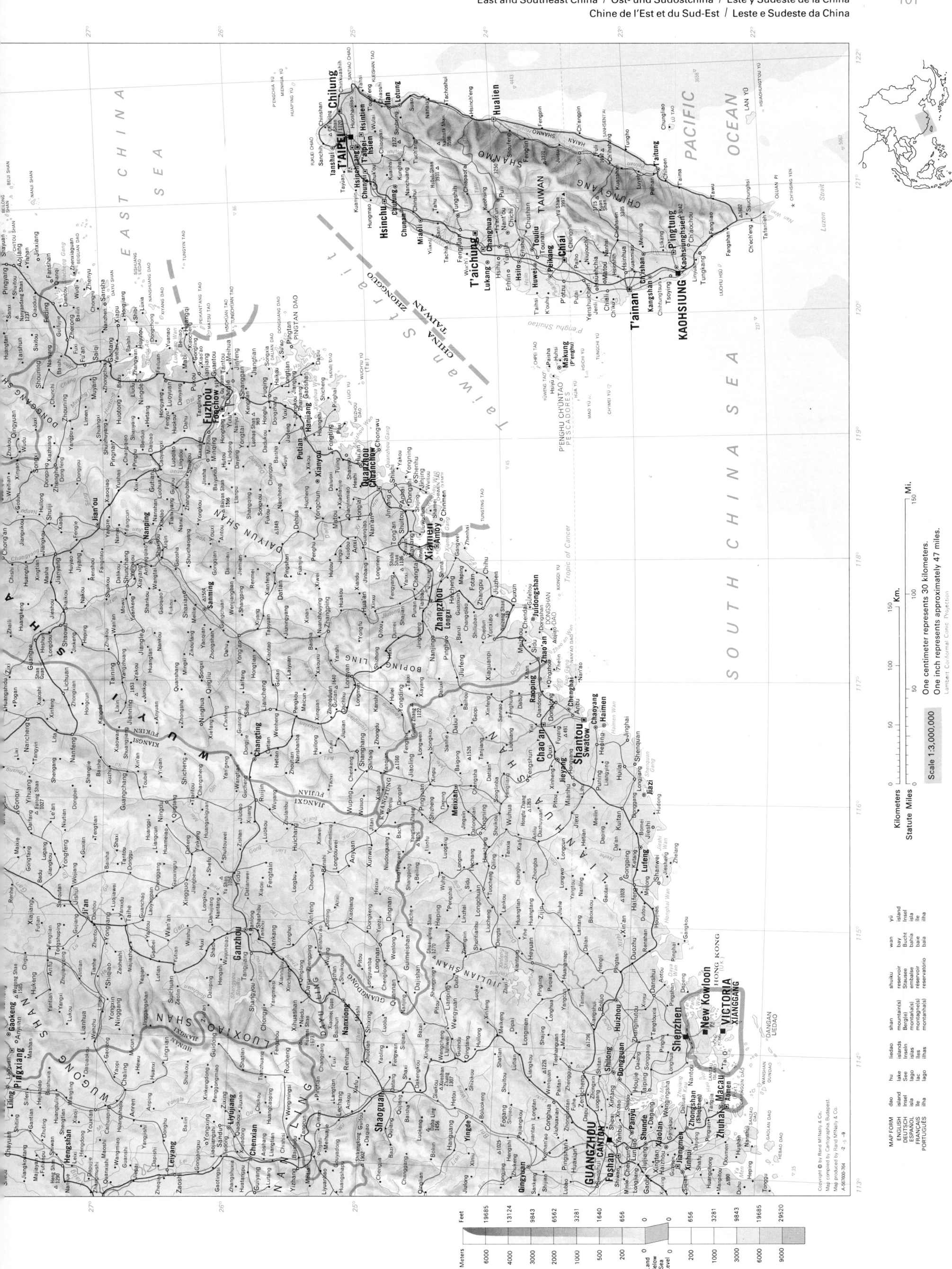
EAST CHINA SEA
PACIFIC OCEAN
SOUTH CHINA SEA
Taiwan Strait
TAIWAN
T'AIPEI
KAOHSIUNG
T'ainan
T'aichung
Chilung
Hualien
PENGHU CH'ÜNTAO
PESCADORES
FUZHOU
Foochow
Xiamen
Amoy
Shantou
Swatow
GUANGZHOU
CANTON
HONG KONG
VICTORIA
XIANGGANG
New Kowloon
Macau
Shenzhen
FUJIAN
JIANGXI
GUANGDONG
WUYI SHAN
NAN LING
DAIYUN SHAN
Tropic of Cancer
Luzon Strait
Scale 1:3,000,000
One centimeter represents 30 kilometers.
One inch represents approximately 47 miles.
Kilometers
Statute Miles
Km.
Mi.
Lambert Conformal Conic Projection
MAP FORM
ENGLISH
DEUTSCH
ESPAÑOL
FRANÇAIS
PORTUGUÊS
dao island Insel isla île ilha
hu lake See lago lac lago
liedao islands Inseln islas îles ilhas
shan mountain(s) Berg(e) montaña(s) montagne(s) montanha(s)
shuiku reservoir Stausee embalse réservoir reservatório
wan bay Bucht bahía baie baía
yü island Insel isla île ilha
Feet
Meters
Land Below Sea Level
Copyright © by Rand McNally & Co.
Map compiled by Cartographia, Budapest.
Map produced by Rand McNally & Co.

Map continues pages 98-99

Map continues page 88

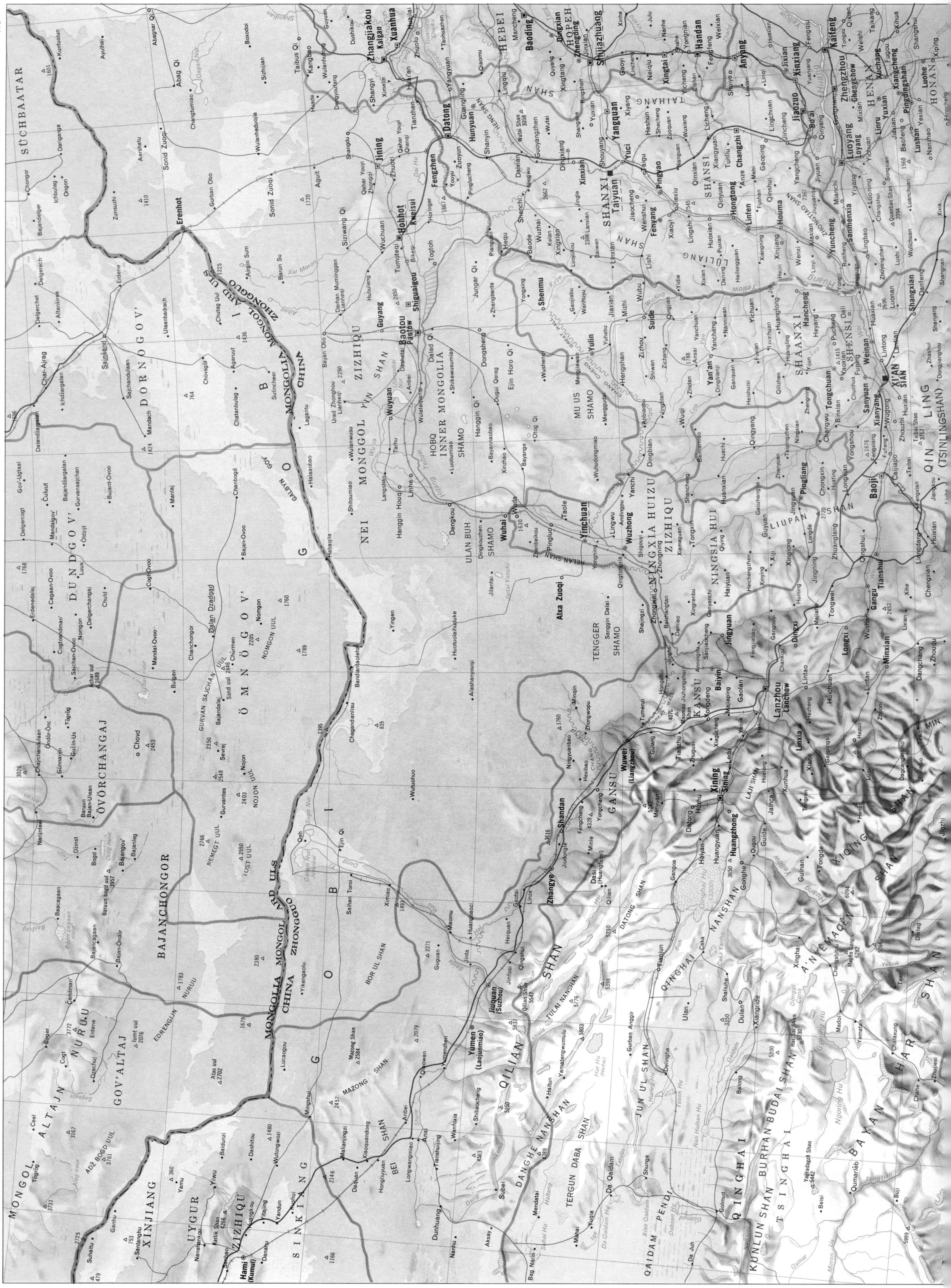
MONGOLIA
CHINA
ZHONGGUO
GOBI
NEI MONGGOL ZIZHIQU
INNER MONGOLIA
NINGXIA HUIZU ZIZHIQU
GANSU
KANSU
QINGHAI
TSINGHAI
SHANXI
SHANSI
SHAANXI
SHENSI
HEBEI
HOPEH
HENAN
HONAN
XINJIANG UYGUR ZIZHIQU
SINKIANG
DORNOGOV'
DUNDGOV'
ÖMNÖGOV'
ÖVÖRCHANGAJ
BAJANCHONGOR
GOV'ALTAJ
SÜCHBAATAR
Lanzhou
Xining
Yinchuan
Baotou
Hohhot
Datong
Taiyuan
Shijiazhuang
Baoding
Zhangjiakou
Erenhot
Jiuquan
Yumen
Zhangye
Wuwei
Dunhuang
Hami
Xi'an
Luoyang
Zhengzhou
Kaifeng
Anyang
Handan
Baoji
Tianshui
QILIAN SHAN
QIN LING
LÜLIANG SHAN
TAIHANG SHAN
BAYAN HAR SHAN
A'NYEMAQEN SHAN
KUNLUN SHAN
QAIDAM PENDI
TENGGER SHAMO
MU US SHAMO
HOBQ SHAMO
BADAIN JARAN SHAMO

Map continues pages 100-101

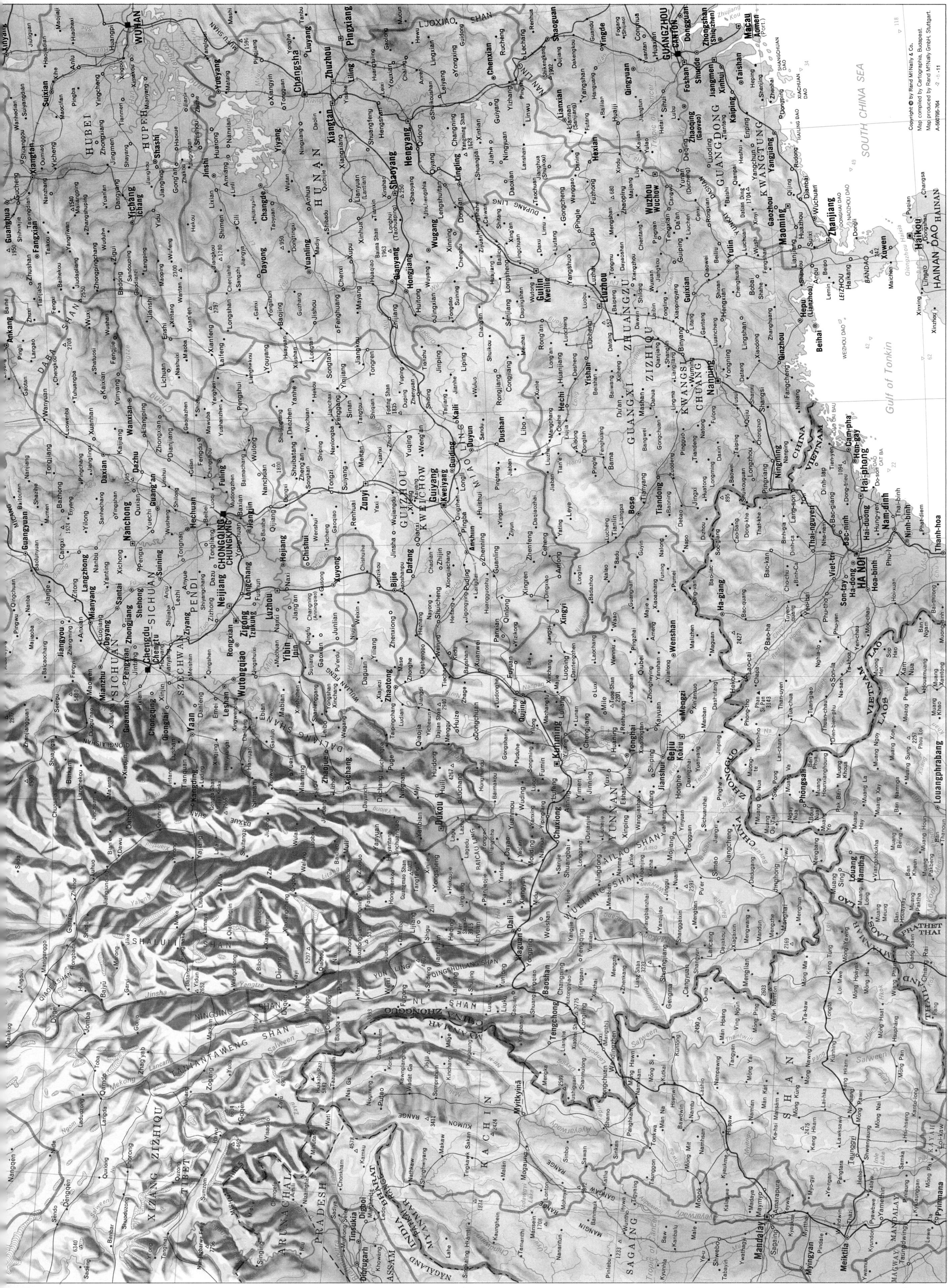
HUBEI
HUPEH
HUNAN
GUANGDONG
KWANGTUNG
GUANGXI ZHUANGZU ZIZHIQU
KWANGSI CHUANG
GUIZHOU
KWEICHOW
SICHUAN
SZECHWAN
YUNNAN
XIZANG ZIZHIQU
TIBET
ARUNACHAL PRADESH
ASSAM
NAGALAND
KACHIN
SAGAING
MANDALAY
MAGWAY
SHAN
KAYAH
VIETNAM
LAOS
THAILAND
PRATHET THAI
MYANMAR
INDIA
CHINA
HAINAN DAO
SOUTH CHINA SEA
Gulf of Tonkin
WUHAN
CHANGSHA
GUANGZHOU
CANTON
CHONGQING
CHUNGKING
CHENGDU
KUNMING
GUIYANG
NANNING
HA NOI
Mandalay
Macau
Aomen
Yangtze
Mekong
Salween
Jinsha
Lancang
MAP FORM | dao | hu | ling | shamo | shan | shuiku
ENGLISH | island | lake | mountains | desert | mountain(s) | reservoir
DEUTSCH | Insel | See | Berge | Wüste | Berg(e) | Stausee
ESPAÑOL | isla | lago | montañas | desierto | montaña(s) | embalse
FRANÇAIS | île | lac | montagnes | désert | montagne(s) | réservoir
PORTUGUÊS | ilha | lago | montanhas | deserto | montanha(s) | reservatório
Kilometers
Statute Miles
Scale 1:6,000,000
One centimeter represents 60 kilometers.
One inch represents approximately 95 miles.
Lambert Conformal Conic Projection
Copyright © by Rand McNally & Co.
Map compiled by Cartographia, Budapest.
Map produced by Rand McNally GmbH, Stuttgart.
A-560795-784
Feet | Meters
19685 | 6000
13124 | 4000
9843 | 3000
6562 | 2000
3281 | 1000
1640 | 500
656 | 200
0 | 0
Land Below Sea Level
656 | 200
3281 | 1000
9843 | 3000
19685 | 6000
29520 | 9000

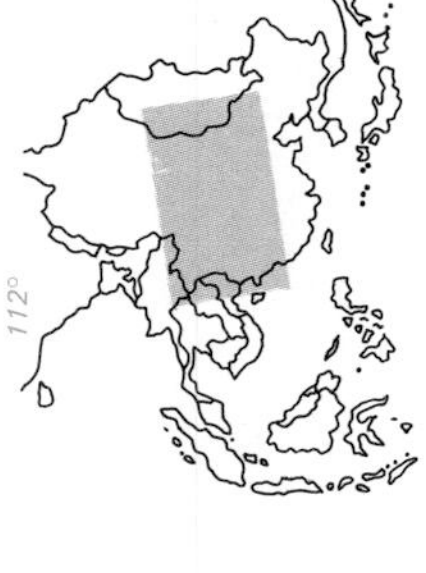

Map continues pages 110-111

Map continues pages 120-121

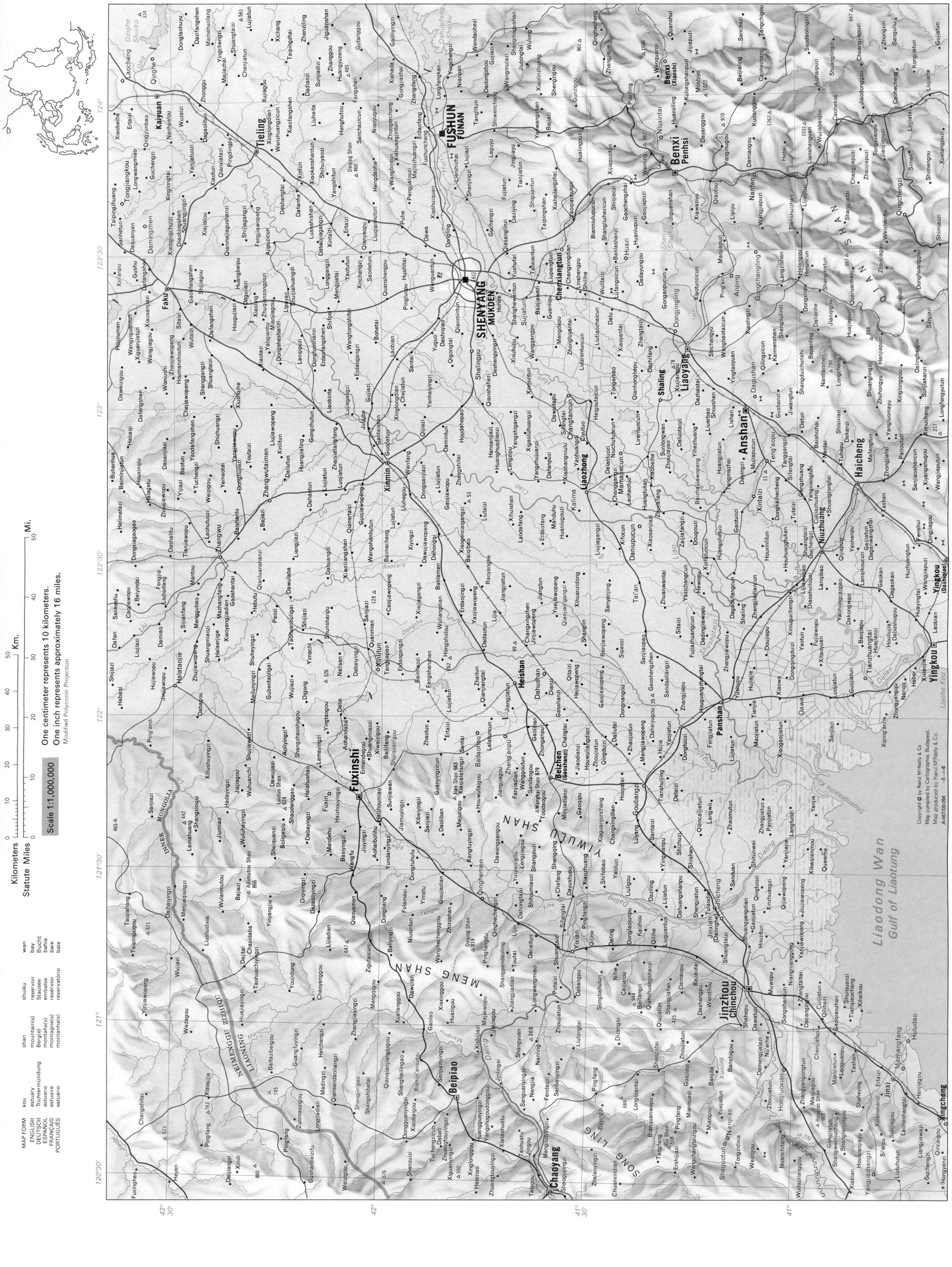
Kilometers 0 10 20 30 40 50 Km.
Statute Miles 0 10 20 30 40 50 Mi.
Scale 1:1,000,000
One centimeter represents 10 kilometers.
One inch represents approximately 16 miles.
Modified Polyconic Projection
MAP FORM kou shan shuku wan
ENGLISH estuary mountain(s) reservoir bay
DEUTSCH Trichtermündung Berg(e) Stausee Bucht
ESPAÑOL estuario montaña(s) embalse bahia
FRANÇAIS estuaire montagne(s) embalse baie
PORTUGUÊS estuário montanha(s) reservatório baía
Copyright © by Rand McNally & Co.
Map compiled by Cartographia, Budapest.
Map produced by Rand McNally & Co.
SHENYANG MUKDEN
FUSHUN
Benxi Penhsi
Anshan
Liaoyang
Tieling
Kaiyuan
Faku
Xinmin
Liaozhong
Heishan
Zhangwu
Fuxinshi
Beipiao
Chaoyang
Jinzhou Chinchow
Jinxi
Xingcheng
Panshan
Haicheng
Yingkou
Niuzhuang
QIAN SHAN
YIWULU SHAN
MENG SHAN
SONG LING
NEIMENGGU ZIZHIQU
LIAONING
INNER MONGOLIA
Liaodong Wan
Gulf of Liaotung

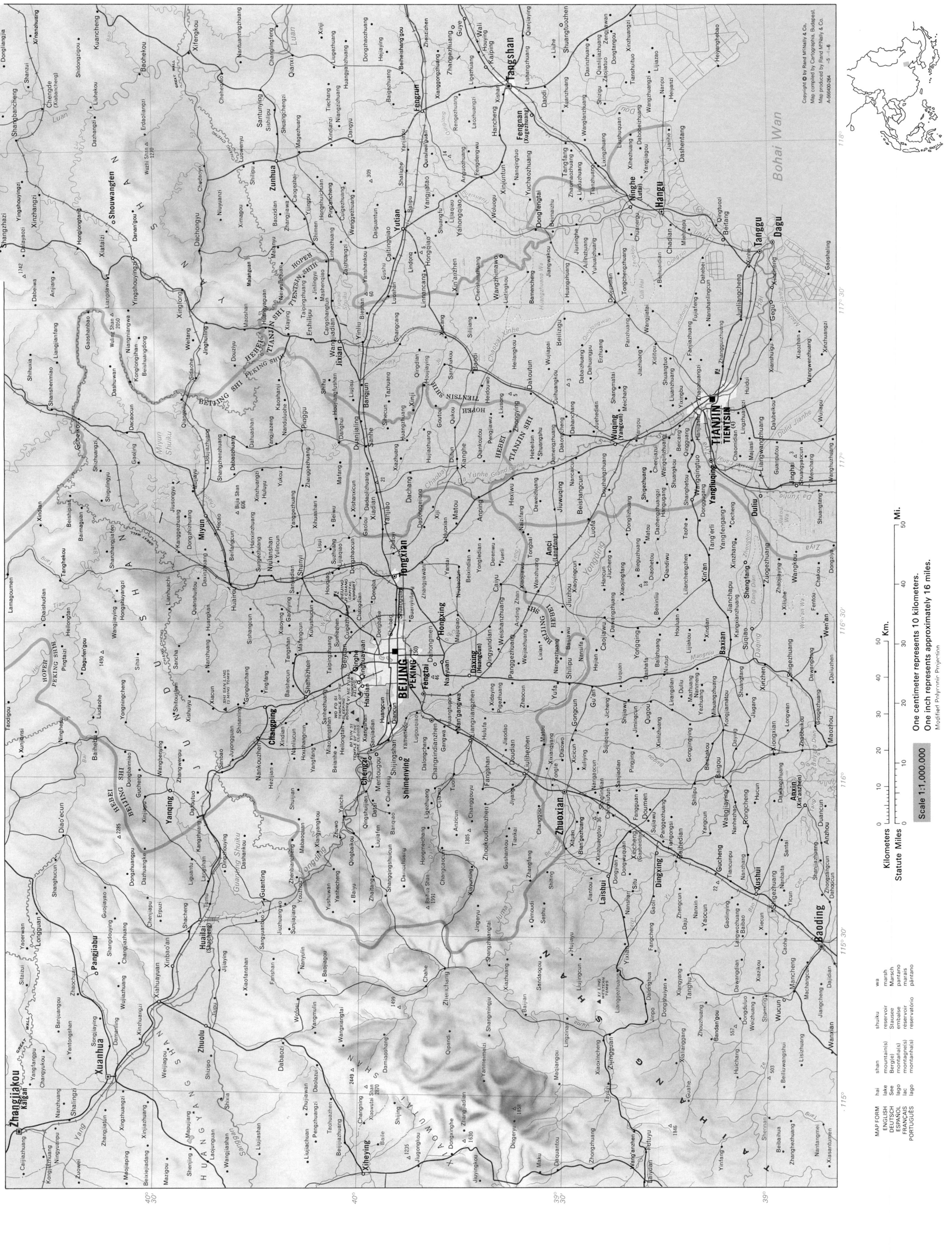
Kilometers
Statute Miles
Scale 1:1,000,000
One centimeter represents 10 kilometers.
One inch represents approximately 16 miles.
Modified Polyconic Projection
MAP FORM hai shan shuiku wa
ENGLISH lake mountain(s) reservoir marsh
DEUTSCH See Berg(e) Stausee Marsch
ESPAÑOL lago montaña(s) embalse pantano
FRANÇAIS lac montagne(s) réservoir marais
PORTUGUÊS lago montanha(s) reservatório pântano
Copyright © by Rand McNally & Co.
Map compiled by Cartographia, Budapest.
Map produced by Rand McNally & Co.
Bohai Wan
BEIJING
PEKING
TIANJIN
TIENTSIN
Tangshan
Baoding
Zhangjiakou
Kalgan
Chengde
Tanggu
Dagu

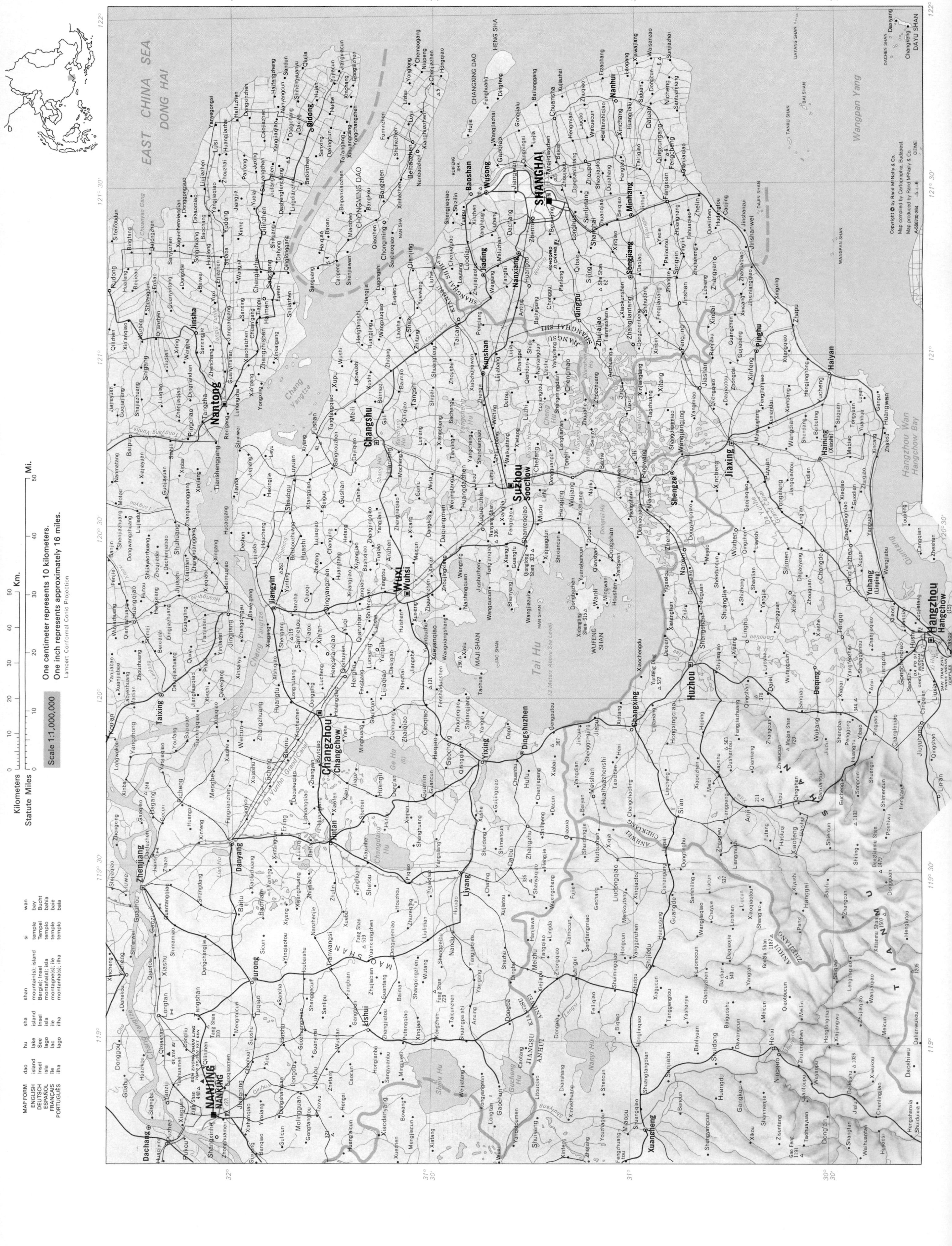
MAP FORM dao hu sha shan si wan
ENGLISH island lake island mountain(s); island temple bay
DEUTSCH Insel See Insel Berg(e); Insel Tempel Bucht
ESPAÑOL isla lago isla montaña(s); isla templo bahía
FRANÇAIS île lac île montagne(s); île temple baie
PORTUGUÊS ilha lago ilha montanha(s); ilha templo baía
Scale 1:1,000,000
One centimeter represents 10 kilometers.
One inch represents approximately 16 miles.
Lambert Conformal Conic Projection
Kilometers
Statute Miles
EAST CHINA SEA
DONG HAI
Tai Hu
SHANGHAI
NANJING
NANKING
Hangzhou Wan
Hangchow Bay

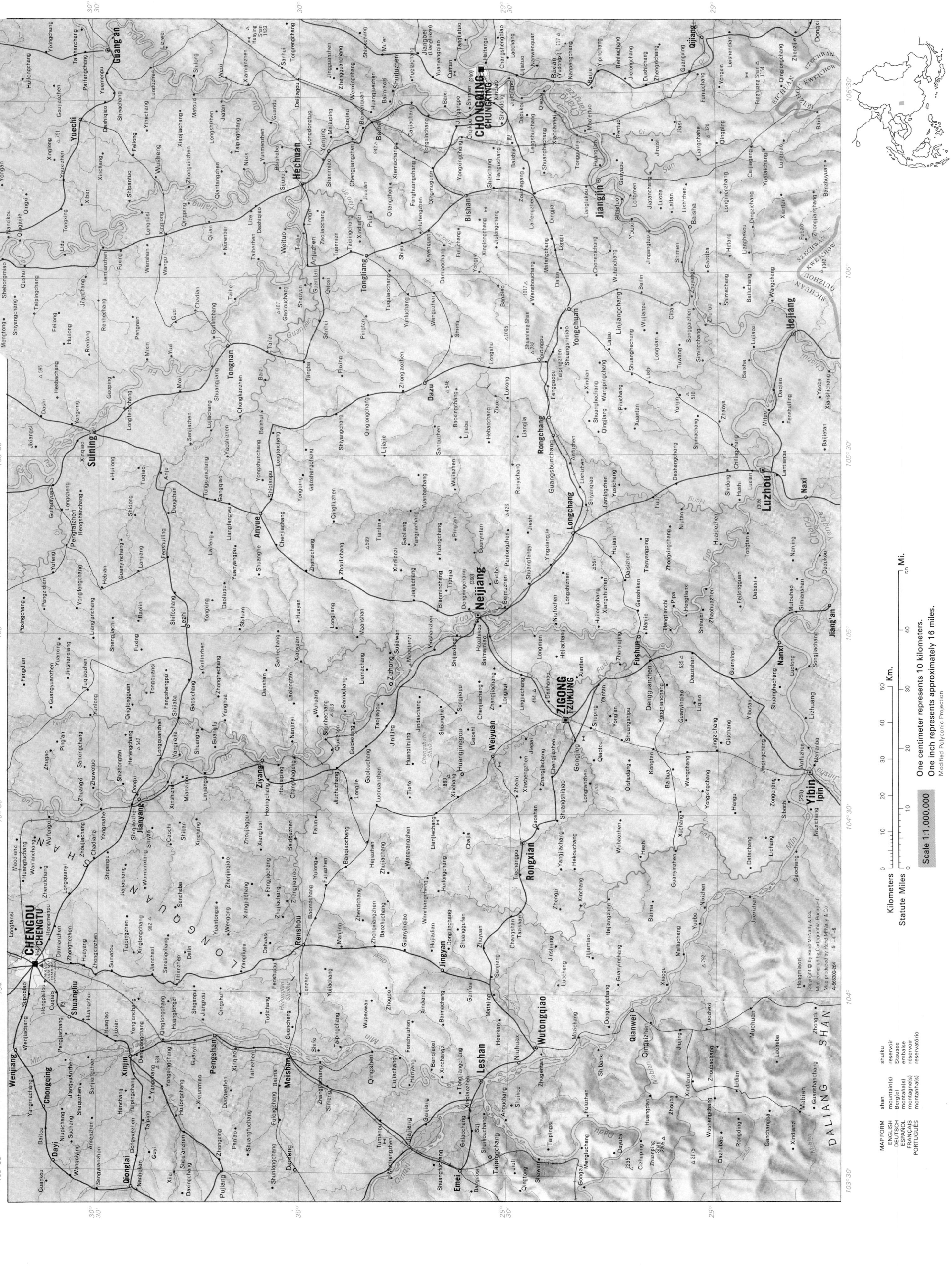
CHONGQING
CHUNGKING
CHENGDU
CHENGTU
ZIGONG
TZUKUNG
Neijiang
Luzhou
Yibin
Ipin
Leshan
Suining
Hechuan
Nanchong
Guang'an
Jiangjin
Yongchuan
Dazu
Tongnan
Anyue
Ziyang
Jianyang
Renshou
Meishan
Pengshan
Emei
Wutongqiao
Rongxian
Fushun
Naxi
Hejiang
Bishan
Tongliang
Weiyuan
Jingyan
Qianwei
Qionglai
Xinjin
Shuangliu
Dayi
Wenjiang
Chongqing
Qijiang
DALIANG SHAN
LONGQUAN SHAN
SICHUAN
GUIZHOU
SZECHWAN
KWEICHOW
MAP FORM
ENGLISH
DEUTSCH
ESPAÑOL
FRANÇAIS
PORTUGUÊS
shan
mountain(s)
Berg(e)
montaña(s)
montagne(s)
montanha(s)
shuiku
reservoir
Stausee
embalse
réservoir
reservatório
Scale 1:1,000,000
Kilometers
Statute Miles
One centimeter represents 10 kilometers.
One inch represents approximately 16 miles.
Modified Polyconic Projection
Copyright © by Rand McNally & Co.
Map compiled by Cartographia, Budapest.
Map produced by Rand McNally & Co.
A-566500-084 -5 -4 -6

Map continues pages 90-91

Map continues pages 118-119

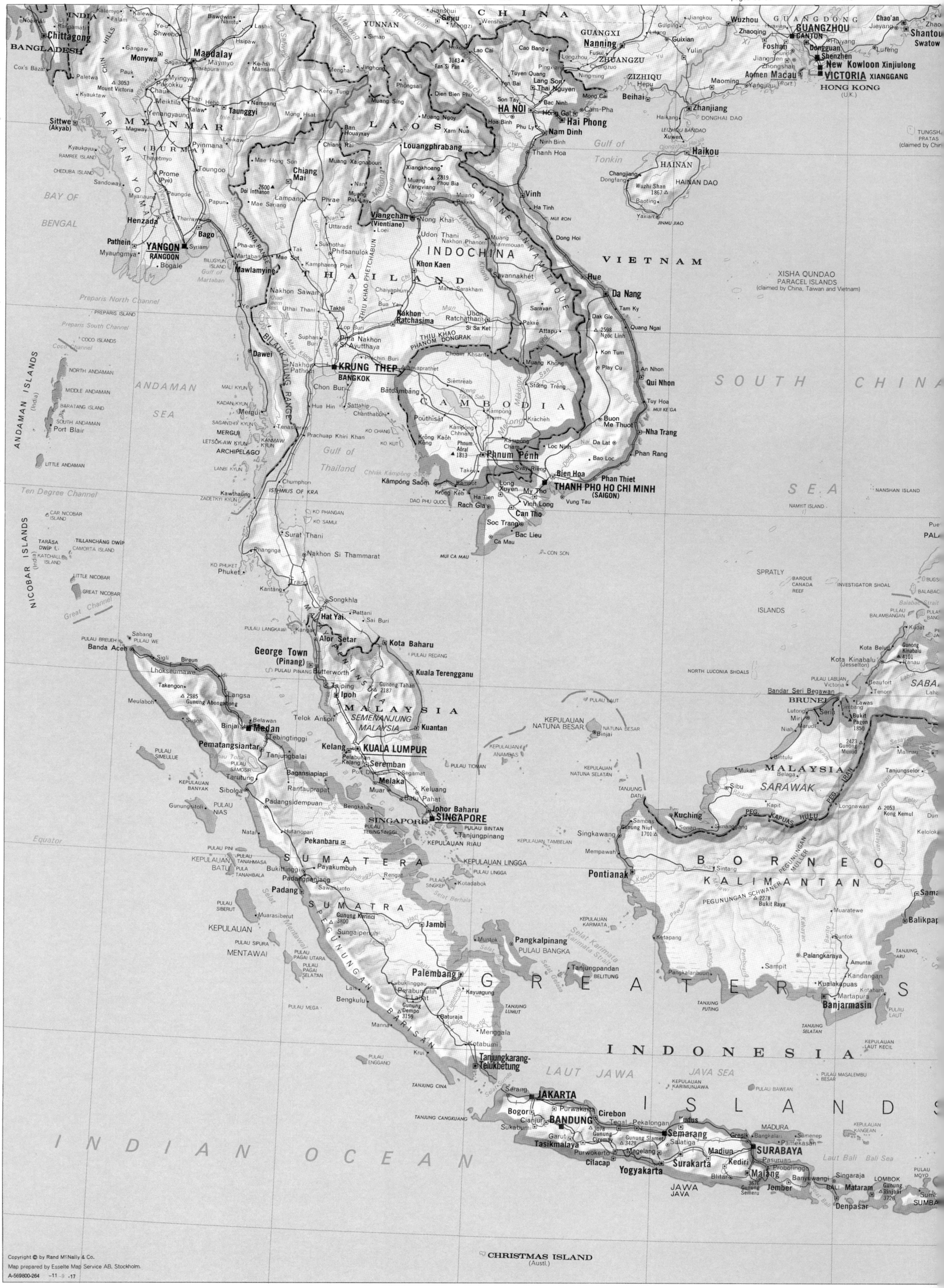
CHINA
YUNNAN
GUANGXI
Nanning
GUANGDONG
GUANGZHOU
Shenzhen
New Kowloon Xinjiulong
VICTORIA XIANGGANG
HONG KONG (U.K.)
Macau
Haikou
HAINAN
Gulf of Tonkin
HA NOI
Hai Phong
VIETNAM
LAOS
Louangphrabang
Viangchan (Vientiane)
INDOCHINA
THAILAND
KRUNG THEP BANGKOK
Chiang Mai
Nakhon Ratchasima
CAMBODIA
Phnum Pénh
THANH PHO HO CHI MINH (SAIGON)
Hue
Da Nang
MYANMAR (BURMA)
Mandalay
YANGON RANGOON
BANGLADESH
Chittagong
BAY OF BENGAL
ANDAMAN SEA
ANDAMAN ISLANDS (India)
NICOBAR ISLANDS (India)
Port Blair
Gulf of Thailand
ISTHMUS OF KRA
MALAYSIA
KUALA LUMPUR
George Town (Pinang)
SINGAPORE
Medan
SUMATERA
SUMATRA
Padang
Palembang
Pekanbaru
Jambi
KEPULAUAN MENTAWAI
Banda Aceh
SOUTH CHINA SEA
XISHA QUNDAO PARACEL ISLANDS (claimed by China, Taiwan and Vietnam)
SPRATLY ISLANDS
KEPULAUAN NATUNA BESAR
BRUNEI
Bandar Seri Begawan
SARAWAK
Kuching
BORNEO
KALIMANTAN
Pontianak
Banjarmasin
GREATER
INDONESIA
ISLANDS
LAUT JAWA JAVA SEA
JAKARTA
BANDUNG
Semarang
SURABAYA
Yogyakarta
JAWA JAVA
Denpasar
Mataram
INDIAN OCEAN
CHRISTMAS ISLAND (Austl.)
Equator



| MAP FORM | gulf | gunung | island | kepulauan | pulau | sea | selat | strait |
|---|---|---|---|---|---|---|---|---|
| ENGLISH | gulf | mountain | island | islands | island | sea | strait | strait |
| DEUTSCH | Golf | Berg | Insel | Inseln | Insel | Meer | Meeresstrasse | Meeresstrasse |
| ESPAÑOL | golfo | montaña | isla | islas | isla | mar | estrecho | estrecho |
| FRANÇAIS | golfe | montagne | île | îles | île | mer | détroit | détroit |
| PORTUGUÊS | golfo | montanha | ilha | ilhas | ilha | mar | estreito | estreito |

PHILIPPINE SEA
PACIFIC OCEAN
PHILIPPINES
LUZON
MINDORO
SAMAR
PANAY
NEGROS
MINDANAO
MANILA
Quezon City
Cebu
Davao
Iloilo
Bacolod
Cagayan de Oro
Zamboanga
TAIWAN
T'AIWAN
NORTHERN MARIANA ISLANDS (U.S.)
MARIANA ISLANDS
GUAM (U.S.)
Agana
FEDERATED STATES OF MICRONESIA
CAROLINE ISLANDS
PALAU BELAU
PALAU ISLANDS
Koror
CELEBES SEA
HALMAHERA
LAUT MALUKU
MOLUCCA SEA
LAUT SERAM
CERAM SEA
LAUT BANDA
BANDA SEA
MOLUCCAS
SERAM
BURU
Ambon
Manado
Gorontalo
KEPULAUAN SULA
KEPULAUAN ARU
KEPULAUAN TANIMBAR
KEPULAUAN KAI
TIMOR
Kupang
Dili
FLORES
SUMBA
TIMOR SEA
ARAFURA SEA
AUSTRALIA
NEW GUINEA
PAPUA NEW GUINEA
PEGUNUNGAN MAOKE
PEGUNUNGAN VAN REES
Puncak Jaya
Jayapura (Sukarnapura)
Teluk Cenderawasih
Gulf of Papua
Torres Strait
Tropic of Cancer
Equator

Map continues pages 160-161

Kilometers 0 200 400 600 Km.
Statute Miles 0 200 400 600 Mi.

Scale 1:12,000,000
One centimeter represents 120 kilometers.
One inch represents approximately 190 miles.
Lambert Conformal Conic Projection

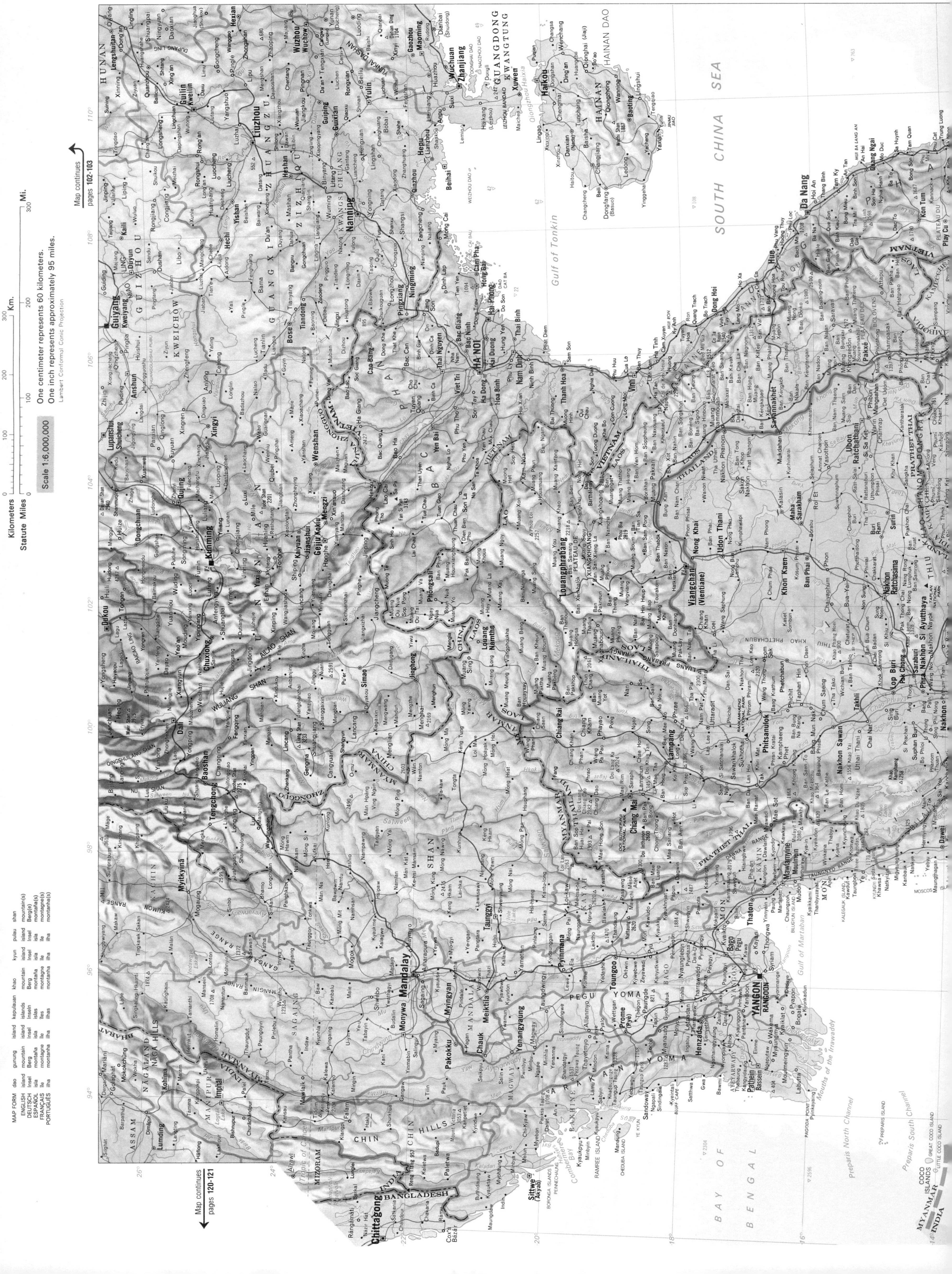
Kilometers 0 100 200 300 Km.
Statute Miles 0 100 200 300 Mi.
Scale 1:6,000,000
One centimeter represents 60 kilometers.
One inch represents approximately 95 miles.
Lambert Conformal Conic Projection
MAP FORM dao gunung island kepulauan khao kyun pulau shan
ENGLISH island mountain island islands mountain island island mountain(s)
DEUTSCH Insel Berg Insel Inseln Berg Insel Insel Berg(e)
ESPAÑOL isla montaña isla islas montaña isla isla montaña(s)
FRANÇAIS île montagne île îles montagne île île montagne(s)
PORTUGUÊS ilha montanha ilha ilhas montanha ilha ilha montanha(s)
Map continues pages 102-103
Map continues pages 120-121
SOUTH CHINA SEA
Gulf of Tonkin
Gulf of Martaban
BAY OF BENGAL
HAINAN DAO
HA NOI
YANGON RANGOON
Mandalay
Vientiane
Da Nang
Chittagong
BANGLADESH
INDIA
MYANMAR

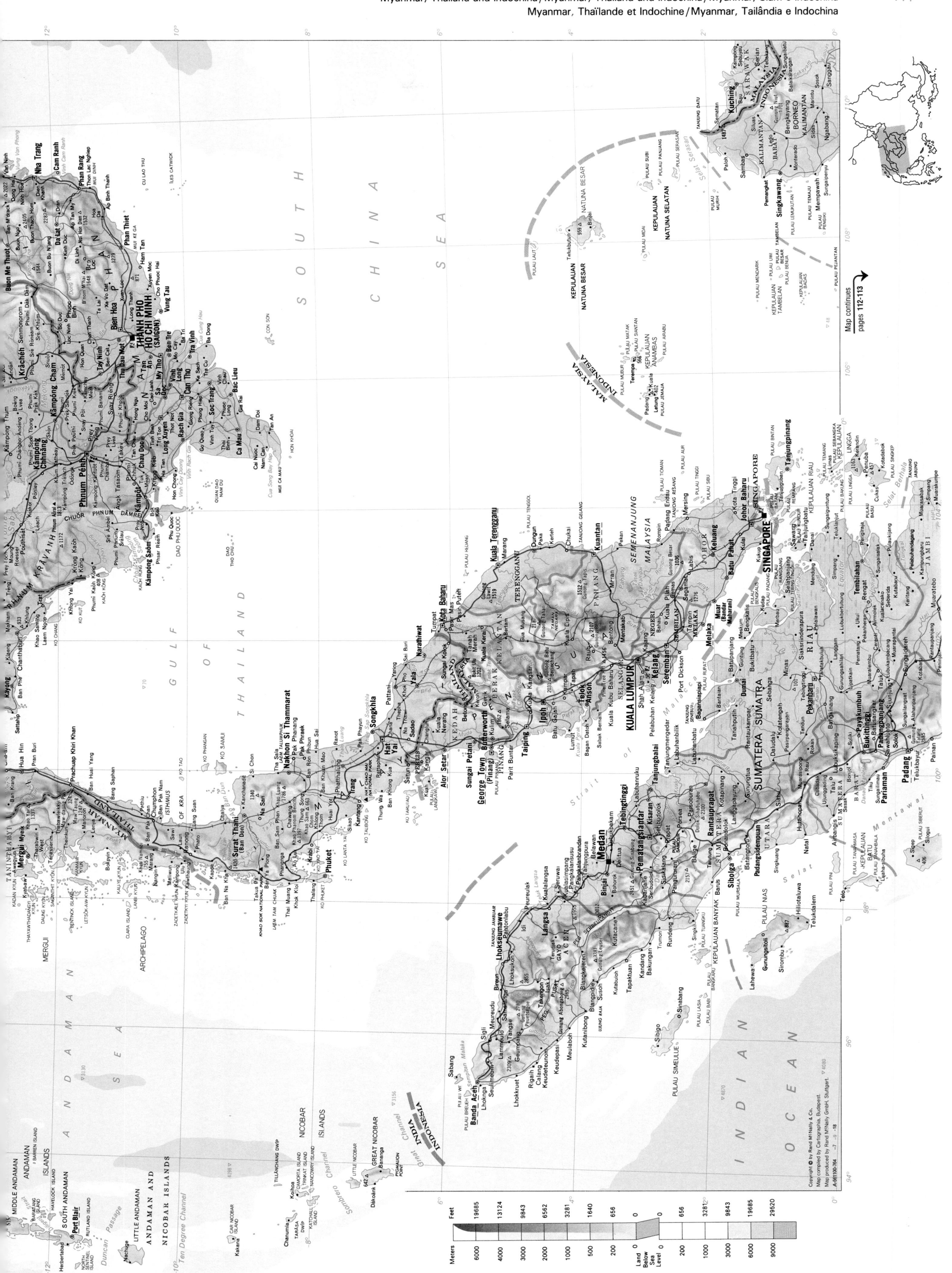

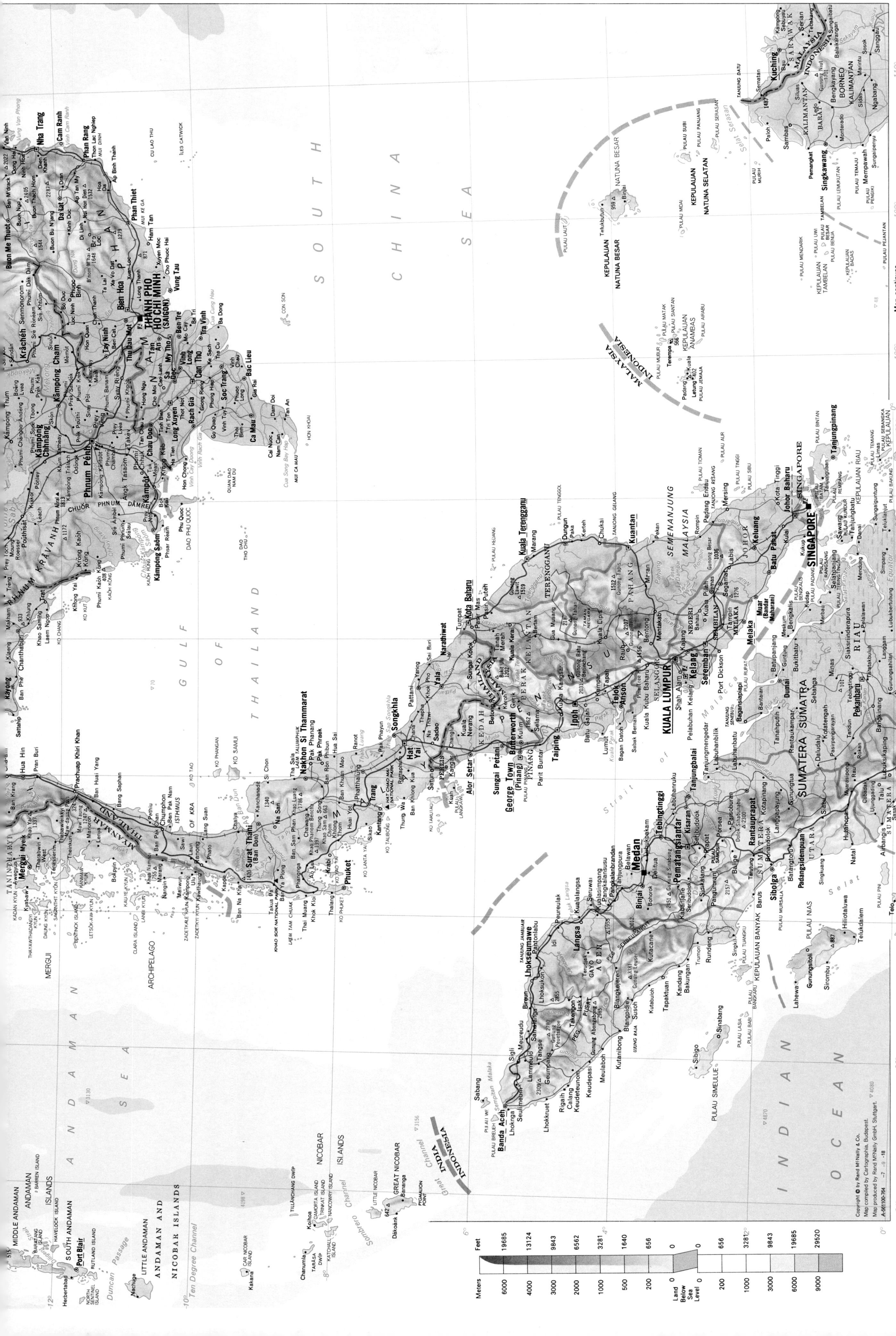
SOUTH CHINA SEA
GULF OF THAILAND
ANDAMAN SEA
INDIAN OCEAN
Strait of Malacca
ANDAMAN AND NICOBAR ISLANDS
MERGUI ARCHIPELAGO
THANH PHO HO CHI MINH (SAIGON)
Phnum Pénh
KUALA LUMPUR
SINGAPORE
SUMATERA SUMATRA
Medan
Padang
Banda Aceh
George Town (Pinang)
Phuket
Map continues pages 112-113
Feet
Meters
Land Below Sea Level
Copyright © by Rand McNally & Co.
Map compiled by Cartographia, Budapest.
Map produced by Rand McNally GmbH, Stuttgart.

# Malaysia and Western Indonesia / Malaysia und westliches Indonesien / Malasia e Indonesia Occidental
# Malaisie et Indonésie Occidentale / Malásia e Indonésia Ocidental

Map continues pages 110-111

SOUTH CHINA SEA
INDIAN OCEAN
LAUT JAWA
SUMATERA
SUMATRA
KALIMANTAN BARAT
JAWA
JAVA
SEMENANJUNG MALAYSIA
THAILAND
MALAYSIA
INDONESIA
SINGAPORE
Kuala Lumpur
JAKARTA
BANDUNG
Palembang
Padang
Pontianak
Kuching
Medan
Pekanbaru
Jambi
Bengkulu
Tanjungkarang-Telukbetung
Semarang
Yogyakarta
Surakarta
Cirebon
Bogor
Ipoh
Kota Baharu
Kuala Terengganu
Kuantan
Melaka
Seremban
Johor Baharu
KEPULAUAN NATUNA BESAR
KEPULAUAN NATUNA SELATAN
KEPULAUAN ANAMBAS
KEPULAUAN TAMBELAN
KEPULAUAN RIAU
KEPULAUAN LINGGA
KEPULAUAN KARIMATA
KEPULAUAN KARIMUNJAWA
KEPULAUAN MENTAWAI
PULAU BANGKA
BELITUNG
PULAU ENGGANO
Selat Sunda / Sunda Strait
Selat Karimata / Karimata Strait
Selat Berhala
Selat Mentawai
Equator
CHRISTMAS ISLAND (Austl.)
Flying Fish Cove
100° 102° 104° 106° 108° 110° 112°
Copyright © by Rand McNally & Co.
Map compiled by Cartographia, Budapest.
Map produced by Rand McNally GmbH, Stuttgart.
A-565500-764

| Meters | Feet |
|---|---|
| 6000 | 19685 |
| 4000 | 13124 |
| 3000 | 9843 |
| 2000 | 6562 |
| 1000 | 3281 |
| 500 | 1640 |
| 200 | 656 |
| 0 Land Below Sea Level | 0 |
| 0 | 0 |
| 200 | 656 |
| 1000 | 3281 |
| 3000 | 9343 |
| 6000 | 19685 |
| 9000 | 29520 |

| MAP FORM | danau | gunung | kepulauan | pegunungan | pulau | selat | tanjung | teluk |
|---|---|---|---|---|---|---|---|---|
| ENGLISH | lake | mountain | islands | mountains | island | strait | cape | bay |
| DEUTSCH | See | Berg | Inseln | Berge | Insel | Meeresstrasse | Kap | Bucht |
| ESPAÑOL | lago | montaña | islas | montañas | isla | estrecho | cabo | bahía |
| FRANÇAIS | lac | montagne | îles | montagnes | île | détroit | cap | baie |
| PORTUGUÊS | lago | montanha | ilhas | montanhas | ilha | estreito | cabo | baía |

Map continues pages 116-117
Map continues pages 164-165
PHILIPPINES
MALAYSIA
SULU SEA
CELEBES SEA
Moro Gulf
MINDANAO
Davao
Zamboanga
Jolo
SABAH
Sandakan
Kota Kinabalu (Jesselton)
BRUNEI
Bandar Seri Begawan
Miri
Tawau
Tarakan
KALIMANTAN TIMUR
BORNEO
KALIMANTAN
Samarinda
Balikpapan
Banjarmasin
KALIMANTAN SELATAN
Makasar Strait
SULAWESI UTARA
Manado
Gorontalo
Palu
SULAWESI TENGAH
SULAWESI SELATAN
SULAWESI CELEBES
SULAWESI TENGGARA
Kendari
Ujungpandang (Makasar)
Teluk Bone
Teluk Tomini
LAUT MALUKU
MOLUCCA SEA
KEPULAUAN SULA
MALUKU
BURU
LAUT BANDA
BANDA SEA
Laut Flores
Flores Sea
Laut Bali
Bali Sea
JAWA SEA
JAWA TIMUR
BALI
Denpasar
LOMBOK
Mataram
SUMBAWA
NUSA TENGGARA BARAT
FLORES
NUSA TENGGARA TIMUR
Ende
SUMBA
Laut Sawu
Sawu Sea
TIMOR
Kupang
Dili
TIMOR TIMUR
TIMOR SEA
Equator

Kilometers 0 100 200 300 Km.

Statute Miles 0 100 200 300 Mi.

Scale 1:6,000,000

One centimeter represents 60 kilometers.

One inch represents approximately 95 miles.

Mercator Projection

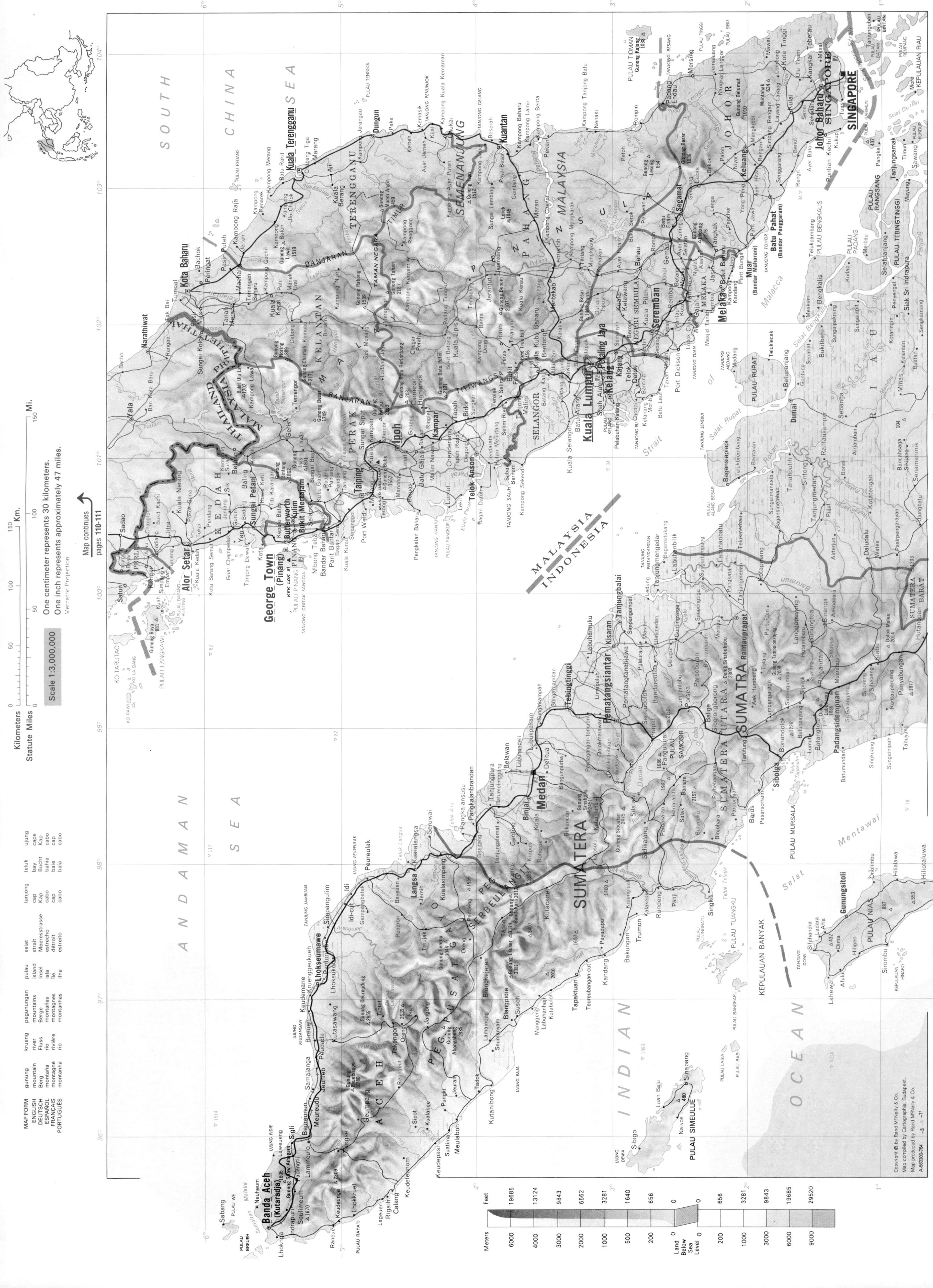
SOUTH CHINA SEA
ANDAMAN SEA
INDIAN OCEAN
Strait of Malacca
MALAYSIA
INDONESIA
THAILAND
MALAYSIA
SUMATERA
SINGAPORE
Kuala Lumpur
George Town (Pinang)
Ipoh
Melaka
Seremban
Kuantan
Kuala Terengganu
Kota Baharu
Alor Setar
Johor Baharu
Medan
Banda Aceh (Kutaradja)
Pematangsiantar
Tebingtinggi
Sibolga
Padangsidempuan
Gunungsitoli
Dumai
Pekanbaru
PULAU NIAS
PULAU SIMEULUE
KEPULAUAN BANYAK
KEPULAUAN RIAU
PULAU LANGKAWI
PULAU RUPAT
PULAU BENGKALIS
ACEH
RIAU
SUMATERA UTARA
SUMATERA BARAT
JOHOR
PAHANG
KEDAH
PERAK
SELANGOR
KELANTAN
TERENGGANU
NEGERI SEMBILAN
MELAKA
PERLIS
Map continues pages 110-111
Map continues pages 112-113
Kilometers 0 50 100 150 Km.
Statute Miles 0 50 100 150 Mi.
Scale 1:3,000,000
One centimeter represents 30 kilometers.
One inch represents approximately 47 miles.
Mercator Projection
MAP FORM: gunung, krueng, pegunungan, pulau, selat, tanjong, teluk, ujung
ENGLISH: mountain, river, mountains, island, strait, cape, bay, cape
DEUTSCH: Berg, Fluss, Berge, Insel, Meeresstrasse, Kap, Bucht, Kap
ESPAÑOL: montaña, rio, montañas, isla, estrecho, cabo, bahia, cabo
FRANÇAIS: montagne, rivière, montagnes, île, détroit, cap, baie, cap
PORTUGUÊS: montanha, rio, montanhas, ilha, estreito, cabo, baia, cabo
Meters 6000 4000 3000 2000 1000 500 200 0 Land Below Sea Level 0 200 1000 3000 6000 9000
Feet 19685 13124 9843 6562 3281 1640 656 0 0 656 3281 9843 19685 29520
Copyright © by Rand McNally & Co.
Map compiled by Cartographia, Budapest.
Map produced by Rand McNally & Co.

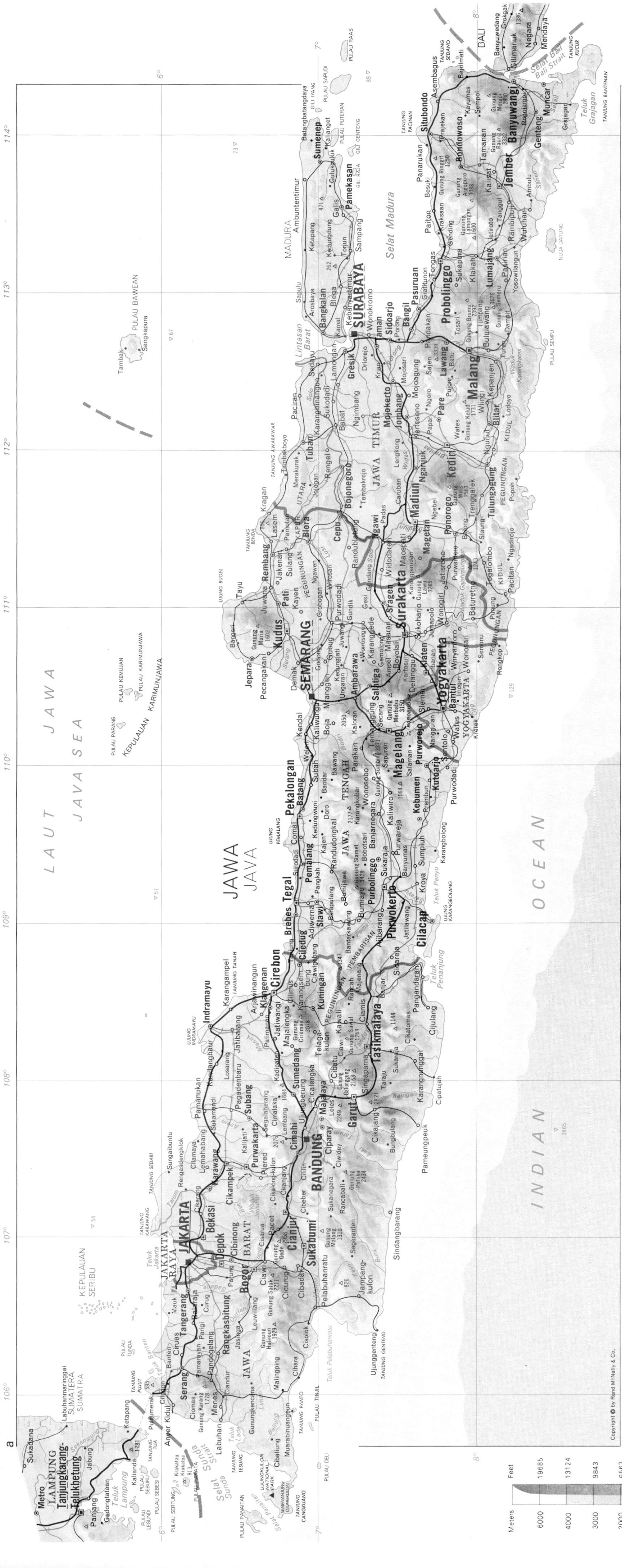
a
JAWA
JAVA
LAUT JAWA
JAVA SEA
INDIAN OCEAN
JAKARTA
BANDUNG
SEMARANG
SURABAYA
MADURA
Copyright © by Rand McNally & Co.

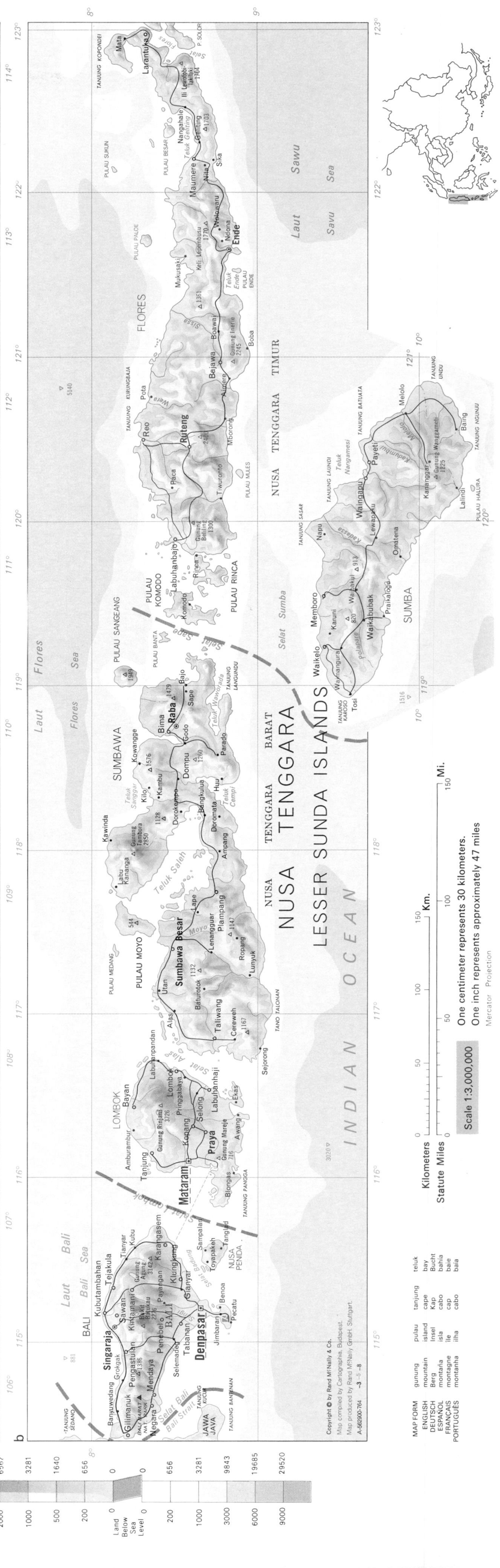
b
NUSA TENGGARA
LESSER SUNDA ISLANDS
INDIAN OCEAN
Laut Flores
Flores Sea
Laut Sawu
Savu Sea
FLORES
SUMBA
SUMBAWA
LOMBOK
BALI
Scale 1:3,000,000
One centimeter represents 30 kilometers.
One inch represents approximately 47 miles
Mercator Projection
Kilometers
Statute Miles
Copyright © by Rand McNally & Co.

Scale 1:3,000,000

One centimeter represents 30 kilometers.
One inch represents approximately 47 miles.
Lambert Conformal Conic Projection

Kilometers 0 50 100 150 Km.
Statute Miles 0 50 100 150 Mi.

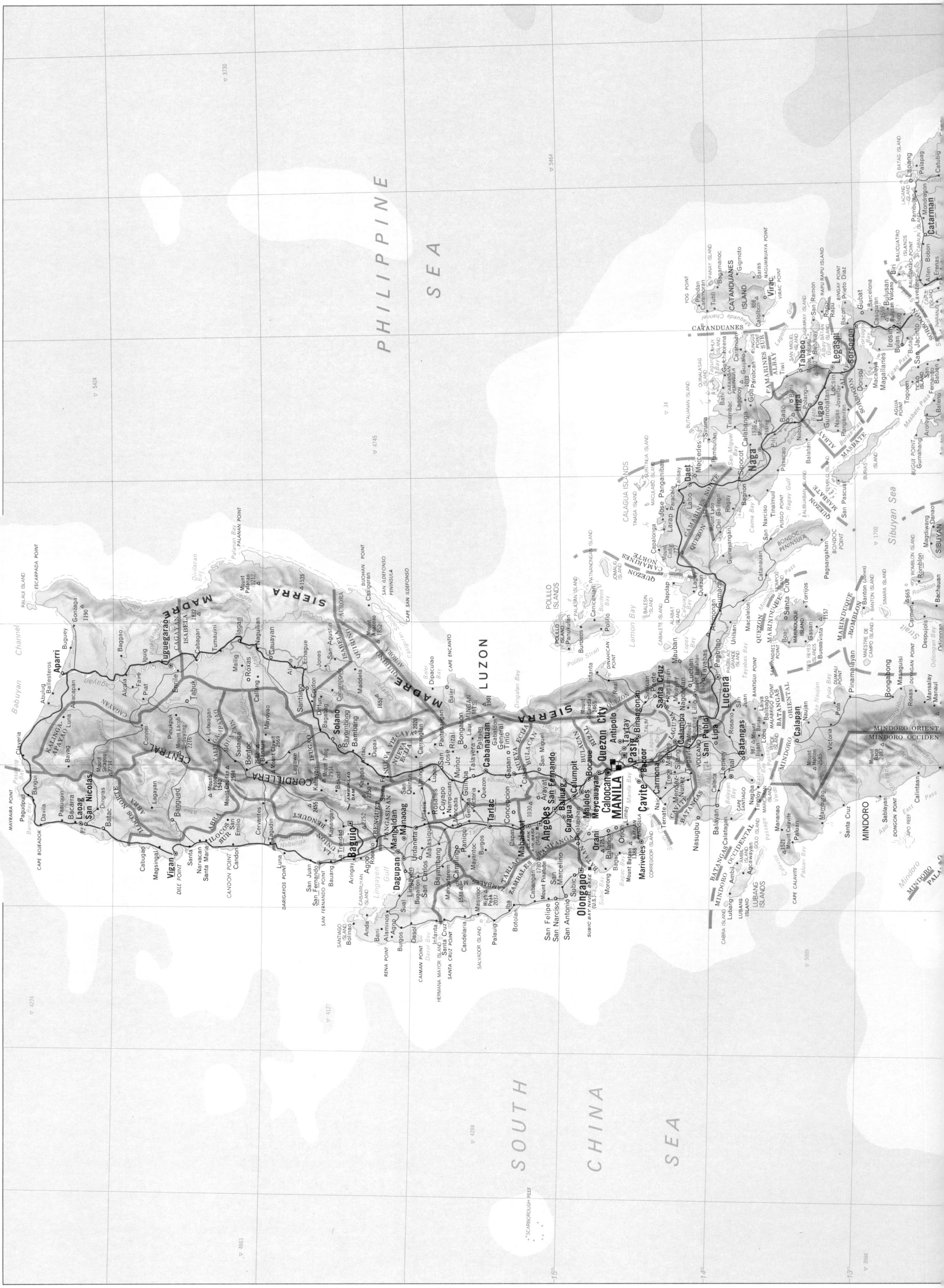
PHILIPPINE SEA
SOUTH CHINA SEA
LUZON
MANILA
Quezon City
Caloocan
Pasay
Cavite
Olongapo
Baguio
Vigan
Laoag
Aparri
Tuguegarao
Dagupan
Cabanatuan
Lucena
Batangas
Naga
Legaspi
Sorsogon
Daet
Virac
Calapan
MINDORO
Catarman
CATANDUANES
BABUYAN ISLANDS
POLILLO ISLANDS
SIERRA MADRE
CORDILLERA CENTRAL
Luzon Strait
Babuyan Channel
Lingayen Gulf
Manila Bay
Lamon Bay
Sibuyan Sea
Tayabas Bay
Ragay Gulf

| MAP FORM | bay | channel | island, i. | mount, mt. | passage | peak, pk. | point | strait |
|---|---|---|---|---|---|---|---|---|
| ENGLISH | bay | channel | island | mount | passage | peak | point | strait |
| DEUTSCH | Bucht | Kanal | Insel | Berg | Durchfahrt | Gipfel | Landspitze | Meeresstrasse |
| ESPAÑOL | bahía | canal | isla | montaña | pasaje | pico | punta | estrecho |
| FRANÇAIS | baie | détroit | île | mont | passage | cime | pointe | détroit |
| PORTUGUÊS | baía | canal | ilha | montanha | passagem | pico | ponta | estreito |

| Feet | 19685 | 13124 | 9843 | 6562 | 3281 | 1640 | 656 | 0 | | 0 | 656 | 3281 | 9843 | 19685 | 29520 |
|---|---|---|---|---|---|---|---|---|---|---|---|---|---|---|---|
| Meters | 6000 | 4000 | 3000 | 2000 | 1000 | 500 | 200 | 0 | Land Below Sea Level | 0 | 200 | 1000 | 3000 | 6000 | 9000 |

SULU SEA
CELEBES SEA
MINDANAO
Moro Gulf
Zamboanga
Davao
Cotabato
Cagayan de Oro
Butuan
Surigao
Iligan
Marawi
Dipolog
Pagadian
Cebu
Mandaue
Lapu-Lapu (Opon)
Tacloban
Iloilo
Bacolod
Roxas
Dumaguete
Tagbilaran
NEGROS
PANAY
BOHOL
PALAWAN
Puerto Princesa
Sandakan
Jolo
Isabela
SULU ARCHIPELAGO
PHILIPPINES PILIPINAS
MALAYSIA
SABAH
BORNEO KALIMANTAN
Map continues pages 112-113
Copyright © by Rand McNally & Co.

Map continues pages 22-23

Map continues pages 134-135

TURKEY
ASIA MINOR
SYRIA
LEBANON
ISRAEL
JORDAN
IRAQ
IRAN
KUWAIT
SAUDI ARABIA
QATAR
BAHRAIN
UNITED ARAB EMIRATES
OMAN
YEMEN
DJIBOUTI
ETHIOPIA
SOMALIA
SUDAN
ERITREA
EGYPT
TURKMENISTAN
AZERBAIJAN
ARMENIA
GEORGIA
CASPIAN SEA
MEDITERRANEAN SEA
RED SEA
Gulf of Aden
Gulf of Oman
Persian Gulf
INDIAN
ARAB
AN NAFŪD
AR RUB' AL KHĀLĪ
NAJD
AL HIJAZ
ASIR
HADRAMAWT
ZUFĀR
DASHT-E KAVĪR
DASHT-E LŪT
KARAKUMY
MAKRAN COAST
OGADEN
Tropic of Cancer
TBILISI
JEREVAN
BAKI
TEHRĀN
BAGHDĀD
DIMASHQ DAMASCUS
BAYRŪT BEIRUT
'AMMĀN
Yerushalayim Jerusalem
Nicosia
AL-KUWAYT
AR-RIYĀD RIYADH
AL-MANĀMAH
AD-DAWHAH Doha
ABŪ ZABY Abu Dhabi
MASQAT Muscat
SAN'Ā'
Adan Aden
Djibouti
Asmera
Aşchabad
Mashhad
Eşfahān
Shīrāz
Makkah Mecca
Al-Madīnah Medina
Jiddah Jeddah
Halab Aleppo
Al-Mawşil Mosul
Al-Başrah Basra
Tabrīz
Ankara
Kayseri
Sivas
Erzurum
Adana
Konya
Hargeysa
Berbera
Dire Dawa
Harer
SUQUTRĀ SOCOTRA (Yemen)
Bandar-e 'Abbās
Kermān
Yazd
Zāhedān

| MAP FORM | gulf | jabal | jazīrat | range | ra's | shan |
|---|---|---|---|---|---|---|
| ENGLISH | gulf | mountain | island | range | cape | mountain(s) |
| DEUTSCH | Golf | Berg | Insel | Gebirge | Kap | Berg(e) |
| ESPAÑOL | golfo | montaña | isla | sierra | cabo | montaña(s) |
| FRANÇAIS | golfe | montagne | île | chaîne | cap | montagne(s) |
| PORTUGUÊS | golfo | montanha | ilha | serra | cabo | montanha(s) |

Kilometers 0 200 400 600 Km.
Statute Miles 0 200 400 600 Mi.

Scale 1:12,000,000

One centimeter represents 120 kilometers.
One inch represents approximately 190 miles.
Lambert Conformal Conic Projection

Map continues
pages 72-73

Map continues
pages 90-91

Map continues
pages 108-109

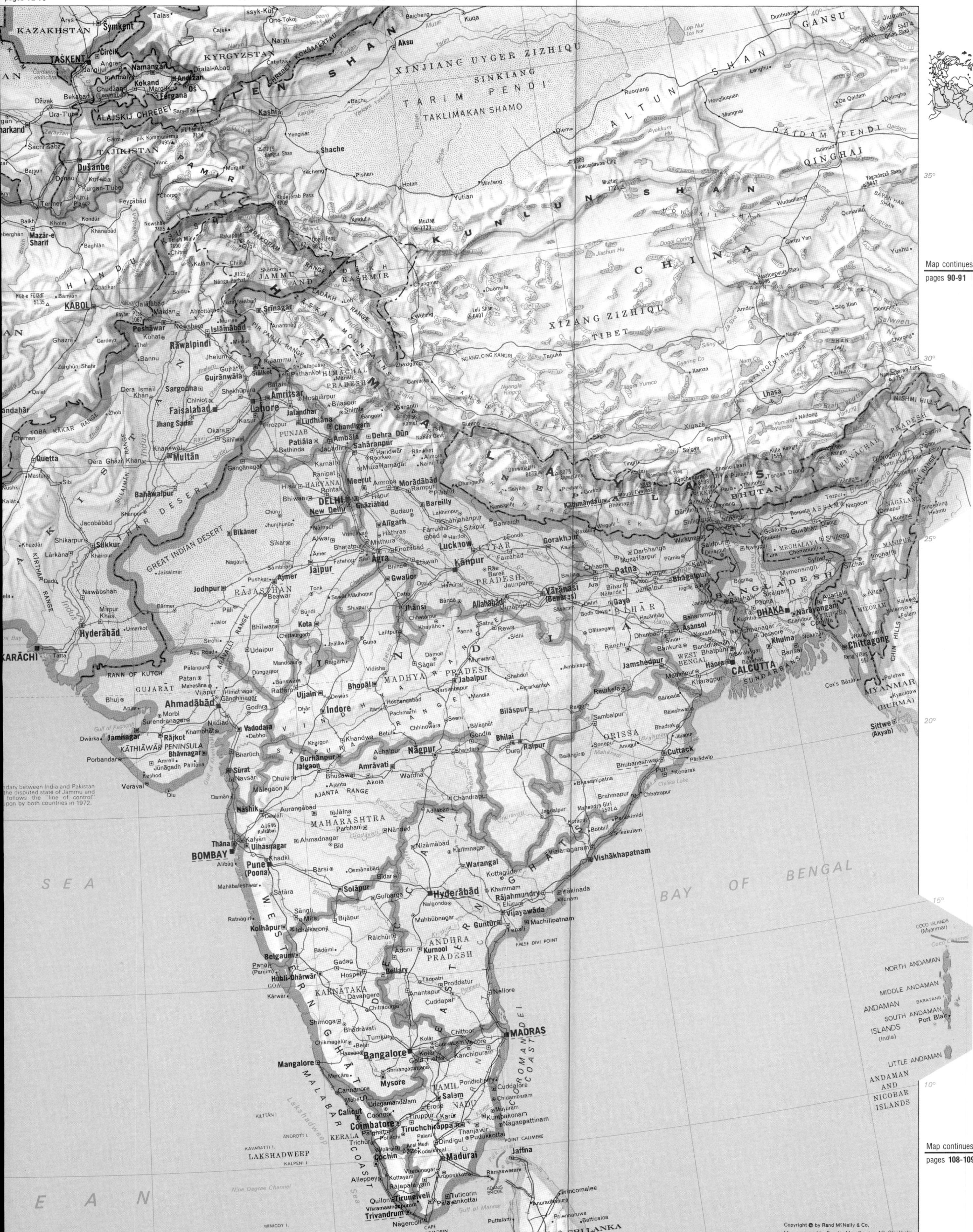
KAZAKHSTAN
KYRGYZSTAN
TAJIKISTAN
XINJIANG UYGER ZIZHIQU
SINKIANG
TARIM PENDI
TAKLIMAKAN SHAMO
TIEN SHAN
ALTUN SHAN
KUNLUN SHAN
QINGHAI
GANSU
QAIDAM PENDI
CHINA
XIZANG ZIZHIQU
TIBET
JAMMU AND KASHMIR
HINDU KUSH
KĀBOL
Peshāwar
Islāmābād
Rāwalpindi
Lahore
Faisalabad
Multān
Quetta
PAKISTAN
Hyderābād
KARĀCHI
THAR DESERT
GREAT INDIAN DESERT
PUNJAB
HARYANA
DELHI
New Delhi
HIMACHAL PRADESH
UTTAR PRADESH
RĀJASTHĀN
Jaipur
Jodhpur
Āgra
Kānpur
Lucknow
Vārānasi
Patna
BIHĀR
NEPAL
Kāthmāndau
BHUTAN
Thimphu
SIKKIM
ASSAM
MEGHALAYA
BANGLADESH
DHAKA
Chittagong
WEST BENGAL
CALCUTTA
ORISSA
Cuttack
MADHYA PRADESH
Bhopāl
Indore
Jabalpur
Nāgpur
GUJARĀT
Ahmadābād
Rājkot
KĀTHIĀWĀR PENINSULA
MAHĀRĀSHTRA
BOMBAY
Pune
Hyderābād
ANDHRA PRADESH
Vishākhapatnam
KARNĀTAKA
Bangalore
Mysore
MADRAS
TAMIL NĀDU
KERALA
Madurai
Trivandrum
Cochin
Calicut
LAKSHADWEEP
SRI LANKA
COLOMBO
Sri Jayawardenepura
(Kotte)
Jaffna
Trincomalee
BAY OF BENGAL
ARABIAN SEA
INDIAN OCEAN
MYANMAR
(BURMA)
Sittwe
(Akyab)
NORTH ANDAMAN
MIDDLE ANDAMAN
SOUTH ANDAMAN
ANDAMAN ISLANDS
(India)
Port Blair
LITTLE ANDAMAN
ANDAMAN AND NICOBAR ISLANDS
COCO ISLANDS
(Myanmar)
Lhasa
Copyright © by Rand McNally & Co.
Map prepared by Esselte Map Service AB, Stockholm.
A-569400-264 -14 -10 -28

Map continues pages 128-129

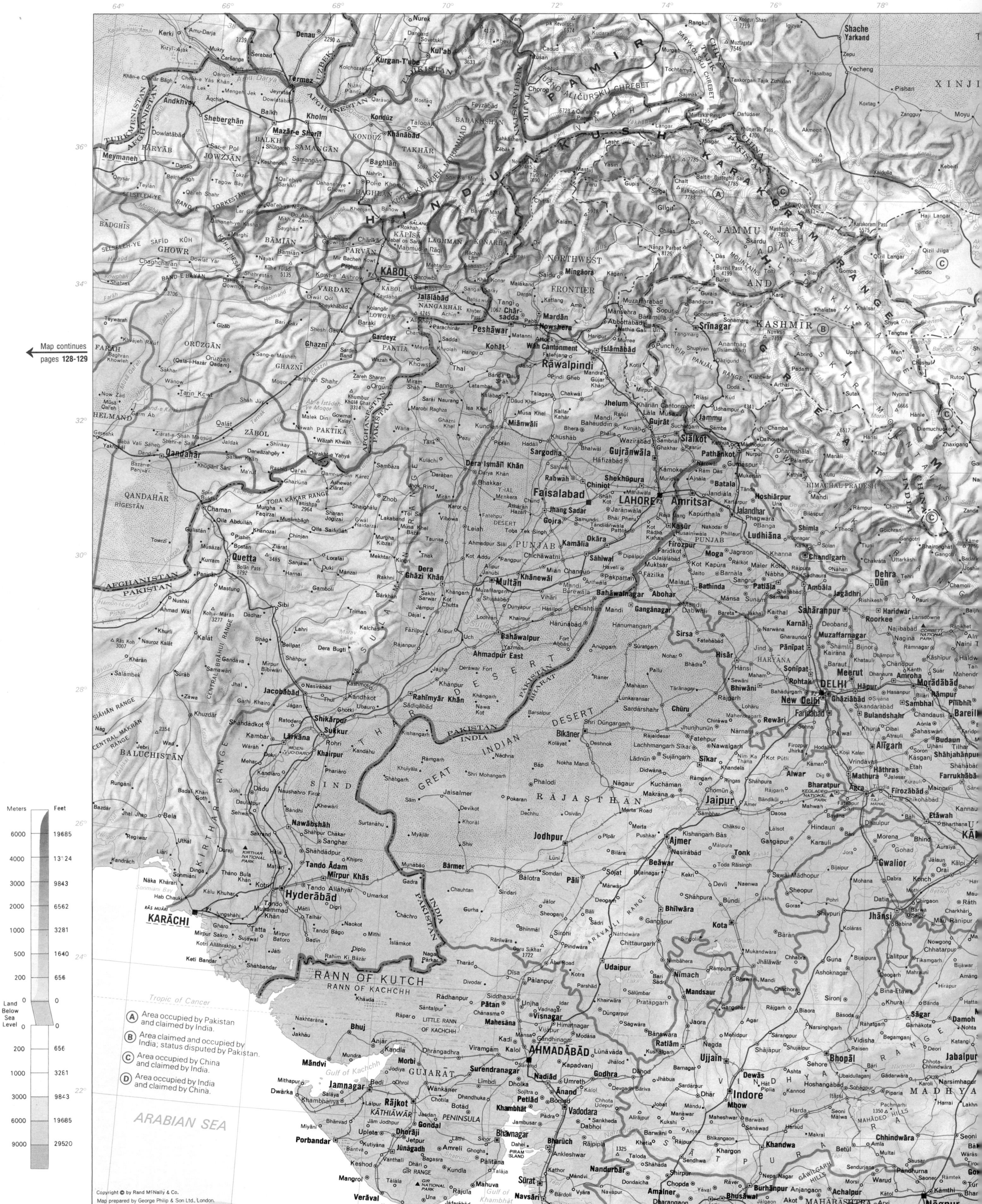
Meters
Feet
6000
19685
4000
13124
3000
9843
2000
6562
1000
3281
500
1640
200
656
0
0
Land Below Sea Level
0
0
200
656
1000
3281
3000
9843
6000
19685
9000
29520
Ⓐ Area occupied by Pakistan and claimed by India.
Ⓑ Area claimed and occupied by India; status disputed by Pakistan.
Ⓒ Area occupied by China and claimed by India.
Ⓓ Area occupied by India and claimed by China.
ARABIAN SEA
KARĀCHI
Hyderābād
Quetta
KĀBOL
Peshāwar
Islāmābād
Rāwalpindi
LAHORE
Amritsar
Faisalabad
Multān
DELHI
New Delhi
Jaipur
Jodhpur
AHMADĀBĀD
Indore
Bhopāl
Nāgpur
Srīnagar
RANN OF KUTCH
GREAT INDIAN DESERT
THAR DESERT
HINDU KUSH
KARAKORAM RANGE
PAMIR
Tropic of Cancer
Copyright © by Rand McNally & Co.
Map prepared by George Philip & Son Ltd., London.
A-565200-764 -8 -T -20

| MAP FORM | co | feng | hu | range | shan | shankou | yumco |
|---|---|---|---|---|---|---|---|
| ENGLISH | lake | peak | lake | range | mountain(s) | pass | lake |
| DEUTSCH | See | Gipfel | See | Gebirge | Berg(e) | Pass | See |
| ESPAÑOL | lago | pico | lago | sierra | montaña(s) | paso | lago |
| FRANÇAIS | lac | cime | lac | chaîne | montagne(s) | col | lac |
| PORTUGUÊS | lago | pico | lago | serra | montanha(s) | passo | lago |

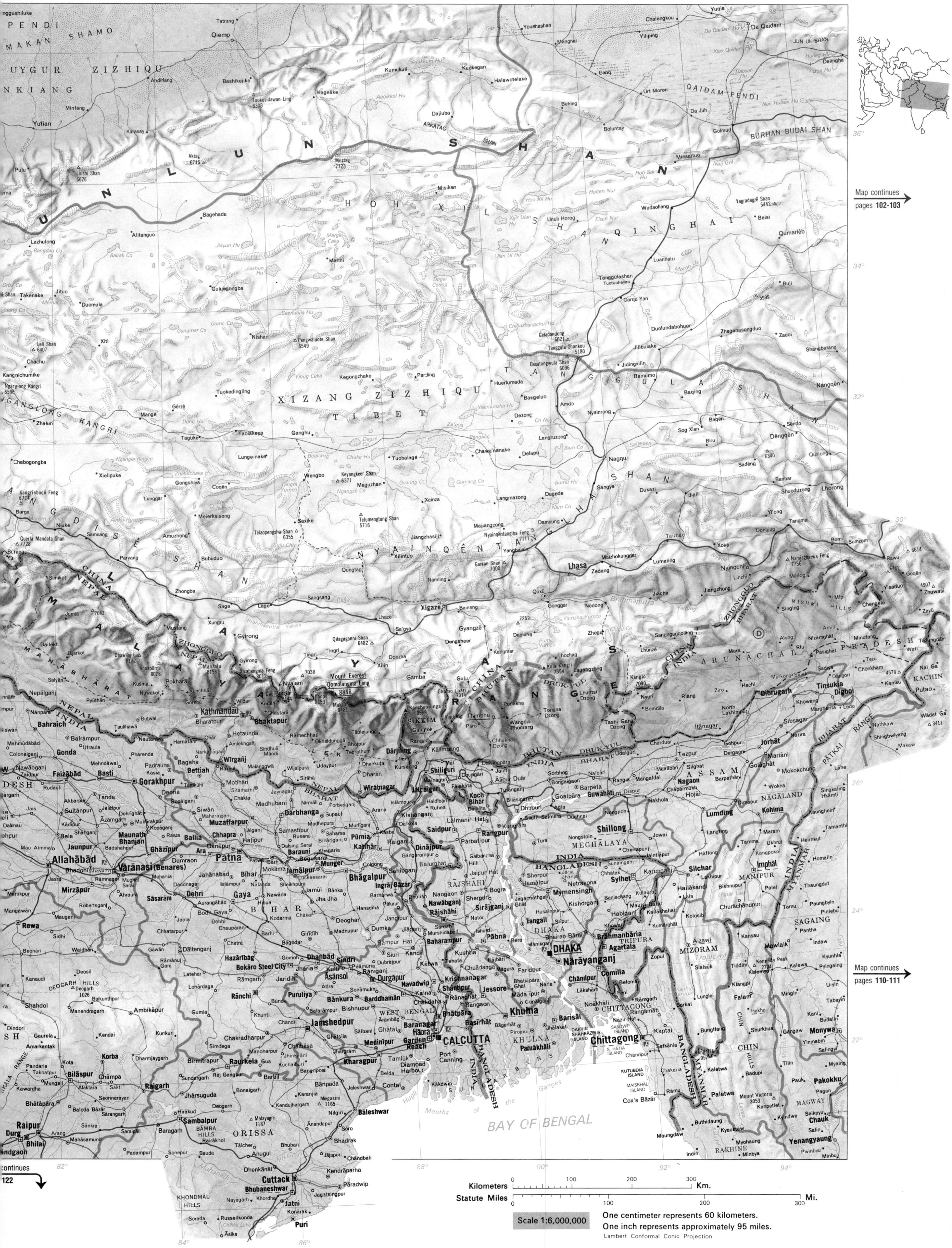
XIZANG ZIZHIQU
TIBET
NYAINQÊNTANGLHA SHAN
HOH XIL SHAN
QAIDAM PENDI
BURHAN BUDAI SHAN
QINGHAI
TANGGULA SHAN
HIMALAYA
GREAT HIMALAYA RANGE
Mount Everest
Qomolangma Feng
8848
Lhasa
Kathmandau
Thimphu
NEPAL
BHUTAN
SIKKIM
BANGLADESH
ARUNACHAL PRADESH
ASSAM
MEGHALAYA
TRIPURA
MANIPUR
NAGALAND
MIZORAM
BIHAR
ORISSA
DHAKA
Calcutta
Patna
Chittagong
Khulna
Allahabad
Vārānasi (Benares)
Gorakhpur
Jamshedpur
Cuttack
Bhubaneshwar
Puri
Shillong
Imphal
Brahmaputra
Ganges
BAY OF BENGAL
Mouths of the Ganges
CHINA
INDIA
MYANMAR

Map continues
pages 102-103

Map continues
pages 110-111

continues
122

Kilometers 0 100 200 300 Km.
Statute Miles 0 100 200 300 Mi.

Scale 1:6,000,000

One centimeter represents 60 kilometers.
One inch represents approximately 95 miles.
Lambert Conformal Conic Projection

# Southern India and Sri Lanka / Südindien und Sri Lanka / India Meridional y Sri Lanka
# Inde Méridionale et Sri Lanka / Índia Meridional e Sri Lanka

Map continues
pages 120-121

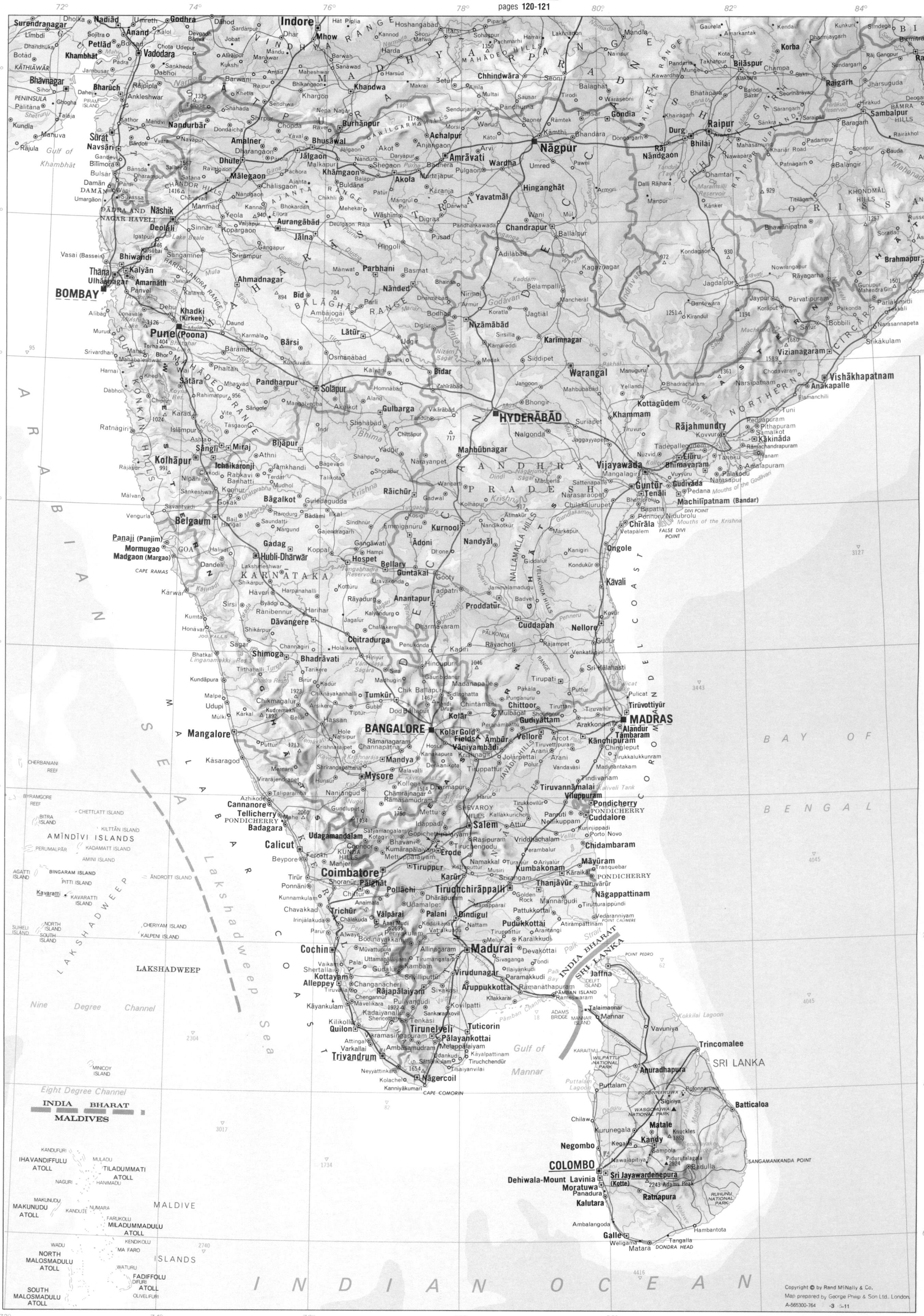
72°
74°
76°
78°
80°
82°
84°
22°
20°
18°
16°
14°
12°
10°
8°
6°
Indore
Mhow
Vadodara
Surat
Nāgpur
Raipur
Bilāspur
Sambalpur
BOMBAY
Pune (Poona)
Nāsik
Aurangābād
Ahmadnagar
Sholāpur
HYDERĀBĀD
Warangal
Vishākhapatnam
Rājahmundry
Vijayawāda
Guntūr
Kolhāpur
Belgaum
Hubli-Dhārwār
Bellary
Kurnool
Nellore
MADRAS
BANGALORE
Mysore
Mangalore
Calicut
Coimbatore
Salem
Tiruchchirāppalli
Madurai
Cochin
Trivandrum
Nāgercoil
Jaffna
Trincomalee
Kandy
COLOMBO
Galle
Batticaloa
SRI LANKA
A R A B I A N   S E A
BAY OF BENGAL
I N D I A N   O C E A N
LAKSHADWEEP
AMĪNDĪVI ISLANDS
Lakshadweep Sea
Nine Degree Channel
Eight Degree Channel
INDIA BHARAT
MALDIVES
MALDIVE ISLANDS
Gulf of Mannar
Palk Strait
Gulf of Khambhāt
CAPE COMORIN
KARNATAKA
ANDHRA PRADESH
ORISSA
V I N D H Y A   R A N G E
COROMANDEL COAST
MALABAR COAST
NORTHERN CIRCARS
Copyright © by Rand McNally & Co.
Map prepared by George Philip & Son Ltd. London
A-565300-764

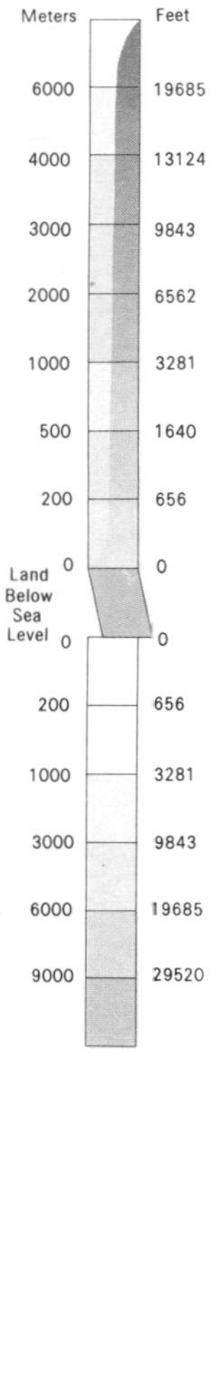
Meters
Feet
6000
19685
4000
13124
3000
9843
2000
6562
1000
3281
500
1640
200
656
0
0
Land Below Sea Level
0
0
200
656
1000
3281
3000
9843
6000
19685
9000
29520

| | | | | | | | |
|---|---|---|---|---|---|---|---|
| ENGLISH | atoll | hills | island | lagoon | lake | range | reservoir |
| DEUTSCH | Atoll | Hügel | Insel | Haff | See | Gebirge | Stausee |
| ESPAÑOL | atolón | colinas | isla | laguna | lago | sierra | embalse |
| FRANÇAIS | atoll | collines | île | lagune | lac | chaîne | réservoir |
| PORTUGUÊS | atol | colinas | ilha | laguna | lago | serra | reservatório |

Kilometers 0 100 200 300 Km.
Statute Miles 0 100 200 300 Mi.

Scale 1:6,000,000
One centimeter represents 60 kilometers.
One inch represents approximately 95 miles.
Lambert Conformal Conic Projection

Map continues page 85

The boundary between India and Pakistan through the disputed state of Jammu and Kashmir follows the line of control agreed to by both countries in 1972.
HINDU KUSH
KUNLUN SHAN
KARAKORAM RANGE
GREAT HIMALAYA RANGE
ZASKAR MOUNTAINS
LADAKH RANGE
DEOSAI MOUNTAINS
NANGA PARBAT RANGE
PIR PANJAL RANGE
SIWALIK RANGE
SALT RANGE
KOHISTAN
BAJAUR
BUNER
DARDISTAN
HUNZA
BALTISTAN
KASHMIR
AFGHANISTAN
PAKISTAN
INDIA
CHINA
THAL
SIND SAGAR DOAB
RECHNA DOAB
BARI DOAB
THAR DESERT
GREAT INDIAN DESERT
Peshāwar
Mardān
Kohāt
Islāmābād
Rāwalpindi
Srīnagar
Jammu
Sargodha
Faisalabad (Lyallpur)
Jhang Sadar
Gujrānwāla
Siālkot
LAHORE
Amritsar
Jalandhar
Ludhiāna
Firozpur
Multān
Bahāwalpur
Dera Ismāīl Khān
Dera Ghāzi Khān
Sāhīwal
Patiāla
Ambāla
Chandīgarh
Shimla
Hisār
Rohtak
DELHI
New Delhi
Copyright © by Rand McNally & Co.
Map prepared by George Philip & Son Ltd. London.
Meters
Feet
6000
19685
4000
13124
3000
9843
2000
6562
1000
3281
500
1640
200
656
0
Land Below Sea Level
9000
29520

Map continues pages 124-125

| MAP FORM | airport | doāb | glacier | pass | range | sar |
|---|---|---|---|---|---|---|
| ENGLISH | airport | upland | glacier | pass | range | mountain |
| DEUTSCH | Flughafen | Bergland | Gletscher | Pass | Gebirge | Berg |
| ESPAÑOL | aeropuerto | tierras altas | glaciar | paso | sierra | montaña |
| FRANÇAIS | aéroport | hautes terres | glacier | col | chaîne | montagne |
| PORTUGUÊS | aeroporto | terras altas | geleira | passo | serra | montanha |

Kilometers 0 50 100 150 Km.
Statute Miles 0 50 100 150 Mi.

Scale 1:3,000,000

One centimeter represents 30 kilometers.
One inch represents approximately 47 miles.
Lambert Conformal Conic Projection

Map continues page 123

Dehra Dūn
Sahāranpur
Muzaffarnagar
Meerut
DELHI
New Delhi
Morādābād
Rāmpur
Bareilly
Alīgarh
Mathura
Āgra
Firozābād
Shāhjahānpur
Farrukhābād
Lucknow
KĀNPUR
Gwalior
Jhānsi
Allahābād
Vārānasi (Benares)
Mirzāpur
Jabalpur
Bhopāl
Sāgar
Rewa
Satna
Bilāspur
CHINA
INDIA
NEPAL
UTTAR PRADESH
MADHYA PRADESH
RĀJASTHĀN
HARYĀNA
PUNJAB
MĀLWA PLATEAU
VINDHYA RANGE
SĀTPURA RANGE
BAGHELKHAND PLATEAU
MAIKALA PLATEAU
Copyright © by Rand McNally & Co.
Map prepared by George Philip & Son Ltd., London
A-567500-764 -6 -12

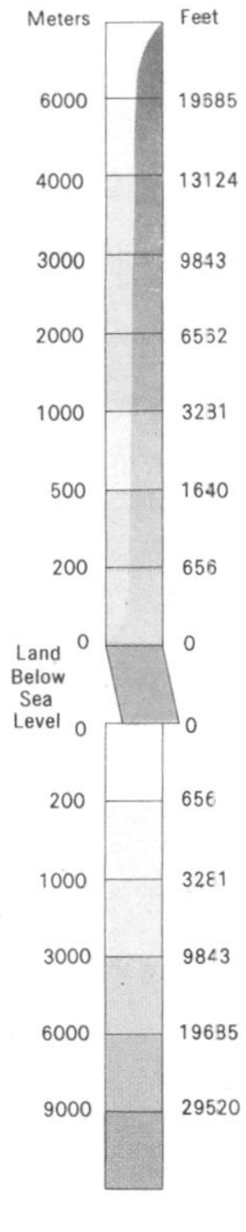
Meters
Feet
6000
19685
4000
13124
3000
9843
2000
6562
1000
3281
500
1640
200
656
0
Land Below Sea Level
9000
29520

| MAP FORM | hills | plains | plateau | range | shan | yumco |
|---|---|---|---|---|---|---|
| ENGLISH | hills | plains | plateau | range | mountains | lake |
| DEUTSCH | Hügel | Ebenen | Hochebene | Gebirge | Berge | See |
| ESPAÑOL | colinas | llanos | meseta | sierra | montañas | lago |
| FRANÇAIS | collines | plaines | plateau | chaîne | montagnes | lac |
| PORTUGUÊS | colinas | planícies | planalto | serra | montanhas | lago |

Kilometers 0 50 100 150 Km.
Statute Miles 0 50 100 150 Mi.

Scale 1:3,000,000

One centimeter represents 30 kilometers.
One inch represents approximately 47 miles.
Lambert Conformal Conic Projection

Lhasa
Kathmandau
Bhaktapur
Pokhara
Hetauda
Mount Everest 8848
Patna
Gaya
Muzaffarpur
Darbhanga
Bhagalpur
Munger
Siliguri
Darjiling
Gangtok
Thimphu
Rangpur
Dinajpur
Rajshahi
Bogra
Pabna
Dhaka (Dacca)
Narayanganj
Comilla
Jessore
Khulna
Barisal
Calcutta
Haora
Kharagpur
Jamshedpur
Ranchi
Asansol
Durgapur
Barddhaman
Dhanbad
Hazaribag
Bokaro Steel City
Raurkela
Sagar Island
Mouths of the Ganges
BAY OF BENGAL
GREAT HIMALAYA RANGE
NYAINQENTANGLHA SHAN
XIZANG
TIBET
BHUTAN
BANGLADESH
INDIA
NEPAL
SIKKIM
MEGHALAYA
ASSAM
WEST BENGAL
BIHAR
ORISSA
GANGES DELTA
SUNDARBANS
84° 85° 86° 87° 88° 89° 90° 91°
29° 28° 27° 26° 25° 24°

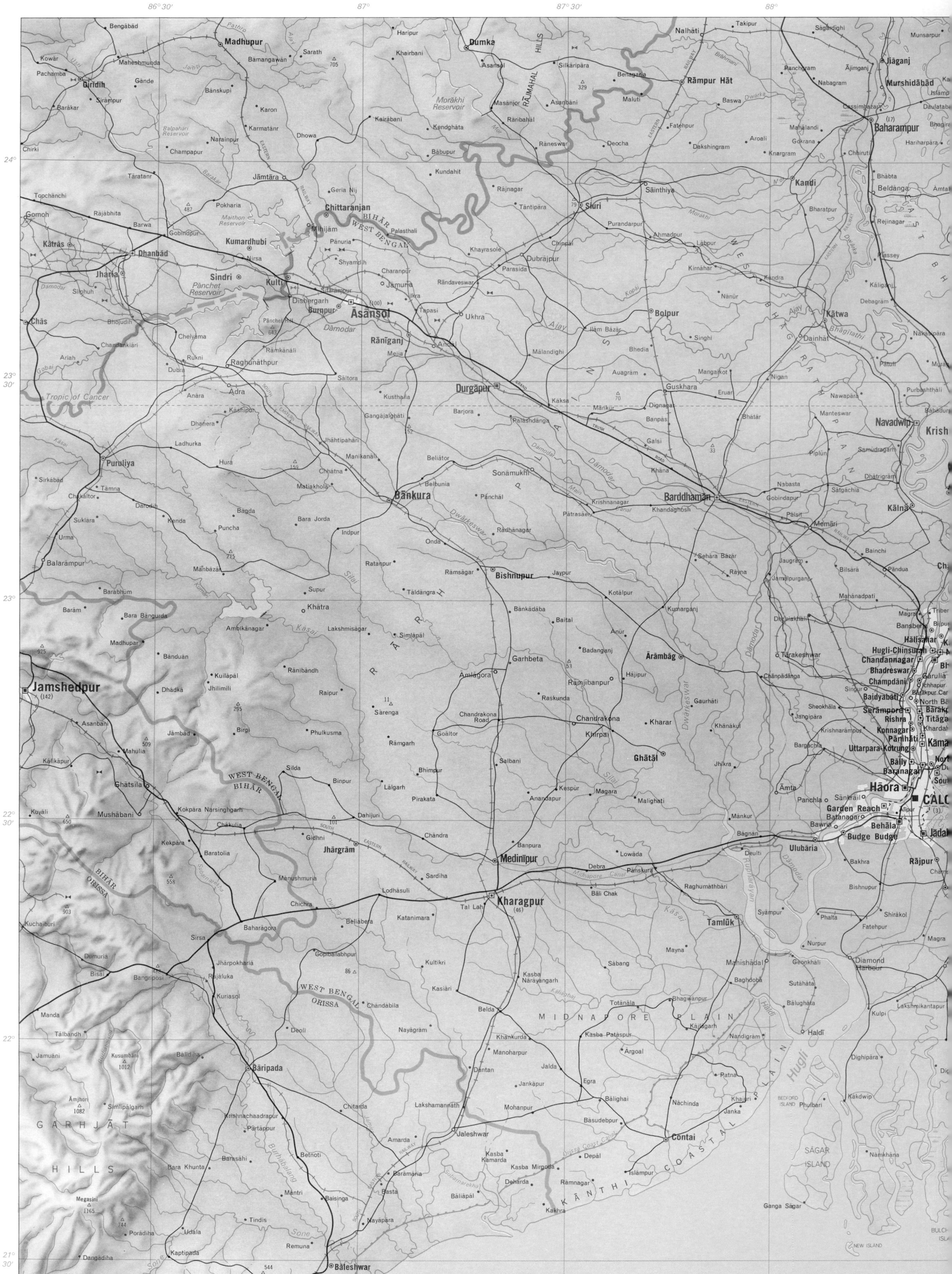
86° 30'
87°
87° 30'
88°
24°
23° 30'
23°
22° 30'
22°
21° 30'
Madhupur
Dumka
Nalhāti
Jiāganj
Murshidābād
Giridih
Rāmpur Hāt
Baharampur
RĀJMAHAL HILLS
Jāmtāra
Chittaranjan
Sūri
Kāndi
Dhanbād
Jharia
Kātrās
Kumardhubi
Sindri
Kulti
Āsansol
Rānīganj
Pānchet Reservoir
Maithon Reservoir
Morākhi Reservoir
Bolpur
Kātwa
Durgāpur
Purūliya
Bānkura
Barddhamān
Navadwīp
Kālna
Bishnupur
Ārāmbāg
Tropic of Cancer
Jamshedpur
Ghātsīla
Medinīpur
Kharagpur
Tamlūk
Hāora
Ulubāria
Garden Reach
Budge Budge
Behāla
Hugli-Chinsura
Chandannagar
Bhadreswar
Champdāni
Serampore
Rishra
Konnagar
Uttarpara-Kotrung
Bally
Baranagar
Bāripada
Jhārgrām
Contai
Jaleshwar
Bāleshwar
Ghātāl
Chandrakona
Diamond Harbour
SĀGAR ISLAND
Ganga Sāgar
NEW ISLAND
WEST BENGAL
BIHĀR
ORISSA
GARHJĀT HILLS
RĀRH
MIDNAPORE PLAIN
KĀNTHI COASTAL PLAIN
Dāmodar
Ajay
Kāsai
Hugli
Bhāgīrathi
Subarnarekha
Rūpnārāyan
Haldi

| MAP FORM | bay | canal | char | delta | island | plain |
|---|---|---|---|---|---|---|
| ENGLISH | bay | canal | island | delta | island | plain |
| DEUTSCH | Bucht | Kanal | Insel | Delta | Insel | Ebene |
| ESPAÑOL | bahía | canal | isla | delta | isla | llanura |
| FRANÇAIS | baie | canal | île | delta | île | plaine |
| PORTUGUÊS | baía | canal | ilha | delta | ilha | planície |

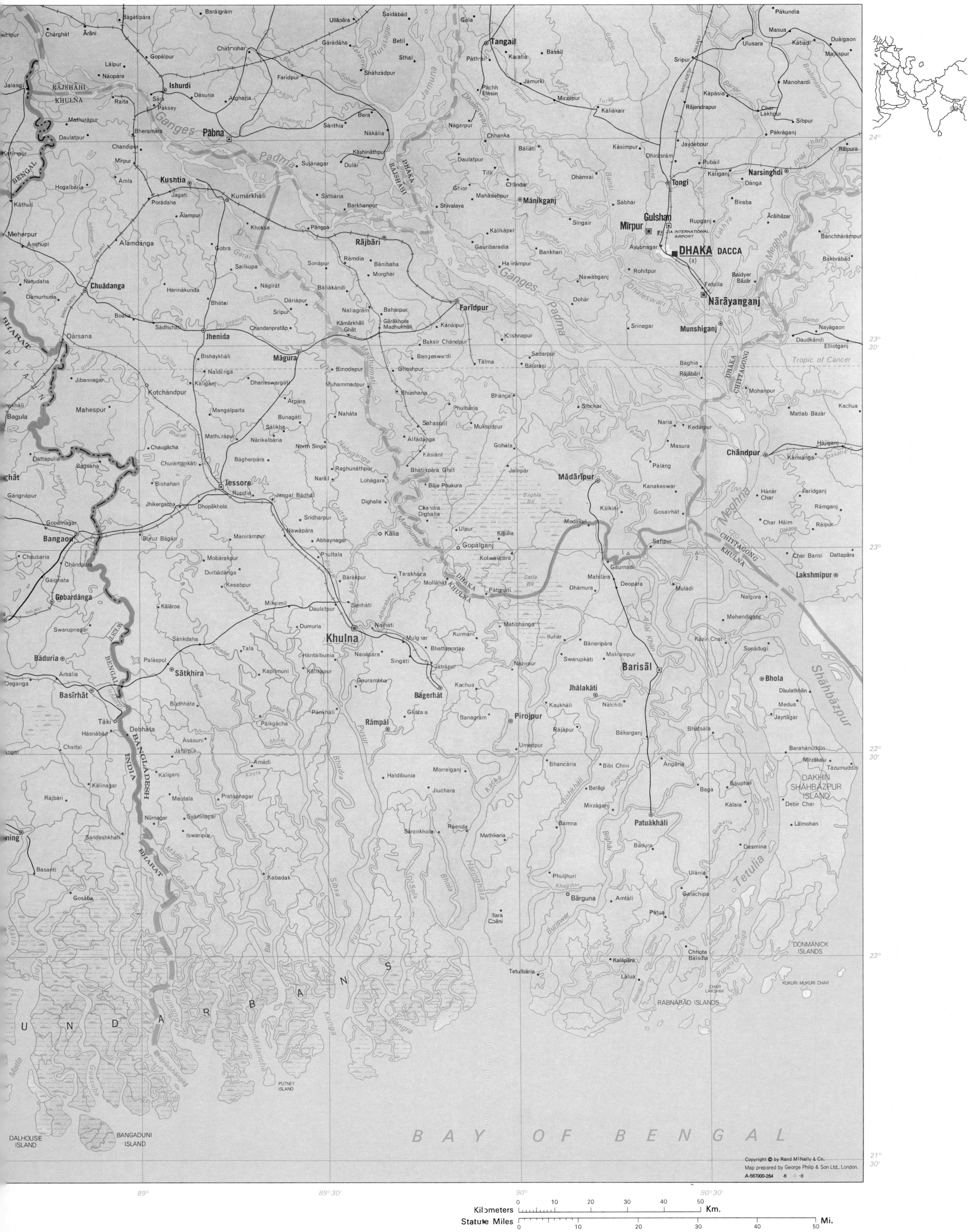
89°
89° 30′
90°
90° 30′
24°
23° 30′
23°
22° 30′
22°
21° 30′
Tropic of Cancer
BAY OF BENGAL
SUNDARBANS
RĀJSHĀHI
KHULNA
DHAKA
RĀJSHĀHI
DHAKA
KHULNA
DHAKA
CHITTAGONG
CHITTAGONG
KHULNA
BENGAL
BHARAT
BANGLADESH
INDIA
Ganges
Padma
Jamuna
Meghna
Dhaleswari
Tetulia
Shāhbāzpur
Madhumati
Pusur
Kālindi
Ichāmati
Baleswar
Āriāl Khān
Tangail
Ishurdi
Pābna
Kushtia
Kumārkhāli
Chuādanga
Jhenida
Māgura
Rājbāri
Farīdpur
Mānikganj
Gulshan
Mirpur
DHAKA DACCA
ZIA INTERNATIONAL AIRPORT
Nārāyanganj
Munshiganj
Tongi
Narsinghdi
Mādārīpur
Chāndpur
Lakshmipur
Jessore
Bangaon
Gobardānga
Bāduria
Basīrhāt
Sātkhira
Khulna
Bāgerhāt
Rāmpāl
Pirojpur
Jhālakāti
Barisāl
Patuākhāli
Bhola
Gopālganj
Kālia
Daulatpur
Nāgarpur
Jaydebpur
Sripur
Kāpāsia
Rāipura
Ulusara
Pākundia
Masua
Kātiadi
Duāigaon
Majlispur
Manohardi
Sibpur
Pākrāganj
DAKHIN SHĀHBĀZPUR ISLAND
DONMĀNICK ISLANDS
RABNABĀD ISLANDS
KUKURI MUKURI CHAR
CHAR LAKSHMI
DALHOUSIE ISLAND
BANGADUNI ISLAND
PUTNEY ISLAND
Copyright © by Rand McNally & Co.
Map prepared by George Philip & Son Ltd., London.
A-567900-264 ·6 ·7 ·8

Kilometers 0 10 20 30 40 50 Km.

Statute Miles 0 10 20 30 40 50 Mi.

Scale 1:1,000,000

One centimeter represents 10 kilometers.
One inch represents approximately 16 miles.

Lambert Conformal Conic Projection

Map continues page 84

Map continues pages 130-131

ANKARA
Kırıkkale
Sivas
Tokat
Erzincan
Erzurum
Kars
JEREVAN
Gäncä
Kayseri
Malatya
Elazığ
Konya
Niğde
Ereğli
Adana
Tarsus
İçel
Osmaniye
Ceyhan
Gaziantep
Şanlıurfa
Diyarbakır
Mardin
Batman
Van
Tabrīz
Orūmīyeh (Rezā'īyeh)
Marāgheh
Mīāneh
Iskenderun
Antioch
Halab Aleppo
Al-Lādhiqīyah Latakia
Nicosia
Gazimağusa Famagusta
Lemesós Limassol
NORTH CYPRUS KUZEY KIBRIS
CYPRUS KÍPROS
The Turkish Republic of Northern Cyprus unilaterally declared its independence on November 15, 1983.
Ḥamāh
Ḥimṣ Homs
Ṭarābulus Tripoli
LEBANON LUBNĀN
BEIRUT BAYRŪT
DIMASHQ DAMASCUS
MEDITERRANEAN SEA
Area occupied by Israel since June 1967
ISRAEL YISRA'EL
'Akko Acre
Hefa Haifa
Netanya
TEL AVIV-YAFO
Yerushalayim Jerusalem
'AMMĀN
Az-Zarqā'
Būr Sa'īd Port Said
Dumyāṭ
Ghazzah Gaza
Al-Ismā'īlīyah
Az-Zaqāzīq
As-Suways Suez
Al-'Arīsh
SYRIA SŪRIYAH
TURKEY TÜRKİYE
Ar-Raqqah
Dayr az-Zawr
Tudmur (Palmyra)
Al-Mawṣil Mosul
Irbīl
Kirkūk
As-Sulaymānīyah
Tall 'Afar
NĪNAWĀ
SALĀH AD-DĪN
AT-TA'MĪM
Sāmarrā'
BAGHDĀD
Ba'qūbah
Al-Fallūjah
Ar-Ramādī
AL-ANBĀR
BĀDIYAT ASH-SHĀM
SYRIAN DESERT
JORDAN AL-URDUN
IRAQ AL-'IRAQ
SAUDI ARABIA AL-'ARABIYAH AS-SU'ŪDIYAH
Karbalā'
Al-Ḥillah
An-Najaf
Ad-Dīwānīyah
As-Samāwah
An-Nāṣirīyah
Al-'Amārah
Al-Kūt
Al-Baṣrah Basra
Az-Zubayr
Kermānshāh (Bakhtarān)
Hamadān
Khorramābād
Sanandaj
Īlām
AL-MUTHANNĀ
AN-NAFŪD
Al-Jawf
Tabūk
Ḥā'il
Buraydah
'Unayzah
AR-RIYĀḌ RIYADH
Al-Madīnah Medina
Yanbu' al-Baḥr
Rābigh
Al-'Aqabah
KUWAIT AL-KUWAYT
Al-Jahrah
Al-Ghurdaqah
Būr Safājah
Al-Quṣayr
SHIBH JAZĪRAT SĪNĀ' SINAI PENINSULA
RED SEA
AL-BAḤR AL-AḤMAR
AL-ḤIJĀZ HEJAZ
AṢ-ṢAḤRĀ' ASH-SHARQĪYAH ARABIAN DESERT
AD-DIBDIBAH
AṢ-ṢUMMĀN
AD-DAHNĀ
Tropic of Cancer
EGYPT MIṢR
SUDAN AS-SŪDĀN
Area administered by Sudan
Administrative Boundary
Meters Feet
6000 19685
4000 13124
3000 9843
2000 6562
1000 3281
500 1640
200 656
0 0
Land Below Sea Level
0 0
200 656
1000 3281
3000 9843
6000 19685
9000 29520

Map continues pages 140-141

Map continues pages 144-145

| MAP FORM | harrat | jabal | jazireh | kūh | ra's | sabkhat | wādī |
|---|---|---|---|---|---|---|---|
| ENGLISH | lava flow | mountain | island | mountain | cape | salt marsh | wadi |
| DEUTSCH | Lavastrom | Berg | Insel | Berg | Kap | Salzmarsch | Wadi |
| ESPAÑOL | corriente de lava | montaña | isla | montaña | cabo | pantano salado | uadi |
| FRANÇAIS | coulée de lave | montagne | île | montagne | cap | marais salé | wadi |
| PORTUGUÊS | corrente de lava | montanha | ilha | montanha | cabo | pântano salgado | uádi |

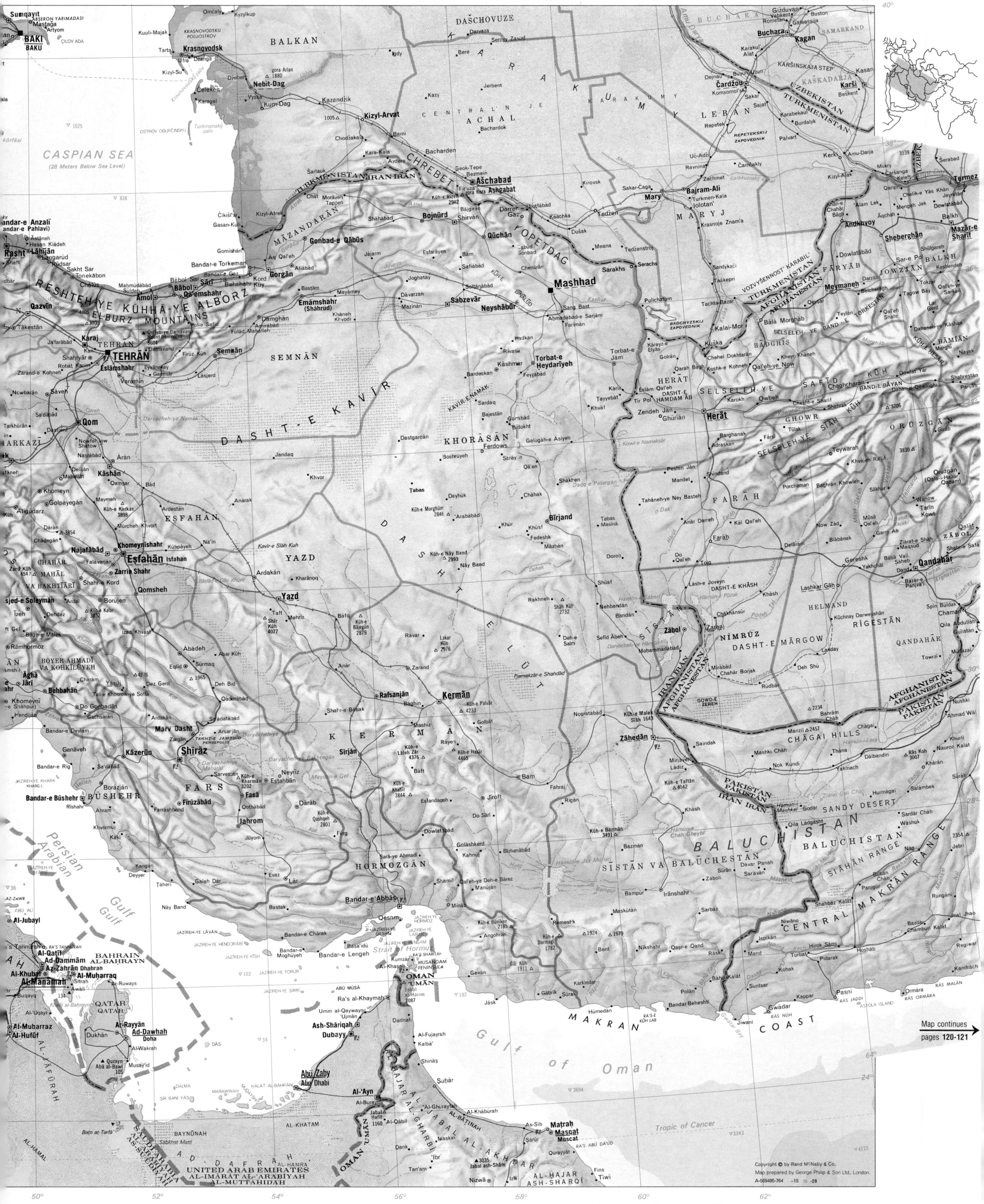
CASPIAN SEA
(28 Meters Below Sea Level)
DASHT-E KAVĪR
DASHT-E LŪT
KHORĀSĀN
SEMNĀN
YAZD
KERMĀN
FĀRS
HORMOZGĀN
SĪSTĀN VA BALŪCHESTĀN
BALUCHISTAN
MAKRAN COAST
Gulf of Oman
Persian Gulf
Arabian Gulf
UNITED ARAB EMIRATES
AL-IMĀRĀT AL-'ARABĪYAH AL-MUTTAḤIDAH
QATAR
BAHRAIN
TEHRĀN
Mashhad
Eşfahān
Shīrāz
Kermān
Herāt
Qandahār
Ašchabad
Dubayy
Abū Zaby
Masqaţ
Tropic of Cancer
Map continues pages 120-121
Copyright © by Rand McNally & Co.
Map prepared by George Philip & Son Ltd., London.

Kilometers 0 100 200 300 Km.
Statute Miles 0 100 200 300 Mi.

Scale 1:6,000,000

One centimeter represents 60 kilometers.
One inch represents approximately 95 miles.
Lambert Conformal Conic Projection

Map continues pages 38-39

B L A C K
M E D I T E R R A N E A N
S E A
Marmara Denizi
Sea of Marmara
TURKEY
BULGARIA
GREECE
ELLÁS
TÜRKİYE
İSTANBUL
ANKARA
İZMİR
Bursa
Konya
Antalya
Eskişehir
Edirne
Çanakkale
Balıkesir
Manisa
Aydın
Denizli
Muğla
Uşak
Afyon
Kütahya
Isparta
Burdur
Zonguldak
Kastamonu
Sakarya
İzmit
Düzce
Bolu
Rodhos
Rhodes
Kárpathos
Khíos
Mitilíni
LÉSVOS
LESBOS
SÁMOS
Nicosia
Lefkoşa
Lefkosia
Lárnax
Lemesós Limassol
Néa Páfos
Paphos
NORTH CYPRUS
KUZEY KIBRIS
CYPRUS
KÍPROS
TAURUS MOUNTAINS
Antalya Körfezi
Gulf of Antalya
Gökova Körfezi
Tuz Gölü
DHODHEKÁNISOS
DODECANESE
PHRYGIA
LYDIA
MYSIA
BITHYNIA
PAPHLAGONIA
GALATIA
LYCAONIA
PISIDIA
PAMPHYLIA
LYCIA
CARIA
The Turkish Republic of Northern Cyprus unilaterally declared its independence on November 15, 1983.


Map prepared by George Philip & Son Ltd., London.
A-563900-764 -7 -8 -14

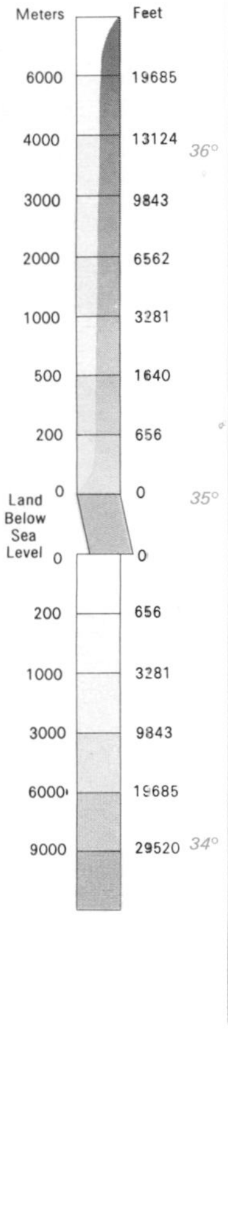
Meters
Feet
6000 19685
4000 13124
3000 9843
2000 6562
1000 3281
500 1640
200 656
0 0
Land Below Sea Level 0
200 656
1000 3281
3000 9843
6000 19685
9000 29520

| MAP FORM | burnu | dağ, dağı | dağları | gölü | jabal | körfezi | sabkhat |
|---|---|---|---|---|---|---|---|
| ENGLISH | cape | mountain | mountains | lake | mountains | bay, gulf | salt marsh |
| DEUTSCH | Kap | Berg | Berge | See | Berge | Bucht, Golf | Salzmarsch |
| ESPAÑOL | cabo | montaña | montañas | lago | montañas | bahía, golfo | pantano salado |
| FRANÇAIS | cap | montagne | montagnes | lac | montagnes | baie, golfe | marais salé |
| PORTUGUÊS | cabo | montanha | montanhas | lago | montanhas | baía, golfo | pântano salgado |

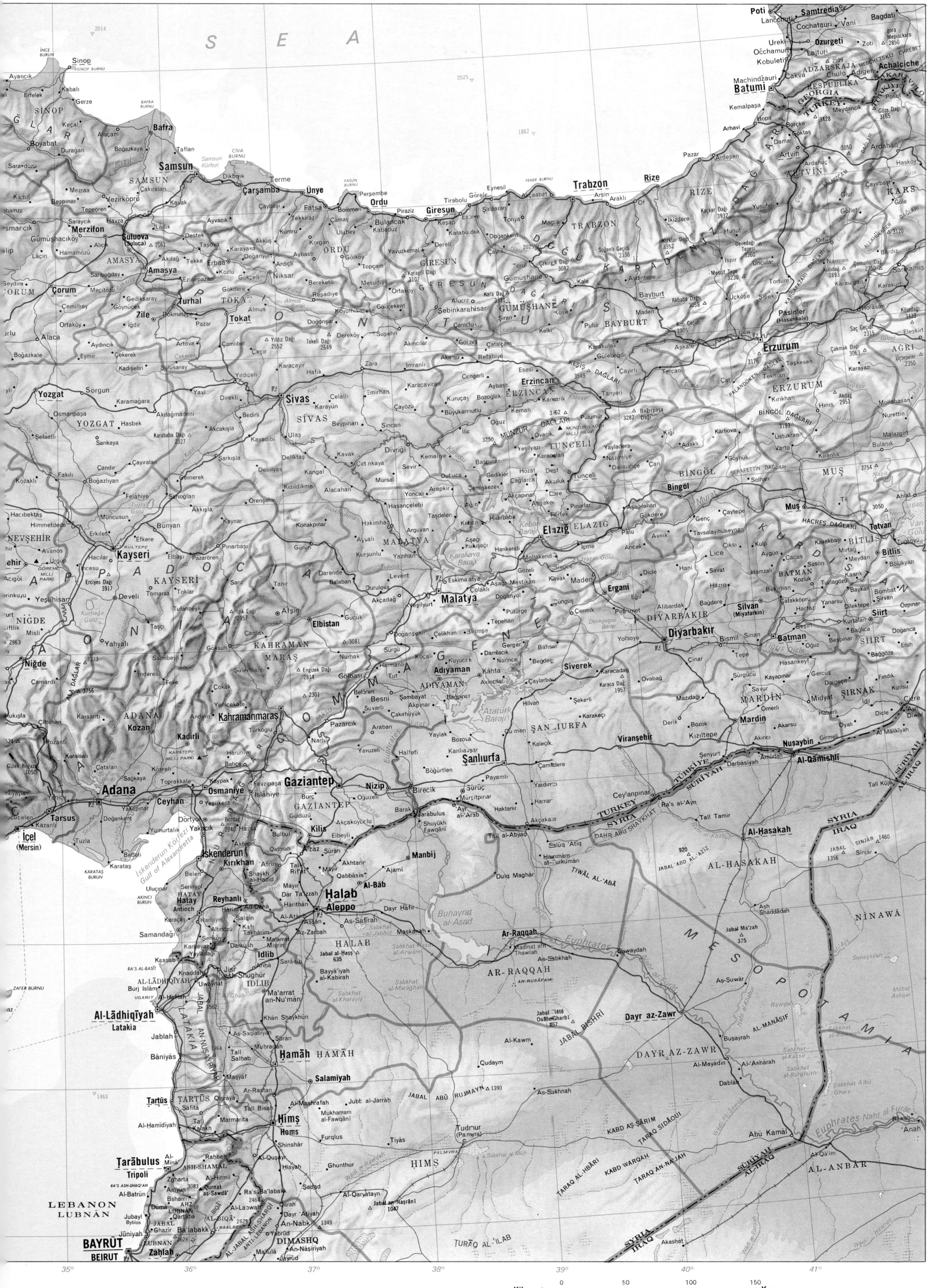
SEA
Sinop
Samsun
Ordu
Giresun
Trabzon
Rize
Batumi
Poti
Çorum
Amasya
Tokat
Sivas
Yozgat
Kayseri
Erzincan
Erzurum
Bayburt
Gümüşhane
Malatya
Elazığ
Tunceli
Bingöl
Muş
Bitlis
Tatvan
Diyarbakır
Siirt
Batman
Mardin
Adıyaman
Kahramanmaraş
Gaziantep
Şanlıurfa
Adana
İçel
(Mersin)
Tarsus
İskenderun
Antakya
Halab
Aleppo
Idlib
Al-Lādhiqīyah
Latakia
Hamāh
Hims
Homs
Ţarţūs
Ţarābulus
Tripoli
BAYRŪT
BEIRUT
DIMASHQ
Ar-Raqqah
Dayr az-Zawr
Al-Hasakah
Al-Qāmishlī
Nusaybin
Abū Kamāl
LEBANON
LUBNĀN
SYRIA
IRAQ
TURKEY
GEORGIA
MESOPOTAMIA
KURDISTAN
CAPPADOCIA
COMMAGENE
Euphrates
Atatürk Barajı
Buhayrat al-Asad
Kilometers 0 50 100 150 Km.
Statute Miles 0 50 100 150 Mi.

Map continues page 84

Map continues pages 128-129

Scale 1:3,000,000

One centimeter represents 30 kilometers.
One inch represents approximately 47 miles.
Conic Projection, Two Standard Parallels

MEDITERRANEAN SEA
Area occupied by Israel.
Area occupied by United Nations Disengagement Observer Force since 1974.
Golan Heights area. Occupied by Israel since 1967. Unilaterally annexed by Israel, 1981.
West Bank area. Occupied by Israel since 1967. Limited autonomy granted to Jericho Area, 1994. Permanent status to be determined.
East Jerusalem portion of West Bank. Unilaterally annexed by Israel, 1980.
Gaza Strip. Occupied by Israel in 1967. Limited autonomy granted, 1994. Permanent status to be determined.

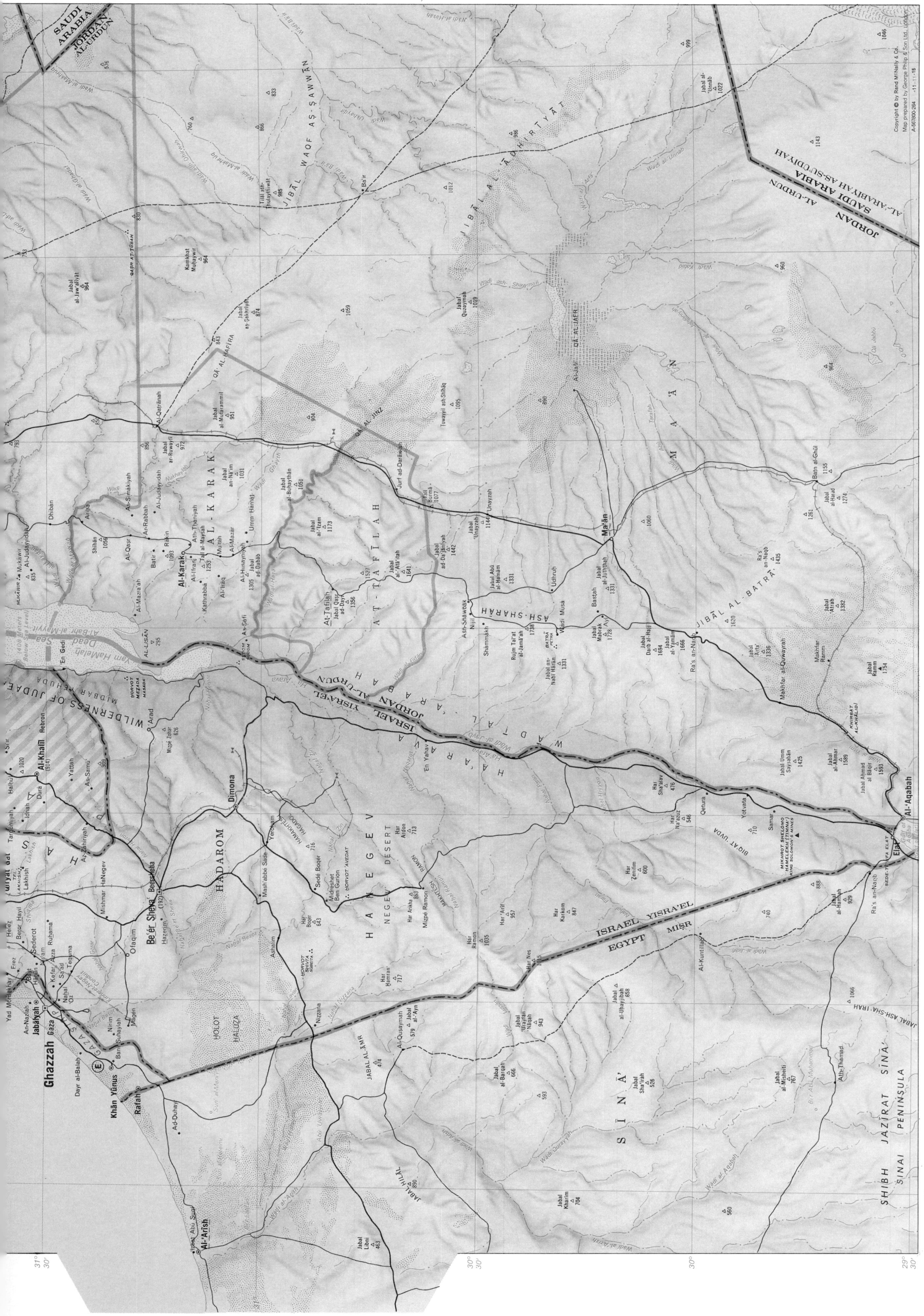
SAUDI ARABIA
JORDAN
AL-URDUN
ISRAEL
YISRA'EL
EGYPT
MIṢR
Ghazzah
Gaza
Khān Yūnus
Rafah
Al-'Arīsh
Be'er Sheva'
Dimona
Al-Karak
Aṭ-Ṭafīlah
Ma'ān
Al-'Aqabah
Elat
WILDERNESS OF JUDAEA
HANEGEV
NEGEV DESERT
HADAROM
AL-KARAK
AṬ-ṬAFĪLAH
MA'ĀN
WĀDĪ AL-'ARABAH
HA'ARAVA
JIBĀL AL-BATRĀ'
JIBĀL AL-'ADHIRIYYĀT
QĀ' AL-JAFR
SĪNĀ'
SHIBH JAZĪRAT SĪNĀ'
SINAI PENINSULA

Kilometers 0 10 20 30 40 50 Km.

Statute Miles 0 10 20 30 40 50 Mi.

Scale 1:1,000,000

One centimeter represents 10 kilometers.
One inch represents approximately 16 miles.
Lambert Conformal Conic Projection

| MAP FORM | har | jabal | nahr | ra's | sede-te'ufa | tall | wādī |
|---|---|---|---|---|---|---|---|
| ENGLISH | mountain | mountain(s) | river | cape | airport | mountain | wadi |
| DEUTSCH | Berg | Berg(e) | Fluss | Kap | Flughafen | Berg | Wadi |
| ESPAÑOL | montaña | montaña(s) | rio | cabo | aeropuerto | montaña | uadi |
| FRANÇAIS | montagne | montagne(s) | rivière | cap | aéroport | montagne | wadi |
| PORTUGUÊS | montanha | montanha(s) | rio | cabo | aeroporto | montanha | uadi |

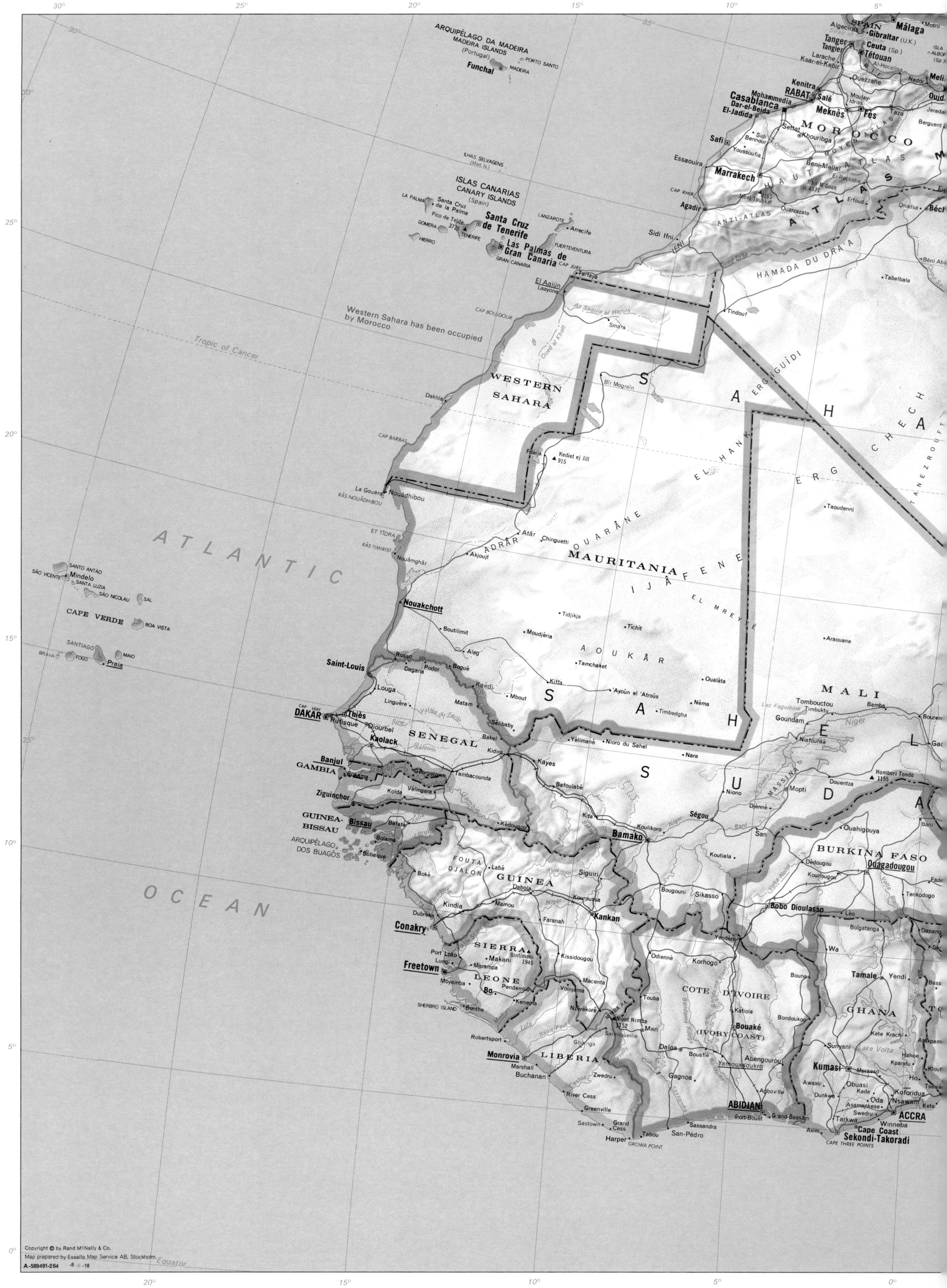
ATLANTIC
OCEAN
ARQUIPÉLAGO DA MADEIRA
MADEIRA ISLANDS
(Portugal)
Funchal
PORTO SANTO
MADEIRA
ILHAS SELVAGENS (Mad. Is.)
ISLAS CANARIAS
CANARY ISLANDS
(Spain)
LA PALMA
Santa Cruz de la Palma
Pico de Teide 3718
GOMERA
HIERRO
TENERIFE
Santa Cruz de Tenerife
Las Palmas de Gran Canaria
GRAN CANARIA
LANZAROTE
Arrecife
FUERTEVENTURA
CAP JUBY
Tarfaya
El Aaiún
Laayoune
CAP BOUJDOUR
Western Sahara has been occupied by Morocco
Tropic of Cancer
As Sagia al Hamra
Smara
WESTERN SAHARA
Dakhla
CAP BARBAS
Bîr Mogreïn
Fdérik
Kediet ej Jill 915
La Gouèra
Nouâdhibou
RÂS NOUÂDHIBOU
ET TÎDRA
RÂS TIMIRIST
Nouâmghâr
ADRAR
Atâr
Chinguetti
Akjoujt
OUARÂNE
MAURITANIA
IJÂFENE
EL MREYYÉ
Nouakchott
Tidjikja
Tichit
Moudjéria
Boutilimit
Aleg
AOUKÂR
Tamchaket
Kiffa
'Ayoûn el 'Atroûs
Néma
Oualâta
Timbedgha
Mbout
Kaédi
Saint-Louis
Rosso
Dagana
Podor
Bogué
Louga
Linguère
Matam
CAP VERT
DAKAR
Thiès
Rufisque
Diourbel
Kaolack
SENEGAL
Sélibaby
Bakel
Kidira
Kayes
Yelimané
Nioro du Sahel
Nara
Banjul
GAMBIA
Georgetown
Tambacounda
Kolda
Vélingara
Ziguinchor
Bafoulabé
Kita
Kédougou
GUINEA-BISSAU
Bissau
Bafatá
Bolama
ARQUIPÉLAGO DOS BIJAGÓS
Bubaque
FOUTA DJALON
Labé
Boké
GUINEA
Dabola
Mamou
Kindia
Dubréka
Conakry
Faranah
Kankan
Siguiri
Kouroussa
Bamako
Koulikoro
Ségou
SIERRA LEONE
Port Loko
Lungi
Makeni
Freetown
Bintimani 1945
Moyamba
Bo
Pendembu
Kenema
SHERBRO ISLAND
Bonthe
Kissidougou
Macenta
Nzérékoré
Voinjama
Robertsport
Monrovia
LIBERIA
Marshall
Buchanan
River Cess
Greenville
Sastown
Grand Cess
Harper
GROWA POINT
Tabou
Sassandra
San-Pédro
Mont Nimba 1752
Man
Danané
Daloa
Gagnoa
CÔTE D'IVOIRE
(IVORY COAST)
Odienné
Korhogo
Touba
Katiola
Bouaké
Bouaflé
Yamoussoukro
Abengourou
ABIDJAN
Port-Bouët
Grand-Bassam
Agboville
Bondoukou
Bouna
Bougouni
Sikasso
Koutiala
Yendéré
Bobo Dioulasso
BURKINA FASO
Ouagadougou
Ouahigouya
Dédougou
Koudougou
Léo
Bolgatanga
Wa
Tamale
Yendi
GHANA
Kete Krachi
Sunyani
Kumasi
Obuasi
Dunkwa
Kade
Oda
Koforidua
Asamankese
Swedru
ACCRA
Winneba
Tarkwa
Axim
Cape Coast
Sekondi-Takoradi
CAPE THREE POINTS
Keta
Tema
Ho
Hohoe
Kpandu
MALI
Tombouctou
Timbuktu
Goundam
Niafounké
Lac Faguibine
Niger
Bamba
Bourem
Hombori Tondo 1155
Douentza
Mopti
Djenné
Niono
San
MASSINA
Araouane
Taoudenni
ERG CHECH
TANEZROUFT
EL HANK
ERG IGUIDI
SAHARA
SAHEL
SUDAN
HAMADA DU DRA'A
Tindouf
Tabelbala
Béni Abbès
Sidi Ifni
IFNI
ANTI-ATLAS
Agadir
CAP RHIR
Essaouira
Marrakech
Jebel Toubkal 4165
HAUT ATLAS
MOYEN ATLAS
Irhil M'Goun 4071
Ouarzazate
Erfoud
Er-Rachidia
Béni-Mellal
Khouribga
Settat
Youssoufia
Sidi Bennour
Safi
El-Jadida
Casablanca
Dar-el-Beida
Mohammedia
RABAT
Salé
Kenitra
Meknès
Fès
Moulay-Idriss
Taza
MOROCCO
Ouezzane
Larache
Ksar-el-Kebir
Al-Hoceima
Tanger
Tangier
Tétouan
Ceuta (Sp.)
Gibraltar (U.K.)
Algeciras
SPAIN
Málaga
Nador
Melilla
Oujda
Jerada
Berguent
Béchar
SANTO ANTÃO
SÃO VICENTE
Mindelo
SANTA LUZIA
SÃO NICOLAU
SAL
CAPE VERDE
BOA VISTA
SANTIAGO
MAIO
BRAVA
FOGO
Praia
Equator
Copyright © by Rand McNally & Co.
Map prepared by Esselte Map Service AB, Stockholm.
A-589491-264

| MAP FORM | bahr, baḥr | chott | jabal | lake | mountains | oued | wahât |
|---|---|---|---|---|---|---|---|
| ENGLISH | river, sea | salt marsh | mountain(s) | lake | mountains | wadi | oasis |
| DEUTSCH | Fluss, Meer | Salzmarsch | Berg(e) | See | Berge | Wadi | Oase |
| ESPAÑOL | río, mar | pantano salado | montaña(s) | lago | montañas | uadi | oasis |
| FRANÇAIS | rivière, mer | marais salé | montagne(s) | lac | montagnes | wadi | oasis |
| PORTUGUÊS | rio, mar | pântano salgado | montanha(s) | lago | montanhas | uádi | oásis |

Map continues pages 22-23

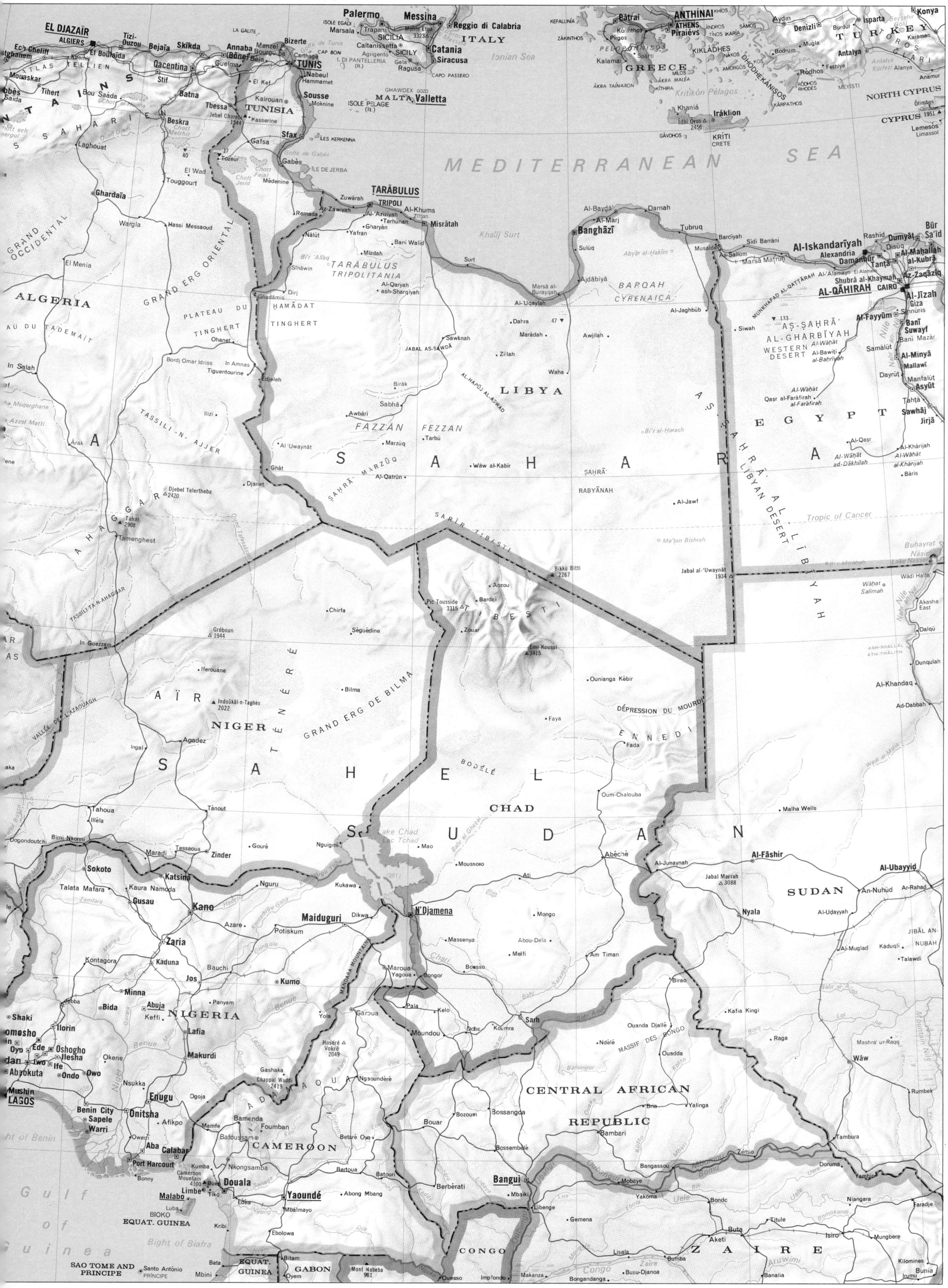
MEDITERRANEAN SEA
Ionian Sea
ALGERIA
TUNISIA
LIBYA
EGYPT
NIGER
CHAD
SUDAN
NIGERIA
CAMEROON
CENTRAL AFRICAN REPUBLIC
ZAIRE
CONGO
GABON
EQUAT. GUINEA
SAO TOME AND PRINCIPE
ITALY
GREECE
TURKEY
CYPRUS
NORTH CYPRUS
MALTA Valletta
SAHARA
SAHEL
SUDAN
TIBESTI
AÏR
TÉNÉRÉ
AHAGGAR
GRAND ERG ORIENTAL
GRAND ERG OCCIDENTAL
GRAND ERG DE BILMA
FAZZĀN FEZZAN
BARQAH CYRENAICA
ṬARĀBULUS TRIPOLITANIA
WESTERN DESERT
LIBYAN DESERT
ENNEDI
BODÉLÉ
DÉPRESSION DU MOURDI
ADAMAOUA
Gulf of Guinea
Bight of Biafra
Bight of Benin
Tropic of Cancer
EL DJAZAÏR ALGIERS
TUNIS
ṬARĀBULUS TRIPOLI
AL-QĀHIRAH CAIRO
Al-Iskandarīyah Alexandria
N'Djamena
Yaoundé
Bangui
Malabo
LAGOS
Palermo
Messina
Catania
Banghāzī
Misrātah
Sfax
Kano
Maiduguri
Al-Fāshir
Lake Chad
Emi Koussi 3415
Pic Toussidé 3315
Bikkū Bitti 2267
Jabal Marrah 3088
Tahat 2908

Map continues pages 136-137

Map continues pages 138-139

Kilometers 0 200 400 600 Km.
Statute Miles 0 200 400 600 Mi.

Scale 1:12,000,000

One centimeter represents 120 kilometers.
One inch represents approximately 190 miles.
Miller Oblated Stereographic Projection

Map continues pages 22-23

Map continues pages 134-135

MEDITERRANEAN SEA
Ionian Sea
ALGERIA
TUNISIA
LIBYA
EGYPT
NIGER
CHAD
SUDAN
NIGERIA
CAMEROON
CENTRAL AFRICAN REPUBLIC
MALI
BENIN
CONGO
GABON
ZAIRE
EQUAT. GUINEA
SAO TOME AND PRINCIPE
GREECE
ITALY
TURKEY
CYPRUS
MALTA
SAHARA
SAHEL
ATLAS MOUNTAINS
TIBESTI
AHAGGAR
AÏR
TÉNÉRÉ
GRAND ERG DE BILMA
GRAND ERG OCCIDENTAL
GRAND ERG ORIENTAL
FEZZAN
BARQAH CYRENAICA
WESTERN DESERT
LIBYAN DESERT
Gulf of Guinea
Bight of Benin
Bight of Biafra
Lake Chad
Tropic of Cancer
EL DJAZAÏR ALGIERS
TUNIS
TARĀBULUS TRIPOLI
AL-QĀHIRAH CAIRO
N'Djamena
LAGOS
Abuja
Yaoundé
Bangui
Malabo
Valletta
ATHÍNAI ATHENS
Banghāzī
Misrātah
Kano
Maiduguri
Douala
Al-Iskandarīyah Alexandria

Map continues pages 138-139

| MAP FORM | bahr, baḥr | chott | jabal | lake | mountains | oued | ra's; ras | wāhāt |
|---|---|---|---|---|---|---|---|---|
| ENGLISH | river, sea | salt marsh | mountain(s) | lake | mountains | wadi | cape | oasis |
| DEUTSCH | Fluss, Meer | Salzmarsch | Berg(e) | See | Berge | Wadi | Kap | Oase |
| ESPAÑOL | río, mar | pantano salado | montaña(s) | lago | montañas | uadi | cabo | oasis |
| FRANÇAIS | rivière, mer | marais salé | montagne(s) | lac | montagnes | wadi | cap | oasis |
| PORTUGUÊS | rio, mar | pântano salgado | montanha(s) | lago | montanhas | uádi | cabo | oásis |

MESOPOTAMIA
SYRIA
IRAQ
IRAN
JORDAN
KUWAYT
QATAR
BAHRAIN
UNITED ARAB EMIRATES
OMAN
SAUDI ARABIA
YEMEN
ERITREA
ETHIOPIA
DJIBOUTI
SOMALIA
KENYA
UGANDA
AN-NAFŪD
NAJD
AD-DAHNĀ'
AR-RUB' AL-KHĀLĪ
HIJĀZ
HADRAMAWT
OGADEN
DASHT-E LŪT
BALUCHISTAN
MAKRAN COAST
ZAGROS
AL-HAMĀD
RED SEA
Persian Gulf
Gulf of Oman
Gulf of Aden
ARABIAN SEA
INDIAN OCEAN
BAGHDĀD
AR-RIYĀD RIYADH
AL-KUWAYT
Ad-Dawhah Doha
Abū Zaby Abu Dhabi
Al-Manāmah
Makkah Mecca
Al-Madīnah Medina
Jiddah Jeddah
Ṣan'ā'
Adan Aden
Asmera
ADIS ABEBA ADDIS ABABA
AL-KHARṬŪM KHARTOUM
Umm Durmān Omdurman
Muqdisho Mogadishu
Djibouti
Hargeysa
Dire Dawa
Bür Südän Port Sudan
Muscat
Dubayy Dubai
Shīrāz
Eşfahān
Tehran
AMMAN
DIMASHQ DAMASCUS
Halab Aleppo
Al-Mawṣil Mosul
Al-Başrah Basra
Ābādān
Al-Hufūf
Salalah
Al-Mukallā
Copyright © by Rand McNally & Co.
Map prepared by Esselte Map Service AB, Stockholm.
A-589391 -264 -12-11-25

Map continues pages 118-119

Kilometers 0 200 400 600 Km.
Statute Miles 0 200 400 600 Mi.

Scale 1:12,000,000

One centimeter represents 120 kilometers.
One inch represents approximately 190 miles.
Miller Oblated Stereographic Projection

# Southern Africa / Südafrika / África Meridional
# Afrique Méridionale / África Meridional

Map continues pages 136-137

ATLANTIC
OCEAN
SAO TOME AND PRINCIPE
EQUATORIAL GUINEA
GABON
CONGO
ZAIRE
ANGOLA
NAMIBIA
BOTSWANA
ZAMBIA
ZIMBABWE
SOUTH AFRICA
LESOTHO
RWANDA
BURUNDI
CAMEROON
CABINDA (Angola)
Libreville
Brazzaville
KINSHASA (LÉOPOLDVILLE)
LUANDA
Lusaka
Windhoek
Gaborone
PRETORIA
JOHANNESBURG
CAPE TOWN KAAPSTAD
Bloemfontein
Kigali
Bujumbura
KATANGA
KALAHARI DESERT
NAMIB DESERT
OVAMBOLAND
DAMARALAND
GREAT NAMAQUALAND
KAOKO VELD
CAPRIVI ZIPFEL
OKAVANGO DELTA
GREAT KARROO
LITTLE KARROO
BUSHMAN LAND
Tropic of Capricorn
Lake Tanganyika
Lake Ngami
Lake Xau
Lake Kariba
Zambezi
Congo

| MAP FORM | cape | île | island | lake | mountains | plateau |
|---|---|---|---|---|---|---|
| ENGLISH | cape | island | island | lake | mountains | plateau |
| DEUTSCH | Kap | Insel | Insel | See | Berge | Hochebene |
| ESPAÑOL | cabo | isla | isla | lago | montañas | meseta |
| FRANÇAIS | cap | île | île | lac | montagnes | plateau |
| PORTUGUÊS | cabo | ilha | ilha | lago | montanhas | planalto |

SOMALIA
KENYA
NAIROBI
Mombasa
Tanga
Zanzibar
DAR ES SALAAM
TANZANIA
Dodoma
SERENGETI PLAIN
MASAI STEPPE
Arusha
Kisumu
Nakuru
Machakos
Lake Nyasa
Lake Malawi
Lilongwe
Blantyre
Zomba
MOZAMBIQUE
Nampula
Nacala
Moçambique
Quelimane
Beira
Inhambane
Inharrime
Pemba
Lindi
Mtwara
COMOROS
Moroni
Dzaoudzi
ARCHIPEL DES COMORES
MAYOTTE (Fr.)
MADAGASCAR
ANTANANARIVO
Antsiranana
Mahajanga
Toamasina
Antsirabe
Fianarantsoa
Toliara
Morondava
Manakara
Farafangana
Tsihombe
Ambovombe
Faradofay
CAP SAINTE-MARIE
CAP D'AMBRE
Mozambique Channel
INDIAN OCEAN
Equator
Tropic of Capricorn
SEYCHELLES
Victoria
MAHÉ ISLAND
PRASLIN ISLAND
LA DIGUE
SILHOUETTE
AMIRANTE ISLANDS (Sey.)
ÎLE DESROCHES (Sey.)
PLATTE ISLAND (Sey.)
COETIVY ISLAND (Sey.)
ALPHONSE ISLAND (Sey.)
PROVIDENCE ISLAND (Sey.)
CERF ISLAND (Sey.)
FARQUHAR GROUP (Sey.)
ALDABRA ISLAND (Sey.)
COSMOLEDO I. (Sey.)
ASSUMPTION ISLAND (Sey.)
ASTOVE ISLAND (Sey.)
SAINT PIERRE ISLAND (Sey.)
AGALEGA ISLANDS (Mauritius)
ÎLES GLORIEUSES (Fr.)
ÎLE TROMELIN (Fr.)
BASSAS DA INDIA (Fr.)
ÎLE EUROPA (Fr.)
ÎLE JUAN DE NOVA (Fr.)
MAURITIUS
Port Louis
Curepipe
Mahébourg
REUNION (Fr.)
Saint-Denis
Le Port
Saint-Paul
Saint-Pierre
MASCARENE ISLANDS
Copyright © by Rand McNally & Co.
Map prepared by Esselte Map Service AB, Stockholm.
A-589200-264

Kilometers 0 200 400 600 Km.

Statute Miles 0 200 400 600 Mi.

Scale 1:12,000,000

One centimeter represents 120 kilometers.
One inch represents approximately 190 miles.
Miller Oblated Stereographic Projection

Map continues pages 128-129

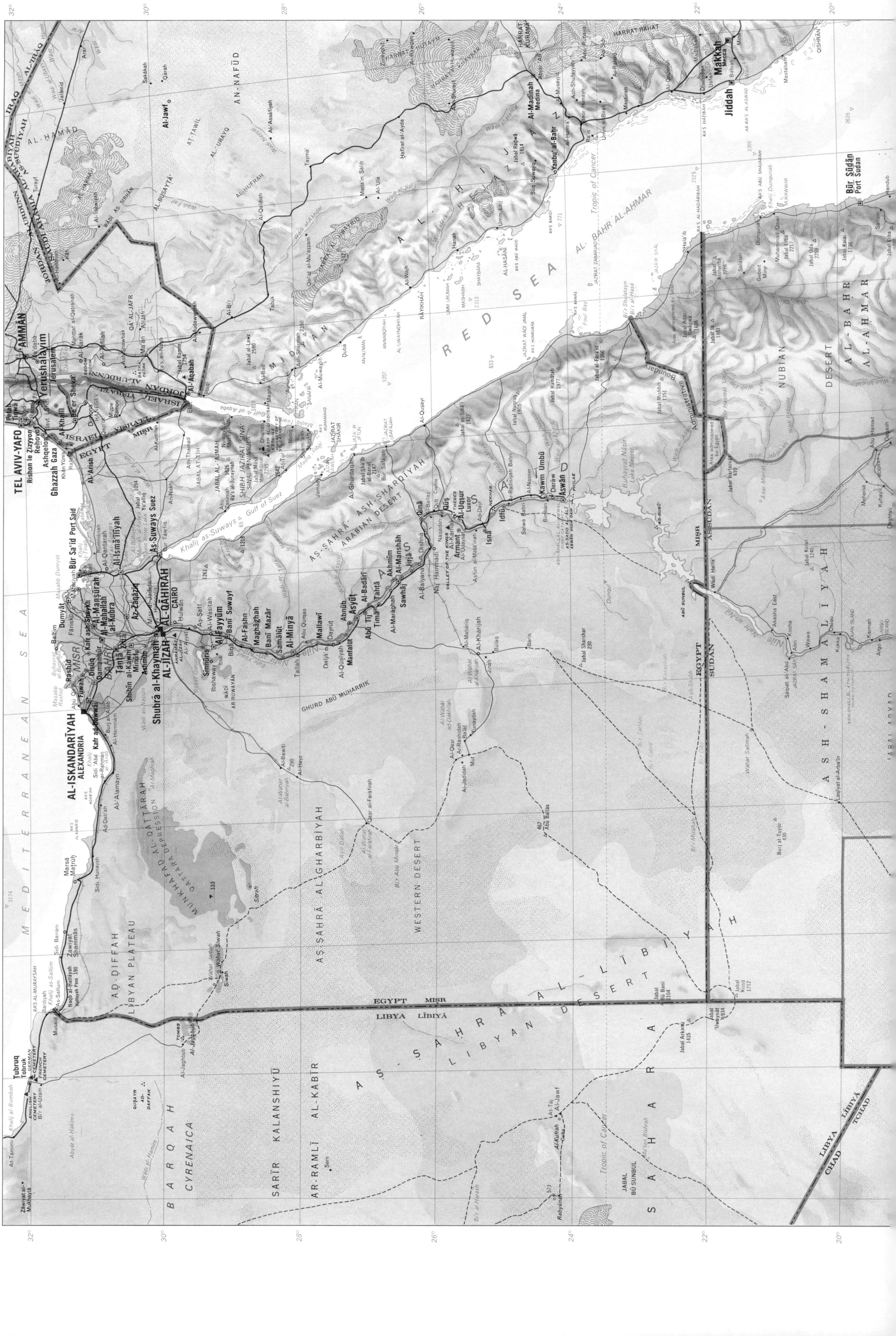
MEDITERRANEAN SEA
RED SEA
AL-BAHR AL-AHMAR
AL-QAHIRAH
CAIRO
AL-ISKANDARIYAH
ALEXANDRIA
AL-JIZAH
TEL AVIV-YAFO
Yerushalayim
Jerusalem
AMMAN
Makkah
Mecca
Jiddah
Al-Madinah
Medina
Bur Sudan
Port Sudan
Bur Sa'id Port Said
As-Suways Suez
Aswan
Luxor
Asyut
Marsa Matruh
Tobruk
WESTERN DESERT
ARABIAN DESERT
NUBIAN DESERT
LIBYAN DESERT
LIBYAN PLATEAU
CYRENAICA
QATTARA DEPRESSION
SINAI PENINSULA
Gulf of Suez
Gulf of Aqaba
Tropic of Cancer
EGYPT
MISR
LIBYA
LIBIYA
SUDAN
AS-SUDAN
ISRAEL
JORDAN
SAUDI ARABIA
CHAD
TCHAD
IRAQ
AN-NAFUD
Nile

Map continues pages 144-145

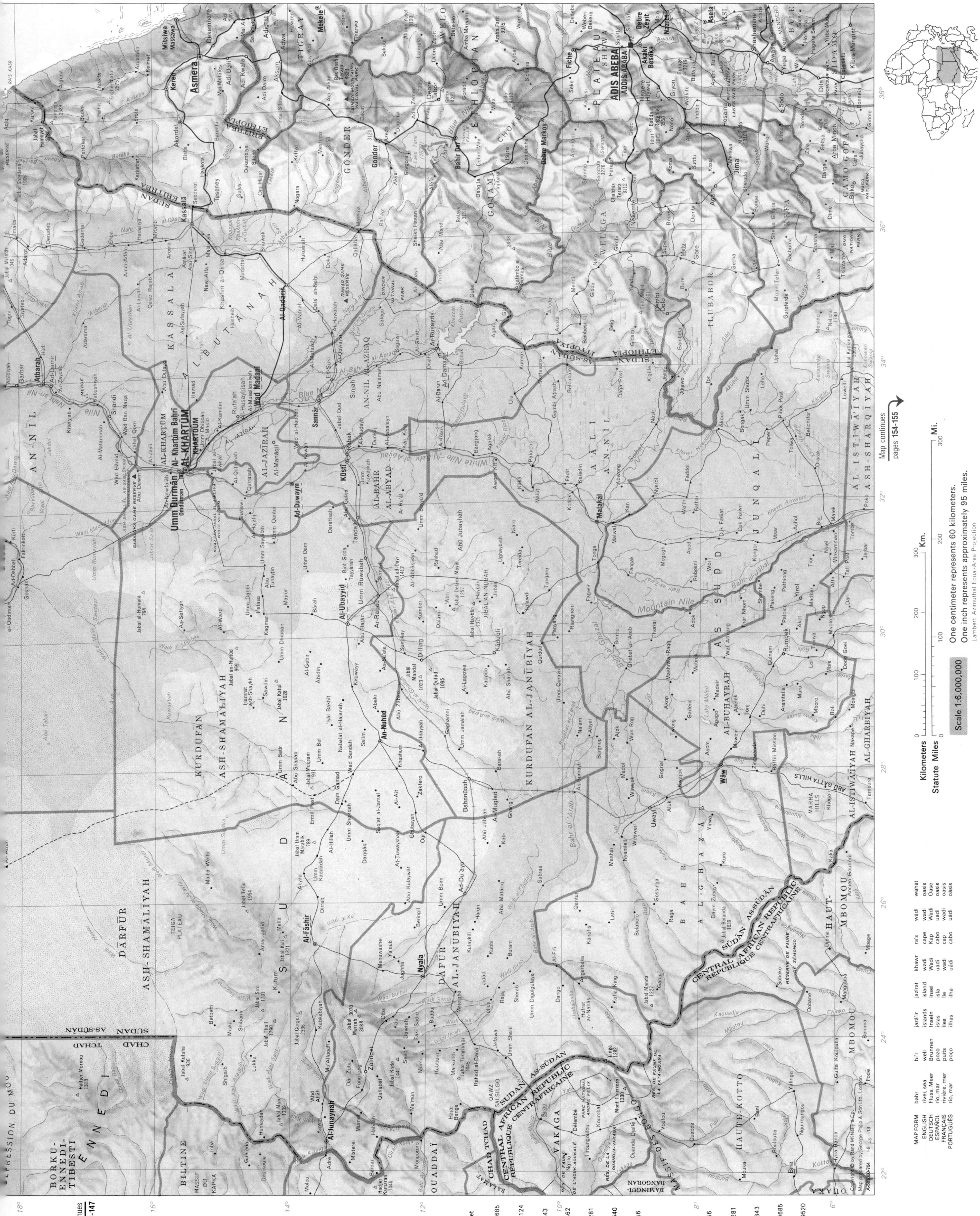
Map continues pages 154-155
Map continues pages 146-147
Scale 1:6,000,000
One centimeter represents 60 kilometers.
One inch represents approximately 95 miles.
Lambert Azimuthal Equal-Area Projection
Kilometers
Statute Miles
Meters
Feet
Land Below Sea Level

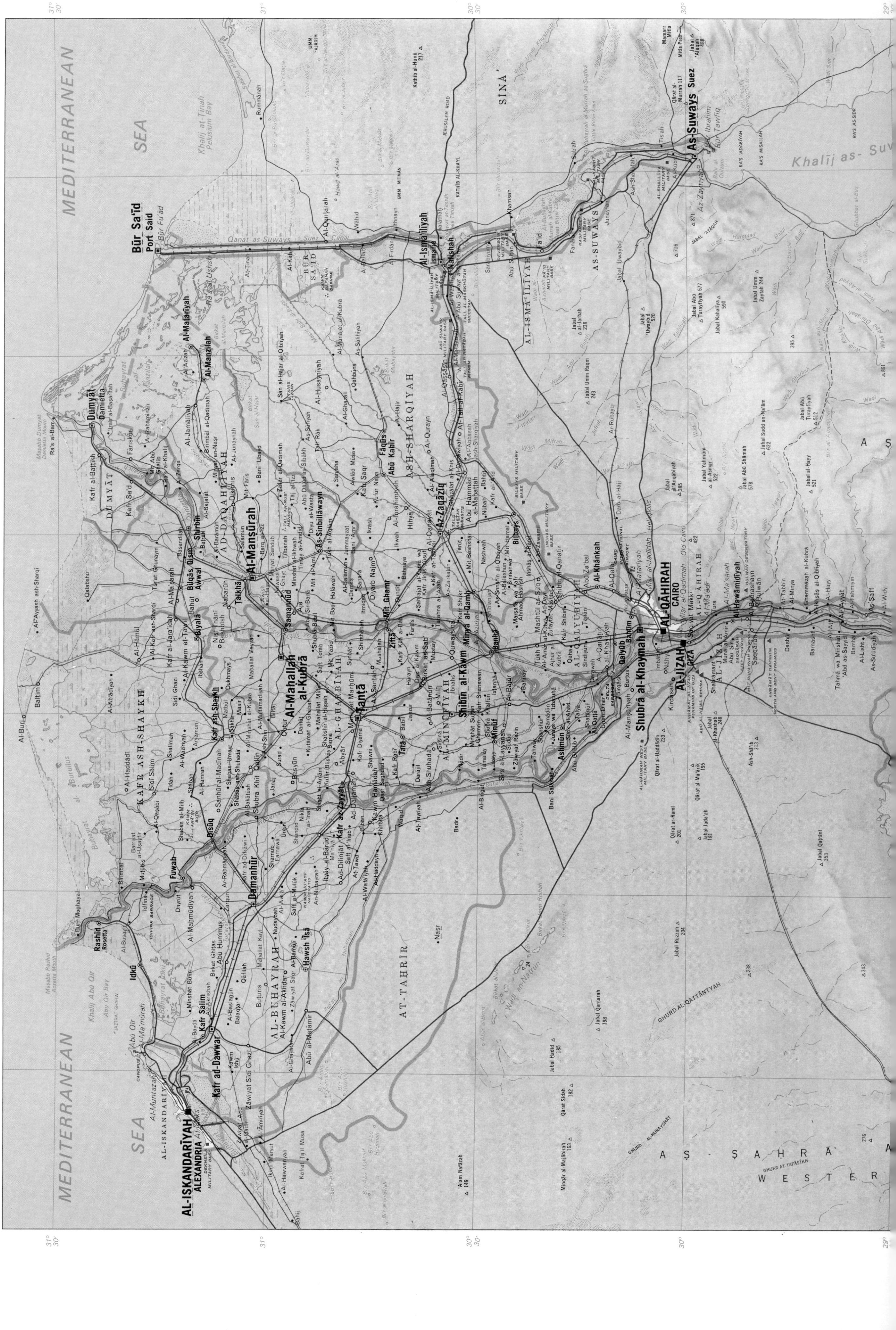
MEDITERRANEAN SEA
Būr Sa'īd
Port Said
Dumyāṭ
Damietta
Al-Manṣūrah
Al-Maḥallah al-Kubrā
Ṭanṭā
Az-Zaqāzīq
Al-Ismā'īlīyah
As-Suways
Suez
Qanāt as-Suways
Suez Canal
AL-QĀHIRAH
CAIRO
AL-JĪZAH
GIZA
Shubrā al-Khaymah
Damanhūr
AL-ISKANDARĪYAH
ALEXANDRIA
Rashīd
Rosetta
Kafr ash-Shaykh
AL-BUḤAYRAH
AT-TAḤRĪR
AD-DAQAHLĪYAH
ASH-SHARQĪYAH
AL-GHARBĪYAH
AL-MINŪFĪYAH
AL-QALYŪBĪYAH
AL-ISMĀ'ĪLĪYAH
AS-SUWAYS
SĪNĀ'
Khalīj as-Suways
AṢ-ṢAḤRĀ' AL-GHARBĪYAH
WESTERN DESERT

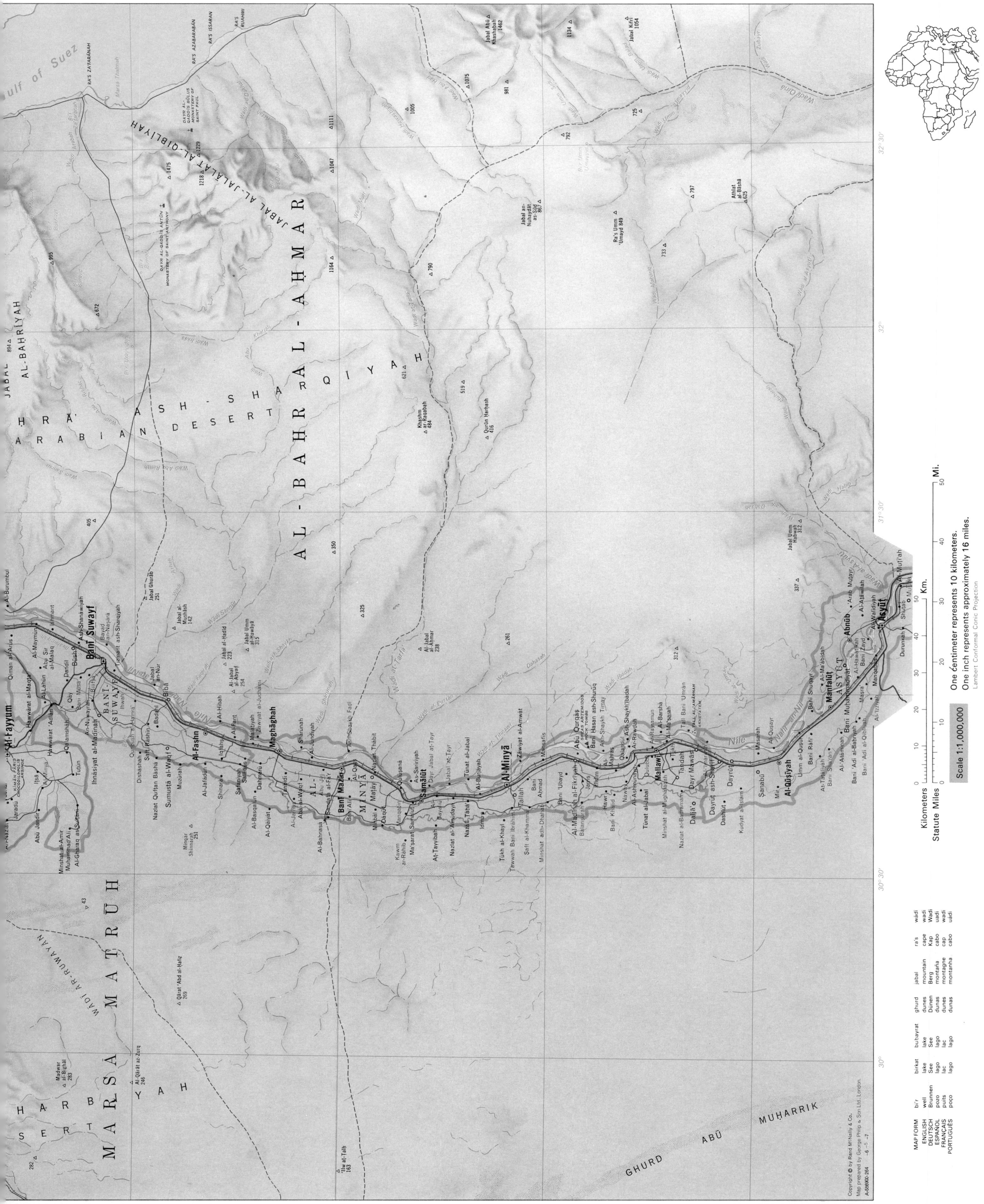
Scale 1:1,000,000
One centimeter represents 10 kilometers.
One inch represents approximately 16 miles.
Lambert Conformal Conic Projection
Kilometers
Statute Miles
Km.
Mi.
MAP FORM bi'r birkat buḥayrat ghurd jabal ra's wādī
ENGLISH well lake lake dunes mountain cape wadi
DEUTSCH Brunnen See See Dünen Berg Kap Wadi
ESPAÑOL pozo lago lago dunas montaña cabo uadi
FRANÇAIS puits lac lac dunes montagne cap wadi
PORTUGUÊS poço lago lago dunas montanha cabo uádi
Copyright © by Rand McNally & Co.
Map prepared by George Philip & Son Ltd., London.
AL-BAḤR AL-AḤMAR
ASH-SHARQIYAH
ARABIAN DESERT
JABAL AL-JALĀLAT AL-QIBLĪYAH
MARSĀ MAṬRŪḤ
GHURD ABŪ MUḤARRIK
Al-Fayyūm
Banī Suwayf
Al-Fashn
Maghāghah
Banī Mazār
Samālūṭ
Al-Minyā
Abū Qurqāṣ
Mallawī
Dayrūṭ
Al-Qūṣīyah
Manfalūṭ
Abnūb
Asyūṭ
Al-Muṭīʽah
Nile

RED SEA
AL-BAHR AL-AHMAR
Gulf of Aden
AR-RUB' AL-KHALI
Jiddah
Makkah
Aden
Asmera
Djibouti
Şan'ā'
NUBIAN DESERT
DAHLAK ARCHIPELAGO
JAZĀ'IR FARASĀN

Map continues pages 128-129

Map continues pages 140-141

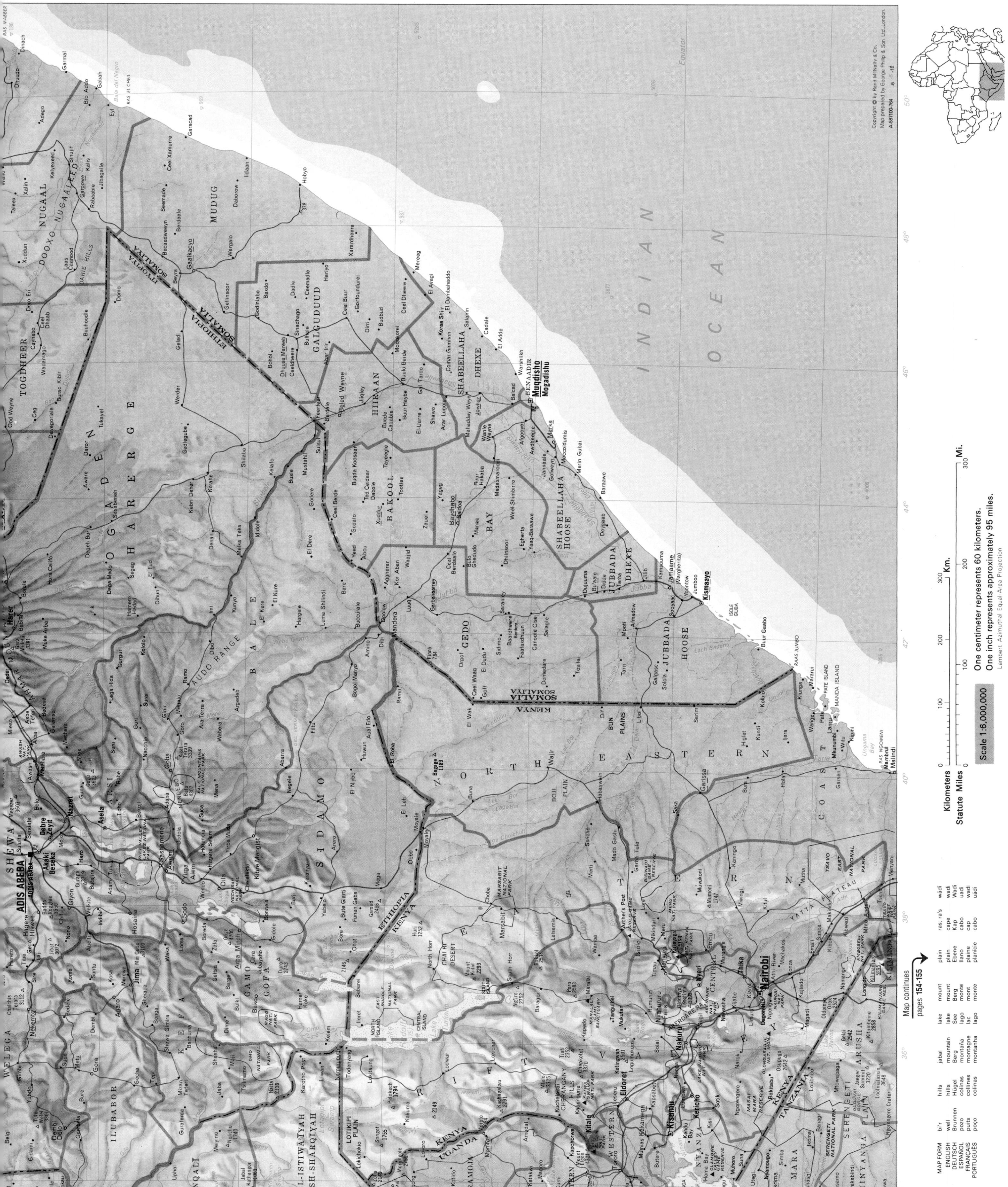
INDIAN OCEAN
ETHIOPIA
SOMALIA
KENYA
Mugdisho
Mogadishu
Nairobi
Kismaayo
Scale 1:6,000,000
One centimeter represents 60 kilometers.
One inch represents approximately 95 miles.
Lambert Azimuthal Equal-Area Projection
Kilometers
Statute Miles
Map continues pages 154-155
Copyright © by Rand McNally & Co.
Map prepared by George Philip & Son Ltd.,London
Meters
Feet
Land Below Sea Level

MEDITERRANEAN SEA
Khalīj Surt
Gulf of Sidra
ṬARĀBULUS
TRIPOLI
Banghāzī
Misrātah
Ṭubruq
Tobruk
Darnah
Al-Bayḍā'
Ajdābiyā
Surt
Sabhā
Marzūq
Ghāt
Ghadāmis
Al-Kufrah
Al-Jaghbūb
As-Sallūm
Zuwārah
Zarzis
Tataouine
Ra's al-Unūf
Jabal Waddān
Waddān
Hūn
Al-Jawf
Awbārī
Murzuq
Tāzirbū
Zillah
Nālūt
Gharyān
Bani Walid
Ajdābiyā
Zaltan
BARQAH
CYRENAICA
ṬARĀBULUS
TRIPOLITANIA
FEZZĀN
AL-ḤARŪJ AL-ASWAD
AS-SAHRĀ' AL-LĪBIYAH
LIBYAN DESERT
SARĪR KALANSHIYŪ
AR-RAMLĪ AL-KABĪR
ṢAḤRĀ' RABYĀNAH
SAḤRĀ' MARZŪQ
ṢAḤRĀ' AWBĀRĪ
ḤAMĀDAT TINGHERT
AL-ḤAMĀDAH AL-ḤAMRĀ'
ḤAMĀDAT ZEGHER
ḤAMĀDAT MARZŪQ
JABAL NAFŪSAH
JABAL BŪ SUNBUL
SARĪR TIBASTI
AD-DIFFAH
LIBYAN PLATEAU
MUNKHAFAD AL-QAṬṬĀRAH
GRAND ERG ORIENTAL
RMEL EL ABIOD
PLATEAU DU TINGHERT
TASSILI N'AJJER
ERG D'ADMER
MESACH MELLET
PLATEAU DU DJADO
PLATEAU DU MANGUÉNI
PLATEAU DU TCHIGAÏ
TÉNÉRÉ DU TAFASSÂSSET
TIBESTI
SAHARA
Tropic of Cancer
EGYPT
MIṢR
LIBYA
LĪBIYĀ
SUDAN
CHAD
TCHAD
NIGER
ALGERIA
ALGÉRIE
TUNISIA
TUNISIE

Map continues
pages 148-149

Map continues pages 140-141



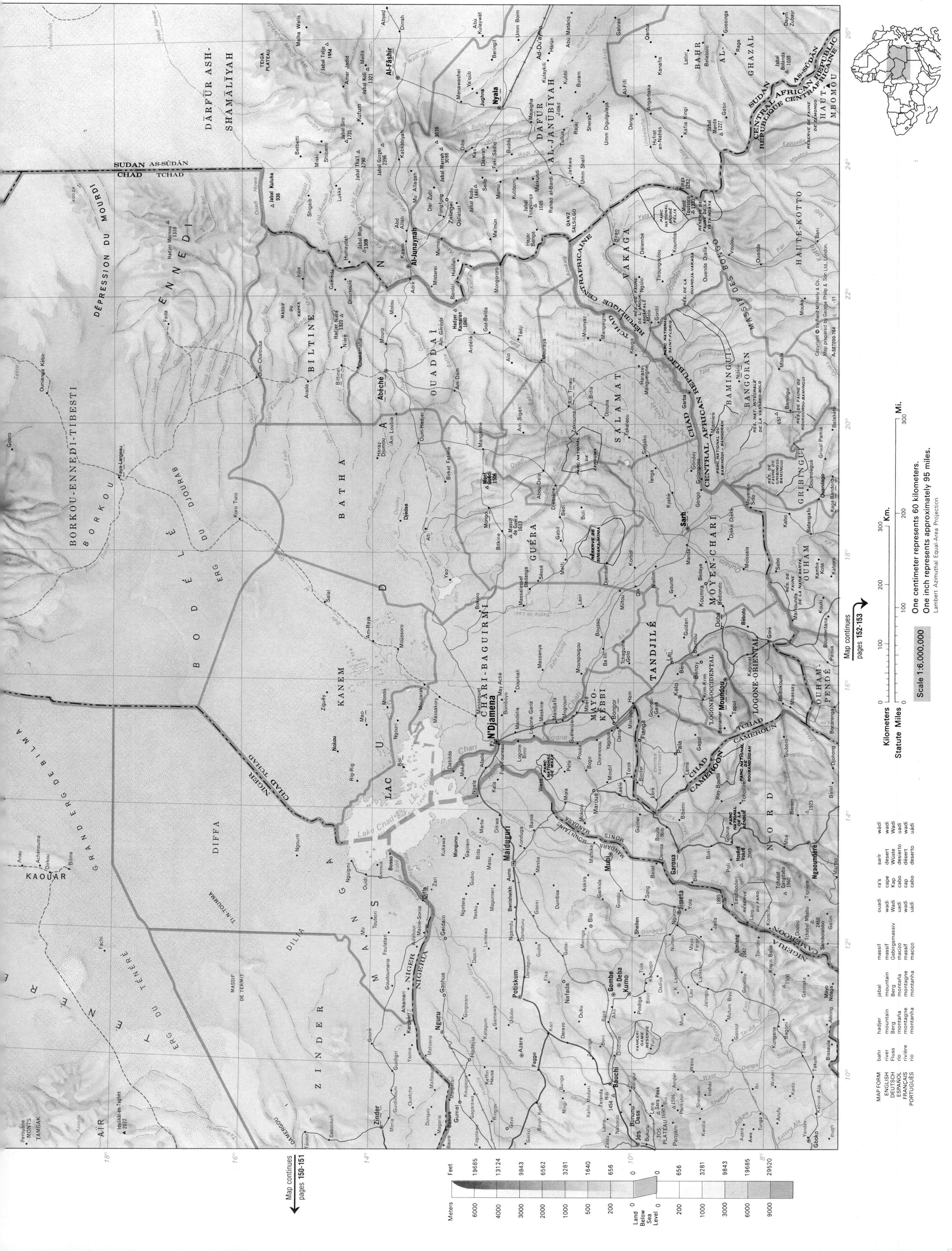
SUDAN AS-SŪDĀN
CHAD TCHAD
BORKOU-ENNEDI-TIBESTI
BATHA
OUADDAÏ
BILTINE
KANEM
LAC
CHARI-BAGUIRMI
GUÉRA
SALAMAT
MAYO-KÉBBI
TANDJILÉ
MOYEN-CHARI
LOGONE-OCCIDENTAL
LOGONE-ORIENTAL
N'Djamena
Abéché
Sarh
Moundou
Lake Chad
Scale 1:6,000,000
One centimeter represents 60 kilometers.
One inch represents approximately 95 miles.
Lambert Azimuthal Equal-Area Projection
Kilometers
Statute Miles
Copyright © by Rand McNally & Co.
Map prepared by George Philip & Son Ltd. London.
Meters
Feet
Land Below Sea Level

Map continues pages 152-153

Map continues pages 150-151

Map continues pages 34-35

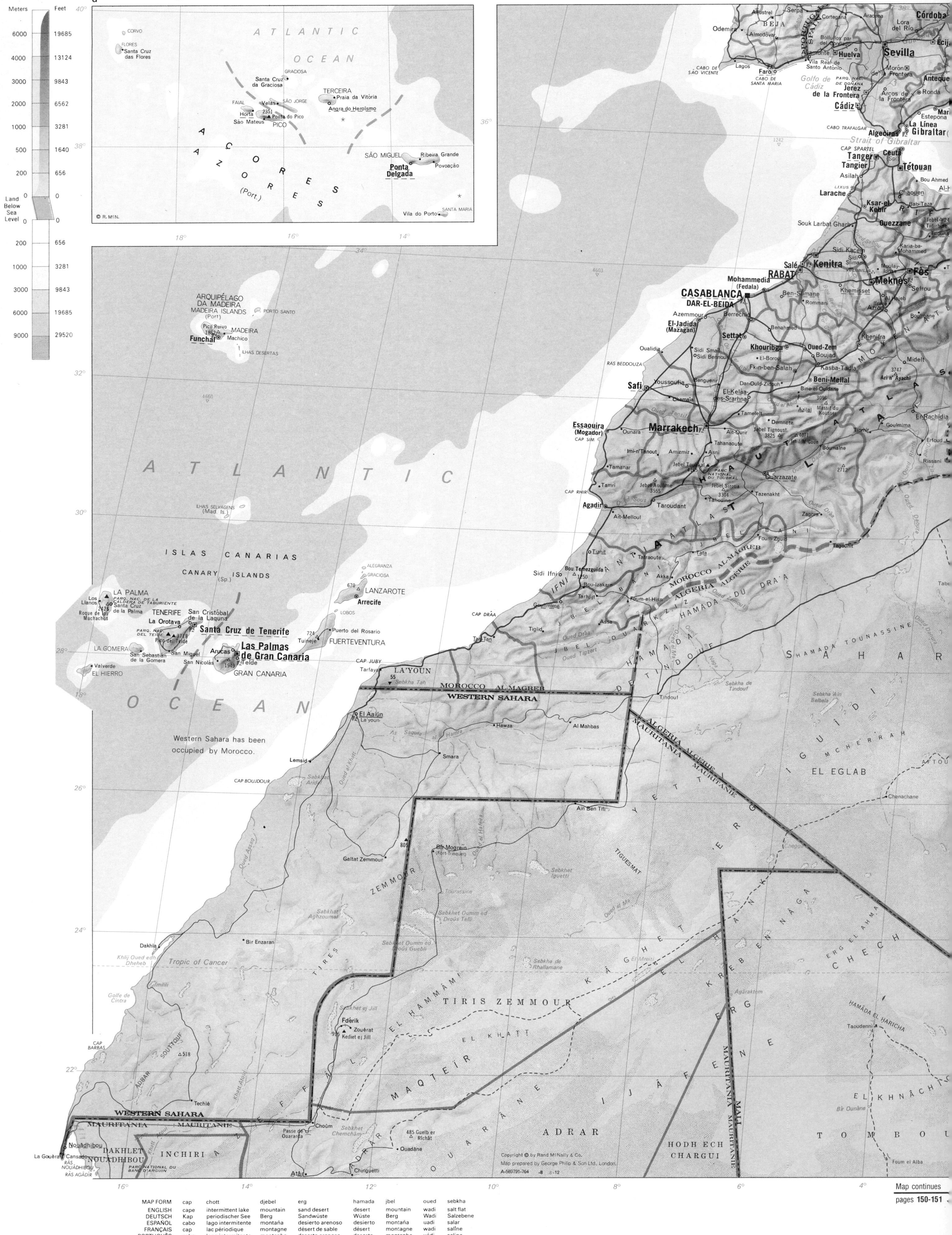
Meters
Feet
6000
19685
4000
13124
3000
9843
2000
6562
1000
3281
500
1640
200
656
Land Below Sea Level
0
0
200
656
1000
3281
3000
9843
6000
19685
9000
29520
a
ATLANTIC OCEAN
CORVO
FLORES
Santa Cruz das Flores
GRACIOSA
Santa Cruz da Graciosa
TERCEIRA
Praia da Vitória
Angra do Heroísmo
FAIAL
Velas
SÃO JORGE
Horta
2351
Ponta do Pico
São Mateus
PICO
AÇORES
AZORES
(Port.)
SÃO MIGUEL
Ribeira Grande
Povoação
Ponta Delgada
SANTA MARIA
Vila do Porto
ARQUIPÉLAGO DA MADEIRA
MADEIRA ISLANDS
(Port.)
PORTO SANTO
Pico Ruivo
1862
MADEIRA
Funchal
Machico
ILHAS DESERTAS
ILHAS SELVAGENS
(Mad. Is.)
ATLANTIC
OCEAN
ISLAS CANARIAS
CANARY ISLANDS
(Sp.)
ALEGRANZA
GRACIOSA
LANZAROTE
Arrecife
LA PALMA
PARQ. NAC. DE LA CALDERA DE TABURIENTE
Los Llanos
Santa Cruz de la Palma
Roque de los Muchachos
TENERIFE
San Cristóbal de la Laguna
La Orotava
PARQ. NAC. DEL TEIDE
Pico del Teide
3718
Santa Cruz de Tenerife
LA GOMERA
San Sebastián de la Gomera
San Miguel
Valverde
EL HIERRO
LOBOS
Puerto del Rosario
FUERTEVENTURA
Tuineje
Arucas
Las Palmas de Gran Canaria
San Nicolás
Telde
1949
GRAN CANARIA
CAP JUBY
Tarfaya
LA'YOUN
MOROCCO AL-MAGREB
WESTERN SAHARA
El Aaiún
La'youn
Hawza
Al Mahbas
Smara
Lemsid
CAP BOUJDOUR
Western Sahara has been occupied by Morocco.
Aïn Ben Tili
Bir Mogrein
(Fort-Trinquet)
Galtat Zemmour
ZEMMOUR
Bir Enzaran
Dakhla
Tropic of Cancer
Golfe de Cintra
CAP BARBAS
TIRIS ZEMMOUR
Fdérik
Zouérat
Kediet ej Jill
MAQTEÏR
ADRAR
Techlé
WESTERN SAHARA
MAURITANIA
MAURITANIE
Nouâdhibou
La Gouèra
DAKHLET NOUÂDHIBOU
INCHIRI
PARC NATIONAL DU BANC D'ARGUIN
RAS NOUÂDHIBOU
RAS AGÂDIR
Choûm
Atâr
Chinguetti
Ouadâne
ADRAR
OUARÂNE
HODH ECH CHARGUI
MAURITANIA
MALI
Odemira
BEJA
PORTUGAL
ESPAÑA
Huelva
Sevilla
Córdoba
Lagos
Faro
CABO DE SÃO VICENTE
Golfo de Cádiz
Jerez de la Frontera
Cádiz
CABO TRAFALGAR
Algeciras
La Línea
Gibraltar
Strait of Gibraltar
CAP SPARTEL
Tanger
Tangier
Ceuta
(Sp.)
Tétouan
Asilah
Larache
Ksar-el-Kebir
Ouezzane
Souk Larbat Gharb
Kenitra
Salé
RABAT
Meknès
Fès
Mohammedia
(Fedala)
CASABLANCA
DAR-EL-BEIDA
Azemmour
El-Jadida
(Mazagan)
Settat
Khouribga
Oued-Zem
Khenifra
Beni-Mellal
Oualidia
Safi
Youssoufia
Essaouira
(Mogador)
Marrakech
Tahanaoute
Jebel Toubkal
4165
Ouarzazate
Agadir
Taroudant
Tiznit
Sidi Ifni
IFNI
Goulimine
Tan-Tan
CAP DRÂA
Tindouf
HAMADA DU DRA'A
ALGERIA ALGÉRIE
MOROCCO AL-MAGREB
ANTI ATLAS
HAUT ATLAS
MOYEN ATLAS
HAMADA DE TINDOUF
Er-Rachidia
Erfoud
SAHARA
EL EGLAB
IGUIDI
Chenachane
YETTI
Taoudenni
TOMBOUCTOU
Copyright © by Rand McNally & Co.
Map prepared by George Philip & Son Ltd., London.

Map continues pages 150-151

| MAP FORM | cap | chott | djebel | erg | hamada | jbel | oued | sebkha |
|---|---|---|---|---|---|---|---|---|
| ENGLISH | cape | intermittent lake | mountain | sand desert | desert | mountain | wadi | salt flat |
| DEUTSCH | Kap | periodischer See | Berg | Sandwüste | Wüste | Berg | Wadi | Salzebene |
| ESPAÑOL | cabo | lago intermitente | montaña | desierto arenoso | desierto | montaña | uadi | salar |
| FRANÇAIS | cap | lac périodique | montagne | désert de sable | désert | montagne | oued | saline |
| PORTUGUÊS | cabo | lago intermitente | montanha | deserto arenoso | deserto | montanha | uádi | salina |

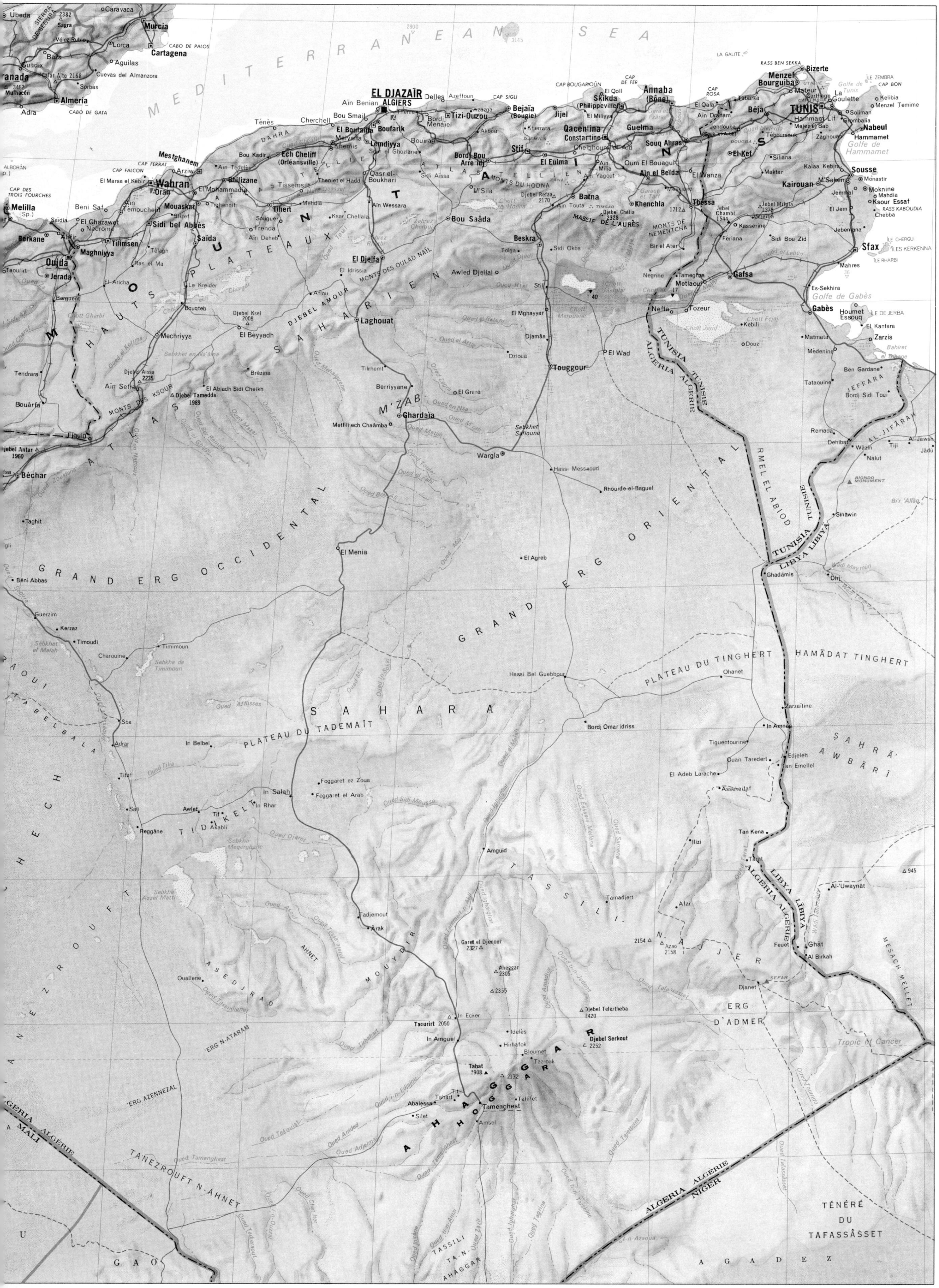
MEDITERRANEAN SEA
EL DJAZAÏR
ALGIERS
TUNIS
Oran
Wahran
Annaba (Bône)
Skikda (Philippeville)
Qacentina Constantine
Bizerte
Sousse
Sfax
Gabès
Kairouan
Gafsa
Tozeur
Bejaïa (Bougie)
Tizi-Ouzou
Blida
Ech Cheliff (Orleansville)
Mostaganem
Tilimsen
Oujda
Melilla
Murcia
Cartagena
Almería
Batna
Biskra
Djelfa
Laghouat
Ghardaïa
Wargla
Touggourt
El Wad
El Menia
Béchar
In Salah
Tamenghest
Ghadāmis
Hassi Messaoud
Bordj Omar Idriss
Amguid
Djanet
HAUTS PLATEAUX
SAHARIEN ATLAS
M'ZAB
GRAND ERG OCCIDENTAL
GRAND ERG ORIENTAL
SAHARA
PLATEAU DU TADEMAÏT
PLATEAU DU TINGHERT
HAMĀDAT TINGHERT
TASSILI
AHAGGAR
TANEZROUFT
ERG D'ADMER
TÉNÉRÉ DU TAFASSÂSSET
AGADEZ
GAO
Tropic of Cancer
TUNISIA TUNISIE
ALGERIA ALGÉRIE
LIBYA LIBYE
MALI
NIGER

Map continues pages 146-147

Kilometers 0 100 200 300 Km.
Statute Miles 0 100 200 300 Mi.

Scale 1:6,000,000
One centimeter represents 60 kilometers.
One inch represents approximately 95 miles.
Lambert Azimuthal Equal-Area Projection

# West Africa / Westafrika / África Occidental
# Afrique Occidentale / África Ocidental

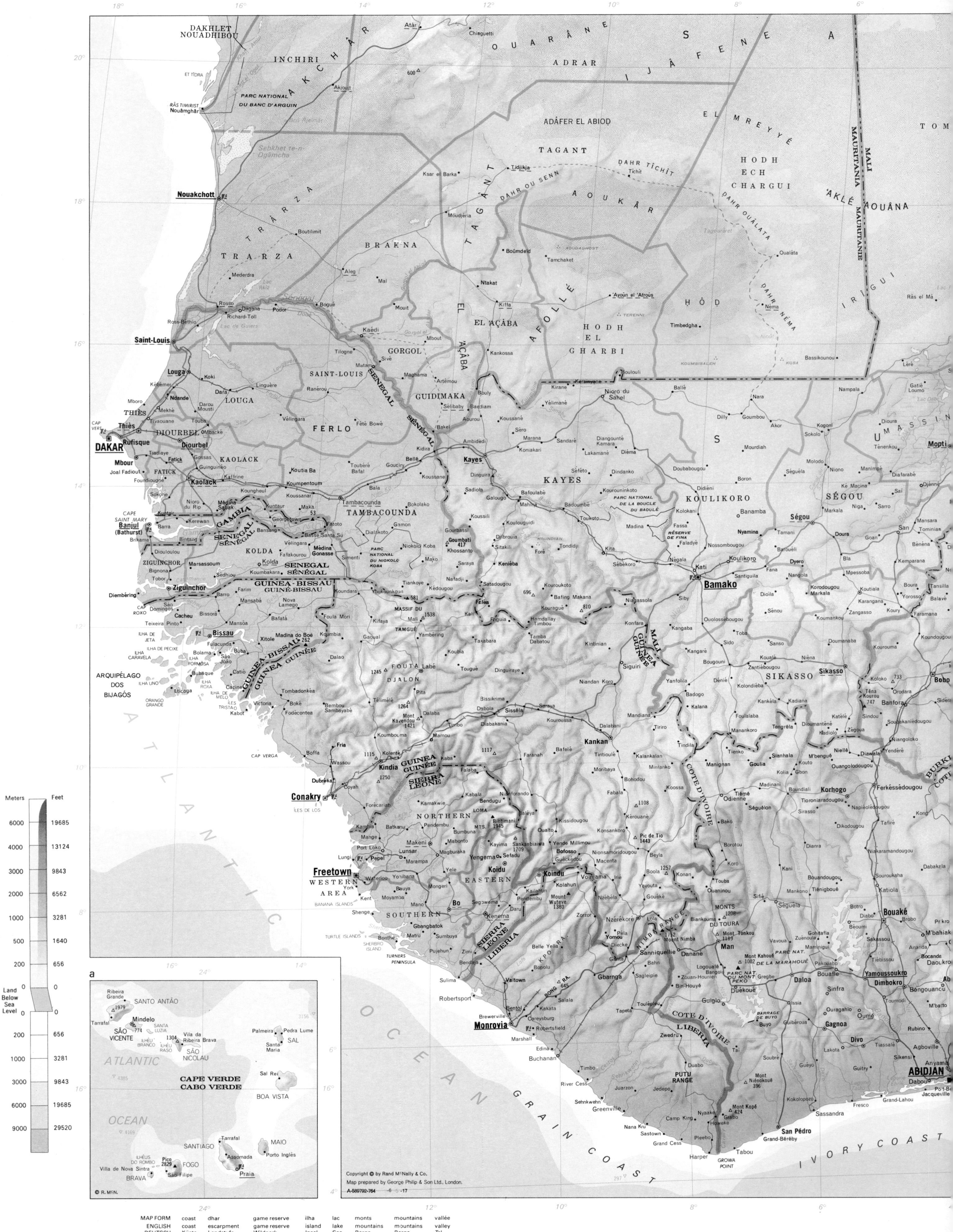

DAKHLET NOUADHIBOU
INCHIRI
AKCHÂR
ADRAR
OUARÂNE
IJÂFENE
ADÂFER EL ABIOḌ
TAGANT
EL MREYYÉ
HODH ECH CHARGUI
TRARZA
BRAKNA
AOUKÂR
DAHR OU SENN
DAHR TÎCHÎT
DAHR OUÂLATA
DAHR NÉMA
ÂKLÉ AOUÂNA
MALI
MAURITANIA
MAURITANIE
PARC NATIONAL DU BANC D'ARGUIN
Nouakchott
Saint-Louis
GORGOL
GUIDIMAKA
EL ÂÇÂBA
HODH EL GHARBI
AFOLLÉ
SAINT-LOUIS
LOUGA
THIÈS
DIOURBEL
KAOLACK
FATICK
FERLO
TAMBACOUNDA
KOLDA
ZIGUINCHOR
DAKAR
Banjul (Bathurst)
GAMBIA
SENEGAL
SÉNÉGAL
GUINEA-BISSAU
GUINÉ-BISSAU
Bissau
ARQUIPÉLAGO DOS BIJAGÓS
GUINEA
GUINÉE
FOUTA DJALON
Conakry
SIERRA LEONE
Freetown
WESTERN AREA
NORTHERN
EASTERN
SOUTHERN
LIBERIA
Monrovia
KAYES
KOULIKORO
SÉGOU
SIKASSO
Bamako
CÔTE D'IVOIRE
ABIDJAN
Yamoussoukro
ATLANTIC OCEAN
GRAIN COAST
IVORY COAST
Meters
Feet
6000
19685
4000
13124
3000
9843
2000
6562
1000
3281
500
1640
200
656
0
Land Below Sea Level
0
200
656
1000
3281
3000
9843
6000
19685
9000
29520
a
CAPE VERDE
CABO VERDE
SANTO ANTÃO
SÃO VICENTE
SÃO NICOLAU
SAL
BOA VISTA
MAIO
SANTIAGO
FOGO
BRAVA
Praia
Mindelo
Copyright © by Rand McNally & Co.
Map prepared by George Philip & Son Ltd., London.
A-589792-764


| MAP FORM | coast | dhar | game reserve | ilha | lac | monts | mountains | vallée |
|---|---|---|---|---|---|---|---|---|
| ENGLISH | coast | escarpment | game reserve | island | lake | mountains | mountains | valley |
| DEUTSCH | Küste | Landstufe | Wildpark | Insel | See | Berge | Berge | Tal |
| ESPAÑOL | costa | escarpa | vedado de caza | isla | lago | montes | montañas | valle |
| FRANÇAIS | côte | escarpement | réserve à gibier | île | lac | monts | montagnes | vallée |
| PORTUGUÊS | costa | escarpa | reserva de caça | ilha | lago | montes | montanhas | vale |

Map continues pages 148-149

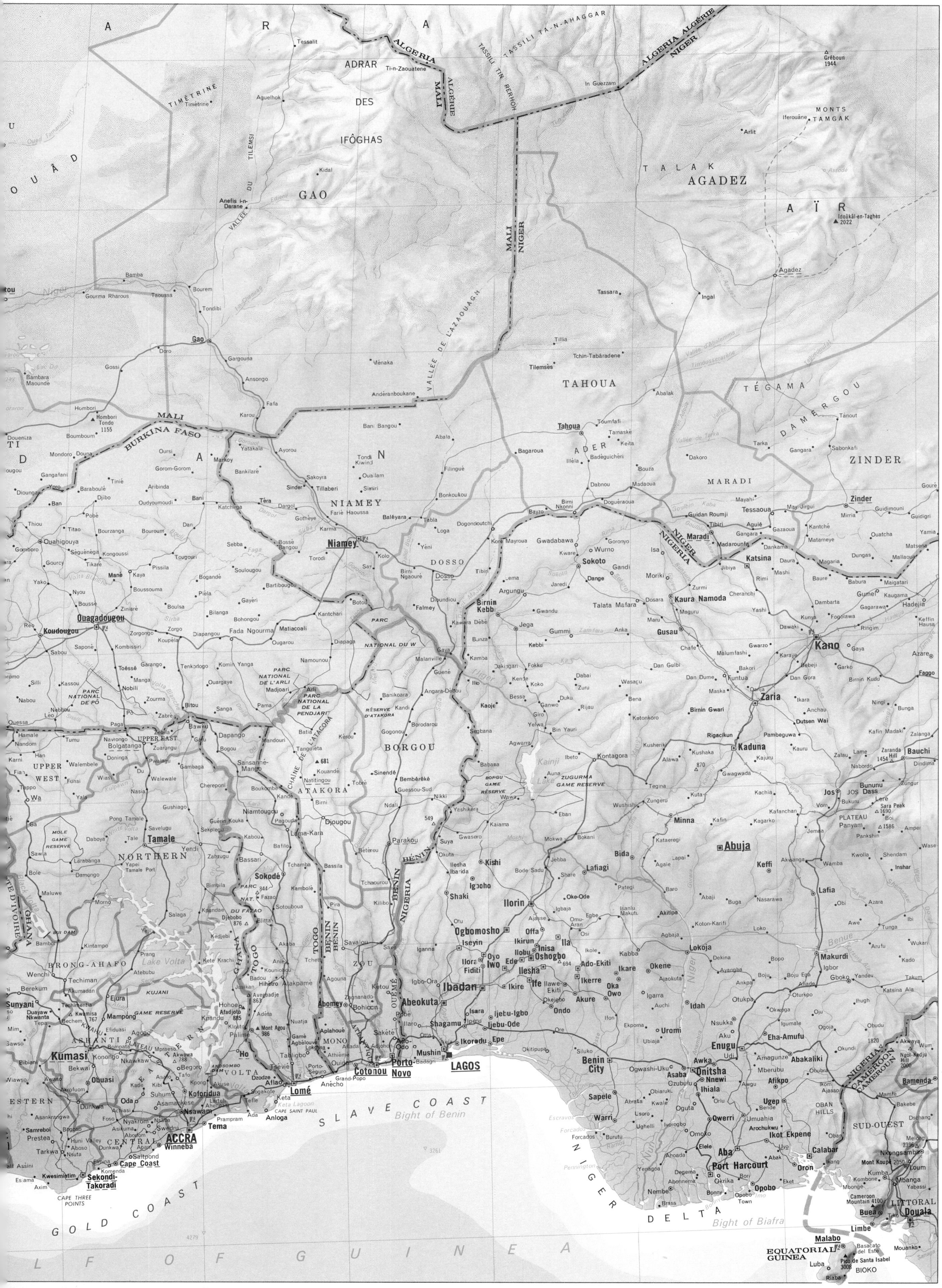
ALGERIA
ALGÉRIE
MALI
NIGER
ADRAR DES IFÔGHAS
TASSILI TA-N-AHAGGAR
TIMÉTRINE
GAO
AGADEZ
AÏR
TAHOUA
TÉGAMA
DAMERGOU
ZINDER
MARADI
NIAMEY
DOSSO
BURKINA FASO
UPPER EAST
UPPER WEST
NORTHERN
BRONG-AHAFO
ASHANTI
EASTERN
CENTRAL
VOLTA
TOGO
BENIN
BÉNIN
BORGOU
ATAKORA
ZOU
OUÉMÉ
NIGERIA
CAMEROON
CAMEROUN
EQUATORIAL GUINEA
BIOKO
SUD-OUEST
LITTORAL
Tessalit
Kidal
Gao
Bourem
Agadez
Arlit
Tahoua
Maradi
Zinder
Niamey
Ouahigouya
Ouagadougou
Koudougou
Tamale
Kumasi
ACCRA
Tema
Cape Coast
Sekondi-Takoradi
Lomé
Cotonou
Porto-Novo
LAGOS
Ibadan
Abeokuta
Ogbomosho
Ilorin
Oshogbo
Abuja
Kaduna
Zaria
Kano
Katsina
Sokoto
Jos
Makurdi
Lokoja
Enugu
Onitsha
Benin City
Warri
Aba
Port Harcourt
Calabar
Douala
Malabo
Kainji Lake
Lake Volta
Niger
Benue
SLAVE COAST
Bight of Benin
GOLD COAST
NIGER DELTA
Bight of Biafra
GULF OF GUINEA
Grébourn 1944
Mont Koupé 2050

Map continues pages 146-147

Map continues pages 152-153

Kilometers 0 100 200 300 Km.
Statute Miles 0 100 200 300 Mi.

Scale 1:6,000,000
One centimeter represents 60 kilometers.
One inch represents approximately 95 miles.
Lambert Azimuthal Equal-Area Projection

Map continues pages 146-147

CENTRAL AFRICAN REPUBLIC
CAMEROON
CONGO
GABON
ZAIRE
EQUATORIAL GUINEA
SAO TOME AND PRINCIPE
Bangui
Yaoundé
Douala
Libreville
Brazzaville
KINSHASA (LÉOPOLDVILLE)
Mbandaka (Coquilhatville)
Bandundu
Ilebo (Port Francqui)
Port Gentil
Malabo
Bata
Enugu
Calabar
Port Harcourt
Bight of Biafra
Gulf of Guinea
Equator

Map continues pages 150-151

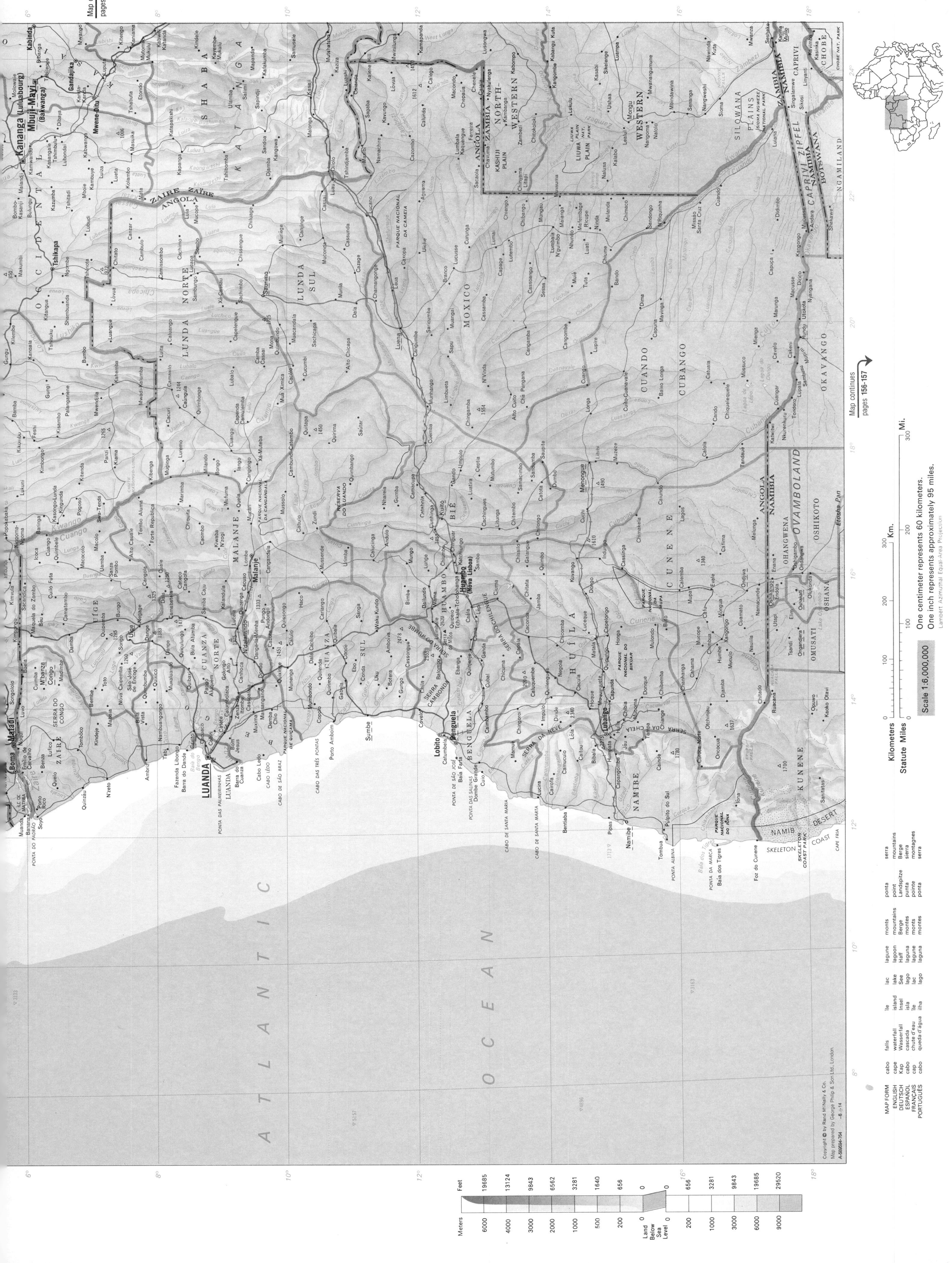
Map continues pages 154-155
Map continues pages 156-157
ATLANTIC OCEAN
Scale 1:6,000,000
One centimeter represents 60 kilometers.
One inch represents approximately 95 miles.
Lambert Azimuthal Equal-Area Projection
Kilometers
Statute Miles
LUANDA
Lobito
Benguela
Huambo (Nova Lisboa)
Kananga (Luluabourg)
Mbuji-Mayi (Bakwanga)
Matadi
Boma
Kabinda
Tshikapa
Namibe
Lubango
Malanje
NAMIBIA
ANGOLA
ZAMBIA
BOTSWANA

KENYA
SOMALIA
ETHIOPIA
UGANDA
TANZANIA
SUDAN
ZAIRE
RWANDA
BURUNDI
CENTRAL AFRICAN REP.
NAIROBI
KAMPALA
DAR ES SALAAM
Mombasa
Kigali
Bujumbura
Kisangani (Stanleyville)
Kalemie (Albertville)
Dodoma
INDIAN OCEAN
Lake Victoria
Lake Tanganyika
KILIMANJARO
SERENGETI PLAIN
MASAI STEPPE

Map continues pages 144-145
Map continues pages 140-141
Map continues pages 152-153

Kilometers 0 100 200 300 Km.
Statute Miles 0 100 200 300 Mi.
Scale 1:6,000,000
One centimeter represents 60 kilometers.
One inch represents approximately 95 miles.
Lambert Azimuthal Equal-Area Projection

| ENGLISH | falls | game reserve | island | lake | mountains | national park | plain | swamp |
|---|---|---|---|---|---|---|---|---|
| DEUTSCH | Wasserfall | Wildreservat | Insel | See | Berge | Nationalpark | Ebene | Sumpf |
| ESPAÑOL | cascada | vedado de caza | isla | lago | montañas | parque nacional | llano | pantano |
| FRANÇAIS | chute d'eau | réserve à gibier | île | lac | montagnes | parc national | plaine | marais |
| PORTUGUÊS | queda d'água | reserva de caça | ilha | lago | montanhas | parque nacional | planície | pântano |

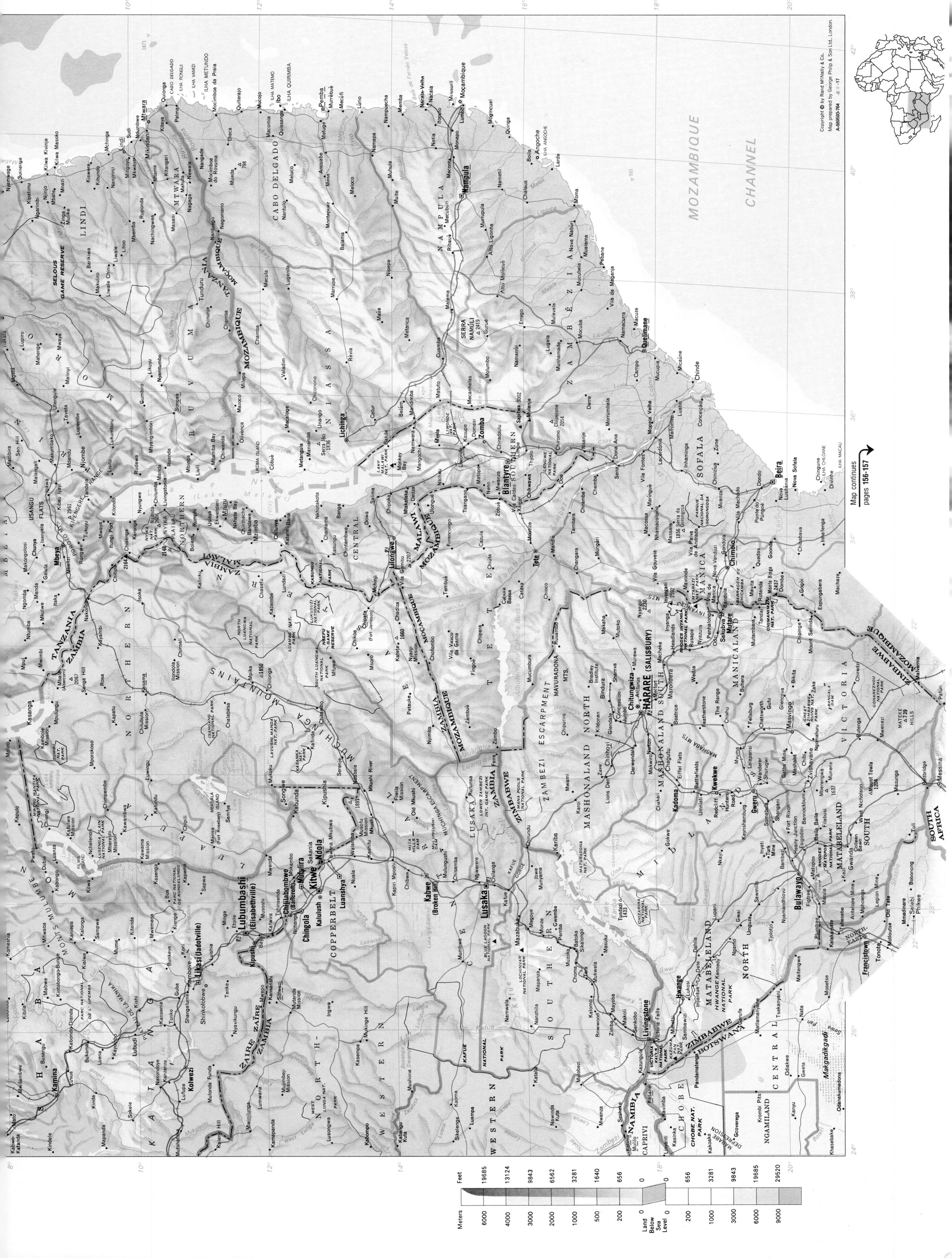
MOZAMBIQUE
CHANNEL
Map continues pages 156-157
Copyright © by Rand McNally & Co.
Map prepared by George Philip & Son Ltd. London.
Lilongwe
Harare (Salisbury)
Lusaka
Lubumbashi (Élisabethville)
Blantyre
Beira
Bulawayo
Nampula
Quelimane
Feet
Meters
Land Below Sea Level

# Southern Africa and Madagascar / Südafrika und Madagaskar / África Meridional y Madagascar
# Afrique Méridionale et Madagascar / África Meridional e Madagascar

Map continues pages 152-153

ATLANTIC
OCEAN
ANGOLA
NAMIBIA
BOTSWANA
SOUTH AFRICA
SÜD-AFRIKA
ZIMBABWE
CAPRIVI ZIPFEL
CAPRIVI STRIP
OVAMBOLAND
OMUSATI
OSHANA
OSHIKOTO
OHANGWENA
OKAVANGO
CUANDO CUBANGO
KUNENE
OTJOZONDJUPA
OMAHEKE
ERONGO
DAMARALAND
KHOMAS
HARDAP
KARAS
GREAT NAMAQUALAND
LITTLE NAMAQUALAND
NAMIB DESERT
KAOKOVELD
SKELETON COAST
KALAHARI DESERT
KGALAGADI
GHANZI
NGAMILAND
KWENENG
CENTRAL
SOUTHERN
SOUTH EAST
BOPHUTHATSWANA
NORTH WEST
FREE STATE
NORTHERN CAPE
WESTERN CAPE
EASTERN CAPE
GRIQUALAND WEST
BECHUANALAND
BUSHMAN LAND
GREAT KAROO
LITTLE KAROO
ETOSHA NATIONAL PARK
Etosha Pan
OKAVANGO DELTA
CENTRAL KALAHARI GAME RESERVE
GEMSBOK NATIONAL PARK
KALAHARI GEMSBOK NATIONAL PARK
Tropic of Capricorn
Windhoek
Swakopmund
Walvis Bay
Lüderitz
Keetmanshoop
Gaborone
Kimberley
Bloemfontein
Upington
CAPE TOWN
KAAPSTAD
Port Elizabeth
Livingstone
Oudtshoorn
George
Stellenbosch
Worcester
CAPE OF GOOD HOPE
CAPE AGULHAS
Meters
Feet
6000 19685
4000 13124
3000 9843
2000 6562
1000 3281
500 1640
200 656
0 0
Land Below Sea Level
200 656
1000 3281
3000 9843
6000 19685
9000 29520
Copyright © by Rand McNally & Co.
Map prepared by George Philip & Son Ltd., London.
A-589292-764


| MAP FORM | bay | berg, berge | cape | game reserve | ilha | lake | national park |
|---|---|---|---|---|---|---|---|
| ENGLISH | bay | mountain, mountains | cape | game reserve | island | lake | national park |
| DEUTSCH | Bucht | Berg, Berge | Kap | Wildpark | Insel | See | Nationalpark |
| ESPAÑOL | bahía | montaña, montañas | cabo | vedado de caza | isla | lago | parque nacional |
| FRANÇAIS | baie | montagne, montagnes | cap | réserve à gibier | île | lac | parc national |
| PORTUGUÊS | baía | montanha, montanhas | cabo | reserva de caça | ilha | lago | parque nacional |

Kilometers 0 100 200 300 Km.

Statute Miles 0 100 200 300 Mi.

Scale 1:6,000,000

One centimeter represents 60 kilometers.
One inch represents approximately 95 miles.
Lambert Azimuthal Equal-Area Projection

Map continues
pages 154-155

a
INDIAN OCEAN
COMOROS
COMORES
Moroni
Mitsamiouli
NJAZIDJA (GRANDE COMORE)
Kartala 2361
Fomboni
MWALI (MOHÉLI)
Mutsamudu
NZWANI (ANJOUAN)
MAYOTTE (Fr.)
Dzaoudzi
Mamoutzou
ARCHIPEL DES COMORES
MOZAMBIQUE CHANNEL
b
MADAGASCAR
MADAGASIKARA
ANTANANARIVO
Antsiranana
Mahajanga
Toamasina
Fianarantsoa
Toliara
Antsirabe
Morondava
Manakara
Farafangana
Faradofay
Nosy Be
MASSIF DU TSARATANANA
Maromokotro 2876
ANKARATRA
Tsiafajavona 2642
MASSIF DU MAKAY
MASSIF DE L'ISALO
MASSIF DE L'IVAKOANY
CHAÎNES ANOSYENNES
PLATEAU DU BEMARAHA
CAP D'AMBRE
CAP SAINTE-MARIE
CAP SAINT-ANDRÉ
CAP EST
Tropic of Capricorn
MOZAMBIQUE CHANNEL
INDIAN OCEAN
c
INDIAN
MAURITIUS
Port Louis
Curepipe
Rose-Hill
Mahébourg
Piton de la Petite Rivière Noire 828
RÉUNION
Saint-Denis
Saint-Pierre
Piton des Neiges 3070
Piton de la Fournaise 2631
MAURITIUS-RÉUNION
MASCARENE ISLANDS
OCEAN
HARARE (SALISBURY)
Chitungwiza
MASHONALAND SOUTH
MIDLANDS
MANICALAND
Mutare
Gweru
Masvingo
VICTORIA
MATABELELAND SOUTH
Bulawayo
Beira
Chimoio
MANICA
SOFALA
Quelimane
ZAMBÉZIA
INHAMBANE
GAZA
Inhambane
Xai-Xai
MAPUTO
ZIMBABWE
MOÇAMBIQUE
SOUTH AFRICA
NORTHERN
Pietersburg
MPUMALANGA
PRETORIA
Nelspruit
Mbabane
SWAZILAND
KWAZULU-NATAL
Pietermaritzburg
DURBAN
Ladysmith
Newcastle
TRANSKEI
Umtata
INDIAN OCEAN
© R. McN.

# South Africa / Republik Südafrika / Sudáfrica
# Afrique du Sud / África do Sul

Map continues pages 156-157

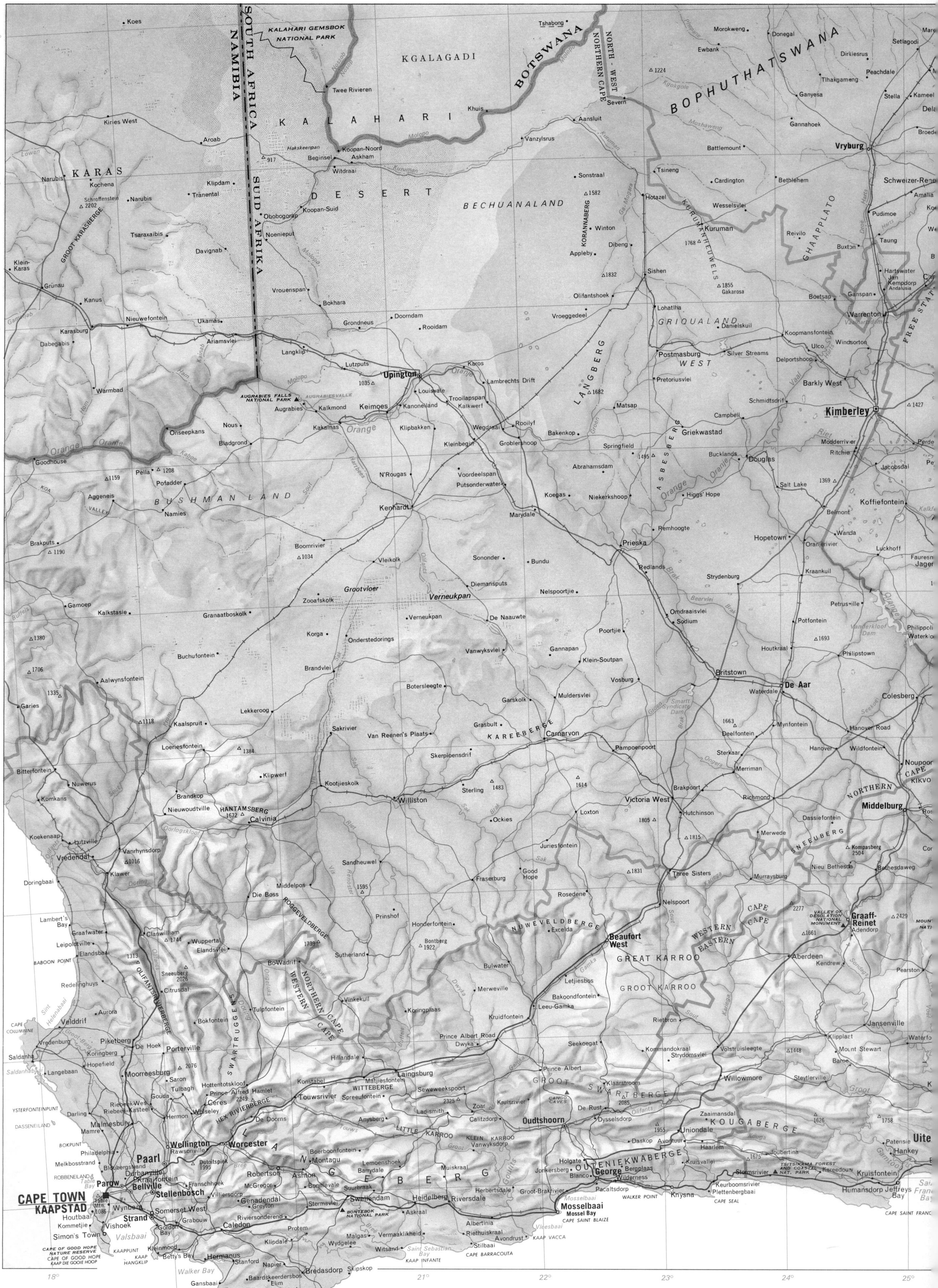
SOUTH AFRICA
SUID AFRIKA
NAMIBIA
BOTSWANA
KALAHARI GEMSBOK NATIONAL PARK
KGALAGADI
KALAHARI
DESERT
BECHUANALAND
BOPHUTHATSWANA
NORTH - WEST
NORTHERN CAPE
KARAS
GROOT KARASBERGE
GRIQUALAND WEST
BUSHMAN LAND
Grootvloer
Verneukpan
KAREEBERGE
NUWEVELDBERGE
GREAT KARROO
GROOT KARROO
WESTERN CAPE
EASTERN CAPE
ROGGEVELDBERGE
HANTAMSBERG
SNEEUBERG
SWARTRUGGENS
OLIFANTSRIVIERBERGE
HEX RIVIERBERGE
WITTEBERGE
LITTLE KARROO
KLEIN KAROO
GROOT SWARTBERGE
KOUGABERGE
OUTENIEKWABERGE
LANGEBERG
Orange
Molopo
Upington
Kimberley
Vryburg
Kuruman
Prieska
Calvinia
Williston
Victoria West
Beaufort West
De Aar
Britstown
Graaff-Reinet
Middelburg
Colesberg
Oudtshoorn
George
Knysna
Mosselbaai
Mossel Bay
Worcester
Wellington
Paarl
Stellenbosch
Bellville
Parow
CAPE TOWN
KAAPSTAD
Simon's Town
Strand
Somerset West
Hermanus
Caledon
Swellendam
Laingsburg
Vredendal
Clanwilliam
Piketberg
Saldanha
CAPE OF GOOD HOPE
KAAP DIE GOEIE HOOP
CAPE AGULHAS
Agulhas
Bredasdorp
Jeffreys Bay
Humansdorp
Kruisfontein
TSITSIKAMMA FOREST AND COASTAL NAT. PARK
AUGRABIES FALLS NATIONAL PARK
BONTEBOK NATIONAL PARK
VALLEY OF DESOLATION NATIONAL MONUMENT
Walker Bay
Valsbaai
Saldanhabaai
Mosselbaai
Vleesbaai
18°
19°
20°
21°
22°
23°
24°
25°
26°
27°
28°
29°
30°
31°
32°
33°
34°

| Meters | Feet |
|---|---|
| 6000 | 19685 |
| 4000 | 13124 |
| 3000 | 9843 |
| 2000 | 6562 |
| 1000 | 3281 |
| 500 | 1640 |
| 200 | 656 |
| 0 | 0 |
| Land Below Sea Level 0 | 0 |
| 200 | 656 |
| 1000 | 3281 |
| 3000 | 9843 |
| 6000 | 19685 |
| 9000 | 29520 |

| MAP FORM | bay | berge | cape | dam | game reserve | national park | pass | point |
|---|---|---|---|---|---|---|---|---|
| ENGLISH | bay | mountains | cape | dam | game reserve | national park | pass | point |
| DEUTSCH | Bucht | Berge | Kap | Damm | Wildpark | Nationalpark | Pass | Landspitze |
| ESPAÑOL | bahía | montañas | cabo | presa | vedado de caza | parque nacional | paso | punta |
| FRANÇAIS | baie | montagnes | cap | barrage | réserve à gibier | parc national | col | pointe |
| PORTUGUÊS | baía | montanhas | cabo | represa | reserva de caça | parque nacional | passo | ponta |

Pretoria
JOHANNESBURG
Soweto
Krugersdorp
Benoni
Germiston
Springs
Vereeniging
Vanderbijlpark
Potchefstroom
Klerksdorp
Kroonstad
Welkom
Virginia
Bethlehem
Harrismith
Ladysmith
Newcastle
Dundee
Pietermaritzburg
DURBAN
Maseru
LESOTHO
DRAKENSBERG
SWAZILAND
Mbabane
Manzini
Maputo
(Lourenço Marques)
MOZAMBIQUE
MOÇAMBIQUE
SOUTH AFRICA
SUID AFRIKA
KWAZULU-NATAL
MPUMALANGA
GAUTENG
ZULULAND
TRANSKEI
KAFFRARIA
CISKEI
EASTERN CAPE
GRIQUALAND EAST
TEMBULAND
PONDOLAND
Umtata
Queenstown
King William's Town
Mdantsane
East London
Oos-Londen
Grahamstown
Port Alfred
Elizabeth
Richard's Bay
Empangeni
Stanger
Port Shepstone
Port Edward
Port Saint Johns
WILD COAST
INDIAN
OCEAN
Copyright © by Rand McNally & Co.
Map prepared by George Philip & Son Ltd., London.
A-584600-764 -7 -8 -15

Kilometers 0 50 100 150 Km.

Statute Miles 0 50 100 150 Mi.

Scale 1:3,000,000

One centimeter represents 30 kilometers.
One inch represents approximately 47 miles.
Lambert Conformal Conic Projection

Map continues
pages 108-109

INDONESIA
JAWA JAVA
Magelang
Madiun
Kediri
Malang
Jember
Cilacap
Yogyakarta
Surakarta
Blitar
Banyuwangi
Singaraja
Mataram
BALI
Denpasar
Praya
LOMBOK
Sumbawa Besar
SUMBAWA
NUSA TENGGARA
LESSER SUNDA ISLANDS
Waingapu
SUMBA
Waikabubak
Baing
TIMOR
Soe
Kupang
Laut Sawu
Savu Sea
PULAU SEMAU
PULAU ROTI
PULAU SAWU
Timor Sea
HIBERNIA REEF
ASHMORE ISLANDS
CARTIER ISLANDS (Austl.)
MELVILLE ISLAND
BATHURST ISLAND
Darwin
Humpty Doo
Rum Jungle
Pine Creek
ARNHEM
POINT BLAZE
Joseph Bonaparte Gulf
CAPE LONDONDERRY
BROWSE ISLAND
SCOTT REEF
BONAPARTE ARCHIPELAGO
BEAGLE REEF
ADÈLE ISLAND
BUCCANEER ARCHIPELAGO
CAPE LEVEQUE
Wyndham
Kununurra
KIMBERLEY PLATEAU
KING LEOPOLD RANGES
DURACK RANGES
Mount Ord 937
Derby
Fitzroy Crossing
Halls Creek
Victoria River Downs
Wave Hill
Broome
ROWLEY SHOALS
CAPE LATOUCHE TREVILLE
La Grange
EIGHTY MILE BEACH
INDIAN OCEAN
NORTHERN TERRITORY
TANAMI DESERT
Lake Gregory
Port Hedland
Goldsworthy
Shay Gap
GREAT SANDY DESERT
DAMPIER ARCHIPELAGO
MONTE BELLO ISLANDS
Dampier
Karratha
Roebourne
BARROW ISLAND
Marble Bar
Nullagine
Lake Mackay
MUIRON ISLANDS
NORTH WEST CAPE
Exmouth
Onslow
Pannawonica
HAMERSLEY RANGE
Wittenoom
Mount Brockman 1132
Mount Bruce 1235
Tom Price
Mount Meharry 1251
Paraburdoo
Newman
Lake Disappointment
Mount Leisler 897
Mount Liebig 1524
POINT CLOATES
WESTERN AUSTRALIA
GIBSON DESERT
Lake Amadeus
CAPE CUVIER
Tropic of Capricorn
Lake Macleod
Mount Augustus 1105
906 Mount Essendon
Mount Olga 1069
Ayers Rock 867
Mount Cockburn 1138
Carnarvon
BERNIER ISLAND
DORRE ISLAND
Peak Hill
ROBINSON RANGE
Lake Carnegie
Mount Aloysius 1085
Mount Woodroffe 1440
DIRK HARTOG ISLAND
STEEP POINT
Denham
Shark Bay
Meekatharra
Wiluna
Nannine
Cue
Lake Austin
Sandstone
Agnew
Mount Redcliffe 562
Laverton
GREAT VICTORIA DESERT
Kalbarri
Mount Magnet
Yalgoo
Northampton
Mullewa
Pindar
Leonora
Malcolm
Lake Carey
HOUTMAN ABROLHOS
Geraldton
Dongara
Three Springs
Lake Barlee
Menzies
Maralinga
Ooldea
Forrest
Deakin
GREEN HEAD
Dalwallinu
Bonnie Rock
Kalgoorlie-Boulder
Coolgardie
Zanthus
Rawlinna
Haig
NULLARBOR PLAIN
Eucla
Moora
Bencubbin
Bullfinch
DARLING RANGE
Southern Cross
Wanneroo
Perth
Fremantle
Northam
York
Kellerberrin
Merredin
Beverley
Brookton
Hyden
Lake Johnston
Norseman
Lake Cowan
Lake Dundas
Eyre
CAPE ADIEU
SAINT PETER
Pinjarra
Narrogin
Newdegate
Wagin
Ravensthorpe
Esperance
CAPE ARID
POINT CULVER
Great Australian Bight
Bunbury
Collie
Nyabing
Katanning
Gnowangerup
Hopetoun
ARCHIPELAGO OF THE RECHERCHE
CAPE NATURALISTE
Busselton
Bridgetown
Manjimup
Bluff Knoll 1096
Mount Barker
Albany
Augusta
Pemberton
Denmark
CAPE LEEUWIN
POINT D'ENTRECASTEAUX
WEST CAPE HOWE
CAPE VANCOUVER
King George Sound
SOUTHERN OCEAN
Copyright © by Rand McNally & Co.
Map prepared by Esselte Map Service AB, Stockholm.
A-590200-264

| | | | | | | | | |
|---|---|---|---|---|---|---|---|---|
| ENGLISH | bay | cape | island | lake | mount | point | range | reef |
| DEUTSCH | Bucht | Kap | Insel | See | Berg | Landspitze | Gebirge | Riff |
| ESPAÑOL | bahía | cabo | isla | lago | montaña | punta | cordillera | arrecife |
| FRANÇAIS | baie | cap | île | lac | mont | pointe | chaîne | récif |
| PORTUGUÊS | baía | cabo | ilha | lago | monte | ponta | cordilheira | recife |

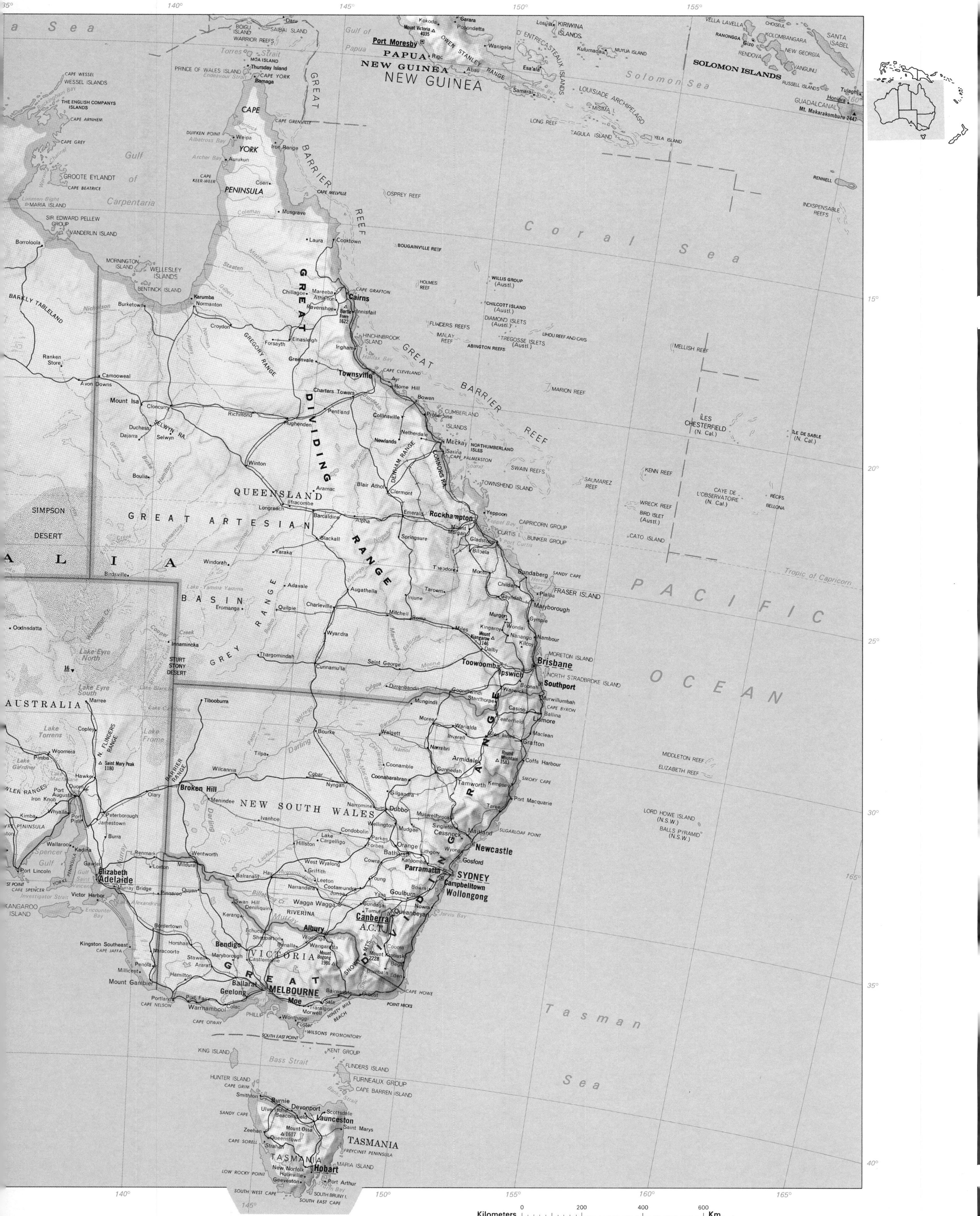
Coral Sea
PACIFIC OCEAN
Tasman Sea
Solomon Sea
Gulf of Carpentaria
Torres Strait
Bass Strait
NEW GUINEA
PAPUA NEW GUINEA
Port Moresby
SOLOMON ISLANDS
Honiara
GUADALCANAL
Mt. Makarakomburu 2447
CAPE YORK PENINSULA
GREAT BARRIER REEF
GREAT DIVIDING RANGE
QUEENSLAND
GREAT ARTESIAN BASIN
GREY RANGE
SIMPSON DESERT
NEW SOUTH WALES
VICTORIA
TASMANIA
Cairns
Townsville
Mackay
Rockhampton
Bundaberg
Maryborough
Brisbane
Ipswich
Toowoomba
Southport
Lismore
Grafton
Coffs Harbour
Armidale
Tamworth
Port Macquarie
Newcastle
Gosford
Parramatta
SYDNEY
Campbelltown
Wollongong
Canberra
A.C.T.
Albury
Bendigo
Ballarat
Geelong
MELBOURNE
Moe
Mount Isa
Cloncurry
Longreach
Charleville
Broken Hill
Dubbo
Orange
Bathurst
Wagga Wagga
Mildura
Adelaide
Elizabeth
Port Augusta
Whyalla
Port Pirie
Mount Gambier
Warrnambool
Launceston
Devonport
Burnie
Hobart
Lake Eyre North
Lake Eyre South
Lake Torrens
Lake Frome
Spencer Gulf
KANGAROO ISLAND
KING ISLAND
FLINDERS ISLAND
Tropic of Capricorn
LORD HOWE ISLAND (N.S.W.)
ÎLES CHESTERFIELD (N. Cal.)

| Kilometers | 0 | 200 | 400 | 600 Km. |
|---|---|---|---|---|
| Statute Miles | 0 | 200 | 400 | 600 Mi. |

Scale 1:12,000,000

One centimeter represents 120 kilometers.
One inch represents approximately 190 miles.
Lambert Conformal Conic Projection

# Western and Central Australia / West-und Mittelaustralien / Australia Centro-occidental
# Australie Occidentale et Centrale / Austrália Ocidental e Central

INDIAN
OCEAN
ROWLEY SHOALS
MONTE BELLO ISLANDS
BARROW ISLAND
DAMPIER ARCHIPELAGO
Port Hedland
Goldsworthy
Shay Gap
Karratha
Roebourne
Wickham
Dampier
Onslow
Exmouth
NORTH WEST CAPE
NINGALOO MARINE PARK
HAMERSLEY
RANGE
HAMERSLEY RANGE NATIONAL PARK
CHICHESTER RANGE
Wittenoom
Tom Price
Paraburdoo
Marble Bar
Nullagine
Newman
OPHTHALMIA RANGE
GREAT SANDY DESERT
LITTLE SANDY DESERT
GIBSON DESERT
W E S T E R N
A U S T R A L I
Broome
Derby
KING LEOPOLD
Fitzroy Crossing
EIGHTY MILE BEACH
RUDALL RIVER NATIONAL PARK
Tropic of Capricorn
Lake Disappointment
Carnarvon
Shark Bay
Denham
DIRK HARTOG ISLAND
BERNIER ISLAND
DORRE ISLAND
KENNEDY RANGE
COLLIER RANGE
ROBINSON RANGE
Peak Hill
Meekatharra
Wiluna
Lake Carnegie
Mount Magnet
Kalbarri
Northampton
Geraldton
HOUTMAN ABROLHOS
Dongara
Leonora
Laverton
Menzies
Kalgoorlie-Boulder
Coolgardie
Norseman
Esperance
Ravensthorpe
Hopetoun
Wanneroo
Stirling
Perth
Fremantle
ROTTNEST ISLAND
Mandurah
Bunbury
Busselton
Margaret River
CAPE LEEUWIN
Albany
Mount Barker
Denmark
STIRLING RANGE
ARCHIPELAGO OF THE RECHERCHE
FITZGERALD RIVER NAT. PARK
Balladonia


| Meters | Feet |
|---|---|
| 6000 | 19685 |
| 4000 | 13124 |
| 3000 | 9843 |
| 2000 | 6562 |
| 1000 | 3281 |
| 500 | 1640 |
| 200 | 656 |
| Land Below Sea Level 0 | 0 |
| 0 | 0 |
| 200 | 656 |
| 1000 | 3281 |
| 3000 | 9843 |
| 6000 | 19685 |
| 9000 | 29520 |

| | | | | | | | | |
|---|---|---|---|---|---|---|---|---|
| ENGLISH | bay | cape | creek, cr. | island, i. | lake, l. | mount | point | range |
| DEUTSCH | Bucht | Kap | Bach | Insel | See | Berg | Landspitze | Gebirge |
| ESPAÑOL | bahía | cabo | riachuelo | isla | lago | montaña | punta | cordillera |
| FRANÇAIS | baie | cap | crique | île | lac | mont | pointe | chaîne |
| PORTUGUÊS | baía | cabo | riacho | ilha | lago | monte | ponta | cordilheira |

Map continues
pages 164-165

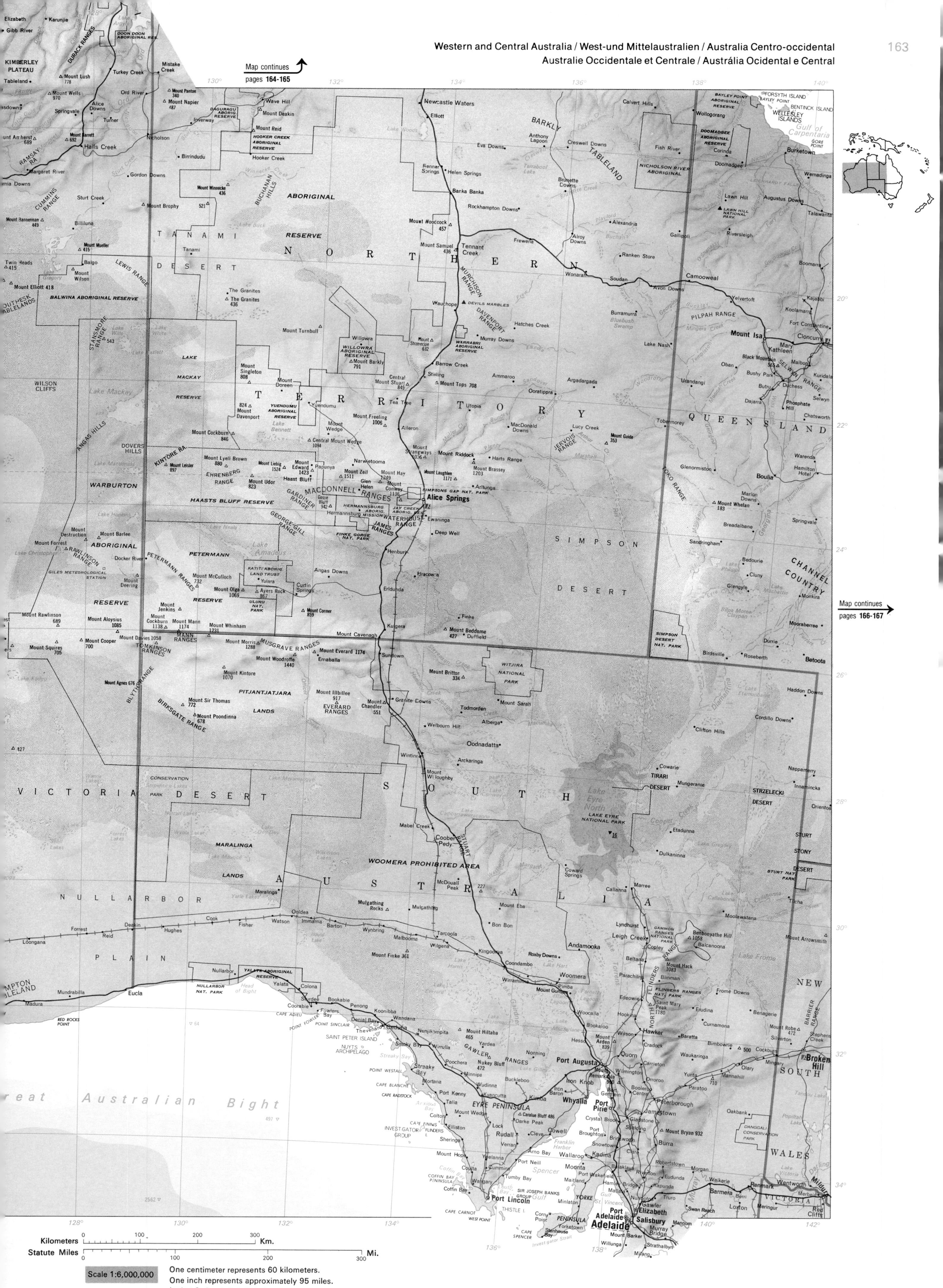
NORTHERN TERRITORY
QUEENSLAND
SOUTH AUSTRALIA
NEW SOUTH WALES
VICTORIA
TANAMI DESERT
SIMPSON DESERT
VICTORIA DESERT
NULLARBOR PLAIN
Great Australian Bight
BARKLY TABLELAND
CHANNEL COUNTRY
Gulf of Carpentaria
Spencer Gulf
Gulf St. Vincent
EYRE PENINSULA
YORKE PENINSULA
MACDONNELL RANGES
MUSGRAVE RANGES
FLINDERS RANGES
GAWLER RANGES
WOOMERA PROHIBITED AREA
Lake Eyre North
Lake Amadeus
Lake Mackay
Lake Torrens
Lake Frome
Lake Gairdner
Alice Springs
Tennant Creek
Mount Isa
Port Augusta
Port Lincoln
Adelaide
Whyalla
Broken Hill
Coober Pedy
Woomera
Oodnadatta
Newcastle Waters
Halls Creek
Camooweal
Cloncurry
Ayers Rock 867
Mount Olga 1069
Eucla
Ceduna
Port Pirie
Burketown
Birdsville
Boulia
Hermannsburg
Yulara
Tanami
Marree
Leigh Creek
Kingoonya
Tarcoola
Cook
Forrest
Mildura
Renmark

Map continues
pages 166-167

Kilometers 0 100 200 300 Km.
Statute Miles 0 100 200 300 Mi.

Scale 1:6,000,000

One centimeter represents 60 kilometers.
One inch represents approximately 95 miles.
Lambert Conformal Conic Projection

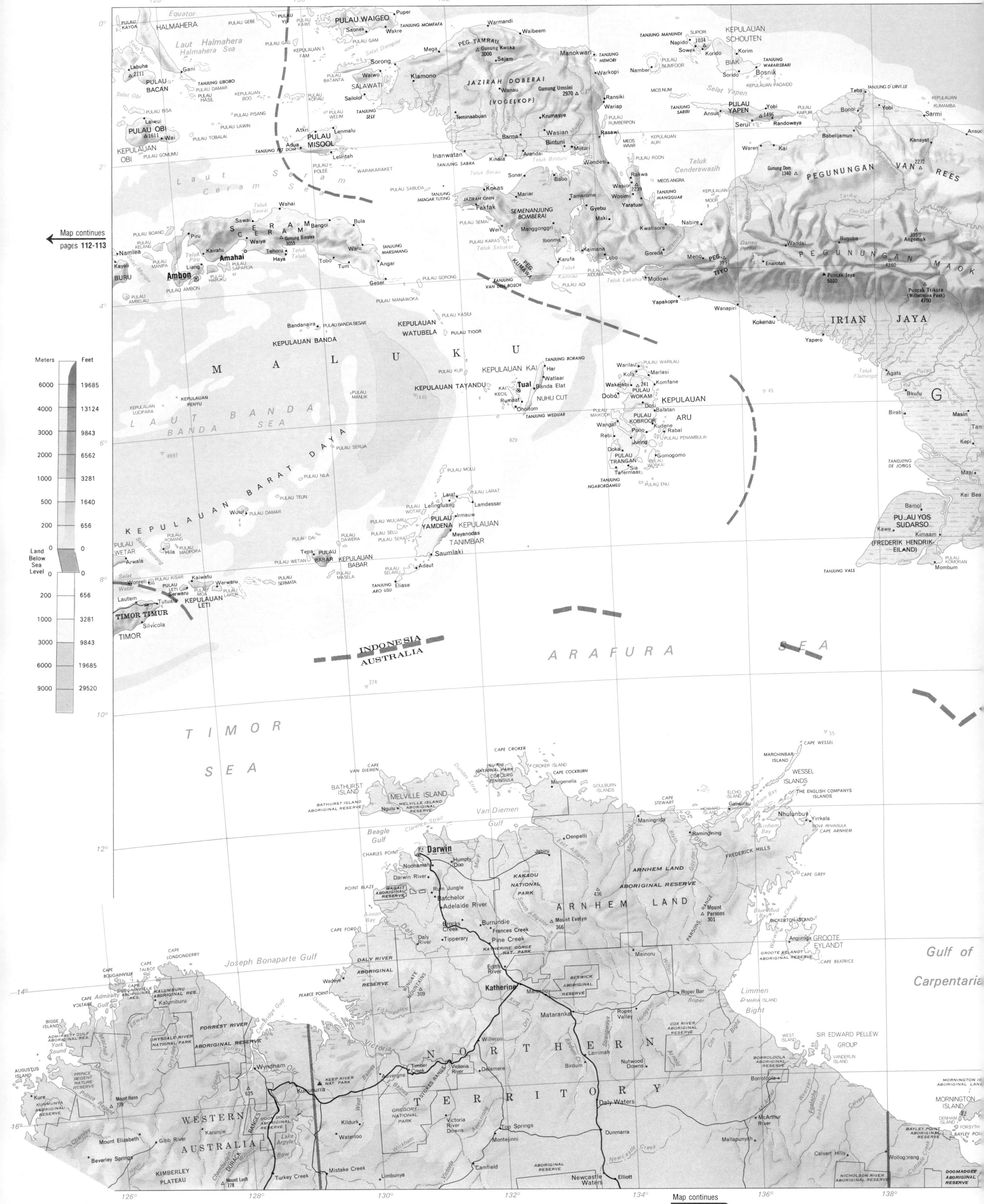
Meters
Feet
6000
19685
4000
13124
3000
9843
2000
6562
1000
3281
500
1640
200
656
0
Land Below Sea Level
HALMAHERA
Laut Halmahera
Halmahera Sea
PULAU WAIGEO
PULAU BACAN
PULAU OBI
KEPULAUAN OBI
PULAU MISOOL
Sorong
Manokwari
JAZIRAH DOBERAI
(VOGELKOP)
KEPULAUAN SCHOUTEN
BIAK
PULAU YAPEN
Teluk Cenderawasih
Laut Seram
Ceram Sea
SERAM
Ambon
Amahai
BURU
Fakfak
SEMENANJUNG BOMBERAI
PEGUNUNGAN VAN REES
PEGUNUNGAN MAOKE
Puncak Jaya 5030
IRIAN JAYA
KEPULAUAN BANDA
KEPULAUAN WATUBELA
MALUKU
KEPULAUAN KAI
Tual
KEPULAUAN TAYANDU
KEPULAUAN ARU
LAUT BANDA
BANDA SEA
KEPULAUAN BARAT DAYA
PULAU WETAR
KEPULAUAN LETI
TIMOR TIMUR
TIMOR
PULAU YAMDENA
KEPULAUAN TANIMBAR
Saumlaki
KEPULAUAN BABAR
PULAU YOS SUDARSO
(FREDERIK HENDRIK EILAND)
INDONESIA
AUSTRALIA
ARAFURA SEA
TIMOR SEA
MELVILLE ISLAND
BATHURST ISLAND
Van Diemen Gulf
Beagle Gulf
Darwin
KAKADU NATIONAL PARK
ARNHEM LAND
ARNHEM LAND ABORIGINAL RESERVE
WESSEL ISLANDS
GROOTE EYLANDT
Gulf of Carpentaria
Joseph Bonaparte Gulf
Katherine
NORTHERN TERRITORY
Daly Waters
Wyndham
Kununurra
WESTERN AUSTRALIA
KIMBERLEY PLATEAU
SIR EDWARD PELLEW GROUP
MORNINGTON ISLAND
Newcastle Waters
Borroloola

Map continues pages 112-113

Map continues pages 162-163

| MAP FORM | bay | cape | island | kepulauan | mount | pulau | range | tanjung |
|---|---|---|---|---|---|---|---|---|
| ENGLISH | bay | cape | island | islands | mount | island | range | cape |
| DEUTSCH | Bucht | Kap | Insel | Inseln | Berg | Insel | Gebirge | Kap |
| ESPAÑOL | bahía | cabo | isla | islas | montaña | isla | cordillera | cabo |
| FRANÇAIS | baie | cap | île | îles | mont | île | chaîne | cap |
| PORTUGUÊS | baía | cabo | ilha | ilhas | monte | ilha | cordilheira | cabo |

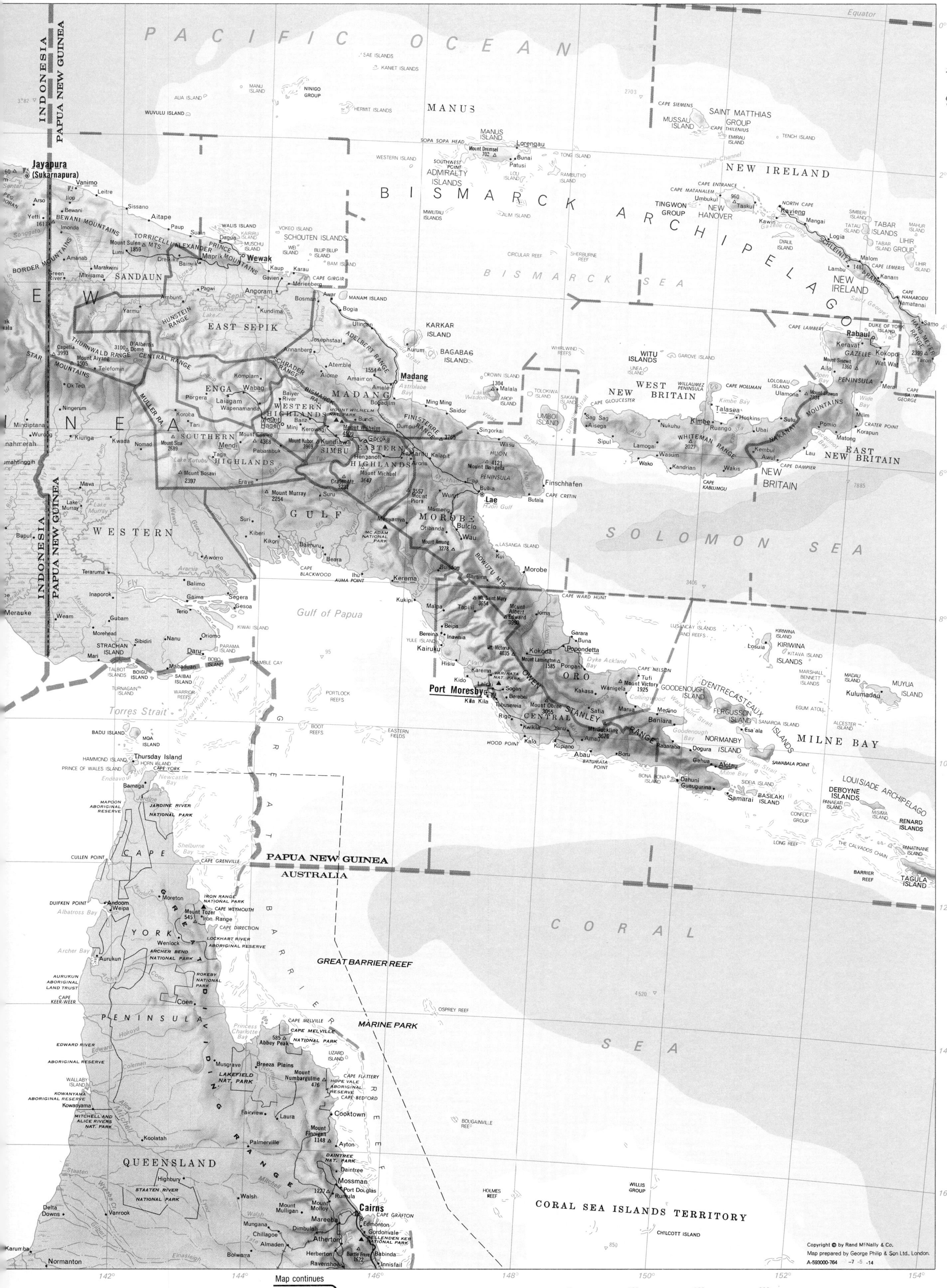
PACIFIC OCEAN
BISMARCK ARCHIPELAGO
BISMARCK SEA
SOLOMON SEA
CORAL SEA
Gulf of Papua
Torres Strait
INDONESIA
PAPUA NEW GUINEA
AUSTRALIA
MANUS
NEW IRELAND
NEW BRITAIN
WEST NEW BRITAIN
EAST NEW BRITAIN
SANDAUN
EAST SEPIK
ENGA
WESTERN HIGHLANDS
SOUTHERN HIGHLANDS
EASTERN HIGHLANDS
SIMBU
MADANG
MOROBE
GULF
WESTERN
CENTRAL
ORO
MILNE BAY
CAPE YORK PENINSULA
QUEENSLAND
GREAT DIVIDING RANGE
GREAT BARRIER REEF
MARINE PARK
CORAL SEA ISLANDS TERRITORY
OWEN STANLEY RANGE
LOUISIADE ARCHIPELAGO
D'ENTRECASTEAUX ISLANDS
SAINT MATTHIAS GROUP
ADMIRALTY ISLANDS
Jayapura (Sukarnapura)
Wewak
Madang
Lae
Port Moresby
Rabaul
Kavieng
Lorengau
Mount Hagen
Goroka
Kundiawa
Mendi
Wabag
Popondetta
Alotau
Kerema
Daru
Thursday Island
Cooktown
Cairns
Equator
Copyright © by Rand McNally & Co.
Map prepared by George Philip & Son Ltd., London.
A-593000-764

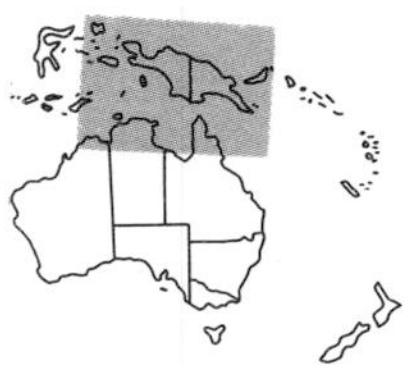

Map continues
pages 166-167

Kilometers 0 100 200 300 Km.
Statute Miles 0 100 200 300 Mi.

Scale 1:6,000,000
One centimeter represents 60 kilometers.
One inch represents approximately 95 miles.
Lambert Conformal Conic Projection

Eastern Australia / Ostaustralien / Australia Oriental
Australie Orientale / Austrália Oriental

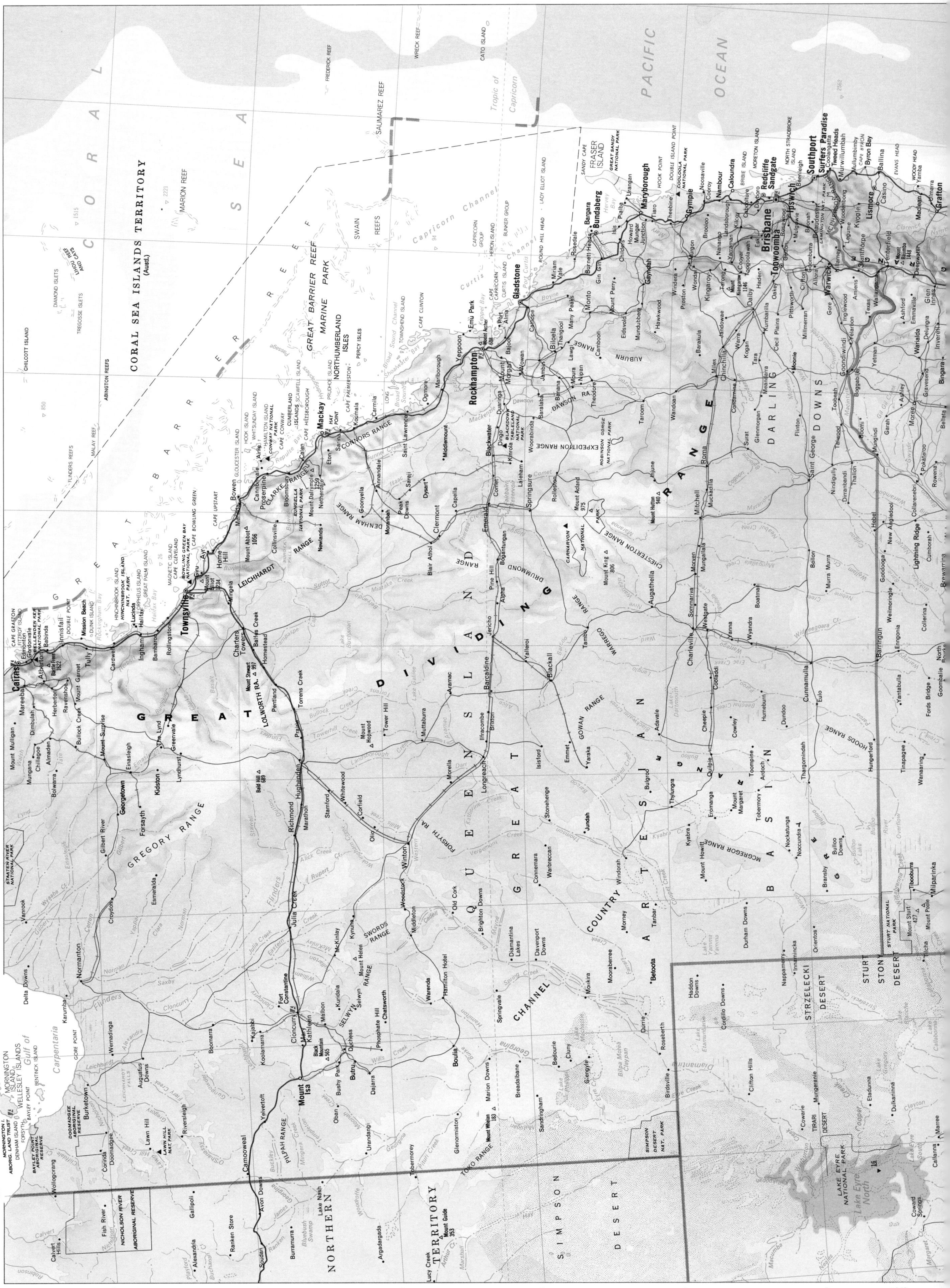
CORAL SEA
CORAL SEA ISLANDS TERRITORY (Austl.)
GREAT BARRIER REEF
GREAT BARRIER REEF MARINE PARK
PACIFIC OCEAN
Tropic of Capricorn
Capricorn Channel
Curtis Channel
FRASER ISLAND
Gulf of Carpentaria
WELLESLEY ISLANDS
MORNINGTON ISLAND
GREAT DIVIDING RANGE
GREAT ARTESIAN BASIN
QUEENSLAND
NORTHERN TERRITORY
SIMPSON DESERT
STRZELECKI DESERT
STURT STONY DESERT
DARLING DOWNS
CHANNEL COUNTRY
GREGORY RANGE
LEICHHARDT RANGE
DENHAM RANGE
CONNORS RANGE
CLARKE RANGE
EXPEDITION RANGE
DAWSON RA.
DRUMMOND RANGE
WARREGO RANGE
GOWAN RANGE
MCGREGOR RANGE
GREY RANGE
SELWYN RANGE
SWORDS RANGE
FORSYTH RA.
LOLWORTH RA.
AUBURN RANGE
CHESTERTON RANGE
PILPAH RANGE
TOKO RANGE
LAKE EYRE NATIONAL PARK
Lake Eyre North
NORTHUMBERLAND ISLES
Cairns
Townsville
Mackay
Rockhampton
Gladstone
Bundaberg
Maryborough
Gympie
Brisbane
Ipswich
Toowoomba
Southport
Surfers Paradise
Warwick
Lismore
Grafton
Mount Isa
Cloncurry
Longreach
Charleville
Roma
Emerald
Winton
Hughenden
Charters Towers
Bowen
Proserpine
Barcaldine
Blackall
Cunnamulla
Normanton
Burketown
Birdsville
Boulia
Camooweal

Map continues pages 164-165

Map continues pages 162-163

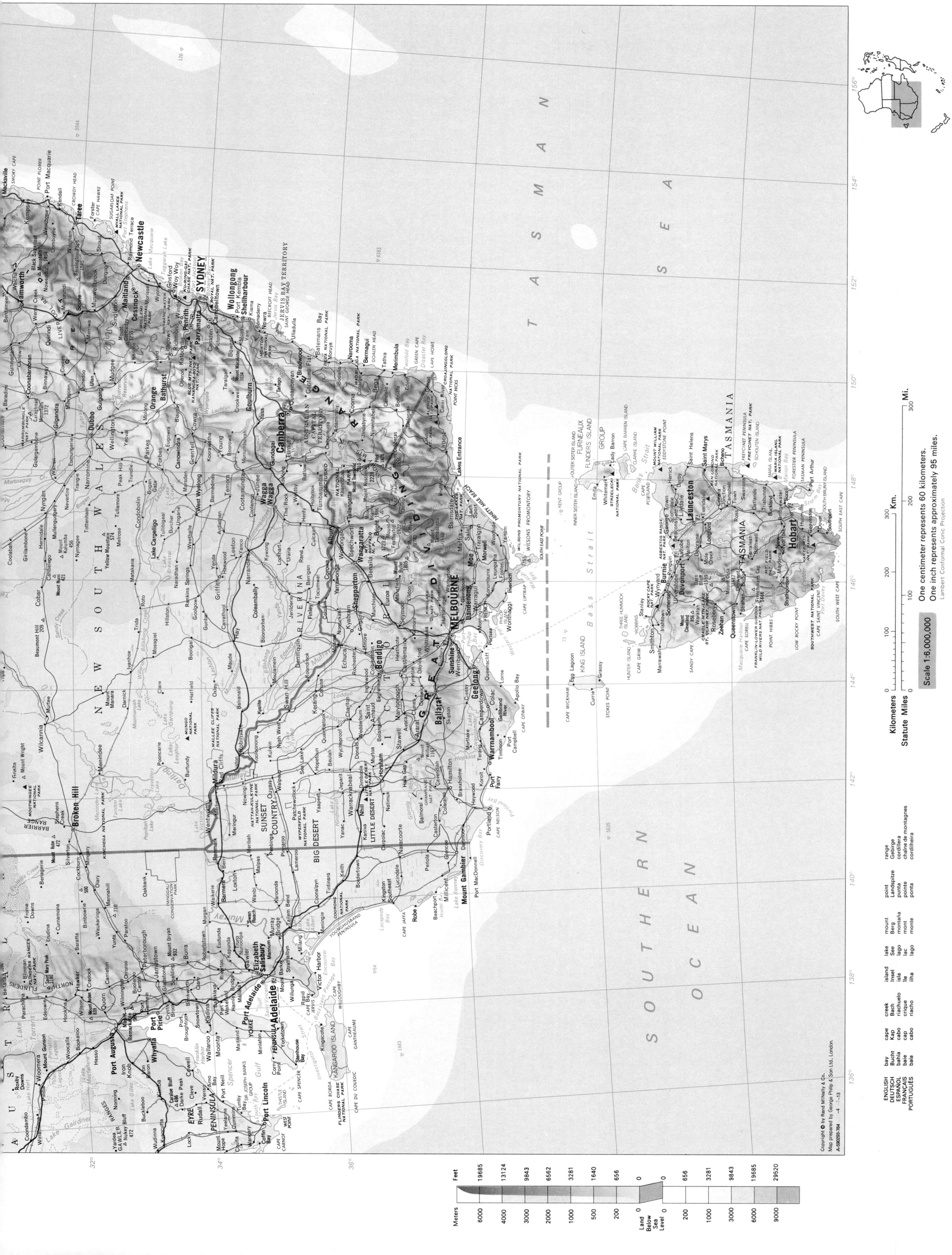
NEW SOUTH WALES
VICTORIA
TASMANIA
TASMAN SEA
SOUTHERN OCEAN
Bass Strait
SYDNEY
Canberra
MELBOURNE
Adelaide
Hobart
Newcastle
Wollongong
Geelong
Ballarat
Bendigo
Launceston
Broken Hill
Mildura
Wagga Wagga
Albury
Dubbo
Bathurst
Orange
Goulburn
Tamworth
Port Augusta
Port Pirie
Whyalla
Port Lincoln
Mount Gambier
Warrnambool
Devonport
Burnie
KANGAROO ISLAND
KING ISLAND
FLINDERS ISLAND
FURNEAUX GROUP
AUSTRALIAN CAPITAL TERRITORY
JERVIS BAY TERRITORY
GREAT DIVIDING RANGE
BIG DESERT
LITTLE DESERT
SUNSET COUNTRY
RIVERINA
EYRE PENINSULA
YORKE PENINSULA
WILSONS PROMONTORY
NINETY MILE BEACH
Scale 1:6,000,000
One centimeter represents 60 kilometers.
One inch represents approximately 95 miles.
Lambert Conformal Conic Projection
Kilometers 0 100 200 300 Km.
Statute Miles 0 100 200 300 Mi.
ENGLISH bay cape creek island lake mount point range
DEUTSCH Bucht Kap Bach Insel See Berg Landspitze Gebirge
ESPAÑOL bahía cabo riachuelo isla lago montaña punta cordillera
FRANÇAIS baie cap ruisseau île lac mont pointe chaîne de montagnes
PORTUGUÊS baía cabo riacho ilha lago monte ponta cordilheira
Copyright © by Rand McNally & Co.
Map prepared by George Philip & Son Ltd., London.
Meters 6000 4000 3000 2000 1000 500 200 0 Land Below Sea Level 0 200 1000 3000 6000 9000
Feet 19685 13124 9843 6562 3281 1640 656 0 0 656 3281 9843 19685 29520

Mount Lofty Ranges
Yorke Peninsula
Gulf Saint Vincent
Investigator Strait
Adelaide
Elizabeth
Gawler
Port Adelaide
Kangaroo Island
Fleurieu Peninsula
Encounter Bay
Lake Alexandrina
Copyright © by Rand McNally & Co.
Map prepared by George Philip & Son Ltd., London

b

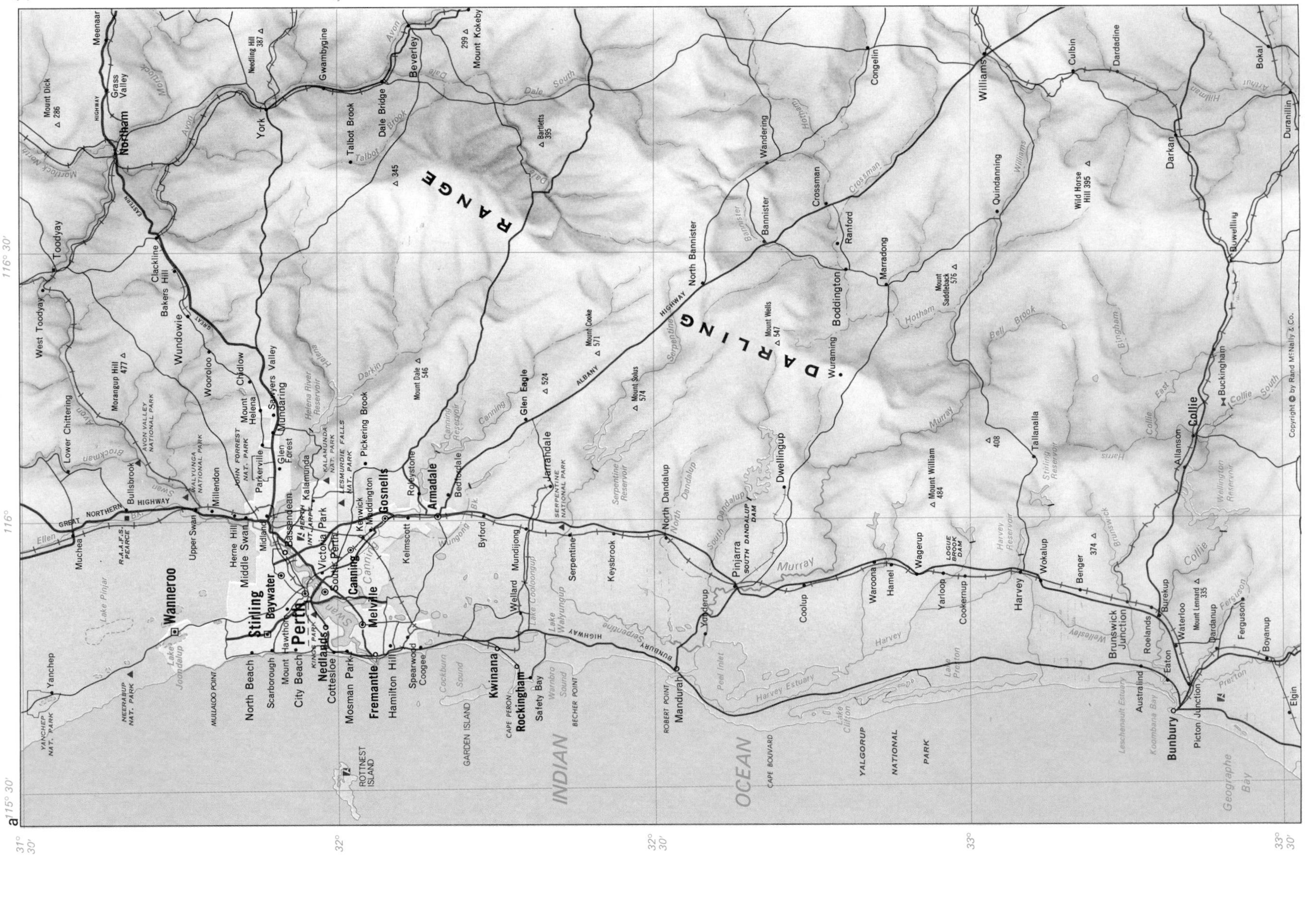
Darling Range
Indian Ocean
Perth
Fremantle
Rockingham
Mandurah
Bunbury
Northam
York
Collie
Copyright © by Rand McNally & Co.

a

Kilometers 0 10 20 30 40 50 Km.

Statute Miles 0 10 20 30 40 50 Mi.

Scale 1:1,000,000

One centimeter represents 10 kilometers.
One inch represents approximately 16 miles.
Lambert Conformal Conic Projection

| | | | | | | | | |
|---|---|---|---|---|---|---|---|---|
| ENGLISH | bay, b. | cape | dam | gulf | island | lake, l. | peninsula | point |
| DEUTSCH | Bucht | Kap | Damm | Golf | Insel | See | Halbinsel | Landspitze |
| ESPAÑOL | bahia | cabo | diques | golfo | isla | lago | península | punta |
| FRANÇAIS | baie | cap | barrage | golfe | île | lac | péninsule | pointe |
| PORTUGUÊS | baia | cabo | barragem | golfo | ilha | lago | península | ponta |

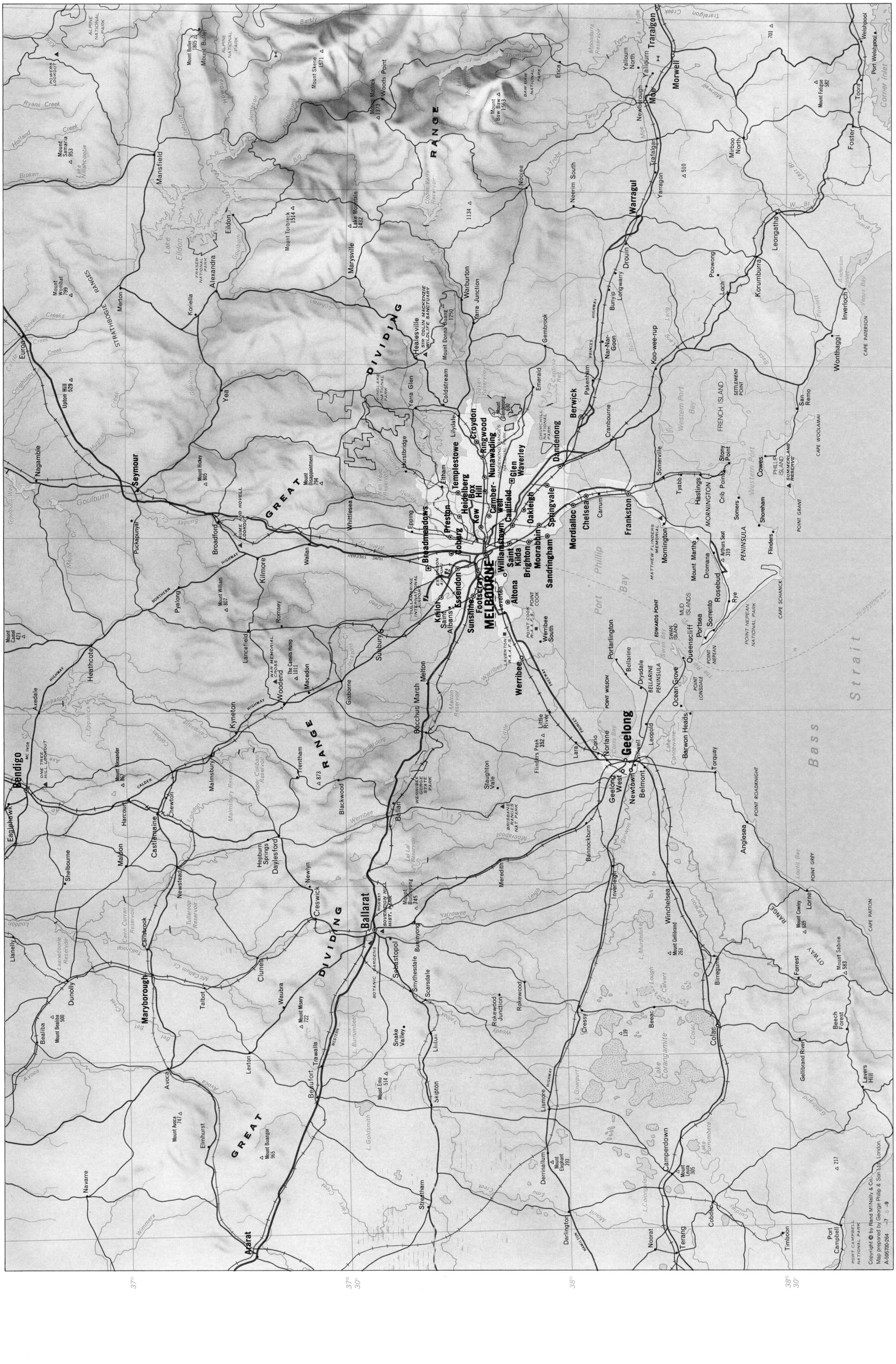
MELBOURNE
Geelong
Ballarat
Bendigo
Port Phillip Bay
Bass Strait
GREAT DIVIDING RANGE
MORNINGTON PENINSULA
FRENCH ISLAND
PHILLIP ISLAND
Copyright © by Rand McNally & Co.
Map prepared by George Philip & Son Ltd. London.
A-596700-264 -7-5-9

Scale 1:1,000,000

One centimeter represents 10 kilometers.
One inch represents approximately 16 miles.

Lambert Conformal Conic Projection

Kilometers 0 10 20 30 40 50 Km.
Statute Miles 0 10 20 30 40 50 Mi.

| ENGLISH | bay, b. | cape | creek, cr. | lake, l. | mount, mt. | point | range, ra. | reservoir, res. |
|---|---|---|---|---|---|---|---|---|
| DEUTSCH | Bucht | Kap | Bach | See | Berg | Landspitze | Gebirge | Stausee |
| ESPAÑOL | bahía | cabo | riachuelo | lago | montaña | punta | cordillera | embalse |
| FRANÇAIS | baie | cap | crique | lac | mont | pointe | chaîne | réservoir |
| PORTUGUÊS | baía | cabo | riacho | lago | monte | ponta | cordilheira | reservatório |

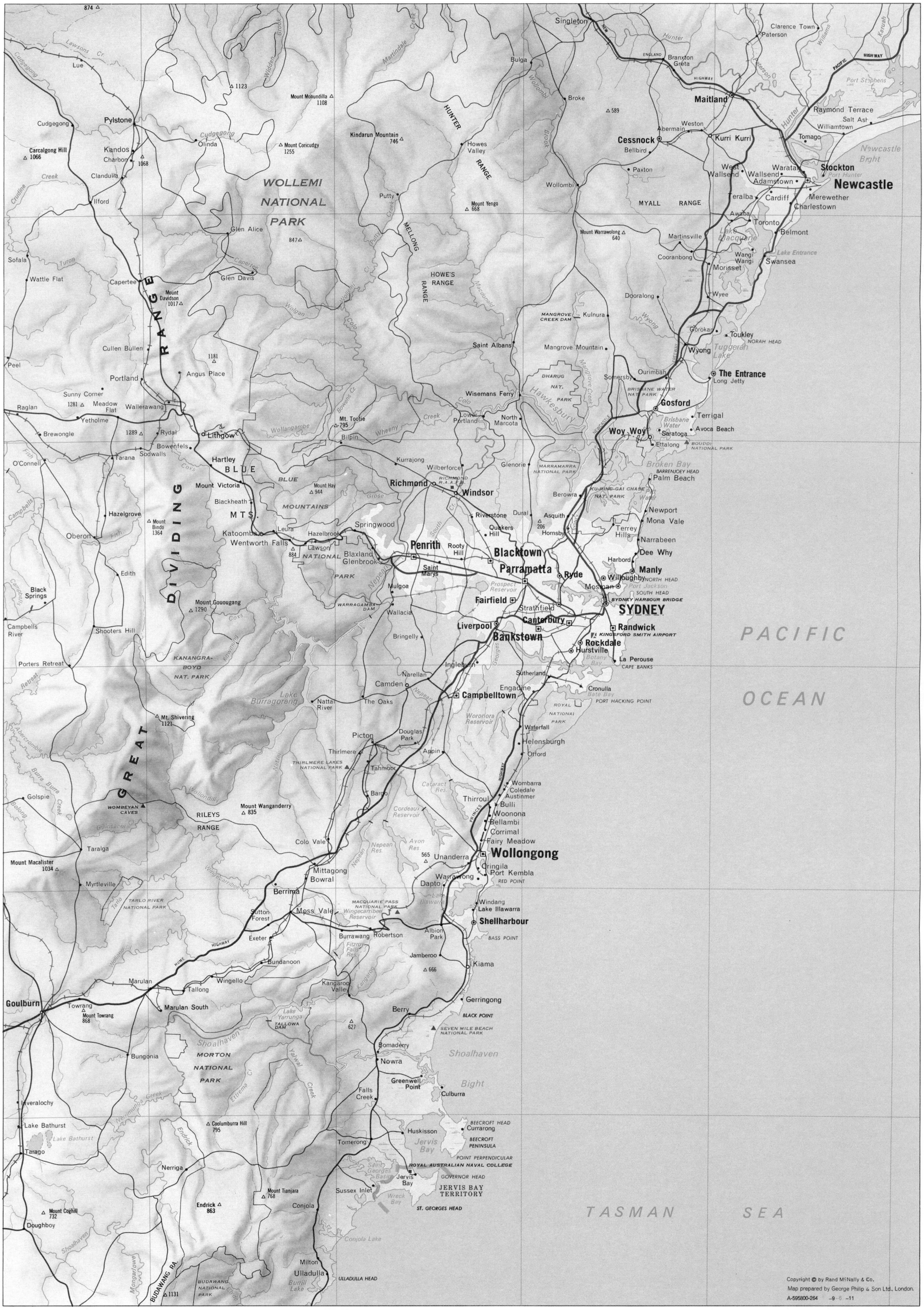

150°
150°30′
151°
151°30′
152°
33°
33° 30′
34°
34° 30′
35°
Singleton
Clarence Town
Paterson
Branxton
Greta
Maitland
Port Stephens
Raymond Terrace
Salt Ash
Williamtown
Tomago
Cessnock
Bellbird
Abermain
Weston
Kurri Kurri
Stockton
Newcastle Bight
Newcastle
Waratah
West Wallsend
Wallsend
Adamstown
Merewether
Charlestown
Cardiff
Teralba
Toronto
Belmont
Lake Macquarie
Swansea
Morisset
Wyee
Wyong
Tuggerah Lake
Toukley
NORAH HEAD
The Entrance
Long Jetty
Gosford
Terrigal
Avoca Beach
Woy Woy
Saratoga
Ettalong
Broken Bay
Palm Beach
Newport
Mona Vale
Narrabeen
Dee Why
Manly
Hornsby
Ryde
Blacktown
Parramatta
Penrith
SYDNEY
Randwick
Rockdale
Hurstville
Botany Bay
La Perouse
CAPE BANKS
Cronulla
PORT HACKING POINT
Sutherland
Liverpool
Bankstown
Canterbury
Fairfield
Campbelltown
Camden
Picton
Wollongong
Port Kembla
RED POINT
Shellharbour
BASS POINT
Kiama
Gerringong
BLACK POINT
Berry
Bomaderry
Nowra
Shoalhaven Bight
Greenwell Point
Culburra
Huskisson
Currarong
BEECROFT HEAD
BEECROFT PENINSULA
Jervis Bay
JERVIS BAY TERRITORY
ROYAL AUSTRALIAN NAVAL COLLEGE
ST. GEORGES HEAD
Sussex Inlet
Conjola
Milton
Ulladulla
ULLADULLA HEAD
PACIFIC
OCEAN
TASMAN
SEA
WOLLEMI NATIONAL PARK
HUNTER RANGE
MYALL RANGE
Windsor
Richmond
Katoomba
Wentworth Falls
Lithgow
Kandos
Pylstone
Portland
Oberon
BLUE MTS.
BLUE MOUNTAINS NATIONAL PARK
GREAT DIVIDING RANGE
KANANGRA-BOYD NAT. PARK
Lake Burragorang
Mittagong
Bowral
Berrima
Moss Vale
Goulburn
Marulan
Bungonia
MORTON NATIONAL PARK
Tarago
Nerriga
Lake Bathurst
Taralga
RILEYS RANGE
Copyright © by Rand McNally & Co.
Map prepared by George Philip & Son Ltd., London.


| ENGLISH | bight | creek, cr. | head | mount | range | reservoir, res. |
|---|---|---|---|---|---|---|
| DEUTSCH | Bucht | Bach | Vorgebirge | Berg | Gebirge | Stausee |
| ESPAÑOL | ensenada pequeña | riachuelo | promontorio | montaña | cordillera | estanque |
| FRANÇAIS | anse | crique | promontoire | mont | chaîne | réservoir |
| PORTUGUÊS | enseada | riacho | promontório | monte | cordilheira | reservatório |

Kilometers 0 10 20 30 40 50 Km.

Statute Miles 0 10 20 30 40 50 Mi.

Scale 1:1,000,000

One centimeter represents 10 kilometers.

One inch represents approximately 16 miles.

Lambert Conformal Conic Projection

a

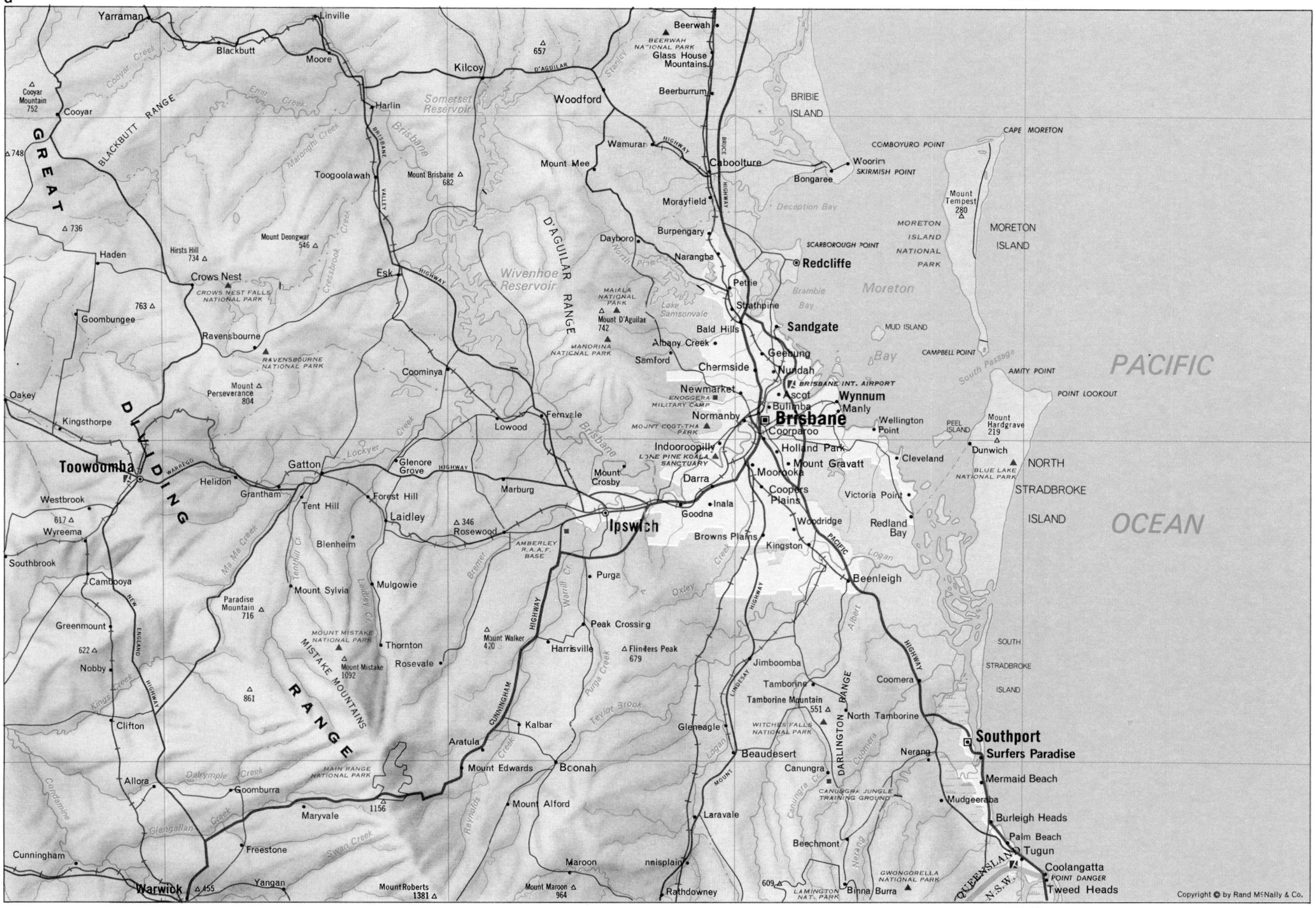

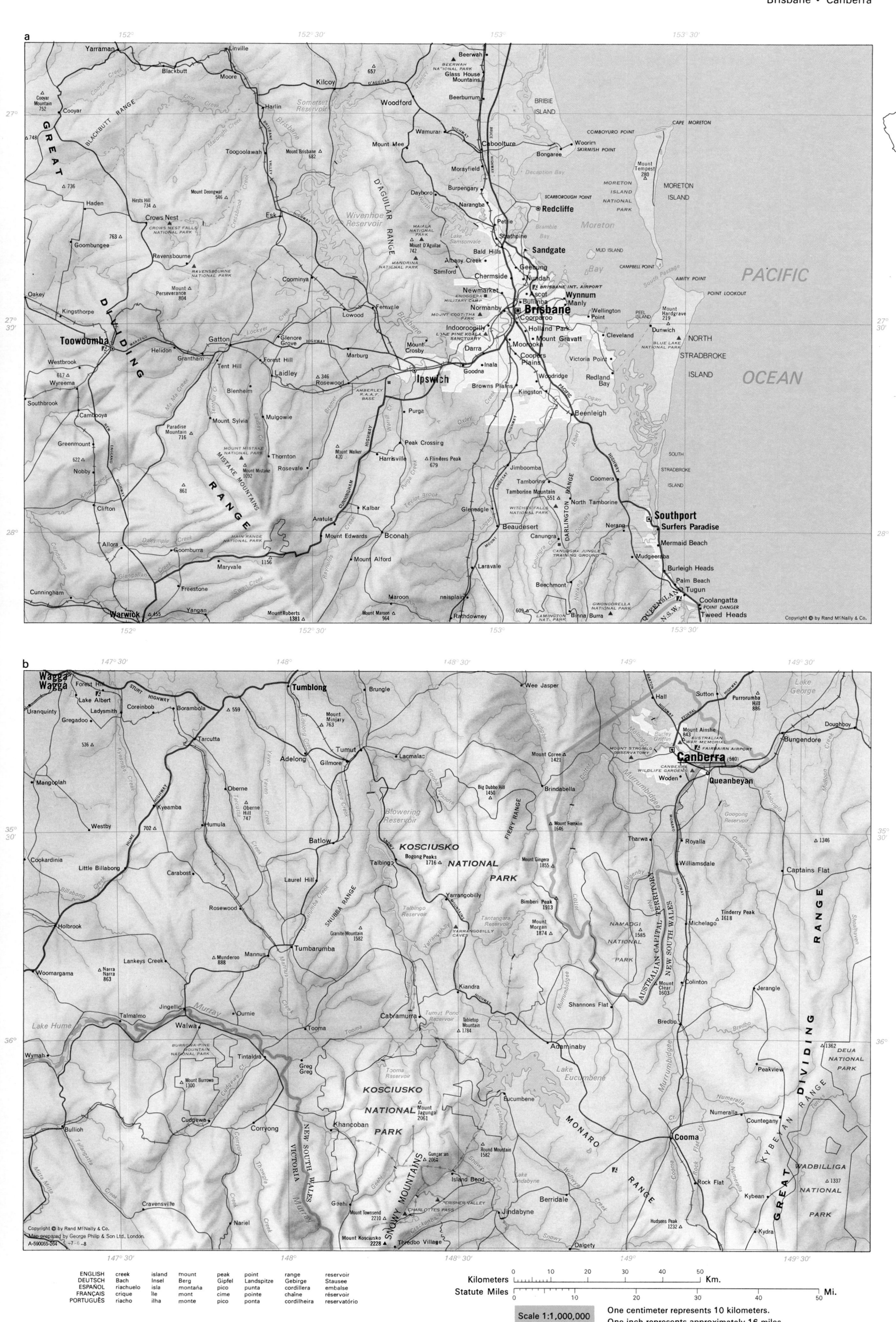

Yarraman
Linville
Blackbutt
Moore
Kilcoy
Beerwah
Glass House Mountains
Woodford
Beerburrum
BRIBIE ISLAND
Cooyar Mountain 752
Cooyar
GREAT DIVIDING RANGE
BLACKBUTT RANGE
Harlin
Somerset Reservoir
Wamuran
Caboolture
Woorim
Bongaree
COMBOYURO POINT
CAPE MORETON
Toogoolawah
Mount Brisbane 682
Mount Mee
D'AGUILAR RANGE
Morayfield
Deception Bay
Mount Tempest 280
MORETON ISLAND
Haden
Hirsts Hill 734
Mount Deongwar 546
Crows Nest
CROWS NEST FALLS NATIONAL PARK
Esk
Wivenhoe Reservoir
Dayboro
Burpengary
Narangba
Redcliffe
SCARBOROUGH POINT
Petrie
Strathpine
Moreton Bay
Goombungee
Ravensbourne
RAVENSBOURNE NATIONAL PARK
Mount D'Aguilar 742
Bald Hills
Sandgate
MUD ISLAND
Albany Creek
Samford
Geebung
Nundah
Chermside
BRISBANE INT. AIRPORT
Newmarket
Ascot
Wynnum
Manly
PACIFIC OCEAN
Mount Perseverance 804
Oakey
Coominya
Kingsthorpe
Bulimba
Normanby
Wellington Point
Brisbane
Coorparoo
Fernvale
Lowood
Dunwich
Toowoomba
Gatton
Glenore Grove
Indooroopilly
Holland Park
Mount Gravatt
Cleveland
NORTH STRADBROKE ISLAND
Helidon
Grantham
Mount Crosby
Darra
Moorooka
Coopers Plains
Victoria Point
Westbrook
Forest Hill
Marburg
Tent Hill
Laidley
Rosewood
Ipswich
Inala
Goodna
Redland Bay
Wyreema
Blenheim
AMBERLEY R.A.A.F. BASE
Browns Plains
Woodridge
Kingston
Southbrook
Cambooya
Purga
Beenleigh
Mount Sylvia
Mulgowie
Paradise Mountain 716
Greenmount
Peak Crossing
Nobby
Thornton
Mount Walker 420
Harrisville
Flinders Peak 679
MISTAKE MOUNTAINS
Mount Mistake 1092
Rosevale
Jimboomba
Tamborine
Coomera
Tamborine Mountain 551
North Tamborine
Clifton
Kalbar
Gleneagle
Southport
Surfers Paradise
Aratula
Beaudesert
Nerang
Mount Edwards
Boonah
Canungra
Mermaid Beach
Allora
Goomburra
MAIN RANGE NATIONAL PARK
Mudgeeraba
Maryvale
Mount Alford
Laravale
Burleigh Heads
Freestone
Beechmont
Palm Beach
Cunningham
Tugun
Maroon
Coolangatta
Warwick
Yangan
Mount Roberts 1381
Mount Maroon 964
Rathdowney
Binna Burra
Tweed Heads
QUEENSLAND
N.S.W.
Copyright © by Rand McNally & Co.


b

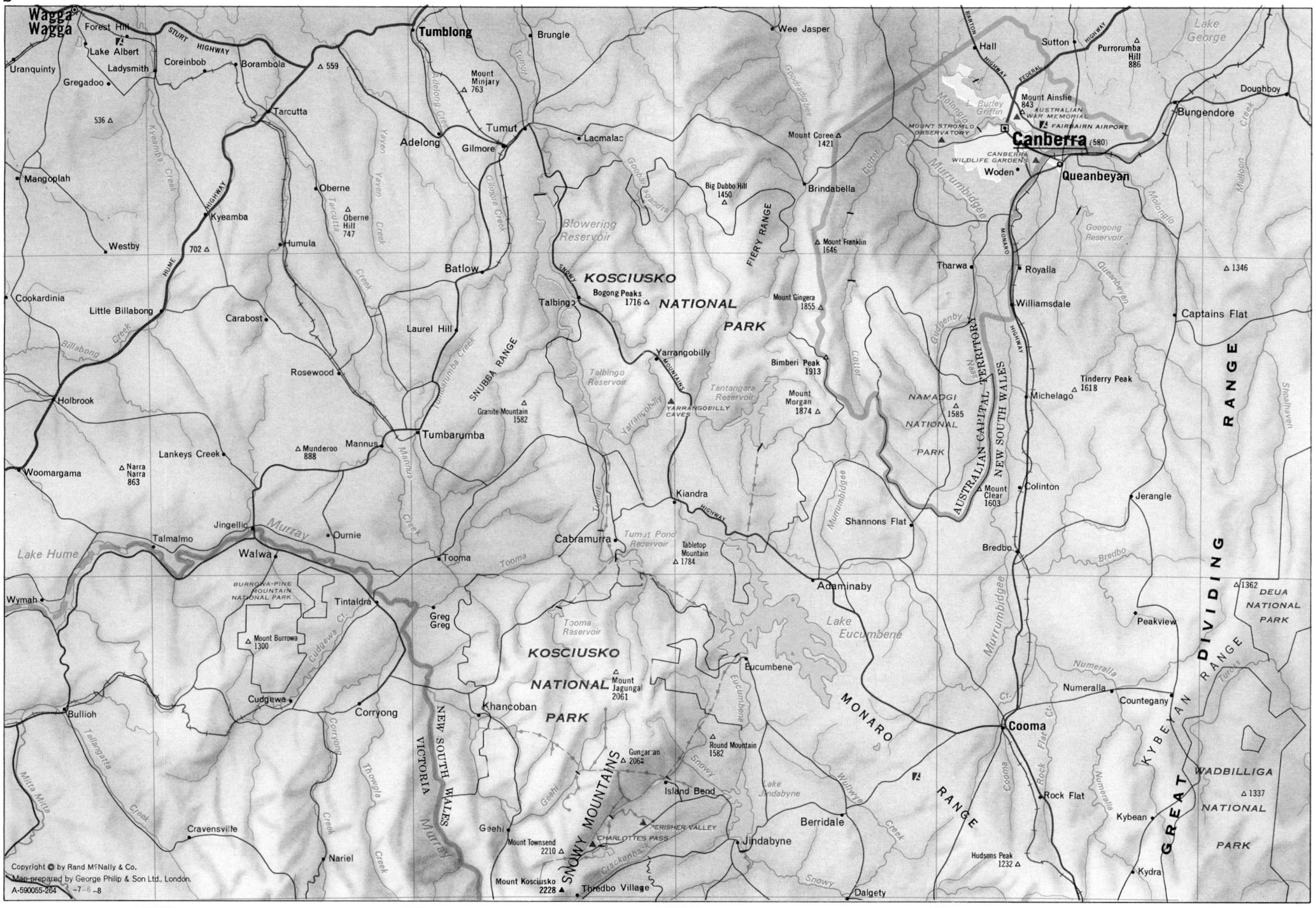

Wagga Wagga
Forest Hill
Lake Albert
Tumblong
Brungle
Wee Jasper
Hall
Sutton
Lake George
Uranquinty
Ladysmith
Coreinbob
Borambola
Gregadoo
Mount Minjary 763
Tarcutta
Tumut
Adelong
Gilmore
Lacmalac
Mount Coree 1421
Canberra
Queanbeyan
Bungendore
Woden
Mangoplah
Oberne
Kyeamba
Big Dubbo Hill 1450
Brindabella
FIERY RANGE
Blowering Reservoir
Westby
Humula
Mount Franklin 1646
Batlow
KOSCIUSKO NATIONAL PARK
Tharwa
Royalla
Cookardinia
Little Billabong
Talbingo
Bogong Peaks 1716
Mount Gingera 1855
Williamsdale
Captains Flat
Carabost
Laurel Hill
Rosewood
Yarrangobilly
Bimberi Peak 1913
AUSTRALIAN CAPITAL TERRITORY
NEW SOUTH WALES
Holbrook
SNUBBA RANGE
Granite Mountain 1582
Mount Morgan 1874
NAMADGI NATIONAL PARK
Tinderry Peak 1618
Michelago
Tumbarumba
Lankeys Creek
Mannus
Woomargama
Kiandra
Colinton
Jerangle
Shannons Flat
Jingellic
Talmalmo
Lake Hume
Walwa
Tooma
Cabramurra
Bredbo
Wymah
Tintaldra
Greg Greg
Adaminaby
Lake Eucumbene
Peakview
KOSCIUSKO NATIONAL PARK
Mount Jagungal 2061
Eucumbene
Numeralla
Countegany
Bullioh
Cudgewa
Corryong
Khancoban
MONARO RANGE
Cooma
GREAT DIVIDING RANGE
KYBEYAN RANGE
WADBILLIGA NATIONAL PARK
DEUA NATIONAL PARK
Gungartan 2068
Round Mountain 1582
Island Bend
Rock Flat
Kybean
SNOWY MOUNTAINS
VICTORIA
Cravensville
Geehi
Jindabyne
Berridale
Nariel
Mount Townsend 2210
Hudsons Peak 1232
Mount Kosciusko 2228
Thredbo Village
Dalgety
Kydra
Copyright © by Rand McNally & Co.
Map prepared by George Philip & Son Ltd. London.


| ENGLISH | creek | island | mount | peak | point | range | reservoir |
|---|---|---|---|---|---|---|---|
| DEUTSCH | Bach | Insel | Berg | Gipfel | Landspitze | Gebirge | Stausee |
| ESPAÑOL | riachuelo | isla | montaña | pico | punta | cordillera | embalse |
| FRANÇAIS | crique | île | mont | cime | pointe | chaîne | réservoir |
| PORTUGUÊS | riacho | ilha | monte | pico | ponta | cordilheira | reservatório |

Kilometers 0 10 20 30 40 50 Km.

Statute Miles 0 10 20 30 40 50 Mi.

Scale 1:1,000,000

One centimeter represents 10 kilometers.

One inch represents approximately 16 miles.

Lambert Conformal Conic Projection

## New Zealand / Neuseeland / Nueva Zelanda
## Nouvelle Zélande / Nova Zelândia

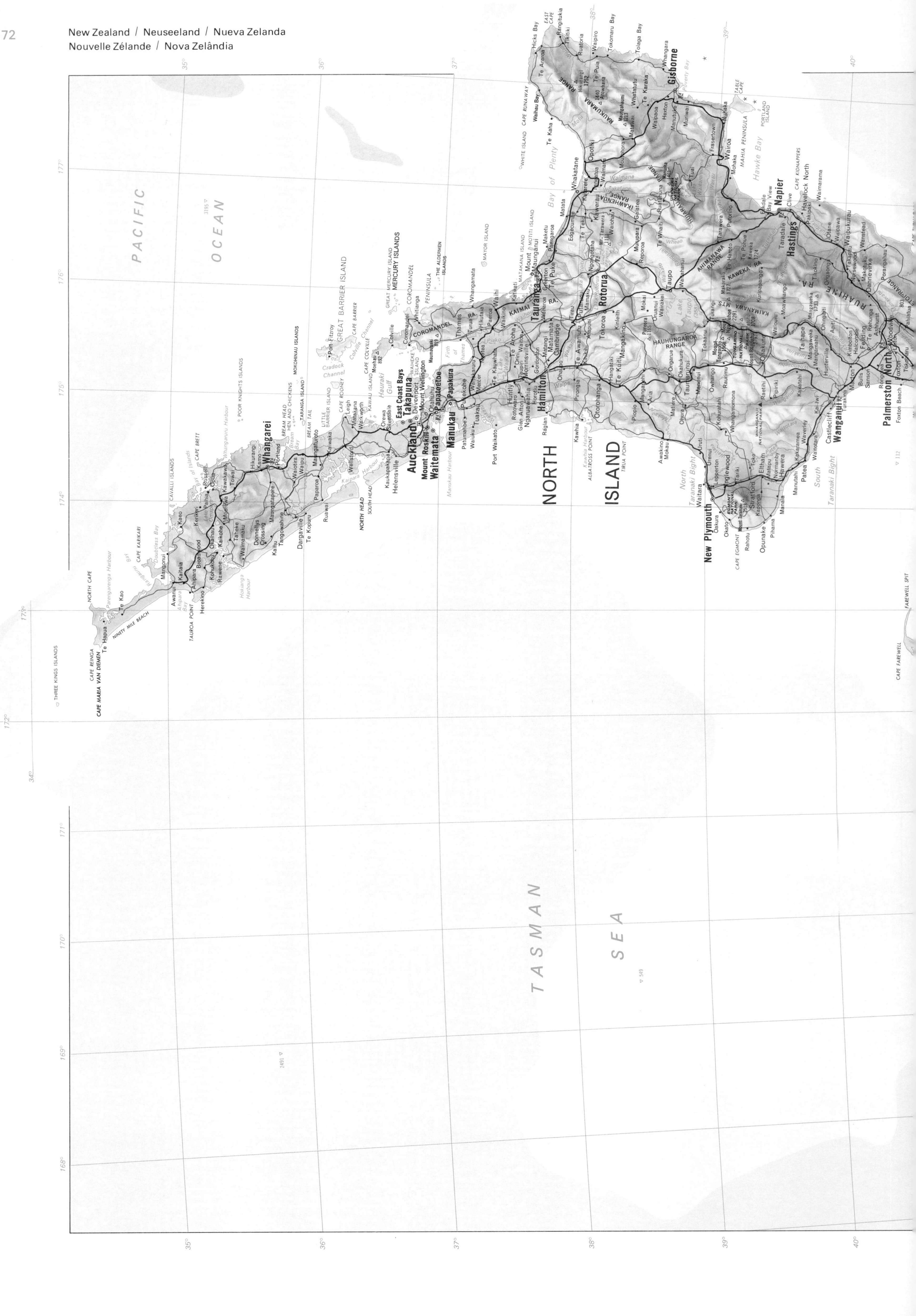

PACIFIC
OCEAN
TASMAN
SEA
NORTH
ISLAND
Auckland
Hamilton
Tauranga
Rotorua
Gisborne
Napier
Hastings
New Plymouth
Wanganui
Palmerston North
Whangarei
Manukau
Takapuna
East Coast Bays
Waitemata
Mount Roskill
Papakura
Papatoetoe
Taupo
Lake Taupo
Bay of Plenty
Hawke Bay
Hauraki Gulf
Firth of Thames
GREAT BARRIER ISLAND
MERCURY ISLANDS
COROMANDEL PENINSULA
CAPE REINGA
CAPE MARIA VAN DIEMEN
NORTH CAPE
NINETY MILE BEACH
THREE KINGS ISLANDS
POOR KNIGHTS ISLANDS
CAVALLI ISLANDS
EAST CAPE
CAPE EGMONT
North Taranaki Bight
South Taranaki Bight
CAPE KIDNAPPERS
MAHIA PENINSULA
KAIMAI RA.
KAWEKA RA.
RUAHINE RA.
KAIMANAWA MTS
HAUHUNGAROA RANGE
RAUKUMARA RANGE
CAPE FAREWELL
FAREWELL SPIT

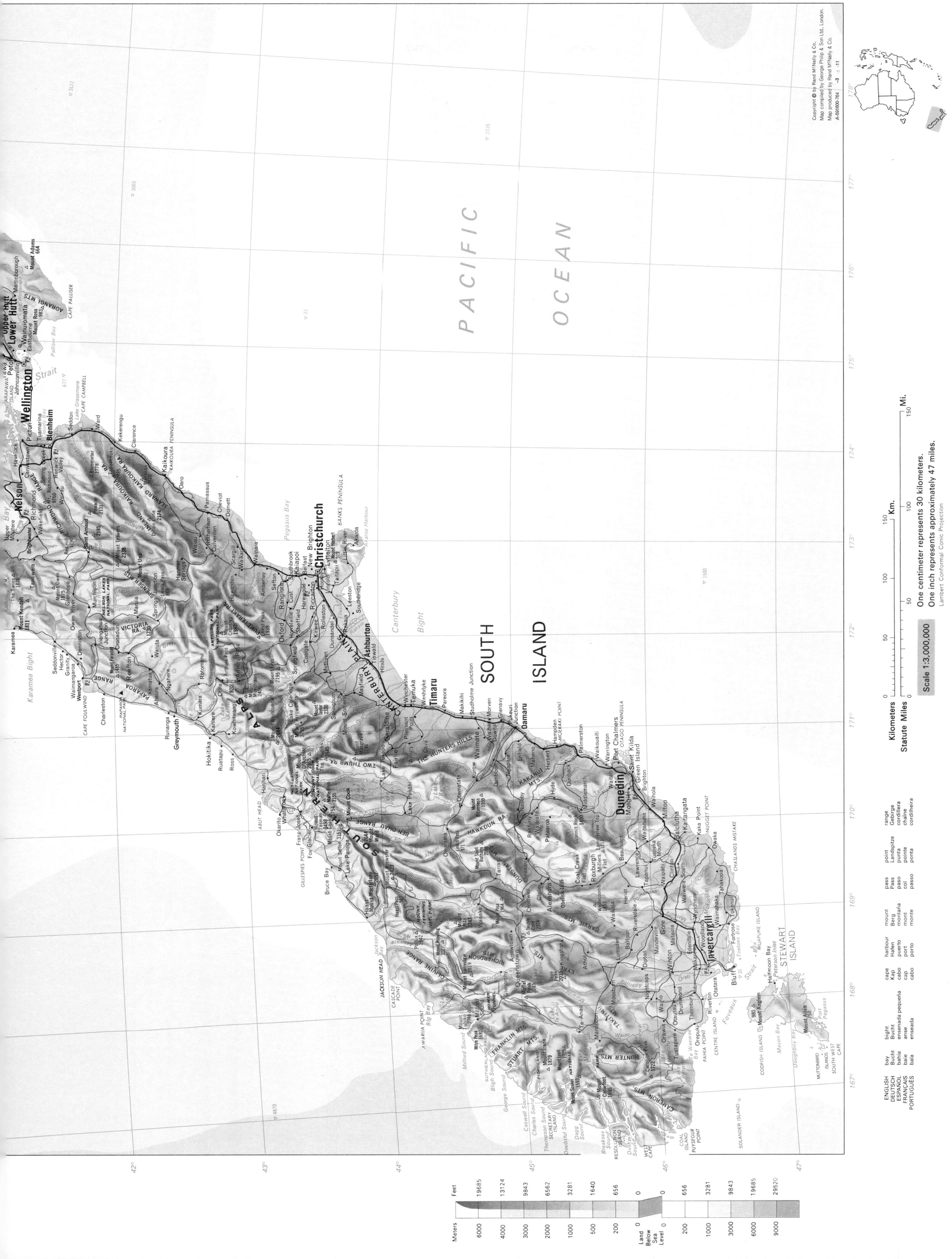
PACIFIC OCEAN
SOUTH ISLAND
STEWART ISLAND
Wellington
Christchurch
Dunedin
Invercargill
Nelson
Blenheim
Timaru
Oamaru
Greymouth
Kaikoura
Foveaux Strait
Canterbury Bight
Karamea Bight
Scale 1:3,000,000
One centimeter represents 30 kilometers.
One inch represents approximately 47 miles.
Lambert Conformal Conic Projection
Kilometers
Statute Miles
ENGLISH bay cape harbour mount pass point range
DEUTSCH Bucht Kap Hafen Berg Pass Landspitze Gebirge
ESPAÑOL bahia cabo puerto montaña paso punta cordillera
FRANÇAIS baie cap port mont col pointe chaîne
PORTUGUÊS baía cabo porto monte passo ponta cordilheira
Meters
Feet
Land Below Sea Level

a

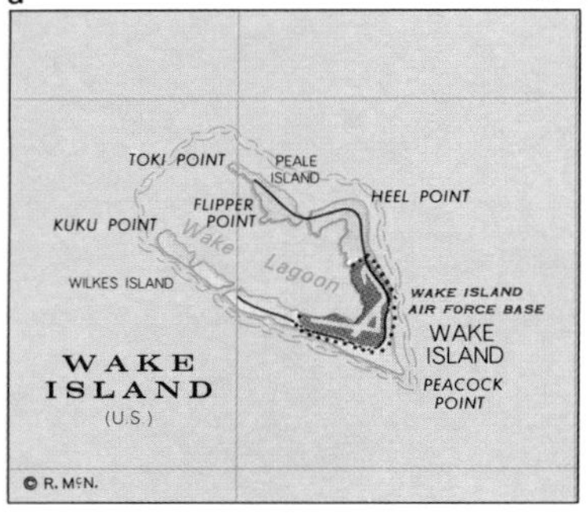
TOKI POINT
PEALE ISLAND
KUKU POINT
FLIPPER POINT
HEEL POINT
WILKES ISLAND
Wake Lagoon
WAKE ISLAND AIR FORCE BASE
WAKE ISLAND
WAKE ISLAND
(U.S.)
PEACOCK POINT
© R. McN.

b

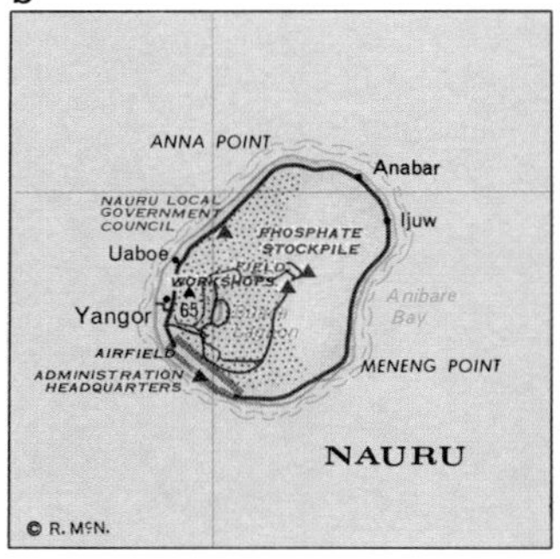
ANNA POINT
Anabar
NAURU LOCAL GOVERNMENT COUNCIL
PHOSPHATE STOCKPILE
Ijuw
Uaboe
Yangor
AIRFIELD
ADMINISTRATION HEADQUARTERS
Anibare Bay
MENENG POINT
NAURU
© R. McN.

c

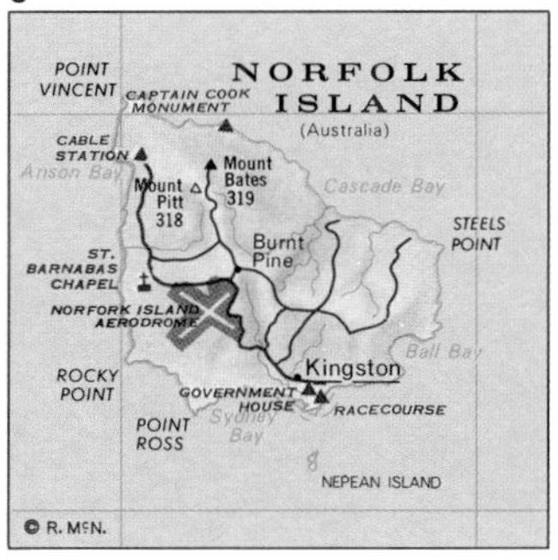
POINT VINCENT
CAPTAIN COOK MONUMENT
NORFOLK ISLAND
(Australia)
CABLE STATION
Anson Bay
Mount Pitt 318
Mount Bates 319
Cascade Bay
ST. BARNABAS CHAPEL
NORFOLK ISLAND AERODROME
Burnt Pine
STEELS POINT
ROCKY POINT
Kingston
GOVERNMENT HOUSE
RACECOURSE
POINT ROSS
Ball Bay
NEPEAN ISLAND
© R. McN.

d

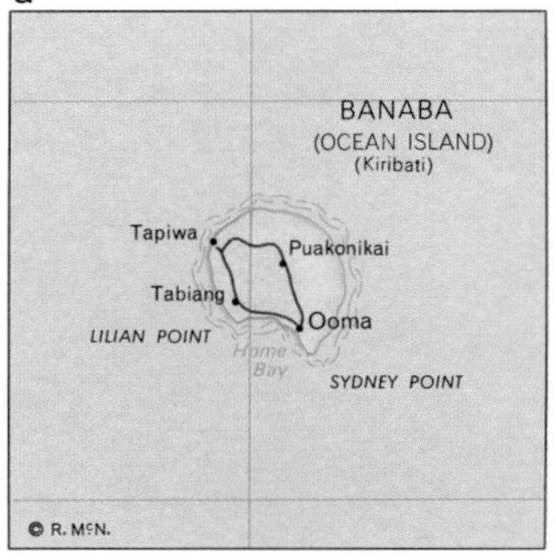
BANABA
(OCEAN ISLAND)
(Kiribati)
Tapiwa
Tabiang
Buakonikai
Ooma
LILIAN POINT
Home Bay
SYDNEY POINT
© R. McN.

e

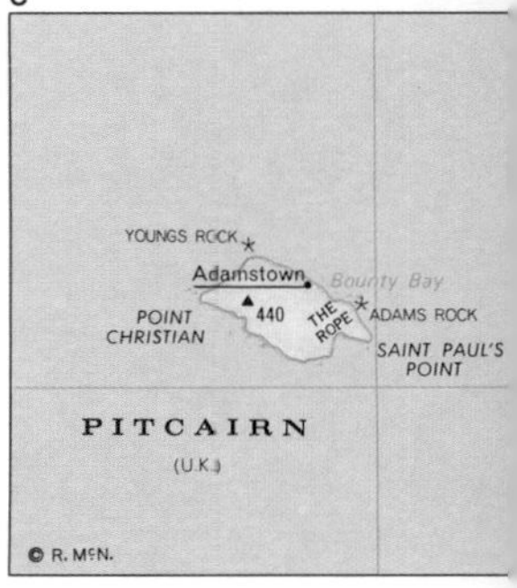
YOUNGS ROCK
Adamstown
Bounty Bay
POINT CHRISTIAN
440
THE ROPE
ADAMS ROCK
SAINT PAUL'S POINT
PITCAIRN
(U.K.)
© R. McN.

f

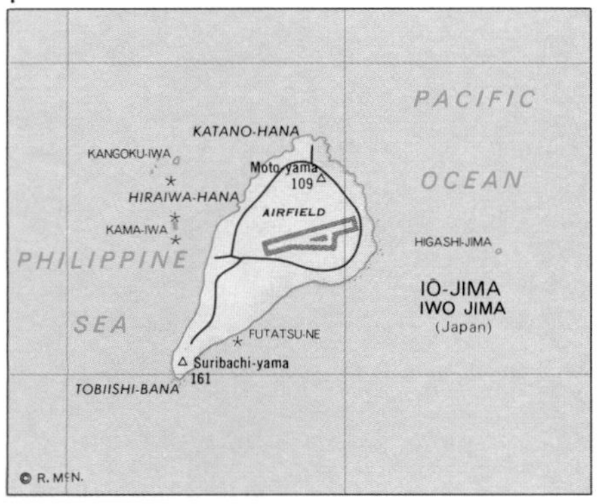
PACIFIC
OCEAN
PHILIPPINE
SEA
KATANO-HANA
KANGOKU-IWA
Moto-yama 109
HIRAIWA-HANA
KAMA-IWA
AIRFIELD
HIGASHI-JIMA
IŌ-JIMA
IWO JIMA
(Japan)
FUTATSU-NE
Suribachi-yama 161
TOBIISHI-BANA
© R. McN.

g

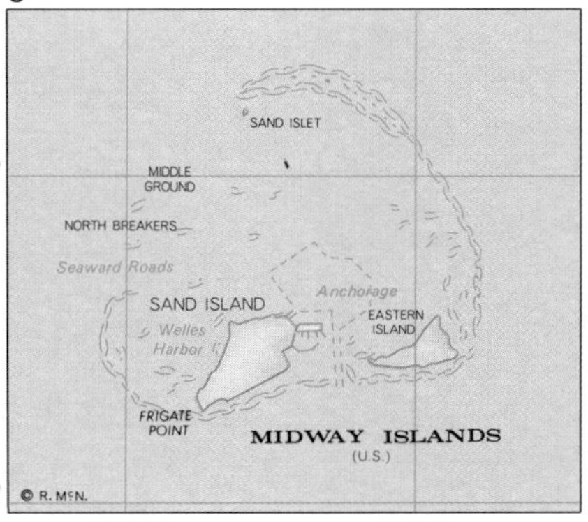
SAND ISLET
MIDDLE GROUND
NORTH BREAKERS
Seaward Roads
SAND ISLAND
Anchorage
Welles Harbor
EASTERN ISLAND
FRIGATE POINT
MIDWAY ISLANDS
(U.S.)
© R. McN.

h

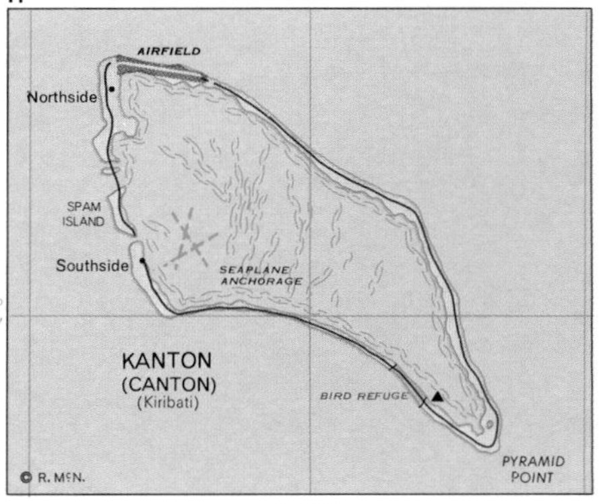
AIRFIELD
Northside
SPAM ISLAND
Southside
SEAPLANE ANCHORAGE
KANTON
(CANTON)
(Kiribati)
BIRD REFUGE
PYRAMID POINT
© R. McN.

k

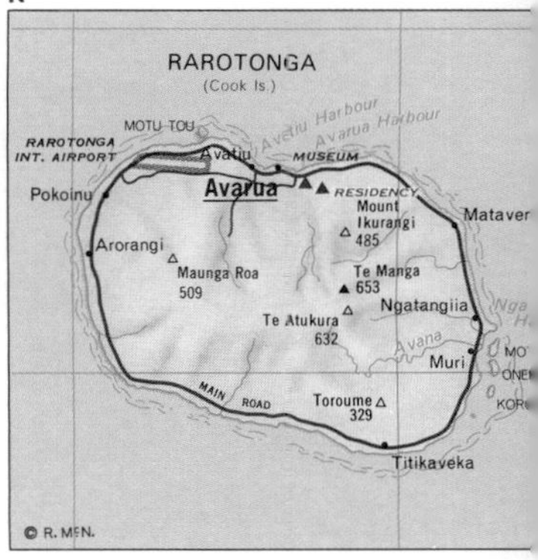
RAROTONGA
(Cook Is.)
MOTU-TOU
RAROTONGA INT. AIRPORT
Avatiu
Avarua
MUSEUM
RESIDENCY
Pokoinu
Matavera
Ikurangi 485
Arorangi
Maunga Roa 509
Te Manga 653
Ngatangiia
Te Atukura 632
Muri
MAIN ROAD
Toroume 329
Titikaveka
© R. McN.

Kilometers 0 5 10 15 Km.

Statute Miles 0 5 10 15 Mi.

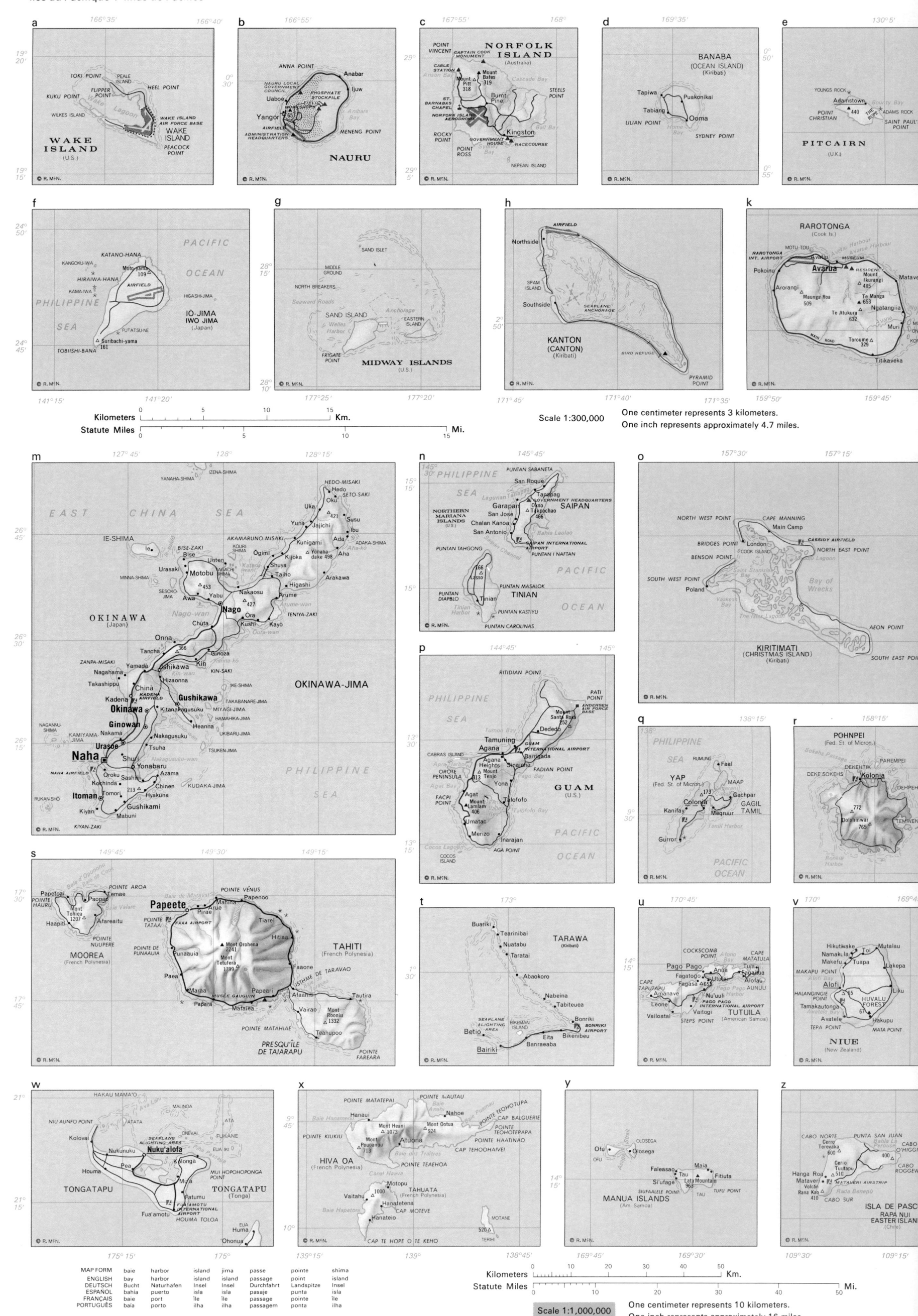

Scale 1:300,000

One centimeter represents 3 kilometers.
One inch represents approximately 4.7 miles.

m

IZENA-SHIMA
YANAHA-SHIMA
HEDO-MISAKI
Hedo
Oku
SETO-SAKI
EAST CHINA SEA
Uka
421
Yuna
Jajichi
Susu
Ibu
IE-SHIMA
AKAMARUNO-MISAKI
Ada
ADAKA-SHIMA
Ie
BISE-ZAKI
Bise
Kunigami
Yonaha-dake 498
Aha
Ogimi
Unten
Kijoka
Urasaki
Motobu
Shuya
Taiho
MINNA-SHIMA
453
Arakawa
SESOKO-JIMA
Awa
Yabu
Nakaosu
Higashi
Nago
427
Arume
Nago-wan
Ora
TENIYA-ZAKI
OKINAWA
(Japan)
Chūta
Kushi
Kayo
Onna
Tancha
366
Ginoza
ZANPA-MISAKI
Yamada
Ishikawa
Kin
Nagahama
KIN-SAKI
Takashippu
China
Hizaonna
IKE-SHIMA
OKINAWA-JIMA
Kadena
KADENA AIRFIELD
Gushikawa
TAKABANARE-JIMA
Okinawa
Kitanakagusuku
MIYAGI-JIMA
Ginowan
HAMAHIKA-JIMA
NAGANNU-SHIMA
Heanna
KAMIYAMA-JIMA
Nakama
Nakagusuku
UKIBARU-JIMA
Urasoe
Tsuha
TSUKEN-JIMA
Naha
Shuri
Yonabaru
NAHA AIRFIELD
Azama
Oroku
Sashiki
Kochinda
Chinen
PHILIPPINE SEA
KUDAKA-JIMA
213
Tomori
Hyakuna
RUKAN-SHŌ
Itoman
Gushikami
Kiyan
Mabuni
KIYAN-ZAKI
© R. McN.

n

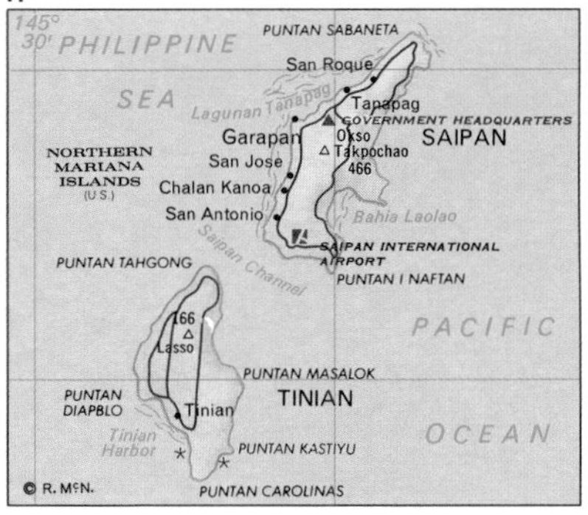
PHILIPPINE SEA
PUNTAN SABANETA
San Roque
Tanapag
GOVERNMENT HEADQUARTERS
Garapan
SAIPAN
NORTHERN MARIANA ISLANDS
(U.S.)
San Jose
Chalan Kanoa
San Antonio
SAIPAN INTERNATIONAL AIRPORT
PUNTAN I NAFTAN
PUNTAN TAHGONG
Saipan Channel
PACIFIC OCEAN
PUNTAN MASALOK
TINIAN
PUNTAN DIAPBLO
Tinian Harbor
PUNTAN KASTIYU
PUNTAN CAROLINAS
© R. McN.

o

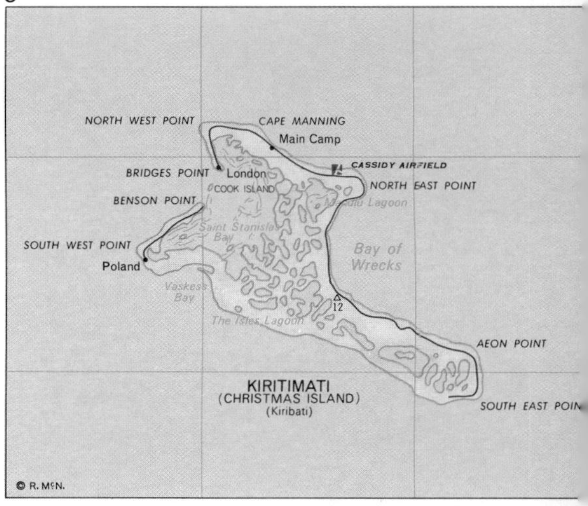
NORTH WEST POINT
CAPE MANNING
Main Camp
BRIDGES POINT
London
CASSIDY AIRFIELD
COOK ISLAND
NORTH EAST POINT
BENSON POINT
SOUTH WEST POINT
Poland
Bay of Wrecks
AEON POINT
KIRITIMATI
(CHRISTMAS ISLAND)
(Kiribati)
SOUTH EAST POINT
© R. McN.

p

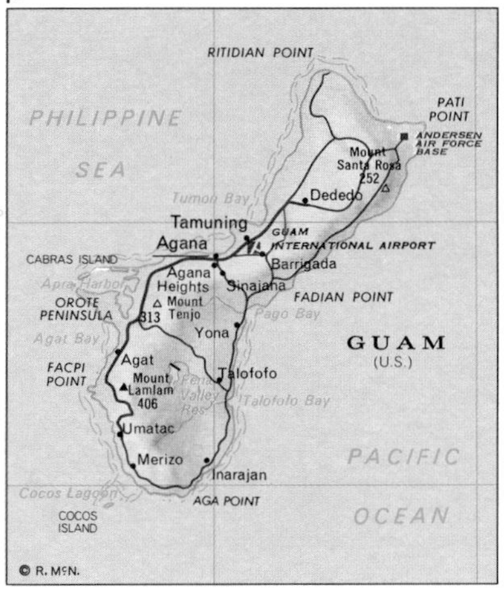
RITIDIAN POINT
PATI POINT
PHILIPPINE SEA
ANDERSEN AIR FORCE BASE
Mount Santa Rosa 252
Tumon Bay
Dededo
Tamuning
Agana
GUAM INTERNATIONAL AIRPORT
CABRAS ISLAND
Barrigada
Agana Heights
Sinajana
FADIAN POINT
OROTE PENINSULA
Mount Tenjo 313
Pago Bay
GUAM
(U.S.)
Yona
FACPI POINT
Agat
Mount Lamlam 406
Talofofo
Umatac
Merizo
Inarajan
PACIFIC OCEAN
Cocos Lagoon
COCOS ISLAND
AGA POINT
© R. McN.

q

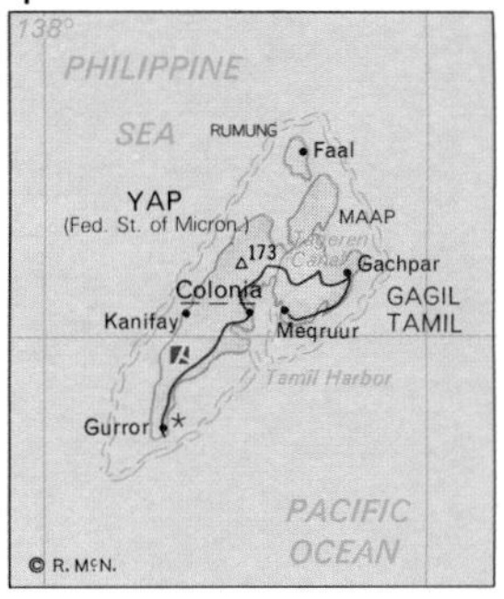
PHILIPPINE SEA
RUMUNG
Faal
YAP
(Fed. St. of Micron.)
MAAP
173
Colonia
Gachpar
GAGIL TAMIL
Kanifay
Meqruur
Tamil Harbor
Gurror
PACIFIC OCEAN
© R. McN.

r

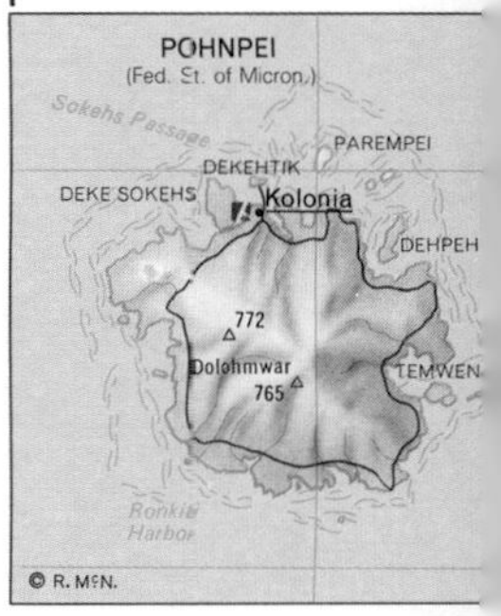
POHNPEI
(Fed. St. of Micron.)
Sokehs Passage
PAREMPEI
DEKEHTIK
DEKE SOKEHS
Kolonia
DEHPEH
772
Dolohmwar 765
TEMWEN
Ronkiti Harbor
© R. McN.

s

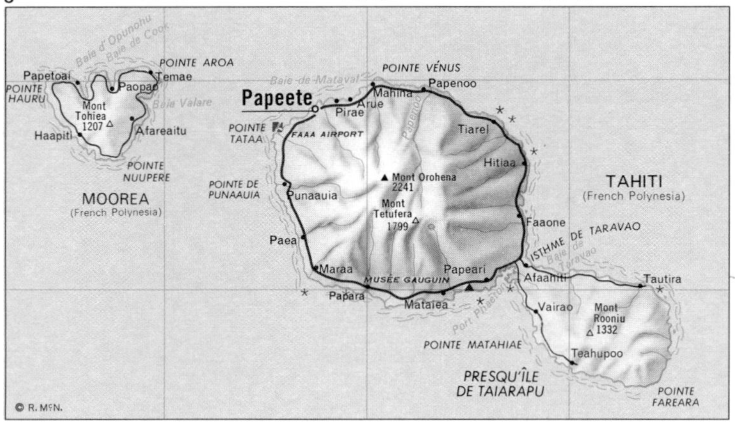
POINTE AROA
Papetoai
Temae
POINTE HAURU
Paopao
Mont Tohiea 1207
Afareaitu
Haapiti
POINTE NUUPERE
MOOREA
(French Polynesia)
POINTE VÉNUS
Papenoo
Papeete
Mahina
Arue
Pirae
POINTE TATAA
FAAA AIRPORT
Tiarei
POINTE DE PUNAAUIA
Punaauia
Mont Orohena 2241
Hitiaa
Mont Tetufera 1799
TAHITI
(French Polynesia)
Paea
Faaone
ISTHME DE TARAVAO
Maraa
Papeari
Papara
MUSÉE GAUGUIN
Afaahiti
Tautira
Mataiea
Vairao
Mont Rooniu 1332
POINTE MATAHIAE
Teahupoo
PRESQU'ÎLE DE TAIARAPU
POINTE FAREARA
© R. McN.

t

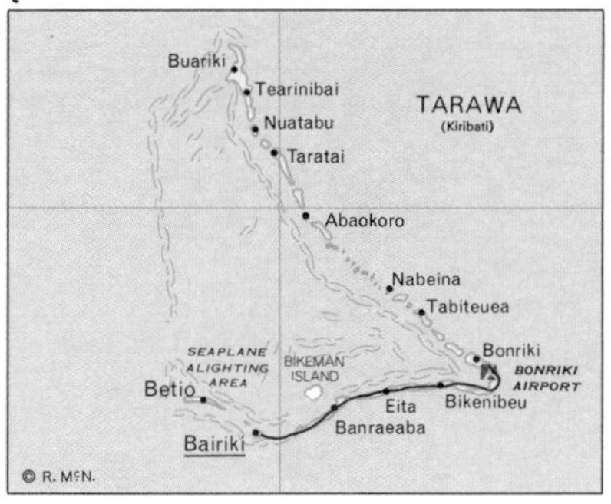
Buariki
Tearinibai
TARAWA
(Kiribati)
Nuatabu
Taratai
Abaokoro
Nabeina
Tabiteuea
SEAPLANE ALIGHTING AREA
BIKEMAN ISLAND
Bonriki
BONRIKI AIRPORT
Betio
Eita
Bikenibeu
Banraeaba
Bairiki
© R. McN.

u

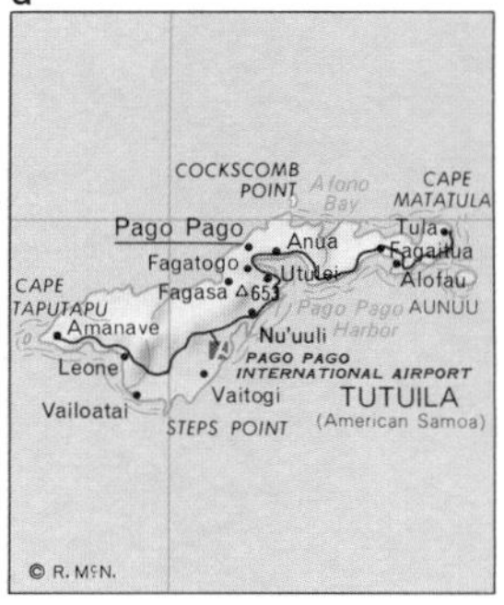
COCKSCOMB POINT
CAPE MATATULA
Pago Pago
Fagatogo
Aoa
Utulei
Fagasa
Alofau
653
CAPE TAPUTAPU
Amanave
Nu'uuli
AUNUU
Leone
PAGO PAGO INTERNATIONAL AIRPORT
Vailoatai
Vaitogi
TUTUILA
STEPS POINT
(American Samoa)
© R. McN.

v

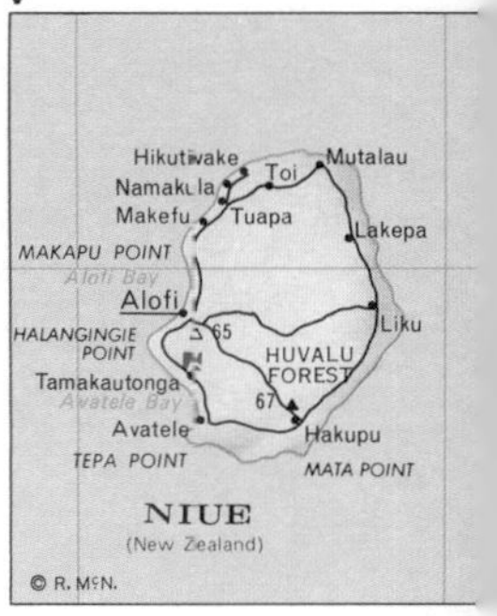
Hikutavake
Toi
Mutalau
Namukulu
Makefu
Tuapa
Lakepa
MAKAPU POINT
Alofi
HALANGINGIE POINT
65
Liku
Tamakautonga
HUVALU FOREST
Avatele
67
Hakupu
TEPA POINT
MATA POINT
NIUE
(New Zealand)
© R. McN.

w

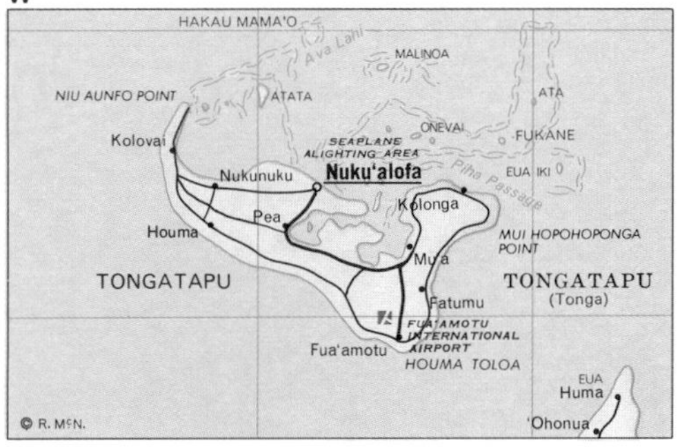
HAKAU MAMA'O
MALINOA
NIU AUFO POINT
ATATA
Kolovai
ONEVAI
FUKAVE
SEAPLANE ALIGHTING AREA
Nukunuku
Nuku'alofa
Pea
Kolonga
Houma
MUI HOPOHOPONGA POINT
TONGATAPU
Mu'a
Fatumu
TONGATAPU
(Tonga)
FUA'AMOTU INTERNATIONAL AIRPORT
Fua'amotu
HOUMA TOLOA
EUA
Huma
'Ohonua
© R. McN.

x

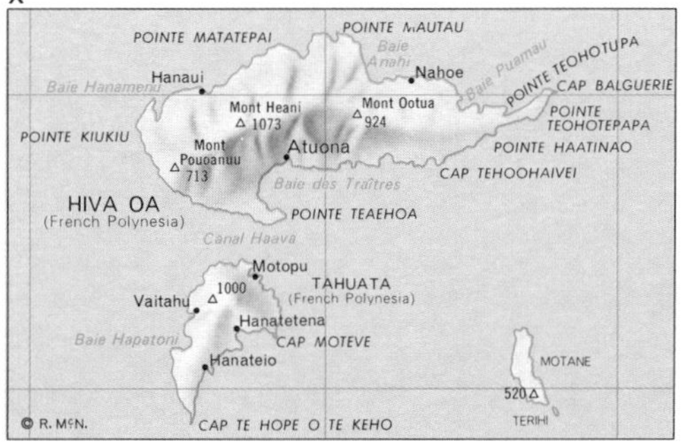
POINTE MATATEPAI
POINTE NAUTAU
Hanaui
Nahoe
POINTE TEOHOTUPA
CAP BALGUERIE
Baie Hanamenu
Mont Heani 1073
Mont Ootua 924
POINTE KIUKIU
Mont Pouoanuu 713
Atuona
POINTE TEOHOTEPAPA
POINTE HAATINAO
CAP TEHOOHAIVEI
Baie des Traîtres
HIVA OA
(French Polynesia)
POINTE TEAEHOA
Canal Havea
Motopu
1000
Vaitahu
TAHUATA
(French Polynesia)
Hanatetena
CAP MOTEVE
Baie Hapatoni
Hanateio
MOTANE
520
CAP TE HOPE O TE KEHO
TERIHI
© R. McN.

y

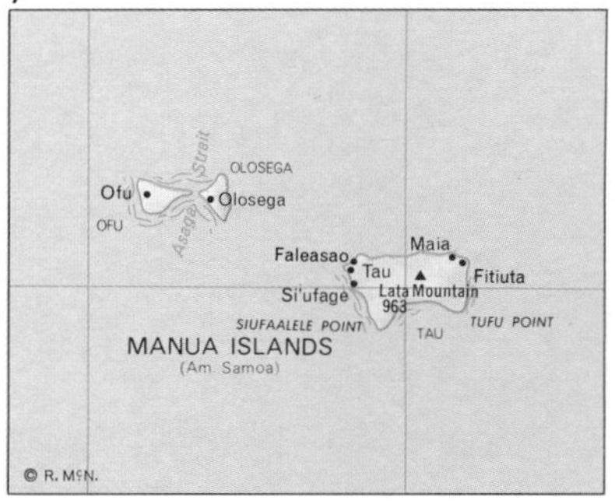
Ofu
OLOSEGA
Olosega
OFU
Maia
Faleasao
Tau
Fitiuta
Si'ufaga
Lata Mountain 963
SIUFAALELE POINT
TUFU POINT
TAU
MANUA ISLANDS
(Am. Samoa)
© R. McN.

z

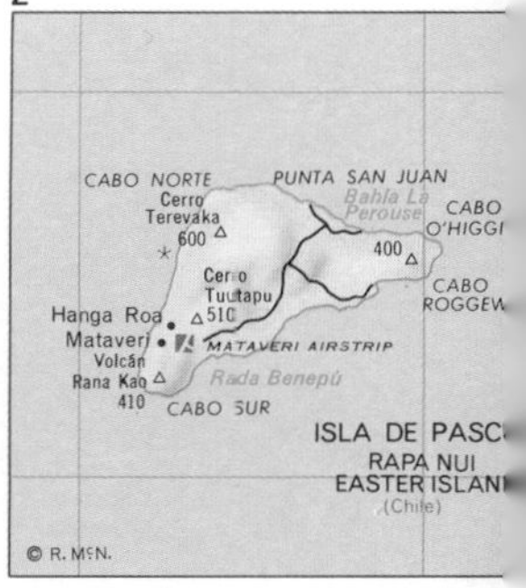
CABO NORTE
PUNTA SAN JUAN
Bahía La Perouse
CABO O'HIGGINS
Cerro Terevaka 600
400
CABO ROGGEVEEN
Cerro Tuutapu 510
Hanga Roa
MATAVERI AIRSTRIP
Mataveri
Volcán Rana Kau 410
Rada Benepú
CABO SUR
ISLA DE PASCUA
RAPA NUI
EASTER ISLAND
(Chile)
© R. McN.

| MAP FORM | baie | harbor | island | jima | passe | pointe | shima |
|---|---|---|---|---|---|---|---|
| ENGLISH | bay | harbor | island | island | passage | point | island |
| DEUTSCH | Bucht | Naturhafen | Insel | Insel | Durchfahrt | Landspitze | Insel |
| ESPAÑOL | bahía | puerto | isla | isla | pasaje | punta | isla |
| FRANÇAIS | baie | port | île | île | passe | pointe | île |
| PORTUGUÊS | baía | porto | ilha | ilha | passagem | ponta | ilha |

Kilometers 0 10 20 30 40 50 Km.

Statute Miles 0 10 20 30 40 50 Mi.

Scale 1:1,000,000

One centimeter represents 10 kilometers.
One inch represents approximately 16 miles.
Transverse Mercator Projection

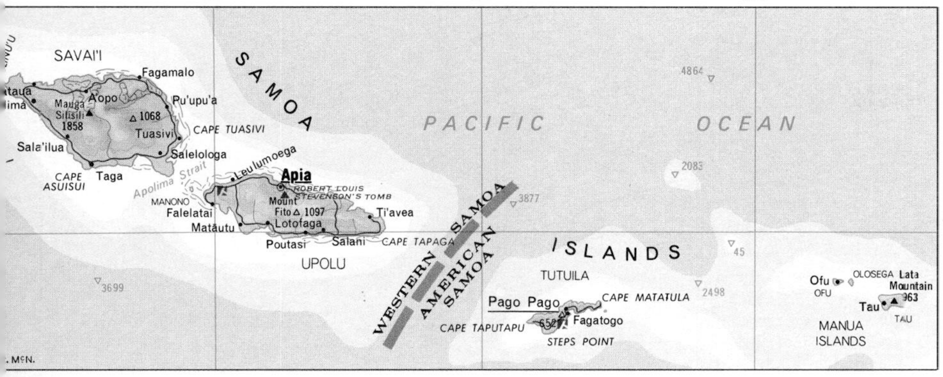
SAVAI'I
Fagamalo
SAMOA
A'opo
Pu'upu'a
Mauga Silisili 1858
1068
Tuasivi
CAPE TUASIVI
Sale'ilua
Salelologa
Leulumoega
Apia
CAPE ASUISUI
Taga
Apolima Strait
Manono
Falelatai
Mataútu
Lotofaga
Ti'avea
Poutasi
Salani
UPOLU
PACIFIC OCEAN
ISLANDS
TUTUILA
WESTERN SAMOA
AMERICAN SAMOA
Pago Pago
CAPE MATATULA
Fagatogo
CAPE TAPUTAPU
STEPS POINT
Ofu
OLOSEGA
Lata Mountain
Tau
MANUA ISLANDS

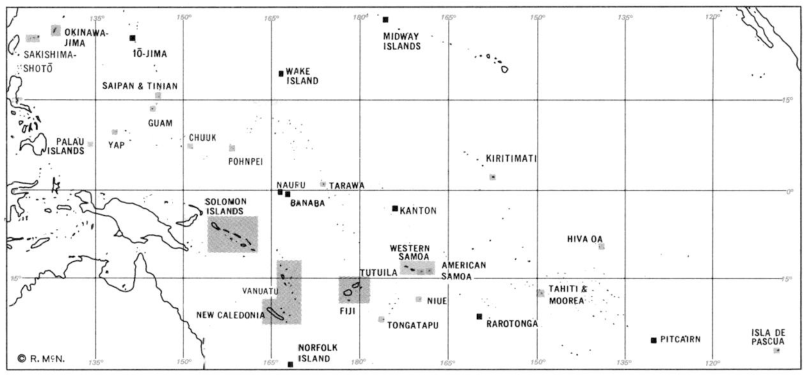
OKINAWA-JIMA
SAKISHIMA-SHOTŌ
IŌ-JIMA
MIDWAY ISLANDS
WAKE ISLAND
SAIPAN & TINIAN
GUAM
PALAU ISLANDS
YAP
CHUUK
POHNPEI
KIRITIMATI
NAURU
TARAWA
BANABA
KANTON
SOLOMON ISLANDS
WESTERN SAMOA
AMERICAN SAMOA
TUTUILA
HIVA OA
VANUATU
FIJI
NIUE
TAHITI & MOOREA
NEW CALEDONIA
TONGATAPU
RAROTONGA
NORFOLK ISLAND
PITCAIRN
ISLA DE PASCUA

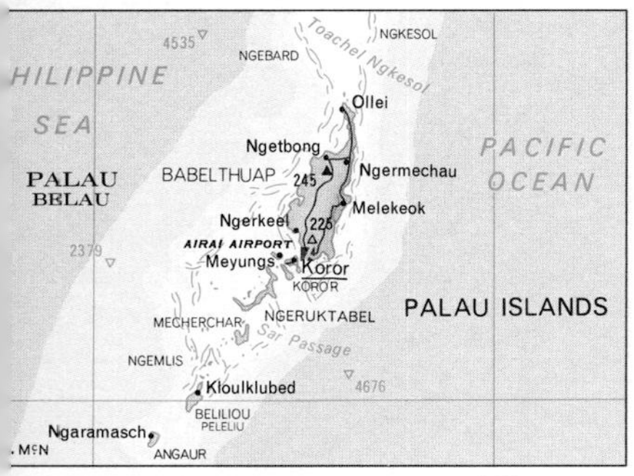
PHILIPPINE SEA
NGKESOL
NGEBARD
Ollei
Ngetbong
Ngermechau
PACIFIC OCEAN
PALAU BELAU
BABELTHUAP
Melekeok
Ngerkeel
AIRAI AIRPORT
Meyungs
Koror
KOROR
PALAU ISLANDS
MECHERCHAR
NGERUKTABEL
NGEMLIS
Kloulklubed
Ngaramasch
ANGAUR

c

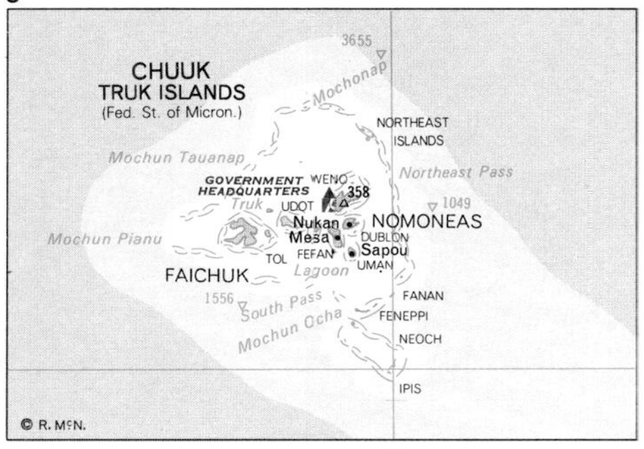
CHUUK
TRUK ISLANDS
(Fed. St. of Micron.)
NORTHEAST ISLANDS
Mochun Tauanap
Northeast Pass
GOVERNMENT HEADQUARTERS
WENO
Mochun Pianu
Nukan
Mesa
NOMONEAS
Sapou
FAICHUK
TOL
FEFAN
UMAN
Lagoon
South Pass
FANAN
FENEPPI
NEOCH
IPIS

d

EAST CHINA SEA
SAKISHIMA-SHOTŌ
IKEMA-JIMA
Karimata
IRABU-JIMA
Irabu
Hirara
SHIMOJI-JIMA
Shimoji
Guskube
MIYAKO-JIMA
MINNA-SHIMA
Tarama
TARAMA-SHIMA
YAEYAMA RETTŌ
MIYAKO-RETTŌ
Hirano
Yonaguni
YONAGUNI-SHIMA
Uehara
IRIOMOTE-JIMA
Kabira
Funakuyā
ISHIGAKI-SHIMA
KOHAMA
Amitori
SHIMA
Miyara
Ishigaki
Ōtomi
Toyohara
OKINAWA
(Japan)
KURO-SHIMA
NAKANOUGAN-JIMA
PHILIPPINE SEA
HATERUMA-SHIMA

Kilometers 0 50 100 150 Km.
Statute Miles 0 50 100 150 Mi.

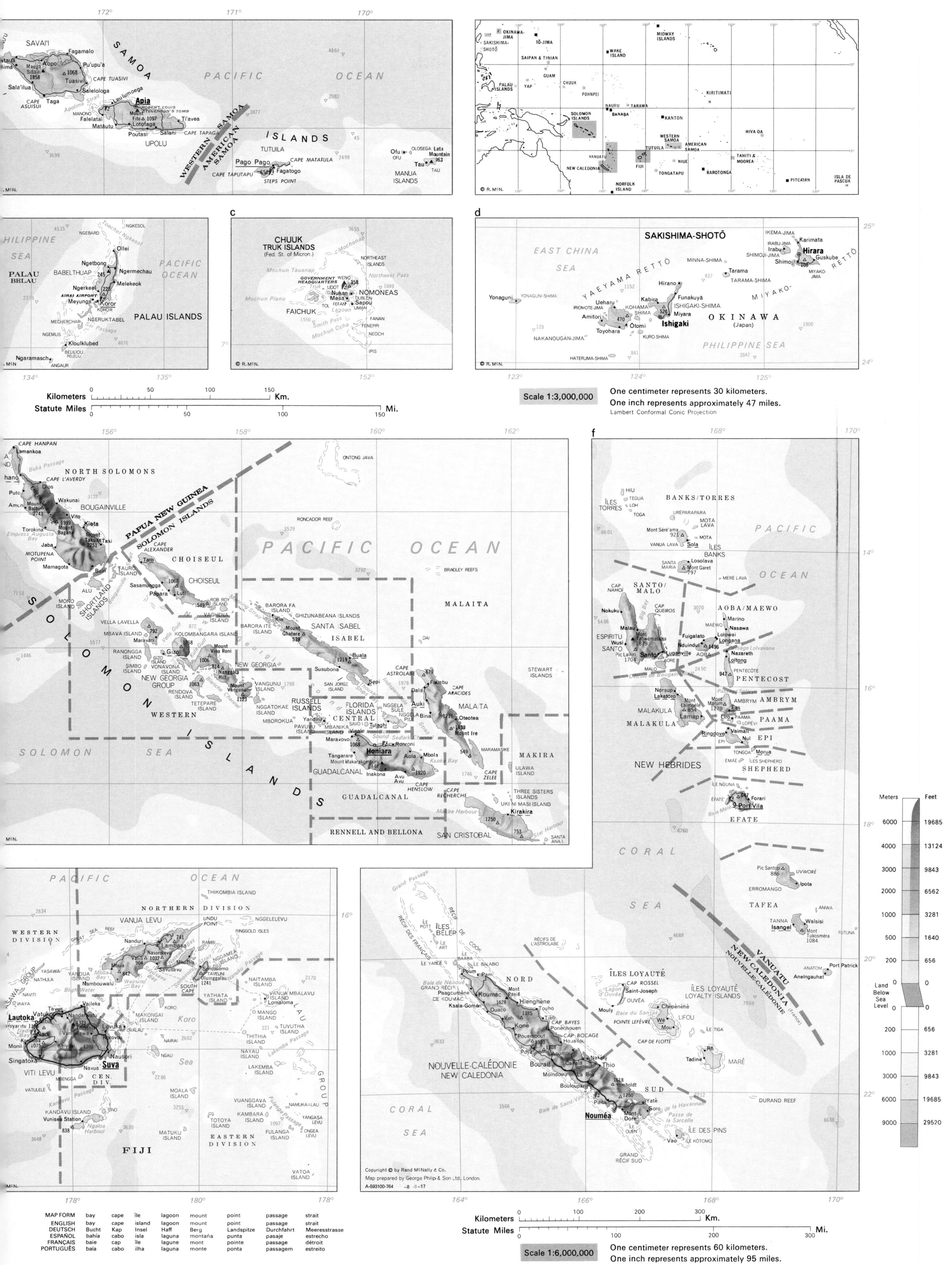

Scale 1:3,000,000

One centimeter represents 30 kilometers.
One inch represents approximately 47 miles.
Lambert Conformal Conic Projection

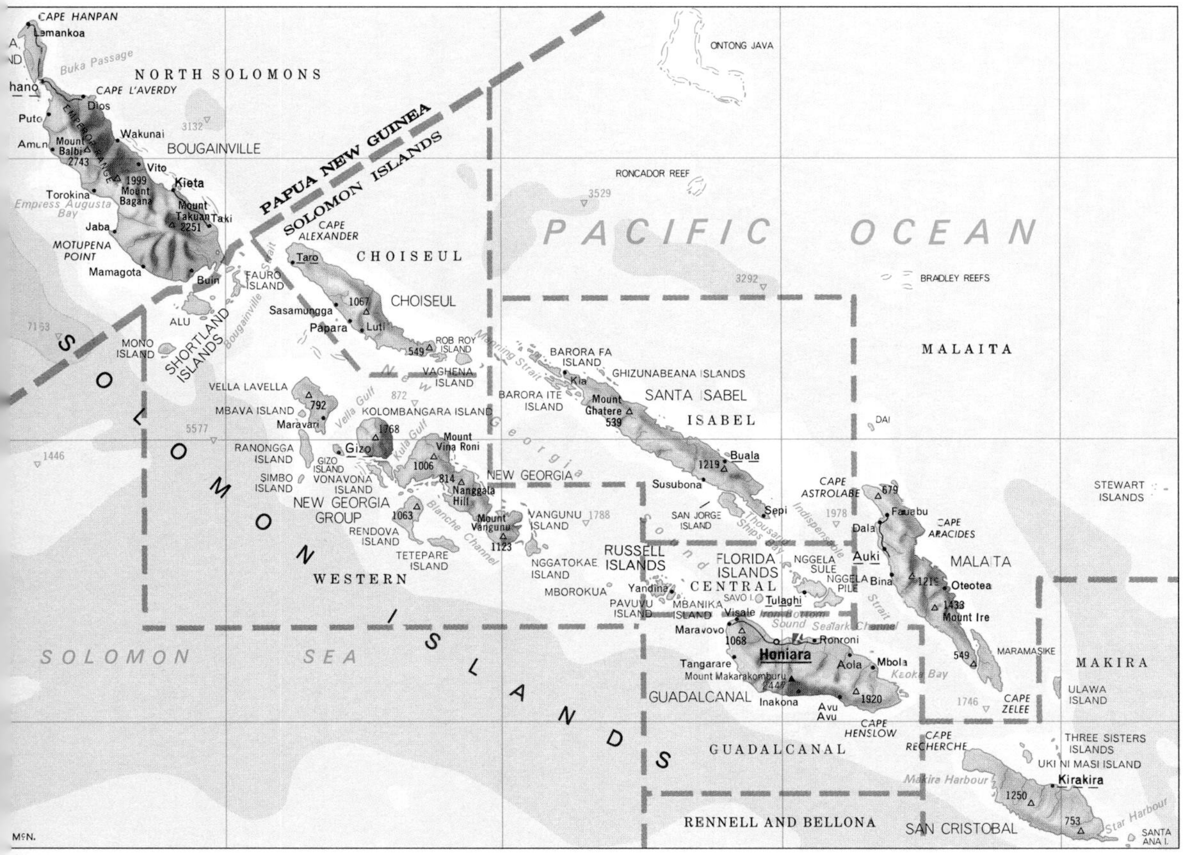
CAPE HANPAN
NORTH SOLOMONS
Buka Passage
CAPE L'AVERDY
Dios
Wakunai
Mount Balbi 2743
BOUGAINVILLE
Vito
Kieta
Torokina
Empress Augusta Bay
Mount Bagana
Mount Takuan 2251
Taki
Jaba
MOTUPENA POINT
Mamagota
PAPUA NEW GUINEA
SOLOMON ISLANDS
CAPE ALEXANDER
Taro
CHOISEUL
RONCADOR REEF
ONTONG JAVA
PACIFIC OCEAN
BRADLEY REEFS
FAURO ISLAND
Buin
Sasamungga
Papara
Luti
SHORTLAND ISLANDS
MONO ISLAND
ALU
ROB ROY ISLAND
VAGHENA ISLAND
BARORA FA ISLAND
GHIZUNABEANA ISLANDS
BARORA ITE ISLAND
SANTA ISABEL
Mount Ghatere
ISABEL
MALAITA
VELLA LAVELLA
MBAVA ISLAND
Maravari
KOLOMBANGARA ISLAND
Gizo
RANONGGA ISLAND
GIZO ISLAND
SIMBO ISLAND
VONAVONA ISLAND
NEW GEORGIA
NEW GEORGIA GROUP
Mount Nangasa Hill
Mount Vangunu
Buala
CAPE ASTROLABE
Fauabu
CAPE ARACIDES
STEWART ISLANDS
RENDOVA ISLAND
TETEPARE ISLAND
VANGUNU ISLAND
SAN JORGE ISLAND
Susubona
Sepi
Dala
Auki
MALAITA
Bina
Oteotea
Mount Ire
WESTERN
NGGATOKAE ISLAND
RUSSELL ISLANDS
FLORIDA ISLANDS
NGGELA SULE
NGGELA PILE
CENTRAL
MBOROKUA
Yandina
SAVO
Tulaghi
PAVUVU ISLAND
MBANIKA ISLAND
Visale
Maravovo
Honiara
Ronconi
MARAMASIKE
MAKIRA
SOLOMON SEA
ISLANDS
Tangarare
Mount Makarakomburu 2447
Aola
Mbolo
GUADALCANAL
Inakona
Avu Avu
CAPE HENSLOW
CAPE ZELEE
ULAWA ISLAND
GUADALCANAL
CAPE RECHERCHE
THREE SISTERS ISLANDS
UKI NI MASI ISLAND
Kirakira
Makira Harbour
RENNELL AND BELLONA
SAN CRISTOBAL
SANTA ANA I.

f

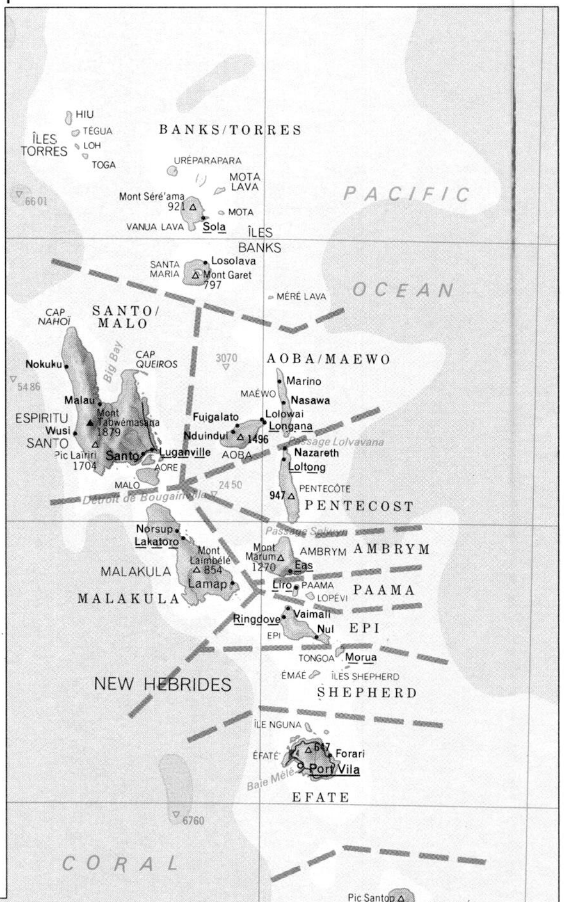
HIU
ÎLES TORRES
TEGUA
LOH
TOGA
BANKS/TORRES
UREPARAPARA
MOTA LAVA
Mont Sérē'ama
VANUA LAVA
Sola
ÎLES BANKS
PACIFIC
OCEAN
SANTA MARIA
Losolava
Mont Garet
MÉRÉ LAVA
CAP NAHOÏ
SANTO/MALO
CAP QUEIROS
Big Bay
Nokuku
AOBA/MAEWO
Marino
MAÉWO
Nasawa
Malau
Mont Tabwemasana 1879
ESPIRITU SANTO
Wusi
Pic Lairiri 1704
Fuigalato
Lolowai
Longana
Nduindui
Santo
Luganville
AOBA
Nazareth
Loltong
MALO
PENTECÔTE
PENTECOST
Norsup
Lakatoro
Mont Lalmbele
Mont Marum
AMBRYM
AMBRYM
MALAKULA
Eas
MALAKULA
Lamap
Ulro
PAAMA
PAAMA
LOPEVI
Ringdove
Vaimali
Nul
EPI
EPI
TONGOA
Morua
NEW HEBRIDES
ÉMAÉ
ÎLES SHEPHERD
SHEPHERD
ÎLE NGUNA
ÉFATÉ
Forari
Port-Vila
EFATE
CORAL
SEA
Pic Santop
UVWORÉ
Ipota
ERROMANGO
TAFEA
ANIWA
TANNA
Waisisi
Isangel
Mont Tukosméra 1084
FUTUNA
ANATOM
Port Patrick
Anelngauhat
VANUATU
NEW CALEDONIA
NOUVELLE-CALÉDONIE (France)

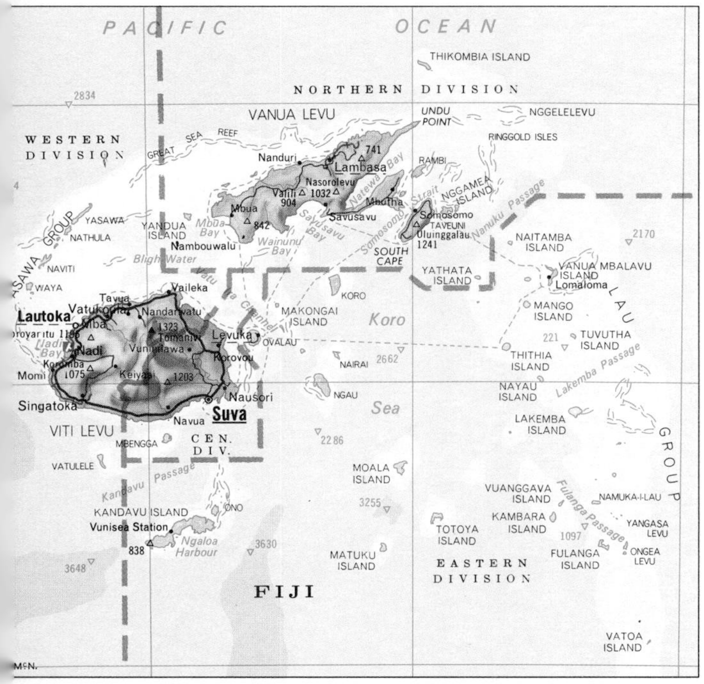
PACIFIC OCEAN
THIKOMBIA ISLAND
NORTHERN DIVISION
VANUA LEVU
UNDU POINT
NGGELELEVU
RINGGOLD ISLES
WESTERN DIVISION
Nanduri
RAMBI
Nasorolevu
Vatili
Mbutha
Savusavu
NGGAMEA
TAVEUNI
Somosomo
Uluinggalau
Nambouwalu
YASAWA
NATHULA
YASAWA GROUP
NAVITI
WAYA
Vaileka
SOUTH CAPE
NAITAMBA ISLAND
YATHATA ISLAND
VANUA MBALAVU
Lomaloma
Lautoka
Vatukoula
Nadi
Nandarivatu
MAKONGAI ISLAND
KORO
Koro
MANGO ISLAND
TUVUTHA ISLAND
Levuka
OVALAU
NAIRAI
THITHIA ISLAND
LAU
Momi
Korovou
NAYAU ISLAND
Singatoka
VITI LEVU
Nausori
Suva
NGAU
LAKEMBA ISLAND
Sea
Navua
CEN. DIV.
MBENGGA
VATULELE
MOALA ISLAND
GROUP
KANDAVU ISLAND
Vunisea Station
Ngaloa Harbour
TOTOYA ISLAND
VUANGGAVA ISLAND
KAMBARA ISLAND
NAMUKA-I-LAU
YANGASA LEVU
ONGEA LEVU
MATUKU ISLAND
EASTERN DIVISION
FULANGA ISLAND
FIJI
VATOA ISLAND

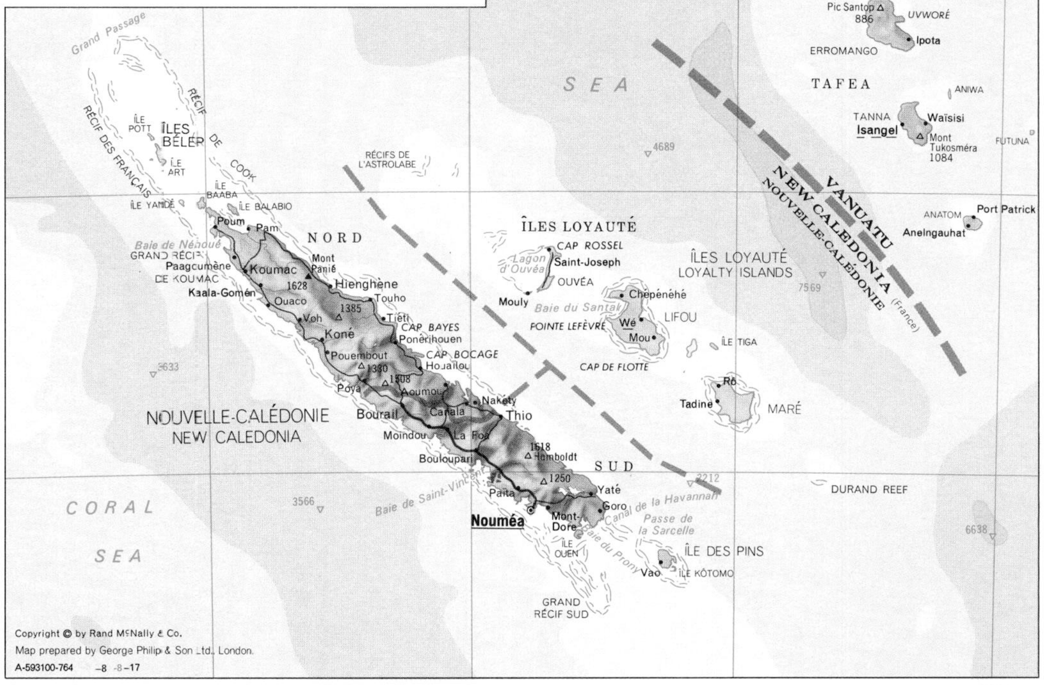
Grand Passage
RÉCIF DES FRANÇAIS
ÎLE POTT
ÎLES BÉLEP
ÎLE ART
RÉCIF DE COOK
RÉCIFS DE L'ASTROLABE
ÎLE YANDÉ
ÎLE BAABA
ÎLE BALABIO
Poum
Pam
NORD
GRAND RÉCIF
Baie de Népoui
Paagoumène
Koumac
Mont Panié
Hienghène
ÎLES LOYAUTÉ
CAP ROSSEL
Saint-Joseph
OUVÉA
ÎLES LOYAUTÉ
LOYALTY ISLANDS
Kaala-Gomen
Ouaco
Touho
Voh
CAP BAYES
Poindimié
Poněrihouen
CAP BOCAGE
Houaïlou
Koné
Pouembout
Poya
Mouly
POINTE LEFÈVRE
Chépénéhé
LIFOU
Wé
Mou
CAP DE FLOTTE
ÎLE TIGA
Kouaoua
Canala
Nakety
Thio
Bourail
Moindou
NOUVELLE-CALÉDONIE
NEW CALEDONIA
Tadine
MARÉ
Bouloupari
Humboldt
SUD
Païta
Yaté
CORAL SEA
Baie de Saint-Vincent
Nouméa
Mont-Dore
Goro
Baie de la Havannah
Passe de la Sarcelle
DURAND REEF
ÎLE OUEN
ÎLE DES PINS
Vao
ÎLE KOTOMO
GRAND RÉCIF SUD
Copyright © by Rand McNally & Co.
Map prepared by George Philip & Son Ltd., London.
A-593100-764

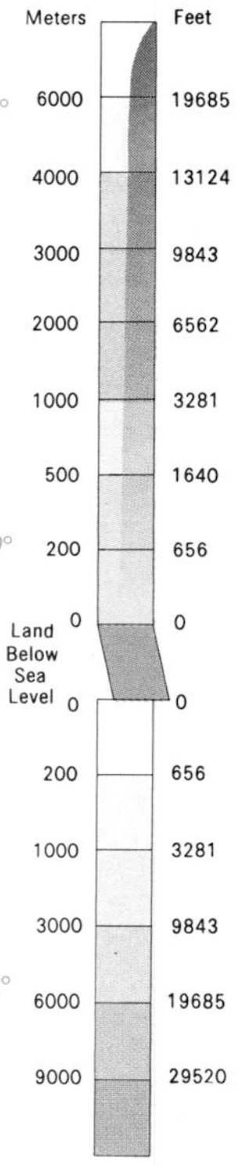
Meters
Feet
6000
19685
4000
13124
3000
9843
2000
6562
1000
3281
500
1640
200
656
Land Below Sea Level
0
0
200
656
1000
3281
3000
9843
6000
19685
9000
29520

| MAP FORM | bay | cape | île | lagoon | mount | point | passage | strait |
|---|---|---|---|---|---|---|---|---|
| ENGLISH | bay | cape | island | lagoon | mount | point | passage | strait |
| DEUTSCH | Bucht | Kap | Insel | Haff | Berg | Landspitze | Durchfahrt | Meeresstrasse |
| ESPAÑOL | bahía | cabo | isla | laguna | montaña | punta | pasaje | estrecho |
| FRANÇAIS | baie | cap | île | lagune | mont | pointe | passage | détroit |
| PORTUGUÊS | baía | cabo | ilha | laguna | monte | ponta | passagem | estreito |

Kilometers 0 100 200 300 Km.
Statute Miles 0 100 200 300 Mi.

Scale 1:6,000,000

One centimeter represents 60 kilometers.
One inch represents approximately 95 miles.
Lambert Conformal Conic Projection

155°
150°
145°
140°
135°
130°
125°
120°
115°
110°
105°
100°
60°
55°
50°
45°
40°
95°
Beaufort Sea
Gulf of Alaska
PACIFIC OCEAN
ALASKA
ALASKA RANGE
UNITED STATES
CANADA
YUKON
NORTHWEST
BANKS ISLAND
VICTORIA ISLAND
MELVILLE ISLAND
PRINCE OF WALES ISLAND
Fairbanks
Anchorage
Whitehorse
Prince Rupert
QUEEN CHARLOTTE ISLANDS
VANCOUVER ISLAND
Vancouver
Victoria
Bellingham
Seattle
Tacoma
Spokane
Portland
Salem
Eugene
COAST MOUNTAINS
ROCKY MOUNTAINS
MACKENZIE MTS
SELWYN MOUNTAINS
PELLY MOUNTAINS
BRITISH COLUMBIA
ALBERTA
SASKATCHEWAN
MANITOBA
Edmonton
Calgary
Lethbridge
Saskatoon
Regina
Winnipeg
Yellowknife
Fort Smith
Fort McMurray
Prince George
Lloydminster
Prince Albert
Moose Jaw
Brandon
Great Falls
Helena
Butte
Billings
Missoula
Boise
Idaho Falls
MONTANA
OREGON
NORTH DAKOTA
SOUTH DAKOTA
MINNESOTA
WYOMING
NEBRASKA
NEVADA
GREAT BASIN
Bismarck
Fargo
Minneapolis
Rapid City
Sioux Falls
Salt Lake City
Ogden
Casper
Cheyenne
Reno
Sacramento
Stockton
SAN FRANCISCO
Oakland
San Jose
Fresno
CASCADE RANGE
SIERRA NEVADA
CALIFORNIA

| | | | | | | | | |
|---|---|---|---|---|---|---|---|---|
| ENGLISH | bay | cape | island | lake, l. | mountains, mts. | point | range | strait |
| DEUTSCH | Bucht | Kap | Insel | See | Berge | Landspitze | Gebirge | Meeresstrasse |
| ESPAÑOL | bahía | cabo | isla | lago | montañas | punta | sierra | estrecho |
| FRANÇAIS | baie | cap | île | lac | montagnes | pointe | chaîne | détroit |
| PORTUGUÊS | baía | cabo | ilha | lago | montanhas | ponta | serra | estreito |

Map continues pages 178-179

GREENLAND
KALAALLIT NUNAAT
(Denmark)
Baffin Bay
Davis Strait
BAFFIN ISLAND
Labrador Sea
ATLANTIC OCEAN
Hudson Bay
Foxe Basin
Ungava Bay
PÉNINSULE D'UNGAVA
LABRADOR
NEWFOUNDLAND
QUÉBEC
ONTARIO
NEW BRUNSWICK
NOVA SCOTIA
PRINCE EDWARD ISLAND
ST. PIERRE AND MIQUELON
James Bay
Gulf of St. Lawrence
Gulf of Maine
All islands within Hudson Bay, James Bay, and Ungava Bay lie within Northwest Territories
MONTREAL
Ottawa
Québec
TORONTO
Halifax
St. John's
BOSTON
NEW YORK
PHILADELPHIA
DETROIT
CHICAGO
Copyright © by Rand McNally & Co.
Map prepared by Rand McNally & Co.
A-520200-264

Kilometers 0 200 400 600 Km.

Statute Miles 0 200 400 600 Mi.

Scale 1:12,000,000

One centimeter represents 120 kilometers.
One inch represents approximately 190 miles.
Lambert Conformal Conic Projection

135°
130°
125°
120°
115°
110°
105°
100°
45°
40°
35°
30°
25°
20°
PACIFIC OCEAN
VANCOUVER ISLAND
BRITISH COLUMBIA
ALBERTA
SASKATCHEWAN
CANADA
UNITED STATES
MONTANA
NORTH DAKOTA
SOUTH DAKOTA
IDAHO
WYOMING
NEBRASKA
OREGON
NEVADA
UTAH
COLORADO
KANSAS
CALIFORNIA
ARIZONA
NEW MEXICO
OKLAHOMA
TEXAS
MEXICO
ROCKY MOUNTAINS
CASCADE RANGE
COAST RANGES
SIERRA NEVADA
GREAT BASIN
SIERRA MADRE OCCIDENTAL
SIERRA MADRE ORIENTAL
Tropic of Cancer
Edmonton
Calgary
Saskatoon
Regina
Vancouver
Victoria
Seattle
Tacoma
Spokane
Portland
Salem
Eugene
Great Falls
Helena
Butte
Billings
Boise
Idaho Falls
Pocatello
Ogden
Salt Lake City
Provo
Reno
Sacramento
SAN FRANCISCO
Oakland
San Jose
Stockton
Modesto
Fresno
Bakersfield
Las Vegas
LOS ANGELES
Long Beach
Santa Ana
Anaheim
Riverside
San Bernardino
San Diego
Tijuana
Mexicali
Ensenada
Phoenix
Tucson
Albuquerque
Santa Fe
El Paso
Ciudad Juárez
Denver
Colorado Springs
Pueblo
Cheyenne
Casper
Rapid City
Bismarck
Amarillo
Lubbock
Odessa
Midland
Abilene
Chihuahua
Hermosillo
Ciudad Obregón
Los Mochis
Culiacán
Mazatlán
Durango
Torreón
Monterrey
Saltillo
Nuevo Laredo
Laredo
Aguascalientes
Zacatecas
San Luis Potosí
Guadalajara
León
Tepic
Copyright © by Rand McNally & Co.
Map prepared by Rand McNally & Co.
A-520500-264 -8 -9 -16

| | | | | | | | | |
|---|---|---|---|---|---|---|---|---|
| ENGLISH | bay | cape | desert | island | lake | mountains | peak | range |
| DEUTSCH | Bucht | Kap | Wüste | Insel | See | Berge | Gipfel | Gebirge |
| ESPAÑOL | bahía | cabo | desierto | isla | lago | montañas | pico | sierra |
| FRANÇAIS | baie | cap | désert | île | lac | montagnes | cime | chaîne |
| PORTUGUÊS | baía | cabo | deserto | ilha | lago | montanhas | pico | serra |

Map continues pages 230-231

Map continues
pages 176-177

ONTARIO
QUÉBEC
ATLANTIC
OCEAN
GULF OF MEXICO
CARIBBEAN SEA
APPALACHIAN MOUNTAINS
WEST INDIES
BAHAMAS
NEW YORK
WASHINGTON
BOSTON
PHILADELPHIA
CHICAGO
DETROIT
TORONTO
MONTRÉAL
LA HABANA
Atlanta
Miami
New Orleans
Jacksonville
Nashville
Memphis
Cincinnati
Cleveland
Pittsburgh
Baltimore
Richmond
Norfolk
Charlotte
Québec
Ottawa
Halifax
BERMUDA (U.K.)
Straits of Florida
Tropic of Cancer
HAITI
DOMINICAN REPUBLIC
SANTO DOMINGO
Port-au-Prince
HISPANIOLA
Santiago de Cuba
CAYMAN IS. (U.K.)
YUCATAN PENINSULA
Mérida
Cancún

Kilometers 0 200 400 600 Km.
Statute Miles 0 200 400 600 Mi.

Scale 1:12,000,000
One centimeter represents 120 kilometers.
One inch represents approximately 190 miles.
Albers Conical Equal-Area Projection

Chukchi Sea
ARCTIC
BERING SEA
Bristol Bay
Norton Sound
Kotzebue Sound
Bering Strait
Anadyrskij zaliv
PACIF
RUSSIA ROSSIJA
UNITED STATES
International Date Line
Arctic Circle
ANADYRSKOJE PLOSKOGORJE
ČUKOTSKIJ AVTONOMNYJ OKRUG
ČUKOTSKIJ POLUOSTROV
SEWARD PENINSULA
LISBURNE PENINSULA
DE LONG MOUNTAINS
BROOK
BAIRD MOUNTAINS
SCHWATKA MOUNTAINS
KUSKOKWIM
AHKLUN MOUNTAINS
KILBUCK MOUNTAINS
TAYLOR MOUNTAINS
ALASKA PENINSULA
ALEUTIAN ISLANDS
ANDREANOF ISLANDS
ISLANDS OF FOUR MOUNTAINS
FOX ISLANDS
KRENITZIN ISLANDS
SHUMAGIN ISLANDS
PRIBILOF ISLANDS
SAINT LAWRENCE ISLAND
SAINT MATTHEW ISLAND
NUNIVAK ISLAND
NELSON ISLAND
UNIMAK ISLAND
UNALASKA ISLAND
UMNAK ISLAND
ATKA ISLAND
ADAK ISLAND
Saint Paul Island
Saint George Island
Anadyr'
Providenija
Uelen
Barrow
Wainwright
Point Hope
Kotzebue
Nome
Unalakleet
Bethel
Dillingham
King Salmon
Port Heiden
Dutch Harbor
Cold Bay
Gambell
Meters
Feet
6000 19685
4000 13124
3000 9843
2000 6562
1000 3281
500 1640
200 656
0 0
Land Below Sea Level
0 0
200 656
1000 3281
3000 9843
6000 19685
9000 29520

| ENGLISH | bay | cape | island, i. | lake, l. | mount, mt. | peak, pk. | point |
|---|---|---|---|---|---|---|---|
| DEUTSCH | Bucht | Kap | Insel | See | Berg | Gipfel | Landspitze |
| ESPAÑOL | bahía | cabo | isla | lago | monte | pico | punta |
| FRANÇAIS | baie | cap | île | lac | mont | cime | pointe |
| PORTUGUÊS | baía | cabo | ilha | lago | monte | pico | ponta |

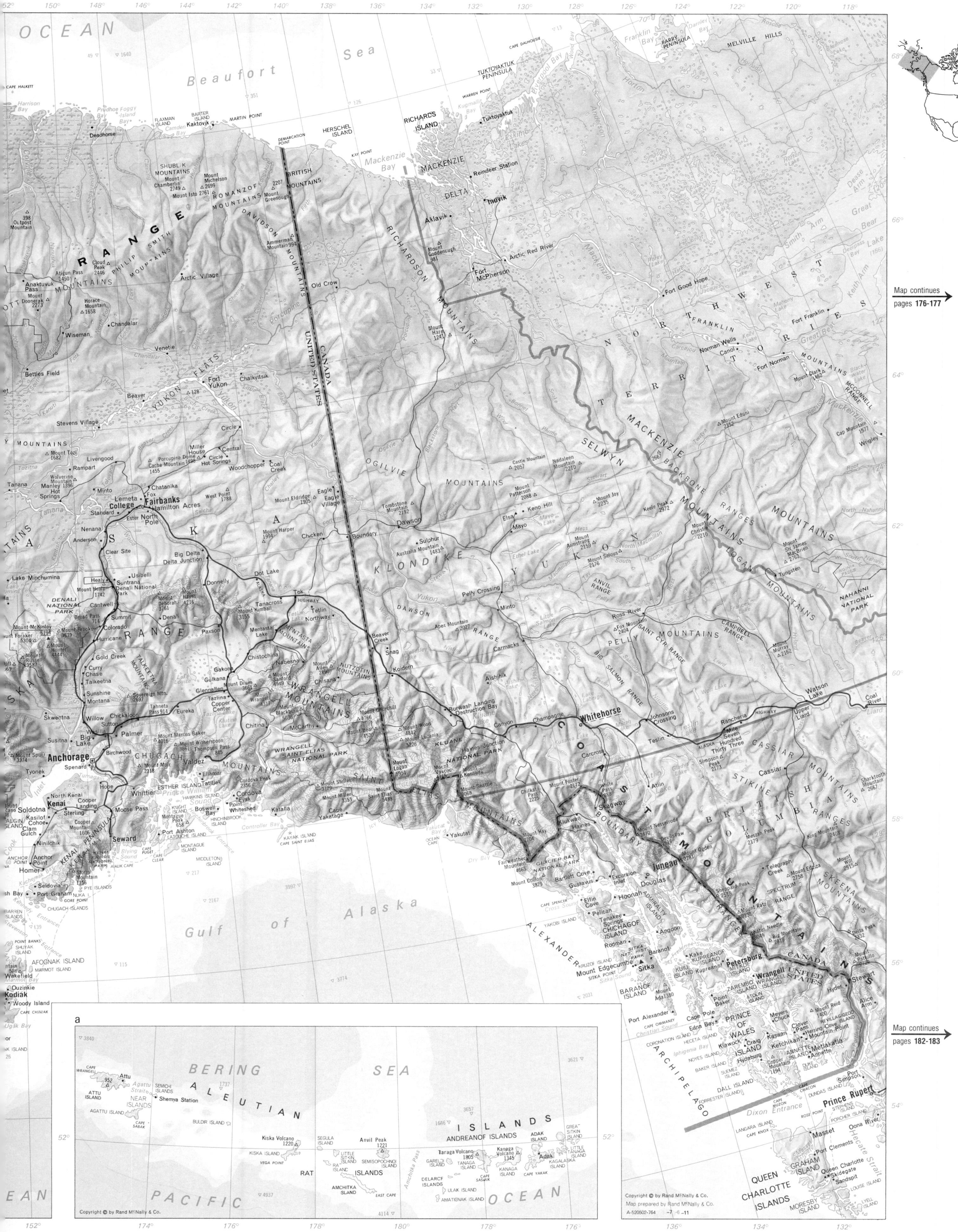
OCEAN
Beaufort Sea
RICHARDS ISLAND
HERSCHEL ISLAND
Mackenzie Bay
MACKENZIE DELTA
Tuktoyaktuk
Inuvik
Aklavik
Fort McPherson
Arctic Red River
Fort Good Hope
Norman Wells
Fort Norman
Fort Franklin
NORTHWEST TERRITORIES
FRANKLIN MOUNTAINS
MACKENZIE MOUNTAINS
SELWYN MOUNTAINS
RICHARDSON MOUNTAINS
BRITISH MOUNTAINS
BROOKS RANGE
PHILIP SMITH MOUNTAINS
ROMANZOF MOUNTAINS
Deadhorse
Kaktovik
Arctic Village
Old Crow
UNITED STATES
CANADA
Wiseman
Chandalar
Venetie
Fort Yukon
Chalkyitsik
YUKON FLATS
Betties Field
Beaver
Stevens Village
Circle
Central
Livengood
Rampart
Tanana
Manley Hot Springs
Chatanika
College
Fairbanks
Hamilton Acres
North Pole
Nenana
Anderson
Clear Site
Big Delta
Delta Junction
Eagle
Eagle Village
Chicken
Boundary
Dawson
OGILVIE MOUNTAINS
KLONDIKE
YUKON
Mayo
Keno Hill
Elsa
Pelly Crossing
Minto
Carmacks
Ross River
PELLY MOUNTAINS
Tok
Tanacross
Tetlin
Northway
Dot Lake
Healy
Cantwell
Denali
Paxson
Mentasta Lake
Chistochina
Gakona
Gulkana
Glennallen
Copper Center
Chitina
WRANGELL MOUNTAINS
Beaver Creek
Koidern
Burwash Landing
Destruction Bay
Haines Junction
KLUANE NATIONAL PARK
Whitehorse
Carcross
Teslin
Watson Lake
Upper Liard
CASSIAR MOUNTAINS
Cassiar
Mount McKinley 6194
DENALI NATIONAL PARK
ALASKA RANGE
TALKEETNA MOUNTAINS
Talkeetna
Willow
Wasilla
Palmer
Sutton
Chickaloon
Eureka
CHUGACH MOUNTAINS
Anchorage
Tyonek
Valdez
Whittier
Cordova
Kenai
Soldotna
Sterling
Seward
Homer
Seldovia
Port Graham
KENAI PENINSULA
Katalla
Yakataga
Yakutat
Mount Logan 6050
Mount Saint Elias 5489
SAINT ELIAS MOUNTAINS
WRANGELL-SAINT ELIAS NATIONAL PARK
Gulf of Alaska
Skagway
Haines
Klukwan
GLACIER BAY NATIONAL PARK
Juneau
Douglas
Gustavus
Hoonah
Pelican
Tenakee Springs
CHICHAGOF ISLAND
BARANOF ISLAND
Sitka
Angoon
Petersburg
Wrangell
Kake
Stewart
Hyder
PRINCE OF WALES ISLAND
Craig
Klawock
Hydaburg
Ketchikan
Metlakatla
ALEXANDER ARCHIPELAGO
COAST MOUNTAINS
SKEENA MOUNTAINS
BRITISH COLUMBIA
Prince Rupert
Dixon Entrance
QUEEN CHARLOTTE ISLANDS
GRAHAM ISLAND
MORESBY ISLAND
Masset
Port Clements
Queen Charlotte
Skidegate
Sandspit
Kodiak
AFOGNAK ISLAND
a
BERING SEA
ALEUTIAN ISLANDS
NEAR ISLANDS
RAT ISLANDS
ANDREANOF ISLANDS
Attu
Shemya Station
Adak
PACIFIC OCEAN
Map continues pages 176-177
Map continues pages 182-183
Copyright © by Rand McNally & Co.
Map prepared by Rand McNally & Co.
A-520502-764

Kilometers 0 100 200 300 Km.
Statute Miles 0 100 200 300 Mi.

Scale 1:6,000,000
One centimeter represents 60 kilometers.
One inch represents approximately 95 miles.
Lambert Conformal Conic Projection

Map continues pages 180-181

Meters
Feet
6000 19685
4000 13124
3000 9843
2000 6562
1000 3281
500 1640
200 656
Land Below Sea Level
0 0
200 656
1000 3281
3000 9843
6000 19685
9000 29520
U.S.
CANADA
Dixon Entrance
QUEEN CHARLOTTE ISLANDS
GRAHAM ISLAND
MORESBY ISLAND
Hecate Strait
Queen Charlotte Sound
Prince Rupert
Kitimat
COAST MOUNTAINS
PACIFIC RANGES
NECHAKO PLATEAU
FRASER PLATEAU
Prince George
Quesnel
VANCOUVER ISLAND
Port Alberni
Nanaimo
VANCOUVER
Victoria
Bellingham
Port Angeles
Strait of Juan de Fuca
UNITED STATES
PACIFIC OCEAN
TWEEDSMUIR PROVINCIAL PARK
STRATHCONA PROVINCIAL PARK
PACIFIC RIM NATIONAL PARK
OLYMPIC NATIONAL PARK



| ENGLISH | creek | Indian reserve | inlet | island | lake, l. | mountain | peak | provincial park | sound |
|---|---|---|---|---|---|---|---|---|---|
| DEUTSCH | Bach | Indianerreservation | Einfahrt | Insel | See | Berg | Gipfel | Provinz-Park | Sund |
| ESPAÑOL | riachuelo | reserva de Indios | abra | isla | lago | montaña | pico | parque de provincia | sonda |
| FRANÇAIS | crique | réserve indienne | bras de mer | île | lac | montagne | cime | parc provincial | détroit |
| PORTUGUÊS | riacho | reserva indígena | enseada | ilha | lago | montanha | pico | parque provincial | estreito |

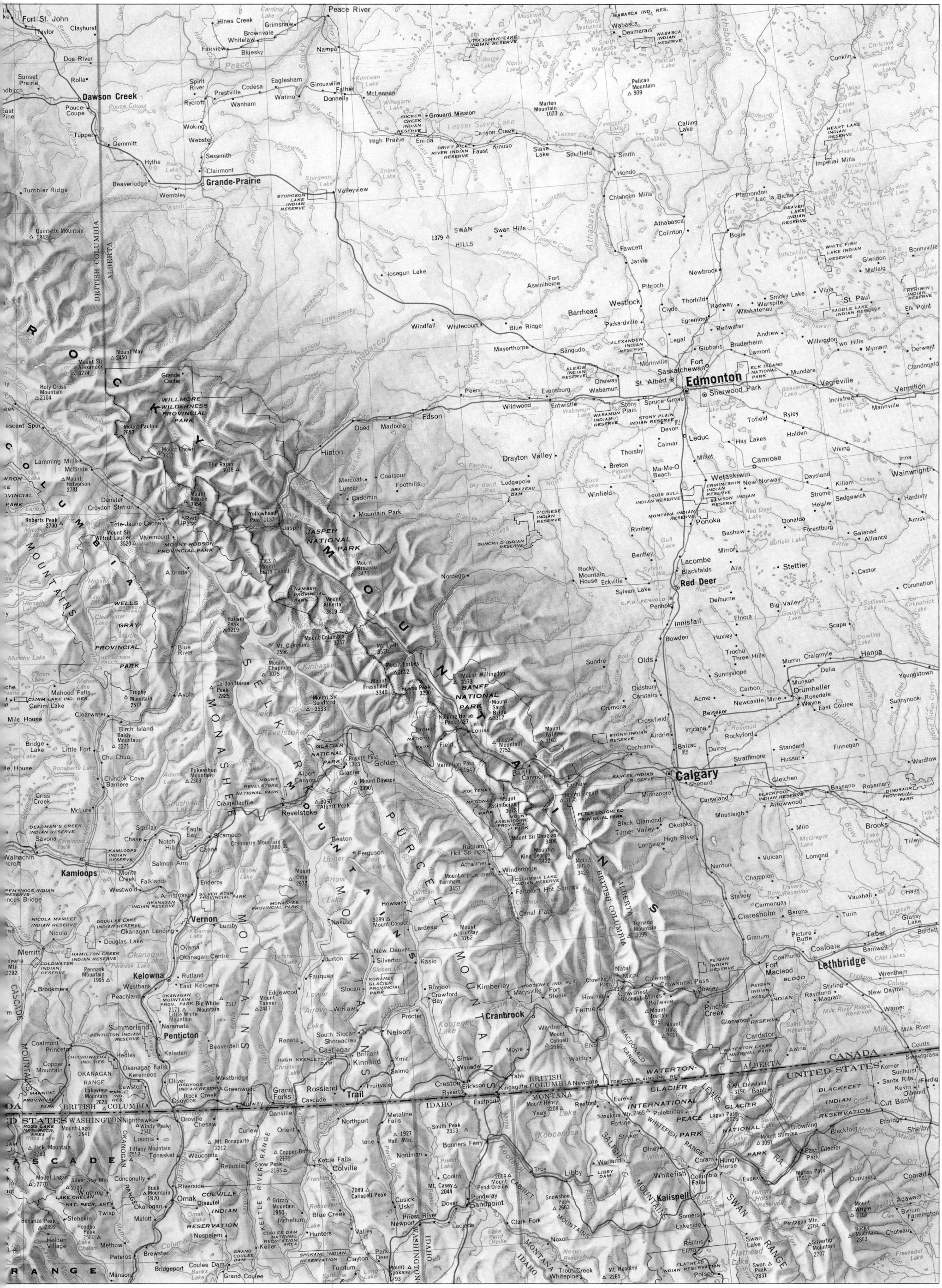
Fort St. John
Dawson Creek
Grande-Prairie
Peace River
Lesser Slave Lake
Slave Lake
SWAN HILLS
Athabasca
Whitecourt
Barrhead
Westlock
St. Albert
Edmonton
Sherwood Park
Fort Saskatchewan
Vegreville
Vermilion
Wainwright
Camrose
Wetaskiwin
Leduc
Ponoka
Edson
Hinton
Jasper
JASPER NATIONAL PARK
Red Deer
Drumheller
Hanna
Calgary
Banff
BANFF NATIONAL PARK
Lethbridge
Fort Macleod
Medicine Hat
Cranbrook
Kamloops
Vernon
Kelowna
Penticton
Revelstoke
Golden
Nelson
Trail
Kalispell
ROCKY MOUNTAINS
COLUMBIA MOUNTAINS
SELKIRK MOUNTAINS
MONASHEE MOUNTAINS
PURCELL MOUNTAINS
BRITISH COLUMBIA
ALBERTA
CANADA
UNITED STATES
WASHINGTON
IDAHO
MONTANA
GLACIER NATIONAL PARK
CASCADE RANGE

Map continues pages 184-185

Map continues pages 202-203

Kilometers 0 50 100 150 Km.
Statute Miles 0 50 100 150 Mi.

Scale 1:3,000,000
One centimeter represents 30 kilometers.
One inch represents approximately 47 miles.
Lambert Conformal Conic Projection

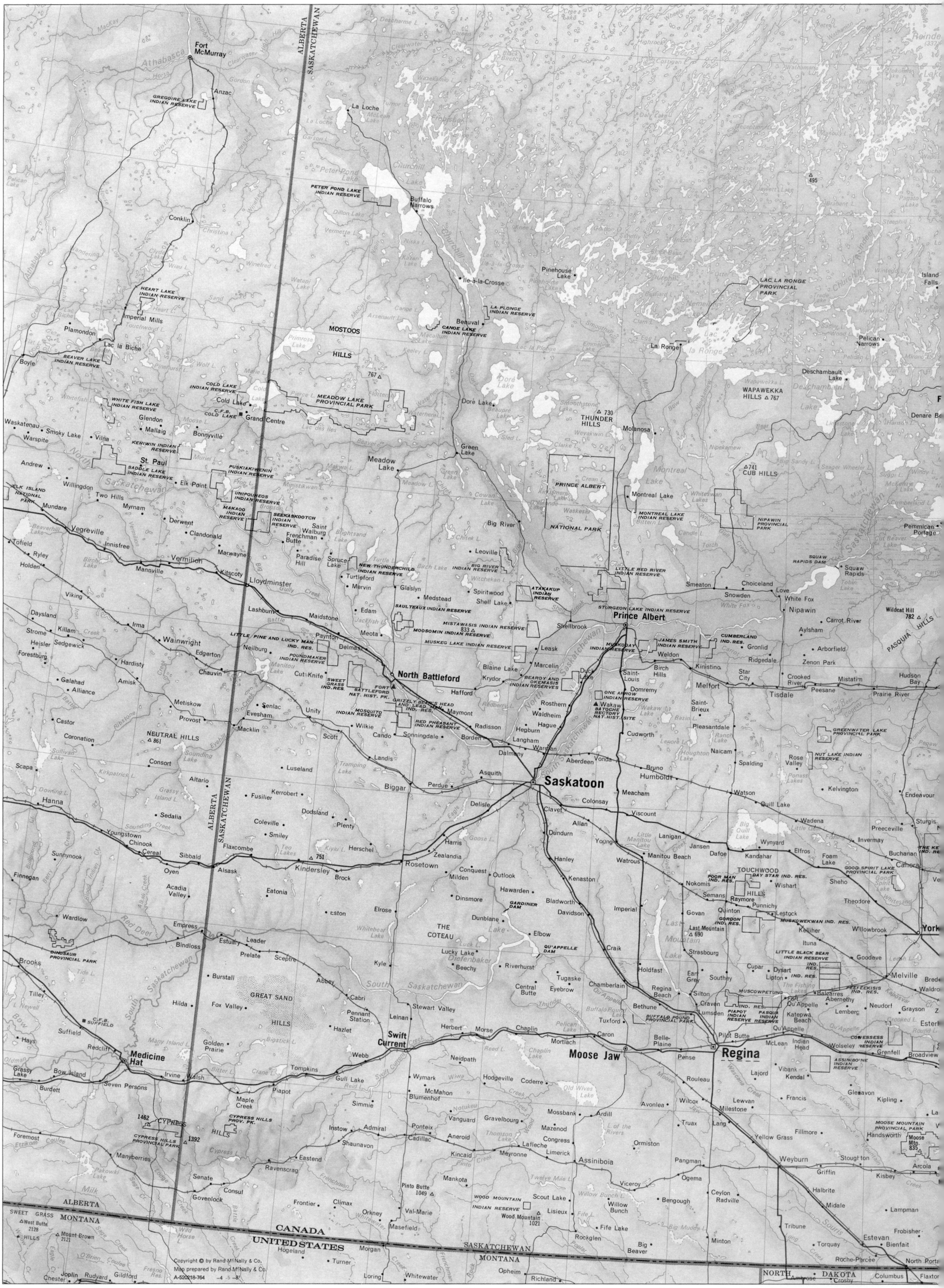
Fort McMurray
La Loche
Buffalo Narrows
Ile-à-la-Crosse
La Ronge
Lac la Ronge
Lac la Biche
Cold Lake
Grand Centre
St. Paul
Lloydminster
North Battleford
Prince Albert
Saskatoon
Moose Jaw
Regina
Swift Current
Medicine Hat
Brooks
Hanna
Kindersley
Biggar
Melfort
Humboldt
Yorkton
Melville
Weyburn
Estevan
Assiniboia
PRINCE ALBERT NATIONAL PARK
MEADOW LAKE PROVINCIAL PARK
CYPRESS HILLS PROV. PK.
GREAT SAND HILLS
MOSTOOS HILLS
THUNDER HILLS
THE COTEAU
ALBERTA
SASKATCHEWAN
CANADA
UNITED STATES
MONTANA
NORTH DAKOTA
Copyright © by Rand McNally & Co.
Map prepared by Rand McNally & Co.

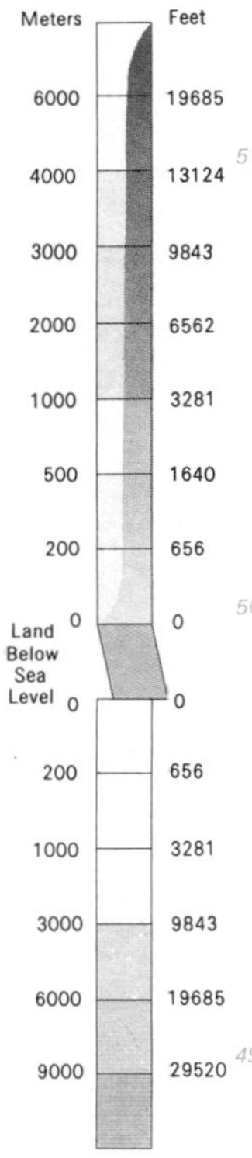
Meters
Feet
6000 19685
4000 13124
3000 9843
2000 6562
1000 3281
500 1640
200 656
0 0
Land Below Sea Level
0 0
200 656
1000 3281
3000 9843
6000 19685
9000 29520

Map continues pages 182-183

Map continues pages 202-203

Map continues pages 198-199

| | | | | | | |
|---|---|---|---|---|---|---|
| ENGLISH | creek, cr. | hills | Indian reserve | island, i. | lake, l. | provincial park |
| DEUTSCH | Bach | Hügel | Indianerreservation | Insel | See | Provinz-Park |
| ESPAÑOL | riachuelo | colinas | reserva de Indios | isla | lago | parque de provincia |
| FRANÇAIS | crique | collines | réserve indienne | île | lac | parc provincial |
| PORTUGUÊS | riacho | colinas | reserva indígena | ilha | lago | parque provincial |

Thompson
Winnipeg
Brandon
Portage-la-Prairie
Kenora
Selkirk
Dauphin
Grand Rapids
Norway House
Cross Lake
Gods Lake
Island Lake
Berens River
Poplar Hill
Pikangikum
Red Lake
Ear Falls
Dryden
Sioux Lookout
International Falls
Gillam
Ilford
Pikwitonei
Thicket Portage
Wabowden
Sherridon
Snow Lake
Oxford House
Shamattawa
Opasquia
York Factory
Port Nelson
South Indian Lake
Nelson House
Lake Winnipeg
Lake Winnipegosis
Lake Manitoba
Cedar Lake
Playgreen Lake
MANITOBA
ONTARIO
MINNESOTA
CANADA
UNITED STATES
WETIKO HILLS
DUCK MOUNTAIN
RIDING MOUNTAIN NATIONAL PARK
WHITESHELL PROVINCIAL PARK
HECLA PROVINCIAL PARK
INTERNATIONAL PEACE GARDEN

Map continues pages 190-191

Kilometers 0 50 100 150 Km.
Statute Miles 0 50 100 150 Mi.

Scale 1:3,000,000

One centimeter represents 30 kilometers.
One inch represents approximately 47 miles.
Lambert Conformal Conic Projection

72° 71° 70° 69° 68° 67° 66° 65° 64° 63°
51° 50° 49° 48° 47° 46° 45° 44°
Sept-Îles
Moisie
Baie de Moisie
Clarke City
Port-Cartier
Rivière-Pentecôte
Islets-Caribou
Baie-Trinité
Godbout
POINTE DES MONTS
Baie-Comeau
Hauterive
Betsiamites
RÉSERVE PORT-CARTIER SEPT-ÎLES
BARRAGE DANIEL-JOHNSON
Magpie
Rivière-au-Tonnerre
Mingan
Havre-St.-Pierre
Lac-Allard
Baie-Johan-Beetz
ÎLES DE MINGAN
MINGAN ARCHIPELAGO NAT. PARK
NEWF.
QUÉ.
Détroit de Jacques-Cartier
Baie-Ste.-Claire
Port-Menier
POINTE DE L'OUEST
CAP HENRI
ÎLE D'ANTICOSTI
POINTE DU SUD-OUEST
Détroit d'Honguedo
Rivière-de-la-Chaloupe
Alma
Kénogami
Arvida
Jonquière
Chicoutimi
La Baie
Forestville
Portneuf-sur-Mer
Sault-au-Mouton
Tadoussac
Saint Lawrence
Matane
Ste.-Félicité
Mont-Joli
Rimouski
Bic
St.-Fabien
Trois-Pistoles
St.-Éloi
Rivière-du-Loup
Cap-Chat
Ste.-Anne-des-Monts
Ste.-Marthe-de-Gaspé
Rivière-à-Claude
Madeleine-Centre
St.-Yvon
Mont Jacques-Cartier 1237
CHIC-CHOCS
PÉNINSULE DE LA GASPÉSIE
Fontenelle
Gaspé
PARC NATIONAL DE FORILLON
Percé
ÎLE BONAVENTURE
Grande-Rivière
Chandler
Newport
POINTE AU MAQUEREAU
Amqui
Causapscal
Nouvelle
New-Richmond
Caplan
Bonaventure
New-Carlisle
Pointe-à-la-Garde
Matapédia
Campbellton
Dalhousie
Jacquet River
Chaleur Bay
Miscou Centre
MISCOU POINT
MISCOU ISLAND
Lamèque
ÎLE LAMÈQUE
Shippegan
Caraquet
Grande-Anse
Beresford
Bathurst
Tracadie
Squaw Cap Mountain 483
Blue Mountain 528
Kedgwick
St.-Quentin
MOUNT CARLETON PROVINCIAL PARK
Mount Carleton 820
Clermont
La Malbaie
Baie-St.-Paul
ÎLE AUX COUDRES
La Pocatière
St.-Jean-Port-Joli
Montmagny
Beaupré
Beauport
Québec
Lauzon
Lévis
Ste.-Foy
Cabano
Dégelis
Edmundston
Madawaska
Fort Kent
Van Buren
Grand Falls
Eagle Lake
Caribou
Presque Isle
Fort Fairfield
Perth-Andover
Houlton
Woodstock
Fredericton
Oromocto
Marysville
Nashwaaksis
Newcastle
Chatham
Miramichi Bay
Neguac
POINT ESCUMINAC
Point Sapin
Richibucto
Rexton
Buctouche
Moncton
Dieppe
Shediac
Sackville
Amherst
Saint John
Sussex
St. Stephen
Calais
St. Andrews
Eastport
GRAND MANAN ISLAND
PRINCE EDWARD ISLAND
Tignish
Alberton
Summerside
Charlottetown
Souris
Montague
Borden
Cape Tormentine
Northumberland Strait
Pictou
New Glasgow
Stellarton
Westville
Truro
Antigonish
Springhill
Parrsboro
Minas Basin
Windsor
Wolfville
Kentville
Digby
Annapolis Royal
Yarmouth
Halifax
Dartmouth
Lunenburg
Bridgewater
Liverpool
Shelburne
Barrington
NOVA SCOTIA
Bay of Fundy
Gulf of Maine
Bangor
Orono
Old Town
Ellsworth
Bar Harbor
ACADIA NATIONAL PARK
Waterville
Augusta
Lewiston
Auburn
Brunswick
Bath
Portland
Biddeford
Saco
Old Orchard Beach
Rockland
Camden
Belfast
Millinocket
Mount Katahdin 1606
BAXTER STATE PARK
Jackman
Lac-Mégantic
St.-Georges
Thetford Mines
APPALACHIAN MOUNTAINS
NOTRE DAME MOUNTAINS
QUÉBEC
NEW BRUNSWICK
MAINE
U.S.
CANADA

| Meters | Feet |
|---|---|
| 6000 | 19685 |
| 4000 | 13124 |
| 3000 | 9843 |
| 2000 | 6562 |
| 1000 | 3281 |
| 500 | 1640 |
| 200 | 656 |
| 0 | 0 |
| Land Below Sea Level 0 | 0 |
| 200 | 656 |
| 1000 | 3281 |
| 3000 | 9843 |
| 6000 | 19685 |
| 9000 | 29520 |

Map continues pages 188-189

| | | | | | | | | |
|---|---|---|---|---|---|---|---|---|
| ENGLISH | bay | cape | dam | island | lake, l. | mountain | point | strait |
| DEUTSCH | Bucht | Kap | Damm | Insel | See | Berg | Landspitze | Meeresstrasse |
| ESPAÑOL | bahía | cabo | presa | isla | lago | montaña | punta | estrecho |
| FRANÇAIS | baie | cap | barrage | île | lac | montagne | pointe | détroit |
| PORTUGUÊS | baía | cabo | represa | ilha | lago | montanha | ponta | estreito |

LABRADOR
SEA
ATLANTIC
OCEAN
NEWFOUNDLAND
LONG RANGE MOUNTAINS
QUÉBEC
NEWF.
NEWFOUNDLAND
CANADA
SAINT PIERRE
AND MIQUELON
(France)
SAINT-PIERRE-
ET-MIQUELON
Saint-Pierre
St. John's
Corner Brook
Gander
Grand Falls
Stephenville
Channel-Port-aux-Basques
St. Anthony
Glace Bay
Sydney
North Sydney
Sydney Mines
CAPE BRETON ISLAND
SABLE ISLAND
(N.S.)
ST. PAUL ISLAND
(N.S.)
Cabot
Strait
AVALON
PENINSULA
BURIN
PENINSULA
GROS MORNE
NATIONAL PARK
TERRA NOVA
NATIONAL PARK
CAPE BRETON
HIGHLANDS
NATIONAL PARK
FORTRESS OF LOUISBOURG
NATIONAL HISTORIC PARK
ÎLES
MONGER
Copyright © by Rand McNally & Co.
Map prepared by Rand McNally & Co.
A-520219-764

Kilometers 0 50 100 150 Km.
Statute Miles 0 50 100 150 Mi.

Scale 1:3,000,000

One centimeter represents 30 kilometers.
One inch represents approximately 47 miles.
Lambert Conformal Conic Projection

Map continues pages 190-191

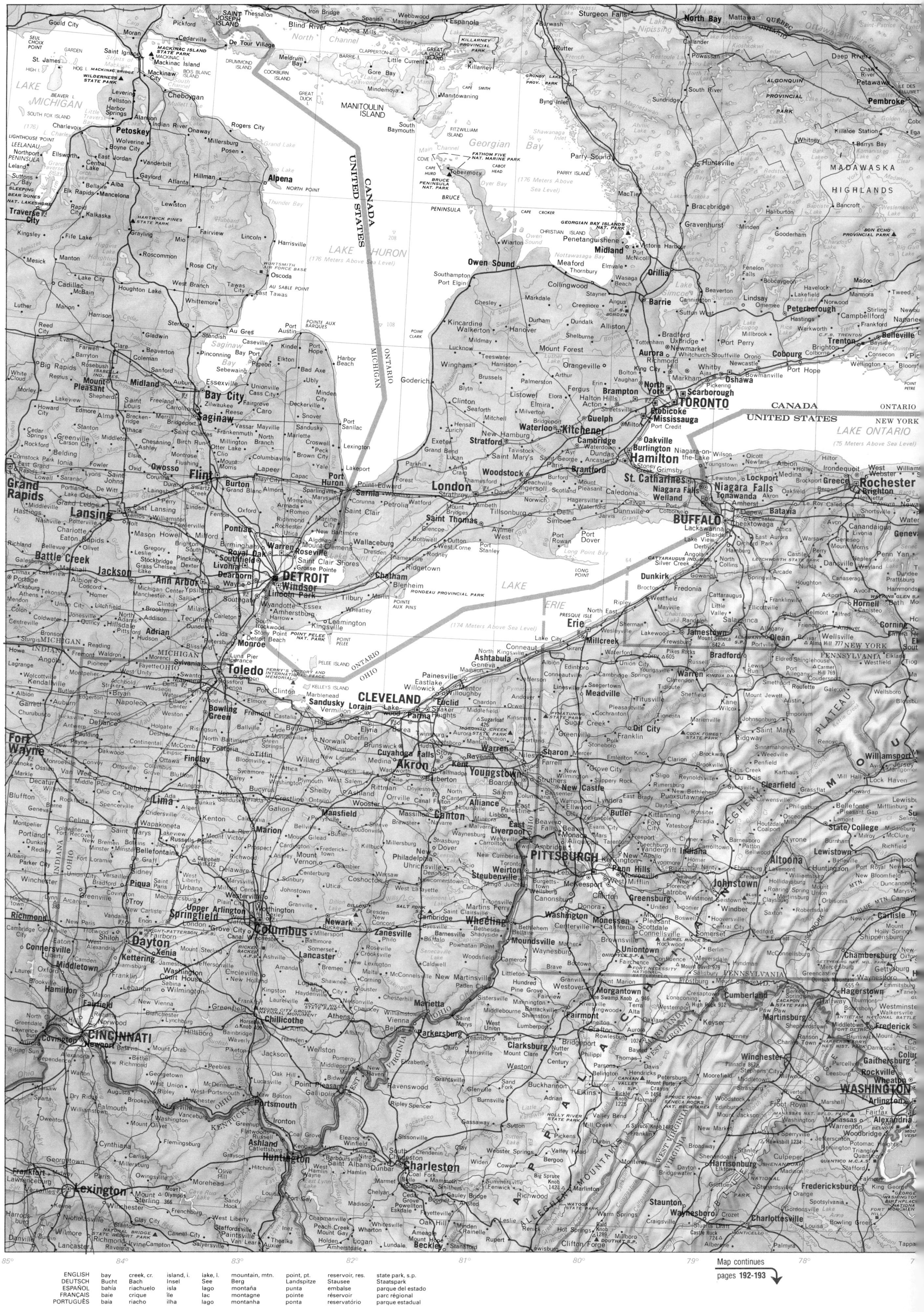
LAKE MICHIGAN
LAKE HURON
(176 Meters Above Sea Level)
Georgian Bay
MANITOULIN ISLAND
CANADA
UNITED STATES
MICHIGAN
ONTARIO
LAKE ONTARIO
(75 Meters Above Sea Level)
LAKE ERIE
(174 Meters Above Sea Level)
NEW YORK
PENNSYLVANIA
OHIO
INDIANA
WEST VIRGINIA
VIRGINIA
MARYLAND
KENTUCKY
ALGONQUIN PROVINCIAL PARK
MADAWASKA HIGHLANDS
DETROIT
TORONTO
CLEVELAND
PITTSBURGH
BUFFALO
CINCINNATI
WASHINGTON
Columbus
Toledo
Lansing
Flint
Saginaw
Grand Rapids
Hamilton
Rochester
Erie
Akron
Dayton
Lexington
Charleston
Huntington
Wheeling
Youngstown
Canton
Ann Arbor
Windsor
London
Kitchener
Niagara Falls
Altoona
Johnstown
Cumberland
ALLEGHENY MOUNTAINS
APPALACHIAN PLATEAU

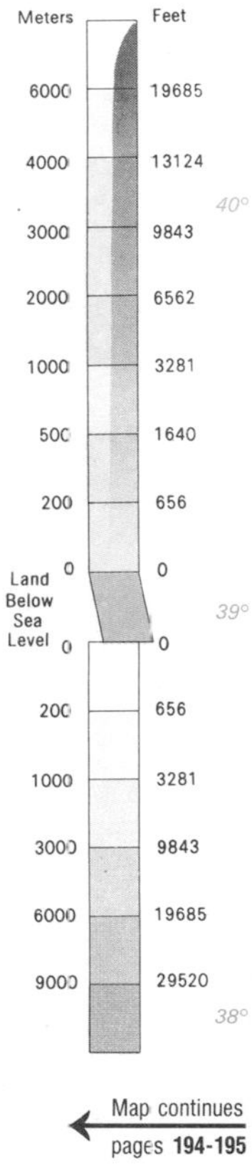
Meters
Feet
6000
19685
4000
13124
3000
9843
2000
6562
1000
3281
500
1640
200
656
0
0
Land Below Sea Level
200
656
1000
3281
3000
9843
6000
19685
9000
29520

Map continues pages 194-195

Map continues pages 192-193

| | | | | | | | | |
|---|---|---|---|---|---|---|---|---|
| ENGLISH | bay | creek, cr. | island, i. | lake, l. | mountain, mtn. | point, pt. | reservoir, res. | state park, s.p. |
| DEUTSCH | Bucht | Bach | Insel | See | Berg | Landspitze | Stausee | Staatspark |
| ESPAÑOL | bahía | riachuelo | isla | lago | montaña | punta | embalse | parque del estado |
| FRANÇAIS | baie | crique | île | lac | montagne | pointe | réservoir | parc régional |
| PORTUGUÊS | baía | riacho | ilha | lago | montanha | ponta | reservatório | parque estadual |

Map continues pages 186-187

Trois-Rivières
Sherbrooke
MONTRÉAL
Ottawa
Portland
Bangor
Augusta
Lewiston
Burlington
Montpelier
Concord
Manchester
Portsmouth
BOSTON
Worcester
Springfield
Hartford
Providence
New Haven
Bridgeport
Albany
Schenectady
Syracuse
Utica
Binghamton
Scranton
Wilkes-Barre
Allentown
Reading
Lancaster
Newark
NEW YORK
Paterson
Trenton
PHILADELPHIA
Camden
Wilmington
Atlantic City
Dover
Gulf of Maine
Massachusetts Bay
Cape Cod Bay
Long Island Sound
ATLANTIC OCEAN
Copyright © by Rand McNally & Co.
Map prepared by Rand McNally & Co.

Kilometers 0 50 100 150 Km.
Statute Miles 0 50 100 150 Mi.

Scale 1:3,000,000
One centimeter represents 30 kilometers.
One inch represents approximately 47 miles.
Albers Conical Equal-Area Projection

Map continues pages 184-185

Map continues pages 198-199

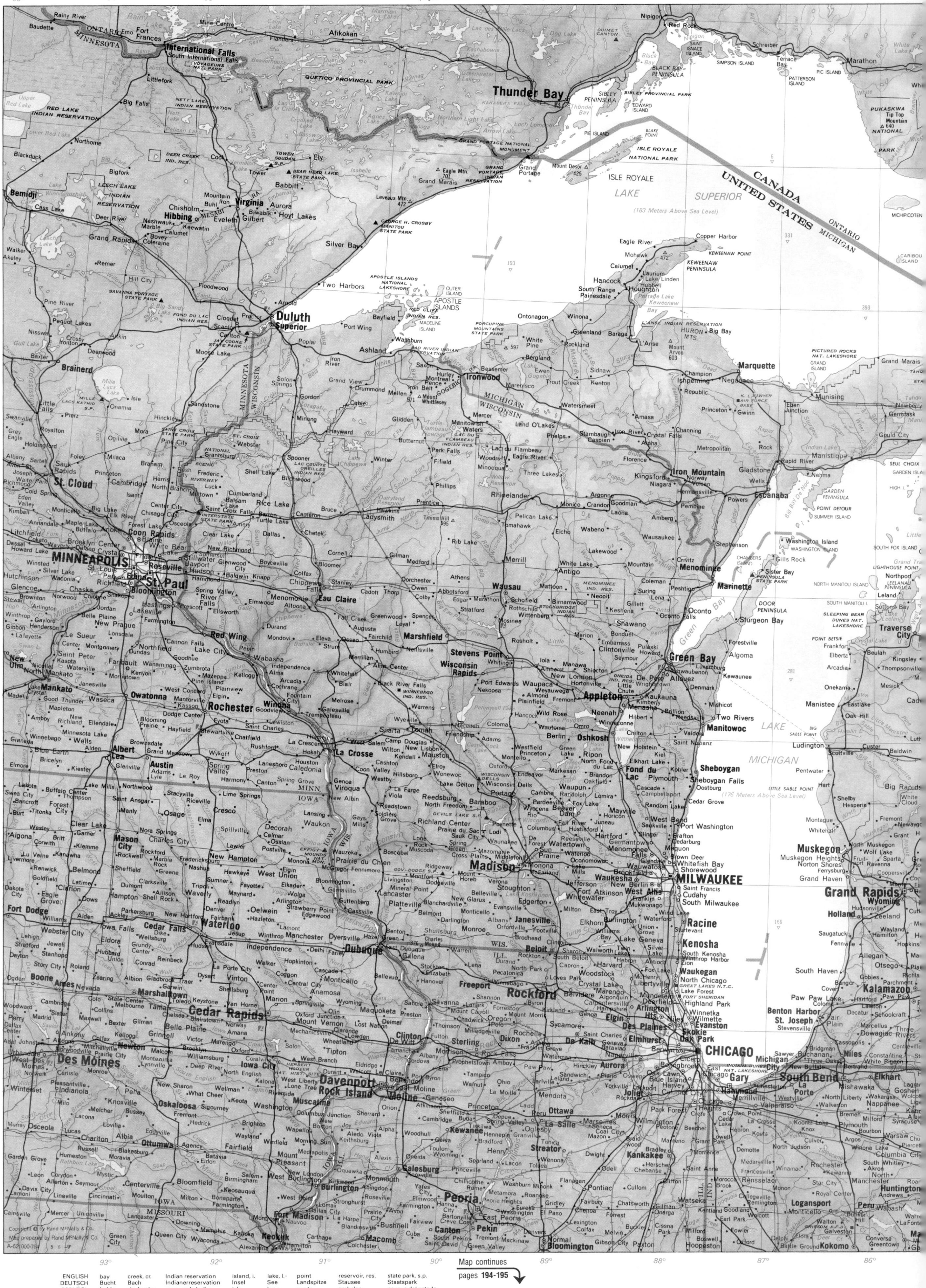
LAKE SUPERIOR
(183 Meters Above Sea Level)
LAKE MICHIGAN
(176 Meters Above Sea Level)
CANADA
UNITED STATES
ONTARIO
MINNESOTA
WISCONSIN
MICHIGAN
IOWA
ILL.
Thunder Bay
Duluth
Superior
MINNEAPOLIS
St. Paul
Rochester
Eau Claire
La Crosse
Green Bay
Appleton
Oshkosh
Madison
MILWAUKEE
Racine
Kenosha
CHICAGO
Rockford
Peoria
Des Moines
Cedar Rapids
Waterloo
Dubuque
Davenport
Rock Island
Moline
Iowa City
Muskegon
Grand Rapids
Kalamazoo
South Bend
Gary
Marquette
Iron Mountain
Escanaba
Marinette
Menominee
Sheboygan
Manitowoc
Wausau
Stevens Point
Wisconsin Rapids
Mankato
Owatonna
St. Cloud
Brainerd
Hibbing
Virginia
International Falls
ISLE ROYALE
Copyright © by Rand McNally & Co.
Map prepared by Rand McNally & Co.

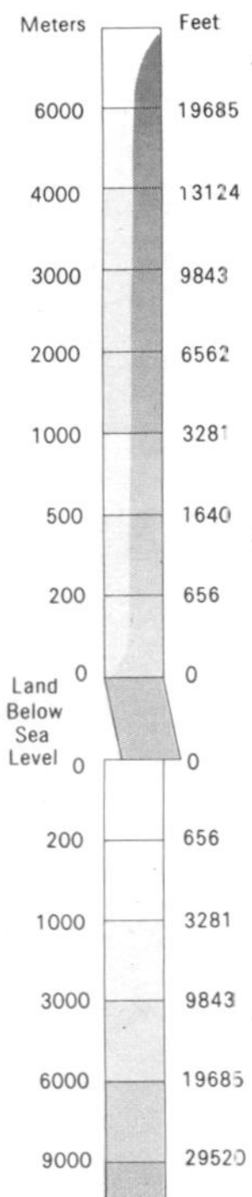
Meters
Feet
6000 19685
4000 13124
3000 9843
2000 6562
1000 3281
500 1640
200 656
0 0
Land Below Sea Level
0 0
200 656
1000 3281
3000 9843
6000 19685
9000 29520

Map continues pages 194-195

| | | | | | | | | | |
|---|---|---|---|---|---|---|---|---|---|
| ENGLISH | bay | creek, cr. | Indian reservation | island, i. | lake, l. | point | reservoir, res. | state park, s.p. |
| DEUTSCH | Bucht | Bach | Indianerreservation | Insel | See | Landspitze | Stausee | Staatspark |
| ESPAÑOL | bahía | riachuelo | reserva de Indios | isla | lago | punta | embalse | parque del estado |
| FRANÇAIS | baie | crique | réserve indienne | île | lac | pointe | réservoir | parc régional |
| PORTUGUÊS | baía | riacho | reserva indígena | ilha | lago | ponta | reservatório | parque estadual |

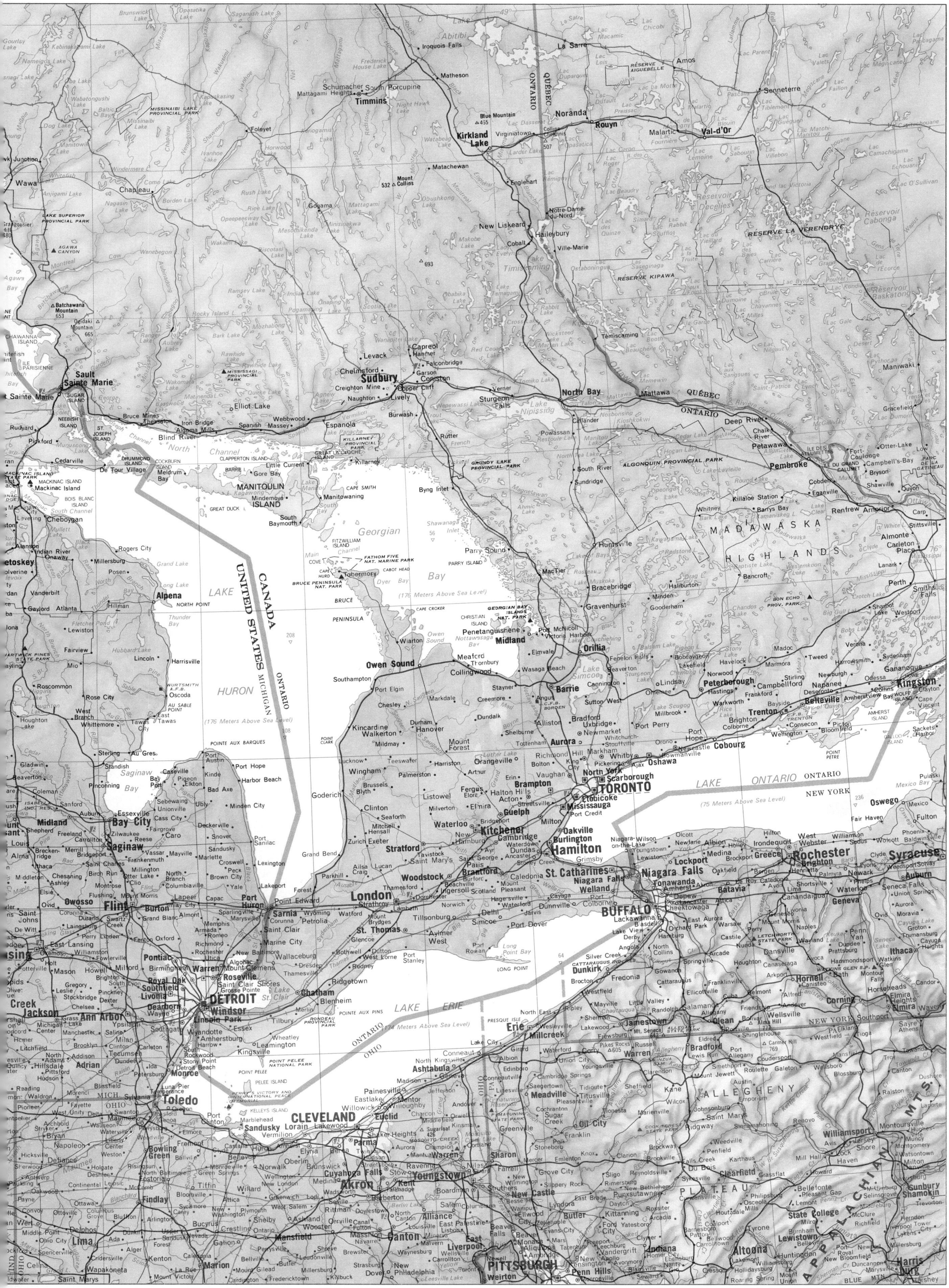
84°
83°
82°
81°
80°
79°
78°
77°
76°
48°
47°
46°
45°
44°
43°
42°
41°
ONTARIO
QUÉBEC
CANADA
UNITED STATES
MICHIGAN
OHIO
NEW YORK
LAKE HURON
(176 Meters Above Sea Level)
Georgian Bay
LAKE ONTARIO
(75 Meters Above Sea Level)
LAKE ERIE
(174 Meters Above Sea Level)
MADAWASKA HIGHLANDS
ALLEGHENY PLATEAU
APPALACHIAN MTS.
MANITOULIN ISLAND
BRUCE PENINSULA
Sault Sainte Marie
Timmins
Kirkland Lake
Rouyn
Noranda
Val-d'Or
Sudbury
North Bay
Pembroke
Kingston
TORONTO
Hamilton
London
Kitchener
St. Catharines
Niagara Falls
BUFFALO
Rochester
Syracuse
Erie
CLEVELAND
Akron
Youngstown
Toledo
DETROIT
Windsor
Flint
Saginaw
Bay City
Sarnia
Port Huron
PITTSBURGH
Owen Sound
Barrie
Orillia
Peterborough
Oshawa
Guelph
Brantford
Alpena
Sault
Wawa
Chapleau

Map continues pages 188-189

Map continues pages 188-189

Kilometers 0 50 100 150 Km.
Statute Miles 0 50 100 150 Mi.

Scale 1:3,000,000
One centimeter represents 30 kilometers.
One inch represents approximately 47 miles.
Albers Conical Equal-Area Projection

Kilometers 0 50 100 150 Km.
Statute Miles 0 50 150 Mi.

Scale 1:3,000,000

One centimeter represents 30 kilometers.
One inch represents approximately 47 miles.

Albers Conical Equal-Area Projection

Map continues pages 188-189

| ENGLISH | bay | cape | creek, cr. | dam | island, i. | lake, l. | mountain, mtn. | state park, s.p. |
|---|---|---|---|---|---|---|---|---|
| DEUTSCH | Bucht | Kap | Bach | Damm | Insel | See | Berg | Staatspark |
| ESPAÑOL | bahía | cabo | riachuelo | presa | isla | lago | montaña | parque del estado |
| FRANÇAIS | baie | cap | crique | barrage | île | lac | montagne | parc régional |
| PORTUGUÊS | baía | cabo | riacho | represa | ilha | lago | montanha | parque estadual |

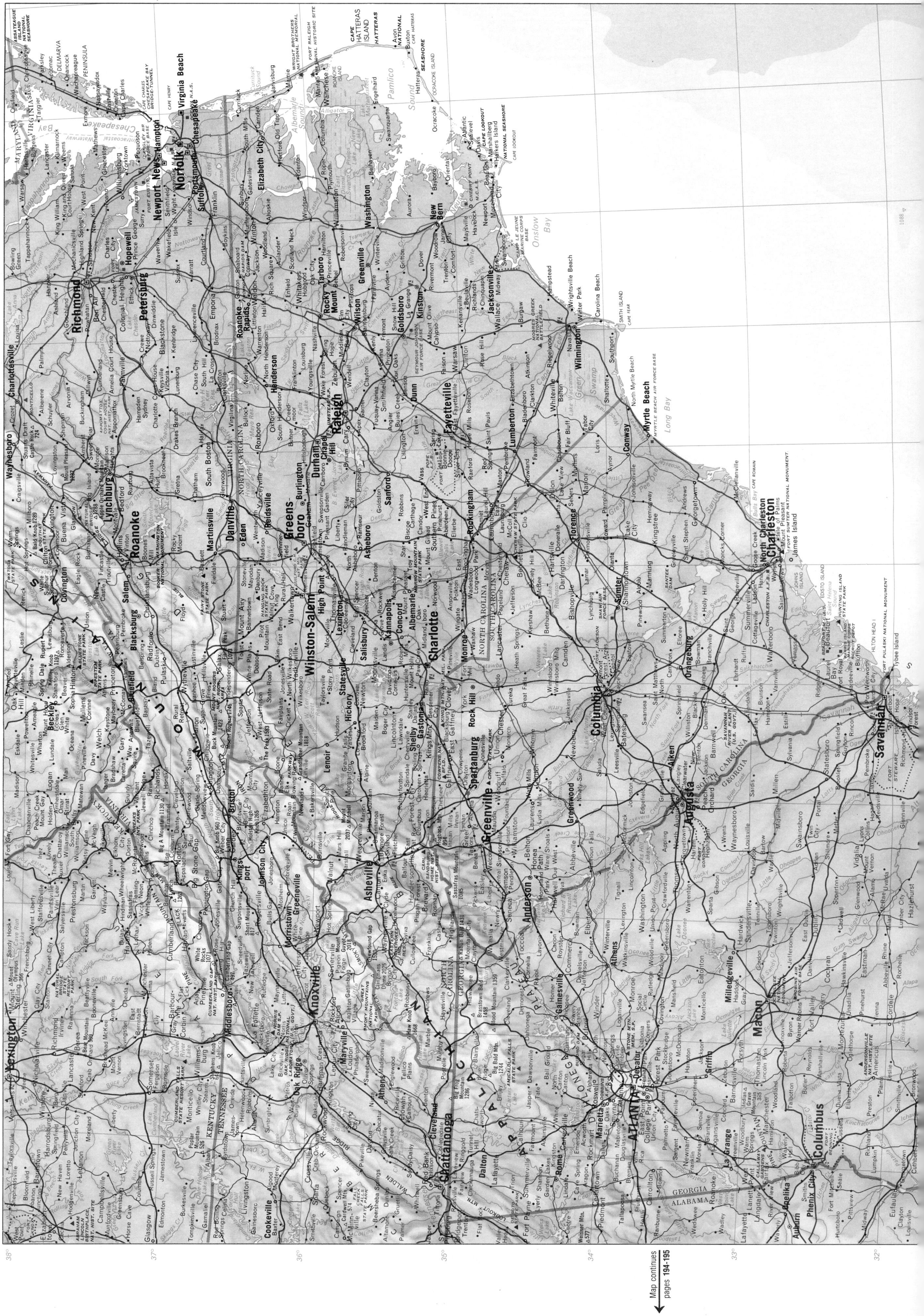
Richmond
Petersburg
Norfolk
Virginia Beach
Chesapeake
Portsmouth
Newport News
Hampton
Lynchburg
Roanoke
Danville
Durham
Raleigh
Greensboro
Winston-Salem
High Point
Charlotte
Fayetteville
Wilmington
Myrtle Beach
Charleston
North Charleston
Columbia
Spartanburg
Greenville
Augusta
Savannah
Macon
Columbus
Atlanta
Athens
Chattanooga
Knoxville
Asheville
Lexington
Pamlico Sound
Onslow Bay
Long Bay

Map continues pages 194-195

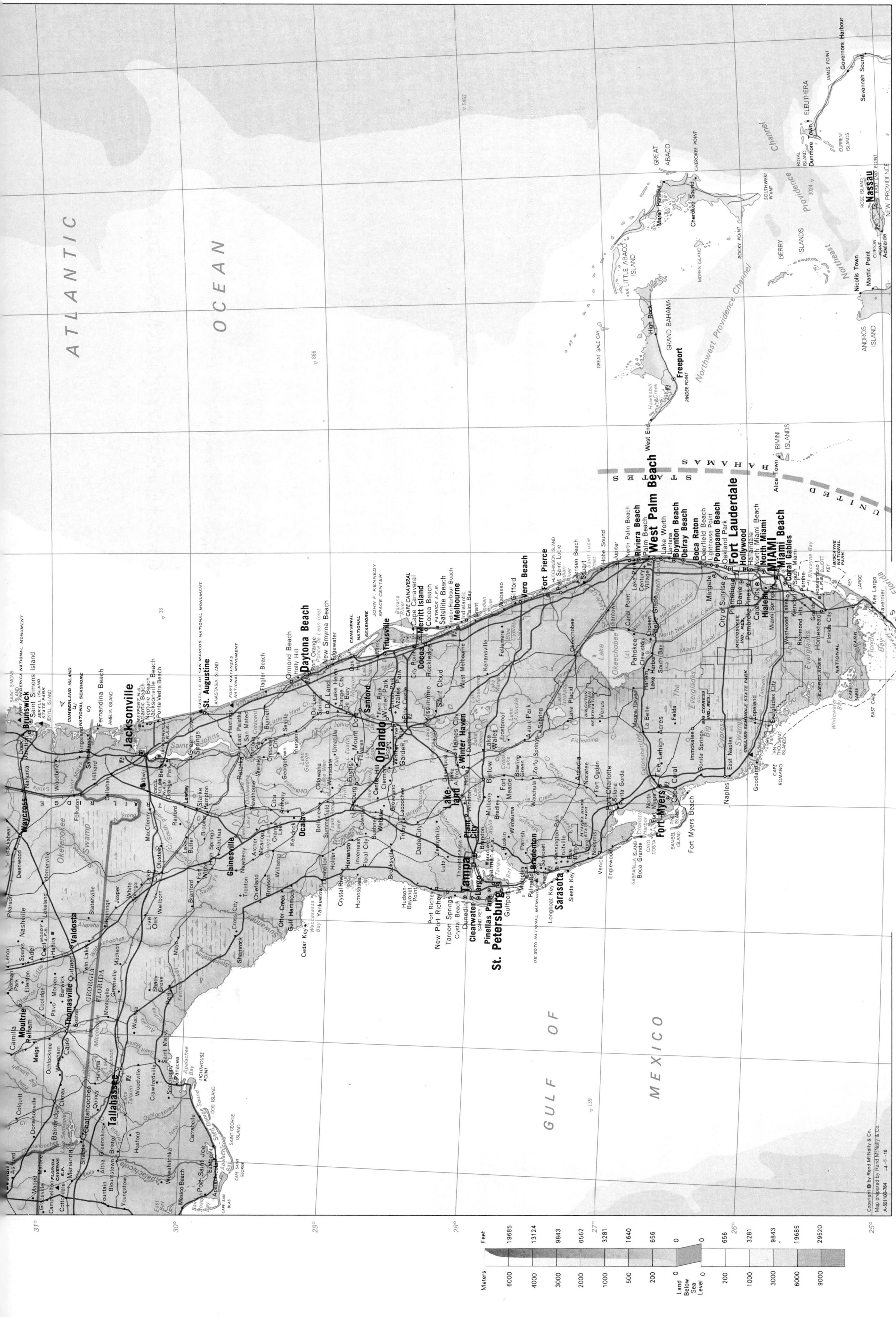
ATLANTIC
OCEAN
GULF OF MEXICO
Jacksonville
Tallahassee
St. Augustine
Daytona Beach
Orlando
Tampa
St. Petersburg
Clearwater
Sarasota
Fort Myers
West Palm Beach
Fort Lauderdale
MIAMI
Miami Beach
Key West
Freeport
Nassau
UNITED STATES
BAHAMAS
Straits of Florida
Map continues
pages 238-239
Copyright © by Rand McNally & Co.

Map continues pages 188-189

Map continues pages 190-191

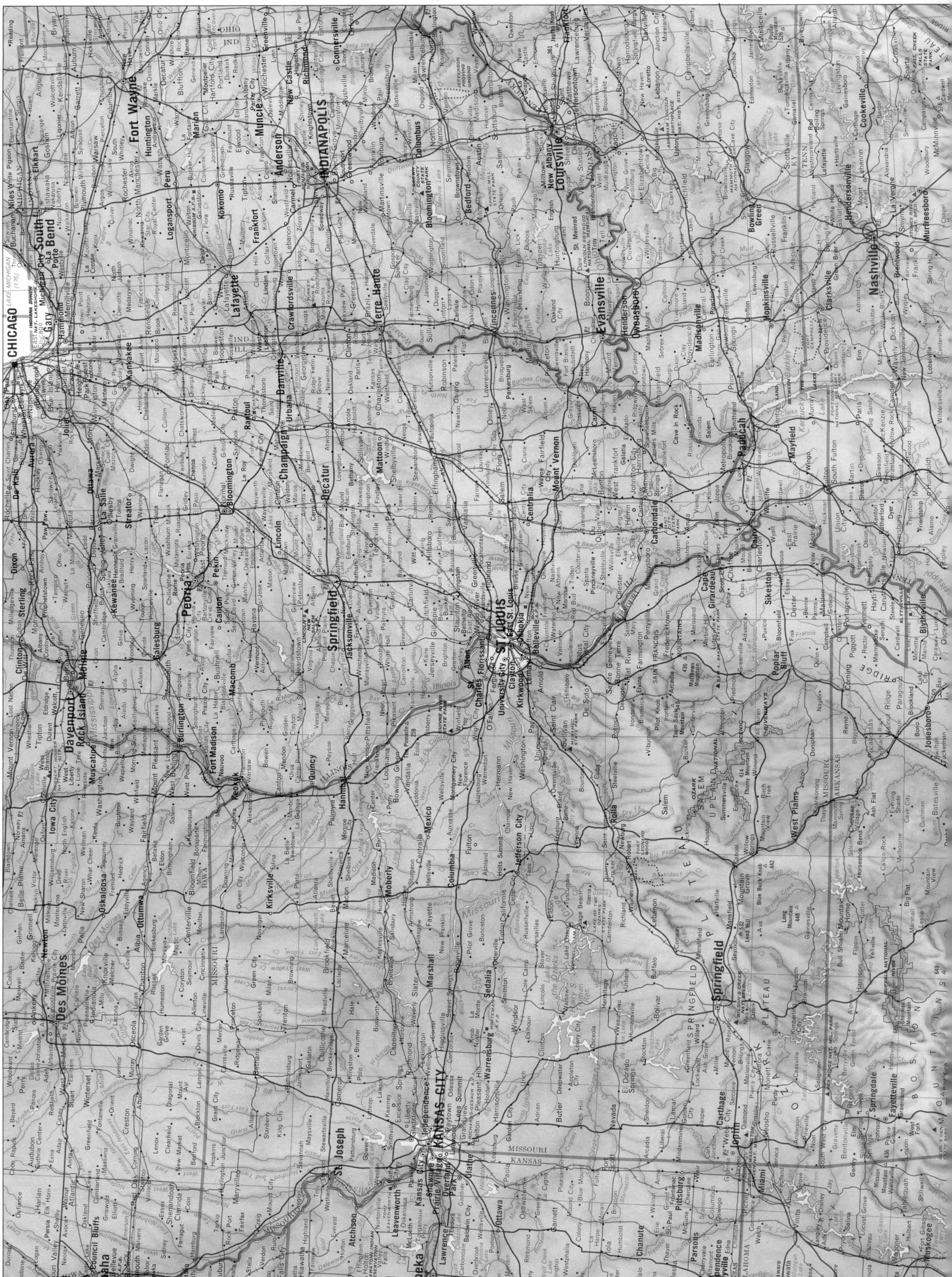
CHICAGO
INDIANAPOLIS
ST. LOUIS
KANSAS CITY
Louisville
Nashville
Des Moines
Omaha
Springfield
Peoria
Fort Wayne
Evansville
Terre Haute
Topeka
St. Joseph
MISSOURI

Map continues pages 198-199

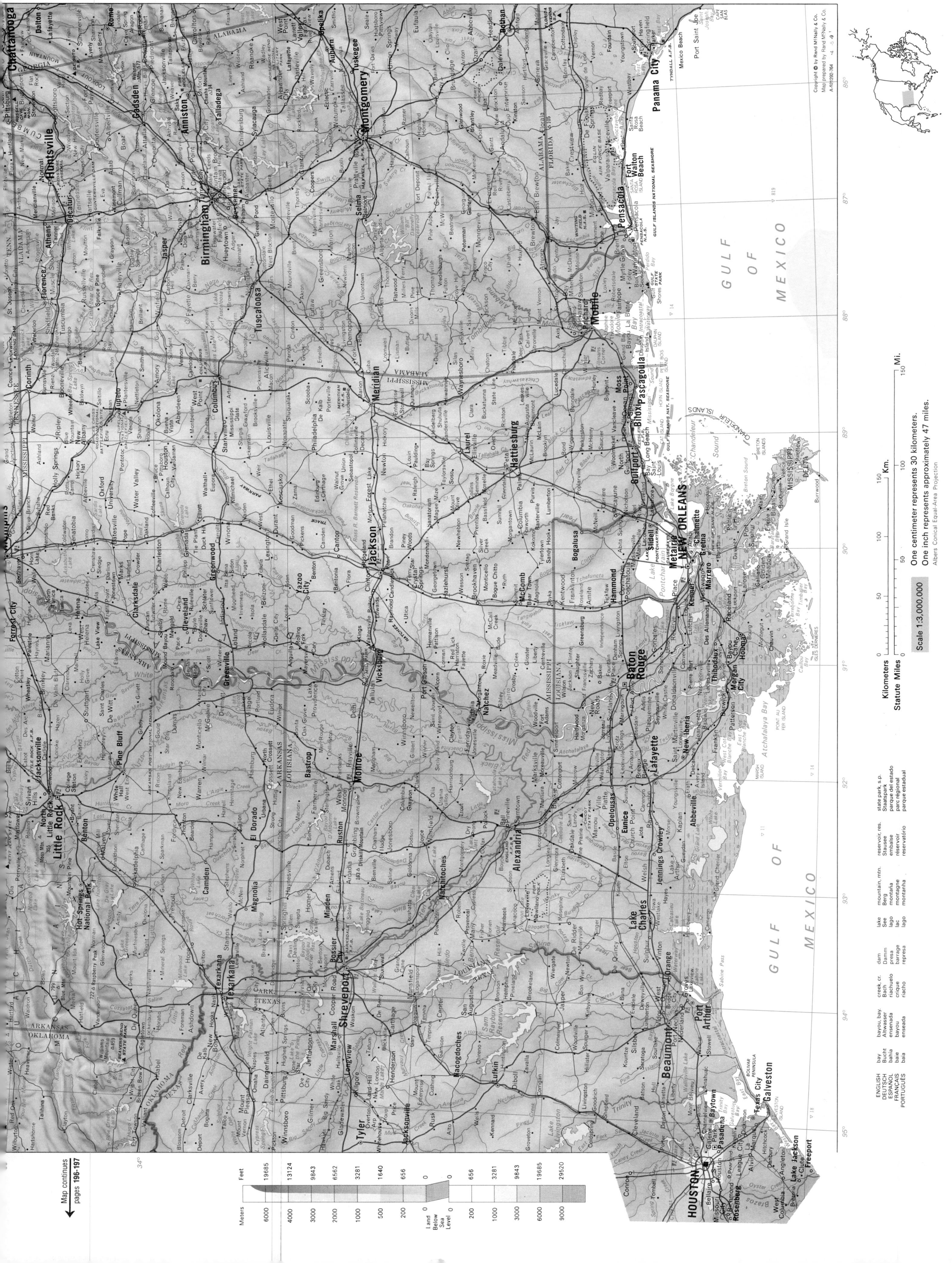
Map continues pages 192-193
Map continues pages 196-197
GULF OF MEXICO
Scale 1:3,000,000
One centimeter represents 30 kilometers.
One inch represents approximately 47 miles.
Albers Conical Equal-Area Projection
Kilometers
Statute Miles
Copyright © by Rand McNally & Co.
ENGLISH bay, bayou, bay, creek, cr., dam, lake, mountain, mtn., reservoir, res., state park, s.p.
DEUTSCH Bucht, Altwasser, Bach, Damm, See, Berg, Stausee, Staatspark
ESPAÑOL bahía, ensenada, riachuelo, presa, lago, montaña, embalse, parque del estado
FRANÇAIS baie, bayou, crique, barrage, lac, montagne, reservoir, parc régional
PORTUGUÊS baía, enseada, riacho, represa, lago, montanha, reservatório, parque estadual
Feet
Meters
Land Below Sea Level
HOUSTON
NEW ORLEANS
Jackson
Montgomery
Birmingham
Shreveport
Little Rock
Memphis
Baton Rouge
Mobile
Chattanooga

Map continues pages 194-195

Map continues pages 198-199

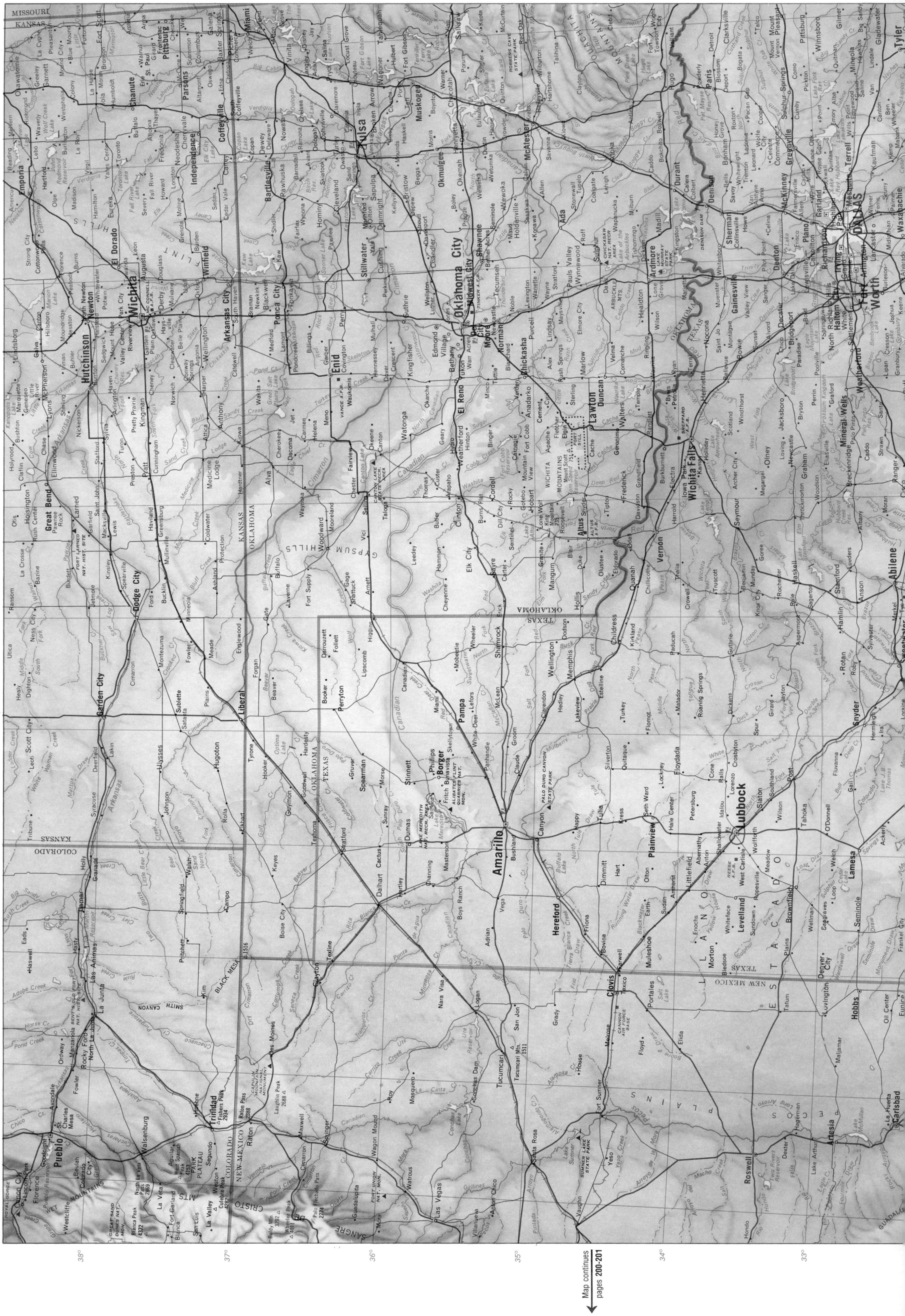
MISSOURI
KANSAS
OKLAHOMA
TEXAS
COLORADO
NEW MEXICO
Wichita
Oklahoma City
Tulsa
Amarillo
Lubbock
Dallas
Fort Worth
Wichita Falls
Dodge City
Pueblo
Trinidad
Clovis
Roswell
Abilene

Map continues pages 200-201

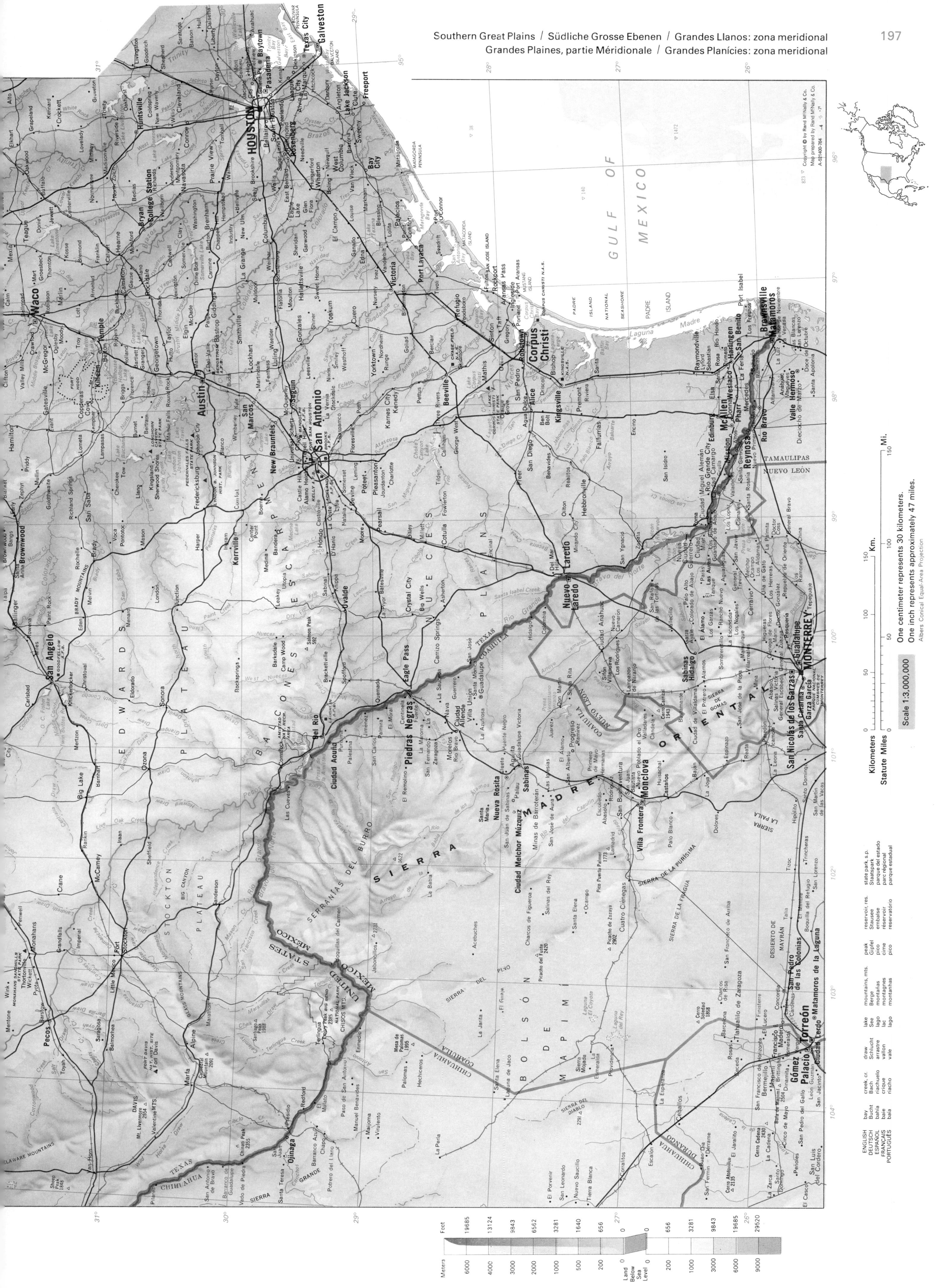
GULF OF MEXICO
Houston
San Antonio
Austin
Corpus Christi
Galveston
Waco
San Angelo
Laredo
Nuevo Laredo
Monterrey
Torreón
Brownsville
Matamoros
Reynosa
EDWARDS PLATEAU
STOCKTON PLATEAU
BALCONES ESCARPMENT
NUECES PLAINS
SIERRA MADRE ORIENTAL
BOLSÓN DE MAPIMÍ
TEXAS
COAHUILA
CHIHUAHUA
NUEVO LEÓN
TAMAULIPAS
DURANGO
UNITED STATES
MEXICO
Scale 1:3,000,000
One centimeter represents 30 kilometers.
One inch represents approximately 47 miles.
Albers Conical Equal-Area Projection
Kilometers
Statute Miles
Copyright © by Rand McNally & Co.
Map prepared by Rand McNally & Co.
ENGLISH
DEUTSCH
ESPAÑOL
FRANÇAIS
PORTUGUÊS
Meters
Feet
Land Below Sea Level

Map continues pages 190-191

Map continues pages 184-185

CANADA
UNITED STATES
MANITOBA
SASKATCHEWAN
ONTARIO
MINNESOTA
NORTH DAKOTA
SOUTH DAKOTA
MONTANA
WYOMING
Winnipeg
Brandon
Portage la Prairie
Grand Forks
Fargo
Moorhead
Bismarck
Mandan
Minot
Jamestown
Aberdeen
Williston
Dickinson
Rapid City
Pierre
Miles City
Bemidji
Brainerd
St. Cloud
Watertown
Devils Lake
COTEAU DU MISSOURI
BADLANDS
BLACK HILLS

Map continues pages 202-203

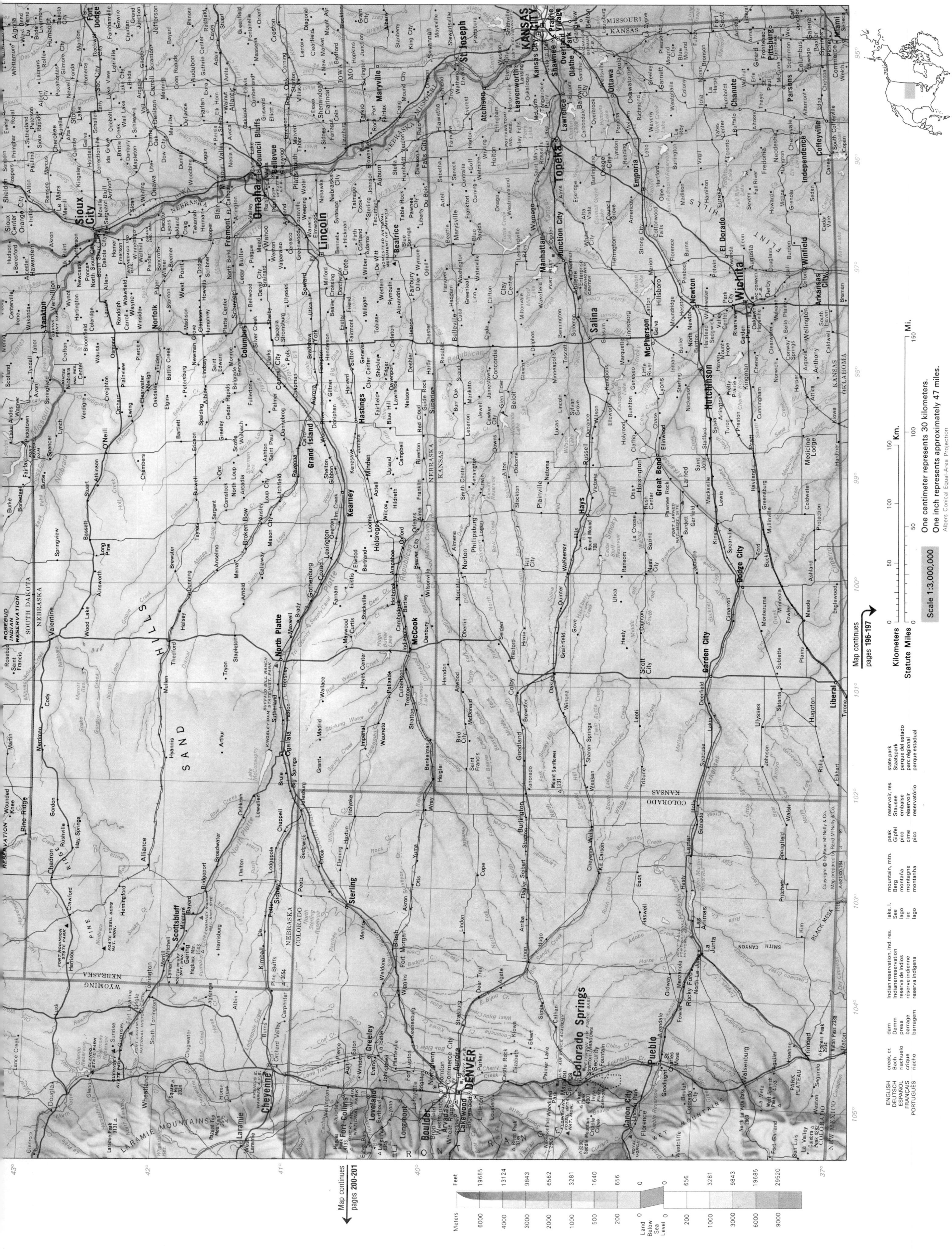
Map continues pages 194-195
Map continues pages 196-197
Map continues pages 200-201
Scale 1:3,000,000
One centimeter represents 30 kilometers.
One inch represents approximately 47 miles.
Albers Conical Equal-Area Projection
Kilometers
Statute Miles
ENGLISH DEUTSCH ESPAÑOL FRANÇAIS PORTUGUÊS
creek, cr. Bach riachuelo crique riacho
dam Damm presa barrage barragem
Indian reservation, Ind. res. Indianerreservation reserva de indios réserve indienne reserva indígena
lake, l. See lago lac lago
mountain, mtn. Berg montaña montagne montanha
peak Gipfel pico cime pico
reservoir, res. Stausee embalse réservoir reservatório
state park Staatspark parque del estado parc régional parque estadual
Copyright © by Rand McNally & Co.
Map prepared by Rand McNally & Co.
Feet
Meters
Land Below Sea Level
NEBRASKA
KANSAS
COLORADO
WYOMING
SOUTH DAKOTA
IOWA
MISSOURI
OKLAHOMA
SAND HILLS
FLINT HILLS
Denver
Colorado Springs
Pueblo
Cheyenne
Omaha
Lincoln
Topeka
Kansas City
Wichita
Sioux City
North Platte

Map continues pages 198-199

Map continues pages 202-203

Casper
Cheyenne
Laramie
Fort Collins
Greeley
Boulder
Longmont
DENVER
Lakewood
Arvada
Colorado Springs
Pueblo
Rock Springs
Grand Junction
Salt Lake City
Ogden
Provo
Orem
Logan
Pocatello
Idaho Falls
Twin Falls
GREAT DIVIDE BASIN
GREAT SALT LAKE DESERT
WYOMING
IDAHO
UTAH
NEVADA
COLORADO

Map continues pages 204-205

Map continues pages 196-197

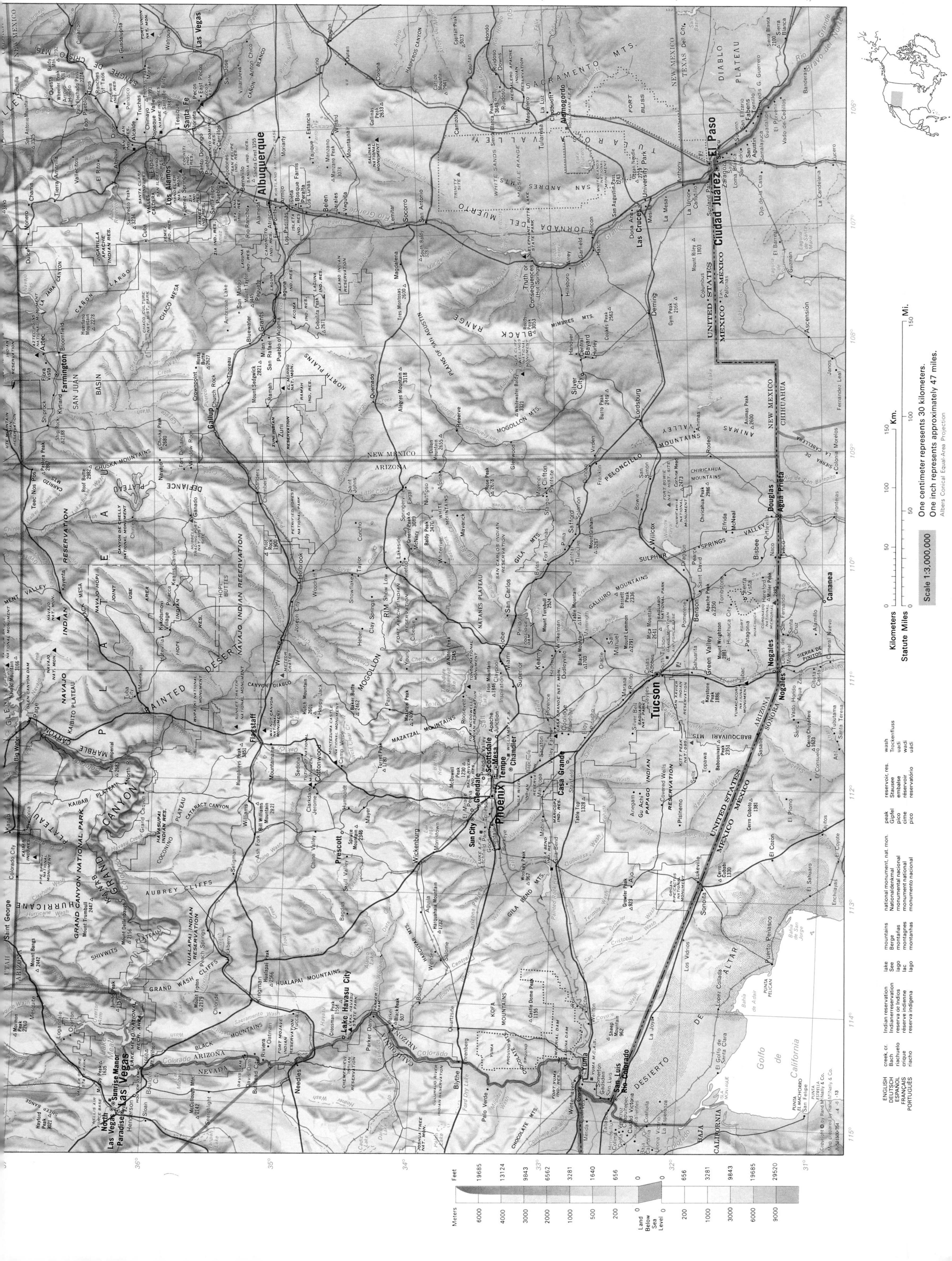
Scale 1:3,000,000
One centimeter represents 30 kilometers.
One inch represents approximately 47 miles.
Albers Conical Equal-Area Projection
Kilometers
Statute Miles
ENGLISH creek, cr. Indian reservation national monument, nat. mon. mountains lake peak reservoir, res. wash
DEUTSCH Bach Indianerreservation Nationaldenkmal Berge See Gipfel Stausee Trockenfluss
ESPAÑOL riachuelo reserva de Indios monumento nacional montañas lago pico embalse uadi
FRANÇAIS crique réserve indienne monument national montagnes lac cime réservoir uadi
PORTUGUÊS riacho reserva indígena monumento nacional montanhas lago pico reservatório uádi
Feet 19685 13124 9843 6562 3281 1640 656 0 0 656 3281 9843 19685 29520
Meters 6000 4000 3000 2000 1000 500 200 0 Land Below Sea Level 0 200 1000 3000 6000 9000
Albuquerque
Santa Fe
El Paso
Ciudad Juárez
Tucson
Phoenix
Las Vegas
Flagstaff
Nogales
GRAND CANYON NATIONAL PARK
NAVAJO INDIAN RESERVATION
UNITED STATES
MEXICO
ARIZONA
NEW MEXICO
Golfo de California
Copyright © by Rand McNally & Co.

Map continues pages 182-183

Meters
Feet
6000
19685
4000
13124
3000
9843
2000
6562
1000
3281
500
1640
200
656
0
Land Below Sea Level
PACIFIC OCEAN
CANADA
UNITED STATES
BRITISH COLUMBIA
WASHINGTON
OREGON
IDAHO
CALIFORNIA
NEVADA
Vancouver
Victoria
Bellingham
Everett
SEATTLE
Tacoma
Olympia
Spokane
Yakima
Wenatchee
Ellensburg
Moses Lake
Richland
Pasco
Kennewick
Walla Walla
Lewiston
Pullman
Moscow
Coeur d'Alene
PORTLAND
Salem
Eugene
Springfield
Corvallis
Albany
Bend
The Dalles
Pendleton
Medford
Ashland
Grants Pass
Roseburg
Klamath Falls
Coos Bay
Eureka
Boise
Nampa
Caldwell
Penticton
Nelson
Cranbrook
Trail
CASCADE RANGE
BLUE MOUNTAINS
COLUMBIA BASIN
HARNEY BASIN
KLAMATH MOUNTAINS
OLYMPIC MTS.
Mount Rainier 4392
Mount Hood 3426
Mount Adams 3742
Mount Shasta 4317
Map continues pages 204-205

| | | | | | | | | |
|---|---|---|---|---|---|---|---|---|
| ENGLISH | creek, cr. | Indian reservation | lake, l. | mountain, mtn. | pass | peak | range | reservoir, res. |
| DEUTSCH | Bach | Indianerreservation | See | Berg | Pass | Gipfel | Gebirge | Stausee |
| ESPAÑOL | riachuelo | reserva de Indios | lago | montaña | paso | pico | sierra | embalse |
| FRANÇAIS | crique | réserve indienne | lac | montagne | col | cime | chaîne | réservoir |
| PORTUGUÊS | riacho | reserva indígena | lago | montanha | passo | pico | serra | reservatório |

Map continues pages 184-185

CANADA
UNITED STATES
ALBERTA
SASKATCHEWAN
MONTANA
WYOMING
IDAHO
UTAH
COLORADO
Great Falls
Helena
Butte
Missoula
Kalispell
Anaconda
Bozeman
Billings
Havre
Lewistown
Miles City
Glasgow
Sheridan
Casper
Rock Springs
Idaho Falls
Pocatello
Twin Falls
Logan
Ogden
Brigham City
Evanston
ROCKY MOUNTAINS
BIG BELT MOUNTAINS
LITTLE BELT MOUNTAINS
ABSAROKA RANGE
BIGHORN MOUNTAINS
BIGHORN BASIN
WIND RIVER RANGE
TETON RANGE
BEAR RIVER RANGE
LOST RIVER RANGE
LEMHI RANGE
BITTERROOT RANGE
MADISON RANGE
GALLATIN RANGE
SNAKE RIVER PLAIN
GREAT DIVIDE BASIN
GREAT SALT LAKE DESERT
YELLOWSTONE NATIONAL PARK
GRAND TETON
FLAMING GORGE NATIONAL RECREATION AREA
Missouri
Yellowstone
Snake
Copyright © by Rand McNally & Co.
Map prepared by Rand McNally & Co.
A-520697-764
114°
113°
112°
111°
110°
109°
108°
107°
106°
48°
47°
46°
45°
44°
43°
42°
41°

Map continues pages 198-199

Map continues pages 200-201

Kilometers 0 50 100 150 Km.
Statute Miles 0 50 100 150 Mi.

Scale 1:3,000,000
One centimeter represents 30 kilometers.
One inch represents approximately 47 miles.
Albers Conical Equal-Area Projection

Map continues pages 200-201

Map continues pages 202-203

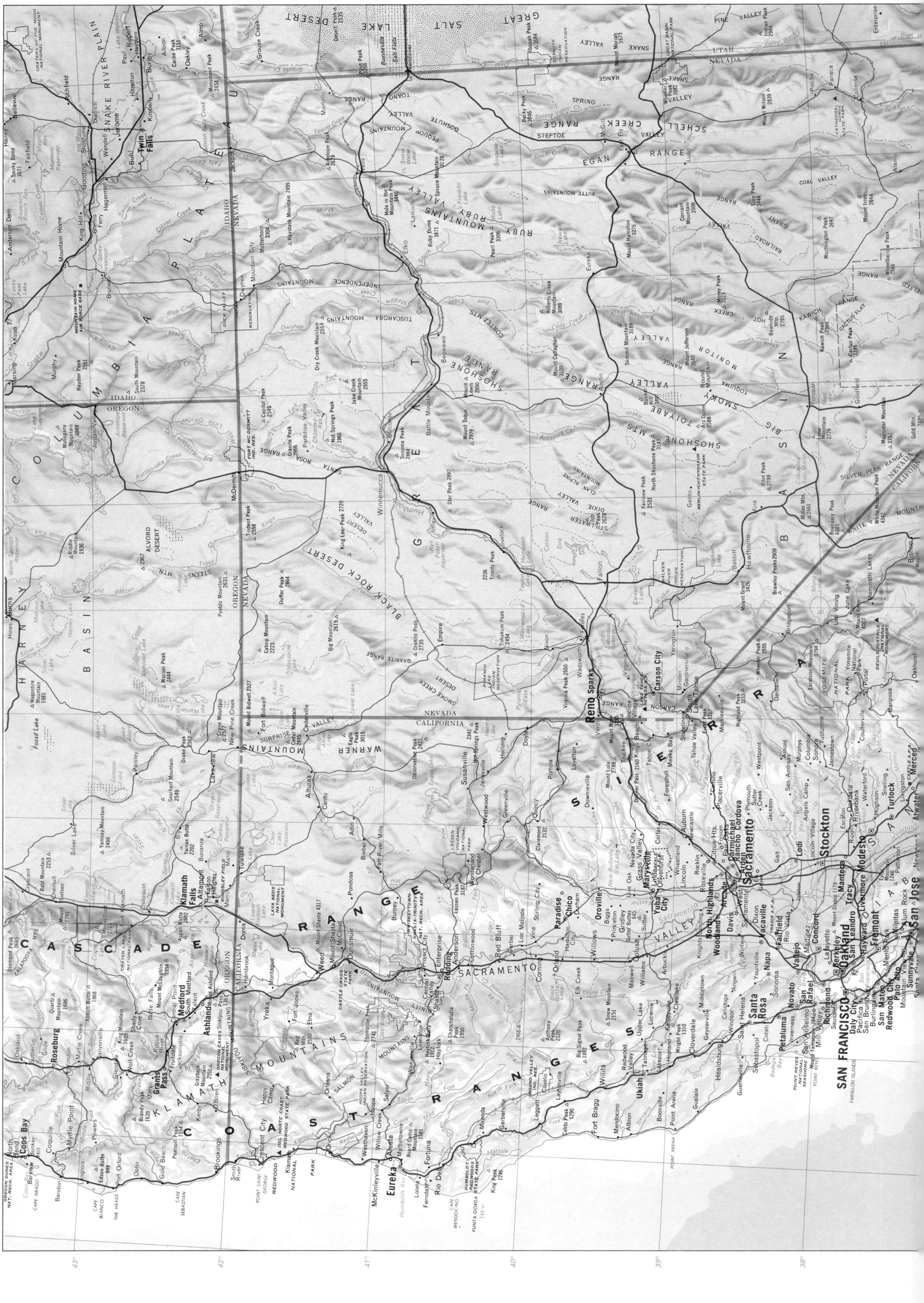
GREAT SALT LAKE DESERT
SNAKE RIVER PLAIN
COLUMBIA PLATEAU
GREAT BASIN
HARNEY BASIN
BLACK ROCK DESERT
CASCADE RANGE
KLAMATH MOUNTAINS
COAST RANGES
SIERRA NEVADA
SACRAMENTO VALLEY
SAN FRANCISCO
Oakland
San Jose
Sacramento
Stockton
Reno
Carson City
Eureka
Redding
Medford
Klamath Falls
Twin Falls
Elko
Winnemucca

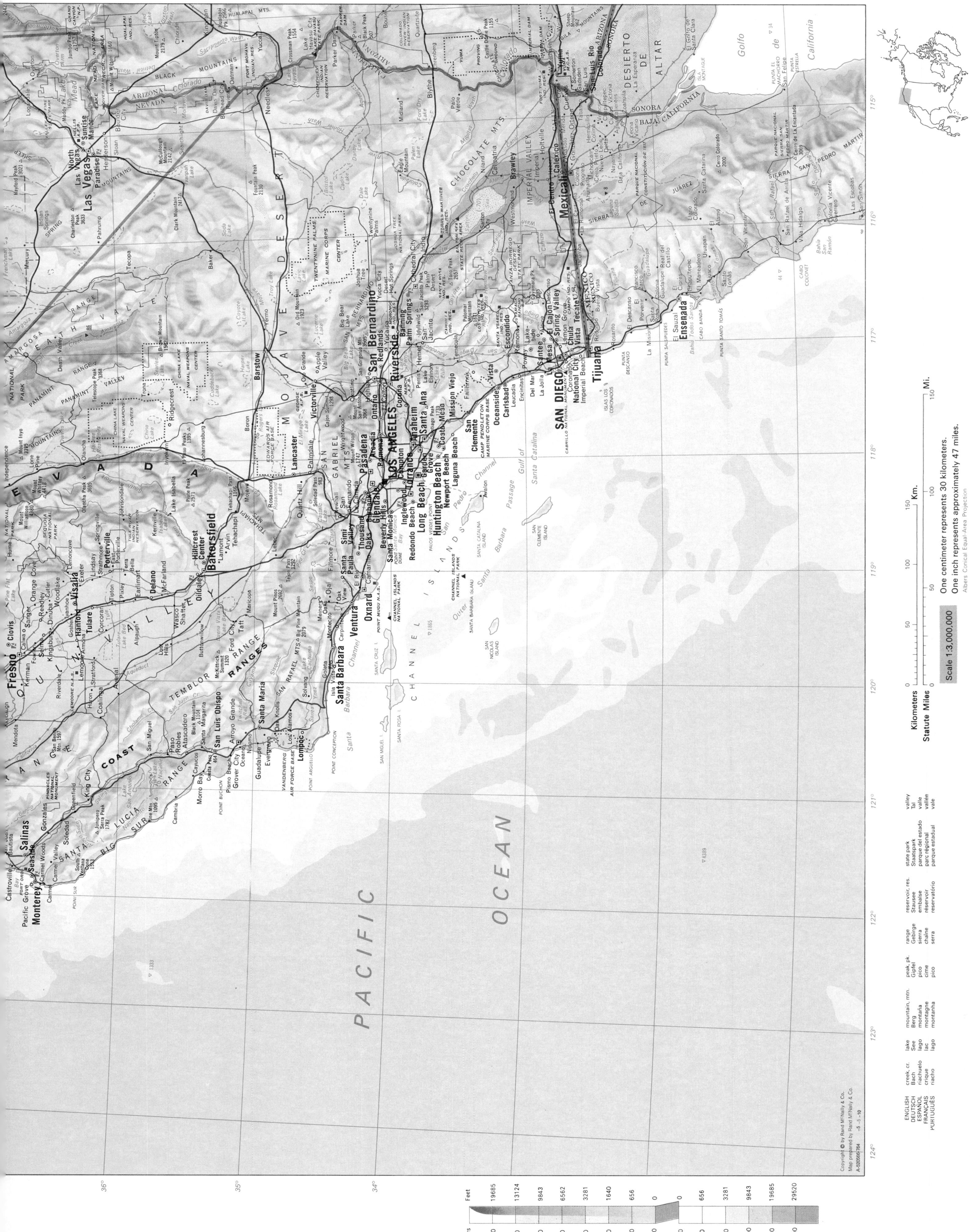
PACIFIC
OCEAN
MOJAVE DESERT
DEATH VALLEY
SAN JOAQUIN VALLEY
IMPERIAL VALLEY
CHOCOLATE MTS.
COAST RANGES
TEMBLOR RANGE
SANTA LUCIA RANGE
CHANNEL ISLANDS
Golfo de California
DESIERTO DE ALTAR
BAJA CALIFORNIA
SONORA
ARIZONA
NEVADA
CALIFORNIA
MEXICO
LOS ANGELES
SAN DIEGO
Las Vegas
Fresno
Bakersfield
San Bernardino
Riverside
Santa Ana
Anaheim
Long Beach
Pasadena
Santa Barbara
Ventura
Oxnard
San Luis Obispo
Salinas
Monterey
Tijuana
Mexicali
Ensenada
Calexico
El Centro
Yuma
Barstow
Lancaster
Palmdale
Victorville
Palm Springs
Oceanside
Escondido
Chula Vista
Visalia
Tulare
Porterville
Santa Maria
Lompoc
Kilometers
Statute Miles
Km.
Mi.
Scale 1:3,000,000
One centimeter represents 30 kilometers.
One inch represents approximately 47 miles.
Albers Conical Equal-Area Projection
ENGLISH creek, cr. lake mountain, mtn. peak, pk. range reservoir, res. state park valley
DEUTSCH Bach See Berg Gipfel Gebirge Stausee Staatspark Tal
ESPAÑOL riachuelo lago montaña pico sierra embalse parque del estado valle
FRANÇAIS crique lac montagne cime chaîne réservoir parc régional vallée
PORTUGUÊS riacho lago montanha pico serra reservatório parque estadual vale
Feet
Meters
Land Below Sea Level
Copyright © by Rand McNally & Co.
Map prepared by Rand McNally & Co.

Québec
Lévis
Lauzon
Beauport
Ste-Foy
Trois-Rivières
Cap-de-la-Madeleine
Shawinigan
Grand-Mère
Sorel
Joliette
St-Jérôme
Laval
MONTRÉAL
Longueuil
Verdun
St-Hyacinthe
Drummondville
Granby
Sherbrooke
Victoriaville
Thetford Mines
Asbestos
St-Jean-sur-Richelieu
Salaberry-de-Valleyfield
Cornwall
Massena
CANADA
UNITED STATES
VERMONT
NEW YORK
NEW HAMPSHIRE
ONTARIO
QUÉBEC
Copyright © by Rand McNally & Co.

| FRANÇAIS | ENGLISH | DEUTSCH | ESPAÑOL | PORTUGUÊS |
|---|---|---|---|---|
| aéroport | airport | Flughafen | aeropuerto | aeroporto |
| barrage | dam | Damm | presa | represa |
| île | island | Insel | isla | ilha |
| lac | lake | See | lago | lago |
| montagne | mountain | Berg | montaña | montanha |
| parc | park | Park | parque | parque |
| réservoir, rés. | reservoir | Stausee | embalse | reservatório |
| rivière, r. | river | Fluss | río | rio |

Kilometers 0 10 20 30 40 50 Km.
Statute Miles 0 10 20 30 40 50 Mi.

Scale 1:1,000,000

One centimeter represents 10 kilometers.
One inch represents approximately 16 miles.
Lambert Conformal Conic Projection

Map continues pages 212-213

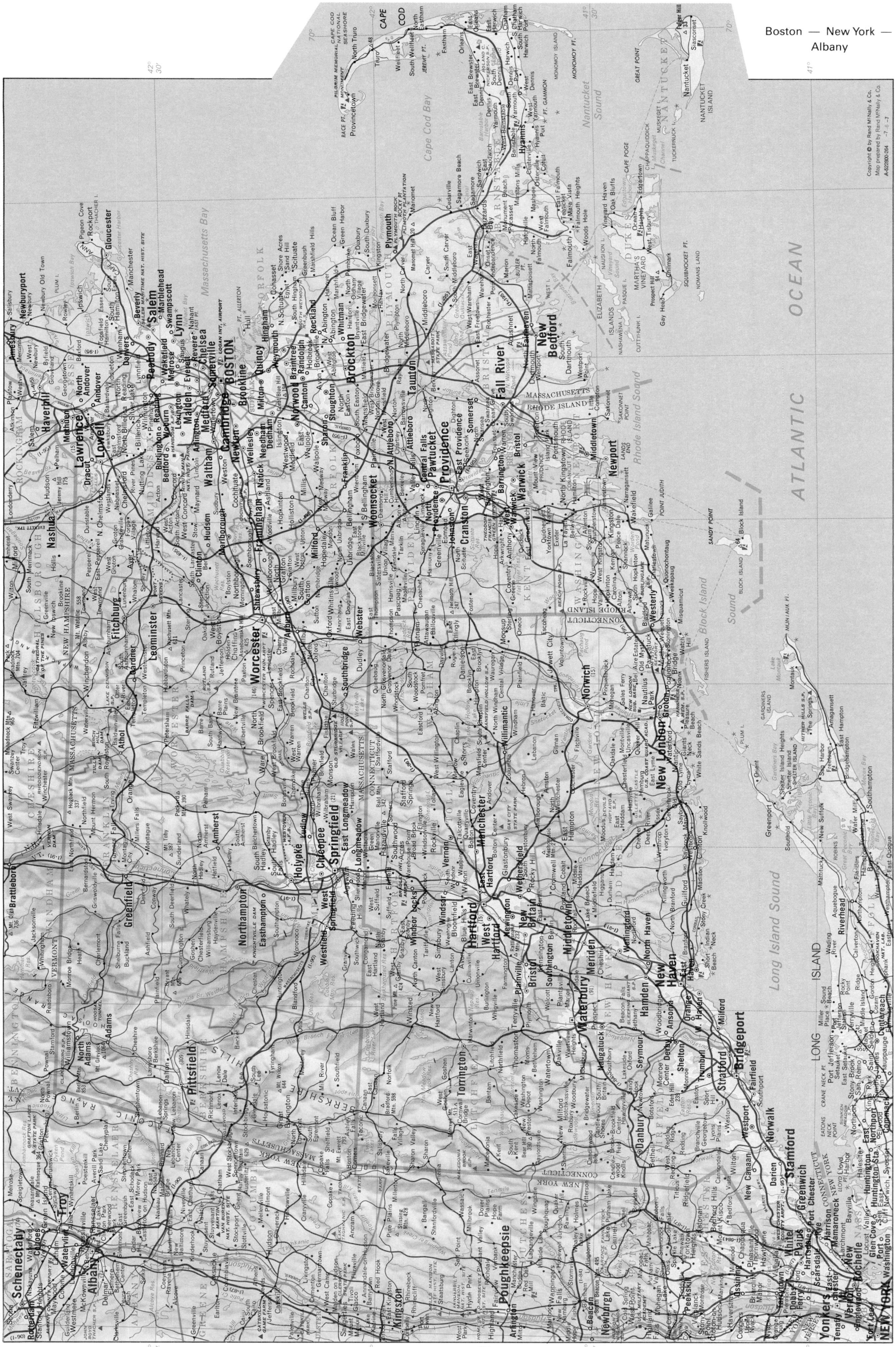
ATLANTIC OCEAN
BOSTON
Providence
Hartford
Springfield
Worcester
New Haven
Bridgeport
Albany
Schenectady
Troy
Poughkeepsie
Long Island Sound
Rhode Island Sound
Block Island Sound
Nantucket Sound
Massachusetts Bay
Cape Cod Bay
LONG ISLAND
CAPE COD

Copyright © by Rand McNally & Co.
Map prepared by Rand McNally & Co.

Map continues pages 208-209

Map continues pages 210-211

| ENGLISH | DEUTSCH | ESPAÑOL | FRANÇAIS | PORTUGUÊS |
|---|---|---|---|---|
| bay | Bucht | bahía | baie | baía |
| island, I. | Insel | isla | île | ilha |
| lake, l. | See | lago | lac | lago |
| mountain, mtn. | Berg | montaña | montagne | montanha |
| point, pt. | Landspitze | punta | pointe | ponta |
| pond | Teich | estanque | étang | lagoa |
| reservoir, res. | Stausee | embalse | réservoir | reservatório |
| sound | Sund | sonda | détroit | estreito |

Kilometers
Statute Miles

Scale 1:1,000,000

One centimeter represents 10 kilometers.
One inch represents approximately 16 miles.
Lambert Conformal Conic Projection

Map continues pages 210-211

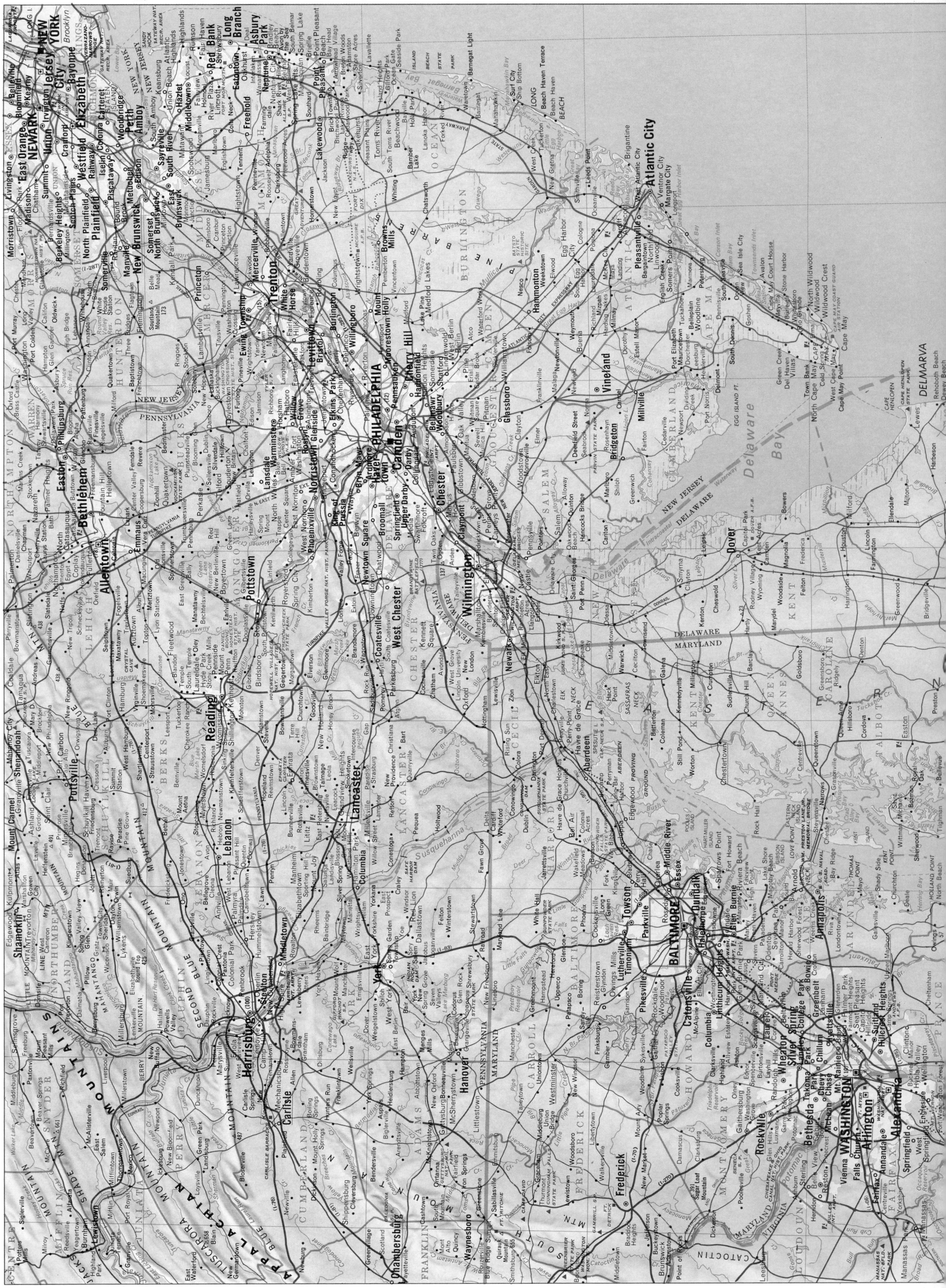
NEW YORK
Jersey City
NEWARK
Elizabeth
Trenton
PHILADELPHIA
Camden
Wilmington
Atlantic City
Vineland
Allentown
Bethlehem
Reading
Lancaster
Harrisburg
York
BALTIMORE
WASHINGTON
Arlington
Alexandria
Delaware Bay
DELMARVA

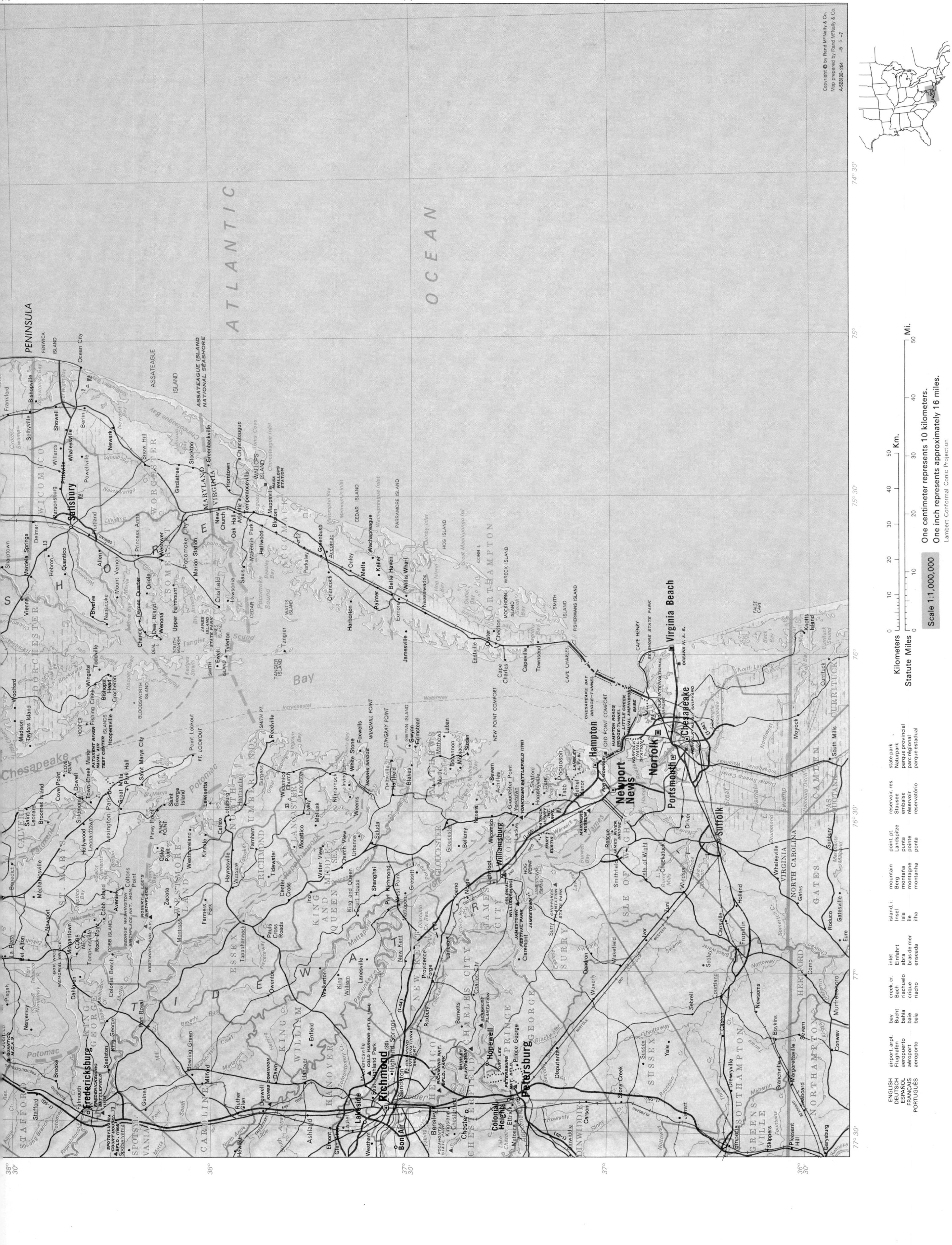

ATLANTIC
OCEAN
Chesapeake
Bay
PENINSULA
ASSATEAGUE ISLAND NATIONAL SEASHORE
MARYLAND
VIRGINIA
NORTH CAROLINA
Fredericksburg
Richmond
Petersburg
Hopewell
Colonial Heights
Williamsburg
Newport News
Hampton
Norfolk
Portsmouth
Chesapeake
Virginia Beach
Suffolk
Salisbury
Ocean City
Chincoteague
Cape Charles
CAPE HENRY
CAPE CHARLES
CHESAPEAKE BAY BRIDGE-TUNNEL
HAMPTON ROADS BRIDGE-TUNNEL
Copyright © by Rand McNally & Co.
Map prepared by Rand McNally & Co.
A-523100-264 -8 -3 -7
Scale 1:1,000,000
Kilometers
Statute Miles
One centimeter represents 10 kilometers.
One inch represents approximately 16 miles.
Lambert Conformal Conic Projection
ENGLISH bay creek, cr. inlet island, i. mountain point, pt. reservoir, res. state park
DEUTSCH Bucht Bach Einfahrt Insel Berg Landspitze Stausee Naturpark
ESPAÑOL bahía riachuelo abra isla montaña punta embalse parque provincial
FRANÇAIS baie crique bras de mer île montagne pointe réservoir parc régional
PORTUGUÊS baía riacho enseada ilha montanha ponta reservatório parque estadual
airport, arpt. Flughafen aeropuerto aéroport aeroporto

Map continues pages 212-213

Map continues pages 214-215

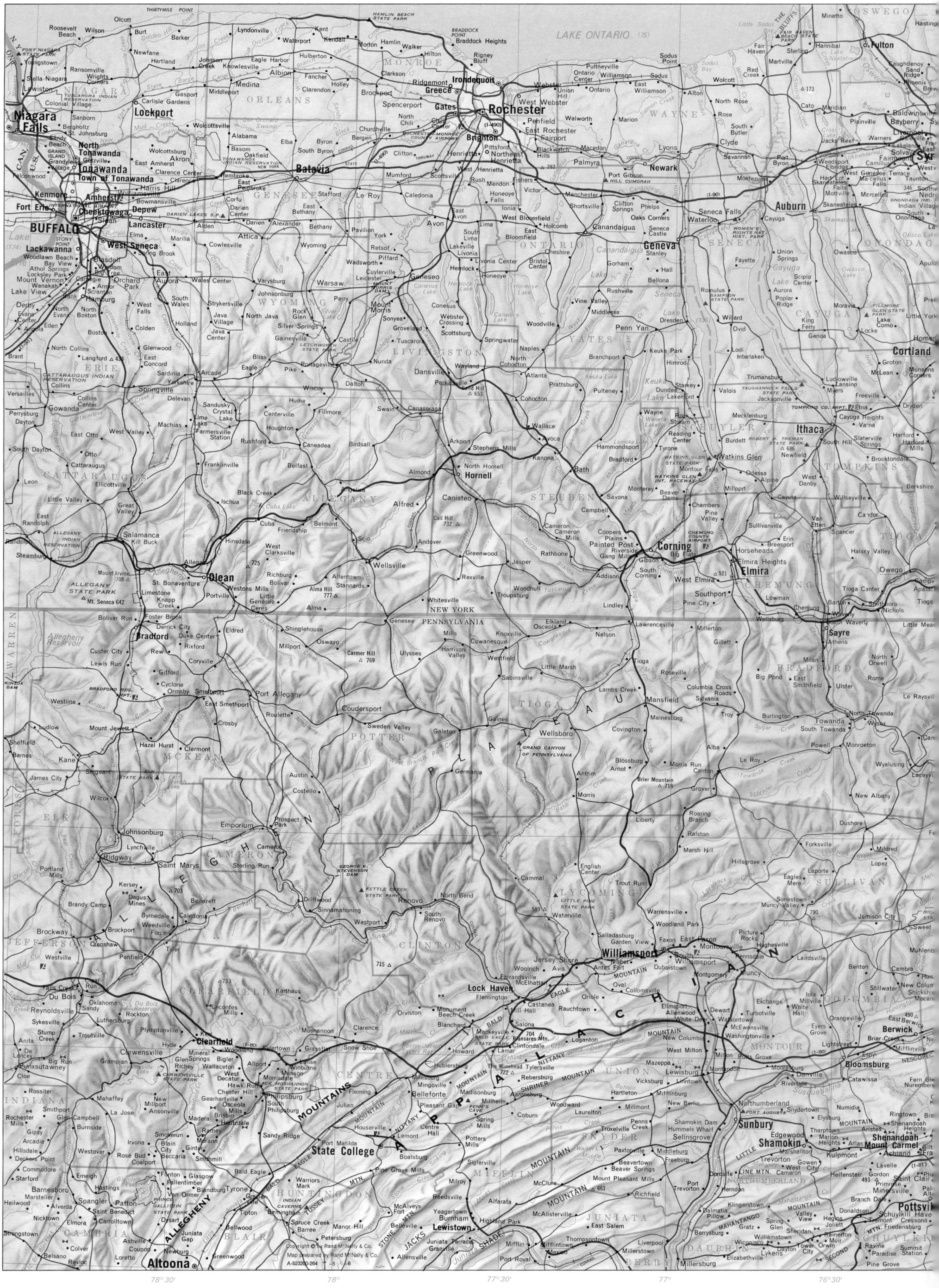
LAKE ONTARIO
Niagara Falls
Lockport
Tonawanda
BUFFALO
Lackawanna
Batavia
Rochester
Irondequoit
Greece
Gates
Brighton
Geneva
Auburn
Cortland
Ithaca
Elmira
Corning
Hornell
Olean
Bradford
Sayre
Wellsboro
Coudersport
Williamsport
Lock Haven
Clearfield
Du Bois
State College
Bellefonte
Altoona
Lewistown
Sunbury
Shamokin
Bloomsburg
Berwick
NEW YORK
PENNSYLVANIA
ALLEGHENY PLATEAU
APPALACHIAN
Copyright © by Rand McNally & Co.
Map prepared by Rand McNally & Co.

| ENGLISH | airport, arpt. | bay | creek, cr. | hill | island | lake | mountain | reservoir | state park, s.p. |
|---|---|---|---|---|---|---|---|---|---|
| DEUTSCH | Flughafen | Bucht | Bach | Hügel | Insel | See | Berg | Stausee | Naturpark |
| ESPAÑOL | aeropuerto | bahía | riachuelo | colina | isla | lago | montaña | embalse | parque provincial |
| FRANÇAIS | aéroport | baie | crique | colline | île | lac | montagne | réservoir | parc régional |
| PORTUGUÊS | aeroporto | baía | riacho | colina | ilha | lago | montanha | reservatório | parque estadual |

ADIRONDACK MOUNTAINS
CATSKILL MOUNTAINS
ATLANTIC OCEAN
Long Island Sound
VERMONT
MASSACHUSETTS
CONNECTICUT
NEW YORK
NEW JERSEY
PENNSYLVANIA
Rome
Utica
Oneida
Gloversville
Amsterdam
Schenectady
Glens Falls
Saratoga Springs
Troy
Albany
Pittsfield
Oneonta
Binghamton
Kingston
Poughkeepsie
Newburgh
Middletown
Danbury
Bridgeport
Stamford
Scranton
Wilkes-Barre
Allentown
Bethlehem
Easton
Paterson
Newark
Jersey City
Elizabeth
NEW YORK
Yonkers
White Plains
Perth Amboy
Map continues page 207
Map continues pages 208-209

Kilometers 0 10 20 30 40 50 Km.
Statute Miles 0 10 20 30 40 50 Mi.

Scale 1:1,000,000

One centimeter represents 10 kilometers.
One inch represents approximately 16 miles.
Lambert Conformal Conic Projection

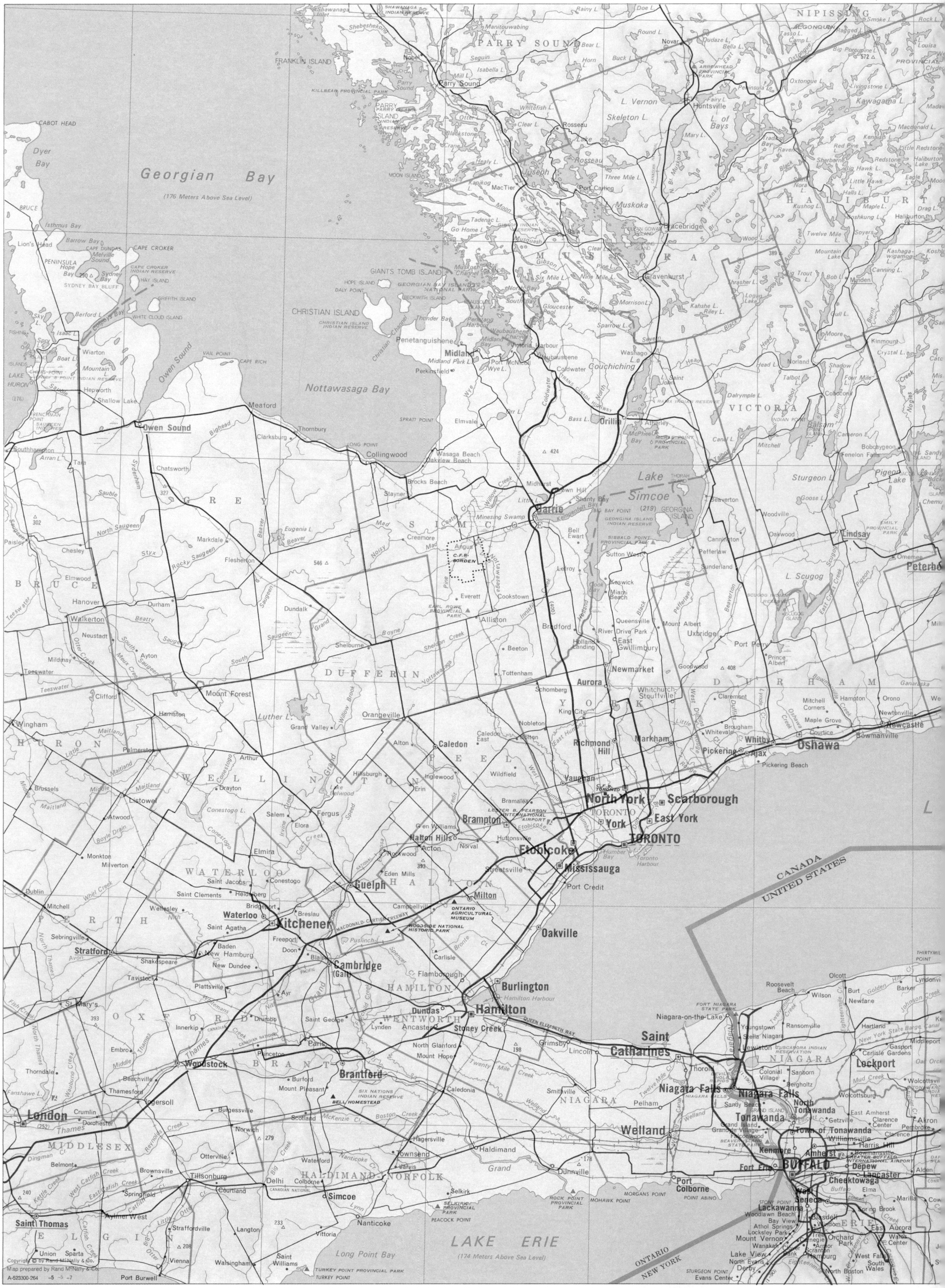
Georgian Bay
(176 Meters Above Sea Level)
Nottawasaga Bay
Lake Simcoe
LAKE ERIE
(174 Meters Above Sea Level)
Long Point Bay
Hamilton Harbour
Toronto Harbour
CANADA
UNITED STATES
ONTARIO
NEW YORK
PARRY SOUND
MUSKOKA
HALIBURTON
VICTORIA
BRUCE
GREY
SIMCOE
DUFFERIN
YORK
DURHAM
PEEL
HURON
WELLINGTON
WATERLOO
HALTON
PERTH
OXFORD
BRANT
HAMILTON
WENTWORTH
MIDDLESEX
ELGIN
HALDIMAND-NORFOLK
NIAGARA
ERIE
Owen Sound
Barrie
Orillia
Midland
Collingwood
Toronto
North York
Scarborough
East York
York
Etobicoke
Mississauga
Brampton
Oakville
Burlington
Hamilton
Kitchener
Waterloo
Guelph
Cambridge (Galt)
Brantford
Woodstock
Stratford
London
Saint Thomas
Simcoe
Saint Catharines
Niagara Falls
Welland
Oshawa
Whitby
Newcastle
Lindsay
Buffalo
Lockport
Tonawanda
Lackawanna
Copyright © by Rand McNally & Co.
Map prepared by Rand McNally & Co.
A-523300-264 -5 -5 -7

| ENGLISH | airport | bay | canal | channel | creek, cr. | Indian reservation | island | lake, l. | point |
|---|---|---|---|---|---|---|---|---|---|
| DEUTSCH | Flughafen | Bucht | Kanal | Kanal | Bach | Indianerreservation | Insel | See | Landspitze |
| ESPAÑOL | aeropuerto | bahía | canal | canal | riachuelo | reserva de Indios | isla | lago | punta |
| FRANÇAIS | aéroport | baie | canal | canal | crique | réserve indienne | île | lac | pointe |
| PORTUGUÊS | aeroporto | baía | canal | canal | riacho | reserva indígena | ilha | lago | ponta |

Map continues pages 214-215

Map continues page 206

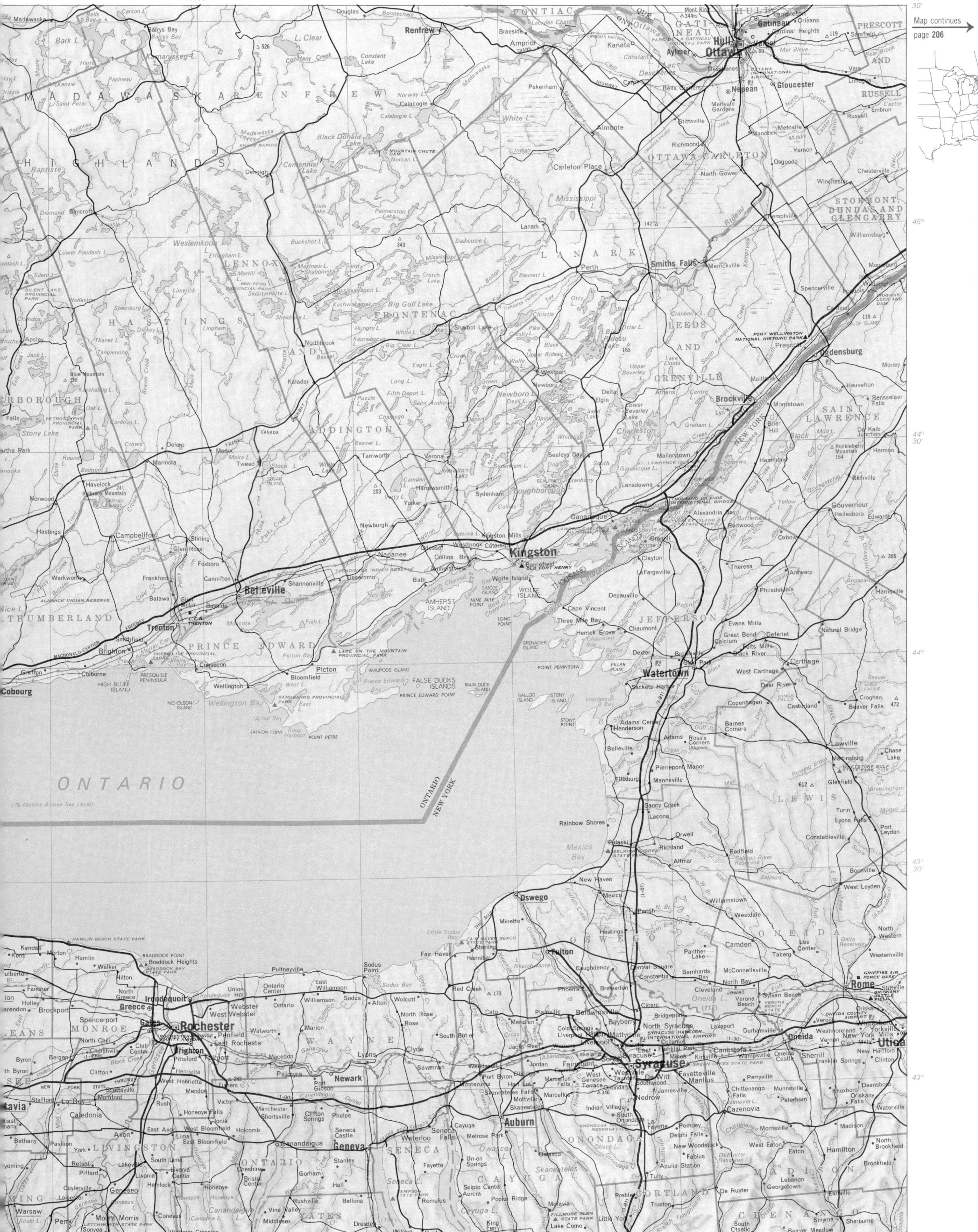
78°
77°30′
77°
76°30′
76°
75°30′
45° 30′
45°
44° 30′
44°
43° 30′
43°
PONTIAC
GATINEAU
Hull
Gatineau
Ottawa
Aylmer
Nepean
Gloucester
Kanata
Arnprior
Renfrew
Pakenham
Almonte
Carleton Place
Smiths Falls
Perth
Lanark
Richmond
Stittsville
OTTAWA-CARLETON
PRESCOTT AND RUSSELL
STORMONT, DUNDAS AND GLENGARRY
MADAWASKA
RENFREW
HIGHLANDS
LENNOX
HASTINGS
FRONTENAC
LANARK
LEEDS AND GRENVILLE
ADDINGTON
Barrys Bay
Bancroft
Denbigh
Madoc
Marmora
Tweed
Havelock
Norwood
Campbellford
Stirling
Frankford
Belleville
Trenton
Brighton
Colborne
Cobourg
Picton
Wellington
Napanee
Deseronto
Kingston
Gananoque
Brockville
Prescott
Ogdensburg
Kemptville
Merrickville
Wolfe Island
PRINCE EDWARD
THUMBERLAND
ONTARIO
(75 Meters Above Sea Level)
ONTARIO
NEW YORK
JEFFERSON
SAINT LAWRENCE
LEWIS
OSWEGO
ONEIDA
ONONDAGA
CAYUGA
SENECA
WAYNE
MONROE
ONTARIO
LIVINGSTON
YATES
CORTLAND
MADISON
CHENANGO
Watertown
Carthage
Lowville
Pulaski
Oswego
Fulton
Syracuse
Rome
Utica
Oneida
Auburn
Geneva
Canandaigua
Newark
Rochester
Greece
Irondequoit
Brighton
Penn Yan
Cortland
Homer
Seneca Falls
Skaneateles
Cazenovia
Hamilton
Camden
Boonville
Sackets Harbor
Clayton
Alexandria Bay
Cape Vincent
Fort Wellington National Historic Park
Thousand Islands

Map continues pages 210-211

Kilometers 0 10 20 30 40 50 Km.

Statute Miles 0 10 20 30 40 50 Mi.

Scale 1:1,000,000

One centimeter represents 10 kilometers.

One inch represents approximately 16 miles.

Lambert Conformal Conic Projection

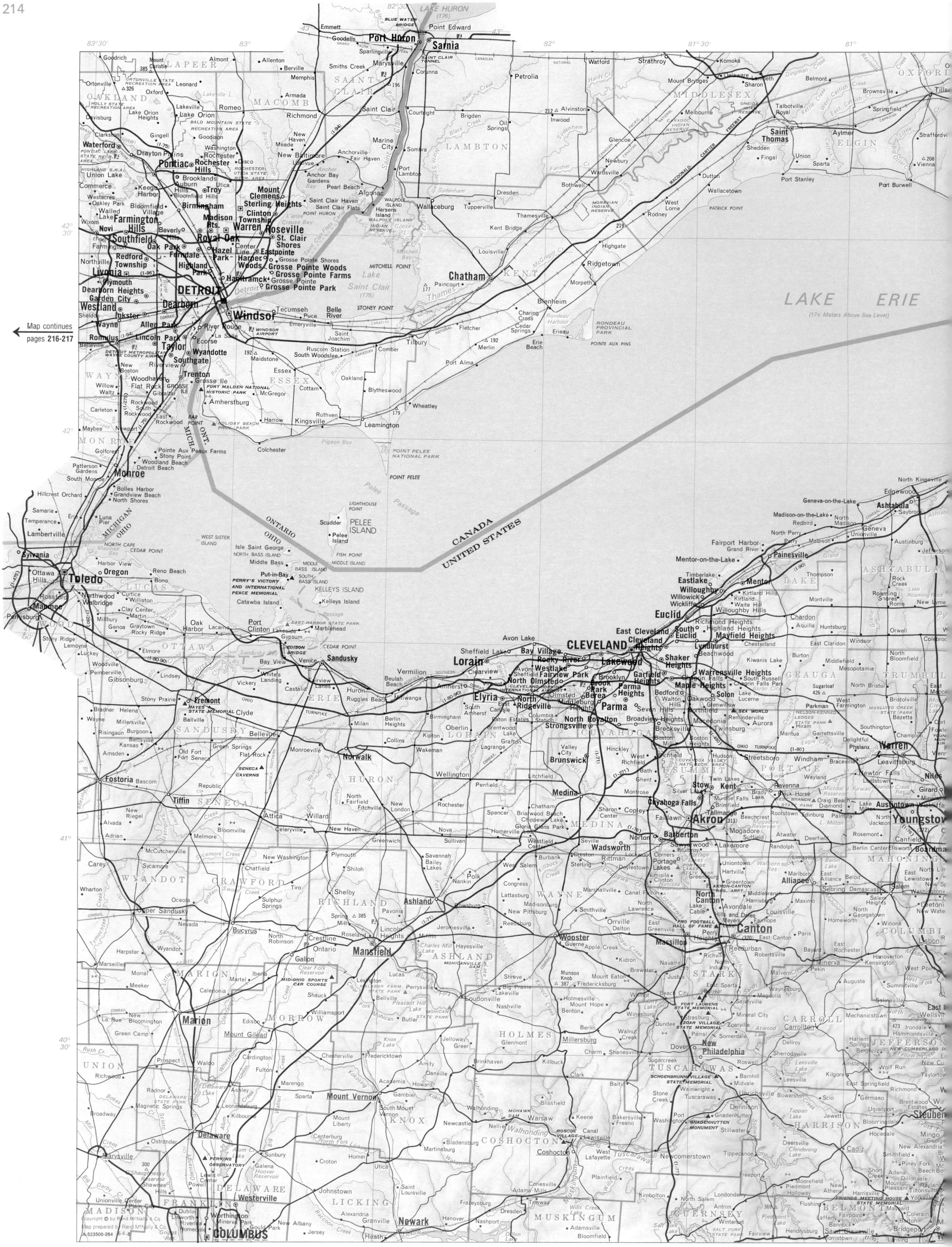
LAKE HURON
LAKE ERIE
(174 Meters Above Sea Level)
Lake Saint Clair
CANADA
UNITED STATES
ONTARIO
OHIO
MICHIGAN
DETROIT
Windsor
Toledo
CLEVELAND
Sarnia
Port Huron
Chatham
Lorain
Elyria
Akron
Canton
Youngstown
Mansfield
Marion
Delaware
Newark
COLUMBUS
Sandusky
Monroe
Ann Arbor
Leamington
Saint Thomas
PELEE ISLAND
KELLEYS ISLAND
Copyright © by Rand McNally & Co.
Map prepared by Rand McNally & Co.
A-523500-264 6-6-8

Map continues pages 216-217

Map continues page 218

| | | | | | | | | |
|---|---|---|---|---|---|---|---|---|
| ENGLISH | airport | creek, cr. | hill | lake, l. | mountain, mtn. | point, pt. | reservoir, res. | state park |
| DEUTSCH | Flughafen | Bach | Hügel | See | Berg | Landspitze | Stausee | Naturpark |
| ESPAÑOL | aeropuerto | riachuelo | colina | lago | montaña | punta | embalse | parque provincial |
| FRANÇAIS | aéroport | crique | colline | lac | montagne | pointe | réservoir | parc régional |
| PORTUGUÊS | aeroporto | riacho | colina | lago | montanha | ponta | reservatório | parque estadual |

Map continues pages 212-213

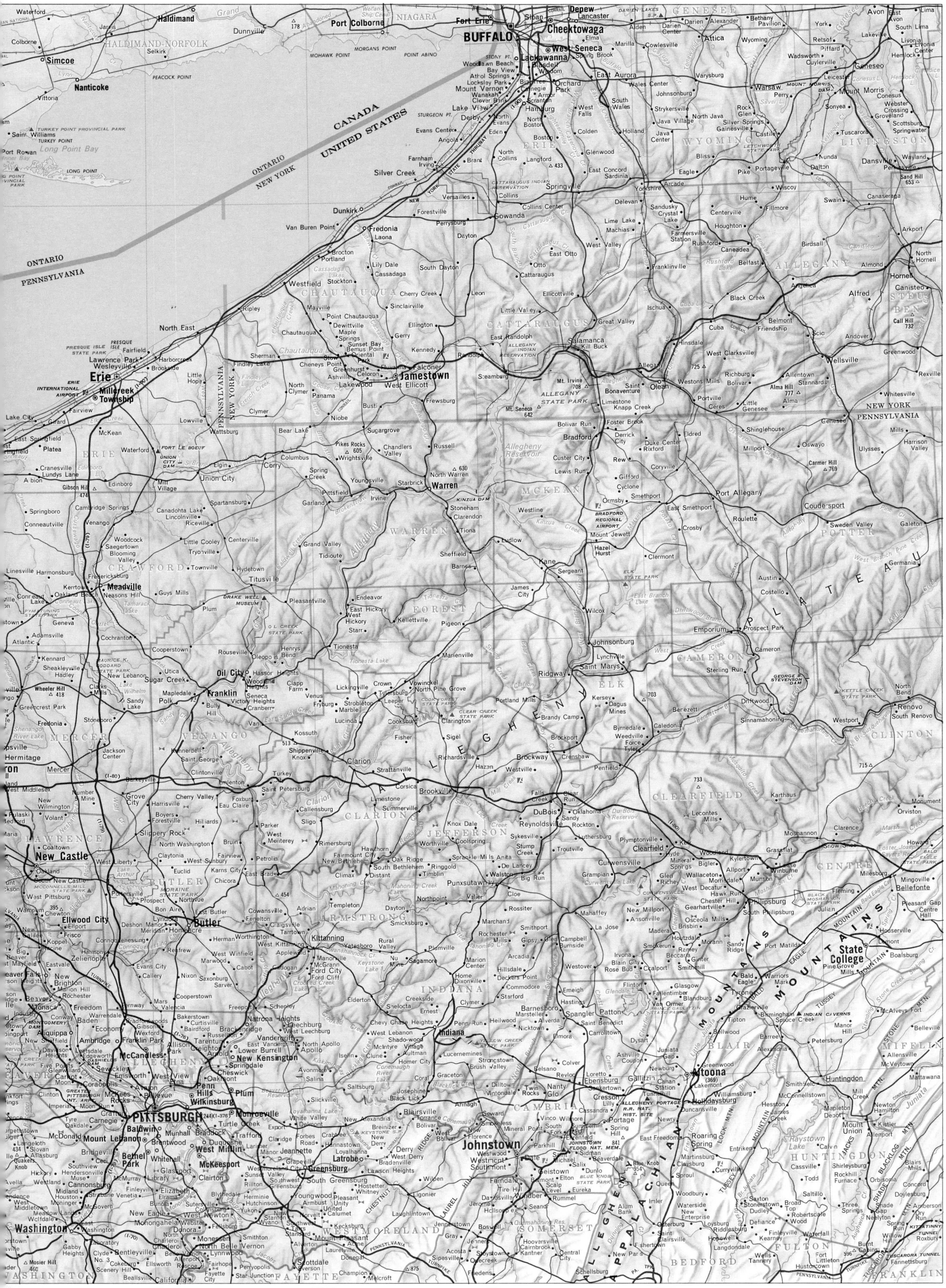

BUFFALO
Erie
Jamestown
Warren
Meadville
Oil City
Franklin
New Castle
Butler
PITTSBURGH
Washington
Johnstown
Altoona
State College
Indiana
Kittanning
Clarion
DuBois
Bradford
Olean
Salamanca
Dunkirk
Fredonia
Hornell
Wellsville
Coudersport
Emporium
Saint Marys
Ridgway
Clearfield
Philipsburg
Bellefonte
Huntingdon
Greensburg
Latrobe
McKeesport
Simcoe
Nanticoke
Haldimand
Port Colborne
Fort Erie
Cheektowaga
Lackawanna
West Seneca
Depew
Lancaster
CANADA
UNITED STATES
ONTARIO
NEW YORK
PENNSYLVANIA
Long Point Bay
ERIE
CHAUTAUQUA
CATTARAUGUS
ALLEGANY
WYOMING
LIVINGSTON
STEUBEN
McKEAN
POTTER
WARREN
CRAWFORD
FOREST
ELK
CAMERON
CLINTON
VENANGO
MERCER
LAWRENCE
BUTLER
CLARION
JEFFERSON
CLEARFIELD
CENTRE
ARMSTRONG
INDIANA
CAMBRIA
BLAIR
HUNTINGDON
MIFFLIN
ALLEGHENY
BEAVER
WESTMORELAND
SOMERSET
BEDFORD
FULTON
FAYETTE
WASHINGTON
FRANKLIN
ALLEGHENY PLATEAU
ALLEGHENY MOUNTAINS
APPALACHIAN
BALD EAGLE MOUNTAIN
Allegheny Reservoir
Allegheny State Park
80°
79°30'
79°
78°30'
78°
42°
41°30'
41°
40°30'


Map continues pages 210-211

Kilometers 0 10 20 30 40 50 Km.

Statute Miles 0 10 20 30 40 50 Mi.

Scale 1:1,000,000

One centimeter represents 10 kilometers.
One inch represents approximately 16 miles.
Lambert Conformal Conic Projection

LAKE MICHIGAN
(176 Meters Above Sea Level)
MILWAUKEE
CHICAGO
Madison
Watertown
Menomonee Falls
Waukesha
Racine
Kenosha
Janesville
Beloit
Rockford
Belvidere
Waukegan
North Chicago
Elgin
Arlington Hts.
Mt. Prospect
Des Plaines
Evanston
Skokie
Schaumburg
Wheaton
Naperville
Aurora
Joliet
Oak Park
Cicero
Hammond
Gary
Michigan City
Valparaiso
Merrillville
Kankakee
Ottawa
La Salle
Streator
Pontiac
Bloomington
Normal
Lafayette
West Lafayette
Rantoul
Benton
Muskegon
WISCONSIN
ILLINOIS
INDIANA
DANE
JEFFERSON
WAUKESHA
WALWORTH
RACINE
KENOSHA
ROCK
GREEN
WINNEBAGO
BOONE
MCHENRY
LAKE
COOK
DU PAGE
KANE
DE KALB
OGLE
LEE
LA SALLE
KENDALL
GRUNDY
WILL
KANKAKEE
LIVINGSTON
IROQUOIS
FORD
MCLEAN
WOODFORD
DE WITT
PIATT
CHAMPAIGN
VERMILION
NEWTON
JASPER
PORTER
LA PORTE
STARKE
PULASKI
WHITE
BENTON
WARREN
TIPPECANOE
CARROLL
CASS
CLINTON
FOUNTAIN
BERRIEN
Copyright © by Rand McNally & Co.
Map prepared by Rand McNally & Co.
A-523000-264


Map continues page 219

| | | | | | | |
|---|---|---|---|---|---|---|
| ENGLISH | airport | creek, cr. | ditch | lake, l. | reservoir | state park, s.p. |
| DEUTSCH | Flughafen | Bach | Graben | See | Stausee | Naturpark |
| ESPAÑOL | aeropuerto | riachuelo | acequia | lago | embalse | parque provincial |
| FRANÇAIS | aéroport | crique | fossé | lac | réservoir | parc régional |
| PORTUGUÊS | aeroporto | riacho | fosso | lago | reservatório | parque estadual |

Grand Rapids
Wyoming
Kalamazoo
Battle Creek
Lansing
East Lansing
Jackson
Ann Arbor
Flint
Pontiac
Detroit
Windsor
Toledo
Fort Wayne
Lima
Elkhart
Marion
Muncie
Kokomo
OTTAWA
KENT
IONIA
CLINTON
SHIAWASSEE
GENESEE
LAPEER
ALLEGAN
BARRY
EATON
INGHAM
LIVINGSTON
OAKLAND
VAN BUREN
KALAMAZOO
CALHOUN
JACKSON
WASHTENAW
WAYNE
CASS
ST. JOSEPH
BRANCH
HILLSDALE
LENAWEE
MONROE
ELKHART
LAGRANGE
STEUBEN
WILLIAMS
FULTON
LUCAS
OTTAWA
NOBLE
DE KALB
DEFIANCE
HENRY
WOOD
SANDUSKY
KOSCIUSKO
WHITLEY
ALLEN
PAULDING
PUTNAM
HANCOCK
SENECA
WABASH
HUNTINGTON
WELLS
ADAMS
VAN WERT
ALLEN
HARDIN
WYANDOT
MIAMI
GRANT
BLACKFORD
JAY
MERCER
AUGLAIZE
LOGAN
HOWARD
TIPTON
MADISON
DELAWARE
RANDOLPH
DARKE
SHELBY
CHAMPAIGN
UNION
MARION
MICHIGAN
OHIO
INDIANA
CANADA
U.S.
LAKE ERIE
(174 Meters Above Sea Level)


Map continues pages 214-215

Map continues page 218

Kilometers 0 10 20 30 40 50 Km.

Statute Miles 0 10 20 30 40 50 Mi.

Scale 1:1,000,000

One centimeter represents 10 kilometers.
One inch represents approximately 16 miles.
Lambert Conformal Conic Projection

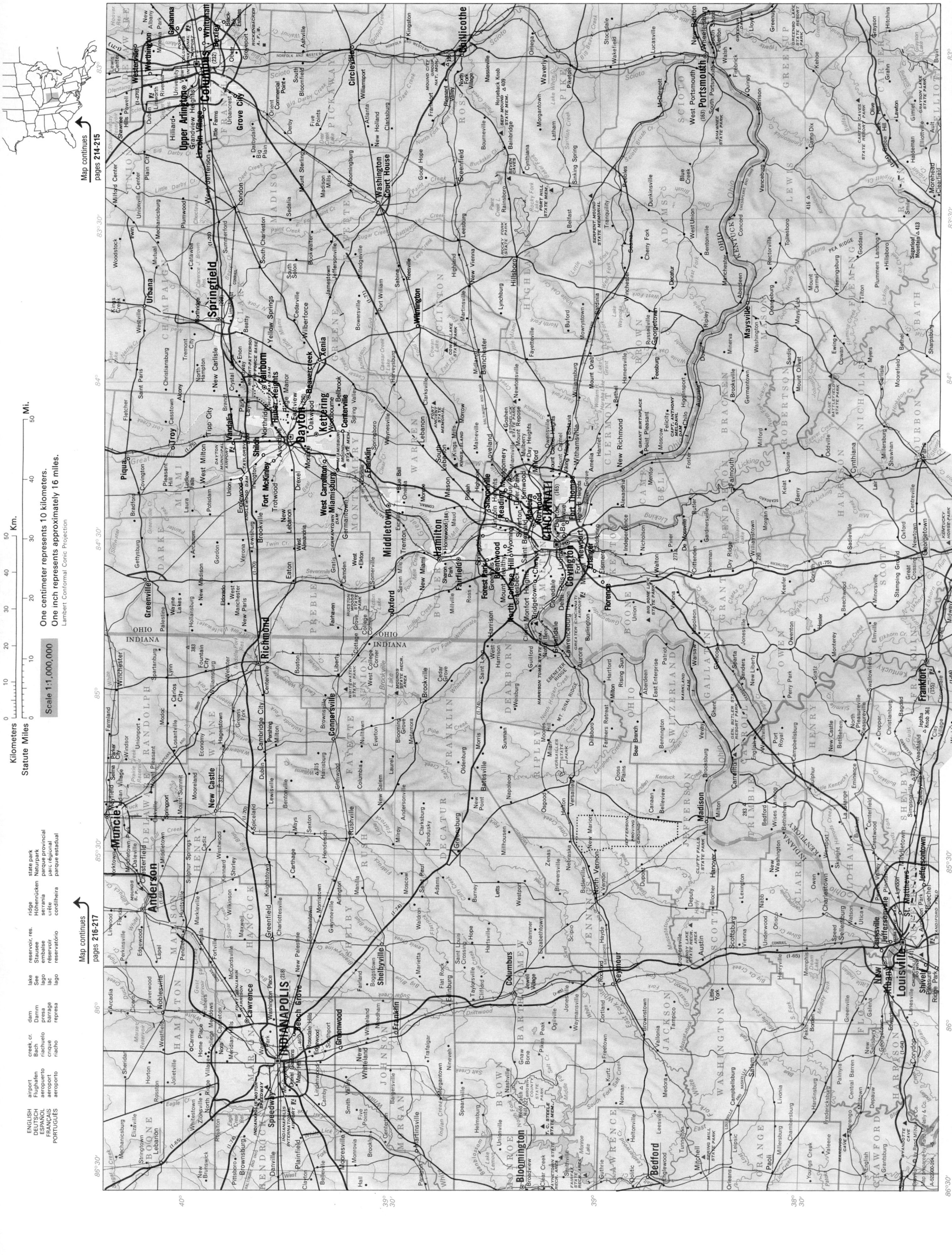
ENGLISH airport creek, cr. dam lake reservoir, res. ridge state park
DEUTSCH Flughafen Bach Damm See Stausee Höhenrücken Naturpark
ESPAÑOL aeropuerto riachuelo presa lago embalse serranía parque provincial
FRANÇAIS aéroport crique barrage lac réservoir crête parc régional
PORTUGUÊS aeroporto riacho represa lago reservatório cordilheira parque estadual
Map continues pages 216-217
Kilometers 0 10 20 30 40 50 Km.
Statute Miles 0 10 20 30 40 50 Mi.
Scale 1:1,000,000
One centimeter represents 10 kilometers.
One inch represents approximately 16 miles.
Lambert Conformal Conic Projection
Map continues pages 214-215
INDIANAPOLIS
CINCINNATI
Louisville
Columbus
Dayton
Springfield
Hamilton
Middletown
Richmond
Muncie
Anderson
Bloomington
Columbus
Frankfort
Portsmouth
Chillicothe
Covington
Newport

Map continues pages 216-217

Springfield
Decatur
Jacksonville
Taylorville
Lincoln
Quincy
Hannibal
Alton
Granite City
Belleville
East St. Louis
St. Louis
St. Charles
Florissant
Centralia
Mount Vernon
Columbia
Jefferson City
Mexico
Fulton
Mississippi
Missouri
Illinois
SANGAMON
MACOUPIN
MADISON
ST. CLAIR
MONTGOMERY
CHRISTIAN
JERSEY
GREENE
PIKE
CALLAWAY
BOONE
GASCONADE
FRANKLIN
WARREN
LINCOLN
AUDRAIN
MARION
RALLS
ADAMS
BROWN
SCOTT
MORGAN
CASS
MENARD
LOGAN
MACON
SHELBY
FAYETTE
BOND
CLINTON
MARION
WASHINGTON
JEFFERSON
MONROE
OSAGE
MARIES
COLE
KNOX
LEWIS
DIVIDING RIDGE
ILLINOIS
MISSOURI

Scale 1:1,000,000

Kilometers 0 10 20 30 40 50 Km.

Statute Miles 0 10 20 30 40 50 Mi.

One centimeter represents 10 kilometers.
One inch represents approximately 16 miles.
Lambert Conformal Conic Projection

| | | | | | | | |
|---|---|---|---|---|---|---|---|
| ENGLISH | creek, cr. | dam | island, I. | lake, L. | lock | reservoir | state park |
| DEUTSCH | Bach | Damm | Insel | See | Schleuse | Stausee | Naturpark |
| ESPAÑOL | riachuelo | presa | isla | lago | esclusa | embalse | parque provincial |
| FRANÇAIS | crique | barrage | île | lac | écluse | réservoir | parc régional |
| PORTUGUÊS | riacho | represa | ilha | lago | eclusa | reservatório | parque estadual |

Kilometers 0 10 20 30 40 50 Km.
Statute Miles 0 10 20 30 40 50 Mi.

Scale 1:1,000,000

One centimeter represents 10 kilometers.
One inch represents approximately 16 miles.
Lambert Conformal Conic Projection

| ENGLISH | DEUTSCH | ESPAÑOL | FRANÇAIS | PORTUGUÊS |
|---|---|---|---|---|
| bay | Bucht | bahía | baie | baía |
| canal | Kanal | canal | canal | canal |
| cape | Kap | cabo | cap | cabo |
| creek, cr. | Bach | riachuelo | crique | riacho |
| inlet | Einfahrt | abra | bras de mer | enseada |
| island | Insel | isla | île | ilha |
| key | Klippe | cayo | caye | recife |
| lake, l. | See | lago | lac | lago |
| swamp | Sumpf | pantano | marais | pântano |

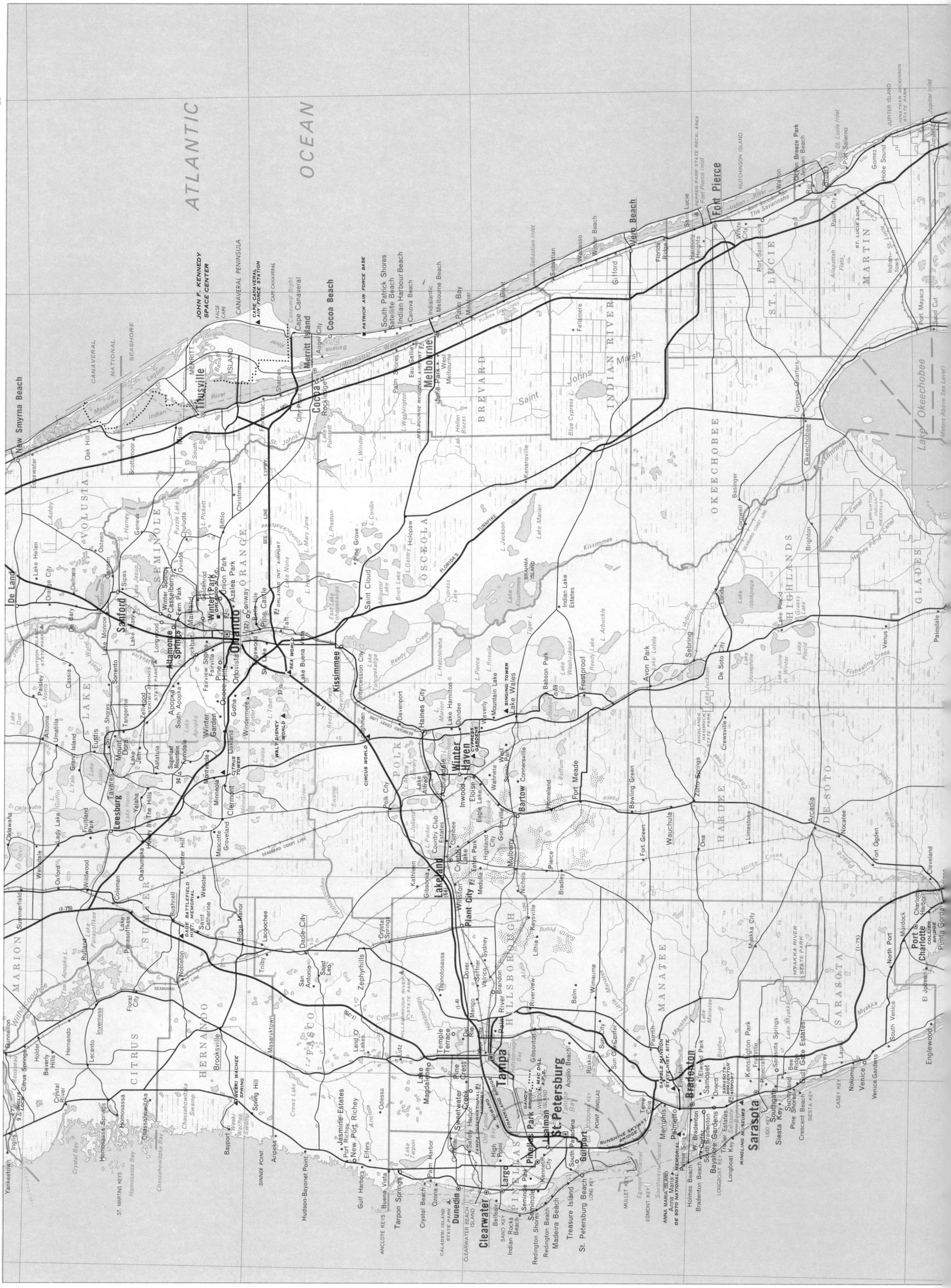
ATLANTIC
OCEAN
Orlando
Tampa
St. Petersburg
Clearwater
Sarasota
Bradenton
Lakeland
Kissimmee
Sanford
Melbourne
Cocoa Beach
Fort Pierce
Vero Beach
Titusville
New Smyrna Beach
De Land
Winter Haven
Leesburg
Lake Okeechobee
JOHN F. KENNEDY SPACE CENTER

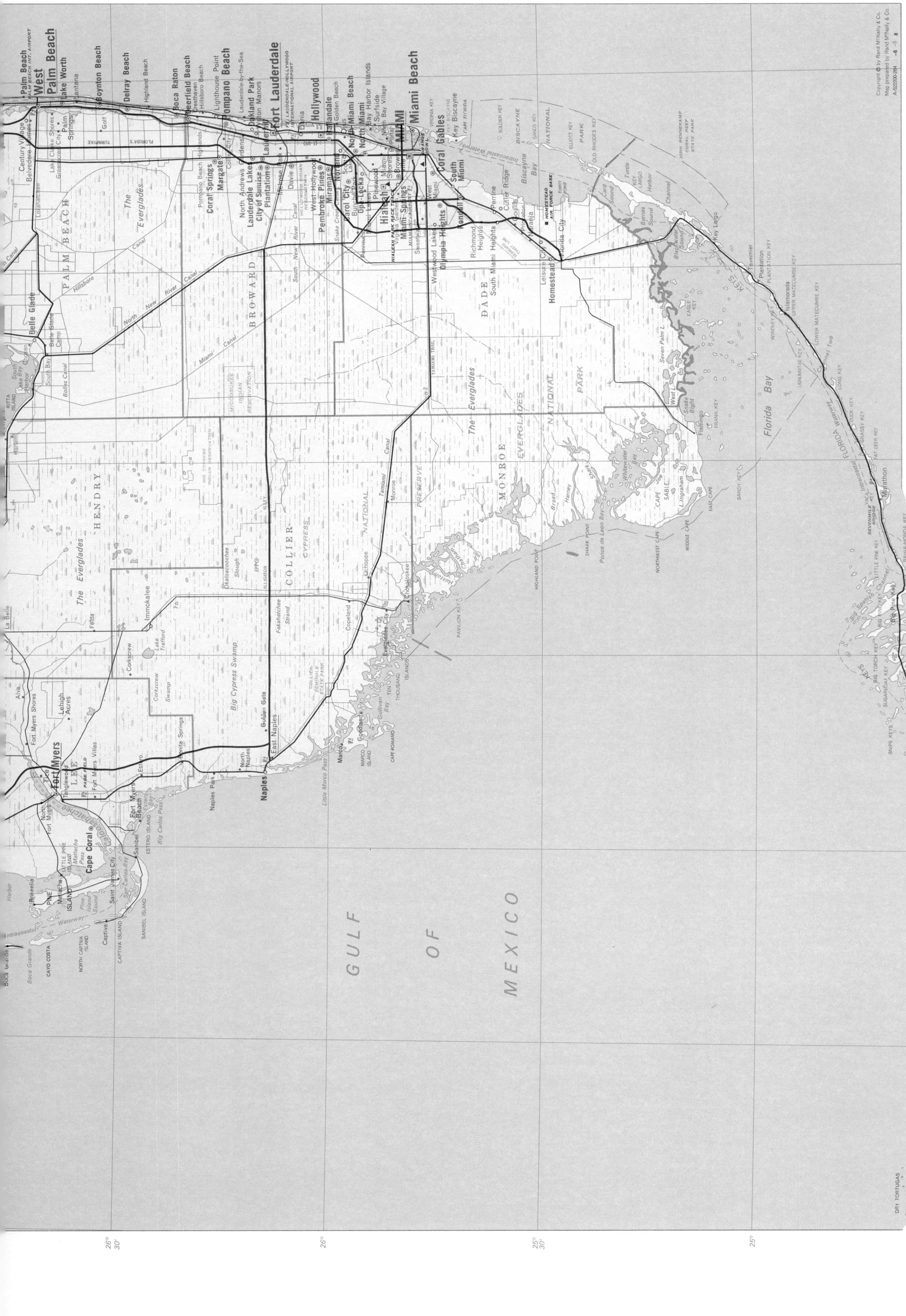
West Palm Beach
Lake Worth
Boynton Beach
Delray Beach
Boca Raton
Deerfield Beach
Pompano Beach
Fort Lauderdale
Hollywood
North Miami Beach
North Miami
Miami Beach
MIAMI
Hialeah
Coral Gables
Miami Springs
South Miami
Homestead
Key Largo
Key West
Marathon
Naples
Fort Myers
Cape Coral
Belle Glade
Immokalee
GULF
OF
MEXICO
Florida Bay
PALM BEACH
BROWARD
DADE
MONROE
COLLIER
HENDRY
LEE
The Everglades
EVERGLADES NATIONAL PARK
Big Cypress Swamp
Biscayne Bay
DRY TORTUGAS
Copyright © by Rand McNally & Co.

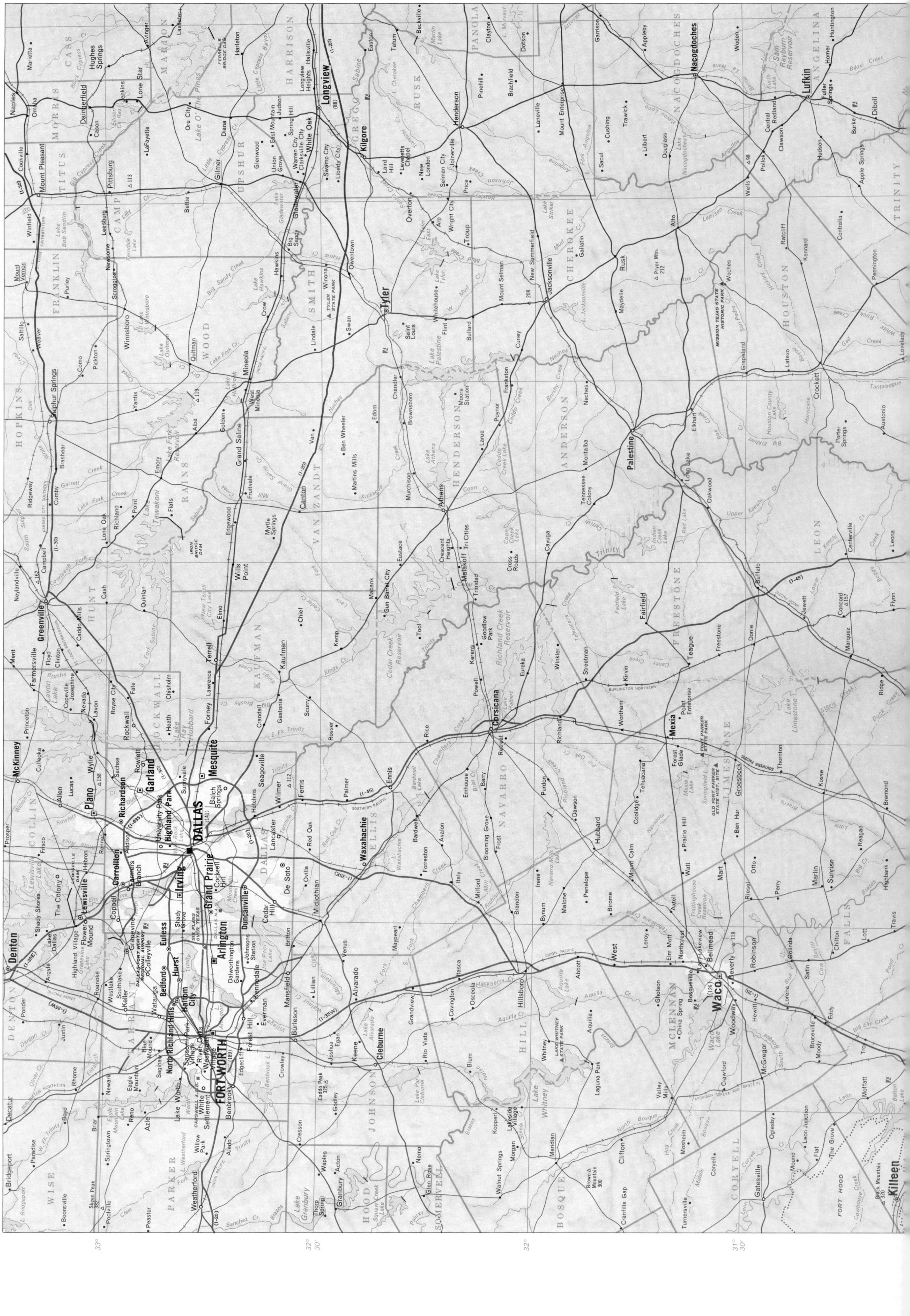
DALLAS
FORT WORTH
Arlington
Garland
Mesquite
Irving
Grand Prairie
Richardson
Plano
McKinney
Denton
Lewisville
Carrollton
Duncanville
Hurst
Euless
Bedford
Waco
Tyler
Longview
Kilgore
Henderson
Nacogdoches
Lufkin
Palestine
Corsicana
Athens
Jacksonville
Mexia
Waxahachie
Ennis
Cleburne
Weatherford
Terrell
Greenville
Sulphur Springs
Mount Pleasant
Killeen
Hillsboro
Crockett
Fairfield
Kaufman
Canton
Mineola
Gilmer
Pittsburg
Daingerfield
Rusk
Marlin
Gatesville
Granbury
Lake Whitney
Richland Creek Reservoir
Cedar Creek Reservoir
Lake Palestine
Lake Tawakoni
Lake Limestone
Sam Rayburn Reservoir
DENTON
COLLIN
HUNT
HOPKINS
FRANKLIN
TITUS
MORRIS
CASS
MARION
HARRISON
UPSHUR
GREGG
RUSK
PANOLA
SMITH
WOOD
RAINS
VAN ZANDT
KAUFMAN
ROCKWALL
DALLAS
ELLIS
NAVARRO
HENDERSON
ANDERSON
CHEROKEE
NACOGDOCHES
ANGELINA
HOUSTON
TRINITY
LEON
FREESTONE
LIMESTONE
MCLENNAN
HILL
JOHNSON
BOSQUE
HOOD
SOMERVELL
PARKER
WISE
CORYELL
FALLS
CAMP

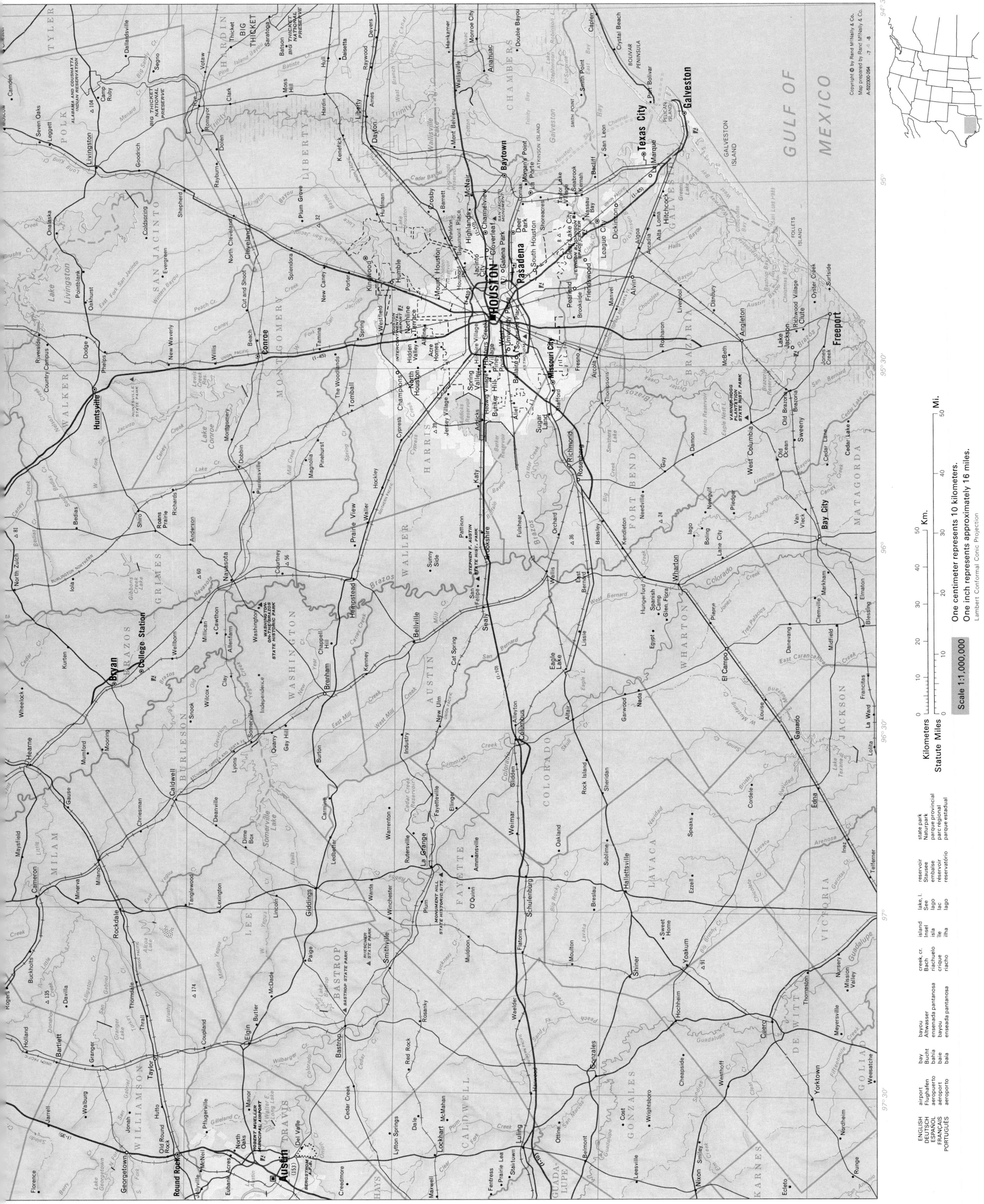
GULF OF MEXICO
HOUSTON
Galveston
Texas City
Pasadena
Baytown
Austin
Bryan
College Station
Huntsville
Conroe
Freeport
Bay City
Scale 1:1,000,000
Kilometers
Statute Miles
One centimeter represents 10 kilometers.
One inch represents approximately 16 miles.
Lambert Conformal Conic Projection
ENGLISH DEUTSCH ESPAÑOL FRANÇAIS PORTUGUÊS
airport Flughafen aeropuerto aéroport aeroporto
bay Bucht bahía baie baía
bayou Altwasser ensenada pantanosa bayou enseada pantanosa
creek, cr. Bach riachuelo crique riacho
island Insel isla île ilha
lake, l. See lago lac lago
reservoir Stausee embalse réservoir reservatório
state park Naturpark parque provincial parc régional parque estadual
Copyright © by Rand McNally & Co.
Map prepared by Rand McNally & Co.

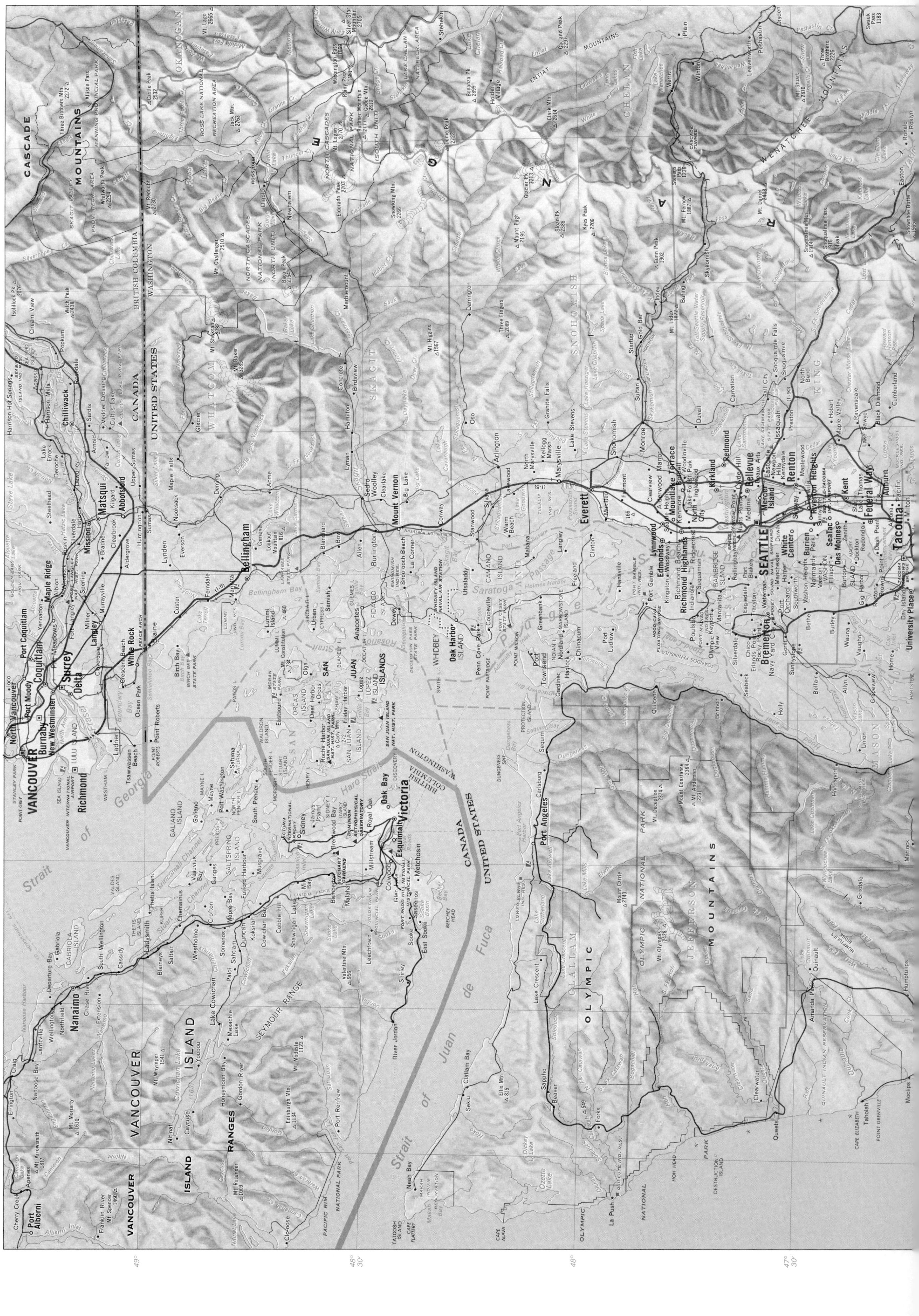
VANCOUVER
Richmond
Burnaby
New Westminster
North Vancouver
Port Moody
Coquitlam
Port Coquitlam
Surrey
Delta
Langley
White Rock
Maple Ridge
Mission
Matsqui
Abbotsford
Chilliwack
CASCADE MOUNTAINS
BRITISH COLUMBIA
WASHINGTON
CANADA
UNITED STATES
Bellingham
Lynden
Ferndale
Blaine
Anacortes
Burlington
Mount Vernon
Sedro Woolley
Oak Harbor
WHIDBEY ISLAND
SAN JUAN ISLANDS
Everett
Marysville
Lynnwood
Edmonds
Mountlake Terrace
Richmond Highlands
Kirkland
Redmond
Bellevue
SEATTLE
Mercer Island
Renton
Bremerton
Federal Way
Kent
Auburn
Tacoma
University Place
Victoria
Esquimalt
Oak Bay
Sidney
Saanich
Nanaimo
Ladysmith
Duncan
Port Alberni
VANCOUVER ISLAND
SEYMOUR RANGE
Strait of Georgia
Strait of Juan de Fuca
Haro Strait
Port Angeles
Sequim
Port Townsend
OLYMPIC MOUNTAINS
OLYMPIC NATIONAL PARK
Forks
La Push
Neah Bay
CLALLAM
JEFFERSON
MASON
KING
SNOHOMISH
SKAGIT
WHATCOM
CHELAN
NORTH CASCADES NATIONAL PARK
Mt. Baker 3285
WENATCHEE MOUNTAINS
Snoqualmie Falls
Issaquah
Snohomish
Monroe
Arlington
Stanwood

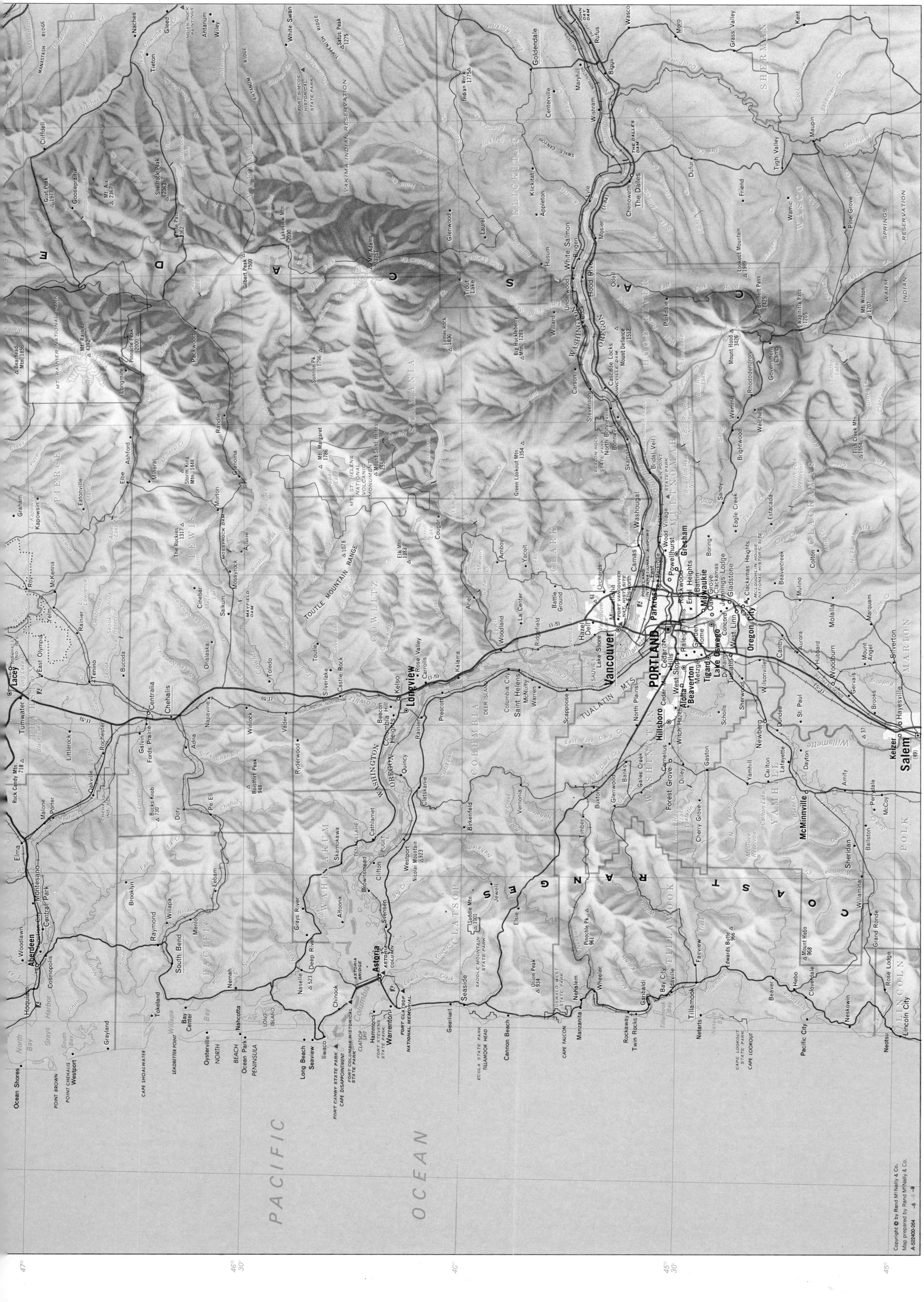
PACIFIC
OCEAN
PORTLAND
Vancouver
Salem
Longview
Kelso
Astoria
Aberdeen
Hoquiam
Centralia
Chehalis
Tumwater
Lacey
The Dalles
Hood River
Goldendale
White Salmon
Gresham
Beaverton
Hillsboro
Tigard
Lake Oswego
Oregon City
McMinnville
Tillamook
Seaside
Warrenton
Long Beach
Ocean Shores
Westport
Raymond
South Bend
Camas
Washougal
Forest Grove
Newberg
Lincoln City
Mt. Rainier
Mt. Adams
Mount Hood
Mount Saint Helens
TOUTLE MOUNTAIN RANGE
TUALATIN MTS
YAKIMA INDIAN RESERVATION
WARM SPRINGS INDIAN RESERVATION
MT. RAINIER NATIONAL PARK
MT. ST. HELENS NATIONAL VOLCANIC MONUMENT
WASHINGTON
OREGON
Columbia
Willamette
PIERCE
LEWIS
COWLITZ
SKAMANIA
KLICKITAT
CLARK
WAHKIAKUM
PACIFIC
CLATSOP
COLUMBIA
WASHINGTON
MULTNOMAH
CLACKAMAS
HOOD RIVER
WASCO
SHERMAN
TILLAMOOK
YAMHILL
POLK
MARION
LINCOLN

Kilometers 0 10 20 30 40 50 Km.

Statute Miles 0 10 20 30 40 50 Mi.

Scale 1:1,000,000

One centimeter represents 10 kilometers.

One inch represents approximately 16 miles.

Lambert Conformal Conic Projection

| ENGLISH | DEUTSCH | ESPAÑOL | FRANÇAIS | PORTUGUÊS |
|---|---|---|---|---|
| bay | Bucht | bahía | baie | baía |
| cape | Kap | cabo | cap | cabo |
| channel | Kanal | canal | canal | canal |
| creek, cr. | Bach | riachuelo | crique | riacho |
| island, I. | Insel | isla | île | ilha |
| lake, l. | See | lago | lac | lago |
| mount | Berg | monte | mont | monte |
| peak | Gipfel | pico | cime | pico |
| strait | Meeresstrasse | estrecho | détroit | estreito |

Reno
Sparks
Sun Valley
Carson City
South Lake Tahoe
Lake Tahoe
SIERRA NEVADA
CARSON RANGE
PINE NUT MOUNTAINS
SWEETWATER MTS.
CATHEDRAL RANGE
YOSEMITE NATIONAL PARK
SACRAMENTO VALLEY
Sacramento
West Sacramento
Stockton
Modesto
Lodi
Davis
Woodland
Yuba City
Marysville
Roseville
Auburn
Placerville
Vacaville
Fairfield
Vallejo
Napa
Santa Rosa
Petaluma
Novato
San Rafael
Richmond
Berkeley
OAKLAND
SAN FRANCISCO
Daly City
Hayward
Fremont
Livermore
Pleasanton
Concord
Walnut Creek
Tracy
Manteca
Turlock
Ceres
Oroville
Willows
Colusa
Clearlake

PACIFIC OCEAN
Monterey Bay
SAN JOAQUIN VALLEY
COAST RANGES
DIABLO RANGE
SANTA LUCIA RANGE
GABILAN RANGE
SIERRA DE SALINAS
SALINAS VALLEY
SANTA CLARA VALLEY
SANTA CRUZ MOUNTAINS
TEMBLOR RANGE
SAN ANDREAS FAULT
KETTLEMAN HILLS
CARRIZO PLAIN
ELK HILLS
MADERA
MERCED
FRESNO
TULARE
KINGS
KERN
SAN BENITO
MONTEREY
SAN LUIS OBISPO
Fresno
Clovis
Madera
Chowchilla
Los Banos
Visalia
Tulare
Hanford
Bakersfield
Delano
Wasco
Shafter
Oildale
Salinas
Monterey
Seaside
Marina
Pacific Grove
Carmel
Watsonville
Santa Cruz
Los Gatos
Gilroy
Morgan Hill
Hollister
King City
Soledad
Greenfield
Gonzales
Coalinga
Avenal
Paso Robles
Atascadero
San Luis Obispo
Morro Bay
Pismo Beach
Cambria
San Simeon
Lemoore
Corcoran
Kerman
Mendota
Firebaugh
Dinuba
Reedley
Selma
Kingsburg
Sanger
San Benito Mtn. 1597
Junipero Serra Peak 1787
Fremont Peak 967
Black Mountain 1104
Mt. Carmel 1346
Lake Nacimiento
Tulare Lake Bed
Scale 1:1,000,000
Kilometers 0 10 20 30 40 50 Km.
Statute Miles 0 10 20 30 40 50 Mi.
One centimeter represents 10 kilometers.
One inch represents approximately 16 miles.
Map continues page 228
ENGLISH bay canal creek, cr. lake, l. mountain, mtn. pass range reservoir slough
DEUTSCH Bucht Kanal Bach See Berg Pass Gebirge Stausee verlandende Wasserfläche
ESPAÑOL bahía canal riachuelo lago montaña paso sierra embalse pantano
FRANÇAIS baie canal crique lac montagne col chaîne réservoir fondrière
PORTUGUÊS baía canal riacho lago montanha passo serra reservatório pântano

Map continues pages 226-227

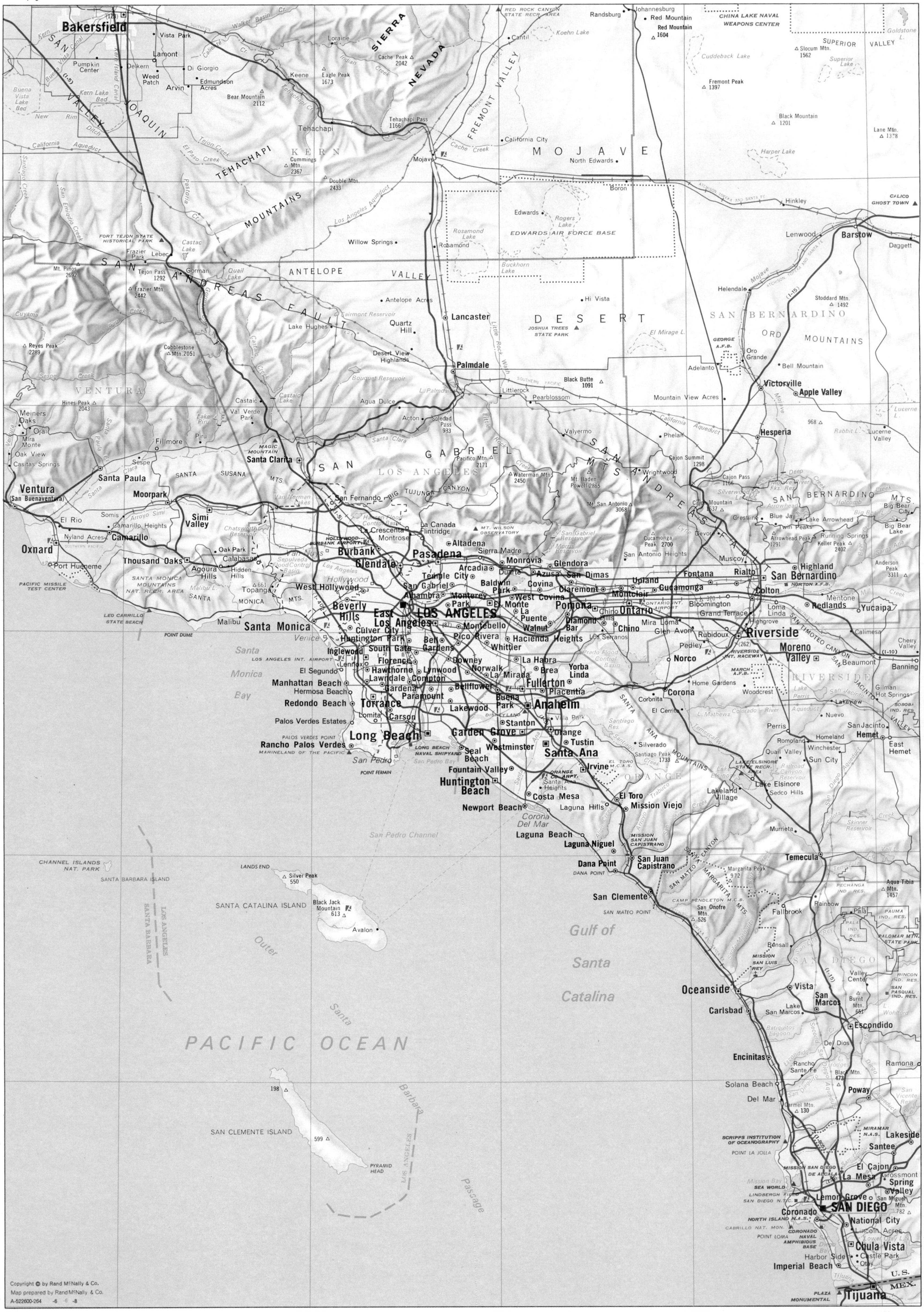
119°
118°30'
118°
117°30'
117°
35°
34° 30'
34°
33° 30'
33°
32° 30'
Bakersfield
SAN JOAQUIN VALLEY
SIERRA NEVADA
TEHACHAPI MOUNTAINS
Tehachapi
Mojave
MOJAVE DESERT
EDWARDS AIR FORCE BASE
CHINA LAKE NAVAL WEAPONS CENTER
ANTELOPE VALLEY
SAN ANDREAS FAULT
Lancaster
Palmdale
Barstow
Victorville
Apple Valley
Hesperia
SAN BERNARDINO MOUNTAINS
SAN GABRIEL MTS.
Ventura (San Buenaventura)
Oxnard
Camarillo
Santa Paula
Santa Clarita
Simi Valley
Thousand Oaks
Burbank
Glendale
Pasadena
LOS ANGELES
Santa Monica
Beverly Hills
Long Beach
Torrance
Anaheim
Santa Ana
Huntington Beach
Newport Beach
Fullerton
Pomona
Ontario
San Bernardino
Riverside
Redlands
Corona
Mission Viejo
San Clemente
Temecula
Oceanside
Escondido
SAN DIEGO
Chula Vista
Tijuana
U.S.
MEX.
PACIFIC OCEAN
Santa Monica Bay
San Pedro Channel
Gulf of Santa Catalina
Outer Santa Barbara Passage
SANTA CATALINA ISLAND
SAN CLEMENTE ISLAND
SANTA BARBARA ISLAND
CHANNEL ISLANDS NAT. PARK
Avalon
Copyright © by Rand McNally & Co.
Map prepared by Rand McNally & Co.
A-522600-264 -6 -8

| ENGLISH | canyon | creek, cr. | lake, l. | mountain, mtn. | pass | peak | point | reservoir, res |
|---|---|---|---|---|---|---|---|---|
| DEUTSCH | Cañon | Bach | See | Berg | Pass | Gipfel | Landspitze | Stausee |
| ESPAÑOL | cañón | riachuelo | lago | montaña | paso | pico | punta | embalse |
| FRANÇAIS | canyon | crique | lac | montagne | col | cime | pointe | réservoir |
| PORTUGUÊS | canhão | riacho | lago | montanha | passo | pico | ponta | reservatório |

Kilometers 0 10 20 30 40 50 Km.

Statute Miles 0 10 20 30 40 50 Mi.

Scale 1:1,000,000

One centimeter represents 10 kilometers.
One inch represents approximately 16 miles.
Lambert Conformal Conic Projection

a

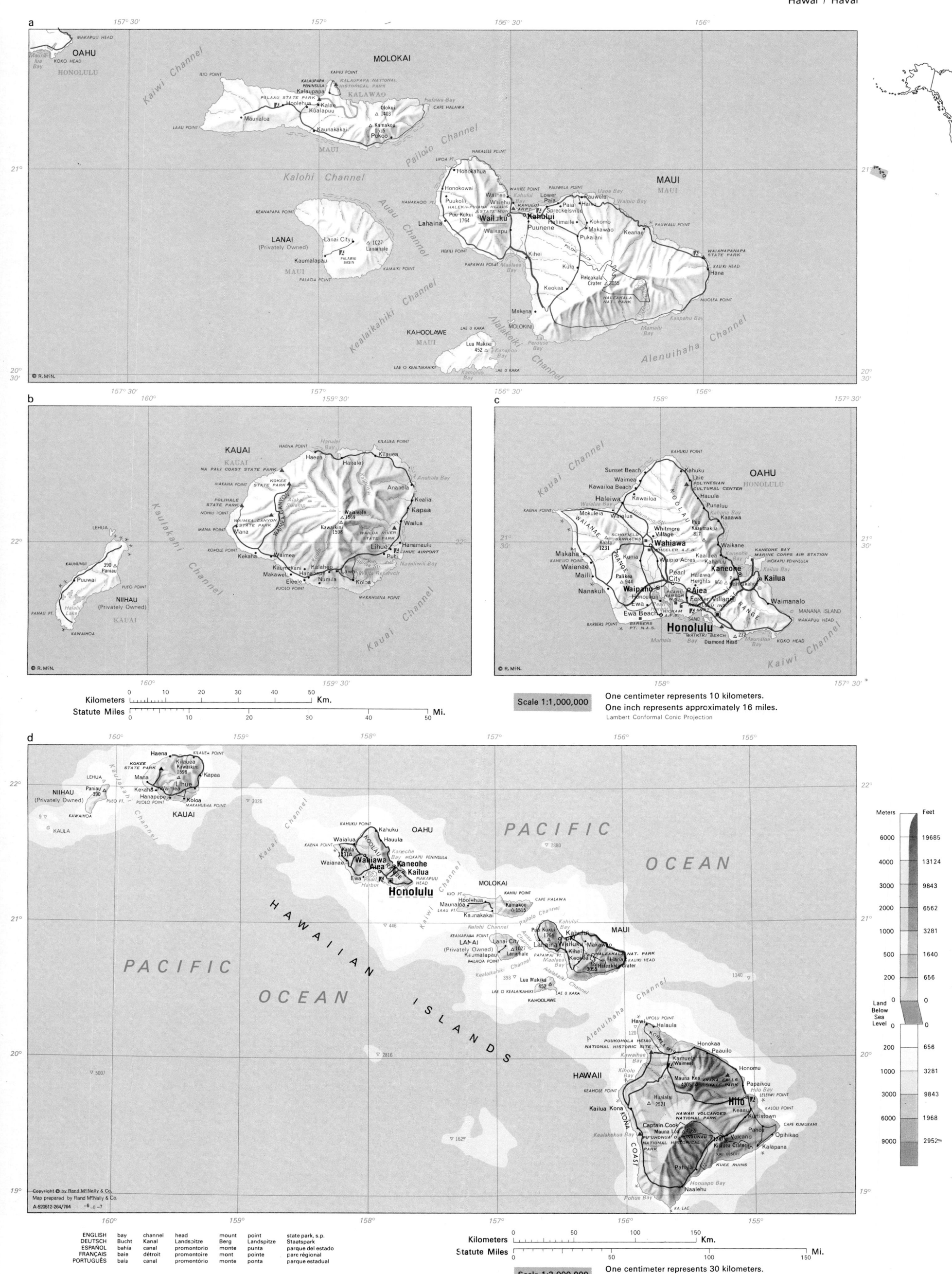

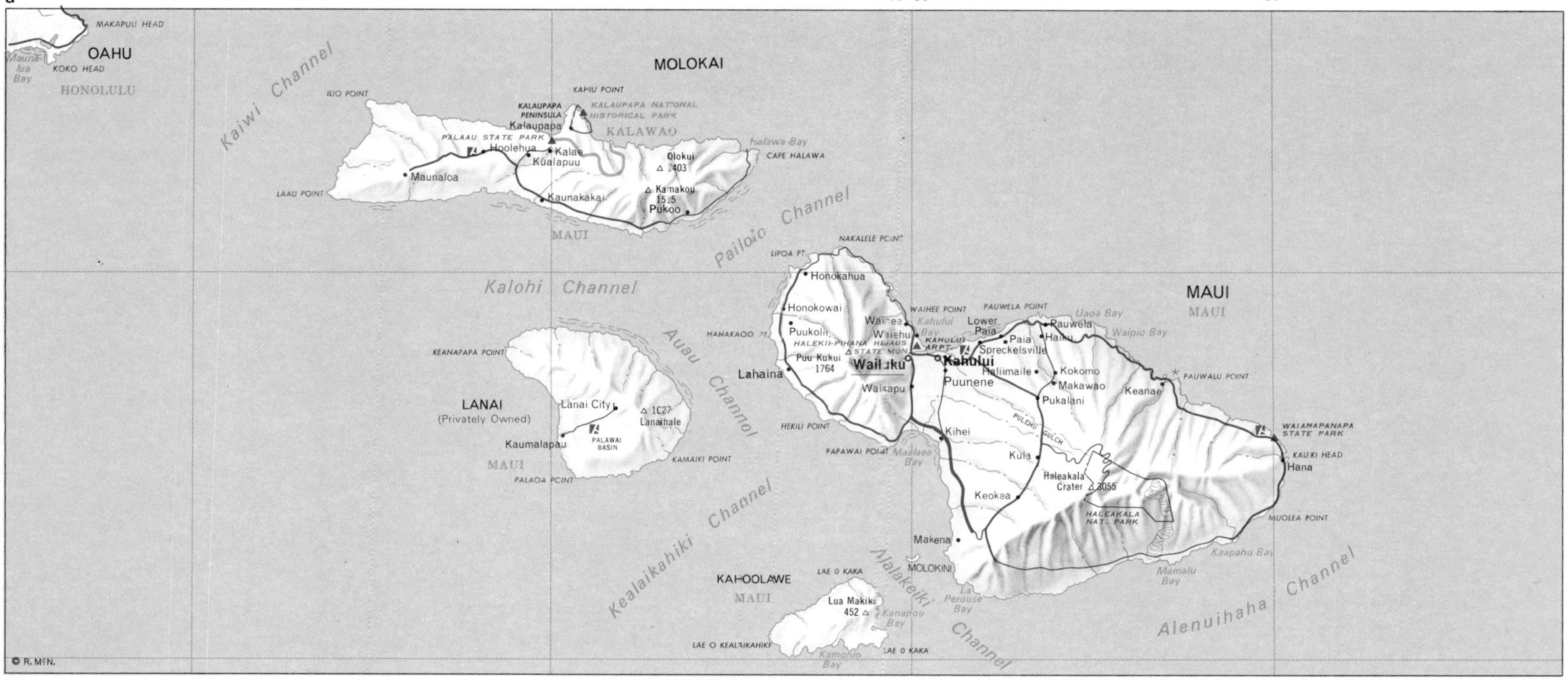
OAHU
HONOLULU
MAKAPUU HEAD
KOKO HEAD
Kaiwi Channel
MOLOKAI
KALAWAO
Kalaupapa
Hoolehua
Kualapuu
Maunaloa
Kaunakakai
Pukoo
CAPE HALAWA
LAAU POINT
ILIO POINT
MAUI
Kalohi Channel
Pailolo Channel
Auau Channel
LANAI
(Privately Owned)
Lanai City
Kaumalapau
Lanaihale
KAHOOLAWE
Lua Makika
452
Kealaikahiki Channel
Alalakeiki Channel
Alenuihaha Channel
Honokahua
Honokowai
Lahaina
Wailuku
Kahului
Puunene
Paia
Haiku
Makawao
Pukalani
Keanae
Hana
Kihei
Kula
Keokea
Makena
Haleakala Crater
3055
HALEAKALA NAT. PARK
Puu Kukui
1764
157° 30'
157°
156° 30'
156°
21°
20° 30'
© R.McN.

b

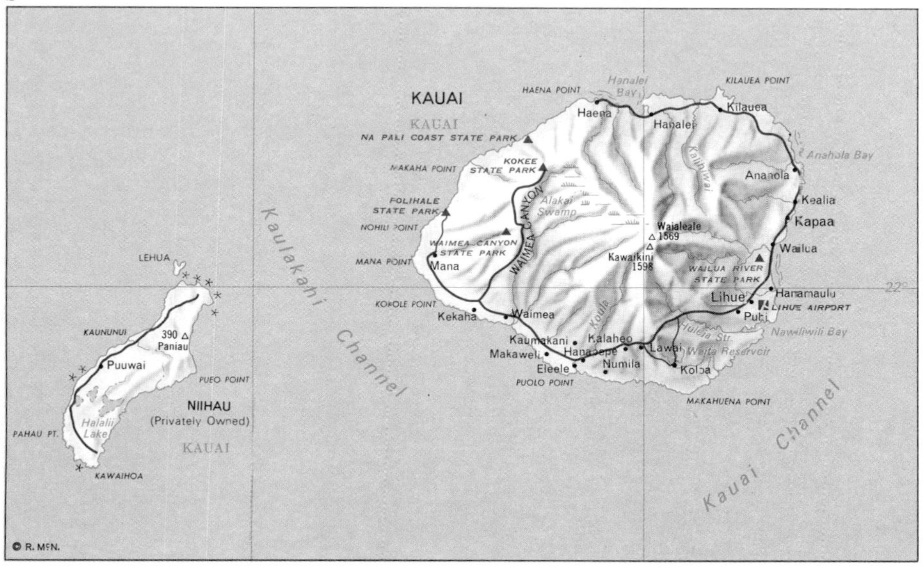
KAUAI
KAUAI
NIIHAU
(Privately Owned)
LEHUA
Puuwai
Paniau
390
Kaulakahi Channel
Kauai Channel
Haena
Hanalei
Kilauea
Anahola
Kealia
Kapaa
Wailua
Lihue
Hanamaulu
Kekaha
Waimea
Kaumakani
Makaweli
Eleele
Hanapepe
Kalaheo
Numila
Lawai
Koloa
Mana
Waialeale
1569
Kawaikini
1598
NA PALI COAST STATE PARK
KOKEE STATE PARK
WAIMEA CANYON STATE PARK
LIHUE AIRPORT
160°
159° 30'
22°
© R.McN.

c

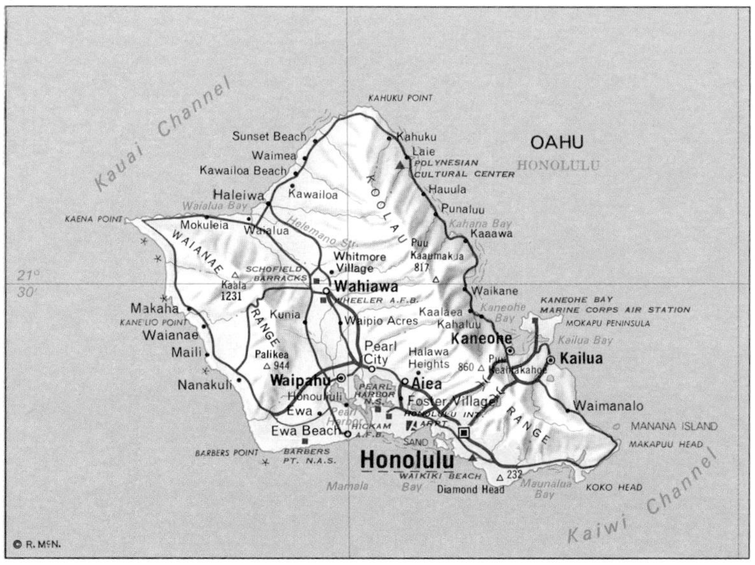
OAHU
HONOLULU
Kauai Channel
Kaiwi Channel
KAHUKU POINT
KAENA POINT
Sunset Beach
Waimea
Kawailoa Beach
Haleiwa
Kawailoa
Mokuleia
Waialua
Kahuku
Laie
POLYNESIAN CULTURAL CENTER
Hauula
Punaluu
Kaaawa
Whitmore Village
Wahiawa
SCHOFIELD BARRACKS
Kaala
1231
Makaha
Waianae
Maili
Nanakuli
Kunia
Waipio Acres
Waipahu
Honouliuli
Ewa
Ewa Beach
Pearl City
Aiea
Halawa Heights
Kaneohe
Kailua
Waimanalo
Honolulu
Diamond Head
232
KOKO HEAD
MAKAPUU HEAD
MANANA ISLAND
WAIANAE RANGE
KOOLAU RANGE
158°
157° 30'
21° 30'
© R.McN.

Kilometers 0 10 20 30 40 50 Km.
Statute Miles 0 10 20 30 40 50 Mi.

Scale 1:1,000,000

One centimeter represents 10 kilometers.
One inch represents approximately 16 miles.
Lambert Conformal Conic Projection

d

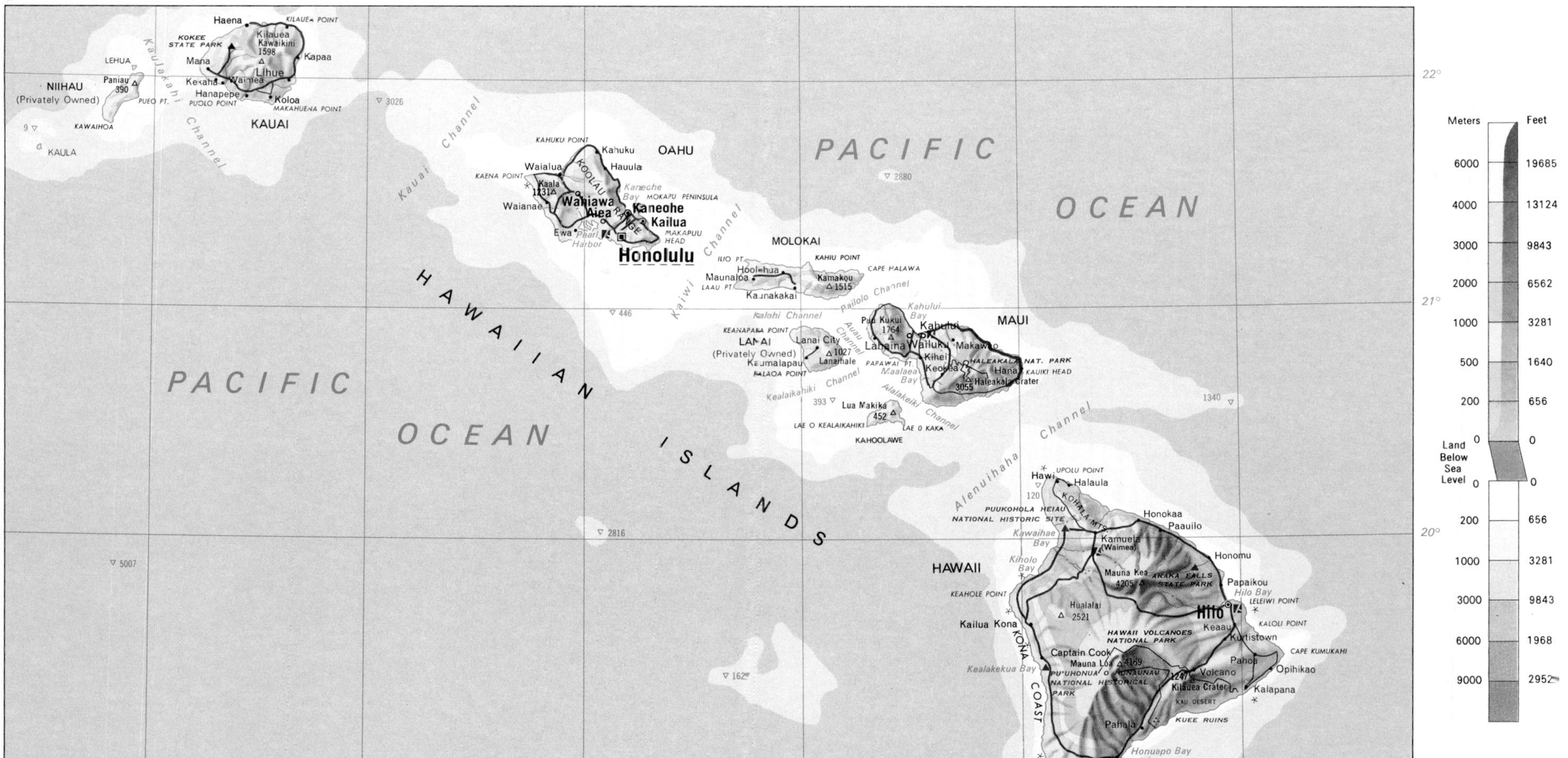
PACIFIC OCEAN
PACIFIC OCEAN
HAWAIIAN ISLANDS
NIIHAU
(Privately Owned)
KAUAI
KAULA
Haena
Kilauea
Kapaa
Lihue
Waimea
Koloa
OAHU
Wahiawa
Kaneohe
Kailua
Honolulu
Waianae
Ewa
Pearl Harbor
MOLOKAI
Kaunakakai
Maunaloa
LANAI
(Privately Owned)
Lanai City
MAUI
Wailuku
Kahului
Lahaina
Hana
KAHOOLAWE
HAWAII
Hawi
Halaula
Honokaa
Paauilo
Kamuela (Waimea)
Mauna Kea
4205
Hualalai
2521
Kailua Kona
Honomu
Papaikou
Hilo
Keaau
Kurtistown
Pahoa
Opihikao
Kalapana
Captain Cook
Mauna Loa
4169
Volcano
Kilauea Crater
Pahala
Naalehu
KONA COAST
HAWAII VOLCANOES NATIONAL PARK
KA LAE
Alenuihaha Channel
Kaiwi Channel
Kauai Channel
160°
159°
158°
157°
156°
155°
22°
21°
20°
19°
Meters
Feet
6000 19685
4000 13124
3000 9843
2000 6562
1000 3281
500 1640
200 656
0 0
Land Below Sea Level
0 0
200 656
1000 3281
3000 9843
6000 1968
9000 2952
Copyright © by Rand McNally & Co.
Map prepared by Rand McNally & Co.
A-520512-264/764

| | | | | | | |
|---|---|---|---|---|---|---|
| ENGLISH | bay | channel | head | mount | point | state park, s.p. |
| DEUTSCH | Bucht | Kanal | Landspitze | Berg | Landspitze | Staatspark |
| ESPAÑOL | bahía | canal | promontorio | monte | punta | parque del estado |
| FRANÇAIS | baie | détroit | promontoire | mont | pointe | parc régional |
| PORTUGUÊS | baía | canal | promontório | monte | ponta | parque estadual |

Kilometers 0 50 100 150 Km.
Statute Miles 0 50 100 150 Mi.

Scale 1:3,000,000

One centimeter represents 30 kilometers.
One inch represents approximately 47 miles.
Lambert Conformal Conic Projection

Map continues
pages 178-179

115°
110°
105°
100°
95°
90°
30°
25°
20°
15°
10°
5°
San Diego
Tijuana
Mexicali
Ensenada
Phoenix
Scottsdale
Tempe
Mesa
Tucson
Albuquerque
Amarillo
Oklahoma City
Tulsa
Springfield
Fort Smith
Little Rock
Memphis
Lubbock
Wichita Falls
Fort Worth
Dallas
Abilene
Midland
Odessa
San Angelo
Shreveport
Waco
Austin
Houston
Beaumont
Port Arthur
New Orleans
Baton Rouge
Jackson
Mobile
Gulfport
Galveston
San Antonio
Corpus Christi
El Paso
Ciudad Juárez
Nogales
Hermosillo
Guaymas
Ciudad Obregón
Chihuahua
Hidalgo del Parral
Los Mochis
Culiacán
Mazatlán
Durango
Torreón
Gómez Palacio
Saltillo
Monterrey
Nuevo Laredo
Laredo
Monclova
Piedras Negras
Reynosa
Brownsville
Matamoros
Ciudad Victoria
Tampico
Zacatecas
San Luis Potosí
Aguascalientes
León
Guadalajara
Tepic
Irapuato
Querétaro
Celaya
Morelia
Colima
Manzanillo
Toluca
CIUDAD DE MÉXICO
MEXICO CITY
Nezahualcóyotl
Cuernavaca
Puebla
Xalapa
Veracruz
Orizaba
Córdoba
Acapulco
Oaxaca
Coatzacoalcos
Villahermosa
Campeche
Mérida
Tuxtla Gutiérrez
Tapachula
Quetzaltenango
GUATEMALA
San Salvador
BELIZE
San Pedro Sula
La Paz
San José del Cabo
Tropic of Cancer
UNITED STATES
MEXICO
ARIZONA
NEW MEXICO
OKLAHOMA
TEXAS
ARKANSAS
LOUISIANA
MISSISSIPPI
EDWARDS PLATEAU
LLANO ESTACADO
SIERRA MADRE OCCIDENTAL
SIERRA MADRE ORIENTAL
SIERRA MADRE DEL SUR
BAJA CALIFORNIA
Golfo de California
GULF OF MEXICO
Bahía de Campeche
Golfo de Tehuantepec
YUCATAN PENINSULA
EL SALVADOR
ISLAS REVILLAGIGEDO
ISLAS MARÍAS
ÎLE CLIPPERTON (Fr.)
PACIFIC OCEAN
Copyright © by Rand McNally & Co.
Map prepared by Esselte Map Service AB, Stockholm.
A-530000-264

| | | | | | | | | | |
|---|---|---|---|---|---|---|---|---|---|
| ESPAÑOL | cabo | cordillera | golfo | isla, i. | lago, l. | punta | sierra | volcán, vol. |
| ENGLISH | cape | mountains | gulf | island | lake | point | mountains | volcano |
| DEUTSCH | Kap | Berge | Golf | Insel | See | Landspitze | Berge | Vulkan |
| FRANÇAIS | cap | montagnes | golfe | île | lac | pointe | montagnes | volcan |
| PORTUGUÊS | cabo | cordilheira | golfo | ilha | lago | ponta | serra | vulcão |

ATLANTIC OCEAN
Sargasso Sea
BERMUDA (U.K.)
Hamilton
Tropic of Cancer
BAHAMAS
Nassau
ANDROS
GRAND BAHAMA
ELEUTHERA
CAT ISLAND
SAN SALVADOR (WATLING ISLAND)
RUM CAY
LONG ISLAND
GREAT EXUMA
CROOKED ISLAND
ACKLINS
MAYAGUANA
GREAT INAGUA
LITTLE INAGUA
TURKS AND CAICOS ISLANDS (U.K.)
Grand Turk
WEST INDIES
GREATER ANTILLES
LA HABANA HAVANA
Matanzas
Cárdenas
Pinar del Río
Santa Clara
Cienfuegos
Sancti-Spíritus
Ciego de Ávila
Camagüey
CUBA
Holguín
Bayamo
Manzanillo
Santiago de Cuba
Guantánamo
ISLA DE LA JUVENTUD
CAYMAN IS. (U.K.)
George Town
JAMAICA
Montego Bay
Kingston
HAITI
Cap-Haïtien
Port-au-Prince
DOMINICAN REPUBLIC
Santiago
SANTO DOMINGO
HISPANIOLA
PUERTO RICO (U.S.)
San Juan
Mayagüez
Ponce
VIRGIN ISLANDS
BRITISH VIRGIN ISLANDS
Road Town
Charlotte Amalie
ANGUILLA (U.K.)
SAINT KITTS AND NEVIS
Basseterre
ANTIGUA AND BARBUDA
Saint John's
MONTSERRAT (U.K.)
Plymouth
GUADELOUPE (Fr.)
Basse-Terre
Pointe-à-Pitre
DOMINICA
Roseau
MARTINIQUE (Fr.)
Fort-de-France
SAINT LUCIA
Castries
SAINT VINCENT AND THE GRENADINES
Kingstown
BARBADOS
Bridgetown
GRENADA
Saint George's
TRINIDAD AND TOBAGO
Port of Spain
LEEWARD IS.
WINDWARD IS.
LESSER ANTILLES
CARIBBEAN SEA
ARUBA (Neth.)
Oranjestad
NETHERLANDS ANTILLES
Willemstad
VENEZUELA
CARACAS
Maracaibo
Valencia
Barquisimeto
Maracay
Barcelona
Cumaná
Maturín
Ciudad Bolívar
Ciudad Guayana
Mérida
San Cristóbal
GUYANA
BRAZIL
Boa Vista
RORAIMA
COLOMBIA
SANTA FE DE BOGOTÁ
Medellín
Cali
Barranquilla
Cartagena
Santa Marta
Bucaramanga
Cúcuta
Manizales
Pereira
Ibagué
Neiva
Popayán
Buenaventura
Villavicencio
AMAZONAS
COSTA RICA
SAN JOSÉ
Puerto Limón
PANAMÁ
Colón
David
NICARAGUA
Bluefields
Puerto Cabezas
FLORIDA
Jacksonville
Tallahassee
Gainesville
Daytona Beach
Orlando
Tampa
St. Petersburg
Sarasota
Fort Myers
West Palm Beach
Fort Lauderdale
Hollywood
Miami
Key West
Straits of Florida
GEORGIA
Atlanta
Macon
Augusta
Savannah
Columbus
Albany
Valdosta
Brunswick
SOUTH CAROLINA
Charleston
Columbia
Greenville
Spartanburg
NORTH CAROLINA
Charlotte
Raleigh
Durham
Greensboro
Winston-Salem
Fayetteville
Wilmington
Asheville
CAPE HATTERAS
CAPE LOOKOUT
CAPE FEAR
VIRGINIA
Norfolk
Newport News
Virginia Beach
Richmond
Roanoke
Lynchburg
Petersburg
Knoxville
APPALACHIAN MTS.

Map continues pages 242-243

Kilometers 0 200 400 600 Km.
Statute Miles 0 200 400 600 Mi.

Scale 1:12,000,000
One centimeter represents 120 kilometers.
One inch represents approximately 190 miles.
Oblique Conic Conformal Projection

San Diego
Tijuana
Mexicali
Yuma
San Luis Rio Colorado
ARIZONA
Tucson
Nogales
El Paso
Ciudad Juárez
NEW MEXICO
Las Cruces
Carlsbad
Hobbs
UNITED STATES
MEXICO
Ensenada
BAJA CALIFORNIA
Golfo de California
Hermosillo
SONORA
Guaymas
Ciudad Obregón
Navojoa
Los Mochis
Chihuahua
CHIHUAHUA
Delicias
Hidalgo del Parral
SIERRA MADRE OCCIDENTAL
Culiacán
SINALOA
Mazatlán
DURANGO
Durango
Torreón
Gómez Palacio
BAJA CALIFORNIA SUR
Santa Rosalía
La Paz
San José del Cabo
Cabo San Lucas
Tropic of Cancer
PACIFIC OCEAN
ISLAS REVILLAGIGEDO (Mex.)
ISLA CLARIÓN (Mex.)
ISLAS MARÍAS
Tepic
NAYARIT
Puerto Vallarta
JALISCO
Guadalajara
Colima
Manzanillo
116°
114°
112°
110°
108°
106°
104°
32°
30°
28°
26°
24°
22°
20°
18°
16°
Copyright © by Rand McNally & Co.
Map prepared by Rand McNally & Co.
A-531600-764 -4 -6 -15

| Meters | Feet |
|---|---|
| 6000 | 19685 |
| 4000 | 13124 |
| 3000 | 9843 |
| 2000 | 6562 |
| 1000 | 3281 |
| 500 | 1640 |
| 200 | 656 |
| 0 | 0 |
| Land Below Sea Level | |
| 0 | 0 |
| 200 | 656 |
| 1000 | 3281 |
| 3000 | 9843 |
| 6000 | 19685 |
| 9000 | 29520 |

| | | | | | | | | |
|---|---|---|---|---|---|---|---|---|
| ESPAÑOL | bahía | cerro | isla | laguna | presa | punta | río | sierra |
| ENGLISH | bay | mountain | island | lagoon | reservoir | point | river | mountains |
| DEUTSCH | Bucht | Berg | Insel | Haff | Stausee | Landspitze | Fluss | Berge |
| FRANÇAIS | baie | montagne | île | lagune | réservoir | pointe | rivière | montagnes |
| PORTUGUÊS | baía | montanha | ilha | laguna | reservatório | ponta | rio | serra |

Kilometers 0 100 200 300 Km.
Statute Miles 0 100 200 300 M

Scale 1:6,000,000

One centimeter represents 60 kilometers.
One inch represents approximately 95 miles.
Lambert Conformal Conic Projection

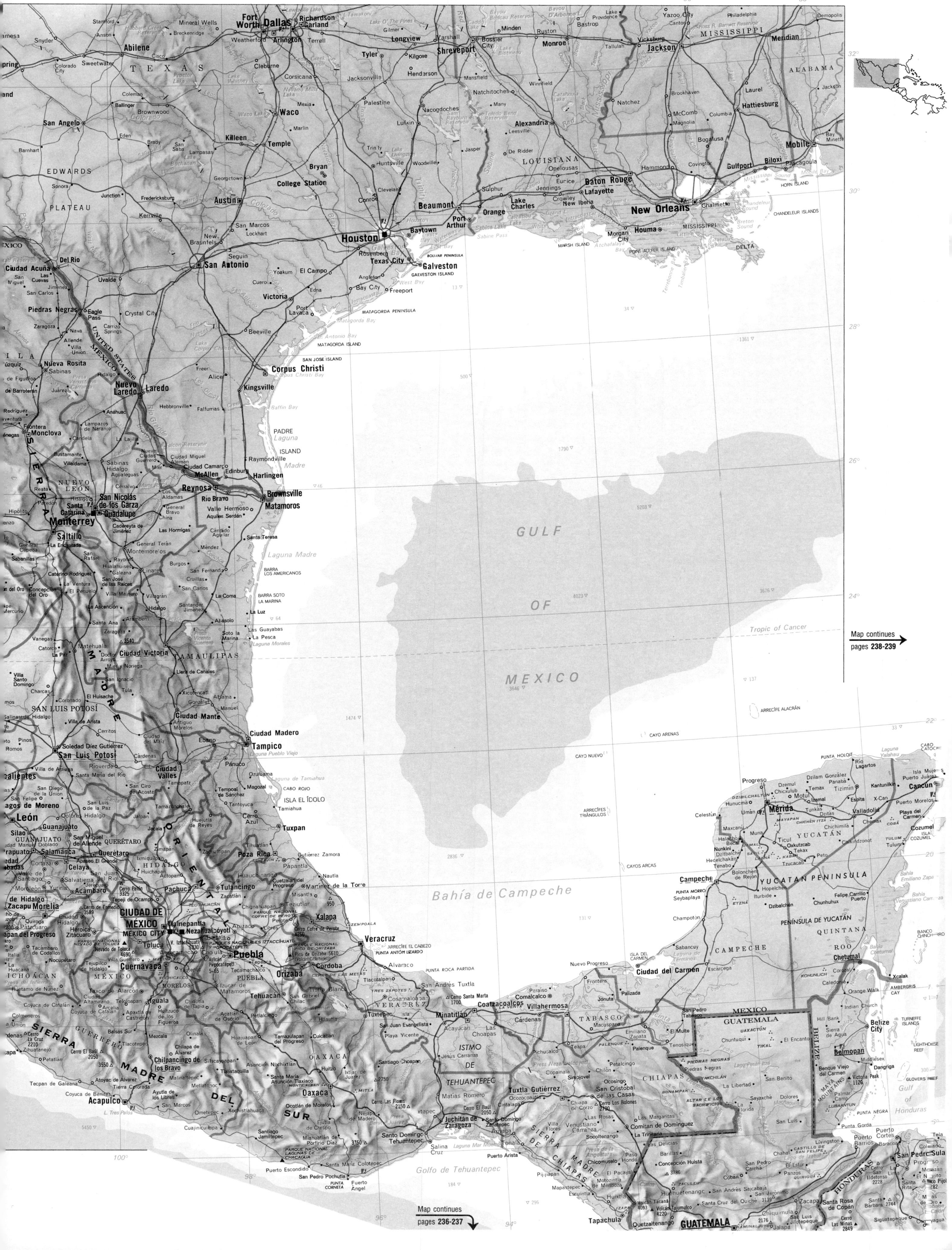
GULF
OF
MEXICO
Bahía de Campeche
Golfo de Tehuantepec
Tropic of Cancer
TEXAS
LOUISIANA
MISSISSIPPI
ALABAMA
EDWARDS
PLATEAU
SIERRA MADRE ORIENTAL
SIERRA MADRE DEL SUR
SIERRA MADRE DE CHIAPAS
YUCATAN PENINSULA
ISTMO DE TEHUANTEPEC
NUEVO LEON
TAMAULIPAS
SAN LUIS POTOSÍ
HIDALGO
PUEBLA
MORELOS
VERACRUZ
OAXACA
TABASCO
CHIAPAS
CAMPECHE
YUCATÁN
QUINTANA ROO
GUATEMALA
BELIZE
HONDURAS
Gulf of Honduras
Dallas
Fort Worth
Abilene
Shreveport
Jackson
Waco
San Angelo
Austin
Houston
Beaumont
Baton Rouge
New Orleans
Mobile
San Antonio
Galveston
Corpus Christi
Laredo
Nuevo Laredo
Monclova
Monterrey
Saltillo
Reynosa
McAllen
Harlingen
Brownsville
Matamoros
Ciudad Victoria
Ciudad Mante
Ciudad Madero
Tampico
San Luis Potosí
León
Guanajuato
Querétaro
Pachuca
Poza Rica
Tuxpan
Xalapa
Veracruz
CIUDAD DE MÉXICO
MEXICO CITY
Toluca
Puebla
Cuernavaca
Orizaba
Córdoba
Acapulco
Oaxaca
Coatzacoalcos
Villahermosa
Tuxtla Gutiérrez
Ciudad del Carmen
Campeche
Mérida
Cancún
Cozumel
Chetumal
Belize City
Belmopan
Tapachula
Quetzaltenango
GUATEMALA
San Pedro Sula

Map continues pages 238-239

Map continues pages 236-237

Map continues pages 232-233

PACIFIC OCEAN
SIERRA MADRE OCCIDENTAL
SIERRA MADRE
Durango
Mazatlán
Tepic
Puerto Vallarta
Manzanillo
Colima
GUADALAJARA
Zacatecas
Aguascalientes
San Luis Potosí
León
Guanajuato
Querétaro
Morelia
Uruapan del Progreso
Lázaro Cárdenas
Acapulco
ISLAS MARÍAS
Meters
Feet
6000
19685
4000
13124
3000
9843
2000
6562
1000
3281
500
1640
200
656
0
Land Below Sea Level
9000
29520
Copyright © by Rand McNally & Co.
Map prepared by Rand McNally & Co.
A-531696-764

| | | | | | | | | | | |
|---|---|---|---|---|---|---|---|---|---|---|
| ESPAÑOL | arroyo | boca | cerro | lago | laguna | punta | río | sierra | volcán |
| ENGLISH | brook | entrance | butte | lake | lagoon | point | river | ranges | volcano |
| DEUTSCH | Bach | Einfahrt | Restberg | See | Haff | Landspitze | Fluss | Bergketten | Vulkan |
| FRANÇAIS | ruisseau | entrée | butte | lac | lagune | pointe | rivière | chaîne | volcan |
| PORTUGUÊS | riacho | entrada | cerro | lago | laguna | ponta | rio | serra | vulcão |

GULF OF MEXICO
Bahía de Campeche
Tropic of Cancer
Golfo de Tehuantepec
Ciudad Victoria
Ciudad Mante
Ciudad Madero
Tampico
Villa Cuauhtémoc
Pánuco
Tuxpan
Poza Rica
Papantla
Martínez de la Torre
Tulancingo
Pachuca
Tezuitlán
Xalapa
Coatepec
Veracruz
Boca del Río
Perote
Apizaco
Tlaxcala
Nezahualcóyotl
Puebla
Atlixco
Izúcar de Matamoros
Tehuacán
Córdoba
Orizaba
Ciudad Mendoza
Fortín
Tierra Blanca
Alvarado
Cosamaloapan
Tlacotalpan
San Andrés Tuxtla
Santiago Tuxtla
Catemaco
Tuxtepec
Acayucan
Coatzacoalcos
Minatitlán
Nanchital
Agua Dulce
Cárdenas
Villahermosa
Comalcalco
Frontera
Teapa
Oaxaca
Juchitán de Zaragoza
Salina Cruz
Santo Domingo Tehuantepec
Tuxtla Gutiérrez
Chiapa de Corzo
San Cristóbal de las Casas
Arriaga
Tonalá
Puerto Escondido
Puerto Ángel
Huejutla de Reyes
Huauchinango
Zacatlán
Teziutlán
Altotonga
Misantla
Nautla
Gutiérrez Zamora
Tuxpan
Tamiahua
Cerro Azul
Naranjos
Tantoyuca
Ozuluama
Tempoal de Sánchez
Ébano
Tamuín
Altamira
Aldama
Soto la Marina
González
Xicoténcatl
TAMAULIPAS
SAN LUIS POTOSÍ
VERACRUZ
HIDALGO
PUEBLA
TLAXCALA
MORELOS
GUERRERO
OAXACA
TABASCO
CHIAPAS
SIERRA MADRE ORIENTAL
SIERRA MADRE DEL SUR
SIERRA MADRE DE CHIAPAS
ISTMO DE TEHUANTEPEC
Tropic of Cancer
Map continues pages 232-233
Map continues pages 236-237

Kilometers 0 50 100 150 Km.
Statute Miles 0 50 100 150 Mi.

Scale 1:3,000,000
One centimeter represents 30 kilometers.
One inch represents approximately 47 miles.
Lambert Conformal Conic Projection

Map continues pages 232-233

Map continues pages 234-235

MEXICO
MÉXICO
GUATEMALA
BELIZE
HONDURAS
EL SALVADOR
PETÉN
ALTA VERAPAZ
BAJA VERAPAZ
IZABAL
QUICHÉ
HUEHUETENANGO
SAN MARCOS
TOTONICAPÁN
QUETZALTENANGO
SOLOLÁ
CHIMALTENANGO
SUCHITEPÉQUEZ
RETALHULEU
ESCUINTLA
SANTA ROSA
JUTIAPA
JALAPA
CHIQUIMULA
ZACAPA
EL PROGRESO
CHIAPAS
SIERRA MADRE DE CHIAPAS
SIERRA DE LAS MINAS
CUCHUMATANES
OCOTEPEQUE
COPÁN
SANTA BÁRBARA
CORTÉS
YORO
ATLÁNTIDA
COMAYAGUA
INTIBUCÁ
LEMPIRA
LA PAZ
FRANCISCO MORAZÁN
EL PARAÍSO
VALLE
CHOLUTECA
CHINANDEGA
ESTELÍ
GUATEMALA
Tapachula
Quetzaltenango
Mazatenango
Retalhuleu
Escuintla
Antigua Guatemala
Cobán
Huehuetenango
Puerto Barrios
Puerto Cortés
San Pedro Sula
La Ceiba
Tela
El Progreso
Tegucigalpa
Santa Ana
San Salvador
Nueva San Salvador
Sonsonate
Acajutla
La Libertad
San Vicente
San Miguel
La Unión
Usulután
Zacatecoluca
Choluteca
Chinandega
León
Managua
Puerto San Jose
Livingston
Gulf of Honduras
Golfo de Fonseca
Comitán de Domínguez
Las Margaritas
Las Rosas
Ocós
Champerico
Puerto Morazán
Corinto
PACIFIC
OCEAN
Copyright © by Rand McNally & Co.
Map prepared by Rand McNally & Co.
A-533600-764

| Meters | Feet |
|---|---|
| 6000 | 19685 |
| 4000 | 13124 |
| 3000 | 9843 |
| 2000 | 6562 |
| 1000 | 3281 |
| 500 | 1640 |
| 200 | 656 |
| 0 | 0 |
| Land Below Sea Level 0 | 0 |
| 200 | 656 |
| 1000 | 3281 |
| 3000 | 9843 |
| 6000 | 19685 |
| 9000 | 29520 |

| | | | | | | | | | |
|---|---|---|---|---|---|---|---|---|---|
| ESPAÑOL | bahía | cerro | cordillera | isla | lago | laguna | punta | sierra | volcán |
| ENGLISH | bay | mountain | mountains | island | lake | lagoon | point | mountains | volcano |
| DEUTSCH | Bucht | Berg | Berge | Insel | See | Haff | Landspitze | Berge | Vulkan |
| FRANÇAIS | baie | montagne | montagnes | île | lac | lagune | pointe | montagnes | volcan |
| PORTUGUÊS | baía | montanha | cordilheira | ilha | lago | laguna | ponta | serra | vulcão |

CARIBBEAN
SEA
LA MOSQUITIA
GRACIAS A DIOS
MONTAÑAS DE COLÓN
COLÓN
HONDURAS
NICARAGUA
JINOTEGA
CORDILLERA ISABELIA
ZELAYA
COSTA DE MOSQUITOS
CORDILLERA DARIENSE
MATAGALPA
BOACO
SERRANÍAS HUAPÍ
CHONTALES
CORDILLERA CHONTALEÑA
SERRANÍAS DE YOLAINA
RÍO SAN JUAN
COSTA RICA
ALAJUELA
HEREDIA
GUANACASTE
CORD. DE GUANACASTE
CORDILLERA CENTRAL
SAN JOSÉ
CARTAGO
LIMÓN
PUNTARENAS
PANAMÁ
BOCAS DEL TORO
ARCHIPIÉLAGO DE BOCAS DEL TORO
CHIRIQUÍ
VERAGUAS
COCLÉ
HERRERA
LOS SANTOS
COLÓN
ISTMO DE PANAMÁ
Golfo de los Mosquitos
Golfo de Panamá
Golfo de Chiriquí
Bahía de Coronado
Bahía de Punta Gorda
Lago de Nicaragua
Cabo Gracias a Dios
CABO GRACIAS A DIOS
CABO CAMARÓN
CABO FALSO
Puerto Lempira
Waspam
San Ramón
Bilwaskarma
Puerto Cabezas
Bonanza
La Rosita
Siuna
Wounta
Prinzapolka
Tungla
La Cruz de Río Grande
La Barra
Rama
Bluefields
El Bluff
San Juan del Norte
Colorado
Puerto Limón
Heredia
Alajuela
SAN JOSÉ
Cartago
Puntarenas
Liberia
Nicoya
Golfito
David
Puerto Armuelles
Santiago
Colón
Panamá
La Chorrera
Balboa
Penonomé
Chitré
Las Tablas
San Andrés
SAN ANDRÉS Y PROVIDENCIA (Colombia)
ISLA DE SAN ANDRÉS
ISLA DE PROVIDENCIA
CAYOS MISKITOS
CAYOS DE ALBUQUERQUE
CAYOS DEL ESTE SUDESTE
ISLAS DEL MAÍZ (Nic.)
CAYO DE SERRANA
CAYOS DE RONCADOR
QUITASUEÑO
CAYO DE SERRANILLA (Colombia)
Edinburgh Channel
85°
84°
83°
82°
81°
80°
15°
14°
13°
12°
11°
10°
9°
8°

Map continues pages 246-247

Kilometers 0 50 100 150 Km.
Statute Miles 0 50 100 150 Mi.

Scale 1:3,000,000
One centimeter represents 30 kilometers.
One inch represents approximately 47 miles.
Lambert Conformal Conic Projection

# Caribbean Region / Mittelamerikanische Inselwelt / Región del Caribe
# Région des Caraïbes / Região do Caribe

Map continues pages 232-233

Map continues pages 236-237

GULF OF MEXICO
Straits of Florida
UNITED STATES
FLORIDA
Miami
Miami Beach
Coral Gables
Fort Lauderdale
Hollywood
Hialeah
West Palm Beach
Fort Myers
Naples
Key West
Key Largo
Florida Bay
FLORIDA KEYS
Everglades
GRAND BAHAMA
Freeport
Nassau
NEW PROVIDENCE
ANDROS
ELEUTHERA
EXUMA
GREAT BAHAMA BANK
LA HABANA
HAVANA
Matanzas
Cárdenas
Pinar del Río
Santa Clara
Cienfuegos
Sancti Spíritus
Ciego de Ávila
Camagüey
Holguín
Bayamo
Manzanillo
Santiago de Cuba
Guantánamo
C U B A
ISLA DE LA JUVENTUD (ISLA DE PINOS)
Golfo de Batabanó
Nicholas Channel
Old Bahama Channel
CAYMAN ISLANDS (U.K.)
George Town
GRAND CAYMAN
LITTLE CAYMAN
CAYMAN BRAC
G R E A T E R
W E S T
JAMAICA
Kingston
Montego Bay
Spanish Town
Port Antonio
Mandeville
C A R I B B E A
YUCATAN PENINSULA
PENÍNSULA DE YUCATÁN
Cancún
Cozumel
MEXICO
QUINTANA ROO
Canal de Yucatán
Gulf of Honduras
ISLAS DE LA BAHÍA
Roatán
HONDURAS
Tegucigalpa
La Ceiba
LA MOSQUITIA
NICARAGUA
Managua
León
Granada
Lago de Nicaragua
Bluefields
COSTA DE MOSQUITOS
SAN ANDRÉS Y PROVIDENCIA (Col.)
COSTA RICA
SAN JOSÉ
Puerto Limón
PANAMÁ
Panamá
Colón
ISTMO DE PANAMÁ
Barranquilla
Cartagena
PACIFIC OCEAN
Copyright © by Rand McNally & Co.
Map prepared by Rand McNally & Co.
A-530100-764 -8 -7 -19


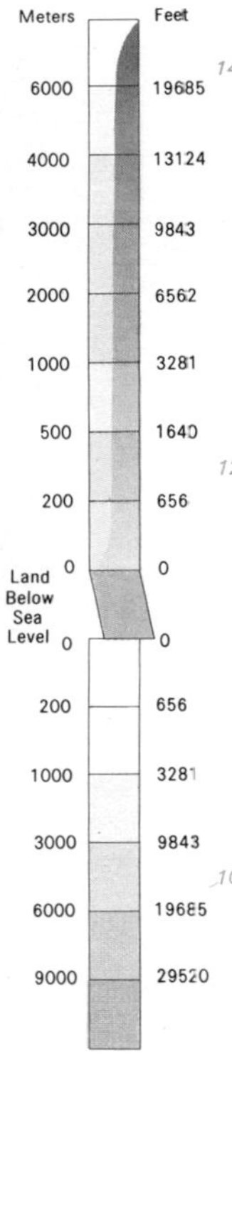

Meters
Feet
6000 19685
4000 13124
3000 9843
2000 6562
1000 3281
500 1640
200 656
0 0
Land Below Sea Level
0 0
200 656
1000 3281
3000 9843
6000 19685
9000 29520


| MAP FORM | bahía | cabo | cerro | channel | golfo | isla | passage | pico | punta |
|---|---|---|---|---|---|---|---|---|---|
| ENGLISH | bay | cape | mountain | channel | gulf | isle | passage | peak | point |
| DEUTSCH | Bucht | Kap | Berg | Kanal | Golf | Insel | Durchfahrt | Gipfel | Landspitze |
| ESPAÑOL | bahía | cabo | cerro | canal | golfo | isla | pasaje | pico | punta |
| FRANÇAIS | baie | cap | montagne | détroit | golfe | île | passage | cime | pointe |
| PORTUGUÊS | baía | cabo | montanha | canal | golfo | ilha | passagem | pico | ponta |

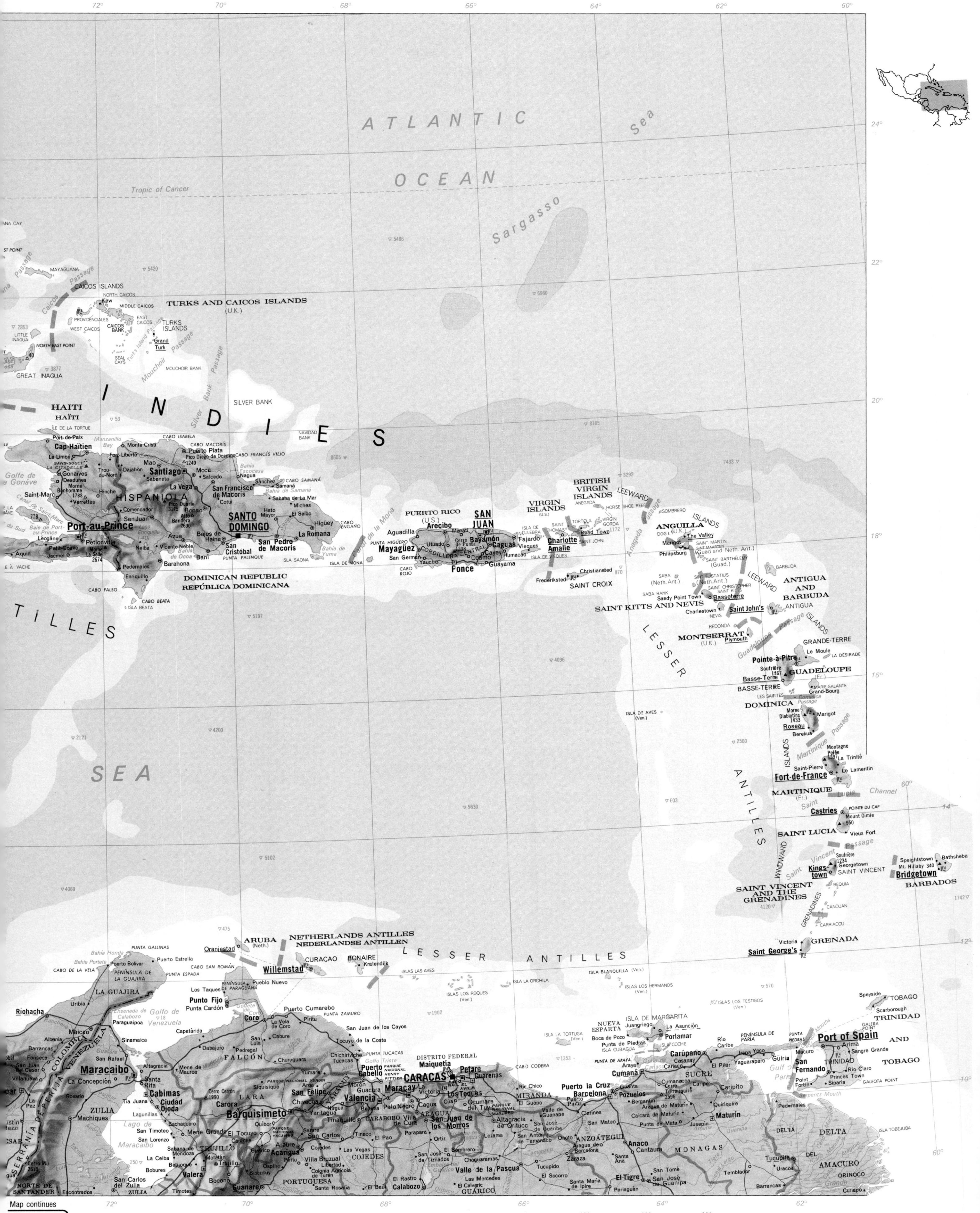
ATLANTIC
OCEAN
Sargasso
Sea
Tropic of Cancer
TURKS AND CAICOS ISLANDS
(U.K.)
CAICOS ISLANDS
NORTH CAICOS
MIDDLE CAICOS
EAST CAICOS
WEST CAICOS
PROVIDENCIALES
TURKS ISLANDS
Grand Turk
Turks Island Passage
Caicos Passage
Mouchoir Passage
Silver Bank Passage
MOUCHOIR BANK
SILVER BANK
NAVIDAD BANK
GREAT INAGUA
LITTLE INAGUA
MAYAGUANA
NORTH EAST POINT
INDIES
HAITI
HAÏTI
ÎLE DE LA TORTUE
Port-de-Paix
Cap-Haïtien
Golfe de la Gonâve
Gonaïves
Saint-Marc
Port-au-Prince
Pétionville
Léogâne
Jacmel
Aquin
HISPANIOLA
Monte Cristi
Puerto Plata
Santiago
La Vega
San Francisco de Macorís
SANTO DOMINGO
San Cristóbal
San Pedro de Macorís
La Romana
Higüey
Barahona
Azua
Baní
Pedernales
Enriquillo
CABO BEATA
ISLA BEATA
CABO FALSO
ISLA SAONA
ISLA DE MONA
CABO ENGAÑO
Samaná
CABO SAMANÁ
CABO ISABELA
CABO FRANCÉS VIEJO
Bahía de Samaná
DOMINICAN REPUBLIC
REPÚBLICA DOMINICANA
Canal de la Mona
PUERTO RICO
(U.S.)
Aguadilla
Arecibo
SAN JUAN
Bayamón
Caguas
Mayagüez
Ponce
Guayama
Humacao
Fajardo
CORDILLERA CENTRAL
VIRGIN ISLANDS
(U.S.)
Charlotte Amalie
Frederiksted
Christiansted
SAINT CROIX
SAINT THOMAS
ISLA DE CULEBRA
Vieques
BRITISH VIRGIN ISLANDS
ANEGADA
TORTOLA
VIRGIN GORDA
Road Town
Anegada Passage
LEEWARD
ISLANDS
ANGUILLA
(U.K.)
The Valley
SOMBRERO
Marigot
SAINT MARTIN
Philipsburg
SAINT BARTHÉLEMY
(Guad.)
SABA
(Neth. Ant.)
SINT EUSTATIUS
SAINT KITTS AND NEVIS
Basseterre
Charlestown
NEVIS
ANTIGUA AND BARBUDA
BARBUDA
ANTIGUA
Saint John's
REDONDA
MONTSERRAT
(U.K.)
Plymouth
LESSER
ANTILLES
GRANDE-TERRE
Le Moule
LA DÉSIRADE
Pointe-à-Pitre
GUADELOUPE
(Fr.)
Basse-Terre
BASSE-TERRE
Guadeloupe Passage
MARIE-GALANTE
Grand-Bourg
LES SAINTES
Dominica Passage
DOMINICA
Roseau
Marigot
ISLA DE AVES
(Ven.)
Martinique Passage
Fort-de-France
MARTINIQUE
(Fr.)
La Trinité
Le Lamentin
Saint Lucia Channel
Castries
SAINT LUCIA
Vieux Fort
Saint Vincent Passage
WINDWARD ISLANDS
Kingstown
Georgetown
SAINT VINCENT
SAINT VINCENT AND THE GRENADINES
BEQUIA
CANOUAN
CARRIACOU
GRENADINES
GRENADA
Saint George's
Bridgetown
BARBADOS
Speightstown
Bathsheba
SEA
CARIBBEAN
TÍLLES
ARUBA
(Neth.)
Oranjestad
NETHERLANDS ANTILLES
NEDERLANDSE ANTILLEN
CURAÇAO
Willemstad
BONAIRE
Kralendijk
LESSER ANTILLES
ISLAS LAS AVES
ISLAS LOS ROQUES
(Ven.)
ISLA LA ORCHILA
ISLA BLANQUILLA
(Ven.)
ISLAS LOS HERMANOS
ISLAS LOS TESTIGOS
ISLA LA TORTUGA
ISLA DE MARGARITA
NUEVA ESPARTA
Porlamar
La Asunción
TOBAGO
Scarborough
TRINIDAD AND TOBAGO
Port of Spain
San Fernando
Arima
Sangre Grande
Princes Town
Siparia
Point Fortin
GALERA POINT
GALEOTA POINT
Gulf of Paria
Serpents Mouth
PENÍNSULA DE PARIA
Güiria
Carúpano
Cumaná
SUCRE
Maturín
MONAGAS
DELTA AMACURO
Tucupita
Orinoco
Barcelona
Puerto La Cruz
ANZOÁTEGUI
El Tigre
Anaco
DISTRITO FEDERAL
CARACAS
Maiquetía
Petare
Guarenas
Los Teques
Maracay
Valencia
Puerto Cabello
CARABOBO
San Felipe
YARACUY
Barquisimeto
LARA
Carora
FALCÓN
Coro
Punto Fijo
Punta Cardón
PENÍNSULA DE PARAGUANÁ
Golfo de Venezuela
LA GUAJIRA
PUNTA GALLINAS
Riohacha
Maracaibo
Cabimas
Ciudad Ojeda
ZULIA
Lago de Maracaibo
COLOMBIA
VENEZUELA
TRUJILLO
Valera
Guanare
PORTUGUESA
Acarigua
COJEDES
San Carlos
GUÁRICO
Calabozo
Valle de la Pascua
San Juan de los Morros
ARAGUA
MIRANDA
NORTE DE SANTANDER
SERRANÍA DE PERIJÁ
Map continues
pages 246-247
72°
70°
68°
66°
64°
62°
60°
24°
22°
20°
18°
16°
14°
12°
10°

Kilometers 0 100 200 300 Km.

Statute Miles 0 100 200 300 Mi.

Scale 1:6,000,000

One centimeter represents 60 kilometers.

One inch represents approximately 95 miles.

Lambert Conformal Conic Projection

# Islands of the West Indies / Westindische Inseln / Islas de las Antillas
# Îles des Antilles / Ilhas do Caribe (Índias Ocidentais)

a

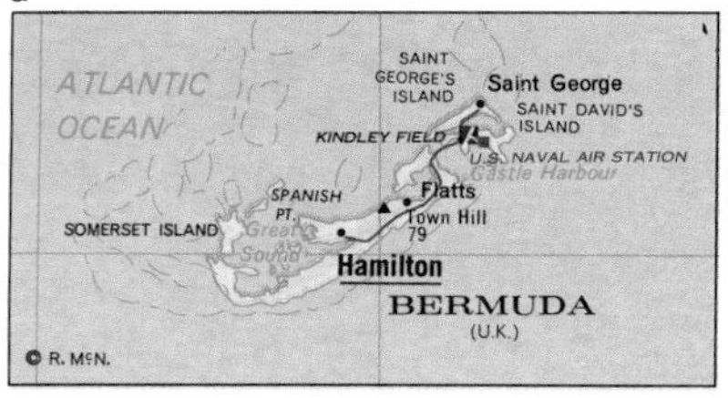

ATLANTIC OCEAN
Saint George
SAINT GEORGE'S ISLAND
SAINT DAVID'S ISLAND
KINDLEY FIELD
U.S. NAVAL AIR STATION
Castle Harbour
SOMERSET ISLAND
SPANISH PT
Flatts
Town Hill
Hamilton
BERMUDA
(U.K.)
© R. McN.


b

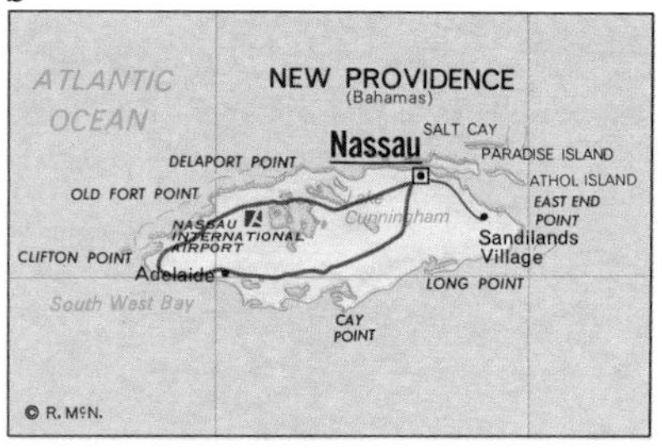

ATLANTIC OCEAN
NEW PROVIDENCE
(Bahamas)
Nassau
DELAPORT POINT
SALT CAY
PARADISE ISLAND
ATHOL ISLAND
OLD FORT POINT
EAST END POINT
NASSAU INTERNATIONAL AIRPORT
CLIFTON POINT
Adelaide
Sandilands Village
LONG POINT
South West Bay
CAY POINT
© R. McN.


c

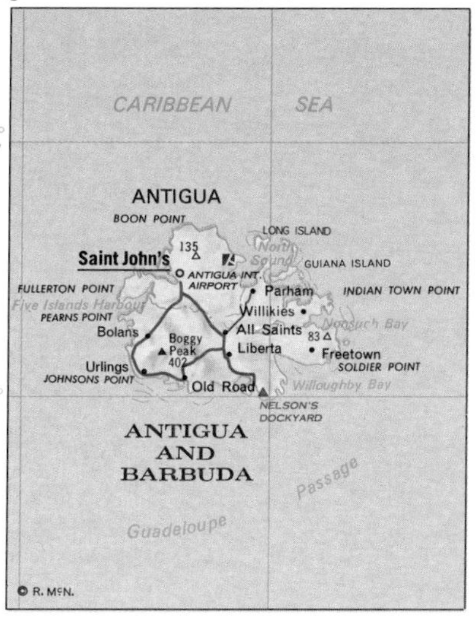

CARIBBEAN SEA
ANTIGUA
BOON POINT
LONG ISLAND
Saint John's
ANTIGUA INT. AIRPORT
GUIANA ISLAND
FULLERTON POINT
Parham
INDIAN TOWN POINT
Five Islands Harbour
PEARNS POINT
Willikies
Bolans
All Saints
Boggy Peak
Liberta
Freetown
Urlings
JOHNSONS POINT
Old Road
SOLDIER POINT
Willoughby Bay
NELSON'S DOCKYARD
ANTIGUA AND BARBUDA
Guadeloupe Passage
© R. McN.


d

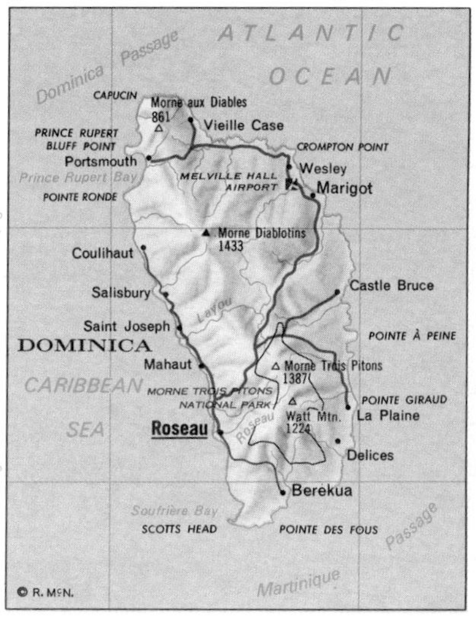

ATLANTIC OCEAN
Dominica Passage
CAPUCIN
Morne aux Diables
Vieille Case
PRINCE RUPERT BLUFF POINT
Portsmouth
Prince Rupert Bay
CROMPTON POINT
MELVILLE HALL AIRPORT
Wesley
Marigot
POINTE RONDE
Morne Diablotins
Coulihaut
Castle Bruce
Salisbury
Saint Joseph
DOMINICA
POINTE À PEINE
Mahaut
Morne Trois Pitons
CARIBBEAN SEA
POINTE GIRAUD
Watt Mtn.
La Plaine
Roseau
Delices
Berekua
Soufrière Bay
SCOTTS HEAD
POINTE DES FOUS
Martinique Passage
© R. McN.


e

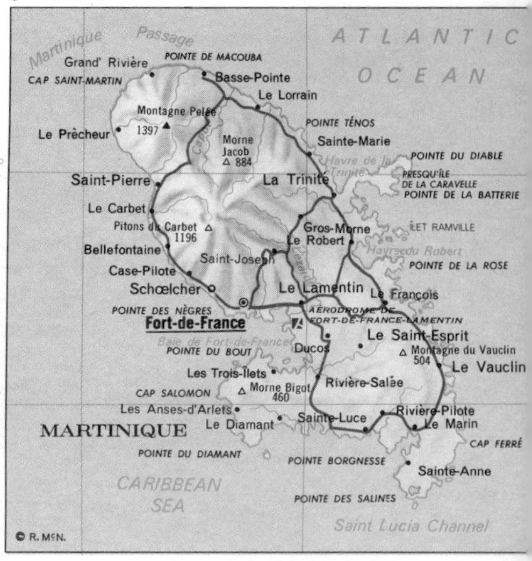

Martinique Passage
ATLANTIC OCEAN
Grand' Rivière
POINTE DE MACOUBA
CAP SAINT-MARTIN
Basse-Pointe
Le Lorrain
Montagne Pelée
Le Prêcheur
POINTE TÉNOS
Sainte-Marie
Morne Jacob
Saint-Pierre
La Trinité
POINTE DU DIABLE
Le Carbet
Pitons du Carbet
Bellefontaine
Gros-Morne
Le Robert
Case-Pilote
Saint-Joseph
Schœlcher
Le Lamentin
Le François
Fort-de-France
Le Saint-Esprit
Ducos
Montagne du Vauclin
Le Vauclin
Les Trois-Ilets
Morne Bigot
Rivière-Salée
CAP SALOMON
Les Anses-d'Arlets
Sainte-Luce
Rivière-Pilote
MARTINIQUE
Le Diamant
Le Marin
CAP FERRÉ
POINTE DU DIAMANT
POINTE BORGNESSE
Sainte-Anne
CARIBBEAN SEA
POINTE DES SALINTS
Saint Lucia Channel
© R. McN.


m

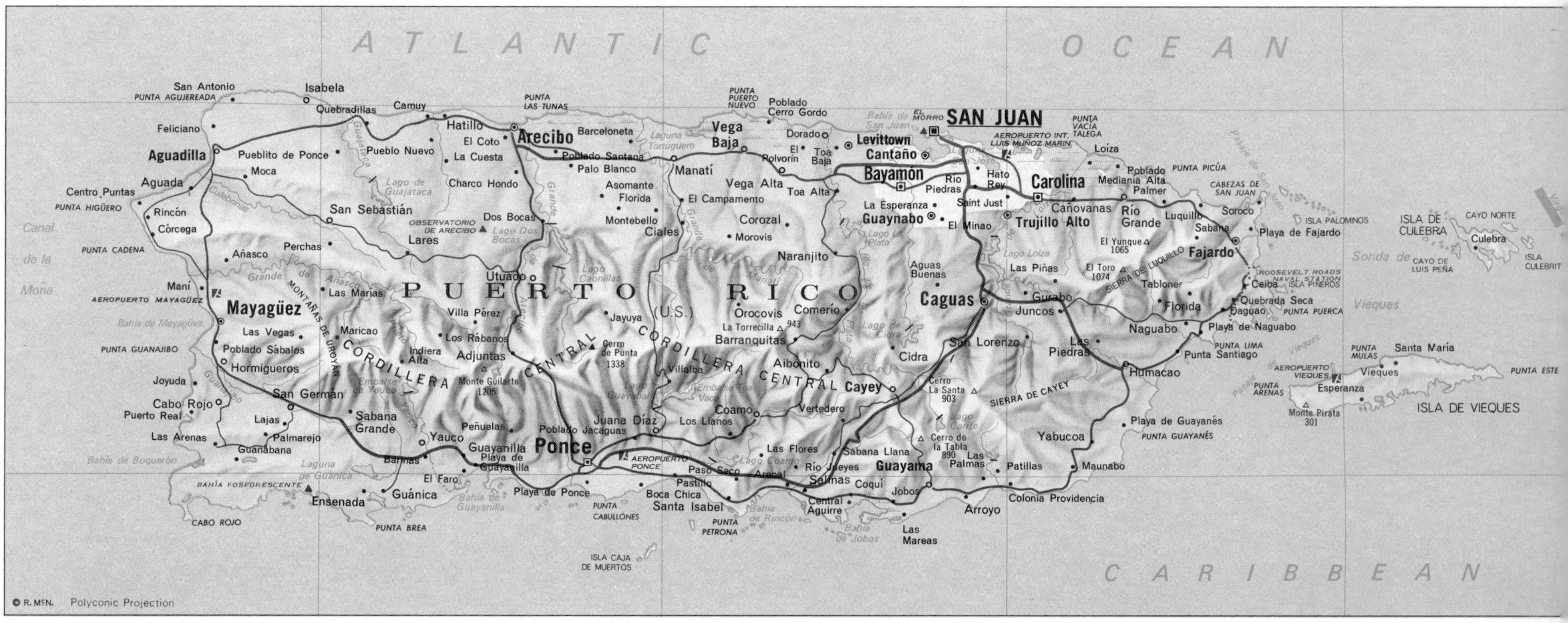

ATLANTIC OCEAN
SAN JUAN
PUERTO RICO (U.S.)
CORDILLERA CENTRAL
Aguadilla
Arecibo
Mayagüez
Ponce
Caguas
Bayamón
Carolina
Guayama
Fajardo
Humacao
ISLA DE CULEBRA
ISLA DE VIEQUES
Canal de la Mona
CARIBBEAN
© R. McN. Polyconic Projection


p

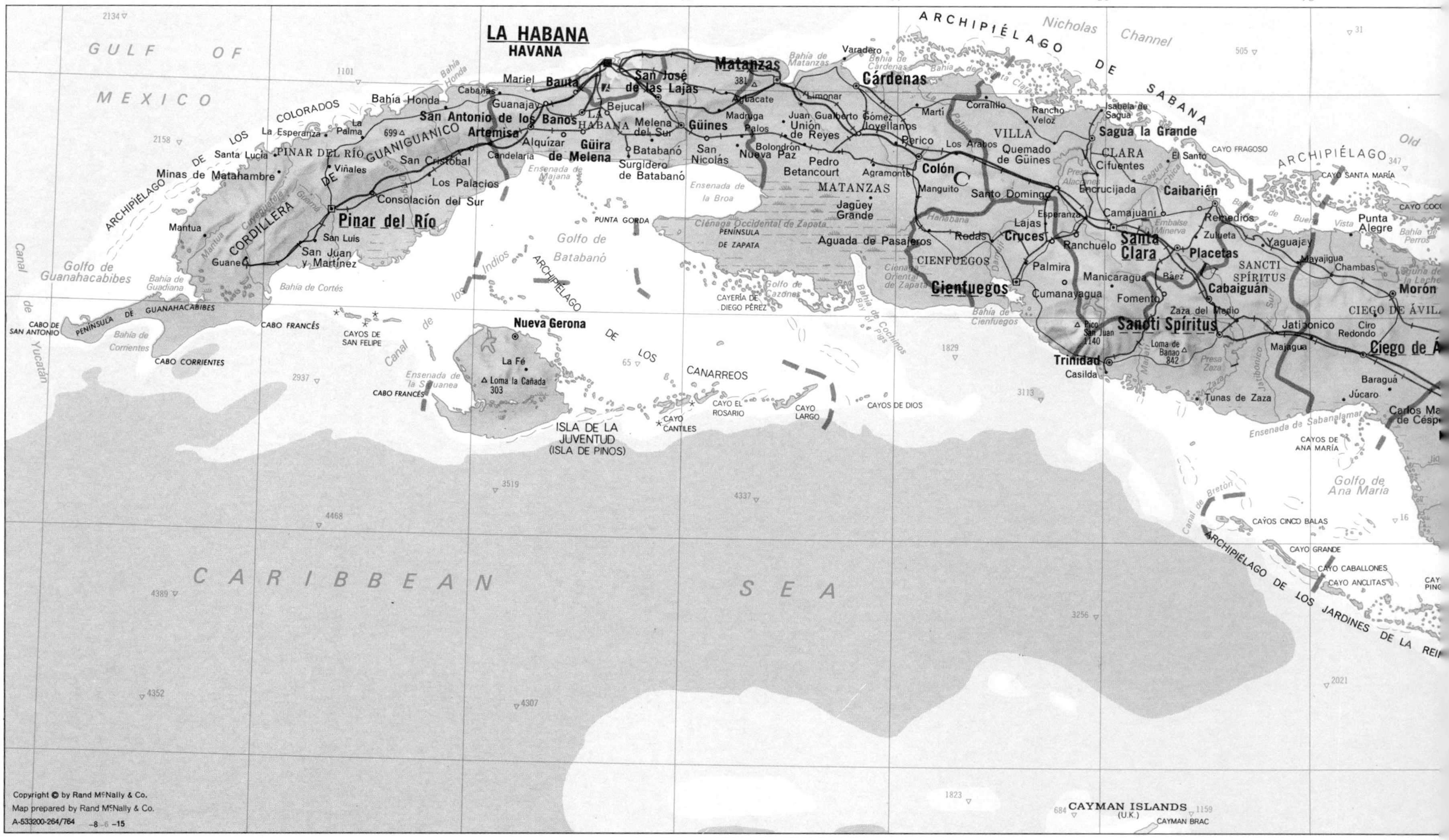

GULF OF MEXICO
LA HABANA
HAVANA
Matanzas
Cárdenas
ARCHIPIÉLAGO DE SABANA
Nicholas Channel
Pinar del Río
Artemisa
San Antonio de los Baños
Güines
Colón
Santa Clara
Cienfuegos
Sancti Spíritus
Trinidad
Ciego de Ávila
Morón
Nueva Gerona
ISLA DE LA JUVENTUD (ISLA DE PINOS)
Golfo de Batabanó
Golfo de Guanahacabibes
CABO DE SAN ANTONIO
CABO CORRIENTES
ARCHIPIÉLAGO DE LOS CANARREOS
Golfo de Ana Maria
ARCHIPIÉLAGO DE LOS JARDINES DE LA REINA
CARIBBEAN SEA
CAYMAN ISLANDS (U.K.)
CAYMAN BRAC
Copyright © by Rand McNally & Co.
Map prepared by Rand McNally & Co.
A-533200-264/764 -8-6-15


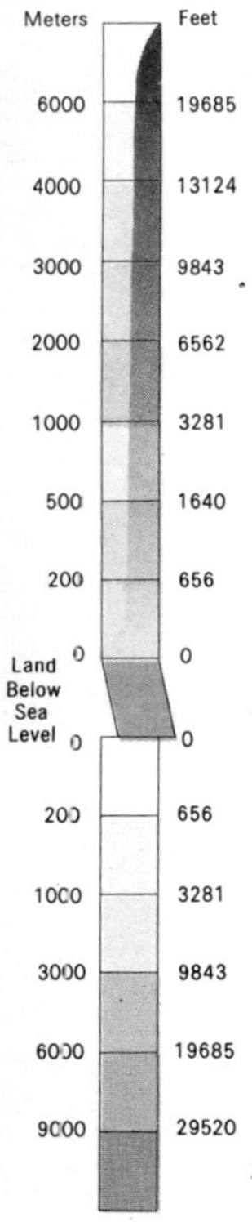

Meters
Feet
6000
19685
4000
13124
3000
9843
2000
6562
1000
3281
500
1640
200
656
Land Below Sea Level
0
0
200
656
1000
3281
3000
9843
6000
19685
9000
29520


| MAP FORM | bahía | cayo | channel | ensenada | golfo | island | mount | passage | point |
|---|---|---|---|---|---|---|---|---|---|
| ENGLISH | bay | cay | channel | bayou | gulf | island | mount | passage | point |
| DEUTSCH | Bucht | Klippe | Kanal | Altwasser | Golf | Insel | Berg | Durchfahrt | Landspitze |
| ESPAÑOL | bahía | cayo | canal | ensenada | golfo | isla | montaña | pasaje | punta |
| FRANÇAIS | baie | caye | détroit | bayou | golfe | île | mont | passage | pointe |
| PORTUGUÊS | baía | baixio | canal | enseada | golfo | ilha | montanha | passagem | ponta |

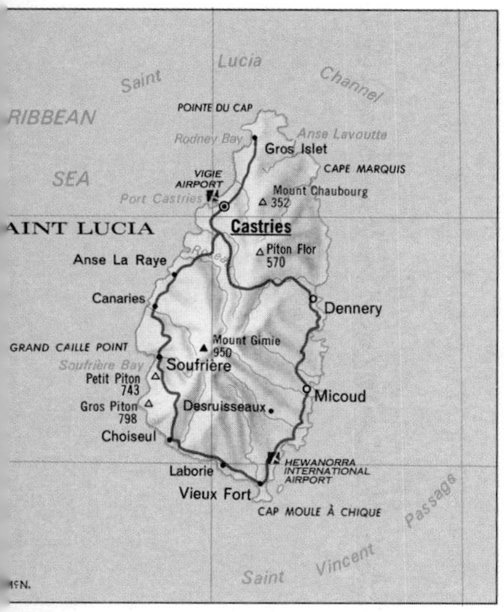
SAINT LUCIA
Castries
Gros Islet
Dennery
Soufrière
Micoud
Vieux Fort
Laborie
Choiseul
Canaries
Anse La Raye
Saint Lucia Channel
Saint Vincent Passage
CARIBBEAN SEA

g

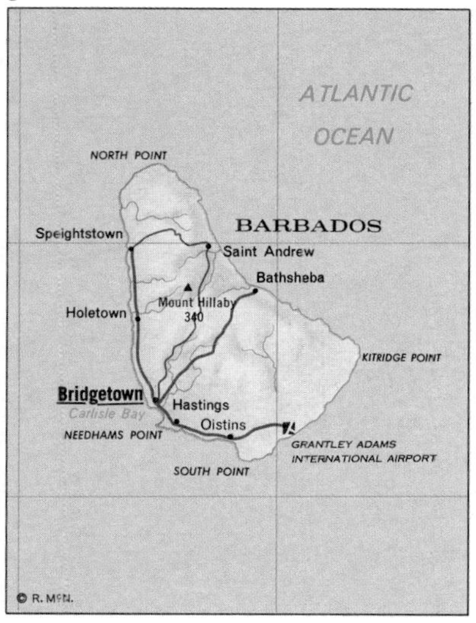
ATLANTIC OCEAN
BARBADOS
Bridgetown
Speightstown
Holetown
Saint Andrew
Bathsheba
Mount Hillaby 340
Hastings
Oistins
NORTH POINT
SOUTH POINT
KITRIDGE POINT
NEEDHAMS POINT
GRANTLEY ADAMS INTERNATIONAL AIRPORT

h

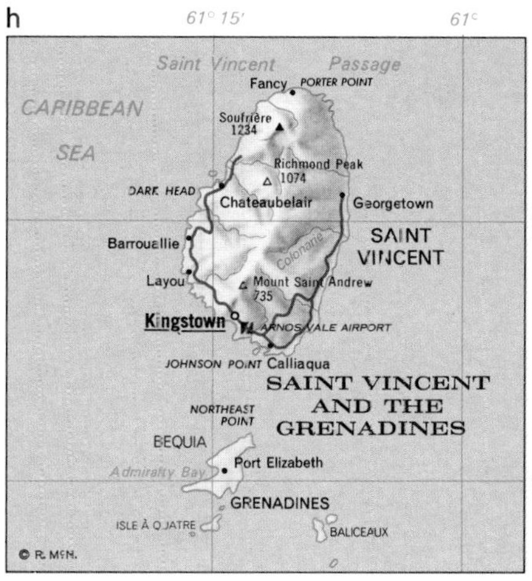
Saint Vincent Passage
CARIBBEAN SEA
Fancy
Soufrière 1234
Richmond Peak 1074
Chateaubelair
Georgetown
SAINT VINCENT
Barrouallie
Layou
Mount Saint Andrew 735
Kingstown
Calliaqua
ARNOS VALE AIRPORT
SAINT VINCENT AND THE GRENADINES
BEQUIA
Port Elizabeth
GRENADINES
Admiralty Bay

k

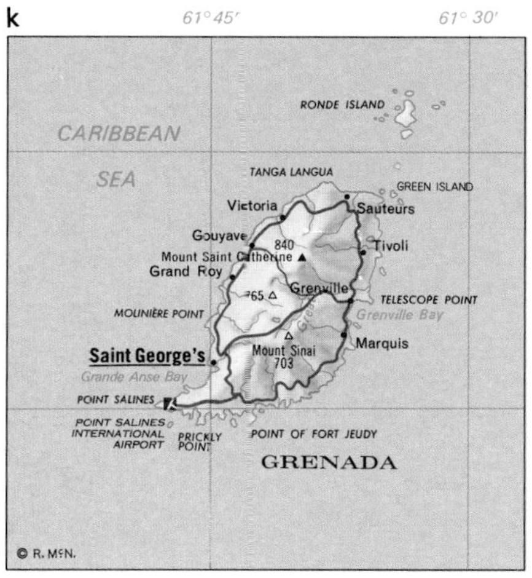
CARIBBEAN SEA
RONDE ISLAND
GREEN ISLAND
Victoria
Sauteurs
Gouyave
Mount Saint Catherine 840
Grand Roy
Tivoli
Grenville
Saint George's
Mount Sinai 703
Marquis
POINT SALINES INTERNATIONAL AIRPORT
GRENADA

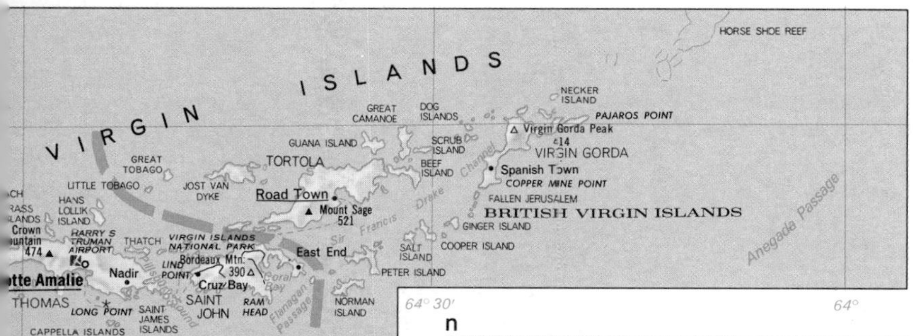
VIRGIN ISLANDS
TORTOLA
Road Town
Mount Sage 521
VIRGIN GORDA
Virgin Gorda Peak 414
Spanish Town
ANEGADA
BRITISH VIRGIN ISLANDS
Charlotte Amalie
SAINT THOMAS
SAINT JOHN
Cruz Bay
East End
Anegada Passage
VIRGIN ISLANDS (U.S.)
S E A

n

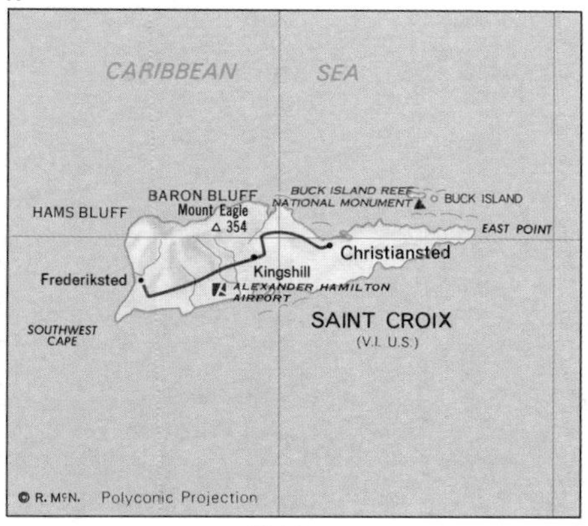
CARIBBEAN SEA
HAMS BLUFF
BARON BLUFF
Mount Eagle 354
BUCK ISLAND REEF NATIONAL MONUMENT
BUCK ISLAND
EAST POINT
Christiansted
Frederiksted
Kingshill
ALEXANDER HAMILTON AIRPORT
SOUTHWEST CAPE
SAINT CROIX (V.I. U.S.)
Polyconic Projection

o

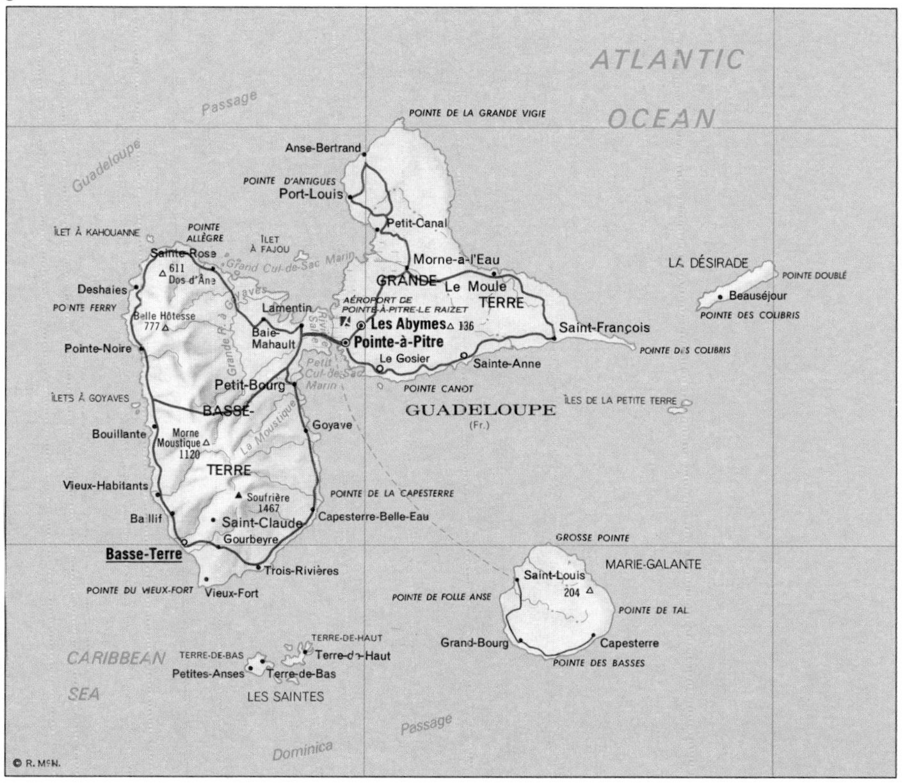
ATLANTIC OCEAN
Guadeloupe Passage
Anse-Bertrand
Port-Louis
Petit-Canal
Morne-a-l'Eau
GRANDE-TERRE
Le Moule
LA DÉSIRADE
Beauséjour
Sainte-Rose
Deshaies
Lamentin
Les Abymes
Pointe-à-Pitre
Saint-François
Baie-Mahault
Le Gosier
Sainte-Anne
Pointe-Noire
Petit-Bourg
BASSE-TERRE
GUADELOUPE (Fr.)
Goyave
Bouillante
Vieux-Habitants
Soufrière 1467
Saint-Claude
Capesterre-Belle-Eau
Basse-Terre
Gourbeyre
Trois-Rivières
Vieux-Fort
MARIE-GALANTE
Saint-Louis
Grand-Bourg
Capesterre
Terre-de-Haut
Terre-de-Bas
LES SAINTES
CARIBBEAN SEA
Dominica Passage

Kilometers 0 10 20 30 40 50 Km.
Statute Miles 0 10 20 30 40 50 Mi.

Scale 1:1,000,000
One centimeter represents 10 kilometers.
One inch represents approximately 16 miles.
Transverse Mercator Projection (except as noted)

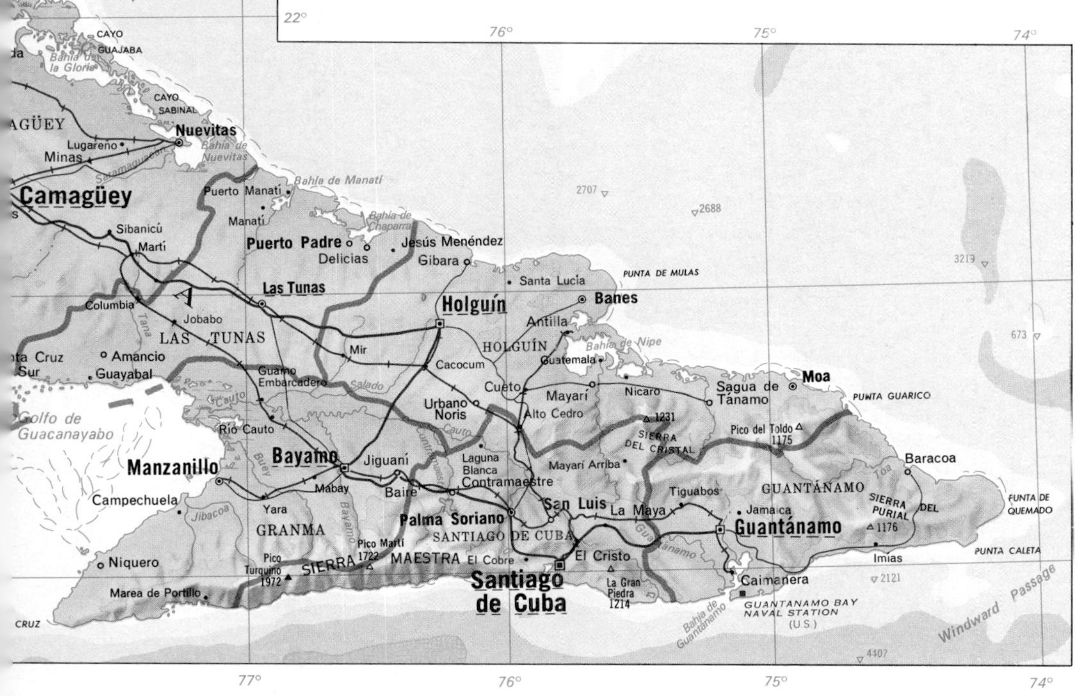
ATLANTIC OCEAN
GREAT BAHAMA BANK
CAMAGÜEY
Nuevitas
Camagüey
Puerto Padre
Las Tunas
Holguín
Banes
Moa
Bayamo
Manzanillo
Palma Soriano
Santiago de Cuba
Guantánamo
Baracoa
SIERRA MAESTRA
GRANMA
GUANTÁNAMO
GUANTÁNAMO BAY NAVAL STATION (U.S.)
Windward Passage
Golfo de Guacanayabo

q

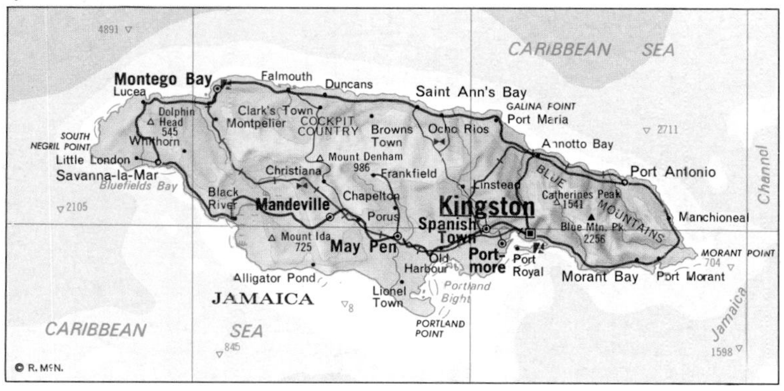
CARIBBEAN SEA
Montego Bay
Falmouth
Saint Ann's Bay
Port Maria
Ocho Rios
Port Antonio
Mandeville
Kingston
Spanish Town
May Pen
Morant Bay
Savanna-la-Mar
BLUE MOUNTAINS
Blue Mtn. Pk. 2256
JAMAICA

r

TOBAGO
Scarborough
CARIBBEAN SEA
Port of Spain
Arima
Sangre Grande
Chaguanas
TRINIDAD
San Fernando
Point Fortin
TRINIDAD AND TOBAGO
Gulf of Paria
ATLANTIC OCEAN
VENEZUELA

s

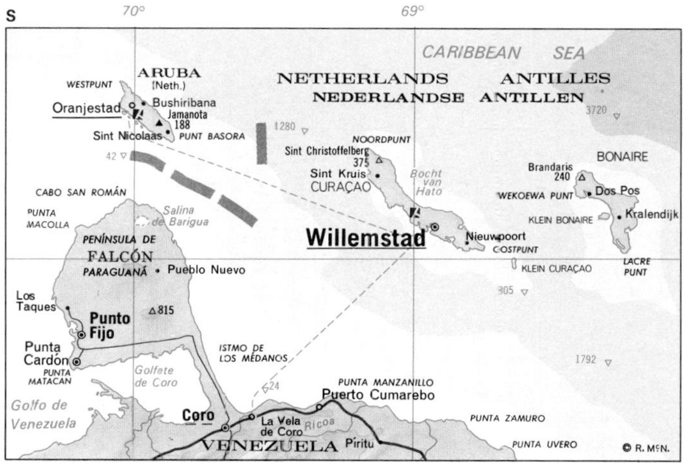
CARIBBEAN SEA
ARUBA (Neth.)
Oranjestad
NETHERLANDS ANTILLES
NEDERLANDSE ANTILLEN
CURAÇAO
Willemstad
BONAIRE
Kralendijk
FALCÓN
Punto Fijo
Coro
Golfo de Venezuela
VENEZUELA

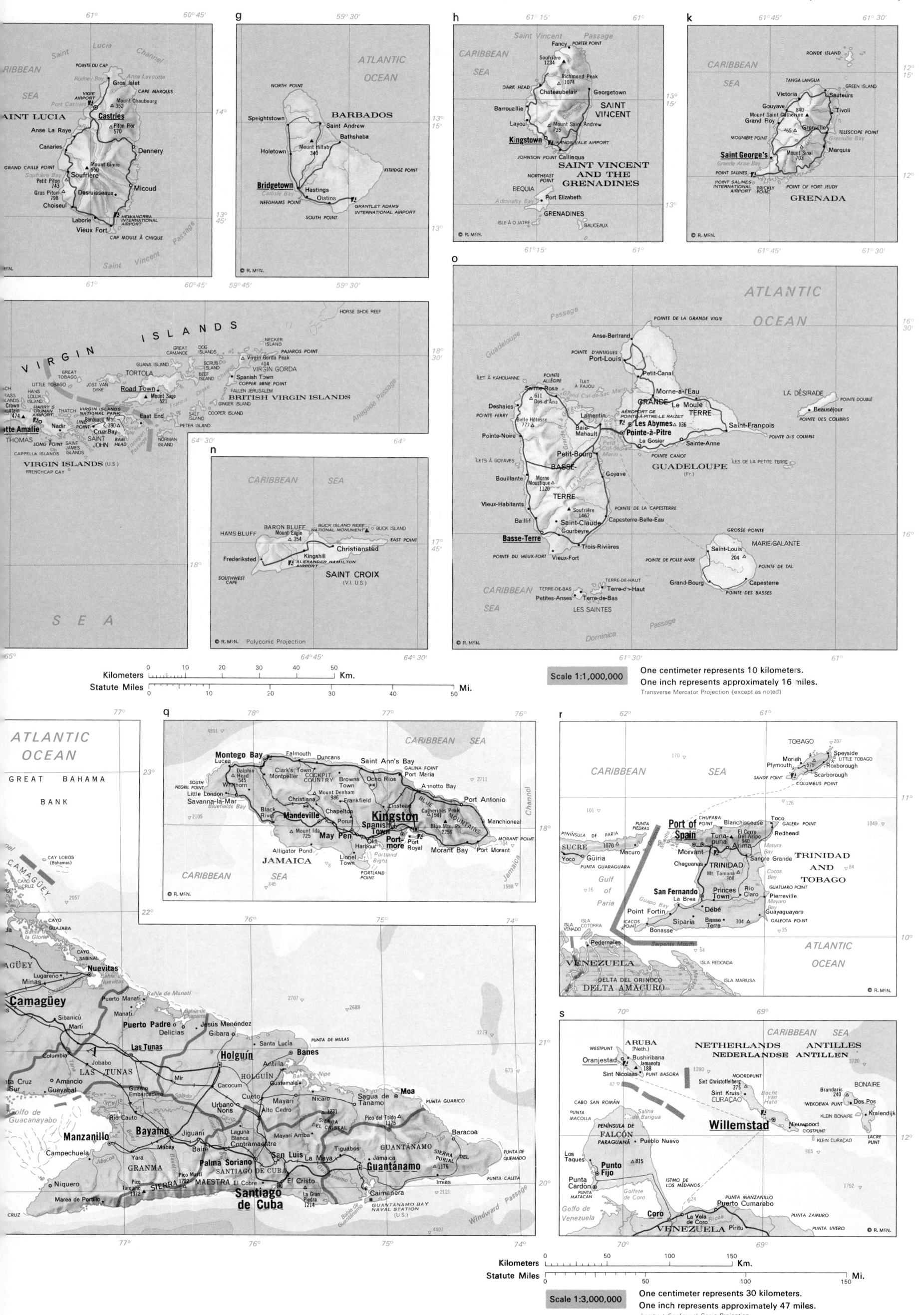

Kilometers 0 50 100 150 Km.
Statute Miles 0 50 100 150 Mi.

Scale 1:3,000,000
One centimeter represents 30 kilometers.
One inch represents approximately 47 miles.
Lambert Conformal Conic Projection

# Northern South America / Südamerika, nördlicher Teil / América del Sur: zona septentrional
# Amérique du Sud Septentrionale / América do Sul: zona setentrional

Map continues pages 230-231

CARIBBEAN SEA
PACIFIC OCEAN
NICARAGUA
Managua
Masaya
Granada
COSTA RICA
SAN JOSÉ
Puerto Limón
Colón
Panamá
ARUBA (Neth.)
Oranjestad
NETHERLANDS ANTILLES
Willemstad
LESSER ANTILLES
SAINT VINCENT AND THE GRENADINES
Barranquilla
Santa Marta
Cartagena
Maracaibo
CARACAS
Valencia
Barquisimeto
Mérida
Cúcuta
San Cristóbal
VENEZUELA
Ciudad Bolívar
Ciudad Guayana
Bucaramanga
Medellín
Manizales
SANTA FE DE BOGOTÁ
COLOMBIA
Villavicencio
Cali
Buenaventura
Popayán
Pasto
LLANOS
Esmeraldas
QUITO
ECUADOR
Guayaquil
Cuenca
Machala
Equator
Iquitos
Leticia
Benjamin Constant
Tumbes
Piura
Sullana
Chiclayo
Trujillo
Chimbote
Huaraz
Callao
LIMA
Huancayo
Ayacucho
Cusco
Ica
Arequipa
PERU
CORDILLERA OCCIDENTAL
CORDILLERA CENTRAL
CORDILLERA ORIENTAL
Pucallpa
Rio Branco
ACRE
Porto Velho
RONDÔNIA
AMAZONAS
SELVA
LA PAZ
BOLIVIA
Cochabamba
Santa Cruz de la Sierra
Sucre
Potosí
Oruro
ALTIPLANO
CORDILLERA REAL
Tacna
Arica
Iquique
CHILE
ARGENTINA
Copyright © by Rand McNally & Co.
Map prepared by Esselte Map Service AB, Stockholm.
A-549100-264 -8 -8 -16
85°
80°
75°
70°
65°
10°
5°
0°
5°
10°
15°
20°


Kilometers 0 200 400 600 Km.

Statute Miles 0 200 400 600 Mi.

Scale 1:12,000,000

One centimeter represents 120 kilometers.
One inch represents approximately 190 miles.
Oblique Conic Conformal Projection

ATLANTIC OCEAN
Equator
Tropic of Capricorn
55°
50°
45°
40°
35°
10°
5°
0°
15°
20°
Georgetown
Paramaribo
Cayenne
SURINAME
FRENCH GUIANA
TUMUC-HUMAC MTS.
ACARAI MTS.
AMAPÁ
Macapá
ILHA DE MARAJÓ
Belém
Amazonas
Amazon
Santarém
PARÁ
Represa de Tucuruí
SERRA DOS CARAJÁS
SERRA DO CACHIMBO
Imperatriz
MARANHÃO
São Luís
Teresina
Parnaíba
Fortaleza
CEARÁ
PIAUÍ
RIO GRANDE DO NORTE
Natal
PARAÍBA
João Pessoa
Campina Grande
PERNAMBUCO
Recife
Olinda
ALAGOAS
Maceió
SERGIPE
Aracaju
BAHIA
Salvador
Feira de Santana
Juazeiro
Petrolina
Represa de Sobradinho
TOCANTINS
Palmas
ILHA DO BANANAL
B R A Z I L
MATO GROSSO
PLANALTO DO MATO GROSSO
Cuiabá
SERRA DO RONCADOR
GOIÁS
BRASÍLIA
PLANALTO CENTRAL
Goiânia
Anápolis
MATO GROSSO DO SUL
Campo Grande
Corumbá
MINAS GERAIS
Belo Horizonte
Uberlândia
Montes Claros
SERRA DO ESPINHAÇO
ESPÍRITO SANTO
Vitória
Vila Velha
Ilhéus
Itabuna
Vitória da Conquista
SÃO PAULO
São Paulo
Santos
Campinas
RIO DE JANEIRO
Niterói
Presidente Prudente
Ribeirão Preto
ATOL DAS ROCAS
ILHA FERNANDO DE NORONHA (Brazil)
CABO DE SÃO ROQUE
CABO ORANGE
CABO MAGUARI

Map continues pages 244-245

| MAP FORM | cerro | cordillera | ilha | lago | nevado | peninsula | serra |
|---|---|---|---|---|---|---|---|
| ENGLISH | mountain | range | island | lake | mountain | peninsula | mountains |
| DEUTSCH | Berg | Gebirge | Insel | See | Berg | Halbinsel | Berge |
| ESPAÑOL | montaña | cordillera | isla | lago | montaña | península | montañas |
| FRANÇAIS | montagne | chaîne | île | lac | montagne | péninsule | montagnes |
| PORTUGUÊS | montanha | cordilheira | ilha | lago | montanha | península | montanhas |

Map continues pages 242-243

PACIFIC
OCEAN
CHILE
ARGENTINA
BOLIVIA
GRAN CHACO
PATAGONIA
ANDES
CORDILLERA DOMEYKO
DESIERTO DE ATACAMA
PUNA DE ATACAMA
Tropic of Capricorn
ISLA SAN FÉLIX (Chile)
ISLA SAN AMBROSIO (Chile)
ARCHIPIÉLAGO JUAN FERNÁNDEZ (Chile)
ISLA ROBINSON CRUSOE
ISLA MÁS A TIERRA
ISLA ALEJANDRO SELKIRK
ISLA MÁS AFUERA
Antofagasta
Calama
Chuquicamata
Tocopilla
Taltal
Chañaral
Copiapó
Vallenar
La Serena
Coquimbo
Ovalle
Valparaíso
Viña del Mar
SANTIAGO
San Bernardo
San Antonio
Rancagua
Talca
Curicó
Chillán
Concepción
Talcahuano
Los Angeles
Temuco
Valdivia
Osorno
Puerto Montt
ISLA GRANDE DE CHILOÉ
ARCHIPIÉLAGO DE LOS CHONOS
PENÍNSULA DE TAITAO
ISLA WELLINGTON
Puerto Natales
Punta Arenas
ISLA GRANDE DE TIERRA DEL FUEGO
Ushuaia
CABO DE HORNOS
ISLA DE LOS ESTADOS
FALKLAND ISLANDS (U.K.)
WEST FALKLAND
Salta
San Salvador de Jujuy
San Miguel de Tucumán
Santiago del Estero
San Fernando del Valle de Catamarca
La Rioja
San Juan
Mendoza
Villa Nueva
San Rafael
Córdoba
Río Cuarto
Santa Fe
Paraná
Rosario
BUENOS AIRES
Resistencia
Corrientes
Formosa
Asunción
Concordia
Mar del Plata
Bahía Blanca
Neuquén
Viedma
San Carlos de Bariloche
Trelew
Rawson
Puerto Madryn
Comodoro Rivadavia
Puerto Deseado
Puerto San Julián
Puerto Santa Cruz
Río Gallegos
Río Grande
Cerro Aconcagua 6959
Golfo San Jorge
Golfo San Matías
PENÍNSULA VALDÉS
Bahía Grande
Estrecho de Magallanes
Copyright © by Rand McNally & Co.
Map prepared by Esselte Map Service AB, Stockholm.
A-549200-264

| MAP FORM | cerro, co. | golfo | ilha | isla | lago | lagoa | monte | salar |
|---|---|---|---|---|---|---|---|---|
| ENGLISH | butte | gulf | island | isle | lake | lake | mountain | saltflat |
| DEUTSCH | Restberg | Golf | Insel | Insel | See | See | Berg | Salzebene |
| ESPAÑOL | cerro | golfo | isla | isla | lago | lago | montaña | salobral |
| FRANÇAIS | butte | golfe | île | île | lac | lac | montagne | salina |
| PORTUGUÊS | colina | golfo | ilha | ilha | lago | lago | montanha | salina |

BRAZIL
PARANÁ
SANTA CATARINA
RIO GRANDE DO SUL
SÃO PAULO
MINAS GERAIS
ESPÍRITO SANTO
RIO DE JANEIRO
SÃO PAULO
RIO DE JANEIRO
Santos
Campinas
Sorocaba
Jundiaí
São José dos Campos
Niterói
Petrópolis
Nova Iguaçu
Volta Redonda
Juiz de Fora
Campos
Ribeirão Preto
Araraquara
São Carlos
Bauru
Marília
Presidente Prudente
Londrina
Maringá
Piracicaba
Limeira
Ponta Grossa
Curitiba
Paranaguá
Joinvile
Blumenau
Itajaí
Florianópolis
Lages
Passo Fundo
Caxias do Sul
São Leopoldo
Porto Alegre
Santa Maria
Pelotas
Rio Grande
Bagé
Foz do Iguaçu
Cascavel
Chapecó
Erexim
Criciúma
Tubarão
MONTEVIDEO
Tropic of Capricorn
ATLANTIC OCEAN
SOUTH GEORGIA AND THE SOUTH SANDWICH ISLANDS (U.K.)
SOUTH GEORGIA
SHAG ROCKS (S. Georgia)
BLACK ROCK (S. Georgia)
BIRD ISLAND
ANNENKOV ISLAND
CAPE DISAPPOINTMENT
CLERKE ROCKS
2934 Mount Paget
TRINDADE (Brazil)
ILHAS MARTIN VAZ (Brazil)
55°
50°
45°
40°
35°
30°
25°
20°
15°

Kilometers 0 200 400 600 Km.

Statute Miles 0 200 400 600 Mi.

Scale 1:12,000,000

One centimeter represents 120 kilometers.
One inch represents approximately 190 miles.
Oblique Conic Conformal Projection

Map continues pages 238-239

CARIBBEAN SEA
PACIFIC OCEAN
NICARAGUA
SAN ANDRÉS Y PROVIDENCIA (Col.)
Barranquilla
Santa Marta
Cartagena
Maracaibo
Medellín
SANTA FE DE BOGOTÁ
Cali
Panamá
Colón
QUITO
Guayaquil
Cuenca
Iquitos
Buenaventura
Cúcuta
Bucaramanga
ARCHIPIÉLAGO DE COLÓN
GALAPAGOS ISLANDS
GALÁPAGOS (Ec.)
PACIFIC OCEAN
Equator
COLOMBIA
ECUADOR
PERU
BRASIL
Amazon
Golfo de Guayaquil
Golfo de Venezuela
Golfo de Panamá
Copyright © by Rand McNally & Co.
Map prepared by Rand McNally & Co.
A-549700-764

| Meters | Feet |
|---|---|
| 6000 | 19685 |
| 4000 | 13124 |
| 3000 | 9843 |
| 2000 | 6562 |
| 1000 | 3281 |
| 500 | 1640 |
| 200 | 656 |
| 0 | 0 |
| Land Below Sea Level | |
| 0 | 0 |
| 200 | 656 |
| 1000 | 3281 |
| 3000 | 9843 |
| 6000 | 19685 |
| 9000 | 29520 |

| MAP FORM | bahía | cabo | cerro, co. | golfo | igarapé | isla, i. | lago, l. | punta | volcán, vol. |
|---|---|---|---|---|---|---|---|---|---|
| ENGLISH | bay | cape | butte | gulf | river | island | lake | point | volcano |
| DEUTSCH | Bucht | Kap | Restberg | Golf | Fluss | Insel | See | Landspitze | Vulkan |
| ESPAÑOL | bahía | cabo | cerro | golfo | río | isla | lago | punta | volcán |
| FRANÇAIS | baie | cap | butte | golfe | rivière | île | lac | pointe | volcan |
| PORTUGUÊS | baía | cabo | colina | golfo | rio | ilha | lago | ponta | vulcão |

Map continues pages 248-249

Map continues
pages 238-239

LESSER ANTILLES
GRENADA
Saint George's
Port of Spain
TRINIDAD
TOBAGO
ATLANTIC
OCEAN
NUEVA ESPARTA
ISLA DE MARGARITA
Porlamar
DISTRITO FEDERAL
CARACAS
Maracay
Valencia
Barcelona
Cumaná
Maturín
MONAGAS
SUCRE
DELTA AMACURO
ANZOÁTEGUI
GUÁRICO
Calabozo
Ciudad Guayana
Ciudad Bolívar
San Fernando
APURE
BOLÍVAR
VENEZUELA
COLOMBIA
Puerto Carreño
Puerto Ayacucho
AMAZONAS
BARIMA-WAINI
CUYUNI-MAZARUNI
Georgetown
New Amsterdam
POTARO-SIPARUNI
UPPER TAKUTU-UPPER ESSEQUIBO
EAST BERBICE-CORENTYNE
SIPALIWINI
NICKERIE
SURINAME
GUYANA
BRASIL
BRAZIL
RORAIMA
Boa Vista
PAKARAIMA MOUNTAINS
SIERRA PARIMA
LA GRAN SABANA
Equator
PARÁ
AMAZONAS
Manaus
Amazon
Negro
Japurá
PARQUE NACIONAL DO JAÚ
Parintins
Coari
Tefé

Map continues
pages 250-251

Kilometers 0 100 200 300 Km.
Statute Miles 0 100 200 300 Mi.

Scale 1:6,000,000

One centimeter represents 60 kilometers.
One inch represents approximately 95 miles.
Oblique Conic Conformal Projection

# Peru, Bolivia and Western Brazil / Peru, Bolivien und westliches Brasilien / Perú, Bolivia y Brasil Occidental
# Pérou, Bolivie et Brésil Occidental / Peru, Bolívia e Brasil Ocidental

80°
78°
76°
74°
72°
70°
82°
6°
8°
10°
12°
14°
16°
18°
20°
PACIFIC
OCEAN
LORETO
AMAZONAS
CAJAMARCA
LAMBAYEQUE
PIURA
DESIERTO DE SECHURA
LIBERTAD
ANCASH
HUÁNUCO
PASCO
JUNÍN
LIMA
HUANCAVELICA
AYACUCHO
APURÍMAC
CUSCO
AREQUIPA
MOQUEGUA
TACNA
PUNO
ICA
UCAYALI
SAN MARTÍN
MADRE DE DIOS
ACRE
CORDILLERA OCCIDENTAL
CORDILLERA CENTRAL
CORDILLERA ORIENTAL
CORDILLERA DE VILCABAMBA
SERRA DO DIVISOR
CORD. ULTRAORIENTAL
PAMPA DEL SACRAMENTO
GRAN PAJONAL
PAMPA DE HUAYURI
ANDES
PERU
BRAZIL
BRASIL
EC.
CHILE
LIMA
Callao
Chiclayo
Trujillo
Chimbote
Piura
Sullana
Cajamarca
Huaraz
Huánuco
Cerro de Pasco
Huancayo
Ayacucho
Cusco
Arequipa
Pucallpa
Iquitos
Juliaca
Puno
Tacna
Arica
Iquique
Tocopilla
Ica
Pisco
Nazca
Mollendo
Camaná
Copyright © by Rand McNally & Co.
Map prepared by Rand McNally & Co.
A-549792-764 -6 -7-9


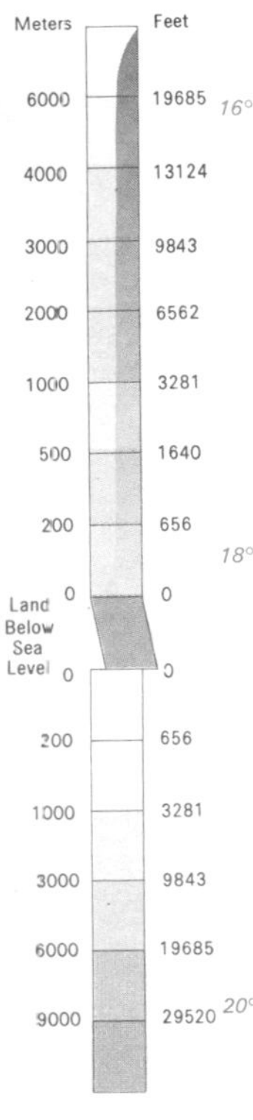

Meters
Feet
6000
19685
4000
13124
3000
9843
2000
6562
1000
3281
500
1640
200
656
0
0
Land Below Sea Level
0
0
200
656
1000
3281
3000
9843
6000
19685
9000
29520


| MAP FORM | cerro | cordillera | isla, i. | lago, l. | nevado | punta | rio | serra |
|---|---|---|---|---|---|---|---|---|
| ENGLISH | mountain | mountains | island | lake | mountain | point | river | mountains |
| DEUTSCH | Berg | Berge | Insel | See | Berg | Landspitze | Fluss | Berge |
| ESPAÑOL | montaña | montañas | isla | lago | nevado | punta | río | sierra |
| FRANÇAIS | montagne | montagnes | île | lac | montagne | pointe | rivière | montagnes |
| PORTUGUÊS | montanha | montanhas | ilha | lago | pico nevado | ponta | rio | serra |

Map continues
pages 246-247

AMAZONAS
SELVAS
PARÁ
SERRA DO CACHIMBO
SERRA DOS APIACÁS
SERRA DO NORTE
SERRA DO TOMBADOR
MATO GROSSO
PLANALTO DO MATO GROSSO
SERRA FORMOSA
CHAPADA DOS PARECIS
RONDÔNIA
PANDO
BENI
COCHABAMBA
SANTA CRUZ
CHUQUISACA
TARIJA
POTOSÍ
CHACO BOREAL
ALTO PARAGUAY
NUEVA ASUNCIÓN
BOQUERÓN
PRESIDENTE HAYES
CONCEPCIÓN
AMAMBAY
SALTA
JUJUY
ARGENTINA
PARAGUAY
BOLIVIA
BRAZIL
BRASIL
Porto Velho
Rio Branco
Humaitá
Lábrea
Ariquemes
Ji-Paraná
Vilhena
Guajará-Mirim
Riberalta
Trinidad
Cochabamba
Oruro
Sucre
Potosí
Tarija
Santa Cruz de la Sierra
Cuiabá
Várzea Grande
Cáceres
Rondonópolis
Corumbá
Campo Grande
Dourados
Ponta Porã
Pedro Juan Caballero
Lago Poopó
Salar de Uyuni
RODOVIA TRANSAMAZÔNICA
Pantanal de São Lourenço
Pantanal do Rio Negro
Laguna Concepción
Bañados del Izozog
SERRANÍA DE SANTIAGO
SERRANÍA DE HUANCHACA
SERRA DE MARACAJU
CORDILLERA REAL
CORDILLERA ORIENTAL

Map continues
pages 250-251

Map continues
page 255

Map continues
pages 252-253

Kilometers 0 100 200 300 Km.
Statute Miles 0 100 200 300 Mi.

Scale 1:6,000,000
One centimeter represents 60 kilometers.
One inch represents approximately 95 miles.
Oblique Conic Conformal Projection

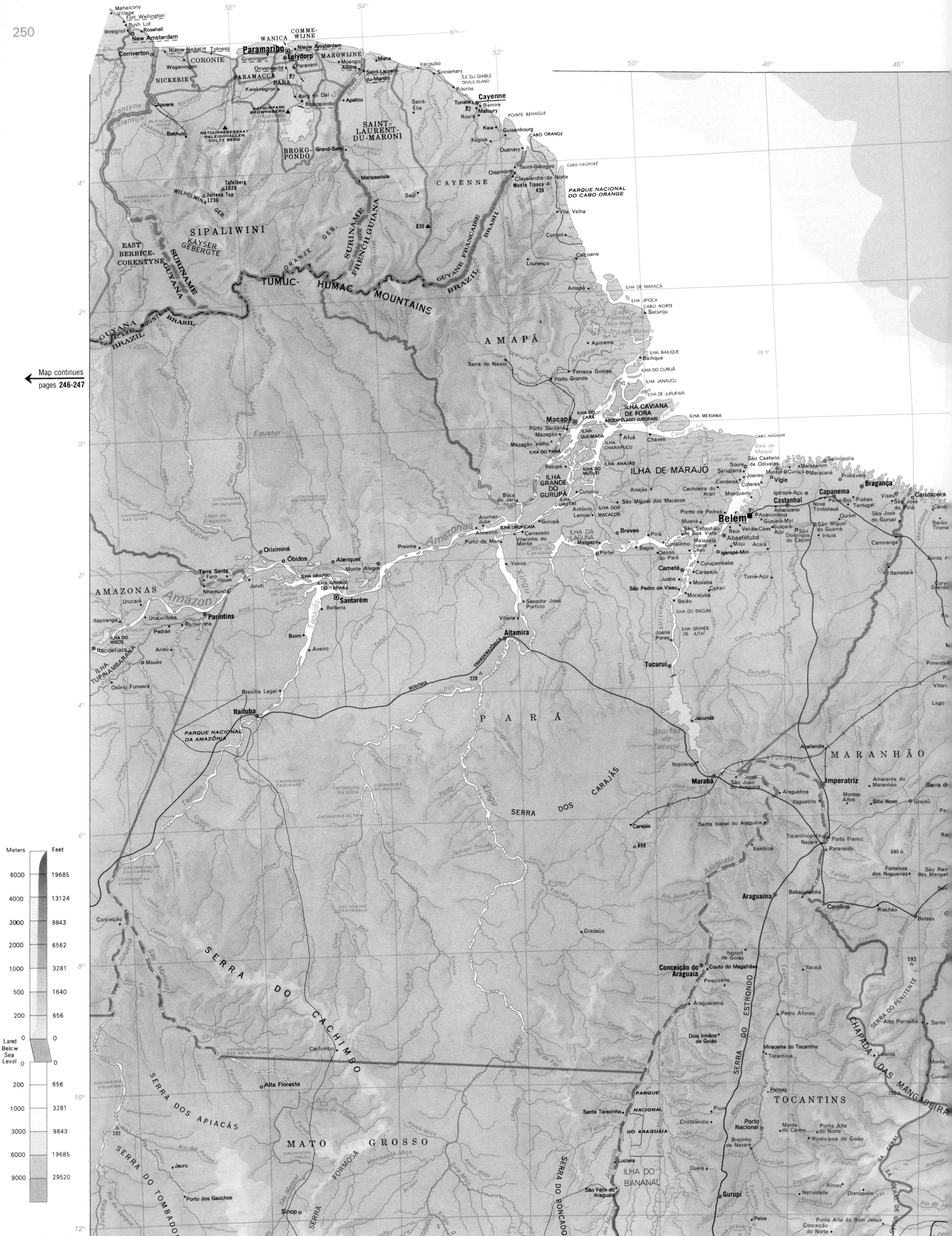
Paramaribo
Cayenne
New Amsterdam
Lelydorp
Corriverton
NICKERIE
CORONIE
SARAMACCA
PARA
MAROWIJNE
COMMEWIJNE
WANICA
BROKOPONDO
SAINT-LAURENT-DU-MARONI
CAYENNE
SIPALIWINI
EAST BERBICE-CORENTYNE
TUMUC-HUMAC MOUNTAINS
GUYANA
SURINAME
FRENCH GUIANA
GUYANE FRANÇAISE
BRASIL
BRAZIL
AMAPÁ
Macapá
ILHA DE MARAJÓ
ILHA CAVIANA DE FORA
ILHA MEXIANA
Belém
Castanhal
Bragança
Capanema
Abaetetuba
Breves
Cametá
Tucuruí
Represa de Tucuruí
Marabá
Imperatriz
MARANHÃO
Equator
Amazonas
Amazon
AMAZONAS
Parintins
Óbidos
Santarém
Altamira
Itaituba
PARQUE NACIONAL DA AMAZÔNIA
P A R Á
SERRA DOS CARAJÁS
Carajás
Conceição do Araguaia
Araguaína
SERRA DO ESTRONDO
SERRA DO CACHIMBO
SERRA DOS APIACÁS
SERRA DO TOMBADOR
MATO GROSSO
SERRA FORMOSA
SERRA DO RONCADOR
ILHA DO BANANAL
PARQUE NACIONAL DO ARAGUAIA
TOCANTINS
Porto Nacional
Gurupi
CHAPADA DAS MANGABEIRAS
Alta Floresta
Sinop
Xingu
Tapajós
Tocantins
Araguaia
Meters
Feet
6000
19685
4000
13124
3000
9843
2000
6562
1000
3281
500
1640
200
656
0
Land Below Sea Level
9000
29520

Map continues pages 246-247

Map continues pages 248-249

Map continues page 255

| MAP FORM | cabo | cachoeira, cach. | ilha, i. | lago, l. | riacho | ribeirão, rão. | rio, r. | serra, sa. |
|---|---|---|---|---|---|---|---|---|
| ENGLISH | cape | waterfall | island | lake | creek | creek | river | mountains |
| DEUTSCH | Kap | Wasserfall | Insel | See | Bach | Bach | Fluss | Berge |
| ESPAÑOL | cabo | cascada | isla | lago | riachuelo | riachuelo | río | montañas |
| FRANÇAIS | cap | chute d'eau | île | lac | crique | crique | rivière | montagnes |
| PORTUGUÊS | cabo | queda d'água | ilha | lago | riacho | riacho | rio | montanhas |

ATLANTIC
OCEAN
Equator
44°
42°
40°
38°
36°
34°
32°
2°
0°
4°
6°
8°
10°
3758
4279
4402
4923
4235
1467
3648
3849
3989
4792
4826
727
ILHA DE SANTANA
PARQUE NACIONAL DOS LENÇÓIS MARANHENSES
PONTA DE JERICOACOARA
ATOL DAS ROCAS
ILHA FERNANDO DE NORONHA (Brazil)
CABO DE SÃO ROQUE
PONTA DO SEIXAS
FORTALEZA
Caucaia
Maranguape
Maracanaú
Pacatuba
Cascavel
Aracati
Mossoró
Natal
Ceará-Mirim
Macaíba
João Pessoa
Santa Rita
Bayeux
Campina Grande
Guarabira
Patos
Sousa
Cajàzeiras
Juazeiro do Norte
Crato
Iguatu
Icó
Quixadá
Crateús
Sobral
Camocim
Parnaíba
Piripiri
Teresina
Timon
Caxias
Codó
Floriano
Picos
Petrolina
Juazeiro
Garanhuns
Caruaru
Arcoverde
Vitória de Santo Antão
Jaboatão
Olinda
RECIFE
Muribeca dos Guararapes
Cabo
Palmares
Maceió
Arapiraca
Penedo
Propriá
Aracaju
São Cristóvão
Estância
Paulo Afonso
Senhor do Bonfim
Alagoinhas
Xique-Xique
Represa de Sobradinho
CEARÁ
RIO GRANDE DO NORTE
PARAÍBA
PERNAMBUCO
ALAGOAS
SERGIPE
PIAUÍ
BAHIA
SERRA GRANDE
CHAPADA DO ARARIPE
PARQUE NACIONAL DA SERRA DA CAPIVARA
Copyright © by Rand McNally & Co.
Map prepared by Rand McNally & Co.
A-540396-764 -6-6-10

Kilometers 0 100 200 300 Km.

Statute Miles 0 100 200 300 Mi.

Scale 1:6,000,000

One centimeter represents 60 kilometers.

One inch represents approximately 95 miles.

Oblique Conic Conformal Projection

Map continues pages 248-249

PACIFIC
OCEAN
Tropic of Capricorn
ANDES
PUNA
ATACAMA
DESIERTO DE ATACAMA
CORDILLERA DOMEYKO
BOLIVIA
CHILE
ARGENTINA
JUJUY
SALTA
TUCUMÁN
CATAMARCA
LA RIOJA
SAN JUAN
MENDOZA
SAN LUIS
CÓRDOBA
SANTIAGO DEL ESTERO
CHACO AUSTRAL
LA PAMPA
NEUQUÉN
RÍO NEGRO
BUENOS AIRES
COQUIMBO
VALPARAÍSO
REGION METROPOLITANA
LIBERTADOR GENERAL BERNARDO O'HIGGINS
MAULE
BIOBÍO
LA ARAUCANÍA
Antofagasta
Tocopilla
Chuquicamata
Calama
Taltal
Chañaral
Copiapó
Vallenar
La Serena
Coquimbo
Ovalle
Viña del Mar
Valparaíso
SANTIAGO
San Antonio
Rancagua
Curicó
Talca
Linares
Chillán
Talcahuano
Concepción
Los Angeles
Temuco
San Salvador de Jujuy
Salta
San Miguel de Tucumán
Santiago del Estero
La Rioja
San Juan
Mendoza
San Luis
Córdoba
Río Cuarto
San Rafael
Santa Rosa
Neuquén
Bahía Blanca
Villa María
Mercedes
Cipolletti
General Roca
Copyright © by Rand McNally & Co.
Map prepared by Rand McNally & Co.
A-540191-764

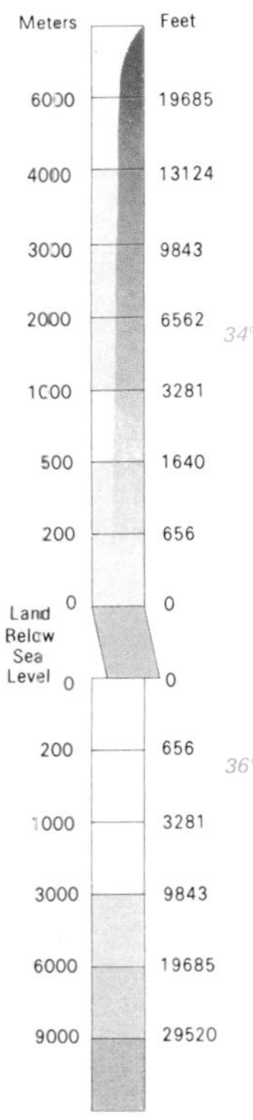
Meters
Feet
6000
19685
4000
13124
3000
9843
2000
6562
1000
3281
500
1640
200
656
Land Below Sea Level
0
9000
29520

Map continues page 254

| MAP FORM | cabo | cerro | cuchilla | ilha | laguna | punta | salar | sierra | volcán |
|---|---|---|---|---|---|---|---|---|---|
| ENGLISH | cape | mountain | hills | island | lagoon; lake | point | saltflat | mountains | volcano |
| DEUTSCH | Kap | Berg | Hügel | Insel | Haff; See | Landspitze | Salzebene | Berge | Vulkan |
| ESPAÑOL | cabo | cerro | cuchilla | isla | laguna | punta | salobral | sierra | volcán |
| FRANÇAIS | cap | montagne | collines | île | lagune; lac | pointe | salina | montagnes | volcan |
| PORTUGUÊS | cabo | montanha | colina | ilha | laguna | ponta | salina | serra | vulcão |

Map continues
page 255

ATLANTIC
OCEAN
SÃO PAULO
Campinas
Santos
Curitiba
Florianópolis
PORTO ALEGRE
Pelotas
Rio Grande
MONTEVIDEO
BUENOS AIRES
La Plata
Mar del Plata
Asunción
Corrientes
Posadas
Encarnación
Londrina
Ponta Grossa
Joinville
Blumenau
Caxias do Sul
Santa Maria
Uruguaiana
Paysandú
Salto
Concordia
PARANÁ
SANTA CATARINA
RIO GRANDE DO SUL
CORRIENTES
MISIONES
MATO GROSSO
SÃO PAULO

Kilometers 0 100 200 300 Km.
Statute Miles 0 100 200 300 Mi.

Scale 1:6,000,000
One centimeter represents 60 kilometers.
One inch represents approximately 95 miles.
Oblique Conic Conformal Projection

# Southern Argentina and Chile / Südliches Argentinien und südliches Chile / Argentina y Chile: zonas meridionales
# Argentine et Chili, parties Méridionales / Argentina e Chile: zonas meridionais

Map continues pages 252-253

PACIFIC OCEAN
ATLANTIC OCEAN
LA PAMPA
BUENOS AIRES
RÍO NEGRO
NEUQUÉN
CHUBUT
SANTA CRUZ
PATAGONIA
ANDES
LA ARAUCANÍA
LOS LAGOS
AISÉN DEL GENERAL CARLOS IBÁÑEZ DEL CAMPO
MAGALLANES Y DE LA ANTÁRTICA CHILENA
ARGENTINA
CHILE
FALKLAND ISLANDS (U.K.)
WEST FALKLAND
EAST FALKLAND
Stanley
ISLA GRANDE DE TIERRA DEL FUEGO
Ushuaia
Río Grande
Punta Arenas
Puerto Natales
Río Gallegos
Puerto Santa Cruz
Puerto San Julián
Puerto Deseado
Comodoro Rivadavia
Trelew
Rawson
Puerto Madryn
Esquel
San Carlos de Bariloche
Neuquén
Bahía Blanca
Viedma
Carmen de Patagones
General Roca
Temuco
Valdivia
Osorno
Puerto Montt
Castro
Coihaique
Golfo San Matías
Golfo San Jorge
Bahía Grande
Strait of Magellan
Estrecho de Le Maire
ISLA DE LOS ESTADOS STATEN ISLAND
CABO DE HORNOS CAPE HORN
ISLA CHILOÉ
ISLA WELLINGTON
ISLA NAVARINO
Copyright © by Rand McNally & Co.
Map prepared by Rand McNally & Co.
A-548400-764


| Meters | Feet |
|---|---|
| 6000 | 19685 |
| 4000 | 13124 |
| 3000 | 9843 |
| 2000 | 6562 |
| 1000 | 3281 |
| 500 | 1640 |
| 200 | 656 |
| 0 | 0 |
| Land Below Sea Level | |
| 0 | 0 |
| 200 | 656 |
| 1000 | 3281 |
| 3000 | 9843 |
| 6000 | 19685 |
| 9000 | 29520 |

| MAP FORM | bahia | cabo | cerro | isla | lago | monte | punta |
|---|---|---|---|---|---|---|---|
| ENGLISH | bay | cape | mountain, hill | isle | lake | mountain | point |
| DEUTSCH | Bucht | Kap | Berg, Hügel | Insel | See | Berg | Landspitze |
| ESPAÑOL | bahía | cabo | cerro | isla | lago | monte | punta |
| FRANÇAIS | baie | cap | montagne, colline | île | lac | montagne | pointe |
| PORTUGUÊS | baía | cabo | montanha, colina | ilha | lago | monte | ponta |

Kilometers 0 100 200 300 Km.

Statute Miles 0 100 200 300 Mi.

Scale 1:6,000,000

One centimeter represents 60 kilometers.
One inch represents approximately 95 miles.
Oblique Conic Conformal Projection

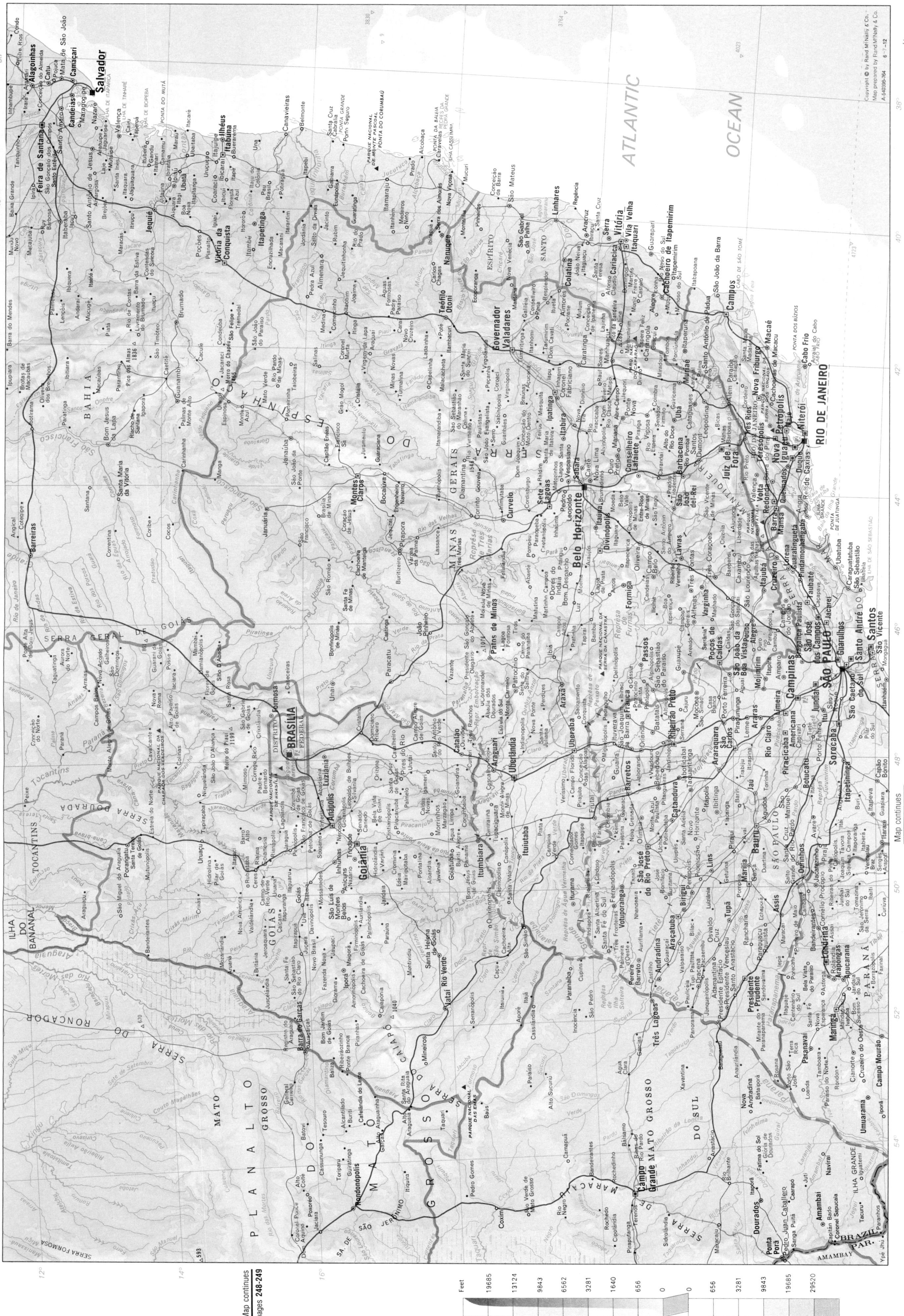
ATLANTIC
OCEAN
BAHIA
MINAS GERAIS
GOIÁS
MATO GROSSO DO SUL
SÃO PAULO
PARANÁ
ESPÍRITO SANTO
RIO DE JANEIRO
DISTRITO FEDERAL
BRASÍLIA
Salvador
Belo Horizonte
São Paulo
Rio de Janeiro
Goiânia
Campo Grande
Vitória
Santos
Campinas
Uberlândia
Uberaba
Ribeirão Preto
Juiz de Fora
Feira de Santana
Ilhéus
Vitória da Conquista
Montes Claros
Governador Valadares
Anápolis
Londrina
Maringá
Bauru
Sorocaba
Campos
Niterói
Petrópolis
Teófilo Otoni
Jequié
Itabuna
Barreiras
Dourados
Presidente Prudente
Araçatuba
São José do Rio Preto
Três Lagoas
SERRA GERAL DE GOIÁS
SERRA DO RONCADOR
PLANALTO DO MATO GROSSO
ILHA DO BANANAL
Rio São Francisco

Map continues pages 250-251
Map continues pages 252-253
Map continues pages 248-249

Scale 1:6,000,000
One centimeter represents 60 kilometers.
One inch represents approximately 95 miles.
Oblique Conic Conformal Projection

Kilometers 0 100 200 300
Statute Miles 0 100 200 300

| MAPFORM | cabo | cachoeira, cach. | ilha, I. | lagoa | parque nacional | ponta | ribeirão, rão. | rio, r. | serra |
|---|---|---|---|---|---|---|---|---|---|
| ENGLISH | cape | waterfall | island | lake | reservation | point | creek | river | mountains |
| DEUTSCH | Kap | Wasserfall | Insel | See | Reservat | Landspitze | Bach | Fluss | Berge |
| ESPAÑOL | cabo | cascada | isla | lago | parque nacional | punta | riachuelo | río | sierra |
| FRANÇAIS | cap | chute d'eau | île | lac | parc national | pointe | crique | rivière | montagnes |
| PORTUGUÊS | cabo | cascata | ilha | lago | parque nacional | ponta | riacho | rio | serra |

| Meters | Feet |
|---|---|
| 6000 | 19685 |
| 4000 | 13124 |
| 3000 | 9843 |
| 2000 | 6562 |
| 1000 | 3281 |
| 500 | 1640 |
| 200 | 656 |
| 0 | 0 |
| Land Below Sea Level 0 | 0 |
| 200 | 656 |
| 1000 | 3281 |
| 3000 | 9843 |
| 6000 | 19685 |
| 9000 | 29520 |

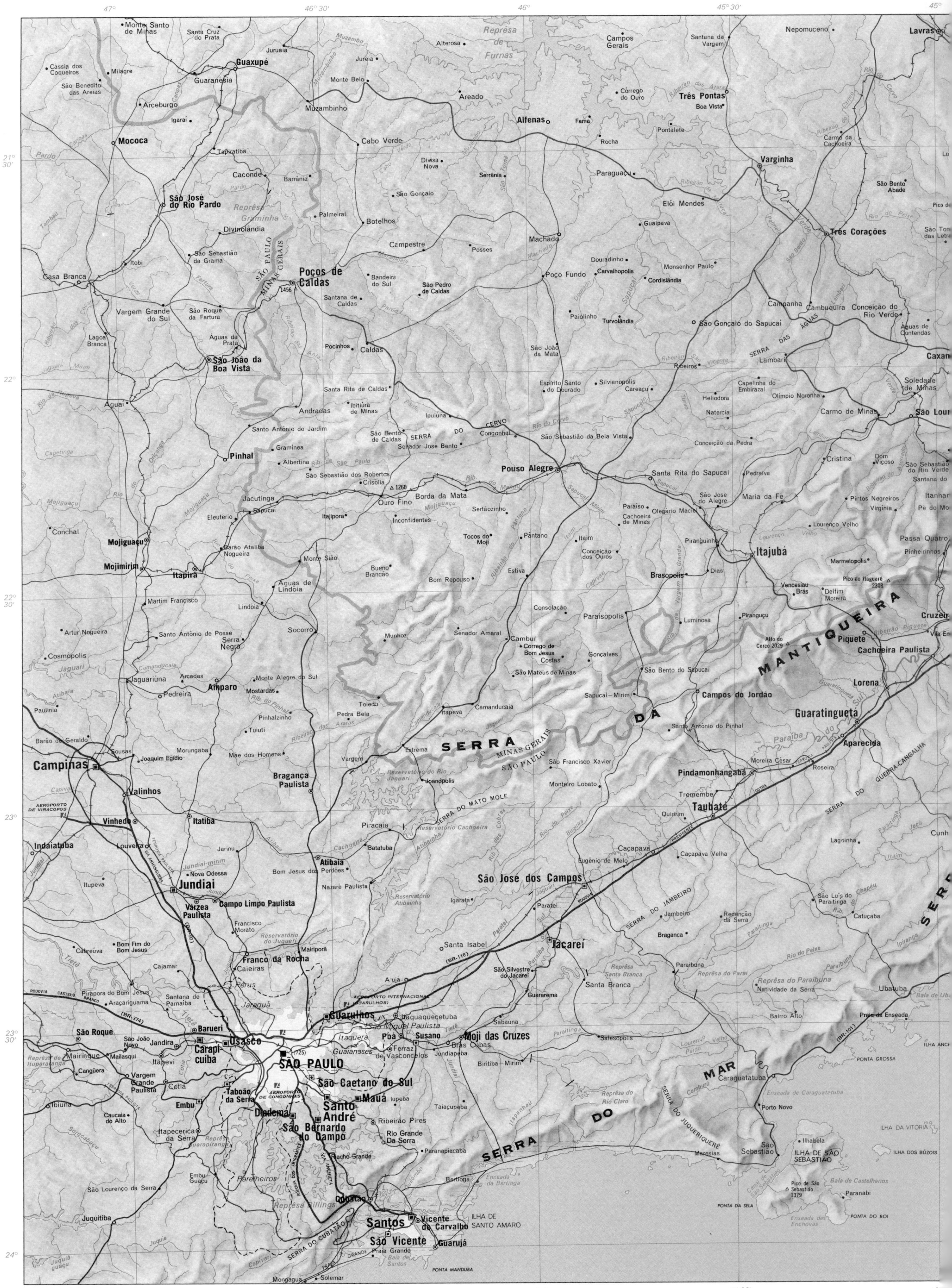
47°
46° 30'
46°
45° 30'
45°
21° 30'
22°
22° 30'
23°
23° 30'
24°
Monte Santo de Minas
Santa Cruz do Prata
Guaxupé
Guaranésia
Juruaia
Jureia
Monte Belo
Muzambinho
Alterosa
Represa de Furnas
Areado
Campos Gerais
Santana da Vargem
Nepomuceno
Lavras
Cassia dos Coqueiros
Milagre
São Benedito das Areias
Arceburgo
Igaraí
Mococa
Alfenas
Fama
Córrego do Ouro
Três Pontas
Boa Vista
Pontalete
Rocha
Carmo da Cachoeira
Tapiratiba
Cabo Verde
Divisa Nova
Serrânia
Paraguaçu
Varginha
Caconde
Barrânia
São Gonçalo
Elói Mendes
São Bento Abade
São José do Rio Pardo
Represa Graminha
Palmeiral
Botelhos
Guaipava
Três Corações
Divinolândia
Campestre
Posses
Machado
São Sebastião da Grama
Itobi
Douradinho
Monsenhor Paulo
Casa Branca
Poços de Caldas
1456
Bandeira do Sul
São Pedro de Caldas
Poço Fundo
Carvalhópolis
Cordislândia
SÃO PAULO
MINAS GERAIS
Santana de Caldas
Campanha
Cambuquira
Conceição do Rio Verde
Vargem Grande do Sul
São Roque da Fartura
Paiolinho
Turvolândia
São Gonçalo do Sapucaí
Águas de Contendas
Lagoa Branca
Águas da Prata
Pocinhos
Caldas
São João da Mata
SERRA DAS ÁGUAS
Lambari
São João da Boa Vista
Ribeiros
Soledade de Minas
Espírito Santo do Dourado
Silvianópolis
Careaçu
Capelinha do Embirazal
Santa Rita de Caldas
Heliodora
Olímpio Noronha
Aguaí
Ibitiura de Minas
Andradas
Ipuiuna
Natércia
Carmo de Minas
Santo Antônio do Jardim
São Bento de Caldas
SERRA DO CERVO
Congonhal
São Sebastião da Bela Vista
Conceição da Pedra
Senador José Bento
Graminea
Pinhal
Albertina
Cristina
Dom Viçoso
Pouso Alegre
Santa Rita do Sapucaí
Pedralva
São Sebastião dos Robertos
Crisólia
1260
Borda da Mata
Jacutinga
Ouro Fino
São José do Alegre
Maria da Fé
Sapucaí
Sertãozinho
Paraíso
Olegário Maciel
Cachoeira de Minas
Conchal
Eleutério
Itajipora
Inconfidentes
Tocos do Moji
Pântano
Itaim
Piranguinho
Itajubá
Mojiguaçu
Barão Ataliba Nogueira
Conceição dos Ouros
Monte Sião
Bueno Brancão
Mojimirim
Itapira
Bom Repouso
Estiva
Brasópolis
Dias
Águas de Lindóia
Marmelópolis
Pico do Itaguaré 2308
Vencesiau Brás
Delfim Moreira
Martim Francisco
Lindóia
Consolação
Paraisópolis
Luminosa
Piranguçu
MANTIQUEIRA
Artur Nogueira
Santo Antônio de Posse
Socorro
Senador Amaral
Munhoz
Cambuí
Córrego do Bom Jesus
Serra Negra
Costas
Gonçalves
Alto do Cerco 2029
Piquete
Cachoeira Paulista
Cosmópolis
São Mateus de Minas
São Bento do Sapucaí
Cruzeiro
Jaguariúna
Arcadas
Amparo
Monte Alegre do Sul
Pedreira
Mostardas
Lorena
Paulínia
Toledo
Itapeva
Camanducaia
Sapucaí-Mirim
Campos do Jordão
Pinhalzinho
Pedra Bela
Guaratinguetá
Tuiuti
DA
Santo Antônio do Pinhal
Barão Geraldo
Sousas
Joaquim Egídio
Morungaba
Mãe dos Homens
SERRA
Extrema
Aparecida
Campinas
Bragança Paulista
Vargem
São Francisco Xavier
Moreira César
Roseira
Reservatório do Rio Jaguari
Joanópolis
Monteiro Lobato
Pindamonhangaba
Valinhos
SERRA DO MATO MOLE
Tremembé
AEROPORTO DE VIRACOPOS
Vinhedo
Itatiba
Piracaia
Reservatório Cachoeira
Quiririm
Taubaté
SERRA DO QUEBRA-CANGALHA
Indaiatuba
Louveira
Jarinu
Batatuba
Caçapava
Lagoinha
Atibaia
Nova Odessa
Bom Jesus dos Perdões
Eugênio de Melo
Caçapava Velha
Itupeva
Jundiaí
Nazaré Paulista
São José dos Campos
Reservatório Atibainha
Várzea Paulista
Campo Limpo Paulista
Igaratá
Paratei
SERRA DO JAMBEIRO
Jambeiro
Redenção da Serra
São Luís do Paraitinga
Catuçaba
Francisco Morato
Reservatório do Juqueri
Cabreúva
Bom Fim do Bom Jesus
Mairiporã
Santa Isabel
Jacareí
Bragança
Franco da Rocha
Caieiras
Cajamar
São Silvestre do Jacareí
Paraibuna
Represa do Paraibuna
Santa Branca
Natividade da Serra
Ubatuba
Perus
Arujá
Pirapora do Bom Jesus
Araçariguama
Santana de Parnaíba
Jaraguá
AEROPORTO INTERNACIONAL (GUARULHOS)
Guararema
Guarulhos
Itaquaquecetuba
Sabaúna
Bairro Alto
Praia da Enseada
São Roque
Barueri
Osasco
São Miguel Paulista
Itaquera
Poá
Suzano
Moji das Cruzes
Salesópolis
São João Novo
Jandira
Carapicuíba
Guaianases
Ferraz de Vasconcelos
Brás Cubas
Jundiapeba
Mairinque
Mailasqui
Itapevi
SÃO PAULO
Biritiba-Mirim
PONTA GROSSA
Cangüera
Vargem Grande Paulista
Cotia
São Caetano do Sul
MAR
Caraguatatuba
Taboão da Serra
AEROPORTO DE CONGONHAS
Mauá
Ibiúna
Embu
Santo André
Diadema
Ribeirão Pires
Taiaçupeba
Represa do Rio Claro
Enseada de Caraguatatuba
Porto Novo
Caucaia do Alto
Itapecerica da Serra
São Bernardo do Campo
Rio Grande da Serra
SERRA DO MAR
SERRA DO JUQUERIQUERÊ
ILHA DA VITÓRIA
Ilhabela
ILHA DOS BÚZIOS
Paranapiacaba
Maresias
São Sebastião
ILHA DE SÃO SEBASTIÃO
Embu Guaçu
Parelheiros
Bertioga
Enseada da Bertioga
Pico de São Sebastião 1379
Baía de Castelhanos
Paranabi
São Lourenço da Serra
Represa Billings
Cubatão
PONTA DA SELA
Juquitiba
Santos
Vicente de Carvalho
ILHA DE SANTO AMARO
PONTA DO BOI
Enseada das Enchovas
São Vicente
Guarujá
SERRA DO CUBATÃO
Praia Grande
PONTA MANDUBA
Mongaguá
Solemar

| MAP FORM | baía | enseada | ilha | pico | ponta | represa | ribeirão | rio | serra |
|---|---|---|---|---|---|---|---|---|---|
| ENGLISH | bay | bay | island | peak | point | reservoir | stream | river | mountains |
| DEUTSCH | Bucht | Bucht | Insel | Gipfel | Landspitze | Stausee | Bach | Fluss | Berge |
| ESPAÑOL | bahía | bahía | isla | pico | punta | estanque | corriente de agua | río | sierra |
| FRANÇAIS | baie | baie | île | cime | pointe | réservoir | cours d'eau | rivière | montagnes |
| PORTUGUÊS | baía | enseada | ilha | pico | ponta | represa | ribeirão | rio | serra |

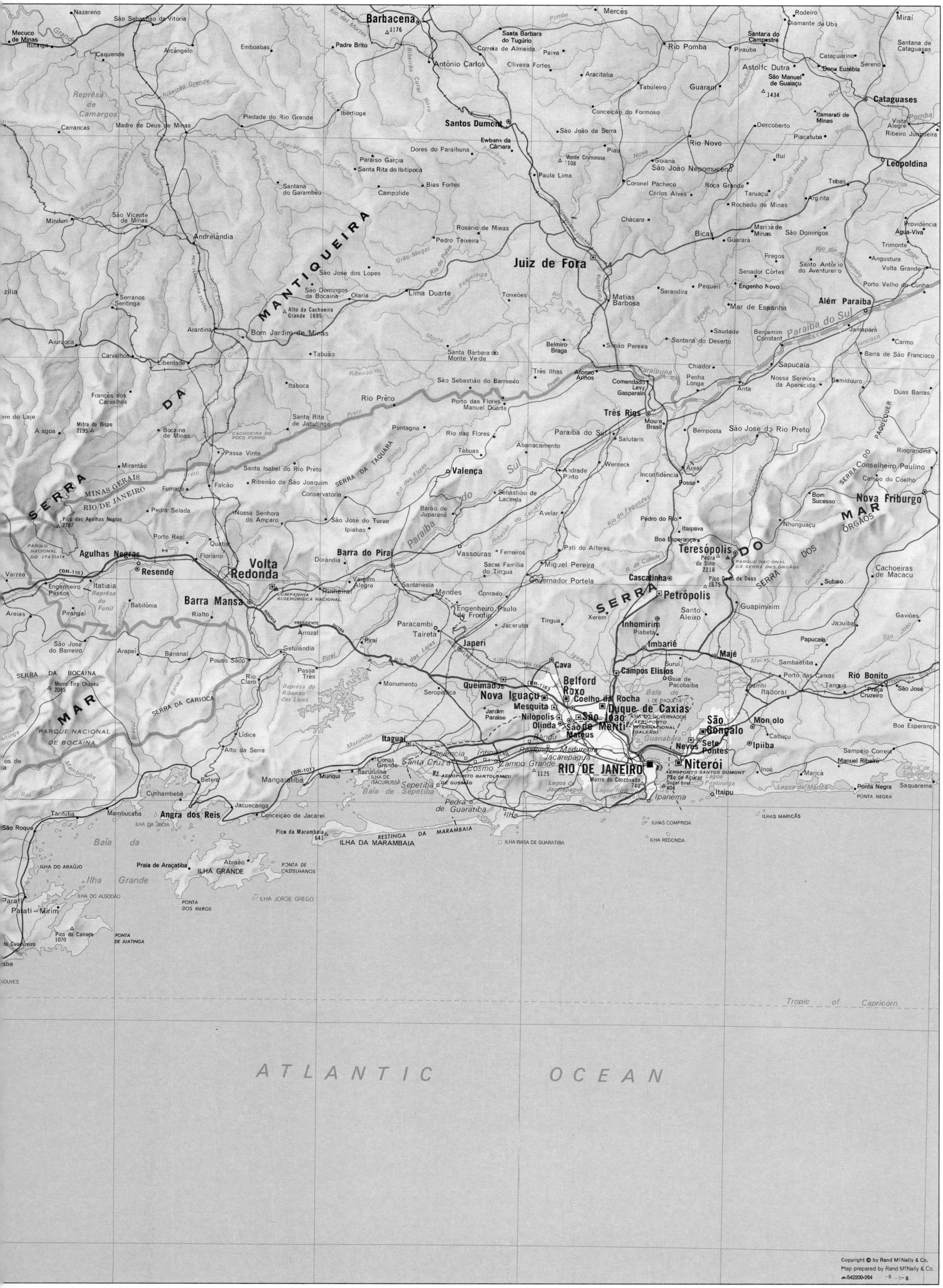
44°30′
44°
43°30′
43°
Barbacena
Santos Dumont
Juiz de Fora
Cataguases
Leopoldina
Muriaé
Andrelândia
SERRA DA MANTIQUEIRA
Três Rios
Paraíba do Sul
Valença
Volta Redonda
Barra Mansa
Resende
Agulhas Negras
Barra do Piraí
Petrópolis
Teresópolis
Nova Friburgo
SERRA DO MAR
Belford Roxo
Nova Iguaçu
Duque de Caxias
São João de Meriti
RIO DE JANEIRO
Niterói
São Gonçalo
Angra dos Reis
ILHA GRANDE
Baía de Sepetiba
Baía da Ilha Grande
ILHA DA MARAMBAIA
Rio Bonito
Cachoeiras de Macacu
Tropic of Capricorn
ATLANTIC OCEAN
21° 30′
22°
22° 30′
23°
23° 30′
24°
44°30′
44°
43°30′
43°
42°30′
Copyright © by Rand McNally & Co.
Map prepared by Rand McNally & Co.

Kilometers 0 10 20 30 40 50 Km.

Statute Miles 0 10 20 30 40 50 Mi.

Scale 1:1,000,000

One centimeter represents 10 kilometers.

One inch represents approximately 16 miles.

Polyconic Projection

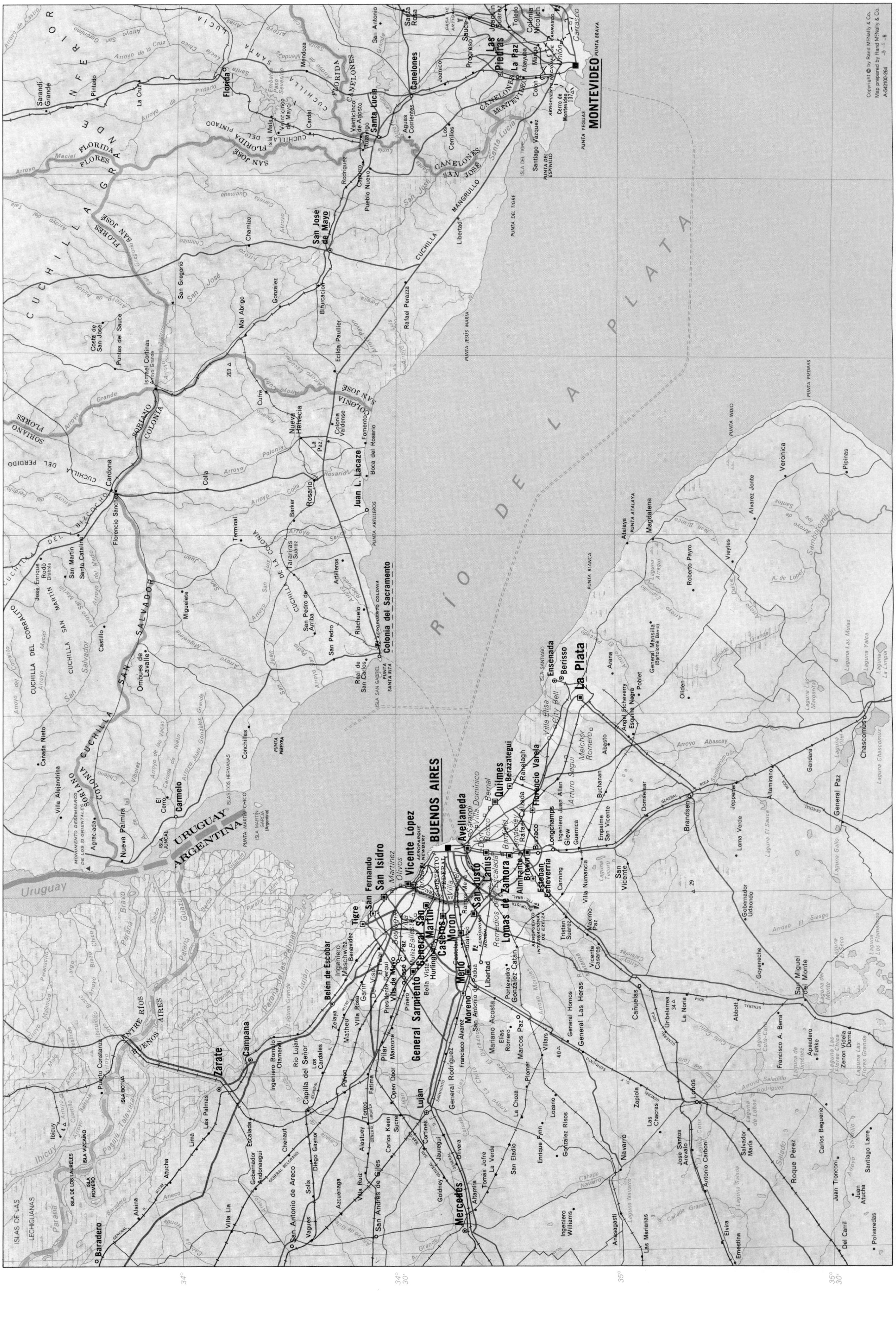
RÍO DE LA PLATA
BUENOS AIRES
MONTEVIDEO
La Plata
Colonia del Sacramento
URUGUAY
ARGENTINA
Uruguay
Canelones
San José de Mayo
Florida
Mercedes
Luján
Zárate
Campana
Copyright © by Rand McNally & Co.
Map prepared by Rand McNally & Co.
A-542100-264

| ESPAÑOL | aerodromo | arroyo, a. | cañada | cuchilla | isla | laguna | punta |
|---|---|---|---|---|---|---|---|
| ENGLISH | airport | brook | brook | hills | island | lake | point |
| DEUTSCH | Flughafen | Bach | Bach | Hügel | Insel | See | Landspitze |
| FRANÇAIS | aéroport | ruisseau | ruisseau | collines | île | lac | point |
| PORTUGUÊS | aeroporto | arroio | riacho | colina | ilha | laguna | ponta |

Kilometers 0 10 20 30 40 50 Km.
Statute Miles 0 10 20 30 40 50 Mi.

Scale 1:1,000,000

One centimeter represents 10 kilometers.
One inch represents approximately 16 miles.
Gauss-Krüger Projection

THIS SECTION CONSISTS of 60 maps of the world's major metropolitan areas, at the scale of 1:300,000. The maps show the generalized land-use patterns in and around each city—the total urban extent, major industrial areas, parks and preserves, and wooded areas. Airports are shown, as are many details of the highway and rail transportation networks. Selected points of interest appear, such as Fisherman's Wharf and Chinatown in San Francisco, the Welcome monument in Jakarta, the Temple of the Jade Buddha in Shanghai, and the Cristo Redentor statue in Rio de Janeiro.

The maps name and locate a great number of towns, villages, and suburbs, and also sections or neighborhoods within limits of the larger cities. Prominent physical features, including elevations, named and unnamed, have been indicated to give a general impression of the local topography. Shaded relief has been omitted, however, to permit display of such details as streams, parks, airport runways, important public buildings and monuments, and the names of major streets. The corporate limits of major cities are also outlined. For the symbols used on these maps see the Legend to Maps.

Maps of major world cities usually vary widely in scale, and heretofore have not been consistent in design and coverage. For this section, a special effort has been made to portray these varied metropolitan areas in as standard and comparable a fashion as possible. However, for a few cities (notably several in Asia) there has not been adequate source material to include certain information, such as major industrial areas and corporate limits.

The order of presentation is generally regional, with some exceptions where for ease of comparison major capitals or industrial centers or cities located in similar physical surroundings have been juxtaposed. Many American cities and some European cities, with their lower densities and more extensive areas, require larger maps than do Asiatic cities of comparable population. The total land area and population within the confines of each map are stated in the margin as a further aid to comparison.

DIESER KARTENTEIL UMFASST 60 Karten der bedeutendsten Stadtregionen der Erde im Massstab 1:300 000. Die Karten zeigen in generalisierter Form die Landnutzung in und um jede Stadt: die gesamte Ausdehnung des verstädterten Gebietes, wichtige Industriegebiete, Parks, Landflächen in Gemeinbesitz und Wald. Flughäfen werden ebenso dargestellt wie viele Einzelheiten des Strassen- und Eisenbahnnetzes. Bekannte Sehenswürdigkeiten sind eingetragen wie die "Fisherman's Wharf" und "Chinatown" in San Francisco, das Willkomm-Denkmal in Jakarta, der Tempel des Jade-Buddhas in Shanghai und die "Cristo Redentor"-Statue in Rio de Janeiro.

Die Karten verzeichnen Name and Lage einer grossen Zahl von Städten, Dörfern, Vororten ebenso wie eingemeindete Ortsteile bei grösseren Städten. Hervortretende physische Formen wie benannte und unbenannte Erhebungen sind aufgenommen, um eine allgemeine Vorstellung des lokalen Reliefs zu geben. Auf die Schummerung wurde jedoch verzichtet, um klar solche Einzelheiten wie Flüsse, Parks, Start- und Landebahnen der Flughäfen, bedeutende öffentliche Gebäude und Denkmäler sowie die Namen der wichtigsten Strassen herausstellen zu können. Eingetragen sind ferner die Gemeindegrenzen der wichtigsten Städte. Zu den auf diesen Karten verwendeten Signaturen siehe "Zeichenerklärung".

Karten der bedeutendsten Weltstädte differieren normalerweise sehr stark in ihren Massstäben und sind daher uneinheitlich in ihrer Gestaltung und Begrenzung. Deshalb wurde in diesem Kartenteil besonderer Wert darauf gelegt, die verschiedenen städtischen Ballungsgebiete in möglichst einheitlicher und vergleichbarer Form darzustellen. Für einige Städte, vor allem mehrere asiatische, war das Quellenmaterial jedoch nicht ausreichend genug, um gewisse Informationen wie Hauptindustriegebiete oder Stadtgrenzen einzutragen.

Im allgemeinen sind diese Karten nach regionalen Gesichtspunkten geordnet. Um Vergleiche zu erleichtern wurden einige Ausnahmen gemacht, indem wichtige Hauptstädte, Industriezentren oder Städte in vergleichbarer landschaftlicher Lage einander gegenübergestellt wurden. Viele americkanische und einige europäische Städte mit ihrer geringen Bevölkerungsdichte, aber ausgedehnteren Fläche erfordern eine grössere Kartenfläche als asiatische Städte von vergleichbarer Bevölkerungszahl. Die gesamte Landfläche und die Bevölkerung innerhalb des dargestellten Gebietes ist am Kartenrand verzeichnet als ein weiteres Hilfsmittel für Vergleiche.

INTEGRAN ESTA SECCION 60 mapas de las áreas metropolitanas más importantes del mundo, a la escala de 1:300 000. Los mapas muestran los patrones de uso del suelo dentro de cada ciudad y en sus alrededores—la extensión total del conglomerado urbano, las principales áreas industriales, parques y reservas, y zonas boscosas. Aparecen los aeropuertos, así como muchos otros detalles de las redes de carreteras y ferrocarriles. Se seleccionaron también puntos de interés, como el Muelle de los Pescadores y el Barrio Chino de San Francisco, el monumento de Bienvenida de Jakarta, el Templo del Buda de Jade de Shanghai y la estatua del Cristo Redentor de Rio de Janeiro.

Los mapas incluyen los nombres y la ubicación de gran número de ciudades, poblaciones menores, suburbios, e inclusive barrios y distritos de algunas de las ciudades más importantes. Las características físicas sobresalientes, e incluso algunas elevaciones con o sin nombre, están indicados para dar una impresión general de la topografía local. Se omitió sin embargo el relieve sombreado, lo cual permite mostrar detalles como ríos y arroyos, parques, pistas de aterrizaje, edificios y monumentos públicos notables y los nombres de las calles principales. También están marcados los límites territoriales de las ciudades más grandes. Para la interpretación de los símbolos usados en estos mapas, véanse Leyendas para Mapas.

Los mapas de las ciudades más importantes del mundo varían generalmente en escala, y hasta ahora no han sido consistentes ni en diseño ni en contenido. En esta sección hemos hecho un esfuerzo de presentar las distintas áreas metropolitanas en la forma más uniforme posible, para facilitar sus comparaciones. Para algunas ciudades (la mayoría de ellas en Asia), no fué posible obtener de las propias fuentes material adecuado para la inclusión de ciertos datos, tales como las mayores áreas industriales y los límites municipales.

Los mapas de áreas metropolitanas se presentan por regiones, a excepción de unos cuantos que aparecen yuxtapuestos para facilitar la comparación entre grandes capitales, o centros comerciales, o ciudades ubicadas en contextos físicos similares. Muchas ciudades de América y algunas ciudades de Europa, por su baja densidad de población y su área extensa, requieren mapas más grandes que los ocupados por ciudades asiáticas con poblaciones comparables. Al margen de cada mapa se anotaron el área total y la población de territorio representado, lo cual facilita también las comparaciones.

CETTE PARTIE COMPREND 60 cartes des principales zones métropolitaines à l'échelle du 1:300 000ᵉ. Les cartes représentent les principaux types d'occupation du sol des villes et de leurs environs, c'est-à-dire de toute la zone urbanisée, les principales zones industrielles, les parcs et réserves naturelles, et les régions boisées. Les aéroports sont aussi représentés ainsi que de nombreux éléments des réseaux routier et ferroviaire. Certains lieux particulièrement intéressants sont indiqués, tels que le quai des pêcheurs et la ville chinoise à San Francisco, le monument de la Bienvenue à Jakarta, le temple du Bouddha de Jade à Shanghai et la statue du Christ Rédempteur à Rio de Janeiro.

Les cartes permettent de localiser un grand nombre de villes, villages et banlieues, ainsi que des quartiers de grandes villes. Les caractéristiques topographiques notables, comme les hauteurs sont indiquées même si elles ne portent pas de nom, pour donner une idée du site de l'aire métropolitaine. L'estompage du relief est omis cependant pour permettre de représenter cours d'eau, parcs, pistes d'envol des aéroports, monuments et bâtiments publics importants, noms des principales rues, ainsi que les limites municipales des grandes villes. (Pour la signification des symboles voir légende.)

En général, les échelles des cartes des grandes villes du monde varient considérablement, et jusqu'ici la présentation et le contenu de ces cartes n'étaient pas comparables. Dans cette partie de l'Atlas, un effort spécial a été fait pour représenter les diverses zones métropolitaines de manière aussi homogène que possible. Cependant, dans certains cas (en Asie notamment), les documents de base n'étaient pas assez complets pour qu'il fût possible d'inclure avec précision des données comme les zones industrielles et les limites municipales.

L'ordre de présentation est régional, avec des exceptions quand, pour faciliter les comparaisons, de grandes capitales de grands centres industriels ou encore des villes possédant un même environnement naturel, sont juxtaposés. Beaucoup de villes américaines et quelques villes européennes ont une faible densité de population et une étendue considérable; elles requièrent, par conséquent, des cartes plus grandes que des villes asiatiques de population similaire. La superficie et la population de chaque carte sont indiquées dans la marge.

INTEGRAM ESTA SEÇÃO 60 mapas das áreas metropolitanas mais importantes do mundo, em escala de 1:300 000. Os mapas mostram os principais tipos de uso do solo em cada cidade e seus arredores, seja, a extensão total da zona urbanizada, as principais áreas industriais, os parques e reservas, e as áreas florestais. Mostram os aeroportos, e muitos detalhes das redês rodo e ferroviária. Indicam também pontos de interesse, selecionados, tais como o Cais dos Pescadores e o Bairro Chinês de San Francisco, o monumento de Boasvindas, em Jakarta, o templo do Buda de Jade, em Shanghai, e a Estátua do Cristo Redentor, no Rio de Janeiro.

Os mapas apresentam o nome e a localização de grande número de cidades, vilas e subúrbios, e incluem bairros das cidades mais importantes. Foram indicadas as características físicas principais, inclusive elevações, com ou sem nome, com o objetivo de proporcionar uma idéia geral da topografia local. No entanto, omitiu-se o sombreado do relevo, para permitir a indicação de detalhes tais como cursos d'água, parques, pistas de aeroportos, edifícios públicos e monumentos notáveis, e os nomes das principais ruas, bem como os limites municipais das grandes cidades. Para a interpretação dos símbolos usados nesses mapas, ver as *Legendas dos mapas*.

Os mapas das cidades mais importantes do mundo variam consideravelmente, de modo geral, quanto à escala, e até o presente não são comparáveis nem na forma de apresentação nem no conteúdo. Nesta seção, fez-se um esforço especial para representar as diversas áreas metropolitanas do modo mais uniforme e comparável possível. No entanto, para algumas cidades, a maioria das quais da Ásia, não foi possível obter fontes fidedignas de informações, tais como áreas industriais principais e limites municipais.

A ordem de apresentação dos mapas das áreas metropolitanas é geralmente regional, exceto em certos casos em que, para facilidade de comparação, capitais ou centros industriais e cidades importantes localizadas em meio físico semelhante foram justapostos. Muitas cidades da América e algumas da Europa, por sua baixa densidade demográfica e áreas mais extensas, exigem mapas maiores que as cidades asiáticas de população comparável. À margem de cada mapa indicam-se a área terrestre e a população total do território representado, também para maior facilidade de comparação.

AREA: 6,400 km²
POPULATION: 10,325,000

| ENGLISH | DEUTSCH | ESPAÑOL | FRANÇAIS | PORTUGUES |
|---|---|---|---|---|
| aerodrome | Flughafen | aeropuerto | aéroport | aeroporto |
| canal | Kanal | canal | canal | canal |
| castle | Burg | castillo | château | castelo |
| palace | Palast | palacio | palais | palácio |
| park | Park | parque | parc | parque |
| race course | Rennbahn | hipódromo | champ de course | hipódromo |
| road | Landstrasse | camino | route | rodovia |
| station | Bahnhof | estación | gare | estação |

Kilometers 0 5 10 15 Km.
Statute Miles 0 5 10 15 Mi.

Scale 1:300,000

One centimeter represents 3 kilometers.
One inch represents approximately 4.7 miles.

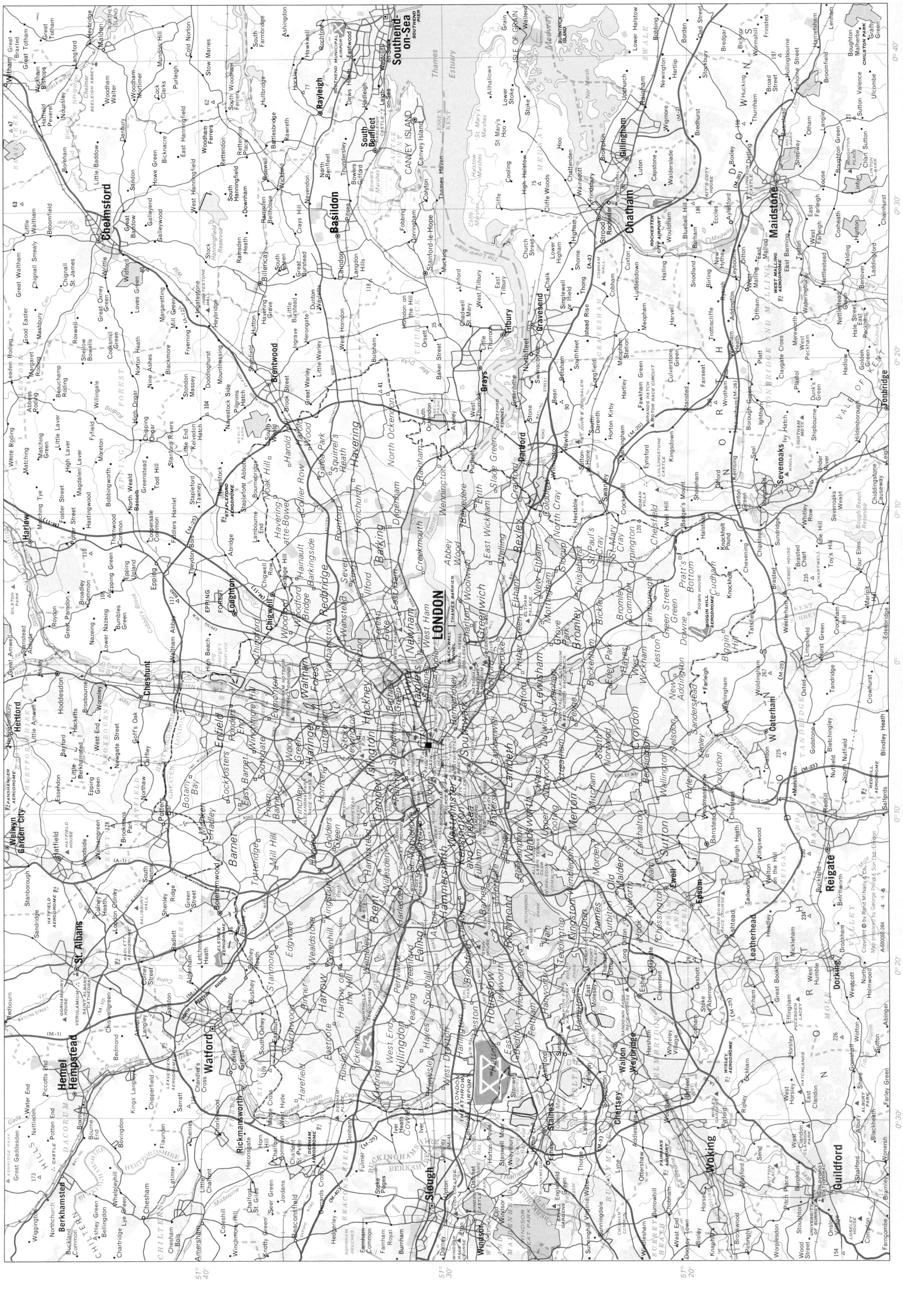
LONDON
Chelmsford
Southend-on-Sea
Basildon
Brentwood
Harlow
Hertford
Welwyn Garden City
St. Albans
Hemel Hempstead
Berkhamsted
Watford
Rickmansworth
Slough
Windsor
Staines
Woking
Guildford
Reigate
Dorking
Epsom
Croydon
Sevenoaks
Tonbridge
Maidstone
Chatham
Gillingham
Rochester
Gravesend
Dartford
Tilbury
Grays
Rayleigh
Cheshunt
Loughton
Chigwell
Thames
Heathrow
Copyright © by Rand McNally & Co.
Map prepared by George Philip & Son Ltd., London

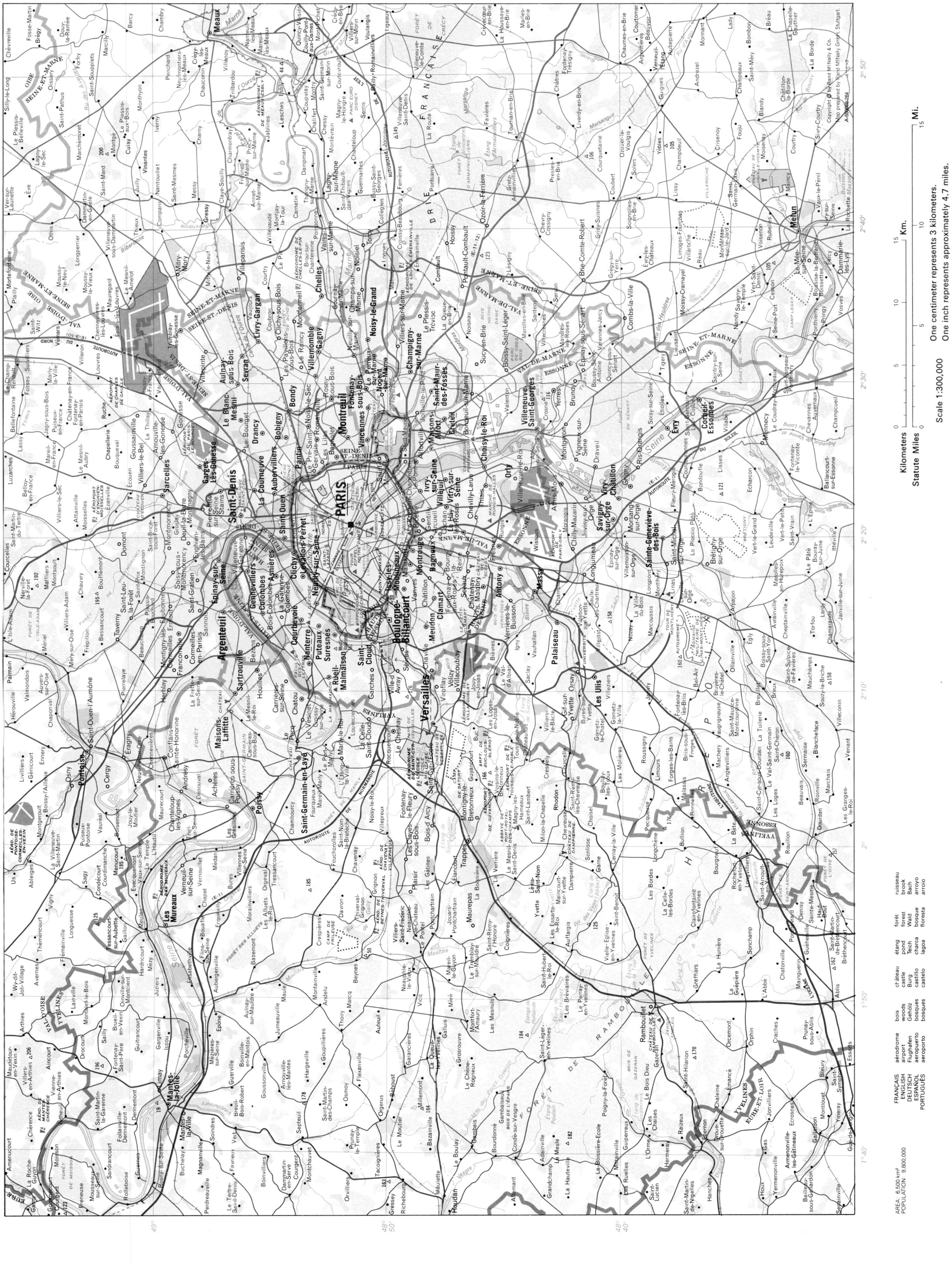

Scale 1:300,000

One centimeter represents 3 kilometers.
One inch represents approximately 4.7 miles.

AREA: 6,500 km²
POPULATION: 9,800,000

| | | | | | | |
|---|---|---|---|---|---|---|
| FRANÇAIS | aérodrome | bois | château | étang | forêt | ruisseau |
| ENGLISH | airport | woods | castle | pond | forest | brook |
| DEUTSCH | Flughafen | Gehölz | Burg | Teich | Wald | Bach |
| ESPAÑOL | aeropuerto | bosques | castillo | charca | bosque | arroyo |
| PORTUGUÊS | aeroporto | bosques | castelo | lagoa | floresta | arroio |

Kilometers 0 5 10 15 Km.

Statute Miles 0 5 10 15 Mi.

Scale 1:300,000

One centimeter represents 3 kilometers.
One inch represents approximately 4.7 miles.

| ENGLISH | DEUTSCH | ESPAÑOL | FRANÇAIS | PORTUGUÊS |
|---|---|---|---|---|
| bank | Bank | banco | banc | banco |
| canal | Kanal | canal | canal | canal |
| hill | Hügel | colina | colline | colina |
| moor | Moor | páramo | lande | charneca |
| park | Park | parque | parc | parque |
| railway station | Bahnhof | terminal ferroviaria | gare | estação ferroviária |
| reservoir | Stausee | estanque | réservoir | reservatório |
| tower | Turm | torre | tour | torre |

AREA: 5,650 km²
POPULATION: 6,275,000

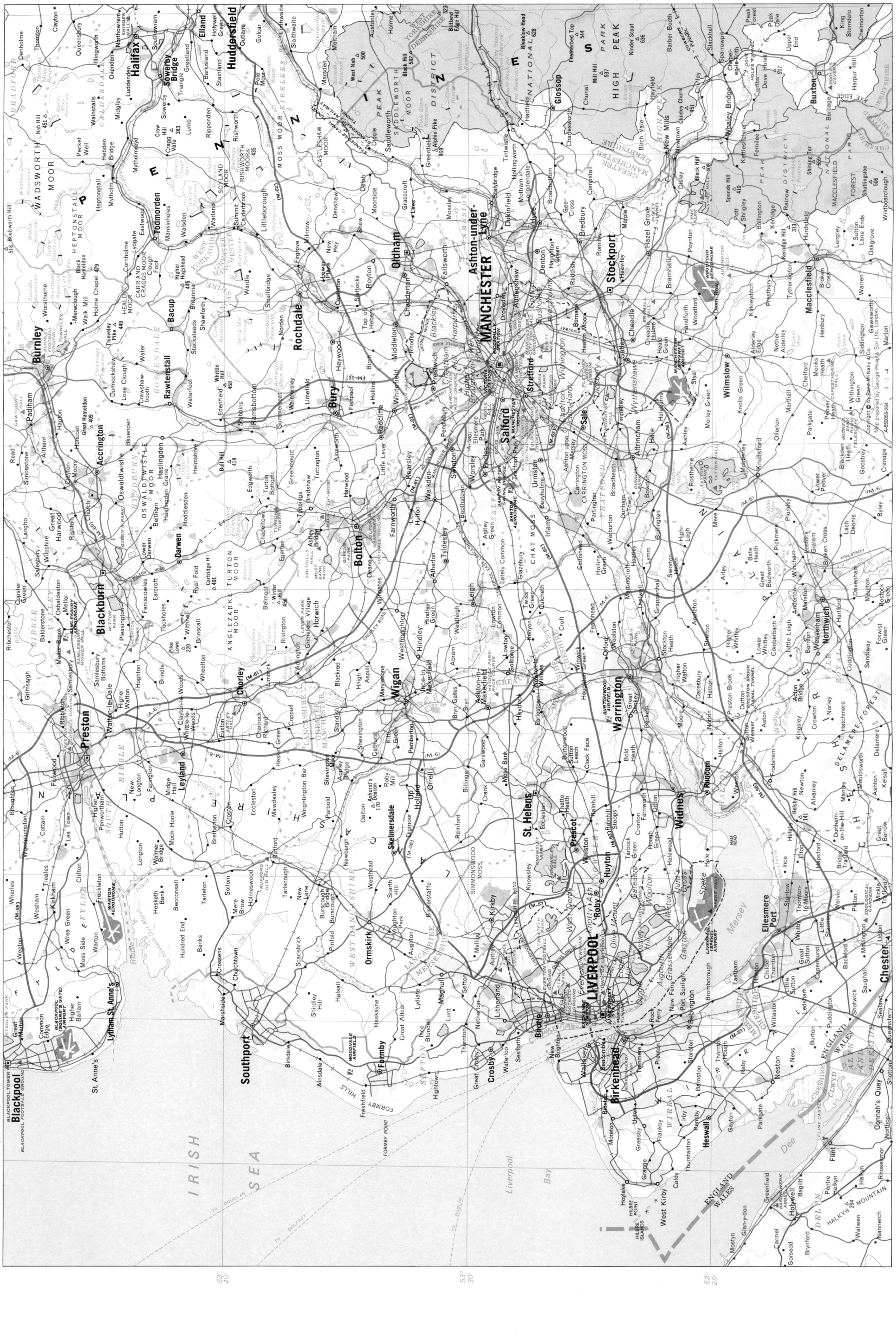

MANCHESTER
LIVERPOOL
Blackpool
Preston
Southport
Burnley
Blackburn
Bolton
Wigan
Warrington
St. Helens
Birkenhead
Chester
Stockport
Oldham
Rochdale
Bury
Salford
Halifax
Huddersfield
Macclesfield
Widnes
Runcorn
Northwich
Ashton-under-Lyne
IRISH SEA
Liverpool Bay

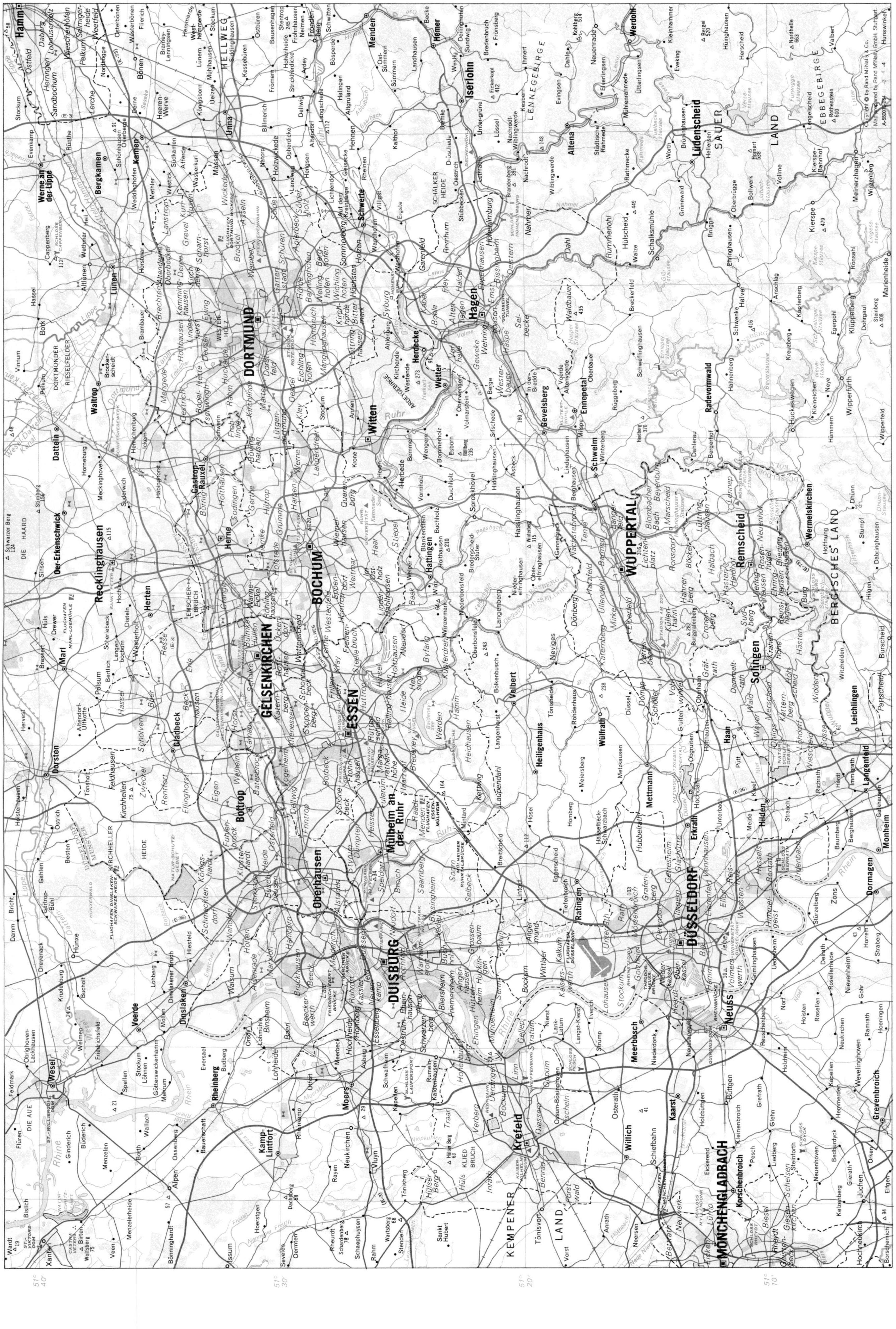
Hamm
Dortmund
Bochum
Gelsenkirchen
Essen
Oberhausen
Duisburg
Düsseldorf
Wuppertal
Hagen
Krefeld
Mönchengladbach
Neuss
Solingen
Remscheid
Copyright © by Rand McNally & Co.
Manufactured by Rand McNally GmbH, Stuttgart.

Kilometers 0 5 10 15 Km.
Statute Miles 0 5 10 15 Mi.
Scale 1:300,000
One centimeter represents 3 kilometers.
One inch represents approximately 4.7 miles.

| DEUTSCH | Bach | Berg | Flughafen | Heide | Kanal | Schloss | Stausee |
|---|---|---|---|---|---|---|---|
| ENGLISH | creek | mountain | airport | heath | canal | castle | reservoir |
| ESPAÑOL | riachuelo | montaña | aeropuerto | matorral | canal | castillo | estanque |
| FRANÇAIS | crique | montagne | aéroport | lande | canal | château | réservoir |
| PORTUGUÊS | riacho | montanha | aeroporto | charneca | canal | castelo | reservatório |

AREA 8,500 km²
POPULATION 8,450,000

a

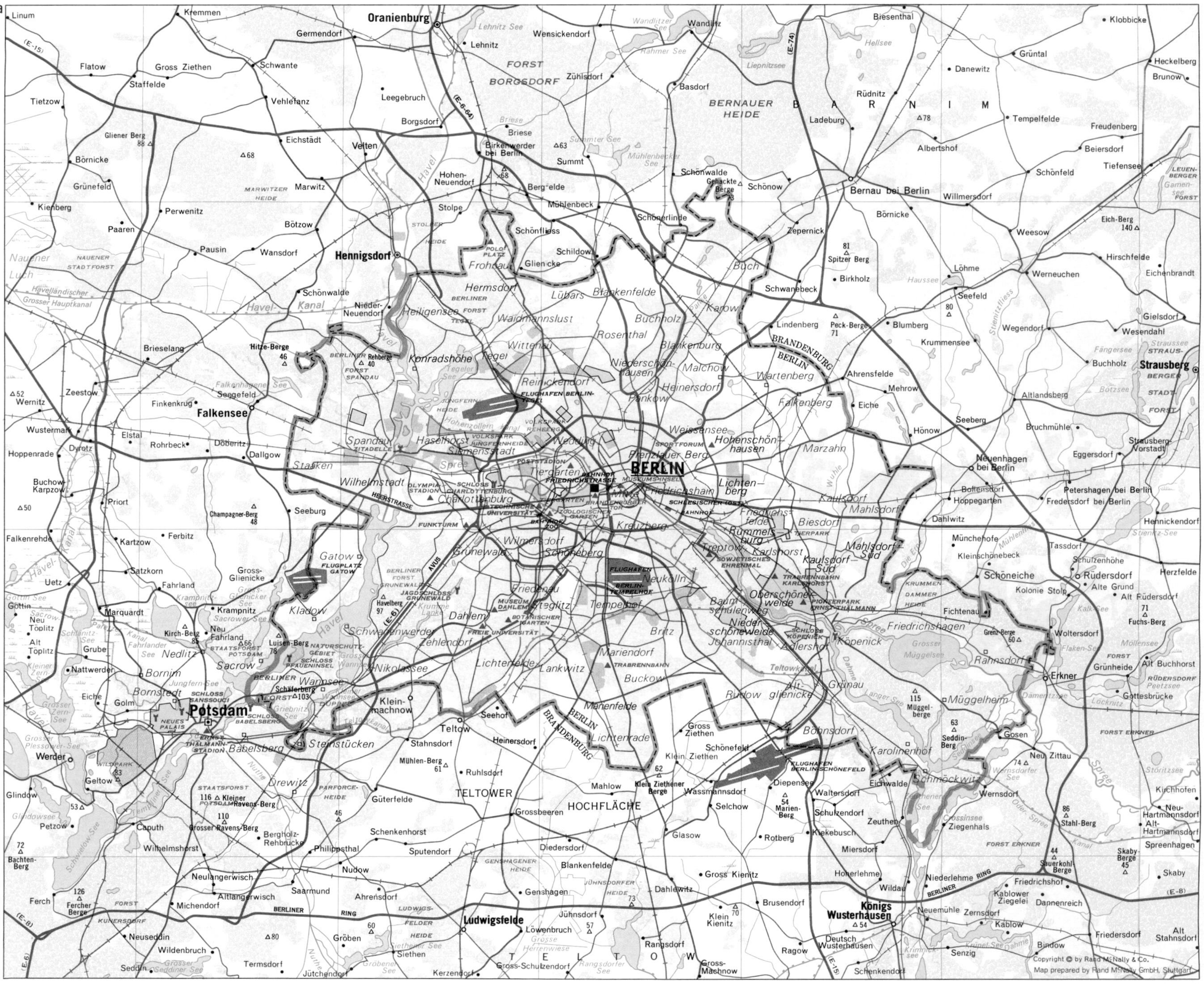
Oranienburg
Hennigsdorf
Falkensee
Potsdam
BERLIN
Spandau
Charlottenburg
Wilmersdorf
Schöneberg
Tempelhof
Neukölln
Kreuzberg
Wedding
Pankow
Reinickendorf
Weissensee
Lichtenberg
Treptow
Köpenick
Zehlendorf
Steglitz
Wannsee
Teltow
Ludwigsfelde
Königs Wusterhausen
Strausberg
Bernau bei Berlin
Erkner
Werder
BARNIM
TELTOWER HOCHFLÄCHE
BERNAUER HEIDE
FLUGHAFEN BERLIN-SCHÖNEFELD
FLUGHAFEN BERLIN-TEGEL
FLUGHAFEN BERLIN-TEMPELHOF
BERLINER RING
Copyright © by Rand McNally & Co.
Map prepared by Rand McNally GmbH, Stuttgart

b

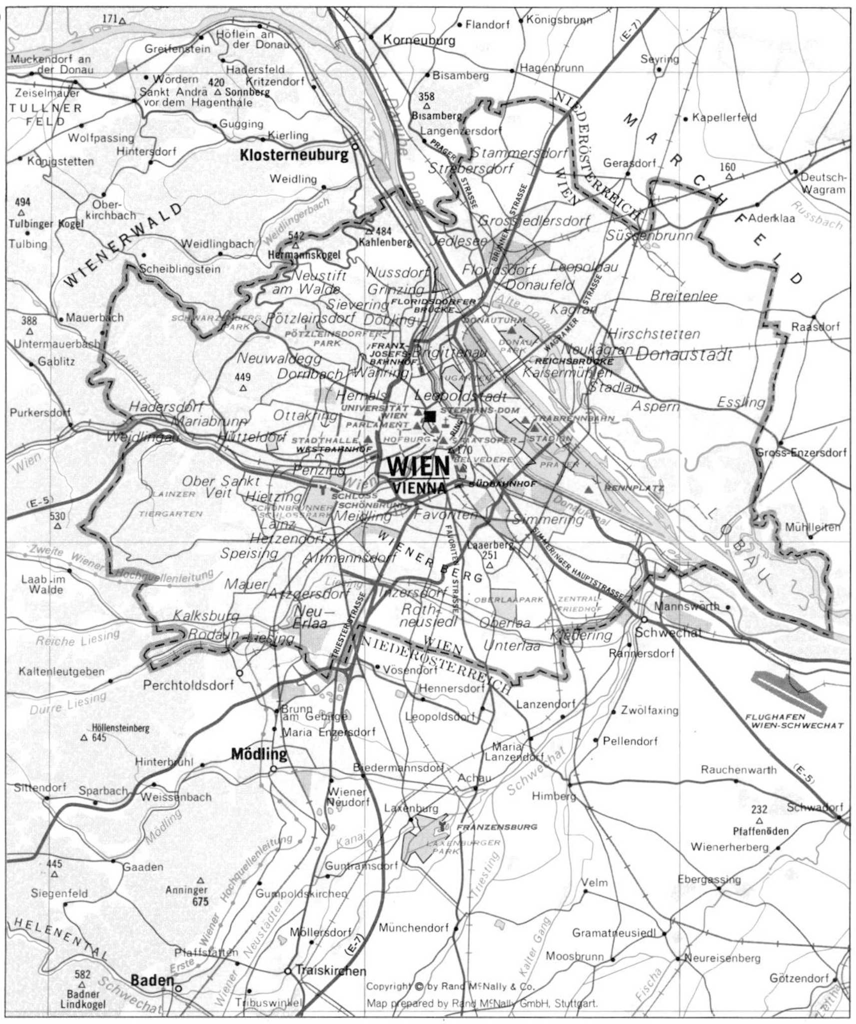
Korneuburg
Klosterneuburg
WIEN
VIENNA
Mödling
Baden
Perchtoldsdorf
WIENERWALD
MARCHFELD
Floridsdorf
Donaustadt
Favoriten
Simmering
Schwechat
FLUGHAFEN WIEN-SCHWECHAT
NIEDERÖSTERREICH
Copyright © by Rand McNally & Co.
Map prepared by Rand McNally GmbH, Stuttgart

c

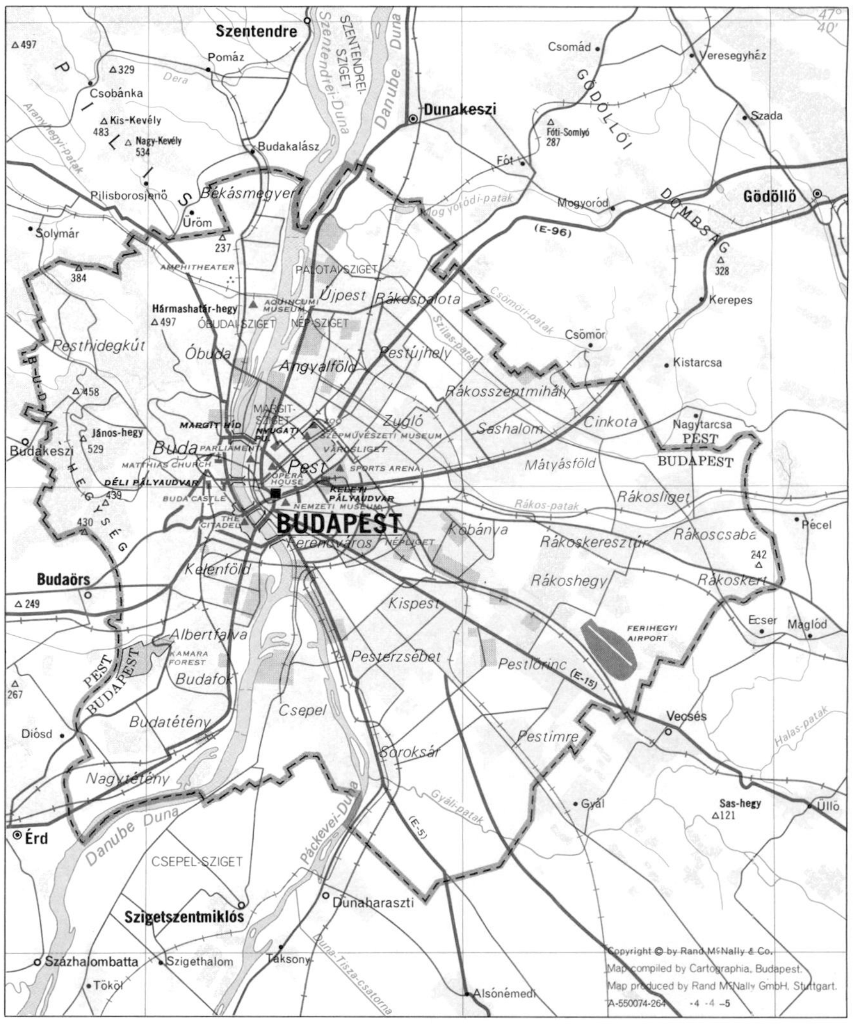
Szentendre
Dunakeszi
Gödöllő
BUDAPEST
Buda
Pest
Óbuda
Újpest
Kispest
Csepel
Budaörs
Érd
Szigetszentmiklós
Vecsés
FERIHEGYI AIRPORT
CSEPEL SZIGET
Danube Duna
GÖDÖLLŐI DOMBSÁG
PILIS
Copyright © by Rand McNally & Co.
Map compiled by Cartographia, Budapest
Map produced by Rand McNally GmbH, Stuttgart
A-550074-264 -4 -4 -5

| | AREA (km²) | POPULATION |
|---|---|---|
| BERLIN | 3,700 | 3,550,000 |
| WIEN | 1,300 | 1,825,000 |
| BUDAPEST | 1,300 | 2,450,000 |

| MAP FORM | Berg | Berge | hegy | Heide | Schloss | See | sziget |
|---|---|---|---|---|---|---|---|
| ENGLISH | hill | hills | mountain | heath | castle | lake | island |
| DEUTSCH | Berg | Berge | Berg | Heide | Schloss | See | Insel |
| ESPAÑOL | colina | colinas | montaña | matorral | castillo | lago | isla |
| FRANÇAIS | colline | collines | montagne | lande | château | lac | île |
| PORTUGUÊS | colina | colinas | montanha | charneca | castelo | lago | ilha |

Kilometers 0 5 10 15 Km.

Statute Miles 0 5 10 15 Mi.

Scale 1:300,000

One centimeter represents 3 kilometers.

One inch represents approximately 4.7 miles.

a

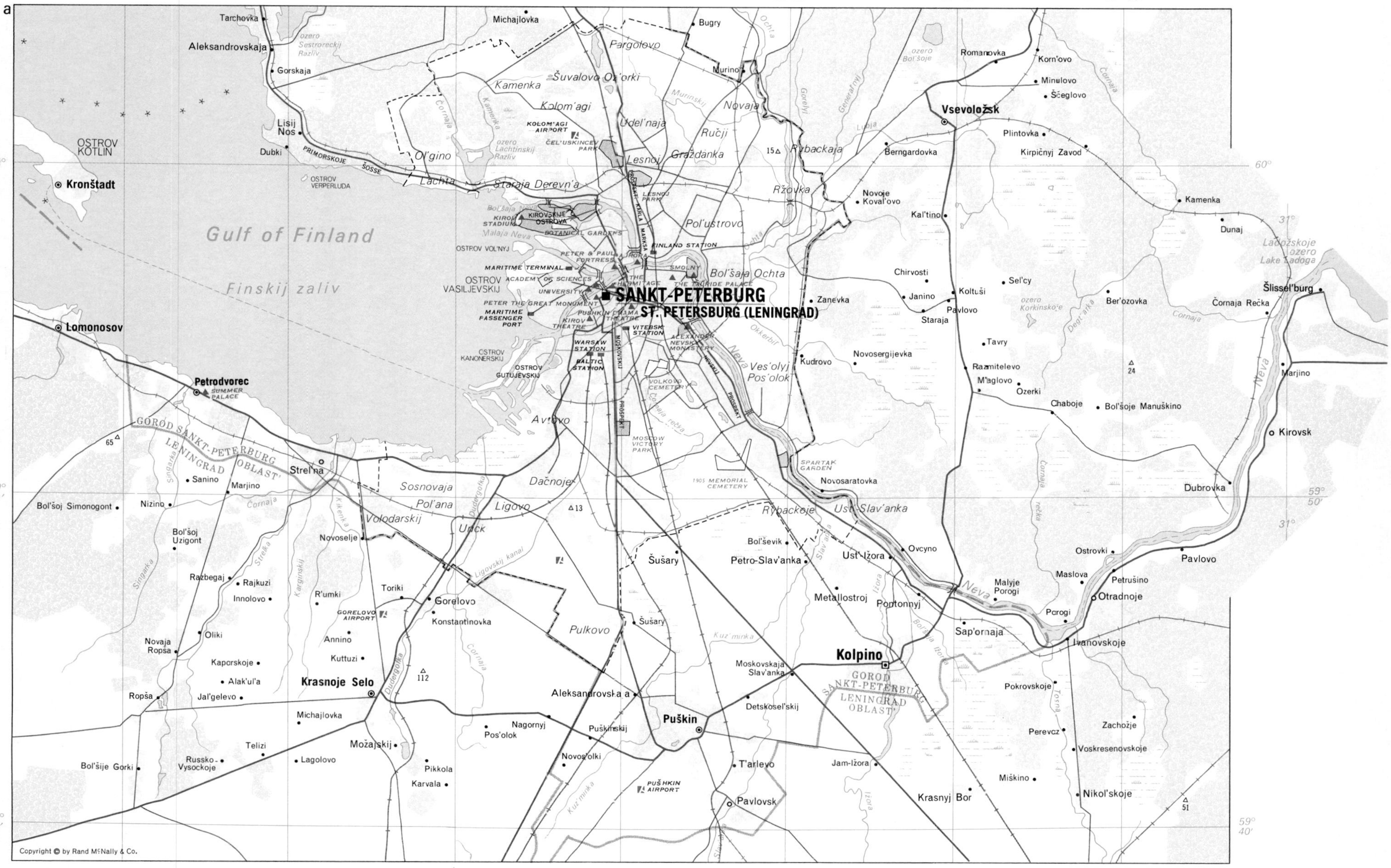

SANKT-PETERBURG
ST. PETERSBURG (LENINGRAD)
Gulf of Finland
Finskij zaliv
OSTROV KOTLIN
Kronštadt
Lomonosov
Petrodvorec
Strel'na
Krasnoje Selo
Puškin
Pavlovsk
Kolpino
Vsevoložsk
Šlissel'burg
Kirovsk
Otradnoje
Sestroreck
Neva
Ladožskoje ozero
Lake Ladoga
GOROD SANKT-PETERBURG
LENINGRAD OBLAST'
PUŠKIN AIRPORT
Copyright © by Rand McNally & Co.


b

MOSKVA MOSCOW
Moskva
GOROD MOSKVA
MOSKVA OBLAST'
Chimki
Mytišči
Kaliningrad
Dolgoprudnyj
Krasnogorsk
Balašicha
Reutov
L'ubercy
Odincovo
Lytkarino
Žukovskij
Železnodorožnyj
Fr'azino
Ščolkovo
Dedovsk
Solncevo
Ivantejevka
Staraja Kupavna
ŠEREMETJEVO AIRPORT
VNUKOVO AIRPORT
BYKOVO AIRPORT
MOSKOVSKAJA KOL'CEVAJA AVTO DOROGA
Copyright © by Rand McNally & Co.
Map compiled by Cartographia, Budapest
Map produced by Rand McNally & Co.


| | AREA (km²) | POPULATION |
|---|---|---|
| SANKT-PETERBURG | 2,800 | 4,850,000 |
| MOSKVA | 3,200 | 9,950,000 |

| MAP FORM | ostrov | ozero | stadion | vodochranilišče | vokzal |
|---|---|---|---|---|---|
| ENGLISH | island | lake | stadium | reservoir | rail terminal |
| DEUTSCH | Insel | See | Stadion | Stausee | Bahnhof |
| ESPAÑOL | isla | lago | estadio | estanque | terminal ferroviaria |
| FRANÇAIS | île | lac | stade | réservoir | gare |
| PORTUGUÊS | ilha | lago | estádio | reservatório | estação ferroviária |

Kilometers 0 5 10 15 Km.

Statute Miles 0 5 10 15 Mi.

Scale 1:300,000

One centimeter represents 3 kilometers.
One inch represents approximately 4.7 miles.

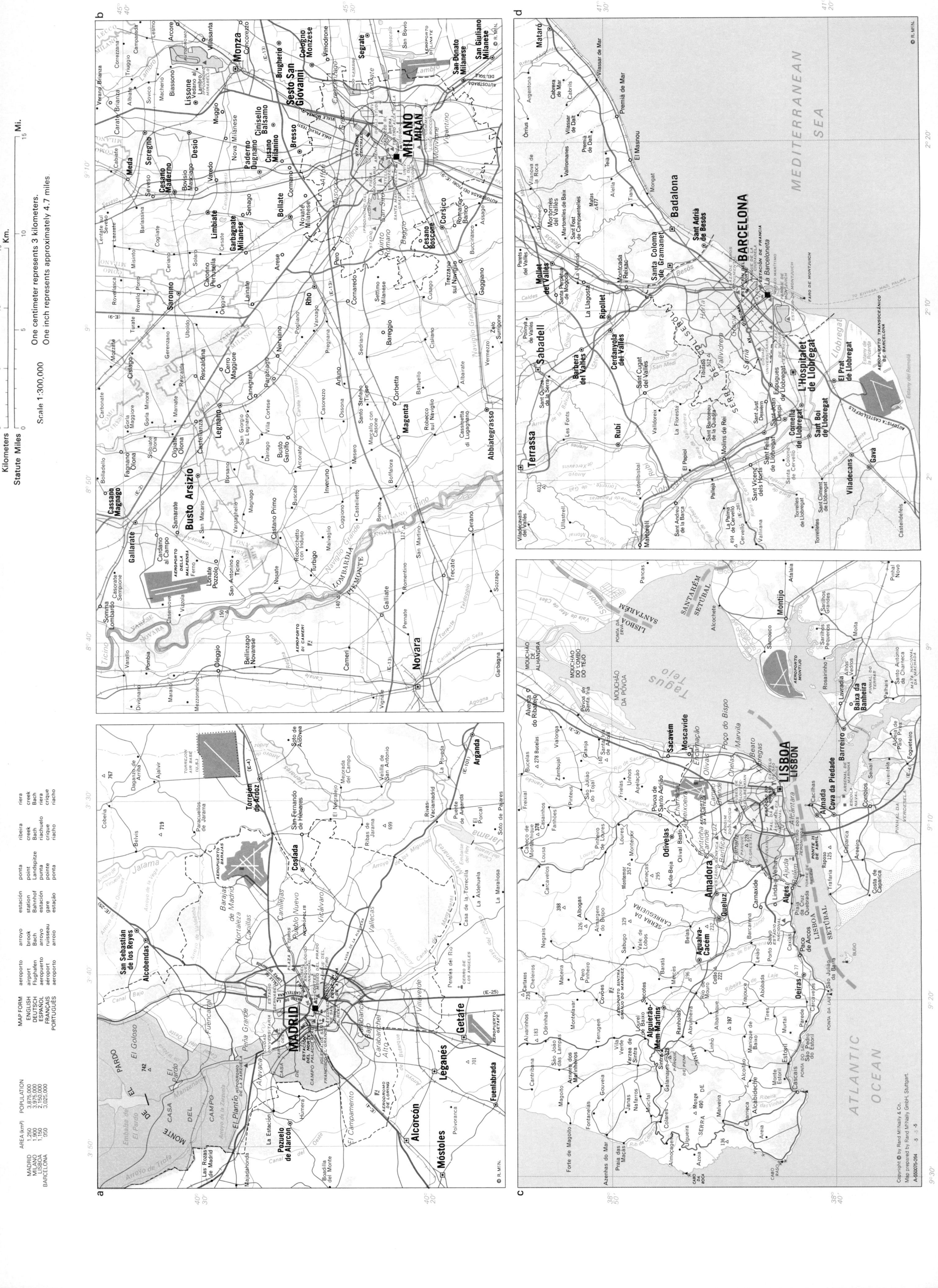
Kilometers
Statute Miles
Scale 1:300,000
One centimeter represents 3 kilometers.
One inch represents approximately 4.7 miles.
MADRID
MILANO
LISBOA
BARCELONA
MILAN
LISBON
MEDITERRANEAN SEA
ATLANTIC OCEAN
Tagus Tejo
Copyright © by Rand McNally & Co.
Map prepared by Rand McNally GmbH, Stuttgart.

b

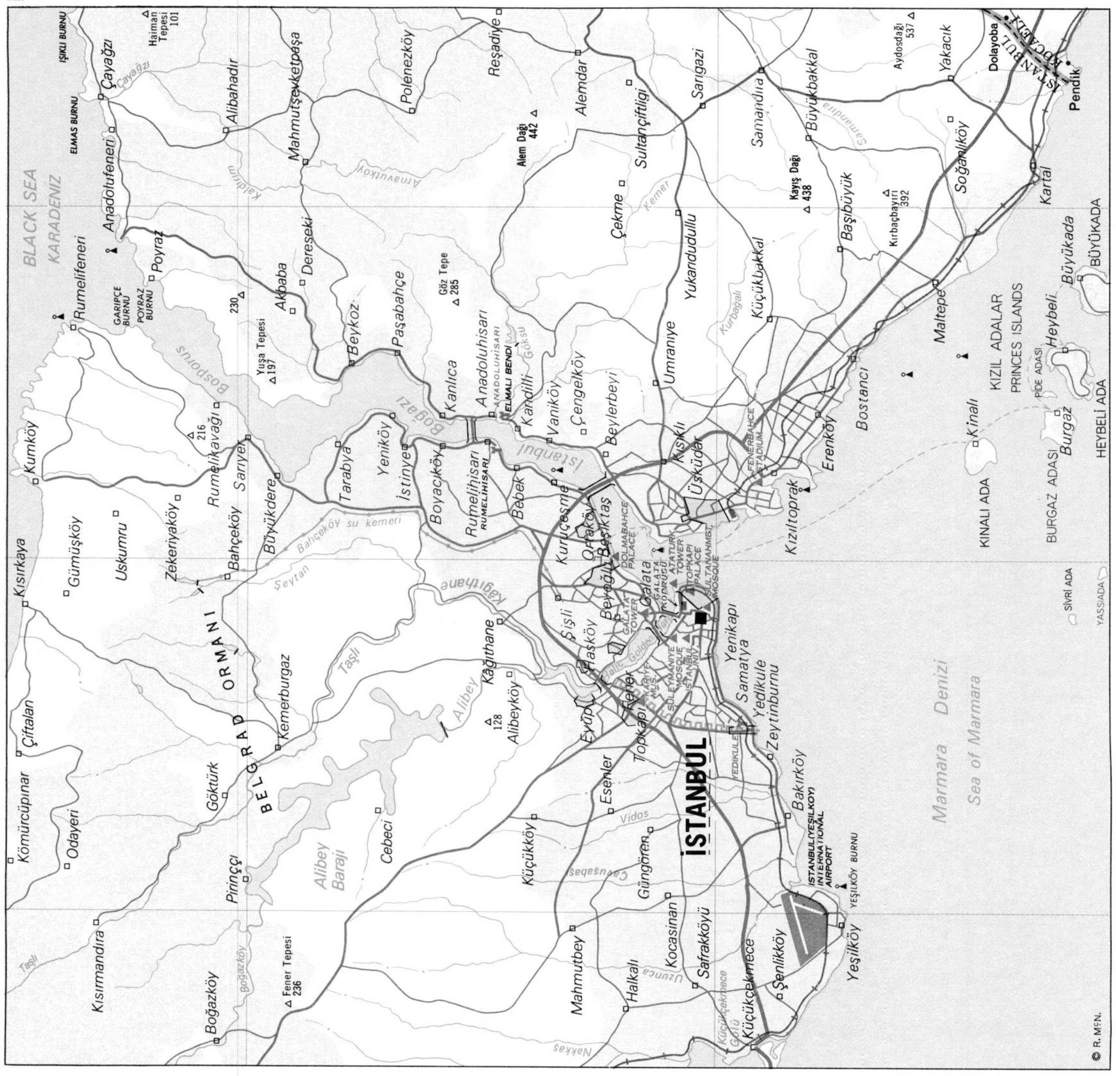
İSTANBUL
BLACK SEA
KARADENİZ
Marmara Denizi
Sea of Marmara
BELGRAD ORMANI
KIZIL ADALAR
PRINCES ISLANDS
© R. M^cN.

d

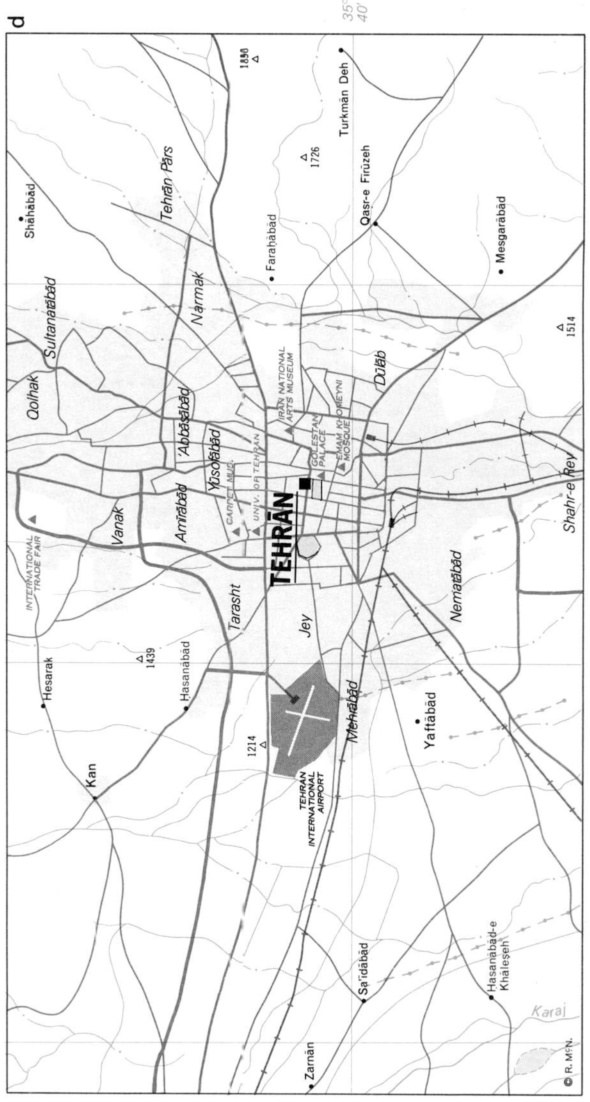
TEHRĀN
TEHRAN INTERNATIONAL AIRPORT
© R. M^cN.

a

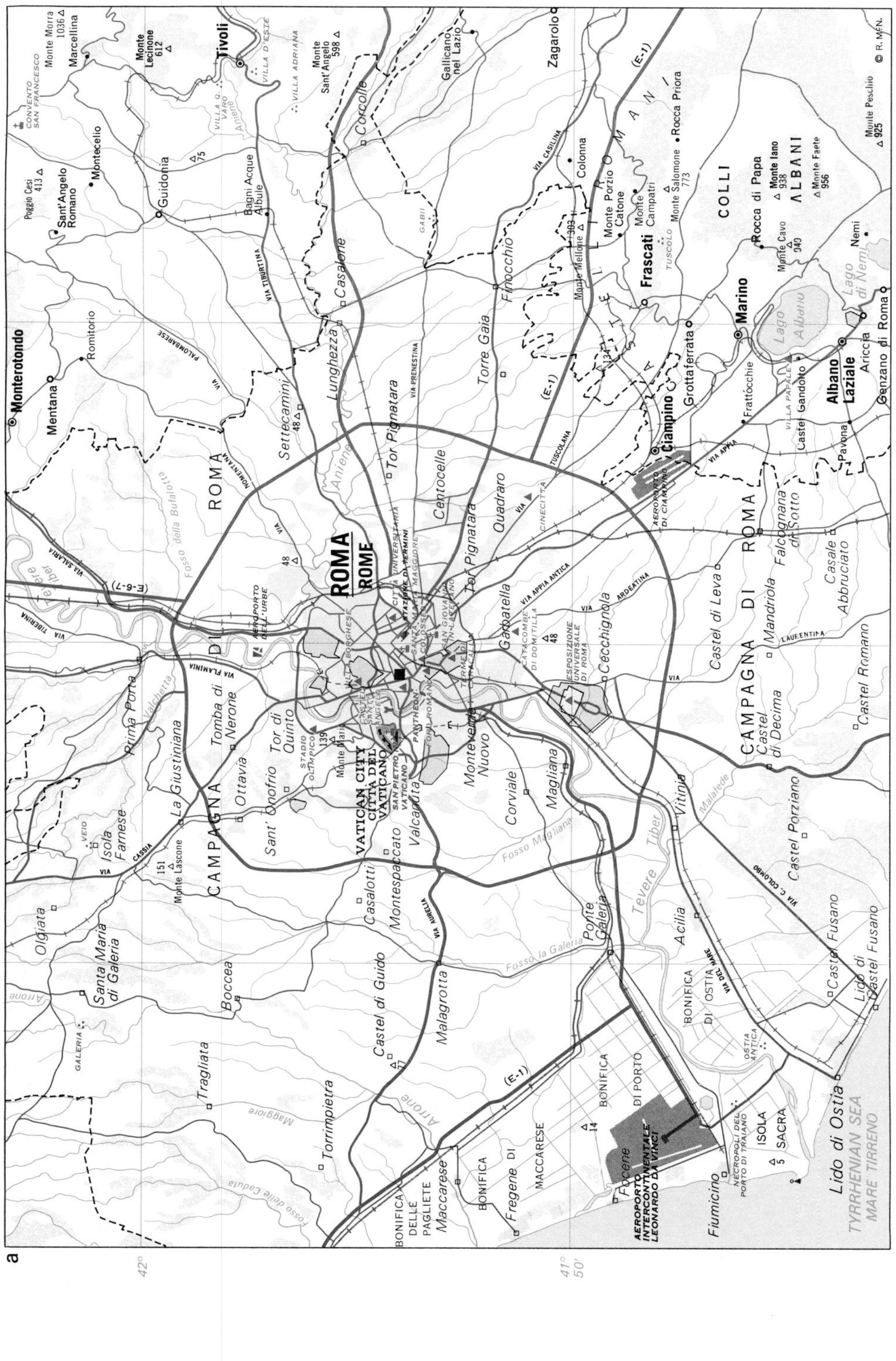
ROMA
ROME
VATICAN CITY
CITTÀ DEL VATICANO
TYRRHENIAN SEA
MARE TIRRENO
© R. M^cN.

c

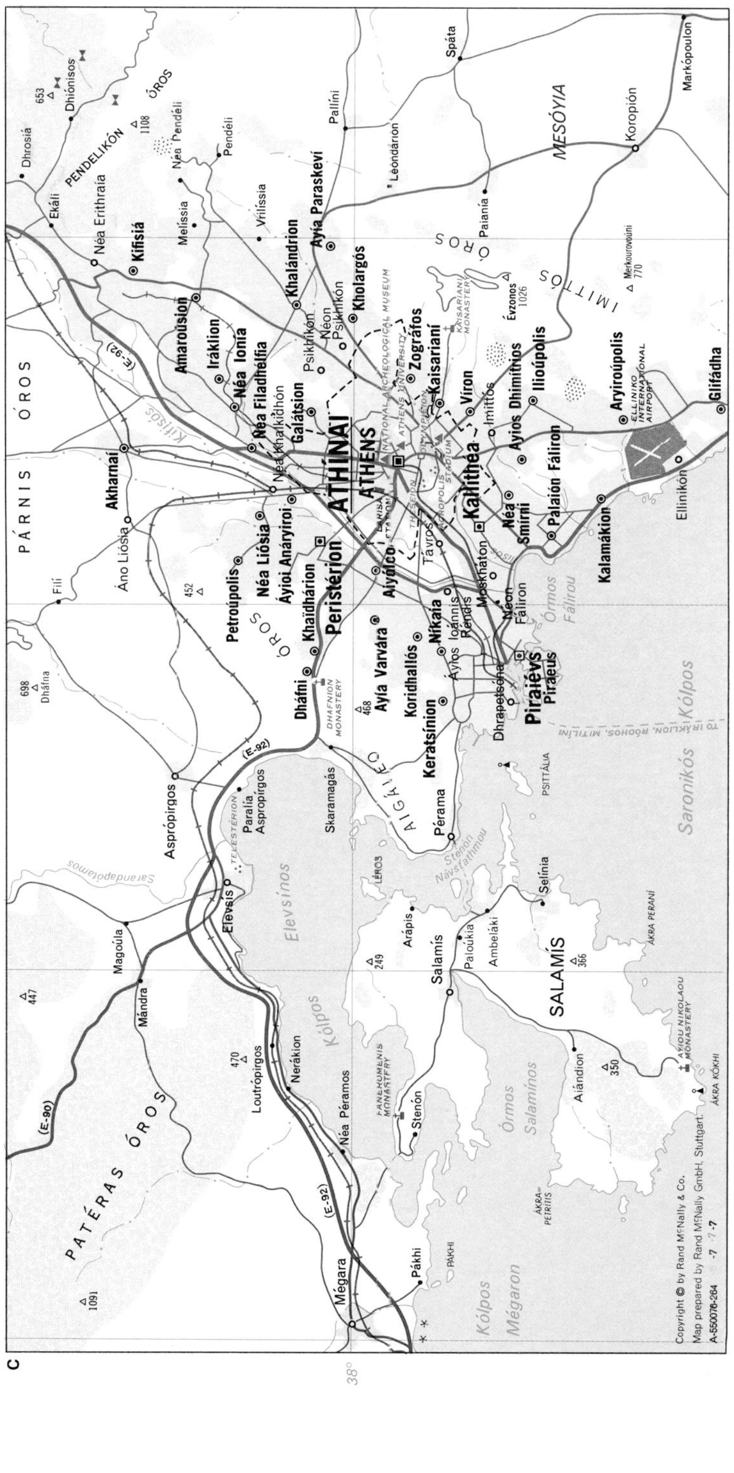
ATHÍNAI
ATHENS
Piraiévs
Piraeus
Saronikós Kólpos
SALAMÍS

| | AREA (km²) | POPULATION |
|---|---|---|
| ROMA | 2,000 | 3,250,000 |
| ATHÍNAI | 1,100 | 3,350,000 |
| İSTANBUL | 1,300 | 4,300,000 |
| TEHRĀN | 950 | 5,200,000 |

| MAP FORM | ada | burnu | camii | deresi | fosso | moni | monte |
|---|---|---|---|---|---|---|---|
| ENGLISH | island | cape | mosque | river | brook | monastery | mount |
| DEUTSCH | Insel | Kap | Moschee | Fluss | Bach | Kloster | Berg |
| ESPAÑOL | isla | cabo | mezquita | río | arroyo | monasterio | monte |
| FRANÇAIS | île | cap | mosquée | rivière | ruisseau | monastère | mont |
| PORTUGUÊS | ilha | cabo | mesquita | rio | arroio | mosteiro | monte |

Kilometers 0 5 10 15 Km.
Statute Miles 0 5 10 15 Mi.

Scale 1:300,000
One centimeter represents 3 kilometers.
One inch represents approximately 4.7 miles.

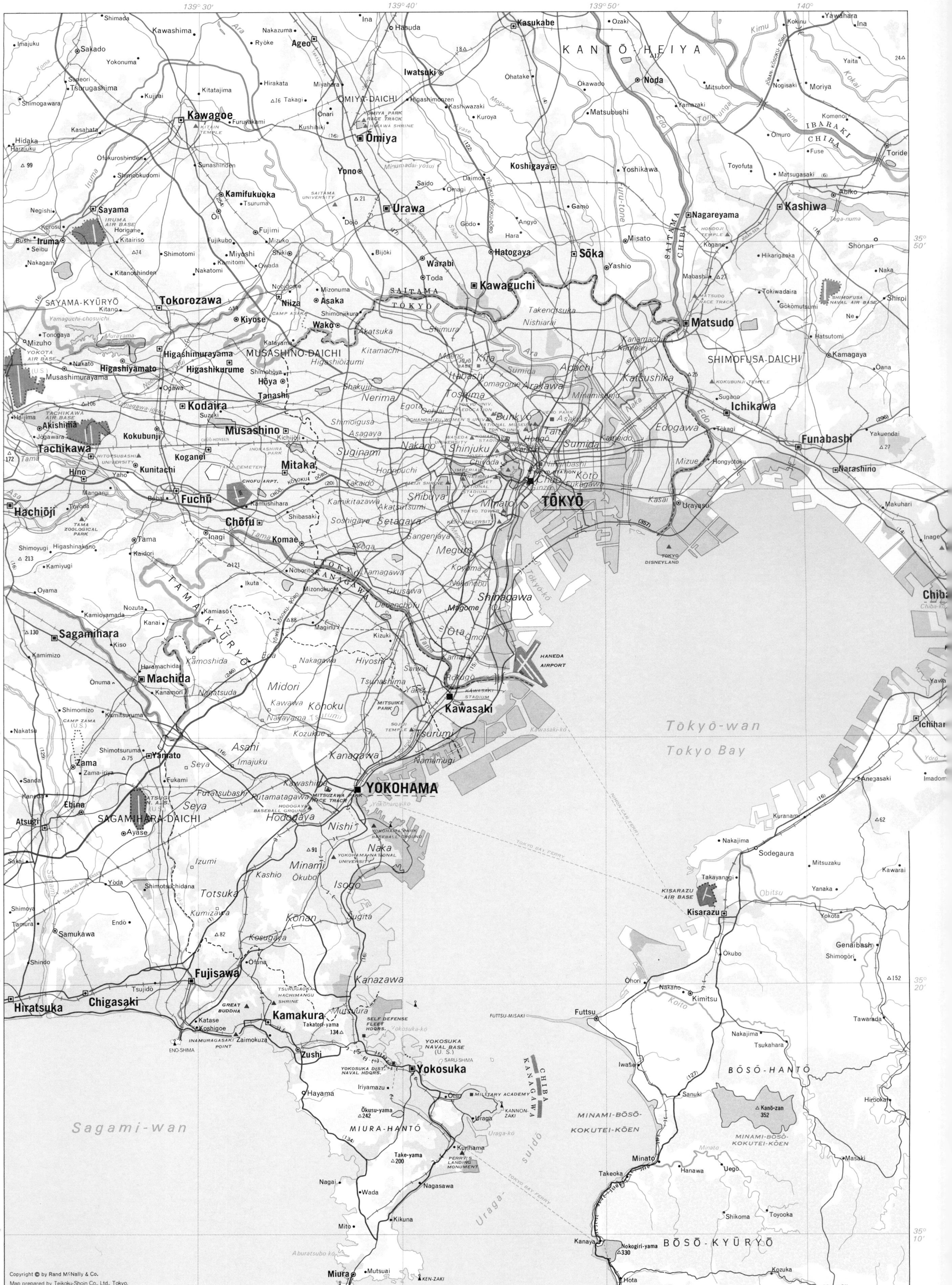
139° 30′
139° 40′
139° 50′
140°
35° 50′
35° 40′
35° 30′
35° 20′
35° 10′
KANTŌ-HEIYA
Kasukabe
Ageo
Iwatsuki
Noda
Kawagoe
Ōmiya
ŌMIYA-DAICHI
Koshigaya
Urawa
Kamifukuoka
Sayama
Iruma
IRUMA AIR BASE
Nagareyama
Kashiwa
Sōka
Hatogaya
Warabi
Kawaguchi
Tokorozawa
SAYAMA-KYŪRYŌ
SAITAMA
TŌKYŌ
Kiyose
Niiza
Asaka
Wakō
Matsudo
SHIMOFUSA-DAICHI
Higashimurayama
Higashiyamato
Higashikurume
MUSASHINO-DAICHI
Hōya
Tanashi
Kodaira
Akishima
Tachikawa
Kokubunji
Musashino
Koganei
Kunitachi
Mitaka
Hino
Fuchū
Hachiōji
Chōfu
Komae
Ichikawa
Funabashi
Narashino
TŌKYŌ
Shinjuku
Shibuya
Minato
Chiyoda
Chūō
Kōtō
Sumida
Taitō
Arakawa
Adachi
Katsushika
Edogawa
Itabashi
Toshima
Bunkyō
Nerima
Suginami
Nakano
Setagaya
Meguro
Shinagawa
Ōta
Urayasu
TOKYO DISNEYLAND
HANEDA AIRPORT
TAMA-KYŪRYŌ
Sagamihara
Machida
Kawasaki
Tōkyō-wan
Tokyo Bay
Yamato
Zama
CAMP ZAMA (U.S.)
Ebina
Atsugi
SAGAMIHARA-DAICHI
Ayase
YOKOHAMA
Fujisawa
Chigasaki
Hiratsuka
Kamakura
Zushi
Yokosuka
YOKOSUKA NAVAL BASE (U.S.)
MIURA-HANTŌ
Sagami-wan
Uraga-suidō
Miura
Kisarazu
KISARAZU AIR BASE
BŌSŌ-HANTŌ
MINAMI-BŌSŌ KOKUTEI-KŌEN
BŌSŌ-KYŪRYŌ
Kanō-zan 352
Nokogiri-yama 330
Futtsu
Kimitsu
Sodegaura
CHIBA
KANAGAWA
IBARAKI
Copyright © by Rand McNally & Co.
Map prepared by Teikoku-Shoin Co., Ltd., Tokyo.
A-560076-264

AREA (km²): 5,350
POPULATION: 24,350,000

| MAP FORM | air base | camp | -daichi | -kō | -shima | temple | -yama |
|---|---|---|---|---|---|---|---|
| ENGLISH | air base | camp | plateau | harbor | island | temple | mountain |
| DEUTSCH | Luftstützpunkt | Lager | Hochebene | Hafen | Insel | Tempel | Berg |
| ESPAÑOL | base aérea | campo | meseta | puerto | isla | templo | montaña |
| FRANÇAIS | base aérienne | camp | plateau | port | île | temple | montagne |
| PORTUGUÊS | base aérea | campo | planalto | porto | ilha | templo | montanha |

Kilometers 0 5 10 15 Km.
Statute Miles 0 5 10 15 Mi.

Scale 1:300,000
One centimeter represents 3 kilometers.
One inch represents approximately 4.7 miles.

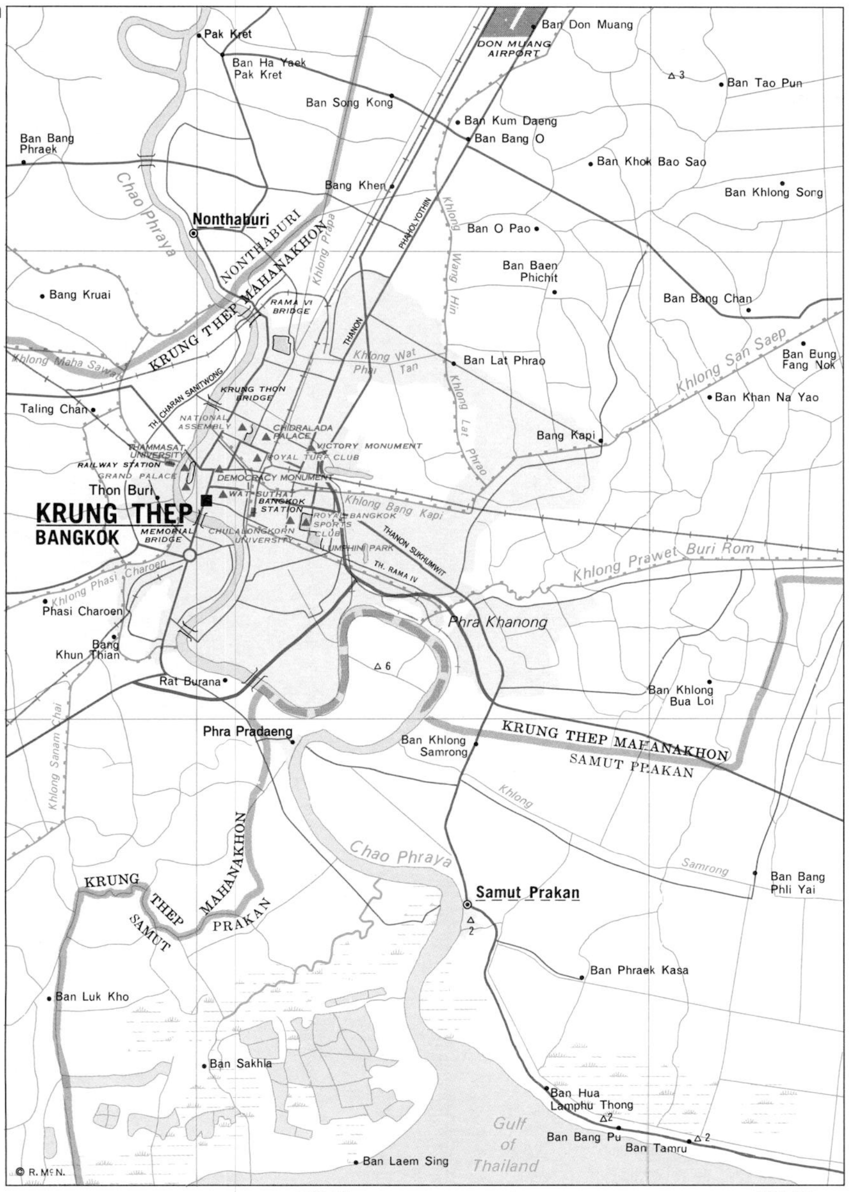
a
KRUNG THEP
BANGKOK
Nonthaburi
Samut Prakan
Chao Phraya
Gulf of Thailand
Phra Khanong
Phra Pradaeng
DON MUANG AIRPORT
KRUNG THEP MAHANAKHON
SAMUT PRAKAN
Ban Don Muang
Pak Kret
Bang Kruai
Taling Chan
Thon Buri
Phasi Charoen
Rat Burana
Ban Luk Kho
Ban Sakhla
Ban Laem Sing
Bang Kapi
Ban Bang Chan
Ban Khlong Song
Ban Tao Pun
Ban Bang Phli Yai
Ban Phraek Kasa
Ban Bang Pu
Ban Tamru
Khlong Prawet Buri Rom
© R. McN.

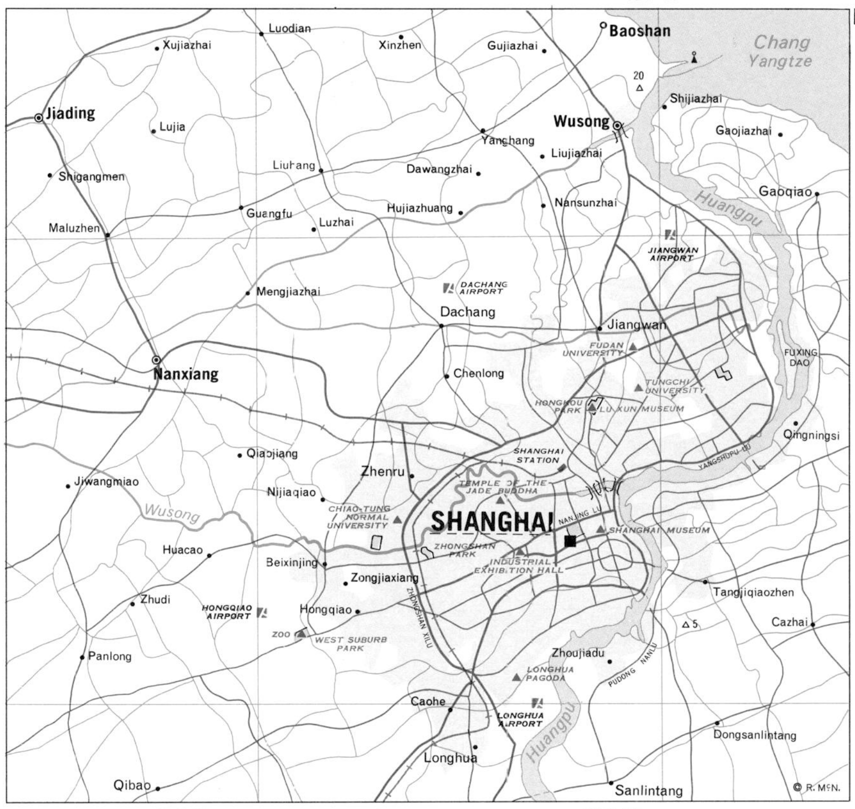
b
SHANGHAI
Baoshan
Wusong
Jiading
Nanxiang
Zhenru
Jiangwan
Dachang
Qibao
Longhua
Sanlintang
Chang Yangtze
Huangpu
Wusong
HONGQIAO AIRPORT
JIANGWAN AIRPORT
DACHANG AIRPORT
SHANGHAI STATION
FUDAN UNIVERSITY
TONGJI UNIVERSITY
Dongsanlintang
Cazhai
Gaoqiao
Qingningsi
© R. McN.

c
THANH PHO HO CHI MINH
(SAIGON)
Thu Duc
Go Vap
Tan Binh
TAN SON NHUT AIRPORT
Sai Gon
Nha Be
Binh Chanh
Hung Long
Tan Kien
Hoa Thoi
Ap Tan Hoa
Binh Hung Hoa
Vinh Loc
Xuan Thoi Thuong
Tan Thoi Nhut
Cho Moi
Long Truong
Phuoc Long Xa
Go Cong
Nhon Trach
Xom Binh Phuoc
Phuoc Khanh
© R. McN.

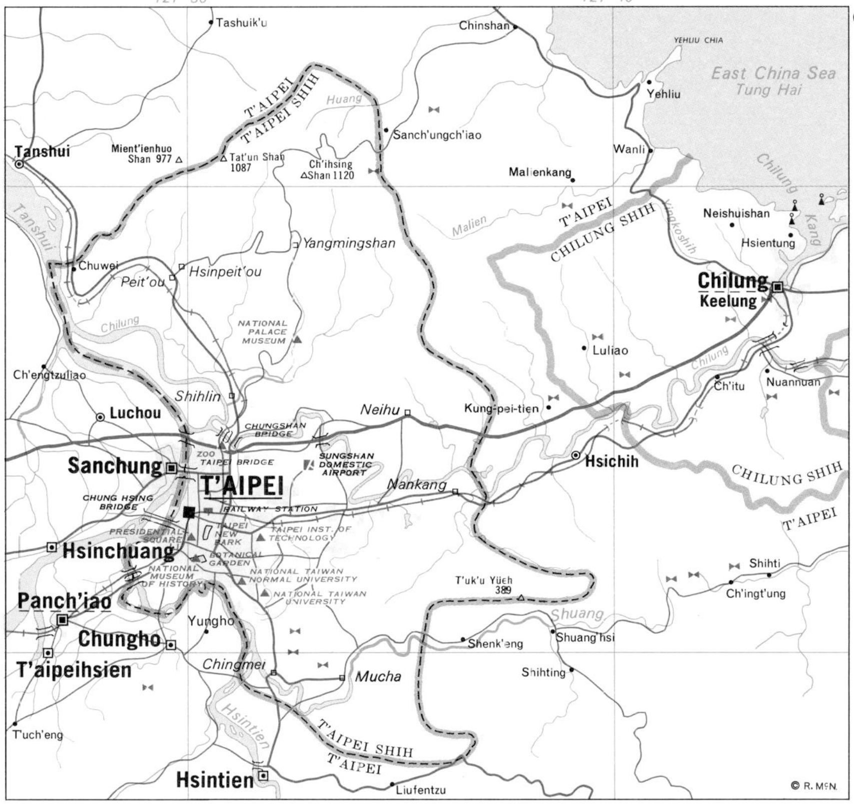
d
T'AIPEI
Tanshui
Sanchung
Hsinchuang
Panch'iao
Chungho
T'aipeihsien
Hsintien
Shihlin
Luchou
Neihu
Nankang
Hsichih
Chilung
Keelung
East China Sea
Tung Hai
SUNGSHAN DOMESTIC AIRPORT
NATIONAL PALACE MUSEUM
Yangmingshan
T'AIPEI SHIH
CHILUNG SHIH
T'AIPEI
Wanli
Yehliu
Chinshan
© R. McN.

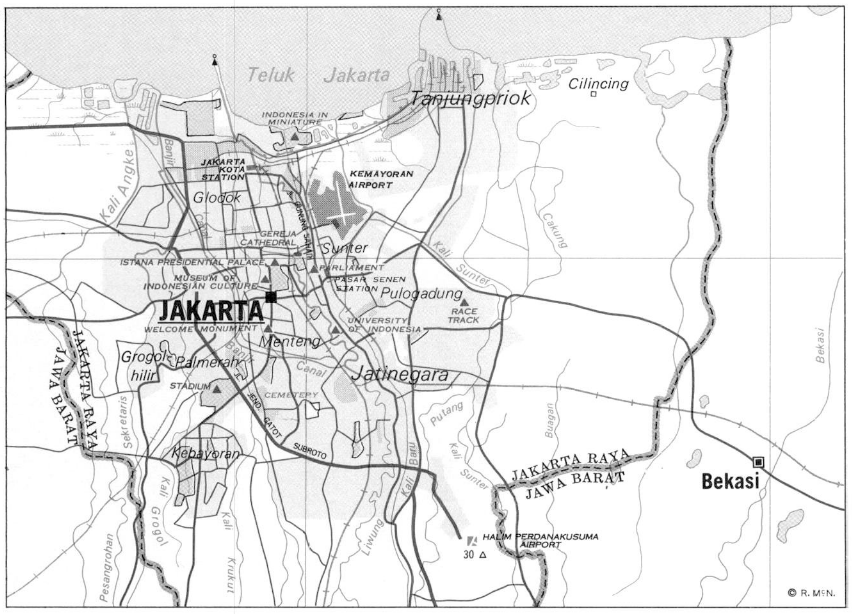
e
JAKARTA
Teluk Jakarta
Tanjungpriok
Cilincing
Glodok
Sunter
Pulogadung
Menteng
Jatinegara
Kebayoran
Bekasi
KEMAYORAN AIRPORT
HALIM PERDANAKUSUMA AIRPORT
JAKARTA RAYA
JAWA BARAT
© R. McN.

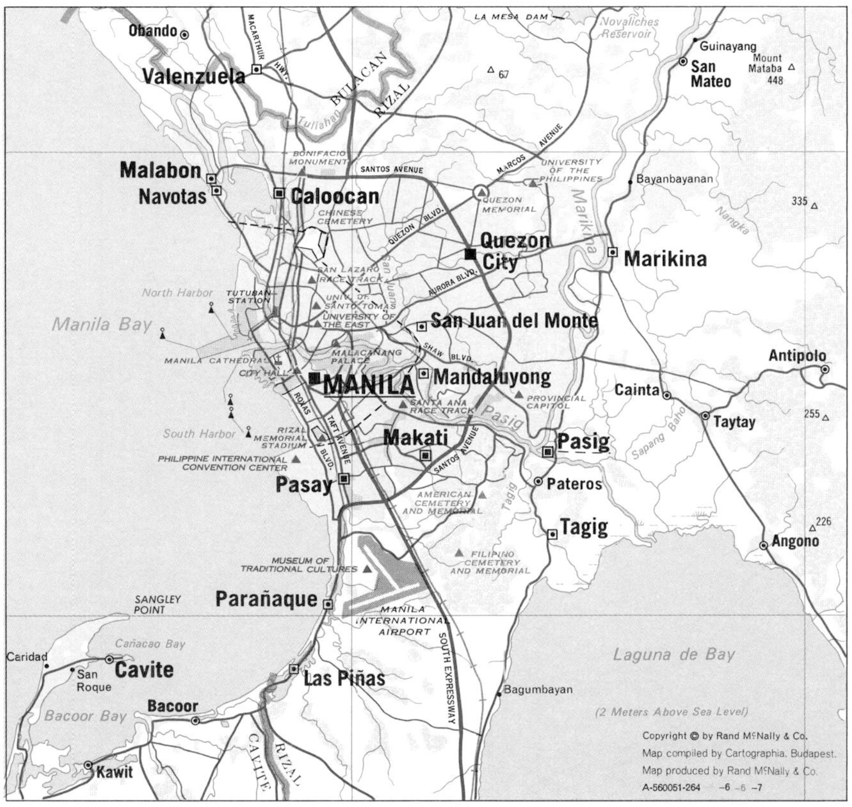
f
MANILA
Quezon City
Caloocan
Malabon
Navotas
Valenzuela
Obando
San Mateo
Marikina
San Juan del Monte
Mandaluyong
Antipolo
Cainta
Taytay
Makati
Pasig
Pateros
Tagig
Pasay
Parañaque
Las Piñas
Cavite
Bacoor
Kawit
Angono
Manila Bay
Laguna de Bay
MANILA INTERNATIONAL AIRPORT
(2 Meters Above Sea Level)
Copyright © by Rand McNally & Co.
Map compiled by Cartographia, Budapest.
Map produced by Rand McNally & Co.
A-560051-264 -6 -6 -7

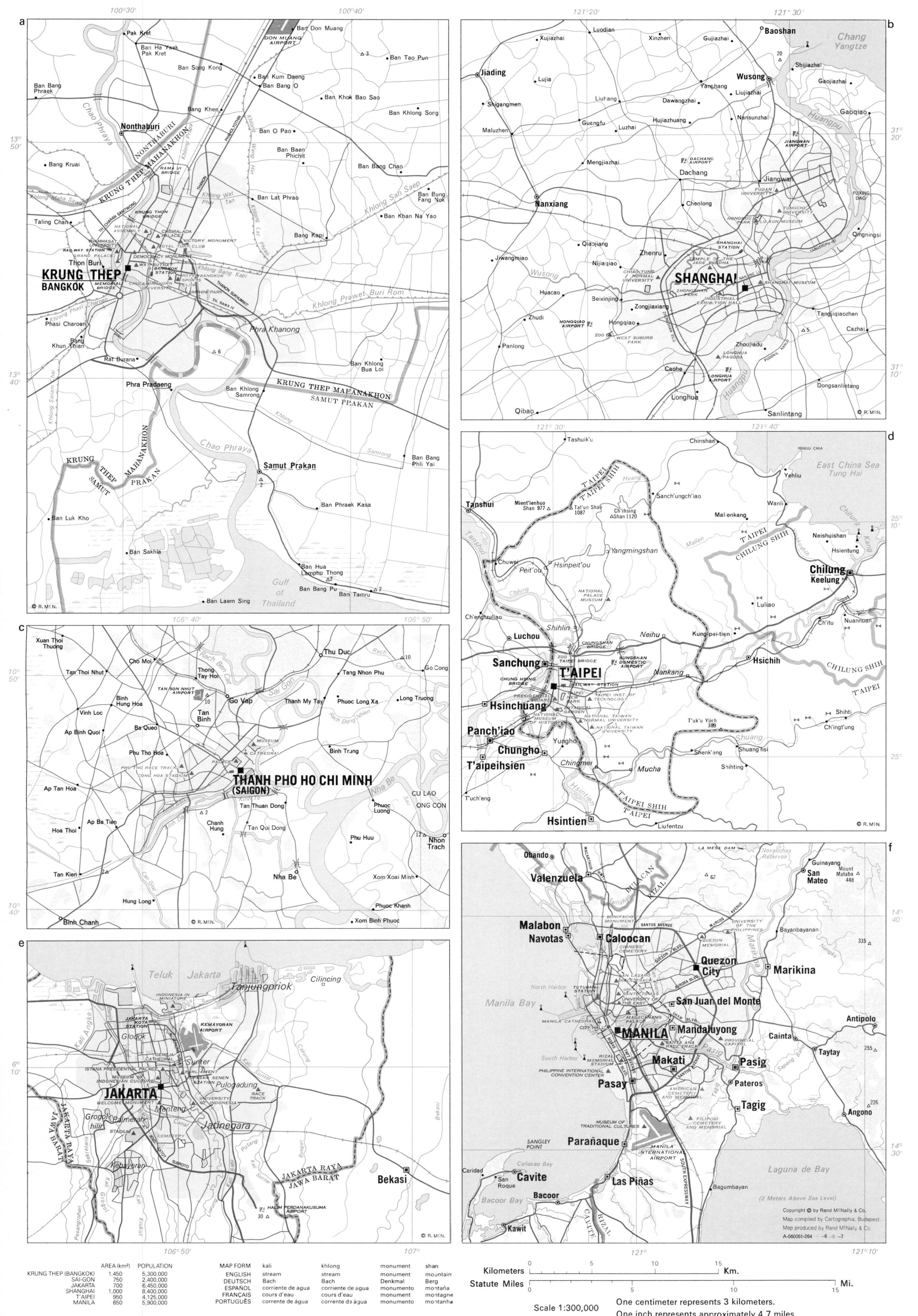

| | AREA (km²) | POPULATION |
|---|---|---|
| KRUNG THEP (BANGKOK) | 1,450 | 5,300,000 |
| SAI-GON | 750 | 2,400,000 |
| JAKARTA | 700 | 6,450,000 |
| SHANGHAI | 1,000 | 8,400,000 |
| T'AIPEI | 950 | 4,125,000 |
| MANILA | 650 | 5,900,000 |

| MAP FORM | kali | khlong | monument | shan |
|---|---|---|---|---|
| ENGLISH | stream | stream | monument | mountain |
| DEUTSCH | Bach | Bach | Denkmal | Berg |
| ESPAÑOL | corriente de agua | corriente de agua | monumento | montaña |
| FRANÇAIS | cours d'eau | cours d'eau | monument | montagne |
| PORTUGUÊS | corrente de água | corrente de água | monumento | montanha |

Kilometers 0 5 10 15 Km.
Statute Miles 0 5 10 15 Mi.

Scale 1:300,000
One centimeter represents 3 kilometers.
One inch represents approximately 4.7 miles.

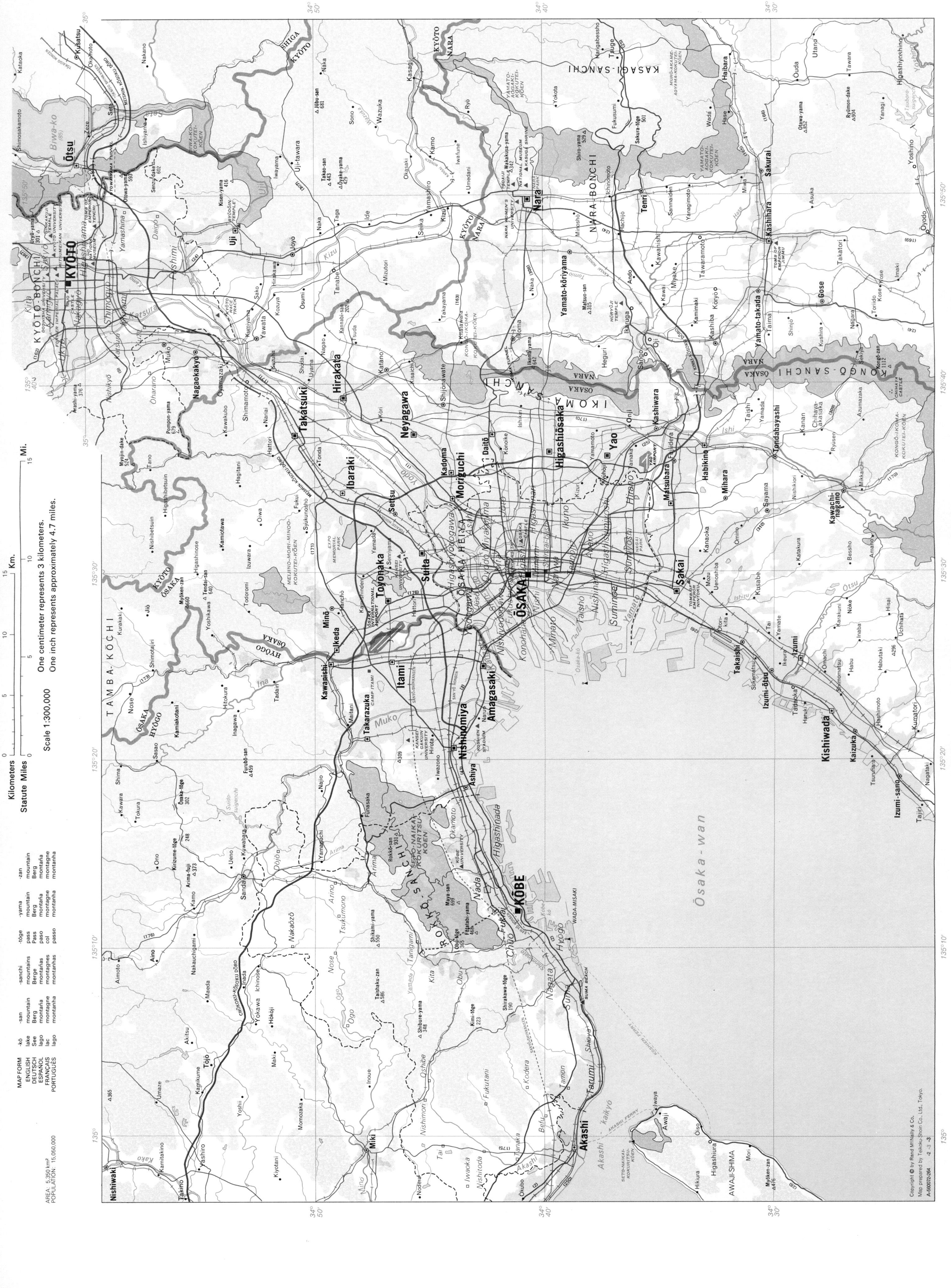
Kilometers 0 5 10 15 Km.
Statute Miles 0 5 10 15 Mi.
Scale 1:300,000
One centimeter represents 3 kilometers.
One inch represents approximately 4.7 miles.
MAP FORM -kō -san -sanchi -tōge -yama -zan
ENGLISH lake mountain mountains pass mountain mountain
DEUTSCH See Berg Berge Pass Berg Berg
ESPAÑOL lago montaña montañas paso montaña montaña
FRANÇAIS lac montagne montagnes col montagne montagne
PORTUGUÊS lago montanha montanhas passo montanha montanha
AREA 5,350 km²
POPULATION 15,050,000
ŌSAKA
KŌBE
KYŌTO
Nara
Sakai
Akashi
Amagasaki
Nishinomiya
Takatsuki
Hirakata
Ōtsu
Uji
Ōsaka-wan
AWAJI-SHIMA
KYŌTO-BONCHI
NARA-BONCHI
ROKKŌ-SANCHI
IKOMA-SANCHI
KONGŌ-SANCHI
KASAGI-SANCHI
TAMBA-KŌCHI
Copyright © by Rand McNally & Co.
Map prepared by Teikoku-Shoin Co., Ltd., Tokyo.

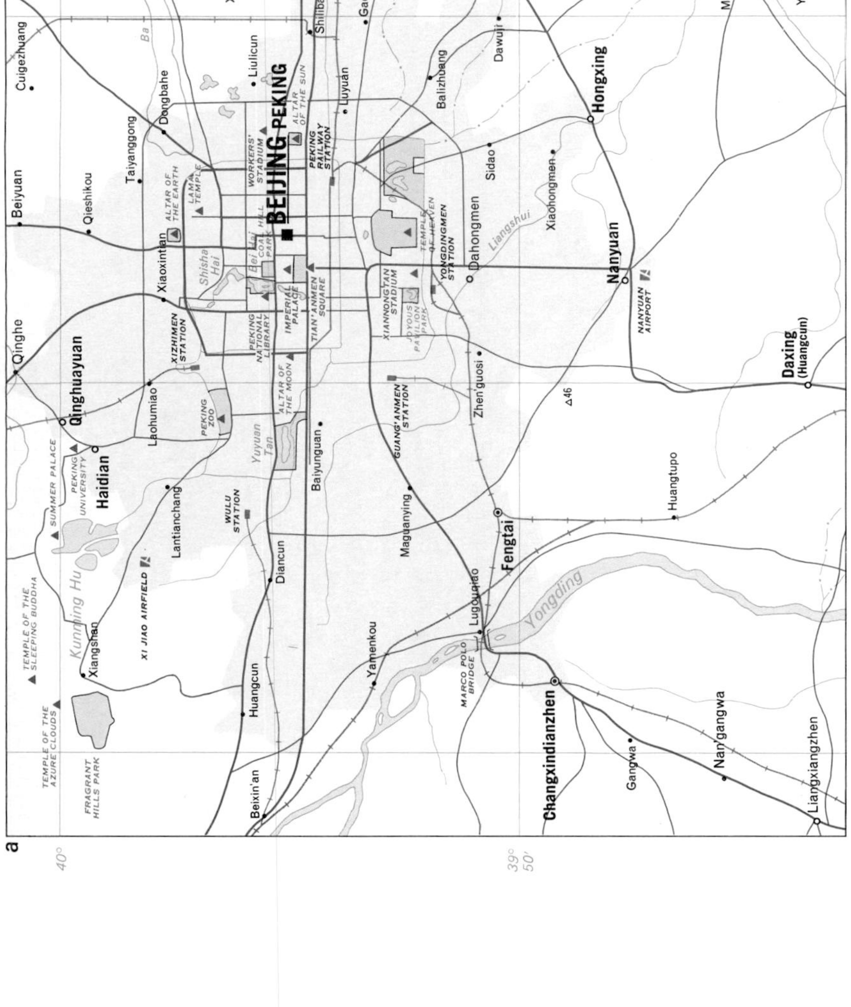
a
BEIJING-PEKING
Haidian
Fengtai
Tongxian
Nanyuan
Daxing (Huangcun)
Changxindianzhen

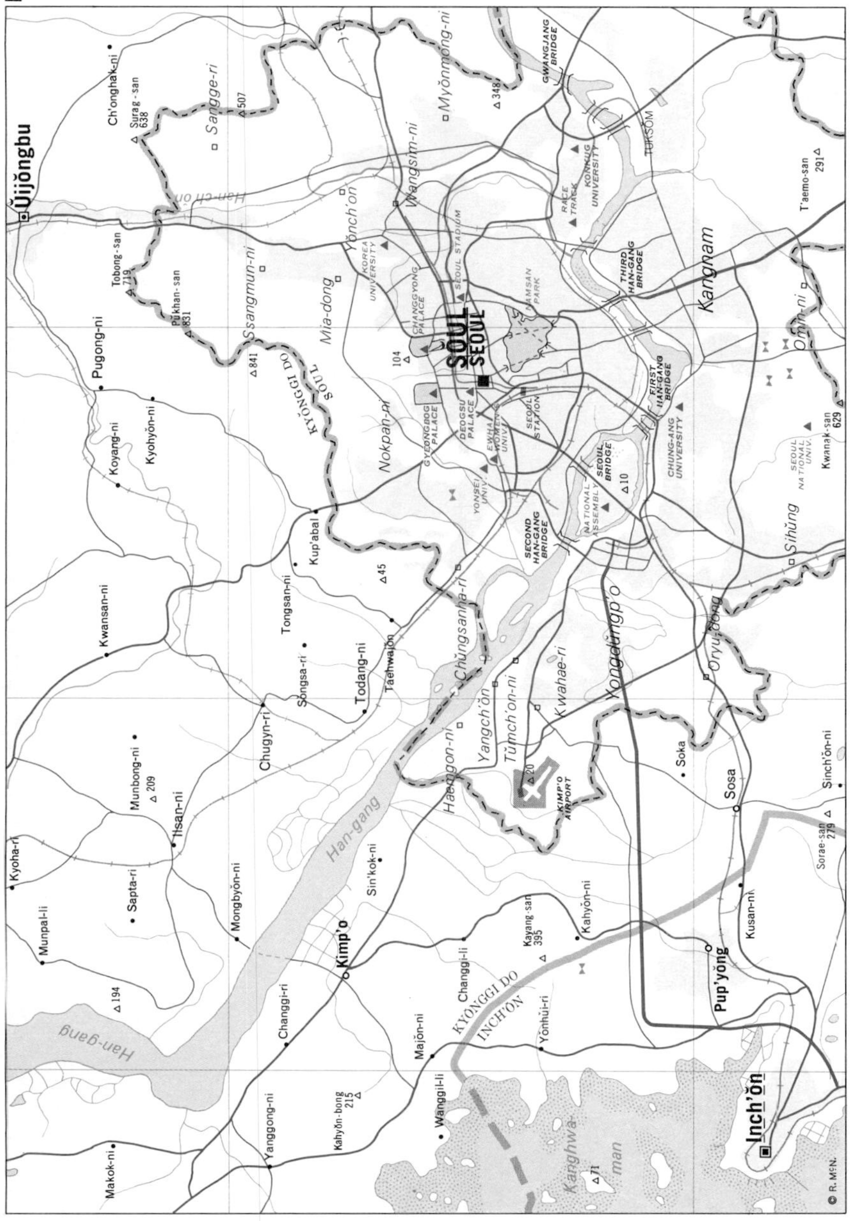
b
SŎUL SEOUL
Ŭijŏngbu
Kimp'o
Inch'ŏn
Han-gang

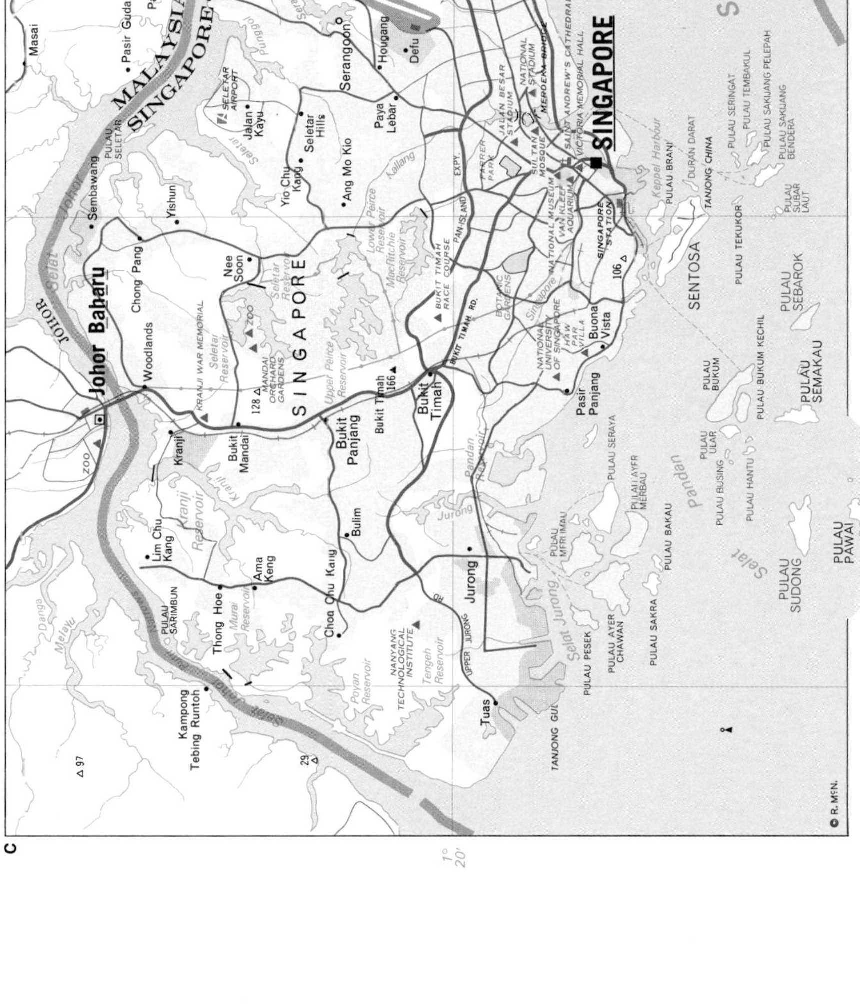
c
SINGAPORE
Johor Baharu
MALAYSIA
SINGAPORE
INDONESIA
Singapore Strait

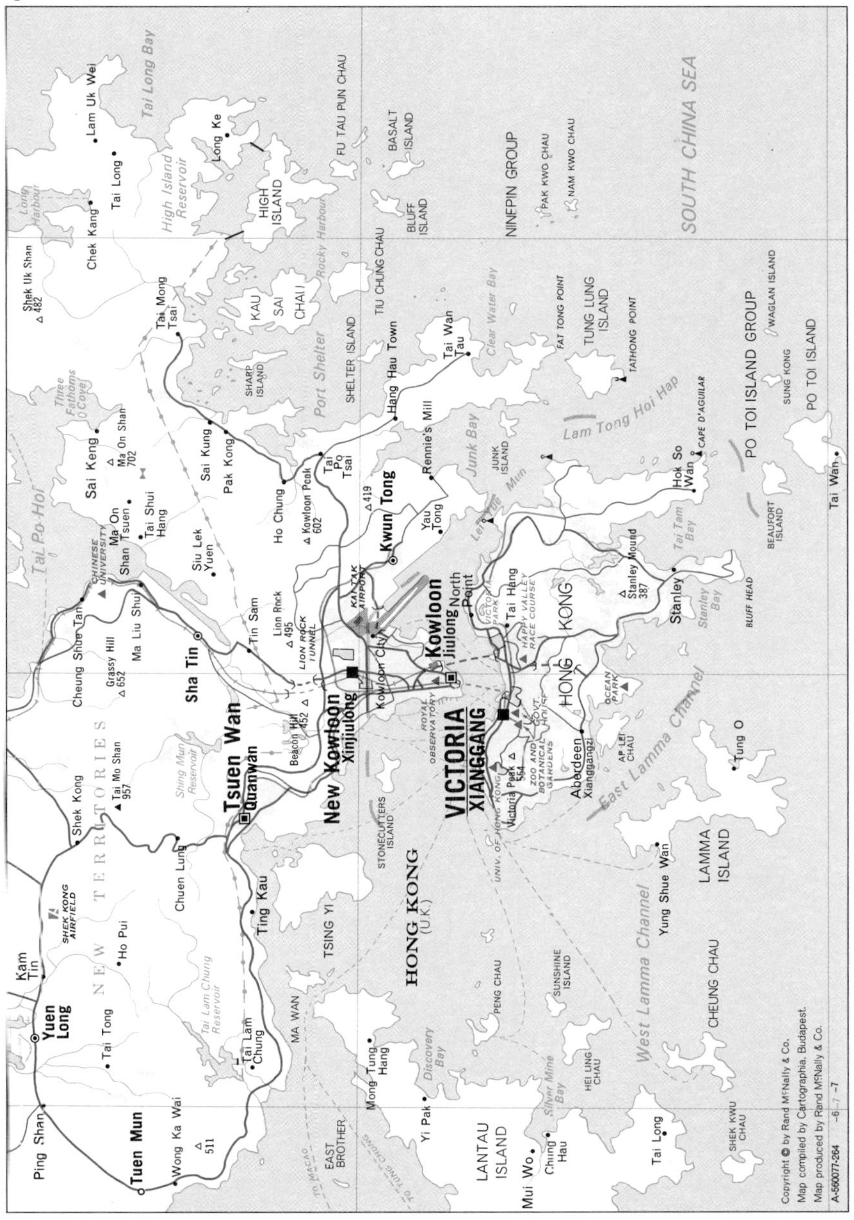
d
VICTORIA XIANGGANG
Kowloon Jiulong
New Kowloon Xinjiulong
Tsuen Wan Quanwan
HONG KONG (U.K.)
SOUTH CHINA SEA
LANTAU ISLAND
Copyright © by Rand McNally & Co.
Map compiled by Cartographia, Budapest.
Map produced by Rand McNally & Co.
A-560077-264 -6-1-7

Kilometers 0 5 10 15 Km.
Statute Miles 0 5 10 15 Mi.

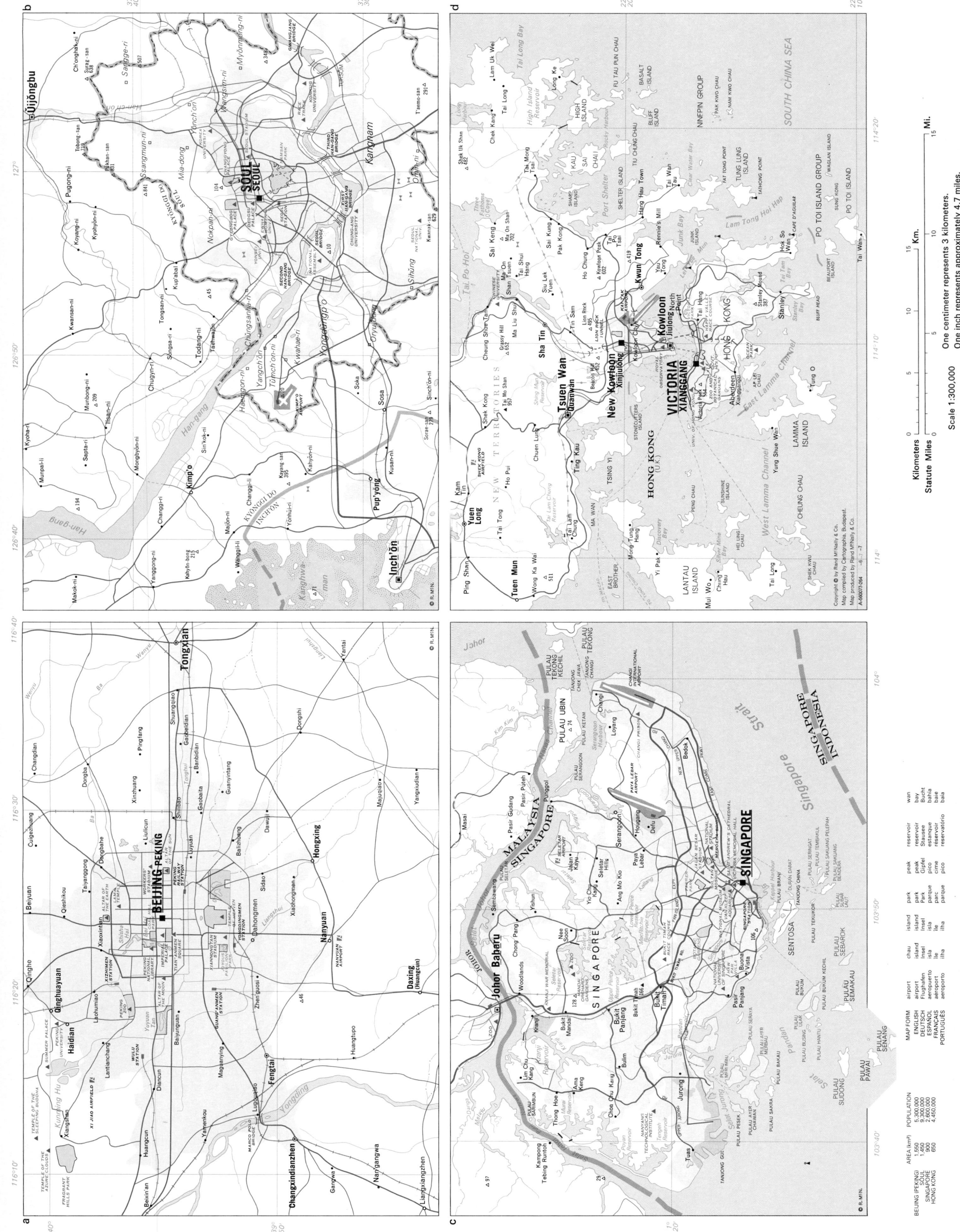

Scale 1:300,000

One centimeter represents 3 kilometers.
One inch represents approximately 4.7 miles.

| | AREA (km²) | POPULATION |
|---|---|---|
| BEIJING (PEKING) | 1,550 | 5,300,000 |
| SŎUL | 1,450 | 9,300,000 |
| SINGAPORE | 900 | 2,600,000 |
| HONG KONG | 650 | 4,450,000 |

| MAP FORM | airport | island | chau | island | park | peak | reservoir | wan |
|---|---|---|---|---|---|---|---|---|
| ENGLISH | airport | island | island | park | peak | reservoir | bay | |
| DEUTSCH | Flughafen | Insel | Insel | Park | Gipfel | Stausee | Bucht | |
| ESPAÑOL | aeropuerto | isla | isla | parque | pico | estanque | bahía | |
| FRANÇAIS | aéroport | île | île | parc | cime | réservoir | baie | |
| PORTUGUÊS | aeroporto | ilha | ilha | parque | pico | reservatório | baía | |

Kilometers 0 5 10 15 Km.
Statute Miles 0 5 10 15 Mi.

Scale 1:300,000
One centimeter represents 3 kilometers.
One inch represents approximately 4.7 miles.

| | AREA (km²) | POPULATION |
|---|---|---|
| DELHI | 1,400 | 5,500,000 |
| BOMBAY | 1,050 | 8,250,000 |
| CALCUTTA | 3,100 | 11,200,000 |

| ENGLISH | airport | dock | island | lake | point | railroad station | road | temple |
|---|---|---|---|---|---|---|---|---|
| DEUTSCH | Flughafen | Dock | Insel | See | Punkt | Bahnhof | Landstrasse | Tempel |
| ESPAÑOL | aeropuerto | muelle | isla | lago | punta | terminal ferroviaria | camino | templo |
| FRANÇAIS | aéroport | quai | île | lac | pointe | gare | route | temple |
| PORTUGUÊS | aeroporto | cais | ilha | lago | ponta | estação ferroviária | rodovia | templo |

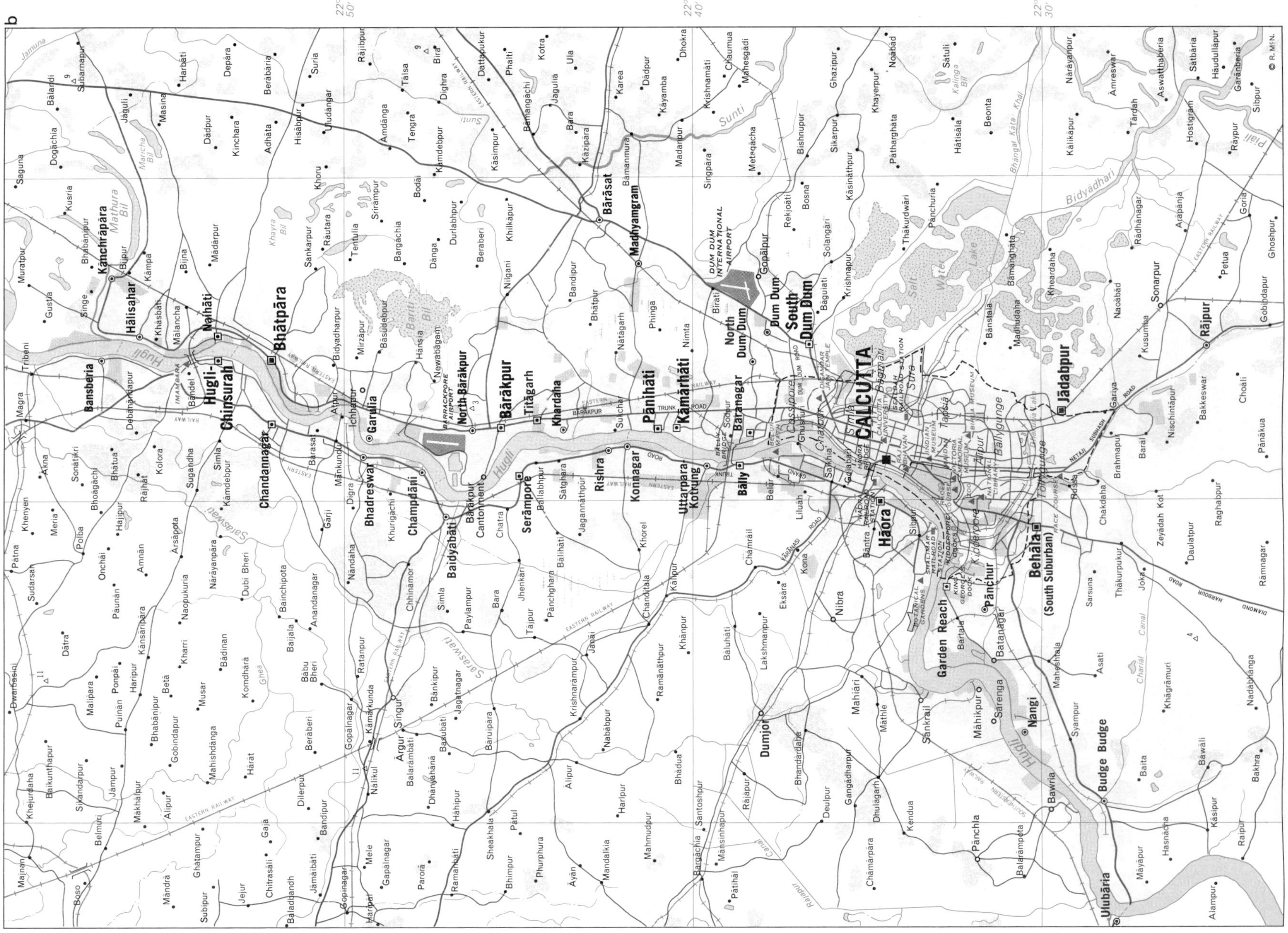
b
CALCUTTA
Hāora
Dum Dum
Bārākpur
Hugli
© R.MᶜN.

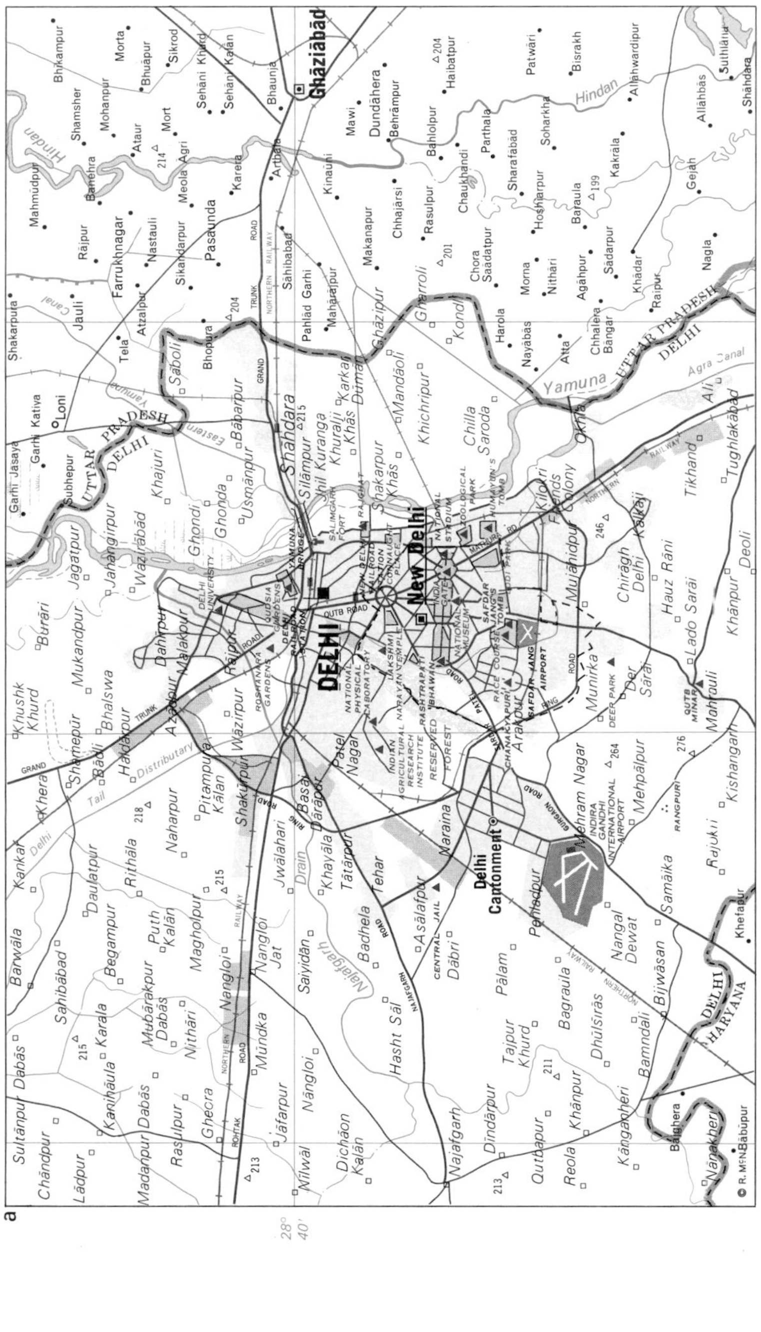
a
DELHI
New Delhi
Delhi Cantonment
Ghaziābād
© R.MᶜN.

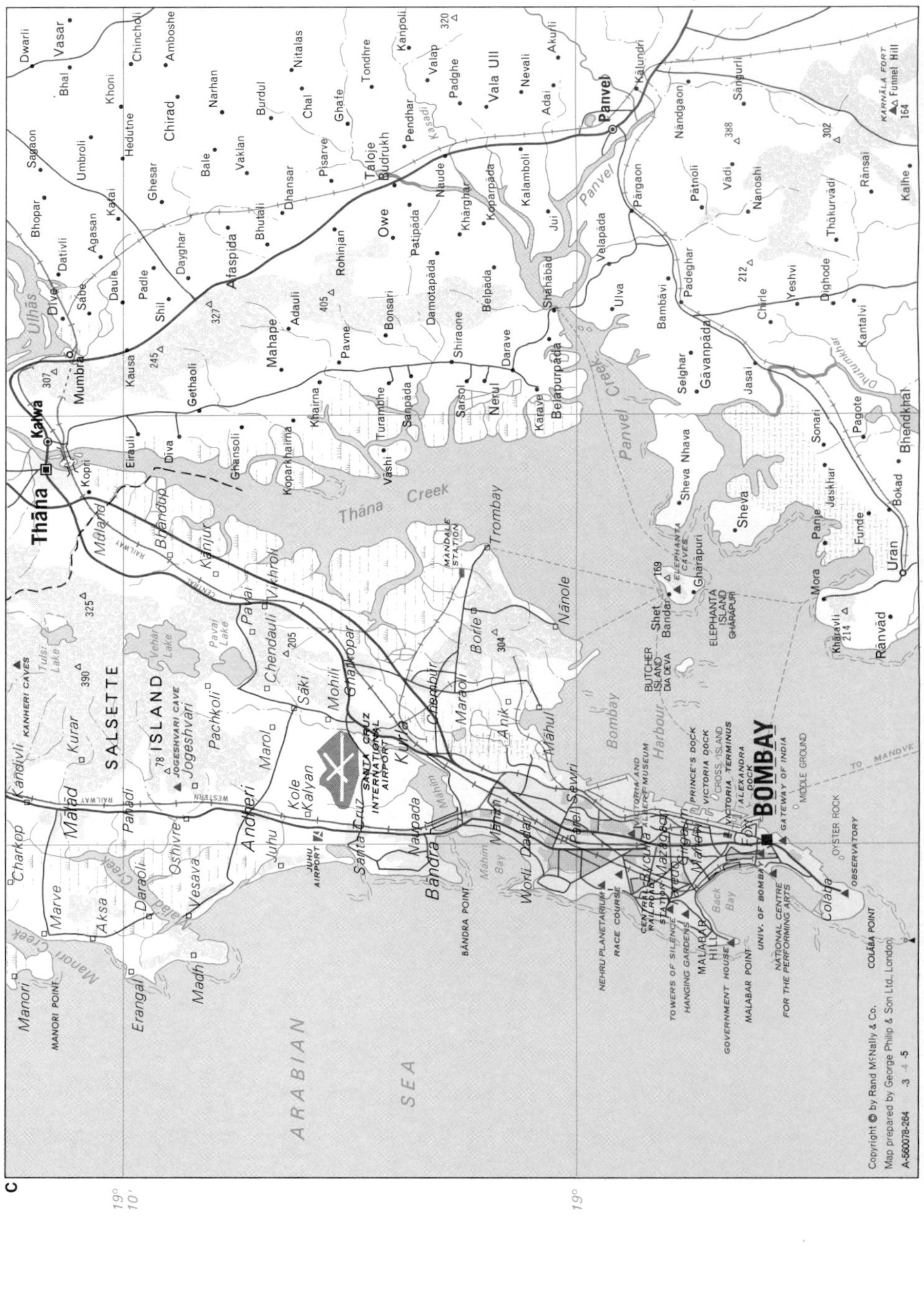
c
BOMBAY
Thāna
SALSETTE ISLAND
ARABIAN SEA
Thāna Creek

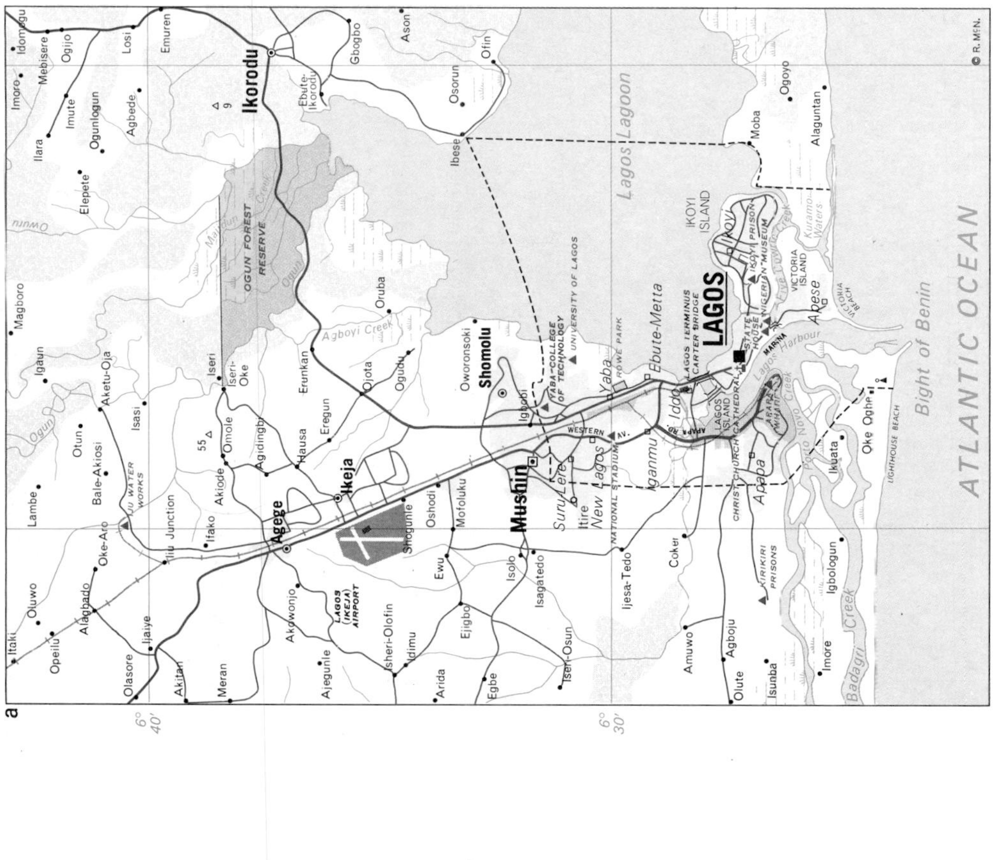
a
LAGOS
Ikeja
Mushin
Ikorodu
Agege
Shomolu
Lagos Lagoon
Bight of Benin
ATLANTIC OCEAN

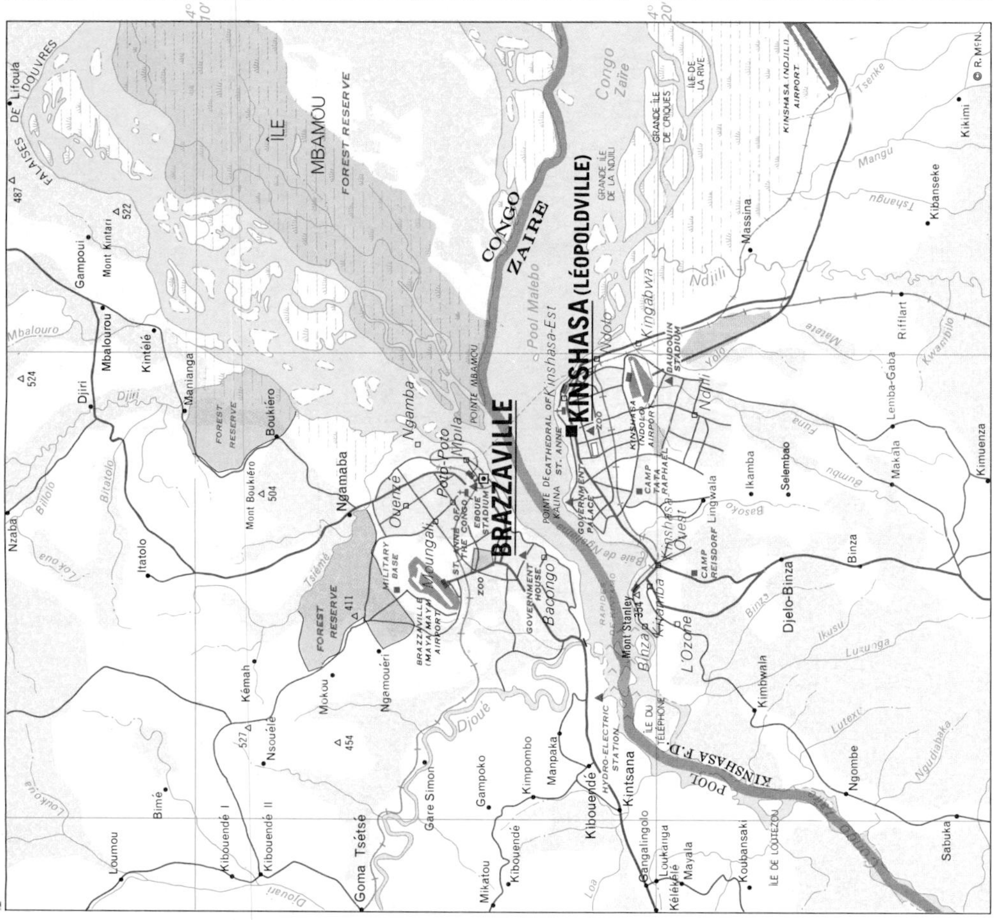
b
BRAZZAVILLE
KINSHASA (LÉOPOLDVILLE)
CONGO
ZAIRE
Pool Malebo
ÎLE MBAMOU

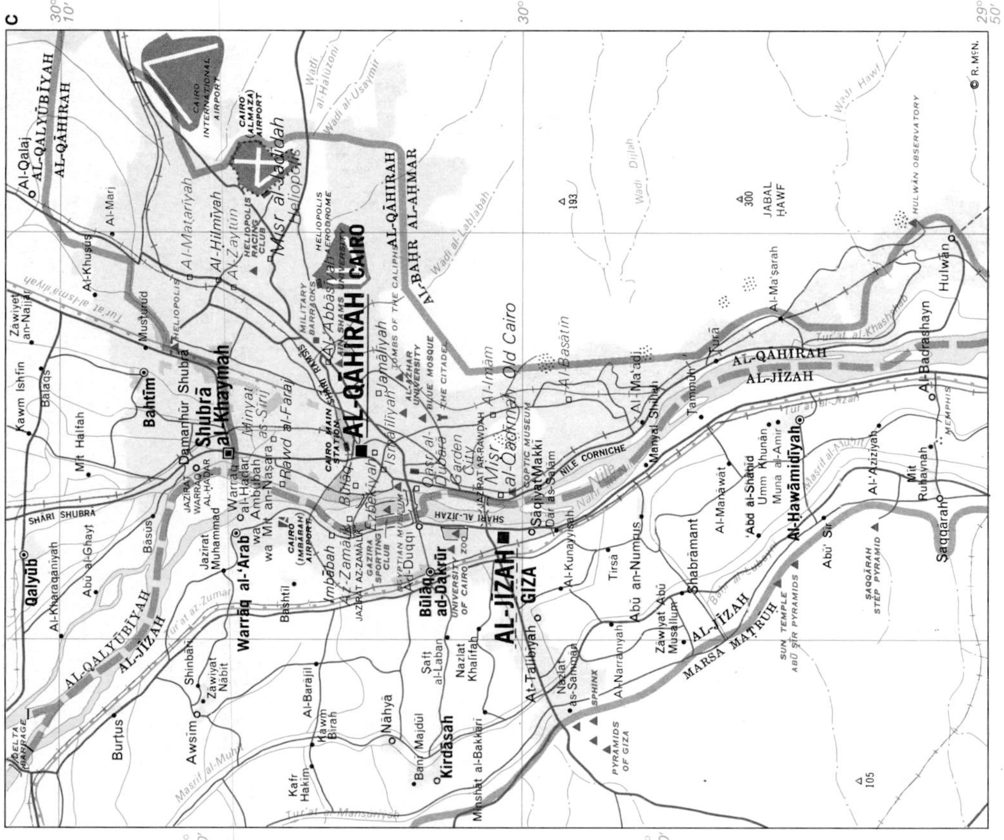
c
AL-QĀHIRAH (CAIRO)
AL-JĪZAH
GIZA
Shubrā al-Khaymah
Qalyūb
Ḥulwān

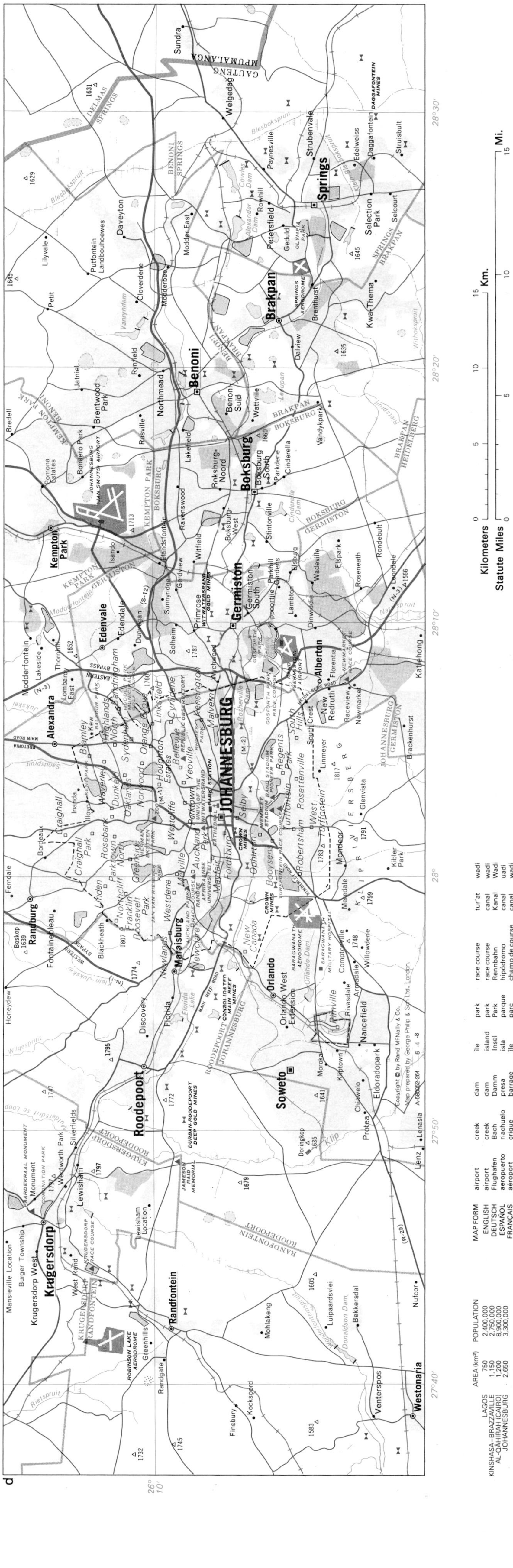
d
JOHANNESBURG
Soweto
Germiston
Benoni
Boksburg
Brakpan
Springs
Krugersdorp
Roodepoort
Randburg
Alberton
Kempton Park
Randfontein
Westonaria

| | AREA (km²) | POPULATION |
|---|---|---|
| LAGOS | 750 | 2,400,000 |
| KINSHASA–BRAZZAVILLE | 1,150 | 2,750,000 |
| AL-QĀHIRAH (CAIRO) | 1,200 | 8,900,000 |
| JOHANNESBURG | 2,650 | 3,300,000 |

| MAP FORM | ENGLISH | DEUTSCH | ESPAÑOL | FRANÇAIS | PORTUGUÊS |
|---|---|---|---|---|---|
| airport | airport | Flughafen | aeropuerto | aéroport | aeroporto |
| creek | creek | Bach | riachuelo | crique | riacho |
| dam | dam | Damm | presa | barrage | represa |
| île | island | Insel | isla | île | ilha |
| park | park | Park | parque | parc | parque |
| race course | race course | Rennbahn | hipódromo | champ de course | hipódromo |
| tur'at | canal | Kanal | canal | canal | canal |
| wadi | wadi | Wadi | uadi | wadi | uadi |

Scale 1:300,000

One centimeter represents 3 kilometers.

One inch represents approximately 4.7 miles.

a

150° 40'
150° 50'
151°
151° 10'
151° 20'
33° 40'
33° 50'
34°
Riverstone
Schofields
Penrith
Blacktown
Parramatta
Fairfield
Liverpool
Bankstown
Campbelltown
SYDNEY
North Sydney
Manly
Ryde
Chatswood
Hornsby
Strathfield
Auburn
Canterbury
Hurstville
Kogarah
Rockdale
Botany
Randwick
Waverley
Woollahra
Mosman
Botany Bay
PACIFIC
OCEAN
ROYAL NATIONAL PARK
KINGSFORD SMITH AIRPORT
Copyright © by Rand McNally & Co.

b

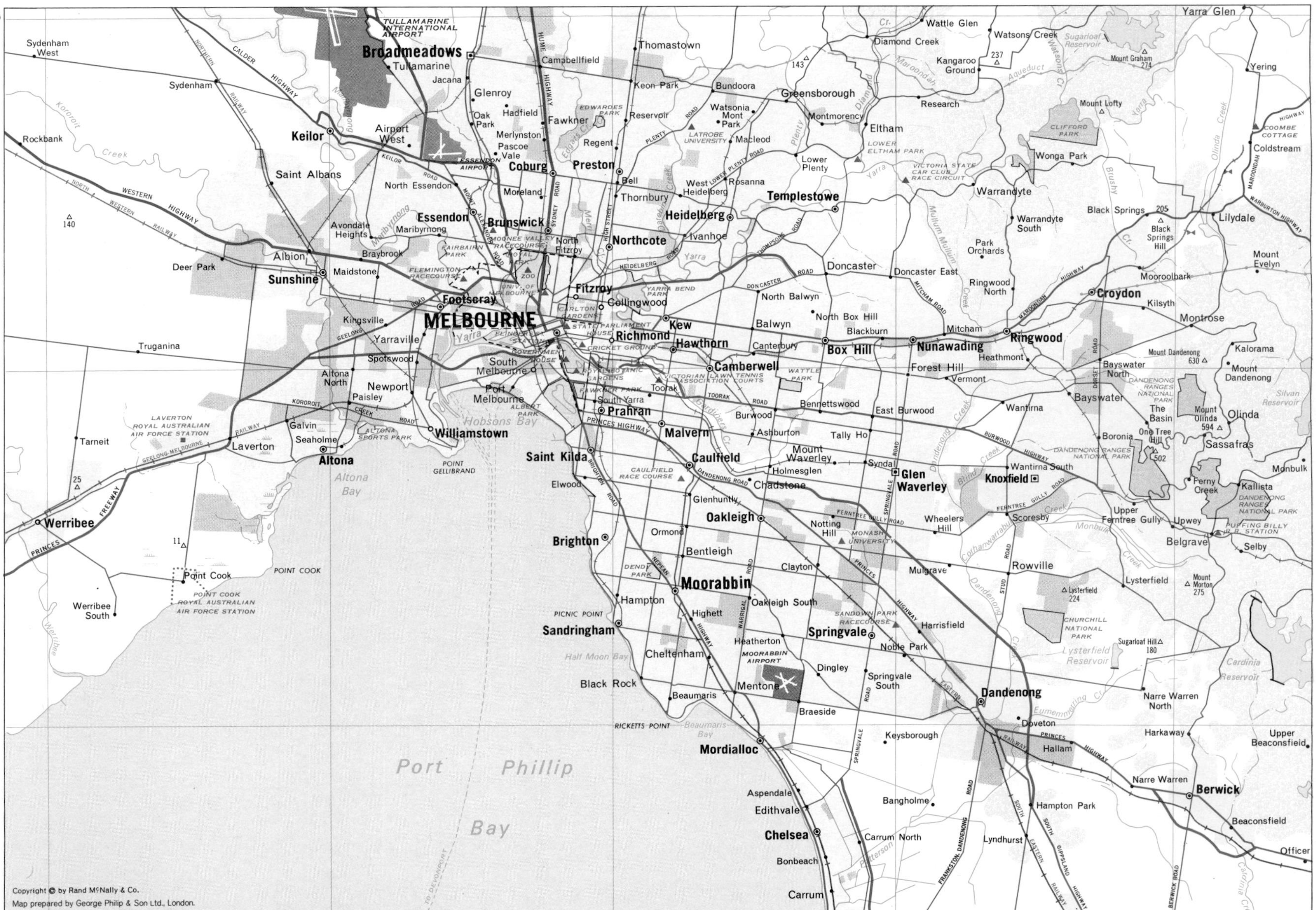
37° 40'
37° 50'
38°
TULLAMARINE INTERNATIONAL AIRPORT
Broadmeadows
Keilor
Coburg
Preston
Essendon
Brunswick
Northcote
Heidelberg
Templestowe
Sunshine
Footscray
MELBOURNE
Fitzroy
Kew
Richmond
Hawthorn
Camberwell
Box Hill
Nunawading
Ringwood
Croydon
Williamstown
Altona
Werribee
Laverton
Saint Kilda
Prahran
Malvern
Caulfield
Glen Waverley
Knoxfield
Oakleigh
Brighton
Moorabbin
Sandringham
Springvale
Dandenong
Mordialloc
Chelsea
Berwick
Port Phillip Bay
Copyright © by Rand McNally & Co.
Map prepared by George Philip & Son Ltd., London.
A-590056-264 -5 -4 -8
144° 40'
144° 50'
145°
145° 10'
145° 20'

| | AREA (km²) | POPULATION |
|---|---|---|
| MELBOURNE | 2,600 | 2,425,000 |
| SYDNEY | 2,800 | 2,850,000 |

| | | | | | | |
|---|---|---|---|---|---|---|
| ENGLISH | bay, b. | bridge | creek, cr. | highway | point | road |
| DEUTSCH | Bucht | Brücke | Bach | Landstrasse | Landspitze | Landstrasse |
| ESPAÑOL | bahía | puente | riachuelo | camino | punta | camino |
| FRANÇAIS | baie | pont | crique | route | pointe | route |
| PORTUGUÊS | baía | ponte | riacho | rodovia | ponta | rodovia |

Kilometers 0 5 10 15 Km.
Statute Miles 0 5 10 15 Mi.

Scale 1:300,000

One centimeter represents 3 kilometers.
One inch represents approximately 4.7 miles.

a

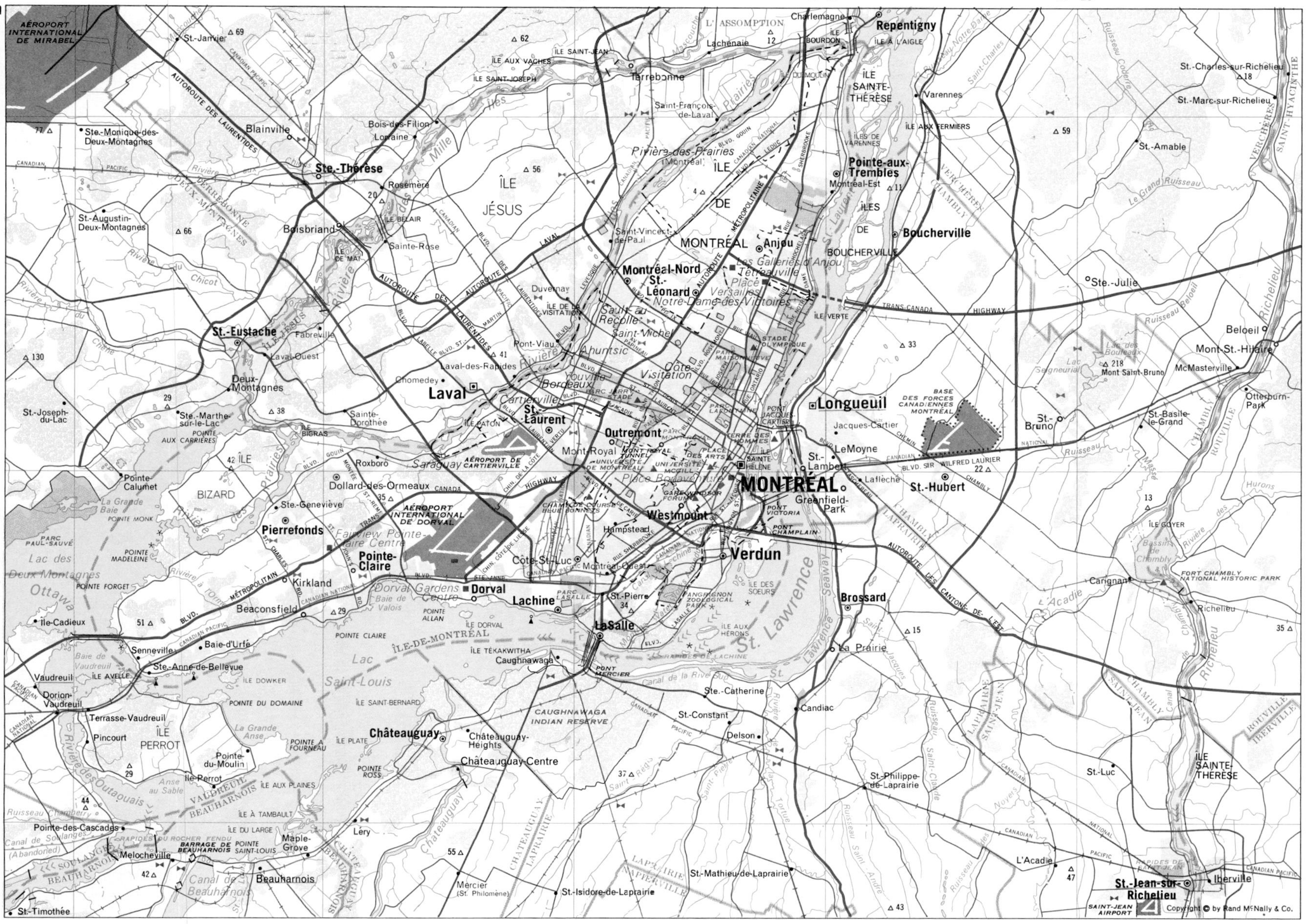
MONTRÉAL
Laval
Longueuil
Verdun
Outremont
Westmount
St.-Laurent
Lachine
LaSalle
Dorval
Pointe-Claire
Pierrefonds
Kirkland
Beaconsfield
Brossard
St.-Hubert
St.-Lambert
Greenfield-Park
Boucherville
Repentigny
Terrebonne
Ste.-Thérèse
Blainville
St.-Eustache
Deux-Montagnes
Châteauguay
Beauharnois
Montréal-Nord
St.-Léonard
Anjou
Pointe-aux-Trembles
Montréal-Est
Côte-St.-Luc
Hampstead
Mont-Royal
Dollard-des-Ormeaux
Ste.-Geneviève
Roxboro
Vaudreuil
Dorion-Vaudreuil
Ste.-Anne-de-Bellevue
Senneville
Baie-d'Urfé
Pincourt
Terrasse-Vaudreuil
Candiac
Delson
Ste.-Catherine
St.-Constant
La Prairie
St.-Jean-sur-Richelieu
Iberville
Chambly
Beloeil
Mont-St.-Hilaire
ÎLE JÉSUS
ÎLE DE MONTRÉAL
ÎLE BIZARD
ÎLE PERROT
Lac des Deux Montagnes
Lac Saint-Louis
St. Lawrence
AÉROPORT INTERNATIONAL DE MIRABEL
AÉROPORT INTERNATIONAL DE DORVAL
AÉROPORT DE CARTIERVILLE
BASE DES FORCES CANADIENNES MONTRÉAL
CAUGHNAWAGA INDIAN RESERVE
FORT CHAMBLY NATIONAL HISTORIC PARK
Copyright © by Rand McNally & Co.

b

TORONTO
North York
York
Etobicoke
Scarborough
East York
Mississauga
Brampton
Vaughan
Markham
Richmond Hill
Pickering
Ajax
Oakville
Port Credit
Streetsville
Malton
Bramalea
Woodbridge
Weston
Agincourt
Don Mills
Leaside
Mimico
New Toronto
Long Branch
LESTER B. PEARSON INTERNATIONAL AIRPORT
BUTTONVILLE AIRFIELD
TORONTO ISLAND AIRPORT
LAKE ONTARIO
(75 Meters Above Sea Level)
CANADA
UNITED STATES
Copyright © by Rand McNally & Co.
Map prepared by Rand McNally & Co.
A-520080-264

| | AREA (km²) | POPULATION |
|---|---|---|
| MONTRÉAL | 3,100 | 2,875,000 |
| TORONTO | 2,100 | 2,850,000 |

| MAP FORM | île | park | rapides | rivière | ruisseau |
|---|---|---|---|---|---|
| ENGLISH | island | park | rapids | river | brook |
| DEUTSCH | Insel | Park | Stromschnellen | Fluss | Bach |
| ESPAÑOL | isla | parque | rápidos | río | arroyo |
| FRANÇAIS | île | parc | rapides | rivière | ruisseau |
| PORTUGUÊS | ilha | parque | rápidos | rio | arroio |

Kilometers 0 5 10 15 Km.
Statute Miles 0 5 10 15 Mi.

Scale 1:300,000

One centimeter represents 3 kilometers.
One inch represents approximately 4.7 miles.

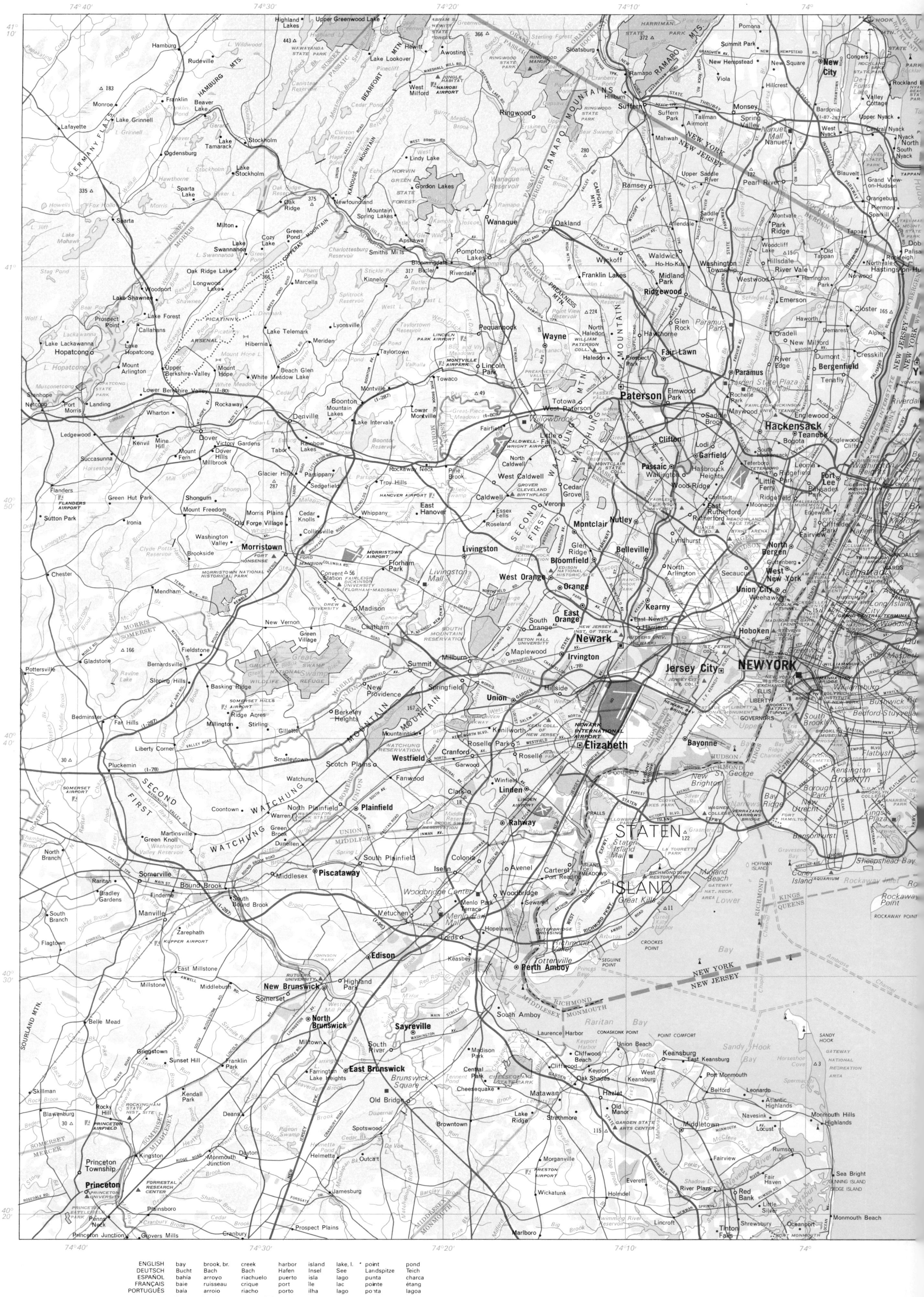
74°40'
74°30'
74°20'
74°10'
74°
41° 10'
41°
40° 50'
40° 40'
40° 30'
40° 20'
NEW YORK
Newark
Elizabeth
Jersey City
Paterson
Hackensack
Passaic
Clifton
Hoboken
Bayonne
STATEN ISLAND
Perth Amboy
New Brunswick
Edison
Plainfield
Morristown
Princeton
Princeton Township
Sayreville
East Brunswick
Rahway
Linden
Union
Westfield
Irvington
East Orange
West Orange
Montclair
Bloomfield
Nutley
Belleville
Kearny
West New York
Union City
North Bergen
Fort Lee
Teaneck
Bergenfield
Paramus
Fair Lawn
Ridgewood
Wayne
Livingston
Dover
Somerville
Bound Brook
Piscataway
Suffern
New City
Nanuet
Spring Valley
Pearl River
Brooklyn
Manhattan
Red Bank
Middletown
Keansburg
Matawan
South Amboy
Raritan Bay
Sandy Hook
Hopatcong
Sparta
Wanaque
Oakland
NEW YORK
NEW JERSEY
RAMAPO MOUNTAINS
WATCHUNG
FIRST
SECOND
SOURLAND MTN.
NEWARK INTERNATIONAL AIRPORT

| ENGLISH | bay | brook, br. | creek | harbor | island | lake, l. | point | pond |
|---|---|---|---|---|---|---|---|---|
| DEUTSCH | Bucht | Bach | Bach | Hafen | Insel | See | Landspitze | Teich |
| ESPAÑOL | bahía | arroyo | riachuelo | puerto | isla | lago | punta | charca |
| FRANÇAIS | baie | ruisseau | crique | port | île | lac | pointe | étang |
| PORTUGUÊS | baía | arroio | riacho | porto | ilha | lago | ponta | lagoa |

For complete glossary see page *I•1*.

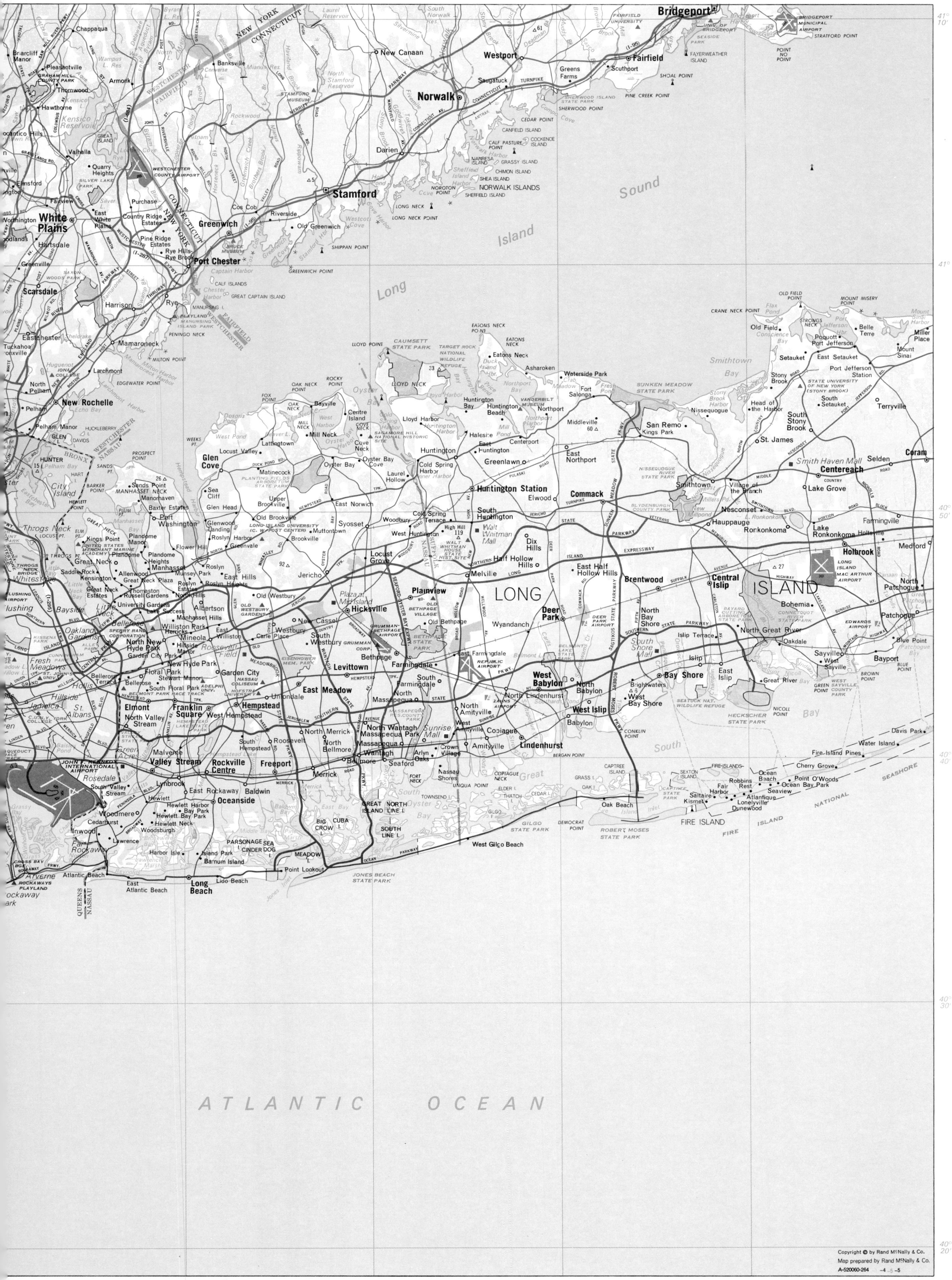

73°40'
73°30'
73°20'
73°10'
41° 10'
41°
40° 50'
40° 40'
40° 30'
40° 20'
NEW YORK
CONNECTICUT
WESTCHESTER
FAIRFIELD
Bridgeport
Fairfield
Westport
Norwalk
New Canaan
Darien
Stamford
Greenwich
Port Chester
Rye
Harrison
White Plains
Scarsdale
Mamaroneck
New Rochelle
Chappaqua
Pleasantville
Armonk
Valhalla
Purchase
Long Island Sound
NORWALK ISLANDS
Oyster Bay
Glen Cove
Huntington
Northport
Smithtown
Commack
Huntington Station
Hicksville
Plainview
Levittown
Hempstead
Freeport
Oceanside
Long Beach
Garden City
Mineola
Valley Stream
Rockville Centre
Elmont
Franklin Square
East Meadow
Massapequa
Amityville
Lindenhurst
West Babylon
Deer Park
Brentwood
Central Islip
Bay Shore
West Islip
Islip
Centereach
Coram
Holbrook
Patchogue
Port Jefferson
Stony Brook
Ronkonkoma
LONG ISLAND
FIRE ISLAND
FIRE ISLAND NATIONAL SEASHORE
South Oyster Bay
Great South Bay
JOHN F. KENNEDY INTERNATIONAL AIRPORT
LONG ISLAND MAC ARTHUR AIRPORT
REPUBLIC AIRPORT
JONES BEACH STATE PARK
ROBERT MOSES STATE PARK
ATLANTIC OCEAN
Copyright © by Rand McNally & Co.
Map prepared by Rand McNally & Co.
A-520060-264 -4 -5 -5


Kilometers 0 5 10 15 Km.

Statute Miles 0 5 10 15 Mi.

Scale 1:300,000

One centimeter represents 3 kilometers.
One inch represents approximately 4.7 miles.

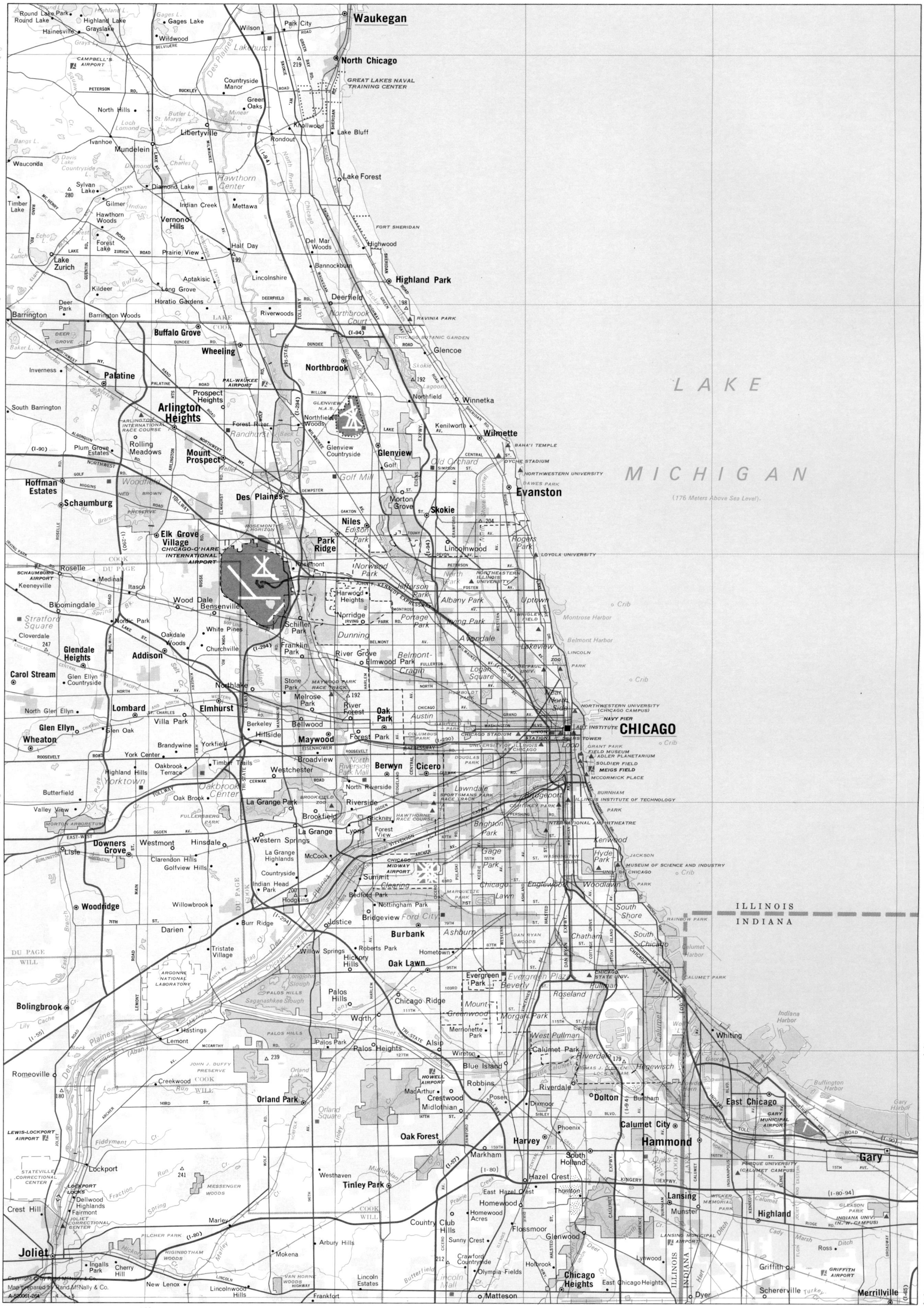
Waukegan
North Chicago
GREAT LAKES NAVAL TRAINING CENTER
Libertyville
Mundelein
Lake Forest
Lake Bluff
FORT SHERIDAN
Highwood
Highland Park
Deerfield
Lake Zurich
Barrington
Buffalo Grove
Wheeling
Northbrook
Glencoe
Winnetka
Palatine
Arlington Heights
Wilmette
Glenview
Mount Prospect
Evanston
Skokie
Niles
Des Plaines
Park Ridge
Elk Grove Village
CHICAGO-O'HARE INTERNATIONAL AIRPORT
Schaumburg
Hoffman Estates
LAKE
MICHIGAN
(176 Meters Above Sea Level)
LOYOLA UNIVERSITY
NORTHWESTERN UNIVERSITY
Roselle
Addison
Elmhurst
Glendale Heights
Carol Stream
Lombard
Glen Ellyn
Wheaton
Oak Park
Maywood
Berwyn
Cicero
CHICAGO
NAVY PEER
SEARS TOWER
Loop
ADLER PLANETARIUM
SOLDIER FIELD
MEIGS FIELD
ILLINOIS INSTITUTE OF TECHNOLOGY
MUSEUM OF SCIENCE AND INDUSTRY
CHICAGO MIDWAY AIRPORT
La Grange
Downers Grove
Woodridge
Burbank
Oak Lawn
Evergreen Park
Bolingbrook
ARGONNE NATIONAL LABORATORY
Blue Island
Harvey
Dolton
Calumet City
Hammond
East Chicago
Gary
Whiting
ILLINOIS
INDIANA
Orland Park
Tinley Park
Oak Forest
Lockport
Romeoville
Joliet
Chicago Heights
Lansing
Highland
Merrillville
Matteson
Homewood
Flossmoor
Mokena
Frankfort
New Lenox
Crest Hill
88°
87° 50'
87° 40'
87° 30'
87° 20'
42° 20'
42° 10'
42°
41° 50'
41° 40'
41° 30'
Copyright by Rand McNally & Co.
Map prepared by Rand McNally & Co.

| | | | | | | |
|---|---|---|---|---|---|---|
| ENGLISH | airport | creek, cr. | harbor | lake, l. | park | woods |
| DEUTSCH | Flughafen | Bach | Hafen | See | Park | Gehölz |
| ESPAÑOL | aeropuerto | riachuelo | puerto | lago | parque | bosques |
| FRANÇAIS | aéroport | crique | port | lac | parc | bois |
| PORTUGUÊS | aeroporto | riacho | porto | lago | parque | bosques |

Kilometers 0 5 10 15 Km.

Statute Miles 0 5 10 15 Mi.

Scale 1:300,000

One centimeter represents 3 kilometers.

One inch represents approximately 4.7 miles.

a

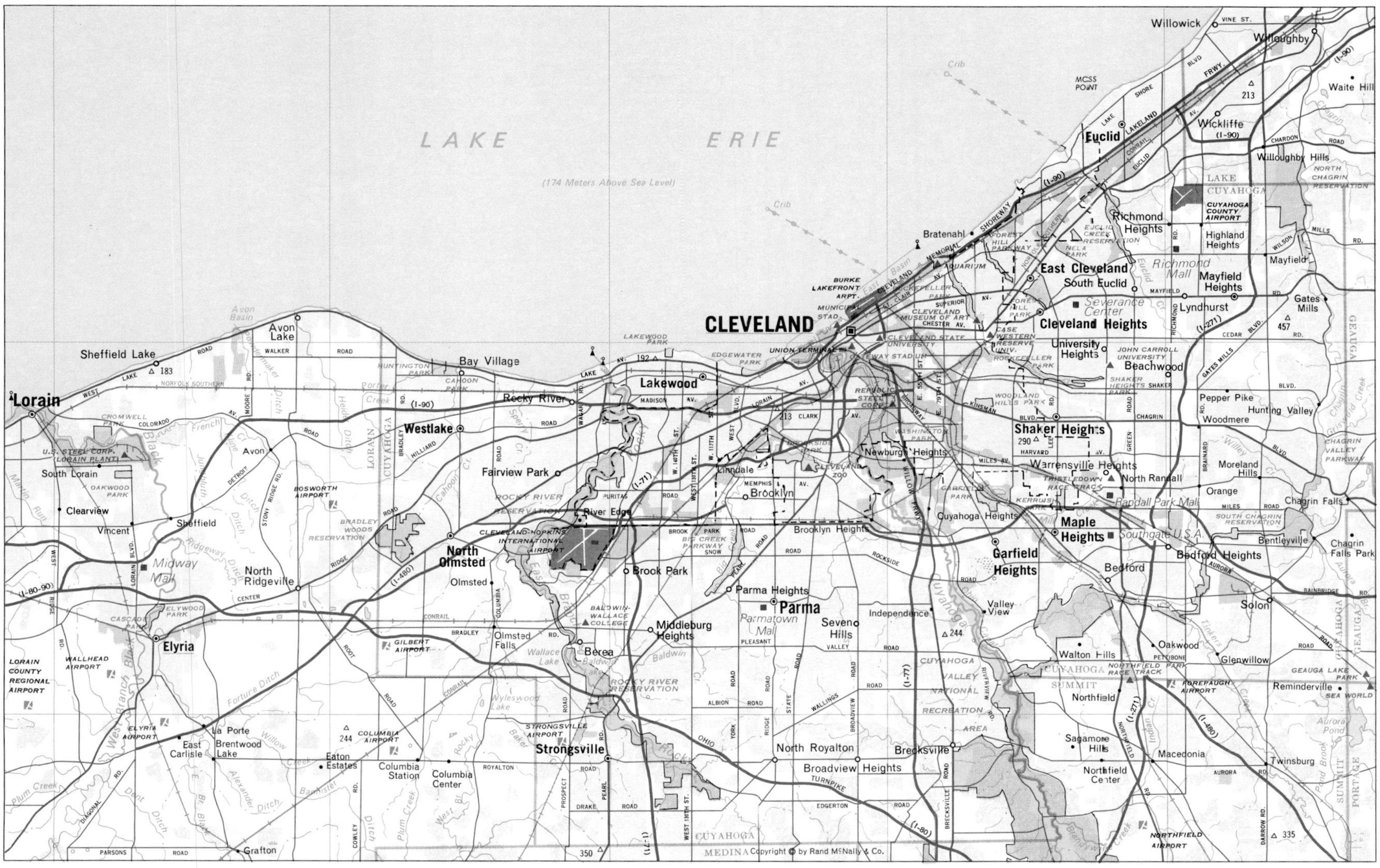
LAKE ERIE
(174 Meters Above Sea Level)
CLEVELAND
Lorain
Sheffield Lake
Avon Lake
Bay Village
Lakewood
Rocky River
Westlake
Euclid
Willowick
Willoughby
Wickliffe
East Cleveland
Cleveland Heights
Shaker Heights
Parma
North Olmsted
Elyria
Strongsville
Berea
Brook Park
Garfield Heights
Maple Heights
Bedford Heights
Solon
Copyright © by Rand McNally & Co.

b

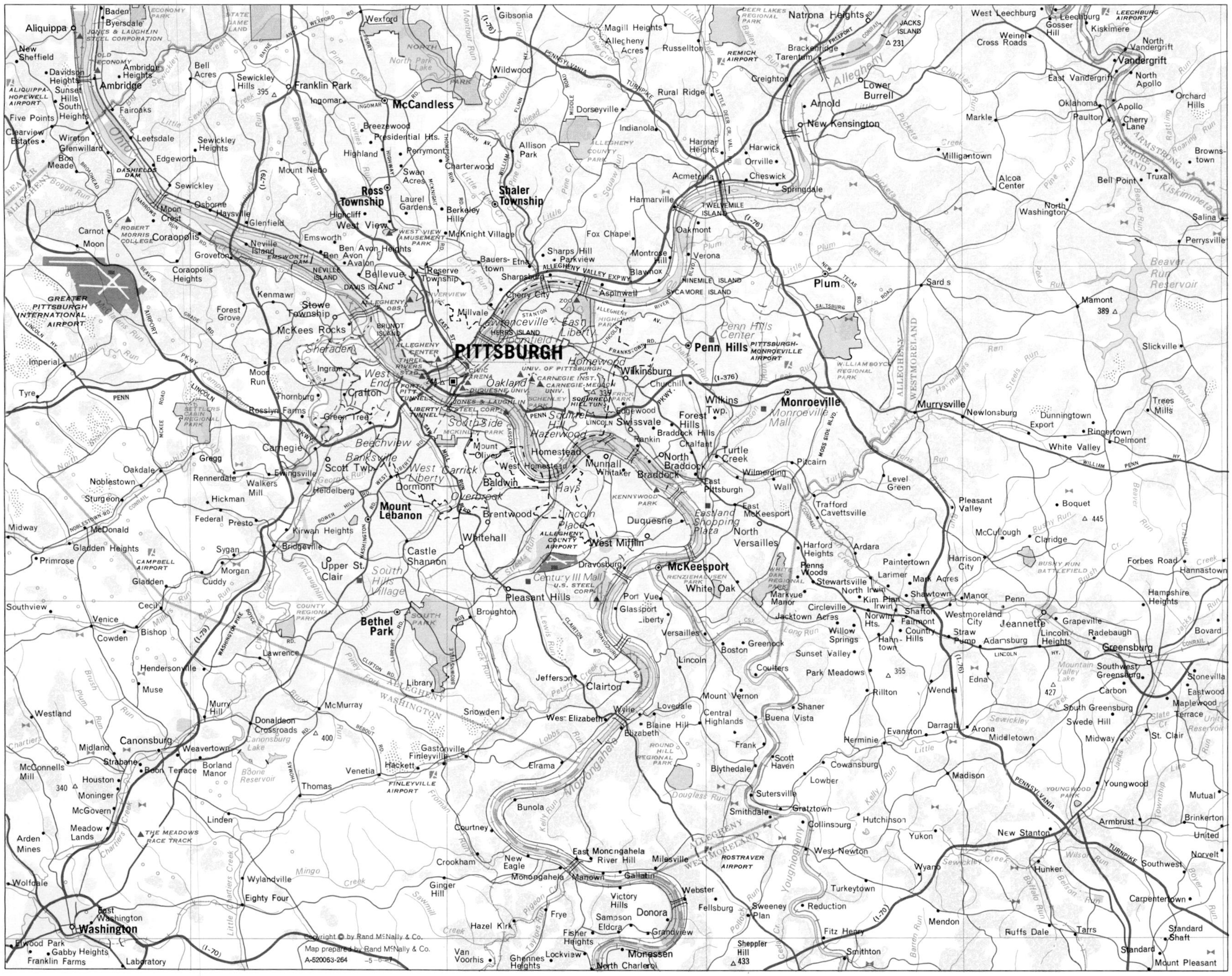
PITTSBURGH
Aliquippa
Ambridge
McCandless
Ross Township
Shaler Township
Coraopolis
Penn Hills
Monroeville
McKeesport
Mount Lebanon
Bethel Park
Canonsburg
Washington
Greensburg
Jeannette
Vandergrift
New Kensington
Clairton
Monessen
Copyright © by Rand McNally & Co.
Map prepared by Rand McNally & Co.

| ENGLISH | creek, cr. | ditch | island | lake, l. | park | reservoir | run |
|---|---|---|---|---|---|---|---|
| DEUTSCH | Bach | Graben | Insel | See | Park | Stausee | Bach |
| ESPAÑOL | riachuelo | acequia | isla | lago | parque | embalse | arroyo |
| FRANÇAIS | crique | fossé | île | lac | parc | réservoir | ruisseau |
| PORTUGUÊS | riacho | fosso | ilha | lago | parque | reservatório | córrego |

Kilometers 0 5 10 15 Km.
Statute Miles 0 5 10 15 Mi.

Scale 1:300,000

One centimeter represents 3 kilometers.
One inch represents approximately 4.7 miles.

Copyright © by Rand McNally & Co.
Map prepared by Rand McNally & Co.

Kilometers 0 5 10 15 Km.
Statute Miles 0 5 10 15 Mi.

Scale 1:300,000
One centimeter represents 3 kilometers.
One inch represents approximately 4.7 miles.

| ENGLISH | canyon | college | creek | dam | hills | mount | park | peak | reservoir |
|---|---|---|---|---|---|---|---|---|---|
| DEUTSCH | Cañon | College | Bach | Damm | Hügel | Berg | Park | Gipfel | Stausee |
| ESPAÑOL | cañon | escuela | riachuelo | diques | colinas | montaña | parque | pico | estanque |
| FRANÇAIS | canyon | collège | crique | barrage | collines | mont | parc | cime | réservoir |
| PORTUGUÊS | canhão | colégio | riacho | represa | colinas | monte | parque | pico | reservatório |

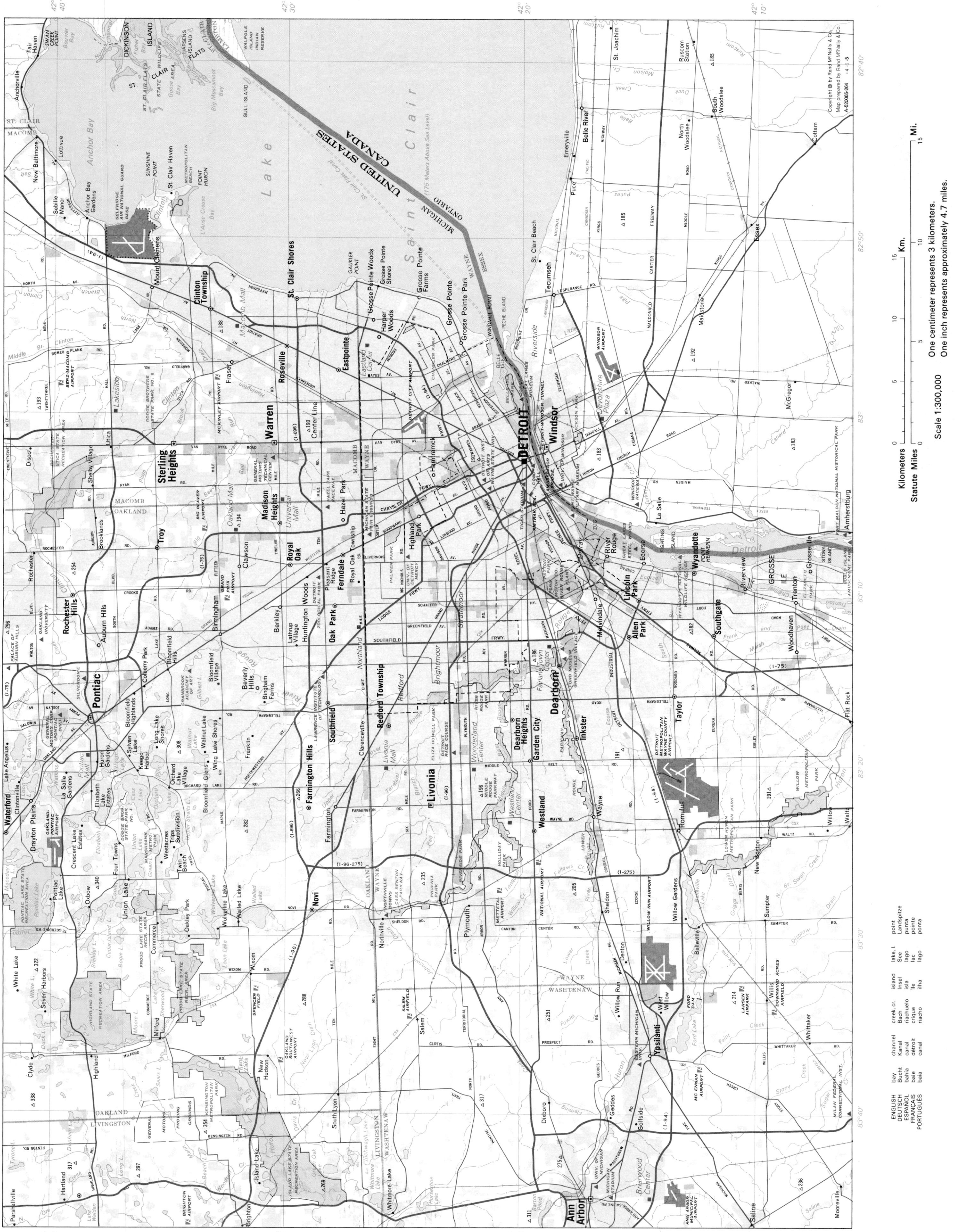
Kilometers 0 5 10 15 Km.
Statute Miles 0 5 10 15 Mi.
Scale 1:300,000
One centimeter represents 3 kilometers.
One inch represents approximately 4.7 miles.
Copyright © by Rand McNally & Co.
Map prepared by Rand McNally & Co.
ENGLISH bay channel creek, cr. island lake, l. point
DEUTSCH Bucht Kanal Bach Insel See Landspitze
ESPAÑOL bahia canal riachuelo isla lago punta
FRANÇAIS baie détroit crique île lac pointe
PORTUGUÊS baia canal riacho ilha lago ponta
UNITED STATES
CANADA
MICHIGAN
ONTARIO
Lake Saint Clair
DETROIT
Windsor
Pontiac
Warren
Sterling Heights
Troy
Dearborn
Livonia
Southfield
Royal Oak
Ann Arbor
Ypsilanti
Wyandotte
Taylor
Westland
Inkster
Wayne
Romulus
Novi
Farmington Hills
Mount Clemens
Clinton Township
St. Clair Shores
Roseville
Eastpointe
Hamtramck
Highland Park
Ferndale
Oak Park
Madison Heights
Rochester Hills
Auburn Hills
Birmingham
Bloomfield Hills
Waterford
Redford Township
Garden City
Dearborn Heights
Lincoln Park
Allen Park
Southgate
Trenton
Grosse Ile
Tecumseh
Amherstburg
Essex
Belle River

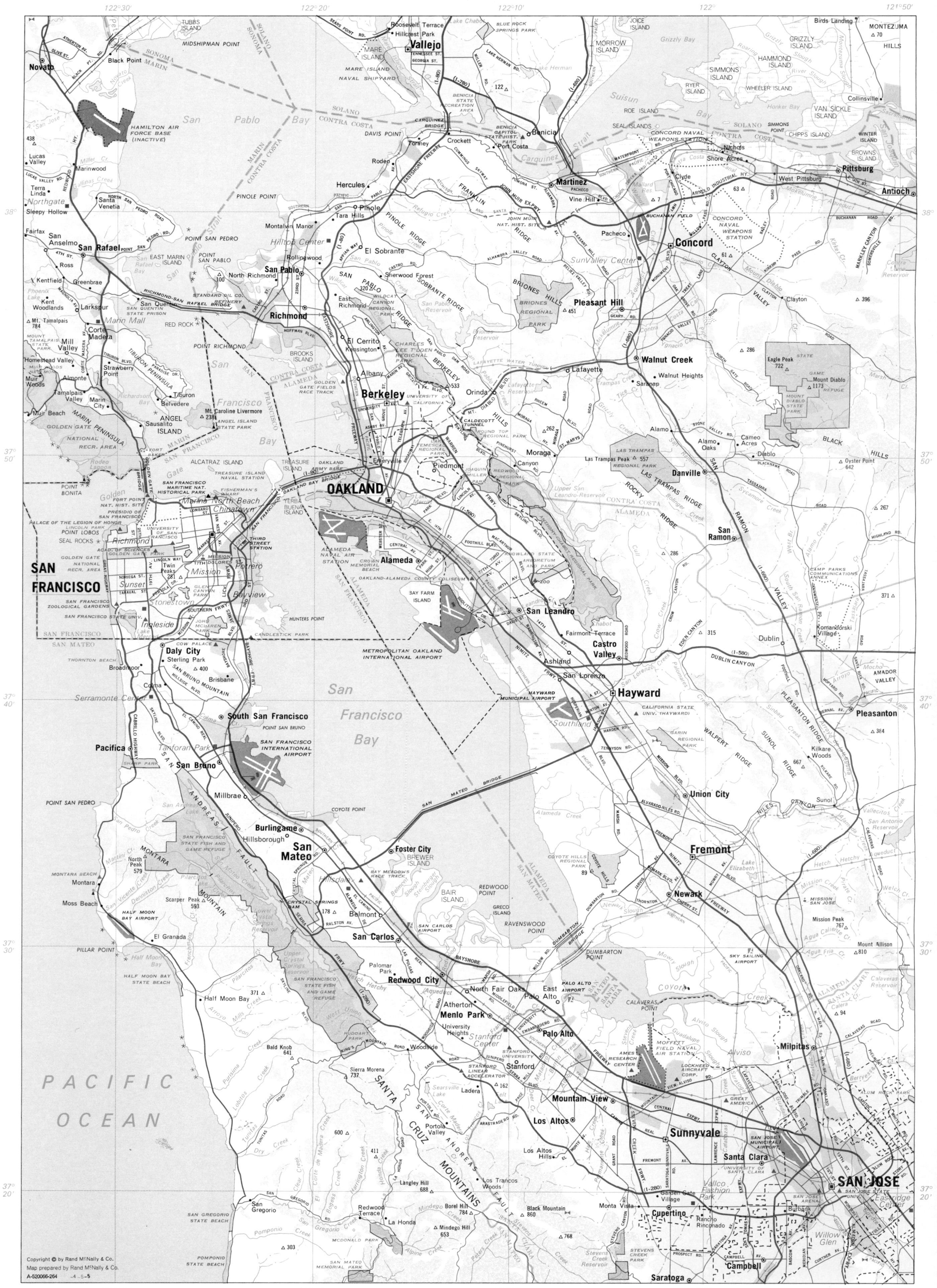
122°30'
122°20'
122°10'
122°
121°50'
38°
37° 50'
37° 40'
37° 30'
37° 20'
Vallejo
Novato
Black Point
SONOMA
MARIN
SOLANO
CONTRA COSTA
MARE ISLAND
MARE ISLAND NAVAL SHIPYARD
TUBBS ISLAND
MIDSHIPMAN POINT
HAMILTON AIR FORCE BASE (INACTIVE)
San Pablo Bay
Benicia
Crockett
Port Costa
Carquinez Strait
Martinez
Suisun Bay
ROE ISLAND
SEAL ISLANDS
CONCORD NAVAL WEAPONS STATION
Pittsburg
West Pittsburg
Antioch
Birds Landing
MONTEZUMA HILLS
GRIZZLY ISLAND
HAMMOND ISLAND
SIMMONS ISLAND
RYER ISLAND
WHEELER ISLAND
Collinsville
VAN SICKLE ISLAND
CHIPPS ISLAND
WINTER ISLAND
BROWNS ISLAND
JOICE ISLAND
MORROW ISLAND
Grizzly Bay
Honker Bay
Nichols
Shore Acres
Clyde
Lucas Valley
Marinwood
Terra Linda
Northgate
Sleepy Hollow
Santa Venetia
Fairfax
San Anselmo
San Rafael
Ross
Kentfield
Greenbrae
Kent Woodlands
Larkspur
Mt. Tamalpais 784
Corte Madera
Mill Valley
Marin Mall
Homestead Valley
Muir Woods
Almonte
Strawberry Point
Tamalpais Valley
Marin City
Tiburon
Belvedere
TIBURON PENINSULA
Muir Beach
Sausalito
ANGEL ISLAND
Mt. Caroline Livermore 781
ANGEL ISLAND STATE PARK
GOLDEN GATE NATIONAL RECR. AREA
MARIN PENINSULA
Rodeo Lagoon
POINT BONITA
Golden Gate
POINT SAN PEDRO
POINT SAN PABLO
EAST MARIN ISLAND
SAN QUENTIN STATE PRISON
San Quentin
RICHMOND-SAN RAFAEL BRIDGE
RED ROCK
POINT RICHMOND
BROOKS ISLAND
Richmond
San Pablo
North Richmond
Rollingwood
El Sobrante
Hilltop Center
Pinole
Hercules
Rodeo
Tara Hills
Montalvin Manor
PINOLE POINT
DAVIS POINT
PINOLE RIDGE
FRANKLIN RIDGE
SOBRANTE RIDGE
Sherwood Forest
San Pablo Reservoir
East Richmond
El Cerrito
Kensington
Albany
Berkeley
UNIVERSITY OF CALIFORNIA
Emeryville
Piedmont
OAKLAND
Orinda
Lafayette
BRIONES HILLS
BRIONES REGIONAL PARK
Pleasant Hill
Pacheco
Concord
SunValley Center
Vine Hill
BUCHANAN FIELD
Walnut Creek
Walnut Heights
Saranap
Clayton
Eagle Peak 722
Mount Diablo 1173
MOUNT DIABLO STATE PARK
BLACK HILLS
Alamo
Alamo Oaks
Cameo Acres
Diablo
Danville
LAS TRAMPAS RIDGE
Las Trampas Peak 557
ROCKY RIDGE
San Ramon
Moraga
Canyon
Upper San Leandro Reservoir
San Francisco Bay
ALCATRAZ ISLAND
TREASURE ISLAND
YERBA BUENA ISLAND
SAN FRANCISCO MARITIME NAT. HISTORICAL PARK
FORT POINT NAT. HIST. SITE
PRESIDIO OF SAN FRANCISCO
PALACE OF THE LEGION OF HONOR
POINT LOBOS
SEAL ROCKS
Marina
North Beach
Chinatown
Richmond
SAN FRANCISCO
Twin Peaks 281
Mission
Potrero
Sunset
Stonestown
Bayview
Ingleside
SAN FRANCISCO ZOOLOGICAL GARDENS
HUNTERS POINT
CANDLESTICK PARK
ALAMEDA NAVAL AIR STATION
Alameda
BAY FARM ISLAND
METROPOLITAN OAKLAND INTERNATIONAL AIRPORT
San Leandro
Fairmont Terrace
Castro Valley
Ashland
San Lorenzo
Hayward
HAYWARD MUNICIPAL AIRPORT
Southland
CALIFORNIA STATE UNIV. (HAYWARD)
Daly City
Sterling Park
Broadmoor
Colma
Brisbane
SAN BRUNO MOUNTAIN
Serramonte Center
South San Francisco
POINT SAN BRUNO
SAN FRANCISCO INTERNATIONAL AIRPORT
Pacifica
Tanforan Park
San Bruno
Millbrae
COYOTE POINT
SAN MATEO BRIDGE
Burlingame
Hillsborough
San Mateo
Foster City
POINT SAN PEDRO
SAN ANDREAS FAULT
Montara
Moss Beach
North Peak 579
MONTARA MOUNTAIN
Scarper Peak 593
HALF MOON BAY AIRPORT
El Granada
PILLAR POINT
Half Moon Bay
Belmont
San Carlos
Redwood City
BAIR ISLAND
GRECO ISLAND
RAVENSWOOD POINT
DUMBARTON POINT
DUMBARTON BRIDGE
North Fair Oaks
Atherton
Menlo Park
East Palo Alto
Palo Alto
Stanford
STANFORD UNIVERSITY
Woodside
Ladera
Portola Valley
Mountain View
Los Altos
Los Altos Hills
Sunnyvale
Santa Clara
SAN JOSE
Milpitas
Alviso
MOFFETT FIELD NAVAL AIR STATION
Cupertino
Monte Vista
Saratoga
Campbell
Willow Glen
Rancho Rinconado
Union City
Fremont
Newark
Sunol
Pleasanton
Dublin
Kilkare Woods
Mission Peak 767
Mount Allison 810
PLEASANTON RIDGE
SUNOL RIDGE
WALPERT RIDGE
PACIFIC OCEAN
SAN GREGORIO STATE BEACH
San Gregorio
POMPONIO STATE BEACH
La Honda
Redwood Terrace
Borel Hill 784
Mindego Hill 653
Langley Hill 688
Bald Knob 641
Sierra Morena 737
Black Mountain 860
SANTA CRUZ MOUNTAINS
Los Trancos Woods
Copyright © by Rand McNally & Co.
Map prepared by Rand McNally & Co.
A-520066-264 -4-5-5

| | | | | | | | |
|---|---|---|---|---|---|---|---|
| ENGLISH | bay | beach | creek, cr. | island | lake | point | reservoir |
| DEUTSCH | Bucht | Strand | Bach | Insel | See | Punkt | Stausee |
| ESPAÑOL | bahia | playa | riachuelo | isla | lago | punta | estanque |
| FRANÇAIS | baie | plage | crique | île | lac | pointe | réservoir |
| PORTUGUÊS | baia | praia | riacho | ilha | lago | ponta | reservatório |

Kilometers 0 5 10 15 Km.

Statute Miles 0 5 10 15 Mi.

Scale 1:300,000

One centimeter represents 3 kilometers.
One inch represents approximately 4.7 miles.

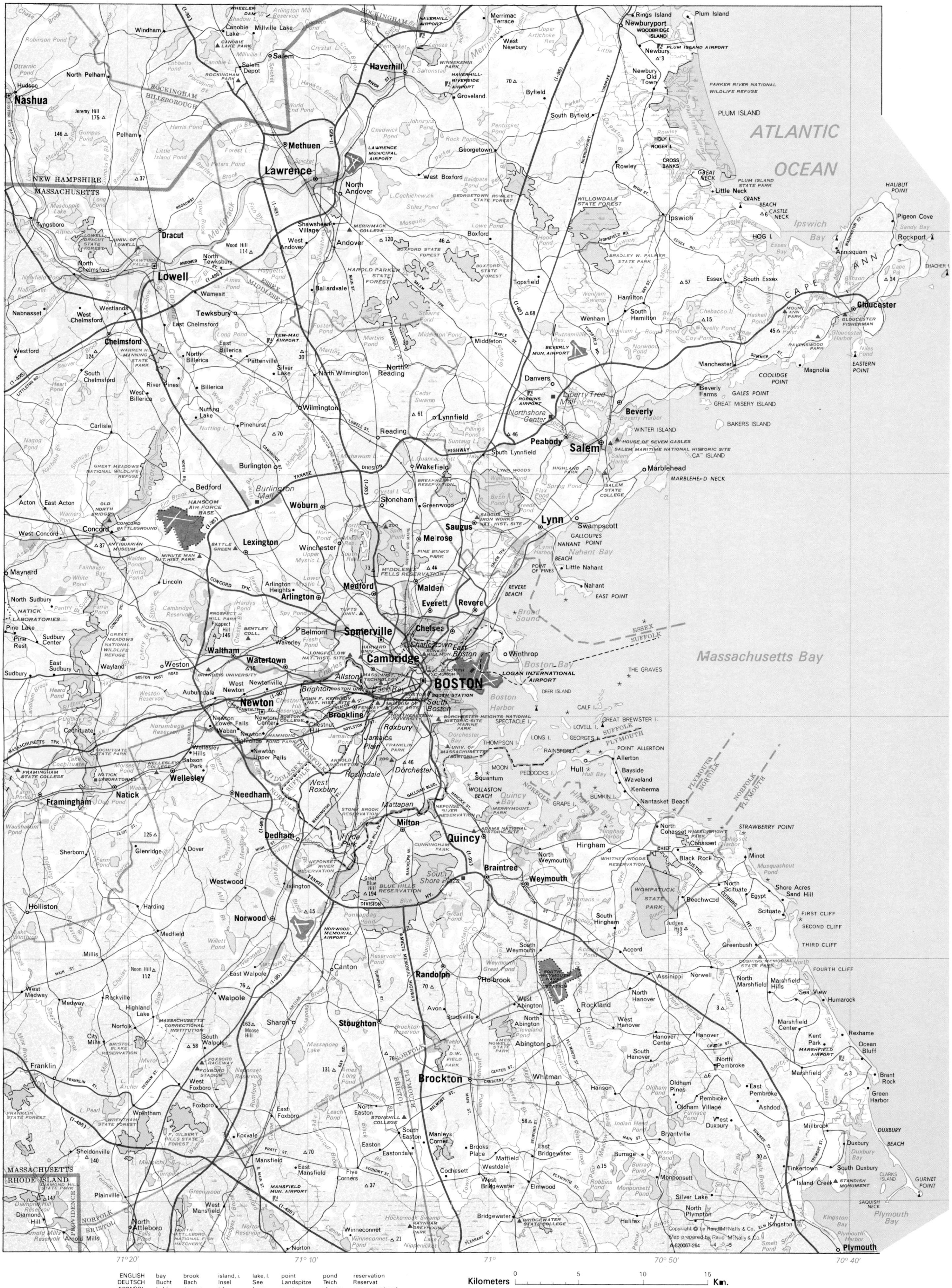
ATLANTIC OCEAN
Massachusetts Bay
BOSTON
Cambridge
Somerville
Lowell
Lawrence
Haverhill
Nashua
Salem
Lynn
Quincy
Brockton
Newton
Waltham
Gloucester
Plymouth
Newburyport
Beverly
Peabody
Framingham
Lexington
Concord
Braintree
Weymouth
Dedham
Norwood
Medford
Malden
Everett
Revere
Chelsea
Winthrop
Hull
Marblehead
Ipswich
Andover
Methuen
NEW HAMPSHIRE
MASSACHUSETTS
RHODE ISLAND
CAPE ANN
LOGAN INTERNATIONAL AIRPORT
Copyright © by Rand McNally & Co.
Map prepared by Rand McNally & Co.
A-520067-264

| ENGLISH | bay | brook | island, i. | lake, l. | point | pond | reservation |
|---|---|---|---|---|---|---|---|
| DEUTSCH | Bucht | Bach | Insel | See | Landspitze | Teich | Reservat |
| ESPAÑOL | bahía | arroyo | isla | lago | punta | charca | parque nacional |
| FRANÇAIS | baie | ruisseau | île | lac | pointe | étang | réservation |
| PORTUGUÊS | baía | arroio | ilha | lago | ponta | lagoa | parque nacional |

Kilometers 0 5 10 15 Km.
Statute Miles 0 5 10 15 Mi.

Scale 1:300,000

One centimeter represents 3 kilometers.
One inch represents approximately 4.7 miles.

| ENGLISH | DEUTSCH | ESPAÑOL | FRANÇAIS | PORTUGUES |
|---|---|---|---|---|
| airport | Flughafen | aeropuerto | aéroport | aeroporto |
| bridge | Brücke | puente | pont | ponte |
| creek, cr. | Bach | riachuelo | crique | riacho |
| island, i. | Insel | isla | île | ilha |
| park | Park | parque | parc | parque |
| point | Landspitze | punta | pointe | ponta |
| run | Bach | arroyo | ruisseau | córrego |
| university | Universität | universidad | université | universidade |

Kilometers 0 5 10 15 Km.
Statute Miles 0 5 10 15 Mi.

Scale 1:300,000
One centimeter represents 3 kilometers.
One inch represents approximately 4.7 miles.

b

BALTIMORE
Towson
Parkville
Catonsville
Dundalk
Essex
Middle River
Columbia
Chesapeake Bay


c

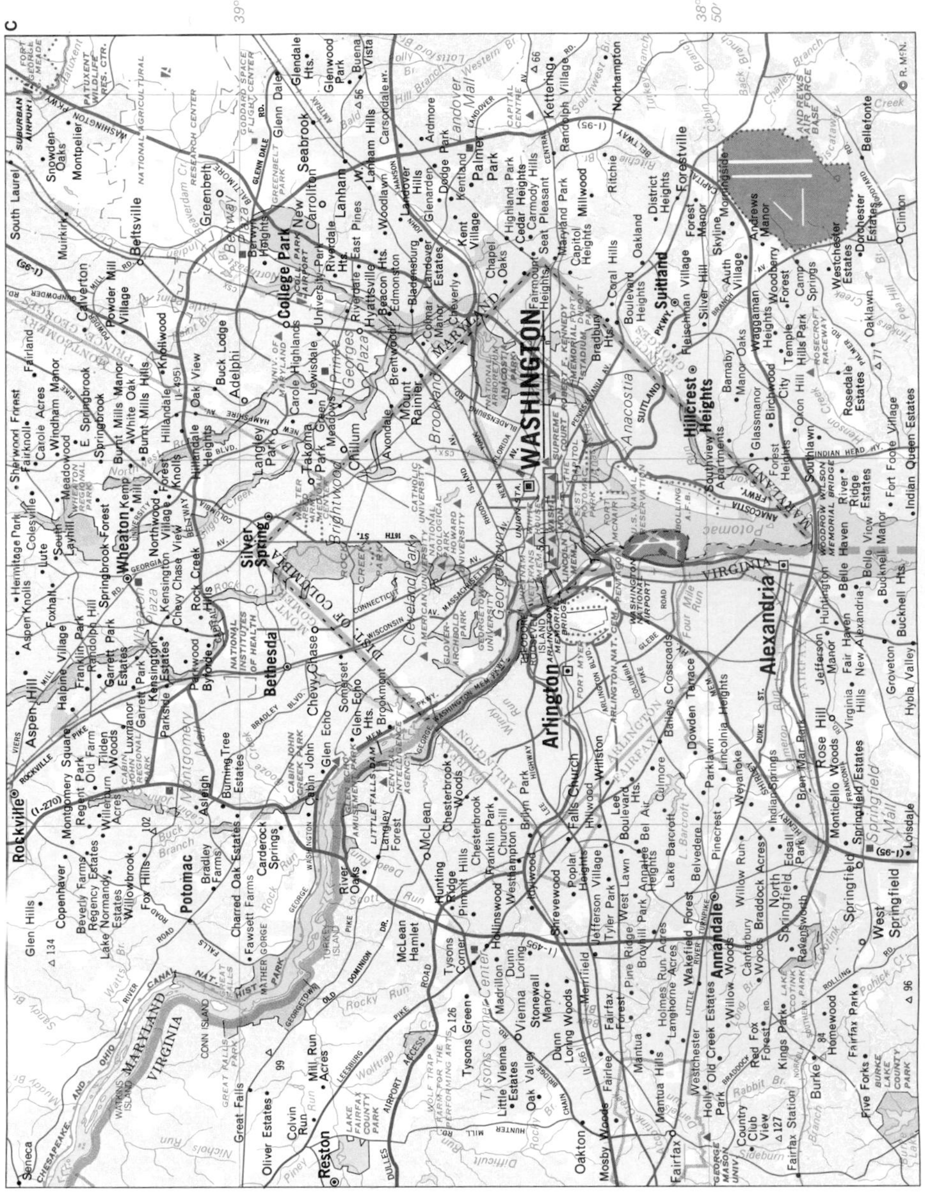

WASHINGTON
Arlington
Alexandria
Silver Spring
Bethesda
Rockville
Wheaton
College Park
Potomac
Annandale


a

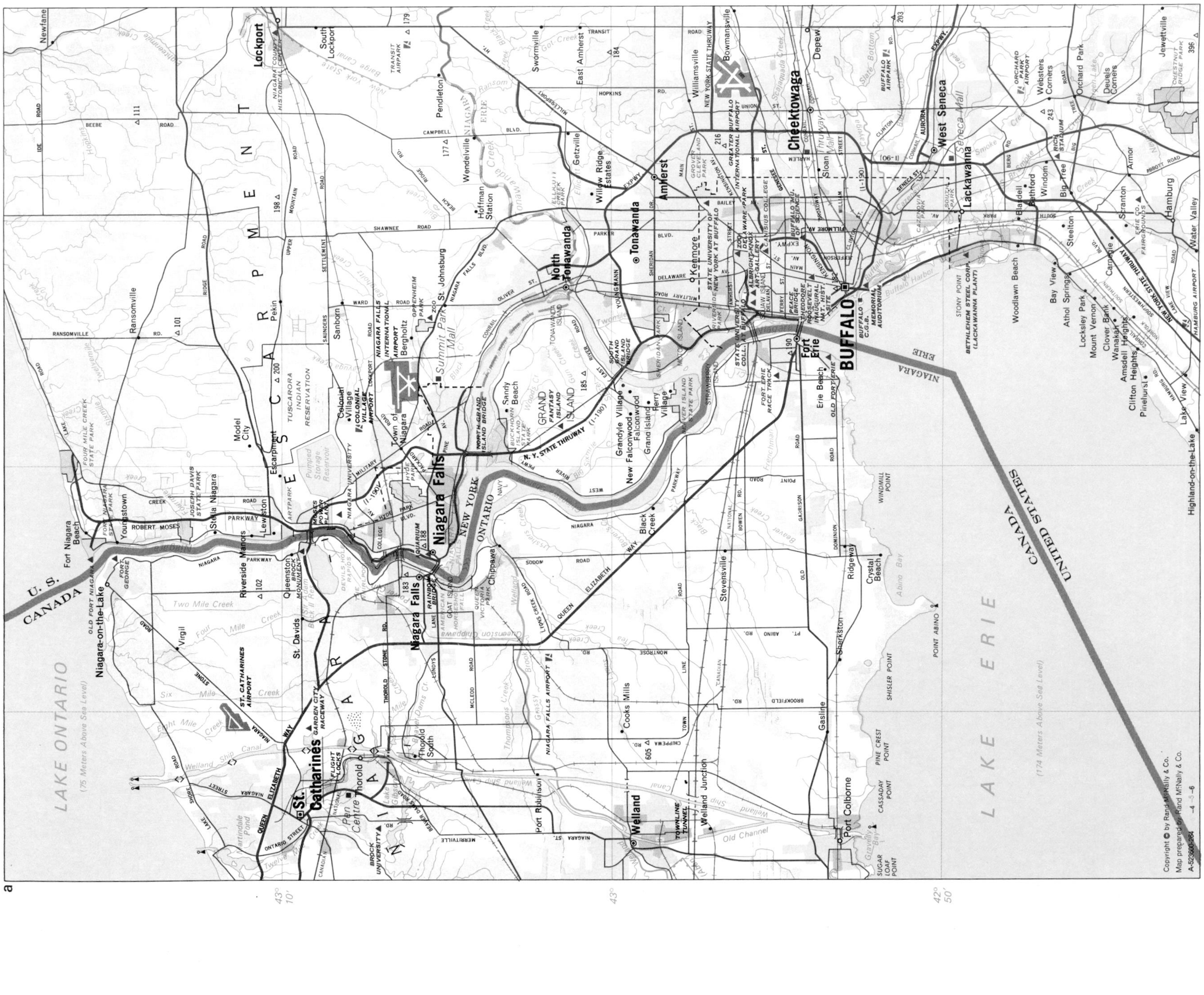

BUFFALO
Niagara Falls
St. Catharines
Lockport
Tonawanda
North Tonawanda
Cheektowaga
Lackawanna
Welland
LAKE ONTARIO
LAKE ERIE
CANADA
UNITED STATES
Copyright © by Rand McNally & Co.

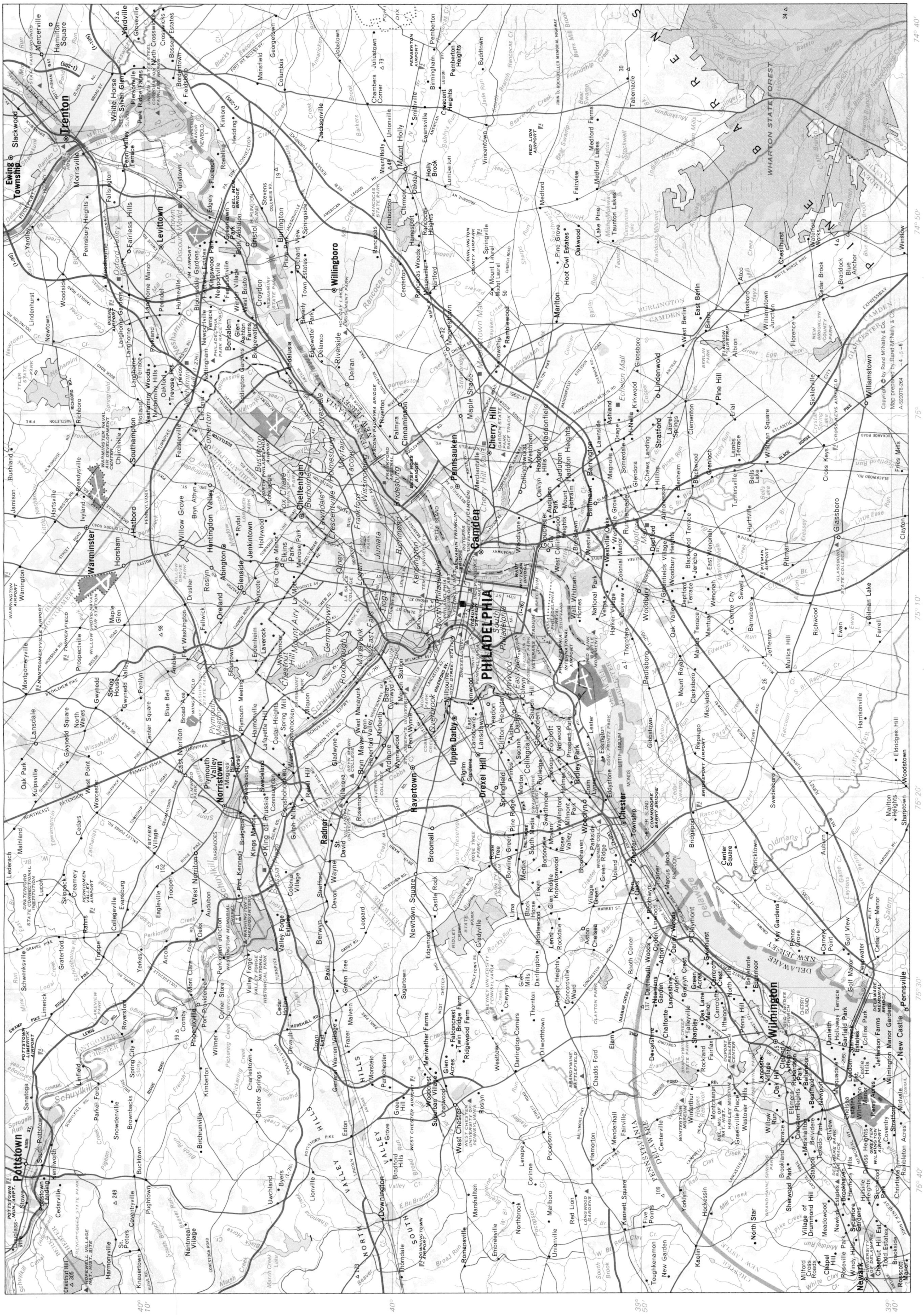

Scale 1:300,000

Kilometers 0 5 10 15

Statute Miles 0 5 10 15

One centimeter represents 3 kilometers.
One inch represents approximately 4.7 miles.

| | | | | | | | |
|---|---|---|---|---|---|---|---|
| ENGLISH | airport | bridge | college | creek, cr. | island, i. | lake, l. | run | state park |
| DEUTSCH | Flughafen | Brücke | College | Bach | Insel | See | Bach | Staatspark |
| ESPAÑOL | aeropuerto | puente | escuela | riachuelo | isla | lago | arroyo | parque del estado |
| FRANÇAIS | aéroport | pont | collége | crique | île | lac | ruisseau | parc régional |
| PORTUGUÊS | aeroporto | ponte | escola | riacho | ilha | lago | córrego | parque estadual |

a

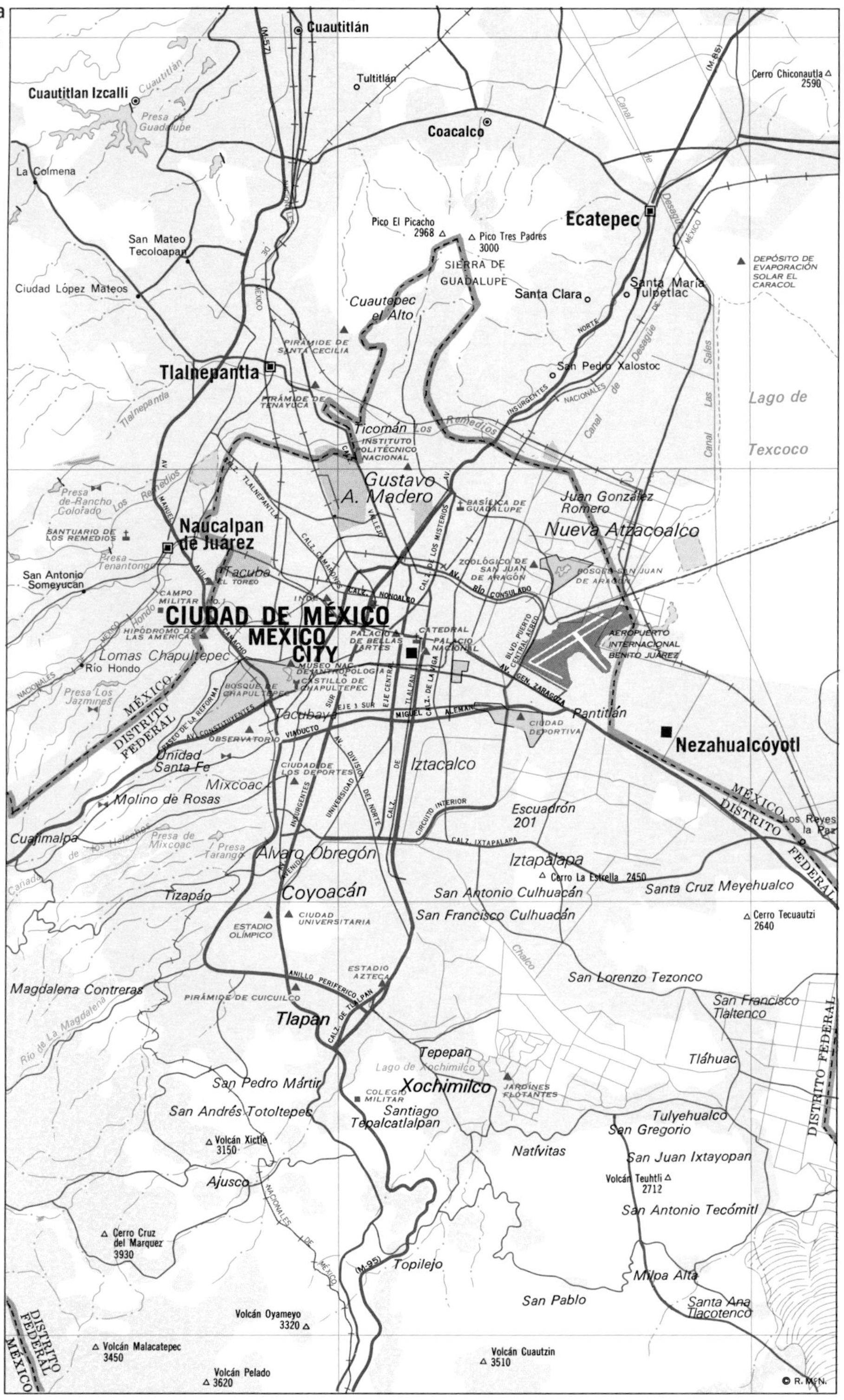
99° 10′
99°
19° 40′
19° 30′
19° 20′
19° 10′
Cuautitlán
Cuautitlan Izcalli
Tultitlán
Coacalco
La Colmena
San Mateo Tecoloapan
Ciudad López Mateos
Ecatepec
Sierra de Guadalupe
Cuautepec el Alto
Santa Clara
Santa María Tulpetlac
San Pedro Xalostoc
Tlalnepantla
Lago de Texcoco
Ticomán
Gustavo A. Madero
Juan González Romero
Nueva Atzacoalco
Naucalpan de Juárez
San Antonio Someyucan
CIUDAD DE MÉXICO
MEXICO CITY
Lomas Chapultepec
Río Hondo
Tacubaya
Pantitlán
Nezahualcóyotl
Unidad Santa Fe
Mixcoac
Iztacalco
Molino de Rosas
Escuadrón 201
Cuajimalpa
Álvaro Obregón
Iztapalapa
Santa Cruz Meyehualco
Tizapán
Coyoacán
San Antonio Culhuacán
San Francisco Culhuacán
Magdalena Contreras
San Lorenzo Tezonco
Tlalpan
San Francisco Tlaltenco
Tepepan
Tláhuac
Xochimilco
San Pedro Mártir
San Andrés Totoltepec
Santiago Tepalcatlalpan
Tulyehualco
San Gregorio
Nativitas
San Juan Ixtayopan
Ajusco
San Antonio Tecómitl
Topilejo
Milpa Alta
San Pablo
Santa Ana Tlacotenco
DISTRITO FEDERAL
MÉXICO

b

82° 30′
82° 20′
23° 10′
23°
GULF OF MEXICO
LA HABANA
HAVANA
Cojímar
Casablanca
Regla
Guanabacoa
Vedado
Miramar
Playa
Marianao
Lawton
San Luis
Mantilla
El Calvario
Santa Fé
Playa Baracoa
Los Pinos
Arroyo Naranjo
Cotorro
Punta Brava
Calabazar
Bauta
Santiago de las Vegas
CIUDAD DE LA HABANA
Laguna de Ariguanabo
Bejucal
Cuatro Caminos

c

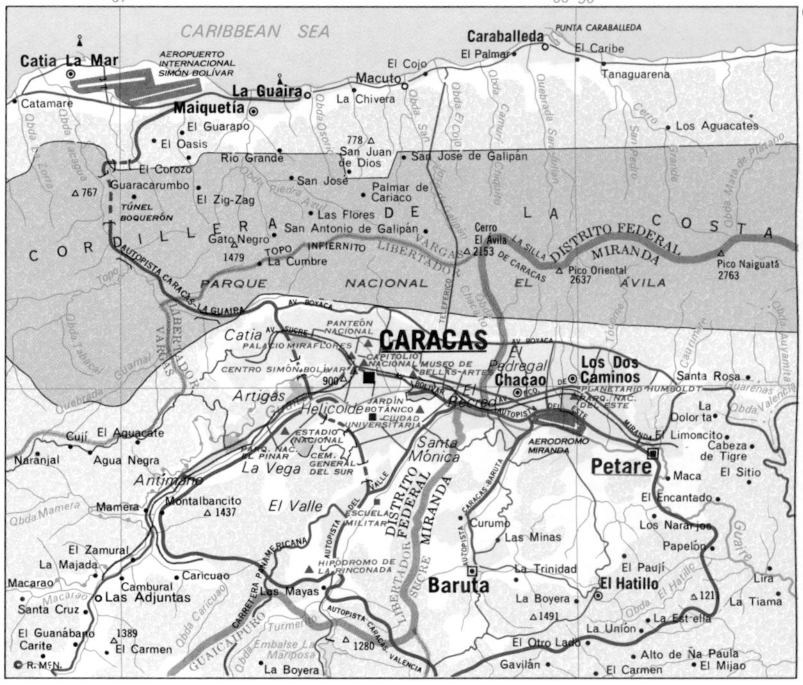
67°
66° 50′
10° 30′
CARIBBEAN SEA
Caraballeda
Catia La Mar
Macuto
La Guaira
Maiquetía
CORDILLERA DE LA COSTA
PARQUE NACIONAL EL ÁVILA
DISTRITO FEDERAL
MIRANDA
CARACAS
Catia
Los Dos Caminos
Chacao
Artigas
Petare
La Vega
El Valle
Antímano
Caricuao
Las Adjuntas
Baruta
El Hatillo

d

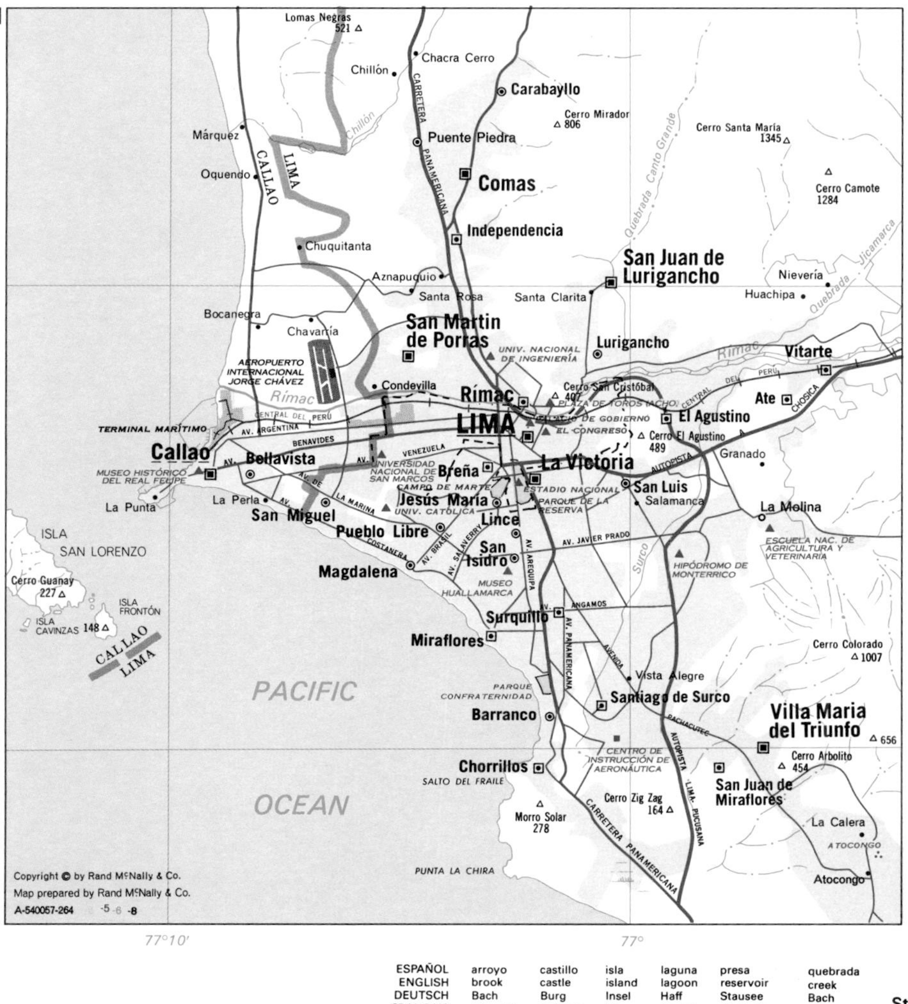
77° 10′
77°
12°
12° 10′
Carabayllo
Puente Piedra
Comas
Independencia
San Juan de Lurigancho
San Martín de Porras
Lurigancho
Vitarte
Rímac
LIMA
CALLAO
Callao
Bellavista
La Perla
San Miguel
Pueblo Libre
Jesús María
Breña
La Victoria
Lince
San Isidro
San Luis
El Agustino
Ate
La Molina
Magdalena
Surquillo
Miraflores
Santiago de Surco
Barranco
Villa María del Triunfo
Chorrillos
San Juan de Miraflores
ISLA SAN LORENZO
PACIFIC OCEAN
Copyright © by Rand McNally & Co.
Map prepared by Rand McNally & Co.
A-540057-264

e

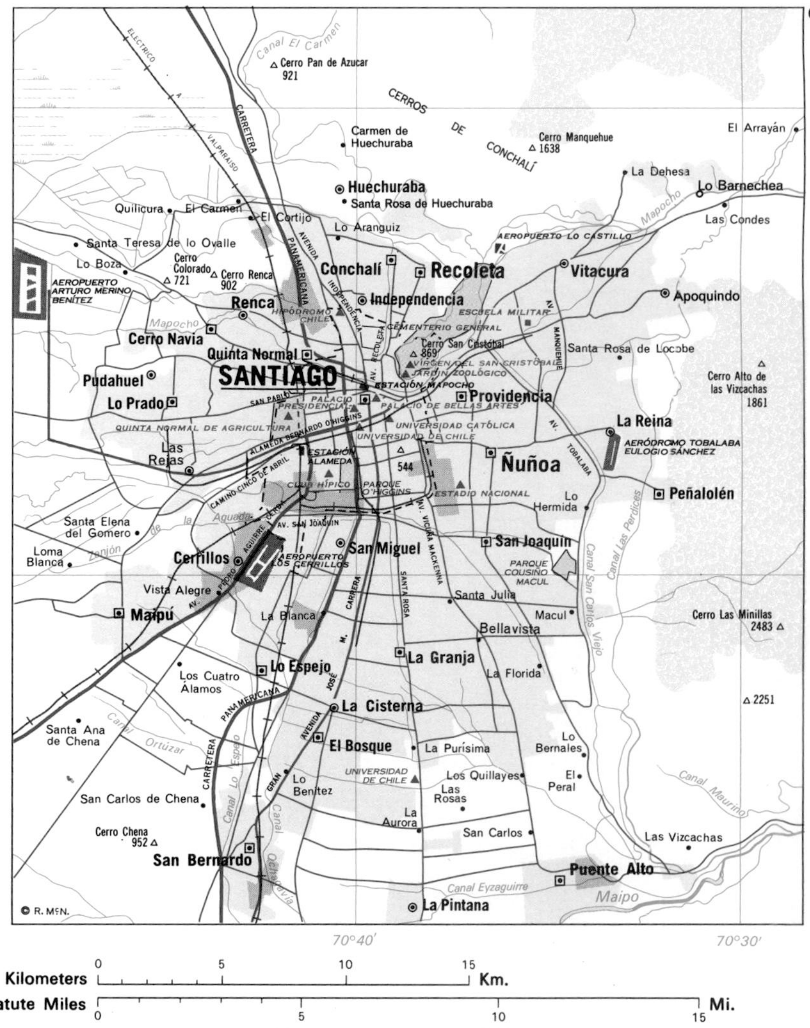
70° 40′
70° 30′
33° 20′
33° 30′
Huechuraba
Lo Barnechea
Las Condes
Conchalí
Recoleta
Vitacura
Independencia
Apoquindo
Renca
Cerro Navia
Quinta Normal
SANTIAGO
Pudahuel
Lo Prado
Providencia
La Reina
Ñuñoa
Peñalolén
San Joaquín
San Miguel
Cerrillos
Maipú
Lo Espejo
La Granja
La Cisterna
El Bosque
San Bernardo
Puente Alto
La Pintana

| ESPAÑOL | arroyo | castillo | isla | laguna | presa | quebrada |
|---|---|---|---|---|---|---|
| ENGLISH | brook | castle | island | lagoon | reservoir | creek |
| DEUTSCH | Bach | Burg | Insel | Haff | Stausee | Bach |
| FRANÇAIS | ruisseau | château | île | lagune | réservoir | crique |
| PORTUGUÊS | arroio | castelo | ilha | laguna | reservatório | riacho |

Kilometers 0 5 10 15 Km.
Statute Miles 0 5 10 15 Mi.

Scale 1:300,000
One centimeter represents 3 kilometers.
One inch represents approximately 4.7 miles.

a

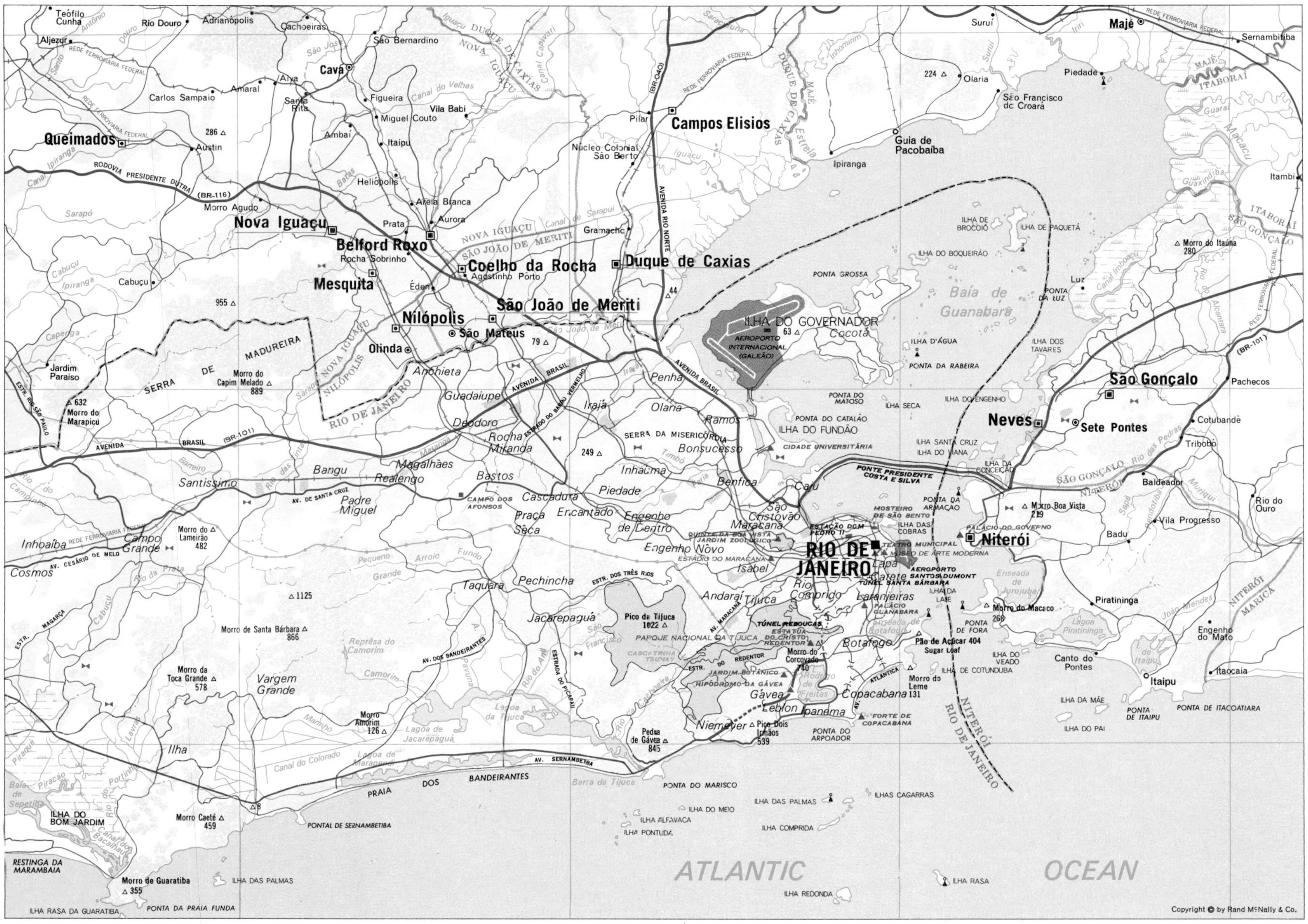
43°30'
43°20'
43°10'
43°
22° 40'
22° 50'
23°
Teófilo Cunha
Rio Douro
Adrianópolis
Cachoeiras
Aljezur
São Bernardino
Cava
Carlos Sampaio
Amaral
Santa Rita
Figueira
Vila Babi
Miguel Couto
Pilar
Campos Elísios
Queimados
Austin
Ambaí
Itaipu
Núcleo Colonial São Bento
Guia de Pacobaíba
Ipiranga
Surui
Majé
Sernambitiba
Olaria
Piedade
São Francisco de Croara
Itambi
RODOVIA PRESIDENTE DUTRA
(BR-116)
Morro Agudo
Heliópolis
Areia Branca
Aurora
Prata
Nova Iguaçu
Belford Roxo
Gramacho
Rocha Sobrinho
Coelho da Rocha
Duque de Caxias
Agostinho Porto
Mesquita
Cabuçu
Éden
São João de Meriti
Nilópolis
São Mateus
Olinda
Anchieta
Jardim Paraíso
SERRA DE MADUREIRA
Morro do Capim Melado 889
Morro do Marapicu 632
Guadalupe
Deodoro
Irajá
Penha
Olaria
Ramos
Rocha Miranda
Bonsucesso
Inhaúma
Magalhães Bastos
Realengo
Bangu
Santíssimo
Cascadura
Piedade
Padre Miguel
Campo Grande
Inhoaíba
Cosmos
Morro do Lameirão 482
Praça Sêca
Encantado
Engenho de Dentro
Engenho Novo
Maracanã
São Cristóvão
Caju
Benfica
Isabel
Taquara
Pechincha
Andaraí
Tijuca
Rio Comprido
RIO DE JANEIRO
Lapa
Catete
Laranjeiras
Botafogo
Jacarepaguá
Pico da Tijuca 1022
Morro de Santa Bárbara 866
Morro da Toca Grande 578
Vargem Grande
Gávea
Leblon
Ipanema
Copacabana
Niemeyer
Pico Dois Irmãos 539
Pedra da Gávea 845
Morro Amorim 126
Ilha
PRAIA DOS BANDEIRANTES
Baía de Sepetiba
ILHA DO BOM JARDIM
Morro Caeté 459
PONTAL DE SERNAMBETIBA
RESTINGA DA MARAMBAIA
Morro de Guaratiba 355
ILHA RASA DA GUARATIBA
PONTA DA PRAIA FUNDA
ILHA DAS PALMAS
PONTA DO MARISCO
ILHA DO MEIO
ILHA ALFAVACA
ILHA PONTUDA
ILHA COMPRIDA
ILHAS CAGARRAS
ILHA REDONDA
ILHA RASA
ATLANTIC OCEAN
ILHA DO GOVERNADOR
AEROPORTO INTERNACIONAL (GALEÃO)
Cocotá
ILHA DO FUNDÃO
CIDADE UNIVERSITÁRIA
PONTE PRESIDENTE COSTA E SILVA
Baía de Guanabara
ILHA DE PAQUETÁ
ILHA DO BOQUEIRÃO
PONTA GROSSA
ILHA D'ÁGUA
PONTA DA RABEIRA
ILHA DOS TAVARES
Luz
PONTA DA LUZ
Neves
Sete Pontes
São Gonçalo
Pachecos
Cotubande
Tribobó
Baldeador
Rio do Ouro
Vila Progresso
Badu
Niterói
Morro Boa Vista 219
Pão de Açúcar 404
Sugar Loaf
Morro do Leme 131
PONTA DO ARPOADOR
Piratininga
Engenho do Mato
Canto do Pontes
Itaipu
Itacoaiara
PONTA DE ITACOATIARA
ILHA DA MÃE
ILHA DO PAI
Morro do Itaúna 280
NITERÓI RIO DE JANEIRO
Copyright © by Rand McNally & Co.

b

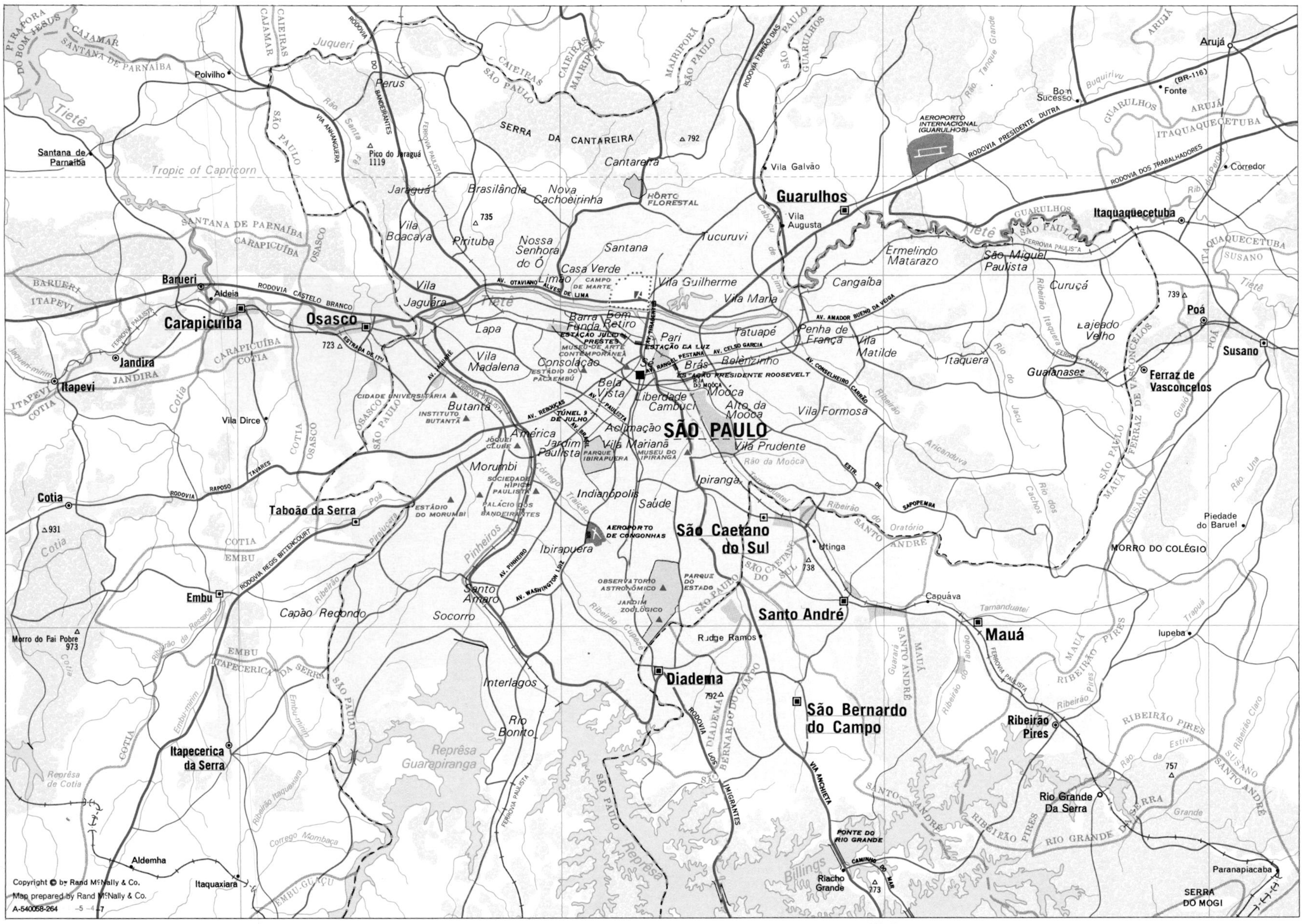
Polvilho
Perus
Pico do Jaraguá 1119
SERRA DA CANTAREIRA
792
Cantareira
Santana de Parnaíba
Tropic of Capricorn
Jaraguá
Brasilândia
Nova Cachoeirinha
HÔRTO FLORESTAL
Vila Galvão
Guarulhos
Vila Augusta
AEROPORTO INTERNACIONAL (GUARULHOS)
Arujá
Bom Sucesso
Fonte
Corredor
Itaquaquecetuba
Vila Boaçava
Pirituba
735
Nossa Senhora do Ó
Santana
Tucuruvi
Ermelino Matarazo
São Miguel Paulista
Barueri
Aldeia
Carapicuíba
Osasco
723
Vila Jaguara
Casa Verde
Vila Guilherme
Vila Maria
Cangaíba
Curuçá
739
Poá
Susano
Lapa
Barra Funda
Bom Retiro
Pari
Tatuapé
Penha de França
Vila Matilde
Lajeado Velho
Itaquera
Guaianases
Ferraz de Vasconcelos
Jandira
Itapevi
Vila Madalena
Consolação
Bela Vista
Brás
Belenzinho
CIDADE UNIVERSITÁRIA
Butantã
Liberdade
Mooca
Cambuci
Alto da Mooca
Vila Formosa
Vila Dirce
América
Jardim Paulista
Aclimação
SÃO PAULO
Vila Mariana
Vila Prudente
Morumbi
Ipiranga
Cotia
931
Taboão da Serra
Indianópolis
Saúde
São Caetano do Sul
Utinga
Piedade do Baruel
MORRO DO COLÉGIO
AEROPORTO DE CONGONHAS
Ibirapuera
Embu
Capão Redondo
Santo Amaro
Socorro
738
Santo André
Capuava
Mauá
Iupeba
Morro do Fai Pobre 973
Rudge Ramos
Diadema
792
São Bernardo do Campo
Interlagos
Rio Bonito
Ribeirão Pires
Itapecerica da Serra
Represa Guarapiranga
757
Rio Grande da Serra
Aldemha
Itaquaxiara
Riacho Grande
773
Paranapiacaba
SERRA DO MOGI
Billings
46°50'
46°40'
46°30'
46°20'
23° 30'
23° 40'
Copyright © by Rand McNally & Co.
Map prepared by Rand McNally & Co.
A-540058-264 -5-4-7

| PORTUGUÊS | ilha | lagoa, l. | morro | ponta | reservatório | ribeirão, rão. |
|---|---|---|---|---|---|---|
| ENGLISH | island | lagoon | hill | point | reservoir | creek |
| DEUTSCH | Insel | Haff | Hügel | Landspitze | Stausee | Bach |
| ESPAÑOL | isla | laguna | colina | punta | embalse | riachuelo |
| FRANÇAIS | île | lagune | colline | pointe | réservoir | crique |

Kilometers 0 5 10 15 Km.

Statute Miles 0 5 10 15 Mi.

Scale 1:300,000

One centimeter represents 3 kilometers.

One inch represents approximately 4.7 miles.

| Kilometers | 0 | 5 | 10 | 15 Km. |
| --- | --- | --- | --- | --- |
| Statute Miles | 0 | 5 | 10 | 15 Mi. |

Scale 1:300,000

One centimeter represents 3 kilometers.
One inch represents approximately 4.7 miles.

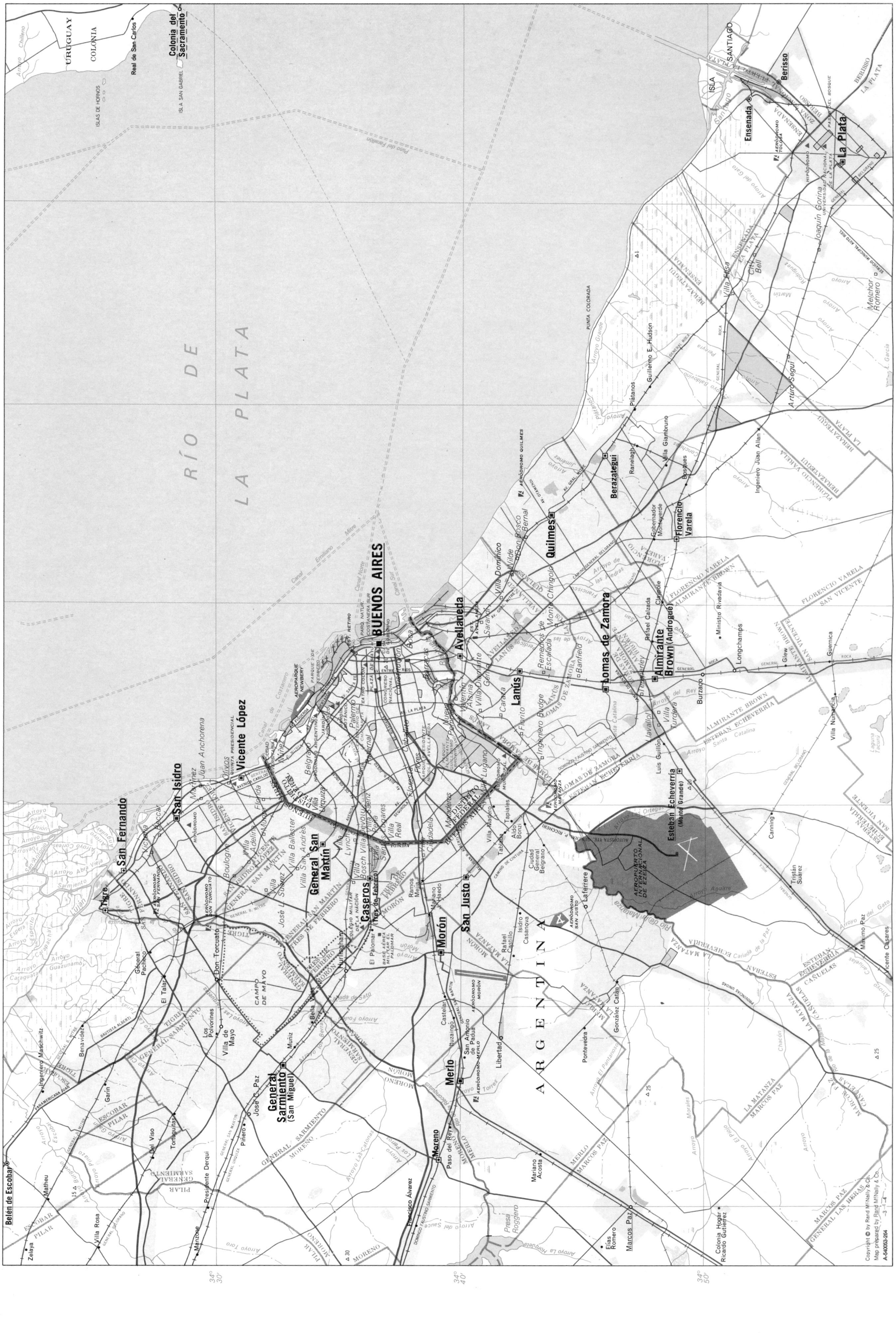
RÍO DE LA PLATA
URUGUAY
COLONIA
Colonia del Sacramento
Real de San Carlos
ISLA SAN GABRIEL
ISLAS DE HORNOS
ARGENTINA
BUENOS AIRES
San Isidro
Vicente López
San Fernando
Tigre
General San Martín
Caseros
Morón
San Justo
Merlo
Moreno
General Sarmiento (San Miguel)
Avellaneda
Lanús
Lomas de Zamora
Almirante Brown (Adrogué)
Esteban Echeverría (Monte Grande)
Quilmes
Florencio Varela
Berazategui
Ensenada
Berisso
La Plata
Belén de Escobar
Copyright © by Rand McNally & Co.
Map prepared by Rand McNally & Co.

| ESPAÑOL | aeropuerto | arroyo | estación | isla | parque | punta |
| --- | --- | --- | --- | --- | --- | --- |
| ENGLISH | airport | brook | station | island | park | point |
| DEUTSCH | Flughafen | Bach | Bahnhof | Insel | Park | Landspitze |
| FRANÇAIS | aéroport | ruisseau | gare | île | parc | pointe |
| PORTUGUÊS | aeroporto | arroio | estação | ilha | parque | ponta |

THE MAP FORM column of the glossary lists in alphabetical order the geographical terms, including any abbreviations, that appear on the maps. Terms preceded by a hyphen are those which commonly appear as endings in map names (for example, -san in Fuji-san, -älven in Dalälven). The languages of the terms are identified by abbreviations in *italics* (see Abbreviations of Language Names below). The glossary provides the English, German, Spanish, French, and Portuguese equivalent for each term.

As a rule, the translations were made from the map form to English, then from English into the other four languages. Since the glossary terms and translations refer to specific map features, some may vary from the customary dictionary definitions of the terms.

IN DER SPALTE "Geographische Begriffe" werden alle Begriffe und Abkürzungen in alphabetischer Ordnung aufgeführt, die in den Karten erscheinen. Begriffe mit vorgesetztem Bindestrich erscheinen normalerweise als Wortendungen in Kartennamen (z.B. -san in Fuji-san, -älven in Dalälven). In *Kursivschrift* sind die jeweiligen Abkürzungen angegeben für die Sprachen, in denen der Begriff wiedergegeben ist (siehe unten: Abkürzungen der Sprachen). Das Verzeichnis gibt für jeden Begriff den entsprechenden Ausdruck in englisch, deutsch, spanisch, französisch, und portugiesisch.

In der Regel wurde der Begriff in der Karte ins Englische übersetzt und dann vom Englischen in die vier anderen Sprachen. Da die Begriffe und Übersetzungen sich auf bestimmte Objekte in der Karte beziehen, können einige von ihnen von den in den üblichen Wörterbüchern aufgeführten Begriffsbestimmungen abweichen.

LOS TÉRMINOS GEOGRÁFICOS que aparecen en los mapas, incluyendo abreviaciones, son presentados en la columna de Términos Geográficas del Glosario, en orden alfabético. Los términos que están precedidos por un guión aparecen frecuentemente como terminaciones de los nombres en los mapas (por ejemplo, -san en Fuji-san, -älvan en Dalälven). Los idiomas que representan los términos están identificados por medio de abreviaciones en *cursiva* (véase abajo, Abreviaciones de los Idiomas Extranjeros). El Glosario provee el equivalente para cada término en inglés, alemán, español, francés y portugués.

Generalmente las traducciones están hechas de las formas originales de la terminología de los mapas que aparecen primero en inglés, y luego se traducen a las otras cuatro lenguas. Algunos términos y traducciones pueden aparecer distintas a las usadas en los diccionarios generales porque se refieren a los rasgos particulares de los mapas.

LE GLOSSAIRE cite par ordre alphabétique les termes géographiques et les abréviations utilisées. Les mots précédés d'un tiret sont des suffixes (par exemple, -san dans Fuji-san, -älven dans Dalälven). La langue d'origine du nom cité est indiquée par une abréviation en *italique* (voir Abréviations des noms de langues, ci-dessous). Le Glossaire donne chaque nom en anglais, allemand, espagnol, français, et portugais.

En général, les termes géographiques des cartes ont d'abord été traduits en anglais, puis de l'anglais dans les quatre autres langues. Les définitions de certains termes sont adaptées aux particularités de l'Atlas. Il peut arriver qu'elles diffèrent des définitions habituelles données par les dictionnaires.

A COLUNA 'TERMINOLOGIA', do *Glossário*, contém todos os termos geográficos que figuram nos mapas, em ordem alfabética e com as respectivas abreviações. Os termos precedidos por um hífen são os que freqüentemente aparecem nos mapas como sufixos de nomes tais como *-san* (em Fuji-san), *-älven* (em Dalälven). As línguas em que os termos são expressos estão identificadas por abreviações em *grifo* (ver abaixo, 'Abreviações das línguas estrangeiras'). O Glossário fornece o equivalente de cada termo em inglês, alemão, espanhol, português e francês.

De modo geral, as traduções foram feitas das formas originais da terminologia usada nos mapas para o inglês, e, em seguida, do inglês para as outras quatro línguas. Uma vez que os termos geográficos e traduções do *Glossário* referem-se a acidentes específicos de cada mapa, é possível que algumas definições sejam diferentes das consignadas nos dicionários gerais das línguas.

## Abbreviations of Language Names / Abkürzungen der Nationalsprachen / Abreviaciones de los Idiomas Extranjeros
## Abréviations des Noms de Langues / Abreviações dos Idiomas Estrangeiros

| | ENGLISH | DEUTSCH | ESPAÑOL | FRANCAIS | PORTUGUÊS |
|---|---|---|---|---|---|
| **Afk.** | Afrikaans | Afrikaans | Africano | Afrikaans | Afrikaans |
| **Alb.** | Albanian | Albanisch | Albanesa | Albanais | Albanês |
| **Ara.** | Arabic | Arabisch | Árabe | Arabe | Árabe |
| **Ber.** | Berber | Berberisch | Bereber | Berbère | Berbere |
| **Ben.** | Bengali | Bengali | Bengali | Bengali | Bengali |
| **Blg.** | Bulgarian | Bulgarisch | Búlgaro | Bulgare | Búlgaro |
| **Bur.** | Burmese | Burmanisch | Birmano | Birman | Birmanês |
| **Cat.** | Catalan | Katalanisch | Catalán | Catalan | Catalão |
| **Cbd.** | Cambodian | Kambodschanisch | Camboyano | Cambodgien | Cambojano |
| **Ch.** | Chinese | Chinesisch | Chino | Chinois | Chinês |
| **Czech** | Czech | Tschechisch | Checo | Tchèque | Tcheco |
| **Dan.** | Danish | Dänisch | Danés | Danois | Dinamarquês |
| **Du.** | Dutch | Niederländisch | Holandés | Néerlandais | Holandês |
| **Eng.** | English | Englisch | Inglés | Anglais | Inglês |
| **Est.** | Estonian | Estnisch | Estonio | Esthonien | Estoniano |
| **Finn.** | Finnish | Finnisch | Finés | Finnois | Finlandês |
| **Flm.** | Flemish | Flämisch | Flamenco | Flamand | Flamengo |
| **Fr.** | French | Französisch | Francés | Français | Francês |
| **Gae.** | Gaelic | Gälisch | Gaélico | Gaélique | Gaélico |
| **Ger.** | German | Deutsch | Alemán | Allemand | Alemão |
| **Gr.** | Greek | Griechisch | Griego | Grec | Grego |
| **Hau.** | Hausa | Haussa | Hausa | Haoussa | Haussa |
| **Heb.** | Hebrew | Hebräisch | Hebreo | Hébreu | Hebraico |
| **Hung.** | Hungarian | Ungarisch | Húngaro | Hongrois | Húngaro |
| **Ice.** | Icelandic | Isländisch | Islandés | Islandais | Islandês |
| **Indon.** | Indonesian | Indonesisch | Indonesio | Indonésien | Indonésio |
| **It.** | Italian | Italienisch | Italiano | Italien | Italiano |
| **Jap.** | Japanese | Japanisch | Japonés | Japonais | Japonês |
| **Kor.** | Korean | Koreanisch | Coreano | Coréen | Coreano |
| **Lao.** | Laotian | Laotisch | Laosiano | Laotien | Laosiano |
| **Lapp.** | Lappish | Lappisch | Lapón | Lapon | Lapão |
| **Latv.** | Latvian | Lettisch | Letón | Letton | Letão |
| **Lith.** | Lithuanian | Litauisch | Lituano | Lithuanien | Lituano |
| **Mal.** | Malay | Malaiisch | Malayo | Malais | Malaio |
| **Mong.** | Mongolian | Mongolisch | Mogol | Mongol | Mongol |
| **Nor.** | Norwegian | Norwegisch | Norvego | Norvégien | Norueguês |
| **Pas.** | Pashto | Paschtu | Pushtu | Pachtou | Pachtu |
| **Per.** | Persian | Persisch | Persa | Persan | Persa |
| **Pol.** | Polish | Polnisch | Polaco | Polonais | Polonês |
| **Poly.** | Polynesian | Polynesisch | Polinesio | Polynésien | Polinésio |
| **Port.** | Portuguese | Portugiesisch | Portugués | Portugais | Português |
| **Rom.** | Romanian | Rumänisch | Rumano | Roumain | Romeno |
| **Rus.** | Russian | Russisch | Ruso | Russe | Russo |
| **S./C.** | Serbo-Croatian | Serbokroatisch | Servio-croata | Serbo-croate | Servo-croata |
| **Sin.** | Sinhalese | Singhalesisch | Cingalés | Cinghalais | Cingalês |
| **Slo.** | Slovak | Slowakisch | Eslovaco | Slovaque | Eslovaco |
| **Sp.** | Spanish | Spanisch | Español | Espagnol | Espanhol |
| **Swe.** | Swedish | Schwedisch | Sueco | Suédois | Sueco |
| **Thai** | Thai | Thai | Tai | Thaï | Tailandês |
| **Tib.** | Tibetan | Tibetisch | Tibetano | Tibétain | Tibetano |
| **Tur.** | Turkish | Türkisch | Turco | Turc | Turco |
| **Ukr.** | Ukrainian | Ukrainisch | Ucranio | Ukrainien | Ucraniano |
| **Viet.** | Vietnamese | Vietnamesisch | Vietnamita | Vietnamien | Vietnamita |
| **Welsh** | Welsh | Walisisch | Galés | Gallois | Galês |

| ENGLISH | DEUTSCH | Map Form<br>Geographische Begriffe<br>Términos Geográficos<br>Termes Géographiques<br>Termos Geográficos | ESPAÑOL | FRANCAIS | PORTUGUÊS |
|---|---|---|---|---|---|
| | | | **A** | | |
| river | Fluss | **-å** *Dan., Nor., Swe.* | río | rivière | rio |
| brook | Bach | **a., arroyo** *Sp.* | arroyo | ruisseau | córrego |
| river | Fluss | **āb** *Per.* | río | rivière | rio |
| army base | Heeres-stützpunkt | **a.b., army base** *Eng.* | base del ejército | base d'armée | base militar |
| well | Brunnen | **ābār** *Ara.* | pozo | puits | poço |
| abbey | Abtei | **abb., abbazia** *It.* | abadía | abbaye | abadia |
| abbey | Abtei | **abbaye** *Fr.* | abadía | abbaye | abadia |
| abbey | Abtei | **abbazia** *It.* | abadía | abbaye | abadia |
| abbey | Abtei | **abbey** *Eng.* | abadía | abbaye | abadia |
| aboriginal reserve | Eingeborenen-schutzgebiet | **aboriginal reserve** *Eng.* | zona de aborígenes | réserve d'indigènes | reserva indígena |
| abbey | Abtei | **Abtei** *Ger.* | abadía | abbaye | abadia |
| ditch | Graben | **acequia** *Sp.* | acequia | fossé | fosso |
| reservoir | Stausee | **ačude** *Port.* | embalse | réservoir | açude |
| island(s) | Insel(n) | **ada(lar)** *Tur.* | isla(s) | île(s) | ilha(s) |
| island | Insel | **adası** *Tur.* | isla | île | ilha |
| mountains | Berge | **adrar** *Ber.* | montañas | montagnes | montanhas |
| Atomic Energy Commission | Atomenergie-kommission | **A.E.C., Atomic Energy Commission** *Eng.* | Comisión de Energía Atomica | Commission de l'Énergie Atomique | Comissão de Energia Atômica |
| airport | Flughafen | **aérd., aérodrome** *Fr.* | aeródromo | aérodrome | aeródromo |
| airport | Flughafen | **aeródromo** *Port., Sp.* | aeródromo | aérodrome | aeródromo |
| airport | Flughafen | **aeroparque** *Sp.* | aeroparque | aéroport | aeroporto |
| airport | Flughafen | **aéroport** *Fr.* | aeropuerto | aéroport | aeroporto |
| airport | Flughafen | **aeroporto** *It., Port.* | aeropuerto | aéroport | aeroporto |
| airport | Flughafen | **aeropuerto** *Sp.* | aeropuerto | aéroport | aeroporto |
| air force base | Luftwaffen-stützpunkt | **a.f.b., air force base** *Eng.* | base aeronáutica | base aérienne | base aérea |
| wadi | Wadi | **ahzar** *Ara.* | uadi | wadi | uádi |
| peak | Gipfel | **aiguille** *Fr.* | pico | aiguille | pico |
| air base | Luftstützpunkt | **air base** *Eng.* | base aérea | base aérienne | base aérea |
| airfield | Flugplatz | **airfield** *Eng.* | camp de aviación | aérodrome | campo de pouso |
| air force base | Luftwaffen-stützpunkt | **air force base** *Eng.* | base aeronáutica | base aérienne | base aérea |
| airport | Flughafen | **airport** *Eng.* | aeropuerto | aéroport | aeroporto |
| cape | Kap | **ákra, akrotírion** *Gr.* | cabo | cap | cabo |
| hill | Hügel | **'alam, 'alāmat** *Ara.* | colina | colline | colina |
| avenue | Allee | **alameda** *Sp.* | alameda | avenue | avenida |
| alps | Alpen | **alpes** *Fr.* | alpes | alpes | alpes |
| alps | Alpen | **alpi** *It.* | alpes | alpes | alpes |
| mountains, hills | Berge, Hügel | **altos** *Sp.* | altos | montagnes, collines | montanhas, colinas |
| river | Fluss | **-älv,-älven** *Swe.* | río | rivière | rio |
| amusement park | Vergnügungs-park | **amusement park** *Eng.* | parque de diversiones | parc récréatif | parque de diversões |
| river | Fluss | **-ån** *Swe.* | río | rivière | rio |
| anchorage | Ankerplatz | **anchorage** *Eng.* | ancladero | ancrage | ancoradouro |
| bay | Bucht | **angra** *Sp.* | angra | baie | baía |
| cove | kleine Bucht | **anse** *Fr.* | ensenada | anse | enseada |
| bay | Bucht | **ao** *Ch.* | bahía | baie | baía |
| bay | Bucht | **ao** *Thai* | bahía | baie | baía |
| acueduct | Aquädukt | **aqueduc** *Fr.* | acueducto | aqueduc | aqueduto |
| aqueduct | Aquädukt | **aqueduct** *Eng.* | acueducto | aqueduc | aqueduto |
| archipelago | Archipel | **archipel** *Fr.* | archipiélago | archipel | arquipélago |
| archipelago | Archipel | **archipelag** *Rus.* | archipiélago | archipel | arquipélago |
| archipelago | Archipel | **archipelago** *Eng.* | archipiélago | archipel | arquipélago |
| archipelago | Archipel | **archipiélago** *Sp.* | archipiélago | archipel | arquipélago |
| arm | Arm | **arm** *Eng.* | brazo | bras | braço de rio |
| army base | Heeres-stützpunkt | **army base** *Eng.* | base del ejército | base d'armée | base militar |
| airport | Flughafen | **arpt., aéroport** *Fr.*<br>**aeroporto**<br>**aeropuerto**<br>**airport** | aeropuerto | aéroport | aeroporto |
| archipelago | Archipel | **arquipélago** *Port.* | archipiélago | archipel | arquipélago |
| reef | Riff | **arrecife** *Sp.* | arrecife | récif | recife |
| brook | Bach | **arroyo** *Sp.* | arroyo | ruisseau | córrego, arroio |
| hills | Hügel | **-ås,-åsen** *Swe.* | colinas | collines | colinas |
| ridge | Höhenrücken | **'assâbet** *Ara.* | sierra | crête | serra |
| atoll | Atoll | **atol** *Port.* | atolón | atoll | atol |
| atoll | Atoll | **atoll** *Eng., Fr.* | atolón | atoll | atol |
| auditorium | Auditorium | **aud., auditorium** *Eng.* | auditorio | auditorium | auditório |
| race course | Rennbahn | **autodrome** *Fr.* | autódromo | autodrome | autódromo |
| race course | Rennbahn | **autodromo** *It.* | autódromo | autodrome | autódromo |
| expressway | Autobahn | **autopista** *Sp.* | autopista | autoroute | via expressa |

| ENGLISH | DEUTSCH | Map Form / Geographische Begriffe / Términos Geográficos / Termes Géographiques / Termos Geográficos | ESPAÑOL | FRANCAIS | PORTUGUÊS |
|---|---|---|---|---|---|
| avenue | Allee | **av., avenida** *Port., Sp.* **avenue** | avenida | avenue | avenida |
| channel | Kanal | **ava** *Poly.* | canal, estrecho | canal, détroit | canal, estreito |
| avenue | Allee | **avenida** *Port., Sp.* | avenida | avenue | avenida |
| spring | Quelle | **'ayn** *Ara.* | manantial | source | manancial, fonte |

## B

| ENGLISH | DEUTSCH | Map Form | ESPAÑOL | FRANCAIS | PORTUGUÊS |
|---|---|---|---|---|---|
| bay | Bucht | **baai** *Du.* | bahía | baie | baía |
| strait | Meeresstrasse | **bab** *Ara.* | estrecho | détroit | estreito |
| brook, creek | Bach | **Bach** *Ger.* | arroyo, riachuelo | ruisseau, crique | córrego, arroio |
| hill | Hügel | **-backen** *Swe.* | colina | colline | colina |
| bay | Bucht | **badia** *Cat.* | bahía | baie | baía |
| desert | Wüste | **bādiyat** *Ara.* | desierto | désert | deserto |
| strait | Meeresstrasse | **bælt** *Dan.* | estrecho | détroit | estreito |
| bay | Bucht | **bahía** *Sp.* | bahía | baie | baía |
| inlet | Einfahrt | **bahiret** *Ara.* | abra | bras de mer | enseada, estuário |
| railroad station | Bahnhof | **Bahnhof** *Ger.* | estacíon de ferrocarril | gare | estação ferroviária |
| river, sea | Fluss, Meer | **bahr, bahr** *Ara.* | río, mar | rivière, mer | rio, mar |
| reservoir | Stausee | **baḥrat** *Ara.* | embalse | réservoir | reservatório |
| bay | Bucht | **baía** *Port.* | bahía | baie | baía |
| bay | Bucht | **baie** *Fr.* | bahía | baie | baía |
| reef, sand bar | Riff, Sandbarre | **bajo** *Sp.* | bajo | récif, banc de sable | recife, banco de areia |
| gorge | Schlucht | **balka** *Rus.* | garganta | gorge | garganta |
| dome | Kuppe | **ballon** *Fr.* | domo | ballon | domo |
| marsh | Marsch | **balta** *Rom.* | pantano | marais | pântano |
| cape | Kap | **-bana** *Jpn.* | cabo | cap | cabo |
| marsh | Marsch | **bañados** *Sp.* | bañados | marais | pântano |
| island | Insel | **-banare** *Jpn.* | isla | île | ilha |
| bank | Bank | **banco** *Sp.* | banco | banc | banco |
| peninsula | Halbinsel | **bandao** *Ch.* | península | péninsule | península |
| bank | Bank | **bank** *Eng.* | banco | banc | banco |
| shoal | Untiefe | **-banken** *Swe.* | bajo | haut-fond | escolho |
| sand bar | Sandbarre | **barra** *Sp.* | barra | banc de sable | banco de areia |
| dam | Damm | **barrage** *Fr.* | presa | barrage | represa |
| ravine | Tobel | **barranca** *Sp.* | barranca | ravin | ravina |
| air base | Luftstützpunkt | **base aérea** *Sp.* | base aérea | base aérienne | base aérea |
| basilica | Basilika | **basílica** *Sp.* | basílica | basilique | basílica |
| basilica | Basilika | **basilique** *Fr.* | basílica | basilique | basílica |
| basin | Becken | **basin** *Eng.* | cuenca | bassin | bacia |
| basin | Becken | **bassin** *Fr.* | cuenca | bassin | bacia |
| marsh | Marsch | **batakliği** *Tur.* | pantano | marais | pântano |
| river | Fluss | **batang** *Indon.* | río | rivière | rio |
| river | Fluss | **batha** *Ara.* | río | rivière | rio |
| marsh | Marsch | **bāṭlāq** *Per.* | pantano | marais | pântano |
| battlefield | Schlachtfeld | **battlefield** *Eng.* | campo de batalla | champ de bataille | campo de batalha |
| mountain | Berg | **batu** *Mal.* | montaña | montagne | montanha |
| bay | Bucht | **bay** *Eng.* | bahía | baie | baía |
| bayou | Altwasser | **bayou** *Fr., Eng.* | ensenada pantanosa | bayou | enseada pantanosa |
| beach | Strand | **beach** *Eng.* | playa | plage | praia |
| mountain | Berg | **bein, beinn** *Gae.* | montaña | montagne | montanha |
| snowcapped mountains | Schneegipfel | **belogorje** *Rus.* | nevados | montagnes neigeuses | picos nevados |
| mountain | Berg | **ben** *Gae.* | montaña | montagne | montanha |
| mountain, hill | Berg | **Berg** *Ger.* | montaña, colina | montagne, colline | montanha, colina |
| mountains | Gebirge | **-berg** *Afk.* | montañas | montagnes | montanhas |
| hill(s), mountain(s) | Hügel, Berg(e) | **-berg** *Swe.* | colina(s), montaña(s) | colline(s), montagne(s) | colina(s), montanha(s) |
| mountains | Berge | **Berge** *Ger.* | montañas | montagnes | montanhas |
| mountains | Berge | **-berge** *Afk.* | montañas | montagnes | montanhas |
| hills, mountains | Hügel, Berge | **-bergen** *Swe.* | colinas, montañas | collines, montagnes | colinas, montanhas |
| hill, mountain | Hügel, Berg | **-berget** *Swe.* | colina, montaña | colline, montagne | colina, montanha |
| upland | Bergland | **Bergland** *Ger.* | tierras altas | hautes terres | terras altas |
| battlefield | Schlachtfeld | **bfld., battlefield** *Eng.* | campo de batalla | champ de bataille | campo de batalha |
| mountain, hill | Berg | **Bg., Berg** *Ger.* | montaña, colina | montagne, colline | montanha, colina |
| bridge | Brücke | **bge., bridge** *Eng.* | puente | pont | ponte |
| bight (bay) | Bucht | **bight** *Eng.* | bahía | baie | baía, enseada |
| bill (point) | Landspitze | **bill** *Eng.* | punta | pointe | ponta |
| valley | Tal | **biq'at** *Heb.* | valle | vallée | vale |
| well | Brunnen | **bi'r** *Ara.* | pozo | puits | poço |
| lake | See | **birkat** *Ara.* | lago | lac | lago |
| mountains | Berge | **bjeshkët** *Alb.* | montañas | montagnes | montanhas |
| brook | Bach | **bk., brook** *Eng.* | arroyo | ruisseau | córrego, arroio |
| upland | Bergland | **blaenau** *Welsh* | tierras altas | hautes terres | terras altas |
| bluff(s) | Steilufer | **bluff(s)** *Eng.* | acantilado(s) | falaise(s) | falésia(s) |
| boulevard | Boulevard | **blvd., boulevard** *Fr., Eng.* | boulevar | boulevard | bulevar |
| mountain | Berg | **b'nom** *Viet.* | montaña | montagne | montanha |
| river mouth | Flussmündung | **boca** *Sp.* | boca | embouchure | foz |
| river mouth, pass | Flussmündung, Pass | **bocca** *It.* | boca, paso | embouchure, col | foz, passo |
| bay | Bucht | **bocht** *Du.* | bahía | baie | baía |
| bay | Bodden | **Bodden** *Ger.* | bahía | baie | baía |
| lake | See | **bœng** *Cbd.* | lago | lac | lago |
| bog | Moor | **bog** *Eng.* | pantano | fondrière | pântano |
| strait | Meeresstrasse | **boğazı** *Tur.* | estrecho | détroit | estreito |
| range | Gebirge | **bogd** *Mong.* | sierra | chaîne | cordilheira |
| woods | Gehölz | **bois** *Fr.* | bosque | bois | bosque |
| enclosed basin | Becken | **bolsón** *Sp.* | bolsón | bassin fermée | bacia fechada |
| forest | Wald | **bory** *Pol.* | bosque | forêt | floresta |
| forest | Wald | **bosque** *Sp.* | bosque | forêt | floresta |
| boulevard | Boulevard | **boulevard** *Fr., Eng.* | boulevar | boulevard | bulevar |
| branch | Arm | **br., branch** *Eng.* | brazo | bras | braço |
| stream distributary | Flussarm | **bratul** *Rom.* | brazo de río | bras | braço de rio |
| breakwater | Wellenbrecher | **breakwater** *Eng.* | rompeolas | brise-lames | quebra-mar |
| glacier | Gletscher | **-breen** *Nor.* | glaciar | glacier | geleira |
| bridge | Brücke | **bridge** *Eng.* | puente | pont | ponte |
| marsh | Bruch | **Bruch** *Ger.* | pantano | marais | pântano |
| bridge | Brücke | **Brücke** *Ger.* | puente | pont | ponte |
| bridge | Brücke | **brug** *Du.* | puente | pont | ponte |
| bay | Bucht | **Bucht** *Ger.* | bahía | baie | baía |
| bay | Bucht | **buchta** *Rus.* | bahía | baie | baía |
| mountain | Berg | **bufa** *Sp.* | bufa | montagne | montanha |
| bay | Bucht | **bugt** *Dan.* | bahía | baie | baía |
| lake | See | **buhayrah** *Ara.* | lago | lac | lago |
| lake, lagoon | See, Lagune, Haff | **buhayrat** *Ara.* | lago, laguna | lac, lagune | lago, laguna |
| mountain, hill | Berg, Hügel | **bukit** *Indon., Mal.* | montaña, colina | montagne, colline | montanha, colina |
| bay | Bucht | **-bukten** *Swe.* | bahía | baie | baía |
| mountain | Berg | **bulu** *Indon.* | montaña | montagne | montanha |
| castle | Burg | **Burg** *Ger.* | castillo | château | castelo |
| hill | Hügel | **burj** *Ara.* | colina | colline | colina |
| brook | Bach | **burn** *Gae.* | riachuelo | crique | riacho |
| cape | Kap | **burnu, burun** *Tur.* | cabo | cap | cabo |
| bay | Busen | **Busen** *Ger.* | bahía | baie | baía |
| butte(s) | Restberg(e) | **butte(s)** *Eng., Fr.* | butte(s) | butte(s) | colina, outeiro |

## C

| ENGLISH | DEUTSCH | Map Form | ESPAÑOL | FRANCAIS | PORTUGUÊS |
|---|---|---|---|---|---|
| cape | Kap | **c. , cabo** *Sp.* **cap cape** | cabo | cap | cabo |
| street | Strasse | **c., calle** *Sp.* | calle | rue | rua |
| peaks | Gipfel | **cabezas** *Sp.* | cabezas | cimes | picos |
| cape | Kap | **cabo** *Port., Sp.* | cabo | cap | cabo |
| waterfall | Wasserfall | **cachoeira** *Port.* | cascada | chute d'eau | cachoeira |
| street | Strasse | **calle** *Sp.* | calle | rue | rua |
| parkway | Ferienstrasse | **calzada** *Sp.* | calzada | allée de parc | alameda de parque |
| mosque | Moschee | **camii** *Tur.* | mezquita | mosqée | mesquita |
| road | Landstrasse | **camino** *Sp.* | camino | route | rodovia |
| camp | Lager | **camp** *Eng., Fr.* | campo | camp | campo |
| plain | Ebene | **campo** *It.* | llanura | plaine | planície |
| brook, ravine | Bach, Tobel | **cañada** *Sp.* | cañada | ruisseau, ravin | ravina |
| canal | Kanal | **canal** *Eng.* | canal | canal | canal |
| canal, channel | Kanal | **canal** *Fr., Port., Sp.* | canal | canal | canal |
| canal, channel | Kanal | **canale** *It.* | canal | canal | canal |
| stream distributary | Flussarm | **caño** *Sp.* | caño | bras | braço de rio, igarapé |
| canyon | Cañon | **cañón** *Sp.* | cañón | canyon | canhão |
| canyon | Cañon | **canyon** *Eng.* | cañón | canyon | canhão |
| plateau | Hochebene | **cao nguyen** *Viet.* | meseta | plateau | planalto |
| cape | Kap | **cap** *Fr., Cat.* | cabo | cap | cabo |
| cape | Kap | **cape** *Eng.* | cabo | cap | cabo |
| capitol | Kapitol | **capitolio** *Sp.* | capitolio | capitole | capitólio |
| cape | Kap | **capo** *It.* | cabo | cap | cabo |
| captain | Kapitän | **capt., captain** *Eng.* | capitán | capitaine | capitão |
| highway | Strasse | **carretera** *Sp.* | carretera | route | rodovia |
| valley | Tal | **carse** *Gae.* | valle | vallée | vale |
| waterfall | Wasserfall | **cascada** *Sp.* | cascada | chute d'eau | queda d'água |
| waterfall | Wasserfall | **cascata** *It.* | cascada | chute d'eau | queda d'água |
| castle | Burg, Schloss | **castel, castello** *It.* | castillo | château | castelo |
| castle | Burg, Schloss | **castelo** *Port.* | castillo | château | castelo |
| castle | Burg, Schloss | **castillo** *Sp.* | castillo | château | castelo |
| castle | Burg, Schloss | **castle** *Eng.* | castillo | château | castelo |
| cataracts | Katarakten | **cataratas** *Port., Sp.* | cataratas | cataractes | cataratas |
| cathedral | Kathedrale | **catedral** *Sp.* | catedral | cathédrale | catedral |
| range | Gebirge | **catena** *Sp.* | catena | chaîne | cordilheira |
| cathedral | Kathedrale | **cathedral** *Eng.* | catedral | cathédrale | catedral |
| causeway | Dammweg | **causeway** *Eng.* | calzada | chaussée | calçada |
| upland | Bergland | **causse** *Fr.* | tierras altas | causse | terras altas |
| cave(s) | Höhle(n) | **cave(s)** *Eng.* | cueva(s) | caverne(s) | caverna(s) |
| cay (islet) | Klippe | **cay** *Eng.* | cayo | caye | baixio |
| cay(s), islet(s) | Klippe(n) | **cayo(s)** *Sp.* | cayo(s) | caye(s) | baixio(s) |
| cemetery | Friedhof | **cementerio** *Sp.* | cementerio | cimetière | cemitério |
| cemetery | Friedhof | **cemetery** *Eng.* | cementerio | cimetière | cemitério |
| mountain(s), hill(s) | Berg(e), Hügel | **cerro(s)** *Sp.* | cerro(s) | montagne(s), colline(s) | montanha(s), colina(s) |
| range | Gebirge | **chaîne** *Fr.* | sierra | chaîne | cordilheira |
| channel | Kanal | **channel** *Eng.* | canal, estrecho | canal, détroit | canal, estreito |
| hills | Hügel | **chapada** *Port.* | colinas | collines | chapada |
| island | Insel | **char** *Ben.* | isla | île | ilha |
| castle | Burg, Schloss | **château** *Fr.* | castillo | château | castelo |
| road | Landstrasse | **chemin** *Fr.* | camino | chemin | rodovia |
| bay | Bucht | **chhâk** *Cbd.* | bahía | baie | baía |
| lake | See | **chi** *Ch.* | lago | lac | lago |
| harbor, harbour | Hafen | **chiang** *Ch.* | puerto | port | porto |
| cape | Kap | **chiao** *Ch.* | cabo | cap | cabo |
| road | Landstrasse | **chin., chemin** *Fr.* | camino | chemin | rodovia |
| river | Fluss | **-ch'ŏn** *Kor.* | río | rivière | rio |
| reservoir | Stausee | **-chŏsuji** *Kor.* | embalse | réservoir | reservatório |
| intermittent lake, salt marsh | periodischer See, Salzmarsch | **chott** *Ara.* | lago intermitente, pantano salado | lac périodique, marais salé | lago intermitente, pântano salgado |
| range | Gebirge | **chr., chrebet** *Rus.* | sierra | chaîne | cordilheira |
| mountains | Berge | **chuŏr phnum** *Cbd.* | montañas | montagnes | montanhas |
| church | Kirche | **church** *Eng.* | iglesia | église | igreja |
| waterfalls | Wasserfälle | **chutes** *Fr.* | cascadas | chutes d'eau | quedas d'água |
| marsh | Marsch | **ciénaga** *Sp.* | ciénaga | marais | pântano |
| peak | Gipfel | **cima** *It., Sp.* | cima | cime | pico |
| peak | Gipfel | **cime** *Fr.* | cima | cime | pico |
| cemetery | Friedhof | **cimetière** *Fr.* | cementerio | cimetière | cemitério |
| city | Stadt | **città** *It.* | ciudad | ville | cidade |
| city | Stadt | **city** *Eng.* | ciudad | ville | cidade |
| city | Stadt | **ciudad** *Sp.* | ciudad | ville | cidade |
| claypan | Tonpfanne | **claypan** *Eng.* | capa de arcilla | couche argilleuse | camada de argila |
| cliff(s) | Kliff(e) | **cliff(s)** *Eng.* | risco(s) | falaise(s) | falésia(s) |
| lake | See | **co** *Tib.* | lago | lac | lago |
| mountain | Berg | **co** *Viet.* | montaña | montagne | montanha |
| mountain, hill | Berg, Hügel | **co., cerro** *Sp.* | cerro | montagne, colline | montanha, colina |
| coast | Küste | **coast** *Eng.* | costa | côte | costa |
| coast guard station | Küstenwacht-station | **coast guard station** *Eng.* | estación de los guardacostas | station des gardescôte | estação de guarda costeira |
| pass | Pass | **col** *Fr.* | paso | col | passo |
| college | Hochschule | **colegio** *Sp.* | colegio | collège | colégio |
| hill(s) | Hügel | **colina(s)** *Sp.* | colina(s) | colline(s) | colina(s) |
| college | Hochschule | **coll., college** *Eng.* | colegio | collège | colégio |
| hills | Hügel | **colli** *It.* | colinas | collines | colinas |
| hills | Hügel | **colline** *It.* | colinas | collines | colinas |
| hills | Hügel | **collines** *Fr.* | colinas | collines | colinas |
| common | Gemeindeland | **common** *Eng.* | campo común | commune | terra comum |
| islands | Inseln | **con** *Viet.* | islas | îles | ilhas |
| plain | Ebene | **conca** *It.* | llanura | plaine | planície |
| convent | Nonnenkloster | **convent** *Eng.* | convento | couvent | convento |
| convent | Nonnenkloster | **convento** *It., Port., Sp.* | convento | couvent | convento |
| range | Gebirge | **cord., cordillera** *Sp.* | cordillera | chaîne | cordilheira |
| mountain | Berg | **corno** *It.* | montaña | montagne | montanha |
| brook | Bach | **córrego** *Port.* | arroyo | ruisseau | córrego |
| coast | Küste | **costa** *Sp.* | costa | côte | costa |
| coast, hills | Küste, Hügel | **côte** *Fr.* | costa, colinas | côte | costa, colinas |
| hills | Hügel | **coteau** *Fr.* | colinas | coteau | colinas |
| coulee | breite Schlucht | **coulee** *Eng.* | rambla | coulée | barranco |
| coulee | breite Schlucht | **coulée** *Fr.* | rambla | coulée | barranco |
| county park | Park | **county park** *Eng.* | parque del condado | parc de comté | parque de condado |
| convent | Nonnenkloster | **couvent** *Fr.* | convento | couvent | convento |
| cove | kleine Bucht | **cove** *Eng.* | ensenada | anse | enseada |
| brook | Bach | **cr., creek** *Eng.* | riachuelo | crique | riacho |
| crag | Felsspitze | **crag** *Eng.* | despeñadero | pointe de rocher | despenhadeiro |
| crater | Krater | **crater** *Eng.* | cráter | cratère | cratera |
| crater | Krater | **cratère** *Fr.* | cráter | cratère | cratera |
| creek | Bach | **creek** *Eng.* | riachuelo | crique | riacho |
| peak | Gipfel | **croda** *It.* | pico | cime | pico |
| canal | Kanal | **csatorna** *Hung.* | canal | canal | canal |
| bay | Bucht | **cua** *Viet.* | bahía | baie | baía |
| hills, ridge | Hügel, Höhenrücken | **cuchilla** *Sp.* | cuchilla | collines, crête | coxilha |
| caves | Höhen | **cuevas** *Sp.* | cuevas | cavernes | cavernas |
| cove | kleine Bucht | **cul-de-sac** *Fr.* | ensenada | cul-de-sac | enseada |
| mountains | Berge | **culmea** *Rom.* | montañas | montagnes | montanhas |
| summit | Gipfel | **cumbre** *Sp.* | cumbre | sommet | cume |

## D

| ENGLISH | DEUTSCH | Map Form | ESPAÑOL | FRANCAIS | PORTUGUÊS |
|---|---|---|---|---|---|
| mountain | Berg | **dağ, dağı** *Tur.* | montaña | montagne | montanha |
| mountains | Berge | **dāgh** *Per.* | montañas | montagnes | montanhas |
| mountains | Berge | **dağlar, dağları** *Tur.* | montañas | montagnes | montanhas |
| hill | Hügel | **ḍahr** *Ara.* | colina | colline | colina |
| plateau | Hochebene | **-dai, -daichi** *Jpn.* | meseta | plateau | planalto |
| mountain | Berg | **-dake** *Jpn.* | montaña | montagne | montanha |
| valley | Tal | **-dal, -dalen** *Nor., Swe.* | valle | vallée | vale |
| dale | weites Tal | **dale** *Eng.* | valle ancho | vallée large | vale aberto |
| dam | Damm | **dam** *Eng.* | presa | barrage | represa |
| lake | See | **danau** *Indon.* | lago | lac | lago |
| island | Insel | **dao** *Ch., Viet.* | isla | île | ilha |
| marsh | Marsch | **daqq** *Per.* | pantano | marais | pântano |
| lake | See | **daryācheh** *Per.* | lago | lac | lago |
| desert | Wüste | **dasht** *Per.* | desierto | désert | deserto |
| monastery | Kloster | **dayr** *Ara.* | monasterio | monastère | mosteiro |
| deep | Tiefe | **deep** *Eng.* | fosa marina | fossé marin | fossa submarina |
| delta | Delta | **delta** *Eng., Fr., Sp.* | delta | delta | delta |

| ENGLISH | DEUTSCH | Map Form Geographische Begriffe Términos Geográficos Termes Géographiques Termos Geográficos | ESPAÑOL | FRANCAIS | PORTUGUÊS |
|---|---|---|---|---|---|
| sea | Meer | **deniz, denizi** *Tur.* | mar | mer | mar |
| monument | Denkmal | **Denkmal** *Ger.* | monumento | monument | monumento |
| pass | Pass | **deo** *Viet.* | paso | col | passo |
| depression | Senke | **depression** *Eng.* | depresión | dépression | depressão |
| river | Fluss | **deresi** *Tur.* | río | rivière | rio |
| desert | Wüste | **desert** *Eng.* | desierto | désert | deserto |
| desert | Wüste | **desierto** *Sp.* | desierto | désert | deserto |
| strait | Meeresstrasse | **détroit** *Fr.* | estrecho | détroit | estreito |
| escarpment | Landstufe | **dhar** *Ara.* | escarpa | escarpement | escarpa |
| canal | Kanal | **dhiórix** *Gr.* | canal | canal | canal |
| lake, marsh | See, Marsch | **dian** *Ch.* | lago, pantano | lac, marais | lago, pântano |
| channel | Kanal | **diep** *Du.* | canal, estrecho | canal, détroit | canal, estreito |
| dike | Deich | **dijk** *Du.* | dique | digue | dique |
| district | Distrikt | **district** *Eng.* | distrito | district | distrito |
| district | Distrikt | **distrito** *Sp.* | distrito | district | distrito |
| ditch | Graben | **ditch** *Eng.* | acequia | fossé | fosso |
| mountain(s) | Berg(e) | **djebel** *Ara.* | montaña(s) | montagne(s) | montanha(s) |
| fjord | Fjord | **-djúp** *Ice.* | fiordo | fjord | fiorde |
| channel, sound | Kanal, Sund | **-djupet** *Swe.* | canal, sonda | canal, détroit | canal, estreito |
| zoo | Zoo | **djurpark** *Swe.* | parque zoológico | zoo | jardim zoológico |
| island | Insel | **-do** *Kor.* | isla | île | ilha |
| interfluve | Erhebung | **doāb** *Per.* | interfluvio | interfluve | interflúvio |
| dock | Dock | **dock** *Eng.* | muelle | quai | doca |
| mountain | Berg | **doi** *Thai* | montaña | montagne | montanha |
| valley | Tal | **dolina** *Rus.* | valle | vallée | vale |
| mountain | Berg | **dolok** *Indon.* | montaña | montagne | montanha |
| hills | Hügel | **dombrovidék** *Hung.* | colinas | collines | colinas |
| hills | Hügel | **dombvidék** *Hung.* | colinas | collines | colinas |
| peak | Gipfel | **dos** *Fr.* | pico | dos | pico |
| downs (hills) | Hügelland | **downs** *Eng.* | colinas | collines | terras baixas (colinas) |
| drive | Fahrweg | **dr., drive** *Eng.* | calzada | avenue | avenida |
| drain (water-course) | Abzugsgraben | **drain** *Eng.* | desaguadero | drainage | escoadouro |
| draw (ravine) | kleines Tal | **draw** *Eng.* | valle pequeño | ravine | bacia, vale |
| drive | Fahrweg | **drive** *Eng.* | calzada | avenue | avenida |
| dry lake | Trockensee | **dry lake** *Eng.* | lago seco | lac asséché | lago seco |
| dunes | Dünen | **dunes** *Eng., Fr.* | dunas | dunes | dunas |

## E

| ENGLISH | DEUTSCH | Map Form | ESPAÑOL | FRANCAIS | PORTUGUÊS |
|---|---|---|---|---|---|
| east | Ost | **e., east** *Eng.* | este | est | leste |
| school | Schule | **école** *Fr.* | escuela | école | escola |
| mountain | Berg | **-egga** *Nor.* | montaña | montagne | montanha |
| memorial | Ehrenmal | **Ehrenmal** *Ger.* | monumento | memorial | monumento |
| river | Fluss | **-elv,-elva** *Nor.* | río | rivière | rio |
| reservoir | Stausee | **embalse** *Sp.* | embalse | réservoir | reservatório |
| pier | Landungsbrücke | **embarcadero** *Sp.* | embarcadero | jetée | cais |
| valley | Tal | **'emeq** *Heb.* | valle | vallée | vale |
| monument | Denkmal | **emlékmű** *Hung.* | monumento | monument | monumento |
| spring | Quelle | **'en** *Heb.* | manantial | source | fonte, manancial |
| cove | kleine Bucht | **enseada** *Port.* | ensenada | anse | enseada |
| cove | kleine Bucht | **ensenada** *Sp.* | ensenada | anse | enseada |
| entrance | Einfahrt | **entrance** *Eng.* | entrada | entrée | entrada |
| forest | Wald | **erdő** *Hung.* | bosque | forêt | floresta |
| sand desert | Sandwüste | **erg** *Ara.* | desierto arenoso | désert de sable | deserto arenoso |
| escarpment | Landstufe | **escarpment** *Eng.* | escarpa | escarpement | escarpa |
| school | Schule | **escuela** *Sp.* | escuela | école | escola |
| highland | Hochland | **espigão** *Port.* | región montañosa | pays montagneux | espigão |
| station | Bahnhof, Stützpunkt | **est., estação** *Port.* **estación** | estación | station | estação |
| stadium | Stadion | **estadio** *Sp.* | estadio | stade | estádio |
| reservoir | Stausee | **estanque** *Sp.* | estanque | réservoir | reservatório |
| estuary | Trichtermündung | **estero** *Sp.* | estero | estuaire | estuário |
| road | Landstrasse | **estr., estrada** *Port.* | camino | route | estrada |
| strait | Meeresstrasse | **estrecho** *Sp.* | estrecho | détroit | estreito |
| estuary | Trichtermündung | **estuary** *Eng.* | estuario | estuaire | estuário |
| pond | Teich | **étang** *Fr.* | charca | étang | lagoa, açude |
| expressway | Autobahn | **expy., expressway** *Eng.* | autopista | autoroute | via expressa |
| island | Insel | **-ey** *Ice.* | isla | île | ilha |
| lake | See | **ežeras** *Lith.* | lago | lac | lago |
| lake | See | **ezers** *Latv.* | lago | lac | lago |

## F

| ENGLISH | DEUTSCH | Map Form | ESPAÑOL | FRANCAIS | PORTUGUÊS |
|---|---|---|---|---|---|
| faculty (school) | Fakultät | **faculté** *Fr.* | facultad | faculté | faculdade |
| fairground | Ausstellungsgelände | **fairground** *Eng.* | campo para ferias | champ de foire | terreno para feiras |
| cliff | Kliff | **falaise** *Fr.* | risco | falaise | falésia |
| fall(s) (waterfall) | Wasserfall | **falls(s)** *Eng.* | cascada | chute d'eau | queda d'água |
| waterfall | Fall | **Fall** *Ger.* | cascada | chute d'eau | queda d'água |
| waterfall | Wasserfall | **-fallet** *Swe.* | cascada | chute d'eau | queda d'água |
| river | Fluss | **far'** *Ara.* | río | rivière | rio |
| lighthouse | Leuchtturm | **faro** *Sp.* | faro | phare | farol |
| upland | Bergland | **farsh** *Ara.* | tierras altas | hautes terres | terras altas |
| fell (mountain, hill) | ödes Hügelland | **fell** *Eng.* | colina rocosa | colline rocheuse | colina rochosa |
| mountain | Berg | **-fell** *Ice.* | montaña | montagne | montanha |
| mountain | Berg | **feng** *Ch.* | montaña | montagne | montanha |
| upland | Bergland | **fennsík** *Hung.* | tierras altas | hautes terres | terras altas |
| ferry | Fähre | **ferry** *Eng.* | balsadera | bac | balsa |
| lake | See | **fertő** *Hung.* | lago | lac | lago |
| fortress | Feste | **Feste** *Ger.* | fortaleza | fort | fortaleza |
| estuary, strait | Trichtermündung, Meeresstrasse | **firth** *Eng.* | estuario, estrecho | estuaire, détroit | estuário, estreito |
| mountain(s) | Berg(e) | **fjäll(en)** *Swe.* | montaña(s) | montagne(s) | montanha(s) |
| mountain | Berg | **fjället** *Swe.* | montaña | montagne | montanha |
| fjord | Fjord | **fjärden** *Swe.* | fiordo | fjord | fiorde |
| mountain | Berg | **-fjell, -fjellet** *Nor.* | montaña | montagne | montanha |
| mountain | Berg | **-fjöll** *Ice.* | montaña | montagne | montanha |
| fjord | Fjord | **-fjord** *Nor.* | fiordo | fjord | fiorde |
| fjord, lake | Fjord, See | **-fjorden** *Nor., Swe.* | fiordo, lago | fjord, lac | fiorde, lago |
| fjord, bay | Fjord, Bucht | **-fjörur** *Ice.* | fiordo, bahía | fjord, baie | fiorde, baía |
| fork | Arm | **fk., fork** *Eng.* | brazo | bras | braço de rio |
| flat | Flachland | **flat** *Eng.* | llano | plat | planície |
| river | Fluss | **-fljót** *Ice.* | río | rivière | rio |
| bay | Bucht | **-flói** *Ice.* | bahía | baie | baía |
| flood control basin | Hochwasserrückhaltebecken | **flood control basin** *Eng.* | cuenca para controlar la inundación | bassin de contrôle d'inondation | bacia de controle de inundações |
| airport | Flugplatz | **Flughafen** *Ger.* | aeropuerto | aéroport | aeroporto |
| airport | Flugplatz | **Flugplatz** *Ger.* | aeropuerto | aérodrome | aeroporto |
| airport | Flughafen | **flygplats** *Swe.* | aeródromo | aérodrome | aeródromo |
| river mouth, pass | Flussmündung, Pass | **foce** *It.* | desembocadura, paso | embouchure, col | desembocadura, foz, passo |
| canal | Kanal | **föcsatorna** *Hung.* | canal | canal | canal |
| glacier | Gletscher | **-fonn** *Nor.* | glaciar | glacier | geleira |
| spring | Quelle | **fontaine** *Fr.* | manantial | fontaine | fonte, manancial |
| pass | Pass | **forca** *It.* | paso | col | passo |
| inlet | Förde | **Förde** *Ger.* | abra | bras de mer | enseada, estuário |
| foreland | Vorland | **foreland** *Eng.* | promontorio | promontoire | promontório |
| forest | Wald | **forest** *Eng.* | bosque | forêt | floresta |
| forest reserve | Waldreservat | **forest reserve** *Eng.* | reserva de bosque | réserve forestière | reserva florestal |
| forest | Wald | **forêt** *Fr.* | bosque | forêt | floresta |
| waterfall | Wasserfall | **-forsen** *Swe.* | cascada | chute d'eau | queda d'água |
| forest | Forst | **Forst** *Ger.* | bosque | forêt | floresta |
| fort | Fort | **fort** *Eng., Fr.* | fuerte | fort | forte |
| waterfall | Wasserfall | **-foss** *Ice.* | cascada | chute d'eau | queda d'água |
| waterfall | Wasserfall | **-fossen** *Nor.* | cascada | chute d'eau | queda d'água |
| brook | Bach | **fosso** *It.* | arroyo | ruisseau | córrego |
| pass | Pass | **foum** *Ara.* | paso | col | passo |
| fracture zone | Bruchzone | **fracture zone** *Eng.* | zona de fractura | zone de faille | zona de fratura |
| freeway | Autobahn | **frwy., freeway** *Eng.* | autopista | autoroute | via expressa |
| fort | Fort | **ft., fort** *Eng., Fr.* | fuerte | fort | forte |
| stream distributary | Flussarm | **furo** *Port.* | brazo de río | bras | furo |

## G

| ENGLISH | DEUTSCH | Map Form | ESPAÑOL | FRANCAIS | PORTUGUÊS |
|---|---|---|---|---|---|
| mountain, hill | Berg, Hügel | **g., gora** *Rus.* | montaña, colina | montagne, colline | montanha, colina |
| mountain | Berg | **g., gunong** *Mal.* **gunung** | montaña | montagne | montanha |
| mountain | Berg | **-gai'sa** *Lapp.* | montaña | montagne | montanha |
| tunnel | Tunnel | **galleria** *It.* | túnel | tunnel | túnel |
| gallery | Galerie | **gallery** *Eng.* | galería | galerie | galeria |
| game farm | Wildfarm | **game farm** *Eng.* | criadero de caza | ferme de gibier | fazenda de caça |
| game park | Wildpark | **game park** *Eng.* | vedado de caza | parc à gibier | parque de caça |
| game refuge | Wildgehege | **game refuge** *Eng.* | refugio de caza | refuge de gibier | refúgio de caça |
| game reserve | Wildreservat | **game reserve** *Eng.* | vedado de caza | réserve à gibier | reserva de caça |
| game sanctuary | Wildschutzgebiet | **game sanctuary** *Eng.* | vedado de caza | réserve à gibier | santuário de caça |
| bay | Bucht | **gang** *Ch.* | bahía | baie | baía |
| river | Fluss | **-gang** *Kor.* | río | rivière | rio |
| gap | Pass | **gap** *Eng.* | paso | col | passo |
| intermittent lake | periodischer See | **garaet** *Ara.* | lago intermitente | lac périodique | lago intermitente |
| garden | Garten | **gard., garden** *Eng.* | jardín | jardin | jardim |
| gardens | Gärten | **gardens** *Eng.* | jardines | jardins | jardins |
| mountain | Berg | **garet** *Ara.* | montaña | montagne | montanha |
| lake | See | **-gata** *Jpn.* | lago | lac | lago |
| gate | Tor | **gate** *Eng.* | puerta | porte | portão |
| mountain torrent | Wildbach | **gave** *Fr.* | torrente | gave | torrente |
| range | Gebirge | **gebergte** *Du.* | sierra | chaîne | cordilheira |
| range | Gebirge | **Gebirge** *Ger.* | sierra | chaîne | cordilheira |
| pass | Pass | **geçidi** *Tur.* | paso | col | passo |
| oasis, well | Oase, Brunnen | **ghadīr** *Ara.* | oasis, pozo | oasis, puits | oásis, poço |
| mountains | Gebirge | **ghar** *Pas.* | montañas | montagnes | montanhas |
| spring | Quelle | **ghayl** *Ara.* | manantial | source | manancial |
| bay | Bucht | **ghubbat** *Ara.* | bahía | baie | baía |
| dunes | Dünen | **ghurd** *Ara.* | dunas | dunes | dunas |
| island | Insel | **gili** *Indon.* | isla | île | ilha |
| peak | Gipfel | **Gipfel** *Ger.* | pico | cime | pico |
| hill | Hügel | **giva't** *Heb.* | colina | colline | colina |
| bay | Bucht | **gji** *Alb.* | bahía | baie | baía |
| glacier | Gletscher | **glacier** *Eng., Fr.* | glaciar | glacier | geleira |
| lake | See | **göl** *Tur.* | lago | lac | lago |
| bald mountains | kahle Berge | **gol'cy** *Rus.* | montañas calvas | monts chauves | montanhas calvas |
| gulf | Golf | **golf** *Cat.* | golfo | golfe | golfo |
| golf course | Golfplatz | **golf course** *Eng.* | campo de golf | champ de golf | campo de golfe |
| gulf | Golf | **golfe** *Fr.* | golfo | golfe | golfo |
| bay | Bucht | **golfete** *Sp.* | golfete | baie | baía |
| gulf | Golf | **golfo** *It., Sp.* | golfo | golfe | golfo |
| lake | See | **gölü** *Tur.* | lago | lac | lago |
| mountain, hill | Berg, Hügel | **gora** *Rus.* | montaña, colina | montagne, colline | montanha, colina |
| mountains | Berge | **gora** *S/C.* | montañas | montagnes | montanhas |
| mountain | Berg | **góra** *Pol.* | montaña | montagne | montanha |
| gorge | Schlucht | **gorge** *Eng., Fr.* | garganta | gorge | garganta |
| mountains, hills | Berge, Hügel | **gorje** *S/C.* | montañas, colinas | montagnes, collines | montanhas, colinas |
| ruins | Ruinen | **gorodišče** *Rus.* | ruinas | ruines | ruínas |
| mountains, hills | Berge, Hügel | **gory** *Rus.* | montañas, colinas | montagnes, collines | montanhas, colinas |
| mountains | Berge | **góry** *Pol.* | montañas | montagnes | montanhas |
| sinkhole | Schluckloch | **gouffre** *Fr.* | sumidero | gouffre | sumidouro |
| wadi | Wadi | **goulbin** *Hau.* | uadi | wadi | uádi |
| ditch | Graben | **Graben** *Ger.* | acequia | fossé | fosso |
| ridge | Höhenrücken | **gr'ada** *Rus.* | sierra | crête | cordilheira |
| mountain | Berg | **gradište** *Blg.* | montaña | montagne | montanha |
| ridges | Höhenrücken | **gr'ady** *Rus.* | sierras | crêtes | cordilheira |
| general | General | **gral., general** *Eng., Sp.* | general | général | geral |
| ridge | Grat | **Grat** *Ger.* | sierra | crête | cordilheira |
| grotto | Grotte | **grotta** *It.* | gruta | grotte | gruta |
| grotto | Grotte | **grotte** *Fr.* | gruta | grotte | gruta |
| group | Gruppe | **group** *Eng.* | grupo | groupe | grupo |
| island | Insel | **-grund** *Swe.* | isla | île | ilha |
| group | Gruppe | **grupo** *Sp.* | grupo | groupe | grupo |
| group | Gruppe | **groppo** *It.* | grupo | groupe | grupo |
| pass | Pass | **guan** *Ch.* | paso | col | passo |
| bay | Bucht | **guba** *Rus.* | bahía | baie | baía |
| mountain | Berg | **guelb** *Ara.* | montaña | montagne | montanha |
| gulch | Wildbachschlucht | **gulch** *Eng.* | quebrada | ravin | quebrada |
| gulf | Golf | **gulf** *Eng.* | golfo | golfe | golfo |
| mountain | Berg | **gunong** *Mal.* | montaña | montagne | montanha |
| mountain | Berg | **gunung** *Indon.* | montaña | montagne | montanha |
| islands | Inseln | **-guntō** *Jpn.* | islas | îles | ilhas |

## H

| ENGLISH | DEUTSCH | Map Form | ESPAÑOL | FRANCAIS | PORTUGUÊS |
|---|---|---|---|---|---|
| upland | Bergland | **hadabat** *Ara.* | tierras altas | hautes terres | terras altas |
| mountain | Berg | **hadjer** *Ara.* | montaña | montagne | montanha |
| lagoon | Haff | **Haff** *Ger.* | laguna | lagune | laguna |
| sea, lake | Meer, See | **hai** *Ch.* | mar, lago | mer, lac | mar, lago |
| strait | Meeresstrasse | **haixia** *Ch.* | estrecho | détroit | estreito |
| reef | Riff | **hakau** *Poly.* | arrecife | récif | recife |
| peninsula | Halbinsel | **Halbinsel** *Ger.* | península | péninsule | península |
| hall | Halle | **hall** *Eng., Fr.* | salón | hall | hall |
| peninsula | Halbinsel | **-halvøya** *Nor.* | península | péninsule | península |
| beach | Strand | **-hama** *Jpn.* | playa | plage | praia |
| desert | Wüste | **hamada** *Ara.* | desierto | désert | deserto |
| plateau | Hochebene | **hammādat** *Ara.* | meseta | plateau | planalto |
| lake, marsh | See, Marsch | **hāmūn** *Per.* | lago, pantano | lac, marais | lago, pântano |
| point | Landspitze | **-hana** *Jpn.* | punta | pointe | ponta |
| peninsula | Halbinsel | **-hantō** *Jpn.* | península | péninsule | península |
| mountain, hill | Berg, Hügel | **har** *Heb.* | montaña, colina | montagne, colline | montanha, colina |
| harbor, harbour | Hafen | **harbor, harbour** *Eng.* | puerto | port | porto |
| mountains, hills | Berge, Hügel | **hare** *Heb.* | montañas, colinas | montagnes, collines | montanhas, colinas |
| ridge | Höhenrücken | **-harju** *Finn.* | sierra | crête | cordilheira |
| lava flow | Lavastrom | **harrat** *Ara.* | corriente de lava | coulée de lave | corrente de lava |
| hills | Hügel | **hauteurs** *Fr.* | colinas | hauteurs | colinas |
| sea, bay | Meer, Bucht | **-hav** *Swe.* | mar, bahía | mer, baie | mar, baía |
| harbor, harbour | Hafen | **havre** *Fr.* | puerto | havre | porto |
| oasis | Oase | **hawd** *Ara.* | oasis | oasis | oásis |
| lake | See | **hawr** *Ara.* | lago | lac | lago |
| harbor, harbour | Hafen | **hbr., harbor, harbour** *Eng.* | puerto | port | porto |
| headquarters | Hauptquartier | **hdqrs., headquarters** *Eng.* | cuartel general | guartier général | quartel-general |
| river | Fluss | **he** *Ch.* | río | rivière | rio |
| head (headland) | Landspitze | **head** *Eng.* | promontorio | promontoire | promontório |

| ENGLISH | DEUTSCH | Map Form / Geographische Begriffe / Términos Geográficos / Termes Géographiques / Termos Geográficos | ESPAÑOL | FRANCAIS | PORTUGUÊS |
|---|---|---|---|---|---|
| heath | Heide | **heath** *Eng.* | matorral | lande | charneca |
| mountain(s) | Berg(e) | **hegy(ség)** *Hung.* | montaña(s) | montagne(s) | montanha(s) |
| heath | Heide | **Heide** *Ger.* | matorral | lande | charneca |
| plain | Ebene | **-heiya** *Jpn.* | llanura | plaine | planície |
| hills | Hügel | **-heuwels** *Afk.* | colinas | collines | colinas |
| highland | Hochland | **highland** *Eng.* | región montañosa | pays montagneux | terras altas |
| highway | Strasse | **highway** *Eng.* | carretera | route | rodovia |
| hill(s) | Hügel | **hill(s)** *Eng.* | colina(s) | colline(s) | colina(s) |
| race course | Rennbahn | **hipòdromo** *Sp.* | hipódromo | hippodrome | hipódromo |
| race course | Rennbahn | **hippodrome** *Fr.* | hipódromo | hippodrome | hipódromo |
| historical | historisch | **hist., historical** *Eng.* | histórico | historique | histórico |
| historical park | historischer Park | **historical park** *Eng.* | parque histórico | parc historique | parque histórico |
| historic(al) site | historische Stätte | **historic(al) site** *Eng.* | sitio histórico | site historique | sítio histórico |
| Her Majesty's Air Station (U.K.) | Luftwaffenstützpunkt (V.K.) | **H.M.A.S., Her Majesty's Air Station** *Eng.* | Real Estación Aeronáutica (R.U.) | Station Aérienne Royale (R.U.) | Estação Aérea Real (R.U.) |
| river | Fluss | **ho** *Ch.* | río | rivière | rio |
| reservoir | Stausee | **-ho** *Kor.* | embalse | réservoir | reservatório |
| mountain | Berg | **-hø** *Nor.* | montaña | montagne | montanha |
| plateau | Hochebene | **Hochebene** *Ger.* | meseta | plateau | planalto |
| forest | Hochwald | **Hochwald** *Ger.* | bosque | forêt | floresta |
| mountain | Berg | **-högarna** *Swe.* | montaña | montagne | montanha |
| height | Höhe | **Höhe** *Ger.* | altura | hauteur | elevação |
| cave(s) | Höhle(n) | **Höhle(n)** *Ger.* | cueva(s) | caverne(s) | caverna(s) |
| island | Insel | **-holm** *Dan.* | isla | île | ilha |
| hook | Haken | **hook** *Eng.* | gancho | crochet | cabo, promontório |
| mountain | Berg | **hora** *Czech, Slo.* | montaña | montagne | montanha |
| mountain, hill | Berg, Hügel | **hora** *Ukr.* | montaña, colina | montagne, colline | montanha, colina |
| point, peak | Horn | **Horn** *Ger.* | punta, pico | pointe, cime | ponta, pico |
| ruin | Ruine | **ḥorva** *Heb.* | ruina | ruine | ruína |
| mountains | Berge | **hory** *Czech, Slo.* | montañas | montagnes | montanhas |
| mountains, hills | Berge, Hügel | **hory** *Ukr.* | montañas, colinas | montagnes, collines | montanhas, colinas |
| hospital | Krankenhaus | **hospital** *Eng., Sp.* | hospital | hôpital | hospital |
| point | Landspitze | **houma** *Poly.* | punta | pointe | ponta |
| house | Haus | **house** *Eng.* | casa | maison | casa |
| island | Insel | **hsü** *Ch.* | isla | île | ilha |
| lake, reservoir | See, Stausee | **hu** *Ch.* | lago, embalse | lac, réservoir | lago, reservatório |
| hill | Hügel | **Hügel** *Ger.* | colina | colline | colina |
| cape | Huk | **Huk** *Ger.* | cabo | cap | cabo |
| cape | Huk | **-huk** *Swe.* | cabo | cap | cabo |
| highway | Strasse | **hy., highway** *Eng.* | carretera | route | rodovia |
| | | | **I** | | |
| island | Insel | **i., isla** *Sp.* **island** | isla | île | ilha |
| icefield | Eisdecke | **icefield** *Eng.* | helero | champ de glace | geleira |
| ice shelf | Schelfeis | **ice shelf** *Eng.* | corniza glacial | barrière de glace | banco de gelo |
| ice tongue | Eiszunge | **ice tongue** *Eng.* | lengua de glaciar | langue glaciaire | língua de geleira |
| dunes | Dünen | **idehan** *Ber.* | dunas | dunes | dunas |
| river | Fluss | **ig., igarapé** *Port.* | río | rivière | igarapé |
| church | Kirche | **iglesia** *Sp.* | iglesia | église | igreja |
| lake | See | **-ike** *Jpn.* | lago | lac | lago |
| island(s) | Insel(n) | **île(s)** *Fr.* | isla(s) | île(s) | ilha(s) |
| islet(s) | kleine Insel(n) | **îlet(s)** *Fr.* | isleta(s) | îlet(s) | ilhota(s) |
| island(s) | Insel(n) | **ilha(s)** *Port.* | isla(s) | île(s) | ilha(s) |
| islet(s) | kleine Insel(n) | **ilhéu(s)** *Port.* | isleta(s) | îlot(s) | ilhéu(s) |
| island | Insel | **illa** *Cat.* | isla | île | ilha |
| islands | Inseln | **illes** *Cat.* | islas | îles | ilhas |
| hill, upland | Hügel, Bergland | **'ilw** *Ara.* | colina, tierras altas | colline, hautes terres | colina, terras altas |
| hill | Hügel | **'ilwat** *Ara.* | colina | colline | colina |
| Indian reservation | Indianer-reservation | **Ind. res., Indian reservation** *Eng.* | reserva de Indios | réserve indienne | reserva indígena |
| inlet | Einfahrt | **inlet** *Eng.* | abra | bras de mer | enseada |
| island(s) | Insel(n) | **Insel(n)** *Ger.* | isla(s) | île(s) | ilha(s) |
| institute | Institut | **inst., institute** *Eng.* | instituto | institut | instituto |
| international | international | **int., international** *Eng.* | internacional | international | internacional |
| race course | Rennbahn | **ippodromo** *It.* | hipódromo | hippodrome | hipódromo |
| wadi | Wadi | **irhazer** *Ber.* | uadi | wadi | uádi |
| dunes | Dünen | **'irq** *Ara.* | dunas | dunes | dunas |
| islands | Inseln | **is., islands** *Eng.* **islas** | islas | îles | ilhas |
| island | Insel | **isla** *Sp.* | isla | île | ilha |
| island(s) | Insel(n) | **island(s)** *Eng.* | isla(s) | île(s) | ilha(s) |
| islands | Inseln | **islas** *Sp.* | islas | îles | ilhas |
| isle(s) | Insel(n) | **isle(s)** *Eng.* | isla(s) | île(s) | ilha(s) |
| islet(s) | kleine Insel(n) | **islet(s)** *Eng.* | isleta(s) | îlot(s) | ilhota(s) |
| islet | kleine Insel | **islote** *Sp.* | islote | îlot | ilhota |
| island | Insel | **isola** *It.* | isla | île | ilha |
| islands | Inseln | **isole** *It.* | islas | îles | ilhas |
| islet | kleine Insel | **isolotto** *It.* | isleta | îlot | ilhota |
| isthmus | Landenge | **isthme** *Fr.* | istmo | isthme | istmo |
| isthmus | Landenge | **isthmus** *Eng.* | istmo | isthme | istmo |
| isthmus | Landenge | **istmo** *Sp.* | istmo | isthme | istmo |
| island | Insel | **-iwa** *Jpn.* | isla | île | ilha |
| | | | **J** | | |
| mountain(s) | Berg(e) | **jabal** *Ara.* | montaña(s) | montagne(s) | montanha(s) |
| cave | Höhle | **jama** *S./C.* | cueva | caverne | caverna |
| caves | Höhlen | **jame** *S./C.* | cuevas | cavernes | cavernas |
| garden | Garten | **jardin** *Fr.* | jardín | jardin | jardim |
| garden | Garten | **jardín** *Sp.* | jardín | jardin | jardim |
| gardens | Gärten | **jardines** *Sp.* | jardines | jardins | jardins |
| lake | See | **järv** *Est.* | lago | lac | lago |
| lake | See | **-järvi** *Finn.* | lago | lac | lago |
| mountains | Berge | **jary** *Rus.* | montañas | montagnes | montanhas |
| lake | See | **-jaur** *Lapp.* | lago | lac | lago |
| islands | Inseln | **jazā'ir** *Ara.* | islas | îles | ilhas |
| peninsula | Halbinsel | **jazirah** *Indon.* | península | péninsule | península |
| island | Insel | **jazīrat** *Ara.* | isla | île | ilha |
| island | Insel | **jazīreh** *Per.* | isla | île | ilha |
| reservoir | Stausee | **jazovir** *Blg.* | embalse | réservoir | reservatório |
| mountain(s) | Berg(e) | **jbel** *Ara.* | montaña(s) | montagne(s) | montanha(s) |
| lake | See | **jezero** *S./C.* | lago | lac | lago |
| lake, lagoon | See, Lagune, Haff | **jezioro** *Pol.* | lago, laguna | lac, lagune | lago, laguna |
| river | Fluss | **jiang** *Ch.* | río | rivière | rio |
| cape | Kap | **jiao** *Ch.* | cabo | cap | cabo |
| mountains | Berge | **jibāl** *Ara.* | montañas | montagnes | montanhas |
| island | Insel | **-jima** *Jpn.* | isla | île | ilha |
| saddle (pass) | Joch | **Joch** *Ger.* | paso | col | passo |
| river | Fluss | **-joki** *Finn.* | río | rivière | rio |
| glacier | Gletscher | **-jøkulen** *Nor.* | glaciar | glacier | geleira |
| glacier | Gletscher | **-jökull** *Ice.* | glaciar | glacier | geleira |
| gulf | Golf | **jūras līcis** *Latv.* | golfo | golfe | golfo |
| islands | Inseln | **juzur** *Ara.* | islas | îles | ilhas |
| | | | **K** | | |
| mountains | Berge | **kabīr** *Per.* | montañas | montagnes | montanhas |
| dunes | Dünen | **kahal** *Ara.* | dunas | dunes | dunas |
| sea | Meer | **-kai** *Jpn.* | mar | mer | mar |
| strait | Meeresstrasse | **-kaikyō** *Jpn.* | estrecho | détroit | estreito |
| mountain | Berg | **-kaise** *Lapp.* | montaña | montagne | montanha |
| navy installation | Anlage de Marine | **ka.j., kaijō-jieitai** *Jpn.* | estación de la marina | installation navale | instalação naval |
| brook | Bach | **kali** *Indon.* | riachuelo | crique | riacho |
| mountain | Berg | **kalns** *Latv.* | montaña | montagne | montanha |
| ridge | Kamm | **Kamm** *Ger.* | sierra | crête | serra |

| ENGLISH | DEUTSCH | Map Form / Geographische Begriffe / Términos Geográficos / Termes Géographiques / Termos Geográficos | ESPAÑOL | FRANCAIS | PORTUGUÊS |
|---|---|---|---|---|---|
| canal | Kanal | **kanaal** *Du.* | canal | canal | canal |
| canal, channel | Kanal | **Kanal** *Ger.* | canal | canal | canal |
| canal, channel | Kanal | **kanal** *Rus., S./C., Swe., Ukr.* | canal | canal | canal |
| canal, channel | Kanal | **kana** *Pol.* | canal | canal | canal |
| canal, channel | Kanal | **kanalen** *Swe.* | canal | canal | canal |
| canal, channel | Kanal | **kanava** *Finn.* | canal | canal | canal |
| pass | Pass | **kandao** *Pas.* | paso | col | passo |
| river | Fluss | **-kang** *Kor.* | río | rivière | rio |
| moor | Moor | **-kangas** *Finn.* | páramo | lande | charneca |
| national park | Nationalpark | **kansallis-puisto** *Finn.* | parque nacional | parc national | parque nacional |
| island | Insel | **kaŏh** *Cbd.* | isla | île | ilha |
| cape | Kap | **Kap** *Ger.* | cabo | cap | cabo |
| gorge | Schlucht | **kapija** *S./C.* | garganta | gorge | garganta |
| cape | Kap | **-kapp** *Nor.* | cabo | cap | cabo |
| dunes | Dünen | **kathīb** *Ara.* | dunas | dunes | dunas |
| desert | Wüste | **kavīr** *Per.* | desierto | désert | deserto |
| mountain | Berg | **kawlat** *Ara.* | montaña | montagne | montanha |
| hill | Hügel | **kawm** *Ara.* | colina | colline | colina |
| mountain | Berg | **kedīet** *Ara.* | montaña | montagne | montanha |
| lake | See | **kenohan** *Indon.* | lago | lac | lago |
| cape | Kap | **kep** *Alb.* | cabo | cap | cabo |
| islands | Inseln | **kepulauan** *Indon.* | islas | îles | ilhas |
| key(s), cay(s) | Klippe(n) | **key(s)** *Eng.* | cayo(s) | caye(s) | baixio(s) |
| intermittent lake | periodischer See | **khabrat** *Ara.* | lago intermitente | lac périodique | lago intermitente |
| gulf | Golf | **khalīj** *Ara.* | golfo | golfe | golfo |
| mountain | Berg | **khao** *Bur., Thai* | montaña | montagne | montanha |
| mountain | Berg | **khashm** *Ara.* | montaña | montagne | montanha |
| wadi | Wadi | **khatt** *Ara.* | uadi | wadi | uádi |
| wadi, river | Wadi, Fluss | **khawr** *Ara.* | uadi, río | wadi, rivière | uádi, rio |
| dam | Damm | **khazzān** *Ara.* | presa | barrage | represa |
| river, canal | Fluss, Kanal | **khlong** *Thai* | río, canal | rivière, canal | rio, canal |
| range | Gebirge | **khrebet** *Ukr.* | sierra | chaîne | cordilheira |
| dunes | Dünen | **khubb** *Ara.* | dunas | dunes | dunas |
| kill (river, channel) | Fluss, Kanal | **kill** *Eng.* | río, canal | rivière, canal | rio, canal |
| cemetery | Friedhof | **kladb., kladbišče** *Rus.* | cementerio | cimetière | cemitério |
| cloister | Kloster | **klasztory** *Pol.* | claustro | cloître | claustro, convento |
| cloister, monastery | Kloster | **Kloster** *Ger.* | claustro, monasterio | cloître, monastère | claustro, mosteiro |
| knob | Kuppe | **knob** *Eng.* | protuberancia | bosse | cerro, colina |
| island | Insel | **ko** *Thai* | isla | île | ilha |
| lake, lagoon | See, Lagune, Haff | **-ko** *Jpn.* | lago, laguna | lac, lagune | lago, laguna |
| harbor, harbour | Hafen | **-kō** *Jpn.* | puerto | port | porto |
| highland | Hochland | **-kōchi** *Jpn.* | región montañosa | pays montagneux | terras altas |
| mountain | Kogel | **Kogel** *Ger.* | montaña | montagne | montanha |
| plateau | Hochebene | **-kogen** *Jpn.* | meseta | plateau | planalto |
| mountains | Berge | **koh** *Per.* | montañas | montagnes | montanhas |
| air force installation | Anlage der Luftwaffe | **ko.j., kōkū-jieitai** *Jpn.* | estación aeronáutica | installation aérienne | instalação da força aérea |
| national park | Nationalpark | **-kokuritsu-kōen** *Jpn.* | parque nacional | parc national | parque nacional |
| national park | Nationalpark | **-kokutei-kōen** *Jpn.* | parque nacional | parc national | parque nacional |
| bay | Bucht | **kólpos** *Gr.* | bahía | baie | baía |
| mountain | Berg | **kong** *Indon.* | montaña | montagne | montanha |
| peak | Kopf | **Kopf** *Ger.* | pico | cime | pico |
| bridge | Brücke | **köprüsü** *Tur.* | puente | pont | ponte |
| gulf, bay | Golf, Bucht | **körfezi** *Tur.* | golfo, bahía | golfe, baie | golfo, baía |
| spit | Landzunge | **kosa** *Rus., Ukr.* | lengua de tierra | flèche | ponta de terra |
| rapids | Stromschnellen | **-koski** *Finn.* | rápidos | rapides | rápidos |
| pass | Pass | **kotal** *Per.* | paso | col | passo |
| basin | Becken | **kotlina** *Pol.* | cuenca | bassin | bacia |
| bay, pass | Bucht, Pass | **kou** *Ch.* | bahía, paso | baie, col | baía, passo |
| ridge | Höhenrücken | **kr'až** *Rus.* | sierra | crête | serra |
| escarpment | Landstufe | **kreb** *Ara.* | escarpa | escarpement | escarpa |
| fort | Fort | **krepost'** *Rus.* | fuerte | fort | forte |
| national park | Nationalpark | **krk., kokuritsu-kōen** *Jpn.* | parque nacional | parc national | parque nacional |
| ridge | Höhenrücken | **kryazh** *Ukr.* | sierra | crête | serra |
| national park | Nationalpark | **ktk., kokutei-kōen** *Jpn.* | parque nacional | parc national | parque nacional |
| bay | Bucht | **kuala** *Mal.* | bahía | baie | baía |
| mountain(s) | Berg(e) | **kūh(ha)** *Per.* | montaña(s) | montagne(s) | montanha(s) |
| hill | Hügel | **-kulle** *Swe.* | colina | colline | colina |
| dome | Kuppe | **Kuppe** *Ger.* | domo | dôme | domo |
| strait | Meeresstrasse | **-kurkku** *Finn.* | estrecho | détroit | estreito |
| channel | Kanal | **kyle** *Gae.* | canal, estrecho | canal, détroit | canal, estreito |
| island | Insel | **kyun** *Bur.* | isla | île | ilha |
| hills | Hügel | **-kyūryū** *Jpn.* | colinas | collines | colinas |
| | | | **L** | | |
| lake | See | **l., lac** *Fr.* **lago lagoa lake** | lago | lac | lago, lagoa |
| pass | Pass | **la** *Tib.* | paso | col | passo |
| province | Provinz | **lääni** *Finn.* | provincia | province | província |
| lake(s) | See(n) | **lac(s)** *Fr.* | lago(s) | lac(s) | lago(s) |
| lake | See | **lacul** *Rom.* | lago | lac | lago |
| cape | Kap | **laem** *Thai* | cabo | cap | cabo |
| lagoon, lake | Lagune, Haff, See | **lag., laguna** *Sp.* | laguna | lagune, lac | laguna |
| lake | See | **lago** *It., Port., Sp.* | lago | lac | lago |
| lake, lagoon | See, Lagune, Haff | **lagoa** *Port.* | lago, laguna | lac, lagune | lagoa |
| lagoon | Lagune, Haff | **lagoon** *Eng.* | laguna | lagune | laguna |
| lakes | Seen | **lagos** *Port., Sp.* | lagos | lacs | lagos |
| lagoon, lake | Lagune, Haff, See | **laguna** *Sp.* | laguna | lagune, lac | laguna, lago |
| lagoon | Lagune, Haff | **lagune** *Fr.* | laguna | lagune | laguna |
| bay | Bucht | **laht** *Est.* | bahía | baie | baía |
| gulf | Golf | **-lahti** *Finn.* | golfo | golfe | golfo |
| lake(s) | See(n) | **lake(s)** *Eng.* | lago(s) | lac(s) | lago(s) |
| county | Grafschaft | **län** *Swe.* | condado | comté | condado |
| lake | Lanke (See) | **Lanke** *Ger.* | lago | lac | lago |
| sea | Meer | **laut** *Indon.* | mar | mer | mar |
| lava flow | Lavastrom | **lava flow** *Eng.* | corriente de lava | coulée de lave | corrente de lava |
| hill, mountain | Hügel, Berg | **law** *Eng.* | colina, montaña | colline, montagne | colina, montanha |
| mountains, forest | Berge, Wald | **les** *Czech* | montañas, bosque | montagnes, forêt | montanhas, floresta |
| forest | Wald | **les** *Rus.* | bosque | forêt | floresta |
| level (plain) | Niveau (Ebene) | **level** *Eng.* | nivel (llano) | niveau (plaine) | planície |
| islands | Inseln | **liedao** *Ch.* | islas | îles | ilhas |
| lighthouse | Leuchtturm | **lighthouse** *Eng.* | faro | phare | farol |
| estuary | Trichter-mündung | **liman** *Rus.* | estuario | estuaire | estuário |
| bay | Bucht | **limanı** *Tur.* | bahía | baie | baía |
| lake | See | **límni** *Gr.* | lago | lac | lago |
| mountain(s), peak | Berg(e), Gipfel | **ling** *Ch.* | montaña(s), pico | montagne(s), pic | montanha(s), pico |
| forest | Wald | **lis** *Ukr.* | bosque | forêt | floresta |
| plain(s) | Ebene(n) | **llano(s)** *Sp.* | llano(s) | plaine(s) | planície(s) |
| lake, reservoir | See, Stausee | **llyn** *Welsh* | lago, embalse | lac, réservoir | lago, reservatório |
| lake, inlet | See, Einfahrt | **loch** *Gae.* | lago, abra | lac, bras de mer | lago, angra |
| lock | Schleuse | **lock** *Eng.* | esclusa | écluse | eclusa |
| lock and dam | Damm mit Schleuse | **lock and dam** *Eng.* | presa y esclusa | écluse et barrage | represa e eclusa |

| ENGLISH | DEUTSCH | Map Form<br>Geographische Begriffe<br>Términos Geográficos<br>Termes Géographiques<br>Termos Geográficos | ESPAÑOL | FRANCAIS | PORTUGUÊS |
|---|---|---|---|---|---|
| gorge | Schlucht | **log** *Rus.* | garganta | gorge | garganta |
| mountain | Berg | **loi** *Bur.* | montaña | montagne | montanha |
| hills | Hügel | **lomas** *Sp.* | lomas | collines | colinas |
| lake | See | **lough** *Gae.* | lago | lac | lago |
| lowland | Tiefland | **lowland** *Eng.* | tierra baja | terrain bas | terras baixas |
| marsh | Luch (Bruch) | **Luch** *Ger.* | pantano | marais | pântano |
| island | Insel | **-luoto** *Finn.* | isla | île | ilha |
| estuary | Trichtermündung | **lyman** *Ukr.* | estuario | estuaire | estuário |

## M

| ENGLISH | DEUTSCH | Map Form<br>Geographische Begriffe<br>Términos Geográficos<br>Termes Géographiques<br>Termos Geográficos | ESPAÑOL | FRANCAIS | PORTUGUÊS |
|---|---|---|---|---|---|
| mountains | Berge | **m., munţii** *Rom.* | montañas | montagnes | montanhas |
| island | Insel | **-maa** *Est.* | isla | île | ilha |
| strait | Meeresstrasse | **madīq** *Ara.* | estrecho | détroit | estreito |
| river | Fluss | **mae** *Thai* | río | rivière | rio |
| depression | Senke | **makhtesh** *Heb.* | depresión | dépression | depressão |
| bay | Bucht | **-man** *Kor.* | bahía | baie | baía |
| monastery | Kloster | **manastir** *S./C.* | monasterio | monastère | mosteiro |
| sea | Meer | **mar** *Sp., It.* | mar | mer | mar |
| marsh | Marsch | **marais** *Fr.* | pantano | marais | pântano |
| sea | Meer | **mare** *It.* | mar | mer | mar |
| marine corps air station | Flugstützpunkt des Marine-Corps | **marine corps air station** *Eng.* | estación aeronáutica de la infantería de marina | station aérienne de fusiliers marins | estação aérea de fuzileiros navais |
| marine corps base | Marine-Corps-Stützpunkt | **marine corps base** *Eng.* | base de la infantería de marina | base de fusiliers marins | base de fuzileiros navais |
| bay | Bucht | **marsā** *Ara.* | bahía | baie | baía |
| marsh | Marsch | **Marsch** *Ger.* | pantano | marais | pântano |
| marsh(es) | Marsch(en) | **marsh(es)** *Eng.* | pantano(s) | marais | pântano(s) |
| river mouth | Flussmündung | **maṣabb** *Ara.* | desembocadura | embouchure | desembocadura |
| canal | Kanal | **maṣrif** *Ara.* | canal | canal | canal |
| massif | Gebirgsmassiv | **massif** *Eng., Fr.* | macizo | massif | maciço |
| marine corps air station | Flugstützpunkt des Marine-Corps | **m.c.a.s., marine corps air station** *Eng.* | estación aeronáutica de la infantería de marina | station aérienne de fusiliers marins | estação aérea de fuzileiros navais |
| marine corps base | Marine-Corps-Stützpunkt | **m.c.b., marine corps base** *Eng.* | base de la infantería de marina | base de fusiliers marins | base de fuzileiros navais |
| meadow | Wiese | **meadow** *Eng.* | prado | prairie | pradaria |
| dunes | Dünen | **médanos** *Sp.* | médanos | dunes | dunas |
| sea, lake | Meer | **Meer** *Ger.* | mar, lago | mer, lac | mar, lago |
| sea, lake | Meer | **-meer** *Afk., Du.* | mar, lago | mer, lac | mar, lago |
| hills | Hügel | **melkosopočnik** *Rus.* | colinas | collines | colinas |
| memorial | Gedenkstätte | **mem., memorial** *Eng.* | monumento | mémorial | monumento |
| peninsula | Halbinsel | **menanjung** *Indon.* | península | péninsule | península |
| sea | Meer | **mer** *Fr.* | mar | mer | mar |
| mesa | Tafelberg | **mesa** *Sp.* | mesa | mesa | mesa |
| plateau | Hochebene | **meseta** *Sp.* | meseta | plateau | planalto |
| middle | Mittel- | **mid., middle** *Eng.* | medio | moyen | médio, central |
| spit | Landzunge | **mierzeja** *Pol.* | lengua de tierra | flèche | ponta de terra |
| bay | Bucht | **mifraẓ** *Heb.* | bahía | baie | baía |
| mines | Bergwerke | **mikhrot** *Heb.* | minas | mines | minas |
| military | militärisch | **mil., military** *Eng.* | militar | militaire | militar |
| harbor, harbour | Hafen | **-minato** *Jpn.* | puerto | port | porto |
| mine | Bergwerk | **mine** *Eng., Fr.* | mina | mine | mina |
| mountain | Berg | **-mine** *Jpn.* | montaña | montagne | montanha |
| cliff | Kliff | **minqār** *Ara.* | risco | falaise | falésia |
| cape | Kap | **-misaki** *Jpn.* | cabo | cap | cabo |
| mission | Mission | **mission** *Eng., Fr.* | misión | mission | missão |
| monument | Denkmal | **mon., monument** *Eng., Fr.* | monumento | monument | monumento |
| monastery | Kloster | **monasterio** *Sp.* | monasterio | monastère | mosteiro |
| monastery | Kloster | **monastero** *It.* | monasterio | monastère | mosteiro |
| monastery | Kloster | **monastery** *Eng.* | monasterio | monastère | mosteiro |
| monastery | Kloster | **moní** *Gr.* | monasterio | monastère | mosteiro |
| mount | Berg | **mont** *Fr.* | monte | mont | monte |
| mountain | Berg | **montagna** *It.* | montaña | montagne | montanha |
| mountain(s) | Berg(e) | **montagne(s)** *Fr.* | montaña(s) | montagne(s) | montanha(s) |
| mountain(s) | Berg(e) | **montaña(s)** *Sp.* | montaña(s) | montagne(s) | montanha(s) |
| mount | Berg | **monte** *It., Port., Sp.* | monte | mont | monte |
| mountains | Berge | **montes** *Port., Sp.* | montes | monts | montes |
| mountains | Berge | **monti** *It.* | montes | monts | montes |
| mountains | Berge | **monts** *Fr.* | montes | monts | montes |
| monument | Denkmal | **monument** *Eng., Fr.* | monumento | monument | monumento |
| moor | Moor | **moor** *Eng.* | páramo | lande | pântano |
| moor | Moor | **Moor** *Ger.* | páramo | lande | pântano |
| sea | Meer | **more** *Rus., Ukr.* | mar | mer | mar |
| mountain | Berg | **-mori** *Jpn.* | montaña | montagne | montanha |
| mountain | Berg | **morne** *Fr.* | montaña | morne | montanha |
| hill, mountain | Hügel, Berg | **morro** *Port., Sp.* | morro | colline, montagne | morro |
| mosque | Moschee | **mosque** *Eng.* | mezquita | mosquée | mesquita |
| island, rock | Insel, Fels | **motu** *Poly.* | isla, roca | île, rocher | ilha, rochedo |
| island | Insel | **mouchão** *Port.* | isla | île | mouchão |
| mound | Erdhügel | **mound** *Eng.* | montículo | tertre | montículo |
| mount | Berg | **mount** *Eng.* | monte | mont | monte |
| mountain(s) | Berg(e) | **mountain(s)** *Eng.* | montaña(s) | montagne(s) | montanha(s) |
| mouth (river mouth) | Mündung | **mouth** *Eng.* | desembocadura | embouchure | desembocadura |
| mount | Berg | **mt., mount** *Eng.* | monte | mont | monte |
| mountain | Berg | **mtn., mountain** *Eng.* | montaña | montagne | montanha |
| mountains | Berge | **mts., mountains** *Eng.* | montañas | montagnes | montanhas |
| point | Landspitze | **mui** *Viet.* | punta | pointe | ponta |
| headland | Landspitze | **mull** *Gae.* | promontorio | promontoire | promontório |
| depression | Senke | **munkhafaḍ** *Ara.* | depresión | dépression | depressão |
| mountain | Berg | **muntele** *Rom.* | montaña | montagne | montanha |
| mountains | Berge | **munţii** *Rom.* | montañas | montagnes | montanhas |
| museum | Museum | **museo** *It., Sp.* | museo | musée | museu |
| museum | Museum | **Museum** *Ger.* | museo | musée | museu |
| museum | Museum | **museum** *Eng.* | museo | musée | museu |
| museum | Museum | **múzeum** *Hung.* | museo | musée | museu |
| museum | Museum | **muzej** *Rus.* | museo | musée | museu |
| cape | Kap | **mys** *Rus., Ukr.* | cabo | cap | cabo |

## N

| ENGLISH | DEUTSCH | Map Form<br>Geographische Begriffe<br>Términos Geográficos<br>Termes Géographiques<br>Termos Geográficos | ESPAÑOL | FRANCAIS | PORTUGUÊS |
|---|---|---|---|---|---|
| north | Nord | **n., north** *Eng.* | norte | nord | norte |
| sea, gulf | Meer, Golf | **-nada** *Jpn.* | mar, golfo | mer, golfe | mar, golfo |
| desert | Wüste | **nafūd** *Ara.* | desierto | désert | deserto |
| plateau, mountains | Hochebene, Berge | **nagorje** *Rus.* | meseta, montañas | plateau, montagnes | planalto, montanhas |
| river | Fluss | **nahr** *Ara.* | río | rivière | rio |
| sea | Meer | **-naikai** *Jpn.* | mar | mer | mar |
| salt flat | Salzebene | **namakzār** *Per.* | salar | saline | salina |
| narrows | Meeresenge | **narrows** *Eng.* | angostura | goulet | estreito |
| peninsula | Halbinsel | **-näs** *Swe.* | península | péninsule | península |
| naval air station | Flugstützpunkt der Marine | **n.a.s., naval air station** *Eng.* | estación aeronáutica de la marina | station de forces aériennes navales | estação aérea da marinha |
| National Aeronautics and Space Administration | Nationale Aeronautik-und Weltraum-Behörde | **N.A.S.A., National Aeronautics and Space Administration** *Eng.* | Administración Nacional Aeronáutica y Espacial | Administration Nationale de l'Espace et Aéronautique | Administração Nacional do Espaço e Aeronáutica |
| national park | Nationalpark | **nasjonal park** *Nor.* | parque nacional | parc national | parque nacional |
| national | national | **nat., national** *Eng., Fr.* | nacional | national | nacional |
| national battlefield site | Schlachtfeld | **national battlefield site** *Eng.* | campo de batalla nacional | champ de bataille national | campo de batalha nacional |
| national cemetery | Nationalfriedhof | **national cemetery** *Eng.* | cementerio nacional | cimetière national | cemitério nacional |
| national forest | Wald in Gemeinbesitz | **national forest** *Eng.* | bosque nacional | forêt nationale | floresta nacional |
| national historical park | Park an historischer Stätte | **national historical park** *Eng.* | parque histórico nacional | parc historique national | parque histórico nacional |
| national historical site | historische Stätte | **national historical site** *Eng.* | lugar histórico nacional | site historique national | sítio histórico nacional |
| national laboratory | staatliche Forschungsanstalt | **national laboratory** *Eng.* | laboratorio nacional | laboratoire national | laboratório nacional |
| national memorial | nationale Gedenkstätte | **national memorial** *Eng.* | monumento nacional | memorial national | monumento nacional |
| national military park | Park bei einem Schlachtfeld | **national military park** *Eng.* | parque militar nacional | parc militaire national | parque militar nacional |
| national monument | Nationaldenkmal | **national monument** *Eng.* | monumento nacional | monument national | monumento nacional |
| national park | Nationalpark | **national park** *Eng.* | parque nacional | parc nationale | parque nacional |
| national recreation area | Ausflugsgebiet | **national recreation area** *Eng.* | campo nacional de recreo | région de récréation national | área de lazer nacional |
| national seashore | öffentlicher Badestrand | **national seashore** *Eng.* | playa nacional | plage nationale | praia nacional |
| national park | Nationalpark | **natsional'nyy park** *Ukr.* | parque nacional | parc nationale | parque nacional |
| reserve | Naturpark | **Naturpark** *Ger.* | reserva natural | réserve naturelle | reserva natural |
| nature reserve | Naturschutzgebiet | **Naturschutzgebiet** *Ger.* | reserva natural | réserve naturelle | reserva natural |
| naval air station | Flugstützpunkt der Marine | **naval air station** *Eng.* | estación aeronáutica de la marina | station de forces aériennes navales | estação aérea da marinha |
| naval base | Flottenstützpunkt | **naval base** *Eng.* | base naval | base navale | base naval |
| naval station | Marinestation | **naval station** *Eng.* | estación naval | station navale | estação naval |
| naval base | Flottenstützpunkt | **n.b., naval base** *Eng.* | base naval | base navale | base naval |
| rock | Fels | **-ne** *Jpn.* | roca | rocher | rochedo |
| neck | Landenge | **neck** *Eng.* | istmo | isthme | istmo |
| necropolis (cemetery) | Friedhof | **necrópolis** *Sp.* | necrópolis | nécropole | necrópole |
| cape | Kap | **neem** *Est.* | cabo | cap | cabo |
| peninsula, point | Halbinsel, Landspitze | **-nes** *Ice., Nor.* | península, punta | péninsule, pointe | península, ponta |
| promontory | Vorgebirge | **ness** *Gae.* | promontorio | promontoire | promontório |
| snowcapped mountain(s) | Schneegipfel | **nev.(s)., nevado(s)** *Sp.* | nevado(s) | montagne(s) neigeuse(s) | pico(s) nevado(s) |
| mountain | Berg | **ngoc** *Viet.* | montaña | montagne | montanha |
| cape | Kap | **nina** *Est.* | cabo | cap | cabo |
| islands | Inseln | **nísoi** *Gr.* | islas | îles | ilhas |
| island | Insel | **nísos** *Gr.* | isla | île | ilha |
| lowland | Tiefland | **nizina** *Rus.* | tierra baja | terrain bas | terras baixas |
| lowland | Tiefland | **nižina** *Slo.* | tierra baja | terrain bas | terras baixas |
| lowland | Tiefland | **nizmennost'** *Rus.* | tierra baja | terrain bas | terras baixas |
| cape | Kap | **nos** *Blg.* | cabo | cap | cabo |
| naval station | Marinestation | **n.s., naval station** *Eng.* | estación naval | station navale | estação naval |
| nature reserve | Naturschutzgebiet | **Nsg., Naturschutzgebiet** *Ger.* | reserva natural | réserve naturelle | reserva natural |
| mountain | Berg | **nui** *Viet.* | montaña | montagne | montanha |
| lake | See | **-numa** *Jpn.* | lago | lac | lago |
| mountains | Berge | **nuruu** *Mong.* | montañas | montagnes | montanhas |
| island | Insel | **nusa** *Indon.* | isla | île | ilha |
| lake | See | **nuur** *Mong.* | lago | lac | lago |
| lowland | Tiefland | **nyzovyna** *Ukr.* | tierra baja | terrain bas | terras baixas |

## O

| ENGLISH | DEUTSCH | Map Form<br>Geographische Begriffe<br>Términos Geográficos<br>Termes Géographiques<br>Termos Geográficos | ESPAÑOL | FRANCAIS | PORTUGUÊS |
|---|---|---|---|---|---|
| island | Insel | **-ø** *Dan., Nor.* | isla | île | ilha |
| island | Insel | **-ö** *Swe.* | isla | île | ilha |
| island | Insel | **o., ostrov** *Rus.* | isla | île | ilha |
| islands | Inseln | **-öarna** *Swe.* | islas | îles | ilhas |
| oasis | Oase | **oasis** *Eng., Fr., Sp.* | oasis | oasis | oásis |
| observatory | Observatorium | **observatorio** *Sp.* | observatorio | observatoire | observatório |
| observatory | Observatorium | **observatory** *Eng.* | observatorio | observatoire | observatório |
| ocean | Ozean | **ocean** *Eng.* | océano | océan | oceano |
| island | Insel | **-ön** *Swe.* | isla | île | ilha |
| mountains | Berge | **óri** *Gr.* | montañas | montagnes | montanhas |
| bay | Bucht | **órmos** *Gr.* | bahía | baie | baía |
| mountain(s) | Berg(e) | **óros** *Gr.* | montaña(s) | montagne(s) | montanha(s) |
| island | Insel | **ostriv** *Ukr.* | isla | île | ilha |
| island(s) | Insel(n) | **ostrov(a)** *Rus.* | isla(s) | île(s) | ilha(s) |
| island | Insel | **ostrovul** *Rom.* | isla | île | ilha |
| islands | Inseln | **otoci** *S./C.* | islas | îles | ilhas |
| island | Insel | **otok** *S./C.* | isla | île | ilha |
| wadi | Wadi | **ouadi** *Ara.* | uadi | wadi | uádi |
| wadi | Wadi | **oued** *Ara.* | uadi | wadi | uádi |
| outlet | Abfluss | **outlet** *Eng.* | desagüe | débouché | escoadouro |
| island | Insel | **-øy, -øya** *Nor.* | isla | île | ilha |
| lake | See | **oz., ozero** *Rus., Ukr.* | lago | lac | lago |
| lakes | Seen | **ozera** *Rus.* | lagos | lacs | lagos |

## P

| ENGLISH | DEUTSCH | Map Form<br>Geographische Begriffe<br>Términos Geográficos<br>Termes Géographiques<br>Termos Geográficos | ESPAÑOL | FRANCAIS | PORTUGUÊS |
|---|---|---|---|---|---|
| hills | Hügel | **pahorkatina** *Czech* | colinas | collines | colinas |
| palace | Palast | **pal., palace** *Eng.* | palacio | palais | palácio |
| palace | Palast | **palacio** *Sp.* | palacio | palais | palácio |
| palace | Palast | **palais** *Fr.* | palacio | palais | palácio |
| palace | Palast | **palazzo** *It.* | palacio | palais | palácio |
| palace | Palast | **paleis** *Du.* | palacio | palais | palácio |
| railroad station | Bahnhof | **pályaudvar** *Hung.* | estacíon ferrocarril | gare | estação ferroviária |
| monument | Denkmal | **pam'atnik** *Rus.* | monumento | monument | monumento |
| plain | Ebene | **pampa** *Sp.* | pampa | plaine | pampa |
| basin | Becken | **pánev** *Czech* | cuenca | bassin | bacia |
| swamp | Sumpf | **pantanal** *Port., Sp.* | pantanal | marais | pantanal |
| marsh, swamp, reservoir | Marsch, Sumpf, Stausee | **pantano** *Sp.* | pantano | marais, réservoir | Pântano |
| moor | Moor | **páramo** *Sp.* | páramo | lande | pântano |
| park | Park | **parc** *Fr.* | parque | parc | parque |
| national park | Nationalpark | **parc national** *Fr.* | parque nacional | parc national | parque nacional |
| park | Park | **parco** *It.* | parque | parc | parque |
| national park | Nationalpark | **parco nazionale** *It.* | parque nacional | parc national | parque nacional |
| provincial park | Naturpark | **parc provincial** *Fr.* | parque de la provincia | parc provincial | parque provincial |
| park | Park | **Park** *Ger.* | parque | parc | parque |
| park | Park | **park** *Eng.* | parque | parc | parque |
| national park | Nationalpark | **park narodowy** *Pol.* | parque nacional | parc national | parque nacional |
| parkway | Ferienstrasse | **parkway** *Eng.* | calzada | allée de parc | alameda de parque |
| park | Park | **parque** *Port., Sp.* | parque | parc | parque |
| national park | Nationalpark | **parq. nac., parque nacional** *Port., Sp.* | parque nacional | parc national | parque nacional |
| beach | Strand | **part** *Hung.* | playa | plage | praia |
| strait | Meeresstrasse | **pas** *Fr.* | estrecho | détroit | estreito |
| passage | Durchfahrt | **pasaje** *Sp.* | pasaje | passage | passagem |
| pass | Pass | **paso** *Sp.* | paso | col | passo |
| pass | Pass | **Pass** *Ger.* | paso | col | passo |
| pass | Pass | **pass** *Eng.* | paso | col | passo |
| passage | Durchfahrt | **passage** *Eng., Fr.* | pasaje | passage | passagem |
| passage | Durchfahrt | **passe** *Fr.* | pasaje | passe | passagem |
| pass | Pass | **passo** *It.* | paso | col | passo |
| pass | Pass | **pasul** *Rom.* | paso | col | passo |
| brook | Bach | **patak** *Hung.* | riachuelo | crique | riacho |
| peak(s) | Gipfel | **peak(s)** *Eng.* | pico(s) | pic(s) | pico(s) |
| cave | Höhle | **pećina** *S./C.* | cueva | caverne | caverna |
| mountain | Berg | **pedra** *Port.* | montaña | montagne | montanha |
| mountains | Berge | **peg., pegunungan** *Indon.* | montañas | montagnes | montanhas |
| sea | Meer | **pélagos** *Gr.* | mar | mer | mar |

| ENGLISH | DEUTSCH | Map Form / Geographische Begriffe / Términos Geográficos / Termes Géographiques / Termos Geográficos | ESPAÑOL | FRANCAIS | PORTUGUÊS |
|---|---|---|---|---|---|
| peninsula | Halbinsel | **pen., peninsula** *Eng.* | península | péninsule | península |
| peak, rock | Gipfel, Fels | **peña** *Sp.* | peña | pic, rocher | penha |
| peak, large rock | Gipfel, grosser Fels | **peñasco** *Sp.* | peñasco | pic, rocher | penhasco |
| basin | Becken | **pendi** *Ch.* | cuenca | bassin | bacia |
| peninsula | Halbinsel | **peninsula** *Eng.* | península | péninsule | península |
| peninsula | Halbinsel | **península** *Sp.* | península | péninsule | península |
| peninsula | Halbinsel | **péninsule** *Fr.* | península | péninsule | península |
| rock | Fels | **peñón** *Sp.* | peñón | rocher | rochedo |
| pass | Pass | **pereval** *Rus., Ukr.* | paso | col | passo |
| strait | Meeresstrasse | **pertuis** *Fr.* | estrecho | pertuis | estreito |
| sand desert | Sandwüste | **peski** *Rus.* | desierto arenoso | désert de sable | deserto arenoso |
| mountain | Berg | **phnum** *Cbd.* | montaña | montagne | montanha |
| mountain | Berg | **phou** *Lao.* | montaña | montagne | montanha |
| mountain | Berg | **phu** *Thai* | montaña | montagne | montanha |
| cape | Kap | **pi** *Ch.* | cabo | cap | cabo |
| plain | Ebene | **piano** *It.* | llanura | plaine | planície |
| peak | Gipfel | **pic** *Fr.* | pico | pic | pico |
| peak | Gipfel | **picacho** *Sp.* | picacho | pic | pico |
| peak | Gipfel | **picco** *It.* | pico | pic | pico |
| peak(s) | Gipfel | **pico(s)** *Port., Sp.* | pico(s) | pic(s) | pico(s) |
| pier | Landungsbrücke | **pier** *Eng.* | embarcadero | jetée | cais |
| mountain | Berg | **-piggen** *Nor.* | montaña | montagne | montanha |
| peak | Gipfel | **pik** *Rus.* | pico | pic | pico |
| forest | Wald | **pinhal** *Port.* | bosque | forêt | pinhal |
| peak | Gipfel | **pique** *Fr.* | pico | pique | pico |
| pyramid | Pyramide | **pirámide** *Sp.* | pirámide | pyramide | pirâmide |
| peak(s) | Gipfel | **piton(s)** *Fr.* | pico(s) | piton(s) | pico(s) |
| peninsula | Halbinsel | **pivostriv** *Ukr.* | península | péninsule | península |
| peak | Gipfel | **piz, pizzo** *It.* | pico | pic | pico |
| peak | Gipfel | **pk., peak** *Eng.* | pico | pic | pico |
| parkway | Ferienstrasse | **pkwy., parkway** *Eng.* | calzada | allée de parc | avenida |
| plain | Ebene | **plain** *Eng.* | llanura | plaine | planície |
| plain | Ebene | **plaine** *Fr.* | llanura | plaine | planície |
| plains | Ebenen | **plains** *Eng.* | llanura | plaines | planícies |
| plateau | Hochebene | **planalto** *Port.* | meseta | plateau | planalto |
| planetarium | Planetarium | **planetario** *Sp.* | planetario | planétarium | planetário |
| planetarium | Planetarium | **planetarium** *Eng.* | planetario | planétarium | planetário |
| mountain, range | Berg, Gebirge | **planina** *S./C.* | montaña, sierra | montagne, chaîne | montanha, cordilheira |
| plateau | Hochebene | **plateau** *Eng., Fr.* | meseta | plateau | planalto |
| plateau | Hochebene | **plato** *Afk., Blg., Rus.* | meseta | plateau | planalto |
| beach | Strand | **playa** *Sp.* | playa | plage | praia |
| square | Platz | **plaza** *Sp.* | plaza | place | praça |
| plateau | Hochebene | **plošina** *Czech* | meseta | plateau | planalto |
| plateau | Hochebene | **ploskogorje** *Rus.* | meseta | plateau | planalto |
| pass | Pass | **poarta** *Rom.* | paso | col | passo |
| hill | Hügel | **poggio** *It.* | colina | colline | colina |
| point | Landspitze | **point** *Eng.* | punta | pointe | ponta |
| point | Landspitze | **pointe** *Fr.* | punta | pointe | ponta |
| island | Insel | **pol** *Du.* | isla | île | ilha |
| plain, basin | Ebene, Becken | **polje** *S./C.* | llanura, cuenca | plaine, bassin | planície, bacia |
| peninsula | Halbinsel | **poluostrov** *Rus.* | península | péninsule | península |
| peninsula | Halbinsel | **poluotok** *S./C.* | península | péninsule | península |
| pond | Teich | **pond** *Eng.* | charca | étang | lago |
| peak | Gipfel | **-pong** *Kor.* | pico | cime | pico |
| bridge | Brücke | **pont** *Fr.* | puente | pont | ponte |
| point | Landspitze | **ponta, pontal** *Port.* | punta | pointe | ponta, pontal |
| bridge | Brücke | **ponte** *Port.* | puente | pont | ponte |
| pool | Tümpel | **pool** *Eng.* | charco | étang | charco |
| rapids | Stromschnellen | **porog** *Rus.* | rápidos | rapides | rápidos |
| port | Hafen | **port** *Eng., Fr.* | puerto | port | porto |
| port | Hafen | **porto** *It.* | puerto | port | porto |
| strait | Meeresstrasse | **porthmós** *Gr.* | estrecho | détroit | estreito |
| provincial park | Naturpark | **p.p., provincial park** *Eng.* | parque de la provincia | parc provincial | parque provincial |
| beach | Strand | **praia** *Port.* | playa | plage | praia |
| reservoir | Stausee | **přehr., přehradová nádrž** *Czech* | embalse | réservoir | reservatório |
| reservoir, dam | Stausee, Damm | **presa** *Sp.* | presa | réservoir, barrage | represa |
| peninsula | Halbinsel | **presqu'île** *Fr.* | península | presqu'île | península |
| reservoir | Stausee | **priehradová nádrz** *Slo.* | embalse | réservoir | reservatório |
| pass | Pass | **priesmyk** *Slo.* | paso | col | passo |
| prison | Gefängnis | **prison** *Eng.* | prisión | prison | prisão |
| pass | Pass | **prohod** *Blg.* | paso | col | passo |
| strait | Meeresstrasse | **proliv** *Rus.* | estrecho | détroit | estreito |
| promontory | Vorgebirge | **promontorio** *It., Sp.* | promontorio | promontoire | promontório |
| promontory | Vorgebirge | **promontory** *Eng.* | promontorio | promontoire | promontório |
| strait | Meeresstrasse | **protoka** *Ukr.* | estrecho | détroit | estreito |
| provincial park | Naturpark | **prov. park, provincial park** *Eng.* | parque de la provincia | parc provincial | parque provincial |
| reservoir | Stausee | **prudy** *Rus.* | embalse | réservoir | reservatório |
| pass | Pass | **průsmyk** *Czech* | paso | col | passo |
| pass | Pass | **przeęcz** *Pol.* | paso | col | passo |
| cape | Kap | **przylądek** *Pol.* | cabo | cap | cabo |
| point | Landspitze | **pt., point** *Eng.* | punta | pointe | ponta |
| railroad station | Bahnhof | **pu., pályaudvar** *Hung.* | estación de ferrocarril | gare | estação ferroviária |
| port | Hafen | **puerto** *Sp.* | puerto | port | porto |
| peak | Gipfel | **puig** *Cat.* | pico | cime | pico |
| island | Insel | **pulau** *Indon., Mal.* | isla | île | ilha |
| upland | Bergland | **puna** *Sp.* | puna | hautes terres | terras altas |
| peak | Gipfel | **puncak** *Indon.* | pico | cime | pico |
| point | Landspitze | **punt** *Du.* | punta | pointe | ponta |
| point, peak | Landspitze, Gipfel | **punta** *It., Sp.* | punta | pointe, cime | ponta |
| point | Landspitze | **puntilla** *Sp.* | puntilla | pointe | ponta pequena |
| forest | Wald | **puszcza** *Pol.* | bosque | forêt | floresta |
| pyramid | Pyramide | **pyramid** *Eng.* | pirámide | pyramide | pirâmide |

## Q

| ENGLISH | DEUTSCH | Map Form | ESPAÑOL | FRANCAIS | PORTUGUÊS |
|---|---|---|---|---|---|
| salt flat | Salzebene | **qāʿ** *Ara.* | salar | saline | salina |
| canal | Kanal | **qanāt** *Ara.* | canal | canal | canal |
| hill | Hügel | **qārat** *Ara.* | colina | colline | colina |
| hills | Hügel | **qārāt** *Ara.* | colinas | collines | colinas |
| dunes | Dünen | **qawz** *Ara.* | dunas | dunes | dunas |
| brook | Bach | **qbda., quebrada** *Sp.* | quebrada | crique | arroio |
| mountain | Berg | **qolleh** *Per.* | montaña | montagne | montanha |
| canal | Kanal | **-qu** *Ch.* | canal | canal | canal |
| quarry | Steinbruch | **quarry** *Eng.* | cantera | carrière | pedreira |
| brook | Bach | **quebrada** *Sp.* | quebrada | crique | arroio |
| rapids | Stromschnellen | **quedas** *Port.* | rápidos | rapides | quedas |
| islands | Inseln | **qundao** *Ch.* | islas | îles | ilhas |
| hill | Hügel | **qūr** *Ara.* | colina | colline | colina |
| mountain | Berg | **qurnat** *Ara.* | montaña | montagne | montanha |

## R

| ENGLISH | DEUTSCH | Map Form | ESPAÑOL | FRANCAIS | PORTUGUÊS |
|---|---|---|---|---|---|
| river | Fluss | **r., rio** *Port.* **río** **river** **rivière** | río | rivière | rio |
| range | Gebirge | **ra., range** *Eng.* | sierra | chaîne | cordilheira |
| Royal Australian Air Force Station | Luftwaffenstützpunkt (Austl.) | **R.A.A.F.S., Royal Australian Air Force Station** *Eng.* | Real Estación Aeronáutica (Austl.) | Station Aérienne Royale (Austl.) | Real Estação da Força Aérea Australiana |
| race course | Rennbahn | **race course** *Eng.* | hipódromo | champ de course | hipódromo |
| race track | Rennbahn | **race track** *Eng.* | hipódromo | champ de course | hipódromo |
| raceway | Rennbahn | **raceway** *Eng.* | hipódromo | champ de course | hipódromo |
| river | Fluss | **rach** *Viet.* | río | rivière | rio |
| anchorage | Ankerplatz | **rada** *Sp.* | rada | ancrage | ancoradouro |
| cape | Kap | **rags** *Latv.* | cabo | cap | cabo |
| railroad | Eisenbahn | **railroad** *Eng.* | ferrocarril | chemin de fer | ferrovia |
| railway | Eisenbahn | **railway** *Eng.* | ferrocarril | chemin de fer | ferrovia |
| railway station | Bahnhof | **railway station** *Eng.* | estacíon de ferrocarril | gare | estação ferroviária |
| dunes | Dünen | **ramlat** *Ara.* | dunas | dunes | dunas |
| range(s) | Gebirge | **range(s)** *Eng.* | sierra(s) | chaîne(s) | cordilheira(s) |
| river | Fluss | **rão., ribeirão** *Port.* | río | rivière | rio, ribeirão |
| rapids | Stromschnellen | **rapides** *Fr.* | rápidos | rapides | rápidos |
| rapids | Stromschnellen | **rapids** *Eng.* | rápidos | rapides | rápidos |
| wadi | Wadi | **raqabat** *Ara.* | uadi | wadi | uádi |
| cape | Kap | **ras, ra's** *Ara.* | cabo | cap | cabo |
| cape | Kap | **rās** *Per.* | cabo | cap | cabo |
| ravine | Tobel | **ravine** *Eng.* | barranca | ravin | ravina |
| plain | Ebene | **ravnina** *Rus.* | llanura | plaine | planície |
| canal | Kanal | **rayyāh** *Ara.* | canal | canal | canal |
| flood plain | Überschwemmungsebene | **razlivy** *Rus.* | llanura de inundación | lit d'inondation | planície de inundação |
| road | Landstrasse | **rd., road** *Eng.* | camino | route | rodovia |
| reef | Riff | **récif** *Fr.* | arrecife | récif | recife |
| reefs | Riffe | **recifes** *Port.* | arrecifes | récifs | recifes |
| reefs | Riffe | **récifs** *Fr.* | arrecifes | récifs | recifes |
| reef(s) | Riff(e) | **reef(s)** *Eng.* | arrecife(s) | récif(s) | recife(s) |
| regional park | Regionalpark | **regional park** *Eng.* | parque regional | parc régional | parque regional |
| mountain | Berg | **-rei** *Jpn.* | montaña | montagne | montanha |
| race course | Rennbahn | **Rennbahn** *Ger.* | hipódromo | champ de course | hipódromo |
| dam, reservoir | Damm, Stausee | **represa** *Port.* | presa, embalse | barrage, réservoir | represa |
| airport | Flughafen | **repülötér** *Hung.* | aeropuerto | aéroport | aeroporto |
| reservoir | Stausee | **res., reservoir** *Eng.* | embalse | réservoir | reservatório |
| reservation | Reservat | **reservation** *Eng.* | reservación | réservation | reserva |
| reservoir | Stausee | **reservatório** *Port.* | embalse | réservoir | reservatório |
| reserve | Reservat | **reserve** *Eng.* | reserva | réserve | reserva |
| reserve | Reservat | **réserve** *Fr.* | reserva | réserve | reserva |
| game reserve | Wildreservat | **réserve de chasse** *Fr.* | vedado de caza | réserve de chasse | reserva de caça |
| reservoir | Stausee | **reservoir** *Eng.* | embalse | réservoir | reservatório |
| reservoir | Stausee | **réservoir** *Fr.* | embalse | réservoir | reservatório |
| beach | Strand | **restinga** *Port.* | playa | plage | praia |
| islands | Inseln | **-retto** *Jpn.* | islas | îles | ilhas |
| ria (inlet) | Ria | **ría** *Sp.* | ría | ria | ria |
| brook | Bach | **riacho** *Port., Sp.* | riacho | crique | riacho |
| brook | Bach | **riachuelo** *Sp.* | riachuelo | crique | riacho |
| brook | Bach | **rib., ribeira** *Port.* | riachuelo | crique | ribeira |
| river | Fluss | **ribeirão** *Port.* | río | rivière | ribeirão |
| ridge | Höhenrücken | **ridge** *Eng.* | sierra | crête | serra |
| moor | Ried | **Ried** *Ger.* | páramo | lande | pântano |
| brook | Bach | **riera** *Sp., Cat.* | riera | crique | riacho |
| national museum | Reichsmuseum | **rijksmuseum** *Du.* | museo nacional | musée national | museu nacional |
| army installation | Anlage des Heeres | **rikujō-jieitai** *Jpn.* | estación del ejército | installation militaire | instalação militar |
| river | Fluss | **rio** *Port.* | río | rivière | rio |
| river | Fluss | **río** *Sp.* | río | rivière | rio |
| river | Fluss | **riozinho** *Port.* | río | rivière | riozinho |
| rise (submarine) | Schwelle (untermeerische) | **rise** *Eng.* | elevación (submarina) | élévation (sous-marine) | elevação (submarina) |
| river | Fluss | **river** *Eng.* | río | rivière | rio |
| brook | Bach | **rivera** *Sp.* | rivera | ruisseau | córrego |
| coast | Küste | **riviera** *It.* | costa | côte | costa |
| river | Fluss | **rivière** *Fr.* | río | rivière | rio |
| army installation | Anlage des Heeres | **r.j., rikujō-jieitai** *Jpn.* | estación del ejército | installation militaire | instalação do exército |
| road | Landstrasse | **road** *Eng.* | camino | route | rodovia |
| roads (anchorage) | Ankerplatz | **roads** *Eng.* | ancladero | ancrage | ancoradouro |
| rock | Fels | **roca** *Sp.* | roca | rocher | rochedo |
| rock, mountain | Fels, Berg | **rocca** *It.* | roca, montaña | rocher, montagne | rochedo, montanha |
| rock(s) | Fels(en) | **rock(s)** *Eng.* | roca(s) | rocher(s) | rochedo(s) |
| cape | Kap | **rt** *S./C.* | cabo | cap | cabo |
| brook | Bach | **rû** *Fr.* | arroyo | rû | córrego |
| mountains | Berge | **rudohorie** *Slo.* | montañas | montagnes | montanhas |
| brook | Bach | **ruisseau** *Fr.* | arroyo | ruisseau | córrego |
| mountain | Berg | **rujm** *Ara.* | montaña | montagne | montanha |
| run (stream) | Bach | **run** *Eng.* | arroyo | ruisseau | córrego |

## S

| ENGLISH | DEUTSCH | Map Form | ESPAÑOL | FRANCAIS | PORTUGUÊS |
|---|---|---|---|---|---|
| south | Süd | **s., south** *Eng.* | sur | sud | sul |
| range | Gebirge | **sa., serra** *Port.* | sierra | chaîne | cordilheira |
| island | Insel | **saar** *Est.* | isla | île | ilha |
| savanna | Savanne | **sabana** *Sp.* | sabana | savane | savana |
| salt marsh, lagoon | Salzmarsch, Lagune, Haff | **sabkhat** *Ara.* | pantano salado, laguna | marais salé, lagune | pântano salgado, laguna |
| dam | Damm | **sadd** *Ara.* | presa | barrage | represa |
| wadi | Wadi | **sagula** *Ara.* | uadi | wadi | uádi |
| desert | Wüste | **ṣaḥrāʾ** *Ara.* | desierto | désert | deserto |
| cape | Kap | **-saki** *Jpn.* | cabo | cap | cabo |
| salt flat | Salzebene | **salar** *Sp.* | salar | saline | salina |
| salt marsh, salt flat | Salzmarsch, Salzebene | **salina(s)** *Sp.* | salina(s) | marais salé, saline | salina(s) |
| salt marsh, salt flat | Salzmarsch, Salzebene | **salines** *Fr.* | pantano salado, salinas, salar | salines | pântano salgado, salinas |
| salt flat | Salzebene | **salt flat** *Eng.* | salar | saline | salina |
| salt lake | Salzsee | **salt lake** *Eng.* | lago salado | lac salé | lago salgado |
| salt marsh | Salzmarsch | **salt marsh** *Eng.* | pantano salado | marais salé | pântano salgado |
| waterfall | Wasserfall | **salto(s)** *Port., Sp.* | salto(s) | chute d'eau | salto(s) |
| reservoir | Stausee | **samudra** *Sin.* | embalse | réservoir | reservatório |
| range | Gebirge | **-sammyaku** *Jpn.* | sierra | chaîne | cordilheira |
| mountain | Berg | **-san** *Jpn., Kor.* | montaña | montagne | montanha |
| mountains | Berge | **-sanchi** *Jpn.* | montañas | montagnes | montanhas |
| mountains | Berge | **-sanmaek** *Kor.* | montañas | montagnes | montanhas |
| shrine | Schrein | **santuario** *It., Sp.* | santuario | châsse | santuário |
| mountain | Berg | **sar** *Pas.* | montaña | montagne | montanha |
| island | Insel | **sari** *Est.* | isla | île | ilha |
| desert | Wüste | **sarīr** *Ara.* | desierto | désert | deserto |
| saddle (pass) | Sattel | **Sattel** *Ger.* | paso | col | passo |
| strait | Meeresstrasse | **šaurums** *Latv.* | estrecho | détroit | estreito |
| waterfall | Wasserfall | **saut** *Fr.* | cascada | saut | queda d'água |
| castle | Schloss | **Schloss** *Ger.* | castillo | château | castelo |
| gorge | Schlucht | **Schlucht** *Ger.* | garganta | gorge | garganta |
| school | Schule | **school** *Eng.* | escuela | école | escola |
| sea | Meer | **sea** *Eng.* | mar | mer | mar |
| seamount | untermeerische Kuppe | **seamount** *Eng.* | montaña submarina | montagne sous-marine | montanha submarina |
| sea scarp | Abbruch | **sea scarp** *Eng.* | cantil | escarpement sous-marin | escarpa submarina |
| dry lake | Trockensee | **sebjet** *Ara.* | lago seco | lac asséché | lago seco |
| salt flat | Salzebene | **sebkha** *Ara.* | salar | saline | salina |
| intermittent lake | periodischer See | **sebkra** *Ara.* | lago intermitente | lac périodique | lago intermitente |
| salt marsh | Salzmarsch | **sebkret** *Ara.* | pantano salado | marais salé | pântano salgado |
| airport | Flughafen | **sede-te'ufa** *Heb.* | aeropuerto | aéroport | aeroporto |
| saddle (pass) | Sattel | **sedlo** *Czech* | paso | col | passo |
| lake(s) | See(n) | **See(n)** *Ger.* | lago(s) | lac(s) | lago(s) |
| strait | Meeresstrasse | **selat** *Indon.* | estrecho | détroit | estreito |
| peninsula | Halbinsel | **semenanjung** *Indon.* | península | péninsule | península |
| seminary | Seminar | **seminary** *Eng.* | seminario | séminaire | seminário |
| mountain | Berg | **-sen** *Jpn.* | montaña | montagne | montanha |
| sound | Sund | **seno** *Sp.* | seno | détroit | estreito |
| mountains | Gebirge | **serra** *Cat.* | montañas | montagnes | montanhas |
| range, mountain | Gebirge, Berg | **serra** *Port.* | sierra | chaîne, montagne | serra |

| ENGLISH | DEUTSCH | Map Form Geographische Begriffe Términos Geográficos Termes Géographiques Termos Geográficos | ESPAÑOL | FRANCAIS | PORTUGUÊS |
|---|---|---|---|---|---|
| ridge(s) | Höhenrücken | **serranía(s)** *Sp.* | serranía(s) | crête(s) | serrania(s) |
| island | Insel | **sha** *Ch.* | isla | île | ilha |
| rapids | Stromschnellen | **shallāl** *Ara.* | rápidos | rapides | rápidos |
| desert | Wüste | **shamo** *Ch.* | desierto | désert | deserto |
| mountain(s), island | Berg(e), Insel | **shan** *Ch.* | montaña(s), isla | montagne(s), île | montanha(s), ilha |
| pass | Pass | **shankou** *Ch.* | paso | col | passo |
| mountains | Berge | **shanmo** *Ch.* | montañas | montagnes | montanhas |
| bay | Bucht | **sharm** *Ara.* | bahía | baie | baía |
| peninsula | Halbinsel | **shibh jazīrat** *Ara.* | península | péninsule | península |
| island | Insel | **-shima** *Jpn.* | isla | île | ilha |
| reef | Riff | **-shō** *Jpn.* | arrecife | récif | recife |
| shoal(s) | Untiefe(n) | **shoal(s)** *Eng.* | bajo(s) | haut-fond(s) | baixio(s) |
| islands | Inseln | **-shotō** *Jpn.* | islas | îles | ilhas |
| shrine | Schrein | **shrine** *Eng.* | santuario | châsse | santuário |
| river | Fluss | **shui** *Ch.* | río | rivière | rio |
| reservoir | Stausee | **shuiku** *Ch.* | embalse | réservoir | reservatório |
| strait | Meeresstrasse | **shuitao** *Ch.* | estrecho | détroit | estreito |
| temple | Tempel | **si** *Ch.* | templo | temple | templo |
| range, ridge | Gebirge, Höhenrücken | **sierra** *Sp.* | sierra | chaîne, crête | serra |
| rapids | Stromschnellen | **šivera** *Rus.* | rápidos | rapides | rápidos |
| lake | See | **-sjø** *Nor.* | lago | lac | lago |
| lakes | Seen | **-sjöarna** *Swe.* | lagos | lacs | lagos |
| lake | See | **-sjøen** *Nor.* | lago | lac | lago |
| lake, bay | See, Bucht | **-sjön** *Swe.* | lago, bahía | lac, baie | lago, baía |
| island | Insel | **skär** *Swe.* | isla | île | ilha |
| forest | Wald | **-skog, -skogen** *Swe.* | bosque | forêt | floresta |
| mountain | Berg | **slieve** *Gae.* | montaña | montagne | montanha |
| castle | Schloss | **slot** *Du.* | castillo | château | castelo |
| castle | Schloss | **slott** *Swe.* | castillo | château | castelo |
| slough (swamp) | verlandende Wasserfläche | **slough** *Eng.* | pantano | fondrière | pântano, brejo |
| ridge | Höhenrücken | **snía., serranía** *Sp.* | serranía | crête | serrania |
| snowfield | Schneefeld | **snowfield** *Eng.* | ventisquero | champ de neige | campo de neve |
| lake | See | **-sø** *Dan.* | lago | lac | lago |
| sound | Sund | **sonda** *Sp.* | sonda | détroit | estreito |
| sound | Sund | **sound** *Eng.* | sonda | détroit | estreito |
| cave, tunnel | Höhle, Tunnel | **souterrain** *Fr.* | cueva, túnel | souterrain | caverna, túnel |
| state park | Naturpark | **s.p., state park** *Eng.* | parque provincial | parc régional | parque estadual |
| cave | Höhle | **špilja** *S./C.* | cueva | caverne | caverna |
| spit | Landzunge | **spit** *Eng.* | lengua de tierra | flèche | ponta de terra |
| peak | Spitze | **Spitze** *Ger.* | pico | cime | pico |
| spring | Quelle | **spr., spring** *Eng.* | manantial | source | fonte, manancial |
| square | Platz | **sq., square** *Eng.* | plaza | place | praça |
| range, ridge | Gebirge, Höhenrücken | **srra., sierra** *Sp.* | sierra | chaîne, crête | serra |
| saint | Sankt | **st., saint** *Eng., Fr.* | san, santa, santo | saint | são, santa, santo |
| street | Strasse | **st., street** *Eng.* | calle | rue | rua |
| saint | Sankt | **sta., santa** *Port., Sp.* | santa | sainte | santa |
| station | Bahnhof, Stützpunkt | **sta., station** *Eng., Fr.* | estación | station | estação |
| stadium | Stadion | **stad., stadium** *Eng.* | estadio | stade | estádio |
| stadium | Stadion | **stadio** *It.* | estadio | stade | estádio |
| stadium | Stadion | **Stadion** *Ger.* | estadio | stade | estádio |
| stadium | Stadion | **stadion** *Rus.* | estadio | stade | estádio |
| stadium | Stadion | **stadium** *Eng.* | estadio | stade | estádio |
| state beach | öffentlicher Badestrand | **state beach** *Eng.* | playa provincial | plage régionale | praia estadual |
| state forest | Wald in Gemeinbesitz | **state forest** *Eng.* | bosque provincial | forêt régionale | floresta estadual |
| state historical park | Park an historischer Stätte | **state historical park** *Eng.* | parque histórico provincial | parc historique régional | parque histórico estadual |
| state park | Naturpark | **state park** *Eng.* | parque provincial | parc régional | parque estadual |
| state recreation area | Ausflugsgebiet | **state recreation area** *Eng.* | zona de recreo provincial | zone récréative regionale | área de lazer estadual |
| station | Bahnhof, Stützpunkt | **station** *Eng., Fr.* | estación | station | estação |
| reservoir | Stausee | **Stausee** *Ger.* | embalse | réservoir | reservatório |
| station | Bahnhof, Stützpunkt | **stazione** *It.* | estación | station | estação |
| saint | Sankt | **ste., sainte** *Fr.* | santa | sainte | santa |
| mountains | Berge | **stěny** *Czech* | montañas | montagnes | montanhas |
| steppe | Steppe | **step'** *Rus.* | estepa | steppe | estepe |
| peak | Gipfel | **štit** *Slo.* | pico | cime | pico |
| saint | Sankt | **sto., santo** *Port., Sp.* | santo | saint | santo |
| strait(s) | Meeresstrasse | **strait(s)** *Eng.* | estrecho | détroit | estreito |
| stream | Strom | **stream** *Eng.* | corriente de agua | cours d'eau | curso d'água |
| street | Strasse | **street** *Eng.* | calle | rue | rua |
| strait | Meeresstrasse | **stretto** *It.* | estrecho | détroit | estreito |
| spit | Landzunge | **strilka** *Ukr.* | lengua de tierra | flèche | ponta de terra |
| stream | Strom | **Strom** *Ger.* | corriente de agua | cours d'eau | curso d'água |
| stream | Strom | **-ström, -strömmen** *Swe.* | corriente de agua | cours d'eau | curso d'água |
| river | Fluss | **-su** *Kor.* | río | rivière | rio |
| channel | Kanal | **-suidō** *Jpn.* | canal, estrecho | canal, détroit | canal, estreito |
| sound | Sund | **Sund** *Ger.* | sonda | détroit | estreito |
| sound | Sund | **-sund** *Swe.* | sonda | détroit | estreito |
| swamp | Sumpf | **swamp** *Eng.* | pantano | marais | pântano |
| ridge | Höhenrücken | **syrt** *Tur.* | sierra | crête | serra |
| island | Insel | **sziget** *Hung.* | isla | île | ilha |

## T

| ENGLISH | DEUTSCH | Map Form | ESPAÑOL | FRANCAIS | PORTUGUÊS |
|---|---|---|---|---|---|
| tableland | Tafelland | **tableland** *Eng.* | mesa, altiplano | plateau | planalto |
| woods | Gehölz | **taillis** *Fr.* | bosque | taillis | bosque |
| reef | Riff | **taka** *Indon.* | arrecife | récif | recife |
| mountain | Berg | **-take** *Jpn.* | montaña | montagne | montanha |
| waterfall | Wasserfall | **-taki** *Jpn.* | cascada | chute d'eau | queda d'água |
| valley | Tal | **Tal** *Ger.* | valle | vallée | vale |
| mountain | Berg | **tall** *Ara.* | montaña | montagne | montanha |
| mountain, hill | Berg, Hügel | **tallat** *Ara.* | montaña, colina | montagne, colline | montanha, colina |
| hills | Hügel | **tallāt** *Ara.* | colinas | collines | colinas |
| dam | Talsperre | **Talsperre** *Ger.* | presa | barrage | represa |
| point | Landspitze | **-tangar, -tangi** *Ice.* | punta | pointe | ponta |
| cape | Kap | **tanjong** *Mal.* | cabo | cap | cabo |
| cape | Kap | **tanjung** *Indon.* | cabo | cap | cabo |
| island | Insel | **tao** *Ch.* | isla | île | ilha |
| hills | Hügel | **taraq** *Ara.* | colinas | collines | colinas |
| lake | See | **tasek** *Mal.* | lago | lac | lago |
| lake | See | **tasik** *Indon.* | lago | lac | lago |
| plateau | Hochebene | **tassili** *Ber.* | meseta | plateau | planalto |
| mountain | Berg | **taung** *Bur.* | montaña | montagne | montanha |
| range | Gebirge | **taungdan** *Bur.* | sierra | chaîne | cordilheira |
| theatre | Theater | **teatro** *It., Sp.* | teatro | théâtre | teatro |
| bay | Bucht | **teluk** *Indon.* | bahía | baie | baía |
| temple | Tempel | **temple** *Eng., Fr.* | templo | temple | templo |
| church | Kirche | **templom** *Hung.* | iglesia | église | igreja |
| desert | Wüste | **ténéré** *Ber.* | desierto | désert | deserto |
| peak, hill | Gipfel, Hügel | **tepe, tepesi** *Tur.* | pico, colina | cime, colline | pico, colina |
| territory | Territorium | **territory** *Eng.* | territorio | territoire | território |
| lagoon | Lagune, Haff | **thale** *Thai* | laguna | lagune | laguna |
| mountains | Berge | **thiu khao** *Thai* | montañas | montagnes | montanhas |
| mountain | Berg | **-tind, -tinderne** *Nor.* | montaña | montagne | montanha |
| ridge | Höhenrücken | **ṭiwāl** *Ara.* | sierra | crête | serra |
| mountain | Berg | **-tjåkko, tjöure** *Lapp.* | montaña | montagne | montanha |
| island | Insel | **-to** *Kor.* | isla | île | ilha |
| island | Insel | **-tō** *Jpn.* | isla | île | ilha |
| lake | See | **tó** *Hung.* | lago | lac | lago |
| pass | Pass | **-tōge** *Jpn.* | paso | col | passo |
| island | Insel | **tokong** *Mal.* | isla | île | ilha |
| lake | See | **tônlé** *Cbd.* | lago | lac | lago |
| mountain torrent | Wildbach | **torrente** *It., Sp.* | torrente | torrent | torrente |
| tower | Turm | **tower** *Eng.* | torre | tour | torre |
| turnpike | gebührenpflichtige Autobahn | **tpk., turnpike** *Eng.* | camino con peaje | grande route à péage | rodovia com pedágio |
| lake | See | **-träsk** *Swe.* | lago | lac | lago |
| trench | Tiefseegraben | **trench** *Eng.* | trinchera | tranchée | fossa submarina |
| trough | Tiefseegraben | **trough** *Eng.* | trinchera | tranchée | fossa submarina |
| volcano | Vulkan | **tulūl** *Ara.* | volcán | volcan | vulcão |
| tunnel | Tunnel | **túnel** *Sp.* | túnel | tunnel | túnel |
| tunnel | Tunnel | **tunnel** *Eng., Fr.* | túnel | tunnel | túnel |
| hill, mountain | Hügel, Berg | **-tunturi** *Finn.* | colina, montaña | colline, montagne | colina, montanha |
| island | Insel | **tuo** *Ch.* | isla | île | ilha |
| canal | Kanal | **tur'at** *Ara.* | canal | canal | canal |
| turnpike | gebührenpflichtige Autobahn | **turnpike** *Eng.* | camino con peaje | grande route à péage | rodovia com pedágio |

## U-V

| ENGLISH | DEUTSCH | Map Form | ESPAÑOL | FRANCAIS | PORTUGUÊS |
|---|---|---|---|---|---|
| cape | Kap | **ujung** *Indon.* | cabo | cap | cabo |
| lagoon | Lagune, Haff | **-umi** *Jpn.* | laguna | lagune | laguna |
| United Nations | Vereinte Nationen | **U.N., United Nations** *Eng.* | Naciones Unidas | Nations Unies | Nações Unidas |
| canal | Kanal | **-unga** *Jpn.* | canal | canal | canal |
| university | Universität | **univ., universidad** *Sp.* **universidade università university** | universidad | université | universidade |
| university | Universität | **Universität** *Ger.* | universidad | université | universidade |
| university | Universität | **université** *Fr.* | universidad | université | universidade |
| university | Universität | **universitet** *Rus.* | universidad | université | universidade |
| upland | Bergland | **upland** *Eng.* | tierras altas | hautes terres | terras altas |
| lake | See | **-ura** *Jpn.* | lago | lac | lago |
| mountain(s) | Berg(e) | **uul** *Mong.* | montaña(s) | montagne(s) | montanha(s) |
| elevation(s) | Höhe(n) | **uval(y)** *Rus.* | altura(s) | élévation(s) | elevação(ões) |
| spring | Quelle | **'uyūn** *Ara.* | manantial | source | fonte, manancial |
| hill | Hügel | **-vaara** *Finn.* | colina | colline | colina |
| strait | Meeresstrasse | **väin** *Est.* | estrecho | détroit | estreito |
| valley | Tal | **val** *Fr., It.* | valle | val | vale |
| valley | Tal | **valle** *It., Sp.* | valle | vallée | vale |
| valley | Tal | **vallée** *Fr.* | valle | vallée | vale |
| waterfall | Wasserfall | **vallen** *Du.* | cascada | chute d'eau | queda d'água |
| valley | Tal | **valley** *Eng.* | valle | vallée | vale |
| valley | Tal | **vallon** *Fr.* | valle | vallon | vale |
| mountain | Berg | **vârful** *Rom.* | montaña | montagne | montanha |
| lake | See | **-vatn** *Ice., Nor.* | lago | lac | lago |
| lake | See | **-vatnet** *Nor.* | lago | lac | lago |
| lake | See | **-vattnett** *Swe.* | lago | lac | lago |
| reservoir | Stausee | **vdchr., vodochranilišče** *Rus.* | embalse | réservoir | reservatório |
| hills | Hügel | **-veden** *Swe.* | colinas | collines | colinas |
| upland | Bergland | **verch** *Rus.* | tierras altas | hautes terres | terras altas |
| lake | See | **-vesi** *Finn.* | lago | lac | lago |
| viaduct | Viadukt | **viaducto** *Sp.* | viaducto | viaduc | viaduto |
| plateau | Hochebene | **-vidda** *Nor.* | meseta | plateau | planalto |
| gulf | Golf | **-viken** *Swe.* | golfo | golfe | golfo |
| bay | Bucht | **vinh** *Viet.* | bahía | baie | baía |
| airport | Flughafen | **vliegveld** *Du.* | aeropuerto | aéroport | aeroporto |
| channel | Kanal | **vliet** *Du.* | canal, estrecho | canal, détroit | canal, estreito |
| canal | Kanal | **vodnyj put'** *Rus.* | canal | canal | canal |
| reservoir | Stausee | **vodochranilišče** *Rus.* | embalse | réservoir | reservatório |
| reservoir | Stausee | **vodoskhovyshche** *Ukr.* | embalse | réservoir | reservatório |
| railroad station | Bahnhof | **vokzal** *Rus.* | estación de ferrocarril | gare | estação ferroviária |
| volcano | Vulkan | **vol., volcán** *Sp.* **volcano** | volcán | volcan | vulcão |
| pass | Pass | **vorota** *Rus.* | paso | col | passo |
| upland | Bergland | **vozvyšennost'** *Rus.* | tierras altas | hautes terres | terras altas |
| mountain | Berg | **vrăh** *Blg.* | montaña | montagne | montanha |
| mountains | Berge | **vrchovina** *Czech, Slo.* | montañas | montagnes | montanhas |
| mountains | Berge | **vrchy** *Slo.* | montañas | montagnes | montanhas |
| peak | Gipfel | **vrh** *S./C.* | pico | cime | pico |
| volcano | Vulkan | **vulkan** *Rus.* | volcán | volcan | vulcão |
| bay | Bucht | **vung** *Viet.* | bahía | baie | baía |
| mountain, hill | Berg, Hügel | **-vuori** *Finn.* | montaña, colina | montagne, colline | montanha, colina |
| upland | Bergland | **vysochyna** *Ukr.* | tierras altas | hautes terres | terras altas |

## W-Z

| ENGLISH | DEUTSCH | Map Form | ESPAÑOL | FRANCAIS | PORTUGUÊS |
|---|---|---|---|---|---|
| west | West | **w., west** *Eng.* | oeste | ouest | oeste |
| marsh | Marsch | **wa** *Ch.* | pantano | marais | pântano |
| wadi | Wadi | **wādī** *Ara.* | uadi | wadi | uádi |
| oasis | Oase | **wāhat, wāḥāt** *Ara.* | oasis | oasis | oásis |
| forest, mountains | Wald | **Wald** *Ger.* | bosque, montañas | forêt, montagnes | floresta, montanhas |
| bay | Bucht | **wan** *Ch., Jap.* | bahía | baie | baía |
| wash | Wadi | **wash** *Eng.* | uadi | wadi | uádi |
| waterfalls | Wasserfälle | **Wasserfälle** *Ger.* | cascadas | chutes d'eau | quedas d'água |
| water (lake, river) | Wasser (See, Fluss) | **water** *Eng.* | agua (lago, río) | eau (lac, rivière) | água (lago, rio) |
| waterway | Wasserstrasse | **waterway** *Eng.* | canal | canal | canal |
| pond | Weiher | **Weiher** *Ger.* | charca | étang | charco |
| well | Brunnen | **well** *Eng.* | pozo | puits | poço |
| bay | Wiek | **Wiek** *Ger.* | bahía | baie | baía |
| woods | Gehölz | **woods** *Eng.* | bosque | bois | bosque |
| water (lake, river) | Wasser (See, Fluss) | **wr., water** *Eng.* | agua (lago, río) | eau (lac, rivière) | água (lago, rio) |
| strait | Meeresstrasse | **xia** *Ch.* | estrecho | détroit | estreito |
| lake, sea | See, Meer | **yam** *Heb.* | lago, mar | lac, mer | lago, mar |
| mountain | Berg | **-yama** *Jpn.* | montaña | montagne | montanha |
| bay | Bucht | **yang** *Ch.* | bahía | baie | baía |
| peninsula | Halbinsel | **yarımadası** *Tur.* | península | péninsule | península |
| mountain | Berg | **yebel** *Ara.* | montaña | montagne | montanha |
| rock, island | Fels, Insel | **yen** *Ch.* | roca, isla | rocher, île | rochedo, ilha |
| mountains | Berge | **yoma** *Bur.* | montañas | montagnes | montanhas |
| island | Insel | **yu** *Ch.* | isla | île | ilha |
| lake | See | **yumco** *Tib.* | lago | lac | lago |
| canal | Kanal | **yunhe** *Ch.* | canal | canal | canal |
| intermittent lake | periodischer See | **zahrez** *Ara.* | lago intermitente | lac périodique | lago intermitente |
| point | Landspitze | **-zaki** *Jpn.* | punta | pointe | ponta |
| lagoon | Lagune, Haff | **zalew** *Pol.* | laguna | lagune | laguna |
| gulf, bay | Golf, Bucht | **zaliv** *Rus.* | golfo, bahía | golfe, baie | golfo, baía |
| reserve | Reservat | **zapov., zapovednik** *Rus.* | reserva | réserve | reserva |
| gulf, bay | Golf, Bucht | **zatoka** *Ukr.* | golfo, bahía | golfe, baie | golfo, baía |
| sea, lake | Meer, See | **zee** *Du.* | mar, lago | mer, lac | mar, lago |
| autonomous province | autonome Provinz | **zizhiqu** *Ch.* | provincia autónoma | province autonome | província autônoma |
| zoo | Zoo | **zoo** *Eng.* | parque zoológico | zoo | jardim zoológico |

THIS TABLE gives the area, population, population density, capital, and political status for every country in the world. The political units listed are categorized by political status in the last column of the table, as follows: A—independent countries; B—internally independent political entities which are under the protection of another country in matters of defense and foreign affairs; C—colonies and other dependent political units; and D—the major administrative subdivisions of Australia, Canada, China, the United Kingdom, and the United States. For comparison, the table also includes the continents and the world. For units categorized B, the names of protecting countries are specified in the political-status column. For units categorized C, the names of administering countries are given in parentheses in the first column.

The populations are estimates for January 1, 1995, made by Rand McNally on the basis of official data, United Nations estimates, and other available information.

IN DIESER ÜBERSICHT sind Fläche, Bevölkerung, Bevölkerungsdichte, Hauptstadt und politischer Status für jedes Land der Erde aufgeführt. Die politischen Einheiten sind in der letzten Spalte der Tabelle nach ihrem politischen Status wie folgt gegliedert: A—souveräne Staaten; B—innenpolitisch unabhängige Länder unter der Protektion eines anderen Landes in Angelegenheiten der Aussenpolitik und Verteidigung; C—Kolonien oder anderweitig abhängige Gebiete; D—die wichtigsten Verwaltungseinheiten von Australien, Kanada, China, dem Vereinigten Königreich und den Vereinigten Staaten. Für Vergleiche enthält die Übersicht auch Angaben über die Kontinente und die Welt. Für die unter B eingestuften Einheiten ist der Name des Schutzstaates in der Spalte Politischer Status aufgeführt. Für die unter C eingestuften Gebiete steht der Name des die Verwaltung ausübenden Landes in Klammern in der ersten Spalte.

Die Bevölkerungsangaben sind Schätzungen zum 1. Januar 1995, die Rand McNally auf der Grundlage amtlicher Zahlen, Schätzungen der Vereinten Nationen und anderer zugänglicher Informationen berechnet hat.

EL CUADRO ABAJO incluye la extensión, población y densidad de población, la capital y el estado político de todos los países del mundo. Las entidades políticas nombradas están clasificadas de acuerdo a su estado político en la última columna de la tabla, de esta manera: A—países independientes; B—entidades políticas internamente independientes las cuales se encuentran bajo la protección de otro país en cuanto a asuntos de defensa nacional y relaciones con el extranjero; C—colonias y otras entidades políticas dependientes; y D—las mayores subdivisiones administrativas de Australia, Canadá, China, el Reino Unido, y los Estados Unidos. Para servir de medida comparativa, el cuadro también incluye los continentes y el mundo. Para las entidades de la clasificación B, los nombres de los países protectores están especificados en la columna de estado político. Para las unidades bajo la categoría C, los nombres de los países administradores se encuentran entre paréntesis en la primera columna.

Las poblaciones son los estimados de Rand McNally, tomados el 1o. de Enero de 1995, en base a datos oficiales, estimados de las Naciones Unidas y varias otras informaciones disponibles.

CETTE TABLE donne, pour chaque pays du monde, les renseignements suivants: superficie, population, densité de population, capitale, statut politique. Les entités politiques sont classées, selon leur statut, dans la dernière colonne du tableau: A—pays indépendants; B—entités politiques indépendants intérieurement, mais qui se trouvent sous la protection d'un autre pays pour leur défense et leurs relations extérieures; C—colonies et autres entités politiques dépendantes; D—principales subdivisions administratives de l'Australie, du Canada, de la Chine, du Royaume-Uni, des États-Unis. Pour permettre les comparaisons, la table comprend aussi les continents et le monde. Pour les entités politiques de la catégorie B, les noms des pays protecteurs sont spécifiés dans la colonne "statut politique". Pour celles de la catégorie C, les noms des pays administrateurs sont mis entre parenthèses dans la première colonne.

Les chiffres concernant la population sont des estimations au 1er janvier 1995, établies par Rand McNally, d'après les sources officielles, les estimations des Nations Unies et autres informations disponibles.

A TABELA que se segue apresenta a área, a população, a densidade demográfica, a capital e o estatuto político de todos os países do mundo. As unidades políticas relacionadas na tabela estão classificadas de acordo com o respectivo estatuto político na última coluna, do seguinte modo: A—países independentes; B—unidades políticas internamente independentes mas que se encontram sob a proteção de outro país no tocante a assuntos de defesa nacional e negócios extrenos; C—colônias e outras unidades políticas dependentes; e D—subdivisões administrativas principais da Austrália, Canadá, China, Reino Unido e Estados Unidos. Para fins de comparabilidade, a tabela também inclui os continentes e o mundo. No tocante ás unidades classificadas em B, os nomes dos países protetores estão especificados na coluna relativa ao estatuto político. Para as unidades da categoria C, os nomes dos países administradores figuram entre parênteses na primeira coluna.

Os dados relativos à população são estimativas de Rand McNally para 1 de janeiro de 1995, com base em dados oficiais, estimativas das Nações Unidas e outras informações disponíveis.

| NAME / NAME / NOMBRE / NOM / NOME<br>English / Englisch<br>Inglés / Anglais / Inglês | NAME / NAME / NOMBRE / NOM / NOME<br>Local / Einheimisch<br>Local / Local / Local | AREA / FLÄCHE<br>AREA / SUPERFICIE / ÁREA<br>sq. km. | AREA / FLÄCHE<br>AREA / SUPERFICIE / ÁREA<br>sq. mi. | POPULATION<br>BEVÖLKERUNG<br>POBLACIÓN<br>POPULATION<br>POPULAÇÃO | DENSITY PER<br>BEVÖLKERUNGSDICHTE<br>PRO / DENSIDAD POR<br>DENSITÉ / DENSIDADE POR<br>sq. km. | DENSITY PER<br>BEVÖLKERUNGSDICHTE<br>PRO / DENSIDAD POR<br>DENSITÉ / DENSIDADE POR<br>sq. mi. | CAPITAL<br>HAUPTSTADT<br>CAPITAL<br>CAPITALE<br>CAPITAL | POLITICAL STATUS<br>POLITISCHER STATUS<br>ESTADO POLITICO<br>STATUS POLITIQUE<br>ESTATUTO POLITICO |
|---|---|---|---|---|---|---|---|---|
| **†Afghanistan** | Afghānestān | 652,225 | 251,826 | 19,715,000 | 30 | 78 | Kābol (Kabul) | A |
| **Africa** | . . . | 30,300,000 | 11,700,000 | 697,600,000 | 23 | 60 | . . . | . . . |
| **Alabama, U.S.** | Alabama | 135,775 | 52,423 | 4,254,000 | 31 | 81 | Montgomery | D |
| **Alaska, U.S.** | Alaska | 1,700,139 | 656,424 | 614,000 | 0.4 | 0.9 | Juneau | D |
| **†Albania** | Shqipëri | 28,748 | 11,100 | 3,394,000 | 118 | 306 | Tiranë | A |
| **Alberta, Can.** | Alberta | 661,190 | 255,287 | 2,632,000 | 4.0 | 10 | Edmonton | D |
| **†Algeria** | Algérie (French) / Djazaïr (Arabic) | 2,381,741 | 919,595 | 27,965,000 | 12 | 30 | El Djazaïr (Algiers) | A |
| **American Samoa (U.S.)** | American Samoa (English) / Amerika Samoa (Samoan) | 199 | 77 | 56,000 | 281 | 727 | Pago Pago | C |
| **†Andorra** | Andorra | 453 | 175 | 59,000 | 130 | 337 | Andorra | B(Sp., Fr.) |
| **†Angola** | Angola | 1,246,700 | 481,354 | 10,690,000 | 8.6 | 22 | Luanda | A |
| **Anguilla** | Anguilla | 91 | 35 | 7,100 | 78 | 203 | The Valley | B(U.K.) |
| **Anhwei, China** | Anhui | 139,000 | 53,668 | 59,490,000 | 428 | 1,108 | Hefei | D |
| **Antarctica** | . . . | 14,000,000 | 5,400,000 | (1) | . . . | . . . | . . . | . . . |
| **†Antigua and Barbuda** | Antigua and Barbuda | 442 | 171 | 67,000 | 152 | 392 | St. John's | A |
| **†Argentina** | Argentina | 2,780,400 | 1,073,519 | 34,083,000 | 12 | 32 | Buenos Aires and Viedma (3) | A |
| **Arizona, U.S.** | Arizona | 295,276 | 114,006 | 4,070,000 | 14 | 36 | Phoenix | D |
| **Arkansas, U.S.** | Arkansas | 137,742 | 53,182 | 2,468,000 | 18 | 46 | Little Rock | D |
| **†Armenia** | Hayastan | 29,800 | 11,506 | 3,794,000 | 127 | 330 | Jerevan | A |
| **Aruba** | Aruba | 193 | 75 | 67,000 | 347 | 893 | Oranjestad | B(Neth.) |
| **Asia** | . . . | 44,900,000 | 17,300,000 | 3,422,700,000 | 76 | 198 | . . . | . . . |
| **†Australia** | Australia | 7,682,300 | 2,966,155 | 18,205,000 | 2.4 | 6.1 | Canberra | A |
| **Australian Capital Territory, Austl.** | Australian Capital Territory | 2,400 | 927 | 309,000 | 129 | 333 | Canberra | D |
| **†Austria** | Österreich | 83,856 | 32,377 | 7,932,000 | 95 | 245 | Wien (Vienna) | A |
| **†Azerbaijan** | Azärbaycan | 86,600 | 33,436 | 7,491,000 | 87 | 224 | Bakı (Baku) | A |
| **†Bahamas** | Bahamas | 13,939 | 5,382 | 275,000 | 20 | 51 | Nassau | A |
| **†Bahrain** | Al-Baḥrayn | 691 | 267 | 563,000 | 815 | 2,109 | Al-Manāmah | A |
| **†Bangladesh** | Bangladesh | 143,998 | 55,598 | 119,370,000 | 829 | 2,147 | Dhaka (Dacca) | A |
| **†Barbados** | Barbados | 430 | 166 | 261,000 | 607 | 1,572 | Bridgetown | A |
| **†Belarus** | Byelarus' | 207,600 | 80,155 | 10,425,000 | 50 | 130 | Minsk | A |
| **†Belgium** | Belgique (French) / België (Flemish) | 30,518 | 11,783 | 10,075,000 | 330 | 855 | Bruxelles (Brussels) | A |
| **†Belize** | Belize | 22,963 | 8,866 | 212,000 | 9.2 | 24 | Belmopan | A |
| **†Benin** | Bénin | 112,600 | 43,475 | 5,433,000 | 48 | 125 | Porto-Novo and Cotonou | A |
| **Bermuda (U.K.)** | Bermuda | 54 | 21 | 61,000 | 1,130 | 2,905 | Hamilton | C |
| **†Bhutan** | Druk-Yul | 46,500 | 17,954 | 1,758,000 | 38 | 98 | Thimphu | B(India) |
| **†Bolivia** | Bolivia | 1,098,581 | 424,165 | 6,790,000 | 6.2 | 16 | La Paz and Sucre | A |
| **†Bosnia and Herzegovina** | Bosna i Hercegovina | 51,129 | 19,741 | 4,481,000 | 88 | 227 | Sarajevo | A |
| **†Botswana** | Botswana | 582,000 | 224,711 | 1,438,000 | 2.5 | 6.4 | Gaborone | A |
| **†Brazil** | Brasil | 8,511,996 | 3,286,500 | 159,690,000 | 19 | 49 | Brasília | A |
| **British Columbia, Can.** | British Columbia (English) / Colombie-Britannique (French) | 947,800 | 365,948 | 3,395,000 | 3.6 | 9.3 | Victoria | D |
| **British Indian Ocean Territory (U.K.)** | British Indian Ocean Territory | 60 | 23 | (1) | . . . | . . . | . . . | C |
| **British Virgin Islands (U.K.)** | British Virgin Islands | 153 | 59 | 13,000 | 85 | 220 | Road Town | C |
| **†Brunei** | Brunei | 5,765 | 2,226 | 289,000 | 50 | 130 | Bandar Seri Begawan | A |
| **†Bulgaria** | Bălgarija | 110,994 | 42,855 | 8,787,000 | 79 | 205 | Sofija (Sofia) | A |
| **†Burkina Faso** | Burkina Faso | 274,000 | 105,792 | 10,275,000 | 38 | 97 | Ouagadougou | A |
| **†Burundi** | Burundi | 27,830 | 10,745 | 6,192,000 | 222 | 576 | Bujumbura | A |
| **California, U.S.** | California | 424,002 | 163,707 | 32,090,000 | 76 | 196 | Sacramento | D |
| **†Cambodia** | Kâmpŭchéa | 181,035 | 69,898 | 9,713,000 | 54 | 139 | Phnum Pénh (Phnom Penh) | A |
| **†Cameroon** | Cameroun (French) / Cameroon (English) | 475,440 | 183,568 | 13,330,000 | 28 | 73 | Yaoundé | A |
| **†Canada** | Canada | 9,970,610 | 3,849,674 | 28,285,000 | 2.8 | 7.3 | Ottawa | A |
| **†Cape Verde** | Cabo Verde | 4,033 | 1,557 | 429,000 | 106 | 276 | Praia | A |
| **Cayman Islands (U.K.)** | Cayman Islands | 259 | 100 | 33,000 | 127 | 330 | George Town | C |
| **†Central African Republic** | République centrafricaine | 622,984 | 240,535 | 3,177,000 | 5.1 | 13 | Bangui | A |
| **†Chad** | Tchad | 1,284,000 | 495,755 | 6,396,000 | 5.0 | 13 | N'Djamena | A |
| **Chekiang, China** | Zhejiang | 101,800 | 39,305 | 43,930,000 | 432 | 1,118 | Hangzhou | D |
| **†Chile** | Chile | 756,626 | 292,135 | 14,050,000 | 19 | 48 | Santiago | A |
| **†China (excl. Taiwan)** | Zhongguo | 9,556,100 | 3,689,631 | 1,196,980,000 | 125 | 324 | Beijing (Peking) | A |
| **Christmas Island (Austl.)** | Christmas Island | 135 | 52 | 1,000 | 7.4 | 19 | Settlement | C |
| **Cocos (Keeling) Islands (Austl.)** | Cocos (Keeling) Islands | 14 | 5.4 | 600 | 43 | 111 | . . . | C |
| **†Colombia** | Colombia | 1,141,748 | 440,831 | 34,870,000 | 31 | 79 | Santa Fe de Bogotá | A |
| **Colorado, U.S.** | Colorado | 269,620 | 104,100 | 3,649,000 | 14 | 35 | Denver | D |
| **†Comoros (excl. Mayotte)** | Comores (French) / Al-Qumur (Arabic) | 2,235 | 863 | 540,000 | 242 | 626 | Moroni | A |
| **†Congo** | Congo | 342,000 | 132,047 | 2,474,000 | 7.2 | 19 | Brazzaville | A |
| **Connecticut, U.S.** | Connecticut | 14,358 | 5,544 | 3,266,000 | 227 | 589 | Hartford | D |
| **Cook Islands** | Cook Islands | 236 | 91 | 19,000 | 81 | 209 | Avarua | B(N.Z.) |
| **†Costa Rica** | Costa Rica | 51,100 | 19,730 | 3,379,000 | 66 | 171 | San José | A |
| **†Cote d'Ivoire** | Côte d'Ivoire | 322,500 | 124,518 | 14,540,000 | 45 | 117 | Abidjan and Yamoussoukro | A |
| **†Croatia** | Hrvatska | 56,538 | 21,829 | 4,801,000 | 85 | 220 | Zagreb | A |
| **†Cuba** | Cuba | 110,861 | 42,804 | 11,560,000 | 104 | 270 | La Habana (Havana) | A |
| **†Cyprus (excl. North Cyprus)** | Kípros (Greek) / Kıbrıs (Turkish) | 5,896 | 2,276 | 551,000 | 93 | 242 | Nicosia (Levkosía) | A |
| **Cyprus, North** | Kuzey Kıbrıs | 3,355 | 1,295 | 182,000 | 54 | 141 | Nicosia (Lefkoşa) | A |
| **†Czech Republic** | Česká Republika | 78,864 | 30,450 | 10,430,000 | 132 | 343 | Praha (Prague) | A |
| **Delaware, U.S.** | Delaware | 6,447 | 2,489 | 709,000 | 110 | 285 | Dover | D |
| **†Denmark** | Danmark | 43,094 | 16,639 | 5,207,000 | 121 | 313 | København (Copenhagen) | A |

| NAME / NAME / NOMBRE / NOM / NOME English / Englisch Inglés / Anglais / Inglês | Local / Einheimisch Local / Local / Local | AREA / FLÄCHE AREA / SUPERFICIE / ÁREA sq. km. | sq. mi. | POPULATION BEVÖLKERUNG POBLACIÓN POPULATION POPULAÇÃO | DENSITY PER BEVÖLKERUNGSDICHTE PRO / DENSIDAD POR DENSITÉ / DENSIDADE POR sq. km. | sq. mi. | CAPITAL HAUPSTADT CAPITAL CAPITALE CAPITAL | POLITICAL STATUS POLITISCHER STATUS ESTADO POLITICO STATUS POLITIQUE ESTATUTO POLITICO |
|---|---|---|---|---|---|---|---|---|
| District of Columbia, U.S. | District of Columbia | 177 | 68 | 575,000 | 3,249 | 8,456 | Washington | D |
| †Djibouti | Djibouti | 23,200 | 8,958 | 557,000 | 24 | 62 | Djibouti | A |
| †Dominica | Dominica | 790 | 305 | 89,000 | 113 | 292 | Roseau | A |
| †Dominican Republic | República Dominicana | 48,442 | 18,704 | 7,896,000 | 163 | 422 | Santo Domingo | A |
| †Ecuador | Ecuador | 272,045 | 105,037 | 11,015,000 | 40 | 105 | Quito | A |
| †Egypt | Mişr | 1,001,449 | 386,662 | 58,100,000 | 58 | 150 | Al-Qāhirah (Cairo) | A |
| †El Salvador | El Salvador | 21,041 | 8,124 | 5,280,000 | 251 | 650 | San Salvador | A |
| England, U.K. | England | 130,410 | 50,352 | 48,730,000 | 374 | 968 | London | D |
| †Equatorial Guinea | Guinea Ecuatorial | 28,051 | 10,831 | 394,000 | 14 | 36 | Malabo | A |
| †Eritrea | Ērtra | 93,679 | 36,170 | 3,458,000 | 37 | 96 | Asmera | A |
| †Estonia | Eesti | 45,100 | 17,413 | 1,515,000 | 34 | 87 | Tallinn | A |
| †Ethiopia | Ītyop'iya | 1,157,603 | 446,953 | 55,070,000 | 48 | 123 | Adis Abeba | A |
| Europe | . . . | 9,900,000 | 3,800,000 | 712,100,000 | 72 | 187 | . . . | . . . |
| Faeroe Islands | Føroyar | 1,399 | 540 | 49,000 | 35 | 91 | Tórshavn | B(Den.) |
| Falkland Islands (U.K.) (2) | Falkland Islands | 12,173 | 4,700 | 2,100 | 0.2 | 0.4 | Stanley | C |
| †Fiji | Fiji (French) / Viti (Fijian) | 18,274 | 7,056 | 775,000 | 42 | 110 | Suva | A |
| †Finland | Suomi (Finnish) / Finland (Swedish) | 338,145 | 130,559 | 5,098,000 | 15 | 39 | Helsinki (Helsingfors) | A |
| Florida, U.S. | Florida | 170,313 | 65,758 | 13,995,000 | 82 | 213 | Tallahassee | D |
| †France (excl. Overseas Departments) | France | 547,026 | 211,208 | 58,010,000 | 106 | 275 | Paris | A |
| French Guiana (Fr.) | Guyane française | 91,000 | 35,135 | 138,000 | 1.5 | 3.9 | Cayenne | C |
| French Polynesia (Fr.) | Polynésie française | 3,521 | 1,359 | 217,000 | 62 | 160 | Papeete | C |
| Fukien, China | Fujian | 120,000 | 46,332 | 31,720,000 | 264 | 685 | Fuzhou | D |
| †Gabon | Gabon | 267,667 | 103,347 | 1,035,000 | 3.9 | 10 | Libreville | A |
| †Gambia | Gambia | 10,689 | 4,127 | 1,082,000 | 101 | 262 | Banjul | A |
| Gaza Strip | . . . | 378 | 146 | 774,000 | 2,048 | 5,301 | . . . | . . . |
| Georgia, U.S. | Georgia | 153,953 | 59,441 | 7,065,000 | 46 | 119 | Atlanta | D |
| †Georgia | Sakartvelo | 69,700 | 26,911 | 5,704,000 | 82 | 212 | Tbilisi | A |
| †Germany | Deutschland | 356,955 | 137,822 | 81,710,000 | 229 | 593 | Berlin and Bonn | A |
| †Ghana | Ghana | 238,533 | 92,098 | 17,210,000 | 72 | 187 | Accra | A |
| Gibraltar (U.K.) | Gibraltar | 6.0 | 2.3 | 32,000 | 5,333 | 13,913 | Gibraltar | C |
| Golan Heights | . . . | 1,176 | 454 | 29,000 | 25 | 64 | . . . | . . . |
| †Greece | Ellás | 131,957 | 50,949 | 10,475,000 | 79 | 206 | Athínai (Athens) | A |
| Greenland | Kalaallit Nunaat (Inuit) / Grønland (Danish) | 2,175,600 | 840,004 | 57,000 | . . . | 0.1 | Godthåb (Nuuk) | B(Den.) |
| †Grenada | Grenada | 344 | 133 | 92,000 | 267 | 692 | St. George's | A |
| Guadeloupe (incl. Dependencies) (Fr.) | Guadeloupe | 1,780 | 687 | 432,000 | 243 | 629 | Basse-Terre | C |
| Guam (U.S.) | Guam | 541 | 209 | 152,000 | 281 | 727 | Agana | C |
| †Guatemala | Guatemala | 108,889 | 42,042 | 10,420,000 | 96 | 248 | Guatemala | A |
| Guernsey (incl. Dependencies) | Guernsey | 78 | 30 | 64,000 | 821 | 2,133 | St. Peter Port | B(U.K.) |
| †Guinea | Guinée | 245,857 | 94,926 | 6,469,000 | 26 | 68 | Conakry | A |
| †Guinea-Bissau | Guiné-Bissau | 36,125 | 13,948 | 1,111,000 | 31 | 80 | Bissau | A |
| †Guyana | Guyana | 214,969 | 83,000 | 726,000 | 3.4 | 8.7 | Georgetown | A |
| Hainan, China | Hainan | 34,000 | 13,127 | 6,945,000 | 204 | 529 | Haikou | D |
| †Haiti | Haïti | 27,750 | 10,714 | 7,069,000 | 255 | 660 | Port-au-Prince | A |
| Hawaii, U.S. | Hawaii | 28,313 | 10,932 | 1,181,000 | 42 | 108 | Honolulu | D |
| Heilungkiang, China | Heilongjiang | 469,000 | 181,082 | 37,345,000 | 80 | 206 | Harbin | D |
| Honan, China | Henan | 167,000 | 64,479 | 90,495,000 | 542 | 1,403 | Zhengzhou | D |
| †Honduras | Honduras | 112,088 | 43,277 | 5,822,000 | 52 | 135 | Tegucigalpa | A |
| Hong Kong (U.K.) | Hong Kong (English) / Xianggang (Chinese) | 1,072 | 414 | 5,927,000 | 5,529 | 14,316 | Hong Kong (Victoria) | C |
| Hopeh, China | Hebei | 190,000 | 73,359 | 64,640,000 | 340 | 881 | Shijiazhuang | D |
| Hunan, China | Hunan | 210,000 | 81,081 | 64,280,000 | 306 | 793 | Changsha | D |
| †Hungary | Magyarország | 93,030 | 35,919 | 10,270,000 | 110 | 286 | Budapest | A |
| Hupeh, China | Hubei | 187,400 | 72,356 | 57,100,000 | 305 | 789 | Wuhan | D |
| †Iceland | Ísland | 103,000 | 39,769 | 265,000 | 2.6 | 6.7 | Reykjavík | A |
| Idaho, U.S. | Idaho | 216,456 | 83,574 | 1,129,000 | 5.2 | 14 | Boise | D |
| Illinois, U.S. | Illinois | 150,007 | 57,918 | 11,870,000 | 79 | 205 | Springfield | D |
| †India (incl. part of Jammu and Kashmir) | India (English) / Bharat (Hindi) | 3,203,975 | 1,237,062 | 909,150,000 | 284 | 735 | New Delhi | A |
| Indiana, U.S. | Indiana | 94,328 | 36,420 | 5,805,000 | 62 | 159 | Indianapolis | D |
| †Indonesia | Indonesia | 1,948,732 | 752,410 | 193,680,000 | 99 | 257 | Jakarta | A |
| Inner Mongolia, China | Nei Monggol | 1,183,000 | 456,759 | 22,745,000 | 19 | 50 | Hohhot | D |
| Iowa, U.S. | Iowa | 145,754 | 56,276 | 2,862,000 | 20 | 51 | Des Moines | D |
| †Iran | Īrān | 1,638,057 | 632,457 | 63,810,000 | 39 | 101 | Tehrān | A |
| †Iraq | Al-'Irāq | 438,317 | 169,235 | 20,250,000 | 46 | 120 | Baghdād | A |
| †Ireland | Ireland (English) / Éire (Gaelic) | 70,285 | 27,137 | 3,546,000 | 50 | 131 | Dublin (Baile Átha Cliath) | A |
| Isle of Man | Isle of Man | 572 | 221 | 72,000 | 126 | 326 | Douglas | B(U.K.) |
| †Israel | Yisra'el (Hebrew) / Isrā'īl (Arabic) | 20,770 | 8,019 | 5,059,000 | 244 | 631 | Yerushalayim (Jerusalem) | A |
| †Italy | Italia | 301,277 | 116,324 | 57,330,000 | 190 | 493 | Roma (Rome) | A |
| †Jamaica | Jamaica | 10,991 | 4,244 | 2,568,000 | 234 | 605 | Kingston | A |
| †Japan | Nihon | 377,801 | 145,870 | 125,360,000 | 332 | 859 | Tōkyō | A |
| Jersey | Jersey | 116 | 45 | 86,000 | 741 | 1,911 | St. Helier | B(U.K.) |
| †Jordan | Al-Urdun | 91,000 | 35,135 | 4,028,000 | 44 | 115 | 'Ammān | A |
| Kansas, U.S. | Kansas | 213,110 | 82,282 | 2,575,000 | 12 | 31 | Topeka | D |
| Kansu, China | Gansu | 450,000 | 173,746 | 23,700,000 | 53 | 136 | Lanzhou | D |
| †Kazakhstan | Kazachstan | 2,717,300 | 1,049,156 | 17,025,000 | 6.3 | 16 | Alma-Ata (Almaty) and Akmola (3) | A |
| Kentucky, U.S. | Kentucky | 104,665 | 40,411 | 3,835,000 | 37 | 95 | Frankfort | D |
| †Kenya | Kenya | 582,646 | 224,961 | 28,380,000 | 49 | 126 | Nairobi | A |
| Kiangsi, China | Jiangxi | 166,600 | 64,325 | 39,980,000 | 240 | 622 | Nanchang | D |
| Kiangsu, China | Jiangsu | 102,600 | 39,614 | 70,980,000 | 692 | 1,792 | Nanjing (Nanking) | D |
| Kiribati | Kiribati | 811 | 313 | 79,000 | 97 | 252 | Bairiki | A |
| Kirin, China | Jilin | 187,000 | 72,201 | 26,095,000 | 140 | 361 | Changchun | D |
| †Korea, North | Chosŏn-minjujuŭi-inmīn-konghwaguk | 120,538 | 46,540 | 23,265,000 | 193 | 500 | P'yŏngyang | A |
| †Korea, South | Taehan-min'guk | 99,016 | 38,230 | 44,655,000 | 451 | 1,168 | Sŏul (Seoul) | A |
| †Kuwait | Al-Kuwayt | 17,818 | 6,880 | 1,866,000 | 105 | 271 | Al-Kuwayt (Kuwait) | A |
| Kwangsi Chuang, China | Guangxi Zhuangzu | 236,300 | 91,236 | 44,765,000 | 189 | 491 | Nanning | D |
| Kwangtung, China | Guangdong | 178,000 | 68,726 | 66,550,000 | 374 | 968 | Guangzhou (Canton) | D |
| Kweichow, China | Guizhou | 170,000 | 65,637 | 34,355,000 | 202 | 523 | Guiyang | D |
| †Kyrgyzstan | Kyrgyzstan | 198,500 | 76,641 | 4,541,000 | 23 | 59 | Biškek (Frunze) | A |
| †Laos | Lao | 236,800 | 91,429 | 4,768,000 | 20 | 52 | Viangchan (Vientiane) | A |
| †Latvia | Latvija | 63,700 | 24,595 | 2,532,000 | 40 | 103 | Rīga | A |
| †Lebanon | Lubnān | 10,400 | 4,015 | 3,660,000 | 352 | 912 | Bayrūt (Beirut) | A |
| †Lesotho | Lesotho | 30,355 | 11,720 | 1,967,000 | 65 | 168 | Maseru | A |
| Liaoning, China | Liaoning | 145,700 | 56,255 | 41,775,000 | 287 | 743 | Shenyang (Mukden) | D |
| †Liberia | Liberia | 99,067 | 38,250 | 2,771,000 | 28 | 72 | Monrovia | A |
| †Libya | Lībiyā | 1,759,540 | 679,362 | 5,148,000 | 2.9 | 7.6 | Ṭarābulus (Tripoli) | A |
| †Liechtenstein | Liechtenstein | 160 | 62 | 30,000 | 188 | 484 | Vaduz | A |
| †Lithuania | Lietuva | 65,300 | 25,212 | 3,757,000 | 58 | 149 | Vilnius | A |
| Louisiana, U.S. | Louisiana | 134,275 | 51,843 | 4,360,000 | 32 | 84 | Baton Rouge | D |
| †Luxembourg | Luxembourg (French) / Lezebuurg (Luxembourgish) | 2,586 | 998 | 396,000 | 153 | 397 | Luxembourg | A |
| Macau (Port.) | Macau | 18 | 7.0 | 396,000 | 22,000 | 56,571 | Macau | C |
| †Macedonia | Makedonija | 25,713 | 9,928 | 2,102,000 | 82 | 212 | Skopje | A |
| †Madagascar | Madagasikara (Malagasy) / Madagascar (French) | 587,041 | 226,658 | 13,645,000 | 23 | 60 | Antananarivo | A |
| Maine, U.S. | Maine | 91,653 | 35,387 | 1,260,000 | 14 | 36 | Augusta | D |
| †Malawi | Malaŵi | 118,484 | 45,747 | 8,984,000 | 76 | 196 | Lilongwe | A |
| †Malaysia | Malaysia | 329,758 | 127,320 | 19,505,000 | 59 | 153 | Kuala Lumpur | A |
| †Maldives | Maldives | 298 | 115 | 251,000 | 842 | 2,183 | Male' | A |
| †Mali | Mali | 1,248,574 | 482,077 | 9,585,000 | 7.7 | 20 | Bamako | A |
| †Malta | Malta | 316 | 122 | 368,000 | 1,165 | 3,016 | Valletta | A |
| Manitoba, Can. | Manitoba | 649,950 | 250,947 | 1,131,000 | 1.7 | 4.5 | Winnipeg | D |
| †Marshall Islands | Marshall Islands | 181 | 70 | 55,000 | 304 | 786 | Majuro (island) | A |
| Martinique (Fr.) | Martinique | 1,100 | 425 | 384,000 | 349 | 904 | Fort-de-France | C |
| Maryland, U.S. | Maryland | 32,135 | 12,407 | 5,045,000 | 157 | 407 | Annapolis | D |
| Massachusetts, U.S. | Massachusetts | 27,337 | 10,555 | 6,117,000 | 224 | 580 | Boston | D |

| NAME / NAME / NOMBRE / NOM / NOME<br>English / Englisch<br>Inglés / Anglais / Inglês | Local / Einheimisch<br>Local / Local / Local | AREA / FLÄCHE<br>AREA / SUPERFICIE / ÁREA<br>sq. km. | sq. mi. | POPULATION<br>BEVÖLKERUNG<br>POBLACIÓN<br>POPULATION<br>POPULAÇÃO | DENSITY PER<br>BEVÖLKERUNGSDICHTE<br>PRO / DENSIDAD POR<br>DENSITÉ / DENSIDADE POR<br>sq. km. | sq. mi. | CAPITAL<br>HAUPSTADT<br>CAPITAL<br>CAPITALE<br>CAPITAL | POLITICAL STATUS<br>POLITISCHER STATUS<br>ESTADO POLITICO<br>STATUS POLITIQUE<br>ESTATUTO POLITICO |
|---|---|---|---|---|---|---|---|---|
| **†Mauritania** | Mauritanie (French) / Mūrītāniyā (Arabic) | 1,025,520 | 395,956 | 2,228,000 | 2.2 | 5.6 | Nouakchott | A |
| **†Mauritius (incl. Dependencies)** | Mauritius | 2,040 | 788 | 1,121,000 | 550 | 1,423 | Port Louis | A |
| **Mayotte (Fr.)** (4) | Mayotte | 374 | 144 | 95,000 | 254 | 660 | Dzaoudzi and Mamoudzou (3) | C |
| **†Mexico** | México | 1,967,183 | 759,534 | 93,860,000 | 48 | 124 | Ciudad de México (Mexico City) | A |
| **Michigan, U.S.** | Michigan | 250,738 | 96,810 | 9,615,000 | 38 | 99 | Lansing | D |
| **†Micronesia, Federated States of** | Federated States of Micronesia | 702 | 271 | 122,000 | 174 | 450 | Kolonia and Paliker (3) | A |
| **Midway Islands (U.S.)** | Midway Islands | 5.2 | 2.0 | 500 | 96 | 250 | . . . | C |
| **Minnesota, U.S.** | Minnesota | 225,182 | 86,943 | 4,595,000 | 20 | 53 | St. Paul | D |
| **Mississippi, U.S.** | Mississippi | 125,443 | 48,434 | 2,678,000 | 21 | 55 | Jackson | D |
| **Missouri, U.S.** | Missouri | 180,546 | 69,709 | 5,330,000 | 30 | 76 | Jefferson City | D |
| **†Moldova** | Moldova | 33,700 | 13,012 | 4,377,000 | 130 | 336 | Chişinău (Kishinev) | A |
| **†Monaco** | Monaco | 1.9 | 0.7 | 31,000 | 16,316 | 44,286 | Monaco | A |
| **†Mongolia** | Mongol Ard Uls | 1,566,500 | 604,829 | 2,462,000 | 1.6 | 4.1 | Ulaanbaatar (Ulan Bator) | A |
| **Montana, U.S.** | Montana | 380,850 | 147,046 | 840,000 | 2.2 | 5.7 | Helena | D |
| **Montserrat (U.K.)** | Montserrat | 102 | 39 | 13,000 | 127 | 333 | Plymouth | C |
| **†Morocco (excl. Western Sahara)** | Al-Magrib | 446,550 | 172,414 | 26,890,000 | 60 | 156 | Rabat | A |
| **†Mozambique** | Moçambique | 799,380 | 308,642 | 17,860,000 | 22 | 58 | Maputo | A |
| **†Myanmar** | Myanmar | 676,577 | 261,228 | 44,675,000 | 66 | 171 | Yangon (Rangoon) | A |
| **†Namibia** | Namibia | 824,272 | 318,253 | 1,623,000 | 2.0 | 5.1 | Windhoek | A |
| **Nauru** | Nauru (English) / Naoero (Nauruan) | 21 | 8.1 | 10,000 | 476 | 1,235 | Yaren District | A |
| **Nebraska, U.S.** | Nebraska | 200,358 | 77,358 | 1,628,000 | 8.1 | 21 | Lincoln | D |
| **†Nepal** | Nepāl | 147,181 | 56,827 | 21,295,000 | 145 | 375 | Kāthmāndau | A |
| **†Netherlands** | Nederland | 41,864 | 16,164 | 15,425,000 | 368 | 954 | Amsterdam and 's-Gravenhage (The Hague) | A |
| **Netherlands Antilles** | Nederlandse Antillen | 800 | 309 | 187,000 | 234 | 605 | Willemstad | B(Neth.) |
| **Nevada, U.S.** | Nevada | 286,368 | 110,567 | 1,444,000 | 5.0 | 13 | Carson City | D |
| **New Brunswick, Can.** | New Brunswick (English) / Nouveau-Brunswick (French) | 73,440 | 28,355 | 764,000 | 10 | 27 | Fredericton | D |
| **New Caledonia (Fr.)** | Nouvelle-Calédonie | 19,058 | 7,358 | 183,000 | 9.6 | 25 | Nouméa | C |
| **Newfoundland, Can.** | Newfoundland (English) / Terre-Neuve (French) | 405,720 | 156,649 | 594,000 | 1.5 | 3.8 | St. John's | D |
| **New Hampshire, U.S.** | New Hampshire | 24,219 | 9,351 | 1,100,000 | 45 | 118 | Concord | D |
| **New Jersey, U.S.** | New Jersey | 22,590 | 8,722 | 7,985,000 | 353 | 916 | Trenton | D |
| **New Mexico, U.S.** | New Mexico | 314,939 | 121,598 | 1,655,000 | 5.3 | 14 | Santa Fe | D |
| **New South Wales, Austl.** | New South Wales | 801,600 | 309,500 | 6,171,000 | 7.7 | 20 | Sydney | D |
| **New York, U.S.** | New York | 141,089 | 54,475 | 18,460,000 | 131 | 339 | Albany | D |
| **†New Zealand** | New Zealand | 270,534 | 104,454 | 3,558,000 | 13 | 34 | Wellington | A |
| **†Nicaragua** | Nicaragua | 129,640 | 50,054 | 4,438,000 | 34 | 89 | Managua | A |
| **†Niger** | Niger | 1,267,000 | 489,191 | 9,125,000 | 7.2 | 19 | Niamey | A |
| **†Nigeria** | Nigeria | 923,768 | 356,669 | 97,300,000 | 105 | 273 | Lagos and Abuja | A |
| **Ningsia Hui, China** | Ningxia Huizu | 66,400 | 25,637 | 4,908,000 | 74 | 191 | Yinchuan | D |
| **Niue** | Niue | 259 | 100 | 1,900 | 7.3 | 19 | Alofi | B(N.Z.) |
| **Norfolk Island (Austl.)** | Norfolk Island | 36 | 14 | 2,700 | 75 | 193 | Kingston | C |
| **North America** | . . . | 24,700,000 | 9,500,000 | 453,300,000 | 18 | 48 | . . . | . . . |
| **North Carolina, U.S.** | North Carolina | 139,397 | 53,821 | 7,065,000 | 51 | 131 | Raleigh | D |
| **North Dakota, U.S.** | North Dakota | 183,123 | 70,704 | 656,000 | 3.6 | 9.3 | Bismarck | D |
| **Northern Ireland, U.K.** | Northern Ireland | 14,144 | 5,461 | 1,636,000 | 116 | 300 | Belfast | D |
| **Northern Mariana Islands** | Northern Mariana Islands | 477 | 184 | 51,000 | 107 | 277 | Saipan (island) | B(U.S.) |
| **Northern Territory, Austl.** | Northern Territory | 1,346,200 | 519,771 | 182,000 | 0.1 | 0.4 | Darwin | D |
| **Northwest Territories, Can.** | Northwest Territories (English) / Territoires du Nord-Ouest (French) | 3,426,320 | 1,322,910 | 57,000 | . . . | . . . | Yellowknife | D |
| **†Norway (incl. Svalbard and Jan Mayen)** | Norge | 386,975 | 149,412 | 4,339,000 | 11 | 29 | Oslo | A |
| **Nova Scotia, Can.** | Nova Scotia (English) / Nouvelle-Écosse (French) | 55,490 | 21,425 | 933,000 | 17 | 44 | Halifax | D |
| **Oceania (incl. Australia)** | . . . | 8,500,000 | 3,300,000 | 28,400,000 | 3.3 | 8.6 | . . . | . . . |
| **Ohio, U.S.** | Ohio | 116,103 | 44,828 | 11,270,000 | 97 | 251 | Columbus | D |
| **Oklahoma, U.S.** | Oklahoma | 181,049 | 69,903 | 3,282,000 | 18 | 47 | Oklahoma City | D |
| **†Oman** | 'Umān | 212,457 | 82,030 | 2,089,000 | 9.8 | 25 | Masqaṭ (Muscat) | A |
| **Ontario, Can.** | Ontario | 1,068,580 | 412,581 | 10,435,000 | 9.8 | 25 | Toronto | D |
| **Oregon, U.S.** | Oregon | 254,819 | 98,386 | 3,098,000 | 12 | 31 | Salem | D |
| **†Pakistan (incl. part of Jammu and Kashmir)** | Pākistān | 879,902 | 339,732 | 129,630,000 | 147 | 382 | Islāmābād | A |
| **†Palau** | Palau (English) / Belau (Palauan) | 508 | 196 | 17,000 | 33 | 87 | Koror and Melekeok (3) | A |
| **†Panama** | Panamá | 75,517 | 29,157 | 2,654,000 | 35 | 91 | Panamá | A |
| **†Papua New Guinea** | Papua New Guinea | 462,840 | 178,704 | 4,057,000 | 8.8 | 23 | Port Moresby | A |
| **†Paraguay** | Paraguay | 406,752 | 157,048 | 4,400,000 | 11 | 28 | Asunción | A |
| **Peking, China** | Beijing | 16,800 | 6,487 | 11,490,000 | 684 | 1,771 | Beijing (Peking) | D |
| **Pennsylvania, U.S.** | Pennsylvania | 119,291 | 46,058 | 12,215,000 | 102 | 265 | Harrisburg | D |
| **†Peru** | Perú | 1,285,216 | 496,225 | 23,095,000 | 18 | 47 | Lima | A |
| **†Philippines** | Philippines (English) / Pilipinas (Pilipino) | 300,000 | 115,831 | 67,910,000 | 226 | 586 | Manila | A |
| **Pitcairn (incl. Dependencies) (U.K.)** | Pitcairn | 49 | 19 | 100 | 2.0 | 5.3 | Adamstown | C |
| **†Poland** | Polska | 313,895 | 121,196 | 38,730,000 | 123 | 320 | Warszawa (Warsaw) | A |
| **†Portugal** | Portugal | 91,985 | 35,516 | 9,907,000 | 108 | 279 | Lisboa (Lisbon) | A |
| **Prince Edward Island, Can.** | Prince Edward Island (English) / Île-du Prince-Édouard (French) | 5,660 | 2,185 | 141,000 | 25 | 65 | Charlottetown | D |
| **Puerto Rico** | Puerto Rico | 9,104 | 3,515 | 3,625,000 | 398 | 1,031 | San Juan | B(U.S.) |
| **†Qatar** | Qaṭar | 11,427 | 4,412 | 519,000 | 45 | 118 | Ad-Dawḥah (Doha) | A |
| **Quebec, Can.** | Québec | 1,540,680 | 594,860 | 7,157,000 | 4.6 | 12 | Québec | D |
| **Queensland, Austl.** | Queensland | 1,727,200 | 666,876 | 3,259,000 | 1.9 | 4.9 | Brisbane | D |
| **Reunion (Fr.)** | Réunion | 2,510 | 969 | 660,000 | 263 | 681 | Saint-Denis | C |
| **Rhode Island, U.S.** | Rhode Island | 4,002 | 1,545 | 1,024,000 | 256 | 663 | Providence | D |
| **†Romania** | România | 237,500 | 91,699 | 22,745,000 | 96 | 248 | Bucureşti (Bucharest) | A |
| **†Russia** | Rossija | 17,075,400 | 6,592,849 | 150,500,000 | 8.8 | 23 | Moskva (Moscow) | A |
| **†Rwanda** | Rwanda | 26,338 | 10,169 | 7,343,000 | 279 | 722 | Kigali | A |
| **St. Helena (incl. Dependencies) (U.K.)** | St. Helena | 314 | 121 | 7,000 | 22 | 58 | Jamestown | C |
| **†St. Kitts and Nevis** | St. Kitts and Nevis | 269 | 104 | 42,000 | 156 | 404 | Basseterre | A |
| **†St. Lucia** | St. Lucia | 616 | 238 | 138,000 | 224 | 580 | Castries | A |
| **St. Pierre and Miquelon (Fr.)** | Saint-Pierre-et-Miquelon | 242 | 93 | 6,700 | 28 | 72 | Saint-Pierre | C |
| **†St. Vincent and the Grenadines** | St. Vincent and the Grenadines | 388 | 150 | 110,000 | 284 | 733 | Kingstown | A |
| **†San Marino** | San Marino | 61 | 24 | 24,000 | 393 | 1,000 | San Marino | A |
| **†Sao Tome and Principe** | São Tomé e Príncipe | 964 | 372 | 127,000 | 132 | 341 | São Tomé | A |
| **Saskatchewan, Can.** | Saskatchewan | 652,330 | 251,866 | 1,018,000 | 1.6 | 4.0 | Regina | D |
| **†Saudi Arabia** | Al-'Arabīyah as-Su'ūdīyah | 2,149,690 | 830,000 | 18,190,000 | 8.5 | 22 | Ar-Riyāḍ (Riyadh) | A |
| **Scotland, U.K.** | Scotland | 78,789 | 30,421 | 5,142,000 | 65 | 169 | Edinburgh | D |
| **†Senegal** | Sénégal | 196,712 | 75,951 | 8,862,000 | 45 | 117 | Dakar | A |
| **†Seychelles** | Seychelles | 453 | 175 | 75,000 | 166 | 429 | Victoria | A |
| **Shanghai, China** | Shanghai | 6,200 | 2,394 | 14,125,000 | 2,278 | 5,900 | Shanghai | D |
| **Shansi, China** | Shanxi | 156,000 | 60,232 | 30,405,000 | 195 | 505 | Taiyuan | D |
| **Shantung, China** | Shandong | 153,000 | 59,074 | 89,400,000 | 584 | 1,513 | Jinan | D |
| **Shensi, China** | Shaanxi | 205,000 | 79,151 | 34,830,000 | 170 | 440 | Xi'an (Sian) | D |
| **†Sierra Leone** | Sierra Leone | 72,325 | 27,925 | 4,690,000 | 65 | 168 | Freetown | A |
| **†Singapore** | Singapore | 636 | 246 | 2,921,000 | 4,593 | 11,874 | Singapore | A |
| **Sinkiang Uighur, China** | Xinjiang Uygur | 1,600,000 | 617,764 | 16,040,000 | 10 | 26 | Ürümqi | D |
| **†Slovakia** | Slovenská Republika | 49,035 | 18,933 | 5,353,000 | 109 | 283 | Bratislava | A |
| **†Slovenia** | Slovenija | 20,253 | 7,820 | 1,993,000 | 98 | 255 | Ljubljana | A |
| **†Solomon Islands** | Solomon Islands | 28,370 | 10,954 | 393,000 | 14 | 36 | Honiara | A |
| **†Somalia** | Somaliya | 637,657 | 246,201 | 7,187,000 | 11 | 29 | Muqdisho (Mogadishu) | A |
| **†South Africa** | South Africa (English) / Suid-Afrika (Afrikaans) | 1,219,909 | 471,010 | 44,500,000 | 36 | 94 | Pretoria, Cape Town, and Bloemfontein | A |

| NAME / NAME / NOMBRE / NOM / NOME — English / Englisch Inglés / Anglais / Inglês | Local / Einheimisch Local / Local / Local | AREA / FLÄCHE AREA / SUPERFICIE / ÁREA sq. km. | sq. mi. | POPULATION BEVÖLKERUNG POBLACIÓN POPULATION POPULAÇÃO | DENSITY PER BEVÖLKERUNGSDICHTE PRO / DENSIDAD POR DENSITÉ / DENSIDADE POR sq. km. | sq. mi. | CAPITAL HAUPSTADT CAPITAL CAPITALE CAPITAL | POLITICAL STATUS POLITISCHER STATUS ESTADO POLÍTICO STATUS POLITIQUE ESTATUTO POLÍTICO |
|---|---|---|---|---|---|---|---|---|
| **South America** | . . . | 17,800,000 | 6,900,000 | 313,900,000 | 18 | 45 | . . . | . . . |
| **South Australia, Austl.** | South Australia | 984,000 | 379,925 | 1,493,000 | 1.5 | 3.9 | Adelaide | D |
| **South Carolina, U.S.** | South Carolina | 82,898 | 32,007 | 3,702,000 | 45 | 116 | Columbia | D |
| **South Dakota, U.S.** | South Dakota | 199,745 | 77,121 | 735,000 | 3.7 | 9.5 | Pierre | D |
| **South Georgia and the South Sandwich Islands (U.K.)** | South Georgia and the South Sandwich Islands | 3,755 | 1,450 | (1) | . . . | . . . | . . . | C |
| **†Spain** | España | 504,750 | 194,885 | 39,260,000 | 78 | 201 | Madrid | A |
| **Spanish North Africa (Sp.) (5)** | Plazas de Soberanía en el Norte de África | 32 | 12 | 146,000 | 4,563 | 12,167 | . . . | C |
| **†Sri Lanka** | Sri Lanka | 64,652 | 24,962 | 18,240,000 | 282 | 731 | Colombo and Sri Jayawardenapura | A |
| **†Sudan** | As-Sūdān | 2,505,813 | 967,500 | 25,840,000 | 10 | 27 | Al-Kharṭūm (Khartoum) | A |
| **†Suriname** | Suriname | 163,820 | 63,251 | 426,000 | 2.6 | 6.7 | Paramaribo | A |
| **†Swaziland** | Swaziland | 17,364 | 6,704 | 889,000 | 51 | 133 | Mbabane and Lobamba | A |
| **†Sweden** | Sverige | 449,964 | 173,732 | 8,981,000 | 20 | 52 | Stockholm | A |
| **Switzerland** | Schweiz (German) / Suisse (French) / Svizzera (Italian) | 41,293 | 15,943 | 7,244,000 | 175 | 454 | Bern (Berne) | A |
| **†Syria** | Sūrīyah | 185,180 | 71,498 | 14,100,000 | 76 | 197 | Dimashq (Damascus) | A |
| **Szechwan, China** | Sichuan | 570,000 | 220,078 | 113,470,000 | 199 | 516 | Chengdu | D |
| **Taiwan** | T'aiwan | 36,002 | 13,900 | 21,150,000 | 587 | 1,522 | T'aipei | A |
| **†Tajikistan** | Tojikiston | 143,100 | 55,251 | 6,073,000 | 42 | 110 | Dušanbe | A |
| **†Tanzania** | Tanzania | 883,749 | 341,217 | 28,350,000 | 32 | 83 | Dar es Salaam and Dodoma | A |
| **Tasmania, Austl.** | Tasmania | 67,800 | 26,178 | 492,000 | 7.3 | 19 | Hobart | D |
| **Tennessee, U.S.** | Tennessee | 109,158 | 42,146 | 5,175,000 | 47 | 123 | Nashville | D |
| **Texas, U.S.** | Texas | 695,676 | 268,601 | 18,330,000 | 26 | 68 | Austin | D |
| **†Thailand** | Prathet Thai | 513,115 | 198,115 | 59,870,000 | 117 | 302 | Krung Thep (Bangkok) | A |
| **Tibet, China** | Xizang | 1,220,000 | 471,045 | 2,275,000 | 1.9 | 4.8 | Lhasa | D |
| **Tientsin, China** | Tianjin | 11,300 | 4,363 | 9,337,000 | 826 | 2,140 | Tianjin (Tientsin) | D |
| **†Togo** | Togo | 56,785 | 21,925 | 4,332,000 | 76 | 198 | Lomé | A |
| **Tokelau (N.Z.)** | Tokelau | 12 | 4.6 | 1,500 | 125 | 326 | . . . | C |
| **Tonga** | Tonga | 747 | 288 | 110,000 | 147 | 382 | Nuku'alofa | A |
| **†Trinidad and Tobago** | Trinidad and Tobago | 5,128 | 1,980 | 1,281,000 | 250 | 647 | Port of Spain | A |
| **Tsinghai, China** | Qinghai | 720,000 | 277,994 | 4,670,000 | 6.5 | 17 | Xining | D |
| **†Tunisia** | Tunisie (French) / Tunis (Arabic) | 163,610 | 63,170 | 8,806,000 | 54 | 139 | Tunis | A |
| **†Turkey** | Türkiye | 779,452 | 300,948 | 62,030,000 | 80 | 206 | Ankara | A |
| **†Turkmenistan** | Türkmenistan | 488,100 | 188,456 | 4,035,000 | 8.3 | 21 | Ašchabad (Ashgabat) | A |
| **Turks and Caicos Islands (U.K.)** | Turks and Caicos Islands | 500 | 193 | 14,000 | 28 | 73 | Grand Turk | C |
| **Tuvalu** | Tuvalu | 26 | 10 | 10,000 | 385 | 1,000 | Funafuti | A |
| **†Uganda** | Uganda | 241,139 | 93,104 | 18,270,000 | 76 | 196 | Kampala | A |
| **†Ukraine** | Ukrayina | 603,700 | 233,090 | 52,140,000 | 86 | 224 | Kyyiv (Kiev) | A |
| **†United Arab Emirates** | Al-Imārāt al-'Arabīyah al-Muttaḥidah | 83,600 | 32,278 | 2,855,000 | 34 | 88 | Abū Ẓaby (Abu Dhabi) | A |
| **†United Kingdom** | United Kingdom | 244,101 | 94,249 | 58,430,000 | 239 | 620 | London | A |
| **†United States** | United States | 9,809,431 | 3,787,425 | 262,530,000 | 27 | 69 | Washington | A |
| **†Uruguay** | Uruguay | 177,414 | 68,500 | 3,317,000 | 19 | 48 | Montevideo | A |
| **Utah, U.S.** | Utah | 219,902 | 84,904 | 1,890,000 | 8.6 | 22 | Salt Lake City | D |
| **†Uzbekistan** | Ŭzbekiston | 447,400 | 172,742 | 22,860,000 | 51 | 132 | Taškent (Toshkent) | A |
| **†Vanuatu** | Vanuatu | 12,190 | 4,707 | 161,000 | 13 | 34 | Port Vila | A |
| **Vatican City** | Città del Vaticano | 0.4 | 0.2 | 1,000 | 2,500 | 5,000 | Città del Vaticano (Vatican City) | A |
| **†Venezuela** | Venezuela | 912,050 | 352,145 | 21,395,000 | 23 | 61 | Caracas | A |
| **Vermont, U.S.** | Vermont | 24,903 | 9,615 | 578,000 | 23 | 60 | Montpelier | D |
| **Victoria, Austl.** | Victoria | 227,600 | 87,877 | 4,570,000 | 20 | 52 | Melbourne | D |
| **†Vietnam** | Viet Nam | 330,036 | 127,428 | 73,760,000 | 223 | 579 | Ha Noi | A |
| **Virginia, U.S.** | Virginia | 110,771 | 42,769 | 6,595,000 | 60 | 154 | Richmond | D |
| **Virgin Islands (U.S.)** | Virgin Islands | 344 | 133 | 97,000 | 282 | 729 | Charlotte Amalie | C |
| **Wake Island (U.S.)** | Wake Island | 7.8 | 3.0 | 300 | 38 | 100 | . . . | C |
| **Wales, U.K.** | Wales | 20,758 | 8,015 | 2,922,000 | 141 | 365 | Cardiff | D |
| **Wallis and Futuna (Fr.)** | Wallis et Futuna | 255 | 98 | 14,000 | 55 | 143 | Mata-Utu | C |
| **Washington, U.S.** | Washington | 184,674 | 71,303 | 5,360,000 | 29 | 75 | Olympia | D |
| **West Bank (incl. Jericho)** | . . . | 6,078 | 2,347 | 1,717,000 | 282 | 732 | . . . | . . . |
| **Western Australia, Austl.** | Western Australia | 2,525,500 | 975,101 | 1,729,000 | 0.7 | 1.8 | Perth | D |
| **Western Sahara** | . . . | 266,000 | 102,703 | 215,000 | 0.8 | 2.1 | El Aaiún (Laayone) | . . . |
| **†Western Samoa** | Western Samoa (English) / Samoa i Sisifo (Samoan) | 2,831 | 1,093 | 172,000 | 61 | 157 | Apia | A |
| **West Virginia, U.S.** | West Virginia | 62,759 | 24,231 | 1,838,000 | 29 | 76 | Charleston | D |
| **Wisconsin, U.S.** | Wisconsin | 169,653 | 65,503 | 5,120,000 | 30 | 78 | Madison | D |
| **Wyoming, U.S.** | Wyoming | 253,349 | 97,818 | 473,000 | 1.9 | 4.8 | Cheyenne | D |
| **†Yemen** | Al-Yaman | 527,968 | 203,850 | 12,910,000 | 24 | 63 | Ṣan'ā' | A |
| **Yugoslavia** | Jugoslavija | 102,173 | 39,449 | 10,765,000 | 105 | 273 | Beograd (Belgrade) | A |
| **Yukon Territory, Can.** | Yukon Territory | 483,450 | 186,661 | 28,000 | 0.1 | 0.2 | Whitehorse | D |
| **Yunnan, China** | Yunnan | 394,000 | 152,124 | 39,140,000 | 99 | 257 | Kunming | D |
| **†Zaire** | Zaïre | 2,344,858 | 905,355 | 43,365,000 | 18 | 48 | Kinshasa | A |
| **†Zambia** | Zambia | 752,618 | 290,587 | 8,809,000 | 12 | 30 | Lusaka | A |
| **†Zimbabwe** | Zimbabwe | 390,757 | 150,872 | 11,075,000 | 28 | 73 | Harare (Salisbury) | A |
| **WORLD** | . . . | 150,100,000 | 57,900,000 | 5,628,000,000 | 37 | 97 | . . . | . . . |

† Member of the United Nations.
. . . None, or not applicable.
(1) No permanent population.
(2) Claimed by Argentina.
(3) Future capital.
(4) Claimed by Comoros.
(5) Comprises Ceuta, Melilla, and several small islands.

† Mitglied der Vereinten Nationen.
. . . Kein(e), oder nicht anwendbar.
(1) Bevölkerungszahl schwankend.
(2) Von Argentinien beansprucht.
(3) Zukünftige Hauptstadt.
(4) Von Komoren beansprucht.
(5) Umfasst Ceuta, Melilla und mehrere kleine Inseln.

† Miembro de las Naciones Unidas.
. . . Ninguno, o no se aplica.
(1) Sin población permanente.
(2) Reclamado por la Argentina.
(3) Capital futura.
(4) Reclamado por las Comores.
(5) Comprende Ceuta, Melilla y various islas pequeñas.

† Membre des Nations Unies.
. . . Pas d'information, ou pas applicable.
(1) Pas de population permanente.
(2) Revendiqué par l'Argentine.
(3) Capitale future.
(4) Revendiqué par les Comores.
(5) Inclus Ceuta, Melilla et plusieurs petites îles.

† Membro das Nações Unidas.
. . . Inexistente ou não aplicável.
(1) Sem população permanente.
(2) Reivindicado pela Argentina.
(3) Capital futuro.
(4) Reivindicado pelas Comores.
(5) Compreende Ceuta, Melilla e várias ilhas pequenas.

THIS TABLE lists the major metropolitan areas of the world according to their estimated population on January l, 1994. For convenience in reference, the areas are grouped by major region with the total for each region given. The number of areas by population classification is given in parentheses with each size group.

For ease of comparison, each metropolitan area has been defined by Rand McNally according to consistent rules. A metropolitan area includes a central city, neighboring communities linked to it by continuous built-up areas, and more distant communities if the bulk of their population is supported by commuters to the central city. Some metropolitan areas have more than one central city; in such cases each central city is listed.

IN DIESER TABELLE sind die Hauptmetropolen der Welt verzeichnet, gemessen nach ihrer Bevölkerung, die nach dem Stand vom 1. Januar 1994 geschätzt wurde. Zur besseren Übersicht sind die Zonen nach grösseren Regionen gruppiert, wobei die Gesamtzahl für jede Region angegeben ist. Die Anzahl der Zonen ist nach Bevölkerung klassifiziert und in Klammern hinter denen nach Grössen sortierten Gruppen angegeben.

Zum einfacheren Vergleich ist jede Metropole von Rand McNally nach übereinstimmenden Massstäben definiert worden. Eine Metropole schliesst eine zentrale Stadt mit benachbarten Gemeinden, die mit ihr durch ununterbrochen bebaute Gebiete verbunden sind ein, sowie weiter entfernte Gemeinden, wenn der grösste Teil ihrer Bevölkerung von den Pendlern unterhalten wird. Einige Metropolen haben mehr als eine zentrale Stadt; in solchen Fällen ist jede dieser zentralen Städte angeführt.

ESTA TABLA indica las principales áreas metropolitanas del mundo, de acuerdo con su población calculada al 1 de enero de 1994. Para facilitar las referencias, las áreas se han agrupado por regiones principales, indicándose el total para cada región. El número de áreas, clasificadas por población, se indica entre paréntesis en los grupos de cada tamaño.

Para facilitar las comparaciones, Rand McNally ha definido cada área metropolitana de acuerdo con reglas consistentes. Un área metropolitana incluye una ciudad central, localidades vecinas vinculadas con ella mediante sectores construídos y contínuos, y localidades más distantes, si el grueso de su población lo constituye un núcleo que diariamente viaja a la ciudad central. Algunas áreas metropolitanas incluyen más de una ciudad central; en tales casos se indica cada una dichas ciudades.

CETTE TABLE contient la liste des aires métropolitaines les plus considérables dans le monde pour ce qui est du peuplement a la date du 1 er janvier 1994. Afin de faciliter la consultation, on a groupé les aires par grandes régions en indiquant la population totale pour chaque région, et, entre parenthéses, le nombre d'aires comprises dans celle-ci.

Afin de rendre plus faciles les comparaisons, Rand McNally a défini chaque aire métropolitaine selorègles cohérentes: une aire métropolitaine englobe une citè centrale ou métropole et l'environnement urbain continu qui s'y rattache; elle inclut également des agglomérations éloignées de la métropole lorsque la population de ces dernières est pour sa májorité constituée d'habitants se rendant quotidiennement dans la cité ou est situé le lieu de travail de ceux-ci. On trouvera quelques aires métropolitaines pourvues de plus d'une métropole. Dans ce cas, chaque métropole est mentionnée.

A TABELA que se segúe relaciona as principais áreas metropolitanas do mundo, de acordo com as respectivas populações, estimadas para 1 de janeiro de 1994. Para facilidade de referência, as áreas metropolitanas foram agrupadas dentro das regiões maiores, indicando-se, entre parênteses, os totais de cada região maior e o número de áreas metropolitanas, classificadas segundo a população, compreendidas em cada uma.

Para fins de comparabilidade, Rand McNally definiu cada área metropolitana de acordo com regras uniformes. Uma área metropolitana inclui uma cidade central, as localidades vizinhas ligadas a ela por áreas construídas contínuas, e as localidades mais distantes, desde que a maior parte de suas respectivas populações dependa economicamente da cidade central e que para ela viaje diariamente. Algumas áreas metropolitanas incluem mais de uma cidade central; em tais casos, indicam-se ambas as cidades.

| CLASSIFICATION<br>KLASSIFIZIERT<br>CLASIFICADAS<br>CLASSIFICATION<br>CLASSIFICAÇÃO | ANGLO-AMERICA<br>ANGLO-AMERIKA<br>AMÉRICA ANGLOSAJONA<br>AMÉRIQUE ANGLO-SAXONNE<br>AMÉRICA ANGLO-SAXÔNICA | LATIN AMERICA<br>LATEIN-AMERIKA<br>AMÉRICA LATINA<br>AMÉRIQUE LATINE<br>AMÉRICA LATINA | EUROPE-RUSSIA<br>EUROPA-RUSSLAND<br>EUROPA-RUSIA<br>EUROPE RUSSIE<br>EUROPA RÚSSIA | ASIA<br>ASIEN<br>ASIA<br>ASIE<br>ÁSIA | AFRICA-OCEANIA<br>AFRIKA-OZEANIEN<br>AFRICA-OCEANÍA<br>AFRIQUE-OCÉANIE<br>ÁFRICA-OCEANIA |
|---|---|---|---|---|---|
| Over 25,000,000 (1) | | | | Tōkyō-Yokohama | |
| 15,000,000-25,000,000 (5) | New York | Ciudad de México (Mexico City)<br>São Paulo | | Ōsaka-Kōbe-Kyōto<br>Sŏul (Seoul) | |
| 10,000,000-15,000,000 (13) | Los Angeles | Buenos Aires<br>Rio de Janeiro | London<br>Moskva (Moscow)<br>Paris | Bombay<br>Calcutta<br>Delhi-New Delhi<br>Jakarta<br>Manila<br>Shanghai | Al-Qāhirah (Cairo) |
| 5,000,000-10,000,000 (22) | Chicago<br>Philadelphia-Trenton-Wilmington<br>San Francisco-Oakland-San Jose<br>Toronto | Lima<br>Santa Fe de Bogotá<br>Santiago | Essen-Dortmund-Duisburg (Ruhr Area)<br>Sankt-Peterburg (St. Petersburg) | Beijing (Peking)<br>Dhaka (Dacca)<br>Hyderābād<br>İstanbul<br>Karāchi<br>Krung Thep (Bangkok)<br>Madras<br>Nagoya<br>T'aipei<br>Tehrān<br>Tianjin (Tientsin)<br>Victoria (Hong Kong) | Lagos |
| 3,000,000-5,000,000 (40) | Boston<br>Dallas-Fort Worth<br>Detroit-Windsor<br>Houston<br>Miami-Fort Lauderdale<br>Montréal<br>San Diego-Tijuana<br>Washington | Belo Horizonte<br>Caracas<br>Guadalajara<br>Porto Alegre | Athínai (Athens)<br>Barcelona<br>Berlin<br>Kyyiv (Kiev)<br>Madrid<br>Mllano (Milan)<br>Roma (Rome) | Ahmadābād<br>Baghdād<br>Bangalore<br>Guangzhou (Canton)<br>Harbin<br>Kuala Lumpur<br>Lahore<br>Pusan<br>Shenyang (Mukden)<br>Singapore<br>Surabaya<br>Thanh Pho Ho Chi Minh (Saigon)<br>Wuhan<br>Yangon (Rangoon) | Al-Iskandarīyah (Alexandria)<br>Casablanca<br>El Djazaïr (Algiers)<br>Johannesburg<br>Kinshasa<br>Melbourne<br>Sydney |
| 2,000,000-3,000,000 (64) | Atlanta<br>Baltimore<br>Cleveland<br>Minneapolis-St. Paul<br>Phoenix<br>Pittsburgh<br>St. Louis<br>Seattle-Tacoma | Curitiba<br>Fortaleza<br>La Habana (Havana)<br>Medellín<br>Monterrey<br>Recife<br>Salvador<br>San Juan<br>Santo Domingo | Amsterdam<br>Birmingham<br>Bruxelles (Brussels)<br>București (Bucharest)<br>Budapest<br>Donets'k-Makiyivka<br>Frankfurt am Main<br>Hamburg<br>Katowice-Bytom-Gliwice<br>Kharkiv<br>Leeds-Bradford<br>Lisboa (Lisbon)<br>Liverpool<br>Manchester<br>München (Munich)<br>Napoli (Naples)<br>Nižnij Novgorod (Gorky)<br>Stuttgart<br>Warszawa (Warsaw)<br>Wien (Vienna) | ʿAmman<br>Ankara<br>Bakı (Baku)<br>Bandung<br>Changchun<br>Chengdu (Chengtu)<br>Chittagong<br>Chongqing (Chungking)<br>Colombo<br>Dalian (Dairen)<br>Dimashq (Damascus)<br>Fukuoka<br>İzmir<br>Kānpur<br>Nanjing (Nanking)<br>Pune (Poona)<br>P'yongyang<br>Sapporo-Otaru<br>Taegu<br>Taškent<br>Tel Aviv-Yafo<br>Xi'an (Sian) | Abidjan<br>Adis Abeba<br>Al-Kharṭūm-Umm Durmān (Khartoum-Omdurman)<br>Cape Town<br>Durban |
| Total/Gesamtzahl<br>Total/Total/Total<br>(145) | 22 | 20 | 32 | 57 | 14 |

ALL URBAN CENTERS of 50,000 or more population and many other important or well-known cities and towns are listed in the following table. The populations are from recent censuses (designated C) or official estimates (designated E) for the dates specified. For a few cities, only unofficial estimates are available (designated U). For comparison, the total population of each country is also given. For each country, the date stated for the total population also applies to the cities, except those for which another date is specified.

Population estimates for 1995 for countries may be found in the World Information Table.

A population figure in parentheses and preceded by a star (★) is the population of a city's entire metropolitan area. To permit meaningful comparisons of metropolitan areas, these have been defined by Rand McNally according to consistent rules (see introduction to Metropolitan Areas Table), and in some cases may differ somewhat from the officially recognized metropolitan areas. Where a town is located within the metropolitan area of another city, that city's name is given in parentheses preceded by a star (★). The capital of a country is denoted by CAPITAL letters.

ALLE STÄDTISCHEN ZENTREN mit 50 000 oder mehr Einwohnern und zahlreiche andere bedeutende oder bekannte Städte sind in der folgenden Tabelle zusammengestellt. Die Bevölkerungszahlen stammen von neuesten Zählungen (mit C gekennzeichnet) oder amtlichen Schätzungen (E) zu den angegebenen Zeitpunkten. Für einige wenige Städte waren lediglich inoffizielle Schätzungen erhältlich (U). Zu Vergleichszwecken ist ferner die Gesamtbevölkerung jedes Landes angegeben. Das Bezugsjahr für die Einwohnerzahl eines Landes betrifft auch die Städte mit Ausnahme jener, bei denen ein anderes Datum angegeben ist.

Schätzungen der Bevölkerungszahlen der Länder für 1995 finden sich in der Welt-Informationstabelle.

Bevölkerungszahlen in Klammern mit vorangestelltem Stern (★) beziehen sich auf die gesamte Stadtregion einer Stadt. Um sinnvolle Vergleiche von Stadtregionen zu ermöglichen, wurden diese von Rand McNally nach einheitlichen Regeln festgelegt (siehe Einleitung: Tabelle der Stadtregionen), weshalb sie in einigen Fällen etwas von der offiziellen Abgrenzung von Stadtregionen abweichen können. Ist eine Stadt in die Stadtregion einer anderen Grossstadt einbezogen, so wird der Name der Stadtregion mit vorangestelltem Stern (★) in Klammern aufgeführt. Die Hauptstadt eines Landes wird durch GROSSBUCHSTABEN hervorgehoben.

TODAS LOS CENTROS URBANOS de 50 000 habitantes o más y muchos otros de importancia así como bien conocidas ciudades y pueblos están incluídos en la tabla que se presenta a continuación. El número de habitantes indicados está tomado del censo más reciente (cifras identificadas con la letra C) o estimados oficiales (E) para las fechas especificadas. Para algunas ciudades, sólo existen informes no oficiales (U). Para medida de comparación, la población total de cada país se encuentra incluída también.

Para permitir una comparación, se da la población total de cada país, referente al mismo año que se usa para las ciudades principles, excepto para aquellas en las que se especifica otra fecha. El número de habitantes para 1995 para los países, se encuentra en la Tabla de Información Mundial.

La segunda cifra para la población que aparece en paréntesis y está precedida por una estrella (★) constituye la población de un área metropolitana entera. Para permitir comparaciones validas de áreas metropolitanas, éstas fueron definidas por Rand McNally siguiendo las reglas establecidas para estos propósitos (véase la Introducción a la Tabla de las Áreas Metropolitanas), y en algunas ocasiones pueden ser un poco distintas de las áreas metropolitanas oficialmente reconocidas. Cuando una población se encuentra dentro de los límites de un área metropolitana de otra ciudad, el nombre de ésta se da entre paréntesis precedido por una (★). La capital de un país se indica con letras MAYÚSCULAS.

TOUTES LES VILLES de plus de 50 000 habitants et des villes moins peuplées, mais cèlèbres ou importantes, sont mentionnées dans la table ci-dessous. Les chiffres donnant la population proviennent de recensements récents (référence C), ou d'estimations officielles (référence E), aux dates indiquées. Pour quelques villes, on dispose seulement d'estimations non officielles (référence U). La population totale de chaque pays est également donnée, ce qui permet des comparaisons. Dans chaque pays, la date des renseignements est identique pour les villes et le pays, sauf indication contraire.

On trouvera dans la table d'informations mondiales les estimations de la population en 1995 pour chaque pays.

Les chiffres entre parenthèses, précédés d'une étoile (★), indiquent la population de l'ensemble de la zone métropolitaine. Pour permettre d'établir des comparaisons significatives entre les zones métropolitaines, ces dernières ont été définies selon des critères uniformes par Rand McNally & Company (voir l'introduction à la table des zones métropolitaines). Parfois, les limites des zones métropolitaines ainsi définies diffèrent des limites officielles. Quand une ville fait partie de la zone métropolitaine d'une autre ville, le nom de celle-ci, précédé d'une étoile (★), est mis entre parenthèses. Le nom des capitales de pays est écrit en lettres MAJUSCULES.

TODOS OS CENTROS URBANOS de 50 000 habitantes e mais, bem como muitas outras cidades e vilas importantes ou muito conhecidas figuram na tabela que se apresenta em sequida. Os dados relativos à população referem-se a censos recentes (identificadas com a letra C), ou a estimativas oficiais (E) nas datas indicadas. Para algumas cidades só existem estimativas não oficiais (U). Para fins de comparabilidade, apresenta-se também a população total de cada país.

Para cada país, a data de referência da população total aplica-se também às cidades exceto quando especificado em contrário. As estimativas da população dos países para 1995 encontra-se na *Tabela de informaçoes mundiais.*

Um dado de população apresentado entre parênteses e precedido por uma estrela (★), refere-se à população de toda a área metropolitana. Para fins de comparabilidade, as áreas metropolitanas foram definidas por Rand McNally segundo regras coerentes (ver a 'Introdução' à *Tabela das áreas metropolitanas),* e em certos casos podem ser um pouco diferentes das áreas metropolitanas oficialmente reconhecidas. Quando um centro urbano esta localizado dentro dos limites da área metropolitana de outro, seu nome figura entre parênteses precedido por uma estrela (★). A capital de um país é indicada por letras MAIÚSCULAS.

**AFGHANISTAN / Afghānestān**

| | |
|---|---:|
| 1988 E | 17,672,000 |
| Herāt | 177,300 |
| Jalālābād (1982E) | 58,000 |
| • KĀBOL | 1,424,400 |
| Kondūz (1982E) | 57,000 |
| Mazār-e Sharīf | 130,600 |
| Qandahār | 225,500 |

**ALBANIA / Shqipëri**

| | |
|---|---:|
| 1989 C | 3,182,400 |
| Durrës | 82,700 |
| Elbasan | 80,700 |
| Korçë | 63,600 |
| Shkodër | 79,900 |
| • TIRANË | 238,100 |
| Vlorë | 71,700 |

**ALGERIA / Algérie / Djazaïr**

| | |
|---|---:|
| 1987 C | 23,038,942 |
| Aïn el Beïda | 61,997 |
| Aïn Oussera | 44,270 |
| Aïn Témouchent | 47,479 |
| Annaba (Bône) | 305,526 |
| Bab Ezzouar (★El Djazaïr) | 55,211 |
| Barika | 56,488 |
| Batna | 181,601 |
| Béchar | 107,311 |
| Bejaïa (Bougie) | 114,534 |
| Beskra | 128,281 |
| Bordj Bou Arreridj | 84,264 |
| Bordj el Kiffan (★El Djazaïr) | 61,035 |
| Boufarik | 41,305 |
| Bou Saâda | 66,688 |
| Ech Cheliff (Orléansville) | 129,976 |
| El Boulaïda | 170,935 |
| • EL DJAZAÏR (ALGIERS) (★2,547,983) | 1,507,241 |
| El Djelfa | 84,207 |
| El Eulma | 67,933 |
| El Wad | 70,073 |
| Ghardaïa | 89,415 |
| Ghilizane | 80,091 |
| Guelma | 77,821 |
| Jijel | 62,793 |
| Khemis | 55,335 |
| Khenchla | 69,743 |
| Laghouat | 67,214 |
| Lemdiyya | 85,195 |
| Maghniyya | 52,275 |
| Messaad | 47,460 |
| Mestghanem | 114,037 |
| Mouaskar | 64,691 |
| M'Sila | 65,805 |
| Qacentina | 440,842 |
| Saïda | 80,825 |
| Sidi bel Abbès | 152,778 |
| Skikda | 128,747 |
| Souq Ahras | 83,015 |
| Stif | 170,182 |
| Tbessa | 107,559 |
| Tihert | 95,821 |
| Tilimsen | 126,882 |
| Tizi-Ouzou | 61,163 |
| Touggourt | 70,645 |
| Wahran | 628,558 |
| Wargla | 81,721 |

**AMERICAN SAMOA / Amerika Samoa**

| | |
|---|---:|
| 1990 C | 46,773 |
| • PAGO PAGO (▲14,295) | 3,518 |

**ANDORRA**

| | |
|---|---:|
| 1991 E | 54,507 |
| • ANDORRA | 20,437 |

**ANGOLA**

| | |
|---|---:|
| 1989 E | 9,739,100 |
| Benguela (1983E) | 155,000 |
| Huambo (Nova Lisboa) (1983E) | 203,000 |
| Lobito (1983E) | 150,000 |
| • LUANDA | 1,459,900 |
| Lubango (1984E) | 95,915 |
| Namibe (1981E) | 100,000 |

**ANGUILLA**

| | |
|---|---:|
| 1984 C | 6,680 |
| South Hill | 961 |
| • THE VALLEY | 1,042 |

**ANTIGUA AND BARBUDA**

| | |
|---|---:|
| 1977 E | 72,000 |
| • SAINT JOHN'S | 24,359 |

**ARGENTINA**

| | |
|---|---:|
| 1991 C | 32,608,560 |
| Almirante Brown (★Buenos Aires) | 448,762 |
| Avellaneda (★Buenos Aires) | 346,620 |
| Bahía Blanca | 255,145 |
| Banda del Río Salí (★San Miguel de Tucumán) | 50,282 |
| Belén de Escobar (★Buenos Aires) | 116,675 |
| Berazategui (★Buenos Aires) | 244,881 |
| Berisso (★Buenos Aires) | 72,703 |
| • BUENOS AIRES (★11,000,000) | 2,960 976 |
| Campana (★Buenos Aires) | 67,267 |
| Caseros (Tres de Febrero) (★Buenos Aires) | 349,221 |
| Chimbas (★San Juan) | 50,514 |
| Comodoro Rivadavia | 124,151 |
| Concordia | 116,491 |
| Córdoba (★1,260,000) | 1,148,305 |
| Corrientes | 257,766 |
| Ensenada (★Buenos Aires) | 47,192 |
| Esteban Echeverría (★Buenos Aires) | 274,303 |
| Florencio Varela (★Buenos Aires) | 249,006 |
| Formosa | 153,855 |
| General San Martín (★Buenos Aires) | 407,506 |
| General Sarmiento (San Miguel) (★Buenos Aires) | 646,891 |
| Godoy Cruz (★Mendoza) | 179,468 |
| Gualeguaychú | 64,620 |
| Junín | 70,138 |
| Lanús (★Buenos Aires) | 466,755 |
| La Plata (★Buenos Aires) | 520,449 |
| La Rioja | 104,494 |
| Las Heras (★Mendoza) | 145,823 |
| Lomas de Zamora (★Buenos Aires) | 572,769 |
| Luján (★Mendoza) | 54,241 |
| Luján (★Buenos Aires) | 66,226 |
| Maipú (★Mendoza) | 71,693 |
| Mar del Plata | 519,707 |
| Mendoza (★770,000) | 121,739 |
| Mercedes | 77,137 |
| Merlo (★Buenos Aires) | 386,304 |
| Moreno (★Buenos Aires) | 285,964 |
| Morón (★Buenos Aires) | 641,541 |
| Necochea | 59,775 |
| Neuquén | 167,076 |
| Olavarría | 72,821 |
| Paraná | 206,848 |
| Pergamino | 78,200 |
| Pilar (★Buenos Aires) | 113,428 |
| Posadas | 201,943 |
| Presidencia Roque Sáenz Peña | 64,476 |
| Punta Alta | 56,165 |
| Quilmes (★Buenos Aires) | 509,445 |
| Rafaela | 67,086 |
| Resistencia (★291,083) | 228,199 |
| Río Cuarto | 134,677 |
| Río Gallegos | 64,628 |
| Rivadavia (★San Juan) | 56,426 |
| Rosario (★1,190,000) | 894 645 |
| Salta | 367,099 |
| San Carlos de Bariloche | 77,750 |
| San Fernando (★Buenos Aires) | 141,496 |
| San Fernando del Valle de Catamarca (★133,050) | 110,269 |
| San Francisco (★58,536) | 55,828 |
| San Isidro (★Buenos Aires) | 299,022 |
| San Juan (★353,476) | 119,492 |
| San Justo (★Buenos Aires) | 1,111,811 |
| San Lorenzo (▲130,242) (★Rosario) | 38,509 |
| San Luis | 110,353 |
| San Martín | 64,821 |
| San Miguel de Tucumán (★622,348) | 470,604 |
| San Nicolás de los Arroyos | 114,752 |
| San Rafael | 94,776 |
| San Salvador de Jujuy | 181,318 |
| Santa Fe (★394,888) | 342,798 |
| Santa Rosa | 75,103 |
| Santiago del Estero (★255,000) | 189,490 |
| San Vicente (★Buenos Aires) | 74,890 |
| Tandil | 90,427 |
| Tigre (★Buenos Aires) | 253,748 |
| Trelew | 78,089 |
| Venado Tuerto | 58,678 |
| Vicente López (★Buenos Aires) | 289,142 |
| Villa Krause (★San Juan) | 83,266 |
| Villa María | 64,763 |
| Villa Nueva (★Mendoza) | 200,595 |
| Zárate (▲91,820) | 77,877 |

**ARMENIA / Hayastan**

| | |
|---|---:|
| 1989 C | 3,283,000 |
| Abovjan (1987E) | 53,000 |
| Ečmiadzin (★Jerevan) (1987E) | 53,000 |
| • JEREVAN (★1,315,000) | 1,199,000 |
| Kirovakan (1987E) | 169,000 |
| Kumajri | 120,000 |
| Razdan (1987E) | 56,000 |

**ARUBA**

| | |
|---|---:|
| 1991 C | 66,687 |
| • ORANJESTAD | 20,045 |

**AUSTRALIA**

| | |
|---|---:|
| 1991 C | 16,850,330 |
| Adelaide (★1,023,597) | 14,843 |
| Albury (★75,905) | 40,154 |
| Auburn (★Sydney) | 48,566 |
| Ballarat (★79,461) | 34,501 |
| Bankstown (★Sydney) | 153,904 |
| Bayswater (★Perth) | 44,010 |
| Bendigo (★67,315) | 30,134 |
| Berwick (★Melbourne) | 69,144 |
| Blacktown (★Sydney) | 211,710 |
| Blue Mountains (★Sydney) | 69,420 |
| Box Hill (★Melbourne) | 45,139 |
| Brisbane (★1,334,017) | 751,115 |
| Broadmeadows (★Melbourne) | 102,996 |
| Brunswick (★Melbourne) | 39,886 |
| Camberwell (★Melbourne) | 83,799 |
| Campbelltown (★Sydney) | 137,879 |
| CANBERRA (★303,846) | 276,162 |
| Canning (★Perth) | 65,967 |
| Canterbury (★Sydney) | 129,232 |
| Caulfield (★Melbourne) | 67,776 |
| Coburg (★Melbourne) | 50,625 |
| Cockburn (★Perth) | 50,380 |
| Coffs Harbour | 51,520 |
| Dandenong (★Melbourne) | 57,275 |
| Darwin (★78,400) | 70,071 |
| Doncaster (★Melbourne) | 102,898 |
| Enfield (★Adelaide) | 61,502 |
| Essendon (★Melbourne) | 52,721 |

▲ Population of an entire municipality, commune, or district, including rural area.
• Largest city in country.
★ Population or designation of the metropolitan area, including suburbs.
**C** Census. **E** Official estimate. **U** Unofficial estimate.

▲ Bevölkerung eines ganzen städtischen Verwaltungsgebietes, eines Kommunalbezirkes oder eines Distrikts, einschliesslich ländlicher Gebiete.
• Grösste Stadt des Landes.
★ Bevölkerung oder Bezeichnung der Stadtregion einschliesslich Vororte.
**C** Volkszählung. **E** Offizielle Schätzung. **U** Inoffizielle Schätzung.

▲ Población de un municipio, comuna o distrito entero, incluyendo sus áreas rurales.
• Ciudad más grande de un país.
★ Población o designación de un área metropolitana, incluyendo los suburbios.
**C** Censo. **E** Estimado oficial. **U** Estimado no oficial.

▲ Population d'une municipalité, d'une commune ou d'un district, zone rurale incluse.
• Ville la plus peuplée du pays.
★ Population de l'agglomération (ou nom de la zone métropolitaine englobante).
**C** Recensement. **E** Estimation officielle. **U** Estimation non officielle.

▲ População de um municipio, comuna ou distrito, inclusive as respectivas áreas rurais.
• Maior cidade de um país.
★ População ou indicação de uma área metropolitana.
**C** Censo. **E** Estimativa oficial. **U** Estimativa não oficial.

| | |
|---|---|
| Fairfield (★Sydney) | 175,099 |
| Footscray (★Melbourne) | 46,844 |
| Frankston (★Melbourne) | 84,986 |
| Geelong (★145,325) | 13,036 |
| Gosford | 128,956 |
| Gosnells (★Perth) | 69,560 |
| Heidelberg (★Melbourne) | 60,468 |
| Hobart (★181,832) | 47,106 |
| Holroyd (★Sydney) | 79,132 |
| Hurstville (★Sydney) | 63,757 |
| Ipswich (★Brisbane) | 73,299 |
| Keilor (★Melbourne) | 106,076 |
| Knox (★Melbourne) | 121,982 |
| Kogarah (★Sydney) | 46,518 |
| Lake Macquarie (★Newcastle) | 162,026 |
| Launceston (★111,438) | 66,747 |
| Leichhardt (★Sydney) | 58,484 |
| Liverpool (★Sydney) | 98,203 |
| Logan (★Brisbane) | 143,107 |
| Mackay (★52,934) | 23,052 |
| Maitland | 46,909 |
| Malvern (★Melbourne) | 41,340 |
| Marion (★Adelaide) | 73,942 |
| Marrickville (★Sydney) | 78,023 |
| Melbourne (★3,022,439) | 60,476 |
| Melville (★Perth) | 84,838 |
| Mitcham (★Adelaide) | 60,939 |
| Moorabbin (★Melbourne) | 94,161 |
| Newcastle (★427,824) | 131,305 |
| Noarlunga (★Adelaide) | 80,882 |
| Northcote (★Melbourne) | 46,547 |
| North Sydney (★Sydney) | 50,446 |
| Nunawading (★Melbourne) | 91,468 |
| Oakleigh (★Melbourne) | 55,151 |
| Parramatta (★Sydney) | 132,798 |
| Penrith (★Sydney) | 149,630 |
| Perth (★1,143,249) | 80,517 |
| Prahran (★Melbourne) | 42,193 |
| Preston (★Melbourne) | 76,996 |
| Randwick (★Sydney) | 115,349 |
| Redcliffe (★Brisbane) | 47,799 |
| Rockdale (★Sydney) | 84,074 |
| Rockhampton (★62,787) | 59,394 |
| Ryde (★Sydney) | 90,197 |
| Saint Kilda (★Melbourne) | 45,481 |
| Salisbury (★Adelaide) | 106,007 |
| Shoalhaven | 68,287 |
| Southport (★268,662) | 157,857 |
| South Sydney (★Sydney) | 77,818 |
| Springvale (★Melbourne) | 89,478 |
| Stirling (★Perth) | 172,731 |
| Sunshine (★Melbourne) | 94,020 |
| • Sydney (★3,538,749) | 13,501 |
| Tea Tree Gully (★Adelaide) | 83,969 |
| Toowoomba | 81,043 |
| Townsville (★116,572) | 87,288 |
| Wagga Wagga | 53,447 |
| Wanneroo (★Perth) | 167,873 |
| Waverley (★Melbourne) | 118,265 |
| Waverley (★Sydney) | 59,095 |
| West Torrens (★Adelaide) | 42,863 |
| Willoughby (★Sydney) | 51,503 |
| Wollongong (★235,966) | 211,417 |
| Woodville (★Adelaide) | 78,824 |
| Woollahra (★Sydney) | 49,904 |

**AUSTRIA / Österreich**

| | |
|---|---|
| 1991 C | 7,795,786 |
| Bruck an der Mur (★50,000) | 14,046 |
| Graz (★265,000) | 237,810 |
| Innsbruck (★200,000) | 118,112 |
| Klagenfurt (★118,000) | 89,415 |
| Leoben (★47,600) | 28,897 |
| Linz (★352,000) | 203,044 |
| Neunkirchen (★45,000) | 10,216 |
| Salzburg (★185,000) | 143,978 |
| Sankt Pölten (★69,500) | 50,026 |
| Steyr (★58,000) | 39,337 |
| Villach (★66,500) | 54,640 |
| Wels (★68,000) | 52,594 |
| • WIEN (VIENNA) (★1,900,000) | 1,539,848 |

**AZERBAIJAN / Azərbaycan**

| | |
|---|---|
| 1991 E | 7,136,600 |
| Äli Bayramlı | 61,500 |
| • BAKI (★2,020,000) | 1,080,500 |
| Gäncä | 282,200 |
| Mingäçevir | 90,900 |
| Naxçıvan | 61,700 |
| Şeki | 63,200 |
| Sumqayıt (★Bakı) | 236,200 |
| Xankändi (Stepanakert) | 55,200 |

**BAHAMAS**

| | |
|---|---|
| 1990 C | 254,685 |
| Freeport (▲171,542) | 28,200 |
| • NASSAU | 141,000 |

**BAHRAIN / Al-Bahrayn**

| | |
|---|---|
| 1988 E | 473,000 |
| • AL-MANĀMAH (★273,000) (1986E) | 82,700 |
| Al-Muharraq (★Al-Manāmah) | 78,000 |
| Jidd Ḥafṣ (★Al-Manāmah) | 48,000 |

**BANGLADESH**

| | |
|---|---|
| 1991 C | 104,766,143 |
| Barisāl | 180,014 |
| Begamganj (1981C) | 69,623 |
| Bhairab Bāzār | 75,747 |
| Bogra | 93,114 |
| Brāhmanbāria | 84,067 |
| Chāndpur | 84,067 |
| Chittagong (★2,342,662) | 1,566,070 |
| Chuādanga | 65,222 |
| Comilla (1981C) | 184,132 |
| • DHAKA (DACCA) (★6,537,308) | 3,637,892 |
| Dinājpur | 136,657 |
| Farīdpur | 72,927 |
| Gopālpur | 45,174 |
| Gulshan (★Dhaka) (1981C) | 215,444 |
| Jamālpur | 108,416 |
| Jessore | 176,398 |
| Jhenida | 69,501 |
| Khulna (★966,096) | 601,051 |
| Kishorganj | 64,676 |
| Kurīgrām | 62,075 |
| Kushtia | 71,706 |
| Mādārīpur | 46,842 |
| Mīrpur (★Dhaka) (1981C) | 349,031 |
| Mymensingh | 138,862 |
| Naogaon | 109,156 |
| Nārāyanganj (★Dhaka) | 288,008 |
| Narsinghdi | 100,120 |
| Nawābganj | 131,260 |
| Noākhāli | 73,766 |
| Pābna | 113,146 |
| Patuākhāli | 50,344 |
| Rājshāhi (★560,013) | 324,532 |
| Rangpur | 220,849 |
| Saidpur | 110,494 |
| Sātkhira | 81,199 |
| Sherpur | 63,030 |
| Sirājganj | 100,003 |
| Sītākunda (★Chittagong) (1981C) | 237,520 |
| Sylhet | 114,284 |
| Tangail | 111,783 |
| Tongi (★Dhaka) | 165,099 |

**BARBADOS**

| | |
|---|---|
| 1990 C | 260,491 |
| • BRIDGETOWN (★125,000) | 5,928 |

**BELARUS / Belarus'**

| | |
|---|---|
| 1991 E | 10,260,400 |
| Babrujsk | 223,000 |
| Baranavičy | 166,700 |
| Barysau | 150,200 |
| Brèst | 277,000 |
| Homel' | 503,300 |
| Hrodna | 284,800 |
| Kobryn | 48,300 |
| Lida | 95,000 |
| Mahilëu | 363,000 |
| Maladzečna | 93,500 |
| Mazyr | 103,000 |
| • MINSK (★1,694,000) | 1,633,600 |
| Navapolack | 96,600 |
| Orša | 125,300 |
| Pinsk | 123,800 |
| Polack | 78,700 |
| Rèčyca | 69,400 |
| Salihorsk | 96,000 |
| Sluck | 60,100 |
| Vicebsk | 361,500 |
| Žlobin | 60,800 |
| Žodzina | 56,000 |

**BELGIUM / België / Belgique**

| | |
|---|---|
| 1991 C | 9,978,681 |
| Aalst (Alost) (★Bruxelles) | 76,382 |
| Anderlecht (★Bruxelles) | 87,884 |
| Antwerpen (★1,140,000) | 467,518 |
| Bastogne (▲12,187) | 7,200 |
| Brugge (Bruges) (★223,000) | 117,063 |
| • BRUXELLES (★2,385,000) | 136,424 |
| Charleroi (★480,000) | 206,214 |
| Etterbeek (★Bruxelles) | 38,894 |
| Forest (★Bruxelles) | 46,437 |
| Genk (★Hasselt) | 61,339 |
| Gent (Gand) (★467,000) | 230,246 |
| Hasselt (★295,000) | 66,611 |
| Ixelles (★Bruxelles) | 72,610 |
| Kortrijk (Courtrai) (★204,000) | 76,141 |
| La Louvière (★150,000) | 76,432 |
| Leuven (Louvain) (★178,000) | 85,018 |
| Liège (Luik) (★747,000) | 194,596 |
| Mechelen (Malines) (★122,000) | 75,313 |
| Molenbeek-St.-Jean (★Bruxelles) | 68,759 |
| Mons (Bergen) (★247,000) | 91,726 |
| Mouscron (★Lille, France) | 53,513 |
| Namur (★149,000) | 130,443 |
| Oostende (Ostende) (★124,000) | 68,500 |
| Roeselare (Roulers) | 52,872 |
| Saint-Gilles (★Bruxelles) | 42,684 |
| Schaerbeek (★Bruxelles) | 102,702 |
| Seraing (★Liège) | 60,838 |
| Sint-Niklaas (Saint-Nicolas) | 68,203 |
| Spa | 10,140 |
| Tournai (Doornik) (▲67,762) | 45,400 |
| Uccle (★Bruxelles) | 73,721 |
| Verviers (★104,000) | 53,482 |
| Waterloo (★Bruxelles) | 27,860 |
| Woluwe-Saint-Lambert (Sint-Lambrechts-Woluwe) (★Bruxelles) | 47,963 |

**BELIZE**

| | |
|---|---|
| 1990 C | 184,340 |
| • Belize City | 43,621 |
| BELMOPAN | 5,256 |

**BENIN / Bénin**

| | |
|---|---|
| 1984 E | 3,825,000 |
| Abomey | 53,000 |
| • COTONOU (1992C) | 533,212 |
| Parakou | 92,000 |
| PORTO-NOVO | 164,000 |

**BERMUDA**

| | |
|---|---|
| 1991 C | 58,460 |
| • HAMILTON (★16,000) | 1,100 |

**BHUTAN / Druk-Yul**

| | |
|---|---|
| 1982 E | 1,333,000 |
| • THIMPHU | 12,000 |

**BOLIVIA**

| | |
|---|---|
| 1992 C | 6,420,792 |
| Cochabamba | 407,825 |
| El Alto (★La Paz) | 405,492 |
| • LA PAZ (★1,120,000) | 713,378 |
| Montero | 52,021 |
| Oruro | 183,422 |
| Potosí | 112,078 |
| Quillacollo | 70,965 |
| Riberalta | 43,454 |
| Santa Cruz de la Sierra | 697,278 |
| SUCRE | 131,769 |
| Tarija | 90,113 |
| Trinidad | 57,328 |

**BOSNIA AND HERZEGOVINA / Bosna i Hercegovina**

| | |
|---|---|
| 1987 E | 4,400,464 |
| Banja Luka (▲193,890) | 130,900 |
| • SARAJEVO (▲479,688) | 341,200 |
| Tuzla (▲129,967) | 67,300 |
| Zenica (▲144,869) | 67,500 |

**BOTSWANA**

| | |
|---|---|
| 1991 C | 1,326,796 |
| Francistown | 65,244 |
| • GABORONE | 133,468 |
| Selebi Phikwe | 39,772 |

**BRAZIL / Brasil**

| | |
|---|---|
| 1991 C | 146,917,459 |
| Abaetetuba (▲100,016) | 55,442 |
| Abreu e Lima (▲76,568) | 70,099 |
| Alagoinhas (▲116,740) | 97,819 |
| Alegrete (▲78,879) | 67,505 |
| Almirante Tamandaré (▲66,090) | 51,240 |
| Altamira (▲120,441) | 48,452 |
| Alvorada (▲142,020) (★Porto Alegre) | 132,582 |
| Americana | 153,592 |
| Ananindeua (▲88,035) | 73,941 |
| Anápolis (▲239,047) | 222,400 |
| Anil (▲695,199) | 81,879 |
| Antônio Bezerra (▲1,765,794) (★Fortaleza) | 193,682 |
| Aparecida de Goiânia (▲178,326) | 48,804 |
| Apucarana (▲94,914) | 80,048 |
| Aracaju | 401,676 |
| Araçatuba (▲159,499) | 146,977 |
| Araguaína (▲103,396) | 81,729 |
| Araguari (▲91,202) | 80,568 |
| Arapiraca (▲165,379) | 131,449 |
| Arapongas (▲64,531) | 59,996 |
| Araraquara (▲166,732) | 101,302 |
| Araras (▲87,355) | 79,002 |
| Araucária (▲61,767) | 53,522 |
| Araxá | 67,919 |
| Assis (▲85,265) | 72,004 |
| Atibaia (▲86,193) | 74,658 |
| Avaré (▲61,063) | 56,232 |
| Bacabal (▲98,875) | 64,844 |
| Bagé (▲118,736) | 89,372 |
| Barbacena (▲99,895) | 80,882 |
| Barra Alegre (▲179,710) | 58,445 |
| Barra do Piraí (▲78,426) | 59,202 |
| Barra Mansa (▲171,671) (★Volta Redonda) | 145,112 |
| Barreiras (▲92,439) | 70,701 |
| Barreiros (▲139,318) (★Florianópolis) | 58,694 |
| Barretos (▲95,538) | 88,935 |
| Barueri (▲130,383) | 66,722 |
| Bauru | 254,690 |
| Bayeux (★João Pessoa) | 77,047 |
| Bebedouro (▲67,752) | 60,792 |
| Belém (★1,355,000) | 765,476 |
| Belford Roxo (▲1,293,611) (★Rio de Janeiro) | 337,698 |
| Belo Horizonte (★3,340,000) | 1,529,566 |
| Betim (★Belo Horizonte) | 162,462 |
| Birigui (▲75,054) | 70,547 |
| Blumenau (▲211,862) | 185,200 |
| Boa Vista (▲142,902) | 118,958 |
| Botucatu (▲90,620) | 81,528 |
| Bragança Paulista (▲108,602) | 88,336 |
| Brás Cubas (▲273,255) | 65,538 |
| BRASÍLIA | 1,513,470 |
| Brusque | 53,438 |
| Cabo (▲126,756) | 68,594 |
| Cabo Frio (▲84,635) | 70,251 |
| Caçapava (▲65,889) | 58,145 |
| Cáceres (▲77,475) | 51,891 |
| Cachoeira do Sul (▲89,148) | 69,780 |
| Cachoeirinha (★Porto Alegre) | 87,976 |
| Cachoeiro de Itapemirim (▲143,763) | 112,099 |
| Camaçari (▲113,615) | 88,302 |
| Camarajibe | 99,431 |
| Cambé (▲73,803) | 66,767 |
| Campina Grande | 298,331 |
| Campinas (★1,290,000) | 759,032 |
| Campo Comprido (▲1,313,094) (★Curitiba) | 105,631 |
| Campo Grande | 516,403 |
| Campo Mourão (▲82,280) | 69,966 |
| Campos (▲388,747) | 277,482 |
| Campos Elísios (▲665,343) (★Rio de Janeiro) | 197,833 |
| Candeias (▲67,936) | 61,432 |
| Canoas (★Porto Alegre) | 269,234 |
| Capuáva (▲615,112) | 92,950 |
| Carapicuíba (▲283,653) (★São Paulo) | 207,264 |
| Carapina (▲221,510) (★Vit2oria) | 141,234 |
| Carazinho (▲58,770) | 49,010 |
| Cariacica (▲274,455) (★Vitória) | 91,888 |
| Carpina (▲65,949) | 50,962 |
| Caruaru (▲213,573) | 180,654 |
| Cascatinha (▲255,261) | 56,890 |
| Cascavel (▲192,884) | 175,332 |
| Castanhal (▲101,963) | 90,364 |
| Catanduva | 88,024 |
| Caucaia (▲165,015) (★Fortaleza) | 66,379 |
| Cava (▲1,293,611) | 59,506 |
| Cavaleiro (▲486,774) (★Recife) | 120,065 |
| Caxias (▲146,730) | 85,332 |
| Caxias do Sul (▲290,969) | 262,983 |
| Chapecó (▲122,889) | 93,697 |
| Codó (▲111,679) | 58,163 |
| Coelho da Rocha (▲424,689) (★Rio de Janeiro) | 152,045 |
| Colatina (▲106,712) | 71,094 |
| Colombo (▲117,658) (★Curitiba) | 110,161 |
| Conselheiro Lafaiete (▲88,843) | 82,619 |
| Contagem (▲448,991) (★Belo Horizonte) | 195,705 |
| Corumbá (▲88,290) | 75,235 |
| Cotia (▲106,822) | 90,469 |
| Coxipó da Ponte (▲401,303) | 140,130 |
| Crato (▲91,413) | 56,374 |
| Criciúma (▲146,162) | 99,375 |
| Cruz Alta (▲68,784) | 61,860 |
| Cruzeiro | 65,935 |
| Cubatão (★Santos) | 90,572 |
| Cuiabá (▲401,303) | 252,784 |
| Curitiba (★1,815,000) | 841,882 |
| Diadema (★São Paulo) | 305,068 |
| Divinópolis (▲151,382) | 141,984 |
| Dourados (▲135,786) | 116,817 |
| Duque de Caxias (▲665,343) (★Rio de Janeiro) | 325,903 |
| Embu (★São Paulo) | 155,851 |
| Erechim (▲72,292) | 61,509 |
| Esteio (★Porto Alegre) | 70,449 |
| Eunápolis (▲70,561) | 63,553 |
| Feira de Santana (▲405,848) | 340,034 |
| Fernandópolis (▲56,125) | 51,216 |
| Ferraz de Vasconcelos (▲95,973) (★São Paulo) | 65,319 |
| Florianópolis (★420,000) | 191,664 |
| Formosa (▲62,974) | 49,135 |
| Fortaleza (★2,040,000) | 743,335 |
| Foz do Iguaçu | 186,362 |
| Franca | 227,613 |
| Francisco Morato | 83,361 |
| Franco da Rocha | 79,534 |
| Garanhuns (▲103,365) | 86,593 |
| Goiabeiras (▲258,243) (★Vitória) | 74,086 |
| Goiânia (★1,130,000) | 912,136 |
| Governador Valadares (▲230,403) | 210,396 |
| Gravataí (▲181,019) (★Porto Alegre) | 166,954 |
| Guaíba (▲83,119) | 72,739 |
| Guarapari (▲61,594) | 54,994 |
| Guarapuava (▲159,692) | 107,046 |
| Guaratinguetá (▲102,005) | 84,660 |
| Guarujá (▲209,814) (★Santos) | 98,918 |
| Guarulhos (▲786,355) (★São Paulo) | 546,417 |
| Gurupi (▲56,741) | 51,005 |
| Hortolândia (▲226,225) | 78,011 |
| Ibes (▲265,251) (★Vitória) | 91,071 |
| Icoraci (▲1,244,688) (★Belém) | 67,458 |
| Igapó (▲606,681) | 117,251 |
| Igarassu (▲79,713) (★Recife) | 48,598 |
| Ijuí (▲75,169) | 58,627 |
| Ilhéus (▲223,482) | 135,117 |
| Imbariê (▲665,343) | 100,687 |
| Imperatriz (▲276,440) | 209,970 |
| Indaiatuba (▲100,816) | 91,752 |
| Inhomirim (▲191,249) | 76,031 |
| Ipatinga (★179,710) | 120,025 |
| Ipiíba (▲778,831) (★Rio de Janeiro) | 121,785 |
| Itabira (▲85,284) | 71,287 |
| Itaboraí (▲161,398) | 72,410 |
| Itabuna (▲185,165) | 170,434 |
| Itaituba (▲116,541) | 62,278 |
| Itajaí | 114,558 |
| Itajubá (▲74,618) | 68,469 |
| Itambi (▲161,398) | 48,891 |
| Itapecerica da Serra (▲92,854) (★São Paulo) | 84,479 |
| Itaperuna (▲78,017) | 55,484 |
| Itapetininga (▲105,071) | 84,703 |
| Itapeva (▲81,858) | 55,658 |
| Itapevi (★São Paulo) | 107,983 |
| Itaquaquecetuba (★São Paulo) | 164,665 |
| Itaquari (▲274,455) (★Vitória) | 169,145 |
| Itatiba (▲61,587) | 54,044 |
| Itaúna | 61,891 |
| Itú (▲107,176) | 88,838 |
| Ituiutaba (▲84,581) | 78,211 |
| Itumbiara (▲79,457) | 68,673 |
| Jaboatão (▲486,774) (★Recife) | 81,178 |
| Jaboticabal (▲59,130) | 53,027 |
| Jacareí (▲163,843) | 144,141 |
| Jandira | 62,573 |
| Japeri (▲1,293,611) | 65,576 |
| Jaraguá do Sul (▲76,994) | 62,578 |
| Jardim Presidente Dutra (▲786,355) (★São Paulo) | 229,987 |
| Jataí (▲65,921) | 53,431 |
| Jaú (▲94,138) | 80,331 |
| Jequié (▲144,572) | 114,542 |
| Ji-Paraná (▲97,719) | 75,384 |
| João Monlevade | 57,413 |
| João Pessoa (★670,000) | 497,308 |
| Joinvile | 326,208 |
| Juàzeiro (▲128,691) (★Petrolina) | 95,676 |
| Juazeiro do Norte | 163,527 |
| Juiz de Fora | 377,538 |
| Jundiaí (▲288,644) | 265,599 |
| Jurema (▲165,015) (★Fortaleza) | 75,463 |
| Justinópolis (▲143,696) (★Belo Horizonte) | 85,452 |
| Lages (▲151,100) | 137,169 |
| Lavras (▲65,857) | 60,690 |
| Leme | 64,525 |
| Limeira (▲207,416) | 177,591 |
| Linhares (▲119,501) | 73,082 |
| Lins (▲59,218) | 54,868 |
| Londrina (▲389,959) | 355,062 |
| Lorena (▲73,187) | 67,766 |
| Luziânia (▲207,425) | 194,128 |
| Macaé (▲100,642) | 57,581 |
| Macapá (▲179,252) | 146,523 |
| Maceió (▲628,241) | 554,727 |
| Manaus | 1,005,634 |
| Marabá (▲122,231) | 102,364 |
| Marília (▲160,872) | 144,906 |
| Maringá | 225,516 |
| Matão | 59,694 |
| Mauá (★São Paulo) | 294,631 |
| Mesquita (▲1,293,611) (★Rio de Janeiro) | 141,326 |
| Messejana (▲1,765,794) (★Fortaleza) | 229,507 |
| Moji das Cruzes (▲273,255) (★São Paulo) | 138,995 |
| Mojiguaçu (▲107,440) | 92,440 |
| Mojimirim (▲64,750) | 57,395 |
| Mondubim (▲1,765,794) (★Fortaleza) | 331,591 |
| Monjolo (▲778,831) (★Rio de Janeiro) | 137,974 |
| Montes Claros (▲249,565) | 223,046 |
| Mossoró (▲191,959) | 177,020 |
| Muriaé (▲84,507) | 65,406 |
| Muribeca dos Guararapes (▲486,774) (★Recife) | 217,905 |
| Natal (▲606,681) | 459,827 |
| Neves (▲778,831) (★Rio de Janeiro) | 151,087 |
| Nilópolis (▲157,936) (★Rio de Janeiro) | 104,671 |
| Niterói (▲435,658) (★Rio de Janeiro) | 400,586 |
| Nossa Senhora do Socorro | 67,443 |
| Nova Brasília (▲178,326) (★Goiânia) | 126,701 |
| Nova Friburgo (▲166,975) | 111,020 |
| Nova Iguaçu (▲1,293,611) (★Rio de Janeiro) | 562,062 |
| Nova Veneza (▲226,225) | 82,203 |
| Novo Hamburgo (★Porto Alegre) | 201,334 |
| Novo Mundo (▲1,313,094) (★Curitiba) | 71,508 |
| Olinda (▲157,936) | 53,265 |
| Olinda (★Recife) | 341,059 |
| Osasco (★São Paulo) | 566,949 |
| Ourinhos (▲76,912) | 70,690 |
| Palhoça (▲68,298) (★Florianópolis) | 58,097 |
| Paracatu (▲62,709) | 49,656 |
| Pará de Minas (▲61,066) | 51,679 |
| Paranaguá (▲107,601) | 88,110 |
| Paranavaí (▲71,173) | 61,043 |
| Parangaba (▲1,765,794) (★Fortaleza) | 267,679 |
| Parnaíba (▲127,992) | 105,131 |
| Parnamirim (▲63,253) | 48,534 |
| Parque Industrial (▲448,991) (★Belo Horizonte) | 223,660 |
| Passo do Sabão (▲169,079) (★Porto Alegre) | 63,140 |
| Passo Fundo (▲147,239) | 135,158 |
| Passos (▲84,618) | 74,218 |
| Patos (▲81,292) | 76,378 |
| Patos de Minas (▲102,766) | 83,670 |

▲ Population of an entire municipality, commune, or district, including rural area.
• Largest city in country.
★ Population or designation of the metropolitan area, including suburbs.
**C** Census. **E** Official estimate. **U** Unofficial estimate.

▲ Bevölkerung eines ganzen städtischen Verwaltungsgebietes, eines Kommunalbezirkes oder eines Distrikts, einschliesslich ländlicher Gebiete.
• Grösste Stadt des Landes.
★ Bevölkerung oder Bezeichnung der Stadtregion einschliesslich Vororte.
**C** Volkszählung. **E** Offizielle Schätzung. **U** Inoffizielle Schätzung.

| | |
|---|---|
| Paulista (▲211,017) (★Recife) | 53,566 |
| Paulo Afonso (▲86,594) | 74,326 |
| Pelotas (▲290,660) | 260,510 |
| Petrolina (★300,000) | 123,857 |
| Petrópolis (▲255,261) (★Rio de Janeiro) | 164,849 |
| Pindamonhangaba (▲101,849) | 71,449 |
| Pinhais (▲106,764) (★Curitiba) | 71,973 |
| Pinheirinho (▲1,313,094) (★Curitiba) | 117,518 |
| Piracicaba (▲283,634) | 223,170 |
| Poá (★São Paulo) | 72,151 |
| Poços de Caldas | 105,223 |
| Ponta Grossa | 219,955 |
| Porto Alegre (★2,850,000) | 1,247,352 |
| Porto Velho (▲161,611) | 56,973 |
| Porto Velho (▲286,471) | 226,196 |
| Pouso Alegre (▲81,776) | 73,875 |
| Praia da Conceição (▲211,017) (★Recife) | 97,635 |
| Praia Grande (▲123,494) | 97,173 |
| Presidente Prudente | 157,618 |
| Queimados (▲1,293,611) (★Rio de Janeiro) | 124,121 |
| Recife (★2,880,000) | 1,296,995 |
| Resende (▲91,605) | 52,261 |
| Ribeirão Pires | 62,240 |
| Ribeirão Preto | 416,486 |
| Rio Branco (▲196,871) | 136,457 |
| Rio Claro | 130,364 |
| Rio de Janeiro (★11,050,000) | 5,473,909 |
| Rio Grande (▲172,408) | 157,608 |
| Rio Verde (▲95,894) | 76,818 |
| Rondonópolis (▲126,082) | 87,307 |
| Salto | 72,076 |
| Salvador (★2,340,000) | 2,070,296 |
| Santa Bárbara d'Oeste | 141,230 |
| Santa Cruz do Sul (▲117,779) | 74,295 |
| Santa Felicidade (▲1,313,094) (★Curitiba) | 53,560 |
| Santa Inês (▲64,655) | 54,006 |
| Santa Maria (▲217,604) | 193,294 |
| Santana do Livramento (▲80,145) | 72,950 |
| Santarém (▲264,779) | 168,153 |
| Santa Rita (▲94,412) (★João Pessoa) | 74,396 |
| Santa Rosa (▲58,262) | 48,211 |
| Santo André (▲615,112) (★São Paulo) | 518,272 |
| Santo Ângelo (▲76,461) | 59,688 |
| Santos (★1,165,000) | 415,554 |
| São Benedito (▲137,686) (★Belo Horizonte) | 91,733 |
| São Bernardo do Campo (★São Paulo) | 550,030 |
| São Borja (▲63,766) | 52,493 |
| São Caetano do Sul (★São Paulo) | 149,203 |
| São Carlos (▲158,186) | 100,502 |
| São Cristóvão | 46,172 |
| São Gabriel (▲59,024) | 47,668 |
| São Gonçalo (▲778,831) (★Rio de Janeiro) | 296,021 |
| São João da Boa Vista (▲69,090) | 60,845 |
| São João del-Rei (▲72,741) | 63,680 |
| São João de Meriti (▲424,689) (★Rio de Janeiro) | 220,742 |
| São José do Rio Preto | 263,454 |
| São José dos Campos (▲442,009) | 385,879 |
| São José dos Pinhais (▲128,170) (★Curitiba) | 99,154 |
| São Leopoldo (★Porto Alegre) | 160,228 |
| São Lourenco da Mata (▲85,889) (★Recife) | 68,479 |
| São Luís (★710,000) | 164,334 |
| São Mateus (▲424,689) | 51,902 |
| • São Paulo (★16,925,000) | 9,393,753 |
| São Vicente (★Santos) | 268,467 |
| Sapiranga (▲58,522) | 51,387 |
| Sapucaia do Sul (★Porto Alegre) | 104,626 |
| Serra (▲221,510) | 62,398 |
| Sertãozinho (▲78,753) | 68,874 |
| Sete Lagoas | 139,910 |
| Sete Pontes (▲778,831) (★Rio de Janeiro) | 71,984 |
| Sobral (▲127,459) | 92,805 |
| Sorocaba | 348,952 |
| Sumaré (▲226,225) | 64,673 |
| Susano (▲159,142) (★São Paulo) | 110,414 |
| Taboão da Serra (★São Paulo) | 159,894 |
| Tatuí (▲76,662) | 68,808 |
| Taubaté (▲206,416) | 185,790 |
| Teixeira de Freitas (▲85,227) | 73,107 |
| Telêmaco Borba (▲64,854) | 50,774 |
| Teófilo Otoni (▲140,676) | 96,382 |
| Teresina (★665,000) | 556,073 |
| Teresópolis (▲120,712) | 96,516 |
| Timon (▲107,394) (★Teresina) | 90,577 |
| Timóteo (▲58,393) | 48,340 |
| Toledo (▲94,857) | 67,343 |
| Três Corações (▲57,053) | 49,138 |
| Três Lagoas (▲68,067) | 60,716 |
| Três Rios (▲81,163) | 60,201 |
| Tubarão (▲95,058) | 83,262 |
| Tupã (▲61,290) | 53,282 |
| Ubá (▲66,422) | 52,673 |
| Uberaba (▲211,358) | 198,565 |
| Uberlândia | 255,191 |
| Umbará (▲1,313,094) (★Curitiba) | 64,523 |
| Umuarama (▲100,185) | 66,995 |
| Uruguaiana (▲117,437) | 103,160 |
| Valinhos (▲67,867) | 59,896 |
| Varginha (▲88,045) | 82,263 |
| Várzea Grande (▲161,611) | 96,379 |
| Várzea Paulista | 67,911 |
| Venda Nova (▲2,017,127) (★Belo Horizonte) | 481,470 |
| Viamão (▲169,079) | 75,782 |
| Vicente de Carvalho (▲209,814) (★Santos) | 110,881 |
| Vila Dirce (▲283,653) | 59,144 |
| Vila Velha (▲265,251) (★Vitória) | 113,664 |
| Vila Xavier (▲166,732) | 50,922 |
| Vitória (★810,000) | 184,157 |
| Vitória da Conquista (▲224,896) | 179,868 |
| Vitória de Santo Antão (▲106,661) | 84,116 |
| Volta Redonda (★430,000) | 219,988 |
| Votorantim | 79,150 |
| Votuporanga (▲66,037) | 59,604 |

**BRITISH VIRGIN ISLANDS**

| | |
|---|---|
| 1980 C | 12,034 |
| • ROAD TOWN | 2,479 |

**BRUNEI**

| | |
|---|---|
| 1981 C | 192,832 |
| • BANDAR SERI BEGAWAN (★64,000) | 22,777 |
| Seria | 23,415 |

**BULGARIA / Bâlgarija**

| | |
|---|---|
| 1992 C | 8,487,317 |
| Asenovgrad | 52,360 |
| Blagoevgrad | 71,476 |
| Burgas | 195,686 |
| Dimitrovgrad | 50,677 |
| Dobrič | 104,494 |
| Gabrovo | 76,522 |
| Haskovo | 80,700 |
| Jambol | 91,497 |
| Kărdžali | 45,793 |
| Kazanlăk | 60,095 |
| Kjustendil | 54,431 |
| Loveč | 48,242 |
| Montana | 52,476 |
| Pazardžik | 82,578 |
| Pernik | 90,549 |
| Pleven | 130,812 |
| Plovdiv | 341,058 |
| Razgrad | 40,933 |
| Ruse | 170,038 |
| Silistra | 48,360 |
| Sliven | 106,212 |
| • SOFIJA (★1,280,000) | 1,190,126 |
| Stara Zagora | 150,518 |
| Šumen | 93,390 |
| Varna | 308,432 |
| Veliko Tărnovo | 67,540 |
| Vidin | 62,691 |
| Vraca | 75,518 |

**BURKINA FASO**

| | |
|---|---|
| 1985 C | 7,964,705 |
| Bobo Dioulasso | 228,668 |
| Koudougou | 51,926 |
| • OUAGADOUGOU | 441,514 |
| Ouahigouya | 38,902 |

**BURUNDI**

| | |
|---|---|
| 1990 C | 5,356,266 |
| • BUJUMBURA | 226,628 |

**CAMBODIA / Kâmpŭchéa**

| | |
|---|---|
| 1990 E | 8,567,582 |
| Bătdâmbâng | 94,412 |
| Kâmpóng Saôm | 67,452 |
| • PHNUM PÉNH | 620,000 |
| Prey Vêng | 41,456 |
| Siĕmréab | 76,434 |
| Ta Khmau | 34,947 |

**CAMEROON / Cameroun**

| | |
|---|---|
| 1987 C | 9,312,429 |
| Bafoussam | 92,331 |
| Bamenda | 95,445 |
| • Douala | 712,251 |
| Edéa | 45,555 |
| Fort-Foureau | 48,620 |
| Foumban | 46,920 |
| Garoua | 122,584 |
| Kumba | 63,911 |
| Maroua | 111,630 |
| Ngaoundéré | 69,682 |
| Nkongsamba | 76,887 |
| YAOUNDÉ | 560,785 |

**CANADA**

| | |
|---|---|
| 1991 C | 27,296,859 |

**CANADA: ALBERTA**

| | |
|---|---|
| 1991 C | 2,545,553 |
| Calgary (★754,033) | 710,677 |
| Edmonton (★839,924) | 616,741 |
| Lethbridge | 60,974 |
| Medicine Hat (★52,681) | 43,625 |
| Red Deer | 58,134 |

**CANADA: BRITISH COLUMBIA**

| | |
|---|---|
| 1991 C | 3,282,061 |
| Burnaby (★Vancouver) | 158,858 |
| Chilliwack (★60,251) | 49,531 |
| Coquitlam (★Vancouver) | 84,021 |
| Delta (★Vancouver) | 88,978 |
| Kamloops (★67,856) | 67,057 |
| Kelowna (★111,846) | 75 950 |
| Nanaimo (★73,547) | 60,129 |
| Prince George | 69,653 |
| Richmond (★Vancouver) | 126,624 |
| Saanich (★Victoria) | 95,577 |
| Surrey (★Vancouver) | 245,173 |
| Vancouver (★1,602,502) | 471,844 |
| Victoria (★287,897) | 71,228 |

**CANADA: MANITOBA**

| | |
|---|---|
| 1991 C | 1,091,942 |
| Winnipeg (★652,354) | 616,790 |

**CANADA: NEW BRUNSWICK**

| | |
|---|---|
| 1991 C | 723,900 |
| Fredericton (★71,869) | 46,466 |
| Moncton (★106,503) | 57,010 |
| Saint John (★124,981) | 74,969 |

**CANADA: NEWFOUNDLAND**

| | |
|---|---|
| 1991 C | 568,474 |
| Saint John's (★171,859) | 95,770 |

**CANADA: NORTHWEST TERRITORIES**

| | |
|---|---|
| 1991 C | 57,649 |
| Yellowknife | 15,179 |

**CANADA: NOVA SCOTIA**

| | |
|---|---|
| 1991 C | 899,942 |
| Dartmouth (★Halifax) | 67,798 |
| Halifax (★320,501) | 114,455 |
| Sydney (★116,100) | 26,063 |

**CANADA: ONTARIO**

| | |
|---|---|
| 1991 C | 10,084,885 |
| Ajax (★Toronto) | 57,350 |
| Barrie (★92,165) | 62,728 |
| Brampton (★Toronto) | 234,445 |
| Brantford (★97,106) | 81,997 |
| Burlington (★Hamilton) | 129,575 |
| Cambridge (Galt) (★Kitchener) | 92,772 |
| Cornwall (★53,545) | 47,137 |
| East York (★Toronto) | 102,696 |
| Etobicoke (★Toronto) | 309,993 |
| Gloucester (★Ottawa) | 101,677 |
| Guelph (★97,213) | 87,976 |
| Hamilton (★599,760) | 318,499 |
| Kingston (★136,401) | 56,597 |
| Kitchener (★356,421) | 168,282 |
| Leamington (★35,792) | 14,182 |
| London (★381,522) | 303,165 |
| Markham (★Toronto) | 153,811 |
| Mississauga (★Toronto) | 463,388 |
| Nepean (★Ottawa) | 107,627 |
| Newcastle | 49,479 |
| Niagara Falls (★Saint Catharines) | 75,399 |
| North Bay (★63,285) | 55,405 |
| North York (★Toronto) | 562,564 |
| Oakville (★Toronto) | 114,670 |
| Oshawa (★240,104) | 129,344 |
| OTTAWA (★920,857) | 313,987 |
| Peterborough (★98,060) | 68,371 |
| Pickering (★Toronto) | 68,631 |
| Richmond Hill (★Toronto) | 80,142 |
| Saint Catharines (★364,552) | 129,300 |
| Sarnia (★87,870) | 74,376 |
| Sault Sainte Marie (★101,800) | 81,476 |
| Scarborough (★Toronto) | 524,598 |
| Stoney Creek (★Hamilton) | 49,968 |
| Sudbury (★157,613) | 92,884 |
| Thunder Bay (★124,427) | 113,946 |
| • Toronto (★3,893,046) | 635,395 |
| Vaughan (★Toronto) | 111,359 |
| Waterloo (★Kitchener) | 71,181 |
| Whitby (★Oshawa) | 61,281 |
| Windsor (★262,075) | 191,435 |
| York (★Toronto) | 140,525 |

**CANADA: PRINCE EDWARD ISLAND**

| | |
|---|---|
| 1991 C | 129,765 |
| Charlottetown (★57,472) | 15,396 |

**CANADA: QUÉBEC**

| | |
|---|---|
| 1991 C | 6,895,963 |
| Beauport (★Québec) | 69,158 |
| Brossard (★Montréal) | 64,793 |
| Charlesbourg (★Québec) | 70,788 |
| Chicoutimi (★160,928) | 62,670 |
| Drummondville (★60,092) | 35,462 |
| Gatineau (★Ottawa) | 92,284 |
| Hull (★Ottawa) | 60,707 |
| Jonquière (★Chicoutimi) | 57,933 |
| La Salle (★Montréal) | 73 804 |
| Laval (★Montréal) | 314,398 |
| Lévis (★Québec) | 39,452 |
| Longueuil (★Montréal) | 129,874 |
| Montréal (★3,127,242) | 1,017,666 |
| Montréal-Nord (★Montréal) | 85,516 |
| Pierrefonds (★Montréal) | 48,735 |
| Québec (★645,550) | 167,517 |
| Repentigny (★Montréal) | 49,630 |
| Sainte-Foy (★Québec) | 71,133 |
| Saint-Hubert (★Montréal) | 74,027 |
| Saint-Jean-sur-Richelieu (★68,378) | 37,607 |
| Saint-Laurent (★Montréal) | 72,402 |
| Saint-Léonard (★Montréal) | 73,120 |
| Shawinigan (★61,672) | 19,931 |
| Sherbrooke (★139,194) | 76,429 |
| Trois-Rivières (★136,303) | 49,426 |
| Verdun (★Montréal) | 61,307 |

**CANADA: SASKATCHEWAN**

| | |
|---|---|
| 1991 C | 988,928 |
| Regina (★191,692) | 179,178 |
| Saskatoon (★210,023) | 186,058 |

**CANADA: YUKON**

| | |
|---|---|
| 1991 C | 27,797 |
| Whitehorse | 17,925 |

**CAPE VERDE / Cabo Verde**

| | |
|---|---|
| 1990 C | 341,491 |
| Mindelo | 47,109 |
| • PRAIA | 61,644 |

**CAYMAN ISLANDS**

| | |
|---|---|
| 1989 C | 25,355 |
| • GEORGE TOWN | 12,921 |

**CENTRAL AFRICAN REPUBLIC / République centrafricaine**

| | |
|---|---|
| 1989 E | 2,841,000 |
| Bambari | 52,100 |
| • BANGUI | 596,800 |
| Berbérati | 45,400 |
| Bouar | 49,200 |

**CHAD / Tchad**

| | |
|---|---|
| 1993 C | 6,288,261 |
| Abéché | 55,715 |
| Moundou | 99,607 |
| • N'DJAMENA | 546,572 |
| Sarh | 77,605 |

**CHILE**

| | |
|---|---|
| 1992 C | 13,348,401 |
| Antofagasta | 225,316 |
| Arica | 161,333 |
| Calama | 103,970 |
| Chillán | 145,759 |
| Concepción (★735,000) | 326,784 |
| Copiapó | 98,188 |
| Coquimbo | 110,879 |
| Coronel (★Concepción) | 79,677 |
| Curicó | 77,733 |
| Iquique | 145,139 |
| La Serena | 109,293 |
| Linares | 59,658 |
| Los Ángeles | 94,716 |
| Lota (★Concepción) | 50,123 |
| Osorno | 114,239 |
| Ovalle | 53,515 |
| Puente Alto (★Santiago) | 254,127 |
| Puerto Montt | 110,139 |
| Punta Arenas | 109,110 |
| Quilpué (★Valparaíso) | 102,233 |
| Rancagua | 179,638 |
| San Antonio | 74,742 |
| San Bernardo (★Santiago) | 179,398 |
| • SANTIAGO (★4,740,000) | 4,295,593 |
| Talca | 15,971 |
| Talcahuano (★Concepción) | 244,034 |
| Temuco | 210,587 |
| Valdivia | 112,712 |
| Vallenar | 42,725 |
| Valparaíso (★690,000) | 274,228 |
| Villa Alemana (★Valparaíso) | 70,663 |
| Viña del Mar (★Valparaíso) | 303,589 |

**CHINA / Zhongguo**

| | |
|---|---|
| 1994 E | 1,185,170,000 |
| Abagnar Qi (▲100,700) (1986E) | 71,700 |
| Acheng (1985E) | 100,304 |
| Aihui (▲135,000) (1986E) | 76,700 |
| Aksu (▲345,900) (1986E) | 143,100 |
| Altay (▲141,700) (1986E) | 62,800 |
| Anci (Langfang) (▲522,800) (1986E) | 122,100 |
| Anda (▲425,500) (1986E) | 130,200 |
| Ankang (1985E) | 89,188 |
| Anqing (▲433,900) (1986E) | 213,200 |
| Anshan (1988E) | 1,330,000 |
| Anshun (▲214,700) (1986E) | 128,800 |
| Anyang (▲541,900) (1986E) | 361,200 |
| Baicheng (▲282,000) (1986E) | 198,600 |
| Baiquan (1985E) | 50,996 |
| Baiyin (▲301,900) (1986E) | 157,100 |
| Baoding (▲535,100) (1986E) | 423,200 |
| Baoji (▲359,500) (1986E) | 286,200 |
| Baoshan (▲688,400) (1986E) | 52,300 |
| Baotou (Paotow) (1988E) | 1,130,000 |
| Baoying (1985E) | 50,479 |
| Bei'an (▲440,500) (1986E) | 199,500 |
| Beihai (▲175,900) (1986E) | 119,000 |
| BEIJING (PEKING) (★7,320,000) | 6,690,000 |
| Beipiao (▲603,700) (1986E) | 180,900 |
| Bengbu (▲612,600) (1986E) | 403,900 |
| Benxi (Penhsi) (1988E) | 860,000 |
| Bijie (1985E) | 54,871 |
| Binxian (▲177,900) (1986E) | 86,700 |
| Binxian (1982C) | 127,326 |
| Boli (1985E) | 61,990 |
| Bose (▲271,400) (1986E) | 82,000 |
| Boshan (1975U) | 100,000 |
| Boxian (1985E) | 63,222 |
| Boxing (1982C) | 57,554 |
| Boyang (1985E) | 60,688 |
| Butha Qi (Zalantun) (▲389,500) (1986E) | 111,300 |
| Cangshan (Bianzhuang) (1982C) | 79,334 |
| Cangzhou (▲293,600) (1986E) | 196,700 |
| Changchun | 2,470,000 |
| Changde (▲220,800) (1986E) | 178,200 |
| Changge (1982C) | 67,002 |
| Changji (▲233,400) (1986E) | 110,500 |
| Changqing (1982C) | 65,094 |
| Changsha | 1,510,000 |
| Changshou (1985E) | 51,923 |
| Changshu (▲998,000) (1986E) | 281,300 |
| Changtu (1985E) | 49,937 |
| Changyi (1982C) | 64,513 |
| Changzhi (▲463,400) (1986E) | 273,000 |
| Changzhou (Changchow) (1986E) | 522,700 |
| Chao'an (▲1,214,500) (1986E) | 265,400 |
| Chaoxian (▲739,500) (1986E) | 116,800 |
| Chaoyang, Guangdong prov. (1985E) | 85,968 |
| Chaoyang, Liaoning prov. (▲318,900) (1986E) | 180,300 |
| Chengde (▲330,400) (1986E) | 226,600 |
| Chengdu (Chengtu) | 2,760,000 |
| Chenghai (1985E) | 50,631 |
| Chenxian (▲191,900) (1986E) | 143,500 |
| Chifeng (Ulanhad) (▲882,900) (1986E) | 299,000 |
| Chongqing (Chungking) | 3,870,000 |
| Chuxian (▲365,000) (1986E) | 113,300 |
| Chuxiong (▲379,400) (1986E) | 67,700 |
| Da'an (1985E) | 70,552 |
| Dachangzhen (1975U) | 50,000 |
| Dalian (Dairen) | 2,400,000 |
| Dandong (1986E) | 579,800 |
| Daqing (▲880,000) (1988E) | 640,000 |
| Dashiqiao (1985E) | 68,898 |
| Datong (1985E) | 55,529 |
| Datong (▲1,040,000) (1988E) | 810,000 |
| Dawa (1985E) | 142,581 |
| Daxian (▲209,400) (1986E) | 142,000 |
| Dehui (1985E) | 60,247 |
| Dengfeng (1982C) | 49,746 |
| Deqing (1982C) | 48,726 |
| Deyang (▲753,400) (1986E) | 184,800 |
| Dezhou (▲276,200) (1986E) | 161,300 |
| Didao (1975U) | 50,000 |
| Dinghai (1985E) | 50,161 |
| Dongchuan (Xincun) (▲275,100) (1986E) | 67,400 |
| Dongguan (▲1,208,500) (1986E) | 254,900 |
| Dongsheng (▲121,300) (1986E) | 57,500 |
| Dongtai (1985E) | 65,788 |
| Dongying (▲514,400) (1986E) | 178,100 |
| Dukou (▲551,200) (1986E) | 380,200 |
| Dunhua (▲448,000) (1986E) | 217,100 |
| Duyun (▲386,600) (1986E) | 123,800 |
| Echeng (▲938,000) (1986E) | 217,400 |
| Enshi (▲679,000) (1986E) | 84,300 |
| Erenhot (1986E) | 7,200 |
| Ergun Zuoqi (1985E) | 55,970 |
| Feixian (1982C) | 73,246 |
| Fengcheng (1985E) | 66,745 |
| Foshan (▲312,700) (1986E) | 243,500 |
| Fujin (1985E) | 60,948 |
| Fuling (▲973,500) (1986E) | 166,300 |
| Fushun (Funan) (1988E) | 1,290,000 |
| Fuxian (Wafangdian) (▲960,700) (1986E) | 246,200 |
| Fuxin (1988E) | 700,000 |
| Fuyang (▲195,200) (1986E) | 143,400 |
| Fuyu, Heilongjiang prov. (1985E) | 48,670 |
| Fuyu, Jilin prov. (1985E) | 98,373 |
| Fuzhou, Fujian prov. | 1,380,000 |
| Fuzhou, Jiangxi prov. (▲171,800) (1986E) | 106,700 |
| Gaixian (1985E) | 67,587 |
| Ganhe (1985E) | 48,128 |
| Ganzhou (▲346,000) (1986E) | 191,600 |
| Gaoqing (Tianzhen) (1982C) | 70,411 |
| Gaoyou (1985E) | 57,844 |
| Gejiu (Kokiu) (▲341,700) (1986E) | 193,600 |
| Golmud (1986E) | 60,300 |
| Gongchangling (1982C) | 49,281 |
| Guanghua (▲420,000) (1986E) | 104,400 |
| Guangyuan (▲805,500) (1986E) | 162,200 |
| Guangzhou (Canton) | 3,750,000 |
| Guanxian, Shandong prov. (1982C) | 49,782 |
| Guanxian, Sichuan prov. (1985E) | 65,039 |
| Guilin (Kweilin) (▲457,500) (1986E) | 324,200 |

▲ Población de un municipio, comuna o distrito entero, incluyendo sus áreas rurales.
• Ciudad más grande de un país.
★ Población o designación de un área metropolitana, incluyendo los suburbios.
**C** Censo. **E** Estimado oficial. **U** Estimado no oficial.

▲ Population d'une municipalité, d'une commune ou d'un district, zone rurale incluse.
• Ville la plus peuplée du pays.
★ Population de l'agglomération (ou nom de la zone métropolitaine englobante).
**C** Recensement. **E** Estimation officielle. **U** Estimation non officielle.

▲ População de um municipio, comuna ou distrito, inclusive as respectivas áreas rurais.
• Maior cidade de um país.
★ População ou indicação de uma área metropolitana.
**C** Censo. **E** Estimativa oficial. **U** Estimativa não oficial.

| | |
|---|---|
| Guixian (1985E) | 61,970 |
| Guiyang (Kweiyang) | 1,080,000 |
| Haicheng (▲984,800) (1986E) | 210,700 |
| Haifeng (1985E) | 50,401 |
| Haikou | 340,000 |
| Hailar (▲163,549) (1986E) | 180,000 |
| Hailin (1985E) | 58,909 |
| Hailong (Meihekou) (▲534,200) (1986E) | 117,500 |
| Hailun (1985E) | 83,448 |
| Haiyang (Dongcun) (1982C) | 77,098 |
| Hami (Kumul) (▲270,300) (1986E) | 146,400 |
| Hancheng (▲304,200) (1986E) | 66,600 |
| Handan (▲1,030,000) (1988E) | 870,000 |
| Hangu (1975U) | 100,000 |
| Hangzhou (Hangchow) | 1,790,000 |
| Hanzhong (▲415,000) (1986E) | 151,700 |
| Harbin | 3,120,000 |
| Hebi (▲321,600) (1986E) | 158,500 |
| Hechi (▲266,800) (1986E) | 74,400 |
| Hechuan (1985E) | 65,237 |
| Hefei | 1,110,000 |
| Hegang (1986E) | 588,300 |
| Helong (1985E) | 62,665 |
| Hengshui (▲286,500) (1986E) | 83,100 |
| Hengyang (▲601,300) (1986E) | 419,200 |
| Heshan (▲109,600) (1986E) | 42,000 |
| Heze (Caozhou) (▲1,001,500) (1986E) | 115,400 |
| Hohhot | 730,000 |
| Hongjiang (▲67,000) (1986E) | 54,300 |
| Horqin Youyi Qianqi (Ulan Hot) (▲192,100) (1986E) | 129,100 |
| Hotan (▲122,800) (1986E) | 71,700 |
| Houma (▲158,500) (1986E) | 67,000 |
| Huadian (1985E) | 75,183 |
| Huai'an (1985E) | 65,673 |
| Huaibei (▲447,200) (1986E) | 252,100 |
| Huaide (▲899,400) (1986E) | 187,600 |
| Huaihua (▲427,100) (1986E) | 102,000 |
| Huainan (▲1,110,000) (1988E) | 700,000 |
| Huaiyin (Wangying) (▲382,500) (1986E) | 201,700 |
| Huanan (1985E) | 66,596 |
| Huanggang (1982C) | 65,961 |
| Huangshi (1986E) | 451,900 |
| Huayun (Huarong) (▲313,500) (1986E) | 81,000 |
| Huinan (Chaoyang) (1985E) | 52,429 |
| Huizhou (▲182,100) (1986E) | 117,000 |
| Hulan (1985E) | 74,989 |
| Hunjiang (Badaojiang) (▲687,700) (1986E) | 442,600 |
| Huzhou (▲964,400) (1986E) | 208,500 |
| Jiading (1985E) | 60,718 |
| Jiamusi (Kiamusze) (▲557,700) (1986E) | 429,800 |
| Ji'an (▲184,300) (1986E) | 132,200 |
| Jiangling (1985E) | 77,887 |
| Jiangmen (▲231,700) (1986E) | 168,800 |
| Jiangyin (1985E) | 66,476 |
| Jiangyou (1985E) | 72,663 |
| Jian'ou (1985E) | 55,180 |
| Jiaohe (1985E) | 51,504 |
| Jiaojiang (▲385,200) (1986E) | 82,300 |
| Jiaoxian (1985E) | 51,869 |
| Jiaozuo (▲509,900) (1986E) | 335,400 |
| Jiawang (1975U) | 50,000 |
| Jiaxing (▲686,500) (1986E) | 210,200 |
| Jiayuguan (▲102,100) (1986E) | 73,800 |
| Jiexiu (1985E) | 51,300 |
| Jieyang (1985E) | 98,531 |
| Jilin (Kirin) (1988E) | 1,200,000 |
| Jinan (Tsinan) | 2,150,000 |
| Jinchang (Baijiazui) (▲136,000) (1986E) | 90,500 |
| Jincheng (▲612,700) (1986E) | 99,900 |
| Jingdezhen (Kingtechen) (▲569,700) (1986E) | 304,000 |
| Jingmen (▲946,500) (1986E) | 227,000 |
| Jinhua (▲799,900) (1986E) | 147,800 |
| Jining, Nei Monggol prov. (1986E) | 163,300 |
| Jining, Shandong prov. (▲765,700) (1986E) | 222,600 |
| Jinshi (▲219,700) (1986E) | 73,700 |
| Jinxi (▲634,300) (1986E) | 223,100 |
| Jinxian (1985E) | 95,761 |
| Jinzhou (Chinchou) (▲810,000) (1988E) | 710,000 |
| Jishou (▲194,500) (1986E) | 59,500 |
| Jishu (1985E) | 75,587 |
| Jiujiang (▲382,300) (1986E) | 248,500 |
| Jiuquan (Suzhou) (▲269,900) (1986E) | 56,300 |
| Jiutai (1985E) | 63,021 |
| Jixi (▲820,000) (1988E) | 700,000 |
| Jixian (1985E) | 59,725 |
| Juancheng (1982C) | 54,110 |
| Junan (Shizilu) (1982C) | 90,222 |
| Junxian (▲423,400) (1986E) | 97,000 |
| Juxian (1982C) | 51,666 |
| Kaifeng (▲629,100) (1986E) | 458,800 |
| Kaili (▲342,100) (1986E) | 96,600 |
| Kaiping (1985E) | 54,145 |
| Kaiyuan (▲342,100) (1986E) | 96,600 |
| Kaiyuan (1985E) | 85,762 |
| Karamay (▲168,868) (1986E) | 185,300 |
| Kashi (▲194,500) (1986E) | 146,300 |
| Keshan (1985E) | 65,088 |
| Korla (▲219,000) (1986E) | 129,400 |
| Kunming | 1,500,000 |
| Kunshan (1985E) | 44,645 |
| Kuytun (1986E) | 60,200 |
| Laiwu (▲1,041,800) (1986E) | 143,500 |
| Langxiang (1985E) | 64,658 |
| Lanxi (1985E) | 53,236 |
| Lanxi (▲606,800) (1986E) | 70,500 |
| Lanzhou (Lanchow) | 1,340,000 |
| Lechang (1986E) | 56,913 |
| Lengshuijiang (▲277,600) (1986E) | 101,700 |
| Lengshuitan (▲362,000) (1986E) | 60,900 |
| Leshan (▲972,300) (1986E) | 307,300 |
| Lhasa (▲107,700) (1986E) | 84,400 |
| Lianyungang (Xinpu) (▲459,400) (1986E) | 288,000 |
| Liaocheng (▲724,300) (1986E) | 119,000 |
| Liaoyang (▲576,900) (1986E) | 442,600 |
| Liaoyuan (1986E) | 370,400 |
| Liling (▲856,300) (1986E) | 107,100 |
| Linfen (▲530,100) (1986E) | 157,600 |
| Lingling (▲515,300) (1986E) | 72,700 |
| Lingyuan (1985E) | 66,825 |
| Linhai (1985E) | 52,653 |
| Linhe (▲365,900) (1986E) | 99,800 |
| Linkou (1985E) | 52,936 |
| Linqing (▲603,000) (1986E) | 87,000 |
| Linqu (1982C) | 84,196 |

| | |
|---|---|
| Linxia (▲150,200) (1986E) | 72,900 |
| Linyi (▲1,365,000) (1986E) | 190,000 |
| Liuzhou (1988E) | 680,000 |
| Longjiang (1985E) | 51,156 |
| Longyan (▲378,500) (1986E) | 114,500 |
| Loudi (▲254,300) (1986E) | 84,200 |
| Lu'an (▲163,400) (1986E) | 122,600 |
| Lufeng (1985E) | 53,015 |
| Luohe (▲159,100) (1986E) | 102,300 |
| Luoyang (Loyang) (▲1,090,000) (1988E) | 760,000 |
| Luzhou (▲360,300) (1986E) | 237,800 |
| Ma'anshan (▲367,000) (1986E) | 258,900 |
| Manzhouli (1986E) | 116,600 |
| Maoming (▲434,900) (1986E) | 118,600 |
| Meixian (▲740,600) (1986E) | 169,000 |
| Mengyin (1982C) | 70,602 |
| Mianyang (▲848,500) (1986E) | 233,900 |
| Minhang (1975U) | 60,000 |
| Mishan (1985E) | 54,919 |
| Mixian (1982C) | 64,776 |
| Mudanjiang (1988E) | 650,000 |
| Nahe (1985E) | 49,725 |
| N'aizishen (1985E) | 51,982 |
| Nancha (1975U) | 50,000 |
| Nanchang | 1,440,000 |
| Nanchong (▲238,100) (1986E) | 158,000 |
| Nanjing (Nanking) | 2,490,000 |
| Nanning | 960,000 |
| Nanpiao (1982C) | 67,274 |
| Nanping (▲420,800) (1986E) | 157,100 |
| Nantong (▲411,000) (1986E) | 308,800 |
| Nanyang (▲294,800) (1986E) | 199,400 |
| Neihuang (1982C) | 56,039 |
| Neijiang (▲298,500) (1986E) | 191,100 |
| Ning'an (1985E) | 49,334 |
| Ningbo | 1,100,000 |
| Ningyang (1982C) | 55,424 |
| Nong'an (1985E) | 55,966 |
| Nunjiang (1985E) | 59,276 |
| Orogen Zizhiqi (1985E) | 48,042 |
| Panshan (▲343,100) (1986E) | 248,100 |
| Panshi (1985E) | 59,270 |
| Pingdingshan (▲819,900) (1986E) | 363,200 |
| Pingliang (▲362,500) (1986E) | 85,400 |
| Pingxiang, Jiangxi prov. (▲1,286,700) (1986E) | 368,700 |
| Pingyi (1982C) | 89,373 |
| Pingyin (1982C) | 62,827 |
| Potou (▲456,100) (1986E) | 59,000 |
| Puqi (1985E) | 65,239 |
| Putian (▲265,400) (1986E) | 64,600 |
| Putuo (1985E) | 50,962 |
| Puyang (▲1,086,100) (1986E) | 131,000 |
| Qian Gorlos (1985E) | 79,494 |
| Qingdao (Tsingtao) | 2,300,000 |
| Qinggang (1985E) | 43,075 |
| Qingjiang, Jiangsu prov. (▲246,617) (1982C) | 150,000 |
| Qingjiang, Jiangxi prov. (1985E) | 42,698 |
| Qingyuan (1985E) | 51,756 |
| Qinhuangdao (Chinwangtao) (▲436,000) (1986E) | 307,500 |
| Qinzhou (▲923,400) (1986E) | 97,100 |
| Qiqihar (Tsitsihar) (▲1,330,000) (1988E) | 1,180,000 |
| Qitaihe (▲309,900) (1986E) | 166,400 |
| Qixia (1982C) | 54,158 |
| Qixian (1982C) | 53,041 |
| Quanzhou (Chuanchou) (▲436,000) (1986E) | 157,000 |
| Qujing (▲758,000) (1986E) | 135,000 |
| Quxian (▲704,800) (1986E) | 124,000 |
| Raoping (1985E) | 54,831 |
| Rizhao (▲970,300) (1986E) | 93,300 |
| Rongcheng (1982C) | 52,878 |
| Rugao (1985E) | 50,643 |
| Rui'an (1985E) | 57,993 |
| Sanmenxia (Shanxian) (▲150,000) (1986E) | 79,000 |
| Sanming (▲214,300) (1986E) | 144,900 |
| • Shanghai (★11,010,000) | 8,930,000 |
| Shangqiu (Zhuji) (▲199,400) (1986E) | 135,400 |
| Shangrao (▲142,500) (1986E) | 113,000 |
| Shangshui (1982C) | 50,191 |
| Shantou (Swatow) (▲790,000) (1988E) | 560,000 |
| Shanwei (1985E) | 61,234 |
| Shaoguan (1986E) | 363,100 |
| Shaowu (▲266,700) (1986E) | 81,400 |
| Shaoxing (▲250,900) (1986E) | 167,100 |
| Shaoyang (▲465,900) (1986E) | 218,600 |
| Shashi (1986E) | 253,700 |
| Shenxian (1982C) | 50,208 |
| Shenyang (Mukden) | 4,050,000 |
| Shenzhen | 640,000 |
| Shiguaigou (1975U) | 50,000 |
| Shihezi (▲549,300) (1987E) | 304,700 |
| Shijiazhuang | 1,610,000 |
| Shiyan (▲332,600) (1986E) | 227,300 |
| Shizuishan (▲317,400) (1986E) | 225,500 |
| Shouguang (1982C) | 83,400 |
| Shuangcheng (1985E) | 91,163 |
| Shuangliao (1985E) | 67,326 |
| Shuangyashan (1986E) | 427,300 |
| Shuicheng (▲2,216,500) (1986E) | 363,500 |
| Shulan (1986E) | 50,582 |
| Shunde (1985E) | 50,262 |
| Siping (▲357,800) (1986E) | 280,100 |
| Sishui (1982C) | 82,990 |
| Songjiang (1985E) | 71,864 |
| Songjianghe (1985E) | 53,023 |
| Suifenhe (▲21,700) (1986E) | 13,900 |
| Suihua (▲732,100) (1986E) | 200,400 |
| Suileng (1985E) | 68,399 |
| Suining (▲1,174,900) (1986E) | 118,500 |
| Suixian (▲1,281,600) (1986E) | 187,700 |
| Suqian (1985E) | 50,742 |
| Suxian (▲218,600) (1986E) | 123,300 |
| Suzhou (Soochow) (1988E) | 740,000 |
| Tai'an (▲1,325,400) (1986E) | 215,900 |
| Taiyuan | 1,720,000 |
| Taizhou (▲210,800) (1987E) | 143,200 |
| Tancheng (1982C) | 61,857 |
| Tangshan (▲1,440,000) (1988E) | 1,080,000 |
| Tao'an (1985E) | 76,269 |
| Tengxian (1985E) | 53,254 |
| Tianjin (Tientsin) | 5,000,000 |
| Tianshui (▲953,200) (1986E) | 209,500 |
| Tiefa (▲146,367) (1982C) | 60,000 |
| Tieli (1985E) | 102,527 |
| Tieling (▲454,100) (1986E) | 326,100 |
| Tongchuan (▲393,200) (1986E) | 268,900 |
| Tonghua (▲367,400) (1986E) | 290,200 |
| Tongliao (▲253,100) (1986E) | 190,100 |
| Tongling (▲216,400) (1986E) | 182,900 |
| Tongren (1985E) | 50,307 |
| Tongxian (1985E) | 97,168 |

| | |
|---|---|
| Tumen (▲99,700) (1986E) | 77,600 |
| Tunxi (▲104,500) (1986E) | 61,800 |
| Turpan (▲196,800) (1986E) | 52,300 |
| Ürümqi | 1,130,000 |
| Wangkui (1985E) | 52,021 |
| Wangqing (1985E) | 61,237 |
| Wanxian (▲280,800) (1986E) | 138,700 |
| Weifang (▲1,042,200) (1986E) | 312,500 |
| Weihai (▲220,800) (1986E) | 83,000 |
| Weinan (▲699,400) (1986E) | 111,300 |
| Weishan (Xiazhen) (1982C) | 57,932 |
| Weixian (Hanting) (1982C) | 50,180 |
| Wenzhou (▲530,600) (1986E) | 372,200 |
| Wuchang (1985E) | 64,403 |
| Wuhai (1986E) | 266,000 |
| Wuhan | 3,870,000 |
| Wuhu (▲502,200) (1986E) | 396,000 |
| Wulian (Hongning) (1982C) | 51,718 |
| Wusong (1982C) | 64,017 |
| Wuwei (Liangzhou) (▲804,000) (1986E) | 115,500 |
| Wuxi (Wuhsi) (1988E) | 880,000 |
| Wuzhong (▲402,400) (1986E) | 48,600 |
| Wuzhou (Wuchow) (▲261,500) (1986E) | 194,800 |
| Xiaguan (▲395,800) (1986E) | 112,100 |
| Xiamen (Amoy) | 470,000 |
| Xi'an (Sian) | 2,410,000 |
| Xiangfan (▲421,200) (1986E) | 314,900 |
| Xiangtan (▲511,100) (1986E) | 389,500 |
| Xianning (▲402,200) (1986E) | 122,200 |
| Xianyang (▲641,800) (1986E) | 285,900 |
| Xiaogan (▲1,204,400) (1986E) | 125,500 |
| Xiaoshan (1985E) | 63,074 |
| Xichang (▲161,000) (1986E) | 105,000 |
| Xinghua (1985E) | 75,573 |
| Xinglongzhen (1982C) | 52,961 |
| Xingtai (▲350,800) (1986E) | 265,600 |
| Xinhui (1985E) | 77,381 |
| Xining (Sining) (1988E) | 620,000 |
| Xinmin (1985E) | 47,900 |
| Xintai (▲1,157,300) (1986E) | 171,400 |
| Xinwen (Suncun) (1975U) | 50,000 |
| Xinxian (▲398,600) (1986E) | 74,200 |
| Xinxiang (▲540,500) (1986E) | 411,000 |
| Xinyang (▲234,200) (1986E) | 169,100 |
| Xinyu (▲610,600) (1986E) | 140,200 |
| Xuancheng (1985E) | 52,387 |
| Xuanhua (1975U) | 140,000 |
| Xuanwei (1982C) | 70,081 |
| Xuchang (▲247,200) (1986E) | 167,800 |
| Xuguit Qi (Yakeshi) (1986E) | 390,000 |
| Xuzhou (Süchow) (1988E) | 860,000 |
| Yaan (▲277,600) (1986E) | 89,200 |
| Yan'an (▲259,800) (1986E) | 86,700 |
| Yancheng (▲1,251,400) (1986E) | 258,400 |
| Yangcheng (1982C) | 57,255 |
| Yangjiang (1986E) | 91,433 |
| Yangquan (▲478,900) (1986E) | 295,100 |
| Yangzhou (▲417,300) (1986E) | 321,500 |
| Yanji (▲216,900) (1986E) | 175,000 |
| Yanji (Longjing) (1985E) | 55,035 |
| Yanling (1982C) | 52,679 |
| Yantai (Chefoo) (▲717,300) (1986E) | 327,000 |
| Yanzhou (1985E) | 48,972 |
| Yaxian (Sanya) (▲321,700) (1986E) | 70,500 |
| Yi'an (1986E) | 54,253 |
| Yibin (Ipin) (▲636,500) (1986E) | 218,800 |
| Yichang (Ichang) (1986E) | 410,500 |
| Yichuan (1982C) | 58,914 |
| Yichun, Heilongjiang prov. (1988E) | 840,000 |
| Yichun, Jiangxi prov. (▲770,200) (1986E) | 132,600 |
| Yidu (1985E) | 54,838 |
| Yilan (1985E) | 50,436 |
| Yima (▲84,800) (1986E) | 53,700 |
| Yinan (Jiehu) (1982C) | 67,803 |
| Yinchuan | 430,000 |
| Yingchengzi (1985E) | 59,072 |
| Yingkou (▲480,000) (1986E) | 366,900 |
| Yingtan (▲116,200) (1986E) | 64,500 |
| Yining (Kuldja) (▲232,000) (1986E) | 153,200 |
| Yiyang (▲365,000) (1986E) | 155,300 |
| Yiyuan (Nanma) (1982C) | 53,800 |
| Yong'an (▲269,000) (1986E) | 105,100 |
| Yongchuan (1985E) | 70,444 |
| Yuci (▲420,700) (1986E) | 171,000 |
| Yueyang (▲411,300) (1986E) | 239,500 |
| Yulin, Guangxi Zhuangzu prov. (▲1,228,800) (1986E) | 115,600 |
| Yulin, Shaanxi prov. (1985E) | 51,610 |
| Yumen (Laojunmiao) (▲160,100) (1986E) | 84,300 |
| Yuncheng, Shandong prov. (1982C) | 54,262 |
| Yuncheng, Shansi prov. (▲434,900) (1986E) | 87,000 |
| Yunyang (1982C) | 54,903 |
| Yushu (1985E) | 57,222 |
| Yuyao (▲772,700) (1986E) | 169,700 |
| Zaozhuang (▲1,592,000) (1986E) | 292,200 |
| Zhangjiakou (Kalgan) (▲640,000) (1988E) | 500,000 |
| Zhangye (▲394,200) (1986E) | 73,000 |
| Zhangzhou (Longxi) (▲310,400) (1986E) | 159,400 |
| Zhanjiang (▲920,900) (1986E) | 335,500 |
| Zhaodong (1985E) | 99,836 |
| Zhaoqing (Gaoyao) (▲187,600) (1986E) | 145,700 |
| Zhaotong (▲546,600) (1986E) | 77,500 |
| Zhaoyuan (1985E) | 42,426 |
| Zhaoyuan (1982C) | 56,389 |
| Zhengzhou (Chengchow) | 1,690,000 |
| Zhenjiang (1986E) | 412,400 |
| Zhongshan (Shiqizhen) (▲1,059,700) (1986E) | 238,700 |
| Zhoucun (1975U) | 50,000 |
| Zhoukouzhen (▲220,400) (1986E) | 110,500 |
| Zhuhai (▲155,000) (1986E) | 88,800 |
| Zhumadian (▲149,500) (1986E) | 99,400 |
| Zhuoxian (1985E) | 54,523 |
| Zhuzhou (Chuchow) (▲499,600) (1986E) | 344,800 |
| Zibo (Zhangdian) (▲2,370,000) (1988E) | 840,000 |
| Zigong (Tzukung) (▲909,300) (1986E) | 361,700 |
| Zixing (▲334,300) (1986E) | 97,100 |
| Ziyang (1985E) | 57,349 |
| Zouping (1982C) | 49,274 |
| Zouxian (1985E) | 61,578 |
| Zunyi (▲347,600) (1986E) | 236,600 |

**COLOMBIA**

| | |
|---|---|
| 1985 C | 27,867,326 |
| Armenia | 187,130 |
| Barrancabermeja | 137,406 |
| Barranquilla (★1,140,000) | 899,781 |
| Bello (★Medellín) | 212,861 |
| Bucaramanga (★550,000) | 352,326 |
| Buenaventura | 160,342 |
| Buga | 82,992 |
| Cali (★1,400,000) | 1,350,565 |
| Cartagena | 531,426 |
| Cartago | 97,791 |
| Ciénaga | 56,860 |
| Cúcuta (★445,000) | 379,478 |
| Dos Quebradas (★Pereira) | 101,480 |
| Duitama | 56,390 |
| Envigado (★Medellín) | 91,391 |
| Florencia | 66,430 |
| Floridablanca (★Bucaramanga) | 143,824 |
| Girardot | 70,078 |
| Ibagué | 292,965 |
| Itagüí (★Medellín) | 137,623 |
| Magangué | 49,160 |
| Maicao | 46,033 |
| Malambo (★Barranquilla) | 52,584 |
| Manizales (★330,000) | 299,352 |
| Medellín (★2,095,000) | 1,468,089 |
| Montería | 157,466 |
| Neiva | 194,556 |
| Ocaña | 51,443 |
| Palmira | 175,186 |
| Pasto | 197,407 |
| Pereira (★390,000) | 233,271 |
| Popayán | 141,964 |
| • SANTA FE DE BOGOTÁ (★4,260,000) | 3,982,941 |
| Santa Marta | 177,922 |
| Sincelejo | 120,537 |
| Soacha (★Santa Fe de Bogotá) | 109,051 |
| Sogamoso | 64,437 |
| Soledad (★Barranquilla) | 165,791 |
| Tuluá | 99,721 |
| Tunja | 93,792 |
| Valledupar | 142,771 |
| Villa Rosario (★Cúcuta) | 63,615 |
| Villavicencio | 178,685 |
| Zipaquirá | 45,676 |

**COMOROS / Al-Qumur / Comores**

| | |
|---|---|
| 1990 E | 452,742 |
| • MORONI | 23,432 |

**CONGO**

| | |
|---|---|
| 1989 C | 2,188,367 |
| • BRAZZAVILLE | 693,712 |
| Dolisie | 57,991 |
| Pointe-Noire | 350,139 |

**COOK ISLANDS**

| | |
|---|---|
| 1991 C | 18,617 |
| • AVARUA | 10,886 |

**COSTA RICA**

| | |
|---|---|
| 1988 E | 2,851,000 |
| Alajuela (▲147,400) (★San José) | 33,800 |
| Desamparados (★San José) (1984C) | 43,352 |
| Puerto Limón (▲62,600) | 40,400 |
| Puntarenas (▲86,400) | 34,100 |
| • SAN JOSÉ (★1,355,000) | 278,600 |

**CÔTE D'IVOIRE (IVORY COAST)**

| | |
|---|---|
| 1988 C | 10,815,694 |
| Abengourou | 59,114 |
| • ABIDJAN | 1,929,079 |
| Agboville | 46,045 |
| Anyama | 56,690 |
| Bouaké | 329,850 |
| Daloa | 121,842 |
| Divo | 72,350 |
| Gagnoa | 85,563 |
| Korhogo | 109,445 |
| Man | 89,575 |
| San Pédro | 70,611 |
| YAMOUSSOUKRO | 106,786 |

**CROATIA / Hrvatska**

| | |
|---|---|
| 1991 C | 4,784,265 |
| Bjelovar | 42,066 |
| Dubrovnik | 55,638 |
| Karlovac | 70,729 |
| Osijek | 129,792 |
| Pula | 69,690 |
| Rijeka | 167,964 |
| Šibenik | 55,842 |
| Sisak | 60,564 |
| Slavonski Brod | 58,531 |
| Split | 200,459 |
| Varaždin | 48,834 |
| Vukovar | 45,963 |
| Zadar | 80,355 |
| • ZAGREB | 867,865 |

**CUBA**

| | |
|---|---|
| 1991 E | 10,694,465 |
| Bayamo | 139,061 |
| Camagüey | 286,404 |
| Cárdenas (▲84,590) | 69,800 |
| Ciego de Ávila | 101,620 |
| Cienfuegos | 136,233 |
| Florida | 51,442 |
| Guantánamo | 215,864 |
| Holguín | 236,967 |
| • LA HABANA (HAVANA) (★2,210,000) | 2,119,059 |
| Las Tunas | 126,678 |
| Manzanillo | 108,668 |
| Matanzas | 119,510 |
| Morón | 49,793 |
| Palma Soriano (▲124,543) | 66,600 |
| Pinar del Río | 136,303 |
| Sancti Spíritus | 97,522 |
| Santa Clara | 203,753 |
| Santiago de Cuba | 434,541 |

**CYPRUS / Kıbrıs / Kípros**

| | |
|---|---|
| 1982 C | 512,097 |
| Lárnax (Larnaca) (★48,330) | 35,823 |
| Lemesós (Limassol) (★107,161) | 74,782 |
| • NICOSIA (LEVKOSÍA) (★185,000) | 48,221 |

**CYPRUS, NORTH / Kuzey Kıbrıs**

| | |
|---|---|
| 1985 E | 160,287 |

▲ Population of an entire municipality, commune, or district, including rural area.
• Largest city in country.
★ Population or designation of the metropolitan area, including suburbs.
**C** Census. **E** Official estimate. **U** Unofficial estimate.

▲ Bevölkerung eines ganzen städtischen Verwaltungsgebietes, eines Kommunalbezirkes oder eines Distrikts, einschliesslich ländlicher Gebiete.
• Grösste Stadt des Landes.
★ Bevölkerung oder Bezeichnung der Stadtregion einschliesslich Vororte.
**C** Volkszählung. **E** Offizielle Schätzung. **U** Inoffizielle Schätzung.

| | |
|---|---|
| Gazimağusa (Famagusta) | 19,428 |
| • NICOSIA (LEFKOŞA) | 37,400 |

**CZECH REPUBLIC / Česká Republika**

| | |
|---|---|
| 1991 C | 10,298,731 |
| Brno (★450,000) | 387,986 |
| Česká Lípa | 39,667 |
| České Budějovice (★114,000) | 97,283 |
| Český Těšín (★Třinec) | 28,737 |
| Cheb | 31,847 |
| Chomutov (★80,000) | 53,191 |
| Děčín (★72,000) | 55,112 |
| Frýdek-Místek (★Ostrava) | 65,067 |
| Havířov (★Ostrava) | 86,267 |
| Hodonín | 30,736 |
| Hradec Králové (★113,000) | 99,889 |
| Jablonec nad Nisou (★Liberec) | 45,918 |
| Jihlava | 52,271 |
| Karlovy Vary (Carlsbad) | 56,291 |
| Karviná (★Ostrava) | 68,368 |
| Kladno (★88,500) | 71,735 |
| Kolín | 31,582 |
| Kroměříž (★38,500) | 28,962 |
| Liberec (★175,000) | 101,934 |
| Litvínov (★Most) | 29,085 |
| Mladá Boleslav | 44,471 |
| Most (★135,000) | 70,675 |
| Nový Jičín | 29,028 |
| Olomouc (★126,000) | 105,690 |
| Opava (★78,000) | 63,601 |
| Orlová (★Ostrava) | 36,307 |
| Ostrava (★760,000) | 327,553 |
| Pardubice | 94,857 |
| Písek | 29,542 |
| Plzeň (★210,000) | 173,129 |
| • PRAHA (★1,328,000) | 1,212,010 |
| Přerov | 51,341 |
| Příbram | 36,869 |
| Prostějov | 50,102 |
| Šumperk | 30,446 |
| Tábor (★55,500) | 36,329 |
| Teplice (★94,000) | 53,039 |
| Třebíč | 39,348 |
| Třinec (★87,500) | 45,189 |
| Trutnov | 31,957 |
| Ústí nad Labem (★115,000) | 99,739 |
| Valašské Meziříčí | 28,153 |
| Vsetín | 31,584 |
| Zlín (★124,000) | 84,634 |
| Znojmo | 39,910 |

**DENMARK / Danmark**

| | |
|---|---|
| 1992 E | 5,162,126 |
| Ålborg (▲156,614) | 115,200 |
| Århus (▲267,873) | 207,300 |
| Ballerup (★København) | 45,476 |
| Esbjerg (▲81,843) | 72,200 |
| Fredericia (▲46,617) | 28,700 |
| Frederiksberg (★København) | 86,372 |
| Gentofte (★København) | 66,077 |
| Gladsakse (★København) | 60,604 |
| Helsingør (Elsinore) (★København) | 56,794 |
| Horsens (▲55,123) | 47,200 |
| Hvidovre (★København) | 48,754 |
| • KØBENHAVN (★1,670,000) | 464,566 |
| Kolding (▲57,982) | 42,700 |
| Kongens Lyngby (★København) | 49,612 |
| Odense (▲179,487) | 142,800 |
| Randers | 61,440 |
| Rønne | 15,236 |
| Roskilde (▲50,158) (★København) | 40,700 |
| Vejle (▲51,845) | 45,700 |

**DJIBOUTI**

| | |
|---|---|
| 1991 E | 508,541 |
| • DJIBOUTI | 329,337 |

**DOMINICA**

| | |
|---|---|
| 1984 E | 77,000 |
| • ROSEAU | 9,348 |

**DOMINICAN REPUBLIC / República Dominicana**

| | |
|---|---|
| 1990 E | 7,169,800 |
| Barahona | 80,400 |
| La Romana | 147,800 |
| La Vega | 192,300 |
| Mao | 58,400 |
| Puerto Plata | 94,900 |
| San Cristóbal | 137,500 |
| San Francisco de Macorís | 165,300 |
| San Juan de la Maguana | 129,700 |
| San Pedro de Macorís | 144,300 |
| Santiago de los Caballeros | 489,500 |
| • SANTO DOMINGO | 2,411,900 |

**ECUADOR**

| | |
|---|---|
| 1990 C | 9,648,189 |
| Ambato | 124,166 |
| Babahoyo | 50,285 |
| Cuenca | 194,981 |
| Eloy Alfaro (★Guayaquil) | 82,359 |
| Esmeraldas | 98,558 |
| • Guayaquil | 1,508,444 |
| Ibarra | 80,991 |
| La Libertad | 50,108 |
| Loja | 94,305 |
| Machala | 144,197 |
| Manta | 125,505 |
| Milagro | 93,637 |
| Portoviejo | 132,937 |
| Quevedo | 86,910 |
| QUITO (★1,300,000) | 1,100,847 |
| Riobamba | 94,505 |
| Santo Domingo de los Colorados | 114,422 |

**EGYPT / Mişr**

| | |
|---|---|
| 1986 C | 48,205,049 |
| Abnūb | 48,302 |
| Abū Kabīr | 68,394 |
| Abū Tīj | 48,518 |
| Akhmīm | 70,494 |
| Al-'Arīsh | 67,337 |
| Al-Fayyūm | 213,070 |
| Al-Ḥawāmidīyah (★Al-Qāhirah) | 73,298 |
| Al-Iskandarīyah (Alexandria) (★3,350,000) | 2,926,859 |
| Al-Ismā'īlīyah (★235,000) | 158,045 |
| Al-Jīzah (Giza) (★Al-Qāhirah) | 1,883,189 |
| Al-Maḥallah al-Kubrā | 306,509 |
| Al-Manṣūrah (★375,000) | 317,508 |
| Al-Manzilah | 54,918 |
| Al-Maṭarīyah | 73,315 |
| Al-Minyā | 179,060 |
| • AL-QĀHIRAH (CAIRO) (★9,300,000) | 6,068,695 |
| Al-Qanāṭir al-Khayrīyah | 49,361 |
| Al-Uqṣur (Luxor) | 126,160 |
| Armant | 54,616 |
| Ashmūn | 54,450 |
| As-Sinbillāwayn | 60,159 |
| As-Suways (Suez) | 327,717 |
| Aswān | 190,579 |
| Asyūṭ | 272,986 |
| Az-Zaqāzīq | 244,354 |
| Bahtīm (★Al-Qāhirah) | 275,807 |
| Banhā | 115,701 |
| Banī Mazār | 47,982 |
| Banī Suwayf | 152,476 |
| Bilbays | 96,511 |
| Bilqās Qism Awwal | 73,040 |
| Biyalā | 47,702 |
| Būlāq ad-Dakrūr (★Al-Qāhirah) | 148,787 |
| Būr Sa'īd (Port Said) | 401,172 |
| Būsh | 54,655 |
| Damanhūr | 188,939 |
| Dikirnis | 48,616 |
| Disūq | 78,316 |
| Dumyāṭ (Damietta) | 89,069 |
| Fāqūs | 48,365 |
| Hawsh 'Īsā | 53,619 |
| Idkū | 70,724 |
| Jirjā | 71,564 |
| Kafr ad-Dawwār (★Al-Iskandarīyah) | 196,244 |
| Kafr ash-Shaykh | 103,301 |
| Kafr az-Zayyāt | 58,276 |
| Kawm Umbū | 52,506 |
| Maghāghah | 50,916 |
| Mallawī | 98,632 |
| Manfalūṭ | 52,281 |
| Marsā Maṭrūḥ | 43,157 |
| Minūf | 69,673 |
| Mīt Ghamr (★100,000) | 91,927 |
| Qalyūb | 84,413 |
| Qinā | 119,917 |
| Rashīd (Rosetta) | 51,789 |
| Samālūṭ | 62,404 |
| Sāqiyat Makkī | 51,062 |
| Sawhāj | 132,649 |
| Shibīn al-Kawm | 132,209 |
| Shubrā al-Khaymah (★Al-Qāhirah) | 714,594 |
| Sinnūris | 55,187 |
| Ṭahṭā | 58,457 |
| Talkhā (★Al-Manṣūrah) | 54,923 |
| Ṭanṭā | 336,517 |
| Ṭimā | 46,824 |
| Warrāq al-'Arab (★Al-Qāhirah) | 127,108 |
| Ziftā (★Mīt Ghamr) | 69,253 |

**EL SALVADOR**

| | |
|---|---|
| 1985 E | 5,337,896 |
| Delgado (★San Salvador) | 67,684 |
| Mejicanos (★San Salvador) | 91,465 |
| Nueva San Salvador (★San Salvador) | 53,688 |
| San Miguel | 88,520 |
| • SAN SALVADOR (★920,000) | 462,652 |
| Santa Ana | 137,879 |
| Soyapango (★San Salvador) | 60,000 |

**EQUATORIAL GUINEA / Guinea Ecuatorial**

| | |
|---|---|
| 1983 C | 300,000 |
| • MALABO | 31,630 |

**ERITREA**

| | |
|---|---|
| 1991 E | 2,951,000 |
| • ASMERA (1990E) | 358,100 |
| Mitsiwa (1986E) | 16,576 |

**ESTONIA / Eesti**

| | |
|---|---|
| 1991 E | 1,581,800 |
| Kohtla-Järve | 74,700 |
| Narva | 83,000 |
| Pärnu | 54,200 |
| • TALLINN | 481,500 |
| Tartu | 115,300 |

**ETHIOPIA / Ityopiya**

| | |
|---|---|
| 1986 E | 44,927,000 |
| • ADIS ABEBA (★1,990,000) (1990E) | 1,912,500 |
| Akaki Beseka (★Adis Abeba) | 58,977 |
| Awasa | 39,593 |
| Bahir Dar | 59,951 |
| Debre Zeyit | 55,706 |
| Dese | 77,459 |
| Dire Dawa (1990E) | 127,400 |
| Gonder | 88,000 |
| Harer | 68,000 |
| Jima | 67,470 |
| Mekele | 66,640 |
| Nazret | 83,091 |

**FAEROE ISLANDS / Føroyar**

| | |
|---|---|
| 1990 E | 47,946 |
| • TÓRSHAVN | 14,767 |

**FALKLAND ISLANDS**

| | |
|---|---|
| 1991 C | 2,050 |
| • STANLEY | 1,557 |

**FIJI**

| | |
|---|---|
| 1986 C | 715,375 |
| Lautoka (★39,057) | 28,728 |
| • SUVA (★141,273) | 69,665 |

**FINLAND / Suomi**

| | |
|---|---|
| 1993 E | 5,054,982 |
| Espoo (Esbo) (★Helsinki) | 179,054 |
| • HELSINKI (HELSINGFORS) (★1,045,000) | 501,514 |
| Joensuu | 48,911 |
| Jyväskylä (★93,000) | 67,609 |
| Kotka | 56,462 |
| Kouvola (★55,300) | 32,151 |
| Kuopio | 82,340 |
| Lahti (★108,300) | 93,784 |
| Lappeenranta | 55,563 |
| Oulu (★122,500) | 103,538 |
| Pori | 76,331 |
| Tampere (★241,200) | 174,859 |
| Turku (Åbo) (★228,500) | 159,916 |
| Vaasa (Vasa) | 54,179 |
| Vantaa (Vanda) (★Helsinki) | 159,213 |

**FRANCE**

| | |
|---|---|
| 1990 C | 56,614,493 |
| Aix-en-Provence (★Marseille) | 123,842 |
| Ajaccio | 58,315 |
| Albi (★54,359) | 46,579 |
| Alès (★76,856) | 41,037 |
| Amiens (★156,120) | 131,872 |
| Angers (★208,282) | 141,404 |
| Angoulême (★102,908) | 42,876 |
| Annecy (★126,729) | 49,644 |
| Antibes (★Cannes) | 63,248 |
| Antony (★Paris) | 57,771 |
| Argenteuil (★Paris) | 93,096 |
| Arles (★54,309) | 39,000 |
| Armentières (★57,738) | 25,219 |
| Arras (★79,607) | 38,983 |
| Asnières [-sur-Seine] (★Paris) | 71,850 |
| Aubervilliers (★Paris) | 67,557 |
| Aulnay-sous-Bois (★Paris) | 82,314 |
| Avignon (★181,136) | 86,939 |
| Bastia (★52,446) | 37,845 |
| Bayonne (★164,378) | 40,051 |
| Beauvais (★57,704) | 54,190 |
| Belfort (★77,844) | 50,125 |
| Besançon (★122,623) | 113,828 |
| Béthune (★261,535) | 24,556 |
| Béziers (★76,304) | 70,996 |
| Blois (★65,132) | 49,318 |
| Bondy (★Paris) | 46,676 |
| Bordeaux (★760,000) | 210,336 |
| Boulogne-Billancourt (★Paris) | 101,743 |
| Boulogne-sur-Mer (★91,249) | 43,678 |
| Bourg-en-Bresse (★55,784) | 40,972 |
| Bourges (★94,731) | 75,609 |
| Brest (★201,480) | 147,956 |
| Brive-la-Gaillarde (★64,379) | 49,765 |
| Bruay-en-Artois (★Béthune) | 24,927 |
| Caen (★191,490) | 112,846 |
| Calais (★101,768) | 75,309 |
| Cambrai (★48,133) | 33,092 |
| Cannes (★335,647) | 68,676 |
| Carcassonne | 43,470 |
| Castres (★46,482) | 44,812 |
| Châlons-sur-Marne (★61,452) | 48,423 |
| Chalon-sur-Saône (★77,764) | 54,575 |
| Chambéry (★103,283) | 54,120 |
| Champigny-sur-Marne (★Paris) | 79,486 |
| Charleville-Mézières (★67,213) | 57,008 |
| Chartres (★85,933) | 39,595 |
| Châteauroux (★67,090) | 50,969 |
| Châtellerault (★36,298) | 34,678 |
| Cherbourg (★92,045) | 27,121 |
| Cholet | 55,132 |
| Clamart (★Paris) | 47,227 |
| Clermont-Ferrand (★254,416) | 136,181 |
| Clichy (★Paris) | 48,030 |
| Cognac (★27,468) | 19,528 |
| Colmar (★83,816) | 63,498 |
| Colombes (★Paris) | 78,513 |
| Compiègne (★67,057) | 41,896 |
| Courbevoie (★Paris) | 65,389 |
| Creil (★97,119) | 31,956 |
| Créteil (★Paris) | 82,088 |
| Denain (★Valenciennes) | 19,544 |
| Dieppe (★43,348) | 35,894 |
| Dijon (★230,451) | 146,703 |
| Douai (★199,562) | 42,175 |
| Drancy (★Paris) | 60,707 |
| Dunkerque (★190,879) | 70,331 |
| Elbeuf (★53,886) | 16,604 |
| Épinal (★62,140) | 36,732 |
| Épinay-sur-Seine (★Paris) | 48,762 |
| Évreux (★57,968) | 49,103 |
| Évry (★Paris) | 45,531 |
| Fontainebleau (★35,706) | 15,714 |
| Fontenay-sous-Bois (★Paris) | 51,868 |
| Forbach (★98,758) | 27,076 |
| Fréjus (★73,967) | 41,486 |
| Gennevilliers (★Paris) | 44,818 |
| Grenoble (★404,733) | 150,758 |
| Hagondange (★112,061) | 8,222 |
| Hayange (★Thionville) | 15,638 |
| Issy-les-Moulineaux (★Paris) | 46,127 |
| Ivry-sur-Seine (★Paris) | 53,619 |
| La Rochelle (★100,264) | 71,094 |
| La Seyne-sur-Mer (★Toulon) | 59,968 |
| Laval (★56,855) | 50,473 |
| Le Blanc-Mesnil (★Paris) | 46,956 |
| Le Havre (★253,627) | 195,854 |
| Le Mans (★189,107) | 145,502 |
| Lens (★323,174) | 35,017 |
| Le Puy (★43,499) | 21,743 |
| Levallois-Perret (★Paris) | 47,548 |
| Lille (★1,050,000) | 172,142 |
| Limoges (★170,065) | 133,464 |
| Longwy (★41,300) | 15,439 |
| Lorient (★115,488) | 59,271 |
| Lourdes | 16,300 |
| Lyon (★1,335,000) | 415,487 |
| Mâcon (★46,714) | 37,275 |
| Maisons-Alfort (★Paris) | 53,375 |
| Mantes-la-Jolie (★Paris) | 45,087 |
| Marseille (★1,225,000) | 800,550 |
| Martigues (★Marseille) | 31,300 |
| Maubeuge (★102,772) | 34,989 |
| Meaux (★63,006) | 48,305 |
| Melun (★107,705) | 35,319 |
| Menton (★Monaco, Monaco) | 29,141 |
| Mérignac (★Bordeaux) | 57,273 |
| Metz (★193,117) | 119,594 |
| Meudon (★Paris) | 45,339 |
| Montargis (★52,804) | 15,020 |
| Montbéliard (★117,510) | 29,005 |
| Montceau-les-Mines (★47,283) | 22,999 |
| Montluçon (★63,018) | 44,248 |
| Montpellier (★248,303) | 207,996 |
| Montreuil-sous-Bois (★Paris) | 94,754 |
| Moulins (★41,715) | 22,799 |
| Moyeuvre-Grande (★Hagondange) | 9,203 |
| Mulhouse (Mülhausen) (★223,856) | 108,357 |
| Nancy (★329,447) | 99,351 |
| Nanterre (★Paris) | 84,565 |
| Nantes (★496,078) | 244,995 |
| Neuilly-sur-Seine (★Paris) | 61,768 |
| Nevers (★58,915) | 41,968 |
| Nice (★516,740) | 342,439 |
| Nîmes (★138,527) | 128,471 |
| Niort (★65,792) | 57,012 |
| Noisy-le-Grand (★Paris) | 54,032 |
| Noisy-le-Sec (★Paris) | 36,309 |
| Orléans (★243,153) | 105,111 |
| Orly (★Paris) | 21,646 |
| Pantin (★Paris) | 47,303 |
| • PARIS (★10,275,000) | 2,152,423 |
| Pau (★144,674) | 82,157 |
| Périgueux (★63,322) | 30,280 |
| Perpignan (★157,873) | 105,983 |
| Pessac (★Bordeaux) | 51,055 |
| Poissy (★Paris) | 36,745 |
| Poitiers (★107,625) | 78,894 |
| Quimper (★65,954) | 59,437 |
| Reims (★206,437) | 180,620 |
| Rennes (★245,065) | 197,536 |
| Roanne (★77,160) | 41,756 |
| Rodez (★39,017) | 24,701 |
| Romans-sur-Isère (★49,212) | 32,734 |
| Roubaix (★Lille) | 97,746 |
| Rouen (★380,161) | 102,723 |
| Rueil-Malmaison (★Paris) | 66,401 |
| Saint-Brieuc (★83,861) | 44,752 |
| Saint-Chamond (★81,795) | 38,878 |
| Saint-Denis (★Paris) | 89,988 |
| Saint-Dizier (★40,097) | 33,552 |
| Saint-Étienne (★313,338) | 199,396 |
| Saint-Lô (★2,760) | 21,546 |
| Saint-Malo | 48,057 |
| Saint-Maur-des-Fossés (★Paris) | 77,206 |
| Saint-Nazaire (★131,511) | 64,812 |
| Saint-Ouen (★Paris) | 42,343 |
| Saint-Quentin (★71,113) | 60,644 |
| Sarcelles (★Paris) | 56,833 |
| Sartrouville (★Paris) | 50,329 |
| Sevran | 48,478 |
| Soissons (★46,168) | 29,829 |
| Strasbourg (★415,000) | 252,338 |
| Suresnes (★Paris) | 35,998 |
| Tarbes (★77,787) | 47,566 |
| Thionville (★132,413) | 39,712 |
| Toulon (★437,553) | 167,619 |
| Toulouse (★650,000) | 358,688 |
| Tourcoing (★Lille) | 93,765 |
| Tours (★282,152) | 129,509 |
| Troyes (★122,763) | 59,255 |
| Valence (★107,965) | 63,437 |
| Valenciennes (★338,392) | 38,441 |
| Vénissieux (★Lyon) | 60,444 |
| Verdun-sur-Meuse (★26,711) | 20,753 |
| Versailles (★Paris) | 87,789 |
| Vichy (★61,566) | 27,714 |
| Villefranche (★55,249) | 29,542 |
| Villejuif (★Paris) | 48,405 |
| Villeneuve-d'Ascq (★Lille) | 65,320 |
| Villeurbanne (★Lyon) | 116,872 |
| Vitry-sur-Seine (★Paris) | 82,400 |
| Wattrelos (★Lille) | 43,675 |

**FRENCH GUIANA / Guyane française**

| | |
|---|---|
| 1982 C | 73,022 |
| • CAYENNE | 38,091 |

**FRENCH POLYNESIA / Polynésie française**

| | |
|---|---|
| 1988 C | 188,814 |
| • PAPEETE (★80,000) | 23,555 |

**GABON**

| | |
|---|---|
| 1985 E | 1,312,000 |
| Franceville | 58,800 |
| Lambaréné | 49,500 |
| • LIBREVILLE | 235,700 |
| Port Gentil | 124,400 |

**GAMBIA**

| | |
|---|---|
| 1993 C | 1,025,867 |
| • BANJUL (★228,945) | 42,407 |
| Brikama | 42,480 |

**GAZA STRIP AND JERICHO AREA**

| | |
|---|---|
| 1992 E | 667,000 |
| ARĪḤĀ (JERICHO) (1967C) | 6,829 |
| • Ghazzah (1986E) | 235,000 |
| Khān Yūnis (1986E) | 98,370 |
| Rafah (1967C) | 49,812 |

**GEORGIA / Sakartvelo**

| | |
|---|---|
| 1991 E | 5,464,200 |
| Batumi | 137,500 |
| Gori | 70,100 |
| Kutaisi | 238,200 |
| Poti | 51,100 |
| Rustavi (★Tbilisi) | 161,900 |
| Suchumi | 120,000 |
| • TBILISI (★1,460,000) | 1,279,000 |
| Zugdidi | 50,600 |

**GERMANY / Deutschland**

| | |
|---|---|
| 1994 E | 81,338,093 |
| Aachen (★550,000) | 246,671 |
| Aalen (★79,000) | 66,333 |
| Ahlen | 55,657 |
| Albstadt | 50,057 |
| Alsdorf (★Aachen) | 46,747 |
| Altenburg | 46,647 |
| Amberg | 44,213 |
| Arnsberg | 77,847 |
| Aschaffenburg (★152,000) | 65,650 |
| Augsburg (★430,000) | 264,764 |
| Baden-Baden | 52,712 |
| Bad Homburg (★Frankfurt am Main) | 51,455 |
| Bad Oeynhausen | 48,365 |
| Bad Salzuflen (★Herford) | 54,979 |
| Bamberg (★122,000) | 70,770 |
| Bautzen | 45,351 |
| Bayreuth (★88,000) | 73,393 |
| Bergheim (★Köln) | 60,121 |
| Bergisch Gladbach (★Köln) | 104,991 |
| Bergkamen (★Essen) | 51,054 |
| BERLIN (★4,200,000) | 3,475,392 |
| Bielefeld (★540,000) | 324,674 |
| Bitterfeld (★105,000) | 17,027 |
| Bocholt | 70,272 |
| Bochum (★Essen) | 401,058 |
| BONN (★580,000) | 296,859 |
| Bottrop (★Essen) | 119,676 |
| Brandenburg | 89,208 |
| Braunschweig (★320,000) | 256,267 |
| Bremen (★790,000) | 551,604 |
| Bremerhaven (★180,000) | 131,492 |
| Castrop-Rauxel (★Essen) | 79,101 |
| Celle | 73,671 |
| Chemnitz (★500,000) | 279,520 |
| Coburg | 44,384 |
| Cottbus | 128,121 |
| Cuxhaven | 56,003 |
| Dachau (★München) | 36,294 |
| Darmstadt (★315,000) | 139,754 |
| Delmenhorst (★Bremen) | 77,127 |
| Dessau (★138,000) | 93,287 |
| Detmold | 72,109 |

▲ Población de un municipio, comuna o distrito entero, incluyendo sus áreas rurales.
• Ciudad más grande de un país.
★ Población o designación de un área metropolitana, incluyendo los suburbios.
C Censo. E Estimado oficial. U Estimado no oficial.

▲ Population d'une municipalité, d'une commune ou d'un district, zone rurale incluse.
• Ville la plus peuplée du pays.
★ Population de l'agglomération (ou nom de la zone métropolitaine englobante).
C Recensement. E Estimation officielle. U Estimation non officielle.

▲ População de um municipio, comuna ou distrito, inclusive as respectivas áreas rurais.
• Maior cidade de um país.
★ População ou indicação de uma área metropolitana.
C Censo. E Estimativa oficial. U Estimativa não oficial.

| | |
|---|---|
| Dinslaken (★Essen) | 67,619 |
| Dormagen (★Köln) | 59,915 |
| Dorsten (★Essen) | 79,941 |
| Dortmund (★Essen) | 601,966 |
| Dresden (★870,000) | 479,273 |
| Duisburg (★Essen) | 536,797 |
| Düren (★110,000) | 89,852 |
| Düsseldorf (★1,225,000) | 574,936 |
| Eberswalde-Finow | 50,730 |
| Eisenach | 42,579 |
| Eisenhüttenstadt | 47,545 |
| Emden | 52,216 |
| Erftstadt (★Köln) | 47,228 |
| Erfurt | 200,799 |
| Erkrath (★Düsseldorf) | 49,299 |
| Erlangen (★Nürnberg) | 102,383 |
| Eschweiler (★Aachen) | 55,791 |
| • Essen (★5,050,000) | 622,380 |
| Esslingen (★Stuttgart) | 91,388 |
| Euskirchen | 51,247 |
| Flensburg (★98,000) | 87,994 |
| Frankenthal (★Mannheim) | 48,099 |
| Frankfurt | 83,850 |
| Frankfurt am Main (★1,950,000) | 659,803 |
| Freiberg | 46,537 |
| Freiburg (★235,400) | 197,384 |
| Friedrichshafen | 56,047 |
| Fulda (★76,000) | 58,711 |
| Fürth (★Nürnberg) | 108,097 |
| Garbsen (★Hannover) | 62,196 |
| Garmisch-Partenkirchen | 26,996 |
| Gelsenkirchen (★Essen) | 295,037 |
| Gera | 122,974 |
| Giessen (★155,000) | 73,705 |
| Gladbeck (★Essen) | 79,931 |
| Göppingen (★155,000) | 56,771 |
| Görlitz | 67,647 |
| Goslar (★72,000) | 46,191 |
| Gotha | 52,265 |
| Göttingen | 128,419 |
| Greifswald | 63,941 |
| Grevenbroich (★Düsseldorf) | 62,737 |
| Gummersbach | 52,374 |
| Gütersloh (★Bielefeld) | 91,634 |
| Hagen (★Essen) | 214,877 |
| Halberstadt | 43,033 |
| Halle (★455,000) | 295,372 |
| Hamburg (★2,440,000) | 1,702,887 |
| Hameln (★65,000) | 59,209 |
| Hamm | 182,390 |
| Hanau (★Frankfurt am Main) | 89,156 |
| Hannover (★1,015,000) | 524,823 |
| Hattingen (★Essen) | 58,481 |
| Heidelberg (★Mannheim) | 139,429 |
| Heidenheim (★83,000) | 52,670 |
| Heilbronn (★250,000) | 122,396 |
| Herford (★123,000) | 65,682 |
| Herne (★Essen) | 180,539 |
| Herten (★Essen) | 69,592 |
| Hilden (★Düsseldorf) | 55,296 |
| Hildesheim (★126,000) | 106,303 |
| Hof | 52,724 |
| Hoyerswerda | 60,894 |
| Hürth (★Köln) | 51,974 |
| Ingolstadt (★150,000) | 109,666 |
| Iserlohn | 98,478 |
| Jena | 100,093 |
| Kaiserslautern (★133,000) | 102,370 |
| Kamen (★Essen) | 46,519 |
| Karlsruhe (★508,000) | 277,998 |
| Kassel (★385,000) | 202,158 |
| Kempten (Allgäu) | 61,669 |
| Kerpen (★Köln) | 60,395 |
| Kiel (★330,000) | 248,931 |
| Kleve | 47,869 |
| Koblenz (★170,000) | 109,807 |
| Köln (★1,820,000) | 962,517 |
| Konstanz | 75,891 |
| Krefeld (★Essen) | 249,565 |
| Landshut | 59,637 |
| Langenfeld (★Düsseldorf) | 56,153 |
| Langenhagen (★Hannover) | 47,609 |
| Leipzig (★720,000) | 490,851 |
| Leverkusen (★Köln) | 161,761 |
| Lingen | 51,338 |
| Lippstadt | 65,822 |
| Lübeck (★255,000) | 217,269 |
| Lüdenscheid | 80,277 |
| Ludwigsburg (★Stuttgart) | 86,216 |
| Ludwigshafen (★Mannheim) | 168,130 |
| Lüneburg | 63,299 |
| Lünen (★Essen) | 89,741 |
| Magdeburg (★400,000) | 270,546 |
| Mainz (★Wiesbaden) | 185,487 |
| Mannheim (★1,530,000) | 318,025 |
| Marburg | 76,582 |
| Marl (★Essen) | 92,590 |
| Meerbusch (★Düsseldorf) | 53,249 |
| Menden | 57,538 |
| Merseburg (★Halle) | 41,528 |
| Minden (★124,000) | 80,423 |
| Moers (★Essen) | 106,631 |
| Mönchengladbach (★420,000) | 265,312 |
| Mülheim an der Ruhr (★Essen) | 177,175 |
| München (Munich) (★1,930,000) | 1,255,623 |
| Münster | 267,367 |
| Neubrandenburg | 85,540 |
| Neumünster | 82,014 |
| Neunkirchen/Saar (★125,000) | 51,997 |
| Neuss (★Düsseldorf) | 148,560 |
| Neustadt an der Weinstrasse | 53,782 |
| Neu-Ulm (★Ulm) | 51,068 |
| Neuwied (★160,000) | 65,740 |
| Norderstedt (★Hamburg) | 69,916 |
| Nordhausen | 44,744 |
| Nordhorn | 50,835 |
| Nürnberg (★1,070,000) | 498,945 |
| Oberhausen (★Essen) | 226,254 |
| Offenbach (★Frankfurt am Main) | 116,870 |
| Offenburg | 54,963 |
| Oldenburg | 147,701 |
| Osnabrück (★275,000) | 168,078 |
| Paderborn | 130,130 |
| Passau | 51,041 |
| Peine | 48,105 |
| Pforzheim (★235,000) | 117,450 |
| Pirmasens | 48,619 |
| Pirna (★Dresden) | 39,958 |
| Plauen | 69,387 |
| Potsdam (★Berlin) | 139,262 |
| Pulheim (★Köln) | 50,474 |
| Rastatt | 48,574 |
| Ratingen (★Düsseldorf) | 90,443 |
| Ravensburg (★75,000) | 47,099 |
| Recklinghausen (★Essen) | 127,150 |
| Regensburg (★185,000) | 125,337 |
| Remscheid (★Wuppertal) | 123,610 |
| Reutlingen (★175,000) | 107,607 |
| Rheine | 73,543 |
| Riesa | 42,656 |
| Rosenheim | 58,553 |
| Rostock | 237,307 |
| Rüsselsheim (★Wiesbaden) | 60,361 |
| Saarbrücken (★365,000) | 190,902 |
| Saarlouis (★115,000) | 38,347 |
| Salzgitter | 117,684 |
| Sankt Augustin (★Bonn) | 53,969 |
| Schwäbisch Gmünd | 63,701 |
| Schwedt | 49,594 |
| Schweinfurt (★105,000) | 55,284 |
| Schwerin | 122,189 |
| Schwerte (★Essen) | 50,955 |
| Siegburg (★175,000) | 36,628 |
| Siegen (★195,000) | 111,845 |
| Sindelfingen (★Stuttgart) | 59,930 |
| Solingen (★Wuppertal) | 166,064 |
| Speyer | 49,310 |
| Stendal | 47,252 |
| Stolberg (★Aachen) | 58,028 |
| Stralsund | 69,230 |
| Stuttgart (★2,020,000) | 594,406 |
| Suhl | 52,386 |
| Trier (★122,000) | 99,183 |
| Troisdorf (★Siegburg) | 67,584 |
| Tübingen | 83,553 |
| Ulm (★220,000) | 114,839 |
| Unna (★Essen) | 64,327 |
| Velbert (★Essen) | 89,643 |
| Viersen (★Mönchengladbach) | 77,204 |
| Villingen-Schwenningen | 81,315 |
| Waiblingen (★Stuttgart) | 50,259 |
| Weimar | 58,807 |
| Wesel | 61,111 |
| Wetzlar (★100,000) | 54,188 |
| Wiesbaden (★800,000) | 270,873 |
| Wilhelmshaven (★122,000) | 91,680 |
| Wismar | 53,149 |
| Witten (★Essen) | 105,807 |
| Wittenberg | 53,374 |
| Wolfenbüttel (★Braunschweig) | 53,812 |
| Wolfsburg | 128,032 |
| Worms (★Mannheim) | 79,155 |
| Wuppertal (★850,000) | 386,625 |
| Würzburg (★195,000) | 128,875 |
| Zweibrücken (★105,000) | 35,704 |
| Zwickau (★180,000) | 107,988 |

**GHANA**

| | |
|---|---|
| 1987 E | 13,577,538 |
| • ACCRA (★1,390,000) | 949,113 |
| Ashiaman (★Accra) (1984C) | 49,427 |
| Cape Coast (1984C) | 86,620 |
| Koforidua (1984C) | 54,400 |
| Kumasi (★540,000) | 385,192 |
| Obuasi (1984C) | 60,146 |
| Sekondi (★175,352) (1984C) | 32,355 |
| Tafo (★Kumasi) (1984C) | 50,432 |
| Takoradi (★Sekondi) (1984C) | 61,527 |
| Tamale (★171,661) | 151,069 |
| Tema (★179,076) (★Accra) | 109,975 |
| Teshie (★Accra) (1984C) | 62,954 |

**GIBRALTAR**

| | |
|---|---|
| 1991 C | 28,074 |
| • GIBRALTAR | 28,074 |

**GREECE / Ellás**

| | |
|---|---|
| 1991 C | 10,259,900 |
| Aiyáleo (★Athínai) | 78,563 |
| Akharnai | 59,698 |
| Amaroúsion (★Athínai) | 64,092 |
| Ampelókipoi (★Thessaloníki) | 40,093 |
| • ATHÍNAI (ATHENS) (★3,150,000) | 772,072 |
| Áyios Dhimítrios (★Athínai) | 57,574 |
| Dráma | 37,604 |
| Ermoúpolis (★16,100) | 13,030 |
| Galátsion (★Athínai) | 57,230 |
| Glifádha (★Athínai) | 63,306 |
| Ilioúpolis (★Athínai) | 75,037 |
| Ioánnina | 56,699 |
| Iráklion (★127,600) | 115,124 |
| Kalámai (★45,100) | 43,625 |
| Kalamariá (★Thessaloníki) | 80,698 |
| Kallithéa (★Athínai) | 114,233 |
| Kardhítsa | 30,289 |
| Kateríni (★48,000) | 43,613 |
| Kavála | 56,571 |
| Keratsínion (★Athínai) | 71,982 |
| Khalándrion (★Athínai) | 66,285 |
| Khalkís | 51,646 |
| Khaniá (★65,500) | 50,077 |
| Khíos (★27,600) | 22,894 |
| Koridhallós (★Athínai) | 63,184 |
| Kórinthos (Corinth) | 27,412 |
| Lárisa (★125,600) | 112,777 |
| Návplion | 11,897 |
| Néa Ionía (★Athínai) | 60,635 |
| Néa Liósia (★Athínai) | 78,326 |
| Neápolis (★Thessaloníki) | 30,568 |
| Néa Smírni (★Athínai) | 69,479 |
| Níkaia (★Athínai) | 87,597 |
| Palaión Fáliron (★Athínai) | 61,371 |
| Pátrai (★172,800) | 152,570 |
| Peristérion (★Athínai) | 137,288 |
| Piraiévs (Piraeus) (★Athínai) | 182,671 |
| Ródhos (Rhodes) | 42,400 |
| Sérrai | 49,380 |
| Spárti (Sparta) (★15,500) | 13,011 |
| Thessaloníki (Salonika) (★755,000) | 383,967 |
| Thívai (Thebes) | 19,505 |
| Tríkala | 44,232 |
| Trípolis | 22,429 |
| Véroia | 37,858 |
| Víron (★Athínai) | 58,523 |
| Vólos (★106,200) | 77,192 |
| Zográfos (★Athínai) | 80,492 |

**GREENLAND / Grønland / Kalaallit Nunaat**

| | |
|---|---|
| 1990 E | 55,558 |
| Egedesminde (Aasiaat) | 3,308 |
| • GODTHÅB (NUUK) | 12,217 |
| Holsteinsborg (Sisimiut) | 4,871 |

**GRENADA**

| | |
|---|---|
| 1991 C | 90,691 |
| • SAINT GEORGE'S (★25,000) | 4,439 |

**GUADELOUPE**

| | |
|---|---|
| 1990 C | 387,034 |
| BASSE-TERRE (★27,500) | 14,082 |
| Les Abymes (★Pointe-à-Pitre) | 62,645 |
| • Pointe-à-Pitre (★84,000) | 26,031 |

**GUAM**

| | |
|---|---|
| 1990 C | 133,152 |
| • AGANA (★50,000) | 1,139 |

**GUATEMALA**

| | |
|---|---|
| 1989 E | 8,935,395 |
| Escuintla | 60,673 |
| • GUATEMALA (★1,400,000) | 1,057,210 |
| Quetzaltenango | 88,769 |

**GUERNSEY**

| | |
|---|---|
| 1991 C | 58,867 |
| • SAINT PETER PORT (★36,000) | 16,648 |

**GUINEA / Guinée**

| | |
|---|---|
| 1986 E | 6,225,000 |
| • CONAKRY | 800,000 |
| Kankan | 100,000 |
| Kindia | 80,000 |
| Labé | 110,000 |
| Nzérékoré (1983C) | 55,356 |

**GUINEA-BISSAU / Guiné-Bissau**

| | |
|---|---|
| 1988 E | 945,000 |
| • BISSAU | 125,000 |

**GUYANA**

| | |
|---|---|
| 1983 E | 918,000 |
| • GEORGETOWN (★188,000) | 78,500 |

**HAITI / Haïti**

| | |
|---|---|
| 1987 E | 5,531,802 |
| Cap-Haïtien | 72,161 |
| Gonaïves | 37,034 |
| • PORT-AU-PRINCE (★880,000) | 797,000 |

**HONDURAS**

| | |
|---|---|
| 1988 C | 4,443,721 |
| Choluteca | 54,481 |
| El Progreso | 60,058 |
| La Ceiba | 68,764 |
| San Pedro Sula (★375,000) | 287,350 |
| • TEGUCIGALPA | 576,661 |

**HONG KONG**

| | |
|---|---|
| 1986 C | 5,395,997 |
| Kowloon (Jiulong) (★Victoria) | 774,781 |
| Kwai Chung (★Victoria) | 131,362 |
| New Kowloon (Xinjiulong) (★Victoria) | 1,526,910 |
| Sha Tin (★Victoria) | 355,810 |
| Sheung Shui | 87,206 |
| Tai Po | 119,679 |
| Tsuen Wan (Quanwan) (★Victoria) | 514,241 |
| Tuen Mun (★Victoria) | 262,458 |
| • VICTORIA (★4,770,000) (1991C) | 1,250,993 |
| Yuen Long | 75,740 |

**HUNGARY / Magyarország**

| | |
|---|---|
| 1994 E | 10,277,000 |
| Békéscsaba | 67,475 |
| • BUDAPEST (★2,515,000) | 1,995,696 |
| Debrecen | 217,706 |
| Dunaújváros | 58,294 |
| Eger | 63,794 |
| Győr | 130,941 |
| Hódmezővásárhely | 50,745 |
| Kaposvár | 70,728 |
| Kecskemét | 105,559 |
| Miskolc | 189,655 |
| Nagykanizsa | 53,060 |
| Nyíregyháza | 115,643 |
| Ózd | 41,868 |
| Pécs | 172,177 |
| Salgótarján | 46,414 |
| Sopron | 56,324 |
| Szeged | 178,878 |
| Székesfehérvár | 109,666 |
| Szolnok | 80,859 |
| Szombathely | 85,932 |
| Tatabánya | 73,505 |
| Vác | 34,283 |
| Veszprém | 65,789 |
| Zalaegerszeg | 62,908 |

**ICELAND / Ísland**

| | |
|---|---|
| 1992 E | 262,193 |
| Akureyri | 14,665 |
| • REYKJAVÍK (★151,779) | 100,850 |

**INDIA / Bharat**

| | |
|---|---|
| 1991 C | 846,302,688 |
| Abohar | 107,163 |
| Achalpur | 96,229 |
| Ādilābād | 84,255 |
| Ādityapur (★Jamshedpur) | 77,803 |
| Ādoni | 136,182 |
| Agartala | 157,358 |
| Āgra (★948,063) | 891,790 |
| Āgra Cantonment (★Āgra) | 49,755 |
| Ahmadābād (★3,312,216) | 2,876,710 |
| Ahmadnagar (★222,088) | 181,339 |
| Aīzawl | 155,240 |
| Ajmer | 402,700 |
| Akola | 328,034 |
| Akot | 65,681 |
| Alandur (★Madras) | 125,244 |
| Alīgarh | 480,520 |
| Ālīpur Duār (★102,815) | 65,241 |
| Allahābād (★844,546) | 792,858 |
| Alleppey (★264,969) | 174,666 |
| Alwal (★Hyderābād) | 66,471 |
| Alwar (★210,146) | 205,086 |
| Amalner | 76,442 |
| Ambājogāi | 57,159 |
| Ambāla (★259,227) | 119,338 |
| Ambāla Cantonment (★Ambāla Sadar) | 49,017 |
| Ambāla Sadar | 90,872 |
| Ambāsamudram (★59,661) | 33,893 |
| Ambattur (★Madras) | 215,424 |
| Ambikāpur (★53,227) | 50,277 |
| Āmbūr | 75,911 |
| Amrāvati | 421,576 |
| Amreli (★69,366) | 67,827 |
| Amritsar | 708,835 |
| Amroha | 137,061 |
| Anakāpalle | 84,356 |
| Ānand (★174,480) | 110,266 |
| Anantapur | 174,924 |
| Anjār | 51,209 |
| Ankleshwar (★78,100) | 51,739 |
| Ara | 157,082 |
| Arakkonam | 71,928 |
| Arcot (★114,760) | 45,205 |
| Arni | 54,898 |
| Aruppukkottai | 78,976 |
| Asansol (★763,939) | 262,188 |
| Ashoknagar-Kalyangarh (★Hābra) | 96,747 |
| Āttūr | 55,667 |
| Auraiya | 50,772 |
| Aurangābād (★592,709) | 573,272 |
| Āvadi (★Madras) | 183,215 |
| Āzamgarh | 78,567 |
| Badagara (★102,430) | 72,434 |
| Bagaha | 64,627 |
| Bāgalkot | 76,903 |
| Bahādurgarh | 56,524 |
| Baharampur (★126,400) | 115,144 |
| Bahraich | 135,400 |
| Baidyabāti (★Calcutta) | 90,081 |
| Bālāghāt (★67,151) | 62,178 |
| Balāngīr | 69,920 |
| Bāleshwar (★101,829) | 85,442 |
| Ballarpur (★92,438) | 83,511 |
| Ballia | 84,063 |
| Bālly (★Calcutta) | 184,474 |
| Bālly (★Calcutta) | 73,322 |
| Balrāmpur | 59,619 |
| Bālurghāt (★126,225) | 119,796 |
| Bānda | 96,795 |
| Bangalore (★4,130,288) | 2,660,088 |
| Bangaon | 79,571 |
| Bānkura | 114,876 |
| Bansberia (★Calcutta) | 93,520 |
| Bānswāra (★67,908) | 66,632 |
| Bāpatla | 62,536 |
| Barākpur (★Calcutta) | 133,265 |
| Bārān | 57,719 |
| Baranagar (★Calcutta) | 224,821 |
| Bārāsat (★Calcutta) | 102,660 |
| Baraut | 67,705 |
| Barddhamān | 245,079 |
| Bareilly (★617,350) | 587,211 |
| Bargarh | 51,205 |
| Bāripada (★69,240) | 49,619 |
| Bārmer | 68,625 |
| Barnāla | 75,430 |
| Bārsi | 88,810 |
| Basīrhāt | 101,409 |
| Basti | 67,371 |
| Batala (★103,367) | 86,006 |
| Bathinda | 159,114 |
| Beāwar (★106,721) | 105,363 |
| Begusarai (★84,018) | 71,424 |
| Bela | 65,945 |
| Belampalli | 66,780 |
| Belgaum (★402,412) | 326,399 |
| Bellary | 245,391 |
| Bettiah | 92,653 |
| Betūl | 63,534 |
| Beypore | 56,505 |
| Bhadohi | 64,010 |
| Bhadrak | 76,435 |
| Bhadrāvati (★149,257) | 55,475 |
| Bhadrāvati New Town (★Bhadrāvati) | 74,928 |
| Bhadreswar (★Calcutta) | 72,474 |
| Bhāgalpur (★260,119) | 253,225 |
| Bhandāra | 71,813 |
| Bharatpur (★156,880) | 148,519 |
| Bharūch (★139,029) | 133,102 |
| Bhātpāra (★Calcutta) | 304,952 |
| Bhavāni (★97,160) | 35,196 |
| Bhāvnagar (★405,225) | 402,338 |
| Bhawānipatna | 51,062 |
| Bhilai (★685,474) | 386,159 |
| Bhīlwāra | 183,965 |
| Bhīmavaram | 121,314 |
| Bhind | 109,755 |
| Bhiwandi (★392,214) | 379,070 |
| Bhiwāni | 121,629 |
| Bhopāl | 1,062,771 |
| Bhubaneshwar | 411,542 |
| Bhuj (★121,009) | 102,176 |
| Bhusāwal (★159,799) | 145,143 |
| Bīd | 112,434 |
| Bīdar (★132,408) | 108,016 |
| Bihār | 201,323 |
| Bijāpur (★193,131) | 186,939 |
| Bijnor (★73,900) | 66,486 |
| Bīkaner | 416,289 |
| Bilāspur (★229,615) | 179,633 |
| Bilimora (★51,039) | 42,052 |
| Birlapur (★65,482) | 20,320 |
| Birnagar (★92,208) | 20,015 |
| Bishnupur | 56,128 |
| Bodhan | 64,406 |
| Bodināyakkanūr | 66,500 |
| Bokāro Steel City (★398,890) | 333,683 |
| Bolpur | 52,760 |
| • Bombay (★12,596,243) | 9,925,891 |
| Botād | 64,603 |
| Brahmapur | 210,418 |
| Brajrajnagar | 69,667 |
| Budaun | 116,695 |
| Budge Budge (★Calcutta) | 72,951 |
| Bulandshahr | 127,201 |
| Buldāna | 52,767 |
| Bulsār (★111,775) | 57,909 |
| Būndi | 65,047 |
| Burhānpur | 172,710 |
| Burnpur (★Āsānsol) | 174,933 |
| Calcutta (★11,021,918) | 4,399,819 |
| Calicut (★801,190) | 419,831 |
| Cannanore (★Tellicherry) | 65,238 |
| Chāībāsa | 56,729 |
| Chākdaha | 74,769 |
| Chakradharpur (★47,666) | 32,737 |
| Chālisgaon | 77,420 |
| Champdāni (★Calcutta) | 101,067 |
| Chandannagar (★Calcutta) | 120,378 |
| Chandausi | 82,748 |
| Chandīgarh (★575,829) | 504,094 |
| Chāndpur | 55,825 |
| Chandrapur | 226,105 |
| Changanācheri | 52,445 |
| Channapatna | 55,209 |
| Chāpra | 136,877 |
| Chās | 65,207 |
| Chhatarpur (★75,594) | 72,824 |
| Chhindwāra (★96,858) | 93,650 |
| Chidambaram (★67,949) | 58,740 |
| Chikmagalūr | 60,816 |
| Chilakalūrupet | 79,142 |
| Chingleput | 54,127 |
| Chintāmani | 50,394 |
| Chīrāla (★142,778) | 80,861 |
| Chitradurga (★103,435) | 87,069 |
| Chittaranjan (★65,689) | 47,186 |

⁂ Population of an entire municipality, commune, or district, including rural area.
• Largest city in country.
★ Population or designation of the metropolitan area, including suburbs.
**C** Census. **E** Official estimate. **U** Unofficial estimate.

⁂ Bevölkerung eines ganzen städtischen Verwaltungsgebietes, eines Kommunalbezirkes oder eines Distrikts, einschliesslich ländlicher Gebiete.
• Grösste Stadt des Landes.
★ Bevölkerung oder Bezeichnung der Stadtregion einschliesslich Vororte.
**C** Volkszählung. **E** Offizielle Schätzung. **U** Inoffizielle Schätzung.

| | |
|---|---|
| Chittaurgarh | 71,569 |
| Chittoor | 133,462 |
| Chopda | 49,234 |
| Chūru | 82,464 |
| Cochin (★1,140,605) | 564,589 |
| Coimbatore (★1,100,746) | 816,321 |
| Contai | 53,484 |
| Coonoor (★100,687) | 48,003 |
| Cuddalore | 144,561 |
| Cuddapah (★215,866) | 121,463 |
| Cuttack (★440,295) | 403,418 |
| Dabgram | 147,217 |
| Dabhoi | 50,641 |
| Dāhod (★96,632) | 66,500 |
| Dāltenganj | 56,323 |
| Damoh (★105,043) | 95,661 |
| Dānāpur (★Patna) | 84,616 |
| Dandeli | 52,701 |
| Darbhanga | 218,391 |
| Darjiling | 73,062 |
| Datia | 64,477 |
| Dāvangere (★287,233) | 266,082 |
| Dehra Dūn (★368,053) | 270,159 |
| Dehri | 93,694 |
| Delhi (★8,419,084) | 7,206,704 |
| Delhi Cantonment (★Delhi) | 94,393 |
| Deoband | 66,208 |
| Deoghar (★85,902) | 76,380 |
| Deolāli (★Nāsik) | 44,331 |
| Deoria | 82,168 |
| Dewās | 164,364 |
| Dhamtari | 69,357 |
| Dhanbad (★815,005) | 151,789 |
| Dhār | 59,246 |
| Dhārāpuram | 48,393 |
| Dharmapuri | 59,318 |
| Dharmavaram | 78,961 |
| Dhaulpur | 68,533 |
| Dholka (★54,352) | 49,860 |
| Dhorāji (★79,479) | 77,748 |
| Dhrāngadhra | 57,961 |
| Dhuburi | 66,216 |
| Dhule | 278,317 |
| Dibrugarh (★125,667) | 120,127 |
| Dimāpur | 57,182 |
| Dindigul | 182,477 |
| Dīsa | 62,435 |
| Dishergarh (★Āsānsol) | 86,832 |
| Dod Ballāpur | 54,609 |
| Dum Dum (★Calcutta) | 40,961 |
| Durg (★Bhilai) | 150,645 |
| Durgāpur | 425,836 |
| Elūru | 212,866 |
| Erode (★361,755) | 159,323 |
| Etah | 78,458 |
| Etāwah | 124,072 |
| Faizābād (★176,922) | 124,437 |
| Farīdābad (★Delhi) | 617,717 |
| Farīdkot | 58,244 |
| Farrukhābād (★208,727) | 194,657 |
| Fatehpur | 117,675 |
| Fathpur | 66,387 |
| Fāzilka | 58,028 |
| Fīrozābād (★270,536) | 215,128 |
| Fīrozpur | 78,738 |
| Fīrozpur Cantonment | 53,094 |
| Gadag | 134,051 |
| Gandhidham | 104,585 |
| Gāndhinagar | 123,359 |
| Ganga Ghat | 50,260 |
| Gangānagar | 161,482 |
| Gangāpur (★68,886) | 53,689 |
| Gangāwati (★85,515) | 64,843 |
| Gangtok | 25,024 |
| Gārulia (★Calcutta) | 80,918 |
| Gaya (★294,427) | 219,675 |
| Ghāziābād (★511,759) | 454,156 |
| Ghāzīpur | 76,547 |
| Girīdīh | 78,097 |
| Godhra (★100,662) | 96,813 |
| Gokāk | 52,080 |
| Gonda | 95,553 |
| Gondal (★81,611) | 80,584 |
| Gondia | 109,470 |
| Gopichettipālaiyam | 48,364 |
| Gorakhpur | 505,566 |
| Gudivāda | 101,656 |
| Gudiyāttam (★90,557) | 83,232 |
| Gūdūr | 55,984 |
| Gulbarga (★310,920) | 304,099 |
| Guna | 100,490 |
| Guntakal | 107,592 |
| Guntūr | 471,051 |
| Gurdāspur | 54,733 |
| Gurgaon (★135,884) | 121,486 |
| Guruvayur (★118,632) | 20,216 |
| Guwāhāti | 584,342 |
| Gwalior (★717,780) | 690,765 |
| Hābra (★196,970) | 100,223 |
| Hājīpur | 87,687 |
| Haldwāni | 104,195 |
| Hālisahar (★Calcutta) | 114,028 |
| Hānsi | 59,653 |
| Hanumāngarh (★82,733) | 78,525 |
| Hāora (★Calcutta) | 950,435 |
| Hāpur | 146,262 |
| Hardoi | 88,651 |
| Haridwār (★187,392) | 147,305 |
| Harihar | 66,647 |
| Hassan (★108,706) | 90,803 |
| Hāthras | 113,285 |
| Hazārībāg | 97,824 |
| Himatnagar | 51,461 |
| Hindaun | 60,780 |
| Hindupur | 104,651 |
| Hinganghāt | 78,715 |
| Hingoli | 54,457 |
| Hisār (★181,255) | 172,677 |
| Hoshangābād | 70,914 |
| Hoshiārpur | 122,705 |
| Hospet (★134,799) | 96,322 |
| Hubli-Dhārwār | 648,298 |
| Hugli-Chinsurah (★Calcutta) | 151,806 |
| Hyderābād (★4,344,437) | 3,043,896 |
| Ichalkaranji (★235,979) | 214,950 |
| Imphāl (★202,839) | 198,535 |
| Indore (★1,109,056) | 1,091,674 |
| Ingrāj Bāzār (★177,164) | 139,204 |
| Itānagar | 16,545 |
| Itārsi (★84,626) | 77,334 |
| Jabalpur (★888,916) | 741,927 |
| Jabalpur Cantonment (★Jabalpur) | 56,124 |
| Jagādhri (★Yamunānagar) | 67,386 |
| Jagdalpur (★84,578) | 66,154 |
| Jagtiāl | 67,591 |
| Jahānābād | 52,332 |
| Jaipur (★1,518,235) | 1,458,483 |
| Jalandhar | 509,510 |
| Jālgaon | 242,193 |
| Jālna | 174,985 |
| Jalpāiguri | 68,732 |
| Jamālpur | 86,112 |
| Jamkhandi | 48,143 |
| Jammu (★223,361) (1981C) | 206,135 |
| Jāmnagar (★381,646) | 341,637 |
| Jamshedpur (★829,171) | 460,577 |
| Jaora (★56,023) | 54,997 |
| Jaunpur | 136,062 |
| Jaypur | 55,246 |
| Jetpur (★95,397) | 73,560 |
| Jhānsi (★368,154) | 300,850 |
| Jharia (★Dhanbād) | 69,641 |
| Jhārsuguda | 65,054 |
| Jhunjhunūn | 72,187 |
| Jīnd | 85,315 |
| Jodhpur | 666,279 |
| Jorhāt (★112,030) | 58,358 |
| Jūnāgadh (★167,110) | 130,484 |
| Kadaiyanallūr | 68,819 |
| Kadiri | 63,378 |
| Kagaznagar | 57,535 |
| Kairāna | 56,079 |
| Kaithal | 71,142 |
| Kākināda (★327,541) | 279,980 |
| Kalamassery (★Cochin) | 54,342 |
| Kālol (★92,550) | 82,137 |
| Kalyān (★Bombay) | 1,014,557 |
| Kāmāreddi | 48,666 |
| Kāmārhāti (★Calcutta) | 266,889 |
| Kambam | 52,435 |
| Kāmthi (★127,151) | 78,612 |
| Kānchipuram (★171,129) | 144,955 |
| Kānchrāpāra (★Calcutta) | 100,194 |
| Kānnangād (★118,214) | 57,165 |
| Kannauj | 58,932 |
| Kānpur (★2,029,889) | 1,874,409 |
| Kānpur Cantonment (★Kānpur) | 95,021 |
| Kapra (★Hyderābād) | 87,747 |
| Kapūrthala | 64,567 |
| Karād | 56,819 |
| Kāraikāl | 61,804 |
| Kāraikkudi (★110,926) | 71,965 |
| Kāranja | 48,866 |
| Karauli | 49,008 |
| Karīmnagar | 148,583 |
| Karnāl (★176,131) | 173,751 |
| Karūr (★113,669) | 73,418 |
| Kārwār | 51,022 |
| Kāsaragod | 50,126 |
| Kāsganj | 75,634 |
| Kāshīpur | 69,870 |
| Katihār (★154,367) | 135,436 |
| Kātwa | 55,541 |
| Kāvali | 65,910 |
| Kāyankulam | 67,151 |
| Keshod | 50,172 |
| Khadki Cantonment (★Pune) | 78,323 |
| Khambhāt (★89,834) | 76,746 |
| Khāmgaon | 73,692 |
| Khammam (★149,077) | 127,992 |
| Khandwa | 145,133 |
| Khanna | 71,990 |
| Kharagpur (★264,842) | 177,989 |
| Kharagpur Railway Settlement (★Kharagpur) | 84,252 |
| Khardaha | 88,358 |
| Khargone | 66,786 |
| Khurja | 80,305 |
| Kishanganj | 64,568 |
| Kishangarh Bās | 81,948 |
| Koch Bihār (★92,820) | 71,215 |
| Kodarma | 53,577 |
| Kohīma | 51,418 |
| Kolār | 83,287 |
| Kolār Gold Fields (★156,746) | 72,485 |
| Kolhāpur (★418,538) | 406,370 |
| Konnagar (★Calcutta) | 62,200 |
| Korba | 124,501 |
| Kota | 537,371 |
| Kot Kapūra | 62,430 |
| Kottagūdem (★102,137) | 80,440 |
| Kottayam (★166,552) | 63,155 |
| Kovilpatti | 78,834 |
| Krishnagiri | 60,315 |
| Krishnanagar | 121,110 |
| Kukatpalle (★Hyderābād) | 186,963 |
| Kulti (★Asansol) | 108,518 |
| Kumārapālaiyam (★Bhavāni) | 57,672 |
| Kumbakonam (★150,540) | 139,483 |
| Kundla (★65,785) | 64,815 |
| Kurasia (★71,708) | 15,898 |
| Kurichi (★Coimbatore) | 64,796 |
| Kurnool (★275,360) | 236,800 |
| Lādnūn | 48,205 |
| Lakhīmpur | 79,951 |
| Lalbahadur Nagar (★Hyderābād) | 155,514 |
| Lalitpur | 79,870 |
| Lātūr | 197,408 |
| Luckeesarai | 53,360 |
| Lucknow (★1,669,204) | 1,619,115 |
| Lucknow Cantonment (★Lucknow) | 50,089 |
| Ludhiāna | 1,042,740 |
| Machilīpatnam (Bandar) | 159,110 |
| Madanapalle | 73,820 |
| Madgaon (Margao) (★72,400) | 58,951 |
| Mādhavaram (★Madras) | 49,258 |
| Madhubani | 53,747 |
| Madhyamgrām (★Calcutta) | 69,252 |
| Madras (★5,421,985) | 3,841,396 |
| Madurai (★1,085,914) | 940,989 |
| Mahbūbnagar | 116,833 |
| Mahesāna (★109,950) | 88,201 |
| Mahoba | 56,247 |
| Mahuva (★64,144) | 59,912 |
| Mainpuri | 76,735 |
| Makrāna (★66,720) | 59,714 |
| Malappuram (★142,204) | 49,692 |
| Malaut | 56,868 |
| Mālegaon | 342,595 |
| Māler Kotla | 88,600 |
| Malkajgiri (★Hyderābād) | 127,178 |
| Malkāpur | 51,311 |
| Mancheriyal | 52,657 |
| Mandsaur | 95,907 |
| Mandya | 120,265 |
| Mangalagiri | 59,152 |
| Mangalore (★426,341) | 273,304 |
| Mango (★Jamshedpur) | 108,100 |
| Manjeri | 69,334 |
| Manmād | 61,312 |
| Mannārgudi | 56,552 |
| Mānsa | 55,089 |
| Mathura (★235,922) | 226,691 |
| Maunath Bhanjan | 136,697 |
| Mawāna | 51,701 |
| Māyūram | 76,837 |
| Medinīpur | 125,498 |
| Meerut (★849,799) | 753,778 |
| Meerut Cantonment (★Meerut) | 96,021 |
| Melappālaiyam (★Tirunelveli) | 68,347 |
| Mettuppālaiyam | 63,479 |
| Mhow (★83,796) | 74,987 |
| Mira Bhayandar (★Bombay) | 175,605 |
| Miraj (★Sāngli) | 121,593 |
| Miryalaguda | 65,879 |
| Mirzāpur | 169,336 |
| Modinagar (★123,279) | 101,660 |
| Moga (★110,958) | 108,304 |
| Mokāma | 59,528 |
| Morādābād (★443,701) | 429,214 |
| Morbi (★120,117) | 90,357 |
| Morena | 147,124 |
| Mormugao (★90,429) | 83,367 |
| Motihāri (★83,255) | 77,432 |
| Mubārakpur (★62,733) | 45,376 |
| Mughal Sarāi (★91,505) | 66,529 |
| Muktsar | 66,383 |
| Munger | 150,112 |
| Murwāra | 163,431 |
| Muzaffarnagar (★247,624) | 240,609 |
| Muzaffarpur | 241,107 |
| Mysore (★653,345) | 480,692 |
| Nābha | 54,421 |
| Nadiād (★170,217) | 167,051 |
| Nagaon | 93,350 |
| Nāgappattinam (★99,745) | 86,489 |
| Nāgaur | 68,194 |
| Nagda | 79,622 |
| Nāgercoil | 190,084 |
| Nagīna | 58,513 |
| Nāgpur (★1,664,006) | 1,624,752 |
| Naihāti (★Calcutta) | 132,701 |
| Najībābād | 66,860 |
| Nalasopara (★Bombay) | 67,732 |
| Nalgonda | 84,910 |
| Nānded (★309,316) | 275,083 |
| Nandurbār | 78,378 |
| Nandyāl | 119,813 |
| Nangi (★Calcutta) | 52,958 |
| Narasapur | 56,362 |
| Narasaraopet | 88,726 |
| Nārnaul | 51,976 |
| Nāshik (★725,341) | 656,925 |
| Navadwīp (★155,905) | 125,037 |
| Navsāri (★190,946) | 126,089 |
| Nawābganj (★77,234) | 64,582 |
| Nawāda | 53,174 |
| Nawalgarh | 51,190 |
| Nedumangād | 49,875 |
| Neemuch (★90,474) | 86,439 |
| Nellore | 316,606 |
| New Bārākpur (★Calcutta) | 63,795 |
| New Bombay (★Bombay) | 304,724 |
| NEW DELHI (★Delhi) | 301,297 |
| Neyveli (★126,889) | 118,080 |
| Nipāni | 51,624 |
| Nirmal | 57,761 |
| Nizāmābād | 241,034 |
| North Bārākpur (★Calcutta) | 100,606 |
| North Dum Dum (★Calcutta) | 149,965 |
| Ongole (★128,648) | 100,836 |
| Orai | 98,716 |
| Osmānābād | 68,019 |
| Pālakodu | 56,969 |
| Palani (★76,209) | 68,907 |
| Pālanpur (★90,269) | 80,657 |
| Pālayankottai (★Tirunelveli) | 98,399 |
| Pālghāt (★180,033) | 123,289 |
| Pāli | 136,842 |
| Pallavaram (★Madras) | 111,866 |
| Palwal | 59,168 |
| Palwancha | 53,102 |
| Panaji (Panjim) (★85,515) | 43,349 |
| Pandharpur | 79,902 |
| Pānihāti (★Calcutta) | 275,990 |
| Pānīpat | 191,212 |
| Panruti | 51,394 |
| Panvel | 58,986 |
| Paramakkudi | 72,321 |
| Parbhani | 190,255 |
| Parli | 72,670 |
| Pātan (★97,025) | 96,112 |
| Pathānkot (★128,198) | 123,930 |
| Patiāla (★253,706) | 238,368 |
| Patna (★1,099,647) | 917,243 |
| Pattukkottai | 58,062 |
| Payyannūr | 64,032 |
| Periyakulam | 46,744 |
| Petlād | 48,552 |
| Phagwāra (★88,316) | 83,163 |
| Pīlībhīt | 106,605 |
| Pilkhua | 51,162 |
| Pimpri-Chinchwad (★Pune) | 517,083 |
| Pollāchi (★127,132) | 86,897 |
| Pondicherry (★401,437) | 203,065 |
| Ponmalai (★Tiruchchirāppalli) | 69,639 |
| Ponnāni | 51,770 |
| Ponnūru Nidubrolu | 54,363 |
| Porbandar (★160,671) | 116,671 |
| Port Blair | 74,955 |
| Proddatūr | 133,914 |
| Pudukkottai | 99,058 |
| Puliyangudi | 53,287 |
| Pune (Poona) (★2,493,987) | 1,566,651 |
| Pune Cantonment (★Pune) | 82,139 |
| Puri | 125,199 |
| Pūrnia (★136,918) | 114,912 |
| Puruliya | 92,386 |
| Pusad | 55,931 |
| Quilon (★362,572) | 139,852 |
| Qutubullapur (★Hyderābād) | 106,591 |
| Rabkavi Banhatti | 60,609 |
| Rāe Bareli | 129,904 |
| Rāichūr (★170,577) | 157,551 |
| Raiganj (★159,266) | 151,045 |
| Raigarh (★90,265) | 86,767 |
| Raipur (★462,694) | 438,639 |
| Rājahmundry (★401,397) | 324,851 |
| Rājapālaiyam | 114,202 |
| Rajendranagar (★Hyderābād) | 84,520 |
| Rajhara-Jharandalli | 55,996 |
| Rājkot (★654,490) | 559,407 |
| Rāj Nāndgaon | 125,371 |
| Rājpur (★86,451) | 60,175 |
| Rājpura | 70,983 |
| Rāmanagaram | 50,437 |
| Rāmanāthapuram | 52,879 |
| Rāmgarh (★82,328) | 51,264 |
| Rāmpur | 243,742 |
| Rānāghāt (★127,035) | 62,532 |
| Rānchi (★614,795) | 599,306 |
| Rānībennur | 67,442 |
| Rānīganj (★155,823) | 61,997 |
| Ratangarh | 55,079 |
| Ratlām (★195,776) | 195,776 |
| Ratnāgiri | 56,529 |
| Raurkela (★398,864) | 215,509 |
| Raurkela Civil Township (★Raurkela) | 142,408 |
| Rāyachoti | 51,931 |
| Rāyagāda | 48,247 |
| Rewa | 128,981 |
| Rewāri | 75,342 |
| Rishīkesh (★71,704) | 44,487 |
| Rishra (★Calcutta) | 102,815 |
| Robertson Pet (★Kolār Gold Fields) | 68,230 |
| Rohtak | 216,096 |
| Roorkee (★91,139) | 80,262 |
| Rudrapur | 61,280 |
| Sāgar (★257,119) | 195,346 |
| Sahāranpur | 374,945 |
| Saharsa | 80,149 |
| Sahaswān | 51,080 |
| Sāhibganj | 49,257 |
| Salem (★578,291) | 366,712 |
| Sāmalkot | 48,760 |
| Sambalpur (★193,297) | 131,138 |
| Sambhal | 150,869 |
| Sangamner | 49,061 |
| Sangareddi | 50,123 |
| Sāngli (★363,751) | 193,197 |
| Sangrūr | 56,419 |
| Sankarankovil | 48,846 |
| Sardārshahr | 67,954 |
| Sarni | 84,379 |
| Sāsarām | 98,122 |
| Sātāra | 95,180 |
| Satna (★160,500) | 156,630 |
| Sawāi Mādhopur (★77,690) | 72,165 |
| Secunderābād Cantonment (★Hyderābād) | 171,148 |
| Sehore | 71,456 |
| Seoni | 64,532 |
| Serampore (★Calcutta) | 137,026 |
| Serilungampalle (★Hyderābād) | 72,320 |
| Shahdol (★60,529) | 55,508 |
| Shāhjahānpur (★260,403) | 237,713 |
| Shāmli | 70,853 |
| Shāntipur | 109,956 |
| Shikohābād | 62,829 |
| Shiliguri | 216,950 |
| Shillong (★223,366) | 131,719 |
| Shimoga (★193,028) | 179,258 |
| Shivpuri | 108,277 |
| Shrīrampur (★79,052) | 71,368 |
| Siddhapur (★51,794) | 50,770 |
| Siddipet | 54,091 |
| Sikandarābād | 60,992 |
| Sīkar | 148,272 |
| Silchar | 115,483 |
| Silvassa | 11,725 |
| Simla (★110,360) | 82,054 |
| Sindri (★Dhānbād) | 72,333 |
| Sircilla | 50,048 |
| Sirsa | 112,841 |
| Sītāmarhi (★67,336) | 44,935 |
| Sītāpur | 121,842 |
| Siuri | 54,298 |
| Sivakāsi (★102,175) | 65,593 |
| Siwān | 63,125 |
| Solāpur (★620,846) | 604,215 |
| Sonīpat | 143,922 |
| South Dum Dum (★Calcutta) | 232,811 |
| Srīkākulam | 88,883 |
| Srikalahasti | 61,578 |
| Srīnagar (★606,002) (1981C) | 594,775 |
| Srīrangam (★Tiruchchirāppalli) | 70,109 |
| Srīvilliputtūr | 68,644 |
| Sujāngarh | 70,843 |
| Sultānpur | 76,533 |
| Sūrat (★1,518,950) | 1,498,817 |
| Surendranagar (★166,466) | 106,110 |
| Suriāpet | 60,630 |
| Tādepallegūdem | 88,878 |
| Tādpatri | 71,068 |
| Talipparamba | 60,226 |
| Tāmbaram (★Madras) | 107,187 |
| Tānda | 70,605 |
| Tanuku | 62,913 |
| Tellicherry (★463,962) | 103,579 |
| Tenāli | 143,726 |
| Tenkāsi | 55,189 |
| Tezpur | 55,064 |
| Thāna (★Bombay) | 803,369 |
| Thānesar | 61,255 |
| Thanjāvūr | 202,013 |
| Theni-Allinagaram | 60,050 |
| Thiruvārūr | 49,195 |
| Thrippunithura (★Cochin) | 51,078 |
| Tīkamgarh | 54,173 |
| Tindivanam | 61,579 |
| Tinsukia | 73,918 |
| Tiruchchirāppalli (★711,862) | 387,223 |
| Tiruchengodu | 63,027 |
| Tirunelveli (★366,869) | 135,825 |
| Tirupati (★188,904) | 174,369 |
| Tiruppattūr | 55,282 |
| Tiruppur (★306,237) | 235,661 |
| Tirūr | 49,453 |
| Tiruvalla | 54,780 |
| Tiruvannāmalai | 109,196 |
| Tiruvottiyūr (★Madras) | 168,642 |
| Titāgarh (★Calcutta) | 114,085 |
| Tonk | 100,079 |
| Trichūr (★275,053) | 74,604 |
| Trivandrum (★826,225) | 524,006 |
| Tiruchchendūr (★75,301) | 27,420 |
| Tumkūr (★179,877) | 138,903 |
| Tuticorin (★280,091) | 199,854 |
| Udagamandalam | 81,763 |
| Udaipur | 308,571 |
| Udamalpet | 58,678 |
| Udgīr | 70,453 |
| Ujjain | 362,266 |
| Ulhāsnagar (★Bombay) | 369,077 |
| Ulubāria | 155,172 |
| Unjha | 51,003 |
| Unnāo | 107,425 |
| Upleta | 51,801 |
| Uppal Kalan (★Hyderābād) | 75,644 |
| Uttarpara-Kotrung (★Calcutta) | 101,268 |
| Vadodara (★1,126,824) | 1,031,346 |
| Vālpārai | 106,523 |
| Vāniyambādi (★92,307) | 72,426 |
| Vārānasi (Benares) (★1,030,863) | 929,270 |
| Vasai (Bassein) (★83,734) | 39,781 |
| Veerappanchattiram (★Erode) | 61,649 |
| Vejalpur (★Ahmadābād) | 92,116 |
| Vellore (★310,776) | 175,061 |
| Verāval (★120,178) | 93,976 |
| Vidisha | 92,922 |
| Vijayawāda (★845,756) | 701,827 |
| Vikramasingapuram | 49,834 |

▲ Población de un municipio, comuna o distrito entero, incluyendo sus áreas rurales.
• Ciudad más grande de un país.
★ Población o designación de un área metropolitana, incluyendo los suburbios.
**C** Censo. **E** Estimado oficial. **U** Estimado no oficial.

▲ Population d'une municipalité, d'une commune ou d'un district, zone rurale incluse.
• Ville la plus peuplée du pays.
★ Population de l'agglomération (ou nom de la zone métropolitaine englobante).
**C** Recensement. **E** Estimation officielle. **U** Estimation non officielle.

▲ População de um município, comuna ou distrito, inclusive as respectivas áreas rurais.
• Maior cidade de um país.
★ População ou indicação de uma área metropolitana.
**C** Censo. **E** Estimativa oficial. **U** Estimativa não oficial.

| | |
|---|---|
| Viluppuram | 88,788 |
| Viramgām | 50,788 |
| Virār (★Bombay) | 57,600 |
| Virudunagar | 70,971 |
| Vishākhapatnam (★1,057,118) | 752,037 |
| Visnagar (★59,647) | 57,869 |
| Vizianagaram (★177,022) | 160,359 |
| Vriddhāchalam | 52,819 |
| Wadhwan (★Surendranager) | 49,791 |
| Warangal (★467,757) | 447,657 |
| Wardha | 102,985 |
| Wāshīm | 49,140 |
| Yamunānagar (★219,754) | 144,346 |
| Yavatmāl (★121,816) | 108,578 |
| Yemmiganur | 65,089 |

**INDONESIA**

| | |
|---|---|
| 1990 C | 179,378,946 |
| Ambon (▲275,888) | 205,193 |
| Balikpapan | 344,147 |
| Banda Aceh (Kuturaja) (▲184,650) | 143,360 |
| Bandung (★2,220,000) | 2,058,122 |
| Banjarmasin | 480,737 |
| Bantul (▲696,944) | 13,700 |
| Banyuwangi (▲1,455,010) | 92,800 |
| Batang (▲591,647) | 55,200 |
| Bekasi (▲951,509) (★Jakarta) | 146,400 |
| Bengkulu | 170,183 |
| Binjai (▲181,866) | 127,184 |
| Blitar (★150,000) | 118,933 |
| Bogor (★620,000) | 271,341 |
| Bojonegoro (▲1,104,031) | 63,700 |
| Brebes (▲1,521,835) | 49,500 |
| Bukittinggi | 83,753 |
| Cianjur (▲1,420,228) | 108,700 |
| Cibinong (▲1,812,734) | 264,100 |
| Cikampek (▲1,152,405) | 91,200 |
| Cilacap (▲1,487,308) | 141,900 |
| Ciledug (▲1,244,151) | 293,000 |
| Cimahi (▲1,909,459) (★Bandung) | 196,900 |
| Ciparay (▲1,909,456) | 135,300 |
| Cirebon (★315,000) | 254,477 |
| Denpasar (▲663,390) | 209,500 |
| Depok (▲1,812,734) (★Jakarta) | 382,000 |
| Dili (▲123,475) | 12,900 |
| Dumai (▲904,375) | 71,500 |
| Garut (▲1,478,757) | 145,900 |
| Genteng (▲1,455,010) | 60,900 |
| Gorontalo (▲119,745) | 94,058 |
| Gresik (▲856,853) | 102,000 |
| Indramayu (▲1,226,609) | 32,700 |
| • JAKARTA (★10,200,000) | 8,227,746 |
| Jambi | 339,786 |
| Jayapura (Sukarnapura) (▲246,389) | 101,200 |
| Jember (▲2,062,554) | 190,000 |
| Jepara (▲827,657) | 36,200 |
| Jombang (▲1,048,805) | 65,700 |
| Karawang (▲1,152,405) | 143,300 |
| Kebumen (▲1,120,982) | 48,300 |
| Kediri | 249,538 |
| Kendari (▲488,471) | 70,700 |
| Kisaran (▲884,594) | 66,600 |
| Klangenang (▲1,035,575) | 291,200 |
| Klaten (▲1,056,135) | 120,400 |
| Kudus (▲631,322) | 182,600 |
| Kuningan (▲739,360) | 33,100 |
| Kupang (▲522,944) | 111,300 |
| Lumajang (▲924,894) | 62,100 |
| Madiun (★200,000) | 170,050 |
| Magelang (★180,000) | 123,156 |
| Majalaya (▲1,909,459) | 176,600 |
| Malang | 695,089 |
| Manado | 320,600 |
| Mataram (▲859,273) | 276,300 |
| Medan | 1,730,052 |
| Mojokerto | 99,707 |
| Muncar (▲1,455,010) | 48,100 |
| Padang (▲631,263) | 477,064 |
| Padangsidempuan (▲954,184) | 72,100 |
| Palangkaraya | 112,511 |
| Palembang | 1,144,047 |
| Palu (▲784,647) | 56,500 |
| Pangkalpinang | 113,129 |
| Pare (▲1,343,125) | 51,400 |
| Parepare (▲101,421) | 84,093 |
| Pasuruan (★190,000) | 152,075 |
| Pati (▲1,064,115) | 54,900 |
| Payakumbuh (▲90,838) | 50,475 |
| Pekalongan (★430,000) | 242,714 |
| Pekanbaru | 398,621 |
| Pemalang (▲1,114,228) | 86,200 |
| Pematangsiantar (★250,000) | 219,316 |
| Perabumulih (▲582,396) | 59,500 |
| Ponorogo (▲837,055) | 59,500 |
| Pontianak | 396,658 |
| Pringsewu (▲1,825,040) | 58,300 |
| Probolinggo (▲176,906) | 131,077 |
| Purwakarta (▲437,327) | 62,300 |
| Purwokerto (▲1,348,825) | 158,300 |
| Purworejo (▲700,788) | 38,600 |
| Salatiga | 98,012 |
| Samarinda (▲407,174) | 334,851 |
| Semarang | 1,249,230 |
| Serang (▲1,201,742) | 84,900 |
| Sibolga | 71,559 |
| Sidoarjo (▲1,167,467) | 76,800 |
| Singaraja (▲540,150) | 59,200 |
| Singkawang (▲574,156) | 64,000 |
| Situbondo (▲574,156) | 63,800 |
| Sorong (▲199,085) | 77,900 |
| Subang (▲1,037,394) | 52,700 |
| Sukabumi (★250,000) | 119,938 |
| Sumedang (▲718,488) | 42,900 |
| Sumenep (▲933,746) | 53,300 |
| Surabaya | 2,473,272 |
| Surakarta (★590,000) | 503,827 |
| Taman (▲1,167,467) | 88,100 |
| Tangerang (▲1,244,151) | 99,100 |
| Tanjungbalai | 107,751 |
| Tanjungkarang-Telukbetung (▲636,418) | 457,927 |
| Tanjungpinang | 105,820 |
| Tarakan (▲232,494) | 61,300 |
| Tasikmalaya (▲1,444,242) | 194,000 |
| Tebingtinggi | 116,749 |
| Tegal (★510,000) | 229,553 |
| Tembilahan (▲4,878,066) | 62,700 |
| Tuban (▲977,716) | 54,700 |
| Tulungagung (▲890,032) | 97,000 |
| Ujungpandang (Makasar) | 944,372 |
| Yogyakarta (★540,000) | 412,059 |

**IRAN / Īrān**

| | |
|---|---|
| 1986 C | 49,445,010 |
| Ābādān | 21,879 |
| Abhar | 62,145 |
| Āghā Jārī | 64,102 |
| Ahvāz | 579,826 |
| Alīgūdarz | 53,843 |
| Āmol | 118,242 |
| Andīmeshk | 56,288 |
| Arāk | 265,349 |
| Ardabīl | 281,973 |
| Bābol | 115,320 |
| Bākhtarān (Kermānshāh) | 560,514 |
| Bam | 50,709 |
| Bandar-e 'Abbās | 201,642 |
| Bandar-e Anzalī (Bandar-e Pahlavī) | 87,063 |
| Bandar-e Būshehr | 120,787 |
| Bandar-e Māh Shahr | 71,808 |
| Behbahān | 78,694 |
| Behshahr | 52,461 |
| Bīrjand | 81,798 |
| Bojnūrd | 93,392 |
| Borāzjān | 67,061 |
| Borūjerd | 183,879 |
| Dezfūl | 151,420 |
| Do Gonbadān | 51,107 |
| Do Rūd | 62,517 |
| Emāmshahr (Shāhrūd) | 78,950 |
| Eṣfahān (★1,175,000) | 986,753 |
| Eslāmābād | 73,362 |
| Eslāmshahr (★Tehrān) | 215,129 |
| Fasā | 64,771 |
| Gonbad-e Qābūs | 87,100 |
| Gorgān | 139,430 |
| Hamadān | 272,499 |
| Īlām | 89,035 |
| Jahrom | 77,174 |
| Karaj (★Tehrān) | 275,100 |
| Kāshān | 138,599 |
| Kāshmar | 49,259 |
| Kāzerūn | 73,444 |
| Kermān | 257,284 |
| Khomeynīshahr (★Eṣfahān) | 104,647 |
| Khorramābād | 208,592 |
| Khorramshahr (1976C) | 146,706 |
| Khvoy | 115,343 |
| Mahābād | 75,238 |
| Malāyer | 103,640 |
| Marāgheh | 100,679 |
| Marand | 71,394 |
| Marv Dasht | 79,132 |
| Mashhad | 1,463,508 |
| Masjed-e Soleymān | 104,787 |
| Mīāndoāb | 59,551 |
| Mīāneh | 65,959 |
| Nahāvand | 52,265 |
| Najafābād | 129,058 |
| Naqadeh | 52,275 |
| Neyshābūr | 109,258 |
| Orūmīyeh (Reẕā'īyeh) | 300,746 |
| Qā'emshahr | 109,288 |
| Qazvīn | 248,591 |
| Qom | 543,139 |
| Qomsheh | 73,367 |
| Qūchān | 66,531 |
| Rafsanjān | 66,498 |
| Rasht | 290,897 |
| Sabzevār | 129,103 |
| Salmās | 50,573 |
| Sanandaj | 204,537 |
| Saqqez | 81,351 |
| Sārī | 141,020 |
| Sāveh | 64,081 |
| Semnān | 64,891 |
| Shahr-e Kord | 75,080 |
| Shīrāz | 848,289 |
| Shīrvān | 48,688 |
| Shūshtar | 65,840 |
| Sīrjān | 90,072 |
| Tabrīz | 971,482 |
| • TEHRĀN (★7,500,000) | 6,042,584 |
| Torbat-e Ḥeydarīyeh | 72,068 |
| Varāmīn | 58,311 |
| Yazd | 230,483 |
| Zābol | 75,105 |
| Zāhedān | 281,923 |
| Zanjān | 215,261 |

**IRAQ / Al 'Irāq**

| | |
|---|---|
| 1985 E | 15,584,987 |
| Ad-Dīwānīyah (1970E) | 62,300 |
| Al-'Amārah | 131,785 |
| Al-Baṣrah | 616,700 |
| Al-Ḥillah | 215,249 |
| Al-Kūt | 73,022 |
| Al-Mawṣil | 570,926 |
| An-Najaf | 242,603 |
| An-Nāṣirīyah | 138,842 |
| Ar-Ramādī | 137,388 |
| As-Samāwah | 75,293 |
| As-Sulaymānīyah | 279,424 |
| • BAGHDĀD (1987C) | 3,841,268 |
| Ba'qūbah | 114,516 |
| Irbīl | 333,903 |
| Karbalā' | 184,574 |
| Kirkūk (1970E) | 207,900 |

**IRELAND / Éire**

| | |
|---|---|
| 1991 C | 3,525,719 |
| Cork (★174,400) | 127,253 |
| • DUBLIN (BAILE ÁTHA CLIATH) (★1,150,000) | 478,389 |
| Dún Laoghaire (★Dublin) | 55,540 |
| Galway | 50,853 |
| Limerick (★75,436) | 52,083 |
| Waterford (★41,853) | 40,328 |

**ISLE OF MAN**

| | |
|---|---|
| 1991 C | 69,788 |
| • DOUGLAS (★30,000) | 22,214 |

**ISRAEL / Isrā'īl / Yisra'el**

| | |
|---|---|
| 1994 E | 5,182,200 |
| 'Akko (Acre) (★Ḥefa) | 45,100 |
| Ashdod | 110,300 |
| Ashqelon | 73,300 |
| Bat Yam (★Tel Aviv-Yafo) | 143,200 |
| Be'ér Sheva'(Beersheba) | 141,400 |
| Bene Beraq (★Tel Aviv-Yafo) | 125,000 |
| Elat | 33,300 |
| Giv'atayim (★Tel Aviv-Yafo) | 47,200 |
| Ḥadera | 56,100 |
| Ḥefa (★460,000) | 246,500 |
| Herzliyya (★Tel Aviv-Yafo) | 84,700 |
| Ḥolon (★Tel Aviv-Yafo) | 162,800 |
| Kefar Sava (★Tel Aviv-Yafo) | 65,800 |
| Lod (Lydda) (★Tel Aviv-Yafo) | 49,500 |
| Nazerat (Nazareth) (★77,000) | 52,200 |
| Netanya (★Tel Aviv-Yafo) | 142,700 |
| Petaḥ Tiqwa (★Tel Aviv-Yafo) | 151,100 |
| Ra'ananna (★Tel Aviv-Yafo) | 56,900 |
| Ramat Gan (★Tel Aviv-Yafo) | 122,800 |
| Ramla (★Tel Aviv-Yafo) | 55,500 |
| Reḥovot (★Tel Aviv-Yafo) | 83,200 |
| Rishon LeẔiyyon (★Tel Aviv-Yafo) | 154,300 |
| • Tel Aviv-Yafo (★1,887,200) | 357,400 |
| YERUSHALAYIM (AL-QUDS) (★604,000) | 567,100 |

**ITALY / Italia**

| | |
|---|---|
| 1991 C | 56,411,290 |
| Afragola (★Napoli) | 59,940 |
| Alessandria (▲93,351) | 74,000 |
| Altamura | 57,462 |
| Ancona | 103,268 |
| Andria | 82,556 |
| Arezzo (▲91,623) | 74,200 |
| Asti (▲74,497) | 62,800 |
| Avellino | 54,343 |
| Aversa (★Napoli) | 50,361 |
| Bari (★475,000) | 341,273 |
| Barletta | 86,215 |
| Benevento (▲62,683) | 51,900 |
| Bergamo (★345,000) | 115,655 |
| Biella | 50,993 |
| Bitonto | 49,792 |
| Bologna (★525,000) | 411,803 |
| Bolzano | 100,380 |
| Brescia | 196,766 |
| Brindisi | 91,778 |
| Busto Arsizio (★Milano) | 77,001 |
| Cagliari (★305,000) | 211,719 |
| Caltanissetta | 62,853 |
| Campobasso (▲51,307) | 44,400 |
| Carpi (▲60,794) | 49,600 |
| Carrara (★Massa) | 68,480 |
| Caserta | 68,811 |
| Casoria (▲79,315) (★Napoli) | 57,800 |
| Castellammare di Stabia (★Napoli) | 68,720 |
| Catania (★550,000) | 330,037 |
| Catanzaro | 103,802 |
| Cava de'Tirreni (★Salerno) | 52,610 |
| Cerignola | 54,971 |
| Cesena (▲89,497) | 72,200 |
| Chieti | 57,535 |
| Cinisello Balsamo (★Milano) | 75,606 |
| Civitavecchia | 50,856 |
| Collegno (★Torino) | 47,192 |
| Cologno Monzese (★Milano) | 50,853 |
| Como (★165,000) | 85,955 |
| Cosenza (★150,000) | 104,483 |
| Cremona | 75,160 |
| Crotone (▲61,813) | 54,300 |
| Cuneo (▲55,838) | 47,900 |
| Empoli (▲42,790) | 32,300 |
| Ercolano (★Napoli) | 60,869 |
| Ferrara (▲140,600) | 110,700 |
| Firenze (★640,000) | 402,316 |
| Foggia | 155,042 |
| Foligno (▲53,518) | 42,500 |
| Forlì (▲109,755) | 90,600 |
| Gela | 79,718 |
| Genova (Genoa) (★805,000) | 675,639 |
| Giugliano in Campania (★Napoli) | 59,091 |
| Grosseto (▲71,373) | 57,000 |
| Imola (▲62,352) | 48,800 |
| Imperia | 41,278 |
| L'Aquila (▲67,818) | 43,100 |
| La Spezia (★185,000) | 101,701 |
| Latina (▲105,543) | 72,700 |
| Lecce | 102,344 |
| Lecco | 45,859 |
| Legnano (★Milano) | 50,068 |
| Livorno | 171,265 |
| Lucca | 86,437 |
| Manfredonia | 58,157 |
| Mantova (▲54,228) | 46,800 |
| Marsala | 77,218 |
| Massa (★145,000) | 67,779 |
| Matera | 54,872 |
| Messina | 274,846 |
| Mestre (▲317,837) (★Venezia) | 181,900 |
| • Milano (Milan) (★3,750,000) | 1,371,008 |
| Modena | 177,501 |
| Molfetta | 66,658 |
| Moncalieri (★Torino) | 58,433 |
| Monopoli (▲43,019) | 33,100 |
| Monza (★Milano) | 121,151 |
| Napoli (Naples) (★2,875,000) | 1,024,601 |
| Nicastro (▲69,660) | 53,700 |
| Nocera Inferiore | 49,021 |
| Novara | 103,349 |
| Padova (★270,000) | 218,186 |
| Palermo | 697,162 |
| Parma | 173,991 |
| Pavia | 80,073 |
| Perugia (▲150,576) | 109,500 |
| Pesaro (▲90,341) | 78,700 |
| Pescara | 128,553 |
| Piacenza | 102,252 |
| Pisa | 101,500 |
| Pistoia (▲87,275) | 73,900 |
| Pordenone | 50,222 |
| Portici (★Napoli) | 67,824 |
| Potenza (▲68,499) | 58,800 |
| Pozzuoli (▲75,706) (★Napoli) | 67,100 |
| Prato (★215,000) | 165,364 |
| Quartu Sant'Elena | 60,852 |
| Ragusa | 69,423 |
| Ravenna (▲136,724) | 87,000 |
| Reggio di Calabria | 178,496 |
| Reggio nell'Emilia (▲131,880) | 108,800 |
| Rho (★Milano) | 51,646 |
| Rimini (▲130,896) | 114,800 |
| Rivoli (★Torino) | 51,884 |
| ROMA (★3,175,000) | 2,693,383 |
| Salerno (★250,000) | 153,436 |
| San Benedetto del Tronto | 45,220 |
| San Giorgio a Cremano (★Napoli) | 62,168 |
| San Remo | 59,247 |
| San Severo | 55,376 |
| Sassari | 120,011 |
| Savona (★112,000) | 68,997 |
| Scandicci (★Firenze) | 53,264 |
| Sesto Fiorentino (★Firenze) | 46,899 |
| Sesto San Giovanni (★Milano) | 85,175 |
| Siena | 57,745 |
| Siracusa | 125,444 |
| Taranto | 232,200 |
| Teramo (▲52,490) | 36,100 |
| Terni (▲109,809) | 93,400 |
| Torino (★1,550,000) | 961,916 |
| Torre Annunziata (★Napoli) | 50,346 |
| Torre del Greco (★Napoli) | 101,456 |
| Trani | 49,337 |
| Trapani (▲69,273) | 59,700 |
| Trento (▲102,124) | 83,100 |
| Treviso | 83,886 |
| Trieste (Triest) (Trst) | 231,047 |
| Udine (★126,000) | 98,322 |
| Varese | 85,461 |
| Venezia (Venice) (★420,000) | 85,100 |
| Vercelli | 50,207 |
| Verona | 258,946 |
| Viareggio (▲60,559) | 51,500 |
| Vicenza | 109,333 |
| Vigevano | 61,380 |
| Viterbo (▲60,213) | 48,700 |
| Vittoria | 56,970 |

**JAMAICA**

| | |
|---|---|
| 1991 C | 2,366,067 |
| • KINGSTON (★890,000) | 587,798 |
| Montego Bay | 83,446 |
| Portmore (★Kingston) | 90,138 |
| Spanish Town (★Kingston) | 92,383 |

**JAPAN / Nihon**

| | |
|---|---|
| 1990 C | 123,611,167 |
| Abiko (★Tōkyō) | 120,628 |
| Ageo (★Tōkyō) | 194,947 |
| Aizu-wakamatsu | 119,080 |
| Akashi (★Ōsaka) | 270,722 |
| Akigawa (★Tōkyō) | 50,387 |
| Akishima (★Tōkyō) | 105,372 |
| Akita | 302,362 |
| Akō | 51,131 |
| Amagasaki (★Ōsaka) | 498,999 |
| Anan (▲59,044) | 47,000 |
| Anjō | 142,251 |
| Aomori | 287,808 |
| Arao (★Ōmuta) | 59,507 |
| Asahikawa | 359,071 |
| Asaka (★Tōkyō) | 103,617 |
| Ashikaga | 167,686 |
| Ashiya (★Ōsaka) | 87,524 |
| Atami | 47,291 |
| Atsugi (★Tōkyō) | 197,282 |
| Ayase (★Tōkyō) | 77,926 |
| Beppu | 130,334 |
| Bisai (★Nagoya) | 55,880 |
| Chiba (★Tōkyō) | 829,455 |
| Chichibu | 60,915 |
| Chigasaki (★Tōkyō) | 201,675 |
| Chikushino (★Fukuoka) | 70,303 |
| Chiryū (★Nagoya) | 54,059 |
| Chita (★Nagoya) | 75,433 |
| Chitose | 78,946 |
| Chōfu (★Tōkyō) | 197,677 |
| Chōshi | 85,138 |
| Daitō (★Ōsaka) | 126,460 |
| Dazaifu (★Fukuoka) | 62,402 |
| Ebetsu (★Sapporo) | 97,201 |
| Ebina (★Tōkyō) | 105,822 |
| Eniwa | 55,615 |
| Fuchū | 45,739 |
| Fuchū | 50,060 |
| Fuchū (★Tōkyō) | 209,396 |
| Fuji (★370,000) | 222,490 |
| Fujieda (★Shizuoka) | 119,815 |
| Fujiidera (★Ōsaka) | 65,922 |
| Fujimi (★Tōkyō) | 94,864 |
| Fujinomiya (★Fuji) | 117,092 |
| Fujioka (▲60,981) | 50,100 |
| Fujisawa (★Tōkyō) | 350,330 |
| Fuji-yoshida | 54,804 |
| Fukaya (▲94,017) | 75,600 |
| Fukuchiyama (▲66,506) | 56,700 |
| Fukui | 252,743 |
| Fukuoka (★1,750,000) | 1,237,062 |
| Fukushima | 277,528 |
| Fukuyama | 365,612 |
| Funabashi (★Tōkyō) | 533,270 |
| Furukawa (▲64,230) | 51,200 |
| Fussa (★Tōkyō) | 58,062 |
| Gamagōri | 84,819 |
| Gifu | 410,324 |
| Ginowan | 75,905 |
| Gotemba | 79,557 |
| Gushikawa | 54,018 |
| Gyōda | 83,181 |
| Habikino (★Ōsaka) | 115,049 |
| Hachinohe | 241,057 |
| Hachiōji (★Tōkyō) | 466,347 |
| Hadano (★Tōkyō) | 155,620 |
| Hagi | 50,618 |
| Hakodate | 307,249 |
| Hamada | 49,135 |
| Hamakita | 81,157 |
| Hamamatsu | 534,620 |
| Hanamaki (▲70,514) | 55,000 |
| Handa (★Nagoya) | 99,550 |
| Hannō (★Tōkyō) | 73,214 |
| Hashima | 61,460 |
| Hasuda (★Tōkyō) | 59,706 |
| Hatogaya (★Tōkyō) | 56,440 |
| Hatsukaichi (★Hiroshima) | 63,441 |
| Hekinan | 65,899 |
| Higashihiroshima (★Hiroshima) | 94,209 |
| Higashikurume (★Tōkyō) | 113,818 |
| Higashimatsuyama | 84,394 |
| Higashimurayama (★Tōkyō) | 134,002 |
| Higashiōsaka (★Ōsaka) | 518,319 |
| Higashiyamato (★Tōkyō) | 75,132 |
| Hikari (★Tokuyama) | 47,611 |
| Hikone | 99,519 |
| Himeji (★660,000) | 454,360 |
| Himi (▲60,766) | 51,400 |
| Hino (★Tōkyō) | 165,928 |
| Hirakata (★Ōsaka) | 390,788 |
| Hiratsuka (★Tōkyō) | 245,950 |
| Hirosaki (▲174,704) | 133,800 |
| Hiroshima (★1,575,000) | 1,085,705 |
| Hita (▲64,695) | 57,100 |
| Hitachi | 202,141 |
| Hōfu | 117,634 |
| Honjō | 59,098 |
| Hōya (★Tōkyō) | 95,146 |
| Hyūga | 58,442 |
| Ibaraki (★Ōsaka) | 254,078 |
| Ichihara (★Tōkyō) | 257,716 |
| Ichikawa (★Tōkyō) | 436,596 |
| Ichinomiya (★Nagoya) | 262,434 |
| Ichinoseki (▲61,967) | 50,100 |
| Iida (▲91,859) | 64,700 |
| Iizuka (★110,000) | 83,131 |
| Ikeda (★Ōsaka) | 104,218 |
| Ikoma (★Ōsaka) | 99,604 |
| Imabari | 123,114 |
| Imari (▲60,882) | 50,000 |
| Ina (▲60,062) | 49,500 |
| Inagi (★Tōkyō) | 58,635 |
| Inazawa (★Nagoya) | 96,274 |
| Inuyama (★Nagoya) | 69,801 |
| Iruma (★Tōkyō) | 137,585 |
| Isahaya | 90,683 |
| Ise (Uji-yamada) | 104,164 |
| Isehara (★Tōkyō) | 89,567 |

▲ Population of an entire municipality, commune, or district, including rural area.
• Largest city in country.
★ Population or designation of the metropolitan area, including suburbs.
**C** Census. **E** Official estimate. **U** Unofficial estimate.

▲ Bevölkerung eines ganzen städtischen Verwaltungsgebietes, eines Kommunalbezirkes oder eines Distrikts, einschliesslich ländlicher Gebiete.
• Grösste Stadt des Landes.
★ Bevölkerung oder Bezeichnung der Stadtregion einschliesslich Vororte.
**C** Volkszählung. **E** Offizielle Schätzung. **U** Inoffizielle Schätzung.

| | |
|---|---|
| Isesaki | 115,938 |
| Ishinomaki | 121,976 |
| Itami (★Ōsaka) | 186,134 |
| Itō | 71,223 |
| Iwaki (Taira) | 355,812 |
| Iwakuni | 109,530 |
| Iwamizawa | 80,417 |
| Iwata | 83,521 |
| Iwatsuki (★Tōkyō) | 106,462 |
| Izumi (★Sendai) | 124,216 |
| Izumi (★Ōsaka) | 146,127 |
| Izumi-ōtsu (★Ōsaka) | 67,035 |
| Izumi-sano (★Ōsaka) | 88,866 |
| Izumo (▲82,679) | 69,600 |
| Joetsu | 130,116 |
| Jōyō (★Ōsaka) | 84,770 |
| Kadoma (★Ōsaka) | 142,297 |
| Kaga | 69,196 |
| Kagoshima | 536,752 |
| Kainan (★Wakayama) | 48,596 |
| Kaizuka (★Ōsaka) | 79,234 |
| Kakamigahara | 129,680 |
| Kakegawa (▲72,795) | 59,000 |
| Kakogawa (★Ōsaka) | 239,803 |
| Kamagaya (★Tōkyō) | 95,052 |
| Kamaishi | 52,484 |
| Kamakura (★Tōkyō) | 174,307 |
| Kameoka | 85,283 |
| Kamifukuoka (★Tōkyō) | 58,761 |
| Kanazawa | 442,868 |
| Kani (★Nagoya) | 80,012 |
| Kanoya (▲77,655) | 61,500 |
| Kanuma (▲90,043) | 74,900 |
| Karatsu (▲79,207) | 70,500 |
| Kariya (★Nagoya) | 120,126 |
| Kasai | 51,784 |
| Kasaoka (▲59,619) | 52,700 |
| Kashihara (★Ōsaka) | 115,554 |
| Kashiwa (★Tōkyō) | 305,058 |
| Kashiwara (★Ōsaka) | 76,819 |
| Kashiwazaki (▲88,309) | 75,300 |
| Kasuga (★Fukuoka) | 88,699 |
| Kasugai (★Nagoya) | 266,599 |
| Kasukabe (★Tōkyō) | 188,823 |
| Katano (★Ōsaka) | 65,308 |
| Katsuta | 109,825 |
| Kawachi-nagano (★Ōsaka) | 108,767 |
| Kawagoe (★Tōkyō) | 304,854 |
| Kawaguchi (★Tōkyō) | 438,680 |
| Kawanishi (★Ōsaka) | 141,253 |
| Kawasaki (★Tōkyō) | 1,173,603 |
| Kesennuma | 65,578 |
| Kimitsu (▲89,242) | 76,100 |
| Kiryū | 126,446 |
| Kisarazu | 123,433 |
| Kishiwada (★Ōsaka) | 188,563 |
| Kitaibaraki | 51,093 |
| Kitakyūshū (★1,525,000) | 1,026,455 |
| Kitami | 107,247 |
| Kitamoto (★Tōkyō) | 63,929 |
| Kiyose (★Tōkyō) | 67,539 |
| Kōbe (★Ōsaka) | 1,477,410 |
| Kōchi | 317,069 |
| Kodaira (★Tōkyō) | 164,013 |
| Kōfu | 200,626 |
| Koga (★Tōkyō) | 58,231 |
| Koganei (★Tōkyō) | 105,899 |
| Kokubunji (★Tōkyō) | 100,982 |
| Komae (★Tōkyō) | 74,189 |
| Komaki (★Nagoya) | 124,441 |
| Komatsu | 106,075 |
| Kōnan (★Nagoya) | 93,837 |
| Kōnosu (★Tōkyō) | 72,435 |
| Kōriyama | 314,642 |
| Koshigaya (★Tōkyō) | 285,259 |
| Kudamatsu (★Tokuyama) | 53,030 |
| Kuki (★Tōkyō) | 66,852 |
| Kumagaya | 152,124 |
| Kumamoto | 579,306 |
| Kunitachi (★Tōkyō) | 65,833 |
| Kurashiki | 414,693 |
| Kure (★Hiroshima) | 216,723 |
| Kuroiso (▲52,344) | 41,900 |
| Kurume | 228,347 |
| Kusatsu (★Ōsaka) | 94,767 |
| Kushiro | 205,639 |
| Kuwana (★Nagoya) | 97,909 |
| Kyōto (★Ōsaka) | 1,461,103 |
| Machida (★Tōkyō) | 349,050 |
| Maebashi | 286,261 |
| Maizuru | 96,333 |
| Marugame | 75,606 |
| Matsubara (★Ōsaka) | 135,919 |
| Matsudo (★Tōkyō) | 456,210 |
| Matsue | 142,956 |
| Matsumoto | 200,715 |
| Matsusaka | 118,725 |
| Matsuyama | 443,322 |
| Mihara | 85,518 |
| Miki (★Ōsaka) | 76,501 |
| Minō (★Ōsaka) | 122,120 |
| Misato (★Tōkyō) | 128,376 |
| Mishima (★Numazu) | 105,418 |
| Mitaka (★Tōkyō) | 165,564 |
| Mito | 234,968 |
| Miura (★Tōkyō) | 52,440 |
| Miyako | 58,503 |
| Miyakonojō (▲130,153) | 106,200 |
| Miyazaki | 287,352 |
| Mobara | 83,437 |
| Moriguchi (★Ōsaka) | 157,372 |
| Morioka | 235,434 |
| Moriyama | 58,561 |
| Mukō (★Ōsaka) | 52,928 |
| Munakata | 68,265 |
| Muroran (★195,000) | 117,855 |
| Musashimurayama (★Tōkyō) | 65,562 |
| Musashino (★Tōkyō) | 139,077 |
| Mutsu | 48,470 |
| Nabari | 68,933 |
| Nagahama | 55,485 |
| Nagano | 347,026 |
| Nagaoka | 185,938 |
| Nagaokakyō (★Ōsaka) | 77,191 |
| Nagareyama (★Tōkyō) | 140,059 |
| Nagasaki | 444,599 |
| Nagoya (★4,800,000) | 2,154,793 |
| Naha | 304,836 |
| Nakama (★Kitakyūshū) | 49,216 |
| Nakatsu | 66,388 |
| Nakatsugawa | 53,722 |
| Nanao | 50,103 |
| Nara (★Ōsaka) | 349,349 |
| Narashino (★Tōkyō) | 151,471 |
| Narita | 86,708 |
| Naruto | 64,575 |
| Naze | 46,306 |
| Neyagawa (★Ōsaka) | 256,524 |
| Niigata | 486,097 |
| Niihama | 129,149 |
| Niitsu (▲63,999) | 55,700 |
| Niiza (★Tōkyō) | 138,919 |
| Nishinomiya (★Ōsaka) | 426,909 |
| Nishio | 95,197 |
| Nobeoka | 130,624 |
| Noboribetsu (★Muroran) | 55,571 |
| Noda (★Tōkyō) | 114,475 |
| Nōgata | 62,530 |
| Noshiro (▲55,915) | 47,800 |
| Numazu (★495,000) | 211,732 |
| Obihiro | 167,384 |
| Ōbu (★Nagoya) | 69,720 |
| Ōdate (▲68,195) | 58,500 |
| Odawara | 193,417 |
| Ōgaki | 148,281 |
| Ōita | 408,501 |
| Ōkawa | 45,704 |
| Okaya | 59,849 |
| Okayama | 593,730 |
| Okazaki | 306,822 |
| Okegawa (★Tōkyō) | 69,029 |
| Okinawa | 105,845 |
| Ōme (★Tōkyō) | 125,960 |
| Ōmi-hachiman (★Ōsaka) | 66,066 |
| Ōmiya (★Tōkyō) | 403,776 |
| Ōmura | 73,435 |
| Ōmuta (★225,000) | 150,453 |
| Ōnojō (★Fukuoka) | 75,214 |
| Onomichi | 97,103 |
| Ōsaka (★16,900,000) | 2,623,801 |
| Ōta | 139,801 |
| Otaru (★Sapporo) | 163,211 |
| Ōtsu (★Ōsaka) | 260,018 |
| Owariashi (★Nagoya) | 65,675 |
| Oyama (▲142,262) | 120,000 |
| Sabae | 62,283 |
| Saga | 169,963 |
| Sagamihara (★Tōkyō) | 531,542 |
| Saijō | 56,821 |
| Saiki | 52,323 |
| Sakado (★Tōkyō) | 95,740 |
| Sakai (★Ōsaka) | 807,765 |
| Sakaide | 63,876 |
| Sakata | 100,811 |
| Saku (▲62,003) | 50,000 |
| Sakura (★Tōkyō) | 144,688 |
| Sakurai | 60,262 |
| Sanda (▲64,560) (★Ōsaka) | 54,500 |
| Sanjō | 85,823 |
| Sano | 83,484 |
| Sapporo (★1,900,000) | 1,671,742 |
| Sasebo | 244,677 |
| Satte | 54,342 |
| Sayama (★Tōkyō) | 157,309 |
| Sayama (★Ōsaka) | 54,319 |
| Seki | 68,386 |
| Sendai, Kagoshima pref. (▲71,735) | 58,000 |
| Sendai, Miyagi pref. (★1,175,000) | 918,398 |
| Sennan (★Ōsaka) | 60,065 |
| Seto | 126,340 |
| Settsu (★Ōsaka) | 87,453 |
| Shibata (▲78,170) | 63,600 |
| Shijōnawate (★Ōsaka) | 50,035 |
| Shiki (★Tōkyō) | 63,491 |
| Shimada (▲73,810) | 64,500 |
| Shimizu (★Shizuoka) | 241,523 |
| Shimodate (▲66,028) | 54,100 |
| Shimonoseki (★Kitakyūshū) | 262,635 |
| Shiogama (★Sendai) | 62,025 |
| Shizuoka (★975,000) | 472,196 |
| Sōka (★Tōkyō) | 206,132 |
| Suita (★Ōsaka) | 345,206 |
| Suwa | 52,464 |
| Suzuka | 174,105 |
| Tachikawa (★Tōkyō) | 152,824 |
| Tagajō (★Sendai) | 58,456 |
| Tagawa | 57,700 |
| Tajimi (★Nagoya) | 94,036 |
| Takaishi (★Ōsaka) | 65,086 |
| Takamatsu | 329,684 |
| Takaoka (★220,000) | 175,466 |
| Takarazuka (★Ōsaka) | 201,862 |
| Takasago (★Ōsaka) | 93,273 |
| Takasaki | 236,461 |
| Takatsuki (★Ōsaka) | 359,867 |
| Takayama | 65,243 |
| Takefu | 70,187 |
| Takikawa | 49,591 |
| Tama (★Tōkyō) | 144,489 |
| Tamano | 73,238 |
| Tanabe (▲69,859) | 59,100 |
| Tanashi (★Tōkyō) | 75,144 |
| Tatebayashi | 76,221 |
| Tenri | 68,815 |
| Tochigi | 86,216 |
| Toda (★Tōkyō) | 87,599 |
| Tōkai (★Nagoya) | 97,358 |
| Toki | 64,946 |
| Tokoname (★Nagoya) | 51,784 |
| Tokorozawa (★Tōkyō) | 303,040 |
| Tokushima | 263,356 |
| Tokuyama (★250,000) | 110,900 |
| • TŌKYŌ (★30,300,000) | 8,163,573 |
| Tomakomai | 160,118 |
| Tondabayashi (★Ōsaka) | 110,447 |
| Toride (★Tōkyō) | 81,665 |
| Tosu | 55,877 |
| Tottori | 142,467 |
| Toyama | 321,254 |
| Toyoake (★Nagoya) | 62,160 |
| Toyohashi | 337,982 |
| Toyokawa | 111,730 |
| Toyonaka (★Ōsaka) | 409,837 |
| Toyota | 332,336 |
| Tsu | 157,177 |
| Tsuchiura | 127,471 |
| Tsuruga | 68,041 |
| Tsuruoka | 99,889 |
| Tsushima (★Nagoya) | 59,343 |
| Tsuyama | 89,400 |
| Ube (★230,000) | 175,053 |
| Ueda | 119,435 |
| Ueno (▲60,242) | 51,400 |
| Uji (★Ōsaka) | 177,010 |
| Uozu | 49,514 |
| Urasoe | 89,994 |
| Urawa (★Tōkyō) | 418,271 |
| Urayasu (★Tōkyō) | 115,675 |
| Usa (▲50,829) | 38,600 |
| Ushiku | 60,693 |
| Utsunomiya | 426,795 |
| Uwajima | 68,034 |
| Wakayama (★495,000) | 396,553 |
| Wakkanai | 48,232 |
| Wakō (★Tōkyō) | 56,890 |
| Warabi (★Tōkyō) | 73,620 |
| Yachiyo (★Tōkyō) | 148,615 |
| Yaizu (★Shizuoka) | 112,186 |
| Yamagata | 249,487 |
| Yamaguchi | 129,461 |
| Yamato (★Tōkyō) | 194,866 |
| Yamato-kōriyama (★Ōsaka) | 92,949 |
| Yamato-takada (★Ōsaka) | 68,237 |
| Yao (★Ōsaka) | 277,568 |
| Yashio (★Tōkyō) | 72,473 |
| Yatsushiro (▲108,135) | 88,300 |
| Yawata (★Ōsaka) | 75,758 |
| Yokkaichi | 274,180 |
| Yokohama (★Tōkyō) | 3,220,331 |
| Yokosuka (★Tōkyō) | 433,358 |
| Yonago | 131,453 |
| Yonezawa | 94,760 |
| Yono (★Tōkyō) | 79,060 |
| Yotsukaidō (★Tōkyō) | 72,157 |
| Yukuhashi | 65,711 |
| Zama (★Tōkyō) | 112,102 |
| Zushi (★Tōkyō) | 56,704 |

**JERSEY**

| | |
|---|---|
| 1991 C | 84,082 |
| • SAINT HELIER (★46,500) | 28,123 |

**JORDAN / Al-Urdun**

| | |
|---|---|
| 1989 E | 3,111,000 |
| Al-Baq'ah (★'Ammān) | 63,985 |
| • 'AMMĀN (★1,625,000) | 936,300 |
| Ar-Ruṣayfah (★'Ammān) | 72,580 |
| As-Salṭ | 47,585 |
| Az-Zarqā' (★'Ammān) | 318,055 |
| Irbid | 167,785 |

**KAZAKHSTAN**

| | |
|---|---|
| 1991 E | 16,793,100 |
| Akmola | 286,000 |
| Aktau | 169,000 |
| Akt'ubinsk | 266,600 |
| • ALMATY (★1,190,000) | 1,156,200 |
| Arkalyk | 64,900 |
| Atyrau | 156,700 |
| Balchaš | 87,600 |
| Džetygara | 48,900 |
| Ekibastuz | 138,900 |
| Karaganda | 608,600 |
| Kentau | 65,100 |
| Kokčetav | 143,300 |
| Kustanaj | 233,900 |
| Kzyl-Orda | 158,200 |
| Leninogorsk | 69,500 |
| Leninsk | 73,000 |
| Pavlodar | 342,500 |
| Petropavlovsk | 248,300 |
| Rudnyj | 128,800 |
| Šachtinsk | 65,300 |
| Saran' | 62,600 |
| Šatpajev | 61,400 |
| Ščučinsk | 56,000 |
| Semipalatinsk | 344,700 |
| Šymkent | 438,800 |
| Taldykorgan | 136,100 |
| Temirtau | 213,100 |
| Turkestan | 81,200 |
| Ural'sk | 214,000 |
| Ust'-Kamenogorsk | 332,900 |
| Žambyl | 312,300 |
| Žanatas | 53,000 |
| Žezkazgan | 111,100 |
| Zyr'anovsk | 53,800 |

**KENYA**

| | |
|---|---|
| 1989 C | 21,397,000 |
| Eldoret | 104,900 |
| Kakamega | 47,300 |
| Kisii | 44,000 |
| Kisumu | 185,100 |
| Kitale | 53,000 |
| Machakos | 116,100 |
| Meru | 78,100 |
| Mombasa (1990E) | 537,000 |
| • NAIROBI (1990E) | 1,505,000 |
| Nakuru | 162,800 |
| Nyeri | 88,600 |
| Thika | 57,100 |

**KIRIBATI**

| | |
|---|---|
| 1990 C | 72,298 |
| BAIRIKI | 2,226 |
| • Bikenibeu | 5,055 |

**KOREA, NORTH / Chosŏn-minjujuŭi-inmīn-konghwaguk**

| | |
|---|---|
| 1981 E | 18,317,000 |
| Ch'ŏngjin | 490,000 |
| Haeju (1983E) | 213,000 |
| Hamhŭng (1970E) | 150,000 |
| Hŭngnam (1976E) | 260,000 |
| Kaesŏng | 259,000 |
| Kanggye (1967E) | 130,000 |
| Kimch'aek (Sŏngjin) (1967E) | 265,000 |
| Namp'o | 241,000 |
| • P'YŎNGYANG | 2,355,000 |
| Sinŭiju | 305,000 |
| Songnim (1944C) | 53,035 |
| Wŏnsan | 398,000 |

**KOREA, SOUTH / Taehan-min'guk**

| | |
|---|---|
| 1990 C | 43,520,199 |
| Andong | 116,932 |
| Ansan (★Sŏul) | 252,157 |
| Anyang (★Sŏul) | 480,668 |
| Bucheon (★Sŏul) | 667,777 |
| Changsŭngp'o | 48,614 |
| Changwŏn (★Masan) | 323,138 |
| Chech'on | 102,037 |
| Cheju | 232,687 |
| Chinhae | 120,207 |
| Chinju | 258,365 |
| Chŏmch'on | 47,802 |
| Ch'ŏnan | 211,382 |
| Ch'ŏngju | 497,429 |
| Chŏnju | 86,850 |
| Chŏnju | 517,104 |
| Ch'unch'ŏn | 174,153 |
| Ch'ungju | 129,994 |
| Ch'ungmu | 92,159 |
| Hanam (★Sŏul) | 101,278 |
| Inch'ŏn (★Sŏul) | 1,818,293 |
| Iri | 203,401 |
| Kangnŭng | 152,605 |
| Kimch'ŏn | 81,349 |
| Kimhae | 106,166 |
| Kimje | 55,136 |
| Kongju | 65,195 |
| Kumi | 206,107 |
| Kŭmsŏng (1985C) | 58,897 |
| Kunp'o (★Sŏul) | 99,956 |
| Kunsan | 218,216 |
| Kwachŏn (★Sŏul) | 72,328 |
| Kwangju | 1,144,695 |
| Kwangmyŏng (★Sŏul) | 328,803 |
| Kyŏngju | 141,895 |
| Kyŏngsan | 60,524 |
| Masan (★625,000) | 496,639 |
| Mikŭm (★Sŏul) | 74,688 |
| Miryang | 52,995 |
| Mokp'o | 253,423 |
| Naju | 55,306 |
| Namwŏn | 63,121 |
| Ŏnyang | 66,379 |
| Osan | 59,492 |
| P'ohang | 318,595 |
| Pusan (★3,800,000) | 3,797,566 |
| P'yŏngt'aek | 79,238 |
| Samch'ŏnp'o | 62,824 |
| Sangju | 51,875 |
| Shihŭng (★Sŏul) | 107,190 |
| Sŏgwipo | 88,292 |
| Sŏkch'o | 73,796 |
| Sŏngnam (★Sŏul) | 540,764 |
| Songtan | 77,460 |
| Sŏsan | 55,930 |
| • SŎUL (★15,850,000) | 10,627,790 |
| Sunch'ŏn | 167,209 |
| Suwŏn (★Sŏul) | 644,968 |
| T'aebaek | 89,770 |
| Taech'ŏn | 56,922 |
| Taegu | 2,228,834 |
| Taejŏn | 1,062,084 |
| Tongduchŏn | 71,448 |
| Tonghae | 89,162 |
| Tongkwang | 70,118 |
| Ŭijŏngbu (★Sŏul) | 212,368 |
| Ŭiwang | 96,892 |
| Ulsan | 682,978 |
| Wŏnju | 173,013 |
| Yŏch'ŏn | 63,802 |
| Yŏngch'ŏn | 48,890 |
| Yŏngju | 84,335 |
| Yŏsu | 173,164 |

**KUWAIT / Al-Kuwayt**

| | |
|---|---|
| 1985 C | 1,697,301 |
| Abraq Khīṭān (★Al-Kuwayt) | 45,120 |
| Al-Aḥmadī (★285,000) | 26,899 |
| Al-Farwānīyah (★Al-Kuwayt) | 68,701 |
| Al-Fuḥayḥīl (★Al-Aḥmadī) | 50,081 |
| Al-Jahrah (★Al-Kuwayt) | 111,222 |
| • AL-KUWAYT (★1,375,000) | 44,335 |
| As-Sālimīyah (★Al-Kuwayt) | 153,359 |
| Aṣ-Ṣulaybīyah (★Al-Kuwayt) | 51,314 |
| Ḥawallī (★Al-Kuwayt) | 145,126 |
| Qalīb ash-Shuyūkh (★Al-Kuwayt) | 114,771 |
| South Khīṭān (★Al-Kuwayt) | 69,256 |
| Subahiya (★Al-Aḥmadī) | 60,787 |

**KYRGYZSTAN**

| | |
|---|---|
| 1991 E | 4,422,200 |
| • BIŠKEK | 631,300 |
| Džalal-Abad | 79,900 |
| Kara-Balta | 55,000 |
| Karakol (Prževal'sk) | 64,300 |
| Oš | 238,200 |
| Tokmak | 71,200 |

**LAOS / Lao**

| | |
|---|---|
| 1985 C | 3,584,803 |
| Savannakhét (1975E) | 53,000 |
| • VIANGCHAN (VIENTIANE) | 377,409 |

**LATVIA / Latvija**

| | |
|---|---|
| 1991 E | 2,680,500 |
| Daugavpils | 129,000 |
| Jelgava | 74,500 |
| Jūrmala (★Rīga) | 66,500 |
| Liepāja | 114,900 |
| • RĪGA (★1,005,000) | 910,200 |
| Ventspils | 50,400 |

**LEBANON / Lubnān**

| | |
|---|---|
| 1982 E | 2,637,000 |
| • BAYRŪT (★1,675,000) | 509,000 |
| Ṣaydā | 105,000 |
| Ṣūr (Tyre) (1970E) | 12,500 |
| Ṭarābulus (Tripoli) | 198,000 |

**LESOTHO**

| | |
|---|---|
| 1986 C | 1,577,536 |
| • MASERU | 109,382 |

**LIBERIA**

| | |
|---|---|
| 1986 E | 2,221,000 |
| • MONROVIA | 465,000 |

**LIBYA / Lībiyā**

| | |
|---|---|
| 1988 E | 3,772,500 |
| Al-Bayḍā (Beida) (1984C) | 67,120 |
| Banghāzī (★472,000) | 446,250 |
| Darnah (1984C) | 62,179 |
| Misrātah (★160,000) | 121,669 |
| • ṬARĀBULUS (TRIPOLI) (★960,000) | 591,062 |
| Ṭubruq (Tobruk) (1984C) | 75,282 |

**LIECHTENSTEIN**

| | |
|---|---|
| 1992 E | 29,386 |
| • VADUZ | 4,887 |

**LITHUANIA / Lietuva**

| | |
|---|---|
| 1992 C | 3,746,400 |
| Alytus | 77,500 |
| Kaunas | 423,000 |
| Klaipėda (Memel) | 208,300 |
| Marijampole | 52,300 |
| Panevėžys | 132,300 |
| Šiauliai | 149,000 |
| • VILNIUS | 596,900 |

**LUXEMBOURG**

| | |
|---|---|
| 1991 C | 384,062 |
| Esch-sur-Alzette (★83,000) | 24,012 |
| • LUXEMBOURG (★136,000) | 75,377 |

▲ Población de un municipio, comuna o distrito entero, incluyendo sus áreas rurales.
• Ciudad más grande de un país.
★ Población o designación de un área metropolitana, incluyendo los suburbios.
**C** Censo. **E** Estimado oficial. **U** Estimado no oficial.

▲ Population d'une municipalité, d'une commune ou d'un district, zone rurale incluse.
• Ville la plus peuplée du pays.
★ Population de l'agglomération (ou nom de la zone métropolitaine englobante).
**C** Recensement. **E** Estimation officielle. **U** Estimation non officielle.

▲ População de um municipio, comuna ou distrito, inclusive as respectivas áreas rurais.
• Maior cidade de um país.
★ População ou indicação de uma área metropolitana.
**C** Censo. **E** Estimativa oficial. **U** Estimativa não oficial.

**MACAU**
1991 C 403,038
• MACAU 342,548

**MACEDONIA / Makedonija**
1994 C 1,936,877
Bitola 75,386
Kumanovo 66,237
Ohrid 41,213
Prilep 67,371
• SKOPJE 440,577
Štip 41,637

**MADAGASCAR / Madagasikara**
1988 E 11,238,000
• ANTANANARIVO 1,250,000
Antsirabe 100,000
Antsiranana 220,000
Fianarantsoa 300,000
Mahajanga 200,000
Toamasina 230,000
Toliara 150,000

**MALAWI / Malaŵi**
1987 C 7,988,507
• Blantyre 333,120
LILONGWE 223,318
Mzuzu 51,904

**MALAYSIA**
1991 C 17,566,982
Alor Setar (★165,113) 125,026
Batu Pahat (★84,538) 71,132
Butterworth (★94,231) (★George Town) 78,672
George Town (Pinang) (★520,000) 219,376
Ipoh (★468,765) 382,633
Johor Baharu (★442,250) (★Singapore, Singapore) 328,646
Kajang (★99,914) 46,269
Kelang (★368,228) 243,698
Keluang (★98,837) 49,043
Kota Baharu (★234,604) 219,713
Kota Kinabalu (Jesselton) (★160,122) 75,787
• KUALA LUMPUR (★1,800,000) 1,145,075
Kuala Terengganu 228,659
Kuantan 198,356
Kuching (★277,346) 147,729
Melaka (★112,873) 74,962
Miri (★102,969) 87,230
Muar (Bandar Maharani) (★70,637) 63,123
Petaling Jaya (★351,719) (★Kuala Lumpur) 254,849
Port Dickson (★47,962) 25,792
Sandakan (★157,180) 126,092
Seremban (★193,009) 182,584
Shah Alam (★Kuala Lumpur) 101,733
Sibu (★133,471) 126,384
Sungai Petani 115,519
Taiping 183,165
Telok Anson (★62,393) 48,350

**MALDIVES**
1990 C 213,215
• MALE' 55,130

**MALI**
1987 C 7,696,348
• BAMAKO 658,275
Gao 55,266
Kayes 50,993
Koutiala 48,698
Mopti 74,771
Ségou 88,135
Sikasso 73,859
Tombouctou (Timbuktu) 31,962

**MALTA**
1991 E 355,910
• VALLETTA (★215,000) 9,199

**MARSHALL ISLANDS**
1988 C 43,380
• Jarej-Uliga-Delap 14,649

**MARTINIQUE**
1990 C 359,579
• FORT-DE-FRANCE (★116,400) 100,072

**MAURITANIA / Mauritanie / Mūrītāniyā**
1987 E 2,007,000
• NOUAKCHOTT 285,000

**MAURITIUS**
1989 E 1,081,669
Beau Bassin-Rose Hill (★Port Louis) 94,236
Curepipe (★Port Louis) 66,704
• PORT LOUIS (★525,000) 141,870
Quatre Bornes (★Port Louis) 65,759
Vacoas-Phoenix (★Port Louis) 56,335

**MAYOTTE**
1985 E 67,205
• DZAOUDZI (★6,979) 5,865

**MEXICO / México**
1990 C 81,249,645
Acámbaro 52,248
Acapulco de Juárez 515,374
Aguascalientes 440,425
Apatzingán de la Constitución 76,643
Apocaca 103,364
Atlixco 74,233
Buenavista 114,653
Campeche 150,518
Cancún 167,730
Cárdenas 61,017
Celaya 214,856
Chalco (★Ciudad de México) 224,190
Chetumal 94,158
Chicoloapan de Juárz 57,306
Chihuahua 516,153
Chilpancingo de los Bravo 97,165
Chimalhuacán 235,587
Cholula de Rivadabia (★Puebla) 53,673
Ciudad Acuña 52,983
Ciudad del Carmen 83,806
• CIUDAD DE MÉXICO (★14,100,000) 8,235,744
Ciudad Guzmán 72,619
Ciudad Hidalgo 48,476
Ciudad Juárez (★El Paso, Tex., U.S.A.) 789,522
Ciudad Lerdo (★Torreón) 46,593
Ciudad López Mateos 315,059
Ciudad Madero (★Tampico) 160,331
Ciudad Mante 76,799
Ciudad Obregón 219,980
Ciudad Valles 91,402
Ciudad Victoria 194,996
Coacalco 151,255
Coatzacoalcos 198,817
Colima 106,967
Comitan de Dominguez 48,299
Córdoba 130,695
Cortazar 45,579
Cuautitlán Izcalli (★Ciudad de México) 313,238
Cuernavaca 279,187
Culiacán 415,046
Delicias 87,412
Durango 348,036
Ecatepec (★Ciudad de México) 1,218,135
Ensenada 169,426
Fresnillo 75,118
Garza García (★Monterrey) 113,017
General Escobedo 96,962
Gómez Palacio (★Torreón) 164,092
Guadalajara (★2,325,000) 1,650,042
Guadalupe (★Monterrey) 535,332
Guadalupe 46,433
Guamúchil 49,635
Guanajuato 73,108
Guasave 49,338
Guaymas 87,484
Hermosillo 406,417
Heroica Zitácuaro 66,983
Hidalgo del Parral 88,197
Iguala 83,412
Irapuato 265,042
Ixtapaluca 115,711
Jiutepec 82,845
Juchitán de Zaragoza 53,666
Lagos de Moreno 63,646
La Paz 137,641
La Piedad de Cabadas 62,625
Las Choapas 43,868
León 758,279
Los Mochis 162,659
Los Reyes la Paz 134,544
Manzanillo 67,697
Matamoros (★Brownsville, Tex., U.S.A.) 266,055
Matehuala 54,713
Mazatlán 262,705
Mérida 523,422
Metepec 116,203
Mexicali (★460,000) 438,377
Minatitlán 142,060
Monclova 177,792
Monterrey (★2,015,000) 1,068,996
Morelia 428,486
Naucalpan de Juárez (★Ciudad de México) 845,960
Navojoa 82,618
Nezahualcóyotl (★Ciudad de México) 1,255,456
Nogales 105,873
Nuevo Laredo (★Laredo, Tex., U.S.A.) 218,413
Oaxaca de Juárez 212,818
Ocotlán 62,595
Orizaba (★215,000) 114,216
Pachuca 174,013
Papantla de Olarte 46,075
Piedras Negras 96,178
Poza Rica 151,739
Puebla (★1,200,000) 1,007,170
Puerto Vallarta 93,503
Querétaro 385,503
Reynosa 265,663
Río Bravo 67,092
Sahuayo de José María Morelos 50,463
Salamanca 123,190
Salina Cruz 61,656
Saltillo 420,947
San Andrés Tuxtla 49,658
San Cristóbal de las Casas 73,388
San Francisco del Rincón 52,291
San Juan del Río 61,652
San Luis Potosí (★600,000) 489,238
San Luis Río Colorado 95,461
San Martín Texmelucan 57,519
San Miguel de Allende 48,935
San Nicolás de los Garza (★Monterrey) 436,603
San Pablo de las Salinas 84,217
Santa Catarina (★Monterrey) 162,707
Silao 50,828
Soledad de Graciano Sanchez 123,943
Tampico (★440,000) 272,690
Tapachula 138,858
Tecomán 60,938
Tehuacán 139,450
Temixco 65,058
Tepatitlán de Morelos 54,036
Tepic 206,967
Texcoco de Mora (★Ciudad de México) 74,194
Tijuana (★San Diego, Calif., U.S.A.) 698,752
Tlalnepantla (★Ciudad de México) 702,270
Tlaquepaque (★Guadalajara) 328,031
Tlaxcala de Xicotencatl 50,486
Toluca de Lerdo 327,865
Tonalá 151,190
Torreón (★690,000) 439,436
Tulancingo 75,477
Tuxpan 69,224
Tuxtepec 62,788
Tuxtla Gutiérrez 289,626
Uruapan del Progreso 187,623
Valle de Santiago 56,009
Veracruz (★540,000) 438,821
Villa Frontera 58,216
Villahermosa 261,231
Villa Nicolás Romero 148,342
Xalapa 279,451
Zacatecas 100,051
Zamora de Hidalgo 109,751
Zapopan (★Guadalajara) 668,323

**MICRONESIA, FEDERATED STATES OF**
1985 C
• KOLONIA 6,169

**MOLDOVA**
1991 E 4,366,300
Bălţi 164,900
• CHIŞINĂU (KISHINEV) 676,700
Rîbniţa (Rybnica) 62,900
Tighina 141,500
Tiraspol 186,000

**MONACO**
1990 C 29,972
• MONACO (★87,000) 29,972

**MONGOLIA / Mongol Ard Uls**
1991 E 2,250,000
Darchan 88,600
Erdene 58,200
• ULAANBAATAR 575,000

**MONTSERRAT**
1980 C 11,606
• PLYMOUTH 1,568

**MOROCCO / Al-Magreb**
1982 C 20,419,555
Agadir 110,479
Beni-Mellal 95,003
Berkane 60,490
• Casablanca (Dar-el-Beida) (★2,475,000) 2,139,204
El-Jadida (Mazagan) 81,455
Fès (★535,000) 448,823
Kenitra 188,194
Khemisset 58,925
Khouribga 127,181
Ksar-el-Kebir 73,541
Larache 63,893
Marrakech (★535,000) 439,728
Meknès (★375,000) 319,783
Mohammedia (Fedala) (★Casablanca) 105,120
Nador 62,040
Oued-Zem 58,744
Oujda 260,082
RABAT (★980,000) 518,616
Safi 197,309
Salé (★Rabat) 289,391
Settat 65,203
Sidi Kacem 55,833
Sidi Slimane 50,457
Tanger (Tangier) (★370,000) 266,346
Tan-Tan 41,451
Taza 77,216
Temera (★Rabat) 48,644
Tétouan 199,615

**MOZAMBIQUE / Moçambique**
1989 E 15,326,476
Beira 291,604
Chimoio (1986E) 86,928
Inhambane (1986E) 64,274
• MAPUTO 1,069,727
Nacala 101,615
Nampula 197,379
Pemba (1986E) 50,215
Quelimane 78,520
Tete (1986E) 56,178
Xai-Xai (1986E) 51,620

**MYANMAR (BURMA)**
1983 C 34,124,908
Bago (Pegu) 150,528
Chauk 51,437
Dawei (Tavoy) 69,882
Henzada 82,005
Kale 52,628
Lashio 88,590
Magway 54,881
Mandalay 532,949
Mawlamyine (Moulmein) 219,961
Maymyo 63,782
Meiktila 96,496
Mergui (Myeik) 88,600
Mogok 49,392
Monywa 106,843
Myingyan 77,060
Myitkyinā 56,427
Nyaunglebin 55,194
Pakokku 71,860
Pathein (Bassein) 144,096
Prome (Pyè) 83,332
Pyinmana 52,962
Sagaing 46,212
Shwebo 52,185
Sittwe (Akyab) 107,621
Taunggyi 108,231
Thaton 61,790
Toungoo 65,861
• YANGON (RANGOON) (★2,650,000) 2,513,023
Yenangyaung 62,582

**NAMIBIA**
1988 E 1,760,000
Walvis Bay (★22,999) (1991C) 12,383
• WINDHOEK 114,500

**NEPAL / Nepāl**
1991 C 18,491,097
Bhaktapur 61,405
Bharatpur 54,670
Butwal 44,272
Dhangaḍhī 44,753
Dharān 66,457
Hetaunḍā 53,836
Janakpur 54,710
• KĀTHMĀNDAU (★520,000) 421,258
Lalitpur 115,865
Mahendranagar 62,050
Nepālgañj 47,819
Pokharā 95,286
Wirātnagar 129,388
Wirgañj 69,005

**NETHERLANDS / Nederland**
1992 E 15,129,150
Alkmaar (★124,000) 91,817
Almelo 63,383
Alphen aan den Rijn 63,573
Amersfoort 104,390
Amstelveen (★Amsterdam) 71,939
• AMSTERDAM (★1,875,000) 713,407
Apeldoorn 148,745
Arnhem (★305,000) 132,928
Assen 50,880
Bergen op Zoom 47,259
Breda (★165,000) 126,709
Delft (★'s-Gravenhage) 90,066
Den Helder 61,225
Deventer 68,004
Dordrecht (★209,000) 111,791
Ede (▲96,044) 50,700
Eindhoven (★384,000) 193,966
Emmen (▲93,107) 37,000
Enschede (★252,000) 147,199
Geleen (★179,000) 33,922
Gouda 67,416
Groningen (★208,000) 169,387
Haarlem (★Amsterdam) 149,788
Haarlemmermeer (▲100,659) (★Amsterdam) 14,000
Heerlen (★267,500) 53,600
Helmond 70,574
Hengelo (★Enschede) 76,726
Hilversum (★Amsterdam) 84,674
Hoorn 59,028
IJmuiden (★Amsterdam) 61,506
Kerkrade (★Heerlen) 53,364
Leeuwarden 86,405
Leiden (★190,000) 112,976
Maastricht (★163,000) 118,152
Nieuwegein (★Utrecht) 58,882
Nijmegen (★242,000) 146,344
Oss 52,132
Purmerend (★Amsterdam) 62,504
Ridderkerk (★Rotterdam) 45,834
Rijswijk (★'s-Gravenhage) 47,456
Roosendaal 61,354
Rotterdam (★1,120,000) 589,707
Schiedam (★Rotterdam) 71,117
'S-GRAVENHAGE (THE HAGUE) (★773,000) 445,287
's-Hertogenbosch (★200,000) 93,171
Soest (★Amersfoort) 41,693
Spijkenisse (★Rotterdam) 69,655
Tilburg (★235,000) 160,618
Utrecht (★528,000) 232,705
Veenendaal 50,791
Venlo (★88,000) 64,890
Vlaardingen (★Rotterdam) 73,893
Vlissingen (Flushing) (▲43,913) 25,000
Zaanstad (★Amsterdam) 131,273
Zeist (★Utrecht) 59,211
Zoetermeer (★'s-Gravenhage) 100,623
Zwolle 97,131

**NETHERLANDS ANTILLES / Nederlandse Antillen**
1990 E 189,687
• WILLEMSTAD (★130,000) (1981C) 31,883

**NEW CALEDONIA / Nouvelle-Calédonie**
1989 C 164,173
• NOUMÉA (★97,581) 65,110

**NEW ZEALAND**
1991 C 3,434,950
• Auckland (★855,571) 315,668
Christchurch (★307,179) 292,858
Dunedin 116,577
Hamilton (★148,625) 101,448
Invercargill 56,148
Lower Hutt (★Wellington) 94,540
Manukau (★Auckland) 226,147
Napier (★110,216) 51,645
Palmerston North (★70,951) 70,318
Rotorua (★53,702) 45,144
Takapuna (★Auckland) 74,360
Tauranga (★70,803) 46,308
Waitemata (★Auckland) 136,716
WELLINGTON (★375,000) 150,301
Whangarei (★44,183) 40,101

**NICARAGUA**
1985 E 3,272,100
Chinandega 75,000
Granada (1981E) 64,642
León 101,000
• MANAGUA 682,000
Masaya 75,000
Matagalpa 68,000

**NIGER**
1988 C 7,220,089
Agadez 49,361
Maradi 104,386
• NIAMEY 392,165
Tahoua 49,948
Zinder 119,838

**NIGERIA**
1987 E 101,907,000
Aba 239,800
Abakaliki 56,800
Abeokuta 341,300
ABUJA (1993U) 250,000
Ado-Ekiti 287,000
Afikpo 65,790
Agege 83,810
Akure 129,600
Amaigbo 53,690
Apomu 49,570
Aramoko 48,280
Asaba 47,410
Awka 88,800
Azare 50,020
Bauchi 68,840
Benin City 183,200
Bida 100,200
Calabar 139,800
Deba 110,600
Duku 52,880
Ede 245,200
Effon-Alaiye 122,300
Ejigbo 84,570
Emure-Ekiti 58,750
Enugu 252,500
Epe 80,560
Erin-Oshogbo 59,940
Eruwa 49,140
Fiditi 49,440
Gboko 49,390
Gbongan 53,990
Gombe 86,120
Gusau 126,200
Ibadan 1,144,000
Idah 50,550
Idanre 56,080
Ife 237,000

▲ Population of an entire municipality, commune, or district, including rural area.
• Largest city in country.
★ Population or designation of the metropolitan area, including suburbs.
**C** Census. **E** Official estimate. **U** Unofficial estimate.

▲ Bevölkerung eines ganzen städtischen Verwaltungsgebietes, eines Kommunalbezirkes oder eines Distrikts, einschliesslich ländlicher Gebiete.
• Grösste Stadt des Landes.
★ Bevölkerung oder Bezeichnung der Stadtregion einschliesslich Vororte.
**C** Volkszählung. **E** Offizielle Schätzung. **U** Inoffizielle Schätzung.

| | |
|---|---|
| Ifon-Oshogbo | 65,980 |
| Igbasa-Odo | 48,040 |
| Igboho | 85,230 |
| Igbo-Ora | 68,060 |
| Igede-Ekiti | 56,570 |
| Ihiala | 73,240 |
| Ijebu-Igbo | 78,680 |
| Ijebu-Ode | 124,900 |
| Ijero-Ekiti | 76,420 |
| Ikare | 112,500 |
| Ikerre | 195,400 |
| Ikire | 94,450 |
| Ikirun | 144,900 |
| Ikole | 71,860 |
| Ikorodu | 147,700 |
| Ikot Ekpene | 69,440 |
| Ila | 210,800 |
| Ilawe-Ekiti | 147,300 |
| Ilesha | 302,100 |
| Ilobu | 159,000 |
| Ilorin | 380,000 |
| Inisa | 95,630 |
| Ipoti-Ekiti | 53,220 |
| Ise-Ekiti | 82,580 |
| Iseyin | 173,500 |
| Iwo | 289,100 |
| Jega (1985E) | 47,000 |
| Jimeta | 66,130 |
| Jos | 164,700 |
| Kaduna | 273,200 |
| Kano | 538,300 |
| Katsina | 165,000 |
| Kaura Namoda | 52,910 |
| Keffi | 57,790 |
| Kishi | 77,210 |
| Kumo | 118,200 |
| Lafia | 97,810 |
| Lafiagi | 57,580 |
| • LAGOS (★3,800,000) | 1,213,000 |
| Lalupon | 56,130 |
| Lere | 49,670 |
| Maiduguri | 255,100 |
| Makurdi | 98,350 |
| Minna | 109,300 |
| Mubi | 51,190 |
| Mushin (★Lagos) | 266,100 |
| Nguru | 78,770 |
| Nsukka | 47,760 |
| Ode-Ekiti | 48,910 |
| Offa | 157,500 |
| Ogbomosho | 582,900 |
| Oka | 114,400 |
| Oke-Mesi | 55,040 |
| Okwe | 52,550 |
| Olupona | 65,720 |
| Ondo | 135,300 |
| Onitsha | 298,200 |
| Opobo | 64,620 |
| Oron | 62,260 |
| Oshogbo | 380,800 |
| Owerri (1985E) | 37,000 |
| Owo | 146,600 |
| Oyan | 50,930 |
| Oyo | 204,700 |
| Pindiga | 64,130 |
| Port Harcourt | 327,300 |
| Potiskum | 56,490 |
| Sapele | 111,200 |
| Shagamu | 93,610 |
| Shaki | 139,000 |
| Shomolu (★Lagos) | 120,700 |
| Sokoto | 163,700 |
| Ugep | 81,910 |
| Umuahia | 52,550 |
| Uyo | 60,500 |
| Warri | 100,700 |
| Zaria | 302,800 |

**NIUE**

| | |
|---|---|
| 1989 C | 2,267 |
| • ALOFI | 706 |

**NORTHERN MARIANA ISLANDS**

| | |
|---|---|
| 1990 C | 43,345 |
| Chalan Kanoa | 2,549 |
| • Garapan | 3,904 |

**NORWAY / Norge**

| | |
|---|---|
| 1993 E | 4,299,231 |
| Bærum (★Oslo) | 89,774 |
| Bergen (▲218,105) | 192,747 |
| Drammen (★58,388) | 49,300 |
| Fredrikstad (★50,077) | 25,748 |
| Hammerfest (▲9,468) | 6,717 |
| Kristiansand (▲67,113) | 55,129 |
| Narvik (▲18,888) | 14,005 |
| • OSLO (★703,896) | 470,204 |
| Skien (▲48,454) | 29,807 |
| Stavanger (★102,267) | 97,721 |
| Tromsø (▲53,382) | 44,030 |
| Trondheim (▲140,718) | 132,301 |

**OMAN / 'Umān**

| | |
|---|---|
| 1983 E | 1,131,000 |
| • MASQAṬ (MUSCAT) | 30,000 |
| Maṭraḥ (1971E) | 14,000 |
| Ṣūr | 30,000 |

**PAKISTAN / Pākistān**

| | |
|---|---|
| 1981 C | 84,253,644 |
| Abbottābād (★65,996) | 32,188 |
| Ahmadpur East | 56,979 |
| Attock (★39,986) | 26,233 |
| Bahāwalnagar | 74,533 |
| Bahāwalpur (★180,263) | 152,009 |
| Bannu (★43,210) | 35,170 |
| Bhakkar | 41,934 |
| Chārsadda | 62,530 |
| Chīchāwatni | 50,241 |
| Chiniot | 105,559 |
| Chishtiān Mandi | 61,959 |
| Daska | 55,555 |
| Dera Ghāzi Khān | 102,007 |
| Dera Ismāīl Khān (★68,145) | 64,358 |
| Drigh Road Cantonment (★Karāchi) | 56,742 |
| Faisalabad (Lyallpur) | 1,104,209 |
| Gojra | 68,000 |
| Gujrānwāla (★658,753) | 600,993 |
| Gujrānwāla Cantonment (★Gujrānwāla) | 57,760 |
| Gujrāt | 155,058 |
| Hāfizābād | 83,464 |
| Hyderābād (★800,000) | 702,539 |
| Hyderābād Cantonment (★Hyderābād) | 48,990 |
| ISLĀMĀBĀD (★Rāwalpindi) | 204,364 |
| Jacobābād | 79,365 |
| Jarānwāla | 69,459 |
| Jhang Sadar | 195,558 |
| Jhelum (★106,462) | 92,646 |
| Kamālia | 61,107 |
| Kāmoke | 71,097 |
| • Karāchi (★5,300,000) | 4,901,627 |
| Karāchi Cantonment (★Karāchi) | 181,981 |
| Kasūr | 155,523 |
| Khairpur | 61,447 |
| Khānewāl | 89,090 |
| Khānpur | 70,589 |
| Khāriān Cantonment (★51,506) | 16,042 |
| Khushāb | 56,274 |
| Kohāt (★77,604) | 55,832 |
| Lahore (★3,025,000) | 2,707,215 |
| Lahore Cantonment (★Lahore) | 245,474 |
| Lārkāna | 123,890 |
| Leiah | 51,482 |
| Malir Cantonment (★Karāchi) | 47,588 |
| Mandi Būrewāla | 86,311 |
| Mardān (★147,977) | 141,842 |
| Miānwāli | 59,159 |
| Mingāora | 88,078 |
| Mīrpur Khās | 124,371 |
| Multān (★732,070) | 696,316 |
| Muzaffargarh | 53,000 |
| Nawābshāh | 102,139 |
| Nowshera (★74,913) | 38,875 |
| Okāra (★153,483) | 127,455 |
| Pākpattan | 69,820 |
| Peshāwar (★566,248) | 506,896 |
| Peshāwar Cantonment (★Peshāwar) | 59,352 |
| Quetta (★285,719) | 244,842 |
| Rahīmyār Khān (★132,635) | 119,036 |
| Rāwalpindi (★1,040,000) | 457,091 |
| Rāwalpindi Cantonment (★Rāwalpindi) | 337,752 |
| Sādiqābād | 63,935 |
| Sāhīwal | 150,954 |
| Sargodha (★291,362) | 231,895 |
| Sargodha Cantonment (★Sargodha) | 59,467 |
| Shekhūpura | 141,168 |
| Shikārpur | 88,138 |
| Shorkot (★50,568) | 18,533 |
| Siālkot (★302,009) | 258,147 |
| Sukkur | 190,551 |
| Tando Ādam | 62,744 |
| Turbat | 52,337 |
| Vihāri | 53,799 |
| Wāh Cantonment | 122,335 |
| Wazīrābād | 62,725 |

**PALAU / Belau**

| | |
|---|---|
| 1990 C | 15,122 |
| • KOROR | 9,018 |

**PANAMA / Panamá**

| | |
|---|---|
| 1990 C | 2,315,047 |
| Balboa (★Panamá) | 1,214 |
| Colón (★96,000) | 54,469 |
| David | 65,635 |
| • PANAMÁ (★770,000) | 411,549 |
| San Miguelito (★Panamá) | 242,529 |

**PAPUA NEW GUINEA**

| | |
|---|---|
| 1990 C | 3,534,038 |
| Lae | 78,265 |
| • PORT MORESBY | 193,242 |
| Rabaul | 16,883 |

**PARAGUAY**

| | |
|---|---|
| 1992 C | 4,123,550 |
| • ASUNCIÓN (★700,000) | 502,426 |
| Caaguazú | 38,200 |
| Capiatá | 83,189 |
| Ciudad del Este | 133,896 |
| Encarnación | 55,359 |
| Fernando de la Mora (★Asunción) | 95,287 |
| Lambaré (★Asunción) | 99,681 |
| Mariano Roque Alonso | 39,240 |
| Pedro Juan Caballero | 53,601 |
| San Lorenzo (★Asunción) | 133,311 |

**PERU / Perú**

| | |
|---|---|
| 1981 C | 17,031,221 |
| Arequipa (★446,942) | 108,023 |
| Ayacucho (★69,533) | 57,432 |
| Barranco (★Lima) | 46,478 |
| Breña (★Lima) | 112,398 |
| Cajamarca | 62,259 |
| Callao (★Lima) | 264,133 |
| Cerro de Pasco (★66,373) | 55,597 |
| Chiclayo (★279,527) | 213,095 |
| Chimbote | 223,341 |
| Chorrillos (★Lima) | 141,881 |
| Chosica | 65,139 |
| Cusco (★184,550) | 89,563 |
| Huacho | 43,398 |
| Huancayo (★164,954) | 84,845 |
| Huánuco | 61,812 |
| Ica | 114,786 |
| Iquitos | 178,738 |
| Jesús María (★Lima) | 83,179 |
| Juliaca | 87,651 |
| La Victoria (★Lima) | 270,778 |
| • LIMA (★4,608,010) | 371,122 |
| Lince (★Lima) | 80,456 |
| Magdalena (★Lima) | 55,535 |
| Miraflores (★Lima) | 103,453 |
| Pisco | 55,604 |
| Piura (★207,934) | 144,609 |
| Pucallpa | 112,263 |
| Pueblo Libre (★Lima) | 83,985 |
| Puno | 67,397 |
| Rímac (★Lima) | 184,484 |
| San Isidro (★Lima) | 71,203 |
| San Martin de Porras (★Lima) | 404,856 |
| Santiago de Surco (★Lima) | 146,636 |
| Sullana | 89,037 |
| Surquillo (★Lima) | 134,158 |
| Tacna | 97,173 |
| Talara | 57,351 |
| Trujillo (★354,301) | 202,469 |
| Tumbes | 47,936 |
| Vitarte (★Lima) | 145,504 |

**PHILIPPINES / Pilipinas**

| | |
|---|---|
| 1990 C | 60,559,116 |
| Angeles | 236,685 |
| Antipolo (▲207,842) | 83,641 |
| Bacolod | 364,180 |
| Bacoor (★Manila) | 159,685 |
| Baguio | 183,102 |
| Baliuag | 89,719 |
| Biñan (★Manila) | 134,553 |
| Binangonan | 127,561 |
| Bislig (▲103,510) | 59,619 |
| Bocaue | 67,243 |
| Butuan (▲227,829) | 100,940 |
| Cabanatuan (▲173,065) | 74,966 |
| Cagayan de Oro (▲339,598) | 252,453 |
| Cainta (★Manila) | 126,839 |
| Calamba (▲173,453) | 97,623 |
| Caloocan (★Manila) | 761,011 |
| Calumpit | 59,042 |
| Catarman (▲50,965) | 21,149 |
| Catbalogan (▲70,470) | 29,233 |
| Cavite (★195,000) | 91,641 |
| Cebu (★825,000) | 610,417 |
| Cotabato | 127,065 |
| Dagupan | 122,247 |
| Davao (▲849,947) | 521,525 |
| Digos (▲96,806) | 37,303 |
| Dumaguete | 80,262 |
| General Santos (Dadiangas) (▲250,389) | 152,907 |
| Guagua | 88,290 |
| Iloilo | 309,505 |
| Isabela (Basilan) (▲59,482) | 13,616 |
| Jolo | 53,055 |
| Kawit (★Cavite) | 47,755 |
| Koronadal (▲108,708) | 44,542 |
| Lapu-Lapu (Opon) | 146,194 |
| Las Piñas (★Manila) | 296,851 |
| Legaspi (▲121,116) | 62,974 |
| Lucena | 150,624 |
| Mabalacat (▲121,115) | 64,261 |
| Macabebe | 55,505 |
| Makati (★Manila) | 452,734 |
| Malabon (★Manila) | 278,380 |
| Malaybalay (▲94,790) | 24,906 |
| Malolos | 125,178 |
| Mandaluyong (★Manila) | 244,538 |
| Mandaue (★Cebu) | 180,285 |
| Mangalcan | 65,947 |
| • MANILA (★9,650,000) | 1,598,918 |
| Marawi | 91,901 |
| Marikina (★Manila) | 310,010 |
| Mariveles (▲60,761) | 52,000 |
| Mati (▲93,023) | 28,504 |
| Meycauayan (★Manila) | 123,982 |
| Muntinglupa (★Manila) | 276,972 |
| Naga | 115,329 |
| Navotas (★Manila) | 186,799 |
| Olongapo | 193,327 |
| Pagadian (▲106,307) | 47,737 |
| Parañaque (★Manila) | 307,717 |
| Pasay (★Manila) | 366,623 |
| Pasig (★Manila) | 397,309 |
| Pateros (★Manila) | 51,401 |
| Polomolok (▲89,372) | 43,399 |
| Puerto Princesa (▲92,147) | 47,461 |
| Pulilan | 48,199 |
| Quezon City (★Manila) | 1,666,766 |
| Sagay (▲105,713) | 47,326 |
| San Fernando | 157,851 |
| San Jose | 40,267 |
| San Juan del Monte (★Manila) | 126,708 |
| San Pablo (▲161,630) | 80,671 |
| San Pedro | 156,486 |
| Santa Cruz | 76,603 |
| Santa Rosa (★Manila) | 94,719 |
| Sorsogon (▲72,871) | 35,058 |
| Surigao (▲100,379) | 38,593 |
| Tacloban | 137,190 |
| Tagbilaran | 56,363 |
| Tagig (★Manila) | 266,080 |
| Tagum (▲135,440) | 60,865 |
| Tarlac (▲208,722) | 46,993 |
| Taytay (★Manila) | 112,403 |
| Valenzuela (★Manila) | 340,050 |
| Zamboanga (▲442,345) | 99,056 |

**PITCAIRN**

| | |
|---|---|
| 1988 C | 59 |
| • ADAMSTOWN | 59 |

**POLAND / Polska**

| | |
|---|---|
| 1993 E | 38,418,100 |
| Będzin (★Katowice) | 64,100 |
| Bełchatów | 58,300 |
| Biała Podlaska | 55,000 |
| Białystok | 274,100 |
| Bielsko-Biała | 179,700 |
| Bydgoszcz | 383,600 |
| Bytom (Beuthen) (★Katowice) | 229,200 |
| Chełm | 68,000 |
| Chorzów (★Katowice) | 128,800 |
| Częstochowa | 299,500 |
| Dąbrowa Górnicza (★Katowice) | 131,600 |
| Dzierżoniów (Reichenbach) (★90,000) | 38,400 |
| Elbląg (Elbing) | 127,300 |
| Ełk | 53,800 |
| Gdańsk (Danzig) (★892,000) | 461,700 |
| Gdynia (★Gdańsk) | 250,200 |
| Gliwice (Gleiwitz) (★Katowice) | 214,400 |
| Głogów | 73,300 |
| Gniezno | 70,600 |
| Gorzów Wielkopolski (Landsberg an der Warthe) | 124,600 |
| Grudziądz | 103,400 |
| Inowrocław | 79,000 |
| Jastrzębie-Zdrój | 104,200 |
| Jaworzno (★Katowice) | 98,500 |
| Jelenia Góra (Hirschberg) | 93,000 |
| Kalisz | 106,600 |
| • Katowice (★2,770,000) | 359,900 |
| Kędzierzyn Kozle | 71,000 |
| Kielce | 213,600 |
| Konin | 81,500 |
| Koszalin (Köslin) | 110,800 |
| Kraków (★823,000) | 744,000 |
| Krosno | 49,400 |
| Kutno | 50,900 |
| Legionowo (★Warszawa) | 50,600 |
| Legnica (Liegnitz) | 106,600 |
| Leszno | 60,200 |
| Łódź (★950,000) | 938,400 |
| Łomża | 61,500 |
| Lubin | 82,800 |
| Lublin (★388,000) | 350,400 |
| Mielec | 63,700 |
| Mysłowice (★Katowice) | 93,200 |
| Nowy Sącz | 80,500 |
| Olsztyn (Allenstein) | 164,900 |
| Opole (Oppeln) | 129,600 |
| Ostrołęka | 52,400 |
| Ostrowiec Świętokrzyski | 79,30 |
| Ostrów Wielkopolski | 74,10 |
| Pabianice (★Łódź) | 76,000 |
| Piekary Śląskie (★Katowice) | 67,800 |
| Piła (Schneidemühl) | 74,400 |
| Piotrków Trybunalski | 81,300 |
| Płock | 125,000 |
| Poznań (★666,000) | 582,900 |
| Pruszków (★Warszawa) | 53,000 |
| Przemyśl | 68,300 |
| Puławy | 54,300 |
| Racibórz (Ratibor) | 64,300 |
| Radom | 230,400 |
| Radomsko | 50,900 |
| Ruda Śląska (★Katowice) | 167,700 |
| Rybnik | 143,100 |
| Rzeszów | 156,700 |
| Siedlce | 73,000 |
| Siemianowice Śląskie (★Katowice) | 79,600 |
| Skarżysko-Kamienna | 51,300 |
| Słupsk (Stolp) | 102,000 |
| Sopot (★Gdańsk) | 45,000 |
| Sosnowiec (★Katowice) | 251,300 |
| Stalowa Wola | 71,200 |
| Starachowice | 57,300 |
| Stargard Szczeciński (Stargard in Pommern) | 72,200 |
| Starogard Gdański | 50,100 |
| Suwałki | 63,900 |
| Świdnica (Schweidnitz) | 64,300 |
| Świętochłowice (★Katowice) | 60,200 |
| Świnoujście (Swinemünde) | 43,300 |
| Szczecin (Stettin) (★448,000) | 416,400 |
| Tarnobrzeg | 49,900 |
| Tarnów | 121,900 |
| Tarnowskie Góry (★Katowice) | 76,900 |
| Tczew | 59,900 |
| Tomaszów Mazowiecki | 69,900 |
| Toruń | 201,800 |
| Tychy (★Katowice) | 136,600 |
| Wałbrzych (Waldenburg) (★207,000) | 140,600 |
| WARSZAWA (★2,312,000) | 1,644,500 |
| Włocławek | 122,300 |
| Wodzisław Śląski | 88,400 |
| Wrocław (Breslau) | 640,700 |
| Zabrze (Hindenburg) (★Katowice) | 203,500 |
| Zamość | 64,300 |
| Zawiercie | 56,500 |
| Zgierz (★Łódź) | 59,000 |
| Zielona Góra (Grünberg) | 115,100 |
| Żory | 66,200 |

**PORTUGAL**

| | |
|---|---|
| 1981 C | 9,833,014 |
| Amadora (★Lisboa) | 95,518 |
| Barreiro (★Lisboa) | 50,863 |
| Braga | 63,033 |
| Coimbra | 74,616 |
| • LISBOA (★2,250,000) | 807,167 |
| Ponta Delgada | 21,187 |
| Porto (★1,225,000) | 327,368 |
| Setúbal | 77,885 |
| Vila Nova de Gaia (★Porto) | 62,469 |

**PUERTO RICO**

| | |
|---|---|
| 1990 C | 3,522,037 |
| Arecibo (★160,500) | 49,545 |
| Bayamón (▲220,262) (★San Juan) | 202,103 |
| Caguas (▲133,447) (★San Juan) | 92,429 |
| Carolina (▲177,806) (★San Juan) | 162,404 |
| Guaynabo (▲92,886) (★San Juan) | 73,385 |
| Mayagüez (★200,600) | 83,010 |
| Ponce (★232,700) | 159,151 |
| • SAN JUAN (★1,877,000) | 426,832 |

**QATAR / Qaṭar**

| | |
|---|---|
| 1986 C | 369,079 |
| • AD-DAWḤAH (DOHA) (★310,000) | 217,294 |
| Ar-Rayyān (★Ad-Dawḥah) | 91,996 |

**REUNION / Réunion**

| | |
|---|---|
| 1982 C | 515,814 |
| • SAINT-DENIS (▲109,072) | 84,400 |

**ROMANIA / România**

| | |
|---|---|
| 1992 C | 22,760,449 |
| Alba Iulia | 71,254 |
| Alexandria | 58,582 |
| Arad | 190,088 |
| Bacău | 204,495 |
| Baia Mare | 148,815 |
| Bistrița | 87,793 |
| Botoșani | 126,204 |
| Brăila | 234,706 |
| • BUCUREȘTI (BUCHAREST) (★2,300,000) | 2,064,474 |
| Buzău | 148,247 |
| Călărași | 76,886 |
| Cluj-Napoca | 328,008 |
| Constanța | 350,476 |
| Craiova | 303,520 |
| Deva | 78,366 |
| Drobeta-Turnu Severin | 115,526 |
| Focșani | 101,296 |
| Galați | 325,788 |
| Giurgiu | 74,236 |
| Hunedoara | 81,198 |
| Iași | 342,994 |
| Lugoj | 50,983 |
| Medgidia | 46,586 |
| Mediaș | 64,488 |
| Miercurea-Ciuc | 46,029 |
| Onești | 59,008 |
| Oradea | 220,848 |
| Petroșani (★76,000) | 52,532 |
| Piatra Neamț | 123,175 |
| Pitești | 179,479 |
| Ploiești (★310,000) | 252,073 |
| Râmnicu Vâlcea | 113,356 |
| Reșița | 96,798 |
| Roman | 80,192 |
| Satu Mare | 131,859 |
| Sfântu Gheorghe | 68,070 |
| Sibiu | 169,696 |
| Slatina | 85,336 |
| Slobozia | 55,614 |
| Suceava | 114,355 |
| Târgoviște | 97,876 |
| Târgu Jiu | 98,267 |
| Târgu Mureș | 163,625 |

▲ Población de un municipio, comuna o distrito entero, incluyendo sus áreas rurales.
• Ciudad más grande de un país.
★ Población o designación de un área metropolitana, incluyendo los suburbios.
**C** Censo. **E** Estimado oficial. **U** Estimado no oficial.

▲ Population d'une municipalité, d'une commune ou d'un district, zone rurale incluse.
• Ville la plus peuplée du pays.
★ Population de l'agglomération (ou nom de la zone métropolitaine englobante).
**C** Recensement. **E** Estimation officielle. **U** Estimation non officielle.

▲ População de um municipio, comuna ou distrito, inclusive as respectivas áreas rurais.
• Maior cidade de um país.
★ População ou indicação de uma área metropolitana.
**C** Censo. **E** Estimativa oficial. **U** Estimativa não oficial.

| | |
|---|---|
| Tecuci | 46,735 |
| Timişoara | 334,278 |
| Tulcea | 97,500 |
| Turda | 61,135 |
| Vaslui | 80,151 |
| Zalău | 68,322 |

**RUSSIA**

| | |
|---|---|
| 1991 E | 148,542,700 |
| Abakan | 157,300 |
| Achtubinsk | 50,800 |
| Ačinsk | 122,000 |
| Alapajevsk | 50,300 |
| Alatyr' | 47,700 |
| Aleksandrov | 68,600 |
| Aleksin | 74,200 |
| Al'metjevsk | 132,700 |
| Amursk | 59,600 |
| Anapa | 55,900 |
| Angarsk | 268,500 |
| Anžero-Sudžensk | 107,000 |
| Apatity | 88,600 |
| Archangel'sk | 420,400 |
| Armavir | 162,200 |
| Arsenjev | 71,200 |
| Art'om | 70,100 |
| Arzamas | 111,800 |
| Asbest | 84,900 |
| Astrachan' | 511,900 |
| Azov | 80,700 |
| Balakovo | 201,300 |
| Balašicha (★Moskva) | 137,600 |
| Balašov | 97,300 |
| Barnaul (★673,000) | 606,800 |
| Batajsk (★Rostov-na-Donu) | 93,300 |
| Belebej | 54,500 |
| Belgorod | 311,400 |
| Belogorsk | 74,300 |
| Belorečensk | 51,900 |
| Beloreck | 73,100 |
| Belovo | 92,900 |
| Berdsk (★Novosibirsk) | 80,400 |
| Berezniki | 199,700 |
| Ber'ozovskij | 51,900 |
| Bijsk | 234,600 |
| Birobidžan | 86,300 |
| Blagoveščensk | 211,000 |
| Bor (★Nižnij Novgorod) | 64,500 |
| Borisoglebsk | 72,100 |
| Boroviči | 62,800 |
| Br'ansk | 458,900 |
| Bratsk | 259,400 |
| Bud'onnovsk | 57,500 |
| Bugul'ma | 91,100 |
| Buguruslan | 54,100 |
| Buj | 62,900 |
| Bujnaksk | 57,900 |
| Buzuluk | 85,100 |
| Čajkovskij | 88,300 |
| Čapajevsk | 96,000 |
| Čebarkul' | 50,700 |
| Čeboksary | 436,000 |
| Čechov | 60,200 |
| Čel'abinsk (★1,325,000) | 1,148,300 |
| Čeremchovo | 73,600 |
| Čerepovec | 315,900 |
| Čerkessk | 117,000 |
| Černogorsk | 79,700 |
| Chabarovsk | 613,300 |
| Chasavjurt | 72,800 |
| Chimki (★Moskva) | 135,500 |
| Cholmsk | 51,800 |
| Čistopol' | 66,600 |
| Čita | 376,300 |
| Čusovoj | 58,000 |
| Dal'negorsk | 50,300 |
| Derbent | 81,500 |
| Dimitrovgrad | 127,000 |
| Dmitrov | 65,600 |
| Dolgoprudnyj (★Moskva) | 71,100 |
| Domodedovo (★Moskva) | 56,300 |
| Doneck | 48,900 |
| Dubna | 67,200 |
| Dzeržinsk (★Nižnij Novgorod) | 286,700 |
| Elektrostal' | 153,000 |
| Elista | 92,700 |
| Engel's (★Saratov) | 183,600 |
| Fr'azino (★Moskva) | 54,000 |
| Furmanov | 45,900 |
| Gatčina (★Sankt-Peterburg) | 80,600 |
| Gelendžik | 48,600 |
| Georgijevsk | 63,700 |
| Georgiu-Dež | 54,600 |
| Glazov | 106,000 |
| Gorno-Altajsk | 47,500 |
| Gr'azi | 47,700 |
| Groznyj | 401,400 |
| Gubkin | 76,400 |
| Gukovo | 67,700 |
| Gus'-Chrustal'nyj | 77,000 |
| Inta | 60,900 |
| Irbit | 51,300 |
| Irkutsk | 640,500 |
| Išim | 65,900 |
| Išimbaj | 71,000 |
| Iskitim | 68,700 |
| Ivanovo | 482,200 |
| Ivantejevka (★Moskva) | 53,200 |
| Iževsk | 646,800 |
| Jakutsk | 193,300 |
| Jarcevo | 54,000 |
| Jaroslavl' | 638,100 |
| Jefremov | 56,600 |
| Jegorjevsk | 74,200 |
| Jejsk | 79,400 |
| Jelec | 121,300 |
| Jelizovo | 48,700 |
| Jermolajevo | 65,600 |
| Jessentuki | 86,300 |
| Joškar-Ola | 247,800 |
| Jurga | 94,000 |
| Južno-Sachalinsk | 164,000 |
| Kaliningrad (★Moskva) | 161,500 |
| Kaliningrad (Königsberg) | 408,100 |
| Kaluga | 315,500 |
| Kamensk-Šachtinskij | 73,100 |
| Kamensk-Ural'skij | 208,700 |
| Kamyšin | 124,400 |
| Kanaš | 56,100 |
| Kandalakša | 54,300 |
| Kansk | 109,900 |
| Kaspijsk | 61,900 |
| Kazan' (★1,165,000) | 1,107,300 |
| Kemerovo | 520,700 |
| Kimry | 62,000 |
| Kinel' | 33,800 |
| Kinešma | 104,900 |
| Kingisepp | 50,600 |
| Kiriši | 53,100 |
| Kirov | 491,200 |
| Kirovo-Čepeck | 95,600 |
| Kisel'ovsk (★Prokopjevsk) | 126,900 |
| Kislovodsk | 116,800 |
| Kizel | 36,600 |
| Klimovsk (★Moskva) | 57,600 |
| Klin | 95,100 |
| Klincy | 71,200 |
| Kogalym | 48,200 |
| Kol'čugino | 45,600 |
| Kolomna | 163,500 |
| Kolpino (★Sankt-Peterburg) | 144,500 |
| Komsomol'sk-na-Amure | 318,800 |
| Kopejsk (★Čel'abinsk) | 78,300 |
| Korkino | 44,800 |
| Korsakov | 45,300 |
| Kostroma | 281,800 |
| Kotlas | 68,900 |
| Kovrov | 161,900 |
| Krasnodar | 631,200 |
| Krasnogorsk (★Moskva) | 91,700 |
| Krasnojarsk | 924,400 |
| Krasnokamensk | 57,800 |
| Krasnokamsk | 67,000 |
| Krasnoturjinsk | 67,200 |
| Krasnoufimsk | 46,100 |
| Krasnoural'sk | 34,800 |
| Krasnyj Sulin | 43,200 |
| Kropotkin | 76,600 |
| Krymsk | 51,100 |
| Kstovo (★Nižnij Novgord) | 65,300 |
| Kujbyšev | 51,600 |
| Kungur | 81,800 |
| Kurgan | 363,800 |
| Kursk | 433,300 |
| Kušva | 43,300 |
| Kuzneck | 100,000 |
| Kyzyl | 88,000 |
| Labinsk | 58,600 |
| Leninogorsk | 63,300 |
| Leninsk-Kuzneckij | 133,400 |
| Lesosibirsk | 69,300 |
| Lipeck | 460,100 |
| Livny | 52,600 |
| Lobn'a (★Moskva) | 61,000 |
| L'ubercy (★Moskva) | 164,900 |
| Lys'va | 77,800 |
| Lytkarino (★Moskva) | 51,700 |
| Machačkala | 333,500 |
| Magadan | 154,900 |
| Magnitogorsk | 443,900 |
| Majkop | 152,500 |
| Mcensk | 49,200 |
| Meleuz | 55,200 |
| Meždurečensk | 107,500 |
| Miass | 169,700 |
| Michajlovka | 58,700 |
| Mičurinsk | 109,400 |
| Mineral'nyje Vody | 72,500 |
| Minusinsk | 74,200 |
| Mončegorsk | 68,100 |
| Moršansk | 50,500 |
| • MOSKVA (MOSCOW) (★13,150,000) | 8,801,500 |
| Murmansk | 472,900 |
| Murom | 126,000 |
| Mytišči (★Moskva) | 153,900 |
| Naberežnyje Čelny | 510,100 |
| Nachodka | 164,500 |
| Nadym | 52,200 |
| Nal'čik | 240,600 |
| Naro-Fominsk | 58,800 |
| Nazarovo | 65,200 |
| Neftejugansk | 65,500 |
| Ner'ungri | 77,200 |
| Nevinnomyssk | 123,300 |
| Nikolo-Berjozovka | 110,500 |
| Nižnekamsk | 196,200 |
| Nižnevartovsk | 247,400 |
| Nižnij Novgorod (Gorky) (★2,025,000) | 1,445,000 |
| Nižnij Tagil | 439,200 |
| Njagan | 59,800 |
| Noginsk | 122,700 |
| Nojabr'sk | 88,500 |
| Noril'sk | 169,000 |
| Novgorod | 233,800 |
| Novoaltajsk (★Barnaul) | 55,200 |
| Novočeboksarsk | 119,300 |
| Novočerkassk | 188,500 |
| Novodvinsk | 50,300 |
| Novokujbyševsk (★Samara) | 113,200 |
| Novokuzneck | 601,900 |
| Novomoskovsk, Tula oblast' (★365,000) | 145,800 |
| Novorossijsk | 188,600 |
| Novošachtinsk | 107,300 |
| Novosibirsk (★1,600,000) | 1,446,300 |
| Novotroick | 107,600 |
| Novyj Urengoj | 93,600 |
| Obninsk | 103,700 |
| Odincovo (★Moskva) | 128,400 |
| Okt'abr'skij | 106,700 |
| Omsk (★1,190,000) | 1,166,800 |
| Orechovo-Zujevo (★205,000) | 136,800 |
| Orel | 345,200 |
| Orenburg | 556,500 |
| Orsk | 272,200 |
| Osinniki | 63,200 |
| Otradnyj | 49,600 |
| Partizansk | 50,000 |
| P'atigorsk | 131,100 |
| Pavlovo | 72,200 |
| Pavlovskij Posad | 70,800 |
| Pečora | 65,500 |
| Penza | 551,100 |
| Perm' (★1,180,000) | 1,110,400 |
| Pervoural'sk | 143,700 |
| Petrodvorec (★Sankt-Peterburg) | 83,800 |
| Petropavlovsk-Kamčatskij | 272,900 |
| Petrozavodsk | 277,400 |
| Podol'sk (★Moskva) | 208,500 |
| Polevskoj | 71,900 |
| Prochladnyj | 58,500 |
| Prokopjevsk (★410,000) | 272,600 |
| Pskov | 207,500 |
| Puškin (★Sankt-Peterburg) | 95,300 |
| Puškino (★Moskva) | 75,800 |
| Ramenskoje | 88,800 |
| Rasskazovo | 49,800 |
| R'azan' | 527,200 |
| Reutov (★Moskva) | 68,900 |
| Revda | 66,000 |
| Roslavl' | 60,700 |
| Rossoš' | 58,900 |
| Rostov-na-Donu (★1,165,000) | 1,027,600 |
| Rubcovsk | 172,500 |
| Ruzajevka | 52,100 |
| Rybinsk | 252,600 |
| Ržev | 70,900 |
| Šachty | 227,700 |
| Šadrinsk | 87,500 |
| Safonovo | 56,300 |
| Sajanogorsk | 53,000 |
| Salavat | 151,400 |
| Sal'sk | 61,700 |
| Samara (★1,505,000) | 1,257,300 |
| Sankt-Peterburg (Saint Petersburg) (★5,525,000) | 4,466,800 |
| Saransk | 319,600 |
| Sarapul | 110,600 |
| Saratov (★1,155,000) | 911,100 |
| Šatka | 51,100 |
| Ščelkovo (★Moskva) | 109,600 |
| Ščokino | 68,800 |
| Šelechov | 48,600 |
| Sergijev Posad (Zagorsk) | 115,600 |
| Serov | 103,800 |
| Serpuchov | 141,200 |
| Severodvinsk | 251,500 |
| Severomorsk | 66,200 |
| Slav'ansk-Na-Kubani | 58,500 |
| Smolensk | 349,800 |
| Soči | 341,500 |
| Sokol | 46,700 |
| Solikamsk | 110,200 |
| Solnečnogorsk (★Moskva) | 56,700 |
| Sosnovyj Bor | 56,700 |
| Spassk-Dal'nij | 61,100 |
| Staryj Oskol | 181,900 |
| Stavropol' | 328,300 |
| Sterlitamak | 252,200 |
| Štupino | 74,600 |
| Šuja | 69,000 |
| Surgut | 261,100 |
| Sverdlovsk (★1,620,000) | 1,375,400 |
| Svetlogorsk | 71,600 |
| Svobodnyj | 80,900 |
| Syktyvkar | 224,000 |
| Syzran' | 174,900 |
| Taganrog | 293,600 |
| Talnach | 65,600 |
| Tambov | 309,600 |
| Tichoreck | 67,600 |
| Tichvin | 71,800 |
| Tobol'sk | 96,800 |
| Toljatti | 654,700 |
| Tomsk | 505,600 |
| Toržok | 50,500 |
| Troick | 89,800 |
| Tuapse | 63,800 |
| Tujmazy | 59,800 |
| Tula (★640,000) | 543,600 |
| Tulun | 53,700 |
| T'umen' | 494,200 |
| Tver' | 455,300 |
| Tyndinskij | 64,700 |
| Uchta | 112,100 |
| Ufa (★1,118,000) | 1,097,000 |
| Uglič | 40,000 |
| Ulan-Ude | 362,400 |
| Uljanovsk | 648,300 |
| Usinsk | 52,300 |
| Usolje-Sibirskoje | 106,800 |
| Ussurijsk | 160,200 |
| Ust'-Ilimsk | 112,200 |
| Ust'-Kut | 61,800 |
| Uzlovaja (★Novomoskovsk) | 34,000 |
| V'az'ma | 59,900 |
| Velikije Luki | 115,400 |
| Verchn'aja Pyšma (★Sverdlovsk) | 53,500 |
| Verchn'aja Salda | 55,100 |
| Vičuga | 49,700 |
| Vidnoje (★Moskva) | 56,900 |
| Vladikavkaz | 306,000 |
| Vladimir | 355,600 |
| Vladivostok | 648,000 |
| Volchov | 50,100 |
| Volgodonsk | 180,700 |
| Volgograd (Stalingrad) (★1,360,000) | 1,007,300 |
| Vologda | 289,200 |
| Vol'sk | 65,500 |
| Volžsk | 62,000 |
| Volžskij (★Volgograd) | 278,400 |
| Vorkuta | 117,400 |
| Voronež | 900,000 |
| Voskresensk | 81,400 |
| Votkinsk | 104,500 |
| Vyborg | 81,100 |
| Vyksa | 62,200 |
| Vyšnij Voločok | 64,600 |
| Zarinsk | 51,800 |
| Zelenograd (★Moskva) | 162,700 |
| Železnodorožnyj (★Moskva) | 99,300 |
| Železnogorsk | 89,200 |
| Žel'onodol'sk | 97,000 |
| Žigulevsk | 45,000 |
| Zlatoust | 208,200 |
| Žukovskij | 101,300 |

**RWANDA**

| | |
|---|---|
| 1991 C | 6,762,145 |
| • KIGALI | 232,733 |

**SAINT HELENA**

| | |
|---|---|
| 1987 C | 5,644 |
| • JAMESTOWN | 1,413 |

**SAINT KITTS AND NEVIS**

| | |
|---|---|
| 1980 C | 44,404 |
| • BASSETERRE | 14,725 |
| Charlestown | 1,771 |

**SAINT LUCIA**

| | |
|---|---|
| 1991 C | 133,308 |
| • CASTRIES (★13,138) | 11,147 |

**SAINT PIERRE AND MIQUELON / Saint-Pierre-et-Miquelon**

| | |
|---|---|
| 1982 C | 6,041 |
| • SAINT-PIERRE | 5,371 |

**SAINT VINCENT AND THE GRENADINES**

| | |
|---|---|
| 1991 C | 106,499 |
| • KINGSTOWN (★26,223) | 15,466 |

**SAN MARINO**

| | |
|---|---|
| 1989 E | 23,000 |
| • SAN MARINO | 2,794 |

**SAO TOME AND PRINCIPE / São Tomé e Príncipe**

| | |
|---|---|
| 1991 C | 117,504 |
| • SÃO TOMÉ | 5,245 |

**SAUDI ARABIA / Al-'Arabīyah as-Su'ūdīyah**

| | |
|---|---|
| 1980 E | 9,229,000 |
| Abhā (1974C) | 30,150 |
| Ad-Dammām | 200,000 |
| Al-Hufūf (1974C) | 101,271 |
| Al-Khubar (1974C) | 48,817 |
| Al-Madīnah (Medina) | 290,000 |
| Al-Mubarraz (1974C) | 54,325 |
| AR-RIYĀD (RIYADH) | 1,250,000 |
| At-Tā'if | 300,000 |
| Buraydah (1974C) | 69,940 |
| Hā'il (1974C) | 40,502 |
| • Jiddah (Jeddah) | 1,300,000 |
| Khamīs Mushayt (1974C) | 49,581 |
| Makkah (Mecca) | 550,000 |
| Najran (1974C) | 47,501 |
| Tabūk (1974C) | 74,825 |

**SENEGAL / Sénégal**

| | |
|---|---|
| 1988 C | 6,892,720 |
| • DAKAR | 1,490,450 |
| Diourbel | 77,548 |
| Kaolack | 152,007 |
| Louga | 52,763 |
| Saint-Louis | 160,689 |
| Thiès | 184,902 |
| Ziguinchor | 124,283 |

**SEYCHELLES**

| | |
|---|---|
| 1984 E | 64,718 |
| • VICTORIA | 23,000 |

**SIERRA LEONE**

| | |
|---|---|
| 1985 C | 3,515,812 |
| Bo | 59,768 |
| • FREETOWN (★525,000) | 469,776 |
| Kenema | 52,473 |
| Koidu | 82,474 |
| Makeni | 49,038 |

**SINGAPORE**

| | |
|---|---|
| 1990 C | 2,690,100 |
| • SINGAPORE (★3,025,000) | 2,690,100 |

**SLOVAKIA / Slovenská Republika**

| | |
|---|---|
| 1991 C | 5,268,935 |
| Banská Bystrica | 85,007 |
| • BRATISLAVA | 441,453 |
| Komárno | 37,370 |
| Košice | 234,840 |
| Martin | 58,338 |
| Michalovce | 38,866 |
| Nitra | 89,888 |
| Nové Zámky | 42,851 |
| Poprad | 52,878 |
| Považská Bystrica | 39,801 |
| Prešov | 87,788 |
| Prievidza | 53,393 |
| Spišská Nová Ves | 39,187 |
| Trenčín | 56,733 |
| Trnava | 71,641 |
| Žilina | 83,853 |
| Zvolen | 41,935 |

**SLOVENIA / Slovenija**

| | |
|---|---|
| 1991 C | 1,974,839 |
| Celje | 42,041 |
| Kranj | 42,988 |
| • LJUBLJANA | 292,589 |
| Maribor | 124,650 |

**SOLOMON ISLANDS**

| | |
|---|---|
| 1986 C | 285,176 |
| • HONIARA | 30,413 |

**SOMALIA / Somaliya**

| | |
|---|---|
| 1984 E | 5,423,000 |
| Berbera | 65,000 |
| Hargeysa | 70,000 |
| Kismaayo | 70,000 |
| Marka | 60,000 |
| • MUQDISHO | 600,000 |

**SOUTH AFRICA / Suid-Afrika**

| | |
|---|---|
| 1991 C | 30,986,920 |
| Alberton (★Johannesburg) | 76,642 |
| Alexandra (★Johannesburg) | 124,586 |
| Atteridgeville (★Pretoria) | 92,008 |
| Bellville (★Cape Town) | 78,822 |
| Benoni (★Johannesburg) | 113,501 |
| Bloemfontein (★280,000) | 126,867 |
| Blue Downs | 60,781 |
| Boksburg (★Johannesburg) | 119,890 |
| Botshabelo (★Bloemfontein) | 117,926 |
| Brakpan (★Johannesburg) | 53,522 |
| CAPE TOWN (KAAPSTAD) (★1,900,000) | 854,616 |
| Carletonville (★175,000) | 118,699 |
| Daveyton (★Johannesburg) | 151,659 |
| Diepmeadow (★Johannesburg) | 241,099 |
| Durban (★1,740,000) | 715,669 |
| East London (Oos-Londen) (★365,000) | 102,325 |
| Edendale (★Pietermaritzburg) | 72,063 |
| Elsies River (★Cape Town) | 82,045 |
| EMbalenhle | 56,502 |
| Evaton (★Vereeniging) | 201,026 |
| Galeshewe (★Kimberley) | 72,118 |
| Ga-Rankuwa (1980C) | 48,300 |
| Germiston (★Johannesburg) | 134,005 |
| Grassy Park (★Cape Town) | 52,675 |
| Guguletu (★Cape Town) | 54,635 |
| Ibhayi (★Port Elizabeth) | 257,054 |
| • Johannesburg (★4,000,000) | 712,507 |
| Kagiso (★Johannesburg) | 61,680 |
| Katlehong (★Johannesburg) | 201,785 |
| Kempton Park (★Johannesburg) | 106,606 |
| Khayelitsa (★Cape Town) | 189,586 |
| Khutsong | 55,834 |
| Kimberley (★160,000) | 80,082 |
| Klerksdorp (★275,000) | 58,923 |
| Krugersdorp (★Johannesburg) | 81,584 |
| Kwa Makuta (★Durban) | 13,609 |
| Kwa Mashu (★Durban) | 156,679 |
| KwaNdengezi (★Durban) | 50,835 |
| KwaNobuhle (★Port Elizabeth) | 92,381 |
| Kwa-Thema (★Johannesburg) | 81,345 |
| Ladysmith (★37,885) | 29,589 |
| Lekoa (Shapeville) (★Vereeniging) | 217,582 |
| Madadeni (★Newcastle) | 95,931 |
| Mafikeng (★16,000) (1980C) | 6,500 |
| Mamelodi (★Pretoria) | 154,845 |

▲ Population of an entire municipality, commune, or district, including rural area.
• Largest city in country.
★ Population or designation of the metropolitan area, including suburbs.
C Census. E Official estimate. U Unofficial estimate.

▲ Bevölkerung eines ganzen städtischen Verwaltungsgebietes, eines Kommunalbezirkes oder eines Distrikts, einschliesslich ländlicher Gebiete.
• Grösste Stadt des Landes.
★ Bevölkerung oder Bezeichnung der Stadtregion einschliesslich Vororte.
C Volkszählung. E Offizielle Schätzung. U Inoffizielle Schätzung.

| | |
|---|---|
| Mangaung (★Bloemfontein) | 125,545 |
| Mdantsane (★East London) (1986E) | 242,823 |
| Midrand (★Pretoria) | 51,107 |
| Motherwell (★Port Elizabeth) | 72,999 |
| Mpumalanga (★Durban) | 62,140 |
| Newtown (★Durban) | 60,696 |
| Ntuzuma (★Durban) | 102,310 |
| Nyanga (★Cape Town) | 92,896 |
| Orange Farm en Omgewing | 49,838 |
| Osizweni (★Durban) | 78,079 |
| Paarl (★Cape Town) | 73,415 |
| Parow (★Cape Town) | 68,081 |
| Pietermaritzburg (★265,000) | 156,473 |
| Pinetown (★Durban) | 70,001 |
| Port Elizabeth (★810,000) | 303,353 |
| PRETORIA (★1,100,000) | 525,583 |
| Randburg (★Johannesburg) | 90,557 |
| Randfontein (★Johannesburg) | 90,557 |
| Roodepoort-Maraisburg (★Johannesburg) | 162,632 |
| Sandton (★Johannesburg) | 101,197 |
| Soshanguve (★Pretoria) | 146,334 |
| Soweto (★Johannesburg) | 596,632 |
| Springs (★Johannesburg) | 72,647 |
| Tembisa (★Johannesburg) | 209,238 |
| Thabong (★Welkom) | 88,547 |
| Uitenhage (★Port Elizabeth) | 67,581 |
| Umlazi (★Durban) | 299,275 |
| Umtata (1978E) | 30,000 |
| Vanderbijlpark (★Vereeniging) | 67,291 |
| Vereeniging (★675,000) | 71,255 |
| Verwoerdburg (★Pretoria) | 80,552 |
| Vosloosrus (★Johannesburg) | 76,015 |
| Welkom (★240,000) | 68,111 |
| Westonaria (★Johannesburg) | 57,117 |

**SPAIN / España**

| | |
|---|---|
| 1988 E | 39,217,804 |
| Alacant (Alicante) | 261,051 |
| Albacete | 125,997 |
| Alcalá de Guadaira | 50,935 |
| Alcalá de Henares (★Madrid) | 150,021 |
| Alcobendas (★Madrid) | 73,455 |
| Alcoi (Alcoy) | 66,074 |
| Alcorcón (★Madrid) | 139,796 |
| Algeciras | 99,528 |
| Almería | 157,644 |
| Avilés (★131,000) | 87,811 |
| Badajoz (▲122,407) | 106,400 |
| Badalona (★Barcelona) | 225,229 |
| Baracaldo (★Bilbao) | 113,502 |
| Barcelona (★4,040,000) | 1,714,355 |
| Bilbao (★985,000) | 384,733 |
| Burgos | 160,561 |
| Cáceres | 71,598 |
| Cádiz (★240,000) | 156,591 |
| Cartagena (▲172,710) | 70,000 |
| Castelló de la Plana | 131,809 |
| Ciudad Real | 56,300 |
| Córdoba | 302,301 |
| Cornellà de Llobregat (★Barcelona) | 86,866 |
| Coslada (★Madrid) | 68,765 |
| Donostia (San Sebastián) (★285,000) | 177,622 |
| Dos Hermanas (▲68,456) | 60,600 |
| Elda | 56,756 |
| El Prat de Llobregat (★Barcelona) | 64,193 |
| El Puerto de Santa María (▲62,285) | 49,900 |
| Elx (Elche) (▲180,256) | 158,300 |
| Ferrol (★129,000) | 86,503 |
| Fuenlabrada (★Madrid) | 128,872 |
| Gernikao (Guernica) (▲17,836) (1981C) | 12,214 |
| Getafe (★Madrid) | 135,367 |
| Gijón | 262,156 |
| Granada | 263,334 |
| Granollers (★Barcelona) | 49,045 |
| Guadalajara | 61,309 |
| Huelva | 137,826 |
| Irún | 54,886 |
| Jaén | 106,435 |
| Jerez de la Frontera (▲183,007) | 156,200 |
| La Coruña | 248,862 |
| La Línea | 60,956 |
| Las Palmas de Gran Canaria (▲366,347) | 319,000 |
| Leganés (★Madrid) | 168,403 |
| León (★159,000) | 136,558 |
| L'Hospitalet de Llobregat (★Barcelona) | 278,449 |
| Linares | 58,622 |
| Lleida (Lérida) (▲109,795) | 91,500 |
| Logroño | 119,038 |
| Lugo (▲78,795) | 68,700 |
| • MADRID (★4,650,000) | 3,102,846 |
| Málaga | 574,456 |
| Manresa | 65,607 |
| Mataró | 100,817 |
| Mérida | 52,368 |
| Móstoles (★Madrid) | 181,648 |
| Murcia (▲314,124) | 149,800 |
| Ourense | 106,042 |
| Oviedo (▲190,073) | 168,900 |
| Palencia | 76,692 |
| Palma (▲314,608) | 249,000 |
| Pamplona | 180,598 |
| Parla (★Madrid) | 66,253 |
| Portugalete (★Bilbao) | 57,813 |
| Puertollano | 52,284 |
| Reus | 83,800 |
| Rubí (★Barcelona) | 48,807 |
| Sabadell (★Barcelona) | 189,489 |
| Salamanca | 159,342 |
| San Baudilio de Llobrega (★Barcelona) | 77,502 |
| San Cristóbal de la Laguna (▲111,533) | 25,900 |
| San Fernando (★Cádiz) | 81,975 |
| San Sebastián de los Reyes (★Madrid) | 51,653 |
| Santa Coloma de Gramanet (★Barcelona) | 136,042 |
| Santa Cruz de Tenerife | 215,228 |
| Santander (▲190,795) | 166,800 |
| Santiago de Compostela (▲88,110) | 68,800 |
| Santurce-Antiguo (★Bilbao) | 52,334 |
| Segovia | 54,402 |
| Sevilla (★945,000) | 663,132 |
| Talavera de la Reina | 68,158 |
| Tarragona (▲109,586) | 63,500 |
| Tarrasa (★Barcelona) | 161,410 |
| Toledo | 59,551 |
| Torrejón de Ardoz (★Madrid) | 83,267 |
| Torrent (★València) | 55,751 |
| València (★1,270,000) | 743,933 |
| Valladolid | 331,461 |
| Vigo (▲271,128) | 179,500 |
| Vitoria (Gasteiz) | 204,264 |
| Zamora | 62,047 |
| Zaragoza | 582,239 |

**SPANISH NORTH AFRICA / Plazas de Soberanía en el Norte de Africa**

| | |
|---|---|
| 1988 E | 122,905 |
| • Ceuta | 67,188 |
| Melilla | 55,717 |

**SRI LANKA**

| | |
|---|---|
| 1989 E | 16,806,000 |
| Battaramulla (★Colombo) (1981C) | 56,535 |
| Batticaloa | 50,000 |
| • COLOMBO (★2,050,000) | 612,000 |
| Dehiwala-Mount Lavinia (★Colombo) | 193,000 |
| Galle | 83,000 |
| Jaffna | 128,000 |
| Kandy | 103,000 |
| Moratuwa (★Colombo) | 166,000 |
| Negombo | 64,000 |
| SRI JAYAWARDENEPURA (KOTTE) (★Colombo) | 108,000 |
| Trincomalee | 49,000 |

**SUDAN / As-Sūdān**

| | |
|---|---|
| 1983 C | 20,594,197 |
| Al-Fāshir | 84,298 |
| • AL-KHARṬŪM (★1,450,000) | 473,597 |
| Al-Kharṭūm Baḥrī (★Al-Kharṭūm) | 340,857 |
| Al-Qaḍārif | 116,876 |
| Al-Ubayyiḍ | 137,582 |
| 'Aṭbarah | 72,836 |
| Būr Sūdān (Port Sudan) | 206,038 |
| Jūbā | 84,377 |
| Kassalā | 141,429 |
| Kūstī | 89,135 |
| Nyala | 111,693 |
| Umm Durmān (Omdurman) (★Al-Kharṭūm) | 526,192 |
| Wad Madanī | 145,015 |
| Wāw | 90,960 |

**SURINAME**

| | |
|---|---|
| 1988 E | 392,000 |
| • PARAMARIBO (★296,000) | 241,000 |
| Wanica (★Paramaribo) | 55,000 |

**SWAZILAND**

| | |
|---|---|
| 1986 C | 712,131 |
| LOBAMBA | |
| Manzini (★30,000) | 18,084 |
| • MBABANE | 38,290 |

**SWEDEN / Sverige**

| | |
|---|---|
| 1991 E | 8,590,630 |
| Borås (▲101,766) | 59,400 |
| Eskilstuna (▲89,765) | 59,800 |
| Gävle (▲88,568) | 67,300 |
| Göteborg (★710,894) | 433,042 |
| Halmstad (▲80,061) | 48,900 |
| Helsingborg (▲109,267) | 82,000 |
| Huddinge (★Stockholm) | 73,829 |
| Järfälla (★Stockholm) | 56,359 |
| Jönköping (▲111,486) | 76,300 |
| Karlstad (▲76,467) | 53,100 |
| Linköping (▲122,268) | 82,700 |
| Luleå (▲68,412) | 42,700 |
| Lund (▲87,681) (★Malmö) | 63,700 |
| Malmö (★475,224) | 233,887 |
| Mölndal (★Göteborg) | 52,028 |
| Nacka (★Stockholm) | 64,056 |
| Norrköping (▲120,522) | 82,600 |
| Örebro (▲120,944) | 86,000 |
| Södertälje (▲81,786) (★Stockholm) | 58,100 |
| Sollentuna (★Stockholm) | 51,377 |
| Solna (★Stockholm) | 51,841 |
| • STOCKHOLM (★1,491,726) | 674,452 |
| Sundsvall (▲93,808) | 50,300 |
| Täby (★Stockholm) | 56,714 |
| Trollhättan (▲51,047) | 41,000 |
| Tumba (★Stockholm) | 38,542 |
| Umeå (▲91,258) | 61,300 |
| Uppsala (▲167,508) | 110,000 |
| Västerås (▲119,761) | 98,300 |
| Växjö (▲69,547) | 48,000 |

**SWITZERLAND / Schweiz / Suisse / Svizzera**

| | |
|---|---|
| 1990 C | 6,873,687 |
| Aarau (★59,500) | 16,481 |
| Arbon (★41,400) | 11,043 |
| Baden (★73,200) | 15,718 |
| Basel (Bâle) (★587,000) | 178,428 |
| BERN (BERNE) (★300,400) | 136,338 |
| Biel (Bienne) (★83,100) | 51,893 |
| Fribourg (Freiburg) (★62,500) | 36,355 |
| Genève (Geneva) (★470,000) | 171,042 |
| Lausanne (★265,000) | 128,112 |
| Locarno (★42,200) | 13,796 |
| Lugano (★94,700) | 25,344 |
| Luzern (★165,000) | 61,034 |
| Neuchâtel (★67,500) | 33,579 |
| Sankt Gallen (★127,000) | 75,237 |
| Schaffhausen (★53,800) | 34,225 |
| Thun (★79,500) | 38,211 |
| Vevey (★65,900) | 15,968 |
| Winterthur (★110,500) | 86,959 |
| Zug (★69,000) | 21,705 |
| • Zürich (★870,000) | 365,043 |

**SYRIA / Sūrīyah**

| | |
|---|---|
| 1994 E | 13,844,000 |
| Al-Hasakah (1981C) | 73,426 |
| Al-Kiswah | 99,050 |
| Al-Lādhiqīyah (Latakia) | 306,535 |
| Al-Qāmishlī (1988E) | 126,236 |
| Ar-Raqqah | 219,016 |
| At-Tall | 66,248 |
| Az-Zabadānī | 49,398 |
| Dar'ā | 180,093 |
| Dārayyā (★Dimashq) (1988E) | 53,204 |
| Dayr az-Zawr | 174,085 |
| • DIMASHQ (DAMASCUS) (★2,230,000) | 1,549,932 |
| Dūmā (★Dimashq) | 131,158 |
| Halab (Aleppo) (★1,640,000) | 1,591,400 |
| Hamāh (1988E) | 222,000 |
| Ḥimṣ | 644,204 |
| Idlib | 113,360 |
| Jaramānah (★Dimashq) | 138,469 |
| Kābir aş Şaghīr (1988E) | 47,728 |
| Madīnat ath Thawrah (1988E) | 58,151 |
| Salamīyah (1988E) | 46,844 |
| Ṭarṭūs | 136,812 |

**TAIWAN / T'aiwan**

| | |
|---|---|
| 1991 E | 20,352,966 |
| Changhua (▲215,224) | 165,000 |
| Chiai (1992E) | 258,713 |
| Chilung (1992E) | 357,000 |
| Chungho (★T'aipei) | 374,339 |
| Chungli | 269,804 |
| Chutung (1988E) | 104,797 |
| Fangshan (★Kaohsiung) | 290,777 |
| Fengyüan (▲151,642) | 121,100 |
| Hsichih (★T'aipei) (1980C) | 70,031 |
| Hsinchu (1992E) | 330,576 |
| Hsinchuang (★T'aipei) | 299,174 |
| Hsintien (★T'aipei) | 225,517 |
| Hualien | 107,552 |
| Ilan (▲81,751) (1980C) | 70,900 |
| Kangshan (1980C) | 78,049 |
| Kaohsiung (★1,845,000) (1992E) | 1,401,239 |
| Lotung (1980C) | 57,925 |
| Lukang (1980C) | 72,019 |
| Miaoli (1980C) | 81,500 |
| Nant'ou (1980C) | 84,038 |
| P'ingchen (★T'aipei) | 147,030 |
| P'ingtung (▲210,801) | 172,400 |
| Sanchung (★T'aipei) | 375,996 |
| Shulin (★T'aipei) | 111,993 |
| Tach'i (1980C) | 67,209 |
| T'aichung (1992E) | 785,182 |
| T'ainan (1992E) | 692,116 |
| • T'AIPEI (★6,130,000) (1992E) | 2,706,453 |
| T'aipeihsien (★T'aipei) | 538,954 |
| T'aitung (▲108,196) | 79,100 |
| Taoyüan | 241,263 |
| T'oufen (1980C) | 66,536 |
| T'uch'eng (▲136,928) (★T'aipei) | 80,300 |
| Yangmei (1980C) | 84,353 |
| Yüanlin (▲121,251) | 53,200 |
| Yungho (★T'aipei) | 249,736 |
| Yungkang (▲136,705) | 70,900 |

**TAJIKISTAN**

| | |
|---|---|
| 1991 E | 5,358,300 |
| Chudžand (Leninabad) | 164,500 |
| • DUŠANBE | 582,400 |
| Kul'ab | 79,300 |
| Kurgan-T'ube | 58,400 |

**TANZANIA**

| | |
|---|---|
| 1985 E | 21,733,000 |
| Arusha (1984E) | 69,000 |
| • DAR ES SALAAM | 1,096,000 |
| DODOMA | 85,000 |
| Iringa (1984E) | 67,000 |
| Kigoma (1978C) | 50,044 |
| Mbeya | 194,000 |
| Morogoro (1984E) | 72,000 |
| Moshi (1984E) | 62,000 |
| Mtwara (1978C) | 48,510 |
| Mwanza | 252,000 |
| Tabora | 214,000 |
| Tanga | 172,000 |
| Ujiji (1967C) | 21,369 |
| Zanzibar | 133,000 |

**THAILAND / Prathet Thai**

| | |
|---|---|
| 1991 E | 56,961,030 |
| Chiang Mai | 161,541 |
| Chon Buri | 45,763 |
| Hat Yai | 142,351 |
| Khon Kaen | 131,478 |
| • KRUNG THEP (BANGKOK) (★7,060,000) | 5,620,591 |
| Nakhon Ratchasima | 202,503 |
| Nakhon Sawan | 108,569 |
| Nakhon Si Thammarat | 74,219 |
| Nonthaburi (★Krung Thep) | 264,201 |
| Pattaya | 64,731 |
| Phitsanulok | 77,672 |
| Phra Nakhon Si Ayutthaya | 60,561 |
| Phuket | 42,913 |
| Sakon Nakhon | 47,869 |
| Samut Prakan (★Krung Thep) | 71,538 |
| Samut Sakhon | 55,509 |
| Saraburi | 64,915 |
| Songkhla | 82,167 |
| Trang | 48,589 |
| Ubon Ratchathani | 98,950 |
| Udon Thani | 78,489 |
| Yala | 68,834 |

**TOGO**

| | |
|---|---|
| 1987 E | 3,148,000 |
| • LOMÉ | 500,000 |
| Sokodé | 55,000 |

**TONGA**

| | |
|---|---|
| 1986 C | 94,535 |
| • NUKU'ALOFA | 21,265 |

**TRINIDAD AND TOBAGO**

| | |
|---|---|
| 1990 C | 1,234,388 |
| • PORT OF SPAIN (★370,000) | 50,878 |
| San Fernando (★75,000) | 30,092 |

**TUNISIA / Tunis / Tunisie**

| | |
|---|---|
| 1984 C | 6,975,450 |
| Ariana (★Tunis) | 98,655 |
| Bardo (★Tunis) | 65,669 |
| Ben Arous (★Tunis) | 52,105 |
| Bizerte | 94,509 |
| Gabès | 92,258 |
| Gafsa | 60,970 |
| Hammam Lif (★Tunis) | 47,009 |
| Houmt Essouk | 92,269 |
| Kairouan | 72,254 |
| Kasserine | 47,606 |
| La Goulette (★Tunis) | 61,609 |
| Menzel Bourguiba | 51,399 |
| Sfax (★310,000) | 231,911 |
| Sousse (★160,000) | 83,509 |
| • TUNIS (★1,225,000) | 596,654 |
| Zarzis | 49,063 |

**TURKEY / Türkiye**

| | |
|---|---|
| 1990 C | 56,473,035 |
| Adana | 916,150 |
| Adıyaman | 100,045 |
| Afyon | 95,643 |
| Ağrı | 58,038 |
| Akhisar | 73,944 |
| Aksaray | 90,698 |
| Akşehir | 51,746 |
| Alanya | 52,450 |
| Amasya | 57,288 |
| ANKARA (★2,650,000) | 2,559,471 |
| Antalya | 378,208 |
| Aydın | 107,011 |
| Bafra | 65,600 |
| Balıkesir | 170,589 |
| Bandırma | 77,444 |
| Batman | 147,347 |
| Bilecik | 23,273 |
| Bolu | 60,789 |
| Burdur | 56,432 |
| Bursa | 834,576 |
| Çanakkale | 53,995 |
| Ceyhan | 85,308 |
| Cizre | 50,023 |
| Çorlu | 74,681 |
| Çorum | 116,810 |
| Darıca | 53,560 |
| Denizli | 204,118 |
| Diyarbakır | 381,144 |
| Düzce | 61,878 |
| Edirne | 102,345 |
| Elazığ | 204,603 |
| Elbistan | 54,741 |
| Ereğli, Konya prov. | 74,283 |
| Ereğli, Zonguldak prov. | 63,987 |
| Erzincan | 91,772 |
| Erzurum | 242,391 |
| Esenyurt (★İstanbul) | 70,280 |
| Eskişehir | 413,082 |
| Gaziantep | 603,434 |
| Gebze (★İstanbul) | 159,116 |
| Gelibolu | 18,670 |
| Gemlik | 50,237 |
| Giresun | 67,604 |
| Gölcük | 64,911 |
| Gümüşhane | 26,014 |
| Hakkâri | 30,407 |
| Hatay (Antioch) | 123,871 |
| İçel (Mersin) | 422,357 |
| İnegöl | 71,120 |
| İskenderun | 154,807 |
| Isparta | 112,117 |
| • İstanbul (★7,550,000) | 6,620,241 |
| İzmir (★1,900,000) | 1,757,414 |
| İzmit | 256,882 |
| Kadirli | 55,061 |
| Kahramanmaraş | 228,129 |
| Karabük | 105,373 |
| Karaman | 76,525 |
| Kars | 78,455 |
| Kastamonu | 51,560 |
| Kayseri | 421,362 |
| Kilis | 82,882 |
| Kırıkkale | 185,431 |
| Kırşehir | 73,538 |
| Kızıltepe | 60,134 |
| Konya | 513,346 |
| Körfez | 65,786 |
| Kozan | 54,451 |
| Kütahya | 130,994 |
| Lüleburgaz | 52,384 |
| Malatya | 281,776 |
| Manisa | 158,928 |
| Mardin | 53,005 |
| Muş | 44,019 |
| Nazilli | 80,277 |
| Nevşehir | 52,719 |
| Niğde | 55,035 |
| Nizip | 58,604 |
| Nusaybin | 49,671 |
| Ödemiş | 51,620 |
| Ordu | 102,107 |
| Osmaniye | 123,307 |
| Polatlı | 60,158 |
| Rize | 52,031 |
| Sakarya | 171,225 |
| Salihli | 70,861 |
| Samsun | 303,979 |
| Şanlıurfa | 276,528 |
| Siirt | 68,320 |
| Silvan (Miyafarkin) | 59,865 |
| Sinop | 25,537 |
| Sivas | 221,512 |
| Siverek | 63,049 |
| Söke | 50,866 |
| Soma | 49,977 |
| Sultanbeyli (★İstanbul) | 82,298 |
| Tarsus | 187,508 |
| Tatvan | 54,071 |
| Tekirdağ | 80,442 |
| Tokat | 83,058 |
| Trabzon | 143,941 |
| Tunceli | 24,513 |
| Turgutlu | 73,634 |
| Turhal | 68,384 |
| Uşak | 105,270 |
| Van | 153,111 |
| Viranşehir | 57,461 |
| Yalova (★İstanbul) | 65,823 |
| Yozgat | 50,335 |
| Zonguldak (★220,000) | 116,725 |

**TURKMENISTAN**

| | |
|---|---|
| 1991 E | 3,714,100 |
| • AŠCHABAD (ASHGABAT) | 412,200 |
| Čardžou | 166,400 |
| Krasnovodsk | 59,500 |
| Mary | 94,900 |
| Nebit-Dag | 89,100 |
| Tašauz | 117,000 |

**TURKS AND CAICOS ISLANDS**

| | |
|---|---|
| 1990 C | 11,465 |
| • GRAND TURK | 3,691 |

**TUVALU**

| | |
|---|---|
| 1979 C | 7,349 |
| • FUNAFUTI | 2,191 |

**UGANDA**

| | |
|---|---|
| 1991 C | 16,582,700 |
| Jinja | 60,979 |
| • KAMPALA | 773,463 |
| Masaka | 49,070 |
| Mbale | 53,634 |

**UKRAINE / Ukrayina**

| | |
|---|---|
| 1991 E | 51,944,400 |

▲ Población de un municipio, comuna o distrito entero, incluyendo sus áreas rurales.
• Ciudad más grande de un país.
★ Población o designación de un área metropolitana, incluyendo los suburbios.
C Censo. E Estimado oficial. U Estimado no oficial.

▲ Population d'une municipalité, d'une commune ou d'un district, zone rurale incluse.
• Ville la plus peuplée du pays.
★ Population de l'agglomération (ou nom de la zone métropolitaine englobante).
C Recensement. E Estimation officielle. U Estimation non officielle.

▲ População de um municipio, comuna ou distrito, inclusive as respectivas áreas rurais.
• Maior cidade de um país.
★ População ou indicação de uma área metropolitana.
C Censo. E Estimativa oficial. U Estimativa não oficial.

| | |
|---|---|
| Alchevs'k | 126,000 |
| Antratsyt (★Krasnyy Luch) | 72,800 |
| Artemivs'k | 90,800 |
| Berdyans'k | 138,700 |
| Berdychivv | 93,400 |
| Bila Tserkva | 204,400 |
| Bilhorod-Dnistrovs'kyy | 56,800 |
| Boryspil' (★Kyyiv) | 52,700 |
| Brovary (★Kyyiv) | 84,800 |
| Bryanka (★Stakhanov) | 64,500 |
| Cherkasy | 302,200 |
| Chernihiv | 305,700 |
| Chernivtsi | 258,800 |
| Chervonohrad | 74,000 |
| Dniprodzerzhyns'k (★Dnipropetrovs'k) | 284,400 |
| Dnipropetrovs'k (★1,600,000) | 1,189,300 |
| Donets'k (★2,125,000) | 1,121,300 |
| Drohobych | 79,200 |
| Druzhkivka (★Kramators'k) | 74,400 |
| Dymytrov (★Krasnoarmiys'k) | 371,800 |
| Dzerzhyns'k (★Horlivka) | 50,500 |
| Dzhankoy | 54,500 |
| Enerhodar | 51,500 |
| Fastiv | 54,400 |
| Feodosiya | 85,600 |
| Horlivka (★700,000) | 336,600 |
| Illichivs'k (★Odesa) | 56,000 |
| Ivano-Frankivs'k | 241,000 |
| Izmayil | 95,100 |
| Izyum | 64,800 |
| Kalush | 69,400 |
| Kam'yanets'-Podil's'kyy | 104,900 |
| Kerch | 178,300 |
| Kharkiv (Kharkov) (★2,050,000) | 1,622,800 |
| Khartsyz'k (★Donets'k) | 69,300 |
| Kherson | 365,400 |
| Khmel'nyts'kyy | 244,500 |
| Kirovohrad | 277,900 |
| Kolomyya | 66,200 |
| Komsomol's'k | 56,000 |
| Konotop | 97,700 |
| Korosten' | 67,500 |
| Kostyantynivka | 107,800 |
| Kovel' | 69,700 |
| Kramators'k (★515,000) | 201,300 |
| Krasnoarmiys'k (★180,000) | 73,300 |
| Krasnodon (★165,000) | 54,800 |
| Krasnyy Luch (★320,000) | 113,400 |
| Kremenchuk | 240,600 |
| Kryvyy Rih | 724,000 |
| • KYYIV (KIEV) (★3,250,000) | 2,635,000 |
| Lozova | 74,100 |
| Lubny | 60,300 |
| Luhans'k (★650,000) | 503,900 |
| Luts'k | 209,500 |
| L'viv | 802,200 |
| Lysychans'k (★415,000) | 126,400 |
| Makiyivka (★Donets'k) | 423,900 |
| Marhanets' | 54,700 |
| Mariupol' (Ždanov) | 521,800 |
| Melitopol' | 176,900 |
| Mukacheve | 88,000 |
| Mykolayiv | 511,600 |
| Nikopol' | 159,000 |
| Nizhyn | 82,000 |
| Nova Kakhovka | 59,000 |
| Novohrad-Volyns'kyy | 56,100 |
| Novomoskovs'k | 76,600 |
| Novovolyns'k | 56,400 |
| Odesa (★1,185,000) | 1,100,700 |
| Okhtyrka | 52,300 |
| Oleksandriya | 104,900 |
| Pavlohrad | 134,300 |
| Pervomays'k (★Stakhanov) | 52,000 |
| Pervomays'k | 83,800 |
| Poltava | 320,100 |
| Pryluky | 72,900 |
| Rivne | 239,300 |
| Romny | 57,700 |
| Roven'ky | 58,500 |
| Rubizhne (★Lysyscans'k) | 75,100 |
| Sevastopol' | 366,200 |
| Shakhtars'k (★Torez) | 73,100 |
| Shepetivka | 51,900 |
| Shostka | 95,200 |
| Simferopol' | 352,600 |
| Slov'yans'k (★Kramators'k) | 137,100 |
| Smila | 81,200 |
| Snizhne (★Torez) | 68,900 |
| Stakhanov (★700,000) | 112,700 |
| Stryy | 68,200 |
| Sumy | 303,300 |
| Sverdlovs'k (★145,000) | 83,700 |
| Svitlovods'k | 57,900 |
| Syeverodonets'k (★Lysychans'k) | 133,300 |
| Ternopil' | 219,200 |
| Torez (★320,000) | 88,100 |
| Uman' | 97,700 |
| Uzhhorod | 122,600 |
| Vinnytsya | 380,900 |
| Yalta | 89,300 |
| Yenakiyeve (★Horlivka) | 120,100 |
| Yevpatoriya | 110,500 |
| Zaporizhzhya | 896,600 |
| Zhovti Vody | 64,900 |
| Zhytomyr | 297,500 |

**UNITED ARAB EMIRATES / Al-Imārāt al-'Arabīyah al-Muttaḥidah**

| | |
|---|---|
| 1980 C | 980,000 |
| ABŪ ẒABY (ABU DHABI) | 242,975 |
| Al-'Ayn | 101,663 |
| Ash-Shāriqah | 125,149 |
| • Dubayy | 265,702 |
| Ra's al-Khaymah | 42,000 |

**UNITED KINGDOM**

| | |
|---|---|
| 1981 C | 55,678,079 |

**UNITED KINGDOM: ENGLAND**

| | |
|---|---|
| 1981 C | 46,220,955 |
| Aldershot (★London) | 53,665 |
| Ashton-under-Lyne (★Manchester) | 43,605 |
| Aylesbury | 51,999 |
| Barnsley | 76,783 |
| Barrow-in-Furness | 50,174 |
| Basildon (★London) | 94,800 |
| Basingstoke | 73,027 |
| Bath | 84,283 |
| Bebington (★Liverpool) | 62,618 |
| Bedford | 75,632 |
| Beeston and Stapleford (★Nottingham) | 64,785 |
| Benfleet (★London) | 50,783 |
| Birkenhead (★Liverpool) | 99,075 |
| Birmingham (★2,675,000) | 1,013,995 |
| Blackburn (★221,900) | 109,564 |
| Blackpool (★280,000) | 146,297 |
| Bognor Regis | 50,323 |
| Bolton (★Manchester) | 143,960 |
| Bootle | 70,860 |
| Bournemouth (★315,000) | 142,829 |
| Bracknell (★London) | 52,257 |
| Bradford (★Leeds) | 293,336 |
| Brentwood (★London) | 51,212 |
| Brighton (★420,000) | 134,581 |
| Bristol (★630,000) | 413,861 |
| Burnley (★160,000) | 76,365 |
| Burton upon Trent | 59,040 |
| Bury (★Manchester) | 61,785 |
| Bury Saint Edmunds | 30,563 |
| Cambridge | 87,111 |
| Cannock (★Birmingham) | 54,503 |
| Canterbury | 34,546 |
| Carlisle | 72,206 |
| Carlton (★Nottingham) | 46,053 |
| Chatham (★London) | 65,835 |
| Cheadle and Gatley (★Manchester) | 59,478 |
| Chelmsford (★London) | 91,109 |
| Cheltenham | 87,188 |
| Cheshunt (★London) | 49,616 |
| Chester | 80,154 |
| Chesterfield (★127,000) | 73,352 |
| Clacton-on-Sea | 39,618 |
| Colchester | 87,476 |
| Corby | 48,704 |
| Coventry (★645,000) | 318,718 |
| Crawley (★London) | 80,113 |
| Crewe | 59,097 |
| Crosby (★Liverpool) | 54,103 |
| Darlington | 85,519 |
| Dartford (★London) | 62,032 |
| Derby (★275,000) | 218,026 |
| Dewsbury (★Leeds) | 49,612 |
| Doncaster | 74,727 |
| Dover | 33,461 |
| Dudley (★Birmingham) | 186,513 |
| Dunstable (★Luton) | 48,436 |
| Durham | 38,105 |
| Eastbourne | 86,715 |
| Eastleigh (★Southampton) | 58,585 |
| Ellesmere Port (★Liverpool) | 65,829 |
| Epsom and Ewell (★London) | 65,830 |
| Esher / Molesey (★London) | 46,688 |
| Exeter | 88,235 |
| Fareham / Portchester (★Portsmouth) | 55,563 |
| Farnborough (★London) | 48,063 |
| Folkestone | 42,949 |
| Frimley and Camberley (★London) | 45,108 |
| Gateshead (★Newcastle) | 91,429 |
| Gillingham (★London) | 92,531 |
| Gloucester (★115,000) | 106,526 |
| Gosport (★Portsmouth) | 69,664 |
| Gravesend (★London) | 53,450 |
| Grays (★London) | 45,881 |
| Greasby / Moreton (★Liverpool) | 56,410 |
| Great Yarmouth | 54,777 |
| Grimsby (★145,000) | 91,532 |
| Guildford (★London) | 61,509 |
| Halesowen (★Birmingham) | 57,533 |
| Halifax | 76,675 |
| Harlow (★London) | 79,150 |
| Harrogate | 63,637 |
| Hartlepool (★Middlesbrough) | 91,749 |
| Hastings | 74,979 |
| Havant (★Portsmouth) | 50,098 |
| Hemel Hempstead (★London) | 80,110 |
| Hereford | 48,277 |
| Hertford (★London) | 21,350 |
| High Wycombe (▲156,800) | 69,575 |
| Hove (★Brighton) | 65,587 |
| Huddersfield (▲377,400) | 147,825 |
| Huyton-with-Roby (★Liverpool) | 62,011 |
| Ipswich | 129,661 |
| Keighley (★Leeds) | 49,188 |
| Kidderminster | 50,385 |
| Kingston upon Hull (★350,000) | 322,144 |
| Kingswood (★Bristol) | 54,736 |
| Kirkby (★Liverpool) | 52,825 |
| Lancaster | 43,902 |
| Leeds (★1,540,000) | 445,242 |
| Leicester (★495,000) | 324,394 |
| Lincoln | 79,980 |
| Littlehampton | 46,028 |
| Liverpool (★1,525,000) | 538,809 |
| • LONDON (★11,100,000) | 6,574,009 |
| Loughborough | 44,895 |
| Lowestoft | 59,430 |
| Luton (★220,000) | 163,209 |
| Macclesfield | 47,525 |
| Maidenhead (★London) | 59,809 |
| Maidstone | 86,067 |
| Manchester (★2,775,000) | 437,612 |
| Mansfield (★198,000) | 71,325 |
| Margate | 53,137 |
| Middlesbrough (★580,000) | 158,516 |
| Middleton (★Manchester) | 51,373 |
| Milton Keynes | 36,886 |
| Newcastle-under-Lyme (★Stoke-on-Trent) | 73,208 |
| Newcastle upon Tyne (★1,300,000) | 199,064 |
| Northampton | 154,172 |
| Norwich (★230,000) | 169,814 |
| Nottingham (★655,000) | 273,300 |
| Nuneaton (★Coventry) | 60,337 |
| Oldbury / Smethwick (★Birmingham) | 153,268 |
| Oldham (★Manchester) | 107,095 |
| Oxford (★230,000) | 113,847 |
| Penzance | 18,501 |
| Peterborough | 113,404 |
| Plymouth (★290,000) | 238,583 |
| Poole (★Bournemouth) | 122,815 |
| Portsmouth (★485,000) | 174,218 |
| Preston (★250,000) | 166,675 |
| Ramsgate | 36,678 |
| Reading (★200,000) | 194,727 |
| Redditch (★Birmingham) | 61,639 |
| Reigate / Redhill (★London) | 48,241 |
| Rochdale (★Manchester) | 97,292 |
| Rotherham (★Sheffield) | 122,374 |
| Royal Leamington Spa (★Coventry) | 56,552 |
| Royal Tunbridge Wells | 57,699 |
| Rugby | 59,039 |
| Runcorn (★Liverpool) | 63,995 |
| Saint Albans (★London) | 76,709 |
| Saint Helens | 114,397 |
| Sale (★Manchester) | 57,872 |
| Salford (★Manchester) | 96,525 |
| Salisbury | 36,890 |
| Scarborough | 36,665 |
| Scunthorpe | 79,043 |
| Sheffield (★710,000) | 470,685 |
| Shrewsbury | 57,731 |
| Slough (★London) | 106,341 |
| Solihull (★Birmingham) | 93,940 |
| Southampton (★415,000) | 211,321 |
| Southend-on-Sea (★London) | 155,720 |
| Southport (★Liverpool) | 88,596 |
| South Shields (★Newcastle) | 86,488 |
| Stafford | 60,915 |
| Staines (★London) | 51,949 |
| Stevenage | 74,757 |
| Stockport (★Manchester) | 135,489 |
| Stockton-on-Tees (★Middlesbrough) | 86,699 |
| Stoke-on-Trent (★440,000) | 272,446 |
| Stourbridge (★Birmingham) | 55,136 |
| Stratford-upon-Avon | 20,941 |
| Stretford (★Manchester) | 47,522 |
| Sunderland (★Newcastle) | 195,064 |
| Sutton Coldfield (★Birmingham) | 102,572 |
| Swindon | 127,348 |
| Tanworth | 63,260 |
| Taunton | 47,793 |
| Torquay (★112,400) | 54,430 |
| Wakefield (★Leeds) | 74,764 |
| Wallasey (★Liverpool) | 62,465 |
| Walsall (★Birmingham) | 177,923 |
| Walton and Weybridge (★London) | 50,031 |
| Warrington | 81,366 |
| Washington (★Newcastle) | 48,856 |
| Waterlooville (★Portsmouth) | 57,296 |
| Watford (★London) | 109,503 |
| West Bromwich (★Birmingham) | 153,725 |
| Weston-super-Mare | 60,821 |
| Widnes | 55,973 |
| Wigan (★Manchester) | 88,725 |
| Woking (★London) | 92,667 |
| Wolverhampton (★Birmingham) | 263,501 |
| Worcester | 75,466 |
| Worthing (★Brighton) | 90,687 |
| York (★145,000) | 123,126 |

**UNITED KINGDOM: NORTHERN IRELAND**

| | |
|---|---|
| 1990 E | 1,589,400 |
| Bangor (★Belfast) | 72,600 |
| Belfast (★685,000) | 295,100 |
| Castlereagh (★Belfast) | 58,100 |
| Londonderry (Derry) | 100,500 |
| Lurgan (★63,000) (1981C) | 20,991 |
| Newtownabbey (★Belfast) | 72,900 |

**UNITED KINGDOM: SCOTLAND**

| | |
|---|---|
| 1990 E | 5,102,400 |
| Aberdeen | 211,080 |
| Ayr (★100,000) (1981C) | 48,493 |
| Clydebank (★Glasgow) (1981C) | 51,832 |
| Coatbridge (1981C) | 50,831 |
| Cumbernauld (★Glasgow) | 50,700 |
| Dundee | 172,860 |
| Dunfermline (★125,817) (1981C) | 52,105 |
| East Kilbride (★Glasgow) | 70,500 |
| Edinburgh (★630,000) | 434,520 |
| Falkirk (★148,171) (1981C) | 36,372 |
| Glasgow (★1,800,000) | 689,210 |
| Greenock (★101,000) (1981C) | 58,436 |
| Hamilton (★Glasgow) (1981C) | 51,666 |
| Irvine (★94,000) | 56,000 |
| Kilmarnock (★84,000) (1981C) | 51,799 |
| Kirkcaldy (★148,171) (1981C) | 46,356 |
| Motherwell (★Glasgow) (1981C) | 30,616 |
| Paisley (★Glasgow) (1981C) | 84,330 |
| Perth (1981C) | 41,916 |
| Stirling (★61,000) (1981C) | 36,640 |

**UNITED KINGDOM: WALES**

| | |
|---|---|
| 1981 C | 2,790,462 |
| Cardiff (★625,000) | 262,313 |
| Cwmbran (★Newport) | 44,592 |
| Llanelli | 45,336 |
| Merthyr Tydfil | 38,893 |
| Neath (★Swansea) | 48,687 |
| Newport (★310,000) | 115,896 |
| Pontypool (★Newport) | 36,064 |
| Port Talbot (★130,000) | 40,078 |
| Rhondda (★Cardiff) | 70,980 |
| Swansea (★275,000) | 172,433 |
| Wrexham | 39,929 |

**UNITED STATES**

| | |
|---|---|
| 1990 C | 248,709,462 |

**UNITED STATES: ALABAMA**

| | |
|---|---|
| 1990 C | 4,040,587 |
| Anniston (★116,034) | 26,623 |
| Auburn (★61,100) | 33,830 |
| Birmingham (★907,810) | 265,968 |
| Decatur (★131,556) | 48,761 |
| Dothan (★130,964) | 53,589 |
| Florence (★131,327) | 36,426 |
| Gadsden (★99,840) | 42,523 |
| Huntsville (★238,912) | 159,789 |
| Mobile (★476,923) | 196,278 |
| Montgomery (★292,517) | 187,106 |
| Tuscaloosa (★150,522) | 77,759 |

**UNITED STATES: ALASKA**

| | |
|---|---|
| 1990 C | 550,043 |
| Anchorage (★248,400) | 226,338 |
| Fairbanks (★59,500) | 30,843 |
| Juneau | 26,751 |

**UNITED STATES: ARIZONA**

| | |
|---|---|
| 1990 C | 3,665,228 |
| Chandler (★Phoenix) | 90,533 |
| Glendale (★Phoenix) | 148,134 |
| Mesa (★Phoenix) | 288,091 |
| Nogales (★Nogales, Mexico) | 19,489 |
| Phoenix (★2,122,101) | 983,403 |
| Scottsdale (★Phoenix) | 130,069 |
| Tempe (★Phoenix) | 141,865 |
| Tucson (★666,880) | 405,390 |
| Yuma (★106,895) | 54,923 |

**UNITED STATES: ARKANSAS**

| | |
|---|---|
| 1990 C | 2,350,725 |
| Fayetteville (★113,409) | 42,099 |
| Fort Smith (★175,911) | 72,798 |
| Hot Springs National Park (★56,500) | 32,462 |
| Jonesboro (★49,300) | 46,535 |
| Little Rock (★513,117) | 175,795 |
| North Little Rock (★Little Rock) | 61,741 |
| Pine Bluff (★85,487) | 57,140 |

**UNITED STATES: CALIFORNIA**

| | |
|---|---|
| 1990 C | 29,760,021 |
| Alameda (★Oakland) | 76,459 |
| Alhambra (★Los Angeles) | 82,106 |
| Anaheim (★2,410,556) (★Los Angeles) | 266,406 |
| Antioch (★Oakland) | 62,195 |
| Arden (★Sacramento) | 62,900 |
| Bakersfield (★543,477) | 174,820 |
| Baldwin Park (★Los Angeles) | 69,330 |
| Bellflower (★Los Angeles) | 61,815 |
| Berkeley (★Oakland) | 102,724 |
| Buena Park (★Anaheim) | 68,784 |
| Burbank (★Los Angeles) | 93,643 |
| Calexico (★Mexicali, Mexico) | 18,633 |
| Camarillo (★Oxnard) | 52,303 |
| Carlsbad (★San Diego) | 63,126 |
| Carmichael (★Sacramento) | 48,702 |
| Carson (★Los Angeles) | 83,995 |
| Cerritos (★Los Angeles) | 53,240 |
| Chico (★182,120) | 40,079 |
| Chino (★Riverside) | 59,682 |
| Chula Vista (★San Diego) | 135,163 |
| Citrus Heights (★Sacramento) | 107,439 |
| Clovis (★Fresno) | 50,323 |
| Compton (★Los Angeles) | 90,454 |
| Concord (★Oakland) | 111,348 |
| Corona (★Riverside) | 76,095 |
| Costa Mesa (★Anaheim) | 96,357 |
| Cucamonga (★Riverside) | 101,409 |
| Daly City (★San Francisco) | 92,311 |
| Diamond Bar (★Los Angeles) | 53,672 |
| Downey (★Los Angeles) | 91,444 |
| East Los Angeles (★Los Angeles) | 126,379 |
| El Cajon (★San Diego) | 88,693 |
| El Monte (★Los Angeles) | 106,209 |
| El Toro (★Anaheim) | 62,685 |
| Escondido (★San Diego) | 108,635 |
| Eureka (★89,800) | 27,025 |
| Fairfield (★Vallejo) | 77,211 |
| Fontana (★Riverside) | 87,535 |
| Fountain Valley (★Anaheim) | 53,691 |
| Fremont (★Oakland) | 173,339 |
| Fresno (★667,490) | 354,202 |
| Fullerton (★Anaheim) | 114,144 |
| Gardena (★Los Angeles) | 49,847 |
| Garden Grove (★Anaheim) | 143,050 |
| Glendale (★Los Angeles) | 180,038 |
| Hacienda Heights (★Los Angeles) | 52,354 |
| Hawthorne (★Los Angeles) | 71,349 |
| Hayward (★Oakland) | 111,498 |
| Hemet (★Riverside) | 36,094 |
| Huntington Beach (★Anaheim) | 181,519 |
| Huntington Park (★Los Angeles) | 56,065 |
| Inglewood (★Los Angeles) | 109,602 |
| Irvine (★Anaheim) | 110,330 |
| La Habra (★Anaheim) | 51,266 |
| Lakewood (★Los Angeles) | 73,557 |
| La Mesa (★San Diego) | 52,931 |
| Lancaster (★189,300) (★Los Angeles) | 97,291 |
| Livermore (★Oakland) | 56,741 |
| Lodi (★Stockton) | 51,874 |
| Lompoc (★Santa Barbara) | 37,649 |
| Long Beach (★Los Angeles) | 429,433 |
| Los Angeles (★14,531,529) | 3,485,398 |
| Lynwood (★Los Angeles) | 61,945 |
| Merced (★178,403) | 56,216 |
| Milpitas (★San Jose) | 50,686 |
| Mission Viejo (★Anaheim) | 72,820 |
| Modesto (★370,522) | 164,730 |
| Montebello (★Los Angeles) | 59,564 |
| Monterey (★Salinas) | 31,954 |
| Monterey Park (★Los Angeles) | 60,738 |
| Mountain View (★San Jose) | 67,460 |
| Napa (★Vallejo) | 61,842 |
| National City (★San Diego) | 54,249 |
| Newport Beach (★Anaheim) | 66,643 |
| Norwalk (★Los Angeles) | 94,279 |
| Oakland (★2,082,914) (★San Francisco) | 372,242 |
| Oceanside (★San Diego) | 128,398 |
| Ontario (★Riverside) | 133,179 |
| Orange (★Anaheim) | 110,658 |
| Oxnard (★669,016) (★Los Angeles) | 142,216 |
| Palm Springs (★Riverside) | 40,181 |
| Palo Alto (★San Jose) | 55,900 |
| Pasadena (★Los Angeles) | 131,591 |
| Pico Rivera (★Los Angeles) | 59,177 |
| Pleasanton (★Oakland) | 50,553 |
| Pomona (★Los Angeles) | 131,723 |
| Porterville (★Visalia) | 29,563 |
| Rancho Cordova (★Sacramento) | 48,731 |
| Redding (★147,036) | 66,462 |
| Redlands (★Riverside) | 60,394 |
| Redondo Beach (★Los Angeles) | 60,167 |
| Redwood City (★San Francisco) | 66,072 |
| Rialto (★Riverside) | 72,388 |
| Richmond (★Oakland) | 87,425 |
| Riverside (★2,588,793) (★Los Angeles) | 226,505 |
| Rosemead (★Los Angeles) | 51,638 |
| Sacramento (★1,481,102) | 369,365 |
| Salinas (★355,660) | 108,777 |
| San Bernardino (★Riverside) | 164,164 |
| San Diego (★2,949,000) | 1,110,549 |
| San Francisco (★6,253,311) | 723,959 |
| San Jose (★1,497,577) (★San Francisco) | 782,248 |
| San Leandro (★Oakland) | 68,223 |
| San Mateo (★San Francisco) | 85,486 |
| Santa Ana (★Anaheim) | 293,742 |
| Santa Barbara (★369,608) | 85,571 |
| Santa Clara (★San Jose) | 93,613 |
| Santa Cruz (★229,734) (★San Francisco) | 49,040 |
| Santa Maria (★Santa Barbara) | 61,284 |
| Santa Monica (★Los Angeles) | 86,905 |
| Santa Rosa (★388,222) (★San Francisco) | 113,313 |
| Santee (★San Diego) | 52,902 |
| Simi Valley (★Oxnard) | 100,217 |
| South Gate (★Los Angeles) | 86,284 |
| South San Francisco (★San Francisco) | 54,312 |
| South Whittier (★Los Angeles) | 51,100 |
| Spring Valley (★San Diego) | 54,600 |
| Stockton (★480,628) | 210,943 |
| Sunnyvale (★San Jose) | 117,229 |
| Thousand Oaks (★Oxnard) | 104,352 |
| Torrance (★Los Angeles) | 133,107 |
| Tustin (★Anaheim) | 50,689 |
| Union City (★Oakland) | 53,762 |
| Upland (★Riverside) | 63,374 |
| Vacaville (★Vallejo) | 71,479 |
| Vallejo (★451,186) (★San Francisco) | 109,199 |

▲ Population of an entire municipality, commune, or district, including rural area.
• Largest city in country.
★ Population or designation of the metropolitan area, including suburbs.
**C** Census. **E** Official estimate. **U** Unofficial estimate.

▲ Bevölkerung eines ganzen städtischen Verwaltungsgebietes, eines Kommunalbezirkes oder eines Distrikts, einschliesslich ländlicher Gebiete.
• Grösste Stadt des Landes.
★ Bevölkerung oder Bezeichnung der Stadtregion einschliesslich Vororte.
**C** Volkszählung. **E** Offizielle Schätzung. **U** Inoffizielle Schätzung.

| | |
|---|---|
| Ventura (San Buenaventura) (★Oxnard) | 92,575 |
| Visalia (★311,921) | 75,636 |
| Vista (★San Diego) | 71,872 |
| Walnut Creek (★Oakland) | 60,569 |
| Watsonville (★Santa Cruz) | 31,099 |
| West Covina (★Los Angeles) | 96,086 |
| Westminster (★Anaheim) | 78,118 |
| Whittier (★Los Angeles) | 77,671 |
| Yorba Linda (★Anaheim) | 52,422 |
| Yuba City (★122,643) | 27,437 |

**UNITED STATES: COLORADO**

| | |
|---|---|
| 1990 C | 3,294,394 |
| Arvada (★Denver) | 89,235 |
| Aurora (★Denver) | 222,103 |
| Boulder (★225,339) (★Denver) | 83,312 |
| Colorado Springs (★397,014) | 281,140 |
| Denver (★1,848,319) | 467,610 |
| Fort Collins (★186,136) | 87,758 |
| Grand Junction (★85,200) | 29,034 |
| Greeley (★131,821) | 60,536 |
| Lakewood (★Denver) | 126,481 |
| Longmont (★Boulder) | 51,555 |
| Loveland (★Fort Collins) | 37,352 |
| Pueblo (★123,051) | 98,640 |
| Thornton (★Denver) | 55,031 |
| Westminster (★Denver) | 74,625 |

**UNITED STATES: CONNECTICUT**

| | |
|---|---|
| 1990 C | 3,287,116 |
| Bridgeport (★443,722) (★New York, N.Y.) | 141,686 |
| Bristol (★79,488) (★Hartford) | 60,640 |
| Danbury (★187,867) (★New York, N.Y.) | 65,585 |
| East Hartford (★Hartford) | 50,452 |
| Fairfield (★Bridgeport) | 53,418 |
| Greenwich (★Stamford) | 58,441 |
| Hamden (★New Haven) | 52,434 |
| Hartford (★1,085,837) | 139,739 |
| Manchester (★Hartford) | 51,618 |
| Meriden (★New Haven) | 59,479 |
| Milford (★Bridgeport) | 48,168 |
| New Britain (★148,188) (★Hartford) | 75,491 |
| New Haven (★530,180) | 130,474 |
| New London (★266,819) | 28,540 |
| Norwalk (★127,378) (★New York, N.Y.) | 78,331 |
| Stamford (★202,557) (★New York, N.Y.) | 108,056 |
| Stratford (★Bridgeport) | 49,389 |
| Torrington (★58,800) | 33,687 |
| Waterbury (★221,629) | 108,961 |
| West Hartford (★Hartford) | 60,110 |
| West Haven (★New Haven) | 54,021 |

**UNITED STATES: DELAWARE**

| | |
|---|---|
| 1990 C | 666,168 |
| Dover (★78,900) | 27,630 |
| Wilmington (★Philadelphia, Pa.) | 71,529 |

**UNITED STATES: DISTRICT OF COLUMBIA**

| | |
|---|---|
| 1990 C | 606,900 |
| WASHINGTON (★3,923,574) | 606,900 |

**UNITED STATES: FLORIDA**

| | |
|---|---|
| 1990 C | 12,937,926 |
| Boca Raton (★West Palm Beach) | 61,492 |
| Brandon (★Tampa) | 57,985 |
| Cape Coral (★Fort Myers) | 74,991 |
| Carol City (★Miami) | 53,331 |
| City of Sunrise (★Fort Lauderdale) | 64,407 |
| Clearwater (★Tampa) | 98,784 |
| Daytona Beach (★370,712) | 61,921 |
| De Land (★Daytona Beach) | 16,491 |
| Fort Lauderdale (★1,255,488) (★Miami) | 149,377 |
| Fort Myers (★335,113) | 45,206 |
| Fort Pierce (★251,071) | 36,830 |
| Fort Walton Beach (★143,776) | 21,471 |
| Gainesville (★204,111) | 84,770 |
| Hialeah (★Miami) | 188,004 |
| Hollywood (★Fort Lauderdale) | 121,697 |
| Jacksonville (★906,727) | 635,230 |
| Kendall (★Miami) | 87,271 |
| Lakeland (★405,382) | 70,576 |
| Largo (★Tampa) | 65,674 |
| Melbourne (★398,978) | 59,646 |
| Miami (★3,192,582) | 358,548 |
| Miami Beach (★Miami) | 92,639 |
| Naples (★152,099) | 19,505 |
| Ocala (★194,833) | 42,045 |
| Orlando (★1,072,748) | 164,693 |
| Panama City (★126,994) | 34,378 |
| Pembroke Pines (★Fort Lauderdale) | 65,452 |
| Pensacola (★344,406) | 58,165 |
| Plantation (★Fort Lauderdale) | 66,692 |
| Pompano Beach (★Fort Lauderdale) | 72,411 |
| Saint Petersburg (★Tampa) | 238,629 |
| Sarasota (★277,776) | 50,961 |
| Tallahassee (★233,598) | 124,773 |
| Tampa (★2,067,959) | 280,015 |
| Venice (★Sarasota) | 16,922 |
| West Palm Beach (★863,518) | 67,643 |
| Winter Haven (★Lakeland) | 24,725 |

**UNITED STATES: GEORGIA**

| | |
|---|---|
| 1990 C | 6,478,216 |
| Albany (★112,561) | 78,122 |
| Athens (★156,267) | 45,734 |
| Atlanta (★2,833,511) | 394,017 |
| Augusta (★396,809) | 44,639 |
| Columbus (★243,072) | 178,681 |
| Macon (★281,103) | 106,612 |
| Rome (★74,900) | 30,326 |
| Savannah (★242,622) | 137,560 |
| Valdosta (★64,000) | 39,806 |
| Warner Robins (★Macon) | 43,726 |

**UNITED STATES: HAWAII**

| | |
|---|---|
| 1990 C | 1,108,229 |
| Hilo (★47,600) | 37,808 |
| Honolulu (★836,231) | 365,272 |

**UNITED STATES: IDAHO**

| | |
|---|---|
| 1990 C | 1,006,749 |
| Boise (★205,775) | 125,738 |
| Idaho Falls (★72,700) | 43,929 |
| Lewiston (★44,300) | 28,082 |
| Nampa (★70,500) | 28,365 |
| Pocatello (★56,700) | 46,080 |

**UNITED STATES: ILLINOIS**

| | |
|---|---|
| 1990 C | 11,430,602 |
| Arlington Heights (★Chicago) | 75,460 |
| Aurora (★356,884) (★Chicago) | 99,581 |
| Bloomington (★129,180) | 51,972 |
| Champaign (★173,025) | 63,502 |
| Chicago (★8,065,633) | 2,783,726 |
| Cicero (★Chicago) | 67,436 |
| Danville (★68,000) | 33,828 |
| Decatur (★117,206) | 83,885 |
| De Kalb (★52,200) | 34,925 |
| Des Plaines (★Chicago) | 53,223 |
| East Saint Louis (★Saint Louis, Mo.) | 40,944 |
| Elgin (★Aurora) | 77,010 |
| Evanston (★Chicago) | 73,233 |
| Galesburg (★40,600) | 33,530 |
| Joliet (★389,650) (★Chicago) | 76,836 |
| Kankakee (★96,255) | 27,575 |
| Mount Prospect (★Chicago) | 53,170 |
| Naperville (★Chicago) | 85,351 |
| Oak Lawn (★Chicago) | 56,182 |
| Oak Park (★Chicago) | 53,648 |
| Peoria (★339,172) | 113,504 |
| Quincy (★50,600) | 39,681 |
| Rockford (★283,719) | 139,426 |
| Schaumburg (★Chicago) | 68,586 |
| Skokie (★Chicago) | 59,432 |
| Springfield (★189,550) | 105,227 |
| Waukegan (★Chicago) | 69,392 |
| Wheaton (★Chicago) | 51,464 |

**UNITED STATES: INDIANA**

| | |
|---|---|
| 1990 C | 5,544,159 |
| Anderson (★130,669) | 59,459 |
| Bloomington (★108,978) | 60,633 |
| Columbus (★59,000) | 31,802 |
| Elkhart (★156,198) | 43,627 |
| Evansville (★278,990) | 126,272 |
| Fort Wayne (★363,811) | 173,072 |
| Gary (★604,526) (★Chicago, Il.) | 116,646 |
| Hammond (★Gary) | 84,236 |
| Indianapolis (★1,249,822) | 731,327 |
| Kokomo (★96,946) | 44,962 |
| Lafayette (★130,598) | 43,764 |
| Marion (★76,900) | 32,618 |
| Michigan City (★55,600) | 33,822 |
| Muncie (★119,659) | 71,035 |
| Richmond (★64,100) | 38,705 |
| South Bend (★247,052) | 105,511 |
| Terre Haute (★130,812) | 57,483 |

**UNITED STATES: IOWA**

| | |
|---|---|
| 1990 C | 2,776,755 |
| Ames (★65,400) | 47,198 |
| Cedar Rapids (★168,767) | 108,751 |
| Clinton (★39,600) | 29,201 |
| Council Bluffs (★Omaha, Ne.) | 54,315 |
| Davenport (★350,861) | 95,333 |
| Des Moines (★392,928) | 193,187 |
| Dubuque (★86,403) | 57,546 |
| Iowa City (★96,119) | 59,738 |
| Mason City | 29,040 |
| Sioux City (★115,018) | 80,505 |
| Waterloo (★146,611) | 66,467 |

**UNITED STATES: KANSAS**

| | |
|---|---|
| 1990 C | 2,477,574 |
| Hutchinson (★46,800) | 39,308 |
| Kansas City (★Kansas City, Mo.) | 149,767 |
| Lawrence (★81,798) | 65,608 |
| Manhattan (★47,400) | 37,712 |
| Olathe (★Kansas City, Mo.) | 63,352 |
| Overland Park (★Kansas City, Mo.) | 111,790 |
| Salina (★42,700) | 42,303 |
| Topeka (★160,976) | 119,883 |
| Wichita (★485,270) | 304,011 |

**UNITED STATES: KENTUCKY**

| | |
|---|---|
| 1990 C | 3,685,296 |
| Bowling Green (★59,100) | 40,641 |
| Covington (★Cincinnati, Oh.) | 43,264 |
| Frankfort | 25,968 |
| Lexington (★348,428) | 225,366 |
| Louisville (★952,662) | 269,063 |
| Owensboro (★87,189) | 53,549 |
| Paducah (★63,000) | 27,256 |

**UNITED STATES: LOUISIANA**

| | |
|---|---|
| 1990 C | 4,219,973 |
| Alexandria (★131,556) | 49,188 |
| Baton Rouge (★528,264) | 219,531 |
| Bossier City (★Shreveport) | 52,721 |
| Houma (★182,842) | 96,982 |
| Kenner (★New Orleans) | 72,033 |
| Lafayette (★208,740) | 94,440 |
| Lake Charles (★168,134) | 70,580 |
| Metairie (★New Orleans) | 149,428 |
| Monroe (★142,191) | 54,909 |
| New Iberia (★49,000) | 31,828 |
| New Orleans (★1,238,816) | 496,938 |
| Shreveport (★334,341) | 198,525 |

**UNITED STATES: MAINE**

| | |
|---|---|
| 1990 C | 1,227,928 |
| Augusta (★56,700) | 21,325 |
| Bangor (★88,745) | 33,181 |
| Lewiston (★88,141) | 39,757 |
| Portland (★215,281) | 64,358 |

**UNITED STATES: MARYLAND**

| | |
|---|---|
| 1990 C | 4,781,468 |
| Annapolis (★Baltimore) | 33,187 |
| Baltimore (★2,382,172) | 736,014 |
| Bethesda (★Washington, D.C.) | 62,936 |
| Columbia (★Baltimore) | 75,883 |
| Cumberland (★101,643) | 23,706 |
| Dundalk (★Baltimore) | 65,800 |
| Hagerstown (★121,393) | 35,445 |
| Salisbury (★72,400) | 20,592 |
| Silver Spring (★Washington, D.C.) | 76,046 |
| Towson (★Baltimore) | 49,445 |
| Wheaton (★Washington, D.C.) (1989) | 58,300 |

**UNITED STATES: MASSACHUSETTS**

| | |
|---|---|
| 1990 C | 6,016,425 |
| Amherst (★44,700) | 17,824 |
| Boston (★4,171,643) | 574,283 |
| Brockton (★189,478) (★Boston) | 92,788 |
| Brookline (★Boston) | 54,718 |
| Cambridge (★Boston) | 95,802 |
| Chicopee (★Springfield) | 56,632 |
| Fall River (★157,272) (★Providence, R.I.) | 92,703 |
| Fitchburg (★102,797) | 41,194 |
| Framingham (★Boston) | 64,994 |
| Haverhill (★Lawrence) | 51,418 |
| Lawrence (★393,516) (★Boston) | 70,207 |
| Lowell (★273,067) (★Boston) | 103,439 |
| Lynn (★Salem) | 81,245 |
| Malden (★Boston) | 53,884 |
| Medford (★Boston) | 57,407 |
| New Bedford (★175,641) | 99,922 |
| Newton (★Boston) | 82,585 |
| Northampton (★Springfield) | 29,289 |
| Pittsfield (★79,250) | 48,622 |
| Quincy (★Boston) | 84,985 |
| Somerville (★Boston) | 76,210 |
| Springfield (★529,519) | 156,983 |
| Taunton (★59,700) | 49,832 |
| Waltham (★Boston) | 57,878 |
| Weymouth (★Boston) | 54,063 |
| Worcester (★436,905) | 169,759 |

**UNITED STATES: MICHIGAN**

| | |
|---|---|
| 1990 C | 9,295,297 |
| Ann Arbor (★282,937) (★Detroit) | 109,592 |
| Battle Creek (★135,982) | 53,540 |
| Benton Harbor (★161,378) | 12,818 |
| Clinton Township (★Detroit) | 85,866 |
| Dearborn (★Detroit) | 89,286 |
| Dearborn Heights (★Detroit) | 60,838 |
| Detroit (★4,665,236) | 1,027,974 |
| East Lansing (★Lansing) | 50,677 |
| Farmington Hills (★Detroit) | 74,652 |
| Flint (★430,459) | 140,761 |
| Grand Rapids (★688,399) | 189,126 |
| Holland (★Grand Rapids) | 30,745 |
| Jackson (★149,756) | 37,446 |
| Kalamazoo (★223,411) | 80,277 |
| Lansing (★432,674) | 127,321 |
| Livonia (★Detroit) | 100,850 |
| Monroe (★62,600) (★Detroit) | 22,902 |
| Muskegon (★158,983) | 40,283 |
| Pontiac (★Detroit) | 71,166 |
| Port Huron (★Sarnia, Canada) | 33,694 |
| Redford Township (★Detroit) | 54,387 |
| Roseville (★Detroit) | 51,412 |
| Royal Oak (★Detroit) | 65,410 |
| Saginaw (★399,320) | 69,512 |
| Saint Clair Shores (★Detroit) | 68,107 |
| Sault Sainte Marie | 14,689 |
| Southfield (★Detroit) | 75,728 |
| Sterling Heights (★Detroit) | 117,810 |
| Taylor (★Detroit) | 70,811 |
| Troy (★Detroit) | 72,884 |
| Warren (★Detroit) | 144,864 |
| Westland (★Detroit) | 84,724 |
| Wyoming (★Grand Rapids) | 63,891 |

**UNITED STATES: MINNESOTA**

| | |
|---|---|
| 1990 C | 4,375,099 |
| Bloomington (★Minneapolis) | 86,335 |
| Brooklyn Park (★Minneapolis) | 56,381 |
| Burnsville (★Minneapolis) | 51,288 |
| Coon Rapids (★Minneapolis) | 52,978 |
| Duluth (★239,971) | 85,493 |
| Mankato (★48,400) | 31,477 |
| Minneapolis (★2,464,124) | 368,383 |
| Plymouth (★Minneapolis) | 50,889 |
| Rochester (★106,470) | 70,745 |
| Saint Cloud (★190,921) | 48,812 |
| Saint Paul (★Minneapolis) | 272,235 |

**UNITED STATES: MISSISSIPPI**

| | |
|---|---|
| 1990 C | 2,573,216 |
| Biloxi (★197,125) | 46,319 |
| Columbus (★52,100) | 23,799 |
| Greenville (★48,500) | 45,226 |
| Gulfport (★Biloxi) | 40,775 |
| Hattiesburg (★71,600) | 41,882 |
| Jackson (★395,396) | 196,637 |
| Laurel (★47,300) | 18,827 |
| Meridian (★60,600) | 41,036 |
| Natchez (★45,700) | 19,460 |
| Pascagoula (★115,243) | 25,899 |
| Vicksburg (★43,500) | 20,908 |

**UNITED STATES: MISSOURI**

| | |
|---|---|
| 1990 C | 5,117,073 |
| Cape Girardeau (★59,100) | 34,438 |
| Columbia (★112,379) | 69,101 |
| Florissant (★Saint Louis) | 51,206 |
| Independence (★Kansas City) | 112,301 |
| Jefferson City (★60,100) | 35,481 |
| Joplin (★134,910) | 40,961 |
| Kansas City (★1,566,280) | 435,146 |
| Saint Charles (★Saint Louis) | 54,555 |
| Saint Joseph (★83,083) | 71,852 |
| Saint Louis (★2,444,099) | 396,685 |
| Springfield (★240,593) | 140,494 |

**UNITED STATES: MONTANA**

| | |
|---|---|
| 1990 C | 799,065 |
| Billings (★113,419) | 81,151 |
| Butte (★33,900) | 33,336 |
| Great Falls (★77,691) | 55,097 |
| Helena | 24,569 |
| Missoula (★65,700) | 42,918 |

**UNITED STATES: NEBRASKA**

| | |
|---|---|
| 1990 C | 1,578,385 |
| Grand Island (★42,200) | 39,386 |
| Lincoln (★213,641) | 191,972 |
| Omaha (★618,262) | 335,795 |

**UNITED STATES: NEVADA**

| | |
|---|---|
| 1990 C | 1,201,833 |
| Carson City | 40,443 |
| Henderson (★Las Vegas) | 64,942 |
| Las Vegas (★741,459) | 258,295 |
| Paradise (★Las Vegas) | 124,682 |
| Reno (★254,667) | 133,850 |
| Sparks (★Reno) | 53,367 |
| Sunrise Manor (★Las Vegas) | 95,362 |

**UNITED STATES: NEW HAMPSHIRE**

| | |
|---|---|
| 1990 C | 1,109,252 |
| Concord (★73,300) | 36,006 |
| Manchester (★147,809) | 99,567 |
| Nashua (★180,557) (★Boston, Ma.) | 79,662 |
| Portsmouth (★223,578) | 25,925 |

**UNITED STATES: NEW JERSEY**

| | |
|---|---|
| 1990 C | 7,730,188 |
| Atlantic City (★319,416) | 37,986 |
| Bayonne (★Jersey City) | 61,444 |
| Bloomfield (★Newark) | 45,061 |
| Brick Township (★New York, N.Y.) | 66,473 |
| Camden (★Philadelphia, Pa.) | 87,492 |
| Cherry Hill (★Philadelphia, Pa.) | 69,319 |
| Clifton (★New York, N.Y.) | 71,742 |
| East Orange (★Newark) | 73,552 |
| Edison (★New York, N.Y.) | 88,680 |
| Elizabeth (★Newark) | 110,002 |
| Irvington (★Newark) | 59,774 |
| Jersey City (★553,099) (★New York, N.Y.) | 228,537 |
| Middletown (★New York, N.Y.) | 62,298 |
| Newark (★1,824,321) (★New York, N.Y.) | 275,221 |
| Passaic (★New York, N.Y.) | 58,041 |
| Paterson (★New York, N.Y.) | 140,891 |
| Trenton (★325,824) (★Philadelphia, Pa.) | 88,675 |
| Union (★Newark) | 50,024 |
| Union City (★Jersey City) | 58,012 |
| Vineland (★138,053) (★Philadelphia, Pa.) | 54,780 |

**UNITED STATES: NEW MEXICO**

| | |
|---|---|
| 1990 C | 1,515,069 |
| Albuquerque (★480,577) | 384,736 |
| Farmington (★50,300) | 33,997 |
| Las Cruces (★135,510) | 62,126 |
| Roswell (★50,600) | 44,654 |
| Santa Fe (★117,043) | 55,859 |

**UNITED STATES: NEW YORK**

| | |
|---|---|
| 1990 C | 17,990,455 |
| Albany (★874,304) | 101,082 |
| Auburn (★52,900) | 31,258 |
| Binghamton (★264,497) | 53,008 |
| Buffalo (★1,189,288) | 328,123 |
| Cheektowaga (★Buffalo) | 84,387 |
| Elmira (★95,195) | 33,724 |
| Glens Falls (★118,539) | 15,023 |
| Hempstead (★New York) | 49,453 |
| Irondequoit (★Rochester) | 52,322 |
| Ithaca (★82,700) | 29,541 |
| Jamestown (★141,895) | 34,681 |
| Kingston (★88,200) | 23,095 |
| Levittown (★New York) | 53,286 |
| Lockport (★57,500) (★Buffalo) | 24,426 |
| Mount Vernon (★New York) | 67,153 |
| Newburgh (★102,300) (★New York) | 26,454 |
| New Rochelle (★New York) | 67,265 |
| • New York (★18,087,251) | 7,322,564 |
| Niagara Falls (★220,756) (★Buffalo) | 61,840 |
| Poughkeepsie (★259,462) | 28,844 |
| Rochester (★1,002,410) | 231,636 |
| Schenectady (★Albany) | 65,566 |
| Syracuse (★659,864) | 163,860 |
| Troy (★Albany) | 54,269 |
| Utica (★316,633) | 68,637 |
| West Seneca (★Buffalo) | 47,866 |
| Yonkers (★New York) | 188,082 |

**UNITED STATES: NORTH CAROLINA**

| | |
|---|---|
| 1990 C | 6,628,637 |
| Asheville (★174,821) | 61,607 |
| Burlington (★108,213) | 39,498 |
| Charlotte (★1,162,093) | 395,934 |
| Durham (★Raleigh) | 136,611 |
| Fayetteville (★274,566) | 75,695 |
| Gastonia (★Charlotte) | 54,732 |
| Goldsboro (★94,200) | 40,709 |
| Greensboro (★942,091) | 183,521 |
| Hickory (★221,700) | 28,301 |
| High Point (★Greensboro) | 69,496 |
| Jacksonville (★149,838) | 30,013 |
| Kannapolis (★Charlotte) | 29,696 |
| Raleigh (★735,480) | 207,951 |
| Rocky Mount (★83,400) | 48,997 |
| Salisbury (★Charlotte) | 23,087 |
| Wilmington (★120,284) | 55,530 |
| Winston-Salem (★Greenboro) | 143,485 |

**UNITED STATES: NORTH DAKOTA**

| | |
|---|---|
| 1990 C | 638,800 |
| Bismarck (★83,831) | 49,256 |
| Fargo (★153,296) | 74,111 |
| Grand Forks (★70,683) | 49,425 |
| Minot (★39,800) | 34,544 |

**UNITED STATES: OHIO**

| | |
|---|---|
| 1990 C | 10,347,115 |
| Akron (★657,575) (★Cleveland) | 223,019 |
| Alliance (★Canton) | 23,376 |
| Ashtabula (★40,900) | 21,633 |
| Brunswick (★Cleveland) | 28,230 |
| Canton (★394,106) | 84,161 |
| Cincinnati (★1,744,124) | 364,040 |
| Cleveland (★2,759,823) | 505,616 |
| Cleveland Heights (★Cleveland) | 54,052 |
| Columbus (★1,377,419) | 632,910 |
| Dayton (★951,270) | 182,044 |
| East Liverpool (★44,400) | 13,654 |
| Elyria (★Lorain) | 56,746 |
| Euclid (★Cleveland) | 54,875 |
| Hamilton (★291,479) (★Cincinnati) | 61,368 |
| Kettering (★Dayton) | 60,569 |
| Lakewood (★Cleveland) | 59,718 |
| Lancaster (★Columbus) | 34,507 |
| Lima (★154,340) | 45,549 |
| Lorain (★271,126) (★Cleveland) | 71,245 |
| Mansfield (★126,137) | 50,627 |
| Marion (★53,900) | 34,075 |
| Middletown (★107,200) (★Cincinnati) | 46,022 |
| Newark (★Columbus) | 44,389 |
| Parma (★Cleveland) | 87,876 |
| Portsmouth (★64,300) | 22,676 |
| Sandusky (★79,800) | 29,764 |
| Springfield (★Dayton) | 70,487 |
| Steubenville (★142,523) | 22,125 |
| Toledo (★614,128) | 332,943 |
| Warren (★Youngstown) | 50,793 |
| Youngstown (★492,619) | 95,732 |
| Zanesville (★67,800) | 26,778 |

▲ Población de un municipio, comuna o distrito entero, incluyendo sus áreas rurales.
• Ciudad más grande de un país.
★ Población o designación de un área metropolitana, incluyendo los suburbios.
**C** Censo. **E** Estimado oficial. **U** Estimado no oficial.

▲ Population d'une municipalité, d'une commune ou d'un district, zone rurale incluse.
• Ville la plus peuplée du pays.
★ Population de l'agglomération (ou nom de la zone métropolitaine englobante).
**C** Recensement. **E** Estimation officielle. **U** Estimation non officielle.

▲ População de um municipio, comuna ou distrito, inclusive as respectivas áreas rurais.
• Maior cidade de um país.
★ População ou indicação de uma área metropolitana.
**C** Censo. **E** Estimativa oficial. **U** Estimativa não oficial.

**UNITED STATES: OKLAHOMA**

| | |
|---|---|
| 1990 C | 3,145,585 |
| Broken Arrow (★Tulsa) | 58,043 |
| Edmond (★Oklahoma City) | 52,315 |
| Enid (★56,735) | 45,309 |
| Lawton (★111,486) | 80,561 |
| Midwest City (★Oklahoma City) | 52,267 |
| Muskogee (★49,500) | 37,708 |
| Norman (★Oklahoma City) | 80,071 |
| Oklahoma City (★958,839) | 444,719 |
| Tulsa (★708,954) | 367,302 |

**UNITED STATES: OREGON**

| | |
|---|---|
| 1990 C | 2,842,321 |
| Beaverton (★Portland) | 53,310 |
| Corvallis (★98,700) | 44,757 |
| Eugene (★282,912) | 112,669 |
| Gresham (★Portland) | 68,235 |
| Medford (★146,389) | 46,951 |
| Portland (★1,477,895) | 437,319 |
| Salem (★278,024) | 107,786 |

**UNITED STATES: PENNSYLVANIA**

| | |
|---|---|
| 1990 C | 11,881,643 |
| Abington (★Philadelphia) | 59,300 |
| Allentown (★686,688) | 105,090 |
| Altoona (★130,542) | 51,881 |
| Bensalem (★Philadelphia) | 56,788 |
| Bethlehem (★Allentown) | 71,428 |
| Bristol (★Philadelphia) | 57,129 |
| Butler (★86,500) | 15,714 |
| Coatesville (★93,400) (★Philadelphia) | 11,038 |
| Erie (★275,572) | 108,718 |
| Hanover (★York) | 14,399 |
| Harrisburg (★587,986) | 52,376 |
| Haverford (★Philadelphia) | 49,848 |
| Hazleton (★Scranton) | 24,730 |
| Johnstown (★241,247) | 28,134 |
| Lancaster (★422,822) | 55,551 |
| Lebanon (★Harrisburg) | 24,800 |
| Lower Merion Township (★Philadelphia) | 58,003 |
| New Castle (★68,400) | 28,334 |
| Oil City (★42,000) | 11,949 |
| Penn Hills (★Pittsburgh) | 51,430 |
| Philadelphia (★5,899,345) | 1,585,577 |
| Pittsburgh (★2,242,798) | 369,879 |
| Pottstown (★88,300) (★Philadelphia) | 21,831 |
| Pottsville (★54,200) | 16,603 |
| Reading (★336,523) | 78,380 |
| Scranton (★734,175) | 81,805 |
| Sharon (★121,003) | 17,493 |
| State College (★123,786) | 38,923 |
| Uniontown (★53,200) (★Pittsburgh) | 12,034 |
| Upper Darby (★Philadelphia) | 84,054 |
| Washington (★66,000) (★Pittsburgh) | 15,864 |
| Wilkes-Barre (★Scranton) | 47,523 |
| Williamsport (★118,710) | 31,933 |
| York (★417,848) | 42,192 |

**UNITED STATES: RHODE ISLAND**

| | |
|---|---|
| 1990 C | 1,003,464 |
| Cranston (★Providence) | 76,060 |
| East Providence (★Providence) | 50,380 |
| Newport (★64,500) | 28,227 |
| Pawtucket (★329,384) (★Providence) | 72,644 |
| Providence (★1,141,510) | 160,728 |
| Warwick (★Providence) | 85,427 |

**UNITED STATES: SOUTH CAROLINA**

| | |
|---|---|
| 1990 C | 3,486,703 |
| Anderson (★145,196) | 26,184 |
| Charleston (★506,875) | 80,414 |
| Columbia (★453,331) | 98,052 |
| Florence (★114,344) | 29,813 |
| Greenville (★640,861) | 58,282 |
| North Charleston (★Charleston) | 70,218 |
| Rock Hill (★Charlotte, N.C.) | 41,643 |
| Spartanburg (★Greenville) | 43,467 |
| Sumter (★90,300) | 41,943 |

**UNITED STATES: SOUTH DAKOTA**

| | |
|---|---|
| 1990 C | 696,004 |
| Pierre | 12,906 |
| Rapid City (★81,343) | 54,523 |
| Sioux Falls (★123,809) | 100,814 |

**UNITED STATES: TENNESSEE**

| | |
|---|---|
| 1990 C | 4,877,185 |
| Bristol (★Johnson City) | 23,421 |
| Chattanooga (★433,210) | 152,466 |
| Clarksville (★169,439) | 75,494 |
| Jackson (★77,982) | 48,949 |
| Johnson City (★436,047) | 49,381 |
| Kingsport (★Johnson City) | 36,365 |
| Knoxville (★604,816) | 165,121 |
| Memphis (★981,747) | 610,337 |
| Murfreesboro (★Nashville) | 44,922 |
| Nashville (★985,026) | 487,969 |

**UNITED STATES: TEXAS**

| | |
|---|---|
| 1990 C | 16,986,510 |
| Abilene (★119,655) | 106,654 |
| Amarillo (★187,547) | 157,615 |
| Arlington (★Fort Worth) | 261,721 |
| Austin (★781,572) | 465,622 |
| Baytown (★Houston) | 63,850 |
| Beaumont (★361,226) | 114,323 |
| Brownsville (★469,000) | 98,962 |
| Bryan (★121,862) | 55,002 |
| Carrollton (★Dallas) | 82,169 |
| College Station (★Bryan) | 52,456 |
| Corpus Christi (★349,894) | 257,453 |
| Dallas (★3,885,415) | 1,006,877 |
| Denton (★Dallas) | 66,270 |
| El Paso (★1,211,300) | 515,342 |
| Fort Worth (★1,332,053) (★Dallas) | 447,619 |
| Freeport (★88,600) (★Houston) | 11,389 |
| Galveston (★217,399) (★Houston) | 59,070 |
| Garland (★Dallas) | 180,650 |
| Grand Prairie (★Dallas) | 99,616 |
| Harlingen (★Brownsville) | 48,735 |
| Houston (★3,711,043) | 1,630,553 |
| Irving (★Dallas) | 155,037 |
| Killeen (★255,301) | 63,535 |
| Laredo (★356,000) | 122,899 |
| Longview (★162,431) | 70,311 |
| Lubbock (★222,636) | 186,206 |
| Lufkin (★56,000) | 30,206 |
| McAllen (★383,545) | 84,021 |
| Mesquite (★Dallas) | 101,484 |
| Midland (★106,611) | 89,443 |
| Odessa (★118,934) | 89,699 |
| Pasadena (★Houston) | 119,363 |
| Plano (★Dallas) | 128,713 |
| Port Arthur (★Beaumont) | 58,724 |
| Richardson (★Dallas) | 74,840 |
| San Angelo (★98,458) | 84,474 |
| San Antonio (★1,302,099) | 935,933 |
| Sherman (★95,021) | 31,601 |
| Temple (★Killeen) | 46,109 |
| Texarkana (★120,132) | 31,656 |
| Tyler (★151,309) | 75,450 |
| Victoria (★74,361) | 55,076 |
| Waco (★189,123) | 103,590 |
| Wichita Falls (★122,378) | 96,259 |

**UNITED STATES: UTAH**

| | |
|---|---|
| 1990 C | 1,722,850 |
| Logan (★60,300) | 32,762 |
| Ogden (★Salt Lake City) | 63,909 |
| Orem (★Provo) | 67,561 |
| Provo (★263,590) | 86,835 |
| Salt Lake City (★1,072,227) | 159,936 |
| Sandy (★Salt Lake City) | 75,058 |
| West Valley City (★Salt Lake City) | 86,976 |

**UNITED STATES: VERMONT**

| | |
|---|---|
| 1990 C | 562,758 |
| Burlington (★131,439) | 39,127 |
| Montpelier (★52,800) | 8,247 |
| Rutland (★53,000) | 18,230 |

**UNITED STATES: VIRGINIA**

| | |
|---|---|
| 1990 C | 6,187,358 |
| Alexandria (★Washington, D.C.) | 111,183 |
| Annandale (★Washington, D.C.) | 50,975 |
| Arlington (★Washington, D.C.) | 170,936 |
| Charlottesville (★131,107) | 40,341 |
| Chesapeake (★Norfolk) | 151,976 |
| Danville (★108,711) | 53,056 |
| Hampton (★Norfolk) | 133,793 |
| Lynchburg (★142,199) | 66,049 |
| Martinsville (★67,100) | 16,162 |
| Newport News (★Norfolk) | 170,045 |
| Norfolk (★1,396,107) | 261,229 |
| Portsmouth (★Norfolk) | 103,907 |
| Richmond (★865,640) | 203,056 |
| Roanoke (★224,477) | 96,397 |
| Suffolk (★Norfolk) | 52,141 |
| Virginia Beach (★Norfolk) | 393,069 |

**UNITED STATES: WASHINGTON**

| | |
|---|---|
| 1990 C | 4,866,692 |
| Bellevue (★Seattle) | 86,874 |
| Bellingham (★127,780) | 52,179 |
| Bremerton (★189,731) | 38,142 |
| Everett (★Seattle) | 69,961 |
| Lakes District (★Tacoma) | 58,412 |
| Longview (★67,100) | 31,499 |
| Olympia (★161,238) | 33,840 |
| Pasco (★Richland) | 20,337 |
| Seattle (★2,559,164) | 516,259 |
| Spokane (★361,364) | 177,196 |
| Tacoma (★586,203) (★Seattle) | 176,664 |
| Yakima (★188,823) | 54,827 |

**UNITED STATES: WEST VIRGINIA**

| | |
|---|---|
| 1990 C | 1,793,477 |
| Beckley (★64,300) | 18,296 |
| Charleston (★250,454) | 57,287 |
| Clarksburg (★53,800) | 18,059 |
| Fairmont (★53,700) | 20,210 |
| Huntington (★312,529) | 54,844 |
| Morgantown (★71,500) | 25,879 |
| Parkersburg (★149,169) | 33,862 |
| Wheeling (★159,301) | 34,882 |

**UNITED STATES: WISCONSIN**

| | |
|---|---|
| 1990 C | 4,891,769 |
| Appleton (★315,121) | 65,695 |
| Beloit (★Janesville) | 35,573 |
| Eau Claire (★137,543) | 56,856 |
| Fond du Lac (★52,400) | 37,757 |
| Green Bay (★194,594) | 96,466 |
| Janesville (★139,510) | 52,133 |
| Kenosha (★128,181) (★Chicago, Il.) | 80,352 |
| La Crosse (★97,904) | 51,003 |
| Madison (★367,085) | 191,262 |
| Manitowoc (★57,300) | 32,520 |
| Milwaukee (★1,607,183) | 628,088 |
| Oshkosh (★Appleton) | 55,006 |
| Racine (★175,034) (★Milwaukee) | 84,298 |
| Sheboygan (★103,877) | 49,676 |
| Waukesha (★Milwaukee) | 56,958 |
| Wausau (★115,400) | 37,060 |
| Wauwatosa (★Milwaukee) | 49,366 |
| West Allis (★Milwaukee) | 63,221 |

**UNITED STATES: WYOMING**

| | |
|---|---|
| 1990 C | 453,588 |
| Casper (★61,226) | 46,742 |
| Cheyenne (★73,142) | 50,008 |

**URUGUAY**

| | |
|---|---|
| 1985 C | 2,955,241 |
| Las Piedras (★Montevideo) | 58,288 |
| Melo | 42,615 |
| Mercedes | 36,702 |
| Minas | 34,661 |
| • MONTEVIDEO (★1,550,000) | 1,251,647 |
| Paysandú | 76,191 |
| Rivera | 57,316 |
| Salto | 80,823 |

**UZBEKISTAN**

| | |
|---|---|
| 1991 E | 20,708,200 |
| Almalyk | 116,400 |
| Andižan | 298,300 |
| Angren | 132,600 |
| Bekabad | 82,800 |
| Buchara | 249,600 |
| Chodžejli | 61,200 |
| Čirčik (★Taškent) | 158,400 |
| Denau | 49,300 |
| Džizak | 110,900 |
| Fergana | 226,500 |
| Gulistan | 56,900 |
| Jangijul' | 56,900 |
| Kagan | 49,800 |
| Karši | 168,000 |
| Kattakurgan | 59,600 |
| Kokand | 175,000 |
| Margilan | 124,900 |
| Namangan | 319,200 |
| Navoi | 111,600 |
| Nukus | 179,600 |
| Šachrichan | 47,600 |
| Šachrisabz | 53,200 |
| Samarkand | 370,500 |
| • TAŠKENT (TASHKENT) (★2,325,000) | 2,113,300 |
| Termez | 90,400 |
| Urgenč | 130,400 |

**VANUATU**

| | |
|---|---|
| 1989 C | 142,944 |
| • PORT VILA (★23,000) | 18,905 |

**VATICAN CITY / Città del Vaticano**

| | |
|---|---|
| 1988 E | 766 |

**VENEZUELA**

| | |
|---|---|
| 1990 C | 18,105,265 |
| Acarigua | 116,551 |
| Anaco | 61,386 |
| Araure | 55,299 |
| Barcelona | 221,792 |
| Barinas | 153,630 |
| Barquisimeto | 625,450 |
| Baruta (★Caracas) | 182,941 |
| Cabimas | 165,755 |
| Cagua | 73,465 |
| Calabozo | 79,578 |
| • CARACAS (★4,000,000) | 1,824,654 |
| Carora | 70,715 |
| Carúpano | 92,333 |
| Catia La Mar (★Caracas) | 100,104 |
| Chacao (★Caracas) | 66,897 |
| Ciudad Bolívar | 225,340 |
| Ciudad Guayana | 453,047 |
| Ciudad Ojeda (Lagunillas) | 73,473 |
| Coro | 124,506 |
| Cumaná | 212,432 |
| El Limón | 90,030 |
| El Tigre | 93,229 |
| Guacara | 100,766 |
| Guanare | 84,904 |
| Guarenas (★Caracas) | 134,158 |
| La Asunción | 16,552 |
| La Victoria | 77,326 |
| Los Dos Caminos (★Caracas) | 59,141 |
| Los Teques (★Caracas) | 140,617 |
| Maiquetía (★Caracas) | 62,834 |
| Maracaibo | 1,249,670 |
| Maracay | 354,196 |
| Mariara | 69,404 |
| Maturín | 206,654 |
| Mérida | 170,902 |
| Palo Negro | 50,718 |
| Petare (★Caracas) | 338,417 |
| Porlamar | 62,732 |
| Pozuelos (1981C) | 80,342 |
| Puerto Ayacucho | 36,107 |
| Puerto Cabello | 128,825 |
| Puerto la Cruz | 115,731 |
| Punto Fijo | 88,681 |
| San Carlos | 50,708 |
| San Cristóbal | 220,675 |
| San Felipe | 65,509 |
| San Fernando | 72,716 |
| San Juan de los Morros | 67,791 |
| Trujillo | 33,241 |
| Tucupita | 41,117 |
| Turmero | 174,280 |
| Valencia | 903,621 |
| Valera | 97,012 |
| Valle de la Pascua | 67,100 |
| Villa de Cura | 51,096 |

**VIETNAM / Viet Nam**

| | |
|---|---|
| 1989 C | 64,411,668 |
| Bac Giang | 50,879 |
| Bac Lieu | 83,483 |
| Bien Hoa | 273,879 |
| Buon Me Thuot | 97,044 |
| Ca Mau | 81,901 |
| Cam Pha | 105,336 |
| Can Tho | 208,078 |
| Chau Doc | 50,935 |
| Da Lat | 102,583 |
| Da Nang | 369,734 |
| Hai Duong | 53,370 |
| Hai Phong (▲1,447,523) | 351,919 |
| HA NOI (★1,275,000) | 905,939 |
| Hoa Binh | 69,323 |
| Hon Gai | 123,102 |
| Hue | 211,718 |
| Long Xuyen | 128,814 |
| Minh Hai (1979C) | 72,517 |
| My Tho | 104,724 |
| Nam Dinh | 165,629 |
| Nha Trang | 213,460 |
| Phan Rang | 71,111 |
| Phan Thiet | 114,236 |
| Play Cu | 76,991 |
| Qui Nhon | 159,852 |
| Rach Gia | 137,784 |
| Sa Dec | 50,733 |
| Soc Trang | 87,899 |
| Soc Trang | 87,899 |
| Tan An | 50,288 |
| Thai Binh | 57,640 |
| Thai Nguyen | 124,871 |
| Thanh Hoa | 84,951 |
| • Thanh Pho Ho Chi Minh (Saigon) (★3,300,000) | 2,796,229 |
| Tra Vinh | 47,785 |
| Tuy Hoa | 54,081 |
| Uong Bi | 49,595 |
| Viet Tri | 73,347 |
| Vinh | 110,793 |
| Vinh Long | 81,620 |
| Vung Tau | 123,528 |
| Yen Bai | 58,645 |

**VIRGIN ISLANDS OF THE UNITED STATES**

| | |
|---|---|
| 1990 C | 101,809 |
| • CHARLOTTE AMALIE (★32,000) | 12,331 |

**WALLIS AND FUTUNA / Wallis et Futuna**

| | |
|---|---|
| 1983 E | 12,408 |
| • MATÂ'UTU | 815 |
| Ono (1976C) | 624 |

**WEST BANK**

| | |
|---|---|
| 1992 E | 1,653,000 |
| • Al-Quds (Jerusalem) (★Yerushalayim, Isreal) | 285,000 |
| Bayt Lahm (Bethlehem) (1971E) | 25,000 |
| Nābulus (1971E) | 64,000 |

**WESTERN SAHARA**

| | |
|---|---|
| 1982 E | 142,000 |
| • EL AAIÚN | 93,875 |

**WESTERN SAMOA / Samoa i Sisifo**

| | |
|---|---|
| 1991 C | 161,298 |
| • APIA | 34,126 |

**YEMEN / Al-Yaman**

| | |
|---|---|
| 1990 E | 15,267,000 |
| 'Adan (★318,000) (1984E) | 176,100 |
| Al-Hudaydah (1986C) | 155,110 |
| Al-Mukallā (1984E) | 58,000 |
| • ṢAN'Ā' (1986C) | 427,150 |
| Ta'izz (1986C) | 178,043 |

**YUGOSLAVIA / Jugoslavija**

| | |
|---|---|
| 1991 C | 10,337,920 |
| • BEOGRAD (★1,554,826) | 1,136,786 |
| Čačak | 72,392 |
| Kragujevac | 146,607 |
| Kraljevo | 56,616 |
| Kruševac | 58,114 |
| Leskovac | 61,963 |
| Niš | 175,555 |
| Novi Pazar | 51,906 |
| Novi Sad | 178,896 |
| Pančevo (★Beograd) | 72,717 |
| Podgorica | 118,059 |
| Priština (▲244,830) (1987E) | 125,400 |
| Šabac | 54,829 |
| Smederevo | 64,257 |
| Sombor | 48,789 |
| Subotica | 100,219 |
| Užice | 53,666 |
| Valjevo | 58,324 |
| Vranje | 51,695 |
| Zrenjanin | 81,382 |

**ZAIRE / Zaïre**

| | |
|---|---|
| 1984 C | 30,729,443 |
| Bandundu | 63,642 |
| Beni | 44,141 |
| Boma | 197,617 |
| Bukavu | 167,950 |
| Bumba | 51,197 |
| Bunia | 59,598 |
| Butembo | 73,312 |
| Gandajika | 64,878 |
| Gbadolite | 27,063 |
| Gemena | 63,052 |
| Goma | 77,908 |
| Ilebo (Port-Francqui) | 53,877 |
| Isiro | 78,268 |
| Kalemie (Albertville) | 73,528 |
| Kamina | 62,789 |
| Kananga (Luluabourg) | 298,693 |
| Kikwit | 149,296 |
| Kindu | 66,812 |
| • KINSHASA (LÉOPOLDVILLE) (1986E) | 3,000,000 |
| Kipushi | 53,207 |
| Kisangani (Stanleyville) | 317,581 |
| Kolwezi | 416,122 |
| Likasi (Jadotville) | 213,862 |
| Lubumbashi (Élisabethville) | 564,830 |
| Matadi | 138,798 |
| Mbandaka (Coquilhatville) | 137,291 |
| Mbuji-Mayi (Bakwanga) | 486,235 |
| Mwene-Ditu | 94,560 |
| Tshikapa | 116,016 |
| Uvira | 74,432 |

**ZAMBIA**

| | |
|---|---|
| 1990 C | 7,818,447 |
| Chililabombwe (Bancroft) (★76,848) | 35,200 |
| Chingola | 167,954 |
| Kabwe (Broken Hill) | 166,519 |
| Kalulushi | 75,197 |
| Kitwe (★338,207) | 247,100 |
| Livingstone | 82,218 |
| Luanshya (★146,275) | 79,500 |
| • LUSAKA | 982,362 |
| Mufulira (★152,944) | 85,000 |
| Ndola | 376,311 |

**ZIMBABWE**

| | |
|---|---|
| 1983 E | 7,740,000 |
| Bulawayo | 429,000 |
| Chitungwiza (★Harare) | 202,000 |
| Gweru (1982C) | 78,940 |
| • HARARE (★955,000) | 681,000 |
| Mutare (1982C) | 75,358 |

▲ Population of an entire municipality, commune, or district, including rural area.
• Largest city in country.
★ Population or designation of the metropolitan area, including suburbs.
C Census. E Official estimate.
U Unofficial estimate.

▲ Bevölkerung eines ganzen städtischen Verwaltungsgebietes, eines Kommunalbezirkes oder eines Distrikts, einschliesslich ländlicher Gebiete.
• Grösste Stadt des Landes.
★ Bevölkerung oder Bezeichnung der Stadtregion einschliess lich Vororte.
C Volkszählung. E Offizielle Schätzung.
U Inoffizielle Schätzung.

▲ Población de un municipio, comuna o distrito entero, incluyendo sus áreas rurales.
• Ciudad más grande de un país.
★ Población o designación de un área metropolitana, incluyendo los suburbios.
C Censo. E Estimado oficial.
U Estimado no oficial.

▲ Population d'une municipalité, d'une commune ou d'un district, zone rurale incluse.
• Ville la plus peuplée du pays.
★ Population de l'agglomération (ou nom de la zone métropolitaine englobante).
C Recensement. E Estimation officielle.
U Estimation non officielle.

▲ População de um município, comuna ou distrito, inclusive as respectivas áreas rurais.
• Maior cidade de um país.
★ População ou indicação de uma área metropolitana.
C Censo. E Estimativa oficial.
U Estimativa não oficial.

The index includes in a single alphabetical list some 170,000 names appearing on the maps. Each name is followed by a page reference to one or more maps and by the location of the feature on the map, in coordinates of latitude and longitude. If a page contains several maps, a lowercase letter identifies the particular map. The page reference for two-page maps is always to the left-hand page.

Most map features are indexed to the largest-scale map on which they appear. However, a feature usually is not indexed to a Metropolitan Area map if it is also shown on another map where it can be seen in a broader setting. Countries, mountain ranges, and other extensive features are generally indexed to the largest-scale map that shows them in their entirety.

The order in which index information is presented is shown in the English, German, Spanish, French, and Portuguese headings at the center of each two-page spread.

For example:

ENGLISH

| Name | Page | Lat.°′ | Long.°′ |
|---|---|---|---|

The features indexed are of three types: *point*, *areal*, and *linear*. For *point* features (for example, cities, mountain peaks, dams), latitude and longitude coordinates give the location of the point on the map. For *areal* features (countries, mountain ranges, etc.), the coordinates generally indicate the approximate center of the feature. For *linear* features (rivers, canals, aqueducts), the coordinates locate a terminating point—for example, the mouth of a river, or the point at which a feature reaches the map margin.

**Name Forms** Names in the index, as on the maps, are generally in the local language and insofar as possible are spelled according to official practice. Diacritical marks are included, except that those used to indicate tone, as in Vietnamese, are usually not shown. Most features that extend beyond the boundaries of one country have no single official name, and these are usually named in English. Many English, German, Spanish, French, and Portuguese names, which may not be shown on the maps, appear in the index as cross references. All cross references are indicated by the symbol →. A name that appears in a shortened version on the map due to space limitations is given in full in the index, with the portion that is omitted on the map enclosed in brackets, for example, Acapulco [de Juárez].

**Transliteration** For names in languages not written in the Roman alphabet, the locally official transliteration system has been used where one exists. Thus, names in Russia and Bulgaria have been transliterated according to the systems adopted by the academies of science of these countries. Similarly, the transliteration for mainland Chinese names follows the Pinyin system, which has been officially adopted in mainland China. For languages with no one locally accepted transliteration system, notably Arabic, transliteration in general follows closely a system adopted by the United States Board on Geographic Names.

**Alphabetization** Names are alphabetized in the order of the letters of the English alphabet. Spanish *ll* and *ch*, for example, are not treated as distinct letters. Furthermore, diacritical marks are disregarded in alphabetization—German or Scandinavian *ä* or *ö* are treated as *a* or *o*.

The names of physical features may appear inverted, since they are always alphabetized under the proper, not the generic, part of the name, thus: "Gibraltar, Strait of Ʉ." Otherwise every entry, whether consisting of one word or more, is alphabetized as a single continuous entity. "Lakeland," for example, appears after "La Crosse" and before "La Salle." Names beginning with articles (Le Havre, Den Helder, Al-Qāhirah, As-Suways) are not inverted. Names beginning with "St." and "Sainte" are alphabetized as though spelled "Saint."

In the case of identical names, towns are listed first, then political divisions, then physical features. Entries that are completely identical (including symbols, discussed below) are distinguished by abbreviations of their official country names and are sequenced alphabetically by country name. The many duplicate names in Canada, the United Kingdom, and the United States are further distinguished by abbreviations of the names of their primary subdivisions. (See list of abbreviations on pages 319-320).

**Abbreviation and Capitalization** Abbreviation and styling have been standardized for all languages. A period is used after every abbreviation even when this may not be the local practice. The abbreviation "St." is used only for "Saint." "Sankt" and other forms of the term are spelled out.

All names are written with an initial capital letter except for a few Dutch names, such as 's-Gravenhage. Capitalization of noninitial words in a name generally follows local practice.

**Symbols** The symbols that appear in the index represent graphically the broad categories of the features named, for example, ▲ for mountain (Everest, Mount ▲). An abbreviated key to the symbols, in the five atlas languages, appears at the foot of each pair of index pages. Superior numbers following some symbols in the index indicate finer distinctions, for example, ▲$^1$ for volcano (Fuji-san ▲$^1$). A complete list of the symbols and superior numbers is given on page I•1.

---

Das Register umfasst in alphabetischer Anordnung etwa 170 000 in den Karten erscheinende Namen. Nach jedem Namen folgt die Seitenangabe zu einer oder mehreren Karten und die Lageangabe des Objektes in der Karte mit geographischer Länge und Breite. Enthält eine Seite mehrere Karten, so wird die betreffende Karte durch einen Kleinbuchstaben gekennzeichnet. Die Seitenangabe für Doppelseiten bezieht sich immer auf die linke Seite.

Die Verweise für die meisten Objekte in den Karten beziehen sich auf die Karte mit dem grössten Massstab. Normalerweise werden jedoch Verweise auf Objekte in den Karten der Stadtregionen nicht gegeben, wenn sie auf einer anderen Karte in grösserem Zusammenhang dargestellt sind. Die Lageangaben für Länder, Gebirgszüge und andere ausgedehnte Objekte beziehen sich allgemein auf die Karte grössten Massstabes, die sie in ihrer ganzen Ausdehnung zeigt.

Die Anordnung, in welcher die Lageangabe erfolgt, geht aus den englischen, deutschen, spanischen, französischen und portugiesischen Überschriften in der Mitte jeder Doppelseite hervor.

Zum Beispiel:

DEUTSCH

| Name | Seite | Breite°′ | Länge°′ E = Ost |
|---|---|---|---|

Die aufgeführten Objekte gliedern sich in drei Gruppen: *punkt-*, *flächen-* und *linienförmige* Objekte. Bei *punktförmigen* Objekten (z.B. Städte, Berge, Dämme) beziehen sich die Angaben nach Länge und Breite auf die Signatur in der Karte. Bei *flächenhaften* Objekten (Länder, Gebirgszüge usw.) verweisen die Koordinaten im allgemeinen auf das ungefähre Zentrum des Objektes. Bei *linienhaften* Objekten (Flüsse, Kanäle, Wasserleitungen) beziehen sich die Koordinaten auf einen bestimmten Punkt, z.B. die Mündung eines Flusses oder den Punkt, an dem das Objekt den Kartenrand schneidet.

**Namengebung** Wie in den Karten so sind auch im Register die Namen im allgemeinen in der örtlichen Namensform wiedergegeben und soweit als möglich in der amtlichen Schreibweise. Diakritische Zeichen wurden gesetzt; sie wurden nur dort weggelassen, wo sie, wie im Vietnamesischen, Tonhöhen kennzeichnen. Meist haben Objekte, die sich über die Grenzen eines Landes hinaus erstrecken, keinen einzigen offiziellen Namen; normalerweise sind sie daher englisch beschriftet. Viele englische, deutsche, spanische, französische und portugiesische Namensformen, die nicht in den Karten enthalten sind, erscheinen im Register als Kreuzverweis. Alle Kreuzverweise werden durch das Symbol → gekennzeichnet. Namen, die aus Platzgründen in abgekürzter Form in der Karte erscheinen, werden im Register voll ausgeschrieben, wobei der auf der Karte weggelassene Teil in Klammern gesetzt ist, z.B. Acapulco [de Juárez].

**Transkription** Für die Transkription von Namen aus Sprachen, die nicht im lateinischen Alphabet geschrieben werden, wurde das offizielle Transkriptionssystem benutzt, sofern ein solches vorhanden ist. So wurden die Namen in Russland und in Bulgarien nach dem von den wissenschaftlichen Akademien dieser Länder angewandten System transkribiert. Entsprechend wurden die Namen auf dem chinesischen Festland nach dem Pinyin-System übertragen, das offiziell in der Volksrepublik China eingeführt wurde. Bei Sprachen, für die ein allgemein anerkanntes Transkriptionssystem nicht vorliegt, vor allem für Arabisch, erfolgte die Transkription in enger Anlehnung an das vom United States Board on Geographic Names angewandte System.

**Alphabetische Ordnung** Die alphabetische Ordnung der Namen entspricht der Reihenfolge der Buchstaben im englischen Alphabet. So werden z.B. das spanische *ll* und *ch* nicht als besondere Buchstaben behandelt. Ferner wurden diakritischen Zeichen beim Alphabetisieren nicht berücksichtigt, das deutsche oder skandinavische *ä* oder *ö* als *a* oder *o* behandelt.

Physische Objekte können umgestellt erscheinen, da sie immer nach dem Eigennamen und nicht nach dem Gattungsbegriff eingeordnet wurden, z.B. "Gibraltar, Strait of Ʉ." Ansonsten wurde jeder Eintrag, ob er aus einem Wort oder aus mehreren besteht, als eine einzige Einheit behandelt. So ist z.B. "Lakeland" nach "La Crosse," aber vor "La Salle" aufgeführt. Namen, die mit einem Artikel beginnen, wurden nicht umgestellt (Le Havre, Den Helder, Al-Qāhirah, As-Suways). Namen, die mit "St." und "Sainte" beginnen, sind der Schreibweise "Saint" nach eingeordnet.

Wo Namensgleichheit besteht, werden zunächst die Städte aufgeführt, dann politische Einheiten und schliesslich physische Objekte. Eintragungen, die vollkommen identisch sind (einschliesslich der weiter unten erläuterten Symbole), werden durch Hinzufügung der Abkürzung des offiziellen Ländernamens unterschieden und sind den Ländernamen nach alphabetisch geordnet. Die zahlreichen identischen Namen in Kanada, dem Vereinigten Königreich und den Vereinigten Staaten sind darüber hinaus noch durch Abkürzungen der obersten Verwaltungseinheit unterschieden. (Siehe Verzeichnis der Abkürzungen, Seite 319-320).

**Abkürzungen und Grossschreibung** Abkürzung und Schreibweise wurden für alle Sprachen vereinheitlicht. Nach jeder Abkürzung steht ein Punkt, auch wenn dies nicht der jeweiligen Gepflogenheit entspricht. Die Abkürzung "St." wird ausschliesslich für "Saint" gebraucht. "Sankt" und andere Formen dieses Begriffes werden ausgeschrieben.

Der erste Buchstabe eines Namens wird gross geschrieben, ausgenommen einige holländische Namen wie 's-Gravenhage. Die Grossschreibung der weiteren Worte eines zusammengesetzten Namens folgt im allgemeinen der landesüblichen Schreibweise.

**Symbole** Die im Register verwendeten Symbole veranschaulichen graphisch die zahlreichen Kategorien der benannten Objekte, z.B. ▲ = Berg (Everest, Mount ▲). Eine kurzgefasste Erläuterung der Symbole erscheint in jeder der fünf Sprachen des Atlas am Fusse jeder Doppelseite des Registers. Hochgestellte Ziffern hinter Symbolen im Register bezeichnen feinere Unterscheidungen, z.B. ▲$^1$ = Vulkan (Fuji-san ▲$^1$). Eine vollständige Übersicht der Symbole und hochgestellten Ziffern findet sich auf Seite I•1.

---

El índice contiene en una sola lista alfabética, alrededor de 170 000 nombres que aparecen en los mapas. Después de cada nombre está indicada la página o las páginas de referencia, en los cuales se encuentran los mismos, y las coordinadas de la latitud y la longitud del lugar del rasgo. Si una página contiene various mapas, letras minúsculas identifican el mapa correspondiente. Para mapas que ocupan dos páginas, la página de referencia siempre es la de la izquierda.

La mayoría de los nombres que figuran en el índice, se efiere a los mapas en la escala más grande. Sin embargo, un nombre no se refiere en un mapa metropolitano si ya aparece en otro mapa, donde se muestra en un marco de mayor proporción. Los países, sierras y otros rasgos extensivos se refieren generalmente en el índice en los mapas de escalas mayores en que se muestran completos.

En orden en que la información del índice se presenta, aparece en un encabezamiento al centro de cada par de páginas, en inglés, alemán, español, francés y portugués.

Por ejemplo:

ESPAÑOL

| Nombre | Página | Lat.°′ | Long.°′ W = Oeste |
|---|---|---|---|

Los rasgos anotados en el índice son de tres tipos: *el punto, el área y la extensión linear*. Para rasgos que indican *el punto* (como por ejemplo, las ciudades, picos de montañas, presas), las coordinadas de latitud y longitud indican la posición exacta del punto sobre el mapa. Respecto a *las áreas* (como países, sierras, etc.), las coordinadas indican usualmente el centro aproximado del rasgo particular. En cuanto a *los rasgos lineares* (ríos, canales, acueductos) las coordinadas indican los puntos terminales, por ejemplo, la boca de un río, o el punto en que un rasgo físico alcanza el margen del mapa.

**Las Formas de los Nombres** Los nombres que aparecen en el índice, así como también en los mapas, se dan en general en el idioma local, y en tanto que es posible siguen la ortografía oficialmente aceptada. Incluímos también marcas diacríticas, excepto las que se usan para indicar tono, como en la lengua vietnamita. A causa de que la mayoría de los rasgos que se extienden más allá de las fronteras de un país no tienen un solo nombre oficial, éstos se denominan usualmente en inglés. Muchos nombres, en inglés, alemán, español, francés y portugués, que pueden no figurar en el mapa, se dan como referencia de una página a otra en el índice. Todas las referencias que pasan a otras páginas se indican con el símbolo →. Un nombre que aparece en el mapa en forma abreviada, debido a la limitación de espacio, en el índice figura en su forma completa, poniendo entre paréntesis angulares la parte omitida en el mapa, por ejemplo Acapulco [de Juárez].

"Trasliteración" Para los nombres escritos en los idiomas que no usan el alfabeto latino, el sistema oficial de trasliteración ha sido utilizado donde localmente existe. Así, los nombres de Rusia y de Bulgaria se trasliteran conforme a los sistemas aceptados por las academias de las ciencias de sus respectivos países. De la misma manera, la trasliteración de los nombres en chino continental siguen el sistema Pinyin que ha sido oficialmente adoptado en este país. Para idiomas sin ningún sistema localmente aceptado de trasliteración, particularmente para el árabe, éstos se trasliteran usando por lo general un sistema adoptado por el United States Board on Geographic Names.

Alfabetización Los nombres se han ordenado de acuerdo con el alfabeto inglés. Las letras del alfabeto en español *ll* y *ch* por ejemplo, no se han considerado letras separadas. Además, los signos diacríticos no se toman en cuenta en la alfabetización — en alemán o escadinavo letras *ä* u *ö* se tratan como *a* u *o*.

Los nombres de los rasgos físicos algunas veces se invierten, ya que se ordenan alfabéticamente según la parte propia y no genérica del nombre. Así por ejemplo, en el caso del Estrecho de Gibraltar aparece: Gibraltar, Strait of ɥ. Por lo demás, cada renglón, sea una palabra o una frase, se alfabetiza como una unidad. Por ejemplo, "Lakeland" aparece después de "La Crosse" y antes de "La Salle." Los nombres que comienzan con artículos (Le Havre, Den Helder, Al-Qāhirah, As-Suways) no están invertidos. Nombres que empiezan con "St." y "Sainte" se alfabetizan como "Saint".

En los casos de nombres idénticos, las poblaciones aparecen primero, las divisiones políticas después y finalmente los rasgos físicos. En caso de ser completamente idénticos (incluyendo los símbolos, discutidos más abajo) se distinguen por medio de abreviaciones de los nombres oficiales de los países a que pertenecen y son puestos en orden alfabético, de acuerdo al nombre de cada país. Hay muchos nombres duplicados en Canadá, el Reino Unido y los Estados Unidos de América, y éstos se distinguen además, por sus subdivisiones primarias. (Vease abajo, la lista de abreviaciones en las páginas 319-320).

Abreviaciones y Mayúsculas Las abreviaciones y el uso de las mayúsculas se han hecho uniformes para todos los idiomas. Se usa un punto al final de la abreviación, aun cuando en algunos casos no sea ésta la práctica local. La abreviación "St." se usa sólo para "Saint." Las otras formas del mismo término, como "Sankt," se escriben completas.

La mayúscula se usa al comienzo de todos los nombres a excepción de algunos holandeses, como 's-Gravenhage. Las palabras que no son iniciales, se dan con mayúscula o minúscula, según la práctica local.

Símbolos Los símbolos que aparecen en el índice representan gráficamente las grandes categorías de los rasgos que se han ido nombrando, por ejemplo, ʌ para montaña (Everest, Mount ʌ). Una clave abreviada para los símbolos aparece en los cinco idiomas del atlas al pie de cada par de páginas del índice. Los números que siguen más arriba del símbolo indican alguna diferencia más precisa, pro ejemplo, ʌ$^1$ para un volcán (Fuji- san ʌ$^1$). Una lista completa de símbolos y números superiores aparece en la página I•1.

---

L'index rassemble en une seule liste alphabétique, quelque 170 000 noms qui figurent sur les cartes. Chaque nom est suivi d'un renvoi à une ou plusieurs pages de cartes et de coordonnées géographiques qui permettent de localiser ce qu'il désigne. Si une page contient plusieurs cartes, une lettre minuscule permet d'identifier chaque carte. Pour les cartes en double page, la référence indiquée est toujours celle de la page de gauche.

En général, l'index renvoie aux cartes où l'information recherchée est reproduite à la plus grande échelle; cependant, les cartes de zones métropolitaines ne sont pas utilisées si le terme géographique figure sur une autre carte dans un contexte plus large. Pour les éléments de grande dimension comme les pays et les chaînes de montagnes, l'index renvoie généralement à la carte à grande échelle qui les représente en entier.

L'ordre des informations de l'index est rappelé en tête de chaque double page dans les cinq langues: anglais, allemand, espagnol, français et portugais.

Par exemple:

FRANÇAIS

| Nom | Page | Lat.°' | Long.°' W = Ouest |
|---|---|---|---|

Les termes de l'index désignent des réalités géographiques de type *ponctuel, spatial* ou *linéaire*. Leur position est déterminée par les coordonnées géographiques du lieu quand les données sont de type *ponctuel* (villes, sommets, barrages, etc.), quand elles sont de type *spatial* (pays, chaînes de montagnes, etc.) par les coordonnées du centre approximatif de la zone considérée, et, quand elles sont du type *linéaire* (aqueducs, canaux, etc.) par les coordonnées soit d'un point terminal comme l'embouchure d'un cours d'eau, soit du point où les limites de la carte les interrompent.

Forme des Toponymes Les noms de l'index comme ceux des cartes sont généralement reproduits dans la langue locale et, dans la mesure du possible, selon leur orthographe officielle. Les signes diacritiques sont conservés, à l'exclusion de ceux qui servent à indiquer le ton, comme en vietnamien. La plupart des données géographiques qui s'étendent au-delà des frontières d'un pays sont nommées souvent en anglais, car elles n'ont pas de nom officiel unique. Beaucoup de noms anglais, allemands, espagnols, français et portugais, qui ne se trouvent pas sur les cartes, sont cités dans l'index sous forme de renvois. Tous les renvois sont signalés par le symbole ( →). Un nom écrit sur la carte sous forme abrégée, par manque de place, figure en entier dans l'index; la partie omise est entre crochets, par exemple: Acapulco [de Juárez].

Transcription des Noms Pour les noms qui viennent de langues n'utilisant pas l'alphabet romain, le système local et officiel de transcription a été utilisé là où il existait. Ainsi, les noms russes et bulgares ont été transcrits selon les systèmes adoptés par les académies des sciences de ces pays. De même, pour la transcription des noms de la Chine continentale, on a employé le système Pinyin, officiellement adopté en Chine continentale. Pour les langues qui n'ont pas de système officiel de transcription en alphabet romain, notamment l'arabe, la transcription suit généralement de près le système adopté par le United States Board on Geographic Names (Comité américain pour les noms géographiques).

Ordre Alphabétique Les noms sont classés dans l'ordre de l'alphabet anglais. Les *ll* et *ch* espagnols, par exemple, ne sont pas traités comme des lettres séparées. De plus, on ne tient pas compte des signes diacritiques: le *ä* et le *ö* allemand ou scandinave correspondent au *a* et *o* sans tréma.

Les noms des données physiques peuvent se trouver inversés car ils sont toujours classés suivant le nom propre. Exemple: "Gibraltar, Strait of ɥ." Par ailleurs, les noms composés d'un ou plusieurs mots sont considérés comme une seule entité. Exemple: "Lakeland" est inscrit après "La Crosse" et avant "La Salle." Les noms qui commencent par un article (Le Havre, Den Helder, Al-Qāhirah, As-Suways) ne sont pas inversés. Les noms qui commencent par "St." ou "Sainte" sont classés comme s'ils s'écrivaient "Saint."

Dans le cas de noms identiques, les villes sont inscrites d'abord, puis les divisions politiques, et ensuite les données physiques. Les noms qui sont tout à fait identiques (y compris les symboles qui s'y rapportent) se distinguent par leur pays d'origine, noté en abrégé dans l'ordre alphabétique. Les noms que l'on rencontre plusieurs fois, au Canada, au Royaume-Uni et aux Etats-Unis se distinguent grâce à l'abréviation de la première subdivision administrative de ce pays (voir la liste des abréviations de la page 319-320).

Abréviations et Majuscules L'usage des abréviations a été standardisé pour toutes les langues. Un point suit chaque abréviation, même quand ce n'est pas l'usage dans certaines langues. L'abréviation "St." sert uniquement pour le mot "Saint." "Ste." et les autres formes du mot "Saint" sont écrites en entier.

Tous les noms commencent par une majuscule, sauf quelques noms des Pays-Bas comme 's-Gravenhage. Certains noms prennent une majuscule, même s'ils ne se trouvent pas au début du terme; on a adopté, en général, l'orthographe locale.

Symboles Les symboles utilisés dans l'index donnent une représentation graphique des réalités géographiques mentionnées. Par exemple, ʌ pour une montagne (Everest, Mount ʌ). Une explication abrégée des symboles dans les cinq langues de l'Atlas se trouve au bas de chaque double page de l'index. Les indices qui accompagnent certains symboles permettent une distinction plus précise. Par exemple, ʌ$^1$ pour volcan (Fujisan ʌ$^1$). Une liste complète des symboles et indices est donnée à la page I•1.

---

O Índice contém, numa só lista alfabética, cerca de 170,000 nomes que figuram nos mapas. Segue-se a cada nome a referência a um ou mais mapas e a localização do acidente geográfico no mapa pelas respectivas coordenadas de latitude e longitude. A referência a mapas que ocupam duas páginas fica sempre na página da esquerda. A maior parte dos acidentes geográficos estão indexados no mapa em que aparecem em escala maior. No entanto, um acidente geográfico não é geralmente indexado num mapa de Área Metropolitana se também figura em outro mapa em que aparece em contexto mais amplo. Os países, cordilheiras e outros acidentes geográficos de maior extensão estão geralmente indexados no mapa em escala maior que os apresente em seu todo.

A ordem em que as informações são apresentadas no Índice figura no cabeçalho, a cada duas páginas, em inglês, alemão, espanhol, francês e PORTUGUÊS.

Por exemplo:

PORTUGUÊS

| Nome | Página | Lat.°' | Long.°' W = Oeste |
|---|---|---|---|

Os acidentes indexados são de três tipos: *Ponto, espacial* (área) e *linear* (extensão). Para acidentes que indicam *pontos* (como, por exemplo, cidades, picos de montanhas, represas), as coordenadas de latitude e longitude indicam a posição exata do ponto no mapa. No que se refere aos *acidentes espaciais* (como países, cordilheiras etc.), as coordenadas geralmente indicam o centro aproximado do acidente específico. Quanto aos *acidentes lineares* (rios, canais, aquedutos), as coordenadas localizam os pontos terminais, como, por exemplo, a foz de um rio, ou o ponto em que um acidente físico atinge a margem do mapa.

Formas dos nomes Os nomes que aparecem no Índice, assim como também nos mapas, são geralmente apresentados na língua local, e tanto quanto possível, seguem a ortografia oficial. Usam-se, também, os sinais diacríticos, exceto os que indicam tom, como na língua vietnamita. A maioria dos acidentes geográficos que se estendem além das fronteiras de um só país não possuem um nome oficial único; nesses casos, estão geralmente indicados em inglês. Muitos nomes em inglês, alemão, espanhol, português e francês podem não figurar nos mapas, mas aparecem no Índice como referências remissivas. Todas essas referências são indicadas pelo símbolo ( →). Um nome que aparece no mapa em forma abreviada devido a limitações de espaço, figura no Índice em sua forma completa, com a parte omitida no mapa entre chaves (por exemplo, Acapulco [de Juárez]).

Transliteração Para os nomes escritos em línguas que não usam o alfabeto latino, foi utilizado o sistema oficial de transliteração, sempre que este existia. Assim, os nomes da Rússia e da Bulgária foram transliterados de acordo com os sistemas adotados pelas academias de ciências desses países. Do mesmo modo, a transliteração dos nomes da China continental seguem o sistema Pinyin, que foi oficialmente adotado nesse país. Para as línguas que não possuem um sistema de transliteração adotado oficialmente, em especial o árabe, a transliteração geralmente segue de perto o sistema adotado pelo Conselho de Nomes Geográficos dos Estados Unidos (United States Board on Geographic Names).

Alfabetação Os nomes foram ordenados de acordo com o alfabeto inglês. Por exemplo, o espanhol *ll* e *ch* não foram considerados como letras separadas. Ademais, os sinais diacríticos não foram considerados na alfabetação. Por exemplo, em alemão ou escandinavo as ietras *ä* ou *ö* foram tratradas como *a* ou *o*.

Os nomes dos acidentes físicos podem aparecer, às vezes, invertidos, já que foram sempre alfabetados pela parte específica e não genérica do nome, como, por exemplo, *Gibraltar, estreito de* ɥ. Por outro lado, cada entrada do Índice, quer constituída por uma só palavra ou mais de uma, foi alfabetada como uma unidade contínua. Por exemplo, "Lakeland" aparece depois de "La Grosse" e antes de "La Salle". Os nomes que começam por artigo (Le Havre, Den Helder, Al-Qāhirah, As-Suways) não são invertidos. Os nomes que começam por "St." e "Sainte" são alfabetados como se fossem soletrados "Saint".

Nos casos de nomes idênticos, as cidades estão relacionadas em primeiro lugar; depois as divisões políticas e em seguida os acidentes físicos. As entradas completamente idênticas (inclusive símbolos, mencionados mais abaixo), distinguem-se pelas abreviaturas dos nomes oficiais dos países a que pertencem e são arrolados na ordem alfabética do nome do país. Os muitos nomes repetidos no Canadá, no Reino Unido e nos Estados Unidos, são ainda diferenciados pelas abreviaturas dos nomes das respectivas subdivisões primárias (Ver a lista de abreviaturas, das páginas 319-320).

Abreviações e uso de maiúsculas As abreviaturas e o estilo foram normalizados em todas as línguas. Usa-se um ponto depois de cada abreviatura, mesmo que não seja essa a prática local. A abreviatura "St." só é usada para "Saint". As outras formas do termo, tal como "Sankt", são escritas por extenso.

Todos os nomes são escritos com a inicial maiúscula exceto em alguns nomes holandeses, como 's-Gravenhage. O uso de maiúsculas em palavras não iniciais de um nome segue geralmente a prática local.

Símbolos Os símbolos que aparecem no Índice representam graficamente as grandes categorias dos acidentes indicados, por exemplo, ʌ para montanha (Everest, Mount ʌ). Uma chave abreviada dos símbolos nas cinco línguas do Atlas figura no pé de cada par de páginas do Índice. Os números altos que acompanham certos símbolos do Índice indicam diferenças mais precisas, como, por examplo, ʌ$^1$ para vulcão (Fuji-san ʌ$^1$). Uma lista completa de símbolos e números altos aparece à pág. I•1.

| | LOCAL NAME | ENGLISH | DEUTSCH | ESPAÑOL | FRANÇAIS | PORTUGUÊS |
|---|---|---|---|---|---|---|
| **Ab., Can.** | Alberta | Alberta | Alberta | Alberta | Alberta | Alberta |
| **Afg.** | Afghānestān | Afghanistan | Afghanistan | Afganistán | Afghanistan | Afeganistão |
| **Afr.** | . . . | Africa | Afrika | Africa | Afrique | África |
| **Ak., U.S.** | Alaska | Alaska | Alaska | Alaska | Alaska | Alasca |
| **Al., U.S.** | Alabama | Alabama | Alabama | Alabama | Alabama | Alabama |
| **Alg.** | Algérie / Djazaïr | Algeria | Algerien | Argelia | Algérie | Argélia |
| **Am. Sam.** | American Samoa / Amerika Samoa | American Samoa | Amerikanisch-Samoa | Samoa Americana | Samoa américaines | Samoa Americana |
| **And.** | Andorra | Andorra | Andorra | Andorra | Andorre | Andorra |
| **Ang.** | Angola | Angola | Angola | Angola | Angola | Angola |
| **Anguilla** | Anguilla | Anguilla | Anguilla | Anguilla | Anguilla | Anguilla |
| **Ant.** | . . . | Antarctica | Antarktis | Antártida | Antarctique | Antártida |
| **Antig.** | Antigua and Barbuda | Antigua and Barbuda | Antigua und Barbuda | Antigua y Barbuda | Antigua-et-Barbuda | Antígua e Barbuda |
| **Ar., U.S.** | Arkansas | Arkansas | Arkansas | Arkansas | Arkansas | Arkansas |
| **Arg.** | Argentina | Argentina | Argentinien | Argentina | Argentine | Argentina |
| **Ar. Su.** | Al-ʿArabīyah as-Suʿūdīyah | Saudi Arabia | Saudi-Arabien | Arabia Saudita | Arabie saoudite | Arábia Saudita |
| **Aruba** | Aruba | Aruba | Aruba | Aruba | Aruba | Aruba |
| **Asia** | . . . | Asia | Asien | Asia | Asie | Ásia |
| **Austl.** | Australia | Australia | Australien | Australia | Australie | Austrália |
| **Az., U.S.** | Arizona | Arizona | Arizona | Arizona | Arizona | Arizona |
| **Azer.** | Azerbaijan | Azerbaijan | Aserbaidschan | Azerbaiján | Azerbaïdjan | Azerbaijão |
| **Ba.** | Bahamas | Bahamas | Bahamas | Bahamas | Bahamas | Bahamas |
| **Bahr.** | Al-Bahrayn | Bahrain | Bahrain | Bahrein | Bahreïn | Bahrein |
| **Barb.** | Barbados | Barbados | Barbados | Barbados | Barbade | Barbados |
| **B.C., Can.** | British Columbia / Colombie-Britannique | British Columbia | Britisch Kolumbien | Columbia Británica | Colombie britannique | Colúmbia Britânica |
| **Bdi.** | Burundi | Burundi | Burundi | Burundi | Burundi | Burundi |
| **Bel.** | Belgique / België | Belgium | Belgien | Bélgica | Belgique | Bélgica |
| **Belize** | Belize | Belize | Belize | Belice | Bélize | Belize |
| **Bela.** | Belarus | Belarus | Belorussland | Bielorrusia | Biélorussie | Bielorrússia |
| **Bénin** | Bénin | Benin | Benin | Benin | Bénin | Benin |
| **Ber.** | Bermuda | Bermuda | Bermuda | Bermudas | Bermudes | Bermudas |
| **B.I.O.T.** | British Indian Ocean Territory | British Indian Ocean Territory | Britisch-Indien Ozean-Territorium | Territorio Británico del Océano Indico | Territoire britannique de l'océan Indien | Território Britânico do Oceano Indico |
| **Blg.** | Bâlgarija | Bulgaria | Bulgarien | Bulgaria | Bulgarie | Bulgária |
| **Bngl.** | Bangladesh | Bangladesh | Bangladesch | Bangladesh | Bangladesh | Bangladesh |
| **Bol.** | Bolivia | Bolivia | Bolivien | Bolivia | Bolivie | Bolívia |
| **Bos.** | Bosna i Hercegovina | Bosnia and Hercegovina | Bosnien und Herzegowina | Bosnia y Herzegovina | Bosnie et Herzégovine | Bósnia e Herzegovina |
| **Bots.** | Botswana | Botswana | Botswana | Botswana | Botswana | Botsuana |
| **Bra.** | Brasil | Brazil | Brasilien | Brasil | Brésil | Brasil |
| **Bru.** | Brunei | Brunei | Brunei | Brunei | Brunéi | Brunei |
| **Br. Vir. Is.** | British Virgin Islands | British Virgin Islands | Britische Jungferninseln | Islas Vírgenes Británicas | Îles Vierges britanniques | Virgens Britânicas, Ilhas |
| **Burkina** | Burkina Faso | Burkina Faso | Burkina Faso | Burkina Faso | Burkina Faso | Burkina Faso |
| **Ca., U.S.** | California | California | Kalifornien | California | Californie | Califórnia |
| **Cam.** | Cameroun / Cameroon | Cameroon | Kamerun | Camerún | Cameroun | Camarão |
| **Can.** | Canada | Canada | Kanada | Canadá | Canada | Canadá |
| **Cay. Is.** | Cayman Islands | Cayman Islands | Caiman-Inseln | Islas Caimán | Îles Caïmanes | Cayman, Ilhas |
| **Centraf.** | République centrafricaine | Central African Republic | Zentralafrikanische Republik | República Centroafricana | République centrafricaine | Centro-Africana, República |
| **Česká Rep.** | Česká Republika | Czech Republic | Tschechische Republik | República Checa | République Tcheque | República Tcheca |
| **Chile** | Chile | Chile | Chile | Chile | Chili | Chile |
| **Christ. I.** | Christmas Island | Christmas Island | Weihnachtsinsel | Isla Christmas | Île Christmas | Christmas, Ilha |
| **C. Iv.** | Côte d'Ivoire | Cote d'Ivoire | Côte d'Ivoire | Côte d'Ivoire | Côte d'Ivoire | Côte d'Ivoire |
| **C.M.I.K.** | Chosŏn-minjujuŭi-inmin-konghwaguk | Korea, North | Nordkorea | Corea del Norte | Corée du Nord | Coréia do Norte |
| **Co., U.S.** | Colorado | Colorado | Colorado | Colorado | Colorado | Colorado |
| **Cocos Is.** | Cocos (Keeling) Islands | Cocos (Keeling) Islands | Cokos-Inseln | Islas Cocos (Keeling) | Îles Cocos (Keeling) | Cocos (Keeling), Ilhas |
| **Col.** | Colombia | Colombia | Kolumbien | Colombia | Colombie | Colômbia |
| **Comores** | Comores / Al-Qumur | Comoros | Komoren | Comoras | Comores | Comores |
| **Congo** | Congo | Congo | Kongo | Congo | Congo | Congo |
| **Cook Is.** | Cook Islands | Cook Islands | Cook-Inseln | Islas Cook | Îles Cook | Cook, Ilhas |
| **C.R.** | Costa Rica | Costa Rica | Costa Rica | Costa Rica | Costa Rica | Costa Rica |
| **Ct., U.S.** | Connecticut | Connecticut | Connecticut | Connecticut | Connecticut | Connecticut |
| **Cuba** | Cuba | Cuba | Kuba | Cuba | Cuba | Cuba |
| **C.V.** | Cabo Verde | Cape Verde | Kap Verde | Cabo Verde | Cap-Vert | Cabo Verde |
| **Dan.** | Danmark | Denmark | Dänemark | Dinamarca | Danemark | Dinamarca |
| **D.C., U.S.** | District of Columbia | District of Columbia | District of Columbia | District of Columbia | District of Columbia | Distrito de Columbia |
| **De., U.S.** | Delaware | Delaware | Delaware | Delaware | Delaware | Delaware |
| **Dji.** | Djibouti | Djibouti | Djibouti | Djibouti | Djibouti | Djibouti |
| **Dom.** | Dominica | Dominica | Dominica | Dominica | Dominique | Dominica |
| **Dtsch.** | Deutschland | Germany | Deutschland | Alemania | Allemagne | Alemanha |
| **D.Y.** | Druk-Yul | Bhutan | Bhutan | Bhután | Bhoutan | Butã |
| **Ec.** | Ecuador | Ecuador | Ecuador | Ecuador | Équateur | Equador |
| **Eesti** | Eesti | Estonia | Estland | Estonia | Estonie | Estónia |
| **Ellás** | Ellás | Greece | Griechenland | Grecia | Grèce | Grécia |
| **El Sal.** | El Salvador | El Salvador | El Salvador | El Salvador | El Salvador | El Salvador |
| **Eng., U.K.** | England | England | England | Inglaterra | Angleterre | Inglaterra |
| **Erit.** | Eritrea | Eritrea | Eritrea | Eritrea | Erythrée | Eritréia |
| **Esp.** | España | Spain | Spanien | España | Espagne | Espanha |
| **Europe** | . . . | Europe | Europa | Europa | Europe | Europa |
| **Falk. Is.** | Falkland Islands | Falkland Islands | Falkland-Inseln | Islas Malvinas | Îles Falkland | Falkland, Ilhas |
| **Fiji** | Fiji | Fiji | Fidschi | Fiji | Fidji | Fiji (Fidji) |
| **Fl., U.S.** | Florida | Florida | Florida | Florida | Floride | Flórida |
| **Før.** | Føroyar | Faeroe Islands | Färöer | Islas Feroe | Îles Féroé | Faeroe, Ilhas |
| **Fr.** | France | France | Frankreich | Francia | France | França |
| **Ga., U.S.** | Georgia | Georgia | Georgia | Georgia | Georgie | Geórgia |
| **Gabon** | Gabon | Gabon | Gabun | Gabón | Gabon | Gabão |
| **Gam.** | Gambia | Gambia | Gambia | Gambia | Gambie | Gâmbia |
| **Gaza** | . . . | Gaza Strip | Gazastreifen | Franja de Gaza | Bande de Gaza | Faixa de Gaza |
| **Ghana** | Ghana | Ghana | Ghana | Ghana | Ghana | Gana |
| **Gib.** | Gibraltar | Gibraltar | Gibraltar | Gibraltar | Gibraltar | Gibraltar |
| **Golan** | . . . | Golan Heights | Golan-Höhen | Alturas de Golán | Hauteurs de Golan | Colinas de Golan |
| **Gren.** | Grenada | Grenada | Grenada | Granada | Grenade | Grenada |
| **Guad.** | Guadeloupe | Guadeloupe | Guadeloupe | Guadalupe | Guadeloupe | Guadalupe |
| **Guam** | Guam | Guam | Guam | Guam | Guam | Guam |
| **Guat.** | Guatemala | Guatemala | Guatemala | Guatemala | Guatemala | Guatemala |
| **Guernsey** | Guernsey | Guernsey | Guernsey | Guernsey | Guernesey | Guernsey |
| **Gui.-B.** | Guiné-Bissau | Guinea-Bissau | Guinea-Bissau | Guinea-Bissau | Guinée-Bissau | Guiné-Bissau |
| **Gui. Ecu.** | Guinea Ecuatorial | Equatorial Guinea | Äquatorial-guinea | Guinea Ecuatorial | Guinée équatoriale | Guiné Equatorial |
| **Guinée** | Guinée | Guinea | Guinea | Guinea | Guinée | Guiné |
| **Guy.** | Guyana | Guyana | Guyana | Guyana | Guyane | Guiana |

| | LOCAL NAME | ENGLISH | DEUTSCH | ESPAÑOL | FRANÇAIS | PORTUGUÊS |
|---|---|---|---|---|---|---|
| **Guy. fr.** | Guyane française | French Guiana | Französisch-Guayana | Guayana Francesa | Guyane française | Guiana Francesa |
| **Haï.** | Haïti | Haiti | Haiti | Haití | Haïti | Haiti |
| **Haya.** | Hayastan | Armenia | Armenien | Armenia | Arménie | Arménia |
| **Hi., U.S.** | Hawaii | Hawaii | Hawaii | Hawaii | Hawaii | Havaí |
| **H.K.** | Hong Kong | Hong Kong | Hongkong | Hong Kong | Hong-Kong | Hong Kong |
| **Hond.** | Honduras | Honduras | Honduras | Honduras | Honduras | Honduras |
| **Hrv.** | Hrvatska | Croatia | Kroatien | Croacia | Croatie | Croácia |
| **Ia., U.S.** | Iowa | Iowa | Iowa | Iowa | Iowa | Iowa |
| **I.A.M.** | Al-Imārāt al-ʿArabīyah al-Muttahidah | United Arab Emirates | Vereinigte Arabische Emirate | Emiratos Arabes Unidos | Émirats arabes unis | Emirados Árabes Unidos |
| **Id., U.S.** | Idaho | Idaho | Idaho | Idaho | Idaho | Idaho |
| **Il., U.S.** | Illinois | Illinois | Illinois | Illinois | Illinois | Illinois |
| **In., U.S.** | Indiana | Indiana | Indiana | Indiana | Indiana | Indiana |
| **India** | India / Bharat | India | Indien | India | Inde | Índia |
| **Indon.** | Indonesia | Indonesia | Indonesien | Indonesia | Indonésie | Indonésia |
| **I. of Man** | Isle of Man | Isle of Man | Insel Man | Isla de Man | Île de Man | Man, Ilha de |
| **Īrān** | Īrān | Iran | Iran | Irán | Iran | Irã |
| **ʿĪrāq** | Al-ʿĪrāq | Iraq | Irak | Iraq | Iraq | Iraque |
| **Ire.** | Ireland / Éire | Ireland | Irland | Irlanda | Irlande | Irlanda |
| **Ísland** | Ísland | Iceland | Island | Islandia | Islande | Islândia |
| **It.** | Italia | Italy | Italien | Italia | Italie | Itália |
| **Ityo.** | Ityopiya | Ethiopia | Äthiopien | Etiopía | Éthiopie | Etiópia |
| **Jam.** | Jamaica | Jamaica | Jamaika | Jamaica | Jamaïque | Jamaica |
| **Jersey** | Jersey | Jersey | Jersey | Jersey | Jersey | Jersey |
| **Jugo.** | Jugoslavija | Yugoslavia | Jugoslawien | Yugoslavia | Yougoslavie | Iugoslávia |
| **Kal. Nun.** | Kalaallit Nunaat / Grønland | Greenland | Grönland | Groenlandia | Groenland | Groenlândia |
| **Kâm.** | Kâmpŭchéa | Cambodia | Kambodscha | Camboya | Cambodge | Camboja |
| **Kaz.** | Kazachstan | Kazakhstan | Kasachstan | Kazajstán | Kazakhstan | Cazaquistão |
| **Kenya** | Kenya | Kenya | Kenia | Kenya | Kenya | Quênia |
| **Kıbrıs** | Kuzey Kıbrıs | Cyprus, North | Türkische Republik Nordzypern | República Turca de Chipre del Norte | République turque du Nord de Chypre | República Turca do Norte de Chipre |
| **Kípros** | Kípros / Kıbrıs | Cyprus | Zypern | Chipre | Chypre | Chipre |
| **Kiribati** | Kiribati | Kiribati | Kiribati | Kiribati | Kiribati | Kiribati |
| **Ks., U.S.** | Kansas | Kansas | Kansas | Kansas | Kansas | Kansas |
| **Kuwayt** | Al-Kuwayt | Kuwait | Kuwait | Kuwait | Koweït | Kuwait |
| **Ky., U.S.** | Kentucky | Kentucky | Kentucky | Kentucky | Kentucky | Kentucky |
| **Kyrg.** | Kyrgyzstan | Kyrgyzstan | Kirgisistan | Kirguizia | Kirghizistan | Quirguistão |
| **La., U.S.** | Louisiana | Louisiana | Louisiana | Luisiana | Louisiane | Louisiana |
| **Lao** | Lao | Laos | Laos | Laos | Laos | Lao |
| **Lat.** | Latvija | Latvia | Lettland | Letonia | Lettonie | Letónia |
| **Leso.** | Lesotho | Lesotho | Lesotho | Lesotho | Lesotho | Lesoto |
| **Liber.** | Liberia | Liberia | Liberia | Liberia | Libéria | Libéria |
| **Lībiyā** | Lībiyā | Libya | Libyen | Libia | Libye | Líbia |
| **Liech.** | Liechtenstein | Liechtenstein | Liechtenstein | Liechtenstein | Liechtenstein | Liechtenstein |
| **Liet.** | Lietuva | Lithuania | Litauen | Lituania | Lithuanie | Lituânia |
| **Lubnān** | Lubnān | Lebanon | Libanon | Líbano | Liban | Líbano |
| **Lux.** | Luxembourg | Luxembourg | Luxemburg | Luxemburgo | Luxembourg | Luxemburgo |
| **Ma., U.S.** | Massachusetts | Massachusetts | Massachusetts | Massachusetts | Massachusetts | Massachusetts |
| **Macau** | Macau | Macao | Macao | Macao | Macao | Macau |
| **Madag.** | Madagasikara / Madagascar | Madagascar | Madagaskar | Madagascar | Madagascar | Madagascar |
| **Magreb** | Al-Magreb | Morocco | Marokko | Marruecos | Maroc | Marrocos |
| **Magy.** | Magyarország | Hungary | Ungarn | Hungría | Hongrie | Hungria |
| **Mak.** | Makedonija | Macedonia | Makedonien | Macedonia | Macédoine | Macedonia |
| **Malaŵi** | Malaŵi | Malawi | Malawi | Malawi | Malawi | Malaui |
| **Malay.** | Malaysia | Malaysia | Malaysia | Malasia | Malaisie | Malásia |
| **Mald.** | Maldives | Maldives | Malediven | Maldivas | Maldives | Maldivas |
| **Mali** | Mali | Mali | Mali | Malí | Mali | Mali |
| **Malta** | Malta | Malta | Malta | Malta | Malte | Malta |
| **Marsh. Is.** | Marshall Islands | Marshall Islands | Marshall Islands | Islas Marshall | Îles Marshall | Marshall Islands |
| **Mart.** | Martinique | Martinique | Martinique | Martinica | Martinique | Martinica |
| **Maur.** | Mauritanie / Mūrītāniyā | Mauritania | Mauretanien | Mauritania | Mauritanie | Mauritânia |
| **Maus.** | Mauritius | Mauritius | Mauritius | Mauricio | Maurice | Maurício |
| **Mayotte** | Mayotte | Mayotte | Mayotte | Mayotte | Mayotte | Mayotte |
| **Mb., Can.** | Manitoba | Manitoba | Manitoba | Manitoba | Manitoba | Manitoba |
| **Md., U.S.** | Maryland | Maryland | Maryland | Maryland | Maryland | Maryland |
| **Me., U.S.** | Maine | Maine | Maine | Maine | Maine | Maine |
| **Méx.** | México | Mexico | Mexiko | México | Mexique | México |
| **Mi., U.S.** | Michigan | Michigan | Michigan | Michigan | Michigan | Michigan |
| **Micron.** | Federated States of Micronesia | Micronesia, Federated States of | Federated States of Micronesia | Estado Federal de Micronesia | États fédérés de Micronésie | Federated States of Micronesia |
| **Mid. Is.** | Midway Islands | Midway Islands | Midway-Inseln | Islas Midway | Îles Midway | Midway, Ilhas |
| **Mişr** | Mişr | Egypt | Ägypten | Egipto | Égypte | Egito |
| **Mn., U.S.** | Minnesota | Minnesota | Minnesota | Minnesota | Minnesota | Minnesota |
| **Mo., U.S.** | Missouri | Missouri | Missouri | Misuri | Missouri | Missouri |
| **Moç.** | Moçambique | Mozambique | Mosambik | Mozambique | Mozambique | Moçambique |
| **Mol.** | Moldova | Moldova | Moldawien | Moldavia | Moldavie | Moldávia |
| **Monaco** | Monaco | Monaco | Monaco | Mónaco | Monaco | Mônaco |
| **Mong.** | Mongol Ard Uls | Mongolia | Mongolei | Mongolia | Mongolie | Mongólia |
| **Monts.** | Montserrat | Montserrat | Montserrat | Montserrat | Montserrat | Montserrat |
| **Ms., U.S.** | Mississippi | Mississippi | Mississippi | Misisipi | Mississippi | Mississipi |
| **Mt., U.S.** | Montana | Montana | Montana | Montana | Montana | Montana |
| **Mya.** | Myanmar | Myanmar | Myanmar | Myanmar | Myanmar | Myanmar |
| **N.A.** | . . . | North America | Nordamerika | América del Norte | Amérique du Nord | América do Norte |
| **Namibia** | Namibia | Namibia | Namibia | Namibia | Namibie | Namíbia |
| **Nauru** | Nauru / Naoero | Nauru | Nauru | Nauru | Nauru | Nauru |
| **N.B., Can.** | New Brunswick / Nouveau-Brunswick | New Brunswick | Neubraunschweig | Nueva Brunswick | Nouveau-Brunswick | Nova Brunswick |
| **N.C., U.S.** | North Carolina | North Carolina | Nord Karolina | Carolina del Norte | Caroline du Nord | Carolina do Norte |
| **N. Cal.** | Nouvelle-Calédonie | New Caledonia | Neukaledonien | Nueva Caledonia | Nouvelle Calédonie | Nova Caledônia |
| **N.D., U.S.** | North Dakota | North Dakota | Nord Dakota | Dakota del Norte | Dakota du Nord | Dakota do Norte |
| **Ne., U.S.** | Nebraska | Nebraska | Nebraska | Nebraska | Nebraska | Nebraska |
| **Ned.** | Nederland | Netherlands | Niederlande | Países Bajos | Pays-Bas | Países Baixos |
| **Ned. Ant.** | Nederlandse Antillen | Netherlands Antilles | Niederländische Antillen | Antillas Neerlandesas | Antilles néerlandaises | Antilhas Holandesas |
| **Nepāl** | Nepāl | Nepal | Nepal | Nepal | Népal | Nepal |
| **Nf., Can.** | Newfoundland / Terre-Neuve | Newfoundland | Neufundland | Terranova | Terre-Neuve | Terra Nova |
| **N.H., U.S.** | New Hampshire | New Hampshire | New Hampshire | Nuevo Hampshire | New Hampshire | Nova Hampshire |
| **Nic.** | Nicaragua | Nicaragua | Nicaragua | Nicaragua | Nicaragua | Nicarágua |
| **Nig.** | Nigeria | Nigeria | Nigeria | Nigeria | Nigéria | Nigéria |
| **Niger** | Niger | Niger | Niger | Níger | Niger | Níger |
| **Nihon** | Nihon | Japan | Japan | Japón | Japon | Japão |
| **N. Ire., U.K.** | Northern Ireland | Northern Ireland | Nordirland | Irlanda del Norte | Irlande du Nord | Irlanda do Norte |
| **Niue** | Niue | Niue | Niue | Niue | Nioué | Niue |

| | LOCAL NAME | ENGLISH | DEUTSCH | ESPAÑOL | FRANÇAIS | PORTUGUÊS |
|---|---|---|---|---|---|---|
| **N.J., U.S.** | New Jersey | New Jersey | New Jersey | Nueva Jersey | New Jersey | Nova Jersey |
| **N.M., U.S.** | New Mexico | New Mexico | New Mexico | Nuevo México | Nouveau-Mexique | Nova México |
| **N. Mar. Is.** | Northern Mariana Islands | Northern Mariana Islands | Northern Mariana Islands | Islas Marianas | Îles Mariannes du Nord | Northern Mariana Islands |
| **Nor.** | Norge | Norway | Norwegen | Noruega | Norvège | Noruega |
| **Norf. I.** | Norfolk Island | Norfolk Island | Norfolk-Insel | Isla Norfolk | Île Norfolk | Norfolk, Ilha |
| **N.S., Can.** | Nova Scotia / Nouvelle-Écosse | Nova Scotia | Neu Schottland | Nueva Escocia | Nouvelle-Écosse | Nova Scotia |
| **N.T., Can.** | Northwest Territories / Territoires du Nord-Ouest | Northwest Territories | Nord-West Territorien | Territorios del Noroeste | Territoires du Nord-Ouest | Territórios do Noroeste |
| **Nv., U.S.** | Nevada | Nevada | Nevada | Nevada | Nevada | Nevada |
| **N.Y., U.S.** | New York | New York | New York | Nueva York | New York | Nova York |
| **N.Z.** | New Zealand | New Zealand | Neuseeland | Nueva Zelanda | Nouvelle-Zélande | Nova Zelândia |
| **Oc.** | . . . | Oceania | Ozeanien | Oceanía | Océanie | Oceania |
| **Oh., U.S.** | Ohio | Ohio | Ohio | Ohio | Ohio | Ohio |
| **Ok., U.S.** | Oklahoma | Oklahoma | Oklahoma | Oklahoma | Oklahoma | Oklahoma |
| **On., Can.** | Ontario | Ontario | Ontario | Ontario | Ontario | Ontário |
| **Or., U.S.** | Oregon | Oregon | Oregon | Oregón | Oregon | Oregon |
| **Öst.** | Österreich | Austria | Österreich | Austria | Autriche | Austria |
| **Pa., U.S.** | Pennsylvania | Pennsylvania | Pennsylvanien | Pensilvania | Pennsylvanie | Pennsylvania |
| **Pāk.** | Pākistān | Pakistan | Pakistan | Pakistán | Pakistan | Paquistão |
| **Palau** | Palau / Belau | Palau | Palau | Palau | Palau (Belau) | Palau |
| **Pan.** | Panamá | Panama | Panama | Panamá | Panama | Panamá |
| **Pap. N. Gui.** | Papua New Guinea | Papua New Guinea | Papua-Neuguinea | Papua Nueva Guinea | Papouasie-Nouvelle Guinée | Papua-Nova Guiné |
| **Para.** | Paraguay | Paraguay | Paraguay | Paraguay | Paraguay | Paraguai |
| **P.E., Can.** | Prince Edward Island / Île-du-Prince-Édouard | Prince Edward Island | Prinz Edward-Insel | Isla Príncipe Eduardo | Île-du-Prince Édouard | Príncipe Eduardo, Ilha do |
| **Perú** | Perú | Peru | Peru | Perú | Pérou | Peru |
| **Pil.** | Pilipinas / Philippines | Philippines | Philippinen | Filipinas | Philippines | Filipinas |
| **Pit.** | Pitcairn | Pitcairn | Pitcairn | Pitcairn | Pitcairn | Pitcairn |
| **Pol.** | Polska | Poland | Polen | Polonia | Pologne | Polônia |
| **Poly. fr.** | Polynésie française | French Polynesia | Französisch-Polynesien | Polinesia Francesa | Polynésie française | Polinésia Francesa |
| **Port.** | Portugal | Portugal | Portugal | Portugal | Portugal | Portugal |
| **P.Q., Can.** | Québec | Quebec | Quebec | Quebec | Québec | Québec |
| **P.R.** | Puerto Rico | Puerto Rico | Puerto Rico | Puerto Rico | Porto Rico | Porto Rico |
| **P.S.N.Á.** | Plazas de Soberanía en el Norte de África | Spanish North Africa | Spanisch-Nordafrika | Plazas de Soberanía en el Norte de África | Afrique du Nord espagnole | África do Norte Espanhola |
| **Qaṭar** | Qaṭar | Qatar | Katar | Qatar | Qatar | Qatar |
| **Rep. Dom.** | República Dominicana | Dominican Republic | Dominikanische Republik | República Dominicana | République dominicaine | Dominicana, República |
| **Réu.** | Réunion | Reunion | Réunion | Reunión | Réunion | Reunião |
| **R.I., U.S.** | Rhode Island | Rhode Island | Rhode Island | Rhode Island | Rhode Island | Rhode Island |
| **Rom.** | România | Romania | Rumänien | Rumania | Roumanie | Romênia |
| **Ross.** | Rossija | Russia | Russland | Rusia | Russie | Rússia |
| **Rw.** | Rwanda | Rwanda | Ruanda | Rwanda | Rwanda | Ruanda |
| **S.A.** | . . . | South America | Südamerika | América del Sur | Amérique du Sud | América do Sul |
| **S. Afr.** | South Africa / Suid-Afrika | South Africa | Südafrika | Sudáfrica | Afrique du Sud | África do Sul |
| **Sak.** | Sakartvelo | Georgia | Georgien | Georgia | Géorgie | Geórgia |
| **S.C., U.S.** | South Carolina | South Carolina | Süd Karolina | Carolina del Sur | Caroline du Sud | Carolina do Sul |
| **Schw.** | Schweiz / Suisse / Svizzera | Switzerland | Schweiz | Suiza | Suisse | Suíça |
| **Scot., U.K.** | Scotland | Scotland | Schottland | Escocia | Écosse | Escócia |
| **S.D., U.S.** | South Dakota | South Dakota | Süd Dakota | Dakota del Sur | Dakota du Sud | Dakota do Sul |
| **Sén.** | Sénégal | Senegal | Senegal | Senegal | Sénégal | Senegal |
| **Sey.** | Seychelles | Seychelles | Seschellen | Seychelles | Seychelles | Seychelles |
| **Shq.** | Shqipëri | Albania | Albanien | Albania | Albanie | Albânia |
| **Sing.** | Singapore | Singapore | Singapur | Singapur | Singapour | Cingapura |
| **Sk., Can.** | Saskatchewan | Saskatchewan | Saskatchewan | Saskatchewan | Saskatchewan | Saskatchewan |
| **S.L.** | Sierra Leone | Sierra Leone | Sierra Leone | Sierra Leona | Sierra Leone | Serra Leoa |
| **S. Lan.** | Sri Lanka | Sri Lanka | Sri Lanka | Sri Lanka | Sri Lanka | Sri Lanka |
| **Slvk.** | Slovensko | Slovakia | Slowakei | Eslovaquia | Slovaquie | Eslováquia |
| **Slvn.** | Slovenija | Slovenia | Slowenien | Eslovenia | Slovénie | Eslovênia |
| **S. Mar.** | San Marino | San Marino | San Marino | San Marino | Saint-Marin | San Marino |
| **Sol. Is.** | Solomon Islands | Solomon Islands | Salomonen | Islas Salomón | Îles Salomon | Salomão, Ilhas |
| **Som.** | Somaliya | Somalia | Somalia | Somalia | Somalie | Somália |
| **St. Hel.** | St. Helena | St. Helena | Sankt Helena | Santa Elena | Sainte-Hélène | Santa Helena |
| **St. K./N.** | St. Kitts and Nevis | St. Kitts and Nevis | Sankt Kitts und Nevis | San Kitts y Nevis | Saint-Kitts-et-Nevis | São Kitts e Nevis |

| | LOCAL NAME | ENGLISH | DEUTSCH | ESPAÑOL | FRANÇAIS | PORTUGUÊS |
|---|---|---|---|---|---|---|
| **St. Luc.** | St. Lucia | St. Lucia | Sankt Lucia | Santa Lucía | Sainte-Lucie | Santa Lúcia |
| **S. Tom./P.** | São Tomé e Príncipe | Sao Tome and Principe | São Tomé und Principe | Santo Tomé y Príncipe | Sao Tomé-et-Principe | São Tomé e Príncipe |
| **St. P./M.** | Saint-Pierre-et-Miquelon | St. Pierre and Miquelon | Saint-Pierre und Miquelon | San Pedro y Miquelón | Saint-Pierre-et-Miquelon | São Pedro e Miquelon |
| **St. Vin.** | St. Vincent and the Grenadines | St. Vincent and the Grenadines | Sankt Vincent und die Grenadinen | San Vicente y las Granadinas | Saint-Vincent-et-Grenadines | São Vicente e Granadinas |
| **Sūd.** | As-Sūdān | Sudan | Sudan | Sudán | Soudan | Sudão |
| **Suomi** | Suomi / Finland | Finland | Finnland | Finlandia | Finlande | Finlândia |
| **Sur.** | Suriname | Suriname | Suriname | Suriname | Suriname | Suriname |
| **Sūrīy.** | Sūrīyah | Syria | Syrien | Siria | Syrie | Síria |
| **Sve.** | Sverige | Sweden | Schweden | Suecia | Suède | Suécia |
| **Swaz.** | Swaziland | Swaziland | Swasiland | Swazilandia | Swaziland | Suazilândia |
| **T.a.a.f.** | Terres australes et antarctiques françaises | French Southern and Antarctic Territories | Französische Süd- und Antarktis-Gebiete | Tierras Australes y Antárticas Francesas | Terres australes et antarctiques françaises | Terras Austrais e Antárticas Francesas |
| **Taehan** | Taehan-min'guk | Korea, South | Südkorea | Corea del Sur | Corée du Sud | Coréia do Sul |
| **T'aiwan** | T'aiwan | Taiwan | Taiwan | Taiwán | Taïwan | Taiwan (Formosa) |
| **Taj.** | Tajikistan | Tajikistan | Tadschikistan | Tadjikistán | Tadjikistan | Tajiquistão |
| **Tan.** | Tanzania | Tanzania | Tansania | Tanzanía | Tanzanie | Tanzânia |
| **Tchad** | Tchad | Chad | Tschad | Chad | Tchad | Tchad |
| **T./C. Is.** | Turks and Caicos Islands | Turks and Caicos Islands | Turks- und Caicos-Inseln | Islas Turcas y Caicos | Îles Turques et Caïques | Turcas e Caicos, Ilhas |
| **Thai** | Prathet Thai | Thailand | Thailand | Tailandia | Thaïlande | Tailândia |
| **Tn., U.S.** | Tennessee | Tennessee | Tennessee | Tennessee | Tennessee | Tennessee |
| **Togo** | Togo | Togo | Togo | Togo | Togo | Togo |
| **Tok.** | Tokelau | Tokelau | Tokelau | Tokelau | Tokélaou | Tokelau |
| **Tonga** | Tonga | Tonga | Tonga | Tonga | Tonga | Tonga |
| **Trin.** | Trinidad and Tobago | Trinidad and Tobago | Trinidad und Tobago | Trinidad y Tabago | Trinité-et-Tobago | Trinidad e Tobago |
| **Tun.** | Tunisie / Tunis | Tunisia | Tunesien | Túnez | Tunisie | Tunísia |
| **Tür.** | Türkiye | Turkey | Türkei | Turquía | Turquie | Turquia |
| **Turk.** | Turkmenistan | Turkmenistan | Turkmenistan | Turkmenia | Turkmenistan | Turquemenistão |
| **Tuvalu** | Tuvalu | Tuvalu | Tuvalu | Tuvalu | Tuvalu | Tuvalu |
| **Tx., U.S.** | Texas | Texas | Texas | Texas | Texas | Texas |
| **Ug.** | Uganda | Uganda | Uganda | Uganda | Ouganda | Uganda |
| **U.K.** | United Kingdom | United Kingdom | Vereinigtes Königreich | Reino Unido | Royaume-Uni | Reino Unido |
| **Ukr.** | Ukraina | Ukraine | Ukraine | Ucrania | Ukraine | Ucrânia |
| **'Umān** | 'Umān | Oman | Oman | Omán | Oman | Omã |
| **Ur.** | Uruguay | Uruguay | Uruguay | Uruguay | Uruguay | Uruguai |
| **Urd.** | Al-Urdun | Jordan | Jordanien | Jordania | Jordanie | Jordânia |
| **U.S.** | United States | United States | Vereinigte Staaten | Estados Unidos | États-Unis | Estados Unidos |
| **Ut., U.S.** | Utah | Utah | Utah | Utah | Utah | Utah |
| **Uzb.** | Uzbekistan | Uzbekistan | Usbekistan | Uzbekistán | Ouzbekistan | Usbequistão |
| **Va., U.S.** | Virginia | Virginia | Virginia | Virginia | Virginie | Virgínia |
| **Vanuatu** | Vanuatu | Vanuatu | Vanuatu | Vanuatu | Vanuatu | Vanuatu |
| **Vat.** | Città del Vaticano | Vatican City | Vatikanstadt | Ciudad del Vaticano | Cité du Vatican | Vaticano |
| **Ven.** | Venezuela | Venezuela | Venezuela | Venezuela | Venezuela | Venezuela |
| **Viet** | Viet Nam | Vietnam | Vietnam | Viet Nam | Viet Nam | Vietnam |
| **Vir. Is., U.S.** | Virgin Islands (U.S.) | Virgin Islands (U.S.) | Amerikanische Jungferninseln | Islas Vírgenes (americanas) | Îles Vierges (américaines) | Virgens Americanas, Ilhas |
| **Vt.** | Vermont | Vermont | Vermont | Vermont | Vermont | Vermont |
| **Wa., U.S.** | Washington | Washington | Washington | Washington | Washington | Washington |
| **Wake I.** | Wake Island | Wake Island | Wake | Isla Wake | Île Wake | Wake |
| **Wales, U.K.** | Wales | Wales | Wales | Gales | Galles | Gales |
| **Wal./F.** | Wallis et Futuna | Wallis and Futuna | Wallis und Futuna | Wallis y Futuna | Wallis et Futuna | Wallis e Futuna |
| **W.B.** | . . . | West Bank | Westufer | Ribera Oeste | Cisjordanie | Margem Oeste |
| **Wi., U.S.** | Wisconsin | Wisconsin | Wisconsin | Wisconsin | Wisconsin | Wisconsin |
| **W. Sah.** | . . . | Western Sahara | Westliche Sahara | Sahara Occidental | Sahara occidental | Saara Ocidental |
| **W. Sam.** | Western Samoa / Samoa i Sisifo | Western Samoa | Westsamoa | Samoa Occidental | Samoa-Occidental | Samoa Ocidental |
| **W.V., U.S.** | West Virginia | West Virginia | West Virginia | Virginia Occidental | Virginie Occidentale | Virgínia Ocidental |
| **Wy., U.S.** | Wyoming | Wyoming | Wyoming | Wyoming | Wyoming | Wyoming |
| **Yaman** | Al-Yaman | Yemen | Jemen | Yemen | Yémen | Iêmen |
| **Yis.** | Yisra'el / Isrā'īl | Israel | Israel | Israel | Israël | Israel |
| **Yk., Can.** | Yukon Territory | Yukon Territory | Yukon | Yukón | Yukon | Yukon |
| **Zaïre** | Zaïre | Zaire | Zaire | Zaire | Zaïre | Zaire |
| **Zam.** | Zambia | Zambia | Sambia | Zambia | Zambie | Zâmbia |
| **Zhg.** | Zhongguo | China | China | China | Chine | China |
| **Zimb.** | Zimbabwe | Zimbabwe | Simbabwe | Zimbabwe | Zimbabwe | Zimbabwe |

## Key to Index Symbols

The symbols below represent the categories into which the physical and cultural features are classified in the Index. Broad categories appear in **boldface** type. Symbols with superior numbers identify subcategories.

## Schlüssel zu den Symbolen des Registers

Die folgenden Symbole veranschaulichen die Kategorien, nach denen physische und kulturgeographische Objekte im Register geordnet sind. Die Oberbegriffe sind in **Fettdruck** hervorgehoben. Symbole mit hochgestellten Nummern kennzeichnen Unterbegriffe.

## Clave de los Símbolos del Índice

Los símbolos abajo representan las categorías dentro de las cuales están clasificados los rasgos físicos y culturales que están incluídos en el Índice. Las grandes categorías aparecen en **negrilla**. Los símbolos que tienen números en su parte superior identifican las subcategorías.

## Signification des Symboles de l'Index

Les symboles ci-dessous représentent les catégories sous lesquelles les données physiques et culturelles sont classées dans l'index. Les symboles en caractèter **gras** correspondent aux catégories principales. Ceux suivis d'un indice désignent les subdivisions d'une même catégorie.

## Chave dos Símbolos do Índice

Os símbolos abaixo representam as categorias em que estão classificados os acidentes físicos e culturais no Índice. As grandes categorias aparecem em **negrito**. Os símbolos acompanhados de números altos identificam as subcategorias.

| ENGLISH | DEUTSCH | ESPAÑOL | FRANÇAIS | PORTUGUÊS |
|---|---|---|---|---|
| ∧ **Mountain** | ∧ **Berg** | ∧ **Montaña** | ∧ **Montagne** | ∧ **Montanha** |
| ∧$^{1}$ Volcano | ∧$^{1}$ Vulkan | ∧$^{1}$ Volcán | ∧$^{1}$ Volcan | ∧$^{1}$ Vulcão |
| ∧$^{2}$ Hill | ∧$^{2}$ Hügel | ∧$^{2}$ Colina | ∧$^{2}$ Colline | ∧$^{2}$ Colina |
| ⋏ **Mountains** | ⋏ **Gebirge** | ⋏ **Montañas** | ⋏ **Montagnes** | ⋏ **Montanhas** |
| ⋏$^{1}$ Plateau | ⋏$^{1}$ Hochebene | ⋏$^{1}$ Meseta | ⋏$^{1}$ Plateau | ⋏$^{1}$ Planalto |
| ⋏$^{2}$ Hills | ⋏$^{2}$ Hügel | ⋏$^{2}$ Colinas | ⋏$^{2}$ Collines | ⋏$^{2}$ Colinas |
| )( **Pass** | )( **Paß** | )( **Paso** | )( **Col** | )( **Passo** |
| V **Valley, Canyon** | V **Tal, Cañon** | V **Valle, Cañón** | V **Vallée, Canyon** | V **Vale, Canhão** |
| ≚ **Plain** | ≚ **Ebene** | ≚ **Llano** | ≚ **Plaine** | ≚ **Planície** |
| ≚$^{1}$ Basin | ≚$^{1}$ Becken | ≚$^{1}$ Cuenca | ≚$^{1}$ Bassin | ≚$^{1}$ Bacia |
| ≚$^{2}$ Delta | ≚$^{2}$ Delta | ≚$^{2}$ Delta | ≚$^{2}$ Delta | ≚$^{2}$ Delta |
| ≻ **Cape** | ≻ **Kap** | ≻ **Cabo** | ≻ **Cap** | ≻ **Cabo** |
| ≻$^{1}$ Peninsula | ≻$^{1}$ Halbinsel | ≻$^{1}$ Península | ≻$^{1}$ Péninsule | ≻$^{1}$ Península |
| ≻$^{2}$ Spit, Sand Bar | ≻$^{2}$ Landzunge, Sandbarre | ≻$^{2}$ Lengua de Tierra, Bajo | ≻$^{2}$ Flèche, Banc de sable | ≻$^{2}$ Ponta de Terra, Banco de Areia |
| I **Island** | I **Insel** | I **Isla** | I **Île** | I **Ilha** |
| I$^{1}$ Atoll | I$^{1}$ Atoll | I$^{1}$ Atolón | I$^{1}$ Atoll | I$^{1}$ Atol |
| I$^{2}$ Rock | I$^{2}$ Fels | I$^{2}$ Roca | I$^{2}$ Rocher | I$^{2}$ Rochedo |
| II **Islands** | II **Inseln** | II **Islas** | II **Îles** | II **Ilhas** |
| II$^{1}$ Rocks | II$^{1}$ Felsen | II$^{1}$ Rocas | II$^{1}$ Rochers | II$^{1}$ Rochedos |
| ≙ **Other Topographic Features** | ≙ **Andere Topographische Objekte** | ≙ **Otros Elementos Topográficos** | ≙ **Autres données topographiques** | ≙ **Outros Acidentes Topográficos** |
| ≙$^{1}$ Continent | ≙$^{1}$ Erdteil | ≙$^{1}$ Continente | ≙$^{1}$ Continent | ≙$^{1}$ Continente |
| ≙$^{2}$ Coast, Beach | ≙$^{2}$ Küste, Strand | ≙$^{2}$ Costa, Playa | ≙$^{2}$ Côte, Plage | ≙$^{2}$ Costa, Praia |
| ≙$^{3}$ Isthmus | ≙$^{3}$ Landenge | ≙$^{3}$ Istmo | ≙$^{3}$ Isthme | ≙$^{3}$ Istmo |
| ≙$^{4}$ Cliff | ≙$^{4}$ Kliff | ≙$^{4}$ Risco | ≙$^{4}$ Falaise | ≙$^{4}$ Falésia |
| ≙$^{5}$ Cave, Caves | ≙$^{5}$ Höhle, Höhlen | ≙$^{5}$ Cueva, Cuevas | ≙$^{5}$ Caverne, Cavernes | ≙$^{5}$ Caverna, Cavernas |
| ≙$^{6}$ Crater | ≙$^{6}$ Krater | ≙$^{6}$ Cráter | ≙$^{6}$ Cratère | ≙$^{6}$ Cratera |
| ≙$^{7}$ Depression | ≙$^{7}$ Senke | ≙$^{7}$ Depresión | ≙$^{7}$ Dépression | ≙$^{7}$ Depressão |
| ≙$^{8}$ Dunes | ≙$^{8}$ Dünen | ≙$^{8}$ Dunas | ≙$^{8}$ Dunes | ≙$^{8}$ Dunas |
| ≙$^{9}$ Lava Flow | ≙$^{9}$ Lavastrom | ≙$^{9}$ Corriente de Lava | ≙$^{9}$ Coulée de lave | ≙$^{9}$ Corrente de Lava |
| ≃ **River** | ≃ **Fluß** | ≃ **Río** | ≃ **Rivière, Fleuve** | ≃ **Rio** |
| ≃$^{1}$ River Channel | ≃$^{1}$ Flussarm | ≃$^{1}$ Brazo de Río | ≃$^{1}$ Bras de rivière | ≃$^{1}$ Canal de Rio |
| ≅ **Canal** | ≅ **Kanal** | ≅ **Canal** | ≅ **Canal** | ≅ **Canal** |
| ≅$^{1}$ Aqueduct | ≅$^{1}$ Aquädukt | ≅$^{1}$ Acueducto | ≅$^{1}$ Aqueduc | ≅$^{1}$ Aqueduto |
| L **Waterfall, Rapids** | L **Wasserfall, Stromschnellen** | L **Cascada, Rápidos** | L **Chute d'eau, Rapides** | L **Quedas d'água, Rápidos** |
| ų **Strait** | ų **Meeresstraße** | ų **Estrecho** | ų **Détroit** | ų **Estreito** |
| ⊂ **Bay, Gulf** | ⊂ **Bucht, Golf** | ⊂ **Bahía, Golfo** | ⊂ **Baie, Golfe** | ⊂ **Baía, Golfo** |
| ⊂$^{1}$ Estuary | ⊂$^{1}$ Trichtermündung | ⊂$^{1}$ Estuario | ⊂$^{1}$ Estuaire | ⊂$^{1}$ Estuário |
| ⊂$^{2}$ Fjord | ⊂$^{2}$ Fjord | ⊂$^{2}$ Fiordo | ⊂$^{2}$ Fjord | ⊂$^{2}$ Fiorde |
| ⊂$^{3}$ Bight | ⊂$^{3}$ Bucht | ⊂$^{3}$ Bahía | ⊂$^{3}$ Baie | ⊂$^{3}$ Enseada |
| ⊜ **Lake, Lakes** | ⊜ **See, Seen** | ⊜ **Lago, Lagos** | ⊜ **Lac, Lacs** | ⊜ **Lago, Lagos** |
| ⊜$^{1}$ Reservoir | ⊜$^{1}$ Stausee | ⊜$^{1}$ Embalse | ⊜$^{1}$ Réservoir, Retenue | ⊜$^{1}$ Reservatório |
| ⁞⁞ **Swamp** | ⁞⁞ **Sumpf** | ⁞⁞ **Pantano** | ⁞⁞ **Marais** | ⁞⁞ **Pântano** |
| ⊓ **Ice Features, Glacier** | ⊓ **Eis- und Gletscherformen** | ⊓ **Accidentes Glaciales, Glaciar** | ⊓ **Formes glaciaires, Glacier** | ⊓ **Acidentes Glaciares, Geleira** |
| ⊤ **Other Hydrographic Features** | ⊤ **Andere Hydrographische Objekte** | ⊤ **Otros Elementos Hidrográficos** | ⊤ **Autres données hydrographiques** | ⊤ **Outros Acidentes Hidrográficos** |
| ⊤$^{1}$ Ocean | ⊤$^{1}$ Ozean | ⊤$^{1}$ Océano | ⊤$^{1}$ Océan | ⊤$^{1}$ Oceano |
| ⊤$^{2}$ Sea | ⊤$^{2}$ Meer | ⊤$^{2}$ Mar | ⊤$^{2}$ Mer | ⊤$^{2}$ Mar |
| ⊤$^{3}$ Anchorage | ⊤$^{3}$ Ankerplatz | ⊤$^{3}$ Ancladero | ⊤$^{3}$ Ancrage | ⊤$^{3}$ Ancoradouro |
| ⊤$^{4}$ Oasis, Well, Spring | ⊤$^{4}$ Oase, Brunnen, Quelle | ⊤$^{4}$ Oasis, Pozo, Manantial | ⊤$^{4}$ Oasis, Puits, Source | ⊤$^{4}$ Oásis, Poço, Fonte, Manancial |

| ENGLISH | DEUTSCH | ESPAÑOL | FRANÇAIS | PORTUGUÊS |
|---|---|---|---|---|
| ✤ **Submarine Features** | ✤ **Untermeerische Objekte** | ✤ **Accidentes Submarinos** | ✤ **Formes de relief sous-marin** | ✤ **Acidentes Submarinos** |
| ✤$^{1}$ Depression | ✤$^{1}$ Senke | ✤$^{1}$ Depresión | ✤$^{1}$ Dépression | ✤$^{1}$ Depressão |
| ✤$^{2}$ Reef, Shoal | ✤$^{2}$ Riff, Untiefe | ✤$^{2}$ Arrecife, Bajo | ✤$^{2}$ Récif, Haut-fond | ✤$^{2}$ Recife, Baixio |
| ✤$^{3}$ Mountain, Mountains | ✤$^{3}$ Berg, Gebirge | ✤$^{3}$ Montaña, Montañas | ✤$^{3}$ Montagne, Montagnes | ✤$^{3}$ Montanha, Montanhas |
| ✤$^{4}$ Slope, Shelf | ✤$^{4}$ Abhang, Schelf | ✤$^{4}$ Talud, Plataforma | ✤$^{4}$ Talus, Plateau continental | ✤$^{4}$ Talude, Plataforma |
| □ **Political Unit** | □ **Politische Einheit** | □ **Unidad Política** | □ **Entité politique** | □ **Unidade Política** |
| □$^{1}$ Independent Nation | □$^{1}$ Unabhängiger Staat | □$^{1}$ Nación Independiente | □$^{1}$ État indépendant | □$^{1}$ País Independente |
| □$^{2}$ Dependency | □$^{2}$ Abhängiges Gebiet | □$^{2}$ Dependencia | □$^{2}$ Dépendance | □$^{2}$ Dependência |
| □$^{3}$ State, Canton, Republic | □$^{3}$ Land, Kanton, Republik | □$^{3}$ Estado, Cantón, República | □$^{3}$ État, Canton, République | □$^{3}$ Estado, Cantão, República |
| □$^{4}$ Province, Region, Oblast | □$^{4}$ Provinz, Landschaft, Oblast | □$^{4}$ Provincia, Región, Oblast | □$^{4}$ Province, Région, Oblast | □$^{4}$ Província, Região, Oblast |
| □$^{5}$ Department, District, Prefecture | □$^{5}$ Département, Distrikt, Präfektur | □$^{5}$ Departamento, Distrito, Prefectura | □$^{5}$ Département, District, Préfecture | □$^{5}$ Departamento, Distrito, Prefeitura |
| □$^{6}$ County | □$^{6}$ Grafschaft | □$^{6}$ Condado | □$^{6}$ Comté | □$^{6}$ Condado |
| □$^{7}$ City, Municipality | □$^{7}$ Stadt, Stadtkreis | □$^{7}$ Ciudad, Municipalidad | □$^{7}$ Ville, Municipalité | □$^{7}$ Cidade, Municipalidade |
| □$^{8}$ Miscellaneous | □$^{8}$ Verschiedenes | □$^{8}$ Misceláneo | □$^{8}$ Divers | □$^{8}$ Diversos |
| □$^{9}$ Historical | □$^{9}$ Historisch | □$^{9}$ Histórico | □$^{9}$ Historique | □$^{9}$ Sítio Histórico |
| ψ **Cultural Institution** | ψ **Kulturelle Institution** | ψ **Institución Cultural** | ψ **Institution culturelle** | ψ **Instituição Cultural** |
| ψ$^{1}$ Religious Institution | ψ$^{1}$ Religiöse Institution | ψ$^{1}$ Institución Religiosa | ψ$^{1}$ Institution religieuse | ψ$^{1}$ Instituição Religiosa |
| ψ$^{2}$ Educational Institution | ψ$^{2}$ Erziehungsinstitution | ψ$^{2}$ Institución Educacional | ψ$^{2}$ Établissement d'éducation | ψ$^{2}$ Estabelecimento de Ensino |
| ψ$^{3}$ Scientific, Industrial Facility | ψ$^{3}$ Wissenschaftliche, Industrielle Anlage | ψ$^{3}$ Institución Científica o Industrial | ψ$^{3}$ Établissement scientifique ou industriel | ψ$^{3}$ Estabelecimento Científico ou Industrial |
| ⊥ **Historical Site** | ⊥ **Historische Stätte** | ⊥ **Sitio Histórico** | ⊥ **Site historique** | ⊥ **Sítio Histórico** |
| ♠ **Recreational Site** | ♠ **Erholungs- und Ferienort** | ♠ **Sitio de Recreo** | ♠ **Centre de loisirs** | ♠ **Área de Lazer** |
| ⊠ **Airport** | ⊠ **Flughafen** | ⊠ **Aeropuerto** | ⊠ **Aéroport** | ⊠ **Aeroporto** |
| ■ **Military Installation** | ■ **Militäranlage** | ■ **Instalación Militar** | ■ **Installation militaire** | ■ **Instalação Militar** |
| ⬥ **Miscellaneous** | ⬥ **Verschiedenes** | ⬥ **Misceláneo** | ⬥ **Divers** | ⬥ **Diversos** |
| ⬥$^{1}$ Region | ⬥$^{1}$ Region | ⬥$^{1}$ Región | ⬥$^{1}$ Région | ⬥$^{1}$ Região |
| ⬥$^{2}$ Desert | ⬥$^{2}$ Wüste | ⬥$^{2}$ Desierto | ⬥$^{2}$ Désert | ⬥$^{2}$ Deserto |
| ⬥$^{3}$ Forest, Moor | ⬥$^{3}$ Wald, Moor | ⬥$^{3}$ Bosque, Páramo | ⬥$^{3}$ Forêt, Lande | ⬥$^{3}$ Floresta, Pântano |
| ⬥$^{4}$ Reserve, Reservation | ⬥$^{4}$ Reservat | ⬥$^{4}$ Reserva, Reservación | ⬥$^{4}$ Réserve | ⬥$^{4}$ Reserva |
| ⬥$^{5}$ Transportation | ⬥$^{5}$ Verkehr | ⬥$^{5}$ Transporte | ⬥$^{5}$ Transport | ⬥$^{5}$ Transporte |
| ⬥$^{6}$ Dam | ⬥$^{6}$ Damm | ⬥$^{6}$ Presa | ⬥$^{6}$ Barrage | ⬥$^{6}$ Represa |
| ⬥$^{7}$ Mine, Quarry | ⬥$^{7}$ Bergwerk, Steinbruch | ⬥$^{7}$ Mina, Cantera | ⬥$^{7}$ Mine, Carrière | ⬥$^{7}$ Mina, Pedreira |
| ⬥$^{8}$ Neighborhood | ⬥$^{8}$ Nachbarschaft | ⬥$^{8}$ Barrio | ⬥$^{8}$ Quartier | ⬥$^{8}$ Arredores, Vizinhança |
| ⬥$^{9}$ Shopping Center | ⬥$^{9}$ Einkaufszentrum | ⬥$^{9}$ Mercado | ⬥$^{9}$ Centre commercial | ⬥$^{9}$ Shopping Center |

## A


| | | | |
|---|---|---|---|
| Aa ≃ | **50** | 51.01 N | 2.06 E |
| Aach | **58** | 47.50 N | 8.51 E |
| Aachen | **56** | 50.47 N | 6.05 E |
| Aach-Linz | **58** | 47.54 N | 9.11 E |
| Aadorf | **58** | 47.30 N | 8.54 E |
| Aaiun | | | |
| → El Aaiún | **148** | 27.09 N | 13.12 W |
| Aalen | **56** | 48.50 N | 10.05 E |
| A'ālī an-Nīl □$^{4}$ | **140** | 9.30 N | 31.00 E |
| Aalsmeer | **52** | 52.16 N | 4.45 E |
| Aalst (Alost), Bel. | **50** | 50.56 N | 4.02 E |
| Aalst, Ned. | **52** | 51.23 N | 5.29 E |
| Aalten | **52** | 51.56 N | 6.35 E |
| Aalter | **50** | 51.05 N | 3.27 E |
| Aalwynsfontein | **158** | 30.27 S | 18.38 E |
| Äänekoski | **26** | 62.36 N | 25.44 E |
| Aansluit | **158** | 26.44 S | 22.28 E |
| Aar ≃ | **56** | 50.23 N | 8.00 E |
| Aarau | **58** | 47.23 N | 8.03 E |
| Aarberg | **58** | 47.03 N | 7.16 E |
| Aarburg | **58** | 47.19 N | 7.54 E |
| Aardenburg | **52** | 51.16 N | 3.27 E |
| Aare ≃ | **58** | 47.37 N | 8.13 E |
| Aareschlucht ♠ | **58** | 46.44 N | 8.12 E |
| Aargau □$^{3}$ | **58** | 47.30 N | 8.10 E |
| Aarle-Rixtel | **52** | 51.31 N | 5.38 E |
| Aaronsburg | **210** | 40.54 N | 77.27 W |
| Aarschot | **56** | 50.59 N | 4.50 E |
| Aarwangen | **58** | 47.15 N | 7.46 E |
| Aazanèn | **34** | 35.13 N | 3.10 W |
| Aba, Nig. | **150** | 5.06 N | 7.21 E |
| Aba, Zaïre | **154** | 3.52 N | 30.14 E |
| Aba, Zhg. | **102** | 33.06 N | 101.59 E |
| Abā al-Bawl, Qurayn ∧$^{2}$ | **128** | 24.56 N | 51.13 E |
| Abā al-Waqf | **142** | 28.35 N | 30.46 E |
| Abā as-Su'ūd | **144** | 17.29 N | 44.08 E |
| Abacaxis ≃ | **242** | 3.54 S | 58.47 W |
| Abaco I | **238** | 26.28 N | 77.05 W |
| Abacou, Pointe ≻ | **238** | 18.03 N | 73.47 W |
| Abadab, Jabal ∧ | **140** | 18.53 N | 35.59 E |
| Ābādān | **128** | 30.20 N | 48.16 E |
| Ābādeh | **128** | 31.10 N | 52.37 E |
| Abadia dos Dourados | **255** | 18.28 S | 47.24 W |
| Abadiânia | **255** | 16.06 S | 48.48 W |
| Abadla | **148** | 31.01 N | 2.44 W |
| Abaeté | **255** | 19.09 S | 45.27 W |
| Abaeté ≃ | **255** | 18.02 S | 45.12 W |
| Abaetetuba | **250** | 1.42 S | 48.54 W |
| Abagajtuj | **88** | 49.35 N | 117.49 E |
| Abagnar Qi | **102** | 43.58 N | 116.04 E |
| Abag Qi | **102** | 43.53 N | 114.33 E |
| Abaí | **252** | 26.01 S | 55.57 W |
| Abaj, Kaz. | **86** | 49.38 N | 72.52 E |
| Abaj, Kaz. | **86** | 50.44 N | 69.30 E |
| Abaj, Ross. | **86** | 50.27 N | 85.05 E |
| Abaji | **150** | 8.28 N | 6.57 E |
| Abajo Mountains ⋏ | **200** | 37.50 N | 109.25 W |
| Abajo Peak ∧ | **200** | 37.51 N | 109.28 W |
| Abak | **150** | 4.57 N | 7.47 E |
| Abakaliki | **150** | 6.21 N | 8.06 E |
| Abakan | **86** | 53.43 N | 91.26 E |
| Abakan ≃ | **86** | 53.43 N | 91.30 E |
| Abakanovo | **76** | 59.18 N | 37.39 E |
| Abakanskij chrebet ⋏ | **86** | 52.20 N | 88.50 E |
| Abala, Congo | **152** | 1.21 S | 15.30 E |
| Abala, Niger | **150** | 14.56 N | 3.26 E |
| Abalak, Niger | **150** | 15.27 N | 6.17 E |
| Abalak, Ross. | **86** | 58.08 N | 68.36 E |
| Abalemma, Vallée d' V | **150** | 15.34 N | 6.23 E |
| Abalessa | **148** | 22.54 N | 4.50 E |
| Aban | **88** | 56.41 N | 96.04 E |
| Abancay | **248** | 13.35 S | 72.55 W |
| Abanga ≃ | **152** | 0.20 S | 10.30 E |
| Abano Terme | **64** | 45.21 N | 11.47 E |
| Abaokoro | **174t** | 1.29 N | 173.02 E |
| Abar Irir | **144** | 4.53 N | 46.10 E |
| Abar Kūh | **128** | 31.08 N | 53.17 E |
| Abarra | **144** | 5.23 N | 39.58 E |
| Abarracamento | **256** | 22.12 S | 43.30 W |
| Abaša | **84** | 42.12 N | 42.13 E |
| Abascay, Arroyo ≃ | **258** | 35.17 S | 58.07 W |
| Abashiri | **92a** | 44.01 N | 144.17 E |
| Abasolo, Méx. | **196** | 27.12 N | 101.24 W |
| Abasolo, Méx. | **196** | 25.57 N | 100.24 W |
| Abasolo, Méx. | **204** | 32.39 N | 115.21 W |
| Abasolo, Méx. | **232** | 25.18 N | 104.40 W |
| Abasolo, Méx. | **232** | 24.04 N | 98.22 W |
| Abasolo, Méx. | **234** | 20.27 N | 101.32 W |
| Abasolo del Valle | **234** | 17.44 N | 95.29 W |
| Abasto | **258** | 34.58 S | 58.06 W |
| Abastumani | **84** | 41.46 N | 42.50 E |
| Abate | **85** | 39.03 N | 77.36 E |
| Abate Alonia, Lago di ⊜ | **68** | 41.01 N | 15.45 E |
| Abatimbo el Gumas | **144** | 10.36 N | 35.13 E |
| Abatskij | **86** | 56.18 N | 70.28 E |
| Abau | **164** | 10.11 S | 148.42 E |
| Abava ≃ | **76** | 57.06 N | 21.54 E |
| Abay | | | |
| → Blue Nile ≃ | **140** | 15.38 N | 32.31 E |
| Abaya, Lake ⊜ | **144** | 6.20 N | 37.55 E |
| Abayuba | **258** | 34.51 S | 56.14 W |
| Abaza | **86** | 52.39 N | 90.06 E |
| Abba | **152** | 5.20 N | 15.11 E |
| Abbabach ≃ | **263** | 51.28 N | 7.41 E |
| Abbadia San Salvatore | **66** | 42.53 N | 11.41 E |
| 'Abbāsābād ⬥$^{8}$ | **267d** | 35.44 N | 51.25 E |
| Abbasanta | **71** | 40.08 N | 8.49 E |
| Abbaye, Étang de l' ⊜ | **261** | 48.41 N | 1.56 E |
| Abbé, Lac (Lake Abe) ⊜ | **144** | 11.06 N | 41.50 E |
| Abbehausen | **52** | 53.29 N | 8.26 E |
| Abbekås | **41** | 55.24 N | 13.36 E |
| Abbensen | **52** | 52.23 N | 10.11 E |
| Abbert ≃ | **48** | 53.25 N | 8.53 W |
| Abbess Roding | **260** | 51.47 N | 0.17 E |
| Abbeville, Fr. | **50** | 50.06 N | 1.50 E |
| Abbeville, Ga., U.S. | **192** | 31.59 N | 83.18 W |
| Abbeville, La., U.S. | **194** | 29.58 N | 92.08 W |
| Abbeville, Ms., U.S. | **194** | 34.30 N | 89.30 W |
| Abbeville, S.C., U.S. | **192** | 34.10 N | 82.22 W |
| Abbey | **184** | 50.43 N | 108.45 W |
| Abbeydorney | **48** | 52.19 N | 9.41 W |
| Abbeyfeale | **48** | 52.24 N | 9.18 W |
| Abbey Head ≻ | **44** | 54.46 N | 3.58 W |
| Abbeyleix | **48** | 52.55 N | 7.20 W |
| Abbey Peak ∧ | **164** | 14.18 S | 144.29 E |
| Abbey Wood ⬥$^{8}$ | **260** | 51.29 N | 0.08 E |
| Abbiategrasso | **62** | 45.24 N | 8.54 E |
| Abbot, Mount ∧ | **166** | 20.03 S | 147.45 E |
| Abbots Bromley | **42** | 52.48 N | 1.52 W |
| Abbotsbury | **42** | 50.40 N | 2.36 W |
| Abbotsford, Austl. | **274a** | 33.51 S | 151.08 E |
| Abbotsford, B.C., Can. | **224** | 49.03 N | 122.17 W |
| Abbotsford, Wi., U.S. | **190** | 44.56 N | 90.18 W |
| Abbots Langley | **42** | 51.43 N | 0.25 W |
| Abbott, Arg. | **258** | 35.17 S | 58.48 W |
| Abbott, Tx., U.S. | **222** | 31.53 N | 97.04 W |
| Abbottābād | **123** | 34.09 N | 73.13 E |
| Abbott Butte ∧ | **202** | 42.57 N | 122.33 W |
| Abbottstown | **208** | 39.53 N | 76.59 W |
| Abchazskaja Respublika □$^{3}$ | **84** | 43.10 N | 41.00 E |
| Abcoude | **52** | 52.16 N | 4.58 E |
| 'Abd al-'Azīz, Jabal ⋏ | **130** | 36.25 N | 40.20 E |
| 'Abd al-Ḥafīẓ, Qārat ∧$^{2}$ | **142** | 28.53 N | 30.08 E |
| 'Abd al-Kūrī I | **118** | 12.12 N | 52.13 E |
| 'Abd Allāh | **140** | 13.30 N | 23.02 E |
| 'Abd Allāh, Khawr ų | **128** | 29.50 N | 48.20 E |
| 'Abd al-Shāhīd | **273c** | 29.55 N | 31.13 E |
| Ābdānān | **128** | 32.58 N | 47.26 E |
| Ábdēra ⊥ | **38** | 40.59 N | 24.58 E |
| Abdrachmanovo | **80** | 54.46 N | 52.30 E |
| Abdul Hakīm | **123** | 30.33 N | 72.07 E |
| Abdulino | **80** | 53.42 N | 53.40 E |
| Abdulovo | **80** | 54.16 N | 53.27 E |
| Abe ≃ | **94** | 34.56 N | 138.24 E |
| Abe, Lake (Lac Abbé) ⊜ | **144** | 11.06 N | 41.50 E |
| Abéché | **146** | 13.49 N | 20.49 E |
| Abéjar | **34** | 41.48 N | 2.47 W |
| Abejonal, Cerro ∧ | **236** | 11.39 N | 86.10 W |
| Abejorral | **246** | 5.47 N | 75.26 W |
| Abekr | **140** | 12.43 N | 28.55 E |
| Abelek | **140** | 7.23 N | 28.46 E |
| Abel Tasman National Park ♠ | **172** | 40.55 S | 173.00 E |
| Abelti | **144** | 8.10 N | 37.34 E |
| Abemama I$^{1}$ | **14** | 0.21 N | 173.51 E |
| Abenberg | **56** | 49.14 N | 10.57 E |
| Abengourou | **150** | 6.44 N | 3.29 W |
| Abeno ⬥$^{8}$ | **270** | 34.38 N | 135.32 E |
| Abenójar | **34** | 38.53 N | 4.21 W |
| Åbenrå | **41** | 55.02 N | 9.26 E |
| Åbenrå Fjord ⊂ | **41** | 55.03 N | 9.34 E |
| Abens ≃ | **60** | 48.51 N | 11.46 E |
| Abensberg | **60** | 48.49 N | 11.51 E |
| Abeokuta | **150** | 7.10 N | 3.26 E |
| Aber | **154** | 2.12 N | 32.21 E |
| Aberaeron | **42** | 52.15 N | 4.15 W |
| Aberaman | **42** | 51.42 N | 3.25 W |
| Aberavon | | | |
| → Port Talbot | **42** | 51.36 N | 3.47 W |
| Abercarn | **42** | 51.39 N | 3.08 W |
| Aberchirder | **46** | 57.33 N | 2.38 W |
| Abercorn, P.Q., Can. | **206** | 45.02 N | 72.40 W |
| Abercorn | | | |
| → Mbala, Zam. | **154** | 8.50 S | 31.22 E |
| Abercrombie ≃ | **170** | 34.09 S | 149.40 E |
| Aberdare | **42** | 51.43 N | 3.27 W |
| Aberdare National Park ♠ | **154** | 0.30 S | 36.45 E |
| Aberdare Range ⋏ | **154** | 0.25 S | 36.38 E |
| Aberdaron | **42** | 52.49 N | 4.43 W |
| Aberdeen, Sk., Can. | **184** | 52.19 N | 106.17 W |
| Aberdeen (Xianggangzi), H.K. | **271d** | 22.15 N | 114.09 E |
| Aberdeen, S. Afr. | **158** | 32.29 S | 24.05 E |
| Aberdeen, Scot., U.K. | **46** | 57.10 N | 2.04 W |
| Aberdeen, Id., U.S. | **202** | 42.56 N | 112.50 W |
| Aberdeen, Md., U.S. | **208** | 39.30 N | 76.09 W |
| Aberdeen, Ms., U.S. | **194** | 33.49 N | 88.32 W |
| Aberdeen, N.C., U.S. | **192** | 35.07 N | 79.25 W |
| Aberdeen, Oh., U.S. | **218** | 38.39 N | 83.45 W |
| Aberdeen, S.D., U.S. | **198** | 45.27 N | 98.29 W |
| Aberdeen, Wa., U.S. | **224** | 46.58 N | 123.48 W |
| Aberdeen Lake ⊜ | **176** | 64.27 N | 99.00 W |
| Aberdeen Lake ⊜$^{1}$ | **194** | 33.55 N | 88.30 W |
| Aberdeen Proving Ground ■ | **208** | 39.25 N | 76.10 W |
| Aberdour | **46** | 56.03 N | 3.19 W |
| Aberdulais | **42** | 51.41 N | 3.48 W |
| Aberdyfi | **42** | 52.33 N | 4.02 W |
| Aberfeldy | **46** | 56.37 N | 3.54 W |
| Aberfoyle | **46** | 56.11 N | 4.23 W |
| Abergavenny | **42** | 51.50 N | 3.00 W |
| Abergele | **44** | 53.17 N | 3.34 W |
| Abergwynfi | **42** | 51.40 N | 3.35 W |
| Abergynolwyn | **42** | 52.40 N | 3.58 W |
| Aberjona ≃ | **283** | 42.27 N | 71.08 W |
| Abermain | **170** | 32.49 S | 151.25 E |
| Abernathy | **196** | 33.50 N | 101.51 W |
| Abernethy, Sk., Can. | **184** | 50.45 N | 103.25 W |
| Abernethy, Scot., U.K. | **46** | 56.20 N | 3.19 W |
| Aberporth | **42** | 52.09 N | 4.33 W |
| Abersoch | **42** | 52.50 N | 4.29 W |
| Abersychan | **42** | 51.44 N | 3.04 W |
| Abert, Lake ⊜ | **202** | 42.38 N | 120.13 W |
| Abertillery | **42** | 51.45 N | 3.09 W |
| Aberuthven | **46** | 56.19 N | 3.39 W |
| Aberystwyth | **42** | 52.25 N | 4.05 W |
| Abessinien, Hochland von | | | |
| → Ethiopian Plateau ⋏$^{1}$ | **144** | 9.00 N | 38.00 E |
| Abetone | **66** | 44.08 N | 10.40 E |
| Abez' | **24** | 66.32 N | 61.42 E |
| Abhā | **144** | 18.13 N | 42.30 E |
| Abhar | **128** | 36.09 N | 49.13 E |
| Abharwat ∧ | **123** | 34.02 N | 74.25 E |
| Abhayāpuri | **124** | 26.20 N | 90.40 E |
| Abhaynagar | **126** | 23.01 N | 89.28 E |
| Abiaca Creek ≃ | **194** | 33.20 N | 90.15 W |
| Abid, Oued el ≃ | **148** | 32.18 N | 7.03 W |
| Ābidīn | **140** | 13.33 N | 29.38 E |
| 'Abīdīyah | **140** | 18.14 N | 33.57 E |
| Abidjan | **150** | 5.19 N | 4.02 W |
| 'Ābid Mār, Tall ∧ | **132** | 32.26 N | 36.42 E |
| Abiengama | **154** | 2.35 N | 27.46 E |
| Abiko | **94** | 35.52 N | 140.03 E |


| | | | | |
|---|---|---|---|---|
| ≃ River | Fluß | Río | Rivière | Rio |
| ≅ Canal | Kanal | Canal | Canal | Canal |
| L Waterfall, Rapids | Wasserfall, Stromschnellen | Cascada, Rápidos | Chute d'eau, Rapides | Cascata, Rápidos |
| ų Strait | Meeresstraße | Estrecho | Détroit | Estreito |
| ⊂ Bay, Gulf | Bucht, Golf | Bahía, Golfo | Baie, Golfe | Baía, Golfo |
| ⊜ Lake, Lakes | See, Seen | Lago, Lagos | Lac, Lacs | Lago, Lagos |
| ⁞⁞ Swamp | Sumpf | Pantano | Marais | Pântano |
| ⊓ Ice Features, Glacier | Eis- und Gletscherformen | Accidentes Glaciales | Formes glaciaires | Acidentes glaciares |
| ⊤ Other Hydrographic Features | Andere Hydrographische Objekte | Otros Elementos Hidrográficos | Autres données hydrographiques | Outros acidentes hidrográficos |

| | | | | |
|---|---|---|---|---|
| ✤ Submarine Features | Untermeerische Objekte | Accidentes Submarinos | Formes de relief sous-marin | Acidentes submarinos |
| □ Political Unit | Politische Einheit | Unidad Politica | Entité politique | Unidade política |
| ψ Cultural Institution | Kulturelle Institution | Institución Cultural | Institution culturelle | Institução cultural |
| ⊥ Historical Site | Historische Stätte | Sitio Histórico | Site historique | Sitio histórico |
| ♠ Recreational Site | Erholungs- und Ferienort | Sitio de Recreo | Centre de loisirs | Area de Lazer |
| ⊠ Airport | Flughafen | Aeropuerto | Aéroport | Aeroporto |
| ■ Military Installation | Militäranlage | Instalación Militar | Installation militaire | Instalação militar |
| ⬥ Miscellaneous | Verschiedenes | Misceláneo | Divers | Diversos |

Abilene, Ks., U.S. 198 38.55 N 97.12 W
Abilene, Tx., U.S. 196 32.26 N 99.43 W
Abingdon, Eng., U.K. 42 51.41 N 1.17 W
Abingdon, Il., U.S. 190 40.48 N 90.24 W
Abingdon, Il., U.S. 194 40.48 N 90.24 W
Abingdon, Va., U.S. 192 36.42 N 81.58 W
Abinger 260 51.12 N 0.24 W
Abington, Ct., U.S. 207 41.51 N 72.00 W
Abington, Ma., U.S. 207 42.06 N 70.56 W
Abington, Pa., U.S. 208 40.07 N 75.07 W
Abington Reefs ✦[2] 166 18.00 S 149.36 E
Abino, Point > 212 42.50 N 79.05 W
Abino Bay c 284a 42.51 N 79.05 W
Abinsk 78 44.52 N 38.09 E
Abiod, Rmel el ⊥[8] 148 31.30 N 9.30 E
Abiquiu 200 36.12 N 106.19 W
Abiquiu Reservoir ⊜[1] 200 36.18 N 106.32 W
Abiseo ≃ 248 7.18 S 76.50 W
Abiseo, Parque Nacional ♦ 248 7.35 S 77.10 W
Abisko 24 68.20 N 18.51 E
Abisko Nationalpark ♦ 24 68.20 N 18.30 E
Abita Springs 194 30.28 N 90.02 W
Abitau ≃ 176 59.53 N 109.03 W
Abitibi ≃ 176 51.03 N 80.55 W
Abitibi, Lake ⊜ 190 48.42 N 79.45 W
Abiy Adi 144 13.26 N 39.05 E
Abiyata, Lake ⊜ 144 7.37 N 38.36 E
Abja-Paluoja 76 58.08 N 25.21 E
Abkhazia → Abchazskaja Respublika □[3] 84 43.10 N 41.00 E
Ableiges 261 49.05 N 1.59 E
Ablis 50 48.31 N 1.50 E
Ablon-sur-Seine 261 48.43 N 2.25 E
Abnūb 142 27.16 N 31.09 E
Åbo → Turku 26 60.27 N 22.17 E
Abóbada 266c 38.43 N 9.20 W
Abodom 150 5.32 N 0.49 W
Abohar 123 30.09 N 74.11 E
Aboisso 150 5.28 N 3.12 W
Abomey 150 7.11 N 1.59 E
Abondance 58 46.17 N 6.44 E
Abong 146 6.59 N 10.44 E
Abongabong, Gunung ∧ 114 4.15 N 96.48 E
Abong Mbang 152 3.59 N 13.10 E
Abonnema 150 4.43 N 6.47 E
Abony 30 47.11 N 20.01 E
Aborigen, pik ∧ 74 61.59 N 149.19 E
Aborlan 116 9.26 N 118.33 E
Aborrebjerg ∧[2] 41 54.59 N 12.32 E
Aboso 150 5.22 N 1.56 W
Abō-tōge )( 94 36.11 N 137.35 E
Abou 144 4.21 N 43.03 E
Abou-Deïa 146 11.27 N 19.17 E
Abounamy ≃ 250 4.24 N 54.26 W
Aboyne 46 57.05 N 2.50 W
Abra □[4] 116 17.35 N 120.50 E
Abra ≃ 116 17.31 N 120.23 E
Abraão 256 23.08 S 44.10 W
Abraham Lake ⊜[1] 182 52.15 N 116.23 W
Abraham Lincoln Birthplace National Historic Site ⊥ 194 37.32 N 85.44 W
Abrahamsdam 158 29.08 S 22.39 E
Abraka 150 5.50 N 6.05 E
Abram 262 53.31 N 2.35 W
Abramcevo 265b 55.50 N 37.50 E
Abramovka 78 51.12 N 41.01 E
Abramovskaja 24 65.11 N 51.43 E
Abram S. Hewitt State Forest ♦ 276 41.11 N 74.22 W
Abrantes 34 39.28 N 8.12 W
Abra Pampa 252 22.43 S 65.42 W
Abraq, Wādī al- V 146 26.27 N 18.48 E
Abrau-D'urso 78 44.43 N 37.37 E
Abra Vieja, Arroyo ≃ 288 34.26 S 58.34 W
Abre-Campo 255 20.18 S 42.29 W
Ábrego 246 8.05 N 73.13 W
Abreojos, Punta > 232 26.42 N 113.35 W
Abreschviller 58 48.38 N 7.06 E
Abreu e Lima 250 7.54 S 34.53 W
'Abrī, Sūd. 140 11.40 N 30.28 E
'Abrī, Sūd. 140 20.48 N 30.20 E
Abriachan 46 57.22 N 4.24 W
Abridge 260 51.39 N 0.07 E
Abriès 62 44.47 N 6.56 E
Abring 123 33.42 N 76.35 E
Abriola 68 40.30 N 15.49 E
Abrova 76 52.30 N 25.34 E
Abrud 38 46.17 N 23.04 E
Abruka saar I 76 58.10 N 22.30 E
Abrunheira 266c 38.46 N 9.21 W
Abruzzi □[4] 66 42.20 N 13.45 E
Abruzzo, Parco Nazionale d' ♦ 66 41.45 N 13.45 E
Absam 64 47.18 N 11.30 E
Absaroka Range ⋏ 202 44.45 N 109.50 W
Absarokee 202 45.31 N 109.26 W
Abscon 50 50.20 N 3.18 E
Absdorf 61 48.24 N 15.59 E
Absecon 208 39.25 N 74.29 W
Absecon Bay c 208 39.24 N 74.28 W
Abşeker 130 38.55 N 39.11 E
Abşeron yarımadası >[1] 84 40.30 N 50.00 E
Abtenau 64 47.33 N 13.21 E
Abtsgmünd 56 48.54 N 10.00 E
Abu 96 34.30 N 131.28 E
Abu ≃ 96 34.25 N 131.24 E
Abū Ahl ⊤[4] 128 34.06 N 43.45 E
Abū 'Alāwī, Wādī V 142 30.07 N 31.51 E
Abū al-Ghayṭ 273c 30.09 N 31.11 E
Abū al-Ḥamām, Jabal ∧ 132 30.27 N 35.38 E
Abū al-Hawl (Sphinx) ⊥ 142 29.59 N 31.08 E
Abū 'Alī I 128 27.20 N 49.33 E
Abū al-Khaṣīb 128 30.27 N 47.59 E
Abū al-Maṭāmīr 142 30.55 N 30.11 E
Abū al-'Urūq, Bi'r ⊤[4] 142 30.45 N 32.23 E
Abū an-Numrus 273c 29.57 N 31.12 E
Abū 'Aradeib, Wādī V 140 14.12 N 23.06 E
Abū 'Arīsh 144 16.57 N 42.50 E
Abū Ballās ∧[2] 140 24.26 N 27.39 E
Abū Daraj, Ra's > 142 29.23 N 32.34 E
Abū Dā'ūd, Ra's > 128 23.19 N 58.55 E
Abū Dā'ūd as-Sibākh 142 30.55 N 31.34 E
Abū Dawm 140 16.16 N 32.36 E
Abū Dawm, Wādī V 140 18.28 N 31.49 E
Abu Dhabi → Abū Ẓaby 128 24.28 N 54.22 E
Abū Dhi'ābah, Wādī V 142 29.37 N 32.06 E
Abū Dīs 140 19.08 N 33.34 E
Abū Dulayq 140 15.54 N 33.49 E
Abufari 248 5.25 S 62.59 W
Abū Gatta Hills ⋏[2] 140 6.06 N 27.44 E
Abū Gelba 140 13.11 N 31.52 E
Abū Ghālib 142 30.16 N 30.56 E
Abū Ḥabl, Khawr V 140 12.49 N 31.15 E
Abū Ḥād, Wādī V 142 28.20 N 32.49 E
Abū Ḥadīmah, Bi'r ⊤[4] 142 30.44 N 29.51 E
Abū Ḥamad 140 19.32 N 33.19 E
Abū Ḥammād al-Mahaṭṭah 142 30.32 N 31.40 E
Abū Ḥarāz, Sūd. 140 12.58 N 29.52 E
Abū Ḥarāz, Sūd. 140 19.04 N 32.07 E
Abū Ḥasan, Jabal ∧ 144 17.42 N 42.54 E
Abū Ḥummuṣ 142 31.06 N 30.19 E
Abū Ḥushsh, Bi'r ⊤[4] 142 30.49 N 29.57 E
Abuja 150 9.12 N 7.11 E
Abū Jābirah 140 11.04 N 26.51 E
Abū Jandīr 142 29.14 N 30.41 E
Abū Jirj 142 28.32 N 30.47 E
Abū Jubayhah 140 11.27 N 31.14 E
Abū Kabīr 142 30.44 N 31.40 E
Abū Kamāl 130 34.27 N 40.55 E
Abū Kharjah, Wādī V 142 28.38 N 31.44 E
Abū Khashabah, Jabal ∧ 142 28.08 N 32.52 E
Abūksāh 142 29.23 N 30.42 E
Abū Kulaywāt 140 12.20 N 26.00 E
Abukuma ≃ 92 38.02 N 140.56 E
Abukuma-kōchi ⋏ 92 37.30 N 140.45 E
Abū Latt I 144 19.58 N 40.08 E
Abulug 116 18.27 N 121.27 E
Abulug ≃ 116 18.29 N 121.25 E
Abū Madd, Ra's > 128 24.50 N 37.07 E
Abū Makhlūf, Bi'r ⊤[4] 142 30.45 N 29.42 E
Abū Maṭāriq 140 10.58 N 26.17 E
Abu Mendi 144 11.47 N 35.43 E
Abū Minqār, Bi'r ⊤[4] 140 26.30 N 27.35 E
Abumombazi 152 3.42 N 22.10 E
Abū Muḥammad, Bi'r ⊤[4] 132 29.43 N 34.13 E
Abū Muḥarrik, Ghurd ⊥[8] 140 27.50 N 29.40 E
Abū Mūsā I 128 25.52 N 55.03 E
Abuna 248 9.42 S 65.23 W
Abuná (Abunã) ≃ 248 9.41 S 65.23 W
Abū Na'āmah 140 12.44 N 34.08 E
Abune Yosef ∧ 144 12.10 N 39.12 E
Abū Qardī, Qā' ≃ 132 32.08 N 37.11 E
Abū Qashsh 132 31.57 N 35.11 E
Abū Qīr ⊸[8] 142 31.19 N 30.04 E
Abū Qīr, Khalīj (Abu Qir Bay) c 142 31.23 N 30.13 E
Abū Qurqāṣ 142 27.56 N 30.50 E
Aburatsubo-kō c 268 35.09 N 139.38 E
Abū Rimth, Wādī V, Miṣr 142 28.45 N 31.27 E
Abū Rimth, Wādī V, Miṣr 142 30.21 N 31.53 E
Abū Rīshat, Wādī V 142 28.54 N 31.37 E
Ābu Road 120 24.29 N 72.47 E
Abū Rubayq 128 23.44 N 39.42 E
Abū Rujmayn, Jabal ⋏ 130 34.52 N 38.20 E
Abū Sanṭ, Wādī V 140 14.11 N 23.06 E
Abū Shajarah, Ra's > 140 21.04 N 37.14 E
Abū Shāmah, Jabal ∧ 142 29.52 N 31.38 E
Abū Shanab, Sūd. 140 10.47 N 29.32 E
Abū Shanab, Sūd. 140 13.57 N 27.47 E
Abū Shaykhāt, Ḍahr ∧[2] 130 36.36 N 39.40 E
Abu Simbel → Abū Sunbul ⊥ 140 22.22 N 31.38 E
Abū Ṣīr 273c 29.53 N 31.13 E
Abu Ṣīr al-Malaq 142 29.15 N 31.05 E
Abū Ṣīr-Banā 142 30.55 N 31.15 E
Abū Ṣīr Pyramids ⊥ 273c 29.54 N 31.12 E
Abū Sulṭan 142 30.25 N 32.19 E
Abū Sunbul ⊥ 140 22.22 N 31.38 E
Abū Ṣuwayr al-Mahaṭṭah 142 30.34 N 32.07 E
Abū Ṣuwayr Military Base ■ 142 30.34 N 32.06 E
Abuta 92a 42.33 N 140.46 E
Abū Ṭabarī ⊤[4] 140 17.35 N 28.31 E
Abū Ṭarafah, Wādī V 132 30.12 N 36.13 E
Abut Head > 172 43.07 S 170.15 E
Abū Tīj 140 27.02 N 31.19 E
Abū Ṭunayṭin 140 14.24 N 31.01 E
Abū Ṭurayfīyah, Jabal ∧, Miṣr 142 29.58 N 32.06 E
Abū Ṭurayfīyah, Jabal ∧, Miṣr 142 29.42 N 31.49 E
Abū 'Uwayjilah ⊤[4] 132 30.50 N 34.07 E
Abuye Meda ∧ 144 10.28 N 39.44 E
Abuyog 116 10.45 N 125.01 E
Abū Zabad 140 12.21 N 29.15 E
Abū Za'bal 142 30.15 N 31.21 E
Abū Ẓaby (Abu Dhabi) 128 24.28 N 54.22 E
Abū Zanīmah 140 29.03 N 33.06 E
Abwong 140 9.07 N 32.12 E
Åby 40 58.40 N 16.11 E
Åby ⊸[8] 41 56.09 N 10.10 E
Aby, Lagune c 150 5.15 N 3.14 W
Abyaḍ 140 13.46 N 26.28 E
Abyaḍ, Al-Bahr al- → White Nile ≃ 140 15.38 N 32.31 E
Abyaḍ, Wādī al- V 142 29.38 N 32.13 E
Åbyälven ≃ 26 65.01 N 21.24 E
Abyār 142 30.50 N 30.52 E
Abyār 'Alī 128 24.25 N 39.32 E
Åbybro 26 57.09 N 9.45 E
Abydos 162 21.25 S 118.54 E
Abyei 140 9.36 N 28.26 E
Åbyggeby 40 60.44 N 17.07 E
Åbytorp 40 59.07 N 15.04 E
Abzanovo 86 53.50 N 58.36 E
Acacías 246 3.59 N 73.46 W
Academia 214 40.25 N 82.28 W
Academy Corners 208 41.57 N 77.23 W
Academy of Sciences ʊ[3] 282 37.46 N 122.28 W
Acadia National Park ♦ 188 44.18 N 68.15 W
Acadia Valley 184 51.08 N 110.13 W
Acahay 252 25.55 S 57.09 W
Açailandia 250 4.57 S 47.29 W
Acajete 234 19.06 N 97.57 W
Acajutiba 250 11.40 S 38.01 W
Acajutla 236 13.36 N 89.50 W
Acala 234 16.34 N 92.48 W
Acalayong 152 1.05 N 9.40 E
Acámbaro 234 20.02 N 100.44 W
Acampo 226 38.10 N 121.13 W
Acandí 246 8.32 N 77.14 W
A Cañiza 34 42.13 N 8.16 W
Acaponeta 234 22.30 N 105.22 W
Acaponeta ≃ 234 22.20 N 105.37 W
Acapulco [de Juárez] 234 16.51 N 99.55 W
Acará 250 1.57 S 48.11 W
Acará ≃ 250 1.40 S 48.25 W
Acará, Lago ⊜ 246 3.39 S 62.40 W
Acaraí ≃ 250 2.02 S 52.15 W
Acarai Mountains ⋏ 246 1.30 N 58.15 W
Acará-Mirim ≃ 250 1.58 S 48.12 W
Acaraú 250 2.53 S 40.07 W
Acaraú ≃ 250 2.51 S 40.08 W
Acaray ≃ 252 25.29 S 54.42 W
Acari, Bra. 250 6.31 S 36.38 W
Acarí, Perú 248 15.26 S 74.37 W
Acari ≃, Bra. 248 5.18 S 59.42 W
Acari ≃, Bra. 255 16.00 S 45.03 W
Acarí ≃, Perú 248 15.39 S 74.39 W
Acarigua 246 9.33 N 69.12 W
Acâș 38 47.33 N 22.47 E
Acate 70 37.02 N 14.28 E
Acate ≃ 70 37.00 N 14.20 E
Acatic 234 20.47 N 102.53 W
Acatlán ≃ 234 18.04 N 98.19 W
Acatlán de Juárez 234 20.26 N 103.38 W
Acatlán de Osorio 234 18.12 N 98.03 W
Acatlán de Pérez Figueroa 234 18.32 N 96.37 W
Acatzingo [de Hidalgo] 234 18.59 N 97.47 W
Acay, Nevado de ∧ 252 24.21 S 66.12 W
Acayucan 234 17.57 N 94.55 W
Accadia 68 41.10 N 15.20 E
Acceglio 62 44.28 N 7.00 E
Aččen, mys > 180 64.45 N 175.30 W
Accettura 68 40.29 N 16.09 E
Ačchoj-Martan 84 43.11 N 45.18 E
Ačči 85 39.57 N 68.14 E
Acciano 66 42.10 N 13.43 E
Accokeek 208 38.40 N 77.02 W
Accomac 208 37.43 N 75.39 W
Accomack □[6] 208 37.45 N 75.40 W
Accord, Ma., U.S. 283 42.10 N 70.53 W
Accord, N.Y., U.S. 210 41.47 N 74.13 W
Accord Brook ≃ 283 42.10 N 70.53 W
Accord Pond ⊜ 283 42.10 N 70.53 W
Accotink Creek ≃ 284c 38.46 N 77.13 W
Accotink Creek, Bear Branch ≃ 284c 38.52 N 77.15 W
Accotink Creek, Long Branch ≃ 284c 38.48 N 77.13 W
Accoville 192 37.46 N 81.50 W
Accra 150 5.33 N 0.13 W
Accra □[4] 150 5.40 N 0.10 W
Accrington 44 53.46 N 2.21 W
Accumoli 66 42.42 N 13.15 E
Acebuches 232 28.15 N 102.43 W
Aceguá 252 31.52 S 54.09 W
Aceh □[4] 114 4.00 N 97.00 E
Aceh ≃ 114 5.36 N 95.20 E
Acerentia ⊥ 68 39.16 N 16.49 E
Acerenza 68 40.48 N 15.57 E
Acerno 68 40.44 N 15.03 E
Acerra 68 40.57 N 14.22 E
Acevedo 252 33.45 S 60.27 W
Achacachi 248 16.03 S 68.43 W
Achaguas 246 7.46 N 68.14 W
Achal □[8] 128 38.30 N 59.00 E
Achalciche 84 41.38 N 42.59 E
Achali-Kindgi 84 42.48 N 41.16 E
Achalkalaki 84 41.25 N 43.29 E
Achalpur 120 21.16 N 77.31 E
Achangaran 85 40.54 N 69.37 E
Achao 254 42.28 S 73.30 W
Achar 252 32.25 S 56.10 W
Acharacle 46 56.44 N 5.47 W
Achar uul ∧ 102 45.10 N 103.45 E
Achau 264b 48.05 N 16.23 E
Achavanich 46 58.22 N 3.24 W
Achelouma, Enneri V 146 21.55 N 13.35 E
Achêne 56 50.16 N 5.03 E
Acheng 89 45.32 N 126.59 E
Achenkirch 64 47.31 N 11.42 E
Achénouma 146 19.08 N 12.55 E
Achen Pass )( 64 47.35 N 11.38 E
Achensee ⊜ 64 47.28 N 11.42 E
Achères 261 48.58 N 2.04 E
Achern 56 48.37 N 8.04 E
Acheron ≃, Austl. 169 37.14 S 145.42 E
Acheron ≃, N.Z. 172 42.24 S 172.58 E
Acheux-en-Amiénois 50 50.04 N 2.32 E
Achhābal 123 33.41 N 75.14 E
Achhnera 124 27.11 N 77.46 E
Achí, Col. 246 8.34 N 74.33 W
Achi, Nihon 94 35.27 N 137.45 E
Achiasi 150 5.52 N 1.00 W
Achicourt 50 50.16 N 2.46 E
Achigan, Lac de l' ⊜ 206 45.56 N 73.58 W
Achiguate ≃ 236 13.55 N 90.55 W
Achill 28 53.56 N 9.54 W
Achilles 208 37.17 N 76.27 W
Achill Head > 48 53.59 N 10.13 W
Achill Island I 48 54.00 N 10.00 W
Achill Sound 48 53.55 N 9.58 W
Achim 52 53.00 N 9.02 E
Achīn 120 34.08 N 70.42 E
Achıras 252 33.10 S 65.00 W
Achir-Ula, gora ∧ 88 50.21 N 94.31 E
Achmeta 84 42.02 N 45.13 E
Achnasaul 46 56.58 N 4.59 W
Achnasheen 46 57.35 N 5.06 W
Achol 140 6.34 N 31.31 E
Achosnich 46 56.45 N 6.06 W
Achterwasser c 54 54.00 N 13.57 E
Achterwehr 41 54.19 N 9.57 E
Achthuizen 52 51.42 N 4.16 E
Achtuba 80 51.37 N 44.22 E
Achtuba ≃ 80 46.42 N 48.00 E
Achtubinsk 80 48.17 N 46.10 E
Achty 84 41.28 N 47.43 E
Achtyrskij 78 44.52 N 38.20 E
Achuapa 236 13.03 N 86.35 W
Achur'an (Arpaçay) ≃ 84 40.06 N 43.39 E
Achwa ≃ 154 3.43 N 31.55 E
Ači 85 41.17 N 73.02 E
Aci Castello 70 37.33 N 15.08 E
Aci Catena 70 37.36 N 15.08 E
Acıgöl 130 38.35 N 34.31 E
Acı Göl ⊜ 130 37.50 N 29.54 E
Acikak 88 54.11 N 106.18 E
Ačikulak 84 44.34 N 44.50 E
Acilia ⊸[8] 267a 41.47 N 12.22 E
Ačimovy Vtoryje 86 60.04 N 75.12 E
Ačinsk 86 56.17 N 90.30 E
Acıpayam 130 37.25 N 29.22 E
Acireale 70 37.37 N 15.10 E
Ačisaj 85 43.35 N 68.53 E
Aci Sant'Antonio 70 37.36 N 15.07 E
Ačisu 84 42.38 N 47.40 E
Ačit 86 56.48 N 57.54 E
Ačit nuur ⊜ 86 49.30 N 90.30 E
Ackerly 196 32.32 N 101.43 W
Ackerman 194 33.18 N 89.10 W
Ackermanville 210 40.49 N 75.17 W
Ackerson Lake 216 42.11 N 84.20 W
Ackley 190 42.33 N 93.03 W
Acklins I 238 22.26 N 73.58 W
Acklins, Bight of c[3] 238 22.30 N 74.15 W
Acland, Mount ∧ 166 24.55 S 148.05 E
Acle 42 52.38 N 1.33 E
Aclimação ⊸[8] 287b 23.34 S 46.37 W
Acme, Ab., Can. 182 51.30 N 113.30 W
Acme, Pa., U.S. 214 40.08 N 79.26 W
Acme, Wa., U.S. 224 48.43 N 122.12 W
Acmetonia 279b 40.32 N 79.49 W
Acobamba 248 12.48 S 74.34 W
Acolla 248 11.44 S 75.34 W
Acoma Indian Reservation ⊸[4] 200 34.52 N 107.40 W
Acomayo, Perú 248 13.55 S 71.41 W
Acomayo, Perú 248 9.46 S 76.05 W
Aconcagua, Cerro ∧ 252 32.39 S 70.01 W
Aconchi 232 29.50 N 110.12 W
Aconibe 152 1.18 N 10.56 E
Acopiara 250 6.06 S 39.27 W
Açores (Azores) II 148a 38.30 N 28.00 W
Acoria 248 12.37 S 74.53 W
Acorizal 248 15.12 S 56.22 W
Acornhoek 156 24.37 S 31.02 E
A Coruña 34 43.22 N 8.23 W
Acosta 214 40.07 N 79.04 W
Acoyapa 236 11.58 N 85.10 W
Acoyapa ≃ 236 11.48 N 85.16 W
Acquabona, Passo di )( 68 39.02 N 16.20 E
Acquacalda 70 38.31 N 14.57 E
Acqualagna 66 43.37 N 12.40 E
Acquanegra sul Chiese 64 45.10 N 10.26 E
Acquapendente 66 42.44 N 11.52 E
Acquappesa 68 39.29 N 15.57 E
Acquarossa 58 46.28 N 8.57 E
Acquasanta Terme 66 42.46 N 13.24 E
Acquasparta 66 42.41 N 12.33 E
Acquaviva 66 43.57 N 12.25 E
Acquaviva delle Fonti 68 40.54 N 16.50 E
Acquaviva Platani 70 37.34 N 13.42 E
Acqui Terme 62 44.41 N 8.28 E
Acra 210 42.19 N 74.03 W
Acraman, Lake ⊜ 162 32.02 S 135.26 E
Acre → 'Akko 132 32.55 N 35.05 E
Acre □[3] 248 9.00 S 70.00 W
Acre ≃ 248 8.45 S 67.22 W
Acre Homes 222 29.53 N 95.27 W
Acri 68 39.29 N 16.23 E
Acropolis ⊥ 267c 37.58 N 23.43 E
Acrotambo, Cerro ∧ 248 8.50 S 76.50 W
Acton, On., Can. 212 43.37 N 80.02 W
Acton, Ca., U.S. 228 34.28 N 118.11 W
Acton, Ma., U.S. 207 42.29 N 71.26 W
Acton, Tx., U.S. 222 32.27 N 97.41 W
Acton ⊸[8] 260 51.30 N 0.16 W
Acton Bridge 262 53.16 N 2.36 W
Acton Homes 158 28.36 S 29.26 E
Acton Lake ⊜ 218 39.34 N 84.45 W
Acton Turville 42 51.32 N 2.17 W
Acton-Vale 206 45.39 N 72.34 W
Actopan 234 20.16 N 98.56 W
Actopan ≃ 234 19.25 N 96.20 W
Açu 250 5.34 S 36.54 W
Açuã ≃ 248 7.12 S 64.11 W
Açucena 255 19.04 S 42.32 W
Acuitzio del Canje 234 19.29 N 101.20 W
Ačujevo 78 45.43 N 37.45 E
Acuña 252 29.55 S 57.58 W
Acurauá ≃ 248 7.37 S 70.48 W
Acurenam 152 1.02 N 10.40 E
Acushnet 207 41.41 N 70.55 W
Acuto 66 41.47 N 13.10 E
Acvež 80 58.21 N 47.46 E
Acworth 192 34.03 N 84.40 W
Ada, Ghana 150 5.47 N 0.24 E
Ada, Jugo. 38 45.48 N 20.08 E
Ada, Nihon 174m 26.44 N 128.19 E
Ada, Mi., U.S. 216 42.57 N 85.29 W
Ada, Mn., U.S. 198 47.18 N 96.31 W
Ada, Oh., U.S. 216 40.46 N 83.49 W
Ada, Ok., U.S. 196 34.46 N 96.40 W
Ada, Mount ∧ 180 56.41 N 134.41 W
Adaba 144 7.00 N 39.24 E
A-da-Beja 266c 38.47 N 9.14 W
'Adabīyah, Ra's > 142 29.52 N 32.30 E
Adachi ⊸[8] 268 35.45 N 139.48 E
Adachi-yama ∧ 96 33.51 N 130.55 E
Adado, Ras > 144 11.20 N 48.40 E
Adâfer el Abiod ⊸[1] 150 19.30 N 10.00 W
Adai 272c 19.01 N 73.08 E
Adalo 144 14.29 N 40.52 E
Adainville 261 48.43 N 1.39 E
Adair, Ia., U.S. 198 41.22 N 94.19 W
Adair, Ok., U.S. 196 36.26 N 95.16 W
Adair □[6] 219 40.08 N 92.22 W
Adair, Bahía de c 200 31.30 N 113.48 W
Adair, Cape > 176 71.24 N 71.13 W
Adairsville 192 34.22 N 84.56 W
Adairville 194 36.40 N 86.51 W
Adaja ≃ 34 41.32 N 4.52 W
Adajevka 86 51.47 N 62.06 E
Adak, Ross. 24 66.30 N 59.38 E
Adak, Ak., U.S. 180 51.54 N 176.35 W
Adaka-shima I 174m 26.45 N 128.20 E
Adak Island I 180 51.45 N 176.40 W
Adaklı 130 39.14 N 40.30 E
Ådalen V 26 63.10 N 17.16 E
Ādam 118 22.24 N 57.32 E
Adam, Mount ∧ 254 51.36 S 59.55 W
Adamantina 255 21.42 S 51.04 W
Adamaoua ⋏ 152 7.00 N 12.00 E
Adamawa → Adamaoua ⋏ 152 7.00 N 12.00 E
Adamclisi 38 44.05 N 27.57 E
Adamello ⋏ 64 46.10 N 10.35 E
Adaminaby 171b 36.03 S 148.43 E
Adami Tulu 144 7.52 N 38.42 E
Adamovka 86 51.32 N 59.56 E
Adamovskoje 82 54.52 N 35.57 E
Adamów 30 51.45 N 22.17 E
Ādampur 123 31.26 N 75.43 E
Adams, In., U.S. 218 39.22 N 85.33 W
Adams, Ma., U.S. 207 42.37 N 73.07 W
Adams, Mn., U.S. 190 43.33 N 92.43 W
Adams, Ne., U.S. 198 40.27 N 96.30 W
Adams, N.Y., U.S. 212 43.48 N 76.01 W
Adams, N.D., U.S. 198 48.25 N 98.04 W
Adams, Tn., U.S. 194 36.34 N 87.03 W
Adams, Wi., U.S. 190 43.57 N 89.49 W
Adams □[6], Il., U.S. 219 39.56 N 91.23 W
Adams □[6], In., U.S. 216 40.50 N 84.56 W
Adams □[6], Oh., U.S. 218 38.48 N 83.32 W
Adams □[6], Pa., U.S. 208 39.48 N 77.15 W
Adams ≃ 182 50.52 N 119.35 W
Adams, Mount ∧, N.Z. 172 41.19 S 175.46 E
Adams, Mount ∧, Wa., U.S. 224 46.12 N 121.28 W
Adams Bridge ✦[2] 122 9.04 N 79.37 E
Adamsburg 279b 40.19 N 79.40 W
Adams Center 212 43.51 N 76.00 W
Adams Creek ≃ 224 46.18 N 121.40 W
Adams Lake ⊜ 182 51.13 N 119.33 W
Adams Mills 214 40.09 N 81.57 W
Adams National Historic Site ⊥ 283 42.15 N 71.01 W
Adams Park 216 42.08 N 85.29 W
Adams Park ♦ 275b 43.48 N 79.09 W
Adams Peak ∧ 122 6.48 N 80.30 E
Adams Rock I[2] 174e 25.04 S 130.05 W
Adamston 208 40.02 N 74.05 W
Adamstown, Austl. 170 32.56 S 151.44 E
Adamstown, Pit. 174e 25.04 S 130.05 W
Adamstown, Md., U.S. 208 39.18 N 77.28 W
Adamstown, Pa., U.S. 208 40.14 N 76.03 W
Adamsville, P.Q., Can. 206 45.17 N 72.47 W
Adamsville, Mi., U.S. 216 41.47 N 86.00 W
Adamsville, Oh., U.S. 214 40.04 N 81.53 W
Adamsville, Pa., U.S. 214 41.31 N 80.22 W
Adamsville, Tn., U.S. 194 35.14 N 88.23 W
'Adan (Aden) 144 12.45 N 45.12 E
Adana 130 37.01 N 35.18 E
Adana □[4] 130 37.20 N 35.45 E
Adanero 34 40.56 N 4.36 W
Adarama 140 17.05 N 34.54 E
Adare 48 52.34 N 8.48 W
Adare, Cape > 9 71.17 S 170.14 E
Adar Gwagwa, Jabal ∧ 140 22.15 N 35.20 E
Adarot 140 17.50 N 36.07 E
Adaševo 80 53.56 N 44.19 E
Adauli 272c 19.06 N 73.02 E
Adaut 164 8.08 S 131.07 E
Adavale 166 25.55 S 144.36 E
Adda ≃, It. 36 45.08 N 9.53 E
Adda ≃, Sūd. 140 9.51 N 24.50 E
Ad-Dab'ah 140 31.02 N 28.26 E
Ad-Dabbah 140 18.03 N 30.57 E
Ad-Dafīnah 128 23.18 N 41.58 E
Aḍ-Ḍafrah ⊸[1] 128 23.25 N 53.25 E
Ad-Dahnā' ⊸[2] 128 24.30 N 48.10 E
Ad-Daljamūn 142 30.48 N 30.50 E
Ad-Damazin 140 11.49 N 34.23 E
Ad-Dāmir 140 17.35 N 33.58 E
Ad-Dammām 128 26.26 N 50.07 E
Ad-Dāmūr 132 33.44 N 35.27 E
Ad-Dānā 130 36.13 N 36.46 E
Ad-Daqahlīyah □[4] 142 31.10 N 31.30 E
Ad-Darb 144 17.43 N 42.15 E
Ad-Dawādimī 128 24.28 N 44.18 E
Ad-Dawḥah (Doha) 128 25.17 N 51.32 E
Ad-Dayr, Miṣr 140 25.20 N 32.35 E
Ad-Dayr, Miṣr 142 30.20 N 31.16 E
Adderbury 42 52.00 N 1.17 W
Ad-Dibdibah ⊸[1] 128 28.00 N 46.30 E
Addicks 222 29.47 N 95.39 W
Addicks Reservoir ⊜[1] 222 29.49 N 95.40 W
Addieville 219 38.23 N 89.29 W
Aḍ-Ḍiffah (Libyan Plateau) ⋏[1] 140 30.30 N 25.30 E
Ad-Dilam 128 23.59 N 47.12 E
Ad-Dilinjāt 142 30.50 N 30.30 E
Ad-Dīmās 132 33.35 N 36.05 E
Addingham 44 53.57 N 1.53 W
Addington 260 51.18 N 0.23 E
Addis 194 30.21 N 91.15 W
Addis Ababa → Adis Abeba 144 9.02 N 38.42 E
Addison, Il., U.S. 216 41.55 N 87.59 W
Addison, Mi., U.S. 216 41.59 N 84.21 W
Addison, N.Y., U.S. 210 42.06 N 77.14 W
Addison, Tx., U.S. 222 32.57 N 96.49 W
Addison Creek ≃ 278 41.51 N 87.51 W
Ad-Dīwānīyah 128 31.59 N 44.56 E
Addlestone 260 51.22 N 0.30 W
Addo 158 33.32 S 25.45 E
Addo Elephant National Park ♦ 158 33.29 S 25.46 E
Ad-Du'ayn 140 11.26 N 26.09 E
Aḍ-Ḍuhayr 132 31.11 N 34.08 E
Ad-Duqqī 273c 30.04 N 31.15 E
Ad-Duwayd 128 30.15 N 42.17 E
Ad-Duwaym 140 14.00 N 32.19 E
Ad-Duwayr 132 33.23 N 35.25 E
Adébour 146 13.20 N 11.54 E
Adego 144 8.58 N 49.35 E
Adel, Ga., U.S. 192 31.08 N 83.25 W
Adel, Ia., U.S. 190 41.36 N 94.01 W
Adelaida → Adelaide 168b 34.55 S 138.35 E
Adelaide, Austl. 166 34.55 S 138.35 E
Adelaide, Austl. 168b 34.55 S 138.35 E
Adelaide, Ba. 240b 25.00 N 77.31 W
Adelaide, S. Afr. 158 32.42 S 26.20 E
Adelaide Airport ⊠ 168b 34.58 S 138.32 E
Adelaide Island I 9 67.15 S 68.30 W
Adelaide Peninsula >[1] 176 68.09 N 97.45 W
Adelaide River 164 13.15 S 131.06 E
Adelanto 228 34.34 N 117.24 W
Adelbert Range ⋏ 164 4.35 S 145.10 E
Adelboden 58 46.30 N 7.33 E
Adelebsen 52 51.34 N 9.45 E
Adèle Island I 160 15.32 S 123.09 E
Adelfia 68 41.00 N 16.52 E
Adélie Coast ⊥[2] 9 67.00 S 139.00 E
Adelong 171b 35.19 S 148.03 E
Adelong Creek ≃ 171b 35.06 S 148.02 E
Adelphi 284c 39.00 N 76.58 W
Adelphia 208 40.13 N 74.15 W
Adelphi University ʊ[2] 276 40.43 N 73.36 W
Adelschlag 60 48.50 N 11.13 E
Adelsheim 56 49.24 N 9.23 E
Adelsö I 40 59.23 N 17.30 E
Adelzhausen 60 48.21 N 11.08 E
Aden → 'Adan 144 12.45 N 45.12 E
Aden, Gulf of c 136 12.30 N 48.00 E
Adena 214 40.13 N 80.52 W
Adenau 56 50.23 N 6.55 E
Adendorf 52 53.17 N 10.26 E
Adendorp 158 32.20 S 24.33 E
Ader ⋏[1] 150 14.50 N 5.15 E
Aderklaa 264b 48.17 N 16.32 E
Adéta 150 7.08 N 0.44 E
Adhāta 272b 22.52 N 88.32 E
'Ādhirīyāt, Jibāl al- ⋏[2] 132 30.25 N 36.48 E
Adi 154 3.24 N 30.48 E
Adi, Pulau I 164 4.18 S 133.26 E
Adiaké 150 5.16 N 3.17 W
Adi Arkay 144 13.27 N 37.57 E
Adi Dairo 144 14.23 N 38.12 E
Adieu, Cape > 162 31.59 S 132.09 E
Adigala 144 10.25 N 42.14 E
Adige (Etsch) ≃ 64 45.10 N 12.20 E
Adigeni 84 41.42 N 42.42 E
Adigrat 144 14.17 N 39.28 E
Adıgüzel Barajı ⊜[1] 130 38.10 N 29.15 E
Adi Keyih 144 14.51 N 39.22 E
Adi Kwala 144 14.38 N 38.50 E
Ādilābād 122 19.40 N 78.32 E
Adilang 154 2.44 N 33.29 E
Adilcevaz 84 38.44 N 42.44 E
Adimi 89 47.20 N 138.56 E
Adin 204 41.11 N 120.56 W
Adinkerke 50 51.04 N 2.36 E
Adirondack Mountains ⋏ 188 44.00 N 74.00 W
Adirondack Park ♦ 188 44.00 N 74.20 W
Adis Abeba (Addis Ababa) 144 9.02 N 38.42 E
Adis Zemen 144 12.07 N 37.47 E
Adi Ugri 144 14.53 N 38.49 E
Adiwerna 115a 6.56 S 109.07 E
Adıyaman 130 37.46 N 38.17 E
Adıyaman □[4] 130 37.45 N 38.30 E
Adjan 112 2.11 N 113.12 E
Adjelman, Oued V 148 22.09 N 3.47 E
Adjohon 150 6.42 N 2.28 E
Adjud 38 46.04 N 27.11 E
Adjumani 154 3.22 N 31.47 E
Adjuntas 240m 18.10 N 66.43 W
Adler 78 43.27 N 39.55 E
Adler Planetarium ʊ 278 41.52 N 87.37 W
Adlershof ⊸[8] 264a 52.26 N 13.33 E
Adlington 44 53.37 N 2.36 W
Adlington Hall ⊥ 262 53.19 N 2.09 W
Adliswil 58 47.19 N 8.32 E
Admer, Erg d' ⊸[2] 148 24.00 N 9.15 E
Admiral 184 49.43 N 108.01 W
Admiralitäts-Inseln → Admiralty Islands II 164 2.10 S 147.00 E
Admiralty Bay c, St. Vin. 241h 13.00 N 61.16 W
Admiralty Bay c, Ak., U.S. 180 70.53 N 155.45 W
Admiralty Gulf c 160 14.20 S 125.50 E
Admiralty Gulf Aboriginal Reserve ⊸[4] 164 14.40 S 125.30 E
Admiralty Inlet c, N.T., Can. 176 73.00 N 86.00 W
Admiralty Inlet c, Wa., U.S. 224 48.05 N 122.39 W
Admiralty Island I, N.T., Can. 176 69.30 N 101.00 W
Admiralty Island I, Ak., U.S. 180 57.50 N 134.30 W
Admiralty Islands II 164 2.10 S 147.00 E
Admiralty Mountains ⋏ 9 71.45 S 168.30 E
Admont 61 47.34 N 14.27 E
Adna 224 46.38 N 123.04 W
Ado ≃ 94 35.19 N 136.05 E
Adobe Creek ≃, Ca., U.S. 282 37.26 N 122.06 W
Adobe Creek ≃, Co., U.S. 198 38.05 N 103.18 W
Ado-Ekiti 150 7.38 N 5.12 E
Adogawa 94 35.20 N 136.02 E
Adok 140 8.11 N 30.19 E
Adolfo López Mateos 232 28.28 N 107.20 W
Adolfo López Mateos, Presa ⊜[1] 232 25.13 N 107.25 W
Adolfsberg 40 59.15 N 15.10 E
Adolphus Reach ⊔ 212 44.05 N 76.55 W
Adonara, Pulau I 112 8.20 S 123.10 E
Ādoni 122 15.38 N 77.17 E
Ado-Odo 150 6.36 N 2.56 E
Adorf 54 50.19 N 12.15 E
Adoua, Korén V 150 14.37 N 6.40 E
Adour ≃ 32 43.32 N 1.32 W
Adowa → Adwa 144 14.10 N 38.55 E
Adra, Esp. 34 36.44 N 3.01 W
Ādra, India 126 23.30 N 86.40 E
'Adrā, Sūrīy. 132 33.37 N 36.30 E
Adranga 154 2.54 N 30.26 E
Adrano 70 37.40 N 14.50 E
Adrar 148 27.54 N 0.17 W
Adrar □[4] 150 20.05 N 11.00 W
Adrâr ⊸[1] 134 20.30 N 13.30 W
Adraskan 128 33.39 N 62.16 E
Adrasman 85 40.38 N 69.58 E
Adré 146 13.28 N 22.12 E
Adrī 146 27.32 N 13.14 E
Adria 64 45.03 N 12.03 E
Adrian, Ga., U.S. 192 32.31 N 82.35 W
Adrian, Mi., U.S. 216 41.53 N 84.02 W
Adrian, Mn., U.S. 198 43.38 N 95.55 W
Adrian, Mo., U.S. 194 38.23 N 94.21 W
Adrian, Oh., U.S. 214 41.03 N 83.20 W
Adrian, Or., U.S. 202 43.44 N 117.04 W
Adrian, Pa., U.S. 214 40.53 N 79.32 W
Adrian, Tx., U.S. 196 35.16 N 102.40 W
Adrian, W.V., U.S. 188 38.54 N 80.16 W
Adrianople → Edirne 130 41.40 N 26.34 E
Adrianópolis 287a 22.39 S 43.30 W
Adrianovka 88 51.34 N 114.30 E
Adriatico, Mar → Adriatic Sea ⊤[2] 22 42.30 N 16.00 E
Adriatic Sea ⊤[2] 22 42.30 N 16.00 E
Adriatique, Mer → Adriatic Sea ⊤[2] 22 42.30 N 16.00 E
Adriatisches Meer → Adriatic Sea ⊤[2] 22 42.30 N 16.00 E
Adrigole 48 51.40 N 9.42 W
Adro 64 45.37 N 9.57 E
Adrogué → Almirante Brown 258 34.48 S 58.23 W
Adstock, Mont ∧ 206 46.02 N 71.12 W
Adua 164 1.55 S 129.50 E
Aduard 52 53.15 N 6.26 E
Adujevo 82 54.59 N 35.59 E
Aduku 154 2.01 N 32.43 E
A Dun ≃ 110 13.24 N 108.28 E
Adur ≃ 42 50.49 N 0.16 W
Adusa 154 1.23 N 28.01 E
Adutiškis 76 55.09 N 26.36 E
Advance 194 37.06 N 89.54 W
Adventure, Bahía ⊔ 254 44.50 S 74.45 W
Advie 46 57.23 N 3.27 W
Advocate Harbour 186 45.20 N 64.47 W
Adwa 144 14.10 N 38.55 E
Adwick le Street 44 53.34 N 1.11 W
Adyča ≃ 74 68.13 N 134.41 E
Adyge 84 44.19 N 41.57 E
Adygea → Adygeja □[3] 72 45.00 N 40.00 E
Adygeja □[3] 72 45.00 N 40.00 E
Adyk 80 45.48 N 45.38 E
Adžarskaja Respublika □[3] 84 41.40 N 42.00 E
Adž Bogd uul ⋏ 102 44.52 N 95.10 E
Adžima 89 48.08 N 139.40 E
Adzopé 150 6.06 N 3.52 W
Adz'va ≃ 24 66.36 N 59.28 E
Adz'vavom 24 66.36 N 59.12 E
Ae, Water of ≃ 44 55.08 N 3.27 W
Æbelø I 41 55.38 N 10.12 E
Aegean Sea ⊤[2] 38 38.30 N 25.00 E
Aegerisee ⊜ 58 47.07 N 8.38 E
Aegina → Aíyina I 38 37.46 N 23.26 E
Aegviidu 76 59.17 N 25.37 E
Aek Humbang 114 1.59 N 99.11 E
Aeknabara 114 1.17 N 99.45 E
Aeon Point > 174o 1.46 N 157.11 W
Aerhuola 89 51.01 N 120.10 E
Aerku Hu ⊜ 120 30.43 N 82.55 E
Ærø I 41 54.53 N 10.20 E
Aeroflots'kyy 78 45.03 N 34.01 E
Aeron ≃ 42 52.14 N 4.16 W
Aeronáutica, Centro de Instrucción de ʊ[2] 286d 12.09 S 77.00 W
Ærøskøbing 41 54.53 N 10.25 E
Aerqi Shan ∧ 89 48.35 N 121.07 E
Aershatu 102 44.11 N 113.36 E
Aerzen 52 52.03 N 9.16 E
Aesch 58 47.28 N 7.36 E
Aeschi 58 46.40 N 7.42 E
A Estrada 34 42.41 N 8.29 W
Aetna 182 49.08 N 113.15 W
Afaahiti 174s 17.43 S 149.19 W
Afadé 146 12.14 N 14.38 E
Afadjoto ∧[2] 150 7.05 N 0.35 E
'Afak 128 32.04 N 45.15 E
Afan ≃ 42 51.35 N 3.48 W
Afanasjevka 78 50.47 N 38.36 E
Afanasjevo, Ross. 24 58.52 N 53.12 E
Afanasjevo, Ross. 82 54.20 N 37.01 E
Afanasjevo, Ross. 82 55.18 N 36.12 E
Afanasjevskoje 86 56.49 N 58.17 E
Afándou 38 36.17 N 28.10 E
Afar 148 25.30 N 8.22 E
Afareaitu 174s 17.33 S 149.47 W
Afars and Issas → Djibouti □[1] 144 11.30 N 43.00 E
Afaspida 272c 19.08 N 73.04 E
Afdem 144 9.28 N 41.00 E
Afferde, Dtsch. 52 52.06 N 9.25 E
Afferde, Dtsch. 263 51.34 N 7.39 E
Afféry 150 6.19 N 3.57 W
Affi 64 45.33 N 10.46 E
Affing 58 48.27 N 10.58 E
Afflisses, Oued V 148 28.29 N 1.09 E
Affoltern am Albis 58 47.17 N 8.27 E
Affori ⊸[8] 266b 45.31 N 9.10 E
Affric ≃ 46 57.19 N 4.50 W
Affric, Glen V 46 57.17 N 4.56 W
Affton 219 38.33 N 90.19 W
Afghānestān → Afghanistan □[1] 118 33.00 N 65.00 E
Afghanistan (Afghānestān) □[1] 118 33.00 N 65.00 E
Afgooye 144 2.09 N 45.07 E
Afia 114 1.23 N 97.32 E
'Afīf 128 23.55 N 42.56 E
Afikpo 150 5.53 N 7.56 E
Afipskij 78 44.55 N 38.50 E
Afiqim 132 32.40 N 35.35 E
Åfjord 26 63.58 N 10.12 E
Aflao 150 6.05 N 1.08 E
Aflenz Kurort 61 47.32 N 15.14 E
Aflou 148 34.07 N 2.06 E
Afmadow 144 0.31 N 42.04 E
Afodo 144 10.14 N 34.39 E
Afogados da Ingazeira 250 7.45 S 37.39 W
Afognak Island I 180 58.15 N 152.30 W
Afollé ⋏[2] 150 16.55 N 10.25 W
Afonicha 24 68.13 N 53.17 E
Afono Bay c 174u 14.15 S 170.39 W
A Fonsagrada 34 43.08 N 7.04 W
Afonso Arinos 256 22.00 S 43.20 W
Afonso Bezerra 250 5.30 S 36.30 W
Afonso Claudio 255 20.05 S 41.08 W
Afonsos, Campo dos ■ 287a 22.53 S 43.23 W
Afragola 68 40.55 N 14.18 E
Afram ≃ 150 7.00 N 0.52 W
Africa ⊥[1] 4 10.00 N 22.00 E
Africa ⊥[1] 10 10.00 N 22.00 E
Africa del Sur → South Africa □[1] 156 30.00 S 26.00 E
Africo 68 38.04 N 15.59 E
Afrika → Africa ⊥[1] 10 10.00 N 22.00 E
Afrikanda 24 67.25 N 32.43 E
'Afrīn 130 36.31 N 36.52 E
'Afrīn ≃ 130 36.22 N 36.28 E
Afrique → Africa ⊥[1] 10 10.00 N 22.00 E
Afrique du Sud (République d') → South Africa □[1] 156 30.00 S 26.00 E
Afritz 64 46.43 N 13.48 E
Afşin 130 38.15 N 36.55 E
Afsluitdijk ⊸[5] 52 53.00 N 5.15 E
Afton, De., U.S. 285 39.49 N 75.29 W
Afton, Ia., U.S. 194 41.01 N 94.11 W
Afton, N.Y., U.S. 210 42.13 N 75.31 W
Afton, Ok., U.S. 196 36.41 N 94.57 W
Afton, Wi., U.S. 216 42.36 N 89.04 W
Afton, Wy., U.S. 200 42.43 N 110.55 W
Aftout ⊸[1] 148 26.40 N 3.48 W
Afuá 250 0.10 S 50.23 W
'Afula 132 32.36 N 35.17 E
'Afula 'Illit 132 32.38 N 35.20 E
Afulu 114 1.17 N 97.15 E
Afyon 130 38.45 N 30.33 E
Afyon □[4] 130 38.40 N 30.30 E


**Symbols** in the index entries represent the broad categories identified in the key at the right. Symbols with superior numbers (⋏[1]) identify subcategories (see complete key on page *I · 1)*.

**Symbole** im Register stellen die rechts im Schlüssel erklärten Kategorien dar. Symbole mit hochgestellten Ziffern (⋏[1]) bezeichnen Unterabteilungen einer Kategorie (vgl. vollständiger Schlüssel auf Seite *I · 1)*.

**Los símbolos** incluídos en el texto del índice representan las grandes categorías identificadas con la clave a la derecha. Los símbolos con numeros en su parte superior (⋏[1]) identifican las subcategorías (véase la clave completa en la página *I · 1)*.

**Les symboles** de l'index représentent les catégories indiquées dans la légende à droite. Les symboles suivis d'un indice (⋏[1]) représentent des sous-catégories (voir légende complète à la page *I · 1)*.

**Os símbolos** incluídos no texto do índice representam as grandes categorias identificadas com a chave à direita. Os símbolos com números em sua parte superior (⋏[1]) identificam as subcategorias (veja-se a chave completa à página *I · 1)*.

| English | Deutsch | Español | Français | Português |
|---|---|---|---|---|
| ∧ Mountain | Berg | Montaña | Montagne | Montanha |
| ⋏ Mountains | Gebirge | Montañas | Montagnes | Montanhas |
| )( Pass | Paß | Paso | Col | Passo |
| V Valley, Canyon | Tal, Cañon | Valle, Cañón | Vallée, Canyon | Vale, Canhão |
| ≃ Plain | Ebene | Llano | Plaine | Planície |
| > Cape | Kap | Cabo | Cap | Cabo |
| I Island | Insel | Isla | Île | Ilha |
| II Islands | Inseln | Islas | Îles | Ilhas |
| ⊥ Other Topographic Features | Andere Topographische Objekte | Otros Elementos Topográficos | Autres données topographiques | Outros acidentes topográficos |

ESPAÑOL — Nombre | Página | Lat.°' | Long.°' W = Oeste
FRANÇAIS — Nom | Page | Lat.°' | Long.°' W = Ouest
PORTUGUÊS — Nome | Página | Lat.°' | Long.°' W = Oeste


| Nombre / Nom / Nome | Página / Page | Lat.°' | Long.°' W = Oeste |
|---|---|---|---|
| Afyonkarahisar → Afyon | 130 | 38.45 N | 30.33 E |
| Afzalgarh | 124 | 29.24 N | 78.41 E |
| Aga, Nor. | 26 | 60.18 N | 6.36 E |
| Aga, Ross. | 88 | 51.12 N | 115.10 E |
| Aga ≃ | 88 | 51.30 N | 115.50 E |
| Agačag | 85 | 44.03 N | 71.58 E |
| Ağaçören | 130 | 38.52 N | 33.56 E |
| Agadez | 150 | 16.58 N | 7.59 E |
| Agadez □[5] | 146 | 19.45 N | 12.00 E |
| Agadez, Ighazer oua-n- V | 150 | 17.28 N | 6.26 E |
| Agadir | 148 | 30.26 N | 9.36 W |
| Agadir □[4] | 148 | 30.40 N | 8.55 W |
| Agâdîr, Râs › | 148 | 20.34 N | 16.32 W |
| Agadyr' | 86 | 48.17 N | 72.53 E |
| Agafonovka | 80 | 50.36 N | 47.26 E |
| Agāhpur | 272a | 28.34 N | 77.22 E |
| Agaie | 150 | 9.03 N | 6.18 E |
| Ägäisches Meer → Aegean Sea ⊤[2] | 38 | 38.30 N | 25.00 E |
| Agalak | 140 | 11.01 N | 32.42 E |
| Agalega Islands II | 138 | 10.24 S | 56.37 E |
| Agal Terara ∧ | 144 | 6.57 N | 40.08 E |
| Agan ≃ | 72 | 61.23 N | 74.35 E |
| Agana | 174p | 13.28 N | 144.45 E |
| Agana Heights | 174p | 13.28 N | 144.45 E |
| Agano ≃ | 92 | 37.57 N | 139.08 E |
| Agapa | 74 | 71.27 N | 89.15 E |
| Aga Point › | 174p | 13.15 N | 144.43 E |
| Agapovka | 86 | 53.18 N | 59.28 E |
| Agar | 120 | 23.42 N | 76.01 E |
| Agara | 84 | 42.03 N | 43.49 E |
| Agâraktem ⊤[4] | 148 | 23.11 N | 6.20 W |
| Ågård | 41 | 55.35 N | 9.26 E |
| Agaro | 144 | 7.50 N | 36.40 E |
| Agartala | 120 | 23.49 N | 91.16 E |
| Agartu | 80 | 49.49 N | 47.06 E |
| Agaru | 140 | 10.59 N | 34.44 E |
| Agaruut | 102 | 43.10 N | 109.26 E |
| Agasan | 272c | 19.11 N | 73.04 E |
| Agassiz | 224 | 49.14 N | 121.46 W |
| Agassiz, Cape › | 9 | 68.29 S | 62.56 W |
| Agassiz Pool ⊖ | 198 | 48.20 N | 95.58 W |
| Agat | 174p | 13.24 N | 144.39 E |
| Agat Bay c | 174p | 13.24 N | 144.39 E |
| Agate | 198 | 39.27 N | 103.56 W |
| Agate Beach | 202 | 44.40 N | 124.03 W |
| Agate Fossil Beds National Monument ♦ | 198 | 42.25 N | 103.43 W |
| Agathonísion I | 38 | 37.28 N | 27.00 E |
| Agats | 164 | 5.33 S | 138.08 E |
| Agatsuma | 94 | 36.34 N | 138.50 E |
| Agatsuma ≃ | 94 | 36.30 N | 139.01 E |
| Agatti Island I | 122 | 10.50 N | 72.12 E |
| Agattu Island I | 181a | 52.25 N | 173.35 E |
| Agattu Strait ʯ | 181a | 52.35 N | 173.25 E |
| Agawa | 96 | 33.34 N | 133.10 E |
| Agawa ≃ | 190 | 47.21 N | 84.38 W |
| Agawa Bay c | 190 | 47.20 N | 84.42 W |
| Agawa Canyon V | 190 | 47.27 N | 84.29 W |
| Agawam, Ma., U.S. | 207 | 42.04 N | 72.36 W |
| Agawam, Mt., U.S. | 182 | 48.00 N | 112.10 W |
| Agay | 62 | 43.26 N | 6.51 E |
| Agazzano | 62 | 44.57 N | 9.31 E |
| Agbaja | 150 | 7.58 N | 6.38 E |
| Agbede | 273a | 6.40 N | 3.29 E |
| Agbélouvé | 150 | 6.40 N | 1.10 E |
| Agboju | 273a | 6.28 N | 3.17 E |
| Agboville | 150 | 5.56 N | 4.13 W |
| Agboyi Creek ≃ | 273a | 6.34 N | 3.25 E |
| Ağcabädi | 84 | 40.03 N | 47.28 E |
| Agcawayan | 116 | 13.46 N | 120.16 E |
| Ağdam | 84 | 39.59 N | 46.57 E |
| Ağdärä | 84 | 40.12 N | 46.48 E |
| Ağdaş | 84 | 40.38 N | 47.28 E |
| Agde | 32 | 43.19 N | 3.28 E |
| Agde, Cap d' › | 32 | 43.16 N | 3.30 E |
| Agege | 273a | 6.37 N | 3.20 E |
| Agejevo | 82 | 54.10 N | 36.29 E |
| Agematsu | 94 | 35.47 N | 137.42 E |
| Agen | 32 | 44.12 N | 0.37 E |
| Agency | 190 | 40.59 N | 92.18 W |
| Agency Lake ⊖ | 202 | 42.32 N | 121.58 W |
| Ageo | 94 | 35.58 N | 139.36 E |
| Agepsta, gora ∧ | 84 | 43.32 N | 40.30 E |
| Ager ≃ | 60 | 48.05 N | 13.51 E |
| Agerbæk | 41 | 55.36 N | 8.48 E |
| Agerskov | 41 | 55.07 N | 9.08 E |
| Agersø I | 41 | 55.12 N | 11.12 E |
| Agery | 168b | 34.10 S | 137.44 E |
| Ágfalva | 61 | 47.41 N | 16.31 E |
| Aggeneis | 158 | 29.03 S | 18.51 E |
| Agger ≃ | 56 | 50.48 N | 7.11 E |
| Aggherar | 144 | 4.03 N | 42.40 E |
| Aggius | 71 | 40.56 N | 9.04 E |
| Aggstein ⊥ | 61 | 48.18 N | 15.25 E |
| Aggteleki Nemzeti Park ♦ | 30 | 48.30 N | 20.32 E |
| Āghā Jārī | 128 | 30.42 N | 49.50 E |
| Aghleam | 48 | 54.08 N | 10.07 W |
| Aghzoumal, Sabkhat ⊖ | 148 | 24.21 N | 12.52 W |
| Agia | 124 | 26.05 N | 90.32 E |
| Agidingbi | 273a | 6.38 N | 3.21 E |
| Agimont | 56 | 50.10 N | 4.48 E |
| Ağın | 130 | 38.57 N | 38.43 E |
| Agincourt ◆[8] | 275b | 43.48 N | 79.17 W |
| Aginskoje, Ross. | 86 | 55.15 N | 94.55 E |
| Aginskoje, Ross. | 88 | 51.06 N | 114.32 E |
| Agira | 70 | 37.39 N | 14.31 E |
| Aglasterhausen | 56 | 49.21 N | 8.59 E |
| Ağlasun | 130 | 37.40 N | 30.32 E |
| Agliana | 66 | 43.54 N | 11.00 E |
| Agliano | 62 | 44.47 N | 8.15 E |
| Aglientu | 71 | 41.05 N | 9.07 E |
| Agly ≃ | 32 | 42.47 N | 3.02 E |
| Agna | 64 | 45.10 N | 11.58 E |
| Agnadello | 62 | 45.26 N | 9.33 E |
| Agnes, Mount ∧ | 162 | 26.51 S | 128.59 E |
| Agnes Lake ⊖ | 190 | 48.13 N | 91.21 W |
| Agnew | 162 | 28.01 S | 120.30 E |
| Agnew Lake ⊖[1] | 190 | 46.22 N | 81.45 W |
| Agnews Hill ∧[2] | 48 | 54.51 N | 5.56 W |
| Agnibilékrou | 150 | 7.08 N | 3.12 W |
| Agnije-Afanasjevskij | 89 | 51.57 N | 138.45 E |
| Agnita | 38 | 45.59 N | 24.38 E |
| Agno, Pil. | 116 | 16.07 N | 119.48 E |
| Agno, Schw. | 58 | 46.00 N | 8.54 E |
| Agno ≃, It. | 64 | 45.31 N | 11.22 E |
| Agno ≃, Pil. | 116 | 16.02 N | 120.08 E |
| Agnone | 66 | 41.48 N | 14.22 E |
| Agnone Bagni ◆[8] | 70 | 37.18 N | 15.06 E |
| Ago | 92 | 34.20 N | 136.51 E |
| Agogna ≃ | 62 | 45.04 N | 8.54 E |
| Agogo, Ghana | 150 | 6.47 N | 1.04 W |
| Agogo, Sūd. | 140 | 7.49 N | 28.52 E |
| Agoo | 116 | 16.20 N | 120.22 E |
| Agordat → Akordat | 144 | 15.33 N | 37.53 E |
| Agordo | 64 | 46.17 N | 12.02 E |
| Agostinho Pôrto | 287a | 22.47 S | 43.23 W |
| Agostitlán | 234 | 19.33 N | 100.41 W |
| Agou, Mont ∧ | 150 | 6.52 N | 0.46 E |
| Agouna | 150 | 7.34 N | 1.42 E |
| Agoura Hills | 228 | 34.08 N | 118.44 W |
| Agout ≃ | 32 | 43.47 N | 1.41 E |
| Agoza ⊥ | 146 | 18.30 N | 23.45 E |
| Āgra | 124 | 27.11 N | 78.01 E |
| Āgra Canal ≍ | 272a | 28.34 N | 77.18 E |
| Agrachanskij poluostrov ›[1] | 84 | 43.42 N | 47.36 E |
| Agraciada | 258 | 33.48 S | 58.15 W |
| Agrado | 246 | 2.15 N | 75.46 W |
| Agraf'novka | 83 | 47.45 N | 39.29 E |
| Agram → Zagreb | 36 | 45.48 N | 15.58 E |
| Agramonte | 240p | 22.41 N | 81.07 W |
| Agrate Brianza | 62 | 45.34 N | 9.21 E |
| Agreda | 34 | 41.51 N | 1.56 W |
| Ağrı | 84 | 39.44 N | 43.03 E |
| Ağrı □[4] | 84 | 39.30 N | 43.15 E |
| Agri ≃ | 68 | 40.13 N | 16.44 E |
| Agri Bavnehøj ∧[2] | 41 | 56.14 N | 10.33 E |
| Ağrı Dağı (Mount Ararat) ∧ | 84 | 39.42 N | 44.18 E |
| Agrigento | 70 | 37.18 N | 13.35 E |
| Agrigento □[4] | 70 | 37.27 N | 13.30 E |
| Agrihan I | 108 | 18.46 N | 145.40 E |
| Agrínion | 38 | 38.37 N | 21.24 E |
| Agrio ≃ | 252 | 38.21 S | 69.43 W |
| Agropoli | 68 | 40.21 N | 15.00 E |
| Agro Pontino ◆[1] | 66 | 41.25 N | 12.55 E |
| Agryz | 80 | 56.33 N | 53.00 E |
| Ağstafa | 84 | 41.08 N | 45.28 E |
| Ağsu | 84 | 40.34 N | 48.24 E |
| Agtuuganon, Mount ∧ | 116 | 7.48 N | 126.12 E |
| Agua, Ilha d' I | 287a | 22.49 S | 43.10 W |
| Agua, Volcán de ∧[1] | 236 | 14.28 N | 90.45 W |
| Água Branca, Bra. | 250 | 9.17 S | 37.55 W |
| Água Branca, Bra. | 250 | 7.31 S | 37.40 W |
| Água Branca, Bra. | 250 | 5.53 S | 42.38 W |
| Agua Brava, Laguna c | 234 | 22.10 N | 105.32 W |
| Agua Caliente, Méx. | 232 | 27.27 N | 108.32 W |
| Agua Caliente, Méx. | 234 | 23.20 N | 105.20 W |
| Agua Caliente Creek ≃ | 282 | 37.29 N | 121.56 W |
| Agua Caliente Grande | 232 | 26.31 N | 108.22 W |
| Aguacate | 240p | 22.59 N | 81.49 W |
| Aguachica | 246 | 8.19 N | 73.38 W |
| Água Clara | 255 | 20.27 S | 52.52 W |
| Aguada | 240m | 18.23 N | 67.11 W |
| Aguada, Zanjón de la ≃ | 286e | 33.30 S | 70.47 W |
| Aguada Cecilio | 254 | 40.51 S | 65.51 W |
| Aguada de Guerra | 254 | 41.04 S | 68.25 W |
| Aguada de Pasajeros | 240p | 22.23 N | 80.51 W |
| Aguadas | 246 | 5.37 N | 75.27 W |
| Aguadilla | 240m | 18.26 N | 67.09 W |
| Água Doce | 252 | 27.00 S | 51.33 W |
| Agua Dulce, Méx. | 234 | 18.08 N | 94.08 W |
| Aguadulce, Pan. | 236 | 8.15 N | 80.33 W |
| Agua Dulce, Ca., U.S. | 228 | 34.30 N | 118.23 W |
| Agua Dulce, Tx., U.S. | 196 | 27.47 N | 97.54 W |
| Agua Fria ≃ | 200 | 33.23 N | 112.21 W |
| Agua Fria Creek ≃ | 282 | 37.28 N | 121.56 W |
| Aguaí | 256 | 22.04 S | 46.58 W |
| Agualeguas | 232 | 26.18 N | 99.34 W |
| Água Limpa | 255 | 18.06 S | 48.46 W |
| Agualva-Cacém | 266c | 38.46 N | 9.18 W |
| Aguán ≃ | 236 | 15.57 N | 85.44 W |
| Aguanaval ≃ | 232 | 25.28 N | 102.53 W |
| Agua Negra | 286c | 10.28 N | 67.01 W |
| Aguanish | 186 | 50.13 N | 62.05 W |
| Aguanus ≃ | 186 | 50.13 N | 62.05 W |
| Aguapeí ≃, Bra. | 248 | 15.53 S | 58.25 W |
| Aguapeí ≃, Bra. | 255 | 21.03 S | 51.47 W |
| Aguapey ≃ | 252 | 29.07 S | 56.36 W |
| Água Preta, Igarapé ≃ | 246 | 1.41 S | 63.48 W |
| Agua Prieta | 232 | 31.18 N | 109.34 W |
| Aguaragüe, Serranía de ⋀ | 248 | 21.30 S | 63.40 W |
| Aguaray | 252 | 22.16 S | 63.44 W |
| Aguaray-Guazú ≃, Para. | 252 | 24.47 S | 57.19 W |
| Aguaray-Guazú ≃, Para. | 252 | 24.05 S | 56.40 W |
| A Guardia | 34 | 41.54 N | 8.53 W |
| Aguarico ≃ | 246 | 0.59 S | 75.11 W |
| Aguaro-Guariquito, Parque Nacional ♦ | 246 | 8.10 N | 66.50 W |
| Aguaruto | 232 | 24.47 N | 107.29 W |
| Aguas ≃ | 34 | 37.09 N | 1.49 W |
| Águas, Serra das ∧ | 256 | 21.55 S | 45.25 W |
| Aguasabon ≃ | 190 | 48.46 N | 87.07 W |
| Águas Belas | 250 | 9.07 S | 37.07 W |
| Aguas Buenas | 240m | 18.15 N | 66.06 W |
| Aguascalientes, Méx. | 200 | 32.18 N | 115.10 W |
| Aguascalientes, Méx. | 234 | 21.53 N | 102.18 W |
| Aguascalientes □[3] | 234 | 22.00 N | 102.30 W |
| Aguascalientes, Río de ≃ | 234 | 21.23 N | 102.28 W |
| Aguas Corrientes | 258 | 34.31 S | 56.24 W |
| Águas da Prata | 256 | 21.56 S | 46.43 W |
| Águas de Contendas | 256 | 21.54 S | 45.01 W |
| Águas de Lindóia | 256 | 22.29 S | 46.39 W |
| Águas Formosas | 255 | 17.05 S | 40.57 W |
| Aguasvivas ≃ | 34 | 41.20 N | 0.25 W |
| Agua Tibia ∧ | 228 | 33.24 N | 116.59 W |
| Água Vermelha, Represa de ⊖[1] | 255 | 20.00 S | 50.00 W |
| Agua-Viva | 256 | 21.41 S | 42.33 W |
| Aguayo | 252 | 31.40 S | 65.54 W |
| Aguaytía ≃ | 248 | 8.08 S | 74.37 W |
| Agua Zarca | 200 | 31.10 N | 110.59 W |
| Agu Bay c | 176 | 70.18 N | 86.30 W |
| A Gudiña | 34 | 42.04 N | 7.08 W |
| Agudos | 255 | 22.28 S | 49.00 W |
| Águeda | 34 | 40.34 N | 8.27 W |
| Águeda ≃ | 34 | 41.02 N | 6.56 W |
| Aguelhok | 150 | 19.28 N | 0.52 E |
| Aguema | 152 | 12.03 S | 21.49 E |
| Aguenier, Lac ⊖ | 186 | 50.43 N | 68.13 W |
| Agugliano | 66 | 43.32 N | 13.23 E |
| Agui | 94 | 34.55 N | 136.55 E |
| Aguié | 150 | 13.30 N | 7.47 E |
| Aguijan I | 108 | 14.51 N | 145.34 E |
| Aguila | 200 | 33.56 N | 113.10 W |
| Aguilar, Esp. | 34 | 37.31 N | 4.39 W |
| Aguilar, Co., U.S. | 198 | 37.24 N | 104.39 W |
| Aguilares, Arg. | 252 | 27.26 S | 65.37 W |
| Aguilares, El Sal. | 236 | 13.58 N | 89.12 W |
| Águilas | 34 | 37.24 N | 1.35 W |
| Aguililla | 234 | 18.44 N | 102.44 W |
| Aguirre ≃ | 246 | 8.28 N | 61.02 W |
| Aguirre, Arroyo ≃ | 288 | 34.46 S | 58.35 W |
| Aguirre, Bahía c | 254 | 54.57 S | 65.50 W |
| Aguit | 102 | 41.52 N | 112.56 E |
| Aguita Zarc | 234 | 23.10 N | 104.28 W |
| Aguja, Cerro ∧ | 254 | 42.11 S | 71.51 W |
| Aguja, Punta › | 248 | 5.48 S | 81.06 W |
| Aguja Point › | 116 | 12.42 N | 123.23 E |
| Agujas, Cabo de las → Agulhas, Cape › | 158 | 34.52 S | 20.00 E |
| Agujereada, Punta › | 240m | 18.31 N | 67.08 W |
| Agujita | 196 | 27.53 N | 101.09 W |
| Agul ≃ | 88 | 55.44 N | 95.41 E |
| Agulai | 144 | 13.41 N | 39.35 E |
| Agulhas | 158 | 34.50 S | 20.00 E |
| Agulhas, Cape › | 158 | 34.52 S | 20.00 E |
| Agulhas Basin ✣[1] | 8 | 47.00 S | 27.00 E |
| Agulhas Negras | 256 | 22.28 S | 44.27 W |
| Agulhas Negras, Pico das ∧ | 256 | 22.23 S | 44.38 W |
| Agulhas Plateau ✣[3] | 10 | 40.00 S | 26.00 E |
| Agung, Gunung ∧ | 115b | 8.21 S | 115.30 E |
| Aguni-jima I | 93b | 26.35 N | 127.14 E |
| Agusan ≃ | 116 | 9.00 N | 125.31 E |
| Agusan del Norte □[4] | 116 | 9.00 N | 125.30 E |
| Agusan del Sur □[4] | 116 | 8.30 N | 125.40 E |
| Agustín Codazzi | 246 | 10.02 N | 73.14 W |
| Agutaya | 116 | 11.09 N | 120.56 E |
| Agutaya Island I | 116 | 11.09 N | 120.58 E |
| Ağva | 130 | 41.09 N | 29.50 E |
| Agvali | 84 | 42.33 N | 46.06 E |
| Agwarra | 150 | 10.42 N | 4.35 E |
| Ägypten → Egypt □[1] | 140 | 27.00 N | 30.00 E |
| Aha | 174m | 26.43 N | 128.17 E |
| Ahaggar (Hoggar) ⋀ | 148 | 23.00 N | 6.30 E |
| Ahaggar, Tassili ta-n- ⋀[1] | 148 | 21.00 N | 6.00 E |
| Aha Hills ⋀[2] | 156 | 19.45 S | 21.10 E |
| Aha-kō c | 174m | 26.43 N | 128.18 E |
| Aham | 60 | 48.32 N | 12.28 E |
| Ahar | 128 | 38.28 N | 47.04 E |
| Ahar ≃ | 128 | 38.32 N | 47.31 E |
| Ahascragh | 48 | 53.24 N | 8.20 W |
| Ahaura | 172 | 42.21 S | 171.32 E |
| Ahaura ≃ | 172 | 42.21 S | 171.31 E |
| Ahaus | 52 | 52.04 N | 7.00 E |
| Aheggar ∧ | 148 | 24.43 N | 5.39 E |
| Ahfir | 148 | 34.57 N | 2.17 W |
| Ahimanawa Range ⋀ | 172 | 39.00 S | 176.27 E |
| Ahipara | 172 | 35.10 S | 173.10 E |
| Ahipara Bay c | 172 | 35.10 S | 173.07 E |
| 'Āhirah | 132 | 32.53 N | 36.28 E |
| Ahırlı | 130 | 37.14 N | 32.08 E |
| Ahklun Mountains ⋀ | 180 | 59.15 N | 161.00 W |
| Ahlat, Tür. | 128 | 38.45 N | 42.29 E |
| Ahlat, Tür. | 130 | 38.45 N | 42.29 E |
| Ahlbeck, Dtsch. | 54 | 53.40 N | 14.11 E |
| Ahlbeck, Dtsch. | 54 | 53.56 N | 14.11 E |
| Ahlem | 52 | 52.23 N | 9.40 E |
| Ahlen | 52 | 51.46 N | 7.53 E |
| Ahlenberg | 263 | 51.25 N | 7.28 E |
| Ahlenmoor ◆[3] | 52 | 53.40 N | 8.45 E |
| Ahlerstedt | 52 | 53.24 N | 9.27 E |
| Ahlhorn | 52 | 52.54 N | 8.14 E |
| Ahlsdorf | 54 | 51.32 N | 11.28 E |
| Ahmadābād | 120 | 23.02 N | 72.37 E |
| Ahmadābād-e Sarjām | 128 | 35.51 N | 59.36 E |
| Ahmad al-Bāqir, Jabal ∧ | 132 | 29.36 N | 35.08 E |
| Ahmadgarh | 123 | 30.41 N | 75.50 E |
| Ahmadnagar | 122 | 19.05 N | 74.44 E |
| Ahmadpur, India | 124 | 23.31 N | 77.13 E |
| Ahmadpur, India | 126 | 23.50 N | 87.42 E |
| Ahmadpur East | 123 | 29.09 N | 71.16 E |
| Ahmadpur Siāl | 123 | 30.41 N | 71.46 E |
| Ahmad Wāl | 120 | 29.25 N | 65.56 E |
| Ahmar, Al-Bahr al- → Red Sea ⊤[2] | 136 | 20.00 N | 38.00 E |
| Ahmar, 'Erg el ◆[2] | 148 | 23.30 N | 4.54 W |
| Ahmar, Jabal al- ∧ | 132 | 29.40 N | 35.09 E |
| Ahmar Mountains ⋀ | 144 | 9.15 N | 41.00 E |
| Ahmedabad → Ahmadābād | 120 | 23.02 N | 72.37 E |
| Ahmetli | 130 | 38.31 N | 27.57 E |
| Ahmic Lake ⊖ | 190 | 45.37 N | 79.42 W |
| Ahnatal | 56 | 51.22 N | 9.24 E |
| Ahnet ⋀ | 148 | 24.58 N | 2.57 E |
| Ahnet, Tanezrouft n- ◆[2] | 148 | 22.15 N | 1.30 E |
| Ahoada | 150 | 5.05 N | 6.38 E |
| Ahoghill | 48 | 54.51 N | 6.22 W |
| Ahome | 232 | 25.55 N | 109.11 W |
| Ahon, Tarso ∧ | 146 | 20.23 N | 18.18 E |
| Ahornspitz ∧ | 64 | 47.08 N | 11.56 E |
| Ahoskie | 192 | 36.17 N | 76.59 W |
| Ahousat | 182 | 49.17 N | 126.04 W |
| Ahr ≃ | 56 | 50.33 N | 7.17 E |
| Ahram | 128 | 28.52 N | 51.16 E |
| Ahrāmāt Dahshūr (North and Bent Pyramids) ⊥ | 142 | 29.48 N | 31.13 E |
| Ahrāmāt Maydūm (Maydūm Pyramid) ⊥ | 142 | 29.23 N | 31.10 E |
| Ahraura | 124 | 25.01 N | 83.01 E |
| Ahrensbök | 54 | 54.00 N | 10.34 E |
| Ahrensburg | 52 | 53.40 N | 10.14 E |
| Ahrensdorf, Dtsch. | 54 | 52.10 N | 14.05 E |
| Ahrensdorf, Dtsch. | 264a | 52.19 N | 13.12 E |
| Ahrensfelde | 264a | 52.35 N | 13.35 E |
| Ahrgebirge ⋀ | 56 | 50.30 N | 6.50 E |
| Ahtanum | 224 | 46.34 N | 120.37 W |
| Ahtanum Creek ≃ | 202 | 46.32 N | 120.31 W |
| Ahtanum Ridge ∧ | 224 | 46.30 N | 120.50 W |
| Ähtäri | 26 | 62.34 N | 24.06 E |
| Ähtärinjärvi ⊖ | 26 | 62.40 N | 24.03 E |
| Ähtävänjoki ≃ | 26 | 63.38 N | 22.48 E |
| Ahtopol | 38 | 42.06 N | 27.57 E |
| Ahu | 98 | 34.27 N | 118.39 E |
| Ahuacatlán, Méx. | 234 | 21.03 N | 104.29 W |
| Ahuacatlán, Méx. | 234 | 20.00 N | 97.52 W |
| Ahuachapán | 236 | 13.55 N | 89.51 W |
| Ahuacuotzingo | 234 | 17.42 N | 98.56 W |
| Ahualulco de Mercado | 234 | 20.42 N | 103.59 W |
| Ahuijullo | 234 | 19.05 N | 103.05 W |
| Ahuijullo ≃ | 234 | 18.49 N | 103.37 W |
| Ahumada, Méx. | 204 | 32.30 N | 115.30 W |
| Ahumada, Méx. | 232 | 30.37 N | 106.31 W |
| Ahun | 32 | 46.05 N | 2.05 E |
| Ahuntsic ◆[8] | 275a | 45.33 N | 73.39 W |
| Ahunui I[1] | 14 | 19.39 S | 140.25 W |
| Ahuriri ≃ | 172 | 44.33 S | 170.11 E |
| Åhus | 26 | 55.55 N | 14.17 E |
| Ahuzhen | 98 | 34.27 N | 118.39 E |
| Ahvāz | 128 | 31.19 N | 48.42 E |
| Ahvenanmaa □[4] | 26 | 60.15 N | 20.00 E |
| Ahwahnee | 226 | 37.21 N | 119.43 W |
| Ahwar | 144 | 13.31 N | 46.42 E |
| Ahwa-ri | 98 | 35.54 N | 129.02 E |
| Ai ≃ | 98 | 40.13 N | 124.30 E |
| Aialik Cape › | 180 | 59.42 N | 149.31 W |
| Aiándion | 267c | 37.55 N | 23.28 E |
| Aiapuá | 246 | 4.29 S | 62.04 W |
| Aiapuá, Lago ⊖ | 246 | 4.27 S | 62.08 W |
| Aibag ≃ | 102 | 42.40 N | 110.42 E |
| Aibonito | 240m | 18.08 N | 66.16 W |
| Aich | 64 | 47.25 N | 13.49 E |
| Aichach | 60 | 48.28 N | 11.08 E |
| Aicha vorm Wald | 60 | 48.41 N | 13.18 E |
| Aichhalden | 58 | 48.16 N | 8.24 E |
| Aichi □[5] | 94 | 35.00 N | 137.15 E |
| Aichi-kōgen-kokutei-kōen ♦ | 94 | 35.10 N | 137.25 E |
| Aichi-yōsui ≍ | 94 | 34.42 N | 136.57 E |
| Aichstetten | 58 | 47.54 N | 10.04 E |
| Aichtal | 56 | 48.38 N | 9.16 E |
| Aidenbach | 60 | 48.34 N | 13.06 E |
| Aidomaggiore | 71 | 40.10 N | 8.51 E |
| Aidone | 70 | 37.25 N | 14.27 E |
| Aidong | 102 | 24.46 N | 107.21 E |
| Aiduma, Pulau I | 164 | 3.58 S | 134.06 E |
| Aiea | 229c | 21.22 N | 157.56 W |
| Aiello Calabro | 68 | 39.07 N | 16.10 E |
| Aigáleo Óros ∧[2] | 267c | 38.00 N | 23.37 E |
| Aigburth ◆[8] | 262 | 53.22 N | 2.55 W |
| Aigen im Mühlkreis | 60 | 48.39 N | 13.58 E |
| Aigenmiao | 89 | 43.36 N | 120.50 E |
| Aigle | 58 | 46.19 N | 6.58 E |
| Aigle, Île à l' I | 275a | 45.42 N | 73.28 W |
| Aigle, Lac à l' ⊖ | 186 | 51.12 N | 65.25 W |
| Aignay-le-Duc | 58 | 47.40 N | 4.44 E |
| Aigre | 32 | 45.54 N | 0.01 E |
| Aiguá | 252 | 34.12 S | 54.45 W |
| Aiguebelette, Lac d' ⊖ | 62 | 45.33 N | 5.48 E |
| Aiguebelette-le-Lac | 62 | 45.32 N | 5.49 E |
| Aiguebelle | 62 | 45.32 N | 6.18 E |
| Aiguebelle, Réserve ♦ | 190 | 48.33 N | 78.45 W |
| Aigueperse | 32 | 46.01 N | 3.12 E |
| Aigues ≃ | 62 | 44.07 N | 4.43 E |
| Aigues-Mortes | 62 | 43.34 N | 4.11 E |
| Aigues-Mortes, Golfe d' c | 62 | 43.31 N | 4.03 E |
| Aigüestortes, Parc National d' ♦ | 34 | 42.30 N | 1.01 E |
| Aigues-Vives | 62 | 43.44 N | 4.10 E |
| Aiguilles | 62 | 44.47 N | 6.52 E |
| Aiguines | 62 | 43.46 N | 6.15 E |
| Aigurande | 32 | 46.26 N | 1.50 E |
| Aihui (Heihe) | 89 | 50.16 N | 127.28 E |
| Aija | 248 | 9.46 S | 77.38 W |
| Aikawa, Nihon | 92 | 38.02 N | 138.15 E |
| Aikawa, Nihon | 94 | 35.32 N | 139.17 E |
| Aiken | 192 | 33.33 N | 81.43 W |
| Aikens Lake ⊖ | 184 | 51.12 N | 95.20 W |
| Ailao Shan ⋀ | 102 | 24.08 N | 101.25 E |
| Ailefroide | 62 | 44.53 N | 6.27 E |
| Aileron | 162 | 22.39 S | 133.20 E |
| Ailette ≃ | 50 | 49.35 N | 3.10 E |
| Aileu | 112 | 8.43 S | 125.34 E |
| Ailimutou Shan ∧ | 104 | 42.19 N | 121.25 E |
| Ailingen | 58 | 47.41 N | 9.29 E |
| Ailinglapalap I[1] | 14 | 7.23 N | 168.46 E |
| Ailinzhuang | 105 | 39.27 N | 117.36 E |
| Aillant-sur-Tholon | 50 | 47.52 N | 3.21 E |
| Aille ≃ | 62 | 43.26 N | 6.30 E |
| Ailly-le-Haut-Clocher | 50 | 50.05 N | 2.00 E |
| Ailly-sur-Noye | 50 | 49.45 N | 2.22 E |
| Ailly-sur-Somme | 50 | 49.55 N | 2.12 E |
| Ailo | 164 | 4.50 S | 151.40 E |
| Ailsa Craig | 190 | 43.08 N | 81.33 W |
| Ailsa Craig I | 44 | 55.16 N | 5.07 W |
| Ailuk I[1] | 14 | 10.20 N | 169.56 E |
| Aim | 74 | 58.50 N | 134.12 E |
| Aimargues | 62 | 43.41 N | 4.12 E |
| Aime | 62 | 45.33 N | 6.39 E |
| Aimere | 115b | 8.50 S | 120.52 E |
| Aimi | 96 | 35.22 N | 133.22 E |
| Aimogasta | 252 | 28.33 S | 66.49 W |
| Aimorés | 255 | 19.30 S | 41.04 W |
| Aimoto | 270 | 34.59 N | 135.10 E |
| Ain □[5] | 32 | 46.10 N | 5.20 E |
| Ain ≃ | 58 | 45.48 N | 5.10 E |
| Aïn Arnat | 34 | 36.11 N | 5.19 E |
| Aïn Azel | 34 | 35.49 N | 5.31 E |
| Ainaži | 76 | 57.52 N | 24.21 E |
| 'Aïn Belbela, Sebkha ≚ | 148 | 27.30 N | 5.20 W |
| Aïn Benian | 148 | 36.48 N | 2.55 E |
| Aïn Ben Tili | 148 | 26.00 N | 9.32 W |
| Aïn Berda | 36 | 36.39 N | 7.35 E |
| Aïn Bessem | 34 | 36.18 N | 3.40 E |
| Aincourt | 261 | 49.04 N | 1.47 E |
| Aïn Defla | 34 | 36.16 N | 1.58 E |
| Aïn Deheb | 148 | 34.51 N | 1.33 E |
| Aïn Draham | 148 | 36.47 N | 8.42 E |
| Aine ≃ | 56 | 50.23 N | 5.31 E |
| Aïn el Beïda | 148 | 35.48 N | 7.24 E |
| Aïn el Hadjel | 34 | 35.40 N | 3.53 E |
| Aïn el Kebira | 34 | 36.22 N | 5.30 E |
| Aïn Milia | 148 | 36.02 N | 6.34 E |
| Aino | 270 | 34.57 N | 135.10 E |
| Aino-shima I, Nihon | 96 | 33.59 N | 130.50 E |
| Aino-shima I, Nihon | 96 | 33.45 N | 130.23 E |
| Aïn Oulmène | 34 | 35.55 N | 5.18 E |
| Ainring | 64 | 47.48 N | 12.56 E |
| Ainsdale | 44 | 53.36 N | 3.02 W |
| Aïn Sefra | 148 | 32.45 N | 0.35 W |
| Ain Shams University ʊ[2] | 273c | 30.03 N | 31.17 E |
| Ainslie, Mount ∧ | 171b | 35.16 S | 149.10 E |
| Ainslie Lake ⊖ | 186 | 46.08 N | 61.12 W |
| Ainsworth, Eng., U.K. | 262 | 53.35 N | 2.22 W |
| Ainsworth, Ne., U.S. | 198 | 42.33 N | 99.51 W |
| Aïn Taghrout | 34 | 36.08 N | 5.05 E |
| Aïn Tedelès | 148 | 36.00 N | 0.18 E |
| Aïn Témouchent | 148 | 35.18 N | 1.08 W |
| Aïn Touta | 148 | 35.23 N | 5.54 E |
| Aintree | 262 | 53.29 N | 2.56 W |
| Aintree Race Course ♦ | 262 | 53.28 N | 2.56 W |
| Aïn Wessara | 148 | 35.27 N | 2.54 E |
| Aïn Yagout | 148 | 35.47 N | 6.25 E |
| Aio | 96 | 34.00 N | 131.26 E |
| Aioi | 96 | 34.48 N | 134.28 E |
| Aiome | 164 | 5.10 S | 144.45 E |
| Aiora | 34 | 39.04 N | 1.03 W |
| Aipe | 246 | 3.13 N | 75.15 W |
| Aiquara | 255 | 14.07 S | 39.52 W |
| Aiquile | 248 | 18.10 S | 65.10 W |
| Aïr ⋀ | 150 | 18.00 N | 8.30 E |
| Airabu, Pulau I | 112 | 2.46 N | 106.14 E |
| Airai Airport ⊠ | 175b | 7.22 N | 134.33 E |
| Airaines | 50 | 49.58 N | 1.57 E |
| Airão | 246 | 1.56 S | 61.22 W |
| Airasca | 62 | 44.55 N | 7.29 E |
| Airbangis | 110 | 0.12 N | 99.23 E |
| Airdikit | 112 | 2.40 S | 101.15 E |
| Airdrie, Ab., Can. | 182 | 51.18 N | 114.02 W |
| Airdrie, Scot., U.K. | 46 | 55.52 N | 3.59 W |
| Aire ≃, Fr. | 56 | 49.19 N | 4.49 E |
| Aire ≃, Eng., U.K. | 44 | 53.44 N | 0.54 W |
| Aire-sur-l'Adour | 32 | 43.42 N | 0.16 W |
| Aire-sur-la-Lys | 50 | 50.38 N | 2.24 E |
| Air Force Island I | 176 | 67.55 N | 74.10 W |
| Airgegas | 112 | 2.42 S | 106.25 E |
| Airgin Sum | 102 | 42.58 N | 111.08 E |
| Airhaji | 112 | 1.57 S | 100.53 E |
| Airjamban | 114 | 1.13 N | 101.14 E |
| Airlie | 166 | 20.16 S | 148.43 E |
| Airmolek | 112 | 0.22 S | 102.17 E |
| Airmont | 276 | 41.06 N | 74.06 W |
| Airola | 68 | 41.04 N | 14.33 E |
| Airole | 62 | 43.52 N | 7.33 E |
| Airolo | 58 | 46.32 N | 8.37 E |
| Airor | 46 | 57.04 N | 5.46 W |
| Airport West | 274b | 37.44 S | 144.53 E |
| Airtenang | 112 | 3.08 S | 101.43 E |
| Airterjun | 114 | 1.20 N | 100.27 E |
| Airuno | 62 | 45.45 N | 9.25 E |
| Airvault | 32 | 46.50 N | 0.08 W |
| Aisch ≃ | 56 | 49.46 N | 11.01 E |
| Aisega | 164 | 5.44 S | 148.21 E |
| Aisén del General Carlos Ibáñez del Campo □[4] | 254 | 46.30 S | 73.30 W |
| Aisey-sur-Seine | 58 | 47.45 N | 4.35 E |
| Aishihik | 180 | 61.35 N | 137.30 W |
| Aishihik Lake ⊖ | 180 | 61.25 N | 137.06 W |
| Ai-shima I | 96 | 34.30 N | 131.17 E |
| Aisinaike | 85 | 39.47 N | 75.47 E |
| Aislingen | 56 | 48.30 N | 10.27 E |
| Aisne □[5] | 50 | 49.30 N | 3.30 E |
| Aisne ≃ | 32 | 49.26 N | 2.50 E |
| Aisne à la Marne, Canal de l' ≍ | 50 | 49.24 N | 3.55 E |
| Aïssa, Djebel ∧ | 148 | 32.51 N | 0.30 W |
| Aïssey | 58 | 47.16 N | 6.20 E |
| Aist ≃ | 61 | 48.14 N | 14.35 E |
| Aisy-sur-Armançon | 50 | 47.39 N | 4.13 E |
| Aitana, Serra d' ∧ | 34 | 38.44 N | 0.16 W |
| Aitape | 164 | 3.08 S | 142.21 E |
| Aiterach ≃ | 60 | 48.54 N | 12.38 E |
| Aiterhofen | 60 | 48.51 N | 12.37 E |
| Aith | 46a | 60.16 N | 1.23 W |
| Aitkin | 190 | 46.31 N | 93.42 W |
| Aït-Melloul | 148 | 30.21 N | 9.31 W |
| Aitolikón | 38 | 38.27 N | 21.22 E |
| Aït-Ourir | 148 | 31.38 N | 7.42 W |
| Aitrach | 58 | 47.56 N | 10.05 E |
| Aitutaki I[1] | 14 | 18.52 S | 159.45 W |
| Ait Youssef ou Ali | 34 | 35.13 N | 3.55 W |
| Aiuaba | 250 | 6.38 S | 40.07 W |
| Aiud | 38 | 46.19 N | 23.44 E |
| Aiún → El Aaiún | 148 | 27.09 N | 13.12 W |
| Aiuruoca | 256 | 21.58 S | 44.36 W |
| Aiuruoca ≃, Bra. | 256 | 21.42 S | 44.22 W |
| Aiuruoca ≃, Bra. | 256 | 21.32 S | 44.26 W |
| Aiva | 287a | 22.42 S | 43.28 W |
| Aiviekste ≃ | 76 | 56.37 N | 25.45 E |
| Aix, Mount ∧ | 224 | 46.47 N | 121.15 W |
| Aix-en-Othe | 50 | 48.13 N | 3.44 E |
| Aix-en-Provence | 62 | 43.32 N | 5.26 E |
| Aix-la-Chapelle → Aachen | 56 | 50.47 N | 6.05 E |
| Aix-les-Bains | 62 | 45.42 N | 5.55 E |
| Aiyáleo | 267c | 37.59 N | 23.41 E |
| Aiyang, Mount ∧ | 164 | 5.05 S | 141.19 E |
| Aiyansh | 182 | 55.17 N | 129.03 W |
| Aíyina | 38 | 37.44 N | 23.27 E |
| Aíyina I | 38 | 37.46 N | 23.26 E |
| Aiyínion | 38 | 40.30 N | 22.33 E |
| Aíyion | 38 | 38.15 N | 22.05 E |
| Āīzawl | 120 | 23.44 N | 92.43 E |
| Aizhaipuzi | 104 | 40.57 N | 124.01 E |
| Aizkraukle | 76 | 56.38 N | 25.13 E |
| Aizpute | 76 | 56.43 N | 21.38 E |
| Aizu-bange | 92 | 37.34 N | 139.49 E |
| Aizu-wakamatsu | 92 | 37.30 N | 139.56 E |
| Aj ≃ | 86 | 56.08 N | 57.40 E |
| Ajā | 142 | 30.57 N | 31.17 E |
| Ajā', Jabal ⋀ | 128 | 27.20 N | 41.45 E |
| 'Ajab Shīr | 128 | 37.28 N | 45.54 E |
| Ajaccio | 36 | 41.55 N | 8.44 E |
| Ajaguz | 86 | 47.56 N | 80.23 E |
| Ajaguz ≃ | 86 | 46.42 N | 79.15 E |
| Ajajú ≃ | 246 | 0.59 N | 72.20 W |
| Ajalpan | 234 | 18.22 N | 97.15 W |
| 'Ajaltūn | 132 | 33.58 N | 35.41 E |
| Ajalvir | 266a | 40.32 N | 3.29 W |
| 'Ajamī | 130 | 36.28 N | 37.42 E |
| Ajan, Ross. | 74 | 56.27 N | 138.10 E |
| Ajan, Ross. | 88 | 54.43 N | 110.55 E |
| Ajan ≃ | 74 | 70.10 N | 95.50 E |
| Ajana | 162 | 27.57 S | 114.38 E |
| Ajanta | 122 | 20.32 N | 75.45 E |
| Ajanta Range ⋀ | 122 | 20.30 N | 76.00 E |
| Ajaokuta | 150 | 7.28 N | 6.39 E |
| Ajarani ≃ | 246 | 1.33 N | 61.16 W |
| Ajasse | 150 | 8.17 N | 4.48 E |
| Ajasso | 150 | 5.52 N | 8.52 E |
| Ajat ≃ | 86 | 52.54 N | 63.02 E |
| Ajax | 212 | 43.51 N | 79.02 W |
| Ajay ≃ | 126 | 23.39 N | 88.08 E |
| Ajbas | 80 | 47.51 N | 49.37 E |
| Ajdābiyā | 146 | 30.48 N | 20.14 E |
| Ajdabul' | 86 | 52.42 N | 68.59 E |
| Ajdar | 78 | 50.03 N | 38.56 E |
| Ajdarkul', ozero ⊖[1] | 72 | 40.45 N | 67.20 E |
| Ajdarly | 86 | 44.32 N | 65.50 E |
| Ajdovščina | 36 | 45.53 N | 13.53 E |
| Ajdyrlinskij | 86 | 52.03 N | 59.50 E |
| Ajegunle | 273a | 6.36 N | 3.17 E |
| Ajgurka ≃ | 80 | 45.46 N | 43.12 E |
| Ajgyrkol', ozero ⊖ | 80 | 48.15 N | 52.50 E |
| Ajhūr al-Kubrā | 142 | 30.18 N | 31.09 E |
| Aji | 96 | 34.23 N | 134.08 E |
| Ajibar | 144 | 10.52 N | 38.40 E |
| Ajibarang | 115a | 7.25 S | 109.04 E |
| Ajigasawa | 92 | 40.47 N | 140.12 E |
| 'Ajīj, Wādī al- V | 130 | 35.19 N | 41.09 E |
| Ajijic | 234 | 20.18 N | 103.17 W |
| Ajil | 114 | 5.05 N | 103.05 E |
| Ājimganj | 126 | 24.14 N | 88.15 E |
| Ajimu | 96 | 33.26 N | 131.21 E |
| Ajipuzicun | 104 | 42.16 N | 123.33 E |
| Ajisu | 96 | 34.00 N | 131.22 E |
| Ajjer, Tassili-n- ⋀[1] | 148 | 25.10 N | 8.00 E |
| Ajka | 30 | 47.07 N | 17.34 E |
| Ajke, ozero ⊖ | 86 | 50.57 N | 61.36 E |
| Ajkino | 24 | 62.15 N | 49.56 E |
| 'Ajlūn | 132 | 32.20 N | 35.45 E |
| Ajlune | 224 | 46.31 N | 122.26 W |
| 'Ajmah, Jabal al- ⋀ | 140 | 29.12 N | 34.02 E |
| Ajmer | 120 | 26.27 N | 74.38 E |
| Ajnāla | 123 | 31.51 N | 74.48 E |
| Ajni | 85 | 39.23 N | 68.32 E |
| Ajo | 200 | 32.22 N | 112.51 W |
| Ajo, Cabo de › | 34 | 43.31 N | 3.35 W |
| Ajok | 140 | 9.15 N | 28.27 E |
| Ajon, ostrov I | 74 | 69.50 N | 168.40 E |
| Ajoya | 232 | 24.04 N | 106.22 W |
| Ajrag nuur ⊖ | 88 | 48.54 N | 93.28 E |
| 'Ajramīyah, Bi'r al- ⊤[4] | 142 | 29.39 N | 31.50 E |
| Ajrum | 84 | 41.13 N | 44.53 E |
| Ajryk | 86 | 50.30 N | 76.48 E |
| Ajtos | 38 | 42.42 N | 27.15 E |
| Ajuchitlán del Progreso | 234 | 18.09 N | 100.29 W |
| Ajuda ◆[8] | 266c | 38.43 N | 9.12 W |
| Ajusco | 204 | 31.35 N | 116.25 W |
| Ajusco ◆[8] | 286a | 19.14 N | 99.12 W |
| Ajuta ≃ | 83 | 47.34 N | 40.07 E |
| Ajuterique | 236 | 14.20 N | 87.43 W |
| Ajutinskij | 83 | 47.46 N | 40.08 E |
| Ajuy | 116 | 11.10 N | 123.01 E |
| Ajuy Bay c | 116 | 11.10 N | 123.02 E |
| Aka ≃ | 92 | 38.54 N | 139.50 E |
| Akaba | 150 | 7.57 N | 1.03 E |
| Akabane | 94 | 34.37 N | 137.12 E |
| Akabira | 92a | 43.34 N | 142.03 E |
| Akabli | 148 | 26.42 N | 1.22 E |
| Akabori | 94 | 36.22 N | 139.14 E |
| Akademii, zaliv c | 89 | 54.15 N | 138.05 E |
| Akagera (Kagera) ≃ | 154 | 0.57 S | 31.47 E |
| Akagera, Parc National de l' ♦ | 154 | 1.30 S | 30.35 E |
| Akagi, Nihon | 94 | 36.33 N | 139.03 E |
| Akagi, Nihon | 96 | 35.00 N | 132.43 E |
| Akagi-san ∧ | 94 | 36.33 N | 139.11 E |
| Akaishi-dake ∧ | 94 | 35.27 N | 138.09 E |
| Akaishi-sammyaku ⋀ | 94 | 35.18 N | 138.07 E |
| Akaka Falls State Park ♦ | 229d | 19.52 N | 155.09 W |
| Akaki Beseka | 144 | 8.52 N | 38.47 E |
| Akālgarh | 123 | 32.16 N | 73.49 E |
| Akalkot | 122 | 17.32 N | 76.13 E |
| Akamaruno-misaki › | 174m | 26.44 N | 128.09 E |
| Akámas, Akrotírion › | 130 | 35.06 N | 32.17 E |
| Akan | 92a | 43.06 N | 144.10 E |
| Akana-tōge )( | 96 | 34.57 N | 132.44 E |
| Akan-kokuritsu-kōen ♦ | 92a | 43.30 N | 144.15 E |
| Akaoka | 96 | 33.32 N | 133.43 E |
| Ak-Aral | 86 | 49.10 N | 90.57 E |
| Akaroa | 172 | 43.48 S | 172.58 E |
| Akaroa Harbour c | 172 | 43.50 S | 172.56 E |
| Åkarp | 41 | 55.39 N | 13.07 E |
| Akarsu, Tür. | 130 | 37.14 N | 41.04 E |
| Akarsu, Tür. | 130 | 39.56 N | 38.38 E |
| Akasaki | 96 | 35.31 N | 133.38 E |
| 'Akasha East | 140 | 21.05 N | 30.43 E |
| Akashat | 130 | 33.45 N | 39.58 E |
| Akashi | 96 | 34.38 N | 134.59 E |
| Akashi ≃ | 270 | 34.38 N | 134.59 E |
| Akashi-kaikyō ʯ | 96 | 34.37 N | 135.02 E |
| Akashina | 94 | 36.21 N | 137.56 E |
| Akatani-ko ⊖[1] | 94 | 36.43 N | 138.54 E |
| Akatjevo | 82 | 54.59 N | 38.45 E |
| Akatova | 76 | 55.09 N | 31.48 E |
| Akatsuka ◆[8] | 268 | 35.46 N | 139.39 E |
| Akatsutsumi ◆[8] | 268 | 35.39 N | 139.39 E |
| Akbaba ◆[8] | 267b | 41.09 N | 29.06 E |
| Akbaba Dağı ∧ | 130 | 40.12 N | 40.51 E |
| Akbajtal | 85 | 38.32 N | 73.49 E |
| Akbajtal, pereval )( | 85 | 38.32 N | 73.40 E |
| Akbarpur, India | 124 | 24.39 N | 83.58 E |
| Akbarpur, India | 124 | 26.25 N | 82.33 E |
| Akbeit | 86 | 51.38 N | 70.02 E |
| Akbou | 148 | 36.28 N | 4.32 E |
| Akbulak, Kaz. | 86 | 49.26 N | 80.28 E |
| Akbulak, Ross. | 86 | 51.01 N | 55.37 E |
| Akbura ≃ | 85 | 40.39 N | 72.36 E |
| Akçaabat | 130 | 41.02 N | 39.34 E |
| Akçadağ | 130 | 38.21 N | 37.59 E |
| Akçakale | 130 | 36.41 N | 38.56 E |
| Akcakışla | 130 | 39.33 N | 36.22 E |
| Akçakoca | 130 | 41.05 N | 31.09 E |
| Akçakoyunlu | 130 | 36.46 N | 37.38 E |
| Akçaova, Tür. | 130 | 37.30 N | 28.02 E |
| Akçaova, Tür. | 130 | 41.03 N | 29.57 E |
| Akçapınar | 130 | 38.57 N | 38.57 E |
| Akčatau | 86 | 47.59 N | 74.02 E |
| Akçay | 130 | 36.36 N | 29.45 E |
| Akçay ≃ | 130 | 37.50 N | 28.15 E |
| Akchâr ◆[1] | 150 | 20.00 N | 14.30 W |
| Akcjabr'ski | 76 | 52.38 N | 28.53 E |
| Akdağ | 130 | 40.43 N | 36.00 E |
| Akdağ ∧ | 130 | 39.29 N | 41.54 E |
| Akdağmadeni | 130 | 39.40 N | 35.54 E |
| Akdala | 86 | 45.02 N | 74.35 E |
| Akdoğan | 130 | 35.06 N | 33.41 E |
| Ak-Dovurak | 86 | 51.16 N | 90.31 E |
| Akechi | 94 | 35.18 N | 137.23 E |
| Akehama | 96 | 33.19 N | 132.26 E |
| Akeley | 190 | 47.00 N | 94.43 W |
| Aken | 54 | 51.51 N | 12.[illegible] E |
| Akeno, Nihon | 94 | 36.15 N | 140.[illegible] E |
| Akeno, Nihon | 94 | 35.46 N | 138.[illegible] E |
| Åker | 40 | 59.15 N | 17.[illegible] E |
| Åkerby | 40 | 60.25 N | 17.4[illegible] E |
| Åkersberga | 40 | 59.29 N | 18.1[illegible] E |
| Akershus □[6] | 26 | 60.00 N | 11.1[illegible] E |
| Akersloot | 52 | 52.34 N | 4.4[illegible] E |
| Akespe | 86 | 46.48 N | 60.3[illegible] E |
| Aketi | 152 | 2.44 N | 23.4[illegible] E |
| Aketilepa | 85 | 39.57 N | 74.03 E |
| Aketu-Oja | 273a | 6.41 N | 3.23 E |
| Åkforsån ≃ | 40 | 58.54 N | 16.28 E |
| Akgöl ⊖ | 130 | 38.58 N | 31.48 E |
| Akharnaí | 38 | 38.05 N | 23.44 E |
| Akhḍar, Al-Jabal al- ⋀, Lībiyā | 146 | 32.30 N | 21.30 |
| Akhḍar, Al-Jabal al- ⋀, 'Umān | 128 | 23.15 N | 57.20 E |
| Akhelóös ≃ | 38 | 38.36 N | 21.14 E |
| Akh Gol ⊖ | 84 | 39.33 N | 44.47 E |
| Akhiok | 180 | 56.57 N | 154.10 W |
| Akhisar | 130 | 38.55 N | 27.51 E |
| Akhmīm | 140 | 26.34 N | 31.44 E |
| Akhnūr | 123 | 32.54 N | 74.44 E |
| Akhtarīn | 130 | 36.31 N | 37.20 E |
| Aki, Nihon | 96 | 33.30 N | 133.54 E |
| Aki, Nihon | 96 | 33.28 N | 131.43 E |
| Aki ≃, Nihon | 94 | 35.41 N | 139.21 E |
| Aki ≃, Nihon | 96 | 33.30 N | 133.55 E |
| Akiachak | 180 | 60.55 N | 161.27 W |
| Akiak | 180 | 60.55 N | 161.12 W |
| Akiéni | 152 | 1.11 S | 13.53 E |
| Akima | 88 | 53.06 N | 115.44 E |
| Akimiski Island I | 176 | 53.00 N | 81.20 W |
| Aki-nada ⊤[2] | 96 | 34.05 N | 132.48 E |
| Akıncı | 130 | 37.10 N | 40.52 E |
| Akıncı Burun › | 130 | 36.19 N | 35.47 E |
| Akıncılar, Tür. | 130 | 40.06 N | 38.21 E |
| Akıncılar, Tür. | 130 | 37.45 N | 38.50 E |
| Akiode | 273a | 6.38 N | 3.21 E |
| Åkirkeby | 26 | 55.04 N | 14.56 E |
| Akishima | 94 | 35.41 N | 139.22 E |
| Akišma ≃ | 89 | 52.08 N | 132.40 E |
| Akita | 92 | 39.43 N | 140.07 E |
| Akita-heiya ≚ | 92 | 39.45 N | 140.10 E |
| Akitan | 273a | 6.39 N | 3.16 E |
| Akitipa | 150 | 8.17 N | 6.16 E |
| Akitkan, chrebet ⋀ | 88 | 57.05 N | 109.05 E |
| Akitsu, Nihon | 96 | 34.19 N | 132.50 E |
| Akitsu, Nihon | 270 | 34.56 N | 135.06 E |
| Akiyama | 94 | 35.34 N | 139.05 E |
| Akiyoshi-dai ⋀[1] | 96 | 34.15 N | 131.15 E |
| Akiyoshi-dai-kokutei-kōen ♦ | 96 | 34.15 N | 131.17 E |
| Akiyoshi-do ≗[5] | 96 | 34.14 N | 131.19 E |
| Akjar | 86 | 51.50 N | 58.14 E |
| Akjoujt | 150 | 19.45 N | 14.23 W |
| Akka | 148 | 29.22 N | 8.14 W |
| Akkala | 86 | 43.43 N | 59.31 E |
| Akkani | 180 | 65.30 N | 171.10 W |
| Akkense | 86 | 46.49 N | 68.20 E |
| Akkerman → Bilhorod-Dnistrovs'kyy | 78 | 46.12 N | 30.20 E |
| Akkermanovka | 86 | 51.11 N | 58.12 E |
| Akkerwoude | 52 | 53.17 N | 5.58 E |
| Akkeshi | 92a | 43.02 N | 144.51 E |
| Akkışla | 130 | 39.00 N | 36.11 E |
| 'Akko (Acre) | 132 | 32.55 N | 35.05 E |
| Akkol', Kaz. | 85 | 43.25 N | 70.47 E |
| Akkol', Kaz. | 86 | 45.02 N | 75.40 E |
| Akkol', Kaz. | 86 | 52.12 N | 75.05 E |
| Akkol', ozero ⊖ | 85 | 43.24 N | 70.40 E |
| Akköy | 130 | 37.29 N | 27.15 E |
| Akkra → Accra | 150 | 5.33 N | 0.13 W |
| Akkrum | 52 | 53.03 N | 5.50 E |
| Ak-Kul' | 85 | 41.41 N | 74.16 E |
| Akkuş | 130 | 40.49 N | 37.01 E |
| Aklan □[4] | 116 | 11.40 N | 122.20 E |
| Aklan ≃ | 116 | 11.44 N | 122.20 E |
| Aklan Point › | 116 | 11.44 N | 122.22 E |
| Aklavik | 180 | 68.12 N | 135.00 W |
| 'Aklé 'Aouâna ◆[1] | 150 | 18.00 N | 5.30 W |
| Akmenrags › | 76 | 56.51 N | 21.03 E |
| Akmeqit | 120 | 37.01 N | 76.59 E |
| Akmeşe | 130 | 40.51 N | 30.12 E |
| Akmola | 86 | 51.10 N | 71.30 E |
| Akmola □[8] | 86 | 51.00 N | 70.00 E |
| Akmuz | 85 | 41.16 N | 76.09 E |
| Ākna | 272b | 22.59 N | 88.21 E |
| Aknet, gora ∧ | 86 | 50.51 N | 75.40 E |
| Aknīste | 76 | 56.10 N | 25.45 E |
| Aknoul | 148 | 34.43 N | 3.49 W |
| Ako, Nig. | 146 | 10.17 N | 10.58 E |
| Akō, Nihon | 96 | 34.45 N | 134.24 E |
| Akoba | 80 | 49.28 N | 47.25 E |
| Akobo | 140 | 7.47 N | 33.01 E |
| Akobo (Akūbū) ≃ | 140 | 7.47 N | 33.03 E |
| Akodiya | 124 | 23.23 N | 76.36 E |
| Akok, Cam. | 152 | 2.46 N | 10.18 E |
| Akok, Gabon | 152 | 0.31 N | 9.45 E |
| Akola | 122 | 20.44 N | 77.00 E |
| Akonolinga | 152 | 3.47 N | 12.15 E |
| Akop | 140 | 8.21 N | 29.05 E |
| Akor | 150 | 14.53 N | 6.58 W |
| Akora | 123 | 34.00 N | 72.08 E |
| Akordat | 144 | 15.33 N | 37.53 E |
| Akören | 130 | 37.27 N | 32.23 E |
| Akosombo Dam ◆[6] | 150 | 6.16 N | 0.03 E |
| Akot, India | 120 | 21.11 N | 77.04 E |
| Akot, Sūd. | 140 | 6.33 N | 30.03 E |
| Akoupé | 150 | 6.23 N | 3.54 W |
| Akowonjo | 273a | 6.37 N | 3.19 E |
| Akpatok Island I | 176 | 60.25 N | 68.00 W |
| Akpınar, Tür. | 130 | 37.34 N | 38.13 E |
| Akpınar, Tür. | 130 | 39.17 N | 33.40 E |
| Akqi | 85 | 40.52 N | 77.58 E |
| Åkrafjorden c[2] | 26 | 59.46 N | 6.06 E |
| Akranes | 24a | 64.18 N | 22.02 W |
| Åkrehamn | 26 | 59.16 N | 5.11 E |
| Akrítas, Ákra › | 38 | 36.43 N | 21.54 E |
| Akrofuom | 150 | 6.07 N | 1.39 W |
| Akrokórinthos ⊥ | 38 | 37.54 N | 22.56 E |
| Akron, Co., U.S. | 198 | 40.09 N | 103.12 W |
| Akron, In., U.S. | 216 | 41.02 N | 86.01 W |
| Akron, Ia., U.S. | 198 | 42.49 N | 96.33 W |
| Akron, N.Y., U.S. | 210 | 43.01 N | 78.29 W |
| Akron, Oh., U.S. | 214 | 41.04 N | 81.31 W |
| Akron, Pa., U.S. | 208 | 40.09 N | 76.12 W |
| Akron-Canton Regional Airport ⊠ | 214 | 40.55 N | 81.27 W |
| Akron City Reservoir ⊖[1] | 214 | 41.20 N | 81.17 W |
| Akrotíri | 130 | 34.36 N | 32.57 E |
| Akša | 88 | 50.16 N | 113.17 E |
| Aksa ◆[8] | 272c | 19.10 N | 72.48 E |
| Aksaj, Kaz. | 80 | 51.09 N | 53.00 E |
| Aksaj, Ross. | 80 | 47.58 N | 43.59 E |
| Aksaj, Ross. | 83 | 47.15 N | 39.52 E |
| Aksaj (Toxkan) ≃, Asia | 85 | 40.55 N | 78.16 E |
| Aksaj ≃, Ross. | 83 | 47.15 N | 39.53 E |
| Aksaj ≃, Ross. | 84 | 43.32 N | 46.51 E |
| Aksakovo | 80 | 54.02 N | 54.09 E |
| Aksaray | 130 | 38.23 N | 34.03 E |
| Aksaray □[4] | 130 | 38.30 N | 34.00 E |
| Aksarka | 74 | 66.36 N | 67.46 E |
| Akšatau | 86 | 49.23 N | 54.36 E |
| Aksaut ≃ | 84 | 43.55 N | 41.42 E |
| Aksay | 102 | 39.28 N | 94.15 E |
| Aksayqin Hu ⊖ | 120 | 35.12 N | 79.50 E |
| Akşehir | 130 | 38.21 N | 31.25 E |
| Akşehir Gölü ⊖ | 130 | 38.30 N | 31.28 E |
| Akseki | 130 | 37.02 N | 31.48 E |
| Aksengir ≃ | 85 | 43.40 N | 76.14 E |
| Aksenkino | 80 | 53.59 N | 53.06 E |
| Aksenovo | 82 | 55.40 N | 38.15 E |
| Aksentjevo | 82 | 55.25 N | 35.54 E |


| | English | Deutsch | Español | Français | Português |
|---|---|---|---|---|---|
| ≃ | River | Fluß | Río | Rivière | Rio |
| ≍ | Canal | Kanal | Canal | Canal | Canal |
| ʟ | Waterfall, Rapids | Wasserfall, Stromschnellen | Cascada, Rápidos | Chute d'eau, Rapides | Cascata, Rápidos |
| ʯ | Strait | Meeresstraße | Estrecho | Détroit | Estreito |
| c | Bay, Gulf | Bucht, Golf | Bahía, Golfo | Baie, Golfe | Baía, Golfo |
| ⊖ | Lake, Lakes | See, Seen | Lago, Lagos | Lac, Lacs | Lago, Lagos |
| ≚ | Swamp | Sumpf | Pantano | Marais | Pântano |
| ⊡ | Ice Features, Glacier | Eis- und Gletscherformen | Accidentes Glaciales | Formes glaciaires | Acidentes glaciares |
| ⊤ | Other Hydrographic Features | Andere Hydrographische Objekte | Otros Elementos Hidrográficos | Autres données hydrographiques | Outros acidentes hidrográficos |
| ✣ | Submarine Features | Untermeerische Objekte | Accidentes Submarinos | Formes de relief sous-marin | Acidentes submarinos |
| □ | Political Unit | Politische Einheit | Unidad Politica | Entité politique | Unidade política |
| ʊ | Cultural Institution | Kulturelle Institution | Institución Cultural | Institution culturelle | Institução cultural |
| ⊥ | Historical Site | Historische Stätte | Sitio Histórico | Site historique | Sitio histórico |
| ♦ | Recreational Site | Erholungs- und Ferienort | Sitio de Recreo | Centre de loisirs | Area de Lazer |
| ⊠ | Airport | Flughafen | Aeropuerto | Aéroport | Aeroporto |
| ■ | Military Installation | Militäranlage | Instalación Militar | Installation militaire | Instalação militar |
| ◆ | Miscellaneous | Verschiedenes | Misceláneo | Divers | Diversos |

ENGLISH · DEUTSCH


| Name | Page | Lat.°′ | Long.°′ |
|---|---|---|---|
| Akšij, Kaz. | **85** | 44.00 N | 76.20 E |
| Akšij, Kaz. | **86** | 47.37 N | 55.56 E |
| Akšijrak, chrebet ∧∧ | **85** | 41.20 N | 74.15 E |
| Aksinjino, Ross. | **82** | 55.44 N | 36.59 E |
| Aksinjino, Ross. | **82** | 56.02 N | 38.12 E |
| Aks'onovo | **88** | 58.51 N | 101.43 E |
| Aks'onovo-Zilovskoje | **88** | 53.04 N | 117.32 E |
| Aksoran, gora ∧ | **86** | 48.27 N | 75.32 E |
| Akstafa ≃ | **84** | 41.15 N | 45.26 E |
| Aksu, Kaz. | **80** | 50.56 N | 53.06 E |
| Aksu, Kaz. | **86** | 52.28 N | 71.59 E |
| Aksu, Kaz. | **86** | 45.37 N | 79.30 E |
| Aksu, Tür. | **130** | 36.58 N | 30.50 E |
| Aksu, Zhg. | **90** | 41.10 N | 80.20 E |
| Aksu ≃, Asia | **85** | 43.22 N | 73.54 E |
| Aksu ≃, Kaz. | **86** | 46.20 N | 78.15 E |
| Aksu ≃, Tür. | **130** | 37.25 N | 36.54 E |
| Aksu ≃, Tür. | **130** | 36.51 N | 30.54 E |
| Aksu-Ajuly | **86** | 48.47 N | 73.40 E |
| Aksuat, Kaz. | **86** | 51.32 N | 64.34 E |
| Aksuat, Kaz. | **86** | 47.45 N | 82.40 E |
| Aksuat, Kaz. | **86** | 48.16 N | 83.50 E |
| Aksubajevo | **80** | 54.52 N | 50.50 E |
| Aksu-Džabaglinskij zapovednik ♣ | **85** | 42.20 N | 70.35 E |
| Aksum | **144** | 14.08 N | 38.43 E |
| Aktag ∧ | **120** | 36.45 N | 84.40 E |
| Aktal | **85** | 41.25 N | 75.03 E |
| Aktanyš | **80** | 55.43 N | 54.05 E |
| Aktas, Kaz. | **85** | 42.57 N | 70.04 E |
| Aktas, Kaz. | **86** | 48.02 N | 66.21 E |
| Aktas, Kaz. | **86** | 49.47 N | 72.59 E |
| Aktaš, Ross. | **86** | 50.18 N | 87.44 E |
| Aktaš, Uzb. | **85** | 41.38 N | 69.44 E |
| Aktaş Gölü ⊜ | **84** | 41.15 N | 43.12 E |
| Aktasty, Kaz. | **86** | 50.06 N | 76.40 E |
| Aktasty, Kaz. | **86** | 50.44 N | 61.43 E |
| Aktau, Kaz. | **72** | 43.35 N | 51.05 E |
| Aktau, Kaz. | **86** | 50.16 N | 73.02 E |
| Aktau, gora ∧ | **86** | 48.00 N | 71.45 E |
| Aktepe | **130** | 36.44 N | 36.27 E |
| Akterek, Kaz. | **85** | 43.22 N | 75.18 E |
| Akterek, Kyrg. | **85** | 42.14 N | 77.45 E |
| Akto | **85** | 39.08 N | 75.57 E |
| Aktobe | **85** | 43.13 N | 67.46 E |
| Aktogaj, Kaz. | **86** | 44.27 N | 76.42 E |
| Aktogaj, Kaz. | **86** | 48.18 N | 74.58 E |
| Aktogaj, Kaz. | **86** | 46.57 N | 79.40 E |
| Aktubek | **86** | 48.37 N | 71.06 E |
| Akt'ubinsk | **86** | 50.17 N | 57.10 E |
| Akt'ubinsk □[8] | **86** | 48.30 N | 58.30 E |
| Akt'ubinskij | **80** | 54.49 N | 52.47 E |
| Aktuluk | **130** | 39.03 N | 39.32 E |
| Aktumsyk | **86** | 46.40 N | 57.19 E |
| Akt'uz | **85** | 42.54 N | 76.07 E |
| Aku | **150** | 6.42 N | 7.20 E |
| Akūbū (Akobo) ≃ | **140** | 7.47 N | 33.03 E |
| Akui ≃ | **96** | 34.06 N | 134.33 E |
| Akula | **152** | 2.22 N | 20.11 E |
| Akuliči Pervyje | **76** | 53.11 N | 33.13 E |
| Akulovo, Ross. | **82** | 55.31 N | 36.42 E |
| Akulovo, Ross. | **82** | 56.05 N | 38.59 E |
| Akumadan | **150** | 7.24 N | 1.57 W |
| Akune | **92** | 32.01 N | 130.11 E |
| Akun Island I | **180** | 54.12 N | 165.35 W |
| Akure | **150** | 7.15 N | 5.12 E |
| Akureyri | **24a** | 65.44 N | 18.08 W |
| Akurli | **272c** | 19.01 N | 73.08 E |
| Akuša | **84** | 42.17 N | 47.21 E |
| Akuse | **150** | 6.06 N | 0.08 E |
| Akuseki-jima I | **93b** | 29.27 N | 129.37 E |
| Akutan | **180** | 54.08 N | 165.46 W |
| Akutan Island I | **180** | 54.10 N | 165.55 W |
| Akutan Pass ʮ | **180** | 54.00 N | 166.10 W |
| Akuticha | **86** | 52.27 N | 84.29 E |
| Akwanga | **150** | 8.55 N | 8.23 E |
| Akwatia | **150** | 6.04 N | 0.49 W |
| Akwawa ∧[2] | **150** | 6.27 N | 0.25 W |
| Akwaya | **152** | 6.30 N | 9.40 E |
| Akyab → Sittwe | **110** | 20.09 N | 92.54 E |
| Akyazı | **130** | 40.41 N | 30.37 E |
| Akyel | **144** | 12.33 N | 37.04 E |
| Akyrtobe | **85** | 42.59 N | 72.07 E |
| Akyurt | **130** | 40.08 N | 33.06 E |
| Akžajkyn, ozero ⊜ | **86** | 44.55 N | 67.46 E |
| Akžal, Kaz. | **86** | 47.47 N | 74.02 E |
| Akžal, Kaz. | **86** | 49.13 N | 81.25 E |
| Akžar, Kaz. | **85** | 43.08 N | 71.38 E |
| Akžar, Kaz. | **86** | 47.35 N | 83.42 E |
| Akžaryk | **86** | 48.34 N | 75.30 E |
| Ål | **26** | 60.38 N | 8.34 E |
| Ala | **64** | 45.45 N | 11.00 E |
| Ala ≃, Bela. | **76** | 52.41 N | 29.39 E |
| Ala ≃, Zhg. | **86** | 42.42 N | 89.12 E |
| Alà, Monti di ∧∧ | **71** | 40.40 N | 9.14 E |
| Al-Abʿādīyah | **142** | 31.22 N | 31.07 E |
| Alabama | **210** | 43.06 N | 78.23 W |
| Alabama □[3], U.S. | **178** | 32.50 N | 87.00 W |
| Alabama □[3], U.S. | **194** | 32.50 N | 87.00 W |
| Alabama ≃ | **194** | 31.08 N | 87.57 W |
| Alabama and Coushatta Indian Reservation ⊸[4] | **222** | 30.43 N | 94.42 W |
| Alabaster | **194** | 33.14 N | 86.48 W |
| Alabat Island I | **116** | 14.07 N | 122.03 E |
| Al-ʿAbbāsah ash-Sharqīyah | **142** | 30.32 N | 31.43 E |
| Al-ʿAbbāsīyah | **140** | 12.10 N | 31.18 E |
| Al-ʿAbbāsīyah ⊸[8] | **273c** | 30.04 N | 31.17 E |
| Alabino | **82** | 55.31 N | 37.01 E |
| Āl-ʿĀbis | **144** | 18.04 N | 43.10 E |
| Alabuga ≃ | **85** | 41.26 N | 74.41 E |
| Ala-Buka | **85** | 41.23 N | 71.30 E |
| Alaca | **130** | 40.10 N | 34.51 E |
| Alacahan | **130** | 39.07 N | 37.37 E |
| Alacalı | **130** | 41.11 N | 29.27 E |
| Alaçam | **130** | 41.37 N | 35.37 E |
| Alaçam Dağları ∧∧ | **130** | 39.20 N | 28.32 E |
| Alacant | **34** | 38.21 N | 0.29 W |
| Alacant □[4] | **34** | 38.30 N | 0.45 W |
| Alaçatı | **130** | 38.16 N | 26.23 E |
| Alachadzy | **84** | 43.14 N | 40.18 E |
| Alachua | **192** | 29.47 N | 82.29 W |
| Alacrán, Arrecife ✣[2] | **232** | 22.24 N | 89.42 W |
| Alacranes, Presa ⊜[1] | **240p** | 22.45 N | 80.08 W |
| Aladağ | **130** | 37.02 N | 32.41 E |
| Aladağ ∧, Tür. | **84** | 40.11 N | 42.49 E |
| Aladağ ∧, Tür. | **130** | 37.44 N | 35.09 E |
| Aladağlar ∧∧, Tür. | **84** | 39.20 N | 43.35 E |
| Ala Dağlar ∧∧, Tür. | **130** | 37.55 N | 35.13 E |
| Al-ʿAdasīyah | **132** | 32.40 N | 35.37 E |
| Alà dei Sardi | **71** | 40.39 N | 9.20 E |
| Aladino | **82** | 54.49 N | 38.12 E |
| Aladinskij, porog ⌞ | **86** | 58.24 N | 95.29 E |
| Ala di Stura | **62** | 45.19 N | 7.19 E |
| Aladjino | **82** | 56.21 N | 37.04 E |
| Aladža manastir ♁[1] | **38** | 43.17 N | 28.01 E |
| Alafia ≃ | **220** | 27.52 N | 82.23 W |
| Alafia, South Prong ≃ | **220** | 27.51 N | 82.08 W |
| Alagbado | **273a** | 6.41 N | 3.18 E |
| Alagna Valsesia | **62** | 45.51 N | 7.56 E |
| Alag nuur ⊜ | **102** | 45.09 N | 94.28 E |
| Alagoa | **256** | 22.10 S | 44.38 W |
| Alagoa Grande | **250** | 7.03 S | 35.38 W |
| Alagoa Nova | **250** | 7.04 S | 35.46 W |
| Alagoas □[3] | **250** | 9.00 S | 36.00 W |
| Alagoinhas | **255** | 12.07 S | 38.26 W |
| Alagón | **34** | 41.46 N | 1.07 W |
| Alagón ≃ | **34** | 39.44 N | 6.53 W |
| Alaguntan | **273a** | 6.26 N | 3.30 E |
| Alah ≃ | **116** | 6.53 N | 124.33 E |
| Alahanpanjang | **112** | 1.05 S | 100.47 E |
| Alahärmä | **26** | 63.14 N | 22.51 E |
| Alaior | **34** | 39.56 N | 4.08 E |
| Al-Ait | **140** | 12.22 N | 27.27 E |
| Al-ʿAjamīyīn | **142** | 29.20 N | 30.43 E |
| Alajärvi | **26** | 63.00 N | 23.49 E |
| Alajku | **85** | 40.18 N | 74.25 E |
| Alajõe | **76** | 59.01 N | 27.26 E |
| Alajskaja dolina V | **85** | 39.30 N | 73.00 E |
| Alajskij chrebet ∧∧ | **85** | 39.45 N | 72.00 E |
| Alajuela | **236** | 10.01 N | 84.13 W |
| Alajuela □[4] | **236** | 10.30 N | 84.30 W |
| Alajuela, Lago ⊜[1] | **236** | 9.15 N | 79.35 W |
| Ālājūjeh | **84** | 38.57 N | 46.41 E |
| Alakai Swamp ≋ | **229b** | 22.08 N | 159.35 W |
| Alakamisy | **157b** | 21.19 S | 47.14 E |
| Alakanuk | **180** | 62.41 N | 164.37 W |
| Alaknanda ≃ | **124** | 30.08 N | 78.36 E |
| Alakol', ozero ⊜ | **86** | 46.10 N | 81.45 E |
| Al-ʿAkrīshah | **142** | 31.08 N | 30.09 E |
| Alaktara | **124** | 22.01 N | 82.26 E |
| Alak'ul'a | **265a** | 59.44 N | 29.56 E |
| Alakurtti | **24** | 66.57 N | 30.18 E |
| Al-ʿĀl | **132** | 32.48 N | 35.44 E |
| Alalakeiki Channel ʮ | **229a** | 20.35 N | 156.30 W |
| Al-ʿAlamayn | **140** | 30.49 N | 28.57 E |
| Al-ʿAlāqimah | **142** | 30.37 N | 31.38 E |
| Alalaú ≃ | **246** | 0.30 S | 61.09 W |
| Al-ʿAmādīyah | **128** | 37.06 N | 43.29 E |
| Alamagan I | **108** | 17.36 N | 145.50 E |
| Al-ʿAmārah | **128** | 31.50 N | 47.09 E |
| Al-ʿAmār al-Kubrā | **142** | 30.21 N | 31.08 E |
| Alamata | **144** | 12.25 N | 39.33 E |
| Alamdānga | **124** | 23.46 N | 88.57 E |
| Alameda, Esp. | **34** | 37.12 N | 4.39 W |
| Alameda, Ca., U.S. | **226** | 37.45 N | 122.14 W |
| Alameda, N.M., U.S. | **200** | 35.11 N | 106.37 W |
| Alameda □[6] | **226** | 37.35 N | 121.55 W |
| Alameda, Estación ⊸[5] | **286e** | 33.27 S | 70.41 W |
| Alameda Creek ≃ | **226** | 37.35 N | 122.09 W |
| Alameda Naval Air Station ■ | **226** | 37.47 N | 122.18 W |
| Alamedin | **85** | 42.54 N | 74.37 E |
| Alamein → Al-ʿAlamayn | **140** | 30.49 N | 28.57 E |
| Alamillo | **200** | 31.02 N | 110.35 W |
| Alaminos | **116** | 16.10 N | 119.59 E |
| Al-ʿĀmirīyah | **142** | 31.01 N | 29.48 E |
| ʿAlam Lek | **128** | 37.02 N | 65.57 E |
| Álamo, Méx. | **234** | 20.55 N | 97.41 W |
| Alamo, Ca., U.S. | **226** | 37.51 N | 122.02 W |
| Alamo, Ga., U.S. | **192** | 32.08 N | 82.46 W |
| Alamo, Mi., U.S. | **216** | 42.22 N | 85.43 W |
| Alamo, Nv., U.S. | **204** | 37.21 N | 115.09 W |
| Alamo, Tn., U.S. | **194** | 35.47 N | 89.07 W |
| Alamo ≃ | **204** | 33.14 N | 115.39 W |
| Alamo Creek ≃ | **282** | 37.42 N | 121.55 W |
| Alamo Creek, West Branch ≃ | **282** | 37.45 N | 121.55 W |
| Alamogordo | **200** | 32.53 N | 105.57 W |
| Alamogordo Creek ≃ | **196** | 34.40 N | 104.23 W |
| Alamo Heights | **196** | 29.29 N | 98.27 W |
| Alamo Indian Reservation ⊸[4] | **200** | 34.30 N | 107.30 W |
| Alamo Lake ⊜[1] | **200** | 34.20 N | 113.30 W |
| Alamo Oaks | **282** | 37.51 N | 121.59 W |
| Alamor | **246** | 4.02 S | 80.02 W |
| Álamos, Méx. | **196** | 26.25 N | 100.25 W |
| Álamos, Méx. | **232** | 27.01 N | 108.56 W |
| Álamos, Río de los ≃ | **196** | 27.53 N | 101.12 W |
| Alamosa | **200** | 37.28 N | 105.52 W |
| Alamosa ≃ | **200** | 37.22 N | 105.46 W |
| Alamosa Creek ≃, N.M., U.S. | **196** | 34.26 N | 103.58 W |
| Alamosa Creek ≃, N.M., U.S. | **200** | 33.20 N | 107.21 W |
| Alamosa East | **200** | 37.28 N | 105.49 W |
| Álamos de Márquez | **232** | 28.40 N | 103.30 W |
| Ālampur, Bngl. | **126** | 23.49 N | 89.06 E |
| Alampur, India | **272b** | 22.25 N | 88.08 E |
| Alanäs | **26** | 64.10 N | 15.42 E |
| Al-ʿĀnāt | **132** | 32.21 N | 36.48 E |
| Al-Anbār □[4] | **128** | 33.45 N | 41.45 E |
| Aland | **122** | 17.34 N | 76.34 E |
| Åland (Ahvenanmaa) II | **26** | 60.15 N | 20.00 E |
| Aland ≃ | **54** | 53.02 N | 11.34 E |
| Åland-Inseln → Åland II | **26** | 60.15 N | 20.00 E |
| Ålands hav ▿[2] | **26** | 60.00 N | 19.30 E |
| Alandur | **122** | 13.02 N | 80.15 E |
| Alangalang | **116** | 11.12 N | 124.51 E |
| Alang-besar, Pulau I | **114** | 2.12 N | 100.39 E |
| Alanje | **236** | 8.24 N | 82.33 W |
| Alano di Piave | **64** | 45.55 N | 11.52 E |
| Alanson | **190** | 45.26 N | 84.47 W |
| Alanya | **130** | 36.33 N | 32.01 E |
| Al-ʿAnz | **132** | 32.23 N | 36.38 E |
| Alaotra, Lac ⊜ | **157b** | 17.30 S | 48.30 E |
| Alapaha | **192** | 31.23 N | 83.13 W |
| Alapaha ≃ | **192** | 30.26 N | 83.06 W |
| Alapajevsk | **86** | 57.52 N | 61.42 E |
| Alaplı | **130** | 41.11 N | 31.24 E |
| Al-ʿAqabah | **132** | 29.31 N | 35.00 E |
| ʿAlaqah, Jabal ∧ | **142** | 29.59 N | 32.53 E |
| Alaquines | **234** | 22.08 N | 99.36 W |
| Al-ʿArabīyah as-Suʿūdīyah → Saudi Arabia □[1] | **118** | 25.00 N | 45.00 E |
| Alarcón | **34** | 39.33 N | 2.05 W |
| Alarcón, Embalse de ⊜[1] | **34** | 39.36 N | 2.10 W |
| Al-ʿArīsh | **132** | 31.08 N | 33.48 E |
| Al-ʿArmah ∧∧[1] | **128** | 25.30 N | 46.30 E |
| Alarobia Vohiposa | **157b** | 20.59 S | 47.09 E |
| Alas | **115b** | 8.32 S | 117.00 E |
| Alas ≃, Indon. | **114** | 3.05 N | 97.55 E |
| Alaš ≃, Ross. | **86** | 51.15 N | 90.54 E |
| Alas, Selat ʮ | **115b** | 8.40 S | 116.40 E |
| Alasan | **112** | 1.45 S | 123.19 E |
| Alasdair, Sgurr ∧ | **46** | 57.12 N | 6.14 W |
| Alaşehir | **130** | 38.21 N | 28.32 E |
| Alashanyouqi | **102** | 40.02 N | 103.33 E |
| Al-ʿAshārah | **130** | 34.55 N | 40.34 E |
| Al-Ashmūnayn | **142** | 27.47 N | 30.49 E |
| Alaska | **216** | 42.50 N | 85.29 W |
| Alaska □[3] | **180** | 65.00 N | 153.00 W |
| Alaska, Gulf of ⊂ | **16** | 58.00 N | 146.00 W |
| Alaska Peninsula ›[1] | **180** | 57.00 N | 158.00 W |
| Alaska Range ∧∧ | **180** | 62.30 N | 150.00 W |
| Al-ʿAssāfīyah | **128** | 28.21 N | 39.08 E |
| Alassio | **62** | 44.00 N | 8.10 E |
| Alastaro | **26** | 60.56 N | 22.55 E |
| Alastuey | **258** | 34.25 S | 59.13 W |
| Älät, Azer. | **84** | 39.57 N | 49.25 E |
| Alat, Uzb. | **128** | 39.26 N | 63.48 E |
| Al-ʿAtāminah | **142** | 27.20 N | 30.50 E |
| Alatan'aola → Xin Barag Youqi | **88** | 48.41 N | 116.53 E |
| Al-Atārib | **130** | 36.08 N | 36.49 E |
| Al-Aṭāwilah | **142** | 27.14 N | 31.13 E |
| Al-ʿAṭf | **142** | 29.39 N | 31.16 E |
| Al-ʿAthāmīn ∧∧ | **128** | 30.22 N | 43.40 E |
| Alatna ≃ | **180** | 66.34 N | 152.34 W |
| Alatri | **66** | 41.43 N | 13.21 E |
| Al-ʿAṭrūn | **140** | 18.11 N | 26.36 E |
| Alatyr' | **80** | 54.51 N | 46.36 E |
| Alatyr' ≃ | **80** | 54.52 N | 46.36 E |
| Alausí | **246** | 2.12 S | 78.50 W |
| Alava, Cape › | **224** | 48.10 N | 124.43 W |
| Alaverdi | **84** | 41.08 N | 44.39 E |
| Alavieska | **26** | 64.10 N | 24.18 E |
| Alavus | **26** | 62.35 N | 23.37 E |
| Alaw ≃ | **44** | 53.18 N | 4.32 W |
| Alaw, Llyn ⊜[1] | **44** | 53.20 N | 4.22 W |
| Alawa | **150** | 10.20 N | 6.39 E |
| Alāwalpur | **123** | 31.26 N | 75.39 E |
| Al-ʿAwjā' | **142** | 30.58 N | 30.32 E |
| Al-ʿAwsajīyah | **128** | 26.49 N | 41.41 E |
| ʿĀlayh | **132** | 33.48 N | 35.36 E |
| Al-ʿAyn | **128** | 24.13 N | 55.46 E |
| Al-ʿAyn ▿[4] | **140** | 16.36 N | 29.19 E |
| Al-ʿAyyāsh ash-Sharqī | **142** | 31.33 N | 31.13 E |
| Al-ʿAyyāṭ | **142** | 29.37 N | 31.15 E |
| Alazani ≃ | **84** | 41.05 N | 46.40 E |
| Alazeja ≃ | **74** | 70.51 N | 153.34 E |
| Al-Azhar University ♁[2] | **273c** | 30.03 N | 31.16 E |
| Alʿ Azīzah | **142** | 31.11 N | 31.57 E |
| Al-ʿAzīzīyah, Lībiyā | **146** | 32.32 N | 13.01 E |
| Al-ʿAzīzīyah, Miṣr | **142** | 30.29 N | 31.18 E |
| Al-ʿAzīzīyah, Miṣr | **273c** | 29.52 N | 31.15 E |
| Al-Azraq ⊸[1] | **132** | 31.52 N | 36.50 E |
| Alb ≃ | **58** | 47.35 N | 8.08 E |
| Alba, It. | **62** | 44.42 N | 8.02 E |
| Alba, Mi., U.S. | **190** | 44.58 N | 84.58 W |
| Alba, Pa., U.S. | **210** | 41.42 N | 76.50 W |
| Alba, Tx., U.S. | **222** | 32.48 N | 95.38 W |
| Alba □[6] | **38** | 46.15 N | 23.30 E |
| Alba, Foum de )( | **148** | 20.27 N | 3.36 W |
| Al-Bāb | **130** | 36.22 N | 37.31 E |
| Albacete | **34** | 38.59 N | 1.51 W |
| Albacete □[4] | **34** | 38.50 N | 1.50 W |
| Albachten | **52** | 51.55 N | 7.31 E |
| Albacina | **66** | 43.21 N | 13.01 E |
| Al-Badʿ | **128** | 28.25 N | 35.04 E |
| Al-Badārī | **140** | 26.59 N | 31.25 E |
| Alba de Tormes | **34** | 40.49 N | 5.31 W |
| Al-Badrashayn | **142** | 29.51 N | 31.16 E |
| Ålbæk | **26** | 57.36 N | 10.25 E |
| Al-Bahnasā | **142** | 28.32 N | 30.39 E |
| Al-Baḥr al-Abyaḍ □[4] | **140** | 13.15 N | 32.25 E |
| Al-Baḥr al-Aḥmar □[4], Miṣr | **142** | 28.45 N | 32.00 E |
| Al-Baḥr al-Aḥmar □[4], Sūd. | **140** | 20.00 N | 35.15 E |
| Al-Baḥrayn → Bahrain □[1] | **128** | 26.00 N | 50.30 E |
| Albaida | **34** | 38.51 N | 0.31 W |
| Albairate | **266b** | 45.25 N | 8.56 E |
| Alba Iulia | **38** | 46.04 N | 23.35 E |
| Al-Bajalāt | **142** | 31.10 N | 31.37 E |
| Al-Bājūr | **142** | 30.26 N | 31.02 E |
| Al-Bakātūsh | **142** | 31.03 N | 30.48 E |
| Al-Balāmūn | **142** | 30.49 N | 31.26 E |
| Al-Balāshūn | **142** | 30.26 N | 31.26 E |
| Al-Ballaḥ | **142** | 30.46 N | 32.19 E |
| Al-Ballāṣ | **140** | 26.01 N | 32.46 E |
| Al-Balqā' □[8] | **132** | 32.00 N | 35.40 E |
| Al-Bālūʿah ⊜ | **130** | 35.55 N | 36.28 E |
| Al-Balyanā | **140** | 26.14 N | 32.00 E |
| Alban | **32** | 43.54 N | 2.28 E |
| Albanel, Lac ⊜ | **176** | 50.55 N | 73.12 W |
| Albanella | **68** | 40.30 N | 15.08 E |
| Albani, Colli ∧∧[2] | **66** | 41.45 N | 12.45 E |
| Albania, Col. | **246** | 1.21 N | 75.57 W |
| Albania, Col. | **246** | 11.01 N | 72.40 W |
| Albania (Shqipëri) □[1], Europe | **22** | 41.00 N | 20.00 E |
| Albania (Shqipëri) □[1], Europe | **38** | 41.00 N | 20.00 E |
| Albanie → Albania □[1] | **38** | 41.00 N | 20.00 E |
| Albanien → Albania □[1] | **38** | 41.00 N | 20.00 E |
| Albano, Lago ⊜ | **66** | 41.45 N | 12.40 E |
| Albano, Monte ∧∧ | **66** | 43.50 N | 10.58 E |
| Albano di Lucania | **68** | 40.35 N | 16.02 E |
| Albano Laziale | **66** | 41.44 N | 12.39 E |
| Albany, Austl. | **162** | 35.02 S | 117.53 E |
| Albany, Ca., U.S. | **226** | 37.53 N | 122.17 W |
| Albany, Ga., U.S. | **192** | 31.34 N | 84.09 W |
| Albany, Il., U.S. | **190** | 41.47 N | 90.13 W |
| Albany, In., U.S. | **216** | 40.18 N | 85.14 W |
| Albany, Ky., U.S. | **194** | 36.41 N | 85.08 W |
| Albany, Mn., U.S. | **190** | 45.37 N | 94.34 W |
| Albany, Mo., U.S. | **194** | 40.14 N | 94.19 W |
| Albany, N.Y., U.S. | **210** | 42.39 N | 73.45 W |
| Albany, Oh., U.S. | **188** | 39.13 N | 82.12 W |
| Albany, Or., U.S. | **202** | 44.38 N | 123.06 W |
| Albany, Tx., U.S. | **196** | 32.43 N | 99.17 W |
| Albany, Wi., U.S. | **190** | 42.42 N | 89.26 W |
| Albany □[6] | **210** | 42.39 N | 73.45 W |
| Albany ≃ | **176** | 52.17 N | 81.31 W |
| Albany County Airport ⊠ | **210** | 42.45 N | 73.48 W |
| Albany Creek | **171a** | 27.21 S | 152.58 E |
| Albany Park ⊸[8] | **278** | 41.58 N | 87.43 W |
| Al-Baqʿah | **132** | 32.05 N | 35.53 E |
| Al-Barājīl | **273c** | 30.04 N | 31.09 E |
| Al-Barāmūn | **142** | 31.07 N | 31.26 E |
| Albardón | **252** | 31.26 S | 68.32 W |
| Albaredo d'Adige | **64** | 45.19 N | 11.16 E |
| Al-Bāriḥah | **132** | 32.34 N | 35.50 E |
| Al-Barnūjī | **142** | 30.56 N | 30.23 E |
| Albaron | **62** | 43.37 N | 4.28 E |
| Albaron ∧ | **62** | 45.20 N | 7.07 E |
| Albarracín | **34** | 40.25 N | 1.26 W |
| Al-Barrah | **128** | 24.55 N | 45.52 E |
| Albarraque | **266c** | 38.46 N | 9.21 W |
| Al-Barshā | **142** | 27.43 N | 30.54 E |
| Al-Barun | **140** | 11.44 N | 33.30 E |
| Al-Basātīn ⊸[8] | **273c** | 29.59 N | 31.16 E |
| Al-Baslaqūn | **142** | 31.06 N | 30.08 E |
| Al-Basqalūn | **142** | 28.42 N | 30.44 E |
| Al-Baṣrah (Basra) | **128** | 30.30 N | 47.47 E |
| Al-Baṣrah □[4] | **128** | 30.20 N | 47.35 E |
| Al-Batānūn | **142** | 30.37 N | 30.59 E |
| Al-Baṭḥā' | **128** | 31.06 N | 45.53 E |
| Al-Bāṭinah ⊸[1] | **128** | 23.45 N | 57.20 E |
| Albatross Bay ⊂ | **164** | 12.45 S | 141.43 E |
| Albatross Point › | **172** | 38.06 S | 174.41 E |
| Al-Batrūn | **130** | 34.15 N | 35.39 E |
| Al-Baṭrūnah | **132** | 33.39 N | 36.02 E |
| Al-Bauga | **140** | 18.16 N | 33.55 E |
| Al-Bawīṭī | **140** | 28.21 N | 28.52 E |
| Albay □[4] | **116** | 13.00 N | 123.40 E |
| Al-Bayahū | **142** | 28.16 N | 30.44 E |
| Al-Bayḍā (Beida), Lībiyā | **146** | 28.22 N | 18.55 E |
| Al-Bayḍā' (Beida), Lībiyā | **146** | 32.46 N | 21.43 E |
| Al-Bayḍā', Miṣr | **142** | 31.10 N | 30.05 E |
| Albay Gulf ⊂ | **116** | 13.10 N | 124.00 E |
| Albazino | **89** | 53.23 N | 124.05 E |
| Albbruck | **58** | 47.35 N | 8.07 E |
| Albegna ≃ | **66** | 42.30 N | 11.11 E |
| Albemarle | **192** | 35.13 N | 80.13 W |
| Albemarle and Chesapeake Canal ≅ | **208** | 36.43 N | 76.15 W |
| Albemarle Sound ʮ | **192** | 36.03 N | 76.12 W |
| Albenga | **62** | 44.03 N | 8.13 E |
| Albens | **62** | 45.47 N | 5.57 E |
| Alberche ≃ | **34** | 39.58 N | 4.46 W |
| Alberdi | **252** | 26.10 S | 58.09 W |
| Alberene | **192** | 37.53 N | 78.37 W |
| Alberga, Austl. | **162** | 27.12 S | 135.28 E |
| Ålberga, Sve. | **40** | 58.44 N | 16.34 E |
| Alberga Creek ≃ | **162** | 27.06 S | 135.33 E |
| Albergaria-a-Velha | **34** | 40.42 N | 8.29 W |
| Alberic | **34** | 39.07 N | 0.31 W |
| Alberni Inlet ⊂ | **182** | 49.07 N | 124.50 W |
| Alberobello | **68** | 40.47 N | 17.15 E |
| Alberona | **68** | 41.26 N | 15.07 E |
| Albero Sole ∧ | **70a** | 35.31 N | 12.32 E |
| Albers | **219** | 38.33 N | 89.37 W |
| Alberschwende | **58** | 47.27 N | 9.49 E |
| Albersloh | **52** | 51.52 N | 7.43 E |
| Albert | **50** | 50.00 N | 2.39 E |
| Albert ≃ | **171a** | 27.42 S | 153.15 E |
| Albert, Lake ⊜, Afr. | **154** | 1.40 N | 31.00 E |
| Albert, Lake ⊜, Austl. | **166** | 35.33 S | 139.17 E |
| Alberta | **194** | 32.13 N | 87.24 W |
| Alberta □[4], Can. | **176** | 54.00 N | 113.00 W |
| Alberta □[4], Can. | **182** | 54.00 N | 113.00 W |
| Alberta, Mount ∧ | **182** | 52.18 N | 117.28 W |
| Albert Canyon | **182** | 51.08 N | 117.52 W |
| Albert City | **198** | 42.46 N | 94.56 W |
| Albert Edward, Mount ∧ | **164** | 8.23 S | 147.24 E |
| Albert Edward Bay ⊂ | **176** | 69.32 N | 103.00 W |
| Albert Falls | **158** | 29.27 S | 30.25 E |
| Albertfalva ⊸[8] | **264c** | 47.27 N | 19.02 E |
| Alberti | **252** | 35.02 S | 60.16 W |
| Albertina | **256** | 22.12 S | 46.37 W |
| Albertinia | **158** | 34.13 S | 21.36 E |
| Albertirsa | **30** | 47.15 N | 19.38 E |
| Albert Kanaal (Canal Albert) ≅ | **56** | 50.39 N | 5.37 E |
| Albert Lea | **190** | 43.38 N | 93.22 W |
| Albert Markham, Mount ∧ | **9** | 81.23 S | 158.12 E |
| Albert Nile ≃ | **154** | 3.36 N | 32.02 E |
| Alberto, Lago → Albert, Lake ⊜ | **154** | 1.40 N | 31.00 E |
| Alberto Eduardo → Albert Edward, Mount ∧ | **164** | 8.23 S | 147.24 E |
| Alberton, P.E., Can. | **186** | 46.49 N | 64.04 W |
| Alberton, S. Afr. | **273d** | 26.16 S | 28.08 E |
| Alberton, Mt., U.S. | **202** | 47.00 N | 114.29 W |
| Albert Park ♣ | **274b** | 37.51 S | 144.57 E |
| Albert Peak ∧ | **182** | 51.02 N | 117.51 W |
| Albertshof | **264a** | 52.42 N | 13.40 E |
| Albertson | **276** | 40.46 N | 73.38 W |
| Albertson Brook ≃ | **285** | 39.41 N | 74.43 W |
| Albertson Brook, Blue Anchor Branch ≃ | **285** | 39.42 N | 74.49 W |
| Albertson Brook, Pump Branch ≃ | **285** | 39.42 N | 74.49 W |
| Albertville, Fr. | **62** | 45.41 N | 6.23 E |
| Albertville, Al., U.S. | **194** | 34.16 N | 86.12 W |
| Albertville — Kalemie, Zaïre | **154** | 5.56 S | 29.12 E |
| Albestroff | **56** | 48.56 N | 6.51 E |
| Albettone | **64** | 45.21 N | 11.35 E |
| Albi | **32** | 43.56 N | 2.09 E |
| Albia, Ia., U.S. | **190** | 41.01 N | 92.48 W |
| Albia, N.Y., U.S. | **210** | 42.43 N | 73.39 W |
| Albiate | **266b** | 45.39 N | 9.15 E |
| Al Bidia | **146** | 10.33 N | 20.13 E |
| Albidona | **68** | 39.55 N | 16.28 E |
| Albignasego | **64** | 45.21 N | 11.52 E |
| Albin | **198** | 41.25 N | 104.05 W |
| Albina | **250** | 5.30 N | 54.03 W |
| Albina, Ponta › | **152** | 15.51 S | 11.44 E |
| Albinea | **64** | 44.37 N | 10.36 E |
| Albino | **62** | 45.46 N | 9.47 E |
| Albion, Austl. | **274b** | 37.47 S | 144.49 E |
| Albion, B.C., Can. | **224** | 49.11 N | 122.33 W |
| Albion, Ca., U.S. | **204** | 39.13 N | 123.46 W |
| Albion, Id., U.S. | **202** | 42.24 N | 113.34 W |
| Albion, Il., U.S. | **194** | 38.22 N | 88.03 W |
| Albion, In., U.S. | **216** | 41.23 N | 85.25 W |
| Albion, Ia., U.S. | **190** | 42.06 N | 92.59 W |
| Albion, Mi., U.S. | **216** | 42.14 N | 84.45 W |
| Albion, Ne., U.S. | **198** | 41.41 N | 98.00 W |
| Albion, N.J., U.S. | **285** | 39.47 N | 74.56 W |
| Albion, N.Y., U.S. | **210** | 43.14 N | 78.11 W |
| Albion, Pa., U.S. | **214** | 41.53 N | 80.22 W |
| Albion, R.I., U.S. | **207** | 41.57 N | 71.27 W |
| Albion, Wa., U.S. | **202** | 46.47 N | 117.14 W |
| Albion, Wi., U.S. | **216** | 42.52 N | 89.04 W |
| Albion Airstrip ⊠ | **285** | 39.46 N | 74.58 W |
| Albion Park | **170** | 34.34 S | 150.47 E |
| Al-Biqāʿ □[4] | **130** | 34.00 N | 36.00 E |
| Al-Biqāʿ V | **128** | 33.50 N | 36.00 E |
| Al-Bi'r | **128** | 28.50 N | 36.19 E |
| Al-Bīrah | **132** | 31.54 N | 35.13 E |
| Al-Birīgāt | **142** | 30.30 N | 30.49 E |
| Al-Birk | **144** | 18.13 N | 41.33 E |
| Al-Birkah | **146** | 24.54 N | 10.11 E |
| Al-Birkah ▿[4] | **144** | 22.12 N | 40.43 E |
| Albisola Marina | **62** | 44.19 N | 8.30 E |
| Albisola Superiore | **62** | 44.20 N | 8.31 E |
| Albizzate | **62** | 45.43 N | 8.44 E |
| Alblasserdam | **52** | 51.52 N | 4.40 E |
| Albo, Monte ∧ | **71** | 40.32 N | 9.35 E |
| Albocàsser | **34** | 40.21 N | 0.02 E |
| Albogas | **266c** | 38.51 N | 9.15 W |
| Alborán, Isla de I | **34** | 35.58 N | 3.02 W |
| Alborán Sea ▿[2] | **34** | 36.00 N | 3.00 W |
| Ålborg | **26** | 57.03 N | 9.56 E |
| Ålborg Bugt ⊂ | **26** | 56.45 N | 10.30 E |
| Alborz, Reshteh-ye Kūhhā-ye (Elburz Mountains) ∧∧ | **128** | 36.00 N | 53.00 E |
| Albreda | **182** | 52.38 N | 119.09 W |
| Albright-Knox Art Gallery ♁ | **284a** | 42.56 N | 78.53 W |
| Albrighton | **42** | 52.38 N | 2.16 W |
| Albstadt | **58** | 48.13 N | 9.01 E |
| Albuch ∧∧ | **56** | 48.15 N | 9.50 E |
| Albuera | **116** | 10.55 N | 124.42 E |
| Albufeira | **34** | 37.05 N | 8.15 W |
| Ālbū Gharz, Sabkhat ⊜ | **130** | 34.45 N | 41.15 E |
| Al-Buḥayrah □[4], Miṣr | **142** | 30.59 N | 30.12 E |
| Al-Buḥayrah □[4], Sūd. | **140** | 7.30 N | 29.30 E |
| Albula ≃ | **58** | 46.42 N | 9.27 E |
| Al-Bunbah | **146** | 32.24 N | 23.08 E |
| Albuñol | **34** | 36.47 N | 3.12 W |
| Albuquerque, Bra. | **248** | 19.23 S | 57.26 W |
| Albuquerque, N.M., U.S. | **200** | 35.05 N | 106.39 W |
| Albuquerque, Cayos de II | **236** | 12.10 N | 81.50 W |
| Al-Buraymī | **128** | 24.15 N | 55.45 E |
| Alburg | **206** | 44.58 N | 73.18 W |
| Al-Burj | **142** | 31.35 N | 30.59 E |
| Al-Burjāyah | **142** | 28.09 N | 30.44 E |
| Alburno, Monte ∧ | **68** | 40.33 N | 15.17 E |
| Alburquerque | **34** | 39.13 N | 7.00 W |
| Alburtis | **208** | 40.31 N | 75.36 W |
| Al-Burumbul | **142** | 29.19 N | 31.14 E |
| Albury, Austl. | **166** | 36.05 S | 146.55 E |
| Albury, N.Z. | **172** | 44.14 S | 170.52 E |
| Albury, Eng., U.K. | **260** | 51.13 N | 0.30 W |
| Albury Park ♣ | **260** | 51.13 N | 0.29 W |
| Al-Buṣaylī | **142** | 31.20 N | 30.24 E |
| Al-Busaytā' ≚ | **128** | 29.30 N | 38.45 E |
| Al-Buṭānah ⊸[1] | **140** | 15.00 N | 34.40 E |
| Al-Buṭaynah | **132** | 32.57 N | 36.42 E |
| Al-Buwayḍah | **132** | 32.28 N | 36.04 E |
| Al-Buzūn | **144** | 15.35 N | 50.55 E |
| Albuzzano | **62** | 45.11 N | 9.16 E |
| Alby, Fr. | **62** | 45.49 N | 6.01 E |
| Alby, Sve. | **26** | 62.30 N | 15.28 E |
| Alca | **248** | 15.08 S | 72.46 W |
| Alcabideche | **266c** | 38.44 N | 9.24 W |
| Alcácer do Sal | **34** | 38.22 N | 8.30 W |
| Alcains | **34** | 39.55 N | 7.27 W |
| Alcala | **116** | 17.54 N | 121.39 E |
| Alcalá de Guadaira | **34** | 37.20 N | 5.50 W |
| Alcalá de Henares | **34** | 40.29 N | 3.22 W |
| Alcalá la Real | **34** | 37.28 N | 3.56 W |
| Alcalde | **200** | 36.05 N | 106.03 W |
| Alcamachi ≃ | **248** | 16.08 S | 66.50 W |
| Alcamo | **70** | 37.59 N | 12.58 E |
| Alčan ≃ | **89** | 46.38 N | 134.22 E |
| Alcanadre ≃ | **34** | 41.37 N | 0.12 W |
| Alcanar | **34** | 40.33 N | 0.29 E |
| Alcañices | **34** | 41.42 N | 6.21 W |
| Alcañiz | **34** | 41.03 N | 0.08 W |
| Alcântara, Bra. | **250** | 2.24 S | 44.24 W |
| Alcántara, Esp. | **34** | 39.43 N | 6.53 W |
| Alcantara, Pil. | **116** | 12.16 N | 122.03 E |
| Alcântara ⊸[8] | **266c** | 38.42 N | 9.10 W |
| Alcantara ≃ | **70** | 37.49 N | 15.16 E |
| Alcántara I, Embalse de ⊜[1] | **34** | 39.45 N | 6.25 W |
| Alcantarilla | **34** | 37.58 N | 1.13 W |
| Alcantilado | **255** | 16.23 S | 53.31 W |
| Alcara li Fusi | **70** | 38.01 N | 14.42 E |
| Alcaraz | **34** | 38.40 N | 2.29 W |
| Alcatraz Island I | **282** | 37.49 N | 122.26 W |
| Alcaudete | **34** | 37.36 N | 4.05 W |
| Alcázar de San Juan | **34** | 39.24 N | 3.12 W |
| Alcazarquivir → Er-Rachidia | **148** | 31.58 N | 4.25 W |
| Alcester, Eng., U.K. | **42** | 52.13 N | 1.52 W |
| Alcester, S.D., U.S. | **198** | 43.01 N | 96.37 W |
| Alcester Island I | **164** | 9.35 S | 152.25 E |
| Alchevs'k | **83** | 48.30 N | 38.47 E |
| Alcira (Gigena) | **252** | 32.45 S | 64.20 W |
| Alcoa | **192** | 35.47 N | 83.58 W |
| Alcoa Center | **279b** | 40.33 N | 79.39 W |
| Alcoa Lake ⊜[1] | **222** | 30.34 N | 97.03 W |
| Alcobaça, Bra. | **255** | 17.30 S | 39.13 W |
| Alcobaça, Port. | **34** | 39.33 N | 8.59 W |
| Alcobaça ≃ | **255** | 17.32 S | 39.12 W |
| Alcobendas | **34** | 40.32 N | 3.38 W |
| Alcochete | **266c** | 38.45 N | 8.58 W |
| Alcockspruit | **158** | 27.55 S | 30.01 E |
| Alcoi | **34** | 38.42 N | 0.28 W |
| Alcoi ≃ | **34** | 38.59 N | 0.09 W |
| Alcoitão | **266c** | 38.44 N | 9.24 W |
| Alcolea del Pinar | **34** | 41.02 N | 2.28 W |
| Alcolu | **192** | 33.45 N | 80.12 W |
| Alcomunga | **234** | 18.25 N | 97.02 W |
| Alconbury Brook ≃ | **42** | 52.19 N | 0.12 W |
| Alconchel | **34** | 38.31 N | 7.04 W |
| Alcony | **218** | 40.01 N | 84.04 W |
| Alcorcón | **266a** | 40.21 N | 3.50 W |
| Alcorn | **194** | 31.52 N | 91.09 W |
| Alcorta | **252** | 33.32 S | 61.07 W |
| Alcoutim | **34** | 37.28 N | 7.28 W |
| Alcova Reservoir ⊜[1] | **200** | 42.32 N | 106.45 W |
| Alcove | **210** | 42.28 N | 73.55 W |
| Alcove Reservoir ⊜[1] | **210** | 42.29 N | 73.57 W |
| Alcovy ≃ | **192** | 33.26 N | 83.50 W |
| Alcubierre | **34** | 41.48 N | 0.27 W |
| Alcúdia | **34** | 39.52 N | 3.07 E |
| Alcúdia, Badia d' ⊂ | **34** | 39.48 N | 3.13 E |
| Alcyon Lake ⊜ | **285** | 39.44 N | 75.08 W |
| Aldabra Island I | **138** | 9.25 S | 46.22 E |
| Aldama, Méx. | **232** | 28.51 N | 105.54 W |
| Aldama, Méx. | **234** | 22.55 N | 98.04 W |
| Aldama, Arroyo ≃ | **286b** | 23.05 N | 82.15 W |
| Aldan, Ross. | **74** | 58.37 N | 125.24 E |
| Aldan, Pa., U.S. | **285** | 39.55 N | 75.17 W |
| Aldan ≃ | **74** | 63.28 N | 129.35 E |
| Aldanskoje nagorje ∧∧[1] | **74** | 57.00 N | 127.00 E |
| Aldbourne | **42** | 51.31 N | 1.37 W |
| Aldbrough | **44** | 53.50 N | 0.07 W |
| Aldbury | **42** | 51.48 N | 0.36 W |
| Alde ≃ | **42** | 52.03 N | 1.28 E |
| Aldea Apeleg | **254** | 44.41 S | 70.51 W |
| Aldeburgh | **42** | 52.09 N | 1.35 E |
| Aldeia de Paio Pires | **266c** | 38.38 N | 9.05 W |
| Aldeia Nova de Santo Bento | **34** | 37.55 N | 7.25 W |
| Aldeia Velha | **256** | 22.47 S | 42.55 W |
| Aldemha | **287b** | 23.45 S | 46.53 W |
| Alden, Il., U.S. | **216** | 42.27 N | 88.31 W |
| Alden, Ia., U.S. | **190** | 42.31 N | 93.22 W |
| Alden, Mn., U.S. | **190** | 43.40 N | 93.34 W |
| Alden, N.Y., U.S. | **210** | 42.54 N | 78.29 W |
| Alden, Pa., U.S. | **210** | 41.10 N | 76.00 W |
| Alden Center | **212** | 42.55 N | 78.32 W |
| Aldenham | **260** | 51.40 N | 0.21 W |
| Aldenhoven | **56** | 50.53 N | 6.16 E |
| Aldenrade ⊸[8] | **263** | 51.31 N | 6.44 E |
| Alder, Ben ∧ | **46** | 56.48 N | 4.28 W |
| Alder Creek ≃ | **202** | 45.50 N | 119.56 W |
| Aldergrove | **224** | 49.04 N | 122.28 W |
| Alder Lake ⊜[1] | **224** | 46.45 N | 122.15 W |
| Alderley Edge | **44** | 53.18 N | 2.15 W |
| Aldermaston | **42** | 51.23 N | 1.09 W |
| Alderney I | **43b** | 49.43 N | 2.12 W |
| Alder Peak ∧ | **226** | 35.53 N | 121.22 W |
| Aldersbach | **60** | 48.36 N | 13.05 E |
| Aldershot | **42** | 51.15 N | 0.47 W |
| Alderson | **192** | 37.44 N | 80.38 W |
| Alderton | **224** | 47.10 N | 122.14 W |
| Alderwood Manor | **224** | 47.49 N | 122.17 W |
| Aldine | **222** | 29.54 N | 95.24 W |
| Aldinga | **168b** | 35.17 S | 138.29 E |
| Aldinga Bay ⊂ | **168b** | 35.20 S | 138.25 E |
| Aldinga Beach | **168b** | 35.18 S | 138.27 E |
| Aldingen | **58** | 48.05 N | 8.41 E |
| Aldino | **64** | 46.23 N | 11.20 E |
| Aldo Bonzi | **288** | 34.42 S | 58.31 W |
| Aldridge | **42** | 52.36 N | 1.55 W |
| Aldwell, Lake ⊜[1] | **224** | 48.05 N | 123.34 W |
| Alechovščina | **76** | 60.25 N | 33.52 E |
| Aled ≃ | **44** | 53.14 N | 3.34 W |
| Aledo, Il., U.S. | **190** | 41.11 N | 90.44 W |
| Aledo, Tx., U.S. | **222** | 32.42 N | 97.36 W |
| Alefa | **144** | 11.57 N | 36.52 E |
| Aleg | **150** | 17.03 N | 13.55 W |
| Alegranza, Isla I | **148** | 29.23 N | 13.30 W |
| Alegre | **255** | 20.46 S | 41.32 W |
| Alegre ≃ | **248** | 15.01 S | 59.57 W |
| Alegres Mountain ∧ | **200** | 34.09 N | 108.11 W |
| Alegrete | **252** | 29.46 S | 55.46 W |
| Alej ≃ | **86** | 52.52 N | 83.36 E |
| Alejandría → Al-Iskandarīyah | **142** | 31.12 N | 29.54 E |
| Alejandro, Isla → Alexander Island I | **9** | 71.00 S | 70.00 W |
| Alejandro Roca | **252** | 33.21 S | 63.43 W |
| Alejandro Selkirk, Isla (Isla Más Afuera) I | **244** | 33.45 S | 80.46 W |
| Alejo Ledesma | **252** | 33.37 S | 62.37 W |
| Alejsk | **86** | 52.28 N | 82.45 E |
| Aleknagik | **180** | 59.17 N | 158.38 W |
| Aleknagik, Lake ⊜ | **180** | 59.20 N | 158.45 W |
| Aleksandrijskaja | **84** | 43.54 N | 47.08 E |
| Aleksandro-Nevskaja | **84** | 43.55 N | 46.35 E |
| Aleksandro-Nevskij | **80** | 53.28 N | 40.13 E |
| Aleksandrov | **82** | 56.24 N | 38.43 E |
| Aleksandrov Gaj | **80** | 50.09 N | 48.34 E |
| Aleksandrovka, Kaz. | **80** | 50.47 N | 52.59 E |
| Aleksandrovka, Kaz. | **85** | 43.27 N | 77.20 E |
| Aleksandrovka, Kaz. | **86** | 53.07 N | 69.50 E |
| Aleksandrovka, Ross. | **78** | 46.47 N | 39.01 E |
| Aleksandrovka, Ross. | **80** | 52.36 N | 50.37 E |
| Aleksandrovka, Ross. | **83** | 47.26 N | 39.13 E |
| Aleksandrovka, Ross. | **86** | 56.32 N | 90.47 E |
| Aleksandrovka, Ross. | **86** | 52.43 N | 54.17 E |
| Aleksandrovskaja, Ross. | **265a** | 60.03 N | 29.59 E |
| Aleksandrovskaja, Ross. | **265a** | 59.44 N | 30.21 E |
| Aleksandrovskij | **78** | 51.03 N | 36.44 E |
| Aleksandrovskij Šl'uz | **86** | 59.26 N | 89.20 E |
| Aleksandrovskij Zavod | **88** | 50.55 N | 117.57 E |
| Aleksandrovskoje, Ross. | **84** | 44.42 N | 43.00 E |
| Aleksandrovskoje, Ross. | **86** | 56.44 N | 85.23 E |
| Aleksandrovskoje, Ross. | **86** | 60.26 N | 77.50 E |
| Aleksandrovsk-Sachalinskij | **89** | 50.54 N | 142.10 E |
| Aleksandrów Kujawski | **30** | 52.52 N | 18.42 E |
| Aleksandrów Łódzki | **30** | 51.49 N | 19.19 E |
| Aleksaskino | **80** | 50.57 N | 47.42 E |
| Aleksejevka, Kaz. | **80** | 50.58 N | 52.25 E |
| Aleksejevka, Kaz. | **86** | 48.25 N | 85.40 E |
| Aleksejevka, Kaz. | **86** | 53.31 N | 69.30 E |
| Aleksejevka, Kaz. | **86** | 51.59 N | 70.59 E |
| Aleksejevka, Kaz. | **86** | 47.16 N | 81.34 E |
| Aleksejevka, Ross. | **78** | 50.37 N | 38.42 E |
| Aleksejevka, Ross. | **80** | 52.35 N | 51.17 E |
| Aleksejevka, Ross. | **80** | 53.15 N | 50.30 E |
| Aleksejevka, Ross. | **80** | 53.02 N | 42.46 E |
| Aleksejevka, Ross. | **80** | 51.49 N | 43.56 E |
| Aleksejevka, Ross. | **80** | 52.18 N | 48.01 E |
| Aleksejevka, Ross. | **82** | 54.41 N | 36.34 E |
| Aleksejevka, Ross. | **83** | 47.38 N | 38.49 E |
| Aleksejevka, Ross. | **83** | 47.41 N | 39.54 E |
| Aleksejevka, Ross. | **86** | 52.30 N | 79.33 E |
| Aleksejevka, Ross. | **86** | 54.31 N | 81.08 E |
| Aleksejevka, Ross. | **86** | 55.22 N | 72.03 E |
| Aleksejevo-Lozovskoje | **78** | 49.24 N | 40.39 E |
| Aleksejevo-Tuzlovka | **83** | 47.50 N | 39.24 E |
| Aleksejevsk | **88** | 57.50 N | 108.23 E |
| Aleksejevskaja | **80** | 50.17 N | 42.11 E |
| Aleksejevskoje | **80** | 55.18 N | 50.06 E |
| Aleksin | **82** | 54.31 N | 37.05 E |
| Aleksinac | **38** | 43.32 N | 21.43 E |
| Alella | **266d** | 41.30 N | 2.18 E |
| Alemanha → Germany □[1] | **30** | 51.00 N | 10.00 E |
| Alemania | **252** | 25.36 S | 65.38 W |
| Alemania → Germany □[1] | **30** | 51.00 N | 10.00 E |
| Alem Dağı ∧ | **267b** | 41.04 N | 29.12 E |
| Alemdar ⊸[8] | **267b** | 41.03 N | 29.14 E |
| Além Paraíba | **256** | 21.52 S | 42.41 W |
| Alençon | **50** | 48.26 N | 0.05 E |
| Alenquer | **250** | 1.56 S | 54.46 W |
| Alentejo □[9] | **34** | 38.00 N | 8.00 W |
| Alenuihaha Channel ʮ | **229a** | 20.26 N | 156.00 W |
| Aléoutiennes, Îles → Aleutian Islands II | **180** | 52.00 N | 176.00 W |
| Alep → Ḥalab | **130** | 36.12 N | 37.10 E |
| Aleppo → Ḥalab | **130** | 36.12 N | 37.10 E |
| Aléria | **36** | 42.05 N | 9.30 E |
| Alert | **16** | 82.29 N | 62.22 W |
| Alert Bay | **182** | 50.35 N | 126.55 W |
| Alès, Fr. | **62** | 44.08 N | 4.05 E |
| Ales, It. | **71** | 39.46 N | 8.49 E |
| Aleşd | **38** | 47.04 N | 22.24 E |
| Alešino, Ross. | **82** | 56.09 N | 37.45 E |
| Alešino, Ross. | **82** | 55.04 N | 36.05 E |
| Aleški | **80** | 51.38 N | 41.46 E |
| Aleškovo | **82** | 54.53 N | 36.23 E |
| Alessandria | **62** | 44.54 N | 8.37 E |
| Alessandria □[4] | **62** | 44.49 N | 8.42 E |
| Alessandria del Carretto | **68** | 39.57 N | 16.23 E |
| Alessandria della Rocca | **70** | 37.34 N | 13.27 E |
| Alessano | **68** | 39.53 N | 18.20 E |
| Ålestrup | **26** | 56.42 N | 9.30 E |
| Ålesund | **26** | 62.28 N | 6.09 E |
| Aletschhorn ∧ | **58** | 46.28 N | 8.00 E |
| Alëuten → Aleutian Islands II | **180** | 52.00 N | 176.00 W |
| Aleutianas, Islas → Aleutian Islands II | **180** | 52.00 N | 176.00 W |
| Aleutian Basin ✣[1] | **16** | 57.00 N | 177.00 E |
| Aleutian Islands II | **180** | 52.00 N | 176.00 W |
| Aleutian Range ∧∧ | **180** | 59.00 N | 155.00 W |
| Aleutian Trench ✣[1] | **6** | 51.00 N | 170.00 W |
| Aleutka | **74** | 45.57 N | 150.10 E |
| Alevina, mys › | **74** | 58.50 N | 151.20 E |
| Ale Water ≃ | **46** | 55.31 N | 2.35 W |
| Alex | **196** | 34.54 N | 97.46 W |
| Alexander, Mb., Can. | **184** | 49.50 N | 100.17 W |
| Alexander, Il., U.S. | **219** | 39.43 N | 90.02 W |
| Alexander, N.Y., U.S. | **210** | 42.54 N | 78.16 W |
| Alexander, N.D., U.S. | **198** | 47.50 N | 103.38 W |
| Alexander ≃ | **132** | 32.24 N | 34.52 E |
| Alexander, Cape › | **175e** | 6.35 S | 156.30 E |
| Alexander, Mount ∧, Austl. | **162** | 22.39 S | 115.32 E |
| Alexander, Mount ∧, Austl. | **169** | 36.59 S | 144.18 E |
| Alexander Archipelago II | **180** | 56.30 N | 134.00 W |
| Alexander Bay | **156** | 28.40 S | 16.30 E |
| Alexander City | **194** | 32.56 N | 85.57 W |
| Alexander Dam ⊜[1] | **273d** | 26.13 S | 28.25 E |
| Alexander Ditch ≅ | **279a** | 41.20 N | 82.05 W |
| Alexander Hamilton Airport ⊠ | **241n** | 17.42 N | 64.48 W |
| Alexander Indian Reserve ⊸[4] | **182** | 53.48 N | 113.58 W |
| Alexander Island I | **9** | 71.00 S | 70.00 W |
| Alexander Nevsky Monastery ♁[1] | **265a** | 59.55 N | 30.24 E |
| Alexandra, Austl. | **169** | 37.12 S | 145.43 E |
| Alexandra, N.Z. | **172** | 45.15 S | 169.24 E |
| Alexandra, S. Afr. | **273d** | 26.06 S | 28.05 E |
| Alexandra ≃ | **166** | 18.14 S | 139.54 E |
| Alexandra Canal ≅ | **274a** | 33.56 S | 151.10 E |
| Alexandra Falls ⌞ | **176** | 60.29 N | 116.18 W |
| Alexandra Park ♣ | **262** | 53.27 N | 2.15 W |
| Alexandra Park Race Course ♣ | **260** | 51.36 N | 0.08 W |
| Alexandretta → İskenderun | **130** | 36.37 N | 36.07 E |
| Alexandretta, Gulf of → İskenderun Körfezi ⊂ | **130** | 36.30 N | 35.40 E |
| Alexandria, Austl. | **166** | 19.05 S | 136.40 E |
| Alexandria, Bra. | **250** | 6.25 S | 38.01 W |
| Alexandria, B.C., Can. | **182** | 52.38 N | 122.27 W |
| Alexandria, On., Can. | **206** | 45.19 N | 74.38 W |
| Alexandria → Al-Iskandarīyah, Miṣr | **142** | 31.12 N | 29.54 E |
| Alexandria, Rom. | **38** | 43.58 N | 25.20 E |
| Alexandria, S. Afr. | **158** | 33.40 S | 26.24 E |
| Alexandria, Scot., U.K. | **46** | 55.59 N | 4.36 W |
| Alexandria, In., U.S. | **216** | 40.15 N | 85.40 W |
| Alexandria, Ky., U.S. | **218** | 38.57 N | 84.23 W |
| Alexandria, La., U.S. | **194** | 31.18 N | 92.26 W |
| Alexandria, Mn., U.S. | **198** | 45.53 N | 95.22 W |
| Alexandria, Mo., U.S. | **194** | 40.21 N | 91.27 W |
| Alexandria, Ne., U.S. | **198** | 40.14 N | 97.23 W |
| Alexandria, Oh., U.S. | **214** | 40.05 N | 82.37 W |
| Alexandria, Pa., U.S. | **214** | 40.34 N | 78.06 W |
| Alexandria, S.D., U.S. | **198** | 43.39 N | 97.46 W |
| Alexandria, Tn., U.S. | **194** | 36.04 N | 86.02 W |
| Alexandria, Va., U.S. | **208** | 38.48 N | 77.02 W |
| Alexandria Bay | **212** | 44.20 N | 75.55 W |
| Alexandrie → Al-Iskandarīyah | **142** | 31.12 N | 29.54 E |
| Alexandrina, Lake ⊜, Austl. | **166** | 35.26 S | 139.10 E |
| Alexandrina, Lake ⊜, Austl. | **168b** | 35.26 S | 139.10 E |
| Alexandroúpolis | **38** | 40.50 N | 25.52 E |
| Alexis | **190** | 41.03 N | 90.33 W |
| Alexis Creek | **182** | 52.05 N | 123.17 W |
| Alexis Indian Reserve ⊸[4] | **182** | 53.46 N | 114.30 W |
| Alezio | **68** | 40.04 N | 18.03 E |
| Alf | **56** | 50.03 N | 7.07 E |
| Ālfādānga | **126** | 23.18 N | 89.42 E |
| Al-Fahmīyīn | **142** | 29.36 N | 31.17 E |
| Al-Fallūjah | **128** | 33.20 N | 43.46 E |
| Alfambra | **34** | 40.33 N | 1.02 W |
| Alfambra ≃ | **34** | 40.21 N | 1.07 W |
| Al-Fant | **142** | 28.46 N | 30.53 E |
| Alfarata | **208** | 40.39 N | 77.27 W |
| Al-Farḍah | **144** | 14.51 N | 48.27 E |
| Alfaro | **34** | 42.11 N | 1.45 W |
| Alfarràs | **34** | 41.49 N | 0.35 E |
| Al-Fāshir | **140** | 13.38 N | 25.21 E |
| Al-Fashn | **142** | 28.49 N | 30.54 E |
| Alfatar | **38** | 43.57 N | 27.17 E |
| Alfavaca, Ilha I | **287a** | 23.02 S | 43.18 W |
| Al-Fāw | **128** | 29.58 N | 48.29 E |
| Al-Fayyūm | **142** | 29.19 N | 30.50 E |
| Al-Fayyūm □[4] | **142** | 29.19 N | 30.48 E |
| Al-Fāzah | **144** | 14.08 N | 43.05 E |
| Alfbach ≃ | **56** | 50.03 N | 7.08 E |
| Alfdorf | **56** | 48.51 N | 9.43 E |
| Alfedena | **66** | 41.44 N | 14.02 E |
| Alfeld, Dtsch. | **52** | 51.59 N | 9.50 E |
| Alfeld, Dtsch. | **60** | 49.26 N | 11.33 E |
| Alfenas | **256** | 21.25 S | 45.57 W |
| Alfhausen | **52** | 52.30 N | 7.57 E |
| Alfianello | **64** | 45.16 N | 10.10 E |
| Al-Fifi | **140** | 10.03 N | 25.01 E |
| Alfiós ≃ | **38** | 37.40 N | 21.33 E |
| Al-Firdān | **142** | 30.41 N | 32.20 E |
| Alföld ≚ | **30** | 47.00 N | 20.00 E |
| Alfonsine | **66** | 44.30 N | 12.03 E |


**Symbols** in the index entries represent the broad categories identified in the key at the right. Symbols with superior numbers (∧∧[1]) identify subcategories (see complete key on page *I · 1).*

**Symbole** im Register stellen die rechts im Schlüssel erklärten Kategorien dar. Symbole mit hochgestellten Ziffern (∧∧[1]) bezeichnen Unterabteilungen einer Kategorie (vgl. vollständiger Schlüssel auf Seite *I · 1).*

**Los símbolos** incluídos en el texto del índice representan las grandes categorías identificadas con la clave a la derecha. Los símbolos con numeros en su parte superior (∧∧[1]) identifican las subcategorías (véase la clave completa en la página *I · 1).*

**Les symboles** de l'index représentent les catégories indiquées dans la légende à droite. Les symboles suivis d'un indice (∧∧[1]) représentent des sous-catégories (voir légende complète à la page *I · 1).*

**Os símbolos** incluídos no texto do índice representam as grandes categorias identificadas com a chave à direita. Os símbolos com números em sua parte superior (∧∧[1]) identificam as subcategorias (veja-se a chave completa à página *I · 1).*

| | English | Deutsch | Español | Français | Português |
|---|---|---|---|---|---|
| ∧ | Mountain | Berg | Montaña | Montagne | Montanha |
| ∧∧ | Mountains | Gebirge | Montañas | Montagnes | Montanhas |
| )( | Pass | Paß | Paso | Col | Passo |
| V | Valley, Canyon | Tal, Cañon | Valle, Cañón | Vallée, Canyon | Vale, Canhão |
| ≚ | Plain | Ebene | Llano | Plaine | Planície |
| › | Cape | Kap | Cabo | Cap | Cabo |
| I | Island | Insel | Isla | Île | Ilha |
| II | Islands | Inseln | Islas | Îles | Ilhas |
| ± | Other Topographic Features | Andere Topographische Objekte | Otros Elementos Topográficos | Autres données topographiques | Outros acidentes topográficos |

ESPAÑOL — Nombre | Página | Lat.°' | Long.°' W = Oeste
FRANÇAIS — Nom | Page | Lat.°' | Long.°' W = Ouest
PORTUGUÊS — Nome | Página | Lat.°' | Long.°' W = Oeste


| | | | |
|---|---|---|---|
| Alford, Austl. | 168b | 33.49 S | 137.49 E |
| Alford, Eng., U.K. | 44 | 53.16 N | 0.10 E |
| Alford, Scot., U.K. | 46 | 57.13 N | 2.42 W |
| Alfortville | 261 | 48.49 N | 2.25 E |
| Ålfotbreen ⊓ | 26 | 61.45 N | 5.40 E |
| Alfred, On., Can. | 206 | 45.34 N | 74.53 W |
| Alfred, Me., U.S. | 188 | 43.28 N | 70.43 W |
| Alfred, N.Y., U.S. | 210 | 42.15 N | 77.47 W |
| Alfred National Park ♠ | 166 | 37.35 S | 149.20 E |
| Alfredo M. Terrazas | 234 | 21.28 N | 98.51 W |
| Alfreton | 44 | 53.06 N | 1.23 W |
| Alfriston | 42 | 50.48 N | 0.10 E |
| Alfta | 26 | 61.21 N | 16.05 E |
| Alfter | 56 | 50.44 N | 7.01 E |
| Al-Fujayrah | 128 | 25.06 N | 56.21 E |
| Al-Fuqahā' | 146 | 27.50 N | 16.22 E |
| Al-Furzul | 132 | 33.52 N | 35.56 E |
| Alga | 86 | 49.46 N | 57.20 E |
| Algabas, Kaz. | 80 | 50.39 N | 52.07 E |
| Algabas, Kaz. | 86 | 44.41 N | 78.06 E |
| Algabas, Kaz. | 86 | 48.21 N | 81.39 E |
| Algači | 88 | 50.43 N | 117.47 E |
| Ålgarås | 40 | 58.48 N | 14.14 E |
| Ålgård | 26 | 58.46 N | 5.51 E |
| Al-Garef | 140 | 12.03 N | 34.19 E |
| Algarrobal | 252 | 28.08 S | 70.39 W |
| Algarrobo, Arg. | 252 | 38.53 S | 63.08 W |
| Algarrobo, Arg. | 252 | 31.44 S | 68.18 W |
| Algarrobo, Chile | 252 | 33.22 S | 71.40 W |
| Algarrobo del Águila | 252 | 36.26 S | 67.09 W |
| Algarve □ 9 | 34 | 37.10 N | 8.15 W |
| Algás ≃ | 34 | 41.13 N | 0.16 E |
| Algasovo | 76 | 53.41 N | 41.40 E |
| Al-Gebir | 140 | 13.43 N | 29.49 E |
| Algeciras, Col. | 246 | 2.35 N | 75.18 W |
| Algeciras, Esp. | 34 | 36.08 N | 5.30 W |
| Algemesí | 34 | 39.11 N | 0.26 W |
| Algena | 144 | 17.19 N | 38.31 E |
| Alger → El Djazaïr, Alg. | 148 | 36.47 N | 3.03 E |
| Alger, Oh., U.S. | 216 | 40.42 N | 83.50 W |
| Alger, Baie d' c | 34 | 36.50 N | 3.15 E |
| Algeria (Algérie) □ 1, Afr. | 134 | 28.00 N | 3.00 E |
| Algeria (Algérie) □ 1, Afr. | 148 | 28.00 N | 3.00 E |
| Algérie → Algeria □ 1 | 148 | 28.00 N | 3.00 E |
| Algerien → Algeria □ 1 | 148 | 28.00 N | 3.00 E |
| Algermissen | 52 | 52.15 N | 9.58 E |
| Algés | 266c | 38.42 N | 9.13 W |
| Al-Ghāb ⊜ | 130 | 35.30 N | 36.18 E |
| Al-Gharaq as-Sulṭānī | 142 | 29.08 N | 30.42 E |
| Al-Gharbīyah □ 4 | 142 | 30.45 N | 31.00 E |
| Al-Ghāriyah | 132 | 32.23 N | 36.39 E |
| Al-Ghāṭ | 128 | 26.00 N | 45.03 E |
| Al-Ghawr V | 132 | 31.50 N | 35.30 E |
| Al-Ghayatah | 142 | 30.57 N | 30.06 E |
| Al-Ghayḍah | 118 | 16.12 N | 52.15 E |
| Al-Ghazālah | 128 | 26.48 N | 41.19 E |
| Al-Ghazālī | 142 | 30.49 N | 31.49 E |
| Al-Ghāzīyah | 132 | 33.31 N | 35.22 E |
| Alghero | 71 | 40.34 N | 8.19 E |
| Al-Ghurayfah | 128 | 24.00 N | 56.29 E |
| Al-Ghurdaqah | 140 | 27.14 N | 33.50 E |
| Algier → El Djazaïr | 148 | 36.47 N | 3.03 E |
| Algiers → El Djazaïr | 148 | 36.47 N | 3.03 E |
| Alginet | 34 | 39.16 N | 0.28 W |
| Algoa | 222 | 29.24 N | 95.11 W |
| Algoabaai c | 158 | 33.50 S | 25.50 E |
| Algodão, Ilha do I | 256 | 23.13 S | 44.36 W |
| Algodón ≃ | 246 | 2.23 S | 71.56 W |
| Algodones | 200 | 35.22 N | 106.28 W |
| Algodor ≃ | 34 | 39.55 N | 3.53 W |
| Algoma | 190 | 44.36 N | 87.25 W |
| Algoma Mills | 190 | 46.10 N | 82.50 W |
| Algona, Ia., U.S. | 190 | 43.04 N | 94.13 W |
| Algona, Wa., U.S. | 224 | 47.16 N | 122.15 W |
| Algonac | 214 | 42.37 N | 82.31 W |
| Algonquin | 216 | 42.09 N | 88.17 W |
| Algonquin Lake ⊜ | 216 | 42.40 N | 85.20 W |
| Algonquin Provincial Park ♠ | 190 | 45.45 N | 78.26 W |
| Algood | 194 | 36.11 N | 85.26 W |
| Algorta, Esp. | 34 | 43.22 N | 3.01 W |
| Algorta, Ur. | 252 | 32.25 S | 57.23 W |
| Alguierão-Mem Martins | 266c | 38.48 N | 9.20 W |
| Al-Ḥaddādī | 142 | 31.20 N | 30.47 E |
| Al-Ḥaddayn | 142 | 30.44 N | 30.38 E |
| Al-Ḥadīthah | 128 | 34.07 N | 42.23 E |
| Al-Ḥaḍr | 128 | 35.35 N | 42.44 E |
| Al-Haffah | 130 | 35.35 N | 36.02 E |
| Al-Ḥafīr Al-Fawqānī | 132 | 33.42 N | 36.28 E |
| Al-Ḥajālīj | 140 | 14.36 N | 31.54 E |
| Al-Ḥajarah ◆ 1 | 128 | 30.00 N | 44.00 E |
| Al-Ḥajar al-Gharbī ⋏ | 128 | 24.10 N | 56.15 E |
| Al-Ḥajar ash-Sharqī ⋏ | 128 | 22.45 N | 59.00 E |
| Al Hajeb | 148 | 33.43 N | 5.13 W |
| Al-Ḥājir | 142 | 30.41 N | 31.49 E |
| Al-Ḥalfāyah | 128 | 31.49 N | 47.26 E |
| Al-Ḥamād ⌓ | 128 | 32.00 N | 39.30 E |
| Alhama de Granada | 34 | 37.00 N | 3.59 W |
| Alhama de Murcia | 34 | 37.51 N | 1.25 W |
| Al-Ḥamal ◆ 1 | 128 | 23.30 N | 49.45 E |
| Alhambra, Ca., U.S. | 228 | 34.05 N | 118.07 W |
| Alhambra, Il., U.S. | 219 | 38.53 N | 89.44 W |
| Al-Ḥamīdīyah | 130 | 34.43 N | 35.56 E |
| Al-Ḥammām | 140 | 30.50 N | 29.23 E |
| Al-Ḥamrā', Ar. Su. | 128 | 23.57 N | 38.52 E |
| 'Al-Ḥamrā', Lubnān | 132 | 33.42 N | 35.27 E |
| Al-Ḥamrah | 142 | 31.10 N | 30.52 E |
| Al-Ḥāmūl | 142 | 31.19 N | 31.10 E |
| Alhandra | 250 | 7.26 S | 34.54 W |
| Alhandra, Mouchão de I | 266c | 38.54 N | 9.00 W |
| Al-Ḥarāk | 132 | 32.44 N | 36.18 E |
| Al-Ḥarīq | 128 | 23.37 N | 46.31 E |
| Al-Ḥārrah | 132 | 33.03 N | 36.00 E |
| Al-Ḥarrah ⌓ 9 | 128 | 31.00 N | 38.30 E |
| Al-Harūj al-Aswad ⋏ 2 | 146 | 27.00 N | 17.10 E |
| Al-Ḥasakah | 130 | 36.29 N | 40.45 E |
| Al-Ḥasakah □ 8 | 130 | 36.30 N | 41.00 E |
| Al-Ḥasānī I | 128 | 24.58 N | 37.05 E |
| Alhaurín el Grande | 34 | 36.38 N | 4.41 W |
| Al-Hawāmidīyah | 273c | 29.54 N | 31.15 E |
| Al-Ḥawātah | 140 | 13.25 N | 34.38 E |
| Al-Hawātikah | 142 | 27.16 N | 31.01 E |
| Al-Ḥawrah | 144 | 13.49 N | 47.37 E |
| Al-Ḥawṭah | 144 | 15.50 N | 48.27 E |
| Al-Hawwārīyah | 142 | 30.58 N | 29.41 E |
| Al-Ḥayy, 'Irāq | 128 | 32.10 N | 46.03 E |
| Al-Ḥayy, Miṣr | 142 | 29.39 N | 31.18 E |
| Al-Ḥayyānīyah | 128 | 28.38 N | 42.45 E |
| Al-Ḥayz | 140 | 28.02 N | 28.39 E |
| Al-Ḥībah | 142 | 28.45 N | 30.55 E |
| Al-Ḥījānah | 132 | 33.21 N | 36.33 E |
| Al-Ḥijāz ◆ 1 | 118 | 24.30 N | 38.30 E |
| Al-Ḥillah, 'Irāq | 128 | 32.29 N | 44.25 E |
| Al-Ḥillah, Sūd. | 140 | 13.27 N | 27.08 E |
| Al-Ḥilmīyah ◆ 8 | 273c | 30.07 N | 31.19 E |
| Al-Hindīyah | 128 | 32.33 N | 44.13 E |
| Al-Hirmil | 130 | 34.23 N | 36.23 E |
| Al-Ḥiṣn | 132 | 32.29 N | 35.52 E |
| Al-Hoceïma | 148 | 35.15 N | 3.55 W |
| Al-Hoceïma □ 4 | 148 | 35.00 N | 4.30 W |
| Al Hoceïma, Baie d' c | 34 | 35.20 N | 3.50 W |
| Alhos Vedros | 266c | 38.39 N | 9.02 W |
| Alhucemas, Peñón de I | 34 | 35.13 N | 3.53 W |
| Al-Ḥudayb | 140 | 13.00 N | 32.50 E |
| Al-Ḥudaydah | 144 | 14.48 N | 42.57 E |
| Al-Ḥufrah | 146 | 29.10 N | 18.02 E |
| Al-Ḥufrah ◆ 1 | 128 | 28.40 N | 38.30 E |
| Al-Hufūf | 128 | 25.22 N | 49.34 E |
| Al-Ḥulwah | 128 | 23.27 N | 46.47 E |
| Al-Ḥumayshah | 144 | 13.41 N | 45.52 E |
| Al-Ḥumrah ◆ 1 | 128 | 23.20 N | 54.30 E |
| Al-Ḥuṣayḥiṣah | 140 | 14.44 N | 33.18 E |
| Al-Ḥusaynīyah | 142 | 30.52 N | 31.55 E |
| Al-Ḥusaynīyah ⊤ 4 | 144 | 17.48 N | 44.27 E |
| Al-Ḥuwaylizah | 132 | 33.02 N | 35.51 E |
| Al-Ḥuwaymī | 144 | 14.05 N | 47.44 E |
| Al-Ḥuwayyiṭ | 128 | 25.36 N | 40.23 E |
| Alì | 70 | 38.02 N | 15.25 E |
| Ali ◆ 8 | 272a | 28.31 N | 77.18 E |
| 'Ālī, As-Sadd al- (Aswān High Dam) ◆ 6 | 140 | 23.58 N | 32.52 E |
| Alía, Esp. | 34 | 39.27 N | 5.13 W |
| Alia, It. | 70 | 37.47 N | 13.43 E |
| Äliabad, Azer. | 84 | 41.29 N | 46.37 E |
| 'Alīābād, Īrān | 128 | 36.57 N | 54.59 E |
| Alīābād, Pāk. | 123 | 36.18 N | 74.37 E |
| Aliade | 150 | 7.16 N | 8.28 E |
| Aliaga, Esp. | 34 | 40.40 N | 0.42 W |
| Aliağa, Tür. | 130 | 38.48 N | 26.59 E |
| Aliákmon ≃ | 38 | 40.30 N | 22.36 E |
| Aliákmonos, Tekhnití Límni ⊜ 1 | 38 | 40.15 N | 22.00 E |
| Aliaksin, Cape > | 180 | 55.30 N | 160.43 W |
| 'Alī al-Gharbī | 128 | 32.27 N | 46.41 E |
| Aliança | 250 | 7.35 S | 35.13 W |
| Aliano | 68 | 40.19 N | 16.14 E |
| Alībāg | 122 | 18.39 N | 72.54 E |
| Alibahadır ◆ 8 | 267b | 41.11 N | 29.12 E |
| Alibardak | 130 | 38.06 N | 40.25 E |
| Alibates Flint Quarries National Monument ♠ | 196 | 35.35 N | 101.39 W |
| Älibäyli | 84 | 41.23 N | 46.49 E |
| Äli Bayramlı | 84 | 39.56 N | 48.56 E |
| Alibey ≃ | 267b | 41.03 N | 28.56 E |
| Alibey, ozero ⊜ | 78 | 45.48 N | 30.02 E |
| Alibey Adası I | 130 | 39.20 N | 26.38 E |
| Alibey Barajı ⊜ 1 | 267b | 41.07 N | 28.55 E |
| Alibeyköy ◆ 8 | 267b | 41.04 N | 28.56 E |
| Alibijaban Island I | 116 | 13.20 N | 122.43 E |
| Alibori ≃ | 150 | 11.56 N | 3.17 E |
| Al-Ibrāhīmīyah | 142 | 30.57 N | 31.35 E |
| Alibunar | 38 | 45.05 N | 20.58 E |
| Alicante → Alacant | 34 | 38.21 N | 0.29 W |
| Alice, S. Afr. | 158 | 32.47 S | 26.50 E |
| Alice, Tx., U.S. | 196 | 27.45 N | 98.04 W |
| Alice ≃, Austl. | 164 | 15.22 S | 141.58 E |
| Alice ≃, Austl. | 166 | 24.02 S | 144.50 E |
| Alice, Punta > | 68 | 39.24 N | 17.10 E |
| Alice Arm | 182 | 55.29 N | 129.29 W |
| Alicedale | 158 | 33.19 S | 26.05 E |
| Alice Downs | 162 | 17.45 S | 127.56 E |
| Alice Springs | 162 | 23.42 S | 133.53 E |
| Alice Superiore | 62 | 45.28 N | 7.47 E |
| Alice Town | 238 | 25.44 N | 79.17 W |
| Aliceville | 194 | 33.07 N | 88.09 W |
| Alicia, Pil. | 116 | 16.45 N | 121.42 E |
| Alicia, Pil. | 116 | 7.30 N | 122.55 E |
| Alıcık | 130 | 40.49 N | 35.21 E |
| Alick Creek ≃ | 166 | 20.25 S | 142.00 E |
| Alicudi, Isola I | 70 | 38.32 N | 14.21 E |
| Alicurá, Embalse de ⊜ 1 | 254 | 40.40 S | 71.00 W |
| Al-'Idwah | 142 | 29.21 N | 30.55 E |
| Alief | 222 | 29.43 N | 95.35 W |
| Alife | 68 | 41.20 N | 14.20 E |
| Al-Ifranj | 132 | 31.11 N | 35.41 E |
| Alīganj, India | 124 | 28.07 N | 80.36 E |
| Alīganj, India | 124 | 27.30 N | 79.11 E |
| Alīgarh | 124 | 27.53 N | 78.05 E |
| Alignements de Carnac ⊥ | 32 | 47.35 N | 3.05 W |
| Alīgūdarz | 128 | 33.24 N | 49.41 E |
| Alijos, Islas II | 232 | 24.57 N | 115.44 W |
| 'Alī Kheyl | 120 | 33.57 N | 69.43 E |
| Al-Ikhṣāṣ al-Qiblīyah | 142 | 29.42 N | 31.17 E |
| Al-Ikhwān II | 118 | 12.08 N | 53.10 E |
| Alikovo | 80 | 55.45 N | 46.45 E |
| Alima ≃ | 152 | 1.36 S | 16.36 E |
| Al-Imām ◆ 8 | 273c | 30.01 N | 31.10 E |
| Al-Imārāt al-'Arabīyah al-Muttaḥidah → United Arab Emirates □ 1 | 128 | 24.00 N | 54.00 E |
| Al-'Imārīyah | 142 | 27.37 N | 30.53 E |
| Alimena | 70 | 37.42 N | 14.07 E |
| Alimini Grande ⊜ | 68 | 40.12 N | 18.27 E |
| Alimini Piccolo ⊜ | 68 | 40.10 N | 18.27 E |
| Aliminusa | 70 | 37.52 N | 13.47 E |
| Alim Island I | 164 | 2.55 S | 147.05 E |
| Alimkent | 85 | 40.58 N | 69.11 E |
| Alimodian | 116 | 10.49 N | 122.26 E |
| Alindao | 152 | 5.02 N | 21.13 E |
| Alingsås | 26 | 57.56 N | 12.31 E |
| Ālīpur, India | 272b | 22.43 N | 88.12 E |
| Alipur, India | 272b | 22.55 N | 88.11 E |
| Alīpur, Pāk. | 123 | 29.23 N | 70.55 E |
| Ālīpur ◆ 8 | 126 | 22.31 N | 88.20 E |
| Ālīpur Duār | 124 | 26.29 N | 89.44 E |
| Alīpur Janūbi | 123 | 30.13 N | 71.18 E |
| Aliquippa | 214 | 40.38 N | 80.14 W |
| Aliquippa-Hopewell Airport ⊠ | 279b | 40.35 N | 80.17 W |
| Alīrājpur | 120 | 22.19 N | 74.21 E |
| Al-'Irāq | 132 | 31.05 N | 35.39 E |
| Al-'Irāq → Iraq □ 1 | 128 | 33.00 N | 44.00 E |
| Al-'Irqah | 144 | 13.30 N | 47.22 E |
| Ali-Sabieh | 144 | 11.09 N | 42.42 E |
| Al-'Īsāwīyah | 128 | 30.38 N | 37.53 E |
| Aliseda | 34 | 39.26 N | 6.41 W |
| Alise-Sainte-Reine | 58 | 47.32 N | 4.29 E |
| Alīshārī | 84 | 39.02 N | 47.15 E |
| Al-Iskandarīyah (Alexandria) | 142 | 31.12 N | 29.54 E |
| Al-Iskandarīyah □ 4 | 142 | 31.10 N | 29.53 E |
| Al-Ismā'īlīyah (Ismailia) | 142 | 30.35 N | 32.16 E |
| Al-Ismā'īlīyah □ 4 | 142 | 30.30 N | 32.15 E |
| Al-Ismā'īlīyah Military Base ■ | 142 | 30.35 N | 32.14 E |
| Aliso Canyon V, Ca., U.S. | 280 | 33.53 N | 117.40 W |
| Aliso Canyon V, Ca., U.S. | 280 | 34.18 N | 118.33 W |
| Aliso Creek ≃ | 228 | 33.31 N | 117.45 W |
| Al-Istiwā'īyah al-Gharbīyah □ 4 | 140 | 5.55 N | 28.15 E |
| Al-Istiwā'īyah ash-Sharqīyah □ 4 | 154 | 4.30 N | 33.00 E |
| Alistráti | 38 | 41.04 N | 23.57 E |
| Alitak, Cape > | 180 | 56.51 N | 154.21 W |
| Alitak Bay c | 180 | 57.00 N | 154.05 W |
| Alitanguo | 120 | 35.10 N | 83.30 E |
| Alì Terme | 70 | 38.01 N | 15.26 E |
| Alivérion | 38 | 38.24 N | 24.02 E |
| Aliwal North | 158 | 30.45 S | 26.45 E |
| Alix | 182 | 52.24 N | 113.11 W |
| Al-'Izzīyah | 142 | 27.13 N | 30.59 E |
| Al-Jabal al-Abyaḍ ∧ 2 | 142 | 28.46 N | 31.00 E |
| Al-Jabal al-Aḥmar ∧ 2 | 142 | 28.19 N | 31.07 E |
| Al-Jabalayn | 140 | 12.36 N | 32.48 E |
| Al-Jadīdah | 140 | 25.34 N | 28.51 E |
| Al-Jafādūn | 142 | 28.50 N | 30.48 E |
| Al-Jafr | 132 | 30.18 N | 36.13 E |
| Al-Jāfūrah ◆ 2 | 128 | 24.14 N | 50.00 E |
| Al-Jaghbūb | 146 | 29.45 N | 24.31 E |
| Al-Jaghbūb ⊤ 4 | 146 | 29.40 N | 24.43 E |
| Al-Jahrah | 128 | 29.20 N | 47.40 E |
| Al-Jamālīyah | 142 | 31.11 N | 31.51 E |
| Al-Jarnūs | 142 | 28.36 N | 30.43 E |
| Al-Jawf, Ar. Su. | 128 | 29.50 N | 39.52 E |
| Al-Jawf, Lībiyā | 146 | 24.11 N | 23.19 E |
| Al-Jawsh | 146 | 32.00 N | 11.40 E |
| Al-Jaylī | 140 | 16.01 N | 32.36 E |
| Al-Jazā'ir → Algeria □ 1 | 148 | 28.00 N | 3.00 E |
| Al-Jazīrah □ 4 | 140 | 14.30 N | 33.20 E |
| Al-Jazīrah ◆ 1 | 140 | 14.25 N | 33.00 E |
| Aljezur, Bra. | 287a | 22.40 S | 43.36 W |
| Aljezur, Port. | 34 | 37.19 N | 8.48 W |
| Al-Jibāb | 132 | 33.06 N | 36.15 E |
| Al-Jifārah | 128 | 23.59 N | 45.11 E |
| Al-Jifārah (Jeffara) ⌓ | 146 | 32.30 N | 11.45 E |
| Al-Jīzah (Giza), Miṣr | 142 | 30.01 N | 31.13 E |
| Al-Jīzah, Urd. | 132 | 31.43 N | 35.58 E |
| Al-Jīzah □ 4 | 142 | 29.46 N | 31.18 E |
| Al-Jubayl | 128 | 27.01 N | 49.40 E |
| Al-Jubayn | 140 | 12.07 N | 35.10 E |
| Al-Judaydah | 132 | 33.54 N | 35.34 E |
| Al-Judayyidah, Urd. | 132 | 31.32 N | 35.39 E |
| Al-Judayyidah, Urd. | 132 | 31.15 N | 35.49 E |
| Al-Jufrah ⊤ 4 | 146 | 29.10 N | 16.00 E |
| Al-Julaydah ⊤ 4 | 128 | 29.03 N | 45.38 E |
| Al-Junaynah, Miṣr | 142 | 31.06 N | 31.41 E |
| Al-Junaynah, Sūd. | 140 | 13.27 N | 22.27 E |
| Al-Junaynah, Sūrīy. | 132 | 32.54 N | 36.44 E |
| Al-Jundīyah | 142 | 28.34 N | 30.50 E |
| Aljustrel | 34 | 37.52 N | 8.10 W |
| Al-Kāb | 142 | 30.57 N | 32.18 E |
| Al-Kabrit Military Base ■ | 142 | 30.15 N | 32.29 E |
| Al-Kafr | 132 | 32.38 N | 36.38 E |
| Al-Kafr ash-Sharqī | 142 | 31.17 N | 31.10 E |
| Al-Kahfah | 128 | 27.04 N | 43.02 E |
| Alkali Creek ≃, Ab., Can. | 184 | 50.52 N | 110.30 W |
| Alkali Creek ≃, Wy., U.S. | 202 | 43.16 N | 107.40 W |
| Alkali Lake | 182 | 51.47 N | 122.14 W |
| Alkali Lake ⊜, Nv., U.S. | 204 | 41.42 N | 119.50 W |
| Alkali Lake ⊜, Or., U.S. | 202 | 42.58 N | 120.02 W |
| Alkamari | 146 | 13.24 N | 11.07 E |
| Al-Kāmilīn | 140 | 15.05 N | 33.11 E |
| Al-Karabah | 140 | 18.33 N | 33.42 E |
| Al-Karak | 132 | 31.11 N | 35.42 E |
| Al-Karak □ 8 | 132 | 31.10 N | 35.45 E |
| Al-Karnak | 140 | 25.43 N | 32.39 E |
| Al-Kawah | 140 | 13.44 N | 32.30 E |
| Al-Kawd | 144 | 13.05 N | 45.22 E |
| Al-Kawm | 130 | 35.11 N | 38.52 E |
| Al-Kawm al-Akhḍar | 142 | 30.58 N | 30.17 E |
| Al-Kawm Aṭ-Ṭawīl | 142 | 31.12 N | 31.05 E |
| Alken | 56 | 50.15 N | 7.26 E |
| Al-Khabrā' | 128 | 26.04 N | 43.33 E |
| Al-Khābūrah | 128 | 23.59 N | 57.08 E |
| Al-Khafaqān ⊜ | 128 | 23.24 N | 40.24 E |
| Al-Khalīl (Hebrón) | 132 | 31.32 N | 35.06 E |
| Al-Khālis | 128 | 33.49 N | 44.32 E |
| Al-Khandaq | 140 | 18.36 N | 30.34 E |
| Al-Khānkah | 142 | 30.13 N | 31.21 E |
| Al-Kharaqānīyah | 273c | 30.10 N | 31.10 E |
| Al-Khārijah | 140 | 25.26 N | 30.33 E |
| Al-Kharṭūm (Khartoum) | 140 | 15.36 N | 32.32 E |
| Al-Kharṭūm □ 4 | 140 | 15.45 N | 32.30 E |
| Al-Kharṭūm Baḥrī | 140 | 15.38 N | 32.33 E |
| Al-Khaṣab | 128 | 26.12 N | 56.15 E |
| Al-Khatam ◆ 1 | 128 | 24.00 N | 55.10 E |
| Al-Khirbah as-Samrā' | 132 | 32.11 N | 36.10 E |
| Al-Khiyām | 132 | 33.19 N | 35.36 E |
| Al-Khubar | 128 | 26.17 N | 50.12 E |
| Al-Khums (Homs) | 146 | 32.39 N | 14.16 E |
| Al-Khuraybah, Urd. | 132 | 32.40 N | 35.52 E |
| Al-Khuraybah, Yaman | 144 | 15.06 N | 48.19 E |
| Al-Khurmah | 144 | 21.54 N | 42.03 E |
| Al-Khushnīyah | 132 | 33.00 N | 35.48 E |
| Al-Khuṣūṣ | 273c | 30.09 N | 31.19 E |
| Al-Kifl | 128 | 32.14 N | 44.22 E |
| Al-Kiswah | 132 | 33.21 N | 36.14 E |
| Alkmaar | 52 | 52.37 N | 4.44 E |
| Alkoven | 61 | 48.17 N | 14.06 E |
| Al-Kūbrī | 142 | 30.02 N | 32.33 E |
| Al-Kūfah | 128 | 32.02 N | 44.24 E |
| Al-Kufrah (Cufra) ⊤ 4 | 146 | 24.20 N | 23.15 E |
| Al-Kunayyisah | 273c | 29.59 N | 31.11 E |
| Al-Kuntillah | 140 | 30.00 N | 34.41 E |
| Al-Kūt | 128 | 32.25 N | 45.49 E |
| Al-Kuwayt | 128 | 29.20 N | 47.59 E |
| Al-Kuwayt → Kuwait □ 1 | 128 | 29.30 N | 47.45 E |
| Alkvettern ⊜ | 40 | 59.25 N | 14.21 E |
| Allaben | 210 | 42.07 N | 74.22 W |
| Al-Labwah | 130 | 34.12 N | 36.21 E |
| Allacapan | 116 | 18.15 N | 121.35 E |
| Allach-Jun' | 74 | 61.08 N | 138.03 E |
| Allada | 150 | 6.39 N | 2.09 E |
| Al-Lādhiqīyah (Latakia) | 130 | 35.31 N | 35.47 E |
| Al-Lādhiqīyah □ 8 | 130 | 35.30 N | 36.00 E |
| Allagash ≃ | 186 | 47.05 N | 69.02 W |
| Allagen | 56 | 51.28 N | 8.14 E |
| Al-Lagowa | 140 | 11.24 N | 29.08 E |
| Allahābād, India | 124 | 25.27 N | 81.51 E |
| Allāhābād, Pāk. | 123 | 28.57 N | 70.53 E |
| Allāhbās | 272a | 28.31 N | 77.25 E |
| Allahüekber Dağları ⋏ | 130 | 40.35 N | 42.32 E |
| Al-Lāhūn | 142 | 29.13 N | 30.59 E |
| Allāhwardipur | 272a | 28.33 N | 77.26 E |
| Allaines | 50 | 48.12 N | 1.50 E |
| Allaire State Park ♠ | 208 | 40.08 N | 74.08 W |
| Allakaket | 180 | 66.34 N | 152.41 W |
| Allaman | 58 | 46.28 N | 6.24 E |
| Allamuchy | 210 | 40.55 N | 74.48 W |
| Allan | 184 | 51.53 N | 106.04 W |
| Allan, Pointe > | 275a | 45.26 N | 73.45 W |
| Allanche | 32 | 45.14 N | 2.56 E |
| Alland | 61 | 48.03 N | 16.05 E |
| Allan Island I | 224 | 48.28 N | 122.42 W |
| Allanmyo | 110 | 19.22 N | 95.13 E |
| Allanridge | 158 | 27.55 S | 26.44 E |
| Allanson | 168a | 33.20 S | 116.06 E |
| Allanton | 46 | 55.47 N | 3.51 W |
| Allan Water ≃ | 46 | 56.08 N | 3.56 W |
| Allapattah Flats ⠿ | 220 | 27.08 N | 80.27 W |
| 'Allāq, Bi'r ⊤ 4 | 146 | 31.05 N | 11.42 E |
| 'Allāqī, Wādī al- V | 140 | 22.42 N | 33.12 E |
| Allard, Lac ⊜ | 186 | 50.32 N | 63.31 W |
| Allardt | 194 | 36.22 N | 84.53 W |
| Allariz | 34 | 42.11 N | 7.48 W |
| Allatoona Lake ⊜ 1 | 192 | 34.08 N | 84.38 W |
| Allauch | 62 | 43.20 N | 5.29 E |
| Al-Layyah | 140 | 16.16 N | 35.25 E |
| Alldays | 156 | 22.44 S | 29.04 E |
| Alle, Bel. | 56 | 49.51 N | 4.58 E |
| Alle, Schw. | 58 | 47.26 N | 7.08 E |
| Älleberg ∧ 2 | 26 | 58.08 N | 13.36 E |
| Allegan | 216 | 42.31 N | 85.51 W |
| Allegan □ 6 | 216 | 42.35 N | 85.53 W |
| Allegan, Lake ⊜ | 216 | 42.33 N | 85.55 W |
| Allegany | 210 | 42.05 N | 78.29 W |
| Allegany □ 6 | 210 | 42.13 N | 78.02 W |
| Allegany Indian Reservation ◆ 4 | 210 | 42.10 N | 78.47 W |
| Allegany State Park ♠ | 210 | 42.04 N | 78.44 W |
| Alleghany | 226 | 39.28 N | 120.51 W |
| Alleghe | 64 | 46.24 N | 12.01 E |
| Allegheny □ 6 | 214 | 40.26 N | 79.59 W |
| Allegheny ≃ | 214 | 40.27 N | 80.00 W |
| Allegheny Acres | 279b | 40.37 N | 79.53 W |
| Allegheny Center ʊ | 279b | 40.27 N | 80.01 W |
| Allegheny County Airport ⊠ | 279b | 40.21 N | 79.56 W |
| Allegheny County Park ♠ | 279b | 40.34 N | 79.55 W |
| Allegheny Mountains ⋏ | 188 | 38.30 N | 80.00 W |
| Allegheny Observatory ʊ 3 | 279b | 40.29 N | 80.01 W |
| Allegheny Plateau ⋏ 1 | 188 | 41.30 N | 78.00 W |
| Allegheny Portage Railroad National Historic Site ⊥ | 214 | 40.28 N | 78.32 W |
| Allegheny Reservoir ⊜ 1 | 214 | 42.00 N | 78.56 W |
| Allègre | 62 | 45.12 N | 3.42 E |
| Allègre, Pointe > | 241o | 16.22 N | 61.45 W |
| Allemagne → Germany □ 1 | 30 | 51.00 N | 10.00 E |
| Allemands, Lac Des ⊜ | 194 | 29.55 N | 90.35 W |
| Allemanskraaldam ⊜ 1 | 158 | 28.16 S | 27.07 E |
| Allemant | 261 | 48.45 N | 1.37 E |
| Allemont | 62 | 45.08 N | 6.02 E |
| Allen, Arg. | 252 | 38.58 S | 67.50 W |
| Allen, Pil. | 116 | 12.30 N | 124.17 E |
| Allen, Md., U.S. | 208 | 38.17 N | 75.41 W |
| Allen, Mi., U.S. | 216 | 41.57 N | 84.46 W |
| Allen, Ne., U.S. | 198 | 42.24 N | 96.50 W |
| Allen, Ok., U.S. | 196 | 34.52 N | 96.24 W |
| Allen, Pa., U.S. | 208 | 40.10 N | 77.05 W |
| Allen, S.D., U.S. | 198 | 43.16 N | 101.55 W |
| Allen, Tx., U.S. | 222 | 33.06 N | 96.40 W |
| Allen, Wa., U.S. | 224 | 48.31 N | 122.23 W |
| Allen □ 6, In., U.S. | 216 | 41.04 N | 85.09 W |
| Allen □ 6, Oh., U.S. | 216 | 40.46 N | 84.06 W |
| Allen ≃ | 44 | 54.58 N | 2.19 W |
| Allen, Lough ⊜ | 48 | 54.08 N | 8.08 W |
| Allen, Mount ∧, N.Z. | 172 | 47.05 S | 167.48 E |
| Allen, Mount ∧, Ak., U.S. | 180 | 62.14 N | 142.13 W |
| Allenby Bridge ◆ 5 | 132 | 31.52 N | 35.52 E |
| Allendale, Il., U.S. | 194 | 38.32 N | 87.43 W |
| Allendale, Mi., U.S. | 216 | 42.58 N | 85.57 W |
| Allendale, N.J., U.S. | 276 | 41.02 N | 74.07 W |
| Allendale, S.C., U.S. | 192 | 33.00 N | 81.18 W |
| Allendale Town | 44 | 54.54 N | 2.15 W |
| Allende, Méx. | 232 | 28.20 N | 100.51 W |
| Allende, Méx. | 234 | 18.09 N | 94.16 W |
| Allendorf | 56 | 51.02 N | 8.38 E |
| Allenfarm | 222 | 30.24 N | 96.14 W |
| All England Lawn Tennis Club ♠ | 260 | 51.26 N | 0.13 W |
| Allen Grove | 216 | 42.35 N | 88.41 W |
| Allen Park | 216 | 42.15 N | 83.12 W |
| Allenport, Pa., U.S. | 214 | 40.20 N | 77.53 W |
| Allenport, Pa., U.S. | 214 | 40.06 N | 79.51 W |
| Allensbach | 58 | 47.43 N | 9.03 E |
| Allenstein → Olsztyn | 30 | 53.48 N | 20.29 E |
| Allensville | 214 | 40.32 N | 77.49 W |
| Allenton, Mi., U.S. | 214 | 42.55 N | 82.57 W |
| Allenton, R.I., U.S. | 207 | 41.32 N | 71.28 W |
| Allentown, N.J., U.S. | 208 | 40.10 N | 74.35 W |
| Allentown, N.Y., U.S. | 210 | 42.05 N | 78.03 W |
| Allentown, Oh., U.S. | 216 | 40.46 N | 84.12 W |
| Allentown, Pa., U.S. | 208 | 40.36 N | 75.28 W |
| Allentsteig | 61 | 48.42 N | 15.20 E |
| Allenwood, N.J., U.S. | 208 | 40.12 N | 74.13 W |
| Allenwood, N.Y., U.S. | 276 | 40.48 N | 73.44 W |
| Allenwood, Pa., U.S. | 210 | 41.07 N | 76.54 W |
| Alleppey | 122 | 9.29 N | 76.19 E |
| Aller ≃ | 30 | 52.57 N | 9.11 E |
| Allerona | 66 | 42.49 N | 11.58 E |
| Allersberg | 60 | 49.15 N | 11.15 E |
| Allershausen | 60 | 48.26 N | 11.36 E |
| Allerslev | 41 | 55.05 N | 12.03 E |
| Allerton, Ia., U.S. | 190 | 40.42 N | 93.21 W |
| Allerton, Ma., U.S. | 283 | 42.18 N | 70.53 W |
| Allerton ◆ 8 | 262 | 53.22 N | 2.53 W |
| Allerton, Point > | 207 | 42.18 N | 70.53 W |
| Allestree | 42 | 52.57 N | 1.29 W |
| Allevard | 62 | 45.24 N | 6.04 E |
| Alley Park ♠ | 276 | 40.45 N | 73.44 W |
| Alleyton | 222 | 29.43 N | 96.29 W |
| Allgäu ◆ 1 | 58 | 47.35 N | 10.10 E |
| Allgäuer Alpen ⋏ | 58 | 47.20 N | 10.25 E |
| Allhallows | 260 | 51.28 N | 0.39 E |
| Alli ≃ | 68 | 38.51 N | 16.40 E |
| Alliance, Ab., Can. | 182 | 52.26 N | 111.47 W |
| Alliance, Ne., U.S. | 198 | 42.12 N | 102.58 W |
| Alliance, Oh., U.S. | 214 | 40.54 N | 81.06 W |
| Allibaudières | 50 | 48.35 N | 4.07 E |
| Al-Lidām | 144 | 20.29 N | 44.50 E |
| Allier □ 5 | 32 | 46.25 N | 3.00 E |
| Allier ≃ | 32 | 46.58 N | 3.04 E |
| Alligator ≃ | 192 | 35.58 N | 75.58 W |
| Alligator Creek ≃, Ga., U.S. | 192 | 31.58 N | 82.22 W |
| Alligator Creek ≃, Tx., U.S. | 222 | 30.42 N | 97.07 W |
| Alligator Lake ⊜ | 220 | 28.13 N | 81.13 W |
| Alligator Pond | 241q | 17.52 N | 77.34 W |
| Alligny-en-Morvan | 50 | 47.12 N | 4.10 E |
| Allihies | 48 | 51.38 N | 10.03 W |
| Allinagaram | 122 | 10.02 N | 77.30 E |
| Allinge | 26 | 55.16 N | 14.49 E |
| Allington Castle ⊥ | 260 | 51.17 N | 0.31 E |
| Al-Lisān > 1 | 132 | 31.17 N | 35.28 E |
| Al-Lisht | 142 | 29.34 N | 31.14 E |
| Allison | 190 | 42.45 N | 92.47 W |
| Allison, Mount ∧ | 282 | 37.30 N | 121.52 W |
| Allison Gulch V | 280 | 34.16 N | 117.44 W |
| Allison Park | 214 | 40.34 N | 79.57 W |
| Alliste | 68 | 39.57 N | 18.05 E |
| Alliston | 212 | 44.09 N | 79.52 W |
| Al-Līth | 144 | 20.09 N | 40.16 E |
| Allmendingen | 58 | 48.20 N | 9.43 E |
| Alloa | 46 | 56.07 N | 3.49 W |
| Allochio, Galleria degli ◆ 5 | 66 | 44.03 N | 11.30 E |
| Allogny | 50 | 47.13 N | 2.19 E |
| Allonby | 44 | 54.46 N | 3.25 W |
| Alloné Abba | 132 | 32.44 N | 35.10 E |
| Allonnes, Fr. | 50 | 48.20 N | 1.40 E |
| Allonnes, Fr. | 50 | 47.58 N | 0.09 E |
| Allora | 171a | 28.02 S | 151.59 E |
| Allos | 62 | 44.14 N | 6.38 E |
| Allos, Col d' )( | 62 | 44.18 N | 6.36 E |
| Allott, Mount ∧ 2 | 162 | 26.06 S | 124.46 E |
| Allouez | 190 | 44.28 N | 88.00 W |
| Alloway | 208 | 39.33 N | 75.21 W |
| Alloway Creek ≃ | 208 | 39.27 N | 75.30 W |
| Allport | 214 | 40.58 N | 78.12 W |
| Allred Peak ∧ | 200 | 40.32 N | 108.33 W |
| All Saints | 240c | 17.03 N | 61.48 W |
| Allschwil | 58 | 47.33 N | 7.33 E |
| Allstedt | 54 | 51.24 N | 11.23 E |
| Allston ◆ 8 | 283 | 42.22 N | 71.08 W |
| Alluets, Forêt des ♠ | 261 | 48.55 N | 1.55 E |
| Al-Luḥayyah | 144 | 15.42 N | 42.42 E |
| Allumette Lake ⊜ | 190 | 45.53 N | 77.13 W |
| Allumettes, Île des I | 190 | 45.50 N | 77.05 W |
| Allumiere | 66 | 42.09 N | 11.54 E |
| Allview Estates | 208 | 39.12 N | 76.51 W |
| Allyn | 224 | 47.23 N | 122.49 W |
| Alm ≃ | 60 | 48.05 N | 13.55 E |
| Alma, N.B., Can. | 186 | 45.36 N | 64.57 W |
| Alma, P.Q., Can. | 186 | 48.33 N | 71.39 W |
| Alma, Ar., U.S. | 194 | 35.28 N | 94.13 W |
| Alma, Ga., U.S. | 192 | 31.32 N | 82.27 W |
| Alma, Il., U.S. | 219 | 38.43 N | 88.55 W |
| Alma, Ks., U.S. | 198 | 39.01 N | 96.17 W |
| Alma, Mi., U.S. | 190 | 43.22 N | 84.39 W |
| Alma, Ne., U.S. | 198 | 40.05 N | 99.21 W |
| Alma, N.Y., U.S. | 210 | 42.01 N | 78.03 W |
| Alma, Wi., U.S. | 190 | 44.19 N | 91.54 W |
| Al-Ma'ābidah | 142 | 27.20 N | 31.01 E |
| Al-Ma'ādī ◆ 8 | 142 | 29.58 N | 31.15 E |
| Alma-Ata → Almaty | 85 | 43.15 N | 76.57 E |
| Alma-Atinskij zapovednik ♠ | 85 | 43.10 N | 77.25 E |
| Alma Center | 190 | 44.26 N | 90.54 W |
| Almada | 34 | 38.41 N | 9.09 W |
| Almaden, Austl. | 166 | 17.20 S | 144.41 E |
| Almadén, Esp. | 34 | 38.46 N | 4.50 W |
| Almadén de la Plata | 34 | 37.52 N | 6.04 W |
| Al-Madīnah (Medina) | 128 | 24.28 N | 39.36 E |
| Al-Madīnah al-Fikrīyah | 142 | 27.56 N | 30.49 E |
| Al-Madwar | 132 | 32.17 N | 36.00 E |
| Al-Mafāzah | 140 | 13.36 N | 34.33 E |
| Al-Mafraq | 132 | 32.21 N | 36.12 E |
| Al-Mafraq □ 8 | 132 | 32.15 N | 36.30 E |
| Almafuerte | 252 | 32.12 S | 64.15 W |
| Al-Maghārīm | 144 | 15.01 N | 47.51 E |
| Al-Maghrah ⊤ 4 | 140 | 30.14 N | 28.56 E |
| Almagor | 132 | 32.55 N | 35.36 E |
| Almagre, Laguna c | 234 | 23.48 N | 97.48 W |
| Al-Magreb → Morocco □ 1 | 148 | 32.00 N | 5.00 W |
| Almagro | 34 | 38.53 N | 3.43 W |
| Almagro Island I | 116 | 11.56 N | 124.18 E |
| Al-Maḥallah al-Kubrā | 142 | 30.58 N | 31.10 E |
| Al-Maḥārīq | 140 | 25.37 N | 30.39 E |
| Al Mahbas | 148 | 27.13 N | 9.44 W |
| Alma Hill ∧ 2 | 210 | 42.03 N | 78.01 W |
| Al-Maḥmūdīyah | 142 | 31.11 N | 30.32 E |
| Al-Maḥraṣ | 142 | 27.49 N | 30.48 E |
| Al-Maḥsamah | 142 | 30.34 N | 32.01 E |
| Al-Majdal | 132 | 32.47 N | 36.30 E |
| Al-Majma'ah | 128 | 25.54 N | 45.20 E |
| Almăjului, Munţii ⋏ | 38 | 44.43 N | 22.12 E |
| Al-Maks ◆ 8 | 142 | 31.09 N | 29.51 E |
| Al-Mālikīyah | 130 | 37.10 N | 42.08 E |
| Almalyk | 85 | 40.50 N | 69.35 E |
| Al-Ma'mūrah ◆ 8 | 142 | 31.18 N | 30.03 E |
| Al-Manāmah | 128 | 26.13 N | 50.35 E |
| Al-Manāqil | 140 | 14.15 N | 32.59 E |
| Al-Manāṣif ◆ 1 | 130 | 35.17 N | 40.50 E |
| Al-Manāwāt | 273c | 29.55 N | 31.14 E |
| Almanor, Lake ⊜ | 204 | 40.15 N | 121.08 W |
| Almansa | 34 | 38.52 N | 1.05 W |
| Al-Manshāh | 140 | 26.28 N | 31.48 E |
| Al-Manṣūrah, Golan | 132 | 33.08 N | 35.48 E |
| Al-Manṣūrah, Miṣr | 142 | 31.03 N | 31.23 E |
| Al-Manṣūrīyah | 142 | 30.08 N | 31.05 E |
| Almanza | 34 | 42.39 N | 5.02 W |
| Al-Manzilah | 142 | 31.09 N | 31.56 E |
| Almanzor ∧ | 34 | 40.15 N | 5.18 W |
| Almanzora ≃ | 34 | 37.14 N | 1.46 W |
| Almar ≃ | 34 | 40.54 N | 5.29 W |
| Al-Marāghah | 140 | 26.42 N | 31.36 E |
| Almargem do Bispo | 266c | 38.51 N | 9.16 W |
| Al-Marj | 146 | 32.30 N | 20.54 E |
| Al-Marj ◆ 8 | 273c | 30.09 N | 31.20 E |
| Almas | 250 | 11.33 S | 47.09 W |
| Almaş ≃ | 38 | 47.14 N | 23.19 E |
| Almas, Pico das ∧ | 255 | 13.33 S | 41.56 W |
| Al-Ma'sarah, Miṣr | 142 | 27.42 N | 30.52 E |
| Al-Ma'sarah, Miṣr | 142 | 31.13 N | 31.19 E |
| Al-Ma'sarah ◆ 8 | 142 | 29.54 N | 31.17 E |
| Al-Mashqūq | 132 | 32.24 N | 36.43 E |
| Al-Mashrafah | 130 | 34.50 N | 36.52 E |
| Al-Masīd | 140 | 15.15 N | 32.57 E |
| Almassora | 34 | 39.57 N | 0.03 W |
| Al-Matammah | 140 | 16.43 N | 33.22 E |
| Al-Maṭarīyah | 142 | 31.11 N | 32.02 E |
| Al-Maṭarīyah ◆ 8 | 142 | 30.07 N | 31.19 E |
| Al-Matnah | 140 | 13.47 N | 35.03 E |
| Almaty (Alma-Ata) | 85 | 43.15 N | 76.57 E |
| Almaty □ 8 | 86 | 44.00 N | 77.00 E |
| Al-Mawṣil (Mosul) | 128 | 36.20 N | 43.08 E |
| Al-Mayādīn | 130 | 35.01 N | 40.27 E |
| Al-Maymūn | 142 | 29.14 N | 31.12 E |
| Almazán | 34 | 41.29 N | 2.32 W |
| Al-Mazār, Urd. | 132 | 31.04 N | 35.42 E |
| Almazar, Uzb. | 85 | 40.59 N | 68.54 E |
| Almaznyj | 83 | 48.02 N | 40.03 E |
| Almazovo | 265b | 55.51 N | 38.02 E |
| Al-Mazra'ah | 132 | 31.16 N | 35.31 E |
| Al-Mazzah | 132 | 33.30 N | 36.15 E |
| Alme | 56 | 51.28 N | 8.37 E |
| Almeer | 52 | 52.20 N | 5.14 E |
| Almeida | 34 | 40.43 N | 6.54 W |
| Almeirim, Bra. | 250 | 1.32 S | 52.34 W |
| Almeirim, Port. | 34 | 39.12 N | 8.38 W |
| Almelo | 52 | 52.21 N | 6.39 E |
| Almena | 198 | 39.53 N | 99.42 W |
| Almenara | 255 | 16.11 S | 40.42 W |
| Almenar de Soria | 34 | 41.41 N | 2.12 W |
| Almendares ≃ | 286b | 23.08 N | 82.25 W |
| Almendra, Embalse de ⊜ 1 | 34 | 41.15 N | 6.10 W |
| Almendralejo | 34 | 38.41 N | 6.24 W |
| Almenêches | 50 | 48.42 N | 0.07 E |
| Al'menevo | 86 | 54.57 N | 63.34 E |
| Almenno San Salvatore | 62 | 45.45 N | 9.35 E |
| Almería | 34 | 36.50 N | 2.27 W |
| Almería □ 4 | 34 | 37.10 N | 2.25 W |
| Almería, Golfo de c | 34 | 36.46 N | 2.30 W |
| Al'metjevsk | 80 | 54.53 N | 52.20 E |
| Al'mež | 24 | 60.03 N | 48.03 E |
| Älmhult | 26 | 56.33 N | 14.08 E |
| Al-Midhnab | 128 | 25.54 N | 44.14 E |
| Al-Mīnā' | 130 | 34.27 N | 35.49 E |
| Almina, Punta de > | 34 | 35.53 N | 5.15 W |
| Almino Afonso | 250 | 6.09 S | 37.46 W |
| Al-Minshāt al-Kubrā | 142 | 31.03 N | 30.54 E |
| Al-Minūfīyah □ 4 | 142 | 30.30 N | 31.00 E |
| Al-Minyā, Miṣr | 142 | 28.06 N | 30.45 E |
| Al-Minyā, Miṣr | 142 | 29.45 N | 31.18 E |
| Al-Minyā, Miṣr | 142 | 29.14 N | 30.45 E |
| Al-Minyā □ 4 | 142 | 28.26 N | 30.42 E |
| Al-Miqdādīyah | 128 | 33.59 N | 44.56 E |
| Almira | 202 | 47.42 N | 118.56 W |
| Almirantazgo, Islas → Admiralty Islands II | 164 | 2.10 S | 147.00 E |
| Almirantazgo, Montes → Admiralty Mountains ⋏ | 9 | 71.45 S | 168.30 E |
| Almirante | 236 | 9.18 N | 82.24 W |
| Almirante, Bahía de c | 236 | 9.20 N | 82.18 W |
| Almirante Brown | 258 | 34.48 S | 58.23 W |
| Almirante Brown □ 5 | 288 | 34.50 S | 58.20 W |
| Almirante Guillermo Brown, Parque ♠ | 288 | 34.40 S | 58.28 W |
| Almirante Latorre | 252 | 29.38 S | 70.58 W |
| Almirante Montt, Golfo ⊔ | 254 | 51.55 S | 72.45 W |
| Almirós | 38 | 39.11 N | 22.46 E |
| Almiroú, Kólpos c | 38 | 35.23 N | 24.20 E |
| Al-Mismīyah | 132 | 33.08 N | 36.23 E |
| Almo | 202 | 42.06 N | 113.37 W |
| Almoçageme | 266c | 38.48 N | 9.28 W |
| Almodôvar | 34 | 37.31 N | 8.04 W |
| Almodóvar del Campo | 34 | 38.43 N | 4.10 W |
| Almolonga | 236 | 14.49 N | 91.30 W |
| Almond, N.Y., U.S. | 210 | 42.19 N | 77.44 W |
| Almond, Wi., U.S. | 190 | 44.15 N | 89.24 W |
| Almond ≃, Scot., U.K. | 46 | 56.25 N | 3.27 W |
| Almond ≃, Scot., U.K. | 46 | 55.58 N | 3.18 W |
| Almondbank | 46 | 56.24 N | 3.33 W |
| Almondsbury | 42 | 51.34 N | 2.34 W |
| Almonesson | 208 | 39.49 N | 75.06 W |
| Almont | 214 | 42.55 N | 83.02 W |
| Almont ≃ | 261 | 48.32 N | 2.40 E |
| Almonte, On., Can. | 212 | 45.14 N | 76.12 W |
| Almonte, Esp. | 34 | 37.15 N | 6.31 W |
| Almonte, Ca., U.S. | 282 | 37.53 N | 122.32 W |
| Almonte ≃ | 34 | 39.42 N | 6.28 W |
| Almora | 124 | 29.37 N | 79.40 E |
| Almsee ⊜ | 64 | 47.45 N | 13.57 E |
| Älmsta | 40 | 59.58 N | 18.48 E |
| Al-Mu'aḍḍamīyah | 132 | 33.45 N | 36.39 E |
| Al-Mubarraz, Ar. Su. | 128 | 25.25 N | 49.35 E |
| Al-Mubarraz, Ar. Su. | 144 | 22.17 N | 46.44 E |
| Al-Mudawwarah | 128 | 29.19 N | 35.59 E |
| Almudévar | 34 | 42.03 N | 0.35 W |
| Al-Muglad | 140 | 11.02 N | 27.44 E |
| Al-Muḥarraq | 128 | 26.16 N | 50.37 E |
| Al-Mukallā | 144 | 14.32 N | 49.08 E |
| Al-Mukhā (Mocha) | 144 | 13.19 N | 43.15 E |
| Al-Munājāt al-Kubrā | 142 | 30.50 N | 32.01 E |
| Almuñécar | 34 | 36.43 N | 3.41 W |
| Almunge | 40 | 59.53 N | 18.03 E |
| Al-Muntazah ◆ 8 | 142 | 31.17 N | 30.01 E |
| Almus | 130 | 40.23 N | 36.5 E |
| Al-Musallamīyah | 140 | 14.34 N | 33.2 E |
| Al-Musayfirah | 132 | 32.37 N | 36.2[illegible] E |
| Al-Musayjīd | 128 | 24.05 N | 39.0[illegible] E |
| Al-Musayyib | 128 | 32.47 N | 44.1[illegible] E |
| Almus Barajı ⊜ 1 | 130 | 40.20 N | 37.0[illegible] E |
| Al-Mushannaf | 132 | 32.44 N | 36.46 E |
| Al-Musharrak Qiblī | 142 | 29.23 N | 30.34 E |
| Al-Mutā'iyah | 132 | 32.29 N | 36.17 E |
| Al-Mu'tamadīyah | 142 | 31.02 N | 31.05 E |
| Al-Mutayn | 132 | 33.54 N | 35.44 [illegible] |
| Al-Muthannā □ 4 | 128 | 30.30 N | 45.15 [illegible] |
| Al-Muṭī'ah | 142 | 27.08 N | 31.18 E |
| Al-Muwaqqar ⊥ | 132 | 31.49 N | 36.06 E |
| Al-Muwassam | 144 | 16.25 N | 42.20 E |
| Al-Muwayh | 144 | 22.45 N | 41.36 E |
| Al-Muwayliḥ | 128 | 27.41 N | 35.27 E |
| Aln ≃ | 44 | 55.23 N | 1.37 W |
| Alnarp | 41 | 55.39 N | 13.05 E |
| Al-Narrānīyah | 273c | 29.58 N | 31.10 E |
| Al'n'aš | 80 | 56.44 N | 54.43 E |
| Alnaši | 80 | 56.11 N | 52.28 E |
| Al-Nasser | 140 | 24.32 N | 32.55 E |
| Alne ≃ | 42 | 52.13 N | 1.52 W |
| Alness | 46 | 57.41 N | 4.15 W |
| Alnmouth | 44 | 55.23 N | 1.36 W |
| Alnön I | 26 | 62.25 N | 17.26 E |
| Alnor | 41 | 54.55 N | 9.36 E |
| Alnwick | 44 | 55.25 N | 1.42 W |
| Alnwick Indian Reserve ◆ 4 | 212 | 44.10 N | 78.06 W |
| Alo | 146 | 11.47 N | 20.53 E |
| Aloândia | 255 | 17.43 S | 49.29 W |
| Alofau | 174u | 14.16 S | 170.36 W |
| Alofi | 174v | 19.01 S | 169.55 W |
| Alofi, Île I | 14 | 14.21 S | 178.02 W |
| Alofi Bay c | 174v | 19.01 S | 169.56 W |
| Aloha | 224 | 45.29 N | 122.51 W |
| Aloha, Lake ⊜ | 226 | 38.52 N | 120.09 W |
| Aloi | 154 | 2.17 N | 33.10 E |
| Aloja | 76 | 57.46 N | 24.53 E |
| Alondra | 280 | 33.55 N | 118.15 W |
| Along | 120 | 28.18 N | 94.39 E |
| Alónnisos | 38 | 39.08 N | 23.50 E |
| Alónnisos I | 38 | 39.13 N | 23.55 E |
| Alor, Kepulauan II | 112 | 8.15 S | 124.30 E |
| Alor, Pulau I | 112 | 8.15 S | 124.45 E |
| Alor, Selat ⊔ | 112 | 8.20 S | 123.48 E |
| Álora | 34 | 36.48 N | 4.42 W |
| Alor Gajah | 114 | 2.23 N | 102.13 E |
| Alor Setar | 114 | 6.07 N | 100.22 E |
| Alor Star → Alor Setar | 114 | 6.07 N | 100.22 E |
| Alorton | 219 | 38.36 N | 90.08 W |
| Al'oškino | 88 | 58.35 N | 100.32 E |
| Al'ošn'a, Ross. | 76 | 53.38 N | 33.29 E |
| Al'ošn'a, Ross. | 82 | 54.14 N | 37.16 E |
| Alosno | 34 | 37.33 N | 7.07 W |
| Alost → Aalst | 50 | 50.56 N | 4.02 E |
| Alotau | 164 | 10.14 S | 150.30 E |
| Alouette ≃ | 224 | 49.16 N | 122.42 W |
| Alouette Lake ⊜ | 224 | 49.19 N | 122.28 W |
| Alovo | 80 | 54.38 N | 46.27 E |
| Aloxe-Corton | 58 | 47.04 N | 4.52 E |
| Aloysius, Mount ∧ | 162 | 26.01 S | 128.34 E |
| Alpachiri | 252 | 37.22 S | 63.46 W |
| Alpaugh | 226 | 35.53 N | 119.29 W |
| Alpen | 52 | 51.35 N | 6.30 E |
| Alpen → Alps ⋏ | 32 | 46.25 N | 10.00 E |
| Alpena, Ar., U.S. | 194 | 36.17 N | 93.17 W |
| Alpena, Mi., U.S. | 190 | 45.03 N | 83.25 W |
| Alpena, S.D., U.S. | 198 | 44.10 N | 98.21 W |
| Alpercatas ≃ | 250 | 6.02 S | 44.19 W |
| Alpes → Alps ⋏ | 32 | 46.25 N | 10.00 E |
| Alpes-de-Haute-Provence □ 5 | 62 | 44.10 N | 6.00 E |
| Alpes Dináricos → Dinara ⋏ | 36 | 43.50 N | 16.35 E |
| Alpes-Maritimes □ 5 | 62 | 44.00 N | 7.10 E |
| Alpes Marítimos → Maritime Alps ⋏ | 62 | 44.15 N | 7.10 E |
| Alpes Transilvanos → Carpaţii Meridionali ⋏ | 38 | 45.30 N | 24.15 E |
| Alpha, Austl. | 166 | 23.39 S | 146.38 E |
| Alpha, Il., U.S. | 190 | 41.12 N | 90.23 W |
| Alpha, Mi., U.S. | 190 | 46.02 N | 88.22 W |
| Alpha, N.J., U.S. | 210 | 40.40 N | 75.09 W |
| Alpharetta | 192 | 34.04 N | 84.17 W |
| Alphen aan den Rijn | 52 | 52.07 N | 4.40 E |
| Alphington | 42 | 50.42 N | 3.31 W |
| Alphin Pike ∧ 2 | 262 | 53.31 N | 2.00 W |
| Alphonse Island I | 138 | 7.00 S | 52.45 E |
| Alpi → Alps ⋏ | 32 | 46.25 N | 10.00 E |
| Alpi, Monte ∧ | 68 | 40.07 N | 15.59 E |
| Alpiarça | 34 | 39.15 N | 8.35 W |
| Alpi Dinariche → Dinara ⋏ | 36 | 43.50 N | 16.35 E |
| Alpignano | 62 | 45.06 N | 7.31 E |
| Alpilles, Chaîne des ⋏ 2 | 62 | 43.45 N | 4.50 E |
| Alpine, Az., U.S. | 200 | 33.50 N | 109.08 W |
| Alpine, Ca., U.S. | 204 | 32.50 N | 116.47 W |
| Alpine, N.J., U.S. | 276 | 40.57 N | 73.55 W |
| Alpine, N.Y., U.S. | 210 | 42.19 N | 76.44 W |
| Alpine, Tx., U.S. | 196 | 30.21 N | 103.39 W |
| Alpine □ 6 | 226 | 38.41 N | 119.47 W |
| Alpine Creek ≃ | 282 | 37.19 N | 122.17 W |
| Alpine National Park ♠ | 166 | 37.00 S | 147.15 E |
| Alpinópolis | 255 | 20.52 S | 46.23 W |
| Alpi Retiche → Rhaetian Alps ⋏ | 58 | 46.30 N | 10.00 E |
| Alpirsbach | 58 | 48.21 N | 8.23 E |
| Alplaus Kill ≃ | 210 | 42.51 N | 73.54 W |
| Alpnachstad | 58 | 46.57 N | 8.17 E |
| Alps ⋏ | 22 | 46.25 N | 10.00 E |
| Alpsee ⊜ | 58 | 47.34 N | 10.10 E |
| Alpu | 130 | 39.47 N | 30.58 E |
| Al-Qābil | 128 | 23.57 N | 55.48 E |
| Al-Qābūn | 132 | 33.33 N | 36.20 E |
| Al-Qadam | 132 | 33.28 N | 36.17 E |
| Al-Qaḍārif | 140 | 14.02 N | 35.24 E |
| Al-Qaḍīmah | 144 | 22.21 N | 39.09 E |
| Al-Qādisīyah □ 4 | 128 | 31.55 N | 45.00 E |
| Al-Qāhirah (Cairo), Miṣr | 142 | 30.03 N | 31.15 E |
| Al-Qāhirah (Cairo), Miṣr | 273c | 30.03 N | 31.15 E |
| Al-Qāhirah □ 4 | 142 | 30.02 N | 31.17 E |
| Al-Qāhirah West Military Base ■ | 142 | 30.06 N | 30.56 E |
| Al-Qaḥmah | 144 | 18.00 N | 41.41 E |
| Al-Qā'im | 128 | 34.21 N | 41.07 E |
| Al-Qā'īyah ⊤ 4 | 128 | 26.27 N | 45.35 E |
| Al-Qāiyāt | 142 | 28.40 N | 30.41 E |
| Al-Qalaj | 142 | 30.11 N | 31.21 E |
| Al-Qalībah | 128 | 28.32 N | 37.42 E |
| Al-Qalyūbīyah □ 4 | 142 | 30.18 N | 31.18 E |
| Al-Qāmishlī | 130 | 37.02 N | 41.14 E |
| Al-Qanāṭir al-Khayrīyah | 142 | 30.12 N | 31.08 E |
| Al-Qanāyāt | 142 | 30.37 N | 31.28 E |
| Al-Qanṭarah | 142 | 30.52 N | 32.19 E |
| Al-Qaryah ash-Sharqīyah | 146 | 30.24 N | 13.36 E |
| Al-Qaryatayn | 130 | 34.14 N | 37.14 E |
| Al-Qaṣabāt | 146 | 32.35 N | 14.03 E |
| Al-Qaṣābī | 142 | 31.16 N | 30.41 E |
| Al-Qaṣr, Miṣr | 140 | 25.42 N | 28.53 E |
| Al-Qaṣr, Urd. | 132 | 31.19 N | 35.45 E |
| Al-Qaṣṣāṣīn | 142 | 30.34 N | 31.56 E |
| Al-Qaṭīf | 128 | 26.33 N | 50.00 E |
| Al-Qaṭrānah | 132 | 31.15 N | 36.03 E |
| Al-Qaṭrūn | 146 | 24.56 N | 14.38 E |
| Al-Qaṭṭā | 142 | 30.13 N | 30.58 E |


| | | | | | |
|---|---|---|---|---|---|
| ≃ River | Fluß | Río | Rivière | Rio | |
| ≊ Canal | Kanal | Canal | Canal | Canal | |
| ⌞ Waterfall, Rapids | Wasserfall, Stromschnellen | Cascada, Rápidos | Chute d'eau, Rapides | Cascata, Rápidos | |
| ⊔ Strait | Meeresstraße | Estrecho | Détroit | Estreito | |
| c Bay, Gulf | Bucht, Golf | Bahía, Golfo | Baie, Golfe | Baía, Golfo | |
| ⊜ Lake, Lakes | See, Seen | Lago, Lagos | Lac, Lacs | Lago, Lagos | |
| ⠿ Swamp | Sumpf | Pantano | Marais | Pântano | |
| ⊓ Ice Features, Glacier | Eis- und Gletscherformen | Accidentes Glaciales | Formes glaciaires | Acidentes glaciares | |
| ⊤ Other Hydrographic Features | Andere Hydrographische Objekte | Otros Elementos Hidrográficos | Autres données hydrographiques | Outros acidentes hidrográficos | |

| | | | | |
|---|---|---|---|---|
| ✢ Submarine Features | Untermeerische Objekte | Accidentes Submarinos | Formes de relief sous-marin | Acidentes submarinos |
| □ Political Unit | Politische Einheit | Unidad Politica | Entité politique | Unidade política |
| ʊ Cultural Institution | Kulturelle Institution | Institución Cultural | Institution culturelle | Instituição cultural |
| ⊥ Historical Site | Historische Stätte | Sitio Histórico | Site historique | Sitio histórico |
| ♠ Recreational Site | Erholungs- und Ferienort | Sitio de Recreo | Centre de loisirs | Area de Lazer |
| ⊠ Airport | Flughafen | Aeropuerto | Aéroport | Aeroporto |
| ■ Military Installation | Militäranlage | Instalación Militar | Installation militaire | Instalação militar |
| ◆ Miscellaneous | Verschiedenes | Misceláneo | Divers | Diversos |

| Name | Page | Lat.°' | Long.°' |
|---|---|---|---|
| Al-Qaṭṭāwīyah | 142 | 30.33 N | 31.40 E |
| Al-Qays | 142 | 28.29 N | 30.47 E |
| Al-Qayṣūmah | 128 | 28.16 N | 46.03 E |
| Al-Qir'awn | 132 | 33.34 N | 35.43 E |
| Al-Qiṣfah | 132 | 32.38 N | 35.52 E |
| Al-Quds → Yerushalayim | 132 | 31.46 N | 35.14 E |
| Alquízar | 240p | 22.48 N | 82.35 W |
| Al-Qun'abah | 132 | 33.08 N | 35.40 E |
| Al-Qunayṭirah | 132 | 33.07 N | 35.49 E |
| Al-Qunayṭirah □[8] | 132 | 33.00 N | 35.50 E |
| Al-Qunfudhah | 144 | 19.08 N | 41.05 E |
| Al-Qurayn | 142 | 30.37 N | 31.44 E |
| Al-Qurayyah | 132 | 32.32 N | 36.36 E |
| Al-Qurnah | 128 | 31.00 N | 47.26 E |
| Al-Quṣaymah | 132 | 30.40 N | 34.22 E |
| Al-Quṣayr, Miṣr | 128 | 26.06 N | 34.17 E |
| Al-Quṣayr, Miṣr | 142 | 27.27 N | 30.52 E |
| Al-Quṣayr, Sūrīy. | 130 | 34.31 N | 36.35 E |
| Al-Qūṣīyah | 142 | 27.26 N | 30.49 E |
| Al-Quṭayfah | 132 | 33.44 N | 36.36 E |
| Al-Quṭaynah | 140 | 14.52 N | 32.21 E |
| Al-Quway'īyah | 128 | 24.03 N | 45.15 E |
| Al-Quwaysī | 140 | 13.20 N | 34.05 E |
| Alrø I | 41 | 55.51 N | 10.05 E |
| Alroy Downs | 162 | 19.18 S | 136.04 E |
| Als I | 41 | 54.59 N | 9.55 E |
| Alsace □[9] | 58 | 48.30 N | 7.30 E |
| Alsace, Ballon d' ∧ | 58 | 47.50 N | 6.51 E |
| Alsager | 44 | 53.06 N | 2.17 W |
| Al'šany | 78 | 52.05 N | 27.20 E |
| Alsask | 184 | 51.23 N | 109.59 W |
| Alsasua | 34 | 42.54 N | 2.10 W |
| Alsdorf | 56 | 50.53 N | 6.10 E |
| Alsea | 202 | 44.22 N | 123.35 W |
| Alsea ≃ | 202 | 44.26 N | 124.05 W |
| Alsek ≃ | 180 | 59.10 N | 138.10 W |
| Alsen | 198 | 48.37 N | 98.42 W |
| Alseno | 64 | 44.54 N | 9.59 E |
| Alsenz | 56 | 49.43 N | 7.49 E |
| Alsenz ≃ | 56 | 49.49 N | 7.51 E |
| Alsey | 219 | 39.34 N | 90.25 W |
| Alsfeld | 56 | 50.45 N | 9.16 E |
| Als Fjord ⊂[2] | 41 | 55.02 N | 9.38 E |
| Alsh, Loch ⊂ | 46 | 57.15 N | 5.39 W |
| Al-Shallūfa Military Base ■ | 142 | 30.03 N | 32.32 E |
| Alsike | 40 | 59.45 N | 17.45 E |
| Alsina | 252 | 33.54 S | 59.23 W |
| Alsip | 216 | 41.40 N | 87.44 W |
| Alsleben | 54 | 51.42 N | 11.41 E |
| Alsónémedi | 264c | 47.19 N | 19.10 E |
| Alstaden ◆[8] | 263 | 51.28 N | 6.50 E |
| Alstäket | 40 | 59.20 N | 18.28 E |
| Alstätte | 52 | 52.08 N | 6.55 E |
| Alstead ≃ | 184 | 55.50 N | 107.26 W |
| Alster | 40 | 59.24 N | 13.36 E |
| Alster ≃ | 52 | 53.36 N | 9.59 E |
| Alsterbro | 26 | 56.57 N | 15.55 E |
| Alstern ⊜ | 40 | 59.40 N | 13.55 E |
| Alston | 44 | 54.49 N | 2.26 W |
| Alsunga | 76 | 56.59 N | 21.34 E |
| Alswede | 52 | 52.20 N | 8.33 E |
| Alt ≃ | 44 | 53.32 N | 3.03 W |
| Alta, Nor. | 24 | 69.55 N | 23.12 E |
| Älta, Sve. | 40 | 59.16 N | 18.11 E |
| Alta, Ca., U.S. | 226 | 39.12 N | 120.49 W |
| Alta, Ia., U.S. | 198 | 42.40 N | 95.17 W |
| Alta, Cachoeira ⌊ | 250 | 5.46 S | 54.28 W |
| Alta, Mount ∧ | 172 | 44.30 S | 168.58 E |
| Altadena | 228 | 34.11 N | 118.07 W |
| Alta Floresta | 250 | 9.57 S | 56.06 W |
| Alta Gracia, Arg. | 252 | 31.40 S | 64.26 W |
| Altagracia, Nic. | 236 | 11.34 N | 85.35 W |
| Altagracia, Ven. | 246 | 10.43 N | 71.32 W |
| Altagracia de Orituco | 246 | 9.52 N | 66.23 W |
| Alta Hill | 226 | 39.14 N | 121.04 W |
| Altai ⋀ | 90 | 48.00 N | 90.00 E |
| Altair | 222 | 29.34 N | 96.28 W |
| Altaj, Mong. | 86 | 48.18 N | 89.35 E |
| Altaj (Jesönbulag), Mong. | 90 | 46.20 N | 96.18 E |
| Altaj, Ross. | 86 | 53.27 N | 91.48 E |
| Altaj □[3] | 86 | 51.00 N | 86.00 E |
| Altajskij | 86 | 51.58 N | 85.22 E |
| Alta Loma | 222 | 29.22 N | 95.04 W |
| Altamaha ≃ | 192 | 31.19 N | 81.17 W |
| Altamira, Arg. | 258 | 34.40 S | 59.22 W |
| Altamira, Bra. | 250 | 3.12 S | 52.12 W |
| Altamira, Chile | 252 | 25.47 S | 69.51 W |
| Altamira, C.R. | 236 | 10.30 N | 84.23 W |
| Altamira, Méx. | 234 | 22.24 N | 97.55 W |
| Altamira, Las Cuevas de ±[5] | 34 | 43.18 N | 4.08 W |
| Altamirano, Arg. | 258 | 35.21 S | 58.09 W |
| Altamirano, Méx. | 196 | 25.55 N | 97.47 W |
| Altamont, Il., U.S. | 219 | 39.03 N | 88.44 W |
| Altamont, Ks., U.S. | 198 | 37.11 N | 95.17 W |
| Altamont, N.Y., U.S. | 210 | 42.42 N | 74.02 W |
| Altamont, Or., U.S. | 202 | 42.12 N | 121.44 W |
| Altamont, Tn., U.S. | 194 | 35.25 N | 85.43 W |
| Altamonte Springs | 220 | 28.39 N | 81.21 W |
| Altamont Pass )( | 226 | 37.45 N | 121.40 W |
| Altamura | 68 | 40.50 N | 16.33 E |
| Altamura, Isla I | 232 | 25.00 N | 108.10 W |
| Altan, Ross. | 88 | 49.31 N | 111.32 E |
| Altan, Ross. | 88 | 49.53 N | 109.04 E |
| Altanbulag, Mong. | 88 | 50.19 N | 106.30 E |
| Altanbulag, Mong. | 88 | 47.41 N | 106.22 E |
| Altan-Cögor | 86 | 49.03 N | 90.27 E |
| Altanširee | 102 | 45.35 N | 110.27 E |
| Altar | 232 | 30.43 N | 111.44 W |
| Altar ≃ | 232 | 30.39 N | 111.53 W |
| Altar, Desierto de ◆[2] | 232 | 31.50 N | 114.15 W |
| Altar de Los Sacrificios ⊥ | 232 | 16.28 N | 90.32 W |
| Altare | 62 | 44.20 N | 8.20 E |
| Altario | 184 | 51.55 N | 110.09 W |
| Altarnun | 42 | 50.37 N | 4.30 W |
| Altar of the Earth ʊ[1] | 271a | 39.57 N | 116.24 E |
| Altar of the Moon ʊ[1] | 271a | 39.55 N | 116.20 E |
| Altar of the Sun ʊ[1] | 271a | 39.54 N | 116.27 E |
| Altar Wash V | 200 | 32.05 N | 111.19 W |
| Altaskij Kraj □[8] | 86 | 52.30 N | 83.00 E |
| Altastenberg | 56 | 51.11 N | 8.28 E |
| Altata, Méx. | 232 | 24.38 N | 107.55 W |
| Altata, Ross. | 80 | 51.07 N | 48.44 E |
| Alta Verapaz □[5] | 236 | 15.40 N | 90.00 W |
| Altavilla Irpina | 68 | 41.00 N | 14.47 E |
| Altavilla Milicia | 70 | 38.02 N | 13.32 E |
| Altavilla Silentina | 68 | 40.32 N | 15.08 E |
| Alta Vista, Ks., U.S. | 198 | 38.51 N | 96.29 W |
| Altavista, Va., U.S. | 192 | 37.06 N | 79.17 W |
| Altay, Ross. | 86 | 60.20 N | 68.58 E |
| Altay, Zhg. | 86 | 47.52 N | 88.07 E |
| Altay → Altaj □[3] | 86 | 51.00 N | 86.00 E |
| Alt Buchhorst | 264a | 52.26 N | 13.51 E |
| Altdöbern | 54 | 51.39 N | 14.02 E |
| Altdorf, Dtsch. | 60 | 48.34 N | 12.07 E |
| Altdorf, Schw. | 58 | 46.53 N | 8.39 E |
| Altdorf bei Nürnberg | 60 | 49.23 N | 11.21 E |
| Alte Donau ⊜ | 264b | 48.14 N | 16.26 E |
| Alteelva ≃ | 24 | 69.58 N | 23.23 E |
| Altefähr | 54 | 54.20 N | 13.07 E |
| Alteglofsheim | 60 | 48.55 N | 12.12 E |
| Alte Grund | 264a | 52.28 N | 13.47 E |
| Altena | 56 | 51.17 N | 7.40 E |
| Altenahr | 56 | 50.31 N | 6.59 E |
| Altenau | 52 | 51.48 N | 10.26 E |
| Altenbeken | 52 | 51.46 N | 8.56 E |
| Altenberg | 54 | 50.46 N | 13.45 E |
| Altenberge | 52 | 52.03 N | 7.27 E |
| Altenbruch | 52 | 53.49 N | 8.46 E |
| Altenbüren | 56 | 51.23 N | 8.30 E |
| Altenburg, Dtsch. | 54 | 50.59 N | 12.26 E |
| Altenburg, Öst. | 61 | 48.38 N | 15.35 E |
| Altenderne Oberbecker ◆[8] | 263 | 51.35 N | 7.33 E |
| Altendorf | 263 | 51.29 N | 7.40 E |
| Altendorf ◆[8] | 263 | 51.25 N | 7.06 E |
| Altendorf-Ulfkotte | 263 | 51.38 N | 7.00 E |
| Altenesch | 52 | 53.08 N | 8.37 E |
| Altenessen ◆[8] | 263 | 51.29 N | 7.00 E |
| Altenfelden | 60 | 48.29 N | 13.58 E |
| Altengamme ◆[8] | 52 | 53.25 N | 10.16 E |
| Altenglan | 56 | 49.33 N | 7.28 E |
| Altenhagen, Dtsch. | 52 | 52.03 N | 8.38 E |
| Altenhagen, Dtsch. | 54 | 53.45 N | 13.06 E |
| Altenhagen ◆[8] | 263 | 51.22 N | 7.28 E |
| Altenhof | 54 | 52.55 N | 13.43 E |
| Altenholz | 41 | 54.24 N | 10.07 E |
| Altenkirchen, Dtsch. | 54 | 54.38 N | 13.20 E |
| Altenkirchen (Westerwald), Dtsch. | 56 | 50.41 N | 7.38 E |
| Altenkrempe | 54 | 54.08 N | 10.49 E |
| Altenkunstadt | 54 | 50.07 N | 11.14 E |
| Altenmarkt an der Alz | 60 | 48.00 N | 12.32 E |
| Altenmünster | 58 | 48.28 N | 10.35 E |
| Altenoythe | 52 | 53.02 N | 7.52 E |
| Altenpleen | 54 | 54.21 N | 12.57 E |
| Altenstadt an der Waldnaab | 60 | 49.48 N | 12.10 E |
| Altensteig | 56 | 48.35 N | 8.37 E |
| Altentreptow | 54 | 53.42 N | 13.14 E |
| Altenvoerde | 263 | 51.18 N | 7.22 E |
| Altenwalde | 52 | 53.49 N | 8.40 E |
| Altenweddingen | 54 | 52.00 N | 11.31 E |
| Alte Oder ≃ | 54 | 52.52 N | 14.09 E |
| Alter do Chão | 34 | 39.12 N | 7.40 W |
| Alterosa | 256 | 21.15 S | 46.08 W |
| Alter Rhein ≃ | 263 | 51.35 N | 6.36 E |
| Altes Land ◆[1] | 52 | 53.33 N | 9.38 E |
| Altevatnet ⊜ | 24 | 68.32 N | 19.30 E |
| Altfraunhofen | 60 | 48.27 N | 12.10 E |
| Altfriedland | 54 | 52.38 N | 14.12 E |
| Altglashütten | 58 | 47.51 N | 8.06 E |
| Alt-Glienicke ◆[8] | 264a | 52.25 N | 13.32 E |
| Altgruland | 263 | 51.27 N | 7.41 E |
| Altha | 192 | 30.34 N | 85.07 W |
| Altham | 262 | 53.47 N | 2.21 W |
| Alt-Hartmannsdorf | 264a | 52.21 N | 13.50 E |
| Althea Lake ⊜ | 283 | 42.40 N | 71.23 W |
| Altheim | 60 | 48.15 N | 13.13 E |
| Altheimer | 194 | 34.19 N | 91.50 W |
| Althofen | 61 | 46.54 N | 14.27 E |
| Altıağaç | 84 | 40.50 N | 48.54 E |
| Altınekin | 130 | 38.19 N | 32.53 E |
| Altinho | 250 | 8.29 S | 36.04 W |
| Altınoluk | 130 | 39.34 N | 26.44 E |
| Altinópolis | 255 | 21.02 S | 47.23 W |
| Altınova | 130 | 39.13 N | 26.47 E |
| Altınözü | 130 | 36.08 N | 36.12 E |
| Altıntaş | 130 | 39.04 N | 30.07 E |
| Altınyaka | 130 | 36.34 N | 30.21 E |
| Altiplano ⋀[1] | 248 | 18.00 S | 68.00 W |
| Alt Käbelich | 54 | 53.29 N | 13.29 E |
| Altkirch | 58 | 47.37 N | 7.15 E |
| Altkirchen | 54 | 50.56 N | 12.21 E |
| Altlandsberg | 54 | 52.33 N | 13.43 E |
| Altlangerwisch | 264a | 52.19 N | 13.04 E |
| Altlewin | 54 | 52.42 N | 14.16 E |
| Altlüdersdorf | 54 | 53.02 N | 13.11 E |
| Altlünen | 52 | 51.38 N | 7.31 E |
| Altmannsdorf ◆[8] | 264b | 48.10 N | 16.20 E |
| Altmannstein | 60 | 48.54 N | 11.39 E |
| Altmar | 212 | 43.31 N | 76.00 W |
| Altmark ◆[1] | 54 | 52.40 N | 11.20 E |
| Alt Meteln | 54 | 53.45 N | 11.21 E |
| Altmittweida | 54 | 50.58 N | 12.57 E |
| Altmühl ≃ | 60 | 48.54 N | 11.54 E |
| Altmünster | 64 | 47.54 N | 13.45 E |
| Altnaharra | 46 | 58.16 N | 4.27 W |
| Alto, Mi., U.S. | 216 | 42.51 N | 85.22 W |
| Alto, Tx., U.S. | 222 | 31.39 N | 95.04 W |
| Alto, Cerro ∧, Méx. | 234 | 20.50 N | 100.22 W |
| Alto, Cerro ∧, Ca., U.S. | 226 | 35.25 N | 120.43 W |
| Alto Anapu ≃ | 250 | 2.15 S | 51.27 W |
| Alto Araguaia | 255 | 17.19 S | 53.12 W |
| Alto Cauale | 152 | 7.34 S | 16.16 E |
| Alto Cedro | 240p | 20.31 N | 75.58 W |
| Alto Chicapa | 152 | 10.53 S | 19.14 E |
| Alto Coité | 255 | 15.47 S | 54.20 W |
| Alto Cuito | 152 | 13.27 S | 18.49 E |
| Alto da Moóca ◆[8] | 287b | 23.34 S | 46.35 W |
| Alto da Serra | 256 | 22.53 S | 44.14 W |
| Alto de las Vizcachas, Cerro ∧ | 286e | 33.25 S | 70.26 W |
| Alto del Carmen | 252 | 28.46 S | 70.30 W |
| Alto de Ña Paula | 286c | 10.24 N | 66.48 W |
| Alto do Rio Doce | 255 | 21.02 S | 43.25 W |
| Altofonte | 70 | 38.03 N | 13.18 E |
| Alto Garças | 255 | 16.56 S | 53.32 W |
| Alto Ligonha | 154 | 15.30 S | 38.20 E |
| Alto Longá | 250 | 5.15 S | 42.12 W |
| Alto Lucero | 234 | 19.37 N | 96.43 W |
| Alto Molócuè | 154 | 15.38 S | 37.42 E |
| Altomonte | 68 | 39.42 N | 16.08 E |
| Altomünster | 60 | 48.23 N | 11.15 E |
| Alton, On., Can. | 212 | 43.52 N | 80.04 W |
| Alton, Eng., U.K. | 42 | 51.09 N | 0.59 W |
| Alton, Il., U.S. | 219 | 38.53 N | 90.11 W |
| Alton, Ia., U.S. | 198 | 42.59 N | 96.00 W |
| Alton, Ks., U.S. | 198 | 39.28 N | 98.56 W |
| Alton, Ky., U.S. | 218 | 38.04 N | 84.55 W |
| Alton, Mo., U.S. | 194 | 36.41 N | 91.23 W |
| Alton, N.H., U.S. | 188 | 43.27 N | 71.13 W |
| Alton, N.Y., U.S. | 210 | 43.13 N | 76.59 W |
| Alton, R.I., U.S. | 207 | 41.26 N | 71.43 W |
| Altona, Austl. | 162 | 27.34 S | 120.00 E |
| Altona, Austl. | 169 | 37.52 S | 144.50 E |
| Altona, Mb., Can. | 184 | 49.06 N | 97.33 W |
| Altona, In., U.S. | 216 | 41.21 N | 85.09 W |
| Altona ◆[8] | 52 | 53.32 N | 9.56 E |
| Altona Bay ⊂ | 274b | 37.53 S | 144.51 E |
| Altona North | 274b | 37.50 S | 144.51 E |
| Altona Sports Park ♦ | 274b | 37.52 S | 144.52 E |
| Altoona, Al., U.S. | 194 | 34.01 N | 86.19 W |
| Altoona, Fl., U.S. | 220 | 28.57 N | 81.38 W |
| Altoona, Ia., U.S. | 190 | 41.39 N | 93.28 W |
| Altoona, Ks., U.S. | 198 | 37.31 N | 95.39 W |
| Altoona, Pa., U.S. | 214 | 40.31 N | 78.23 W |
| Altoona, Wa., U.S. | 224 | 46.16 N | 123.39 W |
| Altoona, Wi., U.S. | 190 | 44.48 N | 91.26 W |
| Alto Pacajá ≃ | 250 | 3.07 S | 50.20 W |
| Alto Paraguai | 248 | 14.30 S | 56.31 W |
| Alto Paraguay □[5] | 248 | 21.00 S | 58.45 W |
| Alto Paraíso de Goiás | 255 | 14.07 S | 47.31 W |
| Alto Paraná □[5] | 252 | 25.00 S | 54.50 W |
| Alto Parnaíba | 250 | 9.06 S | 45.57 W |
| Alto Purús ≃ | 248 | 9.34 S | 70.36 W |
| Alto Río Mayo | 254 | 45.35 S | 71.06 W |
| Alto Río Senguer | 254 | 45.02 S | 70.50 W |
| Altos | 250 | 5.03 S | 42.28 W |
| Alto Santo | 250 | 5.31 S | 38.15 W |
| Alto Sucuriú | 255 | 19.19 S | 52.47 W |
| Altotonga | 234 | 19.46 N | 97.14 W |
| Altötting | 60 | 48.13 N | 12.40 E |
| Alto Volta → Burkina Faso □[1] | 150 | 13.00 N | 1.30 W |
| Alto Yurua ≃ | 248 | 9.24 S | 72.43 W |
| Altrincham | 44 | 53.24 N | 2.21 W |
| Alt Rüdersdorf | 264a | 52.28 N | 13.49 E |
| Alt Ruppin | 54 | 52.56 N | 12.50 E |
| Altshausen | 58 | 47.56 N | 9.32 E |
| Alt Stahnsdorf | 264a | 52.17 N | 13.53 E |
| Altstätten | 58 | 47.23 N | 9.33 E |
| Alt Töplitz | 264a | 52.26 N | 12.55 E |
| Altuchovo | 76 | 52.40 N | 34.20 E |
| Āltūn Kūprī | 128 | 35.45 N | 44.09 E |
| Altun Shan ⋀ | 90 | 38.00 N | 88.00 E |
| Alturas | 204 | 41.29 N | 120.32 W |
| Altus, Ar., U.S. | 194 | 35.26 N | 93.45 W |
| Altus, Ok., U.S. | 196 | 34.38 N | 99.20 W |
| Altus, Lake ⊜[1] | 196 | 34.56 N | 99.18 W |
| Altus Air Force Base ■ | 196 | 34.40 N | 99.16 W |
| Altusried | 58 | 47.48 N | 10.13 E |
| Altyaryk | 85 | 40.23 N | 71.30 E |
| Altykarasu | 86 | 49.12 N | 55.52 E |
| Altynaj | 86 | 57.04 N | 62.00 E |
| Altynasar ⊥ | 86 | 45.10 N | 63.07 E |
| Altynivka | 78 | 51.27 N | 33.10 E |
| Altynkul' | 85 | 40.48 N | 72.10 E |
| Altyntau | 86 | 44.08 N | 68.03 E |
| Altyn-Topkan | 85 | 40.38 N | 69.35 E |
| Alu I | 175e | 7.02 S | 155.47 E |
| Al-Ubayyiḍ | 140 | 13.11 N | 30.13 E |
| Alubijid | 116 | 8.35 N | 124.29 E |
| Alucra | 130 | 40.20 N | 38.46 E |
| Al-'Udaysāt | 140 | 25.35 N | 32.29 E |
| Al-Udayyah | 140 | 12.03 N | 28.17 E |
| Aluk | 140 | 8.26 N | 27.27 E |
| Alūksne | 76 | 57.25 N | 27.03 E |
| Al-'Ulā | 128 | 26.37 N | 37.52 E |
| Alum Bank | 214 | 40.14 N | 78.34 W |
| Alum Creek ≃ | 218 | 39.53 N | 82.54 W |
| Alum Creek Lake ⊜[1] | 214 | 40.15 N | 82.58 W |
| Aluminé | 254 | 39.13 S | 70.57 W |
| Aluminé ≃ | 254 | 39.50 S | 70.53 W |
| Aluminé, Lago ⊜ | 252 | 38.55 S | 71.09 W |
| Alum Rock Park ♦ | 282 | 37.24 N | 121.49 W |
| Alunda | 40 | 60.04 N | 18.05 E |
| Alunitdağ | 84 | 40.32 N | 46.03 E |
| Alupka | 78 | 44.26 N | 34.03 E |
| Al-'Uqaylah | 146 | 30.16 N | 19.12 E |
| Al-'Uqayr | 128 | 25.39 N | 50.12 E |
| Al-Uqṣur (Luxor) | 140 | 25.41 N | 32.39 E |
| Al-'Urayq ±[8] | 128 | 29.10 N | 39.15 E |
| Al-'Urayq ◆[1] | 128 | 24.47 N | 42.55 E |
| Al-Urdun → Jordan □[1] | 128 | 31.00 N | 36.00 E |
| Alushta | 78 | 44.42 N | 34.24 E |
| Al-'Uṭayshān ▾[4] | 140 | 16.25 N | 34.30 E |
| Al-'Uwaynāt | 146 | 25.46 N | 10.34 E |
| Al-'Uwaynidhīyah I | 128 | 26.37 N | 36.05 E |
| Al-'Uyaynah | 128 | 24.54 N | 46.23 E |
| Alva, Scot., U.K. | 46 | 56.09 N | 3.48 W |
| Alva, Fl., U.S. | 220 | 26.42 N | 81.36 W |
| Alva, Ok., U.S. | 196 | 36.48 N | 98.39 W |
| Alva ≃ | 34 | 40.18 N | 8.15 W |
| Alvada | 214 | 41.03 N | 83.24 W |
| Alvaiázere | 34 | 39.49 N | 8.23 W |
| Alvaneu-Bad | 58 | 46.40 N | 9.39 E |
| Älvängen | 26 | 57.58 N | 12.07 E |
| Alvanley | 262 | 53.16 N | 2.45 W |
| Alvarado, Méx. | 234 | 18.46 N | 95.46 W |
| Alvarado, Tx., U.S. | 222 | 32.24 N | 97.12 W |
| Alvarado, Lake ⊜[1] | 222 | 32.23 N | 97.15 W |
| Alvarães | 246 | 3.12 S | 64.50 W |
| Álvarez Jonte | 258 | 35.19 S | 57.28 W |
| Alvarinhos | 266c | 38.54 N | 9.22 W |
| Álvaro Obregón | 234 | 19.50 N | 101.05 W |
| Álvaro Obregón ◆[8] | 286a | 19.21 N | 99.12 W |
| Álvaro Obregón, Presa ⊜[1] | 232 | 27.55 N | 109.52 W |
| Alvastra ⊥ | 26 | 58.18 N | 14.39 E |
| Alvdal | 26 | 62.07 N | 10.39 E |
| Älvdalen | 26 | 61.14 N | 14.02 E |
| Alvear | 252 | 29.06 S | 56.33 W |
| Alvechurch | 42 | 52.21 N | 1.57 W |
| Alverca | 34 | 38.54 N | 9.02 W |
| Alverda | 214 | 40.38 N | 78.52 W |
| Alvernia, Mount ∧[2] | 238 | 24.15 N | 75.24 W |
| Alverton | 214 | 40.08 N | 79.35 W |
| Alves | 46 | 57.38 N | 3.27 W |
| Alvesta | 26 | 56.54 N | 14.33 E |
| Alveston | 42 | 51.36 N | 2.32 W |
| Alviano, Lago di ⊜[1] | 66 | 42.36 N | 12.15 E |
| Ålvik, Nor. | 26 | 60.26 N | 6.26 E |
| Ålvik, Sve. | 26 | 62.25 N | 17.24 E |
| Alvin, Il., U.S. | 216 | 40.19 N | 87.37 W |
| Alvin, Tx., U.S. | 222 | 29.25 N | 95.14 W |
| Alvinópolis | 255 | 20.06 S | 43.03 W |
| Alvinston | 214 | 42.49 N | 81.52 W |
| Alviso ◆[8] | 282 | 37.26 N | 121.58 W |
| Alviso Slough ≃ | 282 | 37.27 N | 122.02 W |
| Alvito, It. | 66 | 41.41 N | 13.45 E |
| Alvito, Port. | 34 | 38.15 N | 7.59 W |
| Älvkarleby | 40 | 60.34 N | 17.27 E |
| Älvkarleö bruk | 40 | 60.32 N | 17.24 E |
| Alvord | 196 | 33.22 N | 97.42 W |
| Alvord Desert ◆[2] | 202 | 42.30 N | 118.25 W |
| Alvord Lake ⊜ | 202 | 42.23 N | 118.36 W |
| Alvordton | 216 | 41.40 N | 84.26 W |
| Alvra, Pass d' )( | 58 | 46.35 N | 9.50 E |
| Älvros | 26 | 62.03 N | 14.39 E |
| Älvsborgs Län □[6] | 26 | 58.00 N | 12.30 E |
| Älvsbyn | 24 | 65.39 N | 20.59 E |
| Älvsnabben ⊥ | 40 | 58.59 N | 18.10 E |
| Al-Wafā'īyah | 142 | 30.46 N | 30.36 E |
| Al-Wajh | 128 | 26.15 N | 36.26 E |
| Al-Wakrah | 128 | 25.10 N | 51.36 E |
| Al-Walīdīyah | 142 | 27.12 N | 31.10 E |
| Alwar | 124 | 27.34 N | 76.36 E |
| Alwar Hills ⋀[2] | 124 | 27.20 N | 76.15 E |
| Al-Wāṣifīyah | 142 | 30.35 N | 32.10 E |
| Al-Wāsiṭah | 142 | 29.20 N | 31.12 E |
| Alwaye | 122 | 10.07 N | 76.21 E |
| Al-Wazīrīyah | 142 | 31.11 N | 30.57 E |
| Al-Wazz | 140 | 15.01 N | 30.10 E |
| Alwen ≃ | 44 | 52.58 N | 3.24 W |
| Al-Widy | 142 | 29.31 N | 31.16 E |
| Alxa Zuoqi | 102 | 38.50 N | 105.32 E |
| Al-Yamāmah → As-Sulaymānīyah | 128 | 24.09 N | 47.19 E |
| Al-Yaman → Yemen □[1] | 144 | 15.00 N | 47.00 E |
| Al Yāmūn | 132 | 32.29 N | 35.14 E |
| Alygdžer | 88 | 53.38 N | 98.16 E |
| Alyn and Deeside □[8] | 262 | 53.16 N | 3.02 W |
| Alypsatar | 86 | 48.03 N | 80.21 W |
| Alyth | 46 | 56.37 N | 3.13 W |
| Alytus | 76 | 54.24 N | 24.03 E |
| Alz ≃ | 60 | 48.16 N | 12.49 E |
| Alzamaj | 88 | 55.33 N | 98.39 E |
| Alzano Lombardo | 62 | 45.44 N | 9.43 E |
| Al-Zarqa | 142 | 31.13 N | 31.38 E |
| Alzenau | 56 | 50.05 N | 9.04 E |
| Alzette ≃ | 56 | 49.52 N | 6.07 E |
| Alzey | 56 | 49.45 N | 8.07 E |
| Alzira (Alcira) | 34 | 39.09 N | 0.26 W |
| Amab, Khawr V | 140 | 17.08 N | 34.51 E |
| Amacayacu, Parque Nacional ♦ | 246 | 3.45 S | 70.10 W |
| Amacuro ≃ | 246 | 8.32 N | 60.28 W |
| Amacuzac ≃ | 234 | 17.53 N | 99.12 W |
| Amadeus, Lake ⊜ | 162 | 24.50 S | 130.45 E |
| Āmādi, Bngl. | 126 | 22.28 N | 89.19 E |
| Amadi, Zaïre | 154 | 3.35 N | 26.47 E |
| Amadjuak Lake ⊜ | 176 | 65.00 N | 71.00 W |
| Amador □[6] | 226 | 38.21 N | 120.46 W |
| Amadora | 266c | 38.45 N | 9.14 W |
| Amador City | 226 | 38.25 N | 120.56 W |
| Amador Valley V | 282 | 37.41 N | 121.51 W |
| Amagansett | 207 | 40.58 N | 72.08 W |
| Amagasaki | 96 | 34.43 N | 135.25 E |
| Amagase | 96 | 33.15 N | 131.02 E |
| Amager I | 41 | 55.37 N | 12.37 E |
| Amagi | 96 | 33.25 N | 130.39 E |
| Amagi-san ∧ | 94 | 34.51 N | 139.00 E |
| Amagi-yugashima | 94 | 34.53 N | 138.56 E |
| Amagoi-dake ∧ | 94 | 35.01 N | 136.23 E |
| Amagunze | 150 | 6.20 N | 7.40 E |
| Amahai | 164 | 3.20 S | 128.55 E |
| Amaichá del Valle | 252 | 26.36 S | 65.55 W |
| Amaimon | 164 | 5.10 S | 145.25 E |
| Amajac ≃ | 234 | 21.15 N | 98.46 W |
| Amaka ≃ | 236 | 14.14 N | 85.07 W |
| Ama Keng | 271c | 1.24 N | 103.42 E |
| Amak Island I | 180 | 55.25 N | 163.07 W |
| Amakusa-nada ▾[2] | 92 | 32.35 N | 130.05 E |
| Amakusa-shotō II | 92 | 32.20 N | 130.15 E |
| Amakuso-Shimo-shima I | 92 | 32.20 N | 130.05 E |
| Amal, Lībiyā | 146 | 29.25 N | 21.10 E |
| Åmål, Sve. | 26 | 59.03 N | 12.42 E |
| Amalāpuram | 122 | 16.35 N | 82.01 E |
| Amalat ≃ | 88 | 54.49 N | 115.12 E |
| Amalfi, Col. | 246 | 6.55 N | 75.04 W |
| Amalfi, It. | 68 | 40.38 N | 14.36 E |
| Amalia | 158 | 27.16 S | 25.03 E |
| Amaliás | 38 | 37.49 N | 21.23 E |
| Amalner | 120 | 21.03 N | 75.04 E |
| Amamaki-zan ∧ | 94 | 36.25 N | 140.09 E |
| Amambaí | 255 | 23.05 S | 55.13 W |
| Amambaí ≃ | 255 | 23.22 S | 53.56 W |
| Amambay □[5] | 252 | 23.00 S | 56.00 W |
| Amami-Ō-shima I | 93b | 28.15 N | 129.20 E |
| Amami-shotō II | 93b | 28.16 N | 129.21 E |
| Amamula | 154 | 0.18 S | 27.50 E |
| Amana | 190 | 41.48 N | 91.52 W |
| Amanã ≃, Bra. | 250 | 4.25 S | 57.34 W |
| Amana ≃, Ven. | 238 | 9.45 N | 62.39 W |
| Amaná, Lago ⊜ | 246 | 2.35 S | 64.40 W |
| Amanab | 164 | 3.35 S | 141.13 E |
| Amanave | 174u | 14.19 S | 170.49 W |
| Amance | 58 | 47.48 N | 6.04 E |
| Amancey | 58 | 47.02 N | 6.05 E |
| Amancio | 240p | 20.49 N | 77.35 W |
| Amanda | 188 | 39.38 N | 82.44 W |
| Amanda Park | 224 | 47.28 N | 123.54 W |
| Amandola | 66 | 42.59 N | 13.21 E |
| Amānganj | 124 | 24.26 N | 80.02 E |
| Amangel'dy, Kaz. | 85 | 43.43 N | 71.07 E |
| Amangel'dy, Kaz. | 86 | 50.10 N | 65.13 E |
| Amangel'dy, Kaz. | 86 | 49.52 N | 59.00 E |
| Åmänningen ⊜ | 40 | 59.57 N | 15.56 E |
| Amano | 270 | 34.26 N | 135.33 E |
| Amanotkel' | 86 | 46.07 N | 61.34 E |
| Amantea | 68 | 39.08 N | 16.05 E |
| Amantogaj | 86 | 50.22 N | 65.33 E |
| Amanu I[1] | 14 | 17.48 S | 140.46 W |
| Amanzimtoti | 158 | 30.03 S | 30.53 E |
| Amapá | 250 | 2.03 N | 50.48 W |
| Amapá □[3] | 250 | 1.00 N | 52.00 W |
| Amapa ≃ | 234 | 18.18 N | 96.19 W |
| Amapala | 236 | 13.17 N | 87.40 W |
| Amapala, Punta de > | 236 | 13.10 N | 87.54 W |
| Amapari ≃ | 250 | 0.43 N | 51.32 W |
| Amaraji | 250 | 8.24 S | 35.27 W |
| Amaral | 287a | 22.42 S | 43.29 W |
| Amaramba, Lago ⊜ | 154 | 14.30 S | 35.55 E |
| Amarante | 250 | 6.14 S | 42.50 W |
| Amarante do Maranhão | 250 | 5.36 S | 46.45 W |
| Amaranth | 184 | 50.36 N | 98.43 W |
| Amarapura | 110 | 21.54 N | 96.03 E |
| Amărăștii de Jos | 38 | 43.59 N | 24.10 E |
| 'Amārat Abū Sinn | 140 | 15.21 N | 35.45 E |
| Amarāvati ≃ | 122 | 10.51 N | 78.11 E |
| Amarda | 126 | 21.47 N | 87.08 E |
| Amareleja | 34 | 38.12 N | 7.14 W |
| Amares | 34 | 41.38 N | 8.21 W |
| Amargosa | 255 | 13.02 S | 39.36 W |
| Amargosa ≃ | 204 | 36.13 N | 116.48 W |
| Amargosa Range ⋀ | 204 | 36.15 N | 116.45 W |
| Amarillo | 196 | 35.13 N | 101.49 W |
| Amarillo, Mar → Yellow Sea ▾[2] | 90 | 36.00 N | 123.00 E |
| 'Amar Jadīd | 140 | 14.28 N | 25.14 E |
| Amarkantak | 124 | 22.40 N | 81.45 E |
| Amarnāth | 122 | 19.11 N | 73.10 E |
| Amarnāth Cave ±[5] | 123 | 34.13 N | 75.31 E |
| Amaro, Monte ∧ | 66 | 42.05 N | 14.05 E |
| Amaroni | 68 | 38.47 N | 16.27 E |
| Amaroúsion | 267c | 38.03 N | 23.49 E |
| Amarpātan | 124 | 24.19 N | 80.59 E |
| Amarube-saki > | 96 | 35.40 N | 134.32 E |
| Amarume | 92 | 38.50 N | 139.55 E |
| Amarwāra | 124 | 22.18 N | 79.10 E |
| Amasa | 190 | 46.13 N | 88.26 W |
| Amaseno ≃ | 66 | 41.19 N | 13.11 E |
| Amasija | 84 | 40.58 N | 43.46 E |
| Amasra | 130 | 41.45 N | 32.24 E |
| Amasya | 130 | 40.39 N | 35.51 E |
| Amasya □[4] | 130 | 40.45 N | 35.30 E |
| Amataurá | 246 | 3.29 S | 68.06 W |
| Amatignak Island I | 181a | 51.15 N | 179.08 W |
| Amatikulu | 158 | 29.06 S | 31.27 E |
| Amatique, Bahía de ⊂ | 236 | 15.55 N | 88.45 W |
| Amatitán | 234 | 20.50 N | 103.43 W |
| Amatitlán | 236 | 14.29 N | 90.37 W |
| Amatitlán, Lago de ⊜ | 236 | 14.27 N | 90.34 W |
| Amatlán de Cañas | 234 | 20.52 N | 104.27 W |
| Amatlán de los Reyes | 234 | 18.50 N | 96.55 W |
| Amatrice | 66 | 42.38 N | 13.17 E |
| Amatsu-kominato | 94 | 35.07 N | 140.10 E |
| Amau | 164 | 10.02 S | 148.34 E |
| Amausi | 124 | 26.46 N | 80.51 E |
| Amawalk | 210 | 41.17 N | 73.46 W |
| Amay | 56 | 50.33 N | 5.19 E |
| Ama-zaki > | 94 | 37.08 N | 136.40 E |
| Amazar | 89 | 53.54 N | 120.53 E |
| Amazon (Solimões) (Amazonas) ≃ | 242 | 0.10 S | 49.00 W |
| Amazonas □[3] | 242 | 5.00 S | 63.00 W |
| Amazonas □[5], Col. | 246 | 1.00 S | 72.00 W |
| Amazonas □[5], Perú | 248 | 5.30 S | 78.00 W |
| Amazonas □[8] | 246 | 3.30 N | 66.00 W |
| Amazonas → Amazon ≃ | 242 | 0.10 S | 49.00 W |
| Amazônia, Parque Nacional da ♦ | 250 | 4.30 S | 56.30 W |
| Amb | 123 | 34.19 N | 72.51 E |
| Ambāh | 124 | 26.43 N | 78.14 E |
| Ambahikily | 157b | 21.36 S | 43.41 E |
| Ambahita | 157b | 24.01 S | 45.16 E |
| Ambaí | 287a | 22.43 S | 43.28 W |
| Ambājogāi | 122 | 18.44 N | 76.23 E |
| Ambakaka | 157b | 24.10 S | 46.17 E |
| Ambāla | 124 | 30.21 N | 76.50 E |
| Ambāla Airport ⊠ | 123 | 30.22 N | 76.50 E |
| Ambalabe | 157b | 18.24 S | 49.10 E |
| Ambalafany | 157b | 22.32 S | 47.36 E |
| Ambalangoda | 122 | 6.14 N | 80.03 E |
| Ambalanjanakomby | 157b | 16.42 S | 47.05 E |
| Ambalavao | 157b | 21.50 S | 46.56 E |
| Ambam | 152 | 2.23 N | 11.17 E |
| Amba Maryam | 144 | 11.26 N | 39.17 E |
| Ambanja | 157b | 13.41 S | 48.27 E |
| Ambar | 248 | 10.44 S | 77.16 W |
| Ambararata | 157b | 15.03 S | 48.33 E |
| Ambarawa | 115a | 7.15 S | 110.24 E |
| Ambarčik, Ross. | 74 | 69.39 N | 162.20 E |
| Ambarčik, Ross. | 88 | 55.09 N | 95.46 E |
| Ambargasta, Salinas de ≚ | 252 | 29.15 S | 64.30 W |
| Ambarijeby | 157b | 14.56 S | 47.41 E |
| Ambarnyj | 24 | 65.56 N | 33.43 E |
| Ambaro, Baie d' ⊂ | 157b | 13.23 S | 48.38 E |
| Ambāsamudram | 122 | 8.42 N | 77.28 E |
| Ambassador Bridge ◆[5] | 281 | 42.20 N | 83.05 W |
| Ambato, Ec. | 246 | 1.15 S | 78.37 W |
| Ambato, Madag. | 157b | 13.24 S | 48.29 E |
| Ambato Boeny | 157b | 16.28 S | 46.43 E |
| Ambatofinandrahana | 157b | 20.33 S | 46.48 E |
| Ambatolampy | 157b | 19.23 S | 47.25 E |
| Ambatomainty | 157b | 17.41 S | 45.40 E |
| Ambatomanoina | 157b | 18.18 S | 47.37 E |
| Ambatondrazaka | 157b | 17.50 S | 48.25 E |
| Ambatosoratra | 157b | 17.34 S | 48.32 E |
| Ambeláki | 267c | 37.57 N | 23.32 E |
| Ambelau, Pulau I | 164 | 3.51 S | 127.12 E |
| Ámbelos, Ákra > | 38 | 39.56 N | 23.55 E |
| Ambenja | 157b | 15.17 S | 46.58 E |
| Amber ≃ | 44 | 53.04 N | 1.29 W |
| Amberes → Antwerpen | 50 | 51.13 N | 4.25 E |
| Amberg, Dtsch. | 60 | 49.27 N | 11.52 E |
| Amberg, Wi., U.S. | 190 | 45.30 N | 87.59 W |
| Ambergris Cay I | 232 | 18.03 N | 87.56 W |
| Ambérieu-en-Bugey | 58 | 45.57 N | 5.21 E |
| Amberley | 172 | 43.10 S | 172.44 E |
| Amberley Royal Australian Air Force Base ■ | 171a | 27.37 S | 152.41 E |
| Amberson | 214 | 40.10 N | 77.41 W |
| Ambert | 62 | 45.33 N | 3.45 E |
| Ambevongo | 157b | 15.27 S | 47.27 E |
| Ambia | 216 | 40.29 N | 87.31 W |
| Ambidédi | 150 | 14.35 N | 11.47 W |
| Ambikānagar | 126 | 22.57 N | 86.46 E |
| Ambikāpur | 124 | 23.07 N | 83.12 E |
| Ambil | 116 | 13.49 N | 120.20 E |
| Ambil Island I | 116 | 13.48 N | 120.18 E |
| Ambilobe | 157b | 13.12 S | 49.04 E |
| Ambinanindrano | 157b | 20.20 S | 48.19 E |
| Ambinanitelo | 157b | 15.21 S | 49.35 E |
| Ambinda | 157b | 16.25 S | 45.52 E |
| Ambivy | 157b | 21.31 S | 44.02 E |
| Ambjörby | 26 | 60.30 N | 13.10 E |
| Ambla | 76 | 59.11 N | 25.51 E |
| Amble | 44 | 55.20 N | 1.34 W |
| Ambler, Ak., U.S. | 180 | 67.05 N | 157.52 W |
| Ambler, Pa., U.S. | 208 | 40.09 N | 75.13 W |
| Ambleside | 44 | 54.26 N | 2.58 W |
| Ambleteuse | 50 | 50.49 N | 1.36 E |
| Amblève ≃ | 56 | 50.28 N | 5.36 E |
| Ambo | 248 | 10.07 S | 76.10 W |
| Amboahangy | 157b | 24.15 S | 46.22 E |
| Amboasary, Madag. | 157b | 18.26 S | 48.16 E |
| Amboasary, Madag. | 157b | 25.02 S | 46.23 E |
| Ambodifototra | 157b | 16.59 S | 49.52 E |
| Ambodilazana | 157b | 18.06 S | 49.10 E |
| Ambodiriana | 157b | 17.55 S | 49.18 E |
| Ambohibary | 157b | 19.20 S | 46.17 E |
| Ambohidratrimo | 157b | 18.50 S | 47.26 E |
| Ambohidray | 157b | 18.36 S | 48.18 E |
| Ambohimahamasina | 157b | 21.56 S | 47.11 E |
| Ambohimahasoa | 157b | 21.07 S | 47.13 E |
| Ambohimanga du Sud | 157b | 20.52 S | 47.36 E |
| Ambohimitombo | 157b | 20.43 S | 47.26 E |
| Amboina → Ambon | 164 | 3.43 S | 128.12 E |
| Amboise | 50 | 47.25 N | 0.59 E |
| Amboíva | 152 | 11.32 S | 14.44 E |
| Ambon | 164 | 3.43 S | 128.12 E |
| Ambon, Pulau I | 164 | 3.40 S | 128.10 E |
| Ambondro | 157b | 25.13 S | 45.44 E |
| Ambonnay | 50 | 49.04 N | 4.10 E |
| Amboseli, Lake ⊜ | 154 | 2.37 S | 37.08 E |
| Amboseli National Park ♦ | 154 | 2.30 S | 37.15 E |
| Amboshe | 272c | 19.09 N | 73.08 E |
| Ambositra | 157b | 20.31 S | 47.15 E |
| Ambovombe | 157b | 25.11 S | 46.05 E |
| Amboy, Il., U.S. | 190 | 41.42 N | 89.19 W |
| Amboy, In., U.S. | 216 | 40.36 N | 85.55 W |
| Amboy, Mn., U.S. | 190 | 43.53 N | 94.09 W |
| Amboy, Wa., U.S. | 224 | 45.54 N | 122.26 W |
| Ambre, Cap d' > | 157b | 11.57 S | 49.17 E |
| Ambre, Montagne d' ∧ | 157b | 12.30 S | 49.10 E |
| Ambridge | 214 | 40.35 N | 80.13 W |
| Ambridge Heights | 279b | 40.36 N | 80.13 W |
| Ambridge Reservoir ⊜[1] | 214 | 40.34 N | 80.21 W |
| Ambrières | 32 | 48.24 N | 0.38 W |
| Ambriz | 152 | 7.50 S | 13.06 E |
| Ambrolauri | 84 | 42.31 N | 43.09 E |
| Ambronay | 58 | 46.00 N | 5.21 E |
| Ambrose | 198 | 48.57 N | 103.28 W |
| Ambrose Brook ≃ | 276 | 40.33 N | 74.32 W |
| Ambrose Channel ⊔ | 276 | 40.32 N | 74.02 W |
| Ambrosia Lake | 200 | 35.25 N | 107.49 W |
| Ambrym □[8] | 175f | 16.15 S | 168.12 E |
| Ambrym I | 175f | 16.15 S | 168.10 E |
| Ambuklao Dam ◆[6] | 116 | 16.28 N | 120.45 E |
| Ambulong Island I | 116 | 12.12 N | 121.01 E |
| Ambulu | 115a | 8.21 S | 113.36 E |
| Ambuntentimur | 115a | 6.54 S | 113.45 E |
| Ambunti | 164 | 4.14 S | 142.50 E |
| Āmbūr | 122 | 12.47 N | 78.42 E |
| Amburambur | 115b | 8.15 S | 116.18 E |
| Amburayan Nabunga ≃ | 116 | 16.55 N | 120.27 E |
| Amby | 56 | 50.53 N | 5.44 E |
| Amchitka Island I | 181a | 51.30 N | 179.00 E |
| Amchitka Pass ⊔ | 181a | 51.30 N | 179.30 W |
| 'Amd | 144 | 15.18 N | 48.00 E |
| Am-Dam | 146 | 12.46 N | 20.29 E |
| Āmdānga | 272b | 22.49 N | 88.31 E |
| Amded, Oued V | 148 | 22.09 N | 3.15 E |
| Amden | 58 | 47.09 N | 9.11 E |
| Amderma | 72 | 69.45 N | 61.39 E |
| Amdo | 120 | 32.18 N | 91.04 E |
| Ameagle | 188 | 37.56 N | 81.25 W |
| Ameca | 234 | 20.33 N | 104.02 W |
| Ameca ≃ | 234 | 20.41 N | 105.18 W |
| Amecameca [de Juárez] | 234 | 19.07 N | 98.46 W |
| Ameghino | 252 | 34.50 S | 62.27 W |
| Ameglia | 64 | 44.04 N | 9.57 E |
| Ameisberg ∧ | 60 | 48.33 N | 13.50 E |
| Ameixoeira ◆[8] | 266c | 38.47 N | 9.10 W |
| Ameland I | 52 | 53.25 N | 5.45 E |
| Amele | 164 | 5.16 S | 145.42 E |
| Amelia, It. | 66 | 42.33 N | 12.25 E |
| Amelia, Oh., U.S. | 218 | 39.01 N | 84.13 W |
| Amelia, Passo d' )( | 66 | 42.36 N | 12.32 E |
| Amelia Court House | 192 | 37.20 N | 77.58 W |
| Amelia Earhart Peak ∧ | 226 | 37.47 N | 119.17 W |
| Amelia Island I | 192 | 30.37 N | 81.27 W |
| Amelinghausen | 52 | 53.08 N | 10.13 E |
| Amelsbüren | 52 | 51.53 N | 7.37 E |
| Amendolara | 68 | 39.57 N | 16.35 E |
| Ameng | 102 | 23.50 N | 104.32 E |
| Amenia | 210 | 41.50 N | 73.33 W |
| Amenucourt | 261 | 49.06 N | 1.39 E |
| Āmer | 120 | 26.59 N | 75.52 E |
| Amerang | 60 | 48.00 N | 12.18 E |
| Amerevo | 265b | 55.55 N | 38.03 E |
| America | 52 | 51.26 N | 5.59 E |
| América del Norte → North America ±[1] | 16 | 45.00 N | 100.00 W |
| América del Sur → South America ±[1] | 18 | 15.00 S | 60.00 W |
| American ≃, Ca., U.S. | 226 | 38.36 N | 121.30 W |
| American ≃, Wa., U.S. | 224 | 46.58 N | 121.08 W |
| American, Middle Fork ≃ | 226 | 38.55 N | 121.02 W |
| American, North Fork ≃ | 226 | 38.43 N | 121.09 W |
| American, South Fork ≃ | 226 | 38.43 N | 121.09 W |
| Americana | 255 | 22.45 S | 47.20 W |
| American Canyon | 226 | 38.10 N | 122.15 W |
| American Cemetery and Memorial ◆ | 269f | 14.33 N | 121.03 E |
| American Falls | 202 | 42.47 N | 112.51 W |
| American Falls ⌊ | 284a | 43.05 N | 79.04 W |
| American Falls Reservoir ⊜[1] | 202 | 42.45 N | 112.45 W |
| American Fork | 200 | 40.22 N | 111.47 W |
| American Highland ⋀[1] | 9 | 72.30 S | 78.00 E |
| American Lake ⊜ | 224 | 47.07 N | 122.34 W |
| American Museum of Natural History ʊ | 276 | 40.47 N | 73.59 W |
| Americano | 250 | 1.19 S | 48.04 W |
| American River | 168b | 35.47 S | 137.47 E |
| American Samoa □[2], Oc. | 14 | 14.20 S | 170.00 W |
| American Samoa □[2], Oc. | 175a | 14.20 S | 170.00 W |
| American University ʊ[2] | 284c | 38.56 N | 77.05 W |
| Américas, Hipódromo de las ♦ | 286a | 19.26 N | 99.13 W |
| Americus, Ga., U.S. | 192 | 32.04 N | 84.13 W |
| Americus, Ks., U.S. | 198 | 38.30 N | 96.15 W |
| Amerikanisches Hochland → American Highland ⋀[1] | 9 | 72.30 S | 78.00 E |
| Ameringkogel ∧ | 61 | 47.04 N | 14.48 E |
| Amérique du Nord → North America ±[1] | 16 | 45.00 N | 100.00 W |
| Amern | 56 | 51.14 N | 6.15 E |
| Amerongen | 52 | 52.00 N | 5.27 E |
| Amersfoort, Ned. | 52 | 52.09 N | 5.24 E |
| Amersfoort, S. Afr. | 158 | 27.01 S | 29.51 E |
| Amersham | 42 | 51.40 N | 0.38 W |
| Amery, Austl. | 162 | 31.09 S | 117.05 E |
| Amery, Mb., Can. | 184 | 56.34 N | 94.03 W |
| Amery, Wi., U.S. | 190 | 45.18 N | 92.21 W |
| Amery Ice Shelf ⊓ | 9 | 69.30 S | 72.00 E |
| Ames, Ia., U.S. | 190 | 42.02 N | 93.37 W |
| Ames, N.Y., U.S. | 210 | 42.50 N | 74.36 W |
| Ames, Tx., U.S. | 222 | 30.03 N | 94.46 W |
| Amesbury, Eng., U.K. | 42 | 51.10 N | 1.45 W |
| Amesbury, Ma., U.S. | 207 | 42.51 N | 70.55 W |
| Ames Long Pond ⊜ | 283 | 42.05 N | 71.07 W |
| Ames Nowell State Park ♦ | 283 | 42.07 N | 70.59 W |
| Ames Pond ⊜ | 283 | 42.38 N | 71.13 W |
| Ames Research Center ʊ[3] | 282 | 37.25 N | 122.04 W |
| Amet Sound ⊔ | 186 | 45.47 N | 63.13 W |
| Amfíklia | 38 | 38.38 N | 22.35 E |
| Amfilokhía | 38 | 38.51 N | 21.10 E |
| Ámfissa | 38 | 38.31 N | 22.24 E |
| Amfreville-la-Campagne | 50 | 49.13 N | 0.57 E |
| Amfreville-les-Champs | 50 | 49.19 N | 1.19 E |
| Amga | 74 | 60.53 N | 132.00 E |
| Amga ≃ | 74 | 62.38 N | 134.32 E |
| Am Géréda | 146 | 12.52 N | 21.10 E |
| Amguema | 180 | 66.58 N | 179.16 W |
| Amguema ≃ | 180 | 68.10 N | 177.40 W |
| Amguid | 148 | 26.26 N | 5.22 E |
| Amgun' ≃ | 89 | 52.56 N | 139.40 E |
| Amherst, N.S., Can. | 186 | 45.49 N | 64.14 W |
| Amherst, Ma., U.S. | 207 | 42.22 N | 72.31 W |
| Amherst, N.H., U.S. | 207 | 42.51 N | 71.37 W |
| Amherst, N.Y., U.S. | 210 | 42.58 N | 78.48 W |
| Amherst, Oh., U.S. | 214 | 41.23 N | 82.13 W |
| Amherst, Tx., U.S. | 196 | 34.01 N | 102.25 W |
| Amherst, Va., U.S. | 192 | 37.35 N | 79.03 W |
| Amherst, Wi., U.S. | 190 | 44.27 N | 89.17 W |
| Amherst, Mount ∧ | 162 | 18.11 S | 126.59 E |
| Amherstburg | 214 | 42.06 N | 83.06 W |
| Amherstdale | 188 | 37.47 N | 81.48 W |
| Amherst Island I | 212 | 44.08 N | 76.45 W |
| Amherstview | 212 | 44.13 N | 76.38 W |
| Ami | 94 | 36.02 N | 140.14 E |
| Amianan Island I | 108 | 21.07 N | 121.57 E |
| Amiata, Monte ∧ | 66 | 42.53 N | 11.37 E |
| Amicalola Falls State Park ♦ | 192 | 34.33 N | 84.15 W |
| Amidon | 198 | 46.28 N | 103.19 W |
| Amiens, Austl. | 166 | 28.35 S | 151.49 E |
| Amiens, Fr. | 50 | 49.54 N | 2.18 E |
| Amili, India | 120 | 28.26 N | 95.52 E |
| Amili, Zhg. | 120 | 28.25 N | 95.52 E |
| Amīn as-Samālūsī, Bi'r ▾[4] | 142 | 29.52 N | 30.02 E |
| Amīndīvi Islands II | 122 | 11.23 N | 72.23 E |
| Aminga | 252 | 28.50 S | 66.54 W |
| Amini Island I | 122 | 11.07 N | 72.44 E |
| Amino, Ityo. | 144 | 4.31 N | 41.49 E |
| Amino, Nihon | 96 | 35.41 N | 135.02 E |
| Aminuis | 156 | 23.43 S | 19.21 E |
| Amīrābād | 128 | 36.04 N | 54.10 E |
| Amīrābād ◆[8] | 267d | 35.43 N | 51.23 E |
| Amirante Islands II | 138 | 6.00 S | 53.10 E |
| Amirauté, Îles de l' → Admiralty Islands II | 164 | 2.10 S | 147.00 E |
| Amisk | 182 | 52.33 N | 111.04 W |
| Amisk Lake ⊜ | 184 | 54.35 N | 102.13 W |
| Amistad, Parque Internacional de la ♦ | 236 | 9.25 N | 83.10 W |
| Amistad, Presa de la (Amistad Reservoir) ⊜[1] | 196 | 29.34 N | 101.15 W |
| Amistad National Recreation Area ♦ | 196 | 29.32 N | 101.12 W |
| Amistad Reservoir (Presa de la Amistad) ⊜[1] | 196 | 29.34 N | 101.15 W |
| Amite | 194 | 30.43 N | 90.30 W |
| Amite ≃ | 194 | 30.12 N | 90.35 W |
| Amite, East Fork ≃ | 194 | 30.58 N | 90.51 W |
| Amiterno ⊥ | 66 | 42.21 N | 13.19 E |
| Amitori | 175d | 24.18 N | 123.41 E |
| Amity, Ar., U.S. | 194 | 34.15 N | 93.27 W |
| Amity, Oh., U.S. | 214 | 40.03 N | 83.17 W |
| Amity, Or., U.S. | 224 | 45.06 N | 123.12 W |
| Amity Point > | 171a | 27.24 S | 153.27 E |
| Amityville | 276 | 40.40 N | 73.25 W |
| Amixtlán | 234 | 20.03 N | 97.48 W |
| Amizmiz | 148 | 31.14 N | 8.14 W |
| Āmjhori ∧ | 126 | 21.51 N | 86.19 E |
| Āmjhupi | 126 | 23.45 N | 88.42 E |
| Āmla, Bngl. | 126 | 23.54 N | 88.56 E |
| Āmla, India | 124 | 21.56 N | 78.07 E |
| Āmlāgora | 126 | 22.50 N | 87.20 E |
| Amlekhgañj | 124 | 27.17 N | 84.59 E |
| Åmli | 26 | 58.47 N | 8.30 E |
| Amlia Island I | 180 | 52.06 N | 173.30 W |
| Amloh | 124 | 30.37 N | 76.14 E |
| Am Loubia | 146 | 13.39 N | 20.08 E |
| Amlwch | 44 | 53.25 N | 4.20 W |
| 'Amm-Adām | 140 | 16.22 N | 36.06 E |
| Ammagan | 85 | 38.56 N | 67.15 E |
| 'Ammān | 132 | 31.57 N | 35.56 E |
| 'Ammān □[8] | 132 | 31.45 N | 36.15 E |
| Ammanford | 42 | 51.48 N | 3.59 W |
| Ämmänsaari | 26 | 64.53 N | 28.55 E |
| Ammansville | 222 | 29.47 N | 96.51 W |
| 'Ammār, Tall ∧[2] | 132 | 32.53 N | 36.29 E |
| Ammarnäs | 24 | 65.56 N | 16.09 E |
| Ammaroo | 162 | 21.45 S | 135.15 E |
| Ämmeberg | 40 | 58.52 N | 15.00 E |
| Ammeloe | 52 | 52.05 N | 6.47 E |
| Ammer ≃ | 64 | 47.57 N | 11.08 E |
| Ammerån ≃ | 26 | 63.09 N | 16.13 E |
| Ammerbuch | 56 | 48.33 N | 8.58 E |
| Ammer Gebirge ⋀ | 64 | 47.35 N | 10.55 E |
| Ammerland ◆[1] | 52 | 53.15 N | 8.00 E |
| Ammerman Mountain ∧ | 180 | 68.21 N | 141.03 W |
| Ammersbek | 52 | 53.42 N | 10.12 E |
| Ammerschwihr | 58 | 48.07 N | 7.17 E |
| Ammersee ⊜ | 60 | 48.00 N | 11.08 E |
| Ammerthal | 60 | 49.26 N | 11.45 E |
| Ammon | 202 | 43.28 N | 111.57 W |
| Ammonoosuc ≃ | 188 | 44.10 N | 72.02 W |
| Amnān | 272b | 22.56 N | 88.18 E |
| Amnat Charoen | 110 | 15.51 N | 104.38 E |
| Amnay ≃ | 116 | 12.58 N | 120.46 E |
| Amne Machin Shan → A'nyêmaqên Shan ⋀ | 102 | 34.30 N | 100.00 E |
| Amnicon ≃ | 190 | 46.41 N | 91.52 W |
| Amnok-kang (Yalu) ≃ | 98 | 39.55 N | 124.22 E |
| Amo ≃, Asia | 124 | 26.16 N | 89.36 E |
| Amo ≃, Zhg. | 102 | 22.58 N | 101.44 E |
| Āmol | 128 | 36.23 N | 52.20 E |
| Amolar | 248 | 18.01 S | 57.30 W |
| Amöneburg | 56 | 50.48 N | 8.55 E |
| Amorbach | 56 | 49.39 N | 9.13 E |
| Amorgós | 38 | 36.50 N | 25.54 E |
| Amorgós I | 38 | 36.50 N | 25.59 E |
| Amorim, Morro ∧[2] | 287a | 23.00 S | 43.26 W |
| Amorinópolis | 255 | 16.36 S | 51.08 W |
| Amorosi | 68 | 41.12 N | 14.28 E |
| Amory | 194 | 33.59 N | 88.29 W |


**Symbols** in the index entries represent the broad categories identified in the key at the right. Symbols with superior numbers (⋀[1]) identify subcategories (see complete key on page *I · 1).*

**Symbole** im Register stellen die rechts im Schlüssel erklärten Kategorien dar. Symbole mit hochgestellten Ziffern (⋀[1]) bezeichnen Unterabteilungen einer Kategorie (vgl. vollständiger Schlüssel auf Seite *I · 1).*

**Los símbolos** incluídos en el texto del índice representan las grandes categorías identificadas con la clave a la derecha. Los símbolos con numeros en su parte superior (⋀[1]) identifican las subcategorías (véase la clave completa en la página *I · 1).*

**Les symboles** de l'index représentent les catégories indiquées dans la légende à droite. Les symboles suivis d'un indice (⋀[1]) représentent des sous-catégories (voir légende complète à la page *I · 1).*

**Os símbolos** incluídos no texto do índice representam as grandes categorias identificadas com a chave à direita. Os símbolos com números em sua parte superior (⋀[1]) identificam as subcategorias (veja-se a chave completa à página *I · 1).*

| Symbol | English | Deutsch | Español | Français | Português |
|---|---|---|---|---|---|
| ∧ | Mountain | Berg | Montaña | Montagne | Montanha |
| ⋀ | Mountains | Gebirge | Montañas | Montagnes | Montanhas |
| )( | Pass | Paß | Paso | Col | Passo |
| V | Valley, Canyon | Tal, Cañon | Valle, Cañón | Vallée, Canyon | Vale, Canhão |
| ≚ | Plain | Ebene | Llano | Plaine | Planície |
| > | Cape | Kap | Cabo | Cap | Cabo |
| I | Island | Insel | Isla | Île | Ilha |
| II | Islands | Inseln | Islas | Îles | Ilhas |
| ± | Other Topographic Features | Andere Topographische Objekte | Otros Elementos Topográficos | Autres données topographiques | Outros acidentes topográficos |

ESPAÑOL

| Nombre | Página | Lat.°′ | Long.°′ W = Oeste |
|---|---|---|---|
| Amos | 190 | 48.35 N | 78.07 W |
| Åmose ≃ | 41 | 55.35 N | 11.18 E |
| Åmot, Nor. | 26 | 59.35 N | 8.00 E |
| Åmot, Nor. | 26 | 59.54 N | 9.54 E |
| Åmotfors | 26 | 59.46 N | 12.22 E |
| Amour → Amur ≃ | 74 | 52.56 N | 141.10 E |
| Amour, Djebel ⩘ | 148 | 34.00 N | 2.15 E |
| Amoy → Xiamen | 100 | 24.28 N | 118.07 E |
| Amozoc | 234 | 19.02 N | 98.03 W |
| Ampana | 112 | 0.51 S | 121.32 E |
| Ampanavoana | 157b | 15.41 S | 50.22 E |
| Ampang | 115b | 8.47 S | 118.00 E |
| Ampanihy | 157b | 24.42 S | 44.45 E |
| Ampaoid, Mount ∧ | 116 | 7.57 N | 125.41 E |
| Amparafaravola | 157b | 17.35 S | 48.13 E |
| Amparihy, Madag. | 157b | 16.40 S | 44.49 E |
| Amparihy, Madag. | 157b | 23.57 S | 47.20 E |
| Amparo | 256 | 22.42 S | 46.45 W |
| Ampasibe | 157b | 22.56 S | 46.58 E |
| Ampasinambo | 157b | 20.31 S | 48.00 E |
| Ampasindava, Baie d' ⊂ | 157b | 13.16 S | 48.43 E |
| Ampasindava, Presq'île d' ›[1] | 157b | 13.45 S | 48.00 E |
| Ampato, Nevado ∧ | 248 | 15.50 S | 71.52 W |
| Ampel | 115a | 7.27 S | 110.32 E |
| Amper | 150 | 9.20 N | 9.43 E |
| Amper ≃ | 60 | 48.30 N | 11.58 E |
| Ampezzo | 64 | 46.25 N | 12.48 E |
| Ampezzo, Valle d' V | 64 | 46.30 N | 12.10 E |
| Ampfing | 60 | 48.16 N | 12.25 E |
| Ampflwang | 64 | 48.05 N | 13.34 E |
| Amphion-les-Bains | 58 | 46.23 N | 6.32 E |
| Ampisikina | 157b | 12.57 S | 49.49 E |
| Ampleforth | 44 | 54.12 N | 1.06 W |
| Ampollino, Lago ◎ | 68 | 39.12 N | 16.37 E |
| Ampombiantambo | 157b | 12.42 S | 48.57 E |
| Amposta | 34 | 40.43 N | 0.35 E |
| Ampotaka | 157b | 25.03 S | 44.41 E |
| Ampoza | 157b | 22.20 S | 44.44 E |
| Ampthill | 42 | 52.02 N | 0.30 W |
| Ampuis | 62 | 45.29 N | 4.49 E |
| Ampus | 62 | 43.36 N | 6.23 E |
| Amqui | 186 | 48.28 N | 67.26 W |
| Āmr, Jabal al- ⩘ | 132 | 30.45 N | 34.20 E |
| Amraoti → Amrāvati | 120 | 20.56 N | 77.45 E |
| Amrāvati | 120 | 20.56 N | 77.45 E |
| Am-Raya | 146 | 14.00 N | 16.35 E |
| Amreli | 120 | 21.37 N | 71.14 E |
| Āmreswar | 272b | 22.28 N | 88.34 E |
| Amriswil | 58 | 47.33 N | 9.18 E |
| Amritsar | 123 | 31.35 N | 74.53 E |
| Amroha | 124 | 28.55 N | 78.28 E |
| Amrūka | 123 | 30.19 N | 73.53 E |
| Amrum I | 30 | 54.39 N | 8.21 E |
| Amsdell Heights | 284a | 42.45 N | 78.54 W |
| Amsden | 214 | 41.13 N | 83.20 W |
| Amsel | 148 | 22.37 N | 5.26 E |
| Åmsele | 26 | 64.32 N | 19.20 E |
| Am Sigan | 146 | 11.41 N | 19.51 E |
| Amsoldingen | 58 | 46.43 N | 7.35 E |
| Amsteg | 58 | 46.46 N | 8.41 E |
| Amstel ≃ | 52 | 52.22 N | 4.54 E |
| Amstelmeer ◎ | 52 | 52.52 N | 4.45 E |
| Amstelveen | 52 | 52.18 N | 4.51 E |
| Amsterdam, Ned. | 52 | 52.22 N | 4.54 E |
| Amsterdam, S. Afr. | 158 | 26.35 S | 30.45 E |
| Amsterdam, N.Y., U.S. | 210 | 42.56 N | 74.11 W |
| Amsterdam, Oh., U.S. | 214 | 40.28 N | 80.55 W |
| Amsterdam, Île I | 6 | 37.52 S | 77.32 E |
| Amsterdam-Rijnkanaal ≊ | 52 | 51.57 N | 5.20 E |
| Amstetten | 61 | 48.07 N | 14.53 E |
| Amston | 207 | 41.37 N | 72.20 W |
| Āmta | 126 | 22.35 N | 88.01 E |
| Amt'ae-do I | 98 | 34.50 N | 126.07 E |
| Āmtala | 126 | 23.55 N | 88.27 E |
| Amtāli | 126 | 22.08 N | 90.14 E |
| Am Timan | 146 | 11.02 N | 20.17 E |
| Amtrak Station ◆[5] | 281 | 42.19 N | 83.04 W |
| Amubri | 236 | 9.31 N | 82.56 W |
| 'Āmūdah | 130 | 37.05 N | 40.54 E |
| Amu-Darja | 128 | 37.53 N | 65.15 E |
| Amu Darya ≃ | 72 | 43.40 N | 59.01 E |
| Amudat | 154 | 1.57 N | 34.57 E |
| Amugulang → Xin Barag Zuoqi | 88 | 48.14 N | 118.18 E |
| Amukta Island I | 180 | 52.29 N | 171.15 W |
| Amukta Pass ⋓ | 180 | 52.25 N | 172.00 W |
| Amulree | 46 | 56.30 N | 3.47 W |
| Amun | 175e | 5.57 S | 154.45 E |
| Amundsen Bay ⊂ | 9 | 66.55 S | 50.00 E |
| Amundsen Gulf ⊂ | 176 | 71.00 N | 124.00 W |
| Amundsen-Scott ʋ[3] | 9 | 90.00 S | 0.00 |
| Amundsen Sea ⍑[2] | 9 | 72.30 S | 112.00 W |
| Amung, Mount ∧ | 164 | 7.26 S | 146.36 E |
| Amungen ◎ | 26 | 61.09 N | 15.39 E |
| Amuntai | 112 | 2.26 S | 115.15 E |
| Amur (Heilong) ≃ | 74 | 52.56 N | 141.10 E |
| 'Amūr, Wādī V | 140 | 18.56 N | 33.34 E |
| Amurang | 112 | 1.11 N | 124.35 E |
| Amuria | 154 | 2.01 N | 33.38 E |
| Amursk | 89 | 50.13 N | 136.52 E |
| Amurskaja Oblast' □[8] | 89 | 53.00 N | 129.00 E |
| Amurskij liman ⊂ | 89 | 52.45 N | 141.40 E |
| Amursko-Zejskaja ravnina ⩘[1] | 89 | 52.30 N | 128.30 E |
| Amurzet | 89 | 47.42 N | 131.05 E |
| Amutag | 116 | 12.23 N | 123.16 E |
| Amuwo | 273a | 6.28 N | 3.18 E |
| Amuyimusu | 98 | 42.25 N | 113.21 E |
| Amuzhong | 120 | 30.33 N | 84.28 E |
| Amvamg | 152 | 1.45 N | 10.29 E |
| Amvrakikós Kólpos ⊂ | 38 | 39.00 N | 21.00 E |
| Amvrosiyivka | 83 | 47.47 N | 38.29 E |
| Amwom, Khawr V | 140 | 7.50 N | 31.13 E |
| Amyl ≃ | 86 | 53.47 N | 92.54 E |
| Amyūn | 130 | 34.18 N | 35.49 E |
| Amz'a | 80 | 56.13 N | 54.23 E |
| Amzi, Oued ti-n- V | 148 | 20.30 N | 4.35 E |
| An | 110 | 19.47 N | 94.02 E |
| Anaa I[1] | 14 | 17.25 S | 145.30 W |
| Anabanua | 112 | 3.57 S | 120.04 E |
| Anabar | 174b | 0.30 S | 166.57 E |
| Anabar ≃ | 74 | 73.08 N | 113.36 E |
| 'Anabtā | 132 | 32.19 N | 35.07 E |
| Anabuki | 96 | 34.02 N | 134.11 E |
| Anacapri | 68 | 40.33 N | 14.13 E |
| Anaco | 246 | 9.27 N | 64.28 W |
| Anacoco | 194 | 31.15 N | 93.20 W |
| Anacoco, Bayou ≃ | 194 | 30.52 N | 93.34 W |
| Anaconda | 202 | 46.07 N | 112.56 W |
| Anaconda Range ⩘ | 202 | 45.55 N | 113.30 W |
| Anacortes | 224 | 48.30 N | 122.36 W |
| Anacostia ◆[8] | 284c | 38.52 N | 76.59 W |
| Anacostia ≃ | 284c | 38.52 N | 77.01 W |
| Anacostia, Little Paint Branch ≃ | 284c | 39.01 N | 76.56 W |
| Anacostia, Northeast Branch ≃ | 284c | 38.57 N | 76.57 W |
| Anacostia, Paint Branch ≃ | 284c | 38.58 N | 76.55 W |
| Anacostia Park ♠ | 284c | 38.54 N | 76.58 W |
| Anacuao, Mount ∧ | 116 | 16.16 N | 121.53 E |
| Anadarko | 196 | 35.04 N | 98.14 W |
| Anadia | 250 | 9.42 S | 36.18 W |
| Anadolufeneri ◆[8] | 267b | 41.12 N | 29.09 E |
| Anadoluhisarı ⊥ | 267b | 41.04 N | 29.03 E |
| Anadyr' | 180 | 64.45 N | 177.29 E |
| Anadyr' ≃ | 74 | 64.55 N | 176.05 E |
| Anadyrskaja nizmennost' ≡ | 180 | 65.30 N | 176.00 E |
| Anadyrskij liman ⊂ | 180 | 64.30 N | 177.45 E |
| Anadyrskij zaliv ⊂ | 180 | 64.00 N | 179.00 W |

FRANÇAIS

| Nom | Page | Lat.°′ | Long.°′ W = Ouest |
|---|---|---|---|
| Anadyrskoje ploskogorje ⩘[1] | 180 | 67.00 N | 174.00 E |
| Anáfi I | 38 | 36.21 N | 25.50 E |
| Anagni | 66 | 41.44 N | 13.09 E |
| 'Ānah | 128 | 34.28 N | 41.56 E |
| Anaheim | 228 | 33.50 N | 117.54 W |
| Anaheim Arena ♠ | 280 | 33.48 N | 117.52 W |
| Anaheim Shopping Center ◆[9] | 280 | 33.51 N | 117.56 W |
| Anaheim Stadium ♠ | 280 | 33.51 N | 117.57 W |
| Anaheim Union Canal ≊ | 280 | 33.54 N | 117.52 W |
| Anahi, Baie ⊂ | 174x | 9.45 S | 138.56 W |
| Anahim Lake | 182 | 52.28 N | 125.18 W |
| Anahola | 229b | 22.08 N | 159.18 W |
| Anahola Bay ⊂ | 229b | 22.09 N | 159.18 W |
| Anáhuac, Méx. | 196 | 25.48 N | 97.45 W |
| Anáhuac, Méx. | 232 | 27.14 N | 100.09 W |
| Anáhuac, Méx. | 232 | 28.25 N | 106.40 W |
| Anahuac, Tx., U.S. | 222 | 29.46 N | 94.41 W |
| Anahuac, Lake ◎ | 222 | 29.48 N | 94.41 W |
| Anaimala | 122 | 10.35 N | 76.56 E |
| Ānai Mudi ∧ | 122 | 10.10 N | 77.04 E |
| Anajás | 250 | 0.59 S | 49.57 W |
| Anajás, Ilha I | 250 | 0.20 S | 50.30 W |
| Anajatuba | 250 | 3.16 S | 44.37 W |
| Anakāpalle | 122 | 17.41 N | 83.01 E |
| Anaklia | 84 | 42.24 N | 41.34 E |
| Anaktuvuk ≃ | 180 | 69.32 N | 151.30 W |
| Anaktuvuk Pass | 180 | 68.10 N | 151.50 W |
| Analalava | 157b | 14.38 S | 47.45 E |
| Analapatsy | 157b | 25.10 S | 46.42 E |
| Analavoka | 157b | 22.33 S | 46.30 E |
| Analomink | 210 | 41.03 N | 75.13 W |
| Anamã | 246 | 3.35 S | 61.22 W |
| Anamã, Lago ◎ | 246 | 3.32 S | 61.35 W |
| Anama Bay | 184 | 51.56 N | 98.05 W |
| Ana María, Cayos de II | 240p | 21.29 N | 78.46 W |
| Ana María, Golfo de ⊂ | 240p | 21.25 N | 78.40 W |
| Anambas, Kepulauan II | 112 | 3.00 N | 106.00 E |
| Anambra ≃ | 150 | 6.11 N | 6.46 E |
| Anamizu | 94 | 37.14 N | 136.54 E |
| Anamoose | 198 | 47.52 N | 100.14 W |
| Anamosa | 190 | 42.06 N | 91.17 W |
| Anamu ≃ | 250 | 0.56 N | 57.03 W |
| Anamur | 130 | 36.06 N | 32.50 E |
| Anamur Burnu › | 130 | 36.03 N | 32.48 E |
| Anan, Nihon | 94 | 35.19 N | 137.49 E |
| Anan, Nihon | 96 | 33.55 N | 134.39 E |
| Ānand | 120 | 22.34 N | 72.56 E |
| Ananda | 150 | 7.17 N | 4.16 W |
| Anandanagar | 272b | 22.51 N | 88.16 E |
| Āndandapur, India | 120 | 21.14 N | 86.07 E |
| Ānandapur, India | 126 | 22.34 N | 87.25 E |
| Anandpur Sahib | 123 | 31.15 N | 76.30 E |
| Ananea | 248 | 14.42 S | 69.33 W |
| Ananindeua | 250 | 1.22 S | 48.23 W |
| Ananjevo | 85 | 42.45 N | 77.40 E |
| Anantapur | 122 | 14.41 N | 77.36 E |
| Anantnāg (Islāmābād) | 123 | 33.44 N | 75.09 E |
| Anan'yiv | 78 | 47.40 N | 29.55 E |
| Anao-aon | 116 | 9.47 N | 125.25 E |
| Anapa | 78 | 44.53 N | 37.19 E |
| Anapo ≃ | 70 | 37.03 N | 15.15 E |
| Anápolis | 255 | 16.20 S | 48.58 W |
| Anapu ≃ | 250 | 1.53 S | 50.53 W |
| Anapurus | 250 | 3.40 S | 43.06 W |
| Anār, Īrān | 128 | 30.53 N | 55.18 E |
| Anar, Kaz. | 86 | 50.38 N | 72.27 E |
| Anāra | 126 | 23.23 N | 86.33 E |
| Anārak | 128 | 33.20 N | 53.42 E |
| Anarchaj | 85 | 44.02 N | 75.15 E |
| Anār Darreh | 128 | 32.46 N | 61.39 E |
| Anaš | 86 | 54.52 N | 91.00 E |
| Anasagasti | 258 | 35.01 S | 59.24 W |
| Añasco | 240m | 18.17 N | 67.08 W |
| Ånäset | 26 | 64.16 N | 21.03 E |
| Anastácio | 255 | 21.31 S | 54.08 W |
| Anastasia Island I | 192 | 29.48 N | 81.16 W |
| Anastasijevka | 83 | 47.34 N | 38.31 E |
| Anastasijevskaja | 78 | 45.13 N | 37.53 E |
| 'Anātā | 132 | 31.49 N | 35.16 E |
| Anatahan I | 108 | 16.22 N | 145.40 E |
| Anatolikí Makedhonía kaí Thráki □[4] | 38 | 41.00 N | 25.00 E |
| Anatolivka | 78 | 46.48 N | 31.13 E |
| Anatom I | 175f | 20.12 S | 169.45 E |
| Añatuya | 252 | 28.28 S | 62.50 W |
| Anauá ≃ | 246 | 0.58 N | 61.21 W |
| Anaurilândia | 255 | 22.03 S | 52.45 W |
| Anavilhanas, Arquipélago das II | 246 | 2.42 S | 60.45 W |
| Anawalt | 192 | 37.20 N | 81.26 W |
| Anbanjing | 102 | 23.57 N | 100.55 E |
| Anbei, Zhg. | 102 | 40.45 N | 96.06 E |
| Anbei, Zhg. | 102 | 40.49 N | 108.56 E |
| Anbianbu | 102 | 37.39 N | 108.11 E |
| Anbo | 98 | 39.51 N | 122.19 E |
| Anbu | 100 | 23.28 N | 116.44 E |
| Anbyŏn | 98 | 39.03 N | 127.32 E |
| Ancarano | 66 | 42.50 N | 13.44 E |
| Ancash □[5] | 248 | 9.30 S | 77.45 W |
| Ancaster, On., Can. | 212 | 43.12 N | 80.00 W |
| Ancaster, Eng., U.K. | 44 | 52.59 N | 0.32 W |
| Ancasti | 252 | 28.49 S | 65.30 W |
| Ancasti, Sierra de ⩘ | 252 | 28.50 S | 65.39 W |
| Ance ≃, Fr. | 62 | 45.17 N | 4.08 E |
| Ance ≃, Fr. | 62 | 44.58 N | 3.40 E |
| Ancenis | 32 | 47.22 N | 1.11 W |
| Ancerville | 58 | 48.38 N | 5.02 E |
| Anchang | 100 | 30.09 N | 120.30 E |
| Anchau | 150 | 10.59 N | 8.23 E |
| Anchieta ◆[8] | 287a | 22.49 S | 43.24 W |
| Anchieta, Ilha I | 256 | 23.33 S | 45.04 W |
| Anch'ing → Anqing | 100 | 30.31 N | 117.02 E |
| Ancho, Canal ⋓ | 254 | 49.54 S | 74.23 W |
| Ancholme ≃ | 44 | 53.41 N | 0.32 W |
| Anchor | 216 | 40.34 N | 88.32 W |
| Anchorage | 180 | 61.13 N | 149.54 W |
| Anchor Bay ⊂ | 214 | 42.38 N | 82.45 W |
| Anchor Bay Gardens | 214 | 42.39 N | 82.49 W |
| Anchorena | 252 | 35.41 S | 65.27 W |
| Anchor Point | 180 | 59.46 N | 151.52 W |
| Anchor Point › | 180 | 59.47 N | 151.52 W |
| Anchorville | 214 | 42.42 N | 82.41 W |
| Anchuras | 34 | 39.29 N | 4.50 W |
| Anci (Langfang) | 105 | 39.31 N | 116.41 E |
| Ancien Ekalla | 152 | 1.27 S | 14.00 E |
| Ancien Goubéré | 140 | 5.51 N | 26.46 E |
| Ancienne-Lorette | 206 | 46.48 N | 71.21 W |
| Anciferovo, Ross. | 76 | 58.58 N | 34.01 E |
| Anciferovo, Ross. | 82 | 55.33 N | 38.49 E |
| Ancipa, Lago di ◎ | 70 | 37.50 N | 14.34 E |
| Anclitas, Cayo I | 240p | 20.48 N | 78.54 W |
| Anclote ≃ | 220 | 39.59 N | 88.49 W |
| Anclote Keys II | 220 | 28.12 N | 82.51 W |
| Ancón, Méx. | 234 | 22.35 N | 101.11 W |
| Ancón, Perú | 248 | 11.47 S | 77.11 W |
| Ancona, It. | 66 | 43.38 N | 13.30 E |
| Ancona, S. Afr. | 158 | 27.40 S | 26.32 E |
| Ancona □[4] | 66 | 43.33 N | 13.10 E |
| Ancón de Sardinas, Bahía de ⊂ | 246 | 1.30 N | 79.00 W |
| Ancoraimes | 248 | 15.54 S | 68.58 W |
| Ancram | 210 | 42.03 N | 73.38 W |
| Ancre ≃ | 50 | 49.54 N | 2.28 E |
| Ancrum | 46 | 55.31 N | 2.35 W |
| Ancuabe | 154 | 12.58 S | 39.54 E |
| Ancud | 254 | 41.52 S | 73.50 W |
| Ancud, Golfo de ⊂ | 254 | 42.05 S | 73.00 W |
| Ancy-le-Franc | 50 | 47.46 N | 4.10 E |
| Ancy-sur-Moselle | 56 | 49.03 N | 6.04 E |
| Anda, Pil. | 116 | 16.17 N | 119.57 E |
| Anda, Zhg. | 89 | 46.24 N | 125.19 E |
| Andacollo, Arg. | 252 | 37.11 S | 70.41 W |
| Andacollo, Chile | 252 | 30.14 S | 71.06 W |

PORTUGUÊS

| Nome | Página | Lat.°′ | Long.°′ W = Oeste |
|---|---|---|---|
| Andahuaylas | 248 | 13.39 S | 73.23 W |
| Andaingo | 157b | 18.12 S | 48.17 E |
| Andāl | 124 | 23.36 N | 87.12 E |
| Andalgalá | 252 | 27.36 S | 66.19 W |
| Andalo | 64 | 46.10 N | 11.00 E |
| Åndalsnes | 26 | 62.34 N | 7.42 E |
| Andalucía □[3] | 34 | 37.30 N | 4.30 W |
| Andalusia, Al., U.S. | 194 | 31.19 N | 86.29 W |
| Andalusia, Pa., U.S. | 285 | 40.04 N | 74.58 W |
| Andaman and Nicobar Islands □[8] | 110 | 11.00 N | 93.00 E |
| Andaman Basin ✢[1] | 12 | 10.00 N | 94.00 E |
| Andamanen → Andaman Islands II | 110 | 12.00 N | 92.45 E |
| Andaman Islands II | 110 | 12.00 N | 92.45 E |
| Andaman Sea ⍑[2] | 110 | 10.00 N | 95.00 E |
| Andamarca, Bol. | 248 | 18.49 S | 67.31 W |
| Andamarca, Perú | 248 | 11.46 S | 74.44 W |
| Andamooka | 166 | 30.27 S | 137.12 E |
| Andance | 62 | 45.14 N | 4.47 E |
| Andapa | 157b | 14.39 S | 49.39 E |
| Andara | 152 | 18.03 S | 21.27 E |
| Andaraí | 255 | 12.48 S | 41.20 W |
| Andaraí ◆[8] | 287a | 22.56 S | 43.15 W |
| Andarax ≃ | 34 | 36.48 N | 2.26 W |
| Andaray | 248 | 15.49 S | 72.50 W |
| Andau | 61 | 47.46 N | 17.02 E |
| Andechs, Kloster ʋ[1] | 64 | 47.58 N | 11.10 E |
| Andeer | 58 | 46.36 N | 9.26 E |
| Andelfingen | 58 | 47.36 N | 8.41 E |
| Andelle ≃ | 50 | 49.19 N | 1.14 E |
| Andelot | 58 | 48.15 N | 5.18 E |
| Andelot-en-Montagne | 58 | 46.51 N | 5.56 E |
| Andelu | 261 | 48.53 N | 1.50 E |
| Anden → Andes ⩘ | 18 | 20.00 S | 67.00 W |
| Andenes | 24 | 69.16 N | 16.08 E |
| Andenne | 56 | 50.29 N | 5.06 E |
| Andéranboukane | 150 | 15.26 N | 3.02 E |
| Ånderdalen Nasjonalpark ♠ | 24 | 69.14 N | 17.17 E |
| Anderlecht | 50 | 50.50 N | 4.18 E |
| Anderlues | 50 | 50.24 N | 4.16 E |
| Andermatt | 58 | 46.38 N | 8.36 E |
| Andernach | 56 | 50.26 N | 7.24 E |
| Andersen Air Force Base ■ | 174p | 13.35 N | 144.56 E |
| Anderslöv | 41 | 55.26 N | 13.22 E |
| Anderson, Al., U.S. | 194 | 34.55 N | 87.15 W |
| Anderson, Ak., U.S. | 180 | 64.21 N | 149.10 W |
| Anderson, Ca., U.S. | 204 | 40.26 N | 122.17 W |
| Anderson, In., U.S. | 218 | 40.06 N | 85.40 W |
| Anderson, Mo., U.S. | 194 | 36.39 N | 94.26 W |
| Anderson, S.C., U.S. | 192 | 34.30 N | 82.39 W |
| Anderson, Tx., U.S. | 222 | 30.29 N | 95.59 W |
| Anderson □[6], Ky., U.S. | 218 | 38.05 N | 84.55 W |
| Anderson □[6], Tx., U.S. | 222 | 31.47 N | 95.40 W |
| Anderson ≃ | 180 | 69.43 N | 128.58 W |
| Anderson, Mount ∧ | 224 | 47.43 N | 123.20 W |
| Anderson Creek ≃ | 194 | 33.18 N | 94.26 W |
| Anderson Dam | 202 | 43.30 N | 115.30 W |
| Anderson Inlet ⊂ | 169 | 38.39 S | 145.48 E |
| Anderson Island I | 224 | 47.10 N | 122.42 W |
| Anderson Lake ◎ | 182 | 50.41 N | 122.07 W |
| Anderson Lake ◎[1] | 226 | 37.11 N | 121.37 W |
| Anderson Peak ∧ | 228 | 34.08 N | 116.53 W |
| Anderson Ranch Reservoir ◎[1] | 202 | 43.25 N | 115.20 W |
| Andersonville | 218 | 39.30 N | 85.17 W |
| Andersonville National Historic Site ⊥ | 192 | 32.12 N | 84.07 W |
| Anderstorp | 26 | 57.17 N | 13.38 E |
| Anderten | 52 | 52.21 N | 9.51 E |
| Anderton | 262 | 53.17 N | 2.32 W |
| Andes, Col. | 246 | 5.40 N | 75.53 W |
| Andes, N.Y., U.S. | 210 | 42.12 N | 74.47 W |
| Andes ⩘ | 18 | 20.00 S | 67.00 W |
| Andes, Lake ◎ | 198 | 43.11 N | 98.27 W |
| Andeville | 50 | 49.15 N | 2.10 E |
| Andevoranto | 157b | 18.57 S | 49.06 E |
| Andfjorden ⋓ | 24 | 69.10 N | 16.20 E |
| Andheri ◆[8] | 272c | 19.07 N | 72.51 E |
| Andhra Lake ◎[1] | 122 | 18.54 N | 73.32 E |
| Andhra Pradesh □[3] | 122 | 16.00 N | 79.00 E |
| Andijk | 52 | 52.45 N | 5.12 E |
| Andijskoje Kojsu ≃ | 84 | 42.47 N | 46.48 E |
| Andikíthira I | 38 | 35.52 N | 23.18 E |
| Andilamena | 157b | 17.01 S | 48.35 E |
| Andimákhia | 38 | 36.48 N | 27.07 E |
| Andīmeshk | 128 | 32.27 N | 48.21 E |
| Andingpu | 102 | 37.58 N | 107.02 E |
| Anding Zhan | 105 | 39.38 N | 116.29 E |
| Andíparos I | 38 | 37.00 N | 25.03 E |
| Andirá ≃ | 250 | 2.45 S | 56.49 W |
| Andirá, Riozinho do ≃ | 248 | 9.2[illegible] S | 67.31 W |
| Andırın | 130 | 37.34 N | 36.20 E |
| Andirlang | 120 | 37.36 N | 83.50 E |
| Ancisleben | 54 | 51.04 N | 10.56 E |
| Ándissa | 38 | 39.14 N | 25.59 E |
| Andižan | 85 | 40.45 N | 72.22 E |
| Andžan □[4] | 85 | 40.45 N | 72.15 E |
| Andkhvoy | 120 | 36.56 N | 65.08 E |
| Andlau-au-Val | 58 | 48.23 N | 7.25 E |
| Ando | 270 | 34.37 N | 135.46 E |
| Andoam | 164 | 12.40 S | 141.55 E |
| Andoas | 246 | 2.50 S | 76.30 W |
| Andoga ≃ | 76 | 59.10 N | 37.27 E |
| Andogskaja gr'ada ∧ | 76 | 59.25 N | 37.30 E |
| Andolsheim | 58 | 48.04 N | 7.25 E |
| Andomskij Pogost | 24 | 61.14 N | 36.36 E |
| Andong, Taehan | 98 | 36.35 N | 128.44 E |
| Andong, Zhg. | 100 | 30.16 N | 121.13 E |
| Andong-chŏsuji ◎[1] | 98 | 36.41 N | 128.49 E |
| Andong-ni | 98 | 39.28 N | 127.27 E |
| Andora | 62 | 43.59 N | 8.03 E |
| Andorf | 60 | 48.23 N | 13.35 E |
| Andorno Micca | 62 | 45.37 N | 8.03 E |
| Andorra | 34 | 42.30 N | 1.31 E |
| Andorra □[1], Europe | 22 | 42.30 N | 1.30 E |
| Andorra □[1], Europe | 34 | 42.30 N | 1.30 E |
| Andorre → Andorra □[1] | 34 | 42.30 N | 1.30 E |
| Andover, Eng., U.K. | 42 | 51.13 N | 1.28 W |
| Andover, Ct., U.S. | 207 | 41.44 N | 72.22 W |
| Andover, Me., U.S. | 188 | 44.38 N | 70.45 W |
| Andover, Ma., U.S. | 207 | 42.39 N | 71.08 W |
| Andover, N.J., U.S. | 210 | 40.59 N | 74.44 W |
| Andover, N.Y., U.S. | 210 | 42.09 N | 77.47 W |
| Andover, Oh., U.S. | 214 | 41.36 N | 80.34 W |
| Andover, S.D., U.S. | 198 | 45.24 N | 97.54 W |
| Andowj | 123 | 37.02 N | 71.27 E |
| Andøya I | 24 | 69.08 N | 15.54 E |
| Andradas | 256 | 22.04 S | 46.34 W |
| Andrade Pinto | 256 | 22.14 S | 43.22 W |
| Andradina | 255 | 20.54 S | 51.23 W |
| Andramasina | 157b | 19.11 S | 47.35 E |
| Andranopasy | 157b | 21.17 S | 43.44 E |
| Andranovory | 157b | 23.08 S | 44.10 E |
| Andrate | 62 | 45.32 N | 7.53 E |
| Andreafsky ≃ | 180 | 62.02 N | 163.16 W |
| Andreafsky, East Fork ≃ | 180 | 62.03 N | 163.07 W |
| Andreanof Islands II | 180 | 52.00 N | 176.00 W |
| Andreapol' | 76 | 56.39 N | 32.15 E |
| Andreas, I. of Man | 44 | 54.22 N | 4.26 W |
| Andreas, Pa., U.S. | 208 | 40.45 N | 75.48 W |
| André Félix, Parc National ♠ | 146 | 9.25 N | 23.20 E |
| Andrejevka, Kaz. | 86 | 52.59 N | 67.23 E |
| Andrejevka, Ross. | 80 | 55.42 N | 54.23 E |
| Andrejevka, Ross. | 80 | 52.19 N | 51.55 E |
| Andrejevka, Ross. | 82 | 55.07 N | 38.37 E |
| Andrejevka, Ross. | 82 | 55.59 N | 37.08 E |
| Andrejevo | 80 | 55.56 N | 41.08 E |
| Andrejevsk | 88 | 58.06 N | 114.08 E |

| | | | |
|---|---|---|---|
| Andrejevskaja | 80 | 47.21 N | 43.02 E |
| Andrejevskoje, Ross. | 82 | 54.23 N | 36.12 E |
| Andrejevskoje, Ross. | 82 | 56.24 N | 39.01 E |
| Andrejevskoje, Ross. | 82 | 55.46 N | 36.35 E |
| Andrejkoviči | 76 | 52.25 N | 33.00 E |
| Andrelândia | 256 | 21.44 S | 44.18 W |
| Andrésy | 261 | 48.59 N | 2.04 E |
| Andretta | 68 | 40.56 N | 15.19 E |
| Andrew | 182 | 53.53 N | 112.21 W |
| Andrew, Mount ∧ | 162 | 32.52 S | 122.56 E |
| Andrews, In., U.S. | 216 | 40.51 N | 85.36 W |
| Andrews, Mi., U.S. | 216 | 41.57 N | 86.22 W |
| Andrews, N.C., U.S. | 192 | 35.12 N | 83.49 W |
| Andrews, S.C., U.S. | 192 | 33.18 N | 79.17 W |
| Andrews, Tx., U.S. | 196 | 32.19 N | 102.32 W |
| Andrews Air Force Base ■ | 208 | 38.48 N | 76.52 W |
| Andrews Manor | 284c | 38.49 N | 76.54 W |
| Andrezel | 261 | 48.37 N | 2.49 E |
| Andrézieux Bouthéon | 62 | 45.32 N | 4.16 E |
| Andria | 68 | 41.13 N | 16.18 E |
| Andriamena | 157b | 17.26 S | 47.30 E |
| Andriandampy | 157b | 22.45 S | 45.41 E |
| Andriba | 157b | 17.36 S | 46.55 E |
| Andrija, Otok I | 36 | 43.02 N | 15.45 E |
| Andrijevica | 38 | 42.44 N | 19.46 E |
| Andriyevo-Ivanivka | 78 | 47.28 N | 30.28 E |
| Andriyivka, Ukr. | 78 | 47.06 N | 36.35 E |
| Andriyivka, Ukr. | 78 | 49.32 N | 36.38 E |
| Andriyivka, Ukr. | 83 | 47.28 N | 37.39 E |
| Andriyivka, Ukr. | 83 | 48.49 N | 37.33 E |
| Androka | 157b | 25.02 S | 44.05 E |
| Andronovskoje | 76 | 60.39 N | 34.46 E |
| Andropov → Rybinsk | 76 | 58.03 N | 38.52 E |
| Ándros | 38 | 37.50 N | 24.57 E |
| Andros I, Ba. | 238 | 24.26 N | 77.57 W |
| Ándros I, Ellás | 38 | 37.45 N | 24.42 E |
| Androscoggin ≃ | 188 | 43.55 N | 69.55 W |
| Androsovka | 80 | 52.41 N | 49.35 E |
| Andros Town | 238 | 24.43 N | 77.47 W |
| Āndrott Island I | 122 | 10.50 N | 73.41 E |
| Andrupene | 76 | 56.11 N | 27.23 E |
| Andrushivka | 78 | 50.01 N | 29.01 E |
| Andr'ušino | 86 | 59.12 N | 62.59 E |
| Andrychów | 30 | 49.52 N | 19.21 E |
| Andudu | 154 | 2.29 N | 28.41 E |
| Andújar | 34 | 38.03 N | 4.04 W |
| Andulo | 152 | 11.30 S | 16.45 E |
| Anduze | 62 | 44.03 N | 3.59 E |
| Andžijevskij | 84 | 44.14 N | 43.05 E |
| Âne, Dos d' ∧ | 241o | 16.19 N | 61.46 W |
| Aneby | 26 | 57.50 N | 14.48 E |
| Anécho | 150 | 6.14 N | 1.36 E |
| Anecón Grande, Cerro ∧ | 254 | 41.25 S | 70.16 W |
| Anefis i-n-Darane | 150 | 18.03 N | 0.36 E |
| Anegada I | 238 | 18.45 N | 64.20 W |
| Anegada, Bahía ⊂ | 254 | 40.15 S | 62.15 W |
| Anegada Passage ⋓ | 238 | 18.30 N | 63.40 W |
| Anegam | 200 | 32.22 N | 112.01 W |
| Anegasaki | 268 | 35.28 N | 140.02 E |
| Anelngauhat | 175f | 20.14 S | 169.44 E |
| Añelo | 252 | 38.21 S | 68.47 W |
| Anenii Noi | 38 | 46.52 N | 29.14 E |
| Anepahan Peak ∧ | 116 | 9.40 N | 118.25 E |
| Aneroid | 184 | 49.43 N | 107.20 W |
| Anet | 50 | 48.51 N | 1.26 E |
| Aneta | 198 | 47.40 N | 97.59 W |
| Aneto, Pico de ∧ | 34 | 42.38 N | 0.40 E |
| Aney | 146 | 19.24 N | 12.56 E |
| Anfeng, Zhg. | 100 | 32.44 N | 120.24 E |
| Anfeng, Zhg. | 100 | 33.06 N | 120.08 E |
| Anfengqiao | 100 | 26.41 N | 118.08 E |
| Anfo | 64 | 45.46 N | 10.29 E |
| Anfu | 100 | 27.23 N | 114.37 E |
| Anfuzhen, Zhg. | 107 | 28.47 N | 104.41 E |
| Anfuzhen, Zhg. | 107 | 29.21 N | 105.28 E |
| Anga | 88 | 53.58 N | 106.12 E |
| Angamacutiro [de la Unión] | 234 | 20.10 N | 101.41 W |
| Angamos, Punta › | 252 | 23.01 S | 70.32 W |
| Angangueo | 234 | 19.37 N | 100.18 W |
| Ang'angxi | 89 | 47.09 N | 123.48 E |
| An'ganka | 89 | 52.18 N | 126.17 E |
| Angao | 100 | 33.08 N | 112.22 E |
| Angar | 164 | 3.39 S | 130.50 E |
| Angara ≃ | 88 | 58.06 N | 93.00 E |
| Angara-Débou | 150 | 11.19 N | 3.03 E |
| Angarbaka | 140 | 9.44 N | 24.44 E |
| Āngāria | 126 | 22.29 N | 90.22 E |
| Angarsk | 88 | 52.34 N | 103.54 E |
| Angas ≃ | 168b | 35.23 S | 138.59 E |
| Angas Downs | 162 | 24.49 S | 132.14 E |
| Angas Hills ⩘[2] | 162 | 22.55 S | 128.00 E |
| Angastaco | 252 | 25.38 S | 66.11 W |
| Angaston | 168b | 34.30 S | 139.02 E |
| Angat ≃ | 116 | 14.53 N | 120.46 E |
| Angatuba | 255 | 23.29 S | 48.25 W |
| Angaul | 88 | 53.49 N | 100.18 E |
| Angaur I | 175b | 6.54 N | 134.09 E |
| Angden Pass )( | 124 | 29.43 N | 86.17 E |
| Angduo | 102 | 32.20 N | 98.55 E |
| Ånge | 26 | 62.31 N | 15.37 E |
| Ángel, Salto (Angel Falls) ⌞ | 246 | 5.57 N | 62.30 W |
| Angel City | 220 | 28.20 N | 80.40 W |
| Ángel de la Guarda, Isla I | 232 | 29.20 N | 113.25 W |
| Angeles | 116 | 15.09 N | 120.35 E |
| Angeles National Forest ♠ | 280 | 34.15 N | 117.56 W |
| Angel Etcheverry | 258 | 35.02 S | 58.04 W |
| Angel Falls → Ángel, Salto ⌞ | 246 | 5.57 N | 62.30 W |
| Ängelholm | 41 | 56.15 N | 12.51 E |
| Ängelholm flygplats ⊠ | 41 | 56.20 N | 12.51 E |
| Angelica | 210 | 42.18 N | 78.00 W |
| Angelina □[6] | 222 | 31.17 N | 94.42 W |
| Angelina ≃ | 194 | 30.53 N | 94.12 W |
| Angelina, East Fork ≃ | 222 | 31.50 N | 94.56 W |
| Angel Island I | 282 | 37.52 N | 122.26 W |
| Angellala Creek ≃ | 166 | 26.40 S | 146.08 E |
| Angeln ◆[1] | 41 | 54.39 N | 9.44 E |
| Angelo ≃ | 162 | 23.43 S | 117.45 E |
| Angel R. Cabada | 234 | 18.35 N | 95.26 W |
| Ängelsberg | 40 | 59.58 N | 16.00 E |
| Angels Camp | 226 | 38.04 N | 120.33 W |
| Angels Creek ≃ | 226 | 38.01 N | 120.33 W |
| Angelus, Lake ◎ | 281 | 42.41 N | 83.20 W |
| Angemuk ∧ | 164 | 3.30 S | 138.34 E |
| Anger, Dtsch. | 64 | 47.48 N | 12.52 E |
| Anger, Öst. | 61 | 47.16 N | 15.42 E |
| Angera | 62 | 45.46 N | 8.35 E |
| Angerbach ≃ | 263 | 51.23 N | 6.44 E |
| Angereb ≃ | 144 | 13.51 N | 36.08 E |
| Angeren | 52 | 51.55 N | 5.58 E |
| Angerhausen ◆[8] | 263 | 51.23 N | 6.44 E |
| Ångermanälven ≃ | 26 | 62.48 N | 17.56 E |
| Ångermanland □[9] | 26 | 63.30 N | 18.05 E |
| Angermund ◆[8] | 263 | 51.20 N | 6.47 E |
| Angermünde | 54 | 53.01 N | 14.00 E |
| Angern, Dtsch. | 54 | 52.21 N | 11.44 E |
| Angern, Öst. | 61 | 48.22 N | 16.50 E |
| Angers | 32 | 47.28 N | 0.33 W |
| Angerville | 50 | 48.19 N | 2.00 E |
| Angervilliers | 261 | 48.36 N | 2.04 E |
| Ängesön I | 26 | 63.43 N | 20.55 E |
| Angevillers | 56 | 49.23 N | 6.02 E |
| Anggowala, Bukit ∧ | 112 | 4.15 S | 121.44 E |
| Anghelu Ruiu, Necropoli ⊥ | 71 | 40.38 N | 8.20 E |
| Anghiari | 66 | 43.32 N | 12.03 E |
| Angical | 255 | 12.00 S | 44.42 W |
| Angical do Piauí | 250 | 6.05 S | 42.44 W |
| Angicos | 250 | 5.40 S | 36.36 W |
| Angier | 192 | 35.30 N | 78.44 W |
| Angijak Island I | 176 | 65.40 N | 62.15 W |
| Angikuni Lake ◎ | 176 | 62.13 N | 99.50 W |

| | | | |
|---|---|---|---|
| Angke, Kali ≃ | 269e | 6.06 S | 106.46 E |
| Angkor Wat ⊥ | 110 | 13.26 N | 103.52 E |
| Ângk Tasaôm | 110 | 11.01 N | 104.41 E |
| Anglais, Baie des ⊂ | 186 | 49.15 N | 68.07 W |
| Anglais, Jardin ♠ | 261 | 48.38 N | 1.49 E |
| Anglais, Rivière des (English) ≃ | 206 | 45.13 N | 73.50 W |
| Angle | 42 | 51.41 N | 5.06 W |
| Angle Inlet | 198 | 49.21 N | 95.04 W |
| Anglem, Mount ∧ | 172 | 46.44 S | 167.56 E |
| Anglesea | 169 | 38.25 S | 144.11 E |
| Anglesey I | 44 | 53.17 N | 4.22 W |
| Anglet | 32 | 43.29 N | 1.31 W |
| Angleterre → England □[8] | 28 | 52.30 N | 1.30 W |
| Angleton | 222 | 29.10 N | 95.25 W |
| Anglezarke Moor ◆[3] | 262 | 53.40 N | 2.33 W |
| Anglezarke Reservoir ◎[1] | 262 | 53.39 N | 2.35 W |
| Angling ≃ | 184 | 56.45 N | 93.36 W |
| Angling Lake ◎ | 184 | 53.55 N | 93.52 W |
| Anglona ◆[1] | 71 | 40.50 N | 8.45 E |
| Anglo-Normandes, Îles → Channel Islands II | 28 | 49.20 N | 2.20 W |
| Anglure | 50 | 48.35 N | 3.49 E |
| Angmagssalik | 176 | 65.36 N | 37.41 W |
| Angmering | 42 | 50.48 N | 0.28 W |
| Ang Mo Kio | 271c | 1.22 N | 103.51 E |
| Ango | 154 | 4.02 N | 25.52 E |
| Angoche | 154 | 16.15 S | 39.54 E |
| Angoche, Ilha I | 154 | 16.20 S | 39.50 E |
| Angohrān | 128 | 26.35 N | 57.54 E |
| Angol | 252 | 37.48 S | 72.43 W |
| Angola, In., U.S. | 216 | 41.38 N | 84.59 W |
| Angola, N.Y., U.S. | 210 | 42.38 N | 79.01 W |
| Angola □[1], Afr. | 138 | 12.30 S | 18.30 E |
| Angola □[1], Afr. | 152 | 12.30 S | 18.30 E |
| Angola Basin ✢[1] | 10 | 15.00 S | 3.00 E |
| Angola Lake Shore | 214 | 42.37 N | 79.05 W |
| Angono | 269f | 14.31 N | 121.09 E |
| Angoon | 180 | 57.30 N | 134.35 W |
| Angora → Ankara | 130 | 39.56 N | 32.52 E |
| Angoram | 164 | 4.04 S | 144.04 E |
| Angostura, Méx. | 232 | 25.22 N | 108.11 W |
| Angostura → Ciudad Bolívar, Ven. | 246 | 8.08 N | 63.33 W |
| Angostura, Presa de la ◎[1] | 234 | 16.10 N | 92.40 W |
| Angostura Reservoir ◎[1] | 198 | 43.18 N | 103.27 W |
| Angoulême | 32 | 45.39 N | 0.09 E |
| Angoumois □[9] | 32 | 45.30 N | 0.05 W |
| Angra, Meos I | 164 | 2.42 S | 134.50 E |
| Angra do Heroísmo | 148a | 38.39 N | 27.13 W |
| Angra do Heroísmo □[5] | 148a | 38.50 N | 27.30 W |
| Angra dos Reis | 256 | 23.00 S | 44.18 W |
| Angren | 85 | 41.01 N | 70.12 E |
| Angren ≃ | 85 | 40.48 N | 68.53 E |
| Angri | 68 | 40.44 N | 14.34 E |
| Angrignon Zoological Park ♠ | 275a | 45.26 N | 73.36 W |
| Angrogna | 62 | 44.50 N | 7.13 E |
| Ängsö | 40 | 59.32 N | 16.51 E |
| Ängsö Nationalpark ♠ | 40 | 59.39 N | 18.44 E |
| Ang Thong | 110 | 14.35 N | 100.27 E |
| Angu | 154 | 3.33 N | 24.28 E |
| Angu ≃ | 256 | 21.48 S | 42.30 W |
| Angualasto | 252 | 30.03 S | 69.09 W |
| Anguang | 89 | 45.31 N | 123.45 E |
| Anguchang | 107 | 29.30 N | 103.39 E |
| Anguciana, Cerro ∧ | 236 | 8.50 N | 83.07 W |
| Anguilas, Arroyo ≃ | 288 | 34.26 S | 58.31 W |
| Anguilla | 194 | 32.58 N | 90.49 W |
| Anguilla □[2], N.A. | 230 | 18.15 N | 63.05 W |
| Anguilla □[2], N.A. | 238 | 18.15 N | 63.05 W |
| Anguilla Cays II | 238 | 23.31 N | 79.33 W |
| Anguillara Sabazia | 66 | 42.05 N | 12.16 E |
| Anguillara Veneta | 64 | 45.08 N | 11.53 E |
| Anguille, Cape › | 186 | 47.55 N | 59.25 W |
| Anguli Nur ◎ | 98 | 41.13 N | 114.32 E |
| Angumu | 154 | 0.07 S | 27.42 E |
| Anguo | 98 | 38.25 N | 115.19 E |
| Anguozhuang | 105 | 39.44 N | 117.59 E |
| Anguruga | 164 | 14.00 S | 136.29 E |
| Angus | 212 | 44.19 N | 79.53 W |
| Angus Place | 170 | 33.20 S | 150.06 E |
| Angustura | 256 | 21.45 S | 42.41 W |
| Angusville | 184 | 50.44 N | 101.01 W |
| Angwa ≃ | 154 | 15.51 S | 30.35 E |
| Angwin | 226 | 38.34 N | 122.26 W |
| Angyalföld ◆[8] | 264c | 47.33 N | 19.05 E |
| Angyō | 268 | 35.51 N | 139.46 E |
| An Hai, Viet | 110 | 15.13 N | 108.56 E |
| Anhai, Zhg. | 100 | 24.45 N | 118.27 E |
| Anhalt □[9] | 54 | 52.00 N | 11.30 E |
| Anholt | 52 | 51.52 N | 6.27 E |
| Anholt I | 26 | 56.42 N | 11.34 E |
| Anhovo | 64 | 46.03 N | 13.37 E |
| Anhua | 102 | 28.18 N | 111.14 E |
| Anhuai | 100 | 33.04 N | 117.50 E |
| Anhui (Anhwei) □[4] | 100 | 32.00 N | 117.00 E |
| Anhŭng | 98 | 36.41 N | 126.10 E |
| Anhwei → Anhui □[4] | 100 | 32.00 N | 117.00 E |
| Aniak | 180 | 61.35 N | 159.33 W |
| Aniak ≃ | 180 | 61.34 N | 159.30 W |
| Aniakchak National Monument ♠ | 180 | 56.50 N | 157.50 W |
| Anibare Bay ⊂ | 174b | 0.32 S | 166.57 E |
| Aniche | 50 | 50.20 N | 3.15 E |
| Anicuns | 255 | 16.28 S | 49.58 W |
| Anié | 150 | 7.45 N | 1.12 E |
| Anié ≃ | 150 | 7.40 N | 1.18 E |
| Anie, Pic d' ∧ | 32 | 42.57 N | 0.43 W |
| Aniene ≃ | 66 | 41.56 N | 12.30 E |
| Anif | 64 | 47.45 N | 13.04 E |
| Anik ◆[8] | 272c | 19.02 N | 72.53 E |
| Anikino, Ross. | 86 | 56.32 N | 73.56 E |
| Anikino, Ross. | 88 | 53.26 N | 120.20 E |
| Anikovo | 76 | 59.23 N | 43.45 E |
| Anil | 250 | 2.32 S | 44.14 W |
| Anil, Rio do ≃ | 287a | 22.59 S | 43.21 W |
| Animas | 200 | 31.56 N | 108.48 W |
| Animas ≃ | 200 | 36.43 N | 108.13 W |
| Animas Peak ∧ | 200 | 31.35 N | 108.47 W |
| Animas Valley V | 200 | 31.45 N | 108.50 W |
| Anin | 110 | 15.40 N | 97.46 E |
| Anina | 38 | 45.05 N | 21.51 E |
| Anipemza | 84 | 40.27 N | 43.37 E |
| Aniskino | 82 | 55.54 N | 38.06 E |
| Añisoc | 152 | 1.51 N | 10.46 E |
| Anita, Ia., U.S. | 198 | 41.26 N | 94.45 W |
| Anita, Pa., U.S. | 214 | 41.00 N | 78.58 W |
| Anıtkaya | 130 | 38.57 N | 30.18 E |
| Aniva | 89 | 46.43 N | 142.32 E |
| Aniva, mys › | 89 | 46.01 N | 143.25 E |
| Aniva, zaliv ⊂ | 89 | 46.16 N | 142.48 E |
| Anivorano | 157b | 18.44 S | 48.58 E |
| Anivorano Nord | 157b | 12.44 S | 49.13 E |
| Aniwa I | 175f | 19.17 S | 169.35 E |
| Anizy-le-Château | 50 | 49.30 N | 3.27 E |
| Anjad | 120 | 22.02 N | 75.03 E |
| Anjan | 26 | 63.41 N | 12.49 E |
| Anjangaon | 120 | 21.10 N | 77.18 E |
| Anjār, India | 120 | 23.08 N | 70.01 E |
| 'Anjar, Lubnān | 132 | 33.42 N | 35.54 E |
| 'Anjarah | 132 | 32.18 N | 35.45 E |
| Anjavimihavana | 157b | 12.32 S | 49.16 E |
| Anji | 106 | 30.43 N | 119.41 E |
| Anjiabe | 157b | 12.07 S | 49.20 E |
| Anjiang | 105 | 40.45 N | 117.38 E |
| Anjigami Lake ◎ | 190 | 47.51 N | 84.34 W |
| Anjō | 94 | 34.57 N | 137.05 E |
| Anjou | 206 | 45.36 N | 73.33 W |
| Anjou □[9] | 32 | 47.20 N | 0.30 W |

| | | | |
|---|---|---|---|
| Anjozorobe | 157b | 18.24 S | 47.5[illegible] E |
| Anju, C.M.I.K. | 98 | 39.36 N | 125.4[illegible] E |
| Anju, Zhg. | 100 | 31.45 N | 113.1[illegible] E |
| Anju, Zhg. | 107 | 30.21 N | 105.2[illegible] E |
| Anjudin | 24 | 62.33 N | 58.1[illegible] E |
| Anjuzhen | 107 | 29.59 N | 106.0[illegible] E |
| Anka | 150 | 12.07 N | 5.55 E |
| Ankang | 102 | 32.42 N | 109.05 E |
| Ankara | 130 | 39.56 N | 32.52 E |
| Ankara □[4] | 130 | 39.50 N | 32.50 E |
| Ankara ≃ | 130 | 39.51 N | 31.55 E |
| Ankaramena | 157b | 21.57 S | 46.39 E |
| Ankaratra ⩘ | 157b | 19.25 S | 47.12 E |
| Ankarimbelo | 157b | 22.08 S | 47.20 E |
| Ankaroaka ∧ | 157b | 17.48 S | 48.32 |
| Ankarsrum | 26 | 57.42 N | 16.19 E |
| Ankasakasa | 157b | 16.21 S | 44.52 E |
| Ankati | 80 | 50.44 N | 51.34 E |
| Ankavandra | 157b | 18.46 S | 45.18 E |
| Ankazoabo | 157b | 22.18 S | 44.31 E |
| Ankazobe | 157b | 18.21 S | 47.07 E |
| Ankazomiriotra | 157b | 19.38 S | 46.32 E |
| Ankeny | 190 | 41.43 N | 93.36 W |
| An Khe | 110 | 13.57 N | 108.39 E |
| Ankilimalinika | 157b | 22.58 S | 43.45 E |
| Ankilizato | 157b | 20.25 S | 45.01 E |
| Anking → Anqing | 100 | 30.31 N | 117.02 E |
| Ankisabe | 157b | 19.17 S | 46.29 E |
| Anklam | 54 | 53.51 N | 13.41 E |
| Ankleshwar | 120 | 21.36 N | 73.00 E |
| Ankober | 144 | 9.35 N | 39.44 E |
| Ankoro | 154 | 6.45 S | 26.57 E |
| Ankororoka | 157b | 25.30 S | 45.11 E |
| Ankou | 100 | 25.03 N | 113.24 E |
| An'kovo | 80 | 56.57 N | 39.57 E |
| Ankpa | 150 | 7.23 N | 7.37 E |
| Ankum | 52 | 52.32 N | 7.52 E |
| Ankwe ≃ | 150 | 8.03 N | 9.26 E |
| Anlinnuoer | 98 | 41.11 N | 114.31 E |
| Anliu | 100 | 23.42 N | 115.42 E |
| Anloga | 150 | 5.47 N | 0.50 E |
| Anlong | 102 | 25.02 N | 105.31 E |
| Ânlóng Vêng | 110 | 14.14 N | 104.05 E |
| Anlu | 100 | 31.17 N | 113.40 E |
| Anma-do I | 98 | 35.21 N | 126.02 E |
| Anmyŏn-do I | 98 | 36.30 N | 126.22 E |
| Ånn ◎ | 26 | 63.16 N | 12.34 E |
| Ann, Cape ›, Ant. | 9 | 66.10 S | 51.22 E |
| Ann, Cape ›, Ma., U.S. | 283 | 42.39 N | 70.38 W |
| Anna, Ross. | 78 | 51.29 N | 40.25 E |
| Anna, Il., U.S. | 194 | 37.27 N | 89.14 W |
| Anna, Oh., U.S. | 216 | 40.23 N | 84.10 W |
| Anna, Tx., U.S. | 196 | 33.21 N | 96.33 W |
| Anna, Lake ◎[1] | 188 | 38.04 N | 77.45 W |
| Annaba (Bône) | 148 | 36.54 N | 7.46 E |
| An-Nabaṭīyah □[4] | 132 | 33.20 N | 35.30 E |
| An-Nabaṭīyah at-Taḥtā | 132 | 33.23 N | 35.29 E |
| Annaberg, Öst. | 61 | 47.52 N | 15.22 E |
| Annaberg, Öst. | 64 | 47.31 N | 13.26 E |
| Annaberg-Buchholz | 54 | 50.35 N | 13.00 E |
| An-Nabī Shīt | 132 | 33.52 N | 36.07 E |
| An-Nabk | 130 | 34.01 N | 36.44 E |
| An-Nabqīyah I | 128 | 26.44 N | 36.01 E |
| Annaburg | 54 | 51.44 N | 13.03 E |
| Annaburger Heide ◆[3] | 54 | 51.40 N | 13.05 E |
| An-Nafūd ◆[2] | 128 | 28.30 N | 41.00 E |
| Annagassan | 48 | 53.53 N | 6.20 W |
| Annahütte | 54 | 51.34 N | 13.53 E |
| An-Najaf | 128 | 31.59 N | 44.20 E |
| An-Najaf □[4] | 128 | 31.00 N | 44.00 E |
| Annaka | 94 | 36.19 N | 138.54 E |
| An-Nakhl, Miṣr | 140 | 29.55 N | 33.45 E |
| An-Nakhl, Sūrīy. | 132 | 33.00 N | 36.07 E |
| Annalee ≃ | 48 | 54.03 N | 7.24 W |
| Annalee Heights | 208 | 38.51 N | 77.10 W |
| Annalong | 48 | 54.06 N | 5.53 W |
| Annam → Trung Phan □[9] | 110 | 15.00 N | 108.00 E |
| Anna Maria | 220 | 27.31 N | 82.44 W |
| Anna Maria Island I | 220 | 27.30 N | 82.43 W |
| An-Nāmir | 132 | 32.47 N | 36.13 E |
| Annamitique, Chaîne ⩘ | 110 | 17.00 N | 106.00 E |
| Annan | 44 | 54.59 N | 3.16 W |
| Annan ≃ | 44 | 54.59 N | 3.16 W |
| Annanberg | 164 | 4.55 S | 144.40 E |
| Annandale, Austl. | 166 | 21.57 S | 148.22 E |
| Annandale, Mn., U.S. | 190 | 45.15 N | 94.07 W |
| Annandale, N.J., U.S. | 210 | 40.38 N | 74.52 W |
| Annandale, Va., U.S. | 208 | 38.49 N | 77.11 W |
| Annandale V | 44 | 55.10 N | 3.25 W |
| Annandale-on-Hudson | 210 | 42.01 N | 73.54 W |
| Anna Pink, Bahía ⊂ | 254 | 45.50 S | 74.50 W |
| Anna Plains | 162 | 19.17 S | 121.37 E |
| Anna Point › | 174b | 0.30 S | 166.56 E |
| Annapolis | 208 | 38.58 N | 76.29 W |
| Annapolis Basin ⊂ | 186 | 44.39 N | 65.42 W |
| Annapolis Royal | 186 | 44.45 N | 65.31 W |
| Annapūrṇa ∧ | 124 | 28.34 N | 83.50 E |
| Annapūrṇapratham ∧ | 124 | 28.31 N | 84.08 E |
| An-Naqīrah ⍑[4] | 126 | 27.53 N | 48.15 E |
| Ann Arbor | 216 | 42.16 N | 83.43 W |
| Ann Arbor Municipal Airport ⊠ | 281 | 42.14 N | 83.45 W |
| Anna Regina | 246 | 7.16 N | 58.30 W |
| Annaricken Brook ≃ | 285 | 40.03 N | 74.42 W |
| An-Nāṣirīyah, 'Īrāq | 128 | 31.02 N | 46.16 E |
| An-Nāṣirīyah, Sūrīy. | 130 | 33.52 N | 36.49 E |
| Annaspan ◎ | 158 | 28.33 S | 25.47 E |
| An-Nawfalāb | 140 | 15.52 N | 32.32 E |
| An-Nawfalīyah | 146 | 30.47 N | 17.50 E |
| An-Nazlah | 132 | 31.32 N | 34.29 E |
| An-Nazlat | 142 | 29.19 N | 30.39 E |
| Annbank | 44 | 55.28 N | 4.30 W |
| Annean, Lake ◎ | 162 | 26.54 S | 118.14 E |
| Anne Arundel □[6] | 208 | 38.59 N | 76.30 W |
| Annebault | 50 | 49.15 N | 0.04 E |
| Annecy | 58 | 45.54 N | 6.07 E |
| Annecy, Lac d' ◎ | 58 | 45.51 N | 6.11 E |
| Annecy-le-Vieux | 58 | 45.55 N | 6.09 E |
| Annemasse | 58 | 46.12 N | 6.15 E |
| Annen | 263 | 51.27 N | 7.22 E |
| Annenkov Island I | 244 | 54.29 S | 37.05 W |
| Annenskij Most | 76 | 60.45 N | 37.10 E |
| Annenskoje | 86 | 53.08 N | 60.26 E |
| Anner ≃ | 48 | 52.22 N | 7.39 W |
| Annestown | 48 | 52.08 N | 7.17 W |
| Annet I | 42a | 49.54 N | 6.21 W |
| Annet-sur-Marne | 261 | 48.56 N | 2.43 E |
| Annette | 182 | 55.03 N | 131.34 W |
| Annette Island I | 182 | 55.10 N | 131.28 W |
| Annevoie-Rouillon | 56 | 50.21 N | 4.50 E |
| Annezin | 50 | 50.32 N | 2.37 E |
| Annfield Plain | 44 | 54.51 N | 1.45 W |
| An Nhon | 110 | 13.53 N | 109.06 E |
| Anniangniang | 89 | 51.33 N | 125.49 E |
| Annicco | 62 | 45.14 N | 9.52 E |
| An-Nīl □[4] | 140 | 19.00 N | 33.00 E |
| An-Nīl al-Azraq □[4] | 140 | 12.00 N | 34.00 E |
| Anning | 102 | 24.59 N | 102.18 E |
| Anningdu | 102 | 36.56 N | 104.31 E |
| Anninger ∧ | 264b | 48.03 N | 16.15 E |
| Annino | 265a | 59.46 N | 30.03 E |
| Anninskije Mineral'nyje Vody | 89 | 52.44 N | 140.12 E |
| Annisquam | 283 | 42.39 N | 70.41 W |
| Annisquam ≃ | 283 | 42.39 N | 70.41 W |
| Anniston | 194 | 33.39 N | 85.49 W |
| Annobón I | 138 | 1.25 S | 5.36 E |
| Annonay | 62 | 45.14 N | 4.40 E |
| Annopol | 30 | 50.54 N | 21.52 E |
| Anno-Rebrikovo | 83 | 49.36 N | 40.12 E |
| Annot | 62 | 43.58 N | 6.40 E |
| Annotto Bay | 241q | 18.16 N | 76.46 W |
| Annsjön ◎ | 40 | 58.48 N | 15.26 E |


| | | | | | |
|---|---|---|---|---|---|
| ≃ River | Fluß | Río | Rivière | Rio | |
| ≊ Canal | Kanal | Canal | Canal | Canal | |
| ⌞ Waterfall, Rapids | Wasserfall, Stromschnellen | Cascada, Rápidos | Chute d'eau, Rapides | Cascata, Rápidos | |
| ⋓ Strait | Meeresstraße | Estrecho | Détroit | Estreito | |
| ⊂ Bay, Gulf | Bucht, Golf | Bahía, Golfo | Baie, Golfe | Baía, Golfo | |
| ◎ Lake, Lakes | See, Seen | Lago, Lagos | Lac, Lacs | Lago, Lagos | |
| ≡ Swamp | Sumpf | Pantano | Marais | Pântano | |
| ⍓ Ice Features, Glacier | Eis- und Gletscherformen | Accidentes Glaciales | Formes glaciaires | Acidentes glaciares | |
| ⍑ Other Hydrographic Features | Andere Hydrographische Objekte | Otros Elementos Hidrográficos | Autres données hydrographiques | Outros acidentes hidrográficos | |

| | | | | |
|---|---|---|---|---|
| ✢ Submarine Features | Untermeerische Objekte | Accidentes Submarinos | Formes de relief sous-marin | Acidentes submarinos |
| □ Political Unit | Politische Einheit | Unidad Política | Entité politique | Unidade política |
| ʋ Cultural Institution | Kulturelle Institution | Institución Cultural | Institution culturelle | Instituição cultural |
| ⊥ Historical Site | Historische Stätte | Sitio Histórico | Site historique | Sitio histórico |
| ♠ Recreational Site | Erholungs- und Ferienort | Sitio de Recreo | Centre de loisirs | Area de Lazer |
| ⊠ Airport | Flughafen | Aeropuerto | Aéroport | Aeroporto |
| ■ Military Installation | Militäranlage | Instalación Militar | Installation militaire | Instalação militar |
| ◆ Miscellaneous | Verschiedenes | Misceláneo | Divers | Diversos |

ENGLISH — Name / Page / Lat.°′ / Long.°′

An-Nubayrah 142 30.54 N 30.35 E
An-Nuhūd 140 12.42 N 28.26 E
An-Nu'mān I 128 27.08 N 35.46 E
An-Nu'mānīyah 128 32.32 N 45.25 E
An-Nuwayrah 142 29.06 N 30.59 E
Annville, Ky., U.S. 192 37.19 N 83.58 W
Annville, Pa., U.S. 208 40.19 N 76.30 W
Annweiler am Trifels 56 49.12 N 7.58 E
Anō 94 34.46 N 136.27 E
Anoia 68 38.27 N 16.05 E
Anoia ≃ 34 41.28 N 1.56 E
Anoka 190 45.11 N 93.23 W
Áno Liósia 267c 38.05 N 23.42 E
Año Nuevo Bay ⊂ 226 37.07 N 122.19 W
Anopino 80 55.42 N 40.40 E
Anori, Bra. 246 3.47 S 61.38 W
Anorí, Col. 246 7.05 N 75.08 W
Anorotsangana 157b 13.56 S 47.55 E
Anosibe 157b 19.26 S 48.13 E
Anosyennes, Chaînes ⋏ 157b 24.30 S 46.50 E
Anotaie ≃ 250 3.29 N 52.04 W
Anpilogovo 78 51.47 N 36.01 E
Anping, Zhg. 98 38.16 N 115.30 E
Anping, Zhg. 98 34.01 N 115.07 E
Anping, Zhg. 100 26.33 N 113.22 E
Anping, Zhg. 104 41.11 N 123.26 E
Anping, Zhg. 105 39.43 N 116.53 E
Anpu 102 21.27 N 110.00 E
'Anqābīyah, Jabal al- ⋏2 142 30.01 N 31.37 E
Anqing 100 30.31 N 117.02 E
Anqiu 98 36.25 N 119.10 E
Anrath 56 51.17 N 6.28 E
Anren, Zhg. 100 28.04 N 119.20 E
Anren, Zhg. 100 26.42 N 113.16 E
Anrenzhen 107 30.31 N 103.38 E
Anröchte 52 51.33 N 8.19 E
Ans, Bel. 56 50.39 N 5.32 E
Ans, Dan. 41 56.19 N 9.36 E
Ansager 41 55.42 N 8.45 E
Ansai 102 36.54 N 109.10 E
'Anṣār 132 33.23 N 35.21 E
Ansbach 56 49.17 N 10.34 E
Anschan → Anshan 104 41.08 N 122.59 E
Anschlag 263 51.10 N 7.29 E
Anse 58 45.56 N 4.43 E
Anseba ≃ 144 17.03 N 37.24 E
Anse-Bertrand 241o 16.29 N 61.31 W
Anse-d'Hainault 238 18.30 N 74.27 W
Anse La Raye 241f 13.57 N 61.03 W
Anselmo 198 41.37 N 99.51 W
Anseremme 56 50.15 N 4.54 E
Anserma 246 5.13 N 75.48 W
Ansfelden 61 48.13 N 14.17 E
Anshan 104 41.08 N 122.59 E
Anshun 102 26.15 N 105.56 E
Ansina 252 31.54 S 55.28 W
Ansley 198 41.17 N 99.22 W
Anson 196 32.45 N 99.53 W
Anson Bay ⊂, Austl. 164 13.20 S 130.06 E
Anson Bay ⊂, Norf. I. 174c 29.01 S 167.55 E
Anson Creek ≃ 212 44.53 N 79.03 W
Ansŏng 98 37.02 N 127.16 E
Ansongo 150 15.40 N 0.30 E
Ansonia, Ct., U.S. 207 41.20 N 73.04 W
Ansonia, Oh., U.S. 216 40.12 N 84.38 W
Ansonville, N.C., U.S. 192 35.06 N 80.06 W
Ansonville, Pa., U.S. 214 40.51 N 78.34 W
Ansouis 62 43.44 N 5.28 E
Ansted 188 38.08 N 81.05 W
Anstey 42 52.40 N 1.11 W
Anstruther 46 56.13 N 2.42 W
Anstruther Lake @ 212 44.45 N 78.12 W
Ansudu 164 2.08 S 139.20 E
Ansus 164 1.44 S 135.49 E
Anta, Bra. 256 22.03 S 42.59 W
Anta, Perú 248 13.29 S 72.09 W
Antabamba 248 14.19 S 72.55 W
Antalaha 157b 14.53 S 50.16 E
Antaliepte 76 55.40 N 25.51 E
Antalivtsi 78 48.38 N 22.31 E
Antalya 130 36.53 N 30.42 E
Antalya □4 130 37.00 N 31.00 E
Antalya, Gulf of ⊂ → Antalya Körfezi ⊂ 130 36.30 N 31.00 E
Antalya Körfezi ⊂ 130 36.30 N 31.00 E
Antambohobe 157b 22.20 S 46.47 E
An Tan 110 15.26 N 108.39 E
Antananambao Manampotsy 157b 19.29 S 48.34 E
Antanambe 157b 16.26 S 49.52 E
Antananarivo 157b 18.55 S 47.31 E
Antananarivo □4 157b 19.00 S 47.00 E
Antanetibe 157b 18.27 S 46.42 E
Antanifotsy 157b 19.39 S 47.19 E
Antanimieva 157b 22.12 S 43.44 E
Antanimora 157b 24.49 S 45.40 E
Antar, Djebel ∧ 148 31.57 N 1.56 W
Antarctica ⊥1 9 87.00 S 60.00 E
Antarctic Peninsula >1 9 69.30 S 65.00 W
Antarctique, Péninsule → Antarctic Peninsula >1 9 69.30 S 65.00 W
Antarktis → Antarctica ⊥1 9 87.00 S 60.00 E
Antártica, Península → Antarctic Peninsula >1 9 69.30 S 65.00 W
Antas 250 10.23 S 38.20 W
Antas, Ribeirão das ≃ 256 21.47 S 46.36 W
Antas, Rio das ≃ 252 29.04 S 51.21 W
An Teallach ∧ 46 57.48 N 5.14 W
Antechamber Bay ⊂ 168b 35.48 S 138.05 E
Antegnate 62 45.29 N 9.47 E
Antelope Acres 228 34.44 N 118.19 W
Antelope Creek ≃, Nv., U.S. 204 40.00 N 117.24 W
Antelope Creek ≃, S.D., U.S. 198 45.19 N 102.27 W
Antelope Creek ≃, Wy., U.S. 198 43.29 N 105.23 W
Antelope Island I 202 40.57 N 112.12 W
Antelope Mine 154 21.02 S 28.27 E
Antelope Peak ∧ 204 41.19 N 114.58 W
Antelope Reservoir @1 202 42.54 N 117.13 W
Antelope Valley V 228 34.45 N 118.20 W
Antelope Wash V 204 39.33 N 116.17 W
Antenor Navarro 250 6.44 S 38.27 W
Antequera, Esp. 34 37.01 N 4.33 W
Antequera, Para. 252 24.08 S 57.07 W
Antero Reservoir @1 200 39.00 N 105.55 W
Anterselva, Lago d' @ 64 46.53 N 12.10 E
Anterselva di Sopra 64 46.52 N 12.08 E
Antes Fort 210 41.12 N 77.14 W
Antetikireja 157b 14.42 S 47.29 E
Antevamena 157b 21.02 S 44.08 E
Antey-Saint-André 62 45.48 N 7.36 E
Anthéor 62 43.26 N 6.53 E
Anthon 198 42.23 N 95.51 W
Anthony, Fl., U.S. 192 29.17 N 82.06 W
Anthony, Ks., U.S. 198 37.09 N 98.01 W
Anthony, N.M., U.S. 200 32.00 N 106.36 W
Anthony, R.I., U.S. 207 41.41 N 71.32 W
Anthony, Tx., U.S. 200 31.59 N 106.36 W
Anthony Chabot Regional Park ♠ 282 37.45 N 122.06 W
Anthony Creek ≃ 188 37.54 N 80.20 W
Anthony Lagoon 162 17.59 S 135.32 E
Anthony Peak ∧ 204 39.51 N 122.58 W
Anti-Atlas ⋏ 148 30.00 N 8.30 W
Antibes 62 43.35 N 7.07 E
Antibes, Cap d' > 62 43.32 N 7.07 E
Anticosti, Île d' I 186 49.30 N 63.00 W
Antiesen ≃ 60 48.22 N 13.24 E
Antietam Creek, West Branch ≃ 208 39.41 N 77.37 W
Antietam National Battlefield ♠ 188 39.24 N 77.47 W
Antifer, Cap d' > 50 49.41 N 0.10 E
Antignano 66 43.30 N 10.19 E
Antigo 190 45.08 N 89.09 W
Antigonish 186 45.35 N 61.55 W
Antigorio, Valle V 58 46.18 N 8.20 E
Antigua I 240c 17.03 N 61.48 W
Antigua and Barbuda □1, N.A. 230 17.03 N 61.48 W
Antigua and Barbuda □1, N.A. 240c 17.03 N 61.48 W
Antigua Guatemala 236 14.34 N 90.44 W
Antigua International Airport ⊗ 240c 17.09 N 61.47 W
Antigues, Pointe d' > 241o 16.26 N 61.33 W
Antiguo Morelos 234 22.33 N 99.05 W
Anti-Lebanon → Sharqī, Al-Jabal ash- ⋏ 132 33.35 N 36.00 E
Antilla, Arg. 252 26.06 S 64.36 W
Antilla, Cuba 240p 20.50 N 75.45 W
Antillas, Archipiélago de las → West Indies II 230 19.00 N 70.00 W
Antillas Holandesas → Netherlands Antilles □2 241s 12.15 N 69.00 W
Antilles hollandaise → Netherlands Antilles □2 241s 12.15 N 69.00 W
Antilles néerlandaises → Netherlands Antilles □2 241s 12.15 N 69.00 W
Antillo 70 37.58 N 15.15 E
Antilyās 132 33.55 N 35.35 E
Antimano ⊕8 286c 10.28 N 66.59 W
Antimony 200 38.07 N 111.59 W
Anting 106 31.18 N 121.09 E
Antioch → Hatay, Tür. 130 36.14 N 36.07 E
Antioch, Ca., U.S. 226 38.00 N 121.48 W
Antioch, Il., U.S. 216 42.28 N 88.05 W
Antioquia 246 6.33 N 75.50 W
Antioquia □5 246 7.00 N 75.30 W
Antipino, Ross. 76 55.55 N 33.16 E
Antipino, Ross. 86 57.49 N 66.34 E
Antipino, Ross. 86 59.01 N 55.10 E
Antipodes Islands II 9 49.40 S 178.47 E
Antipolo 116 14.35 N 121.10 E
Antipovka 80 49.50 N 45.20 E
Antiquarian Museum ⊻ 283 42.27 N 71.20 W
Antique □4 116 11.00 N 121.45 E
Antizana ∧1 246 0.30 S 78.08 W
Antler ≃ 184 49.08 N 101.00 W
Antlers 196 34.13 N 95.37 W
Antoetra 157b 20.46 S 47.20 E
Antofagasta 252 23.39 S 70.24 W
Antofagasta □4 252 23.30 S 69.00 W
Antofagasta de la Sierra 252 26.04 S 67.25 W
Antofalla, Salar de ≐ 252 25.44 S 67.45 W
Antofalla, Volcán ∧1 252 25.34 S 67.55 W
Antoing 50 50.34 N 3.27 E
Antolana ∧ 157b 17.04 S 48.09 E
Antón, Pan. 236 8.24 N 80.16 W
Anton, Tx., U.S. 196 33.49 N 102.10 W
Anton Chico 200 35.12 N 105.08 W
Antongila, Helodrano ⊂ 157b 15.45 S 49.50 E
Antonia 219 38.21 N 90.27 W
Antonibe 157b 15.07 S 47.24 E
Antonina 252 25.27 S 48.43 W
Antonina do Norte 250 6.43 S 39.58 W
Antoniny 78 49.49 N 26.52 E
Antonio Amaro 232 24.16 N 104.01 W
Antonio Carboni 258 35.12 S 59.20 W
Antônio Carlos 256 21.19 S 43.45 W
Antônio de Biedma 254 47.29 S 66.30 W
Antonio Escobedo 234 20.46 N 103.57 W
Antônio Lemos 250 1.22 S 50.50 W
Antônio Prado 252 28.51 S 51.17 W
Antonito 200 37.05 N 106.00 W
Antoniv 78 49.37 N 29.47 E
Antón Lizardo, Punta > 234 19.03 N 95.58 W
Antonovka, Kaz. 86 53.19 N 68.26 E
Antonovka, Kaz. 86 45.38 N 80.15 E
Antonovka, Ross. 80 54.55 N 49.30 E
Antonovo 80 49.23 N 51.47 E
Antony 56 48.45 N 2.18 E
Antopal' 76 52.12 N 24.47 E
Antou 100 26.07 N 118.11 E
Antraigues 62 44.43 N 4.21 E
Antrain 32 48.27 N 1.29 W
Antratsit → Antratsyt 83 48.06 N 39.06 E
Antratsyt 83 48.06 N 39.06 E
Antrim 56 50.54 N 9.15 E
Antrim, N. Ire., U.K. 48 54.43 N 6.13 W
Antrim, Oh., U.S. 214 40.06 N 81.23 W
Antrim, Pa., U.S. 210 41.37 N 77.18 W
Antrodoco 66 42.25 N 13.05 E
Antronapiana 58 46.03 N 8.07 E
Antropologia, Museo Nacional de ⊻ 286a 19.25 N 99.11 W
Antropovo, Ross. 80 58.26 N 43.00 E
Antropovo, Ross. 82 55.15 N 37.39 E
Antsakabary 157b 15.03 S 48.56 E
Antsalova 157b 18.40 S 44.37 E
Antsenavolo 157b 21.24 S 48.03 E
Antsiafabositra 157b 17.18 S 46.57 E
Antsirabe, Madag. 157b 14.00 S 49.59 E
Antsirabe, Madag. 157b 15.57 S 48.58 E
Antsirabe, Madag. 157b 19.51 S 47.02 E
Antsiranana 157b 12.16 S 49.17 E
Antsiranana □4 157b 13.20 S 49.20 E
Antsla 76 57.50 N 26.32 E
Antsohihy 157b 14.52 S 47.59 E
Anttis 24 67.16 N 22.52 E
Antu (Songjiang) 98 42.32 N 128.18 E
Antulai, Jazīrat I 144 15.45 N 42.25 E
Antulai, Gunong ∧ 112 4.40 N 116.21 E
Antun' 89 47.36 N 135.46 E
Antung → Dandong 98 40.08 N 124.20 E
Antuševo, Ross. 76 59.54 N 37.40 E
Antuševo, Ross. 76 59.59 N 42.18 E
Antwerp → Antwerpen, Bel. 50 51.13 N 4.25 E
Antwerp, N.Y., U.S. 212 44.11 N 75.36 W
Antwerp, Oh., U.S. 216 41.10 N 84.44 W
Antwerpen (Anvers) 50 51.13 N 4.25 E
Antwerpen □4 50 51.10 N 4.50 E
Antykan 89 54.55 N 135.12 E
Anua 174u 16.16 S 170.40 W
Anučino, Ross. 80 52.58 N 43.52 E
Anučino, Ross. 89 43.58 N 133.02 E
Anugul 120 20.51 N 85.06 E
Anŭi 98 35.38 N 127.48 E
An'uj ≃ 89 49.18 N 136.27 E
An'ujsk 74 68.18 N 161.38 E
An'ujskij chrebet ⋏, Ross. 74 67.30 N 166.00 E
Anujskij chrebet ⋏, Ross. 86 51.30 N 84.55 E
Anundshögen ⊥ 40 59.38 N 16.32 E
Anūpgarh 123 29.11 N 73.13 E
Anūpshahr 124 28.22 N 78.16 E
Anūr 126 22.55 N 87.39 E
Anuradhapura 122 8.21 N 80.23 E
Anvers → Antwerpen 50 51.13 N 4.25 E
Anversa degli Abruzzi 66 41.59 N 13.48 E
Anvers Island I 9 64.33 S 63.35 W
Anvik 180 62.40 N 160.12 W
Anvik ≃ 180 62.39 N 160.14 W
Anvil Peak ∧ 181a 52.00 N 179.35 E
Anvil Range ⋏ 180 62.30 N 133.50 W
Anvin 50 50.27 N 2.15 E
Anxi, Zhg. 100 25.06 N 118.12 E
Anxi, Zhg. 100 25.15 N 115.06 E
Anxi, Zhg. 102 40.32 N 95.51 E
Anxi, Zhg. 106 30.25 N 120.01 E
Anxian 102 31.40 N 104.32 E
Anxiang 102 29.23 N 112.09 E
Anxin (Xin'anzhen) 105 38.55 N 115.55 E
Anxing 106 31.24 N 119.06 E
Anxious Bay ⊂ 162 33.25 S 134.35 E
Anyama 150 5.30 N 4.03 W
Anyang, Taehan 98 37.23 N 126.55 E
Anyang, Zhg. 98 36.06 N 114.21 E
Anyang ≃ 98 36.01 N 114.46 E
Anyeke 154 2.24 N 32.31 E
A'nyêmaqên Shan ⋏ 102 34.30 N 100.00 E
Anyer Kidul 115a 6.04 S 105.53 E
Anyi 100 28.50 N 115.31 E
Anykščiai 76 55.32 N 25.06 E
Anyox 182 55.25 N 129.49 W
Anysberg 158 33.31 S 20.46 E
Anyuan, Zhg. 100 26.36 N 116.38 E
Anyuan, Zhg. 100 27.37 N 113.54 E
Anyuan, Zhg. 100 25.08 N 115.28 E
Anyuanyi → Tianzhu 102 37.14 N 102.59 E
Anyue 107 30.06 N 105.21 E
Anza ≃, It. 58 46.00 N 8.17 E
Anza ≃, It. 58 46.00 N 8.17 E
Anza-Borrego Desert State Park ♠ 204 33.00 N 116.26 W
Anzac 184 56.27 N 111.02 W
Anzaldo 248 17.50 S 65.55 W
Anzano di Puglia 68 41.07 N 15.17 E
Anzbari ∧ 123 34.40 N 74.50 E
Anze 102 36.11 N 112.16 E
Anžero-Sudžensk 86 56.07 N 86.00 E
Anzhen 106 31.36 N 120.28 E
Anzhou 105 38.52 N 115.49 E
Anzhuang 106 31.04 N 121.01 E
Anzi, It. 68 40.31 N 15.55 E
Anzi, Zaïre 152 0.52 S 23.24 E
Anzicun 105 39.46 N 115.50 E
Anzin 50 50.22 N 3.30 E
Anzio 66 41.27 N 12.37 E
Anzoátegui □3 246 9.00 N 64.30 W
Anzob 85 39.10 N 68.48 E
Anzob, pereval ⨯ 85 39.07 N 68.52 E
Anzola dell'Emilia 64 44.33 N 11.11 E
Anzon ≃ 62 45.45 N 3.57 E
Anžu, ostrova II 74 75.30 N 143.00 E
Aoba I 175f 15.25 S 167.50 E
Aoba / Maewo □8 175f 15.05 S 168.00 E
Aogaki 96 35.14 N 135.00 E
Aoga-shima I 90 32.28 N 139.46 E
Aohaibolihu 104 42.01 N 121.32 E
Aohandaba 104 42.05 N 121.59 E
Aohan Qi (Xinhui) 98 42.19 N 119.59 E
Aoiz 34 42.47 N 1.22 W
Aoji 98 42.31 N 130.23 E
Aojiang 100 27.37 N 120.33 E
Aojiao 100 23.37 N 117.26 E
Aola 175e 9.32 S 160.29 E
Aoliyingzi 104 42.14 N 121.58 E
Ao Luk 110 8.23 N 98.43 E
Aomar 34 36.30 N 3.47 E
Aomen → Macau 100 22.14 N 113.35 E
Aomori 92 40.49 N 140.45 E
Aonla 124 28.17 N 79.09 E
Aono-yama ∧ 96 34.27 N 131.48 E
Aóös (Vijosë) ≃ 38 40.37 N 19.20 E
A'opo 175a 13.29 S 172.30 W
Aôral, Phnum ∧ 110 12.02 N 104.10 E
Aorangi Mountains ⋏ 172 41.26 S 175.20 E
Aore I 175f 15.35 S 167.10 E
Aorere ≃ 172 40.41 S 172.40 E
Aoshang 100 25.46 N 113.19 E
Ao-shima I, Nihon 96 33.44 N 132.29 E
Ao-shima I, Nihon 96 33.55 N 134.44 E
Aosta 62 45.44 N 7.20 E
Aosta □4 58 45.45 N 7.20 E
Aosta, Valle d' V 62 45.46 N 7.25 E
Aoste 62 45.35 N 5.36 E
Aotou 100 22.44 N 114.33 E
Aoudaghost ⊥ 150 17.25 N 10.40 W
Aouderas 150 17.37 N 8.26 E
Aoudour, Oued ≃ 34 35.02 N 5.02 W
Aouk, Bahr ≃ 146 8.51 N 18.53 E
Aoukalé ≃ 146 9.17 N 22.42 E
Aouk-Aoukalé, Réserve de Faune de l' ♠4 146 10.00 N 21.15 E
Aoukâr ⁎1 150 18.00 N 9.30 W
Aoulime, Jebel ∧ 148 30.48 N 8.50 W
Aoumou 175f 21.24 S 165.50 E
Aourou 150 14.57 N 11.35 W
Aoya 96 35.31 N 133.59 E
Aoyama 94 34.40 N 136.11 E
Aoyama-tōge ⨯ 94 34.40 N 136.15 E
Aozi 146 21.04 N 18.41 E
Aozou 146 21.49 N 17.25 E
Apa ≃ 252 22.06 S 58.00 W
Apache 196 34.53 N 98.21 W
Apache Junction 200 33.24 N 111.32 W
Apache Lake @1 200 33.36 N 111.16 W
Apache Peak ∧ 200 31.49 N 110.25 W
Apalachee ≃ 192 33.32 N 83.17 W
Apalachee Bay ⊂ 192 30.00 N 84.13 W
Apalaches → Appalachian Mountains ⋏ 178 41.00 N 77.00 W
Apalachicola 192 29.43 N 84.59 W
Apalachicola ≃ 192 29.44 N 84.59 W
Apalachicola Bay ⊂ 192 29.40 N 85.00 W
Apalachin 210 42.04 N 76.09 W
Apam 150 5.17 N 0.44 W
Apan 234 19.43 N 98.25 W
Apanas, Laguna de @1 236 13.11 N 85.59 W
Apango 234 17.44 N 99.20 W
Apapa ⊕8 273a 6.27 N 3.22 E
Apapa Wharf ⁎5 273a 6.23 N 3.23 E
Apaporis ≃ 246 1.23 S 69.25 W
Aparados da Serra, Parque Nacional de ♠ 252 29.30 S 50.32 W
Aparan 84 40.36 N 44.23 E
Aparecida 256 22.50 S 45.14 W
Aparima ≃ 172 46.20 S 168.01 E
Aparri 116 18.22 N 121.39 E
Apartadó 246 7.54 N 76.39 W
Apaseo El Grande 234 20.33 N 100.41 W
Apastovo 80 55.11 N 48.30 E
Apatin 38 45.40 N 18.59 E
Apatity 24 67.34 N 33.18 E
Apatou 250 5.09 N 54.20 W
Apatzingán de la Constitución 234 19.05 N 102.21 W
Apaxtla de Castrejón 234 18.09 N 99.52 W
Apayacu ≃ 246 3.19 S 71.51 W
Ap Ba Tien 269c 10.44 N 106.36 E
Ap Binh Quoi 269c 10.48 N 106.36 E
Ap Binh Thanh 110 11.11 N 108.42 E
Apcheron, Péninsule de l' → Abşeron yarımadası >1 84 40.30 N 50.00 E
Ape 76 57.32 N 26.40 E
Apeadero Funke 258 35.28 S 58.59 W
Apecchio 66 43.33 N 12.25 E
Ape Dale V 42 52.30 N 2.45 W
Apeganau Lake @ 184 55.35 N 99.35 W
Apelação 266c 38.49 N 9.08 W
Apeldoorn 52 52.13 N 5.58 E
Apeleg, Arroyo ≃ 254 44.58 S 70.07 W
Apen 52 53.13 N 7.48 E
Apenburg 54 52.43 N 11.12 E
Apenes 224 49.16 N 124.41 W
Apeninos → Appennino ⋏ 36 43.00 N 13.00 E
Apenninen → Appennino ⋏ 36 43.00 N 13.00 E
Apennines → Appennino ⋏ 36 43.00 N 13.00 E
Apennins → Appennino ⋏ 36 43.00 N 13.00 E
Apensen 52 53.26 N 9.37 E
Apese ⊕8 273a 6.25 N 3.25 E
Apetlon 61 47.45 N 16.50 E
Apex 192 35.43 N 78.51 W
Apex Mountain ∧ 180 62.28 N 138.04 W
Api 154 3.40 N 25.26 E
Api ∧ 124 30.00 N 80.57 E
Api, Tanjung > 112 0.48 S 121.39 E
Apía, Col. 246 5.05 N 75.58 W
Apia, W. Sam. 175a 13.50 S 171.44 W
Apiacá ≃ 250 9.16 S 57.03 W
Apiacás, Serra dos ⋏1 248 10.15 S 57.15 W
Apiaí 252 24.31 S 48.50 W
Apiaú ≃ 246 2.39 N 61.12 W
Apice 68 41.07 N 14.56 E
Apipilulco 234 18.11 N 99.41 W
Apishapa ≃ 198 38.08 N 103.57 W
Apiti 172 39.58 S 175.53 E
Apizaco 234 19.25 N 98.09 W
Apizolaya 232 24.50 N 102.15 W
Aplahoué 150 6.56 N 1.41 E
Aplao 248 16.05 S 72.31 W
Ap Lei Chau I 271d 22.15 N 114.09 E
Aplerbeck ⊕8 263 51.29 N 7.33 E
Aplinskij, porog ⌊ 88 58.28 N 100.22 E
Apo 234 19.25 N 102.25 W
Apo, Mount ∧ 116 6.59 N 125.16 E
Apodi 250 5.39 S 37.48 W
Apodi ≃ 250 4.56 S 37.10 W
Apo East Pass ⨯ 116 12.40 N 120.40 E
Apoera 250 5.12 N 57.10 W
Apolakkiá 38 36.06 N 27.50 E
Apolda 54 51.01 N 11.31 E
Apolima Strait ⨯ 175a 13.50 S 172.10 W
Apolinario Saravia 252 24.25 S 64.02 W
Apollo 214 40.34 N 79.34 W
Apollo Bay 166 38.45 S 143.40 E
Apollo Beach 220 27.45 N 82.25 W
Apollonia ⊥ 146 32.54 N 21.58 E
Apón ≃ 246 10.06 N 72.23 W
Aponguao ≃ 246 4.48 N 61.36 W
Apopa 236 13.48 N 89.11 W
Apopka 220 28.40 N 81.30 W
Apopka, Lake @ 220 28.37 N 81.38 W
Apoquindo 286e 33.24 S 70.32 W
Aporá 250 11.39 S 38.05 W
Aporé 255 18.58 S 52.01 W
Aporé ≃ 255 19.27 S 50.57 W
Apo Reef ⁂2 116 12.40 N 120.29 E
Aporema 250 1.14 N 50.49 W
Aporo 234 19.41 N 100.25 W
Apostle Islands II 190 46.50 N 90.30 W
Apostle Islands National Lakeshore ♠ 190 46.55 N 91.00 W
Apóstoles 252 27.55 S 55.46 W
Apostolove 78 47.39 N 33.44 E
Appalachen → Appalachian Mountains ⋏ 178 41.00 N 77.00 W
Appalaches, Monts → Appalachian Mountains ⋏ 178 41.00 N 77.00 W
Appalachia 192 36.54 N 82.46 W
Appalachian Mountains ⋏ 178 41.00 N 77.00 W
Äppelbo 40 60.30 N 14.00 E
Appelhülsen 52 51.54 N 7.25 E
Appen 52 53.40 N 9.44 E
Appennino (Apennines) ⋏ 36 43.00 N 13.00 E
Appennino, Galleria dell' ⊕5 66 44.10 N 11.10 E
Appennino Abruzzese ⋏ 66 42.00 N 14.00 E
Appennino Calabrese ⋏ 68 39.00 N 16.30 E
Appennino Campano ⋏ 66 41.30 N 15.00 E
Appennino Ligure ⋏ 62 44.30 N 9.00 E
Appennino Lucano ⋏ 68 40.30 N 16.00 E
Appennino Tosco-Emiliano ⋏ 36 44.00 N 11.30 E
Appennino Umbro-Marchigiano ⋏ 66 43.20 N 12.45 E
Appenweier 58 48.32 N 7.59 E
Appenzell 58 47.20 N 9.25 E
Appenzell-Ausser Rhoden □3 58 47.22 N 9.28 E
Appenzell-Inner Rhoden □3 58 47.18 N 9.25 E
Appiano (Eppan) 64 46.28 N 11.15 E
Appiano Gentile 62 45.44 N 8.59 E
Appin 170 34.12 S 150.47 E
Appingedam 52 53.18 N 6.52 E
Apple ≃, U.S. 190 42.11 N 90.14 W
Apple ≃, Wi., U.S. 190 45.09 N 92.45 W
Appleby, S. Afr. 158 27.39 S 22.36 E
Appleby, Eng., U.K. 44 54.36 N 2.29 W
Appleby, Tx., U.S. 222 31.43 N 94.36 W
Apple Creek 214 40.45 N 81.50 W
Apple Creek ≃, Il., U.S. 219 39.22 N 90.37 W
Apple Creek ≃, Mo., U.S. 194 37.35 N 89.32 W
Apple Creek ≃, N.D., U.S. 198 46.40 N 100.46 W
Applecross 46 57.25 N 5.49 W
Appledore 42 51.03 N 4.10 W
Applegate 226 39.06 N 120.59 W
Applegate ≃ 202 42.26 N 123.27 W
Apple Hill 206 45.13 N 74.46 W
Apple Orchard Mountain ∧ 192 37.31 N 79.31 W
Apples 58 46.34 N 6.25 E
Apple Springs 222 31.13 N 94.58 W
Appleton, Eng., U.K. 262 53.21 N 2.33 W
Appleton, Mn., U.S. 198 45.11 N 96.01 W
Appleton, Wa., U.S. 224 45.48 N 121.16 W
Appleton, Wi., U.S. 190 44.15 N 88.24 W
Appleton City 194 38.11 N 94.01 W
Apple Valley 228 34.30 N 117.11 W
Applewold 214 40.47 N 79.36 W
Appley Bridge 262 53.35 N 2.43 W
Appling 192 33.32 N 82.18 W
Appoigny 50 47.53 N 3.32 E
Appomattox 192 37.21 N 78.49 W
Appomattox ≃ 192 37.18 N 77.18 W
Appomattox Court House National Historical Park ♠ 192 37.23 N 78.48 W
Approuague ≃ 250 4.38 N 51.58 W
Apra Harbor ⊂ 174p 13.27 N 144.38 E
Aprelevka 82 55.33 N 37.04 E
Aprel'sk 88 58.10 N 114.34 E
Aprel'skij 89 53.30 N 126.16 E
Apremont 58 46.13 N 5.40 E
Apremont-la-Forêt 56 48.51 N 5.38 E
Aprica, Passo d' ⨯ 64 46.09 N 10.09 E
Apricena 68 41.47 N 15.27 E
Aprigliano 68 39.14 N 16.20 E
April ≃ 164 4.18 S 142.26 E
Aprilia 66 41.36 N 12.39 E
Apscheron → Abşeron yarımadası >1 84 40.30 N 50.00 E
Apšeronsk 84 44.28 N 39.44 E
Apshawa 276 41.01 N 74.22 W
Apsley 212 44.45 N 78.06 W
Apt 62 43.53 N 5.24 E
Aptakisic 278 42.12 N 87.56 W
Ap Tan Hoa 269c 10.45 N 106.35 E
Ap Tan My 110 11.43 N 108.49 E
Aptos 226 36.58 N 121.53 W
Apuane, Alpi ⋏ 64 44.09 N 10.15 E
Apuaú ≃ 246 2.32 S 60.48 W
Apucarana 255 23.33 S 51.29 W
Apulia Station 210 42.49 N 76.05 W
Apure □3 246 7.10 N 68.50 W
Apure ≃ 246 7.37 N 66.25 W
Apurímac □5 248 14.00 S 73.00 W
Apurímac ≃ 248 11.48 S 74.03 W
Apurito 246 7.56 N 68.27 W
Āq ≃ 84 38.59 N 45.27 E
Aqaba, Gulf of ⊂ 128 29.00 N 34.40 E
'Aqabah, Wādī al- V 132 30.14 N 33.53 E
Āqbolāgh 84 38.54 N 44.32 E
Āqchah 120 36.56 N 66.11 E
'Aqīq 140 18.14 N 38.12 E
'Aqīq, Khalīj ⊂ 140 18.20 N 38.10 E
'Aqīq, Wādī al- V 128 24.17 N 40.10 E
Aq Qal'eh 128 37.01 N 54.30 E
Aqqikkol Hu @ 120 37.05 N 88.05 E
'Aqrabah 132 33.06 N 36.00 E
'Aqrah 128 36.45 N 43.54 E
Aquarius Plateau ⋏1 200 38.05 N 111.40 W
Aquasco 208 38.35 N 76.43 W
Aquashicola 210 40.49 N 75.35 W
Aquashicola Creek ≃ 210 40.47 N 75.37 W
Äquatorial-Guinea → Equatorial Guinea □1 152 2.00 N 9.00 E
Aquebogue 207 40.56 N 72.37 W
Aqueduct Race Track ♠ 276 40.40 N 73.50 W
Aquia Creek ≃ 208 38.23 N 77.18 W
Aquiaulne ≃ 50 47.37 N 2.30 E
Aquidabã 250 10.17 S 37.02 W
Aquidabã ≃ 248 20.58 S 57.50 W
Aquidabán ≃ 252 23.11 S 57.32 W
Aquidauana 248 20.28 S 55.48 W
Aquidauana ≃ 248 19.44 S 56.50 W
Aquila, Méx. 234 18.36 N 103.30 W
Aquila, Schw. 58 46.31 N 8.57 E
Aquileia 64 45.46 N 13.22 E
Aquiles Serdán, Méx. 232 28.36 N 105.53 W
Aquiles Serdán, Méx. 232 25.38 N 97.50 W
Aquili, Cachoeira ⌊ 250 11.08 S 55.22 W
Aquilla, Oh., U.S. 214 41.34 N 81.09 W
Aquilla, Tx., U.S. 222 31.51 N 97.13 W
Aquilla Creek ≃ 222 31.40 N 97.10 W
Aquilla Lake @1 222 31.55 N 97.12 W
Aquilonia 68 41.00 N 15.29 E
Aquin 238 18.17 N 73.24 W
Aquincumi Museum ⊻ 264c 47.34 N 19.03 E
Aquino 66 41.30 N 13.42 E
Aquio ≃ 246 2.42 N 67.34 W
Ara 124 25.34 N 84.40 E
Ara ≃, Esp. 34 42.25 N 0.09 E
Ara ≃, Ire. 48 52.24 N 7.56 W
Ara ≃, Nihon 92 38.09 N 139.25 E
Ara ≃, Nihon 94 35.39 N 139.51 E
Arab 194 34.19 N 86.29 W
'Arab, Baḥr al- ≃ 140 9.02 N 29.28 E
'Arab, Khalīj al- ⊂ 140 30.55 N 29.05 E
Arab, Oued el V 148 34.41 N 6.31 E
Arab, Shatt al- ≃ 128 29.57 N 48.34 E
'Arab, Wādī al- V 132 32.35 N 35.35 E
'Arabābād 128 33.02 N 57.41 E
'Arabah, Wādī V 142 29.07 N 32.39 E
'Arabah, Wādī al- (Ha'Arava) V 132 30.10 N 35.10 E
Arabako □4 34 42.50 N 2.45 W
Araban 130 37.26 N 37.41 E
Arabats'ka zatoka ⊂ 78 45.20 N 35.30 E
Arabba 64 46.30 N 11.52 E
Arabelo 246 4.55 N 64.13 W
Arabi 194 29.57 N 90.00 W
Arabian Basin ⁂1 12 11.30 N 65.00 E
Arabian Desert → Sharqīyah, Aṣ-Ṣaḥrā' ash- ⊕2 140 28.00 N 32.00 E
Arabian Gulf → Persian Gulf ⊂ 128 27.00 N 51.00 E
Arabian Peninsula >1 12 25.00 N 45.00 E
Arabian Sea ⊤2 118 15.00 N 65.00 E
Arabia Saudita → Saudi Arabia □1 118 25.00 N 45.00 E
Arabie, Mer d' → Arabian Sea ⊤2 118 15.00 N 65.00 E
Arabie Saoudite → Saudi Arabia □1 118 25.00 N 45.00 E
Arabique, Péninsule → Arabian Peninsula >1 12 25.00 N 45.00 E
Arabisches Meer → Arabian Sea ⊤2 118 15.00 N 65.00 E
'Arab Muṭayr 142 27.16 N 31.14 E
Ara-Bure, porog ⌊ 88 53.00 N 100.12 E
Äräb Yengicä 84 39.29 N 44.58 E
Araç 130 41.15 N 33.21 E
Araçá ≃ 246 0.25 S 62.55 W
Aracaju 250 10.55 S 37.04 W
Araçariguama 256 23.26 S 47.04 W
Aracataca 246 10.36 N 74.12 W
Aracati 250 4.34 S 37.46 W
Araçatuba 255 21.12 S 50.25 W
Araceli 116 10.33 N 119.59 E
Aracena 34 37.53 N 6.33 W
Arâches-les-Carroz 58 46.02 N 6.39 E
Arachino-seki ⊥ 94 35.33 N 136.05 E
Araci 250 11.20 S 38.57 W
Aracides, Cape > 175e 8.39 S 161.01 E
Aracitaba 256 21.20 S 43.23 W
Aracoiaba 250 4.23 S 38.49 W
Aracruz 255 19.49 S 40.16 W
Araçuaí 255 16.52 S 42.04 W
Araçuaí ≃ 255 16.46 S 42.02 W
Arad, Rom. 38 46.11 N 21.20 E
'Arad, Yis. 132 31.15 N 35.13 E
Arad □6 38 46.20 N 21.40 E
Arada, Hond. 236 14.48 N 88.18 W
Arada, Tchad 146 15.01 N 20.40 E
Aradeo 68 40.08 N 18.08 E
Aradhíppou 130 34.57 N 33.35 E
Arafali 144 15.05 N 39.45 E
Arafune-san ∧ 94 36.12 N 138.38 E
Arafura Sea ⊤2 164 9.00 S 133.00 E
Arafura Shelf ⁂4 14 10.00 S 137.00 E
Aragac, gora ∧ 84 40.32 N 44.14 E
Aragarças 255 15.55 S 52.15 W
Arago, Cape > 202 43.18 N 124.25 W
Aragon 192 34.02 N 85.03 W
Aragón □3 34 41.30 N 0.30 W
Aragón ≃ 34 42.13 N 1.44 W
Aragona 70 37.24 N 13.37 E
Aragua □3 246 10.00 N 67.10 W
Araguacema 250 8.50 S 49.34 W
Araguaçu 255 12.49 S 49.51 W
Aragua de Barcelona 246 9.28 N 64.49 W
Aragua de Maturín 246 9.58 N 63.29 W
Araguaia ≃ 242 5.21 S 48.41 W
Araguaia, Braço Menor ≃ 250 9.50 S 50.10 W
Araguaia, Parque Nacional do ♠ 250 12.00 S 50.20 W
Araguaína 250 7.12 S 48.12 W
Araguainha 255 16.49 S 53.05 W
Araguao, Caño ≃1 246 9.15 N 60.50 W
Araguari 255 18.38 S 48.11 W
Araguari ≃, Bra. 250 1.15 N 49.55 W
Araguari ≃, Bra. 255 18.21 S 48.40 W
Araguatins 250 5.38 S 48.07 W
Aragvi ≃ 84 41.50 N 44.43 E
'Ārah, Ra's al- > 144 12.36 N 43.56 E
Arahal 34 37.16 N 5.33 W
Arai, Nihon 94 34.41 N 137.34 E
Arai, Nihon 94 37.01 N 138.15 E
Ārāihāzar 126 23.47 N 90.40 E
Araioses 250 2.53 S 41.55 W
Ârak, Alg. 148 25.18 N 3.45 E
Arāk, Īrān 128 34.05 N 49.41 E

DEUTSCH — Name / Seite / Breite°′ / Länge°′ E = Ost

Araka 154 4.20 N 30.23 E
Arakamčečen, ostrov I 180 64.45 N 172.30 W
Arakan, porog ⌊ 88 57.35 N 96.36 E
Arakan Yoma ⋏ 110 19.00 N 94.40 E
Arakawa, Nihon 94 35.57 N 139.02 E
Arakawa, Nihon 174m 26.39 N 128.15 E
Arakawa ⊕8 268 35.47 N 139.47 E
Arakawa-dake ∧ 94 35.30 N 138.10 E
Arákhova 38 38.29 N 22.35 E
Árakhthos ≃ 38 39.01 N 21.03 E
Arakkonam 122 13.06 N 79.40 E
Araklı 130 40.57 N 40.03 E
Arakmeer, gora ∧ 84 42.38 N 46.49 E
Arakpur ⊕8 272a 28.35 N 77.10 E
Aral, Kyrg. 85 42.32 N 72.40 E
Aral, Kyrg. 85 41.50 N 73.03 E
Araldy 84 44.18 N 50.24 E
Aral Sea ⊤2 86 45.00 N 60.00 E
Aral'sk 86 46.48 N 61.40 E
Aralsor, ozero @, Kaz. 80 49.05 N 48.12 E
Aralsor, ozero @, Kaz. 80 48.42 N 52.24 E
Aralsul'fat 86 46.50 N 61.58 E
Aramá ≃ 250 1.06 S 50.40 W
Aramac 166 22.59 S 145.14 E
Aramac ≃ 166 23.02 S 144.31 E
Aramari 255 12.04 S 38.30 W
Ārāmbāg 126 22.53 N 87.47 E
Aramberri 232 24.06 N 99.49 W
Aramia ≃ 164 7.55 S 143.22 E
Aramon 62 43.53 N 4.41 E
Arampampa 248 17.55 S 66.04 W
Aramtalla 140 6.47 N 29.13 E
Ārān 128 34.04 N 51.29 E
Arana 258 35.00 S 57.54 W
Arancio, Lago @ 70 37.38 N 13.05 E
Aranda de Duero 34 41.41 N 3.41 W
Arandai 164 2.10 S 133.01 E
Arandas 234 20.42 N 102.21 W
Aranđelovac 38 44.18 N 20.35 E
Arandis 156 22.24 S 15.00 E
Aran Fawddwy ∧ 42 52.47 N 3.41 W
Arang 120 21.12 N 81.58 E
Aranhegyi-patak ≃ 264c 47.34 N 19.04 E
Ārāni, Bngl. 126 24.17 N 88.52 E
Arani, Bol. 248 17.34 S 65.46 W
Ārani, India 122 12.40 N 79.17 E
Aran Island I 48 54.58 N 8.33 W
Aran Islands II 48 53.07 N 9.43 W
Aranjuez 34 40.02 N 3.36 W
Aranos 156 24.09 S 19.09 E
Aransas ≃ 196 28.04 N 97.14 W
Aransas Pass 196 27.54 N 97.08 W
Arantāngi 122 10.10 N 78.59 E
Arantina 256 21.56 S 44.15 W
Aranyaprathet 110 13.41 N 102.30 E
Arao 96 32.57 N 130.28 E
Araouane 150 18.54 N 3.33 W
Arapa, Laguna @ 248 15.10 S 70.01 W
Arapaho 196 35.34 N 98.57 W
Arapahoe 198 40.18 N 99.54 W
Arapaho National Recreation Area ♠ 200 40.07 N 105.48 W
Arāpānja 272b 22.26 N 88.28 E
Arapawa Island I 172 41.11 S 174.19 E
Arapeí 256 22.41 S 44.27 W
Arapey 252 30.58 S 57.32 W
Arapey Chico ≃ 252 30.57 S 57.30 W
Arapey Grande ≃ 252 30.55 S 57.49 W
Arapiraca 250 9.45 S 36.39 W
Arapiri, Ilha I 250 2.04 S 54.56 W
Arápis 267c 37.59 N 23.32 E
Arapiuns ≃ 250 2.18 S 55.00 W
Arapkir 130 39.03 N 38.30 E
Arapongas 255 23.23 S 51.27 W
Arapoti 255 24.08 S 49.50 W
Arapuni 172 38.04 S 175.39 E
Araquil ≃ 34 42.48 N 1.45 W
'Ar'ar 128 30.59 N 41.02 E
'Ar'ar, Wādī V 128 31.23 N 42.26 E
Araracuara 246 0.38 S 72.15 W
Araranguá 252 28.56 S 49.29 W
Araraquara 255 21.47 S 48.10 W
Araras 255 22.22 S 47.23 W
Araras, Açude @1 250 4.20 S 40.28 W
Araras, Ribeirão das ≃, Bra. 256 22.52 S 46.37 W
Araras, Ribeirão das ≃, Bra. 256 21.18 S 45.45 W
Ararat, Austl. 169 37.17 S 142.56 E
Ararat, Haya. 84 39.50 N 44.42 E
Ararat, Mount → Ağrı Dağı ∧ 84 39.42 N 44.18 E
Arari 250 3.28 S 44.47 W
Arari, Lago @ 250 0.37 S 49.07 W
Arāria 124 26.08 N 87.24 E
Araripe 250 7.12 S 40.08 W
Araripe, Chapada do ⋏1 250 7.20 S 40.00 W
Araripina 250 7.33 S 40.34 W
Ararirá ≃ 246 0.30 S 63.33 W
Arar Lugole 144 3.16 N 45.28 E
Araruama, Lagoa de ⊂ 255 22.53 S 42.12 W
Araruna 250 6.32 S 35.44 W
Aras (Araz) ≃ 84 39.56 N 48.28 E
'Aras, Ḥawḍ al- ⊤4 142 30.51 N 32.32 E
Arashi-yama ∧2 270 35.01 N 135.40 E
Åråsviken ⊂ 40 59.02 N 14.01 E
Ara Terra 144 6.38 N 40.57 E
Áratos 38 41.05 N 25.33 E
Aratuípe 255 13.05 S 39.00 W
Aratula 171a 27.59 S 152.32 E
Arau 114 6.26 N 100.16 E
Arauá ≃, Bra. 246 4.06 S 63.36 W
Arauã ≃, Bra. 248 7.59 S 65.14 W
Arauá ≃, Bra. 248 5.40 S 60.48 W
Arauca 246 7.05 N 70.45 W
Arauca □5 246 6.40 N 71.00 W
Arauca ≃ 246 7.24 N 66.35 W
Araucária 252 25.35 S 49.25 W
Arauco 252 37.15 S 73.19 W
Arauco, Golfo de ⊂ 252 37.11 S 73.25 W
Araújo, Ilha do I 256 23.09 S 44.42 W
Araújos 255 19.56 S 45.04 W
Arauquita 246 7.02 N 71.25 W
Araure 246 9.34 N 69.13 W
Aravaca ⊕8 266a 40.28 N 3.46 W
Aravaipa Creek ≃ 200 32.50 N 110.43 W
Arāvalli Range ⋏ 120 25.00 N 73.30 E
Aravan 85 40.32 N 72.30 E
Arawata ≃ 172 44.00 S 168.41 E
Araxá 255 19.35 S 46.55 W
Araya 246 10.34 N 64.15 W
Araya, Punta de > 246 10.38 N 64.18 W
Arayat 116 15.10 N 120.46 E
Araz (Aras) ≃ 84 39.56 N 48.28 E
Arba 144 9.01 N 40.23 E
Arba de Luesia ≃ 34 41.52 N 1.18 W
Arbagar 88 51.56 N 116.15 E
Ārbālia 126 22.41 N 88.47 E
Arba Minch 144 6.02 N 37.33 E
Arbatax 71 39.56 N 9.42 E
Arbaž 80 57.41 N 48.18 E
Arbedo 58 46.12 N 9.03 E
Arbél 132 32.49 N 35.29 E
Arbesbach 61 48.29 N 14.57 E
Arbia ≃ 66 43.08 N 11.28 E
Arboga 40 59.24 N 15.50 E
Arbogaån ≃ 40 59.26 N 16.04 E
Arbois 58 46.54 N 5.46 E
Arboledas 252 36.53 S 61.29 W
Arboletes 246 8.51 N 76.26 W
Arbolito, Cerro ∧2 286d 12.10 S 76.57 W
Arbon 58 47.31 N 9.26 E
Arbonne 50 48.25 N 2.34 E
Arborea 71 39.46 N 8.35 E
Arborea ⊕1 71 39.50 N 8.50 E
Arborfield 184 53.06 N 103.39 W


**Symbols** in the index entries represent the broad categories identified in the key at the right. Symbols with superior numbers (⋏1) identify subcategories (see complete key on page I · 1).

**Symbole** im Register stellen die rechts im Schlüssel erklärten Kategorien dar. Symbole mit hochgestellten Ziffern (⋏1) bezeichnen Unterabteilungen einer Kategorie (vgl. vollständiger Schlüssel auf Seite I · 1).

**Los símbolos** incluídos en el texto del índice representan las grandes categorías identificadas con la clave a la derecha. Los símbolos con numeros en su parte superior (⋏1) identifican las subcategorías (véase la clave completa en la página I · 1).

**Les symboles** de l'index représentent les catégories indiquées dans la légende à droite. Les symboles suivis d'un indice (⋏1) représentent des sous-catégories (voir légende complète à la page I · 1).

**Os símbolos** incluídos no texto do índice representam as grandes categorias identificadas com a chave à direita. Os símbolos com números em sua parte superior (⋏1) identificam as subcategorias (veja-se a chave completa à página I · 1).

| | English | Deutsch | Español | Français | Português |
|---|---|---|---|---|---|
| ∧ | Mountain | Berg | Montaña | Montagne | Montanha |
| ⋏ | Mountains | Gebirge | Montañas | Montagnes | Montanhas |
| ⨯ | Pass | Paß | Paso | Col | Passo |
| V | Valley, Canyon | Tal, Cañon | Valle, Cañón | Vallée, Canyon | Vale, Canhão |
| ≐ | Plain | Ebene | Llano | Plaine | Planície |
| > | Cape | Kap | Cabo | Cap | Cabo |
| I | Island | Insel | Isla | Île | Ilha |
| II | Islands | Inseln | Islas | Îles | Ilhas |
| ⁎ | Other Topographic Features | Andere Topographische Objekte | Otros Elementos Topográficos | Autres données topographiques | Outros acidentes topográficos |

ESPAÑOL

| Nombre | Página | Lat.°′ | Long.°′ W = Oeste |
|---|---|---|---|
| Arborg | 184 | 50.55 N | 97.15 W |
| Arbrå | 26 | 61.29 N | 16.23 E |
| Arbroath | 46 | 56.34 N | 2.35 W |
| Arbu, Monte ∧ | 71 | 39.15 N | 9.27 E |
| Arbuckle | 226 | 39.01 N | 122.03 W |
| Arbuckle, Lake ⊜ | 220 | 27.41 N | 81.24 W |
| Arbuckle Creek ≃ | 220 | 27.26 N | 81.17 W |
| Arbuckle Mountains ⋀ | 196 | 34.25 N | 97.20 W |
| Arbuckles, Lake of the ⊜[1] | 196 | 34.25 N | 97.00 W |
| Arbury Hills | 216 | 41.33 N | 87.51 W |
| Arbus | 71 | 39.32 N | 8.36 E |
| Arbutus Lake ⊜ | 276 | 40.31 N | 74.10 W |
| Arbuzovo | 76 | 56.21 N | 32.27 E |
| Arbuzynka | 78 | 47.53 N | 31.19 E |
| Arc ≃, Fr. | 62 | 43.31 N | 5.07 E |
| Arc ≃, Fr. | 62 | 45.34 N | 6.12 E |
| Arc, Bayou des ≃ | 194 | 35.00 N | 91.30 W |
| Arcachon | 32 | 44.37 N | 1.12 W |
| Arcachon, Bassin d' ⊂ | 32 | 44.40 N | 1.10 W |
| Arcadas | 256 | 22.42 S | 46.52 W |
| Arcade, It. | 64 | 45.47 N | 12.13 E |
| Arcade, Ca., U.S. | 226 | 34.02 N | 118.15 W |
| Arcade, N.Y., U.S. | 210 | 42.32 N | 78.25 W |
| Arcadia, Ca., U.S. | 228 | 34.08 N | 118.02 W |
| Arcadia, Fl., U.S. | 220 | 27.12 N | 81.51 W |
| Arcadia, In., U.S. | 218 | 40.10 N | 86.01 W |
| Arcadia, Ia., U.S. | 198 | 42.01 N | 95.02 W |
| Arcadia, Ks., U.S. | 198 | 37.38 N | 94.37 W |
| Arcadia, La., U.S. | 194 | 32.32 N | 92.55 W |
| Arcadia, Mi., U.S. | 190 | 44.29 N | 86.13 W |
| Arcadia, Mo., U.S. | 194 | 37.35 N | 90.37 W |
| Arcadia, Ne., U.S. | 198 | 41.25 N | 99.07 W |
| Arcadia, Oh., U.S. | 216 | 41.06 N | 83.31 W |
| Arcadia, Pa., U.S. | 214 | 40.47 N | 78.51 W |
| Arcadia, S.C., U.S. | 192 | 34.57 N | 81.59 W |
| Arcadia, Tx., U.S. | 222 | 29.23 N | 95.07 W |
| Arcadia, Wi., U.S. | 190 | 44.15 N | 91.30 W |
| Arcângelo | 256 | 21.18 S | 44.19 W |
| Arcanum | 218 | 39.59 N | 84.33 W |
| Arcas, Cayos II | 232 | 20.12 N | 91.58 W |
| Arcata | 204 | 40.52 N | 124.04 W |
| Arcatao | 236 | 14.05 N | 88.45 W |
| Arc de Triomphe ⊥ | 261 | 48.53 N | 2.17 E |
| Arc Dome ∧ | 204 | 38.50 N | 117.21 W |
| Arce | 66 | 41.35 N | 13.34 E |
| Arceburgo | 256 | 21.22 S | 46.56 W |
| Arčeda ≃ | 80 | 49.52 N | 43.10 E |
| Arčedinsko-Donskije peski ◆[2] | 80 | 49.33 N | 43.15 E |
| Arcelia | 234 | 18.17 N | 100.16 W |
| Arcen | 52 | 51.29 N | 6.11 E |
| Arc-en-Barrois | 58 | 47.57 N | 5.00 E |
| Arces | 50 | 48.05 N | 3.36 E |
| Arc-et-Senans | 58 | 47.02 N | 5.46 E |
| Arcevia | 66 | 43.30 N | 12.56 E |
| Archambault, Lac ⊜ | 206 | 46.18 N | 74.15 W |
| Archangaj □[8] | 88 | 48.00 N | 101.30 E |
| Archangel → Archangel'sk | 24 | 64.34 N | 40.32 E |
| Archangel'sk | 24 | 64.34 N | 40.32 E |
| Archangel'skaja | 78 | 45.41 N | 40.15 E |
| Archangel'sk Oblast' □[4] | 24 | 63.00 N | 42.00 E |
| Archangel'skoje, Ross. | 76 | 53.16 N | 37.42 E |
| Archangel'skoje, Ross. | 78 | 51.27 N | 40.55 E |
| Archangel'skoje, Ross. | 80 | 55.13 N | 44.05 E |
| Archangel'skoje, Ross. | 80 | 54.26 N | 48.40 E |
| Archangel'skoje, Ross. | 82 | 55.19 N | 35.58 E |
| Archangel'skoje, Ross. | 84 | 44.37 N | 44.05 E |
| Archangel'skoje, Ross. | 265b | 55.47 N | 37.18 E |
| Archara | 89 | 49.27 N | 130.07 E |
| Archara ≃ | 89 | 49.13 N | 129.53 E |
| Archbald | 210 | 41.29 N | 75.32 W |
| Archbold | 216 | 41.31 N | 84.18 W |
| Archdale | 192 | 35.54 N | 79.58 W |
| Archer | 192 | 29.31 N | 82.31 W |
| Archer ≃ | 164 | 13.28 S | 141.41 E |
| Archer, Lake ⊜ | 283 | 42.04 N | 71.20 W |
| Archer, Mount ∧ | 166 | 23.20 S | 150.34 E |
| Archer Bay ⊂ | 164 | 13.25 S | 141.43 E |
| Archer Bend National Park ♠ | 164 | 13.30 S | 142.20 E |
| Archer City | 196 | 33.35 N | 98.37 W |
| Archer's Post | 154 | 0.39 N | 37.41 E |
| Arches | 58 | 48.07 N | 6.32 E |
| Arches National Park ♠ | 200 | 38.42 N | 109.45 W |
| Archi | 66 | 42.05 N | 14.23 E |
| Archiac | 32 | 45.31 N | 0.18 W |
| Archidona | 34 | 37.05 N | 4.23 W |
| Archipo-Osipovka | 78 | 44.22 N | 38.33 E |
| Archipovka | 80 | 56.38 N | 41.14 E |
| Archipovo | 24 | 66.26 N | 45.52 E |
| Archonskaja | 84 | 43.07 N | 44.30 E |
| Archshofen | 56 | 49.27 N | 10.04 E |
| Archville | 276 | 41.07 N | 73.52 W |
| Arci, Monte ∧ | 71 | 39.47 N | 8.44 E |
| Arcidosso | 66 | 42.52 N | 11.33 E |
| Arcille | 66 | 42.48 N | 11.15 E |
| Arcinazzo Romano | 66 | 41.48 N | 13.12 E |
| Arcisate | 62 | 45.54 N | 8.52 E |
| Arcis-sur-Aube | 50 | 48.32 N | 4.08 E |
| Arckaringa | 162 | 27.56 S | 134.45 E |
| Arckaringa Creek ≃ | 162 | 28.10 S | 135.22 E |
| Arc-les-Gray | 58 | 47.27 N | 5.35 E |
| Arco, It. | 64 | 45.55 N | 10.53 E |
| Arco, Id., U.S. | 202 | 43.38 N | 113.17 W |
| Arco de Baúlhe | 34 | 41.29 N | 7.58 W |
| Arcola, Sk., Can. | 184 | 49.37 N | 102.30 W |
| Arcola, It. | 64 | 44.07 N | 9.54 E |
| Arcola, Il., U.S. | 194 | 39.41 N | 88.18 W |
| Arcola, In., U.S. | 216 | 41.06 N | 85.17 W |
| Arcola, Ms., U.S. | 194 | 33.16 N | 90.52 W |
| Arcola, Pa., U.S. | 285 | 40.09 N | 75.27 W |
| Arcola, Tx., U.S. | 222 | 29.31 N | 95.27 W |
| Arconate | 266b | 45.32 N | 8.51 E |
| Arcore | 266b | 45.38 N | 9.19 E |
| Arcos | 255 | 20.17 S | 45.32 W |
| Arcos de la Frontera | 34 | 36.45 N | 5.48 W |
| Arcot | 122 | 12.54 N | 79.20 E |
| Arcoverde | 250 | 8.25 S | 37.04 W |
| Arctic Bay | 176 | 73.02 N | 85.11 W |
| Arctic Ocean ⊤[1] | 16 | 85.00 N | 170.00 E |
| Arctic Red ≃ | 180 | 67.27 N | 133.46 W |
| Arctic Red River | 180 | 67.27 N | 133.46 W |
| Arctic Village | 180 | 68.08 N | 145.19 W |
| Arctique, Océan Glacial → Arctic Ocean ⊤[1] | 16 | 85.00 N | 170.00 E |
| Arctowski ʊ[3] | 9 | 62.09 S | 58.28 W |
| Arcturus | 154 | 17.47 S | 31.20 E |
| Arcueil | 261 | 48.48 N | 2.20 E |
| Arcuentu, Monte ∧ | 71 | 39.35 N | 8.33 E |
| Arcvašen | 84 | 40.38 N | 45.32 E |
| Arcy-sur-Cure | 50 | 47.36 N | 3.45 E |
| Ard, Loch ⊜ | 46 | 56.11 N | 4.28 W |
| Ard, Ra's al- ≻ | 128 | 29.21 N | 48.05 E |
| Arda ≃, Europe | 38 | 41.39 N | 26.29 E |
| Arda ≃, It. | 64 | 45.02 N | 10.02 E |
| Ardabīl | 128 | 38.15 N | 48.18 E |
| Ardagger | 61 | 48.11 N | 14.50 E |
| Ardagh | 48 | 52.28 N | 9.04 W |
| Ardahan | 130 | 41.07 N | 42.41 E |
| Ardakān, Īrān | 128 | 30.16 N | 52.01 E |
| Ardakān, Īrān | 128 | 32.19 N | 53.59 E |
| Ardal | 128 | 31.59 N | 50.39 E |
| Ardalanish, Rubh' ≻ | 46 | 56.17 N | 6.18 W |
| Årdalsfjorden ⊂[2] | 26 | 61.12 N | 7.30 E |
| Årdalstangen | 26 | 61.14 N | 7.43 E |

FRANÇAIS

| Nom | Page | Lat.°′ | Long.°′ W = Ouest |
|---|---|---|---|
| Ardanuç | 130 | 41.08 N | 42.04 E |
| Ardara, Ire. | 48 | 54.46 N | 8.25 W |
| Árdara, It. | 71 | 40.37 N | 8.48 E |
| Ardara, Pa., U.S. | 279b | 40.22 N | 79.44 W |
| Ardarroch | 46 | 57.25 N | 5.38 W |
| Ardatov, Ross. | 80 | 55.15 N | 43.06 E |
| Ardatov, Ross. | 80 | 54.51 N | 46.13 E |
| Ardbeg | 46 | 55.39 N | 6.05 W |
| Ardcharnich | 46 | 57.51 N | 5.05 W |
| Ardea | 66 | 41.36 N | 12.33 E |
| Ardèche □[5] | 62 | 44.40 N | 4.20 E |
| Ardèche ≃ | 62 | 44.16 N | 4.39 E |
| Ardee | 48 | 53.52 N | 6.33 W |
| Ardélik | 146 | 12.26 N | 21.25 E |
| Arden, Mb., Can. | 184 | 50.17 N | 99.14 W |
| Arden, Ca., U.S. | 226 | 38.36 N | 121.23 W |
| Arden, De., U.S. | 208 | 39.48 N | 75.29 W |
| Arden, Forest of ◆[3] | 42 | 52.23 N | 1.42 W |
| Arden, Mount ∧ | 166 | 32.09 S | 137.59 E |
| Ardenay-sur-Mérize | 50 | 48.00 N | 0.25 E |
| Arden Mines | 279b | 40.12 N | 80.17 W |
| Ardennes □[5] | 32 | 49.40 N | 4.40 E |
| Ardennes ◆[1] | 56 | 50.10 N | 5.45 E |
| Ardennes, Canal des ≅ | 50 | 49.26 N | 4.02 E |
| Ardenno | 58 | 46.10 N | 9.39 E |
| Ardentinny | 46 | 56.03 N | 4.55 W |
| Ardenza | 66 | 43.31 N | 10.19 E |
| Arderin ∧[2] | 48 | 53.02 N | 7.40 W |
| Ardersier | 46 | 57.34 N | 4.02 W |
| Ardeşen | 130 | 41.12 N | 41.00 E |
| Ardestān | 128 | 33.22 N | 52.23 E |
| Ardey | 263 | 51.28 N | 7.43 E |
| Ardeygebirge ⋀[2] | 263 | 51.25 N | 7.23 E |
| Ardez | 58 | 46.46 N | 10.11 E |
| Ardfern | 46 | 56.10 N | 5.32 W |
| Ardglass | 48 | 54.16 N | 5.37 W |
| Ardgroom | 48 | 51.42 N | 9.52 W |
| Ardıçlı | 130 | 40.40 N | 37.00 E |
| Ardila ≃ | 34 | 38.12 N | 7.28 W |
| Ardill | 184 | 49.53 N | 105.49 W |
| Ardino | 38 | 41.35 N | 25.08 E |
| Ardlethan | 166 | 34.21 S | 146.54 E |
| Ardlui | 46 | 56.18 N | 4.43 W |
| Ardlussa | 46 | 56.02 N | 5.47 W |
| Ardmolich | 46 | 56.49 N | 5.41 W |
| Ardmore, Ire. | 48 | 51.57 N | 7.43 W |
| Ardmore, Al., U.S. | 194 | 34.59 N | 86.50 W |
| Ardmore, In., U.S. | 216 | 41.41 N | 86.19 W |
| Ardmore, Md., U.S. | 284c | 38.56 N | 76.51 W |
| Ardmore, Ok., U.S. | 196 | 34.10 N | 97.08 W |
| Ardmore, Pa., U.S. | 208 | 40.01 N | 75.18 W |
| Ardmore Point ≻, Scot., U.K. | 46 | 56.39 N | 6.07 W |
| Ardmore Point ≻, Scot., U.K. | 46 | 55.42 N | 6.01 W |
| Ardnamurchan ≻[1] | 46 | 56.43 N | 6.00 W |
| Ardnamurchan, Point of ≻ | 46 | 56.44 N | 6.13 W |
| Ardnaree | 48 | 54.06 N | 9.08 W |
| Ardnave Point ≻ | 46 | 55.54 N | 6.20 W |
| Ardoch | 166 | 27.26 S | 144.08 E |
| Ardon, Ross. | 84 | 43.12 N | 44.18 E |
| Ardon, Schw. | 58 | 46.13 N | 7.15 E |
| Ardon ≃ | 84 | 43.17 N | 44.18 E |
| Ardon, Har ∧ | 132 | 30.38 N | 34.57 E |
| Ardooie | 50 | 50.59 N | 3.12 E |
| Ardore | 68 | 38.11 N | 16.10 E |
| Ardoux ≃ | 50 | 47.42 N | 1.35 E |
| Ardoz, Arroyo de ≃ | 266a | 40.26 N | 3.27 W |
| Ardres | 50 | 50.51 N | 1.59 E |
| Ardres ≃ | 50 | 49.18 N | 3.40 E |
| Ardrishaig | 46 | 56.01 N | 5.27 W |
| Ardrossan, Austl. | 168b | 34.25 S | 137.55 E |
| Ardrossan, Scot., U.K. | 46 | 55.39 N | 4.49 W |
| Ardsley, Eng., U.K. | 44 | 53.32 N | 1.28 W |
| Ardsley, N.Y., U.S. | 276 | 41.00 N | 73.50 W |
| Ardtalnaig | 46 | 56.31 N | 4.06 W |
| Arduan Island I | 140 | 19.55 N | 30.22 E |
| Ardusson ≃ | 50 | 48.30 N | 3.32 E |
| Ardvasar | 46 | 57.04 N | 5.54 W |
| Åre | 26 | 63.24 N | 13.04 E |
| Areado | 256 | 21.21 S | 46.09 W |
| Areal | 256 | 22.14 S | 43.07 W |
| Arèches | 62 | 45.41 N | 6.34 E |
| Arecibo | 240m | 18.28 N | 66.43 W |
| Arecibo, Observatorio de ʊ[3] | 240m | 18.20 N | 66.46 W |
| Areco ≃ | 258 | 33.56 S | 59.16 W |
| Areeiro | 266c | 38.39 N | 9.12 W |
| Arefjevo | 86 | 57.01 N | 90.40 E |
| Areguá | 252 | 25.18 S | 57.25 W |
| Arèhausk | 76 | 54.41 N | 30.30 E |
| Areia, Bra. | 250 | 6.58 S | 35.42 W |
| Areia, Port. | 266c | 38.43 N | 9.08 W |
| Areia, Ribeirão da ≃ | 255 | 16.07 S | 45.52 W |
| Areia Branca, Bra. | 250 | 4.56 S | 37.07 W |
| Areia Branca, Bra. | 287a | 22.44 S | 43.25 W |
| Areias | 256 | 22.35 S | 44.42 W |
| Arena | 68 | 38.34 N | 16.13 E |
| Arena, Point ≻ | 204 | 38.57 N | 123.44 W |
| Arena, Punta ≻ | 232 | 23.33 N | 109.28 W |
| Arena de la Ventana, Punta ≻ | 232 | 24.04 N | 109.52 W |
| Arena Island I | 116 | 9.14 N | 120.46 E |
| Arenal, C.R. | 236 | 10.29 N | 84.53 W |
| Arenal, P.R. | 240m | 17.59 N | 66.19 W |
| Arenal, Laguna de ⊜ | 236 | 10.32 N | 84.56 W |
| Arenal, Volcán ∧[1] | 236 | 10.28 N | 84.44 W |
| Arenápolis | 248 | 14.26 S | 56.49 W |
| Arenas, Cayo I | 232 | 22.08 N | 91.24 W |
| Arenas, Punta ≻ | 240m | 18.07 N | 65.35 W |
| Arenas, Punta de ≻ | 254 | 53.09 S | 68.13 W |
| Arenas de San Pedro | 34 | 40.12 N | 5.05 W |
| Arendal | 26 | 58.27 N | 8.48 E |
| Arendonk | 56 | 51.19 N | 5.05 E |
| Arendsee | 54 | 52.53 N | 11.30 E |
| Arendsee ⊜ | 54 | 52.53 N | 11.30 E |
| Arendtsville | 208 | 39.55 N | 77.18 W |
| Arenes, Riera de les ≃ | 266d | 41.29 N | 2.02 E |
| Arenig Fawr ∧ | 42 | 52.55 N | 3.45 W |
| Arenillas | 246 | 3.33 S | 80.04 W |
| Arenosa Creek ≃ | 196 | 28.52 N | 96.44 W |
| Arenys de Mar | 34 | 41.35 N | 2.33 E |
| Arenzano | 62 | 44.24 N | 8.41 E |
| Arenzville | 219 | 39.53 N | 90.22 W |
| Arequipa | 248 | 16.24 S | 71.33 W |
| Arequipa □[5] | 248 | 16.00 S | 72.15 W |
| Arequito | 252 | 33.09 S | 61.28 W |
| Arero | 144 | 4.45 N | 38.49 E |
| Arês, Bra. | 250 | 6.11 S | 35.09 W |
| Arès, Fr. | 32 | 44.46 N | 1.08 W |
| Arèsa ≃ | 76 | 52.33 N | 28.45 E |
| Arese | 266b | 45.33 N | 9.05 E |
| Aresing | 60 | 48.32 N | 11.18 E |
| Åreskutan ∧ | 26 | 63.26 N | 13.06 E |
| Areuse ≃ | 58 | 46.56 N | 6.53 E |
| Arévalo | 34 | 41.04 N | 4.43 W |
| Arezzo | 66 | 43.25 N | 11.53 E |
| Arezzo □[4] | 66 | 43.32 N | 11.50 E |
| Arfa', Jabal ∧ | 132 | 29.51 N | 35.27 E |
| 'Arfā', Wādī al- V | 132 | 30.16 N | 36.34 E |
| Arga ≃ | 34 | 42.18 N | 1.47 W |
| Argada | 88 | 54.14 N | 110.41 E |
| Argadargada | 166 | 21.40 S | 136.40 E |
| Argajaš | 86 | 55.29 N | 60.52 E |
| Argamasilla de Alba | 34 | 39.07 N | 3.06 W |
| Arganda | 34 | 40.18 N | 3.26 W |
| Argao | 116 | 9.52 N | 123.36 E |
| Arga-Sala ≃ | 74 | 68.30 N | 112.12 E |
| Argedeb | 144 | 6.10 N | 41.10 E |
| Argegno | 58 | 45.56 N | 9.08 E |
| Argel → El Djazaïr | 148 | 36.47 N | 3.03 E |
| Argelès-Gazost | 32 | 43.01 N | 0.06 W |
| Argelès-sur-Mer | 32 | 42.33 N | 3.01 E |
| Argelia → Algeria □[1] | 148 | 28.00 N | 3.00 E |

PORTUGUÊS

| Nome | Página | Lat.°′ | Long.°′ W = Oeste |
|---|---|---|---|
| Argen ≃ | 58 | 47.35 N | 9.33 E |
| Argenbühl | 58 | 47.40 N | 9.56 E |
| Argens ≃ | 62 | 43.24 N | 6.44 E |
| Argent | 158 | 26.04 S | 28.50 E |
| Argenta, It. | 66 | 44.37 N | 11.50 E |
| Argenta, Il., U.S. | 219 | 39.58 N | 88.49 W |
| Argentan | 32 | 48.45 N | 0.01 W |
| Argentat | 32 | 45.06 N | 1.56 E |
| Argentera | 62 | 44.24 N | 6.57 E |
| Argentera ∧ | 62 | 44.10 N | 7.18 E |
| Argenteuil | 50 | 48.57 N | 2.15 E |
| Argenteuil □[6] | 206 | 45.45 N | 74.30 W |
| Argentia | 186 | 47.18 N | 53.59 W |
| Argentiera | 71 | 40.44 N | 8.09 E |
| Argentière | 58 | 45.59 N | 6.56 E |
| Argentières | 261 | 48.39 N | 2.52 E |
| Argentina □[1] | 244 | 34.00 S | 64.00 W |
| Argentina ≃ | 62 | 43.50 N | 7.51 E |
| Argentine | 216 | 42.47 N | 83.51 W |
| Argentine → Argentina □[1] | 244 | 34.00 S | 64.00 W |
| Argentine Basin ✢[1] | 18 | 45.00 S | 45.00 W |
| Argentinien → Argentina □[1] | 244 | 34.00 S | 64.00 W |
| Argentino, Hipódromo ♠ | 288 | 34.34 S | 58.26 W |
| Argentino, Lago ⊜ | 254 | 50.13 S | 72.25 W |
| Argentona | 266d | 41.33 N | 2.24 E |
| Argentona, Riera d' ≃ | 266d | 41.31 N | 2.26 E |
| Argenton-Château | 32 | 46.59 N | 0.27 W |
| Argenton-sur-Creuse | 32 | 46.35 N | 1.31 E |
| Argentré | 32 | 48.05 N | 0.39 W |
| Argent-sur-Sauldre | 50 | 47.33 N | 2.27 E |
| Argeş □[6] | 38 | 45.00 N | 24.45 E |
| Argeş ≃ | 38 | 44.04 N | 26.37 E |
| Arghandāb ≃ | 128 | 31.27 N | 64.23 E |
| Arghastān ≃ | 120 | 31.23 N | 65.45 E |
| Argirita | 256 | 21.37 S | 42.50 W |
| Argıthanı | 130 | 38.17 N | 31.43 E |
| Argo | 140 | 19.31 N | 30.25 E |
| Ārgoal | 126 | 21.58 N | 87.38 E |
| Argo Island I | 140 | 19.25 N | 30.27 E |
| Argolikós Kólpos ⊂ | 38 | 37.33 N | 22.45 E |
| Argonia | 198 | 37.15 N | 97.45 W |
| Argonne | 190 | 45.39 N | 88.52 W |
| Argonne ◆[1] | 56 | 49.30 N | 5.00 E |
| Argonne National Laboratory ʊ[3] | 216 | 41.43 N | 87.58 W |
| Argopuro, Gunung ∧ | 115a | 7.57 S | 113.33 E |
| Árgos, Ellás | 38 | 37.39 N | 22.44 E |
| Argos, In., U.S. | 216 | 41.14 N | 86.15 W |
| Árgos Orestikón | 38 | 40.28 N | 21.16 E |
| Argostólion | 38 | 38.10 N | 20.30 E |
| Argoules | 50 | 50.21 N | 1.50 E |
| Argueil | 50 | 49.32 N | 1.31 E |
| Arguello, Point ≻ | 204 | 34.35 N | 120.39 W |
| Argun | 84 | 43.16 N | 45.52 E |
| Argun ≃ | 84 | 43.22 N | 45.55 E |
| Argun' (Ergun) ≃, Asia | 74 | 53.20 N | 121.28 E |
| Argungu | 150 | 12.45 N | 4.31 E |
| Arguni, Teluk ⊂ | 164 | 3.06 S | 133.42 E |
| Ārgur | 272b | 22.48 N | 88.13 E |
| Argut | 86 | 49.51 N | 87.03 E |
| Argut ≃ | 86 | 50.16 N | 86.43 E |
| Arguvan | 130 | 38.47 N | 38.17 E |
| Argyle, Austl. | 162 | 33.32 S | 115.46 E |
| Argyle, Mn., U.S. | 198 | 48.19 N | 96.49 W |
| Argyle, Mo., U.S. | 219 | 38.18 N | 92.02 W |
| Argyle, N.Y., U.S. | 210 | 43.14 N | 73.30 W |
| Argyle, Tx., U.S. | 222 | 33.07 N | 97.11 W |
| Argyle, Lake ⊜[1] | 164 | 16.15 S | 128.45 E |
| 'Arhāb, Wādī V | 142 | 28.55 N | 31.09 E |
| Arhavi | 130 | 41.22 N | 41.16 E |
| Arhéa Epídavros ⊥ | 38 | 37.37 N | 23.02 E |
| Århus | 41 | 56.09 N | 10.13 E |
| Århus □[6] | 41 | 56.15 N | 10.05 E |
| Århus Bugt ⊂ | 41 | 56.09 N | 10.18 E |
| Aria | 172 | 38.33 S | 174.59 E |
| Aria ≃ | 164 | 5.45 S | 149.15 E |
| Ariadnoje | 89 | 45.08 N | 134.25 E |
| Ariah | 126 | 23.33 N | 86.20 E |
| Ariake-kai ⊂ | 92 | 33.00 N | 130.20 E |
| Arial Khān ≃ | 126 | 23.56 N | 90.46 E |
| Ariamácina, Lago di ⊜[1] | 68 | 39.20 N | 16.32 E |
| Ariamsvlei | 156 | 28.07 S | 19.49 E |
| Ariana | 36 | 36.52 N | 10.12 E |
| Ariano, Isola d' I | 64 | 45.00 N | 12.10 E |
| Ariano Irpino | 68 | 41.09 N | 15.05 E |
| Ariano nel Polesine | 64 | 44.56 N | 12.07 E |
| Ariari ≃ | 246 | 2.35 N | 72.47 W |
| Arias | 252 | 33.38 S | 62.25 W |
| Arias, Arroyo de ≃ | 258 | 34.17 S | 56.06 W |
| Arias, Cañada ≃ | 258 | 34.39 S | 58.59 W |
| Ariaú | 250 | 3.11 S | 57.14 W |
| Aribinda | 150 | 14.14 N | 0.52 W |
| Arica, Chile | 248 | 18.29 S | 70.20 W |
| Arica, Col. | 246 | 2.08 S | 71.47 W |
| Arıcak | 130 | 38.33 N | 39.48 E |
| Aricanduva, Ribeirão ≃ | 287b | 23.32 S | 46.33 W |
| Ariccia | 66 | 41.43 N | 12.40 E |
| Arichat | 186 | 45.31 N | 61.01 W |
| Arichuna | 246 | 7.42 N | 67.08 W |
| Arid, Cape ≻ | 162 | 34.00 S | 123.09 E |
| Arida, Nig. | 273a | 6.34 N | 3.16 E |
| Arida, Nihon | 96 | 34.05 N | 135.07 E |
| Arida ≃ | 96 | 34.05 N | 135.06 E |
| Aridal, Sabkhat ⊜ | 148 | 26.12 N | 14.05 W |
| Aridhaía | 38 | 40.59 N | 22.03 E |
| Ariège □[5] | 32 | 43.00 N | 1.30 E |
| Ariège ≃ | 32 | 43.31 N | 1.25 E |
| Ariel, Wa., U.S. | 224 | 45.57 N | 122.34 W |
| Ari'el, W.B. | 132 | 32.06 N | 35.06 E |
| Arienzo | 68 | 41.01 N | 14.30 E |
| Arieş ≃ | 38 | 46.26 N | 23.59 E |
| 'Arif, Har ∧ | 132 | 30.26 N | 34.44 E |
| Ārifwāla | 123 | 30.17 N | 73.04 E |
| Ariguanabo, Laguna de ⊜ | 286b | 22.56 N | 82.33 W |
| Ariguaní ≃ | 246 | 9.35 N | 73.46 W |
| Arīḥā (Jericho), Ariha | 132 | 31.52 N | 35.27 E |
| Arīḥā, Sūrīy. | 130 | 35.48 N | 36.36 E |
| Arīḥā, Urd. | 132 | 31.25 N | 35.47 E |
| Arikaree ≃ | 198 | 40.01 N | 101.56 W |
| Arikaree, North Fork ≃ | 198 | 39.39 N | 102.57 W |
| Arikawa | 92 | 32.59 N | 129.07 E |
| Arikha, Har ∧[2] | 132 | 30.39 N | 34.47 E |
| Arild | 41 | 56.16 N | 12.34 E |
| Arima | 241r | 10.38 N | 61.17 W |
| Arima ◆[8] | 270 | 34.48 N | 135.15 E |
| Arima ≃ | 270 | 34.52 N | 135.15 E |
| Arima-fuji ∧[2] | 270 | 34.55 N | 135.14 E |
| Arimine-dam ◆[6] | 94 | 36.29 N | 137.27 E |
| Arinagour | 46 | 56.37 N | 6.31 W |
| Aringay | 116 | 16.26 N | 120.21 E |
| Arino ◆[8] | 270 | 34.50 N | 135.14 E |
| Arinos ≃ | 248 | 10.25 S | 58.20 W |
| Arinthod | 58 | 46.23 N | 5.34 E |
| Ario de Rosales | 234 | 19.12 N | 101.43 W |
| Ariogala | 76 | 55.16 N | 23.30 E |
| Aripeka | 220 | 28.25 N | 82.39 W |
| Ariporo ≃ | 246 | 6.03 N | 69.54 W |
| Aripuanã | 248 | 9.10 S | 60.38 W |
| Aripuanã ≃ | 248 | 5.07 S | 60.24 W |
| Ariquemes | 248 | 9.56 S | 63.04 W |
| Arisa ≃ | 246 | 7.32 N | 64.00 W |
| Arisaig | 46 | 56.51 N | 5.51 W |
| Arisaig, Sound of ⊂ | 46 | 56.51 N | 5.51 W |
| 'Arīsh, Wādī al- V | 140 | 31.09 N | 33.49 E |
| Arismendi | 246 | 8.29 N | 68.22 W |
| Aristazabal Island I | 182 | 52.30 N | 129.05 W |
| Aristes | 210 | 40.49 N | 76.20 W |
| Aristizábal, Cabo ≻ | 254 | 45.13 S | 66.31 W |
| Aristovo | 82 | 54.37 N | 36.40 E |
| Arıt | 130 | 41.41 N | 32.39 E |
| Aritao | 116 | 16.18 N | 121.02 E |
| Ariton | 194 | 31.36 N | 85.43 W |
| Aritzo | 71 | 39.57 N | 9.12 E |
| Arivonimamo | 157b | 19.01 S | 47.15 E |
| Ariyalūr | 122 | 11.08 N | 79.05 E |
| Arizaro, Salar de ≡ | 252 | 24.42 S | 67.45 W |
| Arizgoiti | 34 | 43.13 N | 2.54 W |
| Arizona | 252 | 35.43 S | 65.18 W |
| Arizona □[3], U.S. | 178 | 34.00 N | 112.00 W |
| Arizona □[3], U.S. | 200 | 34.00 N | 112.00 W |
| Arizpe | 232 | 30.20 N | 110.10 W |
| Arja | 80 | 57.30 N | 46.00 E |
| Årjäng | 26 | 59.23 N | 12.08 E |
| Arjasa | 112 | 6.51 S | 115.16 E |
| Arjawinangun | 115a | 6.39 S | 108.24 E |
| Arjay | 192 | 36.48 N | 83.38 W |
| Arjeplog | 24 | 66.00 N | 17.58 E |
| Arjona, Col. | 246 | 10.15 N | 75.21 W |
| Arjona, Esp. | 34 | 37.56 N | 4.03 W |
| Arka | 74 | 60.03 N | 142.12 E |
| Arkabutla Lake ⊜[1] | 194 | 34.45 N | 90.06 W |
| Arkadak | 80 | 51.58 N | 43.28 E |
| Arkadelphia | 194 | 34.07 N | 93.03 W |
| Arkaig, Loch ⊜ | 46 | 56.58 N | 5.08 W |
| Arkalyk | 86 | 50.13 N | 66.50 E |
| Arkansas □[3], U.S. | 178 | 34.50 N | 92.30 W |
| Arkansas □[3], U.S. | 194 | 34.50 N | 92.30 W |
| Arkansas ≃ | 178 | 33.48 N | 91.04 W |
| Arkansas, Salt Fork ≃ | 196 | 36.36 N | 97.03 W |
| Arkansas City, Ar., U.S. | 194 | 33.36 N | 91.12 W |
| Arkansas City, Ks., U.S. | 198 | 37.03 N | 97.02 W |
| Arkansas Post National Memorial ⊥ | 194 | 33.55 N | 91.26 W |
| Arkanū, Jabal ∧ | 146 | 22.13 N | 24.41 E |
| Arkatag Shan ⋀ | 120 | 36.48 N | 89.10 E |
| Arken-Ahon ∧ | 146 | 20.05 N | 18.25 E |
| Arkhangélos | 38 | 36.12 N | 28.08 E |
| Arkhangel'sk → Archangel'sk | 24 | 64.34 N | 40.32 E |
| Arki | 123 | 31.09 N | 76.58 E |
| Árki I | 38 | 37.22 N | 26.45 E |
| Arkit | 85 | 41.47 N | 71.58 E |
| Arklow | 48 | 52.48 N | 6.09 W |
| Arkoma | 194 | 35.21 N | 94.26 W |
| Arkona, Kap ≻ | 54 | 54.41 N | 13.26 E |
| Arkösund | 26 | 58.30 N | 16.56 E |
| Arkport | 210 | 42.23 N | 77.41 W |
| Arktičeskij, mys ≻ | 74 | 81.15 N | 95.45 E |
| Arktičeskogo Instituta, ostrova II | 74 | 75.20 N | 81.55 E |
| Arkul' | 80 | 57.17 N | 50.03 E |
| Arkville | 210 | 42.08 N | 74.37 W |
| Arkwright | 207 | 41.43 N | 71.33 W |
| Ärla | 40 | 59.17 N | 16.40 E |
| Arlan | 80 | 55.58 N | 54.15 E |
| Arlan, gora ∧ | 128 | 39.40 N | 54.33 E |
| Arlanc | 62 | 45.25 N | 3.44 E |
| Arlanda flygplats ⊠ | 40 | 59.37 N | 17.55 E |
| Arlanza ≃ | 34 | 42.06 N | 4.09 W |
| Arlanzón ≃ | 34 | 42.03 N | 4.17 W |
| Arlbergpass )( | 64 | 47.08 N | 10.12 E |
| Arlberg-Tunnel ◆[5] | 64 | 47.08 N | 10.12 E |
| Arlee | 202 | 47.09 N | 114.05 W |
| Arles | 62 | 43.40 N | 4.38 E |
| Arles à Port de Bouc, Canal d' ≅ | 62 | 43.40 N | 4.37 E |
| Arlesey | 42 | 52.01 N | 0.14 W |
| Arlesheim | 58 | 47.30 N | 7.37 E |
| Arleta ◆[8] | 280 | 34.15 N | 118.26 W |
| Arleux | 50 | 50.17 N | 3.06 E |
| Arley | 262 | 53.19 N | 2.30 W |
| Arli | 150 | 11.35 N | 1.28 E |
| Arli, Parc National de l' ♠ | 150 | 11.35 N | 1.30 E |
| Arlington, S. Afr. | 158 | 28.06 S | 27.54 E |
| Arlington, Ga., U.S. | 192 | 31 26 N | 84.43 W |
| Arlington, In., U.S. | 218 | 39.38 N | 85.34 W |
| Arlington, Ia., U.S. | 190 | 42.44 N | 91.40 W |
| Arlington, Ks., U.S. | 198 | 37.53 N | 98.10 W |
| Arlington, Ky., U.S. | 194 | 36.47 N | 89.00 W |
| Arlington, Ma., U.S. | 207 | 42.24 N | 71.09 W |
| Arlington, Mn., U.S. | 190 | 44.36 N | 94.04 W |
| Arlington, Ne., U.S. | 198 | 41.27 N | 96.21 W |
| Arlington, N.Y., U.S. | 210 | 41.41 N | 73.53 W |
| Arlington, Oh., U.S. | 216 | 40.53 N | 83.39 W |
| Arlington, Or., U.S. | 202 | 45.43 N | 120.11 W |
| Arlington, S.D., U.S. | 198 | 44.21 N | 97.07 W |
| Arlington, Tn., U.S. | 194 | 35.18 N | 89.40 W |
| Arlington, Tx., U.S. | 222 | 32.44 N | 97.06 W |
| Arlington, Vt., U.S. | 210 | 43.04 N | 73.09 W |
| Arlington, Va., U.S. | 208 | 38.52 N | 77.06 W |
| Arlington, Wa., U.S. | 224 | 48.11 N | 122.07 W |
| Arlington □[6] | 284c | 38.50 N | 77.10 W |
| Arlington, Lake ⊜[1] | 222 | 32.42 N | 97.13 W |
| Arlington Heights, Il., U.S. | 216 | 42.05 N | 87.58 W |
| Arlington Heights, Ma., U.S. | 283 | 42.25 N | 71.11 W |
| Arlington International Race Course ♠ | 278 | 42.05 N | 88.00 W |
| Arlington Memorial Bridge ◆[5] | 284c | 38.53 N | 77.03 W |
| Arlington Mill Reservoir ⊜[1] | 283 | 42.48 N | 71.13 W |
| Arlington National Cemetery ◆ | 284c | 38.53 N | 77.04 W |
| Arlit | 150 | 19.00 N | 7.38 E |
| Arlod | 58 | 46.06 N | 5.49 E |
| Arlon | 56 | 49.41 N | 5.49 E |
| Arlöv | 41 | 55.39 N | 13.05 E |
| Arltunga | 162 | 23.26 S | 134.41 E |
| Arl'uk | 86 | 55.26 N | 84.50 E |
| Arluno | 62 | 45.30 N | 8.56 E |
| Arly ≃ | 62 | 45.40 N | 6.23 E |
| Arlyn Oaks | 276 | 40.40 N | 73.27 W |
| Arm ≃ | 184 | 50.46 N | 105.00 W |
| Arma | 198 | 37.32 N | 94.42 W |
| Armação, Ponta da ≻ | 287a | 22.53 S | 43.08 W |
| Armada | 214 | 42.50 N | 82.53 W |
| Armadale, Austl. | 168a | 32.09 S | 116.00 E |
| Armadale, On., Can. | 275b | 43.50 N | 79.15 W |
| Armadale, S. Afr. | 273d | 26.17 S | 27.57 E |
| Armadale, Scot., U.K. | 46 | 55.54 N | 3.42 W |
| Arma di Taggia | 62 | 43.50 N | 7.51 E |
| Armageddon → Tel Megiddo ⊥ | 132 | 32.35 N | 35.11 E |
| Armagh, N. Ire., U.K. | 48 | 54.21 N | 6.39 W |
| Armagh, Pa., U.S. | 214 | 40.27 N | 79.02 W |
| Armagnac □[9] | 32 | 43.45 N | 0.10 E |
| Armah, Wādī V | 144 | 18.12 N | 51.02 E |
| Armainvilliers, Étang d' ⊜ | 261 | 48.45 N | 2.44 E |
| Armainvilliers, Forêt d' ♠ | 261 | 48.45 N | 2.45 E |
| Armance ≃ | 50 | 47.59 N | 3.43 E |
| Armançon ≃, Fr. | 50 | 47.57 N | 3.30 E |
| Armançon ≃, Fr. | 58 | 47.33 N | 4.17 E |
| Armant | 140 | 25.37 N | 32.32 E |
| Armavir | 72 | 45.00 N | 41.08 E |
| Armazém | 252 | 28.16 S | 49.01 W |
| Armbrust | 214 | 40.13 N | 79.33 W |
| Armells Creek ≃ | 202 | 47.37 N | 108.40 W |
| Armenia | 246 | 4.31 N | 75.41 W |
| Armenia □[9] | 84 | 40.30 N | 43.30 E |
| Armenia □[1], Asia | 72 | 40.00 N | 45.00 E |
| Armenia (Hayastan) □[1], Asia | 84 | 40.00 N | 45.00 E |
| Armenija → Armenia □[1] | 72 | 40.00 N | 45.00 E |
| Armeniş | 38 | 45.12 N | 22.19 E |
| Armenistís | 38 | 37.36 N | 26.08 E |
| Armeniya → Armenia □[1] | 72 | 40.00 N | 45.00 E |
| Armeno | 62 | 45.49 N | 8.26 E |
| Armenonville-les-Gâtineaux | 261 | 48.33 N | 1.39 E |
| Armentières | 50 | 50.41 N | 2.53 E |
| Armento | 68 | 40.18 N | 16.04 E |
| Armería | 234 | 18.56 N | 103.58 W |
| Armería ≃ | 234 | 18.52 N | 103.59 W |
| Armero | 246 | 4.58 N | 74.54 W |
| Armidale | 166 | 30.31 S | 151.39 E |
| Armijo | 200 | 35.03 N | 106.40 W |
| Armitage | 42 | 52.44 N | 1.53 W |
| Armit Lake ⊜ | 176 | 64.10 N | 91.32 W |
| Armizonskoje | 86 | 55.57 N | 67.42 E |
| Armona | 226 | 36.19 N | 119.42 W |
| Armonk | 276 | 41.07 N | 73.42 W |
| Armor | 210 | 42.44 N | 78.48 W |
| Armori | 122 | 20.28 N | 79.59 E |
| Armour | 198 | 43.19 N | 98.20 W |
| Armoy, Fr. | 58 | 46.21 N | 6.31 E |
| Armoy, N. Ire., U.K. | 48 | 55.07 N | 6.20 W |
| Armstrong, Arg. | 252 | 32.47 S | 61.36 W |
| Armstrong, B.C., Can. | 182 | 50.27 N | 119.12 W |
| Armstrong, Il., U.S. | 216 | 40.18 N | 87.53 W |
| Armstrong, Ia., U.S. | 198 | 43.23 N | 94.28 W |
| Armstrong, Mo., U.S. | 194 | 39.16 N | 92.42 W |
| Armstrong □[6] | 214 | 40.49 N | 79.32 W |
| Armstrong ≃ | 164 | 16.46 S | 131.12 E |
| Armstrong, Mount ∧ | 180 | 63.12 N | 133.16 W |
| Armstrong Station | 176 | 50.18 N | 89.02 W |
| Armthorpe | 44 | 53.32 N | 1.03 W |
| Ārmūr | 122 | 18.48 N | 78.17 E |
| Armutlu | 130 | 40.31 N | 28.50 E |
| Armyans'k | 78 | 46.07 N | 33.41 E |
| Arnå ≃ | 41 | 54.57 N | 8.53 E |
| Arnaccio | 66 | 43.40 N | 10.27 E |
| Arnaía | 38 | 40.29 N | 23.35 E |
| Arnarfjörður ⊂[2] | 24a | 65.45 N | 23.40 W |
| Årnäs | 40 | 58.41 N | 13.35 E |
| Arnaud ≃ | 176 | 59.59 N | 69.46 W |
| Arnaudville | 194 | 30.24 N | 91.56 W |
| Arnavad, gora ∧ | 85 | 38.33 N | 71.31 E |
| Arnavutköy ≃ | 267b | 41.13 N | 29.12 E |
| Arnay-le-Duc | 58 | 47.08 N | 4.29 E |
| Arnaz | 62 | 45.38 N | 7.43 E |
| Arnborg | 41 | 56.01 N | 8.59 E |
| Arnbruck | 60 | 49.08 N | 13.00 E |
| Arncliffe | 274a | 33.56 S | 151.09 E |
| Arneburg | 54 | 52.40 N | 12.00 E |
| Arnedo | 34 | 42.13 N | 2.06 W |
| Arneiro dos Marinheiros | 266c | 38.51 N | 9.25 W |
| Arneiroz | 250 | 6.20 S | 40.08 W |
| Arnejevo | 82 | 54.58 N | 37.35 E |
| Arnemuiden | 52 | 51.30 N | 3.41 E |
| Årnes | 26 | 60.09 N | 11.28 E |
| Arnett | 196 | 36.08 N | 99.46 W |
| Arney ≃ | 48 | 54.16 N | 7.37 W |
| Arnhem | 52 | 51.59 N | 5.55 E |
| Arnhem, Cape ≻ | 164 | 12.21 S | 136.21 E |
| Arnhem Bay ⊂ | 164 | 12.20 S | 136.12 E |
| Arnhem Land ◆[1] | 164 | 13.10 S | 134.30 E |
| Arnhem Land Aboriginal Reserve ◆[4] | 164 | 13.10 S | 134.30 E |
| Arni | 64 | 44.04 N | 10.15 E |
| Arnis | 41 | 54.38 N | 9.56 E |
| Árnissa | 38 | 40.48 N | 21.50 E |
| Arno I[1] | 14 | 7.05 N | 171.41 E |
| Arno ≃ | 66 | 43.41 N | 10.17 E |
| Arno, Torrente ≃ | 266b | 45.42 N | 8.48 E |
| Arno Bay | 166 | 33.54 S | 136.34 E |
| Arnoia ≃ | 34 | 42.15 N | 8.09 W |
| Arnold, B.C., Can. | 224 | 49.08 N | 122.03 W |
| Arnold, Eng., U.K. | 44 | 53.00 N | 1.08 W |
| Arnold, Ca., U.S. | 204 | 38.15 N | 120.21 W |
| Arnold, Md., U.S. | 208 | 39.01 N | 76.30 W |
| Arnold, Mn., U.S. | 190 | 46.52 N | 92.05 W |
| Arnold, Mo., U.S. | 219 | 38.25 N | 90.22 W |
| Arnold, Ne., U.S. | 198 | 41.25 N | 100.11 W |
| Arnold, Pa., U.S. | 214 | 40.34 N | 79.46 W |
| Arnold ≃ | 164 | 15.19 S | 134.06 E |
| Arnold Arboretum ♠ | 283 | 42.18 N | 71.08 W |
| Arnold Mills | 283 | 41.58 N | 71.23 W |
| Arnold Mills Reservoir ⊜[1] | 283 | 41.59 N | 71.25 W |
| Arnolds Park | 198 | 43.22 N | 95.08 W |
| Arnoldstein | 64 | 46.33 N | 13.43 E |
| Arnon ≃ | 50 | 47.13 N | 2.01 E |
| Arnos Vale Airport ⊠ | 241h | 13.09 N | 61.13 W |
| Arnot | 210 | 41.39 N | 77.07 W |
| Arnouville-lès-Gonesse | 261 | 49.00 N | 2.25 E |
| Arnouville-lès-Mantes | 261 | 48.55 N | 1.44 E |
| Arnprior | 212 | 45.26 N | 76.21 W |
| Arnsberg | 56 | 51.24 N | 8.03 E |
| Arnsberg □[5] | 52 | 51.20 N | 8.00 E |
| Arnsdorf | 54 | 51.05 N | 13.59 E |
| Arnside | 44 | 54.12 N | 2.50 W |
| Arnstadt | 54 | 50.50 N | 10.57 E |
| Arnstein | 56 | 49.58 N | 9.58 E |
| Arnstorf | 60 | 48.34 N | 12.49 E |
| Arnum | 41 | 55.15 N | 8.59 E |
| Årø I | 41 | 55.15 N | 9.45 E |
| Aro ≃ | 246 | 8.01 N | 64.11 W |
| Aroa | 246 | 10.26 N | 68.54 W |
| Aroa ≃ | 246 | 10.40 N | 68.19 W |
| Aroa, Pointe ≻ | 174s | 17.28 S | 149.46 W |
| Aroab | 156 | 26.47 S | 19.40 E |
| Aroali | 126 | 24.03 N | 87.56 E |
| Arochukwu | 150 | 5.23 N | 7.55 E |
| Aroeiras | 250 | 7.31 S | 35.41 W |
| Ar'ofino | 80 | 58.16 N | 39.15 E |
| Arolla | 58 | 46.02 N | 7.29 E |
| Arolsen | 56 | 51.23 N | 9.01 E |
| Aroma | 140 | 15.49 N | 36.08 E |
| Aroma Park | 216 | 41.04 N | 87.48 W |
| Aromas | 226 | 36.53 N | 121.39 W |
| Aromaševo | 86 | 56.52 N | 68.39 E |
| Arona, It. | 62 | 45.46 N | 8.34 E |
| Arona, Pap. N. Gui. | 164 | 6.20 S | 146.00 E |
| Arona, Pa., U.S. | 279b | 40.16 N | 79.39 W |
| Aroostook ≃ | 186 | 46.48 N | 67.45 W |
| Arop Island I | 164 | 5.20 S | 147.05 E |
| Aropuk Lake ⊜ | 180 | 61.12 N | 163.50 W |
| Arorae I | 14 | 2.38 S | 176.49 E |
| Arorangi | 174k | 21.13 S | 159.49 W |
| Aroroy | 116 | 12.31 N | 123.24 E |
| Aros ≃ | 232 | 29.09 N | 109.40 W |
| Arosa | 58 | 46.47 N | 9.41 E |
| Arosbaya | 115a | 6.56 S | 112.51 E |
| Årøsund | 41 | 55.16 N | 9.45 E |
| Arousa, Ría de ⊂[1] | 34 | 42.28 N | 8.57 W |
| Aro Usu, Tanjung ≻ | 164 | 8.20 S | 130.45 E |
| Arowhana ∧ | 172 | 38.07 S | 177.52 E |
| Arp | 222 | 32.13 N | 95.03 W |
| Arpa ≃ | 84 | 39.28 N | 44.57 E |
| Arpaçay | 84 | 40.52 N | 43.20 E |
| Arpaçay (Achur'an) ≃ | 84 | 40.06 N | 43.39 E |
| Arpačin | 83 | 47.14 N | 40.11 E |
| Arpaia | 68 | 41.02 N | 14.33 E |
| Arpajon | 50 | 48.35 N | 2.15 E |
| Ārpāra | 126 | 23.23 N | 89.23 E |
| Arpino | 66 | 41.39 N | 13.36 E |
| Arpoador, Ponta do ≻ | 287a | 22.59 S | 43.12 W |
| Arquà Petrarca | 64 | 45.16 N | 11.43 E |
| Arquà Polesine | 64 | 45.01 N | 11.45 E |
| Arquata del Tronto | 66 | 42.46 N | 13.18 E |
| Arquata Scrivia | 62 | 44.41 N | 8.53 E |
| Arque | 248 | 17.48 S | 66.23 W |
| Arques | 50 | 50.44 N | 2.17 E |
| Arques-la-Bataille | 50 | 49.53 N | 1.08 E |
| Ar-Rabad | 128 | 23.11 N | 39.32 E |
| Ar-Rabbah | 132 | 31.16 N | 35.44 E |
| Arracourt | 58 | 48.44 N | 6.32 E |
| Ar-Radīsīyah Baḥrī | 140 | 24.57 N | 32.53 E |
| Ar-Rafīd | 132 | 32.57 N | 35.53 E |
| Arraga | 252 | 28.04 S | 64.14 W |
| Arrah | 150 | 6.40 N | 3.58 W |
| Ar-Rahad | 140 | 12.43 N | 30.39 E |
| Ar-Raḥāminah | 142 | 31.18 N | 31.45 E |
| Ar-Raḥmānīyah | 142 | 31.06 N | 30.38 E |
| Arraial do Cabo | 255 | 22.58 S | 42.01 W |
| Arraias | 255 | 12.56 S | 46.[illegible] W |
| Arraias ≃, Bra. | 250 | 11.10 S | 53.[illegible] W |
| Arraias ≃, Bra. | 255 | 12.28 S | 47.[illegible] W |
| 'Arrām, Wādī V | 132 | 32.55 N | 36.1[illegible] E |
| Ar-Ramādī | 128 | 33.25 N | 43.1[illegible] E |
| Ar-Ramthā | 132 | 32.34 N | 36.0[illegible] E |
| Arran, Island of I | 46 | 55.35 N | 5.1[illegible] W |
| Ar-Rank | 140 | 11.45 N | 32.4[illegible] E |
| Arran Lake ⊜ | 212 | 44.29 N | 81.16 W |
| Ar-Raqqah | 130 | 35.56 N | 39.01 E |
| Ar-Raqqah □[8] | 130 | 36.00 N | 39.00 E |
| Arras | 50 | 50.17 N | 2.47 E |
| Arras, Nuraghe ⊥ | 71 | 39.40 N | 9.25 E |
| Ar-Rāshidah | 140 | 25.35 N | 28.56 E |
| Ar-Rass | 128 | 25.52 N | 43.28 E |
| Ar-Rastan | 130 | 34.55 N | 36.44 E |
| Arrats ≃ | 32 | 44.06 N | 0.52 E |
| Ar-Rawḍah, Ar. Su. | 128 | 26.05 N | 40.37 E |
| Ar-Rawḍah, Miṣr | 142 | 27.48 N | 30.52 E |
| Ar-Rawḍah, Miṣr | 142 | 29.27 N | 31.00 E |
| Ar-Rawḍah, Yaman | 144 | 14.28 N | 47.17 E |
| Ar-Rāwuk | 144 | 15.45 N | 48.54 E |
| Ar-Rayramūn | 142 | 27.45 N | 30.52 E |
| Ar-Rayyāḥ ar-Minūfīya ≅ | 142 | 30.20 N | 31.00 E |
| Ar-Rayyāḥ at-Tawfīqī ≅ | 142 | 30.11 N | 31.07 E |
| Ar-Rayyān | 128 | 25.18 N | 51.27 E |
| Arrecife | 148 | 28.57 N | 13.32 W |
| Arrecifes | 252 | 34.03 S | 60.07 W |
| Arrée, Montagnes d' ⋀ | 32 | 48.26 N | 3.55 W |
| Arregui, Laguna ⊜ | 258 | 35.05 S | 57.33 W |
| Arrentela | 266c | 38.38 N | 9.06 W |
| Arresø ⊜ | 41 | 55.58 N | 12.08 E |
| Arrey | 200 | 32.50 N | 107.19 W |
| Arriaga | 234 | 16.14 N | 93.54 W |
| Arriba | 198 | 39.17 N | 103.16 W |
| Arrild | 41 | 55.09 N | 8.58 E |
| Ar-Riyāḍ (Riyadh) | 128 | 24.38 N | 46.43 E |
| Arrochar | 46 | 56.12 N | 4.44 W |
| Arroio Grande | 252 | 32.14 S | 53.05 W |
| Arrojado ≃ | 255 | 13.24 S | 44.20 W |
| Arronches | 34 | 39.07 N | 7.17 W |
| Arrone ≃, It. | 66 | 41.52 N | 12.11 E |
| Arrone ≃, It. | 66 | 42.18 N | 11.38 E |
| Arros ≃ | 32 | 43.40 N | 0.02 W |
| Arroscia ≃ | 62 | 44.03 N | 8.11 E |
| Arroux ≃ | 32 | 46.29 N | 3.58 E |
| Arrow ≃, Eng., U.K. | 42 | 52.12 N | 2.43 W |
| Arrow ≃, Eng., U.K. | 42 | 52.09 N | 1.53 W |
| Arrow, Lough ⊜ | 48 | 54.04 N | 8.21 W |
| Arrow Creek ≃ | 202 | 47.43 N | 109.50 W |
| Arrowhead, Lake ⊜[1], Ca., U.S. | 228 | 34.15 N | 117.11 W |
| Arrowhead, Lake ⊜[1], Tx., U.S. | 196 | 33.40 N | 98.20 W |
| Arrowhead Peak ∧ | 228 | 34.13 N | 117.16 W |
| Arrowhead Provincial Park ♠ | 212 | 45.24 N | 79.13 W |
| Arrowhead Village | 208 | 40.04 N | 74.07 W |
| Arrow Lake ⊜ | 190 | 48.08 N | 90.18 W |
| Arrowrock Reservoir ⊜[1] | 202 | 43.36 N | 115.51 W |
| Arrowsmith | 216 | 40.27 N | 88.38 W |
| Arrowsmith, Mount ∧, Austl. | 166 | 30.09 S | 141.50 E |
| Arrowsmith, Mount ∧, B.C., Can. | 224 | 49.13 N | 124.36 W |
| Arrowsmith, Mount ∧, N.Z. | 172 | 43.21 S | 170.59 E |
| Arrowtown | 172 | 44.56 S | 168.50 E |
| Arrowwood | 182 | 50.44 N | 113.09 W |
| Arroyan, Arroyo ≃[1] | 288 | 34.24 S | 58.32 W |
| Arroyito | 252 | 31.25 S | 63.03 W |
| Arroyo | 240m | 17.58 N | 66.04 W |
| Arroyo de la Luz | 34 | 39.29 N | 6.35 W |
| Arroyo Grande, Ca., U.S. | 204 | 35.07 N | 120.35 W |
| Arroyo Grande → Ismael Cortinas, Ur. | 258 | 33.58 S | 57.06 W |
| Arroyo Hondo | 200 | 36.32 N | 105.40 W |
| Arroyo Naranjo ◆[8] | 286b | 23.02 N | 82.23 W |
| Arroyo Seco | 252 | 33.14 S | 60.50 W |
| Arroyo Seco Park ♠ | 280 | 34.06 N | 118.12 W |
| Arroyos y Esteros | 252 | 25.04 S | 57.06 W |
| Arrozal | 256 | 22.37 S | 44.03 W |
| Ar-Ru'at | 140 | 12.21 N | 32.17 E |
| Ar-Rub' al-Khālī ◆[2] | 118 | 20.00 N | 51.00 E |
| Ar-Rubayqī | 142 | 30.10 N | 31.46 E |
| Ar-Ruḥaybah | 132 | 33.45 N | 36.42 E |
| Ar-Rukhaymīyah ⊤[4] | 128 | 29.14 N | 45.35 E |
| Ar-Rumaythah | 128 | 31.32 N | 45.12 E |
| Ar-Rummān | 132 | 32.10 N | 35.50 E |
| Ar-Ruqayyah ⊥ | 132 | 32.47 N | 37.05 E |
| Ar-Ruṣāfah ⊥ | 130 | 35.37 N | 38.45 E |
| Ar-Ruṣayfah | 132 | 32.01 N | 36.03 E |
| Ar-Ruṣayriṣ | 140 | 11.51 N | 34.23 E |
| Ar-Rushaydah | 132 | 32.40 N | 36.50 E |
| Ar-Ruṭbah | 128 | 33.02 N | 40.17 E |
| Ar-Ru'ūs | 142 | 29.21 N | 31.04 E |
| Ar-Ruways | 128 | 26.08 N | 51.13 E |
| Års | 26 | 56.48 N | 9.32 E |
| Aršan, Ross. | 88 | 51.54 N | 102.27 E |
| Aršan, Ross. | 88 | 53.54 N | 99.54 E |
| Arsanjān | 128 | 29.56 N | 53.18 E |
| Aršan'-Zel'men' | 80 | 47.36 N | 44.36 E |
| Ārsāpota | 272b | 22.55 N | 88.18 E |
| Arsbeck | 56 | 51.08 N | 6.12 E |
| Arsenal de Marinha ■ | 266c | 38.39 N | 9.09 W |
| Arsenal Football Club ♠ | 260 | 51.33 N | 0.06 W |
| Arsenault Lake ⊜ | 184 | 55.06 N | 108.30 W |
| Arsenjev | 89 | 44.10 N | 133.15 E |
| Arsenjevka ≃ | 89 | 44.54 N | 133.35 E |
| Arsenjevo | 76 | 53.44 N | 36.40 E |
| Ars-en-Ré | 32 | 46.12 N | 1.31 W |
| Arsi □[4] | 144 | 8.00 N | 39.40 E |
| Arsiè | 64 | 45.59 N | 11.45 E |
| Arsiero | 64 | 45.48 N | 11.21 E |
| Arsikere | 122 | 13.20 N | 76.15 E |
| Arsin | 130 | 40.58 N | 39.56 E |
| Arsintsevo | 78 | 45.17 N | 36.25 E |
| Arsk | 80 | 56.06 N | 49.54 E |
| Arslanbob | 85 | 41.21 N | 72.56 E |
| Årslev | 41 | 55.18 N | 10.29 E |
| Arso | 164 | 2.56 S | 140.47 E |
| Arsoli | 66 | 42.02 N | 13.01 E |
| Ársos | 130 | 34.50 N | 32.46 E |
| Ars-sur-Formans | 58 | 45.59 N | 4.49 E |
| Ars-sur-Moselle | 56 | 49.05 N | 6.04 E |
| Årsta havsbad | 40 | 59.05 N | 18.10 E |
| Arsufhsa ≃ | 84 | 39.08 N | 46.50 E |
| Årsunda | 40 | 60.32 N | 16.44 E |
| Art, Île I | 175f | 19.43 S | 163.38 E |
| Árta, Ellás | 38 | 39.09 N | 20.59 E |
| Artà, Esp. | 34 | 39.42 N | 3.21 E |
| Artarmon | 274a | 33.49 S | 151.11 E |
| Artašat | 84 | 39.59 N | 44.33 E |
| Arta Terme | 64 | 46.28 N | 13.01 E |
| Arteaga | 234 | 18.28 N | 102.25 W |
| Arteche | 116 | 12.17 N | 125.22 E |
| Arte Contemporânea, Museu de ʊ | 287b | 23.32 S | 46.38 W |
| Artegna | 64 | 46.14 N | 13.09 E |
| Artemare | 62 | 45.52 N | 5.42 E |
| Artemisa | 240p | 22.49 N | 82.46 W |
| Artemivka | 78 | 49.46 N | 35.04 E |
| Artemivs'k, Ukr. | 83 | 48.27 N | 38.42 E |
| Artemivs'k, Ukr. | 83 | 48.35 N | 38.00 E |
| Artemón | 38 | 36.59 N | 24.43 E |
| Artémou | 150 | 15.31 N | 12.16 W |
| Artemove | 83 | 48.22 N | 37.53 E |
| Artemovsk → Artemivs'k | 83 | 48.35 N | 38.00 E |
| Artèn | 64 | 46.00 N | 11.50 E |
| Artenay | 50 | 48.05 N | 1.53 E |
| Artern | 54 | 51.22 N | 11.17 E |


| Symbol | English | Deutsch | Español | Français | Português |
|---|---|---|---|---|---|
| ≃ | River | Fluß | Río | Rivière | Rio |
| ≅ | Canal | Kanal | Canal | Canal | Canal |
| ∟ | Waterfall, Rapids | Wasserfall, Stromschnellen | Cascada, Rápidos | Chute d'eau, Rapides | Cascata, Rápidos |
| ⊔ | Strait | Meeresstraße | Estrecho | Détroit | Estreito |
| ⊂ | Bay, Gulf | Bucht, Golf | Bahía, Golfo | Baie, Golfe | Baía, Golfo |
| ⊜ | Lake, Lakes | See, Seen | Lago, Lagos | Lac, Lacs | Lago, Lagos |
| ≡ | Swamp | Sumpf | Pantano | Marais | Pântano |
| ⌂ | Ice Features, Glacier | Eis- und Gletscherformen | Accidentes Glaciales | Formes glaciaires | Acidentes glaciares |
| ⊤ | Other Hydrographic Features | Andere Hydrographische Objekte | Otros Elementos Hidrográficos | Autres données hydrographiques | Outros acidentes hidrográficos |
| ✢ | Submarine Features | Untermeerische Objekte | Accidentes Submarinos | Formes de relief sous-marin | Acidentes submarinos |
| □ | Political Unit | Politische Einheit | Unidad Política | Entité politique | Unidade política |
| ʊ | Cultural Institution | Kulturelle Institution | Institución Cultural | Institution culturelle | Instituição cultural |
| ⊥ | Historical Site | Historische Stätte | Sitio Histórico | Site historique | Sitio histórico |
| ♠ | Recreational Site | Erholungs- und Ferienort | Sitio de Recreo | Centre de loisirs | Area de Lazer |
| ⊠ | Airport | Flughafen | Aeropuerto | Aéroport | Aeroporto |
| ■ | Military Installation | Militäranlage | Instalación Militar | Installation militaire | Instalação militar |
| ◆ | Miscellaneous | Verschiedenes | Misceláneo | Divers | Diversos |

Artesia → Mosomane, Bots. 156 24.04 S 26.15 E
Artesia, Ca., U.S. 280 33.51 N 118.04 W
Artesia, Ms., U.S. 194 33.24 N 88.38 W
Artesia, N.M., U.S. 196 32.50 N 104.24 W
Artesia Lake ⊜ 226 38.57 N 119.22 W
Artesian 198 44.00 N 97.55 W
Arth 58 47.04 N 8.31 E
Arthabaska 206 46.02 N 71.55 W
Arthabaska □6 206 46.05 N 72.00 W
Arthal 123 33.16 N 76.11 E
Arthala 272a 28.40 N 77.24 E
Arthies 261 49.06 N 1.48 E
Arthonnay 50 47.56 N 4.13 E
Arthur, On., Can. 212 43.50 N 80.32 W
Arthur, Il., U.S. 194 39.43 N 88.28 W
Arthur, Ne., U.S. 198 41.34 N 101.41 W
Arthur, N.D., U.S. 198 47.06 N 97.13 W
Arthur, Tn., U.S. 192 36.32 N 83.40 W
Arthur ≐, Austl. 166 41.03 S 144.40 E
Arthur ≐, Austl. 168a 33.31 S 116.50 E
Arthur, Lake ⊜1 214 40.57 N 80.05 W
Arthur Creek ≐ 162 22.55 S 136.45 E
Arthur Kill ≈ 276 40.30 N 74.15 W
Arthurs Pass 172 42.57 S 171.34 E
Arthurs Pass )( 172 42.54 S 171.34 E
Arthur's Pass National Park ♦ 172 42.50 S 171.40 E
Arthurs Seat ∧2 169 38.21 S 144.57 E
Arthur's Town 238 24.38 N 75.42 W
Arthurton 168b 34.16 S 137.45 E
Arti 86 56.26 N 58.32 E
Artibonite ≐ 238 19.15 N 72.47 W
Artico, Océano → Arctic Ocean ∓1 16 85.00 N 170.00 E
Artigas 252 30.24 S 56.28 W
Artigas ✦8 286c 10.30 N 66.56 W
Artigas, Casa de ⊥ 258 34.39 S 56.03 W
Artik 84 40.37 N 43.59 E
Artilleros 258 34.22 S 57.34 W
Artilleros, Punta ⟩ 258 34.28 S 57.32 W
Artillery Lake ⊜ 176 63.09 N 107.52 W
Artlenburg 52 53.22 N 10.29 E
Artney, Glen V 46 56.20 N 4.04 W
Artois □9 50 50.30 N 2.30 E
Artois, Collines de l' ⋀2 50 50.25 N 2.10 E
Art'om 89 43.22 N 132.13 E
Art'omovsk 86 54.21 N 93.26 E
Art'omovskij, Ross. 86 57.21 N 61.54 E
Art'omovskij, Ross. 88 58.12 N 114.45 E
Art'omovskij, Ross. 89 43.27 N 132.22 E
Artova 130 40.03 N 36.19 E
Artpark ♦ 284a 43.10 N 79.03 W
Artrutx, Cap d' ⟩ 34 39.56 N 3.48 E
Artsyz 78 46.00 N 29.26 E
Artuby ≐ 62 43.44 N 6.22 E
Artur Nogueira 256 22.35 S 47.09 W
Arturo Merino Benítez, Aeropuerto ✈ 286e 33.23 S 70.49 W
Arturo Segui ✦8 258 34.51 S 58.09 W
Artvin 130 41.11 N 41.49 E
Artvin □4 130 41.05 N 42.00 E
Artybaš 86 51.48 N 87.16 E
Artyk 74 64.12 N 145.06 E
Artyom 84 40.28 N 50.20 E
Aru, Kepulauan II 164 6.00 S 134.30 E
Aru, Tanjung ⟩ 112 2.10 S 116.34 E
Aru, Teluk ⊂ 114 4.09 N 98.12 E
Arua 154 3.01 N 30.55 E
Aruã ≐ 250 2.39 S 55.38 W
Aruaddin 144 16.15 N 38.43 E
Aruanã 255 14.54 S 51.05 W
Aruângua (Luangwa) ≐ 154 15.36 S 30.25 E
Aruba □2, N.A. 230 12.30 N 69.58 W
Aruba □2, N.A. 241s 12.30 N 69.58 W
Aru Basin ∓1 14 5.00 S 134.00 E
Arucas 148 28.07 N 15.31 W
Arue 174s 17.32 S 149.32 W
Arufu 150 7.50 N 9.14 E
Arujá 256 23.24 S 46.20 W
Arujá □7 287b 23.24 S 46.20 W
Arumanduba 250 1.29 S 52.29 W
Arume 174m 26.36 N 128.07 E
Arume-wan ⊂ 174m 26.35 N 128.08 E
Aruṇ (Pong) ≐, Asia 124 26.49 N 87.09 E
Arun ≐, Eng., U.K. 42 50.48 N 0.33 W
Arunāchal Pradesh □3 120 28.30 N 95.00 E
Arundel, P.Q., Can. 206 45.58 N 74.37 W
Arundel, Eng., U.K. 42 50.51 N 0.34 W
Arun Qi 89 48.07 N 123.28 E
Årup 41 55.23 N 10.04 E
Aruppukkottai 122 9.31 N 78.06 E
Arurandeua ≐ 250 3.43 S 48.50 W
Arusha 154 3.22 S 36.41 E
Arusha □4 154 4.00 S 36.15 E
Arusha Chini 154 3.35 S 37.20 E
Arusha National Park ♦ 154 3.17 S 36.56 E
Arut ≐ 112 2.42 S 111.34 E
Aruvi ≐ 122 8.49 N 79.55 E
Aruwimi ≐ 138 1.13 N 23.36 E
Arvada 200 39.48 N 105.05 W
Arvagh 48 53.55 N 7.34 W
Arvajcheer 90 46.15 N 102.48 E
Arve ≐ 58 46.12 N 6.08 E
Arverne ✦8 276 40.35 N 73.48 W
Arves, Les Aiguilles d' ∧ 62 45.08 N 6.21 E
Arvi 120 20.59 N 78.14 E
Arvida 186 48.25 N 71.11 W
Arvidsjaur 24 65.35 N 19.07 E
Arvier 62 45.42 N 7.11 E
Arvieux 62 44.46 N 6.44 E
Arvika 26 59.39 N 12.36 E
Arvillard 62 45.27 N 6.07 E
Arvin 228 35.12 N 118.49 W
Arvo, Lago ⊜ 68 39.14 N 16.29 E
Arvon, Mount ∧ 190 46.45 N 88.09 W
Arvonia 192 37.40 N 78.20 W
Arvorezinha 252 28.53 S 52.10 W
Arwal 124 25.15 N 84.41 E
Arwala 112 7.41 S 126.49 E
Arxan 89 47.11 N 119.57 E
Aryamūn 142 31.11 N 30.54 E
Aryiroúpolis 267c 37.54 N 23.45 E
Arys' 85 42.26 N 68.48 E
Arys ≐ 85 42.48 N 68.12 E
Arys, ozero ⊜ 86 45.50 N 66.20 E
Arys-Turkestanskij kanal ≅ 85 42.44 N 69.00 E
Arzachena 71 41.05 N 9.23 E
Arzamas 80 55.23 N 43.50 E
Arzana 71 39.55 N 9.31 E
Arzano 68 40.55 N 14.16 E
Arzberg, Dtsch. 54 51.32 N 13.08 E
Arzberg, Dtsch. 60 50.04 N 12.12 E
Arzew, Golfe d' ⊂ 34 35.50 N 0.10 W
Arzew, Salines d' ⊜ 34 35.40 N 0.15 W
Arzfeld 56 50.05 N 6.16 E
Arzignano 64 45.31 N 11.20 E
Arziw 148 35.51 N 0.19 W
Arz Lubnān ✦3 130 34.14 N 36.03 E
Arzni 84 40.19 N 44.36 E
Arzon ≐ 62 45.11 N 3.54 E
Arzúa 34 42.56 N 8.09 W
As, Bel. 56 51.01 N 5.35 E
Aš, Česká Rep. 54 50.10 N 12.10 E
Ås, Nor. 26 59.40 N 10.48 E
Asa, Nihon 96 34.33 N 132.26 E
Aša, Ross. 86 55.00 N 57.16 E
Asa ≐, Nihon 94 35.39 N 139.26 E
Asa ≐, Nihon 96 34.01 N 131.09 E
Asa ≐, Ven. 246 6.50 N 63.18 W
Asab 156 25.29 S 17.59 E
Asaba, Nig. 150 6.12 N 6.44 E
Asaba, Nihon 94 34.42 N 137.56 E
Asad, Buḥayrat al- ⊜1 130 36.00 N 38.10 E
Asadābād, Afg. 120 34.52 N 71.09 E
Asadābād, Īrān 128 34.47 N 48.07 E
Asafo 150 6.11 N 0.28 W
Asaga Strait ≈ 174y 14.11 S 169.40 W
Asagaya ✦8 268 35.42 N 139.38 E
Aşağıbostancı 130 35.10 N 33.00 E
Aşağıçiğil 130 38.03 N 31.52 E
Aşağı Dağ ∧ 84 40.01 N 43.11 E
Aşağı Köynük 84 41.18 N 47.00 E
Aşağı Kuluşağı 130 38.39 N 38.39 E
Aşağılahan 130 38.50 N 39.59 E
Aşağı Mestikân 130 38.25 N 38.46 E
Asahan 114 2.23 N 102.33 E
Asahan ≐ 114 3.02 N 99.52 E
Asahi, Nihon 94 35.14 N 137.22 E
Asahi, Nihon 94 35.43 N 140.39 E
Asahi, Nihon 94 35.59 N 136.07 E
Asahi, Nihon 94 36.05 N 137.21 E
Asahi, Nihon 94 36.14 N 140.31 E
Asahi, Nihon 94 35.02 N 136.40 E
Asahi, Nihon 94 36.07 N 137.52 E
Asahi, Nihon 94 36.57 N 137.34 E
Asahi, Nihon 96 34.59 N 133.50 E
Asahi, Nihon 96 34.51 N 132.16 E
Asahi, Nihon 96 34.17 N 131.28 E
Asahi ✦8, Nihon 268 35.29 N 139.33 E
Asahi ✦8, Nihon 270 34.44 N 135.34 E
Asahi ≐ 96 34.36 N 133.58 E
Asahi-dake ∧, Nihon 92a 43.40 N 142.51 E
Asahi-dake ∧, Nihon 94 37.14 N 139.21 E
Asahigawa → Asahikawa 92a 43.46 N 142.22 E
Asahi-gawa-daiichi-dam ✦6 96 34.53 N 133.22 E
Asahikawa 92a 43.46 N 142.22 E
Asahikawa-chūtonchi, Rikujō-Jieitai- ■ 92a 43.49 N 142.25 E
Asahi-ko ⊜1 96 34.56 N 133.51 E
Asahi-sanchi ⋀ 92 38.25 N 139.50 E
Asaka 94 35.48 N 139.36 E
Asaka, Camp ■ 268 35.47 N 139.36 E
Asakanskij Golec, gora ∧ 88 50.18 N 109.55 E
Asakawa 94 37.05 N 140.25 E
Asake ≐ 94 35.00 N 136.41 E
Asako 96 35.14 N 134.48 E
Asakura 96 33.23 N 130.44 E
Asakusa ✦8 268 35.43 N 139.49 E
Asālafpur ✦8 272a 28.38 N 77.05 E
Asale 144 14.22 N 40.32 E
Asale, Lake ⊜ 144 14.19 N 40.18 E
Asamankese 150 5.52 N 0.42 W
Asama-yama ∧ 94 36.24 N 138.31 E
Asanbani, India 126 22.43 N 86.20 E
Asanbāni, India 126 24.07 N 87.27 E
Asani 154 4.25 S 29.05 E
Asankrangwa 150 5.48 N 2.26 W
Asan-man ⊂ 98 36.56 N 126.51 E
Āsānsol, India 126 24.14 N 87.17 E
Āsānsol, India 126 23.41 N 86.59 E
Ašap 86 57.07 N 56.30 E
Asar 88 47.56 N 117.38 E
Åsarna 26 62.39 N 14.21 E
Asarum 26 56.12 N 14.50 E
Asashina 94 36.16 N 138.25 E
Āsāsuni 126 22.32 N 89.10 E
Asati 272b 22.29 N 88.14 E
Asa-yama ∧ 96 34.47 N 132.23 E
Asayita 144 11.33 N 41.30 E
Asbach 56 50.40 N 7.25 E
Asbeck 263 51.21 N 7.18 E
Asberg 263 51.26 N 6.40 E
Asbesberg ⋀ 158 28.55 S 23.15 E
Asbest 86 57.00 N 61.30 E
Asbestos 206 45.46 N 71.57 W
Asbestos Range National Park ♦ 166 41.08 S 146.39 E
Asbe Teferi 144 9.02 N 40.58 E
Åsbro 40 59.00 N 15.03 E
Asbury 210 40.41 N 75.00 W
Asbury Park 208 40.13 N 74.01 W
Ascea 68 40.08 N 15.11 E
Ascensión 232 31.06 N 107.59 W
Ascension I 10 7.57 S 14.22 W
Ascent 158 27.12 S 29.03 E
Aščerino 265b 55.36 N 37.46 E
Asch 58 47.57 N 10.49 E
Aschabad (Ashgabat) 128 37.57 N 58.23 E
Aschach an der Donau 61 48.22 N 14.02 E
Aschaffenburg 56 49.59 N 9.09 E
Aschbach Markt 61 48.04 N 14.45 E
Ascheberg, Dtsch. 52 51.47 N 7.37 E
Ascheberg, Dtsch. 54 54.08 N 10.20 E
Aschendorf 52 53.04 N 7.22 E
Aschersleben 54 51.45 N 11.27 E
Asciano 66 43.14 N 11.33 E
Aščikol', ozero ⊜ 86 45.05 N 67.15 E
Aščitastysor, ozero ⊜ 86 49.19 N 63.59 E
Ascoli Piceno 66 42.51 N 13.34 E
Ascoli Piceno □4 66 43.01 N 13.34 E
Ascoli Satriano 68 41.12 N 15.34 E
Ascona 58 46.09 N 8.46 E
Ascope 248 7.43 S 79.07 W
Ascot, Austl. 171a 27.26 S 153.04 E
Ascot, Eng., U.K. 42 51.25 N 0.41 W
Ascot ≐ 206 45.21 N 71.51 W
Ascotán 252 21.44 S 68.18 W
Ascros 62 43.55 N 7.01 E
Aščykol', ozero ⊜ 85 43.32 N 70.35 E
Aščyozek ≐ 80 49.12 N 48.06 E
Aščysu ≐ 86 49.54 N 78.58 E
Aseb 144 13.00 N 42.45 E
Åseda 26 57.10 N 15.20 E
Asedjrad ⋀1 148 24.28 N 1.52 E
Asekejevo 80 53.36 N 52.49 E
Asela 144 7.59 N 39.08 E
Åsele 26 64.10 N 17.20 E
Asem ≐ 115a 6.14 S 107.42 E
Asembagus 115a 7.45 S 114.14 E
Asembourg 56 49.43 N 6.02 E
Åsen 26 63.36 N 11.03 E
Asendabo 144 9.50 N 37.33 E
Asendorf 52 52.46 N 9.00 E
Asenovgrad 38 42.01 N 24.52 E
Åsensbruk 26 58.48 N 12.25 E
Aseri 76 59.27 N 26.52 E
Aṣfar, Jabal al- ∧ 132 32.12 N 36.54 E
Asfordby 42 52.46 N 0.57 W
Aṣfūn al-Maṭā'inah 140 25.23 N 32.32 E
Åsgårdstrand 26 59.21 N 10.28 E
Ash, Eng., U.K. 42 51.17 N 1.16 E
Ash, Eng., U.K. 42 51.15 N 0.44 W
Ashalim 132 30.58 N 34.40 E
Ashanti □4 150 6.45 N 1.30 W
'Asharah, Wādī al- V 142 30.21 N 32.15 E
Asharoken 276 40.56 N 73.22 W
Ashaway 207 41.25 N 71.47 W
Ashbourne, Ire. 48 53.31 N 6.24 W
Ashbourne, Eng., U.K. 44 53.02 N 1.44 W
Ash Brook Swamp Reservation ♦ 276 40.37 N 74.21 W
Ashburn, Ga., U.S. 192 31.42 N 83.39 W
Ashburn, Mo., U.S. 219 39.33 N 91.10 W
Ashburn, Va., U.S. 208 39.02 N 77.29 W
Ashburnham 207 42.38 N 71.54 W
Ashburton, Austl. 274b 37.52 S 145.05 E
Ashburton, N.Z. 172 43.55 S 171.45 E
Ashburton, Eng., U.K. 42 50.31 N 3.45 W
Ashburton ≐, Austl. 162 21.40 S 114.56 E
Ashburton ≐, N.Z. 172 44.04 S 171.48 E
Ashburton, North Branch ≐ 172 43.54 S 171.44 E
Ashburton, South Branch ≐ 172 43.44 S 171.32 E
Ashburton Downs 162 23.24 S 117.04 E
Ashby 207 42.40 N 71.49 W
Ashby, Lake ⊜ 220 28.56 N 81.07 W
Ashby-de-la-Zouch 42 52.46 N 1.28 W
Ashchurch 42 52.00 N 2.07 W
Ash Creek ≐, Ca., U.S. 204 41.05 N 121.08 W
Ash Creek ≐, Ct., U.S. 276 41.08 N 73.14 W
Ashcroft 182 50.43 N 121.17 W
Ashdod, Ma., U.S. 283 42.04 N 70.45 W
Ashdod, Yis. 132 31.49 N 34.40 E
Ashdod, Tel ⊥ 132 31.45 N 34.40 E
Ashdot Ya'aqov 132 32.40 N 35.35 E
Ashdown 194 33.40 N 94.07 W
Asheboro 192 35.42 N 79.48 W
Ashern 184 51.11 N 98.21 W
Asherton 196 28.26 N 99.45 W
Asheville 192 35.36 N 82.33 W
Ashewat Ziārat 120 31.22 N 68.32 E
Asheweig ≐ 176 54.17 N 87.12 W
Ashfield, Austl. 274a 33.53 S 151.08 E
Ashfield, Ma., U.S. 207 42.31 N 72.47 W
Ash Flat 194 36.13 N 91.36 W
Ashford, Austl. 166 29.20 S 151.06 E
Ashford, Eng., U.K. 42 51.08 N 0.53 E
Ashford, Eng., U.K. 260 51.26 N 0.27 W
Ashford, Al., U.S. 194 31.10 N 85.14 W
Ashford, Wa., U.S. 224 46.46 N 122.02 W
Ashford Airport ✈ 42 51.04 N 1.01 E
Ash Fork 200 35.13 N 112.28 W
Ash Grove 194 37.18 N 93.35 W
Ashhurst 172 40.18 S 175.45 E
Ashibe 92 33.48 N 129.46 E
Ashibetsu 92a 43.31 N 142.11 E
Ashida ≐ 96 34.26 N 133.25 E
Ashikaga 94 36.20 N 139.27 E
Ashikagga-gakkō ⊥ 94 36.22 N 139.30 E
Ashingdon 260 51.36 N 0.42 E
Ashington 44 55.12 N 1.35 W
Ashino-ko ⊜ 94 35.13 N 139.00 E
Ashio 94 36.38 N 139.27 E
Ashio-sanchi ⋀ 94 36.35 N 139.30 E
Ashippun 216 43.14 N 88.31 W
Ashippun ≐ 216 43.10 N 88.33 W
Ashitaka-yama ∧ 94 35.12 N 138.49 E
Ashiya, Nihon 96 33.53 N 130.40 E
Ashiya, Nihon 96 34.43 N 135.17 E
Ashiya ≐ 270 34.43 N 135.18 E
Ashiyasu 94 35.38 N 138.23 E
Ashiyoro 92a 43.15 N 143.30 E
Ashizuri-misaki ⟩ 92 32.44 N 133.01 E
Ashizuri-Uwakai-kokuritsu-kōen ♦, Nihon 92 32.45 N 132.45 E
Ashizuri-Uwakai-kokuritsu-kōen ♦, Nihon 96 33.07 N 132.27 E
Ashkhabad → Aschabad 128 37.57 N 58.23 E
Ashkum 216 40.53 N 87.57 W
Ashland, Al., U.S. 194 33.16 N 85.50 W
Ashland, Ca., U.S. 226 37.41 N 122.06 W
Ashland, Il., U.S. 219 39.53 N 90.00 W
Ashland, Ks., U.S. 198 37.11 N 99.45 W
Ashland, Ky., U.S. 188 38.28 N 82.38 W
Ashland, Me., U.S. 186 46.37 N 68.24 W
Ashland, Ma., U.S. 207 42.15 N 71.27 W
Ashland, Ms., U.S. 194 34.49 N 89.10 W
Ashland, Mo., U.S. 219 38.46 N 92.15 W
Ashland, Mt., U.S. 202 45.35 N 106.16 W
Ashland, Ne., U.S. 198 41.02 N 96.22 W
Ashland, N.H., U.S. 188 43.41 N 71.37 W
Ashland, N.J., U.S. 285 39.51 N 75.00 W
Ashland, N.Y., U.S. 210 42.18 N 74.20 W
Ashland, Oh., U.S. 214 40.52 N 82.19 W
Ashland, Or., U.S. 202 42.11 N 122.42 W
Ashland, Pa., U.S. 210 40.46 N 76.20 W
Ashland, Va., U.S. 208 37.45 N 77.28 W
Ashland, Wi., U.S. 190 46.35 N 90.53 W
Ashland □6 214 40.52 N 82.19 W
Ashland, Mount ∧ 202 42.05 N 122.43 W
Ashland City 194 36.16 N 87.03 W
Ashley, Austl. 166 29.19 S 149.49 E
Ashley, Eng., U.K. 262 53.21 N 2.20 W
Ashley, Il., U.S. 219 38.20 N 89.11 W
Ashley, In., U.S. 216 41.32 N 85.04 W
Ashley, Mi., U.S. 190 43.11 N 84.28 W
Ashley, Mo., U.S. 219 39.15 N 91.14 W
Ashley, N.D., U.S. 198 46.01 N 99.22 W
Ashley, Oh., U.S. 214 40.24 N 82.57 W
Ashley, Pa., U.S. 210 41.12 N 75.53 W
Ashley ≐ 172 43.16 S 172.43 E
Ashley Creek ≐ 200 40.21 N 109.22 W
Ashley Falls 207 42.03 N 73.20 W
Ashley Green 260 51.44 N 0.35 W
Ashmore 194 39.32 N 88.01 W
Ashmore Islands II 160 12.14 S 123.05 E
Ashmūn 142 30.18 N 30.58 E
Ashokan Reservoir ⊜1 210 41.58 N 74.10 W
Ashoknagar 120 24.34 N 77.43 E
Ashqelon 132 31.40 N 34.35 E
Ashridge Park ♦ 260 51.48 N 0.34 W
Ash-Shabakah 128 30.49 N 43.39 E
Ash-Shabb ∓4 140 22.19 N 29.46 E
Ash-Shaddādah 130 36.02 N 40.45 E
Ash-Shāgūr 132 31.50 N 35.39 E
Ash-Shā'ib ∧2 142 29.50 N 30.56 E
Ash-Shajarah 132 32.39 N 35.56 E
Ash-Shallūfah 142 30.07 N 32.34 E
Ash-Shamāl □4 130 34.30 N 36.00 E
Ash-Shamālīyah □4 140 19.15 N 29.00 E
Ash-Shāmīyah 128 31.57 N 44.36 E
Ash-Shanāwīyah 142 29.08 N 31.08 E
Ash-Sharāh ✦1 132 30.20 N 35.30 E
Ash-Shāriqah 128 25.22 N 55.23 E
Ash-Sharmah 128 28.01 N 35.18 E
Ash-Sharqāṭ 128 35.27 N 43.16 E
Ash-Sharqīyah □4 142 30.48 N 31.48 E
Ash-Sharqīyah ✦1 128 27.00 N 49.00 E
Ash-Shaṭrah 128 31.25 N 46.10 E
Ash-Shawāshinah 142 29.22 N 30.36 E
Ash-Shawbak 132 30.32 N 35.34 E
Ash-Shawmarah 132 33.07 N 35.08 E
Ash-Shaykh Faḍl 142 28.29 N 30.50 E
Ash-Shaykh 'Ibādah 142 27.48 N 30.52 E
Ash-Shaykh Sa'd 132 32.50 N 36.02 E
Ash-Shaykh Timay 142 27.53 N 30.51 E
Ash-Shiḥr 144 14.44 N 49.35 E
Ash-Shīn 142 31.01 N 30.53 E
Ash-Shināfīyah 128 31.35 N 44.39 E
Ash-Shīyāḥ 132 33.51 N 35.30 E
Ash-Shufayyah 128 23.50 N 39.08 E
Ash-Shuhadā' 142 30.36 N 30.54 E
Ash-Shumlul 128 26.31 N 47.19 E
Ash-Shuqayq 144 17.43 N 42.01 E
Ash-Shurayf 128 25.43 N 39.14 E
Ash-Shurayk 140 18.48 N 33.34 E
Ash-Shuwayfāt 132 33.49 N 35.31 E
Ash Slough ≐ 226 37.02 N 120.32 W
Ashta, India 122 16.57 N 74.24 E
Ashta, India 124 23.01 N 76.43 E
Ashtabula 214 41.51 N 80.47 W
Ashtabula □6 214 41.44 N 80.46 W
Ashtabula ≐ 214 41.55 N 80.47 W
Ashtabula, East Branch ≐ 214 41.48 N 80.37 W
Ashtabula, Lake ⊜1 198 47.11 N 97.58 W
Ashtabula, West Branch ≐ 214 41.48 N 80.37 W
Ashtead 42 51.19 N 0.18 W
Ashton, S. Afr. 158 33.50 S 20.05 E
Ashton, Eng., U.K. 262 53.13 N 2.45 W
Ashton, Id., U.S. 202 44.04 N 111.26 W
Ashton, Il., U.S. 190 41.51 N 89.13 W
Ashton, Ia., U.S. 198 43.18 N 95.47 W
Ashton, Md., U.S. 208 39.08 N 77.00 W
Ashton, Ne., U.S. 198 41.14 N 98.47 W
Ashton, R.I., U.S. 207 41.46 N 71.25 W
Ashton-in-Makerfield 44 53.29 N 2.39 W
Ashton-under-Lyne 44 53.29 N 2.06 W
Ashton upon Mersey 262 53.26 N 2.19 W
Ashuanipi Lake ⊜ 176 52.35 N 66.10 W
Ashuelot ≐ 188 42.46 N 72.29 W
Ashurst's Beacon ∧2 262 53.34 N 2.45 W
Ashville, Al., U.S. 194 33.52 N 86.17 W
Ashville, N.Y., U.S. 214 42.06 N 79.23 W
Ashville, Oh., U.S. 218 39.42 N 82.57 W
Ashville, Pa., U.S. 214 40.34 N 78.33 W
Ashwater 42 50.44 N 4.16 W
Ashwaubenon 190 44.30 N 88.06 W
Ashworth Moor Reservoir ⊜1 262 53.38 N 2.16 W
Asi (Nahr al-'Āṣī) ≐ 130 36.02 N 35.58 E
Asia ±1 4 50.00 N 100.00 E
Asia ±1 12 50.00 N 100.00 E
Asia, Kepulauan II 108 1.03 N 131.18 E
Asiago 64 45.52 N 11.30 E
Asia Menor → Asia Minor □9 22 39.00 N 32.00 E
Asia Minor □9 22 39.00 N 32.00 E
Asid Gulf ⊂ 116 12.07 N 123.30 E
Asie → Asia ±1 12 50.00 N 100.00 E
Asie Mineure → Asia Minor □9 22 39.00 N 32.00 E
Asien → Asia ±1 12 50.00 N 100.00 E
āsika 120 19.36 N 84.39 E
Asikuma 150 5.35 N 1.00 W
Asilah 148 35.32 N 6.00 W
Asinara, Golfo dell' ⊂ 71 41.00 N 8.32 E
Asinara, Isola I 71 41.04 N 8.16 E
Asinaro ≐ 70 36.53 N 15.08 E
Asino 86 57.00 N 86.09 E
Asintorf 76 54.42 N 30.39 E
Asipoquobah Lake ⊜ 184 53.40 N 91.15 W
Asipovičy 76 53.18 N 28.38 E
'Asīr ✦1 144 19.00 N 42.00 E
Ašitkovo 82 55.26 N 38.36 E
Aşkale 130 39.55 N 40.42 E
Askam in Furness 44 54.11 N 3.13 W
Askaniya-Nova 78 46.27 N 33.52 E
Askarovo 86 53.21 N 58.30 E
Askeaton 48 52.36 N 8.58 W
Asker 26 59.50 N 10.26 E
Askern 44 53.37 N 1.09 W
Askersund 40 58.53 N 14.54 E
Askham 158 26.59 S 20.47 E
Askim 26 59.35 N 11.10 E
Askino 86 56.05 N 56.34 E
Askira 146 10.39 N 12.55 E
Askival ∧ 46 56.59 N 6.17 W
Askiz 86 53.08 N 90.32 E
Askja ∧1 24a 65.00 N 16.48 W
Askø I 41 54.54 N 11.30 E
Äsköping 40 59.09 N 16.04 E
Askov 41 55.28 N 9.06 E
Askraal 158 34.09 S 20.52 E
Askrigg 44 54.19 N 2.04 W
Askvoll 26 61.21 N 5.04 E
Aslanapa 130 39.13 N 29.52 E
Aslan-Sara 84 39.02 N 48.16 E
Aslantaş Barajı ⊜1 130 37.20 N 36.15 E
Asleigh 284c 39.01 N 77.10 W
Åsljunga 41 56.19 N 13.22 E
Ašlyk 86 57.33 N 68.40 E
Ašlyk ≐ 86 57.50 N 69.12 E
Asmār 120 35.02 N 71.22 E
Asmara → Asmera 144 15.20 N 38.53 E
Asmera 144 15.20 N 38.53 E
Ašmjanskae uzvyšša ⋀1 76 54.20 N 26.00 E
Ašmjany 76 54.25 N 25.56 E
Asmundtorp 41 55.53 N 12.56 E
Asnæs 41 55.49 N 11.31 E
Asnæs ⟩1 41 55.40 N 11.00 E
Asnebumskit Hill ∧2 207 42.18 N 71.54 W
Åsnen ⊜ 26 56.38 N 14.42 E
Asni 148 31.14 N 7.55 W
Asnières [-sur-Seine] 50 48.55 N 2.17 E
Asō, Nihon 94 35.59 N 140.29 E
Aso, Nihon 96 32.58 N 131.02 E
Aso ≐ 66 43.06 N 13.51 E
Asoc 152 1.26 N 11.18 E
Aso-kokuritsu-kōen ♦ 92 33.00 N 131.07 E
Asola 64 45.13 N 10.24 E
Asolo 64 45.48 N 11.54 E
Asomante 240m 18.23 N 66.36 W
Ason 273a 6.34 N 3.31 E
Asosa 144 10.03 N 34.32 E
Aso-san ∧ 92 32.53 N 131.06 E
Asoteriba, Jabal ∧ 140 21.51 N 36.30 E
Asotin 202 46.20 N 117.02 W
Asouf, Oued V 148 25.51 N 1.33 E
Asowsches Meer → Azov, Sea of ∓2 78 46.00 N 36.00 E
Asp 34 38.21 N 0.46 W
Aspach, Dtsch. 56 48.58 N 9.24 E
Aspach, Öst. 60 48.11 N 13.18 E
Aspach-le-Bas 58 47.46 N 7.09 E
Aspang Markt 61 47.33 N 16.06 E
Aspara ≐ 85 43.17 N 73.28 E
Aspatria 44 54.46 N 3.20 W
Aspe, Gave d' ≐ 32 43.12 N 0.36 W
Aspen 200 39.11 N 106.49 W
Aspen Butte ∧ 202 42.19 N 122.05 W
Aspendale 274b 38.02 S 145.07 E
Aspendos ⊥ 130 37.00 N 31.10 E
Aspen Hill 284c 39.04 N 77.04 W
Aspen Knolls 284c 39.05 N 77.05 W
Aspen Lake ⊜ 202 42.18 N 122.00 W
Asperg 56 48.54 N 9.07 E
Aspermont 196 33.08 N 100.13 W
Aspern ✦8 264b 48.13 N 16.29 E
Aspers 208 39.59 N 77.13 W
Asperup 41 55.29 N 9.55 E
Aspid, Mount ∧ 180 53.30 N 167.33 W
Aspindza 84 41.36 N 43.15 E
Aspinwall → Colón, Pan. 236 9.22 N 79.54 W
Aspinwall, Pa., U.S. 279b 40.29 N 79.54 W
Aspiring, Mount ∧ 172 44.23 S 168.44 E
Aspö 40 59.29 N 17.02 E
Aspres-sur-Buëch 62 44.31 N 5.45 E
Aspromonte ⋀ 68 38.10 N 15.55 E
Asprópirgos 267c 38.04 N 23.35 E
Aspull 262 53.34 N 2.35 W
Aspy Bay ⊂ 186 46.55 N 60.25 W
Asquins 50 47.29 N 3.45 E
Asquith, Austl. 274a 33.41 S 151.06 E
Asquith, Sk., Can. 184 52.08 N 107.13 W
Asralt chajrchan ∧ 88 48.29 N 107.24 E
Asrāni 123 29.31 N 72.07 E
Assa, Kaz. 85 43.02 N 71.10 E
Assa, Magreb 148 28.34 N 9.27 W
Assa ≐, Kaz. 85 43.55 N 70.25 E
Assa ≐, Ross. 84 43.13 N 45.25 E
As-Sa'ata 140 13.37 N 29.59 E
Assab → Aseb 144 13.00 N 42.45 E
Assabet ≐ 283 42.28 N 71.21 W
As-Sabkhah 130 35.48 N 39.15 E
Aṣ-Ṣadārah 144 14.30 N 48.04 E
As-Sa'dīyah 128 34.11 N 45.07 E
Aṣ-Ṣaff 140 29.34 N 31.17 E
As-Saffānīyah 128 27.58 N 48.47 E
Aṣ-Ṣāfī 132 31.02 N 35.28 E
As-Safīrah 130 36.04 N 37.22 E
Aṣ-Ṣāfiyah 140 15.31 N 30.07 E
Assago 266b 45.24 N 9.08 E
Assaí 255 23.22 S 50.49 W
Aṣ-Ṣa'īd □9 140 26.00 N 32.00 E
Assaikwatamo ≐ 184 56.52 N 95.50 W
Assal, Lac ⊜ 144 11.41 N 42.25 E
'Assāl al-Ward 132 33.52 N 36.24 E
Aṣ-Ṣāliḥīyah 142 30.47 N 31.59 E
As-Salīmah 144 14.02 N 45.46 E
As-Sallūm 140 31.34 N 25.09 E
As-Salmān 128 30.30 N 44.32 E
As-Salṭ 132 32.03 N 35.44 E
Assam □3 120 26.00 N 93.00 E
As-Samāwah 128 31.18 N 45.17 E
As-Samū' 132 31.24 N 35.04 E
Assam Valley V 124 26.30 N 90.30 E
'Assān 130 36.05 N 37.14 E
Aṣ-Ṣanāfīn Al-Qiblīyah 142 30.27 N 31.18 E
Aṣ-Ṣanamayn 132 33.05 N 36.10 E
As-Sanṭah 142 30.45 N 31.08 E
Assaq, Oued V 148 25.41 N 14.40 W
Aṣ-Ṣaqlabiyah 130 35.22 N 36.23 E
Aṣ-Ṣarafand 132 33.27 N 35.18 E
Assaré 250 6.52 S 39.52 W
Aṣ-Ṣarīḥ 132 32.30 N 35.54 E
As-Sarīrīyah 142 28.20 N 30.45 E
Assateague Island I 208 38.05 N 75.10 W
Assateague Island National Seashore ♦ 208 38.00 N 75.15 W
Assawoman Bay ⊂ 208 38.25 N 75.05 W
Assawoman Canal ≅ 208 38.31 N 75.04 W
Assawompset Pond ⊜ 207 41.50 N 70.55 W
Asse 50 50.55 N 4.12 E
Asse ≐ 62 43.53 N 5.53 E
Assean Lake ⊜ 184 56.13 N 96.30 W
Assebroek 50 51.12 N 3.16 E
Assekaifaf 148 27.08 N 8.50 E
Assel 52 53.41 N 9.25 E
Asseln ✦8 263 51.32 N 7.35 E
Assembleia Nacional, Palacio da ⊛ 266c 38.43 N 9.09 W
Assemini 71 39.17 N 9.00 E
Assen 52 52.59 N 6.34 E
Assendelft 52 52.27 N 4.45 E
Assenede 50 51.14 N 3.45 E
Assens 41 55.16 N 9.55 E
Asserbo 41 56.01 N 12.01 E
Assergi 66 42.25 N 13.30 E
Asseria ⊥ 36 44.02 N 15.39 E
As-Sīb 128 23.41 N 58.11 E
As-Sidr 128 23.27 N 39.45 E
As-Sijn 132 32.47 N 36.28 E
As-Simākīyah 132 31.18 N 35.48 E
As-Sinbillāwayn 142 30.53 N 31.27 E
Assíni ⊥ 38 37.36 N 22.48 E
Assiniboia 184 49.38 N 105.59 W
Assiniboine ≐ 184 49.53 N 97.08 W
Assiniboine, Mount ∧ 182 50.52 N 115.39 W
Assiniboine Indian Reserve ✦4 184 50.21 N 103.28 W
Assinika ≐ 184 52.37 N 96.10 W
Assinippi 283 42.09 N 70.51 W
Assis, Bra. 252 22.40 S 50.25 W
Assis, Bra. 255 22.40 S 50.25 W
Assis Chateaubriand 252 24.29 S 53.32 W
Assiscunk Creek ≐ 208 40.05 N 74.51 W
Assisi 66 43.04 N 12.37 E
Asslar 56 50.35 N 8.28 E
Assling 60 48.00 N 12.00 E
Asso 62 45.52 N 9.16 E
Assodé ∓4 150 18.26 N 8.28 E
Assomada 150a 15.06 N 23.41 W
Assonet 207 41.47 N 71.04 W
Assoro 70 37.37 N 14.25 E
As-Subū' ⊥ 140 22.45 N 32.34 E
As-Sūdān → Sudan □1 140 15.00 N 30.00 E
As-Sudd ✦1 140 8.00 N 31.00 E
As-Sufāl 144 14.06 N 48.42 E
Aṣ-Ṣufayyah 140 15.30 N 34.42 E
Aṣ-Ṣūfīyah 142 30.55 N 31.46 E
As-Sukhnah, Sūrīy. 130 34.52 N 38.52 E
As-Sukhnah, Urd. 132 32.08 N 36.04 E
As-Sulaymānīyah, Ar. Su. 128 24.09 N 47.19 E
As-Sulaymānīyah, 'Irāq 128 35.33 N 45.26 E
As-Sulaymānīyah □4 128 35.30 N 45.25 E
As-Sulaymī 128 26.17 N 41.21 E
As-Sulayyil 144 20.27 N 45.34 E
As-Sulṭān 146 31.07 N 17.10 E
As-Sumayḥ 140 9.49 N 27.39 E
Aṣ-Ṣummān ✦1 128 25.00 N 47.00 E
As-Summāqīyāt 132 32.26 N 36.24 E
Assumption, Il., U.S. 219 39.31 N 89.02 W
Assumption, Oh., U.S. 216 41.40 N 83.54 W
Assumption Island I 138 9.45 S 46.30 E
Assunpink Creek ≐ 285 40.13 N 74.46 W
As-Su'ūdīyah 142 29.33 N 31.14 E
Aṣ-Ṣuwār 130 35.30 N 40.39 E
As-Suwaydā' 132 32.42 N 36.34 E
As-Suwaydā' □8 132 32.45 N 36.45 E
As-Suways (Suez) 142 29.58 N 32.33 E
As-Suways □4 142 30.12 N 32.30 E
Assynt, Loch ⊜ 46 58.11 N 5.06 W
Ašt 85 40.41 N 70.20 E
Asta, Cima d' ∧ 64 46.10 N 11.36 E
Astaffort 32 44.04 N 0.40 E
Astakós 38 38.32 N 21.05 E
Āstāneh, Īrān 128 37.17 N 49.59 E
Āstāneh, Īrān 128 33.53 N 49.22 E
Astara, Azer. 84 38.28 N 48.52 E
Āstārā, Īrān 128 38.26 N 48.52 E
Aštarak 84 40.18 N 44.22 E
Astaškovo 82 55.32 N 38.38 E
Astatula 220 28.43 N 81.44 W
Asten, Ned. 52 51.24 N 5.45 E
Asten, Öst. 61 48.13 N 14.25 E
Asti 62 44.54 N 8.12 E
Asti □4 62 44.55 N 8.10 E
Astica 252 30.56 S 67.23 W
Astico ≐ 64 45.37 N 11.37 E
Astipálaia 38 36.30 N 26.30 E
Astipálaia I 38 36.35 N 26.25 E
Astley Bridge 262 53.36 N 2.26 W
Astley Green 262 53.29 N 2.27 W
Astley Hall ⊥ 262 53.39 N 2.38 W
Astola Island I 128 25.07 N 63.51 E
Astolfo Dutra 256 21.19 S 42.52 W
Aston, Eng., U.K. 262 53.18 N 2.40 W
Aston, Pa., U.S. 285 39.52 N 75.26 W
Aston Clinton 42 51.48 N 0.44 W
Aston-on-Trent 42 52.52 N 1.23 W
Astor 123 35.22 N 74.51 E
Astor ≐ 123 35.34 N 74.41 E
Astorga, Bra. 255 23.13 S 51.40 W
Astorga, Esp. 34 42.27 N 6.03 W
Astorga, Pil. 116 6.54 N 125.27 E
Astoria, Il., U.S. 219 40.13 N 90.21 W
Astoria, Or., U.S. 224 46.11 N 123.49 W
Astoria ✦8 276 40.46 N 73.55 W
Astoria Bridge ✦5 224 46.13 N 123.52 W
Astoria Column ⊥ 224 46.11 N 123.50 W
Åstorp 41 56.08 N 12.57 E
Astove Island I 138 10.06 S 47.45 E
Astra 254 45.44 S 67.30 W
Astrachan' 80 46.21 N 48.03 E
Astrachanka 86 51.33 N 69.47 E
Astrachan' Oblast' □4 80 47.00 N 47.30 E
Astrachanskij 80 46.12 N 47.16 E
Astrachanskij zapovednik ✦4 80 46.00 N 48.32 E
Astrakhan → Astrachan' 80 46.21 N 48.03 E
Astrašycki Haradok 76 54.04 N 27.42 E
Astravec 76 54.37 N 25.57 E
Astrodome ♦ 222 29.41 N 95.25 W
Astrolabe, Cape ⟩ 175e 8.20 S 160.34 E
Astrolabe, Récifs de l' ∓2 175f 19.48 S 165.37 E
Astrolabe Bay ⊂ 164 5.20 S 145.50 E
Astrouna 76 55.08 N 29.53 E
Astryna 76 53.44 N 24.32 E
Astudillo 34 42.12 N 4.18 W
Astura, Torre ⊥ 66 41.24 N 12.46 E
Asturias 116 10.34 N 123.43 E
Asturias □3 34 43.20 N 6.00 W
Asturias □4 34 43.20 N 6.00 W
Astwood Bank 42 52.15 N 1.56 W
Asubulak 86 49.31 N 83.03 E
Asuisui, Cape ⟩ 175a 13.47 S 172.29 W
Asuka 96 34.28 N 135.50 E
Asuka ⊛3 9 71.32 S 24.08 E
Asuke 94 35.08 N 137.19 E
Asunción 252 25.16 S 57.40 W
Asunción, Bahía ⊂ 232 27.06 N 114.11 W
Asuncion Island I 108 19.40 N 145.24 E
Asunción Ixtaltepec 234 16.30 N 95.03 W
Asunción Mita 236 14.20 N 89.43 W
Asunción Nochixtlán 234 17.28 N 97.14 W
Åsunden ⊜, Sve. 26 57.58 N 15.50 E
Åsunden ⊜, Sve. 26 57.44 N 13.22 E
Asunga, Wādī V 146 13.21 N 22.17 E
Asuni 71 39.52 N 8.56 E
'Āṣūr, Tall ∧ 132 31.59 N 35.17 E
Asuwa 94 36.01 N 136.16 E
Asuwa ≐ 94 36.04 N 136.11 E
Asveja 76 56.01 N 28.06 E
Asvejskae, vozero ⊜ 76 56.03 N 28.08 E
Aswad, Ar-Ra's al- ⟩ 144 21.22 N 39.08 E
Aswān 140 24.05 N 32.53 E
Aswān High Dam → 'Ālī, As-Sadd al- ✦6 140 23.58 N 32.52 E
Aswatthaberia 272b 22.26 N 88.32 E
Asy ≐ 85 43.31 N 78.20 E
Asyūṭ 142 27.11 N 31.11 E
Asyūṭ □4 142 27.20 N 30.50 E
Asyūṭī, Wādī al- V 142 27.11 N 31.16 E
Aszód 30 47.39 N 19.31 E
'Ata I, Tonga 14 22.20 S 176.12 W
Ata I, Tonga 174w 21.03 S 175.00 W
Atabaj 85 43.30 N 68.20 E
Atabapo ≐ 246 4.03 N 67.42 W
Atabasca → Athabasca ≐ 176 58.40 N 110.50 W
Atabasca, Lago → Athabasca, Lake ⊜ 176 59.07 N 110.00 W
Atabey 130 37.57 N 30.39 E
Atacama □4 252 27.30 S 70.00 W
Atacama, Desierto de ✦2 18 24.30 S 69.15 W
Atacama, Puna de ⋀1 252 24.30 S 67.30 W
Atacama, Salar de ≚ 252 23.30 S 68.15 W
Ataco 246 3.35 N 75.23 W
Atacora, Chaîne de l' ⋀ 150 10.45 N 1.30 E
Atacuari ≐ 246 3.47 S 70.44 W
Atafu I1 14 8.33 S 172.30 W
Atagaj 88 55.06 N 99.23 E
Atago-yama ∧, Nihon 94 35.07 N 139.59 E
Atago-yama ∧, Nihon 96 35.03 N 135.37 E
Ātāi ≐1 126 22.51 N 89.33 E
'Aṭā'iṭah, Jabal al- ∧ 132 30.40 N 35.39 E
Atakakup Indian Reserve ✦4 184 53.24 N 106.55 W
Atakano-seki ⊥ 94 36.24 N 136.25 E
Atakora □5 150 10.00 N 1.35 E
Atakora, Réserve d' ✦4 150 11.30 N 2.10 E
Atakpamé 150 7.32 N 1.08 E
Atalaia, Bra. 250 9.31 S 36.02 W
Atalaia, Port. 266c 38.42 N 8.55 W
Atalándi 38 38.39 N 23.00 E
Atalanka 88 54.50 N 103.05 E
Atalaya, Arg. 258 35.02 S 57.32 W
Atalaya, Pan. 236 8.03 N 80.56 W
Atalaya, Perú 248 10.44 S 73.45 W
Atalaya, Cerro ∧, Chile 254 52.45 S 72.42 W
Atalaya, Cerro ∧, Perú 248 12.38 S 71.56 W
Atalaya, Punta ⟩ 258 35.01 S 57.31 W
Atamanovka 88 51.56 N 113.37 E
Atamanovo 86 56.24 N 93.36 E
Atambua 112 9.07 S 124.54 E
Atami 94 35.05 N 139.04 E
Atapupu 112 9.00 S 124.51 E
'Atāq 144 14.33 N 46.48 E
'Atāqah, Jabal ⋀ 142 29.58 N 32.20 E
Atâr 150 20.31 N 13.03 W
Ataram, 'Erg n- ✦2 148 23.46 N 1.44 E
Atarés, Castillo de ⊥ 286b 23.08 N 82.21 W
Atāri 123 31.36 N 74.35 E
Atary 80 57.32 N 49.18 E
Atascadero 226 35.29 N 120.40 W
Atascosa ≐ 196 28.26 N 98.12 W
At'aševo 80 54.36 N 46.06 E
Atasu 86 48.42 N 71.38 E
Atas uul ∧ 102 43.18 N 96.36 E
Atata I 174w 21.03 S 175.15 W
Atatürk Barajı ⊜1 130 37.30 N 38.30 E
Ataturk Tower ⊥ 267b 41.00 N 28.59 E
Ataur 272a 28.43 N 77.24 E
Atauro, Pulau I 112 8.13 S 125.35 E
Atbara ('Aṭbarah) ≐ 140 17.40 N 33.56 E
'Aṭbarah 140 17.42 N 33.59 E
'Aṭbarah (Atbara) ≐ 140 17.40 N 33.56 E
Atbasar 86 51.48 N 68.20 E
At-Baši 85 41.10 N 75.48 E
Atbaši ≐ 85 41.24 N 75.38 E
Atbaši, chrebet ⋀ 85 40.55 N 75.40 E
Atchafalaya ≐ 194 29.53 N 91.28 W
Atchafalaya Bay ⊂ 194 29.25 N 91.20 W
Atchison 198 39.33 N 95.07 W
Atco 208 39.46 N 74.53 W
Ate 286d 12.03 S 76.58 W
Atebubu 150 7.45 N 0.59 W
Ateca 34 41.20 N 1.47 W
Atelchu ≐ 255 12.05 S 53.46 W
Ateleta 66 41.51 N 14.12 E
Ateli 124 28.06 N 76.17 E
Atella 68 40.52 N 15.39 E
Atemajac de Brizuela 234 20.11 N 103.42 W
Atemar 80 54.11 N 45.24 E
Atemble 164 5.05 S 144.45 E
Atena Lucana 68 40.27 N 15.33 E
Atenango del Río 234 18.05 N 99.06 W
Atenas → Athínai 38 37.58 N 23.43 E
Atencingo 234 18.30 N 98.36 W
Atengo ≐ 234 21.50 N 104.43 W
Atenguillo 234 20.25 N 104.31 W
Atenguillo ≐ 234 20.55 N 104.38 W
Atenquique 234 19.31 N 103.30 W
Atepcevo 82 55.20 N 36.46 E
Aterno ≐ 66 42.11 N 13.51 E
Aterrado, Ribeirão do ≐ 256 22.09 S 45.03 W
Atessa 66 42.04 N 14.27 E
Aṭfīḥ 142 29.24 N 31.15 E
Aṭfīḥī, Wādī al- V 142 29.23 N 31.16 E
Ātgharia 126 24.06 N 89.14 E
Atglen 208 39.57 N 75.58 W
Ath 50 50.38 N 3.47 E
Athabasca 182 54.43 N 113.17 W
Athabasca ≐ 176 58.40 N 110.50 W
Athabasca, Lake ⊜ 176 59.07 N 110.00 W
Athalmer 182 50.32 N 116.02 W
Athapapuskow Lake ⊜ 184 54.33 N 101.40 W
Athārabānki ≐1 126 22.49 N 89.39 E
Athārān Hazāri 123 31.11 N 72.06 E
Athboy 48 53.37 N 6.55 W
Athea 48 52.28 N 9.17 W
Athen → Athínai 38 37.58 N 23.43 E
Athena 202 45.48 N 118.29 W
Athènes → Athínai 38 37.58 N 23.43 E
Athenry 48 53.18 N 8.45 W
Athens, On., Can. 212 44.38 N 75.57 W
Athens → Athínai, Ellás 38 37.58 N 23.43 E
Athens, Al., U.S. 194 34.48 N 86.58 W
Athens, Ga., U.S. 192 33.57 N 83.22 W
Athens, Il., U.S. 219 39.57 N 89.43 W


**Symbols** in the index entries represent the broad categories identified in the key at the right. Symbols with superior numbers (⋀1) identify subcategories (see complete key on page *I · 1).*

**Symbole** im Register stellen die rechts im Schlüssel erklärten Kategorien dar. Symbole mit hochgestellten Ziffern (⋀1) bezeichnen Unterabteilungen einer Kategorie (vgl. vollständiger Schlüssel auf Seite *I · 1).*

**Los símbolos** incluídos en el texto del índice representan las grandes categorías identificadas con la clave a la derecha. Los símbolos con numeros en su parte superior (⋀1) identifican las subcategorías (véase la clave completa en la página *I · 1).*

**Les symboles** de l'index représentent les catégories indiquées dans la légende à droite. Les symboles suivis d'un indice (⋀1) représentent des sous-catégories (voir légende complète à la page *I · 1).*

**Os símbolos** incluídos no texto do índice representam as grandes categorias identificadas com a chave à direita. Os símbolos com números em sua parte superior (⋀1) identificam as subcategorias (veja-se a chave completa à página *I · 1).*

| | | | | |
|---|---|---|---|---|
| ∧ Mountain | Berg | Montaña | Montagne | Montanha |
| ⋀ Mountains | Gebirge | Montañas | Montagnes | Montanhas |
| )( Pass | Paß | Paso | Col | Passo |
| V Valley, Canyon | Tal, Cañon | Valle, Cañón | Vallée, Canyon | Vale, Canhão |
| ≚ Plain | Ebene | Llano | Plaine | Planície |
| ⟩ Cape | Kap | Cabo | Cap | Cabo |
| I Island | Insel | Isla | Île | Ilha |
| II Islands | Inseln | Islas | Îles | Ilhas |
| ± Other Topographic Features | Andere Topographische Objekte | Otros Elementos Topográficos | Autres données topographiques | Outros acidentes topográficos |

ESPAÑOL

| Nombre | Página | Lat.°′ | Long.°′ W = Oeste |
|---|---|---|---|
| Athens, La., U.S. | 194 | 32.39 N | 93.01 W |
| Athens, Mi., U.S. | 216 | 42.05 N | 85.14 W |
| Athens, N.Y., U.S. | 210 | 42.15 N | 73.48 W |
| Athens, Oh., U.S. | 188 | 39.19 N | 82.06 W |
| Athens, Pa., U.S. | 210 | 41.57 N | 76.31 W |
| Athens, Tn., U.S. | 132 | 35.26 N | 84.35 W |
| Athens, Tx., U.S. | 222 | 32.12 N | 95.51 W |
| Athens, W.V., U.S. | 192 | 37.25 N | 81.00 W |
| Athens, Wi., U.S. | 190 | 45.01 N | 90.04 W |
| Athens, Lake ⊜[1] | 222 | 32.14 N | 95.45 W |
| Athenstedt | 54 | 51.56 N | 10.55 E |
| Athens University ◙[2] | 267c | 37.59 N | 23.44 E |
| Atherley | 212 | 44.36 N | 79.22 W |
| Atherstone | 42 | 52.35 N | 1.31 W |
| Atherton, Austl. | 166 | 17.16 S | 145.29 E |
| Atherton, Eng., U.K. | 44 | 53.31 N | 2.31 W |
| Atherton, Ca., U.S. | 226 | 37.27 N | 122.11 W |
| Athi ≃ | 154 | 2.59 S | 38.31 E |
| Athiaínou | 130 | 35.04 N | 33.32 E |
| Athiémé | 150 | 6.35 N | 1.40 E |
| Athies-sous-Laon | 50 | 49.34 N | 3.41 E |
| Athínai (Athens), Ellás | 38 | 37.58 N | 23.43 E |
| Athínai (Athens), Ellás | 267c | 37.58 N | 23.43 E |
| Äthiopien → Ethiopia □[1] | 144 | 9.00 N | 39.00 E |
| Athi River | 154 | 1.27 S | 36.59 E |
| Athis-Mons | 261 | 48.43 N | 2.24 E |
| Athlat al-Bāshā ∧[2] | 142 | 27.31 N | 32.20 E |
| Athleague | 48 | 53.34 N | 8.15 W |
| Athlone | 48 | 53.25 N | 7.56 W |
| Athni | 122 | 16.44 N | 75.04 E |
| Athok | 110 | 17.12 N | 95.05 E |
| Athol, N.Z. | 172 | 45.31 S | 168.35 E |
| Athol, Ma., U.S. | 207 | 42.35 N | 72.13 W |
| Athol Bay ⊂ | 212 | 43.53 N | 77.15 W |
| Athol Island I | 240b | 25.05 N | 77.16 W |
| Atholl, Forest of ◆[3] | 46 | 56.50 N | 4.00 W |
| Athol Springs | 210 | 42.46 N | 78.52 W |
| Áthos ∧ | 38 | 40.09 N | 24.19 E |
| Ath-Tha'lah | 132 | 32.42 N | 36.26 E |
| Ath-Thamad | 140 | 29.41 N | 34.18 E |
| Ath-Thanīyah | 132 | 31.10 N | 35.43 E |
| Athus | 56 | 49.34 N | 5.50 E |
| Athy | 48 | 53.00 N | 7.00 W |
| Ati | 146 | 13.13 N | 18.20 E |
| Atiak | 154 | 3.15 N | 32.07 E |
| Atibaia | 256 | 23.07 S | 46.33 W |
| Atibainha ≃ | 256 | 22.42 S | 47.17 W |
| Atibainha, Reservatório ⊜[1] | 256 | 23.10 S | 46.20 W |
| Atico | 248 | 16.14 S | 73.39 W |
| Aticonipi, Lac ⊜ | 186 | 51.52 N | 59.22 W |
| Atienza | 34 | 41.12 N | 2.52 W |
| Atigun Pass )( | 180 | 68.08 N | 149.29 W |
| Atik Lake ⊜ | 184 | 55.16 N | 96.00 W |
| Atikokan | 190 | 48.45 N | 91.37 W |
| Atikonak Lake ⊜ | 176 | 52.40 N | 64.30 W |
| Atil | 200 | 30.50 N | 111.35 W |
| Atimari ≃ | 248 | 9.04 S | 67.23 W |
| Atimonan | 116 | 14.00 N | 121.55 E |
| Atina | 66 | 41.37 N | 13.48 E |
| Atiparaná ≃[1] | 246 | 1.51 S | 65.37 W |
| Atiquizaya | 236 | 13.58 N | 89.46 W |
| Atirāmpattinam | 122 | 10.21 N | 79.24 E |
| Atitlán, Lago de ⊜ | 236 | 14.42 N | 91.12 W |
| Atitlán, Volcán ∧[1] | 236 | 14.35 N | 91.11 W |
| Atiu I | 14 | 20.02 S | 158.07 W |
| Atka, Ross. | 74 | 60.50 N | 151.48 E |
| Atka, Ak., U.S. | 180 | 52.12 N | 174.12 W |
| Atka Island I | 180 | 52.15 N | 174.30 W |
| Atkaracalar | 130 | 40.50 N | 33.04 E |
| Atkarsk | 80 | 51.52 N | 45.00 E |
| Atkins | 194 | 35.14 N | 92.56 W |
| Atkinson, Il., U.S. | 190 | 41.25 N | 90.00 W |
| Atkinson, Ne., U.S. | 198 | 42.31 N | 98.58 W |
| Atkinson, N.H., U.S. | 207 | 42.50 N | 71.08 W |
| Atkinson, N.C., U.S. | 192 | 34.31 N | 78.10 W |
| Atkinson Island I | 222 | 29.40 N | 94.58 W |
| Atkinson Lake ⊜ | 184 | 55.59 N | 94.48 W |
| Atkri | 164 | 1.44 S | 130.04 E |
| Atlacomulco | 234 | 19.48 N | 99.53 W |
| Atlanta, Ga., U.S. | 192 | 33.44 N | 84.23 W |
| Atlanta, Il., U.S. | 194 | 40.15 N | 89.14 W |
| Atlanta, Mi., U.S. | 190 | 45.00 N | 84.08 W |
| Atlanta, Mo., U.S. | 194 | 39.53 N | 92.28 W |
| Atlanta, N.Y., U.S. | 210 | 42.33 N | 77.28 W |
| Atlanta, Oh., U.S. | 218 | 39.34 N | 83.11 W |
| Atlanta, Tx., U.S. | 194 | 33.06 N | 94.09 W |
| Atlantic, Ia., U.S. | 198 | 41.24 N | 95.00 W |
| Atlantic, N.C., U.S. | 192 | 34.53 N | 76.20 W |
| Atlantic, Pa., U.S. | 214 | 41.30 N | 80.21 W |
| Atlantic, Va., U.S. | 208 | 37.54 N | 75.30 W |
| Atlantic □[6] | 208 | 39.27 N | 74.44 W |
| Atlantic Beach, Fl., U.S. | 192 | 30.20 N | 81.23 W |
| Atlantic Beach, N.Y., U.S. | 276 | 40.35 N | 73.44 W |
| Atlantic City | 208 | 39.21 N | 74.25 W |
| Atlantic Highlands | 208 | 40.24 N | 74.02 W |
| Atlantic-Indian Basin ✣[1] | 6 | 60.00 S | 15.00 E |
| Atlantic-Indian Ridge ✣[3] | 4 | 53.00 S | 15.00 E |
| Atlántico □[5] | 246 | 10.45 N | 75.00 W |
| Atlántico, Océano → Atlantic Ocean ⚲[1] | 8 | 5.00 S | 25.00 W |
| Atlantic Ocean ⚲[1] | 4 | 5.00 S | 25.00 W |
| Atlantic Ocean ⚲[1] | 8 | 5.00 S | 25.00 W |
| Atlantic Peak ∧ | 200 | 42.37 N | 109.00 W |
| Atlántida | 252 | 34.46 S | 55.45 W |
| Atlántida □[5] | 236 | 15.40 N | 87.00 W |
| Atlantique | 276 | 40.39 N | 73.10 W |
| Atlantique □[5] | 150 | 6.35 N | 2.15 E |
| Atlantique, Océan → Atlantic Ocean ⚲[1] | 8 | 5.00 S | 25.00 W |
| Atlantischer Ozean → Atlantic Ocean ⚲[1] | 8 | 5.00 S | 25.00 W |
| Atlas, Mi., U.S. | 216 | 42.56 N | 83.32 W |
| Atlas, Pa., U.S. | 208 | 40.48 N | 76.26 W |
| Atlasburg | 214 | 40.20 N | 80.23 W |
| Atlas Mountains ⋏ | 148 | 33.00 N | 2.00 W |
| Atlasova, ostrov I | 74 | 50.53 N | 155.27 E |
| Atlasovo | 92a | 46.01 N | 142.09 E |
| Atlas Saharien ⋏ | 148 | 33.25 N | 1.20 E |
| Atlas Tellien ⋏ | 148 | 36.00 N | 3.00 E |
| Atlin | 180 | 59.35 N | 133.42 W |
| Atlin Lake ⊜ | 180 | 59.20 N | 133.45 W |
| 'Atlit | 132 | 32.41 N | 34.56 E |
| Atlixco | 234 | 18.54 N | 98.26 W |
| Ātmakūr | 122 | 15.53 N | 78.35 E |
| Atmanov Ugol | 80 | 53.07 N | 41.23 E |
| Atmis | 80 | 53.28 N | 43.57 E |
| Atmore | 194 | 31.01 N | 87.29 W |
| Ätna → Etna, Monte ∧[1] | 70 | 37.46 N | 15.00 E |
| Atna ≃ | 26 | 61.44 N | 10.49 E |
| Atna Peak ∧ | 182 | 53.57 N | 128.03 W |
| Atnarko ≃ | 182 | 52.22 N | 126.04 W |
| Atnis | 86 | 58.48 N | 69.38 E |
| Atnosen | 26 | 61.44 N | 10.49 E |
| Atō | 96 | 34.24 N | 131.43 E |
| Atocha | 248 | 20.56 S | 66.14 W |
| Atocha, Estación de ◆[5] | 266a | 40.24 N | 3.41 W |
| Atocongo | 286d | 12.08 S | 76.56 W |
| Atocongo ⊥ | 286d | 12.12 S | 76.55 W |
| Atoka | 196 | 34.23 N | 96.07 W |
| Atotonilco | 232 | 24.15 N | 102.45 W |
| Atotonilco, Cerro ∧ | 196 | 26.08 N | 104.43 W |
| Atotonilco, Lago ⊜ | 234 | 20.22 N | 103.39 W |
| Atotonilco de Tula | 234 | 20.00 N | 99.13 W |
| Atotonilco El Alto | 234 | 20.33 N | 102.31 W |
| Atoui, Khaṭṭ V | 150 | 20.04 N | 15.59 W |
| Atoyac | 234 | 20.01 N | 103.32 W |
| Atoyac ≃, Méx. | 234 | 17.05 N | 100.29 W |
| Atoyac ≃, Méx. | 234 | 18.10 N | 98.31 W |
| Atoyac ≃, Méx. | 234 | 16.30 N | 97.31 W |

FRANÇAIS

| Nom | Page | Lat.°′ | Long.°′ W = Ouest |
|---|---|---|---|
| Atoyac ≃, Méx. | 234 | 19.02 N | 96.08 W |
| Atoyac de Álvarez | 234 | 17.12 N | 100.26 W |
| Atoyaquillo ≃ | 234 | 16.37 N | 97.41 W |
| Atpur | 272b | 22.50 N | 88.23 E |
| Atrå | 26 | 59.59 N | 8.45 E |
| 'Atrah, Jabal ∧ | 132 | 29.40 N | 35.34 E |
| Atrai ≃ | 124 | 24.29 N | 89.03 E |
| Atrak (Atrek) ⊜ | 128 | 37.28 N | 53.57 E |
| Ätran ≃ | 26 | 56.53 N | 12.30 E |
| Atrato ≃ | 246 | 8.17 N | 76.58 W |
| Atrauli | 124 | 28.02 N | 78.17 E |
| Atrek (Atrak) ≃ | 128 | 37.28 N | 53.57 E |
| Atri | 66 | 42.35 N | 13.58 E |
| Atripalda | 68 | 40.55 N | 14.50 E |
| Atrisco | 200 | 34.59 N | 106.41 W |
| Atrop ◆[8] | 263 | 51.24 N | 6.43 E |
| Atsion Lake ⊜ | 285 | 39.44 N | 74.44 W |
| Atsugi | 94 | 35.27 N | 139.22 E |
| Atsugi-hikōjō ■ | 94 | 35.28 N | 139.27 E |
| Atsumi, Nihon | 92 | 38.37 N | 139.35 E |
| Atsumi, Nihon | 94 | 34.37 N | 137.07 E |
| Atsumi-hantō ›[1] | 94 | 34.39 N | 137.15 E |
| Atta | 272a | 28.34 N | 77.20 E |
| At-Tabbīn | 142 | 29.47 N | 31.18 E |
| Aṭ-Ṭafīlah | 132 | 30.50 N | 35.36 E |
| Aṭ-Ṭafīlah □[8] | 132 | 30.45 N | 35.45 E |
| At-Tahrīr □[4] | 142 | 30.40 N | 30.15 E |
| Aṭ-Ṭā'if | 144 | 21.16 N | 40.24 E |
| Attainville | 261 | 49.03 N | 2.21 E |
| At-Tāj | 146 | 24.13 N | 23.18 E |
| Aṭ-Ṭalibīyah | 273c | 30.00 N | 31.11 E |
| At-Tall | 132 | 33.36 N | 36.18 E |
| Attalla | 194 | 34.01 N | 86.05 W |
| At-Tall al-Kabīr | 142 | 30.34 N | 31.47 E |
| At-Ta'mīm □[4] | 128 | 35.25 N | 44.20 E |
| At-Tamīmī | 146 | 32.20 N | 23.04 E |
| Attapu | 110 | 14.48 N | 106.50 E |
| Attar, Oued el V | 148 | 33.27 N | 5.26 E |
| At-Tatālīyah | 142 | 27.20 N | 30.50 E |
| Attáviros ∧ | 38 | 36.12 N | 27.52 E |
| Attawapiskat | 176 | 52.55 N | 82.26 W |
| Attawapiskat ≃ | 176 | 52.57 N | 82.18 W |
| Attawapiskat Lake ⊜ | 176 | 52.18 N | 87.54 W |
| Attawaugan | 207 | 41.52 N | 71.52 W |
| At-Tawd | 142 | 30.47 N | 30.37 E |
| At-Tawīl ⋏ | 128 | 29.20 N | 39.35 E |
| Aṭ-Ṭayrīyah | 142 | 30.39 N | 30.46 E |
| At-Taysīyah ⊞ | 128 | 28.00 N | 44.00 E |
| Aṭ-Ṭayyibah, Miṣr | 142 | 28.16 N | 30.39 E |
| Aṭ-Ṭayyibah, Sūrīy. | 132 | 32.33 N | 36.14 E |
| Aṭ-Ṭayyibah, Sūrīy. | 132 | 32.48 N | 36.46 E |
| Aṭ-Ṭayyibah, Urd. | 132 | 32.33 N | 35.43 E |
| Attel ≃ | 64 | 48.01 N | 12.11 E |
| Attendorn | 56 | 51.07 N | 7.54 E |
| Attenhausen | 58 | 47.59 N | 10.20 E |
| Attenkirchen | 60 | 48.30 N | 11.46 E |
| Atterbury | 219 | 40.04 N | 89.55 W |
| Attersee | 64 | 47.55 N | 13.33 E |
| Attersee ⊜ | 64 | 47.52 N | 13.33 E |
| Attert ≃ | 56 | 49.52 N | 6.05 E |
| Attica, In., U.S. | 216 | 40.17 N | 87.14 W |
| Attica, Ks., U.S. | 198 | 37.14 N | 98.13 W |
| Attica, N.Y., U.S. | 210 | 42.51 N | 78.16 W |
| Attica, Oh., U.S. | 214 | 41.03 N | 82.53 W |
| Attica → Attikí □[9] | 38 | 38.10 N | 23.20 E |
| Attichy | 50 | 49.25 N | 3.03 E |
| Attigliano | 66 | 42.31 N | 12.17 E |
| Attigny | 56 | 49.29 N | 4.35 E |
| Attikí □[4] | 38 | 38.00 N | 23.45 E |
| Attikí □[9] | 38 | 38.10 N | 23.20 E |
| 'Attīl | 132 | 32.22 N | 35.04 E |
| Attimis | 64 | 46.11 N | 13.16 E |
| At-Tīnah | 142 | 31.03 N | 32.18 E |
| Attingal | 122 | 8.41 N | 76.50 E |
| Attir | 140 | 6.04 N | 30.50 E |
| Attleboro | 207 | 41.56 N | 71.17 W |
| Attleborough | 42 | 52.31 N | 1.01 E |
| Attnang | 60 | 48.01 N | 13.43 E |
| Attock | 123 | 33.54 N | 72.15 E |
| Attoyac ≃ | 194 | 31.29 N | 94.18 W |
| Attu | 181a | 52.56 N | 173.14 E |
| At-Tubah | 144 | 12.40 N | 43.30 E |
| Attu Island I | 181a | 52.55 N | 173.00 E |
| Aṭ-Ṭunayb | 132 | 31.48 N | 35.57 E |
| Āttūr, India | 122 | 11.36 N | 78.37 E |
| Aṭ-Ṭūr, Miṣr | 140 | 28.14 N | 33.37 E |
| Aṭ-Ṭuwayshah | 140 | 12.21 N | 26.32 E |
| Aṭ-Ṭuwayyah | 128 | 27.36 N | 41.13 E |
| Attymon | 48 | 53.19 N | 8.35 W |
| Atucatiquini ≃ | 248 | 7.44 S | 67.57 W |
| Atucha | 258 | 33.58 S | 59.18 W |
| Atuel ≃ | 252 | 36.17 S | 66.50 W |
| Atuel, Bañados del ≡ | 252 | 36.30 S | 66.55 W |
| Atuntaqui | 246 | 0.20 N | 78.13 W |
| Atuona | 174x | 9.48 S | 139.02 W |
| At'urjevo | 80 | 54.21 N | 43.19 E |
| Atushi | 85 | 39.43 N | 76.08 E |
| Åtvidaberg | 26 | 58.12 N | 16.00 E |
| Atwater, Sk., Can. | 184 | 50.47 N | 102.10 W |
| Atwater, Ca., U.S. | 226 | 37.20 N | 120.36 W |
| Atwater, Il., U.S. | 219 | 39.20 N | 89.44 W |
| Atwater, Mn., U.S. | 198 | 45.08 N | 94.46 W |
| Atwater, Oh., U.S. | 214 | 41.01 N | 81.10 W |
| Atwood, On., Can. | 212 | 43.40 N | 81.01 W |
| Atwood, Ca., U.S. | 280 | 33.52 N | 117.50 W |
| Atwood, Il., U.S. | 194 | 39.48 N | 88.28 W |
| Atwood, In., U.S. | 216 | 41.15 N | 85.58 W |
| Atwood, Ks., U.S. | 198 | 39.48 N | 101.02 W |
| Atwood, Tn., U.S. | 194 | 35.58 N | 88.40 W |
| Atwood Lake ⊜[1] | 214 | 40.33 N | 81.13 W |
| Atyrau (Gurjev) | 80 | 47.07 N | 51.56 E |
| Atyrau □[4] | 80 | 47.30 N | 51.00 E |
| Atzalpur | 272a | 28.43 N | 77.21 E |
| Atzendorf | 54 | 51.55 N | 11.35 E |
| Atzgersdorf ◆[8] | 264b | 48.09 N | 16.18 E |
| Au | 58 | 47.19 N | 9.59 E |
| Auagrām | 126 | 23.31 N | 87.41 E |
| Auaiá-Miçu ≃ | 250 | 10.51 S | 53.08 W |
| Aua Island I | 164 | 1.27 S | 143.04 E |
| Aual Edo | 144 | 4.14 N | 40.37 E |
| Auari ≃ | 246 | 3.33 N | 63.48 W |
| Auau Channel ⊻ | 229a | 20.51 N | 156.45 W |
| Aub | 56 | 49.33 N | 10.04 E |
| Aubá | 112 | 9.02 S | 125.22 E |
| Aubagne | 62 | 43.17 N | 5.34 E |
| Aubange | 56 | 49.35 N | 5.48 E |
| Aube □[5] | 32 | 48.15 N | 4.05 E |
| Aube ≃ | 32 | 48.34 N | 3.43 E |
| Aubenas | 62 | 44.37 N | 4.23 E |
| Aubenton | 50 | 49.50 N | 4.12 E |
| Aubepierre | 261 | 48.38 N | 2.53 E |
| Aubergenville | 261 | 48.58 N | 1.51 E |
| Auberive | 58 | 47.47 N | 5.03 E |
| Auberry | 226 | 37.04 N | 119.29 W |
| Aubervilliers | 50 | 48.55 N | 2.23 E |
| Aubetin ≃ | 50 | 48.49 N | 3.01 E |
| Aubette ≃ | 261 | 49.00 N | 1.54 E |
| Aubigny-en-Artois | 50 | 50.21 N | 2.35 E |
| Aubigny-sur-Nère | 50 | 47.29 N | 2.26 E |
| Aubin | 32 | 44.32 N | 2.14 E |
| Aubinadong ≃ | 190 | 46.51 N | 83.22 W |
| Aubonne | 58 | 46.28 N | 6.24 E |
| Auboué | 56 | 49.13 N | 5.59 E |
| Aubrac ⋏ | 32 | 44.40 N | 3.00 E |
| Aubrey Cliffs ⊥[4] | 200 | 35.45 N | 113.00 W |
| Aubrey Lake ⊜[1] | 190 | 46.54 N | 83.11 W |
| Aubrives | 56 | 50.06 N | 4.46 E |
| Aubry Lake ⊜ | 180 | 67.23 N | 126.30 W |
| Auburn, Austl. | 168b | 34.01 S | 138.41 E |
| Auburn, Austl. | 274a | 33.51 S | 151.02 E |
| Auburn, Al., U.S. | 194 | 32.36 N | 85.28 W |
| Auburn, Ca., U.S. | 226 | 38.53 N | 121.04 W |
| Auburn, Il., U.S. | 219 | 39.35 N | 89.44 W |
| Auburn, In., U.S. | 216 | 41.22 N | 85.03 W |
| Auburn, Ky., U.S. | 194 | 37.02 N | 86.54 W |
| Auburn, Me., U.S. | 188 | 44.05 N | 70.13 W |
| Auburn, Ma., U.S. | 207 | 42.11 N | 71.50 W |
| Auburn, Mi., U.S. | 190 | 43.36 N | 84.04 W |
| Auburn, Ne., U.S. | 198 | 40.23 N | 95.50 W |

PORTUGUÊS

| Nome | Página | Lat.°′ | Long.°′ W = Oeste |
|---|---|---|---|
| Auburn, N.J., U.S. | 285 | 39.42 N | 75.22 W |
| Auburn, N.Y., U.S. | 210 | 42.55 N | 76.33 W |
| Auburn, Pa., U.S. | 208 | 40.35 N | 76.05 W |
| Auburn, Wa., U.S. | 224 | 47.18 N | 122.13 W |
| Auburn ≃ | 166 | 25.38 S | 151.12 E |
| Auburndale, Fl., U.S. | 220 | 28.03 N | 81.47 W |
| Auburndale, Ma., U.S. | 283 | 42.21 N | 71.22 W |
| Auburn Hills | 214 | 42.38 N | 83.13 W |
| Auburn Hills, Palace of ♠ | 281 | 42.41 N | 83.14 W |
| Auburn Range ⋏ | 166 | 25.10 S | 150.30 E |
| Auburn Ravine V | 226 | 38.51 N | 121.31 W |
| Auburn Southeast | 210 | 42.54 N | 76.32 W |
| Aubusson | 32 | 45.57 N | 2.11 E |
| Auby-sur-Semois | 56 | 49.49 N | 5.10 E |
| Auca Mahuida | 252 | 37.53 S | 68.31 W |
| Auca Mahuida, Cerro ∧ | 252 | 37.45 S | 68.56 W |
| Aucará | 248 | 14.15 S | 74.05 W |
| Auce | 76 | 56.28 N | 22.53 E |
| Auch | 32 | 43.39 N | 0.35 E |
| Auchel | 50 | 50.30 N | 2.28 E |
| Auchenblae | 46 | 56.54 N | 2.26 W |
| Auchencairn | 44 | 54.51 N | 3.53 W |
| Auchi | 150 | 7.02 N | 6.14 E |
| Auchinleck | 44 | 55.28 N | 4.17 W |
| Auchterarder | 46 | 56.18 N | 3.43 W |
| Auchterderran | 46 | 56.09 N | 3.16 W |
| Auchtermuchty | 46 | 56.17 N | 3.15 W |
| Aucilla ≃ | 192 | 30.05 N | 83.59 W |
| Auckland | 172 | 36.52 S | 174.46 E |
| Auckland Islands II | 9 | 50.40 S | 166.30 E |
| Auckland Park ◆[8] | 273d | 26.11 S | 28.00 E |
| Auckland Park Race Course ♠ | 273d | 26.11 S | 28.00 E |
| Aude □[5] | 32 | 43.05 N | 2.30 E |
| Aude ≃ | 32 | 43.13 N | 3.14 E |
| Audenge | 32 | 44.41 N | 1.00 W |
| Audenshaw | 262 | 53.28 N | 2.08 W |
| Audenshaw Reservoirs ⊜[1] | 262 | 53.28 N | 2.08 W |
| Auderghem | 50 | 50.49 N | 4.26 E |
| Audeux | 58 | 47.16 N | 5.53 E |
| Audierne | 32 | 48.01 N | 4.32 W |
| Audincourt | 58 | 47.29 N | 6.50 E |
| Audley | 44 | 53.03 N | 2.18 W |
| Audo Range ⋏ | 144 | 6.30 N | 41.30 E |
| Audrain □[6] | 219 | 39.12 N | 91.50 W |
| Audresselles | 50 | 50.49 N | 1.36 E |
| Audruicq | 50 | 50.53 N | 2.05 E |
| Audubon, Ia., U.S. | 198 | 41.43 N | 94.55 W |
| Audubon, N.J., U.S. | 208 | 39.53 N | 75.04 W |
| Audubon, Pa., U.S. | 285 | 40.07 N | 75.27 W |
| Audubon Lake ⊜[1] | 198 | 47.35 N | 101.10 W |
| Audubon Park, Ky., U.S. | 218 | 38.12 N | 85.43 W |
| Audubon Park, N.J., U.S. | 285 | 39.54 N | 75.05 W |
| Audun-le-Roman | 56 | 49.22 N | 5.53 E |
| Aue | 54 | 50.35 N | 12.42 E |
| Aue ≃ | 52 | 53.11 N | 7.41 E |
| Auer → Ora | 64 | 46.21 N | 11.18 E |
| Auerbach, Dtsch. | 54 | 50.41 N | 12.54 E |
| Auerbach, Dtsch. | 54 | 50.30 N | 12.23 E |
| Auerbach, Dtsch. | 60 | 48.48 N | 13.06 E |
| Auerbach in der Oberpfalz | 60 | 49.42 N | 11.38 E |
| Auersberg ∧ | 54 | 50.27 N | 12.39 E |
| Auerswalde | 54 | 50.54 N | 12.55 E |
| Auezov | 86 | 49.46 N | 81.38 E |
| Auf dem Kreinberge | 263 | 51.27 N | 7.36 E |
| Auffargis | 261 | 48.42 N | 1.53 E |
| Auffay | 50 | 49.43 N | 1.06 E |
| Aufsess | 60 | 49.54 N | 11.13 E |
| Augarten ♠ | 264b | 48.14 N | 16.23 E |
| Augathella | 166 | 25.48 S | 146.35 E |
| Augher | 48 | 54.26 N | 7.09 W |
| Aughnacloy | 48 | 54.25 N | 6.58 W |
| Aughrim | 48 | 52.51 N | 6.17 W |
| Aughton, Eng., U.K. | 44 | 53.22 N | 1.18 W |
| Aughton, Eng., U.K. | 262 | 53.32 N | 2.56 W |
| Aughton Park | 262 | 53.33 N | 2.53 W |
| Aughwick Creek ≃ | 214 | 40.22 N | 77.50 W |
| Auglaize □[6] | 216 | 40.34 N | 84.12 W |
| Auglaize ≃ | 216 | 41.17 N | 84.21 W |
| Augrabies | 158 | 28.37 S | 20.20 E |
| Augrabies Falls National Park ♠ | 158 | 28.35 S | 20.19 E |
| Augrabiesvalle ⌞ | 158 | 28.35 S | 20.19 E |
| Au Gres | 190 | 44.02 N | 83.41 W |
| Au Gres ≃ | 190 | 44.02 N | 83.40 W |
| Au Gres, East Branch ≃ | 190 | 44.05 N | 83.41 W |
| Augsburg | 58 | 48.23 N | 10.53 E |
| Augšligatne | 76 | 57.14 N | 25.02 E |
| Augusta, Austl. | 162 | 34.19 S | 115.10 E |
| Augusta, It. | 70 | 37.13 N | 15.13 E |
| Augusta, Ar., U.S. | 194 | 35.16 N | 91.21 W |
| Augusta, Ga., U.S. | 192 | 33.28 N | 82.01 W |
| Augusta, Il., U.S. | 194 | 40.13 N | 90.57 W |
| Augusta, Ks., U.S. | 198 | 37.41 N | 97.58 W |
| Augusta, Ky., U.S. | 218 | 38.46 N | 84.00 W |
| Augusta, Me., U.S. | 188 | 44.18 N | 69.46 W |
| Augusta, Mi., U.S. | 216 | 42.20 N | 85.21 W |
| Augusta, Mo., U.S. | 219 | 38.34 N | 90.53 W |
| Augusta, Mt., U.S. | 202 | 47.29 N | 112.23 W |
| Augusta, N.J., U.S. | 210 | 41.07 N | 74.43 W |
| Augusta, Oh., U.S. | 214 | 40.41 N | 81.01 W |
| Augusta, Wi., U.S. | 190 | 44.40 N | 91.07 W |
| Augusta, Golfo di ⊂ | 70 | 37.12 N | 15.13 E |
| Augustdorf | 52 | 51.53 N | 8.43 E |
| Augustenborg | 41 | 54.57 N | 9.53 E |
| Augustine Island I | 180 | 59.22 N | 153.28 W |
| Augusto Severo | 250 | 5.52 S | 37.19 W |
| Augustów | 30 | 53.51 N | 22.59 E |
| Augustowski, Kanał ≚ | 76 | 53.54 N | 23.26 E |
| Augustus, Mount ∧ | 162 | 24.20 S | 116.50 E |
| Augustusburg | 54 | 50.49 N | 13.06 E |
| Augustus Downs | 166 | 18.33 S | 139.52 E |
| Augustus Island I | 164 | 15.20 S | 124.30 E |
| Auila, Ribeirão ≃ | 255 | 12.09 S | 53.20 W |
| Au in der Hallertau | 60 | 48.33 N | 11.45 E |
| Aujon ≃ | 58 | 48.09 N | 4.48 E |
| Auki | 175e | 8.46 S | 160.42 E |
| Aulander | 192 | 36.13 N | 77.06 W |
| Aulanko | 26 | 61.02 N | 24.27 E |
| Auld, Lake ⊜ | 162 | 22.32 S | 123.44 E |
| Auldearn | 46 | 57.34 N | 3.49 W |
| Aulendorf | 58 | 47.57 N | 9.38 E |
| Aulestad | 26 | 61.13 N | 10.17 E |
| Auletta | 68 | 40.34 N | 15.25 E |
| Aulla | 64 | 44.12 N | 9.58 E |
| Aulnay | 32 | 46.01 N | 0.21 W |
| Aulnay-sous-Bois | 50 | 48.57 N | 2.31 E |
| Aulnay-sur-Mauldre | 261 | 48.56 N | 1.51 E |
| Aulne ≃ | 32 | 48.17 N | 4.16 W |
| Aulneau Peninsula ›[1] | 184 | 49.23 N | 94.29 W |
| Aulnois-sur-Seille | 56 | 48.52 N | 6.19 E |
| Aulnoye-Aymeries | 50 | 50.12 N | 3.50 E |
| Ault, Fr. | 50 | 50.06 N | 1.27 E |
| Ault, Co., U.S. | 200 | 40.34 N | 104.43 W |
| Ault, Ky., U.S. | 218 | 38.12 N | 83.14 W |
| Aultbea | 46 | 57.50 N | 5.35 W |
| Aultman | 214 | 40.34 N | 79.16 W |
| Aultshire | 216 | 40.13 N | 85.19 W |
| Auma | 54 | 50.42 N | 11.54 E |
| Aumale | 50 | 49.46 N | 1.45 E |
| Auma Point › | 164 | 7.55 S | 145.25 E |
| Aumetz | 56 | 49.25 N | 5.56 E |
| Aumont-Aubrac | 32 | 44.43 N | 3.17 E |
| Aumühle | 52 | 53.31 N | 10.19 E |
| Auna | 150 | 10.12 N | 4.45 E |
| Auneau | 50 | 48.27 N | 1.46 E |
| Auneuil | 50 | 49.22 N | 2.00 E |
| Auning | 26 | 56.26 N | 10.23 E |
| Auno | 146 | 11.50 N | 12.53 E |
| Aunuu I | 174u | 14.17 S | 170.33 W |
| Auob ≃ | 156 | 26.25 S | 20.35 E |
| Auponhia | 112 | 1.56 S | 125.29 E |
| Aups | 62 | 43.37 N | 6.14 E |
| Aur, Pulau I | 112 | 2.27 N | 104.31 E |
| Aura | 26 | 60.36 N | 22.34 E |
| Aurach | 56 | 49.15 N | 10.25 E |
| Aurach ≃, Dtsch. | 56 | 49.34 N | 10.59 E |
| Aurach ≃, Dtsch. | 56 | 49.51 N | 10.56 E |
| Aurachmat | 85 | 41.34 N | 70.07 E |
| Auraiya | 124 | 26.28 N | 79.31 E |
| Aurangābād, India | 122 | 19.53 N | 75.20 E |
| Aurangābād, India | 124 | 24.45 N | 84.22 E |
| Auray | 32 | 47.40 N | 2.59 W |
| Aurdal | 26 | 60.56 N | 9.24 E |
| Aure | 26 | 63.16 N | 8.32 E |
| Aurelia | 198 | 42.42 N | 95.26 W |
| Aurelius | 216 | 42.31 N | 84.31 W |
| Aurès, Massif de l' ⋏ | 148 | 35.08 N | 6.30 E |
| Auri, Kepulauan II | 164 | 1.59 S | 134.42 E |
| Aurich | 52 | 53.28 N | 7.29 E |
| Auriesville Shrine ◙[1] | 210 | 42.54 N | 74.19 W |
| Auriflama | 255 | 20.41 S | 50.34 W |
| Aurigny → Alderney I | 43b | 49.43 N | 2.12 W |
| Aurilândia | 255 | 16.44 S | 50.28 W |
| Aurillac | 32 | 44.56 N | 2.26 E |
| Aurina, Valle V | 64 | 47.00 N | 12.00 E |
| Aurine, Alpi (Zillertaler Alpen) ⋏ | 64 | 47.00 N | 11.55 E |
| Aurino ≃ | 64 | 46.48 N | 11.55 E |
| Auriol | 62 | 43.23 N | 5.38 E |
| Aurisina | 64 | 45.45 N | 13.41 E |
| Aurlandsfjorden ⊂[2] | 26 | 61.05 N | 7.02 E |
| Aurlandsvangen | 26 | 60.54 N | 7.11 E |
| Aurolzmünster | 60 | 48.15 N | 13.27 E |
| Auron | 62 | 44.14 N | 6.56 E |
| Auronzo di Cadore | 64 | 46.33 N | 12.26 E |
| Aurora, Bra. | 250 | 6.57 S | 38.58 W |
| Aurora, Bra. | 287a | 22.46 S | 43.24 W |
| Aurora, On., Can. | 212 | 44.00 N | 79.28 W |
| Aurora, S. Afr. | 158 | 32.42 S | 18.29 E |
| Aurora, Co., U.S. | 200 | 39.43 N | 104.49 W |
| Aurora, Il., U.S. | 216 | 41.45 N | 88.19 W |
| Aurora, In., U.S. | 218 | 39.03 N | 84.54 W |
| Aurora, Me., U.S. | 188 | 44.51 N | 68.19 W |
| Aurora, Mn., U.S. | 190 | 47.31 N | 92.14 W |
| Aurora, Mo., U.S. | 194 | 36.58 N | 93.43 W |
| Aurora, Ne., U.S. | 198 | 40.52 N | 98.00 W |
| Aurora, N.Y., U.S. | 210 | 42.45 N | 76.42 W |
| Aurora, N.C., U.S. | 192 | 35.18 N | 76.47 W |
| Aurora, Oh., U.S. | 214 | 41.19 N | 81.20 W |
| Aurora, Or., U.S. | 224 | 45.13 N | 122.45 W |
| Aurora, Ut,. U.S. | 200 | 38.55 N | 111.56 W |
| Aurora, W.V., U.S. | 188 | 39.19 N | 79.33 W |
| Aurora □[4] | 116 | 16.00 N | 121.40 E |
| Aurora ◙ | 265a | 59.57 N | 30.21 E |
| Aurora do Norte | 255 | 12.43 S | 46.24 W |
| Aurora Pond ⊜ | 279a | 41.20 N | 81.23 W |
| Auroux | 62 | 44.45 N | 3.44 E |
| Aursunden ⊜ | 26 | 62.40 N | 11.40 E |
| Aurukun | 164 | 13.19 S | 141.45 E |
| Aurukun Aboriginal Land Trust ◆[4] | 164 | 13.45 S | 141.45 E |
| Aurunci, Monti ⋏ | 66 | 41.22 N | 13.40 E |
| Aus | 156 | 26.40 S | 16.15 E |
| Ausable ≃, On., Can. | 190 | 43.19 N | 81.46 W |
| Au Sable ≃, Mi., U.S. | 190 | 44.25 N | 83.20 W |
| Au Sable, North Branch ≃ | 190 | 44.40 N | 84.23 W |
| Au Sable, South Branch ≃ | 190 | 44.40 N | 84.23 W |
| Au Sable Forks | 188 | 44.26 N | 73.40 W |
| Au Sable Point › | 190 | 44.20 N | 83.20 W |
| Auschwitz → Oświęcim | 30 | 50.03 N | 19.12 E |
| Ausevik ⊥ | 26 | 61.32 N | 5.16 E |
| Auskerry I | 46 | 59.02 N | 2.34 W |
| Ausleben | 54 | 52.05 N | 11.07 E |
| Ausoni, Monti ⋏ | 66 | 41.25 N | 13.20 E |
| Ausserferrera | 58 | 46.33 N | 9.26 E |
| Ausserfragant | 64 | 46.56 N | 13.06 E |
| Aussig → Ústí nad Labem | 54 | 50.40 N | 14.02 E |
| Aussois | 62 | 45.14 N | 6.45 E |
| Aust-Agder □[6] | 26 | 58.50 N | 8.00 E |
| Austerlitz → Slavkov u Brna, Česká Rep. | 61 | 49.09 N | 16.52 E |
| Austerlitz, Ned. | 52 | 52.05 N | 5.19 E |
| Austerlitz, N.Y., U.S. | 210 | 42.19 N | 73.28 W |
| Austerlitz, Gare ◆[5] | 261 | 48.50 N | 2.22 E |
| Austin, Bra. | 287a | 22.43 S | 43.32 W |
| Austin, Mb., Can. | 184 | 49.57 N | 98.56 W |
| Austin, In., U.S. | 218 | 38.45 N | 85.48 W |
| Austin, Mn., U.S. | 190 | 43.40 N | 92.58 W |
| Austin, Nv., U.S. | 204 | 39.29 N | 117.04 W |
| Austin, Pa., U.S. | 214 | 41.37 N | 78.05 W |
| Austin, Tx., U.S. | 222 | 30.16 N | 97.44 W |
| Austin □[6] | 222 | 29.53 N | 96.15 W |
| Austin ◆[8] | 278 | 41.54 N | 87.45 W |
| Austin, Lake ⊜ | 162 | 27.40 S | 118.00 E |
| Austin, Lake ⊜[1] | 222 | 30.19 N | 97.46 W |
| Austin Bayou ≃ | 222 | 29.07 N | 95.18 W |
| Austinburg | 214 | 41.46 N | 80.51 W |
| Austin Channel ⊻ | 176 | 75.35 N | 103.25 W |
| Austin Lake ⊜ | 216 | 42.11 N | 85.33 W |
| Austinmer | 170 | 34.18 S | 150.56 E |
| Austin's Post | 158 | 29.32 S | 25.49 E |
| Austintown | 214 | 41.06 N | 80.45 W |
| Austinville | 192 | 36.51 N | 80.54 W |
| Austnes | 26 | 62.38 N | 6.16 E |
| Austonio | 222 | 31.11 N | 95.38 W |
| Austonley | 262 | 53.34 N | 1.50 W |
| Austral | 274a | 33.56 S | 150.48 E |
| Australes, Îles II | 14 | 23.00 S | 150.00 W |
| Australia □[1] | 160 | 25.00 S | 135.00 E |
| Australia Mountain ∧ | 180 | 63.36 N | 138.08 W |
| Australian Capital Territory □[8] | 171b | 35.30 S | 149.00 E |
| Australian War Memorial ⊥ | 171b | 35.17 S | 149.09 E |
| Australia Plains | 168b | 34.06 S | 139.09 E |
| Australie → Australia □[1] | 160 | 25.00 S | 135.00 E |
| Australien → Australia □[1] | 160 | 25.00 S | 135.00 E |
| Australind | 168a | 33.16 S | 115.44 E |
| Austral Seamounts ✣[3] | 14 | 22.40 S | 152.45 W |
| Austråt | 26 | 63.43 N | 9.45 E |
| Austria (Österreich) □[1], Europe | 22 | 47.20 N | 13.20 E |
| Austria (Österreich) □[1], Europe | 30 | 47.20 N | 13.20 E |
| Austvågøya I | 24 | 68.20 N | 14.36 E |
| Autazes | 246 | 3.35 S | 59.08 W |
| Auteuil, Fr. | 50 | 49.21 N | 2.05 E |
| Auteuil, Fr. | 261 | 48.50 N | 1.49 E |
| Autheuil | 50 | 49.06 N | 1.17 E |
| Authie ≃ | 50 | 50.21 N | 1.38 E |
| Authon | 62 | 44.14 N | 6.08 E |
| Authon-du-Perche | 50 | 48.12 N | 0.55 E |
| Authon-la-Plaine | 50 | 48.27 N | 1.57 E |
| Auth Village | 284c | 38.49 N | 76.55 W |
| Autlán de Navarro | 234 | 19.46 N | 104.22 W |
| Autore, Monte ∧ | 66 | 41.58 N | 13.12 E |
| Autrey-lès-Gray | 58 | 47.29 N | 5.30 E |
| Autriche → Austria □[1] | 30 | 47.20 N | 13.20 E |
| Autumn Hill | 284b | 39.16 N | 76.48 W |
| Autun | 32 | 46.57 N | 4.18 E |
| Auve | 56 | 49.02 N | 4.42 E |
| Auvergne | 164 | 15.41 S | 130.01 E |
| Auvergne □[9] | 32 | 45.25 N | 2.30 E |
| Auvernaux | 261 | 48.32 N | 2.30 E |
| Auvers-sur-Oise | 50 | 49.04 N | 2.10 E |
| Auvézère ≃ | 32 | 45.12 N | 0.51 E |
| Aux Cayes → Les Cayes | 238 | 18.12 N | 73.45 W |
| Auxerre | 50 | 47.48 N | 3.34 E |
| Auxier | 192 | 37.44 N | 82.45 W |
| Auxi-le-Château | 50 | 50.14 N | 2.07 E |
| Auxon | 50 | 48.06 N | 3.55 E |
| Auxonne | 58 | 47.12 N | 5.23 E |
| Aux Sable Creek ≃ | 216 | 41.23 N | 88.20 W |
| Auxvasse | 219 | 39.01 N | 91.53 W |
| Auxvasse Creek ≃ | 219 | 38.41 N | 91.49 W |
| Auxy | 58 | 46.57 N | 4.24 E |
| Auyamita, Quebrada ≃ | 286c | 10.30 N | 66.46 W |
| Auyán Tepuy ∧ | 246 | 5.55 N | 62.32 W |
| Auzances | 32 | 46.02 N | 2.30 E |
| Auzangate, Nevado ∧ | 248 | 13.48 S | 71.14 W |
| Auzon ≃, Fr. | 58 | 48.30 N | 4.20 E |
| Auzon ≃, Fr. | 62 | 44.02 N | 4.54 E |
| Ava, Il., U.S. | 194 | 37.53 N | 89.29 W |
| Ava, Mo., U.S. | 194 | 36.57 N | 92.39 W |
| Avadchara | 84 | 43.31 N | 40.39 E |
| Avadh Plains ⊞ | 124 | 26.20 N | 82.00 E |
| Avaí | 255 | 22.08 S | 49.22 W |
| Āvaj | 128 | 35.34 N | 49.13 E |
| Avakubi | 154 | 1.20 N | 27.34 E |
| Aval' | 85 | 40.19 N | 71.50 E |
| Aval, Falaise d' ⊥[4] | 50 | 49.45 N | 0.10 E |
| Avala ⊥ | 38 | 44.45 N | 20.35 E |
| Avaldsnes | 26 | 59.21 N | 5.16 E |
| Avallon | 50 | 47.29 N | 3.54 E |
| Avaloirs, Les ∧[2] | 32 | 48.28 N | 0.07 W |
| Avalon, Ca., U.S. | 228 | 33.20 N | 118.19 W |
| Avalon, N.J., U.S. | 208 | 39.06 N | 74.43 W |
| Avalon, Pa., U.S. | 214 | 40.30 N | 80.04 W |
| Avalon, Tx., U.S. | 222 | 32.12 N | 96.48 W |
| Avalon, Wi., U.S. | 216 | 42.38 N | 88.52 W |
| Avalon Peninsula ›[1] | 186 | 47.30 N | 53.30 W |
| Ávalos | 232 | 28.35 N | 106.00 W |
| Avana ≃ | 174k | 21.14 S | 159.43 W |
| Avanos | 130 | 38.43 N | 34.51 E |
| Avant | 196 | 36.29 N | 96.03 W |
| Avaré, Bra. | 252 | 23.05 S | 48.55 W |
| Avaré, Bra. | 255 | 23.05 S | 48.55 W |
| Avarskoje Kojsu ≃ | 84 | 42.47 N | 46.48 E |
| Avarua | 174k | 21.12 S | 159.46 W |
| Avarua Harbour ⊂ | 174k | 21.11 S | 159.46 W |
| Avatanak Island I | 180 | 54.03 N | 165.19 W |
| Avatele | 174v | 19.06 S | 169.55 W |
| Avatele Bay ⊂ | 174v | 19.05 S | 169.56 W |
| Avatiu | 174k | 21.12 S | 159.47 W |
| Avatiu Harbour ⊂ | 174k | 21.11 S | 159.47 W |
| Avčala | 84 | 41.48 N | 44.48 E |
| Avdiyivka | 83 | 48.08 N | 37.46 E |
| Ave ≃ | 34 | 41.20 N | 8.45 W |
| Avebury | 42 | 51.27 N | 1.51 W |
| Avebury Stone Circle ⊥ | 42 | 51.28 N | 1.51 W |
| 'Avedat, Ḥorvot ⊥ | 132 | 30.48 N | 34.46 E |
| Avegbadje ∧ | 150 | 7.14 N | 0.38 E |
| Aveiro, Bra. | 250 | 3.15 S | 55.10 W |
| Aveiro, Port. | 34 | 40.38 N | 8.39 W |
| Aveiro, Ria de ≃[1] | 34 | 40.38 N | 8.44 W |
| Avelar | 256 | 22.20 S | 43.25 W |
| Avelengo | 64 | 46.38 N | 11.13 E |
| Aveley | 260 | 51.30 N | 0.16 E |
| Avelgem | 50 | 50.46 N | 3.26 E |
| Avella, It. | 68 | 40.58 N | 14.36 E |
| Avella, Pa., U.S. | 214 | 40.16 N | 80.27 W |
| Avellaneda, Arg. | 252 | 34.39 S | 58.23 W |
| Avellaneda, Arg. | 252 | 29.07 S | 59.40 W |
| Avellaneda, Arg. | 258 | 34.39 S | 58.23 W |
| Avellaneda □[5] | 288 | 34.40 S | 58.20 W |
| Avellaneda, Estacion ◆[5] | 288 | 34.41 S | 58.22 W |
| Avelle, Île I | 275a | 45.24 N | 74.00 W |
| Avellino | 68 | 40.54 N | 14.47 E |
| Avellino □[4] | 68 | 41.00 N | 15.10 E |
| Avenal | 226 | 36.00 N | 120.07 W |
| Avenal Creek ≃ | 226 | 35.47 N | 120.04 W |
| Aven Armand ⊥[5] | 32 | 44.15 N | 3.22 E |
| Avenas | 58 | 46.12 N | 4.37 E |
| Avenches | 58 | 46.53 N | 7.02 E |
| Avenel | 276 | 40.34 N | 74.17 W |
| Aventureiro, Rio do ≃ | 256 | 21.52 S | 42.39 W |
| Avenue | 208 | 38.15 N | 76.46 W |
| Averbode | 56 | 51.02 N | 4.59 E |
| Averbode, Abbaye d' ◙[1] | 56 | 51.02 N | 4.59 E |
| Averill Lake ⊜ | 206 | 44.59 N | 71.44 W |
| Averill Park | 210 | 42.38 N | 73.33 W |
| Avern ⊜ | 40 | 58.54 N | 15.32 E |
| Avernakø I | 41 | 55.01 N | 10.17 E |
| Avernes | 261 | 49.05 N | 1.52 E |
| Avernes, Ru des ≃ | 261 | 49.04 N | 2.51 E |
| Averøya I | 26 | 63.01 N | 7.34 E |
| Aversa | 68 | 40.58 N | 14.12 E |
| Avery, Ca., U.S. | 226 | 38.13 N | 120.22 W |
| Avery, Id., U.S. | 202 | 47.15 N | 115.48 W |
| Avery, Tx., U.S. | 194 | 33.33 N | 94.47 W |
| Avery Island | 194 | 29.54 N | 91.54 W |
| Aves, Isla de I | 238 | 15.42 N | 63.38 W |
| Avesnelles | 50 | 50.07 N | 3.57 E |
| Avesnes-le-Comte | 50 | 50.17 N | 2.32 E |
| Avesnes-lès-Aubert | 50 | 50.12 N | 3.23 E |
| Avesnes-sur-Helpe | 50 | 50.07 N | 3.56 E |
| Avesta | 40 | 60.09 N | 16.12 E |
| Aveto ≃ | 62 | 44.42 N | 9.23 E |
| Avetrana | 68 | 40.21 N | 17.43 E |
| Aveyron □[5] | 32 | 44.15 N | 2.40 E |
| Aveyron ≃ | 32 | 44.05 N | 1.16 E |
| Avezzano | 66 | 42.02 N | 13.25 E |
| Avgustovka | 80 | 52.16 N | 50.44 E |
| Aviano | 64 | 46.04 N | 12.36 E |
| Avich, Loch ⊜ | 46 | 56.16 N | 5.20 W |
| Aviemore | 46 | 57.12 N | 3.50 W |
| Avigliana | 62 | 45.05 N | 7.23 E |
| Avigliano | 68 | 40.44 N | 15.44 E |
| Avignon | 62 | 43.57 N | 4.49 E |
| Ávila | 34 | 40.39 N | 4.42 W |
| Ávila □[4] | 34 | 40.35 N | 5.00 W |
| Avila Beach | 226 | 35.10 N | 120.43 W |
| Avilés | 34 | 43.33 N | 5.55 W |
| Avilla | 216 | 41.22 N | 85.14 W |
| Avilley | 58 | 47.26 N | 6.16 E |
| Aviña | 34 | 43.36 N | 8.08 W |
| Avinger | 222 | 32.54 N | 94.33 W |
| Avinurme | 76 | 58.59 N | 26.51 E |
| Avio | 64 | 45.44 N | 10.56 E |
| Avion | 50 | 50.24 N | 2.50 E |
| Avioth | 56 | 49.34 N | 5.24 E |
| Avis | 210 | 41.11 N | 77.18 W |
| Avisio ≃ | 64 | 46.07 N | 11.05 E |
| Avispa, Cerro ∧ | 246 | 1.16 N | 65.51 W |
| Aviston | 219 | 38.36 N | 89.36 W |
| Aviz | 34 | 39.03 N | 7.53 W |
| Avize | 50 | 48.58 N | 4.01 E |
| Avlan Gölü ⊜ | 130 | 36.34 N | 29.57 E |
| Avlum | 41 | 56.16 N | 8.48 E |
| Avnbøl | 41 | 54.58 N | 9.39 E |
| Avnik | 130 | 38.39 N | 40.20 E |
| Avoca, Austl. | 169 | 37.05 S | 143.28 E |
| Avoca, Ia., U.S. | 198 | 41.28 N | 95.20 W |
| Avoca, N.Y., U.S. | 210 | 42.24 N | 77.25 W |
| Avoca, Pa., U.S. | 210 | 41.20 N | 75.44 W |
| Avoca ≃, Austl. | 166 | 35.42 S | 143.44 E |
| Avoca ≃, Ire. | 48 | 52.48 N | 6.09 W |
| Avoca, Mount ∧ | 169 | 37.07 S | 143.21 E |
| Avoca Beach | 170 | 33.29 S | 151.29 E |
| Avocado Heights | 280 | 34.08 N | 117.54 W |
| Avola, B.C., Can. | 182 | 51.47 N | 119.19 W |
| Avola, It. | 70 | 36.54 N | 15.08 E |
| Avon, Austl. | 168b | 34.17 S | 138.20 E |
| Avon, Fr. | 50 | 48.24 N | 2.43 E |
| Avon, Ct., U.S. | 207 | 41.48 N | 72.49 W |
| Avon, Il., U.S. | 190 | 40.39 N | 90.26 W |
| Avon, Ma., U.S. | 207 | 42.07 N | 71.02 W |
| Avon, Mn., U.S. | 190 | 45.36 N | 94.27 W |
| Avon, Mt., U.S. | 202 | 46.35 N | 112.36 W |
| Avon, N.Y., U.S. | 210 | 42.54 N | 77.44 W |
| Avon, N.C., U.S. | 192 | 35.21 N | 75.30 W |
| Avon, Oh., U.S. | 214 | 41.27 N | 82.02 W |
| Avon, Pa., U.S. | 208 | 40.22 N | 76.23 W |
| Avon, S.D., U.S. | 198 | 43.00 N | 98.[illegible]3 W |
| Avon □[6] | 42 | 51.30 N | 2.[illegible]0 W |
| Avon ≃, Austl. | 168a | 31.40 S | 116.[illegible] E |
| Avon ≃, N.S., Can. | 186 | 45.10 N | 64.[illegible] W |
| Avon ≃, On., Can. | 212 | 43.18 N | 81.1[illegible] W |
| Avon ≃, Eng., U.K. | 42 | 51.30 N | 2.4[illegible] W |
| Avon ≃, Eng., U.K. | 42 | 50.17 N | 3.5[illegible] W |
| Avon ≃, Eng., U.K. | 42 | 50.43 N | 1.4[illegible] W |
| Avon ≃, Eng., U.K. | 42 | 52.25 N | 1.3[illegible] W |
| Avon ≃, Eng., U.K. | 42 | 51.59 N | 2.1[illegible] W |
| Avon ≃, Scot., U.K. | 46 | 56.01 N | 3.4[illegible] W |
| Avon ≃, Scot., U.K. | 46 | 57.25 N | 3.23 W |
| Avon, Ben ∧ | 46 | 57.05 N | 3.27 W |
| Avon, Ru d' ≃ | 261 | 48.39 N | 2.46 E |
| Avon Basin ⊂ | 279a | 41.30 N | 82.03 W |
| Avon by the Sea | 208 | 40.11 N | 74.00 W |
| Avondale, Az., U.S. | 200 | 33.26 N | 112.20 W |
| Avondale, Co., U.S. | 198 | 38.14 N | 104.21 W |
| Avondale, Md., U.S. | 284c | 38.56 N | 76.59 W |
| Avondale, Oh., U.S. | 214 | 39.47 N | 84.08 W |
| Avondale Heights | 274b | 37.46 S | 144.51 E |
| Avon Downs | 166 | 20.05 S | 137.30 E |
| Avondrust | 158 | 34.21 S | 21.51 E |
| Avon Lake | 214 | 41.30 N | 82.01 W |
| Avonlea | 184 | 50.00 N | 105.04 W |
| Avonmore, On., Can. | 206 | 45.10 N | 74.58 W |
| Avonmore, Pa., U.S. | 214 | 40.31 N | 79.27 W |
| Avonmore ≃ | 48 | 52.50 N | 6.13 W |
| Avonmouth | 42 | 51.31 N | 2.42 W |
| Avon Park | 220 | 27.35 N | 81.30 W |
| Avon Reservoir ⊜[1] | 170 | 34.24 S | 150.40 E |
| Avontuur | 158 | 33.44 S | 23.11 E |
| Avon Valley National Park ♠ | 168a | 31.41 S | 116.06 E |
| Avon Water ≃ | 46 | 55.47 N | 4.01 W |
| Avoudrey | 58 | 47.08 N | 6.26 E |
| Avrainville | 261 | 48.34 N | 2.15 E |
| Avranches | 32 | 48.41 N | 1.22 W |
| Avranlo | 84 | 41.39 N | 43.52 E |
| Avre ≃, Fr. | 50 | 49.53 N | 2.20 E |
| Avre ≃, Fr. | 50 | 48.47 N | 1.22 E |
| Avrieux | 62 | 45.13 N | 6.43 E |
| Avroult | 50 | 50.38 N | 2.09 E |
| Avtatkuul' ≃ | 180 | 64.06 N | 178.10 E |
| Avtovo ◆[8] | 265a | 59.52 N | 30.15 E |
| Avu Avu | 175e | 9.50 S | 160.23 E |
| Awa, Nihon | 96 | 34.04 N | 134.12 E |
| Awa, Nihon | 174m | 26.36 N | 127.56 E |
| Awaba | 170 | 33.01 S | 151.33 E |
| A'waj, Nahr al- ≃ | 132 | 33.20 N | 36.34 E |
| Awaji | 96 | 34.35 N | 135.01 E |
| Awaji-shima I | 96 | 34.21 N | 134.51 E |
| Awakino | 172 | 38.39 S | 174.38 E |
| 'Awālī | 128 | 26.05 N | 50.33 E |
| Awang | 115b | 8.54 S | 116.24 E |
| Awano | 94 | 36.31 N | 139.41 E |
| Awanui | 172 | 35.03 S | 173.15 E |
| Awar | 164 | 4.09 S | 144.51 E |
| Awara | 94 | 36.13 N | 136.12 E |
| Awarawar, Tanjung › | 115a | 6.45 S | 111.56 E |
| Aware | 144 | 8.15 N | 44.10 E |
| Awarua Point › | 172 | 44.15 S | 168.03 E |
| Awasa | 144 | 6.45 N | 38.15 E |
| Awasa, Lake ⊜ | 144 | 7.05 N | 38.25 E |
| Awasan Bay ⊂ | 116 | 9.56 N | 125.36 E |
| Awash | 144 | 8.59 N | 40.10 E |
| Awash ≃ | 144 | 11.45 N | 41.05 E |
| Awa-shima I, Nihon | 92 | 38.27 N | 139.14 E |
| Awa-shima I, Nihon | 96 | 34.16 N | 133.38 E |
| Awash National Park ♠ | 144 | 9.05 N | 40.00 E |
| Awaso | 150 | 6.14 N | 2.16 W |
| Awatere ≃ | 172 | 41.37 S | 174.10 E |
| Awbārī | 146 | 26.35 N | 12.46 E |
| Awbārī, Ṣaḥrā' ⊥[8] | 146 | 28.00 N | 11.30 E |
| Awdheegle | 144 | 1.59 N | 44.50 E |
| Awe | 150 | 8.09 N | 9.07 E |
| Awe, Loch ⊜ | 46 | 56.15 N | 5.17 W |
| Awegyun | 110 | 12.44 N | 98.44 E |
| Awgu | 150 | 6.04 N | 7.29 E |
| Awīsh al-Ḥajar | 142 | 31.01 N | 31.19 E |
| 'Awjā', Wādī al- V | 132 | 31.56 N | 35.31 E |
| Awjilah | 146 | 29.09 N | 21.15 E |
| Awka | 150 | 6.12 N | 7.05 E |
| Awlād Mūsā | 142 | 30.48 N | 31.44 E |
| Awled Djellal | 148 | 34.28 N | 5.02 E |
| Awlef | 148 | 26.58 N | 1.05 E |
| Aworo Kit | 140 | 10.59 N | 32.38 E |
| Aworro | 164 | 7.45 S | 143.10 E |
| Awosting | 276 | 41.09 N | 74.20 W |
| Awsīm | 273c | 30.07 N | 31.08 E |
| Awul | 164 | 6.00 S | 151.00 E |
| Awuna ≃ | 180 | 69.04 N | 155.30 W |
| Awwal, Ash-Shallāl al- (First Cataract) ⌞ | 140 | 24.01 N | 32.52 E |
| Awwalī, Nahr al- ≃ | 132 | 33.35 N | 35.23 E |
| Axamilpa ≃ | 234 | 18.35 N | 98.11 W |
| Axams | 64 | 47.14 N | 11.18 E |
| Axat | 32 | 42.48 N | 2.14 E |
| Axbridge | 42 | 51.18 N | 2.49 W |
| Axe ≃, Eng., U.K. | 42 | 51.19 N | 2.59 W |
| Axe ≃, Eng., U.K. | 42 | 50.42 N | 3.03 W |
| Axe Creek ≃ | 169 | 36.46 S | 144.30 E |
| Axedale | 169 | 36.47 S | 144.30 E |
| Axe Edge ⋏[2] | 262 | 53.14 N | 1.57 W |
| Axel | 52 | 51.16 N | 3.55 E |
| Axel Heiberg Island I | 16 | 79.45 N | 91.00 W |
| Axim | 150 | 4.52 N | 2.14 W |
| Axinim | 246 | 4.02 S | 59.22 W |
| Axiós (Vardar) ≃ | 38 | 40.35 N | 22.50 E |
| Axis | 194 | 30.55 N | 88.01 W |
| Axixá | 250 | 2.51 S | 44.04 W |
| Ax-les-Thermes | 32 | 42.43 N | 1.50 E |
| Axminster | 42 | 50.47 N | 3.00 W |
| Axmouth | 42 | 50.42 N | 3.02 W |
| Axochiapan | 234 | 18.30 N | 98.46 W |
| Axtell, Ks., U.S. | 198 | 39.52 N | 96.15 W |
| Axtell, Ne., U.S. | 198 | 40.28 N | 99.07 W |
| Axtell, Tx., U.S. | 222 | 31.39 N | 96.58 W |
| Aÿ | 50 | 49.03 N | 4.00 E |
| Ayabaca | 246 | 4.38 S | 79.43 W |
| Ayabe | 96 | 35.18 N | 135.15 E |
| Ayachi, Ari n' ∧ | 148 | 32.29 N | 4.57 W |
| Ayacucho, Arg. | 252 | 37.09 S | 58.29 W |
| Ayacucho, Bol. | 248 | 17.51 S | 63.20 W |
| Ayacucho, Perú | 248 | 13.07 S | 74.13 W |
| Ayacucho □[5] | 248 | 14.00 S | 74.00 W |
| Ayakkum Hu ⊜ | 120 | 37.30 N | 89.20 E |
| Ayamé | 150 | 5.37 N | 3.11 W |
| Ayamiken | 152 | 2.07 N | 10.01 E |
| Ayamonte | 34 | 37.13 N | 7.24 W |
| Āyān | 272b | 22.43 N | 88.09 E |
| Ayancık | 130 | 41.57 N | 34.36 E |
| Ayangba | 150 | 7.30 N | 7.08 E |
| Ayapel | 246 | 8.19 N | 75.09 W |
| Ayarza, Laguna de ⊜ | 236 | 14.25 N | 90.08 W |
| Ayas, It. | 62 | 45.50 N | 7.41 E |
| Ayaş, Tür. | 130 | 40.01 N | 32.21 E |
| Ayase | 94 | 35.26 N | 139.26 E |
| Ayase ≃ | 268 | 35.45 N | 139.49 E |
| Ayauta | 96 | 34.13 N | 133.53 E |
| Ayaviri | 248 | 14.52 S | 70.35 W |
| Ayaviri ≃ | 248 | 15.01 S | 70.22 W |
| 'Aybaāl, Jabal ∧ | 132 | 32.14 N | 35.16 E |
| Aybastı, Tür. | 130 | 39.42 N | 39.02 E |
| Aybastı, Tür. | 130 | 40.41 N | 37.24 E |
| Aydar ≃ | 78 | 48.42 N | 39.13 E |
| Aydar-Mykolayivka | 83 | 48.58 N | 38.58 E |
| Ayden | 192 | 35.28 N | 77.24 W |
| Aydere | 128 | 38.24 N | 56.45 E |
| Aydın | 130 | 37.51 N | 27.51 E |
| Aydın □[4] | 130 | 37.45 N | 28.00 E |
| Aydıncık, Tür. | 130 | 36.08 N | 33.19 E |
| Aydıncık, Tür. | 130 | 40.08 N | 35.18 E |
| Aydın Dağları ⋏ | 130 | 38.00 N | 28.00 E |
| Aydınkent | 130 | 37.06 N | 31.36 E |
| Aydıntepe | 130 | 40.24 N | 40.09 E |
| Aydin Ula ∧ | 86 | 42.55 N | 87.35 E |
| Aydosdağı ∧ | 267b | 40.56 N | 29.15 E |


| | | | | | |
|---|---|---|---|---|---|
| ≃ River | Fluß | Río | Rivière | Rio | |
| ≚ Canal | Kanal | Canal | Canal | Canal | |
| ⌞ Waterfall, Rapids | Wasserfall, Stromschnellen | Cascada, Rápidos | Chute d'eau, Rapides | Cascata, Rápidos | |
| ⊻ Strait | Meeresstraße | Estrecho | Détroit | Estreito | |
| ⊂ Bay, Gulf | Bucht, Golf | Bahía, Golfo | Baie, Golfe | Baía, Golfo | |
| ⊜ Lake, Lakes | See, Seen | Lago, Lagos | Lac, Lacs | Lago, Lagos | |
| ≡ Swamp | Sumpf | Pantano | Marais | Pântano | |
| ✻ Ice Features, Glacier | Eis- und Gletscherformen | Accidentes Glaciales | Formes glaciaires | Acidentes glaciares | |
| ⚲ Other Hydrographic Features | Andere Hydrographische Objekte | Otros Elementos Hidrográficos | Autres données hydrographiques | Outros acidentes hidrográficos | |

| | | | | |
|---|---|---|---|---|
| ✣ Submarine Features | Untermeerische Objekte | Accidentes Submarinos | Formes de relief sous-marin | Acidentes submarinos |
| □ Political Unit | Politische Einheit | Unidad Politica | Entité politique | Unidade política |
| ◙ Cultural Institution | Kulturelle Institution | Institución Cultural | Institution culturelle | Instituição cultural |
| ⊥ Historical Site | Historische Stätte | Sitio Histórico | Site historique | Sitio histórico |
| ♠ Recreational Site | Erholungs- und Ferienort | Sitio de Recreo | Centre de loisirs | Area de Lazer |
| ⊠ Airport | Flughafen | Aeropuerto | Aéroport | Aeroporto |
| ■ Military Installation | Militäranlage | Instalación Militar | Installation militaire | Instalação militar |
| ◆ Miscellaneous | Verschiedenes | Misceláneo | Divers | Diversos |

ENGLISH — Name | Page | Lat.°′ | Long.°′
DEUTSCH — Name | Seite | Breite°′ | Länge°′ E = Ost


Ayelu ∧ 144 10.04 N 40.46 E
Ayer, Schw. 58 46.11 N 7.36 E
Ayer, Ma., U.S. 207 42.33 N 71.35 W
Ayer Baloi 114 1.35 N 103.20 E
Ayer Chawan, Pulau I 271c 1.17 N 103.42 E
Ayer Hitam, Malay. 114 1.55 N 103.11 E
Ayer Hitam, Malay. 114 2.56 N 102.24 E
Ayer Jerneh 114 4.24 N 103.24 E
Ayer Kuning Selatan 114 2.30 N 102.28 E
Ayer Merbau, Pulau I 271c 1.16 N 103.43 E
Ayers Cliff 206 45.10 N 72.03 W
Ayers Rock (Uluru) ∧ 162 25.23 S 131.05 E
Ayersville 216 41.14 N 84.17 W
Ayeyarwady □[8] 110 17.00 N 95.00 E
Ayeyarwady (Irrawaddy) ≃ 110 15.50 N 95.06 E
Aygün 130 38.26 N 41.17 E
Ayía Marína 38 37.09 N 26.52 E
Ayía Paraskeví, Ellás 38 39.15 N 26.16 E
Ayía Paraskeví, Ellás 267c 38.01 N 23.50 E
Ayiássos 38 39.05 N 26.23 E
Ayía Varvára 267c 37.59 N 23.39 E
Ayina ≃ 152 1.48 N 13.10 E
Aying 64 47.58 N 11.47 E
Áyioi Anáryiroi 267c 38.02 N 23.43 E
Áyion Óros □[8] 38 40.15 N 24.15 E
Áyion Óros >[1] 38 40.15 N 24.15 E
Áyios Dhimítrios 267c 37.56 N 23.44 E
Áyios Evstrátios I 38 39.31 N 25.00 E
Áyios Ioánnis Réndis 267c 37.58 N 23.40 E
Áyios Kírikos 38 37.37 N 26.14 E
Áyios Nikólaos 38 35.11 N 25.42 E
Ayiou Nikolaou Monastery ⊍[1] 267c 37.53 N 23.27 E
Ayíou Órous, Kólpos ⊂ 38 40.12 N 24.03 E
Ayl 132 30.13 N 35.32 E
Aylesbury 42 51.50 N 0.50 W
Aylesford 42 51.18 N 0.29 E
Aylesham 42 51.13 N 1.13 E
Aylmer 188 45.26 N 75.50 W
Aylmer, Lake ⊜ 206 45.50 N 71.22 W
Aylmer, Mount ∧ 182 51.19 N 115.26 W
Aylmer-East 212 45.26 N 75.50 W
Aylmer Lake ⊜ 176 64.05 N 108.30 W
Aylmer West 212 42.46 N 80.59 W
Aylsham, Sk., Can. 184 53.11 N 103.49 W
Aylsham, Eng., U.K. 42 52.49 N 1.15 E
ʿAyn al-ʿArab 130 36.54 N 38.21 E
ʿAyn Dār 128 25.59 N 49.23 E
ʿAyn Dīwār 130 37.17 N 42.11 E
ʿAynīn ⊤[4] 144 20.48 N 41.39 E
Aynor 192 33.59 N 79.11 W
ʿAynūnah 128 28.05 N 35.08 E
Ayo 248 15.41 S 72.16 W
Ayo Ayo 248 17.05 S 68.00 W
Ayod 140 8.07 N 31.26 E
Ayodhya 124 26.48 N 82.12 E
Ayo El Chico 234 20.32 N 102.21 W
Ayom 140 7.52 N 28.23 E
Ayorou 150 14.44 N 0.55 E
Ayos 152 3.54 N 12.31 E
'Ayoûn el 'Atroûs 150 16.40 N 9.37 W
Ay-Petri, hora ∧ 78 44.27 N 34.03 E
Ayr, Austl. 166 19.35 S 147.24 E
Ayr, On., Can. 212 43.17 N 80.27 W
Ayr, Scot., U.K. 44 55.28 N 4.38 W
Ayr ≃ 44 55.29 N 4.28 W
ʿAyrah 132 32.37 N 36.32 E
Ayrancı 130 37.22 N 33.42 E
Ayre, Point of > 44 54.26 N 4.22 W
Aysgarth 44 54.17 N 2.00 W
Aysha 144 10.46 N 42.37 E
ʿAytā al-Fakhkhār 132 33.38 N 35.54 E
ʿAytanīt 132 33.34 N 35.40 E
Ayton, Austl. 164 15.56 S 145.22 E
Ayton, On., Can. 212 44.03 N 80.56 W
Ayton, Eng., U.K. 44 54.14 N 0.29 W
Ayu, Kepulauan II 108 0.28 N 131.03 E
Ayubnagar 126 23.46 N 90.23 E
Ayulhai 102 44.36 N 115.36 E
Ayuñgon 116 9.51 N 123.08 E
Ayuquila ≃ 234 19.23 N 103.51 W
Ayutla 234 20.07 N 104.22 W
Ayutla de los Libres 234 16.54 N 99.13 W
Ayvacık, Tür. 130 39.36 N 26.24 E
Ayvacık, Tür. 130 41.00 N 36.39 E
Ayvalı 130 38.44 N 37.38 E
Ayvalık 130 39.18 N 26.41 E
Aywaille 56 50.28 N 5.40 E
Azabarabān, Ra's > 142 28.51 N 32.43 E
Azacualpa, Hond. 236 14.27 N 86.09 W
Azacualpa, Hond. 236 15.19 N 88.33 W
Azādpur ◆[8] 272a 28.43 N 77.11 E
Azai 94 35.26 N 136.18 E
Azaila 34 41.17 N 0.29 W
Azalea Park 220 28.32 N 81.18 W
Azama 174m 26.11 N 127.49 E
Azamatovo 80 53.18 N 53.28 E
Azambuja 34 39.04 N 8.52 W
Āzamgarh 124 26.04 N 83.11 E
Azamiga-dake ∧ 96 34.20 N 131.47 E
Azángaro 248 14.55 S 70.13 W
Azángaro ≃ 248 15.17 S 70.10 W
Azanka 86 58.02 N 64.48 E
Azao ∧ 148 25.12 N 8.08 E
Azaouâd ◆[1] 150 19.00 N 3.00 W
Azaouagh, Vallée de l' V 150 15.30 N 3.18 E
Azapa, Quebrada de ≃ 248 18.30 S 70.17 W
Azar V 150 16.02 N 4.04 E
Azara 150 8.21 N 9.12 E
Āzārbāyjān-e Gharbī □[4] 128 37.40 N 45.00 E
Āzārbāyjān-e Sharqī □[4] 128 38.00 N 47.00 E
Azare 150 11.40 N 10.11 E
Āzar Shahr 128 37.45 N 45.59 E
Azaryčy 76 52.28 N 29.16 E
Azas ≃ 88 52.26 N 96.15 E
Azat, gora ∧[2] 86 46.55 N 69.00 E
Azay-le-Rideau 50 47.16 N 0.28 E
Azay-sur-Cher 50 47.21 N 0.51 E
Azay-sur-Indre 50 47.12 N 0.57 E
Aʿzāz 130 36.35 N 37.03 E
Azazga 148 36.44 N 4.22 E
Azcuénaga 258 34.23 S 59.21 W
Aždaak, gora ∧ 84 40.13 N 44.56 E
Azdavay 130 41.39 N 33.18 E
Azdzjacičy 76 54.06 N 28.50 E
Azeffâl ⫠[8] 148 21.00 N 14.45 W
Azeffoun 148 36.53 N 4.25 E
Azejevo 80 54.41 N 42.02 E
Azemmour 148 33.20 N 8.25 W
Azenhas do Mar 266c 38.50 N 9.28 W
Azennezal, 'Erg V 148 22.50 N 0.25 E
Azerbaidzhan → Azerbaijan □[1] 22 40.30 N 47.30 E
Azerbaijan (Azärbaycan) □[1], Asia 72 40.30 N 47.30 E
Azerbaijan (Azärbaycan) □[1], Asia 84 40.30 N 47.30 E
Azerbajdžan → Azerbaijan □[1] 72 40.30 N 47.30 E
Azerbaydzan → Azerbaijan □[1] 72 40.30 N 47.30 E
Azergues ≃ 58 45.56 N 4.44 E
Azëry 76 53.43 N 24.11 E
Azezo 144 12.35 N 37.28 E
Azgir 80 47.50 N 47.54 E
Azhikode 122 11.59 N 75.21 E
Azilal 148 31.58 N 6.34 W
Azilal □[4] 148 31.55 N 6.30 W
Azile 154 3.32 N 29.52 E
Azincourt 50 50.28 N 2.08 E
Azle 222 32.53 N 97.32 W
Aznakajevo 80 54.53 N 53.04 E
Aznapuquio 286d 11.59 S 77.04 W
Azogues 246 2.44 S 78.50 W
Azoia 266c 38.46 N 9.29 W
Azor 132 32.01 N 34.48 E
Azores → Açores II 148a 38.30 N 28.00 W
Azores-Gibraltar Ridge ✢[3] 10 37.00 N 16.00 W
Azores Plateau ✢[3] 10 39.00 N 30.00 W
Azoum, Bahr (Wādī ʿAẓūm) V 146 10.53 N 20.15 E
Azov 83 47.07 N 39.25 E
Azov, Sea of ⊤[2] 78 46.00 N 36.00 E
Azovs'ke 78 45.34 N 34.34 E
Azovskij kanal ≊ 83 47.07 N 39.27 E
Azoyú 234 16.43 N 98.44 W
Azpeitia 34 43.11 N 2.16 W
Azraq, Al-Baḥr al- → Blue Nile ≃ 140 15.38 N 32.31 E
Azraq, Bahr ≃ 146 10.52 N 20.35 E
Azraq, Wādī al- V 140 10.33 N 28.40 E
Azraq ash-Shīshān 132 31.50 N 36.48 E
Azrou 148 33.27 N 5.14 W
Aztalan State Park ♦ 216 43.04 N 88.51 W
Aztec 200 36.49 N 107.59 W
Azteca, Estadio ♦ 286a 19.18 N 99.09 W
Aztec Peak ∧ 200 33.48 N 110.55 W
Aztec Ruins National Monument ♦ 200 36.51 N 108.10 W
Azua 238 18.27 N 70.44 W
Azuaga 34 38.16 N 5.41 W
Azuay □[4] 246 3.00 S 79.00 W
Azucena 252 37.29 S 59.18 W
Azuchi 94 35.09 N 136.08 E
Azuchi-jō ⊥ 94 35.10 N 136.08 E
Azuer ≃ 34 39.08 N 3.36 W
Azuero, Península de >[1] 246 7.40 N 80.35 W
Azufre, Volcán ∧[1] 252 25.11 S 68.31 W
Azuga 38 45.27 N 25.33 E
Azul 252 36.47 S 59.51 W
Azul, Cerro ∧, C.R. 236 9.54 N 85.14 W
Azul, Cerro ∧, Ec. 246a 0.54 S 91.21 W
Azul, Cerro ∧, Hond. 236 14.32 N 88.23 W
Azul, Cordillera ⋏ 248 8.30 S 76.10 W
Azul Casa, Cerro ∧ 252 22.29 S 65.20 W
ʿAẓūm, Wādī (Bahr Azoum) V 146 10.53 N 20.15 E
Azuma, Nihon 94 36.31 N 139.19 E
Azuma, Nihon 94 36.33 N 138.54 E
Azuma, Nihon 94 35.56 N 140.28 E
Azuma, Nihon 94 36.36 N 138.20 E
Azumaya-san ∧ 94 36.32 N 138.25 E
Azumazaka 270 34.26 N 135.39 E
Azumi 94 36.11 N 137.47 E
Azur, Côte d' ⫠[2] 62 43.30 N 7.00 E
Azurduy 248 19.59 S 64.29 W
Azure Clouds, Temple of the ⊍[1] 271a 40.00 N 116.11 E
Azure Lake ⊜ 182 52.23 N 120.00 W
Azusa 228 34.08 N 117.54 W
Azusa ≃ 94 36.17 N 137.56 E
Ažu-Tajga, gora ∧ 86 51.35 N 88.45 E
Az-Zabābidah 132 32.23 N 35.20 E
Az-Zabadānī 132 33.43 N 36.05 E
Az-Zāb al-Kabīr → Great Zab ≃ 128 36.00 N 43.21 E
Az-Zāb aṣ-Ṣaghīr → Little Zab ≃ 128 35.12 N 43.25 E
Aẓ-Ẓāhirīyah 132 31.25 N 34.58 E
Aẓ-Ẓahrān (Dhahran) 128 26.18 N 50.08 E
Az-Zamālik ◆[8] 273c 30.04 N 31.13 E
Azzanello 64 45.18 N 9.55 E
Az-Zankalūn 142 30.33 N 31.27 E
Azzano Decimo 64 45.53 N 12.43 E
Az-Zaqāzīq 142 30.35 N 31.31 E
Az-Zarbah 130 36.04 N 36.59 E
Az-Zarqāʾ 132 32.05 N 36.06 E
Az-Zarqāʾ □[8] 132 32.00 N 36.45 E
Az-Zawāmil 142 30.21 N 31.26 E
Az-Zāwiyah 146 32.45 N 12.44 E
Az-Zaydāb 140 17.26 N 33.53 E
Az-Zaydīyah 144 15.18 N 43.04 E
Az-Zaytīyah ◆[8] 142 29.58 N 32.31 E
Az-Zaytūn ◆[8] 273c 30.06 N 31.19 E
Azzel Matti, Sebkha ≃ 148 25.55 N 0.56 E
Az-Zilfī 128 26.18 N 44.48 E
Az-Zrārīyah 132 33.21 N 35.20 E
Az-Zubayr 128 30.23 N 47.43 E
ʿAzzūn 132 32.11 N 35.03 E
Azzurra, Grotta (Blue Grotto) ⫠[5] 68 40.35 N 14.14 E

**B**

Ba ≃, Viet 110 13.02 N 109.03 E
Ba ≃, Zhg. 100 30.25 N 115.02 E
Ba ≃, Zhg. 102 31.03 N 107.08 E
Ba ≃, Zhg. 271a 39.57 N 116.38 E
Ba, Loch ⊜ 46 56.36 N 4.44 W
Baa 112 10.43 S 123.03 E
Baaba, Île I 175f 20.03 S 163.59 E
Baacagaan 102 45.35 N 99.27 E
Baad 58 47.19 N 10.07 E
Baah 112 10.28 S 121.59 E
Baak 263 51.25 N 7.10 E
Baal 56 51.02 N 6.17 E
Baao 116 13.27 N 123.22 E
Baar 58 47.12 N 8.32 E
Baar ◆[1] 58 48.00 N 8.30 E
Baarbach ≃ 263 51.27 N 7.39 E
Baardheere (Bardera) 144 2.20 N 42.17 E
Baardskeerdersbos 158 34.34 S 19.35 E
Baargaal 144 11.17 N 51.04 E
Baarle-Hertog 56 51.27 N 4.56 E
Baarle-Nassau 52 51.27 N 4.53 E
Baarlo 52 51.20 N 6.05 E
Baarn 52 52.13 N 5.16 E
Baasrode 50 51.02 N 4.10 E
Baba 246 1.47 S 79.40 W
Baba ≃ 152 6.25 N 17.07 E
Baba Burnu >, Tür. 130 39.29 N 26.04 E
Baba Burnu >, Tür. 130 41.17 N 31.24 E
Babaçulândia 250 7.13 S 47.46 W
Babadag, Rom. 38 44.54 N 28.43 E
Babadağ, Tür. 130 37.48 N 28.52 E
Babadağ ∧ 84 41.02 N 48.19 E
Babaeski 130 41.26 N 27.06 E
Babahoyo 246 1.49 S 79.31 W
Babaī (Sarju) ≃ 124 27.42 N 81.16 E
Babailiqiao 100 32.26 N 118.57 E
Babajevo 76 59.23 N 35.56 E
Babajurt 84 43.36 N 46.47 E
Babak 112 7.08 N 125.41 E
Babakin 162 32.07 S 118.01 E
Babana 150 10.26 N 3.50 E
Babanango 158 28.30 S 31.00 E
Babanka 78 48.43 N 30.26 E
Babanūsah 140 11.20 N 27.48 E
Babar, Kepulauan II 164 7.50 S 129.45 E
Babar, Pulau I 164 7.55 S 129.45 E
Bābarpur ◆[8] 272a 28.41 N 77.17 E
Babat, Indon. 112 2.45 S 103.38 E
Babat, Indon. 115a 7.06 S 112.10 E
Babatag, chrebet ⋏ 85 38.15 N 68.20 E
Babati 154 4.13 S 35.45 E
Bābā Valī Ṣāḥeb 120 31.40 N 65.40 E
Babaykivka 78 49.01 N 34.32 E
Babb 182 48.51 N 113.26 W
Babbacombe Bay ⊂ 42 50.30 N 3.25 W
Babb Creek ≃ 210 41.33 N 77.23 W
Babbitt, Mn., U.S. 190 47.43 N 91.57 W
Babbitt, Nv., U.S. 204 38.32 N 118.38 W
Bʿabdā 132 33.50 N 35.32 E
Bʿabdāt 132 33.53 N 35.40 E
Babel, Mont de ∧ 186 51.27 N 68.42 W
Babelijamun 164 2.04 S 137.43 E
Bab el Mandeb → Mandeb, Bab el Ц 144 12.40 N 43.20 E
Babelsberg ◆[8] 264a 52.24 N 13.05 E
Babelsberg, Schloss ⊥ 264a 52.24 N 13.05 E
Babelthuap I 175b 7.30 N 134.36 E
Babenhausen, Dtsch. 56 49.57 N 8.56 E
Babenhausen, Dtsch. 58 48.09 N 10.15 E
Babenki 82 55.21 N 37.11 E
Babeyru 154 1.52 N 27.27 E
Babi, Pulau I 114 2.05 N 96.39 E
Babia, Arroyo de la ≃ 196 28.25 N 101.45 W
Babian ≃ 102 22.58 N 101.44 E
Babičy 76 52.17 N 30.00 E
Bābil 142 30.41 N 31.00 E
Bābil □[4] 128 32.40 N 44.35 E
Bābil, Aṭlāl (Babylon) ⊥ 128 32.33 N 44.24 E
Babile 144 9.15 N 42.19 E
Babilônia 256 22.33 S 44.28 W
Babimost 30 52.10 N 15.51 E
Babīna 124 25.15 N 78.28 E
Babina Greda 38 45.07 N 18.33 E
Babinda 166 17.20 S 145.55 E
Babine 182 55.19 N 126.37 W
Babine ≃ 182 55.42 N 127.40 W
Babine Lake ⊜ 182 54.45 N 126.00 W
Babine Range ⋏ 182 55.00 N 126.25 W
Babino, Ross. 76 59.50 N 40.49 E
Babino, Ross. 76 56.44 N 34.17 E
Babino, Ross. 76 59.14 N 31.26 E
Babino, Ross. 80 57.22 N 48.45 E
Babiogórski Park Narodowy ♦ 30 49.35 N 19.30 E
Babo 164 2.33 S 133.25 E
Bābol 128 36.34 N 52.42 E
Bābol Sar 128 36.43 N 52.39 E
Baboon Point > 158 32.19 S 18.20 E
Baboquivari Mountains ⋏ 200 31.45 N 111.35 W
Baboquivari Peak ∧ 200 31.46 N 111.35 W
Babor, Djebel ∧ 34 36.30 N 5.28 E
Baborów 30 50.09 N 17.59 E
Babošino 82 54.13 N 37.08 E
Baboua 152 5.48 N 14.49 E
Babrongan Tower ∧[2] 162 18.36 S 123.33 E
Babrujsk 76 53.09 N 29.14 E
Babson Park, Fl., U.S. 220 27.49 N 81.31 W
Babson Park, Ma., U.S. 283 42.18 N 71.23 W
Babson Reservoir ⊜[1] 283 42.38 N 70.40 W
Babstovo 89 48.07 N 132.27 E
Bab-Taza 148 35.03 N 5.14 W
Bābu Bheri 272b 22.51 N 88.14 E
Bābupur, India 126 24.01 N 87.10 E
Bābūpur, India 272a 28.30 N 76.59 E
Babura 150 12.46 N 9.01 E
Bābūsar Pass )( 123 35.09 N 74.03 E
Babuškin 88 51.41 N 105.54 E
Babuškin ◆[8] 265b 55.52 N 37.42 E
Babuyan 116 10.00 N 118.54 E
Babuyan Channel Ц 116 18.44 N 121.40 E
Babuyan Island I 108 19.32 N 121.57 E
Babuyan Islands II 108 19.15 N 121.40 E
Babylon 210 40.41 N 73.19 W
Babylon → Bābil, Aṭlāl ⊥ 128 32.33 N 44.24 E
Babynino 76 54.23 N 35.43 E
Bača ≃ 64 46.09 N 13.48 E
Bacaadweeyn 144 7.12 N 47.32 E
Bacabal 250 4.14 S 44.47 W
Bacacay 116 13.18 N 123.47 E
Bacadéhuachi 232 29.44 N 109.10 W
Bacajaí ≃ 250 3.27 S 51.53 W
Bacalhau, Canal do ≊ 287a 23.03 S 43.35 W
Bacaligo 84 42.33 N 44.57 E
Bačalino 86 57.46 N 67.17 E
Bacan, Pulau I 164 0.35 S 127.30 E
Bacao 116 10.27 N 119.48 E
Bacarra 116 18.15 N 120.35 E
Bacatuba 250 5.40 S 43.42 W
Bacău 38 46.34 N 26.55 E
Bacău □[6] 38 46.30 N 26.45 E
Baccalieu Island I 186 48.08 N 52.48 W
Bac Can 110 22.08 N 105.50 E
Baccarat 58 48.27 N 6.45 E
Bacchiglione ≃ 64 45.11 N 12.14 E
Bacchus Marsh 169 37.41 S 144.27 E
Bačėjkava 76 55.01 N 29.09 E
Baceno 58 46.16 N 8.19 E
Bacerac 232 30.18 N 108.50 W
Bacevičy 76 53.24 N 29.14 E
Bac Giang 110 21.16 N 106.12 E
Bach 58 47.16 N 10.24 E
Bachagou 98 40.36 N 122.54 E
Bachaquero 246 9.56 N 71.08 W
Bacharach 56 50.04 N 7.46 E
Bacharden 128 38.26 N 57.25 E
Bachardok 128 38.46 N 58.30 E
Bachauan 116 12.28 N 122.06 E
Bache 106 31.05 N 120.40 E
Bacheng 106 31.27 N 120.52 E
Bachi 100 24.48 N 115.49 E
Bachiniva 232 28.45 N 107.15 W
Bach Ma 110 16.12 N 107.52 E
Bachmetjevka 80 51.06 N 44.46 E
Bachmutovo 76 56.22 N 34.03 E
Bacho 114 6.37 N 101.39 E
Bachok 114 6.04 N 102.24 E
Bacht 85 40.43 N 68.42 E
Bachta, Ross. 74 62.28 N 89.00 E
Bachta, Ross. 86 55.45 N 92.26 E
Bachtemir ≃ 80 45.43 N 47.38 E
Bachten-Berg ∧[2] 264a 52.20 N 12.54 E
Bachty 86 46.39 N 82.42 E
Bachu 90 39.50 N 78.20 E
Bachuma 144 6.48 N 35.53 E
Back ≃, N.T., Can. 176 67.15 N 95.15 W
Back ≃, Va., U.S. 208 37.06 N 76.17 W
Bačka ◆[1] 38 45.50 N 19.30 E
Bačka Palanka 38 45.15 N 19.24 E
Bačka Topola 38 45.49 N 19.38 E
Back Bay ◆[8] 283 42.21 N 71.05 W
Back Bay ⊂, India 272c 18.56 N 72.49 E
Back Bay ⊂, Va., U.S. 208 36.35 N 75.57 W
Backberg 40 60.37 N 16.37 E
Backbone Ranges ⋏ 180 63.30 N 129.00 W
Back Branch ≃ 284c 38.50 N 76.48 W
Back Brook ≃ 276 40.26 N 74.39 W
Back Channel ≃[1] 279b 40.30 N 80.05 W
Back Creek ≃ 188 38.02 N 79.54 W
Backe 26 63.49 N 16.24 E
Bäckefors 26 58.48 N 12.10 E
Bäckehagen 40 60.39 N 15.34 E
Backford 262 53.15 N 2.54 W
Bäckhammar 40 59.10 N 14.11 E
Bački Petrovac 38 45.22 N 19.35 E
Backnang 56 48.56 N 9.25 E
Back River ⊂ 208 39.16 N 76.27 W
Back River Neck >[1] 284b 39.18 N 76.26 W
Backstairs Passage Ц 168b 35.42 S 138.05 E
Bac Lieu 110 9.17 N 105.44 E
Bacliff 222 29.31 N 94.59 W
Bac Ninh 110 21.11 N 106.03 E
Baco, Mount ∧ 116 12.49 N 121.10 E
Bacoachi 232 30.38 N 109.56 W
Bacoli 68 40.48 N 14.05 E
Bacolod 116 10.40 N 122.57 E
Bacon 116 13.03 N 124.03 E
Baconga ◆[8] 273b 4.18 S 15.16 E
Bacon Peak ∧ 224 48.39 N 121.31 W
Bacons Run ≃ 285 40.06 N 74.41 W
Baconton 192 31.22 N 84.09 W
Bacoor 116 14.28 N 120.56 E
Bacoor Bay ⊂ 269f 14.28 N 120.54 E
Bac Phan □[9] 110 22.00 N 105.00 E
Bac Quang 110 22.29 N 104.52 E
Bacqueville-en-Caux 50 49.47 N 1.00 E
Bácsalmás 30 46.08 N 19.20 E
Bács-Kiskun □[6] 30 46.30 N 19.25 E
Bacton 42 52.52 N 1.28 E
Bâcu ≃ 38 46.55 N 29.28 E
Bacuag 116 9.37 N 125.38 E
Bacuit Bay ⊂ 116 11.07 N 119.23 E
Bácum 232 27.33 N 110.05 W
Bacungan 116 9.56 N 118.42 E
Bacup 44 53.43 N 2.12 W
Bacuranao ≃ 286b 23.10 N 82.14 W
Bacuranao, Presa ⊜[1] 286b 23.07 N 82.13 W
Bacuri, Cachoeira do ∟ 250 5.29 S 54.18 W
Bacuri, Ilha do I 250 2.55 S 49.43 W
Bacuri, Lago do ⊜ 250 3.16 S 42.15 W
Bačurka 24 68.32 N 56.57 E
Bacuyangan 116 9.39 N 122.27 E
Bād 128 33.41 N 52.01 E
Bad ≃, Mi., U.S. 190 43.18 N 84.06 W
Bad ≃, S.D., U.S. 198 44.22 N 100.22 W
Bad ≃, Wi., U.S. 190 46.38 N 90.40 W
Badʿ, Wādī V 142 29.41 N 32.20 E
Bada 88 51.23 N 109.54 E
Bad Abbach 60 48.56 N 12.03 E
Badagara 122 11.36 N 75.35 E
Badagri 150 6.27 N 2.55 E
Badagri Creek ⊂ 273a 6.25 N 3.18 E
Badahl 142 28.56 N 30.54 E
Bad Aibling 64 47.52 N 12.00 E
Bada Jāmda 124 22.09 N 85.23 E
Badajia 100 33.57 N 120.17 E
Badajós ≃ 246 3.15 S 63.02 W
Badajós, Lago ⊜ 246 3.15 S 62.47 W
Badajoz 34 38.53 N 6.58 W
Badajoz □[4] 34 38.40 N 6.00 W
Badakani 152 4.46 S 14.52 E
Badakhshān □[4] 120 36.45 N 72.00 E
Badal Khān Goth 120 26.31 N 67.06 E
Badalona 34 41.27 N 2.15 E
Badalucco 62 43.55 N 7.51 E
Badam 85 42.23 N 69.15 E
Bādāmi 122 15.55 N 75.41 E
Bādāmpahār 124 22.06 N 86.06 E
Badana, Lach V 144 0.50 S 42.04 E
Badanah 128 30.59 N 41.02 E
Badanga 146 11.36 N 17.26 E
Badanganj 126 22.54 N 87.33 E
Badaohao 104 41.47 N 121.57 E
Badaohe, Zhg. 98 40.24 N 118.42 E
Badaohe, Zhg. 98 40.02 N 122.17 E
Badarīnāth 124 30.44 N 79.29 E
Badarma 88 57.46 N 102.36 E
Badas 112 4.36 N 114.27 E
Badas, Kepulauan II 112 0.35 N 107.06 E
Badata, gora ∧ 88 51.55 N 111.35 E
Bad Aussee 64 47.36 N 13.47 E
Bad Axe 190 43.48 N 83.00 W
Badaying 98 41.22 N 117.28 E
Badazhou 102 24.36 N 105.04 E
Bad Bentheim 52 52.19 N 7.10 E
Badbergen 52 52.38 N 7.59 E
Bad Bergzabern 56 49.07 N 8.00 E
Bad Berka 54 50.54 N 11.17 E
Bad Berleburg 56 51.03 N 8.23 E
Bad Berneck 60 50.03 N 11.40 E
Bad Bertrich 56 50.04 N 7.02 E
Bad Bevensen 52 53.05 N 10.34 E
Bad Bibra 54 51.12 N 11.35 E
Bad Birnbach 60 48.27 N 13.01 E
Bad Blankenburg 54 50.41 N 11.16 E
Bad Bocklet 56 50.16 N 10.05 E
Bad Brambach 54 50.13 N 12.19 E
Bad Bramstedt 52 53.55 N 9.53 E
Bad Breisig 56 50.31 N 7.18 E
Bad Brückenau 56 50.18 N 9.47 E
Bad Buchau 58 48.03 N 9.36 E
Bad Camberg 56 50.18 N 8.16 E
Bad Creek ≃ 216 41.25 N 83.57 W
Baddā 132 33.41 N 36.26 E
Badda Rogghie ∧ 144 8.43 N 37.41 E
Baddeck 186 46.07 N 60.45 W
Bad Ditzenbach 56 48.35 N 9.41 E
Baddo ≃ 128 27.59 N 64.21 E
Bad Doberan 54 54.06 N 11.53 E
Baddomalhi 123 31.59 N 74.40 E
Bad Dreibergen 52 53.12 N 8.01 E
Bad Driburg 52 51.44 N 9.01 E
Bad Düben 54 51.36 N 12.34 E
Bad Dürkheim 56 49.28 N 8.10 E
Bad Dürrenberg 54 51.18 N 12.04 E
Bad Dürrheim 58 48.01 N 8.32 E
Badé, Centraf. 152 6.41 N 17.07 E
Bade, Indon. 164 7.10 S 139.35 E
Badeggi 150 9.05 N 6.08 E
Badéguichéri 150 14.31 N 5.22 E
Bad Eilsen 52 52.14 N 9.06 E
Bad Elster 54 50.17 N 12.14 E
Bad Ems 56 50.20 N 7.43 E
Baden, On., Can. 212 43.24 N 80.39 W
Baden, Dtsch. 52 53.00 N 9.04 E
Baden, Erit. 144 17.00 N 38.00 E
Baden, Öst. 61 48.00 N 16.14 E
Baden, Schw. 58 47.29 N 8.18 E
Baden, Pa., U.S. 214 40.38 N 80.13 W
Baden-Baden 56 48.46 N 8.14 E
Bad Endbach 56 50.45 N 8.32 E
Bad Endorf 64 47.54 N 12.18 E
Badenoch □[9] 46 56.57 N 4.19 W
Baden-Powell, Mount ∧ 228 34.21 N 117.46 W
Badenweiler 58 47.48 N 7.40 E
Baden-Württemberg □[3] 30 48.30 N 9.00 E
Badenyon 46 57.15 N 3.05 W
Baderna 64 45.12 N 13.46 E
Badersleben 54 51.59 N 10.53 E
Bad Essen 52 52.19 N 8.20 E
Bad Feilnbach 64 47.46 N 12.00 E
Badfish Creek ≃ 216 42.50 N 89.10 W
Bad Frankenhausen 54 51.21 N 11.06 E
Bad Freienwalde 54 52.47 N 14.01 E
Bad Friedrichshall 56 49.14 N 9.11 E
Bad Fusch 64 47.12 N 12.51 E
Bad Füssingen 60 48.22 N 13.17 E
Badgam 123 34.01 N 74.43 E
Bad Gandersheim 52 51.52 N 10.01 E
Badgastein 64 47.07 N 13.08 E
Badger, Nf., Can. 186 48.59 N 56.02 W
Badger, Mn., U.S. 198 48.46 N 96.00 W
Badger Creek ≃, Co., U.S. 198 40.17 N 103.42 W
Badger Creek ≃, Co., U.S. 200 38.28 N 105.52 W
Badger Creek ≃, Or., U.S. 224 45.16 N 121.11 W
Badger Pass )( 226 37.40 N 119.39 W
Badger's Mount 260 51.20 N 0.09 E
Badgery's Creek 274a 33.53 S 150.44 E
Badgerys Creek ≃ 274a 33.51 S 150.46 E
Bādghīs □[4] 128 35.00 N 63.45 E
Bad Gleichenberg 61 46.52 N 15.54 E
Bad Godesberg 56 50.41 N 7.10 E
Bad Goisern 64 47.38 N 13.37 E
Bad Gottleuba 54 50.51 N 13.56 E
Bad Grund 52 51.48 N 10.14 E
Bad Hall 61 48.02 N 14.13 E
Bad Harzburg 54 51.53 N 10.33 E
Bad Heilbrunn 64 47.45 N 11.28 E
Badhela ◆[8] 272a 28.38 N 77.04 E
Bad Helmstedt 54 52.14 N 11.03 E
Bad Herrenalb 56 48.48 N 8.26 E
Bad Hersfeld 56 50.52 N 9.42 E
Badhoevedorp 52 52.21 N 4.46 E
Bad Hofgastein 64 47.10 N 13.06 E
Bad Homburg vor der Höhe 56 50.13 N 8.37 E
Bad Honnef 56 50.39 N 7.13 E
Bad Hönningen 56 50.31 N 7.19 E
Bādī ≃ 124 27.55 N 83.27 E
Badia (Abtei) 64 46.37 N 11.54 E
Badia, Val V 64 46.40 N 11.53 E
Badia Calavena 64 45.34 N 11.09 E
Badia Polesine 64 45.05 N 11.29 E
Badia Prataglia 66 43.47 N 11.52 E
Badia Tedalda 66 43.42 N 12.11 E
Bad Iburg 52 52.09 N 8.02 E
Badile Camuno, Pizzo ∧ 58 46.01 N 10.25 E
Badīn 120 24.39 N 68.50 E
Bādinan 272b 22.54 N 88.14 E
Badinko ≃ 150 13.42 N 9.35 W
Badin Lake ⊜[1] 192 35.27 N 80.06 W
Badiraguato 232 25.22 N 107.31 W
Bad Ischl 64 47.43 N 13.37 E
Bad Karlshafen 52 51.38 N 9.27 E
Bad Kissingen 56 50.12 N 10.04 E
Bad Kleinen 54 53.46 N 11.28 E
Bad Kleinkirchheim 64 46.49 N 13.49 E
Bad Klosterlausnitz 54 50.55 N 11.52 E
Bad Kohlgrub 64 47.40 N 11.03 E
Bad König 56 49.45 N 9.01 E
Bad Königshofen im Grabfeld, Dtsch. 54 50.18 N 10.29 E
Bad Königshofen im Grabfeld, Dtsch. 56 50.18 N 10.29 E
Bad Kösen 54 51.08 N 11.43 E
Bad Köstritz 54 50.56 N 12.01 E
Bad Kreuznach 56 49.52 N 7.51 E
Bad Krozingen 58 47.55 N 7.43 E
Bādkulla 126 23.17 N 88.32 E
Bad Laasphe 56 50.56 N 8.24 E
Bad Laer 52 52.06 N 8.05 E
Badlands ⋏[2], U.S. 198 46.45 N 103.30 W
Badlands ⋏[2], S.D., U.S. 198 43.30 N 102.20 W
Badlands National Park ♦ 198 43.47 N 102.15 W
Bad Langensalza 56 51.06 N 10.38 E
Bad Lauchstädt 54 51.23 N 11.52 E
Bad Lausick 54 51.08 N 12.38 E
Bad Lauterberg [im Harz] 52 51.38 N 10.28 E
Bad Leonfelden 61 48.33 N 14.19 E
Bādli ◆[8] 272a 28.45 N 77.09 E
Bad Liebenstein 54 50.49 N 10.21 E
Bad Liebenwerda 54 51.31 N 13.23 E
Bad Liebenzell 56 48.46 N 8.44 E
Bad Lippspringe 52 51.46 N 8.49 E
Bad Marienberg 56 50.39 N 7.57 E
Bad Meinberg 52 51.53 N 8.58 E
Bad Mergentheim 56 49.30 N 9.46 E
Bad Mitterndorf 60 47.33 N 13.55 E
Bad Mukran 54 54.26 N 13.35 E
Bad Münder 52 52.12 N 9.27 E
Bad Münster am Stein-Ebernburg 56 49.49 N 7.51 E
Bad Münstereifel 56 50.33 N 6.46 E
Bad Muskau 54 51.32 N 14.43 E
Bad Nauheim 56 50.22 N 8.44 E
Bad Nenndorf 52 52.20 N 9.22 E
Badnera 122 20.52 N 77.44 E
Badner Lindkogel ∧ 264b 48.01 N 16.11 E
Bad Neuenahr-Ahrweiler 56 50.33 N 7.08 E
Bad Neustadt an der Saale 56 50.19 N 10.13 E
Bad Niedernau 58 48.27 N 8.53 E
Bad Oeynhausen 52 52.12 N 8.48 E
Badogo 150 11.02 N 8.13 W
Badolato 68 38.34 N 16.31 E
Bad Oldesloe 52 53.48 N 10.22 E
Ba Dong, Viet 110 9.40 N 106.34 E
Badong, Zhg. 102 31.02 N 110.20 E
Badonviller 58 48.30 N 6.54 E
Bad Orb 56 50.14 N 9.20 E
Badou, Togo 150 7.35 N 0.36 E
Badou, Zhg. 98 36.27 N 117.55 E
Badouling 100 32.10 N 117.36 E
Badoumbé 150 13.38 N 10.13 W
Bad Peterstal-Griesbach 58 48.26 N 8.12 E
Badplaas 158 25.57 S 30.35 E
Bad Pyrmont 52 51.59 N 9.15 E
Badr 142 30.33 N 30.43 E
Bad Radkersburg 61 46.41 N 15.59 E
Bad Ragaz 58 47.00 N 9.30 E
Bad Rappenau 56 49.14 N 9.06 E
Bad Rehburg 52 52.26 N 9.13 E
Bad Reichenhall 64 47.43 N 12.52 E
Badr Ḥunayn 128 23.44 N 38.46 E
Bad Rippoldsau 58 48.26 N 8.19 E
Bad River Indian Reservation ◆[4] 190 46.33 N 90.40 W
Bad Rothenfelde 52 52.06 N 8.09 E
Bad Saarow 54 52.17 N 14.03 E
Bad Sachsa 54 51.36 N 10.32 E
Bad Säckingen 58 47.33 N 7.56 E
Bad Salzdetfurth 52 52.03 N 10.01 E
Bad Salzig 56 50.12 N 7.38 E
Bad Salzschlirf 56 50.37 N 9.29 E
Bad Salzuflen 52 52.05 N 8.44 E
Bad Salzungen 56 50.48 N 10.13 E
Bad Sankt Leonhard im Lavanttal 61 46.58 N 14.48 E
Bad Sassendorf 52 51.35 N 8.10 E
Bad Schandau 54 50.55 N 14.10 E
Bad Schmiedeberg 54 51.41 N 12.44 E
Bad Schönborn 56 49.13 N 8.39 E
Bad Schwalbach 56 50.08 N 8.04 E
Bad Schwartau 54 53.55 N 10.40 E
Bad Segeberg 52 53.56 N 10.17 E
Bādshāhpur 124 25.47 N 82.49 E
Bad Soden 56 50.08 N 8.30 E
Bad Soden-Salmünster 56 50.17 N 9.22 E
Bad Sooden-Allendorf 56 51.16 N 9.58 E
Bad Steben 54 50.22 N 11.38 E
Bad Stuer 54 53.22 N 12.19 E
Bad Suderode 54 51.44 N 11.07 E
Bad Sulza 54 51.05 N 11.37 E
Bad Sülze 54 54.06 N 12.38 E
Bad Tatzmannsdorf 61 47.20 N 16.13 E
Bad Teinach 56 48.41 N 8.41 E
Bad Tennstedt 54 51.09 N 10.50 E
Bad Tölz 64 47.46 N 11.34 E
Badu, Bra. 287a 22.54 S 43.04 W
Badu, Zhg. 100 26.51 N 119.35 E
Badu, Zhg. 100 28.32 N 117.57 E
Badu, Zhg. 102 24.15 N 105.41 E
Badu Island I 164 10.07 S 142.08 E
Badulla 122 6.59 N 81.03 E
Badung, Selat Ц 115b 8.40 S 115.22 E
Badupi 120 21.36 N 93.25 E
Bādura 126 22.16 N 90.21 E
Bad Urach 58 48.29 N 9.23 E
Bāduria 126 22.44 N 88.47 E
Badvel 122 14.45 N 79.03 E
Bad Vellach 61 46.26 N 14.33 E
Bad Vilbel 56 50.12 N 8.42 E
Bad Vöslau 61 47.57 N 16.16 E
Bad Waldsee 58 47.55 N 9.45 E
Badwater Creek ≃ 202 43.17 N 108.08 W
Bad Westernkotten 52 51.38 N 8.21 E
Bad Wiessee 64 47.43 N 11.43 E
Bad Wildbad im Schwarzwald 56 48.45 N 8.32 E
Bad Wildungen 56 51.07 N 9.07 E
Bad Wilsnack 54 52.57 N 11.57 E
Bad Wimpfen 56 49.14 N 9.09 E
Bad Windsheim 56 49.31 N 10.25 E
Bad Wörishofen 58 48.00 N 10.36 E
Bad Wurzach 58 47.54 N 9.54 E
Badžalskij chrebet ⋏ 89 50.40 N 134.50 E
Bad Zwesten 56 51.03 N 9.10 E
Bad Zwischenahn 52 53.11 N 8.00 E
Baediam 150 15.03 N 11.51 W
Bække 41 55.34 N 9.09 E
Baena 34 37.37 N 4.19 W
Baependi 256 21.57 S 44.53 W
Baependi ≃ 256 21.52 S 45.04 W
Baer Field ⊠ 216 40.59 N 85.11 W
Baerl ◆[8] 263 51.29 N 6.41 E
Baesweiler 56 50.54 N 6.11 E
Báez 240p 22.13 N 79.45 W
Baeza, Ec. 246 0.27 S 77.53 W
Baeza, Esp. 34 37.59 N 3.28 W
Baezaeko ≃ 182 53.09 N 123.48 W
Bafang 152 5.09 N 10.11 E
Bafatá 150 12.10 N 14.40 W
Bafelé 150 10.09 N 10.08 W
Baffa 123 34.26 N 73.13 E
Baffin Basin ✢[1] 16 73.15 N 67.00 W
Baffin Bay ⊂, N.A. 16 73.00 N 66.00 W
Baffin Bay ⊂, Tx., U.S. 196 27.15 N 97.33 W
Baffin Island I 176 68.00 N 70.00 W
Bafia 152 4.44 N 11.16 E
Bafilo 150 9.21 N 1.16 E
Bafing ≃, Afr. 150 13.49 N 10.50 W
Bafing ≃, Mali 150 12.27 N 7.07 W
Bafing Makana 150 12.33 N 10.15 W
Bafoulabé 150 13.48 N 10.50 W
Bafoussam 152 5.29 N 10.24 E
Bāfq 128 31.35 N 55.24 E
Bafra 130 41.34 N 35.56 E
Bafra Burnu > 130 41.44 N 35.58 E
Bāft 128 29.14 N 56.38 E
Bafuku 154 4.15 N 27.54 E
Bafwabaka 154 2.07 N 27.40 E
Bafwabalinga 154 0.51 N 27.04 E
Bafwaboli 154 0.39 N 26.10 E
Bafwangbe 154 1.39 N 26.51 E
Bafwapada 154 0.56 N 26.57 E
Bafwasende 154 1.05 N 27.16 E
Bafwasomboli 154 1.27 N 27.01 E
Baga 126 22.26 N 90.28 E
Bagabag 116 16.37 N 121.15 E
Bagabag Island I 164 4.50 S 146.15 E
Baga-Burul 80 46.00 N 44.36 E
Bagac 116 14.36 N 120.23 E
Bagacay Point > 116 8.58 N 124.48 E
Bagac Bay ⊂ 116 14.36 N 120.22 E
Bagaces 236 10.31 N 85.15 W
Baga Chentej nuruu ⋏ 88 48.30 N 107.30 E
Bagage ∧ 154 3.23 N 40.12 E
Bagagem ≃, Bra. 250 11.37 S 48.12 W
Bagagem ≃, Bra. 255 13.58 S 48.21 W
Bagaha 124 27.06 N 84.05 E
Bagahak ∧ 116 5.03 N 118.44 E
Bagajevskij 78 47.19 N 40.23 E
Bāgalkot 122 16.11 N 75.42 E
Bagamanoc 116 13.57 N 124.17 E
Bagamoyo 154 6.26 S 38.54 E
Bagan 86 54.06 N 77.40 E
Bagana 80 54.22 N 51.25 E
Bagana, Mount ∧ 175e 6.09 S 155.12 E
Bagan Datoh 114 3.59 N 100.47 E
Bagañga 116 7.35 N 126.34 E
Bagan Serai 114 5.01 N 100.32 E
Bagansiapiapi 114 2.09 N 100.49 E
Bagansinembah 114 1.46 N 100.29 E
Bagansitukang 114 2.38 N 100.15 E
Baganza ≃ 64 44.47 N 10.19 E
Bagara 85 40.55 N 68.26 E
Bağarası 130 37.42 N 27.33 E
Bagaroua 150 14.38 N 4.21 E
Bagasra 120 21.29 N 70.57 E
Bagata 152 3.44 S 17.57 E
Bāgātipāra 126 24.18 N 88.57 E
Bagawi 140 12.19 N 34.21 E
Bagband 52 53.21 N 7.36 E
Bagbe ≃ 150 8.42 N 11.15 W
Bagbele 154 4.21 N 29.17 E
Bāgda 126 23.13 N 86.41 E
Bagdad → Baghdād, ʿĪrāq 128 33.21 N 44.25 E
Bagdad, Az., U.S. 200 34.34 N 113.12 W
Bagdad, Fl., U.S. 194 30.35 N 87.01 W
Bagdad, Ky., U.S. 218 38.15 N 85.03 W
Bagdaha 126 23.13 N 88.53 E
Bagdanga 126 24.02 N 88.32 E
Bagdarin 88 54.26 N 113.36 E
Bagdati 84 42.06 N 42.48 E
Bağdere 130 38.07 N 40.44 E
Bagé 252 31.20 S 54.06 W
Bagehadu 120 35.25 N 84.50 E
Bâgé-le-Châtel 58 46.18 N 4.56 E
Bagenkop 41 54.45 N 10.41 E
Bāgerhāt 124 22.40 N 89.48 E
Bages et de Sigean, Étang de ⊂ 32 43.05 N 3.03 E
Bāgevādi 122 16.35 N 75.58 E
Baggao 116 17.56 N 121.46 E
Baggeryd 24 57.30 N 14.07 E
Baggetorp 40 59.01 N 16.04 E
Baggio ◆[8] 266b 45.27 N 9.06 E
Bağgöze 130 37.43 N 41.55 E
Baggs 200 41.02 N 107.39 W
Baggy Point > 42 51.09 N 4.16 W
Bāgh 123 33.59 N 73.47 E
Baghdād 128 33.21 N 44.25 E
Baghdād □[4] 128 33.30 N 44.30 E
Baghdobā 126 22.08 N 87.54 E
Baghelkhand Plateau ⋏[1] 124 23.45 N 82.20 E
Bāgh-e Malek 128 31.32 N 49.55 E
Bagheria 70 38.05 N 13.30 E
Bāgherpāra 126 23.14 N 89.21 E
Bāghia 126 23.27 N 90.29 E
Baghia Bīl ≋ 126 23.07 N 90.03 E
Bāghīn 128 30.12 N 56.48 E
Baghlān 120 36.13 N 68.46 E
Baghlān □[4] 120 35.45 N 69.00 E
Bāghmundi 124 23.12 N 86.03 E
Bāghpat 124 28.57 N 77.13 E
Baghrān Khowleh 120 33.01 N 64.58 E
Bagillt 262 53.16 N 3.10 W
Bağırpaşa Dağı ∧ 130 39.30 N 40.06 E
Bağırsak (Sājūr) ≃ 130 36.40 N 38.05 E
Bağkonak 130 38.12 N 31.17 E
Bagley 198 47.31 N 95.23 W
Bāgli 124 22.39 N 76.21 E
Bağlıca 130 37.53 N 41.46 E
Bağlum 130 40.03 N 32.51 E
Bāgmāri ◆[8] 272b 22.34 N 88.25 E
Bāgmatī □[8] 124 27.45 N 85.30 E
Bāgmatī ≃ 124 25.31 N 86.44 E
Bagn 26 60.49 N 9.34 E
Bagnacavallo 66 44.25 N 12.00 E
Bagnaia 66 42.25 N 12.09 E
Bāgnān 126 22.28 N 87.59 E
Bagnara Calabra 68 38.18 N 15.49 E
Bagnara di Romagna 66 44.23 N 11.49 E
Bag Narin 102 38.57 N 94.08 E
Bagnasco 62 44.18 N 8.02 E
Bagnell Dam ◆[6] 194 38.11 N 92.39 W
Bagnères-de-Bigorre 32 43.04 N 0.09 E
Bagnères-de-Luchon 32 42.47 N 0.36 E
Bagnes, Vallée de V 58 46.03 N 7.18 E
Bagneux 261 48.48 N 2.18 E
Bagni Acque Albule 66 41.57 N 12.43 E
Bagni del Masino 58 46.15 N 9.36 E
Bagni di Lucca 66 44.01 N 10.35 E
Bagni di Rabbi 64 46.24 N 10.48 E
Bagno a Ripoli 66 43.45 N 11.19 E
Bagno di Romagna 66 43.50 N 11.57 E
Bagnolet 261 48.52 N 2.25 E
Bagnoli del Trigno 66 41.42 N 14.27 E
Bagnoli di Sopra 64 45.11 N 11.53 E
Bagnoli Irpino 68 40.50 N 15.04 E
Bagnolo in Piano 64 44.46 N 10.40 E
Bagnolo Mella 64 45.26 N 10.10 E
Bagnols-en-Forêt 62 43.32 N 6.42 E
Bagnols-les-Bains 62 44.30 N 3.40 E
Bagnols-sur-Cèze 62 44.10 N 4.37 E
Bagñon 116 13.44 N 122.50 E
Bagnone 64 44.19 N 10.00 E
Bagnoregio 66 42.37 N 12.05 E
Bagno Vignoni 66 43.02 N 11.39 E


**Symbols** in the index entries represent the broad categories identified in the key at the right. Symbols with superior numbers (⋏[1]) identify subcategories (see complete key on page *I* · *1*).

**Symbole** im Register stellen die rechts im Schlüssel erklärten Kategorien dar. Symbole mit hochgestellten Ziffern (⋏[1]) bezeichnen Unterabteilungen einer Kategorie (vgl. vollständiger Schlüssel auf Seite *I* · *1*).

**Los símbolos** incluídos en el texto del índice representan las grandes categorías identificadas con la clave a la derecha. Los símbolos con numeros en su parte superior (⋏[1]) identifican las subcategorías (véase la clave completa en la página *I* · *1*).

**Les symboles** de l'index représentent les catégories indiquées dans la légende à droite. Les symboles suivis d'un indice (⋏[1]) représentent des sous-catégories (voir légende complète à la page *I* · *1*).

**Os símbolos** incluídos no texto do índice representam as grandes categorias identificadas com a chave à direita. Os símbolos com números em sua parte superior (⋏[1]) identificam as subcategorias (veja-se a chave completa à página *I* · *1*).

| | | | | | |
|---|---|---|---|---|---|
| ∧ | Mountain | Berg | Montaña | Montagne | Montanha |
| ⋏ | Mountains | Gebirge | Montañas | Montagnes | Montanhas |
| )( | Pass | Paß | Paso | Col | Passo |
| V | Valley, Canyon | Tal, Cañon | Valle, Cañón | Vallée, Canyon | Vale, Canhão |
| ≃ | Plain | Ebene | Llano | Plaine | Planície |
| > | Cape | Kap | Cabo | Cap | Cabo |
| I | Island | Insel | Isla | Île | Ilha |
| II | Islands | Inseln | Islas | Îles | Ilhas |
| ⫠ | Other Topographic Features | Andere Topographische Objekte | Otros Elementos Topográficos | Autres données topographiques | Outros acidentes topográficos |

ESPAÑOL — FRANÇAIS — PORTUGUÊS

| Nombre / Nom / Nome | Página / Page | Lat.°′ | Long.°′ W = Oeste / W = Ouest |
|---|---|---|---|
| Bago (Pegu) | 110 | 17.20 N | 96.29 E |
| Bago □[8] | 110 | 18.00 N | 96.00 E |
| Bågø I | 41 | 55.18 N | 9.49 E |
| Bago ≃ | 116 | 10.33 N | 122.50 E |
| Bagod | 61 | 46.53 N | 16.45 E |
| Bagodar | 124 | 24.05 N | 85.52 E |
| Bagodo | 152 | 6.25 N | 13.23 E |
| Bagoé ≃ | 150 | 12.36 N | 6.34 W |
| Bagolino | 64 | 45.49 N | 10.28 E |
| Bagoni | 146 | 7.53 N | 10.43 E |
| Bagot □[6] | 206 | 45.40 N | 72.45 W |
| Bagotville, Base des Forces canadiennes ■ | 186 | 48.20 N | 70.58 W |
| Bağpınar | 130 | 37.35 N | 38.19 E |
| Bagrationovsk | 76 | 54.23 N | 20.39 E |
| Bagrauła ◆[8] | 272a | 28.34 N | 77.04 E |
| Bagre | 250 | 1.54 S | 50.12 W |
| Bagshot | 42 | 51.22 N | 0.42 W |
| Bag Tal | 89 | 43.20 N | 122.16 E |
| Bāguiati | 272b | 22.36 N | 88.26 E |
| Baguio | 116 | 16.25 N | 120.36 E |
| Bagula | 126 | 23.19 N | 88.39 E |
| Bagumbayan | 269f | 14.28 N | 121.03 E |
| Bagyrlaj ≃ | 80 | 48.08 N | 51.14 E |
| Bāh | 124 | 26.53 N | 78.36 E |
| Bāhādurābād Ghāt | 124 | 25.09 N | 89.42 E |
| Bāhādurgarh | 124 | 28.41 N | 76.56 E |
| Bāhādurpur | 126 | 23.25 N | 88.28 E |
| Bahaia, Monte ʌ | 144 | 11.20 N | 49.45 E |
| Baha'i Temple ʊ[1] | 278 | 42.05 N | 87.41 W |
| Bahamas □[1], N.A. | 230 | 24.15 N | 76.00 W |
| Bahamas □[1], N.A. | 238 | 24.15 N | 76.00 W |
| Bahār | 128 | 34.54 N | 48.26 E |
| Baharāgora | 126 | 22.17 N | 86.43 E |
| Baharampur | 126 | 24.06 N | 88.15 E |
| Baharpur | 126 | 23.41 N | 89.34 E |
| Bahata Cherneshchyna | 78 | 48.59 N | 35.35 E |
| Bahau | 114 | 2.49 N | 102.25 E |
| Bahau ≃ | 112 | 2.34 N | 116.20 E |
| Bahāwalnagar | 123 | 29.59 N | 73.16 E |
| Bahāwalpur | 123 | 29.24 N | 71.41 E |
| Bahçe | 130 | 37.14 N | 36.34 E |
| Bahçeköy ◆[8] | 267b | 41.11 N | 28.59 E |
| Bahçeköy su kemeri ≅[1] | 267b | 41.03 N | 28.59 E |
| Bahechuan | 98 | 40.59 N | 124.49 E |
| Baheri | 124 | 28.47 N | 79.30 E |
| Baherove | 78 | 45.23 N | 36.17 E |
| Bahi, Pil. | 116 | 13.53 N | 123.38 E |
| Bahi, Tan. | 154 | 5.59 S | 35.19 E |
| Bahía → Salvador | 255 | 12.59 S | 38.31 W |
| Bahia □[3] | 250 | 11.00 S | 42.00 W |
| Bahía, Islas de la II | 236 | 16.20 N | 86.30 W |
| Bahía Azul | 236 | 9.11 N | 81.54 W |
| Bahía Blanca | 252 | 38.43 S | 62.17 W |
| Bahía Bustamante | 254 | 45.08 S | 66.32 W |
| Bahía Erasmo, Parque Nacional ♦ | 254 | 46.05 S | 73.35 W |
| Bahía Honda | 240p | 22.54 N | 83.10 W |
| Bahia Honda Key I | 220 | 24.40 N | 81.16 W |
| Bahia Honda Point › | 116 | 9.24 N | 118.07 E |
| Bahía Kino | 232 | 28.50 N | 111.55 W |
| Bahía Laura | 254 | 48.24 S | 66.29 W |
| Bahīj | 142 | 30.56 N | 29.35 E |
| Bahir Dar | 144 | 11.35 N | 37.28 E |
| Bahi Swamp ≋ | 154 | 6.05 S | 35.10 E |
| Bahjoi | 124 | 28.24 N | 78.37 E |
| Bahl | 123 | 28.38 N | 75.38 E |
| Bahlolpur | 272a | 28.37 N | 77.24 E |
| Bahn | 150 | 7.05 N | 8.45 W |
| Bahnāy | 142 | 30.23 N | 31.04 E |
| Bahnayā | 142 | 30.41 N | 31.23 E |
| Baḩrah | 144 | 21.24 N | 39.29 E |
| Bahraich | 124 | 27.35 N | 81.36 E |
| Bahrain (Al-Baḩrayn) □[1], Asia | 118 | 26.00 N | 50.30 E |
| Bahrain (Al-Baḩrayn) □[1], Asia | 128 | 26.00 N | 50.30 E |
| Baḩr al-Ghazāl □[4] | 140 | 8.30 N | 26.00 E |
| Bahrām Chāh | 128 | 29.26 N | 64.03 E |
| Baḩrānī, Ḩālat al- I | 128 | 24.23 N | 54.14 E |
| Bahranivtsi | 78 | 49.17 N | 27.56 E |
| Baḩrayn, Khalīj al c | 128 | 25.45 N | 50.40 E |
| Bahrdorf | 54 | 52.23 N | 11.00 E |
| Bahrein → Bahrain □[1] | 128 | 26.00 N | 50.30 E |
| Baḩrīyah, Al-Wāḩāt al- ₸[4] | 140 | 28.15 N | 28.57 E |
| Bahser | 130 | 37.57 N | 39.18 E |
| Bahtīm | 142 | 30.08 N | 31.17 E |
| Baḩṭīṭ | 142 | 30.29 N | 31.38 E |
| Bāhū Kalāt | 128 | 25.43 N | 61.25 E |
| Bāhū Kalāt ≃ | 128 | 25.11 N | 61.31 E |
| Bahulu, Pulau I | 112 | 3.33 S | 122.18 E |
| Bahu-mbelu | 112 | 2.13 S | 121.41 E |
| Bahušėŭsk | 76 | 54.51 N | 30.13 E |
| Bahūt | 142 | 31.10 N | 31.19 E |
| Baï | 150 | 13.38 N | 3.22 W |
| Bai ≃, Zhg. | 102 | 32.10 N | 112.20 E |
| Bai ≃, Zhg. | 105 | 40.43 N | 116.33 E |
| Baia | 68 | 40.49 N | 14.04 E |
| Baia de Aramă | 38 | 45.00 N | 22.49 E |
| Baía dos Tigres | 152 | 16.36 S | 11.43 E |
| Baía Farta | 152 | 12.40 S | 13.11 E |
| Baia Mare | 38 | 47.40 N | 23.35 E |
| Baiano | 68 | 40.57 N | 14.37 E |
| Baião | 250 | 2.41 S | 49.41 W |
| Baiardo | 62 | 43.54 N | 7.43 E |
| Baía Rica ≃ | 248 | 12.40 S | 63.04 W |
| Baia Sprie | 38 | 47.40 N | 23.42 E |
| Baibao | 105 | 39.04 N | 115.31 E |
| Baibei | 100 | 27.47 N | 115.53 E |
| Baïbokoum | 146 | 7.46 N | 15.43 E |
| Baibuting | 106 | 30.33 N | 120.46 E |
| Baicang | 124 | 30.14 N | 90.44 E |
| Baicao | 98 | 41.13 N | 116.07 E |
| Baicaochang | 102 | 32.08 N | 103.59 E |
| Baicao Ling ʎ | 102 | 26.10 N | 101.20 E |
| Baicha | 100 | 29.11 N | 115.37 E |
| Baicheng, Zhg. | 89 | 45.38 N | 122.46 E |
| Baicheng, Zhg. | 90 | 41.46 N | 81.52 E |
| Baidian | 106 | 30.47 N | 119.14 E |
| Baidiao | 102 | 28.07 N | 101.28 E |
| Baidoa → Baydhabo | 144 | 3.07 N | 43.39 E |
| Baidunzi | 102 | 43.11 N | 95.19 E |
| Baidyabāti | 126 | 22.47 N | 88.20 E |
| Baidyanāth | 124 | 24.29 N | 86.42 E |
| Baidyer Bāzār | 126 | 23.39 N | 90.37 E |
| Baie-Comeau | 186 | 49.13 N | 68.10 W |
| Baie-Comeau-Hauterive, Réserve ♦ | 186 | 50.05 N | 68.00 W |
| Baie-des-Ha! Ha! | 186 | 50.56 N | 58.56 W |
| Baie-de-Shawinigan | 206 | 46.34 N | 72.45 W |
| Baie-des-Moutons | 186 | 50.47 N | 59.02 W |
| Baie-du-Renard | 186 | 49.17 N | 61.50 W |
| Baie-d'Urfé | 206 | 45.25 N | 73.55 W |
| Baie-Johan-Beetz | 186 | 50.17 N | 62.48 W |
| Baie-Mahault | 241o | 16.16 N | 61.35 W |
| Baienfurt | 64 | 47.49 N | 9.38 E |
| Baiersbronn | 58 | 48.30 N | 8.22 E |
| Baiersdorf | 60 | 49.39 N | 11.01 E |
| Baies, Lac des ⊜ | 190 | 47.18 N | 77.40 W |
| Baie-Sainte-Claire | 186 | 49.54 N | 64.30 W |
| Baie-Saint-Paul | 186 | 47.27 N | 70.30 W |
| Baie-Trinité | 186 | 49.25 N | 67.18 W |
| Baie Verte | 186 | 49.56 N | 56.11 W |
| Baieville | 206 | 46.08 N | 72.43 W |
| Baigezhuang | 105 | 39.54 N | 118.09 E |
| Baigneux-les-Juifs | 58 | 47.36 N | 4.38 E |
| Baigong | 100 | 24.18 N | 116.14 E |
| Baigou | 105 | 39.07 N | 116.01 E |
| Baigou ≃ | 105 | 39.06 N | 116.00 E |
| Baiguoshu | 106 | 30.45 N | 119.07 E |
| Baigusi | 102 | 33.10 N | 103.52 E |
| Baihāli Jot ʌ | 123 | 32.51 N | 76.32 E |
| Baihar | 124 | 22.06 N | 80.33 E |
| Baihe, Zhg. | 100 | 29.12 N | 120.55 E |
| Baihe, Zhg. | 102 | 32.17 N | 110.02 E |
| Baihebu | 105 | 40.39 N | 116.10 E |
| Baihegang | 106 | 31.16 N | 121.08 E |
| Baihekou | 102 | 31.46 N | 110.13 E |
| Baihou | 100 | 24.18 N | 116.48 E |
| Baihua | 107 | 29.07 N | 104.37 E |
| Baihua Shan ʌ | 105 | 39.50 N | 115.35 E |
| Baijala | 272b | 22.51 N | 88.16 E |
| Baijian | 105 | 39.36 N | 115.16 E |
| Baijiang | 100 | 29.51 N | 119.20 E |
| Baijiawu | 105 | 39.30 N | 116.28 E |
| Baijie | 107 | 29.17 N | 106.31 E |
| Baijietan | 107 | 28.44 N | 105.30 E |
| Baijnāth | 124 | 29.55 N | 79.37 E |
| Baiju | 100 | 33.04 N | 120.20 E |
| Baikal, Lago → Bajkal, ozero ⊜ | 88 | 53.00 N | 107.40 E |
| Baikal, Lake → Bajkal, ozero ⊜ | 88 | 53.00 N | 107.40 E |
| Baikal-See → Bajkal, ozero ⊜ | 88 | 53.00 N | 107.40 E |
| Baikeshu | 106 | 30.26 N | 118.55 E |
| Baikonur → Bajkonyr | 86 | 47.50 N | 66.03 E |
| Baikunthapur | 272b | 22.59 N | 88.13 E |
| Baikunthpur | 124 | 23.15 N | 82.33 E |
| Bailadores | 246 | 8.15 N | 71.50 W |
| Bailaiqiao | 100 | 32.40 N | 118.23 E |
| Bailang | 89 | 46.57 N | 120.05 E |
| Baildon | 44 | 53.52 N | 1.46 W |
| Baile | 105 | 39.55 N | 114.51 E |
| Baile Átha Luain → Athlone | 48 | 53.25 N | 7.56 W |
| Băile Govora | 38 | 45.05 N | 24.11 E |
| Băile Herculane | 38 | 44.54 N | 22.25 E |
| Bailén | 34 | 38.06 N | 3.46 W |
| Băile Olănești | 38 | 45.11 N | 24.16 E |
| Băilești | 38 | 44.02 N | 23.21 E |
| Bailey | 192 | 35.46 N | 78.07 W |
| Bailey Lakes | 214 | 40.57 N | 82.21 W |
| Bailey Run ≃ | 279b | 40.35 N | 79.47 W |
| Baileys Crossroads | 284c | 38.51 N | 77.08 W |
| Bail Hongal | 122 | 15.49 N | 74.52 E |
| Bailian | 102 | 24.09 N | 112.22 E |
| Bailicun | 102 | 25.45 N | 110.33 E |
| Bailieborough | 48 | 53.54 N | 6.59 W |
| Bailin, Zhg. | 100 | 27.12 N | 120.10 E |
| Bailin, Zhg. | 100 | 26.20 N | 113.18 E |
| Bailin, Zhg. | 107 | 29.11 N | 105.57 E |
| Bailin, Zhg. | 107 | 28.45 N | 106.26 E |
| Bailingmiao → Darhan Muminggan Lianheqi | 102 | 41.50 N | 110.27 E |
| Bailique | 250 | 0.58 N | 50.04 W |
| Bailique, Ilha I | 250 | 1.02 N | 49.58 W |
| Bailleau-sous-Gallardon | 261 | 48.32 N | 1.39 E |
| Bailleul | 50 | 50.44 N | 2.44 E |
| Ba Illi | 146 | 10.30 N | 16.34 E |
| Baillie ≃ | 176 | 65.10 N | 104.24 W |
| Baillie Islands II | 176 | 70.33 N | 128.10 W |
| Baillif | 241o | 16.01 N | 61.45 W |
| Bailly-Romainvilliers | 261 | 48.50 N | 2.49 E |
| Bailong ≃ | 102 | 32.18 N | 105.42 E |
| Bailonggang | 106 | 31.15 N | 121.44 E |
| Bailu ≃ | 100 | 32.25 N | 115.34 E |
| Bailuchang | 107 | 28.56 N | 105.57 E |
| Bailu Hu ⊜ | 100 | 30.03 N | 113.06 E |
| Bailundo | 152 | 12.12 S | 15.52 E |
| Bailuoji | 100 | 29.37 N | 113.15 E |
| Baima, Zhg. | 106 | 31.35 N | 119.10 E |
| Baima, Zhg. | 107 | 30.03 N | 103.44 E |
| Baima, Zhg. | 107 | 29.09 N | 104.16 E |
| Baimachang, Zhg. | 102 | 29.18 N | 107.30 E |
| Baimachang, Zhg. | 104 | 41.59 N | 122.30 E |
| Baimachang, Zhg. | 107 | 29.40 N | 103.54 E |
| Baimaguan | 105 | 40.41 N | 116.52 E |
| Baimakou | 102 | 25.55 N | 102.06 E |
| Baimamiao, Zhg. | 102 | 36.58 N | 108.08 E |
| Baimamiao, Zhg. | 107 | 29.33 N | 104.59 E |
| Baimao, Zhg. | 106 | 31.39 N | 120.52 E |
| Baimao, Zhg. | 106 | 31.35 N | 120.54 E |
| Baima Shan ʌ | 102 | 27.12 N | 110.32 E |
| Baimashi | 100 | 29.15 N | 118.42 E |
| Baimazhai | 100 | 28.06 N | 115.50 E |
| Baimiaozi, Zhg. | 89 | 46.18 N | 123.35 E |
| Baimiaozi, Zhg. | 98 | 40.34 N | 120.36 E |
| Baimiaozi, Zhg. | 104 | 41.55 N | 122.12 E |
| Baimiaozi, Zhg. | 107 | 29.47 N | 106.29 E |
| Baimuqiao | 106 | 32.01 N | 120.19 E |
| Baimuru | 164 | 7.30 S | 144.49 E |
| Bain ≃ | 44 | 53.05 N | 0.12 W |
| Baïna Bondio | 152 | 5.10 N | 16.33 E |
| Bainang | 120 | 29.11 N | 89.12 E |
| Bainbridge, Ga., U.S. | 192 | 30.54 N | 84.34 W |
| Bainbridge, N.Y., U.S. | 210 | 42.17 N | 75.28 W |
| Bainbridge, Oh., U.S. | 218 | 39.13 N | 83.16 W |
| Bainbridge, Pa., U.S. | 208 | 40.05 N | 76.40 W |
| Bainbridge Island I | 224 | 47.37 N | 122.33 W |
| Bainchi | 126 | 23.07 N | 88.14 E |
| Bainchipota | 272b | 22.52 N | 88.16 E |
| Bain-de-Bretagne | 32 | 47.50 N | 1.41 W |
| Baindt | 58 | 47.51 N | 9.40 E |
| Baing | 115b | 10.14 S | 120.34 E |
| Bainiqiao | 100 | 29.35 N | 114.09 E |
| Bains-les-Bains | 58 | 48.00 N | 6.16 E |
| Bainville | 198 | 48.08 N | 104.13 W |
| Bainyik | 164 | 3.40 S | 143.00 E |
| Baio Grande | 34 | 43.09 N | 8.58 W |
| Baiona | 34 | 42.07 N | 8.51 W |
| Baipeng | 102 | 24.09 N | 109.25 E |
| Baipu | 106 | 32.15 N | 120.46 E |
| Baiqibao | 104 | 41.48 N | 122.30 E |
| Baiqiu | 100 | 32.44 N | 112.38 E |
| Baiquan, Zhg. | 89 | 47.36 N | 126.07 E |
| Baiquan, Zhg. | 100 | 30.06 N | 122.08 E |
| Baiqueyuan | 100 | 31.48 N | 115.05 E |
| Bair, Pa., U.S. | 208 | 39.54 N | 76.50 W |
| Bā'ir, Urd. | 132 | 30.46 N | 36.41 E |
| Bā'ir, Wādī V | 132 | 30.58 N | 37.09 E |
| Bairab Co ⊜ | 120 | 35.00 N | 83.03 E |
| Baird | 196 | 32.23 N | 99.23 W |
| Baird, Mount ʌ | 202 | 43.22 N | 111.06 W |
| Bairdford | 214 | 40.37 N | 79.52 W |
| Baird Inlet c | 180 | 60.45 N | 164.00 W |
| Baird Mountains ʎ | 180 | 67.35 N | 161.30 W |
| Baire | 240p | 20.19 N | 76.20 W |
| Bairiki | 174t | 1.20 N | 173.01 E |
| Bairin Zuoqi | 90 | 44.00 N | 119.00 E |
| Bair Island I | 282 | 37.32 N | 122.13 W |
| Bairkum | 85 | 42.05 N | 68.11 E |
| Bairnsdale | 166 | 37.50 S | 147.38 E |
| Bairoil | 200 | 42.14 N | 107.33 W |
| Bairrinho | 256 | 22.36 S | 47.06 W |
| Bairro Alto | 256 | 23.29 S | 45.21 W |
| Bairuopu | 100 | 28.12 N | 112.46 E |
| Bais, Fr. | 32 | 48.15 N | 0.22 W |
| Bais, Pil. | 116 | 9.35 N | 123.07 E |
| Baïse ≃ | 32 | 44.17 N | 0.18 E |
| Baisha, Zhg. | 100 | 29.26 N | 119.16 E |
| Baisha, Zhg. | 100 | 25.40 N | 118.59 E |
| Baisha, Zhg. | 100 | 25.24 N | 117.16 E |
| Baisha, Zhg. | 100 | 34.22 N | 112.32 E |
| Baisha, Zhg. | 100 | 26.58 N | 115.22 E |
| Baisha, Zhg. | 100 | 24.39 N | 113.31 E |
| Baisha, Zhg. | 100 | 34.20 N | 113.14 E |
| Baisha, Zhg. | 107 | 28.55 N | 105.45 E |
| Baisha, Zhg. | 107 | 29.04 N | 106.07 E |
| Baisha, Zhg. | 110 | 19.17 N | 109.27 E |
| Baishaba | 107 | 30.03 N | 106.21 E |
| Bai Shan I | 106 | 30.35 N | 121.43 E |
| Baishanji | 100 | 33.48 N | 116.40 E |
| Baishantu | 104 | 42.21 N | 122.35 E |
| Baishapu | 100 | 29.58 N | 115.04 E |
| Baishatan | 98 | 36.52 N | 121.38 E |
| Baishe | 100 | 27.02 N | 116.20 E |
| Baishecun | 105 | 40.10 N | 116.18 E |
| Baishi, Zhg. | 100 | 27.18 N | 119.45 E |
| Baishi, Zhg. | 100 | 26.48 N | 119.46 E |
| Baishi, Zhg. | 102 | 22.36 N | 110.55 E |
| Baishidu | 100 | 25.26 N | 113.01 E |
| Baishiyi | 107 | 29.29 N | 106.22 E |
| Baishizhai | 104 | 40.57 N | 122.58 E |
| Baishui, Zhg. | 100 | 28.42 N | 113.04 E |
| Baishui, Zhg. | 106 | 30.34 N | 119.39 E |
| Baishui, Zhg. | 107 | 30.06 N | 105.38 E |
| Baishuifan | 100 | 30.17 N | 115.43 E |
| Baishuijiang | 102 | 33.29 N | 106.01 E |
| Baishun | 100 | 25.12 N | 114.01 E |
| Baishuxia | 100 | 27.22 N | 113.41 E |
| Baisinga | 126 | 21.39 N | 86.54 E |
| Baisley Pond ⊜ | 276 | 40.41 N | 73.47 W |
| Baisogala | 76 | 55.38 N | 23.43 E |
| Bāisrasi | 126 | 23.27 N | 90.02 E |
| Baita, India | 272b | 22.27 N | 88.11 E |
| Baita, Zhg. | 106 | 31.48 N | 119.35 E |
| Baitadī | 124 | 29.32 N | 80.26 E |
| Baital | 126 | 22.57 N | 87.28 E |
| Baitazi | 98 | 42.19 N | 120.19 E |
| Baitazibeigou | 104 | 42.17 N | 120.48 E |
| Bai Thuong | 110 | 19.54 N | 105.23 E |
| Baitings Reservoir ⊜[1] | 262 | 53.40 N | 1.59 W |
| Baitou | 107 | 30.37 N | 103.36 E |
| Baitoutan | 102 | 32.30 N | 106.56 E |
| Baitu | 106 | 31.59 N | 119.21 E |
| Baitugang | 100 | 33.28 N | 112.22 E |
| Baiwang | 102 | 24.14 N | 108.32 E |
| Baiwen | 102 | 38.15 N | 111.06 E |
| Baixa da Banheira | 266c | 38.39 N | 9.03 W |
| Baixa Grande | 255 | 11.57 S | 40.11 W |
| Baixi | 107 | 29.39 N | 106.28 E |
| Baixiang | 98 | 37.32 N | 114.34 E |
| Baixingt | 89 | 43.08 N | 121.03 E |
| Baixio | 250 | 6.44 S | 38.43 W |
| Baixo Longa | 152 | 15.42 S | 18.50 E |
| Baiyan, Zhg. | 100 | 28.04 N | 120.02 E |
| Baiyan, Zhg. | 106 | 31.08 N | 119.38 E |
| Baiyang | 100 | 34.25 N | 112.12 E |
| Baiyang Dian ⊜ | 98 | 38.53 N | 116.00 E |
| Baiyanghe | 86 | 43.13 N | 88.28 E |
| Baiyan Shan ʌ | 100 | 26.05 N | 118.25 E |
| Baiyer River | 164 | 5.35 S | 144.10 E |
| Baiyin | 102 | 36.47 N | 104.07 E |
| Baiyinheshuo | 89 | 44.31 N | 119.51 E |
| Baiyintaohai | 89 | 43.12 N | 120.23 E |
| Baiyü, Zhg. | 102 | 31.18 N | 98.49 E |
| Baiyu, Zhg. | 105 | 40.01 N | 115.37 E |
| Baiyundu | 100 | 26.10 N | 118.47 E |
| Baiyunguan | 271a | 39.54 N | 116.19 E |
| Baizhongpu | 100 | 33.22 N | 114.50 E |
| Baizi | 107 | 30.06 N | 105.43 E |
| Baja | 30 | 46.11 N | 18.57 E |
| Baja, Punta › | 232 | 29.58 N | 115.49 W |
| Baja California | 200 | 32.18 N | 115.12 W |
| Baja California □[3] | 232 | 30.00 N | 115.00 W |
| Baja California ›[1] | 232 | 28.00 N | 113.30 W |
| Baja California Seamount Province ✦ | 16 | 26.00 N | 124.00 W |
| Baja California Sur □[3] | 232 | 26.00 N | 112.00 W |
| Bajada del Agrio | 252 | 38.23 S | 70.02 W |
| Baján | 196 | 26.32 N | 101.15 W |
| Bajan Adraga | 88 | 48.32 N | 111.03 E |
| Bajan Agt | 88 | 49.02 N | 102.05 E |
| Bajanaul | 86 | 50.47 N | 75.42 E |
| Bajancagaan | 102 | 45.00 N | 98.59 E |
| Bajan Chajrchan | 88 | 49.18 N | 96.20 E |
| Bajanchongor | 90 | 46.08 N | 100.43 E |
| Bajanchongor □[4] | 102 | 45.00 N | 99.30 E |
| Bajancogt | 88 | 45.54 N | 106.10 E |
| Bajandaj | 88 | 53.04 N | 105.30 E |
| Bajandalaj | 102 | 43.28 N | 103.28 E |
| Bajandelger, Mong. | 88 | 47.44 N | 108.07 E |
| Bajandelger, Mong. | 102 | 45.40 N | 112.20 E |
| Bajan Dün | 88 | 49.13 N | 113.23 E |
| Bajandžargalan | 102 | 45.40 N | 107.59 E |
| Bajan Dzürch | 88 | 50.12 N | 98.58 E |
| Bajan-Enger | 86 | 48.25 N | 90.50 E |
| Bajango | 88 | 48.55 N | 106.06 E |
| Bajangol, Ross. | 88 | 50.44 N | 103.27 E |
| Bajan-Gol, Ross. | 88 | 52.49 N | 99.54 E |
| Bajangov' | 102 | 44.44 N | 100.24 E |
| Bajanleg | 102 | 44.33 N | 100.50 E |
| Bajan Nuur | 86 | 48.54 N | 91.14 E |
| Bajanölgij □[4] | 86 | 48.20 N | 89.50 E |
| Bajan-Öndör | 102 | 44.47 N | 98.39 E |
| Bajan-Ovoo, Mong. | 88 | 47.47 N | 112.05 E |
| Bajan-Ovoo, Mong. | 102 | 42.57 N | 106.07 E |
| Bajánsenye | 30 | 46.48 N | 16.23 E |
| Bajan Tümen | 88 | 48.04 N | 114.24 E |
| Bajan Uul, Mong. | 88 | 47.40 N | 101.30 E |
| Bajan Uul, Mong. | 88 | 49.10 N | 112.50 E |
| Bajan Uul, Mong. | 88 | 49.41 N | 96.20 E |
| Bājaur □[9] | 123 | 34.50 N | 71.30 E |
| Baja Verapaz □[5] | 236 | 15.05 N | 90.20 W |
| Bajawa | 115b | 8.47 S | 120.59 E |
| Bajbičetau ʎ | 85 | 41.12 N | 75.15 E |
| Baj-Chak | 88 | 51.13 N | 94.34 E |
| Bajčunas | 80 | 47.14 N | 52.55 E |
| Bajčurovo | 80 | 51.20 N | 42.41 E |
| Bajdarackaja guba c | 72 | 69.00 N | 67.30 E |
| Bajconovo | 88 | 54.17 N | 104.38 E |
| Bajdrag ≃ | 102 | 45.38 N | 99.15 E |
| Bājegūn, Kūh-e ʌ | 128 | 31.28 N | 55.51 E |
| Bājengdoba | 124 | 25.54 N | 90.31 E |
| Bāje Phukura | 126 | 23.09 N | 89.45 E |
| Bajer | 88 | 55.44 N | 99.30 E |
| Bajestān | 128 | 34.31 N | 58.10 E |
| Bajevo | 86 | 53.17 N | 80.46 E |
| Bajganin | 86 | 48.43 N | 55.53 E |
| Bajgekum | 86 | 44.18 N | 66.28 E |
| Bajghera | 272a | 28.32 N | 77.01 E |
| Bājgīrān | 128 | 37.36 N | 58.24 E |
| Bajgul | 80 | 48.49 N | 49.08 E |
| Bajiaotai | 104 | 41.14 N | 121.14 E |
| Bajiazi, Zhg. | 104 | 42.17 N | 122.37 E |
| Bajiazi, Zhg. | 104 | 42.21 N | 121.27 E |
| Bajiazi, Zhg. | 104 | 41.36 N | 123.53 E |
| Bājil | 144 | 15.04 N | 43.16 E |
| Bajimba, Mount ʌ | 166 | 29.18 S | 152.07 E |
| Bajina Bašta | 38 | 43.58 N | 19.34 E |
| Bajkadam | 85 | 43.44 N | 69.55 E |
| Bajkal | 88 | 51.53 N | 104.47 E |
| Bajkal, ozero (Lake Baikal) ⊜ | 88 | 53.00 N | 107.40 E |
| Bajkalovo, Ross. | 86 | 57.24 N | 63.46 E |
| Bajkalovo, Ross. | 86 | 57.45 N | 67.40 E |
| Bajkal'sk | 88 | 51.33 N | 104.05 E |
| Bajkal'skij chrebet ʎ | 88 | 55.00 N | 108.40 E |
| Bajkal'skij zapovednik ♦ | 88 | 51.25 N | 105.10 E |
| Bajkal'skoje | 88 | 55.21 N | 109.12 E |
| Bajkit | 74 | 61.41 N | 96.25 E |
| Bajkonur | 86 | 47.50 N | 66.03 E |
| Bajkovo | 80 | 54.47 N | 44.51 E |
| Bajmak | 86 | 52.36 N | 58.19 E |
| Bajmok | 38 | 45.58 N | 19.25 E |
| Bajnazar | 86 | 48.32 N | 73.42 E |
| Bajo, Indon. | 112 | 0.27 N | 120.48 E |
| Bajo, Indon. | 115b | 8.35 S | 119.01 E |
| Bajo, Canal ≅ | 266a | 40.27 N | 3.43 W |
| Bajo Baudó | 246 | 4.58 N | 77.22 W |
| Bajo Boquete | 236 | 8.47 N | 82.26 W |
| Bajool | 166 | 23.39 S | 150.39 E |
| Bajos de Haina | 238 | 18.25 N | 70.02 W |
| Bajos del Balsamar | 234 | 17.34 N | 100.48 W |
| Bajr'aki | 80 | 54.43 N | 53.24 E |
| Bajram-Ali | 128 | 37.37 N | 62.10 E |
| Bajsa | 88 | 53.58 N | 113.33 E |
| Bajseit | 85 | 43.35 N | 78.20 E |
| Baj-Sot | 88 | 51.42 N | 95.22 E |
| Bajsun | 85 | 38.14 N | 67.12 E |
| Bajtajlak | 86 | 45.15 N | 75.00 E |
| Bajulmati | 115a | 7.56 S | 114.23 E |
| Bajžansaj | 85 | 43.13 N | 69.56 E |
| Bak | 61 | 46.43 N | 16.51 E |
| Bakacak | 130 | 40.12 N | 27.06 E |
| Bakal | 86 | 54.56 N | 58.48 E |
| Bakala | 152 | 6.11 N | 20.22 E |
| Bakaldy | 80 | 55.39 N | 44.44 E |
| Bakali ≃ | 152 | 4.34 S | 17.06 E |
| Bakaly | 80 | 55.10 N | 53.48 E |
| Bakambe | 152 | 5.39 S | 23.37 E |
| Bakanas | 86 | 44.50 N | 76.15 E |
| Bakanas ≃ | 86 | 47.05 N | 79.18 E |
| Bakap | 114 | 4.26 N | 101.04 E |
| Bakar | 116 | 7.09 N | 125.42 E |
| Bākarganj | 124 | 22.33 N | 90.21 E |
| Bakaruma | 124 | 22.32 N | 83.25 E |
| Bakau, Pulau I | 271c | 1.16 N | 103.43 E |
| Bakbakty | 86 | 44.35 N | 76.40 E |
| Bakčar | 86 | 57.01 N | 82.05 E |
| Bakčar ≃ | 86 | 57.37 N | 82.18 E |
| Bake | 112 | 3.03 S | 100.16 E |
| Bakebe | 152 | 5.35 N | 9.33 E |
| Bakel | 150 | 14.54 N | 12.27 W |
| Bakem | 112 | 1.58 S | 105.54 E |
| Bakenkop | 158 | 28.01 S | 23.02 E |
| Bakeoven Creek ≃ | 224 | 45.12 N | 121.05 W |
| Baker, Ca., U.S. | 204 | 35.15 N | 116.04 W |
| Baker, Fl., U.S. | 194 | 30.47 N | 86.40 W |
| Baker, La., U.S. | 194 | 30.35 N | 91.10 W |
| Baker, Mt., U.S. | 198 | 46.22 N | 104.17 W |
| Baker, Or., U.S. | 202 | 44.46 N | 117.49 W |
| Baker ≃, Chile | 254 | 47.49 S | 73.37 W |
| Baker ≃, Wa., U.S. | 224 | 48.38 N | 121.41 W |
| Baker, Canal ɥ | 254 | 48.00 S | 74.00 W |
| Baker, Mount ʌ | 224 | 48.47 N | 121.49 W |
| Baker Butte ʌ | 200 | 34.27 N | 111.22 W |
| Baker Canyon V | 280 | 33.47 N | 117.38 W |
| Baker Creek ≃, B.C., Can. | 182 | 52.59 N | 122.30 W |
| Baker Creek ≃, Oh., U.S. | 279a | 41.21 N | 81.54 W |
| Baker Creek ≃, Or., U.S. | 224 | 45.15 N | 123.14 W |
| Baker Island I, Oc. | 14 | 0.15 N | 176.27 W |
| Baker Island I, Ak., U.S. | 182 | 55.20 N | 133.36 W |
| Baker Lake | 176 | 64.15 N | 96.00 W |
| Baker Lake ⊜, Austl. | 162 | 26.54 S | 126.05 E |
| Baker Lake ⊜, N.T., Can. | 176 | 64.10 N | 95.30 W |
| Baker Lake ⊜, Il., U.S. | 278 | 42.08 N | 88.07 W |
| Baker Lake ⊜[1] | 224 | 48.43 N | 121.37 W |
| Bakersfield | 226 | 35.22 N | 119.01 W |
| Bakersfield South | 228 | 35.20 N | 119.03 W |
| Bakers Hill | 168a | 31.45 S | 116.27 E |
| Bakers Island I | 283 | 42.32 N | 70.47 W |
| Bakerstown | 214 | 40.39 N | 79.56 W |
| Baker Street | 260 | 51.30 N | 0.21 E |
| Bakersville, N.C., U.S. | 192 | 36.00 N | 82.09 W |
| Bakersville, Oh., U.S. | 214 | 40.21 N | 81.39 W |
| Bakerville | 158 | 26.00 S | 26.06 E |
| Bakeshu | 98 | 42.26 N | 124.37 E |
| Bâ Kêv | 110 | 13.42 N | 107.12 E |
| Bakewell | 44 | 53.13 N | 1.40 W |
| Bakhchysaray | 78 | 44.45 N | 33.51 E |
| Bakhmach | 78 | 51.13 N | 32.46 E |
| Bakhmut ≃ | 83 | 48.56 N | 38.03 E |
| Bakhmutivka | 83 | 48.52 N | 39.03 E |
| Bakhra | 126 | 22.24 N | 88.11 E |
| Bākhrābād | 126 | 23.43 N | 90.53 E |
| Bakhri | 124 | 25.35 N | 86.16 E |
| Bākhtarān (Kermānshāh) | 128 | 34.19 N | 47.04 E |
| Bakhtarān □[4] | 128 | 34.30 N | 47.00 E |
| Bakhtegān, Daryācheh-ye ⊜ | 128 | 29.20 N | 54.05 E |
| Bakhtiyārpur | 124 | 25.28 N | 85.31 E |
| Bakhuis | 250 | 4.42 N | 56.49 W |
| Bakı (Baku) | 84 | 40.23 N | 49.51 E |
| Bakile | 154 | 13.58 S | 35.15 E |
| Bakino | 82 | 56.20 N | 38.59 E |
| Bakinskaja | 78 | 44.46 N | 39.18 E |
| Bakır ≃ | 130 | 38.55 N | 27.00 E |
| Bakitabu | 154 | 1.29 S | 35.34 E |
| Bakkafjörður | 24a | 66.04 N | 14.45 W |
| Bakkaflói c | 24a | 66.10 N | 14.45 W |
| Bakkagerði | 24a | 65.32 N | 13.48 W |
| Bakkeswar | 272b | 22.25 N | 88.22 E |
| Bakkeveen | 52 | 53.05 N | 6.15 E |
| Baklan | 130 | 37.58 N | 29.36 E |
| Baklanka | 76 | 58.43 N | 40.06 E |
| Bakloh | 123 | 32.28 N | 75.55 E |
| Bakluši | 80 | 52.07 N | 43.22 E |
| Bako, C. Iv. | 150 | 9.09 N | 7.37 W |
| Bako, Ityo. | 144 | 5.50 N | 36.40 E |
| Bakony ʎ | 30 | 47.15 N | 17.50 E |
| Bakool □[4] | 144 | 4.00 N | 44.00 E |
| Bakoondfontein | 158 | 32.43 S | 22.30 E |
| Bakori | 150 | 11.34 N | 7.27 E |
| Bakou → Bakı | 84 | 40.23 N | 49.51 E |
| Bakouma | 152 | 5.42 N | 22.47 E |
| Bakovka | 265b | 55.41 N | 37.20 E |
| Bakoy ≃ | 150 | 13.49 N | 10.50 W |
| Bakruz'ak | 86 | 52.59 N | 58.42 E |
| Baksan | 84 | 43.40 N | 43.32 E |
| Baksan ≃ | 84 | 43.42 N | 43.32 E |
| Bakšejevo, Ross. | 80 | 55.44 N | 39.53 E |
| Bakšejevo, Ross. | 86 | 57.26 N | 73.00 E |
| Baksir Chāndpur | 126 | 23.30 N | 89.44 E |
| Bakšty | 76 | 53.56 N | 26.11 E |
| Baksuk ≃ | 86 | 51.50 N | 69.30 E |
| Baku → Bakı | 84 | 40.23 N | 49.51 E |
| Bakulin Point › | 116 | 8.33 N | 126.22 E |
| Bakum | 52 | 52.45 N | 8.11 E |
| Bakumpai | 112 | 1.26 S | 113.05 E |
| Bakun | 120 | 32.32 N | 80.26 E |
| Bakung, Pulau I | 112 | 0.04 N | 104.27 E |
| Bakungan | 114 | 2.56 N | 97.30 E |
| Bakuriani | 84 | 41.46 N | 43.32 E |
| Bakury | 80 | 52.22 N | 44.42 E |
| Bakwa-Kenge | 152 | 4.51 S | 22.04 E |
| Bakwanga → Mbuji-Mayi | 152 | 6.09 S | 23.38 E |
| Bakyrly | 86 | 44.21 N | 67.48 E |
| Bal ≃ | 126 | 21.58 N | 89.21 E |
| Bala, On., Can. | 212 | 45.01 N | 79.37 W |
| Bala, Sén. | 150 | 14.02 N | 13.10 W |
| Balâ, Tür. | 130 | 39.34 N | 33.08 E |
| Bala, Wales, U.K. | 42 | 52.54 N | 3.35 W |
| Balabac | 116 | 7.59 N | 117.04 E |
| Balabac Island I | 116 | 7.57 N | 117.01 E |
| Balabac Strait ɥ | 112 | 7.35 N | 117.00 E |
| Bālā Bāgh | 120 | 34.24 N | 70.14 E |
| Ba'labakk | 130 | 34.00 N | 36.12 E |
| Balabalagan, Kepulauan II | 112 | 2.20 S | 117.25 E |
| Balaban | 130 | 38.28 N | 37.36 E |
| Balabanovo | 82 | 55.11 N | 36.40 E |
| Balabio, Île I | 175f | 20.07 S | 164.11 E |
| Balabyne | 78 | 47.44 N | 35.13 E |
| Balachčin | 86 | 54.09 N | 89.23 E |
| Balachna | 80 | 56.30 N | 43.36 E |
| Balachta | 86 | 55.24 N | 91.37 E |
| Balachtison, gora ʌ | 86 | 54.36 N | 93.50 E |
| Balaci | 38 | 44.21 N | 24.55 E |
| Bala-Cynwyd | 285 | 40.00 N | 75.14 W |
| Balad | 128 | 34.01 N | 44.09 E |
| Baladbandh | 272b | 22.52 N | 88.07 E |
| Balad'ok | 89 | 53.41 N | 133.07 E |
| Balagansk | 88 | 53.57 N | 103.02 E |
| Bālāghāt | 120 | 21.48 N | 80.11 E |
| Bālāghāt Range ʎ | 122 | 18.45 N | 76.30 E |
| Balagny-sur-Thérain | 50 | 49.18 N | 2.20 E |
| Balaguer | 34 | 41.47 N | 0.49 E |
| Balaikarangan | 112 | 0.50 N | 110.26 E |
| Balaiselasa | 112 | 1.48 S | 100.50 E |
| Balaisepuah | 112 | 0.27 N | 111.13 E |
| Balaj | 86 | 55.52 N | 93.59 E |
| Balaka | 152 | 4.51 S | 19.57 E |
| Balakän | 84 | 41.43 N | 46.26 E |
| Balakété | 152 | 6.56 N | 19.54 E |
| Balakirevo | 82 | 56.30 N | 38.51 E |
| Balaklava, Austl. | 168b | 34.09 S | 138.25 E |
| Balaklava, Ukr. | 78 | 44.30 N | 33.36 E |
| Balakliya, Ukr. | 78 | 49.14 N | 31.44 E |
| Balakliya, Ukr. | 78 | 49.27 N | 36.52 E |
| Bālākot | 123 | 34.33 N | 73.21 E |
| Balakovo | 80 | 52.02 N | 47.47 E |
| Balal, Laga ≃ | 154 | 3.25 N | 37.15 E |
| Balallan | 46 | 58.05 N | 6.35 W |
| Balama, Moç. | 154 | 13.20 S | 38.30 E |
| Bal'amā, Urd. | 132 | 32.14 N | 36.05 E |
| Balamban | 116 | 10.30 N | 123.42 E |
| Balambangan, Pulau I | 112 | 7.15 N | 116.55 E |
| Bālā Morghāb | 128 | 35.35 N | 63.20 E |
| Bālandi | 272b | 22.58 N | 88.32 E |
| Balanga | 116 | 14.41 N | 120.32 E |
| Balangala | 152 | 0.24 N | 19.45 E |
| Ba Lang An, Mui › | 110 | 15.14 N | 108.56 E |
| Balangero | 62 | 45.16 N | 7.31 E |
| Balangiga | 116 | 11.07 N | 125.23 E |
| Balāngīr | 122 | 20.43 N | 83.29 E |
| Balanguingui Island I | 116 | 6.01 N | 121.41 E |
| Bālān Şafar 'Ali | 128 | 38.59 N | 47.27 E |
| Balanşūrah | 142 | 27.55 N | 30.41 E |
| Balantak, Gunung ʌ | 112 | 0.45 S | 123.20 E |
| Balapulang | 115a | 7.03 S | 109.05 E |
| Bālāpur | 122 | 20.40 N | 76.46 E |
| Balaqs | 273c | 30.10 N | 31.17 E |
| Balaqṭar | 142 | 31.05 N | 30.13 E |
| Balaraja | 115a | 6.12 S | 106.27 E |
| Balarāmbāti | 272b | 22.48 N | 88.13 E |
| Balarāmpota | 272b | 22.31 N | 88.08 E |
| Balarāmpur | 126 | 23.07 N | 86.13 E |
| Balaruc-le-Vieux | 62 | 43.27 N | 3.41 E |
| Balaši | 80 | 51.24 N | 49.55 E |
| Balašicha | 82 | 55.49 N | 37.58 E |
| Balašov | 80 | 51.32 N | 43.08 E |
| Balassagyarmat | 30 | 48.05 N | 19.18 E |
| Balāṭ | 140 | 25.33 N | 29.16 E |
| Balatan, Indon. | 164 | 6.05 S | 134.45 E |
| Balatan, Pil. | 116 | 13.20 N | 123.10 E |
| Balatina | 38 | 47.42 N | 27.21 E |
| Balaton | 198 | 44.14 N | 95.52 W |
| Balaton ⊜ | 30 | 46.50 N | 17.45 E |
| Balaurin | 112 | 8.15 S | 123.43 E |
| Balavé | 150 | 12.23 N | 4.09 W |
| Balaxanı | 84 | 40.29 N | 49.54 E |
| Balayan | 116 | 13.57 N | 120.44 E |
| Balayan Bay c | 116 | 13.51 N | 120.47 E |
| Balazote | 34 | 38.53 N | 2.08 W |
| Balbi, Mount ʌ[1] | 175e | 5.55 S | 154.59 E |
| Balbieriškis | 76 | 54.32 N | 23.52 E |
| Balbigny | 62 | 45.49 N | 4.11 E |
| Balbina, Represa ⊜[1] | 246 | 1.20 S | 59.40 W |
| Balboa | 236 | 8.57 N | 79.34 W |
| Balbriggan | 48 | 53.37 N | 6.11 W |
| Balcad | 144 | 2.23 N | 45.23 E |
| Balcanoona | 166 | 30.31 S | 139.18 E |
| Balcarce | 252 | 37.50 S | 58.15 W |
| Balcarres | 184 | 50.48 N | 103.33 W |
| Bălcești | 38 | 44.37 N | 23.56 E |
| Balchaš | 86 | 46.49 N | 74.59 E |
| Balchaš, ozero (Lake Balkhash) ⊜ | 86 | 46.00 N | 74.00 E |
| Balch Springs | 222 | 32.43 N | 96.37 W |
| Balcı | 130 | 38.43 N | 34.06 E |
| Balčik | 38 | 43.25 N | 28.10 E |
| Balclutha | 172 | 46.14 S | 169.44 E |
| Balcombe | 42 | 51.04 N | 0.08 W |
| Balcones Escarpment ⏏[4] | 196 | 29.30 N | 99.15 W |
| Balde | 252 | 33.20 S | 66.38 W |
| Baldeador | 287a | 22.53 S | 43.02 W |
| Bald Eagle | 214 | 40.42 N | 78.12 W |
| Bald Eagle Creek ≃ | 210 | 41.08 N | 77.24 W |
| Bald Eagle Mountain ʌ | 214 | 41.00 N | 77.45 W |
| Bald Eagle State Park ♦ | 214 | 41.00 N | 77.40 W |
| Baldegger See ⊜ | 58 | 47.12 N | 8.16 E |
| Baldeneysee ⊜ | 263 | 51.24 N | 7.03 E |
| Balderschwang | 58 | 47.28 N | 10.06 E |
| Balderstone | 262 | 53.47 N | 2.34 W |
| Balderton | 44 | 53.03 N | 0.47 W |
| Bald Head › | 162 | 35.07 S | 118.01 E |
| Bald Hill ʌ[2] | 166 | 20.18 S | 144.06 E |
| Bald Hill Branch ≃ | 284c | 18.55 N | 76.49 W |
| Baldhill Creek ≃ | 198 | 47.09 N | 98.03 W |
| Bald Hills | 171a | 27.19 S | 153.01 E |
| Baldichieri d'Asti | 62 | 44.54 N | 8.07 E |
| Baldim | 255 | 19.17 S | 43.57 W |
| Bald Island I | 162 | 34.55 S | 118.27 E |
| Bald Knob | 194 | 35.18 N | 91.34 W |
| Bald Knob ʌ, Ca., U.S. | 282 | 37.25 N | 122.21 W |
| Bald Knob ʌ, Va., U.S. | 192 | 37.56 N | 79.51 W |
| Bald Knoll ʌ | 200 | 42.24 N | 110.29 W |
| Bald Mountain ʌ, Ct., U.S. | 207 | 41.59 N | 72.25 W |
| Bald Mountain ʌ, Nv., U.S. | 226 | 38.33 N | 119.07 W |
| Bald Mountain ʌ, Or., U.S. | 202 | 43.16 N | 121.21 W |
| Bald Mountain ʌ, Or., U.S. | 202 | 44.36 N | 117.53 W |
| Bald Mountain ʌ, Or., U.S. | 202 | 44.48 N | 123.33 W |
| Bald Mountain ʌ, Vt., U.S. | 210 | 42.55 N | 73.09 W |
| Bald Mountain State Recreation Area ♦ | 216 | 42.46 N | 83.14 W |
| Baldo, Monte ʌ | 64 | 45.47 N | 10.48 E |
| Baldock | 42 | 51.59 N | 0.12 W |
| Baldock Lake ⊜ | 184 | 56.33 N | 97.57 W |
| Baldone | 76 | 56.45 N | 24.24 E |
| Baldovino, Arroyo ≃ | 288 | 34.46 S | 58.07 W |
| Baldoyle | 48 | 53.24 N | 6.08 W |
| Baldpate Pond ⊜ | 283 | 42.42 N | 71.00 W |
| Balduinstein | 56 | 50.20 N | 7.58 E |
| Baldur | 184 | 49.23 N | 99.15 W |
| Baldwin, Fl., U.S. | 192 | 30.18 N | 81.58 W |
| Baldwin, La., U.S. | 194 | 29.50 N | 91.32 W |
| Baldwin, Mi., U.S. | 190 | 43.54 N | 85.51 W |
| Baldwin, N.Y., U.S. | 210 | 40.39 N | 73.36 W |
| Baldwin, Pa., U.S. | 214 | 40.23 N | 79.57 W |
| Baldwin, Wi., U.S. | 190 | 44.58 N | 92.22 W |
| Baldwin Bay c | 276 | 40.38 N | 73.35 W |
| Baldwin City | 198 | 38.46 N | 95.11 W |
| Baldwin Creek ≃ | 279a | 41.22 N | 81.51 W |
| Baldwin Hills ʎ[2] | 280 | 34.00 N | 118.22 W |
| Baldwin Lake ⊜ | 279a | 41.21 N | 81.51 W |
| Baldwin Park | 228 | 34.05 N | 117.57 W |
| Baldwin Peninsula ›[1] | 180 | 66.44 N | 162.15 W |
| Baldwinsville | 210 | 43.09 N | 76.19 W |
| Baldwinville | 207 | 42.36 N | 72.04 W |
| Baldwin-Wallace College ʊ[2] | 279a | 41.23 N | 81.51 W |
| Baldwyn | 194 | 34.31 N | 88.38 W |
| Baldy Mountain ʌ, B.C., Can. | 182 | 51.28 N | 120.02 W |
| Baldy Mountain ʌ, Mb., Can. | 184 | 51.28 N | 100.44 W |
| Baldy Mountain ʌ, Mt., U.S. | 202 | 48.09 N | 109.39 W |
| Baldy Mountain ʌ, N.M., U.S. | 200 | 36.38 N | 105.13 W |
| Baldy Peak ʌ | 200 | 33.55 N | 109.35 W |
| Bale, Hrv. | 64 | 45.02 N | 13.48 E |
| Bale, India | 272c | 19.08 N | 73.06 E |
| Bâle → Basel, Schw. | 58 | 47.33 N | 7.35 E |
| Bale □[4] | 144 | 6.20 N | 41.30 E |
| Bale-Akiosi | 273a | 6.41 N | 3.21 E |
| Balearen → Balears, Illes II | 34 | 39.30 N | 3.00 E |
| Baléares, Îles → Balears, Illes II | 34 | 39.30 N | 3.00 E |
| Balearic Islands → Balears, Illes II | 34 | 39.30 N | 3.00 E |
| Balears □[3] | 34 | 39.30 N | 3.00 E |
| Balears, Illes (Balearic Islands) II | 34 | 39.30 N | 3.00 E |
| Balease, Gunung ʌ | 112 | 2.24 S | 120.3[illegible] E |
| Balegane | 158 | 26.04 S | 31.34 E |
| Baleh ≃ | 112 | 2.01 N | 113.01 E |
| Baleia, Ponta da › | 255 | 17.40 S | 39.07 W |
| Baleine, Grande rivière de la ≃ | 176 | 55.16 N | 77.47 W |
| Baleine, Petite rivière de la ≃ | 176 | 56.00 N | 76.45 W |
| Baleine, Rivière à la ≃ | 176 | 58.15 N | 67.40 W |
| Balej | 88 | 51.36 N | 116.38 E |
| Balelasberg ʎ | 158 | 27.30 S | 30.07 E |
| Bale Mountains National Park ♦ | 144 | 7.00 N | 39.40 E |
| Bâle-Mulhouse, Aéroport ⊠ | 58 | 47.35 N | 7.32 E |
| Balen | 56 | 51.10 N | 5.09 E |
| Balena | 152 | 0.55 N | 20.00 E |
| Baleno | 116 | 12.28 N | 123.30 E |
| Baler | 116 | 15.46 N | 121.34 E |
| Baler Bay c | 116 | 15.50 N | 121.35 E |
| Baleshare I | 46 | 57.31 N | 7.22 W |
| Bāleshwar | 126 | 21.30 N | 86.56 E |
| Balesin Island I | 116 | 14.26 N | 122.02 E |
| Balestrand | 26 | 61.12 N | 6.32 E |
| Balestrate | 70 | 38.03 N | 13.00 E |
| Baléya | 150 | 9.15 N | 10.29 W |
| Baléyara | 150 | 13.47 N | 2.57 E |
| Balezino | 80 | 57.58 N | 53.00 E |
| Balfate | 236 | 15.48 N | 86.25 W |
| Balfes Creek | 166 | 20.13 S | 145.55 E |
| Balfour, N.Z. | 172 | 45.50 S | 168.35 E |
| Balfour, S. Afr. | 158 | 26.44 S | 28.31 E |
| Balfour, Scot., U.K. | 46 | 59.01 N | 2.55 W |
| Balfour, N.C., U.S. | 192 | 35.20 N | 82.28 W |
| Balfour Downs | 162 | 22.50 S | 120.50 E |
| Balfour Park ♦ | 273d | 26.08 S | 28.06 E |
| Balfron | 46 | 56.04 N | 4.20 W |
| Balgach | 58 | 47.25 N | 9.35 E |
| Bălgarija → Bulgaria □[1] | 38 | 43.00 N | 25.00 E |
| Balgazyn | 88 | 51.08 N | 95.00 E |
| Balgo | 162 | 20.09 S | 127.48 E |
| Balgowlah | 274a | 33.48 S | 151.16 E |
| Balguerie, Cap › | 174x | 9.45 S | 138.47 W |
| Balhannah | 168b | 35.00 S | 138.50 E |
| Bāli | 120 | 25.11 N | 73.17 E |
| Bali □[4] | 115b | 8.30 S | 115.00 E |
| Bali I | 115b | 8.20 S | 115.00 E |
| Bali, Laut (Bali Sea) ₸[2] | 112 | 7.45 S | 115.30 E |
| Bali, Selat ɥ | 112 | 8.18 S | 114.25 E |
| Bāliākāndi | 126 | 23.38 N | 89.33 E |
| Baliangao | 116 | 8.40 N | 123.36 E |
| Bāliāpāl | 126 | 21.40 N | 87.17 E |
| Bāliāti | 126 | 23.59 N | 90.03 E |
| Balibago | 116 | 13.37 N | 121.18 E |
| Bali Barat National Park ♦ | 115b | 8.15 S | 114.40 E |
| Baliceaux I | 241h | 12.57 N | 61.08 W |
| Bāli Chak | 126 | 22.22 N | 87.33 E |
| Balicuatro Islands II | 116 | 12.39 N | 124.24 E |
| Balicuatro Point › | 116 | 12.35 N | 124.16 E |
| Balidianzi | 98 | 41.13 N | 124.49 E |
| Bālidiha | 126 | 21.58 N | 86.38 E |
| Balige | 114 | 2.20 N | 99.04 E |
| Bālighai | 126 | 21.52 N | 87.35 E |
| Balihan | 98 | 41.29 N | 118.41 E |
| Bālihāti | 272b | 22.44 N | 88.19 E |
| Balıkesir | 130 | 39.39 N | 27.53 E |
| Balıkesir □[4] | 130 | 39.45 N | 27.50 E |
| Balık Gölü ⊜ | 84 | 39.47 N | 43.34 E |
| Balīkh ≃ | 130 | 35.52 N | 39.12 E |
| Balıklıtohma ≃ | 130 | 38.50 N | 37.41 E |
| Balikpapan | 112 | 1.17 S | 116.50 E |
| Balikumbat | 152 | 5.54 N | 10.23 E |
| Balimbing, Indon. | 112 | 5.55 S | 104.34 E |
| Balimbing, Pil. | 116 | 5.05 N | 119.58 E |
| Balimo | 164 | 8.03 S | 142.56 E |
| Balin | 89 | 48.19 N | 122.19 E |
| Balincollig | 48 | 51.53 N | 8.35 W |
| Balindong (Watu) | 116 | 7.55 N | 124.12 E |
| Baling | 114 | 5.40 N | 100.55 E |
| Balingasag | 116 | 8.45 N | 124.47 E |
| Balingen | 58 | 48.16 N | 8.51 E |
| Balingian | 112 | 2.55 N | 112.32 E |
| Balingup | 162 | 33.48 S | 115.58 E |
| Balintang Channel ɥ | 108 | 19.49 N | 121.40 E |
| Balintore | 46 | 57.45 N | 3.54 W |
| Balipu | 105 | 39.53 N | 117.48 E |
| Balışeyh | 130 | 39.56 N | 33.43 E |
| Baliuag | 116 | 14.57 N | 120.54 E |
| Baliung ≃ | 115a | 6.50 S | 105.52 E |
| Baliungan Island I | 116 | 5.09 N | 120.12 E |
| Baliyingzi | 104 | 41.59 N | 121.14 E |
| Baliza | 255 | 16.15 S | 52.25 W |
| Balizhuang, Zhg. | 105 | 39.16 N | 116.28 E |
| Balizhuang, Zhg. | 271a | 39.52 N | 116.28 E |
| Balk | 52 | 52.54 N | 5.34 E |
| Balkach, Lago → Balchaš, ozero ⊜ | 86 | 46.00 N | 74.00 E |
| Balkan □[8] | 128 | 39.30 N | 55.00 E |
| Balkan Mountains → Stara Planina ʎ | 38 | 42.45 N | 25.00 E |
| Balkan Peninsula ›[1] | 10 | 44.00 N | 23.00 E |
| Balkaria → Kabardino-Balkarija □[3] | 84 | 43.30 N | 43.30 E |
| Balkašino | 86 | 52.31 N | 68.46 E |
| Balkbrug | 52 | 52.36 N | 6.24 E |
| Balkh | 120 | 36.46 N | 66.54 E |
| Balkh □[4] | 120 | 36.30 N | 67.00 E |
| Balkh ≃ | 120 | 36.39 N | 66.56 E |
| Balkhash → Balchaš | 86 | 46.49 N | 74.59 E |
| Balkhash, Lake → Balchaš, ozero ⊜ | 86 | 46.00 N | 74.00 E |
| Balky | 78 | 47.23 N | 34.57 E |
| Ball | 194 | 31.24 N | 92.24 W |
| Balla | 48 | 53.48 N | 9.09 W |
| Balla Balla | 154 | 20.26 S | 29.02 E |
| Ballabhpur | 272b | 22.44 N | 88.21 E |
| Ballachulish | 46 | 56.40 N | 5.10 W |
| Balladonia | 162 | 32.27 S | 123.51 E |
| Ballagh | 48 | 52.35 N | 7.59 W |
| Ballaghaderreen | 48 | 53.55 N | 8.36 W |
| Ballālpur | 122 | 19.50 N | 79.22 E |
| Ballan | 169 | 37.36 S | 144.14 E |
| Ballancourt | 50 | 48.31 N | 2.23 E |
| Ballangen | 24 | 68.20 N | 16.50 E |
| Ballantine | 202 | 45.56 N | 108.08 W |
| Ballantrae | 44 | 55.06 N | 5.00 W |
| Ballao | 71 | 39.33 N | 9.22 E |
| Ballarat, Austl. | 166 | 37.34 S | 143.52 E |
| Ballarat, Austl. | 169 | 37.34 S | 143.52 E |
| Ballard, Lake ⊜ | 162 | 29.27 S | 120.55 E |
| Ballardvale | 207 | 42.37 N | 71.09 W |
| Ballata | 70 | 37.58 N | 12.41 E |
| Ballater | 46 | 57.03 N | 3.03 W |
| Ballaugh | 44 | 54.20 N | 4.32 W |
| Ball Bay c | 174c | 29.03 S | 167.59 E |
| Ballé | 150 | 15.20 N | 8.35 W |
| Ballen | 41 | 55.49 N | 10.39 E |
| Ballenas, Bahía de c | 232 | 26.45 N | 113.26 W |
| Ballenato, Punta › | 286b | 23.06 N | 82.30 W |
| Ballengeich | 158 | 27.52 S | 29.59 E |
| Ballenita, Punta › | 252 | 25.46 S | 70.44 W |
| Ballenstedt | 54 | 51.43 N | 11.14 E |
| Balleny Basin ✦[1] | 9 | 67.00 S | 170.00 E |
| Balleny Islands II | 9 | 66.35 S | 162.50 E |
| Balleroy | 32 | 49.11 N | 0.50 W |


| Symbol | English | Deutsch | Español | Français | Português |
|---|---|---|---|---|---|
| ≃ | River | Fluß | Río | Rivière | Rio |
| ≅ | Canal | Kanal | Canal | Canal | Canal |
| ∟ | Waterfall, Rapids | Wasserfall, Stromschnellen | Cascada, Rápidos | Chute d'eau, Rapides | Cascata, Rápidos |
| ɥ | Strait | Meeresstraße | Estrecho | Détroit | Estreito |
| c | Bay, Gulf | Bucht, Golf | Bahía, Golfo | Baie, Golfe | Baía, Golfo |
| ⊜ | Lake, Lakes | See, Seen | Lago, Lagos | Lac, Lacs | Lago, Lagos |
| ≋ | Swamp | Sumpf | Pantano | Marais | Pântano |
| ⊓ | Ice Features, Glacier | Eis- und Gletscherformen | Accidentes Glaciales | Formes glaciaires | Acidentes glaciares |
| ₸ | Other Hydrographic Features | Andere Hydrographische Objekte | Otros Elementos Hidrográficos | Autres données hydrographiques | Outros acidentes hidrográficos |
| ✦ | Submarine Features | Untermeerische Objekte | Accidentes Submarinos | Formes de relief sous-marin | Acidentes submarinos |
| □ | Political Unit | Politische Einheit | Unidad Politica | Entité politique | Unidade política |
| ʊ | Cultural Institution | Kulturelle Institution | Institución Cultural | Institution culturelle | Instituição cultural |
| ⊥ | Historical Site | Historische Stätte | Sitio Histórico | Site historique | Sitio histórico |
| ♦ | Recreational Site | Erholungs- und Ferienort | Sitio de Recreo | Centre de loisirs | Area de Lazer |
| ⊠ | Airport | Flughafen | Aeropuerto | Aéroport | Aeroporto |
| ■ | Military Installation | Militäranlage | Instalación Militar | Installation militaire | Instalação militar |
| ◆ | Miscellaneous | Verschiedenes | Misceláneo | Divers | Diversos |

| ENGLISH Name | Page | Lat.°′ | Long.°′ |
|---|---|---|---|
| Ballerup | 41 | 55.44 N | 12.22 E |
| Ballesteros, Arg. | 252 | 32.33 S | 62.59 W |
| Ballesteros, Pil. | 116 | 18.25 N | 121.31 E |
| Balleza | 232 | 26.57 N | 106.21 W |
| Balleza ≃ | 232 | 27.23 N | 106.17 W |
| Ball Ground | 192 | 34.20 N | 84.22 W |
| Ballı | 130 | 40.50 N | 27.03 E |
| Ballia | 124 | 25.45 N | 84.10 E |
| Ballico | 226 | 37.27 N | 120.42 W |
| Ballidu | 162 | 30.36 S | 116.46 E |
| Ballina, Austl. | 166 | 28.52 S | 153.33 E |
| Ballina, Ire. | 48 | 54.07 N | 9.09 W |
| Ballina, Ire. | 48 | 52.49 N | 8.26 W |
| Ballinakill | 48 | 52.53 N | 7.18 W |
| Ballinalack | 48 | 53.37 N | 7.28 W |
| Ballinascarty | 48 | 51.40 N | 8.51 W |
| Ballinasloe | 48 | 53.20 N | 8.13 W |
| Ballinderry ≃ | 48 | 54.40 N | 6.31 W |
| Ballindine | 48 | 53.39 N | 8.59 W |
| Ballineen | 48 | 51.44 N | 8.56 W |
| Ballingarry | 48 | 52.29 N | 8.52 W |
| Ballingeary | 48 | 51.49 N | 9.13 W |
| Ballinger | 196 | 31.44 N | 99.56 W |
| Ballingry | 46 | 56.09 N | 3.20 W |
| Ballingslöv | 41 | 56.13 N | 13.51 E |
| Ballinluig | 46 | 56.38 N | 3.39 W |
| Ballino | 64 | 45.58 N | 10.48 E |
| Ballinrobe | 48 | 53.37 N | 9.13 W |
| Ballinskelligs Bay c | 48 | 51.50 N | 10.15 W |
| Ballintoy | 48 | 55.14 N | 6.22 W |
| Ballintra | 48 | 54.35 N | 8.08 W |
| Balloch | 46 | 57.29 N | 4.07 W |
| Ballon | 50 | 48.10 N | 0.14 E |
| Ballona Creek ≃ | 280 | 33.58 N | 118.27 W |
| Ballouville | 207 | 41.52 N | 71.51 W |
| Ballsh | 38 | 40.36 N | 19.44 E |
| Balls Pyramid I | 160 | 31.45 S | 159.15 E |
| Ballston | 224 | 45.04 N | 123.19 W |
| Ballston Lake | 210 | 42.54 N | 73.52 W |
| Ballston Spa | 210 | 43.00 N | 73.50 W |
| Ballville | 214 | 41.20 N | 83.09 W |
| Ballwin | 219 | 38.35 N | 90.32 W |
| Bālly, India | 272b | 22.38 N | 88.21 E |
| Bally, Pa., U.S. | 208 | 40.24 N | 75.35 W |
| Bālly -•-[8] | 272b | 22.39 N | 88.21 E |
| Ballybay | 48 | 54.08 N | 6.54 W |
| Ballybofey | 48 | 54.48 N | 7.47 W |
| Ballybogy | 48 | 55.07 N | 6.34 W |
| Bālly Bridge -•-[5] | 272b | 22.39 N | 88.21 E |
| Ballybunnion | 48 | 52.31 N | 9.40 W |
| Ballycanew | 48 | 52.36 N | 6.19 W |
| Ballycastle, Ire. | 48 | 54.16 N | 9.23 W |
| Ballycastle, N. Ire., U.K. | 48 | 55.12 N | 6.15 W |
| Ballyclare | 48 | 54.45 N | 6.00 W |
| Ballyconneely | 48 | 53.26 N | 10.02 W |
| Ballyconnell | 48 | 54.07 N | 7.35 W |
| Ballycotton | 48 | 51.50 N | 8.01 W |
| Ballycroy | 48 | 54.01 N | 9.51 W |
| Ballyduff, Ire. | 48 | 52.09 N | 8.03 W |
| Ballyduff, Ire. | 48 | 52.27 N | 9.40 W |
| Ballyferriter | 48 | 52.09 N | 10.26 W |
| Ballyfinboy ≃ | 48 | 53.02 N | 8.15 W |
| Ballygar | 48 | 53.32 N | 8.20 W |
| Ballygawley | 48 | 54.28 N | 7.02 W |
| Ballygorman | 48 | 55.22 N | 7.21 W |
| Ballygowan | 48 | 54.30 N | 5.48 W |
| Ballygunge -•-[8] | 272b | 22.31 N | 88.21 E |
| Ballyhaise | 48 | 54.03 N | 7.19 W |
| Ballyhalbert | 48 | 54.30 N | 5.28 W |
| Ballyhaunis | 48 | 53.46 N | 8.46 W |
| Ballyhoura Mountains ⩚ | 48 | 52.20 N | 8.35 W |
| Ballyjamesduff | 48 | 53.52 N | 7.12 W |
| Ballylongford | 48 | 52.33 N | 9.28 W |
| Ballymacoda | 48 | 51.57 N | 7.54 W |
| Ballymahon | 48 | 53.34 N | 7.45 W |
| Ballymakeery (Ballyvourney) | 48 | 51.55 N | 9.09 W |
| Ballymena | 48 | 54.52 N | 6.17 W |
| Ballymoe | 48 | 53.42 N | 8.29 W |
| Ballymoney | 48 | 55.04 N | 6.31 W |
| Ballymote | 48 | 54.06 N | 8.31 W |
| Ballymurray | 48 | 53.35 N | 8.08 W |
| Ballynahinch | 48 | 54.24 N | 5.54 W |
| Ballyneety | 48 | 52.35 N | 8.33 W |
| Ballynoe | 48 | 52.03 N | 8.05 W |
| Ballyquintin Point › | 48 | 54.20 N | 5.30 W |
| Ballyragget | 48 | 52.47 N | 7.20 W |
| Ballysadare | 48 | 54.13 N | 8.31 W |
| Ballyshannon | 48 | 54.30 N | 8.11 W |
| Ballyteige Bay c | 48 | 52.11 N | 6.39 W |
| Ballyvaghan | 48 | 53.07 N | 9.07 W |
| Ballyvoy | 48 | 55.12 N | 6.12 W |
| Ballywalter | 48 | 54.33 N | 5.30 W |
| Balm | 220 | 27.45 N | 82.15 W |
| Balmaceda | 254 | 45.55 S | 71.41 W |
| Balmaceda, Cerro ∧ | 254 | 51.25 S | 73.11 W |
| Balmain | 274a | 33.51 S | 151.11 E |
| Balme | 62 | 45.18 N | 7.13 E |
| Balmerino | 46 | 56.24 N | 3.02 W |
| Balmertown | 184 | 51.04 N | 93.44 W |
| Balmhorn ∧ | 58 | 46.25 N | 7.43 E |
| Balmoral, Austl. | 166 | 37.15 S | 141.51 E |
| Balmoral, S. Afr. | 158 | 25.52 S | 28.59 E |
| Balmoral Castle ⊥ | 46 | 57.02 N | 3.14 W |
| Balmorhea | 196 | 30.59 N | 103.45 W |
| Balmville | 210 | 41.32 N | 74.00 W |
| Balnacra | 46 | 57.28 N | 5.23 W |
| Balnearia | 252 | 31.00 S | 62.40 W |
| Balobanovo | 82 | 55.51 N | 38.14 E |
| Balobe | 154 | 0.05 N | 28.00 E |
| Baloda Bāzār | 120 | 21.40 N | 82.10 E |
| Balombo | 152 | 12.21 S | 14.46 E |
| Balong, Indon. | 115a | 7.57 S | 111.26 E |
| Balong, Zhg. | 102 | 36.17 N | 97.20 E |
| Balonne ≃ | 166 | 28.47 S | 147.56 E |
| Bālotra | 120 | 25.50 N | 72.14 E |
| Baloži | 76 | 56.53 N | 24.06 E |
| Balpahari Reservoir ⊜[1] | 126 | 24.04 N | 86.28 E |
| Balrāmpur | 124 | 27.26 N | 82.11 E |
| Balranald | 166 | 34.38 S | 143.33 E |
| Balș | 38 | 44.21 N | 24.06 E |
| Balsam Lake | 190 | 45.27 N | 92.27 W |
| Balsam Lake ⊜ | 212 | 44.35 N | 78.50 W |
| Bálsamo | 255 | 20.27 S | 53.57 W |
| Balsas | 250 | 7.31 S | 46.02 W |
| Balsas ≃ | 234 | 17.55 N | 102.10 W |
| Balsas, Rio das ≃, Bra. | 250 | 9.58 S | 47.52 W |
| Balsas, Rio das ≃, Bra. | 250 | 7.14 S | 44.33 W |
| Balsas Sur | 234 | 17.59 N | 99.47 W |
| Bal'šavik | 76 | 52.34 N | 30.53 E |
| Balseiro ≃ | 250 | 5.51 S | 43.44 W |
| Balsham | 42 | 52.08 N | 0.20 E |
| Balsorano | 66 | 41.49 N | 13.34 E |
| Bålsta | 40 | 59.35 N | 17.30 E |
| Balsthal | 58 | 47.19 N | 7.42 E |
| Balta | 78 | 47.55 N | 29.37 E |
| Baltaj | 80 | 52.28 N | 46.38 E |
| Baltanás | 34 | 41.56 N | 4.15 W |
| Baltasar Brum | 252 | 30.44 S | 57.19 W |
| Baltasi | 80 | 56.21 N | 50.12 E |
| Baltasound | 46a | 60.45 N | 0.52 W |
| Baltazar, Arroyo ≃ | 258 | 33.47 S | 58.58 W |
| Bălți | 38 | 47.46 N | 27.56 E |
| Baltic, Ct., U.S. | 207 | 41.37 N | 72.05 W |
| Baltic, Oh., U.S. | 214 | 40.26 N | 81.41 W |
| Baltic Bay c | 190 | 48.22 N | 83.43 W |
| Baltico, Mar → Baltic Sea ▾[2] | 24 | 57.00 N | 19.00 E |
| Baltic Sea ▾[2] | 24 | 57.00 N | 19.00 E |
| Baltic Station -•-[5] | 265a | 59.55 N | 30.18 E |
| Baltijsk | 76 | 54.39 N | 19.55 E |
| Baltijskaja kosa ›[2] | 32 | 54.25 N | 19.35 E |
| Balṭīm | 142 | 31.33 N | 31.05 E |
| Baltimore, Ire. | 48 | 51.29 N | 9.22 W |
| Baltimore, S. Afr. | 156 | 23.15 S | 28.20 E |
| Baltimore, Md., U.S. | 208 | 39.17 N | 76.36 W |
| Baltimore, Md., U.S. | 284b | 39.17 N | 76.36 W |
| Baltimore, Oh., U.S. | 188 | 39.50 N | 82.36 W |
| Baltimore □[6] | 208 | 39.22 N | 76.36 W |
| Baltimore, University of ⊍[2] | 284b | 39.18 N | 76.37 W |
| Baltimore Airpark ⊠ | 284b | 39.24 N | 76.25 W |
| Baltimore Highlands | 284b | 39.13 N | 76.38 W |
| Baltimore-Washington International Airport ⊠ | 208 | 39.11 N | 76.40 W |
| Baltinglass | 48 | 52.55 N | 6.41 W |
| Baltique, Mer → Baltic Sea ▾[2] | 24 | 57.00 N | 19.00 E |
| Baltistān -•-[1] | 123 | 35.18 N | 75.37 E |
| Baltit | 123 | 36.20 N | 74.40 E |
| Baltoji-Vokė | 76 | 54.28 N | 25.06 E |
| Baltoro Glacier ⊓ | 123 | 35.42 N | 76.10 E |
| Baltra, Isla I | 246a | 0.26 S | 90.16 W |
| Baltrum I | 52 | 53.44 N | 7.23 E |
| Bālu ≃, Bngl. | 126 | 23.44 N | 90.30 E |
| Ba Lu ≃, Viet | 110 | 14.18 N | 107.52 E |
| Baluarte ≃ | 234 | 22.49 N | 106.02 W |
| Baluarte, Arroyo V | 196 | 27.09 N | 98.07 W |
| Baluchistān □[4] | 120 | 29.00 N | 67.00 E |
| Baluchistan □[9] | 128 | 28.00 N | 63.00 E |
| Balud | 116 | 12.02 N | 123.12 E |
| Bālughāta | 126 | 22.05 N | 88.01 E |
| Bāluhāti | 272b | 22.39 N | 88.16 E |
| Balui ≃ | 112 | 2.42 N | 113.47 E |
| Balukbaluk Island I | 116 | 6.40 N | 121.43 E |
| Balupe ≃ | 76 | 56.57 N | 26.55 E |
| Bālurghāt | 124 | 25.13 N | 88.46 E |
| Balut Island I | 116 | 5.24 N | 125.23 E |
| Balvano | 68 | 40.39 N | 15.31 E |
| Balve | 56 | 51.20 N | 7.51 E |
| Balvi | 76 | 57.08 N | 27.17 E |
| Balvicar | 46 | 56.14 N | 5.38 W |
| Balwina Aboriginal Reserve -•-[4] | 162 | 20.30 S | 128.00 E |
| Balwyn | 274b | 37.49 S | 145.05 E |
| Balxuca, Arroyo de la ≃ | 266d | 41.31 N | 2.06 E |
| Balya | 130 | 39.45 N | 27.35 E |
| Balygyčan | 74 | 63.56 N | 154.12 E |
| Balykči | 85 | 40.54 N | 71.50 E |
| Balyksa | 86 | 53.25 N | 89.05 E |
| Balykši | 80 | 47.05 N | 51.54 E |
| Balyktyg-Chem ≃ | 88 | 51.15 N | 96.54 E |
| Balyn | 78 | 48.52 N | 26.40 E |
| Balzac | 182 | 51.10 N | 114.01 W |
| Balzar | 246 | 1.22 S | 79.54 W |
| Balzers | 58 | 47.04 N | 9.30 E |
| Bal'zino | 88 | 51.03 N | 113.35 E |
| Balzola | 62 | 45.11 N | 8.24 E |
| Bām, Īrān | 128 | 36.58 N | 57.59 E |
| Bam, Īrān | 128 | 29.06 N | 58.21 E |
| Bama, Nig. | 146 | 11.30 N | 13.41 E |
| Bama, Zhg. | 102 | 24.21 N | 107.08 E |
| Bamaga | 164 | 10.52 S | 142.24 E |
| Bamaji Lake ⊜ | 184 | 51.09 N | 91.25 W |
| Bamako | 150 | 12.39 N | 8.00 W |
| Bāmangāchi | 272b | 22.46 N | 88.31 E |
| Bāmangawān | 126 | 24.14 N | 86.49 E |
| Bāmanghāra | 272b | 22.31 N | 88.28 E |
| Bāmanmura | 272b | 22.42 N | 88.31 E |
| Bamao | 100 | 29.26 N | 120.59 E |
| Bamata | 152 | 1.00 S | 21.06 E |
| Bamba, Mali | 150 | 17.02 N | 1.24 W |
| Bamba, Zaïre | 152 | 5.45 S | 18.23 E |
| Bambamarca | 248 | 6.41 S | 78.32 W |
| Bambana ≃ | 236 | 13.27 N | 83.50 W |
| Bambang | 116 | 16.23 N | 121.06 E |
| Bambannan Island I | 116 | 5.37 N | 120.17 E |
| Bambara Maoundé | 150 | 15.51 N | 2.47 W |
| Bambari | 152 | 5.45 N | 20.40 E |
| Bambaroo | 166 | 18.52 S | 146.12 E |
| Bambāvi | 272c | 18.58 N | 73.03 E |
| Bamberg, Dtsch. | 56 | 49.53 N | 10.53 E |
| Bamberg, S.C., U.S. | 192 | 33.17 N | 81.02 W |
| Bamber Lake | 208 | 39.54 N | 74.19 W |
| Bamberton | 224 | 48.35 N | 123.31 W |
| Bambesa | 154 | 3.28 N | 25.43 E |
| Bambesi | 144 | 9.45 N | 34.38 E |
| Bambezi | 154 | 20.00 S | 28.56 E |
| Bambili | 154 | 3.39 N | 26.07 E |
| Bambinga | 152 | 3.42 S | 18.54 E |
| Bambio | 152 | 3.54 N | 16.59 E |
| Bamboesberg ⩚ | 158 | 31.30 S | 26.10 E |
| Bamboi | 150 | 8.10 N | 2.02 W |
| Bamboo Creek | 162 | 20.56 S | 120.13 E |
| Bamboo Springs | 162 | 22.04 S | 119.38 E |
| Bambouti | 154 | 5.24 N | 27.12 E |
| Bambuí | 255 | 20.01 S | 45.58 W |
| Bambujka | 88 | 55.47 N | 115.48 E |
| Bambula | 154 | 1.17 S | 25.38 E |
| Bamburgh | 44 | 55.36 N | 1.42 W |
| Bamburral ≃ | 248 | 20.10 S | 58.07 W |
| Bambuto ≃ | 200 | 30.51 N | 110.52 W |
| Bam Co ⊜ | 120 | 31.30 N | 91.05 E |
| Bamencheng | 105 | 39.35 N | 117.37 E |
| Bamenda | 152 | 5.56 N | 10.10 E |
| Bamendjou | 152 | 5.24 N | 10.19 E |
| Bamfield | 182 | 48.50 N | 125.08 W |
| Bamhā | 142 | 29.35 N | 31.14 E |
| Bami | 128 | 38.44 N | 56.48 E |
| Bāmīān | 120 | 34.50 N | 67.50 E |
| Bāmīān □[4] | 120 | 34.45 N | 67.15 E |
| Bamiancheng | 89 | 43.13 N | 124.02 E |
| Bamingui | 152 | 7.34 N | 20.11 E |
| Bamingui ≃ | 146 | 8.33 N | 19.05 E |
| Bamingui-Bangoran □[5] | 146 | 8.15 N | 20.15 E |
| Bamingui-Bangoran, Parc National du ♦ | 146 | 8.00 N | 19.40 E |
| Bam Island I | 164 | 3.35 S | 144.50 E |
| Bāmna | 126 | 22.19 N | 90.06 E |
| Bamndali -•-[8] | 272a | 28.33 N | 77.03 E |
| Bamol | 164 | 7.38 S | 138.37 E |
| Bampton, Eng., U.K. | 42 | 51.00 N | 3.29 W |
| Bampton, Eng., U.K. | 42 | 51.44 N | 1.33 W |
| Bampūr | 128 | 27.12 N | 60.27 E |
| Bampūr ≃ | 128 | 27.18 N | 59.06 E |
| Bāmra Hills ⩚[2] | 120 | 21.30 N | 84.30 E |
| Bamu ≃ | 164 | 8.01 S | 143.33 E |
| Bamumo | 120 | 32.30 N | 93.15 E |
| Ban | 150 | 14.05 N | 2.27 W |
| Bana, Malaŵi | 154 | 12.25 S | 34.08 E |
| Ba Na, Viet | 110 | 15.59 N | 107.59 E |
| Banā, Wādī V | 144 | 13.03 N | 45.24 E |
| Banaba (Ocean Island) I | 174d | 0.52 S | 169.35 E |
| Banabuiú ≃ | 250 | 5.07 S | 38.06 W |
| Banabuiú, Açude ⊜[1] | 250 | 5.20 S | 39.05 W |
| Ban Aen | 110 | 18.02 N | 98.37 E |
| Banagher | 48 | 53.11 N | 7.59 W |
| Banagi | 154 | 2.16 S | 34.51 E |
| Banago | 116 | 7.30 N | 124.07 E |
| Banagrām | 126 | 22.35 N | 89.55 E |
| Banahao, Mount ∧ | 116 | 14.04 N | 121.29 E |
| Banalia | 154 | 1.33 N | 25.20 E |
| Banamba | 150 | 13.33 N | 7.27 W |
| Banana, Austl. | 166 | 24.28 S | 150.07 E |
| Banana, Zaïre | 152 | 6.01 S | 12.24 E |
| Banana Creek ≃ | 220 | 28.36 N | 80.38 W |
| Banana Islands II | 150 | 8.07 N | 13.13 W |
| Bananal | 256 | 22.41 S | 44.19 W |
| Bananal ≃, Bra. | 250 | 8.33 S | 49.26 W |
| Bananal ≃, Bra. | 256 | 22.32 S | 44.11 W |
| Bananal, Ilha do I | 250 | 11.30 S | 50.15 W |
| Banana River c | 220 | 28.25 N | 80.38 W |
| Bananeiras | 250 | 6.45 S | 35.37 W |
| Bananga | 110 | 6.56 N | 93.54 E |
| Banao, Loma de ∧ | 240p | 21.51 N | 78.36 W |
| Bānār ≃ | 124 | 24.04 N | 90.38 E |
| Banaras → Vārānasi | 124 | 25.20 N | 83.00 E |
| Banari | 70 | 43.34 N | 8.42 E |
| Bānāripāra | 126 | 22.47 N | 90.10 E |
| Banarlı | 130 | 41.04 N | 27.20 E |
| Banās ≃ | 120 | 25.54 N | 76.45 E |
| Banās, Ra's › | 140 | 23.54 N | 35.48 E |
| Banat □[9] | 38 | 45.20 N | 20.40 E |
| Banate Bay c | 116 | 10.58 N | 122.48 E |
| Banaue | 116 | 16.55 N | 121.04 E |
| Banavie | 46 | 56.47 N | 5.07 W |
| Banay, Mount ∧ | 116 | 13.42 N | 121.10 E |
| Banaz | 130 | 38.46 N | 29.46 E |
| Ban Baen Phichit | 269a | 13.50 N | 100.40 E |
| Ban Ban | 110 | 19.38 N | 103.34 E |
| Ban Bang Chan | 269a | 13.49 N | 100.42 E |
| Ban Bang O | 269a | 13.53 N | 100.36 E |
| Ban Bang Phli Yai | 269a | 13.36 N | 100.42 E |
| Ban Bang Phraek | 269a | 13.53 N | 100.26 E |
| Ban Bang Pu | 269a | 13.31 N | 100.39 E |
| Banbar | 120 | 30.49 N | 94.59 E |
| Ban Bat | 110 | 13.13 N | 108.39 E |
| Banbidian | 271a | 39.54 N | 116.32 E |
| Ban Blech | 110 | 13.12 N | 108.13 E |
| Ban Bonèng | 110 | 17.58 N | 104.35 E |
| Ban Bouang-nom | 110 | 15.47 N | 106.47 E |
| Banbridge | 48 | 54.21 N | 6.16 W |
| Ban Bua Chum | 110 | 15.15 N | 101.12 E |
| Banbuji | 100 | 33.34 N | 116.44 E |
| Ban Bung Fang Nok | 269a | 13.48 N | 100.43 E |
| Ban Bung Na Rang | 110 | 16.11 N | 100.09 E |
| Ban Bungxai | 110 | 15.42 N | 106.14 E |
| Banbury | 42 | 52.04 N | 1.20 W |
| Bancahsaga | 114 | 0.49 N | 101.07 E |
| Bancalan Island I | 116 | 8.14 N | 117.06 E |
| Banc d'Arguin, Parc National du ♦ | 150 | 20.00 N | 16.20 W |
| Ban Chak | 110 | 14.17 N | 105.25 E |
| Ban Cha La | 110 | 17.11 N | 106.05 E |
| Bānchhārāmpur | 126 | 23.46 N | 90.48 E |
| Banchory | 46 | 57.03 N | 2.31 W |
| Banco, Punta › | 236 | 8.23 N | 83.09 W |
| Bancos, Isla → Banks Island I | 176 | 73.15 N | 121.30 W |
| Bancroft, On., Can. | 212 | 45.03 N | 77.51 W |
| Bancroft, Id., U.S. | 202 | 42.43 N | 111.53 W |
| Bancroft, Ia., U.S. | 190 | 43.17 N | 94.13 W |
| Bancroft, Mi., U.S. | 216 | 42.52 N | 84.03 W |
| Bancroft, Ne., U.S. | 198 | 42.00 N | 96.34 W |
| Bancroft → Chililabombwe, Zam. | 154 | 12.18 S | 27.43 E |
| Bancun | 106 | 30.53 N | 118.48 E |
| Banda, India | 124 | 24.03 N | 78.57 E |
| Bānda, India | 124 | 25.29 N | 80.20 E |
| Banda, Zaïre | 154 | 4.11 N | 27.04 E |
| Banda, Kepulauan II | 164 | 4.35 S | 129.55 E |
| Banda, Laut (Banda Sea) ▾[2] | 108 | 5.00 S | 128.00 E |
| Banda Aceh (Kuturaja) | 114 | 5.34 N | 95.20 E |
| Bandabe | 157b | 15.31 S | 49.04 E |
| Banda Besar, Pulau I | 164 | 4.34 S | 129.55 E |
| Bānda Dāūd Shāh | 123 | 33.16 N | 71.11 E |
| Banda del Río Salí | 252 | 26.50 S | 65.10 W |
| Banda Elat | 164 | 5.39 S | 132.59 E |
| Bandahara, Gunung ∧ | 114 | 3.45 N | 97.47 E |
| Bandai-Asahi-kokuritsu-kōen ♦ | 92 | 38.16 N | 139.57 E |
| Bandai-san ∧ | 92 | 37.36 N | 140.04 E |
| Bandak ⊜ | 26 | 59.24 N | 8.15 E |
| Bandama ≃ | 150 | 5.10 N | 5.00 W |
| Bandama Blanc ≃ | 150 | 6.54 N | 5.31 W |
| Bandama Rouge ≃ | 150 | 6.54 N | 5.31 W |
| Bandān, Īrān | 128 | 31.23 N | 60.44 E |
| Ban Dan, Thai | 110 | 15.19 N | 105.30 E |
| Bandanaira | 164 | 4.32 S | 129.54 E |
| Bandan'gou | 105 | 39.08 N | 115.11 E |
| Ban Dangtai | 110 | 17.06 N | 104.57 E |
| Ban Dan Lan Hoi | 110 | 17.00 N | 99.35 E |
| Bandar → Machilīpatnam, India | 122 | 16.10 N | 81.08 E |
| Bandar, Indon. | 115a | 7.02 S | 109.47 E |
| Bandar Baharu | 114 | 5.08 N | 100.30 E |
| Bandar Beheshtī | 128 | 25.18 N | 60.37 E |
| Bandardurian | 114 | 2.21 N | 99.44 E |
| Bandar-e 'Abbās | 128 | 27.11 N | 56.17 E |
| Bandar-e Anzalī (Bandar-e Pahlavī) | 128 | 37.28 N | 49.27 E |
| Bandar-e Būshehr | 128 | 28.59 N | 50.50 E |
| Bandar-e Chārak | 128 | 26.43 N | 54.16 E |
| Bandar-e Deylam | 128 | 30.04 N | 50.10 E |
| Bandar-e Gaz | 128 | 36.47 N | 53.59 E |
| Bandar-e Khomeynī (Bandar-e Shāhpūr) | 128 | 30.25 N | 49.05 E |
| Bandar-e Lengeh | 128 | 26.33 N | 54.53 E |
| Bandar-e Māh Shahr | 128 | 30.33 N | 49.12 E |
| Bandar-e Moghūyeh | 128 | 26.35 N | 54.31 E |
| Bandar-e Rīg | 128 | 29.29 N | 50.38 E |
| Bandar-e Torkeman | 128 | 36.56 N | 54.06 E |
| Bandar Penggaram → Batu Pahat | 114 | 1.51 N | 102.56 E |
| Bandarpulau | 114 | 2.41 N | 99.31 E |
| Bandar Seri Begawan | 112 | 4.56 N | 114.55 E |
| Bandawe | 154 | 11.57 S | 34.10 E |
| Bande | 34 | 42.02 N | 7.58 W |
| Banded Peak ∧ | 200 | 37.06 N | 106.38 W |
| Bandeira, Pico da ∧ | 255 | 20.26 S | 41.47 W |
| Bandeira do Sul | 256 | 21.47 S | 46.23 W |
| Bandeirantes, Bra. | 255 | 13.41 S | 50.48 W |
| Bandeirantes, Bra. | 255 | 19.53 S | 54.23 W |
| Bandeirantes, Bra. | 255 | 23.06 S | 50.21 W |
| Bandeirantes, Palácio dos ⊍ | 287b | 23.36 S | 46.43 W |
| Bandeirantes, Praia dos ±[2] | 287a | 23.01 S | 43.25 W |
| Bandéko | 152 | 1.56 N | 17.28 E |
| Bāndel | 272b | 22.56 N | 88.22 E |
| Bandeli | 157a | 12.55 S | 45.13 E |
| Bandelier National Monument ♦ | 200 | 35.45 N | 106.20 W |
| Bandera, Arg. | 252 | 28.54 S | 62.16 W |
| Bandera, Tx., U.S. | 196 | 29.44 N | 99.04 W |
| Bandera, Alto ∧ | 238 | 18.49 N | 70.37 W |
| Banderas | 200 | 31.01 N | 105.35 W |
| Banderas, Bahía de c | 234 | 20.40 N | 105.25 W |
| Banderilla | 234 | 19.36 N | 96.56 W |
| Bāndhi | 120 | 26.35 N | 68.18 E |
| Bandholm | 41 | 54.50 N | 11.29 E |
| Bandiagara | 150 | 14.21 N | 3.37 W |
| Bandiantaolehai | 102 | 41.41 N | 104.06 E |
| Bāndīkūi | 124 | 27.03 N | 76.34 E |
| Bandipur, India | 272b | 22.44 N | 88.26 E |
| Bandipur, India | 272b | 22.51 N | 88.10 E |
| Bandipura | 123 | 34.25 N | 74.39 E |
| Bandırma | 130 | 40.20 N | 27.58 E |
| Bandırma Körfezi c | 130 | 40.25 N | 28.00 E |
| Bando | 152 | 15.00 S | 20.30 E |
| Bandol | 62 | 43.08 N | 5.45 E |
| Bandon, Ire. | 48 | 51.45 N | 8.45 W |
| Ban Don → Surat Thani, Thai | 110 | 9.08 N | 99.19 E |
| Bandon, Or., U.S. | 202 | 43.07 N | 124.24 W |
| Ban Don, Viet | 110 | 12.53 N | 107.48 E |
| Bandon ≃ | 48 | 51.42 N | 8.30 W |
| Ban Don, Ao c | 110 | 9.20 N | 99.25 E |
| Ban Donhiang | 110 | 18.05 N | 101.48 E |
| Ban Dônko | 110 | 16.12 N | 106.17 E |
| Ban Don Muang | 269a | 13.55 N | 100.36 E |
| Bāndra -•-[8] | 272c | 19.03 N | 72.49 E |
| Bāndra Point › | 272c | 19.03 N | 72.49 E |
| Bānduān | 126 | 22.53 N | 86.31 E |
| Bandula | 156 | 19.02 S | 33.07 E |
| Ban Dulad V | 144 | 8.26 N | 45.54 E |
| Bandundu | 152 | 3.18 S | 17.20 E |
| Bandundu □[4] | 152 | 4.00 S | 18.00 E |
| Bandung | 115a | 6.54 S | 107.36 E |
| Banegas | 248 | 17.09 S | 62.50 W |
| Bāneh | 128 | 35.59 N | 45.53 E |
| Banehra | 272a | 28.44 N | 77.23 E |
| Banes | 240p | 20.58 N | 75.43 W |
| Banff, Ab., Can. | 182 | 51.10 N | 115.34 W |
| Banff, Scot., U.K. | 46 | 57.40 N | 2.33 W |
| Banff National Park ♦ | 182 | 51.38 N | 116.22 W |
| Banfield -•-[8] | 258 | 34.44 S | 58.23 W |
| Banfora | 150 | 10.38 N | 4.46 W |
| Banga, India | 123 | 31.11 N | 75.59 E |
| Banga, Pil. | 116 | 11.38 N | 122.20 E |
| Banga, Zaïre | 152 | 5.27 S | 20.28 E |
| Banga ≃ | 116 | 6.44 N | 124.34 E |
| Bañgad | 116 | 12.10 N | 123.24 E |
| Bangaduni Island I | 126 | 21.34 N | 88.52 E |
| Bangala Dam -•-[6] | 154 | 20.40 S | 31.15 E |
| Bangall | 210 | 41.53 N | 73.42 W |
| Bangalore | 122 | 12.58 N | 77.36 E |
| Bangalur → Bangalore | 122 | 12.58 N | 77.36 E |
| Bangangté | 152 | 5.09 N | 10.31 E |
| Bangaon | 126 | 23.04 N | 88.49 E |
| Bangassou | 152 | 4.50 N | 23.07 E |
| Bangda | 102 | 27.59 N | 98.40 E |
| Bangdag Co ⊜ | 120 | 34.59 N | 81.35 E |
| Bangeluo | 120 | 32.27 N | 90.35 E |
| Bangeswardi | 126 | 23.29 N | 89.44 E |
| Bangeta, Mount ∧ | 164 | 6.15 S | 147.04 E |
| Banggai (Luwuk) | 112 | 1.34 S | 123.30 E |
| Banggai, Kepulauan II | 112 | 1.30 S | 123.15 E |
| Banggai, Pulau I | 112 | 1.37 S | 123.33 E |
| Banggi, Pulau I | 116 | 7.17 N | 117.12 E |
| Banggong Co ⊜ | 120 | 33.45 N | 79.30 E |
| Banghāzī | 146 | 32.07 N | 20.04 E |
| Banghiang ≃ | 110 | 16.03 N | 105.15 E |
| Bangholme | 274b | 38.02 S | 145.11 E |
| Bangi → Bangui | 152 | 4.22 N | 18.35 E |
| Bangil | 115a | 7.36 S | 112.47 E |
| Bangjang | 140 | 11.23 N | 32.42 E |
| Bangjun | 105 | 39.59 N | 117.16 E |
| Bangka, Pulau I, Indon. | 112 | 2.15 S | 106.00 E |
| Bangka, Pulau I, Indon. | 112 | 1.48 N | 125.09 E |
| Bangka, Selat ⋓ | 112 | 2.20 S | 105.45 E |
| Bangkalan | 115a | 7.02 S | 112.44 E |
| Bang Kapi | 269a | 13.46 N | 100.39 E |
| Bang Kapi, Khlong ≅ | 269a | 13.45 N | 100.36 E |
| Bangkaru, Pulau I | 114 | 2.04 N | 97.07 E |
| Bang Khen | 269a | 13.52 N | 100.36 E |
| Bang Khun Thian | 269a | 13.42 N | 100.28 E |
| Bangkinang | 112 | 0.21 N | 101.02 E |
| Bangkir | 112 | 0.48 N | 120.14 E |
| Bangko | 112 | 2.05 S | 102.17 E |
| Bangkog Co ⊜ | 120 | 31.42 N | 89.30 E |
| Bangkok → Krung Thep | 110 | 13.45 N | 100.31 E |
| Bangkok Station -•-[5] | 269a | 13.44 N | 100.32 E |
| Bangkou | 106 | 31.40 N | 121.26 E |
| Bang Krathum | 110 | 16.34 N | 100.18 E |
| Bang Kruai | 269a | 13.48 N | 100.29 E |
| Bangkulu, Pulau I | 112 | 1.50 S | 123.06 E |
| Bangkulua | 115b | 8.41 S | 118.13 E |
| Bangladesch → Bangladesh □[1] | 120 | 24.00 N | 90.00 E |
| Bangladesh □[1], Asia | 118 | 24.00 N | 90.00 E |
| Bangladesh □[1], Asia | 120 | 24.00 N | 90.00 E |
| Bang Lamung | 110 | 12.58 N | 100.54 E |
| Bang Mun Nak | 110 | 16.02 N | 100.23 E |
| Ban Gnômmarat Kèo | 110 | 17.36 N | 105.10 E |
| Bangolo | 150 | 7.01 N | 7.29 W |
| Bangor, Ire. | 48 | 54.09 N | 9.45 W |
| Bangor, N. Ire., U.K. | 44 | 54.40 N | 5.40 W |
| Bangor, N. Ire., U.K. | 48 | 54.40 N | 5.40 W |
| Bangor, Wales, U.K. | 44 | 53.13 N | 4.08 W |
| Bangor, Ca., U.S. | 226 | 39.23 N | 121.24 W |
| Bangor, Me., U.S. | 188 | 44.48 N | 68.46 W |
| Bangor, Mi., U.S. | 216 | 42.18 N | 86.06 W |
| Bangor, Pa., U.S. | 210 | 40.51 N | 75.12 W |
| Bangoran ≃ | 146 | 8.42 N | 19.06 E |
| Bang Pa In | 110 | 14.14 N | 100.35 E |
| Bāngra ≃ | 126 | 21.48 N | 89.43 E |
| Bangriposi | 126 | 22.10 N | 86.32 E |
| Bangs | 196 | 31.43 N | 99.08 W |
| Bangs, Mount ∧ | 200 | 36.48 N | 113.51 W |
| Bang Saphan | 110 | 11.12 N | 99.31 E |
| Bangshi | 98 | 40.23 N | 122.46 E |
| Bangs Lake ⊜ | 278 | 42.16 N | 88.08 W |
| Bangsri | 115a | 6.30 S | 110.45 E |
| Bangu -•-[8] | 256 | 22.52 S | 43.27 W |
| Bangué | 152 | 3.01 N | 15.07 E |
| Bangued | 116 | 17.36 N | 120.37 E |
| Bangui, Centraf. | 152 | 4.22 N | 18.35 E |
| Bangui, Pil. | 116 | 18.32 N | 120.46 E |
| Bangui Bay c | 116 | 18.34 N | 120.44 E |
| Bangunpurba | 114 | 3.23 N | 98.50 E |
| Banguru | 154 | 0.27 N | 27.17 E |
| Bangwei | 102 | 23.46 N | 107.34 E |
| Bangweulu, Lake ⊜ | 154 | 11.05 S | 29.45 E |
| Bangweulu Swamps ⩸ | 154 | 11.30 S | 30.15 E |
| Bangzhen | 106 | 31.39 N | 121.29 E |
| Banhā | 142 | 30.28 N | 31.11 E |
| Ban Hatgnao | 110 | 14.40 N | 106.35 E |
| Ban Hatkiang | 110 | 18.11 N | 102.40 E |
| Ban Hat Yai → Hat Yai | 110 | 7.01 N | 100.28 E |
| Ban Ha Yaek Pak Kret | 269a | 13.54 N | 100.31 E |
| Ban Hèt | 110 | 14.44 N | 107.29 E |
| Banhine, Parque Nacional de ♦ | 156 | 22.45 S | 32.50 E |
| Ban Hin Heup | 110 | 18.38 N | 102.20 E |
| Ban Hom | 110 | 15.33 N | 98.46 E |
| Ban Hong | 110 | 18.18 N | 98.50 E |
| Ban Hong Muang | 110 | 17.04 N | 105.12 E |
| Ban Houayxay | 110 | 20.18 N | 100.26 E |
| Ban Huai Yang | 110 | 11.36 N | 99.40 E |
| Ban Hua Lamphu Thong | 269a | 13.32 N | 100.38 E |
| Bani, Burkina | 150 | 14.02 N | 0.02 W |
| Bani, Centraf. | 152 | 7.07 N | 22.49 E |
| Bani, Pil. | 116 | 16.11 N | 119.52 E |
| Baní, Rep. Dom. | 238 | 18.17 N | 70.20 W |
| Bani ≃ | 150 | 14.30 N | 4.12 W |
| Bani, Jbel ⩚ | 148 | 29.30 N | 8.00 W |
| Bania | 152 | 4.00 N | 16.07 E |
| Baniachang | 120 | 24.31 N | 91.22 E |
| Banī 'Adī al-Baḥrīyah | 142 | 27.15 N | 30.55 E |
| Banī 'Adī al-Qiblīyah | 142 | 27.15 N | 30.56 E |
| Banī Aḥmad | 142 | 28.03 N | 30.46 E |
| Banī 'Alī | 142 | 28.29 N | 30.43 E |
| Baniara, Indon. | 114 | 2.31 N | 98.39 E |
| Baniara, Pap. N. Gui. | 164 | 9.46 S | 149.53 E |
| Bānibaha | 126 | 23.42 N | 89.37 E |
| Bani Bangou | 150 | 15.03 N | 2.42 E |
| Banie | 30 | 53.08 N | 14.38 E |
| Banifing ≃ | 150 | 12.43 N | 6.25 W |
| Banihāl Pass )( | 123 | 33.31 N | 75.13 E |
| Banī Ḥasan ash-Shurūq | 142 | 27.54 N | 30.51 E |
| Banī Khālid | 142 | 27.50 N | 30.44 E |
| Banikoara | 150 | 11.18 N | 2.26 E |
| Banima | 152 | 5.26 N | 23.54 E |
| Banī Majdūl | 273c | 30.02 N | 31.07 E |
| Banī Mazār | 142 | 28.30 N | 30.48 E |
| Banī Muḥammadīyāt | 142 | 27.17 N | 31.05 E |
| Banī Mūsā | 142 | 29.08 N | 31.03 E |
| Banīnah | 146 | 32.05 N | 20.16 E |
| Banio, Lagune c | 152 | 3.35 S | 11.00 E |
| Baniou | 34 | 35.25 N | 4.21 E |
| Banī Rāfi' | 142 | 27.22 N | 30.53 E |
| Banī Salāmah | 142 | 30.19 N | 30.51 E |
| Banī Sha'rān | 142 | 27.19 N | 30.51 E |
| Banī Shuqayr | 142 | 27.23 N | 30.59 E |
| Banister ≃ | 192 | 36.42 N | 78.48 W |
| Banī Suhaylah | 132 | 31.20 N | 34.20 E |
| Banī Suwayf | 142 | 29.05 N | 31.05 E |
| Banī Suwayf □[4] | 142 | 29.03 N | 31.02 E |
| Banī 'Ubayd, Miṣr | 142 | 31.01 N | 31.39 E |
| Banī 'Ubayd, Miṣr | 142 | 27.57 N | 30.46 E |
| Banī Walīd | 146 | 31.45 N | 14.01 E |
| Bāniyās, Golan | 142 | 33.15 N | 35.41 E |
| Bāniyās, Sūriy. | 130 | 35.11 N | 35.57 E |
| Banī Zayd | 142 | 27.13 N | 31.09 E |
| Banja Luka | 36 | 44.46 N | 17.11 E |
| Banjar | 115a | 7.22 S | 108.32 E |
| Banjarmasin | 112 | 3.20 S | 114.35 E |
| Banjarnegara | 115a | 7.23 S | 109.41 E |
| Banjin | 106 | 32.19 N | 120.24 E |
| Banjir Kanal ≅ | 269e | 6.07 S | 106.45 E |
| Banjita | 104 | 41.11 N | 120.52 E |
| Banjščice ⩚[1] | 64 | 46.04 N | 13.42 E |
| Banjuangou | 105 | 40.44 N | 115.11 E |
| Banjul (Bathurst) | 150 | 13.28 N | 16.39 W |
| Bankä, Azer. | 84 | 39.25 N | 49.15 E |
| Bānka, India | 124 | 24.53 N | 86.55 E |
| Ban'ka ≃ | 265b | 55.49 N | 37.22 E |
| Banka Banka | 162 | 18.48 S | 134.01 E |
| Bānkādāba | 126 | 22.58 N | 87.21 E |
| Bankana | 152 | 4.25 S | 16.11 E |
| Bankas | 150 | 14.04 N | 3.31 W |
| Ban Katèp | 110 | 16.48 N | 105.52 E |
| Ban Kavak | 110 | 17.18 N | 105.37 E |
| Bankberg ⩚ | 158 | 32.22 S | 25.26 E |
| Ban Kèngkabao | 110 | 16.48 N | 104.45 E |
| Ban Kèngkok | 110 | 16.26 N | 105.12 E |
| Ban Kèngtangan | 110 | 16.05 N | 105.22 E |
| Bankeryd | 26 | 57.51 N | 14.07 E |
| Bankfoot | 46 | 56.30 N | 3.30 W |
| Ban Khamphô | 110 | 14.38 N | 106.17 E |
| Ban Khan Na Yao | 269a | 13.47 N | 100.41 E |
| Bankhari | 126 | 23.44 N | 90.03 E |
| Ban Kheun | 110 | 20.13 N | 101.07 E |
| Ban Khlong Bua Loi | 269a | 13.41 N | 100.41 E |
| Ban Khlong Kua | 110 | 6.57 N | 100.08 E |
| Ban Khlong Samrong | 269a | 13.39 N | 100.36 E |
| Ban Khlong Song | 269a | 13.51 N | 100.43 E |
| Ban Khok Bao Sao | 269a | 13.52 N | 100.39 E |
| Ban Khuan Mao | 110 | 7.58 N | 99.37 E |
| Bankilaré | 150 | 14.35 N | 0.44 E |
| Bankim | 152 | 6.05 N | 11.30 E |
| Bānkipur | 272b | 22.48 N | 88.14 E |
| Ban Kota Baru | 114 | 6.27 N | 101.21 E |
| Ban Krang | 110 | 12.52 N | 99.18 E |
| Ban Kruat | 110 | 14.25 N | 103.07 E |
| Banks, Eng., U.K. | 44 | 53.41 N | 2.55 W |
| Banks, Al., U.S. | 194 | 31.48 N | 85.50 W |
| Banks, Or., U.S. | 224 | 45.37 N | 123.06 W |
| Banks, Cape › | 274a | 34.00 S | 151.15 E |
| Banks, Îles II | 175f | 13.50 S | 167.30 E |
| Banks, Point › | 180 | 58.36 N | 152.18 W |
| Banksian ≃ | 184 | 53.41 N | 94.10 W |
| Banks Island I, B.C., Can. | 182 | 53.25 N | 130.10 W |
| Banks Island I, N.T., Can. | 176 | 73.15 N | 121.30 W |
| Banks Lake ⊜[1] | 202 | 47.45 N | 119.15 W |
| Banksmeadow | 274a | 33.58 S | 151.13 E |
| Banks Peninsula ›[1] | 172 | 43.45 S | 173.00 E |
| Banks Strait ⋓ | 166 | 40.40 S | 148.07 E |
| Banks / Torres □[8] | 175f | 13.50 S | 167.20 E |
| Bankstown | 170 | 33.55 S | 151.02 E |
| Bankstown Aerodrome ⊠ | 274a | 33.55 S | 150.59 E |
| Banksville | 276 | 41.09 N | 73.38 W |
| Banksville -•-[8] | 279b | 40.24 N | 80.03 W |
| Ban Kum Daeng | 269a | 13.53 N | 100.36 E |
| Bankumuna | 152 | 4.28 S | 19.57 E |
| Bānkura | 126 | 23.15 N | 87.04 E |
| Ban Laem Sing | 269a | 13.30 N | 100.34 E |
| Banlamen | 104 | 41.51 N | 122.27 E |
| Banlashanzi | 104 | 41.26 N | 123.28 E |
| Ban Lat Phrao | 269a | 13.47 N | 100.36 E |
| Ban Le Kathe | 110 | 15.49 N | 98.53 E |
| Banliyuan | 106 | 30.50 N | 118.58 E |
| Ban Luk Kho | 269a | 13.34 N | 100.27 E |
| Ban Mae La Luang | 110 | 18.32 N | 97.56 E |
| Ban Mae Mo | 110 | 18.15 N | 99.42 E |
| Bānmankhi Bazar | 124 | 25.53 N | 87.11 E |
| Banmauk | 110 | 24.24 N | 95.51 E |
| Ban M'diap | 110 | 12.56 N | 108.43 E |
| Ban M'drack | 110 | 12.42 N | 108.47 E |
| Banmian | 100 | 26.02 N | 118.06 E |
| Ban Mit | 110 | 18.51 N | 101.55 E |
| Ban Muangngat | 110 | 19.05 N | 104.04 E |
| Ban Muang Yot | 110 | 19.22 N | 100.34 E |
| Bann ≃ | 48 | 55.10 N | 6.46 W |
| Banna ≃ | 62 | 45.11 N | 7.51 E |
| Ban Nadou | 110 | 15.51 N | 105.38 E |
| Ban Nagnom | 110 | 17.02 N | 105.44 E |
| Ban Nahin | 110 | 18.14 N | 104.13 E |
| Bannaja | 88 | 57.05 N | 108.12 E |
| Ban Nakala | 110 | 16.17 N | 105.11 E |
| Ban Na Kha | 110 | 9.26 N | 98.28 E |
| Ban Nalan | 110 | 15.50 N | 106.04 E |
| Ban Nalè | 110 | 18.42 N | 101.34 E |
| Ban Namcha | 110 | 19.09 N | 102.53 E |
| Ban Nam Chan | 110 | 18.01 N | 103.53 E |
| Ban Namnga | 110 | 20.22 N | 102.19 E |
| Ban Nam Tao | 110 | 17.50 N | 101.15 E |
| Ban Nam Thaeng | 110 | 15.34 N | 105.30 E |
| Ban Naxon | 110 | 18.12 N | 103.05 E |
| Ban Naxouang | 110 | 18.25 N | 104.29 E |
| Bannay | 50 | 47.23 N | 2.53 E |
| Banner Elk | 192 | 36.09 N | 81.52 W |
| Bannerman, Mount ∧[2] | 162 | 19.26 S | 127.10 E |
| Banner Park ♦ | 284b | 39.19 N | 76.42 W |
| Bannertown | 192 | 36.29 N | 80.34 W |
| Bannesdorf | 54 | 54.28 N | 11.13 E |
| Bannewitz | 54 | 51.00 N | 13.43 E |
| Ban Ngam | 110 | 20.11 N | 104.53 E |
| Bannikovo | 86 | 56.07 N | 70.17 E |
| Banning | 228 | 33.55 N | 116.52 W |
| Banningville → Bandundu | 152 | 3.18 S | 17.20 E |
| Bannister | 168a | 32.40 S | 116.33 E |
| Bannister ≃ | 168a | 32.49 S | 116.29 E |
| Bannister Ditch ≅ | 279a | 41.18 N | 82.01 W |
| Bannock | 214 | 40.06 N | 80.59 W |
| Bannockburn, Austl. | 169 | 38.03 S | 144.10 E |
| Bannockburn, Scot., U.K. | 46 | 56.06 N | 3.55 W |
| Bannockburn, Il., U.S. | 278 | 42.12 N | 87.52 W |
| Bannockburn, Zimb. | 154 | 20.16 S | 29.51 E |
| Bannockburn Battlesite ⊥ | 46 | 56.06 N | 3.54 W |
| Bannock Creek ≃ | 202 | 42.53 N | 112.40 W |
| Bannock Peak ∧ | 202 | 42.36 N | 112.42 W |
| Ban Nong Lumphuk | 110 | 14.40 N | 102.43 E |
| Ban Nong Takhian | 110 | 13.08 N | 101.24 E |
| Bannovka | 86 | 53.45 N | 62.57 E |
| Bannu | 123 | 32.59 N | 70.36 E |
| Bánokszentgyörgy | 61 | 46.33 N | 16.47 E |
| Banon | 62 | 44.02 N | 5.38 E |
| Ban O Pao | 269a | 13.50 N | 100.38 E |
| Baños, Ec. | 246 | 1.24 S | 78.25 W |
| Baños, Perú | 248 | 10.05 S | 76.45 W |
| Banow | 120 | 35.38 N | 69.15 E |
| Ban Pak Bong | 110 | 18.32 N | 98.56 E |
| Ban Pak Chan | 110 | 10.32 N | 98.51 E |
| Ban Pakha | 110 | 14.38 N | 107.24 E |
| Ban Pakkhop | 110 | 19.49 N | 100.36 E |
| Ban Pak Nam | 110 | 10.26 N | 99.15 E |
| Ban Pakneun | 110 | 19.14 N | 101.50 E |
| Banpās | 126 | 23.24 N | 87.45 E |
| Ban Phai, Thai | 110 | 16.04 N | 102.44 E |
| Ban Phai, Thai | 110 | 17.33 N | 103.00 E |
| Ban Phe | 110 | 12.38 N | 101.26 E |
| Ban Pho | 110 | 13.36 N | 101.05 E |
| Ban Phon | 110 | 15.25 N | 106.42 E |
| Ban Phông Pho | 110 | 14.36 N | 105.52 E |
| Banphot Phisai | 110 | 15.56 N | 99.59 E |
| Ban Phraek Kasa | 269a | 13.34 N | 100.38 E |
| Ban Phya | 110 | 21.35 N | 102.55 E |
| Ban Pong | 110 | 13.49 N | 99.53 E |
| Banpu | 98 | 34.28 N | 119.18 E |
| Banpura | 126 | 22.27 N | 87.22 E |
| Banqiao, Zhg. | 100 | 30.06 N | 120.27 E |
| Banqiao, Zhg. | 100 | 31.46 N | 112.31 E |
| Banqiao, Zhg. | 100 | 33.21 N | 116.41 E |
| Banqiao, Zhg. | 105 | 39.56 N | 115.51 E |
| Banqiao, Zhg. | 106 | 31.55 N | 118.59 E |
| Banqiao, Zhg. | 107 | 29.31 N | 115.59 E |
| Banqiaochang | 107 | 29.54 N | 104.21 E |

| DEUTSCH Name | Seite | Breite°′ | Länge°′ E = Ost |
|---|---|---|---|
| Banqiaoji | 100 | 32.19 N | 116.37 E |
| Banqiaoxi | 107 | 29.41 N | 103.47 E |
| Banquan | 98 | 35.07 N | 118.42 E |
| Banraeaba | 174t | 1.20 N | 173.02 E |
| Ban Ron Phibun | 110 | 8.09 N | 99.51 E |
| Ban Sa-ang | 110 | 17.26 N | 105.44 E |
| Ban Saen To | 110 | 16.05 N | 99.51 E |
| Ban Sakhla | 269a | 13.32 N | 100.30 E |
| Bansalan | 116 | 6.47 N | 125.14 E |
| Ban Salik | 110 | 18.30 N | 100.45 E |
| Ban Samang | 110 | 19.43 N | 102.36 E |
| Ban Sam Phan | 110 | 8.33 N | 99.09 E |
| Ban Sam Pong | 110 | 18.32 N | 102.47 E |
| Ban Samrong | 110 | 14.23 N | 102.50 E |
| Bansang | 150 | 13.26 N | 14.39 W |
| Ban San Xieng La | 110 | 19.27 N | 102.26 E |
| Bansberia | 126 | 22.58 N | 88.24 E |
| Bānsda | 120 | 20.45 N | 73.22 E |
| Bansha | 48 | 52.28 N | 8.04 W |
| Banshadhāra ≃ | 122 | 18.21 N | 84.08 E |
| Banshanpu | 100 | 27.42 N | 113.24 E |
| Banshi | 100 | 25.20 N | 115.23 E |
| Banshigou | 104 | 41.09 N | 120.58 E |
| Bānsi | 124 | 27.11 N | 82.56 E |
| Bansi ≃ | 126 | 23.50 N | 90.15 E |
| Ban Signo | 110 | 17.51 N | 105.04 E |
| Bansin | 54 | 53.57 N | 14.07 E |
| Banská Bystrica | 30 | 48.44 N | 19.07 E |
| Banská Štiavnica | 30 | 48.28 N | 18.56 E |
| Bansko | 38 | 41.50 N | 23.29 E |
| Bānskupi | 126 | 24.10 N | 86.41 E |
| Ban Songkhon | 110 | 17.58 N | 105.10 E |
| Ban Song Kong | 269a | 13.53 N | 100.34 E |
| Ban Sop Huai Hai | 110 | 19.33 N | 98.05 E |
| Ban Sôppheung | 110 | 18.33 N | 104.17 E |
| Banstala | 272b | 22.32 N | 88.25 E |
| Banstead | 42 | 51.19 N | 0.12 W |
| Bānswāra | 120 | 23.33 N | 74.27 E |
| Banta | 226 | 37.45 N | 121.22 W |
| Banta, Pulau I | 115b | 8.25 S | 119.14 E |
| Bantaeng | 112 | 5.32 S | 119.56 E |
| Bantaian | 114 | 1.56 N | 100.54 E |
| Bantaji | 100 | 32.41 N | 118.35 E |
| Ban Takhlo | 110 | 15.27 N | 100.44 E |
| Bantam | 207 | 41.43 N | 73.14 W |
| Bantam Lake ⊜ | 207 | 41.42 N | 73.13 W |
| Ban Tamru | 269a | 13.31 N | 100.41 E |
| Ban Tao Pun | 269a | 13.53 N | 100.41 E |
| Bantarkawung | 115a | 7.13 S | 108.55 E |
| Bantayan | 116 | 11.10 N | 123.43 E |
| Bantayan Island I | 116 | 11.13 N | 123.44 E |
| Banteer | 48 | 52.07 N | 8.54 W |
| Banteln | 52 | 52.04 N | 9.44 E |
| Banten | 115a | 6.03 S | 106.09 E |
| Banten, Teluk c | 115a | 6.00 S | 106.10 E |
| Bantenan, Tanjung › | 115a | 8.47 S | 114.33 E |
| Ban Teung | 110 | 17.54 N | 105.29 E |
| Ban Thabôk | 110 | 18.22 N | 103.12 E |
| Ban Thanoun | 110 | 19.50 N | 101.29 E |
| Ban Thapayi | 110 | 16.19 N | 105.41 E |
| Bantheville | 56 | 49.21 N | 5.05 E |
| Ban Thieng | 110 | 19.08 N | 102.12 E |
| Ban Tian Sa | 110 | 18.43 N | 103.14 E |
| Bantigui Point › | 116 | 13.41 N | 121.28 E |
| Banting | 114 | 2.49 N | 101.30 E |
| Banton (Jones) | 116 | 12.57 N | 122.05 E |
| Ban Tong Khop | 110 | 17.04 N | 104.16 E |
| Banton Island I | 116 | 12.56 N | 122.04 E |
| Bāntra | 272b | 22.35 N | 88.19 E |
| Bantry | 48 | 51.41 N | 9.27 W |
| Bantry Bay c | 48 | 51.38 N | 9.48 W |
| Bantul | 115a | 7.54 S | 110.20 E |
| Bāntva | 120 | 21.29 N | 70.05 E |
| Banūr | 124 | 30.34 N | 76.43 E |
| Ban Van Hom | 110 | 18.44 N | 104.01 E |
| Ban Vat | 110 | 16.54 N | 106.25 E |
| Banwell | 42 | 51.20 N | 2.52 W |
| Banwy ≃ | 42 | 52.42 N | 3.16 W |
| Ban Xènkhalôk | 110 | 19.42 N | 101.54 E |
| Banxiancun | 106 | 30.33 N | 119.42 E |
| Ban Xot | 110 | 18.11 N | 104.05 E |
| Banya, Punta de la › | 34 | 40.34 N | 0.38 E |
| Banyak, Kepulauan II | 114 | 2.10 N | 97.15 E |
| Ban Ya Plong | 110 | 8.53 N | 98.35 E |
| Banyo | 152 | 6.45 N | 11.49 E |
| Banyoles | 34 | 42.07 N | 2.46 E |
| Banyumas | 115a | 7.31 S | 109.17 E |
| Banyuwangi | 115a | 8.12 S | 114.21 E |
| Banyuwedang | 115b | 8.08 S | 114.36 E |
| Banz | 164 | 5.47 S | 144.37 E |
| Banzare Coast ±[2] | 9 | 67.00 S | 126.00 E |
| Banzhuyuan | 107 | 28.44 N | 106.18 E |
| Banzi, It. | 68 | 40.52 N | 16.01 E |
| Banzi, Zhg. | 100 | 24.18 N | 117.19 E |
| Banzkow | 54 | 53.32 N | 11.31 E |
| Bao ≃, Zhg. | 100 | 33.40 N | 116.33 E |
| Bao ≃, Zhg. | 105 | 39.02 N | 115.39 E |
| Bao ≃, Zhg. | 105 | 40.31 N | 118.17 E |
| Bao, Ouadi V | 146 | 16.36 N | 23.55 E |
| Bao'an, Zhg. | 100 | 30.11 N | 114.43 E |
| Baoan → Zhuolu, Zhg. | 105 | 40.22 N | 115.12 E |
| Baoan, Zhg. | 106 | 31.46 N | 121.21 E |
| Baoancun | 89 | 48.13 N | 125.52 E |
| Baochang → Taibus Qi, Zhg. | 98 | 41.56 N | 115.22 E |
| Baochang, Zhg. | 106 | 32.04 N | 121.25 E |
| Baocheng | 102 | 33.08 N | 107.09 E |
| Baode | 102 | 39.06 N | 111.11 E |
| Baodi | 105 | 39.44 N | 117.17 E |
| Baoding | 105 | 38.52 N | 115.29 E |
| Baofeng | 100 | 33.55 N | 113.02 E |
| Baofu | 106 | 30.31 N | 119.29 E |
| Baoguosi | 107 | 29.35 N | 103.25 E |
| Bao Ha | 110 | 22.11 N | 104.21 E |
| Baohekou | 105 | 40.32 N | 118.15 E |
| Baoji, Zhg. | 100 | 33.08 N | 118.19 E |
| Baoji, Zhg. | 102 | 34.23 N | 107.09 E |
| Baojiagou | 105 | 40.05 N | 115.22 E |
| Baojiapu | 104 | 40.51 N | 122.14 E |
| Baojiatou | 106 | 30.11 N | 119.48 E |
| Baojiawazi | 104 | 41.38 N | 123.24 E |
| Baojing | 102 | 28.43 N | 109.25 E |
| Baokang → Horqin Zuoyi Zhongqi | 89 | 44.07 N | 123.18 E |
| Bao Lac, Viet | 110 | 22.57 N | 105.40 E |
| Bao Lac, Viet | 110 | 11.32 N | 107.48 E |
| Baolin | 107 | 30.24 N | 105.02 E |
| Baolizhen | 89 | 42.56 N | 123.46 E |
| Baolunyuan | 102 | 32.22 N | 105.40 E |
| Baomachang | 107 | 29.58 N | 104.12 E |
| Baon | 116 | 6.47 N | 126.05 E |
| Baonian | 106 | 31.55 N | 119.21 E |
| Baoning | 102 | 23.31 N | 106.24 E |
| Baoqing | 89 | 46.21 N | 132.14 E |
| Baoquan | 98 | 36.16 N | 119.04 E |
| Baoro | 152 | 5.40 N | 15.58 E |
| Baoshan, Zhg. | 100 | 32.39 N | 113.54 E |
| Baoshan, Zhg. | 102 | 26.19 N | 104.27 E |
| Baoshan, Zhg. | 102 | 25.09 N | 99.09 E |
| Baoshan, Zhg. | 106 | 31.25 N | 121.29 E |
| Baoting | 110 | 18.42 N | 109.45 E |
| Baotou (Paotow) | 102 | 40.40 N | 109.59 E |
| Baotun | 104 | 42.29 N | 122.52 E |
| Baoulé ≃ | 150 | 13.33 N | 9.54 W |
| Baowei | 102 | 22.39 N | 106.50 E |
| Baoxikou | 100 | 23.16 N | 115.14 E |
| Baoxingchang | 107 | 29.38 N | 105.41 E |
| Baoxinji | 100 | 32.35 N | 115.00 E |
| Baoyi | 100 | 32.13 N | 116.42 E |
| Baoying | 100 | 33.16 N | 119.20 E |
| Baozhuchang | 107 | 29.48 N | 104.15 E |
| Baozidian | 105 | 40.11 N | 117.48 E |
| Bāp | 120 | 27.23 N | 72.21 E |
| Bapanling | 104 | 40.58 N | 123.08 E |
| Bāpatla | 122 | 15.54 N | 80.28 E |
| Bapaume | 50 | 50.06 N | 2.51 E |
| Bapchule | 200 | 33.08 N | 111.52 W |
| Bapsfontein | 158 | 26.08 S | 28.25 E |
| Baptiste Lake ⊜ | 212 | 45.07 N | 78.02 W |


**Symbols** in the index entries represent the broad categories identified in the key at the right. Symbols with superior numbers (⩚[1]) identify subcategories (see complete key on page *I · 1*).

**Symbole** im Register stellen die rechts im Schlüssel erklärten Kategorien dar. Symbole mit hochgestellten Ziffern (⩚[1]) bezeichnen Unterabteilungen einer Kategorie (vgl. vollständiger Schlüssel auf Seite *I · 1*).

**Los símbolos** incluídos en el texto del índice representan las grandes categorías identificadas con la clave a la derecha. Los símbolos con numeros en su parte superior (⩚[1]) identifican las subcategorías (véase la clave completa en la página *I · 1*).

**Les symboles** de l'index représentent les catégories indiquées dans la légende à droite. Les symboles suivis d'un indice (⩚[1]) représentent des sous-catégories (voir légende complète à la page *I · 1*).

**Os símbolos** incluídos no texto do índice representam as grandes categorias identificadas com a chave à direita. Os símbolos com números em sua parte superior (⩚[1]) identificam as subcategorias (veja-se a chave completa à página *I · 1*).

| | | | | |
|---|---|---|---|---|
| ∧ Mountain | Berg | Montaña | Montagne | Montanha |
| ⩚ Mountains | Gebirge | Montañas | Montagnes | Montanhas |
| )( Pass | Paß | Paso | Col | Passo |
| V Valley, Canyon | Tal, Cañon | Valle, Cañón | Vallée, Canyon | Vale, Canhão |
| ⩦ Plain | Ebene | Llano | Plaine | Planície |
| › Cape | Kap | Cabo | Cap | Cabo |
| I Island | Insel | Isla | Île | Ilha |
| II Islands | Inseln | Islas | Îles | Ilhas |
| ± Other Topographic Features | Andere Topographische Objekte | Otros Elementos Topográficos | Autres données topographiques | Outros acidentes topográficos |

ESPAÑOL · FRANÇAIS · PORTUGUÊS


| Nombre / Nom / Nome | Página / Page | Lat.°′ | Long.°′ W = Oeste / W = Ouest |
|---|---|---|---|
| Baptistown | 208 | 40.31 N | 75.00 W |
| Bāqa el Gharbīya | 132 | 32.25 N | 35.03 E |
| Baqar, Maṣrif Baḥr al- ≡ | 142 | 31.05 N | 32.08 E |
| Baqar, Wādī al- V | 146 | 27.49 N | 18.37 E |
| Baqên | 120 | 31.56 N | 94.00 E |
| Baqing | 120 | 32.15 N | 93.30 E |
| B'aqlīn | 132 | 33.41 N | 35.33 E |
| Ba'qūbah | 128 | 33.45 N | 44.38 E |
| Baquedano | 252 | 23.20 S | 69.51 W |
| Ba Queo | 269c | 10.48 N | 106.38 E |
| Bar, Jugo. | 38 | 42.05 N | 19.05 E |
| Bar, Ross. | 88 | 51.17 N | 107.33 E |
| Bar, Ukr. | 78 | 49.04 N | 27.40 E |
| Bar ≃ | 56 | 49.42 N | 4.50 E |
| Bāra, India | 124 | 25.13 N | 87.22 E |
| Bara, India | 272b | 22.43 N | 88.31 E |
| Bara, India | 272b | 22.46 N | 88.17 E |
| Bara, Nig. | 146 | 10.22 N | 10.44 E |
| Baraawe | 144 | 1.06 N | 44.03 E |
| Barabai | 112 | 2.35 S | 115.23 E |
| Bara Bāngurda | 126 | 22.57 N | 86.24 E |
| Bāra Banki | 124 | 26.55 N | 81.12 E |
| Barabanovo | 82 | 54.43 N | 38.10 E |
| Barābhūm | 126 | 23.02 N | 86.22 E |
| Barabinsk | 86 | 55.21 N | 78.21 E |
| Barabinskaja step' ≋ | 86 | 55.00 N | 79.00 E |
| Baraboo | 190 | 43.28 N | 89.44 W |
| Baraboo ≃ | 190 | 43.29 N | 89.26 W |
| Baraboulé | 150 | 14.12 N | 1.51 W |
| Baracaju ≃ | 255 | 12.21 S | 51.00 W |
| Barachit | 144 | 14.39 N | 39.27 E |
| Barachois Pond Provincial Park ♠ | 186 | 48.30 N | 58.14 W |
| Baracoa, Cuba | 240p | 20.21 N | 74.30 W |
| Baracoa, Hond. | 236 | 15.43 N | 87.52 W |
| Baradā ≃ | 132 | 33.30 N | 36.28 E |
| Baradero | 258 | 33.48 S | 59.30 W |
| Baradero ≃ | 258 | 33.55 S | 59.16 W |
| Baradili | 71 | 39.43 N | 8.54 E |
| Baradine | 166 | 30.56 S | 149.04 E |
| Bara Doāni | 126 | 22.06 N | 89.59 E |
| Baraga | 190 | 46.46 N | 88.29 W |
| Baragaon → Nālanda | 124 | 25.07 N | 85.25 E |
| Baragarh | 120 | 21.20 N | 83.37 E |
| Baragiano | 68 | 40.41 N | 15.35 E |
| Baragoi | 154 | 1.47 N | 36.47 E |
| Baraguá | 240p | 21.41 N | 78.38 W |
| Baragwanath Aerodrome ⊠ | 273d | 26.15 S | 27.59 E |
| Baragwanath Military Hospital ʋ | 273d | 26.16 S | 27.56 E |
| Bārah | 140 | 13.42 N | 30.22 E |
| Barahānuddin | 126 | 22.30 N | 90.43 E |
| Barahona | 238 | 18.12 N | 71.06 W |
| Barāigrām | 126 | 24.19 N | 89.10 E |
| Bara Issa ≃ | 150 | 16.09 N | 3.28 W |
| Barajas, Aeropuerto ⊠ | 266a | 40.28 N | 3.34 W |
| Barajas de Madrid ◆[8] | 266a | 40.28 N | 3.35 E |
| Bara Jorda | 126 | 23.10 N | 86.50 E |
| Barak | 130 | 36.51 N | 37.59 E |
| Barāk ≃ | 120 | 24.52 N | 92.30 E |
| Baraka | 154 | 4.06 S | 29.06 E |
| Baraka (Khawr Barakah) V | 144 | 18.13 N | 37.35 E |
| Barakah | 140 | 10.58 N | 27.59 E |
| Barakah, Khawr (Baraka) V | 144 | 18.13 N | 37.35 E |
| Barakaldo | 34 | 43.18 N | 2.59 W |
| Barākar | 126 | 24.07 N | 86.14 E |
| Barakār ≃ | 126 | 23.42 N | 86.48 E |
| Bara Khunta | 126 | 21.43 N | 86.38 E |
| Baraki | 120 | 33.56 N | 68.55 E |
| Barakloj | 86 | 52.12 N | 67.49 E |
| Bārākpur, Bngl. | 126 | 22.55 N | 89.32 E |
| Bārākpur, India | 126 | 22.46 N | 88.21 E |
| Bārākpur Cantonment | 272b | 22.46 N | 88.22 E |
| Barakula | 166 | 26.26 S | 150.31 E |
| Barāl | 272b | 22.27 N | 88.22 E |
| Baral ≃ | 126 | 24.10 N | 89.27 E |
| Baralaba | 166 | 24.11 S | 149.49 E |
| Barām | 126 | 22.57 N | 86.18 E |
| Baram ≃ | 112 | 4.36 N | 113.59 E |
| Baram, Tanjong › | 112 | 4.35 N | 113.59 E |
| Barama ≃ | 246 | 7.40 N | 59.15 W |
| Barāmāria | 126 | 21.42 N | 87.04 E |
| Bārāmati | 122 | 18.09 N | 74.35 E |
| Bāramūla | 123 | 34.12 N | 74.21 E |
| Baran', Bela. | 76 | 54.30 N | 28.40 E |
| Baran', Bela. | 76 | 54.29 N | 30.18 E |
| Bārān, India | 124 | 25.06 N | 76.31 E |
| Baranagar | 126 | 22.38 N | 88.22 E |
| Baranakovo | 86 | 58.08 N | 82.58 E |
| Baranavičy | 76 | 53.08 N | 26.02 E |
| Barancevo | 82 | 55.04 N | 37.38 E |
| Baranello | 66 | 41.32 N | 14.34 E |
| Barangbarang | 112 | 6.24 S | 120.28 E |
| Barangeon ≃ | 50 | 47.12 N | 2.10 E |
| Barani | 150 | 13.10 N | 3.53 W |
| Baraniki | 80 | 46.31 N | 41.50 E |
| Baranivka | 78 | 50.18 N | 27.40 E |
| Baranoa | 246 | 10.48 N | 74.55 W |
| Barano d'Ischia | 68 | 40.42 N | 13.55 E |
| Baranof | 180 | 57.05 N | 134.50 W |
| Baranof Island I | 180 | 57.00 N | 135.00 W |
| Baranovskoje | 82 | 55.25 N | 38.45 E |
| Barany, Ross. | 76 | 57.20 N | 29.09 E |
| Barany, Ross. | 80 | 57.38 N | 52.16 E |
| Baranya □[6] | 30 | 46.05 N | 18.15 E |
| Baranykivka | 83 | 49.10 N | 39.50 E |
| Barão Ataliba Nogueira | 256 | 22.24 S | 46.45 W |
| Barão de Geraldo | 256 | 22.49 S | 47.06 W |
| Barão de Grajaú | 250 | 6.45 S | 43.01 W |
| Barão de Juparanã | 256 | 22.21 S | 43.41 W |
| Barão de Melgaço | 248 | 16.13 S | 55.58 W |
| Barão de Tromai | 250 | 1.29 S | 45.36 W |
| Baraolt | 38 | 46.05 N | 25.36 E |
| Baraque de Fraiture ∧ | 56 | 50.15 N | 5.44 E |
| Baras | 116 | 13.40 N | 124.22 E |
| Barasāhi | 126 | 21.43 N | 86.44 E |
| Bārāsat, India | 126 | 22.43 N | 88.29 E |
| Bārāsat, India | 272b | 22.51 N | 88.22 E |
| Baraševo | 80 | 54.32 N | 42.53 E |
| Barashi | 78 | 50.43 N | 28.01 E |
| Baraški | 24 | 65.40 N | 52.10 E |
| Barat, Lintasan ᴗ | 115a | 7.08 S | 112.40 E |
| Baratā | 266c | 38.48 N | 9.19 W |
| Baratang Island I | 110 | 12.13 N | 92.45 E |
| Barataria | 194 | 29.43 N | 90.07 W |
| Barataria Bay C | 194 | 29.22 N | 89.57 W |
| Barat Daya, Kepulauan II | 108 | 7.25 S | 128.00 E |
| Barate | 112 | 9.54 S | 123.38 E |
| Bar'atino, Ross. | 76 | 54.19 N | 34.31 E |
| Bar'atino, Ross. | 82 | 54.43 N | 36.49 E |
| Baratolia | 126 | 22.25 N | 86.37 E |
| Baratta | 166 | 31.59 S | 139.06 E |
| Barauana ≃ | 246 | 1.14 N | 60.41 W |
| Baraula | 272a | 28.34 N | 77.22 E |
| Barauni | 124 | 25.29 N | 85.59 E |
| Baraut | 124 | 29.06 N | 77.16 E |
| Baravuḥa | 76 | 55.36 N | 28.37 E |
| Baraya | 246 | 3.10 N | 75.04 W |
| Barbacena | 256 | 21.14 S | 43.46 W |
| Barbacoas | 246 | 1.41 N | 78.09 W |
| Barbades → Barbados □[1] | 241g | 13.10 N | 59.32 W |
| Barbadillo del Mercado | 34 | 42.02 N | 3.21 W |
| Barbadoes Island I | 285 | 40.07 N | 75.22 W |
| Barbados □[1], N.A. | 230 | 13.10 N | 59.32 W |
| Barbados □[1], N.A. | 241g | 13.10 N | 59.32 W |
| Barbagia ◆[1] | 71 | 39.55 N | 9.12 E |
| Barbalha | 250 | 7.19 S | 39.17 W |
| Barbar | 140 | 18.01 N | 33.59 E |
| Barbarano Vicentino | 64 | 45.24 N | 11.32 E |
| Barbarasco | 64 | 44.14 N | 9.56 E |
| Barbareta, Isla I | 236 | 16.26 N | 86.09 W |
| Barbaria, Cap de › | 34 | 38.38 N | 1.23 E |
| Barbaros | 130 | 40.54 N | 27.27 E |
| Barbas, Cap › | 148 | 22.18 N | 16.41 W |
| Barbaši | 76 | 57.42 N | 28.24 E |
| Barbastro | 34 | 42.02 N | 0.08 E |
| Barbate | 34 | 36.12 N | 5.55 W |
| Barbate ≃ | 34 | 36.11 N | 5.55 W |
| Barbeau Peak ∧ | 16 | 81.54 N | 75.01 W |
| Barbentane | 62 | 43.54 N | 4.45 E |
| Barberà del Vallès | 266d | 41.31 N | 2.08 E |
| Barber Booth | 262 | 53.22 N | 1.50 W |
| Barberena | 236 | 14.18 N | 90.22 W |
| Barberena ≃ | 234 | 22.34 N | 97.52 W |
| Barberino di Mugello | 66 | 44.00 N | 11.15 E |
| Barberino Val d'Elsa | 66 | 43.32 N | 11.10 E |
| Barbers Point › | 229c | 21.18 N | 158.07 W |
| Barbers Point Naval Air Station ■ | 229c | 21.19 N | 158.04 W |
| Barberton, S. Afr. | 156 | 25.48 S | 31.03 E |
| Barberton, Oh., U.S. | 214 | 41.00 N | 81.36 W |
| Barbezieux | 32 | 45.28 N | 0.09 W |
| Bar Bigha | 124 | 25.13 N | 85.44 E |
| Barbil | 124 | 22.06 N | 85.20 E |
| Barbis | 54 | 51.37 N | 10.25 E |
| Barbizon | 50 | 48.27 N | 2.36 E |
| Barbosa, Col. | 246 | 6.26 N | 75.20 W |
| Barbosa, Col. | 246 | 5.57 N | 73.37 W |
| Barboursville | 188 | 38.24 N | 82.17 W |
| Barbourville | 192 | 36.51 N | 83.53 W |
| Barbuda I | 238 | 17.38 N | 61.48 W |
| Barbuise ≃ | 50 | 48.33 N | 3.58 E |
| Barby | 54 | 51.58 N | 11.53 E |
| Bârca | 38 | 43.58 N | 23.37 E |
| Barčadiv | 85 | 38.19 N | 72.29 E |
| Barca Grande ≃ | 258 | 34.09 S | 58.23 W |
| Barcaldine | 166 | 23.33 S | 145.17 E |
| Barcarena | 266c | 38.44 N | 9.17 W |
| Barcarena, Ribeira de ≃ | 266c | 38.42 N | 9.27 W |
| Barcarrota | 34 | 38.31 N | 6.51 W |
| Barcău (Berettyó) ≃ | 38 | 46.59 N | 21.07 E |
| Barce → Al-Marj | 146 | 32.30 N | 20.54 E |
| Barcellona Pozzo di Gotto | 70 | 38.09 N | 15.13 E |
| Barcelona, Esp. | 34 | 41.23 N | 2.11 E |
| Barcelona, Esp. | 266d | 41.23 N | 2.11 E |
| Barcelona, Méx. | 232 | 26.12 N | 103.25 W |
| Barcelona, Pil. | 116 | 12.52 N | 124.09 E |
| Barcelona, Ven. | 246 | 10.08 N | 64.42 W |
| Barcelona □[4] | 34 | 41.40 N | 2.00 E |
| Barcelona, Aeropuerto Transoceánico de ⊠ | 266d | 41.18 N | 2.05 E |
| Barcelone → Barcelona | 34 | 41.23 N | 2.11 E |
| Barceloneta | 240m | 18.27 N | 66.32 W |
| Barcelonnette | 62 | 44.23 N | 6.39 E |
| Barcelos, Bra. | 246 | 0.58 S | 62.57 W |
| Barcelos, Port. | 34 | 41.32 N | 8.37 W |
| Barchaticha | 80 | 57.34 N | 45.13 E |
| Barchyn ≃ | 88 | 48.43 N | 110.17 E |
| Barcillonnette | 62 | 44.26 N | 5.55 E |
| Barcin | 30 | 52.52 N | 17.57 E |
| Barcis | 64 | 46.11 N | 12.33 E |
| Barclay | 208 | 39.08 N | 75.51 W |
| Barclay Brook ≃ | 276 | 40.19 N | 74.22 W |
| Barcoo ≃ | 166 | 25.30 S | 142.50 E |
| Barcroft, Lake ⊜[1] | 284c | 38.51 N | 77.09 W |
| Barcs | 30 | 45.58 N | 17.28 E |
| Barcy | 261 | 49.01 N | 2.53 E |
| Barczewo | 30 | 53.50 N | 20.42 E |
| Bard | 62 | 45.36 N | 7.45 E |
| Bärdä, Azer. | 84 | 40.23 N | 47.08 E |
| Barda, Ross. | 86 | 56.54 N | 55.38 E |
| Barda del Medio | 252 | 38.43 S | 68.10 W |
| Bardagué, Enneri V | 146 | 22.06 N | 16.28 E |
| Bardai, Sūd. | 140 | 12.43 N | 21.53 E |
| Bardaï, Tchad | 146 | 21.22 N | 16.59 E |
| Bardawīl, Sabkhat al- ≋ | 140 | 31.10 N | 33.10 E |
| Barddhamān | 126 | 23.15 N | 87.51 E |
| Bardejov | 30 | 49.18 N | 21.16 E |
| Bardenas Reales ⋏[1] | 34 | 42.10 N | 1.25 W |
| Bardeskan | 128 | 35.12 N | 57.58 E |
| Bardi | 62 | 44.38 N | 9.44 E |
| Bardīyah | 146 | 31.46 N | 25.06 E |
| Bardız | 130 | 40.26 N | 42.20 E |
| Bardney | 44 | 53.12 N | 0.21 W |
| Bardo | 36 | 36.50 N | 10.06 E |
| Bardoc | 162 | 30.20 S | 121.17 E |
| Bārdoli | 120 | 21.07 N | 73.07 E |
| Bardolino | 64 | 45.33 N | 10.43 E |
| Bardonecchia | 62 | 45.05 N | 6.42 E |
| Bardonia | 276 | 41.07 N | 74.00 W |
| Bardoux, Lac ⊜ | 186 | 51.09 N | 67.50 W |
| Bardowick | 52 | 53.18 N | 10.23 E |
| Bardsey Island I | 42 | 52.45 N | 4.45 W |
| Bardsey Sound ᴗ | 42 | 52.47 N | 4.45 W |
| Bardstown | 194 | 37.48 N | 85.28 W |
| Bardu | 24 | 68.52 N | 18.21 E |
| Bardufoss | 24 | 69.04 N | 18.30 E |
| Bardwell, Ky., U.S. | 194 | 36.52 N | 89.00 W |
| Bardwell, Tx., U.S. | 222 | 32.16 N | 96.42 W |
| Bardwell Lake ⊜[1] | 222 | 32.16 N | 96.39 W |
| Bare | 144 | 4.42 N | 42.47 E |
| Bareggio | 266b | 45.29 N | 9.00 E |
| Barei, Wādī V | 140 | 13.27 N | 23.57 E |
| Bareilly | 124 | 28.21 N | 79.25 E |
| Bareli | 124 | 23.00 N | 78.14 E |
| Barenburg | 52 | 52.37 N | 8.47 E |
| Barendrecht | 52 | 51.51 N | 4.32 E |
| Bärenklau | 54 | 51.56 N | 14.34 E |
| Bärenstein, Dtsch. | 54 | 50.30 N | 13.02 E |
| Bärenstein, Dtsch. | 54 | 50.48 N | 13.47 E |
| Barentin | 50 | 49.33 N | 0.57 E |
| Barents Sea ⚲[2] | 12 | 74.00 N | 36.00 E |
| Barents Trough ✢[1] | 12 | 75.00 N | 29.00 E |
| Barentu | 144 | 15.04 N | 37.37 E |
| Bareo | 112 | 3.45 N | 115.27 E |
| Baresville | 208 | 39.48 N | 76.57 W |
| Bareta | 123 | 29.52 N | 75.42 E |
| Barfleur | 32 | 49.40 N | 1.15 W |
| Barfleur, Pointe de › | 32 | 49.42 N | 1.16 W |
| Barga | 64 | 44.04 N | 10.29 E |
| Bargāchia, India | 126 | 22.39 N | 88.07 E |
| Bargāchia, India | 272b | 22.48 N | 88.27 E |
| Bargagli | 62 | 44.27 N | 9.05 E |
| Bargaintown | 208 | 39.22 N | 70.35 W |
| Bargara | 166 | 24.49 S | 152.27 E |
| Bargas | 34 | 39.56 N | 4.03 W |
| Barge, It. | 62 | 44.43 N | 7.20 E |
| Barge, Ityo. | 144 | 6.14 N | 36.58 E |
| Barg-e Maṯāl | 120 | 35.40 N | 71.21 E |
| Bargemon | 62 | 43.37 N | 6.32 E |
| Bargen | 58 | 47.48 N | 8.37 E |
| Bargersville | 218 | 39.31 N | 86.10 W |
| Barghanak | 128 | 33.56 N | 62.26 E |
| Bargnop | 140 | 9.30 N | 28.28 E |
| Bargo | 170 | 34.18 S | 150.35 E |
| Bargoed | 42 | 51.43 N | 3.15 W |
| Bargteheide | 52 | 53.44 N | 10.16 E |
| Bārguna | 126 | 22.09 N | 90.07 E |
| Barguzin | 88 | 53.37 N | 109.37 E |
| Barguzin ≃ | 88 | 53.27 N | 109.00 E |
| Barguzinskij chrebet ⋏ | 88 | 54.30 N | 110.20 E |
| Barguzinskij zapovednik ♠ | 88 | 54.25 N | 109.40 E |
| Bārh | 124 | 25.29 N | 85.43 E |
| Barhaj | 124 | 26.17 N | 83.44 E |
| Bar Harbor | 188 | 44.23 N | 68.12 W |
| Barharwa | 124 | 24.52 N | 87.47 E |
| Barhau | 112 | 5.19 S | 102.10 E |
| Barhi | 124 | 24.18 N | 85.25 E |
| Bar Hill | 42 | 52.15 N | 0.01 E |
| Barhiya | 124 | 25.17 N | 86.02 E |
| Bāri, India | 124 | 23.03 N | 78.05 E |
| Bāri, India | 124 | 26.39 N | 77.36 E |
| Bari, It. | 68 | 41.07 N | 16.52 E |
| Bari, Zaïre | 152 | 3.19 N | 19.23 E |
| Bari □[4], It. | 68 | 40.56 N | 16.40 E |
| Bari □[4], Som. | 144 | 10.00 N | 50.00 E |
| Baria ≃ | 246 | 1.56 N | 66.35 W |
| Baricella | 64 | 44.39 N | 11.32 E |
| Barichara | 246 | 6.38 N | 73.14 W |
| Barīdī, Ra's › | 128 | 24.17 N | 37.31 E |
| Bāri Doāb ⋏[1] | 123 | 30.25 N | 73.00 E |
| Barī Gāv | 120 | 33.52 N | 67.49 E |
| Barigazzo | 64 | 44.16 N | 10.39 E |
| Barigua, Salina de ≋ | 241s | 12.08 N | 69.59 W |
| Barika | 34 | 35.23 N | 5.22 E |
| Barika, Oued ≃ | 34 | 35.22 N | 5.18 E |
| Barikiwa | 154 | 9.28 S | 37.54 E |
| Barīkowṯ | 120 | 35.18 N | 71.32 E |
| Barile | 68 | 40.57 N | 15.40 E |
| Barillas | 236 | 15.48 N | 91.18 W |
| Bariloche → San Carlos de Bariloche | 254 | 41.09 S | 71.18 W |
| Barilo-Krepinskaja | 83 | 47.45 N | 39.32 E |
| Barīm (Perim) I | 144 | 12.39 N | 43.25 E |
| Barima ≃ | 246 | 8.33 N | 60.25 W |
| Barima-Waini □[4] | 246 | 7.45 N | 59.30 W |
| Barin | 84 | 39.13 N | 44.28 E |
| Barinas, P.R. | 240m | 18.01 N | 66.51 W |
| Barinas, Ven. | 246 | 8.38 N | 70.12 W |
| Barinas □[3] | 246 | 8.10 N | 69.50 W |
| Baring | 224 | 47.46 N | 121.29 W |
| Baring, Cape › | 176 | 70.05 N | 117.20 W |
| Baringa, Zaïre | 152 | 6.17 S | 16.55 E |
| Baringa, Zaïre | 152 | 0.45 N | 20.52 E |
| Baringo, Lake ⊜ | 154 | 0.38 N | 36.05 E |
| Båring Vig C | 41 | 55.32 N | 9.56 E |
| Barinitas | 246 | 8.45 N | 70.25 W |
| Bāripada | 126 | 21.56 N | 86.43 E |
| Bariri | 255 | 22.04 S | 48.44 W |
| Bārīs | 140 | 24.40 N | 30.36 E |
| Barisacho | 84 | 42.28 N | 44.54 E |
| Bari Sādri | 120 | 24.25 N | 74.28 E |
| Barisāl | 124 | 22.42 N | 90.22 E |
| Barisan, Pegunungan ⋏ | 112 | 3.00 S | 102.15 E |
| Bari Sardo | 71 | 39.50 N | 9.38 E |
| Barisciano | 66 | 42.19 N | 13.35 E |
| Bariti Bil ⊜ | 272b | 22.48 N | 88.26 E |
| Barito ≃ | 112 | 3.32 S | 114.29 E |
| Baritú, Parque Nacional ♠ | 252 | 22.30 S | 64.35 W |
| Barjā | 132 | 33.39 N | 35.26 E |
| Barjac | 62 | 44.18 N | 4.21 E |
| Barjols | 62 | 43.33 N | 6.00 E |
| Barjora | 126 | 23.26 N | 87.17 E |
| Barjūj, Wādī V | 146 | 25.57 N | 13.12 E |
| Bark ≃ | 216 | 42.55 N | 88.50 W |
| Barka Kāna | 124 | 23.37 N | 85.29 E |
| Barkal | 120 | 22.44 N | 92.23 E |
| Barkam | 102 | 31.50 N | 102.40 E |
| Barkava | 76 | 56.43 N | 26.36 E |
| Barkelsby | 41 | 54.30 N | 9.50 E |
| Barker, N.Y., U.S. | 210 | 43.19 N | 78.33 W |
| Barker, Ur. | 258 | 34.16 S | 57.27 W |
| Barker Point › | 276 | 40.51 N | 73.44 W |
| Barker Reservoir ⊜[1] | 222 | 29.44 N | 95.44 W |
| Barkers Brook ≃ | 285 | 40.03 N | 74.45 W |
| Barkerville | 182 | 53.04 N | 121.31 W |
| Barkerville Historic Park ♠ | 182 | 53.04 N | 121.30 W |
| Barkeyville | 214 | 41.12 N | 79.58 W |
| Barkhamsted Reservoir ⊜[1] | 207 | 41.57 N | 72.57 W |
| Bārkhān | 120 | 29.54 N | 69.31 E |
| Barkhanpur | 126 | 23.50 N | 89.33 E |
| Barking ◆[8] | 42 | 51.33 N | 0.06 E |
| Barkingside ◆[8] | 260 | 51.36 N | 0.05 E |
| Barki Saraiya | 124 | 24.10 N | 85.53 E |
| Barkisland | 262 | 53.41 N | 1.55 W |
| Bark Lake ⊜, On., Can. | 190 | 46.54 N | 82.28 W |
| Bark Lake ⊜, On., Can. | 212 | 45.27 N | 77.51 W |
| Barkley, Lake ⊜[1] | 194 | 36.40 N | 87.55 W |
| Barkley Sound ᴗ | 182 | 48.53 N | 125.20 W |
| Barkly ≃ | 169 | 37.32 S | 146.32 E |
| Barkly, Mount ∧[2] | 162 | 21.34 S | 132.28 E |
| Barkly East | 158 | 30.58 S | 27.33 E |
| Barkly Tableland ⋏[1] | 162 | 18.00 S | 136.00 E |
| Barkly West | 158 | 28.05 S | 24.31 E |
| Barkol | 90 | 43.50 N | 93.30 E |
| Barksdale | 196 | 29.44 N | 100.02 W |
| Barkuhi | 124 | 22.13 N | 78.42 E |
| Barla | 130 | 38.01 N | 30.47 E |
| Bârlad | 38 | 46.14 N | 27.40 E |
| Bârlad ≃ | 38 | 45.36 N | 27.31 E |
| Barlassina | 266b | 45.39 N | 9.08 E |
| Barlaston | 42 | 52.57 N | 2.10 W |
| Barlby | 44 | 53.48 N | 1.03 W |
| Barleben | 54 | 52.12 N | 11.37 E |
| Bar-le-Duc | 56 | 48.47 N | 5.10 E |
| Barlee, Lake ⊜ | 162 | 29.10 S | 119.30 E |
| Barlee, Mount ∧[2] | 162 | 24.37 S | 128.06 E |
| Barlee Range ⋏ | 162 | 23.35 S | 116.00 E |
| Barles | 62 | 44.16 N | 6.16 E |
| Barletta | 68 | 41.19 N | 16.17 E |
| Barlin | 50 | 50.27 N | 2.37 E |
| Barlinek | 30 | 53.00 N | 15.12 E |
| Barling | 194 | 35.19 N | 94.18 W |
| Barlow | 194 | 37.03 N | 89.02 W |
| Barluk | 88 | 54.32 N | 101.43 E |
| Barma | 164 | 1.54 S | 133.00 E |
| Barmancak, ozero ⊜ | 80 | 48.02 N | 44.40 E |
| Barmashove | 78 | 47.07 N | 32.26 E |
| Barmedman | 166 | 34.09 S | 147.23 E |
| Barmen ◆[8] | 263 | 51.17 N | 7.13 E |
| Bārmer | 120 | 25.45 N | 71.23 E |
| Barmera | 166 | 34.15 S | 140.28 E |
| Barmouth | 42 | 52.43 N | 4.03 W |
| Barmouth Bay C | 42 | 52.42 N | 4.08 W |
| Barmstedt | 52 | 53.47 N | 9.46 E |
| Barnaby Manor Oaks | 284c | 38.50 N | 76.58 W |
| Barnagar | 120 | 23.03 N | 75.22 E |
| Barnāla | 123 | 30.23 N | 75.33 E |
| Barnard Castle | 44 | 54.33 N | 1.55 W |
| Barnasht | 142 | 29.41 N | 31.15 E |
| Bärnau | 60 | 49.49 N | 12.26 E |
| Barnaul | 86 | 53.22 N | 83.45 E |
| Bärnbach | 61 | 47.05 N | 15.06 E |
| Barn Bluff ∧ | 166 | 41.43 S | 145.56 E |
| Barneberg | 54 | 52.08 N | 11.03 E |
| Barnegat | 208 | 39.45 N | 74.13 W |
| Barnegat Bay C | 208 | 39.52 N | 74.07 W |
| Barnegat Light | 208 | 39.45 N | 74.06 W |
| Barne Inlet C | 9 | 80.15 S | 160.15 E |
| Barnes | 214 | 41.40 N | 79.01 W |
| Barnes ◆[8] | 260 | 51.28 N | 0.15 W |
| Barnesboro | 214 | 40.39 N | 78.46 W |
| Barnes Corners | 212 | 43.49 N | 75.49 W |
| Barnes Ice Cap ⊓ | 176 | 70.00 N | 73.15 W |
| Barnes Lake ⊜ | 184 | 56.23 N | 98.06 W |
| Barnes Sound ᴗ | 220 | 25.14 N | 80.23 W |
| Barnesville, Ga., U.S. | 192 | 33.03 N | 84.09 W |
| Barnesville, Mn., U.S. | 198 | 46.39 N | 96.25 W |
| Barnesville, Oh., U.S. | 188 | 39.59 N | 81.10 W |
| Barnet ◆[8] | 42 | 51.40 N | 0.13 W |
| Barnetby le Wold | 44 | 53.35 N | 0.25 W |
| Barnett | 219 | 39.16 N | 89.42 W |
| Barnetts | 208 | 37.22 N | 77.09 W |
| Barneveld, Ned. | 52 | 52.08 N | 5.35 E |
| Barneveld, N.Y., U.S. | 210 | 43.16 N | 75.12 W |
| Barneville-Carteret | 32 | 49.23 N | 1.47 W |
| Barnhart, Mo., U.S. | 219 | 38.20 N | 90.23 W |
| Barnhart, Tx., U.S. | 196 | 31.08 N | 101.10 W |
| Barnhill | 214 | 40.27 N | 81.21 W |
| Barnim ◆[1] | 54 | 52.40 N | 13.45 E |
| Barnoldswick | 44 | 53.55 N | 2.11 W |
| Barnówko | 54 | 52.48 N | 14.45 E |
| Barnsboro | 285 | 39.46 N | 75.09 W |
| Barnsdall | 196 | 36.33 N | 96.09 W |
| Barnsley | 44 | 53.34 N | 1.28 W |
| Barnstable | 207 | 41.42 N | 70.18 W |
| Barnstable □[6] | 207 | 41.42 N | 70.18 W |
| Barnstable Harbor C | 207 | 41.43 N | 70.18 W |
| Barnstaple | 42 | 51.05 N | 4.04 W |
| Barnstaple Bay C | 42 | 51.05 N | 4.20 W |
| Barnston | 262 | 53.21 N | 3.05 W |
| Barnstorf | 52 | 52.42 N | 8.30 E |
| Barnt Green | 42 | 52.22 N | 1.59 W |
| Barnton | 262 | 53.16 N | 2.33 W |
| Barntrup | 52 | 51.59 N | 9.06 E |
| Barnum Island | 276 | 40.36 N | 73.39 W |
| Barnwell, Ab., Can. | 182 | 49.46 N | 112.15 W |
| Barnwell, S.C., U.S. | 192 | 33.14 N | 81.21 W |
| Baro | 150 | 8.37 N | 6.25 E |
| Baro ≃ | 144 | 8.26 N | 33.13 E |
| Barobo | 116 | 8.33 N | 126.07 E |
| Baroda → Vadodara, India | 122 | 22.18 N | 73.12 E |
| Baroda, India | 124 | 25.30 N | 76.39 E |
| Baroda, Mi., U.S. | 216 | 41.57 N | 86.29 W |
| Baroe | 158 | 33.13 S | 24.33 E |
| Barometer ∧ | 172 | 41.50 S | 173.39 E |
| Baron Bluff ≗[4] | 241n | 17.47 N | 64.47 W |
| Baronissi | 68 | 40.44 N | 14.45 E |
| Baron'ki | 76 | 53.09 N | 32.08 E |
| Barons | 182 | 50.00 N | 113.05 W |
| Barora Fa Island I | 175e | 7.30 S | 158.20 E |
| Barora Ite Island I | 175e | 7.35 S | 158.24 E |
| Barossa Reservoir ⊜[1] | 168b | 34.39 S | 138.51 E |
| Barotac Nuevo | 116 | 10.54 N | 122.42 E |
| Barotac Viejo | 116 | 11.03 N | 122.51 E |
| Barouéli | 150 | 13.04 N | 6.50 W |
| Barpathār | 120 | 26.17 N | 93.53 E |
| Barpeta | 120 | 26.19 N | 91.00 E |
| Bar Point › | 214 | 42.03 N | 83.06 W |
| Barqa | 120 | 30.57 N | 81.20 E |
| Barqah (Cyrenaica) □[9] | 146 | 31.00 N | 22.30 E |
| Barqah, Jabal al- ∧ | 132 | 30.25 N | 34.18 E |
| Barq al-'Izz | 142 | 31.01 N | 31.26 E |
| Barque Canada Reef ✢[2] | 108 | 8.12 N | 113.19 E |
| Barques, Pointe aux › | 190 | 44.04 N | 82.58 W |
| Barquisimeto | 246 | 10.04 N | 69.19 W |
| Barr | 58 | 48.24 N | 7.27 E |
| Barra, Bra. | 250 | 11.05 S | 43.10 W |
| Barra, Gam. | 150 | 13.20 N | 16.36 W |
| Barra I | 46 | 56.58 N | 7.29 W |
| Barra, Ponta da › | 156 | 23.47 S | 35.32 E |
| Barra, Sound of ᴗ | 46 | 57.05 N | 7.25 W |
| Barraba | 166 | 30.22 S | 150.36 E |
| Barracas ◆[8] | 288 | 34.38 S | 58.22 W |
| Barrackpore → Bārākpur | 126 | 22.46 N | 88.21 E |
| Barrackpore Airport ⊠ | 272b | 22.47 N | 88.22 E |
| Barrackville | 188 | 39.30 N | 80.10 W |
| Barracouta, Cape › | 158 | 34.26 S | 21.22 E |
| Barra da Estiva | 255 | 13.38 S | 41.19 W |
| Barra de Santo Antônio | 250 | 9.24 S | 35.30 W |
| Barra de São Francisco | 256 | 21.58 S | 42.42 W |
| Barra do Bugres | 248 | 15.05 S | 57.11 W |
| Barra do Corda | 250 | 5.30 S | 45.15 W |
| Barra do Cuanza | 152 | 9.09 S | 13.00 E |
| Barra do Dande | 152 | 8.28 S | 13.22 E |
| Barra do Garças | 255 | 15.53 S | 52.15 W |
| Barra do Mendes | 255 | 11.43 S | 42.04 W |
| Barra do Piraí | 256 | 22.28 S | 43.49 W |
| Barra do Ribeiro | 252 | 30.18 S | 51.18 W |
| Barra dos Coqueiros | 250 | 10.54 S | 37.03 W |
| Barra Falsa, Ponta da › | 156 | 22.55 S | 35.37 E |
| Barrafranca | 70 | 37.22 N | 14.12 E |
| Barra Funda ◆[8] | 287b | 23.31 S | 46.39 W |
| Barra Head › | 46 | 56.46 N | 7.38 W |
| Barrali | 71 | 39.28 N | 9.06 E |
| Barra Mansa | 256 | 22.32 S | 44.11 W |
| Barranca, Perú | 248 | 10.45 S | 77.46 W |
| Barranca, Perú | 248 | 4.50 S | 76.42 W |
| Barrancabermeja | 246 | 7.03 N | 73.52 W |
| Barrancas, Col. | 246 | 10.57 N | 72.50 W |
| Barrancas, Ven. | 246 | 8.46 N | 70.06 W |
| Barrancas, Ven. | 246 | 8.42 N | 62.11 W |
| Barrancas ≃ | 252 | 36.52 S | 69.45 W |
| Barranco | 286d | 12.09 S | 77.02 W |
| Barranco Azul | 196 | 29.21 N | 104.17 W |
| Barranco de Guadalupe | 196 | 30.02 N | 104.44 W |
| Barranco do Velho | 34 | 37.14 N | 7.56 W |
| Barrancos | 34 | 38.08 N | 6.59 W |
| Barrânia | 256 | 21.33 S | 46.32 W |
| Barranqueras | 252 | 27.29 S | 58.56 W |
| Barranquilla | 246 | 10.59 N | 74.48 W |
| Barranquitas | 240m | 18.11 N | 66.18 W |
| Barras | 250 | 4.15 S | 42.18 W |
| Barrax | 34 | 39.03 N | 2.12 W |
| Barre, Ma., U.S. | 207 | 42.25 N | 72.06 W |
| Barre, Vt., U.S. | 188 | 44.11 N | 72.30 W |
| Barrea | 66 | 41.45 N | 13.59 E |
| Barreal | 252 | 31.38 S | 69.28 W |
| Barree | 214 | 40.35 N | 78.06 W |
| Barre Falls Dam ◆[6] | 207 | 42.26 N | 72.02 W |
| Barreiras | 255 | 12.08 S | 45.00 W |
| Barreirinha | 250 | 2.47 S | 57.03 W |
| Barreirinhas | 250 | 2.45 S | 42.50 W |
| Barreiro | 34 | 38.40 N | 9.05 W |
| Barreiro ≃, Bra. | 255 | 15.43 S | 52.45 W |
| Barreiro ≃, Bra. | 287a | 22.52 S | 43.34 W |
| Barreiros | 250 | 8.49 S | 35.12 W |
| Barrême | 62 | 43.57 N | 6.22 E |
| Barren ≃ | 194 | 37.11 N | 86.37 W |
| Barren, Nosy II | 157b | 18.25 S | 43.40 E |
| Barren Island I | 110 | 12.16 N | 93.51 E |
| Barren Islands II | 180 | 58.55 N | 152.15 W |
| Barrenjoey Head › | 170 | 33.34 S | 151.20 E |
| Barren River Lake ⊜[1] | 194 | 36.45 N | 86.02 W |
| Barren Run ≃ | 279b | 40.09 N | 79.42 W |
| Barre Plains | 207 | 42.22 N | 72.06 W |
| Barret-le-Bas | 62 | 44.16 N | 5.44 E |
| Barretos | 255 | 20.33 S | 48.33 W |
| Barrett | 222 | 29.53 N | 95.04 W |
| Barrett, Mount ∧ | 162 | 18.10 S | 127.33 E |
| Barrhead, Ab., Can. | 182 | 54.08 N | 114.24 W |
| Barrhead, Scot., U.K. | 46 | 55.48 N | 4.24 W |
| Barrhill | 44 | 55.07 N | 4.46 W |
| Barrie | 212 | 44.24 N | 79.40 W |
| Barriefield | 212 | 44.14 N | 76.28 W |
| Barrie Island I | 190 | 45.55 N | 82.40 W |
| Barrien | 52 | 52.56 N | 8.49 E |
| Barrier, Cape › | 172 | 36.21 S | 175.31 E |
| Barrière | 182 | 51.11 N | 120.07 W |
| Barrier Range ⋏ | 166 | 31.25 S | 141.25 E |
| Barrier Reef ✢[2] | 164 | 11.36 S | 153.00 E |
| Barrigada | 174p | 13.28 N | 144.48 E |
| Barrilla Draw V | 196 | 31.21 N | 103.23 W |
| Barr Ilyās | 132 | 33.46 N | 35.54 E |
| Barrington, N.S., Can. | 186 | 43.34 N | 65.34 W |
| Barrington, Il., U.S. | 216 | 42.09 N | 88.08 W |
| Barrington, N.J., U.S. | 285 | 39.51 N | 75.03 W |
| Barrington, R.I., U.S. | 207 | 41.44 N | 71.18 W |
| Barrington Hills | 216 | 42.07 N | 88.09 W |
| Barrington Lake ⊜ | 184 | 56.55 N | 100.15 W |
| Barrington Tops ∧ | 166 | 32.00 S | 151.28 E |
| Barrington Woods | 278 | 42.09 N | 88.04 W |
| Barringun | 166 | 29.01 S | 145.43 E |
| Barrio de la Soledad | 234 | 16.48 N | 95.15 W |
| Barrita Vieja | 236 | 13.55 N | 90.54 W |
| Barrīyat al-Uṣayfir | 142 | 31.18 N | 30.40 E |
| Barro, Bra. | 250 | 7.11 S | 38.47 W |
| Barro, Gui.-B. | 150 | 12.24 N | 15.30 W |
| Barro Alto | 255 | 15.04 S | 48.58 W |
| Barron | 190 | 45.24 N | 91.50 W |
| Barron Creek ≃ | 282 | 37.27 N | 122.05 W |
| Barron Lake | 216 | 41.51 N | 86.11 W |
| Barrouallie | 241h | 13.14 N | 61.17 W |
| Barrow, Arg. | 252 | 38.18 S | 60.14 W |
| Barrow, Ak., U.S. | 180 | 71.17 N | 156.34 W |
| Barrow ≃ | 48 | 52.15 N | 7.00 W |
| Barrow, Point › | 180 | 71.23 N | 156.30 W |
| Barrow Bay C | 212 | 44.58 N | 81.13 W |
| Barrow Creek | 162 | 21.33 S | 133.53 E |
| Barrowford | 44 | 53.52 N | 2.13 W |
| Barrow-in-Furness | 44 | 54.07 N | 3.14 W |
| Barrow Island I | 162 | 20.48 S | 115.23 E |
| Barrows | 184 | 52.49 N | 101.27 W |
| Barrow Strait ᴗ | 176 | 74.21 N | 94.10 W |
| Barrowsville | 207 | 41.56 N | 71.12 W |
| Barrow upon Humber | 44 | 53.41 N | 0.23 W |
| Barry, Wales, U.K. | 42 | 51.24 N | 3.18 W |
| Barry, Il., U.S. | 219 | 39.41 N | 91.02 W |
| Barry, Tx., U.S. | 222 | 32.06 N | 96.38 W |
| Barry □[6] | 216 | 42.35 N | 85.18 W |
| Barrydale | 158 | 33.55 S | 20.43 E |
| Barrys Bay | 212 | 45.29 N | 77.41 W |
| Barrys Bay C | 212 | 45.28 N | 77.42 W |
| Barryton | 190 | 43.45 N | 85.08 W |
| Barrytown | 210 | 42.00 N | 73.56 W |
| Barryville | 210 | 41.28 N | 74.54 W |
| Barsakel'mes, ostrov I | 86 | 45.40 N | 59.58 E |
| Barsalpur | 120 | 28.10 N | 72.15 E |
| Baršatas | 86 | 48.13 N | 78.21 E |
| Barsbüttel | 52 | 53.34 N | 10.10 E |
| Bårse | 41 | 55.07 N | 11.58 E |
| Bārsi | 122 | 18.14 N | 75.42 E |
| Barsinghausen | 52 | 52.18 N | 9.27 E |
| Baršino | 86 | 49.45 N | 69.36 E |
| Barskaun | 85 | 42.10 N | 77.37 E |
| Barsø I | 41 | 55.07 N | 9.34 E |
| Barssel | 52 | 53.10 N | 7.44 E |
| Barst | 56 | 49.04 N | 6.50 E |
| Barstow, Ca., U.S. | 228 | 34.53 N | 117.01 W |
| Barstow, Tx., U.S. | 196 | 31.28 N | 103.24 W |
| Barsuki | 82 | 54.15 N | 37.30 E |
| Bar-sur-Aube | 58 | 48.14 N | 4.43 E |
| Bar-sur-Seine | 50 | 48.07 N | 4.22 E |
| Bart | 208 | 39.56 N | 76.05 W |
| Bārta ≃ | 76 | 56.24 N | 21.03 E |
| Bartala | 272b | 22.33 N | 88.16 E |
| Bartang ≃ | 120 | 37.56 N | 71.34 E |
| Bartazuga, Jabal ∧ | 140 | 21.44 N | 33.33 E |
| Bartelso | 219 | 38.32 N | 89.28 W |
| Bartenheim | 58 | 47.38 N | 7.28 E |
| Bartenstein | 56 | 49.21 N | 9.53 E |
| Barter Island I | 180 | 70.08 N | 143.35 W |
| Barth | 54 | 54.22 N | 12.43 E |
| Barthe ≃ | 54 | 54.22 N | 12.41 E |
| Barthélemy, Deo )( | 110 | 19.26 N | 104.06 E |
| Bartholomew □[6] | 218 | 39.13 N | 85.55 W |
| Bartholomew, Bayou ≃ | 194 | 32.43 N | 92.04 W |
| Bartibougou | 150 | 12.52 N | 0.48 E |
| Bartica | 246 | 6.24 N | 58.37 W |
| Bartın | 130 | 41.38 N | 32.21 E |
| Bartle Frere ∧ | 166 | 17.23 S | 145.49 E |
| Bartlesville | 196 | 36.44 N | 95.58 W |
| Bartlett, Il., U.S. | 216 | 41.59 N | 88.11 W |
| Bartlett, Ne., U.S. | 198 | 41.53 N | 98.33 W |
| Bartlett, N.H., U.S. | 188 | 44.04 N | 71.17 W |
| Bartlett, Tn., U.S. | 194 | 35.12 N | 89.52 W |
| Bartlett, Tx., U.S. | 222 | 30.48 N | 97.26 W |
| Bartlett Brook ≃ | 283 | 42.42 N | 71.13 W |
| Bartlett Cove | 180 | 58.27 N | 135.55 W |
| Bartlett Reservoir ⊜[1] | 200 | 33.52 N | 111.37 W |
| Bartletts ∧[2] | 168a | 32.19 S | 116.43 E |
| Bartletts Harbour | 186 | 50.57 N | 57.00 W |
| Bartley | 198 | 40.14 N | 100.18 W |
| Bartolomé Bavio → General Mansilla | 258 | 35.05 S | 57.45 W |
| Bartolomé de las Casas | 252 | 25.24 S | 59.34 W |
| Bartolomeu de Gusmão, Aeroporto ⊠ | 256 | 22.56 S | 43.43 W |
| Bartolomeu Dias | 156 | 21.10 S | 35.09 E |
| Barton, Austl. | 162 | 30.31 S | 132.39 E |
| Barton, N.Y., U.S. | 210 | 42.03 N | 76.27 W |
| Barton, Oh., U.S. | 214 | 40.06 N | 80.50 W |
| Barton, Vt., U.S. | 188 | 44.44 N | 72.10 W |
| Barton Aerodrome ⊠ | 262 | 53.28 N | 2.23 W |
| Barton Lake | 216 | 42.06 N | 85.35 W |
| Barton Lake ⊜ | 184 | 52.00 N | 94.06 W |
| Barton-le-Clay | 42 | 51.57 N | 0.25 W |
| Barton Mills | 42 | 52.20 N | 0.31 E |
| Barton Park ♠ | 274a | 33.57 S | 151.09 E |
| Barton Run ≃ | 285 | 39.53 N | 74.51 W |
| Barton-under-Needwood | 42 | 52.45 N | 1.43 W |
| Barton-upon-Humber | 44 | 53.41 N | 0.27 W |
| Bartonville | 190 | 40.39 N | 89.39 W |
| Barton Water Swing Bridge ◆[5] | 262 | 53.28 N | 2.21 W |
| Bartoszyce | 30 | 54.16 N | 20.49 E |
| Bartow, Fl., U.S. | 220 | 27.53 N | 81.50 W |
| Bartow, Ga., U.S. | 192 | 32.52 N | 82.28 W |
| Baru, Kali ≡ | 269e | 6.10 S | 106.51 E |
| Barú, Volcán ∧[1] | 236 | 8.48 N | 82.33 W |
| Barueri | 256 | 23.31 S | 46.53 W |
| Barugo | 116 | 11.20 N | 124.44 E |
| Bāruipāra | 272b | 22.46 N | 88.14 E |
| Bāruipur | 126 | 22.21 N | 88.27 E |
| Bārūk, Jabal al- ∧ | 132 | 33.43 N | 35.45 E |
| Barumini | 71 | 39.42 N | 9.00 E |
| Barumun ≃ | 114 | 2.30 N | 100.09 E |
| Barun Bogd uul ∧ | 90 | 44.57 N | 100.15 E |
| Barung, Nusa I | 115a | 8.28 S | 113.20 E |
| Barun Su | 102 | 42.27 N | 111.01 E |
| Barun-Torej, ozero ⊜ | 88 | 50.10 N | 115.30 E |
| Baruntse ∧ | 124 | 27.51 N | 86.59 E |
| Barus | 114 | 2.00 N | 98.24 E |
| Baruta | 286c | 10.26 N | 66.53 W |
| Baruth | 54 | 52.03 N | 13.30 E |
| Baruun Bajan-Ulaan | 102 | 45.10 N | 101.24 E |
| Baruun bogd uul ∧ | 102 | 44.57 N | 100.15 E |
| Baruun-Urt | 90 | 46.42 N | 113.15 E |
| Barva, Volcán ∧[1] | 236 | 10.08 N | 84.06 W |
| Barvas | 46 | 58.22 N | 6.32 W |
| Barver | 52 | 52.37 N | 8.35 E |
| Barvicha | 265b | 55.44 N | 37.16 E |
| Barview | 202 | 43.21 N | 124.18 W |
| Barvinkove | 78 | 48.54 N | 37.02 E |
| Barwa | 126 | 23.51 N | 86.26 E |
| Barwāh | 120 | 22.16 N | 76.03 E |
| Barwāla ◆[8] | 272a | 28.46 N | 77.04 E |
| Barwāni | 120 | 22.02 N | 74.54 E |
| Barwa Sāgar | 124 | 25.23 N | 78.44 E |
| Barwell | 42 | 52.32 N | 1.21 W |
| Barwice | 30 | 53.45 N | 16.22 E |
| Barwick | 192 | 30.54 N | 83.44 W |
| Barwidgee | 162 | 27.02 S | 120.54 E |
| Barwon ≃, Austl. | 166 | 30.00 S | 148.05 E |
| Barwon ≃, Austl. | 169 | 38.13 S | 144.25 E |
| Barwon Heads (South Barwon) | 169 | 38.17 S | 144.30 E |
| Barybino, Ross. | 82 | 55.16 N | 37.54 E |
| Barybino, Ross. | 82 | 54.56 N | 37.47 E |
| Barycz ≃ | 30 | 51.42 N | 16.15 E |
| Barykova, mys › | 180 | 63.02 N | 179.29 E |
| Barykovo | 82 | 54.38 N | 38.48 E |
| Barynino | 82 | 55.47 N | 36.21 E |
| Baryš | 80 | 53.39 N | 47.08 E |
| Baryš ≃ | 80 | 54.35 N | 46.48 E |
| Barysau | 76 | 54.15 N | 28.30 E |
| Baryševo | 86 | 54.58 N | 83.11 E |
| Baryshivka | 78 | 50.22 N | 31.19 E |
| Baryšniki | 80 | 56.57 N | 46.33 E |
| Barzah | 132 | 33.34 N | 36.19 E |
| Barzas | 86 | 55.43 N | 86.19 E |
| Barzio | 58 | 45.57 N | 9.27 E |
| Basacato del Este | 152 | 3.37 N | 8.54 E |
| Basai Dārāpur ◆[8] | 272a | 28.40 N | 77.08 E |
| Bāsa' Īdū | 128 | 26.39 N | 55.17 E |
| Basail, Arg. | 252 | 27.52 S | 59.18 W |
| Bāsāil, Bngl. | 126 | 24.14 N | 90.0[illegible] E |
| Basakin | 80 | 48.11 N | 42.1[illegible] E |
| Basāl | 123 | 33.33 N | 72.1[illegible] E |
| Basalt ≃ | 166 | 19.38 S | 145.5[illegible] E |
| Basalt Island I | 271d | 22.19 N | 114.2[illegible] E |
| Basaluzzo | 62 | 44.46 N | 8.4[illegible] E |
| Basandīlah | 142 | 31.12 N | 31.2[illegible] E |
| Basankusu | 152 | 1.14 N | 19.4[illegible] E |
| Bašanta | 80 | 46.05 N | 41.5[illegible] E |
| Basanti | 126 | 22.12 N | 88.4[illegible] E |
| Basarabeasca | 78 | 46.20 N | 28.5[illegible] E |
| Basarabi | 38 | 44.10 N | 28.24 E |
| Basatongwula Shan ∧ | 120 | 33.05 N | 91.30 E |
| Basavakalyān | 122 | 17.52 N | 76.57 E |
| Basavilbaso | 252 | 32.22 S | 58.53 W |
| Baščelakskij chrebet ⋏ | 86 | 51.15 N | 84.30 E |
| Baschi | 66 | 42.40 N | 12.13 E |
| Basco | 108 | 20.27 N | 121.58 E |
| Bascom | 214 | 41.07 N | 83.17 W |
| Bascuñán, Cabo › | 252 | 28.51 S | 71.30 W |
| Basdahl | 52 | 53.26 N | 8.59 E |
| Basdorf | 54 | 52.44 N | 13.26 E |
| Basekpio | 154 | 4.44 N | 24.40 E |
| Basel (Bâle) | 58 | 47.33 N | 7.35 E |
| Baselga di Pinè | 64 | 46.08 N | 11.14 E |
| Baselice | 68 | 41.24 N | 14.58 E |
| Basel-Land □[3] | 58 | 47.30 N | 7.50 E |
| Basel-Stadt □[3] | 58 | 47.38 N | 7.40 E |
| Basen ≃ | 96 | 34.48 N | 132.51 E |
| Bas-en-Basset | 62 | 45.18 N | 4.06 E |
| Basentello ≃ | 68 | 40.40 N | 16.23 E |
| Basento ≃ | 68 | 40.21 N | 16.50 E |
| Başeu ≃ | 38 | 47.44 N | 27.15 E |
| Basey | 116 | 11.17 N | 125.04 E |
| Bashaw | 182 | 52.35 N | 112.58 W |
| Basher Kill ≃ | 210 | 41.27 N | 74.35 W |
| Bashi Channel ᴗ | 108 | 22.00 N | 121.00 E |
| Bashikejike | 120 | 37.30 N | 85.50 E |
| Bashiqiao | 106 | 31.40 N | 120.22 E |
| Bashkortostan → Baškirija □[3] | 86 | 54.00 N | 56.00 E |
| Bashtanka | 78 | 47.24 N | 32.25 E |
| Bashtīl | 273c | 30.05 N | 31.11 E |
| Basi, India | 123 | 30.36 N | 76.50 E |
| Basi, India | 123 | 30.41 N | 76.24 E |
| Basiad Bay C | 116 | 14.16 N | 122.19 E |
| Basiano | 112 | 1.16 S | 122.50 E |
| Basibasy | 157b | 22.10 S | 43.40 E |
| Başıbüyük ◆[8] | 267b | 40.57 N | 29.08 E |
| Basicò | 70 | 38.04 N | 15.04 E |
| Basid | 85 | 38.07 N | 72.09 E |
| Basilaki Island I | 164 | 10.35 S | 151.00 E |
| Basilan □[4] | 116 | 6.35 N | 121.55 E |
| Basilan Island I | 116 | 6.34 N | 122.03 E |
| Basilan Peak ∧ | 116 | 6.33 N | 122.04 E |
| Basilan Strait ᴗ | 116 | 6.49 N | 122.05 E |
| Basildon | 42 | 51.35 N | 0.25 E |
| Basildon □[8] | 260 | 51.35 N | 0.29 E |
| Basile | 194 | 30.29 N | 92.35 W |
| Basiliano | 64 | 46.01 N | 13.06 E |
| Basilicata □[4] | 68 | 40.30 N | 16.10 E |
| Basiluzzo, Isola I | 70 | 38.39 N | 15.07 E |
| Basin, Mt., U.S. | 202 | 46.16 N | 112.15 W |
| Basin, Wy., U.S. | 202 | 44.22 N | 108.02 W |
| Bäsingen ⊜ | 40 | 60.09 N | 16.20 E |
| Basinger | 220 | 27.24 N | 81.01 W |
| Basingstoke | 42 | 51.15 N | 1.05 W |
| Basingstoke Canal ≡ | 260 | 51.21 N | 0.29 W |
| Basingwerk Abbey ʋ[1] | 262 | 53.17 N | 3.12 W |
| Basin Lake ⊜ | 184 | 52.38 N | 105.18 W |
| Basīrhāt | 126 | 22.40 N | 88.53 E |
| Basīrpur | 123 | 30.35 N | 73.50 E |
| Basīṭ, Ra's al- › | 130 | 35.51 N | 35.48 E |
| Basiyingzi | 104 | 42.05 N | 121.37 E |
| Basja ≃ | 76 | 53.46 N | 31.01 E |
| Basjanovskij | 86 | 58.19 N | 60.44 E |
| Baška | 36 | 44.58 N | 14.46 E |
| Baskahegan Lake ⊜ | 188 | 45.30 N | 67.48 W |
| Baskakovka | 76 | 54.36 N | 34.19 E |
| Başkale | 128 | 38.02 N | 44.00 E |
| Baskatong, Réservoir ⊜[1] | 190 | 46.48 N | 75.50 W |
| Baškaus ≃ | 86 | 51.09 N | 87.43 E |
| Basket Lake ⊜ | 184 | 49.43 N | 92.00 W |
| Basking Ridge | 276 | 40.42 N | 74.32 W |
| Baškino | 82 | 55.18 N | 36.41 E |
| Baškirija □[3], Ross. | 72 | 54.00 N | 56.00 E |
| Baškirija □[3], Ross. | 86 | 54.00 N | 56.00 E |
| Baškirskij zapovednik ♠ | 86 | 53.30 N | 57.58 E |
| Baskomutan Milli Parkı ♠ | 130 | 38.50 N | 30.05 E |
| Başköy | 84 | 39.53 N | 44.32 E |
| Baskuduk | 86 | 49.43 N | 61.32 E |
| Baš-Kugandy | 85 | 42.00 N | 74.39 E |
| Baskunčak, ozero ⊜ | 80 | 48.12 N | 46.54 E |
| Baslow | 44 | 53.15 N | 1.38 W |
| Başmakçı | 130 | 37.54 N | 30.01 E |
| Bašmakovo | 80 | 53.12 N | 43.02 E |
| Basmat | 122 | 19.19 N | 77.10 E |
| Bäsna | 40 | 60.32 N | 15.12 E |
| Bāsoda | 124 | 23.51 N | 77.56 E |
| Basoko | 152 | 1.14 N | 23.36 E |
| Basoko ≃ | 273b | 4.19 S | 15.16 E |
| Basoli | 123 | 32.30 N | 75.49 E |
| Basom | 210 | 43.04 N | 78.24 W |
| Basongo | 152 | 4.20 S | 20.24 E |
| Basora, Punt › | 241s | 12.25 N | 69.52 W |
| Basovizza | 64 | 45.38 N | 13.52 E |
| Başpınar | 130 | 39.12 N | 38.42 E |
| Basque Lands → Euskal Herriko □[3] | 34 | 43.00 N | 2.30 W |
| Basra → Al-Başrah | 128 | 30.30 N | 47.47 E |
| Bas-Rhin □[5] | 32 | 48.35 N | 7.40 E |
| Bass ≃ | 169 | 38.30 S | 145.26 E |
| Bassano | 182 | 50.47 N | 112.28 W |
| Bassano del Grappa | 64 | 45.46 N | 11.44 E |
| Bassari | 150 | 9.15 N | 0.47 E |
| Bassas da India ✢[2] | 138 | 21.25 S | 39.42 E |
| Bass Creek ≃ | 216 | 42.37 N | 89.04 W |
| Basse-Californie → Baja California ›[1] | 232 | 28.00 N | 113.30 W |
| Bassecourt | 58 | 47.20 N | 7.15 E |
| Bassein → Pathein | 110 | 16.47 N | 94.44 E |
| Bassein ≃[1] | 110 | 15.56 N | 94.18 E |
| Basse-Kotto □[5] | 152 | 5.00 N | 21.30 E |
| Bassella | 34 | 42.01 N | 1.18 E |
| Bassen | 52 | 53.04 N | 9.04 E |
| Bassendean | 168a | 31.55 S | 115.56 E |
| Bassenthwaite | 44 | 54.41 N | 3.12 W |
| Bassenthwaite Lake ⊜ | 44 | 54.38 N | 3.13 W |
| Basse-Pointe | 240e | 14.52 N | 61.07 W |
| Basses, Pointe des › | 241o | 15.52 N | 61.17 W |
| Basse Santa Su | 150 | 13.19 N | 14.13 W |
| Basse-Terre, Guad. | 241o | 16.00 N | 61.44 W |
| Basseterre, St. K.-N. | 238 | 17.18 N | 62.43 W |
| Basse Terre, Trin. | 241r | 10.08 N | 61.18 W |
| Basse-Terre I | 241o | 16.10 N | 61.40 W |
| Bassett, Ne., U.S. | 198 | 42.35 N | 99.32 W |
| Bassett, Va., U.S. | 192 | 36.45 N | 79.59 W |
| Bassett Creek ≃ | 194 | 31.25 N | 87.56 W |
| Bassett Peak ∧ | 200 | 32.30 N | 110.17 W |
| Bassfield | 194 | 31.30 N | 89.44 W |
| Bass Harbor | 188 | 44.14 N | 68.20 W |
| Bass Hill | 274a | 33.54 S | 151.00 E |
| Bassignana | 62 | 45.00 N | 8.44 E |
| Bassikounou | 150 | 15.52 N | 5.57 W |
| Bassila | 150 | 9.01 N | 1.40 E |
| Bassin des Aghlabites ⊥ | 36 | 35.43 N | 10.10 E |
| Bassingbourn | 42 | 52.04 N | 0.03 W |
| Bass Lake, Ca., U.S. | 226 | 37.19 N | 119.33 W |


| Symbol | English | Deutsch | Español | Français | Português |
|---|---|---|---|---|---|
| ≃ | River | Fluß | Río | Rivière | Rio |
| ≡ | Canal | Kanal | Canal | Canal | Canal |
| ⌊ | Waterfall, Rapids | Wasserfall, Stromschnellen | Cascada, Rápidos | Chute d'eau, Rapides | Cascata, Rápidos |
| ᴗ | Strait | Meeresstraße | Estrecho | Détroit | Estreito |
| C | Bay, Gulf | Bucht, Golf | Bahía, Golfo | Baie, Golfe | Baía, Golfo |
| ⊜ | Lake, Lakes | See, Seen | Lago, Lagos | Lac, Lacs | Lago, Lagos |
| ≋ | Swamp | Sumpf | Pantano | Marais | Pântano |
| ⊓ | Ice Features, Glacier | Eis- und Gletscherformen | Accidentes Glaciales | Formes glaciaires | Acidentes glaciares |
| ⚲ | Other Hydrographic Features | Andere Hydrographische Objekte | Otros Elementos Hidrográficos | Autres données hydrographiques | Outros acidentes hidrográficos |
| ✢ | Submarine Features | Untermeerische Objekte | Accidentes Submarinos | Formes de relief sous-marin | Acidentes submarinos |
| □ | Political Unit | Politische Einheit | Unidad Politica | Entité politique | Unidade politica |
| ʋ | Cultural Institution | Kulturelle Institution | Institución Cultural | Institution culturelle | Instituição cultural |
| ⊥ | Historical Site | Historische Stätte | Sitio Histórico | Site historique | Sitio histórico |
| ♠ | Recreational Site | Erholungs- und Ferienort | Sitio de Recreo | Centre de loisirs | Area de Lazer |
| ⊠ | Airport | Flughafen | Aeropuerto | Aéroport | Aeroporto |
| ■ | Military Installation | Militäranlage | Instalación Militar | Installation militaire | Instalação militar |
| ◆ | Miscellaneous | Verschiedenes | Misceláneo | Divers | Diversos |

Bass Lake, In., U.S. 216 41.12 N 86.36 W
Bass Lake ⊜, On., Can. 212 44.49 N 76.08 W
Bass Lake ⊜, In., U.S. 216 41.13 N 86.36 W
Bass Lake ⊜[1] 226 37.19 N 119.34 W
Bass Point › 170 34.36 S 150.54 E
Bass River 186 45.25 N 63.47 W
Bass Strait ⩌ 166 39.20 S 145.30 E
Bassum 52 52.51 N 8.43 E
Basswood Lake ⊜, On., Can. 190 46.20 N 83.23 W
Basswood Lake ⊜, N.A. 190 48.06 N 91.40 W
Basta 126 21.41 N 87.03 E
Båstad 26 56.26 N 12.51 E
Basṭah 132 30.14 N 35.32 E
Bastak 128 27.14 N 54.22 E
Basṭām 128 36.29 N 55.04 E
Bastei ♠ 54 50.58 N 14.04 E
Bastelica 36 42.00 N 9.02 E
Basti 124 26.48 N 82.43 E
Bastia, Fr. 36 42.42 N 9.27 E
Bastia, It. 66 43.04 N 12.33 E
Bastian 192 37.09 N 81.09 W
Bastiglia 64 44.43 N 11.00 E
Bastimentos 236 9.21 N 82.12 W
Bastimentos, Isla I 236 9.18 N 82.08 W
Bastogne 56 50.00 N 5.43 E
Bastrop, La., U.S. 194 32.46 N 91.54 W
Bastrop, Tx., U.S. 222 30.06 N 97.18 W
Bastrop □[6] 222 33.00 N 97.18 W
Bastrop, Lake ⊜[1] 222 30.09 N 97.18 W
Bastrop Bay ⊂ 222 29.06 N 95.11 W
Bastrop State Park ♠ 222 30.07 N 97.17 W
Bastuträsk 26 64.47 N 20.02 E
Basu, Pulau I 112 0.18 S 103.36 E
Basubāti 272b 22.47 N 88.12 E
Bāsudebpur, India 126 21.49 N 87.38 E
Bāsudebpur, India 272b 22.49 N 88.25 E
Basuo → Dongfang 110 19.05 N 108.39 E
Bāsūs 273c 30.08 N 31.13 E
Baswa 126 24.08 N 87.52 E
Basyūn 142 30.57 N 30.49 E
Bas-Zaïre □[4] 152 5.30 S 14.30 E
Bata 152 1.51 N 9.45 E
Bataan □[4] 116 14.40 N 120.25 E
Bataan, Mount ∧ 116 14.31 N 120.28 E
Bataan Peninsula ›[1] 116 14.40 N 120.25 E
Batabanó 240p 22.43 N 82.17 W
Batabanó, Golfo de ⊂ 240p 22.15 N 82.30 W
Batac 116 18.05 N 120.35 E
Batad 116 11.25 N 123.06 E
Batagaj 74 67.38 N 134.38 E
Batagaj-Alyta 74 67.48 N 130.25 E
Batag Island I 116 12.38 N 125.04 E
Batagol 88 52.22 N 100.45 E
Bataguassu 255 21.42 S 52.22 W
Bataiporã 255 22.20 S 53.17 W
Batajsk 83 47.10 N 39.44 E
Batak 38 41.57 N 24.13 E
Batak, Jazovir ⊜[1] 38 41.59 N 24.11 E
Batakan 112 4.05 S 114.38 E
Batala 123 31.48 N 75.12 E
Batalha, Bra. 250 9.41 S 37.08 W
Batalha, Bra. 250 4.01 S 42.05 W
Batalha, Port. 34 39.39 N 8.50 W
Bataly 86 52.52 N 62.00 E
Batam, Pulau I 112 1.05 N 104.03 E
Batama, Ross. 88 53.53 N 101.36 E
Batama, Zaïre 154 0.56 N 26.39 E
Batamaj 74 63.31 N 129.27 E
Batamšinskij 86 50.36 N 58.16 E
Batan, Pil. 116 11.35 N 122.30 E
Batan, Zhg. 98 34.10 N 120.04 E
Batanagar 126 22.31 N 88.15 E
Batang, Indon. 115a 6.55 S 109.45 E
Batang, Zhg. 102 30.02 N 99.02 E
Batangafo 152 7.18 N 18.18 E
Batangas 116 13.45 N 121.03 E
Batangas □[4] 116 13.50 N 121.00 E
Batangas Bay ⊂ 116 13.43 N 121.00 E
Batangbatangdaya 115a 6.56 S 113.59 E
Batang Berjuntai 114 3.23 N 101.25 E
Batang Kali 114 3.28 N 101.38 E
Batangtoru 114 1.29 N 99.03 E
Batan Island I, Pil. 108 20.26 N 121.58 E
Batan Island I, Pil. 116 13.15 N 124.00 E
Batan Islands II 108 20.30 N 121.50 E
Batanta, Pulau I 164 0.50 S 130.40 E
Batas ≃ 287a 22.44 S 43.24 W
Batas Island I 116 11.10 N 119.36 E
Bátaszék 30 46.12 N 18.44 E
Batatais 255 20.53 S 47.37 W
Batatuba 256 23.04 S 46.25 W
Batavia, Arg. 252 34.47 S 65.41 W
Batavia, Il., U.S. 216 41.51 N 88.18 W
Batavia, Ia., U.S. 190 40.59 N 92.10 W
Batavia, Mi., U.S. 216 41.55 N 85.06 W
Batavia, N.Y., U.S. 210 42.59 N 78.11 W
Batavia, Oh., U.S. 218 39.04 N 84.10 W
Batawa 212 44.10 N 77.36 W
Batbatan Island I 116 11.28 N 121.55 E
Batcengel 88 47.47 N 101.58 E
Batchawana ≃ 190 46.55 N 84.32 W
Batchawana Mountain ∧ 190 47.04 N 84.24 W
Batchawanna Island I 190 46.53 N 84.30 W
Batchelor 164 13.04 S 131.01 E
Bătdâmbâng 110 13.06 N 103.12 E
Bate Bay ⊂ 170 34.04 S 151.12 E
Bateckij 76 58.39 N 30.19 E
Bate Heath 262 53.19 N 2.28 W
Batéké, Plateaux ⩘[1] 152 3.30 S 15.45 E
Batemans Bay 166 35.43 S 150.11 E
Batenbrock ◆[8] 263 51.31 N 6.57 E
Batepito ≃ 200 30.48 N 109.11 W
Bates, Mount ∧ 174c 29.01 S 167.56 E
Batesburg 192 33.54 N 81.32 W
Bates Creek ≃ 200 42.41 N 106.37 W
Bates Range ⩘ 162 27.25 S 121.13 E
Batesville, Ar., U.S. 194 35.46 N 91.38 W
Batesville, In., U.S. 218 39.18 N 85.13 W
Batesville, Ms., U.S. 194 34.18 N 89.56 W
Batesville, Tx., U.S. 196 28.57 N 99.37 W
Bath, N.B., Can. 186 46.31 N 67.36 W
Bath, On., Can. 212 44.11 N 76.47 W
Bath, Eng., U.K. 42 51.23 N 2.22 W
Bath, Il., U.S. 219 40.11 N 90.08 W
Bath, Me., U.S. 188 43.54 N 69.49 W
Bath, Mi., U.S. 216 42.49 N 84.26 W
Bath, N.Y., U.S. 210 42.20 N 77.19 W
Bath, Oh., U.S. 214 41.11 N 81.38 W
Bath, Pa., U.S. 208 40.43 N 75.23 W
Bath □[6] 218 38.14 N 83.48 W
Batha □[5] 146 14.00 N 19.00 E
Batha ≃ 146 12.47 N 17.34 E
Bath Addition 285 40.06 N 74.52 W
Bathgate, Scot., U.K. 46 55.55 N 3.39 W
Bathgate, N.D., U.S. 198 48.52 N 97.28 W
Bathinda 123 30.12 N 74.57 E
Bathsheba 241g 13.13 N 59.31 W
Bathurst, Austl. 166 33.25 S 149.35 E
Bathurst, N.B., Can. 186 47.36 N 65.39 W
Bathurst → Banjul, Gam. 150 13.28 N 16.39 W
Bathurst, S. Afr. 158 33.30 S 26.50 E
Bathurst, Cape › 176 70.35 N 128.00 W
Bathurst, Lake ⊜ 170 35.04 S 149.44 E
Bathurst Inlet 176 66.50 N 108.01 W
Bathurst Inlet ⊂ 176 68.10 N 108.50 W
Bathurst Island I, Austl. 164 11.37 S 130.23 E
Bathurst Island I, N.T., Can. 16 76.00 N 100.30 W
Bathurst Island Aboriginal Reserve ◆[4] 164 11.37 S 130.23 E
Bati 144 11.10 N 40.02 E
Batia 150 10.54 N 1.29 E
Batiāgarh 124 24.07 N 79.21 E
Batié 150 9.53 N 2.55 W
Bāṭin, Wādī al- V 128 29.35 N 47.00 E
Batina 38 45.51 N 18.51 E
Batiquitos Lagoon ⊂ 228 33.05 N 117.18 W
Batīr 132 31.16 N 35.42 E
Batiscan ≃ 206 46.31 N 72.15 W
Batiste Creek ≃ 222 30.04 N 94.28 W
Batkanu 150 9.05 N 12.25 W
Batken 85 40.03 N 70.50 E
Batley 44 53.44 N 1.37 W
Batlow 171b 35.31 S 148.09 E
Batman 130 37.52 N 41.07 E
Batman □[4] 130 38.00 N 41.15 E
Batna 148 35.34 N 6.11 E
Baṭn al-Ghūl 132 29.44 N 35.52 E
Batnorov 88 47.55 N 111.30 E
Batō, Nihon 94 36.44 N 140.10 E
Bato, Pil. 116 10.20 N 124.47 E
Ba To, Viet 110 14.46 N 108.44 E
Bato, Lake ⊜ 116 13.19 N 123.21 E
Batoala 152 0.48 N 13.27 E
Batoche Rectory National Historic Site ⊥ 184 52.41 N 106.02 W
Batoka 154 16.47 S 27.15 E
Baton Rouge 194 30.27 N 91.09 W
Bator 123 33.06 N 75.19 E
Batorampon Point › 116 7.07 N 121.54 E
Batouri 152 4.26 N 14.22 E
Batovi 255 15.53 S 53.24 W
Batpajsagyr, peski ◆[2] 80 47.20 N 48.40 E
Baṭrā (Petra) ⊥ 132 30.20 N 35.26 E
Baṭrā', Jibāl al- ⩘ 132 29.53 N 35.38 E
Baṭrah 142 31.10 N 31.27 E
Ba Tri 110 10.02 N 106.36 E
Batsawul 120 34.15 N 70.52 E
Batson 222 30.15 N 94.37 W
Batsto ≃ 285 39.39 N 74.39 W
Batsto, Skit Branch ≃ 285 39.46 N 74.41 W
Batsto State Historic Site ⊥ 208 39.39 N 74.39 W
Bat Sûmber 88 48.29 N 106.42 E
Battaglia Terme 64 45.17 N 11.47 E
Battambang → Bătdâmbâng 110 13.06 N 103.12 E
Battenberg 56 51.01 N 8.38 E
Batten Kill ≃ 188 43.06 N 73.35 W
Batterie, Pointe de la › 240e 14.44 N 60.54 W
Bätterkinden 58 47.08 N 7.32 E
Battersea ◆[8] 260 51.28 N 0.10 W
Battersea Park ♠ 260 51.29 N 0.09 W
Batticaloa 122 7.43 N 81.42 E
Battice 56 50.39 N 5.49 E
Battin 224 45.29 N 122.34 W
Battipaglia 68 40.37 N 14.58 E
Battle 42 50.55 N 0.29 E
Battle ≃ 176 52.43 N 108.15 W
Battle Creek, Ia., U.S. 198 42.18 N 95.35 W
Battle Creek, Mi., U.S. 216 42.19 N 85.10 W
Battle Creek, Ne., U.S. 198 41.59 N 97.35 W
Battle Creek ≃, N.A. 202 48.36 N 109.11 W
Battle Creek ≃, Ca., U.S. 204 40.21 N 122.11 W
Battle Creek ≃, Id., U.S. 202 42.14 N 116.32 W
Battle Creek ≃, Mi., U.S. 216 42.19 N 85.12 W
Battle Creek ≃, Tx., U.S. 196 32.50 N 98.58 W
Battle Creek, North Fork ≃ 204 40.26 N 122.00 W
Battle Creek, South Fork ≃ 204 40.26 N 122.00 W
Battlefields 154 18.31 S 29.52 E
Battle Green ⊥ 283 42.27 N 71.14 W
Battle Ground, In., U.S. 216 40.30 N 86.50 W
Battle Ground, Wa., U.S. 224 45.46 N 122.31 W
Battle Harbour 176 52.16 N 55.35 W
Battle Lake 198 46.16 N 95.42 W
Battlement Mesa ∧ 200 39.20 N 108.00 W
Battlemount 158 26.57 S 23.46 E
Battle Mountain 204 40.38 N 116.56 W
Battle Mountain ∧ 200 41.02 N 107.16 W
Battlesbridge 260 51.37 N 0.34 E
Battonya 30 46.17 N 21.01 E
Battuello 266b 45.27 N 8.56 E
Batu 115a 7.52 S 112.31 E
Batu ∧ 144 6.55 N 39.46 E
Batu, Bukit ∧ 112 2.16 N 113.43 E
Batu, Kepulauan II 110 0.18 S 98.28 E
Batuan 116 12.25 N 123.47 E
Batu Arang 114 3.19 N 101.28 E
Batuata, Pulau I 112 6.12 S 122.42 E
Batuata, Tanjung › 115b 9.37 S 120.29 E
Batu-Batu 112 4.09 S 119.52 E
Batu Berinchang, Gunong ∧ 114 4.30 N 101.24 E
Batubetumpang 112 2.53 S 106.09 E
Batubrok, Bukit ∧ 112 1.10 N 114.36 E
Batu Caves 114 3.14 N 101.40 E
Batudaka, Pulau I 112 0.28 S 121.48 E
Batu Enam 114 2.35 N 102.43 E
Batu Gajah 114 4.28 N 101.03 E
Batui 112 1.17 S 122.33 E
Batui, Pegunungan ⩘ 112 1.15 S 122.10 E
Batuidu 112 10.38 S 123.25 E
Batukau, Bukit ∧ 115b 8.20 S 115.05 E
Batukelau 112 0.48 N 115.01 E
Batu Laut 114 2.41 N 101.31 E
Batulicin 112 3.27 S 116.00 E
Batumata Point › 164 10.17 S 148.57 E
Batumi 84 41.38 N 41.38 E
Batumundan 114 1.17 N 98.50 E
Batu Pahat (Bandar Penggaram) 114 1.51 N 102.56 E
Batupanjang 114 1.43 N 101.31 E
Batu Puteh, Gunong ∧ 114 4.13 N 101.27 E
Batuputih 112 1.24 N 118.29 E
Baturaja 112 4.08 S 104.10 E
Batu Rakit 114 5.27 N 103.03 E
Baturetno 115a 7.59 S 110.56 E
Baturino, Ross. 86 57.48 N 85.12 E
Baturino, Ross. 265b 55.35 N 37.31 E
Baturinskaja 78 45.47 N 39.22 E
Baturité 250 4.20 S 38.53 W
Baturotok 115b 8.42 S 117.10 E
Baturusa 112 2.02 S 106.07 E
Baturyn 78 51.21 N 32.51 E
Batusangkar 112 0.27 S 100.35 E
Batutinggi 112 1.55 S 113.19 E
Bat Yam 132 32.01 N 34.45 E
Batyrevo 80 55.04 N 47.38 E
Batyr-Mala, ozero ⊜ 80 47.35 N 44.45 E
Bau 112 1.25 N 110.08 E
Baú ≃ 250 7.26 S 54.47 W
Bauang 116 16.31 N 120.20 E
Baubašata, gory ⩘ 85 41.20 N 72.45 E
Baubau 112 5.28 S 122.38 E
Baucina 70 37.55 N 13.32 E
Baud 32 47.52 N 3.01 W
Bauda 120 20.50 N 84.19 E
Baudette 190 48.42 N 94.35 W
Baudó ≃ 246 4.57 N 77.22 W
Baudouin Stadium ♠ 273b 4.20 S 15.20 E
Baudour 50 50.29 N 3.49 E
Bauernschaft 263 51.34 N 6.33 E
Bauerstown 279b 40.30 N 79.59 W
Baugo Creek ≃ 216 41.40 N 86.04 W
Baukau 112 8.27 S 126.27 E
BAuland ◆[1] 56 49.31 N 9.29 E
Bauld, Cape › 186 51.38 N 55.25 W
Baulkham Hills 274a 33.46 S 151.00 E
Baulmes 58 46.48 N 6.32 E
Bauma 58 47.23 N 8.53 E
Baumberg 263 51.07 N 6.54 E
Baume ≃ 62 44.26 N 4.20 E
Baume-les-Dames 58 47.21 N 6.22 E
Baumholder 56 49.37 N 7.20 E
Baumschulenweg ◆[8] 264a 52.28 N 13.29 E
Baun 112 10.18 S 123.43 E
Baunach 56 49.59 N 10.50 E
Baunach ≃ 56 49.59 N 10.51 E
Baunatal 56 51.16 N 9.25 E
Baunei 71 40.02 N 9.40 E
Baunt 88 55.16 N 113.08 E
Baunt, ozero ⊜ 88 55.12 N 113.00 E
Bāuphal 126 22.25 N 90.33 E
Baure 150 12.50 N 8.45 E
Baures 248 13.35 S 63.35 W
Baures ≃ 248 12.30 S 64.18 W
Bauru 255 22.19 S 49.04 W
Baús 255 18.19 S 53.10 W
Bausendorf 56 50.01 N 6.59 E
Bausenhagen 263 51.31 N 7.48 E
Bauska 76 56.24 N 24.14 E
Bauta 240p 22.59 N 82.33 W
Bauta □[7] 286b 22.59 N 82.33 W
Bautino 84 44.33 N 50.15 E
Bautzen 54 51.11 N 14.26 E
Bauxite 194 34.33 N 92.31 W
Bauya 150 8.11 N 12.34 W
Bavans 58 47.29 N 6.44 E
Bavari 62 44.26 N 9.01 E
Bavaria → Bayern □[3] 30 49.00 N 11.30 E
Bavarian Alps → Bayerische Alpen ⩘ 64 47.30 N 11.00 E
Bavay 50 50.18 N 3.47 E
Båven ⊜ 40 59.01 N 16.56 E
Baveno 58 45.55 N 8.30 E
Bavilliers 58 47.37 N 6.50 E
Bavispe 232 30.24 N 108.50 W
Bavispe ≃ 232 29.15 N 109.11 W
Bavleny 80 56.24 N 39.34 E
Bavly 80 54.25 N 53.17 E
Bavnhöj ∧[2] 41 55.55 N 10.07 E
Bavtugaj 84 43.11 N 46.49 E
Baw 110 23.19 N 95.50 E
Bāwal 124 28.05 N 76.35 E
Bawal, Pulau I 112 2.44 S 110.06 E
Bāwāli 272b 22.25 N 88.12 E
Bawang 115a 7.06 S 109.55 E
Baw Baw, Mount ∧ 169 37.50 S 146.17 E
Baw Baw National Park ♠ 169 37.55 S 146.22 E
Baw Beese Lake ⊜ 216 41.54 N 84.36 W
Bawdeswell 42 52.45 N 1.01 E
Bawdwin 110 23.06 N 97.18 E
Bawean, Pulau I 115a 5.46 S 112.40 E
Baweigang 106 31.57 N 120.14 E
Bawinkel 52 52.36 N 7.25 E
Bawku 150 11.05 N 0.14 W
Bawlake 110 19.11 N 97.21 E
Bawmi 110 17.19 N 94.35 E
Bawria 126 22.29 N 88.10 E
Bawtry 44 53.26 N 1.01 W
Baxdo 144 5.46 N 47.15 E
Baxenden 262 53.44 N 2.20 W
Baxian, Zhg. 105 39.06 N 116.23 E
Baxian (Yudongxi), Zhg. 107 29.23 N 106.32 E
Baxley 192 31.46 N 82.20 W
Baxter, Ia., U.S. 190 41.49 N 93.09 W
Baxter, Mn., U.S. 190 46.20 N 94.17 W
Baxter, Tn., U.S. 194 36.09 N 85.38 W
Baxter Estates 276 40.50 N 73.42 W
Baxter Springs 198 37.02 N 94.44 W
Baxter State Park ♠ 188 46.00 N 68.58 W
Baxterville 194 31.05 N 89.35 W
Bay 194 35.44 N 90.33 W
Bay □[4] 144 2.30 N 43.30 E
Bay, Laguna de ⊜ 116 14.23 N 121.15 E
Baya, Zaïre 152 4.57 N 19.43 E
Baya, Zaïre 154 11.52 S 27.27 E
Bayāḍah, Wādī al- V 146 26.08 N 18.35 E
Bayāḍ an-Naṣārā 142 29.04 N 31.08 E
Bayag 116 18.16 N 121.02 E
Bayala 158 27.47 S 32.08 E
Bay al-Kabīr, Wādī V 146 31.15 N 15.57 E
Bayambang 116 15.49 N 120.27 E
Bayamo 240p 20.23 N 76.39 W
Bayamo ≃ 240p 20.34 N 76.44 W
Bayamón 240m 18.24 N 66.09 W
Bayan, Azer. 84 40.34 N 46.09 E
Bayan, Indon. 115b 8.16 S 116.26 E
Bayan, Zhg. 89 46.05 N 127.24 E
Bāyan, Band-e ⩘ 120 34.20 N 65.30 E
Bayāna 124 26.54 N 77.17 E
Bayanbayanan 269f 14.39 N 121.06 E
Bayanchagan 89 47.19 N 124.03 E
Bayang 116 7.48 N 124.12 E
Bayanga 152 2.53 N 16.19 E
Bayange 102 39.19 N 107.31 E
Bayan Har Shan ⩘ 102 33.48 N 98.10 E
Bayanheshuomiao 89 48.51 N 119.46 E
Bayanjie 89 49.36 N 124.37 E
Bayanluke 89 50.52 N 119.33 E
Bayannaobao 102 39.44 N 107.40 E
Bayano, Lago ⊜[1] 246 9.10 N 78.40 W
Bayan Obo 102 41.58 N 110.02 E
Bayan Tal 89 43.44 N 123.16 E
Bayard, Ia., U.S. 198 41.51 N 94.33 W
Bayard, Ne., U.S. 198 41.45 N 103.19 W
Bayard, N.M., U.S. 200 32.45 N 108.07 W
Bayard, Oh., U.S. 214 40.46 N 81.04 W
Bayard, W.V., U.S. 188 39.16 N 79.21 W
Bayard, Col )( 62 44.37 N 6.05 E
Bayard Cutting Arboretum State Park ♠ 276 40.45 N 73.10 W
Bayat, Indon. 112 2.06 S 103.38 E
Bayat, Tür. 130 38.59 N 30.56 E
Bayat, Tür. 130 40.39 N 34.15 E
Bayawan 116 9.22 N 122.48 E
Bayawan ≃ 116 9.22 N 122.48 E
Baybay 116 10.41 N 124.48 E
Bayberry 210 43.08 N 76.13 W
Bayble 46 58.12 N 6.13 W
Bayboro 192 35.08 N 76.46 W
Bay Bulls 186 47.19 N 52.49 W
Bayburt 130 40.16 N 40.15 E
Bayburt □[4] 130 40.15 N 40.00 E
Bay Center 224 46.37 N 123.57 W
Bay City, Mi., U.S. 190 43.35 N 83.53 W
Bay City, Or., U.S. 224 45.31 N 123.53 W
Bay City, Tx., U.S. 222 28.58 N 95.58 W
Bay Creek ≃, Il., U.S. 194 37.16 N 88.31 W
Bay Creek ≃, Il., U.S. 219 39.20 N 90.46 W
Baydā', Bi'r ⊤[4] 142 29.45 N 32.13 E
Bay de Verde 186 48.05 N 52.54 W
Baydhabo (Baidoa) 144 3.07 N 43.39 E
Bay du Nord ≃ 186 47.44 N 55.25 W
Bayel 58 48.12 N 4.47 E
Bayerische Alpen ⩘ 64 47.30 N 11.00 E
Bayerisch Eisenstein 60 49.07 N 13.12 E
Bayerischer Wald ⩘ 60 49.00 N 12.40 E
Bayerischer Wald, Nationalpark ♠ 60 48.56 N 13.28 E
Bayern □[3] 30 49.00 N 11.30 E
Bayes, Cap › 175f 20.57 S 165.25 E
Bayeuen 114 4.36 N 97.53 E
Bayeux, Bra. 250 7.08 S 34.56 W
Bayeux, Fr. 32 49.16 N 0.42 W
Bay Farm Island I 282 37.43 N 122.14 W
Bayfield, Co., U.S. 200 37.13 N 107.35 W
Bayfield, Wi., U.S. 190 46.48 N 90.49 W
Bayfield, Île I 186 51.13 N 58.23 W
Bayford 260 51.46 N 0.06 W
'Bayh 132 33.44 N 35.31 E
Bayhān al-Qaṣāḍ 144 14.48 N 45.43 E
Bay Harbor Islands 220 25.53 N 80.08 W
Bayhead, Scot., U.K. 46 57.33 N 7.24 W
Bay Head, N.J., U.S. 208 40.04 N 74.03 W
Bayiji 98 34.18 N 117.41 E
Bayındır 130 38.13 N 27.40 E
Bayingzi 104 41.28 N 120.46 E
Baykan 130 38.09 N 41.47 E
Baykonur → Bajkonyr 86 47.50 N 66.03 E
Bay Kurt 85 39.58 N 75.33 E
Bay L'Argent 186 47.33 N 54.54 W
Bayley Point › 164 16.56 S 139.02 E
Baylis 219 39.44 N 90.54 W
Bay Meadows Race Track ♠ 282 37.32 N 122.18 W
Bay Minette 194 30.52 N 87.46 W
Baynūnah ◆[1] 128 23.50 N 52.50 E
Bayombong 116 16.29 N 121.09 E
Bayon 58 48.29 N 6.19 E
Bayonne, Fr. 32 43.29 N 1.29 W
Bayonne, N.J., U.S. 210 40.40 N 74.06 W
Bayonne ≃ 206 46.05 N 73.10 W
Bayonne Bridge ◆[5] 276 40.38 N 74.09 W
Bayons 62 44.20 N 6.10 E
Bayou Bodcau Reservoir ⊜[1] 194 32.45 N 93.30 W
Bayou Cane 194 29.37 N 90.45 W
Bayou D'Arbonne Lake ⊜[1] 194 32.45 N 92.25 W
Bayou La Batre 194 30.24 N 88.14 W
Bayovar 248 5.50 S 81.03 W
Bay Park 276 40.38 N 73.40 W
Bayport, Fl., U.S. 220 28.33 N 82.39 W
Bay Port, Mi., U.S. 190 43.50 N 83.22 W
Bayport, Mn., U.S. 190 45.01 N 92.46 W
Bayport, N.Y., U.S. 210 40.44 N 73.03 W
Bayramiç 130 39.48 N 26.37 E
Bayramören 130 40.57 N 33.12 E
Bayreuth 60 49.57 N 11.35 E
Bay Ridge 208 38.56 N 76.27 W
Bay Ridge ◆[8] 276 40.37 N 74.02 W
Bay Ridge Channel ⩌ 276 40.39 N 74.02 W
Bayrischzell 64 47.40 N 12.00 E
Bay Roberts 186 47.36 N 53.16 W
Bayrūt (Beirut) 130 33.53 N 35.30 E
Bayrūt □[4] 132 33.56 N 35.30 E
Bays, Lake of ⊜ 212 45.15 N 79.04 W
Bay Saint Louis 194 30.18 N 89.19 W
Bay Shore 210 40.43 N 73.14 W
Bayshore Gardens 220 27.25 N 82.35 W
Bayside, On., Can. 212 44.07 N 77.30 W
Bayside, Ma., U.S. 283 42.18 N 70.53 W
Bayside, Wi., U.S. 216 43.10 N 87.54 W
Bayside ◆[8] 276 40.46 N 73.46 W
Bay Springs 194 31.58 N 89.17 W
Bay Springs Lake ⊜[1] 194 34.35 N 88.20 W
Bayston Hill 42 52.40 N 2.45 W
Bayswater 274b 37.51 S 145.16 E
Bayswater North 274b 37.49 S 145.17 E
Bayt ad-Dīn 132 33.42 N 35.35 E
Bayt al-Faqīh 144 14.32 N 43.20 E
Bayt Ḥānūn 132 31.32 N 34.33 E
Bayt Jālā 132 31.43 N 35.11 E
Bayt Jinn 132 33.19 N 35.53 E
Bayt Laḥm (Bethlehem) 132 31.43 N 35.12 E
Bayt Mirī 132 33.52 N 35.36 E
Baytown 222 29.44 N 94.58 W
Bayt Sāḥūr 132 31.42 N 35.13 E
Bayt Sīrā 132 31.53 N 35.03 E
Bayunglencir 112 2.03 S 103.41 E
Bayview, Austl. 274a 33.40 S 151.18 E
Bay View, N.Z. 172 39.25 S 176.53 E
Bay View, N.Y., U.S. 210 42.47 N 78.51 W
Bay View, Oh., U.S. 214 41.28 N 82.50 W
Bayview ◆[8] 282 37.44 N 122.23 W
Bay Village 214 41.29 N 81.55 W
Bayville, N.J., U.S. 208 39.54 N 74.09 W
Bayville, N.Y., U.S. 210 40.54 N 73.33 W
Baywater 168a 31.55 S 115.56 E
Baywood Park 226 35.20 N 120.50 W
Bayyāḍah, Ra's al- › 132 33.10 N 35.10 E
Bayyā'īyah al-Kabīrah 130 35.42 N 37.09 E
Bayyūḍah ⊤[4] 140 17.32 N 32.07 E
Bayzo 150 13.52 N 4.45 E
Baza 34 37.29 N 2.46 W
Bazai 100 24.32 N 114.10 E
Bazainville 261 48.48 N 1.40 E
Bazaliya 78 49.43 N 26.27 E
Bazar 88 53.58 N 116.05 E
Bazarčaj 84 39.40 N 45.48 E
Bazarčulan 80 49.04 N 51.56 E
Bazardüzü dağ ∧ 84 41.13 N 47.51 E
Bāzār-e Panjvā'ī 120 31.32 N 65.28 E
Bazargic → Dobrič 38 43.34 N 27.50 E
Bazar-Kurgan 85 41.02 N 72.45 E
Bazarnyje Mataki 80 54.56 N 49.56 E
Bazarnyj Karabulak 80 52.16 N 46.25 E
Bazarnyj Syzgan 80 53.45 N 46.46 E
Bazarovo 82 54.47 N 38.10 E
Bazartobe 80 49.23 N 51.50 E
Bazaruto, Ilha do I 156 21.40 S 35.28 E
Bazas 32 44.26 N 0.13 W
Bazavluk ≃ 78 47.34 N 34.04 E
Bazdār 120 26.21 N 65.03 E
Bazeilles 56 49.40 N 4.59 E
Bazemont 261 48.56 N 1.52 E
Bazetta 214 41.20 N 80.47 W
Bazhong 102 31.51 N 106.39 E
Bazi 100 24.46 N 113.10 E
Baziège 32 43.27 N 1.37 E
Bažigan 84 44.33 N 45.41 E
Bazine 198 38.26 N 99.41 W
Baziqiao 106 32.07 N 119.52 E
Bazkovskaja 80 49.36 N 41.43 E
Bazmān 128 27.49 N 60.12 E
Bazmān, Kūh-e ∧ 128 28.04 N 60.00 E
Bazoches-les-Gallerandes 50 48.10 N 2.03 E
Bazoches-sur-Hoëne 50 48.33 N 0.28 E
Bazoj 86 55.45 N 83.22 E
Bazzano 64 44.30 N 11.05 E
Be ≃ 110 11.06 N 106.58 E
Be, Nosy I 157b 13.20 S 48.15 E
Beach, Il., U.S. 216 42.26 N 87.50 W
Beach, N.D., U.S. 198 46.55 N 104.00 W
Beach, Tx., U.S. 222 30.20 N 95.29 W
Beach Channel ⩌ 276 40.35 N 73.50 W
Beach City 214 40.39 N 81.34 W
Beach City Lake ⊜[1] 214 40.41 N 81.36 W
Beach Glen 276 40.56 N 74.29 W
Beach Haven, N.J., U.S. 208 39.33 N 74.14 W
Beach Haven, Pa., U.S. 210 41.04 N 76.11 W
Beach Haven Terrace 208 39.35 N 74.13 W
Beach Lake 210 41.36 N 75.09 W
Beach Lake ⊜ 281 42.33 N 83.43 W
Beach Pond State Park ♠ 207 41.35 N 71.45 W
Beachport 166 37.30 S 140.01 E
Beachville 212 43.05 N 80.49 W
Beachwood, N.J., U.S. 208 39.56 N 74.11 W
Beachwood, Oh., U.S. 214 41.27 N 81.30 W
Beachy Head › 42 50.44 N 0.16 E
Beacon, Austl. 162 30.26 S 117.51 E
Beacon, N.Y., U.S. 210 41.30 N 73.58 W
Beacon Falls 207 41.26 N 73.03 W
Beacon Heights 284c 38.57 N 76.54 W
Beacon Hill, Austl. 274a 33.45 S 151.15 E
Beacon Hill, Wa., U.S. 224 46.08 N 122.57 W
Beacon Hill ∧[2], H.K. 271d 22.21 N 114.09 E
Beacon Hill ∧[2], Wales, U.K. 42 52.23 N 3.12 W
Beacon Rock State Park ♠ 224 45.38 N 122.03 W
Beaconsfield, Austl. 166 41.12 S 146.48 E
Beaconsfield, Austl. 274b 38.03 S 145.22 E
Beaconsfield, P.Q., Can. 206 45.26 N 73.50 W
Beaconsfield, Eng., U.K. 42 51.37 N 0.39 W
Beaconsfield □[8] 260 51.34 N 0.35 W
Beadle Lake 216 42.18 N 85.12 W
Beagh, Slieve ∧[2] 48 54.21 N 7.12 W
Beagle, Canal ⩌ 254 54.53 S 68.10 W
Beagle Bay 162 16.58 S 122.40 E
Beagle Gulf ⊂ 164 12.00 S 130.20 E
Beagle Reef ✦[2] 160 15.20 S 123.29 E
Bealanana 157b 14.33 S 48.44 E
Beale, Cape › 182 48.44 N 125.20 W
Beale, Lake ⊜[1] 122 19.45 N 73.44 E
Beale Air Force Base ■ 226 39.08 N 121.20 W
Bealiba 169 36.48 S 143.33 E
Bealiba, Mount ∧[2] 169 36.49 S 143.38 E
Beallsville 214 40.04 N 80.01 W
Beals Creek ≃ 196 32.10 N 100.51 W
Beam ≃ 260 51.31 N 0.10 E
Beaminster 42 50.49 N 2.45 W
Bean 260 51.25 N 0.17 E
Beanblossom Creek ≃ 194 39.20 N 86.39 W
Bean Creek ≃ 216 41.35 N 84.19 W
Bear ≃, Sk., Can. 184 54.33 N 103.58 W
Bear ≃, U.S. 200 41.30 N 112.08 W
Bear ≃, Ca., U.S. 226 38.57 N 121.35 W
Bear, Mount ∧ 180 61.17 N 141.09 W
Beara 164 7.30 S 144.50 E
Bear Bay ⊂ 176 75.47 N 87.00 W
Bear Branch 218 38.55 N 85.05 W
Bear Brook ≃, On., Can. 212 45.25 N 75.10 W
Bear Brook ≃, N.J., U.S. 276 41.02 N 74.03 W
Bear Brook State Park ♠ 188 43.05 N 71.26 W
Bear Butte ∧ 198 44.28 N 103.26 W
Bear Canyon V 280 34.14 N 118.07 W
Bear Cove 182 50.44 N 127.27 W
Bear Creek 210 41.11 N 75.45 W
Bear Creek ≃, On., Can. 214 42.44 N 82.23 W
Bear Creek ≃, U.S. 194 34.46 N 88.05 W
Bear Creek ≃, U.S. 196 37.45 N 101.23 W
Bear Creek ≃, U.S. 216 41.17 N 83.57 W
Bear Creek ≃, Al., U.S. 194 33.11 N 88.05 W
Bear Creek ≃, Ca., U.S. 226 38.56 N 122.20 W
Bear Creek ≃, Ca., U.S. 226 38.02 N 121.18 W
Bear Creek ≃, Ca., U.S. 226 37.17 N 120.50 W
Bear Creek ≃, Ca., U.S. 228 34.10 N 117.01 W
Bear Creek ≃, Ca., U.S. 280 34.14 N 117.53 W
Bear Creek ≃, Co., U.S. 200 39.40 N 105.00 W
Bear Creek ≃, Il., U.S. 219 39.33 N 89.23 W
Bear Creek ≃, Il., U.S. 219 40.07 N 91.29 W
Bear Creek ≃, Md., U.S. 284b 39.13 N 76.30 W
Bear Creek ≃, Mo., U.S. 219 39.03 N 91.14 W
Bear Creek ≃, N.D., U.S. 198 46.10 N 98.06 W
Bear Creek ≃, Oh., U.S. 218 39.39 N 84.17 W
Bear Creek ≃, Or., U.S. 202 44.06 N 120.46 W
Bear Creek ≃, Or., U.S. 202 42.26 N 122.58 W
Bear Creek ≃, Pa., U.S. 214 41.23 N 78.50 W
Bear Creek ≃, Wy., U.S. 198 41.41 N 104.13 W
Bear Creek, South Fork ≃ 219 40.09 N 91.18 W
Bear Creek, West Fork ≃ 280 34.16 N 117.53 W
Bearden 194 33.43 N 92.36 W
Beardmore 176 49.36 N 87.57 W
Beardmore Glacier ⊓ 9 83.45 S 171.00 E
Beardsley Lake ⊜[1] 226 38.13 N 120.03 W
Beardstown, Il., U.S. 219 40.01 N 90.25 W
Beardstown, In., U.S. 216 41.08 N 86.36 W
Beardy and Okemasis Indian Reserves ◆[4] 184 52.48 N 106.20 W
Bearfort Mountain ∧ 276 41.09 N 74.23 W
Bear Head Creek ≃ 194 30.18 N 93.35 W
Bear Head Lake ⊜ 184 55.33 N 96.10 W
Bear Head Lake State Park ♠ 190 47.49 N 92.04 W
Bearhead Mountain ∧ 224 47.02 N 121.53 W
Bear Hill ∧[2], Ct., U.S. 207 41.39 N 73.24 W
Bear Hill ∧[2], N.Y., U.S. 210 41.18 N 74.00 W
Bear-in-the-Lodge Creek ≃ 198 43.41 N 101.50 W
Bear Island I, Ant. 9 74.30 S 110.45 W
Bear Island I, Mb., Can. 184 54.53 N 98.04 W
Bear Island I, Ire. 48 51.40 N 9.48 W
Bear Island → Bjørnøya I, Nor. 12 74.25 N 19.00 E
Bear Island I, Va., U.S. 284c 38.59 N 77.14 W
Bear Lake, B.C., Can. 182 56.11 N 126.51 W
Bear Lake, Pa., U.S. 214 42.00 N 79.30 W
Bear Lake ⊜, Ab., Can. 182 55.16 N 119.00 W
Bear Lake ⊜, B.C., Can. 182 56.06 N 126.45 W
Bear Lake ⊜, Mb., Can. 184 55.08 N 96.00 W
Bear Lake ⊜, On., Can. 212 45.26 N 79.35 W
Bear Lake ⊜, U.S. 200 42.00 N 111.20 W
Bear Mountain ∧, Ca., U.S. 228 35.12 N 118.38 W
Bear Mountain ∧, Ky., U.S. 192 37.32 N 84.16 W
Bear Mountain ∧, Or., U.S. 202 43.51 N 122.53 W
Bear Mountain ∧[2] 210 41.18 N 74.01 W
Bear Mountain State Park ♠ 210 41.17 N 74.00 W
Béarn □[9] 32 43.20 N 0.45 W
Bear Pond ⊜ 276 40.58 N 74.40 W
Bear River 186 44.34 N 65.39 W
Bear River Range ⩘ 200 41.50 N 111.30 W
Bear Run ≃ 279b 40.33 N 80.04 W
Bearsden 46 55.56 N 4.20 W
Bears Paw Mountains ⩘ 202 48.15 N 109.30 W
Bearstead 260 51.16 N 0.35 E
Bearsville 210 42.02 N 74.09 W
Bear Swamp ≃ 285 39.54 N 74.47 W
Bear Swamp ≡ 285 39.53 N 74.45 W
Bear Swamp Brook ≃ 276 41.04 N 74.13 W
Bear Swamp Lake ⊜ 276 41.06 N 74.13 W
Beartooth Mountains ⩘ 202 45.00 N 109.30 W
Beartooth Pass )( 202 44.58 N 109.28 W
Bear Town 194 31.13 N 90.27 W
Beās 123 31.31 N 75.17 E
Beās ≃ 123 31.10 N 74.59 E
Beasain 34 43.03 N 2.11 W
Beas de Segura 34 38.15 N 2.53 W
Beasley 222 29.30 N 95.55 W
Beasley Bay ⊂ 208 37.51 N 75.44 W
Beason 219 40.09 N 89.12 W
Beata, Cabo › 238 17.36 N 71.25 W
Beata, Isla I 238 17.35 N 71.31 W
Beatenberg 58 46.42 N 7.48 E
Beato ◆[8] 266c 38.44 N 9.06 W
Beaton 182 50.44 N 117.44 W
Beatrice, Al., U.S. 194 31.44 N 87.12 W
Beatrice, Ne., U.S. 198 40.16 N 96.44 W
Beatrice, Zimb. 154 18.15 S 30.55 E
Beatrice, Cape › 164 14.15 S 136.59 E
Beattie 198 39.51 N 96.25 W
Beattock 44 55.18 N 3.28 W
Beatton ≃ 176 56.10 N 120.25 W
Beatty, Nv., U.S. 204 36.54 N 116.45 W
Beatty, Oh., U.S. 218 39.53 N 83.50 W
Beatty Saugeen ≃ 212 44.08 N 81.02 W
Beattyville 192 37.34 N 83.42 W
Beaubru 56 49.46 N 5.05 E
Beaucaire 62 43.48 N 4.38 E
Beauce ◆[1] 50 48.22 N 1.50 E
Beauceville 188 46.12 N 70.46 W
Beauchamp 261 49.01 N 2.12 E
Beauchamp Roding 260 51.46 N 0.18 E
Beauchêne, Lac ⊜ 190 46.39 N 78.55 W
Beauchêne Island I 254 52.55 S 59.12 W
Beaucoup Creek ≃, Il., U.S. 194 37.47 N 89.17 W
Beaucoup Creek ≃, Il., U.S. 219 38.13 N 89.20 W
Beaucourt 58 47.29 N 6.55 E
Beaudesert 171a 27.59 S 153.00 E
Beaudette ≃ 206 45.12 N 74.19 W
Beaudry, Lac ⊜ 190 47.44 N 78.55 W
Beauduc, Pointe de › 62 43.22 N 4.34 E
Beaufays 56 50.34 N 5.38 E
Beaufort, Austl. 169 37.26 S 143.23 E
Beaufort, Fr. 58 46.34 N 5.26 E
Beaufort, Fr. 62 45.43 N 6.35 E
Beaufort, Lux. 56 49.51 N 6.18 E
Beaufort, Malay. 112 5.20 N 115.45 E
Beaufort, Mo., U.S. 219 38.26 N 91.12 W
Beaufort, N.C., U.S. 192 34.43 N 76.39 W
Beaufort, S.C., U.S. 192 32.25 N 80.40 W
Beaufort, Cape › 162 34.26 S 115.32 E
Beaufort, Massif de ⩘[1] 62 45.44 N 6.35 E
Beaufort Castle → Qal'at ash-Shaqīf ⊥ 132 33.19 N 35.32 E
Beaufort Island I 271d 22.11 N 114.15 E
Beaufort Marine Corps Air Station ■ 192 32.30 N 80.44 W
Beaufort Sea ⊤[2] 16 73.00 N 140.00 W
Beaufort West 158 32.18 S 22.36 E
Beaugency 50 47.47 N 1.38 E
Beauharnois 206 45.19 N 73.52 W
Beauharnois □[6] 206 45.15 N 74.00 W
Beauharnois, Barrage de ◆[6] 275a 45.19 N 73.55 W
Beauharnois, Canal de ≡ 206 45.19 N 73.54 W
Beaujeu 58 46.09 N 4.36 E
Beaujolais □[9] 32 46.05 N 4.10 E
Beaulieu 42 50.49 N 1.27 W
Beaulieu-lès-Loches 50 47.07 N 1.01 E
Beaulieu-sur-Mer 62 43.42 N 7.20 E
Beauly 46 57.29 N 4.29 W
Beauly ≃ 46 57.28 N 4.28 W
Beauly Firth ⊂[1] 46 57.30 N 4.23 W
Beaumaris, Austl. 274b 37.59 S 145.02 E
Beaumaris, Wales, U.K. 44 53.16 N 4.05 W
Beaumaris Bay ⊂ 274b 38.00 S 145.03 E
Beaumes-de-Venise 62 44.07 N 5.02 E
Beaumesnil 50 49.01 N 0.43 E
Beaumetz-lès-Loges 50 50.14 N 2.39 E
Beaumont, Bel. 50 50.14 N 4.14 E
Beaumont, Nf., Can. 186 49.37 N 55.41 W
Beaumont, Fr. 32 49.40 N 1.51 W
Beaumont, N.Z. 172 45.49 S 169.32 E
Beaumont, Ca., U.S. 228 33.55 N 116.58 W
Beaumont, Ms., U.S. 194 31.10 N 88.55 W
Beaumont, Tx., U.S. 194 30.05 N 94.06 W
Beaumont-du-Gâtinais 50 48.08 N 2.29 E
Beaumont-en-Argonne 56 49.32 N 5.03 E
Beaumont Hill ∧[2] 166 31.33 S 145.13 E
Beaumont-la-Ronce 50 47.34 N 0.40 E
Beaumont-le-Roger 50 49.05 N 0.47 E
Beaumont Place 222 29.50 N 95.14 W
Beaumont-sur-Oise 50 49.08 N 2.17 E
Beaumont-sur-Sarthe 50 48.13 N 0.08 E
Beaune 58 47.02 N 4.50 E
Beaune-la-Rolande 50 48.04 N 2.26 E
Beauport 206 46.52 N 71.11 W
Beaupré 186 47.03 N 70.54 W
Beaupréau 32 47.12 N 1.00 W
Beaupre Island I 212 44.26 N 76.19 W
Beaupré Lake ⊜ 184 54.30 N 107.10 W
Beauraing 56 50.07 N 4.58 E
Beaurepaire 62 45.20 N 5.03 E
Beaurepaire-en-Bresse 58 46.40 N 5.23 E
Beaurières 62 44.35 N 5.33 E
Beaurivage 206 46.25 N 71.14 W
Beaurivage ≃ 206 46.42 N 71.16 W
Beauséjour, Mb., Can. 184 50.04 N 96.33 W
Beauséjour, Guad. 241o 16.18 N 61.04 W
Beausoleil 62 43.45 N 7.26 E
Beausoleil Island I 212 44.51 N 79.52 W
Beautor 50 49.39 N 3.20 E
Beauvais, Fr. 50 49.26 N 2.05 E
Beauvais, Fr. 261 48.32 N 2.03 E
Beauvais Creek ≃ 202 45.29 N 107.45 W
Beauvais-Tillé, Aéroport ⊠ 50 49.28 N 2.07 E
Beauval, Sk., Can. 184 55.09 N 107.37 W
Beauval, Fr. 50 50.06 N 2.20 E
Beauvezer 62 44.09 N 6.36 E
Beauville 32 44.17 N 0.52 E
Beauvoir 261 48.39 N 2.52 E
Beauvoir-sur-Mer 32 46.55 N 2.02 W
Beauvoir-sur-Niort 32 46.11 N 0.28 W
Beaux Arts 224 47.35 N 122.11 W
Beaver, Ak., U.S. 180 66.22 N 147.24 W
Beaver, Ok., U.S. 196 36.48 N 100.31 W
Beaver, Or., U.S. 224 45.16 N 123.49 W
Beaver, Pa., U.S. 214 40.41 N 80.18 W
Beaver, Ut., U.S. 200 38.16 N 112.38 W
Beaver, Wa., U.S. 224 48.03 N 124.19 W
Beaver, W.V., U.S. 192 37.44 N 81.08 W
Beaver □[6] 214 40.40 N 80.25 W
Beaver ≃, Can. 176 59.43 N 124.16 W
Beaver ≃, Can. 184 55.25 N 107.45 W
Beaver ≃, On., Can. 212 44.34 N 80.27 W
Beaver ≃, U.S. 196 36.35 N 99.30 W
Beaver ≃, N.Y., U.S. 188 43.54 N 75.30 W
Beaver ≃, Pa., U.S. 214 40.40 N 80.18 W
Beaver ≃, Ut., U.S. 200 39.10 N 112.57 W
Beaver Brook 210 40.55 N 75.59 W
Beaver Brook ≃, U.S. 207 42.40 N 71.19 W
Beaver Brook ≃, Ma., U.S. 283 42.03 N 70.58 W
Beaver Brook ≃, Ma., U.S. 283 42.36 N 71.21 W
Beaver Brook ≃, Ma., U.S. 283 42.23 N 71.14 W
Beaver Brook ≃, N.J., U.S. 276 40.54 N 74.30 W
Beaver Brook ≃, N.J., U.S. 276 40.58 N 74.35 W
Beaver City 198 40.08 N 99.49 W
Beaver Creek, Yk., Can. 180 62.22 N 140.52 W
Beavercreek, Oh., U.S. 218 39.43 N 84.03 W

**Symbols** in the index entries represent the broad categories identified in the key at the right. Symbols with superior numbers (⩘[1]) identify subcategories (see complete key on page *I · 1)*.

**Symbole** im Register stellen die rechts im Schlüssel erklärten Kategorien dar. Symbole mit hochgestellten Ziffern (⩘[1]) bezeichnen Unterabteilungen einer Kategorie (vgl. vollständiger Schlüssel auf Seite *I · 1)*.

**Los símbolos** incluídos en el texto del índice representan las grandes categorías identificadas con la clave a la derecha. Los símbolos con numeros en su parte superior (⩘[1]) identifican las subcategorías (véase la clave completa en la página *I · 1)*.

**Les symboles** de l'index représentent les catégories indiquées dans la légende à droite. Les symboles suivis d'un indice (⩘[1]) représentent des sous-catégories (voir légende complète à la page *I · 1)*.

**Os símbolos** incluídos no texto do índice representam as grandes categorias identificadas com a chave à direita. Os símbolos com números em sua parte superior (⩘[1]) identificam as subcategorias (veja-se a chave completa à página *I · 1)*.

| | | | | | |
|---|---|---|---|---|---|
| ∧ Mountain | Berg | Montaña | Montagne | Montanha |
| ⩘ Mountains | Gebirge | Montañas | Montagnes | Montanhas |
| )( Pass | Paß | Paso | Col | Passo |
| V Valley, Canyon | Tal, Cañon | Valle, Cañón | Vallée, Canyon | Vale, Canhão |
| ≌ Plain | Ebene | Llano | Plaine | Planície |
| › Cape | Kap | Cabo | Cap | Cabo |
| I Island | Insel | Isla | Île | Ilha |
| II Islands | Inseln | Islas | Îles | Ilhas |
| ⊥ Other Topographic Features | Andere Topographische Objekte | Otros Elementos Topográficos | Autres données topographiques | Outros acidentes topográficos |

ESPAÑOL / FRANÇAIS / PORTUGUÊS


| Nombre / Nom / Nome | Página / Page | Lat.°′ | Long.°′ W = Oeste / W = Ouest |
|---|---|---|---|
| Beavercreek, Or., U.S. | 224 | 45.17 N | 122.32 W |
| Beaver Creek ≃, On., Can. | 212 | 44.30 N | 77.42 W |
| Beaver Creek ≃, On., Can. | 212 | 44.44 N | 76.58 W |
| Beaver Creek ≃, On., Can. | 275b | 43.51 N | 79.20 W |
| Beaver Creek ≃, On., Can. | 284a | 42.58 N | 79.01 W |
| Beaver Creek ≃, U.S. | 198 | 47.20 N | 103.39 W |
| Beaver Creek ≃, U.S. | 198 | 40.04 N | 99.20 W |
| Beaver Creek ≃, U.S. | 198 | 43.25 N | 103.59 W |
| Beaver Creek ≃, U.S. | 216 | 40.58 N | 87.49 W |
| Beaver Creek ≃, Ak., U.S. | 180 | 66.15 N | 147.32 W |
| Beaver Creek ≃, Ca., U.S. | 226 | 38.12 N | 120.19 W |
| Beaver Creek ≃, Co., U.S. | 198 | 38.22 N | 104.58 W |
| Beaver Creek ≃, Co., U.S. | 198 | 40.20 N | 103.33 W |
| Beaver Creek ≃, Il., U.S. | 216 | 42.16 N | 88.56 W |
| Beaver Creek ≃, Il., U.S. | 219 | 38.33 N | 89.30 W |
| Beaver Creek ≃, Ky., U.S. | 218 | 38.31 N | 84.11 W |
| Beaver Creek ≃, Md., U.S. | 208 | 39.32 N | 77.42 W |
| Beaver Creek ≃, Mo., U.S. | 194 | 36.38 N | 93.02 W |
| Beaver Creek ≃, Mt., U.S. | 202 | 48.29 N | 107.24 W |
| Beaver Creek ≃, Ne., U.S. | 198 | 40.42 N | 97.20 W |
| Beaver Creek ≃, Ne., U.S. | 198 | 41.26 N | 97.42 W |
| Beaver Creek ≃, N.J., U.S. | 285 | 39.45 N | 75.23 W |
| Beaver Creek ≃, N.Y., U.S. | 212 | 44.36 N | 75.22 W |
| Beaver Creek ≃, N.D., U.S. | 198 | 46.15 N | 100.29 W |
| Beaver Creek ≃, Oh., U.S. | 216 | 41.25 N | 83.51 W |
| Beaver Creek ≃, Oh., U.S. | 216 | 40.34 N | 84.45 W |
| Beaver Creek ≃, Oh., U.S. | 218 | 39.57 N | 83.46 W |
| Beaver Creek ≃, Ok., U.S. | 196 | 34.00 N | 97.57 W |
| Beaver Creek ≃, Or., U.S. | 224 | 44.56 N | 121.22 W |
| Beaver Creek ≃, Pa., U.S. | 285 | 40.00 N | 75.42 W |
| Beaver Creek ≃, Tx., U.S. | 196 | 33.53 N | 98.49 W |
| Beaver Creek ≃, Wy., U.S. | 202 | 42.58 N | 108.26 W |
| Beaver Creek State Park ♦ | 214 | 40.44 N | 80.35 W |
| Beaver Crossing | 198 | 40.46 N | 97.16 W |
| Beaverdale | 214 | 40.19 N | 78.41 W |
| Beaver Dam, Ky., U.S. | 194 | 37.24 N | 86.52 W |
| Beaverdam, Oh., U.S. | 216 | 40.50 N | 83.59 W |
| Beaver Dam, Wi., U.S. | 190 | 43.27 N | 88.50 W |
| Beaverdam Brook ≃ | 276 | 40.26 N | 74.28 W |
| Beaverdam Creek ≃, U.S. | 284c | 38.55 N | 76.57 W |
| Beaverdam Creek ≃, Md., U.S. | 284c | 39.01 N | 76.54 W |
| Beaverdam Creek ≃, N.J., U.S. | 285 | 39.56 N | 74.45 W |
| Beaver Dams | 210 | 42.17 N | 76.58 W |
| Beaver Dams Creek ≃ | 284a | 43.06 N | 79.11 W |
| Beaver Dam Wash V | 200 | 36.54 N | 114.55 W |
| Beaverdell | 182 | 49.26 N | 119.05 W |
| Beaver Falls, N.Y., U.S. | 212 | 43.53 N | 75.25 W |
| Beaver Falls, Pa., U.S. | 214 | 40.45 N | 80.19 W |
| Beaverhead ≃ | 202 | 45.31 N | 112.21 W |
| Beaverhead Mountains ⋏ | 202 | 45.00 N | 113.20 W |
| Beaverhill Lake ⊜, Ab., Can. | 182 | 53.27 N | 112.32 W |
| Beaver Hill Lake ⊜, Mb., Can. | 184 | 54.16 N | 94.53 W |
| Beaverhouse Lake ⊜ | 190 | 48.32 N | 92.05 W |
| Beaver Island I | 190 | 45.40 N | 85.31 W |
| Beaver Island State Park ♦ | 210 | 42.58 N | 78.57 W |
| Beaver Kill ≃ | 210 | 41.59 N | 75.08 W |
| Beaver Lake | 210 | 41.07 N | 74.33 W |
| Beaver Lake ⊜, Ab., Can. | 182 | 54.43 N | 111.50 W |
| Beaver Lake ⊜, On., Can. | 212 | 44.30 N | 77.02 W |
| Beaver Lake ⊜, On., Can. | 212 | 44.44 N | 78.17 W |
| Beaver Lake ⊜, N.J., U.S. | 276 | 41.05 N | 74.33 W |
| Beaver Lake ⊜, N.Y., U.S. | 276 | 40.53 N | 73.34 W |
| Beaver Lake ⊜[1] | 194 | 36.20 N | 93.55 W |
| Beaver Lake Indian Reserve ◆[4] | 182 | 54.39 N | 111.54 W |
| Beaverlodge | 182 | 55.13 N | 119.26 W |
| Beaver Meadow | 210 | 42.40 N | 75.41 W |
| Beaver Meadows | 210 | 40.55 N | 75.54 W |
| Beaver Mountains ⋏ | 180 | 62.54 N | 156.58 W |
| Beaver Run ≃, N.J., U.S. | 276 | 41.11 N | 74.36 W |
| Beaver Run ≃, Pa., U.S. | 279b | 40.34 N | 79.33 W |
| Beaver Run ≃, Pa., U.S. | 285 | 40.10 N | 75.40 W |
| Beaver Run Reservoir ⊜[1] | 214 | 40.29 N | 79.33 W |
| Beavers Bend State Park ♦ | 194 | 34.08 N | 94.42 W |
| Beaver Springs | 208 | 40.45 N | 77.13 W |
| Beaver Swamp Brook ≃ | 276 | 40.57 N | 73.43 W |
| Beaverton, On., Can. | 212 | 44.26 N | 79.09 W |
| Beaverton, Mi., U.S. | 190 | 43.52 N | 84.29 W |
| Beaverton, Or., U.S. | 224 | 45.29 N | 122.48 W |
| Beaverton ≃ | 212 | 44.26 N | 79.10 W |
| Beavertown | 210 | 40.45 N | 77.10 W |
| Beaverville | 216 | 40.57 N | 87.39 W |
| Beāwar | 120 | 26.06 N | 74.19 E |
| Beazley | 252 | 33.45 S | 66.39 W |
| Bebao | 157b | 17.22 S | 44.33 E |
| Bebar ≃ | 114 | 3.07 N | 103.27 E |
| Bebedouro | 255 | 20.56 S | 48.28 W |
| Bebeji | 150 | 11.40 N | 8.19 E |
| Bebek ◆[8] | 267b | 41.04 N | 29.02 E |
| Bebelevo | 82 | 54.32 N | 36.30 E |
| Bebeli | 130 | 36.41 N | 35.27 E |
| Beberibe | 250 | 4.11 S | 38.08 W |
| Bebertal | 54 | 52.15 N | 11.18 E |
| Bebington | 44 | 53.23 N | 3.01 W |
| Béboto | 146 | 8.16 N | 16.56 E |
| Bebra | 56 | 50.58 N | 9.47 E |
| Becal | 232 | 20.27 N | 90.02 W |
| Bécancour | 206 | 46.20 N | 72.26 W |
| Bécancour ≃ | 206 | 46.22 N | 72.27 W |
| Beccar ◆[8] | 288 | 34.28 S | 58.31 W |
| Beccaria | 214 | 40.46 N | 78.27 W |
| Beccles | 42 | 52.28 N | 1.34 E |
| Becconsall | 262 | 53.42 N | 2.50 W |
| Bečej | 38 | 45.37 N | 20.03 E |
| Beceni | 38 | 45.23 N | 26.46 E |
| Becerra Creek ≃ | 196 | 28.05 N | 98.55 W |
| Becerreá | 34 | 42.51 N | 7.10 W |
| Becerro, Cayos II | 236 | 15.57 N | 83.17 W |
| Béchar | 148 | 31.37 N | 2.13 W |
| Becharof Lake ⊜ | 180 | 58.00 N | 156.30 W |
| Bechater | 36 | 37.18 N | 9.45 E |
| Bechem | 150 | 7.05 N | 2.02 W |
| Becher Bay ⊂ | 224 | 48.19 N | 123.37 W |
| Becher Point ≻ | 168a | 32.23 S | 115.44 E |
| Bechet | 38 | 43.46 N | 23.58 E |
| Bechevin Bay ⊂ | 180 | 55.00 N | 163.27 W |
| Bechhofen | 56 | 49.09 N | 10.33 E |
| Bechtelsville | 208 | 40.22 N | 75.38 W |
| Bechuanaland ◆[1] | 158 | 27.10 S | 22.10 E |
| Bechyně | 30 | 49.18 N | 14.29 E |
| Becke | 263 | 51.24 N | 7.47 E |
| Beckemeyer | 219 | 38.36 N | 89.26 W |
| Beckenham ◆[8] | 260 | 51.24 N | 0.02 W |
| Beckenried | 58 | 46.58 N | 8.29 E |
| Becket | 207 | 42.19 N | 73.05 W |
| Beckhausen ◆[8] | 263 | 51.34 N | 7.02 E |
| Beckingen | 56 | 49.24 N | 6.42 E |
| Beckington | 42 | 51.16 N | 2.18 W |
| Beck Lake ⊜ | 278 | 42.04 N | 87.52 W |
| Beckler ≃ | 224 | 47.43 N | 121.21 W |
| Beckley | 188 | 37.46 N | 81.11 W |
| Beck Pond ⊜ | 283 | 42.36 N | 70.49 W |
| Becks Creek ≃ | 219 | 39.08 N | 88.56 W |
| Beckum | 52 | 51.45 N | 8.02 E |
| Beckville | 222 | 32.14 N | 94.27 W |
| Beckwith Island I | 212 | 44.52 N | 80.08 W |
| Becky Peak ʌ | 204 | 39.58 N | 114.36 W |
| Beclean | 38 | 47.11 N | 24.10 E |
| Bečov nad Teplou | 54 | 50.02 N | 12.19 E |
| Becsehely | 61 | 46.27 N | 16.48 E |
| Bedale | 44 | 54.17 N | 1.35 W |
| Bédarieux | 32 | 43.37 N | 3.09 E |
| Bédarrides | 62 | 44.02 N | 4.54 E |
| Bédaya | 146 | 8.55 N | 17.52 E |
| Bedburdyck | 56 | 51.07 N | 6.34 E |
| Bedburg | 56 | 50.59 N | 6.35 E |
| Bedburg-Hau | 52 | 51.45 N | 6.10 E |
| Beddgelert | 44 | 53.01 N | 4.06 W |
| Beddingestrand | 41 | 55.21 N | 13.29 E |
| Beddington ◆[8] | 260 | 51.22 N | 0.08 W |
| Beddome, Mount ʌ | 162 | 25.50 S | 134.22 E |
| Beddouza, Ras ≻ | 148 | 32.34 N | 9.19 W |
| Bedele | 144 | 8.33 N | 36.23 E |
| Beden Brook ≃ | 276 | 40.25 N | 74.38 W |
| Bedeque Bay ⊂ | 186 | 46.22 N | 63.53 W |
| Beder | 41 | 56.04 N | 10.13 E |
| Bederkesa | 52 | 53.38 N | 8.50 E |
| Bederwanak | 144 | 9.34 N | 44.23 E |
| Bedesa | 144 | 8.54 N | 40.47 E |
| Bedford, P.Q., Can. | 206 | 45.07 N | 72.59 W |
| Bedford, S. Afr. | 158 | 32.41 S | 26.05 E |
| Bedford, Eng., U.K. | 42 | 52.08 N | 0.29 W |
| Bedford, In., U.S. | 218 | 38.51 N | 86.29 W |
| Bedford, Ia., U.S. | 198 | 40.40 N | 94.43 W |
| Bedford, Ky., U.S. | 218 | 38.35 N | 85.19 W |
| Bedford, Ma., U.S. | 207 | 42.29 N | 71.16 W |
| Bedford, Mi., U.S. | 216 | 42.23 N | 85.13 W |
| Bedford, N.Y., U.S. | 210 | 41.12 N | 73.39 W |
| Bedford, Oh., U.S. | 214 | 41.23 N | 81.32 W |
| Bedford, Pa., U.S. | 188 | 40.01 N | 78.30 W |
| Bedford, Tx., U.S. | 222 | 32.50 N | 97.08 W |
| Bedford, Va., U.S. | 192 | 37.20 N | 79.31 W |
| Bedford □[6] | 214 | 40.09 N | 78.30 W |
| Bedford, Cape ≻ | 164 | 15.14 S | 145.21 E |
| Bedfordale | 168a | 32.10 S | 116.03 E |
| Bedford Harbour ⊂ | 162 | 33.35 S | 120.35 E |
| Bedford Heights | 279a | 41.25 N | 81.31 W |
| Bedford Hills | 210 | 41.14 N | 73.41 W |
| Bedford Island I | 126 | 21.51 N | 88.05 E |
| Bedford Level ≍ | 42 | 52.27 N | 0.02 W |
| Bedford Park | 278 | 41.46 N | 87.49 W |
| Bedford Park ◆[8] | 276 | 40.52 N | 73.53 W |
| Bedfordshire □[6] | 42 | 52.05 N | 0.30 W |
| Bedford-Stuyvesant ◆[8] | 276 | 40.41 N | 73.55 W |
| Bedi, India | 120 | 22.30 N | 70.02 E |
| Bédi, Tchad | 146 | 11.06 N | 18.33 E |
| Bedias | 222 | 30.46 N | 95.57 W |
| Bedias Creek ≃ | 222 | 30.54 N | 95.37 W |
| Bedinggong | 112 | 2.42 S | 106.13 E |
| Bédiondo | 146 | 8.39 N | 17.12 E |
| Bedirli | 130 | 39.35 N | 36.38 E |
| Bedlington | 44 | 55.08 N | 1.35 W |
| Bedminster, N.J., U.S. | 276 | 40.40 N | 74.38 W |
| Bedminster, Pa., U.S. | 208 | 40.26 N | 75.11 W |
| Bedmond | 260 | 51.43 N | 0.25 W |
| Bednodemjanovsk | 80 | 53.56 N | 43.10 E |
| Bedoba | 88 | 58.48 N | 97.12 E |
| Bédoin | 62 | 44.07 N | 5.10 E |
| Bedok | 271c | 1.19 N | 103.57 E |
| Bedong | 114 | 5.44 N | 100.31 E |
| Bedonia | 62 | 44.30 N | 9.38 E |
| Bedourie | 166 | 24.21 S | 139.28 E |
| Bedum | 52 | 53.17 N | 6.36 E |
| Bedwas | 42 | 51.35 N | 3.13 W |
| Bedworth | 42 | 52.28 N | 1.29 W |
| Beeac | 169 | 38.12 S | 143.38 E |
| Beebe, P.Q., Can. | 206 | 45.01 N | 72.09 W |
| Beebe, Ar., U.S. | 194 | 35.04 N | 91.52 W |
| Beech ≃ | 194 | 35.37 N | 88.10 W |
| Beechal Creek ≃ | 166 | 27.24 S | 145.13 E |
| Beech Bottom | 214 | 40.13 N | 80.39 W |
| Beech Brook ≃ | 276 | 41.08 N | 74.18 W |
| Beech Creek | 194 | 37.10 N | 87.03 W |
| Beech Creek ≃ | 210 | 41.04 N | 77.34 W |
| Beechcrest | 214 | 41.05 N | 81.20 W |
| Beecher, Il., U.S. | 216 | 41.20 N | 87.37 W |
| Beecher, Mi., U.S. | 216 | 43.05 N | 83.42 W |
| Beecher City | 219 | 39.11 N | 88.47 W |
| Beecher Falls | 206 | 45.00 N | 71.30 W |
| Beechey Head ≻ | 224 | 48.19 N | 123.39 W |
| Beech Forest | 169 | 38.38 S | 143.34 E |
| Beech Fork ≃ | 194 | 37.46 N | 85.41 W |
| Beech Grove | 218 | 39.43 N | 86.05 W |
| Beechmont | 171a | 28.07 S | 153.11 E |
| Beechview ◆[8] | 279b | 40.25 N | 80.02 W |
| Beechwood, Ky., U.S. | 218 | 38.24 N | 84.44 W |
| Beechwood, Ma., U.S. | 283 | 42.12 N | 70.49 W |
| Beechwood, Mi., U.S. | 216 | 46.09 N | 88.46 W |
| Beechworth | 166 | 36.22 S | 146.41 E |
| Beechy | 184 | 50.51 N | 107.25 W |
| Beeck ◆[8] | 263 | 51.29 N | 6.44 E |
| Beeckerwerth ◆[8] | 263 | 51.29 N | 6.41 E |
| Beecroft | 274a | 33.45 S | 151.04 E |
| Beecroft Head ≻ | 170 | 35.01 S | 150.51 E |
| Beecroft Peninsula ≻[1] | 170 | 35.02 S | 150.50 E |
| Beedenbostel | 52 | 52.38 N | 10.16 E |
| Beef Island I | 240m | 18.27 N | 64.31 W |
| Beek, Ned. | 52 | 51.51 N | 5.54 E |
| Beek, Ned. | 52 | 51.32 N | 5.38 E |
| Beek, Ned. | 56 | 50.56 N | 5.49 E |
| Beela ≃ | 44 | 54.13 N | 2.47 W |
| Beeleigh Abbey ʊ[1] | 260 | 51.44 N | 0.40 E |
| Beelen | 52 | 51.55 N | 8.07 E |
| Beelitz | 54 | 52.14 N | 12.58 E |
| Beemer | 198 | 41.55 N | 96.48 W |
| Beemster ◆[1] | 52 | 52.35 N | 4.55 E |
| Beendorf | 54 | 52.14 N | 11.05 E |
| Beenleigh | 171a | 27.43 S | 153.12 E |
| Beerburrum | 171a | 26.58 S | 152.58 E |
| Beerfelden | 56 | 49.34 N | 8.58 E |
| Bee Ridge | 220 | 27.17 N | 82.28 W |
| Beeringgnurding Hill ʌ[2] | 162 | 29.53 S | 117.55 E |
| Beernem | 50 | 51.09 N | 3.20 E |
| Beerse | 56 | 51.19 N | 4.52 E |
| Beersheba → Be'ér Sheva' | 132 | 31.14 N | 34.47 E |
| Beersheba Springs | 194 | 35.28 N | 85.39 W |
| Be'ér Sheva' (Beersheba) | 132 | 31.14 N | 34.47 E |
| Be'er Sheva', Naḥal V | 132 | 31.11 N | 34.35 E |
| Beerta | 52 | 53.10 N | 7.05 E |
| Be'ér Toviyya | 132 | 31.44 N | 34.44 E |
| Beervlei Brak ≃ | 158 | 29.58 S | 23.12 E |
| Beerwah | 171a | 26.51 S | 152.58 E |
| Beerwah National Park ♦ | 171a | 26.54 S | 152.53 E |
| Be'er Ya'agov | 132 | 31.56 N | 34.50 E |
| Beesenlaublingen | 54 | 51.42 N | 11.41 E |
| Beeskow | 54 | 52.10 N | 14.14 E |
| Beestekraal | 156 | 25.23 S | 27.38 E |
| Beesten | 52 | 52.26 N | 7.30 E |
| Beeston | 42 | 52.56 N | 1.12 W |
| Beet ≃ | 115a | 6.16 S | 107.15 E |
| Beethoven Peninsula ≻[1] | 9 | 71.40 S | 73.45 W |
| Beeton | 212 | 44.05 N | 79.47 W |
| Beetsterzwaag | 52 | 53.03 N | 6.05 E |
| Beetz, Lac ⊜ | 186 | 50.34 N | 62.42 W |
| Beetzendorf | 54 | 52.42 N | 11.05 E |
| Beeville | 196 | 28.24 N | 97.44 W |
| Beevor, Mount ʌ[2] | 168b | 34.56 S | 139.02 E |
| Befale | 152 | 0.28 N | 20.58 E |
| Befandriana | 157b | 15.16 S | 48.32 E |
| Befandriana Atsimo | 157b | 22.06 S | 43.54 E |
| Befasy | 157b | 20.33 S | 44.23 E |
| Befori | 152 | 0.06 N | 22.17 E |
| Befotaka, Madag. | 157b | 13.15 S | 48.16 E |
| Befotaka, Madag. | 157b | 14.32 S | 48.01 E |
| Befotaka, Madag. | 157b | 23.49 S | 46.59 E |
| Befotaka, Madag. | 157b | 21.29 S | 44.44 E |
| Befu ◆[8] | 270 | 34.40 N | 135.02 E |
| Beg, Lough ⊜ | 48 | 54.47 N | 6.28 W |
| Bega | 166 | 36.40 S | 149.50 E |
| Bega (Begej) ≃ | 38 | 45.13 N | 20.19 E |
| Begamganj, Bngl. | 124 | 22.49 N | 91.07 E |
| Begamganj, India | 124 | 23.36 N | 78.20 E |
| Begampur ◆[8] | 272a | 28.44 N | 77.04 E |
| Beğdeş | 130 | 37.51 N | 39.05 E |
| Begej (Bega) ≃ | 38 | 45.13 N | 20.19 E |
| Beger | 102 | 45.42 N | 97.10 E |
| Beggs | 196 | 35.44 N | 96.04 W |
| Begičevskij | 76 | 53.47 N | 38.15 E |
| Beginsel | 158 | 26.57 S | 20.39 E |
| Beglickaja, kosa ≻[2] | 83 | 47.07 N | 38.35 E |
| Begna ≃ | 26 | 60.10 N | 10.16 E |
| Begonias, Presa ⊜[1] | 234 | 20.55 N | 100.50 W |
| Begoro | 150 | 6.23 N | 0.23 W |
| Begovat → Bekabad | 85 | 40.13 N | 69.14 E |
| Begunicy | 76 | 59.35 N | 29.19 E |
| Begur, Cap de ≻ | 34 | 41.57 N | 3.14 E |
| Begusarai | 124 | 25.25 N | 86.08 E |
| Behāla | 126 | 22.31 N | 88.19 E |
| Behauge, Pointe ≻ | 250 | 4.40 N | 51.54 W |
| Behbahān | 128 | 30.35 N | 50.14 E |
| Behleg | 120 | 36.47 N | 91.41 E |
| Behm Canal ◡ | 182 | 55.41 N | 131.35 W |
| Beho | 56 | 50.13 N | 6.00 E |
| Béhoust | 261 | 48.50 N | 1.43 E |
| Behrāmpur | 272a | 28.38 N | 77.24 E |
| Behren-lès-Forbach | 56 | 49.10 N | 6.57 E |
| Behring, Détroit de → Bering Strait ◡ | 180 | 65.30 N | 169.00 W |
| Behringen, Dtsch. | 52 | 53.07 N | 9.58 E |
| Behringen, Dtsch. | 54 | 51.01 N | 10.31 E |
| Behshahr | 128 | 36.43 N | 53.34 E |
| Beht, Oued ≃ | 148 | 34.25 N | 6.26 W |
| Bei ≃ | 90 | 23.09 N | 112.48 E |
| Bei'an | 89 | 48.16 N | 126.36 E |
| Beianhe | 105 | 40.04 N | 116.06 E |
| Beibaihua | 105 | 38.57 N | 114.51 E |
| Beibaozhen | 106 | 31.33 N | 121.38 E |
| Beibei | 107 | 29.49 N | 106.26 E |
| Beicai | 106 | 31.12 N | 121.34 E |
| Beicang | 105 | 39.13 N | 117.07 E |
| Beida → Al-Bayḍā' | 146 | 32.46 N | 21.43 E |
| Beida ≃ | 102 | 40.18 N | 99.26 E |
| Beida, Chott ⊜ | 34 | 35.56 N | 5.49 E |
| Beidaihe | 98 | 39.54 N | 119.29 E |
| Beidaoqiao | 86 | 44.12 N | 89.38 E |
| Beidouzhen | 107 | 30.02 N | 104.26 E |
| Beidun | 100 | 26.42 N | 118.57 E |
| Beierfeld | 54 | 50.33 N | 12.47 E |
| Beiersdorf | 264a | 52.42 N | 13.47 E |
| Beifangcun | 105 | 40.20 N | 116.42 E |
| Beifangzi | 104 | 41.22 N | 121.03 E |
| Beigang | 100 | 29.20 N | 113.41 E |
| Beighton | 44 | 53.20 N | 1.20 W |
| Beigi | 144 | 9.20 N | 34.29 E |
| Beiguan Dao I | 100 | 27.10 N | 120.32 E |
| Beiguo | 106 | 31.47 N | 120.33 E |
| Beihai | 102 | 21.29 N | 109.05 E |
| Bei Hai ⊜ | 271a | 39.56 N | 116.22 E |
| Beihedian | 105 | 39.13 N | 115.45 E |
| Beiheishang'gou | 105 | 39.53 N | 118.15 E |
| Beihuaidian | 105 | 39.16 N | 117.33 E |
| Beijialing | 104 | 41.08 N | 124.02 E |
| Beijiao | 100 | 26.22 N | 119.58 E |
| Beijiean | 106 | 32.15 N | 121.12 E |
| Beijijiazhuang | 105 | 40.01 N | 114.51 E |
| Beijing (Peking), Zhg. | 105 | 39.55 N | 116.25 E |
| Beijing (Peking), Zhg. | 271a | 39.55 N | 116.25 E |
| Beijing Ji Chang (Capitol Airport) ⊠ | 105 | 40.03 N | 116.35 E |
| Beijing Shi (Peking Shih) □[7] | 98 | 40.15 N | 116.30 E |
| Beiji Shan I | 100 | 27.38 N | 121.12 E |
| Beijuma ≃ | 105 | 39.30 N | 115.56 E |
| Beikan | 100 | 32.23 N | 121.21 E |
| Beilen | 52 | 52.52 N | 6.31 E |
| Beili | 110 | 19.10 N | 108.43 E |
| Beilifang | 104 | 41.59 N | 121.57 E |
| Beiling | 100 | 24.36 N | 115.20 E |
| Beiliu | 102 | 22.42 N | 110.22 E |
| Beiliuwangshui | 105 | 38.57 N | 115.03 E |
| Beilizigu | 105 | 39.30 N | 117.28 E |
| Beilngries | 60 | 49.02 N | 11.29 E |
| Beilong Shan I | 100 | 27.40 N | 120.58 E |
| Beilrode | 54 | 51.35 N | 13.03 E |
| Beilstein, Dtsch. | 56 | 49.02 N | 9.18 E |
| Beilstein, Dtsch. | 56 | 50.06 N | 7.14 E |
| Beimaizhu | 105 | 39.31 N | 117.44 E |
| Beiminjiatun | 104 | 42.38 N | 122.43 E |
| Beimuzhen | 107 | 29.31 N | 105.05 E |
| Beinamar | 146 | 8.40 N | 15.23 E |
| Beine-Nauroy | 50 | 49.15 N | 4.13 E |
| Beinette | 62 | 44.22 N | 7.39 E |
| Beinwil | 58 | 47.22 N | 7.35 E |
| Beinwil am See | 58 | 47.16 N | 8.13 E |
| Beipa | 164 | 8.30 S | 146.35 E |
| Beipan ≃ | 102 | 25.05 N | 106.00 E |
| Beipanxiaozhen | 106 | 31.44 N | 121.26 E |
| Beipiao | 104 | 41.49 N | 120.46 E |
| Beipo | 102 | 21.14 N | 109.53 E |
| Beiqi | 98 | 40.27 N | 122.20 E |
| Beiqiao | 106 | 31.03 N | 121.24 E |
| Beira | 156 | 19.49 S | 34.52 E |
| Beira Baixa □[9] | 34 | 39.45 N | 7.30 W |
| Beira Litoral □[9] | 34 | 40.15 N | 8.25 W |
| Beiru ≃ | 100 | 33.43 N | 113.35 E |
| Beirut → Bayrūt | 130 | 33.53 N | 35.30 E |
| Beirut International Airport ⊠ | 132 | 33.49 N | 35.30 E |
| Beisanjia | 98 | 42.04 N | 124.42 E |
| Beiseker | 182 | 51.23 N | 113.32 W |
| Beishakou | 105 | 39.08 N | 116.07 E |
| Beishan | 102 | 24.28 N | 108.35 E |
| Bei Shan ⋏ | 102 | 41.30 N | 96.00 E |
| Beishangcun | 105 | 39.28 N | 116.58 E |
| Beishipian | 105 | 40.43 N | 116.55 E |
| Beishuangdong | 105 | 40.32 N | 117.24 E |
| Beishuiquan | 98 | 40.05 N | 114.40 E |
| Beisi | 102 | 34.59 N | 95.07 E |
| Beisu | 98 | 38.13 N | 114.46 E |
| Beitaitou | 98 | 37.06 N | 118.31 E |
| Beitang | 105 | 39.07 N | 117.42 E |
| Beitanshiqiao | 106 | 31.05 N | 121.38 E |
| Beitbridge, Zimb. | 154 | 22.13 S | 30.00 E |
| Beitbridge, Zimb. | 156 | 22.13 S | 30.00 E |
| Beith | 46 | 55.45 N | 4.38 W |
| Beitstadfjorden ⊂[2] | 26 | 63.53 N | 11.00 E |
| Beiuș | 38 | 46.40 N | 22.21 E |
| Beiwei | 106 | 32.05 N | 121.12 E |
| Beiwenquan | 107 | 29.51 N | 106.24 E |
| Beiwu | 105 | 40.04 N | 116.48 E |
| Beiwudu | 100 | 33.39 N | 113.39 E |
| Beixiadai | 106 | 32.12 N | 120.08 E |
| Beixiejiadang | 105 | 40.30 N | 114.50 E |
| Beixili | 89 | 51.47 N | 125.45 E |
| Beixin'an | 271a | 39.55 N | 116.08 E |
| Beixindian | 105 | 39.44 N | 116.44 E |
| Beixing | 89 | 48.29 N | 125.40 E |
| Beixinjing | 106 | 31.13 N | 121.22 E |
| Beixinliu | 105 | 39.16 N | 116.31 E |
| Beixinzhen | 106 | 31.49 N | 121.31 E |
| Beiyan | 98 | 36.33 N | 118.42 E |
| Beiyi ≃ | 105 | 39.19 N | 115.39 E |
| Beiyin | 106 | 31.07 N | 120.47 E |
| Beiyindai | 104 | 42.35 N | 122.22 E |
| Beiyuan | 105 | 40.01 N | 116.24 E |
| Beizhaijiawopeng | 104 | 41.14 N | 122.41 E |
| Beizhen, Zhg. | 98 | 37.22 N | 118.01 E |
| Beizhen (Gaoshanzi), Zhg. | 104 | 41.36 N | 121.47 E |
| Beizhouzhuang | 106 | 31.52 N | 120.24 E |
| Beizifu | 98 | 42.09 N | 120.29 E |
| Beja, Bra. | 250 | 1.36 S | 48.47 W |
| Beja, Port. | 34 | 38.01 N | 7.52 W |
| Beja, Ross. | 86 | 53.03 N | 90.54 E |
| Béja, Tun. | 148 | 36.44 N | 9.11 E |
| Beja □[5] | 34 | 37.50 N | 8.00 W |
| Bejaïa (Bougie) | 148 | 36.45 N | 5.05 E |
| Bejaïa, Golfe de ⊂ | 34 | 36.45 N | 5.25 E |
| Béjar | 34 | 40.23 N | 5.46 W |
| Bejhi ≃ | 120 | 29.47 N | 67.58 E |
| Bejneu | 86 | 45.15 N | 55.07 E |
| Bejsug ≃ | 78 | 45.54 N | 38.56 E |
| Bejsugskij liman ⊂ | 78 | 46.07 N | 38.25 E |
| Bejtonovo | 89 | 53.14 N | 124.27 E |
| Bejucal | 240p | 22.56 N | 82.23 W |
| Bejucal □[7] | 286b | 22.56 N | 82.23 W |
| Bejuco | 236 | 8.36 N | 79.53 W |
| Bejucos ≃ | 234 | 18.36 N | 100.40 W |
| Bejuma | 246 | 10.11 N | 68.16 W |
| Bek ≃ | 152 | 2.29 N | 15.15 E |
| Béka | 146 | 9.04 N | 12.53 E |
| Bekaa Valley → Al-Biqā' V | 128 | 33.50 N | 36.00 E |
| Bekabad | 85 | 40.13 N | 69.14 E |
| Bekancan | 114 | 3.18 N | 98.24 E |
| Bekasi | 115a | 6.14 S | 106.59 E |
| Bekasi ≃ | 269e | 6.10 S | 107.02 E |
| Békásmegyer ◆[8] | 264c | 47.36 N | 19.03 E |
| Bekasovo | 82 | 55.26 N | 36.49 E |
| Bekdaš | 72 | 41.34 N | 52.32 E |
| Békés | 30 | 46.46 N | 21.08 E |
| Békés □[6] | 30 | 46.46 N | 21.08 E |
| Békéscsaba | 30 | 46.41 N | 21.06 E |
| Beketovo | 89 | 53.13 N | 125.01 E |
| Bekilli | 130 | 38.14 N | 29.26 E |
| Bekily | 157b | 24.13 S | 45.19 E |
| Bekirhan | 130 | 38.10 N | 41.19 E |
| Bekisopa | 157b | 21.40 S | 45.54 E |
| Bekitro | 157b | 24.33 S | 45.18 E |
| Bekkaria | 36 | 35.22 N | 8.15 E |
| Bekkersdal | 273d | 26.18 S | 27.42 E |
| Bekkevoort | 56 | 50.57 N | 4.58 E |
| Beklemiševo, Ross. | 80 | 53.52 N | 47.25 E |
| Beklemiševo, Ross. | 88 | 52.07 N | 112.40 E |
| Bekodoka | 157b | 16.58 S | 45.07 E |
| Bekoji | 144 | 7.34 N | 39.17 E |
| Bekok | 114 | 2.18 N | 103.08 E |
| Bekopaka | 157b | 19.09 S | 44.48 E |
| Bekovo | 80 | 52.28 N | 43.43 E |
| Bektauata, gora ʌ | 86 | 47.30 N | 74.50 E |
| Bektyševo | 82 | 56.34 N | 39.14 E |
| Bekwai | 150 | 6.27 N | 1.35 W |
| Bela, India | 124 | 25.56 N | 81.59 E |
| Bela, Pāk. | 120 | 26.14 N | 66.19 E |
| Bela, Zaïre | 154 | 0.38 N | 29.14 E |
| Belaazërsk | 76 | 52.28 N | 25.11 E |
| Bélabo | 152 | 5.00 N | 13.20 E |
| Belabolo | 140 | 8.57 N | 25.51 E |
| Bela Crkva | 38 | 44.54 N | 21.26 E |
| Bela Cruz | 250 | 3.03 S | 40.11 W |
| Belaga | 108 | 2.42 N | 113.47 E |
| Bel'agaš | 86 | 50.48 N | 80.44 E |
| Bel-Air, Fr. | 261 | 48.37 N | 2.10 E |
| Bel Air, Md., U.S. | 208 | 39.32 N | 76.20 W |
| Bel Air, Va., U.S. | 284c | 38.52 N | 77.10 W |
| Bel Air ◆[8] | 280 | 34.05 N | 118.27 W |
| Bélair, Île I | 275a | 45.37 N | 73.48 W |
| Bel Aire Estates | 207 | 41.23 N | 72.00 W |
| Belair Recreation Park ♦ | 168b | 35.01 S | 138.39 E |
| Belaja, Ross. | 78 | 51.03 N | 35.43 E |
| Belaja, Ross. | 80 | 57.59 N | 51.42 E |
| Belaja ≃, Ross. | 78 | 45.04 N | 39.23 E |
| Belaja ≃, Ross. | 84 | 44.45 N | 39.50 E |
| Belaja ≃, Ross. | 86 | 55.54 N | 53.33 E |
| Belaja ≃, Ross. | 180 | 65.45 N | 173.20 E |
| Belaja, gora ʌ, Ross. | 88 | 53.10 N | 119.50 E |
| Belaja, gora ʌ, Ross. | 180 | 65.50 N | 174.40 E |
| Belaja Ber'ozka | 76 | 52.23 N | 33.29 E |
| Belaja Cholunica | 86 | 58.50 N | 50.48 E |
| Belaja Gora | 76 | 58.31 N | 31.45 E |
| Belaja Kalitva | 78 | 48.11 N | 40.46 E |
| Bel'ajevka, Ross. | 86 | 57.28 N | 55.28 E |
| Bel'ajevka, Ross. | 86 | 51.24 N | 56.26 E |
| Bel'ajevo | 76 | 55.31 N | 31.06 E |
| Belalcázar | 34 | 38.34 N | 5.10 W |
| Bel Alton | 208 | 38.27 N | 76.58 W |
| Belambanganumpu | 112 | 4.54 S | 105.03 E |
| Belampalli | 122 | 19.02 N | 79.30 E |
| Bělá nad Radbuzou | 60 | 49.36 N | 12.44 E |
| Belang | 112 | 0.57 N | 124.47 E |
| Bélanger ≃ | 184 | 53.26 N | 97.40 W |
| Bel'aninovo | 265b | 55.57 N | 37.39 E |
| Bel'anskij | 80 | 47.45 N | 41.33 E |
| Bela Palanka | 38 | 43.13 N | 22.19 E |
| Bělá pod Bezdězem | 54 | 50.30 N | 14.50 E |
| Belapurpāda | 272c | 19.01 N | 73.02 E |
| Belarus □[1], Europe | 22 | 53.50 N | 28.00 E |
| Belarus (Belarus') □[1], Europe | 76 | 53.50 N | 28.00 E |
| Belaruskaja hrada ʌ | 76 | 53.40 N | 27.00 E |
| Belarus Station ◆[5] | 265b | 55.47 N | 37.35 E |
| Belas | 266c | 38.47 N | 9.16 W |
| Belau → Palau □[1] | 14 | 5.00 N | 137.00 E |
| Belavenona | 157b | 24.50 S | 47.04 E |
| Bela Vista, Ang. | 152 | 7.50 S | 13.40 E |
| Bela Vista, Bra. | 252 | 22.06 S | 56.31 W |
| Bela Vista, Moç. | 156 | 26.20 S | 32.40 E |
| Bela Vista ◆[8] | 287b | 23.33 S | 46.38 W |
| Bela Vista de Goiás | 255 | 16.58 S | 48.57 W |
| Bela Vista do Paraíso | 255 | 23.00 S | 51.12 W |
| Belavuša | 78 | 51.57 N | 26.56 E |
| Belawan | 114 | 3.47 N | 98.41 E |
| Belaya ʌ | 144 | 11.25 N | 36.12 E |
| Belayan ≃ | 112 | 0.14 S | 116.36 E |
| Belaya Tserkov → Bila Tserkva | 78 | 49.49 N | 30.07 E |
| Belbo ≃ | 62 | 44.54 N | 8.31 E |
| Belbubulo | 140 | 9.57 N | 34.04 E |
| Belbunia | 126 | 23.17 N | 87.09 E |
| Belcamp | 208 | 39.28 N | 76.14 W |
| Belcastro | 68 | 39.02 N | 16.47 E |
| Bełchatów | 30 | 51.22 N | 19.21 E |
| Belchen ʌ | 58 | 47.49 N | 7.50 E |
| Belcher | 194 | 32.44 N | 93.49 W |
| Belcherāgh | 120 | 35.50 N | 65.14 E |
| Belcher Creek ≃ | 276 | 41.08 N | 74.23 W |
| Belcher Islands II | 176 | 56.20 N | 79.30 W |
| Belchertown | 207 | 42.16 N | 72.24 W |
| Belchite | 34 | 41.18 N | 0.45 W |
| Bělčice | 60 | 49.30 N | 13.53 E |
| Belcoo | 48 | 54.17 N | 7.52 W |
| Belcourt | 198 | 48.50 N | 99.44 W |
| Belda | 126 | 22.05 N | 87.21 E |
| Beldānga | 126 | 23.56 N | 88.15 E |
| Bel'd'ažki | 76 | 52.39 N | 35.42 E |
| Belding | 216 | 43.05 N | 85.13 W |
| Bele, ozero ⊜ | 86 | 54.39 N | 90.12 E |
| Belebej | 80 | 54.07 N | 54.07 E |
| Belebelka | 76 | 57.34 N | 30.56 E |
| Belecke | 52 | 51.29 N | 8.20 E |
| Beled Weyne | 144 | 4.45 N | 45.12 E |
| Bélel, Cam. | 152 | 7.03 N | 14.26 E |
| Belel, Nig. | 146 | 9.38 N | 13.12 E |
| Belém, Bra. | 250 | 1.27 S | 48.29 W |
| Belém, Moç. | 154 | 14.13 S | 35.58 E |
| Belém ◆[8] | 266c | 38.42 N | 9.12 W |
| Belém, Torre de ⊥ | 266c | 38.42 N | 9.13 W |
| Belém de São Francisco | 250 | 8.46 S | 38.58 W |
| Belén, Arg. | 252 | 27.39 S | 67.02 W |
| Belén, Bol. | 248 | 19.48 S | 65.33 W |
| Belén, Chile | 248 | 18.29 S | 69.31 W |
| Belén, Col. | 246 | 6.00 N | 72.55 W |
| Belén, Nic. | 236 | 11.30 N | 85.53 W |
| Belén, Para. | 252 | 23.30 S | 57.06 W |
| Belen, Tür. | 130 | 36.32 N | 36.10 E |
| Belen, N.M., U.S. | 200 | 34.39 N | 106.46 W |
| Belén, Ur. | 252 | 30.47 S | 57.47 W |
| Belén ≃ | 252 | 28.00 S | 66.52 W |
| Belén de Escobar | 258 | 34.21 S | 58.47 W |
| Belén del Refugio | 234 | 21.31 N | 102.25 W |
| Belene | 38 | 43.39 N | 25.07 E |
| Belenichino | 78 | 50.56 N | 36.37 E |
| Belènzinho ◆[8] | 287b | 23.32 S | 46.35 W |
| Bélep, Îles II | 175f | 19.45 S | 163.40 E |
| Beles ≃ | 144 | 11.10 N | 36.10 E |
| Belesar, Embalse de ⊜[1] | 34 | 42.45 N | 7.40 W |
| Belet Uen → Beled Weyne | 144 | 4.45 N | 45.12 E |
| Belews Lake ⊜[1] | 192 | 36.17 N | 80.03 W |
| Belfair | 224 | 47.27 N | 122.49 W |
| Belfast, N.Z. | 172 | 43.27 S | 172.38 E |
| Belfast, S. Afr. | 156 | 25.43 S | 30.03 E |
| Belfast, N. Ire., U.K. | 48 | 54.35 N | 5.55 W |
| Belfast, Me., U.S. | 188 | 44.25 N | 69.00 W |
| Belfast, N.Y., U.S. | 210 | 42.20 N | 78.06 W |
| Belfast, Oh., U.S. | 218 | 39.03 N | 83.32 W |
| Belfast (Aldergrove) Airport ⊠ | 48 | 54.38 N | 6.12 W |
| Belfast Lough ⊂ | 48 | 54.40 N | 5.50 W |
| Belfeld | 52 | 51.19 N | 6.06 E |
| Belfield, Austl. | 274a | 33.54 S | 151.05 E |
| Belfield, N.D., U.S. | 198 | 46.53 N | 103.11 W |
| Belfiore | 64 | 45.23 N | 11.12 E |
| Belford, Eng., U.K. | 44 | 55.36 N | 1.49 W |
| Belford, N.J., U.S. | 276 | 40.25 N | 74.05 W |
| Belford Roxo | 256 | 22.46 S | 43.24 W |
| Belfort | 58 | 47.38 N | 6.52 E |
| Belfort □[8] | 58 | 47.38 N | 6.55 E |
| Belforte del Chienti | 66 | 43.10 N | 13.14 E |
| Belfry, Ky., U.S. | 192 | 37.37 N | 82.16 W |
| Belfry, Mt., U.S. | 202 | 45.08 N | 109.00 W |
| Belgaum | 122 | 15.52 N | 74.31 E |
| Belgern | 54 | 51.29 N | 13.07 E |
| Bélgica → Belgium □[1] | 30 | 50.50 N | 4.00 E |
| Belgica Mountains ⋏ | 9 | 72.35 S | 31.10 E |
| België → Belgium □[1] | 30 | 50.50 N | 4.00 E |
| Belgien → Belgium □[1] | 30 | 50.50 N | 4.00 E |
| Belgioioso | 62 | 45.10 N | 9.19 E |
| Belgique → Belgium □[1] | 30 | 50.50 N | 4.00 E |
| Belgium □[1], Europe | 22 | 50.50 N | 4.00 E |
| Belgium □[1], Europe | 30 | 50.50 N | 4.00 E |
| Belgodère | 36 | 42.35 N | 9.01 E |
| Belgorod | 78 | 50.36 N | 36.35 E |
| Belgorod Oblast' □[4] | 78 | 50.45 N | 37.30 E |
| Belgrad → Beograd | 38 | 44.50 N | 20.30 E |
| Belgrade → Beograd, Jugo. | 38 | 44.50 N | 20.30 E |
| Belgrade, Mn., U.S. | 198 | 45.27 N | 95.00 W |
| Belgrade, Mt., U.S. | 202 | 45.46 N | 111.10 W |
| Belgrade, Ne., U.S. | 198 | 41.28 N | 98.04 W |
| Belgrado → Beograd | 38 | 44.50 N | 20.30 E |
| Belgrad Ormanı ◆[3] | 267b | 41.10 N | 28.55 E |
| Belgrano ◆[8] | 288 | 34.34 S | 58.28 W |
| Belgrano ≃ | 254 | 48.15 S | 71.14 W |
| Belgrano, Lago ⊜ | 254 | 47.50 S | 72.09 W |
| Belgrano II ʊ[3] | 9 | 77.46 S | 38.11 W |
| Belgrave | 274b | 37.55 S | 145.21 E |
| Belhar | 124 | 24.55 N | 86.36 E |
| Belhaven | 192 | 35.32 N | 76.37 W |
| Belhus Park ♦ | 260 | 51.31 N | 0.17 E |
| Beliābera | 126 | 22.17 N | 86.57 E |
| Beliātor | 126 | 23.20 N | 87.13 E |
| Belica, Hrv. | 61 | 46.26 N | 16.27 E |
| Belica, Ross. | 78 | 51.07 N | 35.34 E |
| Belice → Belize City | 232 | 17.30 N | 88.12 W |
| Belice → Belize □[1] | 232 | 17.15 N | 88.45 W |
| Belice ≃ | 70 | 37.35 N | 12.52 E |
| Belichifor | 140 | 6.33 N | 33.16 E |
| Belici ≃ | 70 | 37.31 N | 13.50 E |
| Beličij, ostrov I | 89 | 54.26 N | 137.51 E |
| Belick | 76 | 52.55 N | 30.27 E |
| Beli Drim ≃ | 38 | 42.06 N | 20.25 E |
| Beliling, Gunung ʌ | 115b | 8.37 S | 119.59 E |
| Beliliou (Peleliu) I | 175b | 7.01 N | 134.15 E |
| Beli Manastir | 38 | 45.46 N | 18.36 E |
| Belin | 32 | 44.30 N | 0.47 W |
| Belinga | 152 | 1.13 N | 13.12 E |
| Belington | 188 | 39.01 N | 79.56 W |
| Belinskij | 80 | 52.58 N | 43.26 E |
| Belinyu | 112 | 1.38 S | 105.46 E |
| Belitung I | 112 | 2.50 S | 107.55 E |
| Belize □[1], N.A. | 230 | 17.15 N | 88.45 W |
| Belize □[1], N.A. | 232 | 17.15 N | 88.45 W |
| Belize ≃ | 232 | 17.32 N | 88.14 W |
| Belize City | 232 | 17.30 N | 88.12 W |
| Belize Inlet ⊂ | 182 | 51.08 N | 127.15 W |
| Belknap Crater ⊥[6] | 202 | 44.17 N | 121.50 W |
| Belkofski | 180 | 55.05 N | 162.02 W |
| Bel'kovo | 82 | 56.15 N | 38.48 E |
| Bel'kovskij, Ostrov I | 74 | 75.32 N | 135.44 E |
| Bell, Austl. | 274b | 37.45 S | 145.00 E |
| Bell, S. Afr. | 158 | 33.15 S | 27.23 E |
| Bell, Ca., U.S. | 280 | 33.58 N | 118.11 W |
| Bell □[6] | 222 | 31.03 N | 97.27 W |
| Bell ≃, P.Q., Can. | 176 | 49.48 N | 77.38 W |
| Bell ≃, Yk., Can. | 180 | 67.17 N | 137.46 W |
| Bella | 68 | 40.45 N | 15.32 E |
| Bella Bella | 182 | 52.09 N | 128.07 W |
| Bellac | 32 | 46.07 N | 1.02 E |
| Bella Coola | 182 | 52.22 N | 126.46 W |
| Bella Coola ≃ | 182 | 52.22 N | 126.43 W |
| Bell Acres | 279b | 40.36 N | 80.10 W |
| Bella Flor | 248 | 11.09 S | 67.49 W |
| Bellagio | 58 | 45.59 N | 9.15 E |
| Bellahy | 48 | 53.58 N | 8.48 W |
| Bellair | 192 | 30.10 N | 81.44 W |
| Bellaire, Mi., U.S. | 190 | 44.58 N | 85.12 W |
| Bellaire, Oh., U.S. | 188 | 40.00 N | 80.45 W |
| Bellaire, Tx., U.S. | 222 | 29.42 N | 95.27 W |
| Bella Isla, Estrecho de → Belle Isle, Strait of ◡ | 176 | 51.35 N | 56.30 W |
| Bella Lake ⊜ | 212 | 45.27 N | 79.02 W |
| Bellambi | 170 | 34.21 S | 150.55 E |
| Bellamy, Al., U.S. | 194 | 32.26 N | 88.08 W |
| Bellamy, Va., U.S. | 208 | 37.24 N | 76.34 W |
| Bellano | 58 | 46.03 N | 9.18 E |
| Bellaria | 66 | 44.09 N | 12.28 E |
| Bellarine | 169 | 38.08 S | 144.37 E |
| Bellarine Peninsula ≻[1] | 169 | 38.13 S | 144.35 E |
| Bellariva | 68 | 41.55 N | 15.58 E |
| Bellary | 122 | 15.09 N | 76.56 E |
| Bellas Artes, Museo de ʊ | 286c | 10.30 N | 66.53 W |
| Bellas Artes, Palacio de ʊ | 286a | 19.26 N | 99.08 W |
| Bellata | 166 | 29.55 S | 149.47 E |
| Bella Tola ʌ | 58 | 46.15 N | 7.39 E |
| Bella Unión | 252 | 30.15 S | 57.35 W |
| Bella Vista, Arg. | 252 | 28.30 S | 59.03 W |
| Bella Vista, Arg. | 252 | 27.02 S | 65.18 W |
| Bella Vista, Arg. | 258 | 34.33 S | 58.41 W |
| Bellavista, Chile | 286e | 33.31 S | 70.37 W |
| Bella Vista, Para. | 252 | 22.08 S | 56.31 W |
| Bellavista, Perú | 248 | 4.54 S | 80.42 W |
| Bellavista, Perú | 248 | 7.04 S | 76.35 W |
| Bellavista, Perú | 286d | 12.04 S | 77.08 W |
| Bellbird | 170 | 32.51 S | 151.21 E |
| Bellbrook, Austl. | 166 | 30.49 S | 152.31 E |
| Bellbrook, Oh., U.S. | 218 | 39.38 N | 84.04 W |
| Bell Brook ≃ | 168a | 33.01 S | 116.15 E |
| Bell Crags ʌ[2] | 44 | 55.03 N | 2.22 W |
| Bell Creek ≃, Ca., U.S. | 280 | 34.12 N | 118.36 W |
| Bell Creek ≃, In., U.S. | 218 | 40.09 N | 85.27 W |
| Bellé, Sén. | 150 | 14.25 N | 12.18 W |
| Belle, Mo., U.S. | 219 | 38.17 N | 91.43 W |
| Belle, W.V., U.S. | 188 | 38.13 N | 81.32 W |
| Belle ≃, On., Can. | 214 | 42.17 N | 82.43 W |
| Belle ≃, Mi., U.S. | 214 | 42.43 N | 82.30 W |
| Belleair | 220 | 27.55 N | 82.48 W |
| Belleau | 50 | 49.06 N | 3.18 E |
| Belle Ayr Mountain ʌ | 210 | 42.07 N | 74.29 W |
| Belle Bay ⊂ | 186 | 47.36 N | 55.18 W |
| Belle Center | 216 | 40.30 N | 83.44 W |
| Belledonne, Chaîne de ⋏ | 62 | 45.18 N | 6.08 E |
| Belle-Église | 50 | 49.12 N | 2.13 E |
| Belleek | 48 | 54.28 N | 8.06 W |
| Belle Farm Estates | 208 | 39.23 N | 76.45 W |
| Bellefontaine, Fr. | 58 | 46.33 N | 6.04 E |
| Bellefontaine, Fr. | 261 | 49.06 N | 2.28 E |
| Bellefontaine, Mart. | 240e | 14.40 N | 61.10 W |
| Bellefontaine, Oh., U.S. | 216 | 40.21 N | 83.45 W |
| Bellefontaine Neighbors | 219 | 38.44 N | 90.13 W |
| Bellefonte, De., U.S. | 208 | 39.45 N | 75.30 W |
| Bellefonte, Md., U.S. | 284c | 38.47 N | 76.52 W |
| Bellefonte, Pa., U.S. | 214 | 40.54 N | 77.46 W |
| Belle Fourche | 198 | 44.40 N | 103.51 W |
| Belle Fourche ≃ | 198 | 44.26 N | 102.19 W |
| Belle Fourche Reservoir ⊜[1] | 198 | 44.44 N | 103.42 W |
| Bellegarde, Fr. | 58 | 46.06 N | 5.49 E |
| Bellegarde, Fr. | 62 | 43.45 N | 4.31 E |
| Bellegarde-du-Loiret | 50 | 47.59 N | 2.26 E |
| Bellegem | 50 | 50.47 N | 3.16 E |
| Belle Glade | 220 | 26.41 N | 80.40 W |
| Belle Glade Camp | 220 | 26.40 N | 80.41 W |
| Bellegrove | 208 | 40.22 N | 76.33 W |
| Belle Haven, Va., U.S. | 208 | 37.33 N | 75.49 W |
| Belle Haven, Va., U.S. | 284c | 38.47 N | 77.04 W |
| Belleherbe | 58 | 47.16 N | 6.40 E |
| Belle Hôtesse ʌ | 241o | 16.16 N | 61.46 W |
| Belle-Île I | 32 | 47.20 N | 3.10 W |
| Belle Isle | 220 | 28.27 N | 81.21 W |
| Belle Isle I, Nf., Can. | 176 | 51.55 N | 55.20 W |
| Belle Isle I, Mi., U.S. | 281 | 42.20 N | 82.58 W |
| Belle Isle, Strait of ◡ | 176 | 51.35 N | 56.30 W |
| Belle Isle Park ♦ | 281 | 42.20 N | 82.59 W |
| Bellelay | 58 | 47.16 N | 7.10 E |
| Bellême | 50 | 48.22 N | 0.34 E |
| Belle Mead | 208 | 40.28 N | 74.39 W |
| Bellemoor | 285 | 39.43 N | 75.35 W |
| Bellencombre | 50 | 49.42 N | 1.14 E |
| Bellenden Ker National Park ♦ | 164 | 17.15 S | 145.53 E |
| Belleoram | 186 | 47.31 N | 55.25 W |
| Belleplain | 208 | 39.16 N | 74.52 W |
| Belle-Plaine, Sk., Can. | 184 | 50.24 N | 105.09 W |
| Belle Plaine, Ia., U.S. | 190 | 41.53 N | 92.16 W |
| Belle Plaine, Ks., U.S. | 198 | 37.23 N | 97.16 W |
| Belle Plaine, Mn., U.S. | 190 | 44.37 N | 93.46 W |
| Belle Rive | 219 | 38.14 N | 88.45 W |
| Belle River | 214 | 42.18 N | 82.43 W |
| Bellerose | 276 | 40.44 N | 73.43 W |
| Bellerose ◆[8] | 276 | 40.45 N | 73.43 W |
| Bellerose Terrace | 276 | 40.43 N | 73.43 W |
| Belle Terre | 276 | 40.58 N | 73.04 W |
| Bellevaux-Ligneuville | 56 | 50.24 N | 6.00 E |
| Belle Vernon | 214 | 40.07 N | 79.52 W |
| Bellevesvre | 58 | 46.50 N | 5.22 E |
| Belleview, Fl., U.S. | 192 | 29.03 N | 82.03 W |
| Belleview, In., U.S. | 218 | 38.53 N | 85.23 W |
| Belle View, Va., U.S. | 208 | 38.46 N | 77.03 W |
| Belleville, On., Can. | 212 | 44.10 N | 77.23 W |
| Belleville, Fr. | 56 | 48.49 N | 6.06 E |
| Belleville, Il., U.S. | 219 | 38.31 N | 89.59 W |
| Belleville, In., U.S. | 218 | 39.41 N | 86.29 W |
| Belleville, Ks., U.S. | 198 | 39.49 N | 97.37 W |
| Belleville, Mi., U.S. | 216 | 42.12 N | 83.29 W |
| Belleville, N.J., U.S. | 210 | 40.47 N | 74.09 W |
| Belleville, N.Y., U.S. | 212 | 43.47 N | 76.07 W |
| Belleville, Pa., U.S. | 214 | 40.36 N | 77.43 W |
| Belleville, R.I., U.S. | 207 | 41.33 N | 71.28 W |
| Belleville, Wi., U.S. | 216 | 42.51 N | 89.32 W |
| Belleville Lake ⊜ | 281 | 42.12 N | 83.29 W |
| Belleville-sur-Meuse | 56 | 49.11 N | 5.23 E |
| Belleville-sur-Saône | 58 | 46.06 N | 4.45 E |
| Bellevue, Ab., Can. | 182 | 49.35 N | 114.22 W |
| Bellevue, Fr. | 50 | 49.53 N | 4.12 E |
| Bellevue, Id., U.S. | 202 | 43.27 N | 114.15 W |
| Bellevue, Ia., U.S. | 190 | 42.15 N | 90.25 W |
| Bellevue, Ky., U.S. | 218 | 39.06 N | 84.28 W |
| Bellevue, Md., U.S. | 208 | 38.42 N | 76.11 W |
| Bellevue, Mi., U.S. | 216 | 42.26 N | 85.01 W |
| Bellevue, Ne., U.S. | 198 | 41.08 N | 95.53 W |
| Bellevue, Oh., U.S. | 214 | 41.16 N | 82.50 W |
| Bellevue, Pa., U.S. | 214 | 40.29 N | 80.03 W |
| Bellevue, Tx., U.S. | 196 | 33.38 N | 98.01 W |
| Bellevue, Wa., U.S. | 224 | 47.36 N | 122.11 W |
| Bellevue ◆[8] | 273d | 26.11 S | 28.05 E |
| Belle Vue Zoological Gardens ♦ | 262 | 53.28 N | 2.11 W |
| Bell Ewart | 212 | 44.16 N | 79.33 W |
| Belley | 62 | 45.46 N | 5.41 E |
| Belleydoux | 58 | 46.15 N | 5.46 E |
| Belle Yella | 150 | 7.22 N | 10.00 W |
| Bellflower, Ca., U.S. | 228 | 33.52 N | 118.06 W |
| Bellflower, Il., U.S. | 216 | 40.20 N | 88.32 W |
| Bellflower, Mo., U.S. | 219 | 39.00 N | 91.21 W |
| Bell Gardens | 228 | 33.57 N | 118.09 W |
| Bellheim | 56 | 49.11 N | 8.16 E |
| Bell Hill ʌ[2] | 210 | 43.09 N | 75.07 W |
| Bell Homestead ⊥ | 212 | 43.04 N | 80.18 W |
| Bellicourt | 50 | 49.57 N | 3.14 E |
| Bellingdon | 260 | 51.44 N | 0.38 W |
| Bellinge | 41 | 55.20 N | 10.20 E |
| Bellingen | 166 | 30.27 S | 152.54 E |
| Bellingham, Eng., U.K. | 44 | 55.09 N | 2.16 W |
| Bellingham, Ma., U.S. | 207 | 42.05 N | 71.28 W |
| Bellingham, Mn., U.S. | 198 | 45.08 N | 96.17 W |
| Bellingham, Wa., U.S. | 224 | 48.45 N | 122.29 W |
| Bellingham Bay ⊂ | 224 | 48.45 N | 122.35 W |
| Bellingshausen ʊ[3] | 9 | 62.12 S | 58.58 W |
| Bellingshausen Sea ⊤[2] | 9 | 71.00 S | 85.00 W |
| Bellingwolde | 52 | 53.07 N | 7.09 E |
| Bellinzago Novarese | 62 | 45.34 N | 8.38 E |


| | | | | |
|---|---|---|---|---|
| ≃ River | Fluß | Río | Rivière | Rio |
| Canal | Kanal | Canal | Canal | Canal |
| Waterfall, Rapids | Wasserfall, Stromschnellen | Cascada, Rápidos | Chute d'eau, Rapides | Cascata, Rápidos |
| Strait | Meeresstraße | Estrecho | Détroit | Estreito |
| ⊂ Bay, Gulf | Bucht, Golf | Bahía, Golfo | Baie, Golfe | Baía, Golfo |
| ⊜ Lake, Lakes | See, Seen | Lago, Lagos | Lac, Lacs | Lago, Lagos |
| Swamp | Sumpf | Pantano | Marais | Pântano |
| Ice Features, Glacier | Eis- und Gletscherformen | Accidentes Glaciales | Formes glaciaires | Acidentes glaciares |
| ⊤ Other Hydrographic Features | Andere Hydrographische Objekte | Otros Elementos Hidrográficos | Autres données hydrographiques | Outros acidentes hidrográficos |

| | | | | |
|---|---|---|---|---|
| Submarine Features | Untermeerische Objekte | Accidentes Submarinos | Formes de relief sous-marin | Acidentes submarinos |
| □ Political Unit | Politische Einheit | Unidad Política | Entité politique | Unidade política |
| ʊ Cultural Institution | Kulturelle Institution | Institución Cultural | Institution culturelle | Instituição cultural |
| ⊥ Historical Site | Historische Stätte | Sitio Histórico | Site historique | Sítio histórico |
| ♦ Recreational Site | Erholungs- und Ferienort | Sitio de Recreo | Centre de loisirs | Area de Lazer |
| ⊠ Airport | Flughafen | Aeropuerto | Aéroport | Aeroporto |
| ■ Military Installation | Militäranlage | Instalación Militar | Installation militaire | Instalação militar |
| ◆ Miscellaneous | Verschiedenes | Misceláneo | Divers | Diversos |

ENGLISH


| Name | Page | Lat.°′ | Long.°′ |
| --- | --- | --- | --- |
| Bellinzona | 58 | 46.11 N | 9.02 E |
| Bell Island I, Nf., Can. | 186 | 47.36 N | 52.58 W |
| Bell Island I, Nf., Can. | 186 | 50.44 N | 55.35 W |
| Bell Island Hot Springs | 182 | 55.56 N | 131.34 W |
| Bellmawr | 208 | 39.52 N | 75.05 W |
| Bellmead | 222 | 31.35 N | 97.06 W |
| Bellmore | 276 | 40.40 N | 73.31 W |
| Bell Mountain | 228 | 34.35 N | 117.15 W |
| Bellnhausen | 56 | 50.42 N | 8.43 E |
| Bello, Col. | 246 | 6.20 N | 75.33 W |
| Bello, Cuba | 286b | 23.07 N | 82.24 W |
| Bello Horizonte → Belo Horizonte | 255 | 19.55 S | 43.56 W |
| Bellona | 210 | 42.46 N | 77.01 W |
| Bellona, Récifs ✣[2] | 160 | 21.30 S | 159.00 E |
| Bellona Plateau ✣[3] | 14 | 20.30 S | 158.30 E |
| Bellone, Cap › | 157b | 16.14 S | 49.51 E |
| Bellosguardo | 68 | 40.25 N | 15.19 E |
| Bellot Strait ɥ | 176 | 71.58 N | 94.45 W |
| Bellows Falls | 188 | 43.08 N | 72.26 W |
| Belloy-en-France | 261 | 49.05 N | 2.22 E |
| Bellpat | 120 | 28.59 N | 68.00 E |
| Bell Peninsula ›[1] | 176 | 63.50 N | 82.00 W |
| Bell Point | 279b | 40.33 N | 79.33 W |
| Bells, Tn., U.S. | 194 | 35.43 N | 89.05 W |
| Bells, Tx., U.S. | 196 | 33.37 N | 96.25 W |
| Bellsbank | 44 | 55.18 N | 4.23 W |
| Bells Bay c | 212 | 45.30 N | 77.51 W |
| Bells Corners | 212 | 45.19 N | 75.50 W |
| Bellshill | 46 | 55.49 N | 4.01 W |
| Bells Lake | 285 | 39.44 N | 75.02 W |
| Bells Lake ⊜ | 285 | 39.45 N | 75.04 W |
| Belltown, De., U.S. | 208 | 38.44 N | 75.10 W |
| Belltown, Il., U.S. | 219 | 39.23 N | 90.25 W |
| Belluno | 64 | 46.09 N | 12.13 E |
| Belluno □[4] | 64 | 46.15 N | 12.08 E |
| Bellvale | 210 | 41.15 N | 74.18 W |
| Bell Ville, Arg. | 252 | 32.37 S | 62.42 W |
| Bellville, S. Afr. | 158 | 33.53 S | 18.36 E |
| Bellville, Oh., U.S. | 214 | 40.37 N | 82.30 W |
| Bellville, Tx., U.S. | 222 | 29.57 N | 96.15 W |
| Bellwood, Il., U.S. | 278 | 41.52 N | 87.52 W |
| Bellwood, Ne., U.S. | 198 | 41.20 N | 97.14 W |
| Bellwood, Pa., U.S. | 214 | 40.36 N | 78.19 W |
| Bellwood, Lake ⊜ | 212 | 43.46 N | 80.20 W |
| Belly ≐ | 182 | 49.46 N | 113.02 W |
| Bellyk | 86 | 54.32 N | 91.17 E |
| Belm | 52 | 52.18 N | 8.08 E |
| Belmar, Md., U.S. | 284b | 39.21 N | 76.32 W |
| Belmar, N.J., U.S. | 208 | 40.10 N | 74.01 W |
| Bélmez | 34 | 38.16 N | 5.12 W |
| Belmiro Braga | 256 | 21.57 S | 43.25 W |
| Belmond | 190 | 42.50 N | 93.36 W |
| Belmont, Austl. | 169 | 38.10 S | 144.21 E |
| Belmont, Austl. | 170 | 33.02 S | 151.40 E |
| Belmont, Mb., Can. | 184 | 49.24 N | 99.27 W |
| Belmont, N.S., Can. | 186 | 45.25 N | 63.23 W |
| Belmont, On., Can. | 212 | 42.53 N | 81.05 W |
| Belmont, S. Afr. | 158 | 29.28 S | 24.22 E |
| Belmont, Eng., U.K. | 262 | 53.38 N | 2.30 W |
| Belmont, Ca., U.S. | 226 | 37.31 N | 122.16 W |
| Belmont, Ma., U.S. | 283 | 42.23 N | 71.10 W |
| Belmont, Mi., U.S. | 216 | 43.05 N | 85.37 W |
| Belmont, Ms., U.S. | 194 | 34.30 N | 88.12 W |
| Belmont, N.H., U.S. | 188 | 43.26 N | 71.28 W |
| Belmont, N.Y., U.S. | 210 | 42.13 N | 78.02 W |
| Belmont, Pa., U.S. | 214 | 40.17 N | 78.53 W |
| Belmont, S.C., U.S. | 192 | 34.02 N | 81.01 W |
| Belmont, Tx., U.S. | 222 | 29.31 N | 97.41 W |
| Belmont, Wi., U.S. | 190 | 42.44 N | 90.20 W |
| Belmont □[6] | 214 | 40.05 N | 80.54 W |
| Belmonte, Bra. | 255 | 15.51 S | 38.54 W |
| Belmonte, Esp. | 34 | 43.17 N | 6.14 W |
| Belmonte, Esp. | 34 | 39.34 N | 2.42 W |
| Belmonte, Port. | 34 | 40.21 N | 7.21 W |
| Belmonte Calabro | 68 | 39.09 N | 16.05 E |
| Belmonte Mezzagno | 70 | 38.02 N | 13.23 E |
| Belmont Harbor c | 278 | 41.57 N | 87.38 W |
| Belmont Lake ⊜, On., Can. | 212 | 44.30 N | 77.50 W |
| Belmont Lake ⊜, N.Y., U.S. | 276 | 40.44 N | 73.20 W |
| Belmont Lake State Park ♠ | 276 | 40.43 N | 73.20 W |
| Belmont Park | 214 | 41.10 N | 80.39 W |
| Belmont Park Race Track ♠ | 276 | 40.43 N | 73.43 W |
| Belmont Reservoir ⊜[1] | 262 | 53.39 N | 2.30 W |
| Belmont Slough ≐ | 282 | 37.33 N | 122.14 W |
| Belmopan | 232 | 17.15 N | 88.46 W |
| Belmore, Austl. | 274a | 33.55 S | 151.05 E |
| Belmore, Oh., U.S. | 216 | 41.09 N | 83.56 W |
| Belmullet | 48 | 54.14 N | 10.00 W |
| Belmuri | 272b | 22.57 N | 88.09 E |
| Belo | 157b | 19.42 S | 44.33 E |
| Belœil, Bel. | 50 | 50.33 N | 3.43 E |
| Beloeil, P.Q., Can. | 206 | 45.34 N | 73.12 W |
| Belœil, Château de ʊ | 50 | 50.35 N | 3.44 E |
| Beloeil, Ruisseau ≐ | 275a | 45.39 N | 73.12 W |
| Beloglazovo | 86 | 56.05 N | 72.40 E |
| Belogorje | 78 | 50.30 N | 40.01 E |
| Belogorka | 80 | 50.42 N | 53.27 E |
| Belogornoje | 80 | 52.25 N | 47.35 E |
| Belogorode | 82 | 54.23 N | 38.31 E |
| Belogorsk, Ross. | 86 | 55.05 N | 88.28 E |
| Belogorsk, Ross. | 89 | 50.57 N | 128.25 E |
| Belogorskij | 86 | 49.27 N | 83.10 E |
| Belogorskoje | 80 | 53.35 N | 48.12 E |
| Belogradčik | 38 | 43.38 N | 22.41 E |
| Beloha | 157b | 25.10 S | 45.03 E |
| Belo Horizonte | 255 | 19.55 S | 43.56 W |
| Beloit, Ks., U.S. | 198 | 39.27 N | 98.06 W |
| Beloit, Oh., U.S. | 214 | 40.55 N | 80.59 W |
| Beloit, Wi., U.S. | 216 | 42.30 N | 89.01 W |
| Belo Jardim | 250 | 8.20 S | 36.26 W |
| Belojarsk | 86 | 53.28 N | 83.54 E |
| Beloje, Kaz. | 86 | 48.55 N | 82.58 E |
| Beloje, Ross. | 80 | 58.23 N | 39.24 E |
| Beloje, ozero ⊜ | 76 | 60.11 N | 37.37 E |
| Beloje more (White Sea) ⊤[2] | 24 | 65.30 N | 38.00 E |
| Belokuricha | 86 | 51.59 N | 84.59 E |
| Belomestnaja | 76 | 52.24 N | 37.37 E |
| Belomestnaja Dvojn'a | 80 | 52.42 N | 41.03 E |
| Belomorsk | 24 | 64.32 N | 34.48 E |
| Belomorsko-Baltijskij kanal ≍ | 24 | 62.48 N | 34.48 E |
| Belondo | 152 | 0.16 S | 19.31 E |
| Belonge | 152 | 2.06 S | 19.32 E |
| Belonia | 124 | 23.15 N | 91.27 E |
| Beloomut | 76 | 54.57 N | 39.20 E |
| Belorado | 34 | 42.25 N | 3.11 W |
| Beloreč ensk | 78 | 44.46 N | 39.52 E |
| Beloreck | 86 | 53.58 N | 58.24 E |
| Belören, Tür. | 130 | 40.51 N | 33.30 E |
| Belören, Tür. | 130 | 37.39 N | 37.34 E |
| Belören, Tür. | 130 | 37.12 N | 32.33 E |
| Belorussia → Belarus □[1] | 22 | 53.35 N | 28.00 E |
| Belorussija → Belarus □[1] | 72 | 53.50 N | 28.00 E |
| Belorussiya → Belarus □[1] | 72 | 53.50 N | 28.00 E |
| Beloščelje | 24 | 64.52 N | 46.56 E |
| Belo-sur-mer | 157b | 20.44 S | 44.00 E |
| Belot, Lac ⊜ | 180 | 66.55 N | 126.18 W |
| Belousovka | 86 | 50.08 N | 82.33 E |
| Belousovo | 82 | 55.05 N | 36.40 E |
| Bel'ov | 76 | 53.48 N | 36.08 E |
| Belo Vale | 255 | 20.25 S | 44.01 W |
| Belovo, Ross. | 86 | 52.57 N | 82.16 E |
| Belovo, Ross. | 86 | 54.25 N | 86.18 E |
| Belovodskoje | 85 | 42.50 N | 74.06 E |
| Beloz'orsk | 76 | 60.02 N | 37.48 E |
| Belp | 58 | 46.53 N | 7.30 E |
| Belpāda | 272c | 19.02 N | 73.03 E |
| Belpasso | 70 | 37.35 N | 14.58 E |
| Belper | 44 | 53.01 N | 1.29 W |
| Belpre | 188 | 39.16 N | 81.34 W |
| Belrose | 274a | 33.44 S | 151.13 E |
| Belsano | 214 | 40.31 N | 78.52 W |
| Belsele | 50 | 51.09 N | 4.05 E |
| Bel'skoje, Ross. | 80 | 54.44 N | 40.22 E |
| Bel'skoje, Ross. | 86 | 57.49 N | 92.09 E |
| Belson Run ≐ | 279b | 40.12 N | 79.37 W |
| Belspring | 192 | 37.11 N | 80.36 W |
| Belt | 202 | 47.23 N | 110.55 W |
| Beltana | 166 | 30.48 S | 138.25 E |
| Belt Creek ≐ | 202 | 47.36 N | 111.02 W |
| Belted Range ⋏ | 204 | 37.25 N | 116.10 W |
| Belterra | 250 | 2.38 S | 54.57 W |
| Belthorn | 262 | 53.43 N | 2.26 W |
| Beltinci | 61 | 46.36 N | 16.15 E |
| Belton, Eng., U.K. | 42 | 52.34 N | 1.41 E |
| Belton, Eng., U.K. | 44 | 53.33 N | 0.49 W |
| Belton, Mo., U.S. | 194 | 38.48 N | 94.31 W |
| Belton, S.C., U.S. | 192 | 34.31 N | 82.29 W |
| Belton, Tx., U.S. | 222 | 31.03 N | 97.27 W |
| Belton Lake ⊜[1] | 222 | 31.08 N | 97.32 W |
| Beltra | 48 | 54.13 N | 8.37 W |
| Beltrán | 252 | 27.50 S | 64.04 W |
| Beltsville, Md., U.S. | 208 | 39.02 N | 76.54 W |
| Beltsvilie, Md., U.S. | 284c | 39.02 N | 76.54 W |
| Belturbet | 48 | 54.06 N | 7.28 W |
| Beltway Plaza ●[9] | 284c | 39.00 N | 76.54 W |
| Bel'tyrskij | 86 | 53.02 N | 90.16 E |
| Beltzville Lake ⊜[1] | 210 | 40.52 N | 75.37 W |
| Beltzville State Park ♠ | 210 | 40.52 N | 75.36 W |
| Belucha, gora ∧ | 86 | 49.48 N | 86.40 E |
| Belugino | 82 | 54.47 N | 37.54 E |
| Belumut, Gunong ∧ | 114 | 2.02 N | 103.34 E |
| Belūr, India | 122 | 13.10 N | 75.52 E |
| Belur, India | 272b | 22.38 N | 88.18 E |
| Beluran | 112 | 5.54 N | 117.33 E |
| Belur Math ʊ[1] | 272b | 22.38 N | 88.22 E |
| Belušje | 24 | 66.54 N | 47.31 E |
| Belvedere, It. | 64 | 45.44 N | 13.23 E |
| Belvedere, Ca., U.S. | 226 | 37.52 N | 122.28 W |
| Belvedere, Va., U.S. | 284c | 38.50 N | 77.10 W |
| Belvedere ●[8] | 260 | 51.29 N | 0.09 E |
| Belvedere ʊ | 264b | 48.11 N | 16.23 E |
| Belvedere di Spinello | 68 | 39.12 N | 16.53 E |
| Belvedere Homes | 220 | 26.43 N | 80.06 W |
| Belvedere Marittimo | 68 | 39.37 N | 15.52 E |
| Belvedere Ostrense | 66 | 43.34 N | 13.09 E |
| Belvès | 32 | 44.47 N | 1.00 E |
| Belvidere, De., U.S. | 208 | 39.43 N | 75.37 W |
| Belvidere, Il., U.S. | 216 | 42.15 N | 88.50 W |
| Belvidere, N.J., U.S. | 210 | 40.49 N | 75.04 W |
| Belview | 198 | 44.36 N | 95.19 W |
| Belvis | 266a | 40.33 N | 3.33 W |
| Belvís de la Jara | 34 | 39.45 N | 4.57 W |
| Belvoir → Kokhav HaYarden ⊥ | 132 | 32.36 N | 35.31 E |
| Belvoir, Vale of V | 42 | 52.57 N | 0.53 W |
| Belyando ≐ | 166 | 21.38 S | 146.50 E |
| Belyj | 76 | 55.50 N | 32.56 E |
| Belyj, ostrov I | 74 | 73.10 N | 70.45 E |
| Belyje Berega | 76 | 53.12 N | 34.40 E |
| Belyje Kolodezi | 82 | 54.55 N | 38.42 E |
| Belyje Stolby | 82 | 55.20 N | 37.52 E |
| Belyje Vody | 85 | 42.25 N | 69.50 E |
| Belyj Gorodok | 76 | 56.58 N | 37.30 E |
| Belyj Jar, Ross. | 80 | 53.57 N | 48.58 E |
| Belyj Jar, Ross. | 86 | 53.36 N | 91.24 E |
| Belyj Jar, Ross. | 86 | 58.26 N | 85.01 E |
| Belyj Kalodez' | 78 | 50.02 N | 38.40 E |
| Belyj Luch ≐ | 80 | 57.43 N | 43.42 E |
| Belyj Rast | 82 | 56.08 N | 37.26 E |
| Belz, Fr. | 32 | 47.41 N | 3.10 W |
| Belz, Ukr. | 78 | 50.23 N | 24.01 E |
| Bełżec | 30 | 50.24 N | 23.26 E |
| Belzig | 54 | 52.08 N | 12.35 E |
| Belzoni | 194 | 33.11 N | 90.29 W |
| Bełżyce | 30 | 51.11 N | 22.18 E |
| Bem | 219 | 38.15 N | 91.28 W |
| Bemaraha, Plateau du ⋏[1] | 157b | 19.15 S | 45.00 E |
| Bemarivo, Madag. | 157b | 16.56 S | 44.21 E |
| Bemarivo, Madag. | 157b | 21.45 S | 44.45 E |
| Bemarivo ≐, Madag. | 157b | 15.27 S | 47.40 E |
| Bemarivo ≐, Madag. | 157b | 14.09 S | 50.09 E |
| Bemavo | 157b | 21.37 S | 45.24 E |
| Bembe | 152 | 7.02 S | 14.18 E |
| Bembéréké | 150 | 10.13 N | 2.40 E |
| Bembézar ≐ | 34 | 37.45 N | 5.13 W |
| Bembezi ≐ | 154 | 18.57 S | 27.47 E |
| Bembou Sambayabé | 150 | 10.55 N | 13.44 W |
| Bembridge | 42 | 50.41 N | 1.05 W |
| Bement | 194 | 39.55 N | 88.34 W |
| Bemidji | 190 | 47.28 N | 94.52 W |
| Bemis | 194 | 35.34 N | 88.49 W |
| Bemmel | 52 | 51.54 N | 5.54 E |
| Bemclanga | 157b | 17.44 S | 45.06 E |
| Bemposta | 256 | 22.09 S | 43.07 W |
| Bemus Point | 214 | 42.09 N | 79.23 W |
| Bemyž | 80 | 56.08 N | 51.44 E |
| Ben, Kinh ≍ | 269c | 10.43 N | 106.37 E |
| Bena | 150 | 11.18 N | 5.55 E |
| Benaadir □[4] | 144 | 2.07 N | 45.24 E |
| Benāb | 128 | 37.20 N | 46.04 E |
| Bena-Dibele | 152 | 4.07 S | 22.50 E |
| Benagaria | 126 | 24.11 N | 87.37 E |
| Benagerie | 166 | 31.25 S | 140.24 E |
| Benahmed | 148 | 33.07 N | 7.17 W |
| Benain ≐ | 112 | 9.39 S | 124.59 E |
| Bena-Leka | 152 | 5.08 S | 22.10 E |
| Benalla | 166 | 36.33 S | 145.59 E |
| Benamejí | 34 | 37.16 N | 4.32 W |
| Benara ∧ | 157a | 12.53 S | 45.10 E |
| Benares → Vārānasi | 124 | 25.20 N | 83.00 E |
| Bénat, Cap › | 62 | 43.05 N | 6.22 E |
| Benátky nad Jizerou | 54 | 50.17 N | 14.51 E |
| Bena-Tshadi | 152 | 4.40 S | 22.49 E |
| Benavarri | 34 | 42.07 N | 0.29 E |
| Benavente, Esp. | 34 | 42.00 N | 5.41 W |
| Benavente, Port. | 34 | 38.59 N | 8.48 W |
| Benavides | 196 | 27.35 N | 98.24 W |
| Benavidez | 258 | 34.25 S | 58.42 W |
| Ben Avon | 279b | 40.31 N | 80.05 W |
| Ben Avon Heights | 279b | 40.31 N | 80.04 W |
| Ben Badis | 34 | 34.57 N | 0.55 W |
| Benbane Head › | 48 | 55.15 N | 6.28 W |
| Benbecula I | 46 | 57.26 N | 7.21 W |
| Ben Bolt | 196 | 27.39 N | 98.05 W |
| Benbonyathe Hill ∧ | 166 | 30.24 S | 139.11 E |
| Benbrook | 222 | 32.40 N | 97.27 W |
| Benbrook Lake ⊜[1] | 222 | 32.38 N | 97.27 W |
| Ben Cat | 110 | 11.09 N | 106.36 E |
| Ben Cat, Rach ≐ | 269c | 10.50 N | 106.42 E |
| Bencha, Khao Phanom ∧ | 110 | 8.17 N | 98.56 E |
| Ben-Chicao, Col de )( | 34 | 36.12 N | 2.45 E |
| Bencubbin | 162 | 30.48 S | 117.52 E |
| Bend | 202 | 44.03 N | 121.18 W |
| Benda, Tanjung › | 115a | 6.37 S | 111.29 E |
| Bendaja | 150 | 7.10 N | 11.15 W |
| Bende | 150 | 5.36 N | 7.39 E |
| Bendela | 152 | 3.18 S | 17.36 E |
| Bendeleben, Mount ∧ | 180 | 65.10 N | 164.03 W |
| Bendemeer | 166 | 30.53 S | 151.10 E |
| Bender Beyla | 144 | 9.29 N | 50.49 E |
| Benderge ∧ | 158 | 31.06 S | 27.58 E |
| Bendersville | 208 | 39.59 N | 77.15 W |
| Bendigo | 169 | 36.46 S | 144.17 E |
| Bendimahi ≐ | 84 | 38.56 N | 43.38 E |
| Bendorf | 56 | 50.25 N | 7.34 E |
| Bendugu | 150 | 9.32 N | 10.57 W |
| Bēne | 76 | 56.29 N | 23.04 E |
| Bene Beraq | 132 | 32.05 N | 34.50 E |
| Benedict | 208 | 38.30 N | 76.40 W |
| Benediktbeuern | 64 | 47.42 N | 11.25 E |
| Benediktenwand ≗[4] | 64 | 47.39 N | 11.28 E |
| Beneditinos | 250 | 5.27 S | 42.22 W |
| Benedito Leite | 250 | 7.13 S | 44.34 W |
| Bénéna | 150 | 13.07 N | 4.22 W |
| Benenitra | 157b | 23.27 S | 45.05 E |
| Benepú, Rada ⊤[3] | 174z | 27.10 S | 109.25 W |
| Beneraird ∧[2] | 44 | 55.04 N | 4.57 W |
| Benešov | 30 | 49.47 N | 14.43 E |
| Benešov nad Ploučnicí | 54 | 50.45 N | 14.22 E |
| Bénestroff | 56 | 48.55 N | 6.45 E |
| Benetutti | 71 | 40.27 N | 9.10 E |
| Beneuvre | 58 | 47.42 N | 4.57 E |
| Bene Vagienna | 62 | 44.33 N | 7.50 E |
| Bénévent-l'Abbaye | 32 | 46.07 N | 1.38 E |
| Benevento | 68 | 41.08 N | 14.45 E |
| Benevento □[4] | 68 | 41.15 N | 14.17 E |
| Benezett | 214 | 41.19 N | 78.23 W |
| Benfeld | 58 | 48.22 N | 7.36 E |
| Benfica ●[8], Bra. | 287a | 22.53 S | 43.15 W |
| Benfica ●[8], Port. | 266c | 38.45 N | 9.12 W |
| Benfica, Estádio ♠ | 266c | 38.45 N | 9.11 W |
| Bèng ≐, Lao | 110 | 19.53 N | 101.08 E |
| Beng ≐, Zhg. | 98 | 35.05 N | 118.24 E |
| Benga | 154 | 13.19 S | 34.16 E |
| Bengābād | 126 | 24.18 N | 86.21 E |
| Bengal, Bay of c | 12 | 15.00 N | 90.00 E |
| Bengala, Golfo del → Bengal, Bay of c | 12 | 15.00 N | 90.00 E |
| Bengalen, Golf von → Bengal, Bay of c | 12 | 15.00 N | 90.00 E |
| Bengamisa | 154 | 0.57 N | 25.10 E |
| Bengara | 112 | 3.11 N | 117.12 E |
| Ben Gardane | 148 | 33.08 N | 11.13 E |
| Bengasi → Banghāzī | 146 | 32.07 N | 20.04 E |
| Bengbis | 152 | 3.27 N | 12.27 E |
| Bengbu | 100 | 32.58 N | 117.24 E |
| Benger | 168a | 33.11 S | 115.52 E |
| Benghazi → Banghāzī | 146 | 32.07 N | 20.04 E |
| Ben Giang | 110 | 15.41 N | 107.47 E |
| Bengkalis | 114 | 1.28 N | 102.07 E |
| Bengkalis, Pulau I | 114 | 1.30 N | 102.15 E |
| Bengkalis, Selat ɥ | 114 | 1.30 N | 102.00 E |
| Bengkayang | 112 | 0.50 N | 109.29 E |
| Bengkoka ≐ | 116 | 6.50 N | 117.03 E |
| Bengkulu | 112 | 3.48 S | 102.16 E |
| Bengkulu □[4] | 112 | 4.00 S | 102.30 E |
| Bengo □[5] | 152 | 8.30 S | 13.20 E |
| Bengo ≐ | 152 | 8.45 S | 13.24 E |
| Bengo, Baía do c | 152 | 8.43 S | 13.21 E |
| Bengoi | 164 | 3.01 S | 130.12 E |
| Bengough | 184 | 49.24 N | 105.08 W |
| Bengtsfors | 26 | 59.02 N | 12.13 E |
| Benguela | 152 | 12.35 S | 13.25 E |
| Benguela □[5] | 152 | 12.45 S | 14.30 E |
| Benguerir | 148 | 32.14 N | 7.57 W |
| Benguet □[4] | 116 | 16.30 N | 120.40 E |
| Bengut, Cap › | 34 | 36.55 N | 3.54 E |
| Benha → Banhā | 142 | 30.28 N | 31.11 E |
| Benham | 192 | 36.57 N | 82.56 W |
| Ben Hur | 222 | 31.30 N | 96.44 W |
| Beni, Nig. | 146 | 10.27 N | 10.24 E |
| Beni, Zaïre | 154 | 0.30 N | 29.28 E |
| Beni □[5] | 248 | 14.00 S | 65.30 W |
| Beni ≐ | 248 | 10.58 S | 66.09 W |
| Béni Abbas | 148 | 30.08 N | 2.10 W |
| Benicarló | 34 | 40.25 N | 0.26 E |
| Benicia | 226 | 38.02 N | 122.09 W |
| Benicia Capitol State Historic Park ♠ | 282 | 38.03 N | 122.09 W |
| Benicia State Recreation Area ♠ | 282 | 38.05 N | 122.13 W |
| Benicito ≐ | 248 | 11.32 S | 65.47 W |
| Benidorm | 34 | 38.32 N | 0.06 W |
| Beni-Mellal | 148 | 32.22 N | 6.29 W |
| Beni-Mellal □[4] | 148 | 32.22 N | 6.27 W |
| Benin (Bénin) □[1], Afr. | 134 | 9.30 N | 2.15 E |
| Benin (Bénin) □[1], Afr. | 150 | 9.30 N | 2.15 E |
| Benin ≐ | 150 | 5.45 N | 5.04 E |
| Benin, Bight of c[3] | 150 | 5.30 N | 3.00 E |
| Benin City | 150 | 6.19 N | 5.41 E |
| Beni Saf | 148 | 35.19 N | 1.23 W |
| Benisheikh | 146 | 11.49 N | 12.29 E |
| Benissa | 34 | 38.34 N | 0.03 E |
| Beni Suef → Banī Suwayf | 142 | 29.05 N | 31.05 E |
| Benito | 184 | 51.55 N | 101.31 W |
| Benito Juárez, Arg. | 252 | 37.40 S | 59.48 W |
| Benito Juárez, Méx. | 234 | 19.14 N | 100.28 W |
| Benito Juárez, Méx. | 234 | 17.50 N | 92.32 W |
| Benito Juárez, Aeropuerto Internacional ⊠ | 286a | 19.26 N | 99.04 W |
| Benito Juárez, Presa ⊜[1] | 234 | 16.27 N | 95.30 W |
| Benit Point › | 116 | 9.54 N | 125.17 E |
| Benjakoni | 76 | 54.15 N | 25.22 E |
| Benjamim Constant | 256 | 21.57 S | 42.53 W |
| Benjamin | 196 | 33.35 N | 99.48 W |
| Benjamín, Isla I | 254 | 44.40 S | 74.08 W |
| Benjamín Aceval | 252 | 24.58 S | 57.34 W |
| Benjamin Constant | 246 | 4.22 S | 70.02 W |
| Benjamin Franklin Bridge ●[5] | 285 | 39.57 N | 75.08 W |
| Benjamín Hill | 232 | 30.10 N | 111.10 W |
| Benjamín Zorrilla | 252 | 39.06 S | 65.29 W |
| Benkelman | 198 | 40.02 N | 101.31 W |
| Benken | 54 | 52.10 N | 12.28 E |
| Benkovac | 36 | 44.02 N | 15.37 E |
| Benld | 219 | 39.05 N | 89.48 W |
| Benllech | 44 | 53.19 N | 4.13 W |
| Ben Lomond | 226 | 37.05 N | 122.05 W |
| Ben Lomond National Park ♠ | 166 | 41.34 S | 147.11 E |
| Ben Mehidi | 36 | 36.46 N | 7.54 E |
| Benmore, Lake ⊜[1] | 172 | 44.25 S | 170.15 E |
| Benndale | 194 | 30.52 N | 88.48 W |
| Benndorf | 54 | 51.34 N | 11.29 E |
| Benneckenstein | 54 | 51.40 N | 10.45 E |
| Bennekom | 52 | 52.00 N | 5.40 E |
| Bennet | 198 | 40.40 N | 96.30 W |
| Bennett, Lake ⊜ | 162 | 22.55 S | 130.57 E |
| Bennetta, ostrov I | 74 | 76.21 N | 148.56 E |
| Bennett Lake ⊜, Can. | 180 | 60.05 N | 134.50 W |
| Bennett Lake ⊜, Mb., Can. | 184 | 53.28 N | 96.05 W |
| Bennett Lake ⊜, On., Can. | 212 | 44.55 N | 76.27 W |
| Bennett Pass )( | 224 | 45.18 N | 121.39 W |
| Bennettsbridge | 48 | 52.36 N | 7.12 W |
| Bennetts Creek ≐ | 210 | 42.16 N | 77.35 W |
| Bennettsville | 192 | 34.37 N | 79.41 W |
| Bennettswood | 274b | 37.51 S | 145.07 E |
| Bennigsen | 52 | 52.14 N | 9.40 E |
| Benninghofen ●[8] | 263 | 51.29 N | 7.31 E |
| Bennington, In., U.S. | 218 | 38.52 N | 85.08 W |
| Bennington, Ks., U.S. | 198 | 39.01 N | 97.35 W |
| Bennington, Vt., U.S. | 210 | 42.52 N | 73.11 W |
| Bennington □[6] | 207 | 42.50 N | 73.08 W |
| Bennington Battle Monument ⊥ | 210 | 42.53 N | 73.13 W |
| Benniu | 106 | 31.52 N | 119.48 E |
| Bennstedt | 54 | 51.29 N | 11.50 E |
| Beno | 152 | 3.37 S | 17.48 E |
| Benoa | 115b | 8.46 S | 115.13 E |
| Ben Ohau Range ⋏ | 172 | 44.00 S | 170.00 E |
| Benoit | 194 | 33.39 N | 91.00 W |
| Benom, Gunong ∧ | 114 | 3.49 N | 102.04 E |
| Benoni, S. Afr. | 156 | 26.11 S | 28.19 E |
| Benoni, S. Afr. | 158 | 26.11 S | 28.19 E |
| Benoni □[5] | 273d | 26.08 S | 28.22 E |
| Benoni-Suid | 273d | 26.13 S | 28.18 E |
| Bénoué (Benue) ≐ | 134 | 7.48 N | 6.46 E |
| Bénoué, Parc National de la ♠ | 146 | 8.20 N | 13.50 E |
| Benover | 260 | 51.13 N | 0.26 E |
| Bénoy | 146 | 8.59 N | 16.19 E |
| Benque Viejo del Carmen | 232 | 17.05 N | 89.08 W |
| Benrad ●[8] | 263 | 51.20 N | 6.30 E |
| Benrath ●[8] | 56 | 51.10 N | 6.51 E |
| Benrath, Schloss ⊥ | 263 | 51.10 N | 6.52 E |
| Bensalem | 285 | 40.04 N | 74.56 W |
| Bensbach ≐ | 164 | 9.08 S | 141.00 E |
| Bensberg | 56 | 50.58 N | 7.09 E |
| Bensdorf | 54 | 52.24 N | 12.20 E |
| Ben Sekka, Rass › | 36 | 37.21 N | 9.45 E |
| Bensenville | 278 | 41.57 N | 87.56 W |
| Bensersiel | 52 | 53.40 N | 7.34 E |
| Benshausen | 54 | 50.38 N | 10.35 E |
| Bensheim | 56 | 49.41 N | 8.37 E |
| Bensley | 208 | 37.26 N | 77.26 W |
| Ben-Slimane | 148 | 33.41 N | 7.10 W |
| Ben-Slimane □[4] | 148 | 33.40 N | 7.10 W |
| Ben Smih | 36 | 36.23 N | 7.31 E |
| Benson, Eng., U.K. | 42 | 51.38 N | 1.05 W |
| Benson, Az., U.S. | 200 | 31.58 N | 110.17 W |
| Benson, Md., U.S. | 208 | 39.30 N | 76.23 W |
| Benson, Mn., U.S. | 198 | 45.18 N | 95.35 W |
| Benson, N.C., U.S. | 192 | 35.22 N | 78.32 W |
| Bensonhurst ●[8] | 276 | 40.35 N | 73.59 W |
| Benson Point › | 174o | 1.56 N | 157.29 W |
| Bens Run ≐ | 284b | 39.19 N | 76.48 W |
| Bent | 128 | 26.17 N | 59.31 E |
| Benta | 114 | 4.01 N | 101.58 E |
| Benteng (Salayar) | 112 | 6.08 S | 120.27 E |
| Bentheim, Dtsch. | 52 | 52.17 N | 7.10 E |
| Bentheim, Mi., U.S. | 216 | 42.42 N | 85.55 W |
| Ben Thuy | 110 | 18.39 N | 105.42 E |
| Bentiaba | 152 | 14.15 S | 12.21 E |
| Bentiaba ≐ | 152 | 14.29 S | 12.50 E |
| Bentinck Island I, Austl. | 164 | 17.04 S | 139.30 E |
| Bentinck Island I, Mya. | 110 | 11.45 N | 98.03 E |
| Bentiu | 140 | 9.14 N | 29.50 E |
| Bentleigh | 274b | 37.55 S | 145.02 E |
| Bentley, Ab., Can. | 182 | 52.28 N | 114.04 W |
| Bentley, Eng., U.K. | 44 | 53.33 N | 1.09 W |
| Bentley College ʊ[2] | 283 | 42.23 N | 71.13 W |
| Bentleyville, Oh., U.S. | 279a | 41.25 N | 81.26 W |
| Bentleyville, Pa., U.S. | 214 | 40.07 N | 80.00 W |
| Bento Gomes ≐ | 248 | 16.40 S | 57.12 W |
| Bento Gonçalves | 252 | 29.10 S | 51.31 W |
| Bentol | 150 | 6.26 N | 10.36 W |
| Benton, Ar., U.S. | 194 | 34.33 N | 92.35 W |
| Benton, Il., U.S. | 194 | 37.59 N | 88.55 W |
| Benton, In., U.S. | 216 | 41.30 N | 85.45 W |
| Benton, Ky., U.S. | 194 | 36.51 N | 88.21 W |
| Benton, La., U.S. | 194 | 32.41 N | 93.44 W |
| Benton, Ms., U.S. | 194 | 32.49 N | 90.15 W |
| Benton, Mo., U.S. | 194 | 37.05 N | 89.33 W |
| Benton, Oh., U.S. | 214 | 40.36 N | 81.51 W |
| Benton, Pa., U.S. | 210 | 41.11 N | 76.23 W |
| Benton, Tn., U.S. | 192 | 35.10 N | 84.39 W |
| Benton, Wi., U.S. | 190 | 42.34 N | 90.22 W |
| Benton □[6] | 216 | 40.37 N | 87.19 W |
| Benton City, Mo., U.S. | 219 | 39.08 N | 91.45 W |
| Benton City, Wa., U.S. | 202 | 46.15 N | 119.29 W |
| Bentong | 114 | 3.32 N | 101.55 E |
| Benton Harbor | 216 | 42.07 N | 86.26 W |
| Benton Heights | 216 | 42.07 N | 86.24 W |
| Bentonia | 194 | 32.38 N | 90.21 W |
| Benton Lake ⊜ | 202 | 47.40 N | 111.20 W |
| Benton Ridge | 216 | 41.00 N | 83.47 W |
| Bentonville, Ar., U.S. | 194 | 36.22 N | 94.12 W |
| Bentonville, In., U.S. | 218 | 39.45 N | 85.15 W |
| Bentonville, Oh., U.S. | 218 | 38.45 N | 83.37 W |
| Ben Tre | 110 | 10.14 N | 106.23 E |
| Bent's Old Fort National Historic Site ⊥ | 198 | 38.05 N | 103.28 W |
| Benua, Pulau I | 112 | 0.56 N | 107.27 E |
| Benue (Bénoué) ≐ | 134 | 7.48 N | 6.46 E |
| Benut | 114 | 1.38 N | 103.16 E |
| Benwee ∧ | 48 | 53.35 N | 9.31 W |
| Benwee Head › | 48 | 54.20 N | 9.50 W |
| Ben Wheeler | 222 | 32.27 N | 95.42 W |
| Benxi (Penhsi), Zhg. | 104 | 41.18 N | 123.45 E |
| Benxi (Xiaoshi), Zhg. | 104 | 41.17 N | 124.07 E |
| Benza | 152 | 6.16 S | 12.57 E |
| Beograd (Belgrade) | 38 | 44.50 N | 20.30 E |
| Beohāri | 124 | 24.03 N | 81.23 E |
| Beonta | 272b | 22.31 N | 88.31 E |
| Béoumi | 150 | 7.40 N | 5.34 W |
| Beowawe | 204 | 40.35 N | 116.28 W |
| Beppu | 96 | 33.17 N | 131.30 E |
| Beppu-wan c | 96 | 33.18 N | 131.35 E |
| Bequia I | 241h | 13.01 N | 61.13 W |
| Bequimão | 250 | 2.26 S | 44.47 W |
| Bera | 126 | 24.05 N | 89.37 E |
| Berābāria | 272b | 22.52 N | 88.34 E |
| Beraberi, India | 272b | 22.46 N | 88.27 E |
| Berāberi, India | 272b | 22.51 N | 88.12 E |
| Beraketa, Madag. | 157b | 24.11 S | 45.42 E |
| Beraketa, Madag. | 157b | 23.07 S | 44.25 E |
| Beramanja | 157b | 13.13 S | 48.56 E |
| Bérandjoko | 152 | 3.06 N | 17.17 E |
| Berāsi | 124 | 23.36 N | 81.51 E |
| Berasia | 124 | 23.38 N | 77.26 E |
| Berat | 38 | 40.42 N | 19.57 E |
| Beratzhausen | 60 | 49.06 N | 11.48 E |
| Berau | 58 | 47.42 N | 8.15 E |
| Berau ≐ | 112 | 2.10 N | 117.42 E |
| Berau, Teluk c | 164 | 2.30 S | 132.30 E |
| Beravina | 157b | 18.10 S | 45.14 E |
| Berazategui | 258 | 34.46 S | 58.13 W |
| Berazategui □[5] | 288 | 34.50 S | 58.10 W |
| Berazino, Bela. | 76 | 53.49 N | 28.59 E |
| Berazino, Bela. | 76 | 54.54 N | 28.12 E |
| Berbenno di Valtellina | 64 | 46.10 N | 9.44 E |
| Berbera | 144 | 10.25 N | 45.02 E |
| Berbérati | 152 | 4.16 N | 15.47 E |
| Berbice ≐ | 246 | 6.17 N | 57.32 W |
| Berceto | 64 | 44.31 N | 9.59 E |
| Berchem, Bel. | 50 | 51.12 N | 4.26 E |
| Berchem, Bel. | 50 | 50.47 N | 3.30 E |
| Berchem-Sainte-Agathe | 56 | 50.52 N | 4.17 E |
| Berchidda | 71 | 40.47 N | 9.10 E |
| Berching | 60 | 49.07 N | 11.27 E |
| Berchtesgaden | 64 | 47.38 N | 13.01 E |
| Berchtesgaden, Nationalpark ♠ | 64 | 47.30 N | 13.00 E |
| Berchum ●[8] | 263 | 51.23 N | 7.32 E |
| Berck | 50 | 50.24 N | 1.34 E |
| Berclair | 196 | 28.32 N | 97.36 W |
| Berčogur | 86 | 48.25 N | 58.44 E |
| Bercu | 50 | 50.31 N | 3.17 E |
| Berd | 84 | 40.53 N | 45.23 E |
| Berda ≐ | 78 | 46.48 N | 36.52 E |
| Berdaale | 144 | 7.04 N | 47.51 E |
| Berdale | 144 | 4.56 N | 45.02 E |
| Berd'auš | 86 | 55.09 N | 59.09 E |
| Berdigest'ach | 74 | 62.06 N | 126.40 E |
| Berdniki | 80 | 57.25 N | 46.33 E |
| Berdorf | 56 | 49.50 N | 6.21 E |
| Berdsk | 86 | 54.47 N | 83.02 E |
| Berd'užje | 86 | 55.48 N | 68.19 E |
| Berdyans'k | 78 | 46.45 N | 36.49 E |
| Berdyans'ka kosa ›[2] | 78 | 46.42 N | 36.48 E |
| Berdyans'ka zatoka c | 78 | 46.42 N | 36.35 E |
| Berdychiv | 78 | 49.54 N | 28.36 E |
| Béré, Tchad | 146 | 9.20 N | 16.09 E |
| Bere, Turk. | 128 | 39.47 N | 58.06 E |
| Berea, Ky., U.S. | 192 | 37.34 N | 84.17 W |
| Berea, Oh., U.S. | 214 | 41.21 N | 81.51 W |
| Berea, S.C., U.S. | 192 | 34.53 N | 82.27 W |
| Bere Alston | 42 | 50.29 N | 4.11 W |
| Berebei | 164 | 9.31 S | 147.27 E |
| Beregajevo | 86 | 57.10 N | 87.32 E |
| Beregovoj | 86 | 55.12 N | 78.51 E |
| Bereguardo | 62 | 45.15 N | 9.01 E |
| Berehomet | 78 | 48.12 N | 25.21 E |
| Berehove | 78 | 48.13 N | 22.39 E |
| Bereina | 164 | 8.40 S | 146.30 E |
| Bereka ≐ | 78 | [illegible] | 36.59 E |
| Bereketli | 130 | 40.31 N | 37.18 E |
| Bereku | 154 | 4.27 S | 35.44 E |
| Berekua | 240d | 15.14 N | 61.19 W |
| Berekum | 150 | 7.27 N | 2.37 W |
| Bérem | 152 | 7.33 N | 13.55 E |
| Beren, liman ⊜ | 80 | 46.52 N | 44.55 E |
| Berenda Slough ≐ | 226 | 37.00 N | 120.29 W |
| Berendejevo | 82 | 56.36 N | 39.01 E |
| Berens ≐ | 184 | 52.21 N | 97.02 W |
| Berens Island I | 184 | 52.18 N | 97.17 W |
| Berens River | 184 | 52.22 N | 97.02 W |
| Bere Regis | 42 | 50.46 N | 2.14 W |
| Beresford, N.B., Can. | 186 | 47.42 N | 65.42 W |
| Beresford, S.D., U.S. | 198 | 43.04 N | 96.46 W |
| Berestechko | 78 | 50.23 N | 25.07 E |
| Berești | 38 | 46.06 N | 27.53 E |
| Berettyó (Barcău) ≐ | 38 | 46.59 N | 21.07 E |
| Berettyóújfalu | 30 | 47.14 N | 21.32 E |
| Berevo, Madag. | 157b | 17.14 S | 44.17 E |
| Berevo, Madag. | 157b | 19.44 S | 44.58 E |
| Berezajka | 76 | 57.59 N | 33.54 E |
| Berezan' | 78 | 50.19 N | 31.30 E |
| Berezanskaja | 78 | 45.43 N | 39.34 E |
| Berezans'kyy lyman c[1] | 78 | 46.43 N | 31.30 E |
| Berezdiv | 78 | 50.27 N | 27.05 E |
| Bereze | 78 | 51.44 N | 33.52 E |
| Berezhany, Ukr. | 78 | 51.27 N | 26.27 E |
| Berezhany, Ukr. | 78 | 49.27 N | 24.56 E |
| Berezino | 80 | 50.06 N | 48.52 E |
| Berezivka, Ukr. | 78 | 47.12 N | 30.55 E |
| Berezivka, Ukr. | 78 | 47.49 N | 32.28 E |
| Berezivka, Ukr. | 78 | 45.35 N | 33.20 E |
| Berezna | 78 | 51.34 N | 31.47 E |
| Berezn'agi | 78 | 49.59 N | 41.06 E |
| Berezne | 78 | 51.00 N | 26.45 E |
| Bereznehuvate | 78 | 47.20 N | 32.49 E |
| Bereznik | 24 | 62.51 N | 42.40 E |
| Berezniki | 86 | 59.24 N | 56.46 E |
| Bereznyaky, Ukr. | 78 | 49.09 N | 31.57 E |
| Bereznyaky, Ukr. | 78 | 49.51 N | 33.01 E |
| Berezova Rudka | 78 | 50.19 N | 32.14 E |
| Berezove | 78 | 51.35 N | 27.20 E |
| Berezyne | 78 | 46.14 N | 29.12 E |
| Berford Lake ⊜ | 212 | 44.48 N | 81.11 W |
| Berg, Dtsch. | 60 | 49.20 N | 11.26 E |
| Berg, Dtsch. | 64 | 47.58 N | 11.21 E |
| Berg, Lux. | 56 | 49.49 N | 6.05 E |
| Berg, Nor. | 24 | 69.26 N | 17.15 E |
| Berg, Öst. | 64 | 46.45 N | 13.09 E |
| Berga, Dtsch. | 54 | 50.45 N | 12.10 E |
| Berga, Dtsch. | 54 | 51.27 N | 11.00 E |
| Berga, Esp. | 34 | 42.06 N | 1.51 E |
| Berga, Sve. | 40 | 59.21 N | 16.26 E |
| Bergama | 130 | 39.07 N | 27.11 E |
| Bergambacht | 52 | 51.56 N | 4.46 E |
| Bergamo | 62 | 45.41 N | 9.43 E |
| Bergamo □[4] | 64 | 45.50 N | 9.48 E |
| Bergan Point › | 276 | 40.40 N | 73.20 W |
| Bergantín | 246 | 10.01 N | 64.22 W |
| Bergantino | 64 | 45.05 N | 11.15 E |
| Bergara | 34 | 43.07 N | 2.25 W |
| Bergbau Museum ʊ | 263 | 51.29 N | 7.13 E |
| Bergby | 26 | 60.56 N | 17.02 E |
| Berge, Dtsch. | 52 | 52.37 N | 7.44 E |
| Berge, Dtsch. | 54 | 53.15 N | 11.50 E |
| Berge, Dtsch. | 263 | 51.21 N | 7.22 E |
| Bergedorf ●[8] | 52 | 53.29 N | 10.13 E |
| Bergei ∧[2] | 263 | 51.13 N | 7.46 E |
| Bergeijk | 52 | 51.19 N | 5.22 E |
| Bergen → Mons, Bel. | 50 | 50.27 N | 3.56 E |
| Bergen, Dtsch. | 52 | 52.48 N | 9.58 E |
| Bergen, Dtsch. | 54 | 52.53 N | 10.58 E |
| Bergen, Dtsch. | 64 | 47.48 N | 12.35 E |
| Bergen, Ned. | 52 | 52.40 N | 4.41 E |
| Bergen, Nor. | 26 | 60.23 N | 5.20 E |
| Bergen, N.Y., U.S. | 210 | 43.05 N | 77.56 W |
| Bergen □[6] | 210 | 40.53 N | 74.03 W |
| Bergen aan Zee | 52 | 52.38 N | 4.37 E |
| Bergen [auf Rügen] | 54 | 54.25 N | 13.26 E |
| Bergen Basin c | 276 | 40.39 N | 73.49 W |
| Bergen-Belsen-Denkmal ⊥ | 52 | 52.46 N | 9.55 E |
| Berg en Dal | 250 | 5.09 N | 55.04 W |
| Bergenfield | 210 | 40.55 N | 73.59 W |
| Bergen Mall ●[9] | 276 | 40.55 N | 74.04 W |
| Bergen op Zoom | 52 | 51.30 N | 4.17 E |
| Berger | 219 | 38.40 N | 91.20 W |
| Bergerac | 32 | 44.51 N | 0.29 E |
| Bergères-lès-Vertus | 50 | 48.53 N | 4.00 E |
| Bergerhof | 263 | 51.12 N | 7.21 E |
| Bergfelde | 54 | 52.40 N | 13.19 E |
| Berggiesshübel | 54 | 50.52 N | 13.57 E |
| Berghausen, Dtsch. | 263 | 51.18 N | 7.17 E |
| Berghausen, Dtsch. | 263 | 51.07 N | 6.55 E |
| Bergheim, Dtsch. | 56 | 50.55 N | 6.38 E |
| Bergheim, Fr. | 58 | 48.12 N | 7.22 E |
| Bergheim, Öst. | 64 | 47.50 N | 13.02 E |
| Berghem | 52 | 51.46 N | 5.34 E |
| Berghofen ●[8] | 263 | 51.29 N | 7.32 E |
| Bergholtz | 210 | 43.06 N | 78.53 W |
| Bergholtz Creek ≐ | 284a | 43.05 N | 78.57 W |
| Bergholz | 214 | 40.31 N | 80.53 W |
| Bergholz-Rehbrücke | 54 | 52.20 N | 13.05 E |
| Bergisches Land ●[1] | 56 | 51.00 N | 7.30 E |
| Bergisch Gladbach | 56 | 50.59 N | 7.07 E |
| Bergkamen | 52 | 51.38 N | 7.38 E |
| Bergkvara | 26 | 56.23 N | 16.05 E |
| Bergland | 190 | 46.35 N | 89.34 W |
| Bergneustadt | 56 | 51.01 N | 7.39 E |
| Bergnicourt | 50 | 49.25 N | 4.15 E |
| Bergö I | 26 | 62.58 N | 21.11 E |
| Bergoo | 188 | 38.29 N | 80.18 W |
| Bergplaas | 158 | 33.54 S | 22.40 E |
| Bergrheinfeld | 56 | 50.00 N | 10.10 E |
| Bergsäng | 40 | 60.06 N | 13.33 E |
| Bergsbrunna | 40 | 59.49 N | 17.43 E |
| Bergsche Maas ≐ | 52 | 51.45 N | 5.08 E |
| Bergshamra | 40 | 59.38 N | 18.37 E |
| Bergsjö | 26 | 61.59 N | 17.04 E |
| Bergslagen ●[1] | 40 | 59.55 N | 15.00 E |
| Bergstrom Air Force Base ■ | 222 | 30.12 N | 97.40 W |
| Bergtheim | 56 | 49.54 N | 10.04 E |
| Berguent | 148 | 34.03 N | 2.02 W |
| Bergues | 50 | 50.58 N | 2.26 E |
| Bergum | 52 | 53.11 N | 5.59 E |
| Bergün | 58 | 46.38 N | 9.45 E |
| Bergville | 158 | 28.52 S | 29.18 E |
| Bergvreten | 40 | 60.31 N | 16.26 E |
| Bergwitz | 54 | 51.48 N | 12.35 E |
| Berhala, Selat ɥ | 112 | 0.48 S | 104.25 E |
| Beri | 124 | 28.42 N | 76.35 E |
| Berici, Monti ⋏ | 64 | 45.26 N | 11.31 E |
| Berikul'skij | 86 | 55.32 N | 88.08 E |
| Beringa, ostrov I | 74 | 55.00 N | 165.15 E |
| Beringen | 56 | 51.03 N | 5.13 E |
| Bering Glacier ⊓ | 180 | 60.15 N | 143.30 W |
| Beringhausen | 56 | 51.24 N | 8.46 E |
| Beringil | 140 | 12.10 N | 25.41 E |
| Beringin | 112 | 3.41 S | 104.18 E |
| Beringovskij | 180 | 63.03 N | 179.19 E |
| Bering Sea ⊤[2] | 16 | 60.00 N | 175.00 W |
| Bering Strait ɥ | 180 | 65.30 N | 169.00 W |
| Berinsfield | 42 | 51.40 N | 1.11 W |
| Berisso | 258 | 34.52 S | 57.53 W |
| Berisso □[5] | 288 | 34.55 S | 57.53 W |
| Berja | 34 | 36.51 N | 2.57 W |
| Berkåk | 26 | 62.50 N | 10.00 E |
| Berkakit | 74 | 56.34 N | 124.48 E |
| Berkane | 148 | 34.59 N | 2.20 W |
| Berkel ≐ | 52 | 52.09 N | 6.12 E |
| Berkeley, Eng., U.K. | 42 | 51.42 N | 2.27 W |
| Berkeley, Ca., U.S. | 226 | 37.52 N | 122.16 W |
| Berkeley, Mo., U.S. | 219 | 38.45 N | 90.20 W |
| Berkeley, R.I., U.S. | 207 | 41.55 N | 71.25 W |
| Berkeley, Vale of V | 42 | 51.45 N | 2.25 W |
| Berkeley Heights | 210 | 40.41 N | 74.26 W |
| Berkeley Hills | 279b | 40.32 N | 80.00 W |


DEUTSCH


| Name | Seite | Breite°′ | Länge°′ E = Ost |
| --- | --- | --- | --- |
| Berkeley Hills ⋏[2] | 282 | 37.54 N | 122.16 W |
| Berkeley Plantation ⊥ | 208 | 37.19 N | 77.10 W |
| Berkeley Springs | 188 | 39.37 N | 78.13 W |
| Berkhamsted | 42 | 51.46 N | 0.35 W |
| Berkheim | 58 | 48.02 N | 10.04 E |
| Berkley, Ma., U.S. | 207 | 41.50 N | 71.05 W |
| Berkley, Mi., U.S. | 281 | 42.30 N | 83.11 W |
| Berkner Island I | 9 | 79.30 S | 49.30 W |
| Berks □[6] | 208 | 40.20 N | 75.50 W |
| Berkshire, Ma., U.S. | 207 | 42.30 N | 73.11 W |
| Berkshire, N.Y., U.S. | 210 | 42.18 N | 76.11 W |
| Berkshire □[6], Eng., U.K. | 42 | 51.30 N | 1.20 W |
| Berkshire □[6], Ma., U.S. | 207 | 42.27 N | 73.15 W |
| Berkshire Downs ⋏[1] | 42 | 51.33 N | 1.24 W |
| Berkshire Hills ⋏[2] | 207 | 42.20 N | 73.10 W |
| Berlaar | 56 | 51.07 N | 4.39 E |
| Berlaimont | 50 | 50.12 N | 3.49 E |
| Berland ≐ | 182 | 54.01 N | 116.50 W |
| Berlanga de Duero | 34 | 41.28 N | 2.51 W |
| Berlenga I | 34 | 39.25 N | 9.30 W |
| Berlengas ≐ | 250 | 5.39 S | 42.19 W |
| Berlevåg | 24 | 70.51 N | 29.06 E |
| Berlicum | 52 | 51.42 N | 5.23 E |
| Berlikum | 52 | 53.15 N | 5.39 E |
| Berlin, Dtsch. | 54 | 52.31 N | 13.24 E |
| Berlin, Dtsch. | 264a | 52.31 N | 13.24 E |
| Berlin, S. Afr. | 158 | 32.54 S | 27.35 E |
| Berlin, Ct., U.S. | 207 | 41.37 N | 72.44 W |
| Berlin, Md., U.S. | 208 | 38.19 N | 75.13 W |
| Berlin, Ma., U.S. | 207 | 42.22 N | 71.38 W |
| Berlin, N.H., U.S. | 188 | 44.28 N | 71.11 W |
| Berlin, N.J., U.S. | 208 | 39.47 N | 74.55 W |
| Berlin, N.Y., U.S. | 210 | 42.42 N | 73.23 W |
| Berlin, Oh., U.S. | 214 | 40.34 N | 81.48 W |
| Berlin, Pa., U.S. | 188 | 39.55 N | 78.57 W |
| Berlin, Wi., U.S. | 190 | 43.58 N | 88.56 W |
| Berlin □[3] | 54 | 52.33 N | 13.30 E |
| Berlin, Mount ∧ | 9 | 76.03 S | 135.52 W |
| Berlin Center | 214 | 41.01 N | 80.57 W |
| Berlinchen | 54 | 53.13 N | 12.34 E |
| Berliner Brücke ●[5] | 263 | 51.27 N | 6.47 E |
| Berlinguet Inlet c | 176 | 71.10 N | 85.35 W |
| Berlin Heights | 214 | 41.20 N | 82.30 W |
| Berlin-Ichthyosaur State Park ♠ | 204 | 38.51 N | 117.35 W |
| Berlin Lake ⊜[1] | 214 | 41.00 N | 81.00 W |
| Berlin Mountain ∧ | 210 | 42.42 N | 73.17 W |
| Berlin Park ♠ | 285 | 39.47 N | 74.57 W |
| Berlin-Schönefeld, Flughafen ⊠ | 54 | 52.23 N | 13.31 E |
| Berlinsville | 210 | 40.47 N | 75.35 W |
| Berlin-Tegel, Flughafen ⊠ | 54 | 52.34 N | 13.18 E |
| Berlin-Tempelhof, Flughafen ⊠ | 54 | 52.29 N | 13.25 E |
| Berlstedt | 54 | 51.04 N | 11.15 E |
| Bermagui | 166 | 36.25 S | 150.04 E |
| Bermamyt, gora ∧ | 84 | 43.41 N | 42.27 E |
| Bermejillo | 232 | 25.53 N | 103.37 W |
| Bermejito ≐ | 252 | 25.39 S | 60.11 W |
| Bermejo | 252 | 31.37 S | 67.39 W |
| Bermejo ≐, Arg. | 252 | 31.52 S | 67.22 W |
| Bermejo ≐, S.A. | 252 | 26.51 S | 58.23 W |
| Bermejo, Paso del )( | 252 | 32.50 S | 70.05 W |
| Bermen, Lac ⊜ | 176 | 53.35 N | 68.55 W |
| Bermeo | 34 | 43.26 N | 2.43 W |
| Bermillo de Sayago | 34 | 41.22 N | 6.06 W |
| Bermo | 124 | 23.47 N | 85.57 E |
| Bermondsey ●[8] | 260 | 51.30 N | 0.04 W |
| Bermuda □[2], N.A. | 230 | 32.20 N | 64.45 W |
| Bermuda □[2], N.A. | 240a | 32.20 N | 64.45 W |
| Bermuda Rise ✣[3] | 16 | 32.30 N | 65.00 W |
| Bermudes → Bermuda □[2] | 240a | 32.20 N | 64.45 W |
| Bermudian Creek ≐ | 208 | 40.01 N | 76.55 W |
| Bern (Berne) | 58 | 46.57 N | 7.26 E |
| Bern (Berne) □[3] | 58 | 46.55 N | 7.35 E |
| Bern, Flughafen ⊠ | 58 | 46.55 N | 7.30 E |
| Berna → Bern | 58 | 46.57 N | 7.26 E |
| Bernabéu, Estadio ♠ | 266a | 40.27 N | 3.41 W |
| Bernal ●[8] | 258 | 34.42 S | 58.17 W |
| Bernalda | 68 | 40.24 N | 16.41 E |
| Bernalillo | 200 | 35.18 N | 106.33 W |
| Bernam ≐ | 114 | 3.48 N | 100.57 E |
| Bernardo O'Higgins, Parque ♠ | 286e | 33.28 S | 70.40 W |
| Bernardston | 207 | 42.40 N | 72.33 W |
| Bernardsville | 210 | 40.43 N | 74.34 W |
| Bernasconi | 252 | 37.54 S | 63.43 W |
| Bernate | 266b | 45.29 N | 8.49 E |
| Bernau am Chiemsee | 64 | 47.48 N | 12.22 E |
| Bernau bei Berlin | 54 | 52.40 N | 13.35 E |
| Bernauer Heide ●[3] | 264a | 52.43 N | 13.30 E |
| Bernaville | 50 | 50.08 N | 2.10 E |
| Bernay | 50 | 49.06 N | 0.36 E |
| Bernbeuren | 58 | 47.44 N | 10.46 E |
| Bernburg | 54 | 51.48 N | 11.44 E |
| Berndorf | 61 | 47.57 N | 16.08 E |
| Berne, Dtsch. | 52 | 53.11 N | 8.29 E |
| Berne → Bern, Schw. | 58 | 46.57 N | 7.26 E |
| Berne, In., U.S. | 216 | 40.39 N | 84.57 W |
| Berne, N.Y., U.S. | 210 | 42.38 N | 74.08 W |
| Berneburg | 56 | 51.04 N | 9.53 E |
| Berner Alpen ⋏ | 58 | 46.30 N | 7.30 E |
| Berneray I, Scot., U.K. | 46 | 56.47 N | 7.38 W |
| Berneray I, Scot., U.K. | 46 | 57.43 N | 7.12 W |
| Berneval-le-Grand | 50 | 49.57 N | 1.12 E |
| Berngardovka | 265a | 60.01 N | 30.36 E |
| Bernhardina | 158 | 27.53 S | 28.40 E |
| Bernhards Bay | 210 | 43.15 N | 75.56 W |
| Bernhardsthal | 61 | 48.41 N | 16.52 E |
| Bernhardswald | 60 | 49.06 N | 12.15 E |
| Bernice | 194 | 32.49 N | 92.39 W |
| Bernie | 194 | 36.40 N | 89.58 W |
| Bernier Bay c | 176 | 71.00 N | 87.30 W |
| Bernier Island I | 162 | 24.52 S | 113.08 E |
| Bernina ⋏ | 58 | 46.22 N | 9.50 E |
| Bernina, Passo del )( | 58 | 46.24 N | 10.03 E |
| Bernina, Piz ∧ | 58 | 46.21 N | 9.51 E |
| Bernisdale | 46 | 57.27 N | 6.24 W |
| Bernkastel-Kues | 56 | 49.55 N | 7.04 E |
| Bernried | 64 | 47.52 N | 11.17 E |
| Bernsbach | 54 | 50.34 N | 12.46 E |
| Bernsdorf | 54 | 51.22 N | 14.04 E |
| Bernsfelden | 56 | 49.34 N | 9.53 E |
| Bernstadt | 54 | 51.03 N | 14.50 E |
| Bernville | 208 | 40.26 N | 76.07 W |
| Bero ≐ | 152 | 15.10 S | 12.09 E |
| Beroga | 114 | 2.56 N | 101.55 E |
| Berolzheim | 56 | 49.28 N | 9.32 E |
| Beromünster | 58 | 47.12 N | 8.11 E |
| Berón de Astrada | 252 | 27.33 S | 57.32 W |
| Beror Hayil | 132 | 31.33 N | 34.38 E |
| Beroroha | 157b | 21.41 S | 45.10 E |
| Beroun | 30 | 49.58 N | 14.04 E |
| Berounka ≐ | 30 | 50.00 N | 14.24 E |
| Berovo | 38 | 41.42 N | 22.51 E |
| Berowra | 170 | 33.37 S | 151.09 E |
| Ber'ožnoje | 76 | 59.55 N | 39.17 E |
| Ber'ozovaja ≐ | 80 | 48.31 N | 41.03 E |
| Ber'ozovka, Kaz. | 80 | 51.11 N | 53.16 E |
| Ber'ozovka, Ross. | 24 | 65.00 N | 56.26 E |
| Ber'ozovka, Ross. | 76 | 53.26 N | 38.53 E |
| Ber'ozovka, Ross. | 80 | 52.06 N | 45.07 E |
| Ber'ozovka, Ross. | 86 | 51.51 N | 82.58 E |
| Ber'ozovka, Ross. | 86 | 56.03 N | 93.07 E |
| Ber'ozovka, Ross. | 86 | 54.02 N | 76.35 E |
| Ber'ozovka, Ross. | 86 | 59.24 N | 82.38 E |
| Ber'ozovka, Ross. | 86 | 59.35 N | 56.02 E |
| Ber'ozovka, Ross. | 89 | 50.35 N | 127.52 E |
| Ber'ozovo, Ross. | 265a | 59.56 N | 29.48 E |
| Ber'ozovo, Ross. | 74 | 63.56 N | 65.02 E |
| Ber'ozovo, Ross. | 80 | 51.56 N | 48.28 E |


**Symbols** in the index entries represent the broad categories identified in the key at the right. Symbols with superior numbers (⋏[1]) identify subcategories (see complete key on page *I · 1*).

**Symbole** im Register stellen die rechts im Schlüssel erklärten Kategorien dar. Symbole mit hochgestellten Ziffern (⋏[1]) bezeichnen Unterabteilungen einer Kategorie (vgl. vollständiger Schlüssel auf Seite *I · 1*).

**Los símbolos** incluídos en el texto del índice representan las grandes categorías identificadas con la clave a la derecha. Los símbolos con numeros en su parte superior (⋏[1]) identifican las subcategorías (véase la clave completa en la página *I · 1*).

**Les symboles** de l'index représentent les catégories indiquées dans la légende à droite. Les symboles suivis d'un indice (⋏[1]) représentent des souscatégories (voir légende complète à la page *I · 1*).

**Os símbolos** incluídos no texto do índice representam as grandes categorias identificadas com a chave à direita. Os símbolos com números em sua parte superior (⋏[1]) identificam as subcategorias (veja-se a chave completa à página *I · 1*).

| | | | | | |
| --- | --- | --- | --- | --- | --- |
| ∧ Mountain | Berg | Montaña | Montagne | Montanha |
| ⋏ Mountains | Gebirge | Montañas | Montagnes | Montanhas |
| )( Pass | Paß | Paso | Col | Passo |
| V Valley, Canyon | Tal, Cañon | Valle, Cañón | Vallée, Canyon | Vale, Canhão |
| ≐ Plain | Ebene | Llano | Plaine | Planície |
| › Cape | Kap | Cabo | Cap | Cabo |
| I Island | Insel | Isla | Île | Ilha |
| II Islands | Inseln | Islas | Îles | Ilhas |
| ✣ Other Topographic Features | Andere Topographische Objekte | Otros Elementos Topográficos | Autres données topographiques | Outros acidentes topográficos |

ESPAÑOL

| Nombre | Página | Lat.°′ | Long.°′ W = Oeste |
|---|---|---|---|
| Ber'ozovo, Ross. | 82 | 54.03 N | 36.24 E |
| Ber'ozovo, Ross. | 82 | 54.19 N | 38.17 E |
| Ber'ozovskaja | 80 | 50.16 N | 43.59 E |
| Ber'ozovskij | 86 | 55.39 N | 86.16 E |
| Ber'ozovskij R'adok | 76 | 58.06 N | 34.29 E |
| Ber'ozovskoje | 86 | 55.50 N | 89.36 E |
| Berra | 64 | 44.59 N | 11.58 E |
| Berras, Arroyo los ≃ | 288 | 34.34 S | 58.40 W |
| Berre ≃ | 62 | 44.24 N | 4.40 E |
| Berre, Étang de ⊂ | 62 | 43.27 N | 5.08 E |
| Berrechid | 148 | 33.17 N | 7.35 W |
| Berre-des-Alpes | 62 | 43.50 N | 7.19 E |
| Berre-l'Étang | 62 | 43.28 N | 5.11 E |
| Ber Remad, Oued V | 148 | 31.45 N | 1.10 E |
| Berri | 166 | 34.17 S | 140.36 E |
| Berridale | 171b | 36.22 S | 148.50 E |
| Berriedale | 46 | 58.11 N | 3.29 W |
| Berrien □[6] | 216 | 41.59 N | 86.30 W |
| Berrien Springs | 216 | 41.56 N | 86.20 W |
| Berrigan | 166 | 35.40 S | 145.49 E |
| Berrima | 170 | 34.30 S | 150.20 E |
| Berriozábal | 234 | 16.48 N | 93.16 W |
| Berriyyane | 148 | 32.50 N | 3.46 E |
| Berrouaghia | 34 | 36.08 N | 2.55 E |
| Berrugosa Point > | 116 | 10.23 N | 125.33 E |
| Berry, Austl. | 170 | 34.47 S | 150.42 E |
| Berry, Al., U.S. | 194 | 33.39 N | 87.36 W |
| Berry, Ky., U.S. | 218 | 38.31 N | 84.23 W |
| Berry □[9] | 50 | 47.20 N | 2.10 E |
| Berry, Canal du ≊ | 50 | 47.17 N | 1.25 E |
| Berry-au-Bac | 50 | 49.24 N | 3.54 E |
| Berry Creek ≃, Ab., Can. | 182 | 50.50 N | 111.36 W |
| Berry Creek ≃, Tx., U.S. | 222 | 30.40 N | 97.36 W |
| Berryessa, Lake ⊜[1] | 226 | 38.35 N | 122.14 W |
| Berryessa Creek ≃ | 282 | 37.24 N | 121.53 W |
| Berryessa Peak ∧ | 226 | 38.40 N | 122.11 W |
| Berry Islands II | 238 | 25.34 N | 77.45 W |
| Berry Mountain ∧ | 208 | 40.31 N | 77.02 W |
| Berrysburg | 208 | 40.36 N | 76.49 W |
| Berrys Creek ≃ | 276 | 40.47 N | 74.05 W |
| Berryville | 194 | 36.21 N | 93.34 W |
| Berseba | 156 | 26.00 S | 17.46 E |
| Bersenbrück | 52 | 52.33 N | 7.56 E |
| Bershad' | 78 | 48.23 N | 29.30 E |
| Bersut | 80 | 55.32 N | 50.54 E |
| Berta ≃ | 130 | 41.09 N | 41.53 E |
| Bertam | 114 | 5.09 N | 102.03 E |
| Berté, Lac ⊜ | 186 | 50.48 N | 68.30 W |
| Bertha | 198 | 46.16 N | 95.03 W |
| Berthåga | 40 | 59.52 N | 17.35 E |
| Berthelsdorf | 54 | 51.05 N | 14.13 E |
| Berthier □[6] | 206 | 46.30 N | 73.45 W |
| Berthierville | 206 | 46.05 N | 73.10 W |
| Berthold | 198 | 48.18 N | 101.44 W |
| Berthoud | 200 | 40.18 N | 105.04 W |
| Berthoud Pass )( | 200 | 39.45 N | 105.45 W |
| Bertincourt | 50 | 50.05 N | 2.59 E |
| Bertinoro | 66 | 44.09 N | 12.08 E |
| Bertioga | 256 | 23.51 S | 46.09 W |
| Bertioga, Enseada da ⊂ | 256 | 23.50 S | 46.08 W |
| Bertkow | 54 | 52.43 N | 11.54 E |
| Bertlich | 263 | 51.37 N | 7.04 E |
| Bertogne | 56 | 50.05 N | 5.40 E |
| Bertolínia | 250 | 7.38 S | 43.57 W |
| Bertoua | 152 | 4.35 N | 13.41 E |
| Bertram | 196 | 30.45 N | 98.03 W |
| Bertrand, Mi., U.S. | 216 | 41.46 N | 86.15 W |
| Bertrand, Ne., U.S. | 198 | 40.31 N | 99.38 W |
| Bertrix | 56 | 49.51 N | 5.15 E |
| Bertry | 50 | 50.05 N | 3.27 E |
| Beru I | 14 | 1.20 S | 176.00 E |
| Beruas | 114 | 4.30 N | 100.47 E |
| Beruri | 246 | 3.54 S | 61.22 W |
| Berville | 214 | 42.55 N | 82.53 W |
| Berville-sur-Mer | 50 | 49.26 N | 0.22 E |
| Berwang | 58 | 47.24 N | 10.45 E |
| Berwick, Austl. | 169 | 38.02 S | 145.21 E |
| Berwick, N.S., Can. | 186 | 45.03 N | 64.44 W |
| Berwick, La., U.S. | 194 | 29.41 N | 91.13 W |
| Berwick, Me., U.S. | 188 | 43.15 N | 70.51 W |
| Berwick, Pa., U.S. | 210 | 41.03 N | 76.14 W |
| Berwick-upon-Tweed | 44 | 55.46 N | 2.00 W |
| Berwyn, Il., U.S. | 216 | 41.51 N | 87.47 W |
| Berwyn, Pa., U.S. | 208 | 40.02 N | 75.26 W |
| Berwyn ⩘ | 42 | 52.53 N | 3.24 W |
| Berwyn Heights | 284c | 38.59 N | 76.54 W |
| Beryslav | 78 | 46.51 N | 33.26 E |
| Bērze ≃ | 76 | 56.41 N | 23.37 E |
| Berzé-la-Ville | 58 | 46.22 N | 4.42 E |
| Berz-Macomb Airport ⊠ | 281 | 42.40 N | 82.58 W |
| Bès ≃ | 62 | 44.08 N | 6.14 E |
| Besalampy | 157b | 16.45 S | 44.30 E |
| Besana in Brianza | 62 | 45.42 N | 9.17 E |
| Besançon | 58 | 47.15 N | 6.02 E |
| Besani | 124 | 24.08 N | 80.17 E |
| Bešankovičy | 76 | 55.03 N | 29.27 E |
| Besar, Gunong ∧, Malay. | 114 | 5.10 N | 101.18 E |
| Besar, Gunong ∧, Malay. | 114 | 2.30 N | 103.10 E |
| Besar, Gunung ∧ | 112 | 2.43 S | 115.37 E |
| Besar, Pulau I | 115b | 8.28 S | 122.22 E |
| Besar Hantu, Gunong ∧ | 114 | 3.12 N | 102.02 E |
| Besaya ≃ | 34 | 43.21 N | 4.04 W |
| Besbes | 36 | 36.42 N | 7.51 E |
| Besedino | 78 | 51.42 N | 36.28 E |
| Besedy | 265b | 55.37 N | 37.47 E |
| Besedz' ≃ | 76 | 52.38 N | 31.09 E |
| Besenfeld | 56 | 48.35 N | 8.25 E |
| Beserah | 114 | 3.52 N | 103.22 E |
| Besigheim | 56 | 49.00 N | 9.08 E |
| Besikama | 112 | 9.36 S | 124.57 E |
| Beşiktaş ◆[8] | 267b | 41.03 N | 29.01 E |
| Beşiri | 130 | 37.55 N | 41.18 E |
| Besitang | 114 | 4.02 N | 98.12 E |
| Beškent | 128 | 38.49 N | 65.39 E |
| Beskid Mountains ⩘ | 30 | 49.40 N | 20.00 E |
| Beşkonak | 130 | 37.08 N | 31.12 E |
| Beskra | 148 | 34.51 N | 5.44 E |
| Beškube | 85 | 39.50 N | 68.18 E |
| Beskudnikovo ◆[8] | 265b | 55.52 N | 37.34 E |
| Beslan | 84 | 43.12 N | 44.33 E |
| Beslenej | 84 | 44.14 N | 41.44 E |
| Besnard Lake ⊜ | 184 | 55.24 N | 106.05 W |
| Besni | 130 | 37.41 N | 37.52 E |
| Besor, Naḥal V | 132 | 31.28 N | 34.22 E |
| Besós ≃ | 266d | 41.25 N | 2.04 E |
| Besozzo | 62 | 45.51 N | 8.39 E |
| Besp'atovo | 82 | 54.45 N | 38.54 E |
| Beşpınar, Tür. | 130 | 41.09 N | 35.14 E |
| Beşpınar, Tür. | 130 | 37.51 N | 41.36 E |
| Besputa ≃ | 82 | 54.50 N | 37.58 E |
| Bessacarr | 44 | 53.30 N | 1.04 W |
| Bessancourt | 261 | 49.02 N | 2.13 E |
| Bessans | 62 | 45.19 N | 7.00 E |
| Bessarabia □[9] | 38 | 47.00 N | 28.30 E |
| Bessarabka | 86 | 53.37 N | 73.17 E |
| Bessaz, gora ∧ | 85 | 43.49 N | 68.40 E |
| Bessbrook | 48 | 54.12 N | 6.25 W |
| Besse, Dtsch. | 56 | 51.13 N | 9.23 E |
| Besse, Nig. | 150 | 11.15 N | 4.30 E |
| Bessèges | 62 | 44.17 N | 4.06 E |
| Bessemer, Al., U.S. | 194 | 33.24 N | 86.57 W |
| Bessemer, Mi., U.S. | 190 | 46.28 N | 90.03 W |
| Bessemer, Pa., U.S. | 214 | 40.58 N | 80.29 W |
| Bessemer City | 192 | 35.17 N | 81.17 W |
| Besser | 41 | 55.52 N | 10.39 E |
| Bessé-sur-Braye | 50 | 47.50 N | 0.45 E |
| Bessheim | 26 | 61.31 N | 8.51 E |
| Besshiyama | 96 | 33.50 N | 133.23 E |
| Bessho | 270 | 34.27 N | 135.31 E |
| Bessonovka | 80 | 53.18 N | 45.03 E |
| Best | 52 | 51.31 N | 5.24 E |
| Best'ach | 74 | 61.52 N | 129.55 E |
| Bestamak, Kaz. | 86 | 49.43 N | 55.07 E |

FRANÇAIS

| Nom | Page | Lat.°′ | Long.°′ W = Ouest |
|---|---|---|---|
| Bestamak, Kaz. | 86 | 49.13 N | 78.21 E |
| Beštau, gora ∧ | 84 | 44.06 N | 43.01 E |
| Besten | 263 | 51.39 N | 6.54 E |
| Bestensee | 54 | 52.15 N | 13.37 E |
| Bestfield | 285 | 39.43 N | 75.36 W |
| Bestobe | 86 | 52.30 N | 73.05 E |
| Beštor, gora ∧ | 85 | 42.03 N | 70.50 E |
| Bestuževo | 24 | 61.37 N | 43.58 E |
| Bestwig, Dtsch. | 52 | 51.22 N | 8.24 E |
| Bestwig, Dtsch. | 56 | 51.22 N | 8.24 E |
| Besuki | 115a | 7.45 S | 113.41 E |
| Besut ≃ | 114 | 5.48 N | 102.35 E |
| Beswick Aboriginal Reserve ◆[4] | 164 | 14.30 S | 133.10 E |
| Betā | 272b | 22.55 N | 88.14 E |
| Betafo | 157b | 19.50 S | 46.51 E |
| Betāgi | 126 | 22.25 N | 90.11 E |
| Bet Alfa | 132 | 32.31 N | 35.26 E |
| Beta Main Canal ≊ | 226 | 36.34 N | 120.11 W |
| Betamba | 152 | 2.13 S | 21.23 E |
| Betang Melaka | 114 | 2.28 N | 102.25 E |
| Betano | 112 | 9.10 S | 125.43 E |
| Betanzos, Bol. | 248 | 19.34 S | 65.27 W |
| Betanzos, Esp. | 34 | 43.17 N | 8.12 W |
| Betanzos, Ría de ⊂[1] | 34 | 43.23 N | 8.15 W |
| Betaré Oya | 152 | 5.36 N | 14.05 E |
| Betarsjön ⊜ | 26 | 63.44 N | 16.52 E |
| Bet Bet Creek ≃ | 169 | 36.52 S | 143.52 E |
| Betbetti | 140 | 15.06 N | 24.12 E |
| Betchworth | 260 | 51.14 N | 0.16 W |
| Bet Dagan | 132 | 32.00 N | 34.50 E |
| Bete Hor | 144 | 11.37 N | 39.02 E |
| Betém | 256 | 22.52 S | 44.17 W |
| Bétera | 34 | 39.35 N | 0.27 W |
| Bétérou | 150 | 9.12 N | 2.16 E |
| Bet Guvrin | 132 | 31.36 N | 34.54 E |
| Bet Ha'arava | 132 | 31.48 N | 35.32 E |
| Bethal | 158 | 26.27 S | 29.28 E |
| Bethalto | 219 | 38.54 N | 90.02 W |
| Bethanien | 156 | 26.32 S | 17.11 E |
| Bethany, Ct., U.S. | 207 | 41.25 N | 72.59 W |
| Bethany, Il., U.S. | 219 | 39.38 N | 88.44 W |
| Bethany, Mo., U.S. | 194 | 40.16 N | 94.01 W |
| Bethany, N.Y., U.S. | 210 | 42.55 N | 78.08 W |
| Bethany, Ok., U.S. | 196 | 35.31 N | 97.37 W |
| Bethany, Pa., U.S. | 210 | 41.37 N | 75.21 W |
| Bethany, W.V., U.S. | 214 | 40.12 N | 80.33 W |
| Bethany Reservoir ⊜[1] | 226 | 37.47 N | 121.37 W |
| Bet HaShitta | 132 | 32.33 N | 35.26 E |
| Bethel, Ak., U.S. | 180 | 60.48 N | 161.46 W |
| Bethel, Ct., U.S. | 207 | 41.22 N | 73.24 W |
| Bethel, De., U.S. | 208 | 38.27 N | 75.21 W |
| Bethel, Ky., U.S. | 218 | 38.14 N | 83.52 W |
| Bethel, Me., U.S. | 188 | 44.24 N | 70.47 W |
| Bethel, Mo., U.S. | 219 | 39.52 N | 92.01 W |
| Bethel, N.Y., U.S. | 210 | 41.41 N | 74.52 W |
| Bethel, N.C., U.S. | 192 | 35.48 N | 77.22 W |
| Bethel, Oh., U.S. | 218 | 38.57 N | 84.04 W |
| Bethel, Pa., U.S. | 208 | 40.28 N | 76.18 W |
| Bethel, Wa., U.S. | 224 | 47.32 N | 122.38 W |
| Bethel Acres | 196 | 35.19 N | 97.00 W |
| Bethel Island | 226 | 38.01 N | 121.39 W |
| Bethel Manor | 208 | 37.06 N | 76.25 W |
| Bethel Park | 214 | 40.18 N | 80.02 W |
| Bethelsdorp | 158 | 33.52 S | 25.34 E |
| Bethel Springs | 194 | 35.14 N | 88.36 W |
| Béthencourt-sur-Mer | 50 | 50.05 N | 1.30 E |
| Bethersden | 42 | 51.08 N | 0.48 E |
| Bethesda, Wales, U.K. | 44 | 53.11 N | 4.03 W |
| Bethesda, Md., U.S. | 208 | 38.58 N | 77.06 W |
| Bethesda, Oh., U.S. | 188 | 40.00 N | 81.04 W |
| Bethesdaweg | 158 | 31.55 S | 24.45 E |
| Bethford | 284a | 42.48 N | 78.48 W |
| Bethgate | 284b | 39.18 N | 76.51 W |
| Béthisy-Saint-Pierre | 50 | 49.18 N | 2.49 E |
| Bethlehem, S. Afr. | 156 | 28.15 S | 28.15 E |
| Bethlehem, S. Afr. | 158 | 27.10 S | 24.00 E |
| Bethlehem, S. Afr. | 158 | 28.15 S | 28.15 E |
| Bethlehem, Ct., U.S. | 207 | 41.38 N | 73.12 W |
| Bethlehem, In., U.S. | 218 | 38.32 N | 85.25 W |
| Bethlehem, Ky., U.S. | 218 | 38.24 N | 85.04 W |
| Bethlehem, Pa., U.S. | 210 | 40.37 N | 75.22 W |
| Bethlehem, W.V., U.S. | 188 | 40.02 N | 80.41 W |
| Bethlehem → Bayt Laḥm, W.B. | 132 | 31.43 N | 35.12 E |
| Bethlehem Center | 210 | 42.40 N | 73.42 W |
| Bethlehem Steel Corporation ⚜[3], Md., U.S. | 284b | 39.13 N | 76.29 W |
| Bethlehem Steel Corporation (Lackawanna Plant) ⚜[3], N.Y., U.S. | 284a | 42.49 N | 78.52 W |
| Bethnal Green ◆[8] | 260 | 51.32 N | 0.03 W |
| Bethoncourt | 58 | 47.32 N | 6.48 E |
| Bethpage | 210 | 40.44 N | 73.28 W |
| Bethpage State Park ♦ | 210 | 40.45 N | 73.27 W |
| Bethulie | 158 | 30.32 S | 25.59 E |
| Bethune, Sk., Can. | 184 | 50.43 N | 105.08 W |
| Béthune, Fr. | 50 | 50.32 N | 2.38 E |
| Bethune, S.C., U.S. | 192 | 34.24 N | 80.20 W |
| Béthune ≃ | 50 | 49.53 N | 1.09 E |
| Betijoque | 246 | 9.23 N | 70.44 W |
| Betil | 126 | 24.14 N | 89.43 E |
| Betio | 174t | 1.21 N | 172.56 E |
| Betioky | 157b | 23.42 S | 44.22 E |
| Betis ≃ | 114 | 4.53 N | 101.48 E |
| Betlica | 76 | 54.01 N | 33.57 E |
| Betna ≃ | 126 | 22.34 N | 89.12 E |
| Bet Netofa, Biq'at ⊻ | 132 | 32.49 N | 35.19 E |
| Betnoti | 126 | 21.44 N | 86.51 E |
| Beton-Bazoches | 50 | 48.42 N | 3.15 E |
| Betong, Malay. | 112 | 1.24 N | 111.31 E |
| Betong, Thai | 110 | 5.45 N | 101.05 E |
| Betoota | 166 | 25.42 S | 140.44 E |
| Bétou | 152 | 3.03 N | 18.31 E |
| Betpak-Dala ◆[2] | 86 | 46.00 N | 70.00 E |
| Betroka | 157b | 23.16 S | 46.06 E |
| Betsham | 260 | 51.25 N | 0.19 E |
| Bet Sh'ean | 132 | 32.30 N | 35.30 E |
| Bet She'arim, Ḥorbat ⊥ | 132 | 32.42 N | 35.08 E |
| Bet Shemesh | 132 | 31.45 N | 35.00 E |
| Betsiamites | 186 | 48.56 N | 68.38 W |
| Betsiamites ≃ | 186 | 48.56 N | 68.38 W |
| Betsiamites, Barrage ◆[6] | 186 | 49.22 N | 69.47 W |
| Betsiamites, Pointe de > | 186 | 48.55 N | 68.37 W |
| Betsiamites, Réserve indienne de ◆[4] | 186 | 49.05 N | 68.37 W |
| Betsiboka ≃ | 157b | 16.03 S | 46.36 E |
| Betsie, Point > | 190 | 44.42 N | 86.16 W |
| Betsioky | 157b | 21.31 S | 44.28 E |
| Betsukai | 92a | 43.23 N | 145.17 E |
| Betsy Layne | 192 | 37.33 N | 82.38 W |
| Betsy Ross Bridge ◆[5] | 285 | 39.59 N | 75.04 W |
| Bettembourg | 56 | 49.32 N | 6.02 E |
| Bettendorf | 190 | 41.31 N | 90.30 W |
| Betterton | 208 | 39.21 N | 76.03 W |
| Bettiah | 124 | 26.48 N | 84.30 E |
| Bettie | 222 | 32.48 N | 94.58 W |
| Bettles Field | 180 | 66.55 N | 151.30 W |
| Bettola | 62 | 44.47 N | 9.36 E |
| Bettona | 66 | 43.01 N | 12.29 E |
| Bettrath ◆[8] | 263 | 51.13 N | 6.26 E |
| Bettsville | 214 | 41.14 N | 83.14 W |
| Bettyhill | 46 | 58.32 N | 4.14 W |
| Betty's Bay | 158 | 34.22 S | 18.52 E |
| Betūl | 124 | 21.55 N | 77.54 E |
| Betumbe-Bongo | 152 | 2.11 S | 18.46 E |
| Betung, Indon. | 112 | 1.52 S | 103.16 E |
| Betung, Indon. | 112 | 2.50 S | 104.14 E |
| Betuwe ◆[1] | 52 | 51.55 N | 5.30 E |

PORTUGUÊS

| Nome | Página | Lat.°′ | Long.°′ W = Oeste |
|---|---|---|---|
| Betwa ≃ | 124 | 25.55 N | 80.12 E |
| Betws-y-Coed | 44 | 53.05 N | 3.48 W |
| Betz | 50 | 49.09 N | 2.57 E |
| Betz ≃ | 50 | 48.09 N | 2.45 E |
| Betzdorf | 56 | 50.47 N | 7.53 E |
| Betzenstein | 60 | 49.41 N | 11.25 E |
| Béu | 152 | 6.14 S | 15.28 E |
| Beucha | 54 | 51.19 N | 12.34 E |
| Beugneux | 50 | 49.14 N | 3.25 E |
| Beuil | 62 | 44.06 N | 6.59 E |
| Beulah, Austl. | 166 | 35.56 S | 142.26 E |
| Beulah, Co., U.S. | 200 | 38.04 N | 104.59 W |
| Beulah, Mi., U.S. | 190 | 44.37 N | 86.05 W |
| Beulah, Ms., U.S. | 194 | 33.47 N | 90.58 W |
| Beulah, N.D., U.S. | 198 | 47.15 N | 101.46 W |
| Beulah, Lake ⊜ | 216 | 42.49 N | 88.23 W |
| Beulah Beach | 214 | 41.25 N | 82.22 W |
| Beulah Reservoir ⊜[1] | 202 | 43.56 N | 118.09 W |
| Beulaville | 192 | 34.55 N | 77.46 W |
| Beult ≃ | 42 | 51.14 N | 0.25 E |
| Beure | 58 | 47.12 N | 6.00 E |
| Beureunun | 114 | 5.18 N | 95.59 E |
| Beuron | 58 | 48.03 N | 8.58 E |
| Beuthen → Bytom | 30 | 50.22 N | 18.54 E |
| Beuvron ≃, Fr. | 50 | 47.28 N | 3.31 E |
| Beuvron ≃, Fr. | 50 | 47.29 N | 1.15 E |
| Beuvronne ≃ | 261 | 48.56 N | 2.44 E |
| Beuvry | 50 | 50.31 N | 2.41 E |
| Beuzeville | 50 | 49.20 N | 0.21 E |
| Bevagna | 66 | 42.56 N | 12.36 E |
| Bever ≃ | 52 | 52.01 N | 7.46 E |
| Bevera ≃ | 62 | 43.49 N | 7.34 E |
| Beveren | 50 | 51.13 N | 4.15 E |
| B. Everett Jordan Lake ⊜[1] | 192 | 35.45 N | 79.00 W |
| Beverino | 62 | 44.14 N | 9.47 E |
| Beverley, Austl. | 168a | 32.06 S | 116.56 E |
| Beverley, Eng., U.K. | 44 | 53.52 N | 0.26 W |
| Beverley Minster ⚜[1] | 44 | 53.50 N | 0.27 W |
| Beverley Springs | 162 | 16.43 S | 125.28 E |
| Beverlo | 56 | 51.05 N | 5.12 E |
| Beverly, Ma., U.S. | 207 | 42.33 N | 70.52 W |
| Beverly, N.J., U.S. | 208 | 40.03 N | 74.55 W |
| Beverly, Tx., U.S. | 222 | 31.30 N | 97.10 W |
| Beverly ◆[8] | 278 | 41.43 N | 87.41 W |
| Beverly Farms, Md., U.S. | 284c | 39.04 N | 77.11 W |
| Beverly Farms, Ma., U.S. | 283 | 42.34 N | 70.49 W |
| Beverly Harbor ⊂ | 283 | 42.32 N | 70.53 W |
| Beverly Hills, Austl. | 274a | 33.57 S | 151.05 E |
| Beverly Hills, Ca., U.S. | 228 | 34.04 N | 118.23 W |
| Beverly Hills, Fl., U.S. | 220 | 28.56 N | 82.28 W |
| Beverly Hills, Mi., U.S. | 216 | 42.31 N | 83.13 W |
| Beverly Lake ⊜ | 176 | 64.36 N | 100.30 W |
| Beverly Municipal Airport ⊠ | 283 | 42.35 N | 70.55 W |
| Beverly Run ≃ | 208 | 37.55 N | 77.11 W |
| Beverly Shores | 216 | 41.41 N | 86.58 W |
| Bevern | 52 | 51.51 N | 9.29 E |
| Beverstausee ⊜[1] | 263 | 51.09 N | 7.23 E |
| Beverstedt | 52 | 53.26 N | 8.49 E |
| Beverungen | 52 | 51.39 N | 9.22 E |
| Beverwijk | 52 | 52.28 N | 4.40 E |
| Bevier | 194 | 39.45 N | 92.34 W |
| Bevin, Lac ⊜ | 206 | 45.57 N | 74.35 W |
| Bevoalavo | 157b | 25.13 S | 45.26 E |
| Bewani | 164 | 3.02 S | 141.10 E |
| Bewani Mountains ⩘ | 164 | 3.10 S | 141.25 E |
| Bewār | 124 | 27.13 N | 79.18 E |
| Bewdley, On., Can. | 212 | 44.05 N | 78.19 W |
| Bewdley, Eng., U.K. | 42 | 52.22 N | 2.19 W |
| Bewl Water ⊜[1] | 42 | 51.04 N | 0.24 E |
| Bex | 58 | 46.15 N | 7.01 E |
| Bexbach | 56 | 49.21 N | 7.16 E |
| Bexhill | 42 | 50.50 N | 0.29 E |
| Bexley, Austl. | 274a | 33.57 S | 151.08 E |
| Bexley, Oh., U.S. | 218 | 39.58 N | 82.56 W |
| Bexley ◆[8] | 42 | 51.26 N | 0.10 E |
| Beyazköy | 130 | 41.21 N | 27.42 E |
| Beybach ≃ | 56 | 50.13 N | 7.23 E |
| Beyçayırı | 130 | 40.15 N | 26.55 E |
| Beycuma | 130 | 41.19 N | 31.59 E |
| Bey Dağları ⩘ | 130 | 36.40 N | 30.15 E |
| Beydağları Olimpos Milli Parkı ♦ | 130 | 36.40 N | 30.25 E |
| Beydili | 130 | 40.10 N | 31.01 E |
| Beyenburg ◆[8] | 263 | 51.15 N | 7.18 E |
| Beykoz ◆[8] | 267b | 41.08 N | 29.05 E |
| Beyla | 150 | 8.41 N | 8.37 W |
| Beyläqan | 84 | 39.47 N | 47.37 E |
| Beylerbeyi ◆[8] | 267b | 41.03 N | 29.03 E |
| Beylikahır | 130 | 39.42 N | 31.13 E |
| Beylul | 144 | 13.10 N | 42.26 E |
| Beynes | 261 | 48.51 N | 1.53 E |
| Beynes-Thiverval, Aérodrome de ⊠ | 261 | 48.51 N | 1.54 E |
| Beyoğlu ◆[8] | 267b | 41.02 N | 28.59 E |
| Beypazarı | 130 | 40.10 N | 31.56 E |
| Beypınarı | 130 | 39.31 N | 37.44 E |
| Beypore | 122 | 11.11 N | 75.49 E |
| Beyra | 144 | 6.57 N | 47.19 E |
| Beyrouth → Bayrūt | 130 | 33.53 N | 35.30 E |
| Beyşehir | 130 | 37.41 N | 31.43 E |
| Beyşehir Gölü ⊜ | 130 | 37.40 N | 31.30 E |
| Beytüşşebap | 128 | 37.34 N | 43.10 E |
| Bezaha | 157b | 23.30 S | 44.31 E |
| Bežanickaja vozvyšennost' ⩘[1] | 76 | 56.54 N | 29.20 E |
| Bežanicy | 76 | 56.58 N | 29.53 E |
| Bezau | 58 | 47.23 N | 9.54 E |
| Bezavona ∧ | 157b | 15.02 S | 49.52 E |
| Bezděz ∧ | 54 | 50.32 N | 14.43 E |
| Bezděz ⊥ | 54 | 50.32 N | 14.46 E |
| Bezdzež | 76 | 52.19 N | 25.18 E |
| Bèze | 58 | 47.28 N | 5.16 E |
| Bežeck | 76 | 57.47 N | 36.39 E |
| Bežeckij Verch ⩘[1] | 76 | 57.36 N | 36.54 E |
| Bezenčuk | 80 | 52.59 N | 49.26 E |
| Bezerra ≃ | 255 | 13.16 S | 47.31 W |
| Bezerros | 250 | 8.14 S | 35.45 W |
| Bezet | 132 | 33.05 N | 35.08 E |
| Béziers | 32 | 43.21 N | 3.15 E |
| Bezimenne | 83 | 47.06 N | 37.56 E |
| Bezmein | 128 | 38.05 N | 58.12 E |
| Bezmenšur | 80 | 56.29 N | 51.17 E |
| Bezno | 54 | 50.22 N | 14.48 E |
| Bezons | 261 | 48.56 N | 2.13 E |
| Bežta | 84 | 42.08 N | 46.08 E |
| Bezwada → Vijayawāda | 122 | 16.31 N | 80.37 E |
| Bezym'anka | 80 | 49.56 N | 43.15 E |
| Bezym'annaja | 80 | 51.20 N | 46.26 E |
| Bezzecca | 64 | 45.55 N | 10.43 E |
| Bezzubovo | 82 | 55.27 N | 38.55 E |
| Bhabānipur, India | 272b | 22.57 N | 88.27 E |
| Bhabānipur, India | 272b | 22.56 N | 88.13 E |
| Bhabhua | 124 | 25.03 N | 83.37 E |
| Bhābta | 126 | 23.59 N | 88.15 E |
| Bhadarwāh | 123 | 32.59 N | 75.43 E |
| Bhadaur | 123 | 30.29 N | 75.19 E |
| Bhādgāon → Bhaktapur | 124 | 27.42 N | 85.27 E |
| Bhadohi | 124 | 25.25 N | 82.34 E |
| Bhādra | 123 | 29.07 N | 75.10 E |
| Bhadra ≃[1] | 126 | 22.19 N | 89.31 E |
| Bhadrāchalam | 122 | 17.40 N | 80.53 E |
| Bhadrak | 120 | 21.03 N | 86.30 E |
| Bhadrapur | 124 | 26.32 N | 88.06 E |
| Bhadra Reservoir ⊜[1] | 122 | 13.40 N | 75.35 E |
| Bhadrāvati | 122 | 13.52 N | 75.43 E |
| Bhadreswar | 126 | 22.50 N | 88.21 E |
| Bhādua | 272b | 22.41 N | 88.12 E |
| Bhāg | 120 | 29.02 N | 67.49 E |
| Bhagaiya | 124 | 25.12 N | 87.29 E |
| Bhāgalpur | 124 | 25.15 N | 87.00 E |

| | | | |
|---|---|---|---|
| Bhāgīrathi ≃, India | 124 | 30.08 N | 78.35 E |
| Bhāgīrathi ≃, India | 126 | 23.25 N | 88.23 E |
| Bhagirathpur | 126 | 24.05 N | 88.29 E |
| Bhagwānpur | 126 | 22.07 N | 87.45 E |
| Bhainsa | 122 | 19.06 N | 77.58 E |
| Bhāi Pheru | 123 | 31.12 N | 73.57 E |
| Bhairab ≃[1] | 126 | 22.51 N | 89.34 E |
| Bhairab Bāzār | 120 | 24.04 N | 90.58 E |
| Bhairhawā | 124 | 27.31 N | 83.24 E |
| Bhaironghāti | 120 | 31.01 N | 78.53 E |
| Bhakkar | 123 | 31.38 N | 71.04 E |
| Bhākra Dam ◆[6] | 123 | 31.24 N | 76.30 E |
| Bhaktapur | 124 | 27.42 N | 85.27 E |
| Bhal | 272c | 19.11 N | 73.08 E |
| Bhālki | 122 | 18.02 N | 77.13 E |
| Bhalswa ◆[8] | 272a | 28.44 N | 77.10 E |
| Bhalwāl | 123 | 32.16 N | 72.54 E |
| Bhamdūn | 132 | 33.48 N | 35.39 E |
| Bhamo | 110 | 24.16 N | 97.14 E |
| Bhandāra | 120 | 21.10 N | 79.39 E |
| Bhandārdaha | 272b | 22.37 N | 88.13 E |
| Bhandāria | 126 | 22.29 N | 90.04 E |
| Bhānder | 124 | 25.44 N | 78.45 E |
| Bhander Plateau ⩘[1] | 124 | 24.10 N | 80.20 E |
| Bhāndup ◆[8] | 272c | 19.09 N | 72.57 E |
| Bhānga | 126 | 23.22 N | 89.59 E |
| Bhāngar | 126 | 22.31 N | 88.37 E |
| Bhāngar Kāta Khāl ≃ | 272b | 22.31 N | 88.33 E |
| Bhanvad | 120 | 21.56 N | 69.47 E |
| Bhārat → India □[1] | 118 | 20.00 N | 77.00 E |
| Bharatpur, India | 124 | 27.13 N | 77.29 E |
| Bharatpur, India | 126 | 23.53 N | 88.05 E |
| Bharatpur, Nepāl | 124 | 27.14 N | 84.21 E |
| Bharthana | 124 | 26.45 N | 79.14 E |
| Bharūch | 120 | 21.42 N | 72.58 E |
| Bhātai | 126 | 23.36 N | 89.11 E |
| Bhātāpāra | 120 | 21.44 N | 81.56 E |
| Bhātār | 126 | 23.25 N | 87.54 E |
| Bhatgaon → Bhaktapur | 124 | 27.42 N | 85.27 E |
| Bhātghar Lake ⊜[1] | 122 | 18.12 N | 73.49 E |
| Bhātiāpāra Ghāt | 124 | 23.13 N | 89.42 E |
| Bhatkal | 122 | 13.58 N | 74.34 E |
| Bhātpāra | 126 | 22.52 N | 88.24 E |
| Bhātpur | 272b | 22.43 N | 88.25 E |
| Bhātsāla | 126 | 22.33 N | 90.30 E |
| Bhattapratāp | 126 | 22.45 N | 89.48 E |
| Bhattiprolu | 122 | 16.06 N | 80.47 E |
| Bhātua | 272b | 22.57 N | 88.22 E |
| Bhaun | 123 | 32.52 N | 72.45 E |
| Bhaunja | 272a | 28.40 N | 77.25 E |
| Bhavāni | 122 | 11.27 N | 77.41 E |
| Bhāvnagar | 122 | 21.46 N | 72.09 E |
| Bhawānīgarh | 124 | 30.16 N | 76.02 E |
| Bhawani Mandi | 120 | 24.25 N | 75.50 E |
| Bhawānipatna | 122 | 19.54 N | 83.10 E |
| Bhedia | 126 | 23.36 N | 87.42 E |
| Bheigeir, Beinn ∧[2] | 46 | 55.44 N | 6.05 W |
| Bhendkhal | 272c | 18.53 N | 72.59 E |
| Bhera | 123 | 32.29 N | 72.55 E |
| Bheramara | 126 | 24.02 N | 88.58 E |
| Bherī □[8] | 124 | 28.30 N | 81.45 E |
| Bherī ≃ | 124 | 28.44 N | 81.16 E |
| Bheula, Beinn ∧ | 46 | 56.08 N | 4.58 W |
| Bhīkampur | 272a | 28.45 N | 77.27 E |
| Bhīkangaon | 120 | 21.52 N | 75.57 E |
| Bhilai | 120 | 21.13 N | 81.26 E |
| Bhilainagar → Bhilai | 120 | 21.13 N | 81.26 E |
| Bhīlwāra | 120 | 25.21 N | 74.38 E |
| Bhīma ≃ | 122 | 16.24 N | 77.18 E |
| Bhīmavaram | 122 | 16.32 N | 81.32 E |
| Bhimbar | 123 | 32.59 N | 74.04 E |
| Bhīmphedī | 124 | 27.32 N | 85.07 E |
| Bhīmpur, India | 126 | 22.37 N | 87.08 E |
| Bhimpur, India | 272b | 22.46 N | 88.08 E |
| Bhind | 124 | 26.34 N | 78.48 E |
| Bhinga | 124 | 27.43 N | 81.56 E |
| Bhīnmāl | 120 | 25.00 N | 72.15 E |
| Bhiwandi | 122 | 19.18 N | 73.04 E |
| Bhiwāni | 124 | 28.47 N | 76.08 E |
| Bhoāgāchi | 272b | 22.57 N | 88.20 E |
| Bhojpur | 124 | 27.10 N | 87.03 E |
| Bhojudih | 126 | 23.38 N | 86.27 E |
| Bhokardan | 122 | 20.16 N | 75.46 E |
| Bhola | 124 | 22.41 N | 90.39 E |
| Bhola ≃[1] | 126 | 22.04 N | 89.49 E |
| Bhongaon | 124 | 27.15 N | 79.11 E |
| Bhongīr | 122 | 17.31 N | 78.53 E |
| Bhonrāsa | 124 | 22.59 N | 76.12 E |
| Bhopāl | 124 | 23.16 N | 77.24 E |
| Bhopar | 272c | 19.12 N | 73.05 E |
| Bhopura | 272a | 28.42 N | 77.20 E |
| Bhoutan → Bhutan □[1] | 120 | 27.30 N | 90.30 E |
| Bhowali | 124 | 29.23 N | 79.31 E |
| Bhuāpur | 272a | 28.43 N | 77.26 E |
| Bhuban | 120 | 20.53 N | 85.50 E |
| Bhubaneshwar | 120 | 20.14 N | 85.50 E |
| Bhucho | 123 | 30.13 N | 75.06 E |
| Bhuj | 120 | 23.16 N | 69.40 E |
| Bhunarheri | 124 | 30.13 N | 76.27 E |
| Bhunya | 158 | 26.32 S | 31.01 E |
| Bhusāwal | 120 | 21.03 N | 75.46 E |
| Bhūshana | 126 | 23.24 N | 89.40 E |
| Bhutali | 272c | 19.07 N | 73.04 E |
| Bhutan (Druk-Yul) □[1], Asia | 118 | 27.30 N | 90.30 E |
| Bhutan (Druk-Yul) □[1], Asia | 120 | 27.30 N | 90.30 E |
| Bia ≃, Afr. | 150 | 5.21 N | 3.11 W |
| Biá ≃, Bra. | 246 | 3.28 S | 67.23 W |
| Bia, Phou ∧ | 110 | 18.59 N | 103.09 E |
| Biābānak | 128 | 32.11 N | 64.11 E |
| Biabo ≃ | 248 | 6.58 S | 76.23 W |
| Biacesa | 64 | 45.56 N | 10.47 E |
| Biache-Saint-Vaast | 50 | 50.18 N | 2.57 E |
| Biadene | 64 | 45.47 N | 12.04 E |
| Biafra, Bight of ⊂[3] | 134 | 4.00 N | 8.00 E |
| Biak I | 164 | 1.00 S | 136.00 E |
| Biała | 30 | 50.23 N | 17.40 E |
| Biała ≃ | 30 | 50.03 N | 20.55 E |
| Biała Piska | 30 | 53.37 N | 22.04 E |
| Biała Podlaska | 30 | 52.02 N | 23.06 E |
| Biała Podlaska □[4] | 30 | 52.00 N | 23.00 E |
| Biała Rawska | 30 | 51.49 N | 20.29 E |
| Białobrzegi | 30 | 51.40 N | 20.57 E |
| Białogard | 30 | 54.01 N | 16.00 E |
| Białowieski Park Narodowy ♦ | 30 | 52.40 N | 23.50 E |
| Biały Bór | 30 | 53.54 N | 16.51 E |
| Białystok | 30 | 53.09 N | 23.09 E |
| Białystok □[4] | 30 | 53.00 N | 23.00 E |
| Bian ≃ | 164 | 8.07 S | 139.56 E |
| Bian, Bidean nam ∧ | 46 | 56.38 N | 5.02 W |
| Biancavilla | 70 | 37.38 N | 14.52 E |
| Bianchi | 68 | 39.06 N | 16.24 E |
| Bianco | 68 | 38.05 N | 16.09 E |
| Bianco, Canale ≊ | 64 | 45.02 N | 12.05 E |
| Bianco, Capo > | 70 | 37.23 N | 13.16 E |
| Bianco, Monte (Mont Blanc) ∧ | 62 | 45.50 N | 6.52 E |
| Bian'er | 102 | 31.14 N | 101.28 E |
| Bianga | 152 | 4.51 N | 20.25 E |
| Bian'gezhuang | 105 | 39.28 N | 115.53 E |
| Biankouma | 150 | 7.44 N | 7.37 W |
| Bianlinzhen | 98 | 37.26 N | 116.32 E |
| Bianminchang | 107 | 29.41 N | 105.04 E |
| Bianniulupucun | 104 | 41.30 N | 123.42 E |
| Bianquanwopu | 104 | 41.21 N | 120.48 E |
| Bianzè | 62 | 45.18 N | 8.07 E |
| Biaora | 124 | 23.55 N | 76.54 E |
| Biaro, Pulau I | 112 | 2.05 N | 125.20 E |
| Biarritz | 32 | 43.29 N | 1.34 W |
| Biasca | 58 | 46.22 N | 8.58 E |
| Bias Fortes | 256 | 21.36 S | 43.46 W |
| Biassono | 62 | 45.37 N | 9.16 E |
| Biaza | 86 | 56.38 N | 78.18 E |
| Bibā | 142 | 28.55 N | 30.59 E |

| | | | |
|---|---|---|---|
| Bibai | 92a | 43.19 N | 141.52 E |
| Bibala | 152 | 14.46 S | 13.21 E |
| Bībān | 142 | 30.47 N | 30.40 E |
| Bibane, Bahiret el ⊂ | 148 | 33.16 N | 11.19 E |
| Bibanga | 152 | 6.15 S | 23.56 E |
| Bibban, Khawr V | 140 | 11.00 N | 32.41 E |
| Bibb City | 192 | 32.30 N | 84.59 W |
| Bibbiano | 64 | 44.40 N | 10.28 E |
| Bibbiena | 66 | 43.42 N | 11.49 E |
| Bibbona | 66 | 43.16 N | 10.35 E |
| Bibei ≃ | 34 | 42.24 N | 7.13 W |
| Bibémi | 146 | 9.19 N | 13.53 E |
| Biberach | 58 | 48.20 N | 8.02 E |
| Biberach an der Riss | 58 | 48.06 N | 9.47 E |
| Biberbach | 56 | 48.31 N | 10.48 E |
| Biberonne ≃ | 261 | 48.59 N | 2.41 E |
| Bibert ≃ | 56 | 49.27 N | 10.59 E |
| Bibertal | 58 | 48.24 N | 10.12 E |
| Bibiani | 150 | 6.28 N | 2.20 W |
| Bībi Chīni | 126 | 22.28 N | 90.12 E |
| Bibione | 64 | 45.38 N | 13.00 E |
| Bibir'ovo | 76 | 54.28 N | 33.08 E |
| Biblián | 246 | 2.42 S | 78.52 W |
| Biblis | 56 | 49.41 N | 8.27 E |
| Bibo | 102 | 29.02 N | 99.20 E |
| Bibrka | 78 | 49.38 N | 24.18 E |
| Bic | 186 | 48.22 N | 68.42 W |
| Biča | 86 | 57.53 N | 70.37 E |
| Bicas | 256 | 21.43 S | 43.04 W |
| Bicaz | 38 | 46.54 N | 26.05 E |
| Biccari | 68 | 41.24 N | 15.11 E |
| Bicester | 42 | 51.54 N | 1.09 W |
| Bičevinka | 76 | 59.44 N | 37.40 E |
| Biche, Lac la ⊜ | 182 | 54.50 N | 112.03 W |
| Bichena | 144 | 10.27 N | 38.12 E |
| Bicheno | 166 | 41.53 S | 148.18 E |
| Bichhia | 124 | 22.27 N | 80.42 E |
| Bichl | 64 | 47.43 N | 11.24 E |
| Bichlbach | 58 | 47.25 N | 10.47 E |
| Bichota Canyon V | 280 | 34.16 N | 117.48 W |
| Biči ≃ | 89 | 52.10 N | 139.50 E |
| Bičigt | 88 | 47.06 N | 95.05 E |
| Bickerstaffe | 262 | 53.32 N | 2.50 W |
| Bickerton, Cape > | 9 | 66.20 S | 136.56 E |
| Bickerton Island I | 164 | 13.45 S | 136.12 E |
| Bickle Knob ∧ | 188 | 38.56 N | 79.44 W |
| Bickley ◆[8] | 260 | 51.24 N | 0.03 E |
| Bicknacre, Eng., U.K. | 42 | 51.41 N | 0.35 E |
| Bicknacre, Eng., U.K. | 260 | 51.41 N | 0.35 E |
| Bicknell, In., U.S. | 194 | 38.46 N | 87.18 W |
| Bicknell, Ut,. U.S. | 200 | 38.20 N | 111.32 W |
| Bicknor | 260 | 51.18 N | 0.40 E |
| Bicol ≃ | 116 | 13.44 N | 123.07 E |
| Bicske | 30 | 47.29 N | 18.37 E |
| Bicudo ≃ | 255 | 18.04 S | 44.33 W |
| Bičura | 88 | 50.36 N | 107.35 E |
| Bičurina | 86 | 56.51 N | 55.25 E |
| Bīd | 122 | 18.59 N | 75.46 E |
| Bida, Nig. | 146 | 12.20 N | 13.25 E |
| Bida, Nig. | 150 | 9.05 N | 6.01 E |
| Bīdar | 122 | 17.54 N | 77.33 E |
| Bidde | 144 | 0.58 N | 42.37 E |
| Biddeford | 188 | 43.29 N | 70.27 W |
| Biddenden | 42 | 51.07 N | 0.39 E |
| Biddiyā | 132 | 32.07 N | 35.05 E |
| Biddulph | 44 | 53.08 N | 2.10 W |
| Bideford | 42 | 51.01 N | 4.13 W |
| Bidente ≃ | 66 | 44.24 N | 12.12 E |
| Bidford-on-Avon | 42 | 52.10 N | 1.51 W |
| Bidhūna | 124 | 26.49 N | 79.31 E |
| Bidian | 100 | 32.38 N | 113.03 E |
| Bīdokht | 128 | 34.21 N | 58.46 E |
| Bidoni | 71 | 40.07 N | 8.56 E |
| Bidor | 114 | 4.07 N | 101.17 E |
| Bidston | 262 | 53.24 N | 3.05 W |
| Bidwell | 188 | 38.55 N | 82.17 W |
| Bidwell, Mount ∧ | 204 | 41.58 N | 120.10 W |
| Bidya ≃[1] | 126 | 21.56 N | 88.42 E |
| Bidyādhari ≃ | 272b | 22.23 N | 88.35 E |
| Bidyādharpur | 272b | 22.50 N | 88.24 E |
| Bidžan | 89 | 47.58 N | 131.58 E |
| Bidžan ≃ | 89 | 47.44 N | 132.19 E |
| Bie | 40 | 59.05 N | 16.12 E |
| Bié □[5] | 152 | 12.30 S | 17.15 E |
| Biebelried | 56 | 49.46 N | 10.04 E |
| Bieber, Dtsch. | 56 | 50.09 N | 9.19 E |
| Bieber, Ca., U.S. | 204 | 41.07 N | 121.08 W |
| Biebrza ≃ | 30 | 53.13 N | 22.25 E |
| Biecz | 30 | 49.44 N | 21.14 E |
| Biedenkopf | 56 | 50.55 N | 8.32 E |
| Biederitz | 54 | 52.09 N | 11.43 E |
| Biedermannsdorf | 264b | 48.05 N | 16.21 E |
| Bieguzhuang | 105 | 39.19 N | 116.39 E |
| Biei | 92a | 43.35 N | 142.28 E |
| Biel (Bienne) | 58 | 47.10 N | 7.12 E |
| Bielawa | 30 | 50.41 N | 16.38 E |
| Bielawski, Mount ∧ | 226 | 37.13 N | 122.06 W |
| Bielefeld | 52 | 52.01 N | 8.31 E |
| Bieler Lake ⊜ | 176 | 70.20 N | 73.00 W |
| Bielersee ⊜ | 58 | 47.05 N | 7.10 E |
| Bielin | 54 | 52.47 N | 14.28 E |
| Biella | 62 | 45.34 N | 8.03 E |
| Biella □[4] | 62 | 45.35 N | 8.50 E |
| Bielsk | 30 | 52.40 N | 19.49 E |
| Bielsko-Biała | 30 | 49.49 N | 19.02 E |
| Bielsko-Biała □[4] | 30 | 49.40 N | 19.10 E |
| Bielsk Podlaski | 30 | 52.47 N | 23.12 E |
| Biemenhorst | 52 | 51.49 N | 6.36 E |
| Bienenbüttel | 52 | 53.08 N | 10.29 E |
| Bienfait | 184 | 49.08 N | 102.47 W |
| Bien Hoa | 110 | 10.57 N | 106.49 E |
| Bienne → Biel | 58 | 47.10 N | 7.12 E |
| Bienne ≃, Fr. | 50 | 48.15 N | 0.04 E |
| Bienne ≃, Fr. | 58 | 46.20 N | 5.38 E |
| Bienno | 64 | 45.56 N | 10.18 E |
| Bientina | 66 | 43.42 N | 10.37 E |
| Bienville | 194 | 32.21 N | 92.58 W |
| Bienville, Lac ⊜ | 176 | 55.05 N | 72.40 W |
| Biere, Dtsch. | 54 | 51.58 N | 11.39 E |
| Bière, Schw. | 58 | 46.33 N | 6.20 E |
| Bierné | 28 | 47.49 N | 0.32 W |
| Bieruń Stary | 30 | 50.06 N | 19.06 E |
| Bierutów | 30 | 51.08 N | 17.32 E |
| Bierwart | 56 | 50.34 N | 5.01 E |
| Biesbos ◆[1] | 52 | 51.45 N | 4.50 E |
| Biesdorf ◆[8] | 264a | 52.31 N | 13.33 E |
| Biese ≃ | 54 | 52.45 N | 11.37 E |
| Biesel ◆[8] | 263 | 51.10 N | 6.29 E |
| Biesenthal | 54 | 52.46 N | 13.37 E |
| Bieshan | 105 | 39.58 N | 117.29 E |
| Biesiesvlei | 158 | 26.22 S | 25.55 E |
| Biesles | 58 | 48.05 N | 5.18 E |
| Biessenhofen, Dtsch. | 58 | 47.50 N | 10.38 E |
| Biessenhofen, Dtsch. | 64 | 47.50 N | 10.38 E |
| Bieszczadzki Park Narodowy ♦ | 30 | 49.05 N | 22.45 E |
| Bieteluobaoluosika | 89 | 48.35 N | 119.56 E |
| Bietigheim | 56 | 48.54 N | 8.14 E |
| Bietigheim-Bissingen | 56 | 48.58 N | 9.07 E |
| Bietschhorn ∧ | 58 | 46.24 N | 7.51 E |
| Bièvre | 56 | 49.56 N | 5.01 E |
| Bièvre ≃ | 261 | 48.47 N | 2.20 E |
| Bièvres | 261 | 48.45 N | 2.13 E |
| Biferno ≃ | 66 | 41.59 N | 15.02 E |
| Bifoun | 152 | 0.22 S | 10.23 E |
| Bifuka | 92a | 44.29 N | 142.21 E |
| Bifurcación | 258 | 34.19 S | 56.48 W |
| Big ≃, Austl. | 169 | 37.18 S | 146.02 E |
| Big ≃, N.T., Can. | 176 | 72.30 N | 125.14 W |
| Big ≃, Sk., Can. | 184 | 53.50 N | 107.02 W |
| Big ≃, Ak., U.S. | 180 | 63.00 N | 154.56 W |
| Big ≃, Mo., U.S. | 219 | 38.28 N | 90.37 W |
| Biga | 130 | 40.13 N | 27.14 E |
| Bigadiç | 130 | 39.23 N | 28.08 E |
| Big A Mountain ∧ | 192 | 37.03 N | 82.02 W |
| Big Annemessex River ⊂ | 208 | 38.03 N | 75.50 W |
| Big Antelope Creek ≃ | 202 | 42.28 N | 117.13 W |

| | | | |
|---|---|---|---|
| Big Bald Mountain ∧, N.B., Can. | 186 | 47.12 N | 66.25 W |
| Big Bald Mountain ∧, Ga., U.S. | 192 | 34.45 N | 84.19 W |
| Big Baldy ∧ | 202 | 44.47 N | 115.13 W |
| Big Baldy Mountain ∧ | 202 | 46.58 N | 110.37 W |
| Big Bar Creek | 182 | 51.12 N | 122.06 W |
| Big Basin Redwoods State Park ♦ | 226 | 37.09 N | 122.17 W |
| Big Bay | 190 | 46.49 N | 87.44 W |
| Big Bay ⊂, N.Z. | 172 | 44.18 S | 168.05 E |
| Big Bay ⊂, Vanuatu | 175f | 15.06 S | 166.54 E |
| Big Bay De Noc ⊂ | 190 | 45.46 N | 86.43 W |
| Big Bay Point > | 212 | 44.24 N | 79.31 W |
| Big Bear City | 228 | 34.15 N | 116.50 W |
| Big Bear Lake | 228 | 34.15 N | 116.53 W |
| Big Bear Lake ⊜ | 228 | 34.15 N | 116.55 W |
| Big Beaver, Sk., Can. | 184 | 49.08 N | 105.10 W |
| Big Beaver, Pa., U.S. | 214 | 40.50 N | 80.20 W |
| Big Beaver Airport ⊠ | 281 | 42.33 N | 83.06 W |
| Big Beaver Creek ≃, Mi., U.S. | 281 | 42.32 N | 83.01 W |
| Big Beaver Creek ≃, Oh., U.S. | 218 | 39.01 N | 83.03 W |
| Big Beaver Creek ≃, Wa., U.S. | 224 | 48.40 N | 121.08 W |
| Big Bell | 162 | 27.21 S | 117.40 E |
| Big Belt Mountains ⩘ | 202 | 46.40 N | 111.25 W |
| Big Bend, Swaz. | 158 | 26.50 S | 31.57 E |
| Big Bend, Wi., U.S. | 216 | 42.52 N | 88.12 W |
| Big Bend National Park ♦ | 196 | 29.12 N | 103.12 W |
| Big Bend Reservoir ⊜[1] | 182 | 52.57 N | 115.37 W |
| Big Black ≃ | 194 | 32.00 N | 91.05 W |
| Big Blue ≃, U.S. | 198 | 39.11 N | 96.32 W |
| Big Blue ≃, In., U.S. | 218 | 39.20 N | 85.59 W |
| Big Blue, West Fork ≃ | 198 | 40.42 N | 96.59 W |
| Big Bone Lick State Park ♦ | 218 | 38.53 N | 84.45 W |
| Big Bonito Creek ≃ | 200 | 33.34 N | 109.56 W |
| Big Brook ≃ | 276 | 40.19 N | 74.10 W |
| Big Brushy Creek ≃, Tx., U.S. | 222 | 32.32 N | 96.20 W |
| Big Brushy Creek ≃, Tx., U.S. | 222 | 29.12 N | 96.55 W |
| Big Bureau Creek ≃ | 194 | 41.17 N | 89.21 W |
| Bigbury Bay ⊂ | 42 | 50.16 N | 3.48 W |
| Big Cabin Creek ≃ | 194 | 36.26 N | 95.08 W |
| Big Canyon V | 196 | 30.05 N | 101.55 W |
| Big Carlos Pass ⊂ | 220 | 26.24 N | 81.52 W |
| Big Cedar Lake ⊜ | 212 | 44.37 N | 78.10 W |
| Big Chino Wash V | 200 | 34.52 N | 112.28 W |
| Big Clear Lake ⊜ | 212 | 44.43 N | 76.55 W |
| Big Clifty | 194 | 37.32 N | 86.09 W |
| Big Coulee Creek ≃ | 202 | 46.17 N | 108.56 W |
| Big Cow Creek ≃ | 194 | 30.34 N | 93.44 W |
| Big Creek, B.C., Can. | 182 | 51.44 N | 123.03 W |
| Big Creek, Ca., U.S. | 226 | 37.12 N | 119.14 W |
| Big Creek ≃, B.C., Can. | 182 | 51.40 N | 122.50 W |
| Big Creek ≃, On., Can. | 214 | 42.19 N | 82.27 W |
| Big Creek ≃, On., Can. | 214 | 42.36 N | 80.27 W |
| Big Creek ≃, Ar., U.S. | 194 | 34.21 N | 91.03 W |
| Big Creek ≃, Ca., U.S. | 226 | 37.12 N | 119.19 W |
| Big Creek ≃, Ca., U.S. | 226 | 36.53 N | 119.15 W |
| Big Creek ≃, Id., U.S. | 202 | 45.06 N | 114.44 W |
| Big Creek ≃, Il., U.S. | 219 | 39.07 N | 88.52 W |
| Big Creek ≃, In., U.S. | 216 | 40.38 N | 86.46 W |
| Big Creek ≃, In., U.S. | 218 | 38.48 N | 85.39 W |
| Big Creek ≃, Ks., U.S. | 198 | 38.47 N | 98.55 W |
| Big Creek ≃, La., U.S. | 194 | 32.10 N | 91.53 W |
| Big Creek ≃, Mo., U.S. | 194 | 40.02 N | 94.07 W |
| Big Creek ≃, Mo., U.S. | 219 | 38.52 N | 90.50 W |
| Big Creek ≃, Oh., U.S. | 279a | 41.27 N | 81.41 W |
| Big Creek ≃, Or., U.S. | 224 | 46.11 N | 123.35 W |
| Big Creek ≃, Tx., U.S. | 222 | 29.22 N | 95.34 W |
| Big Creek ≃, Tx., U.S. | 222 | 31.09 N | 96.52 W |
| Big Creek ≃, Wa., U.S. | 224 | 47.15 N | 121.10 W |
| Big Creek, East Fork ≃ | 194 | 40.16 N | 94.03 W |
| Big Creek, West Fork ≃ | 194 | 40.16 N | 94.03 W |
| Big Creek Parkway ♦ | 279a | 41.24 N | 81.45 W |
| Big Creek Peak ∧ | 202 | 44.28 N | 113.32 W |
| Big Crow Island I | 276 | 40.37 N | 73.33 W |
| Big Cypress Creek ≃ | 222 | 33.00 N | 94.51 W |
| Big Cypress Indian Reservation ◆[4] | 220 | 26.14 N | 80.49 W |
| Big Cypress National Preserve ♦ | 220 | 25.55 N | 81.10 W |
| Big Cypress Swamp ⁝ | 220 | 26.10 N | 81.38 W |
| Big Dalton Canyon V | 280 | 34.10 N | 117.48 W |
| Big Dalton Wash V | 280 | 34.04 N | 117.58 W |
| Big Darby Creek ≃ | 218 | 39.37 N | 82.58 W |
| Big Delta | 180 | 64.09 N | 145.50 W |
| Big Desert ◆[2] | 166 | 35.40 S | 141.00 E |
| Big Diomede Island → Ratmanova, ostrov I | 180 | 65.46 N | 169.02 W |
| Big Ditch ≊ | 216 | 40.13 N | 88.22 W |
| Big Dry Creek ≃ | 202 | 47.30 N | 106.19 W |
| Big Dubbo Hill ∧ | 171b | 35.25 S | 148.36 E |
| Big Eau Pleine ≃ | 190 | 44.48 N | 90.00 W |
| Big Elk Creek ≃ | 208 | 39.35 N | 75.52 W |
| Big Elkhart Creek ≃ | 222 | 31.22 N | 95.41 W |
| Big Elm Creek ≃ | 222 | 30.53 N | 96.56 W |
| Bigelow Bight ⊂[3] | 188 | 43.15 N | 70.30 W |
| Big Escambia Creek ≃ | 194 | 30.58 N | 87.14 W |
| Big Falls | 190 | 48.11 N | 93.48 W |
| Big Flat | 194 | 36.00 N | 92.24 W |
| Big Flat Creek ≃ | 194 | 31.33 N | 87.31 W |
| Big Flats | 210 | 42.08 N | 76.56 W |
| Bigfork, Mn., U.S. | 190 | 47.44 N | 93.39 W |
| Bigfork, Mt., U.S. | 202 | 48.04 N | 114.04 W |
| Big Fork ≃ | 190 | 48.31 N | 93.43 W |
| Big Four Ditch ≊ | 216 | 40.27 N | 88.10 W |
| Big Frog Mountain ∧ | 192 | 35.00 N | 84.32 W |
| Biggar, Sk., Can. | 184 | 52.04 N | 108.00 W |
| Biggar, Scot., U.K. | 46 | 55.38 N | 3.32 W |
| Biggarsberg ⩘ | 158 | 28.12 S | 29.48 E |
| Bigge | 56 | 51.21 N | 8.28 E |
| Bigge Island I | 164 | 14.35 S | 125.10 E |
| Biggers | 194 | 36.19 N | 90.48 W |
| Biggestausee ⊜[1] | 56 | 51.05 N | 7.55 E |
| Biggin Hill ◆[8] | 42 | 51.18 N | 0.04 E |
| Biggin Hill Aerodrome ⊠ | 260 | 51.19 N | 0.03 E |
| Biggleswade | 42 | 52.05 N | 0.17 W |
| Biggs, Ca., U.S. | 226 | 39.24 N | 121.42 W |
| Biggs, Or., U.S. | 224 | 45.40 N | 120.50 W |
| Big Gull Lake ⊜ | 212 | 44.50 N | 76.58 W |
| Big Gully Creek ≃ | 184 | 53.13 N | 109.03 W |
| Bighāi ≃[1] | 126 | 22.10 N | 90.13 E |
| Big Hawk Lake ⊜ | 212 | 45.10 N | 78.44 W |
| Bighead ≃ | 212 | 44.36 N | 80.35 W |
| Big Hole ≃ | 202 | 45.34 N | 112.20 W |
| Big Hole National Battlefield ⊥ | 202 | 45.35 N | 113.35 W |
| Bighorn ≃ | 202 | 46.09 N | 107.28 W |


| | | | | | | |
|---|---|---|---|---|---|---|
| ≃ River | Fluß | Río | Rivière | Rio | | |
| ≊ Canal | Kanal | Canal | Canal | Canal | | |
| ∟ Waterfall, Rapids | Wasserfall, Stromschnellen | Cascada, Rápidos | Chute d'eau, Rapides | Cascata, Rápidos | | |
| ‖ Strait | Meeresstraße | Estrecho | Détroit | Estreito | | |
| ⊂ Bay, Gulf | Bucht, Golf | Bahía, Golfo | Baie, Golfe | Baía, Golfo | | |
| ⊜ Lake, Lakes | See, Seen | Lago, Lagos | Lac, Lacs | Lago, Lagos | | |
| ⁝ Swamp | Sumpf | Pantano | Marais | Pântano | | |
| ⊓ Ice Features, Glacier | Eis- und Gletscherformen | Accidentes Glaciales | Formes glaciaires | Acidentes glaciares | | |
| ⊤ Other Hydrographic Features | Andere Hydrographische Objekte | Otros Elementos Hidrográficos | Autres données hydrographiques | Outros acidentes hidrográficos | | |
| ✦ Submarine Features | Untermeerische Objekte | Accidentes Submarinos | Formes de relief sous-marin | Acidentes submarinos | | |
| □ Political Unit | Politische Einheit | Unidad Politica | Entité politique | Unidade política | | |
| ⚜ Cultural Institution | Kulturelle Institution | Institución Cultural | Institution culturelle | Institução cultural | | |
| ⊥ Historical Site | Historische Stätte | Sitio Histórico | Site historique | Sitio histórico | | |
| ♦ Recreational Site | Erholungs- und Ferienort | Sitio de Recreo | Centre de loisirs | Area de Lazer | | |
| ⊠ Airport | Flughafen | Aeropuerto | Aéroport | Aeroporto | | |
| ■ Military Installation | Militäranlage | Instalación Militar | Installation militaire | Instalação militar | | |
| ◆ Miscellaneous | Verschiedenes | Misceláneo | Divers | Diversos | | |

| Name | Page | Lat.°′ | Long.°′ |
|---|---|---|---|
| Bighorn Basin ≚[1] | 202 | 44.15 N | 108.10 W |
| Bighorn Canyon National Recreation Area ♦ | 202 | 45.00 N | 108.15 W |
| Big Horn Lake ⊜[1] | 202 | 45.06 N | 108.08 W |
| Bighorn Mountains ⋏ | 202 | 44.00 N | 107.30 W |
| Bight, Head of c | 162 | 31.30 S | 131.10 E |
| Big Huckleberry Mountain ∧ | 224 | 45.51 N | 121.47 W |
| Big Island | 192 | 37.32 N | 79.21 W |
| Big Island I, N.T., Can. | 176 | 62.43 N | 70.43 W |
| Big Island I, On., Can. | 184 | 49.10 N | 94.40 W |
| Big Island I, On., Can. | 212 | 44.33 N | 78.30 W |
| Big Knob ∧ | 192 | 36.40 N | 82.31 W |
| Big Koniuji Island I | 180 | 55.06 N | 159.33 W |
| Big Lake, Ak., U.S. | 180 | 61.33 N | 149.52 W |
| Big Lake, Mn., U.S. | 190 | 45.19 N | 93.44 W |
| Big Lake, Tx., U.S. | 196 | 31.11 N | 101.27 W |
| Big Lake, Wa., U.S. | 224 | 48.24 N | 122.14 W |
| Big Lake ⊜, Me., U.S. | 188 | 45.10 N | 67.40 W |
| Big Lake ⊜, Wa., U.S. | 224 | 48.23 N | 122.12 W |
| Bigler | 214 | 40.59 N | 78.19 W |
| Biglerville | 208 | 39.55 N | 77.14 W |
| Big Lick Creek ≃ | 216 | 40.22 N | 85.27 W |
| Big Lookout Mountain ∧ | 202 | 44.37 N | 117.17 W |
| Big Lost ≃ | 202 | 43.50 N | 112.44 W |
| Big Monon Ditch ≍ | 216 | 40.52 N | 86.46 W |
| Big Mossy Point › | 184 | 53.41 N | 97.57 W |
| Big Mountain ∧, B.C., Can. | 180 | 56.53 N | 131.31 W |
| Big Mountain ∧, Nv., U.S. | 204 | 41.17 N | 119.04 W |
| Big Mountain Creek ≃ | 182 | 55.04 N | 118.39 W |
| Big Muddy ≃ | 194 | 37.35 N | 89.31 W |
| Big Muddy, Casey Fork ≃ | 194 | 38.06 N | 88.57 W |
| Big Muddy Creek ≃, Mt., U.S. | 198 | 48.08 N | 104.36 W |
| Big Muddy Creek ≃, N.D., U.S. | 198 | 46.37 N | 101.24 W |
| Big Muddy Lake ⊜ | 184 | 49.08 N | 104.54 W |
| Big Muscamoot Bay c | 281 | 42.33 N | 82.40 W |
| Bignasco | 58 | 46.20 N | 8.36 E |
| Big Nasty Creek ≃ | 198 | 45.41 N | 102.51 W |
| Big Nemaha, North Fork ≃ | 198 | 40.04 N | 95.43 W |
| Bignona | 150 | 12.49 N | 16.14 W |
| Big Oak Flat | 226 | 37.49 N | 120.16 W |
| Bigot, Morne ∧[2] | 240e | 14.31 N | 61.04 W |
| Big Otter ≃ | 192 | 37.07 N | 79.23 W |
| Big Otter Creek ≃ | 212 | 42.38 N | 80.48 W |
| Big Ox Creek ≃ | 218 | 38.44 N | 85.52 W |
| Big Pine | 204 | 37.09 N | 118.17 W |
| Big Pine Creek ≃ | 216 | 40.18 N | 87.15 W |
| Big Pine Key | 220 | 24.40 N | 81.21 W |
| Big Pine Key I | 220 | 24.42 N | 81.23 W |
| Big Pine Mountain ∧ | 204 | 34.42 N | 119.39 W |
| Big Piney | 200 | 42.32 N | 110.06 W |
| Big Piney ≃ | 194 | 37.53 N | 92.04 W |
| Big Piney Creek ≃ | 194 | 35.20 N | 93.20 W |
| Big Pipe Creek ≃ | 208 | 39.36 N | 77.17 W |
| Big Plain | 218 | 39.50 N | 83.17 W |
| Big Pocono State Park ♦ | 210 | 41.03 N | 75.19 W |
| Bigpoint | 194 | 30.35 N | 88.28 W |
| Big Pond | 210 | 41.53 N | 76.43 W |
| Big Porcupine Creek ≃ | 202 | 46.16 N | 106.43 W |
| Big Porcupine Lake ⊜ | 212 | 45.27 N | 78.36 W |
| Big Prairie | 214 | 40.40 N | 82.06 W |
| Big Prairie Creek ≃ | 194 | 32.35 N | 87.45 W |
| Big Quilcene ≃ | 224 | 47.49 N | 122.52 W |
| Big Quill Lake ⊜ | 184 | 51.55 N | 104.22 W |
| Big Raccoon Creek ≃ | 194 | 39.46 N | 87.22 W |
| Big Rapids | 190 | 43.41 N | 85.29 W |
| Bigras, Île I | 275a | 45.31 N | 73.51 W |
| Big Rib ≃ | 190 | 44.56 N | 89.41 W |
| Big Rideau Lake ⊜ | 212 | 44.45 N | 76.14 W |
| Big River | 184 | 53.50 N | 107.01 W |
| Big River Indian Reserve ◆[4] | 184 | 53.33 N | 107.10 W |
| Big Rock | 216 | 41.46 N | 88.33 W |
| Big Rock Creek ≃ | 216 | 41.38 N | 88.32 W |
| Big Rocky Creek ≃ | 222 | 29.34 N | 96.50 W |
| Big Run | 214 | 40.58 N | 78.52 W |
| Big Sable ≃ | 190 | 44.02 N | 86.31 W |
| Big Sable Point › | 190 | 44.03 N | 86.31 W |
| Big Salmon ≃ | 180 | 61.52 N | 134.56 W |
| Big Salmon Range ⋏ | 180 | 61.10 N | 133.45 W |
| Big Sand Lake ⊜ | 176 | 57.45 N | 99.42 W |
| Big Sandy, Mt., U.S. | 202 | 48.10 N | 110.06 W |
| Big Sandy, Tn., U.S. | 194 | 36.14 N | 88.05 W |
| Big Sandy, Tx., U.S. | 222 | 32.35 N | 95.07 W |
| Big Sandy ≃, U.S. | 188 | 38.25 N | 82.36 W |
| Big Sandy ≃, Az., U.S. | 200 | 34.19 N | 113.31 W |
| Big Sandy ≃, Tn., U.S. | 194 | 36.15 N | 88.06 W |
| Big Sandy ≃, Wy., U.S. | 202 | 41.51 N | 109.47 W |
| Big Sandy Creek ≃, Ca., U.S. | 226 | 35.47 N | 120.43 W |
| Big Sandy Creek ≃, Co., U.S. | 198 | 38.06 N | 102.29 W |
| Big Sandy Creek ≃, Ga., U.S. | 192 | 32.42 N | 82.57 W |
| Big Sandy Creek ≃, Mt., U.S. | 202 | 48.34 N | 109.48 W |
| Big Sandy Creek ≃, Ne., U.S. | 198 | 40.13 N | 97.18 W |
| Big Sandy Creek ≃, Tx., U.S. | 196 | 33.11 N | 97.40 W |
| Big Sandy Creek ≃, Tx., U.S. | 222 | 32.33 N | 95.05 W |
| Big Sandy Creek ≃, Tx., U.S. | 222 | 30.31 N | 94.28 W |
| Big Sandy Lake ⊜, Sk., Can. | 184 | 54.26 N | 104.04 W |
| Big Sandy Lake ⊜, Mn., U.S. | 190 | 46.45 N | 93.17 W |
| Big Sandy Reservoir ⊜[1] | 200 | 42.16 N | 109.26 W |
| Big Satilla Creek ≃ | 192 | 31.27 N | 82.03 W |
| Bigsby Island I | 184 | 49.04 N | 94.35 W |
| Big Sewickley Creek ≃ | 279b | 40.35 N | 80.13 W |
| Big Shawnee Creek ≃ | 216 | 40.15 N | 87.18 W |
| Big Sheep Mountain ∧ | 202 | 47.03 N | 105.43 W |
| Big Signal Peak ∧ | 204 | 39.31 N | 123.06 W |
| Big Sinking Creek ≃ | 194 | 37.55 N | 86.31 W |
| Big Sioux ≃ | 198 | 42.30 N | 96.25 W |
| Big Sixmile Creek ≃ | 284a | 43.02 N | 79.01 W |
| Big Sky | 202 | 45.17 N | 111.17 W |
| Big Slough ≃ | 192 | 30.56 N | 84.33 W |
| Big Smoky Valley V | 204 | 38.30 N | 117.15 W |
| Big Snowy Mountains ⋏ | 202 | 46.50 N | 109.30 W |
| Big Southern Butte ∧ | 202 | 43.23 N | 113.01 W |
| Big Spanish Channel ꓵ | 220 | 24.44 N | 81.20 W |
| Bigspring, Mo., U.S. | 219 | 38.38 N | 91.28 W |
| Big Spring, Tx., U.S. | 196 | 32.15 N | 101.28 W |
| Big Springs | 198 | 41.03 N | 102.04 W |
| Big Spruce Knob ∧ | 188 | 38.16 N | 80.12 W |
| Big Squaw Mountain ∧ | 188 | 45.30 N | 69.45 W |
| Bigstick Lake ⊜ | 184 | 50.16 N | 109.20 W |
| Bigstone ≃ | 184 | 55.55 N | 94.36 W |
| Big Stone City | 198 | 45.17 N | 96.27 W |
| Big Stone Gap | 192 | 36.52 N | 82.44 W |
| Bigstone Lake ⊜, Mb., Can. | 184 | 53.42 N | 95.44 W |
| Big Stone Lake ⊜, U.S. | 198 | 45.25 N | 96.40 W |
| Big Sunflower ≃ | 194 | 32.40 N | 90.40 W |
| Big Sur | 226 | 36.16 N | 121.48 W |
| Big Sur ≃ | 226 | 36.17 N | 121.51 W |
| Big Sur ◆[1] | 226 | 35.45 N | 121.20 W |
| Big Swamp Creek ≃ | 194 | 32.19 N | 86.49 W |
| Big Swan Creek ≃ | 194 | 35.46 N | 87.24 W |
| Big Thicket National Preserve ♦ | 222 | 32.35 N | 94.40 W |
| Big Thompson ≃ | 200 | 40.21 N | 104.45 W |
| Big Timber | 202 | 45.50 N | 109.57 W |
| Big Timber Creek ≃ | 285 | 39.53 N | 75.08 W |
| Big Timber Creek, North Branch ≃ | 285 | 39.50 N | 75.05 W |
| Big Timber Creek, South Branch ≃ | 285 | 39.50 N | 75.05 W |
| Big Torch Key I | 220 | 24.43 N | 81.26 W |
| Big Tree | 210 | 42.46 N | 78.49 W |
| Big Trout Lake ⊜, On., Can. | 176 | 53.45 N | 90.00 W |
| Big Trout Lake ⊜, On., Can. | 212 | 44.56 N | 78.56 W |
| Big Tujunga Canyon V | 228 | 34.16 N | 118.18 W |
| Big Tujunga Dam ◆[6] | 280 | 34.18 N | 118.12 W |
| Biguaçu | 252 | 27.30 S | 48.40 W |
| Big Valley | 182 | 52.02 N | 112.46 W |
| Bigwa | 154 | 7.13 S | 39.09 E |
| Big Walnut Creek ≃, In., U.S. | 194 | 39.30 N | 86.57 W |
| Big Walnut Creek ≃, Oh., U.S. | 218 | 39.48 N | 83.01 W |
| Big Warrambool ≃ | 166 | 30.05 S | 147.33 E |
| Big Water | 200 | 37.05 N | 111.41 W |
| Big Wells | 196 | 28.34 N | 99.34 W |
| Big White Mountain ∧ | 182 | 49.42 N | 118.58 W |
| Big Wills Creek ≃ | 194 | 33.59 N | 86.00 W |
| Big Wood ≃ | 202 | 42.52 N | 114.54 W |
| Bihać | 36 | 44.49 N | 15.52 E |
| Bīhar | 124 | 25.11 N | 85.31 E |
| Bihār □[3] | 124 | 25.00 N | 86.00 E |
| Biharamulo | 154 | 2.38 S | 31.20 E |
| Bihārīganj | 124 | 25.44 N | 86.59 E |
| Bihor □[6] | 38 | 47.00 N | 22.15 E |
| Bihor, Vârful ∧ | 38 | 46.27 N | 22.42 E |
| Bihoro | 92a | 43.49 N | 144.07 E |
| Bihosava | 76 | 55.49 N | 27.43 E |
| Bihu | 100 | 28.21 N | 119.48 E |
| Bihun | 78 | 51.24 N | 28.17 E |
| Bija ≃ | 86 | 52.25 N | 85.05 E |
| Bijagós, Arquipélago dos II | 150 | 11.25 N | 16.20 W |
| Bijainagar | 120 | 25.56 N | 74.38 E |
| Bijaipur | 124 | 26.03 N | 77.22 E |
| Bijaipura | 124 | 24.46 N | 77.48 E |
| Bijāpur | 122 | 16.50 N | 75.42 E |
| Bījār | 128 | 35.52 N | 47.36 E |
| Bijāwar | 124 | 24.38 N | 79.30 E |
| Bijbān Chāh | 128 | 26.54 N | 64.42 E |
| Bījbiāra | 123 | 33.48 N | 75.06 E |
| Bijeljina | 38 | 44.45 N | 19.13 E |
| Bijelo Polje | 38 | 43.02 N | 19.44 E |
| Bijiang | 110 | 26.30 N | 98.55 E |
| Bijia Shan ∧ | 105 | 40.17 N | 116.50 E |
| Bijie | 102 | 27.18 N | 105.20 E |
| Bijlikol', ozero ⊜ | 85 | 43.03 N | 70.41 E |
| Bijna | 272b | 22.55 N | 88.27 E |
| Bijni | 124 | 26.31 N | 90.40 E |
| Bijnor | 124 | 29.22 N | 78.08 E |
| Bijōki | 268 | 35.49 N | 139.39 E |
| Bijou Creek ≃ | 198 | 40.17 N | 103.52 W |
| Bijpur | 126 | 22.56 N | 88.26 E |
| Bijsk | 86 | 52.34 N | 85.15 E |
| Bijwāsan ◆[8] | 272a | 28.32 N | 77.03 E |
| Bīkāner | 120 | 28.01 N | 73.18 E |
| Bīkaner Canal ≍ | 123 | 30.08 N | 73.57 E |
| Bikar I[1] | 14 | 12.15 N | 170.06 E |
| Bikbulovo | 80 | 55.39 N | 53.26 E |
| Bike | 144 | 9.30 N | 41.18 E |
| Bikeman Island I | 174t | 1.22 N | 173.00 E |
| Bikenibeu | 174t | 1.21 N | 173.07 E |
| Bikeqi | 102 | 40.45 N | 111.17 E |
| Bikeru | 112 | 5.15 S | 120.07 E |
| Bikfayyā | 132 | 33.55 N | 35.41 E |
| Bikié | 152 | 3.06 S | 13.52 E |
| Bikin | 89 | 46.48 N | 134.16 E |
| Bikin ≃ | 89 | 46.51 N | 134.02 E |
| Bikini I[1] | 14 | 11.35 N | 165.23 E |
| Bikita | 154 | 20.06 S | 31.41 E |
| Bīkkū Bīttī ∧ | 146 | 22.00 N | 19.12 E |
| Bikl'an' | 80 | 55.37 N | 52.10 E |
| Bikoro | 152 | 0.45 S | 18.07 E |
| Bikuar, Parque Nacional do ♦ | 152 | 15.12 S | 14.42 E |
| Bila ≃, Indon. | 114 | 2.30 N | 100.08 E |
| Bila ≃, Ukr. | 83 | 49.18 N | 38.52 E |
| Bila ≃, Ukr. | 83 | 48.35 N | 39.10 E |
| Bilaa Point › | 116 | 9.49 N | 125.26 E |
| Bilac | 255 | 21.24 S | 50.28 W |
| Bilād Zahrān ◆[1] | 144 | 20.16 N | 41.14 E |
| Bílá hora ⊥ | 54 | 50.05 N | 14.20 E |
| Bila Krynytsya, Ukr. | 78 | 47.21 N | 33.10 E |
| Bila Krynytsya, Ukr. | 78 | 50.38 N | 29.29 E |
| Bilang, Teluk c | 112 | 1.15 N | 121.25 E |
| Bilanga | 150 | 12.32 N | 0.02 E |
| Bilāra | 120 | 26.10 N | 73.42 E |
| Bilāri | 124 | 28.38 N | 78.48 E |
| Bil'arsk | 80 | 54.58 N | 50.22 E |
| Bilāsipāra | 124 | 26.14 N | 90.14 E |
| Bilāspur, India | 123 | 31.20 N | 76.45 E |
| Bilāspur, India | 124 | 28.53 N | 79.16 E |
| Bilāspur, India | 124 | 22.05 N | 82.09 E |
| Biläsuvar, Azer. | 84 | 39.24 N | 48.24 E |
| Biläsuvar (Pushkino), Azer. | 84 | 39.27 N | 48.33 E |
| Bilatan Island I | 116 | 4.59 N | 120.00 E |
| Bilato | 112 | 0.32 N | 122.38 E |
| Bila Tserkva | 78 | 49.49 N | 30.07 E |
| Bilauktaung Range ⋏ | 110 | 13.00 N | 99.00 E |
| Bilbao | 34 | 43.15 N | 2.58 W |
| Bilbays | 142 | 30.25 N | 31.34 E |
| Bilbays Military Base ■ | 142 | 30.24 N | 31.36 E |
| Bilbilis ⊥ | 34 | 41.25 N | 1.39 W |
| Bil'čir | 88 | 51.02 N | 110.34 E |
| Bile | 83 | 48.31 N | 39.04 E |
| Bileća | 38 | 42.53 N | 18.26 E |
| Bilecik | 130 | 40.09 N | 29.59 E |
| Bilecik □[4] | 130 | 40.10 N | 30.10 E |
| Bilen'ka ≃ | 83 | 48.53 N | 38.29 E |
| Bilen'ke, Ukr. | 78 | 47.37 N | 35.03 E |
| Bilen'ke, Ukr. | 83 | 48.46 N | 37.38 E |
| Biles Island I | 285 | 40.10 N | 74.45 W |
| Biłgoraj | 30 | 50.34 N | 22.43 E |
| Bilgrām | 124 | 27.11 N | 80.02 E |
| Bilhorod-Dnistrovs'kyy | 78 | 46.12 N | 30.20 E |
| Bili | 154 | 4.09 N | 25.10 E |
| Bili ≃ | 136 | 4.09 N | 22.29 E |
| Bilian | 100 | 28.21 N | 120.33 E |
| Bilifyā | 142 | 29.07 N | 31.03 E |
| Bīlimora | 120 | 20.45 N | 72.57 E |
| Bilin | 110 | 17.14 N | 97.15 E |
| Bilin ≃ | 110 | 17.05 N | 97.08 E |
| Bílina | 54 | 50.35 N | 13.45 E |
| Bílina ≃ | 54 | 50.40 N | 14.02 E |
| Bilioso ≃ | 68 | 40.39 N | 16.24 E |
| Biliran Island I | 116 | 11.35 N | 124.28 E |
| Biliran Strait ꓵ | 116 | 11.30 N | 124.28 E |
| Biliri | 146 | 9.52 N | 11.13 E |
| Biliu ≃ | 98 | 39.30 N | 122.36 E |
| Bilk ◆[8] | 263 | 51.12 N | 6.47 E |
| Bilky | 78 | 50.49 N | 28.11 E |
| Billabong Creek ≃ | 166 | 35.06 S | 144.02 E |
| Billeberga | 41 | 55.53 N | 13.00 E |
| Billerbeck | 52 | 51.59 N | 7.17 E |
| Billerica | 207 | 42.33 N | 71.16 W |
| Billericay | 42 | 51.38 N | 0.25 E |
| Billesdon | 42 | 52.37 N | 0.55 W |
| Billesholm | 41 | 56.03 N | 13.00 E |
| Billiat | 58 | 46.04 N | 5.47 E |
| Billigheim | 56 | 49.21 N | 9.15 E |
| Billiluna | 162 | 19.37 S | 127.41 E |
| Billinge, Sve. | 41 | 55.58 N | 13.21 E |
| Billinge, Eng., U.K. | 262 | 53.30 N | 2.42 W |
| Billingen ⋏[2] | 26 | 58.24 N | 13.45 E |
| Billingham | 44 | 54.36 N | 1.17 W |
| Billings, Mo., U.S. | 194 | 37.04 N | 93.33 W |
| Billings, Mt., U.S. | 202 | 45.46 N | 108.30 W |
| Billings, Ok., U.S. | 196 | 36.31 N | 97.26 W |
| Billings, Reprêsa ⊜[1] | 256 | 23.47 S | 46.37 W |
| Billingsfors | 26 | 58.59 N | 12.15 E |
| Billings Heights | 202 | 45.50 N | 108.32 W |
| Billingshurst | 42 | 51.01 N | 0.28 W |
| Billmerich | 263 | 51.30 N | 7.41 E |
| Billolo ≃ | 273b | 4.07 S | 15.19 E |
| Billom | 32 | 45.44 N | 3.21 E |
| Billund | 41 | 55.44 N | 9.07 E |
| Bill Williams ≃ | 200 | 34.17 N | 114.03 W |
| Bill Williams Mountain ∧ | 200 | 35.12 N | 112.12 W |
| Billy Chinook, Lake ⊜[1] | 202 | 44.33 N | 121.20 W |
| Billy-Montigny | 50 | 50.25 N | 2.52 E |
| Bilma | 146 | 18.41 N | 12.56 E |
| Biloela | 166 | 24.24 S | 150.30 E |
| Bilo Gora ⋏ | 36 | 46.06 N | 16.46 E |
| Bilohirs'k | 78 | 45.03 N | 34.36 E |
| Bilohir'ya | 78 | 50.01 N | 26.25 E |
| Bilohorivka | 83 | 48.55 N | 38.15 E |
| Bilohorodka | 78 | 50.00 N | 26.39 E |
| Bilokurakine | 83 | 49.33 N | 38.44 E |
| Biloluts'k | 83 | 49.41 N | 39.02 E |
| Bilopillya | 78 | 51.09 N | 34.18 E |
| Bilousivka | 78 | 49.57 N | 32.20 E |
| Bilovods'k | 83 | 49.12 N | 39.35 E |
| Biloxi | 194 | 30.23 N | 88.53 W |
| Biloxi ≃ | 194 | 30.26 N | 89.00 W |
| Biloxi Creek ≃ | 222 | 31.05 N | 94.37 W |
| Bilozerka | 78 | 46.37 N | 32.27 E |
| Bilozers'ke | 78 | 48.33 N | 37.04 E |
| Bilozir'ya, Ukr. | 78 | 49.29 N | 31.35 E |
| Bilozir'ya, Ukr. | 78 | 49.18 N | 31.54 E |
| Bilpa Morea Claypan ≚ | 166 | 25.00 S | 140.00 E |
| Bilpin | 170 | 33.30 S | 150.31 E |
| Bilqās Qism Awwal | 142 | 31.13 N | 31.21 E |
| Bilsārā | 126 | 23.05 N | 88.10 E |
| Bil'sha Kam'yanka ≃ | 83 | 48.22 N | 40.04 E |
| Bilshausen | 52 | 51.37 N | 10.10 E |
| Bil'shivtsi | 78 | 49.12 N | 24.44 E |
| Bilsi | 124 | 28.08 N | 78.55 E |
| Bil's'ka Volya | 78 | 51.27 N | 25.49 E |
| Bilston | 42 | 52.34 N | 2.04 W |
| Biltāj | 142 | 31.00 N | 30.59 E |
| Bilthoven | 52 | 52.07 N | 5.17 E |
| Biltine | 146 | 14.32 N | 20.55 E |
| Biltine □[5] | 146 | 15.00 N | 21.00 E |
| Biltmore Forest | 192 | 35.32 N | 82.31 W |
| Bilugyun Island I | 110 | 16.24 N | 97.32 E |
| Bilwaskarma | 236 | 14.45 N | 83.53 W |
| Bilyayivka | 78 | 46.29 N | 30.12 E |
| Bilychi | 78 | 50.29 N | 30.19 E |
| Bilyky | 78 | 49.15 N | 34.16 E |
| Bilyts'ke | 83 | 48.25 N | 37.13 E |
| Bilyy Kolodyaz' | 78 | 50.12 N | 37.08 E |
| Bilzen | 56 | 50.52 N | 5.31 E |
| Bima | 115b | 8.28 S | 118.43 E |
| Bimbān | 140 | 24.26 N | 32.53 E |
| Bimbe | 152 | 11.49 S | 15.49 E |
| Bimberi Peak ∧ | 171b | 35.40 S | 148.47 E |
| Bimbila | 150 | 8.51 N | 0.04 E |
| Bimbo | 152 | 4.18 N | 18.33 E |
| Bimbowrie | 166 | 32.03 S | 140.09 E |
| Bimé | 273b | 4.09 S | 15.11 E |
| Bimini Islands II | 192 | 25.42 N | 79.15 W |
| Bin ≃ | 100 | 23.40 N | 112.58 E |
| Bina | 175e | 8.55 S | 160.46 E |
| Bīna-Etāwa | 124 | 24.11 N | 78.11 E |
| Binaiya, Gunung ∧ | 164 | 3.11 S | 129.26 E |
| Binalbagan | 116 | 10.12 N | 122.50 E |
| Binalbagan ≃ | 116 | 10.12 N | 122.51 E |
| Bin'an | 89 | 45.50 N | 127.45 E |
| Binanga | 114 | 1.24 N | 99.46 E |
| Binangonan | 116 | 14.28 N | 121.11 E |
| Binas | 50 | 47.54 N | 1.28 E |
| Binasco | 62 | 45.20 N | 9.06 E |
| Binau | 56 | 49.22 N | 9.04 E |
| Binche | 50 | 50.24 N | 4.10 E |
| Binchuan | 102 | 25.46 N | 100.33 E |
| Bindal | 24 | 65.06 N | 12.30 E |
| Binder, Mong. | 88 | 48.35 N | 110.36 E |
| Binder, Tchad | 146 | 9.58 N | 14.28 E |
| Bindki | 124 | 26.02 N | 80.36 E |
| Bindlach | 60 | 49.59 N | 11.37 E |
| Bindloss | 184 | 50.52 N | 110.16 W |
| Bindo, Mount ∧ | 170 | 33.40 S | 150.01 E |
| Bindow | 264a | 52.17 N | 13.45 E |
| Bindura | 154 | 17.19 S | 31.20 E |
| Bine-el-Ouidane | 148 | 32.07 N | 6.26 W |
| Binéfar | 34 | 41.51 N | 0.18 E |
| Binford | 198 | 47.33 N | 98.20 W |
| Binga, Pil. | 116 | 10.45 N | 119.19 E |
| Binga, Zaïre | 152 | 2.23 N | 20.30 E |
| Binga, Monte ∧ | 156 | 19.45 S | 33.04 E |
| Bingara | 166 | 29.52 S | 150.34 E |
| Bingaram Island I | 122 | 10.56 N | 72.17 E |
| Bingay Point › | 116 | 13.04 N | 124.11 E |
| Bingcha | 100 | 32.30 N | 120.52 E |
| Bingen, Dtsch. | 56 | 49.57 N | 7.54 E |
| Bingen, Wa., U.S. | 224 | 45.42 N | 121.27 W |
| Binger | 196 | 35.18 N | 98.20 W |
| Bingerbrück | 56 | 49.58 N | 7.53 E |
| Bingerville | 150 | 5.21 N | 3.54 W |
| Bingfang | 106 | 32.15 N | 121.20 E |
| Bingham, Eng., U.K. | 42 | 52.57 N | 0.57 W |
| Bingham, Me., U.S. | 188 | 45.03 N | 69.52 W |
| Bingham ≃ | 168a | 33.20 S | 116.16 E |
| Bingham Farms | 281 | 42.32 N | 83.16 W |
| Binghamton | 210 | 42.05 N | 75.55 W |
| Bin Ghashīr | 146 | 32.41 N | 13.11 E |
| Bin Ghunaymah, Jabal ⋏ | 146 | 25.00 N | 15.30 E |
| Bingi | 154 | 0.24 S | 29.05 E |
| Bingley | 44 | 53.51 N | 1.50 W |
| Bingöl | 130 | 38.53 N | 40.29 E |
| Bingöl □[4] | 130 | 39.00 N | 40.40 E |
| Bingöl Dağları ⋏ | 130 | 39.20 N | 41.20 E |
| Binhai (Dongkan) | 100 | 34.03 N | 119.51 E |
| Binh Ca | 110 | 21.48 N | 105.18 E |
| Binh Chanh | 269c | 10.40 N | 106.34 E |
| Binh Gia | 110 | 21.59 N | 106.21 E |
| Binh Hung Hoa | 269c | 10.49 N | 106.37 E |
| Binh Khe | 110 | 13.57 N | 108.51 E |
| Binh Kieu | 110 | 15.35 N | 108.04 E |
| Bin-Houyé | 150 | 6.47 N | 8.19 W |
| Binh Son | 110 | 15.18 N | 108.46 E |
| Binh Trung | 269c | 10.47 N | 106.46 E |
| Binigsian Point › | 116 | 9.50 N | 122.23 E |
| Bining | 56 | 49.02 N | 7.15 E |
| Binjai, Indon. | 112 | 3.48 N | 108.14 E |
| Binjai, Indon. | 114 | 3.36 N | 98.30 E |
| Binjohara | 114 | 2.12 N | 98.12 E |
| Bīnlūd, Kūh-e ⋏ | 128 | 36.28 N | 58.49 E |
| Binna Burra | 171a | 28.13 S | 153.14 E |
| Binnah, Ras › | 144 | 11.08 N | 51.10 E |
| Binnaway | 166 | 31.33 S | 149.23 E |
| Binnian, Slieve ∧ | 48 | 54.08 N | 5.58 W |
| Binningen | 58 | 47.32 N | 7.34 E |
| Binodepur | 126 | 23.26 N | 89.30 E |
| Binongko, Pulau I | 112 | 5.57 S | 124.02 E |
| Binpur | 126 | 22.36 N | 86.55 E |
| Binscarth | 184 | 50.37 N | 101.16 W |
| Binsheim ◆[8] | 263 | 51.31 N | 6.42 E |
| Bintan, Pulau I | 112 | 1.05 N | 104.30 E |
| Bintang | 150 | 13.10 N | 16.08 W |
| Bintang, Gunong ∧ | 114 | 5.25 N | 100.52 E |
| Bintauna | 112 | 0.53 N | 123.33 E |
| Bint Goda | 140 | 13.17 N | 31.33 E |
| Bintimani ∧ | 150 | 9.13 N | 11.07 W |
| Bint Jubayl | 132 | 33.07 N | 35.26 E |
| Bintuhan | 112 | 4.48 S | 103.22 E |
| Bintulu | 112 | 3.10 N | 113.02 E |
| Bintuni | 164 | 2.07 S | 133.32 E |
| Bintuni, Teluk c | 164 | 2.20 S | 133.30 E |
| Binxian, Zhg. | 89 | 45.44 N | 127.29 E |
| Binxian, Zhg. | 98 | 37.28 N | 117.56 E |
| Binxian, Zhg. | 102 | 35.00 N | 108.08 E |
| Binyamina | 132 | 32.31 N | 34.57 E |
| Binyang | 102 | 23.18 N | 108.46 E |
| Bin Yauri | 150 | 10.47 N | 4.50 E |
| Binz | 54 | 54.24 N | 13.36 E |
| Binza | 273b | 4.21 S | 15.14 E |
| Binza ◆[8] | 273b | 4.20 S | 15.14 E |
| Binza ≃ | 273b | 4.21 S | 15.14 E |
| Bio Addo | 144 | 8.18 N | 49.48 E |
| Bíobío □[4] | 252 | 37.00 S | 72.30 W |
| Bíobío ≃, Chile | 252 | 36.49 S | 73.10 W |
| Bíobío ≃, Chile | 252 | 31.38 S | 71.34 W |
| Biodi | 154 | 3.19 N | 28.35 E |
| Biograd | 36 | 43.56 N | 15.27 E |
| Biogradska Gora Nacionalni Park ♦ | 38 | 42.57 N | 19.40 E |
| Bioko □[4] | 152 | 3.30 N | 8.40 E |
| Bioko I | 152 | 3.30 N | 8.40 E |
| Biola | 226 | 36.48 N | 120.00 W |
| Bionaz | 62 | 45.52 N | 7.25 E |
| Biondo | 154 | 0.23 S | 25.13 E |
| Biondo Monument ⊥ | 146 | 31.25 N | 10.15 E |
| Biot | 62 | 43.38 N | 7.06 E |
| Bipindi | 152 | 3.05 N | 10.25 E |
| Bippen | 52 | 52.35 N | 7.44 E |
| Bippus | 216 | 40.56 N | 85.37 W |
| Biqiao | 106 | 31.02 N | 119.02 E |
| Bir, Ras › | 144 | 11.59 N | 43.22 E |
| Bira, India | 272b | 22.47 N | 88.34 E |
| Bira, Ross. | 89 | 49.15 N | 137.16 E |
| Bira, Ross. | 89 | 49.02 N | 132.30 E |
| Bira ≃ | 89 | 48.07 N | 133.21 E |
| Birab | 164 | 6.12 S | 138.25 E |
| Bīraba | 126 | 23.51 N | 90.34 E |
| Birāk | 146 | 27.32 N | 14.16 E |
| Birakan | 89 | 49.01 N | 131.42 E |
| Bi'r 'Alī | 144 | 14.01 N | 48.19 E |
| Bi'r al-Uzam | 146 | 31.54 N | 23.58 E |
| Birandža | 89 | 54.35 N | 136.18 E |
| Birao | 146 | 10.17 N | 22.47 E |
| Birati | 272b | 22.39 N | 88.27 E |
| Birava | 154 | 2.21 S | 28.54 E |
| Bircao → Buur Gaabo | 144 | 1.12 S | 41.51 E |
| Birch | 262 | 53.34 N | 2.13 W |
| Birch ≃, Ab., Can. | 176 | 58.30 N | 112.15 W |
| Birch ≃, W.V., U.S. | 188 | 38.35 N | 80.53 W |
| Birch Bay | 224 | 48.55 N | 122.45 W |
| Birch Bay c | 224 | 48.53 N | 122.47 W |
| Birch Bay State Park ♦ | 224 | 49.54 N | 123.47 W |
| Birch Cliff ◆[8] | 275b | 43.41 N | 79.17 W |
| Birch Creek ≃, Ak., U.S. | 180 | 66.30 N | 146.30 W |
| Birch Creek ≃, Id., U.S. | 202 | 43.51 N | 112.43 W |
| Birch Creek ≃, Mt., U.S. | 202 | 48.26 N | 112.15 W |
| Birch Creek ≃, Mt., U.S. | 202 | 47.45 N | 109.34 W |
| Birch Hill Dam ◆[6] | 207 | 42.38 N | 72.09 W |
| Birch Hills | 184 | 52.59 N | 105.25 W |
| Birchington | 42 | 51.23 N | 1.19 E |
| Birch Island | 182 | 51.36 N | 119.55 W |
| Birch Island I | 184 | 52.25 N | 99.55 W |
| Birch Lake ⊜, Ab., Can. | 182 | 53.19 N | 111.35 W |
| Birch Lake ⊜, On., Can. | 184 | 51.24 N | 92.20 W |
| Birch Lake ⊜, Sk., Can. | 184 | 53.28 N | 108.07 W |
| Birch Mountains ⋏[2] | 176 | 57.30 N | 112.30 W |
| Bir Chouhada | 34 | 35.53 N | 6.18 E |
| Birch Pond ⊜ | 283 | 42.28 N | 71.00 W |
| Birch Reservoir ⊜[1] | 196 | 36.31 N | 96.12 W |
| Birch River | 184 | 52.23 N | 101.06 W |
| Birch Run | 190 | 43.15 N | 83.47 W |
| Birch Run ≃ | 285 | 40.09 N | 75.37 W |
| Birchrunville | 285 | 40.08 N | 75.39 W |
| Birch Tree | 194 | 36.59 N | 91.29 W |
| Birch Vale | 262 | 53.23 N | 1.57 W |
| Birchwood, Eng., U.K. | 44 | 53.13 N | 0.36 W |
| Birchwood, Ak., U.S. | 180 | 61.28 N | 149.22 W |
| Birchwood, Wi., U.S. | 190 | 45.39 N | 91.33 W |
| Birchwood City | 284c | 38.49 N | 76.59 W |
| Birchwood Park, De., U.S. | 285 | 39.22 N | 75.39 W |
| Birchwood Park, N.J., U.S. | 208 | 40.06 N | 74.09 W |
| Birchy Bay | 186 | 49.21 N | 54.44 W |
| Bird City | 198 | 39.45 N | 101.31 W |
| Bird Creek ≃ | 196 | 36.13 N | 95.44 W |
| Bird Island | 198 | 44.46 N | 94.53 W |
| Bird Island I, S. Afr. | 158 | 33.51 S | 26.18 E |
| Bird Island I, S. Geor. | 244 | 54.00 S | 38.05 W |
| Bird Island ʊ[3] | 9 | 54.00 S | 38.03 W |
| Bird Islet I | 160 | 22.10 S | 155.28 E |
| Bird River c | 284b | 39.23 N | 76.23 W |
| Birdsall | 210 | 42.23 N | 77.55 W |
| Birdsboro | 208 | 40.15 N | 75.48 W |
| Birds Landing | 282 | 38.08 N | 121.52 W |
| Birdsview | 224 | 48.32 N | 121.52 W |
| Birdsville | 166 | 25.54 S | 139.22 E |
| Birdtail Creek ≃ | 184 | 50.16 N | 101.12 W |
| Birdum | 164 | 15.39 S | 133.13 E |
| Birdum Creek ≃ | 164 | 15.14 S | 133.00 E |
| Birdwood | 168b | 34.49 S | 138.57 E |
| Birecik | 130 | 37.02 N | 37.58 E |
| Bire Kpatua Game Reserve ◆[4] | 154 | 5.12 N | 27.36 E |
| Bir el Ater | 148 | 34.44 N | 8.03 E |
| Bir Enzaran | 148 | 23.56 N | 14.33 W |
| Bireuen | 114 | 5.12 N | 96.41 E |
| Bir Ghbalou | 34 | 36.16 N | 3.35 E |
| Birgi | 126 | 22.42 N | 86.41 E |
| Birgi Vecchi | 70 | 37.53 N | 12.29 E |
| Biri | 116 | 12.41 N | 124.22 E |
| Birigui | 255 | 21.18 S | 50.19 W |
| Biri Island I | 116 | 12.40 N | 124.22 E |
| Birikčul' | 86 | 53.20 N | 89.56 E |
| Biril'ussy | 86 | 57.07 N | 90.32 E |
| Birimbāl | 142 | 31.21 N | 30.30 E |
| Birimbāl al-Qadīmah | 142 | 31.10 N | 31.44 E |
| Birimşe | 130 | 38.03 N | 38.32 E |
| Biritiba-Mirim | 256 | 23.35 S | 46.02 W |
| Bīrjand | 128 | 32.53 N | 59.13 E |
| Birkat as-Sab' | 142 | 30.38 N | 31.05 E |
| Birkat Ghiṭās | 142 | 31.07 N | 30.16 E |
| Birkdale | 262 | 53.37 N | 3.02 W |
| Birkeland | 26 | 58.20 N | 8.14 E |
| Birken | 182 | 50.29 N | 122.36 W |
| Birkenau | 56 | 49.34 N | 8.43 E |
| Birkendorf | 58 | 47.45 N | 8.18 E |
| Birkenfeld, Dtsch. | 56 | 48.52 N | 8.38 E |
| Birkenfeld, Dtsch. | 56 | 49.51 N | 9.42 E |
| Birkenfeld, Dtsch. | 56 | 49.39 N | 7.10 E |
| Birkenfeld, Or., U.S. | 224 | 45.59 N | 123.20 W |
| Birkenhead | 44 | 53.24 N | 3.02 W |
| Birkenhead Park ♦ | 262 | 53.24 N | 3.02 W |
| Birkenwerder bei Berlin | 54 | 52.41 N | 13.16 E |
| Birkerød | 41 | 55.50 N | 12.26 E |
| Birket Fatimé | 146 | 12.54 N | 19.05 E |
| Birkfeld | 61 | 47.21 N | 15.42 E |
| Birkholz | 264a | 52.38 N | 13.34 E |
| Birkkarspitze ∧ | 64 | 47.25 N | 11.25 E |
| Birk-Nack › | 41 | 54.48 N | 9.55 E |
| Birksgate Range ⋏ | 162 | 27.10 S | 129.45 E |
| Birky | 78 | 49.42 N | 36.02 E |
| Birla Museum ʊ | 272b | 22.32 N | 88.22 E |
| Birlik, Kaz. | 80 | 47.28 N | 50.32 E |


ENGLISH


| Name | Page | Lat.°′ | Long.°′ |
|---|---|---|---|
| Birlik, Kaz. | 86 | 44.05 N | 73.31 E |
| Birling | 260 | 51.19 N | 0.25 E |
| Birling ∧[2] | 274a | 33.57 S | 150.43 E |
| Birmā | 142 | 30.51 N | 30.54 E |
| Birmania → Myanmar □[1] | 110 | 22.00 N | 98.00 E |
| Birmanie → Myanmar □[1] | 110 | 22.00 N | 98.00 E |
| Birmingham, Eng., U.K. | 42 | 52.28 N | 1.55 W |
| Birmingham, Al., U.S. | 194 | 33.31 N | 86.48 W |
| Birmingham, Ia., U.S. | 190 | 40.52 N | 91.56 W |
| Birmingham, Mi., U.S. | 216 | 42.32 N | 83.12 W |
| Birmingham, N.J., U.S. | 285 | 39.58 N | 74.42 W |
| Birmingham, Oh., U.S. | 214 | 41.20 N | 82.21 W |
| Birmingham, Pa., U.S. | 214 | 40.38 N | 78.13 W |
| Birmingham Airport ⊠ | 42 | 52.27 N | 1.45 W |
| Birmitrapur | 124 | 22.24 N | 84.46 E |
| Bîr Mogreïn (Fort-Trinquet) | 148 | 25.14 N | 11.35 W |
| Birnagar | 126 | 23.14 N | 88.33 E |
| Birnamwood | 190 | 44.56 N | 89.12 W |
| Birnbaum | 64 | 46.41 N | 12.54 E |
| Birni | 150 | 10.00 N | 1.31 E |
| Birnie I[1] | 14 | 3.35 S | 171.31 W |
| Birni Ngaouré | 150 | 13.05 N | 2.54 E |
| Birnin Gwari | 150 | 11.01 N | 6.48 E |
| Birnin Kebbi | 150 | 12.32 N | 4.12 E |
| Birni Nkonni | 150 | 13.48 N | 5.15 E |
| Birnin Kudu | 150 | 11.27 N | 9.30 E |
| Birobidžan | 89 | 48.48 N | 132.57 E |
| Birobijan → Jevrej □[3] | 89 | 48.30 N | 132.00 E |
| Birofel'd | 89 | 48.26 N | 132.47 E |
| Birome | 222 | 31.49 N | 96.58 W |
| Birqāsh | 142 | 30.10 N | 31.02 E |
| Birr | 48 | 53.05 N | 7.54 W |
| Birregurra | 169 | 38.20 S | 143.48 E |
| Birrie ≃ | 166 | 29.43 S | 146.37 E |
| Birrindudu | 162 | 18.22 S | 129.27 E |
| Birs (Birse) ≃ | 58 | 47.22 N | 7.22 E |
| Birsk | 86 | 55.25 N | 55.32 E |
| Birstall | 42 | 52.41 N | 1.07 W |
| Birstein | 56 | 50.21 N | 9.19 E |
| Birštonas | 76 | 54.37 N | 24.02 E |
| Birten | 263 | 51.38 N | 6.29 E |
| Birtle | 184 | 50.25 N | 101.03 W |
| Birtley | 44 | 54.54 N | 1.34 W |
| Biru | 120 | 31.30 N | 93.51 E |
| Bir'učij | 83 | 46.53 N | 39.33 E |
| Bir'učja ≃ | 83 | 47.23 N | 39.07 E |
| Birufu | 164 | 5.52 S | 138.24 E |
| Bir'ul'ka | 88 | 53.52 N | 106.21 E |
| Bir'ul'ovo ◆[8] | 265b | 55.35 N | 37.40 E |
| Birungu, Parc des ♦ | 154 | 1.25 S | 29.30 E |
| Birūr | 122 | 13.37 N | 75.58 E |
| Bir'usa | 88 | 57.10 N | 96.30 E |
| Bir'usa (Ona) ≃ | 88 | 57.43 N | 95.24 E |
| Bir'usinsk | 88 | 55.57 N | 97.49 E |
| Biryukove | 83 | 47.57 N | 39.44 E |
| Biržai | 76 | 56.12 N | 24.45 E |
| Bîrzava ≃ | 38 | 45.16 N | 20.49 E |
| Birżebbuġa | 36 | 35.49 N | 14.32 E |
| Bisa, Pulau I | 164 | 1.15 S | 127.28 E |
| Bisaccia | 68 | 41.01 N | 15.22 E |
| Bisacquino | 70 | 37.42 N | 13.15 E |
| Bisāi, India | 126 | 22.10 N | 86.24 E |
| Bisai, Nihon | 94 | 35.16 N | 136.44 E |
| Bīsalpur | 124 | 28.18 N | 79.48 E |
| Bisamberg | 264b | 48.20 N | 16.22 E |
| Bisamberg ∧[2] | 264b | 48.19 N | 16.22 E |
| Bisan-shotō II | 96 | 34.24 N | 133.50 E |
| Bisbee, Az., U.S. | 200 | 31.26 N | 109.55 W |
| Bisbee, N.D., U.S. | 198 | 48.37 N | 99.22 W |
| Biscarrosse | 32 | 44.24 N | 1.10 W |
| Biscarrosse et de Parentis, Lac de c | 32 | 44.20 N | 1.10 W |
| Biscay, Bay of c | 32 | 44.00 N | 4.00 W |
| Biscayne, Key I | 220 | 25.42 N | 80.10 W |
| Biscayne Bay c | 220 | 25.33 N | 80.15 W |
| Biscayne National Park ♦ | 220 | 25.25 N | 80.12 W |
| Bisceglie | 68 | 41.14 N | 16.31 E |
| Bischheim | 58 | 48.37 N | 7.45 E |
| Bischofsgrün | 60 | 50.03 N | 11.47 E |
| Bischofsheim, Dtsch. | 56 | 50.24 N | 10.01 E |
| Bischofsheim, Dtsch. | 56 | 49.59 N | 8.22 E |
| Bischofshofen | 64 | 47.25 N | 13.13 E |
| Bischofsmais | 60 | 48.55 N | 13.05 E |
| Bischofswerda | 54 | 51.07 N | 14.10 E |
| Bischofswiesen | 64 | 47.39 N | 12.57 E |
| Bischofszell | 58 | 47.29 N | 9.15 E |
| Bischwald, Étang de ⊜ | 56 | 49.00 N | 6.42 E |
| Bischwiller | 56 | 48.46 N | 7.52 E |
| Biscoe, Ar., U.S. | 194 | 34.49 N | 91.24 W |
| Biscoe, N.C., U.S. | 192 | 35.21 N | 79.46 W |
| Biscoe Islands II | 9 | 66.00 S | 66.30 W |
| Biscotasi Lake ⊜ | 190 | 47.19 N | 82.07 W |
| Biscucuy | 246 | 9.22 N | 69.59 W |
| Bise | 174m | 26.42 N | 127.54 E |
| Bisei | 96 | 34.41 N | 133.33 E |
| Bisentina, Isola I | 66 | 42.35 N | 11.54 E |
| Bisenzio ≃ | 66 | 43.46 N | 11.06 E |
| Biser | 86 | 58.25 N | 58.53 E |
| Biserovo | 265b | 55.47 N | 38.07 E |
| Biserovskoje, ozero ⊜ | 265b | 55.46 N | 38.07 E |
| Bisert' ≃ | 86 | 56.39 N | 57.55 E |
| Bise-zaki › | 174m | 26.43 N | 127.53 E |
| Bisha | 144 | 15.28 N | 37.34 E |
| Bīshah, Wādī V | 144 | 21.24 N | 43.26 E |
| Bishahari | 126 | 23.10 N | 89.01 E |
| Bishan | 107 | 29.37 N | 106.13 E |
| Bishanga | 152 | 4.31 S | 21.02 E |
| Bishaykhāli | 126 | 23.28 N | 89.09 E |
| Bishkek → Biškek | 85 | 42.54 N | 74.36 E |
| Bishkhāli ≃[1] | 126 | 21.59 N | 89.59 E |
| Bishkin' ≃ | 83 | 49.15 N | 39.35 E |
| Bishnāh | 123 | 32.37 N | 74.52 E |
| Bishnupur, India | 120 | 24.38 N | 93.46 E |
| Bishnupur, India | 126 | 22.23 N | 88.16 E |
| Bishnupur, India | 126 | 23.05 N | 87.19 E |
| Bishnupur, India | 272b | 22.37 N | 88.31 E |
| Bisho | 158 | 32.50 S | 27.20 E |
| Bishop, Ca., U.S. | 204 | 37.21 N | 118.23 W |
| Bishop, Pa., U.S. | 279b | 40.19 N | 80.12 W |
| Bishop, Tx., U.S. | 196 | 27.35 N | 97.47 W |
| Bishop Airport ⊠ | 216 | 42.58 N | 83.44 W |
| Bishop Auckland | 44 | 54.40 N | 1.40 W |
| Bishop Rock I[2] | 42a | 49.52 N | 6.27 W |
| Bishop's Castle | 42 | 52.29 N | 3.00 W |
| Bishop's Cleeve | 42 | 51.57 N | 2.04 W |
| Bishop's Falls | 186 | 49.01 N | 55.30 W |
| Bishops Frome | 42 | 52.08 N | 2.29 W |
| Bishops Head | 208 | 38.16 N | 76.04 W |
| Bishops Lydeard | 42 | 51.04 N | 3.12 W |
| Bishop's Stortford | 42 | 51.53 N | 0.09 E |
| Bishopsteignton | 42 | 50.34 N | 3.31 W |
| Bishopstoke | 42 | 50.59 N | 1.19 W |
| Bishopston | 42 | 51.35 N | 4.03 W |
| Bishop's Waltham | 42 | 50.58 N | 1.12 W |
| Bishopthorpe | 44 | 53.55 N | 1.06 W |
| Bishopton | 206 | 45.35 N | 71.35 W |
| Bishopville, Md., U.S. | 208 | 38.26 N | 75.11 W |
| Bishopville, S.C., U.S. | 192 | 34.13 N | 80.14 W |
| Bishrah, Ma'ṭan ⊤[4] | 146 | 22.58 N | 22.39 E |
| Bishrī, Jabal ∧ | 130 | 35.20 N | 39.20 E |
| Bisignano | 68 | 39.31 N | 16.17 E |
| Bisina, Lake ⊜ | 154 | 1.38 N | 33.56 E |
| Bisinadi Game Reserve ◆[4] | 154 | 0.10 N | 38.20 E |
| Bisingen | 58 | 48.18 N | 8.55 E |
| Biskamža | 86 | 53.30 N | 89.30 E |


DEUTSCH


| Name | Seite | Breite°′ | Länge°′ E = Ost |
|---|---|---|---|
| Biskaya, Golf von → Biscay, Bay of c | 32 | 44.00 N | 4.00 W |
| Biškek (Frunze) | 85 | 42.54 N | 74.36 E |
| Biskintā | 132 | 33.57 N | 35.48 E |
| Biskupiec | 30 | 53.52 N | 20.58 E |
| Bisley, Eng., U.K. | 42 | 51.45 N | 2.08 W |
| Bisley, Eng., U.K. | 260 | 51.20 N | 0.38 W |
| Bislich | 263 | 51.41 N | 6.29 E |
| Bislig | 116 | 8.13 N | 126.19 E |
| Bislig Bay c | 116 | 8.14 N | 126.22 E |
| Bismarck, Il., U.S. | 216 | 40.16 N | 87.37 W |
| Bismarck, Mo., U.S. | 194 | 37.46 N | 90.37 W |
| Bismarck, N.D., U.S. | 198 | 46.48 N | 100.47 W |
| Bismarck Archipelago II | 164 | 5.00 S | 150.00 E |
| Bismarck Range ⋏ | 164 | 5.30 S | 144.45 E |
| Bismarck Sea ⊤[2] | 164 | 4.00 S | 148.00 E |
| Bismark | 54 | 52.39 N | 11.32 E |
| Bismil | 130 | 37.51 N | 40.40 E |
| Bismo | 26 | 61.53 N | 8.16 E |
| Bismuna, Laguna c | 236 | 14.45 N | 83.20 W |
| Biso | 154 | 1.46 N | 31.25 E |
| Bison | 198 | 45.31 N | 102.27 W |
| Bison Peak ∧ | 200 | 39.14 N | 105.30 W |
| Bispberg | 40 | 60.22 N | 15.47 E |
| Bispgården | 26 | 63.02 N | 16.37 E |
| Bispingen | 52 | 53.05 N | 10.00 E |
| Bisrakh | 272a | 28.34 N | 77.26 E |
| Bisrāmpur | 124 | 24.15 N | 83.56 E |
| Bissa, Djebel ∧ | 34 | 36.26 N | 1.28 E |
| Bissau | 150 | 11.51 N | 15.35 W |
| Bissaula | 146 | 7.00 N | 10.27 E |
| Bissegem | 50 | 50.49 N | 3.13 E |
| Bissendorf, Dtsch. | 52 | 52.14 N | 8.10 E |
| Bissendorf, Dtsch. | 52 | 52.31 N | 9.45 E |
| Bissett | 184 | 51.02 N | 95.40 W |
| Bissigh, Lach ≃ | 144 | 0.45 N | 41.33 E |
| Bissikrima | 150 | 10.51 N | 10.56 W |
| Bissingen | 56 | 48.43 N | 10.37 E |
| Bissingheim ◆[8] | 263 | 51.21 N | 7.31 E |
| Bissorã | 150 | 12.14 N | 15.31 W |
| Bistcho Lake ⊜ | 176 | 59.40 N | 118.40 W |
| Bistineau, Lake ⊜[1] | 194 | 32.25 N | 93.22 W |
| Bistra ≃ | 38 | 45.29 N | 22.11 E |
| Bistreț | 38 | 43.54 N | 23.30 E |
| Bistrica | 61 | 46.33 N | 16.16 E |
| Bistrița | 38 | 47.08 N | 24.30 E |
| Bistrița ≃ | 38 | 46.30 N | 26.57 E |
| Bistrița-Năsăud □[6] | 38 | 47.15 N | 24.30 E |
| Biswān | 124 | 27.30 N | 81.00 E |
| Bisztynek | 30 | 54.06 N | 20.55 E |
| Bitadton | 116 | 11.30 N | 122.05 E |
| Bitam | 152 | 2.05 N | 11.29 E |
| Bitam, Oued ≃ | 34 | 35.15 N | 5.11 E |
| Bitatolo ≃ | 273b | 4.09 S | 15.19 E |
| Bitburg | 56 | 49.58 N | 6.31 E |
| Bitca | 265b | 55.34 N | 37.37 E |
| Bitca ≃ | 265b | 55.34 N | 37.37 E |
| Bitche | 56 | 49.03 N | 7.26 E |
| Bitchū | 96 | 34.47 N | 133.27 E |
| Bitéa, Ouadi V | 146 | 13.11 N | 20.10 E |
| Bitetto | 68 | 41.02 N | 16.45 E |
| Bithia ⊥ | 71 | 38.53 N | 8.52 E |
| Bithlo | 220 | 28.33 N | 81.06 W |
| Bithynia □[9] | 130 | 40.10 N | 30.15 E |
| Bitia, Wādī V | 140 | 17.34 N | 32.15 E |
| Bitik | 80 | 50.09 N | 50.30 E |
| Bitkine | 146 | 11.59 N | 18.13 E |
| Bitlis | 130 | 38.22 N | 42.06 E |
| Bitlis □[4] | 128 | 38.30 N | 42.10 E |
| Bitola | 38 | 41.01 N | 21.20 E |
| Bitolj → Bitola | 38 | 41.01 N | 21.20 E |
| Bitonto | 68 | 41.06 N | 16.42 E |
| Bitou | 150 | 11.16 N | 0.18 W |
| Bitra Island I | 122 | 11.33 N | 72.09 E |
| Bitritto | 68 | 41.03 N | 16.50 E |
| Bitschwiller-lès-Thann | 58 | 47.50 N | 7.05 E |
| Bitter Creek ≃, Ut,. U.S. | 200 | 39.58 N | 109.25 W |
| Bitter Creek ≃, Wy., U.S. | 200 | 41.31 N | 109.27 W |
| Bitterfeld | 54 | 51.37 N | 12.20 E |
| Bitterfontein | 158 | 31.00 S | 18.32 E |
| Bitter Lake ⊜ | 184 | 50.08 N | 109.48 W |
| Bittermark ◆[8] | 263 | 51.27 N | 7.28 E |
| Bitterness, Mount ∧ | 172 | 44.45 S | 170.18 E |
| Bittern Lake ⊜ | 184 | 53.55 N | 105.50 W |
| Bitterroot ≃ | 202 | 46.52 N | 114.06 W |
| Bitterroot, East Fork ≃ | 202 | 45.57 N | 114.08 W |
| Bitterroot, West Fork ≃ | 202 | 45.57 N | 114.08 W |
| Bitterroot Range ⋏ | 202 | 47.06 N | 115.10 W |
| Bitterwater Creek ≃ | 226 | 35.41 N | 119.58 W |
| Bitti | 71 | 40.29 N | 9.23 E |
| Bit'ug ≃ | 78 | 50.37 N | 39.55 E |
| Bitung | 112 | 1.27 N | 125.11 E |
| Bitupitá | 250 | 2.54 S | 41.16 W |
| Bituruna | 252 | 26.10 S | 51.34 W |
| Biu | 146 | 10.35 N | 12.13 E |
| Bivalve | 208 | 38.18 N | 75.53 W |
| Bivins | 194 | 33.01 N | 94.12 W |
| Bivio | 58 | 46.28 N | 9.38 E |
| Bivona | 70 | 37.37 N | 13.26 E |
| Bivongi | 68 | 38.28 N | 16.27 E |
| Biwabik | 190 | 47.31 N | 92.20 W |
| Biwa-ko ⊜ | 94 | 35.15 N | 136.05 E |
| Biwa-ko-kokutei-kōen ♦ | 94 | 35.10 N | 136.00 E |
| Biwa-ko-ōhashi ◆[5] | 94 | 35.08 N | 135.56 E |
| Bixby | 196 | 35.56 N | 95.52 W |
| Biyalā | 142 | 31.10 N | 31.13 E |
| Biyang | 100 | 32.44 N | 113.20 E |
| Biysk → Bijsk | 86 | 52.34 N | 85.15 E |
| Biyuk-Karasu ≃ | 78 | 45.27 N | 34.47 E |
| Bi Yun Si (Temple of the Azure Clouds) ʊ[1] | 105 | 40.00 N | 116.11 E |
| Biz'aki | 80 | 55.56 N | 52.28 E |
| Bizana | 158 | 30.58 S | 29.52 E |
| Biz'ar | 86 | 57.31 N | 56.09 E |
| Bizard, Île I | 275a | 45.29 N | 73.54 W |
| Bižbul'ak | 80 | 53.43 N | 54.16 E |
| Bizcocho, Cuchilla del ⋏[2] | 258 | 33.45 S | 57.30 W |
| Bizen | 96 | 34.44 N | 134.09 E |
| Bizerte | 148 | 37.17 N | 9.52 E |
| Bizerte, Lac de ⊜ | 36 | 37.12 N | 9.52 E |
| Bīzhanābād | 128 | 27.55 N | 58.03 E |
| Bizkaiko □[4] | 34 | 43.20 N | 2.45 W |
| Bjæverskov | 41 | 55.27 N | 12.02 E |
| Bjahoml' | 76 | 54.44 N | 28.04 E |
| Bjala, Blg. | 38 | 42.53 N | 27.53 E |
| Bjala, Blg. | 38 | 43.27 N | 25.44 E |
| Bjala Slatina | 38 | 43.28 N | 23.56 E |
| Bjalyničy | 76 | 53.59 N | 29.42 E |
| Bjalynkavičy | 76 | 53.15 N | 32.08 E |
| Bjarèzina ≃, Bela. | 76 | 52.33 N | 30.14 E |
| Bjarèzina ≃, Bela. | 76 | 53.48 N | 25.59 E |
| Bjarezinski Bijasferny zapavednik ♦ | 76 | 54.40 N | 28.15 E |
| Bjargtangar › | 24a | 65.31 N | 24.32 W |
| Bjärnum | 41 | 56.17 N | 13.42 E |
| Bjaroza | 76 | 52.32 N | 24.59 E |
| Bjarozauka | 76 | 53.43 N | 25.30 E |
| Bjärred | 41 | 55.43 N | 13.01 E |
| Bjärsjölagård | 41 | 55.44 N | 13.41 E |
| Bjästa | 26 | 63.12 N | 18.30 E |
| Bjelaja → Belaja ≃ | 72 | 55.54 N | 53.33 E |
| Bjelovar | 36 | 45.54 N | 16.51 E |
| Bjernede | 41 | 55.27 N | 11.38 E |
| Bjerre Skov ∧[2] | 41 | 55.47 N | 9.53 E |
| Bjerringbro | 26 | 56.23 N | 9.40 E |
| Björbo | 40 | 60.28 N | 14.42 E |
| Bjørkelangen | 26 | 59.53 N | 11.34 E |
| Björklinge | 40 | 60.02 N | 17.33 E |
| Björknäs | 40 | 59.19 N | 18.14 E |


**Symbols** in the index entries represent the broad categories identified in the key at the right. Symbols with superior numbers (⋏[1]) identify subcategories (see complete key on page *I* · *1*).

**Symbole** im Register stellen die rechts im Schlüssel erklärten Kategorien dar. Symbole mit hochgestellten Ziffern (⋏[1]) bezeichnen Unterabteilungen einer Kategorie (vgl. vollständiger Schlüssel auf Seite *I* · *1*).

**Los símbolos** incluídos en el texto del índice representan las grandes categorías identificadas con la clave a la derecha. Los símbolos con numeros en su parte superior (⋏[1]) identifican las subcategorías (véase la clave completa en la página *I* · *1*).

**Les symboles** de l'index représentent les catégories indiquées dans la légende à droite. Les symboles suivis d'un indice (⋏[1]) représentent des sous-catégories (voir légende complète à la page *I* · *1*).

**Os símbolos** incluídos no texto do índice representam as grandes categorias identificadas com a chave à direita. Os símbolos com números em sua parte superior (⋏[1]) identificam as subcategorias (veja-se a chave completa à página *I* · *1*).

| | | | | |
|---|---|---|---|---|
| ∧ Mountain | Berg | Montaña | Montagne | Montanha |
| ⋏ Mountains | Gebirge | Montañas | Montagnes | Montanhas |
| )( Pass | Paß | Paso | Col | Passo |
| V Valley, Canyon | Tal, Cañon | Valle, Cañón | Vallée, Canyon | Vale, Canhão |
| ≚ Plain | Ebene | Llano | Plaine | Planície |
| › Cape | Kap | Cabo | Cap | Cabo |
| I Island | Insel | Isla | Île | Ilha |
| II Islands | Inseln | Islas | Îles | Ilhas |
| ⊥ Other Topographic Features | Andere Topographische Objekte | Otros Elementos Topográficos | Autres données topographiques | Outros acidentes topográficos |

Björkö I 40 59.53 N 19.00 E
Björköby 26 63.21 N 21.19 E
Björköfjärden c 40 59.53 N 18.56 E
Björkvik 40 58.50 N 16.31 E
Björna 26 63.34 N 18.33 E
Bjørnafjorden c² 26 60.06 N 5.22 E
Björndammen 40 59.52 N 16.49 E
Björneborg → Pori, Suomi 26 61.29 N 21.47 E
Björneborg, Sve. 40 59.15 N 14.15 E
Bjornesfjorden ⊜ 26 60.10 N 7.41 E
Björnlunda 40 59.04 N 17.09 E
Bjørnøya (Bear Island) I 12 74.25 N 19.00 E
Bjurholm 26 63.56 N 19.13 E
Bjuv 41 56.05 N 12.54 E
Bkāsīn 132 33.34 N 35.35 E
Bla 150 12.57 N 5.46 W
Blaby 42 52.34 N 1.09 W
Blace 38 43.17 N 21.18 E
Black (Lixian) (Da) ≃, Asia 110 21.15 N 105.20 E
Black ≃, Mb., Can. 184 50.49 N 96.20 W
Black ≃, On., Can. 190 48.42 N 80.38 W
Black ≃, On., Can. 190 48.36 N 86.16 W
Black ≃, On., Can. 212 44.32 N 77.22 W
Black ≃, On., Can. 212 44.20 N 79.20 W
Black ≃, On., Can. 212 44.42 N 79.19 W
Black ≃, U.S. 194 35.38 N 91.19 W
Black ≃, Ak., U.S. 180 66.39 N 144.50 W
Black ≃, Az., U.S. 200 33.44 N 110.13 W
Black ≃, La., U.S. 194 31.16 N 91.50 W
Black ≃, Mi., U.S. 190 43.00 N 82.25 W
Black ≃, Mi., U.S. 190 45.39 N 84.29 W
Black ≃, Mi., U.S. 190 46.40 N 90.03 W
Black ≃, Mi., U.S. 214 43.00 N 82.25 W
Black ≃, N.M., U.S. 196 32.14 N 104.05 W
Black ≃, N.Y., U.S. 188 43.59 N 76.04 W
Black ≃, N.C., U.S. 192 34.35 N 78.16 W
Black ≃, Oh., U.S. 214 41.28 N 82.11 W
Black ≃, S.C., U.S. 192 33.24 N 79.15 W
Black ≃, Vt., U.S. 188 43.16 N 72.27 W
Black ≃, Vt., U.S. 188 44.55 N 72.13 W
Black ≃, Wa., U.S. 224 46.49 N 123.13 W
Black ≃, Wi., U.S. 190 43.57 N 91.22 W
Black, East Branch ≃ 214 41.22 N 82.07 W
Black, East Fork ≃ 190 44.26 N 90.42 W
Black, Middle Branch ≃ 216 42.25 N 86.14 W
Black, South Branch ≃ 216 42.25 N 86.15 W
Black, West Branch ≃ 214 41.22 N 82.07 W
Blackadder Water ≃ 46 55.46 N 2.15 W
Blackall 166 24.25 S 145.28 E
Black Bay c 190 48.40 N 88.30 W
Black Bay Peninsula ≻¹ 190 48.38 N 88.21 W
Black Bear Creek ≃ 196 36.25 N 96.38 W
Black Bear Island Lake ⊜ 184 55.38 N 105.40 W
Blackberry Creek ≃ 216 41.38 N 88.27 W
Blackberry Heights 216 41.45 N 88.23 W
Black Birch Lake ⊜ 184 56.54 N 107.45 W
Black Brook ≃, Ma., U.S. 283 41.59 N 71.03 W
Black Brook ≃, Ma., U.S. 283 42.38 N 71.21 W
Black Brook ≃, N.J., U.S. 276 40.42 N 74.31 W
Black Bullock Hill ∧² 168b 35.37 S 138.12 E
Blackburn, Austl. 274b 37.49 S 145.09 E
Blackburn, Eng., U.K. 44 53.45 N 2.29 W
Blackburn, Scot., U.K. 46 55.52 N 3.38 W
Blackburn □⁸ 262 53.42 N 2.28 W
Blackburn, Mount ∧ 180 61.44 N 143.26 W
Blackbutt 171a 26.53 S 152.06 E
Black Butte ∧, Ca., U.S. 228 34.33 N 117.43 W
Black Butte ∧, Mt., U.S. 202 44.54 N 111.51 W
Black Butte ∧, Mt., U.S. 202 46.47 N 110.56 W
Black Butte Lake ⊜¹ 204 39.45 N 122.20 W
Blackbutt Range ∧ 171a 27.00 S 152.00 E
Black Canyon of the Gunnison National Monument ♦ 200 38.32 N 107.42 W
Blackcraig Hill ∧ 44 55.20 N 4.08 W
Black Creek, B.C., Can. 182 49.50 N 125.08 W
Black Creek, On., Can. 284a 43.00 N 79.01 W
Black Creek, N.Y., U.S. 210 42.17 N 78.14 W
Black Creek ≃, On., Can. 214 42.43 N 82.21 W
Black Creek ≃, On., Can. 275b 43.41 N 79.32 W
Black Creek ≃, On., Can. 284a 42.59 N 79.01 W
Black Creek ≃, Az., U.S. 200 35.16 N 109.14 W
Black Creek ≃, Mi., U.S. 216 41.49 N 83.54 W
Black Creek ≃, Mi., U.S. 216 43.11 N 86.14 W
Black Creek ≃, Ms., U.S. 194 33.01 N 90.21 W
Black Creek ≃, Ms., U.S. 194 30.39 N 88.39 W
Black Creek ≃, Mo., U.S. 219 39.41 N 91.55 W
Black Creek ≃, N.Y., U.S. 210 43.19 N 75.04 W
Black Creek ≃, N.Y., U.S. 210 43.06 N 77.41 W
Black Creek ≃, N.Y., U.S. 284a 43.03 N 78.42 W
Black Creek ≃, N.Y., U.S. 284a 43.03 N 78.57 W
Black Creek ≃, Pa., U.S. 210 41.00 N 76.10 W
Black Creek ≃, S.C., U.S. 192 34.18 N 79.37 W
Black Creek Park ♦ 275b 43.46 N 79.31 W
Black Creek Pioneer Village ♦ 275b 43.47 N 79.32 W
Black Cypress Creek ≃ 222 32.53 N 94.26 W
Blackden Heath 262 53.14 N 2.20 W
Black Devon ≃ 46 56.06 N 3.47 W
Black Diamond, Ab., Can. 182 50.42 N 114.14 W
Black Diamond, Wa., U.S. 224 47.18 N 122.00 W
Black Donald Lake ⊜¹ 212 45.13 N 76.55 W
Black Down Hills ∧² 42 50.57 N 3.09 W
Blackdown Tableland National Park ♦ 166 23.43 S 149.05 E
Blackduck 190 47.43 N 94.32 W
Black Duck ≃ 176 56.51 N 89.02 W
Black Eagle 202 47.31 N 111.16 W
Black Esk ≃ 44 55.12 N 3.10 W
Blackfalds 182 52.23 N 113.47 W
Blackfeet Indian Reservation ✦⁴ 202 48.40 N 113.00 W
Blackfoot, Id., U.S. 202 43.11 N 112.20 W
Blackfoot, Mt., U.S. 202 48.34 N 112.52 W
Blackfoot ≃, Id., U.S. 202 43.08 N 112.30 W
Blackfoot ≃, Mt., U.S. 202 46.52 N 113.53 W
Blackfoot, North Fork ≃ 202 46.59 N 113.07 W
Blackfoot Indian Reserve ✦⁴ 182 50.45 N 113.00 W
Blackfoot Reservoir ⊜¹ 202 42.55 N 111.35 W

Blackford 46 56.15 N 3.46 W
Blackford □⁶ 216 40.27 N 85.22 W
Black Forest → Schwarzwald ∧ 58 48.00 N 8.15 E
Blackhall Colliery 44 54.44 N 1.14 W
Blackhall Mountain ∧ 200 41.02 N 106.41 W
Black Hameldon ∧² 262 53.44 N 2.08 W
Black Hawk 184 48.48 N 93.59 W
Black Hawk Creek ≃ 190 42.30 N 92.21 W
Black Head ≻, Ire. 48 53.08 N 9.17 W
Black Head ≻, Eng., U.K. 42 50.01 N 5.06 W
Blackhead Bay c 186 48.34 N 53.15 W
Blackheath, Austl. 170 33.38 S 150.17 E
Blackheath, S. Afr. 273d 26.08 S 27.58 E
Blackheath, Eng., U.K. 260 51.12 N 0.31 W
Black Hill ∧², Eng., U.K. 262 53.20 N 2.01 W
Black Hill ∧², Eng., U.K. 262 53.33 N 1.53 W
Black Hills ∧ 198 44.00 N 104.00 W
Black Hills ∧² 282 37.50 N 121.52 W
Blackhope Scar ∧ 46 55.44 N 3.05 W
Black Horse, Oh., U.S. 214 41.09 N 81.18 W
Black Horse, Pa., U.S. 285 39.55 N 75.25 W
Black Horse, Pa., U.S. 285 40.06 N 75.19 W
Black Horse Creek ≃ 285 40.05 N 75.43 W
Black Island I 184 51.10 N 96.30 W
Black Isle ≻¹ 46 57.35 N 4.15 W
Black Jack 219 38.47 N 90.16 W
Black Jack Mountain ∧ 228 33.23 N 118.24 W
Black-Lake 206 46.03 N 71.21 W
Black Lake ⊜, On., Can. 212 44.46 N 76.18 W
Black Lake ⊜, Sk., Can. 176 59.10 N 105.20 W
Black Lake ⊜, Mi., U.S. 190 45.28 N 84.15 W
Black Lake ⊜, N.Y., U.S. 212 44.31 N 75.35 W
Black Lake ⊜, Wa., U.S. 224 47.00 N 122.58 W
Black Lake Bayou ≃ 194 32.01 N 93.09 W
Blacklegs Creek ≃ 214 40.30 N 79.27 W
Blackley ✦⁸ 262 53.31 N 2.13 W
Black Lick 214 40.28 N 79.11 W
Blacklick Creek ≃ 214 40.28 N 79.13 W
Blacklick Creek, North Branch ≃ 214 40.29 N 78.55 W
Blacklick Estates 218 39.54 N 83.22 W
Blacklog Mountain ∧ 214 40.20 N 77.45 W
Blacklunans 46 56.44 N 3.22 W
Black Mesa ∧, U.S. 196 37.05 N 103.10 W
Black Mesa ∧, Az., U.S. 200 36.35 N 110.20 W
Blackmoor ∧¹ 42 50.24 N 4.46 W
Blackmoorfoot Reservoir ⊜¹ 262 53.37 N 1.51 W
Blackmoor Vale V 42 50.56 N 2.25 W
Blackmore 260 51.41 N 0.19 E
Blackmore, Mount ∧ 202 45.27 N 111.01 W
Black Moshannon State Park ♦ 214 40.54 N 78.03 W
Black Mountain 192 35.37 N 82.19 W
Black Mountain ∧, D.Y. 124 27.17 N 90.23 E
Black Mountain ∧, Wales, U.K. 42 51.52 N 3.46 W
Black Mountain ∧, U.S. 192 36.54 N 82.54 W
Black Mountain ∧, Az., U.S. 200 32.46 N 110.57 W
Black Mountain ∧, Ca., U.S. 226 35.24 N 120.21 W
Black Mountain ∧, Ca., U.S. 228 35.08 N 117.14 W
Black Mountain ∧, Ca., U.S. 282 37.19 N 122.09 W
Black Mountain ∧, Id., U.S. 202 46.53 N 115.33 W
Black Mountain ∧, Mt., U.S. 202 46.44 N 112.31 W
Black Mountain ∧, Or., U.S. 202 45.13 N 119.17 W
Black Mountain ∧, Wy., U.S. 202 44.45 N 107.22 W
Black Mountain ∧², Austl. 166 21.08 S 139.41 E
Black Mountain ∧², Ca., U.S. 228 32.59 N 117.07 W
Black Mountain ∧², Tx., U.S. 222 31.09 N 97.44 W
Black Mountains ∧, Wales, U.K. 42 51.57 N 3.08 W
Black Mountains ∧, Az., U.S. 200 35.30 N 114.30 W
Black Nossob ≃ 156 23.05 S 18.45 E
Black Peak ∧ 200 34.08 N 114.13 W
Black Pine Peak ∧ 202 42.08 N 113.08 W
Black Pipe Creek ≃ 198 43.47 N 101.14 W
Black Point 226 38.07 N 122.31 W
Black Point ≻, Austl. 168b 34.37 S 137.54 E
Black Point ≻, Austl. 170 34.47 S 150.50 E
Black Point ≻, Ak., U.S. 180 57.00 N 153.18 W
Blackpool 44 53.50 N 3.03 W
Blackpool □⁸ 262 53.47 N 3.02 W
Blackpool (Squire's Gate) Airport ✈ 262 53.47 N 3.02 W
Blackpool Football Ground ♦ 262 53.49 N 3.03 W
Blackpool Tower ♦ 262 53.49 N 3.03 W
Black Range ∧ 200 33.20 N 107.50 W
Black River, Jam. 241q 18.01 N 77.51 W
Black River, N.Y., U.S. 212 44.00 N 75.47 W
Black River Bay c 212 43.58 N 76.07 W
Black River Falls 190 44.17 N 90.51 W
Black Rock, Austl. 274b 37.59 S 145.01 E
Black Rock, Ar., U.S. 194 36.06 N 91.05 W
Black Rock, Ma., U.S. 283 42.14 N 70.49 W
Black Rock I², Ire. 48 54.05 N 10.22 W
Black Rock I², S. Geor. 244 53.39 S 41.48 W
Black Rock Desert ✦² 204 41.10 N 119.00 W
Blackrod 262 53.35 N 2.35 W
Blacksburg, S.C., U.S. 192 35.07 N 81.30 W
Blacksburg, Va., U.S. 192 37.13 N 80.24 W
Blacks Creek ≃ 285 40.08 N 74.43 W
Black Sea ⊤² 22 43.00 N 35.00 E
Blacks Fork ≃ 200 41.24 N 109.38 W
Blacks Harbour 186 45.03 N 66.47 W
Blackshear 192 31.18 N 82.14 W
Blackshear, Lake ⊜¹ 192 31.56 N 83.56 W
Blacksod Bay c 48 54.08 N 10.00 W
Black Springs, Austl. 170 33.52 S 149.42 E
Black Springs, Austl. 274b 37.46 S 145.19 E
Black Springs Hill ∧² 274b 37.46 S 145.19 E
Black Star Canyon V 280 33.47 N 117.39 W
Blackstone, Ma., U.S. 207 42.01 N 71.32 W
Blackstone, Va., U.S. 192 37.04 N 77.59 W
Blackstone ≃, Ab., Can. 182 52.50 N 116.07 W
Blackstone ≃, Yk., Can. 180 65.51 N 137.12 W
Blackstone Lake ⊜ 212 45.14 N 79.53 W
Black Sugarloaf Mountain ∧ 166 31.20 S 151.33 E
Black Thunder Creek ≃ 198 43.33 N 104.41 W
Blacktown 170 33.46 S 150.55 E
Blackville 192 33.21 N 81.16 W

Black Volta (Volta Noire) ≃ 150 8.41 N 1.33 W
Blackwall Tunnel ✦⁵ 260 51.30 N 0.01 E
Black Warrior ≃ 194 32.32 N 87.51 W
Blackwalnut Point ≻ 208 38.40 N 76.20 W
Blackwatch Hills 210 43.05 N 77.27 W
Blackwater, Austl. 166 23.35 S 148.53 E
Blackwater, Ire. 48 52.26 N 6.21 W
Blackwater ≃, Europe 48 54.31 N 6.34 W
Blackwater ≃, Ire. 48 51.51 N 7.50 W
Blackwater ≃, Ire. 48 53.39 N 6.43 W
Blackwater ≃, Eng., U.K. 42 51.45 N 1.00 E
Blackwater ≃, U.S. 194 30.36 N 87.02 W
Blackwater ≃, Md., U.S. 208 38.21 N 76.01 W
Blackwater ≃, Mo., U.S. 194 38.56 N 92.51 W
Blackwater ≃, Va., U.S. 208 36.33 N 76.55 W
Blackwater Creek ≃, Austl. 166 25.56 S 144.20 E
Black Water Creek ≃, Fl., U.S. 220 28.51 N 81.24 W
Blackwater Draw V 196 33.35 N 101.50 W
Blackwaterfoot 46 55.30 N 5.19 W
Blackwater Lake ⊜ 180 64.00 N 123.05 W
Blackwater Reservoir ⊜¹, Scot., U.K. 46 56.41 N 4.46 W
Blackwater Reservoir ⊜¹, Scot., U.K. 46 56.44 N 3.14 W
Blackwater Sound ⊔ 220 25.10 N 80.25 W
Blackwell, Ok., U.S. 196 36.48 N 97.16 W
Blackwell, Tx., U.S. 196 32.05 N 100.19 W
Blackwood, Austl. 168b 35.02 S 138.37 E
Blackwood, Austl. 169 37.29 S 144.19 E
Blackwood, N.J., U.S. 285 39.48 N 75.03 W
Blackwood ≃ 162 34.19 S 115.11 E
Blackwood, Cape ≻ 164 7.50 S 144.30 E
Blackwood Terrace 285 39.48 N 75.05 W
Bladel 52 51.23 N 5.13 E
Bladenboro 192 34.32 N 78.47 W
Bladensburg, Md., U.S. 284c 38.56 N 76.56 W
Bladensburg, Oh., U.S. 214 40.17 N 82.17 W
Blades 208 38.38 N 75.36 W
Bladgrond 158 28.52 S 19.57 E
Bladnoch ≃ 44 54.51 N 4.25 W
Bladworth 184 51.18 N 106.09 W
Blaenau Ffestiniog 42 52.59 N 3.56 W
Blaenavon 42 51.48 N 3.05 W
Bláfell ∧ 24a 64.32 N 19.53 W
Blagaj 36 43.15 N 17.50 E
Blagdon 42 51.20 N 2.43 W
Blagodarnoje 86 47.03 N 82.10 E
Blagodarnyj 72 45.06 N 43.27 E
Blagodatnoje, Kaz. 86 51.18 N 72.49 E
Blagodatnoje, Ross. 78 51.32 N 34.54 E
Blagodatovka 80 52.14 N 50.27 E
Blagoevgrad 38 42.01 N 23.06 E
Blagoveščenka, Kaz. 85 43.18 N 74.12 E
Blagoveščenka, Kaz. 86 52.22 N 66.58 E
Blagoveščenka, Ross. 80 51.19 N 44.03 E
Blagoveščenka, Ross. 86 52.50 N 79.52 E
Blagoveščensk, Ross. 86 55.01 N 55.59 E
Blagoveščensk, Ross. 89 50.17 N 127.32 E
Blagoveščenskoje 86 56.08 N 62.58 E
Blåhø ∧ 26 62.45 N 9.19 E
Blahodatne, Ukr. 83 47.42 N 37.25 E
Blahodatne, Ukr. 83 47.53 N 38.29 E
Blåhøj 41 55.51 N 9.01 E
Blaichach 58 47.34 N 10.15 E
Blaikfjället ∧ 26 64.33 N 16.12 E
Blain, Fr. 32 47.29 N 1.46 W
Blain, Pa., U.S. 208 40.20 N 77.31 W
Blaina 42 51.46 N 3.10 W
Blain City 214 40.45 N 78.34 W
Blaine, Mn., U.S. 190 45.09 N 93.14 W
Blaine, Wa., U.S. 224 48.59 N 122.44 W
Blaine Creek ≃ 188 38.11 N 82.37 W
Blaine Hill 279b 40.16 N 79.53 W
Blaine Lake 184 52.50 N 106.54 W
Blaineys 224 48.53 N 123.47 W
Blainville 206 45.40 N 73.52 W
Blainville-sur-l'Eau 58 48.33 N 6.24 E
Blair, On., Can. 212 43.23 N 80.23 W
Blair, Ne., U.S. 198 41.32 N 96.07 W
Blair, Ok., U.S. 196 34.46 N 99.20 W
Blair, Wi., U.S. 190 44.18 N 91.14 W
Blair □⁶ 214 40.30 N 78.25 W
Blair Athol 166 22.42 S 147.33 E
Blair Atholl 46 56.46 N 3.51 W
Blairgowrie 46 56.36 N 3.21 W
Blairs Mills 214 40.17 N 77.43 W
Blairstown, Ia., U.S. 190 41.54 N 92.05 W
Blairstown, N.J., U.S. 210 40.59 N 74.57 W
Blairsville, Ga., U.S. 192 34.52 N 83.57 W
Blairsville, Pa., U.S. 214 40.25 N 79.15 W
Blaise ≃, Fr. 50 48.46 N 1.25 E
Blaise ≃, Fr. 58 48.38 N 4.43 E
Blaisy-Bas 58 47.22 N 4.44 E
Blaj 38 46.11 N 23.55 E
Blakehurst 274a 33.59 S 151.07 E
Blakeley Canal ≍ 226 36.09 N 119.48 W
Blakely, Ga., U.S. 192 31.22 N 84.56 W
Blakely, Pa., U.S. 210 41.28 N 75.35 W
Blakely Island I 224 48.33 N 122.50 W
Blakeney, Eng., U.K. 42 52.58 N 1.00 E
Blakeney, Eng., U.K. 42 51.46 N 2.29 W
Blake Plateau ✦⁴ 16 31.00 N 79.00 W
Blake Point ≻ 190 48.12 N 88.25 W
Blake Ridge ✦³ 16 29.00 N 73.30 W
Blakes 208 37.30 N 76.22 W
Blakesburg 190 40.57 N 92.38 W
Blakeslee, Oh., U.S. 216 41.31 N 84.44 W
Blakeslee, Pa., U.S. 210 41.06 N 75.36 W
Blalock Island I 202 45.53 N 119.41 W
Blâmont, Fr. 58 48.35 N 6.51 E
Blamont, Fr. 58 47.23 N 6.51 E
Blanc, Cap → Nouâdhibou, Râs ≻, Afr. 148 20.46 N 17.03 W
Blanc, Cap ≻, Tun. 36 37.20 N 9.51 E
Blanc, Mont ∧, P.Q., Can. 186 48.47 N 66.52 W
Blanc, Mont (Monte Bianco) ∧, Europe 62 45.50 N 6.52 E
Blanca 200 37.27 N 105.31 W
Blanca, Bahía c 252 38.55 S 62.10 W
Blanca, Isla I 248 9.06 S 78.38 W
Blanca, Laguna ⊜ 254 52.25 S 71.10 W
Blanca, Punta ≻, Arg. 258 34.57 S 57.40 W
Blanca, Punta ≻, Chile 252 25.06 S 70.30 W
Blanca, Sierra ∧ 200 31.15 N 105.26 W
Blanca Lake ⊜ 224 47.53 N 121.22 W
Blanca Peak ∧ 200 37.35 N 105.29 W
Blancas, Peñas ∧ 236 13.15 N 85.41 W
Blanc du Cheilon, Mont ∧ 58 45.59 N 7.25 E
Blanchard, Ok., U.S. 196 35.08 N 97.39 W
Blanchard, Pa., U.S. 210 41.04 N 77.36 W
Blanchard ≃ 216 41.02 N 84.18 W
Blanchardville 190 42.48 N 89.51 W
Blanche ≃, On., Can. 190 47.34 N 79.32 W
Blanche ≃, P.Q., Can. 206 46.40 N 72.08 W
Blanche, Cape ≻ 162 33.01 S 134.09 E
Blanche, Dent ∧ 58 46.03 N 7.36 E
Blanche, Lake ⊜, Austl. 162 22.25 S 123.17 E

Blanche, Lake ⊜, Austl. 166 29.15 S 139.39 E
Blanche, Mer → Beloje more ⊤² 24 65.30 N 38.00 E
Blanche Channel ⊔ 175e 8.30 S 157.30 E
Blancheface 261 48.32 N 2.06 E
Blanche Marie Val ∟ 250 4.44 N 56.53 W
Blanchester 218 39.17 N 83.59 W
Blanchisseuse 241r 10.47 N 61.18 W
Blanco, S. Afr. 158 33.57 S 22.24 E
Blanco, Tx., U.S. 196 30.06 N 98.25 W
Blanco ≃, Arg. 252 30.12 S 69.05 W
Blanco ≃, Arg. 254 47.22 S 71.12 W
Blanco ≃, Bol. 248 13.09 S 63.46 W
Blanco ≃, Ec. 246 0.28 N 79.25 W
Blanco ≃, Tx., U.S. 196 29.51 N 97.55 W
Blanco, Cabo → Nouâdhibou, Râs ≻, Afr. 148 20.46 N 17.03 W
Blanco, Cabo ≻, C.R. 236 9.34 N 85.07 W
Blanco, Cañon V 200 35.20 N 105.05 W
Blanco, Cape ≻ 202 42.50 N 124.34 W
Blanco, Lago ⊜ 254 54.03 S 69.00 W
Blanco, Mar → Beloje more ⊤² 24 65.30 N 38.00 E
Blanco, Monte → Blanc, Mont ∧ 62 45.50 N 6.52 E
Blanco, Río ≃ 200 37.07 N 107.03 W
Blanco Creek ≃ 196 28.19 N 97.19 W
Blanc-Sablon 186 51.25 N 57.07 W
Bland, Mo., U.S. 219 38.18 N 91.37 W
Bland, Va., U.S. 192 37.06 N 81.06 W
Blanda ≃ 24a 65.39 N 20.18 W
Blandburg 214 40.41 N 78.24 W
Blandford 207 42.10 N 72.55 W
Blandford Forum 42 50.52 N 2.11 W
Blanding 200 37.37 N 109.28 W
Blandinsville 190 40.33 N 90.51 W
Blandon 208 40.26 N 75.53 W
Blandy 261 48.34 N 2.47 E
Blanes 34 41.41 N 2.48 E
Blangkejeren 114 3.59 N 97.20 E
Blangpidie 114 3.45 N 96.51 E
Blangy-le-Château 50 49.14 N 0.17 E
Blangy-sur-Bresle 50 49.56 N 1.38 E
Blanice ≃ 61 49.05 N 14.03 E
Blankenberg 56 50.45 N 7.22 E
Blankenberge 50 51.19 N 3.08 E
Blankenburg 54 51.48 N 10.58 E
Blankenburg ✦⁸ 264a 52.35 N 13.28 E
Blankenese ✦⁸ 52 53.33 N 9.48 E
Blankenfelde 54 52.20 N 13.23 E
Blankenfelde ✦⁸ 264a 52.37 N 13.23 E
Blankenhain 54 50.51 N 11.21 E
Blankenheim, Dtsch. 54 51.31 N 11.25 E
Blankenheim, Dtsch. 56 50.26 N 6.39 E
Blankensee 54 52.14 N 13.08 E
Blankenstein 263 51.24 N 7.14 E
Blanket 196 31.49 N 98.47 W
Blanquilla, Isla I 246 11.51 N 64.37 W
Blansko 30 49.22 N 16.39 E
Blanský Les ✦³ 61 48.52 N 14.16 E
Blantyre 154 15.47 S 35.00 E
Blanzac 62 45.07 N 3.51 E
Blanzy 58 46.42 N 4.23 E
Blaricum 52 52.16 N 5.15 E
Blarney 48 51.56 N 8.34 W
Blarney Castle ⊥ 48 51.56 N 8.34 W
Blasdell 210 42.47 N 78.49 W
Blasheim 52 52.18 N 8.34 E
Błaszki 30 51.39 N 18.27 E
Blatná 60 49.26 N 13.53 E
Blatten 58 46.25 N 7.50 E
Blau ≃ 58 48.23 N 9.49 E
Blaubeuren 58 48.24 N 9.47 E
Blauen ∧ 58 47.47 N 7.42 E
Blauer Nil → Blue Nile ≃ 140 15.38 N 32.31 E
Blaufelden 56 49.18 N 9.58 E
Blaustein 58 48.25 N 9.53 E
Blauvelt 276 41.03 N 73.57 W
Blauvelt State Park ♦ 276 41.04 N 73.56 W
Blawenburg 276 40.24 N 74.42 W
Blawnox 279b 40.29 N 79.51 W
Blaxland 274a 33.45 S 150.36 E
Blaxland Creek ≃ 274a 33.48 S 150.46 E
Blaydon 44 54.58 N 1.42 W
Blaye-et-Sainte-Luce 32 45.08 N 0.39 W
Blayney 166 33.32 S 149.15 E
Blaze, Point ≻ 164 12.56 S 130.12 E
Błażowa 30 49.54 N 22.05 E
Bleaker Island I 254 52.13 S 58.53 W
Bleaklow Head ∧ 262 53.28 N 1.50 W
Blean 42 51.19 N 1.02 E
Bleckede 54 53.17 N 10.44 E
Bled 36 46.22 N 14.06 E
Bledsoe 196 33.38 N 103.01 W
Bleecker 210 43.10 N 74.22 W
Blefjell ∧ 26 59.48 N 9.10 E
Blega 115a 7.08 S 113.03 E
Bleiberg ob Villach 64 46.37 N 13.41 E
Bleiburg 61 46.35 N 14.48 E
Bleicherode 54 51.26 N 10.34 E
Blekendorf 54 54.16 N 10.38 E
Blekinge □⁹ 26 56.20 N 15.05 E
Blekinge Län □⁶ 26 56.20 N 15.20 E
Bléneau 50 47.42 N 2.57 E
Blenheim, Austl. 171a 27.39 S 152.20 E
Blenheim, On., Can. 214 42.20 N 82.00 W
Blenheim, N.Z. 172 41.31 S 173.57 E
Blenheim, N.J., U.S. 285 39.48 N 75.05 W
Blenheim Palace ♦ 42 51.47 N 1.21 W
Blenio, Val V 58 46.27 N 8.58 E
Blénod-lès-Pont-à-Mousson 56 48.53 N 6.03 E
Blénod-lès-Toul 58 48.36 N 5.50 E
Bléone ≃ 62 44.03 N 6.00 E
Blérancourt 50 49.31 N 3.09 E
Bléré 50 47.20 N 1.00 E
Blerick 52 51.23 N 6.10 E
Blériot-Plage 50 50.57 N 1.50 E
Blesbokspruit ≃ 273d 26.17 S 28.29 E
Blessing 222 28.52 N 96.13 W
Blessington 48 53.10 N 6.32 W
Bletchingley 260 51.14 N 0.06 W
Bletchley 42 52.00 N 0.46 W
Bletterans 58 46.45 N 5.27 E
Bleu → Chang ≃ 90 31.48 N 121.10 E
Bleue, Mer ≡ 212 45.24 N 75.30 W
Bleury 261 48.31 N 1.45 E
Bleus, Monts ∧ 154 1.30 N 30.30 E
Blevio 62 45.50 N 9.05 E
Blewett Falls Lake ⊜¹ 192 35.03 N 79.54 W
Blexen 52 53.32 N 8.32 E
Blidö I 40 59.37 N 18.54 E
Blidworth 44 53.06 N 1.07 W
Bliedinghausen ✦⁸ 263 51.09 N 7.12 E
Bliersheim ✦⁸ 263 51.23 N 6.43 E
Blies ≃ 56 49.07 N 7.04 E
Blieskastel 56 49.14 N 7.16 E
Bligh Sound ⊔ 172 44.50 S 167.32 E
Bligh Water ⊔ 175g 17.00 S 178.00 E
Bligny 50 49.11 N 3.52 E
Bligny-sur-Ouche 58 47.06 N 4.40 E
Blik, Mount ∧ 116 6.58 N 124.15 E
Blina 162 17.46 S 124.32 E
Blind ≃ 276 40.57 N 73.42 W
Blind Creek ≃ 274b 37.54 S 145.12 E
Blindley Heath 260 51.12 N 0.04 W
Blind River 190 46.10 N 82.58 W
Blinman 166 31.06 S 138.41 E
Blinnenhorn ∧ 58 46.26 N 8.19 E
Blinovskij 80 49.23 N 42.19 E
Bliss 210 42.34 N 78.15 W
Blissfield, Mi., U.S. 216 41.49 N 83.51 W
Blissfield, Oh., U.S. 214 40.24 N 81.58 W
Blitar 115a 8.06 S 112.09 E
Blithe ≃ 42 52.45 N 1.50 W

Blithfield Reservoir ⊜¹ 42 52.48 N 1.53 W
Blitta 150 8.19 N 0.59 E
Blois 50 47.35 N 1.20 E
Blokhus 26 57.15 N 9.35 E
Blokzijl 52 52.44 N 5.57 E
Blombacher Bach ✦⁸ 263 51.15 N 7.14 E
Blombacka 40 59.37 N 13.47 E
Blomberg 52 51.56 N 9.05 E
Blomstermåla 26 56.59 N 16.20 E
Blönduós 24a 65.39 N 20.15 W
Blongas 115b 8.53 S 116.02 E
Blonville-sur-Mer 50 49.19 N 0.02 E
Blood Indian Creek ≃ 184 50.55 N 111.03 W
Blood Indian Reserve ✦⁴ 182 49.30 N 113.10 W
Blood Mountain ∧ 192 34.44 N 83.56 W
Blood River ⊥ 158 28.20 S 30.35 E
Bloodsworth Island I 208 38.10 N 76.03 W
Bloodvein ≃ 184 51.45 N 96.44 W
Bloody Foreland ≻ 48 55.09 N 8.17 W
Bloomdale 216 41.10 N 83.33 W
Bloomer 190 45.06 N 91.29 W
Bloomfield, On., Can. 212 43.59 N 77.14 W
Bloomfield, Ct., U.S. 207 41.49 N 72.43 W
Bloomfield, In., U.S. 194 39.01 N 86.56 W
Bloomfield, Ia., U.S. 190 40.45 N 92.24 W
Bloomfield, Ky., U.S. 194 37.54 N 85.19 W
Bloomfield, Mo., U.S. 194 36.53 N 89.55 W
Bloomfield, Ne., U.S. 198 42.35 N 97.38 W
Bloomfield, N.J., U.S. 210 40.48 N 74.11 W
Bloomfield, N.M., U.S. 200 36.42 N 107.59 W
Bloomfield, Oh., U.S. 214 40.03 N 81.44 W
Bloomfield ✦⁸ 279b 40.27 N 79.56 W
Bloomfield Glens 281 42.33 N 83.20 W
Bloomfield Highlands 281 42.36 N 83.16 W
Bloomfield Hills 216 42.35 N 83.14 W
Bloomfield Village 216 42.33 N 83.15 W
Bloomingburg, N.Y., U.S. 210 41.33 N 74.26 W
Bloomingburg, Oh., U.S. 218 39.36 N 83.23 W
Bloomingdale, Il., U.S. 278 41.57 N 88.04 W
Bloomingdale, Mi., U.S. 216 42.22 N 85.57 W
Bloomingdale, N.J., U.S. 210 41.00 N 74.19 W
Bloomingdale, Oh., U.S. 214 40.21 N 80.49 W
Blooming Glen 208 40.22 N 75.15 W
Blooming Grove, In., U.S. 218 39.30 N 85.04 W
Blooming Grove, N.Y., U.S. 210 41.25 N 74.11 W
Blooming Grove, Pa., U.S. 210 41.21 N 75.09 W
Blooming Grove, Tx., U.S. 222 32.06 N 96.43 W
Blooming Prairie 190 43.52 N 93.03 W
Bloomington, Ca., U.S. 228 34.04 N 117.23 W
Bloomington, Il., U.S. 216 40.29 N 88.59 W
Bloomington, In., U.S. 218 39.09 N 86.31 W
Bloomington, Mn., U.S. 190 44.50 N 93.17 W
Bloomington, N.Y., U.S. 210 41.53 N 74.03 W
Bloomington, Tx., U.S. 196 28.38 N 96.53 W
Bloomington, Wi., U.S. 190 42.53 N 90.55 W
Bloomington, Lake ⊜¹ 216 40.37 N 88.55 W
Blooming Valley 214 41.40 N 80.03 W
Bloomsburg 210 41.00 N 76.27 W
Bloomsbury, Austl. 166 20.43 S 148.35 E
Bloomsbury, N.J., U.S. 210 40.39 N 75.05 W
Bloomsdale Gardens 285 40.07 N 74.52 W
Bloomville, N.Y., U.S. 210 42.20 N 74.48 W
Bloomville, Oh., U.S. 214 41.03 N 83.00 W
Blora 115a 6.57 S 111.25 E
Bloserville 208 40.12 N 77.24 W
Blossburg 210 41.40 N 77.03 W
Blossom 196 33.39 N 95.23 W
Blossom Hill 208 40.05 N 76.19 W
Blötberget 40 60.07 N 15.04 E
Blotzheim 58 47.36 N 7.29 E
Blouberg ∧ 156 23.08 S 28.56 E
Blouberg ∧ 156 23.01 S 28.59 E
Bloubergstrand 158 33.47 S 18.28 E
Blouin, Lac ⊜ 190 48.10 N 77.44 W
Bloumet 148 23.27 N 6.05 E
Blounstown 192 30.26 N 85.02 W
Blountsville 194 34.04 N 86.35 W
Blountville 192 36.31 N 82.19 W
Blovice 60 49.35 N 13.33 E
Blovstrød 41 55.52 N 12.24 E
Blowering Reservoir ⊜¹ 171b 35.30 S 148.15 E
Blowing Rock 192 36.08 N 81.40 W
Bloxham 42 52.02 N 1.22 W
Bloxom 208 37.49 N 75.37 W
Blšanka ≃ 54 50.10 N 13.34 E
Blšany 54 50.10 N 13.29 E
Bludenz 58 47.09 N 9.49 E
Bludnaja ≃ 88 51.24 N 110.39 E
Blue ≃, Az., U.S. 200 33.13 N 109.11 W
Blue ≃, Co., U.S. 200 40.03 N 106.24 W
Blue ≃, In., U.S. 216 41.07 N 85.30 W
Blue ≃, In., U.S. 218 38.11 N 86.19 W
Blue ≃, Ok., U.S. 196 33.53 N 95.56 W
Blue, Middle Fork ≃ 218 38.33 N 86.07 W
Blue, South Fork ≃ 218 38.26 N 86.11 W
Blue, West Fork ≃ 218 38.33 N 86.07 W
Blue Anchor 285 39.41 N 74.54 W
Blue Anchor Brook ≃ 285 39.42 N 74.49 W
Blue Ash 218 39.13 N 84.22 W
Blue Ball 218 39.29 N 84.21 W
Blue Bell 208 40.09 N 75.16 W
Bluebell Hill 260 51.20 N 0.30 E
Blue Bonnets, Champ de Course ♦ 275a 45.29 N 73.39 W
Blue Brook ≃ 276 40.40 N 74.25 W
Blue Buck Knob ∧² 194 36.57 N 92.07 W
Bluebush Swamp ≡ 162 20.30 S 137.25 E
Blue Creek, Oh., U.S. 218 38.47 N 83.20 W
Blue Creek, Wa., U.S. 182 48.19 N 117.49 W
Blue Creek, Wa., U.S. 202 48.19 N 117.49 W
Blue Creek ≃, Ca., U.S. 226 38.28 N 120.22 W
Blue Creek ≃, Id., U.S. 202 42.02 N 116.08 W
Blue Creek ≃, Ne., U.S. 198 41.19 N 102.10 W

Blue Creek ≃, Oh., U.S. 216 41.07 N 84.26 W
Blue Creek ≃, Ut., U.S. 200 41.31 N 112.24 W
Blue Cypress Lake ⊜ 220 27.44 N 80.45 W
Blue Earth 190 43.38 N 94.06 W
Blue Earth ≃ 190 44.09 N 94.02 W
Bluefield, Va., U.S. 192 37.15 N 81.16 W
Bluefield, W.V., U.S. 192 37.16 N 81.13 W
Bluefields 236 12.00 N 83.45 W
Bluefields, Bahía de c 236 12.02 N 83.44 W
Bluefields Bay c 241q 18.10 N 78.03 W
Blue Grass Airport ✈ 218 38.02 N 84.36 W
Blue Grotto → Azzurra, Grotta ±⁵ 68 40.35 N 14.14 E
Blue Hill, Me., U.S. 188 44.24 N 68.35 W
Blue Hill, Ne., U.S. 198 40.19 N 98.26 W
Blue Hill Bay c 188 44.15 N 68.30 W
Blue Hills 207 41.40 N 72.56 W
Blue Hills of Couteau ∧² 186 47.59 N 57.43 W
Blue Hills Reservation ♦ 283 42.13 N 71.05 W
Blue Island 216 41.39 N 87.40 W
Blue Jay 228 34.15 N 117.13 W
Bluejoint Lake ⊜ 202 42.35 N 119.40 W
Blue Knob ∧ 214 40.17 N 78.34 W
Blue Knob State Park ♦ 214 40.16 N 78.35 W
Blue Lagoon National Park ♦ 154 15.30 S 27.25 E
Blue Lake National Park ♦ 171a 27.31 S 153.29 E
Blue Licks Battlefield State Park ♦ 218 38.26 N 84.00 W
Blue Marsh Lake ⊜¹ 208 40.25 N 76.05 W
Blue Mesa Reservoir ⊜¹ 200 38.27 N 107.10 W
Blue Mosque ♦¹ 273c 30.02 N 31.15 E
Blue Mound, Il., U.S. 219 39.42 N 89.07 W
Blue Mound, Ks., U.S. 198 38.05 N 95.00 W
Blue Mound, Tx., U.S. 222 32.51 N 97.19 W
Blue Mountain, Ms., U.S. 194 34.40 N 89.01 W
Blue Mountain, N.Y., U.S. 210 42.07 N 74.01 W
Blue Mountain ∧, N.B., Can. 186 47.49 N 66.19 W
Blue Mountain ∧, Nf., Can. 186 50.24 N 57.10 W
Blue Mountain ∧, Ar., U.S. 194 34.41 N 94.03 W
Blue Mountain ∧, Mt., U.S. 198 47.16 N 104.10 W
Blue Mountain ∧, N.H., U.S. 188 44.47 N 71.28 W
Blue Mountain ∧, Pa., U.S. 188 40.15 N 77.30 W
Blue Mountain ∧², On., Can. 190 48.15 N 80.07 W
Blue Mountain ∧², On., Can. 212 44.30 N 77.58 W
Blue Mountain Peak ∧ 241q 18.03 N 76.35 W
Blue Mountains ∧, Austl. 170 33.37 S 150.17 E
Blue Mountains ∧, Jam. 241q 18.06 N 76.40 W
Blue Mountains ∧, U.S. 202 45.30 N 118.15 W
Blue Mountains ∧, Me., U.S. 188 44.50 N 70.35 W
Blue Mountains National Park ♦ 170 33.40 S 150.25 E
Blue Mud Bay c 164 13.26 S 135.56 E
Blue Nile (Al-Bahr al-Azraq) (Abay) ≃ 140 15.38 N 32.31 E
Bluenose Lake ⊜ 180 68.25 N 119.45 W
Blue Point 276 40.45 N 73.02 W
Blue Point ≻ 276 40.44 N 73.02 W
Blue Rapids 198 39.40 N 96.39 W
Blue Ridge, Ab., Can. 182 54.08 N 115.22 W
Blue Ridge, Ga., U.S. 192 34.51 N 84.19 W
Blue Ridge, Il., U.S. 216 40.17 N 88.29 W
Blue Ridge ∧ 178 37.00 N 82.00 W
Blue Ridge Summit 208 39.43 N 77.28 W
Blue River 182 52.05 N 119.17 W
Blue Rock Springs Park ♦ 282 38.08 N 122.12 W
Bluesky 182 56.04 N 118.14 W
Blue Springs 198 40.08 N 96.39 W
Blue Stack Mountains ∧ 48 54.45 N 8.05 W
Bluestone ≃ 192 37.34 N 80.59 W
Bluestone Dam ✦⁶ 192 37.36 N 80.53 W
Bluestone Lake ⊜¹ 192 37.30 N 80.50 W
Bluestone State Park ♦ 192 37.37 N 80.56 W
Bluewater 200 35.15 N 107.59 W
Blue Water Bridge ✦⁵ 214 43.00 N 82.25 W
Bluff, N.Z. 172 46.36 S 168.20 E
Bluff, Ut,. U.S. 200 37.17 N 109.33 W
Bluff Cape ≻ 110 18.00 N 94.26 E
Bluff City, Il., U.S. 219 38.57 N 89.02 W
Bluff City, Tn., U.S. 192 36.28 N 82.15 W
Bluff Cove c 280 33.48 N 118.24 W
Bluff Creek ≃, U.S. 196 36.58 N 97.26 W
Bluff Creek ≃, Ks., U.S. 198 37.02 N 99.29 W
Bluff Dale 196 32.21 N 98.01 W
Bluff Head ≻ 271d 22.11 N 114.12 E
Bluff Island I 271d 22.19 N 114.21 E
Bluff Knoll ∧ 162 34.23 S 118.20 E
Bluff Park 194 33.24 N 86.51 W
Bluff Point ≻ 162 27.50 S 114.06 E
Bluffs 219 39.45 N 90.32 W
Bluff Springs 219 39.59 N 90.21 W
Bluffton, In., U.S. 216 40.44 N 85.10 W
Bluffton, Oh., U.S. 216 40.53 N 83.53 W
Bluffton, S.C., U.S. 192 32.14 N 80.51 W
Bluffy Lake ⊜ 184 50.47 N 92.55 W
Bluford 219 38.20 N 88.45 W
Blum 222 32.09 N 97.24 W
Blumberg, Dtsch. 54 52.36 N 13.37 E
Blumberg, Dtsch. 58 47.50 N 8.31 E
Blumenau 252 26.56 S 49.03 W
Blumenhof 184 50.01 N 107.41 W
Blumenthal 54 53.05 N 12.22 E
Blümlisalp ∧ 58 46.30 N 7.47 E
Blunt 198 44.30 N 99.59 W
Blup Blup Island I 164 3.30 S 144.37 E
Bly 202 42.24 N 121.02 W
Blying Sound ⊔ 180 59.40 N 149.15 W
Blyth, Austl. 168b 33.51 S 138.29 E
Blyth, On., Can. 190 43.44 N 81.26 W
Blyth, Eng., U.K. 44 55.07 N 1.30 W
Blyth ≃, Austl. 164 12.04 S 134.35 E
Blyth ≃, Eng., U.K. 42 52.18 N 1.40 E
Blyth ≃, Eng., U.K. 44 55.08 N 1.31 W
Blyth Bridge 46 55.42 N 3.24 W
Blythe 204 33.36 N 114.35 W
Blythedale 214 40.21 N 79.48 W
Blytheswood 214 42.07 N 82.36 W
Blytheville 194 35.55 N 89.55 W
Blytheville Air Force Base ■ 194 35.57 N 89.57 W
Blyth Range ∧ 162 26.50 S 129.00 E
Blyznyuky 78 48.52 N 36.33 E
Bnei Braq → Bene Beraq 132 32.05 N 34.50 E
Bø, Nor. 24 68.37 N 14.33 E
Bø, Nor. 26 59.25 N 9.04 E
Bo, S.L. 150 7.56 N 11.21 W
Boa 154 10.32 S 28.06 E
Boac 116 13.27 N 121.50 E


| Symbol | English | Deutsch | Español | Français | Português |
|---|---|---|---|---|---|
| ≃ | River | Fluß | Río | Rivière | Rio |
| ≍ | Canal | Kanal | Canal | Canal | Canal |
| ∟ | Waterfall, Rapids | Wasserfall, Stromschnellen | Cascada, Rápidos | Chute d'eau, Rapides | Cascata, Rápidos |
| ⊔ | Strait | Meeresstraße | Estrecho | Détroit | Estreito |
| c | Bay, Gulf | Bucht, Golf | Bahía, Golfo | Baie, Golfe | Baía, Golfo |
| ⊜ | Lake, Lakes | See, Seen | Lago, Lagos | Lac, Lacs | Lago, Lagos |
| ≡ | Swamp | Sumpf | Pantano | Marais | Pântano |
| ✱ | Ice Features, Glacier | Eis- und Gletscherformen | Accidentes Glaciales | Formes glaciaires | Acidentes glaciares |
| ⊤ | Other Hydrographic Features | Andere Hydrographische Objekte | Otros Elementos Hidrográficos | Autres données hydrographiques | Outros acidentes hidrográficos |
| ✦ | Submarine Features | Untermeerische Objekte | Accidentes Submarinos | Formes de relief sous-marin | Acidentes submarinos |
| □ | Political Unit | Politische Einheit | Unidad Politica | Entité politique | Unidade política |
| ♦ | Cultural Institution | Kulturelle Institution | Institución Cultural | Institution culturelle | Instituição cultural |
| ⊥ | Historical Site | Historische Stätte | Sitio Histórico | Site historique | Sitio histórico |
| ♦ | Recreational Site | Erholungs- und Ferienort | Sitio de Recreo | Centre de loisirs | Area de Lazer |
| ✈ | Airport | Flughafen | Aeropuerto | Aéroport | Aeroporto |
| ■ | Military Installation | Militäranlage | Instalación Militar | Installation militaire | Instalação militar |
| ✦ | Miscellaneous | Verschiedenes | Misceláneo | Divers | Diversos |

Boaco 236 12.28 N 85.40 W
Boaco □[5] 236 12.30 N 85.30 W
Boadilla del Monte 266a 40.24 N 3.53 W
Boa Esperança, Bra. 255 21.05 S 45.34 W
Boa Esperança, Bra. 256 22.48 S 42.34 W
Boa Esperança, Bra. 256 22.24 S 43.05 W
Boa Esperança, Represa ⊜[1] 250 6.50 S 44.00 W
Bo'ai 102 35.10 N 113.04 E
Boali 152 4.48 N 18.07 E
Boalia 126 23.35 N 88.57 E
Boalsburg 214 40.46 N 77.48 W
Boane 156 26.06 S 32.19 E
Boano, Pulau I 164 2.56 S 127.56 E
Boa Nova 255 14.22 S 40.10 W
Bo'ao 110 19.14 N 110.34 E
Boara Pisani 64 45.08 N 11.47 E
Boara Polesine 64 45.07 N 11.48 E
Board Camp Mountain ∧ 204 40.42 N 123.43 W
Boardman 214 41.01 N 80.39 W
Boardman ≐ 190 44.46 N 85.38 W
Boarhills 46 56.19 N 2.42 W
Boario Terme 64 45.54 N 10.10 E
Boat Basin 182 49.29 N 126.25 W
Boat Channel ꓤ 212 44.10 N 76.31 W
Boath 46 57.44 N 4.23 W
Boat Lake ⊜ 212 44.44 N 81.13 W
Boatman 166 27.16 S 146.55 E
Boat of Garten 46 57.20 N 3.44 W
Boa Viagem 250 5.07 S 39.44 W
Boa Vista, Bra. 246 2.49 N 60.40 W
Boa Vista, Bra. 256 21.25 S 45.35 W
Boa Vista I 150a 16.05 N 22.50 W
Boa Vista, Morro ∧[2] 287a 22.53 S 43.06 W
Boavita 246 6.20 N 72.35 W
Boawai 115b 8.46 S 121.10 E
Boayan Island I 116 10.34 N 119.09 E
Boaz 194 34.12 N 86.09 W
Boba 115b 8.57 S 121.04 E
Bobai 102 22.12 N 109.52 E
Bobbau 54 51.41 N 12.16 E
Bobbili 122 18.34 N 83.22 E
Bobbing 260 51.21 N 0.43 E
Bobbingworth 260 51.44 N 0.13 E
Bobbin Head 274a 33.39 S 151.08 E
Bobbio 62 44.46 N 9.23 E
Bobbio Pellice 62 44.48 N 7.07 E
Bobbys Run ≐ 285 39.58 N 74.48 W
Bobcaygeon 212 44.33 N 78.33 W
Bobenheim-Roxheim 56 49.35 N 8.21 E
Bobigny 50 48.54 N 2.27 E
Böbingen, Dtsch. 56 48.49 N 9.54 E
Bobingen, Dtsch. 58 48.16 N 10.50 E
Bobitz 54 53.47 N 11.20 E
Bob Lake ⊜ 212 44.55 N 78.47 W
Böblingen 56 48.41 N 9.01 E
Boblo Island Amusement Park ♦ 281 42.06 N 83.07 W
Bobo Dioulasso 150 11.12 N 4.18 W
Boboiob, gora ∧ 85 40.52 N 70.21 E
Bobo Island I 164 9.08 S 143.14 E
Bobolice 30 53.57 N 16.36 E
Bobonaza ≐ 246 2.36 S 76.38 W
Bobonong 156 21.58 S 28.17 E
Bobos ≐ 234 20.15 N 96.47 W
Bobotsari 115a 7.18 S 109.22 E
Bobr 76 54.20 N 29.16 E
Bobr ≐, Bela. 76 54.03 N 28.51 E
Bóbr ≐, Pol. 30 52.04 N 15.04 E
Bobrov 78 51.06 N 40.02 E
Bobrovytsya 78 50.44 N 31.22 E
Bobrujsk → Babrujsk 76 53.09 N 29.14 E
Bobryk ≐ 76 52.08 N 26.46 E
Bobrykove 83 47.56 N 39.13 E
Bobrynets' 78 48.03 N 32.09 E
Bob Sandlin, Lake ⊜[1] 222 33.05 N 95.03 W
Bobs Creek ≐ 219 38.57 N 90.42 W
Bobs Lake ⊜ 212 44.40 N 76.35 W
Bobtown 188 39.45 N 79.58 W
Bobuk 140 11.30 N 34.05 E
Bobures 246 9.15 N 71.11 W
Boby, Pic ∧ 157b 22.12 S 46.55 E
Boca ≐[8] 288 34.38 S 58.21 W
Bôca, Cachoeira da ⊥ 250 5.27 S 54.24 W
Boca Brava, Isla I 236 8.13 N 82.16 W
Boca Chica 240m 17.59 N 66.32 W
Boca Chica Key I 220 24.34 N 81.42 W
Bôca da Mata 250 9.41 S 36.11 W
Boca del Monte 236 8.21 N 82.07 W
Boca del Rio 234 19.06 N 96.06 W
Boca del Rosario 258 34.26 S 57.17 W
Boca de Pozo 246 11.00 N 64.23 W
Boca de Quadra ꓤ 182 55.08 N 130.50 W
Bôca do Acre 248 8.45 S 67.23 W
Bôca do Jari 250 1.07 S 51.58 W
Bocage, Cap ≻ 175f 21.12 S 165.35 E
Boca Grande 220 26.44 N 82.15 W
Boca Grande Channel ꓤ 220 24.34 N 82.03 W
Boca Grande Key I 220 24.32 N 82.00 W
Bocaina ≐ 256 22.40 S 45.00 W
Bocaina, Parque Nacional de ♦ 256 23.00 S 44.15 W
Bocaina, Serra da ∧ 256 22.43 S 44.40 W
Bocaina de Minas 256 22.10 S 44.24 W
Bocaiúva 255 17.07 S 43.49 W
Bocanda 150 7.04 N 4.30 W
Bocanegra 286d 12.01 S 77.07 W
Bocaranga 152 6.59 N 15.39 E
Boca Raton 220 26.21 N 80.05 W
Boca Reservoir ⊜[1] 226 39.24 N 120.06 W
Bocas del Toro 236 9.20 N 82.15 W
Bocas del Toro □[4] 236 8.50 N 82.10 W
Bocas del Toro, Archipiélago de II 236 9.20 N 82.10 W
Bocaue 116 14.48 N 120.55 E
Bocay 236 14.19 N 85.10 W
Bocay ≐ 236 14.20 N 85.10 W
Boccaleone 66 44.39 N 11.48 E
Boccea ≐[8] 267a 41.58 N 12.19 E
Bocchigliero 68 39.25 N 16.45 E
Bocconi 64 44.01 N 11.46 E
Bochan 88 53.09 N 103.48 E
Bochil 234 16.59 N 92.55 W
Böch Möron 86 49.40 N 90.20 E
Bochnia 30 49.58 N 20.26 E
Bocholt, Bel. 56 51.10 N 5.35 E
Bocholt, Dtsch. 52 51.50 N 6.36 E
Bocholtz 56 50.49 N 6.00 E
Bochov 54 50.06 N 13.02 E
Bochum, Dtsch. 56 51.28 N 7.13 E
Bochum, Dtsch. 263 51.28 N 7.13 E
Bochum, S. Afr. 156 23.17 S 29.07 E
Bockel 52 53.12 N 9.17 E
Böckel ≐[8] 263 51.13 N 7.12 E
Bockenem 52 52.00 N 10.07 E
Bockhorn 52 53.23 N 8.01 E
Böckstein 64 47.05 N 13.07 E
Bockum ≐[8], Dtsch. 263 51.21 N 6.38 E
Bockum ≐[8], Dtsch. 263 51.28 N 7.44 E
Bockum-Hövel 52 51.42 N 7.46 E
Bocognano 36 42.05 N 9.03 E
Bocón, Caño ≐ 246 3.42 N 67.53 W
Boconó 246 9.15 N 70.16 W
Bocq ≐ 56 50.20 N 4.53 E
Bocşa 38 45.23 N 21.47 E
Boczów 54 52.19 N 14.58 E
Boda, Centraf. 152 4.19 N 17.28 E
Böda, Sve. 26 57.15 N 17.03 E
Boda, Sve. 26 61.01 N 15.13 E
Bodafors 26 57.30 N 14.42 E
Boda Glasbruk 26 56.44 N 15.40 E
Bodāi 272b 22.48 N 88.29 E
Bodajbo 88 57.51 N 114.10 E
Bodalangi 152 3.14 N 22.14 E
Bodalla 166 36.05 S 150.03 E
Bodallin 162 31.22 S 118.52 E
Bodåsgruvan 40 60.25 N 16.26 E
Bodcau Creek ≐ 194 33.01 N 93.31 W
Boddam, Scot., U.K. 46 57.28 N 1.47 W
Boddam, Scot., U.K. 46a 59.55 N 1.17 W
Boddington 168a 32.48 S 116.28 E
Bode 198 42.52 N 94.17 W
Bode ≐ 54 51.50 N 11.46 E
Bodega Bay c 204 38.15 N 123.00 W
Bodegraven 52 52.05 N 4.45 E
Bodélé ≐[1] 146 16.30 N 16.30 E
Bodelschwingh ≐[8] 263 51.33 N 7.22 E
Bodelshausen 58 48.24 N 8.58 E
Boden → Fleres, It. 64 46.58 N 11.21 E
Boden, Sve. 26 65.50 N 21.42 E
Bodenburg 52 52.01 N 10.01 E
Bodenfelde 52 51.38 N 9.33 E
Bodenheim 56 49.56 N 8.18 E
Bodenmais 60 49.04 N 13.06 E
Bodensee (Lake Constance) ⊜ 58 47.35 N 9.25 E
Bodenteich 54 52.50 N 10.41 E
Bodenwerder 52 51.59 N 9.31 E
Bodenwies ∧ 61 47.45 N 14.34 E
Bodenwöhr 60 49.16 N 12.19 E
Boderg, Lough ⊜ 48 53.52 N 7.58 W
Bode Sadu 150 9.00 N 4.47 E
Bodhan 122 18.40 N 77.54 E
Bodh Gaya 124 24.42 N 84.59 E
Bodiam 42 51.00 N 0.33 E
Bodināyakkanūr 122 10.01 N 77.21 E
Bodine, Mount ∧ 182 55.37 N 125.49 W
Bodjoki 152 2.59 N 22.18 E
Bodjokola 152 3.54 N 20.17 E
Bodmin 42 50.29 N 4.43 W
Bodmin Moor ≐[3] 42 50.33 N 4.33 W
Bodø 24 67.17 N 14.23 E
Bodocó 250 7.47 S 39.55 W
Bodoquena, Serra da ∧[1] 248 21.00 S 56.50 W
Bodoukpa 152 5.43 N 17.36 E
Bodri ≐ 115a 6.52 S 110.10 E
Bodrog ≐ 30 48.07 N 21.25 E
Bodrum 130 37.02 N 27.26 E
Bodstedt 54 54.22 N 12.37 E
Bo Duc 110 11.58 N 106.48 E
Bodzentyn 30 50.56 N 20.57 E
Boè, Piz ∧ 64 46.31 N 11.48 E
Boëge 58 46.13 N 6.25 E
Boekelo 52 52.13 N 6.47 E
Boele ≐[8] 263 51.24 N 7.28 E
Boémbé 152 2.54 S 15.39 E
Boende 152 0.13 S 20.52 E
Boeng Lvea 110 12.36 N 105.34 E
Boeni 157a 12.55 S 45.06 E
Boën-sur-Lignon 62 45.44 N 3.59 E
Boeo, Capo ≻ 70 37.48 N 12.25 E
Boerboonfontein 158 33.43 S 20.32 E
Boerne 196 29.47 N 98.43 W
Boeslunde 41 55.18 N 11.17 E
Boesmans ≐, S. Afr. 158 28.46 S 30.09 E
Boesmans ≐, S. Afr. 158 33.42 S 26.39 E
Boesmansriviermond 158 33.42 S 26.39 E
Boetsap 158 27.59 S 24.30 E
Boeuf ≐ 194 31.52 N 91.47 W
Boeuf Creek ≐ 219 38.36 N 91.09 W
Boffa 150 10.10 N 14.02 W
Boffalora 266b 45.28 N 8.50 E
Boffzen 52 51.45 N 9.23 E
Bofoku 152 0.57 S 20.53 E
Bofors 40 59.20 N 14.32 E
Bofosso 150 8.40 N 9.42 W
Bŏfu → Hōfu 96 34.03 N 131.34 E
Boga 154 1.03 N 29.56 E
Bogachiel ≐ 224 47.55 N 124.28 W
Bogadjim 164 5.25 S 145.45 E
Bogal, Lagh ≐ 154 0.45 N 40.50 E
Bogale 110 16.17 N 95.24 E
Bogalusa 194 30.47 N 89.50 W
Bogan ≐ 166 29.57 S 146.21 E
Bogandé 150 12.59 N 0.08 W
Bog and Vly Meadows ≋ 276 40.56 N 74.19 W
Bogan Gate 166 33.07 S 147.48 E
Bogangolo 152 5.34 N 18.15 E
Bogantungan 166 23.39 S 147.18 E
Bogart, Mount ∧ 182 50.55 N 115.14 W
Bogastow Brook ≐ 283 42.12 N 71.22 W
Bogata 196 33.28 N 95.13 W
Bogatišćevo-Jepišino 82 54.47 N 38.25 E
Bogatoje 80 53.04 N 51.24 E
Bogatyje Saby 80 56.01 N 50.27 E
Bogatyr' 84 53.15 N 50.02 E
Bogatyrevo 80 50.22 N 48.46 E
Bogazkale 130 40.02 N 34.37 E
Bogazkaya 130 41.27 N 35.54 E
Bogazköy ≐[8] 267b 41.11 N 28.46 E
Bogazköy ≐ 267b 41.10 N 28.49 E
Bogazliyan 130 39.12 N 35.15 E
Bogbonga 152 1.35 N 19.25 E
Bogcang ≐ 120 31.56 N 87.24 E
Bogd 102 45.11 N 100.43 E
Bogdanovič 86 56.47 N 62.02 E
Bogdanovka, Ross. 80 52.42 N 50.46 E
Bogdanovka, Ross. 80 52.10 N 52.37 E
Bogda Shan ∧ 90 43.35 N 89.45 E
Bogdo Ula ∧ 86 43.50 N 88.20 E
Bogel 56 50.11 N 7.48 E
Bogembaj 86 52.29 N 72.20 E
Bogen 60 48.55 N 12.43 E
Bogense 41 55.34 N 10.06 E
Boger City 192 35.29 N 81.12 W
Bogess Creek ≐ 282 37.18 N 122.19 W
Bogetići 36 42.41 N 18.58 E
Boggabilla 166 28.37 S 150.21 E
Boggabri 166 30.42 S 150.02 E
Boggeragh Mountains ∧ 48 52.03 N 8.55 W
Boggola, Mount ∧ 162 23.48 S 117.40 E
Boggs Run ≐ 279b 40.32 N 80.14 W
Boggstown 218 39.34 N 85.55 W
Boggy Creek ≐ 222 33.45 N 95.33 W
Boggy Peak ∧ 240c 17.03 N 61.51 W
Boghra ≐ 164 4.15 S 144.55 E
Bogia 164 4.16 S 144.58 E
Bogie Lake ⊜ 281 42.37 N 83.31 W
Bogilima 152 3.34 N 19.16 E
Bogliasco 62 44.23 N 9.04 E
Bognanco Fonti 58 46.07 N 8.12 E
Bognes 24 68.10 N 16.00 E
Bognor Regis 42 50.47 N 0.41 W
Bogny-sur-Meuse 56 49.51 N 4.46 E
Bogo, Cam. 146 10.44 N 14.36 E
Bogo, Pil. 116 11.03 N 124.00 E
Bogø I 41 54.56 N 12.04 E
Bogo Bay c 116 11.05 N 124.01 E
Bogol Manyo 144 4.31 N 41.32 E
Bogol'ubovo, Ross. 76 55.12 N 32.57 E
Bogol'ubovo, Ross. 80 56.13 N 40.31 E
Bogomila 38 41.36 N 21.28 E
Bogong, Mount ∧ 166 36.45 S 147.18 E
Bogong Peaks ∧ 171b 35.34 S 148.28 E
Bogor 115a 6.35 S 106.47 E
Bogoria, Lake ⊜ 154 0.15 N 36.06 E
Bogoro 154 1.24 N 30.17 E
Bogorodick 80 53.46 N 38.08 E
Bogorodickoje 80 46.20 N 41.10 E
Bogorodsk, Ross. 24 62.16 N 52.28 E
Bogorodsk, Ross. 80 56.06 N 43.31 E
Bogorodskoje, Ross. 80 57.51 N 50.45 E
Bogorodskoje, Ross. 80 46.20 N 43.53 E
Bogorodskoje, Ross. 80 55.55 N 49.05 E
Bogorodskoje, Ross. 82 55.26 N 36.14 E
Bogorodskoje, Ross. 89 52.25 N 140.34 E
Bogorodskoje ≐[8] 265b 55.49 N 37.44 E
Bogoso 150 5.34 N 2.01 W
Bogosskij chrebet ∧ 84 42.15 N 46.05 E
Bogotá → Santa Fe de Bogotá, Col. 246 4.36 N 74.05 W
Bogota, N.J., U.S. 276 40.52 N 74.01 W
Bogotol 86 56.12 N 89.33 E
Bogou 150 10.39 N 0.11 E
Bogovarovo 24 58.59 N 47.01 E
Bogra 124 24.51 N 89.22 E
Bograd 86 54.13 N 90.51 E
Bogue Hill ∧[2] 44 55.08 N 3.55 W
Bogučany 88 58.23 N 97.29 E
Bogučar 78 49.57 N 40.33 E
Bogučar ≐ 78 49.57 N 40.39 E
Bogué 150 16.35 N 14.16 W
Bogue Chitto 194 31.26 N 90.27 W
Bogue Chitto ≐ 194 30.35 N 89.49 W
Bogue Chitto Creek ≐ 194 32.10 N 87.14 W
Bogue Phalia ≐ 194 33.15 N 90.44 W
Bogues Bay c 208 37.52 N 75.29 W
Bŏğürtlen 130 37.10 N 38.04 E
Bogustan 85 41.41 N 70.05 E
Bo Hai (Gulf of Chihli) c 98 38.30 N 120.00 E
Bohai Haixia ꓤ 98 38.15 N 121.00 E
Bohain-en-Vermandois 50 49.59 N 3.27 E
Bohai Wan c 98 38.40 N 118.20 E
Bohan 56 49.52 N 4.53 E
Bohannon 208 37.24 N 76.22 W
Böheimkirchen 61 48.12 N 15.46 E
Bohemia 210 40.46 N 73.06 W
Bohemia → Čechy □[9] 30 49.50 N 14.00 E
Bohemia ≐ 208 39.29 N 75.55 W
Bohemia Downs 162 18.53 S 126.14 E
Bohemian Forest ∧ 30 49.15 N 12.45 E
Bohetai 104 42.01 N 123.13 E
Bohicon 150 7.12 N 2.04 E
Bohin 144 11.44 N 51.15 E
Bohinjska Bistrica 36 46.17 N 13.57 E
Bohinjsko Jezero ⊜ 64 46.17 N 13.50 E
Bohlen 54 51.12 N 12.23 E
Böhlitz-Ehrenberg 54 51.21 N 12.17 E
Böhme ≐ 52 52.46 N 9.28 E
Böhmen → Čechy □[9] 30 49.50 N 14.00 E
Böhmenkirch 56 48.41 N 9.55 E
Böhmerwald → Bohemian Forest ∧ 30 49.15 N 12.45 E
Bohmte 52 52.22 N 8.19 E
Bohners Lake 216 42.37 N 88.17 W
Böhnsdorf ≐[8] 264a 52.24 N 13.33 E
Bohodou 150 9.46 N 9.04 W
Bohodukhiv 78 50.10 N 35.30 E
Bohol 144 5.45 N 46.09 E
Bohol □[4] 116 9.50 N 124.10 E
Bohol I 116 9.50 N 124.10 E
Bohol Sea ⊤[2] 116 9.10 N 124.25 E
Bohongou 150 12.30 N 0.42 E
Bohorg 152 6.23 N 15.37 E
Bohorodchany 78 48.48 N 24.32 E
Bohorok 114 3.30 N 98.12 E
Bohusián □[9] 26 58.15 N 11.50 E
Bohuslav 78 49.33 N 30.53 E
Bohušovice nad Ohří 54 50.29 N 14.07 E
Bohutin 60 49.40 N 13.55 E
Boi 150 9.34 N 9.27 E
Boi, Ponta do ≻ 256 23.58 S 45.15 W
Boiaçu 246 0.27 S 61.46 W
Boiano 66 41.29 N 14.29 E
Boiceville 210 41.59 N 74.15 W
Boiestown 186 46.27 N 66.25 W
Boigu Island I 164 9.16 S 142.13 E
Boila 154 16.10 S 39.50 E
Boiling Springs, N.C., U.S. 192 35.30 N 81.37 W
Boiling Springs, Pa., U.S. 208 40.08 N 77.07 W
Boim 250 2.49 S 55.10 W
Boinville-en-Mantois 261 48.56 N 1.46 E
Boinvilliers 261 48.55 N 1.40 E
Boipeba, Ilha de I 255 13.39 S 38.55 W
Boiro 34 42.39 N 8.54 W
Bois, Lac des ⊜, N.T., Can. 180 66.40 N 125.15 W
Bois, Lac des → Woods, Lake of the ⊜, N.A. 184 49.15 N 94.45 W
Bois, Rio dos ≐ 255 18.35 S 50.02 W
Bois Blanc Island I 190 45.45 N 84.28 W
Boisbriand 275a 45.37 N 73.51 W
Bois Brule ≐ 190 46.45 N 91.37 W
Boischâtel 206 46.54 N 71.08 W
Bois-Colombes 261 48.55 N 2.16 E
Bois-d'Arcy 261 48.48 N 2.02 E
Bois d'Arc Creek ≐ 196 33.50 N 95.50 W
Bois-d'Arcy 261 48.48 N 2.01 E
Bois-des-Filion 206 45.40 N 73.45 W
Bois de Sioux ≐ 198 46.16 N 96.36 W
Boise 202 43.36 N 116.12 W
Boise ≐ 202 43.49 N 117.01 W
Boise, Middle Fork ≐ 202 43.42 N 115.44 W
Boise, North Fork ≐ 202 43.42 N 115.38 W
Boise, South Fork ≐ 202 43.33 N 115.51 W
Boise City 196 36.43 N 102.30 W
Boisemont 261 49.01 N 2.00 E
Bois-Guillaume 50 49.28 N 1.08 E
Bois-le-Roi 50 48.28 N 2.42 E
Boissettes 261 48.31 N 2.37 E
Boissevain 184 49.14 N 100.03 W
Boissise-la-Bertrand 261 48.32 N 2.35 E
Boissy-l'Aillerie 261 49.05 N 2.02 E
Boissy-Saint-Léger 50 48.45 N 2.31 E
Boissy-sous-Saint-Yon 261 48.34 N 2.13 E
Boistfort Peak ∧ 224 46.29 N 123.12 W
Boitzenburg 54 53.15 N 13.37 E
Boizenburg 54 53.22 N 10.43 E
Boja 115a 7.06 S 110.16 E
Bojadła 30 51.57 N 15.50 E
Bojarkino 82 54.57 N 38.31 E
Bojarsk 88 56.19 N 106.04 E
Bojayá ≐ 246 6.35 N 76.54 W
Bojeador, Cape ≻ 116 18.30 N 120.34 E
Bojkovice 30 49.03 N 17.48 E
Bojevo 78 51.24 N 39.19 E
Boji Plain ≐ 154 1.30 N 39.45 E
Bojizhang 98 41.49 N 117.46 E
Bojnūrd 128 37.28 N 57.19 E
Bojonegoro 115a 7.09 S 111.52 E
Boju 150 7.25 N 7.52 E
Boju Ega 150 7.24 N 8.04 E
Bojuru 252 31.39 S 51.26 W
Boka 272c 18.53 N 72.59 E
Bokada 152 4.08 N 19.23 E
Bokal 168a 33.29 S 116.54 E
Bokala, Zaïre 152 3.07 S 17.02 E
Bokala, Zaïre 152 2.03 S 18.59 E
Bokani 150 9.26 N 5.13 E
Bokaro Steel City 124 23.45 N 86.07 E
Bokatola 152 0.38 S 18.46 E
Bokchito 196 34.01 N 96.08 W
Boké, Guinée 150 10.56 N 14.18 W
Boke, Kaz. 86 49.05 N 81.38 E
Bokeelia 220 26.42 N 82.09 W
Bokele 152 0.13 N 21.51 E
Bokela 152 1.03 S 21.56 E
Bokes Creek ≐ 214 40.24 N 83.08 W
Bokfontein 158 32.48 S 19.12 E
Bokhara 158 27.57 S 20.30 E
Bokhara ≐ 166 29.55 S 146.42 E
Boki 146 8.48 N 13.32 E
Bokito 152 4.34 N 11.07 E
Bokkol ∧ 154 1.50 N 37.02 E
Bok Koŭ 110 10.37 N 104.03 E
Böklund 52 54.35 N 9.35 E
Boknafjorden c[2] 26 59.10 N 5.35 E
Boko 152 4.47 S 14.38 E
Bokod 116 16.30 N 120.50 E
Bokodo 152 3.58 N 19.29 E
Bokolako 150 13.36 N 12.33 W
Bokonbajevskoje 85 42.07 N 77.00 E
Bokondji 152 2.22 N 18.42 E
Bokondo 152 0.15 N 22.32 E
Bokong 112 9.58 S 124.04 E
Bokoro 146 12.23 N 17.03 E
Boko Songo 152 4.26 S 13.37 E
Bokota 152 0.51 S 22.18 E
Bokote 152 0.05 S 20.08 E
Bokovo-Antratsit → Antratsyt 83 48.06 N 39.06 E
Bokovskaja 80 49.15 N 41.49 E
Bokpunt ≻ 158 33.34 S 18.19 E
Bokpyin 110 11.16 N 98.46 E
Boksburg 158 26.12 S 28.14 E
Boksburg □[5] 273d 26.12 S 28.14 E
Boksburg-Noord 273d 26.12 S 28.15 E
Boksburg South 273d 26.14 S 28.15 E
Boksburg-West 273d 26.13 S 28.14 E
Boksitogorsk 76 59.28 N 33.51 E
Bokungu 152 0.41 S 22.19 E
Bol, Hrv. 36 43.16 N 16.40 E
Bol, Tchad 146 13.28 N 14.43 E
Bolaang Mongondow 112 0.56 N 124.10 E
Bolama, Gui.-B. 150 11.35 N 15.28 W
Bolama, Zaïre 152 1.57 N 22.58 E
Bolaman 130 41.03 N 37.37 E
Bolān ≐ 120 28.38 N 67.42 E
Bolanda, Jabal ∧ 140 7.44 N 25.28 E
Bol'andikik ≐ 85 39.11 N 72.17 E
Bolangum 166 36.46 S 142.53 E
Bolaños 234 21.41 N 103.47 W
Bolaños ≐ 234 21.14 N 104.08 W
Bolaños de Calatrava 34 38.54 N 3.40 W
Bolān Pass ⨯ 120 29.45 N 67.35 E
Bolans 240c 17.02 N 61.53 W
Bolay I 152 4.20 N 17.21 E
Bolayır 130 40.31 N 26.45 E
Bolbec 50 49.34 N 0.29 E
Bolcali 84 40.38 N 46.18 E
Bolčary 86 59.49 N 68.48 E
Bolchov 76 53.27 N 36.01 E
Bolchuny 80 47.59 N 46.25 E
Bolda ≐ 80 46.10 N 48.14 E
Boldasevo 80 54.43 N 45.33 E
Boldekow 54 53.43 N 13.35 E
Bolderslev 41 54.59 N 9.18 E
Bold Heath 262 53.24 N 2.42 W
Boldon 44 54.57 N 1.27 W
Bol'dužan 85 38.19 N 69.40 E
Bole, Ghana 150 9.02 N 2.29 W
Bole, Zhg. 86 44.53 N 82.05 E
Bolekhiv 78 49.04 N 23.52 E
Boleko 152 1.31 S 19.53 E
Bolero 154 10.59 S 33.45 E
Boles 194 34.46 N 94.02 W
Bolesławiec 30 51.16 N 15.34 E
Boleszkowice 30 52.44 N 14.36 E
Boletice nad Labem 54 50.45 N 14.13 E
Boley 196 35.29 N 96.29 W
Bolgart 162 31.16 S 116.30 E
Bolgatanga 150 10.46 N 0.52 W
Bolhrad 78 45.41 N 28.36 E
Boli, Süd. 140 6.01 N 28.43 E
Boli, Tchad 150 10.46 N 18.43 E
Boli, Zhg. 89 45.46 N 130.31 E
Bolia 152 1.36 S 18.23 E
Boliden 26 64.52 N 20.23 E
Boligee 194 32.45 N 88.01 W
Boligeqiu 104 42.14 N 121.42 E
Bolikov 61 49.02 N 15.22 E
Bolinao 116 16.23 N 119.54 E
Boling 226 37.54 N 122.42 W
Boling 222 29.15 N 95.56 W
Bolingbrook 216 41.41 N 88.04 W
Bolinger Creek ≐ 282 37.47 N 122.00 W
Bolingo 152 3.30 S 21.43 E
Bolishan 89 43.50 N 123.31 E
Bolivar, Austl. 168b 34.46 S 138.36 E
Bolívar, Col. 246 5.50 N 76.01 W
Bolívar, Col. 246 4.21 N 76.18 W
Bolívar, Col. 246 1.50 N 76.58 W
Bolívar, Perú 248 7.18 S 77.48 W
Bolivar, Mo., U.S. 194 37.36 N 93.24 W
Bolivar, N.Y., U.S. 210 42.04 N 78.10 W
Bolivar, Oh., U.S. 214 40.39 N 81.27 W
Bolivar, Pa., U.S. 214 40.23 N 79.09 W
Bolivar, Tn., U.S. 194 35.15 N 88.59 W
Bolívar □[3] 246 6.20 N 63.30 W
Bolívar □[4] 246 1.35 S 79.00 W
Bolívar □[5] 246 9.00 N 74.40 W
Bolívar, Cerro ∧ 246 7.28 N 63.25 W
Bolívar, Pico ∧ 246 8.30 N 71.02 W
Bolivar Peninsula ≻[1] 196 29.27 N 94.39 W
Bolivar Run 214 41.59 N 78.39 W
Bolivia □[1], S.A. 242 17.00 S 65.00 W
Bolivia □[1], S.A. 248 17.00 S 65.00 W
Bolivie → Bolivia □[1] 248 17.00 S 65.00 W
Bolivien → Bolivia □[1] 248 17.00 S 65.00 W
Boljarovo 38 42.09 N 26.49 E
Boljevac 38 43.50 N 21.58 E
Bolkar Dağları ∧ 130 37.15 N 34.20 E
Bölkenbusch 263 51.21 N 7.06 E
Boll 56 48.38 N 9.37 E
Bolladello 266b 45.41 N 8.50 E
Bollate 62 45.33 N 9.07 E
Böllberg ∧[2] 263 51.23 N 7.19 E
Bollendorf 56 49.51 N 6.22 E
Bollène 62 44.17 N 4.45 E
Bollensdorf 264a 52.31 N 13.43 E
Bolles Canal ≋ 220 26.38 N 80.34 W
Bolles Harbor 216 41.51 N 83.24 W
Bollin ≐ 44 53.23 N 2.28 W
Bolling Air Force Base ■ 284c 38.51 N 77.02 W
Bollington, Eng., U.K. 44 53.18 N 2.06 W
Bollington, Eng., U.K. 262 53.22 N 2.25 W
Bollnäs 26 61.21 N 16.25 E
Bollon 166 28.05 S 147.15 E
Bollstabruk 26 63.00 N 17.39 E
Bollstanäs 40 59.30 N 17.56 E
Bollullos par del Condado 34 37.20 N 6.32 W
Bollwerk 263 51.10 N 7.35 E
Bolmen ⊜ 26 56.55 N 13.40 E
Bolnisi 84 41.28 N 44.33 E
Bolo 144 8.50 N 39.22 E
Bolobo 152 2.10 S 16.14 E
Bolochovo 82 54.05 N 37.50 E
Bologna 64 44.29 N 11.20 E
Bologna □[4] 64 44.28 N 11.26 E
Bologne, Fr. 58 48.12 N 5.08 E
Bologne → Bologna, It. 64 44.29 N 11.20 E
Bolognesi 248 6.35 S 73.10 W
Bolognetta 70 37.58 N 13.27 E
Bolognola 66 42.59 N 13.14 E
Bologoje 76 57.54 N 34.02 E
Bologovo 76 56.54 N 31.52 E
Bolomba 152 0.29 N 19.12 E
Bolombo 152 3.59 S 23.08 E
Bolombo ≐ 152 1.32 N 21.14 E
Bolon' 89 49.55 N 136.22 E
Bolon', ozero ⊜ 89 49.51 N 136.22 E
Bolonchén de Rejón 232 20.00 N 89.49 W
Bolondo 152 1.39 N 9.44 E
Bolondrón 240p 22.46 N 81.27 W
Bolong ≐ 170 34.15 S 149.36 E
Bolonia → Bologna 64 44.29 N 11.20 E
Bolótana 71 40.20 N 8.57 E
Bolotnoje 86 55.41 N 84.33 E
Boloto 82 54.10 N 36.20 E
Bolotovskoje 88 58.33 N 62.28 E
Bolovens, Plateaus des ∧[1] 110 15.20 N 106.20 E
Bolpur 124 23.40 N 87.43 E
Bolqār (Bolgarçay) ≐ 84 39.28 N 48.36 E
Bolqarçay (Bolqār) ≐ 84 39.28 N 48.36 E
Bol'šaja 76 59.36 N 41.48 E
Bol'šaja ≐ 80 48.35 N 41.50 E
Bol'šaja Atn'a 80 56.15 N 49.27 E
Bol'šaja Balachn'a ≐ 74 73.37 N 107.05 E
Bol'šaja Brembola 82 56.45 N 38.55 E
Bol'šaja Bukon' 86 48.53 N 82.43 E
Bol'šaja Čalykla ≐ 80 51.51 N 49.34 E
Bol'šaja Černigovka 80 52.07 N 50.52 E
Bol'šaja Chalan' 78 50.56 N 37.26 E
Bol'šaja Cheta ≐ 74 69.33 N 84.15 E
Bol'šaja Chobda ≐ 86 50.56 N 54.34 E
Bol'šaja Chundala 76 60.04 N 34.18 E
Bol'šaja Čuja ≐ 88 58.56 N 112.13 E
Bol'šaja Čurakovka 86 53.03 N 64.20 E
Bol'šaja Dmitrijevka 80 51.21 N 45.15 E
Bol'šaja Dora 76 59.05 N 37.38 E
Bol'šaja Džalga 80 45.59 N 42.41 E
Bol'šaja Glušica 80 52.24 N 50.28 E
Bol'šaja Ižora 76 59.56 N 29.34 E
Bol'šaja Ižorka ≐ 265a 59.48 N 30.36 E
Bol'šaja Kakša ≐ 80 57.53 N 45.28 E
Bol'šaja Kamenka 80 53.39 N 50.31 E
Bol'šaja Kandala 80 54.32 N 49.22 E
Bol'šaja Kaskara 86 57.11 N 65.58 E
Bol'šaja Ket' ≐ 86 57.39 N 91.45 E
Bol'šaja Kinel' ≐ 80 53.14 N 50.30 E
Bol'šaja Kirsanovka 83 47.40 N 38.54 E
Bol'šaja Kokšaga ≐ 80 56.08 N 47.47 E
Bol'šaja Konkudera ≐ 88 57.34 N 112.30 E
Bol'šaja Kugul'ta ≐ 80 45.41 N 41.57 E
Bol'šaja Kuonamka ≐ 74 70.45 N 113.24 E
Bol'šaja Laba ≐ 84 44.16 N 40.53 E
Bol'šaja Lipovica 80 52.33 N 41.20 E
Bol'šaja Martynovka 80 47.17 N 41.40 E
Bol'šaja Murta 86 55.55 N 93.07 E
Bol'šaja Neva ≐ 265a 59.58 N 30.13 E
Bol'šaja Norja 80 56.41 N 52.43 E
Bol'šaja Ochta ≐[8] 265a 59.57 N 30.25 E
Bol'šaja Ol'šanka 80 51.32 N 44.17 E
Bol'šaja Orlovka 80 47.20 N 41.16 E
Bol'šaja Osinovaja ≐ 180 66.30 N 174.00 E
Bol'šaja Pas'ma 80 58.38 N 43.53 E
Bol'šaja Rečka 88 51.57 N 104.44 E
Bol'šaja Ržaksa 80 52.08 N 42.13 E
Bol'šaja Sestra ≐ 82 56.16 N 35.56 E
Bol'šaja Smedva ≐ 82 54.50 N 38.34 E
Bol'šaja Sosnova 80 57.40 N 54.36 E
Bol'šaja Talovaja 78 46.58 N 40.37 E
Bol'šaja Tarel' 88 53.45 N 106.40 E
Bol'šaja Tavoložka 80 52.07 N 49.04 E
Bol'šaja Uča 80 56.37 N 52.05 E
Bol'šaja Usa 86 56.44 N 55.06 E
Bol'šaja Ussurka ≐ 89 45.57 N 133.42 E
Bol'šaja Višera 76 58.55 N 32.08 E
Bol'šaja Vladimirovka 86 50.53 N 79.31 E
Bolsa Knolls 226 36.44 N 121.38 W
Bol'šakovo, Ross. 76 54.53 N 21.40 E
Bol'šakovo, Ross. 265b 55.54 N 37.17 E
Bol'šekrepinskaja 83 47.36 N 39.22 E
Bol'šelig 24 62.07 N 52.25 E
Bolsena 66 42.39 N 11.59 E
Bolsena, Lago di ⊜ 66 42.36 N 11.56 E
Bol'šenarymskoje 86 49.16 N 84.32 E
Bol'šerečje 86 56.06 N 74.38 E
Bol'šereck 74 52.25 N 156.24 E
Bol'šetroickoje 78 50.33 N 37.17 E
Bol'šeustjikinskoje 86 55.57 N 58.16 E
Bol'ševik, Ross. 74 62.44 N 147.30 E
Bol'ševik, Ross. 265a 59.49 N 30.30 E
Bol'ševik, ostrov I 74 78.40 N 102.30 E
Bol'šezemel'skaja Tundra ≐[1] 24 67.30 N 56.00 E
Bolshoi Theatre ⅎ 265b 55.46 N 37.37 E
Bol'šije Algaši 80 55.22 N 46.29 E
Bol'šije Belyniči 82 54.38 N 38.50 E
Bol'šije Bereźniki 80 54.11 N 45.58 E
Bol'šije Gorki, Ross. 82 56.28 N 35.51 E
Bol'šije Gorki, Ross. 265a 59.42 N 29.51 E
Bol'šije Kajbicy 80 55.25 N 48.13 E
Bol'šije Kizi, ozero ⊜ 89 51.38 N 140.20 E
Bol'šije Kl'uči 80 55.59 N 48.47 E
Bol'šije Kl'uščí 80 54.08 N 48.14 E
Bol'šije Liachvi ≐ 84 41.58 N 44.06 E
Bol'šije Michalicyny 80 58.29 N 48.14 E
Bol'šije Ozerki 80 52.36 N 46.33 E
Bol'šije Pom'aly 80 56.42 N 46.40 E
Bol'šije Ruči 82 56.36 N 36.58 E
Bol'šije Saly 83 47.24 N 39.41 E
Bol'šije Tarchany 80 54.42 N 48.34 E
Bol'šije Ugli 88 57.47 N 112.51 E
Bol'šije Uki 86 56.57 N 72.37 E
Bol'šije Ždanovy 80 58.40 N 49.05 E
Bol'šoj 80 50.13 N 43.26 E
Bol'šoj Aksuat, ozero ⊜ 86 51.24 N 64.28 E
Bol'šoj An'uj ≐ 74 68.30 N 160.49 E
Bol'šoj Azbulat, ozero ⊜ 86 53.17 N 77.25 E
Bol'šoj Begičev, ostrov I 74 74.20 N 112.30 E
Bol'šoj Bogdo, gora ∧[2] 80 48.08 N 46.52 E
Bol'šoj Boktybaj, gora ∧ 86 48.27 N 58.30 E
Bol'šoj Čeremšan ≐ 80 54.11 N 49.39 E
Bol'šoj Civil' ≐ 80 55.54 N 47.28 E
Bol'šoje, ozero ⊜ 265a 60.04 N 30.39 E
Bol'šoje Aksu 84 43.20 N 79.35 E
Bol'šoje Alekseievskoje 82 55.14 N 38.12 E
Bol'šoje Boldino 80 54.59 N 45.19 E
Bol'šoje Bun'kovo 82 55.51 N 38.37 E
Bol'šoje Goloustnoje 88 52.01 N 105.25 E
Bol'šoje Gorodišče, Ross. 76 57.17 N 30.31 E
Bol'šoje Gorodišče, Ross. 78 50.37 N 37.06 E
Bol'šoje Ignatovo 80 55.02 N 45.34 E
Bol'šoje Jarovoje, ozero ⊜ 86 52.53 N 78.36 E
Bol'šoje Jašaltinskoje, ozero ⊜ 80 46.17 N 42.27 E
Bol'šoje Kibejevo 80 56.55 N 47.05 E
Bol'šoje Korovino 82 54.30 N 39.02 E
Bol'šoje Manuškino 265a 59.53 N 30.49 E
Bol'šoje Michajlovskoje 82 56.47 N 38.04 E
Bol'šoje Mikuškino 80 53.56 N 51.36 E
Bol'šoje Muraškino 80 55.47 N 44.46 E
Bol'šoje Nagatkino 80 54.33 N 48.24 E
Bol'šoje Nurkejevo 80 54.48 N 49.52 E
Bol'šoje Nyrsy 80 55.44 N 50.19 E
Bol'šoje Ogar'ovo 76 53.33 N 37.43 E
Bol'šoje Pikino 80 56.25 N 44.22 E
Bol'šoje Polpino 76 53.16 N 34.22 E
Bol'šoje Ramenje 76 58.21 N 36.40 E
Bol'šoje Rybuškino 76 56.54 N 31.42 E
Bol'šoje Sazonovo 76 58.56 N 35.24 E
Bol'šoje Šelo 76 57.43 N 38.56 E
Bol'šoje Šem'akino 80 54.31 N 46.38 E
Bol'šoje Soldatskoje 78 51.21 N 35.31 E
Bol'šoje Sudačje 80 50.45 N 44.15 E
Bol'šoje Topol'noje, ozero ⊜ 86 53.20 N 78.00 E
Bol'šoje Uro 88 53.32 N 109.48 E
Bol'šoje Zagorje 76 57.51 N 28.57 E
Bol'šoje Žokovo 82 54.45 N 38.27 E
Bol'šoj Gašun ≐ 80 47.22 N 42.43 E
Bol'šoj Golec, gora ∧ 88 51.52 N 119.24 E
Bol'šoj Irgiz ≐ 80 52.01 N 47.24 E
Bol'šoj Jenisej (Bij-Chem) ≐ 88 51.43 N 94.26 E
Bol'šoj Jugan ≐ 86 60.55 N 73.40 E
Bol'šoj Kamen' 89 43.06 N 132.21 E
Bol'šoj Kandarat' 80 54.25 N 47.00 E
Bol'šoj Kanym, gora ∧ 86 50.13 N 88.20 E
Bol'šoj Karagaj 86 57.57 N 70.15 E
Bol'šoj Karaman ≐ 80 51.40 N 46.38 E
Bol'šoj Ketmen' 86 43.27 N 80.24 E
Bol'šoj Kujaš 86 55.50 N 61.06 E
Bol'šoj Kundyš ≐ 80 56.32 N 47.23 E
Bol'šoj Kuvaj 80 54.37 N 47.05 E
Bol'šoj Kymynej, gora ∧ 180 66.34 N 172.32 W
Bol'šoj L'achovskij, ostrov I 74 73.35 N 142.00 E
Bol'šoj Lug 88 52.07 N 104.10 E
Bol'šoj Matačynaj, gora ∧ 180 66.28 N 179.25 W
Bol'šoj Melik 80 51.38 N 43.18 E
Bol'šoj Nesvetaj ≐ 83 47.27 N 39.54 E
Bol'šoj Onguren 88 53.38 N 107.36 E
Bol'šoj Patom ≐ 88 59.15 N 113.56 E
Bol'šoj Pit ≐ 86 59.01 N 91.44 E
Bol'šoj Porog 86 52.35 N 92.18 E
Bol'šoj Šagan 80 50.57 N 51.08 E
Bol'šoj Sajan ∧ 88 52.00 N 99.30 E
Bol'šoj Salym ≐ 86 60.55 N 70.25 E
Bol'šoj Santar, ostrov I 89 55.00 N 137.42 E
Bol'šoj Šatan, gora ∧ 86 53.41 N 57.36 E
Bol'šoj Simonogont 265a 59.50 N 29.49 E
Bol'šoj Sorokino 86 56.38 N 63.53 E
Bol'šoj Sundyr' 80 56.07 N 46.46 E
Bol'šoj Tal'cy 76 59.13 N 33.00 E
Bol'šoj Tolkaj 80 53.30 N 51.57 E
Bol'šoj T'uters, ostrov I 76 59.51 N 27.13 E
Bol'šoj Uluj 86 56.39 N 90.36 E
Bol'šoj Uran ≐ 80 52.24 N 53.15 E
Bol'šoj Uvat, ozero ⊜ 86 57.35 N 70.30 E
Bol'šoj Uzen' ≐ 80 48.50 N 49.40 E
Bol'šoj Uzigont 265a 59.48 N 29.53 E
Bol'šoj Vjass 80 53.48 N 45.30 E
Bol'šoj Vlasjevo 89 53.24 N 140.55 E
Bol'šoj Zelenčuk ≐ 84 44.36 N 41.56 E
Bolsover 44 53.14 N 1.18 W
Bolsward 52 53.03 N 5.31 E
Boltaña 34 42.27 N 0.04 E
Boltigen 58 46.38 N 7.24 E
Boltino 265b 55.58 N 37.41 E
Bolton, On., Can. 212 43.53 N 79.44 W
Bolton, Eng., U.K. 262 53.35 N 2.26 W
Bolton, Ct., U.S. 207 41.46 N 72.26 W
Bolton, Ms., U.S. 194 32.20 N 90.27 W
Bolton, N.C., U.S. 192 34.19 N 78.24 W
Bolton □[8] 262 53.34 N 2.28 W
Bolton Abbey 44 53.59 N 1.53 W
Bolton Abbey ⅎ[1] 44 53.59 N 1.54 W
Bolton Center 207 41.47 N 72.26 W
Bolton Creek ≐ 212 44.58 N 76.23 W
Bolton Lake ⊜ 184 54.16 N 95.47 W
Bolton-le-Sands 44 54.06 N 2.47 W
Bolton upon Dearne 44 53.31 N 1.19 W
Bolton Wanderers Football Ground ♦ 262 53.34 N 2.25 W
Bolu 130 40.44 N 31.37 E
Bolu □[4] 130 40.40 N 31.30 E
Bölükyazı 130 38.18 N 42.10 E
Boluntay 120 36.34 N 92.38 E
Boluo, Zhg. 100 23.11 N 114.17 E
Boluo, Zhg. 100 24.27 N 113.03 E
Boluochi 98 41.24 N 119.56 E
Boluokeng 100 24.05 N 113.22 E
Bolus Head ≻ 48 51.46 N 10.21 W
Bolva ≐ 76 53.17 N 34.20 E
Bolvadin 130 38.42 N 31.04 E
Bolwarra 166 17.24 S 144.11 E
Bőly 30 45.58 N 18.32 E
Bolyčevo 82 55.46 N 35.43 E
Bolzaneto 62 44.27 N 8.54 E
Bolzano (Bozen) 64 46.31 N 11.22 E
Bolzano □[4] 64 46.43 N 11.30 E
Boma 152 5.51 S 13.03 E
Bomaderry 170 34.51 S 150.37 E
Bomal 56 50.23 N 5.32 E
Bomandjokou 152 0.34 N 14.23 E
Bomaneh 152 1.18 N 23.47 E
Bomarsund 26 60.13 N 20.15 E
Bomate 152 1.10 S 19.41 E
Bomba 66 42.02 N 14.22 E
Bombakabo 152 3.04 N 19.42 E
Bombala 166 36.54 S 149.14 E
Bombarral 34 39.16 N 9.09 W
Bombay 130 38.08 N 42.18 E
Bombay, India 122 18.58 N 72.50 E
Bombay, India 272c 18.58 N 72.50 E
Bombay, N.Y., U.S. 206 44.56 N 74.34 W
Bombay, University of ⅎ[2] 272c 18.57 N 72.50 E
Bombay Harbour c 272c 18.57 N 72.52 E
Bombeeraj Semenanjung ≻[1] 164 3.00 S 133.00 E
Bombetoka, Baie de c 157b 15.50 S 46.17 E
Bombimba 152 0.31 N 19.24 E
Bombo 154 0.35 N 32.32 E
Bombo ≐ 152 3.58 S 15.59 E
Bombo-Kasanji 152 5.54 S 21.51 E
Bomboma 152 2.25 N 18.54 E
Bombo-Makuka 152 5.26 S 16.19 E
Bombombwa 154 1.21 N 25.30 E
Bombon 261 48.34 N 2.52 E
Bomboyo 146 12.01 N 15.28 E
Bom Conselho 250 9.10 S 36.41 W
Bom Despacho 255 19.43 S 45.15 W
Bomdila 120 27.27 N 92.17 E
Bomei 100 22.57 N 115.46 E
Bom Fim do Bom Jesus 256 23.17 S 47.02 W
Bomhus 40 60.41 N 17.13 E
Bomili 154 1.40 N 27.01 E
Bom Jardim, Ilha do I 287a 23.02 S 43.35 W
Bom Jardim de Goiás 255 16.17 S 52.07 W
Bom Jardim de Minas 256 21.57 S 44.11 W
Bom Jesus, Ang. 152 9.09 S 13.34 E
Bom Jesus, Bra. 250 9.04 S 44.22 W
Bom Jesus da Lapa 255 13.15 S 43.25 W
Bom Jesus de Goiás 255 18.12 S 49.44 W
Bom Jesus dos Perdões 256 23.08 S 46.28 W
Bømlafjorden c[2] 26 59.39 N 5.20 E
Bomlitz 52 52.54 N 9.38 E
Bømlo I 26 59.46 N 5.12 E
Bommerholz 263 51.23 N 7.18 E
Bommern 263 51.25 N 7.20 E
Bomnak 88 54.44 N 128.51 E
Bomokandi ≐ 154 3.39 N 26.08 E
Bomongo 152 1.22 N 18.21 E
Bomotu 152 4.05 N 19.24 E
Bompata 150 6.38 N 1.04 W
Bompietro 70 37.44 N 14.06 E
Bomputu 152 1.20 S 20.06 E
Bom Repouso 256 22.28 S 46.09 W
Bom Retiro 252 27.48 S 49.31 W
Bom Retiro ≐[8] 287b 23.32 S 46.38 W
Bom Sucesso, Bra. 248 15.43 S 56.07 W
Bom Sucesso, Bra. 256 21.02 S 44.45 W
Bom Sucesso, Bra. 256 22.17 S 42.49 W
Bom Sucesso, Bra. 287b 23.25 S 46.23 W
Bomu (Mbomou) ≐ 136 4.08 N 22.26 E
Bon, Cap ≻ 36 37.05 N 11.03 E
Bona 56 47.16 N 4.40 E
Bona Bona Island I 164 10.30 S 149.50 E
Bon Accord 158 25.37 S 28.13 E
Bonaduz 58 46.49 N 9.25 E
Bonaero Park 273d 26.07 S 28.16 E
Bonai 114 1.16 N 100.52 E
Bonaigarh 120 21.50 N 84.57 E
Bon Air 208 37.31 N 77.33 W
Bon Aire 214 40.52 N 79.55 W
Bonaire I 241s 12.10 N 68.15 W
Bonampak ⊥ 232 16.44 N 91.05 W
Bonan 40 60.44 N 17.18 E
Bonandolok 114 1.47 N 98.48 E
Bonanza, Nic. 236 14.01 N 84.35 W
Bonanza, Or., U.S. 202 42.11 N 121.24 W
Bonanza, Ut., U.S. 200 40.01 N 109.10 W


**Symbols** in the index entries represent the broad categories identified in the key at the right. Symbols with superior numbers (∧[1]) identify subcategories (see complete key on page I · 1).

**Symbole** im Register stellen die rechts im Schlüssel erklärten Kategorien dar. Symbole mit hochgestellten Ziffern (∧[1]) bezeichnen Unterabteilungen einer Kategorie (vgl. vollständiger Schlüssel auf Seite I · 1).

**Los símbolos** incluidos en el texto del índice representan las grandes categorías identificadas con la clave a la derecha. Los símbolos con numeros en su parte superior (∧[1]) identifican las subcategorías (véase la clave completa en la página I · 1).

**Les symboles** de l'index représentent les catégories indiquées dans la légende à droite. Les symboles suivis d'un indice (∧[1]) représentent des sous-catégories (voir légende complète à la page I · 1).

**Os símbolos** incluídos no texto do índice representam as grandes categorias identificadas com a chave à direita. Os símbolos com números em sua parte superior (∧[1]) identificam as subcategorias (veja-se a chave completa à página I · 1).

| ENGLISH | DEUTSCH | ESPAÑOL | FRANÇAIS | PORTUGUÊS |
|---|---|---|---|---|
| ∧ Mountain | Berg | Montaña | Montagne | Montanha |
| ∧ Mountains | Gebirge | Montañas | Montagnes | Montanhas |
| ⨯ Pass | Paß | Paso | Col | Passo |
| V Valley, Canyon | Tal, Cañon | Valle, Cañón | Vallée, Canyon | Vale, Canhão |
| ≐ Plain | Ebene | Llano | Plaine | Planície |
| ≻ Cape | Kap | Cabo | Cap | Cabo |
| I Island | Insel | Isla | Île | Ilha |
| II Islands | Inseln | Islas | Îles | Ilhas |
| ⊥ Other Topographic Features | Andere Topographische Objekte | Otros Elementos Topográficos | Autres données topographiques | Outros acidentes topográficos |

| ESPAÑOL Nombre / FRANÇAIS Nom / PORTUGUÊS Nome | Página / Page / Página | Lat.°′ | Long.°′ W = Oeste / W = Ouest / W = Oeste |
|---|---|---|---|
| Bonanza Peak ∧ | 224 | 48.14 N | 120.52 W |
| Bonao | 238 | 18.56 N | 70.25 W |
| Bonaparte | 190 | 40.41 N | 91.48 W |
| Bonaparte ≃ | 182 | 50.46 N | 121.17 W |
| Bonaparte, Lake ⊜ | 212 | 44.09 N | 75.23 W |
| Bonaparte, Mount ∧ | 202 | 48.45 N | 119.08 W |
| Bonaparte | | | |
| Archipelago II | 160 | 14.17 S | 125.18 E |
| Bonaparte Lake ⊜ | 182 | 51.16 N | 120.35 W |
| Bonar Bridge | 46 | 57.53 N | 4.21 W |
| Bonarcado | 71 | 40.04 N | 8.38 E |
| Bonasila Dome ∧ | 180 | 62.19 N | 160.30 W |
| Bonasse | 241r | 10.05 N | 61.52 W |
| Bonassola | 62 | 44.11 N | 9.35 E |
| Bonaventure | 186 | 48.03 N | 65.29 W |
| Bonaventure ≃ | 186 | 48.02 N | 65.28 W |
| Bonaventure, Île I | 186 | 48.30 N | 64.10 W |
| Bonavista | 186 | 48.39 N | 53.07 W |
| Bonavista, Cape › | 186 | 48.42 N | 53.05 W |
| Bonavista Bay c | 186 | 48.45 N | 53.20 W |
| Bonawe | 46 | 56.26 N | 5.13 W |
| Bonawon | 116 | 9.08 N | 122.55 E |
| Bonbeach | 274b | 38.04 S | 145.08 E |
| Bonboillon | 58 | 47.20 N | 5.42 E |
| Bon Bon | 162 | 30.26 S | 135.28 E |
| Bonbonon Point › | 116 | 9.03 N | 123.08 E |
| Bonchester Bridge | 44 | 55.24 N | 2.40 W |
| Boncourt | 58 | 47.30 N | 6.56 E |
| Boncuk Dağı ∧ | 130 | 36.53 N | 29.17 E |
| Bond | 194 | 30.54 N | 89.10 W |
| Bond □[6] | 219 | 38.53 N | 89.25 W |
| Bondari | 80 | 52.57 N | 42.04 E |
| Bondarivka | 83 | 49.23 N | 39.37 E |
| Bondeno | 64 | 44.53 N | 11.25 E |
| Bondi | 274a | 33.53 S | 151.17 E |
| Bondo, Zaïre | 152 | 1.22 S | 23.53 E |
| Bondo, Zaïre | 152 | 3.49 N | 23.40 E |
| Bondoc Peninsula ›[1] | 116 | 13.30 N | 122.30 E |
| Bondoc Point › | 116 | 13.10 N | 122.36 E |
| Bondorf | 58 | 48.31 N | 8.49 E |
| Bondoufle | 261 | 48.37 N | 2.23 E |
| Bondoukou | 150 | 8.02 N | 2.48 W |
| Bondowoso | 115a | 7.55 S | 113.49 E |
| Bondsville | 207 | 42.12 N | 72.20 W |
| Bonduel | 190 | 44.44 N | 88.26 W |
| Bondues | 50 | 50.42 N | 3.06 E |
| Bondy | 261 | 48.54 N | 2.28 E |
| Bondy, Forêt de ♠ | 261 | 48.55 N | 2.35 E |
| Bône | | | |
| → Annaba, Alg. | 148 | 36.54 N | 7.46 E |
| Bone, Indon. | 112 | 4.46 S | 122.52 E |
| Bone | | | |
| → Watampone, | | | |
| Indon. | 112 | 4.32 S | 120.20 E |
| Bone, Indon. | 112 | 5.09 S | 122.37 E |
| Bone, Teluk c | 112 | 4.00 S | 120.40 E |
| Bonebone | 112 | 2.36 S | 120.33 E |
| Bon Echo Provincial | | | |
| Park ♠ | 212 | 44.52 N | 77.15 W |
| Bonefro | 66 | 41.42 N | 14.56 E |
| Bone Island I | 212 | 44.56 N | 79.51 W |
| Bonelipu | 112 | 4.50 S | 123.11 E |
| Bonelohe | 112 | 5.48 S | 120.27 E |
| Bönen | 52 | 51.36 N | 7.44 E |
| Boneogeh | 112 | 7.16 S | 120.48 E |
| Bonerate, Pulau I | 112 | 7.22 S | 121.08 E |
| Bon Espérance, Cap | | | |
| de | | | |
| → Good Hope, | | | |
| Cape of › | 158 | 34.24 S | 18.30 E |
| Bo'ness | 46 | 56.01 N | 3.37 W |
| Bonesteel | 198 | 43.04 N | 98.56 W |
| Bonete, Cerro ∧ | 252 | 27.51 S | 68.47 W |
| Bonete Chico, Cerro | | | |
| ∧ | 252 | 28.01 S | 68.45 W |
| Bonětice | 60 | 49.41 N | 12.49 E |
| Bonfield | 216 | 41.09 N | 88.03 W |
| Bonfinópolis de | | | |
| Minas | 255 | 16.28 S | 45.59 W |
| Bonfol | 58 | 47.29 N | 7.09 E |
| Bonga | 144 | 7.17 N | 36.15 E |
| Bongabon | 116 | 15.38 N | 121.08 E |
| Bongabon ≃ | 116 | 12.40 N | 121.33 E |
| Bongabong | 116 | 12.45 N | 121.29 E |
| Bongaigaon | 124 | 26.28 N | 90.34 E |
| Bongak | 140 | 7.27 N | 33.14 E |
| Bongandanga | 152 | 1.30 N | 21.03 E |
| Bongao Island I | 116 | 5.01 N | 119.46 E |
| Bongaree | 171a | 27.05 S | 153.10 E |
| Bonggaw | 116 | 5.02 N | 119.46 E |
| Bongka | 112 | 0.58 S | 121.27 E |
| Bongka ≃ | 112 | 0.59 S | 121.05 E |
| Bong Mieu | 110 | 15.25 N | 108.24 E |
| Bongo, Ang. | 152 | 8.48 S | 17.49 E |
| Bongo, Gabon | 152 | 2.10 S | 10.12 E |
| Bongo, Massif des ⋏ | 146 | 8.40 N | 22.25 E |
| Bongo I | 152 | 3.01 N | 20.06 E |
| Bongo II | 152 | 1.47 S | 17.41 E |
| Bongo Island I | 116 | 7.20 N | 124.02 E |
| Bongolu | 152 | 2.48 N | 22.29 E |
| Bongon | 112 | 6.35 N | 116.52 E |
| Bongor | 146 | 10.17 N | 15.22 E |
| Bongou ≃ | 140 | 6.42 N | 22.04 E |
| Bongouanou | 150 | 6.39 N | 4.12 W |
| Bong Range ⋏ | 150 | 6.50 N | 10.00 W |
| Bong Son | 110 | 14.26 N | 109.01 E |
| Bonham | 196 | 33.34 N | 96.10 W |
| Bonheiden | 56 | 51.02 N | 4.32 E |
| Bonhomme, Col du )( | 58 | 48.10 N | 7.06 E |
| Bonhomme, Morne ∧ | 238 | 19.05 N | 72.18 W |
| Bonhomme Island I | 219 | 38.42 N | 90.36 W |
| Bonifacio, Fr. | 36 | 41.23 N | 9.10 E |
| Bonifacio, Pil. | 116 | 8.03 N | 123.37 E |
| Bonifacio, Strait of Ц | 36 | 41.20 N | 9.15 E |
| Bonifacio Monument | | | |
| ⊥ | 269f | 14.39 N | 120.59 E |
| Bonifati | 68 | 39.35 N | 15.54 E |
| Bonifati, Capo › | 68 | 39.35 N | 15.52 E |
| Bonifay | 194 | 30.47 N | 85.40 W |
| Bonifica del Volturno | | | |
| ≚ | 68 | 41.01 N | 14.00 E |
| Bonilla Island I | 182 | 53.29 N | 130.36 W |
| Bonin Islands | | | |
| → Ogasawara- | | | |
| guntō II | 14 | 27.00 N | 142.10 E |
| Bonita | 194 | 32.55 N | 91.40 W |
| Bonita, Point › | 282 | 37.49 N | 122.32 W |
| Bonita Springs | 220 | 26.20 N | 81.46 W |
| Bonito, Bra. | 248 | 21.08 S | 56.28 W |
| Bonito, Bra. | 250 | 8.29 S | 35.44 W |
| Bonito, It. | 68 | 41.06 N | 15.00 E |
| Bonito ≃, Bra. | 255 | 16.31 S | 51.23 W |
| Bonito ≃, Bra. | 256 | 22.12 S | 43.02 W |
| Bonito ≃, Bra. | 256 | 22.09 S | 43.40 W |
| Bonito, Pico ∧ | 236 | 15.38 N | 86.55 W |
| Bonito, Rio ≃ | 200 | 33.23 N | 105.16 W |
| Bonito de Santa Fé | 250 | 7.19 S | 38.31 W |
| Bonjol | 112 | 0.01 S | 100.13 E |
| Bonkoukou | 150 | 14.01 N | 3.13 E |
| Bon Meade | 279b | 40.33 N | 80.14 W |
| Bonn | 56 | 50.44 N | 7.05 E |
| Bonnanaro | 71 | 40.32 N | 8.45 E |
| Bonndorf im | | | |
| Schwarzwald | 58 | 47.49 N | 8.20 E |
| Bonneauville | 208 | 39.46 N | 77.10 W |
| Bonne Bay (Woody | | | |
| Point) | 186 | 49.30 N | 57.56 W |
| Bonne Bay c | 186 | 49.33 N | 57.55 W |
| Bonnebosq | 50 | 49.12 N | 0.05 E |
| Bonnechere ≃ | 190 | 45.31 N | 76.33 W |
| Bonneia | 144 | 5.41 N | 37.45 E |
| Bonnelles | 261 | 48.37 N | 2.02 E |
| Bonner | 202 | 46.52 N | 113.51 W |
| Bonners Ferry | 202 | 48.41 N | 116.18 W |
| Bonne-sur-Ménoge | 58 | 46.10 N | 6.20 E |
| Bonnet, Lac du ⊜ | 184 | 50.22 N | 95.55 W |
| Bonnétable | 50 | 48.11 N | 0.26 E |
| Bonne Terre | 194 | 37.55 N | 90.33 W |
| Bonnet Plume ≃ | 180 | 65.55 N | 134.58 W |
| Bonneuil-sur-Marne | 261 | 48.46 N | 2.29 E |
| Bonneval | 50 | 48.11 N | 1.24 E |
| Bonneval-sur-Arc | 62 | 45.22 N | 7.03 E |
| Bonnevaux | 58 | 46.18 N | 6.40 E |
| Bonneville, Fr. | 58 | 46.05 N | 6.25 E |
| Bonneville, Or., U.S. | 224 | 45.38 N | 121.57 W |
| Bonneville Dam ◆[6] | 224 | 45.39 N | 121.56 W |
| Bonneville Peak ∧ | 202 | 42.46 N | 112.08 W |
| Bonneville Salt Flats | | | |
| ≚ | 200 | 40.45 N | 113.52 W |
| Bonney, Lake ⊜ | 166 | 37.48 S | 140.22 E |
| Bonney Lake | 224 | 47.10 N | 122.11 W |
| Bonnie Doone | 192 | 35.05 N | 78.57 W |
| Bonnières | 50 | 49.02 N | 1.35 E |
| Bonnie Rock | 162 | 30.32 S | 118.21 E |
| Bonnieux | 62 | 43.49 N | 5.18 E |
| Bonnievale | 158 | 33.57 S | 20.06 E |
| Bönnigheim | 56 | 49.03 N | 9.06 E |
| Bönninghardt | 263 | 51.35 N | 6.28 E |
| Bonnots Mill | 219 | 38.34 N | 91.58 W |
| Bonny | 150 | 4.27 N | 7.10 E |
| Bonny ≃[1] | 150 | 4.20 N | 7.10 E |
| Bonnyrigg, Austl. | 274a | 33.54 S | 150.54 E |
| Bonnyrigg, Scot., | | | |
| U.K. | 46 | 55.52 N | 3.08 W |
| Bonny-sur-Loire | 50 | 47.34 N | 2.50 E |
| Bonnyville | 182 | 54.16 N | 110 44 W |
| Bono, It. | 71 | 40.25 N | 9.02 E |
| Bono, Ar., U.S. | 194 | 35.54 N | 90.48 W |
| Bono, Oh., U.S. | 214 | 41.38 N | 83.16 W |
| Bonoi | 164 | 1.51 S | 137.48 E |
| Bonorva | 71 | 40.25 N | 8.46 E |
| Bonoua | 150 | 5.16 N | 3.36 W |
| Bonpas Creek ≃ | 194 | 38.16 N | 87.59 W |
| Bonriki | 174t | 1.23 N | 173.09 E |
| Bonriki Airport ⊠ | 174t | 1.22 N | 173.10 E |
| Bons | 58 | 46.16 N | 6.23 E |
| Bonsall | 228 | 33.17 N | 117.13 W |
| Bonsari | 272c | 19.04 N | 73.02 E |
| Bon Secour | 194 | 30.18 N | 87.43 W |
| Bon-Secours, Bel. | 50 | 50.30 N | 3.36 E |
| Bonsecours, Fr. | 50 | 49.26 N | 1.08 E |
| Bonshaw | 186 | 46.12 N | 63.21 W |
| Bonsucesso ◆[8] | 287a | 22.52 S | 43.15 W |
| Bontang | 112 | 0.08 N | 117.30 E |
| Bontberg ∧ | 158 | 32.21 S | 21.04 E |
| Bontebok National | | | |
| Park ♠ | 158 | 34.07 S | 20.23 E |
| Bonthe | 150 | 7.32 N | 12.30 W |
| Bontoc | 116 | 17.05 N | 120.58 E |
| Bon Wier | 194 | 30.44 N | 93.39 W |
| Bonyhád | 30 | 46.19 N | 18.32 E |
| Boo, Kepulauan II | 164 | 1.12 S | 129.24 E |
| Booby Point › | 284b | 39.17 N | 76.23 W |
| Boock | 54 | 53.29 N | 14.15 E |
| Boody | 219 | 39.46 N | 89.03 W |
| Boogardie | 162 | 28.02 S | 117.47 E |
| Booischot | 56 | 51.03 N | 4.46 E |
| Bookabie | 162 | 31.50 S | 132.41 E |
| Bookaloo | 166 | 31.55 S | 137.22 E |
| Book Cliffs ⋏[4] | 200 | 39.20 N | 109.00 W |
| Booke | 152 | 2.33 S | 22.00 E |
| Booker | 196 | 36.27 N | 100.32 W |
| Booker T. | | | |
| Washington | | | |
| National Monument | | | |
| ♠ | 192 | 37.01 N | 79.45 W |
| Bookwalter | 218 | 39.42 N | 83.32 W |
| Boola | 150 | 8.22 N | 8.43 W |
| Boolaloo | 162 | 22.35 S | 115.51 E |
| Booleroo Centre | 166 | 32.53 S | 138.21 E |
| Booligal | 166 | 33.52 S | 144.53 E |
| Boologooro | 162 | 24.21 S | 114.02 E |
| Boom | 50 | 51.05 N | 4.22 E |
| Boomarra | 166 | 19.33 S | 140.20 E |
| Boomer | 188 | 38.09 N | 81.17 W |
| Boomi | 166 | 28.44 S | 149.35 E |
| Boomrivier | 158 | 29.33 S | 20.27 E |
| Boonah | 171a | 28.00 S | 152.41 E |
| Böön cagaan nuur ⊜ | 102 | 45.35 N | 99.09 E |
| Boone, Ia., U.S. | 190 | 42.03 N | 93.52 W |
| Boone, N.C., U.S. | 192 | 36.13 N | 81.40 W |
| Boone □[6], Il., U.S. | 216 | 42.15 N | 88.50 W |
| Boone □[6], In., U.S. | 218 | 40.03 N | 86.28 W |
| Boone □[6], Ky., U.S. | 218 | 38.57 N | 84.45 W |
| Boone □[6], Mo., U.S. | 219 | 38.55 N | 92.15 W |
| Boone ≃ | 190 | 42.19 N | 93.56 W |
| Boone Draw V | 196 | 33.51 N | 103.42 W |
| Boone Grove | 216 | 41.21 N | 87.08 W |
| Boone Lake ⊜[1] | 192 | 36.25 N | 82.25 W |
| Boone Reservoir ⊜[1] | 279b | 40.15 N | 80.08 W |
| Boones Mill | 192 | 37.06 N | 79.57 W |
| Booneville, Ar., U.S. | 194 | 35.08 N | 93.55 W |
| Booneville, Ky., U.S. | 192 | 37.28 N | 83.40 W |
| Booneville, Ms., U.S. | 194 | 34.39 N | 88.34 W |
| Boon Point › | 240c | 17.10 N | 61.50 W |
| Boons | 158 | 25.59 S | 27.13 E |
| Boonsboro | 208 | 39.30 N | 77.39 W |
| Boonsville | 222 | 33.04 N | 97.52 W |
| Boonton | 210 | 40.54 N | 74.24 W |
| Boonton Reservoir | | | |
| ⊜[1] | 276 | 40.53 N | 74.25 W |
| Boonville, Ca., U.S. | 204 | 39.00 N | 123.21 W |
| Boonville, In., U.S. | 194 | 38.02 N | 87.16 W |
| Boonville, Mo., U.S. | 194 | 38.58 N | 92.44 W |
| Boonville, N.Y., U.S. | 212 | 43.29 N | 75.20 W |
| Boopi ≃ | 248 | 15.41 S | 67.15 W |
| Boorabbin National | | | |
| Park ♠ | 162 | 31.13 S | 120.10 E |
| Boorama | 144 | 9.56 N | 43.11 E |
| Boorindal | 166 | 30.21 S | 146.08 E |
| Booroorban | 166 | 34.56 S | 144.46 E |
| Boorowa | 166 | 34.26 S | 148.43 E |
| Boos | 50 | 49.23 N | 1.12 E |
| Boosaaso | 144 | 11.17 N | 49.11 E |
| Boossen | 54 | 52.22 N | 14.29 E |
| Boot | 44 | 54.24 N | 3.17 W |
| Bootahnie Indian | | | |
| Reserve ◆[4] | 182 | 50.24 N | 121.31 W |
| Booth | 194 | 32.30 N | 86.34 W |
| Booth, Lac ⊜ | 190 | 46.45 N | 78.34 W |
| Boothbay Harbor | 188 | 43.51 N | 69.37 W |
| Boothby, Cape › | 9 | 66.34 S | 57.16 E |
| Booth Corner | 285 | 39.51 N | 75.29 W |
| Boothia, Gulf of c | 176 | 71.00 N | 91.00 W |
| Boothia Peninsula ›[1] | 176 | 70.30 N | 95.00 W |
| Boothstown | 262 | 53.30 N | 2.25 W |
| Boothville | 194 | 29.20 N | 89.25 W |
| Booth Wood | | | |
| Reservoir ⊜[1] | 262 | 53.38 N | 1.58 W |
| Boothwyn | 285 | 39.49 N | 75.26 W |
| Bootle | 44 | 53.28 N | 3.00 W |
| Boot Reefs ✢[2] | 164 | 10.00 S | 144.40 E |
| Booué | 152 | 0.06 S | 11.56 E |
| Booysens ◆[8] | 273d | 26.14 S | 28.01 E |
| Booze Creek ≃ | 284c | 38.59 N | 77.07 W |
| Bopfingen | 56 | 48.51 N | 10.21 E |
| Bo Phloi | 110 | 14.19 N | 99.31 E |
| Bophuthatswana □[9] | 156 | 26.00 S | 25.35 E |
| Boping | 98 | 36.36 N | 116.07 E |
| Boping Ling ⋏ | 100 | 25.00 N | 117.00 E |
| Bopo | 150 | 7.37 N | 7.52 E |
| Bopolu | 150 | 7.03 N | 10.32 W |
| Boppard | 56 | 50.14 N | 7.35 E |
| Boqér, Har ∧ | 132 | 30.52 N | 34.43 E |
| Boqueirão, Ilha do I | 287a | 22.46 S | 43.09 W |
| Boqueirão, Serra do | | | |
| ⋏[2] | 250 | 11.30 S | 43.45 W |
| Boquerón | 236 | 8.30 N | 82.34 W |
| Boquerón □[5] | 252 | 21.30 S | 60.00 W |
| Boquerón, Bahía de | | | |
| c | 240m | 18.01 N | 67.12 W |
| Boquerón, Túnel ◆[5] | 286c | 10.34 N | 67.00 W |
| Boquet | 279b | 40.23 N | 79.36 W |
| Boquilla, Presa de la | | | |
| ⊜[1] | 232 | 27.30 N | 105.30 W |
| Boquilla del Refugio | 196 | 25.33 N | 102.28 W |
| Boquillas del Carmen | 232 | 29.17 N | 102.53 W |
| Boquim | 250 | 11.09 S | 37.37 W |
| Bor, Česká Rep. | 60 | 49.43 N | 12.47 E |
| Bor, Jugo. | 38 | 44.05 N | 22.07 E |
| Bor, Ross. | 24 | 63.00 N | 42.38 E |
| Bor, Ross. | 80 | 56.22 N | 44.05 E |
| Bor, Sūd. | 140 | 6.12 N | 31.33 E |
| Bor, Tür. | 130 | 37.54 N | 34.34 E |
| Bor, Lak ≃ | 154 | 1.18 N | 40.40 E |
| Bora-Bora I | 14 | 16.30 S | 151.45 W |
| Borabu | 110 | 16.02 N | 103.07 E |
| Boracay Island I | 116 | 11.59 N | 121.55 E |
| Boraha, Nosy I | 157b | 16.50 S | 49.55 E |
| Borah Peak ∧ | 202 | 44.08 N | 113.48 W |
| Boraldaj ≃ | 85 | 42.33 N | 69.07 E |
| Borale | 144 | 9.10 N | 42.35 E |
| Borambola | 171b | 35.12 S | 147.41 E |
| Borang, Tanjung › | 164 | 5.16 S | 133.07 E |
| Borås | 26 | 57.43 N | 12.55 E |
| Borāzjān | 128 | 29.16 N | 51.12 E |
| Borba, Bra. | 246 | 4.24 S | 59.35 W |
| Borba, Port. | 34 | 38.48 N | 7.27 W |
| Borbeck ◆[8] | 263 | 51.29 N | 6.57 E |
| Borbera ≃ | 62 | 44.42 N | 8.52 E |
| Borca di Cadore | 64 | 46.26 N | 12.13 E |
| Borcea, Braţul ≃ | 38 | 44.40 N | 27.53 E |
| Borchen | 52 | 51.39 N | 8.44 E |
| Borçka | 130 | 41.22 N | 41.40 E |
| Borculo, Ned. | 52 | 52.07 N | 6.31 E |
| Borculo, Mi., U.S. | 216 | 42.53 N | 86.01 W |
| Borda, Cape › | 166 | 35.45 S | 136.34 E |
| Borda da Mata | 256 | 22.16 S | 46.10 W |
| Bordeaux, Fr. | 32 | 44.50 N | 0.34 W |
| Bordeaux, S. Afr. | 273d | 26.06 S | 28.01 E |
| Bordeaux ◆[8] | 275a | 45.33 N | 73.41 W |
| Bordeaux Mountain | | | |
| ∧[2] | 240m | 18.20 N | 64.44 W |
| Borden, Austl. | 162 | 34.05 S | 118.16 E |
| Borden, Sk., Can. | 184 | 52.25 N | 107.13 W |
| Borden, Eng., U.K. | 260 | 51.20 N | 0.42 E |
| Borden, In., U.S. | 218 | 38.28 N | 85.57 W |
| Borden, Canadian | | | |
| Forces Base ■ | 212 | 44.17 N | 79.55 W |
| Borden Lake ⊜ | 190 | 47.50 N | 83.18 W |
| Borden Peninsula ›[1] | 176 | 73.00 N | 83.00 W |
| Bordentown | 208 | 40.08 N | 74.42 W |
| Border Mountains ⋏ | 164 | 3.40 S | 141.05 E |
| Borders □[4] | 46 | 55.37 N | 3.15 W |
| Bordertown | 166 | 36.19 S | 140.47 E |
| Bordesholm | 30 | 54.11 N | 10.01 E |
| Bordeyri | 24a | 65.15 N | 21.10 W |
| Bordighera | 62 | 43.46 N | 7.39 E |
| Bording | 41 | 56.12 N | 9.17 E |
| Bording Kirkeby | 41 | 56.10 N | 9.15 E |
| Bordino, Fiume di ≃ | 70 | 37.53 N | 12.37 E |
| Bordj Bou Arreridj | 148 | 36.04 N | 4.46 E |
| Bordj Bounaama | 34 | 35.51 N | 1.36 E |
| Bordj Menaïel | 148 | 36.44 N | 3.43 E |
| Bordj Omar Idriss | 148 | 28.09 N | 6.43 E |
| Bordj Sidi Toui | 148 | 32.44 N | 11.22 E |
| Bordunskij | 85 | 42.40 N | 75.37 E |
| Bore, It. | 62 | 44.43 N | 9.47 E |
| Bore, Ityo. | 144 | 4.40 N | 37.40 E |
| Boré, Mali | 150 | 15.08 N | 3.29 W |
| Boreda | 144 | 6.32 N | 37.48 E |
| Boreham | 260 | 51.46 N | 0.33 E |
| Borehamwood | 42 | 51.40 N | 0.16 W |
| Borel Hill ∧ | 282 | 37.19 N | 122.12 W |
| Borello | 66 | 44.03 N | 12.11 E |
| Borensberg | 26 | 58.34 N | 15.17 E |
| Boreray I | 46 | 57.42 N | 7.18 W |
| Boretto | 64 | 44.54 N | 10.33 E |
| Borgå | | | |
| → Porvoo | 26 | 60.24 N | 25.40 E |
| Borgallo, Galleria del | | | |
| ◆[5] | 62 | 44.25 N | 9.53 E |
| Borgarnes | 24a | 64.35 N | 21.53 W |
| Borgata Costiera | 70 | 37.43 N | 12.39 E |
| Børgefjell | | | |
| Nasjonalpark ♠ | 24 | 65.10 N | 14.00 E |
| Borgentreich | 52 | 51.34 N | 9.14 E |
| Börger, Dtsch. | 52 | 52.54 N | 7.32 E |
| Borger, Ned. | 52 | 52.55 N | 6.46 E |
| Borger, Tx., U.S. | 196 | 35.40 N | 101.23 W |
| Borgerhout | 50 | 51.13 N | 4.26 E |
| Borgetto | 70 | 38.03 N | 13.08 E |
| Borggård | 40 | 58.44 N | 15.32 E |
| Borghetto | 64 | 45.41 N | 10.56 E |
| Borghetto di Vara | 62 | 44.13 N | 9.43 E |
| Borghetto Lodigiano | 62 | 45.13 N | 9.30 E |
| Borghetto Santo | | | |
| Spirito | 62 | 44.06 N | 8.14 E |
| Borgholm | 26 | 56.53 N | 16.39 E |
| Borgholzhausen | 52 | 52.06 N | 8.18 E |
| Borghorst | 52 | 52.07 N | 7.23 E |
| Borgia | 68 | 38.49 N | 16.30 E |
| Borgio-Verezzi | 62 | 44.10 N | 8.18 E |
| Borgloon | 56 | 50.48 N | 5.20 E |
| Borg Mountain ∧ | 9 | 72.42 S | 3.30 W |
| Borgne, Lake c | 194 | 30.05 N | 89.40 W |
| Borgnesse, Pointe › | 240e | 14.27 N | 60.54 W |
| Borgo | 64 | 46.03 N | 11.27 E |
| Borgo alla Collina | 66 | 43.45 N | 11.43 E |
| Borgo a Mozzano | 66 | 43.59 N | 10.33 E |
| Borgo Cerreto | 66 | 42.49 N | 12.54 E |
| Borgo d'Ale | 62 | 45.21 N | 8.03 E |
| Borgoforte | 64 | 45.03 N | 10.45 E |
| Borgofranco d'Ivrea | 62 | 45.30 N | 7.51 E |
| Borgolavezzaro | 62 | 45.19 N | 8.42 E |
| Borgomanero | 62 | 45.42 N | 8.28 E |
| Borgomaro | 62 | 43.58 N | 7.56 E |
| Borgonovo Val | | | |
| Tidone | 62 | 45.01 N | 9.26 E |
| Borgo Pace | 66 | 43.39 N | 12.17 E |
| Borgoricco | 64 | 45.32 N | 11.58 E |
| Borgorose | 66 | 42.11 N | 13.13 E |
| Borgo San Dalmazzo | 62 | 44.20 N | 7.30 E |
| Borgo San Giacomo | 64 | 45.21 N | 9.58 E |
| Borgo San Lorenzo | 66 | 43.57 N | 11.23 E |
| Borgosatollo | 64 | 45.28 N | 10.14 E |
| Borgosesia | 62 | 45.43 N | 8.16 E |
| Borgo Tossignano | 66 | 44.16 N | 11.35 E |
| Borgou □[5] | 150 | 10.30 N | 2.50 E |
| Borgo Val di Taro | 62 | 44.29 N | 9.46 E |
| Borgo Vercelli | 62 | 45.21 N | 8.28 E |
| Borgsdorf | 54 | 52.42 N | 13.14 E |
| Borgsdorf, Forst ◆[3] | 264a | 52.42 N | 13.19 E |
| Borgu Game Reserve | | | |
| ◆[4] | 150 | 10.15 N | 4.10 E |
| Borgund ʊ[1] | 26 | 61.03 N | 7.49 E |
| Bori | 150 | 4.42 N | 7.21 E |
| Borig Delijn els ◆[2] | 88 | 50.00 N | 94.00 E |
| Borikhan | 110 | 18.33 N | 103.43 E |
| Borilovo | 76 | 53.22 N | 35.58 E |
| Borinage □[9] | 50 | 50.30 N | 4.00 E |
| Boring, Md., U.S. | 208 | 39.31 N | 76.49 W |
| Boring, Or., U.S. | 224 | 45.25 N | 122.22 W |
| Borinskoje | 76 | 52.27 N | 39.22 E |
| Borisoglebsk | 80 | 51.23 N | 42.06 E |
| Borisoglebskij | 80 | 57.16 N | 39.09 E |
| Borisovka, Ross. | 76 | 52.50 N | 39.58 E |
| Borisovka, Ross. | 78 | 50.36 N | 36.01 E |
| Borisovo | 82 | 55.25 N | 36.03 E |
| Borisovo ◆[8] | 265b | 55.38 N | 37.45 E |
| Borisovo-Sudskoje | 76 | 59.54 N | 36.01 E |
| Borisovskaja | 76 | 60.12 N | 39.48 E |
| Borivs'ke | 83 | 48.51 N | 38.34 E |
| Borja, Esp. | 34 | 41.50 N | 1.32 W |
| Borja, Perú | 246 | 4.26 S | 77.33 W |
| Bork | 52 | 51.40 N | 7.28 E |
| Borkavičy | 76 | 55.40 N | 28.20 E |
| Borken, Dtsch. | 52 | 51.51 N | 6.51 E |
| Borken, Dtsch. | 56 | 51.03 N | 9.16 E |
| Borkenwirthe | 52 | 51.53 N | 6.50 E |
| Borki | 86 | 59.08 N | 82.15 E |
| Borkoldoj, chrebet ⋏ | 85 | 41.25 N | 77.50 E |
| Børkop | 41 | 55.39 N | 9.39 E |
| Borkou ◆[1] | 146 | 18.15 N | 18.50 E |
| Borkou-Ennedi- | | | |
| Tibesti □[5] | 146 | 18.15 N | 18.50 E |
| Borkum | 52 | 53.35 N | 6.40 E |
| Borkum I | 52 | 53.35 N | 6.41 E |
| Borland Manor | 279b | 40.15 N | 80.09 W |
| Borlänge | 40 | 60.29 N | 15.25 E |
| Borle ◆[8] | 272c | 19.02 N | 72.55 E |
| Borlu | 130 | 38.44 N | 28.27 E |
| Bormes-les-Mimosas | 62 | 43.09 N | 6.20 E |
| Bormida ≃ | 62 | 44.56 N | 8.40 E |
| Bormida di Millesimo | | | |
| ≃ | 62 | 44.40 N | 8.20 E |
| Bormida di Spigno ≃ | 62 | 44.40 N | 8.20 E |
| Bormio | 64 | 46.28 N | 10.22 E |
| Born, Dtsch. | 54 | 52.22 N | 11.28 E |
| Born, Dtsch. | 54 | 54.23 N | 12.32 E |
| Borna, Dtsch. | 54 | 51.19 N | 13.11 E |
| Borna, Dtsch. | 54 | 51.07 N | 12.30 E |
| Borndiep c | 52 | 53.25 N | 5.35 E |
| Borne | 52 | 52.18 N | 6.45 E |
| Borne ≃ | 62 | 45.03 N | 3.54 E |
| Borneo (Kalimantan) I | 112 | 0.30 N | 114.00 E |
| Bornheim | 56 | 50.46 N | 6.59 E |
| Bornholm I | 26 | 55.10 N | 15.00 E |
| Bornholte | 52 | 51.52 N | 8.29 E |
| Bornhöved | 54 | 54.04 N | 10.16 E |
| Börnicke, Dtsch. | 54 | 52.41 N | 12.56 E |
| Börnicke, Dtsch. | 264a | 52.40 N | 13.38 E |
| Börnig ◆[8] | 263 | 51.33 N | 7.16 E |
| Bornim ◆[8] | 264a | 52.26 N | 13.00 E |
| Borno | 64 | 45.56 N | 10.12 E |
| Bornos, Embalse de | | | |
| ⊜[1] | 34 | 36.50 N | 5.30 W |
| Bornsdorf | 54 | 51.46 N | 13.41 E |
| Bornstedt ◆[8] | 264a | 52.25 N | 13.02 E |
| Boro ≃ | 140 | 8.52 N | 26.11 E |
| Borobudur ⊥ | 115a | 7.36 S | 110.12 E |
| Borodarou | 150 | 10.59 N | 2.53 E |
| Borodino, Ross. | 82 | 55.32 N | 35.50 E |
| Borodino, Ross. | 82 | 56.53 N | 37.00 E |
| Borodino, Ross. | 88 | 55.55 N | 94.55 E |
| Borodino, Ukr. | 78 | 46.18 N | 29.13 E |
| Borodulicha | 86 | 50.43 N | 80.55 E |
| Borodulino | 80 | 57.59 N | 54.20 E |
| Borodyanka | 78 | 50.39 N | 29.56 E |
| Borogoncy | 74 | 62.42 N | 131.08 E |
| Borohoro Shan ⋏ | 86 | 44.06 N | 83.10 E |
| Boroko | 112 | 0.55 N | 123.16 E |
| Boromlya | 78 | 50.37 N | 34.59 E |
| Boromo | 150 | 11.45 N | 2.56 W |
| Boron, Mali | 150 | 14.01 N | 7.30 W |
| Boron, Ca., U.S. | 228 | 34.59 N | 117.38 W |
| Boronga Islands II | 110 | 19.58 N | 93.06 E |
| Borongan | 116 | 11.37 N | 125.26 E |
| Boronia | 274b | 37.52 S | 145.17 E |
| Borore | 71 | 40.13 N | 8.48 E |
| Borotou | 150 | 8.44 N | 7.30 W |
| Boroughbridge | 44 | 54.06 N | 1.23 W |
| Borough Green | 42 | 51.17 N | 0.19 E |
| Borough Park ◆[8] | 276 | 40.38 N | 74.00 W |
| Borova, Ukr. | 78 | 50.12 N | 30.07 E |
| Borova, Ukr. | 83 | 49.24 N | 37.40 E |
| Borova ≃ | 83 | 48.58 N | 38.24 E |
| Borovan | 38 | 43.26 N | 23.45 E |
| Borovany | 61 | 48.54 N | 14.39 E |
| Borove | 78 | 51.06 N | 27.13 E |
| Boroviči | 76 | 58.24 N | 33.55 E |
| Borovka ≃ | 80 | 52.54 N | 52.00 E |
| Borovl'anka | 86 | 52.38 N | 84.29 E |
| Borovoj | 24 | 59.55 N | 51.38 E |
| Borovoje | 86 | 53.04 N | 70.19 E |
| Borovsk | 82 | 55.12 N | 36.30 E |
| Borovskaja | 24 | 60.46 N | 41.06 E |
| Borovskij | 86 | 57.03 N | 65.44 E |
| Borovskoj | 86 | 53.48 N | 64.12 E |
| Borovskoje | 86 | 52.39 N | 82.08 E |
| Borovy | 60 | 49.33 N | 13.18 E |
| Borovyk ≃ | 83 | 49.11 N | 38.33 E |
| Borozdino | 82 | 54.07 N | 38.22 E |
| Borraan | 144 | 10.14 N | 48.44 E |
| Borrachudo ≃ | 255 | 18.12 S | 45.16 W |
| Borrazópolis | 255 | 23.56 S | 51.36 W |
| Borrby | 26 | 55.27 N | 14.10 E |
| Borre | 41 | 55.00 N | 12.28 E |
| Borre ⊥ | 26 | 59.23 N | 10.28 E |
| Borreby | 41 | 55.14 N | 11.19 E |
| Borriana, Esp. | 34 | 39.53 N | 0.05 W |
| Borriana, It. | 62 | 45.30 N | 8.02 E |
| Borris | 48 | 52.35 N | 6.55 W |
| Borrisokane | 48 | 52.59 N | 8.07 W |
| Borrisoleigh | 48 | 52.45 N | 7.57 W |
| Borroloola | 164 | 16.04 S | 136.17 E |
| Borroloola Aboriginal | | | |
| Reserve ◆[4] | 164 | 16.00 S | 136.15 E |
| Borrowdale | 44 | 54.31 N | 3.10 W |
| Börry | 52 | 52.01 N | 9.27 E |
| Borş | 38 | 47.07 N | 21.49 E |
| Borşa, Rom. | 38 | 47.39 N | 24.40 E |
| Borşa, Rom. | 38 | 46.56 N | 23.40 E |
| Borsad | 120 | 22.25 N | 72.54 E |
| Borsano | 266b | 45.35 N | 8.51 E |
| Borschemich | 263 | 51.04 N | 6.25 E |
| Borščovo | 82 | 56.30 N | 36.51 E |
| Borščovočnyj chrebet | | | |
| ⋏ | 88 | 52.00 N | 117.00 E |
| Borsdorf | 54 | 51.21 N | 12.32 E |
| Borshchiv | 78 | 48.48 N | 26.03 E |
| Borskoje | 80 | 53.02 N | 51.43 E |
| Borsod-Abaúj- | | | |
| Zemplén □[6] | 30 | 48.15 N | 21.00 E |
| Börssum | 54 | 52.04 N | 10.35 E |
| Borstendorf | 54 | 50.46 N | 13.10 E |
| Bortala ≃ | 86 | 44.50 N | 82.45 E |
| Borth, Dtsch. | 52 | 51.36 N | 6.33 E |
| Borth, Wales, U.K. | 42 | 52.29 N | 4.03 W |
| Borthwick Water ≃ | 44 | 55.24 N | 2.50 W |
| Bortigali | 71 | 40.17 N | 8.50 E |
| Bortigiadas | 71 | 40.53 N | 9.02 E |
| Bort-les-Orgues | 32 | 45.24 N | 2.30 E |
| Bortnychi | 78 | 50.22 N | 30.41 E |
| Borto | 88 | 53.35 N | 111.53 E |
| Bortondale | 285 | 39.54 N | 79.24 W |
| Boru | 164 | 10.14 S | 148.50 E |
| Boruca | 236 | 9.00 N | 83.20 W |
| Borūjen | 128 | 31.59 N | 51.18 E |
| Borūjerd | 128 | 33.54 N | 48.46 E |
| Bor Ul Shan ⋏ | 102 | 41.20 N | 98.55 E |
| Borve | 46 | 56.58 N | 7.32 W |
| Borysiv | 78 | 50.11 N | 26.31 E |
| Boryslav | 78 | 49.16 N | 23.27 E |
| Boryspil' | 78 | 50.21 N | 30.57 E |
| Borz'a | 88 | 50.24 N | 116.31 E |
| Borz'a ≃ | 88 | 50.38 N | 115.38 E |
| Borzna | 78 | 51.15 N | 32.25 E |
| Boržomi | 84 | 41.50 N | 43.21 E |
| Boržomskij | | | |
| zapovednik ♠ | 84 | 41.50 N | 43.10 E |
| Borzonasca | 62 | 44.25 N | 9.23 E |
| Borzyszkowy | 30 | 54.03 N | 17.22 E |
| Bosa | 71 | 40.18 N | 8.30 E |
| Bosaga | 86 | 47.55 N | 72.58 E |
| Bosambi | 152 | 2.24 N | 22.39 E |
| Bosanska Dubica | 36 | 45.11 N | 16.49 E |
| Bosanska Gradiška | 36 | 45.09 N | 17.15 E |
| Bosanska Krupa | 36 | 44.53 N | 16.10 E |
| Bosanski Novi | 36 | 45.03 N | 16.23 E |
| Bosanski Petrovac | 36 | 44.33 N | 16.22 E |
| Bosanski Šamac | 38 | 45.03 N | 18.28 E |
| Bosansko Grahovo | 36 | 44.11 N | 16.22 E |
| Bősárkány | 61 | 47.41 N | 17.14 E |
| Bosau | 54 | 54.06 N | 10.25 E |
| Bosavi, Mount ∧ | 164 | 6.35 S | 142.50 E |
| Boscastle | 42 | 50.41 N | 4.42 W |
| Bosco, It. | 66 | 44.53 N | 12.14 E |
| Bosco, It. | 66 | 43.08 N | 12.28 E |
| Boscobel | 190 | 43.08 N | 90.42 W |
| Bosco Chiesanuova | 64 | 45.37 N | 11.02 E |
| Bosco Marengo | 62 | 44.49 N | 8.41 E |
| Boscoreale | 68 | 40.46 N | 14.28 E |
| Bose | 102 | 23.54 N | 106.37 E |
| Bösel | 52 | 53.00 N | 7.58 E |
| Bosencheve, Parque | | | |
| Nacional ♠ | 234 | 19.36 N | 100.15 W |
| Bosenge | 152 | 1.18 N | 22.19 E |
| Bósforo, Estrecho del | | | |
| → İstanbul Boğazı | | | |
| Ц | 130 | 41.06 N | 29.04 E |
| Bosham | 42 | 50.49 N | 0.52 W |
| Boshan | 98 | 36.29 N | 117.50 E |
| Boshkung Lake ⊜ | 212 | 45.04 N | 78.44 W |
| Boshoek | 156 | 25.30 S | 27.09 E |
| Boshof | 158 | 28.34 S | 25.04 E |
| Boshrūyeh | 128 | 33.53 N | 57.26 E |
| Bosilegrad | 38 | 42.29 N | 22.28 E |
| Bösingen | 58 | 48.14 N | 8.34 E |
| Bosjökloster | 41 | 55.54 N | 13.31 E |
| Boškajnar | 85 | 38.13 N | 68.51 E |
| Boskol' | 86 | 53.45 N | 61.12 E |
| Boskop | 158 | 26.34 S | 27.08 E |
| Boskop ∧ | 273d | 26.05 S | 27.57 E |
| Boskovice | 30 | 49.29 N | 16.40 E |
| Boskuil | 158 | 27.23 S | 25.51 E |
| Bosman | 164 | 4.10 S | 144.40 E |
| Bosna | 272b | 22.37 N | 88.30 E |
| Bosna ≃ | 36 | 45.04 N | 18.29 E |
| Bosna-Hercegovina | | | |
| → Bosnia and | | | |
| Herzegovina □[1] | 36 | 44.15 N | 17.30 E |
| Bošn'akovo | 89 | 49.38 N | 142.10 E |
| Bosnia and | | | |
| Herzegovina □[1] | 22 | 44.15 N | 17.30 E |
| Bosnik | 164 | 1.10 S | 136.14 E |
| Boso | 272b | 22.58 N | 88.08 E |
| Bosobolo | 152 | 4.11 N | 19.54 E |
| Boso-Djafo | 152 | 1.06 N | 19.14 E |
| Bosogo | 85 | 41.09 N | 76.25 E |
| Bōsō-hantō ›[1] | 94 | 35.18 N | 140.10 E |
| Bōsō-kyūryō ⋏[2] | 268 | 35.08 N | 139.56 E |
| Bososama | 152 | 4.18 N | 20.00 E |
| Bösperde | 263 | 51.28 N | 7.46 E |
| Bosphore, Détroit du | | | |
| → İstanbul Boğazı | | | |
| Ц | 130 | 41.06 N | 29.04 E |
| Bosporus | | | |
| → İstanbul Boğazı | | | |
| Ц | 130 | 41.06 N | 29.04 E |
| Bosque □[6] | 222 | 31.55 N | 97.35 W |
| Bosque, Paseo del ♠ | 288 | 34.55 S | 57.56 W |
| Bosque Farms | 200 | 34.53 N | 106.40 W |
| Bosques | 288 | 34.49 S | 58.14 W |
| Bosques Petrificados, | | | |
| Monumento | | | |
| Natural ♠ | 254 | 47.39 S | 68.07 W |
| Bosqueville | 222 | 31.38 N | 97.13 W |
| Bossangoa | 152 | 6.29 N | 17.27 E |
| Bossdorf | 54 | 51.59 N | 12.40 E |
| Bossé Bangou | 150 | 13.21 N | 1.18 E |
| Bossembélé | 152 | 5.16 N | 17.39 E |
| Bossentele | 152 | 5.41 N | 16.38 E |
| Bossert Estates | 285 | 40.09 N | 74.44 W |
| Bossier City | 194 | 32.30 N | 93.43 W |
| Bossley Park | 274a | 33.52 S | 150.54 E |
| Bosso | 146 | 13.42 N | 13.19 E |
| Bosso, Dallol V | 150 | 12.25 N | 2.50 E |
| Bossolasco | 62 | 44.32 N | 8.02 E |
| Bossut, Cape › | 162 | 18.43 S | 121.38 E |
| Bostān, Īrān | 128 | 31.43 N | 48.00 E |
| Bostān, Pāk. | 120 | 30.26 N | 67.02 E |
| Bostancı ◆[8] | 267b | 40.57 N | 29.05 E |
| Bostandyk | 80 | 49.38 N | 48.54 E |
| Bosten Hu ⊜ | 90 | 42.00 N | 87.00 E |
| Bostock Green | 262 | 53.13 N | 2.30 W |
| Boston, Pil. | 116 | 7.52 N | 126.22 E |
| Boston, Eng., U.K. | 44 | 52.59 N | 0.01 W |
| Boston, Ga., U.S. | 192 | 30.47 N | 83.47 W |
| Boston, In., U.S. | 218 | 39.44 N | 84.51 W |
| Boston, Ma., U.S. | 207 | 42.21 N | 71.03 W |
| Boston, Ma., U.S. | 283 | 42.21 N | 71.03 W |
| Boston, N.Y., U.S. | 210 | 42.38 N | 78.44 W |
| Boston, Pa., U.S. | 279b | 40.18 N | 79.49 W |
| Boston Bar | 182 | 49.52 N | 121.26 W |
| Boston Bay c | 283 | 42.22 N | 70.54 W |
| Boston Brook ≃ | 283 | 42.37 N | 71.00 W |
| Boston College ʊ[2] | 283 | 42.20 N | 71.10 W |
| Boston Common ♠ | 283 | 42.21 N | 71.05 W |
| Boston Corners | 210 | 42.03 N | 73.31 W |
| Boston Creek ≃ | 212 | 43.02 N | 79.56 W |
| Boston Harbor | 224 | 47.08 N | 122.54 W |
| Boston Harbor c | 283 | 42.20 N | 70.58 W |
| Boston Heights | 214 | 41.15 N | 81.30 W |
| Boston Mill | 214 | 41.16 N | 81.34 W |
| Boston Mountains ⋏ | 194 | 35.50 N | 93.20 W |
| Boston Spa | 44 | 53.54 N | 1.21 W |
| Boston University ʊ[2] | 283 | 42.21 N | 71.07 W |
| Bosumtwi, Lake ⊜ | 150 | 6.30 N | 1.25 W |
| Bosut ≃ | 38 | 44.57 N | 19.22 E |
| Boswell, In., U.S. | 216 | 40.31 N | 87.22 W |
| Boswell, Ok., U.S. | 196 | 34.01 N | 95.52 W |
| Boswell, Pa., U.S. | 214 | 40.09 N | 79.01 W |
| Boswell Bay | 180 | 60.24 N | 146.08 W |
| Bosworth | 194 | 39.28 N | 93.20 W |
| Bosworth Airport ⊠ | 279a | 41.26 N | 82.00 W |
| Bosworth Field ⊥ | 42 | 52.36 N | 1.25 W |
| Botād | 120 | 22.10 N | 71.40 E |
| Botafogo ◆[8] | 287a | 22.57 S | 43.11 W |
| Botafogo, Enseada | | | |
| de c | 287a | 22.57 S | 43.10 W |
| Botany | 274a | 33.57 S | 151.12 E |
| Botany Bay ◆[8] | 260 | 51.41 N | 0.07 W |
| Botany Bay c | 170 | 33.59 S | 151.12 E |
| Botelhos | 256 | 21.39 S | 46.24 W |
| Botera | 152 | 11.37 S | 14.17 E |
| Botersleegte | 158 | 30.35 S | 21.22 E |
| Botesdale | 42 | 52.20 N | 1.01 E |
| Boteti ≃ | 156 | 20.08 S | 23.23 E |
| Botev ∧ | 38 | 42.43 N | 24.55 E |
| Botevgrad | 38 | 42.54 N | 23.47 E |
| Botha's Hill | 158 | 29.45 S | 30.45 E |
| Bothaville | 158 | 27.27 S | 26.36 E |
| Bothel | 52 | 53.04 N | 9.30 E |
| Bothell | 224 | 47.45 N | 122.12 W |
| Bothe-Napa Valley | | | |
| State Park ♠ | 226 | 38.32 N | 122.32 W |
| Bothnia, Gulf of c | 26 | 63.00 N | 20.00 E |
| Bothwell, Austl. | 166 | 42.23 S | 147.00 E |
| Bothwell, On., Can. | 214 | 42.38 N | 81.52 W |
| Boticas | 34 | 41.41 N | 7.40 W |
| Botija, Ilha da I | 246 | 3.58 S | 62.53 W |
| Botija, Isla I | 258 | 33.52 S | 59.02 W |
| Botiyeve | 78 | 46.41 N | 35.52 E |
| Botkins | 216 | 40.28 N | 84.10 W |
| Botkul', ozero ⊜ | 80 | 48.46 N | 46.40 E |
| Botkyrka | 40 | 59.14 N | 17.49 E |
| Botlich | 84 | 42.39 N | 46.14 E |
| Bot Makak | 152 | 4.00 N | 10.55 E |
| Botnia, Golfo de | | | |
| → Bothnia, Gulf of | | | |
| c | 26 | 63.00 N | 20.00 E |
| Botola | 152 | 1.17 S | 18.13 E |
| Botolan | 116 | 15.17 N | 120.01 E |
| Botoşani | 38 | 47.45 N | 26.40 E |
| Botoşani □[6] | 38 | 48.00 N | 26.45 E |
| Botoşaniţa | 38 | 47.53 N | 26.07 E |
| Botou | 150 | 12.40 N | 2.03 E |
| Botovo | 82 | 56.03 N | 38.26 E |
| Bo Trach | 110 | 17.35 N | 106.32 E |
| Botrange ∧ | 56 | 50.30 N | 6.08 E |
| Botricello | 68 | 38.56 N | 16.51 E |
| Botro | 150 | 7.51 N | 5.19 W |
| Botsford | 210 | 41.21 N | 73.15 W |
| Botswana □[1], Afr. | 138 | 22.00 S | 24.00 E |
| Botswana □[1], Afr. | 156 | 22.00 S | 24.00 E |
| Botte Donato, Monte | | | |
| ∧ | 68 | 39.17 N | 16.26 E |
| Bottenhavet | | | |
| (Selkämeri) c | 26 | 62.00 N | 20.00 E |
| Bottenviken | | | |
| (Perämeri) c | 26 | 65.00 N | 23.00 E |
| Bottesford | 42 | 52.56 N | 0.48 W |
| Bottineau | 198 | 48.49 N | 100.26 W |
| Bottisham | 42 | 52.13 N | 0.16 E |
| Bottnischer | | | |
| Meerbusen | | | |
| → Bothnia, Gulf of | | | |
| c | 26 | 63.00 N | 20.00 E |
| Bottoms Reservoir | | | |
| ⊜[1] | 262 | 53.28 N | 1.58 W |
| Bottrop | 52 | 51.31 N | 6.55 |
| Botucatu | 255 | 22.52 S | 48.26 W |
| Botwood | 186 | 49.09 N | 55.21 W |
| Boty | 88 | 52.24 N | 118.32 E |
| Bötzingen | 58 | 48.04 N | 7.44 E |
| Bötzow | 54 | 52.39 N | 13.08 E |
| Bötzsee ⊜ | 264a | 52.34 N | 13.50 E |
| Bouaflé, C. Iv. | 150 | 6.59 N | 5.45 W |
| Bouafle, Fr. | 261 | 48.58 N | 1.54 E |
| Bou Ahmed | 148 | 35.25 N | 5.00 W |
| Bouaké | 150 | 7.41 N | 5.02 W |
| Bou Ali, Oued V | 148 | 31.14 N | 4.16 E |
| Bouânane | 148 | 32.03 N | 3.03 W |
| Bouandougou | 150 | 8.13 N | 5.40 W |
| Bouar | 152 | 5.57 N | 15.36 E |
| Bou Arada | 36 | 36.20 N | 9.38 E |
| Bou Areg, Sebkha c | 34 | 35.10 N | 2.45 W |
| Bouârfa | 148 | 32.30 N | 1.59 W |
| Bouaye | 32 | 47.09 N | 1.42 W |
| Boubandjidah, Parc | | | |
| National de ♠ | 146 | 8.45 N | 14.45 E |
| Bou Bernous | 148 | 27.18 N | 2.59 W |
| Boubín ∧ | 60 | 48.59 N | 13.51 E |
| Bouca | 152 | 6.30 N | 18.17 E |
| Bouchain | 50 | 50.17 N | 3.19 E |
| Bouchegouf | 36 | 36.28 N | 7.44 E |
| Boucher ≃ | 186 | 49.10 N | 69.06 W |
| Boucher, Lac ⊜ | 186 | 51.07 N | 59.35 W |
| Boucherville | 206 | 45.36 N | 73.27 W |
| Boucherville, Îles de II | 275a | 45.37 N | 73.28 W |
| Bouches-du-Rhône | | | |
| □[5] | 62 | 43.30 N | 5.00 E |
| Bouchoir | 50 | 49.45 N | 2.41 E |
| Bouclans | 58 | 47.14 N | 6.15 E |
| Boucle du Baoulé, | | | |
| Parc National de la | | | |
| ♠ | 150 | 13.50 N | 9.00 W |
| Bouddi National Park | | | |
| ♠ | 170 | 33.31 S | 131.24 E |
| Boudjellil | 34 | 36.20 N | 4.21 E |
| Boudnib | 148 | 31.57 N | 4.38 W |
| Boudouaou | 34 | 36.43 N | 3.25 E |
| Boudry | 58 | 46.57 N | 6.50 E |
| Boué | 50 | 50.01 N | 3.42 E |
| Bouenza □[5] | 152 | 4.00 S | 13.45 E |
| Boufarik | 148 | 36.34 N | 2.55 E |
| Bouffémont | 261 | 49.03 N | 2.18 E |
| Bou Ficha | 36 | 36.18 N | 10.29 E |
| Bougaa | 34 | 36.20 N | 5.05 E |
| Bougainville I | 175e | 6.00 S | 155.00 E |
| Bougainville, Cape › | 164 | 13.54 S | 126.06 E |
| Bougainville, Détroit | | | |
| de Ц | 175f | 15.50 S | 167.10 E |
| Bougainville Reef ✢[2] | 164 | 15.30 S | 147.06 E |
| Bougainville Strait Ц | 175e | 6.40 S | 156.10 E |
| Bougar'oûn, Cap › | 34 | 37.06 N | 6.28 E |
| Bough Beech | | | |
| Reservoir ⊜[1] | 260 | 51.13 N | 0.08 E |
| Boughton | 44 | 53.12 N | 1.00 W |
| Boughton Green | 260 | 51.14 N | 0.32 E |
| Boughton Malherbe | 260 | 51.13 N | 0.42 E |
| Boughton Place ʊ | 260 | 51.13 N | 0.32 E |
| Bougie | | | |
| → Bejaïa | 148 | 36.45 N | 5.05 E |
| Bougou | 152 | 3.45 S | 11.12 E |
| Bougouni | 150 | 11.25 N | 7.29 W |
| Bougouriba ≃ | 150 | 10.42 N | 2.56 W |
| Bougzoul | 34 | 35.42 N | 2.51 E |
| Bou Hadjar | 36 | 36.30 N | 8.06 E |
| Bou Hajar | 36 | 35.42 N | 10.48 E |
| Bouillante | 241o | 16.06 N | 61.45 W |
| Bouillon | 56 | 49.48 N | 5.04 E |
| Bouilly | 50 | 48.12 N | 4.00 E |
| Bouïra | 148 | 36.23 N | 3.54 E |
| Bouisy, Ru de ≃ | 261 | 48.34 N | 2.45 E |
| Bou Izakarn | 148 | 29.09 N | 9.44 W |
| Boujad | 148 | 32.48 N | 6.26 W |
| Boujailles | 58 | 46.53 N | 6.05 E |
| Boujdour, Cap › | 148 | 26.08 N | 14.30 W |
| Bouka ≃ | 150 | 11.00 N | 10.50 W |
| Bou Kadir | 148 | 36.04 N | 1.07 E |
| Bou Khadra | 36 | 35.45 N | 8.02 E |
| Boukiéro | 273b | 4.12 S | 15.18 E |
| Boukiéro, Mont ∧[2] | 273b | 4.11 S | 15.17 E |
| Boukombé | 150 | 10.11 N | 1.06 E |
| Boula Ibib | 146 | 9.34 N | 13.46 E |
| Boulaide | 56 | 49.54 N | 5.49 E |
| Boularderie Island I | 186 | 46.15 N | 60.30 W |
| Boulay-Moselle | 56 | 49.11 N | 6.30 E |
| Boulbon | 62 | 43.52 N | 4.41 E |
| Boulder, Co., U.S. | 200 | 40.00 N | 105.16 W |
| Boulder, Mt., U.S. | 202 | 46.14 N | 112.07 W |
| Boulder ≃ | 202 | 45.52 N | 111.57 W |
| Boulder City | 204 | 35.58 N | 114.49 W |
| Boulder Creek | 226 | 37.07 N | 122.07 W |
| Boulder Creek ≃ | 200 | 37.47 N | 111.22 W |
| Boulder Hill | 216 | 41.41 N | 88.25 W |
| Bouleaux, Lac des ⊜ | 275a | 45.33 N | 73.19 W |
| Bouli ≃ | 150 | 13.15 N | 0.03 E |
| Boulia | 166 | 22.54 S | 139.54 E |
| Bouligny | 56 | 49.17 N | 5.45 E |
| Boullay-les-Troux | 261 | 48.41 N | 2.03 E |
| Boulmane | 148 | 33.22 N | 4.45 W |
| Boulmane □[4] | 148 | 33.00 N | 4.00 W |
| Boulogne ◆[8] | 258 | 34.31 S | 58.34 W |
| Boulogne, Bois de ♠ | 261 | 48.50 N | 2.15 E |
| Boulogne-Billancourt | 50 | 48.50 N | 2.15 E |
| Boulogne-sur-Gesse | 32 | 43.18 N | 0.39 E |
| Boulogne-sur-Mer | 50 | 50.43 N | 1.37 E |
| Bouloire | 50 | 47.58 N | 0.33 E |
| Boulouli | 150 | 15.34 N | 9.21 W |
| Bouloupari | 175f | 21.52 S | 166.04 E |
| Boulouris-sur-Mer | 62 | 43.25 N | 6.48 E |
| Boulsa | 150 | 12.39 N | 0.34 W |
| Boulsworth Hill ∧ | 44 | 53.48 N | 2.06 W |
| Bouly | 150 | 15.19 N | 11.48 W |
| Bou Maad, Djebel ∧ | 34 | 36.26 N | 2.08 E |
| Boumalne | 148 | 31.32 N | 5.27 W |
| Boumba ≃ | 152 | 2.02 N | 15.12 E |
| Boumbé I ≃ | 152 | 4.04 N | 15.23 E |
| Boumbé II ≃ | 152 | 4.08 N | 15.08 E |
| Boumboum | 150 | 15.01 N | 1.42 W |
| Boûmdeïd | 150 | 17.26 N | 9.50 W |
| Bou Medfaa | 34 | 36.22 N | 2.28 E |
| Boumentana | 152 | 6.59 N | 16.56 E |
| Boumnyebe | 152 | 3.52 N | 10.49 E |
| Boumou | 146 | 9.02 N | 16.26 E |
| Bouna | 150 | 9.16 N | 3.00 W |
| Boundary | 180 | 64.04 N | 141.06 W |
| Boundary Bay c | 224 | 49.00 N | 122.58 W |
| Boundary Peak ∧ | 204 | 37.51 N | 118.21 W |
| Boundary Ranges ⋏ | 180 | 59.00 N | 134.00 W |
| Bound Brook | 210 | 40.34 N | 74.32 W |
| Bound Brook ≃, Ma., | | | |
| U.S. | 283 | 42.13 N | 70.47 W |
| Bound Brook ≃, | | | |
| N.J., U.S. | 276 | 40.35 N | 74.30 W |
| Boundiali | 150 | 9.31 N | 6.29 W |
| Boun Nua | 110 | 21.38 N | 101.54 E |
| Bountiful | 200 | 40.53 N | 111.52 W |
| Bounty Bay c | 174e | 25.04 S | 130.05 W |
| Bounty Islands II | 14 | 47.42 S | 179.04 E |
| Bounty Trough ✢[1] | 14 | 46.00 S | 178.00 E |
| Bouqteb | 148 | 34.02 N | 0.05 E |
| Bouquet Reservoir | | | |
| ⊜[1] | 228 | 34.35 N | 118.24 W |
| Bouqueval | 261 | 49.01 N | 2.26 E |
| Boura | 150 | 12.25 N | 4.33 W |
| Bouradière | 62 | 43.58 N | 5.19 E |
| Bourail | 175f | 21.34 S | 165.30 E |
| Bouray-sur-Juine | 261 | 48.31 N | 2.18 E |
| Bourbeuse ≃ | 194 | 38.24 N | 90.53 W |
| Bourbeuse, Dry Fork | | | |
| ≃ | 194 | 38.16 N | 91.26 W |


| Symbol | English | Deutsch | Español | Français | Português |
|---|---|---|---|---|---|
| ≃ | River | Fluß | Río | Rivière | Rio |
| ≍ | Canal | Kanal | Canal | Canal | Canal |
| ᒪ | Waterfall, Rapids | Wasserfall, Stromschnellen | Cascada, Rápidos | Chute d'eau, Rapides | Cascata, Rápidos |
| Ц | Strait | Meeresstraße | Estrecho | Détroit | Estreito |
| c | Bay, Gulf | Bucht, Golf | Bahía, Golfo | Baie, Golfe | Baía, Golfo |
| ⊜ | Lake, Lakes | See, Seen | Lago, Lagos | Lac, Lacs | Lago, Lagos |
| ≚ | Swamp | Sumpf | Pantano | Marais | Pântano |
| ⊓ | Ice Features, Glacier | Eis- und Gletscherformen | Accidentes Glaciales | Formes glaciaires | Acidentes glaciares |
| ⊤ | Other Hydrographic Features | Andere Hydrographische Objekte | Otros Elementos Hidrográficos | Autres données hydrographiques | Outros acidentes hidrográficos |
| ✢ | Submarine Features | Untermeerische Objekte | Accidentes Submarinos | Formes de relief sous-marin | Acidentes submarinos |
| □ | Political Unit | Politische Einheit | Unidad Politica | Entité politique | Unidade política |
| ʊ | Cultural Institution | Kulturelle Institution | Institución Cultural | Institution culturelle | Institução cultural |
| ⊥ | Historical Site | Historische Stätte | Sitio Histórico | Site historique | Sitio histórico |
| ♠ | Recreational Site | Erholungs- und Ferienort | Sitio de Recreo | Centre de loisirs | Area de Lazer |
| ⊠ | Airport | Flughafen | Aeropuerto | Aéroport | Aeroporto |
| ■ | Military Installation | Militäranlage | Instalación Militar | Installation militaire | Instalação militar |
| ◆ | Miscellaneous | Verschiedenes | Misceláneo | Divers | Diversos |

ENGLISH / DEUTSCH


| Name (Name) | Page (Seite) | Lat.°′ (Breite°′) | Long.°′ (Länge°′ E = Ost) |
|---|---|---|---|
| Bourbon, In., U.S. | 216 | 41.17 N | 86.06 W |
| Bourbon, Mo., U.S. | 194 | 38.09 N | 91.14 W |
| Bourbon □[6] | 218 | 38.14 N | 84.14 W |
| Bourbon ≃ | 206 | 46.17 N | 71.55 W |
| Bourbon-Lancy | 32 | 46.38 N | 3.46 E |
| Bourbonnais | 216 | 41.08 N | 87.52 W |
| Bourbonnais □[9] | 32 | 46.20 N | 3.00 E |
| Bourbonne-les-Bains | 58 | 47.57 N | 5.45 E |
| Bourbourg | 50 | 50.57 N | 2.12 E |
| Bourbre ≃ | 62 | 45.47 N | 5.11 E |
| Bourdeaux | 62 | 44.35 N | 5.08 E |
| Bourdon, Île I | 275a | 45.43 N | 73.29 W |
| Bourdon, Réservoir du ⊜[1] | 50 | 47.36 N | 3.07 E |
| Bourdonné | 261 | 48.45 N | 1.40 E |
| Bou Regreg, Oued ≃ | 148 | 34.03 N | 6.50 W |
| Bourem | 150 | 16.57 N | 0.21 W |
| Bourg | 194 | 29.33 N | 90.36 W |
| Bourg-Achard | 50 | 49.21 N | 0.49 E |
| Bourganeuf | 32 | 45.57 N | 1.46 E |
| Bourg-Argental | 62 | 45.18 N | 4.33 E |
| Bourg-de-Péage | 62 | 45.02 N | 5.03 E |
| Bourg-en-Bresse | 58 | 46.12 N | 5.13 E |
| Bourges | 32 | 47.05 N | 2.24 E |
| Bourget | 206 | 45.26 N | 75.09 W |
| Bourget, Lac du ⊜ | 62 | 45.44 N | 5.52 E |
| Bourg-la-Reine | 261 | 48.47 N | 2.19 E |
| Bourg-Lastic | 32 | 45.39 N | 2.33 E |
| Bourg-lés-Valence | 62 | 44.57 N | 4.53 E |
| Bourgneuf | 261 | 48.36 N | 2.00 E |
| Bourgneuf-en-Retz | 32 | 47.02 N | 1.57 W |
| Bourgogne | 50 | 49.21 N | 4.04 E |
| Bourgogne (Burgundy) □[9] | 32 | 47.00 N | 4.30 E |
| Bourgogne, Canal de ≅ | 32 | 47.58 N | 3.30 E |
| Bourgoin-Jallieu | 62 | 45.35 N | 5.17 E |
| Bourg-Saint-Andéol | 62 | 44.22 N | 4.39 E |
| Bourg-Saint-Maurice | 62 | 45.37 N | 6.46 E |
| Bourg-Saint-Pierre | 58 | 45.57 N | 7.12 E |
| Bourgtheroulde | 50 | 49.18 N | 0.53 E |
| Bourgueil | 50 | 47.17 N | 0.10 E |
| Bou Rjeïmât ⊤[4] | 150 | 19.04 N | 15.08 W |
| Bourke | 166 | 30.05 S | 145.56 E |
| Bourmont | 58 | 48.12 N | 5.35 E |
| Bourne | 42 | 52.46 N | 0.23 W |
| Bourne ≃, Fr. | 62 | 45.04 N | 5.15 E |
| Bourne ≃, Eng., U.K. | 42 | 51.02 N | 1.47 W |
| Bournebridge | 260 | 51.38 N | 0.11 E |
| Bourne End | 260 | 51.45 N | 0.32 W |
| Bournemouth | 42 | 50.43 N | 1.54 W |
| Bourneville, Fr. | 50 | 49.23 N | 0.37 E |
| Bourneville, Oh., U.S. | 218 | 39.17 N | 83.09 W |
| Bourn Vincent Memorial Park ♠ | 48 | 52.01 N | 9.30 W |
| Bouroum | 150 | 13.37 N | 0.39 W |
| Bourron-Marlotte | 50 | 48.20 N | 2.42 E |
| Bourscheid | 56 | 49.55 N | 6.04 E |
| Bourtange | 52 | 53.00 N | 7.11 E |
| Bourtanger Moor ◈[3] | 52 | 52.50 N | 7.06 E |
| Bourton-on-the-Water | 42 | 51.53 N | 1.45 W |
| Bourzanga | 150 | 13.41 N | 1.33 W |
| Bou Saâda | 148 | 35.12 N | 4.11 E |
| Bou Salem | 36 | 36.36 N | 8.59 E |
| Bousbecque | 50 | 50.46 N | 3.05 E |
| Bouse | 200 | 33.55 N | 114.00 W |
| Bou Sellam, Oued ≃ | 34 | 36.26 N | 4.34 E |
| Bouse Wash V | 200 | 34.02 N | 114.20 W |
| Bou Smail | 148 | 36.38 N | 2.41 E |
| Boussac | 32 | 46.21 N | 2.13 E |
| Boussé, Burkina | 150 | 12.39 N | 1.53 W |
| Bousse, Fr. | 56 | 49.17 N | 6.12 E |
| Boussières | 58 | 47.09 N | 5.54 E |
| Bousso | 146 | 10.29 N | 16.43 E |
| Boussois | 50 | 50.17 N | 4.03 E |
| Boussouma | 150 | 12.55 N | 1.05 W |
| Boussu | 50 | 50.26 N | 3.48 E |
| Boussy-Saint-Antoine | 261 | 48.41 N | 2.32 E |
| Bout, Pointe du › | 240e | 14.34 N | 61.03 W |
| Bouteille, Lac de la ⊜ | 206 | 46.42 N | 73.41 W |
| Bouteldja | 36 | 36.47 N | 8.12 E |
| Bou Temezguida ∧ | 148 | 29.21 N | 9.55 W |
| Boutilimit | 150 | 17.33 N | 14.42 W |
| Bouttencourt | 50 | 49.56 N | 1.38 E |
| Bouvard, Cape › | 168a | 32.41 S | 115.37 E |
| Bouvetøya I | 9 | 54.26 S | 3.24 E |
| Bouvier Bay c | 281 | 42.39 N | 82.38 W |
| Bouvières | 62 | 44.30 N | 5.13 E |
| Bouxières-aux-Dames | 56 | 48.45 N | 6.10 E |
| Bouxwiller | 56 | 48.49 N | 7.29 E |
| Bouyon | 62 | 43.50 N | 7.07 E |
| Bouza | 150 | 14.25 N | 6.02 E |
| Bou Zadjar | 34 | 35.35 N | 1.09 W |
| Bouzonville | 56 | 49.18 N | 6.32 E |
| Bov | 41 | 54.50 N | 9.23 E |
| Bova | 68 | 38.00 N | 15.56 E |
| Bøvågen | 26 | 60.40 N | 4.58 E |
| Bovalino Marina | 68 | 38.10 N | 16.11 E |
| Bova Marina | 68 | 37.56 N | 15.55 E |
| Bovard | 279b | 40.19 N | 79.30 W |
| Bovec | 36 | 46.20 N | 13.33 E |
| Bovegno | 64 | 45.48 N | 10.16 E |
| Bovenden | 52 | 51.35 N | 9.55 E |
| Bovenkarspel | 52 | 52.42 N | 5.15 E |
| Bøverdal | 26 | 61.43 N | 8.21 E |
| Boves, Fr. | 50 | 49.51 N | 2.23 E |
| Boves, It. | 62 | 44.19 N | 7.33 E |
| Bovey | 190 | 47.17 N | 93.25 W |
| Bovey ≃ | 42 | 50.34 N | 3.37 W |
| Bovey Tracey | 42 | 50.36 N | 3.40 W |
| Bovill | 202 | 46.51 N | 116.23 W |
| Boville Ernica | 66 | 41.38 N | 13.28 E |
| Bovina | 196 | 34.31 N | 102.53 W |
| Bovina Center | 210 | 42.16 N | 74.47 W |
| Bovingdon | 42 | 51.44 N | 0.32 W |
| Bövinghausen ◈[8] | 263 | 51.31 N | 7.19 E |
| Bovington Camp | 42 | 50.42 N | 2.14 W |
| Bovino | 68 | 41.15 N | 15.20 E |
| Bovisio Masciago | 266b | 45.37 N | 9.09 E |
| Bovolenta | 64 | 45.16 N | 11.56 E |
| Bovolone | 64 | 45.15 N | 11.07 E |
| Bovril | 252 | 31.21 S | 59.26 W |
| Bovrup | 41 | 54.59 N | 9.36 E |
| Bow | 224 | 48.33 N | 122.23 W |
| Bow ≃, Austl. | 162 | 16.32 S | 128.39 E |
| Bow ≃, Ab., Can. | 182 | 49.56 N | 111.42 W |
| Bow ≃, Sk., Can. | 184 | 54.56 N | 105.13 W |
| Bo-Wadrif | 158 | 32.26 S | 20.07 E |
| Bowang | 106 | 31.34 N | 118.50 E |
| Bowbells | 198 | 48.48 N | 102.14 W |
| Bow Brook ≃ | 42 | 52.04 N | 2.07 W |
| Bowburn | 44 | 54.43 N | 1.31 W |
| Bow Creek ≃ | 198 | 39.35 N | 99.14 W |
| Bowden | 182 | 51.55 N | 114.02 W |
| Bowdle | 198 | 45.27 N | 99.39 W |
| Bowdoin, Lake ⊜ | 202 | 48.24 N | 107.41 W |
| Bowdon, Eng., U.K. | 262 | 53.23 N | 2.22 W |
| Bowdon, Ga., U.S. | 192 | 33.32 N | 85.15 W |
| Bowdon, N.D., U.S. | 198 | 47.28 N | 99.42 W |
| Bowelling | 168a | 33.25 S | 116.29 E |
| Bowen, Arg. | 252 | 35.00 S | 67.31 W |
| Bowen, Austl. | 166 | 20.01 S | 148.15 E |
| Bowen, Il., U.S. | 194 | 40.14 N | 91.04 W |
| Bowen ≃ | 166 | 20.24 S | 147.21 E |
| Bowenfels | 170 | 33.31 S | 150.07 E |
| Bowens Creek ≃ | 170 | 33.21 S | 150.35 E |
| Bowers | 208 | 39.15 N | 75.36 W |
| Bowers Gifford | 260 | 51.34 N | 0.32 E |
| Bowers Mansion ⊥ | 226 | 39.17 N | 119.50 W |
| Bowers Marshes ≡ | 260 | 51.33 N | 0.32 E |
| Bowers Ridge ✢[3] | 16 | 54.00 N | 179.00 E |
| Bowerston | 214 | 40.25 N | 81.11 W |
| Bowersville | 218 | 39.34 N | 83.43 W |
| Bowgreave | 44 | 53.52 N | 2.45 W |
| Bowie, Az., U.S. | 200 | 32.19 N | 109.29 W |
| Bowie, Md., U.S. | 208 | 39.00 N | 76.46 W |
| Bowie, Tx., U.S. | 196 | 33.33 N | 97.50 W |
| Bowie Creek ≃ | 194 | 31.26 N | 89.24 W |
| Bow Island | 184 | 49.52 N | 111.22 W |
| Bowland, Forest of ◈[3] | 44 | 53.58 N | 2.32 W |
| Bowles Creek ≃ | 222 | 32.02 N | 94.59 W |
| Bowley Bar ›[2] | 284b | 39.18 N | 76.23 W |
| Bowleys Quarters | 284b | 39.19 N | 76.24 W |
| Bowling Green, Fl., U.S. | 220 | 27.38 N | 81.49 W |
| Bowling Green, Ky., U.S. | 194 | 36.59 N | 86.26 W |
| Bowling Green, Mo., U.S. | 219 | 39.20 N | 91.11 W |
| Bowling Green, Oh., U.S. | 216 | 41.22 N | 83.39 W |
| Bowling Green, Pa., U.S. | 285 | 39.55 N | 75.23 W |
| Bowling Green, Va., U.S. | 208 | 38.02 N | 77.20 W |
| Bowling Green, Cape › | 166 | 19.19 S | 147.25 E |
| Bowling Green Bay National Park ♠ | 166 | 19.28 S | 147.14 E |
| Bowman, Ca., U.S. | 226 | 38.57 N | 121.03 W |
| Bowman, Ga., U.S. | 192 | 34.12 N | 83.01 W |
| Bowman, N.D., U.S. | 198 | 46.10 N | 103.23 W |
| Bowman, S.C., U.S. | 192 | 33.20 N | 80.40 W |
| Bowman, Mount ∧ | 182 | 51.10 N | 121.55 W |
| Bowman Creek ≃, Pa., U.S. | 210 | 41.31 N | 75.58 W |
| Bowman Creek ≃, Wa., U.S. | 224 | 45.50 N | 121.03 W |
| Bowman-Haley Lake ⊜[1] | 198 | 46.00 N | 103.20 W |
| Bowman Island I | 9 | 65.17 S | 103.08 E |
| Bowman Lake ⊜[1] | 226 | 39.27 N | 120.38 W |
| Bowmans | 168b | 34.09 S | 138.16 E |
| Bowmansdale | 208 | 40.10 N | 76.59 W |
| Bowmanstown | 208 | 40.48 N | 75.40 W |
| Bowmansville, N.Y., U.S. | 212 | 42.56 N | 78.41 W |
| Bowmansville, Pa., U.S. | 208 | 40.10 N | 76.04 W |
| Bowmanville | 212 | 43.55 N | 78.41 W |
| Bowmanville Creek ≃ | 212 | 43.53 N | 78.40 W |
| Bowmont Water ≃ | 44 | 55.34 N | 2.09 W |
| Bowmore | 46 | 55.45 N | 6.17 W |
| Bowness-on-Windermere | 44 | 54.22 N | 2.55 W |
| Bowokan, Kepulauan II | 112 | 2.05 S | 123.35 E |
| Bowral | 170 | 34.28 S | 150.25 E |
| Bowraville | 166 | 30.39 S | 152.51 E |
| Bowron ≃ | 182 | 54.04 N | 121.48 W |
| Bowron Lake Provincial Park ♠ | 182 | 53.10 N | 121.06 W |
| Bowsman | 184 | 52.14 N | 101.14 W |
| Bowwood | 154 | 17.07 S | 26.17 E |
| Box | 42 | 51.26 N | 2.15 W |
| Boxberg, Dtsch. | 54 | 51.24 N | 14.34 E |
| Boxberg, Dtsch. | 56 | 49.29 N | 9.38 E |
| Box Butte Creek ≃ | 198 | 42.28 N | 102.37 W |
| Box Creek ≃, Tx., U.S. | 222 | 31.33 N | 95.43 W |
| Box Creek ≃, Tx., U.S. | 222 | 31.35 N | 95.10 W |
| Box Elder | 202 | 48.19 N | 110.00 W |
| Boxelder Creek ≃, U.S. | 198 | 45.59 N | 103.57 W |
| Box Elder Creek ≃, Co., U.S. | 198 | 40.23 N | 104.28 W |
| Boxelder Creek ≃, Co., U.S. | 198 | 40.33 N | 105.00 W |
| Box Elder Creek ≃, Mt., U.S. | 202 | 46.57 N | 108.04 W |
| Boxelder Creek ≃, S.D., U.S. | 198 | 44.01 N | 102.27 W |
| Boxey | 186 | 47.25 N | 55.34 W |
| Boxey Point › | 186 | 47.24 N | 55.35 W |
| Boxford | 207 | 42.39 N | 70.59 W |
| Boxford State Forest ♠ | 283 | 42.39 N | 71.02 W |
| Box Grove | 275b | 43.51 N | 79.14 W |
| Box Hill | 169 | 37.49 S | 145.08 E |
| Boxholm | 26 | 58.12 N | 15.03 E |
| Boxian | 100 | 33.53 N | 115.45 E |
| Boxing | 98 | 37.08 N | 118.07 E |
| Boxley | 260 | 51.18 N | 0.33 E |
| Boxmeer | 52 | 51.39 N | 5.57 E |
| Boxmoor | 260 | 51.45 N | 0.29 W |
| Boxodoi | 98 | 42.34 N | 115.18 E |
| Boxtel | 52 | 51.35 N | 5.20 E |
| Boyabat | 130 | 41.28 N | 34.47 E |
| Boyabo | 152 | 3.43 N | 18.46 E |
| Boyacá □[5] | 246 | 5.30 N | 73.30 W |
| Boyacıköy ◈[8] | 267b | 41.06 N | 29.02 E |
| Boyalı | 130 | 41.02 N | 33.19 E |
| Boyalık | 130 | 41.15 N | 28.37 E |
| Boyang | 100 | 28.59 N | 116.40 E |
| Boyanup | 168a | 33.29 S | 115.44 E |
| Boyarka | 78 | 50.19 N | 30.19 E |
| Boyasengese | 152 | 3.29 N | 20.33 E |
| Boyce | 194 | 31.23 N | 92.40 W |
| Boyceville | 190 | 45.02 N | 92.02 W |
| Boyd, Mn., U.S. | 198 | 44.50 N | 95.54 W |
| Boyd, Tx., U.S. | 222 | 33.05 N | 97.34 W |
| Boyd ≃ | 166 | 29.51 S | 152.35 E |
| Boyd's Cove | 186 | 49.27 N | 54.39 W |
| Boydton | 192 | 36.40 N | 78.23 W |
| Boyenge | 152 | 0.25 N | 18.51 E |
| Boyer ≃ | 198 | 41.28 N | 95.55 W |
| Boyera | 152 | 0.38 S | 19.25 E |
| Boyer Aḥmadī va Kohkīlūyeh □[4] | 128 | 30.40 N | 50.40 E |
| Boyer Run ≃ | 279b | 40.13 N | 79.32 W |
| Boyers | 214 | 41.06 N | 79.54 W |
| Boyer's Creek ≃ | 284a | 43.00 N | 79.02 W |
| Boyertown | 208 | 40.20 N | 75.38 W |
| Boyes Hot Springs | 226 | 38.19 N | 122.29 W |
| Boykins | 208 | 36.34 N | 77.12 W |
| Boyle, Ab., Can. | 182 | 54.35 N | 112.49 W |
| Boyle, Ire. | 48 | 53.58 N | 8.18 W |
| Boyle, Ms., U.S. | 194 | 33.42 N | 90.50 W |
| Boyle Drain ≃ | 212 | 43.42 N | 81.06 W |
| Boyle Heights ◈[8] | 280 | 34.02 N | 118.13 W |
| Boylston, Al., U.S. | 194 | 32.26 N | 86.17 W |
| Boylston, Ma., U.S. | 207 | 42.23 N | 71.42 W |
| Boyne | 275b | 43.29 N | 79.50 W |
| Boyne ≃, Austl. | 166 | 23.56 S | 151.21 E |
| Boyne ≃, Mb., Can. | 184 | 49.34 N | 97.52 W |
| Boyne ≃, On., Can. | 212 | 44.10 N | 79.49 W |
| Boyne ≃, Ire. | 48 | 53.43 N | 6.15 W |
| Boyne Battlesite ⊥ | 48 | 53.42 N | 6.23 W |
| Boyne City | 190 | 45.12 N | 85.00 W |
| Boynton | 196 | 35.38 N | 95.39 W |
| Boynton Beach | 220 | 26.31 N | 80.04 W |
| Boyo | 152 | 5.43 N | 21.33 E |
| Boyolali | 115a | 7.32 S | 110.35 E |
| Boysen Reservoir ⊜[1] | 202 | 43.19 N | 108.11 W |
| Boysen State Park ♠ | 202 | 43.23 N | 108.07 W |
| Boys Ranch | 196 | 35.32 N | 102.15 W |
| Boyuibe | 248 | 20.25 S | 63.17 W |
| Böyük Hinaldağ ∧ | 84 | 40.20 N | 45.57 E |
| Böyük Kirs dağ ∧ | 84 | 39.41 N | 46.44 E |
| Boyup Brook | 162 | 33.50 S | 116.24 E |
| Bozburun | 130 | 36.41 N | 28.04 E |
| Boz Burun › | 130 | 40.32 N | 28.46 E |
| Bozburun Yarımadası ›[1] | 130 | 36.40 N | 28.10 E |
| Bozcaada | 130 | 39.50 N | 26.04 E |
| Boz Dağ ∧, Tür. | 130 | 37.18 N | 29.12 E |
| Boz Dağ ∧, Tür. | 130 | 38.19 N | 28.08 E |
| Bozdağ ∧, Tür. | 130 | 36.50 N | 36.22 E |
| Boz Dağlar ∧∧ | 130 | 38.20 N | 27.45 E |
| Bozdoğan | 130 | 37.40 N | 28.19 E |
| Bozel | 62 | 45.27 N | 6.39 E |
| Bozeman | 202 | 45.40 N | 111.02 W |
| Bozen → Bolzano | 64 | 46.31 N | 11.22 E |
| Bozene | 152 | 2.56 N | 19.12 E |
| Bozhen | 98 | 38.07 N | 116.32 E |
| Boží Dar | 54 | 50.24 N | 12.55 E |
| Bozkır | 130 | 37.11 N | 32.15 E |
| Bozkurt, Tür. | 130 | 37.49 N | 29.37 E |
| Bozkurt, Tür. | 130 | 41.57 N | 34.01 E |
| Bozman | 208 | 38.46 N | 76.16 W |
| Bozoğlak | 130 | 39.38 N | 38.49 E |
| Bozok | 130 | 37.18 N | 40.22 E |
| Bozoum | 152 | 6.19 N | 16.23 E |
| Bozova, Tür. | 130 | 37.22 N | 38.31 E |
| Bozova, Tür. | 130 | 37.13 N | 30.18 E |
| Bozovici | 38 | 44.55 N | 21.59 E |
| Bozšakol' | 86 | 51.50 N | 74.20 E |
| Bozum | 52 | 53.05 N | 5.42 E |
| Bozüyük | 130 | 39.54 N | 30.03 E |
| Bozzolo | 64 | 45.06 N | 10.29 E |
| Bra | 62 | 44.42 N | 7.51 E |
| Braan ≃ | 46 | 56.33 N | 3.35 W |
| Braås | 26 | 57.04 N | 15.03 E |
| Brabant □[4] | 56 | 50.45 N | 4.30 E |
| Brabante, Isla de → Brabant Island I | 9 | 64.15 S | 62.20 W |
| Brabant Island I | 9 | 64.15 S | 62.20 W |
| Brabant Lake ⊜ | 184 | 56.00 N | 103.43 W |
| Brabrand | 41 | 56.09 N | 10.07 E |
| Brač, Otok I | 36 | 43.20 N | 16.40 E |
| Bracadale, Loch c | 46 | 57.19 N | 6.30 W |
| Bracciano | 66 | 42.06 N | 12.10 E |
| Bracciano, Lago di ⊜ | 66 | 42.07 N | 12.14 E |
| Bracco, Passo del )( | 62 | 44.15 N | 9.34 E |
| Bracebridge | 212 | 45.02 N | 79.19 W |
| Bracebridge Heath | 44 | 53.13 N | 0.33 W |
| Braceville, Il., U.S. | 216 | 41.14 N | 88.16 W |
| Braceville, Oh., U.S. | 214 | 41.14 N | 80.58 W |
| Brachfield | 222 | 32.03 N | 94.39 W |
| Bracieux | 50 | 47.33 N | 1.33 E |
| Bracigliano | 68 | 40.49 N | 14.42 E |
| Bracigovo | 38 | 42.01 N | 24.22 E |
| Bräcke | 26 | 62.43 N | 15.27 E |
| Brackel ◈[8] | 263 | 51.32 N | 7.33 E |
| Bracken □[6] | 218 | 38.40 N | 84.06 W |
| Brackendale | 182 | 49.46 N | 123.09 W |
| Brackenheim | 56 | 49.05 N | 9.03 E |
| Brackenhurst | 273d | 26.19 S | 28.06 E |
| Bracken Lake ⊜ | 184 | 53.37 N | 99.50 W |
| Brackenridge | 214 | 40.36 N | 79.44 W |
| Brackett Field ⊠ | 280 | 34.05 N | 117.47 W |
| Brackettville | 196 | 29.18 N | 100.25 W |
| Brački Kanal ɥ | 36 | 43.24 N | 16.40 E |
| Brackley | 42 | 52.02 N | 1.09 W |
| Bracknell | 42 | 51.26 N | 0.45 W |
| Bracktown | 218 | 38.04 N | 84.31 W |
| Brackwede | 52 | 51.59 N | 8.31 E |
| Braco | 46 | 56.15 N | 3.53 W |
| Braço do Norte | 252 | 28.17 S | 49.11 W |
| Bracuí ≃ | 256 | 22.57 S | 44.24 W |
| Brad | 38 | 46.08 N | 22.47 E |
| Bradano ≃ | 68 | 40.23 N | 16.51 E |
| Bradbury | 280 | 34.08 N | 117.59 W |
| Bradbury Heights | 284c | 38.52 N | 76.56 W |
| Braddock, N.J., U.S. | 285 | 39.42 N | 74.53 W |
| Braddock, Pa., U.S. | 214 | 40.24 N | 79.52 W |
| Braddock Acres | 284c | 38.49 N | 77.10 W |
| Braddock Heights, Md., U.S. | 208 | 39.25 N | 77.30 W |
| Braddock Heights, N.Y., U.S. | 210 | 43.19 N | 77.42 W |
| Braddock Hills | 279b | 40.25 N | 79.51 W |
| Braddock Point › | 210 | 43.19 N | 77.43 W |
| Braddocks Millpond ⊜ | 285 | 39.49 N | 74.51 W |
| Braden ≃ | 220 | 27.30 N | 82.32 W |
| Bradenton | 220 | 27.29 N | 82.34 W |
| Bradenton Beach | 220 | 27.28 N | 82.42 W |
| Bradenville | 214 | 40.19 N | 79.20 W |
| Braderup | 41 | 54.50 N | 8.53 E |
| Bradford, On., Can. | 212 | 44.07 N | 79.34 W |
| Bradford, Eng., U.K. | 44 | 53.48 N | 1.45 W |
| Bradford, Ar., U.S. | 194 | 35.25 N | 91.27 W |
| Bradford, Il., U.S. | 190 | 41.10 N | 89.39 W |
| Bradford, N.Y., U.S. | 210 | 42.22 N | 77.07 W |
| Bradford, Oh., U.S. | 218 | 40.08 N | 84.26 W |
| Bradford, Pa., U.S. | 214 | 41.57 N | 78.38 W |
| Bradford, R.I., U.S. | 207 | 41.23 N | 71.44 W |
| Bradford, Tn., U.S. | 194 | 36.04 N | 88.48 W |
| Bradford, Vt., U.S. | 188 | 43.59 N | 72.09 W |
| Bradford □[6] | 210 | 41.56 N | 78.40 W |
| Bradford □[8] | 262 | 53.47 N | 1.52 W |
| Bradford Hills | 285 | 40.01 N | 75.39 W |
| Bradford Mountain ∧ | 207 | 41.59 N | 73.18 W |
| Bradford-on-Avon | 42 | 51.20 N | 2.15 W |
| Bradford Regional Airport ⊠ | 214 | 41.48 N | 78.38 W |
| Bradfordwoods | 214 | 40.38 N | 80.05 W |
| Brading | 42 | 50.41 N | 1.09 W |
| Bradley, Ar., U.S. | 194 | 33.05 N | 93.39 W |
| Bradley, Ca., U.S. | 226 | 35.51 N | 120.47 W |
| Bradley, Fl., U.S. | 220 | 27.48 N | 81.59 W |
| Bradley, Il., U.S. | 216 | 41.08 N | 87.51 W |
| Bradley, Mi., U.S. | 216 | 42.38 N | 85.39 W |
| Bradley, S.D., U.S. | 198 | 45.05 N | 97.38 W |
| Bradley Beach | 208 | 40.12 N | 74.01 W |
| Bradley Farms | 284c | 39.00 N | 77.11 W |
| Bradley Gardens | 276 | 40.34 N | 74.39 W |
| Bradley Institute | 154 | 17.02 S | 31.27 E |
| Bradley International Airport ⊠ | 207 | 41.55 N | 72.40 W |
| Bradley Reefs ✢[2] | 175e | 6.52 S | 160.48 E |
| Bradley Woods Reservation ♠ | 279a | 41.25 N | 81.58 W |
| Bradley W. Palmer State Park ♠ | 283 | 42.39 N | 70.54 W |
| Bradner, B.C., Can. | 224 | 49.06 N | 122.25 W |
| Bradner, Oh., U.S. | 214 | 41.19 N | 83.26 W |
| Bradninch | 42 | 50.50 N | 3.25 W |
| Bradore-Bay | 186 | 51.28 N | 57.14 W |
| Bradshaw, Eng., U.K. | 262 | 53.36 N | 2.24 W |
| Bradshaw, Md., U.S. | 208 | 39.25 N | 76.22 W |
| Bradshaw, Ne., U.S. | 198 | 40.53 N | 97.44 W |
| Bradshaw, W.V., U.S. | 192 | 37.21 N | 81.47 W |
| Bradwell-on-Sea | 42 | 51.44 N | 0.54 E |
| Bradworthy | 42 | 50.54 N | 4.22 W |
| Brady, Mt., U.S. | 202 | 48.02 N | 111.50 W |
| Brady, Ne., U.S. | 198 | 41.01 N | 100.22 W |
| Brady, Tx., U.S. | 196 | 31.08 N | 99.20 W |
| Brady Creek ≃ | 196 | 31.07 N | 98.59 W |
| Brady Lake | 214 | 41.09 N | 81.19 W |
| Brady Mountains ∧∧[2] | 196 | 31.20 N | 99.40 W |
| Brae | 46a | 60.23 N | 1.21 W |
| Brædstrup | 41 | 55.58 N | 9.37 E |
| Braemar | 46 | 57.01 N | 3.23 W |
| Braeside, Austl. | 162 | 21.12 S | 121.01 E |
| Braeside, Austl. | 274b | 37.59 S | 145.07 E |
| Braeside, On., Can. | 212 | 45.28 N | 76.24 W |
| Braga | 34 | 41.33 N | 8.26 W |
| Bragado | 252 | 35.08 S | 60.30 W |
| Bragança, Bra. | 250 | 1.03 S | 46.46 W |
| Braganca, Bra. | 256 | 23.18 S | 45.38 W |
| Bragança, Port. | 34 | 41.49 N | 6.45 W |
| Bragança Paulista | 256 | 22.57 S | 46.34 W |
| Bragar | 46 | 58.24 N | 6.40 W |
| Braham | 190 | 45.43 N | 93.10 W |
| Brahetrolleborg ⊥ | 41 | 55.09 N | 10.22 E |
| Brahin | 78 | 51.47 N | 30.14 E |
| Brahinka ≃ | 78 | 51.22 N | 30.24 E |
| Brahma Island I | 220 | 27.52 N | 81.15 W |
| Brāhmanbāria | 120 | 23.59 N | 91.07 E |
| Brāhmani ≃, India | 120 | 20.39 N | 86.46 E |
| Brāhmani ≃, India | 126 | 24.09 N | 88.01 E |
| Brahmapur, India | 122 | 19.19 N | 84.47 E |
| Brahmapur, India | 272b | 22.28 N | 88.22 E |
| Brahmaputra (Yarlung) ≃ | 120 | 24.02 N | 90.59 E |
| Brāhmaur | 123 | 32.27 N | 76.32 E |
| Brahynivka | 78 | 48.29 N | 36.21 E |
| Braich y Pwll › | 42 | 52.48 N | 4.36 W |
| Braidwood, Austl. | 166 | 35.27 S | 149.48 E |
| Braidwood, Il., U.S. | 216 | 41.15 N | 88.12 W |
| Braies (Prags) | 64 | 46.42 N | 12.08 E |
| Brăila | 38 | 45.16 N | 27.58 E |
| Brăila □[6] | 38 | 45.00 N | 27.40 E |
| Brain ≃ | 42 | 51.48 N | 0.39 E |
| Brainard, Ne., U.S. | 198 | 41.11 N | 97.00 W |
| Brainard, N.Y., U.S. | 210 | 42.30 N | 73.31 W |
| Braine | 50 | 49.20 N | 3.32 E |
| Braine-l'Alleud | 50 | 50.41 N | 4.22 E |
| Braine-le-Château | 50 | 50.41 N | 4.16 E |
| Braine-le-Comte | 50 | 50.36 N | 4.08 E |
| Brainerd | 190 | 46.21 N | 94.12 W |
| Braint ≃ | 44 | 53.08 N | 4.19 W |
| Braintree, Eng., U.K. | 42 | 51.53 N | 0.32 E |
| Braintree, Ma., U.S. | 207 | 42.13 N | 71.00 W |
| Braintree □[8] | 260 | 51.47 N | 0.36 E |
| Brak ≃, S. Afr. | 158 | 31.32 S | 21.33 E |
| Brak ≃, S. Afr. | 158 | 29.35 S | 22.55 E |
| Brake, Dtsch. | 52 | 53.19 N | 8.28 E |
| Brake, Dtsch. | 52 | 52.04 N | 8.35 E |
| Brake, Dtsch. | 52 | 52.01 N | 8.55 E |
| Brakel, Bel. | 50 | 50.48 N | 3.46 E |
| Brakel, Dtsch. | 52 | 51.43 N | 9.10 E |
| Brakna □[4] | 150 | 17.30 N | 13.30 W |
| Brakpan | 158 | 26.14 S | 28.22 E |
| Brakpan □[5] | 273d | 26.16 S | 28.21 E |
| Brakpoort | 158 | 31.20 S | 23.22 E |
| Brakputs | 158 | 29.29 S | 18.24 E |
| Brakwater | 156 | 22.24 S | 17.06 E |
| Brålanda | 26 | 58.34 N | 12.22 E |
| Bralorne | 182 | 50.47 N | 122.49 W |
| Bramalea | 212 | 43.44 N | 79.43 W |
| Bramall Hall ⊥ | 262 | 53.23 N | 2.09 W |
| Braman | 196 | 36.55 N | 97.20 W |
| Brambauer | 263 | 51.35 N | 7.27 E |
| Bramberg am Wildkogel | 64 | 47.16 N | 12.21 E |
| Bramble Bay c | 171a | 27.17 S | 153.05 E |
| Bramble Cay I | 164 | 9.08 S | 143.52 E |
| Bramdrupdam | 41 | 55.31 N | 9.28 E |
| Bramey-Lenningsen | 263 | 51.34 N | 7.46 E |
| Bramfeld ◈[8] | 52 | 53.37 N | 10.04 E |
| Bramford | 42 | 52.04 N | 1.06 E |
| Bramhall | 262 | 53.22 N | 2.10 W |
| Bramhope | 44 | 53.53 N | 1.37 W |
| Bramley | 260 | 51.12 N | 0.34 W |
| Bramley ◈[8] | 273d | 26.08 S | 28.05 E |
| Bramley Mountain ∧ | 210 | 42.18 N | 74.49 W |
| Bramming | 41 | 55.28 N | 8.42 E |
| Brampton, On., Can. | 212 | 43.41 N | 79.46 W |
| Brampton, Eng., U.K. | 42 | 52.19 N | 0.14 W |
| Brampton, Eng., U.K. | 44 | 54.57 N | 2.43 W |
| Brampton Airfield ⊠ | 275b | 43.40 N | 79.47 W |
| Bramsche | 52 | 52.24 N | 7.58 E |
| Bramsöfjärden ⊜ | 40 | 60.20 N | 17.10 E |
| Bramstedt | 52 | 53.22 N | 8.41 E |
| Brancaleone Marina | 68 | 37.58 N | 16.06 E |
| Brancaster | 42 | 52.58 N | 0.39 E |
| Brancaster Roads ⊤[3] | 42 | 53.00 N | 0.41 E |
| Branch | 186 | 46.53 N | 53.57 W |
| Branch □[6] | 216 | 41.55 N | 85.03 W |
| Branch Brook Park ♠ | 276 | 40.46 N | 74.10 W |
| Branch Dale | 208 | 40.41 N | 76.20 W |
| Branchport | 210 | 42.36 N | 77.09 W |
| Branchville, Ct., U.S. | 207 | 41.16 N | 73.26 W |
| Branchville, N.J., U.S. | 210 | 41.08 N | 74.45 W |
| Branchville, S.C., U.S. | 192 | 33.15 N | 80.48 W |
| Branchville, Va., U.S. | 208 | 36.34 N | 77.14 W |
| Branco | 152 | 12.30 S | 20.32 E |
| Branco ≃, Bra. | 246 | 1.24 S | 61.51 W |
| Branco ≃, Bra. | 248 | 10.03 S | 67.51 W |
| Branco ≃, Bra. | 248 | 7.44 S | 61.46 W |
| Branco ≃, Bra. | 248 | 9.12 S | 64.22 W |
| Branco ≃, Bra. | 248 | 9.37 S | 60.33 W |
| Branco ≃, Bra. | 248 | 21.00 S | 57.48 W |
| Branco ≃, Bra. | 250 | 7.01 S | 51.42 W |
| Branco ≃, Bra. | 250 | 12.00 S | 44.56 W |
| Branco, Ilhéu I | 150a | 16.39 N | 24.41 W |
| Brand, Dtsch. | 56 | 50.43 N | 6.09 E |
| Brand, Öst. | 58 | 47.06 N | 9.44 E |
| Brandamore | 208 | 40.03 N | 75.50 W |
| Brandaris ∧[2] | 241s | 12.17 N | 68.24 W |
| Brandberg ∧ | 156 | 21.10 S | 14.33 E |
| Brandbu | 26 | 60.28 N | 10.30 E |
| Brande | 41 | 55.57 N | 9.07 E |
| Brandebourg → Brandenburg | 54 | 52.24 N | 12.32 E |
| Brandeis University Ψ[2] | 283 | 42.22 N | 71.16 W |
| Brandenberg | 64 | 47.29 N | 11.53 E |
| Brandenberg ∧[2] | 263 | 51.20 N | 7.37 E |
| Brandenburg, Dtsch. | 54 | 52.24 N | 12.32 E |
| Brandenburg, Ky., U.S. | 194 | 38.00 N | 86.10 W |
| Brandenburg □[3] | 54 | 52.30 N | 13.30 E |
| Brandenburger Tor ⊥ | 264a | 52.31 N | 13.23 E |
| Brand-Erbisdorf | 54 | 50.52 N | 13.19 E |
| Brandfort | 158 | 28.47 S | 26.30 E |
| Br'andino | 80 | 54.23 N | 49.23 E |
| Brandis | 54 | 51.20 N | 12.36 E |
| Brandizzo | 62 | 45.11 N | 7.51 E |
| Brandkop | 158 | 31.13 S | 19.13 E |
| Brandon, Mb., Can. | 184 | 49.50 N | 99.57 W |
| Brandon, Eng., U.K. | 42 | 52.27 N | 0.37 E |
| Brandon, Eng., U.K. | 44 | 54.46 N | 1.39 W |
| Brandon, Fl., U.S. | 220 | 27.56 N | 82.17 W |
| Brandon, Ms., U.S. | 194 | 32.16 N | 89.59 W |
| Brandon, S.D., U.S. | 198 | 43.35 N | 96.34 W |
| Brandon, Tx., U.S. | 222 | 32.03 N | 96.58 W |
| Brandon, Vt., U.S. | 188 | 43.47 N | 73.05 W |
| Brandon, Wi., U.S. | 190 | 43.44 N | 88.46 W |
| Brandon Bay c | 48 | 52.15 N | 10.05 W |
| Brandon Head › | 48 | 52.16 N | 10.14 W |
| Brandon Mountain ∧ | 48 | 52.14 N | 10.15 W |
| Brandon Road Lock and Dam ◈[5] | 278 | 41.30 N | 88.06 W |
| Brandonville | 210 | 40.52 N | 76.10 W |
| Brand Park ♠ | 280 | 34.11 N | 118.16 W |
| Brandsen | 258 | 35.10 S | 58.14 W |
| Brands Hatch Motor Race Circuit ♠ | 260 | 51.22 N | 0.16 E |
| Brandsø I | 41 | 55.21 N | 9.43 E |
| Brandt | 218 | 39.54 N | 84.05 W |
| Brandvlei | 158 | 30.25 S | 20.30 E |
| Brandy Camp | 214 | 41.19 N | 78.41 W |
| Brandy Peak ∧ | 202 | 42.36 N | 123.53 W |
| Brandýsek | 54 | 50.10 N | 14.10 E |
| Brandýs nad Labem | 54 | 50.10 N | 14.41 E |
| Brandywine Battlefield ⊥ | 208 | 39.53 N | 75.35 W |
| Brandywine Creek ≃, U.S. | 285 | 39.44 N | 75.32 W |
| Brandywine Creek ≃, In., U.S. | 218 | 39.31 N | 85.52 W |
| Brandywine Creek ≃, Oh., U.S. | 279a | 41.17 N | 81.34 W |
| Brandywine Creek, East Branch ≃ | 208 | 39.55 N | 75.39 W |
| Brandywine Creek, West Branch ≃ | 208 | 39.55 N | 75.39 W |
| Brandywine Creek State Park ♠ | 285 | 39.48 N | 75.35 W |
| Brandywine Park ♠ | 285 | 39.45 N | 75.33 W |
| Brandywine Springs Park ♠ | 285 | 39.45 N | 75.38 W |
| Branford, Ct., U.S. | 207 | 41.16 N | 72.48 W |
| Branford, Fl., U.S. | 192 | 29.57 N | 82.55 W |
| Brani, Pulau I | 271c | 1.15 N | 103.50 E |
| Braniewo | 30 | 54.24 N | 19.50 E |
| Branka, Česká Rep. | 60 | 49.50 N | 12.33 E |
| Br'anka, Ross. | 86 | 59.08 N | 93.27 E |
| Branlin ≃ | 50 | 47.51 N | 3.06 E |
| Brannenburg | 64 | 47.44 N | 12.05 E |
| Branquinho ≃ | 248 | 5.45 S | 71.27 W |
| Bransby | 166 | 28.14 S | 142.04 E |
| Bransfield Strait ɥ | 9 | 63.00 S | 59.00 W |
| Bransgore | 42 | 50.47 N | 1.44 W |
| Brańsk, Pol. | 30 | 52.45 N | 22.51 E |
| Br'ansk, Ross. | 76 | 53.15 N | 34.22 E |
| Br'anskaja Kosa, mys › | 84 | 44.22 N | 47.00 E |
| Br'ansk Oblast' □[4] | 76 | 53.00 N | 34.00 E |
| Branson | 194 | 36.38 N | 93.13 W |
| Brant | 210 | 42.35 N | 79.01 W |
| Brant □[6] | 212 | 43.10 N | 80.20 W |
| Brant ≃ | 44 | 53.09 N | 0.35 W |
| Br'anta ≃ | 89 | 54.27 N | 127.42 E |
| Brantas ≃ | 115a | 7.28 S | 112.25 E |
| Brantford | 212 | 43.08 N | 80.16 W |
| Brantingham Lake ⊜ | 212 | 43.42 N | 75.17 W |
| Brant Lake | 188 | 43.40 N | 73.45 W |
| Brantley | 194 | 31.34 N | 86.15 W |
| Brantôme | 32 | 45.22 N | 0.39 E |
| Brant Rock | 283 | 42.05 N | 70.38 W |
| Brantville | 186 | 47.22 N | 64.58 W |
| Branxholme | 166 | 37.51 S | 141.47 E |
| Branxton | 170 | 32.39 S | 151.22 E |
| Branzi | 64 | 46.00 N | 9.46 E |
| Brás ◈[8] | 287b | 23.32 S | 46.36 W |
| Brás Cubas | 256 | 23.32 S | 46.13 W |
| Bras d'Or Lake ⊜ | 186 | 45.52 N | 60.50 W |
| Brashear | 222 | 33.07 N | 95.44 W |
| Brasil → Brazil □[1] | 242 | 10.00 S | 55.00 W |
| Brasilândia ◈[8] | 287b | 23.28 S | 46.41 W |
| Brasiléia | 248 | 11.00 S | 68.44 W |
| Brasília | 255 | 15.47 S | 47.55 W |
| Brasília, Parque Nacional de ♠ | 255 | 15.36 S | 48.08 W |
| Brasília de Minas | 255 | 16.12 S | 44.26 W |
| Brasília Legal | 250 | 3.49 S | 55.36 W |
| Brasilien → Brazil □[1] | 242 | 10.00 S | 55.00 W |
| Braslau | 76 | 55.38 N | 27.02 E |
| Brasopolis | 256 | 22.28 S | 45.37 W |
| Brașov | 38 | 45.39 N | 25.37 E |
| Brașov □[6] | 38 | 45.45 N | 25.15 E |
| Brass | 150 | 4.19 N | 6.14 E |
| Brass Castle | 210 | 40.47 N | 74.58 W |
| Brasschaat | 50 | 51.17 N | 4.27 E |
| Brassert | 263 | 51.40 N | 7.05 E |
| Brassey, Banjaran ∧∧ | 112 | 4.54 N | 117.30 E |
| Brassey, Mount ∧ | 162 | 23.05 S | 134.38 E |
| Brass Islands II | 240m | 18.24 N | 64.58 W |
| Brassó → Brașov | 38 | 45.39 N | 25.37 E |
| Brasstown Bald ∧ | 192 | 34.52 N | 83.48 W |
| Brastad | 26 | 58.23 N | 11.29 E |
| Brasted | 260 | 51.16 N | 0.06 E |
| Brasted Chart | 260 | 51.16 N | 0.06 E |
| Břasy | 60 | 49.50 N | 13.35 E |
| Bratca | 38 | 46.56 N | 22.37 E |
| Bratcevo ◈[8] | 265b | 55.51 N | 37.24 E |
| Bratejevo ◈[8] | 265b | 55.38 N | 37.45 E |
| Bratenahl | 279a | 41.32 N | 81.37 W |
| Brateș, Lacul ⊜ | 38 | 45.30 N | 28.05 E |
| Bratislava | 30 | 48.09 N | 17.07 E |
| Bratol'ubovka | 86 | 51.13 N | 66.46 E |
| Bratsk | 88 | 56.05 N | 101.48 E |
| Bratskaja Kada | 88 | 55.02 N | 102.06 E |
| Brats'ke | 78 | 47.52 N | 31.34 E |
| Bratskoje vodochranilišče ⊜[1] | 88 | 56.10 N | 102.10 E |
| Bratslav | 78 | 48.50 N | 28.55 E |
| Brattfors | 40 | 59.40 N | 14.01 E |
| Brattleboro | 207 | 42.51 N | 72.33 W |
| Bratto | 64 | 45.55 N | 10.04 E |
| Brattvåg | 26 | 62.36 N | 6.27 E |
| Braubach | 56 | 50.16 N | 7.40 E |
| Braulio Carrillo, Parque Nacional ♠ | 236 | 10.10 N | 84.00 W |
| Braúnas | 255 | 19.04 S | 42.43 W |
| Braunau am Inn | 60 | 48.15 N | 13.02 E |
| Braunfels | 56 | 50.31 N | 8.23 E |
| Braunlage | 54 | 51.44 N | 10.37 E |
| Bräunlingen | 58 | 47.55 N | 8.26 E |
| Braunsbedra | 54 | 51.15 N | 11.49 E |
| Braunschweig, Dtsch. | 52 | 52.16 N | 10.31 E |
| Braunschweig, S. Afr. | 158 | 32.48 S | 27.22 E |
| Braunschweig □[5] | 52 | 52.00 N | 10.20 E |
| Braunston | 42 | 52.17 N | 1.12 W |
| Braunton | 42 | 51.07 N | 4.10 W |
| Braunwald | 58 | 46.56 N | 9.00 E |
| Brava I | 150a | 14.52 N | 24.43 W |
| Brava, Costa ⊥[2] | 34 | 41.45 N | 3.04 E |
| Brava, Laguna ⊜ | 252 | 28.22 S | 68.50 W |
| Brava, Punta › | 258 | 34.56 S | 56.10 W |
| Brave | 188 | 39.44 N | 80.16 W |
| Bravicea | 38 | 47.22 N | 28.26 E |
| Bråviken c | 40 | 58.38 N | 16.32 E |
| Bravo, Cerro ∧, Bol. | 248 | 17.40 S | 64.35 W |
| Bravo, Cerro ∧, Perú | 248 | 5.32 S | 79.15 W |
| Bravo del Norte (Rio Grande) ≃ | 178 | 25.55 N | 97.09 W |
| Brawley | 204 | 32.58 N | 115.31 W |
| Brawley Peaks ∧∧ | 204 | 38.15 N | 118.55 W |
| Brawley Wash V | 200 | 32.34 N | 111.26 W |
| Bray, Bel. | 50 | 50.26 N | 4.06 E |
| Bray, Ire. | 48 | 53.12 N | 6.06 W |
| Bray ≃ | 42 | 50.59 N | 3.53 W |
| Bray, Pays de ◈[1] | 50 | 49.46 N | 1.26 E |
| Braybrook | 274b | 37.47 S | 144.51 E |
| Bray-Dunes | 50 | 51.05 N | 2.31 E |
| Braye ≃ | 50 | 47.45 N | 0.42 E |
| Bray Head › | 48 | 51.53 N | 10.26 W |
| Brayiliv | 78 | 49.06 N | 28.09 E |
| Bray Island I | 176 | 69.20 N | 76.45 W |
| Braymer | 194 | 39.35 N | 93.47 W |
| Braysur-Seine | 50 | 48.25 N | 3.14 E |
| Bray-sur-Somme | 50 | 49.56 N | 2.43 E |
| Brayton | 44 | 53.46 N | 1.05 W |
| Brazeau ≃ | 182 | 52.55 N | 115.15 W |
| Brazeau, Mount ∧ | 182 | 52.33 N | 117.21 W |
| Brazeau Dam ◈[6] | 182 | 52.45 N | 115.30 W |
| Brazen Head › | 158 | 31.43 S | 29.25 E |
| Brazey-en-Plaine | 58 | 47.08 N | 5.13 E |
| Brazil | 194 | 39.31 N | 87.07 W |
| Brazil (Brasil) □[1] | 242 | 10.00 S | 55.00 W |
| Brazil Basin ✢[1] | 8 | 15.00 S | 25.00 W |
| Brazo Chico, Arroyo ≃ | 258 | 33.45 S | 58.32 W |
| Brazo Largo, Arroyo ≃ | 258 | 33.47 S | 58.36 W |
| Brazoria | 222 | 29.02 N | 95.34 W |
| Brazoria □[6] | 222 | 29.12 N | 95.25 W |
| Brazoria Reservoir ⊜[1] | 222 | 29.05 N | 95.01 W |
| Brazos □[6] | 222 | 30.40 N | 96.18 W |
| Brazos ≃ | 196 | 28.53 N | 95.23 W |
| Brazos, Clear Fork ≃ | 196 | 33.01 N | 98.40 W |
| Brazos, Double Mountain Fork ≃ | 196 | 33.15 N | 100.00 W |
| Brazos, Salt Fork ≃ | 196 | 33.15 N | 100.00 W |
| Brazo Sur [del Rio Coig] ≃ | 254 | 51.32 S | 70.04 W |
| Brazzaville, Congo | 152 | 4.16 S | 15.17 E |
| Brazzaville, Congo | 273b | 4.16 S | 15.17 E |
| Brazzaville (Maya Maya) Airport ⊠ | 273b | 4.15 S | 15.15 E |
| Brčko | 38 | 44.53 N | 18.48 E |
| Brda ≃ | 30 | 53.07 N | 18.08 E |
| Brdy ∧∧ | 60 | 49.40 N | 13.50 E |
| Bré → Bray | 48 | 53.12 N | 6.06 W |
| Brea | 228 | 33.55 N | 117.53 W |
| Brea, Punta › | 240m | 17.56 N | 66.55 W |
| Brea Canyon V | 280 | 33.55 N | 117.55 W |
| Brea Creek ≃ | 280 | 33.53 N | 117.59 W |
| Breadalbane | 166 | 23.49 S | 139.35 E |
| Brea Dam ◈[6] | 280 | 33.54 N | 117.56 W |
| Breaden Bluff ∧[2] | 162 | 26.56 S | 124.32 E |
| Breadysville | 285 | 40.13 N | 75.04 W |
| Breakenridge, Mount ∧ | 182 | 49.43 N | 121.56 W |
| Breakheart Reservation ♠ | 283 | 42.29 N | 71.02 W |
| Breaksea Sound ɥ | 172 | 45.35 S | 166.40 E |
| Breaks Interstate Park ♠ | 192 | 37.17 N | 82.18 W |
| Bream | 42 | 51.45 N | 2.34 W |
| Bream Bay c | 172 | 35.55 S | 174.30 E |
| Bream Head › | 172 | 35.51 S | 174.35 E |
| Breamish ≃ | 44 | 55.31 N | 1.56 W |
| Bream Tail › | 172 | 36.03 S | 174.35 E |
| Brea Pozo | 252 | 28.15 S | 63.57 W |
| Breaston | 44 | 52.54 N | 1.19 W |
| Bréau | 261 | 48.34 N | 2.53 E |
| Breaux Bridge | 194 | 30.16 N | 91.53 W |
| Breaza | 38 | 45.11 N | 25.40 E |
| Brebes | 115a | 6.53 S | 109.03 E |
| Brécey | 32 | 48.44 N | 1.10 W |
| Brechen | 56 | 50.20 N | 8.14 E |
| Brechfa | 42 | 51.57 N | 4.09 W |
| Brechin | 46 | 56.44 N | 2.40 W |
| Brecht | 56 | 51.21 N | 4.38 E |
| Brechten ◈[8] | 263 | 51.35 N | 7.28 E |
| Breckenridge, Co., U.S. | 200 | 39.28 N | 106.02 W |
| Breckenridge, Mi., U.S. | 190 | 43.24 N | 84.28 W |
| Breckenridge, Mn., U.S. | 198 | 46.15 N | 96.35 W |
| Breckenridge, Mo., U.S. | 194 | 39.45 N | 93.48 W |
| Breckenridge, Tx., U.S. | 196 | 32.45 N | 98.54 W |
| Breckerfeld | 56 | 51.16 N | 7.28 E |
| Breckland ◈[1] | 42 | 52.28 N | 0.37 E |
| Brecknock → Brecon | 42 | 51.57 N | 3.24 W |
| Brecknock, Península ›[1] | 254 | 54.35 S | 71.50 W |
| Brecksville | 214 | 41.19 N | 81.37 W |
| Břeclav | 30 | 48.46 N | 16.53 E |
| Brecon | 42 | 51.57 N | 3.24 W |
| Brecon Beacons ∧ | 42 | 51.53 N | 3.31 W |
| Brecon Beacons National Park ♠ | 42 | 51.52 N | 3.25 W |
| Bred | 41 | 55.22 N | 10.07 E |
| Breda, Ned. | 52 | 51.35 N | 4.46 E |
| Breda, Ia., U.S. | 198 | 42.10 N | 94.58 W |
| Bredaryd | 26 | 57.10 N | 13.44 E |
| Bredasdorp | 158 | 34.32 S | 20.02 E |
| Bredbo | 171b | 35.57 S | 149.10 E |
| Bredbo ≃ | 171b | 35.58 S | 149.08 E |
| Bredbury | 262 | 53.25 N | 2.06 W |
| Bredbyn | 26 | 63.27 N | 18.06 E |
| Breddin | 54 | 52.52 N | 12.13 E |
| Brede ≃ | 41 | 55.09 N | 8.42 E |
| Bredebro | 41 | 55.03 N | 8.49 E |
| Bredell | 273d | 26.05 S | 28.17 E |
| Bredenbeck | 52 | 52.15 N | 9.37 E |
| Bredenbruch | 263 | 51.21 N | 7.45 E |
| Bredenbury | 184 | 50.57 N | 102.03 W |
| Bredene | 50 | 51.14 N | 2.58 E |
| Bredeney ◈[8] | 263 | 51.24 N | 6.59 E |
| Bredenscheid-Stüter | 263 | 51.22 N | 7.11 E |
| Bredereiche | 54 | 53.08 N | 13.14 E |
| Bredgar | 260 | 51.18 N | 0.42 E |
| Bredhurst | 260 | 51.20 N | 0.35 E |
| Bredon Hill ∧[2] | 42 | 52.06 N | 2.03 W |
| Bredsjö | 40 | 59.50 N | 14.44 E |
| Bredsjön ⊜ | 40 | 60.13 N | 13.55 E |
| Bredstedt | 41 | 54.37 N | 8.59 E |
| Bredsten | 41 | 55.42 N | 9.24 E |
| Bredy | 86 | 52.26 N | 60.21 E |
| Bree | 56 | 51.08 N | 5.36 E |
| Breë ≃ | 158 | 34.24 S | 20.50 E |
| Breeches, Lac ⊜ | 206 | 45.54 N | 71.28 W |
| Breedoge ≃ | 48 | 53.55 N | 8.27 W |
| Breeds Pond ⊜ | 283 | 42.28 N | 70.59 W |
| Breedsville | 216 | 42.21 N | 86.08 W |
| Breese | 219 | 38.36 N | 89.31 W |
| Breesport | 210 | 42.10 N | 76.44 W |
| Breeza Plains | 164 | 14.50 S | 144.07 E |
| Breezewood | 279b | 40.34 N | 80.03 W |
| Breg ≃ | 58 | 47.57 N | 8.31 E |
| Bregalnica ≃ | 38 | 41.43 N | 22.09 E |
| Breganze | 64 | 45.42 N | 11.34 E |
| Bregenz | 58 | 47.30 N | 9.46 E |
| Bregenzer Wald ∧∧ | 58 | 47.20 N | 10.00 E |
| Bregninge, Dan. | 41 | 55.41 N | 11.19 E |
| Bregninge, Dan. | 41 | 55.01 N | 10.37 E |
| Bregovo | 38 | 44.09 N | 22.39 E |
| Breguzzo | 64 | 46.00 N | 10.42 E |
| Brégy | 261 | 49.05 N | 2.52 E |
| Bréhal | 32 | 48.54 N | 1.31 W |
| Brehna | 54 | 51.33 N | 12.12 E |
| Breiðafjörður c | 24a | 65.15 N | 23.15 W |
| Breidbach | 158 | 32.54 S | 27.27 E |
| Breidenbach, Dtsch. | 56 | 50.55 N | 8.28 E |
| Breidenbach, Fr. | 56 | 49.08 N | 7.25 E |
| Breil-sur-Roya | 62 | 43.56 N | 7.30 E |
| Breinizer | 214 | 40.24 N | 79.16 W |
| Breisach | 58 | 48.01 N | 7.40 E |
| Breisgau □[9] | 58 | 47.45 N | 7.45 E |
| Breitenbrunn, Dtsch. | 54 | 50.29 N | 12.46 E |
| Breitenbrunn, Dtsch. | 60 | 49.05 N | 11.37 E |
| Breitenfelde | 52 | 53.36 N | 10.38 E |
| Breitenfurt bei Wien | 61 | 48.08 N | 16.08 E |
| Breitengüssbach | 56 | 49.58 N | 10.53 E |
| Breitenlee ◈[8] | 264b | 48.15 N | 16.30 E |
| Breitenstein | 54 | 51.37 N | 10.56 E |
| Breitenworbis | 54 | 51.24 N | 10.25 E |
| Breithorn ∧ | 58 | 45.56 N | 7.45 E |
| Breitlingsee ⊜ | 54 | 52.23 N | 12.28 E |
| Breitscheid, Dtsch. | 56 | 50.41 N | 8.11 E |
| Breitscheid, Dtsch. | 56 | 51.22 N | 6.52 E |
| Breitsetten | 61 | 48.12 N | 16.42 E |
| Breitungen | 54 | 50.45 N | 10.20 E |
| Brejinho de Nazaré | 250 | 11.01 S | 48.34 W |
| Brejo | 250 | 3.41 S | 42.47 W |
| Brejões | 255 | 13.06 S | 39.48 W |
| Brejo Grande | 250 | 10.26 S | 36.28 W |
| Brejo Santo | 250 | 7.29 S | 39.00 W |
| Brejtovo | 76 | 58.18 N | 37.52 E |
| Brekken | 26 | 62.39 N | 11.53 E |
| Brekstad | 26 | 63.41 N | 9.41 E |
| Breloh | 52 | 53.01 N | 10.04 E |
| Bremangerlandet I | 26 | 61.51 N | 5.02 E |
| Brembio | 62 | 45.13 N | 9.34 E |
| Brembo ≃ | 62 | 45.35 N | 9.32 E |
| Brême → Bremen | 52 | 53.04 N | 8.49 E |
| Bremelau | 58 | 48.20 N | 9.32 E |
| Bremen, Dtsch. | 52 | 53.04 N | 8.49 E |
| Bremen, Ga., U.S. | 192 | 33.43 N | 85.08 W |
| Bremen, In., U.S. | 216 | 41.26 N | 86.08 W |
| Bremen, Oh., U.S. | 188 | 39.42 N | 82.25 W |
| Bremen □[3] | 52 | 53.05 N | 8.50 E |
| Bremen, Flughafen ⊠ | 52 | 53.03 N | 8.46 E |
| Bremer ≃, Austl. | 168b | 35.23 S | 139.02 E |
| Bremer ≃, Austl. | 171a | 27.39 S | 152.45 E |
| Bremer Bay | 162 | 34.24 S | 119.22 E |
| Bremer Bay c | 162 | 34.23 S | 119.25 E |
| Bremerhaven | 52 | 53.33 N | 8.34 E |
| Bremerton | 224 | 47.34 N | 122.37 W |
| Bremerton East | 224 | 47.35 N | 122.38 W |
| Bremervörde | 52 | 53.29 N | 9.08 E |
| Bremgarten | 58 | 47.21 N | 8.21 E |
| Bremke, Dtsch. | 52 | 52.07 N | 9.06 E |
| Bremke, Dtsch. | 56 | 51.15 N | 8.12 E |
| Bremke, Dtsch. | 263 | 51.23 N | 7.41 E |
| Bremner ≃ | 190 | 48.41 N | 85.31 W |
| Bremond | 222 | 31.09 N | 96.40 W |
| Brem River | 182 | 50.26 N | 124.39 W |
| Breña | 286d | 12.04 S | 77.04 W |
| Brendel Lake ⊜ | 281 | 42.38 N | 83.30 W |
| Brenderup | 41 | 55.29 N | 9.59 E |
| Brendlorenzen | 56 | 50.20 N | 10.13 E |
| Brendon Hills ∧∧[2] | 42 | 51.07 N | 3.25 W |
| Brenham | 222 | 30.10 N | 96.23 W |
| Brenig, Llyn ⊜[1] | 44 | 53.05 N | 3.32 W |
| Brenish | 46 | 58.08 N | 7.08 W |
| Brenish, Aird › | 46 | 58.08 N | 7.08 W |
| Bren Mar Park | 284c | 38.48 N | 77.09 W |
| Brenne ≃, Fr. | 50 | 47.38 N | 4.16 E |
| Brenne ≃, Fr. | 50 | 47.24 N | 0.51 E |
| Brennero (Brenner) | 64 | 47.00 N | 11.30 E |
| Brennero, Passo del → Brenner Pass )( | 64 | 47.00 N | 11.30 E |
| Brenner Pass )( | 64 | 47.00 N | 11.30 E |
| Breno, It. | 64 | 45.57 N | 10.18 E |
| Breno, Schw. | 58 | 46.02 N | 8.53 E |
| Brénod | 58 | 46.04 N | 5.36 E |
| Brent, Al., U.S. | 194 | 32.56 N | 87.09 W |
| Brent, Fl., U.S. | 194 | 30.28 N | 87.14 W |


**Symbols** in the index entries represent the broad categories identified in the key at the right. Symbols with superior numbers (∧∧[1]) identify subcategories (see complete key on page *I · 1).*

**Symbole** im Register stellen die rechts im Schlüssel erklärten Kategorien dar. Symbole mit hochgestellten Ziffern (∧∧[1]) bezeichnen Unterabteilungen einer Kategorie (vgl. vollständiger Schlüssel auf Seite *I · 1).*

**Los símbolos** incluídos en el texto del índice representan las grandes categorías identificadas con la clave a la derecha. Los símbolos con numeros en su parte superior (∧∧[1]) identifican las subcategorías (véase la clave completa en la página *I · 1).*

**Les symboles** de l'index représentent les catégories indiquées dans la légende à droite. Les symboles suivis d'un indice (∧∧[1]) représentent des sous-catégories (voir légende complète à la page *I · 1).*

**Os símbolos** incluídos no texto do índice representam as grandes categorias identificadas com a chave à direita. Os símbolos com números em sua parte superior (∧∧[1]) identificam as subcategorias (veja-se a chave completa à página *I · 1).*

| | English | Deutsch | Español | Français | Português |
|---|---|---|---|---|---|
| ∧ | Mountain | Berg | Montaña | Montagne | Montanha |
| ∧∧ | Mountains | Gebirge | Montañas | Montagnes | Montanhas |
| )( | Pass | Paß | Paso | Col | Passo |
| V | Valley, Canyon | Tal, Cañon | Valle, Cañón | Vallée, Canyon | Vale, Canhão |
| ≚ | Plain | Ebene | Llano | Plaine | Planície |
| › | Cape | Kap | Cabo | Cap | Cabo |
| I | Island | Insel | Isla | Île | Ilha |
| II | Islands | Inseln | Islas | Îles | Ilhas |
| ⊥ | Other Topographic Features | Andere Topographische Objekte | Otros Elementos Topográficos | Autres données topographiques | Outros acidentes topográficos |

ESPAÑOL: Nombre · Página · Lat.°′ · Long.°′ W = Oeste
FRANÇAIS: Nom · Page · Lat.°′ · Long.°′ W = Ouest
PORTUGUÊS: Nome · Página · Lat.°′ · Long.°′ W = Oeste


| Nombre / Nom / Nome | Página / Page | Lat.°′ | Long.°′ |
|---|---|---|---|
| Brent -♦-[8] | 42 | 51.34 N | 0.17 W |
| Brent ≃ | 260 | 51.28 N | 0.18 W |
| Brenta ≃ | 64 | 45.11 N | 12.18 E |
| Brenta, Gruppo di ⋏ | 64 | 46.11 N | 10.54 E |
| Brentford -♦-[8] | 260 | 51.29 N | 0.18 W |
| Brenthurst | 273d | 26.16 S | 28.23 E |
| Brentino | 64 | 45.40 N | 10.55 E |
| Brentonico | 64 | 45.49 N | 10.57 E |
| Brent Reservoir ◎[1] | 260 | 51.35 N | 0.15 W |
| Brentwood, Eng., U.K. | 42 | 51.38 N | 0.18 E |
| Brentwood, Eng., U.K. | 260 | 51.38 N | 0.18 E |
| Brentwood, Ca., U.S. | 226 | 37.55 N | 121.41 W |
| Brentwood, Md., U.S. | 208 | 38.56 N | 76.57 W |
| Brentwood, N.Y., U.S. | 210 | 40.46 N | 73.14 W |
| Brentwood, Oh., U.S. | 218 | 39.13 N | 84.31 W |
| Brentwood, Pa., U.S. | 214 | 40.22 N | 79.58 W |
| Brentwood, Tn., U.S. | 194 | 36.01 N | 86.46 W |
| Brentwood □[8] | 260 | 51.37 N | 0.20 E |
| Brentwood Bay | 224 | 48.35 N | 123.28 W |
| Brentwood Estates | 214 | 40.25 N | 80.45 W |
| Brentwood Heights -♦-[8] | 280 | 34.04 N | 118.30 W |
| Brentwood Lake | 214 | 41.19 N | 82.05 W |
| Brentwood Park | 273d | 26.08 S | 28.18 E |
| Brenz ≃ | 56 | 48.34 N | 10.24 E |
| Breo | 62 | 44.23 N | 7.49 E |
| Bréon, Ruisseu du ≃ | 261 | 48.40 N | 2.49 E |
| Brera, Palazzo di ʋ | 266b | 45.28 N | 9.11 E |
| Brereton Park | 158 | 26.55 S | 30.30 E |
| Brescello | 64 | 44.54 N | 10.31 E |
| Brescia | 64 | 45.33 N | 10.15 E |
| Brescia □[4] | 64 | 45.38 N | 10.18 E |
| Bresewitz | 54 | 54.24 N | 12.40 E |
| Brésil → Brazil □[1] | 242 | 10.00 S | 55.00 W |
| Breskens | 52 | 51.24 N | 3.34 E |
| Breslau, On., Can. | 212 | 43.28 N | 80.25 W |
| Breslau → Wrocław, Pol. | 30 | 51.06 N | 17.00 E |
| Breslau, Tx., U.S. | 222 | 29.31 N | 97.00 W |
| Bresle ≃ | 50 | 50.04 N | 1.22 E |
| Bresles | 50 | 49.25 N | 2.15 E |
| Bresnahan, Mount ∧ | 162 | 23.50 S | 117.55 E |
| Bressanone (Brixen) | 64 | 46.43 N | 11.39 E |
| Bressay I | 46a | 60.08 N | 1.05 W |
| Bressay Sound ꭒ | 46a | 60.07 N | 1.09 W |
| Bresse -♦-[1] | 58 | 46.30 N | 5.15 E |
| Bresso | 266b | 45.32 N | 9.11 E |
| Bressuire | 32 | 46.51 N | 0.30 W |
| Brest, Blg. | 38 | 43.38 N | 24.35 E |
| Brèst, Bela. | 76 | 52.06 N | 23.42 E |
| Brest, Fr. | 32 | 48.24 N | 4.29 W |
| Brest' □[8] | 76 | 52.30 N | 25.30 E |
| Brestanica | 36 | 45.59 N | 15.29 E |
| Bretagne (Brittany) □[9] | 32 | 48.00 N | 3.00 W |
| Bretenoux | 32 | 44.55 N | 1.50 E |
| Breteuil | 50 | 49.38 N | 2.18 E |
| Breteuil-sur-Iton | 50 | 48.50 N | 0.55 E |
| Bréthencourt | 261 | 48.30 N | 1.55 E |
| Bretherton | 262 | 53.41 N | 2.48 W |
| Brétigny ■ | 261 | 48.35 N | 2.20 E |
| Brétigny-sur-Orge | 50 | 48.37 N | 2.19 E |
| Bretnig | 54 | 51.08 N | 14.04 E |
| Breton | 182 | 53.07 N | 114.28 W |
| Bretón, Canal de ꭒ | 240p | 21.10 N | 79.30 W |
| Breton, Pertuis ꭒ | 32 | 46.25 N | 1.20 W |
| Breton Bay ⊂ | 208 | 38.16 N | 76.39 W |
| Breton Islands II | 194 | 29.28 N | 89.11 W |
| Breton Sound ꭒ | 194 | 29.30 N | 89.30 W |
| Breton Woods | 208 | 40.02 N | 74.06 W |
| Brett ≃ | 42 | 51.58 N | 0.58 E |
| Brett, Cape › | 172 | 35.10 S | 174.20 E |
| Bretten | 56 | 49.02 N | 8.42 E |
| Breu, Rio do ≃ | 246 | 3.29 S | 66.20 W |
| Breuberg | 56 | 49.49 N | 9.03 E |
| Breueh, Pulau I | 110 | 5.41 N | 95.05 E |
| Breuil-Bois-Robert | 261 | 48.57 N | 1.43 E |
| Breuil-Cervinia | 58 | 45.56 N | 7.38 E |
| Breuillet | 261 | 48.34 N | 2.10 E |
| Breuilpont | 50 | 48.58 N | 1.26 E |
| Breukelen | 52 | 52.10 N | 5.00 E |
| Breux | 261 | 48.34 N | 2.11 E |
| Brevard | 192 | 35.14 N | 82.44 W |
| Brevard □[6] | 220 | 28.18 N | 80.42 W |
| Brévenne ≃ | 62 | 45.51 N | 4.40 E |
| Brevens bruk | 40 | 59.01 N | 15.35 E |
| Breves | 250 | 1.40 S | 50.29 W |
| Brevig Mission | 180 | 65.20 N | 166.29 W |
| Brevik, Nor. | 26 | 59.04 N | 9.42 E |
| Brevik, Sve. | 40 | 59.21 N | 18.12 E |
| Brevoort Island I | 176 | 63.30 N | 64.20 W |
| Brewarrina | 166 | 29.57 S | 146.52 E |
| Brewer | 188 | 44.47 N | 68.45 W |
| Brewer Island I | 282 | 37.33 N | 122.16 W |
| Brewersville | 218 | 39.05 N | 85.37 W |
| Brewerton | 210 | 43.14 N | 76.08 W |
| Brewerville | 150 | 6.26 N | 10.47 W |
| Brewongle | 170 | 33.29 S | 149.43 E |
| Brewood | 42 | 52.41 N | 2.10 W |
| Brewster, Ks., U.S. | 198 | 39.22 N | 101.22 W |
| Brewster, Ma., U.S. | 207 | 41.45 N | 70.05 W |
| Brewster, Mn., U.S. | 198 | 43.41 N | 95.28 W |
| Brewster, Ne., U.S. | 198 | 41.56 N | 99.51 W |
| Brewster, N.Y., U.S. | 210 | 41.23 N | 73.37 W |
| Brewster, Oh., U.S. | 214 | 40.42 N | 81.35 W |
| Brewster, Wa., U.S. | 202 | 48.05 N | 119.46 W |
| Brewster, Kap › | 16 | 70.19 N | 22.05 W |
| Brewster, Lake ◎ | 166 | 33.28 S | 146.00 E |
| Brewster, Mount ∧ | 172 | 44.04 S | 169.27 E |
| Brewton | 194 | 31.06 N | 87.04 W |
| Breyten | 158 | 26.16 S | 30.00 E |
| Břežany | 61 | 48.52 N | 16.20 E |
| Brežice | 36 | 45.54 N | 15.36 E |
| Brézina | 148 | 33.04 N | 1.14 E |
| Brézins | 62 | 45.21 N | 5.19 E |
| Březnice | 60 | 49.33 N | 13.57 E |
| Breznik | 38 | 42.44 N | 22.54 E |
| Březno, Česká Rep. | 54 | 50.24 N | 13.26 E |
| Brezno, Slvk. | 30 | 48.50 N | 19.39 E |
| Brézolles | 50 | 48.41 N | 1.04 E |
| Březová | 54 | 50.06 N | 12.39 E |
| Březové Hory | 60 | 49.41 N | 13.58 E |
| Bria | 152 | 6.32 N | 21.59 E |
| Brian Boru Peak ∧ | 182 | 55.05 N | 127.35 W |
| Briançon | 62 | 44.54 N | 6.39 E |
| Brian Head ∧ | 200 | 37.41 N | 112.50 W |
| Brianza □[9] | 62 | 45.40 N | 9.10 E |
| Briar | 222 | 33.00 N | 97.34 W |
| Briarcliff Manor | 210 | 41.08 N | 73.49 W |
| Briar Creek | 210 | 40.10 N | 76.46 W |
| Briar Creek ≃ | 222 | 32.06 N | 96.22 W |
| Briare | 50 | 47.38 N | 2.44 E |
| Briare, Canal de ≊ | 50 | 48.02 N | 2.43 E |
| Briarres-sur-Essonne | 50 | 48.14 N | 2.25 E |
| Briarwood Beach | 214 | 41.06 N | 81.54 W |
| Briarwood Center -♦-[9] | 281 | 42.14 N | 83.45 W |
| Briatico | 68 | 38.43 N | 16.02 E |
| Bribano | 64 | 46.06 N | 12.05 E |
| Bribie Island I | 171a | 27.00 S | 153.07 E |
| Bricelyn | 190 | 43.33 N | 93.48 W |
| Briceni | 38 | 48.22 N | 27.04 E |
| Brice Run ≃ | 284b | 39.19 N | 76.50 W |
| Brices Cross Roads National Battlefield Site ⊥ | 194 | 34.31 N | 88.41 W |
| Briceville | 192 | 36.10 N | 84.11 W |
| Bricherasio | 62 | 44.49 N | 7.18 E |
| Bricht | 263 | 51.41 N | 6.51 E |
| Brickebacken | 40 | 59.15 N | 15.15 E |
| Brick Lake ◎ | 220 | 28.10 N | 81.12 W |
| Brick Township | 208 | 40.04 N | 74.08 W |
| Briçonnet, Lac ◎ | 186 | 51.27 N | 60.11 W |
| Bricquebec | 32 | 49.28 N | 1.38 W |
| Bridal Veil | 224 | 45.33 N | 122.10 W |
| Bridalveil Fall ∟ | 226 | 37.43 N | 119.39 W |
| Bride | 44 | 54.22 N | 4.22 W |
| Bride ≃ | 48 | 52.04 N | 7.52 W |
| Bridesburg -♦-[8] | 285 | 40.00 N | 75.04 W |
| Brides-les-Bains | 62 | 45.27 N | 6.34 E |
| Bridge | 42 | 51.14 N | 1.07 E |
| Bridge ≃ | 182 | 50.45 N | 121.55 W |
| Bridge City | 194 | 30.01 N | 93.50 W |
| Bridge Creek ≃ | 224 | 48.26 N | 120.52 W |
| Bridgehampton | 207 | 40.56 N | 72.18 W |
| Bridge Lake | 182 | 51.29 N | 120.43 W |
| Bridgend, Scot., U.K. | 46 | 55.48 N | 6.16 W |
| Bridgend, Scot., U.K. | 46 | 56.48 N | 2.45 W |
| Bridgend, Wales, U.K. | 42 | 51.31 N | 3.35 W |
| Bridgenorth | 212 | 44.23 N | 78.23 W |
| Bridge of Allan | 46 | 56.09 N | 3.57 W |
| Bridge of Gaur | 46 | 56.41 N | 4.27 W |
| Bridge of Orchy | 46 | 56.30 N | 4.46 W |
| Bridge of Weir | 46 | 55.52 N | 4.35 W |
| Bridgeport, On., Can. | 212 | 43.29 N | 80.29 W |
| Bridgeport, Al., U.S. | 194 | 34.56 N | 85.42 W |
| Bridgeport, Ca., U.S. | 226 | 38.10 N | 119.13 W |
| Bridgeport, Ct., U.S. | 207 | 41.10 N | 73.12 W |
| Bridgeport, Il., U.S. | 194 | 38.42 N | 87.45 W |
| Bridgeport, Mi., U.S. | 190 | 43.21 N | 83.52 W |
| Bridgeport, Ne., U.S. | 198 | 41.39 N | 103.05 W |
| Bridgeport, N.J., U.S. | 285 | 39.48 N | 75.20 W |
| Bridgeport, N.Y., U.S. | 210 | 43.09 N | 75.58 W |
| Bridgeport, Oh., U.S. | 214 | 40.04 N | 80.44 W |
| Bridgeport, Pa., U.S. | 285 | 40.06 N | 75.21 W |
| Bridgeport, Tx., U.S. | 222 | 33.12 N | 97.45 W |
| Bridgeport, Wa., U.S. | 202 | 48.00 N | 119.40 W |
| Bridgeport, W.V., U.S. | 188 | 39.17 N | 80.15 W |
| Bridgeport -♦-[8] | 278 | 41.51 N | 87.39 W |
| Bridgeport, Lake ◎[1] | 222 | 33.13 N | 97.48 W |
| Bridgeport, University of ʋ[2] | 276 | 41.10 N | 73.12 W |
| Bridgeport Airport ✈ | 285 | 39.47 N | 75.20 W |
| Bridgeport Harbor ⊂ | 276 | 41.10 N | 73.11 W |
| Bridgeport Municipal Airport ✈ | 276 | 41.10 N | 73.08 W |
| Bridgeport Reservoir ◎[1] | 226 | 38.22 N | 119.14 W |
| Bridger | 202 | 45.17 N | 108.54 W |
| Bridge River Indian Reserve -♦-[4] | 182 | 50.45 N | 122.00 W |
| Bridger Peak ∧ | 200 | 41.12 N | 107.02 W |
| Bridges Point › | 174o | 1.58 N | 157.28 W |
| Bridgeton, Mo., U.S. | 219 | 38.44 N | 90.24 W |
| Bridgeton, N.J., U.S. | 208 | 39.25 N | 75.14 W |
| Bridgetown, Austl. | 162 | 33.57 S | 116.08 E |
| Bridgetown, Barb. | 241g | 13.06 N | 59.37 W |
| Bridgetown, N.S., Can. | 186 | 44.51 N | 65.18 W |
| Bridgetown, Oh., U.S. | 218 | 39.09 N | 84.38 W |
| Bridge Trafford | 262 | 53.14 N | 2.49 W |
| Bridgeview | 278 | 41.45 N | 87.48 W |
| Bridgeville, De., U.S. | 208 | 38.44 N | 75.36 W |
| Bridgeville, Pa., U.S. | 214 | 40.21 N | 80.06 W |
| Bridgewater, Austl. | 166 | 42.44 S | 147.14 E |
| Bridgewater, Austl. | 168b | 35.02 S | 138.47 E |
| Bridgewater, N.S., Can. | 186 | 44.23 N | 64.31 W |
| Bridgewater, Ct., U.S. | 210 | 41.32 N | 73.22 W |
| Bridgewater, Me., U.S. | 186 | 46.25 N | 67.50 W |
| Bridgewater, Ma., U.S. | 207 | 41.59 N | 70.58 W |
| Bridgewater, N.Y., U.S. | 210 | 42.58 N | 75.15 W |
| Bridgewater, Pa., U.S. | 285 | 40.05 N | 74.55 W |
| Bridgewater, S.D., U.S. | 198 | 43.33 N | 97.30 W |
| Bridgewater, Va., U.S. | 188 | 38.22 N | 78.58 W |
| Bridgewater Canal ≊ | 262 | 53.20 N | 2.45 W |
| Bridgewater State College ʋ[2] | 283 | 41.59 N | 70.58 W |
| Bridgman | 216 | 41.57 N | 86.33 W |
| Bridgnorth | 42 | 52.33 N | 2.25 W |
| Bridgton | 188 | 44.03 N | 70.42 W |
| Bridgwater | 42 | 51.08 N | 3.00 W |
| Bridgwater Bay ⊂ | 42 | 51.16 N | 3.12 W |
| Bridlington | 44 | 54.05 N | 0.12 W |
| Bridlington Bay ⊂ | 44 | 54.04 N | 0.08 W |
| Bridport | 42 | 50.44 N | 2.46 W |
| Brie -♦-[1] | 50 | 48.40 N | 3.20 E |
| Briec | 32 | 48.06 N | 4.00 W |
| Brie-Comte-Robert | 50 | 48.41 N | 2.37 E |
| Brie Française -♦-[1] | 261 | 48.48 N | 2.46 E |
| Brieg → Brzeg | 30 | 50.52 N | 17.27 E |
| Brielle, Ned. | 52 | 51.54 N | 4.10 E |
| Brielle, N.J., U.S. | 208 | 40.06 N | 74.03 W |
| Brienne-le-Château | 58 | 48.24 N | 4.32 E |
| Brienne-sur-Aisne | 50 | 49.26 N | 4.03 E |
| Brienno | 58 | 45.55 N | 9.07 E |
| Brienon-sur-Armançon | 50 | 48.00 N | 3.37 E |
| Brien Run ≃ | 284b | 39.20 N | 76.28 W |
| Brienz | 58 | 46.46 N | 8.03 E |
| Brienza | 68 | 40.29 N | 15.37 E |
| Brienzer Rothorn ∧ | 58 | 46.48 N | 8.04 E |
| Brienzersee ◎ | 58 | 46.43 N | 7.57 E |
| Brier Creek ≃ | 192 | 32.47 N | 81.26 W |
| Brierfield | 44 | 53.50 N | 2.14 W |
| Brier Hill | 212 | 44.32 N | 75.40 W |
| Brier Island I | 186 | 44.16 N | 66.22 W |
| Brierley Hill | 42 | 52.29 N | 2.07 W |
| Brier Mountain ∧ | 210 | 41.37 N | 77.02 W |
| Briese | 264a | 52.42 N | 13.18 E |
| Briese ≃ | 264a | 52.41 N | 13.15 E |
| Brieselang | 54 | 52.35 N | 13.00 E |
| Briesen | 54 | 52.20 N | 14.16 E |
| Brieske | 54 | 51.29 N | 13.57 E |
| Brieskow-Finkenheerd | 54 | 52.16 N | 14.35 E |
| Briey | 56 | 49.15 N | 5.56 E |
| Brig | 58 | 46.19 N | 8.00 E |
| Brigach ≃ | 58 | 47.58 N | 8.30 E |
| Brigantine | 208 | 39.24 N | 74.21 W |
| Brig Bay | 186 | 51.04 N | 56.55 W |
| Brigden | 214 | 42.49 N | 82.17 W |
| Brigg | 44 | 53.34 N | 0.30 W |
| Briggs | 196 | 30.53 N | 97.56 W |
| Brigham City | 200 | 41.30 N | 112.00 W |
| Brighouse | 44 | 53.42 N | 1.47 W |
| Brighstone | 42 | 50.38 N | 1.24 W |
| Bright | 166 | 36.44 S | 146.58 E |
| Brightlingsea | 42 | 51.49 N | 1.02 E |
| Brightmoor -♦-[8] | 281 | 42.24 N | 83.14 W |
| Brighton, Austl. | 168b | 35.01 S | 138.31 E |
| Brighton, Austl. | 169 | 37.55 S | 145.00 E |
| Brighton, On., Can. | 212 | 44.02 N | 77.44 W |
| Brighton, N.Z. | 172 | 45.57 S | 170.20 E |
| Brighton, Eng., U.K. | 42 | 50.50 N | 0.08 W |
| Brighton, Co., U.S. | 200 | 39.59 N | 104.49 W |
| Brighton, Fl., U.S. | 220 | 27.14 N | 81.06 W |
| Brighton, Il., U.S. | 219 | 39.02 N | 90.08 W |
| Brighton, Ia., U.S. | 190 | 41.10 N | 91.49 W |
| Brighton, Md., U.S. | 284b | 39.21 N | 76.43 W |
| Brighton, Mi., U.S. | 216 | 42.31 N | 83.46 W |
| Brighton, N.Y., U.S. | 210 | 43.08 N | 77.33 W |
| Brighton -♦-[8] | 283 | 42.21 N | 71.08 W |
| Brighton Airport ✈ | 281 | 42.34 N | 83.47 W |
| Brighton Downs | 166 | 23.22 S | 141.34 E |
| Brighton Indian Reservation -♦-[4] | 220 | 27.04 N | 81.05 W |
| Brighton-Le-Sands | 274a | 33.58 S | 151.09 E |
| Brighton Park -♦-[8] | 278 | 41.49 N | 87.42 W |
| Brighton State Recreation Area ♦ | 216 | 42.30 N | 83.48 W |
| Brightsand Lake ◎ | 184 | 53.36 N | 108.52 W |
| Brightwater | 172 | 41.23 S | 173.07 E |
| Brightwaters | 276 | 40.43 N | 73.16 W |
| Brightwood | 224 | 45.23 N | 122.01 W |
| Brightwood -♦-[8] | 284c | 38.58 N | 77.02 W |
| Brigittenau -♦-[8] | 264b | 48.14 N | 16.22 E |
| Brignoles | 62 | 43.24 N | 6.04 E |
| Brignoud | 62 | 45.15 N | 5.54 E |
| Brig o'Turk | 46 | 56.13 N | 4.22 W |
| Brigstock | 42 | 52.27 N | 0.36 W |
| Brigus | 186 | 47.32 N | 53.13 W |
| Brihuega | 34 | 40.45 N | 2.52 W |
| Briis-sous-Forges | 261 | 48.38 N | 2.07 E |
| Brijuni (Brioni) | 64 | 44.55 N | 13.46 E |
| Brijuni I | 64 | 44.55 N | 13.46 E |
| Brikama | 150 | 13.15 N | 16.39 W |
| Brilhante ≃ | 255 | 21.58 S | 54.18 W |
| Brill | 42 | 51.49 N | 1.03 W |
| Brilliant, B.C., Can. | 182 | 49.19 N | 117.38 W |
| Brilliant, Al., U.S. | 194 | 34.01 N | 87.45 W |
| Brilliant, Oh., U.S. | 214 | 40.15 N | 80.37 W |
| Brillion | 190 | 44.10 N | 88.03 W |
| Brilon | 56 | 51.24 N | 8.34 E |
| Brilyn Park | 284c | 38.54 N | 77.10 W |
| Brimfield, Eng., U.K. | 42 | 52.18 N | 2.42 W |
| Brimfield, In., U.S. | 216 | 41.27 N | 85.24 W |
| Brimfield, Ma., U.S. | 207 | 42.07 N | 72.12 W |
| Brimfield, Oh., U.S. | 214 | 41.06 N | 81.21 W |
| Brimington | 44 | 53.16 N | 1.23 W |
| Brindabella | 171b | 35.23 S | 148.45 E |
| Brindisi | 68 | 40.38 N | 17.56 E |
| Brindisi □[4] | 68 | 40.35 N | 17.40 E |
| Brindisi Montagna | 68 | 40.37 N | 15.57 E |
| Brindle | 262 | 53.43 N | 2.36 W |
| Bringelly | 170 | 33.56 S | 150.44 E |
| Bringelly Creek ≃ | 274a | 33.58 S | 150.38 E |
| Brinje | 36 | 45.00 N | 15.08 E |
| Brinkerton | 279b | 40.13 N | 79.32 W |
| Brinkhaven | 214 | 40.28 N | 82.12 W |
| Brinkleigh | 284b | 39.18 N | 76.50 W |
| Brinkley, Austl. | 168b | 35.14 S | 139.13 E |
| Brinkley, Ar., U.S. | 194 | 34.53 N | 91.11 W |
| Brinkum | 52 | 53.00 N | 8.47 E |
| Brinkworth | 166 | 33.42 S | 138.24 E |
| Brinnon | 224 | 47.40 N | 122.53 W |
| Brinon-sur-Beuvron | 50 | 47.17 N | 3.30 E |
| Brins, Ābār al- ⊤[4] | 142 | 30.29 N | 30.05 E |
| Brinscall | 262 | 53.41 N | 2.34 W |
| Brinyan | 46 | 59.07 N | 2.59 W |
| Brion, Île I | 186 | 47.48 N | 61.28 W |
| Brione | 58 | 46.18 N | 8.47 E |
| Briones Hills ⋏[2] | 282 | 37.56 N | 122.08 W |
| Briones Regional Park ♦ | 282 | 37.56 N | 122.08 W |
| Briones Reservoir ◎[1] | 282 | 37.55 N | 122.12 W |
| Brionne | 50 | 49.12 N | 0.43 E |
| Brion-sur-Ource | 58 | 47.55 N | 4.39 E |
| Brioude | 32 | 45.18 N | 3.23 E |
| Briouze | 32 | 48.42 N | 0.22 W |
| Brisbane, Austl. | 171a | 27.28 S | 153.02 E |
| Brisbane, Ca., U.S. | 226 | 37.41 N | 122.24 W |
| Brisbane ≃ | 171a | 27.24 S | 153.09 E |
| Brisbane, Mount ∧ | 171a | 27.05 S | 152.32 E |
| Brisbane International Airport ✈ | 171a | 27.27 S | 153.11 E |
| Brisbane Ranges National Park ♦ | 169 | 37.52 S | 144.14 E |
| Brisbane Water ⊂ | 170 | 33.28 S | 151.20 E |
| Brisbane Water National Park ♦ | 170 | 33.30 S | 151.15 E |
| Brisben | 210 | 42.22 N | 75.41 W |
| Brisbin | 214 | 40.50 N | 78.21 W |
| Briseñas | 234 | 20.16 N | 102.33 W |
| Brisighella | 66 | 44.13 N | 11.46 E |
| Brissac | 62 | 43.52 N | 3.42 E |
| Brissago | 58 | 46.07 N | 8.43 E |
| Bristol, Eng., U.K. | 42 | 51.27 N | 2.35 W |
| Bristol, Ct., U.S. | 207 | 41.41 N | 72.57 W |
| Bristol, Fl., U.S. | 192 | 30.25 N | 84.58 W |
| Bristol, Il., U.S. | 216 | 41.39 N | 88.27 W |
| Bristol, In., U.S. | 216 | 41.43 N | 85.49 W |
| Bristol, N.H., U.S. | 188 | 43.35 N | 71.44 W |
| Bristol, Pa., U.S. | 208 | 40.06 N | 74.51 W |
| Bristol, R.I., U.S. | 207 | 41.40 N | 71.16 W |
| Bristol, S.D., U.S. | 198 | 45.20 N | 97.44 W |
| Bristol, Tn., U.S. | 192 | 36.35 N | 82.11 W |
| Bristol, Vt., U.S. | 188 | 44.08 N | 73.04 W |
| Bristol, Va., U.S. | 192 | 36.35 N | 82.11 W |
| Bristol, Wi., U.S. | 216 | 42.33 N | 88.02 W |
| Bristol □[6], Ma., U.S. | 207 | 41.54 N | 71.06 W |
| Bristol □[6], R.I., U.S. | 207 | 41.42 N | 71.18 W |
| Bristol (Lulsgate) Airport ✈ | 42 | 51.23 N | 2.43 W |
| Bristol Bay ⊂ | 180 | 58.00 N | 159.00 W |
| Bristol-Blake Reservation ♦ | 283 | 42.06 N | 71.19 W |
| Bristol Center | 210 | 42.49 N | 77.23 W |
| Bristol Channel ꭒ | 42 | 51.20 N | 4.00 W |
| Bristol Lake ◎ | 204 | 34.28 N | 115.41 W |
| Bristolville | 214 | 41.23 N | 80.52 W |
| Bristow | 196 | 35.49 N | 96.23 W |
| Britânia | 255 | 15.14 S | 51.09 W |
| Británicas, Islas → British Isles II | 4 | 54.00 N | 4.00 W |
| Britannia, On., Can. | 275b | 43.37 N | 79.41 W |
| Britannia, Eng., U.K. | 262 | 53.41 N | 2.11 W |
| Britannia Beach | 182 | 49.38 N | 123.12 W |
| Britische Jungfern-Inseln → British Virgin Islands □[2] | 240m | 18.30 N | 64.30 W |
| British Columbia □[4], Can. | 176 | 54.00 N | 125.00 W |
| British Columbia □[4], Can. | 182 | 54.00 N | 125.00 W |
| British Honduras → Belize □[1] | 232 | 17.15 N | 88.45 W |
| British Indian Ocean Territory □[2] | 12 | 7.00 S | 72.00 E |
| British Isles II | 4 | 54.00 N | 4.00 W |
| British Mountains ⋏ | 180 | 69.00 N | 140.20 W |
| British Museum ʋ | 260 | 51.31 N | 0.08 W |
| British Solomon Islands → Solomon Islands □[1] | 175e | 8.00 S | 159.00 E |
| British Virgin Islands □[2], N.A. | 230 | 18.30 N | 64.30 W |
| British Virgin Islands □[2], N.A. | 240m | 18.30 N | 64.30 W |
| Britland Edge Hill ∧[2] | 262 | 53.31 N | 1.50 W |
| Briton Ferry | 42 | 51.38 N | 3.49 W |
| Brits | 158 | 25.42 S | 27.45 E |
| Britstown | 158 | 30.37 S | 23.30 E |
| Britt | 190 | 43.05 N | 93.48 W |
| Brittany → Bretagne □[9] | 32 | 48.00 N | 3.00 W |
| Brittas | 48 | 53.14 N | 6.27 W |
| Britten | 158 | 27.42 S | 25.17 E |
| Brittingham | 196 | 25.45 N | 103.24 W |
| Britton, Mi., U.S. | 216 | 41.59 N | 83.49 W |
| Britton, S.D., U.S. | 198 | 45.47 N | 97.45 W |
| Britton, Tx., U.S. | 222 | 32.33 N | 97.04 W |
| Britton, Mount ∧[2] | 162 | 26.31 S | 134.43 E |
| Britz | 54 | 52.53 N | 13.49 E |
| Britz -♦-[8] | 264a | 52.27 N | 13.26 E |
| Brive-la-Gaillarde | 32 | 45.10 N | 1.32 E |
| Brives-Charensac | 62 | 45.03 N | 3.56 E |
| Briviesca | 34 | 42.33 N | 3.19 W |
| Brivio | 62 | 45.44 N | 9.27 E |
| Brixen im Thale | 64 | 47.27 N | 12.15 E |
| Brixham | 42 | 50.24 N | 3.30 W |
| Brixlegg | 64 | 47.25 N | 11.53 E |
| Brixton | 166 | 23.32 S | 144.57 E |
| Brixworth | 42 | 52.20 N | 0.54 W |
| Brlik | 85 | 43.40 N | 73.49 E |
| Brloh | 61 | 48.56 N | 14.13 E |
| Brno | 30 | 49.12 N | 16.37 E |
| Bro | 40 | 59.31 N | 17.38 E |
| Broa, Ensenada de la ⊂ | 240p | 22.35 N | 82.00 W |
| Broad ≃, U.S. | 192 | 34.00 N | 81.04 W |
| Broad ≃, Fl., U.S. | 220 | 25.28 N | 81.09 W |
| Broad ≃, Ga., U.S. | 192 | 33.59 N | 82.39 W |
| Broadalbin | 210 | 43.03 N | 74.11 W |
| Broad Arrow | 162 | 30.20 S | 121.27 E |
| Broad Axe | 285 | 40.10 N | 75.15 W |
| Broadback ≃ | 176 | 51.21 N | 78.52 W |
| Broad Bay ⊂ | 46 | 58.15 N | 6.15 W |
| Broadbottom | 262 | 53.26 N | 2.01 W |
| Broad Brook | 207 | 41.54 N | 72.32 W |
| Broad Chalke | 42 | 51.02 N | 1.57 W |
| Broadclyst | 42 | 50.46 N | 3.26 W |
| Broad Creek ⊂ | 208 | 38.45 N | 76.15 W |
| Broad Creek ≃ | 208 | 39.42 N | 76.14 W |
| Broadford, Austl. | 169 | 37.13 S | 145.03 E |
| Broadford, Scot., U.K. | 46 | 57.14 N | 5.54 W |
| Broad Haven ⊂ | 48 | 54.18 N | 9.55 W |
| Broadheath | 262 | 53.24 N | 2.21 W |
| Broadhurst Range ⋏ | 162 | 22.23 S | 122.09 E |
| Broadkill ≃ | 208 | 38.47 N | 75.10 W |
| Broad Law ∧ | 46 | 55.30 N | 3.22 W |
| Broadley Common | 260 | 51.45 N | 0.04 E |
| Broadmeadows | 169 | 37.40 S | 144.54 E |
| Broadmoor | 226 | 37.41 N | 122.29 W |
| Broad Neck ›[1] | 208 | 39.03 N | 76.27 W |
| Broad Oak | 42 | 50.57 N | 0.36 E |
| Broad Pass )( | 180 | 63.18 N | 149.09 W |
| Broad Run ≃, Pa., U.S. | 285 | 39.56 N | 75.41 W |
| Broad Run ≃, Pa., U.S. | 285 | 39.59 N | 75.40 W |
| Broad Run ≃, Va., U.S. | 208 | 38.41 N | 77.29 W |
| Broad Sound ꭒ, Austl. | 166 | 22.10 S | 149.45 E |
| Broad Sound ꭒ, Ma., U.S. | 283 | 42.25 N | 70.58 W |
| Broad Sound Channel ꭒ | 166 | 22.05 S | 150.20 E |
| Broadstairs | 42 | 51.22 N | 1.27 E |
| Broad Street | 260 | 51.17 N | 0.38 E |
| Broad Top | 214 | 40.12 N | 78.08 W |
| Broadus | 198 | 45.26 N | 105.24 W |
| Broadview, Sk., Can. | 184 | 50.20 N | 102.30 W |
| Broadview, Il., U.S. | 216 | 41.51 N | 87.51 W |
| Broadview, In., U.S. | 218 | 39.10 N | 87.33 W |
| Broadview Heights | 214 | 41.18 N | 81.41 W |
| Broadwater | 198 | 41.35 N | 102.51 W |
| Broadway, Eng., U.K. | 42 | 52.02 N | 1.51 W |
| Broadway, Oh., U.S. | 214 | 40.20 N | 83.24 W |
| Broadway, Va., U.S. | 188 | 38.38 N | 78.46 W |
| Broadwell | 219 | 40.04 N | 89.27 W |
| Broadwindsor | 42 | 50.49 N | 2.48 W |
| Broadwood | 172 | 35.16 S | 173.23 E |
| Broager | 41 | 54.53 N | 9.41 E |
| Brobo | 150 | 7.43 N | 4.42 W |
| Broby | 26 | 56.15 N | 14.05 E |
| Brobyværk | 41 | 55.14 N | 10.15 E |
| Broc | 58 | 46.36 N | 7.06 E |
| Brocēni | 76 | 56.42 N | 22.35 E |
| Brochel | 46 | 57.26 N | 6.01 W |
| Brochet | 176 | 57.53 N | 101.40 W |
| Brochet, Lac au ◎ | 186 | 49.40 N | 69.37 W |
| Brochterbeck | 52 | 52.13 N | 7.44 E |
| Brock | 184 | 51.27 N | 108.42 W |
| Brock ≃ | 44 | 53.52 N | 2.47 W |
| Brock Creek ≃ | 285 | 40.15 N | 74.50 W |
| Brocken ∧ | 54 | 51.48 N | 10.36 E |
| Brockenhurst | 42 | 50.49 N | 1.34 W |
| Brockenscheidt | 263 | 51.38 N | 7.25 E |
| Brockhagen | 52 | 51.59 N | 8.20 E |
| Brockham | 260 | 51.14 N | 0.17 W |
| Brockman ≃ | 168a | 31.41 S | 116.07 E |
| Brockman, Mount ∧ | 162 | 22.28 S | 117.18 E |
| Brock Monument ⊥ | 284a | 43.09 N | 79.04 W |
| Brockport, N.Y., U.S. | 210 | 43.12 N | 77.56 W |
| Brockport, Pa., U.S. | 214 | 41.16 N | 78.44 W |
| Brocks Beach | 212 | 44.27 N | 80.06 W |
| Brocks Creek | 164 | 13.28 S | 131.25 E |
| Brockton, Ma., U.S. | 207 | 42.05 N | 71.01 W |
| Brockton, Mt., U.S. | 198 | 48.09 N | 104.54 W |
| Brockton, Pa., U.S. | 208 | 40.45 N | 76.04 W |
| Brockton Reservoir ◎[1] | 283 | 42.07 N | 71.03 W |
| Brock University ʋ[2] | 284a | 43.07 N | 79.15 W |
| Brockville | 212 | 44.35 N | 75.41 W |
| Brockway | 214 | 41.15 N | 78.47 W |
| Brockworth | 42 | 51.51 N | 2.09 W |
| Brocoió, Ilha de I | 287a | 22.45 S | 43.07 W |
| Brocton | 214 | 42.23 N | 79.26 W |
| Brod, Česká Rep. | 60 | 49.51 N | 12.45 E |
| Brod, Mak. | 38 | 41.31 N | 21.12 E |
| Broddbo | 40 | 59.59 N | 16.28 E |
| Brodenbach | 56 | 50.14 N | 7.26 E |
| Brodeur Peninsula ›[1] | 176 | 73.00 N | 88.00 W |
| Brodhead, Ky., U.S. | 192 | 37.24 N | 84.24 W |
| Brodhead, Wi., U.S. | 190 | 42.37 N | 89.22 W |
| Brodhead Creek ≃ | 210 | 40.59 N | 75.08 W |
| Brodheadsville | 210 | 40.55 N | 75.24 W |
| Brodick | 46 | 55.35 N | 5.09 W |
| Brodnax | 192 | 36.42 N | 78.01 W |
| Brodnica | 30 | 53.16 N | 19.23 E |
| Brodokalmak | 86 | 55.35 N | 62.06 E |
| Brody, Pol. | 30 | 51.45 N | 14.45 E |
| Brody, Ukr. | 78 | 50.06 N | 25.10 E |
| Broedersput | 158 | 26.49 S | 25.08 E |
| Broek [op Langendijk] | 52 | 52.40 N | 4.48 E |
| Brogan | 202 | 44.14 N | 117.30 W |
| Broglie | 50 | 49.01 N | 0.32 E |
| Brohlbach ≃ | 56 | 50.29 N | 7.20 E |
| Broich -♦-[8] | 263 | 51.25 N | 6.51 E |
| Broichweiden | 56 | 50.49 N | 6.09 E |
| Brok | 30 | 52.43 N | 21.52 E |
| Brok ∧ | 123 | 34.32 N | 76.35 E |
| Brokdorf | 52 | 53.52 N | 9.19 E |
| Broke | 170 | 32.45 S | 151.06 E |
| Broke Inlet ⊂ | 162 | 34.55 S | 116.25 E |
| Broken ≃ | 169 | 36.41 S | 146.00 E |
| Broken Arrow | 196 | 36.03 N | 95.47 W |
| Broken Bay ⊂ | 170 | 33.34 S | 151.18 E |
| Broken Bow, Ne., U.S. | 198 | 41.24 N | 99.38 W |
| Broken Bow, Ok., U.S. | 194 | 34.01 N | 94.44 W |
| Broken Bow Lake ◎[1] | 194 | 34.10 N | 94.40 W |
| Broken Cross, Eng., U.K. | 262 | 53.15 N | 2.29 W |
| Broken Cross, Eng., U.K. | 262 | 53.15 N | 2.10 W |
| Brokenhead ≃ | 184 | 50.25 N | 96.40 W |
| Broken Hill, Austl. | 166 | 31.57 S | 141.27 E |
| Broken Hill → Kabwe, Zam. | 154 | 14.27 S | 28.27 E |
| Broken Ridge ✦[3] | 12 | 31.30 S | 95.00 E |
| Brokenstraw Creek ≃ | 214 | 41.51 N | 79.09 W |
| Broken Sword Creek ≃ | 214 | 40.46 N | 83.11 W |
| Brokopondo | 250 | 5.04 N | 54.58 W |
| Brokopondo □[5] | 250 | 4.40 N | 55.00 W |
| Brokopondo Stuwmeer ◎[1] | 250 | 4.45 N | 55.00 W |
| Brölbach ≃ | 56 | 50.47 N | 7.18 E |
| Brolo | 70 | 38.09 N | 14.50 E |
| Bromberg → Bydgoszcz | 30 | 53.08 N | 18.00 E |
| Bromborough | 262 | 53.19 N | 2.59 W |
| Brome, P.Q., Can. | 206 | 45.12 N | 72.34 W |
| Brome, Dtsch. | 54 | 52.36 N | 10.56 E |
| Brome □[6] | 206 | 45.10 N | 72.30 W |
| Brome, Lac ◎ | 206 | 45.15 N | 72.30 W |
| Brome, Mont ∧ | 206 | 45.17 N | 72.38 W |
| Bromham | 42 | 52.09 N | 0.31 W |
| Bromley -♦-[8] | 42 | 51.24 N | 0.02 E |
| Bromley Common -♦-[8] | 260 | 51.22 N | 0.03 E |
| Bromley Plateau ✦[3] | 18 | 32.00 S | 35.00 W |
| Bromma -♦-[8] | 40 | 59.21 N | 17.55 E |
| Bromma flygplats ✈ | 40 | 59.21 N | 17.55 E |
| Brommö I | 40 | 58.50 N | 13.41 E |
| Bromo, Gunung ∧ | 115a | 7.57 S | 112.57 E |
| Bromölla | 26 | 56.04 N | 14.28 E |
| Brompton, Eng., U.K. | 44 | 54.22 N | 1.25 W |
| Brompton, Eng., U.K. | 260 | 51.23 N | 0.33 E |
| Brompton, Lac ◎ | 206 | 45.27 N | 72.09 W |
| Bromptonville | 206 | 45.28 N | 71.57 W |
| Bromsgrove | 42 | 52.20 N | 2.03 W |
| Bromyard | 42 | 52.11 N | 2.30 W |
| Bron | 62 | 45.44 N | 4.55 E |
| Brønderslev | 26 | 57.16 N | 9.58 E |
| Bronevskaja | 24 | 61.43 N | 39.10 E |
| Brong-Ahafo □[4] | 150 | 7.45 N | 1.30 W |
| Broni | 62 | 45.04 N | 9.16 E |
| Bronkhorstspruit | 158 | 25.48 S | 28.44 E |
| Bronkhorstspruitdam ◎[1] | 158 | 25.55 S | 28.42 E |
| Bronkow | 54 | 51.40 N | 13.55 E |
| Bronllys | 42 | 52.01 N | 3.16 W |
| Bronlund Peak ∧ | 176 | 57.26 N | 126.38 W |
| Bronn | 60 | 49.44 N | 11.28 E |
| Bronnae | 76 | 52.19 N | 30.29 E |
| Bronnicy | 82 | 55.25 N | 38.16 E |
| Bronnikovo | 86 | 58.32 N | 68.25 E |
| Brønnøysund | 24 | 65.30 N | 12.10 E |
| Bronnzell | 56 | 50.31 N | 9.41 E |
| Brøns | 41 | 55.11 N | 8.44 E |
| Bronson, Fl., U.S. | 192 | 29.26 N | 82.38 W |
| Bronson, Ks., U.S. | 198 | 37.54 N | 95.04 W |
| Bronson, Mi., U.S. | 216 | 41.52 N | 85.11 W |
| Bronson, Tx., U.S. | 194 | 31.21 N | 94.01 W |
| Bronson Lake ◎ | 184 | 53.52 N | 109.43 W |
| Bronte, It. | 70 | 37.47 N | 14.50 E |
| Bronte, Tx., U.S. | 196 | 31.53 N | 100.18 W |
| Bronte Creek ≃ | 212 | 43.23 N | 79.43 W |
| Bronwood | 192 | 31.49 N | 84.21 W |
| Bronx □[6] | 210 | 40.49 N | 73.56 W |
| Bronx -♦-[8] | 276 | 40.49 N | 73.56 W |
| Bronx ≃ | 276 | 40.49 N | 73.52 W |
| Bronx Park ♦ | 276 | 40.52 N | 73.53 W |
| Bronxville | 276 | 40.56 N | 73.49 W |
| Bronx-Whitestone Bridge -♦-[5] | 276 | 40.48 N | 73.50 W |
| Bronx Zoo ♦ | 276 | 40.51 N | 73.53 W |
| Bronyts'ka Huta | 78 | 50.56 N | 27.19 E |
| Bronzolo (Branzoll) | 64 | 46.24 N | 11.19 E |
| Brooch, Lac ◎ | 186 | 50.44 N | 67.58 W |
| Broodsnyersplaas | 158 | 26.03 S | 29.29 E |
| Brook | 216 | 40.51 N | 87.21 W |
| Brooke | 208 | 38.23 N | 77.22 W |
| Brooke □[6] | 214 | 40.18 N | 80.33 W |
| Brookeborough | 48 | 54.19 N | 7.24 W |
| Brookeland | 194 | 31.09 N | 94.00 W |
| Brooker | 192 | 29.53 N | 82.19 W |
| Brooke's Point | 116 | 8.47 N | 117.50 E |
| Brookfield, N.S., Can. | 186 | 45.15 N | 63.17 W |
| Brookfield, Ct., U.S. | 207 | 41.28 N | 73.24 W |
| Brookfield, Il., U.S. | 216 | 41.49 N | 87.51 W |
| Brookfield, Ma., U.S. | 207 | 42.12 N | 72.06 W |
| Brookfield, Mi., U.S. | 216 | 42.27 N | 84.47 W |
| Brookfield, Mo., U.S. | 194 | 39.47 N | 93.04 W |
| Brookfield, N.Y., U.S. | 210 | 42.48 N | 75.19 W |
| Brookfield, Oh., U.S. | 214 | 41.14 N | 80.34 W |
| Brookfield, Wi., U.S. | 216 | 43.03 N | 88.06 W |
| Brookfield Center | 207 | 41.27 N | 73.23 W |
| Brookfield Zoo ♦ | 278 | 41.50 N | 87.50 W |
| Brookford | 192 | 35.42 N | 81.20 W |
| Brookhaven, De., U.S. | 285 | 39.42 N | 75.41 W |
| Brookhaven, Ms., U.S. | 194 | 31.34 N | 90.26 W |
| Brookhaven, Pa., U.S. | 285 | 39.52 N | 75.22 W |
| Brookhaven National Laboratory ʋ[3] | 207 | 40.54 N | 72.52 W |
| Brookings, Or., U.S. | 202 | 42.03 N | 124.16 W |
| Brookings, S.D., U.S. | 198 | 44.18 N | 96.47 W |
| Brookland, Eng., U.K. | 42 | 50.59 N | 0.50 E |
| Brookland, Ar., U.S. | 194 | 35.54 N | 90.34 W |
| Brookland -♦-[8] | 284c | 38.56 N | 76.59 W |
| Brooklands | 214 | 42.38 N | 83.06 W |
| Brookland Terrace | 285 | 39.44 N | 75.37 W |
| Brooklandville | 284b | 39.25 N | 76.40 W |
| Brooklawn | 285 | 39.52 N | 75.07 W |
| Brooklet | 192 | 32.22 N | 81.39 W |
| Brooklin | 212 | 43.57 N | 78.57 W |
| Brookline, Ma., U.S. | 207 | 42.21 N | 71.07 W |
| Brookline, N.H., U.S. | 207 | 42.44 N | 71.39 W |
| Brooklyn, N.S., Can. | 186 | 44.03 N | 64.42 W |
| Brooklyn, Ct., U.S. | 207 | 41.47 N | 71.57 W |
| Brooklyn, Il., U.S. | 219 | 40.14 N | 90.46 W |
| Brooklyn, In., U.S. | 218 | 39.32 N | 86.22 W |
| Brooklyn, Ia., U.S. | 190 | 41.44 N | 92.26 W |
| Brooklyn, Mi., U.S. | 216 | 42.06 N | 84.14 W |
| Brooklyn, Ms., U.S. | 194 | 31.03 N | 89.11 W |
| Brooklyn, Oh., U.S. | 214 | 41.26 N | 81.44 W |
| Brooklyn, Pa., U.S. | 210 | 41.45 N | 75.48 W |
| Brooklyn, Wa., U.S. | 224 | 46.47 N | 123.31 W |
| Brooklyn, Wi., U.S. | 216 | 42.51 N | 89.22 W |
| Brooklyn -♦-[8], Md., U.S. | 284b | 39.14 N | 76.36 W |
| Brooklyn -♦-[8], N.Y., U.S. | 210 | 40.42 N | 74.00 W |
| Brooklyn Battery Tunnel -♦-[5] | 276 | 40.42 N | 74.01 W |
| Brooklyn Bridge -♦-[5] | 276 | 40.42 N | 74.00 W |
| Brooklyn Center | 190 | 45.04 N | 93.19 W |
| Brooklyn Heights | 279a | 41.24 N | 81.40 W |
| Brooklyn Marine Park ♦ | 276 | 40.35 N | 73.55 W |
| Brooklyn Museum ʋ | 276 | 40.40 N | 73.58 W |
| Brookmans Park | 260 | 51.43 N | 0.12 W |
| Brookmere | 182 | 49.49 N | 120.53 W |
| Brookmont | 284c | 38.57 N | 77.07 W |
| Brookneal | 192 | 37.03 N | 78.56 W |
| Brook Park | 214 | 41.23 N | 81.48 W |
| Brookport | 194 | 37.07 N | 88.37 W |
| Brooks, Ab., Can. | 182 | 50.35 N | 111.53 W |
| Brooks, Ca., U.S. | 226 | 38.45 N | 122.09 W |
| Brooks, Me., U.S. | 188 | 44.33 N | 69.07 W |
| Brooks, Or., U.S. | 224 | 45.02 N | 122.57 W |
| Brooks, Mount ∧ | 180 | 63.11 N | 150.40 W |
| Brooks Air Force Base ■ | 196 | 29.21 N | 98.25 W |
| Brooks Bay ⊂ | 182 | 50.13 N | 127.55 W |
| Brooksburg | 218 | 38.44 N | 85.15 W |
| Brookshire | 222 | 29.47 N | 95.57 W |
| Brookside, De., U.S. | 285 | 39.40 N | 75.43 W |
| Brookside, N.J., U.S. | 276 | 40.48 N | 74.34 W |
| Brookside, Pa., U.S. | 214 | 42.08 N | 80.00 W |
| Brookside, Tx., U.S. | 222 | 29.35 N | 95.18 W |
| Brookside Park ♦ | 279a | 41.27 N | 81.43 W |
| Brooks Island I | 282 | 37.54 N | 122.21 W |
| Brooks Mountain ∧ | 180 | 65.33 N | 167.09 W |
| Brooks Place | 283 | 42.02 N | 71.01 W |
| Brooks Range ⋏ | 180 | 68.00 N | 154.00 W |
| Brookston | 216 | 40.36 N | 86.52 W |
| Brook Street | 260 | 51.37 N | 0.17 E |
| Brooksville, Fl., U.S. | 220 | 28.33 N | 82.23 W |
| Brooksville, Ky., U.S. | 218 | 38.40 N | 84.03 W |
| Brooksville, Ms., U.S. | 194 | 33.14 N | 88.34 W |
| Brookton | 162 | 32.22 S | 117.01 E |
| Brooktondale | 210 | 42.23 N | 76.24 W |
| Brookvale | 274a | 33.46 S | 151.17 E |
| Brookview | 210 | 42.32 N | 73.43 W |
| Brookville, In., U.S. | 218 | 39.25 N | 85.00 W |
| Brookville, Ma., U.S. | 207 | 42.07 N | 71.00 W |
| Brookville, N.Y., U.S. | 276 | 40.48 N | 73.34 W |
| Brookville, Oh., U.S. | 218 | 39.50 N | 84.24 W |
| Brookville, Pa., U.S. | 214 | 41.09 N | 79.05 W |
| Brookville Lake ◎[1] | 218 | 39.30 N | 85.00 W |
| Brookwood | 260 | 51.18 N | 0.38 W |
| Brooloo | 166 | 26.29 S | 152.42 E |
| Broom, Little Loch ⊂ | 46 | 57.54 N | 5.22 W |
| Broom, Loch ⊂ | 46 | 57.52 N | 5.08 W |
| Broomall | 285 | 39.58 N | 75.21 W |
| Broome | 162 | 17.58 S | 122.14 E |
| Broome □[6] | 210 | 42.08 N | 75.54 W |
| Broome County Airport ✈ | 210 | 42.13 N | 75.59 W |
| Broomes Island | 208 | 38.25 N | 76.32 W |
| Broomfield, Eng., U.K. | 260 | 51.46 N | 0.[illegible]8 E |
| Broomfield, Eng., U.K. | 260 | 51.14 N | 0.[illegible]8 E |
| Broomfield, Co., U.S. | 200 | 39.55 N | 105.[illegible]5 W |
| Broons | 32 | 48.19 N | 2.[illegible]6 W |
| Brooten | 198 | 45.30 N | 95.[illegible]7 W |
| Brophy, Mount ∧[2] | 162 | 19.11 S | 128.[illegible]1 E |
| Brora | 46 | 58.01 N | 3.[illegible] W |
| Brora ≃ | 46 | 58.01 N | 3.[illegible] W |
| Brørup | 41 | 55.29 N | 9.[illegible] E |
| Broseley | 42 | 52.37 N | 2.2[illegible] W |
| Brosewere Bay ⊂ | 276 | 40.37 N | 73.4[illegible] W |
| Broshniv-Osada | 78 | 49.00 N | 24.1[illegible] E |
| Brosna ≃ | 48 | 53.13 N | 7.5[illegible] W |
| Brossac | 32 | 45.20 N | 0.0[illegible] W |
| Brossard | 206 | 45.26 N | 73.2[illegible] W |
| Brossasco | 62 | 44.34 N | 7.21 E |
| Brosso | 62 | 45.30 N | 7.4[illegible] E |
| Brotas de Macaúbas | 255 | 12.00 S | 42.38 W |
| Brothers Brook ≃ | 276 | 41.02 N | 73.36 W |
| Brötjärna | 40 | 60.30 N | 15.01 E |
| Broto | 34 | 42.36 N | 0.06 W |
| Brotton | 44 | 54.34 N | 0.56 W |
| Brou | 50 | 48.13 N | 1.11 E |
| Brough, Eng., U.K. | 44 | 54.32 N | 2.19 W |
| Brough, Eng., U.K. | 44 | 53.44 N | 0.35 W |
| Brough, Scot., U.K. | 46 | 58.39 N | 3.20 W |
| Brougham | 212 | 43.55 N | 79.06 W |
| Brough Head › | 46 | 59.08 N | 3.17 W |
| Broughshane | 48 | 54.54 N | 6.12 W |
| Broughton, Eng., U.K. | 42 | 52.23 N | 0.46 W |
| Broughton, Eng., U.K. | 44 | 53.34 N | 0.33 W |
| Broughton, Eng., U.K. | 44 | 53.49 N | 2.44 W |
| Broughton, Eng., U.K. | 262 | 53.49 N | 2.44 W |
| Broughton, Scot., U.K. | 46 | 55.37 N | 3.25 W |
| Broughton, Wales, U.K. | 44 | 53.10 N | 2.59 W |
| Broughton, Pa., U.S. | 214 | 40.21 N | 79.59 W |
| Broughton in Furness | 44 | 54.17 N | 3.12 W |
| Broughton Island I | 176 | 67.35 N | 63.50 W |
| Broughtown | 46 | 59.15 N | 2.36 W |
| Broughty Ferry | 46 | 56.28 N | 2.53 W |
| Broumov | 30 | 50.35 N | 16.20 E |
| Brousseval | 58 | 48.29 N | 4.58 E |
| Brou-sur-Chantereine | 261 | 48.53 N | 2.38 E |
| Brouvelieures | 58 | 48.14 N | 6.44 E |
| Brouwersdam -♦-[6] | 52 | 51.46 N | 3.51 E |
| Brouwershaven | 52 | 51.44 N | 3.54 E |
| Brovary | 78 | 50.31 N | 30.46 E |
| Brovst | 26 | 57.06 N | 9.32 E |
| Broward □[6] | 220 | 26.09 N | 80.29 W |
| Browerville | 198 | 46.05 N | 94.51 W |
| Brown □[6], Il., U.S. | 219 | 39.59 N | 90.45 W |
| Brown □[6], In., U.S. | 218 | 39.12 N | 86.15 W |
| Brown □[6], Oh., U.S. | 218 | 38.52 N | 83.54 W |
| Brown, Mount ∧ | 202 | 48.52 N | 111.09 W |
| Brown, Point › | 224 | 46.56 N | 124.10 W |
| Brownbacks | 285 | 40.11 N | 75.37 W |
| Brown City | 190 | 43.12 N | 82.59 W |
| Brown Clee Hill ∧[2] | 42 | 52.28 N | 2.35 W |
| Brown County State Park ♦ | 218 | 39.09 N | 86.14 W |
| Brown Creek ≃ | 276 | 40.43 N | 73.04 W |
| Browndale | 210 | 41.40 N | 75.27 W |
| Brown Deer | 216 | 43.09 N | 87.57 W |
| Browne Bay ⊂ | 176 | 73.08 N | 97.30 W |
| Brownfield | 196 | 33.10 N | 102.16 W |
| Brown Gelly ∧[2] | 42 | 50.32 N | 4.32 W |
| Brownhills | 42 | 52.39 N | 1.55 W |
| Browning, Il., U.S. | 219 | 40.08 N | 90.22 W |
| Browning, Mo., U.S. | 194 | 40.02 N | 93.09 W |
| Browning, Mt., U.S. | 202 | 48.33 N | 113.00 W |
| Browning Entrance ⊂ | 182 | 53.41 N | 130.30 W |
| Browning Island I | 212 | 45.00 N | 79.25 W |
| Brown Lake ◎ | 176 | 65.55 N | 91.15 W |
| Brownlee Park | 216 | 42.18 N | 85.05 W |
| Brownlee Reservoir ◎[1] | 202 | 44.40 N | 117.05 W |
| Brown Mountain ∧, Ca., U.S. | 204 | 35.41 N | 117.01 W |
| Brown Mountain ∧, Ca., U.S. | 280 | 34.14 N | 118.08 W |
| Brown Mountain ∧[2] | 222 | 31.51 N | 97.39 W |
| Brown Point › | 276 | 40.43 N | 73.04 W |
| Brownsberg, Natuurpark ♦ | 250 | 4.50 N | 55.10 W |
| Brownsboro | 222 | 32.18 N | 95.37 W |
| Browns Brook ≃ | 276 | 41.09 N | 73.17 W |
| Brownsburg, P.Q., Can. | 206 | 45.41 N | 74.25 W |
| Brownsburg, In., U.S. | 218 | 39.50 N | 86.23 W |
| Browns Canyon ∨ | 280 | 34.18 N | 118.35 W |
| Brownsdale | 190 | 43.44 N | 92.52 W |
| Browns Island I | 282 | 38.02 N | 121.52 W |
| Browns Lake | 216 | 42.42 N | 88.14 W |
| Brownsmead | 224 | 46.13 N | 123.32 W |
| Browns Mills | 208 | 39.58 N | 74.35 W |
| Browns Point | 224 | 47.18 N | 122.21 W |
| Browns Town, Jam. | 241q | 18.24 N | 77.22 W |
| Brownstown, Il., U.S. | 219 | 38.59 N | 88.57 W |
| Brownstown, In., U.S. | 218 | 38.52 N | 86.02 W |
| Brownstown, Pa., U.S. | 208 | 40.08 N | 76.13 W |
| Brownstown Creek ≃ | 281 | 42.06 N | 83.13 W |
| Browns Valley, Ca., U.S. | 226 | 39.15 N | 121.23 W |
| Browns Valley, Mn., U.S. | 198 | 45.35 N | 96.49 W |
| Brownsville, On., Can. | 212 | 42.52 N | 80.50 W |
| Brownsville, Ca., U.S. | 226 | 39.28 N | 121.16 W |
| Brownsville, Fl., U.S. | 220 | 25.50 N | 80.17 W |
| Brownsville, In., U.S. | 218 | 39.39 N | 85.00 W |
| Brownsville, Ky., U.S. | 194 | 37.11 N | 86.16 W |
| Brownsville, La., U.S. | 194 | 32.30 N | 92.10 W |
| Brownsville, Or., U.S. | 202 | 44.23 N | 122.59 W |
| Brownsville, Pa., U.S. | 188 | 40.01 N | 79.53 W |
| Brownsville, Tn., U.S. | 194 | 35.35 N | 89.15 W |
| Brownsville, Tx., U.S. | 196 | 25.54 N | 97.29 W |
| Brownton | 190 | 44.43 N | 94.21 W |
| Browntown | 276 | 40.24 N | 74.19 W |
| Brownvale | 182 | 56.08 N | 117.53 W |
| Brownville, Al., U.S. | 194 | 33.23 N | 87.45 W |
| Brownville, Me., U.S. | 188 | 45.18 N | 69.02 W |
| Brownville, Ne., U.S. | 198 | 40.23 N | 95.39 W |
| Brownville, N.Y., U.S. | 212 | 44.00 N | 75.59 W |
| Brownville Junction | 188 | 45.21 N | 69.03 W |
| Brown Willy ∧[2] | 42 | 50.35 N | 4.36 W |
| Brownwood | 196 | 31.42 N | 98.59 W |
| Brownwood, Lake ◎[1] | 196 | 31.51 N | 99.02 W |
| Browse Island I | 160 | 14.07 S | 123.33 E |
| Broxbourne | 260 | 51.45 N | 0.01 W |
| Broxbourne □[8] | 260 | 51.44 N | 0.04 W |
| Broxton | 192 | 31.37 N | 82.53 W |
| Broye ≃ | 58 | 46.55 N | 7.02 E |
| Broyhill Park | 284c | 38.51 N | 77.11 W |
| Broža | 76 | 52.57 N | 29.07 E |
| Brozas | 34 | 39.37 N | 6.46 W |
| Brozzo | 64 | 45.43 N | 10.14 E |
| Brtonigla | 64 | 45.23 N | 13.38 E |
| Brû | 58 | 48.21 N | 6.41 E |
| Bruay-en-Artois | 50 | 50.29 N | 2.33 E |
| Bruay-sur-l'Escaut | 50 | 50.23 N | 3.32 E |
| Bruce, Ms., U.S. | 194 | 33.59 N | 89.20 W |
| Bruce, S.D., U.S. | 198 | 44.26 N | 96.53 W |
| Bruce, Wi., U.S. | 190 | 45.27 N | 91.16 W |
| Bruce □[6] | 212 | 44.30 N | 81.15 W |
| Bruce, Mount ∧ | 162 | 22.36 S | 118.08 E |
| Bruce Bay | 172 | 43.35 S | 169.41 E |
| Bruce Creek ≃ | 275b | 43.52 N | 79.18 W |
| Bruce Lake | 184 | 50.48 N | 93.24 W |
| Bruce Lake ◎ | 184 | 50.49 N | 93.20 W |


| Symbol | English | Deutsch | Español | Français | Português |
|---|---|---|---|---|---|
| ≃ | River | Fluß | Río | Rivière | Rio |
| ≊ | Canal | Kanal | Canal | Canal | Canal |
| ∟ | Waterfall, Rapids | Wasserfall, Stromschnellen | Cascada, Rápidos | Chute d'eau, Rapides | Cascata, Rápidos |
| ꭒ | Strait | Meeresstraße | Estrecho | Détroit | Estreito |
| ⊂ | Bay, Gulf | Bucht, Golf | Bahía, Golfo | Baie, Golfe | Baía, Golfo |
| ◎ | Lake, Lakes | See, Seen | Lago, Lagos | Lac, Lacs | Lago, Lagos |
| ⩸ | Swamp | Sumpf | Pantano | Marais | Pântano |
| ≋ | Ice Features, Glacier | Eis- und Gletscherformen | Accidentes Glaciales | Formes glaciaires | Acidentes glaciares |
| ⊤ | Other Hydrographic Features | Andere Hydrographische Objekte | Otros Elementos Hidrográficos | Autres données hydrographiques | Outros acidentes hidrográficos |
| ✦ | Submarine Features | Untermeerische Objekte | Accidentes Submarinos | Formes de relief sous-marin | Acidentes submarinos |
| □ | Political Unit | Politische Einheit | Unidad Politica | Entité politique | Unidade política |
| ʋ | Cultural Institution | Kulturelle Institution | Institución Cultural | Institution culturelle | Institução cultural |
| ⊥ | Historical Site | Historische Stätte | Sitio Histórico | Site historique | Sitio histórico |
| ♦ | Recreational Site | Erholungs- und Ferienort | Sitio de Recreo | Centre de loisirs | Area de Lazer |
| ✈ | Airport | Flughafen | Aeropuerto | Aéroport | Aeroporto |
| ■ | Military Installation | Militäranlage | Instalación Militar | Installation militaire | Instalação militar |
| -♦- | Miscellaneous | Verschiedenes | Misceláneo | Divers | Diversos |

| Name | Page | Lat.°′ | Long.°′ |
| --- | --- | --- | --- |
| Bruce Mines | **190** | 46.18 N | 83.48 W |
| Bruce Museum ʊ | **276** | 41.01 N | 73.37 W |
| Bruce Peninsula ≻[1] | **190** | 44.50 N | 81.20 W |
| Bruce Peninsula National Park ♦ | **190** | 45.12 N | 81.40 W |
| Bruce Rock | **162** | 31.53 S | 118.09 E |
| Bruceville | **222** | 31.19 N | 97.14 W |
| Bruchberg ʌ | **54** | 51.47 N | 10.29 E |
| Bruche ≃ | **58** | 48.34 N | 7.43 E |
| Bruchhausen | **56** | 51.26 N | 8.01 E |
| Bruchhausen-Vilsen | **52** | 52.50 N | 9.00 E |
| Bruchmühlbach-Miesau | **56** | 49.24 N | 7.26 E |
| Bruchmühle | **264a** | 52.33 N | 13.47 E |
| Br'uchoveckaja | **78** | 45.48 N | 38.59 E |
| Bruchsal | **56** | 49.07 N | 8.35 E |
| Brück, Dtsch. | **54** | 52.12 N | 12.46 E |
| Bruck, Öst. | **64** | 47.17 N | 12.49 E |
| Bruck an der Leitha | **61** | 48.02 N | 16.47 E |
| Bruck an der Mur | **61** | 47.25 N | 15.16 E |
| Bruckberg | **60** | 48.31 N | 12.00 E |
| Bruckhausen ●[8] | **263** | 51.29 N | 6.44 E |
| Bruck in der Oberpfalz | **60** | 49.15 N | 12.18 E |
| Brückl | **61** | 46.45 N | 14.32 E |
| Bruckmühl | **64** | 47.53 N | 11.54 E |
| Brucoli ●[8] | **70** | 37.17 N | 15.11 E |
| Brudager | **41** | 55.07 N | 10.41 E |
| Bruderheim | **182** | 53.47 N | 112.56 W |
| Brue ≃ | **42** | 51.13 N | 3.00 W |
| Brue-Auriac | **62** | 43.32 N | 5.57 E |
| Brueil-en-Vexin | **261** | 49.02 N | 1.49 E |
| Brüel | **54** | 53.44 N | 11.43 E |
| Bruff | **48** | 52.29 N | 8.33 W |
| Bruges → Brugge | **50** | 51.13 N | 3.14 E |
| Brugg | **58** | 47.29 N | 8.12 E |
| Brugge (Bruges), Bel. | **50** | 51.13 N | 3.14 E |
| Brügge, Dtsch. | **263** | 51.13 N | 7.34 E |
| Brüggen | **56** | 51.14 N | 6.11 E |
| Brugherio | **62** | 45.33 N | 9.18 E |
| Brugnato | **62** | 44.14 N | 9.43 E |
| Brühl | **56** | 50.48 N | 6.54 E |
| Bruin, Ky., U.S. | **218** | 38.11 N | 83.01 W |
| Bruin, Pa., U.S. | **214** | 41.04 N | 79.44 W |
| Bruinisse | **52** | 51.40 N | 4.06 E |
| Bruin Point ʌ | **200** | 39.39 N | 110.22 W |
| Bruit, Pulau I | **112** | 2.35 N | 111.20 E |
| Bruja, Cerro ʌ | **236** | 9.29 N | 79.34 W |
| Brule | **198** | 41.05 N | 101.53 W |
| Brule ≃ | **190** | 45.57 N | 88.12 W |
| Brûlé, Lac ⊜, Can. | **176** | 52.17 N | 63.52 W |
| Brûlé, Lac ⊜, P.Q., Can. | **190** | 46.57 N | 77.12 W |
| Brule Lake ⊜ | **212** | 45.03 N | 77.04 W |
| Brûly | **50** | 49.58 N | 4.31 E |
| Brumadinho | **255** | 20.08 S | 44.13 W |
| Brumado | **255** | 14.13 S | 41.40 W |
| Brumath | **56** | 48.44 N | 7.43 E |
| Brumby Creek ≃ | **162** | 24.09 S | 118.39 E |
| Brummen | **52** | 52.05 N | 6.09 E |
| Brumunddal | **26** | 60.53 N | 10.56 E |
| Bruna ≃ | **66** | 42.45 N | 10.53 E |
| Brunate | **62** | 45.49 N | 9.06 E |
| Brunau | **54** | 52.45 N | 11.28 E |
| Brundall | **42** | 52.37 N | 1.26 E |
| Brundby | **41** | 55.49 N | 10.37 E |
| Brundidge | **194** | 31.43 N | 85.48 W |
| Brune ≃ | **50** | 49.45 N | 3.47 E |
| Bruneau | **202** | 42.52 N | 115.47 W |
| Bruneau ≃ | **202** | 42.57 N | 115.58 W |
| Brunei → Bandar Seri Begawan | **112** | 4.56 N | 114.55 E |
| Brunei □[1], Asia | **108** | 4.30 N | 114.40 E |
| Brunei □[1], Asia | **112** | 4.30 N | 114.40 E |
| Brunei, Teluk c | **112** | 5.05 N | 115.18 E |
| Brünen | **52** | 51.43 N | 6.39 E |
| Brunette Creek ≃ | **162** | 18.47 S | 135.41 E |
| Brunette Downs | **162** | 18.38 S | 135.57 E |
| Brunette Island I | **186** | 47.16 N | 55.54 W |
| Brunflo | **26** | 63.05 N | 14.49 E |
| Brungle | **171b** | 35.10 S | 148.14 E |
| Brunico (Bruneck) | **64** | 46.48 N | 11.56 E |
| Brünigpass )( | **58** | 46.46 N | 8.09 E |
| Brüninghausen | **263** | 51.13 N | 7.41 E |
| Brunkeberg | **26** | 59.26 N | 8.29 E |
| Brünn → Brno, Česká Rep. | **30** | 49.12 N | 16.37 E |
| Brünn, Dtsch. | **54** | 50.27 N | 10.51 E |
| Brunn, Dtsch. | **54** | 53.40 N | 13.22 E |
| Brunna | **40** | 59.51 N | 17.26 E |
| Brunn am Gebirge | **61** | 48.07 N | 16.17 E |
| Brunnen, Dtsch. | **60** | 48.38 N | 11.18 E |
| Brunnen, Schw. | **58** | 47.00 N | 8.36 E |
| Brunner, Lake ⊜ | **172** | 42.37 S | 171.27 E |
| Brunnerville | **208** | 40.11 N | 76.17 W |
| Brunni | **58** | 47.03 N | 8.42 E |
| Brunnsvik | **40** | 60.12 N | 15.08 E |
| Bruno | **184** | 52.15 N | 105.30 W |
| Brunot Island I | **279b** | 40.28 N | 80.03 W |
| Brunow | **264a** | 52.44 N | 13.52 E |
| Brunoy | **50** | 48.42 N | 2.30 E |
| Brunsbüttel | **52** | 53.54 N | 9.07 E |
| Brunsbüttelkoog | **52** | 53.54 N | 9.08 E |
| Brunson | **192** | 32.55 N | 81.11 W |
| Brunssum | **56** | 50.56 N | 5.59 E |
| Brunswick, Austl. | **274b** | 37.46 S | 144.58 E |
| Brunswick → Braunschweig, Dtsch. | **52** | 52.16 N | 10.31 E |
| Brunswick, Ga., U.S. | **192** | 31.08 N | 81.29 W |
| Brunswick, Me., U.S. | **188** | 43.54 N | 69.57 W |
| Brunswick, Md., U.S. | **208** | 39.18 N | 77.37 W |
| Brunswick, Mo., U.S. | **194** | 39.25 N | 93.07 W |
| Brunswick, Oh., U.S. | **214** | 41.14 N | 81.50 W |
| Brunswick ≃ | **168a** | 33.15 S | 115.45 E |
| Brunswick, Península ≻[1] | **254** | 53.30 S | 71.25 W |
| Brunswick Junction | **168a** | 33.15 S | 115.51 E |
| Brunswick Lake ⊜ | **190** | 49.00 N | 83.23 W |
| Brunswick Naval Air Station ■ | **188** | 43.54 N | 69.56 W |
| Brunswick Square ●[9] | **276** | 40.25 N | 74.23 W |
| Bruntál | **30** | 49.59 N | 17.28 E |
| Bruree | **48** | 52.26 N | 8.36 W |
| Brus, Laguna de c | **236** | 15.50 N | 84.35 W |
| Brus'any | **80** | 53.13 N | 49.24 E |
| Brusasco | **62** | 45.09 N | 8.04 E |
| Bruselas → Bruxelles | **50** | 50.50 N | 4.20 E |
| Brusendorf | **264a** | 52.19 N | 13.31 E |
| Brush | **198** | 40.15 N | 103.37 W |
| Brush Creek ≃, Oh., U.S. | **216** | 41.26 N | 84.24 W |
| Brush Creek ≃, Pa., U.S. | **279b** | 40.23 N | 79.46 W |
| Brush Run ≃, Pa., U.S. | **279b** | 40.18 N | 80.07 W |
| Brush Run ≃, Pa., U.S. | **279b** | 40.16 N | 80.10 W |
| Brush Valley | **214** | 40.32 N | 79.04 W |
| Brushy Creek ≃, Austl. | **274b** | 37.43 S | 145.17 E |
| Brushy Creek ≃, Ok., U.S. | **196** | 34.55 N | 95.34 W |
| Brushy Creek ≃, Tx., U.S. | **222** | 32.59 N | 96.12 W |
| Brushy Creek ≃, Tx., U.S. | **222** | 30.48 N | 95.09 W |
| Brushy Creek ≃, Tx., U.S. | **222** | 31.55 N | 95.26 W |
| Brushy Creek ≃, Tx., U.S. | **222** | 30.43 N | 97.03 W |
| Brushy Creek ≃, Tx., U.S. | **222** | 29.04 N | 96.34 W |
| Brusio | **58** | 46.14 N | 10.07 E |
| Brus Laguna | **236** | 15.47 N | 84.35 W |
| Brusovo | **76** | 57.51 N | 35.24 E |
| Brusque | **252** | 27.06 S | 48.56 W |
| Brussel → Bruxelles | **50** | 50.50 N | 4.20 E |
| Brussels → Bruxelles, Bel. | **50** | 50.50 N | 4.20 E |
| Brussels, On., Can. | **212** | 43.44 N | 81.15 W |
| Brussels, Il., U.S. | **219** | 38.57 N | 90.36 W |
| Brusson | **62** | 45.45 N | 7.44 E |
| Brüssow | **54** | 53.24 N | 14.07 E |
| Brusy | **30** | 53.53 N | 17.45 E |
| Brusyliv | **78** | 50.17 N | 29.32 E |
| Brutelles | **50** | 50.08 N | 1.31 E |
| Bruthen | **166** | 37.43 S | 147.48 E |
| Bruton | **42** | 51.07 N | 2.27 W |
| Brüx → Most | **54** | 50.32 N | 13.39 E |
| Bruxelles (Brussels) (Brussel) | **56** | 50.50 N | 4.20 E |
| Bruxelles National, Aéroport ⊠ | **50** | 50.54 N | 4.30 E |
| Bruyères | **58** | 48.12 N | 6.43 E |
| Bruyères-le-Châtel | **261** | 48.36 N | 2.11 E |
| Bruzual | **246** | 8.03 N | 69.19 W |
| Bruzzano Zeffirio | **68** | 38.02 N | 16.05 E |
| Brwinów | **30** | 52.09 N | 20.43 E |
| Bryan, Oh., U.S. | **216** | 41.28 N | 84.33 W |
| Bryan, Tx., U.S. | **222** | 30.40 N | 96.22 W |
| Bryan, Mount ʌ | **166** | 33.26 S | 138.59 E |
| Bryan Coast ±[2] | **9** | 73.45 S | 82.00 W |
| Bryanka | **83** | 48.29 N | 38.39 E |
| Bryansk → Br'ansk | **76** | 53.15 N | 34.22 E |
| Bryans Road | **208** | 38.37 N | 77.04 W |
| Bryant, Ar., U.S. | **194** | 34.35 N | 92.29 W |
| Bryant, In., U.S. | **216** | 40.32 N | 84.58 W |
| Bryant, S.D., U.S. | **198** | 44.35 N | 97.28 W |
| Bryant Creek ≃ | **194** | 36.36 N | 92.17 W |
| Bryant Mountain ʌ | **207** | 42.28 N | 72.58 W |
| Bryantville | **207** | 42.02 N | 70.50 W |
| Bryas, Lac ⊜ | **206** | 46.44 N | 73.05 W |
| Bryce Canyon National Park ♦ | **200** | 37.29 N | 112.12 W |
| Bryher I | **42a** | 49.57 N | 6.20 W |
| Brykalansk | **24** | 65.30 N | 54.12 E |
| Brykovka | **80** | 52.32 N | 48.35 E |
| Bryli | **76** | 53.54 N | 30.33 E |
| Brymbo | **44** | 53.06 N | 3.04 W |
| Bryn | **262** | 53.30 N | 2.39 W |
| Brynamman | **42** | 51.49 N | 3.52 W |
| Bryn Athyn | **285** | 40.08 N | 75.04 W |
| Bryn Brawd ʌ[2] | **42** | 52.09 N | 3.54 W |
| Bryncethin | **42** | 51.33 N | 3.34 W |
| Bryne | **26** | 58.44 N | 5.39 E |
| Brynford | **262** | 53.16 N | 3.14 W |
| Bryn Gates | **262** | 53.30 N | 2.37 W |
| Bryn'kovskaja | **78** | 46.02 N | 38.35 E |
| Brynmawr, Wales, U.K. | **42** | 51.49 N | 3.11 W |
| Bryn Mawr, Pa., U.S. | **208** | 40.01 N | 75.18 W |
| Bryn Mawr College ʊ[2] | **285** | 40.02 N | 75.19 W |
| Bryrup | **41** | 56.01 N | 9.31 E |
| Bryson, P.Q., Can. | **188** | 45.41 N | 76.37 W |
| Bryson, Tx., U.S. | **196** | 33.10 N | 98.23 W |
| Bryson City | **192** | 35.25 N | 83.26 W |
| Brza Palanka | **38** | 44.28 N | 22.27 E |
| Brzeg | **30** | 50.52 N | 17.27 E |
| Brześć Kujawski | **30** | 52.37 N | 18.55 E |
| Brześć nad Bugiem → Brèst | **76** | 52.06 N | 23.42 E |
| Brzesko | **30** | 49.59 N | 20.36 E |
| Brzeszcze | **30** | 49.59 N | 19.08 E |
| Brzeziny | **30** | 51.48 N | 19.46 E |
| Brzozów | **30** | 49.42 N | 22.02 E |
| Bsharrī | **130** | 34.15 N | 36.01 E |
| Bua ≃ | **154** | 12.42 S | 34.13 E |
| Bu'aale | **144** | 1.05 N | 42.35 E |
| Buada Lagoon c | **174b** | 0.31 S | 166.55 E |
| Buad Island I | **116** | 11.40 N | 124.51 E |
| Buagan ≃ | **269e** | 6.17 S | 106.55 E |
| Buala | **175e** | 8.08 S | 159.35 E |
| Bū al-Ḥīdān, Wādī V | **146** | 27.25 N | 19.22 E |
| Buangor, Mount ʌ | **169** | 37.18 S | 143.13 E |
| Buapinang | **112** | 4.46 S | 121.34 E |
| Buariki | **174t** | 1.36 N | 172.58 E |
| Buatan | **114** | 0.44 N | 101.51 E |
| Bua Yai | **110** | 15.35 N | 102.25 E |
| Buayan ≃ | **116** | 6.06 N | 125.14 E |
| Bu'ayrāt al-Ḥasūn | **146** | 31.24 N | 15.44 E |
| Buba | **150** | 11.36 N | 14.55 W |
| Bubai | **268** | 35.40 N | 139.29 E |
| Bū Bānī, Jabal ʌ | **140** | 22.38 N | 25.00 E |
| Bubanza | **154** | 3.06 S | 29.23 E |
| Bubaque | **150** | 11.17 N | 15.50 W |
| Bubendorf | **58** | 47.27 N | 7.44 E |
| Bubenreuth | **60** | 49.38 N | 11.01 E |
| Bubia | **164** | 6.40 S | 146.55 E |
| Būbiyān I | **128** | 29.45 N | 48.15 E |
| Bubu ≃ | **154** | 6.03 S | 35.19 E |
| Bubu, Gunong ʌ | **114** | 4.42 N | 100.47 E |
| Bubuan Island I, Pil. | **116** | 6.21 N | 121.58 E |
| Bubuan Island I, Pil. | **116** | 6.11 N | 120.58 E |
| Bubuduo | **120** | 30.06 N | 84.38 E |
| Buburu | **152** | 1.26 N | 18.03 E |
| Bubye ≃ | **154** | 22.20 S | 31.07 E |
| Buc | **261** | 48.46 N | 2.08 E |
| Bucak | **130** | 37.28 N | 30.36 E |
| Bucakkışla | **130** | 36.57 N | 33.02 E |
| Bucaramanga | **246** | 7.08 N | 73.09 W |
| Bucarest → București | **38** | 44.26 N | 26.06 E |
| Bucas Grande Island I | **116** | 9.40 N | 125.57 E |
| Buccaneer Archipelago II | **160** | 16.17 S | 123.20 E |
| Buccheri | **70** | 37.08 N | 14.51 E |
| Bucchianico | **66** | 42.18 N | 14.11 E |
| Buccinasco | **266b** | 45.24 N | 9.07 E |
| Buccino | **68** | 40.37 N | 15.23 E |
| Buccurale | **144** | 4.31 N | 42.01 E |
| Bucelas | **266c** | 38.54 N | 9.07 W |
| Bucelas ʌ[2] | **266c** | 38.53 N | 9.07 W |
| Buch | **58** | 48.14 N | 10.11 E |
| Buch ●[8] | **264a** | 52.38 N | 13.30 E |
| Buchach | **78** | 49.04 N | 25.23 E |
| Buchanan, Arg. | **258** | 34.58 S | 58.13 W |
| Buchanan, Sk., Can. | **184** | 51.43 N | 102.45 W |
| Buchanan, Liber. | **150** | 5.57 N | 10.02 W |
| Buchanan, Ga., U.S. | **192** | 33.48 N | 85.11 W |
| Buchanan, Mi., U.S. | **216** | 41.49 N | 86.21 W |
| Buchanan, N.Y., U.S. | **210** | 41.16 N | 73.56 W |
| Buchanan, Va., U.S. | **192** | 37.31 N | 79.40 W |
| Buchanan, Lake ⊜ | **166** | 21.28 S | 145.52 E |
| Buchanan, Lake ⊜[1] | **196** | 30.48 N | 98.25 W |
| Buchanan Creek ≃ | **162** | 19.11 S | 136.16 E |
| Buchanan Field ⊠ | **282** | 37.59 N | 122.03 W |
| Buchanan Hills ⋏[2] | **162** | 18.53 S | 131.02 E |
| Buchan Ness ≻ | **46** | 57.28 N | 1.45 W |
| Buchans | **186** | 48.49 N | 56.52 W |
| Buchara | **128** | 39.48 N | 64.25 E |
| Buchara □[8] | **128** | 40.00 N | 64.00 E |
| Bucharest → București | **38** | 44.26 N | 26.06 E |
| Buchbach | **60** | 48.19 N | 12.17 E |
| Buchelay | **261** | 48.59 N | 1.40 E |
| Büchen, Dtsch. | **52** | 53.29 N | 10.36 E |
| Buchen, Dtsch. | **56** | 49.32 N | 9.17 E |
| Buchenberg | **58** | 47.42 N | 10.14 E |
| Büchenbeuren | **56** | 49.55 N | 7.16 E |
| Buchenwald-Denkmal ⊥ | **54** | 51.01 N | 11.15 E |
| Buchholz, Dtsch. | **54** | 52.10 N | 12.55 E |
| Buchholz, Dtsch. | **56** | 50.41 N | 7.23 E |
| Buchholz, Dtsch. | **263** | 51.23 N | 7.15 E |
| Buchholz, Dtsch. | **264a** | 52.35 N | 13.47 E |
| Buchholz ●[8], Dtsch. | **263** | 51.23 N | 6.46 E |
| Buchholz ●[8], Dtsch. | **264a** | 52.36 N | 13.26 E |
| Buchholz in der Nordheide | **52** | 53.20 N | 9.52 E |
| Büchlberg | **60** | 48.40 N | 13.30 E |
| Buchloe | **58** | 48.02 N | 10.44 E |
| Buchmany | **78** | 51.04 N | 28.04 E |
| Bucholt | **263** | 51.39 N | 6.43 E |
| Buchon, Point ≻ | **226** | 35.15 N | 120.54 W |
| Buchow-Karpzow | **264a** | 52.31 N | 12.57 E |
| Buchs, Schw. | **58** | 47.23 N | 8.04 E |
| Buchs, Schw. | **58** | 47.10 N | 9.28 E |
| Buchtarminskoje vodochranilišče ⊜[1] | **86** | 49.15 N | 84.20 E |
| Buchufontein | **158** | 30.18 S | 19.36 E |
| Buchy | **50** | 49.35 N | 1.22 E |
| Bučina | **60** | 48.58 N | 13.36 E |
| Bucine | **66** | 43.29 N | 11.37 E |
| Buck, Lake ⊜ | **162** | 19.38 S | 130.21 E |
| Buckatunna | **194** | 31.32 N | 88.31 W |
| Buckatunna Creek ≃ | **194** | 31.30 N | 88.32 W |
| Buck Branch ≃ | **284b** | 39.01 N | 77.10 W |
| Buck Creek | **216** | 40.29 N | 86.46 W |
| Buck Creek ≃, U.S. | **196** | 34.35 N | 99.58 W |
| Buck Creek ≃, In., U.S. | **218** | 39.37 N | 85.56 W |
| Buck Creek ≃, In., U.S. | **218** | 40.11 N | 85.30 W |
| Buck Creek ≃, Ky., U.S. | **192** | 36.59 N | 84.29 W |
| Buck Creek ≃, Oh., U.S. | **218** | 39.56 N | 83.51 W |
| Buck Creek ≃, Pa., U.S. | **285** | 40.15 N | 74.50 W |
| Buckden, Eng., U.K. | **42** | 52.17 N | 0.16 W |
| Buckden, Eng., U.K. | **44** | 54.12 N | 2.05 W |
| Bückeburg | **52** | 52.16 N | 9.02 E |
| Bücken | **52** | 52.46 N | 9.07 E |
| Buckeye | **200** | 33.22 N | 112.34 W |
| Buckeye Creek ≃ | **226** | 38.54 N | 121.55 W |
| Buckeye Lake | **188** | 39.56 N | 82.28 W |
| Buckeystown | **208** | 39.20 N | 77.25 W |
| Buckfastleigh | **42** | 50.29 N | 3.46 W |
| Buckhannon | **188** | 38.59 N | 80.13 W |
| Buckhaven | **46** | 56.11 N | 3.03 W |
| Buck Hill Falls | **210** | 41.11 N | 75.15 W |
| Buck Hollow ≃ | **224** | 45.10 N | 120.50 W |
| Buckholts | **222** | 30.52 N | 97.08 W |
| Buckhorn ≃ | **180** | 66.13 N | 161.10 W |
| Buckhorn Draw V | **196** | 30.39 N | 100.52 W |
| Buckhorn Island State Park ♦ | **284a** | 43.03 N | 78.59 W |
| Buckhorn Lake ⊜, On., Can. | **212** | 44.28 N | 78.23 W |
| Buckhorn Lake ⊜, Ca., U.S. | **228** | 34.50 N | 117.59 W |
| Buckie | **46** | 57.40 N | 2.58 W |
| Buckingham, Austl. | **168a** | 33.24 S | 116.19 E |
| Buckingham, P.Q., Can. | **188** | 45.35 N | 75.25 W |
| Buckingham, Eng., U.K. | **42** | 52.00 N | 1.00 W |
| Buckingham, Pa., U.S. | **208** | 40.18 N | 75.01 W |
| Buckingham, Va., U.S. | **192** | 37.32 N | 78.37 W |
| Buckingham Bay c | **164** | 12.10 S | 135.46 E |
| Buckingham Palace ʊ | **260** | 51.30 N | 0.08 W |
| Buckinghamshire □[6] | **42** | 51.45 N | 0.48 W |
| Buck Island I | **241n** | 17.48 N | 64.37 W |
| Buck Island Reef National Monument ♦ | **241n** | 17.48 N | 64.37 W |
| Buck Lake ⊜, Ab., Can. | **182** | 53.00 N | 114.45 W |
| Buck Lake ⊜, On., Can. | **212** | 45.25 N | 79.24 W |
| Buckland, Austl. | **166** | 42.37 S | 147.43 E |
| Buckland, Eng., U.K. | **260** | 51.15 N | 0.15 W |
| Buckland, Ak., U.S. | **180** | 65.59 N | 161.07 W |
| Buckland, Ma., U.S. | **207** | 42.35 N | 72.47 W |
| Buckland, Oh., U.S. | **216** | 40.37 N | 84.16 W |
| Buckland Brewer | **42** | 50.57 N | 4.14 W |
| Buckland Common | **260** | 51.45 N | 0.39 W |
| Bucklands | **158** | 29.03 S | 23.44 E |
| Buckleboo | **166** | 32.55 S | 136.12 E |
| Buckley, Wales, U.K. | **44** | 53.09 N | 3.04 W |
| Buckley, Il., U.S. | **216** | 40.36 N | 88.02 W |
| Buckley, Wa., U.S. | **224** | 47.09 N | 122.01 W |
| Buckley ≃ | **166** | 20.22 S | 137.57 E |
| Buckley Bay c | **9** | 68.16 S | 148.12 E |
| Bucklin, Ks., U.S. | **198** | 37.32 N | 99.38 W |
| Bucklin, Mo., U.S. | **194** | 39.46 N | 92.53 W |
| Buck Lodge | **284c** | 39.01 N | 76.58 W |
| Buck Mountain ʌ, Va., U.S. | **192** | 36.40 N | 81.15 W |
| Buck Mountain ʌ, Wa., U.S. | **202** | 48.26 N | 119.50 W |
| Bucknell Heights | **284c** | 38.46 N | 77.04 W |
| Bucknell Manor | **208** | 38.46 N | 77.04 W |
| Buckner | **218** | 38.23 N | 85.26 W |
| Buckner Creek ≃ | **198** | 38.11 N | 99.34 W |
| Buckner Mountain ʌ | **224** | 48.30 N | 121.00 W |
| Buckners Creek ≃ | **222** | 29.53 N | 96.53 W |
| Buckow | **54** | 52.34 N | 14.04 E |
| Buckow ●[8] | **264a** | 52.25 N | 13.26 E |
| Bucks □[6] | **208** | 40.19 N | 75.08 W |
| Bucksburn | **46** | 57.12 N | 2.18 W |
| Buckshot Lake ⊜ | **212** | 45.00 N | 77.04 W |
| Buckskin Creek ≃ | **218** | 39.14 N | 83.17 W |
| Buckskin Gulch V | **200** | 37.01 N | 111.52 W |
| Bucks Knob ʌ | **224** | 46.41 N | 123.20 W |
| Bucksport | **188** | 44.34 N | 68.47 W |
| Bucktown | **285** | 40.10 N | 75.43 W |
| Bückwitz | **54** | 52.52 N | 12.29 E |
| Buc-Louis-Blériot, Aérodrome de ⊠ | **261** | 48.45 N | 2.05 E |
| Bucoda | **224** | 46.47 N | 122.52 W |
| Bucovăț | **38** | 47.13 N | 28.27 E |
| Buco Zau | **152** | 4.46 S | 12.33 E |
| Bucquoy | **50** | 50.08 N | 2.42 E |
| Buctouche | **186** | 46.28 N | 64.43 W |
| Bucun | **98** | 36.37 N | 117.27 E |
| București (Bucharest) | **38** | 44.26 N | 26.06 E |
| București □[7] | **38** | 44.30 N | 26.15 E |
| Bucutua Island I | **116** | 6.09 N | 121.49 E |
| Bucy-lès-Pierrepont | **50** | 49.39 N | 3.54 E |
| Bucyrus | **214** | 40.48 N | 82.58 W |
| Bud | **26** | 62.55 N | 6.55 E |
| Buda, Il., U.S. | **190** | 41.19 N | 89.40 W |
| Buda, Tx., U.S. | **196** | 30.05 N | 97.51 W |
| Buda ●[8] | **264c** | 47.30 N | 19.02 E |
| Buda Castle ⊥ | **264c** | 47.30 N | 19.02 E |
| Budafok ●[8] | **264c** | 47.26 N | 19.02 E |
| Budagovo | **88** | 54.38 N | 100.08 E |
| Budai-hegység ⋏ | **264c** | 47.31 N | 18.58 E |
| Budakalász | **264c** | 47.37 N | 19.03 E |
| Buda-Kašalëva | **76** | 52.43 N | 30.34 E |
| Budakeszi | **264c** | 47.31 N | 18.56 E |
| Budalin | **110** | 22.22 N | 95.08 E |
| Budaörs | **264c** | 47.27 N | 18.58 E |
| Budapest, Magy. | **30** | 47.30 N | 19.05 E |
| Budapest, Magy. | **264c** | 47.30 N | 19.05 E |
| Budapest □[7] | **264c** | 47.30 N | 19.05 E |
| Búđardalur | **24a** | 65.10 N | 21.42 W |
| Budarin | **80** | 47.54 N | 42.36 E |
| Budarino | **80** | 50.31 N | 51.04 E |
| Budatétény ●[8] | **264c** | 47.25 N | 19.01 E |
| Budaun | **124** | 28.03 N | 79.07 E |
| Budawang National Park ♦ | **170** | 35.26 S | 150.02 E |
| Budawang Range ⋏ | **170** | 35.20 S | 150.03 E |
| Budayuan | **98** | 40.56 N | 125.19 E |
| Budberg | **263** | 51.32 N | 6.38 E |
| Budbud | **144** | 4.11 N | 46.28 E |
| Budd Coast ±[2] | **9** | 66.30 S | 113.00 E |
| Büddenstedt | **54** | 52.11 N | 11.02 E |
| Buddh Gaya → Bodh Gaya | **124** | 24.42 N | 84.59 E |
| Budd Inlet c | **224** | 47.06 N | 122.54 W |
| Budd Lake | **210** | 40.52 N | 74.44 W |
| Buddtown | **285** | 39.56 N | 74.42 W |
| Buddu | **140** | 11.54 N | 24.08 E |
| Buddusò | **71** | 40.35 N | 9.15 E |
| Bude, Eng., U.K. | **42** | 50.50 N | 4.33 W |
| Bude, Ms., U.S. | **194** | 31.27 N | 90.51 W |
| Bude Bay c | **42** | 50.50 N | 4.37 W |
| Budel | **52** | 51.17 N | 5.35 E |
| Budelli, Isola I | **71** | 41.17 N | 9.21 E |
| Büdelsdorf | **41** | 54.18 N | 9.40 E |
| Büderich | **52** | 51.37 N | 6.34 E |
| Budești | **38** | 44.14 N | 26.28 E |
| Budge Budge | **126** | 22.27 N | 88.10 E |
| Budhāthum | **124** | 28.04 N | 84.50 E |
| Budhhāta | **126** | 22.36 N | 89.10 E |
| Budhī Gaṇḍakī ≃ | **124** | 27.48 N | 84.45 E |
| Budhlāda | **123** | 29.56 N | 75.34 E |
| Budi | **152** | 3.04 S | 23.56 E |
| Büdingen | **56** | 50.17 N | 9.07 E |
| Búđir | **24a** | 64.56 N | 13.58 W |
| Budišov nad Budišovkou | **30** | 49.47 N | 17.38 E |
| Budjala | **152** | 2.39 N | 19.42 E |
| Budkov | **61** | 49.03 N | 15.39 E |
| Budleigh Salterton | **42** | 50.38 N | 3.20 W |
| Budogošč' | **76** | 59.17 N | 32.27 E |
| Budogoviščі | **76** | 53.36 N | 36.18 E |
| Budoni | **71** | 40.43 N | 9.42 E |
| Bud'onnovka | **80** | 50.52 N | 52.48 E |
| Bud'onnovsk | **84** | 44.46 N | 44.09 E |
| Bud'onnovskaja | **80** | 46.56 N | 41.33 E |
| Bud'onnyj, Kyrg. | **85** | 42.30 N | 72.35 E |
| Bud'onnyj, Ross. | **83** | 47.27 N | 39.46 E |
| Budrio | **64** | 44.32 N | 11.32 E |
| Budslau | **76** | 54.47 N | 27.27 E |
| Budweis → České Budějovice | **30** | 48.59 N | 14.28 E |
| Budworth Mere ⊜ | **262** | 53.17 N | 2.31 W |
| Budy | **78** | 49.53 N | 36.02 E |
| Budy ka | **78** | 50.30 N | 34.26 E |
| Budyně nad Ohří | **54** | 50.22 N | 14.09 E |
| Budzhak ⋏[1] | **78** | 46.10 N | 29.00 E |
| Buea | **152** | 4.09 N | 9.14 E |
| Buëch ≃ | **62** | 44.12 N | 5.57 E |
| Buechel | **218** | 38.11 N | 85.39 W |
| Buehl Airport ⊠ | **285** | 40.11 N | 74.54 W |
| Buell | **50** | 48.56 N | 1.27 E |
| Buela | **152** | 5.55 S | 14.33 E |
| Buell | **219** | 39.02 N | 91.27 W |
| Bue Marino, Grotta del ±[5] | **71** | 40.15 N | 9.38 E |
| Buena | **208** | 39.30 N | 74.55 W |
| Buena Esperanza | **252** | 34.45 S | 65.15 W |
| Buena Esperanza, Cabo de → Good Hope, Cape of ≻ | **158** | 34.24 S | 18.30 E |
| Buena Park, Ca., U.S. | **228** | 33.52 N | 117.59 W |
| Buena Park, Wi., U.S. | **216** | 42.48 N | 88.14 W |
| Buenaventura, Col. | **246** | 3.53 N | 77.04 W |
| Buenaventura, Méx. | **232** | 29.51 N | 107.29 W |
| Buena Vista, Bol. | **248** | 17.27 S | 63.40 W |
| Buena Vista, Méx. | **204** | 32.32 N | 116.44 W |
| Buenavista, Méx. | **234** | 22.36 N | 100.09 W |
| Buena Vista, Para. | **252** | 26.08 S | 56.03 W |
| Buenavista, Pil. | **116** | 8.59 N | 125.24 E |
| Buenavista, Pil. | **116** | 13.15 N | 121.57 E |
| Buenavista, Pil. | **116** | 10.04 N | 118.49 E |
| Buenavista, Pil. | **116** | 7.15 N | 122.16 E |
| Buena Vista, Co., U.S. | **200** | 38.50 N | 106.07 W |
| Buena Vista, Fl., U.S. | **220** | 28.11 N | 82.44 W |
| Buena Vista, Ga., U.S. | **192** | 32.19 N | 84.31 W |
| Buena Vista, Md., U.S. | **284c** | 38.57 N | 76.50 W |
| Buena Vista, Ms., U.S. | **194** | 33.53 N | 88.50 W |
| Buena Vista, Pa., U.S. | **279b** | 40.17 N | 79.48 W |
| Buena Vista, Va., U.S. | **192** | 37.44 N | 79.21 W |
| Buena Vista, Bahía de c | **240p** | 22.30 N | 79.08 W |
| Buena Vista Canal ≊ | **228** | 35.21 N | 119.06 W |
| Buenavista de Cuéllar | **234** | 18.27 N | 99.25 W |
| Buena Vista Lake Bed ⊜ | **204** | 35.11 N | 119.17 W |
| Buenavista Tomatlán | **234** | 19.12 N | 102.36 W |
| Buen Día | **196** | 26.21 N | 104.32 W |
| Buendia, Embalse de ⊜[1] | **34** | 40.25 N | 2.43 W |
| Buenga ≃ | **152** | 6.07 S | 15.58 E |
| Bueno ≃ | **254** | 40.13 S | 73.43 W |
| Bueno Brandão | **256** | 22.27 S | 46.21 W |
| Buenópolis | **255** | 17.54 S | 44.11 W |
| Buenos Aires, Arg. | **258** | 34.36 S | 58.27 W |
| Buenos Aires, Arg. | **288** | 34.36 S | 58.27 W |
| Buenos Aires, Col. | **246** | 3.02 N | 76.38 W |
| Buenos Aires, C.R. | **236** | 9.10 N | 83.20 W |
| Buenos Aires □[4] | **252** | 36.00 S | 60.00 W |
| Buenos Aires, Lago (Lago General Carrera) ⊜ | **254** | 46.35 S | 72.00 W |
| Buen Pasto | **254** | 45.05 S | 69.28 W |
| Buer ●[8] | **263** | 51.36 N | 7.03 E |
| Buerarema | **255** | 14.57 S | 39.19 W |
| Buerāt, Bi'r ⊤[4] | **142** | 28.59 N | 32.10 E |
| Buertuokai | **85** | 39.35 N | 74.58 E |
| Buesaco | **246** | 1.23 N | 77.09 W |
| Buescher State Park ♦ | **222** | 30.02 N | 97.09 W |
| Buet, Le ʌ | **58** | 46.02 N | 6.52 E |
| Buey ≃ | **240p** | 20.28 N | 77.05 W |
| Bufalotta, Fosso della ≃ | **267a** | 41.59 N | 12.30 E |
| Buffalo, Il., U.S. | **219** | 39.51 N | 89.25 W |
| Buffalo, In., U.S. | **216** | 40.53 N | 86.45 W |
| Buffalo, Ks., U.S. | **198** | 37.42 N | 95.41 W |
| Buffalo, Mn., U.S. | **190** | 45.10 N | 93.52 W |
| Buffalo, Mo., U.S. | **194** | 37.38 N | 93.05 W |
| Buffalo, N.Y., U.S. | **210** | 42.53 N | 78.52 W |
| Buffalo, N.Y., U.S. | **284a** | 42.53 N | 78.52 W |
| Buffalo, Oh., U.S. | **188** | 39.54 N | 81.31 W |
| Buffalo, Ok., U.S. | **196** | 36.50 N | 99.37 W |
| Buffalo, S.C., U.S. | **192** | 34.43 N | 81.41 W |
| Buffalo, S.D., U.S. | **198** | 45.35 N | 103.32 W |
| Buffalo, Tx., U.S. | **222** | 31.28 N | 96.04 W |
| Buffalo, Wy., U.S. | **202** | 44.20 N | 106.41 W |
| Buffalo ≃, Can. | **176** | 60.55 N | 115.00 W |
| Buffalo ≃, S. Afr. | **158** | 28.43 S | 30.37 E |
| Buffalo ≃, Ar., U.S. | **194** | 36.10 N | 92.26 W |
| Buffalo ≃, Mn., U.S. | **198** | 47.06 N | 96.49 W |
| Buffalo ≃, Ms., U.S. | **194** | 31.04 N | 91.34 W |
| Buffalo ≃, N.Y., U.S. | **284a** | 42.53 N | 78.53 W |
| Buffalo ≃, Tn., U.S. | **194** | 36.00 N | 87.50 W |
| Buffalo ≃, Wi., U.S. | **190** | 44.22 N | 91.55 W |
| Buffalo, State University College at ʊ[2] | **284a** | 42.56 N | 78.53 W |
| Buffalo Airpark ⊠ | **284a** | 42.52 N | 78.43 W |
| Buffalo Bayou ≃ | **222** | 29.46 N | 95.05 W |
| Buffalo Bill Ranch State Historical Park ♦ | **198** | 41.10 N | 100.48 W |
| Buffalo Bill Reservoir ⊜[1] | **202** | 44.29 N | 109.13 W |
| Buffalo Bill State Park ♦ | **202** | 44.30 N | 109.14 W |
| Buffalo Center | **190** | 43.23 N | 93.56 W |
| Buffalo Coast Guard Base ■ | **284a** | 42.52 N | 78.54 W |
| Buffalo Creek ≃, U.S. | **198** | 45.57 N | 102.56 W |
| Buffalo Creek ≃, U.S. | **214** | 40.16 N | 80.37 W |
| Buffalo Creek ≃, Il., U.S. | **278** | 42.08 N | 87.55 W |
| Buffalo Creek ≃, Ia., U.S. | **190** | 42.06 N | 91.18 W |
| Buffalo Creek ≃, Ks., U.S. | **198** | 39.35 N | 97.43 W |
| Buffalo Creek ≃, Ky., U.S. | **218** | 38.28 N | 83.03 W |
| Buffalo Creek ≃, Mn., U.S. | **198** | 44.51 N | 94.00 W |
| Buffalo Creek ≃, N.Y., U.S. | **210** | 42.52 N | 78.47 W |
| Buffalo Creek ≃, Ok., U.S. | **196** | 36.47 N | 99.15 W |
| Buffalo Creek ≃, Pa., U.S. | **208** | 40.29 N | 77.08 W |
| Buffalo Creek ≃, Pa., U.S. | **210** | 40.58 N | 76.53 W |
| Buffalo Creek ≃, Pa., U.S. | **214** | 40.40 N | 79.41 W |
| Buffalo Grove | **216** | 42.09 N | 87.57 W |
| Buffalo Harbor c | **284a** | 42.51 N | 78.52 W |
| Buffalo Lake | **198** | 44.44 N | 94.37 W |
| Buffalo Lake ⊜, Ab., Can. | **182** | 52.27 N | 112.54 W |
| Buffalo Lake ⊜, N.T., Can. | **176** | 60.10 N | 115.30 W |
| Buffalo Lake ⊜[1] | **196** | 34.54 N | 102.07 W |
| Buffalo Museum of Science ʊ | **284a** | 42.54 N | 78.51 W |
| Buffalo Narrows | **184** | 55.51 N | 108.30 W |
| Buffalo National River ♦ | **194** | 35.58 N | 92.53 W |
| Buffalo Pound Lake ⊜ | **184** | 50.39 N | 105.30 W |
| Buffalo Pound Provincial Park ♦ | **184** | 50.36 N | 105.30 W |
| Buffalo Run ≃ | **279b** | 40.12 N | 79.37 W |
| Buffalo Zoo ♦ | **284a** | 42.56 N | 78.51 W |
| Buffels ≃, S. Afr. | **156** | 29.41 S | 17.03 E |
| Buffels ≃, S. Afr. | **158** | 33.45 S | 21.11 E |
| Buffington Harbor c | **278** | 41.38 N | 87.25 W |
| Buffum, Lake ⊜ | **220** | 27.48 N | 81.40 W |
| Buford, Ga., U.S. | **192** | 34.07 N | 84.00 W |
| Buford, Oh., U.S. | **218** | 39.04 N | 83.50 W |
| Buford Dam ●[6] | **192** | 34.11 N | 84.03 W |
| Buftea | **38** | 44.34 N | 25.57 E |
| Bug ≃ | **22** | 52.31 N | 21.05 E |
| Buga, Col. | **246** | 3.54 N | 76.17 W |
| Buga, Nig. | **150** | 8.30 N | 7.21 E |
| Bugajevka | **83** | 49.39 N | 39.42 E |
| Bugalagrande | **246** | 4.11 N | 76.09 W |
| Bugala Island I | **154** | 0.40 S | 32.20 E |
| Bugallon | **116** | 15.57 N | 120.13 E |
| Buganga | **154** | 0.03 S | 31.59 E |
| Bugasong | **116** | 11.03 N | 122.04 E |
| Bugat, Mong. | **86** | 48.59 N | 90.10 E |
| Bugat, Mong. | **88** | 47.55 N | 101.16 E |
| Bugbrooke | **42** | 52.12 N | 1.01 W |
| Bug Catooti | **144** | 10.44 N | 50.35 E |
| Buğdaylı | **130** | 40.13 N | 27.46 E |
| Bugeat | **32** | 45.35 N | 1.59 E |
| Bugel, Ujung ≻ | **115a** | 6.26 S | 111.03 E |
| Bugene | **154** | 1.35 S | 31.08 E |
| Bugey ●[1] | **58** | 45.55 N | 5.30 E |
| Buggenhout | **50** | 51.01 N | 4.12 E |
| Buggerru | **71** | 39.24 N | 8.24 E |
| Bugio I | **266c** | 38.39 N | 9.18 W |
| Bugiri | **154** | 0.34 N | 33.45 E |
| Bugle | **42** | 50.24 N | 4.47 W |
| Bug Méridional → Pivdennyy Buh ≃ | **78** | 46.59 N | 31.58 E |
| Bugojno | **36** | 44.03 N | 17.27 E |
| Bugøynes | **24** | 69.58 N | 29.39 E |
| Bugrino | **24** | 68.48 N | 49.09 E |
| Bugry, Ross. | **76** | 58.46 N | 35.15 E |
| Bugry, Ross. | **265a** | 60.04 N | 30.24 E |
| Bugsanga ≃ | **116** | 12.26 N | 120.59 E |
| Bugsuk Island I | **116** | 8.15 N | 117.18 E |
| Bugt, Zhg. | **89** | 48.46 N | 121.57 E |
| Bugt, Zhg. | **98** | 42.20 N | 120.43 E |
| Buguba | **164** | 3.41 S | 137.30 E |
| Buguey | **116** | 18.17 N | 121.50 E |
| Bugui Point ≻ | **116** | 12.36 N | 123.14 E |
| Bugul'dejka | **88** | 52.33 N | 106.05 E |
| Bugul'ma | **80** | 54.33 N | 52.48 E |
| Bugul'minsko-Belebejevskaja vozvyšennost' ⋏[1] | **80** | 54.54 N | 52.42 E |
| Bugun' ≃ | **85** | 42.58 N | 68.35 E |
| Bugun'skoje vodochranilišče ⊜[1] | **85** | 42.45 N | 69.05 E |
| Buguruslan | **80** | 53.39 N | 52.26 E |
| Buh ≃ | **102** | 36.58 N | 99.48 E |
| Buhanhua | **104** | 42.39 N | 122.46 E |
| Bū Ḥashīshah, Thamad ⊤[4] | **146** | 26.23 N | 18.47 E |
| Buhayivka | **83** | 49.28 N | 37.23 E |
| Buḥayrah, Rayyāḥ al- ≊ | **142** | 30.43 N | 30.45 E |
| Buḥaythān, Jabal al- ʌ | **132** | 30.55 N | 35.53 E |
| Buhera | **154** | 19.18 S | 31.29 E |
| Buhi | **116** | 13.26 N | 123.31 E |
| Buhi, Lake ⊜ | **116** | 13.26 N | 123.31 E |
| Bühl, Dtsch. | **56** | 48.42 N | 8.08 E |
| Buhl, Fr. | **58** | 47.56 N | 7.11 E |
| Buhl, Id., U.S. | **202** | 42.35 N | 114.45 W |
| Buhl, Mn., U.S. | **190** | 47.29 N | 92.46 W |
| Buhler | **198** | 38.08 N | 97.46 W |
| Bühler ≃ | **56** | 49.10 N | 9.47 E |
| Bühlertal | **56** | 48.41 N | 8.10 E |
| Buhuai | **120** | 33.22 N | 80.36 E |
| Buhuși | **38** | 46.43 N | 26.41 E |
| Bui Dam ●[6] | **150** | 8.22 N | 2.10 W |
| Buie, Loch c | **46** | 56.20 N | 5.52 W |
| Buile Hill Park ♦ | **262** | 53.29 N | 2.18 W |
| Builth Wells | **42** | 52.09 N | 3.24 W |
| Buin, Chile | **252** | 33.44 S | 70.45 W |
| Buin, Pap. N. Gui. | **175e** | 6.50 S | 155.44 E |
| Buin, Piz ʌ | **58** | 46.50 N | 10.08 E |
| Buinen | **52** | 52.55 N | 6.50 E |
| Buinsk, Ross. | **80** | 55.12 N | 47.03 E |
| Buinsk, Ross. | **80** | 54.57 N | 48.17 E |
| Buíque | **250** | 8.37 S | 37.09 W |
| Buis-les-Baronnies | **62** | 44.16 N | 5.16 E |
| Buitenpost | **52** | 53.15 N | 6.09 E |
| Buj | **80** | 58.30 N | 41.30 E |
| Buj ≃ | **80** | 56.13 N | 54.12 E |
| Bujaki | **24** | 59.03 N | 48.40 E |
| Bujalance | **34** | 37.54 N | 4.22 W |
| Bujant, Mong. | **86** | 48.33 N | 89.34 E |
| Bujant, Mong. | **86** | 48.10 N | 91.55 E |
| Bujant ≃ | **88** | 47.08 N | 97.38 E |
| Bujant-Ovoo | **102** | 44.58 N | 107.05 E |
| Bujaraloz | **34** | 41.30 N | 0.09 W |
| Buje | **36** | 45.24 N | 13.40 E |
| Buji | **102** | 33.58 N | 95.22 E |
| Bujnaksk | **84** | 42.49 N | 47.07 E |
| Bujnavičy | **78** | 51.52 N | 28.33 E |
| Bujr nuur ⊜ | **88** | 47.48 N | 117.42 E |
| Bujukly | **89** | 49.30 N | 142.47 E |
| Bujumbura | **154** | 3.23 S | 29.22 E |
| Bük, Magy. | **61** | 47.23 N | 16.45 E |
| Buk, Pol. | **30** | 52.22 N | 16.31 E |
| Buka | **85** | 40.48 N | 69.11 E |
| Bukačača | **88** | 52.59 N | 116.55 E |
| Bukachivtsi | **78** | 49.15 N | 24.29 E |
| Buka Island I | **175e** | 5.15 S | 154.35 E |
| Bukama | **154** | 9.12 S | 25.51 E |
| Būkān, Īrān | **128** | 36.31 N | 46.12 E |
| Bukan', Ross. | **76** | 53.55 N | 34.42 E |
| Bukanovskaja | **80** | 49.42 N | 42.18 E |
| Buka Passage ⋃ | **175e** | 5.25 S | 154.41 E |
| Bukarest → București | **38** | 44.26 N | 26.06 E |
| Bukarevo | **82** | 55.57 N | 36.44 E |
| Bukavu | **154** | 2.30 S | 28.52 E |
| Bukene | **154** | 4.14 S | 32.53 E |
| Bukhara → Buchara | **128** | 39.48 N | 64.25 E |
| Bukhayt, Bi'r ⊤[4] | **142** | 29.13 N | 32.17 E |
| Bukide, Pulau I | **112** | 3.47 N | 125.36 E |
| Bukidnon □[4] | **116** | 8.00 N | 125.00 E |
| Bukima | **154** | 1.48 S | 33.25 E |
| Bukit Baharu | **114** | 2.13 N | 102.16 E |
| Bukitbatu | **114** | 1.27 N | 102.00 E |
| Bukit Betong | **114** | 4.15 N | 101.56 E |
| Bukit Fraser | **114** | 3.43 N | 101.45 E |
| Bukit Kachi | **114** | 6.24 N | 100.32 E |
| Bukit Mandai | **271c** | 1.25 N | 103.45 E |
| Bukit Mertajam | **114** | 5.22 N | 100.28 E |
| Bukit Panjang | **271c** | 1.23 N | 103.46 E |
| Bukit Serok | **114** | 2.55 N | 102.50 E |
| Bukit Timah | **271c** | 1.20 N | 103.47 E |
| Bukit Timah Race Course ♦ | **271c** | 1.20 N | 103.48 E |
| Bukittinggi | **112** | 0.19 S | 100.22 E |
| Bükk ⋏ | **30** | 48.05 N | 20.30 E |
| Bukoba | **154** | 1.20 S | 31.49 E |
| Bukombe | **154** | 3.31 S | 32.03 E |
| Bukovica ●[1] | **36** | 44.10 N | 15.40 E |
| Bukovina □[9] | **78** | 48.00 N | 25.30 E |
| Bukrino | **82** | 54.48 N | 36.14 E |
| Bukuka | **88** | 51.11 N | 116.39 E |
| Bukukun | **88** | 49.27 N | 111.08 E |
| Bukum, Pulau I | **271c** | 1.14 N | 103.47 E |
| Bukumbirwa | **154** | 0.46 S | 28.44 E |
| Bukum Kechil, Pulau I | **271c** | 1.14 N | 103.46 E |
| Bukunga | **154** | 7.41 S | 25.56 E |
| Bukuru | **150** | 9.48 N | 8.51 E |
| Bukuya | **154** | 0.41 N | 31.50 E |
| Bula | **164** | 3.06 S | 130.30 E |
| Bula ≃ | **80** | 55.12 N | 48.23 E |
| Bula Atumba | **152** | 8.40 S | 14.48 E |
| Bulacan □[4] | **116** | 15.00 N | 121.05 E |
| Bulacaue Point ≻ | **116** | 11.36 N | 123.09 E |
| Bülach | **58** | 47.31 N | 8.32 E |
| Bulajevo | **86** | 54.54 N | 70.26 E |
| Bulak | **88** | 51.02 N | 115.21 E |
| Bulaka ≃ | **164** | 8.06 S | 139.12 E |
| Bulak Gölü ⊜ | **130** | 38.32 N | 32.55 E |
| Bulalacao | **116** | 12.20 N | 121.20 E |
| Bulalacao Island I | **116** | 11.45 N | 120.10 E |
| Bulalaqui Point ≻ | **116** | 11.17 N | 124.03 E |
| Bulan, Pil. | **116** | 6.44 N | 124.47 E |
| Bulan, Pil. | **116** | 12.40 N | 123.52 E |
| Bulan, Ky., U.S. | **192** | 37.18 N | 83.09 W |
| Bulanaš | **86** | 57.16 N | 62.00 E |
| Bulancak | **130** | 40.57 N | 38.14 E |
| Bulandshahr | **124** | 28.24 N | 77.51 E |
| Bulanicha | **86** | 52.48 N | 84.57 E |
| Bulanık | **130** | 39.05 N | 42.15 E |
| Bulan Island I | **116** | 6.08 N | 121.50 E |
| Bulanovo | **86** | 52.27 N | 55.10 E |
| Būlāq | **140** | 25.12 N | 30.32 E |
| Būlāq ●[8] | **273c** | 30.04 N | 31.14 E |
| Būlāq ad-Dakrūr | **273c** | 30.02 N | 31.11 E |
| Bulava | **89** | 51.55 N | 140.25 E |
| Bulawa, Gunung ʌ | **112** | 0.30 N | 123.34 E |
| Bulawayo | **154** | 20.09 S | 28.36 E |
| Bulbjerg ʌ[2] | **26** | 57.09 N | 9.02 E |
| Bulbul | **130** | 36.46 N | 36.49 E |
| Bulbul, Wādī V | **140** | 10.59 N | 24.33 E |
| Bulcherry Island I | **126** | 21.33 N | 88.31 E |
| Buldan | **130** | 38.03 N | 28.51 E |
| Buldāna | **122** | 20.32 N | 76.11 E |
| Buldern | **52** | 51.52 N | 7.22 E |
| Buldibuyo | **248** | 8.07 S | 77.22 W |
| Buldir Island I | **181a** | 52.21 N | 175.54 E |
| Buldon | **116** | 7.33 N | 124.25 E |
| Buldurta | **80** | 50.05 N | 53.11 E |
| Buldyrty ≃ | **80** | 49.48 N | 52.34 E |
| Bulembu | **158** | 25.56 S | 31.06 E |
| Bulga | **170** | 32.39 S | 151.01 E |
| Bulgakovo | **76** | 55.14 N | 32.08 E |
| Bulgan, Mong. | **86** | 46.53 N | 91.05 E |
| Bulgan, Mong. | **88** | 48.45 N | 103.34 E |
| Bulgan, Mong. | **102** | 44.05 N | 103.32 E |
| Bulgan □[4] | **88** | 49.00 N | 103.30 E |
| Bulgar | **80** | 54.57 N | 49.05 E |
| Bulgaria (Bălgarija) □[1], Europe | **22** | 43.00 N | 25.00 E |
| Bulgaria (Bălgarija) □[1], Europe | **38** | 43.00 N | 25.00 E |
| Bulgarie → Bulgaria □[1] | **38** | 43.00 N | 25.00 E |
| Bulgarien → Bulgaria □[1] | **38** | 43.00 N | 25.00 E |
| Bulger | **214** | 40.23 N | 80.20 W |
| Bulgnéville | **58** | 48.13 N | 5.50 E |
| Bulgroo | **166** | 25.48 S | 143.59 E |
| Bulhale | **144** | 5.20 N | 46.29 E |
| Buliluyan | **116** | 8.20 N | 117.12 E |
| Buliluyan, Cape ≻ | **116** | 8.20 N | 117.11 E |
| Bulim | **271c** | 1.22 N | 103.43 E |
| Bulimba | **171a** | 27.25 S | 153.04 E |
| Bulki | **144** | 6.10 N | 36.40 E |
| Bulkington | **42** | 52.29 N | 1.25 W |
| Bulkley ≃ | **182** | 55.13 N | 127.40 W |
| Bulkley Ranges ⋏ | **182** | 54.30 N | 127.30 W |
| Bull ≃ | **182** | 49.28 N | 115.26 W |
| Bullabulling | **162** | 31.01 S | 120.32 E |
| Bullaque ≃ | **34** | 38.59 N | 4.17 W |
| Bullara | **162** | 22.40 S | 114.03 E |
| Bullard | **222** | 32.08 N | 95.19 W |
| Bulla Regia ⊥ | **36** | 36.34 N | 8.46 E |
| Bullas | **34** | 38.03 N | 1.40 W |
| Bullaxaar | **144** | 10.23 N | 44.25 E |
| Bullay | **56** | 50.03 N | 7.08 E |
| Bull Creek ≃, Nv., U.S. | **204** | 38.43 N | 115.34 W |
| Bull Creek ≃, N.Y., U.S. | **284a** | 43.03 N | 78.50 W |
| Bull Creek ≃, Oh., U.S. | **214** | 40.42 N | 80.32 W |
| Bull Creek ≃, S.D., U.S. | **198** | 43.41 N | 99.28 W |
| Bull Creek ≃, S.D., U.S. | **198** | 45.40 N | 103.18 W |
| Bull Creek ≃, Tx., U.S. | **196** | 32.36 N | 101.10 W |
| Bulldog | **164** | 7.45 S | 146.25 E |
| Bulle | **58** | 46.37 N | 7.04 E |
| Buller ≃ | **172** | 41.44 S | 171.35 E |
| Buller, Mount ʌ | **169** | 37.09 S | 146.26 E |
| Bullfinch | **162** | 30.59 S | 119.06 E |
| Bullfrog Creek ≃ | **200** | 37.19 N | 110.44 W |
| Bull Harbour | **182** | 50.54 N | 127.55 W |
| Bullhead | **198** | 45.45 N | 101.04 W |
| Bullhead City | **204** | 35.08 N | 114.34 W |
| Bull Hide Creek ≃ | **222** | 31.23 N | 97.01 W |
| Bull Hill ʌ[2] | **262** | 53.40 N | 2.21 W |
| Bulli | **170** | 34.20 S | 150.55 E |
| Bullicame ⊥ | **66** | 42.22 N | 12.04 E |
| Büllingen | **56** | 50.25 N | 6.16 E |
| Bullioh | **171b** | 36.12 S | 147.20 E |
| Bullion | **261** | 48.37 N | 2.00 E |
| Bull Lake ⊜[1] | **202** | 43.11 N | 109.07 W |
| Bull Lake Creek ≃ | **202** | 43.14 N | 109.02 W |
| Bull Mountain ʌ | **202** | 46.05 N | 112.04 W |
| Bullock | **192** | 36.30 N | 78.33 W |
| Bullock Creek | **166** | 17.43 S | 144.31 E |
| Bullock Creek ≃ | **166** | 21.40 S | 145.09 E |
| Bulloo ≃ | **166** | 28.43 S | 142.30 E |
| Bulloo Downs | **166** | 28.31 S | 142.57 E |
| Bulloo Lake ⊜ | **166** | 28.43 S | 142.25 E |
| Bulloo River Overflow ≚ | **166** | 28.50 S | 142.40 E |
| Bullpound Creek ≃ | **182** | 51.05 N | 111.58 W |
| Bull Run ≃, Or., U.S. | **224** | 45.26 N | 122.15 W |
| Bull Run ≃, Va., U.S. | **208** | 38.43 N | 77.23 W |
| Bull Run Lake ⊜ | **224** | 45.27 N | 121.50 W |
| Bull Run Reservoir Number 2 ⊜[1], Or., U.S. | **224** | 45.28 N | 122.10 W |
| Bull Run Reservoir Number 1 ⊜[1], Or., U.S. | **224** | 45.30 N | 122.04 W |
| Bullrun Rock ʌ | **202** | 44.21 N | 118.17 W |
| Bulls | **172** | 40.10 S | 175.23 E |
| Bulls Bay c | **192** | 32.59 N | 79.33 W |
| Bullsbrook | **168a** | 31.40 S | 116.01 E |
| Bulls Gap | **192** | 36.15 N | 83.05 W |
| Bull Shoals | **194** | 36.23 N | 92.34 W |
| Bull Shoals Lake ⊜[1] | **194** | 36.30 N | 92.50 W |
| Bullskin Creek ≃ | **218** | 38.10 N | 85.19 W |
| Bullville | **210** | 41.33 N | 74.22 W |


**Symbols** in the index entries represent the broad categories identified in the key at the right. Symbols with superior numbers (⋏[1]) identify subcategories (see complete key on page *I · 1).*

**Symbole** im Register stellen die rechts im Schlüssel erklärten Kategorien dar. Symbole mit hochgestellten Ziffern (⋏[1]) bezeichnen Unterabteilungen einer Kategorie (vgl. vollständiger Schlüssel auf Seite *I · 1).*

**Los símbolos** incluídos en el texto del índice representan las grandes categorías identificadas con la clave a la derecha. Los símbolos con numeros en su parte superior (⋏[1]) identifican las subcategorías (véase la clave completa en la página *I · 1).*

**Les symboles** de l'index représentent les catégories indiquées dans la légende à droite. Les symboles suivis d'un indice (⋏[1]) représentent des sous-catégories (voir légende complète à la page *I · 1).*

**Os símbolos** incluídos no texto do índice representam as grandes categorias identificadas com a chave à direita. Os símbolos com números em sua parte superior (⋏[1]) identificam as subcategorias (veja-se a chave completa à página *I · 1).*

| | | | | | |
| --- | --- | --- | --- | --- | --- |
| ʌ Mountain | Berg | Montaña | Montagne | Montanha |
| ⋏ Mountains | Gebirge | Montañas | Montagnes | Montanhas |
| )( Pass | Paß | Paso | Col | Passo |
| V Valley, Canyon | Tal, Cañon | Valle, Cañón | Vallée, Canyon | Vale, Canhão |
| ≚ Plain | Ebene | Llano | Plaine | Planície |
| ≻ Cape | Kap | Cabo | Cap | Cabo |
| I Island | Insel | Isla | Île | Ilha |
| II Islands | Inseln | Islas | Îles | Ilhas |
| ± Other Topographic Features | Andere Topographische Objekte | Otros Elementos Topográficos | Autres données topographiques | Outros acidentes topográficos |

ESPAÑOL

| Nombre | Página | Lat.°′ | Long.°′ W = Oeste |
|---|---|---|---|
| Bully Creek ≃ | 202 | 43.58 N | 117.15 W |
| Bully Hill | 214 | 41.22 N | 79.50 W |
| Bully-les-Mines | 50 | 50.26 N | 2.43 E |
| Bulmke-Hüllen ⊸[8] | 263 | 51.31 N | 7.06 E |
| Bulnaj nuruu ⋏ | 88 | 49.05 N | 98.30 E |
| Bulnes | 252 | 36.44 S | 72.18 W |
| Bulo Ghedudo | 144 | 2.52 N | 43.01 E |
| Bulolo | 164 | 7.10 S | 146.40 E |
| Bulpham | 260 | 51.33 N | 0.22 E |
| Bulpitt | 219 | 39.35 N | 89.26 W |
| Bulsār | 122 | 20.38 N | 72.56 E |
| Bulstrode ≃ | 206 | 46.02 N | 72.15 W |
| Bultei | 71 | 40.27 N | 9.03 E |
| Bultfontein | 158 | 28.20 S | 26.05 E |
| Buluan | 116 | 6.44 N | 124.47 E |
| Buluan ≃ | 116 | 6.47 N | 124.47 E |
| Buluan, Lake ⊜ | 116 | 6.40 N | 124.49 E |
| Buluduku | 114 | 2.20 N | 98.14 E |
| Bulugansk | 88 | 52.24 N | 110.23 E |
| Bulukumba | 112 | 5.33 S | 120.11 E |
| Bulukuto | 152 | 0.12 S | 21.42 E |
| Bululawang | 115a | 8.05 S | 112.38 E |
| Bulungu, Zaïre | 152 | 6.04 S | 21.54 E |
| Bulungu, Zaïre | 152 | 4.33 S | 18.36 E |
| Bulupayung | 114 | 1.38 N | 99.11 E |
| Bulusan | 116 | 12.45 N | 124.08 E |
| Bulusan Volcano ∧ | 116 | 12.46 N | 124.03 E |
| Bulwater | 158 | 32.29 S | 21.48 E |
| Bulwer | 158 | 29.46 S | 29.47 E |
| Bulyčevo | 82 | 55.06 N | 37.15 E |
| Bulyee | 162 | 32.22 S | 117.31 E |
| Bumba | 152 | 2.11 N | 22.28 E |
| Bumbah, Khalīj al- ⊂ | 146 | 32.20 N | 23.10 E |
| Bumbire Island I | 154 | 1.40 S | 31.53 E |
| Bumbles Green | 260 | 51.44 N | 0.02 E |
| Bumbo | 152 | 6.55 S | 19.16 E |
| Bumbu ≃ | 273b | 4.23 S | 15.18 E |
| Bumbulan | 112 | 0.29 N | 122.04 E |
| Bumbun, Pulau I | 112 | 4.27 N | 118.40 E |
| Bumbuna | 150 | 9.03 N | 11.44 W |
| Bumbunga Lake ⊜ | 168b | 33.54 S | 138.11 E |
| Bumiayu | 115a | 7.15 S | 109.00 E |
| Bumijawa | 115a | 7.10 S | 109.07 E |
| Bumkin Island I | 283 | 42.17 N | 70.54 W |
| Bumping ≃ | 224 | 46.59 N | 121.06 W |
| Bumping Lake ⊜ | 224 | 46.52 N | 121.19 W |
| Bumpus, Mount ∧[2] | 176 | 69.33 N | 112.40 W |
| Bumtang ≃ | 124 | 26.56 N | 90.51 E |
| Bumu Hu ⊜ | 120 | 31.15 N | 91.10 E |
| Buna, Kenya | 154 | 2.47 N | 39.31 E |
| Buna, Pap. N. Gui. | 164 | 8.40 S | 148.25 E |
| Buna, Tx., U.S. | 194 | 30.26 N | 93.58 W |
| Buna, Zaïre | 152 | 3.15 S | 18.59 E |
| Bunagāti | 126 | 23.19 N | 89.25 E |
| Bunai | 164 | 2.11 S | 147.14 E |
| Bunaj | 85 | 38.26 N | 71.32 E |
| Bun'atino | 82 | 56.24 N | 37.15 E |
| Bunavista | 196 | 35.39 N | 101.28 W |
| Bunawan | 116 | 8.12 N | 125.57 E |
| Bunazi | 154 | 1.13 S | 31.24 E |
| Bunbeg | 48 | 55.03 N | 8.18 W |
| Bunbury | 168a | 33.19 S | 115.38 E |
| Bunceton | 194 | 38.47 N | 92.47 W |
| Bunclody | 48 | 52.38 N | 6.40 W |
| Buncrana | 48 | 55.08 N | 7.27 W |
| Bundaberg | 166 | 24.52 S | 152.21 E |
| Bundanoon | 170 | 34.39 S | 150.18 E |
| Bundarra | 166 | 30.10 S | 151.05 E |
| Bunde, Dtsch. | 52 | 53.11 N | 7.16 E |
| Bünde, Dtsch. | 52 | 52.12 N | 8.35 E |
| Bunde, Ned. | 56 | 50.54 N | 5.45 E |
| Bundeena | 274a | 34.05 S | 151.09 E |
| Bundey ≃ | 162 | 21.46 S | 135.37 E |
| Bündheim | 54 | 51.53 N | 10.32 E |
| Būndi, India | 120 | 25.27 N | 75.39 E |
| Bundi, Pap. N. Gui. | 164 | 5.40 S | 145.15 E |
| Bundick Creek ≃ | 194 | 30.36 N | 92.57 W |
| Bundoora | 274b | 37.42 S | 145.04 E |
| Bundoran | 48 | 54.28 N | 8.17 W |
| Būndu, India | 124 | 23.11 N | 85.35 E |
| Bundu, S. Afr. | 158 | 29.45 S | 22.02 E |
| Bunduqiyah | 154 | 5.06 N | 30.53 E |
| Bund'ur | 86 | 57.32 N | 82.01 E |
| Buner □[9] | 123 | 34.35 N | 72.35 E |
| Bunessan | 46 | 56.19 N | 6.14 W |
| Bunga | 150 | 11.04 N | 9.38 E |
| Bunga ≃ | 150 | 11.23 N | 9.56 E |
| Bungamas | 112 | 3.42 S | 102.23 E |
| Bungay | 42 | 52.28 N | 1.26 E |
| Bungbulang | 115a | 7.27 S | 107.35 E |
| Bunge | 26 | 57.51 N | 19.01 E |
| Bungegep | 164 | 7.48 S | 139.52 E |
| Bungendore | 171b | 35.15 S | 149.27 E |
| Bunger Hills ⋏[2] | 9 | 66.17 S | 100.47 E |
| Bung Kan | 110 | 18.23 N | 103.37 E |
| Bungku | 112 | 2.33 S | 121.58 E |
| Bungo | 152 | 7.26 S | 15.23 E |
| Bungoma | 154 | 0.34 N | 34.34 E |
| Bungonia | 170 | 34.51 S | 149.57 E |
| Bungo-suidō ɥ | 92 | 33.00 N | 132.13 E |
| Bungo-takada | 96 | 33.33 N | 131.27 E |
| Bungsberg ∧[2] | 54 | 54.12 N | 10.43 E |
| Bungtlang | 120 | 22.20 N | 92.46 E |
| Bungu | 154 | 7.38 S | 39.03 E |
| Buni ≃ | 115a | 7.26 S | 106.47 E |
| Bunia | 154 | 1.34 N | 30.15 E |
| Bunianga | 152 | 3.34 S | 20.06 E |
| Būnīken, Kūh-e ∧ | 128 | 26.46 N | 58.12 E |
| Buninyong | 169 | 37.39 S | 143.53 E |
| Buninyong, Mount ∧ | 169 | 37.39 S | 143.56 E |
| Bunji | 123 | 35.40 N | 74.36 E |
| Bunkeflo strand | 41 | 55.33 N | 12.57 E |
| Bunker | 194 | 37.27 N | 91.12 W |
| Bunker Group II | 166 | 23.48 S | 152.20 E |
| Bunker Hill, Il., U.S. | 219 | 39.02 N | 89.57 W |
| Bunker Hill, In., U.S. | 216 | 40.40 N | 86.06 W |
| Bunker Hill, Or., U.S. | 202 | 43.21 N | 124.12 W |
| Bunker Hill, Tx., U.S. | 222 | 29.46 N | 95.32 W |
| Bunker Hill ∧ | 204 | 39.15 N | 117.08 W |
| Bunker Hill Monument ⊥ | 283 | 42.22 N | 71.04 W |
| Bunkeya | 154 | 10.07 S | 27.17 E |
| Bunkie | 194 | 30.57 N | 92.10 W |
| Bunkyō ⊸[8] | 268 | 35.43 N | 139.45 E |
| Bunnahowen | 48 | 54.11 N | 9.54 W |
| Bunnell | 192 | 29.27 N | 81.15 W |
| Bunnik | 52 | 52.04 N | 5.12 E |
| Bünningstedt | 52 | 53.41 N | 10.13 E |
| Bunola | 214 | 40.14 N | 79.56 W |
| Bun Plains ≚ | 154 | 0.44 N | 40.42 E |
| Bunratty Castle ⊥ | 48 | 52.42 N | 8.48 W |
| Bunschoten | 52 | 52.14 N | 5.22 E |
| Bunsuru ≃ | 150 | 13.21 N | 6.23 E |
| Bunta | 112 | 0.48 S | 122.10 E |
| Buntine | 162 | 29.59 S | 116.34 E |
| Buntingford | 42 | 51.57 N | 0.01 W |
| Buntok | 112 | 1.42 S | 114.48 E |
| Bununu Dass | 150 | 10.00 N | 9.31 E |
| Bunut | 112 | 0.46 N | 112.30 E |
| Bunyambili | 154 | 2.21 S | 29.25 E |
| Bünyan | 130 | 38.51 N | 35.52 E |
| Bunyip | 169 | 38.06 S | 145.43 E |
| Bunyip ≃ | 169 | 38.13 S | 145.27 E |
| Bunyolo | 34 | 39.25 N | 0.47 W |
| Bunyrevo | 82 | 54.34 N | 37.09 E |
| Bunyu, Pulau I | 112 | 3.30 N | 117.50 E |
| Bunza | 150 | 12.08 N | 4.00 E |
| Buochs | 58 | 46.58 N | 8.22 E |
| Buol | 112 | 1.10 N | 121.26 E |
| Buolkalach | 74 | 72.56 N | 119.50 E |
| Buonalbergo | 68 | 41.13 N | 14.59 E |
| Buona Vista | 271c | 1.16 N | 103.47 E |
| Buon Bu N'jang | 110 | 12.06 N | 107.40 E |
| Buonconvento | 66 | 43.08 N | 11.29 E |
| Buon Me Thuot | 110 | 12.40 N | 108.03 E |
| Buon Mrong | 110 | 12.48 N | 108.28 E |
| Buon Ngo | 110 | 12.30 N | 108.28 E |
| Buon Thach Hom | 110 | 12.17 N | 108.48 E |
| Buon Ya Soup | 110 | 13.05 N | 107.52 E |
| Buor-Chaja, guba ⊂ | 74 | 71.30 N | 131.00 E |

FRANÇAIS

| Nom | Page | Lat.°′ | Long.°′ W = Ouest |
|---|---|---|---|
| Buor-Chaja, mys › | 74 | 71.56 N | 132.40 E |
| Bupul | 164 | 7.31 S | 140.52 E |
| Buqay'āwīyah, Qā' al- ≚ | 132 | 32.03 N | 37.07 E |
| Buqayq | 128 | 25.56 N | 49.40 E |
| Buqda Koosaar | 144 | 4.31 N | 44.49 E |
| Buqde Caqable | 144 | 4.04 N | 45.15 E |
| Buquira ≃ | 256 | 23.10 S | 45.54 W |
| Buquirivu ≃ | 287b | 23.28 S | 46.28 W |
| Buqūm, Ḥarrat al- ⋏[9] | 144 | 20.54 N | 42.00 E |
| Bur | 88 | 58.47 N | 107.01 E |
| Bura, Kenya | 154 | 3.30 S | 38.18 E |
| Bura, Kenya | 154 | 1.06 S | 39.57 E |
| Bura Gaurānga ≃[1] | 126 | 22.00 N | 90.33 E |
| Burakin | 162 | 30.31 S | 117.10 E |
| Buraly | 80 | 55.04 N | 52.52 E |
| Buram | 140 | 10.49 N | 25.10 E |
| Buran | 86 | 48.04 N | 85.15 E |
| Burangulovo | 86 | 53.26 N | 58.23 E |
| Buranhém ≃ | 255 | 16.27 S | 39.04 W |
| Burankol' | 86 | 46.14 N | 54.12 E |
| Burannoje | 86 | 50.59 N | 54.28 E |
| Burano ≃ | 66 | 43.37 N | 12.40 E |
| Burao Kibir | 144 | 8.42 N | 45.29 E |
| Burāq | 132 | 33.10 N | 36.29 E |
| Burāri ⊸[8] | 272a | 28.46 N | 77.12 E |
| Buras | 194 | 29.21 N | 89.31 W |
| Buraševo | 82 | 56.44 N | 35.52 E |
| Burauen | 116 | 10.58 N | 124.53 E |
| Burayd, Bi'r ⊤[4] | 142 | 29.08 N | 32.07 E |
| Buraydah | 128 | 26.20 N | 43.59 E |
| Burayk | 146 | 26.33 N | 13.08 E |
| Buraykah | 132 | 32.50 N | 36.34 E |
| Burbach | 56 | 50.45 N | 8.05 E |
| Burbage, Eng., U.K. | 42 | 51.20 N | 1.40 W |
| Burbage, Eng., U.K. | 262 | 53.15 N | 1.56 W |
| Burbank, Ca., U.S. | 226 | 37.19 N | 121.55 W |
| Burbank, Ca., U.S. | 228 | 34.10 N | 118.18 W |
| Burbank, Il., U.S. | 216 | 41.45 N | 87.45 W |
| Burbank, Il., U.S. | 278 | 41.45 N | 87.46 W |
| Burbank, Oh., U.S. | 214 | 40.59 N | 81.59 W |
| Burbank, Wa., U.S. | 202 | 46.12 N | 119.00 W |
| Burbank Studios ʊ[3] | 280 | 34.09 N | 118.21 W |
| Burbure | 50 | 50.32 N | 2.28 E |
| Burç | 130 | 37.02 N | 37.10 E |
| Burcei | 71 | 39.21 N | 9.21 E |
| Burcevo | 82 | 55.02 N | 38.09 E |
| Burcher | 166 | 33.32 S | 147.18 E |
| Burcin | 62 | 45.26 N | 5.26 E |
| Burco | 144 | 9.31 N | 45.34 E |
| Burda | 124 | 25.50 N | 77.35 E |
| Burdalyk | 128 | 38.25 N | 64.20 E |
| Burdekin ≃ | 166 | 19.39 S | 147.30 E |
| Burdekin Falls ∟ | 166 | 20.39 S | 147.09 E |
| Burden | 198 | 37.18 N | 96.45 W |
| Burdeos → Bordeaux, Fr. | 32 | 44.50 N | 0.34 W |
| Burdeos, Pil. | 116 | 14.51 N | 121.58 E |
| Burdeos Bay ⊂ | 116 | 14.44 N | 122.06 E |
| Burdett, Ab., Can. | 182 | 49.50 N | 111.32 W |
| Burdett, Ks., U.S. | 198 | 38.11 N | 99.31 W |
| Burdett, N.Y., U.S. | 210 | 42.25 N | 76.50 W |
| Burdul | 272c | 19.07 N | 73.07 E |
| Burdur | 130 | 37.43 N | 30.17 E |
| Burdur □[4] | 130 | 37.30 N | 30.00 E |
| Burdur Gölü ⊜ | 130 | 37.44 N | 30.12 E |
| Burdwood Bank ✣[3] | 18 | 54.15 S | 59.00 W |
| Bure, Ityo. | 144 | 8.15 N | 35.09 E |
| Bure, Ityo. | 144 | 10.47 N | 37.06 E |
| Bure ≃ | 42 | 52.37 N | 1.43 E |
| Bure, Pic de ∧ | 62 | 44.38 N | 5.56 E |
| Bureå | 26 | 64.37 N | 21.12 E |
| Bureälven ≃ | 26 | 64.37 N | 21.13 E |
| Bureg Changaj | 88 | 48.14 N | 103.57 E |
| Bureinskij chrebet ⋏ | 89 | 50.35 N | 133.35 E |
| Bureja | 89 | 49.52 N | 129.48 E |
| Bureja ≃ | 89 | 49.25 N | 129.35 E |
| Burekup | 168a | 33.19 S | 115.49 E |
| Büren, Dtsch. | 52 | 51.33 N | 8.33 E |
| Büren, Mong. | 88 | 47.13 N | 95.54 E |
| Büren an der Aare | 58 | 47.08 N | 7.23 E |
| Büren Chaan | 88 | 49.29 N | 99.14 E |
| Bürengijn nuruu ⋏ | 88 | 49.15 N | 104.30 E |
| Bures | 261 | 48.57 N | 1.58 E |
| Bures-sur-Yvette | 261 | 48.42 N | 2.10 E |
| Burey-en-Vaux | 58 | 48.34 N | 5.40 E |
| Burfjord | 24 | 69.56 N | 22.00 E |
| Burford, On., Can. | 212 | 43.06 N | 80.26 W |
| Burford, Eng., U.K. | 42 | 51.49 N | 1.38 W |
| Būr Fu'ād ⊸[8] | 142 | 31.15 N | 32.19 E |
| Burg, Dtsch. | 54 | 51.49 N | 14.08 E |
| Burg, Dtsch. | 54 | 52.16 N | 11.51 E |
| Burg, Dtsch. | 56 | 50.42 N | 8.19 E |
| Burg ⊸[8] | 263 | 51.08 N | 7.09 E |
| Burg, Schloss ⊥ | 263 | 51.08 N | 7.10 E |
| Burga | 76 | 58.45 N | 32.29 E |
| Burgas | 38 | 42.30 N | 27.28 E |
| Burgas □[4], Blg. | 38 | 42.36 N | 26.41 E |
| Burgas □[4], Blg. | 130 | 42.10 N | 27.00 E |
| Burgaski Zaliv ⊂ | 38 | 42.30 N | 27.33 E |
| Burgau | 58 | 48.26 N | 10.25 E |
| Burg [auf Fehmarn] | 54 | 54.26 N | 11.12 E |
| Burgaw | 192 | 34.33 N | 77.55 W |
| Burgaz ⊸[8] | 267b | 40.53 N | 29.03 E |
| Burgaz Adası I | 267b | 40.53 N | 29.04 E |
| Burgbernheim | 56 | 49.27 N | 10.19 E |
| Burgdorf, Dtsch. | 52 | 52.27 N | 10.00 E |
| Burgdorf, Schw. | 58 | 47.04 N | 7.37 E |
| Burgebrach | 56 | 49.50 N | 10.44 E |
| Bürgel | 54 | 50.56 N | 11.45 E |
| Burgenland □[3] | 61 | 47.30 N | 16.20 E |
| Burgeo | 186 | 47.37 N | 57.37 W |
| Burgersdorp | 158 | 31.00 S | 26.20 E |
| Burger Township | 273d | 26.05 S | 27.46 E |
| Burges, Mount ∧[2] | 162 | 30.50 S | 121.06 E |
| Burgess | 208 | 37.53 N | 76.21 W |
| Burgess Hill | 42 | 50.57 N | 0.07 W |
| Burgessville | 212 | 43.01 N | 80.39 W |
| Burgettstown | 214 | 40.22 N | 80.23 W |
| Burggrafenberg ∧[2] | 263 | 51.13 N | 7.07 E |
| Burghaun | 56 | 50.42 N | 9.44 E |
| Burghausen | 60 | 48.09 N | 12.49 E |
| Burghead | 46 | 57.42 N | 3.30 W |
| Burgheim | 60 | 48.42 N | 11.01 E |
| Burgh Heath | 260 | 51.18 N | 0.13 W |
| Burghill | 214 | 41.22 N | 80.34 W |
| Burgh le Marsh | 44 | 53.09 N | 0.15 E |
| Burghūth, Sabkhat al- ⊜ | 130 | 34.58 N | 41.06 E |
| Burgin | 194 | 37.45 N | 84.46 W |
| Burgio | 70 | 37.36 N | 13.17 E |
| Burgjoss | 56 | 50.12 N | 9.29 E |
| Burgkirchen, Dtsch. | 64 | 48.10 N | 12.44 E |
| Burgkirchen, Öst. | 60 | 48.12 N | 13.06 E |
| Burgkunstadt | 54 | 50.08 N | 11.14 E |
| Bürglen, Schw. | 58 | 46.53 N | 8.40 E |
| Bürglen, Schw. | 58 | 47.33 N | 9.09 E |
| Burglengenfeld | 60 | 49.13 N | 12.03 E |
| Burgo de Osma | 34 | 41.35 N | 3.04 W |
| Burgoon | 214 | 41.16 N | 83.15 W |
| Burgos, Esp. | 34 | 42.21 N | 3.42 W |
| Burgos, It. | 71 | 40.23 N | 8.59 E |
| Burgos, Méx. | 232 | 24.57 N | 98.47 W |
| Burgos, Pil. | 116 | 16.04 N | 119.52 E |
| Burgos, Pil. | 116 | 15.30 N | 120.24 E |
| Burgos □[4] | 34 | 42.20 N | 3.40 W |
| Burgsinn | 56 | 50.09 N | 9.38 E |
| Burgstädt | 54 | 50.55 N | 12.49 E |
| Burgstall, Dtsch. | 54 | 52.24 N | 11.41 E |
| Burgstall → Postal, It. | 64 | 46.36 N | 11.11 E |
| Burg Stargard | 54 | 53.29 N | 13.18 E |
| Burgsvik | 26 | 57.03 N | 18.16 E |
| Burgueño, Arroyo ≃ | 288 | 34.24 S | 58.47 W |
| Burgund → Bourgogne □[9] | 32 | 47.00 N | 4.30 E |
| Burgundy → Bourgogne □[9] | 32 | 47.00 N | 4.30 E |
| Burgusio (Burgeis) | 64 | 46.42 N | 10.31 E |
| Burgwedel | 52 | 52.29 N | 9.51 E |

PORTUGUÊS

| Nome | Página | Lat.°′ | Long.°′ W = Oeste |
|---|---|---|---|
| Burgwindheim | 56 | 49.49 N | 10.35 E |
| Burhābalang ≃ | 126 | 21.28 N | 87.04 E |
| Burham | 260 | 51.20 N | 0.29 E |
| Burhan Budai Shan ⋏ | 102 | 36.00 N | 96.00 E |
| Burhaniye, Tür. | 130 | 37.57 N | 28.45 E |
| Burhaniye, Tür. | 130 | 39.30 N | 26.58 E |
| Burhānpur | 120 | 21.18 N | 76.14 E |
| Burhar | 124 | 23.13 N | 81.32 E |
| Burhave | 52 | 53.34 N | 8.21 E |
| Burholme ⊸[8] | 285 | 40.03 N | 75.05 W |
| Buri | 255 | 23.48 S | 48.35 W |
| Burias Island I | 116 | 12.57 N | 123.08 E |
| Burias Pass ɥ | 116 | 13.00 N | 123.15 E |
| Buribaj | 86 | 51.57 N | 58.11 E |
| Būr Ibrāhīm ⊸[8] | 142 | 29.57 N | 32.34 E |
| Burica, Punta › | 236 | 8.03 N | 82.53 W |
| Burien | 224 | 47.28 N | 122.20 W |
| Burigi, Lake ⊜ | 154 | 2.05 S | 31.15 E |
| Burila Mare | 38 | 44.27 N | 22.34 E |
| Burin | 186 | 47.02 N | 55.10 W |
| Burin Peninsula ›[1] | 186 | 47.00 N | 55.40 W |
| Buri Ram | 110 | 15.00 N | 103.07 E |
| Buriswar ≃[1] | 126 | 21.58 N | 90.02 E |
| Buritama | 255 | 21.03 S | 50.08 W |
| Buriti, Bra. | 250 | 3.55 S | 42.57 W |
| Buriti, Bra. | 255 | 16.27 S | 53.27 W |
| Buriti ≃ | 248 | 12.50 S | 58.28 W |
| Buriti Alegre | 255 | 18.09 S | 49.03 W |
| Buriti Bravo | 250 | 5.50 S | 43.50 W |
| Buriticupu ≃ | 250 | 4.13 S | 46.33 W |
| Buriti dos Lopes | 250 | 3.10 S | 41.52 W |
| Buritizeiro | 255 | 17.21 S | 44.58 W |
| Būriya | 124 | 30.09 N | 77.21 E |
| Burj al-'Arab | 140 | 30.55 N | 29.32 E |
| Burjassot | 34 | 39.31 N | 0.25 W |
| Burjatija □[3], Ross. | 74 | 53.00 N | 109.00 E |
| Burjatija □[3], Ross. | 88 | 53.00 N | 109.00 E |
| Burji | 144 | 5.20 N | 37.57 E |
| Burj Islām | 130 | 35.41 N | 35.48 E |
| Burj Mughayzil | 142 | 31.27 N | 30.23 E |
| Burkan ≃ | 85 | 41.43 N | 76.46 E |
| Burkau | 54 | 51.10 N | 14.10 E |
| Burkburnett | 196 | 34.05 N | 98.34 W |
| Burke, S.D., U.S. | 198 | 43.10 N | 99.17 W |
| Burke, Tx., U.S. | 222 | 31.14 N | 94.46 W |
| Burke, Va., U.S. | 284c | 38.47 N | 77.16 W |
| Burke ≃ | 166 | 23.12 S | 139.33 E |
| Burke Channel ɥ | 182 | 52.07 N | 127.38 W |
| Burke Island I | 9 | 73.15 S | 104.35 W |
| Burke Lake ⊜[1] | 284c | 38.46 N | 77.18 W |
| Burke Lake County Park ♠ | 284c | 38.45 N | 77.18 W |
| Burke Lakefront Airport ⊠ | 279a | 41.31 N | 81.41 W |
| Burkesville | 194 | 36.47 N | 85.22 W |
| Burket | 216 | 41.09 N | 85.58 W |
| Burketown | 166 | 17.43 S | 139.34 E |
| Burkett Gardens | 226 | 37.57 N | 121.15 W |
| Burkettsville | 216 | 40.21 N | 84.39 W |
| Burkhardtsdorf | 54 | 50.44 N | 12.55 E |
| Burkina Faso □[1], Afr. | 134 | 13.00 N | 1.30 W |
| Burkina Faso □[1], Afr. | 150 | 13.00 N | 1.30 W |
| Burkit | 80 | 47.03 N | 50.42 E |
| Burksville | 219 | 38.16 N | 90.09 W |
| Burla | 86 | 53.19 N | 78.21 E |
| Burla ≃ | 86 | 53.20 N | 78.02 E |
| Burladingen | 58 | 48.17 N | 9.07 E |
| Burleigh | 208 | 39.02 N | 74.51 W |
| Burleigh Falls | 212 | 44.34 N | 78.13 W |
| Burleigh Heads | 171a | 28.06 S | 153.27 E |
| Burleson | 222 | 32.32 N | 97.19 W |
| Burleson □[6] | 222 | 30.30 N | 96.43 W |
| Burley, Id., U.S. | 202 | 42.32 N | 113.47 W |
| Burley, Wa., U.S. | 224 | 47.25 N | 122.37 W |
| Burley Griffin, Lake ⊜ | 171b | 35.13 S | 149.05 E |
| Burli | 86 | 53.36 N | 61.55 E |
| Burlin | 80 | 51.25 N | 52.44 E |
| Burlingame, Ca., U.S. | 226 | 37.35 N | 122.21 W |
| Burlingame, Ks., U.S. | 198 | 38.45 N | 95.00 W |
| Burlingame State Park ♠ | 207 | 41.22 N | 71.43 W |
| Burlington, Nf., Can. | 186 | 49.45 N | 56.02 W |
| Burlington, On., Can. | 212 | 43.19 N | 79.47 W |
| Burlington, Co., U.S. | 198 | 39.18 N | 102.16 W |
| Burlington, Ct., U.S. | 207 | 41.46 N | 72.57 W |
| Burlington, Il., U.S. | 216 | 42.03 N | 88.33 W |
| Burlington, In., U.S. | 216 | 40.29 N | 86.24 W |
| Burlington, Ia., U.S. | 190 | 40.48 N | 91.06 W |
| Burlington, Ks., U.S. | 198 | 38.11 N | 95.44 W |
| Burlington, Ky., U.S. | 218 | 39.01 N | 84.43 W |
| Burlington, Ma., U.S. | 207 | 42.30 N | 71.11 W |
| Burlington, Mi., U.S. | 216 | 42.06 N | 85.05 W |
| Burlington, N.J., U.S. | 208 | 40.04 N | 74.51 W |
| Burlington, N.C., U.S. | 192 | 36.05 N | 79.26 W |
| Burlington, N.D., U.S. | 198 | 48.16 N | 101.25 W |
| Burlington, Pa., U.S. | 210 | 41.47 N | 76.37 W |
| Burlington, Tx., U.S. | 222 | 31.01 N | 96.60 W |
| Burlington, Vt., U.S. | 188 | 44.28 N | 73.12 W |
| Burlington, Wa., U.S. | 224 | 48.28 N | 122.19 W |
| Burlington, Wi., U.S. | 216 | 42.40 N | 88.16 W |
| Burlington, Wy., U.S. | 202 | 44.26 N | 108.25 W |
| Burlington □[6] | 208 | 39.50 N | 74.47 W |
| Burlington Beach | 216 | 41.30 N | 87.03 W |
| Burlington County Airpark ⊠ | 285 | 39.56 N | 74.50 W |
| Burlington Island I | 285 | 40.05 N | 74.51 W |
| Burlington Junction | 194 | 40.26 N | 95.03 W |
| Burlington Mall ⊸[9] | 283 | 42.29 N | 71.13 W |
| Burlit | 89 | 46.33 N | 134.14 E |
| Burluk | 80 | 50.34 N | 44.33 E |
| Burma → Myanmar □[1] | 110 | 22.00 N | 98.00 E |
| Burmā, Tall ∧ | 132 | 30.38 N | 35.50 E |
| Burmakino | 80 | 57.27 N | 40.20 E |
| Burn ≃ | 44 | 54.12 N | 1.38 W |
| Burnaby | 224 | 49.15 N | 122.57 W |
| Burnaby Island I | 182 | 52.24 N | 131.20 W |
| Burnage | 262 | 53.26 N | 2.12 W |
| Burnas, ozero ⊜ | 78 | 45.52 N | 30.08 E |
| Burnet | 196 | 30.45 N | 98.13 W |
| Burnett ≃ | 166 | 24.46 S | 152.25 E |
| Burnett Bay ⊂ | 176 | 73.53 N | 124.00 W |
| Burnett Brook ≃ | 276 | 40.46 N | 74.38 W |
| Burnett Heads | 166 | 24.46 S | 152.25 E |
| Burnettsville | 216 | 40.46 N | 86.36 W |
| Burney, Ca., U.S. | 204 | 40.52 N | 121.39 W |
| Burney, In., U.S. | 218 | 39.19 N | 85.38 W |
| Burnham, Eng., U.K. | 42 | 51.33 N | 0.39 W |
| Burnham, Il., U.S. | 278 | 41.39 N | 87.34 W |
| Burnham, Pa., U.S. | 208 | 40.38 N | 77.34 W |
| Burnham Beeches ⊸[3] | 260 | 51.34 N | 0.38 W |
| Burnham Market | 42 | 52.57 N | 0.44 E |
| Burnham-on-Crouch | 42 | 51.38 N | 0.49 E |
| Burnham-on-Sea | 42 | 51.15 N | 3.00 W |
| Burnhamthorpe | 275b | 43.37 N | 79.36 W |
| Burnhaven | 46 | 57.29 N | 1.47 W |
| Burnie | 166 | 41.04 S | 145.54 E |
| Burning Tree Estates | 284c | 39.01 N | 77.12 W |
| Burnips | 216 | 42.44 N | 85.50 W |
| Burniston | 44 | 54.19 N | 0.26 W |
| Burnley | 44 | 53.48 N | 2.14 W |
| Burnley □[8] | 262 | 53.46 N | 2.15 W |
| Burnley Creek ≃ | 212 | 44.13 N | 77.51 W |
| Burnley Football Ground ♠ | 262 | 53.48 N | 2.14 W |
| Burnmouth | 46 | 55.50 N | 2.04 W |
| Burnoje | 85 | 42.37 N | 70.46 E |
| Burnookt'abr'skoje | 85 | 42.42 N | 70.49 E |
| Burnpur | 126 | 23.40 N | 86.57 E |
| Burns, Ks., U.S. | 198 | 38.05 N | 96.53 W |
| Burns, Or., U.S. | 202 | 43.35 N | 119.03 W |
| Burns, Tn., U.S. | 194 | 36.03 N | 87.18 W |
| Burns, Wy., U.S. | 198 | 41.11 N | 104.21 W |
| Burns Creek ≃ | 198 | 47.22 N | 104.25 W |
| Burns Flat | 196 | 35.20 N | 99.10 W |
| Burns Harbor | 216 | 41.37 N | 87.10 W |
| Burnside, Austl. | 168b | 34.57 S | 138.40 E |
| Burnside, Ky., U.S. | 192 | 36.59 N | 84.36 W |
| Burnside, Pa., U.S. | 214 | 40.49 N | 78.47 W |
| Burnside ≃ | 176 | 66.51 N | 108.04 W |
| Burnside, Lake ⊜ | 162 | 25.33 S | 123.02 E |
| Burns Lake | 182 | 54.14 N | 125.46 W |
| Burnsville, Al., U.S. | 194 | 32.28 N | 86.53 W |
| Burnsville, Ms., U.S. | 194 | 34.50 N | 88.18 W |
| Burnsville, N.C., U.S. | 192 | 35.55 N | 82.18 W |
| Burnsville, W.V., U.S. | 188 | 38.51 N | 80.39 W |
| Burnt ≃, On., Can. | 212 | 44.35 N | 78.46 W |
| Burnt ≃, Or., U.S. | 202 | 44.22 N | 117.14 W |
| Burnt Cabins | 214 | 40.05 N | 77.54 W |
| Burnt Corn Creek ≃ | 194 | 31.06 N | 87.04 W |
| Burnt Hills | 210 | 42.54 N | 73.53 W |
| Burnt Island, Nf., Can. | 186 | 47.36 N | 58.53 W |
| Burntisland, Scot., U.K. | 46 | 56.03 N | 3.15 W |
| Burnt Meadow Brook ≃ | 276 | 41.05 N | 74.18 W |
| Burnt Mills, Lake ⊜ | 208 | 36.50 N | 76.38 W |
| Burnt Mills Hills | 284c | 39.02 N | 77.00 W |
| Burnt Mills Manor | 284c | 39.02 N | 77.00 W |
| Burnt Mountain ∧ | 228 | 33.12 N | 117.04 W |
| Burntop | 158 | 26.49 S | 30.54 E |
| Burnt Pine | 174c | 29.02 S | 167.56 E |
| Burnt Pond ⊜ | 186 | 48.11 N | 57.24 W |
| Burntwick Island I | 260 | 51.25 N | 0.41 E |
| Burntwood | 42 | 52.41 N | 1.56 W |
| Burntwood ≃ | 184 | 56.08 N | 96.30 W |
| Burntwood Lake ⊜ | 184 | 55.29 N | 100.07 W |
| Burnyj, porog ∟ | 86 | 57.43 N | 95.18 E |
| Buro | 144 | 11.28 N | 49.41 E |
| Buron | 84 | 42.48 N | 44.03 E |
| Buronzo | 62 | 45.29 N | 8.16 E |
| Burow | 54 | 53.46 N | 13.16 E |
| Burpengary | 171a | 27.10 S | 152.57 E |
| Burpham | 260 | 51.15 N | 0.33 W |
| Burqin | 86 | 47.43 N | 86.53 E |
| Burqin ≃ | 86 | 47.40 N | 86.55 E |
| Burra | 166 | 33.40 S | 138.56 E |
| Burra Burra Creek ≃ | 170 | 34.10 S | 149.38 E |
| Burracoppin | 162 | 31.23 S | 118.29 E |
| Burra Creek ≃ | 168b | 33.51 S | 139.18 E |
| Burrage | 283 | 42.02 N | 70.51 W |
| Burrage Pond ⊜ | 283 | 42.01 N | 70.52 W |
| Burragorang, Lake ⊜[1] | 170 | 33.57 S | 150.26 E |
| Burramurra | 166 | 20.30 S | 137.20 E |
| Burravoe | 46a | 60.32 N | 1.28 W |
| Burrawang | 170 | 34.36 S | 150.31 E |
| Burray I | 46 | 58.51 N | 2.54 W |
| Burrel, Shq. | 38 | 41.37 N | 20.00 E |
| Burrel, Ca., U.S. | 226 | 36.30 N | 119.59 W |
| Burrendong Reservoir ⊜[1] | 166 | 32.39 S | 149.15 E |
| Burren Junction | 166 | 30.06 S | 148.58 E |
| Burrill Lake ⊂ | 170 | 35.23 S | 150.27 E |
| Burrinjuck Reservoir ⊜[1] | 166 | 35.00 S | 148.45 E |
| Burro, Serranías del ⋏ | 196 | 29.10 N | 102.05 W |
| Burr Oak, In., U.S. | 216 | 41.15 N | 86.25 W |
| Burr Oak, Ks., U.S. | 198 | 39.51 N | 98.18 W |
| Burr Oak, Mi., U.S. | 216 | 41.50 N | 85.19 W |
| Burro Burro ≃ | 246 | 4.48 N | 58.51 W |
| Burro Creek ≃ | 200 | 34.32 N | 113.35 W |
| Burro Peak ∧ | 200 | 32.35 N | 108.26 W |
| Burrowa, Mount ∧ | 171b | 36.05 S | 147.42 E |
| Burrowa-Pine Mountain National Park ♠ | 171b | 36.06 S | 147.44 E |
| Burrow Head › | 44 | 54.41 N | 4.24 W |
| Burrowhill | 260 | 51.21 N | 0.36 W |
| Burrows | 216 | 40.40 N | 86.30 W |
| Burrows Island I | 224 | 48.29 N | 122.42 W |
| Burr Ridge | 278 | 41.46 N | 87.55 W |
| Burrs Mill Brook ≃ | 285 | 39.53 N | 74.42 W |
| Burrton | 198 | 38.01 N | 97.40 W |
| Burrumbeet, Lake ⊜ | 169 | 37.30 S | 143.39 E |
| Burrundie | 164 | 13.32 S | 131.42 E |
| Burruyacú | 252 | 26.30 S | 64.45 W |
| Burrwood | 194 | 28.58 N | 89.22 W |
| Burry Holms I | 42 | 51.37 N | 4.18 W |
| Burry Port | 42 | 51.42 N | 4.15 W |
| Bürs | 58 | 47.09 N | 9.48 E |
| Bursa | 130 | 40.11 N | 29.04 E |
| Bursa □[4] | 130 | 40.10 N | 29.00 E |
| Būr Safājah | 140 | 26.44 N | 33.56 E |
| Būr Sa'īd (Port Said) | 142 | 31.16 N | 32.18 E |
| Būr Sa'īd □[4] | 142 | 30.36 N | 32.15 E |
| Burscheid | 56 | 51.05 N | 7.06 E |
| Burscough | 262 | 53.35 N | 2.51 W |
| Burscough Bridge | 44 | 53.36 N | 2.52 W |
| Bursey, Mount ∧ | 9 | 76.00 S | 132.40 W |
| Burshtyn | 78 | 49.17 N | 24.37 E |
| Bursol' | 86 | 53.11 N | 78.27 E |
| Bürstadt | 56 | 49.38 N | 8.27 E |
| Burstall | 184 | 50.40 N | 109.54 W |
| Būr Sūdān (Port Sudan) | 140 | 19.37 N | 37.14 E |
| Burt, Ia., U.S. | 190 | 43.11 N | 94.13 W |
| Burt, N.Y., U.S. | 210 | 43.19 N | 78.43 W |
| Būr Tawfīq ⊸[8] | 128 | 29.57 N | 32.34 E |
| Burtenbach | 58 | 48.20 N | 10.26 E |
| Burt Lake ⊜ | 190 | 45.27 N | 84.40 W |
| Burtnieks ezers ⊜ | 76 | 57.45 N | 25.16 E |
| Burton, B.C., Can. | 182 | 49.59 N | 117.54 W |
| Burton, Eng., U.K. | 42 | 50.44 N | 1.45 W |
| Burton, Eng., U.K. | 262 | 53.16 N | 3.01 W |
| Burton, Il., U.S. | 219 | 39.55 N | 91.15 W |
| Burton, Mi., U.S. | 216 | 43.01 N | 84.16 W |
| Burton, Mi., U.S. | 216 | 43.02 N | 83.36 W |
| Burton, Oh., U.S. | 214 | 41.28 N | 81.08 W |
| Burton, Tx., U.S. | 222 | 30.11 N | 96.36 W |
| Burton, Wa., U.S. | 224 | 47.23 N | 122.27 W |
| Burton, Lake ⊜[1] | 192 | 34.50 N | 83.33 W |
| Burton Fleming | 44 | 54.08 N | 0.20 W |
| Burton Latimer | 42 | 52.23 N | 0.41 W |
| Burtons Bridge | 216 | 42.17 N | 88.14 W |
| Burton Seamount ✣[3] | 14 | 32.00 S | 171.45 W |
| Burtonsville | 208 | 39.07 N | 76.56 W |
| Burton upon Stather | 44 | 53.39 N | 0.41 W |
| Burton upon Trent | 42 | 52.49 N | 1.36 W |
| Burtonwood | 262 | 53.26 N | 2.39 W |
| Burtonwood Airfield ⊠ | 262 | 53.24 N | 2.39 W |
| Burträsk | 26 | 64.31 N | 20.39 E |
| Burtundy | 166 | 33.44 S | 142.16 E |
| Burṭus | 142 | 30.09 N | 31.08 E |
| Buru I | 108 | 3.24 S | 126.40 E |
| Buruanga | 116 | 11.51 N | 121.53 E |
| Burukan | 89 | 53.02 N | 136.03 E |
| Buruldaj | 85 | 42.48 N | 75.52 E |
| Burullus, Buḥayrat al- ⊜ | 142 | 31.30 N | 30.50 E |
| Burūm | 144 | 14.22 N | 48.57 E |
| Burundaj | 85 | 43.23 N | 76.51 E |
| Burundi □[1], Afr. | 138 | 3.15 S | 30.00 E |
| Burundi □[1], Afr. | 154 | 3.15 S | 30.00 E |
| Burundučicha | 80 | 58.21 N | 46.07 E |
| Burun-Šibertuj, gora ∧ | 88 | 49.42 N | 109.59 E |
| Bururi | 154 | 3.57 S | 29.37 E |
| Burutu | 150 | 5.21 N | 5.31 E |
| Buruz Bāgān | 126 | 23.03 N | 89.00 E |
| Burwash | 190 | 46.19 N | 80.48 W |
| Burwash Landing | 180 | 61.21 N | 139.00 W |
| Burwell, Eng., U.K. | 42 | 52.16 N | 0.19 E |
| Burwell, Ne., U.S. | 198 | 41.46 N | 99.07 W |
| Burwell Bay ⊂ | 208 | 37.04 N | 76.38 W |
| Burwick | 46 | 58.44 N | 2.57 W |
| Burwood, Austl. | 274a | 33.53 S | 151.06 E |
| Burwood, Austl. | 274b | 37.51 S | 145.06 E |
| Bury, P.Q., Can. | 206 | 45.28 N | 71.30 W |
| Bury, Eng., U.K. | 42 | 50.54 N | 0.34 W |
| Bury, Eng., U.K. | 44 | 53.36 N | 2.17 W |
| Bury □[8] | 262 | 53.35 N | 2.19 W |
| Buryatia → Burjatija □[3] | 88 | 53.00 N | 109.00 E |
| Buryn' | 78 | 51.13 N | 33.49 E |
| Bury Saint Edmunds | 42 | 52.15 N | 0.43 E |
| Burzaco | 258 | 34.49 S | 58.24 W |
| Burzet | 62 | 44.44 N | 4.15 E |
| Burzil | 123 | 34.52 N | 75.07 E |
| Burzil Pass )( | 123 | 34.54 N | 75.06 E |
| Būṣ, Ghubbat al- ⊂ | 142 | 29.36 N | 32.22 E |
| Busa, Mount ∧ | 116 | 6.08 N | 124.39 E |
| Busachi | 71 | 40.02 N | 8.54 E |
| Busalla | 62 | 44.34 N | 8.57 E |
| Busambra, Rocca ∧ | 70 | 37.51 N | 13.24 E |
| Busan → Pusan | 98 | 35.06 N | 129.03 E |
| Busana | 64 | 44.22 N | 10.19 E |
| Busanga | 152 | 0.51 S | 22.04 E |
| Busanga Swamp ≋ | 154 | 14.10 S | 25.50 E |
| Busangu | 154 | 8.32 S | 25.31 E |
| Buṣayrah | 130 | 35.09 N | 40.26 E |
| Busby, Austl. | 274a | 33.54 S | 150.53 E |
| Busby, Mt., U.S. | 202 | 45.32 N | 106.57 W |
| Busca | 62 | 44.31 N | 7.29 E |
| Buscate | 266b | 45.32 N | 8.49 E |
| Buscbusc ≃ | 144 | 1.08 S | 41.49 E |
| Buschberg ∧[2] | 61 | 48.34 N | 16.23 E |
| Busche | 64 | 46.02 N | 11.59 E |
| Busch Gardens ♠ | 280 | 34.13 N | 118.28 W |
| Buschhausen ⊸[8] | 263 | 51.30 N | 6.51 E |
| Busdorf | 41 | 54.29 N | 9.32 E |
| Buseck | 56 | 50.36 N | 8.47 E |
| Buseto Palizzolo | 70 | 38.01 N | 12.43 E |
| Būsh | 142 | 29.09 N | 31.08 E |
| Bush ≃, N. Ire., U.K. | 44 | 55.13 N | 6.32 W |
| Bush ≃, S.C., U.S. | 192 | 34.08 N | 81.36 W |
| Būshehr □[4] | 128 | 28.50 N | 51.20 E |
| Bushenyi | 154 | 0.32 S | 30.11 E |
| Bushey | 42 | 51.39 N | 0.22 W |
| Bushey Heath | 260 | 51.38 N | 0.20 W |
| Bushi | 268 | 35.50 N | 139.22 E |
| Bushimaie ≃ | 152 | 6.02 S | 23.45 E |
| Bushiribana | 241s | 12.33 N | 69.58 W |
| Bushkill | 210 | 41.06 N | 75.00 W |
| Bush Kill ≃ | 210 | 41.05 N | 74.59 W |
| Bushkill Falls ∟ | 210 | 41.09 N | 75.01 W |
| Bushland | 196 | 35.11 N | 102.04 W |
| Bush Lot | 246 | 6.12 N | 57.16 W |
| Bushman Land □[9] | 158 | 29.15 S | 20.00 E |
| Bushmills | 48 | 55.12 N | 6.32 W |
| Bushnell, Fl., U.S. | 220 | 28.39 N | 82.06 W |
| Bushnell, Il., U.S. | 190 | 40.33 N | 90.30 W |
| Bush River ≃ | 208 | 39.21 N | 76.14 W |
| Bushton | 198 | 38.30 N | 98.23 W |
| Bushtyna | 78 | 48.04 N | 23.27 E |
| Bū Shubayrim, Wādī ∨ | 146 | 27.07 N | 19.30 E |
| Bushwick ⊸[8] | 276 | 40.42 N | 73.55 W |
| Bushy Park | 166 | 21.16 S | 139.43 E |
| Bushy Park ♠ | 260 | 51.25 N | 0.20 W |
| Bushy Run ≃ | 279b | 40.20 N | 79.40 W |
| Bushy Run Battlefield ⊥ | 279b | 40.21 N | 79.38 W |
| Busia | 154 | 0.28 N | 34.05 E |
| Busigny | 50 | 50.02 N | 3.28 E |
| Busing, Pulau I | 271c | 1.14 N | 103.45 E |
| Businga | 152 | 3.20 N | 20.53 E |
| Büsingen | 58 | 47.42 N | 8.41 E |
| Busira ≃ | 152 | 0.15 S | 18.59 E |
| Busjön ⊜, Sve. | 40 | 60.06 N | 13.28 E |
| Busjön ⊜, Sve. | 40 | 60.31 N | 13.58 E |
| Bus'k | 78 | 49.58 N | 24.37 E |
| Buskerud □[6] | 26 | 60.25 N | 9.12 E |
| Buskhyttan | 40 | 58.40 N | 16.56 E |
| Busko Zdrój | 30 | 50.28 N | 20.44 E |
| Busle | 144 | 5.28 N | 44.25 E |
| Busoga □[5] | 154 | 0.40 N | 33.30 E |
| Busovača | 36 | 44.06 N | 17.53 E |
| Buṣrā al-Ḥarīrī (Bosor) | 132 | 32.50 N | 36.20 E |
| Buṣrā ash-Shām | 132 | 32.31 N | 36.29 E |
| Bussana | 62 | 43.49 N | 7.51 E |
| Bussang | 58 | 47.53 N | 6.51 E |
| Bussang, Col de )( | 58 | 47.54 N | 6.54 E |
| Busselton | 162 | 33.39 S | 115.20 E |
| Busseri ≃ | 140 | 7.41 N | 28.03 E |
| Busseto | 64 | 44.59 N | 10.02 E |
| Bussey | 190 | 41.12 N | 92.52 W |
| Bussières | 62 | 45.50 N | 4.16 E |
| Bussi sul Tirino | 66 | 42.12 N | 13.49 E |
| Busskoje | 84 | 43.50 N | 44.37 E |
| Bussolengo | 64 | 45.28 N | 10.51 E |
| Bussoleno | 62 | 45.08 N | 7.09 E |
| Bussum | 52 | 52.16 N | 5.10 E |
| Bussy-Rabutin, Château de ⊥ | 58 | 47.35 N | 4.31 E |
| Bussy-Saint-Georges | 261 | 48.51 N | 2.42 E |
| Bustamante, Méx. | 232 | 26.33 N | 100.30 W |
| Bustamante, Méx. | 234 | 23.26 N | 99.47 W |
| Bustān, Wādī al- ∨ | 142 | 28.24 N | 30.49 E |
| Buštěhrad | 54 | 50.09 N | 14.10 E |
| Buşteni | 38 | 45.25 N | 25.32 E |
| Busti | 214 | 42.02 N | 79.17 W |
| Bustleton ⊸[8] | 285 | 40.05 N | 75.02 W |
| Busto Arsizio | 62 | 45.37 N | 8.51 E |
| Busto Garolfo | 62 | 45.33 N | 8.53 E |
| Buston, Taj. | 85 | 40.31 N | 69.19 E |
| Buston, Uzb. | 128 | 40.04 N | 64.49 E |
| Busu-Adula | 152 | 2.05 N | 21.40 E |
| Busuanga | 116 | 12.10 N | 119.55 E |
| Busuanga Island I | 116 | 12.05 N | 120.05 E |
| Busu-Djanoa | 152 | 1.43 N | 21.23 E |
| Bušuicha | 76 | 59.02 N | 40.26 E |
| Bušulej | 88 | 52.45 N | 117.13 E |
| Büsum | 30 | 54.08 N | 8.51 E |
| Busu-Melo | 152 | 1.48 N | 20.15 E |
| Bū Sunbul, Jabal ⋏[2] | 146 | 23.10 N | 22.21 E |
| Buta, Ross. | 80 | 55.02 N | 51.57 E |
| Buta, Zaïre | 154 | 2.48 N | 24.44 E |
| Butag | 116 | 12.38 N | 123.56 E |
| Butajira | 144 | 8.07 N | 38.22 E |
| Butala | 164 | 6.42 S | 147.37 E |
| Butan | 38 | 43.39 N | 23.45 E |
| Bután → Bhutan □[1] | 120 | 27.30 N | 90.30 E |
| Butand State Park ♠ | 226 | 37.13 N | 122.20 W |
| Butantã ⊸[8] | 287b | 23.34 S | 46.43 W |
| Butantã, Instituto ʊ[3] | 287b | 23.34 S | 46.43 W |
| Buta Ranquil | 252 | 37.03 S | 69.50 W |
| Butare | 154 | 2.36 S | 29.44 E |
| Butaritari I[1] | 14 | 3.07 N | 172.48 E |
| Butarque, Arroyo de ≃ | 266a | 40.19 N | 3.39 W |
| Butauanan Island I | 116 | 14.07 N | 123.17 E |
| Butchart Gardens ♠ | 224 | 48.33 N | 123.28 W |
| Butcher Island (Dia Deva) I | 272c | 18.58 N | 72.54 E |
| Bute | 168b | 33.52 S | 138.01 E |
| Bute, Island of I | 46 | 55.50 N | 5.06 W |
| Bute, Kyles of ɥ | 46 | 55.53 N | 5.13 W |
| Bute, Sound of ɥ | 46 | 55.44 N | 5.12 W |
| Büteelijn nuruu ⋏ | 88 | 50.00 N | 104.50 E |
| Bute Giarti | 144 | 4.33 N | 37.45 E |
| Bute Inlet ⊂ | 182 | 50.37 N | 124.53 W |
| Butemba | 154 | 1.09 N | 31.36 E |
| Butembo | 154 | 0.09 N | 29.17 E |
| Butera | 70 | 37.11 N | 14.11 E |
| Butere | 154 | 0.13 N | 34.30 E |
| Bütgenbach | 56 | 50.26 N | 6.12 E |
| Butha Buthe | 158 | 28.45 S | 28.15 E |
| Butha Qi (Zalantun) | 89 | 48.02 N | 122.43 E |
| Buthidaung | 110 | 20.52 N | 92.32 E |
| Buthier ≃ | 62 | 45.44 N | 7.22 E |
| Buthroton ⊥ | 38 | 39.46 N | 20.00 E |
| Buti | 66 | 43.44 N | 10.35 E |
| Butiá | 252 | 30.07 S | 51.58 W |
| Butiaba | 154 | 1.49 N | 31.19 E |
| Butig Mountains ⋏ | 116 | 7.39 N | 124.20 E |
| Butka | 86 | 56.47 N | 63.47 E |
| Butler, Al., U.S. | 194 | 32.05 N | 88.13 W |
| Butler, Ga., U.S. | 192 | 32.33 N | 84.14 W |
| Butler, Il., U.S. | 219 | 39.12 N | 89.32 W |
| Butler, In., U.S. | 216 | 41.25 N | 84.52 W |
| Butler, Ky., U.S. | 218 | 38.47 N | 84.22 W |
| Butler, Mo., U.S. | 194 | 38.15 N | 94.19 W |
| Butler, N.J., U.S. | 210 | 41.00 N | 74.20 W |
| Butler, Oh., U.S. | 214 | 40.35 N | 82.[illegible]5 W |
| Butler, Ok., U.S. | 196 | 35.38 N | 99.[illegible]1 W |
| Butler, Pa., U.S. | 214 | 40.51 N | 79.[illegible]3 W |
| Butler, Tx., U.S. | 222 | 30.19 N | 97.[illegible]8 W |
| Butler, Wi., U.S. | 216 | 43.06 N | 88.[illegible]4 W |
| Butler □[6], Oh., U.S. | 218 | 39.26 N | 84.[illegible] W |
| Butler □[6], Pa., U.S. | 214 | 40.52 N | 79.[illegible] W |
| Butler, Lake ⊜ | 220 | 28.28 N | 81.[illegible] W |
| Butler Lake ⊜ | 278 | 42.17 N | 87.[illegible] W |
| Butler Point › | 207 | 41.40 N | 70.4[illegible] W |
| Butler Reservoir ⊜[1] | 276 | 40.59 N | 74.2[illegible] W |
| Butlers Bridge | 48 | 54.02 N | 7.2[illegible] W |
| Butlerville | 218 | 39.02 N | 85.3[illegible] W |
| Butmīyah | 132 | 32.56 N | 35.5[illegible] E |
| Butnau Lake ⊜ | 184 | 56.13 N | 95.2[illegible] W |
| Butner | 192 | 36.07 N | 78.4[illegible] W |
| Buto | 152 | 15.46 S | 15.0[illegible] E |
| Buton, Pulau I | 112 | 5.00 S | 122.55 [illegible] |
| Butong | 112 | 1.06 S | 114.50 [illegible] |
| Butru | 166 | 21.30 S | 139.43 [illegible] |
| Butsha | 154 | 0.57 N | 29.13 [illegible] |
| Buttapietra | 64 | 45.20 N | 11.00 [illegible] |
| Butte, Mt., U.S. | 202 | 46.00 N | 112.32 [illegible] |
| Butte, Ne., U.S. | 198 | 42.54 N | 98.50 [illegible] |
| Butte □[6] | 226 | 39.27 N | 121.30 [illegible] |
| Butte City | 226 | 39.28 N | 121.59 [illegible] |
| Butte Creek ≃, Ca., U.S. | 204 | 39.12 N | 121.56 [illegible] |
| Butte Creek ≃, Or., U.S. | 224 | 45.09 N | 122.46 [illegible] |
| Butte du Lion ⊥ | 50 | 50.40 N | 4.24 E |
| Butte Falls | 202 | 42.32 N | 122.33 W |
| Buttelstedt | 54 | 51.05 N | 11.20 E |
| Butte Mountains ⋏ | 204 | 39.50 N | 115.05 W |
| Butten | 56 | 48.58 N | 7.13 E |
| Butter Brook ≃ | 283 | 42.31 N | 71.24 W |
| Butter Creek ≃ | 202 | 45.52 N | 119.19 W |
| Butterfield, Il., U.S. | 278 | 41.50 N | 88.02 W |
| Butterfield, Mn., U.S. | 198 | 43.57 N | 94.47 W |
| Butterfield Creek ≃ | 278 | 41.33 N | 87.37 W |
| Butterfield Lake ⊜ | 212 | 44.19 N | 75.46 W |
| Butterley Reservoir ⊜[1] | 262 | 53.35 N | 1.56 W |
| Buttermere | 44 | 54.33 N | 3.17 W |
| Butternut | 190 | 46.00 N | 90.29 W |
| Butternut Creek ≃, N.Y., U.S. | 210 | 42.25 N | 75.22 W |
| Butternut Creek ≃, N.Y., U.S. | 210 | 43.06 N | 76.00 W |
| Butterwick | 44 | 52.59 N | 0.05 E |
| Butterworth, Malay. | 114 | 5.25 N | 100.24 E |
| Butterworth, S. Afr. | 158 | 32.23 S | 28.04 E |
| Buttevant | 48 | 52.14 N | 8.40 W |
| Büttgen | 56 | 51.12 N | 6.36 E |
| Buttlar | 56 | 50.45 N | 9.57 E |
| Buttle Lake ⊜ | 182 | 49.46 N | 125.36 W |
| Button Islands II | 176 | 60.35 N | 64.45 W |
| Buttonville | 275b | 43.52 N | 79.22 W |
| Buttonville Airfield ⊠ | 275b | 43.52 N | 79.23 W |
| Buttonwillow | 226 | 35.24 N | 119.28 W |
| Buttrio | 64 | 46.01 N | 13.20 E |
| Buttstädt | 54 | 51.07 N | 11.25 E |
| Butty Head › | 162 | 33.54 S | 121.38 E |
| Buttzville | 210 | 40.49 N | 75.00 W |
| Butuan | 116 | 8.57 N | 125.33 E |
| Butuan Bay ⊂ | 116 | 9.06 N | 125.20 E |
| Butuj | 88 | 53.27 N | 112.22 E |
| Bū Tumayyim, Wādī ∨ | 146 | 26.56 N | 19.13 E |
| Buṭūris | 142 | 31.00 N | 30.15 E |
| Buturlino, Ross. | 80 | 55.34 N | 44.55 E |
| Buturlino, Ross. | 82 | 54.55 N | 37.29 E |
| Buturlinovka | 78 | 50.50 N | 40.36 E |
| Butwal | 124 | 27.42 N | 83.27 E |
| Butylicy | 80 | 55.32 N | 41.31 E |
| Butzbach | 56 | 50.26 N | 8.40 E |
| Bützfleth | 52 | 53.39 N | 9.28 E |
| Bützow | 54 | 53.50 N | 11.59 E |
| Bützsee ⊜ | 54 | 52.49 N | 12.53 E |
| Butztown | 208 | 40.39 N | 75.22 W |
| Buuhoodle | 144 | 8.15 N | 46.20 E |
| Buulo Berde | 144 | 3.51 N | 45.34 E |
| Buur Gaabo | 144 | 1.12 S | 41.51 E |
| Buurgplaatz ∧ | 56 | 50.10 N | 6.01 E |
| Buur Hakaba | 144 | 2.47 N | 44.05 E |
| Buur Haybe | 144 | 3.57 N | 45.07 E |
| Buwarah, Sabkhat al- ≋ | 130 | 35.09 N | 41.12 E |
| Buwayḍān | 132 | 33.12 N | 36.26 E |
| Buxar | 124 | 25.35 N | 83.59 E |
| Buxheim, Dtsch. | 58 | 48.00 N | 10.08 E |
| Buxheim, Dtsch. | 64 | 48.00 N | 10.08 E |
| Buxtehude | 52 | 53.28 N | 9.41 E |
| Buxton, Guy. | 246 | 6.47 N | 58.02 W |
| Buxton, S. Afr. | 158 | 27.38 S | 24.42 E |
| Buxton, Eng., U.K. | 44 | 53.15 N | 1.55 W |
| Buxton, N.C., U.S. | 192 | 35.16 N | 75.32 W |
| Buxton, N.D., U.S. | 198 | 47.36 N | 97.05 W |
| Buxton, Or., U.S. | 224 | 45.41 N | 123.11 W |
| Buxton, Mount ∧ | 182 | 51.35 N | 127.55 W |
| Buxy | 58 | 46.43 N | 4.41 E |
| Buye | 154 | 4.38 N | 27.30 E |
| Buyiqiao | 106 | 31.47 N | 119.48 E |
| Buyo | 150 | 6.16 N | 7.03 W |
| Buyo, Barrage de ⊸[6] | 150 | 6.15 N | 7.05 W |
| Buyuan ≃ | 102 | 21.51 N | 101.13 E |
| Büyükada | 130 | 40.52 N | 29.07 E |
| Büyükada I | 267b | 40.52 N | 29.07 E |
| Büyükarmutlu | 130 | 39.35 N | 38.26 E |
| Büyükbakkal ⊸[8] | 267b | 40.59 N | 29.11 E |
| Büyükçeçeli | 130 | 39.43 N | 33.52 E |
| Büyükçekmece | 130 | 41.01 N | 28.34 E |
| Büyükdere ⊸[8] | 267b | 41.09 N | 29.02 E |
| Büyükeceli | 130 | 36.11 N | 33.40 E |
| Büyükkale | 130 | 38.01 N | 27.34 E |
| Büyükkarıştıran | 130 | 41.18 N | 27.32 E |
| Büyükkemikli Burnu › | 130 | 40.18 N | 26.14 E |
| Büyükmenderes ≃ | 130 | 37.28 N | 27.11 E |
| Büyükzap → Great Zab ≃ | 128 | 36.00 N | 43.21 E |
| Buyun Shan ∧ | 98 | 40.06 N | 122.42 E |
| Buyun Uzun | 128 | 39.13 N | 63.19 E |
| Buzan ≃ | 80 | 46.18 N | 49.06 E |
| Buzanaj, peski ⊸[2] | 80 | 47.30 N | 49.50 E |
| Buzançais | 32 | 46.53 N | 1.25 E |
| Buzancy | 56 | 49.25 N | 4.57 E |
| Bužaninovo | 82 | 56.23 N | 38.18 E |
| Bužarovo | 82 | 55.59 N | 36.47 E |
| Buzău | 38 | 45.09 N | 26.49 E |
| Buzău □[6] | 38 | 45.15 N | 26.45 E |
| Buzău ≃ | 38 | 45.26 N | 27.44 E |
| Buzen | 96 | 33.37 N | 131.08 E |
| Búzi ≃ | 156 | 19.50 S | 34.43 E |
| Buziaş | 38 | 45.39 N | 21.36 E |
| Buziji | 100 | 33.49 N | 118.14 E |
| Buzinovka | 80 | 48.32 N | 43.53 E |
| Búzios, Ilha dos I | 256 | 23.48 S | 45.08 W |
| Búzios, Ponta dos › | 255 | 22.44 S | 41.53 W |
| Buz'kyy lyman ⊂[1] | 78 | 46.45 N | 31.55 E |
| Buzlanovo | 265b | 55.46 N | 37.13 E |
| Buzovna | 84 | 40.31 N | 50.04 E |
| Buzuluk, Kaz. | 86 | 51.55 N | 66.16 E |
| Buzuluk, Ross. | 80 | 52.47 N | 52.15 E |
| Buzuluk ≃, Ross. | 80 | 50.13 N | 42.12 E |
| Buzuluk ≃, Ross. | 80 | 52.47 N | 52.16 E |
| Buzzards Bay | 207 | 41.44 N | 70.37 W |
| Buzzards Bay ⊂ | 207 | 41.33 N | 70.47 W |
| Bwana Mkubwa | 154 | 13.01 S | 28.42 E |
| Bwasa | 152 | 3.53 S | 18.25 E |
| Bwendi | 154 | 4.01 N | 26.41 E |
| Bwlch | 42 | 51.54 N | 3.15 W |
| By | 40 | 60.12 N | 16.28 E |
| Byādgi | 122 | 14.41 N | 75.29 E |
| Byam Channel ɥ | 176 | 75.20 N | 105.20 W |
| Byam Martin Channel ɥ | 176 | 75.45 N | 104.00 W |
| Byam Martin Island I | 176 | 75.15 N | 104.00 W |
| Byberry Creek ≃ | 285 | 40.04 N | 74.59 W |


| English | Deutsch | Español | Français | Português |
|---|---|---|---|---|
| ≃ River | Fluß | Río | Rivière | Rio |
| ≍ Canal | Kanal | Canal | Canal | Canal |
| ∟ Waterfall, Rapids | Wasserfall, Stromschnellen | Cascada, Rápidos | Chute d'eau, Rapides | Cascata, Rápidos |
| ɥ Strait | Meeresstraße | Estrecho | Détroit | Estreito |
| ⊂ Bay, Gulf | Bucht, Golf | Bahía, Golfo | Baie, Golfe | Baía, Golfo |
| ⊜ Lake, Lakes | See, Seen | Lago, Lagos | Lac, Lacs | Lago, Lagos |
| ≋ Swamp | Sumpf | Pantano | Marais | Pântano |
| ⌂ Ice Features, Glacier | Eis- und Gletscherformen | Accidentes Glaciales | Formes glaciaires | Acidentes glaciares |
| ⊤ Other Hydrographic Features | Andere Hydrographische Objekte | Otros Elementos Hidrográficos | Autres données hydrographiques | Outros acidentes hidrográficos |

| English | Deutsch | Español | Français | Português |
|---|---|---|---|---|
| ✣ Submarine Features | Untermeerische Objekte | Accidentes Submarinos | Formes de relief sous-marin | Acidentes submarinos |
| □ Political Unit | Politische Einheit | Unidad Politica | Entité politique | Unidade política |
| ʊ Cultural Institution | Kulturelle Institution | Institución Cultural | Institution culturelle | Institução cultural |
| ⊥ Historical Site | Historische Stätte | Sitio Histórico | Site historique | Sitio histórico |
| ♠ Recreational Site | Erholungs- und Ferienort | Sitio de Recreo | Centre de loisirs | Area de Lazer |
| ⊠ Airport | Flughafen | Aeropuerto | Aéroport | Aeroporto |
| ■ Military Installation | Militäranlage | Instalación Militar | Installation militaire | Instalação militar |
| ⊸ Miscellaneous | Verschiedenes | Misceláneo | Divers | Diversos |

| | | | |
|---|---|---|---|
| Byblos → Jubayl | 130 | 34.07 N | 35.39 E |
| Bycen' | 76 | 52.54 N | 25.29 E |
| Bychawa | 30 | 51.01 N | 22.32 E |
| Bychok ≃ | 83 | 48.26 N | 37.47 E |
| Byčki, Ross. | 76 | 54.15 N | 34.39 E |
| Byčki, Ross. | 80 | 53.38 N | 40.54 E |
| Byculla ✦[8] | 272c | 18.58 N | 72.49 E |
| Byčyha | 76 | 55.41 N | 29.58 E |
| Byczyna | 30 | 51.07 N | 18.11 E |
| Bydalen | 26 | 63.06 N | 13.47 E |
| Bydgoszcz | 30 | 53.08 N | 18.00 E |
| Bydgoszcz □[4] | 30 | 53.15 N | 18.00 E |
| Byelorussia → Belarus □[1] | 72 | 53.50 N | 28.00 E |
| Byers, Pa., U.S. | 285 | 40.05 N | 75.41 W |
| Byers, Tx., U.S. | 196 | 34.04 N | 98.11 W |
| Byersdale | 279b | 40.37 N | 80.13 W |
| Byers Run ≃ | 279b | 40.24 N | 79.42 W |
| Byesville | 188 | 39.58 N | 81.32 W |
| Byfang ✦[8] | 263 | 51.24 N | 7.06 E |
| Byfield, Eng., U.K. | 42 | 52.11 N | 1.14 W |
| Byfield, Ma., U.S. | 207 | 42.45 N | 70.56 W |
| Byfleet | 42 | 51.20 N | 0.29 W |
| Byford | 168a | 32.13 S | 116.00 E |
| Byforde | 284c | 39.01 N | 77.05 W |
| Bygdeå | 26 | 64.04 N | 20.51 E |
| Bygdeträsket ⊜ | 26 | 64.26 N | 20.32 E |
| Bygdin | 26 | 61.20 N | 8.48 E |
| Bygdin ⊜ | 26 | 61.21 N | 8.36 E |
| Bygi | 80 | 57.13 N | 53.44 E |
| Byglandsfjord | 26 | 58.41 N | 7.48 E |
| Byglandsfjorden ⊜ | 26 | 58.48 N | 7.50 E |
| Byhalia | 194 | 34.52 N | 89.41 W |
| Byhaŭ | 76 | 53.32 N | 30.12 E |
| Bykivka | 78 | 50.17 N | 27.58 E |
| Bykle | 26 | 59.21 N | 7.20 E |
| Bykov | 89 | 47.21 N | 142.32 E |
| Bykovka | 82 | 55.29 N | 37.40 E |
| Bykovo, Ross. | 80 | 49.47 N | 45.22 E |
| Bykovo, Ross. | 82 | 54.01 N | 37.54 E |
| Bykovo, Ross. | 82 | 55.37 N | 38.04 E |
| Bykovo Airport ⊠ | 265b | 55.36 N | 38.05 E |
| Bylas | 200 | 33.08 N | 110.07 W |
| Bylbasivka | 83 | 48.51 N | 37.30 E |
| Bylderup | 41 | 54.57 N | 9.07 E |
| Byley | 262 | 53.13 N | 2.25 W |
| Bylkyldak | 86 | 48.38 N | 75.16 E |
| Bylnice | 30 | 49.04 N | 18.01 E |
| Bylot Island I | 176 | 73.13 N | 78.34 W |
| Byng Inlet | 190 | 45.46 N | 80.33 W |
| Bynum, Mt., U.S. | 182 | 47.58 N | 112.18 W |
| Bynum, N.C., U.S. | 192 | 35.46 N | 79.08 W |
| Bynum, Tx., U.S. | 222 | 31.58 N | 97.00 W |
| Byōdōin Temple ʋ[1] | 270 | 34.53 N | 135.48 E |
| Byram ≃ | 276 | 40.59 N | 73.39 W |
| Byramgore Reef ✧[2] | 122 | 11.54 N | 71.49 E |
| Byram Lake Reservoir ⊜[1] | 276 | 41.10 N | 73.41 W |
| Byrd, Lac ⊜ | 190 | 47.01 N | 76.56 W |
| Byrdstown | 194 | 36.34 N | 85.07 W |
| Byrka | 88 | 50.39 N | 118.31 E |
| Byrne Arena ♦ | 276 | 40.49 N | 74.05 W |
| Byrnedale | 214 | 41.17 N | 78.30 W |
| Byro | 162 | 26.05 S | 116.09 E |
| Byrock | 166 | 30.40 S | 146.24 E |
| Byron, Ca., U.S. | 226 | 37.52 N | 121.38 W |
| Byron, Ga., U.S. | 192 | 32.39 N | 83.45 W |
| Byron, Il., U.S. | 190 | 42.07 N | 89.15 W |
| Byron, Mi., U.S. | 216 | 42.49 N | 83.57 W |
| Byron, N.Y., U.S. | 210 | 43.04 N | 78.03 W |
| Byron, Wy., U.S. | 202 | 44.47 N | 108.30 W |
| Byron, Cape › | 166 | 28.39 S | 153.38 E |
| Byron, Isla I | 254 | 47.47 S | 75.12 W |
| Byron Bay | 166 | 28.39 S | 153.37 E |
| Byron Center | 216 | 42.49 N | 85.42 W |
| Byrranga, gory ⋏ | 74 | 75.00 N | 104.00 E |
| Byryuchyy Ostriv, kosa ›[2] | 78 | 46.08 N | 35.05 E |
| Byšice-Liblice | 54 | 50.19 N | 14.38 E |
| Bysjön ⊜ | 40 | 60.23 N | 14.30 E |
| Byske | 26 | 64.57 N | 21.12 E |
| Byskeälven ≃ | 26 | 64.57 N | 21.13 E |
| Bystraja ≃ | 80 | 47.58 N | 41.00 E |
| Bystřany | 54 | 50.38 N | 13.51 E |
| Bystrica ≃ | 80 | 58.38 N | 49.05 E |
| Bystřice | 30 | 49.45 N | 14.41 E |
| Bystřice pod Hostýnem | 30 | 49.24 N | 17.40 E |
| Bystrij Tanyp ≃ | 86 | 55.46 N | 54.35 E |
| Bystrovka | 85 | 42.47 N | 75.43 E |
| Bystryj | 86 | 57.50 N | 73.58 E |
| Bystryj Istok | 86 | 52.23 N | 84.24 E |
| Bystrzyca Kłodzka | 30 | 50.18 N | 16.38 E |
| Bytantaj ≃ | 74 | 68.46 N | 134.20 E |
| Bytča, Bela. | 76 | 54.18 N | 28.24 E |
| Bytča, Slvk. | 30 | 49.14 N | 18.36 E |
| Bytkiv | 78 | 48.38 N | 24.26 E |
| Bytom (Beuthen) | 30 | 50.22 N | 18.54 E |
| Bytoš' | 76 | 53.50 N | 34.06 E |
| Bytów | 30 | 54.11 N | 17.30 E |
| Byumba | 154 | 1.35 S | 30.04 E |
| Byval'ki | 78 | 51.51 N | 30.37 E |
| Byxelkrok | 26 | 57.20 N | 17.00 E |
| Bzyb' ≃ | 84 | 43.12 N | 40.18 E |
| Bzybskij chrebet ⋏ | 84 | 43.18 N | 40.41 E |

C

| | | | |
|---|---|---|---|
| Ca ≃ | 110 | 18.46 N | 105.47 E |
| Čaa-Chol' | 86 | 51.32 N | 92.23 E |
| Caacupé | 252 | 25.23 S | 57.09 W |
| Čaadajevka | 80 | 53.09 N | 45.56 E |
| Čaadajevo | 80 | 55.40 N | 42.02 E |
| Caaguazú | 252 | 25.26 S | 56.02 W |
| Caaguazú □[5] | 252 | 25.00 S | 55.45 W |
| Caála | 152 | 12.51 S | 15.33 E |
| Caamaño Sound ⋃ | 182 | 52.49 N | 129.28 W |
| Caapiranga | 246 | 3.18 S | 61.13 W |
| Caapucú | 252 | 26.13 S | 57.12 W |
| Caarapó | 255 | 22.38 S | 54.48 W |
| Caatinga | 255 | 17.10 S | 45.53 W |
| Caazapá | 252 | 26.09 S | 56.24 W |
| Caazapá □[5] | 252 | 26.10 S | 56.00 W |
| Cabaçal ≃ | 248 | 16.00 S | 57.42 W |
| Cabadbaran | 116 | 9.10 N | 125.38 E |
| Cabadiangan Plateau ⋏[1] | 116 | 9.50 N | 122.36 E |
| Cabagan | 116 | 17.26 N | 121.46 E |
| Cabaiguán | 240p | 22.05 N | 79.30 W |
| Cabalete Island I | 116 | 14.17 N | 121.50 E |
| Cabalian | 116 | 10.16 N | 125.10 E |
| Cabaliana, Lago ⊜ | 246 | 3.20 S | 60.50 W |
| Cabalian Bay ⊂ | 116 | 10.13 N | 125.10 E |
| Cabalian Point › | 116 | 12.06 N | 122.01 E |
| Caballero Creek ≃ | 280 | 34.11 N | 118.32 W |
| Caballito ✦[8] | 288 | 34.37 S | 58.27 W |
| Caballones, Cayo I | 240p | 20.52 N | 79.00 W |
| Caballo Reservoir ⊜[1] | 200 | 32.58 N | 107.18 W |
| Cabana | 248 | 8.24 S | 78.02 W |
| Cabanaconde | 248 | 15.37 S | 71.59 W |
| Cabañas | 240p | 22.58 N | 82.55 W |
| Cabanatuan | 116 | 15.29 N | 120.58 E |
| Cabangan | 116 | 15.10 N | 120.03 E |
| Cabano | 186 | 47.41 N | 68.53 W |
| Cabarroguis | 116 | 16.33 N | 121.32 E |
| Cabarruyan Island I | 116 | 16.18 N | 119.59 E |
| Cabaun Island I | 116 | 12.34 N | 124.30 E |
| Cabeceiras | 255 | 15.48 S | 46.59 W |
| Cabeço de Montachique | 266c | 38.54 N | 9.11 W |
| Cabellera, Sierra de la ⋏ | 200 | 30.55 N | 109.07 W |
| Cabery | 216 | 41.00 N | 88.12 W |
| Cabeza del Buey | 34 | 38.43 N | 5.13 W |
| Cabeza de Tigre | 286c | 10.28 N | 66.46 W |
| Cabezas | 248 | 18.46 S | 63.24 W |
| Cabiao | 116 | 15.15 N | 120.51 E |
| Cabiate | 266b | 45.40 N | 9.10 E |
| Cabildo, Arg. | 252 | 38.29 S | 61.54 W |
| Cabildo, Chile | 252 | 32.26 S | 71.05 W |
| Cabimas | 246 | 10.23 N | 71.28 W |
| Cabin Branch ≃, Md., U.S. | 284b | 39.13 N | 76.35 W |
| Cabin Branch ≃, Md., U.S. | 284c | 38.51 N | 76.48 W |
| Cabin Creek ≃ | 198 | 46.55 N | 104.52 W |
| Cabinda | 152 | 5.33 S | 12.12 E |
| Cabinda □[5] | 152 | 5.00 S | 12.30 E |
| Cabinet Mountains ⋏ | 202 | 48.20 N | 116.00 W |
| Cabingaan Island I | 116 | 5.41 N | 121.03 E |
| Cabin John | 208 | 38.58 N | 77.09 W |
| Cabin John Creek ≃ | 284b | 38.58 N | 77.09 W |
| Cabin John Creek Park ♦ | 284c | 38.59 N | 77.09 W |
| Cabin John Regional Park ♦ | 284c | 39.02 N | 77.09 W |
| Cabiri | 152 | 8.52 S | 13.39 E |
| Cabixi ≃ | 248 | 13.41 S | 60.44 W |
| Cable | 190 | 46.12 N | 91.17 W |
| Cable Airport ⊠ | 280 | 34.08 N | 117.41 W |
| Cables | 162 | 27.59 S | 123.23 E |
| Cabo | 250 | 8.17 S | 35.02 W |
| Cabo Blanco | 254 | 47.12 S | 65.45 W |
| Cabo de Hornos, Parque Nacional ♦ | 250 | 55.45 S | 67.25 W |
| Cabo Delgado □[5] | 154 | 12.35 S | 39.00 E |
| Cabo Frio | 255 | 22.53 S | 42.01 W |
| Cabo Gracias a Dios | 236 | 14.59 N | 83.10 W |
| Cabo Ledo | 152 | 9.39 S | 13.17 E |
| Cabonga, Réservoir ⊜[1] | 190 | 47.20 N | 76.35 W |
| Cabool | 194 | 37.07 N | 92.06 W |
| Caboolture | 166 | 27.05 S | 152.57 E |
| Cabo Orange, Parque Nacional do ♦ | 250 | 3.00 N | 51.00 W |
| Cabo Raso | 254 | 44.21 S | 65.14 W |
| Caborca | 232 | 30.37 N | 112.06 W |
| Cabo Rojo | 240m | 18.05 N | 67.09 W |
| Cabot, Ar., U.S. | 194 | 34.58 N | 92.00 W |
| Cabot, Pa., U.S. | 214 | 40.46 N | 79.46 W |
| Cabot, Mount ∧ | 188 | 44.31 N | 71.24 W |
| Cabot Head › | 212 | 45.14 N | 81.17 W |
| Cabot Strait ⋃ | 186 | 47.20 N | 59.30 W |
| Cabo Verde | 256 | 21.28 S | 46.24 W |
| Cabo Verde → Cape Verde □[1] | 150a | 16.00 N | 24.00 W |
| Cabo Verde ≃ | 256 | 21.28 S | 46.17 W |
| Cabra | 34 | 37.28 N | 4.27 W |
| Cabra Corral, Embalse ⊜[1] | 252 | 25.15 S | 65.25 W |
| Cabra Island I | 116 | 13.53 N | 120.02 E |
| Cabramatta | 274a | 33.54 S | 150.56 E |
| Cabramatta Creek ≃ | 274a | 33.54 S | 150.57 E |
| Cabramurra | 171b | 35.58 S | 148.23 E |
| Cabras | 71 | 39.56 N | 8.32 E |
| Cabras, Stagno di ⊜ | 71 | 39.57 N | 8.29 E |
| Cabras Island I | 174p | 13.27 N | 144.40 E |
| Cabrayıl | 84 | 39.23 N | 47.02 E |
| Cabrel | 234 | 20.06 N | 105.14 W |
| Cabrera ≃, Col. | 246 | 3.26 N | 75.07 W |
| Cabrera ≃, Esp. | 34 | 42.25 N | 6.49 W |
| Cabrera, Illa de I | 34 | 39.09 N | 2.56 E |
| Cabrera de Mar | 266d | 41.32 N | 2.24 E |
| Cabreúva | 256 | 23.18 S | 47.08 W |
| Cabri | 184 | 50.37 N | 108.28 W |
| Cabria | 64 | 45.54 N | 13.35 E |
| Cabriel ≃ | 34 | 39.14 N | 1.03 W |
| Cabrillo National Monument ♦ | 228 | 32.41 N | 117.15 W |
| Cabrils | 266d | 41.32 N | 2.22 E |
| Cabrobó | 250 | 8.31 S | 39.19 W |
| Cabruta | 246 | 7.38 N | 66.15 W |
| Cabucgayan | 116 | 11.29 N | 124.34 E |
| Cabuçu | 256 | 22.50 S | 42.55 W |
| Cabuçu ≃, Bra. | 287a | 22.59 S | 43.37 W |
| Cabuçu ≃, Bra. | 287a | 22.48 S | 43.37 W |
| Cabuçu de Cima ≃ | 287b | 23.31 S | 46.33 W |
| Cabugao | 116 | 17.48 N | 120.27 E |
| Cabulauan Island I | 116 | 11.23 N | 120.06 E |
| Cabullónes, Punta › | 240m | 17.58 N | 66.35 W |
| Cabulo | 152 | 10.15 S | 16.40 E |
| Cabure | 246 | 11.08 N | 69.38 W |
| Čabusy | 76 | 52.49 N | 28.06 E |
| Cabuta | 152 | 9.50 S | 14.48 E |
| Cabuya | 236 | 9.36 N | 85.06 W |
| Cabuyal | 236 | 10.40 N | 85.40 W |
| Cabuyaro | 246 | 4.18 N | 72.49 W |
| Caca | 80 | 48.11 N | 44.40 E |
| Çaçador | 252 | 26.47 S | 51.00 W |
| Čačak | 38 | 43.53 N | 20.21 E |
| Cacaohatán | 236 | 14.59 N | 92.10 W |
| Cacaoui, Lac ⊜ | 186 | 50.53 N | 66.58 W |
| Caçapava | 256 | 23.06 S | 45.42 W |
| Caçapava do Sul | 252 | 30.30 S | 53.30 W |
| Caçapava Velha | 256 | 23.07 S | 45.39 W |
| Cacapon ≃ | 188 | 39.37 N | 78.16 W |
| Cacapon State Park ♦ | 188 | 39.32 N | 78.23 W |
| Cacas | 130 | 38.23 N | 41.17 E |
| Caccamo | 70 | 37.56 N | 13.40 E |
| Caccia, Capo › | 71 | 40.34 N | 8.09 E |
| Çaccuri | 68 | 39.14 N | 16.47 E |
| Čačenka ≃ | 265b | 55.46 N | 37.18 E |
| Cacequi | 252 | 29.53 S | 54.49 W |
| Cáceres, Bra. | 248 | 16.04 S | 57.41 W |
| Cáceres, Col. | 246 | 7.35 N | 75.20 W |
| Cáceres, Esp. | 34 | 39.29 N | 6.22 W |
| Çáceres □[4] | 34 | 39.40 N | 6.05 E |
| Čačèrsk | 76 | 52.55 N | 30.55 E |
| Čačèvičy | 76 | 53.31 N | 29.51 E |
| Cachan | 261 | 48.48 N | 2.20 E |
| Cacharí | 252 | 36.24 S | 59.32 W |
| Cache | 196 | 34.37 N | 98.37 W |
| Cache ≃, Ar., U.S. | 194 | 34.42 N | 91.20 W |
| Cache ≃, Il., U.S. | 194 | 37.04 N | 89.10 W |
| Caché, Lac ⊜ | 206 | 46.21 N | 74.39 W |
| Cache Creek | 182 | 50.48 N | 121.19 W |
| Cache Creek ≃, Ca., U.S. | 226 | 38.42 N | 121.42 W |
| Cache Creek ≃, Ca., U.S. | 228 | 35.06 N | 117.58 W |
| Cache Creek, North Fork ≃ | 226 | 38.59 N | 122.30 W |
| Cache la Poudre ≃ | 200 | 40.25 N | 104.36 W |
| Cache la Poudre, North Fork ≃ | 198 | 40.54 N | 105.22 W |
| Cache Mountain ∧ | 180 | 65.31 N | 147.20 W |
| Cache Peak ∧, Ca., U.S. | 228 | 35.13 N | 118.15 W |
| Cache Peak ∧, Id., U.S. | 202 | 42.11 N | 113.40 W |
| Cache Slough ≃ | 226 | 38.11 N | 121.40 W |
| Cacheu | 150 | 12.16 N | 16.10 W |
| Cacheu ⊂[1] | 150 | 12.10 N | 16.21 W |
| Cachí | 252 | 25.06 S | 66.11 W |
| Cachimbo | 250 | 9.24 S | 54.56 W |
| Cachimbo, Serra do ⋏ | 250 | 8.30 S | 55.50 W |
| Cachimo | 152 | 8.21 S | 21.20 E |
| Cachingues | 152 | 13.05 S | 16.43 E |
| Cachir | 88 | 48.06 N | 98.52 E |
| Cachkadzor | 84 | 40.33 N | 44.43 E |
| Cachoeira ≃ | 256 | 23.06 S | 46.29 W |
| Cachoeira, Reservatório ⊜[1] | 256 | 23.03 S | 46.15 W |
| Cachoeira, Rio da ≃ | 287a | 23.00 S | 43.18 W |
| Cachoeira Alta | 255 | 18.48 S | 50.58 W |
| Cachoeira de Goiás | 255 | 16.44 S | 50.38 W |
| Cachoeira de Manteiga | 255 | 16.39 S | 45.16 W |
| Cachoeira de Minas | 256 | 22.21 S | 45.47 W |
| Cachoeira do Arari | 250 | 1.01 S | 48.58 W |
| Cachoeira do Sul | 252 | 30.02 S | 52.54 W |
| Cachoeira Grande, Alto da ∧ | 256 | 21.54 S | 44.06 W |
| Cachoeira Paulista | 256 | 22.40 S | 45.01 W |
| Cachoeiras | 287a | 22.39 S | 43.28 W |
| Cachoeiras de Macacu | 256 | 22.28 S | 42.39 W |
| Cachoeirinha | 250 | 8.29 S | 36.14 W |
| Cachoeiro de Itapemirim | 255 | 20.51 S | 41.06 W |
| Cachos, Punta › | 252 | 27.39 S | 71.02 W |
| Çachos, Rio dos ≃ | 287b | 23.36 S | 46.26 W |
| Čachrov | 60 | 49.16 N | 13.18 E |
| Cachuela Esperanza | 248 | 10.32 S | 65.38 W |
| Cachuma, Lake ⊜[1] | 204 | 34.35 N | 119.55 W |
| Cacilhas | 266c | 38.41 N | 9.09 W |
| Cacine | 150 | 11.08 N | 14.57 W |
| Caciporé ≃ | 250 | 3.51 N | 51.08 W |
| Caciporé, Cabo › | 250 | 3.55 N | 51.07 W |
| Căciulați | 38 | 44.38 N | 26.10 E |
| Cacnipa Island I | 116 | 10.30 N | 119.04 E |
| Cacocum | 240p | 20.44 N | 76.23 W |
| Cacólo | 152 | 10.07 S | 19.17 E |
| Caconda | 152 | 13.43 S | 15.06 E |
| Caconde | 256 | 21.33 S | 46.38 W |
| Cacra | 248 | 12.48 S | 75.48 W |
| Cactus | 196 | 36.04 N | 102.00 W |
| Cactus Flat ≚ | 204 | 37.45 N | 116.45 W |
| Cactus Peak ∧ | 204 | 37.47 N | 116.53 W |
| Caçu | 255 | 18.37 S | 51.04 W |
| Cacuaco | 152 | 8.47 S | 13.22 E |
| Cacula | 152 | 14.29 S | 14.10 E |
| Caculé | 255 | 14.30 S | 42.13 W |
| Caculuvar ≃ | 152 | 16.46 S | 14.36 E |
| Cacuri, Ang. | 152 | 8.14 S | 18.20 E |
| Cacuri, Ven. | 246 | 4.48 N | 65.21 W |
| Cacuso | 152 | 9.26 S | 15.43 E |
| Çadale | 144 | 2.45 N | 46.19 E |
| Čadan | 86 | 51.17 N | 91.35 E |
| Cadaqués | 34 | 42.17 N | 3.17 E |
| Çadariri ≃ | 248 | 6.20 S | 57.46 W |
| Čadca | 30 | 49.26 N | 18.48 E |
| Caddington | 42 | 51.51 N | 0.27 W |
| Caddo, Ok., U.S. | 196 | 34.07 N | 96.15 W |
| Caddo, Tx., U.S. | 196 | 32.38 N | 98.40 W |
| Caddo ≃ | 194 | 34.10 N | 93.03 W |
| Caddo Creek ≃, Ok., U.S. | 196 | 34.14 N | 96.59 W |
| Caddo Creek ≃, Tx., U.S. | 222 | 32.02 N | 95.26 W |
| Caddo Creek Lake ⊜[1] | 222 | 32.05 N | 95.39 W |
| Caddo Lake ⊜[1] | 194 | 32.42 N | 94.01 W |
| Caddo Mills | 222 | 33.04 N | 96.14 W |
| Caddo Peak ∧ | 222 | 32.29 N | 97.24 W |
| Caddy Vista | 216 | 42.50 N | 87.54 W |
| Cadell ≃ | 166 | 22.51 S | 141.55 E |
| Cadena, Arroyo de la ≃ | 196 | 26.17 N | 104.00 W |
| Cadena, Cerro ∧ | 196 | 25.50 N | 104.04 W |
| Cadena, Punta › | 240m | 18.18 N | 67.14 W |
| Cadenberge | 52 | 53.46 N | 9.04 E |
| Cadenet | 62 | 43.44 N | 5.22 E |
| Cadeo | 62 | 44.58 N | 9.48 E |
| Cadereyta de Jiménez | 232 | 25.36 N | 100.00 W |
| Cader Idris ∧ | 42 | 52.42 N | 3.54 W |
| Cadibarrawirracanna, Lake ⊜ | 162 | 28.52 S | 135.27 E |
| Cadig, Mount ∧ | 116 | 14.09 N | 122.27 E |
| Cadillac, Sk., Can. | 184 | 49.44 N | 107.43 W |
| Cadillac, Fr. | 32 | 44.38 N | 0.19 W |
| Cadillac, Mi., U.S. | 190 | 44.15 N | 85.24 W |
| Cadipietra (Steinhaus) | 64 | 46.59 N | 11.59 E |
| Cadishead | 262 | 53.25 N | 2.26 W |
| Cadix → Cádiz | 34 | 36.32 N | 6.18 W |
| Cádiz, Esp. | 34 | 36.32 N | 6.18 W |
| Cadiz, Pil. | 116 | 10.57 N | 123.18 E |
| Cadiz, In., U.S. | 218 | 39.57 N | 85.30 W |
| Cadiz, Ky., U.S. | 194 | 36.51 N | 87.50 W |
| Cadiz, Oh., U.S. | 214 | 40.16 N | 80.59 W |
| Cádiz □[4] | 34 | 36.35 N | 5.50 W |
| Cádiz, Bahía de ⊂ | 34 | 36.32 N | 6.16 W |
| Cádiz, Golfo de ⊂ | 34 | 36.50 N | 7.10 W |
| Cadiz Lake ⊜ | 204 | 34.18 N | 115.24 W |
| Cadlao Island I | 116 | 11.13 N | 119.21 E |
| Çadnam | 42 | 50.55 N | 1.35 W |
| Čadobec | 88 | 58.40 N | 98.51 E |
| Čadobec ≃ | 88 | 58.40 N | 98.50 E |
| Cadogan | 214 | 40.45 N | 79.34 W |
| Cadolzburg | 56 | 49.28 N | 10.51 E |
| Cadomin | 182 | 53.02 N | 117.20 W |
| Cadoneghe | 64 | 45.26 N | 11.55 E |
| Cadore ✦[1] | 64 | 46.30 N | 12.20 E |
| Cadosia | 210 | 41.58 N | 75.16 W |
| Cadott | 190 | 44.56 N | 91.09 W |
| Cadoux | 162 | 30.47 S | 117.08 E |
| Caduruan Point › | 116 | 11.45 N | 124.05 E |
| Caduta, Fosso delle ≃ | 267a | 41.56 N | 12.12 E |
| Cadwell | 192 | 32.20 N | 83.02 W |
| Cady Marsh Ditch ≅ | 278 | 41.33 N | 87.29 W |
| Cady Mountain ∧[2] | 224 | 48.33 N | 123.07 W |
| Cadzand | 52 | 51.22 N | 3.25 E |
| Caen | 32 | 49.11 N | 0.21 W |
| Caengo (Kwenge) ≃ | 152 | 4.50 S | 18.42 E |
| Caerano di San Marco | 64 | 45.47 N | 12.00 E |
| Caere ⊥ | 66 | 42.02 N | 12.07 E |
| Caergwrle | 44 | 53.07 N | 3.03 W |
| Caerleon | 42 | 51.37 N | 2.57 W |
| Caernarfon | 44 | 53.08 N | 4.16 W |
| Caernarfon Bay ⊂ | 44 | 53.05 N | 4.30 W |
| Caernarfon Castle ⊥ | 44 | 53.08 N | 4.16 W |
| Caerphilly | 42 | 51.35 N | 3.14 W |
| Caerphilly Castle ⊥ | 42 | 51.34 N | 3.14 W |
| Caersws | 42 | 52.31 N | 3.25 W |
| Caesar Creek ≃ | 218 | 39.29 N | 84.03 W |
| Caesar Creek, Anderson Fork ≃ | 218 | 39.33 N | 83.58 W |
| Caesar Creek Lake ⊜[1] | 218 | 39.30 N | 84.00 W |
| Cæsarea → Qesari, Horbat ⊥ | 132 | 32.30 N | 34.53 E |
| Caetanópolis | 255 | 19.18 S | 44.24 W |
| Caeté | 255 | 19.54 S | 43.40 W |
| Caeté ≃ | 248 | 9.03 S | 68.39 W |
| Caeté, Morro ∧[2] | 287a | 23.03 S | 43.31 W |
| Caetité | 255 | 14.04 S | 42.29 W |
| Cafayate | 252 | 26.05 S | 65.58 W |
| Cafelândia do Leste | 255 | 16.40 S | 53.25 W |
| Cafima | 152 | 16.39 S | 16.27 E |
| Cafu | 152 | 16.27 S | 15.14 E |
| Cafuini ≃ | 246 | 1.17 N | 57.11 W |
| Cagaan Chajrchan | 88 | 49.25 N | 94.15 E |
| Cagaan Gol | 86 | 48.57 N | 89.07 E |
| Cagaan Nuur, Mong. | 86 | 49.32 N | 89.42 E |
| Cagaannuur, Mong. | 88 | 50.20 N | 105.03 E |
| Cagaan-Ovoo | 102 | 45.51 N | 105.17 E |
| Cagaan Uul | 88 | 49.28 N | 98.30 E |
| Cagaan-Üür | 88 | 50.32 N | 101.30 E |
| Çágado ≃ | 256 | 22.02 S | 43.09 W |
| Čagan ≃ | 80 | 51.12 N | 51.20 E |
| Cagan-Aman | 80 | 47.34 N | 46.43 E |
| Cagan-Churtej, chrebet ⋏ | 88 | 51.32 N | 110.00 E |
| Cagarras, Ilhas II | 287a | 23.02 S | 43.12 W |
| Cagayan □[4] | 116 | 18.00 N | 121.50 E |
| Cagayan ≃ | 116 | 18.22 N | 121.37 E |
| Cagayancillo | 116 | 9.34 N | 121.12 E |
| Cagayan de Oro | 116 | 8.29 N | 124.39 E |
| Cagayan de Tawi-Tawi | 116 | 7.01 N | 118.30 E |
| Cagayan Island I | 116 | 9.36 N | 121.14 E |
| Cagayan Islands II | 116 | 9.40 N | 121.16 E |
| Çagayan Sulu Island I | 116 | 7.01 N | 118.30 E |
| Čagda | 74 | 58.45 N | 130.37 E |
| Cageri | 84 | 42.39 N | 42.45 E |
| Caggiano | 68 | 40.34 N | 15.29 E |
| Çağış | 130 | 39.30 N | 28.01 E |
| Çağlarca | 130 | 39.05 N | 39.10 E |
| Cagli | 66 | 43.33 N | 12.39 E |
| Cagliari | 71 | 39.13 N | 9.07 E |
| Cagliari □[4] | 71 | 39.30 N | 8.45 E |
| Cagliari, Golfo di ⊂ | 71 | 39.08 N | 9.11 E |
| Çagliari, Stagno di ⊜ | 71 | 39.13 N | 9.02 E |
| Čaglinka ≃ | 86 | 53.59 N | 69.47 E |
| Cagnano Varano | 68 | 41.49 N | 15.47 E |
| Çagnes-sur-Mer | 62 | 43.40 N | 7.09 E |
| Čagoda | 76 | 59.10 N | 35.17 E |
| Čagoda ≃ | 76 | 59.05 N | 35.18 E |
| Čagodošča ≃ | 76 | 58.57 N | 36.35 E |
| Čagojan | 89 | 52.08 N | 128.15 E |
| Čagra ≃ | 80 | 52.37 N | 48.15 E |
| Cagraray Island I | 116 | 13.18 N | 123.52 E |
| Cagua | 246 | 10.11 N | 67.27 W |
| Caguán ≃ | 246 | 0.08 S | 74.18 W |
| Caguas | 240m | 18.14 N | 66.02 W |
| Cagveri | 84 | 41.48 N | 43.29 E |
| Cagwait | 116 | 8.55 N | 126.18 E |
| Cahaba ≃ | 194 | 32.20 N | 87.05 W |
| Cahabón | 236 | 15.34 N | 89.49 W |
| Cahabón ≃ | 236 | 15.25 N | 89.36 W |
| Cahama | 152 | 16.17 S | 14.19 E |
| Caha Mountains ⋏ | 48 | 51.45 N | 9.45 W |
| Caher | 48 | 52.21 N | 7.56 W |
| Caherdaniel | 48 | 51.45 N | 10.05 W |
| Cahersiveen | 48 | 51.57 N | 10.13 W |
| Cahokia | 219 | 38.34 N | 90.11 W |
| Cahokia Creek ≃ | 219 | 38.47 N | 90.01 W |
| Cahokia Mounds State Park ♦ | 219 | 38.39 N | 90.03 W |
| Cahoon Creek ≃ | 279a | 41.29 N | 81.55 W |
| Cahoon Park ♦ | 279a | 41.29 N | 81.56 W |
| Cahoonzie | 210 | 41.26 N | 74.43 W |
| Cahora Bassa | 154 | 15.35 S | 32.48 E |
| Cahora Bassa, Albufeira de ⊜[1] | 154 | 15.40 S | 31.40 E |
| Cahore Point › | 48 | 52.34 N | 6.11 W |
| Cahors | 32 | 44.27 N | 1.26 E |
| Cahto Peak ∧ | 204 | 39.41 N | 123.35 W |
| Cahuilla Indian Reservation ✦[4] | 204 | 33.30 N | 116.43 W |
| Cahuinari ≃ | 246 | 1.21 S | 70.44 W |
| Cahuita, Punta › | 236 | 9.45 N | 82.49 W |
| Cahul | 38 | 45.54 N | 28.11 E |
| Caí ≃ | 252 | 29.56 S | 51.16 W |
| Caia ≃ | 34 | 38.50 N | 7.05 W |
| Caianda | 152 | 11.02 S | 23.31 E |
| Caiapó ≃, Bra. | 250 | 8.52 S | 49.36 W |
| Caiapó ≃, Bra. | 255 | 15.49 S | 51.53 W |
| Caiapó, Serra do ⋏ | 255 | 17.00 S | 52.00 W |
| Caiapônia | 255 | 16.57 S | 51.49 W |
| Caiazzo | 68 | 41.11 N | 14.22 E |
| Caibarién | 240p | 22.31 N | 79.28 W |
| Cai Bau, Dao I | 110 | 21.10 N | 107.27 E |
| Caibiran | 116 | 11.34 N | 124.35 E |
| Caiçara, Bra. | 250 | 6.36 S | 35.29 W |
| Caiçara, Bra. | 255 | 15.34 S | 50.12 W |
| Caicara, Caño ≃ | 246 | 7.44 N | 69.04 W |
| Caicara de Maturín | 246 | 9.49 N | 63.36 W |
| Caicara de Orinoco | 246 | 7.37 N | 66.10 W |
| Caicedonia | 246 | 4.20 N | 75.50 W |
| Caicó | 250 | 6.27 S | 37.06 W |
| Caicos Bank ✧[4] | 238 | 21.35 N | 71.55 W |
| Caicos Islands II | 238 | 21.56 N | 71.58 W |
| Caicos Passage ⋃ | 238 | 22.00 N | 72.30 W |
| Caieiras | 256 | 23.22 S | 46.44 W |
| Caieiras □[7] | 287b | 23.23 S | 46.41 W |
| Caigou | 100 | 33.16 N | 114.32 E |
| Caiguna | 162 | 32.17 S | 125.25 E |
| Caihuaping | 100 | 26.54 N | 113.23 E |
| Caijiachang | 107 | 29.44 N | 106.29 E |
| Caijiagang | 107 | 28.55 N | 106.21 E |
| Caijialou | 104 | 41.24 N | 121.06 E |
| Caijiapo | 102 | 34.17 N | 107.39 E |
| Caijiazhuang | 105 | 40.48 N | 114.44 E |
| Caille | 62 | 43.46 N | 6.44 E |
| Cailloma | 248 | 15.12 S | 71.46 W |
| Caillou Bay ⊂ | 194 | 29.06 N | 90.56 W |
| Caima Bay ⊂ | 116 | 13.42 N | 122.48 E |
| Caimán, Islas → Cayman Islands □[2] | 238 | 19.30 N | 80.40 W |
| Caimanera | 240p | 19.59 N | 75.09 W |
| Caïmanes → Cayman Islands □[2] | 238 | 19.30 N | 80.40 W |
| Caiman Point › | 116 | 15.55 N | 119.46 E |
| Caimbambo | 152 | 12.58 S | 14.01 E |
| Cain ≃ | 42 | 52.46 N | 3.08 W |
| Cain Creek ≃ | 198 | 44.17 N | 98.10 W |
| Cainde | 152 | 15.42 S | 13.12 E |
| Caine ≃ | 248 | 18.23 S | 65.21 W |
| Caino | 64 | 45.38 N | 10.18 E |
| Cains ≃ | 186 | 46.40 N | 65.47 W |
| Cainsdorf | 54 | 50.41 N | 12.29 E |
| Cainsville | 194 | 40.28 N | 93.59 W |
| Cainta | 269f | 14.35 N | 121.07 E |
| Cai Nuoc | 110 | 8.56 N | 105.01 E |
| Cairano | 68 | 40.54 N | 15.22 E |
| Cairari | 250 | 2.33 S | 49.07 W |
| Caird Coast ⏚[2] | 9 | 76.00 S | 24.30 W |
| Caire, Le → Al-Qāhirah | 142 | 30.03 N | 31.15 E |
| Cairnbrook | 214 | 40.07 N | 78.49 W |
| Cairn Curran Reservoir ⊜[1] | 169 | 37.04 S | 143.59 E |
| Cairndow | 46 | 56.15 N | 4.56 W |
| Cairngorm Mountains ⋏ | 46 | 57.04 N | 3.50 W |
| Cairn Mountain ∧ | 180 | 61.10 N | 155.20 W |
| Cairnryan | 44 | 54.58 N | 5.02 W |
| Cairns | 166 | 16.55 S | 145.46 E |
| Cairns Lake ⊜ | 184 | 51.42 N | 94.30 W |
| Cairnsmore of Carsphairn ∧ | 44 | 55.15 N | 4.12 W |
| Cairnsmore of Fleet ∧ | 44 | 54.59 N | 4.20 W |
| Cairn Table ∧ | 44 | 55.29 N | 4.02 W |
| Cairn Water ≃ | 44 | 55.07 N | 3.45 W |
| Cairo → Al-Qāhirah, Mişr | 142 | 30.03 N | 31.15 E |
| Cairo, Ga., U.S. | 192 | 30.52 N | 84.12 W |
| Cairo, Il., U.S. | 194 | 37.00 N | 89.10 W |
| Cairo, Ne., U.S. | 198 | 41.00 N | 98.36 W |
| Cairo, N.Y., U.S. | 210 | 42.17 N | 73.59 W |
| Cairo, Oh., U.S. | 216 | 40.49 N | 84.05 W |
| Cairo, W.V., U.S. | 188 | 39.12 N | 81.09 W |
| Cairo (Almaza) Airport ⊠, Mişr | 273c | 30.06 N | 31.22 E |
| Cairo (Imbābah) Airport ⊠, Mişr | 273c | 30.04 N | 31.12 E |
| Cairo, University of ʋ[2] | 273c | 30.02 N | 31.12 E |
| Cairoçu, Pico do ∧ | 256 | 23.18 S | 44.36 W |
| Cairofa | 152 | 14.05 S | 12.54 E |
| Cairo International Airport ⊠ | 142 | 30.08 N | 31.24 E |
| Cairo Main Station ✦[5] | 273c | 30.04 N | 31.15 E |
| Cairo Montenotte | 62 | 44.24 N | 8.16 E |
| Cairu | 255 | 13.30 S | 39.03 W |
| Caister-on-Sea | 42 | 52.39 N | 1.44 E |
| Caistor | 44 | 53.30 N | 0.20 W |
| Caitingqiao | 105 | 39.54 N | 117.39 E |
| Caitou | 152 | 14.28 S | 13.06 E |
| Caiundo | 152 | 15.46 S | 17.28 E |
| Caivano | 68 | 40.57 N | 14.18 E |
| Caiwan | 102 | 25.50 N | 110.50 E |
| Caixi | 100 | 25.15 N | 116.28 E |
| Caiyu | 105 | 39.39 N | 116.37 E |
| Caizhuang | 98 | 34.17 N | 114.08 E |
| Çaizi Hu ⊜ | 100 | 30.48 N | 117.05 E |
| Čaja ≃, Ross. | 86 | 58.08 N | 82.57 E |
| Čaja ≃, Ross. | 88 | 58.15 N | 109.35 E |
| Cajabamba, Ec. | 246 | 1.42 S | 78.45 W |
| Cajabamba, Perú | 248 | 7.37 S | 78.03 W |
| Cajacay | 248 | 10.10 S | 77.26 W |
| Caja de Muertos, Isla I | 240m | 17.54 N | 66.32 W |
| Cajamar | 256 | 23.21 S | 46.53 W |
| Cajamarca | 248 | 7.10 S | 78.31 W |
| Çajamarca □[5] | 248 | 6.15 S | 78.50 W |
| Čajan | 85 | 43.02 N | 69.23 E |


ENGLISH


| Name | Page | Lat.°′ | Long.°′ |
|---|---|---|---|
| Čajan ≃ | 85 | 42.52 N | 68.56 E |
| Cajapió | 250 | 2.58 S | 44.48 W |
| Cajarc | 32 | 44.29 N | 1.50 E |
| Cajari | 250 | 3.20 S | 45.01 W |
| Cajari ≃ | 250 | 0.48 S | 51.43 W |
| Çajatambo | 248 | 10.29 S | 77.02 W |
| Čajatyn, chrebet ⋏ | 89 | 52.25 N | 138.25 E |
| Cajàzeiras | 250 | 6.54 S | 38.34 W |
| Čajek | 85 | 41.56 N | 74.30 E |
| Čajkovskij | 80 | 56.47 N | 54.09 E |
| Čajniče | 38 | 43.33 N | 19.04 E |
| Cajones ≃ | 234 | 17.45 N | 95.55 W |
| Cajones, Cayos ✧[2] | 236 | 16.05 N | 83.12 W |
| Cajon Mountain ∧ | 228 | 34.16 N | 117.25 W |
| Cajon Pass )( | 228 | 34.19 N | 117.26 W |
| Cajon Summit )( | 228 | 34.21 N | 117.27 W |
| Caju ✦[8] | 287a | 22.53 S | 43.13 W |
| Cajuru | 255 | 21.17 S | 47.18 W |
| Caka | 102 | 36.48 N | 99.19 E |
| Çaka Yanhu ⊜ | 102 | 36.40 N | 99.20 E |
| Čakčar, chrebet ⋏ | 85 | 38.35 N | 67.28 E |
| Cakeni | 152 | 17.48 S | 19.27 E |
| Cakir | 88 | 50.27 N | 103.35 E |
| Çakıralan | 130 | 41.10 N | 35.47 E |
| Çakırgöl Dağı ∧ | 130 | 40.34 N | 39.42 E |
| Çakırhüyük | 130 | 37.34 N | 37.50 E |
| Çakmak | 130 | 37.37 N | 34.19 E |
| Çakmak Dağı ∧ | 130 | 39.46 N | 42.12 E |
| Čakovec | 61 | 46.23 N | 16.26 E |
| Čakovice ✦[8] | 54 | 50.08 N | 14.31 E |
| Cakung ≃ | 269e | 6.06 S | 106.56 E |
| Çal | 130 | 38.05 N | 29.24 E |
| Çala, S. Afr. | 158 | 31.30 S | 27.37 E |
| Cala, Tür. | 84 | 41.05 N | 43.21 E |
| Cala, Embalse de ⊜[1] | 34 | 37.50 N | 6.00 W |
| Calabacillas | 234 | 23.13 N | 99.45 W |
| Calabanga | 116 | 13.42 N | 123.12 E |
| Calabar | 150 | 4.57 N | 8.19 E |
| Calabasas | 228 | 34.09 N | 118.38 W |
| Calabasas, Arroyo ≃ | 280 | 34.12 N | 118.36 W |
| Calabazar ✦[8] | 286b | 23.01 N | 82.22 W |
| Calabazas Creek ≃ | 282 | 37.25 N | 121.58 W |
| Calabernardo | 70 | 36.52 N | 15.08 E |
| Calabogie | 212 | 45.18 N | 76.43 W |
| Calabogie Lake ⊜ | 212 | 45.16 N | 76.45 W |
| Calabozo | 246 | 8.56 N | 67.26 W |
| Calabozo, Ensenada de ⊂ | 246 | 11.30 N | 71.45 W |
| Calabria □[4] | 68 | 39.00 N | 16.30 E |
| Calabria, Parco Nazionale di ♦ | 68 | 38.09 N | 15.54 E |
| Calabritto | 68 | 40.47 N | 15.13 E |
| Calabro ≃ | 70 | 37.53 N | 14.11 E |
| Calabugdong Island I | 116 | 11.06 N | 119.41 E |
| Calaca | 116 | 13.56 N | 120.49 E |
| Calacuccia | 36 | 42.20 N | 9.03 E |
| Caladang, Mount ∧ | 116 | 14.49 N | 121.21 E |
| Caladesi Island I | 220 | 28.02 N | 82.49 W |
| Caladesi Island State Park ♦ | 220 | 28.02 N | 82.48 W |
| Cala d'Oliva | 71 | 41.05 N | 8.20 E |
| Calafat | 38 | 43.59 N | 22.56 E |
| Calafquén, Lago ⊜ | 254 | 39.31 S | 72.10 W |
| Calagnaan Island I | 116 | 11.29 N | 123.13 E |
| Cala Gonone | 71 | 40.18 N | 9.38 E |
| Calagua Islands II | 116 | 14.27 N | 122.55 E |
| Calahorra | 34 | 42.18 N | 1.58 W |
| Calais, Fr. | 50 | 50.57 N | 1.50 E |
| Calais, Me., U.S. | 188 | 45.11 N | 67.16 W |
| Calais, Canal de ≅ | 50 | 50.57 N | 1.51 E |
| Calais, Pas de (Strait of Dover) ⋃ | 50 | 51.00 N | 1.30 E |
| Calala | 152 | 12.59 S | 23.30 E |
| Calalaste, Sierra de ⋏ | 252 | 25.30 S | 67.30 W |
| Calalzo di Cadore | 64 | 46.27 N | 12.23 E |
| Calama | 252 | 22.28 S | 68.56 W |
| Calamar, Col. | 246 | 10.15 N | 74.55 W |
| Calamar, Col. | 246 | 1.58 N | 72.41 W |
| Calamarca | 248 | 16.55 S | 68.09 W |
| Calamba, Pil. | 116 | 14.13 N | 121.10 E |
| Calamba, Pil. | 116 | 8.35 N | 123.39 E |
| Calamian Group II | 116 | 12.00 N | 120.00 E |
| Calamity Creek ≃ | 196 | 29.41 N | 103.42 W |
| Calamocha | 34 | 40.55 N | 1.18 W |
| Calamonaci | 70 | 37.31 N | 13.17 E |
| Calamus ≃ | 198 | 41.48 N | 99.09 W |
| Calañas | 34 | 37.39 N | 6.53 W |
| Calanca, Val V | 58 | 46.22 N | 9.07 E |
| Calanda | 34 | 40.56 N | 0.14 W |
| Calandagan Island I | 116 | 10.39 N | 120.15 E |
| Calang | 114 | 4.38 N | 95.34 E |
| Calangianus | 71 | 40.56 N | 9.11 E |
| Calanna | 68 | 38.11 N | 15.43 E |
| Calapan | 116 | 13.25 N | 121.10 E |
| Calape | 116 | 9.54 N | 123.52 E |
| Calapooia ≃ | 202 | 44.38 N | 123.08 W |
| Calapooya Mountains ⋏ | 202 | 43.30 N | 122.50 W |
| Calar Alto ∧ | 34 | 37.15 N | 2.25 W |
| Călărași, Mol. | 38 | 47.16 N | 28.19 E |
| Călărași, Rom. | 38 | 44.11 N | 27.20 E |
| Călărași □[6] | 38 | 44.20 N | 27.10 E |
| Calarcá | 246 | 4.31 N | 75.38 W |
| Calascibetta | 70 | 37.35 N | 14.16 E |
| Calasetta | 71 | 39.07 N | 8.22 E |
| Calatabiano | 70 | 37.49 N | 15.14 E |
| Calatafimi | 70 | 37.55 N | 12.52 E |
| Calatagan | 116 | 13.50 N | 120.38 E |
| Calatayud | 34 | 41.21 N | 1.38 W |
| Calau | 54 | 51.45 N | 13.56 E |
| Calauag Bay ⊂ | 116 | 14.02 N | 122.13 E |
| Calavà, Capo › | 70 | 38.11 N | 14.55 E |
| Calaveras □[6] | 226 | 38.12 N | 120.41 W |
| Calaveras ≃ | 226 | 37.58 N | 121.22 W |
| Calaveras, North Fork ≃ | 226 | 38.12 N | 120.43 W |
| Calaveras Big Trees State Park ♦ | 226 | 38.16 N | 120.19 W |
| Calaveras Point › | 282 | 37.28 N | 122.03 W |
| Calaveras Reservoir ⊜[1] | 226 | 37.28 N | 121.49 W |
| Calaveritas Creek ≃ | 226 | 38.10 N | 120.40 W |
| Calavino | 64 | 46.03 N | 10.59 E |
| Calavite, Cape › | 116 | 13.27 N | 120.18 E |
| Calavite, Mount ∧ | 116 | 13.29 N | 120.24 E |
| Calavite Passage ⋃ | 116 | 13.36 N | 120.25 E |
| Calavon ≃ | 62 | 43.52 N | 5.35 E |
| Calawah ≃ | 224 | 47.56 N | 124.27 W |
| Calawah, North Fork ≃ | 224 | 47.58 N | 124.20 W |
| Calawah, South Fork ≃ | 224 | 47.58 N | 124.20 W |
| Calayan | 116 | 19.16 N | 121.28 E |
| Çalayan Island I | 116 | 19.20 N | 121.27 E |
| Čalba | 89 | 52.43 N | 131.27 E |
| Calbayog | 116 | 12.04 N | 124.36 E |
| Calbe | 54 | 51.54 N | 11.46 E |
| Calberlah | 54 | 52.25 N | 10.37 E |
| Calbiga | 116 | 11.38 N | 125.01 E |
| Calbuco | 254 | 41.46 S | 73.08 W |
| Calca | 248 | 13.20 S | 71.57 W |
| Calçado ≃ | 256 | 22.05 S | 43.04 W |
| Calcasieu ≃ | 194 | 30.05 N | 93.20 W |
| Calcasieu Lake ⊜ | 194 | 29.50 N | 93.17 W |
| Calceta | 246 | 0.51 S | 80.10 W |
| Calcha | 248 | 21.06 S | 67.31 W |
| Calchaquí | 252 | 29.54 S | 60.18 W |
| Calchaquí ≃ | 252 | 26.03 S | 65.50 W |
| Calciano | 68 | 40.35 N | 16.11 E |
| Calcinaia | 66 | 43.41 N | 10.37 E |
| Calcinato | 64 | 45.27 N | 10.24 E |
| Calcio | 62 | 45.30 N | 9.50 E |
| Calcium | 212 | 44.01 N | 75.51 W |
| Calçoene | 250 | 2.30 N | 50.57 W |
| Calçoene ≃ | 250 | 2.30 N | 50.50 W |
| Calcutta, India | 126 | 22.32 N | 88.22 E |
| Calcutta, India | 272b | 22.32 N | 88.22 E |
| Calcutta, Oh., U.S. | 214 | 40.40 N | 80.34 W |
| Calcutta University ʋ[2] | 272b | 22.35 N | 88.22 E |
| Caldaro (Kaltern) | 64 | 46.25 N | 11.14 E |


DEUTSCH


| Name | Seite | Breite°′ | Länge°′ E = Ost |
|---|---|---|---|
| Caldarola | 66 | 43.08 N | 13.13 E |
| Caldas, Bra. | 256 | 21.56 S | 46.23 W |
| Caldas, Col. | 246 | 6.05 N | 75.38 W |
| Caldas □[5] | 246 | 5.15 N | 75.30 W |
| Caldas da Rainha | 34 | 39.24 N | 9.08 W |
| Caldas de Reis | 34 | 42.36 N | 8.38 W |
| Caldas Novas | 255 | 17.45 S | 48.38 W |
| Caldè | 58 | 45.57 N | 8.38 E |
| Caldecott Tunnel ✦[5] | 282 | 37.52 N | 122.12 W |
| Calden | 56 | 51.25 N | 9.24 E |
| Calder ≃, Eng., U.K. | 44 | 53.44 N | 1.21 W |
| Calder ≃, Eng., U.K. | 262 | 53.49 N | 2.24 W |
| Calder, Loch ⊜ | 46 | 58.31 N | 3.36 W |
| Caldera | 252 | 27.04 S | 70.50 W |
| Caldera de Taburiente, Parque Nacional de la ♦ | 148 | 28.48 N | 17.52 W |
| Calder and Hebble Navigation Canal ≅ | 262 | 53.43 N | 1.54 W |
| Calder Bridge | 44 | 54.27 N | 3.29 W |
| Calderbrook | 262 | 53.39 N | 2.05 W |
| Calderdale □[8] | 262 | 53.44 N | 2.00 W |
| Calderstones Park ♦ | 262 | 53.23 N | 2.54 W |
| Caldes | 64 | 46.22 N | 10.56 E |
| Caldes ≃ | 266d | 41.31 N | 2.13 E |
| Caldew ≃ | 44 | 54.54 N | 2.56 W |
| Caldey Island I | 42 | 51.38 N | 4.41 W |
| Caldicot | 42 | 51.36 N | 2.45 W |
| Caldiero | 64 | 45.22 N | 11.11 E |
| Çaldıran | 84 | 39.09 N | 43.55 E |
| Čaldonazzo | 64 | 45.59 N | 11.16 E |
| Caldonazzo, Lago di ⊜ | 64 | 46.01 N | 11.15 E |
| Čaldonka | 88 | 53.47 N | 119.12 E |
| Caldwell, Id., U.S. | 202 | 43.39 N | 116.41 W |
| Caldwell, Ks., U.S. | 198 | 37.01 N | 97.36 W |
| Caldwell, N.J., U.S. | 276 | 40.51 N | 74.17 W |
| Caldwell, Oh., U.S. | 188 | 39.44 N | 81.31 W |
| Caldwell, Tx., U.S. | 222 | 30.31 N | 96.41 W |
| Caldwell □[6] | 222 | 29.50 N | 97.40 W |
| Caldwell Creek ≃ | 214 | 41.37 N | 79.37 W |
| Caldwell-Wright Airport ⊠ | 276 | 40.53 N | 74.17 W |
| Caldy | 262 | 53.21 N | 3.10 W |
| Cale ≃ | 42 | 50.59 N | 2.20 W |
| Caledon, On., Can. | 212 | 43.52 N | 80.00 W |
| Caledon, S. Afr. | 158 | 34.12 S | 19.23 E |
| Caledon (Mohokare) ≃ | 158 | 30.31 S | 26.05 E |
| Caledon East | 212 | 43.52 N | 79.52 W |
| Caledonia, Belize | 232 | 18.14 N | 88.29 W |
| Caledonia, N.S., Can. | 186 | 44.22 N | 65.02 W |
| Caledonia, On., Can. | 212 | 43.04 N | 79.56 W |
| Caledonia, Il., U.S. | 216 | 42.22 N | 88.53 W |
| Caledonia, Mi., U.S. | 216 | 42.47 N | 85.31 W |
| Caledonia, Mn., U.S. | 190 | 43.38 N | 91.29 W |
| Caledonia, Ms., U.S. | 194 | 33.40 N | 88.19 W |
| Caledonia, N.Y., U.S. | 210 | 42.58 N | 77.51 W |
| Caledonia, Oh., U.S. | 214 | 40.38 N | 82.58 W |
| Caledonia, Pa., U.S. | 214 | 41.17 N | 78.27 W |
| Caledonian Canal ≅ | 46 | 56.50 N | 5.06 W |
| Caledonia State Park ♦ | 208 | 39.56 N | 77.29 W |
| Calego | 152 | 12.10 S | 23.36 E |
| Calella | 34 | 41.37 N | 2.40 E |
| Calemba | 152 | 16.04 S | 15.44 E |
| Calen | 166 | 20.54 S | 148.46 E |
| Calendžicha | 84 | 42.37 N | 42.04 E |
| Calenzano | 66 | 43.51 N | 11.09 E |
| Calera, Al., U.S. | 194 | 33.06 N | 86.45 W |
| Calera, Ok., U.S. | 196 | 33.56 N | 96.25 W |
| Calera Creek ≃ | 282 | 37.27 N | 121.54 W |
| Caleta, Punta › | 240p | 20.04 N | 74.18 W |
| Caleta Olivia | 254 | 46.26 S | 67.32 W |
| Caleufú | 252 | 35.35 S | 64.33 W |
| Calexico | 204 | 32.40 N | 115.29 W |
| Calf Island I | 283 | 42.20 N | 70.54 W |
| Calf Islands II | 276 | 40.59 N | 73.38 W |
| Calfkiller ≃ | 194 | 35.49 N | 85.29 W |
| Calf of Man I | 44 | 54.03 N | 4.48 W |
| Calfpasture ≃ | 188 | 37.58 N | 79.28 W |
| Calf Pasture Point › | 276 | 41.05 N | 73.24 W |
| Calgary | 182 | 51.03 N | 114.05 W |
| Calhan | 198 | 39.02 N | 104.17 W |
| Calhariz ✦[8] | 266c | 38.44 N | 9.12 W |
| Calhoun, Al., U.S. | 194 | 32.03 N | 86.32 W |
| Calhoun, Ga., U.S. | 192 | 34.30 N | 84.57 W |
| Calhoun, Ky., U.S. | 194 | 37.32 N | 87.15 W |
| Calhoun, Mo., U.S. | 194 | 38.28 N | 93.37 W |
| Calhoun, Tn., U.S. | 192 | 35.17 N | 84.44 W |
| Calhoun □[6], Il., U.S. | 219 | 39.09 N | 90.37 W |
| Calhoun □[6], Mi., U.S. | 216 | 42.14 N | 85.00 W |
| Calhoun City | 194 | 33.51 N | 89.18 W |
| Calhoun Falls | 192 | 34.05 N | 82.35 W |
| Cali, Col. | 246 | 3.27 N | 76.31 W |
| Çalı, Tür. | 130 | 40.10 N | 28.54 E |
| Čalian Point › | 116 | 6.07 N | 125.42 E |
| Calicoan Island I | 116 | 10.59 N | 125.48 E |
| Calico Ghost Town ⊥ | 228 | 34.57 N | 116.52 W |
| Calico Rock | 194 | 36.07 N | 92.08 W |
| Calicut | 122 | 11.15 N | 75.46 E |
| Caliente | 204 | 37.36 N | 114.30 W |
| Caliente Creek ≃ | 228 | 35.17 N | 118.48 W |
| Califon | 210 | 40.43 N | 74.50 W |
| California, Mo., U.S. | 194 | 38.37 N | 92.33 W |
| California, Pa., U.S. | 214 | 40.03 N | 79.53 W |
| California □[3], U.S. | 178 | 37.30 N | 119.30 W |
| California □[3], U.S. | 204 | 37.30 N | 119.30 W |
| California, Golfo de ⊂ | 232 | 28.00 N | 112.00 W |
| California, University of ʋ[2] | 282 | 37.52 N | 122.15 W |
| California Aqueduct ≅[1] | 204 | 33.52 N | 117.12 W |
| California City | 228 | 35.08 N | 117.58 W |
| California Creek ≃ | 196 | 33.05 N | 99.33 W |
| California Institute of Technology ʋ[2] | 280 | 34.08 N | 118.08 W |
| California Institution for Men ʋ | 280 | 33.59 N | 117.40 W |
| California Institution for Women ʋ | 280 | 33.57 N | 117.38 W |
| California-Los Angeles, University of (U.C.L.A.) ʋ[2] | 280 | 34.04 N | 118.26 W |
| California State Polytechnic University ʋ[2] | 280 | 34.04 N | 117.49 W |
| California State University (Northridge) ʋ[2], Ca., U.S. | 280 | 34.14 N | 118.32 W |
| California State University (Los Angeles) ʋ[2], Ca., U.S. | 280 | 34.04 N | 118.10 W |
| California State University (Dominguez Hills) ʋ[2], Ca., U.S. | 280 | 33.52 N | 118.17 W |
| California State University (Fullerton) ʋ[2], Ca., U.S. | 280 | 33.53 N | 117.53 W |
| California State University (Long Beach) ʋ[2], Ca., U.S. | 280 | 33.47 N | 118.06 W |
| California State University (Hayward) ʋ[2], Ca., U.S. | 282 | 37.39 N | 122.04 W |
| Calihualá | 234 | 17.35 N | 98.10 W |
| Cäliilabad | 84 | 39.14 N | 48.31 E |
| Calilegua | 252 | 23.47 S | 64.47 W |
| Calilegua, Parque Nacional ♦ | 252 | 23.40 S | 64.50 W |
| Călimănești | 38 | 45.14 N | 24.20 E |
| Călimani, Munții ⋏ | 38 | 47.07 N | 25.03 E |
| Calimera | 68 | 40.15 N | 18.17 E |
| Calimere, Point › | 122 | 10.18 N | 79.52 E |
| Calimesa | 228 | 34.00 N | 117.03 W |


**Symbols** in the index entries represent the broad categories identified in the key at the right. Symbols with superior numbers (⋏[1]) identify subcategories (see complete key on page *I · 1).*

**Symbole** im Register stellen die rechts im Schlüssel erklärten Kategorien dar. Symbole mit hochgestellten Ziffern (⋏[1]) bezeichnen Unterabteilungen einer Kategorie (vgl. vollständiger Schlüssel auf Seite *I · 1).*

**Los símbolos** incluídos en el texto del índice representan las grandes categorías identificadas con la clave a la derecha. Los símbolos con numeros en su parte superior (⋏[1]) identifican las subcategorías (véase la clave completa en la página *I · 1).*

**Les symboles** de l'index représentent les catégories indiquées dans la légende à droite. Les symboles suivis d'un indice (⋏[1]) représentent des sous-catégories (voir légende complète à la page *I · 1).*

**Os símbolos** incluídos no texto do índice representam as grandes categorias identificadas com a chave à direita. Os símbolos com números em sua parte superior (⋏[1]) identificam as subcategorias (veja-se a chave completa à página *I · 1).*

| | | | | | |
|---|---|---|---|---|---|
| ∧ | Mountain | Berg | Montaña | Montagne | Montanha |
| ⋏ | Mountains | Gebirge | Montañas | Montagnes | Montanhas |
| )( | Pass | Paß | Paso | Col | Passo |
| V | Valley, Canyon | Tal, Cañon | Valle, Cañón | Vallée, Canyon | Vale, Canhão |
| ≚ | Plain | Ebene | Llano | Plaine | Planície |
| › | Cape | Kap | Cabo | Cap | Cabo |
| I | Island | Insel | Isla | Île | Ilha |
| II | Islands | Inseln | Islas | Îles | Ilhas |
| ⏚ | Other Topographic Features | Andere Topographische Objekte | Otros Elementos Topográficos | Autres données topographiques | Outros acidentes topográficos |

ESPAÑOL

| Nombre | Página | Lat.°′ | Long.°′ W = Oeste |
|---|---|---|---|
| Calindó ≃ | 255 | 14.26 S | 43.51 W |
| Calingasta | 252 | 31.19 S | 69.25 W |
| Calingiri | 162 | 31.06 S | 116.27 E |
| Calinog | 116 | 11.07 N | 122.32 E |
| Calintaan | 116 | 12.35 N | 120.56 E |
| Calion | 194 | 33.19 N | 92.32 W |
| Calipatria | 204 | 33.07 N | 115.30 W |
| Calispell Peak ∧ | 202 | 48.26 N | 117.30 W |
| Calistoga | 226 | 38.34 N | 122.34 W |
| Calitri | 68 | 40.54 N | 15.27 E |
| Calitzdorp | 158 | 33.33 S | 21.42 E |
| Calizzano | 62 | 44.14 N | 8.07 E |
| Calka | 84 | 41.37 N | 44.05 E |
| Calkinskoje vodochranilišče ⊜[1] | 84 | 41.38 N | 44.03 E |
| Čalkojdy | 85 | 40.44 N | 73.39 E |
| Calla | 226 | 37.46 N | 121.11 W |
| Callabonna, Lake ⊜ | 166 | 29.45 S | 140.04 E |
| Callabonna Creek ≃ | 166 | 29.38 S | 140.08 E |
| Callac | 32 | 48.24 N | 3.26 W |
| Callaghan, Mount ∧ | 204 | 39.42 N | 116.57 W |
| Callahan | 192 | 30.33 N | 81.49 W |
| Callahan, Mount ∧ | 200 | 39.26 N | 108.07 W |
| Callahans | 276 | 40.58 N | 74.37 W |
| Callan | 48 | 52.33 N | 7.23 W |
| Callander, On., Can. | 190 | 46.13 N | 79.23 W |
| Callander, Scot., U.K. | 46 | 56.15 N | 4.14 W |
| Callang | 116 | 17.02 N | 121.38 E |
| Callanish | 46 | 58.12 N | 6.43 W |
| Callanmarca | 248 | 12.52 S | 74.38 W |
| Callanna | 166 | 29.38 S | 137.55 E |
| Callantsoog | 52 | 52.49 N | 4.41 E |
| Callao, Perú | 248 | 12.04 S | 77.09 W |
| Callao, Va., U.S. | 208 | 37.58 N | 76.33 W |
| Callao □[4] | 286d | 12.04 S | 77.09 W |
| Callaquén, Volcán ∧[1] | 252 | 37.54 S | 71.26 W |
| Callas | 62 | 43.35 N | 6.32 E |
| Callaway | 198 | 41.17 N | 99.55 W |
| Callaway □[6] | 219 | 38.50 N | 91.52 W |
| Callaway Gardens ♦ | 192 | 32.51 N | 84.52 W |
| Calle | 56 | 51.20 N | 8.13 E |
| Callensburg | 214 | 41.08 N | 79.33 W |
| Callery | 214 | 40.45 N | 80.02 W |
| Call Hill ∧[2] | 210 | 42.13 N | 77.40 W |
| Calliano, It. | 62 | 45.00 N | 8.15 E |
| Calliano, It. | 64 | 45.56 N | 11.05 E |
| Calliaqua | 241h | 13.08 N | 61.12 W |
| Callicoon | 210 | 41.46 N | 75.03 W |
| Callicoon Center | 210 | 41.50 N | 74.57 W |
| Calliham | 196 | 28.29 N | 98.21 W |
| Calling Lake | 182 | 55.15 N | 113.12 W |
| Calling Lake ⊜ | 182 | 55.13 N | 113.15 W |
| Callington, Austl. | 168b | 35.07 S | 139.02 E |
| Callington, Eng., U.K. | 42 | 50.30 N | 4.18 W |
| Calliope | 166 | 24.00 S | 151.12 E |
| Callosa d'En Sarrià | 34 | 38.39 N | 0.07 W |
| Callosa de Segura | 34 | 38.08 N | 0.52 W |
| Calloway Canal ≋ | 226 | 35.24 N | 119.01 W |
| Calmar, Ab., Can. | 182 | 53.16 N | 113.49 W |
| Calmar → Kalmar, Sve. | 26 | 56.40 N | 16.22 E |
| Calmar, Ia., U.S. | 190 | 43.11 N | 91.51 W |
| Călmățui ≃ | 38 | 44.50 N | 27.50 E |
| Calmazzo | 66 | 43.40 N | 12.46 E |
| Calmbach | 56 | 48.46 N | 8.35 E |
| Calm Lake ⊜ | 190 | 48.46 N | 92.04 W |
| Čal'mny-Varre | 24 | 67.10 N | 37.33 E |
| Čalna | 24 | 61.55 N | 34.01 E |
| Calnali | 234 | 20.55 N | 98.35 W |
| Calne | 42 | 51.27 N | 2.00 W |
| Calobre | 236 | 8.19 N | 80.51 W |
| Calola | 152 | 16.30 S | 17.51 E |
| Calolbon | 116 | 13.36 N | 124.06 E |
| Calólo | 152 | 10.00 S | 14.53 E |
| Calolziocorte | 62 | 45.48 N | 9.26 E |
| Calonne-Ricouart | 50 | 50.29 N | 2.29 E |
| Caloocan | 116 | 14.39 N | 120.58 E |
| Caloosahatchee ≃ | 220 | 26.31 N | 82.01 W |
| Caloosahatchee Canal ≋ | 220 | 26.46 N | 81.27 W |
| Caloote | 168b | 34.58 S | 139.16 E |
| Calore ≃, It. | 68 | 40.31 N | 15.01 E |
| Calore ≃, It. | 68 | 41.11 N | 14.28 E |
| Caloundra | 166 | 26.48 S | 153.09 E |
| Calouste-Gulbenkian, Museu de ⊍ | 266c | 38.44 N | 9.08 W |
| Caloveto | 68 | 39.30 N | 16.45 E |
| Calp | 34 | 38.39 N | 0.03 E |
| Calpulalpan | 234 | 19.35 N | 98.35 W |
| Čalpy | 80 | 55.05 N | 53.06 E |
| Calshot | 42 | 50.49 N | 1.19 W |
| Calstock | 42 | 50.30 N | 4.12 W |
| Caltabellotta | 70 | 37.34 N | 13.13 E |
| Caltagirone | 70 | 37.14 N | 14.31 E |
| Caltagirone ≃ | 70 | 37.21 N | 14.42 E |
| Caltanissetta | 70 | 37.29 N | 14.04 E |
| Caltanissetta □[4] | 70 | 37.29 N | 14.04 E |
| Caltavuturo | 70 | 37.49 N | 13.53 E |
| Çaltılıbük | 130 | 39.57 N | 28.36 E |
| Caltra | 48 | 53.26 N | 8.25 W |
| Čaltyr' | 83 | 47.17 N | 39.30 E |
| Caluango | 152 | 8.21 S | 19.40 E |
| Calubian | 116 | 11.27 N | 124.26 E |
| Calucinga | 152 | 11.18 S | 16.12 E |
| Călugăreni | 38 | 44.07 N | 26.01 E |
| Caluire-et-Cuire | 62 | 45.48 N | 4.51 E |
| Calumbolaca | 152 | 9.09 S | 13.48 E |
| Calumet, Mi., U.S. | 190 | 47.14 N | 88.27 W |
| Calumet, Mn., U.S. | 190 | 47.19 N | 93.16 W |
| Calumet, Pa., U.S. | 214 | 40.13 N | 79.28 W |
| Calumet ≃ | 278 | 41.44 N | 87.32 W |
| Calumet, Lake ⊜ | 216 | 41.41 N | 87.35 W |
| Calumet City | 216 | 41.36 N | 87.31 W |
| Calumet Harbor c | 278 | 41.44 N | 87.32 W |
| Calumet Park | 278 | 41.39 N | 87.39 W |
| Calumet Park ♦ | 278 | 41.43 N | 87.32 W |
| Calumet Sag Channel ≋ | 278 | 41.42 N | 87.57 W |
| Calumpit | 116 | 14.55 N | 120.46 E |
| Calunda | 152 | 12.06 S | 23.23 E |
| Caluquembe | 152 | 13.47 S | 14.44 E |
| Calusa Island I | 116 | 9.37 N | 121.01 E |
| Caluso | 62 | 45.18 N | 7.53 E |
| Caluula | 144 | 11.58 N | 50.45 E |
| Caluula, Raasiga › | 144 | 11.59 N | 50.47 E |
| Caluya Island I | 116 | 11.55 N | 121.34 E |
| Calvados □[5] | 32 | 49.10 N | 0.30 W |
| Calvello | 68 | 40.28 N | 15.51 E |
| Calver | 44 | 53.16 N | 1.38 W |
| Calvera | 68 | 40.09 N | 16.09 E |
| Calvert, Al., U.S. | 194 | 31.09 N | 88.01 W |
| Calvert, Tx., U.S. | 222 | 30.58 N | 96.40 W |
| Calvert □[6] | 208 | 38.33 N | 76.35 W |
| Calvert ≃ | 164 | 16.17 S | 137.44 E |
| Calvert, Lough ⊜ | 169 | 38.11 S | 143.42 E |
| Calvert City | 194 | 37.02 N | 88.21 W |
| Calvert Hills | 166 | 17.15 S | 137.20 E |
| Calvert Island I | 182 | 51.35 N | 128.00 W |
| Calverton, Eng., U.K. | 44 | 53.02 N | 1.05 W |
| Calverton, Md., U.S. | 284c | 39.03 N | 76.56 W |
| Calverton, N.Y., U.S. | 207 | 40.55 N | 72.45 W |
| Calvi | 36 | 42.34 N | 8.45 E |
| Calvi, Monte ∧ | 66 | 43.05 N | 10.37 E |
| Calvia | 34 | 39.34 N | 2.31 E |
| Calvi dell'Umbria | 66 | 42.24 N | 12.34 E |
| Calvillo | 234 | 21.51 N | 102.43 W |
| Calvin, Ok., U.S. | 196 | 34.58 N | 96.14 W |
| Calvin, Pa., U.S. | 214 | 40.20 N | 78.02 W |
| Calvinia | 158 | 31.25 S | 19.45 E |
| Calvisano | 64 | 45.20 N | 10.20 E |
| Calvo, Monte ∧ | 68 | 41.44 N | 15.46 E |
| Calvörde | 54 | 52.23 N | 11.17 E |
| Calw | 56 | 48.43 N | 8.44 E |
| Calwa | 226 | 36.42 N | 119.45 W |
| Calypso | 192 | 35.09 N | 78.06 W |
| Calzada | 248 | 6.02 S | 77.02 W |
| Cam ≃ | 42 | 52.21 N | 0.15 E |
| Camabatela | 152 | 8.11 S | 15.22 E |
| Camaçã ≃ | 248 | 6.35 S | 66.27 W |
| Camaçari | 255 | 12.41 S | 38.18 W |

FRANÇAIS

| Nom | Page | Lat.°′ | Long.°′ W = Ouest |
|---|---|---|---|
| Camachigama, Lac ⊜ | 190 | 47.50 N | 76.19 W |
| Camacupa | 152 | 12.03 S | 17.30 E |
| Camaguán | 246 | 8.06 N | 67.36 W |
| Camagüey | 240p | 21.23 N | 77.55 W |
| Camagüey □[4] | 240p | 21.30 N | 78.00 W |
| Camagüey, Archipiélago de II | 240p | 22.30 N | 78.10 W |
| Camaiore | 64 | 43.56 N | 10.18 E |
| Camaiú ≃ | 248 | 5.30 S | 59.42 W |
| Camajuaní | 240p | 22.28 N | 79.44 W |
| Camaldoli, Eremo di ⊍[1] | 66 | 43.46 N | 11.47 E |
| Camamu | 255 | 13.57 S | 39.07 W |
| Camaná | 248 | 16.37 S | 72.42 W |
| Camaná ≃ | 248 | 16.39 S | 72.46 W |
| Camanaú ≃ | 246 | 1.51 S | 61.14 W |
| Camanche | 190 | 41.47 N | 90.15 W |
| Camanche Reservoir ⊜[1] | 226 | 38.13 N | 120.58 W |
| Camandag Island I | 116 | 11.59 N | 124.25 E |
| Camanducaia | 256 | 22.46 S | 46.09 W |
| Camanducaia ≃, Bra. | 256 | 22.39 S | 46.58 W |
| Camanducaia ≃, Bra. | 256 | 22.55 S | 46.25 W |
| Camano Island I | 224 | 48.10 N | 122.30 W |
| Camaoí ≃ | 250 | 3.12 S | 48.04 W |
| Camapuã | 255 | 19.30 S | 54.05 W |
| Camaquã | 252 | 30.51 S | 51.49 W |
| Camaquã ≃ | 252 | 31.17 S | 51.47 W |
| Camará | 246 | 3.55 S | 62.44 W |
| Camarajibe | 250 | 8.01 S | 34.58 W |
| Camararé ≃ | 248 | 12.15 S | 58.55 W |
| Camarat, Cap › | 62 | 43.12 N | 6.41 E |
| Camarda | 66 | 42.23 N | 13.29 E |
| Çamardı | 130 | 37.50 N | 35.00 E |
| Camarès | 32 | 43.49 N | 2.53 E |
| Camargo, Bol. | 248 | 20.39 S | 65.13 W |
| Camargo, Méx. | 232 | 27.40 N | 105.10 W |
| Camargos, Represa de ⊜[1] | 256 | 21.25 S | 44.30 W |
| Camargue ✦[1] | 62 | 43.34 N | 4.34 E |
| Camargue, Parc Naturel Regional de ♦ | 62 | 43.30 N | 4.28 E |
| Camarillo | 228 | 34.12 N | 119.02 W |
| Camarillo Heights | 228 | 34.14 N | 119.02 W |
| Camarina ⊥ | 70 | 36.52 N | 14.27 E |
| Camariñas | 34 | 43.07 N | 9.10 W |
| Camarines Norte □[4] | 116 | 14.10 N | 122.40 E |
| Camarines Sur □[4] | 116 | 13.35 N | 123.20 E |
| Camarón, Arroyo ≃ | 196 | 27.08 N | 100.00 W |
| Camarón, Cabo › | 236 | 16.00 N | 85.05 W |
| Camarones | 254 | 44.48 S | 65.42 W |
| Camarones, Bahía c | 254 | 44.45 S | 65.34 W |
| Camas, Esp. | 34 | 37.24 N | 6.02 W |
| Çamaş, Tür. | 130 | 40.55 N | 37.32 E |
| Camas, Wa., U.S. | 224 | 45.35 N | 122.23 W |
| Camas Creek ≃, Id., U.S. | 202 | 43.20 N | 114.24 W |
| Camas Creek ≃, Id., U.S. | 202 | 44.53 N | 114.44 W |
| Camas Creek ≃, Id., U.S. | 202 | 43.53 N | 112.21 W |
| Camas Creek ≃, Or., U.S. | 202 | 45.01 N | 118.59 W |
| Camastra | 70 | 37.15 N | 13.47 E |
| Camatagua, Embalse de ⊜[1] | 246 | 9.50 N | 67.00 W |
| Camatambo | 152 | 6.30 S | 15.18 E |
| Ca Mau | 110 | 9.11 N | 105.08 E |
| Ca Mau, Mui › | 110 | 8.38 N | 104.44 E |
| Camaxilo | 152 | 8.21 S | 18.56 E |
| Camba | 112 | 4.54 S | 119.50 E |
| Camba Cassai | 152 | 9.40 S | 19.18 E |
| Cambados | 34 | 42.30 N | 8.48 W |
| Cambará | 255 | 23.03 S | 50.05 W |
| Čambarak | 84 | 40.36 N | 45.21 E |
| Camberley | 42 | 51.21 N | 0.45 W |
| Camberwell | 169 | 37.50 S | 145.04 E |
| Camberwell ✦[8] | 260 | 51.28 N | 0.05 W |
| Cambiano | 62 | 44.58 N | 7.47 E |
| Cambo | 44 | 55.10 N | 1.57 W |
| Cambo ≃ | 152 | 7.40 S | 17.17 E |
| Cambodia (Kâmpŭchéa) □[1], Asia | 108 | 13.00 N | 105.00 E |
| Cambodia (Kâmpŭchéa) □[1], Asia | 110 | 13.00 N | 105.00 E |
| Cambois | 44 | 55.10 N | 1.31 W |
| Cambonda, Serra ⋏ | 152 | 12.06 S | 14.00 E |
| Camboon | 166 | 25.03 S | 150.26 E |
| Cambooya | 171a | 27.42 S | 151.52 E |
| Camboriú | 252 | 27.01 S | 48.38 W |
| Camborne | 42 | 50.12 N | 5.19 W |
| Cambra | 210 | 41.11 N | 76.18 W |
| Cambrai, Austl. | 168b | 34.39 S | 139.17 E |
| Cambrai, Fr. | 50 | 50.10 N | 3.14 E |
| Cambremer | 50 | 49.09 N | 0.03 E |
| Cambria, Ca., U.S. | 226 | 35.33 N | 121.04 W |
| Cambria, In., U.S. | 216 | 40.22 N | 86.33 W |
| Cambria, Mi., U.S. | 216 | 41.49 N | 84.39 W |
| Cambria, Wi., U.S. | 190 | 43.32 N | 89.06 W |
| Cambria □[6] | 214 | 40.29 N | 79.16 W |
| Cambria Ice Field ⊓ | 182 | 55.55 N | 129.30 W |
| Cambrian Mountains ⋏ | 28 | 52.35 N | 3.35 W |
| Cambrian Park | 226 | 37.15 N | 121.55 W |
| Cambridge (Galt), On., Can. | 212 | 43.22 N | 80.19 W |
| Cambridge, N.Z. | 172 | 37.53 S | 175.28 E |
| Cambridge, Eng., U.K. | 42 | 52.13 N | 0.08 E |
| Cambridge, Id., U.S. | 202 | 44.34 N | 116.41 W |
| Cambridge, Il., U.S. | 190 | 41.18 N | 90.11 W |
| Cambridge, Ia., U.S. | 190 | 41.53 N | 93.31 W |
| Cambridge, Md., U.S. | 208 | 38.33 N | 76.04 W |
| Cambridge, Ma., U.S. | 207 | 42.22 N | 71.06 W |
| Cambridge, Mn., U.S. | 190 | 45.34 N | 93.13 W |
| Cambridge, Ne., U.S. | 198 | 40.16 N | 100.09 W |
| Cambridge, N.Y., U.S. | 210 | 43.01 N | 73.22 W |
| Cambridge, Oh., U.S. | 188 | 40.02 N | 81.35 W |
| Cambridge, Wi., U.S. | 216 | 43.00 N | 89.01 W |
| Cambridge Bay | 176 | 69.03 N | 105.05 W |
| Cambridge City | 218 | 39.48 N | 85.10 W |
| Cambridge Fiord c[2] | 176 | 71.20 N | 74.44 W |
| Cambridge Gulf c | 164 | 14.55 S | 128.15 E |
| Cambridge Park | 274a | 33.45 S | 150.43 E |
| Cambridge Reservoir ⊜[1] | 283 | 42.24 N | 71.16 W |
| Cambridgeshire □[6] | 42 | 52.20 N | 0.05 E |
| Cambridge Springs | 214 | 41.48 N | 80.03 W |
| Cambrils | 34 | 41.04 N | 1.03 E |
| Cambriú, Ponta de › | 252 | 25.10 S | 47.55 W |
| Cambuci ✦[8] | 287b | 23.34 S | 46.37 W |
| Cambuí | 256 | 22.37 S | 46.04 W |
| Cambulo | 152 | 7.48 S | 21.14 E |
| Cambundi-Catembo | 152 | 10.09 S | 17.31 E |
| Cambuquira | 256 | 21.51 S | 45.18 W |
| Cambural | 286c | 10.26 N | 66.59 W |
| Camburg | 54 | 51.03 N | 11.42 E |
| Camburú ≃ | 256 | 23.41 S | 45.28 W |
| Camby | 218 | 39.40 N | 86.19 W |
| Čamčakly | 128 | 37.56 N | 63.06 E |
| Camden, Austl. | 170 | 34.03 S | 150.42 E |
| Camden, S. Afr. | 158 | 26.38 S | 30.07 E |
| Camden, Al., U.S. | 194 | 31.59 N | 87.17 W |
| Camden, Ar., U.S. | 194 | 33.35 N | 92.50 W |
| Camden, De., U.S. | 208 | 39.06 N | 75.32 W |
| Camden, Il., U.S. | 219 | 40.09 N | 90.46 W |
| Camden, In., U.S. | 216 | 40.36 N | 86.32 W |
| Camden, Me., U.S. | 188 | 44.12 N | 69.03 W |
| Camden, Mi., U.S. | 216 | 41.45 N | 84.45 W |
| Camden, Ms., U.S. | 194 | 32.46 N | 89.50 W |
| Camden, N.J., U.S. | 208 | 39.55 N | 75.07 W |
| Camden, N.Y., U.S. | 210 | 43.20 N | 75.44 W |
| Camden, N.C., U.S. | 192 | 36.19 N | 76.10 W |
| Camden, Oh., U.S. | 218 | 39.37 N | 84.38 W |
| Camden, S.C., U.S. | 192 | 34.14 N | 80.36 W |
| Camden, Tn., U.S. | 194 | 36.03 N | 88.05 W |

PORTUGUÊS

| Nome | Página | Lat.°′ | Long.°′ W = Oeste |
|---|---|---|---|
| Camden, Tx., U.S. | 222 | 30.55 N | 94.44 W |
| Camden □[6], N.J., U.S. | 208 | 39.57 N | 75.07 W |
| Camden □[6], N.C., U.S. | 208 | 36.28 N | 76.21 W |
| Camden ✦[8] | 260 | 51.33 N | 0.10 W |
| Camden, Grupo II | 254 | 54.40 S | 71.58 W |
| Camden Aerodrome ⊠ | 274a | 34.03 S | 150.41 E |
| Camden Bay c | 180 | 70.00 N | 145.00 W |
| Camden Hills State Park ♦ | 188 | 44.17 N | 69.05 W |
| Camden Lake ⊜ | 212 | 44.25 N | 76.52 W |
| Camden Station ✦[5] | 284b | 39.17 N | 76.37 W |
| Camdenton | 194 | 38.00 N | 92.44 W |
| Camedo | 58 | 46.09 N | 8.37 E |
| Cameia, Parque Nacional da ♦ | 152 | 11.45 S | 21.20 E |
| Camel ≃ | 42 | 50.33 N | 4.55 W |
| Camel, Mount ∧[2] | 169 | 36.45 S | 144.43 E |
| Camelback Mountain ∧, Ak., U.S. | 180 | 62.33 N | 157.20 W |
| Camelback Mountain ∧, Pa., U.S. | 210 | 41.03 N | 75.21 W |
| Camelford | 42 | 50.37 N | 4.41 W |
| Çameli | 130 | 37.05 N | 29.20 E |
| Camels Hump ∧ | 188 | 44.19 N | 72.53 W |
| Camenca | 38 | 48.03 N | 28.42 E |
| Cameo Acres | 282 | 37.51 N | 121.58 W |
| Camerano | 66 | 43.32 N | 13.33 E |
| Cameri | 62 | 45.30 N | 8.39 E |
| Cameri, Aeroporto di ⊠ | 266b | 45.32 N | 8.40 E |
| Camerino | 66 | 43.08 N | 13.04 E |
| Cameron, La., U.S. | 194 | 29.47 N | 93.19 W |
| Cameron, Mo., U.S. | 194 | 39.44 N | 94.14 W |
| Cameron, N.Y., U.S. | 210 | 42.12 N | 77.24 W |
| Cameron, Pa., U.S. | 214 | 41.27 N | 78.10 W |
| Cameron, S.C., U.S. | 192 | 33.33 N | 80.42 W |
| Cameron, Tx., U.S. | 222 | 30.51 N | 96.58 W |
| Cameron, W.V., U.S. | 188 | 39.49 N | 80.34 W |
| Cameron, Wi., U.S. | 190 | 45.24 N | 91.44 W |
| Cameron □[6] | 214 | 41.31 N | 78.14 W |
| Cameron ≃ | 224 | 49.17 N | 124.38 W |
| Cameron, Lac ⊜ | 206 | 46.06 N | 74.50 W |
| Cameron Highlands | 114 | 4.29 N | 101.27 E |
| Cameron Hills ⋏[2] | 176 | 59.48 N | 118.00 W |
| Cameron Lake ⊜, B.C., Can. | 224 | 49.17 N | 124.37 W |
| Cameron Lake ⊜, On., Can. | 212 | 44.34 N | 78.45 W |
| Cameron Mills | 210 | 42.11 N | 77.22 W |
| Cameron Mountains ⋏ | 172 | 46.00 S | 167.00 E |
| Cameron Park | 226 | 38.39 N | 120.56 W |
| Cameron Run ≃ | 284c | 38.48 N | 77.04 W |
| Cameroon (Cameroun) □[1] | 134 | 6.00 N | 12.00 E |
| Cameroon Mountain ∧ | 152 | 4.12 N | 9.11 E |
| Camerota | 68 | 40.02 N | 15.23 E |
| Cameroun → Cameroon □[1] | 134 | 6.00 N | 12.00 E |
| Camerún → Cameroon □[1] | 134 | 6.00 N | 12.00 E |
| Cametá | 250 | 2.15 S | 49.30 W |
| Camfield | 164 | 17.09 S | 131.21 E |
| Çamiçi Gölü ⊜ | 130 | 37.30 N | 27.25 E |
| Camiguin □[4] | 116 | 9.15 N | 124.40 E |
| Camiguin Island I, Pil. | 116 | 18.56 N | 121.55 E |
| Camiguin Island I, Pil. | 116 | 9.11 N | 124.42 E |
| Camiling | 116 | 15.42 N | 120.24 E |
| Camilla | 192 | 31.13 N | 84.12 W |
| Camillus | 210 | 43.02 N | 76.19 W |
| Camin | 54 | 53.27 N | 10.58 E |
| Camiña | 248 | 19.18 S | 69.26 W |
| Caminha | 34 | 41.52 N | 8.50 W |
| Camino | 226 | 38.44 N | 120.40 W |
| Camiranga | 250 | 1.48 S | 46.17 W |
| Camiri | 248 | 20.03 S | 63.31 W |
| Camisano Vicentino | 64 | 45.31 N | 11.43 E |
| Camisea ≃ | 248 | 11.35 S | 72.58 W |
| Çamissombo | 152 | 8.10 S | 20.39 E |
| Čamjarysy | 78 | 51.42 N | 30.24 E |
| Camlad ≃ | 42 | 52.36 N | 3.10 W |
| Çamlıbel | 130 | 40.05 N | 36.29 E |
| Çamlıdere, Tür. | 130 | 37.08 N | 39.03 E |
| Çamlıdere, Tür. | 130 | 40.30 N | 32.29 E |
| Çamlıyayla | 130 | 37.09 N | 34.36 E |
| Cam Lo | 110 | 16.49 N | 106.59 E |
| Čamlyk ≃ | 84 | 44.45 N | 40.45 E |
| Cammal | 210 | 41.24 N | 77.28 W |
| Cammarata | 70 | 37.38 N | 13.38 E |
| Cammarta, Monte ∧ | 70 | 37.37 N | 13.36 E |
| Camoapa | 236 | 12.23 N | 85.31 W |
| Camocim | 250 | 2.54 S | 40.50 W |
| Camogli | 62 | 44.21 N | 9.09 E |
| Çamoluk | 130 | 40.08 N | 38.45 E |
| Camonica, Val V | 64 | 46.00 N | 10.20 E |
| Camooweal | 166 | 19.55 S | 138.07 E |
| Camopi ≃ | 250 | 3.11 N | 52.20 W |
| Camorim ≃ | 287a | 22.59 S | 43.25 W |
| Camorim, Represa do ⊜[1] | 287a | 22.58 S | 43.27 W |
| Camorta Island I | 110 | 8.08 N | 93.30 E |
| Camote, Cerro ∧ | 286d | 11.57 S | 77.06 W |
| Camotes Islands II | 116 | 10.40 N | 124.24 E |
| Camotes Sea ⊤[2] | 116 | 10.30 N | 124.15 E |
| Camotlán ≃ | 234 | 22.01 N | 104.15 W |
| Camowen ≃ | 48 | 54.36 N | 7.18 W |
| Camp □[6] | 222 | 33.00 N | 94.58 W |
| Campagna | 68 | 40.40 N | 15.08 E |
| Campagna di Roma ✦[1] | 66 | 41.50 N | 12.35 E |
| Campagna Lupia | 64 | 45.21 N | 12.06 E |
| Campagnano di Roma | 66 | 42.08 N | 12.23 E |
| Campagnatico | 66 | 42.53 N | 11.16 E |
| Campagne-lès-Hesdin | 50 | 50.24 N | 1.52 E |
| Campaign | 194 | 35.46 N | 85.37 W |
| Campamento | 236 | 14.33 N | 86.42 W |
| Campana, Arg. | 258 | 34.10 S | 58.57 W |
| Campana, It. | 68 | 39.24 N | 16.50 E |
| Campana, Isla I | 254 | 48.20 S | 75.15 W |
| Campanario | 34 | 38.52 N | 5.37 W |
| Campanario, Cerro de ∧ | 248 | 5.57 S | 77.31 W |
| Campanella, Punta › | 68 | 40.34 N | 14.19 E |
| Campanero, Cerro ∧ | 246 | 5.54 N | 65.12 W |
| Campanha | 256 | 21.50 S | 45.24 W |
| Campania □[4] | 68 | 40.55 N | 14.50 E |
| Campania Island I | 182 | 53.05 N | 129.30 W |
| Camparada | 266b | 45.39 N | 9.19 E |
| Campaspe ≃, Austl. | 166 | 21.00 S | 146.24 E |
| Campaspe ≃, Austl. | 169 | 36.41 S | 144.31 E |
| Campbell, S. Afr. | 158 | 28.48 S | 23.44 E |
| Campbell, Ca., U.S. | 226 | 37.17 N | 121.56 W |
| Campbell, Mn., U.S. | 198 | 46.05 N | 96.24 W |
| Campbell, Mo., U.S. | 194 | 36.29 N | 90.04 W |
| Campbell, Ne., U.S. | 198 | 40.18 N | 98.44 W |
| Campbell, N.Y., U.S. | 210 | 42.13 N | 77.11 W |
| Campbell, Oh., U.S. | 214 | 41.04 N | 80.35 W |
| Campbell, Tx., U.S. | 222 | 33.09 N | 95.57 W |
| Campbell □[6] | 218 | 38.55 N | 84.20 W |
| Campbell, Cape › | 172 | 41.44 S | 174.17 E |
| Campbell Airport ⊠ | 279b | 40.21 N | 80.11 W |
| Campbellfield | 274b | 37.41 S | 144.57 E |
| Campbellford | 212 | 44.18 N | 77.48 W |
| Campbell Hall | 210 | 41.27 N | 74.16 W |
| Campbell Hill ∧[2] | 216 | 40.22 N | 83.43 W |
| Campbell Island I | 9 | 52.30 S | 169.05 E |
| Campbell Lake ⊜ | 182 | 50.01 N | 125.27 W |
| Campbell Plateau ✣[3] | 9 | 51.00 S | 170.00 E |
| Campbell Point › | 171a | 27.22 S | 153.55 E |
| Campbellpore | 123 | 33.46 N | 72.22 E |
| Campbell Range ∧ | 180 | 61.08 N | 129.45 W |
| Campbell River | 182 | 50.01 N | 125.15 W |
| Campbells Creek | 170 | 33.42 S | 149.37 E |
| Campbell's Airport ⊠ | 278 | 42.20 N | 83.04 W |
| Campbell's-Bay | 188 | 45.44 N | 76.36 W |
| Campbellsburg, In., U.S. | 218 | 38.39 N | 86.15 W |
| Campbellsburg, Ky., U.S. | 218 | 38.31 N | 85.12 W |
| Campbell Slough ≃ | 226 | 39.22 N | 121.51 W |
| Campbellsport | 190 | 43.35 N | 88.16 W |
| Campbells River | 170 | 33.54 S | 149.37 E |
| Campbells Run ≃ | 279b | 40.24 N | 80.05 W |
| Campbellsville | 194 | 37.20 N | 85.20 W |
| Campbellton, N.B., Can. | 186 | 48.00 N | 66.40 W |
| Campbellton, Nf., Can. | 186 | 49.17 N | 54.56 W |
| Campbellton, P.E., Can. | 186 | 46.47 N | 64.18 W |
| Campbellton, Fl., U.S. | 192 | 30.56 N | 85.24 W |
| Campbell Town, Austl. | 166 | 41.56 S | 147.29 E |
| Campbelltown, Austl. | 168b | 34.53 S | 138.40 E |
| Campbelltown, Austl. | 170 | 34.04 S | 150.49 E |
| Campbelltown, Pa., U.S. | 208 | 40.17 N | 76.35 W |
| Campbellville | 212 | 43.29 N | 79.59 W |
| Campbeltown | 46 | 55.26 N | 5.36 W |
| Camp Creek ≃, Ca., U.S. | 226 | 38.38 N | 120.40 W |
| Camp Creek ≃, Mo., U.S. | 219 | 39.02 N | 91.12 W |
| Camp Creek Lake ⊜[1] | 222 | 31.03 N | 96.19 W |
| Camp David ⊍ | 208 | 39.38 N | 77.28 W |
| Camp de Frileuse ■ | 261 | 48.52 N | 1.55 E |
| Camp de Satory ■ | 261 | 48.47 N | 2.06 E |
| Camp Dix | 218 | 38.29 N | 83.17 W |
| Camp Douglas | 190 | 43.55 N | 90.16 W |
| Campeche | 232 | 19.51 N | 90.32 W |
| Campeche □[3], Méx. | 232 | 19.00 N | 90.30 W |
| Campeche □[3], Méx. | 232 | 19.00 N | 90.30 W |
| Campeche, Bahía de c | 232 | 20.00 N | 94.00 W |
| Campeche Bank ✣[4] | 16 | 22.00 N | 90.00 W |
| Campechuela | 240p | 20.14 N | 77.17 W |
| Campegine | 64 | 44.45 N | 10.32 E |
| Campello Monti | 58 | 45.56 N | 8.15 E |
| Câmpeni | 38 | 46.22 N | 23.03 E |
| Camperdown, Austl. | 169 | 38.14 S | 143.09 E |
| Camperdown, S. Afr. | 158 | 29.42 S | 30.33 E |
| Camperville | 184 | 51.59 N | 100.09 W |
| Campestre | 256 | 21.43 S | 46.15 W |
| Cam Pha | 110 | 21.01 N | 107.19 E |
| Camp Hill, Al., U.S. | 194 | 32.48 N | 85.39 W |
| Camp Hill, Pa., U.S. | 208 | 40.14 N | 76.55 W |
| Câmpia Turzii | 38 | 46.33 N | 23.54 E |
| Campi Bisenzio | 66 | 43.49 N | 11.08 E |
| Campidano ✦[1] | 71 | 39.30 N | 8.47 E |
| Campiglia dei Fosci | 66 | 43.27 N | 11.03 E |
| Campiglia Marittima | 66 | 43.03 N | 10.37 E |
| Campillo de Llerena | 34 | 38.30 N | 5.50 W |
| Campillos | 34 | 37.03 N | 4.51 W |
| Câmpina | 38 | 45.08 N | 25.44 E |
| Campina ✦[1] | 34 | 37.45 N | 4.45 W |
| Campina Grande | 250 | 7.13 S | 35.53 W |
| Campinas | 256 | 22.54 S | 47.05 W |
| Campina Verde | 255 | 19.31 S | 49.28 W |
| Campinho, Rio do ≃ | 287a | 22.52 S | 43.37 W |
| Campione | 58 | 45.58 N | 8.58 E |
| Campione del Garda | 64 | 45.45 N | 10.45 E |
| Campi Salentina | 68 | 40.24 N | 18.01 E |
| Campitello | 64 | 46.28 N | 11.44 E |
| Camp King | 150 | 4.55 N | 7.58 W |
| Camp Lake | 216 | 42.32 N | 88.09 W |
| Camp Lake ⊜ | 212 | 45.27 N | 78.54 W |
| Camp Leger ■ | 261 | 48.34 N | 2.34 E |
| Camp Lejeune Marine Corps Base ■ | 192 | 34.40 N | 77.21 W |
| Campli | 66 | 42.43 N | 13.41 E |
| Camplong | 112 | 10.02 S | 123.55 E |
| Campo, Cam. | 152 | 2.22 N | 9.49 E |
| Campo, Moç. | 156 | 17.44 S | 36.21 E |
| Campo, Co., U.S. | 198 | 37.06 N | 102.34 W |
| Campo, Réserve de ✦[4] | 152 | 2.35 N | 9.57 E |
| Campoalegre | 246 | 2.41 N | 75.20 W |
| Campo Alegre ≃ | 250 | 9.19 S | 50.06 W |
| Campo Alegre de Goiás | 255 | 17.39 S | 47.45 W |
| Campobasso | 66 | 41.34 N | 14.39 E |
| Campobasso □[4] | 66 | 41.38 N | 14.35 E |
| Campobello di Licata | 70 | 37.15 N | 13.55 E |
| Campobello di Mazara | 70 | 37.38 N | 12.45 E |
| Campobello Island I | 186 | 44.53 N | 66.55 W |
| Campo Belo | 255 | 20.53 S | 45.16 W |
| Campo Blenio | 58 | 46.34 N | 8.56 E |
| Campocologno | 58 | 46.13 N | 10.08 E |
| Campodarsego | 64 | 45.30 N | 11.54 E |
| Campo de Criptana | 34 | 39.24 N | 3.07 W |
| Campo de la Cruz | 246 | 10.23 N | 74.53 W |
| Campo de Marte ♦ | 286d | 12.04 S | 77.03 W |
| Campo de Marte ■ | 287b | 23.30 S | 46.37 W |
| Campo de Mayo ■ | 288 | 34.32 S | 58.38 W |
| Campo di Giove | 66 | 42.01 N | 14.03 E |
| Campo di Trens (Trens) | 64 | 46.52 N | 11.29 E |
| Campo do Coelho | 256 | 22.15 S | 42.39 W |
| Campodolcino | 58 | 46.24 N | 9.21 E |
| Campo Erê | 252 | 26.23 S | 53.03 W |
| Campofelice di Fitalia | 70 | 37.50 N | 13.29 E |
| Campofelice di Roccella | 70 | 37.59 N | 13.53 E |
| Campofiorito | 70 | 37.45 N | 13.16 E |
| Campo Florido | 255 | 19.47 S | 48.35 W |
| Campoformido | 64 | 46.01 N | 13.09 E |
| Campo Formoso | 250 | 10.31 S | 40.20 W |
| Campofranco | 70 | 37.30 N | 13.43 E |
| Campogalliano | 64 | 44.41 N | 10.50 E |
| Campo Gallo | 252 | 26.35 S | 62.51 W |
| Campo Grande, Arg. | 252 | 27.13 S | 54.58 W |
| Campo Grande, Bra. | 255 | 20.27 S | 54.37 W |
| Campo Grande ✦[8], Bra. | 256 | 22.54 S | 43.34 W |
| Campo Grande ✦[8], Port. | 266c | 38.45 N | 9.09 W |
| Campo Indian Reservation ✦[4] | 204 | 32.40 N | 116.20 W |
| Campo Largo, Arg. | 252 | 26.48 S | 60.50 W |
| Campo Largo, Bra. | 252 | 25.26 S | 49.32 W |
| Campolaro | 64 | 45.55 N | 10.20 E |
| Campolasta (Astfeld) | 64 | 46.40 N | 11.22 E |
| Campolato, Capo › | 70 | 37.17 N | 15.12 E |
| Campo Libertad ■ | 286b | 23.05 N | 82.26 W |
| Campolide | 256 | 21.36 S | 43.53 W |
| Campolieto | 66 | 41.38 N | 14.46 E |
| Campo Ligure | 62 | 44.32 N | 8.42 E |
| Campo Limpo Paulista | 256 | 23.12 S | 46.48 W |
| Campo Maior, Bra. | 250 | 4.49 S | 42.10 W |
| Campo Maior, Port. | 34 | 39.01 N | 7.04 W |
| Campomarino | 66 | 41.57 N | 15.02 E |
| Campo Militar Número Uno ■ | 286a | 19.27 N | 99.14 W |
| Campomorone | 62 | 44.30 N | 8.53 E |
| Campo Mourão | 255 | 24.03 S | 52.22 W |
| Campo Novo | 252 | 27.42 S | 53.48 W |
| Campo Pequeno ♦ | 266c | 38.44 N | 9.08 W |
| Campo Quijano | 252 | 24.55 S | 65.39 W |
| Campora | 68 | 40.19 N | 15.17 E |
| Camporeale | 70 | 37.54 N | 13.06 E |
| Camporgiano | 64 | 44.09 N | 10.20 E |
| Camporredondo | 248 | 6.07 S | 78.21 W |
| Campos | 255 | 21.45 S | 41.18 W |
| Campos Altos | 255 | 19.41 S | 46.10 W |
| Camposampiero | 64 | 45.34 N | 11.56 E |
| Campo Santo, Arg. | 252 | 24.40 S | 65.06 W |
| Camposanto, It. | 64 | 44.47 N | 11.08 E |
| Campos Belos | 255 | 13.03 S | 46.53 W |
| Campos de Cunha | 256 | 22.55 S | 44.49 W |
| Campos do Jordão | 256 | 22.44 S | 45.35 W |
| Campos Elisios | 256 | 22.42 S | 43.17 W |
| Campos Gerais | 256 | 21.14 S | 45.46 W |
| Campos Novos | 252 | 27.24 S | 51.12 W |
| Campos Sales | 250 | 7.04 S | 40.23 W |
| Campo Tencia, Pizzo ∧ | 58 | 46.26 N | 8.43 E |
| Campotosto | 66 | 42.33 N | 13.22 E |
| Campotosto, Lago di ⊜ | 66 | 42.32 N | 13.22 E |
| Campo Tures (Sand in Taufers) | 64 | 46.55 N | 11.57 E |
| Campovalano | 66 | 42.44 N | 13.40 E |
| Camp Parks Communications Annex ■ | 282 | 37.44 N | 121.54 W |
| Camp Pendleton Marine Corps Base ■ | 228 | 33.19 N | 117.18 W |
| Camp Point | 219 | 40.02 N | 91.04 W |
| Camp Ruby | 222 | 30.42 N | 94.45 W |
| Campsie | 274a | 33.55 S | 151.06 E |
| Campsie Fells ⋏[2] | 46 | 56.02 N | 4.12 W |
| Camp Springs | 208 | 38.48 N | 76.54 W |
| Campti | 194 | 31.53 N | 93.07 W |
| Campton | 192 | 37.44 N | 83.32 W |
| Camptonville | 226 | 39.27 N | 121.03 W |
| Camptown | 210 | 41.43 N | 76.14 W |
| Câmpulung | 38 | 45.16 N | 25.03 E |
| Câmpulung Moldovenesc | 38 | 47.31 N | 25.34 E |
| Campus | 216 | 41.01 N | 88.18 W |
| Campuya ≃ | 246 | 1.43 S | 73.30 W |
| Camp Verde | 200 | 34.33 N | 111.51 W |
| Campville | 210 | 42.06 N | 76.09 W |
| Camp Wood | 196 | 29.40 N | 100.01 W |
| Cam Ranh | 110 | 11.54 N | 109.09 E |
| Cam Ranh, Vinh c | 110 | 11.53 N | 109.10 E |
| Camrose, Ab., Can. | 182 | 53.01 N | 112.50 W |
| Camrose, Wales, U.K. | 42 | 51.51 N | 5.01 W |
| Camsell ≃ | 176 | 65.40 N | 118.07 W |
| Camu ≃ | 250 | 1.15 N | 57.09 W |
| Camucia | 66 | 43.16 N | 11.58 E |
| Camucuio | 152 | 14.12 S | 13.20 E |
| Camurí Chiquito, Quebrada ≃ | 286c | 10.37 N | 66.52 W |
| Çamurlu Dağ ∧ | 130 | 40.21 N | 42.26 E |
| Camuy | 240m | 18.29 N | 66.51 W |
| Cam Xuyen | 110 | 18.15 N | 106.00 E |
| Çamyndy | 85 | 41.37 N | 74.20 E |
| Čamzinka | 80 | 54.24 N | 45.47 E |
| Çan, Tür. | 130 | 40.02 N | 27.03 E |
| Çan, Tür. | 130 | 39.09 N | 40.13 E |
| Can ≃ | 42 | 51.44 N | 0.28 E |
| Canaan, Ct., U.S. | 207 | 42.01 N | 73.19 W |
| Canaan, Fl., U.S. | 220 | 28.48 N | 81.14 W |
| Canaan, In., U.S. | 218 | 38.52 N | 85.25 W |
| Canaan, N.Y., U.S. | 210 | 42.25 N | 73.27 W |
| Canaan, Vt., U.S. | 206 | 44.59 N | 71.32 W |
| Canaan ≃ | 186 | 45.55 N | 65.47 W |
| Canaan Lake ⊜ | 276 | 40.47 N | 73.01 W |
| Canaan Valley State Park ♦ | 188 | 39.02 N | 79.32 W |
| Cana-brava ≃, Bra. | 255 | 13.11 S | 48.11 W |
| Cana-brava ≃, Bra. | 255 | 12.12 S | 48.40 W |
| Cañacao Bay c | 269f | 14.29 N | 120.55 E |
| Canaçarí, Lago ⊜ | 250 | 2.57 S | 58.15 W |
| Canada □[1] | 176 | 60.00 N | 95.00 W |
| Cañada, Loma la ∧[2] | 240p | 21.41 N | 82.57 W |
| Canada Bay c | 186 | 50.43 N | 56.10 W |
| Cañada de Caracheo | 234 | 20.22 N | 100.57 W |
| Cañada de Gómez | 252 | 32.49 S | 61.24 W |
| Cañada Honda | 252 | 31.59 S | 68.33 W |
| Canada Lake ⊜ | 210 | 43.10 N | 74.32 W |
| Cañada Nieto | 258 | 33.43 S | 58.05 W |
| Canadarago Lake ⊜ | 210 | 42.48 N | 75.01 W |
| Canada's Wonderland ♦ | 275b | 43.51 N | 79.33 W |
| Cañada Verde → Villa Huidobro | 252 | 34.50 S | 64.35 W |
| Canadaway Creek ≃ | 214 | 42.28 N | 79.22 W |
| Canadensis | 210 | 41.11 N | 75.15 W |
| Canadian | 196 | 35.54 N | 100.22 W |
| Canadian ≃, U.S. | 196 | 35.27 N | 95.03 W |
| Canadian ≃, Co., U.S. | 200 | 40.53 N | 106.20 W |
| Canadian, Deep Fork ≃ | 196 | 35.28 N | 95.50 W |
| Canadian Forces Base Trenton ■ | 212 | 44.07 N | 77.33 W |
| Canadice Lake ⊜ | 210 | 42.43 N | 77.34 W |
| Cañadón Seco | 254 | 46.33 S | 67.35 W |
| Canaguá ≃ | 246 | 7.57 N | 69.36 W |
| Canaima | 246 | 6.14 N | 62.52 W |
| Canaima, Parque Nacional ♦ | 246 | 4.27 N | 62.00 W |
| Canajoharie | 210 | 42.54 N | 74.34 W |
| Çanakkale | 130 | 40.09 N | 26.24 E |
| Çanakkale □[4] | 130 | 40.10 N | 26.45 E |
| Çanakkale Boğazı (Dardanelles) ⋈ | 130 | 40.15 N | 26.25 E |
| Canal, Islas del → Channel Islands II | 28 | 49.20 N | 2.20 W |
| Canala | 175f | 21.32 S | 165.57 E |
| Canale | 62 | 44.48 N | 8.00 E |
| Canale, Val V | 64 | 46.29 N | 13.30 E |
| Canalejas | 234 | 19.57 N | 99.39 W |
| Canal Flats | 182 | 50.09 N | 115.48 W |
| Canal Fulton | 214 | 40.53 N | 81.35 W |
| Canal Lake ⊜ | 212 | 44.34 N | 79.03 W |
| Canal Lewisville | 214 | 40.18 N | 81.50 W |
| Canal Point | 220 | 26.51 N | 80.38 W |
| Canals | 252 | 33.33 S | 62.53 W |
| Canal Winchester | 188 | 39.51 N | 82.48 W |
| Canamã ≃ | 248 | 8.45 S | 59.15 W |
| Canandaigua | 210 | 42.52 N | 77.20 W |
| Canandaigua Lake ⊜ | 210 | 42.49 N | 77.16 W |
| Canandaigua Outlet ≃ | 210 | 43.04 N | 77.00 W |
| Cananea | 232 | 30.57 N | 110.18 W |
| Cananéia | 252 | 25.01 S | 47.57 W |
| Canan Station | 214 | 40.28 N | 78.26 W |
| Canapine, Forca ⋈ | 66 | 42.45 N | 13.12 E |
| Canápolis | 255 | 18.44 S | 49.13 W |
| Canapville | 50 | 49.19 N | 0.08 E |
| Cañar | 246 | 2.33 S | 78.56 W |
| Cañar □[4] | 246 | 2.30 S | 79.00 W |
| Canard ≃ | 214 | 42.09 N | 83.06 W |
| Canard, Lac au ⊜ | 206 | 45.48 N | 71.31 W |
| Canarias, Islas (Canary Islands) II | 148 | 28.00 N | 15.30 W |
| Canaries | 241f | 13.55 N | 61.04 W |
| Canaro | 64 | 44.56 N | 11.40 E |
| Canarreos, Archipiélago de los II | 240p | 21.50 N | 82.30 W |
| Canarsie ✦[8] | 276 | 40.38 N | 73.53 W |
| Canarsie Park ♦ | 276 | 40.38 N | 73.53 W |
| Canarsie Polder I | 276 | 40.37 N | 73.52 W |
| Canary Basin ✣[1] | 10 | 30.00 N | 25.00 W |
| Canary Islands → Canarias, Islas II | 148 | 28.00 N | 15.30 W |
| Cañas | 236 | 10.25 N | 85.07 W |
| Canaseraga | 210 | 42.27 N | 77.46 W |
| Canaseraga Creek ≃ | 210 | 42.45 N | 77.50 W |
| Cañasgordas | 246 | 6.45 N | 76.01 W |
| Canastota | 210 | 43.04 N | 75.45 W |
| Canatlán | 232 | 24.31 N | 104.47 W |
| Canaveral, Cape › | 220 | 28.27 N | 80.32 W |
| Canaveral Bight c[3] | 220 | 28.26 N | 80.33 W |
| Canaveral National Seashore ♦ | 220 | 28.45 N | 80.45 W |
| Canaveral Peninsula ›[1] | 220 | 28.28 N | 80.34 W |
| Cañaveras | 34 | 40.22 N | 2.24 W |
| Canavese ✦[9] | 62 | 45.20 N | 7.40 E |
| Canavieiras | 255 | 15.39 S | 38.57 W |
| Cañazas | 236 | 8.19 N | 81.13 W |
| Canazei | 64 | 46.28 N | 11.46 E |
| Canbelego | 166 | 31.33 S | 146.[illegible] E |
| Canberra | 171b | 35.17 S | 149.[illegible] E |
| Canberra Wildlife Gardens ♦ | 171b | 35.20 S | 149.[illegible] E |
| Canby, Ca., U.S. | 204 | 41.26 N | 120.5[illegible] W |
| Canby, Mn., U.S. | 198 | 44.42 N | 96.1[illegible] W |
| Canby, Or., U.S. | 224 | 45.15 N | 122.4[illegible] W |
| Cancajanang, Mount ∧ | 116 | 11.04 N | 124.4[illegible] E |
| Cancale | 32 | 48.41 N | 1.5[illegible] W |
| Cancano, Lago di ⊜ | 64 | 46.31 N | 10.18 E |
| Cance ≃ | 62 | 45.12 N | 4.48 E |
| Cancellara | 68 | 40.44 N | 15.56 E |
| Cancello e Arnone | 68 | 41.04 N | 14.03 E |
| Canchaque | 248 | 5.24 S | 79.36 W |
| Canche ≃ | 50 | 50.31 N | 1.39 E |
| Cancon | 32 | 44.32 N | 0.38 E |
| Cancún | 232 | 21.05 N | 86.46 W |
| Čančur | 88 | 53.49 N | 106.59 E |
| Canda | 64 | 45.03 N | 11.30 E |
| Candala → Qandala | 144 | 11.28 N | 49.52 E |
| Candarave | 248 | 17.16 S | 70.15 W |
| Çandarlı | 130 | 38.56 N | 26.56 E |
| Çandarlı Körfezi c | 130 | 38.52 N | 26.55 E |
| Candás | 34 | 43.35 N | 5.46 W |
| Candé | 32 | 47.34 N | 1.02 W |
| Candeias, Bra. | 255 | 12.40 S | 38.33 W |
| Candeias, Bra. | 255 | 20.47 S | 45.16 W |
| Candeias ≃ | 248 | 8.39 S | 63.31 W |
| Candela, It. | 68 | 41.08 N | 15.31 E |
| Candela, Méx. | 232 | 26.50 N | 100.40 W |
| Candela, Río de ≃ | 196 | 27.16 N | 100.18 W |
| Candelaria, Arg. | 252 | 27.28 S | 55.44 W |
| Candelaria, Arg. | 252 | 32.04 S | 65.49 W |
| Candelária, Bra. | 252 | 29.40 S | 52.48 W |
| Candelaria, Col. | 246 | 3.25 N | 76.20 W |
| Candelaria, Cuba | 240p | 22.44 N | 82.58 W |
| Candelaria, Pil. | 116 | 15.38 N | 119.56 E |
| Candelaria ≃ | 232 | 18.37 N | 91.14 W |
| Candelaria Loxicha | 234 | 15.54 N | 96.31 W |
| Candelaro ≃ | 68 | 41.34 N | 15.53 E |
| Candeleda | 34 | 40.09 N | 5.14 W |
| Candelo, Austl. | 166 | 36.46 S | 149.42 E |
| Candelo, It. | 62 | 45.33 N | 8.07 E |
| Candia → Iráklion | 38 | 35.20 N | 25.09 E |
| Candiac | 206 | 45.23 N | 73.31 W |
| Candia Canavese | 62 | 45.20 N | 7.53 E |
| Candia Lomellina | 62 | 45.11 N | 8.36 E |
| Cándido Aguilar | 232 | 25.30 N | 98.02 W |
| Cândido de Abreu | 252 | 24.35 S | 51.20 W |
| Cândido Mendes | 250 | 1.27 S | 45.43 W |
| Candies Creek ≃ | 192 | 35.18 N | 84.51 W |
| Candijay | 116 | 9.49 N | 124.30 E |
| Çandır, Tür. | 130 | 40.16 N | 33.29 E |
| Çandır, Tür. | 130 | 39.15 N | 35.32 E |
| Candle | 180 | 65.55 N | 161.56 W |
| Candle Lake ⊜ | 184 | 53.50 N | 105.18 W |
| Candlemas Islands II | 18 | 57.03 S | 26.40 W |
| Candlestick | 194 | 32.15 N | 90.20 W |
| Candlestick Park ♦ | 282 | 37.43 N | 122.23 W |
| Candlewood, Lake ⊜ | 207 | 41.32 N | 73.27 W |
| Candlewood Isle | 207 | 41.29 N | 73.27 W |
| Candlewood Knolls | 207 | 41.28 N | 73.27 W |
| Candlewood Shores | 207 | 41.28 N | 73.26 W |
| Čandman', Mong. | 86 | 50.02 N | 92.03 E |
| Čandman', Mong. | 102 | 45.20 N | 97.59 E |
| Cando, Ang. | 152 | 16.30 S | 18.19 E |
| Cando, Sk., Can. | 184 | 52.23 N | 108.14 W |
| Cando, N.D., U.S. | 198 | 48.29 N | 99.12 W |
| Candombé ≃ | 152 | 16.54 S | 21.52 E |
| Candon | 116 | 17.12 N | 120.27 E |
| Candon Point › | 116 | 17.13 N | 120.24 E |
| Candor, N.Y., U.S. | 210 | 42.13 N | 76.20 W |
| Candor, N.C., U.S. | 192 | 35.17 N | 79.44 W |
| Candover | 158 | 27.28 S | 31.57 E |
| Cane ≃, Austl. | 162 | 21.33 S | 115.23 E |
| Cane ≃, La., U.S. | 194 | 31.31 N | 92.43 W |
| Cane ≃, N.C., U.S. | 192 | 36.00 N | 82.16 W |
| Canea → Khaniá | 38 | 35.31 N | 24.02 E |
| Caneadea | 210 | 42.23 N | 78.09 W |
| Caneças | 266c | 38.49 N | 9.14 W |
| Cane Creek ≃ | 194 | 36.29 N | 90.28 W |
| Canegrate | 266b | 45.34 N | 8.56 E |
| Canela | 252 | 29.22 S | 50.50 W |
| Canelas | 232 | 25.06 N | 106.34 W |
| Canelles, Embalse de ⊜[1] | 34 | 42.10 N | 0.30 E |
| Canelli | 62 | 44.43 N | 8.17 E |
| Canelones | 258 | 34.32 S | 56.17 W |
| Canelones □[5] | 258 | 34.35 S | 56.15 W |
| Canelón Grande, Arroyo ≃ | 258 | 34.30 S | 56.24 W |
| Cane Run ≃ | 218 | 38.13 N | 84.37 W |
| Cañete, Chile | 252 | 37.48 S | 73.24 W |
| Cañete, Esp. | 34 | 40.03 N | 1.35 W |
| Caneva | 64 | 45.58 N | 12.26 E |
| Caney | 198 | 37.00 N | 95.56 W |
| Caney ≃ | 196 | 36.20 N | 95.42 W |
| Caney Brook ≃ | 276 | 41.07 N | 73.50 W |
| Caney Creek ≃, Ar., U.S. | 194 | 33.46 N | 93.07 W |
| Caney Creek ≃, Tx., U.S. | 196 | 28.46 N | 95.39 W |
| Caney Creek ≃, Tx., U.S. | 222 | 32.48 N | 95.33 W |
| Caney Creek ≃, Tx., U.S. | 222 | 30.28 N | 95.38 W |
| Caney Creek ≃, Tx., U.S. | 222 | 30.04 N | 96.08 W |
| Caney Creek ≃, Tx., U.S. | 222 | 31.52 N | 96.13 W |
| Caney Creek ≃, Tx., U.S. | 222 | 31.03 N | 94.33 W |
| Caney Creek ≃, Tx., U.S. | 222 | 30.53 N | 95.48 W |
| Caney Creek ≃, Tx., U.S. | 222 | 30.07 N | 95.10 W |
| Canfield | 214 | 41.01 N | 80.45 W |
| Canfield Island I | 276 | 41.06 N | 73.23 W |
| Canfranc-Estación | 34 | 42.43 N | 0.31 W |
| Cangaíba ✦[8] | 287b | 23.30 S | 46.31 W |
| Cangallo | 248 | 13.33 S | 74.12 W |
| Cangamba | 152 | 13.40 S | 19.54 E |
| Cangandala | 152 | 9.45 S | 16.33 E |
| Cangandala, Parque Nacional da ♦ | 152 | 9.45 S | 16.50 E |
| Cangas, Bra. | 248 | 16.05 S | 56.33 W |
| Cangas, Esp. | 34 | 42.16 N | 8.47 W |
| Cangas de Narcea | 34 | 43.11 N | 6.33 W |
| Cangas de Onís | 34 | 43.21 N | 5.07 W |
| Cangbu | 100 | 30.49 N | 114.35 E |
| Can Gioc ≃ | 269c | 10.42 N | 106.37 E |
| Cangkuang, Tanjung › | 115a | 6.51 S | 105.15 E |
| Cangniutun | 105 | 39.23 N | 115.54 E |
| Cango Caves ⊥[5] | 158 | 33.23 S | 22.14 E |
| Cangola | 152 | 7.58 S | 15.52 E |
| Cangombe | 152 | 14.24 S | 19.59 E |
| Cangongo | 152 | 9.24 S | 17.30 E |
| Cangqian, Zhg. | 106 | 30.17 N | 120.25 E |
| Cangqian, Zhg. | 106 | 30.18 N | 120.00 E |
| Cangshangtun | 105 | 40.03 N | 117.32 E |
| Canguaretama | 250 | 6.24 S | 35.08 W |
| Canguçu | 252 | 31.24 S | 52.41 W |
| Canguera | 256 | 23.36 S | 47.09 W |
| Cangumbe | 152 | 12.00 S | 19.17 E |
| Cangwu | 102 | 23.22 N | 111.13 E |
| Cangxi | 102 | 31.48 N | 105.57 E |
| Cangyrtas | 85 | 40.53 N | 72.50 E |
| Cangyuan | 102 | 23.12 N | 99.16 E |
| Cangzhou | 98 | 38.19 N | 116.51 E |
| Canhoca | 152 | 9.15 S | 14.41 E |
| Canhotinho | 250 | 8.53 S | 36.12 W |
| Caniapiscau ≃ | 176 | 57.40 N | 69.30 W |
| Caniapiscau, Lac ⊜ | 176 | 54.10 N | 69.55 W |
| Canicanian | 116 | 14.46 N | 122.01 E |
| Canicattì | 70 | 37.21 N | 13.51 E |


| | | | | |
|---|---|---|---|---|
| ≃ River | Fluß | Río | Rivière | Rio |
| ≋ Canal | Kanal | Canal | Canal | Canal |
| ⌊ Waterfall, Rapids | Wasserfall, Stromschnellen | Cascada, Rápidos | Chute d'eau, Rapides | Cascata, Rápidos |
| ⋈ Strait | Meeresstraße | Estrecho | Détroit | Estreito |
| c Bay, Gulf | Bucht, Golf | Bahía, Golfo | Baie, Golfe | Baía, Golfo |
| ⊜ Lake, Lakes | See, Seen | Lago, Lagos | Lac, Lacs | Lago, Lagos |
| ≡ Swamp | Sumpf | Pantano | Marais | Pântano |
| ⊓ Ice Features, Glacier | Eis- und Gletscherformen | Accidentes Glaciales | Formes glaciaires | Acidentes glaciares |
| ⊤ Other Hydrographic Features | Andere Hydrographische Objekte | Otros Elementos Hidrográficos | Autres données hydrographiques | Outros acidentes hidrográficos |

| | | | | |
|---|---|---|---|---|
| ✣ Submarine Features | Untermeerische Objekte | Accidentes Submarinos | Formes de relief sous-marin | Acidentes submarinos |
| □ Political Unit | Politische Einheit | Unidad Política | Entité politique | Unidade política |
| ⊍ Cultural Institution | Kulturelle Institution | Institución Cultural | Institution culturelle | Instituição cultural |
| ⊥ Historical Site | Historische Stätte | Sitio Histórico | Site historique | Sítio histórico |
| ♦ Recreational Site | Erholungs- und Ferienort | Sitio de Recreo | Centre de loisirs | Área de Lazer |
| ⊠ Airport | Flughafen | Aeropuerto | Aéroport | Aeroporto |
| ■ Military Installation | Militäranlage | Instalación Militar | Installation militaire | Instalação militar |
| ✦ Miscellaneous | Verschiedenes | Misceláneo | Divers | Diversos |

ENGLISH / DEUTSCH

| Name | Page (Seite) | Lat.°′ (Breite°′) | Long.°′ (Länge°′ E = Ost) |
|---|---|---|---|
| Canicattini Bagni | 70 | 37.02 N | 15.04 E |
| Canigao Channel ⊔ | 116 | 10.15 N | 124.42 E |
| Canigou, Pic du ∧ | 32 | 42.31 N | 2.27 E |
| Canillas ●[8] | 266a | 40.28 N | 3.38 W |
| Canillejas ●[8] | 266a | 40.27 N | 3.37 W |
| Canim Lake | 182 | 51.46 N | 120.54 W |
| Canim Lake ⊜ | 182 | 51.52 N | 120.45 W |
| Canim Lake Indian Reserve ●[4] | 182 | 51.47 N | 121.00 W |
| Canindé | 250 | 4.22 S | 39.19 W |
| Canindé ≃ | 250 | 6.15 S | 42.52 W |
| Canindeyú □[5] | 252 | 24.15 S | 55.15 W |
| Canino | 66 | 42.28 N | 11.45 E |
| Canipaan | 116 | 8.35 N | 117.16 E |
| Canipo Island I | 116 | 10.59 N | 120.57 E |
| Canisius College ʋ[2] | 284a | 42.55 N | 78.52 W |
| Canisp ∧ | 46 | 58.07 N | 5.03 W |
| Canistear Reservoir ⊜[1] | 276 | 41.08 N | 74.29 W |
| Canisteo | 210 | 42.16 N | 77.36 W |
| Canisteo ≃ | 210 | 42.07 N | 77.08 W |
| Canistota | 198 | 43.35 N | 97.17 W |
| Cañitas de Felipe Pescador | 234 | 23.36 N | 102.43 W |
| Canjáyar | 34 | 37.00 N | 2.44 W |
| Canjinge | 152 | 10.12 S | 21.17 E |
| Cankhor | 144 | 10.46 N | 46.13 E |
| Çankırı | 130 | 40.36 N | 33.37 E |
| Çankırı □[4] | 130 | 40.45 N | 33.25 E |
| Canlaon | 116 | 10.22 N | 123.12 E |
| Canlaon Volcano ∧[1] | 116 | 10.25 N | 123.08 E |
| Canley Vale | 274a | 33.53 S | 150.57 E |
| Canmore | 182 | 51.05 N | 115.21 W |
| Canna | 68 | 40.05 N | 16.30 E |
| Canna I | 46 | 57.04 N | 6.34 W |
| Canna, Sound of ⊔ | 46 | 57.03 N | 6.25 W |
| Cannanore | 122 | 11.51 N | 75.22 E |
| Cannara | 66 | 43.00 N | 12.35 E |
| Canne ⊥ | 68 | 41.18 N | 16.09 E |
| Cannel City | 192 | 37.47 N | 83.16 W |
| Cannelton | 194 | 37.54 N | 86.44 W |
| Canner ≃ | 56 | 49.24 N | 6.16 E |
| Cannero-Riviera | 58 | 46.01 N | 8.41 E |
| Cannes | 62 | 43.33 N | 7.01 E |
| Cannes, Bayou des ≃ | 194 | 30.12 N | 92.35 W |
| Canneto, It. | 66 | 43.12 N | 10.44 E |
| Canneto, It. | 70 | 38.29 N | 14.58 E |
| Canneto sull'Oglio | 64 | 45.09 N | 10.25 E |
| Cannich | 46 | 57.21 N | 4.46 W |
| Cannich ≃ | 46 | 57.21 N | 4.44 W |
| Cannifton | 212 | 44.12 N | 77.23 W |
| Canning, Arg. | 288 | 34.53 S | 58.30 W |
| Canning, Austl. | 168a | 32.02 S | 115.56 E |
| Canning, N.S., Can. | 186 | 45.09 N | 64.25 W |
| Canning ≃, Austl. | 168a | 32.01 S | 115.51 E |
| Canning ≃, Ak., U.S. | 180 | 70.05 N | 145.30 W |
| Canning Hill ∧[2] | 162 | 28.50 S | 117.49 E |
| Canning Lake ⊜ | 212 | 44.56 N | 78.38 W |
| Canning Reservoir ⊜[1] | 168a | 32.10 S | 116.09 E |
| Cannington, On., Can. | 212 | 44.21 N | 79.02 W |
| Cannington, Eng., U.K. | 42 | 51.09 N | 3.04 W |
| Cannobio | 58 | 46.04 N | 8.42 E |
| Cannock | 42 | 52.42 N | 2.09 W |
| Cannock Chase ●[1] | 42 | 52.43 N | 2.00 W |
| Cannon ≃ | 190 | 44.35 N | 92.33 W |
| Cannon Air Force Base ■ | 196 | 34.23 N | 103.18 W |
| Cannon Bali | 198 | 46.23 N | 100.35 W |
| Cannonball ≃ | 198 | 46.26 N | 100.38 W |
| Cannon Beach | 224 | 45.53 N | 123.57 W |
| Cannondale | 207 | 41.12 N | 73.25 W |
| Cannon Falls | 190 | 44.30 N | 92.54 W |
| Cannonsburg | 216 | 43.03 N | 85.28 W |
| Cannonsville Reservoir ⊜[1] | 210 | 42.08 N | 75.19 W |
| Cannonvale | 166 | 20.17 S | 148.42 E |
| Cann River | 166 | 37.34 S | 149.10 E |
| Caño, Isla del I | 236 | 8.44 N | 83.53 W |
| Canoas | 252 | 29.56 S | 51.11 W |
| Canoas ≃, Bra. | 252 | 27.36 S | 51.25 W |
| Canoas ≃, Bra. | 256 | 21.30 S | 47.09 W |
| Canobie Lake | 283 | 42.48 N | 71.14 W |
| Canobie Lake ⊜ | 283 | 42.49 N | 71.15 W |
| Canobie Lake Park ♦ | 283 | 42.48 N | 71.15 W |
| Canoe | 182 | 50.45 N | 119.13 W |
| Canoe ≃, B.C., Can. | 182 | 52.09 N | 118.27 W |
| Canoe ≃, Ma., U.S. | 283 | 41.58 N | 71.08 W |
| Canoe Brook ≃ | 276 | 40.45 N | 74.22 W |
| Canoe Brook Reservoirs ⊜[1] | 276 | 40.45 N | 74.21 W |
| Canoe Creek Indian Reserve ●[4] | 182 | 51.32 N | 122.15 W |
| Canoe Lake ⊜ | 184 | 55.11 N | 108.15 W |
| Canoe Lake Indian Reserve ●[4] | 184 | 55.08 N | 108.12 W |
| Canoga Park ●[8] | 280 | 34.12 N | 118.35 W |
| Canoinhas | 252 | 26.10 S | 50.24 W |
| Canol | 180 | 65.14 N | 126.56 W |
| Canon | 192 | 34.21 N | 83.07 W |
| Canon ≃ | 224 | 46.36 N | 123.53 W |
| Canonbie | 44 | 55.05 N | 2.57 W |
| Canon City | 200 | 38.24 N | 105.13 W |
| Cañón del Sumidero, Parque Nacional ♦ | 234 | 16.45 N | 93.05 W |
| Caño Negro | 236 | 10.54 N | 84.44 W |
| Canonsburg | 214 | 40.15 N | 80.11 W |
| Canonsburg Lake ⊜ | 279b | 40.16 N | 80.07 W |
| Canoochee ≃ | 192 | 31.59 N | 81.18 W |
| Canoole Cise | 144 | 2.02 N | 42.19 E |
| Canopus ⊥ | 142 | 31.18 N | 30.03 E |
| Canora | 184 | 51.37 N | 102.26 W |
| Canosa di Puglia | 68 | 41.13 N | 16.04 E |
| Canossa ⊥ | 64 | 44.35 N | 10.27 E |
| Canot, Pointe › | 241o | 16.12 N | 61.28 W |
| Canouan I | 238 | 12.43 N | 61.20 W |
| Canova | 198 | 43.52 N | 97.30 W |
| Canova Beach | 220 | 28.08 N | 80.34 W |
| Cañovanas | 240m | 18.23 N | 65.54 W |
| Cánoves ≃ | 266d | 41.37 N | 2.22 E |
| Canow | 54 | 53.12 N | 12.54 E |
| Canowindra | 166 | 33.34 S | 148.38 E |
| Can Quer, Torrente de ≃ | 266d | 41.31 N | 2.11 E |
| Cansado | 148 | 20.51 N | 17.02 W |
| Cansanção | 250 | 10.41 S | 39.31 W |
| Canso | 186 | 45.20 N | 61.00 W |
| Canso, Strait of ⊔ | 186 | 45.37 N | 61.25 W |
| Canta | 248 | 11.25 S | 76.38 W |
| Cantabria | 234 | 19.50 N | 101.44 W |
| Cantabria □[3] | 34 | 43.15 N | 4.00 W |
| Cantabria (Santander) □[4] | 34 | 43.15 N | 4.00 W |
| Cantábrica, Cordillera ⋏ | 34 | 43.00 N | 5.00 W |
| Cantabriques → Cantábrica, Cordillera ⋏ | 34 | 43.00 N | 5.00 W |
| Cantagalo | 255 | 21.58 S | 42.22 W |
| Cantagalo, Cachoeira L | 250 | 7.18 S | 54.52 W |
| Cantal □[5] | 32 | 45.05 N | 2.45 E |
| Cantalejo | 34 | 41.15 N | 3.55 W |
| Cantalupo in Sabina | 66 | 42.18 N | 12.39 E |
| Cantalupo nel Sannio | 66 | 41.31 N | 14.24 E |
| Čantal'vejergyn ≃ | 180 | 67.38 N | 179.22 W |
| Cantanhede, Bra. | 250 | 3.39 S | 44.24 W |
| Cantanhede, Port. | 34 | 40.21 N | 8.36 W |
| Cantareira ●[8] | 287b | 23.27 S | 46.37 W |
| Cantareira, Serra da ∧ | 287b | 23.25 S | 46.39 W |
| Cantaura | 246 | 9.19 N | 64.21 W |
| Cant Clough Reservoir ⊜[1] | 262 | 53.46 N | 2.09 W |
| Canteleu | 50 | 49.27 N | 1.02 E |
| Canterbury, Austl. | 274a | 33.55 S | 151.07 E |
| Canterbury, Austl. | 274b | 37.49 S | 145.05 E |
| Canterbury, N.B., Can. | 186 | 45.53 N | 67.29 W |
| Canterbury, Eng., U.K. | 42 | 51.17 N | 1.05 E |
| Canterbury Bight c[3] | 172 | 44.15 S | 171.38 E |
| Canterbury Cathedral ʋ[1] | 42 | 51.17 N | 1.05 E |
| Canterbury Park Racecourse ♦ | 274a | 33.54 S | 151.07 E |
| Canterbury Plains ≚ | 172 | 44.00 S | 171.45 E |
| Canterbury Woods | 284c | 38.49 N | 77.15 W |
| Can Tho | 110 | 10.02 N | 105.47 E |
| Cantiano | 66 | 43.28 N | 12.38 E |
| Cantil | 228 | 35.18 N | 117.58 W |
| Cantiles, Cayo I | 240p | 21.36 N | 82.02 W |
| Cantin Lake ⊜ | 184 | 53.27 N | 95.10 W |
| Canto do Buriti | 250 | 8.07 S | 42.58 W |
| Canto do Pontes | 287a | 22.58 S | 43.04 W |
| Canto Grande, Quebrada V | 286d | 11.59 S | 77.01 W |
| Cantoira | 62 | 45.21 N | 7.23 E |
| Canton, Ct., U.S. | 207 | 41.49 N | 72.53 W |
| Canton, Ga., U.S. | 192 | 34.14 N | 84.29 W |
| Canton, Il., U.S. | 190 | 40.33 N | 90.02 W |
| Canton, Ks., U.S. | 198 | 38.23 N | 97.25 W |
| Canton, Ma., U.S. | 207 | 42.09 N | 71.08 W |
| Canton, Mn., U.S. | 190 | 43.31 N | 91.55 W |
| Canton, Ms., U.S. | 194 | 32.36 N | 90.02 W |
| Canton, Mo., U.S. | 219 | 40.07 N | 91.37 W |
| Canton, N.J., U.S. | 208 | 39.28 N | 75.24 W |
| Canton, N.Y., U.S. | 188 | 44.35 N | 75.10 W |
| Canton, N.C., U.S. | 192 | 35.31 N | 82.50 W |
| Canton, Oh., U.S. | 214 | 40.47 N | 81.22 W |
| Canton, Ok., U.S. | 196 | 36.03 N | 98.35 W |
| Canton, Pa., U.S. | 210 | 41.39 N | 76.51 W |
| Canton, S.D., U.S. | 198 | 43.18 N | 96.35 W |
| Canton, Tx., U.S. | 222 | 32.33 N | 95.51 W |
| Canton → Guangzhou, Zhg. | 100 | 23.06 N | 113.16 E |
| Canton → Kanton I | 174h | 2.50 S | 171.40 W |
| Canton Airport ⊠ | 174h | 2.46 S | 171.43 W |
| Canton Lake ⊜[1] | 196 | 36.08 N | 98.36 W |
| Canton Lake State Recreational Area ♦ | 196 | 36.08 N | 98.39 W |
| Cantonment | 194 | 30.36 N | 87.20 W |
| Cantorbéry → Canterbury | 42 | 51.17 N | 1.05 E |
| Cantrall | 219 | 39.56 N | 89.41 W |
| Cantribana | 266c | 38.53 N | 9.25 W |
| Cantù | 62 | 45.44 N | 9.08 E |
| Cantu ≃ | 252 | 24.46 S | 52.54 W |
| Cantua Creek | 226 | 36.33 N | 120.22 W |
| Cantua Creek ≃ | 226 | 36.28 N | 120.17 W |
| Cantwell | 180 | 63.23 N | 148.57 W |
| Cañuelas | 258 | 35.03 S | 58.44 W |
| Cañuelas □[5] | 288 | 34.56 S | 58.41 W |
| Cañuelas, Arroyo ≃ | 258 | 34.55 S | 58.38 W |
| Canumã | 246 | 4.02 S | 59.04 W |
| Canumã ≃ | 246 | 3.55 S | 59.10 W |
| Canungra | 171a | 28.01 S | 153.10 E |
| Canungra Creek ≃ | 171a | 27.55 S | 153.06 E |
| Canungra Jungle Training Ground ■ | 171a | 28.02 S | 153.10 E |
| Canutama | 248 | 6.32 S | 64.20 W |
| Canutillo | 200 | 31.54 N | 106.35 W |
| Canvastown | 172 | 41.18 S | 173.40 E |
| Canvey Island | 42 | 51.32 N | 0.36 E |
| Canvey Island I | 42 | 51.33 N | 0.34 E |
| Čany | 86 | 55.19 N | 76.46 E |
| Čany, ozero ⊜ | 86 | 54.50 N | 77.30 E |
| Cany-Barville | 50 | 49.47 N | 0.38 E |
| Canyon, Yk., Can. | 180 | 60.52 N | 137.02 W |
| Canyon, Ca., U.S. | 282 | 37.49 N | 122.09 W |
| Canyon, Tx., U.S. | 196 | 34.58 N | 101.55 W |
| Canyon City | 202 | 44.23 N | 118.56 W |
| Canyon Creek | 182 | 55.22 N | 115.05 W |
| Canyon Creek ≃, Az., U.S. | 200 | 33.49 N | 110.40 W |
| Canyon Creek ≃, Ca., U.S. | 226 | 39.22 N | 120.45 W |
| Canyon Creek ≃, Id., U.S. | 202 | 42.59 N | 115.59 W |
| Canyon Creek ≃, Wa., U.S. | 224 | 45.57 N | 122.22 W |
| Canyon Creek ≃, Wa., U.S. | 224 | 48.43 N | 120.55 W |
| Canyon de Chelly National Monument ♦ | 200 | 36.01 N | 109.26 W |
| Canyon Ferry Lake ⊜[1] | 202 | 46.33 N | 111.37 W |
| Canyon Lake ⊜[1] | 196 | 29.52 N | 98.16 W |
| Canyonlands National Park ♦ | 200 | 38.10 N | 110.00 W |
| Canyonville | 202 | 42.55 N | 123.16 W |
| Canzar | 152 | 7.38 S | 21.32 E |
| Canzo | 62 | 45.51 N | 9.16 E |
| Cao ≃, Zhg. | 98 | 40.29 N | 124.08 E |
| Cao ≃, Zhg. | 105 | 38.52 N | 115.46 E |
| Cao Bang | 110 | 22.40 N | 106.15 E |
| Caochi | 107 | 30.19 N | 104.24 E |
| Caocun | 106 | 31.42 N | 118.56 E |
| Caodian, Zhg. | 100 | 28.39 N | 120.23 E |
| Caodian, Zhg. | 100 | 33.21 N | 112.39 E |
| Caodian, Zhg. | 102 | 32.32 N | 111.11 E |
| Cao'e | 100 | 30.01 N | 120.52 E |
| Cao'e ≃ | 100 | 30.06 N | 120.46 E |
| Caofang | 100 | 26.04 N | 116.35 E |
| Caogezhai | 105 | 40.09 N | 117.50 E |
| Caohe, Zhg. | 105 | 38.57 N | 115.32 E |
| Caohe, Zhg. | 269b | 31.09 N | 121.25 E |
| Caohecheng | 104 | 40.46 N | 124.02 E |
| Caohekou | 104 | 40.54 N | 123.53 E |
| Caohezhang | 104 | 41.04 N | 124.03 E |
| Caojian | 102 | 25.38 N | 99.07 E |
| Caojiawopeng | 104 | 42.00 N | 122.20 E |
| Caojiawopu | 104 | 42.37 N | 122.19 E |
| Caojiawu | 105 | 39.24 N | 116.31 E |
| Caojiazhen | 106 | 31.55 N | 121.38 E |
| Caojiezi | 107 | 29.53 N | 106.24 E |
| Caojing | 106 | 30.47 N | 121.24 E |
| Caojun | 100 | 29.41 N | 116.17 E |
| Cao Lanh | 110 | 10.27 N | 105.38 E |
| Caolaoji | 100 | 33.06 N | 117.22 E |
| Caolisport, Loch c | 46 | 55.54 N | 5.37 W |
| Caomaji | 98 | 34.52 N | 116.17 E |
| Caombo | 152 | 8.43 S | 16.51 E |
| Caonao ≃ | 240p | 22.05 N | 78.05 W |
| Caonian | 100 | 32.56 N | 120.20 E |
| Caonillas, Lago ⊜ | 240m | 18.16 N | 66.39 W |
| Caopeng | 106 | 31.44 N | 121.17 E |
| Caoping | 100 | 28.48 N | 118.22 E |
| Caopu | 98 | 34.34 N | 118.52 E |
| Caoqiao | 106 | 31.32 N | 119.59 E |
| Caorle | 64 | 45.36 N | 12.53 E |
| Caorso | 62 | 45.03 N | 9.52 E |
| Caoshi, Zhg. | 98 | 42.17 N | 125.16 E |
| Caoshi, Zhg. | 100 | 33.32 N | 116.29 E |
| Caota | 100 | 29.42 N | 120.08 E |
| Caotang | 106 | 31.16 N | 118.59 E |
| Caoxi | 100 | 28.42 N | 117.18 E |
| Caoxian | 98 | 34.53 N | 115.33 E |
| Caoyangxi | 100 | 26.34 N | 118.47 E |
| Cap, Le → Cape Town | 158 | 33.55 S | 18.22 E |
| Cap, Pointe du › | 241f | 14.07 N | 60.57 W |
| Capac | 190 | 43.00 N | 82.55 W |
| Capaccio | 68 | 40.25 N | 15.05 E |
| Capacciotti, Lago di ⊜[1] | 68 | 41.10 N | 15.47 E |
| Capaci | 70 | 38.10 N | 13.14 E |
| Capage | 152 | 13.21 S | 21.05 E |
| Čapajevka | 82 | 54.38 N | 35.50 E |
| Čapajevka ≃ | 80 | 53.08 N | 49.37 E |
| Čapajevo | 80 | 50.12 N | 51.10 E |
| Čapajevsk | 80 | 52.58 N | 49.41 E |
| Capala | 152 | 13.37 S | 14.45 E |
| Capalbio | 66 | 42.27 N | 11.25 E |
| Capalonga | 116 | 14.20 N | 122.30 E |
| Capanaparo ≃ | 246 | 7.01 N | 67.07 W |
| Capanema, Bra. | 250 | 1.12 S | 47.11 W |
| Capanema, Bra. | 252 | 25.40 S | 53.48 W |
| Capangombe | 152 | 15.05 S | 13.08 E |
| Capanne, Monte ∧ | 66 | 42.46 N | 10.10 E |
| Capannoli | 66 | 43.35 N | 10.41 E |
| Capannori | 66 | 43.50 N | 10.34 E |
| Capão Bonito | 255 | 24.01 S | 48.20 W |
| Capão Doce, Morro do ∧ | 252 | 26.43 S | 51.25 W |
| Capão Redondo ●[8] | 287b | 23.40 S | 46.46 W |
| Capaotigamau, Lac ⊜ | 186 | 50.18 N | 68.14 W |
| Caparaó, Parque Nacional do ♦ | 255 | 20.33 S | 41.45 W |
| Caparica | 266c | 38.40 N | 9.12 W |
| Caparo Viejo ≃ | 246 | 7.46 N | 70.23 W |
| Capas | 116 | 15.20 N | 120.35 E |
| Capatárida | 246 | 11.11 N | 70.37 W |
| Cap-aux-Meules (Grindstone Island) | 186 | 47.23 N | 61.52 W |
| Cap aux Meules, Île du I | 186 | 47.23 N | 61.54 W |
| Capay | 226 | 38.32 N | 122.03 W |
| Cap-Chat | 186 | 49.06 N | 66.42 W |
| Cap-de-la-Madeleine | 206 | 46.22 N | 72.31 W |
| Cape ≃ | 166 | 20.49 S | 146.51 E |
| Cape Arid National Park ♦ | 162 | 33.40 S | 123.25 E |
| Cape Barren Island I | 166 | 40.25 S | 148.12 E |
| Cape Basin ✚[1] | 8 | 37.00 S | 7.00 E |
| Cape Bougainville Aboriginal Reserve ●[4] | 164 | 14.10 S | 126.30 E |
| Cape Breton Highlands National Park ♦ | 186 | 46.45 N | 60.45 W |
| Cape Breton Island I | 186 | 46.00 N | 60.30 W |
| Cape Broyle | 186 | 47.06 N | 52.57 W |
| Cape Canaveral | 220 | 28.24 N | 80.36 W |
| Cape Canaveral Air Force Station ■ | 220 | 28.29 N | 80.35 W |
| Cape Charles | 208 | 37.16 N | 76.01 W |
| Cape Coast | 150 | 5.05 N | 1.15 W |
| Cape Cod Bay c | 207 | 41.52 N | 70.22 W |
| Cape Cod Canal ≖ | 207 | 41.47 N | 70.30 W |
| Cape Cod National Seashore ♦ | 207 | 41.56 N | 70.00 W |
| Cape Comorin → Kanniyākumari | 122 | 8.05 N | 77.34 E |
| Cape Coral | 220 | 26.33 N | 81.56 W |
| Cape Croker Indian Reserve ●[4] | 212 | 44.55 N | 81.01 W |
| Cape Dorset | 176 | 64.14 N | 76.32 W |
| Cape Elizabeth | 188 | 43.33 N | 70.12 W |
| Cape Fear ≃ | 192 | 33.53 N | 78.00 W |
| Cape Girardeau | 194 | 37.18 N | 89.31 W |
| Cape Hatteras National Seashore ♦ | 192 | 35.30 N | 76.35 W |
| Cape Henlopen State Park ♦ | 208 | 38.45 N | 75.06 W |
| Cape Jervis | 168b | 35.36 S | 138.06 E |
| Cape Johnson Tablemount ✚[3] | 14 | 17.08 N | 177.15 W |
| Cape Krusenstern National Monument ♦ | 180 | 67.30 N | 163.40 W |
| Capela | 250 | 10.30 S | 37.04 W |
| Cape LaHave Island I | 186 | 44.12 N | 64.22 W |
| Cape la Hune | 186 | 47.33 N | 56.52 W |
| Capel Curig | 44 | 53.06 N | 3.54 W |
| Capelengue | 152 | 9.12 S | 19.43 E |
| Capelinha | 255 | 17.42 S | 42.31 W |
| Capelinha do Embirazal | 256 | 22.02 S | 45.26 W |
| Cape Lisburne | 180 | 68.52 N | 166.05 W |
| Capel'ka | 76 | 58.03 N | 28.59 E |
| Capella | 166 | 23.05 S | 148.02 E |
| Capella ∧ | 164 | 5.00 S | 141.05 E |
| Capelle [aan de IJssel] | 52 | 51.55 N | 4.35 E |
| Capellen | 56 | 49.38 N | 5.59 E |
| Capelongo | 152 | 14.54 S | 15.08 E |
| Cape Lookout National Seashore ♦ | 192 | 34.40 N | 76.23 W |
| Cape Lookout State Park ♦ | 224 | 45.21 N | 123.59 W |
| Capel Saint Mary | 42 | 52.00 N | 1.04 E |
| Cape May | 208 | 38.56 N | 74.54 W |
| Cape May □[6] | 208 | 38.56 N | 74.55 W |
| Cape May Coast Guard Air Station ■ | 208 | 38.57 N | 74.53 W |
| Cape May Court House | 208 | 39.04 N | 74.49 W |
| Cape May Point | 208 | 39.09 N | 74.46 W |
| Capembé ≃ | 152 | 16.10 S | 21.00 E |
| Cape Melville National Park ♦ | 164 | 14.20 S | 144.30 E |
| Capenda Camulemba | 152 | 9.24 S | 18.27 E |
| Capenga ≃ | 287a | 22.49 S | 43.37 W |
| Capenhurst | 262 | 53.15 N | 2.57 W |
| Cape of Good Hope Nature Reserve ●[4] | 158 | 34.18 S | 18.26 E |
| Cape Pole | 180 | 55.58 N | 133.48 W |
| Cape Pond ⊜ | 283 | 42.38 N | 70.38 W |
| Cape Porpoise | 188 | 43.22 N | 70.26 W |
| Cape Range National Park ♦ | 162 | 22.10 S | 113.55 E |
| Cape Rise ✚[3] | 8 | 42.00 S | 15.00 E |
| Capernaum → Kefar Naḥum ⊥ | 132 | 32.53 N | 35.34 E |
| Cape Romanzof | 180 | 61.49 N | 165.56 W |
| Capertee | 170 | 33.09 S | 149.59 E |
| Capertee ≃ | 170 | 33.12 S | 150.28 E |
| Cape Sable Island I | 186 | 43.25 N | 65.37 W |
| Cape Scott Provincial Park ♦ | 182 | 50.45 N | 128.20 W |
| Capesterre | 241o | 15.54 N | 61.13 W |
| Capesterre, Pointe de la › | 241o | 16.03 N | 61.33 W |
| Capesterre-Belle-Eau | 241o | 16.03 N | 61.34 W |
| Capesthorne Hall ⊥ | 262 | 53.15 N | 2.14 W |
| Capestrano | 66 | 42.16 N | 13.46 E |
| Capetinga ≃ | 256 | 22.04 S | 47.14 W |
| Cape Tormentine | 186 | 46.08 N | 63.47 W |
| Cape Town (Kaapstad) | 158 | 33.55 S | 18.22 E |
| Cape Verde (Cabo Verde) □[1], Afr. | 134 | 16.00 N | 24.00 W |
| Cape Verde (Cabo Verde) □[1], Afr. | 150a | 16.00 N | 24.00 W |
| Cape Verde Basin ✚[1] | 8 | 15.00 N | 30.00 W |
| Cape Verde Islands → Cape Verde □[1] | 150a | 16.00 N | 24.00 W |
| Cape Verde Terrace ✚[3] | 10 | 18.00 N | 20.00 W |
| Capeville | 208 | 37.12 N | 75.57 W |
| Cape Vincent | 212 | 44.07 N | 76.19 W |
| Cape Yakataga | 180 | 60.04 N | 142.26 W |
| Cape York Peninsula ›[1] | 164 | 14.00 S | 142.30 E |
| Cap-Haïtien | 238 | 19.45 N | 72.12 W |
| Capilla de Farruco | 252 | 32.53 S | 55.25 W |
| Capilla del Monte | 252 | 30.51 S | 64.31 W |
| Capilla del Señor | 258 | 34.18 S | 59.06 W |
| Capim ≃ | 250 | 1.40 S | 47.47 W |
| Capim Melado, Morro do ∧ | 287a | 22.50 S | 43.29 W |
| Capinas Point › | 116 | 11.05 N | 125.14 E |
| Capinópolis | 255 | 18.41 S | 49.35 W |
| Capinota | 248 | 17.43 S | 66.14 W |
| Capinzal | 252 | 27.20 S | 51.36 W |
| Capira | 236 | 8.45 N | 79.53 W |
| Cap Island I | 116 | 5.57 N | 120.06 E |
| Capistrano, Bra. | 250 | 4.28 S | 38.55 W |
| Capistrano, It. | 68 | 38.41 N | 16.17 E |
| Capistrello | 66 | 41.57 N | 13.23 E |
| Capitachouane ≃ | 190 | 47.36 N | 76.54 W |
| Capitachouane, Lac ⊜ | 190 | 48.05 N | 75.55 W |
| Capital Airport ⊠ | 219 | 39.51 N | 89.41 W |
| Capital Centre ♦ | 284c | 38.54 N | 76.51 W |
| Capital City Airport ⊠ | 216 | 42.47 N | 84.35 W |
| Capitan | 200 | 33.32 N | 105.34 W |
| Capitán Aracena, Isla I | 254 | 54.10 S | 71.20 W |
| Capitán Arturo Prat ʋ[3] | 9 | 62.30 S | 59.41 W |
| Capitán Bado | 255 | 23.16 S | 55.32 W |
| Capitán Bermúdez | 252 | 32.49 S | 60.43 W |
| Capitán Meza | 252 | 26.55 S | 55.15 W |
| Capitan Peak ∧ | 200 | 33.36 N | 105.16 W |
| Capitán Sarmiento | 252 | 34.10 S | 59.48 W |
| Capitão de Campos | 250 | 4.28 S | 41.57 W |
| Capitão Enéas | 255 | 16.21 S | 43.43 W |
| Capitola | 226 | 36.58 N | 121.57 W |
| Capitol Heights | 208 | 38.53 N | 76.54 W |
| Capitol Park | 208 | 39.08 N | 75.30 W |
| Capitol Peak ∧ | 204 | 41.50 N | 117.18 W |
| Capitol Reef National Park ♦ | 200 | 38.11 N | 111.20 W |
| Capitol View | 192 | 33.57 N | 80.56 W |
| Capivari | 255 | 23.00 S | 47.31 W |
| Capivari ≃, Bra. | 248 | 19.16 S | 57.10 W |
| Capivari ≃, Bra. | 255 | 12.30 S | 39.55 W |
| Capivari ≃, Bra. | 256 | 24.09 S | 46.48 W |
| Capivari ≃, Bra. | 256 | 22.14 S | 44.57 W |
| Capivari ≃, Bra. | 256 | 21.53 S | 46.15 W |
| Capivari ≃, Bra. | 256 | 22.26 S | 45.47 W |
| Capivari ≃, Bra. | 256 | 22.56 S | 47.16 W |
| Capivari ≃, Bra. | 256 | 21.30 S | 44.20 W |
| Capivari ≃, Bra. | 256 | 21.12 S | 44.52 W |
| Capivari, Canal ≖ | 287a | 22.42 S | 43.21 W |
| Capiz → Roxas | 116 | 11.35 N | 122.45 E |
| Capiz □[4] | 116 | 11.30 N | 122.30 E |
| Capizzi | 70 | 37.51 N | 14.29 E |
| Caplan | 186 | 48.06 N | 65.41 W |
| Caplen | 222 | 29.29 N | 94.33 W |
| Caples Lake ⊜[1] | 226 | 38.42 N | 120.03 W |
| Čaplina ≃ | 248 | 18.14 S | 70.33 W |
| Čaplino | 180 | 64.25 N | 172.15 W |
| Čapljina | 36 | 43.07 N | 17.42 E |
| Caplone, Monte ∧ | 64 | 45.48 N | 10.38 E |
| Čaplygin | 76 | 53.14 N | 39.58 E |
| Cap Mountain ∧ | 180 | 63.25 N | 123.29 W |
| Capnoyan Island I | 116 | 10.44 N | 120.54 E |
| Capoche ≃ | 154 | 15.23 S | 32.53 E |
| Capodichino, Aeroporto di ⊠ | 68 | 40.50 N | 14.17 E |
| Capodimonte | 66 | 42.33 N | 11.55 E |
| Capo di Ponte | 64 | 46.02 N | 10.21 E |
| Capo d'Orlando | 70 | 38.10 N | 14.53 E |
| Capoeira, Corredeira L | 250 | 6.48 S | 58.21 W |
| Capolago | 58 | 45.55 N | 8.59 E |
| Capoliveri | 66 | 42.45 N | 10.22 E |
| Caporolo ≃ | 152 | 12.56 S | 13.00 E |
| Caposele | 68 | 40.49 N | 15.13 E |
| Capostrada | 66 | 43.57 N | 10.54 E |
| Capot ≃ | 240e | 14.51 N | 61.05 W |
| Capoterra | 71 | 39.11 N | 8.58 E |
| Capoti-an, Mount ∧ | 116 | 11.45 N | 125.15 E |
| Capotoan, Mount ∧ | 116 | 12.09 N | 124.57 E |
| Cappadocia □[9] | 130 | 38.30 N | 36.00 E |
| Cappamore | 48 | 52.37 N | 8.20 W |
| Cap-Pelé | 186 | 46.13 N | 64.18 W |
| Cappella Islands II | 240m | 18.17 N | 64.54 W |
| Cappelle | 66 | 42.03 N | 13.22 E |
| Cappelle sul Tavo | 66 | 42.28 N | 14.06 E |
| Cappeln | 52 | 52.48 N | 8.07 E |
| Cappenberg | 263 | 51.39 N | 7.32 E |
| Cappenberg, Schloss ⊥ | 263 | 51.39 N | 7.32 E |
| Cappercleuch | 44 | 55.29 N | 3.12 W |
| Cappoquin | 48 | 52.08 N | 7.50 W |
| Capracotta | 66 | 41.50 N | 14.16 E |
| Capraia | 66 | 43.03 N | 9.50 E |
| Capraia, Isola I | 66 | 42.08 N | 15.31 E |
| Capraia, Isola di I | 66 | 43.02 N | 9.49 E |
| Capranica | 66 | 42.15 N | 12.11 E |
| Caprara, Punta › | 71 | 41.07 N | 8.19 E |
| Caprarola | 66 | 42.19 N | 12.14 E |
| Capreol | 190 | 46.43 N | 80.56 W |
| Caprera, Isola I | 71 | 41.12 N | 9.28 E |
| Caprese Michelangelo | 66 | 43.39 N | 11.59 E |
| Capri | 68 | 40.33 N | 14.14 E |
| Capri, Isola di I | 68 | 40.33 N | 14.13 E |
| Capriati a Volturno | 68 | 41.28 N | 14.08 E |
| Capricorn, Cape › | 166 | 23.30 S | 151.13 E |
| Capricorn Channel ⊔ | 166 | 23.00 S | 152.20 E |
| Capricorn Group II | 166 | 23.28 S | 152.00 E |
| Capri Leone | 70 | 38.05 N | 14.44 E |
| Caprino Veronese | 64 | 45.36 N | 10.47 E |
| Caprivi □[4] | 156 | 18.00 S | 23.00 E |
| Caprivi Zipfel (Caprivi Strip) □[9] | 156 | 17.59 S | 23.00 E |
| Caprolace, Lago di ⊜ | 66 | 41.21 N | 12.58 E |
| Capron, Il., U.S. | 216 | 42.24 N | 88.44 W |
| Capron, Va., U.S. | 208 | 36.42 N | 77.12 W |
| Cap Saint Jacques → Vung Tau | 110 | 10.21 N | 107.04 E |
| Cap-Santé | 206 | 46.40 N | 71.47 W |
| Capstone | 260 | 51.21 N | 0.34 E |
| Captain Anthony Meldahl Dam ●[6] | 218 | 38.48 N | 84.11 W |
| Captain Cook | 229d | 19.29 N | 155.55 W |
| Captain Cook Bridge ●[5] | 274a | 34.00 S | 151.08 E |
| Captain Cook Landing Place Park ♦ | 274a | 34.00 S | 151.14 E |
| Captain Cook Monument ⊥ | 174c | 29.00 S | 167.56 E |
| Captain Daniel Wright Woods ♦ | 278 | 42.13 N | 87.56 W |
| Captain Harbor c | 276 | 41.00 N | 73.36 W |
| Captain Pond ⊜ | 283 | 42.48 N | 71.10 W |
| Captains Flat | 171b | 35.35 S | 149.27 E |
| Captieux | 32 | 44.18 N | 0.16 W |
| Captina Creek ≃ | 188 | 39.52 N | 80.48 W |
| Captiva | 220 | 26.31 N | 82.11 W |
| Captiva Island I | 220 | 26.31 N | 82.11 W |
| Captree Island I | 276 | 40.39 N | 73.16 W |
| Captree State Park ♦ | 276 | 40.39 N | 73.16 W |
| Capua | 68 | 41.06 N | 14.12 E |
| Capual Island I | 116 | 6.02 N | 121.24 E |
| Capuáva | 287b | 23.39 S | 46.29 W |
| Capuça I | 152 | 17.22 S | 21.18 E |
| Capucapu ≃ | 246 | 1.45 S | 58.35 W |
| Capucin › | 240d | 15.38 N | 61.28 W |
| Capul | 116 | 12.25 N | 124.11 E |
| Capulín, Río del ≃ | 196 | 27.31 N | 101.33 W |
| Capulin Mountain National Monument ♦ | 196 | 36.48 N | 103.55 W |
| Capul Island I | 116 | 12.26 N | 124.10 E |
| Capuna | 152 | 15.38 S | 19.43 E |
| Capunda | 152 | 14.57 S | 14.03 E |
| Capurro | 258 | 34.25 S | 56.28 W |
| Capurso | 68 | 41.03 N | 16.55 E |
| Caputh | 54 | 52.21 N | 13.00 E |
| Cap-Vert → Cape Verde □[1] | 150a | 16.00 N | 24.00 W |
| Caquende | 256 | 21.20 S | 44.33 W |
| Caquetá □[8] | 246 | 1.00 N | 74.00 W |
| Caquetá (Japurá) ≃ | 246 | 3.08 S | 64.46 W |
| Caquiaviri | 248 | 17.03 S | 68.38 W |
| Čar ≃ | 86 | 50.22 N | 80.55 E |
| Čara, Ityo. | 144 | 5.52 N | 37.12 E |
| Čara, Ross. | 88 | 56.54 N | 118.12 E |
| Čara ≃ | 74 | 60.22 N | 120.50 E |
| Cará, Ilha do I | 250 | 0.01 S | 50.50 W |
| Caraballeda | 286c | 10.37 N | 66.50 W |
| Caraballeda, Punta › | 286c | 10.37 N | 66.50 W |
| Carabanchel Alto ●[8] | 266a | 40.22 N | 3.45 W |
| Carabanchel Bajo ●[8] | 266a | 40.23 N | 3.47 W |
| Carabao Island I | 116 | 12.04 N | 121.56 E |
| Carabaya ≃ | 248 | 14.43 S | 70.17 W |
| Carabaya, Cordillera de ⋏ | 248 | 13.50 S | 70.45 W |
| Carabayllo | 286d | 11.52 S | 77.02 W |
| Carabelas Grande ≃ | 253 | 34.15 S | 58.43 W |
| Carabinani ≃ | 246 | 1.58 S | 61.31 W |
| Carabobo □[3] | 246 | 10.10 N | 68.05 W |
| Carabost | 171b | 35.36 S | 147.44 E |
| Caracal | 38 | 44.07 N | 24.21 E |
| Caracalla, Terme di ⊥ | 267a | 41.53 N | 12.29 E |
| Caracaraí | 246 | 1.50 N | 61.08 W |
| Caracas, Ven. | 246 | 10.30 N | 66.56 W |
| Caracas, Ven. | 286c | 10.30 N | 66.56 W |
| Čarach | 86 | 59.03 N | 62.15 E |
| Carache | 246 | 9.38 N | 70.14 W |
| Caracol, Bra. | 250 | 9.17 S | 43.20 W |
| Caracol, Bra. | 252 | 22.01 S | 57.02 W |
| Caracollo | 248 | 17.39 S | 67.10 W |
| Caracorum → Karakoram Range ⋏ | 120 | 35.30 N | 77.00 E |
| Carácuaro de Morelos | 234 | 18.46 N | 101.02 W |
| Caradoc Indian Reserve ●[4] | 214 | 42.48 N | 81.29 W |
| Caraffa di Catanzaro | 68 | 38.53 N | 16.29 E |
| Caraga | 116 | 7.20 N | 126.34 E |
| Caraga ≃ | 116 | 7.20 N | 126.34 E |
| Caragh, Lough ⊜ | 48 | 52.03 N | 9.52 W |
| Caraghnan Mountain ∧ | 166 | 31.20 S | 149.03 E |
| Caraglio | 62 | 44.25 N | 7.26 E |
| Caraguata, Arroyo ≃ | 288 | 34.24 S | 58.38 W |
| Caraguatatuba | 256 | 23.37 S | 45.25 W |
| Caraguatatuba, Enseada de c | 256 | 23.40 S | 45.20 W |
| Caraguatay | 252 | 25.14 S | 56.52 W |
| Caraí | 255 | 17.12 S | 41.42 W |
| Caraibamba | 248 | 14.24 S | 73.09 W |
| Caraïbes, Îles des → West Indies II | 230 | 19.00 N | 70.00 W |
| Caraïbes, Mer des → Caribbean Sea ⊤[2] | 230 | 15.00 N | 73.00 W |
| Caraigres, Cerro ∧ | 236 | 9.43 N | 84.05 W |
| Caraíva ≃ | 255 | 16.48 S | 39.08 W |
| Carajari ≃ | 250 | 4.45 S | 54.20 W |
| Carajás | 250 | 6.06 S | 50.23 W |
| Carajás, Serra dos ⋏ | 250 | 5.50 S | 51.20 W |
| Caralue Bluff ∧[2] | 166 | 33.26 S | 136.16 E |
| Caramagna-Piemonte | 62 | 44.46 N | 7.44 E |
| Caramanico Terme | 66 | 42.09 N | 14.00 E |
| Caramay | 116 | 10.11 N | 119.14 E |
| Caramoan | 116 | 13.46 N | 123.52 E |
| Caramoan Peninsula ›[1] | 116 | 13.48 N | 123.40 E |
| Caramoran | 116 | 13.59 N | 124.08 E |
| Caramy ≃ | 62 | 43.26 N | 6.12 E |
| Caranavi | 248 | 15.46 S | 67.36 W |
| Carandaí | 255 | 20.57 S | 43.48 W |
| Carandayti | 248 | 20.45 S | 63.04 W |
| Carangola | 255 | 20.44 S | 42.02 W |
| Carano | 64 | 46.16 N | 11.27 E |
| Caransebeș | 38 | 45.25 N | 22.13 E |
| Carapá ≃ | 252 | 24.30 S | 54.20 W |
| Carapachay ≃[1] | 288 | 34.25 S | 58.35 W |
| Carapajó | 250 | 2.16 S | 49.22 W |
| Cara-Paraná ≃ | 246 | 1.45 S | 73.13 W |
| Carapeguá | 252 | 25.48 S | 57.14 W |
| Carapelle ≃ | 68 | 41.30 N | 15.55 E |
| Carapicuíba | 256 | 23.31 S | 46.50 W |
| Carapicuíba □[7] | 287b | 23.31 S | 46.53 W |
| Carapo ≃ | 246 | 7.30 N | 64.02 W |
| Caraquet | 186 | 47.48 N | 64.57 W |
| Caráquez | 246 | 0.36 S | 80.25 W |
| Carare ≃ | 246 | 6.48 N | 74.06 W |
| Carasco | 62 | 44.21 N | 9.21 E |
| Caraș-Severin □[6] | 38 | 45.00 N | 22.00 E |
| Caratasca, Laguna de c | 236 | 15.23 N | 83.55 W |
| Carate Brianza | 62 | 45.41 N | 9.14 E |
| Caratinga | 255 | 19.47 S | 42.08 W |
| Carauari | 246 | 4.52 S | 66.54 W |
| Caraúbas | 250 | 5.47 S | 37.34 W |
| Caravaca de la Cruz | 34 | 38.06 N | 1.51 W |
| Caravaggio | 62 | 45.30 N | 9.38 E |
| Caravela, Ilha I | 150 | 11.30 N | 16.20 W |
| Caravelas | 255 | 17.45 S | 39.15 W |
| Caravelí | 248 | 15.46 S | 73.22 W |
| Caravelle, Presqu'île de la ›[1] | 240e | 14.45 N | 60.55 W |
| Caravius, Monte is ∧ | 71 | 39.09 N | 8.49 E |
| Caraway | 194 | 35.45 N | 90.19 W |
| Carayaó | 252 | 25.10 S | 56.26 W |
| Caraz | 248 | 9.03 S | 77.45 W |
| Caraza ●[8] | 288 | 34.42 S | 58.26 W |
| Carazinho | 252 | 28.18 S | 52.48 W |
| Carazo □[5] | 236 | 11.45 N | 86.15 W |
| Carballiño | 34 | 42.26 N | 8.04 W |
| Carballo | 34 | 43.13 N | 8.41 W |
| Carberry | 184 | 49.52 N | 99.20 W |
| Carbet, Pitons du ⋏ | 240e | 14.42 N | 61.07 W |
| Carbo | 232 | 29.42 N | 110.58 W |
| Carbol ≃ | 70 | 37.32 N | 12.59 E |
| Carbon, Ab., Can. | 182 | 51.29 N | 113.09 W |
| Carbon, Pa., U.S. | 279b | 40.17 N | 79.34 W |
| Carbon, Tx., U.S. | 196 | 32.16 N | 98.50 W |
| Carbon □[6] | 210 | 40.52 N | 75.45 W |
| Carbon ≃ | 224 | 47.07 N | 122.13 W |
| Carbon, Cap › | 34 | 36.47 N | 5.06 E |
| Carbonado | 224 | 47.04 N | 122.03 W |
| Carbonara, Capo › | 71 | 39.06 N | 9.31 E |
| Carbonara, Pizzo ∧ | 70 | 37.54 N | 14.02 E |
| Carbonare | 64 | 45.56 N | 11.13 E |
| Carbonate | 266b | 45.41 N | 8.56 E |
| Carbon-Blanc | 32 | 44.53 N | 0.31 W |
| Carbon Canyon Dam ●[6] | 280 | 33.55 N | 117.50 W |
| Carbon Creek ≃ | 280 | 33.49 N | 118.04 W |
| Carbondale, Co., U.S. | 200 | 39.24 N | 107.12 W |
| Carbondale, Il., U.S. | 194 | 37.43 N | 89.13 W |
| Carbondale, Ks., U.S. | 198 | 38.49 N | 95.41 W |
| Carbondale, Pa., U.S. | 210 | 41.34 N | 75.30 W |
| Carbone | 68 | 40.09 N | 16.05 E |
| Carbonear | 186 | 47.45 N | 53.13 W |
| Carboneras de Guadazaon | 34 | 39.53 N | 1.48 W |
| Carbon Hill | 194 | 33.53 N | 87.31 W |
| Carbonia | 71 | 39.10 N | 8.31 E |
| Carbonin (Schluderbach) | 64 | 46.37 N | 12.13 E |
| Carbost | 46 | 57.18 N | 6.22 W |
| Carcaixent | 34 | 39.08 N | 0.27 W |
| Carcajou ≃ | 180 | 65.37 N | 128.43 W |
| Carcalgong Hill ∧ | 170 | 32.52 S | 149.41 E |
| Carcans, Lac de c | 32 | 45.08 N | 1.08 W |
| Carcar | 116 | 10.06 N | 123.38 E |
| Carcarañá | 252 | 32.51 S | 61.09 W |
| Carcarañá ≃ | 252 | 32.27 S | 60.48 W |
| Carcare | 62 | 44.21 N | 8.18 E |
| Carcar Point › | 116 | 10.05 N | 123.41 E |
| Carcassonne | 32 | 43.13 N | 2.21 E |
| Carcastillo | 34 | 42.23 N | 1.26 W |
| Carcavelos, Port. | 266c | 38.41 N | 9.20 W |
| Carcavelos, Port. | 266c | 38.53 N | 9.14 W |
| Carceri, Eremo delle ʋ[1] | 66 | 43.05 N | 12.42 E |
| Carcès | 62 | 43.28 N | 6.11 E |
| Carchi □[4] | 246 | 0.45 N | 78.00 W |
| Carcroft | 44 | 53.34 N | 1.11 W |
| Carcross | 180 | 60.10 N | 134.42 W |
| Cardabia | 162 | 23.06 S | 113.48 E |
| Çardak, Tür. | 130 | 38.06 N | 36.49 E |
| Čardak, Uzb. | 85 | 41.37 N | 69.56 E |
| Cardal | 258 | 34.18 S | 56.24 W |
| Cardano al Campo | 266b | 45.39 N | 8.47 E |
| Čardara | 85 | 41.17 N | 67.55 E |
| Čardara, step' ⋏[1] | 85 | 42.00 N | 68.00 E |
| Čardarinskoje vodochranilišče ⊜[1] | 85 | 41.10 N | 68.15 E |
| Cardeña | 34 | 38.13 N | 4.19 W |
| Cárdenas, Cuba | 240p | 23.02 N | 81.12 W |
| Cárdenas, Méx. | 234 | 22.00 N | 99.40 W |
| Cárdenas, Méx. | 234 | 17.59 N | 93.22 W |
| Cárdenas, Nic. | 236 | 11.12 N | 85.31 W |
| Cárdenas, Bahía de c | 240p | 23.05 N | 81.10 W |
| Cardener ≃ | 34 | 41.41 N | 1.51 E |
| Carderock Springs | 284c | 38.59 N | 77.10 W |
| Cardiel, Lago ⊜ | 254 | 48.55 S | 71.15 W |
| Cardiff, Austl. | 170 | 32.57 S | 151.41 E |
| Cardiff, Wales, U.K. | 42 | 51.29 N | 3.13 W |
| Cardiff, Md., U.S. | 208 | 39.43 N | 76.20 W |
| Cardiff, N.J., U.S. | 208 | 39.24 N | 74.35 W |
| Cardigan, P.E., Can. | 186 | 46.14 N | 62.37 W |
| Cardigan, Wales, U.K. | 42 | 52.06 N | 4.40 W |
| Cardigan Bay c, P.E., Can. | 186 | 46.10 N | 62.30 W |
| Cardigan Bay c, Wales, U.K. | 42 | 52.30 N | 4.20 W |
| Cardigan Island I | 42 | 52.08 N | 4.41 W |
| Cardigan State Park ♦ | 188 | 43.38 N | 71.54 W |
| Cardinal | 212 | 44.47 N | 75.23 W |
| Cardinale | 68 | 38.38 N | 16.23 E |
| Cardinal Heights | 212 | 45.27 N | 75.37 W |
| Cardinal Lake ⊜ | 182 | 56.14 N | 117.44 W |
| Cardington, S. Afr. | 158 | 27.11 S | 23.30 E |
| Cardington, Oh., U.S. | 214 | 40.30 N | 82.53 W |
| Cardinia Creek ≃ | 274b | 38.12 S | 145.23 E |
| Cardinia Reservoir ⊜[1] | 169 | 37.58 S | 145.25 E |
| Cardona | 258 | 33.53 S | 57.23 W |
| Cardonal, Punta › | 232 | 28.28 N | 111.45 W |
| Cardoso | 255 | 20.04 S | 49.54 W |
| Cardozo | 252 | 32.38 S | 56.21 W |
| Card Sound ⊔ | 220 | 25.20 N | 80.18 W |
| Cardston | 182 | 49.12 N | 113.18 W |
| Cardwell, Austl. | 166 | 18.16 S | 146.02 E |
| Cardwell, Mo., U.S. | 194 | 36.02 N | 90.17 W |
| Cardwell Mountain ∧ | 194 | 35.41 N | 85.41 W |
| Čardžou | 128 | 39.06 N | 63.34 E |
| Careaçu | 256 | 22.02 S | 45.42 W |
| Careen Lake ⊜ | 184 | 57.00 N | 108.10 W |
| Carega, Cima ∧ | 64 | 45.44 N | 11.08 E |
| Carei | 38 | 47.42 N | 22.28 E |
| Careiro | 246 | 3.12 S | 59.45 W |
| Careiro, Ilha do I | 246 | 3.10 S | 59.44 W |
| Čarėja | 76 | 54.37 N | 29.17 E |
| Carén | 252 | 30.51 S | 70.47 W |
| Čarencavan | 84 | 40.24 N | 44.38 E |
| Carencro | 194 | 30.19 N | 92.02 W |
| Carentan | 32 | 49.18 N | 1.14 W |
| Careri | 68 | 38.10 N | 16.07 E |
| Cares ≃ | 34 | 43.19 N | 4.36 W |
| Caresana | 62 | 45.13 N | 8.30 E |
| Caretta | 192 | 37.20 N | 81.40 W |
| Carevičina | 80 | 52.27 N | 46.43 E |
| Carey | 214 | 40.57 N | 83.22 W |
| Carey, Lake ⊜ | 162 | 29.05 S | 122.15 E |
| Carey Downs | 162 | 25.38 S | 115.27 E |
| Careysburg | 150 | 6.30 N | 10.32 W |
| Cargados Carajos Shoals II | 12 | 16.38 S | 59.38 E |
| Cargill | 46 | 56.30 N | 3.22 W |
| Carhaix-Plouguer | 32 | 48.17 N | 3.35 W |
| Carhuamayo | 248 | 10.55 S | 76.02 W |
| Carhuanca | 248 | 13.45 S | 73.48 W |
| Carhuaz | 248 | 9.16 S | 77.38 W |
| Carhué | 252 | 37.11 S | 62.44 W |
| Caria □[9] | 130 | 37.30 N | 28.00 E |
| Cariacica | 255 | 20.16 S | 40.25 W |
| Cariaco | 246 | 10.29 N | 63.33 W |
| Cariaco, Golfo de c | 246 | 10.30 N | 64.00 W |
| Cariamanga | 246 | 4.20 S | 79.35 W |
| Cariango | 152 | 10.37 S | 15.20 E |
| Cariati | 68 | 39.30 N | 16.56 E |
| Caribana, Punta › | 246 | 8.37 N | 76.52 W |
| Caribbean Sea ⊤[2] | 230 | 15.00 N | 73.00 W |
| Caribe, Mar → Caribbean Sea ⊤[2] | 230 | 15.00 N | 73.00 W |
| Cariboo ≃ | 182 | 52.40 N | 121.40 W |
| Cariboo Mountains ⋏ | 182 | 53.00 N | 121.00 W |
| Caribou, N.S., Can. | 186 | 45.44 N | 62.42 W |
| Caribou, Me., U.S. | 186 | 46.51 N | 68.00 W |
| Caribou ≃ | 176 | 59.20 N | 94.44 W |
| Caribou, Lac du ⊜ | 206 | 46.56 N | 72.50 W |
| Caribou Island I | 190 | 47.22 N | 85.49 W |
| Caribou Mountain ∧, Id., U.S. | 202 | 43.06 N | 111.18 W |
| Caribou Mountain ∧, Me., U.S. | 188 | 45.26 N | 70.38 W |
| Caribou Mountains ⋏ | 176 | 59.12 N | 115.40 W |
| Caribou Range ⋏ | 202 | 43.05 N | 111.15 W |
| Carichic | 232 | 27.56 N | 107.03 W |
| Caricuao | 286c | 10.27 N | 66.59 W |
| Caricuao, Quebrada ≃ | 286c | 10.26 N | 66.59 W |
| Caricyn → Volgograd | 80 | 48.44 N | 44.25 E |
| Caridad, Pil. | 116 | 10.50 N | 124.45 E |
| Caridad, Pil. | 269f | 14.29 N | 120.53 E |
| Caridade | 250 | 4.13 S | 39.12 W |
| Carife | 68 | 41.01 N | 15.12 E |
| Carigara | 116 | 11.18 N | 124.41 E |
| Carigara Bay c | 116 | 11.24 N | 124.40 E |
| Carignan, P.Q., Can. | 275a | 45.27 N | 73.18 W |
| Carignan, Fr. | 56 | 49.38 N | 5.10 E |
| Carignano, It. | 62 | 44.55 N | 7.40 E |
| Carignano, It. | 66 | 43.49 N | 12.56 E |
| Cari Laufquen Grande, Lago ⊜ | 254 | 41.07 S | 69.30 W |
| Carinda | 166 | 30.28 S | 147.41 E |
| Cariñena | 34 | 41.20 N | 1.13 W |
| Caringbah | 274a | 34.03 S | 151.08 E |
| Carinhanha | 255 | 14.18 S | 43.47 W |
| Carinhanha ≃ | 255 | 14.20 S | 43.47 W |
| Carini | 70 | 38.08 N | 13.11 E |
| Carini, Golfo di c | 70 | 38.12 N | 13.22 E |
| Carinish | 46 | 57.31 N | 7.18 W |
| Carinola | 68 | 41.11 N | 13.58 E |
| Carioca, Serra da ∧ | 256 | 22.47 S | 44.18 W |
| Caripe | 246 | 10.12 N | 63.29 W |
| Caripi ≃ | 250 | 3.56 N | 51.27 W |
| Caripito | 246 | 10.08 N | 63.06 W |
| Carira | 250 | 10.21 S | 37.42 W |
| Cariré | 250 | 3.57 S | 40.27 W |
| Caririaçu | 250 | 7.02 S | 39.17 W |
| Carisbrook | 169 | 37.02 S | 143.49 E |
| Carisbrooke | 42 | 50.41 N | 1.19 W |
| Carisolo | 64 | 46.10 N | 10.45 E |
| Carite | 286c | 10.24 N | 67.01 W |
| Carite, Lago ⊜ | 240m | 18.04 N | 66.06 W |
| Cariús | 250 | 6.32 S | 39.30 W |
| Čarkesar | 85 | 41.02 N | 70.53 E |
| Carlentini | 70 | 37.16 N | 15.01 E |
| Carle Place | 276 | 40.45 N | 73.36 W |
| Carles | 116 | 11.34 N | 123.08 E |
| Carlet | 34 | 39.14 N | 0.31 W |
| Carleton, Mi., U.S. | 216 | 42.03 N | 83.23 W |
| Carleton, Ne., U.S. | 198 | 40.18 N | 97.40 W |
| Carleton, Mount ∧ | 186 | 47.23 N | 66.53 W |
| Carleton Place | 212 | 45.08 N | 76.09 W |
| Carletonville | 158 | 26.23 S | 27.22 E |
| Cârlibaba | 38 | 47.35 N | 25.07 E |
| Carlin | 204 | 40.42 N | 116.06 W |
| Carling | 56 | 49.10 N | 6.43 E |
| Carlingford | 274a | 33.47 S | 151.03 E |
| Carlingford Lough c | 48 | 54.04 N | 6.10 W |
| Carlinville | 219 | 39.16 N | 89.52 W |
| Carlinville, Lake ⊜[1] | 219 | 39.14 N | 89.51 W |
| Carlisle, On., Can. | 212 | 43.23 N | 79.59 W |
| Carlisle, Eng., U.K. | 44 | 54.54 N | 2.55 W |
| Carlisle, Ar., U.S. | 194 | 34.46 N | 91.44 W |
| Carlisle, In., U.S. | 194 | 38.58 N | 87.24 W |
| Carlisle, Ia., U.S. | 190 | 41.30 N | 93.29 W |
| Carlisle, Ky., U.S. | 218 | 38.18 N | 84.01 W |


**Symbols** in the index entries represent the broad categories identified in the key at the right. Symbols with superior numbers (⋏[1]) identify subcategories (see complete key on page *I · 1*).

**Symbole** im Register stellen die rechts im Schlüssel erklärten Kategorien dar. Symbole mit hochgestellten Ziffern (⋏[1]) bezeichnen Unterabteilungen einer Kategorie (vgl. vollständiger Schlüssel auf Seite *I · 1*).

**Los símbolos** incluídos en el texto del índice representan las grandes categorías identificadas con la clave a la derecha. Los símbolos con numeros en su parte superior (⋏[1]) identifican las subcategorías (véase la clave completa en la página *I · 1*).

**Les symboles** de l'index représentent les catégories indiquées dans la légende à droite. Les symboles suivis d'un indice (⋏[1]) représentent des sous-catégories (voir légende complète à la page *I · 1*).

**Os símbolos** incluídos no texto do índice representam as grandes categorias identificadas com a chave à direita. Os símbolos com números em sua parte superior (⋏[1]) identificam as subcategorias (veja-se a chave completa à página *I · 1*).

| Symbol | English | Deutsch | Español | Français | Português |
|---|---|---|---|---|---|
| ∧ | Mountain | Berg | Montaña | Montagne | Montanha |
| ⋏ | Mountains | Gebirge | Montañas | Montagnes | Montanhas |
| )( | Pass | Paß | Paso | Col | Passo |
| V | Valley, Canyon | Tal, Cañon | Valle, Cañón | Vallée, Canyon | Vale, Canhão |
| ≚ | Plain | Ebene | Llano | Plaine | Planície |
| › | Cape | Kap | Cabo | Cap | Cabo |
| I | Island | Insel | Isla | Île | Ilha |
| II | Islands | Inseln | Islas | Îles | Ilhas |
| ⊥ | Other Topographic Features | Andere Topographische Objekte | Otros Elementos Topográficos | Autres données topographiques | Outros acidentes topográficos |

Carlisle, Ma., U.S. 283 42.31 N 71.21 W
Carlisle, N.Y., U.S. 210 42.45 N 74.27 W
Carlisle, Oh., U.S. 218 39.35 N 84.20 W
Carlisle, Pa., U.S. 208 40.12 N 77.11 W
Carlisle Barracks ■ 208 40.13 N 77.11 W
Carlisle Bay c 241g 13.05 N 59.37 W
Carlisle Gardens 210 43.11 N 78.39 W
Carlisle Island I 180 52.52 N 170.02 W
Carlisle Springs 208 40.16 N 77.10 W
Carl Junction 194 37.10 N 94.33 W
Carlls ≃ 276 40.41 N 73.20 W
Carloforte 71 39.08 N 8.18 E
Carlopoli 68 39.03 N 16.27 E
Carlópolis 255 23.25 S 49.41 W
Carlos, Isla I 254 54.03 S 73.20 W
Carlos Alves 256 21.37 S 43.07 W
Carlos Barbosa 252 29.18 S 51.30 W
Carlos Beguerie 258 35.29 S 59.06 W
Carlos Casares 252 35.38 S 61.21 W
Carlos Chagas 255 17.43 S 40.45 W
Carlos City 218 40.02 N 85.02 W
Carlos Forseca Amador 236 11.59 N 86.31 W
Carlos Keen 258 34.29 S 59.14 W
Carlos Manuel de Céspedes 240p 21.35 N 78.17 W
Carlos Pellegrini 252 32.03 S 61.48 W
Carlos Reyles 252 33.03 S 56.29 W
Carlos Sampaio 287a 22.42 S 43.31 W
Carlos Tejedor 252 35.23 S 62.25 W
Carlow, Dtsch. 54 53.46 N 10.56 E
Carlow, Ire. 48 52.50 N 6.55 W
Carlow □6 48 52.40 N 6.50 W
Carloway 46 58.17 N 6.48 W
Carl Sandburg Home National Historic Site ⊥1 192 35.16 N 82.27 W
Carlsbad → Karlovy Vary, Česká Rep. 54 50.11 N 12.52 E
Carlsbad, Ca., U.S. 228 33.09 N 117.20 W
Carlsbad, N.M., U.S. 196 32.25 N 104.13 W
Carlsbad, Tx., U.S. 196 31.36 N 100.38 W
Carlsbad Caverns National Park ♦ 196 32.08 N 104.35 W
Carlsberg Ridge ✢3 12 6.00 N 61.00 E
Carlsborg 224 48.05 N 123.10 W
Carlsfeld 54 50.26 N 12.35 E
Carlstadt 276 40.50 N 74.05 W
Carlton, Austl. 274a 33.58 S 151.08 E
Carlton, Eng., U.K. 42 52.58 N 1.05 W
Carlton, Eng., U.K. 44 53.42 N 1.01 W
Carlton, Mn., U.S. 190 46.39 N 92.25 W
Carlton, Or., U.S. 224 45.18 N 123.11 W
Carlton, Tx., U.S. 196 31.55 N 98.10 W
Carlton Gardens ♦ 274b 37.48 S 144.59 E
Carlton Lake @ 224 45.18 N 123.11 W
Carluke 46 55.45 N 3.51 W
Carlyle, Sk., Can. 184 49.38 N 102.16 W
Carlyle, Il., U.S. 219 38.36 N 89.22 W
Carlyle Lake @1 219 38.40 N 89.18 W
Carmacks 180 62.05 N 136.18 W
Carmagnola 62 44.51 N 7.43 E
Carman 184 49.32 N 98.00 W
Carmanah Creek ≃ 224 48.37 N 124.44 W
Carmangay 182 50.08 N 113.07 W
Carmanville 186 49.24 N 54.17 W
Carmarthen 42 51.52 N 4.19 W
Carmarthen Bay c 42 51.40 N 4.30 W
Carmaux 56 44.03 N 2.09 E
Carmel, Wales, U.K. 262 53.17 N 3.15 W
Carmel, Ca., U.S. 226 36.33 N 121.55 W
Carmel, In., U.S. 218 39.58 N 86.07 W
Carmel, N.J., U.S. 208 39.26 N 75.07 W
Carmel, N.Y., U.S. 210 41.26 N 73.41 W
Carmel ≃ 226 36.32 N 121.56 W
Carmel, Mount ∧, Ca., U.S. 226 36.23 N 121.47 W
Carmel, Mount → Karmel, Har ∧, Yis. 132 32.44 N 35.02 E
Carmel Bay c 226 36.33 N 121.57 W
Carmel Head > 44 53.24 N 4.34 W
Carmel Highlands 226 36.30 N 121.56 W
Carmel Hills 226 36.32 N 121.53 W
Carmel Mountain ∧2 228 32.55 N 117.13 W
Carmelo 258 34.00 S 58.17 W
Carmel Point 226 36.31 N 122.55 W
Carmel Valley 226 36.29 N 121.43 W
Carmel Woods 226 36.34 N 121.54 W
Carmen → Ciudad del Carmen, Méx. 232 18.38 N 91.50 W
Carmen, Pil. 116 8.59 N 125.17 E
Carmen, Pil. 116 9.50 N 124.12 E
Carmen, Pil. 116 10.35 N 124.01 E
Carmen, Pil. 116 12.37 N 122.07 E
Carmen, Ok., U.S. 196 36.34 N 98.27 W
Carmen, Ur. 252 33.15 S 56.01 W
Carmen, Isla I 232 25.57 N 111.12 W
Carmen, Isla del I 232 18.42 N 91.40 W
Carmen, Río del ≃ 252 28.45 S 70.30 W
Carmen Alto 252 23.11 S 69.40 W
Carmen de Apicalá 246 4.09 N 74.44 W
Carmen de Areco 252 34.22 S 59.49 W
Carmen de Huechuraba 286e 33.21 S 70.40 W
Carmen de Patagones 252 40.48 S 62.59 W
Carmer Hill ∧2 214 41.54 N 77.58 W
Carmi 194 38.05 N 88.09 W
Carmi, Lake @ 206 44.58 N 72.53 W
Carmiano 68 40.21 N 18.03 E
Carmichael 226 38.37 N 121.19 W
Carmignano di Brenta 64 45.38 N 11.42 E
Carmila 166 21.55 S 149.25 E
Carmine 222 30.09 N 96.41 W
Carmo 256 21.56 S 42.37 W
Carmo, Monte ∧ 62 44.11 N 8.11 E
Carmo, Ribeirão do ≃ 256 21.20 S 45.10 W
Carmo, Rio do ≃ 250 5.02 S 37.12 W
Carmo da Cachoeira 256 21.28 S 45.13 W
Carmo de Minas 256 22.07 S 45.08 W
Carmo do Paranaíba 255 18.59 S 46.21 W
Carmo do Rio Verde 255 15.21 S 49.42 W
Carmody Hills 284c 38.54 N 76.54 W
Carmona, Esp. 34 37.28 N 5.38 W
Carmona, Pil. 116 14.19 N 121.03 E
Carmópolis de Minas 255 20.33 S 44.38 W
Carmzow 54 53.23 N 14.02 E
Carnaíba 250 7.48 S 37.49 W
Carnamah 162 29.42 S 115.53 E
Carnarvon, Austl. 162 24.53 S 113.40 E
Carnarvon, S. Afr. 158 30.56 S 22.08 E
Carnarvon → Caernarfon, Wales, U.K. 44 53.08 N 4.16 W
Carnarvon National Park ♦ 166 25.00 S 148.00 E
Carnatic □9 118 12.30 N 78.15 E
Carnation 224 47.38 N 121.54 W
Carnaval, Arroyo ≃ 288 34.52 S 58.02 W
Carnaxide 266c 38.43 N 9.15 W
Carncastle 48 54.54 N 5.53 W
Carndonagh 48 55.15 N 7.15 W
Carnduff 184 49.10 N 101.50 W
Carnedd Llewelyn ∧ 44 53.10 N 3.58 W
Carnedd Wen ∧ 42 52.41 N 3.35 W
Carnegie, Austl. 162 25.43 S 122.59 E
Carnegie, N.Y., U.S. 210 42.45 N 78.51 W
Carnegie, Ok., U.S. 196 35.06 N 98.36 W
Carnegie, Pa., U.S. 214 40.24 N 80.05 W
Carnegie, Lake @ 162 26.10 S 122.30 E
Carnegie Institute ʋ2 279b 40.27 N 79.57 W
Carnegie-Mellon University ʋ2 279b 40.27 N 79.57 W
Carnegie Ridge ✢3 18 1.00 S 85.00 W
Carnelian Bay 226 39.14 N 120.05 W
Carnetin 261 48.54 N 2.42 E
Carnew 48 52.43 N 6.30 W
Carneys Point 208 39.42 N 75.28 W
Carnforth 44 54.08 N 2.46 W
Carnia 64 46.22 N 13.08 E
Carnia ✦1 64 46.25 N 13.00 E
Carniche, Alpi (Karnische Alpen) ⋏ 64 46.40 N 13.00 E
Car Nicobar Island I 110 9.10 N 92.47 E
Carnide ✦8 266c 38.46 N 9.11 W
Carnières 50 50.10 N 3.21 E
Carniques → Karnische Alpen ⋏ 64 46.40 N 13.00 E
Carnlough 48 54.59 N 6.00 W
Carno 42 52.33 N 3.31 W
Carnon-Plage 62 43.32 N 3.59 E
Carnot, Centraf. 152 4.56 N 15.52 E
Carnot, Pa., U.S. 214 40.31 N 80.13 W
Carnot, Cape > 166 34.57 S 135.38 E
Carnoules 62 43.18 N 6.11 E
Carnoustie 46 56.30 N 2.44 W
Carnsore Point > 48 52.10 N 6.22 W
Carnwath 46 55.43 N 3.38 W
Carnwath ≃ 180 68.26 N 128.50 W
Caro 190 43.29 N 83.23 W
Caroga Creek ≃ 210 42.58 N 74.38 W
Caroga Lake 210 43.08 N 74.29 W
Carol Beach Estates 216 42.31 N 87.49 W
Carol City 220 25.56 N 80.14 W
Carole Acres 284c 39.04 N 77.00 W
Caroleen 192 35.16 N 81.47 W
Carole Highlands 284c 38.58 N 76.59 W
Carolei 68 39.15 N 16.13 E
Carolina, Bra. 250 7.20 S 47.28 W
Carolina, Col. 246 6.43 N 75.17 W
Carolina, El Sal. 236 13.51 N 88.19 W
Carolina, P.R. 240m 18.23 N 65.57 W
Carolina, S. Afr. 158 26.05 S 30.06 E
Carolina, R.I., U.S. 207 41.27 N 71.39 W
Carolina Beach 192 34.02 N 77.53 W
Carolinas, Puntan > 174n 14.55 N 145.38 E
Caroline □6, Md., U.S. 208 38.53 N 75.50 W
Caroline □6, Va., U.S. 208 38.00 N 77.20 W
Caroline I1 14 9.58 S 150.13 W
Caroline du Nord → North Carolina □3 192 35.30 N 80.00 W
Caroline du Sud → South Carolina □3 192 34.00 N 81.00 W
Caroline Islands II 14 8.00 N 147.00 E
Caroline Livermore, Mount ∧2 282 37.52 N 122.26 W
Caroline Peak ∧ 172 45.56 S 167.13 E
Carol Stream 216 41.54 N 88.08 W
Caron 184 50.28 N 105.52 W
Caron, Lac @ 190 48.00 N 78.53 W
Çarona 64 46.01 N 9.47 E
Čaronda 76 60.34 N 38.59 E
Caroní ≃ 246 8.21 N 62.43 W
Caronia 70 38.01 N 14.26 E
Caronia ≃ 70 38.03 N 14.26 E
Caronno Pertusella 266b 45.36 N 9.03 E
Carora 246 10.11 N 70.05 W
Carosino 68 40.27 N 17.23 E
Carouge 58 46.11 N 6.09 E
Car'ov 80 48.40 N 45.22 E
Carovigno 68 40.42 N 17.39 E
Carovilli 66 41.43 N 14.17 E
Car'ovščina 80 53.37 N 44.45 E
Čarozero 76 60.28 N 38.39 E
Carp 212 45.21 N 76.02 W
Carp ≃, On., Can. 212 45.29 N 76.14 W
Carp ≃, Mi., U.S. 190 46.02 N 84.42 W
Carpaneto Piacentino 62 44.55 N 9.47 E
Carpanzano 68 39.09 N 16.18 E
Carpates → Carpathian Mountains ⋏ 22 48.00 N 24.00 E
Carpathian Mountains ⋏ 22 48.00 N 24.00 E
Carpaţii Meridionali ⋏ 38 45.30 N 24.15 E
Cárpatos → Carpathian Mountains ⋏ 22 48.00 N 24.00 E
Carpegna 66 43.47 N 12.20 E
Carpenedolo 64 45.22 N 10.26 E
Carpentaria, Gulf of c 164 14.00 S 139.00 E
Carpenter 198 41.02 N 104.21 W
Carpenter Creek ≃ 216 40.54 N 87.12 W
Carpenter Lake @ 182 50.50 N 122.30 W
Carpentersville 216 42.07 N 88.15 W
Carpentertown 279b 40.11 N 79.31 W
Carpentras 62 44.03 N 5.03 E
Carpet Museum ʋ 267d 35.43 N 51.24 E
Carpi 64 44.47 N 10.53 E
Carpignano Sesia 62 45.32 N 8.25 E
Carpina 250 7.51 S 35.15 W
Cărpineni 38 46.47 N 28.22 E
Carpineti 64 44.28 N 10.31 E
Carpineto Romano 66 41.36 N 13.05 E
Carpino 68 41.51 N 15.51 E
Carpinone 66 41.35 N 14.19 E
Carpinteria 204 34.23 N 119.31 W
Carpio 198 48.26 N 101.42 W
Carp Lake @ 182 54.45 N 123.20 W
Carpolac 166 36.44 S 141.19 E
Carquefou 32 47.18 N 1.30 W
Carqueiranne 62 43.05 N 6.05 E
Carquinez Bridge ✦5 282 38.04 N 122.14 W
Carquinez Strait ⊔ 282 38.02 N 122.12 W
Carra, Lough @ 48 53.42 N 9.16 W
Carrabelle 192 29.51 N 84.39 W
Carradale 46 55.35 N 5.28 W
Carramar 274a 33.53 S 150.58 E
Carrancas 256 21.30 S 44.39 W
Carr and Craggs Moor ✦3 262 53.43 N 2.09 W
Carranglan 116 15.58 N 121.04 E
Carranza, Cabo > 252 35.36 S 72.38 W
Carrao ≃ 246 6.17 N 62.51 W
Carrara 64 44.05 N 10.06 E
Carrascal 116 9.22 N 125.56 E
Carrasco ✦8 258 34.54 S 56.05 W
Carrasco, Aeropuerto Nacional de ⊠ 258 34.52 S 56.02 W
Carrathool 166 34.24 S 145.26 E
Carrauntoohil ∧ 48 51.59 N 9.45 W
Carrazedo 250 1.36 S 51.54 W
Carrboro 192 35.54 N 79.04 W
Carr Bridge 46 57.17 N 3.49 W
Carrcroft 285 39.47 N 75.30 W
Carrcroft Crest 285 39.47 N 75.30 W
Carrefour Pompadour ♦ 261 48.46 N 2.26 E
Carregueira, Serra da ⋏2 266c 38.48 N 9.15 W
Carreria 252 21.59 S 58.35 W
Carreta, Punta > 248 14.13 S 76.18 W
Carreta Quemada, Arroyo ≃ 258 34.21 S 56.41 W
Carriacou I 238 12.30 N 61.27 W
Carrick ✦8 279b 40.23 N 79.59 W
Carrick ✦1 44 55.12 N 4.38 W
Carrickart 48 55.10 N 7.47 W
Carrickfergus 48 54.43 N 5.49 W
Carrickmacross 48 53.58 N 6.43 W
Carrick on Shannon 48 53.57 N 8.05 W
Carrick on Suir 48 52.21 N 7.25 W
Carrie, Mount ∧ 224 47.53 N 123.39 W
Carriere 194 30.37 N 89.39 W
Carrière, Lac @ 190 47.14 N 77.12 W
Carrières, Pointe aux > 275a 45.31 N 73.54 W
Carrières-sous-Bois 261 48.57 N 2.07 E
Carrières-sous-Poissy 261 48.57 N 2.03 E
Carrières-sur-Seine 261 48.55 N 2.11 E
Carriers Mills 194 37.41 N 88.38 W
Carrieton 166 32.26 S 138.32 E
Carrigahorig 48 53.04 N 8.09 W
Carrigaline 48 51.48 N 8.24 W
Carrigallen 48 53.59 N 7.39 W
Carrillo, C.R. 236 9.52 N 85.30 W
Carrillo, Méx. 232 26.54 N 103.55 W
Carrington, Eng., U.K. 262 53.26 N 2.24 W
Carrington, N.D., U.S. 198 47.26 N 99.07 W
Carrington Island I 202 41.00 N 112.37 W
Carrington Moss ✦3 262 53.25 N 2.23 W
Carr Inlet c 224 47.17 N 122.42 W
Carrión ≃ 34 41.53 N 4.32 W
Carrión de los Condes 34 42.20 N 4.36 W
Carrizal ≃ 234 23.03 N 97.46 W
Carrizal, Cerro ∧ 196 26.43 N 100.36 W
Carrizal Bajo 252 28.05 S 71.10 W
Carrizo 34 42.35 N 5.50 W
Carrizo Creek ≃, U.S. 196 36.05 N 102.36 W
Carrizo Creek ≃, N.M., U.S. 196 35.40 N 103.43 W
Carrizo Mountain ∧ 200 33.41 N 105.42 W
Carrizo Mountains ⋏ 200 36.45 N 109.10 W
Carrizo Plain ≚ 226 35.25 N 120.00 W
Carrizo Springs 196 28.31 N 99.51 W
Carrizo Wash V, U.S. 200 34.36 N 109.26 W
Carrizo Wash V, Ca., U.S. 204 33.05 N 115.56 W
Carrizozo 200 33.38 N 105.52 W
Carro 62 43.20 N 5.02 E
Carrodano 62 44.14 N 9.39 E
Carroll, Ia., U.S. 198 42.03 N 94.52 W
Carroll, Ne., U.S. 198 42.16 N 97.11 W
Carroll □6, In., U.S. 216 40.36 N 86.41 W
Carroll □6, Ky., U.S. 218 38.39 N 85.06 W
Carroll □6, Md., U.S. 208 39.35 N 77.00 W
Carroll □6, Oh., U.S. 214 40.34 N 81.05 W
Carroll Lake @ 184 51.07 N 95.05 W
Carroll Park ♦ 284b 39.17 N 76.39 W
Carrolls 224 46.05 N 122.52 W
Carrollton, Al., U.S. 194 33.10 N 88.06 W
Carrollton, Ga., U.S. 192 33.35 N 85.05 W
Carrollton, Il., U.S. 219 39.18 N 90.24 W
Carrollton, Ky., U.S. 218 38.40 N 85.10 W
Carrollton, Mi., U.S. 190 43.27 N 83.55 W
Carrollton, Ms., U.S. 194 33.30 N 89.55 W
Carrollton, Mo., U.S. 194 39.21 N 93.29 W
Carrollton, Oh., U.S. 214 40.34 N 81.05 W
Carrollton, Tx., U.S. 222 32.57 N 96.53 W
Carrollton Manor 208 39.05 N 76.35 W
Carrolltown 214 40.36 N 78.43 W
Carrollwood 284b 39.20 N 76.23 W
Carron ≃, Austl. 166 17.42 S 141.06 E
Carron ≃, Scot., U.K. 46 57.25 N 5.27 W
Carron ≃, Scot., U.K. 46 57.53 N 4.21 W
Carron ≃, Scot., U.K. 46 56.02 N 3.44 W
Carron, Loch c 46 57.22 N 5.31 W
Carronbridge 44 55.16 N 3.48 W
Carron Valley Reservoir @1 46 56.02 N 4.05 W
Carros 62 43.48 N 7.11 E
Carrot ≃ 184 53.50 N 101.17 W
Carrot River 184 53.17 N 103.35 W
Carrouges 28 48.34 N 0.09 W
Carrowmore Lake @ 48 54.12 N 9.47 W
Carrsville 208 36.43 N 76.50 W
Carrù 62 44.29 N 7.52 E
Carrum 169 38.05 S 145.08 E
Carrum Downs 274b 38.06 S 145.11 E
Carrum North 274b 38.03 S 145.09 E
Carrville 194 32.32 N 85.52 W
Carryduff 48 54.31 N 5.53 W
Carry Falls Reservoir @1 188 44.25 N 74.45 W
Carry-le-Rouet 62 43.20 N 5.09 E
Carsaig 46 56.17 N 6.00 W
Çarşamba 130 41.12 N 36.44 E
Čaršanga 128 37.30 N 66.01 E
Carseland 182 50.51 N 113.28 W
Çarshalton ✦8 260 51.22 N 0.10 W
Čarsk 86 49.35 N 81.05 E
Carsoli 66 42.06 N 13.05 E
Carson, Ca., U.S. 228 33.49 N 118.16 W
Carson, N.D., U.S. 198 46.25 N 101.33 W
Carson, Va., U.S. 208 37.02 N 77.23 W
Carson, Wa., U.S. 224 45.43 N 121.49 W
Carson ≃ 204 39.45 N 118.40 W
Carson, East Fork ≃ 226 38.59 N 119.49 W
Carson, West Fork ≃ 226 38.59 N 119.49 W
Carson City, Mi., U.S. 190 43.10 N 84.50 W
Carson City, Nv., U.S. 226 39.10 N 119.46 W
Carsondale 284c 38.57 N 76.50 W
Carson Lake @, On., Can. 212 45.31 N 77.46 W
Carson Lake @, Nv., U.S. 204 39.19 N 118.43 W
Carson Range ⋏ 226 39.15 N 119.50 W
Carson Sink @ 204 39.45 N 118.30 W
Carson Valley V 226 39.00 N 119.48 W
Carstairs, Ab., Can. 182 51.34 N 114.06 W
Carstairs, Scot., U.K. 46 55.42 N 3.42 W
Carstensz-Toppen → Jaya, Puncak ∧ 164 4.05 S 137.11 E
Carswell Air Force Base ■ 222 32.47 N 97.26 W
Cartagena, Chile 252 33.33 S 71.37 W
Cartagena, Col. 246 10.25 N 75.32 W
Cartagena, Esp. 34 37.36 N 0.59 W
Cartago, Col. 246 4.45 N 75.55 W
Cartago, C.R. 236 9.52 N 83.55 W
Çartago □4 236 9.50 N 83.45 W
Čartak 85 41.05 N 71.50 E
Cartaxo 34 39.09 N 8.47 W
Cartaxos ∧2 266c 38.54 N 9.20 W
Cartaya 34 37.17 N 7.09 W
Carter 196 35.13 N 99.30 W
Carter □6 218 38.20 N 83.05 W
Carter Bridge ✦5 273a 6.28 N 3.23 E
Carter Caves State Resort Park ♦ 218 38.22 N 83.10 W
Carteret 210 40.34 N 74.13 W
Carter Lake 198 41.17 N 95.55 W
Carter Mountain ∧ 202 44.12 N 109.25 W
Carters Lake @1 192 34.35 N 84.35 W
Cartersville 192 34.09 N 84.48 W
Carterton, N.Z. 172 41.02 S 175.31 E
Carterton, Eng., U.K. 42 51.45 N 1.35 W
Carterville 194 37.45 N 89.04 W
Carthage, Tun. 148 36.51 N 10.21 E
Carthage, Ar., U.S. 194 34.04 N 92.33 W
Carthage, Il., U.S. 190 40.24 N 91.08 W
Carthage, In., U.S. 218 39.44 N 85.34 W
Carthage, Ms., U.S. 194 32.43 N 89.32 W
Carthage, Mo., U.S. 194 37.10 N 94.18 W
Carthage, N.Y., U.S. 212 43.58 N 75.36 W
Carthage, N.C., U.S. 192 35.20 N 79.25 W
Carthage, S.D., U.S. 198 44.10 N 97.42 W
Carthage, Tn., U.S. 194 36.15 N 85.57 W
Carthage, Tx., U.S. 194 32.09 N 94.20 W
Carthage ⊥ 36 36.52 N 10.20 E
Cartier Islands II 160 12.32 S 123.32 E
Cartierville ✦8 275a 45.32 N 73.42 W
Cartierville, Aéroport de ⊠ 275a 45.31 N 73.43 W
Cartridge Hill ∧2 262 53.41 N 2.30 W
Cartura 64 45.16 N 11.50 E
Cartwright, Mb., Can. 184 49.06 N 99.20 W
Cartwright, Nf., Can. 176 53.42 N 57.01 W
Caruaru 250 8.17 S 35.58 W
Čarumas 248 16.49 S 70.43 W
Carúngol 88 49.14 N 106.29 E
Carunjamba ≃ 152 13.57 S 12.25 E
Carúpano 246 10.40 N 63.14 W
Caruray 116 10.20 N 119.00 E
Carutapera 250 1.13 S 46.01 W
Caruthers 226 36.32 N 119.50 W
Caruthersville 194 36.11 N 89.39 W
Carutu ≃ 246 5.05 N 63.28 W
Carvalhopolis 256 21.47 S 46.51 W
Carvalhos 256 22.00 S 44.28 W
Carver 207 41.53 N 70.45 W
Carversville 208 40.23 N 75.04 W
Carvin 50 50.29 N 2.58 E
Carvoeiro 246 1.24 S 61.59 W
Carvoeiro, Cabo > 34 39.21 N 9.24 W
Carwitzer See @ 54 53.18 N 13.28 E
Cary, Il., U.S. 216 42.12 N 88.14 W
Cary, Ms., U.S. 194 32.48 N 90.55 W
Cary, N.C., U.S. 192 35.47 N 78.46 W
Cary ≃ 42 51.09 N 2.59 W
Caryčelekskij zapovednik ♦ 85 41.50 N 71.55 E
Çaryk, ozero @ 80 46.13 N 42.43 E
Čarymovo 86 58.31 N 77.42 E
Čaryn 86 43.46 N 79.24 E
Čaryš ≃ 86 52.22 N 83.45 E
Čaryšskoje 86 51.24 N 83.35 E
Caryville, Fl., U.S 194 30.46 N 85.48 W
Caryville, Tn., U.S. 192 36.17 N 84.13 W
Casablanca (Dar-el-Beida) 148 33.39 N 7.35 W
Casablanca □4 148 33.35 N 7.30 W
Casablanca ✦8 286b 23.09 N 82.20 W
Casabona 68 39.15 N 16.57 E
Casa Branca 256 21.46 S 47.04 W
Casacalenda 68 41.44 N 14.51 E
Casa de la Torrecilla 266a 40.19 N 3.37 W
Casa del Campo ♦ 266a 40.32 N 3.47 W
Casa de Piedra, Embalse @1 252 38.15 S 67.20 W
Casa Grande 200 32.52 N 111.45 W
Casa Grande National Monument ♦ 200 32.59 N 111.32 W
Casainhos 266c 38.53 N 9.10 W
Casalanguida 66 42.03 N 14.30 E
Casalattico 66 41.37 N 13.43 E
Casalbordino 66 42.09 N 14.35 E
Casalbuono 68 40.13 N 15.41 E
Casalbuttano 64 45.15 N 9.58 E
Casal di Principe 68 41.00 N 14.08 E
Casale Abbruciato ✦8 267a 41.44 N 12.33 E
Casalecchio di Reno 64 44.28 N 11.16 E
Casale Monferrato 62 45.08 N 8.27 E
Casale sul Sile 64 45.36 N 12.19 E
Casaletto Spartano 68 40.09 N 15.37 E
Casalmaggiore 64 44.59 N 10.26 E
Casalmorano 62 45.17 N 9.54 E
Casalnuovo Monterotaro 68 41.37 N 15.06 E
Casa Loma ʋ 275b 43.41 N 79.25 W
Casalone ✦8 267a 41.56 N 12.41 E
Casalotti ✦8 267a 41.55 N 12.22 E
Casalpusterlengo 62 45.11 N 9.39 E
Casal Velino 68 40.11 N 15.06 E
Casalvieri 66 41.38 N 13.43 E
Casamance ≃ 150 12.33 N 16.46 W
Casamari, Abbazia di ʋ1 66 41.41 N 13.29 E
Casamassima 68 40.57 N 16.55 E
Casamicciola Terme 68 40.45 N 13.54 E
Casanare □3 246 5.45 N 72.00 W
Casanare ≃ 246 6.02 N 69.51 W
Casanay 246 10.30 N 63.25 W
Casa Nova 250 9.07 S 40.58 W
Casarano 68 40.00 N 18.10 E
Casar de Cáceres 34 39.34 N 6.25 W
Casarsa della Delizia 64 45.57 N 12.50 E
Casas 234 23.44 N 98.45 W
Casas Adobes 200 32.19 N 110.59 W
Casas Grandes ≃ 232 31.22 N 107.31 W
Casas-Ibáñez 34 39.17 N 1.28 W
Casasimarro 34 39.22 N 2.02 W
Casauman ≃ 116 7.16 N 126.31 E
Casa Verde ✦8 287b 23.30 S 46.39 W
Casavieja 34 40.17 N 4.46 W
Casbas 252 36.45 S 62.30 W
Casca 252 28.34 S 51.59 W
Casca, Rio da ≃ 248 14.52 S 55.52 W
Cascadas Basaseachic, Parque Nacional ♦ 232 28.10 N 108.22 W
Cascade, B.C., Can. 182 49.01 N 118.13 W
Cascade, Id., U.S. 202 44.30 N 116.02 W
Cascade, Ia., U.S. 190 42.17 N 91.00 W
Cascade, Mi., U.S. 216 42.55 N 85.30 W
Cascade, Mt., U.S. 202 47.16 N 111.41 W
Cascade, Wi., U.S. 190 43.39 N 88.00 W
Cascade ≃, N.Z. 172 44.02 S 168.22 E
Cascade ≃, Wa., U.S. 224 48.32 N 121.26 W
Cascade Bay c 174c 29.01 S 167.58 E
Cascade Locks 224 45.40 N 121.53 W
Cascade Mountains (Cascade Range) ⋏ 202 45.00 N 121.30 W
Cascade Park ♦ 279a 41.23 N 82.06 W
Cascade Point > 172 44.00 S 168.22 E
Cascade Range ⋏ 178 45.00 N 121.30 W
Cascade Reservoir @1 202 44.35 N 116.06 W
Cascade Tunnel ✦5 224 47.40 N 121.03 W
Cascadura ✦8 287a 22.53 S 43.20 W
Cascais 34 38.42 N 9.25 W
Cascalho Rico 255 18.34 S 47.52 W
Cascapédia ≃ 186 48.11 N 65.54 W
Cascatinha 256 22.29 S 43.09 W
Cascavel, Bra. 250 4.07 S 38.14 W
Cascavel, Bra. 252 24.57 S 53.28 W
Cascia 66 42.43 N 13.01 E
Casciana Terme 66 43.31 N 10.32 E
Cascina 66 43.41 N 10.33 E
Casco Bay c 188 43.40 N 70.00 W
Çascumpec Bay c 186 46.45 N 64.03 W
Čascy 82 55.37 N 36.52 E
Casei Gerola 62 45.00 N 8.55 E
Case Inlet c 224 47.19 N 122.53 W
Casekow 54 53.12 N 14.12 E
Casella 62 44.32 N 9.00 E
Caselle, Aeroporto di ⊠ 62 45.13 N 7.40 E
Caselle in Pittari 68 40.10 N 15.33 E
Caselle Torinese 62 45.10 N 7.39 E
Cà Selva, Lago di @1 64 46.16 N 12.40 E
Casenove 66 42.58 N 12.50 E
Casentino V 66 43.40 N 11.50 E
Casenuove 266b 45.38 N 8.42 E
Case-Pilote 240e 14.38 N 61.08 W
Caseros 258 34.36 S 58.33 W
Caserta 68 41.04 N 14.20 E
Caserta □4 68 41.14 N 14.10 E
Caseville 190 43.56 N 83.16 W
Case Western Reserve University ʋ2 279a 41.30 N 81.36 W
Casey, Il., U.S. 194 39.17 N 87.59 W
Casey, Ia., U.S. 198 41.30 N 94.31 W
Casey ʋ3 9 66.17 S 110.32 E
Casey, Mount ∧ 202 48.26 N 116.42 W
Casey Bay c 9 67.20 S 48.00 E
Casey Key I 220 27.10 N 82.29 W
Caseyville 219 38.38 N 90.02 W
Cash 222 32.59 N 96.07 W
Cashel, Ire. 48 52.31 N 7.53 W
Cashel, Ire. 48 53.25 N 9.48 W
Cashie ≃ 192 35.53 N 76.49 W
Cashiers 192 35.06 N 83.06 W
Cashmere 202 47.31 N 120.28 W
Cashmere Downs 162 28.58 S 119.35 E
Cashton 190 43.44 N 90.46 W
Cashtown 208 39.53 N 77.22 W
Casigua 246 8.46 N 72.30 W
Casiguran, Pil. 116 16.17 N 122.07 E
Casiguran, Pil. 116 12.52 N 124.00 E
Casiguran Sound ⊔ 116 16.06 N 121.58 E
Casilda, Arg. 252 33.03 S 61.10 W
Casilda, Cuba 240p 21.46 N 79.59 W
Casimcea 38 44.43 N 28.23 E
Casimiro Castillo 234 19.38 N 104.28 W
Casina 64 44.30 N 10.30 E
Casino 166 28.52 S 153.03 E
Casiquiare ≃ 246 2.01 N 67.07 W
Casita 200 31.00 N 110.53 W
Çasitas Springs 228 34.22 N 119.18 W
Čáslav 30 49.54 N 15.23 E
Çasma 248 9.28 S 78.19 W
Čašniki 76 54.52 N 29.08 E
Čašnikovo 265b 55.59 N 37.25 E
Časnočor, gora ∧ 24 67.45 N 33.25 E
Casola in Lunigiana 64 44.14 N 10.10 E
Casola Valsenio 66 44.13 N 11.37 E
Casole d'Elsa 66 43.20 N 11.02 E
Casoli 66 42.07 N 14.18 E
Cason 222 33.02 N 94.49 W
Casorate Primo 62 45.19 N 9.01 E
Casorate Sempione 62 45.40 N 8.44 E
Casorezzo 266b 45.31 N 8.54 E
Çasoria 68 40.54 N 14.17 E
Časovo 24 62.01 N 50.36 E
Caspe 34 41.14 N 0.02 W
Casper 200 42.52 N 106.18 W
Casper Creek, Middle Fork ≃ 200 43.01 N 106.29 W
Caspian 190 46.03 N 88.37 W
Caspian Sea ⊤2 72 42.00 N 50.30 E
Caspienne, Mer → Caspian Sea ⊤2 72 42.00 N 50.30 E
Caspio, Depresión del → Prikaspijskaja nizmennost' ≚ 80 48.00 N 52.00 E
Caspio, Mar → Caspian Sea ⊤2 72 42.00 N 50.30 E
Caspoggio 64 46.16 N 9.52 E
Cass □6, Il., U.S. 219 39.57 N 90.13 W
Cass □6, In., U.S. 216 40.45 N 86.21 W
Cass □6, Mi., U.S. 216 41.55 N 86.01 W
Cass □6, Tx., U.S. 222 33.05 N 94.32 W
Cass ≃ 190 43.23 N 83.59 W
Cassadaga 214 42.20 N 79.18 W
Cassadaga Creek ≃ 214 42.05 N 79.08 W
Cassadaga Lakes @ 214 42.21 N 79.19 W
Cassaday Point > 284a 42.52 N 79.13 W
Cassagnas 62 44.16 N 3.45 E
Cassai 152 10.33 S 21.59 E
Cassai (Kasai) ≃ 152 3.02 S 16.57 E
Cassamba 152 13.06 S 20.18 E
Cassandra 214 40.24 N 78.38 W
Cassanje ≃ 248 17.06 S 57.23 W
Cassano allo Ionio 68 39.47 N 16.20 E
Cassano d'Adda 62 45.32 N 9.31 E
Cassano delle Murge 68 40.53 N 16.46 E
Cassano Magnago 62 45.41 N 8.50 E
Cassaro 70 37.07 N 14.56 E
Cass Benton Parkway ♦ 281 42.25 N 83.28 W
Cass City 190 43.36 N 83.10 W
Cassel 50 50.48 N 2.29 E
Casselberry 220 28.40 N 81.19 W
Cassella 216 40.25 N 84.34 W
Casselman 206 45.19 N 75.05 W
Casselton 198 46.54 N 97.12 W
Cássia, Bra. 255 20.36 S 46.56 W
Cassia, Fl., U.S. 220 28.53 N 81.28 W
Cássia dos Coqueiros 256 21.17 S 47.10 W
Cassiar 180 59.16 N 129.40 W
Cassiar Mountains ⋏ 176 59.00 N 129.00 W
Cassibile ≃ 70 36.57 N 15.11 E
Cassidy 224 49.04 N 123.53 W
Cassidy Airfield ⊠ 174o 1.57 N 157.18 W
Cassilândia 255 19.09 S 51.45 W
Cassimbazar 126 24.07 N 88.16 E
Cassine 62 44.45 N 8.31 E
Cassinetta di Lugagnano 266b 45.25 N 8.54 E
Cassinga 152 15.08 S 16.05 E
Cassino, Bra. 252 32.11 S 52.10 W
Cassino, It. 66 41.30 N 13.49 E
Cassio 64 44.35 N 10.02 E
Cassipore ✦8 272b 22.37 N 88.22 E
Cassis 62 43.13 N 5.32 E
Cass Lake 190 47.22 N 94.36 W
Cass Lake @, Mi., U.S. 281 42.36 N 83.22 W
Cass Lake @, Mn., U.S. 190 47.25 N 94.32 W
Cassley ≃ 46 57.58 N 4.35 W
Cassoalala 152 9.30 S 14.22 E
Cassoango 152 13.42 S 20.56 E
Cassolnovo 62 45.22 N 8.48 E
Cassone 64 45.44 N 10.46 E
Cassongue 152 11.51 S 15.03 E
Cassopolis 216 41.54 N 86.00 W
Casstown 218 40.03 N 84.07 W
Cassumba, Ilha I 255 17.46 S 39.17 W
Cassunda 152 10.57 S 21.03 E
Cassununga 255 16.03 S 53.38 W
Cassville, In., U.S. 216 40.33 N 86.08 W
Cassville, Mo., U.S. 194 36.40 N 93.52 W
Cassville, N.Y., U.S. 210 42.57 N 75.15 W
Cassville, Pa., U.S. 214 40.18 N 78.02 W
Cassville, Wi., U.S. 190 42.42 N 90.59 W
Castac Lake @ 228 34.50 N 118.51 W
Castagnaro 64 45.07 N 11.24 E
Castagneto Carducci 66 43.10 N 10.36 E
Castaic 228 34.30 N 118.37 W
Castaic Creek ≃ 228 34.25 N 118.37 W
Castaic Lake @1 228 34.32 N 118.37 W
Castalia 214 41.24 N 82.48 W
Castanea 210 41.07 N 77.25 W
Castanhal 250 1.18 S 47.55 W
Castanheira de Pêra 34 40.00 N 8.13 W
Castaños 196 26.47 N 101.25 W
Castañones, Punta > 236 12.28 N 87.11 W
Castano Primo 62 45.33 N 8.47 E
Casteggio 62 45.00 N 9.07 E
Castel 43b 49.28 N 2.34 W
Castelar 258 34.40 S 58.40 W
Castel Baronia 68 41.03 N 15.11 E
Castel Bolognese 66 44.19 N 11.48 E
Castelbuono 70 37.56 N 14.05 E
Castelcivita 68 40.30 N 15.15 E
Casteldaccia 70 38.03 N 13.32 E
Castel d'Ario 64 45.11 N 10.58 E
Casteldarne (Ehrenburg) 64 46.48 N 11.50 E
Casteldelfino 62 44.35 N 7.04 E
Castel del Monte 66 42.22 N 13.43 E
Castel del Piano 66 42.53 N 11.32 E
Castel del Rio 66 44.12 N 11.30 E
Castel di Decima ✦8 267a 41.45 N 12.26 E
Castel di Guido ✦8 267a 41.54 N 12.17 E
Castel di Ieri 66 42.06 N 13.44 E
Castel di Iudica 70 37.30 N 14.38 E
Castel di Leva ✦8 267a 41.47 N 12.32 E
Castel di Lucio 70 37.53 N 14.19 E
Castel di Sangro 66 41.47 N 14.06 E
Castel di Tora 66 42.13 N 12.58 E
Castelfidardo 66 43.28 N 13.33 E
Castelfiorentino 66 43.36 N 10.58 E
Castelfondo 64 46.27 N 11.07 E
Castelforte 66 41.18 N 13.49 E
Castelfranco Emilia 64 44.37 N 11.03 E
Castelfranco in Miscano 68 41.18 N 15.05 E
Castelfranco Veneto 64 45.40 N 11.55 E
Castel Frentano 66 42.12 N 14.22 E
Castel Fusano ✦8 267a 41.44 N 12.19 E
Castel Gandolfo 66 41.45 N 12.39 E
Castel Giorgio 66 42.42 N 11.59 E
Castelgrande 68 40.47 N 15.26 E
Castelhanos, Baía de c 256 23.51 S 45.[illegible] W
Castelhanos, Ponta dos > 256 23.10 S 44.[illegible] W
Castellabate 68 40.17 N 14.5[illegible] E
Castell'Alfero 62 44.59 N 8.1[illegible] E
Castellalto 66 42.40 N 13.4[illegible] E
Castellammare, Golfo di c 70 38.08 N 12.5[illegible] E
Castellammare del Golfo 70 38.01 N 12.5[illegible] E
Castellammare di Stabia 68 40.42 N 14.29 E
Castellamonte 62 45.23 N 7.42 E
Castellana, Grotte di ⊥5 68 40.53 N 17.07 E
Castellana Grotte 68 40.53 N 17.11 E
Castellana Sicula 70 37.47 N 14.02 E
Castellane 62 43.51 N 6.31 E
Castellaneta 68 40.37 N 16.57 E
Castellanza 62 45.37 N 8.54 E
Castellarano 64 44.30 N 10.44 E
Castell'Arquato 62 44.51 N 9.52 E
Castell'Azzara 66 42.46 N 11.42 E
Castellazzo Bormida 62 44.51 N 8.34 E
Castellbisbal 266d 41.29 N 1.59 E
Castelldefels 266d 41.17 N 1.59 E
Castelleone 62 45.18 N 9.46 E
Castelletto 266b 45.30 N 8.48 E
Castelletto di Brenzone 64 45.41 N 10.45 E
Castelli, Arg. 252 36.06 S 57.47 W
Castelli, It. 66 42.29 N 13.43 E
Castellina in Chianti 66 43.28 N 11.17 E
Castellina Marittima 66 43.25 N 10.35 E
Castelli Romani ✦1 267a 41.48 N 12.42 E
Castelló □4 34 40.10 N 0.10 W
Castello, Monte ∧2 66 43.03 N 9.49 E
Castello d'Annone 62 44.53 N 8.19 E
Castello di Fiemme 64 46.17 N 11.26 E
Castello Lavazzo 64 46.17 N 12.18 E
Castellón de la Plana 34 39.59 N 0.02 W
Castellote 34 40.48 N 0.19 W
Castello Tesino 64 46.04 N 11.38 E
Castellucchio 64 45.09 N 10.39 E
Castelluccio 68 40.00 N 15.58 E
Castell'Umberto 70 38.05 N 14.48 E
Castelluzzo 70 38.06 N 12.44 E
Castel Madama 66 41.58 N 12.52 E
Castel Maggiore 64 44.34 N 11.22 E
Castelmagno 62 44.24 N 7.13 E
Castelmassa 64 45.01 N 11.18 E
Castelmauro 66 41.50 N 14.43 E
Castelmezzano 68 40.32 N 16.03 E
Castelmoron-sur-Lot 32 44.24 N 0.30 E
Castelnaudary 32 43.19 N 1.57 E
Castelnau-Montratier 32 44.16 N 1.21 E
Castelnovo di Sotto 64 44.49 N 10.34 E
Castelnovo ne'Monti 64 44.26 N 10.24 E
Castelnuovo 64 45.26 N 10.47 E
Castelnuovo Berardenga 66 43.21 N 11.30 E
Castelnuovo dell'Abate 66 43.00 N 11.31 E
Castelnuovo della Daunia 68 41.35 N 15.07 E
Castelnuovo di Garfagnana 64 44.06 N 10.24 E
Castelnuovo di Porto 66 42.07 N 12.30 E
Castelnuovo di Val di Cecina 66 43.12 N 10.59 E
Castelnuovo Don Bosco 62 45.03 N 7.58 E
Castelnuovo Nigra 62 45.26 N 7.41 E
Castelnuovo Rangone 64 44.33 N 10.56 E
Castelnuovo Scrivia 62 44.59 N 8.53 E
Castelo 255 20.36 S 41.12 W
Castelo Branco 34 39.49 N 7.30 W
Castelo do Piauí 250 5.20 S 41.33 W
Castel Pagano 68 41.24 N 14.48 E
Castel Porziano ✦8 267a 41.44 N 12.24 E
Castelraimondo 66 43.12 N 13.04 E
Castel Romano ✦8 267a 41.44 N 12.27 E
Castel San Gimignano 66 43.24 N 11.00 E
Castel San Giorgio 68 40.47 N 14.42 E
Castel San Giovanni 62 45.04 N 9.26 E
Castel San Lorenzo 68 40.25 N 15.14 E
Castel San Pietro Terme 66 44.24 N 11.35 E
Castel Sant'Elia 66 42.15 N 12.22 E
Castelsaraceno 68 40.10 N 16.00 E
Castelsardo 71 40.55 N 8.43 E
Castelsarrasin 32 44.02 N 1.06 E
Castelsilano 68 39.16 N 16.46 E
Casteltermini 70 37.32 N 13.39 E
Castelvecchio Subequo 66 42.08 N 13.44 E
Castelvetere in Val Fortore 68 41.27 N 14.56 E
Castelvetrano 70 37.41 N 12.47 E
Castelvetro di Modena 64 44.30 N 10.57 E
Castelvetro Piacentino 64 45.05 N 9.59 E
Castel Viscardo 66 42.45 N 12.00 E
Castel Volturno 68 41.02 N 13.56 E
Castenaso 64 44.30 N 11.28 E
Castenedolo 64 45.28 N 10.18 E
Casterton 166 37.35 S 141.24 E
Castets 32 43.53 N 1.09 W
Castiglioncello 66 43.24 N 10.24 E
Castiglione Chiavarese 62 44.16 N 9.21 E
Castiglione d'Adda 62 45.13 N 9.41 E
Castiglione dei Pepoli 66 44.08 N 11.09 E
Castiglione del Lago 66 43.07 N 12.03 E
Castiglione della Pescaia 66 42.46 N 10.53 E
Castiglione delle Stiviere 64 45.23 N 10.29 E
Castiglione di Sicilia 70 37.53 N 15.07 E
Castiglione d'Orcia 66 43.00 N 11.37 E
Castiglione d'Ossola 58 46.03 N 8.13 E
Castiglione Messer Marino 66 41.52 N 14.27 E
Castiglione Olona 62 45.46 N 8.52 E
Castiglion Fibocchi 66 43.32 N 11.46 E
Castiglion Fiorentino 66 43.20 N 11.55 E
Castile 210 42.37 N 78.03 W
Castilho 255 20.52 S 51.29 W
Castilla 248 5.12 S 80.38 W
Castilla, Playa de ⊥2 34 37.00 N 6.33 W
Castilla-La Mancha □3 34 39.30 N 3.00 W
Castilla la Nueva □9 34 40.00 N 3.45 W
Castilla la Vieja □9 34 41.30 N 4.00 W
Castilla-León □3 34 41.30 N 5.00 W
Castillo 258 33.53 S 57.40 W
Castillo, Cerro ∧ 254 43.03 S 71.57 W
Castillo, Pampa del ≚ 254 45.58 S 68.24 W
Castillo de San Marcos National Monument ♦ 192 29.44 N 81.20 W
Castillo Incaico de Ingapirca ⊥ 246 2.34 S 78.50 W
Castillon-la-Bataille 32 44.51 N 0.03 W
Castillos 252 34.12 S 53.50 W
Castillos, Laguna de @ 252 34.20 S 53.54 W
Castine 188 44.23 N 68.48 W
Castione della Presolana 64 45.54 N 10.04 E
Castions di Strada 64 45.54 N 13.11 E
Castle Acre 42 52.42 N 0.41 E
Castle Air Force Base ■ 226 37.22 N 120.34 W
Castlebar 48 53.52 N 9.17 W
Castlebay 46 56.57 N 7.28 W


| Symbol | English | Deutsch | Español | Français | Português |
|---|---|---|---|---|---|
| ≃ | River | Fluß | Río | Rivière | Rio |
| ≡ | Canal | Kanal | Canal | Canal | Canal |
| ⌊ | Waterfall, Rapids | Wasserfall, Stromschnellen | Cascada, Rápidos | Chute d'eau, Rapides | Cascata, Rápidos |
| ⊔ | Strait | Meeresstraße | Estrecho | Détroit | Estreito |
| c | Bay, Gulf | Bucht, Golf | Bahía, Golfo | Baie, Golfe | Baía, Golfo |
| @ | Lake, Lakes | See, Seen | Lago, Lagos | Lac, Lacs | Lago, Lagos |
| ≚ | Swamp | Sumpf | Pantano | Marais | Pântano |
| ⊟ | Ice Features, Glacier | Eis- und Gletscherformen | Accidentes Glaciales | Formes glaciaires | Acidentes glaciares |
| ⊤ | Other Hydrographic Features | Andere Hydrographische Objekte | Otros Elementos Hidrográficos | Autres données hydrographiques | Outros acidentes hidrográficos |
| ✢ | Submarine Features | Untermeerische Objekte | Accidentes Submarinos | Formes de relief sous-marin | Acidentes submarinos |
| □ | Political Unit | Politische Einheit | Unidad Política | Entité politique | Unidade política |
| ʋ | Cultural Institution | Kulturelle Institution | Institución Cultural | Institution culturelle | Instituição cultural |
| ⊥ | Historical Site | Historische Stätte | Sitio Histórico | Site historique | Sítio histórico |
| ♦ | Recreational Site | Erholungs- und Ferienort | Sitio de Recreo | Centre de loisirs | Área de Lazer |
| ⊠ | Airport | Flughafen | Aeropuerto | Aéroport | Aeroporto |
| ■ | Military Installation | Militäranlage | Instalación Militar | Installation militaire | Instalação militar |
| ✦ | Miscellaneous | Verschiedenes | Misceláneo | Divers | Diversos |

ENGLISH — Name, Page, Lat.°′, Long.°′
DEUTSCH — Name, Seite, Breite°′, Länge°′ E = Ost


| Name | Page | Lat.°′ | Long.°′ |
|---|---|---|---|
| Castlebellingham | 48 | 53.54 N | 6.23 W |
| Castleberry | 194 | 31.17 N | 87.01 W |
| Castleblayney | 48 | 54.07 N | 6.44 W |
| Castle Bruce | 240d | 15.26 N | 61.16 W |
| Castle Cape ➤ | 180 | 56.15 N | 158.06 W |
| Castle Cary | 42 | 51.06 N | 2.31 W |
| Castlecliff | 172 | 39.57 S | 174.59 E |
| Castlecomer | 48 | 52.48 N | 7.12 W |
| Castleconnell | 48 | 52.43 N | 8.30 W |
| Castlecrag | 274a | 33.48 S | 151.13 E |
| Castle Crags State Park ♦ | 204 | 41.10 N | 122.20 W |
| Castle Creek | 210 | 42.14 N | 75.55 W |
| Castle Creek ≐, Austl. | 169 | 36.41 S | 145.29 E |
| Castle Creek ≐, Id., U.S. | 202 | 43.06 N | 116.16 W |
| Castle Dale | 200 | 39.23 N | 110.27 W |
| Castledawson | 48 | 54.47 N | 6.33 W |
| Castlederg | 48 | 54.42 N | 7.36 W |
| Castledermot | 48 | 52.55 N | 6.50 W |
| Castle Dome Peak ∧ | 200 | 33.05 N | 114.08 W |
| Castle Donington | 42 | 52.51 N | 1.19 W |
| Castle Douglas | 44 | 54.57 N | 3.56 W |
| Castlefinn | 48 | 54.47 N | 7.35 W |
| Castleford | 44 | 53.44 N | 1.21 W |
| Castlegar | 182 | 49.19 N | 117.40 W |
| Castle Harbour ⊂ | 240a | 32.21 N | 64.40 W |
| Castle Hill | 274a | 33.44 S | 151.00 E |
| Castle Hills, De., U.S. | 208 | 39.41 N | 75.33 W |
| Castle Hills, Tx., U.S. | 196 | 29.32 N | 98.31 W |
| Castleisland | 48 | 52.14 N | 9.27 W |
| Castlemaine, Austl. | 169 | 37.04 S | 144.13 E |
| Castlemaine, Ire. | 48 | 52.09 N | 9.43 W |
| Castlemartyr | 48 | 51.55 N | 8.03 W |
| Castlemore | 275b | 43.47 N | 79.41 W |
| Castle Mountain ∧, Ab., Can. | 182 | 51.18 N | 115.55 W |
| Castle Mountain ∧, Yk., Can. | 180 | 64.32 N | 135.25 W |
| Castle Mountain ∧, Ca., U.S. | 226 | 35.56 N | 120.20 W |
| Castle Neck ➤[1] | 283 | 42.41 N | 70.45 W |
| Castle Neck ≐ | 283 | 42.40 N | 70.44 W |
| Castle Park | 228 | 32.36 N | 117.04 W |
| Castle Peak ∧, Co., U.S. | 200 | 39.01 N | 106.52 W |
| Castle Peak ∧, Id., U.S. | 202 | 44.02 N | 114.35 W |
| Castle Peak ∧, Wa., U.S. | 224 | 48.58 N | 120.51 W |
| Castlepoint | 172 | 40.54 S | 176.13 E |
| Castle Point □[8] | 260 | 51.33 N | 0.35 E |
| Castlepollard | 48 | 53.40 N | 7.17 W |
| Castlerea | 48 | 53.46 N | 8.29 W |
| Castlereagh ≐ | 166 | 30.12 S | 147.32 E |
| Castle Rock, Co., U.S. | 200 | 39.22 N | 104.51 W |
| Castle Rock, Pa., U.S. | 285 | 39.58 N | 75.26 W |
| Castle Rock, Wa., U.S. | 224 | 46.16 N | 122.54 W |
| Castle Rock ∧, Or., U.S. | 202 | 44.02 N | 118.11 W |
| Castle Rock ∧, Va., U.S. | 192 | 37.57 N | 78.44 W |
| Castle Rock Butte ∧ | 198 | 45.00 N | 103.27 W |
| Castle Rock Lake ⊜[1] | 190 | 43.56 N | 89.58 W |
| Castle Shannon | 279b | 40.21 N | 80.01 W |
| Castleshaw Moor ◆[3] | 262 | 53.36 N | 2.00 W |
| Castleside | 44 | 54.50 N | 1.52 W |
| Castleton, Eng., U.K. | 44 | 53.21 N | 1.46 W |
| Castleton, Eng., U.K. | 44 | 54.28 N | 0.56 W |
| Castleton, Eng., U.K. | 262 | 53.35 N | 2.11 W |
| Castleton, In., U.S. | 218 | 39.54 N | 86.03 W |
| Castleton, Vt., U.S. | 188 | 43.36 N | 73.10 W |
| Castleton on Hudson | 210 | 42.32 N | 73.45 W |
| Castletown, I. of Man | 44 | 54.04 N | 4.40 W |
| Castletown, Scot., U.K. | 46 | 58.35 N | 3.23 W |
| Castletown Bearhaven (Castletown Bere) | 48 | 51.39 N | 9.55 W |
| Castletown Bere → Castletown Bearhaven | 48 | 51.39 N | 9.55 W |
| Castletown Geoghegan | 48 | 53.26 N | 7.38 W |
| Castletownroche | 48 | 52.10 N | 8.28 W |
| Castletownshend | 48 | 51.32 N | 9.11 W |
| Castlewellan | 48 | 54.16 N | 5.57 W |
| Castlewood, Ky., U.S. | 218 | 38.04 N | 84.27 W |
| Castlewood, S.D., U.S. | 198 | 44.43 N | 97.01 W |
| Castlewood, Va., U.S. | 192 | 36.53 N | 82.16 W |
| Častoje | 82 | 54.11 N | 37.47 E |
| Častooz'ornoje | 86 | 55.34 N | 67.53 E |
| Castor | 182 | 52.13 N | 111.53 W |
| Castor ≐, On., Can. | 212 | 45.18 N | 75.10 W |
| Castor ≐, Mo., U.S. | 194 | 36.51 N | 89.44 W |
| Castorano | 66 | 42.54 N | 13.43 E |
| Castor Creek ≐ | 194 | 31.47 N | 92.22 W |
| Castorland | 212 | 43.53 N | 75.30 W |
| Castra Vetera ⊥ | 263 | 51.39 N | 6.28 E |
| Castres | 32 | 43.36 N | 2.15 E |
| Castricum | 52 | 52.33 N | 4.39 E |
| Castries, Fr. | 62 | 43.40 N | 3.59 E |
| Castries, St. Luc. | 241f | 14.01 N | 61.00 W |
| Castries, Port ⊂ | 241f | 14.01 N | 61.01 W |
| Castro, Bra. | 252 | 24.47 S | 50.00 W |
| Castro, Chile | 254 | 42.29 S | 73.46 W |
| Castro, It. | 64 | 45.48 N | 10.04 E |
| Castro, Arroyo de ≐ | 258 | 33.37 S | 56.10 W |
| Castro, Punta ➤ | 254 | 43.22 S | 65.03 W |
| Castro Barros | 252 | 30.35 S | 65.44 W |
| Castrocaro Terme | 66 | 44.10 N | 11.57 E |
| Castrocielo | 66 | 41.32 N | 13.42 E |
| Castro Daire | 34 | 40.54 N | 7.56 W |
| Castro dei Volsci | 66 | 41.30 N | 13.24 E |
| Castro del Río | 34 | 37.41 N | 4.28 W |
| Castrofilippo | 70 | 37.21 N | 13.46 E |
| Castrojeriz | 34 | 42.17 N | 4.08 W |
| Castro Marim | 34 | 37.13 N | 7.26 W |
| Castronuño | 34 | 41.23 N | 5.16 W |
| Castronuovo di Sant'Andrea | 68 | 40.11 N | 16.11 E |
| Castronuovo di Sicilia | 70 | 37.41 N | 13.36 E |
| Castropol | 34 | 43.32 N | 7.02 W |
| Castrop-Rauxel | 52 | 51.34 N | 7.18 E |
| Castroreale | 70 | 38.06 N | 15.12 E |
| Castro-Urdiales | 34 | 43.23 N | 3.13 W |
| Castro Valley | 226 | 37.41 N | 122.05 W |
| Castro Verde | 34 | 37.42 N | 8.05 W |
| Castrovillari | 68 | 39.49 N | 16.13 E |
| Castroville, Ca., U.S. | 226 | 36.45 N | 121.45 W |
| Castroville, Tx., U.S. | 196 | 29.21 N | 98.52 W |
| Castrovirreyna | 248 | 13.16 S | 75.19 W |
| Castuera | 34 | 38.43 N | 5.33 W |
| Čast uul ∧ | 86 | 48.40 N | 90.45 E |
| Častyje | 80 | 57.19 N | 54.59 E |
| Casummit Lake | 184 | 51.28 N | 92.24 W |
| Casupá | 252 | 34.07 S | 55.39 W |
| Caswell Sound ⨃ | 172 | 45.00 S | 167.10 E |
| Çat | 130 | 39.40 N | 41.00 E |
| Cat ≐ | 184 | 51.07 N | 91.25 W |
| Catabola | 152 | 12.09 S | 17.16 E |
| Cataby | 162 | 30.43 S | 115.31 E |
| Catacamas | 236 | 14.48 N | 85.54 W |
| Catacaos | 248 | 5.16 S | 80.41 W |
| Catacocha | 246 | 4.04 S | 79.38 W |
| Cataguarino | 256 | 21.18 S | 42.43 W |
| Cataguases | 256 | 21.24 S | 42.41 W |
| Catahoula Lake ⊜ | 194 | 31.30 N | 92.06 W |
| Çatak | 128 | 38.01 N | 43.07 E |
| Çatakköprü | 130 | 38.09 N | 41.12 E |
| Catalaban Island I | 116 | 11.51 N | 125.28 E |
| Çatalan | 130 | 37.14 N | 35.16 E |
| Catalão | 255 | 18.10 S | 47.57 W |
| Catalão, Ponta do ➤ | 287a | 22.51 S | 43.13 W |
| Çatalca | 130 | 41.09 N | 28.27 E |
| Çatalçam | 130 | 40.00 N | 38.51 E |
| Catalfaro ≐ | 70 | 37.22 N | 14.43 E |
| Catalina, Nf., Can. | 186 | 48.31 N | 53.05 W |
| Catalina, Chile | 252 | 25.13 S | 69.43 W |
| Catalina → Santa Catalina Island I | 228 | 33.23 N | 118.24 W |
| Catalina, Punta ➤ | 254 | 52.32 S | 68.47 W |
| Catalonia → Catalunya □[4] | 34 | 41.40 N | 1.30 E |
| Catalunya □[3] | 34 | 41.40 N | 1.30 E |
| Catalzeytin | 130 | 41.57 N | 34.13 E |
| Catamarca □[4] | 252 | 27.00 S | 67.00 W |
| Catamare | 286c | 10.36 N | 67.02 W |
| Catamayo | 246 | 3.59 S | 79.21 W |
| Catamayo ≐ | 246 | 4.18 S | 80.09 W |
| Catanauan | 116 | 13.36 N | 122.19 E |
| Catanduanes □[4] | 116 | 13.47 N | 124.16 E |
| Catanduanes Island I | 116 | 13.45 N | 124.15 E |
| Catanduva | 255 | 21.08 S | 48.58 W |
| Catane → Catania | 70 | 37.30 N | 15.06 E |
| Catania | 70 | 37.30 N | 15.06 E |
| Catania □[4] | 70 | 37.23 N | 14.40 E |
| Catania, Golfo di ⊂ | 70 | 37.24 N | 15.09 E |
| Catania, Piana di ≚ | 70 | 37.25 N | 14.51 E |
| Cataño | 240m | 18.27 N | 66.07 W |
| Catanzaro | 68 | 38.54 N | 16.36 E |
| Catanzaro □[4] | 68 | 38.54 N | 16.36 E |
| Catanzaro Lido | 68 | 38.49 N | 16.36 E |
| Cataonia □[9] | 130 | 38.00 N | 35.00 E |
| Catára ≐ | 152 | 13.34 S | 12.35 E |
| Cataract Canyon V | 200 | 36.03 N | 112.35 W |
| Cataract Reservoir ⊜[1] | 170 | 34.16 S | 150.48 E |
| Catarama | 246 | 1.35 S | 79.28 W |
| Cataraqui | 212 | 44.16 N | 76.32 W |
| Cataraqui ≐ | 212 | 44.13 N | 76.28 W |
| Catarina | 250 | 6.12 S | 39.54 W |
| Catarman, Pil. | 116 | 9.08 N | 124.40 E |
| Catarman, Pil. | 116 | 12.30 N | 124.38 E |
| Catarroja | 34 | 39.24 N | 0.24 W |
| Catasauqua | 208 | 40.39 N | 75.29 W |
| Catatumbo ≐ | 246 | 9.22 N | 71.45 W |
| Catawba | 218 | 40.00 N | 83.37 W |
| Catawba ≐ | 192 | 34.36 N | 80.54 W |
| Catawba Island | 214 | 41.35 N | 82.50 W |
| Catawissa, Mo., U.S. | 219 | 38.25 N | 90.47 W |
| Catawissa, Pa., U.S. | 210 | 40.57 N | 76.27 W |
| Catawissa Creek ≐ | 210 | 40.57 N | 76.28 W |
| Cataxa | 154 | 15.58 S | 33.12 E |
| Cat Ba, Dao I | 110 | 20.50 N | 107.00 E |
| Catbalogan | 116 | 11.46 N | 124.53 E |
| Catchabutan, Punta ➤ | 236 | 15.50 N | 86.32 W |
| Catchacoma Lake ⊜ | 212 | 44.45 N | 78.20 W |
| Cateco Cangola | 152 | 8.27 S | 15.48 E |
| Catedral, Cerro ∧[2] | 252 | 34.23 S | 54.40 W |
| Cateel | 116 | 7.48 N | 126.27 E |
| Cateel ≐ | 116 | 7.47 N | 126.27 E |
| Cateel Bay ⊂ | 116 | 7.54 N | 126.25 E |
| Catemaco | 234 | 18.25 N | 95.07 W |
| Catemaco, Laguna ⊜ | 234 | 18.25 N | 95.05 W |
| Catembe | 156 | 26.00 S | 32.33 E |
| Catenanuova | 70 | 37.34 N | 14.41 E |
| Caterham | 42 | 51.17 N | 0.04 W |
| Caterino Rodriguez | 232 | 24.51 N | 100.19 W |
| Catete | 152 | 9.06 S | 13.43 E |
| Catete ◆[8] | 287a | 22.55 S | 43.10 W |
| Catete ≐ | 250 | 6.04 S | 54.09 W |
| Catfish Creek ≐, On., Can. | 212 | 42.39 N | 81.01 W |
| Catfish Creek ≐, N.Y., U.S. | 212 | 43.31 N | 76.19 W |
| Catfish Creek ≐, Tx., U.S. | 222 | 31.47 N | 95.56 W |
| Catford ◆[8] | 260 | 51.27 N | 0.01 W |
| Catharine Creek ≐ | 210 | 42.21 N | 76.51 W |
| Cathcart | 158 | 32.18 S | 27.09 E |
| Cathead Mountain ∧ | 210 | 43.17 N | 74.17 W |
| Cathedral City | 204 | 33.46 N | 116.27 W |
| Cathedral Gorge State Park ♦ | 204 | 37.50 N | 114.30 W |
| Cathedral Mountain ∧ | 196 | 30.10 N | 103.40 W |
| Cathedral of the Pines ψ[1] | 207 | 42.47 N | 71.58 W |
| Cathedral Provincial Park ♦ | 202 | 49.05 N | 120.10 W |
| Cathedral Range ⋏ | 226 | 37.47 N | 119.21 W |
| Catherines Peak ∧ | 241q | 18.04 N | 76.42 W |
| Catheys Valley | 226 | 37.25 N | 120.06 W |
| Cathlamet | 224 | 46.12 N | 123.22 W |
| Catholic University ψ[2] | 284c | 38.56 N | 77.00 W |
| Catia ◆[8] | 286c | 10.31 N | 66.57 W |
| Catia La Mar | 286c | 10.36 N | 67.02 W |
| Ca' Tiepolo | 66 | 44.56 N | 12.22 E |
| Catignano | 66 | 42.21 N | 13.57 E |
| Catió | 150 | 11.13 N | 15.10 W |
| Catirina, Punta ∧ | 71 | 40.29 N | 9.32 E |
| Cat Island I, Ba. | 238 | 24.27 N | 75.30 W |
| Cat Island I, Ma., U.S. | 283 | 42.31 N | 70.49 W |
| Cat Island I, Ms., U.S. | 194 | 30.13 N | 89.06 W |
| Čatkal ≐ | 85 | 41.38 N | 70.01 E |
| Čatkal'skij chrebet ⋏ | 85 | 41.40 N | 71.05 E |
| Cat Lake ⊜ | 184 | 51.40 N | 91.50 W |
| Catlettsburg | 188 | 38.24 N | 82.36 W |
| Catlin | 194 | 40.03 N | 87.42 W |
| Catlins ≐ | 172 | 46.29 S | 169.43 E |
| Catlodge | 46 | 57.00 N | 4.15 W |
| Catnip Mountain ∧ | 204 | 41.52 N | 119.23 W |
| Cato | 210 | 43.10 N | 76.34 W |
| Catoche, Cabo ➤ | 232 | 21.35 N | 87.05 W |
| Catoctin Creek ≐ | 208 | 39.18 N | 77.33 W |
| Catoctin Mountain ∧ | 208 | 39.26 N | 77.31 W |
| Cato Island I | 166 | 23.15 S | 155.32 E |
| Catolé do Rocha | 250 | 6.21 S | 37.45 W |
| Católica, Universidad ψ[2], Chile | 286e | 33.27 S | 70.39 W |
| Católica, Universidad ψ[2], Perú | 286d | 12.04 S | 77.05 W |
| Caton | 44 | 54.04 N | 2.43 W |
| Catonsville | 208 | 39.16 N | 76.43 W |
| Catonsville Manor | 284b | 39.18 N | 76.44 W |
| Catoosa | 196 | 36.11 N | 95.44 W |
| Catorce | 234 | 23.42 N | 100.54 W |
| Catorce, Sierra de ⋏ | 234 | 23.36 N | 100.52 W |
| Catota | 152 | 13.52 S | 17.15 E |
| Catria, Monte ∧ | 66 | 43.28 N | 12.42 E |
| Catriló | 252 | 36.26 S | 63.24 W |
| Catrimani ≐ | 246 | 0.28 N | 61.44 W |
| Catrine | 46 | 55.30 N | 4.20 W |
| Cats, Mont des ∧[2] | 50 | 50.47 N | 2.40 E |
| Catshill | 42 | 52.22 N | 2.03 W |
| Catskill | 210 | 42.13 N | 73.51 W |
| Catskill Aqueduct ≐ | 276 | 41.11 N | 73.48 W |
| Catskill Creek ≐ | 210 | 42.12 N | 73.51 W |
| Catskill Game Farm ♦ | 210 | 42.15 N | 74.01 W |
| Catskill Mountains ⋏ | 210 | 42.10 N | 74.30 W |
| Catskill Park ♦ | 210 | 42.00 N | 74.30 W |
| Cat Spring | 222 | 29.51 N | 96.20 W |
| Catt, Mount ∧ | 182 | 54.21 N | 128.47 W |
| Cattai Creek ≐ | 274a | 33.40 S | 150.56 E |
| Cattaraugus | 210 | 42.19 N | 78.52 W |
| Cattaraugus □[6] | 214 | 42.15 N | 78.45 W |
| Cattaraugus Creek ≐ | 214 | 42.35 N | 79.10 W |
| Cattaraugus Creek, South Branch ≐ | 214 | 42.26 N | 78.53 W |
| Cattaraugus Indian Reservation ◆[4] | 210 | 42.33 N | 78.56 W |
| Cattenom | 56 | 49.25 N | 6.15 E |
| Catterick | 44 | 54.22 N | 1.38 W |
| Catterick Garrison | 44 | 54.22 N | 1.43 W |
| Cattle Canyon V | 280 | 34.14 N | 117.46 W |
| Cattolica | 66 | 43.58 N | 12.44 E |
| Cattolica del Sacro Cuore, Università ψ[2] | 266b | 45.27 N | 9.11 E |
| Cattolica Eraclea | 70 | 37.26 N | 13.24 E |
| Catton | 44 | 54.55 N | 2.15 W |
| Catu | 255 | 12.21 S | 38.23 W |
| Catuala | 152 | 16.29 S | 19.03 E |
| Catuane | 156 | 26.48 S | 32.18 E |
| Catubig | 116 | 12.24 N | 125.03 E |
| Catubig ≐ | 116 | 12.34 N | 125.01 E |
| Catuçaba | 256 | 23.15 S | 45.12 W |
| Catumbela | 152 | 12.25 S | 13.34 E |
| Catumbela ≐ | 152 | 12.27 S | 13.29 E |
| Catur | 154 | 13.45 S | 35.30 E |
| Catus | 32 | 44.34 N | 1.20 E |
| Çatwick, Îles II | 110 | 10.00 N | 109.00 E |
| Čatyr-K'ol', ozero ⊜ | 85 | 40.38 N | 75.17 E |
| Čatyrtaš | 85 | 40.55 N | 76.26 E |
| Cau ≐ | 110 | 21.07 N | 106.18 E |
| Cau, Rach ≐ | 269c | 10.51 N | 106.49 E |
| Cauaburi ≐ | 246 | 0.17 S | 65.56 W |
| Cauayan, Pil. | 116 | 16.56 N | 121.46 E |
| Cauayan, Pil. | 116 | 9.58 N | 122.37 E |
| Caubvick, Mount (Mont d'Iberville) ∧ | 176 | 58.53 N | 63.43 W |
| Cauca □[5] | 246 | 2.30 N | 76.50 W |
| Cauca ≐ | 246 | 8.54 N | 74.28 W |
| Caucaia | 250 | 3.42 S | 38.39 W |
| Caucaia do Alto | 256 | 23.41 S | 47.02 W |
| Caucase, Monts du → Caucasus ⋏ | 84 | 42.30 N | 45.00 E |
| Caucasia | 246 | 8.00 N | 75.12 W |
| Caucaso → Caucasus ⋏ | 84 | 42.30 N | 45.00 E |
| Caucasus (Bol'šoj Kavkaz) ⋏ | 84 | 42.30 N | 45.00 E |
| Caucete | 252 | 31.39 S | 68.17 W |
| Cauchari, Salar de ≚ | 252 | 23.50 S | 66.50 W |
| Cauchon Lake ⊜ | 184 | 55.25 N | 96.30 W |
| Caudebec-en-Caux | 50 | 49.32 N | 0.44 E |
| Caudebec-lés-Elbeuf | 50 | 49.17 N | 1.02 E |
| Caudry | 50 | 50.08 N | 3.25 E |
| Caughdenoy | 210 | 43.16 N | 76.12 W |
| Caughnawaga | 275a | 45.25 N | 73.41 W |
| Caughnawaga Indian Reserve ◆[4] | 206 | 45.23 N | 73.41 W |
| Cauitan, Mount ∧ | 116 | 17.16 N | 121.00 E |
| Cauit Point ➤, Pil. | 116 | 12.16 N | 122.38 E |
| Cauit Point ➤, Pil. | 116 | 9.18 N | 126.12 E |
| Cauldcleuch Head ∧ | 44 | 55.18 N | 2.51 W |
| Caulfield | 169 | 37.53 S | 145.03 E |
| Caulfield Racecourse ♦ | 274b | 37.53 S | 145.02 E |
| Caulkerbush | 44 | 54.54 N | 3.40 W |
| Caulonia | 68 | 38.23 N | 16.25 E |
| Caumont-sur-Durance | 62 | 43.54 N | 4.57 E |
| Caumsett State Park ♦ | 276 | 40.55 N | 73.28 W |
| Çaúngula | 152 | 8.25 S | 18.40 E |
| Čaunskaja guba ⊂ | 74 | 69.20 N | 170.00 E |
| Cauquenes | 252 | 35.58 S | 72.21 W |
| Caura ≐ | 246 | 7.38 N | 64.53 W |
| Caurés ≐ | 246 | 1.21 S | 62.20 W |
| Caurimare ≐ | 286c | 10.28 N | 66.48 W |
| Căușani | 38 | 46.38 N | 29.25 E |
| Çausapscal | 186 | 48.22 N | 67.14 W |
| Čausovo | 82 | 54.49 N | 36.55 E |
| Caussade | 32 | 44.10 N | 1.32 E |
| Cautário ≐ | 248 | 12.13 S | 64.34 W |
| Caution, Cape ➤ | 182 | 51.10 N | 127.47 W |
| Çauto ≐ | 240p | 20.33 N | 77.14 W |
| Čauvaj | 85 | 40.08 N | 72.13 E |
| Caux, Pays de ◆[1] | 50 | 49.40 N | 0.40 E |
| Cava | 256 | 22.41 S | 43.26 W |
| Cava de' Tirreni | 68 | 40.42 N | 14.42 E |
| Cávado ≐ | 34 | 41.32 N | 8.48 W |
| Cavaglià | 62 | 45.24 N | 8.05 E |
| Cavaillon | 62 | 43.50 N | 5.02 E |
| Cavalaire-sur-Mer | 62 | 43.10 N | 6.32 E |
| Cavalcante | 255 | 13.48 S | 47.30 W |
| Cavalese | 64 | 46.17 N | 11.27 E |
| Cavalheiro | 255 | 17.15 S | 48.02 W |
| Cavalier | 198 | 48.47 N | 97.37 W |
| Cavalière | 62 | 43.09 N | 6.26 E |
| Cavalla (Cavally) ≐ | 150 | 4.22 N | 7.32 W |
| Cavalleria, Cap de ➤ | 34 | 40.05 N | 4.05 E |
| Cavallermaggiore | 62 | 44.43 N | 7.41 E |
| Cavalli Islands II | 172 | 35.02 S | 173.58 E |
| Cavallino, Litorale di ±[2] | 64 | 45.27 N | 12.30 E |
| Cavallo, Île I | 71 | 41.21 N | 9.16 E |
| Cavallo, Monte ∧ | 64 | 46.08 N | 12.30 E |
| Cavally (Cavalla) ≐ | 150 | 4.22 N | 7.32 W |
| Cavalos, Ribeirão dos ≐ | 256 | 21.29 S | 44.13 W |
| Cava Manara | 62 | 45.08 N | 9.07 E |
| Cavan | 48 | 54.00 N | 7.21 W |
| Cavan □[6] | 48 | 53.55 N | 7.15 W |
| Çavanaugh, Lake ⊜ | 224 | 48.23 N | 122.00 W |
| Čavan'ga | 24 | 66.06 N | 37.47 E |
| Cavarzere | 64 | 45.08 N | 12.05 E |
| Cavaso del Tomba | 64 | 45.51 N | 11.52 E |
| Çavdır | 130 | 37.09 N | 29.42 E |
| Cave, It. | 66 | 41.49 N | 12.56 E |
| Cave, N.Z. | 172 | 44.19 S | 170.57 E |
| Cave City, Ar., U.S. | 194 | 35.56 N | 91.32 W |
| Cave City, Ky., U.S. | 194 | 37.08 N | 85.57 W |
| Cave Creek ≐ | 200 | 33.34 N | 112.07 W |
| Cave del Predil | 64 | 46.26 N | 13.34 E |
| Cavedine | 64 | 45.59 N | 10.59 E |
| Cave In Rock | 194 | 37.29 N | 88.10 W |
| Caveiras ≐ | 252 | 27.35 S | 50.56 W |
| Cavelo | 152 | 17.33 S | 19.21 E |
| Cavendish | 166 | 37.31 S | 142.02 E |
| Cavernago | 62 | 45.38 N | 9.46 E |
| Cavertitz | 54 | 51.23 N | 13.08 E |
| Cave Run Lake ⊜[1] | 188 | 38.03 N | 83.30 W |
| Cave Spring | 192 | 34.14 N | 85.20 W |
| Cavettsville | 279b | 40.22 N | 79.46 W |
| Cavezzo | 64 | 44.50 N | 11.02 E |
| Cavi | 62 | 44.17 N | 9.22 E |
| Caviana de Fora, Ilha I | 250 | 0.10 N | 50.10 W |
| Cavili Island I | 116 | 9.17 N | 120.50 E |
| Cavinzas, Isla I | 286d | 12.07 S | 77.13 W |
| Cavite | 116 | 14.29 N | 120.55 E |
| Çavite □[4] | 116 | 14.15 N | 120.50 E |
| Čavka | 84 | 41.44 N | 41.45 E |
| Čavlisaj | 85 | 41.08 N | 69.44 E |
| Cavo, Monte ∧ | 267a | 41.45 N | 12.42 E |
| Cavoli, Isola dei I | 71 | 39.05 N | 9.33 E |
| Cavonne ≐ | 68 | 40.17 N | 16.47 E |
| Cavour | 62 | 44.47 N | 7.22 E |
| Cavour, Canale ≊ | 62 | 45.11 N | 7.54 E |
| Cavriago | 64 | 44.42 N | 10.31 E |
| Cavriana | 64 | 45.21 N | 10.36 E |
| Cavtat | 38 | 42.35 N | 18.13 E |
| Çavuş | 130 | 37.36 N | 31.56 E |
| Çavuşbaşı ≐ | 267b | 40.58 N | 28.51 E |
| Çavuşçu Gölü ⊜ | 130 | 38.25 N | 31.53 E |
| Čavusy | 76 | 53.48 N | 30.58 E |
| Cawatose, Lac ⊜ | 190 | 47.20 N | 77.07 W |
| Cawayan | 116 | 11.56 N | 123.46 E |
| Cawdor | 46 | 57.31 N | 3.56 W |
| Cawker City | 198 | 39.30 N | 98.26 W |
| Cawnpore → Kānpur | 124 | 26.28 N | 80.21 E |
| Cawood, Eng., U.K. | 44 | 53.50 N | 1.07 W |
| Cawood, Ky., U.S. | 192 | 36.47 N | 83.13 W |
| Cawston, B.C., Can. | 182 | 49.11 N | 119.45 W |
| Cawston, Eng., U.K. | 42 | 52.46 N | 1.10 E |
| Cawthon | 222 | 30.25 N | 96.14 W |
| Caxambu | 256 | 21.59 S | 44.56 W |
| Caxias, Bra. | 250 | 4.50 S | 43.21 W |
| Caxias, Port. | 266c | 38.42 N | 9.16 W |
| Caxias do Sul | 252 | 29.10 S | 51.11 W |
| Caxinas, Punta ➤ | 236 | 16.01 N | 86.02 W |
| Caxito | 152 | 8.33 S | 13.36 E |
| Caxiuana, Baía de ⊂ | 250 | 1.45 S | 51.20 W |
| Caxopa | 152 | 11.52 S | 20.52 E |
| Çay | 130 | 38.35 N | 31.02 E |
| Çayacal, Punta ➤ | 234 | 17.56 N | 102.11 W |
| Çayağzı ◆[8] | 267b | 41.13 N | 29.12 E |
| Çayağzı ≐ | 267b | 41.14 N | 29.12 E |
| Çayambe | 246 | 0.03 N | 78.08 W |
| Cayambe ∧[1] | 246 | 0.00 | 77.59 W |
| Cayapoñga | 116 | 5.48 N | 125.33 E |
| Çaybaşı | 130 | 41.02 N | 37.06 E |
| Çayce | 192 | 33.57 N | 81.04 W |
| Çaycuma | 130 | 41.25 N | 32.05 E |
| Çaycuse | 224 | 48.53 N | 124.22 W |
| Caycuse ≐ | 224 | 48.48 N | 124.41 W |
| Cay Duong, Vinh ⊂ | 110 | 10.10 N | 104.45 E |
| Cayenne | 250 | 4.56 N | 52.20 W |
| Cayenne □[8] | 250 | 4.00 N | 52.30 W |
| Cayes → Les Cayes | 238 | 18.12 N | 73.45 W |
| Cayeux-sur-Mer | 50 | 50.11 N | 1.29 E |
| Cayey | 240m | 18.07 N | 66.10 W |
| Cayey, Sierra de ⋏ | 240m | 18.07 N | 66.02 W |
| Çayıralan | 130 | 39.18 N | 35.40 E |
| Çayırbaşı | 130 | 40.53 N | 42.36 E |
| Çayırhan | 130 | 40.06 N | 31.37 E |
| Çayırlı | 130 | 39.48 N | 40.01 E |
| Çaylarbası | 130 | 37.41 N | 39.00 E |
| Çaylus | 32 | 44.14 N | 1.46 E |
| Cayman Brac I | 238 | 19.43 N | 79.49 W |
| Cayman Islands □[2], N.A. | 230 | 19.30 N | 80.40 W |
| Cayman Islands □[2], N.A. | 238 | 19.30 N | 80.40 W |
| Cayman Trench ⊹[1] | 16 | 19.00 N | 80.00 W |
| Cayna | 248 | 10.11 S | 76.20 W |
| Caynabo | 144 | 8.57 N | 46.26 E |
| Cayo Agua, Isla I | 236 | 9.09 N | 82.02 W |
| Çayözü | 130 | 39.36 N | 38.11 E |
| Cay Point ➤ | 240b | 24.59 N | 77.25 W |
| Çayra | 130 | 40.41 N | 39.06 E |
| Çayres | 62 | 44.55 N | 3.48 E |
| Cay Sal Bank ⊹[2] | 238 | 23.45 N | 80.00 W |
| Çaytepe | 130 | 38.48 N | 40.41 E |
| Çayucos | 226 | 35.27 N | 120.54 W |
| Cayuga, In., U.S. | 194 | 39.56 N | 87.27 W |
| Cayuga, N.Y., U.S. | 210 | 42.55 N | 76.44 W |
| Cayuga, N.D., U.S. | 198 | 46.04 N | 97.23 W |
| Cayuga, Tx., U.S. | 222 | 31.57 N | 95.57 W |
| Cayuga □[6] | 210 | 42.56 N | 76.34 W |
| Cayuga and Seneca Canal ≊ | 210 | 42.56 N | 76.44 W |
| Cayuga Creek ≐, N.Y., U.S. | 210 | 42.52 N | 78.47 W |
| Cayuga Creek ≐, N.Y., U.S. | 284a | 43.04 N | 78.57 W |
| Cayuga Heights | 210 | 42.27 N | 76.29 W |
| Cayuga Lake ⊜ | 210 | 42.45 N | 76.45 W |
| Cayuta | 210 | 42.17 N | 76.42 W |
| Cayuta Creek ≐ | 210 | 41.59 N | 76.30 W |
| Cazaclia | 38 | 46.00 N | 28.37 E |
| Cazage | 152 | 11.02 S | 20.45 E |
| Cazalla de la Sierra | 34 | 37.56 N | 5.45 W |
| Căzănești | 38 | 44.37 N | 27.01 E |
| Cazaux et de Sanguinet, Lac de ⊂ | 32 | 44.30 N | 1.10 W |
| Cazenovia | 210 | 42.55 N | 75.51 W |
| Cazenovia Creek ≐ | 210 | 42.52 N | 78.50 W |
| Cazenovia Creek, East Branch ≐ | 210 | 42.46 N | 78.38 W |
| Cazenovia Creek, West Branch ≐ | 210 | 42.46 N | 78.39 W |
| Cazenovia Lake ⊜ | 210 | 42.57 N | 75.53 W |
| Cazenovia Park ♦ | 284a | 42.51 N | 78.48 W |
| Cazères | 32 | 43.13 N | 1.05 E |
| Cazhai | 269b | 31.12 N | 121.34 E |
| Cazin | 36 | 44.58 N | 15.57 E |
| Çazis | 58 | 46.43 N | 9.25 E |
| Čazma | 36 | 45.45 N | 16.37 E |
| Cazombo | 152 | 11.54 S | 22.52 E |
| Cazones ≐ | 234 | 20.44 N | 97.12 W |
| Cazones, Golfo de ⊂ | 240p | 21.55 N | 81.20 W |
| Cazorla, Esp. | 34 | 37.55 N | 3.00 W |
| Cazorla, Ven. | 246 | 8.01 N | 67.00 W |
| Cazula | 154 | 15.25 S | 33.40 E |
| Ccapi | 248 | 13.52 S | 72.05 W |
| Cchaltubo | 84 | 42.20 N | 42.35 E |
| Cchenisckali ≐ | 84 | 42.07 N | 42.18 E |
| Çchinvali | 84 | 42.13 N | 43.56 E |
| Čchorocku | 84 | 42.32 N | 42.07 E |
| Cchunkuri | 84 | 42.23 N | 42.34 E |
| Cea ≐ | 34 | 42.00 N | 5.36 W |
| Ceanannus Mór (Kells) | 48 | 53.44 N | 6.53 W |
| Ceará → Fortaleza | 250 | 3.43 S | 38.30 W |
| Ceará □[3] | 250 | 5.00 S | 40.00 W |
| Ceará-Mirim | 250 | 5.38 S | 35.26 W |
| Ceará-Mirim ≐ | 250 | 5.40 S | 35.13 W |
| Ceatharlach → Carlow | 48 | 52.50 N | 6.55 W |
| Cebaco, Isla De I | 246 | 7.32 N | 81.09 W |
| Ceballos | 232 | 26.32 N | 104.09 W |
| Čebarkul' | 86 | 54.58 N | 60.25 E |
| Çebeci ◆[8] | 267b | 41.07 N | 28.52 E |
| Čeboksarskoje vodochranilišče ⊜[1] | 24 | 56.10 N | 46.00 E |
| Čeboksary | 80 | 56.09 N | 47.15 E |
| Cebolla Creek ≐ | 200 | 38.29 N | 107.13 W |
| Cebollar | 252 | 29.06 S | 66.33 W |
| Cebollas | 234 | 23.23 N | 104.50 W |
| Cebollatí | 252 | 33.16 S | 53.47 W |
| Cebollatí ≐ | 252 | 33.09 S | 53.38 W |
| Cebollita Peak ∧ | 200 | 34.43 N | 107.51 W |
| Céboruco, Volcán ∧[1] | 234 | 21.09 N | 104.30 W |
| Čebotovka, Ross. | 83 | 48.42 N | 39.51 E |
| Čebotovka, Ross. | 83 | 48.41 N | 40.00 E |
| Cebreros | 34 | 40.27 N | 4.28 W |
| Čebsara | 76 | 59.12 N | 38.50 E |
| Cebu | 116 | 10.18 N | 123.54 E |
| Cebu □[4] | 116 | 10.20 N | 123.45 E |
| Cebu I | 116 | 10.20 N | 123.45 E |
| Čeburgol' | 78 | 45.34 N | 38.07 E |
| Cebu Strait ⨃ | 116 | 9.45 N | 123.40 E |
| Ceccano | 66 | 41.34 N | 13.20 E |
| Cecchignola ◆[8] | 267a | 41.49 N | 12.29 E |
| Çeceda | 196 | 26.04 N | 103.25 W |
| Čečen', ostrov I | 84 | 43.58 N | 47.45 E |
| Cecer Chaan → Öndörchaan | 88 | 47.19 N | 110.39 E |
| Cecerleg, Mong. | 88 | 48.52 N | 101.14 E |
| Cecerleg, Mong. | 88 | 47.30 N | 101.27 E |
| Cecerleg, Mong. | 88 | 49.30 N | 97.36 E |
| Çecheng | 105 | 39.06 N | 116.48 E |
| Čechov, Ross. | 82 | 55.09 N | 37.27 E |
| Čechov, Ross. | 89 | 47.28 N | 141.59 E |
| Čechova, gora ∧ | 89 | 47.03 N | 142.50 E |
| Čechtice | 30 | 49.37 N | 15.03 E |
| Čechy □[9] | 30 | 49.50 N | 14.00 E |
| Cecil, Ga., U.S. | 192 | 31.02 N | 83.23 W |
| Cecil, Oh., U.S. | 216 | 41.13 N | 84.35 W |
| Cecil, Pa., U.S. | 214 | 40.19 N | 80.10 W |
| Cecil □[6] | 208 | 39.36 N | 75.50 W |
| Cecil Field Naval Air Station ■ | 192 | 30.12 N | 81.52 W |
| Cecilia | 194 | 37.39 N | 85.57 W |
| Cecilia, Mount ∧[2] | 162 | 20.45 S | 120.55 E |
| Cecil Park | 274a | 33.52 S | 150.51 E |
| Cecil Plains | 166 | 27.32 S | 151.12 E |
| Cecil Rhodes, Mount ∧ | 162 | 25.26 S | 121.26 E |
| Cecilton | 208 | 39.24 N | 75.52 W |
| Cecina | 66 | 43.19 N | 10.31 E |
| Cecina ≐ | 66 | 43.18 N | 10.29 E |
| Çecita, Lago di ⊜ | 68 | 39.24 N | 16.30 E |
| Čečnja-Ingušetija □[3] | 84 | 43.15 N | 45.40 E |
| Čečuj ≐ | 88 | 58.12 N | 109.18 E |
| Čečujsk | 88 | 58.05 N | 108.42 E |
| Cedar ≐, U.S. | 190 | 41.17 N | 91.21 W |
| Cedar ≐, Mi., U.S. | 190 | 43.53 N | 84.29 W |
| Cedar ≐, Mi., U.S. | 190 | 45.25 N | 87.21 W |
| Cedar ≐, Ne., U.S. | 198 | 41.22 N | 97.57 W |
| Cedar ≐, N.Y., U.S. | 188 | 43.51 N | 74.11 W |
| Cedar ≐, Wa., U.S. | 224 | 47.30 N | 122.12 W |
| Cedar, Middle Branch ≐ | 216 | 42.38 N | 84.05 W |
| Cedar, West Branch ≐ | 216 | 42.41 N | 84.09 W |
| Cedar, West Fork ≐ | 190 | 42.37 N | 92.29 W |
| Cedar Bayou ≐ | 222 | 29.41 N | 94.56 W |
| Cedar Beach | 284b | 39.17 N | 76.25 W |
| Cedar Bluff Reservoir ⊜[1] | 198 | 38.47 N | 99.47 W |
| Cedar Bluffs | 198 | 41.23 N | 96.36 W |
| Cedar Breaks National Monument ♦ | 200 | 37.29 N | 112.53 W |
| Cedar Brook | 208 | 39.42 N | 74.54 W |
| Cedar Brook ≐, N.J., U.S. | 276 | 40.19 N | 74.33 W |
| Cedar Brook ≐, N.J., U.S. | 276 | 40.23 N | 74.23 W |
| Cedar Brook ≐, N.J., U.S. | 285 | 39.40 N | 74.43 W |
| Cedar Brook Park ♦ | 275b | 43.45 N | 79.14 W |
| Cedarburg | 190 | 43.17 N | 87.59 W |
| Cedar City, Mo., U.S. | 219 | 38.35 N | 92.10 W |
| Cedar City, Ut,. U.S. | 200 | 37.40 N | 113.03 W |
| Cedar Creek | 222 | 30.05 N | 97.30 W |
| Cedar Creek ≐, Al., U.S. | 194 | 32.13 N | 87.06 W |
| Cedar Creek ≐, Az., U.S. | 200 | 33.48 N | 110.18 W |
| Cedar Creek ≐, Ct., U.S. | 276 | 41.09 N | 73.13 W |
| Cedar Creek ≐, De., U.S. | 208 | 38.55 N | 75.20 W |
| Cedar Creek ≐, Ga., U.S. | 194 | 34.08 N | 85.19 W |
| Cedar Creek ≐, Id., U.S. | 202 | 42.24 N | 114.49 W |
| Cedar Creek ≐, In., U.S. | 216 | 41.12 N | 85.02 W |
| Cedar Creek ≐, Ia., U.S. | 190 | 40.58 N | 91.40 W |
| Cedar Creek ≐, Ia., U.S. | 198 | 42.24 N | 94.59 W |
| Cedar Creek ≐, Ky., U.S. | 218 | 38.25 N | 84.53 W |
| Cedar Creek ≐, Mo., U.S. | 219 | 38.38 N | 92.13 W |
| Cedar Creek ≐, N.D., U.S. | 198 | 46.07 N | 101.18 W |
| Cedar Creek ≐, Oh., U.S. | 214 | 41.38 N | 83.17 W |
| Cedar Creek ≐, Pa., U.S. | 279b | 40.10 N | 79.47 W |
| Cedar Creek ≐, Tx., U.S. | 196 | 32.53 N | 98.37 W |
| Cedar Creek ≐, Tx., U.S. | 222 | 30.51 N | 96.12 W |
| Cedar Creek ≐, Tx., U.S. | 222 | 32.04 N | 96.05 W |
| Cedar Creek ≐, Tx., U.S. | 222 | 30.02 N | 97.17 W |
| Cedar Creek ≐, Wa., U.S. | 224 | 45.56 N | 122.37 W |
| Cedar Creek Reservoir ⊜[1], Tx., U.S. | 222 | 32.20 N | 96.10 W |
| Cedar Creek Reservoir ⊜[1], Tx., U.S. | 222 | 29.56 N | 96.44 W |
| Cedar Crest Manor | 285 | 39.41 N | 75.28 W |
| Cedaredge | 200 | 38.54 N | 107.55 W |
| Cedar Falls | 190 | 42.31 N | 92.26 W |
| Cedar Grove, On., Can. | 275b | 43.52 N | 79.12 W |
| Cedar Grove, In., U.S. | 218 | 39.21 N | 84.56 W |
| Cedar Grove, N.J., U.S. | 276 | 40.51 N | 74.13 W |
| Cedar Grove, W.V., U.S. | 188 | 38.13 N | 81.25 W |
| Cedar Grove, Wi., U.S. | 190 | 43.34 N | 87.49 W |
| Cedar Grove Reservoir ⊜[1] | 276 | 40.52 N | 74.13 W |
| Cedar Heights, Md., U.S. | 284c | 38.54 N | 76.54 W |
| Cedar Heights, Pa., U.S. | 285 | 40.05 N | 75.17 W |
| Cedar Hill, Mo., U.S. | 219 | 38.21 N | 90.39 W |
| Cedar Hill, N.Y., U.S. | 210 | 42.33 N | 73.47 W |
| Cedar Hill, Tn., U.S. | 194 | 36.33 N | 86.59 W |
| Cedar Hill, Tx., U.S. | 222 | 32.35 N | 96.57 W |
| Cedar Hills | 224 | 45.30 N | 122.47 W |
| Cedar Hollow | 285 | 40.04 N | 75.31 W |
| Cedarhurst, Md., U.S. | 208 | 39.07 N | 76.41 W |
| Cedarhurst, N.Y., U.S. | 276 | 40.37 N | 73.43 W |
| Cedar Island I, Md., U.S. | 208 | 37.56 N | 75.52 W |
| Cedar Island I, N.Y., U.S. | 276 | 40.38 N | 73.21 W |
| Cedar Island I, Va., U.S. | 208 | 37.39 N | 75.36 W |
| Cedar Island Lake ⊜ | 281 | 42.38 N | 83.28 W |
| Cedar Key | 192 | 29.08 N | 83.02 W |
| Cedar Knolls | 276 | 40.49 N | 74.26 W |
| Cedar Lake, In., U.S. | 216 | 41.21 N | 87.26 W |
| Cedar Lake, Tx., U.S. | 222 | 28.54 N | 95.35 W |
| Cedar Lake ⊜, On., Can. | 190 | 46.02 N | 78.30 W |
| Cedar Lake ⊜, In., U.S. | 216 | 41.22 N | 87.26 W |
| Cedar Lake ⊜, N.J., U.S. | 276 | 40.55 N | 74.28 W |
| Cedar Lake ⊜, Tx., U.S. | 196 | 32.49 N | 102.17 W |
| Cedar Lake ⊜[1] | 184 | 53.15 N | 100.10 W |
| Cedar Lake Creek ≐ | 222 | 28.50 N | 95.35 W |
| Cedar Lane | 222 | 28.54 N | 95.38 W |
| Cedar Mill | 224 | 45.32 N | 122.51 W |
| Cedarmont | 158 | 26.50 S | 29.01 E |
| Cedar Mountain ∧ | 204 | 41.36 N | 120.16 W |
| Cedar Point | 216 | 41.16 N | 89.08 W |
| Cedar Point ➤, Ct., U.S. | 276 | 41.06 N | 73.22 W |
| Cedar Point ➤, Oh., U.S. | 214 | 41.42 N | 83.20 W |
| Cedar Point ➤, Oh., U.S. | 214 | 41.30 N | 82.41 W |
| Cedar Pond ⊜ | 276 | 41.07 N | 74.06 W |
| Cedar Rapids, Ia., U.S. | 190 | 41.59 N | 91.40 W |
| Cedar Rapids, Ne., U.S. | 198 | 41.34 N | 98.09 W |
| Cedar Ridge | 226 | 39.12 N | 121.01 W |
| Cedar Run ≐ | 208 | 38.41 N | 77.29 W |
| Cedars | 285 | 40.13 N | 75.22 W |
| Cedars of Lebanon → Arz Lubnān ◆[3] | 130 | 34.14 N | 36.03 E |
| Cedar Springs, On., Can. | 214 | 42.17 N | 82.02 W |
| Cedar Springs, Mi., U.S. | 190 | 43.13 N | 85.33 W |
| Cedar Swamp ≡, Ma., U.S. | 283 | 42.33 N | 71.05 W |
| Cedar Swamp ≡, N.J., U.S. | 285 | 39.48 N | 75.20 W |
| Cedartown | 192 | 34.03 N | 85.15 W |
| Cedarvale, B.C., Can. | 182 | 55.01 N | 128.20 W |
| Cedar Vale, Ks., U.S. | 198 | 37.06 N | 96.30 W |
| Cedarville, S. Afr. | 158 | 30.23 S | 29.03 E |
| Cedarville, Ca., U.S. | 204 | 41.31 N | 120.10 W |
| Cedarville, In., U.S. | 216 | 41.12 N | 85.01 W |
| Cedarville, Ma., U.S. | 207 | 41.48 N | 70.33 W |
| Cedarville, Mi., U.S. | 190 | 46.00 N | 84.22 W |
| Cedarville, N.J., U.S. | 208 | 39.19 N | 75.12 W |
| Cedarville, N.Y., U.S. | 210 | 42.56 N | 75.07 W |
| Cedarville, Oh., U.S. | 218 | 39.44 N | 83.48 W |
| Cedarville, Pa., U.S. | 285 | 40.14 N | 75.40 W |
| Cedarville Reservoir ⊜[1] | 216 | 41.12 N | 85.01 W |
| Cedar Wash V | 200 | 35.53 N | 111.25 W |
| Cedarwood Park | 208 | 40.03 N | 74.08 W |
| Cedegolo | 64 | 46.05 N | 10.21 E |
| Çedeira | 34 | 43.39 N | 8.03 W |
| Čeder | 88 | 51.25 N | 94.45 E |
| Cedillo, Embalse de ⊜[1] | 34 | 39.40 N | 7.25 W |
| Cedral | 234 | 23.48 N | 100.44 W |
| Cedrino ≐ | 71 | 40.23 N | 9.44 E |
| Cedro | 250 | 6.36 S | 39.03 W |
| Cedro, Cerro ∧ | 234 | 18.35 N | 99.42 W |
| Cedros, Hond. | 236 | 14.35 N | 87.08 W |
| Cedros, Méx. | 232 | 24.41 N | 101.47 W |
| Cedros, Isla I | 232 | 28.12 N | 115.15 W |
| Ceduna | 162 | 32.07 S | 133.40 E |
| Cedynia | 30 | 52.50 N | 14.14 E |
| Ceel | 102 | 45.36 N | 95.51 E |
| Ceelaayo | 144 | 11.15 N | 48.54 E |
| Ceel Afweyne | 144 | 9.55 N | 47.15 E |
| Ceel Berdaale | 144 | 3.14 N | 43.11 E |
| Ceel Berde | 144 | 4.50 N | 43.39 E |
| Ceel Buur | 144 | 4.40 N | 46.37 E |
| Ceel Dhaab | 144 | 8.56 N | 46.30 E |
| Ceel Dheere, Som. | 144 | 3.51 N | 47.12 E |
| Ceeldheere, Som. | 144 | 5.22 N | 46.11 E |
| Ceel Doofaar | 144 | 10.38 N | 49.02 E |
| Ceel Waaq | 144 | 2.44 N | 41.01 E |
| Ceel Xamurre | 144 | 7.13 N | 48.54 E |
| Ceemadle | 144 | 5.14 N | 46.56 E |
| Ceepeecee | 182 | 49.52 N | 126.43 W |
| Ceerigaabo | 144 | 10.37 N | 47.22 E |
| Cefalà Diana | 70 | 37.54 N | 13.28 E |
| Cefalonia → Kefallinía I | 38 | 38.15 N | 20.35 E |
| Cefalù | 70 | 38.02 N | 14.01 E |
| Cefni ≐ | 44 | 53.12 N | 4.23 W |
| Cefn-mawr | 42 | 52.58 N | 3.04 W |
| Ceg | 144 | 8.58 N | 45.20 E |
| Çega ≐ | 34 | 41.33 N | 4.46 W |
| Čeganly | 80 | 53.54 N | 53.34 E |
| Čegdomyn | 89 | 51.07 N | 133.05 E |
| Čegem ≐ | 84 | 43.38 N | 43.48 E |
| Čegem Pervyj | 84 | 43.34 N | 43.35 E |
| Čegitun' | 180 | 66.34 N | 171.06 W |
| Cegléd | 30 | 47.10 N | 19.48 E |
| Ceglie Messapico | 68 | 40.39 N | 17.31 E |
| Cehegín | 34 | 38.06 N | 1.48 W |
| Ceheng | 102 | 25.10 N | 105.48 E |
| Cehnice | 60 | 49.12 N | 14.02 E |
| Cehu Silvaniei | 38 | 47.25 N | 23.11 E |
| Ceiba | 240m | 18.16 N | 65.39 W |
| Ceibo ≐ | 258 | 33.57 S | 58.27 W |
| Ceilán → Sri Lanka □[1] | 122 | 7.00 N | 81.00 E |
| Ceiriog ≐ | 42 | 52.57 N | 3.02 W |
| Çeirw ≐ | 44 | 52.59 N | 3.27 W |
| Čejč | 61 | 48.57 N | 16.57 E |
| Čekalin | 82 | 54.06 N | 36.15 E |
| Čekan | 80 | 54.51 N | 53.34 E |
| Čekanovskij | 88 | 56.13 N | 101.25 E |
| Çekerek | 130 | 40.04 N | 35.31 E |
| Çekerek ≐ | 130 | 40.34 N | 35.46 E |
| Čekmaguš | 86 | 55.08 N | 54.40 E |
| Çekme ◆[8] | 267b | 41.03 N | 29.10 E |
| Čekšino | 76 | 59.39 N | 40.33 E |
| Čekujevo | 24 | 63.34 N | 38.56 E |
| Čekunda | 89 | 50.48 N | 132.10 E |
| Čel'abinsk | 86 | 55.10 N | 61.24 E |
| Čel'abinsk Oblast' □[4] | 86 | 54.30 N | 60.30 E |
| Čelákovice | 54 | 50.10 N | 14.46 E |
| Celâlli | 130 | 39.42 N | 37.26 E |
| Celano | 66 | 42.05 N | 13.33 E |
| Celanova | 34 | 42.09 N | 7.58 W |
| Çelaya | 234 | 20.31 N | 100.49 W |
| Čelbas ≐ | 78 | 46.06 N | 38.59 E |
| Čelbasskaja | 78 | 45.59 N | 39.22 E |
| Celbridge | 48 | 53.20 N | 6.33 W |
| Celebes → Sulawesi I | 112 | 2.00 S | 121.00 E |
| Celebes Basin ⊹[1] | 14 | 4.00 N | 122.00 E |
| Çelebes Sea ⊤[2] | 112 | 3.00 N | 122.00 E |
| Čeleken | 128 | 39.26 N | 53.07 E |
| Celendín | 248 | 6.52 S | 78.09 W |
| Celenza sul Trigno | 66 | 41.52 N | 14.35 E |
| Celenza Valfortore | 68 | 41.34 N | 14.58 E |
| Celerina | 58 | 46.31 N | 9.51 E |
| Celeryville | 214 | 41.02 N | 82.45 W |
| Celeste | 196 | 33.18 N | 96.12 W |
| Celestún | 232 | 20.52 N | 90.24 W |
| Celica | 246 | 4.07 S | 79.59 W |
| Celico | 68 | 39.19 N | 16.20 E |
| Çelikhan | 130 | 38.02 N | 38.15 E |
| Čelina, Ross. | 80 | 46.32 N | 41.02 E |
| Celina, Oh., U.S. | 216 | 40.32 N | 84.34 W |
| Celina, Tn., U.S. | 194 | 36.33 N | 85.30 W |
| Celina, Tx., U.S. | 196 | 33.19 N | 96.47 W |
| Celinnoje, Ross. | 86 | 53.04 N | 85.40 E |
| Celinnoje, Ross. | 86 | 54.31 N | 63.39 E |
| Celinnyj | 80 | 46.40 N | 44.32 E |
| Celinograd → Akmola | 86 | 51.10 N | 71.30 E |
| Celjahany | 76 | 52.31 N | 25.51 E |
| Çelje | 36 | 46.14 N | 15.16 E |
| Čelkar, Kaz. | 80 | 50.32 N | 51.51 E |
| Čelkar, Kaz. | 86 | 47.50 N | 59.36 E |
| Cellar Head ➤ | 46 | 58.26 N | 6.10 W |
| Celldömölk | 30 | 47.16 N | 17.09 E |
| Celle | 52 | 52.37 N | 10.05 E |
| Celle, Ruisseau la ≐ | 261 | 48.35 N | 2.01 E |
| Celle Ligure | 62 | 44.20 N | 8.33 E |
| Celles | 56 | 50.14 N | 5.01 E |
| Celles-sur-Plaine | 58 | 48.28 N | 6.57 E |
| Cellettes | 50 | 47.32 N | 1.23 E |
| Cellina ≐ | 64 | 46.02 N | 12.47 E |
| Cellino Attanasio | 66 | 42.36 N | 13.52 E |
| Çellino San Marco | 68 | 40.28 N | 17.58 E |
| Čelmozero | 24 | 64.18 N | 31.48 E |
| Čelno-Veršiny | 80 | 54.26 N | 51.06 E |
| Čelobitjevo | 265b | 55.55 N | 37.40 E |
| Celone ≐ | 68 | 41.36 N | 15.41 E |
| Celorico da Beira | 34 | 40.38 N | 7.23 W |
| Celoron | 214 | 42.06 N | 79.17 W |
| Celtic Sea ⊤[2] | 28 | 51.00 N | 6.30 W |
| Celtic Shelf ⊹[4] | 10 | 49.15 N | 7.00 W |
| Çeltikçi, Tür. | 130 | 40.20 N | 32.28 E |
| Çeltikçi, Tür. | 130 | 37.32 N | 30.29 E |
| Čel'uš | 86 | 51.32 N | 87.46 E |
| Čel'uskin, mys ➤ | 74 | 77.45 N | 104.20 E |
| Čel'uskincev park ♦ | 265a | 60.01 N | 30.19 E |
| Cemaes Head ➤ | 42 | 52.07 N | 4.44 W |
| Čemal | 86 | 51.25 N | 86.01 E |
| Čembilej | 80 | 55.19 N | 45.43 E |
| Cembra | 64 | 46.10 N | 11.13 E |
| Cembra, Val di V | 64 | 46.10 N | 11.13 E |
| Cement | 196 | 34.55 N | 98.08 W |
| Cement City | 216 | 42.04 N | 84.19 W |
| Cementon, N.Y., U.S. | 210 | 42.09 N | 73.55 W |
| Çementon, Pa., U.S. | 208 | 40.41 N | 75.30 W |
| Čemerno | 36 | 43.11 N | 18.37 E |
| Cemesskaja buchta ⊂ | 78 | 44.40 N | 37.50 E |
| Cemilbey | 130 | 40.21 N | 35.04 E |
| Çemişkezek | 130 | 39.04 N | 38.55 E |
| Cemmaes | 42 | 52.37 N | 3.42 W |
| Čemolgan | 85 | 43.23 N | 76.37 E |
| Cempi, Teluk ⊂ | 115b | 8.44 S | 118.25 E |
| Cenajo, Embalse de ⊜[1] | 34 | 38.25 N | 2.00 W |
| Čenča | 88 | 55.57 N | 110.59 E |
| Cencenighe | 64 | 46.21 N | 11.58 E |
| Çenchermandal | 88 | 47.37 N | 109.05 E |
| Čency | 82 | 56.03 N | 36.01 E |
| Cenderawasih, Teluk ⊂ | 164 | 2.30 S | 135.20 E |
| Cendras | 62 | 44.09 N | 4.04 E |
| Cene | 62 | 45.47 N | 9.49 E |
| Cenepa ≐ | 246 | 4.35 S | 78.12 W |
| Čengel | 86 | 48.56 N | 89.10 E |
| Čengel'dy | 85 | 41.51 N | 68.59 E |
| Çengelköy ◆[8] | 267b | 41.03 N | 29.03 E |
| Çengerli | 130 | 39.48 N | 38.52 E |
| Cengles, Croda di ∧ | 64 | 46.34 N | 10.38 E |
| Ceno ≐ | 36 | 44.41 N | 10.05 E |
| Cenovo | 38 | 43.32 N | 25.39 E |


**Symbols** in the index entries represent the broad categories identified in the key at the right. Symbols with superior numbers (⋏[1]) identify subcategories (see complete key on page *I · 1).*

**Symbole** im Register stellen die rechts im Schlüssel erklärten Kategorien dar. Symbole mit hochgestellten Ziffern (⋏[1]) bezeichnen Unterabteilungen einer Kategorie (vgl. vollständiger Schlüssel auf Seite *I · 1).*

**Los símbolos** incluídos en el texto del índice representan las grandes categorías identificadas con la clave a la derecha. Los símbolos con numeros en su parte superior (⋏[1]) identifican las subcategorías (véase la clave completa en la página *I · 1).*

**Les symboles** de l'index représentent les catégories indiquées dans la légende à droite. Les symboles suivis d'un indice (⋏[1]) représentent des sous-catégories (voir légende complète à la page *I · 1).*

**Os símbolos** incluídos no texto do índice representam as grandes categorias identificadas com a chave à direita. Os símbolos com números em sua parte superior (⋏[1]) identificam as subcategorias (veja-se a chave completa à página *I · 1).*

| | English | Deutsch | Español | Français | Português |
|---|---|---|---|---|---|
| ∧ | Mountain | Berg | Montaña | Montagne | Montanha |
| ⋏ | Mountains | Gebirge | Montañas | Montagnes | Montanhas |
| )( | Pass | Paß | Paso | Col | Passo |
| V | Valley, Canyon | Tal, Cañon | Valle, Cañón | Vallée, Canyon | Vale, Canhão |
| ≚ | Plain | Ebene | Llano | Plaine | Planície |
| ➤ | Cape | Kap | Cabo | Cap | Cabo |
| I | Island | Insel | Isla | Île | Ilha |
| II | Islands | Inseln | Islas | Îles | Ilhas |
| ± | Other Topographic Features | Andere Topographische Objekte | Otros Elementos Topográficos | Autres données topographiques | Outros acidentes topográficos |

ESPAÑOL

| Nombre | Página | Lat.°′ | Long.°′ W = Oeste |
|---|---|---|---|
| Cenrana | 112 | 3.18 S | 118.50 E |
| Censeau | 58 | 46.49 N | 6.04 E |
| Centallo | 62 | 44.30 N | 7.35 E |
| Centenario | 252 | 38.48 S | 68.08 W |
| Centenário do Sul | 255 | 22.48 S | 51.37 W |
| Centennial Lake ⊜ | 285 | 39.50 N | 74.51 W |
| Centennial Lake ⊜[1] | 212 | 45.10 N | 72.05 W |
| Centennial Mountains ⋌ | 202 | 44.35 N | 111.55 W |
| Centennial Park ♦, Austl. | 274a | 33.54 S | 151.14 E |
| Centennial Park ♦, On., Can. | 275b | 43.39 N | 79.35 W |
| Centennial Wash V | 200 | 33.14 N | 112.46 W |
| Centeno | 66 | 42.48 N | 11.49 E |
| Center, Co., U.S. | 200 | 37.45 N | 106.06 W |
| Center, In., U.S. | 216 | 40.26 N | 86.04 W |
| Center, Mo., U.S. | 219 | 39.30 N | 91.31 W |
| Center, Ne., U.S. | 198 | 42.36 N | 97.52 W |
| Center, N.D., U.S. | 198 | 47.06 N | 101.17 W |
| Center, Tx., U.S. | 194 | 31.47 N | 94.10 W |
| Centerbrook | 207 | 41.21 N | 72.24 W |
| Center Brunswick | 210 | 42.45 N | 73.37 W |
| Centerburg | 214 | 40.18 N | 82.41 W |
| Center City | 190 | 45.23 N | 92.48 W |
| Center Cross | 208 | 37.48 N | 76.46 W |
| Centereach | 210 | 40.51 N | 73.06 W |
| Centerfield | 218 | 38.21 N | 83.24 W |
| Center Hill | 220 | 28.38 N | 81.59 W |
| Center Hill Lake ⊜[1] | 194 | 36.00 N | 85.45 W |
| Center Line | 214 | 42.29 N | 83.01 W |
| Center Moriches | 188 | 40.48 N | 72.47 W |
| Center Mountain ∧ | 202 | 45.06 N | 115.13 W |
| Center Point, Al., U.S. | 194 | 33.37 N | 86.41 W |
| Center Point, Ia., U.S. | 190 | 42.11 N | 91.47 W |
| Center Point, Tx., U.S. | 196 | 29.57 N | 99.02 W |
| Centerport, N.Y., U.S. | 210 | 40.54 N | 73.22 W |
| Centerport, Pa., U.S. | 208 | 40.29 N | 76.01 W |
| Center Square, N.J., U.S. | 285 | 39.46 N | 75.23 W |
| Center Square, Pa., U.S. | 208 | 40.10 N | 75.18 W |
| Centerton, In., U.S. | 218 | 39.30 N | 86.23 W |
| Centerton, N.J., U.S. | 285 | 39.31 N | 75.10 W |
| Center Valley | 208 | 40.32 N | 75.24 W |
| Centerville, De., U.S. | 285 | 39.49 N | 75.37 W |
| Centerville, In., U.S. | 218 | 39.49 N | 84.59 W |
| Centerville, Ia., U.S. | 190 | 40.43 N | 92.52 W |
| Centerville, Ma., U.S. | 207 | 41.38 N | 70.20 W |
| Centerville, Mo., U.S. | 194 | 37.26 N | 90.57 W |
| Centerville, N.Y., U.S. | 210 | 42.29 N | 78.15 W |
| Centerville, Oh., U.S. | 218 | 39.37 N | 84.09 W |
| Centerville, Pa., U.S. | 188 | 40.02 N | 79.58 W |
| Centerville, S.D., U.S. | 198 | 43.07 N | 96.57 W |
| Centerville, Tn., U.S. | 194 | 35.46 N | 87.28 W |
| Centerville, Tx., U.S. | 222 | 31.15 N | 95.58 W |
| Centerville, Ut,. U.S. | 200 | 40.55 N | 111.52 W |
| Centerville, Wa., U.S. | 224 | 45.45 N | 120.54 W |
| Centinela | 196 | 28.47 N | 100.34 W |
| Cento | 64 | 44.43 N | 11.17 E |
| Centocelle ◆-[8] | 267a | 41.53 N | 12.34 E |
| Cento Croci, Passo di )( | 62 | 44.25 N | 9.37 E |
| Centola | 68 | 40.04 N | 15.19 E |
| Central, Bra. | 250 | 11.08 S | 42.08 W |
| Central, Ak., U.S. | 180 | 65.34 N | 144.48 W |
| Central, Az., U.S. | 200 | 32.52 N | 109.47 W |
| Central, N.M., U.S. | 200 | 32.46 N | 108.08 W |
| Central, S.C., U.S. | 192 | 34.43 N | 82.46 W |
| Central, Tx., U.S. | 222 | 31.26 N | 94.49 W |
| Central □[4], Ghana | 150 | 5.30 N | 1.00 W |
| Central □[4], Kenya | 154 | 0.45 S | 37.00 E |
| Central □[4], Malaŵi | 154 | 13.00 S | 34.00 E |
| Central □[4], Sol.Is. | 175e | 9.10 S | 159.50 E |
| Central □[4], Scot., U.K. | 46 | 56.05 N | 4.20 W |
| Central □[4], Zam. | 154 | 14.30 S | 29.00 E |
| Central □[5], Bots. | 156 | 21.30 S | 26.00 E |
| Central □[5], Pap. N. Gui. | 164 | 9.00 S | 147.00 E |
| Central □[5], Para. | 252 | 25.30 S | 57.30 W |
| Central □[5], Ug. | 154 | 0.10 N | 32.00 E |
| Central, Cordillera ⋌, Col. | 246 | 5.00 N | 75.00 W |
| Central, Cordillera ⋌, C.R. | 236 | 10.10 N | 84.05 W |
| Central, Cordillera ⋌, Pan. | 236 | 8.30 N | 81.30 W |
| Central, Cordillera ⋌, Perú | 248 | 8.00 S | 77.00 W |
| Central, Cordillera ⋌, Pil. | 116 | 17.20 N | 120.57 E |
| Central, Cordillera ⋌, P.R. | 240m | 18.10 N | 66.35 W |
| Central, Macizo → Central, Massif ⋌ | 32 | 45.00 N | 3.10 E |
| Central, Massif ⋌ | 32 | 45.00 N | 3.10 E |
| Central, Planalto ⋌[1] | 242 | 18.00 S | 47.00 W |
| Central, Sistema ⋌ | 34 | 40.30 N | 5.00 W |
| Central African Republic □[1] | 136 | 7.00 N | 21.00 E |
| Central Aguirre | 240m | 17.57 N | 66.13 W |
| Central Arizona Project ≅[1] | 200 | 32.25 N | 111.08 W |
| Central Barren | 218 | 38.22 N | 86.06 W |
| Central Brāhui Range ⋌ | 120 | 29.20 N | 66.55 E |
| Central Bridge | 210 | 42.42 N | 74.20 W |
| Central Butte | 184 | 50.47 N | 106.30 W |
| Central City, Il., U.S. | 219 | 38.32 N | 89.07 W |
| Central City, Ia., U.S. | 190 | 42.12 N | 91.31 W |
| Central City, Ky., U.S. | 194 | 37.17 N | 87.07 W |
| Central City, Ne., U.S. | 198 | 41.06 N | 98.00 W |
| Central City, Pa., U.S. | 214 | 40.06 N | 78.48 W |
| Central Division □[5] | 175g | 18.05 S | 178.30 E |
| Centrale, Stazione ◆-[5] | 266b | 45.29 N | 9.12 E |
| Central Falls | 207 | 41.53 N | 71.23 W |
| Central Heights | 200 | 33.24 N | 110.48 W |
| Central Highlands | 279b | 40.16 N | 79.50 W |
| Centralia, Il., U.S. | 219 | 38.31 N | 89.08 W |
| Centralia, Ks., U.S. | 198 | 39.43 N | 96.07 W |
| Centralia, Mo., U.S. | 219 | 39.12 N | 92.08 W |
| Centralia, Tx., U.S. | 222 | 31.16 N | 95.02 W |
| Centralia, Wa., U.S. | 224 | 46.42 N | 122.57 W |
| Centralia, Lake ⊜ | 219 | 38.32 N | 88.59 W |
| Centralia Draw V | 196 | 31.27 N | 101.16 W |
| Centralia Reservoir ⊜[1] | 219 | 38.32 N | 89.08 W |
| Centralina | 255 | 18.34 S | 49.13 W |
| Central Intelligence Agency ʊ | 284c | 38.57 N | 77.09 W |
| Central Island I | 154 | 3.30 N | 36.03 E |
| Central Islip | 210 | 40.47 N | 73.12 W |
| Central Kalahari Game Reserve ◆-[4] | 156 | 22.15 S | 23.45 E |
| Central Lake | 190 | 45.04 N | 85.15 W |
| Central Makrān Range ⋌ | 128 | 26.40 N | 64.30 E |
| Central'nolesnoj zapovednik ◆-[4] | 76 | 56.32 N | 32.50 E |
| Central Nyack | 276 | 41.06 N | 73.57 W |
| Central'nyj, Ross. | 76 | 53.41 N | 39.38 E |
| Central'nyj, Ross. | 86 | 55.12 N | 87.40 E |
| Central'nyj, Ross. | 86 | 58.45 N | 84.28 E |
| Central'nyj, Ross. | 86 | 57.41 N | 80.57 E |
| Central'nyj, Ross. | 265b | 55.53 N | 37.52 E |
| Central'nyje Karakumy ◆-[2] | 128 | 39.00 N | 60.00 E |
| Central Pacific Basin -✦-[1] | 14 | 5.00 N | 175.00 W |

FRANÇAIS

| Nom | Page | Lat.°′ | Long.°′ W = Ouest |
|---|---|---|---|
| Central Park, N.J., U.S. | 276 | 40.26 N | 74.18 W |
| Central Park, Wa., U.S. | 224 | 46.58 N | 123.41 W |
| Central Park ♦ | 276 | 40.47 N | 73.58 W |
| Central Point | 202 | 42.22 N | 122.54 W |
| Central Railroad Station ◆-[5] | 272c | 18.58 N | 72.50 E |
| Central Range ⋌, Leso. | 158 | 29.35 S | 28.35 E |
| Central Range ⋌, Pap. N. Gui. | 164 | 5.00 S | 142.30 E |
| Central Square | 210 | 43.17 N | 76.08 W |
| Central Utah Canal ≅ | 200 | 39.35 N | 112.12 W |
| Central Valley, Ca., U.S. | 204 | 40.40 N | 122.22 W |
| Central Valley, N.Y., U.S. | 210 | 41.19 N | 74.07 W |
| Central Village | 207 | 41.43 N | 71.54 W |
| Centre | 194 | 34.09 N | 85.40 W |
| Centre □[6] | 210 | 40.55 N | 77.47 W |
| Centre, Canal du ≅ | 32 | 46.27 N | 4.07 E |
| Centre Atomique de Marcoule ʊ[3] | 62 | 44.08 N | 4.42 E |
| Centre City | 285 | 39.46 N | 75.10 W |
| Centre d'Énergie de Pierrelatte ʊ[3] | 62 | 44.21 N | 4.44 E |
| Centre Hall | 214 | 40.50 N | 77.41 W |
| Centre Island | 276 | 40.54 N | 73.32 W |
| Centre Island I | 172 | 46.28 S | 167.51 E |
| Centre Island Park ♦ | 275b | 43.37 N | 79.23 W |
| Centre Lake ⊜ | 212 | 44.36 N | 75.51 W |
| Centre Peak ∧ | 182 | 55.41 N | 126.26 W |
| Centre-Sud □[4] | 152 | 4.10 N | 12.00 E |
| Centreville, Al., U.S. | 194 | 32.56 N | 87.08 W |
| Centreville, Il., U.S. | 219 | 38.35 N | 90.07 W |
| Centreville, Ky., U.S. | 218 | 38.13 N | 84.24 W |
| Centreville, Md., U.S. | 208 | 39.02 N | 76.04 W |
| Centreville, Mi., U.S. | 216 | 41.55 N | 85.31 W |
| Centreville, Ms., U.S. | 194 | 31.05 N | 91.04 W |
| Centreville, Va., U.S. | 208 | 38.50 N | 77.25 W |
| Centro Puntas | 240m | 18.22 N | 67.16 W |
| Centro Simón Bolívar ◆-[9] | 286c | 10.30 N | 66.55 W |
| Centuripe | 70 | 37.37 N | 14.44 E |
| Century, Fl., U.S. | 194 | 30.58 N | 87.15 W |
| Century, W.V., U.S. | 188 | 39.05 N | 80.11 W |
| Century City ◆-[8] | 280 | 34.03 N | 118.26 W |
| Century III Mall ◆-[9] | 279b | 40.21 N | 79.57 W |
| Century Village | 220 | 26.42 N | 80.05 W |
| Cenxi | 102 | 22.59 N | 111.00 E |
| Čepca | 80 | 57.54 N | 53.25 E |
| Čepca ≃ | 80 | 58.36 N | 50.04 E |
| Čepeckij | 80 | 58.29 N | 51.12 E |
| Čepelare | 38 | 41.44 N | 24.41 E |
| Čepel'ovo | 82 | 55.11 N | 37.30 E |
| Čepovan | 64 | 46.03 N | 13.47 E |
| Cepoy | 50 | 48.03 N | 2.44 E |
| Ceprano | 66 | 41.33 N | 13.31 E |
| Čepřovice | 60 | 49.10 N | 13.59 E |
| Ceptia | 152 | 12.56 S | 17.35 E |
| Cepu | 115a | 7.09 S | 111.35 E |
| Čerahoŭka | 76 | 52.13 N | 31.27 E |
| Ceraino | 64 | 45.35 N | 10.50 E |
| Ceram → Seram I | 164 | 3.00 S | 129.00 E |
| Cerami | 70 | 37.49 N | 14.30 E |
| Cerami ≃ | 70 | 37.42 N | 14.29 E |
| Ceram Sea → Seram, Laut ⊤[2] | 108 | 2.30 S | 128.00 E |
| Cerano, It. | 62 | 45.25 N | 8.47 E |
| Cerano, Méx. | 234 | 20.07 N | 101.23 W |
| Ceraso | 68 | 40.11 N | 15.15 E |
| Cerbicale, Îles II | 71 | 41.34 N | 9.24 E |
| Čerčany | 30 | 49.51 N | 14.43 E |
| Cerchiara di Calabria | 68 | 39.51 N | 16.23 E |
| Čerchov ∧ | 60 | 49.23 N | 12.47 E |
| Cercié | 58 | 46.07 N | 4.40 E |
| Cerco, Alto do ∧ | 256 | 22.38 S | 45.22 W |
| Cerda | 70 | 37.54 N | 13.49 E |
| Čerdakly | 80 | 54.23 N | 48.51 E |
| Cerdanyola del Vallès | 266d | 41.30 N | 2.09 E |
| Cerdas | 248 | 20.48 S | 66.29 W |
| Cerdeña, Isla de → Sardegna I | 71 | 40.00 N | 9.00 E |
| Čerdojak | 86 | 48.48 N | 84.00 E |
| Cerdon, Fr. | 50 | 47.38 N | 2.22 E |
| Cerdon, Fr. | 58 | 46.05 N | 5.28 E |
| Čerdyn' | 24 | 60.23 N | 56.24 E |
| Cère ≃ | 32 | 44.55 N | 1.53 E |
| Cerea | 64 | 45.12 N | 11.13 E |
| Cereal | 184 | 51.25 N | 110.48 W |
| Cereales | 252 | 36.49 S | 63.51 W |
| Čerecha ≃ | 76 | 57.46 N | 28.21 E |
| Cereglio | 64 | 44.18 N | 11.04 E |
| Čerek ≃ | 84 | 43.42 N | 44.03 E |
| Čeremchovo | 88 | 53.09 N | 103.05 E |
| Čeremisinovo | 78 | 51.54 N | 37.15 E |
| Čeremšan, Ross. | 80 | 55.15 N | 48.07 E |
| Čeremšan, Ross. | 80 | 54.40 N | 51.30 E |
| Čeremšanka, Ross. | 86 | 59.10 N | 76.51 E |
| Čeremšanka, Ross. | 86 | 56.07 N | 60.19 E |
| Čeremšany | 89 | 44.42 N | 135.43 E |
| Cerenti | 112 | 0.30 S | 101.52 E |
| Čerepanovka | 80 | 57.07 N | 54.10 E |
| Čerepanovo | 86 | 54.13 N | 83.22 E |
| Čerepaška, ostrov I | 83 | 47.11 N | 38.59 E |
| Čerepet' | 82 | 54.07 N | 36.23 E |
| Čerepkovo ◆-[8] | 265b | 55.46 N | 37.23 E |
| Čerepovec | 76 | 59.08 N | 37.54 E |
| Ceres, Arg. | 252 | 29.53 S | 61.57 W |
| Ceres, Bra. | 255 | 15.17 S | 49.35 W |
| Ceres, It. | 62 | 45.19 N | 7.23 E |
| Ceres, S. Afr. | 158 | 33.21 S | 19.18 E |
| Ceres, Ca., U.S. | 226 | 37.35 N | 120.57 W |
| Ceres, N.Y., U.S. | 210 | 42.00 N | 78.16 W |
| Ceresco, Mi., U.S. | 216 | 42.16 N | 85.04 W |
| Ceresco, Ne., U.S. | 198 | 41.03 N | 96.38 W |
| Ceresole Reale | 62 | 45.26 N | 7.15 E |
| Céreste | 62 | 43.51 N | 5.35 E |
| Céret | 32 | 42.29 N | 2.45 E |
| Cereté | 246 | 8.53 N | 75.48 W |
| Čerevkovo | 24 | 61.46 N | 45.12 E |
| Cereweh | 115b | 8.52 S | 116.51 E |
| Cerf Island I | 138 | 9.32 S | 50.59 E |
| Čerga | 86 | 51.35 N | 85.38 E |
| Cergy | 261 | 49.02 N | 2.04 E |
| Ceri ≃ | 42 | 52.03 N | 4.29 W |
| Ceriale | 62 | 44.06 N | 8.14 E |
| Ceriana | 62 | 43.53 N | 7.46 E |
| Ceriano | 266b | 45.38 N | 9.05 E |
| Cerignola | 68 | 41.16 N | 15.54 E |
| Cérilly | 32 | 46.37 N | 2.49 E |
| Cerisano | 68 | 39.16 N | 16.11 E |
| Cerisiers | 50 | 48.08 N | 3.29 E |
| Čerkašina | 88 | 58.37 N | 108.30 E |
| Čerkasovo | 82 | 54.33 N | 36.48 E |
| Čerkasskoje | 80 | 52.26 N | 47.13 E |
| Čerkassy | 76 | 52.41 N | 38.43 E |
| Çerkeş | 130 | 40.50 N | 32.54 E |
| Čerkesovskij | 80 | 50.41 N | 42.34 E |
| Čerkessk | 84 | 44.14 N | 42.04 E |
| Çerkezköy | 130 | 41.17 N | 28.00 E |
| Čerkizovo, Ross. | 82 | 55.12 N | 38.45 E |
| Čerkizovo, Ross. | 265b | 55.58 N | 37.48 E |
| Čerkizovo, Ross. | 265b | 55.57 N | 37.22 E |
| Cerknica | 36 | 45.48 N | 14.22 E |
| Čerkovišče | 76 | 55.54 N | 30.51 E |
| Čerlak | 86 | 54.09 N | 74.48 E |
| Čerlakskij | 86 | 53.47 N | 74.31 E |
| Cermei | 38 | 46.33 N | 21.51 E |
| Čermen | 84 | 43.11 N | 44.42 E |
| Cermignano | 66 | 42.35 N | 13.47 E |
| Çermik | 130 | 38.09 N | 39.27 E |
| Čermoz | 86 | 58.53 N | 56.08 E |
| Čern' | 76 | 53.27 N | 36.55 E |
| Cerna, Hrv. | 38 | 45.11 N | 18.42 E |
| Cerna, Rom. | 38 | 45.04 N | 28.18 E |
| Čern'achovsk (Insterburg) | 76 | 54.38 N | 21.49 E |

PORTUGUÊS

| Nome | Página | Lat.°′ | Long.°′ W = Oeste |
|---|---|---|---|
| Černá hora ∧ | 60 | 48.58 N | 13.48 E |
| Černaja Rečka | 85 | 43.00 N | 74.55 E |
| Čern'ajevo | 89 | 52.45 N | 126.00 E |
| Černak | 85 | 43.24 N | 68.02 E |
| Čern'anka | 78 | 50.55 N | 37.49 E |
| Černaučycy | 76 | 52.13 N | 23.44 E |
| Cernăuți → Chernivtsi | 78 | 48.18 N | 25.56 E |
| Černava | 76 | 53.37 N | 39.09 E |
| Černavka, Ross. | 80 | 52.18 N | 47.14 E |
| Černavka, Ross. | 80 | 52.11 N | 42.25 E |
| Cernavodă | 38 | 44.21 N | 28.01 E |
| Černá v Pošumavi | 61 | 48.44 N | 14.07 E |
| Cernay | 58 | 47.49 N | 7.10 E |
| Cernay-la-Ville | 50 | 48.40 N | 1.58 E |
| Cerne Abbas | 42 | 50.49 N | 2.29 W |
| Černeckoje | 82 | 55.15 N | 37.20 E |
| Cernei, Munții ⋌ | 38 | 45.02 N | 22.31 E |
| Černigovka, Kaz. | 86 | 50.28 N | 71.27 E |
| Černigovka, Ross. | 89 | 49.37 N | 129.57 E |
| Černigovka, Ross. | 89 | 44.21 N | 132.33 E |
| Černigovskaja | 78 | 44.41 N | 39.40 E |
| Černi Vrăh ∧ | 38 | 42.34 N | 23.17 E |
| Cernobbio | 62 | 45.50 N | 9.04 E |
| Černogolovka | 82 | 56.00 N | 38.22 E |
| Černogorsk | 86 | 53.49 N | 91.18 E |
| Černokol'skaja | 86 | 56.42 N | 72.49 E |
| Černorečje | 84 | 43.15 N | 45.41 E |
| Černoreckoje | 86 | 52.45 N | 76.40 E |
| Černošín | 60 | 49.49 N | 12.53 E |
| Čerňovice | 60 | 49.49 N | 13.06 E |
| Černovka, Ross. | 86 | 56.47 N | 76.28 E |
| Černovka, Ross. | 89 | 51.43 N | 128.12 E |
| Čern'ovo, Ross. | 76 | 58.39 N | 28.14 E |
| Čern'ovo, Ross. | 82 | 54.43 N | 38.36 E |
| Čern'ovo, Ross. | 265b | 55.50 N | 37.18 E |
| Černovskije Kopi | 88 | 52.00 N | 113.15 E |
| Černovskoje, Ross. | 80 | 58.42 N | 47.23 E |
| Černovskoje, Ross. | 80 | 57.29 N | 54.36 E |
| Černucha | 80 | 55.36 N | 43.46 E |
| Cernusco sul Naviglio | 62 | 45.31 N | 9.19 E |
| Černuška, Ross. | 86 | 56.29 N | 56.03 E |
| Černuška, Ross. | 88 | 52.58 N | 101.55 E |
| Cerny-en-Laonnois | 50 | 49.27 N | 3.40 E |
| Černyševsk | 88 | 52.35 N | 117.00 E |
| Černyševskij | 74 | 63.00 N | 112.15 E |
| Černyškovskij | 80 | 48.27 N | 42.14 E |
| Černyšova, gr'ada ⋌ | 24 | 66.30 N | 59.00 E |
| Čer'omuchova | 80 | 54.57 N | 51.09 E |
| Čer'omuski ◆-[8] | 265b | 55.41 N | 37.35 E |
| Cerralvo | 232 | 26.06 N | 99.37 W |
| Cerralvo, Isla I | 232 | 24.15 N | 109.55 W |
| Cerreto, Passo del )( | 64 | 44.18 N | 10.13 E |
| Cerreto d'Esi | 66 | 43.19 N | 12.59 E |
| Cerreto Guidi | 66 | 43.45 N | 10.53 E |
| Cerreto Sannita | 68 | 41.17 N | 14.33 E |
| Cerrigydrudion | 44 | 53.02 N | 3.33 W |
| Cërrik | 38 | 41.02 N | 19.57 E |
| Cerrillos, Arg. | 252 | 24.54 S | 65.29 W |
| Cerrillos, Chile | 286e | 33.30 S | 70.43 W |
| Cerrillos, N.M., U.S. | 200 | 35.26 N | 106.07 W |
| Cerrina | 62 | 45.07 N | 8.13 E |
| Cerritos, Méx. | 234 | 22.26 N | 100.17 W |
| Cerritos, Ca., U.S. | 280 | 33.52 N | 118.05 W |
| Cerro | 58 | 45.54 N | 8.36 E |
| Cerro, Forca di )( | 66 | 42.45 N | 12.47 E |
| Cerro Azul, Arg. | 252 | 27.38 S | 55.29 W |
| Cerro Azul, Bra. | 252 | 24.50 S | 49.15 W |
| Cerro Azul, Méx. | 234 | 21.12 N | 97.44 W |
| Cerro Azul, Perú | 248 | 13.02 S | 76.30 W |
| Cerro Chato | 252 | 33.06 S | 55.08 W |
| Cerro Colorado | 252 | 33.52 S | 55.33 W |
| Cerro Corá | 250 | 6.03 S | 36.21 W |
| Cerro de las Mesas ⊥ | 234 | 18.47 N | 96.05 W |
| Cerro de los Angeles ʊ[1] | 266a | 40.19 N | 3.41 W |
| Cerro de Pasco | 248 | 10.41 S | 76.16 W |
| Cerro Gordo | 219 | 39.53 N | 88.43 W |
| Cerro Grande ≃ | 286c | 10.37 N | 66.49 W |
| Cerro Largo | 252 | 28.09 S | 54.45 W |
| Cerro Maggiore | 266b | 45.36 N | 8.58 E |
| Cerro Moreno | 252 | 23.28 S | 70.25 W |
| Cerrón, Cerro ∧ | 246 | 10.19 N | 70.39 W |
| Cerro Navia | 286e | 33.25 S | 70.43 W |
| Cerrón Grande, Embalse ⊜[1] | 236 | 14.00 N | 89.00 W |
| Cerro Prieto | 204 | 32.27 N | 115.17 W |
| Cerros Colorados, Embalse ⊜[1] | 252 | 38.35 S | 68.40 W |
| Cerros de Amotape, Parque Nacional ♦ | 246 | 4.10 S | 80.30 W |
| Cerro Tololo, Observatorio ʊ[3] | 252 | 30.05 S | 71.00 W |
| Cerro Vera | 252 | 33.11 S | 57.28 W |
| Čerskij | 74 | 68.45 N | 161.45 E |
| Čerskogo, chrebet ⋌, Ross. | 74 | 65.00 N | 144.00 E |
| Čerskogo, chrebet ⋌, Ross. | 88 | 52.00 N | 114.00 E |
| Čerskogo, gora ∧ | 88 | 55.05 N | 108.40 E |
| Cersosimo | 68 | 40.03 N | 16.21 E |
| Certaldo | 66 | 43.33 N | 11.02 E |
| Čertanovka ≃ | 265b | 55.38 N | 37.47 E |
| Čertanovo ◆-[8] | 265b | 55.38 N | 37.37 E |
| Čertkovo | 83 | 49.23 N | 40.10 E |
| Čertolino | 76 | 56.12 N | 33.54 E |
| Certosa (Karthaus) | 64 | 46.42 N | 10.54 E |
| Certosa di Pavia | 62 | 45.15 N | 9.09 E |
| Čerusti | 76 | 55.33 N | 40.01 E |
| Červ'anka | 88 | 57.41 N | 99.33 E |
| Cervantes, Austl. | 162 | 30.30 S | 115.04 E |
| Cervantes, Pil. | 116 | 16.59 N | 120.44 E |
| Cervarezza | 64 | 44.23 N | 10.20 E |
| Cervaro | 66 | 41.29 N | 13.54 E |
| Cervaro ≃ | 68 | 41.30 N | 15.52 E |
| Cervati, Monte ∧ | 68 | 40.17 N | 15.29 E |
| Cervelló | 266d | 41.24 N | 1.57 E |
| Cervello, Cozzo ∧ | 68 | 39.24 N | 16.05 E |
| Cervelló, Riera de ≃ | 266d | 41.24 N | 2.01 E |
| Čèrven' | 76 | 53.42 N | 28.26 E |
| Červen Brjag | 38 | 43.16 N | 24.06 E |
| Červený Kostelec | 30 | 50.29 N | 16.06 E |
| Cervera | 34 | 41.40 N | 1.17 E |
| Cervera del Río Alhama | 34 | 42.01 N | 1.57 W |
| Cervera de Pisuerga | 34 | 42.52 N | 4.30 W |
| Cerveteri | 66 | 42.00 N | 12.06 E |
| Cervi, Monte dei ∧ | 70 | 37.53 N | 13.58 E |
| Cervia | 66 | 44.15 N | 12.22 E |
| Cervialto, Monte ∧ | 68 | 40.47 N | 15.08 E |
| Cervignano del Friuli | 64 | 45.49 N | 13.20 E |
| Cervin, Mont → Matterhorn ∧ | 58 | 45.59 N | 7.43 E |
| Cervinara | 68 | 41.01 N | 14.37 E |
| Cervino (Matterhorn) ∧ | 58 | 45.59 N | 7.43 E |
| Cervione | 36 | 42.20 N | 9.31 E |
| Červl'onnaja | 84 | 43.30 N | 45.54 E |
| Cervo, Esp. | 34 | 43.40 N | 7.25 W |
| Cervo, It. | 62 | 43.55 N | 8.07 E |
| Cervo ≃ | 62 | 45.22 N | 8.24 E |
| Cervo, Capo › | 62 | 43.55 N | 8.08 E |
| Cervo, Rio do ≃, Bra. | 256 | 21.12 S | 45.10 W |
| Cervo, Rio do ≃, Bra. | 256 | 22.07 S | 45.49 W |
| Cervo, Serra do ∧ | 256 | 22.06 S | 46.07 W |
| Čèrykaŭ | 76 | 53.34 N | 31.23 E |
| Cesana Torinese | 62 | 44.57 N | 6.47 E |
| Cesano, It. | 66 | 42.07 N | 12.21 E |
| Cesano, It. | 66 | 43.45 N | 13.10 E |
| Cesano ≃ | 66 | 43.45 N | 13.10 E |
| Cesano Boscone | 266b | 45.27 N | 9.06 E |
| Cesano Maderno | 62 | 45.38 N | 9.08 E |
| Cesar □[5] | 246 | 9.20 N | 73.30 W |
| Cesar ≃ | 246 | 9.00 N | 73.58 W |
| Cesarò | 70 | 37.50 N | 14.43 E |
| Cesate | 266b | 45.36 N | 9.05 E |
| Cesena | 66 | 44.08 N | 12.15 E |
| Cesenatico | 66 | 44.12 N | 12.24 E |
| Cesi, Poggio ∧[2] | 267a | 42.02 N | 12.44 E |
| Cesiomaggiore | 64 | 46.05 N | 11.59 E |
| Cēsis | 76 | 57.18 N | 25.15 E |
| Česká Kamenice | 54 | 50.47 N | 14.26 E |
| Česká Kublice | 60 | 49.22 N | 12.52 E |
| Česká Lípa | 54 | 50.42 N | 14.32 E |
| Česká Třebová | 30 | 49.54 N | 16.27 E |
| České Budějovice | 61 | 48.59 N | 14.28 E |
| České středohoří ⋌ | 54 | 50.35 N | 14.09 E |
| Českomoravská vrchovina ⋌[1] | 30 | 49.20 N | 15.30 E |
| Český Brod | 54 | 50.02 N | 14.58 E |
| Český Krumlov | 61 | 48.49 N | 14.19 E |
| Česma | 86 | 53.50 N | 60.40 E |
| Çeşme | 130 | 38.18 N | 26.19 E |
| Cessalto | 64 | 45.42 N | 12.36 E |
| Češskaja guba c | 24 | 67.30 N | 46.30 E |
| Cessnock | 170 | 32.50 S | 151.21 E |
| Cesson | 261 | 48.34 N | 2.36 E |
| Cestos ≃ | 150 | 5.40 N | 9.10 W |
| Cesvaine | 76 | 56.58 N | 26.19 E |
| Čet' ≃ | 86 | 56.51 N | 86.48 E |
| Cetara | 68 | 40.39 N | 14.42 E |
| Cetate | 38 | 44.06 N | 23.03 E |
| Cetatea Albă → Bilhorod-Dnistrovs'kyy | 78 | 46.12 N | 30.20 E |
| Četbulak | 85 | 41.17 N | 73.58 E |
| Cetian | 100 | 25.44 N | 116.22 E |
| Cetina ≃ | 36 | 43.26 N | 16.42 E |
| Cetinje | 38 | 42.23 N | 18.55 E |
| Çetinkaya | 130 | 39.15 N | 37.38 E |
| Cetona | 66 | 42.58 N | 11.54 E |
| Cetona, Monte ∧ | 66 | 42.56 N | 11.52 E |
| Cetraro | 68 | 39.31 N | 15.56 E |
| Cetronia | 208 | 40.35 N | 75.31 W |
| Céüse, Montagne de ∧ | 62 | 44.31 N | 5.57 E |
| Ceuta | 34 | 35.53 N | 5.19 W |
| Ceva | 62 | 44.23 N | 8.02 E |
| Cevedale, Monte (Zufallspitze) ∧ | 64 | 46.27 N | 10.37 E |
| Cevennen → Cévennes ◆-[1] | 32 | 44.00 N | 3.30 E |
| Cévennes ◆-[1] | 32 | 44.00 N | 3.30 E |
| Cévennes, Parc National des ♦ | 32 | 44.15 N | 3.40 E |
| Cevins | 62 | 45.35 N | 6.28 E |
| Cevio | 58 | 46.19 N | 8.36 E |
| Cevizli | 130 | 37.12 N | 31.45 E |
| Ceyhan | 130 | 37.04 N | 35.47 E |
| Ceyhan ≃ | 130 | 36.45 N | 35.41 E |
| Ceylanpınar | 130 | 36.51 N | 40.02 E |
| Çeyldağ | 84 | 40.17 N | 49.18 E |
| Ceylon, Sk., Can. | 184 | 49.28 N | 104.36 W |
| Ceylon, Mn., U.S. | 198 | 43.32 N | 94.37 W |
| Ceylon → Sri Lanka □[1] | 122 | 7.00 N | 81.00 E |
| Ceyzériat | 58 | 46.10 N | 5.19 E |
| Cèze ≃ | 62 | 44.06 N | 4.42 E |
| Chaam, Ned. | 52 | 51.31 N | 4.52 E |
| Cha-am, Thai | 110 | 12.48 N | 99.58 E |
| Chaanling | 100 | 29.39 N | 113.49 E |
| Chaatl Island I | 182 | 53.00 N | 132.25 W |
| Chabanais | 32 | 45.52 N | 0.43 E |
| Chabang Tiga | 114 | 5.19 N | 103.08 E |
| Chabaricha | 24 | 65.50 N | 52.16 E |
| Chabařovice | 54 | 50.40 N | 13.56 E |
| Chabarovo | 72 | 69.39 N | 60.24 E |
| Chabarovsk | 89 | 48.27 N | 135.06 E |
| Chabarovsk Kraj □[8] | 89 | 52.00 N | 138.00 E |
| Chabarowsk → Chabarovsk | 89 | 48.27 N | 135.06 E |
| Chabary | 86 | 53.37 N | 79.33 E |
| Chabás | 252 | 33.15 S | 61.22 W |
| Chabeuil | 62 | 44.54 N | 5.01 E |
| Chabez | 84 | 44.02 N | 41.47 E |
| Chābi | 124 | 22.49 N | 80.41 E |
| Chabjuwardoo Bay c | 162 | 22.57 S | 113.48 E |
| Chablais ◆-[1] | 58 | 46.18 N | 6.39 E |
| Chablis | 50 | 47.49 N | 3.48 E |
| Chabogongba | 120 | 31.47 N | 81.14 E |
| Chaboje | 265a | 59.53 N | 30.46 E |
| Chabot, Lake ⊜, Ca., U.S. | 282 | 38.08 N | 122.14 W |
| Chabot, Lake ⊜, Ca., U.S. | 282 | 37.43 N | 122.07 W |
| Chabris | 50 | 47.15 N | 1.39 E |
| Chabuchaer | 86 | 43.42 N | 81.04 E |
| Chabu-Rabot, pereval )( | 85 | 38.40 N | 70.43 E |
| Chacabuco | 252 | 34.38 S | 60.29 W |
| Chacaito, Quebrada ≃ | 286c | 10.29 N | 66.52 W |
| Chacaltianguis | 234 | 18.20 N | 95.50 W |
| Chacao | 286c | 10.30 N | 66.51 W |
| Chácara | 256 | 21.41 S | 43.13 W |
| Chacarita, Cementerio de la ◆- | 288 | 34.33 S | 58.28 W |
| Chacarrão, Cachoeira do ʟ | 250 | 6.32 S | 58.12 W |
| Chacayán | 248 | 10.24 S | 76.25 W |
| Chachani, Nevado ∧ | 248 | 16.12 S | 71.33 W |
| Chachapoyas, Perú | 242 | 6.13 S | 77.51 W |
| Chachapoyas, Perú | 248 | 6.13 S | 77.51 W |
| Chachas | 248 | 15.30 S | 72.16 W |
| Chachoengsao | 110 | 13.42 N | 101.05 E |
| Chāchora | 124 | 24.10 N | 76.59 E |
| Chāchro | 120 | 25.07 N | 70.15 E |
| Chachu | 120 | 33.16 N | 81.41 E |
| Chaclacayo | 248 | 11.59 S | 76.46 W |
| Chaco □[4] | 252 | 26.25 S | 60.30 W |
| Chaco □[5] | 248 | 20.00 S | 60.30 W |
| Chaco ≃ | 200 | 36.46 N | 108.39 W |
| Chaco Austral ◆-[1] | 252 | 26.30 S | 61.30 W |
| Chaco Boreal ◆-[1] | 252 | 23.00 S | 60.00 W |
| Chaco Central ◆-[1] | 252 | 25.00 S | 59.45 W |
| Chaco Culture National Historical Park ♦ | 200 | 36.06 N | 108.00 W |
| Chaco Mesa ∧ | 200 | 35.47 N | 107.35 W |
| Chacón, Arroyo ≃ | 288 | 34.53 S | 58.39 W |
| Chacon, Cape › | 182 | 54.42 N | 132.00 W |
| Chacra Cerro | 286d | 11.55 S | 77.04 W |
| Chacuaco Creek ≃ | 196 | 37.34 N | 103.38 W |
| Chad (Tchad) □[1], Afr. | 136 | 15.00 N | 19.00 E |
| Chad (Tchad) □[1], Afr. | 146 | 15.00 N | 19.00 E |
| Chad, Lake (Lac Tchad) ⊜ | 146 | 13.20 N | 14.00 E |
| Chada-Bulak | 88 | 50.38 N | 116.18 E |
| Chadbourn | 192 | 34.19 N | 78.49 W |
| Chadderton | 44 | 53.33 N | 2.08 W |
| Chadds Ford | 285 | 39.52 N | 75.35 W |
| Chādegān | 128 | 32.46 N | 50.39 E |
| Chadian, Zhg. | 102 | 26.48 N | 105.48 E |
| Chadian, Zhg. | 105 | 39.14 N | 117.45 E |
| Chadian, Zhg. | 107 | 30.14 N | 105.56 E |
| Chadianzi | 107 | 30.31 N | 104.22 E |
| Chadiza | 154 | 14.05 S | 32.28 E |
| Chadron | 198 | 42.49 N | 103.00 W |
| Chadstone | 274b | 37.53 S | 145.05 E |
| Chadwell Saint Mary | 260 | 51.29 N | 0.22 E |
| Chadwick | 190 | 42.01 N | 89.53 W |
| Chadwick Manor | 284b | 39.19 N | 76.46 W |
| Chadwick Pond ⊜ | 283 | 42.44 N | 71.05 W |
| Chadwicks | 210 | 43.01 N | 75.16 W |
| Chadyžensk | 78 | 44.25 N | 39.33 E |
| Chadžalmachi | 84 | 42.26 N | 47.13 E |
| Chae Hom | 110 | 18.43 N | 99.35 E |
| Chaem ≃ | 110 | 18.11 N | 98.38 E |
| Chaersen | 89 | 46.19 N | 121.54 E |
| Chaeryŏng | 98 | 38.24 N | 125.36 E |
| Chafarinas, Islas II | 34 | 35.11 N | 2.26 W |
| Chafe | 150 | 11.56 N | 6.55 E |
| Chaffee | 194 | 37.10 N | 89.39 W |
| Chaffins | 207 | 42.21 N | 71.51 W |
| Chāgai | 128 | 29.18 N | 64.42 E |
| Chāgai Hills ⋌[2] | 128 | 29.30 N | 64.15 E |
| Chagandianlisu | 102 | 41.47 N | 103.29 E |
| Chagang Do □[4] | 98 | 40.50 N | 126.30 E |
| 'Chaghcharān | 120 | 34.32 N | 65.15 E |
| Chagny | 58 | 46.55 N | 4.45 E |
| Chagos Archipelago II | 12 | 6.00 S | 72.00 E |
| Chagos-Laccadive Plateau -✦-[3] | 12 | 3.00 N | 73.00 E |
| Chagrin ≃ | 214 | 41.40 N | 81.27 W |
| Chagrin, Aurora Branch ≃ | 279a | 41.25 N | 81.25 W |
| Chagrin Falls | 214 | 41.26 N | 81.24 W |
| Chagrin Falls Park | 214 | 41.21 N | 81.32 W |
| Chagrin Valley Parkway ♦ | 279a | 41.26 N | 81.25 W |
| Chaguanas | 241r | 10.31 N | 61.25 W |
| Chaguaramas | 246 | 9.20 N | 66.16 W |
| Chahaignes | 50 | 47.44 N | 0.31 E |
| Chāhak | 128 | 33.17 N | 58.54 E |
| Chahal | 236 | 15.45 N | 89.34 W |
| Chahancheluo | 98 | 41.39 N | 114.22 E |
| Chahanwusu → Dulan | 102 | 36.16 N | 98.28 E |
| Chahār Borjak | 128 | 30.17 N | 62.03 E |
| Chahār Deh-ye Ghowrband | 120 | 34.59 N | 68.44 E |
| Chahār Maḥāl va Bakhtīārī □[4] | 128 | 32.00 N | 51.00 E |
| Chahayang | 89 | 48.24 N | 124.15 E |
| Chahe, Zhg. | 100 | 33.16 N | 119.02 E |
| Chahe, Zhg. | 102 | 33.48 N | 97.22 E |
| Chahe, Zhg. | 105 | 39.50 N | 115.21 E |
| Chāh Gheybī, Hāmūn-e ≋ | 128 | 28.06 N | 60.50 E |
| Chahuamiao | 100 | 33.00 N | 115.56 E |
| Chahuites | 234 | 16.17 N | 94.11 W |
| Chai ≃ | 104 | 42.20 N | 123.52 E |
| Chai Badan | 110 | 15.04 N | 101.05 E |
| Chāībāsa | 124 | 22.34 N | 85.49 E |
| Chaigou | 98 | 36.15 N | 119.36 E |
| Chaihe | 89 | 44.47 N | 129.42 E |
| Chaijiawan | 100 | 29.10 N | 113.06 E |
| Chaillé-les-Marais | 32 | 46.24 N | 1.01 W |
| Chailley | 50 | 48.05 N | 3.42 E |
| Chailly-en-Bière | 50 | 48.28 N | 2.35 E |
| Chai Nat | 110 | 15.11 N | 100.08 E |
| Chainhurst | 260 | 51.12 N | 0.29 E |
| Chain O'Lakes State Park ♦, Il., U.S. | 216 | 42.27 N | 88.11 W |
| Chain O'Lakes State Park ♦, In., U.S. | 216 | 41.20 N | 85.26 W |
| Chainpur | 124 | 23.08 N | 84.15 E |
| Chaipudyrskaja guba c | 24 | 68.30 N | 59.30 E |
| Chaiqiao | 100 | 29.51 N | 121.56 E |
| Chairel, Laguna de c | 234 | 22.17 N | 97.57 W |
| Chaishudian | 105 | 40.46 N | 116.30 E |
| Chaiši | 84 | 42.57 N | 42.12 E |
| Chait | 85 | 39.11 N | 70.53 E |
| Chaital | 126 | 22.31 N | 88.47 E |
| Chaitén | 254 | 42.55 S | 72.43 W |
| Chaiwopu | 86 | 43.33 N | 87.59 E |
| Chaiya | 110 | 9.23 N | 99.14 E |
| Chaiyaphum | 110 | 15.48 N | 102.02 E |
| Chajarí | 252 | 30.46 S | 57.59 W |
| Chajdarken | 85 | 39.57 N | 71.21 E |
| Chajia | 107 | 29.37 N | 104.27 E |
| Chajian | 100 | 32.40 N | 118.46 E |
| Chajianling | 98 | 39.14 N | 114.36 E |
| Chajiaqiao | 100 | 34.00 N | 120.07 E |
| Chajrchan | 88 | 48.35 N | 101.56 E |
| Chajrchandulaan | 102 | 45.57 N | 102.03 E |
| Chajul | 236 | 15.30 N | 91.02 W |
| Chaka | 154 | 4.49 N | 31.14 E |
| Chakachamna Lake ⊜ | 180 | 61.13 N | 152.35 W |
| Chakāltor | 126 | 23.14 N | 86.22 E |
| Chak Amru | 123 | 32.22 N | 75.11 E |
| Chakari | 154 | 18.05 S | 29.51 E |
| Chakaria | 120 | 21.45 N | 92.05 E |
| Chakarnaba | 146 | 14.13 N | 20.51 E |
| Chakasija □[3], Ross. | 72 | 53.00 N | 90.00 E |
| Chakasija □[3], Ross. | 86 | 53.00 N | 90.00 E |
| Chākdaha, India | 126 | 23.05 N | 88.31 E |
| Chakdaha, India | 272b | 22.20 N | 88.20 E |
| Chake Chake | 154 | 5.15 S | 39.46 E |
| Chakhānsūr | 128 | 31.10 N | 62.04 E |
| Chākia | 124 | 26.25 N | 85.03 E |
| Chakkarat | 110 | 15.00 N | 102.16 E |
| Chakou, Zhg. | 98 | 38.03 N | 113.36 E |
| Chakou, Zhg. | 105 | 38.53 N | 116.41 E |
| Chakradharpur | 124 | 22.42 N | 85.38 E |
| Chakrāta | 120 | 30.42 N | 77.51 E |
| Chāksu | 120 | 26.36 N | 75.57 E |
| Chākulia | 126 | 22.29 N | 86.43 E |
| Chakwadām | 102 | 27.29 N | 98.31 E |
| Chakwāl | 123 | 32.56 N | 72.52 E |
| Chal | 272c | 19.06 N | 73.08 E |
| Chala | 248 | 15.52 S | 74.16 W |
| Chalabesa | 154 | 11.22 S | 31.01 E |
| Chalais | 32 | 45.16 N | 0.02 E |
| Chālakuda | 122 | 10.18 N | 76.20 E |
| Chalamont | 58 | 46.00 N | 5.10 E |
| Chalampé | 58 | 47.49 N | 7.33 E |
| Chalan Kanoa | 174n | 15.08 N | 145.43 E |
| Chalatenango | 236 | 14.03 N | 88.56 W |
| Chalaua | 154 | 16.06 S | 39.11 E |
| Chalaux ≃ | 50 | 47.23 N | 3.54 E |
| Chalaxung | 102 | 34.10 N | 97.44 E |
| Chalbi Desert ◆-[2] | 154 | 3.00 N | 37.20 E |
| Chalchgol | 88 | 48.11 N | 114.54 E |
| Chalchihuites | 234 | 23.29 N | 103.53 W |
| Chalchis Terara ∧ | 144 | 9.08 N | 36.44 E |
| Chalchuapa | 236 | 13.59 N | 89.41 W |
| Chalchyn ≃ | 88 | 47.55 N | 117.47 E |
| Chalcis → Khalkís | 38 | 38.28 N | 23.36 E |
| Chalco ≃ | 286a | 19.19 N | 99.08 W |
| Chaldon | 260 | 51.17 N | 0.07 W |
| Chaleine | 261 | 48.36 N | 1.43 E |
| Chalengkou | 120 | 38.02 N | 93.54 E |
| Châlette-sur-Loing | 50 | 48.01 N | 2.44 E |
| Chaleur Bay c | 186 | 48.00 N | 65.45 W |
| Chalfant | 279b | 40.25 N | 79.52 W |
| Chalfant Run ≃ | 279b | 40.25 N | 79.48 W |
| Chalfont | 208 | 40.17 N | 75.13 W |
| Chalfont Common | 260 | 51.38 N | 0.33 W |
| Chalfonte | 285 | 39.49 N | 75.31 W |
| Chalfont Saint Giles | 260 | 51.38 N | 0.34 W |
| Chalfont Saint Peter | 42 | 51.37 N | 0.33 W |
| Chalford | 42 | 51.45 N | 2.09 W |
| Chalhuanca | 248 | 14.17 S | 73.15 W |
| Chalía ≃ | 254 | 49.35 S | 69.34 W |
| Chalifert | 261 | 48.53 N | 2.46 E |
| Chalilovo | 86 | 51.24 N | 58.04 E |
| Chalindrey | 58 | 47.48 N | 5.26 E |
| Chaling | 100 | 26.47 N | 113.33 E |
| Chālisgaon | 122 | 20.28 N | 75.01 E |
| Chalisi | 102 | 32.55 N | 102.04 E |
| Chaliun | 88 | 48.50 N | 103.59 E |
| Chalk | 260 | 51.26 N | 0.25 E |
| Chalkabad | 86 | 42.42 N | 59.43 E |
| Chalk Draw V | 196 | 29.36 N | 103.15 W |
| Chalk River | 190 | 46.01 N | 77.27 W |
| Chalkyitsik | 180 | 66.39 N | 143.43 W |
| Challakere | 122 | 14.19 N | 76.39 E |
| Challans | 32 | 46.51 N | 1.53 W |
| Challapata | 248 | 18.54 S | 66.47 W |
| Challenge | 226 | 39.29 N | 121.13 W |
| Challenger, Mount ∧ | 224 | 48.50 N | 121.20 W |
| Challenger Deep -✦-[1] | 14 | 11.21 N | 142.12 E |
| Challes-les-Eaux | 62 | 45.33 N | 5.59 E |
| Challis | 202 | 44.30 N | 114.13 W |
| Challviri, Salar de ≋ | 248 | 22.32 S | 67.34 W |
| Chal'mer-Ju | 24 | 67.58 N | 64.50 E |
| Chalmers | 216 | 40.39 N | 86.52 W |
| Chalmette | 194 | 29.56 N | 89.57 W |
| Chalone Creek ≃ | 226 | 36.21 N | 121.14 W |
| Chalonnes-sur-Loire | 32 | 47.21 N | 0.46 W |
| Châlons-sur-Marne | 50 | 48.57 N | 4.22 E |
| Chalon-sur-Saône | 58 | 46.47 N | 4.51 E |
| Chalosse ◆-[1] | 32 | 43.45 N | 0.30 W |
| Chalt | 123 | 36.15 N | 74.20 E |
| Chaltel, Cerro (Monte Fitzroy) ∧ | 254 | 49.17 S | 73.05 W |
| Chaluhe | 89 | 43.43 N | 126.00 |
| Châlus, Fr. | 32 | 45.39 N | 0.59 E |
| Chālūs, Īrān | 128 | 36.38 N | 51.26 E |
| Cham, Dtsch. | 60 | 49.13 N | 12.41 E |
| Cham, Schw. | 58 | 47.11 N | 8.28 E |
| Cham ≃ | 60 | 49.13 N | 12.42 E |
| Chama | 200 | 36.54 N | 106.34 W |
| Chama ≃ | 246 | 9.03 N | 71.40 W |
| Chama, Rio ≃ | 200 | 36.03 N | 106.05 W |
| Chamah, Gunong ∧ | 114 | 5.13 N | 101.33 E |
| Chamaicó | 252 | 35.03 S | 64.58 W |
| Chamama | 154 | 12.55 S | 33.43 E |
| Chamamat'urt | 84 | 43.36 N | 46.30 E |
| Chaman | 120 | 30.55 N | 66.27 E |
| Chamangonge | 152 | 11.16 S | 20.24 E |
| Chamao, Khao ∧ | 110 | 12.57 N | 101.45 E |
| Chamarande | 261 | 48.31 N | 2.13 E |
| Chamar-Daban, chrebet ⋌ | 88 | 51.15 N | 105.00 E |
| Chāmārpāra | 272b | 22.35 N | 88.08 E |
| Chamaya ≃ | 248 | 5.44 S | 78.39 W |
| Chamba, India | 123 | 32.34 N | 76.08 E |
| Chamba, Moç. | 154 | 12.07 S | 36.57 E |
| Chamba, Tan. | 154 | 11.35 S | 36.58 E |
| Chambal ≃ | 120 | 26.30 N | 79.15 E |
| Chambaran, Plateau de ⋌[1] | 62 | 45.15 N | 5.15 E |
| Chambas | 240p | 22.12 N | 78.55 W |
| Chamberlain, Sk., Can. | 184 | 50.50 N | 105.34 W |
| Chamberlain, S.D., U.S. | 198 | 43.48 N | 99.19 W |
| Chamberlain ≃ | 164 | 15.08 S | 128.06 E |
| Chamberlain Lake ⊜ | 186 | 46.17 N | 69.20 W |
| Chamberlin, Mount ∧ | 180 | 69.16 N | 144.55 W |
| Chamberry, Ruisseau ≃ | 275a | 45.20 N | 73.58 W |
| Chambers, Az., U.S. | 200 | 35.11 N | 109.25 W |
| Chambers, Ne., U.S. | 198 | 42.12 N | 98.44 W |
| Chambers, N.Y., U.S. | 210 | 42.16 N | 76.57 W |
| Chambers □[6] | 222 | 29.42 N | 94.40 W |
| Chambers Brook ≃ | 276 | 40.35 N | 74.41 W |
| Chambersburg, Il., U.S. | 219 | 39.49 N | 90.39 W |
| Chambersburg, In., U.S. | 218 | 38.31 N | 86.24 W |
| Chambersburg, Pa., U.S. | 208 | 39.56 N | 77.39 W |
| Chambers Corner | 285 | 40.01 N | 74.44 W |
| Chambers Creek ≃ | 222 | 31.58 N | 96.10 W |
| Chambers Creek, North Fork ≃ | 222 | 32.16 N | 96.58 W |
| Chambers Creek, South Fork ≃ | 222 | 32.16 N | 96.58 W |
| Chambers Island I | 190 | 45.11 N | 87.21 W |
| Chambéry | 62 | 45.34 N | 5.56 E |
| Chambeshi ≃ | 154 | 11.21 S | 30.37 E |
| Chambi, Jebel ∧ | 148 | 35.11 N | 8.42 E |
| Chambira ≃, Perú | 246 | 4.28 S | 74.50 W |
| Chambira ≃, Perú | 246 | 3.55 S | 73.45 W |
| Chamblee | 192 | 33.53 N | 84.17 W |
| Chambley-Bussières | 56 | 49.03 N | 5.54 E |
| Chambly, P.Q., Can. | 206 | 45.27 N | 73.17 W |
| Chambly, Fr. | 50 | 49.10 N | 2.15 E |
| Chambly □[6] | 206 | 45.30 N | 73.20 W |
| Chambly, Bassin de ⊜ | 206 | 45.27 N | 73.17 W |
| Chambly, Canal de ≅ | 275a | 45.25 N | 73.15 W |
| Chambois | 50 | 48.48 N | 0.07 E |
| Chambon-sur-Dolore | 62 | 45.30 N | 3.37 E |
| Chambon-sur-Voueize | 32 | 46.11 N | 2.25 E |
| Chambord, Château de ⊥ | 50 | 47.37 N | 1.31 E |
| Chambourcy | 261 | 48.54 N | 2.03 E |
| Chambri Lake ⊜ | 164 | 4.16 S | 143.08 E |
| Chambry | 261 | 49.00 N | 2.54 E |
| Chamburi Kalāt | 128 | 26.09 N | 64.43 E |
| Chamdo → Qamdo | 102 | 31.11 N | 97.15 E |
| Chāme, Nepāl | 124 | 28.33 N | 84.15 E |
| Chame, Pan. | 236 | 8.35 N | 79.53 W |
| Chame, Punta › | 236 | 8.39 N | 79.42 W |
| Chamela | 234 | 19.32 N | 105.05 W |
| Chamelecón | 236 | 15.24 N | 88.01 W |
| Chamelecón ≃ | 236 | 15.51 N | 87.49 W |
| Chamical | 252 | 30.21 S | 66.19 W |
| Chamizo | 258 | 34.10 S | 56.41 W |
| Chamizo, Arroyo ≃ | 258 | 34.15 S | 56.44 W |
| Chamkanī | 120 | 33.48 N | 69.49 E |
| Chāmlūjā ≃ | 124 | 29.38 N | 80.24 E |
| Chamo, Lake ⊜ | 144 | 5.50 N | 37.33 E |
| Chamois, It. | 62 | 45.50 N | 7.37 E |
| Chamois, Mo., U.S. | 219 | 38.40 N | 91.46 W |
| Chamojie | 89 | 49.25 N | 124.45 E |
| Chamoli | 124 | 30.24 N | 79.21 E |
| Chamonix-Mont-Blanc | 58 | 45.55 N | 6.52 E |
| Chamousset | 62 | 45.33 N | 6.12 E |
| Chamoux-sur-Gelon | 62 | 45.32 N | 6.13 E |
| Chāmpa | 124 | 22.03 N | 82.39 E |
| Champagne, Yk., Can. | 180 | 60.47 N | 136.29 W |
| Champagne, Fr. | 62 | 45.16 N | 4.48 E |
| Champagne □[9] | 32 | 49.00 N | 4.30 E |
| Champagne Castle ∧ | 158 | 29.06 S | 29.20 E |
| Champagne-en-Valromay | 58 | 45.54 N | 5.41 E |
| Champagner-Berg ∧[2] | 264a | 52.31 N | 13.05 E |
| Champagne-sur-Seine | 50 | 48.24 N | 2.48 E |
| Champagney | 58 | 47.42 N | 6.41 E |
| Champagnole | 58 | 46.45 N | 5.55 E |
| Champagny | 62 | 45.27 N | 6.42 E |
| Chāmpāhāti | 126 | 22.23 N | 88.29 E |
| Champaign | 194 | 40.06 N | 88.14 W |
| Champaign □[6], Il., U.S. | 216 | 40.07 N | 88.12 W |
| Champaign □[6], Oh., U.S. | 218 | 40.07 N | 83.45 W |
| Champapur | 126 | 24.02 N | 86.31 E |
| Champaquí, Cerro ∧ | 252 | 31.59 S | 64.56 W |
| Champasak | 110 | 14.53 N | 105.52 E |
| Champāwat | 124 | 29.20 N | 80.06 E |
| Champcueil | 261 | 48.31 N | 2.27 E |
| Champdāni | 126 | 22.48 N | 88.21 E |
| Champdeniers | 32 | 46.29 N | 0.24 W |
| Champdepraz | 62 | 45.41 N | 7.39 E |
| Champdeuil | 261 | 48.37 N | 2.44 E |
| Champdor | 58 | 46.01 N | 5.36 E |
| Champdoré, Lac ⊜ | 176 | 55.55 N | 65.49 W |
| Champeaux | 50 | 48.35 N | 2.48 E |
| Champeix | 32 | 45.36 N | 3.08 E |
| Champerico | 236 | 14.18 N | 91.55 W |
| Champéry | 58 | 46.10 N | 6.52 E |
| Champex | 58 | 46.02 N | 7.07 E |
| Champier | 62 | 45.27 N | 5.17 E |
| Champigneulles | 56 | 48.44 N | 6.10 E |
| Champigny-sur-Marne | 261 | 48.49 N | 2.31 E |
| Champion, Ab., Can. | 182 | 50.14 N | 113.09 W |
| Champion, Mi., U.S. | 190 | 46.30 N | 87.57 W |
| Champion, Oh., U.S. | 214 | 41.17 N | 80.51 W |
| Champion, Pa., U.S. | 214 | 40.05 N | 79.21 W |
| Champions | 222 | 29.59 N | 95.31 W |
| Champlain | 206 | 44.59 N | 73.26 W |
| Champlain □[6] | 206 | 46.45 N | 72.35 W |
| Champlain ≃ | 206 | 46.27 N | 72.17 W |
| Champlain, Lake ⊜ | 188 | 44.45 N | 73.15 W |
| Champlain, Pont ◆-[5] | 206 | 45.28 N | 73.32 W |
| Champlain Canal ≅ | 210 | 43.20 N | 73.34 W |
| Champlan | 261 | 48.43 N | 2.16 E |
| Champlin Creek ≃ | 276 | 40.43 N | 73.12 W |
| Champlitte-et-le-Prélot | 58 | 47.37 N | 5.31 E |
| Champlon | 56 | 50.07 N | 5.28 E |


| | | | | |
|---|---|---|---|---|
| ≃ River | Fluß | Río | Rivière | Rio |
| ≅ Canal | Kanal | Canal | Canal | Canal |
| ʟ Waterfall, Rapids | Wasserfall, Stromschnellen | Cascada, Rápidos | Chute d'eau, Rapides | Cascata, Rápidos |
| ⊻ Strait | Meeresstraße | Estrecho | Détroit | Estreito |
| c Bay, Gulf | Bucht, Golf | Bahía, Golfo | Baie, Golfe | Baía, Golfo |
| ⊜ Lake, Lakes | See, Seen | Lago, Lagos | Lac, Lacs | Lago, Lagos |
| ≋ Swamp | Sumpf | Pantano | Marais | Pântano |
| ⁂ Ice Features, Glacier | Eis- und Gletscherformen | Accidentes Glaciales | Formes glaciaires | Acidentes glaciares |
| ⊤ Other Hydrographic Features | Andere Hydrographische Objekte | Otros Elementos Hidrográficos | Autres données hydrographiques | Outros acidentes hidrográficos |

| | | | | |
|---|---|---|---|---|
| -✦- Submarine Features | Untermeerische Objekte | Accidentes Submarinos | Formes de relief sous-marin | Acidentes submarinos |
| □ Political Unit | Politische Einheit | Unidad Política | Entité politique | Unidade política |
| ʊ Cultural Institution | Kulturelle Institution | Institución Cultural | Institution culturelle | Instituição cultural |
| ⊥ Historical Site | Historische Stätte | Sitio Histórico | Site historique | Sítio histórico |
| ♦ Recreational Site | Erholungs- und Ferienort | Sitio de Recreo | Centre de loisirs | Área de Lazer |
| ✈ Airport | Flughafen | Aeropuerto | Aéroport | Aeroporto |
| ■ Military Installation | Militäranlage | Instalación Militar | Installation militaire | Instalação militar |
| ◆- Miscellaneous | Verschiedenes | Misceláneo | Divers | Diversos |

| Name | Page | Lat.°′ | Long.°′ |
|---|---|---|---|
| Champoluc | 62 | 45.50 N | 7.44 E |
| Champotón | 232 | 19.21 N | 90.43 W |
| Champrond-en-Gâtine | 50 | 48.24 N | 1.05 E |
| Champs | 50 | 47.44 N | 3.36 E |
| Champs-sur-Marne | 261 | 48.51 N | 2.36 E |
| Chāmpua | 124 | 22.05 N | 85.40 E |
| Champvans | 58 | 47.06 N | 5.26 E |
| Chāmrāil | 272b | 22.38 N | 88.18 E |
| Chāmrājnagar Rāmasamudram | 122 | 11.55 N | 76.57 E |
| Chamrousse | 62 | 45.08 N | 5.52 E |
| Chamsara ≃ | 88 | 52.42 N | 95.46 E |
| Chamusca | 34 | 39.21 N | 8.29 W |
| Chamza Chakimzada | 85 | 40.26 N | 71.30 E |
| Chana | 110 | 6.55 N | 100.44 E |
| Chanabadskij | 85 | 40.49 N | 72.58 E |
| Chanakyapuri ▫[9] | 272a | 28.36 N | 77.11 E |
| Chañar | 252 | 30.32 S | 65.58 W |
| Chañaral | 252 | 26.21 S | 70.37 W |
| Chañaral, Isla I | 252 | 29.02 S | 71.35 W |
| Chanas | 62 | 45.18 N | 4.49 E |
| Chānasma | 120 | 23.43 N | 72.07 E |
| Chanbogd | 102 | 43.12 N | 107.10 E |
| Chancay | 248 | 11.35 S | 77.16 W |
| Chancay ≃ | 248 | 11.37 S | 77.15 W |
| Chance | 208 | 38.10 N | 75.56 W |
| Chanceaux | 58 | 47.31 N | 4.42 E |
| Chanceaux-sur-Choisille | 50 | 47.28 N | 0.42 E |
| Chanch | 88 | 51.30 N | 100.40 E |
| Chanchelulla Peak ∧ | 204 | 40.28 N | 122.59 W |
| Chanchiang → Zhanjiang | 102 | 21.16 N | 110.28 E |
| Chanchöchij uul ⋀ | 88 | 49.30 N | 94.30 E |
| Chanchongor | 102 | 43.50 N | 104.25 E |
| Chanco | 252 | 35.44 S | 72.32 W |
| Chancy | 58 | 46.08 N | 6.00 E |
| Chanda → Chandrapur, India | 122 | 19.57 N | 79.18 E |
| Chanda, Ross. | 88 | 55.00 N | 107.14 E |
| Chanda ≃ | 88 | 55.00 N | 107.14 E |
| Chāndābila | 126 | 22.05 N | 87.00 E |
| Chandagajty | 86 | 50.44 N | 92.03 E |
| Chandalar | 180 | 67.30 N | 148.30 W |
| Chandalar ≃ | 180 | 66.36 N | 145.48 W |
| Chandalar, East Fork ≃ | 180 | 67.05 N | 147.16 W |
| Chandalar, Middle Fork ≃ | 180 | 67.10 N | 148.19 W |
| Chandalar, North Fork ≃ | 180 | 67.10 N | 148.19 W |
| Chandan Chauki | 124 | 28.33 N | 80.47 E |
| Chandankiāri | 126 | 23.34 N | 86.22 E |
| Chandannagar | 126 | 22.51 N | 88.21 E |
| Chandanpratāp | 126 | 23.33 N | 89.24 E |
| Chāndar | 126 | 23.54 N | 89.58 E |
| Chandausi | 124 | 28.27 N | 78.46 E |
| Chāndbāli | 120 | 20.47 N | 86.46 E |
| Chandeleur Islands II | 194 | 29.48 N | 88.51 W |
| Chandeleur Sound ʯ | 194 | 29.55 N | 89.10 W |
| Chanderi | 124 | 24.43 N | 78.08 E |
| Chandernagore → Chandannagar | 126 | 22.51 N | 88.21 E |
| Chandīgarh | 123 | 30.44 N | 76.55 E |
| Chandīgarh ▫[8] | 123 | 30.45 N | 76.50 E |
| Chāndil | 124 | 22.58 N | 86.03 E |
| Chandīpur | 126 | 23.59 N | 89.01 E |
| Chanditala | 272b | 22.41 N | 88.16 E |
| Chandla | 124 | 25.05 N | 80.12 E |
| Chandler, P.Q., Can. | 186 | 48.21 N | 64.41 W |
| Chandler, Az., U.S. | 200 | 33.18 N | 111.50 W |
| Chandler, In., U.S. | 194 | 38.02 N | 87.22 W |
| Chandler, Ok., U.S. | 196 | 35.42 N | 96.52 W |
| Chandler, Tx., U.S. | 222 | 32.18 N | 95.29 W |
| Chandler ≃ | 180 | 69.27 N | 151.30 W |
| Chandler, Mount ∧[2] | 162 | 27.00 S | 133.20 E |
| Chandler Lake ⊜ | 180 | 68.15 N | 152.43 W |
| Chandler Park ♦ | 281 | 42.24 N | 82.58 W |
| Chandler's Cross | 260 | 51.40 N | 0.27 W |
| Chandler's Ford | 42 | 50.59 N | 1.23 W |
| Chandlers Valley | 214 | 41.56 N | 79.18 W |
| Chandlerville | 219 | 40.02 N | 90.09 W |
| Chandless ≃ | 248 | 9.08 S | 69.51 W |
| Chāndor Hills ⋀[2] | 122 | 20.30 N | 74.00 E |
| Chandos Lake ⊜ | 212 | 44.49 N | 78.00 W |
| Chāndpara | 126 | 22.58 N | 88.47 E |
| Chāndpur, Bngl. | 120 | 22.08 N | 91.55 E |
| Chāndpur, Bngl. | 124 | 23.13 N | 90.39 E |
| Chāndpur, India | 124 | 29.09 N | 78.16 E |
| Chāndpur ➤[8] | 272a | 28.45 N | 77.01 E |
| Chāndra | 126 | 22.28 N | 87.09 E |
| Chandrabhāga ≃ | 123 | 32.59 N | 76.25 E |
| Chandra Dighalia | 126 | 23.04 N | 89.46 E |
| Chandrakona | 126 | 22.44 N | 87.31 E |
| Chandrakona Road | 126 | 22.44 N | 87.21 E |
| Chandrapur | 122 | 19.57 N | 79.18 E |
| Chāndvad | 122 | 20.20 N | 74.15 E |
| Chandyga | 74 | 62.40 N | 135.36 E |
| Chanfang | 105 | 39.56 N | 115.55 E |
| Chang (Yangtze) ≃, Zhg. | 90 | 31.48 N | 121.10 E |
| Chang ≃, Zhg. | 100 | 28.59 N | 116.42 E |
| Chang ≃, Zhg. | 100 | 26.53 N | 119.41 E |
| Chang, Ko I | 110 | 12.05 N | 102.20 E |
| Changa | 84 | 44.27 N | 50.36 E |
| Changaj | 88 | 47.52 N | 99.28 E |
| Changajn nuruu ⋀ | 90 | 47.30 N | 100.00 E |
| Changal | 88 | 49.19 N | 104.24 E |
| Changalane | 156 | 26.17 S | 32.11 E |
| Chang'an, Zhg. | 102 | 26.00 N | 109.34 E |
| Changan → Xi'an, Zhg. | 102 | 34.15 N | 108.52 E |
| Changanācheri | 122 | 9.28 N | 76.33 E |
| Changane ≃ | 156 | 24.43 S | 33.32 E |
| Chang'anzhen | 106 | 30.28 N | 120.27 E |
| Changara | 154 | 16.54 S | 33.14 E |
| Changarul'skij chrebet ⋀ | 88 | 51.10 N | 103.00 E |
| Changbai | 98 | 41.26 N | 128.11 E |
| Changbai Shan ⋀ | 98 | 41.40 N | 128.00 E |
| Changbu | 100 | 23.48 N | 115.26 E |
| Changcaocun | 105 | 39.49 N | 115.47 E |
| Changchaoling | 106 | 31.00 N | 119.40 E |
| Changcheng, Zhg. | 100 | 31.49 N | 116.54 E |
| Changcheng, Zhg. | 110 | 19.24 N | 108.42 E |
| Chang Cheng (Great Wall) ⊥ | 98 | 40.30 N | 116.30 E |
| Chang Chenmo ≃ | 120 | 34.17 N | 78.19 E |
| Changchiak'ou → Zhangjiakou | 105 | 40.50 N | 114.53 E |
| Ch'angchih → Changzhi | 102 | 36.11 N | 113.08 E |
| Changchou → Zhangzhou | 100 | 24.33 N | 117.39 E |
| Changchow → Changzhou | 106 | 31.47 N | 119.57 E |
| Changchun | 89 | 43.53 N | 125.19 E |
| Changchunling | 89 | 45.22 N | 125.28 E |
| Changdan | 98 | 37.56 N | 126.45 E |
| Changdang Hu ⊜ | 106 | 31.35 N | 119.35 E |
| Changdao (Sihou) | 98 | 37.56 N | 120.42 E |
| Changde | 102 | 29.02 N | 111.41 E |
| Changdian | 105 | 40.01 N | 116.32 E |
| Ch'angdo | 98 | 38.30 N | 127.40 E |
| Ch'ang-dong | 98 | 39.03 N | 126.34 E |
| Change Islands | 186 | 49.40 N | 54.25 W |
| Changeon ≃ | 50 | 47.16 N | 0.05 E |
| Changfeng | 100 | 32.27 N | 117.09 E |
| Changgang | 100 | 24.38 N | 113.05 E |
| Changgangzi | 104 | 41.26 N | 122.41 E |
| Changge | 100 | 34.15 N | 113.50 E |
| Changgi-ap › | 98 | 36.05 N | 129.34 E |
| Changgi-li | 271b | 37.35 N | 126.44 E |
| Changgi-ri | 271b | 37.38 N | 126.41 E |
| Changgou | 105 | 39.34 N | 115.53 E |
| Changgouyu | 105 | 39.44 N | 115.52 E |
| Changguandian | 100 | 32.58 N | 115.16 E |
| Changguowei | 100 | 29.15 N | 121.56 E |
| Changgye-ri | 98 | 34.33 N | 126.49 E |
| Changgyong Palace ⊍ | 271b | 37.36 N | 127.00 E |
| Changhai, Zhg. | 98 | 39.18 N | 122.35 E |
| Chang-hai → Shanghai, Zhg. | 106 | 31.14 N | 121.28 E |
| Changhang | 98 | 36.01 N | 126.40 E |
| Changhe | 106 | 30.11 N | 120.11 E |
| Changhowŏn | 98 | 37.08 N | 127.39 E |
| Chang Hu ⊜ | 100 | 30.15 N | 112.35 E |
| Changhua, T'aiwan | 100 | 24.05 N | 120.32 E |
| Changhua, Zhg. | 100 | 30.11 N | 119.13 E |
| Changhŭng | 98 | 34.41 N | 126.52 E |
| Changhŭng-ni | 98 | 40.24 N | 128.19 E |
| Changi | 271c | 1.23 N | 103.59 E |
| Changi, Tanjong › | 271c | 1.23 N | 104.00 E |
| Changi International Airport ⊠ | 271c | 1.22 N | 103.59 E |
| Changi Prison ⊍ | 271c | 1.22 N | 103.58 E |
| Changji | 86 | 44.01 N | 87.19 E |
| Changjiang, Zhg. | 100 | 25.19 N | 113.56 E |
| Changjiang, Zhg. | 110 | 19.17 N | 109.02 E |
| Changjiangbu | 100 | 30.52 N | 113.43 E |
| Changjiapuzi | 104 | 40.51 N | 123.43 E |
| Changjiazhuang | 105 | 40.35 N | 115.24 E |
| Changjie | 100 | 29.16 N | 121.40 E |
| Changjing | 106 | 31.45 N | 120.29 E |
| Changjin-gang ≃ | 98 | 41.24 N | 127.45 E |
| Changjin-ŭp | 98 | 40.23 N | 127.15 E |
| Changkai | 100 | 28.04 N | 116.18 E |
| Changkalajier | 85 | 40.09 N | 76.59 E |
| Changkeng | 106 | 30.19 N | 121.57 E |
| Changkiakow → Zhangjiakou | 105 | 40.50 N | 114.53 E |
| Changlapod Pass )( | 124 | 30.08 N | 87.06 E |
| Changle, Zhg. | 98 | 36.42 N | 118.49 E |
| Changle, Zhg. | 100 | 29.25 N | 120.37 E |
| Changle, Zhg. | 100 | 26.00 N | 119.31 E |
| Changlejie | 100 | 28.52 N | 113.19 E |
| Changleqiao | 106 | 30.21 N | 119.51 E |
| Changlezhen | 106 | 31.56 N | 121.15 E |
| Changli, Zhg. | 98 | 39.43 N | 119.11 E |
| Changli, Zhg. | 98 | 36.57 N | 119.45 E |
| Changling | 89 | 44.15 N | 123.58 E |
| Changlingfeng | 105 | 40.11 N | 118.24 E |
| Changlingji | 100 | 32.30 N | 114.54 E |
| Changlingzi, Zhg. | 98 | 39.47 N | 122.43 E |
| Changlingzi, Zhg. | 98 | 39.33 N | 121.19 E |
| Changlinhe | 100 | 31.40 N | 117.29 E |
| Changlun | 114 | 6.26 N | 100.26 E |
| Changmar | 120 | 34.15 N | 79.45 E |
| Changmong-ni | 98 | 34.58 N | 128.41 E |
| Changning, Zhg. | 102 | 26.19 N | 112.21 E |
| Changning, Zhg. | 102 | 24.55 N | 99.35 E |
| Changning (Anningqiao), Zhg. | 102 | 28.21 N | 104.53 E |
| Changning, Zhg. | 105 | 39.59 N | 114.55 E |
| Ch'angnyŏng | 98 | 35.33 N | 128.29 E |
| Changnyŏn-ni | 98 | 38.37 N | 125.16 E |
| Changokurt | 72 | 61.58 N | 64.18 E |
| Ch'angpin | 100 | 23.19 N | 121.27 E |
| Changping | 105 | 40.14 N | 116.14 E |
| Changputong | 102 | 28.05 N | 98.29 E |
| Ch'angp'yŏng-dong | 98 | 41.27 N | 127.31 E |
| Changqiao, Zhg. | 100 | 24.15 N | 117.39 E |
| Changqiao, Zhg. | 100 | 26.49 N | 118.50 E |
| Changqing | 98 | 36.34 N | 116.43 E |
| Changsa | 102 | 19.51 N | 110.53 E |
| Changsan-got › | 98 | 38.08 N | 124.39 E |
| Changsha, Zhg. | 100 | 28.12 N | 112.58 E |
| Changsha, Zhg. | 100 | 24.13 N | 116.07 E |
| Changshaba Shuiku ⊜[1] | 107 | 29.42 N | 104.40 E |
| Changshageng | 107 | 30.00 N | 104.35 E |
| Changshan, Zhg. | 98 | 36.54 N | 117.50 E |
| Changshan, Zhg. | 100 | 28.55 N | 118.30 E |
| Changshan, Zhg. | 107 | 29.30 N | 104.13 E |
| Changshan ≃ | 100 | 28.57 N | 118.50 E |
| Changshan Qundao II | 98 | 39.00 N | 122.45 E |
| Changsheng | 100 | 26.16 N | 116.01 E |
| Changshengqiao | 107 | 29.31 N | 106.39 E |
| Changshitai | 104 | 42.33 N | 120.43 E |
| Changshitou | 102 | 35.03 N | 99.11 E |
| Changshou | 102 | 29.51 N | 107.06 E |
| Changshoudian | 100 | 31.26 N | 112.35 E |
| Changshoujie | 100 | 28.44 N | 113.57 E |
| Changshu | 106 | 31.39 N | 120.45 E |
| Changshui | 102 | 34.21 N | 111.29 E |
| Changsŏng | 98 | 35.20 N | 126.49 E |
| Changsŏng-ni | 98 | 40.58 N | 127.04 E |
| Changsu | 98 | 35.40 N | 127.32 E |
| Changtai, Zhg. | 100 | 28.34 N | 118.37 E |
| Changtai, Zhg. | 100 | 24.40 N | 117.46 E |
| Changtai, Zhg. | 104 | 41.34 N | 122.00 E |
| Changtancun | 104 | 41.33 N | 123.02 E |
| Ch'angte → Changde | 102 | 29.02 N | 111.41 E |
| Changteh → Anyang | 98 | 36.06 N | 114.21 E |
| Changting, Zhg. | 89 | 44.32 N | 128.47 E |
| Changting, Zhg. | 100 | 25.52 N | 116.20 E |
| Changtumiao | 102 | 43.30 N | 114.34 E |
| Changuinola | 236 | 9.25 N | 82.32 W |
| Changuinola ≃ | 236 | 9.28 N | 82.27 W |
| Changwu, Zhg. | 89 | 46.00 N | 125.36 E |
| Changwu, Zhg. | 102 | 35.09 N | 107.42 E |
| Changxindianzhen | 105 | 39.49 N | 116.12 E |
| Changxing | 106 | 31.01 N | 119.54 E |
| Changxing Dao I, Zhg. | 98 | 39.34 N | 121.23 E |
| Changxing Dao I, Zhg. | 106 | 31.24 N | 121.42 E |
| Changxingdian, Zhg. | 104 | 41.27 N | 121.44 E |
| Changxingdian, Zhg. | 104 | 41.33 N | 123.23 E |
| Changxingzhen | 104 | 41.40 N | 122.14 E |
| Changxuanling | 100 | 31.08 N | 114.20 E |
| Changyi | 98 | 36.51 N | 119.23 E |
| Changyŏn | 98 | 38.15 N | 125.06 E |
| Changyuan | 98 | 35.13 N | 114.39 E |
| Changyukou | 105 | 40.46 N | 115.08 E |
| Changzhi | 102 | 36.11 N | 113.08 E |
| Changzhou (Changchow) | 106 | 31.47 N | 119.57 E |
| Chanhanga | 152 | 16.04 S | 14.07 E |
| Chanh Hung | 269c | 10.44 N | 106.41 E |
| Chani | 88 | 57.05 N | 120.58 E |
| Chani ≃ | 88 | 57.02 N | 120.59 E |
| Chanino | 76 | 54.13 N | 36.37 E |
| Chanka, ozero (Xingkai Hu) ⊜ | 89 | 45.00 N | 132.24 E |
| Chankiang → Zhanjiang | 102 | 21.16 N | 110.28 E |
| Chankou | 102 | 35.52 N | 104.27 E |
| Channagiri | 122 | 14.02 N | 75.56 E |
| Channahon | 216 | 41.26 N | 88.14 W |
| Channapatna | 122 | 12.39 N | 77.13 E |
| Channel Country ➤[1] | 166 | 24.45 S | 141.00 E |
| Channel Islands II, Europe | 43b | 49.20 N | 2.20 W |
| Channel Islands II, Ca., U.S. | 204 | 33.30 N | 119.15 W |
| Channel Islands National Park ♦ | 204 | 33.28 N | 119.02 W |
| Channel Lake | 216 | 42.29 N | 88.08 W |
| Channel-Port-aux-Basques | 186 | 47.34 N | 59.09 W |
| Channel Tunnel ➤[5] | 50 | 51.00 N | 1.35 E |
| Channelview | 222 | 29.46 N | 95.06 W |
| Channing, Mi., U.S. | 190 | 46.08 N | 88.05 W |
| Channing, Tx., U.S. | 196 | 35.41 N | 102.20 W |
| Chānpādānga | 126 | 22.50 N | 87.58 E |
| Chantada | 34 | 42.37 N | 7.46 W |
| Chantajskoje, ozero ⊜ | 74 | 68.20 N | 91.00 E |
| Chantajskoje vodochranilišče ⊜[1] | 72 | 68.00 N | 88.00 E |
| Chantang | 100 | 33.41 N | 117.37 E |
| Chantau | 86 | 44.13 N | 73.51 E |
| Chanteloup | 261 | 48.51 N | 2.44 E |
| Chanteloup-les-Vignes | 261 | 48.59 N | 2.02 E |
| Chan-Tengri, pik ∧ | 72 | 42.15 N | 80.10 E |
| Chanthaburi | 110 | 12.36 N | 102.09 E |
| Chantilly | 50 | 49.12 N | 2.28 E |
| Chantraine | 58 | 48.10 N | 6.26 E |
| Chantrans | 58 | 47.03 N | 6.09 E |
| Chantrey Inlet ⊂ | 176 | 67.48 N | 96.20 W |
| Chanty-Mansijsk | 74 | 61.00 N | 69.06 E |
| Chanty-Mansijskij Avtonomnyj Okrug ▫[8] | 86 | 60.15 N | 70.45 E |
| Chanujn ≃ | 88 | 49.22 N | 102.22 E |
| Chanumla | 110 | 8.19 N | 93.05 E |
| Chanute | 198 | 37.40 N | 95.27 W |
| Chanute Air Force Base ■ | 216 | 40.18 N | 88.09 W |
| Chanuwāla | 123 | 32.44 N | 73.08 E |
| Chao ≃ | 105 | 40.36 N | 117.08 E |
| Chao, Isla I | 248 | 8.45 S | 78.47 W |
| Chao'an | 100 | 23.41 N | 116.38 E |
| Chaobai ≃ | 105 | 39.48 N | 117.08 E |
| Chaobai Xinhe ≃ | 105 | 39.37 N | 117.26 E |
| Chaocheng | 98 | 36.05 N | 115.35 E |
| Ch'aochou, T'aiwan | 100 | 22.33 N | 120.32 E |
| Ch'aochou → Chao'an, Zhg. | 100 | 23.41 N | 116.38 E |
| Chao Hu ⊜ | 100 | 31.31 N | 117.33 E |
| Chaomidian | 105 | 39.04 N | 117.01 E |
| Chao Phraya ≃ | 110 | 13.32 N | 100.36 E |
| Chaor ≃ | 89 | 46.48 N | 123.37 E |
| Chaoshui, Zhg. | 89 | 49.44 N | 127.21 E |
| Chaoshui, Zhg. | 98 | 37.42 N | 120.55 E |
| Chaouen | 148 | 35.10 N | 5.16 W |
| Chaouen ▫[4] | 148 | 35.15 N | 5.00 W |
| Chaource | 50 | 48.04 N | 4.08 E |
| Chaoxian | 100 | 31.36 N | 117.52 E |
| Chaoyang, Zhg. | 89 | 44.34 N | 126.20 E |
| Chaoyang, Zhg. | 100 | 23.17 N | 116.37 E |
| Chaoyang, Zhg. | 104 | 41.35 N | 120.28 E |
| Chaoyangchuan | 98 | 42.54 N | 129.21 E |
| Chaoyangcun | 89 | 50.02 N | 124.16 E |
| Chaoyanggou | 104 | 42.07 N | 121.04 E |
| Chaoyangpo | 89 | 43.37 N | 124.42 E |
| Chaoyangshan | 89 | 43.02 N | 125.40 E |
| Chaozhuang | 98 | 34.18 N | 114.56 E |
| Chapada dos Guimarães | 248 | 15.26 S | 55.45 W |
| Chapada dos Veadeiros, Parque Nacional da ♦ | 255 | 13.58 S | 47.30 W |
| Chapadinha | 250 | 3.44 S | 43.21 W |
| Chapala | 234 | 20.18 N | 103.12 W |
| Chapala, Laguna de ⊜ | 234 | 20.15 N | 103.00 W |
| Chapare ≃, Bol. | 248 | 15.58 S | 64.42 W |
| Chapare ≃, Bol. | 248 | 16.25 S | 64.35 W |
| Chapareillan | 62 | 45.28 N | 5.58 E |
| Chāparmukh | 120 | 26.12 N | 92.32 E |
| Chaparra, Bahía de ⊂ | 240p | 21.13 N | 76.31 W |
| Chaparral | 246 | 3.43 N | 75.28 W |
| Chapayeve | 78 | 49.21 N | 35.54 E |
| Chapayevka, Ukr. | 78 | 49.33 N | 32.06 E |
| Chapayevka, Ukr. | 78 | 47.29 N | 36.20 E |
| Chapčeranga | 88 | 49.42 N | 112.24 E |
| Chapeauroux | 62 | 44.50 N | 3.44 E |
| Chapecó | 252 | 27.06 S | 52.36 W |
| Chapel-en-le-Frith | 44 | 53.20 N | 1.54 W |
| Chapelfell Top ∧ | 44 | 54.41 N | 2.13 W |
| Chapelhall | 46 | 55.50 N | 3.56 W |
| Chapel Hill, De., U.S. | 285 | 39.42 N | 75.44 W |
| Chapel Hill, N.C., U.S. | 192 | 35.54 N | 79.03 W |
| Chapel Hill, Tn., U.S. | 194 | 35.37 N | 86.41 W |
| Chapel Hill Channel ʯ | 276 | 40.32 N | 74.02 W |
| Chapelle Creek ≃ | 198 | 44.16 N | 99.55 W |
| Chapellerie | 261 | 49.02 N | 2.26 E |
| Chapel Oaks | 284c | 38.54 N | 76.55 W |
| Chapel Point › | 42 | 50.16 N | 4.46 W |
| Chapel Saint Leonards | 44 | 53.13 N | 0.19 E |
| Chapelton | 241q | 18.05 N | 77.16 W |
| Chapeltown, Eng., U.K. | 44 | 53.28 N | 1.28 W |
| Chapeltown, Eng., U.K. | 262 | 53.38 N | 2.24 W |
| Chapet | 261 | 48.58 N | 1.56 E |
| Chapéu, Morro do ∧ | 255 | 14.55 S | 42.31 W |
| Chapéu, Ribeirão do ≃ | 256 | 23.14 S | 45.18 W |
| Chapicuy | 252 | 31.39 S | 57.54 W |
| Chapimarca | 248 | 13.58 S | 73.04 W |
| Chapin | 219 | 39.46 N | 90.24 W |
| Chapin, Lake ⊜ | 216 | 41.56 N | 86.21 W |
| Chaplain, Lake ⊜[1] | 224 | 47.57 N | 121.51 W |
| Chapleau | 190 | 47.50 N | 83.24 W |
| Chapleau ≃ | 190 | 48.29 N | 82.57 W |
| Chapleau, Lac ⊜ | 206 | 46.14 N | 74.57 W |
| Chaplin, Sk., Can. | 184 | 50.28 N | 106.40 W |
| Chaplin, Ct., U.S. | 207 | 41.47 N | 72.07 W |
| Chaplin ≃ | 194 | 37.50 N | 85.11 W |
| Chaplin Lake ⊜ | 184 | 50.18 N | 106.35 W |
| Chapliyivka | 78 | 51.43 N | 33.12 E |
| Chaplyne | 78 | 48.09 N | 36.14 E |
| Chaplynka | 78 | 46.23 N | 33.32 E |
| Chapman, Ks., U.S. | 198 | 38.58 N | 97.01 W |
| Chapman, Ne., U.S. | 198 | 41.01 N | 98.09 W |
| Chapman, Pa., U.S. | 208 | 40.46 N | 75.24 W |
| Chapman, Cape › | 176 | 69.12 N | 88.59 W |
| Chapman, Mount ∧ | 182 | 51.50 N | 118.20 W |
| Chapman College ⊍[2] | 280 | 33.47 N | 117.51 W |
| Chapman Creek ≃ | 198 | 38.58 N | 97.00 W |
| Chapman Lake ⊜ | 184 | 56.58 N | 98.12 W |
| Chapman's (Okwa) ≃ | 156 | 22.30 S | 23.00 E |
| Chapmanville | 188 | 37.58 N | 82.01 W |
| Chapman Woods | 280 | 34.08 N | 118.05 W |
| Chapo | 196 | 29.17 N | 104.20 W |
| Chaponval | 261 | 49.04 N | 2.09 E |
| Chappaqua | 210 | 41.09 N | 73.45 W |
| Chappell | 198 | 41.05 N | 102.28 W |
| Chappell Hill | 222 | 30.09 N | 96.16 W |
| Chāpra | 126 | 23.32 N | 88.33 E |
| Chapry | 83 | 47.14 N | 39.31 E |
| Chaptico Bay ⊂ | 208 | 38.21 N | 76.49 W |
| Chapultepec, Méx. | 204 | 31.50 N | 116.38 W |
| Chapultepec, Méx. | 204 | 32.22 N | 115.05 W |
| Chapultepec, Bosque de ♦ | 286a | 19.25 N | 99.12 W |
| Chapultepec, Castillo de ⊥ | 286a | 19.25 N | 99.11 W |
| Chá Pungana | 152 | 13.44 S | 18.39 E |
| Chaqui | 248 | 19.36 S | 65.32 W |
| Chaquiago | 252 | 27.32 S | 66.21 W |
| Char ≃ | 42 | 50.44 N | 2.53 W |
| Char ⫪[4] | 148 | 21.31 N | 12.51 W |
| Charaa ≃ | 88 | 49.38 N | 105.49 E |
| Charabali | 80 | 47.24 N | 47.16 E |
| Chara-Chužar | 88 | 52.30 N | 99.39 E |
| Charadai | 252 | 27.38 S | 59.54 W |
| Charagauli | 84 | 42.01 N | 43.12 E |
| Charagua | 248 | 19.48 S | 63.13 W |
| Charagun | 88 | 51.36 N | 111.05 E |
| Char-Ajrag | 102 | 45.49 N | 109.17 E |
| Charal | 88 | 51.58 N | 96.39 E |
| Charalá | 246 | 6.17 N | 73.10 W |
| Charām | 128 | 30.45 N | 50.44 E |
| Charaña | 248 | 17.36 S | 69.28 W |
| Charanor | 88 | 50.05 N | 116.40 E |
| Charanpur | 126 | 23.45 N | 87.02 E |
| Charapán | 234 | 19.41 N | 102.06 W |
| Charapucu, Ilha I | 250 | 0.18 S | 50.48 W |
| Charata | 252 | 27.13 S | 61.12 W |
| Charauz | 88 | 52.16 N | 106.17 E |
| Charavines-les-Bains | 62 | 45.26 N | 5.31 E |
| Charazani → Amarete | 248 | 15.14 S | 68.58 W |
| Charazargaj | 88 | 52.57 N | 104.41 E |
| Charbala | 74 | 64.07 N | 120.19 E |
| Char Bansi | 126 | 22.59 N | 90.43 E |
| Charbatovo | 88 | 53.46 N | 106.00 E |
| Charbon | 170 | 32.54 S | 149.58 E |
| Charcana | 248 | 15.15 S | 73.04 W |
| Charcas | 234 | 23.08 N | 101.07 W |
| Charco Azul, Bahía de ⊂ | 236 | 8.15 N | 82.45 W |
| Charco Hondo | 240m | 18.25 N | 66.43 W |
| Charcos de Figueroa | 232 | 27.45 N | 102.11 W |
| Charcos de Risa | 232 | 26.15 N | 103.10 W |
| Charcot Island I | 9 | 69.45 S | 75.15 W |
| Chard | 42 | 50.53 N | 2.58 W |
| Chardon | 214 | 41.36 N | 81.08 W |
| Charduār | 120 | 26.52 N | 92.46 E |
| Chardzhou → Čardžou | 128 | 39.06 N | 63.34 E |
| Charef, Oued ∨ | 148 | 34.07 N | 2.05 W |
| Charente ▫[5] | 32 | 45.40 N | 0.10 E |
| Charente ≃ | 32 | 45.57 N | 1.05 W |
| Charente-Maritime ▫[5] | 32 | 45.30 N | 0.45 W |
| Charenton-du-Cher | 32 | 46.44 N | 2.38 E |
| Charenton-le-Pont | 261 | 48.49 N | 2.25 E |
| Charentonne ≃ | 50 | 49.07 N | 0.44 E |
| Charest ≃ | 206 | 46.36 N | 72.14 W |
| Chārghāt | 126 | 24.17 N | 88.45 E |
| Char Hāim | 126 | 23.04 N | 90.38 E |
| Chari ≃ | 146 | 12.58 N | 14.31 E |
| Chariāl Canal ≍ | 272b | 22.28 N | 88.11 E |
| Chari-Baguirmi ▫[5] | 146 | 11.30 N | 16.30 E |
| Charik | 88 | 54.15 N | 101.39 E |
| Chārīkār | 120 | 35.01 N | 69.11 E |
| Charing | 42 | 51.13 N | 0.48 E |
| Charing Cross | 214 | 42.20 N | 82.06 W |
| Charino, Ross. | 76 | 59.57 N | 43.44 E |
| Charino, Ross. | 82 | 54.33 N | 37.52 E |
| Charistvala | 84 | 42.26 N | 43.02 E |
| Chariton | 190 | 41.00 N | 93.18 W |
| Chariton ≃ | 194 | 39.19 N | 92.57 W |
| Chariton, Mussel Fork ≃ | 194 | 39.24 N | 92.55 W |
| Charitonovo, Ross. | 24 | 61.27 N | 47.28 E |
| Charitonovo, Ross. | 82 | 56.52 N | 36.44 E |
| Charity | 246 | 7.24 N | 58.36 W |
| Charkhāri | 124 | 25.24 N | 79.45 E |
| Charkhi Dādri | 124 | 28.37 N | 76.16 E |
| Char'kin | 80 | 48.46 N | 51.49 E |
| Charkop ➤[8] | 272c | 19.13 N | 72.49 E |
| Charkow → Kharkiv | 78 | 50.00 N | 36.15 E |
| Char Lākhpur | 126 | 24.04 N | 90.40 E |
| Charland, Lac ⊜ | 206 | 46.52 N | 74.11 W |
| Charlbury | 42 | 51.53 N | 1.29 W |
| Charl Cilliers | 158 | 26.39 S | 29.12 E |
| Charlemagne | 206 | 45.43 N | 73.29 W |
| Charlemont | 207 | 42.37 N | 72.52 W |
| Charleroi, Bel. | 50 | 50.25 N | 4.26 E |
| Charleroi, Pa., U.S. | 214 | 40.08 N | 79.53 W |
| Charleroi à Bruxelles, Canal de ≍ | 50 | 50.51 N | 4.19 E |
| Charles ▫[6] | 208 | 38.32 N | 76.59 W |
| Charles ≃ | 207 | 42.22 N | 71.03 W |
| Charles, Cape › | 208 | 37.08 N | 75.58 W |
| Charles, Lake ⊜ | 278 | 42.15 N | 87.58 W |
| Charles, Peak ∧ | 162 | 32.52 S | 121.11 E |
| Charlesbourg | 206 | 46.51 N | 71.16 W |
| Charles Branch ≃ | 284c | 38.47 N | 76.48 W |
| Charles City, Ia., U.S. | 190 | 43.03 N | 92.40 W |
| Charles City, Va., U.S. | 208 | 37.20 N | 77.04 W |
| Charles City ▫[6] | 208 | 37.20 N | 77.02 W |
| Charles de Gaulle, Aéroport ⊠ | 50 | 49.01 N | 2.33 E |
| Charles Island I | 176 | 62.40 N | 74.15 W |
| Charles Lee Tilden Regional Park ♦ | 282 | 37.54 N | 122.15 W |
| Charles Mill Lake ⊜[1] | 214 | 40.45 N | 82.22 W |
| Charles Mound ∧[2] | 190 | 42.30 N | 90.14 W |
| Charles Point › | 164 | 12.23 S | 130.36 E |
| Charles Sound ʯ | 172 | 45.02 S | 167.04 E |
| Charleston, Austl. | 168b | 34.55 S | 138.54 E |
| Charleston, N.Z. | 172 | 41.54 S | 171.26 E |
| Charleston, Ar., U.S. | 194 | 35.17 N | 94.02 W |
| Charleston, Il., U.S. | 194 | 39.29 N | 88.10 W |
| Charleston, Ms., U.S. | 194 | 34.00 N | 90.03 W |
| Charleston, Mo., U.S. | 194 | 36.55 N | 89.21 W |
| Charleston, S.C., U.S. | 192 | 32.46 N | 79.55 W |
| Charleston, W.V., U.S. | 188 | 38.20 N | 81.37 W |
| Charleston Air Force Base ■ | 192 | 32.55 N | 80.03 W |
| Charleston Lake ⊜ | 212 | 44.32 N | 76.00 W |
| Charleston Peak ∧ | 204 | 36.16 N | 115.42 W |
| Charlestown, Austl. | 170 | 32.58 S | 151.42 E |
| Charlestown, Ire. | 48 | 53.57 N | 8.49 W |
| Charlestown, St. K.-N. | 238 | 17.08 N | 62.37 W |
| Charlestown, S. Afr. | 158 | 27.30 S | 29.55 E |
| Charlestown, In., U.S. | 218 | 38.27 N | 85.40 W |
| Charlestown, Md., U.S. | 208 | 39.34 N | 75.58 W |
| Charlestown, N.H., U.S. | 188 | 43.14 N | 72.25 W |
| Charlestown, Pa., U.S. | 285 | 40.06 N | 75.33 W |
| Charlestown, R.I., U.S. | 207 | 41.22 N | 71.38 W |
| Charles Town, W.V., U.S. | 188 | 39.17 N | 77.51 W |
| Charlestown ➤[8] | 283 | 42.23 N | 71.04 W |
| Charlestown of Aberlour | 46 | 57.28 N | 3.14 W |
| Charlesworth | 262 | 53.26 N | 1.59 W |
| Charleville, Austl. | 166 | 26.24 S | 146.15 E |
| Charleville → Ráth Luirc, Ire. | 48 | 52.21 N | 8.41 W |
| Charleville-Mézières | 56 | 49.46 N | 4.43 E |
| Charlevoix | 190 | 45.19 N | 85.15 W |
| Charlevoix, Lake ⊜ | 190 | 45.15 N | 85.08 W |
| Charley ≃ | 180 | 65.20 N | 142.49 W |
| Charlie Bluff | 216 | 42.50 N | 88.58 W |
| Charlie Creek ≃ | 220 | 27.21 N | 81.49 W |
| Charlie Lake | 182 | 56.16 N | 120.57 W |
| Charlieu | 32 | 46.10 N | 4.10 E |
| Charlotte, Mi., U.S. | 216 | 42.33 N | 84.50 W |
| Charlotte, N.C., U.S. | 192 | 35.13 N | 80.50 W |
| Charlotte, Tn., U.S. | 194 | 36.10 N | 87.20 W |
| Charlotte, Tx., U.S. | 196 | 28.51 N | 98.42 W |
| Charlotte ▫[6] | 220 | 26.54 N | 81.58 W |
| Charlotte Amalie | 240m | 18.21 N | 64.56 W |
| Charlotte Court House | 192 | 37.03 N | 78.39 W |
| Charlotte Creek ≃ | 210 | 42.27 N | 75.01 W |
| Charlotte Harbor | 220 | 26.57 N | 82.04 W |
| Charlotte Harbor ⊂ | 220 | 26.45 N | 82.12 W |
| Charlotte Lake ⊜ | 182 | 52.11 N | 125.20 W |
| Charlottenberg | 26 | 59.53 N | 12.17 E |
| Charlottenburg ➤[8] | 264a | 52.31 N | 13.16 E |
| Charlottenburg, Schloss ⊥ | 264a | 52.31 N | 13.14 E |
| Charlottesburg Reservoir ⊜[1] | 276 | 41.02 N | 74.26 W |
| Charlottes Pass ♦ | 171b | 36.25 S | 145.20 E |
| Charlottesville, In., U.S. | 218 | 39.47 N | 85.36 W |
| Charlottesville, Va., U.S. | 192 | 38.01 N | 78.28 W |
| Charlottetown | 186 | 46.14 N | 63.08 W |
| Charlotteville | 210 | 42.33 N | 74.40 W |
| Charlovka | 24 | 68.47 N | 37.15 E |
| Charlton, Austl. | 166 | 36.16 S | 143.21 E |
| Charlton, Ma., U.S. | 207 | 42.08 N | 71.58 W |
| Charlton ➤[8] | 260 | 51.29 N | 0.02 E |
| Charlton City | 207 | 42.08 N | 71.59 W |
| Charlton Island I | 176 | 52.00 N | 79.30 W |
| Charlton Kings | 42 | 51.53 N | 2.03 W |
| Charlu | 24 | 61.48 N | 30.52 E |
| Charly-sur-Marne | 50 | 48.58 N | 3.17 E |
| Charm | 214 | 40.30 N | 81.47 W |
| Charmentray | 261 | 48.57 N | 2.47 E |
| Charmes | 58 | 48.22 N | 6.17 E |
| Charmes-sur-Rhône | 62 | 44.52 N | 4.50 E |
| Charmey | 58 | 46.38 N | 7.10 E |
| Charminster | 42 | 50.43 N | 2.28 W |
| Charmois-l'Orgueilleux | 58 | 48.06 N | 6.16 E |
| Charmont-en-Beauce | 50 | 48.14 N | 2.06 E |
| Charmouth | 42 | 50.45 N | 2.55 W |
| Charnay-lès-Mâcon | 58 | 46.18 N | 4.47 E |
| Charneca | 266c | 38.44 N | 9.27 W |
| Charneca ➤[8] | 266c | 38.47 N | 9.08 W |
| Charnley ≃ | 164 | 16.25 S | 124.57 E |
| Charnock Richard | 262 | 53.38 N | 2.41 W |
| Char nuur ⊜, Mong. | 88 | 48.06 N | 93.12 E |
| Char nuur ⊜, Mong. | 88 | 48.20 N | 96.05 E |
| Charnwood Forest ➤[3] | 42 | 52.43 N | 1.15 W |
| Charny, P.Q., Can. | 206 | 46.43 N | 71.16 W |
| Charny, Fr. | 50 | 47.53 N | 3.06 E |
| Charny, Fr. | 261 | 48.58 N | 2.46 E |
| Charny-sur-Meuse | 56 | 49.12 N | 5.22 E |
| Charo | 234 | 19.45 N | 101.03 W |
| Charolles | 32 | 46.26 N | 4.17 E |
| Charouine | 148 | 29.01 N | 0.16 W |
| Charovsk | 76 | 59.59 N | 40.11 E |
| Charpi ≃ | 89 | 49.40 N | 136.10 E |
| Charquemont | 58 | 47.13 N | 6.49 E |
| Charred Oak Estates | 284c | 39.00 N | 77.10 W |
| Charrette Creek ≃ | 219 | 38.37 N | 91.03 W |
| Charron Lake ⊜ | 184 | 52.45 N | 95.15 W |
| Charroux | 32 | 46.09 N | 0.24 E |
| Chars | 50 | 49.10 N | 1.56 E |
| Chārsadda | 123 | 34.09 N | 71.44 E |
| Charter Oak, Ca., U.S. | 280 | 34.06 N | 117.52 W |
| Charter Oak, Ia., U.S. | 198 | 42.04 N | 95.35 W |
| Charters Towers | 166 | 20.05 S | 146.16 E |
| Charterwood | 279b | 40.33 N | 80.00 W |
| Chartiers Creek ≃ | 214 | 40.28 N | 80.03 W |
| Chartiers Run ≃, Pa., U.S. | 279b | 40.36 N | 79.43 W |
| Chartiers Run ≃, Pa., U.S. | 279b | 40.15 N | 80.12 W |
| Chartley | 207 | 41.56 N | 71.13 W |
| Chartres | 50 | 48.27 N | 1.30 E |
| Chartrettes | 50 | 48.29 N | 2.42 E |
| Chartridge | 260 | 51.44 N | 0.39 W |
| Chart Sutton | 260 | 51.13 N | 0.35 E |
| Chartwell ⊥ | 260 | 51.14 N | 0.05 E |
| Char Us nuur ⊜ | 90 | 48.00 N | 92.10 E |
| Charutajuvom | 24 | 66.49 N | 59.30 E |
| Chās | 126 | 23.38 N | 86.10 E |
| Chasav'urt | 84 | 43.15 N | 46.37 E |
| Chascomús | 258 | 35.34 S | 58.01 W |
| Chascomús, Laguna ⊜ | 258 | 35.36 S | 58.01 W |
| Chašdala | 85 | 39.42 N | 67.07 E |
| Chase, B.C., Can. | 182 | 50.49 N | 119.41 W |
| Chase, Ak., U.S. | 180 | 62.27 N | 150.07 W |
| Chase, Ks., U.S. | 198 | 38.21 N | 98.20 W |
| Chase, Md., U.S. | 208 | 39.21 N | 76.22 W |
| Chase, Mount ∧ | 188 | 46.07 N | 68.29 W |
| Chase Brook ≃ | 283 | 42.48 N | 71.27 W |
| Chase City | 192 | 36.47 N | 78.27 W |
| Chase Field Naval Air Station ■ | 196 | 28.21 N | 97.40 W |
| Chasefu | 154 | 11.55 S | 33.08 E |
| Chase Lake | 212 | 43.46 N | 75.19 W |
| Chase River | 224 | 49.08 N | 123.55 W |
| Chashma Barrage ➤[6] | 123 | 32.26 N | 71.23 E |
| Chasicó | 254 | 40.18 S | 68.58 W |
| Chasidaba | 104 | 42.19 N | 121.19 E |
| Chasiv Yar | 83 | 48.35 N | 37.50 E |
| Chaska | 190 | 44.47 N | 93.36 W |
| Chaslands Mistake › | 172 | 46.38 S | 169.22 E |
| Chasŏng | 98 | 41.27 N | 126.37 E |
| Chasŏngganggu | 98 | 41.34 N | 126.36 E |
| Chassahowitzka | 220 | 28.43 N | 82.34 W |
| Chassahowitzka Bay ⊂ | 220 | 28.41 N | 82.40 W |
| Chassahowitzka Swamp ≡ | 220 | 28.38 N | 82.37 W |
| Chasseron, Mont ∧ | 58 | 46.51 N | 6.33 E |
| Chasse-sur-Rhône | 62 | 45.34 N | 4.49 E |
| Chassezac ≃ | 62 | 44.26 N | 4.19 E |
| Chašuri | 84 | 42.00 N | 43.36 E |
| Chasurta | 88 | 52.17 N | 108.52 E |
| Chasuta | 248 | 6.35 S | 76.11 W |
| Chāt | 128 | 37.59 N | 55.16 E |
| Chatanbulag | 102 | 43.09 N | 109.08 E |
| Chatanga | 74 | 71.58 N | 102.30 E |
| Chatanga ≃ | 74 | 72.55 N | 106.00 E |
| Chatangskij zaliv ⊂ | 74 | 73.30 N | 109.00 E |
| Chatanika | 180 | 65.07 N | 147.31 W |
| Chatanika ≃ | 180 | 65.04 N | 149.18 W |
| Château-Arnoux | 62 | 44.06 N | 6.00 E |
| Chateaubelair | 241h | 13.17 N | 61.15 W |
| Châteaubriant | 32 | 47.43 N | 1.23 W |
| Château-Chinon | 32 | 47.04 N | 3.56 E |
| Château d'Oex | 58 | 46.28 N | 7.08 E |
| Château-du-Loir | 50 | 47.42 N | 0.25 E |
| Châteaudun | 50 | 48.05 N | 1.20 E |
| Châteaufort | 261 | 48.44 N | 2.06 E |
| Chateaugay | 206 | 44.55 N | 74.04 W |
| Château-Gontier | 32 | 47.50 N | 0.42 W |
| Châteauguay | 206 | 45.23 N | 73.45 W |
| Châteauguay ▫[6] | 206 | 45.15 N | 73.45 W |
| Châteauguay ≃ | 188 | 45.24 N | 73.45 W |
| Châteauguay-Centre | 206 | 45.21 N | 73.45 W |
| Châteauguay Heights | 275a | 45.23 N | 73.44 W |
| Château-Landon | 50 | 48.09 N | 2.42 E |
| Château-la-Vallière | 50 | 47.33 N | 0.19 E |
| Châteaulin | 32 | 48.12 N | 4.05 W |
| Châteaumeillant | 32 | 46.34 N | 2.12 E |
| Châteauneuf | 62 | 43.23 N | 5.10 E |
| Châteauneuf-de-Randon | 62 | 44.39 N | 3.40 E |
| Châteauneuf-du-Pape | 62 | 44.03 N | 4.50 E |
| Châteauneuf-du-Rhône | 62 | 44.29 N | 4.43 E |
| Châteauneuf-en-Thymerais | 50 | 48.35 N | 1.15 E |
| Châteauneuf-sur-Charente | 32 | 45.36 N | 0.03 W |
| Châteauneuf-sur-Loire | 50 | 47.52 N | 2.14 E |
| Châteauneuf-sur-Sarthe | 32 | 47.41 N | 0.30 W |
| Châteauneuf-Val-de-Bargis | 50 | 47.17 N | 3.14 E |
| Château-Porcien | 50 | 49.32 N | 4.15 E |
| Château-Queyras | 62 | 44.45 N | 6.47 E |
| Châteauredon | 62 | 44.01 N | 6.13 E |
| Châteaurenard, Fr. | 50 | 47.56 N | 2.56 E |
| Châteaurenard, Fr. | 62 | 43.53 N | 4.51 E |
| Château-Renault | 50 | 47.35 N | 0.55 E |
| Château-Richer | 186 | 46.58 N | 71.01 W |
| Châteauroux | 32 | 46.49 N | 1.42 E |
| Château-Salins | 56 | 48.49 N | 6.30 E |
| Château-Thierry | 50 | 49.03 N | 3.24 E |
| Châteauvillain | 58 | 48.02 N | 4.55 E |
| Châtel | 58 | 46.17 N | 6.50 E |
| Châtel-Censoir | 50 | 47.31 N | 3.38 E |
| Châtelet | 50 | 50.24 N | 4.31 E |
| Châtelineau | 56 | 50.25 N | 4.31 E |
| Châtellerault | 32 | 46.49 N | 0.33 E |
| Châtel-Saint-Denis | 58 | 46.32 N | 6.54 E |
| Châtel-sur-Moselle | 58 | 48.18 N | 6.24 E |
| Châtelus-Malvaleix | 32 | 46.18 N | 2.01 E |
| Châtenay-en-France | 261 | 49.04 N | 2.27 E |
| Châtenay-Malabry | 261 | 48.46 N | 2.17 E |
| Châtenois, Fr. | 58 | 48.18 N | 5.50 E |
| Châtenois, Fr. | 58 | 48.16 N | 7.24 E |
| Châtenois-les-Forges | 58 | 47.34 N | 6.51 E |
| Chater ≃ | 42 | 52.38 N | 0.32 W |
| Chatfield, Mn., U.S. | 190 | 43.50 N | 92.11 W |
| Chatfield, Oh., U.S. | 214 | 40.57 N | 82.56 W |
| Chatgal | 88 | 50.26 N | 100.09 E |
| Chatham, N.B., Can. | 186 | 47.02 N | 65.28 W |
| Chatham, On., Can. | 214 | 42.24 N | 82.11 W |
| Chatham, Eng., U.K. | 42 | 51.23 N | 0.32 E |
| Chatham, Il., U.S. | 219 | 39.40 N | 89.42 W |
| Chatham, La., U.S. | 194 | 32.18 N | 92.27 W |
| Chatham, Ma., U.S. | 207 | 41.40 N | 69.57 W |
| Chatham, N.J., U.S. | 210 | 40.44 N | 74.23 W |
| Chatham, N.Y., U.S. | 210 | 42.21 N | 73.35 W |
| Chatham, Oh., U.S. | 214 | 41.06 N | 82.01 W |
| Chatham, Pa., U.S. | 208 | 39.51 N | 75.49 W |
| Chatham, Va., U.S. | 192 | 36.49 N | 79.23 W |
| Chatham ➤[8] | 278 | 41.45 N | 87.37 W |
| Chatham ≃ | 220 | 25.42 N | 81.17 W |
| Chatham, Isla I | 254 | 50.40 S | 74.20 W |
| Chatham Head | 186 | 47.00 N | 65.33 W |
| Chatham Islands II | 14 | 43.55 S | 176.30 W |
| Chatham Rise ✣[3] | 14 | 43.30 S | 178.00 W |
| Chatham Sound ʯ | 182 | 54.32 N | 130.35 W |
| Chatham Strait ʯ | 180 | 57.30 N | 134.45 W |
| Chatian | 100 | 27.54 N | 118.58 E |
| Châtillon, Fr. | 261 | 48.48 N | 2.17 E |
| Châtillon, It. | 62 | 45.45 N | 7.37 E |
| Châtillon-Coligny | 50 | 47.50 N | 2.51 E |
| Châtillon-en-Bazois | 32 | 47.03 N | 3.40 E |
| Châtillon-en-Diois | 62 | 44.41 N | 5.28 E |
| Châtillon-la-Borde | 261 | 48.33 N | 2.49 E |
| Châtillon-sur-Chalaronne | 58 | 46.07 N | 4.58 E |
| Châtillon-sur-Indre | 32 | 46.59 N | 1.11 E |
| Châtillon-sur-Loire | 50 | 47.35 N | 2.45 E |
| Châtillon-sur-Marne | 50 | 49.06 N | 3.45 E |
| Châtillon-sur-Seine | 58 | 47.51 N | 4.33 E |
| Chating | 106 | 31.21 N | 119.25 E |
| Chātmohar | 126 | 24.13 N | 89.15 E |
| Chat Moss ➤[3] | 262 | 53.27 N | 2.27 W |
| Chato, Cerro ∧ | 254 | 42.29 S | 72.01 W |
| Chatom | 194 | 31.27 N | 88.15 W |
| Chatonville | 261 | 48.33 N | 1.52 E |
| Chatou | 261 | 48.54 N | 2.09 E |
| Chatpur ➤[8] | 272b | 22.36 N | 88.22 E |
| Chatra, India | 124 | 24.13 N | 84.52 E |
| Chatra, India | 272b | 22.46 N | 88.20 E |
| Châtres | 261 | 48.43 N | 2.49 E |
| Chats, Lac des ⊜ | 212 | 45.28 N | 76.23 W |
| Chatsquot Mountain ∧ | 182 | 53.08 N | 127.30 W |
| Chatswood | 274a | 33.48 S | 151.12 E |
| Chatsworth, Austl. | 166 | 21.58 S | 140.19 E |
| Chatsworth, On., Can. | 212 | 44.27 N | 80.54 W |
| Chatsworth, Ga., U.S. | 192 | 34.45 N | 84.46 W |
| Chatsworth, Il., U.S. | 216 | 40.45 N | 88.17 W |
| Chatsworth, N.J., U.S. | 208 | 39.49 N | 74.32 W |
| Chatsworth, Zimb. | 154 | 19.38 S | 31.13 E |
| Chatsworth ➤[8] | 280 | 34.15 N | 118.36 W |
| Chatsworth House ⊍ | 44 | 53.13 N | 1.36 W |
| Chatsworth Reservoir ⊜[1] | 228 | 34.14 N | 118.37 W |
| Chattahoochee | 192 | 30.42 N | 84.50 W |
| Chattahoochee ≃ | 192 | 30.52 N | 84.57 W |
| Chattanooga, Oh., U.S. | 216 | 40.38 N | 84.47 W |
| Chattanooga, Tn., U.S. | 194 | 35.02 N | 85.18 W |
| Chattaroy | 192 | 37.42 N | 82.16 W |
| Chattenden | 260 | 51.25 N | 0.32 E |
| Chatteris | 42 | 52.27 N | 0.03 E |
| Châttillon-de-Michaille | 58 | 46.08 N | 5.47 E |
| Chattolanee | 284b | 39.24 N | 76.45 W |
| Chatton | 44 | 55.33 N | 1.55 W |
| Chatun' | 82 | 55.00 N | 37.50 E |
| Chaturat | 110 | 15.34 N | 101.51 E |
| Chatwood | 208 | 39.58 N | 75.35 W |
| Chatyrka | 74 | 62.03 N | 175.15 E |
| Chaubaria | 126 | 22.59 N | 88.40 E |
| Chaubourg, Mount ∧[2] | 241f | 14.02 N | 60.57 W |
| Chauconin | 261 | 48.58 N | 2.51 E |
| Chaudes-Aigues | 32 | 44.51 N | 3.00 E |
| Chaudfontaine | 56 | 50.35 N | 5.38 E |
| Chaudière ≃ | 186 | 46.45 N | 71.17 W |
| Chau Doc | 110 | 10.42 N | 105.07 E |
| Chauekuktuli, Lake ⊜ | 180 | 60.03 N | 158.45 W |
| Chauffayer | 62 | 44.45 N | 6.01 E |
| Chaugācha, Bngl. | 126 | 23.16 N | 89.01 E |
| Chaugācha, Bngl. | 126 | 23.16 N | 89.01 E |
| Chauhtan | 120 | 25.29 N | 71.04 E |
| Chauk | 110 | 20.54 N | 94.50 E |
| Chaukhandi | 272a | 28.37 N | 77.24 E |
| Chaullay | 248 | 12.57 S | 72.39 W |
| Chaulnes | 50 | 49.49 N | 2.48 E |
| Chaumergy | 58 | 46.51 N | 5.29 E |
| Chaumes-en-Brie | 261 | 48.40 N | 2.51 E |
| Chaumont, Fr. | 58 | 48.07 N | 5.08 E |
| Chaumont, N.Y., U.S. | 212 | 44.04 N | 76.07 W |
| Chaumont ≃ | 212 | 44.04 N | 76.08 W |
| Chaumont Bay ⊂ | 212 | 44.02 N | 76.13 W |
| Chaumont-en-Vexin | 50 | 49.16 N | 1.53 E |
| Chaumont-Porcien | 50 | 49.39 N | 4.15 E |
| Chaumont-sur-Aire | 56 | 48.56 N | 5.15 E |
| Chaumont-sur-Loire | 50 | 47.29 N | 1.11 E |
| Chaumont-sur-Tharonne | 50 | 47.37 N | 1.54 E |
| Chaumua | 272b | 22.39 N | 88.33 E |
| Chauncey | 188 | 39.23 N | 82.07 W |
| Chaŭn-do I | 98 | 34.53 N | 126.03 E |
| Chaungwabyin | 110 | 13.41 N | 98.22 E |
| Chaungzon | 110 | 16.22 N | 97.32 E |
| Chauny | 50 | 49.37 N | 3.13 E |
| Chaupāran | 124 | 24.23 N | 85.15 E |
| Chaussin | 58 | 46.58 N | 5.25 E |
| Chausu-yama ∧ | 94 | 35.14 N | 137.39 E |
| Chausuyama-kofun ⊥ | 94 | 36.25 N | 139.50 E |
| Chautārā | 124 | 27.46 N | 85.42 E |
| Chautauqua | 214 | 42.12 N | 79.28 W |
| Chautauqua ▫[6] | 214 | 42.15 N | 79.30 W |
| Chautauqua Creek ≃ | 214 | 42.20 N | 79.36 W |
| Chautauqua Lake ⊜ | 214 | 42.12 N | 79.27 W |
| Chautengo, Laguna ⊂ | 234 | 16.37 N | 99.07 W |
| Chauvigny | 32 | 46.34 N | 0.39 E |
| Chauvin, Ab., Can. | 184 | 52.42 N | 110.07 W |
| Chauvin, La., U.S. | 194 | 29.26 N | 90.35 W |
| Chauvirey-le-Châtel | 58 | 47.47 N | 5.45 E |
| Chauvry | 261 | 49.03 N | 2.16 E |
| Chavakkad | 122 | 10.32 N | 76.06 E |
| Chaval | 250 | 3.02 S | 41.15 W |
| Chavanges | 58 | 48.31 N | 4.34 E |
| Chavannes, Lac ⊜ | 190 | 46.51 N | 77.10 W |
| Chavarría, Arg. | 252 | 28.57 S | 58.35 W |
| Chavarría, Perú | 286d | 12.01 S | 77.05 W |
| Chavast | 85 | 40.13 N | 68.50 E |
| Chavenay | 261 | 48.51 N | 1.59 E |
| Chavenay-Villepreux, Aérodrome de ⊠ | 261 | 48.51 N | 1.58 E |
| Chavertovo | 82 | 54.17 N | 39.12 E |
| Chaves, Bra. | 250 | 0.10 S | 49.55 W |
| Chaves, Port. | 34 | 41.44 N | 7.28 W |
| Chaville | 261 | 48.48 N | 2.10 E |
| Chaviña | 248 | 14.59 S | 73.50 W |
| Cháviva | 246 | 4.22 N | 72.20 W |
| Chavki | 82 | 54.20 N | 38.13 E |
| Chavornay | 58 | 46.43 N | 6.34 E |
| Chavuma | 152 | 13.05 S | 22.40 E |
| Chawa'nanake | 120 | 31.36 N | 89.41 E |
| Chawang | 110 | 8.25 N | 99.30 E |
| Chawinda | 123 | 32.21 N | 74.42 E |
| Chay ≃ | 110 | 21.39 N | 105.12 E |
| Chayanta | 248 | 18.27 S | 66.30 W |
| Chayuan, Zhg. | 100 | 29.20 N | 121.34 E |
| Chayuan, Zhg. | 100 | 27.40 N | 112.57 E |
| Chayue | 106 | 30.49 N | 119.21 E |
| Chazay-d'Azergues | 62 | 45.53 N | 4.37 E |
| Chazelles-sur-Lyon | 62 | 45.38 N | 4.23 E |
| Chazratišoch, chrebet ⋀ | 85 | 38.30 N | 70.15 E |
| Chazy | 188 | 44.53 N | 73.26 W |
| Chbar ≃ | 110 | 13.19 N | 107.05 E |
| Cheadle, Eng., U.K. | 42 | 52.59 N | 1.59 W |
| Cheadle, Eng., U.K. | 44 | 53.24 N | 2.13 W |
| Cheadle Hulme | 262 | 53.22 N | 2.12 W |
| Cheaha Mountain ∧ | 194 | 33.30 N | 85.47 W |
| Cheakamus Indian Reserve ➤[4] | 182 | 49.48 N | 123.11 W |
| Cheam ➤[8] | 260 | 51.21 N | 0.13 W |
| Cheam View | 224 | 49.15 N | 121.41 W |
| Cheapside | 222 | 29.17 N | 97.24 W |
| Cheat ≃ | 188 | 39.45 N | 79.54 W |
| Cheat, Shavers Fork ≃ | 188 | 39.06 N | 79.33 W |


**Symbols** in the index entries represent the broad categories identified in the key at the right. Symbols with superior numbers (⋀[1]) identify subcategories (see complete key on page *I · 1).*

**Symbole** im Register stellen die rechts im Schlüssel erklärten Kategorien dar. Symbole mit hochgestellten Ziffern (⋀[1]) bezeichnen Unterabteilungen einer Kategorie (vgl. vollständiger Schlüssel auf Seite *I · 1).*

**Los símbolos** incluídos en el texto del índice representan las grandes categorías identificadas con la clave a la derecha. Los símbolos con numeros en su parte superior (⋀[1]) identifican las subcategorías (véase la clave completa en la página *I · 1).*

**Les symboles** de l'index représentent les catégories indiquées dans la légende à droite. Les symboles suivis d'un indice (⋀[1]) représentent des sous-catégories (voir légende complète à la page *I · 1).*

**Os símbolos** incluídos no texto do índice representam as grandes categorias identificadas com a chave à direita. Os símbolos com números em sua parte superior (⋀[1]) identificam as subcategorias (veja-se a chave completa à página *I · 1).*

| | English | Deutsch | Español | Français | Português |
|---|---|---|---|---|---|
| ∧ | Mountain | Berg | Montaña | Montagne | Montanha |
| ⋀ | Mountains | Gebirge | Montañas | Montagnes | Montanhas |
| )( | Pass | Paß | Paso | Col | Passo |
| ∨ | Valley, Canyon | Tal, Cañon | Valle, Cañón | Vallée, Canyon | Vale, Canhão |
| ≃ | Plain | Ebene | Llano | Plaine | Planície |
| › | Cape | Kap | Cabo | Cap | Cabo |
| I | Island | Insel | Isla | Île | Ilha |
| II | Islands | Inseln | Islas | Îles | Ilhas |
| ⊥ | Other Topographic Features | Andere Topographische Objekte | Otros Elementos Topográficos | Autres données topographiques | Outros acidentes topográficos |

ESPAÑOL — Nombre | Página | Lat.°′ | Long.°′ W = Oeste

FRANÇAIS — Nom | Page | Lat.°′ | Long.°′ W = Ouest

PORTUGUÊS — Nome | Página | Lat.°′ | Long.°′ W = Oeste



| | | | |
|---|---|---|---|
| Cheb | 54 | 50.01 N | 12.25 E |
| Chebacco Lake ⊜ | 283 | 42.37 N | 70.48 W |
| Chebanse | 216 | 41.00 N | 87.54 W |
| Chebba | 148 | 35.14 N | 10.02 E |
| Chebeigou | 89 | 43.28 N | 127.04 E |
| Chebogue Point › | 186 | 43.45 N | 66.07 W |
| Cheboksary → Čeboksary | 80 | 56.09 N | 47.15 E |
| Cheboygan | 190 | 45.38 N | 84.28 W |
| Chech, Erg ◆[2] | 148 | 25.00 N | 2.15 W |
| Chechel'nyk | 78 | 48.14 N | 29.21 E |
| Ch'ech'eng | 100 | 22.05 N | 120.42 E |
| Chechnya → Čečnja-Ingušetija □[3] | 84 | 43.15 N | 45.40 E |
| Chech'on | 98 | 37.08 N | 128.12 E |
| Chęciny | 30 | 50.48 N | 20.28 E |
| Checleset Bay ϲ | 182 | 50.03 N | 127.40 W |
| Checotah | 196 | 35.28 N | 95.31 W |
| Chedabucto Bay ϲ | 186 | 45.23 N | 61.10 W |
| Chedaoyu | 105 | 40.22 N | 117.57 E |
| Cheddar | 42 | 51.17 N | 2.46 W |
| Cheddleton | 44 | 53.04 N | 2.02 W |
| Cheduba Island I | 110 | 18.48 N | 93.38 E |
| Cheduba Strait ʯ | 110 | 18.56 N | 93.45 E |
| Chedun | 100 | 24.09 N | 117.19 E |
| Chée ≃ | 56 | 48.45 N | 4.39 E |
| Cheektowaga | 210 | 42.55 N | 78.46 W |
| Cheepie | 166 | 26.39 S | 145.01 E |
| Cheesequake | 276 | 40.25 N | 74.17 W |
| Cheesequake Creek ≃ | 276 | 40.28 N | 74.16 W |
| Cheesequake State Park ♦ | 276 | 40.26 N | 74.16 W |
| Cheetham Hill ◆[8] | 262 | 53.31 N | 2.15 W |
| Chefang, Zhg. | 104 | 41.35 N | 121.26 E |
| Chefang, Zhg. | 106 | 31.15 N | 120.45 E |
| Chef-Boutonne | 32 | 46.07 N | 0.04 W |
| Chefoo → Yantai | 98 | 37.33 N | 121.20 E |
| Chefornak | 180 | 60.13 N | 164.12 W |
| Chefumage ≃ | 152 | 12.15 S | 22.19 E |
| Chegar Perah | 114 | 4.25 N | 101.56 E |
| Chegga ⍑[4] | 148 | 25.30 N | 5.46 W |
| Chegutu | 154 | 18.10 S | 30.14 E |
| Chehalis | 224 | 46.39 N | 122.57 W |
| Chehalis ≃ | 224 | 46.57 N | 123.50 W |
| Chehalis, Point › | 224 | 46.55 N | 124.07 W |
| Chehalis, South Fork ≃ | 224 | 46.40 N | 123.15 W |
| Chehalis Indian Reservation ◆[4] | 224 | 46.49 N | 123.13 W |
| Chehe | 102 | 25.00 N | 107.38 E |
| Chehel Dokhtarān | 128 | 35.06 N | 62.19 E |
| Cheheqiao | 105 | 40.21 N | 118.16 E |
| Cheil, Ras el › | 144 | 7.44 N | 49.50 E |
| Cheine | 54 | 52.52 N | 11.04 E |
| Cheiron, Cime du ʌ | 62 | 43.49 N | 6.58 E |
| Chejiatun | 104 | 41.57 N | 123.01 E |
| Chejiawopeng | 104 | 42.29 N | 123.07 E |
| Cheju | 90 | 33.31 N | 126.32 E |
| Cheju-do I | 90 | 33.20 N | 126.30 E |
| Chekiang → Zhejiang □[4] | 100 | 29.00 N | 120.00 E |
| Chek Jawa, Tanjong › | 271c | 1.24 N | 104.00 E |
| Chek Kang | 271d | 22.26 N | 114.21 E |
| Chela, Serra da ʌ | 152 | 16.00 S | 13.10 E |
| Chelan | 202 | 47.50 N | 120.00 W |
| Chelan □[6] | 224 | 47.56 N | 120.52 W |
| Chelan, Lake ⊜ | 202 | 48.05 N | 120.30 W |
| Chelas ◆[8] | 266c | 38.45 N | 9.07 W |
| Cheleiros | 266c | 38.53 N | 9.20 W |
| Cheleiros, Ribeira de ≃ | 266c | 38.54 N | 9.22 W |
| Chelelektu | 144 | 6.00 N | 38.09 E |
| Chelford | 262 | 53.16 N | 2.16 W |
| Chelforó | 252 | 39.04 S | 66.32 W |
| Chelghoum el Aïd | 148 | 36.10 N | 6.10 E |
| Chélia, Djebel ʌ | 148 | 35.17 N | 6.40 E |
| Chéliff, Oued ≃ | 148 | 36.01 N | 0.07 E |
| Chelīk-e Yās Khān | 120 | 37.05 N | 66.14 E |
| Chellaston | 42 | 52.53 N | 1.27 W |
| Chelles | 50 | 48.53 N | 2.36 E |
| Chelles-le-Pin, Aérodrome de ⊠ | 261 | 48.55 N | 2.35 E |
| Chełm | 30 | 51.10 N | 23.28 E |
| Chełm □[4] | 30 | 51.20 N | 23.20 E |
| Chelmer ≃ | 42 | 51.44 N | 0.42 E |
| Chelmer and Blackwater Navigation ≍ | 260 | 51.44 N | 0.43 E |
| Chełmno | 30 | 53.22 N | 18.26 E |
| Chelmorton | 262 | 53.13 N | 1.50 W |
| Chelmsford, On., Can. | 190 | 46.35 N | 81.12 W |
| Chelmsford, Eng., U.K. | 42 | 51.44 N | 0.28 E |
| Chelmsford, Ma., U.S. | 207 | 42.35 N | 71.21 W |
| Chelmsford □[8] | 260 | 51.44 N | 0.30 E |
| Chelmsford Dam ⊜[1] | 158 | 28.02 S | 29.52 E |
| Chełmża | 30 | 53.12 N | 18.37 E |
| Chelsea, Austl. | 169 | 38.03 S | 145.07 E |
| Chelsea, Ia., U.S. | 190 | 41.55 N | 92.23 W |
| Chelsea, Ma., U.S. | 207 | 42.23 N | 71.02 W |
| Chelsea, Mi., U.S. | 216 | 42.19 N | 84.01 W |
| Chelsea, Ok., U.S. | 196 | 36.32 N | 95.25 W |
| Chelsea, Pa., U.S. | 285 | 39.52 N | 75.28 W |
| Chelsea, Vt., U.S. | 188 | 43.59 N | 72.26 W |
| Chelsea Estates | 208 | 39.41 N | 75.36 W |
| Chelsfield ◆[8] | 260 | 51.21 N | 0.08 E |
| Cheltenham, Austl. | 274a | 33.46 S | 151.05 E |
| Cheltenham, Austl. | 274b | 37.58 S | 145.03 E |
| Cheltenham, Eng., U.K. | 42 | 51.54 N | 2.04 W |
| Cheltenham, Md., U.S. | 208 | 38.44 N | 76.49 W |
| Cheltenham, Pa., U.S. | 208 | 40.03 N | 75.05 W |
| Chel'ul'ja | 26 | 61.44 N | 30.41 E |
| Chelvand | 128 | 38.18 N | 48.50 E |
| Chelyabinsk → Čel'abinsk | 86 | 55.10 N | 61.24 E |
| Chelyāma | 126 | 23.37 N | 86.33 E |
| Chelyan | 188 | 38.11 N | 81.29 W |
| Chemaïa | 148 | 32.05 N | 8.37 W |
| Chemainus | 224 | 48.55 N | 123.43 W |
| Chemainus ⊜ | 224 | 48.53 N | 123.41 W |
| Chemaogang | 106 | 31.33 N | 121.52 E |
| Chemax | 232 | 20.39 N | 87.56 W |
| Chemba | 154 | 17.08 S | 34.52 E |
| Chembūr ◆[8] | 272c | 19.04 N | 72.54 E |
| Chemchâm, Sebkhet ⊜ | 148 | 21.05 N | 12.05 W |
| Chemčik ≃ | 86 | 51.47 N | 92.00 E |
| Chemehuevi Indian Reservation ◆[4] | 204 | 34.30 N | 114.23 W |
| Chemer | 78 | 51.07 N | 31.13 E |
| Chemerivtsi | 78 | 49.01 N | 26.21 E |
| Chemillé | 32 | 47.13 N | 0.44 W |
| Chemin | 58 | 46.59 N | 5.19 E |
| Cheminis, Colline ʌ[2] | 190 | 48.08 N | 79.31 W |
| Chemnitz | 54 | 50.50 N | 12.55 E |
| Chemnitz ≃ | 54 | 50.59 N | 12.47 E |
| Chemor | 114 | 4.43 N | 101.07 E |
| Chemulpo → Inch'ŏn | 98 | 37.28 N | 126.38 E |
| Chemult | 202 | 43.13 N | 121.46 W |
| Chemung, Il., U.S. | 216 | 42.25 N | 88.40 W |
| Chemung, N.Y., U.S. | 210 | 42.01 N | 76.37 W |
| Chemung □[6] | 210 | 42.06 N | 76.49 W |
| Chemung ≃ | 210 | 41.55 N | 76.31 W |
| Chemung County Airport ⊠ | 210 | 42.10 N | 76.53 W |
| Chemung Lake ⊜ | 212 | 44.25 N | 78.22 W |
| Chena, Cerro ʌ | 286e | 33.36 N | 70.45 W |
| Chenāb ≃ | 123 | 29.23 N | 71.02 E |
| Chenachane | 148 | 26.00 N | 4.15 W |
| Chenail Ecarté ≃[1] | 214 | 42.28 N | 82.29 W |
| Chenango □[6] | 210 | 42.32 N | 75.31 W |
| Chenango ≃ | 210 | 42.05 N | 75.55 W |
| Chenango Bridge | 210 | 42.10 N | 75.51 W |
| Chenango Forks | 210 | 42.14 N | 75.50 W |
| Chenango Valley State Park ♦ | 210 | 42.14 N | 75.50 W |
| Chenārān | 128 | 36.39 N | 59.06 E |
| Chenaut | 258 | 34.15 S | 59.13 W |
| Chen Barag Qi | 89 | 49.21 N | 119.31 E |
| Chenbofang | 98 | 37.27 N | 115.18 E |
| Chencai | 100 | 29.37 N | 120.22 E |
| Chenchiang → Zhenjiang | 106 | 32.13 N | 119.26 E |
| Chencun | 100 | 22.58 N | 113.13 E |
| Chendai | 100 | 23.48 N | 117.24 E |
| Chendauli ◆[8] | 272c | 19.07 N | 72.54 E |
| Chenderiang | 114 | 4.16 N | 101.14 E |
| Chenderoh, Tasek ⊜ | 114 | 4.58 N | 100.57 E |
| Chêne, Rivière du ≃, P.Q., Can. | 206 | 46.34 N | 72.00 W |
| Chêne, Rivière du ≃, P.Q., Can. | 206 | 45.33 N | 73.54 W |
| Chenele | 152 | 12.54 S | 23.54 E |
| Chenequa | 216 | 43.06 N | 88.23 W |
| Chénéville | 206 | 45.53 N | 75.03 W |
| Cheney, Ks., U.S. | 198 | 37.37 N | 97.46 W |
| Cheney, Wa., U.S. | 202 | 47.29 N | 117.34 W |
| Cheney Reservoir ⊜[1] | 198 | 37.45 N | 97.50 W |
| Cheneys Point | 214 | 42.08 N | 79.24 W |
| Cheneyville | 194 | 31.00 N | 92.17 W |
| Chenfang | 100 | 28.01 N | 117.32 E |
| Cheng'an | 98 | 36.27 N | 114.41 E |
| Chengannūr | 122 | 9.20 N | 76.38 E |
| Chengbu | 102 | 26.18 N | 110.13 E |
| Chengchow → Zhengzhou | 102 | 34.48 N | 113.39 E |
| Chengde (Xiabancheng), Zhg. | 105 | 40.47 N | 118.08 E |
| Chengde, Zhg. | 105 | 40.58 N | 117.53 E |
| Chengdu (Chengtu) | 107 | 30.39 N | 104.04 E |
| Chengele | 120 | 28.47 N | 96.16 E |
| Chenggang | 100 | 26.32 N | 115.26 E |
| Chenggu | 102 | 33.10 N | 107.22 E |
| Chenghai | 100 | 23.30 N | 116.46 E |
| Cheng Hu ⊜ | 106 | 31.13 N | 120.49 E |
| Chenghuang | 102 | 22.32 N | 109.39 E |
| Chengjia | 100 | 24.50 N | 112.50 E |
| Chengjiahe | 100 | 32.18 N | 112.27 E |
| Chengjiang | 102 | 24.45 N | 102.54 E |
| Chengjiangzhen | 107 | 29.52 N | 106.23 E |
| Chengjiazhen | 107 | 29.24 N | 104.36 E |
| Chengkou | 102 | 31.54 N | 108.41 E |
| Chenglingji | 100 | 29.26 N | 113.09 E |
| Chenglong | 100 | 24.51 N | 114.41 E |
| Chengmai | 110 | 19.48 N | 110.02 E |
| Chengmao | 106 | 31.10 N | 120.53 E |
| Chengpu | 100 | 25.46 N | 118.48 E |
| Chengqian | 98 | 35.21 N | 117.21 E |
| Chengqianwei | 100 | 28.09 N | 116.13 E |
| Chengshan Jiao › | 98 | 37.24 N | 122.42 E |
| Chengteh → Chengde | 105 | 40.58 N | 117.53 E |
| Chengtu → Chengdu | 107 | 30.39 N | 104.04 E |
| Ch'engtzuliao | 269d | 25.06 N | 121.27 E |
| Chengwu | 98 | 34.58 N | 115.52 E |
| Chengxian | 102 | 33.43 N | 105.41 E |
| Chengxi Hu ⊜ | 100 | 32.24 N | 116.15 E |
| Chengyang, Zhg. | 98 | 36.18 N | 120.22 E |
| Chengyang, Zhg. | 100 | 29.59 N | 119.44 E |
| Chengzi, Zhg. | 98 | 41.57 N | 117.16 E |
| Chengzi, Zhg. | 105 | 39.58 N | 116.02 E |
| Chengzitan | 98 | 39.30 N | 122.30 E |
| Ch'enhsien → Chenxian | 100 | 25.48 N | 112.59 E |
| Chen Hu ⊜ | 100 | 30.29 N | 113.22 E |
| Chenies | 260 | 51.41 N | 0.32 W |
| Chenil, Lac ⊜ | 186 | 51.51 N | 59.41 W |
| Cheniménil | 58 | 48.08 N | 6.36 E |
| Chenji | 100 | 33.50 N | 119.11 E |
| Chenjiachang, Zhg. | 107 | 30.04 N | 105.15 E |
| Chenjiachang, Zhg. | 107 | 29.35 N | 104.52 E |
| Chenjiagang | 98 | 34.25 N | 119.49 E |
| Chenjiahe | 102 | 29.28 N | 109.59 E |
| Chenjiaji | 100 | 30.42 N | 114.21 E |
| Chenjiapang | 106 | 31.14 N | 119.42 E |
| Chenjiapu | 105 | 40.31 N | 115.37 E |
| Chenjiaqiao | 106 | 31.27 N | 121.16 E |
| Chenjiatun, Zhg. | 104 | 42.20 N | 124.06 E |
| Chenjiatun, Zhg. | 104 | 40.57 N | 121.01 E |
| Chenjiawan | 106 | 31.02 N | 120.35 E |
| Chenjiaxiang | 100 | 31.29 N | 113.45 E |
| Chenjiazhen | 106 | 31.30 N | 121.48 E |
| Chenjiazui | 105 | 39.17 N | 116.59 E |
| Chenkeng | 100 | 25.06 N | 116.15 E |
| Chenlingjiao | 106 | 30.23 N | 118.47 E |
| Chenliu | 98 | 34.43 N | 114.31 E |
| Chenlong | 269b | 31.17 N | 121.25 E |
| Chennevières | 261 | 49.00 N | 2.07 E |
| Chennevières-lès-Louvres | 261 | 49.03 N | 2.33 E |
| Chenoa | 216 | 40.44 N | 88.43 W |
| Chenonceaux | 50 | 47.20 N | 1.04 E |
| Chenonceaux, Château de ⊥ | 50 | 47.20 N | 1.04 E |
| Chenôve | 58 | 47.17 N | 5.00 E |
| Chenoweth | 224 | 45.37 N | 121.13 W |
| Chenqiao | 98 | 34.58 N | 114.32 E |
| Chenquingqiao | 89 | 49.08 N | 127.16 E |
| Chenshanzhuang | 105 | 39.43 N | 117.30 E |
| Chenshichang | 107 | 29.17 N | 106.00 E |
| Chens-sur-Léman | 58 | 46.20 N | 6.16 E |
| Chentang | 102 | 23.54 N | 110.39 E |
| Chentejn nuruu ⋏ | 88 | 48.30 N | 108.30 E |
| Chentij | 88 | 48.05 N | 109.45 E |
| Chentij □[4] | 88 | 48.00 N | 110.30 E |
| Chenxi | 102 | 27.51 N | 109.59 E |
| Chenxian | 100 | 25.48 N | 112.59 E |
| Chenxiangtun | 104 | 41.36 N | 123.30 E |
| Chenyang, Zhg. | 100 | 33.47 N | 120.10 E |
| Chenyang → Shenyang, Zhg. | 104 | 41.48 N | 123.27 E |
| Cheonan → Ch'ŏnan | 98 | 36.48 N | 127.09 E |
| Cheongju → Ch'ŏngju | 98 | 36.39 N | 127.31 E |
| Cheo Reo | 110 | 13.24 N | 108.27 E |
| Chepachet | 207 | 41.54 N | 71.40 W |
| Chepaúa | 152 | 12.58 S | 22.43 E |
| Chepén | 248 | 7.13 S | 79.27 W |
| Chépénéhé | 175f | 20.47 S | 167.09 E |
| Chepes | 252 | 31.21 S | 66.36 W |
| Chepil' | 78 | 49.19 N | 36.55 E |
| Chepkotet ʌ | 154 | 1.15 N | 35.26 E |
| Chepo | 246 | 9.10 N | 79.06 W |
| Chepstow | 42 | 51.39 N | 2.41 W |
| Cheptainville | 261 | 48.33 N | 2.16 E |
| Cher □[5] | 32 | 47.05 N | 2.30 E |
| Cher ≃ | 32 | 47.21 N | 0.29 E |
| Cheradi, Isole II | 68 | 40.27 N | 17.10 E |
| Cherain | 56 | 50.11 N | 5.52 E |
| Cherán | 234 | 19.41 N | 101.57 W |
| Chéran ≃ | 62 | 45.53 N | 5.56 E |
| Cheranchi | 150 | 12.40 N | 7.42 E |
| Cherangany Hills ⋏[2] | 154 | 1.15 N | 35.27 E |
| Cherasco | 62 | 44.39 N | 7.51 E |
| Cherāt | 123 | 33.49 N | 71.53 E |
| Cheraw | 192 | 34.41 N | 79.53 W |
| Cheraw State Park ♦ | 192 | 34.36 N | 79.55 W |
| Cherbaniani Reef ✣[2] | 122 | 12.18 N | 71.53 E |
| Cherbourg | 32 | 49.39 N | 1.39 W |
| Cherchell | 148 | 36.36 N | 2.12 E |
| Cheremkhovo → Čeremchovo | 88 | 53.09 N | 103.05 E |
| Cheremosh ≃ | 78 | 48.23 N | 25.37 E |
| Chérence | 261 | 49.05 N | 1.41 E |
| Chereponi | 150 | 10.09 N | 0.17 E |
| Cherepovets → Čerepovec | 76 | 59.08 N | 37.54 E |
| Chergui, Chott ech ⊜ | 148 | 34.21 N | 0.30 E |
| Chergui, Île I | 148 | 34.44 N | 11.14 E |
| Chergui, Zahrez ⊜ | 148 | 35.12 N | 3.32 E |
| Cheribon → Cirebon | 115a | 6.44 S | 108.34 E |
| Cherio ≃ | 64 | 45.34 N | 9.51 E |
| Cherita, Sebkhet ⊜ | 36 | 35.21 N | 10.19 E |
| Cheriton | 208 | 37.17 N | 75.58 W |
| Cheriyam Island I | 122 | 10.09 N | 73.40 E |
| Cherkas'ke, Ukr. | 78 | 48.44 N | 35.22 E |
| Cherkas'ke, Ukr. | 83 | 48.50 N | 37.23 E |
| Cherkasy | 78 | 49.26 N | 32.04 E |
| Cherkasy □[4] | 78 | 49.30 N | 31.30 E |
| Cherkessia → Karačajevo-Čerkesija □[3] | 84 | 44.00 N | 42.00 E |
| Cherkessk → Čerkessk | 84 | 44.14 N | 42.04 E |
| Cherlen → Kerulen ≃ | 90 | 48.48 N | 117.00 E |
| Chermside | 171a | 27.23 S | 153.02 E |
| Chernelytsya | 78 | 48.48 N | 25.26 E |
| Chernigov → Chernihiv | 78 | 51.30 N | 31.18 E |
| Chernihiv | 78 | 51.30 N | 31.18 E |
| Chernihiv □[4] | 78 | 51.15 N | 32.00 E |
| Chernihivka | 78 | 47.13 N | 36.14 E |
| Chernivtsi, Ukr. | 78 | 48.33 N | 28.09 E |
| Chernivtsi, Ukr. | 78 | 48.18 N | 25.56 E |
| Chernivtsi □[8] | 78 | 43.30 N | 26.00 E |
| Chernobyl → Chornobyl' | 78 | 51.16 N | 30.14 E |
| Chernofski | 180 | 53.24 N | 167.33 W |
| Chernogorsk → Černogorsk | 86 | 53.49 N | 91.18 E |
| Chernovtsy → Chernivtsi | 78 | 48.18 N | 25.56 E |
| Chernyakhiv | 78 | 50.27 N | 28.39 E |
| Chero ≃ | 62 | 45.03 N | 9.51 E |
| Cherokee, Al., U.S. | 194 | 34.45 N | 87.58 W |
| Cherokee, Ia., U.S. | 198 | 42.44 N | 95.33 W |
| Cherokee, Ks., U.S. | 198 | 37.20 N | 94.48 W |
| Cherokee, Ok., U.S. | 196 | 36.45 N | 98.21 W |
| Cherokee, Tx., U.S. | 196 | 30.59 N | 98.43 W |
| Cherokee □[6] | 222 | 31.48 N | 95.10 W |
| Cherokee, Lake ⊜[1] | 222 | 32.21 N | 94.39 W |
| Cherokee Canal ≍ | 226 | 39.18 N | 121.55 W |
| Cherokee Lake ⊜[1] | 192 | 36.16 N | 83.20 W |
| Cherokee Point › | 192 | 26.16 N | 77.03 W |
| Cherokee Ranch | 208 | 40.25 N | 75.55 W |
| Cherokees, Lake O' The ⊜[1] | 194 | 36.39 N | 94.49 W |
| Cherokee Village | 194 | 36.17 N | 91.30 W |
| Chéroy | 50 | 48.12 N | 3.00 E |
| Cherpuči | 89 | 53.01 N | 138.52 E |
| Cherquenco | 252 | 38.41 S | 72.00 W |
| Cherrabun | 162 | 18.29 S | 125.19 E |
| Cherrapunji | 120 | 25.18 N | 91.42 E |
| Cherry Brook ≃, Ma., U.S. | 283 | 42.23 N | 71.17 W |
| Cherry Brook ≃, N.J., U.S. | 276 | 41.01 N | 74.00 W |
| Cherry City | 279b | 40.29 N | 79.58 W |
| Cherry Creek, B.C., Can. | 224 | 49.17 N | 124.47 W |
| Cherry Creek, N.Y., U.S. | 214 | 42.17 N | 79.06 W |
| Cherry Creek ≃, Az., U.S. | 200 | 33.41 N | 110.49 W |
| Cherry Creek ≃, Ca., U.S. | 226 | 37.53 N | 119.58 W |
| Cherry Creek ≃, Co., U.S. | 198 | 39.45 N | 105.01 W |
| Cherry Creek ≃, Mt., U.S. | 198 | 46.48 N | 105.15 W |
| Cherry Creek ≃, N.D., U.S. | 198 | 47.41 N | 103.02 W |
| Cherry Creek ≃, S.D., U.S. | 198 | 44.36 N | 101.30 W |
| Cherry Creek ≃, Tx., U.S. | 196 | 31.13 N | 103.34 W |
| Cherry Creek, East Fork ≃ | 226 | 38.06 N | 119.47 W |
| Cherry Creek, West Fork ≃ | 226 | 38.04 N | 119.54 W |
| Cherry Fork | 218 | 38.53 N | 83.37 W |
| Cherry Grove, N.Y., U.S. | 210 | 40.39 N | 73.06 W |
| Cherry Grove, Or., U.S. | 224 | 45.26 N | 123.14 W |
| Cherry Hill, Il., U.S. | 278 | 41.32 N | 88.02 W |
| Cherry Hill, N.J., U.S. | 208 | 39.56 N | 75.01 W |
| Cherry Hill ◆[8] | 284b | 39.15 N | 76.38 W |
| Cherry Hill Mall ◆[9] | 285 | 39.56 N | 75.02 W |
| Cherry Island I | 285 | 39.43 N | 75.31 W |
| Cherry Lake ⊜[1] | 226 | 38.00 N | 119.54 W |
| Cherryland | 226 | 37.41 N | 122.06 W |
| Cherry Lane | 279b | 40.34 N | 79.33 W |
| Cherryplain | 210 | 42.38 N | 73.22 W |
| Cherry Point Marine Corps Air Station ■ | 192 | 34.54 N | 76.54 W |
| Cherryvale | 198 | 37.16 N | 95.33 W |
| Cherry Valley, Ar., U.S. | 194 | 35.24 N | 90.45 W |
| Cherry Valley, Ca., U.S. | 228 | 33.57 N | 116.53 W |
| Cherry Valley, Il., U.S. | 216 | 42.14 N | 88.56 W |
| Cherry Valley, Ma., U.S. | 207 | 42.14 N | 71.52 W |
| Cherry Valley, N.Y., U.S. | 210 | 42.47 N | 74.45 W |
| Cherry Valley, Pa., U.S. | 214 | 41.10 N | 79.48 W |
| Cherry Valley Creek ≃ | 210 | 42.35 N | 74.56 W |
| Cherryville, N.C., U.S. | 192 | 35.22 N | 81.22 W |
| Cherryville, Pa., U.S. | 208 | 40.45 N | 75.33 W |
| Cherrywood | 275b | 43.52 N | 79.08 W |
| Chertsey | 42 | 51.24 N | 0.30 W |
| Chervona Kam'yanka | 78 | 48.38 N | 33.26 E |
| Chervonapopivka | 83 | 49.08 N | 38.09 E |
| Chervone, Ukr. | 78 | 51.46 N | 34.04 E |
| Chervone, Ukr. | 78 | 49.57 N | 28.53 E |
| Chervonoarmiys'k, Ukr. | 78 | 50.08 N | 25.16 E |
| Chervonoarmiys'k, Ukr. | 78 | 50.28 N | 28.14 E |
| Chervonohrad | 78 | 50.24 N | 24.14 E |
| Chervonooskils'ke vodoskhovyshche ⊜[1] | 83 | 49.17 N | 37.37 E |
| Chervonopartyzans'k | 83 | 48.04 N | 39.50 E |
| Chervonyy Donets' | 78 | 49.29 N | 36.34 E |
| Chervonyy Oskil | 83 | 49.11 N | 37.26 E |
| Chervonyy Zhovten' | 83 | 48.56 N | 39.23 E |
| Cherwell ≃ | 42 | 51.44 N | 1.15 W |
| Chesaco Park | 284b | 39.19 N | 76.30 W |
| Chesaning | 190 | 43.11 N | 84.06 W |
| Chesapeake | 208 | 36.49 N | 76.16 W |
| Chesapeake and Delaware Canal ≍ | 208 | 39.32 N | 75.51 W |
| Chesapeake and Ohio Canal National Historical Park ♦ | 208 | 39.03 N | 77.16 W |
| Chesapeake Bay ϲ | 208 | 38.40 N | 76.25 W |
| Chesapeake Bay Bridge-Tunnel ◆[5] | 208 | 37.00 N | 76.02 W |
| Chesapeake Beach | 208 | 38.41 N | 76.32 W |
| Chesaw | 182 | 48.56 N | 119.03 W |
| Chesdin, Lake ⊜[1] | 208 | 37.15 N | 77.33 W |
| Cheseaux | 58 | 46.35 N | 6.36 E |
| Chesham | 42 | 51.43 N | 0.38 W |
| Chesham Bois | 260 | 51.41 N | 0.37 W |
| Cheshire, Ct., U.S. | 207 | 41.29 N | 72.54 W |
| Cheshire, Ma., U.S. | 207 | 42.33 N | 73.09 W |
| Cheshire, N.Y., U.S. | 210 | 42.49 N | 77.20 W |
| Cheshire □[6], Eng., U.K. | 44 | 53.23 N | 2.30 W |
| Cheshire □[6], N.H., U.S. | 207 | 42.50 N | 72.15 W |
| Cheshire Plain ≚ | 44 | 53.17 N | 2.40 W |
| Cheshire Reservoir ⊜[1] | 207 | 42.32 N | 73.11 W |
| Chesht-e Sharīf | 128 | 34.21 N | 63.44 E |
| Cheshunt | 42 | 51.43 N | 0.02 W |
| Chesil Beach ⩡[2] | 42 | 50.38 N | 2.33 W |
| Chesilhurst | 285 | 39.43 N | 74.52 W |
| Cheslatta Lake ⊜ | 182 | 53.44 N | 125.18 W |
| Chesley | 212 | 44.17 N | 81.05 W |
| Chesnee | 192 | 35.08 N | 81.51 W |
| Chess ≃ | 260 | 51.38 N | 0.27 W |
| Chessington ◆[8] | 260 | 51.21 N | 0.18 W |
| Chessy | 261 | 48.53 N | 2.46 E |
| Chest Creek ≃ | 214 | 40.53 N | 78.44 W |
| Chester, Eng., U.K. | 44 | 53.12 N | 2.54 W |
| Chester, Ca., U.S. | 204 | 40.18 N | 121.13 W |
| Chester, Ct., U.S. | 207 | 41.24 N | 72.27 W |
| Chester, Il., U.S. | 194 | 37.54 N | 89.49 W |
| Chester, Md., U.S. | 208 | 38.58 N | 76.17 W |
| Chester, Ma., U.S. | 207 | 42.16 N | 72.58 W |
| Chester, Mt., U.S. | 202 | 48.30 N | 110.58 W |
| Chester, Ne., U.S. | 198 | 40.00 N | 97.37 W |
| Chester, N.J., U.S. | 210 | 40.47 N | 74.41 W |
| Chester, Ok., U.S. | 196 | 36.12 N | 98.55 W |
| Chester, Pa., U.S. | 208 | 39.50 N | 75.21 W |
| Chester, S.C., U.S. | 192 | 34.42 N | 81.12 W |
| Chester, Tx., U.S. | 222 | 30.55 N | 94.36 W |
| Chester, Vt., U.S. | 188 | 43.15 N | 72.35 W |
| Chester, Va., U.S. | 208 | 37.21 N | 77.26 W |
| Chester, W.V., U.S. | 214 | 40.36 N | 80.33 W |
| Chester □[6] | 208 | 39.58 N | 75.36 W |
| Chester □[8] | 262 | 53.16 N | 2.52 W |
| Chester ≃ | 208 | 39.00 N | 76.10 W |
| Chester Basin | 186 | 44.34 N | 64.19 W |
| Chesterbrook | 284c | 38.55 N | 77.09 W |
| Chester Brook ≃ | 283 | 42.23 N | 71.14 W |
| Chesterbrook Woods | 284c | 38.56 N | 77.08 W |
| Chester Creek ≃ | 208 | 39.50 N | 75.22 W |
| Chester Creek, East Branch ≃ | 285 | 39.56 N | 75.32 W |
| Chester Creek, West Branch ≃ | 285 | 39.54 N | 75.27 W |
| Chesterfield, Eng., U.K. | 44 | 53.15 N | 1.25 W |
| Chesterfield, Ct., U.S. | 207 | 41.24 N | 72.11 W |
| Chesterfield, Il., U.S. | 219 | 39.15 N | 90.04 W |
| Chesterfield, In., U.S. | 218 | 40.06 N | 85.35 W |
| Chesterfield, Ma., U.S. | 207 | 42.23 N | 72.50 W |
| Chesterfield, S.C., U.S. | 192 | 34.44 N | 80.05 W |
| Chesterfield, Va., U.S. | 192 | 37.22 N | 77.30 W |
| Chesterfield □[6] | 208 | 37.20 N | 77.25 W |
| Chesterfield, Îles II | 160 | 19.30 S | 158.00 E |
| Chesterfield, Nosy I | 157b | 16.20 S | 43.58 E |
| Chesterfield Inlet | 176 | 63.21 N | 90.42 W |
| Chesterfield Inlet ϲ | 176 | 63.25 N | 90.45 W |
| Chester Heights | 285 | 39.53 N | 75.28 W |
| Chester Hill, Austl. | 274a | 33.53 S | 151.00 E |
| Chesterhill, Oh., U.S. | 188 | 39.29 N | 81.51 W |
| Chester Hill, Pa., U.S. | 214 | 40.53 N | 78.14 W |
| Chester Island I | 285 | 39.50 N | 75.21 W |
| Chesterland | 214 | 41.31 N | 81.21 W |
| Chester-le-Street | 44 | 54.52 N | 1.34 W |
| Chester Morse Lake ⊜[1] | 224 | 47.23 N | 121.42 W |
| Chesters | 44 | 55.23 N | 2.36 W |
| Chester Springs | 285 | 40.06 N | 75.37 W |
| Chesterton | 216 | 41.36 N | 87.03 W |
| Chesterton Range ⋏ | 166 | 25.30 S | 147.27 E |
| Chestertown | 208 | 39.12 N | 76.04 W |
| Chesterville, On., Can. | 212 | 45.06 N | 75.14 W |
| Chesterville, Oh., U.S. | 214 | 40.29 N | 82.41 W |
| Chestnut | 219 | 40.03 N | 89.11 W |
| Chestnut Hill, Ma., U.S. | 283 | 42.20 N | 71.10 W |
| Chestnut Hill, Pa., U.S. | 210 | 40.04 N | 75.12 W |
| Chestnut Hill ◆[8] | 285 | 40.04 N | 75.13 W |
| Chestnut Hill ʌ[2] | 285 | 40.13 N | 75.45 W |
| Chestnut Hill Estates | 285 | 39.40 N | 75.42 W |
| Chestnut Hill Reservoir ⊜[1] | 283 | 42.20 N | 71.10 W |
| Chestnut Ridge ʌ | 214 | 40.09 N | 79.24 W |
| Chestnut Ridge Park ♦ | 284a | 42.43 N | 78.46 W |
| Chest Peak ʌ | 172 | 43.06 S | 172.01 E |
| Chesuncook Lake ⊜ | 188 | 46.00 N | 69.20 W |
| Cheswick | 214 | 40.32 N | 79.47 W |
| Cheswold | 208 | 39.13 N | 75.35 W |
| Chet ≃ | 42 | 52.33 N | 1.32 E |
| Cheta ≃ | 74 | 71.54 N | 102.06 E |
| Chetaibi | 36 | 37.04 N | 7.23 E |
| Chetco ≃ | 202 | 42.03 N | 124.16 W |
| Chetek | 190 | 45.18 N | 91.39 W |
| Chéticamp | 186 | 46.38 N | 61.01 W |
| Chet Iter, Oued V | 148 | 21.39 N | 2.30 E |
| Chetopa | 198 | 37.02 N | 95.05 W |
| Chettlatt Island I | 122 | 11.42 N | 72.42 E |
| Chetumal | 232 | 18.30 N | 88.18 W |
| Chetumal, Bahía ϲ | 232 | 18.20 N | 88.05 W |
| Chetwynd | 182 | 55.42 N | 121.40 W |
| Cheung Chau I | 271d | 22.12 N | 114.01 E |
| Cheung Shue Tan | 271d | 22.26 N | 114.12 E |
| Chevak | 180 | 61.39 N | 165.17 W |
| Cheval Blanc, Sommet du ʌ | 62 | 44.07 N | 6.26 E |
| Chevannes | 261 | 48.32 N | 2.27 E |
| Chevelon Creek ≃ | 200 | 34.57 N | 110.31 W |
| Chevening | 260 | 51.18 N | 0.08 E |
| Chevenoz | 58 | 46.20 N | 6.39 E |
| Cheverly | 284c | 38.55 N | 76.54 W |
| Cheverny | 50 | 47.30 N | 1.28 E |
| Chevillon | 58 | 48.32 N | 5.08 E |
| Chevilly-Larue | 261 | 48.46 N | 2.21 E |
| Cheviot, N.Z. | 172 | 42.49 S | 173.16 E |
| Cheviot, Oh., U.S. | 218 | 39.09 N | 84.36 W |
| Cheviot Hills ⋏[2] | 44 | 55.22 N | 2.22 W |
| Chevreuse | 50 | 48.42 N | 2.03 E |
| Chèvreville | 261 | 49.07 N | 2.51 E |
| Chevril, Lac du ⊜ | 62 | 45.29 N | 6.56 E |
| Chevry-Cossigny | 261 | 48.43 N | 2.40 E |
| Chevy Chase | 284c | 38.58 N | 77.04 W |
| Chevy Chase Heights | 214 | 40.36 N | 79.08 W |
| Chevy Chase View | 284c | 39.01 N | 77.05 W |
| Chewaucan ≃ | 202 | 42.30 N | 120.18 W |
| Chew Bahir (Lake Stefanie) ⊜ | 144 | 4.40 N | 36.50 E |
| Chewelah | 202 | 48.16 N | 117.42 W |
| Chew Magna | 42 | 51.22 N | 2.35 W |
| Chew Reservoir ⊜[1] | 262 | 53.31 N | 1.56 W |
| Chews Landing | 285 | 39.50 N | 75.04 W |
| Chewton, Austl. | 169 | 37.05 S | 144.16 E |
| Chewton, Pa., U.S. | 214 | 40.53 N | 80.20 W |
| Chexbres | 58 | 46.29 N | 6.47 E |
| Cheyenne, Ok., U.S. | 196 | 35.36 N | 99.40 W |
| Cheyenne, Wy., U.S. | 200 | 41.08 N | 104.49 W |
| Cheyenne ≃ | 198 | 44.40 N | 101.15 W |
| Cheyenne, Dry Fork ≃ | 198 | 43.25 N | 105.23 W |
| Cheyenne River Indian Reservation ◆[4] | 198 | 45.00 N | 100.40 W |
| Cheyenne Wells | 198 | 38.49 N | 102.21 W |
| Cheyne Bay ϲ | 162 | 34.35 S | 118.50 E |
| Cheyne Point › | 162 | 33.58 S | 122.34 E |
| Cheyney | 285 | 39.56 N | 75.31 W |
| Cheyney University of Pennsylvania ʊ[2] | 285 | 39.56 N | 75.32 W |
| Chezhen | 98 | 37.54 N | 117.37 E |
| Chhabra | 124 | 24.40 N | 76.50 E |
| Chhachhrauli | 124 | 30.15 N | 77.22 E |
| Chhajārsi | 272a | 28.38 N | 77.23 E |
| Chhalera Bāngar | 272a | 28.33 N | 77.20 E |
| Chhanka | 126 | 23.59 N | 89.55 E |
| Chhapra | 124 | 25.46 N | 84.45 E |
| Chhātak | 120 | 25.02 N | 91.40 E |
| Chhatarpur, India | 124 | 24.23 N | 84.11 E |
| Chhatarpur, India | 124 | 24.55 N | 79.36 E |
| Chhātna | 126 | 23.18 N | 86.58 E |
| Chhatrapur | 122 | 19.21 N | 84.59 E |
| Chhattīsgarh ≚ | 122 | 21.15 N | 82.00 E |
| Chhay Arêng ≃ | 110 | 11.31 N | 103.25 E |
| Chhêb Kândal | 110 | 13.45 N | 105.24 E |
| Chhibrāmau | 124 | 27.09 N | 79.31 E |
| Chhināmor | 272b | 22.48 N | 88.18 E |
| Chhindwāra | 124 | 22.04 N | 78.56 E |
| Chhiruti | 126 | 24.01 N | 88.11 E |
| Chhitauni | 124 | 27.09 N | 83.58 E |
| Chhlong ≃ | 110 | 12.15 N | 105.58 E |
| Chhota Bāisdia | 126 | 22.00 N | 90.27 E |
| Chhota-Chhindwāra | 124 | 23.03 N | 79.29 E |
| Chhota Udepur | 120 | 22.19 N | 74.01 E |
| Chhukha Dzong | 124 | 27.09 N | 89.36 E |
| Chi ≃, Thai | 110 | 15.18 N | 103.31 E |
| Chi ≃, Thai | 110 | 15.11 N | 104.43 E |
| Chi ≃, Zhg. | 100 | 32.51 N | 117.59 E |
| Chía | 246 | 4.52 N | 74.04 W |
| Chia, Laguna ⊜ | 234 | 22.10 N | 98.02 W |
| Chiador | 256 | 22.01 S | 43.03 W |
| Chiahsien | 100 | 23.05 N | 120.35 E |
| Chiahsing → Jiaxing | 106 | 30.46 N | 120.45 E |
| Chiai | 100 | 23.29 N | 120.27 E |
| Chialamberto | 62 | 45.22 N | 7.21 E |
| Chiali | 100 | 23.10 N | 120.10 E |
| Chiambala ≃ | 152 | 16.22 S | 11.49 E |
| Chiampo | 64 | 45.33 N | 11.17 E |
| Chiampo ≃ | 64 | 45.20 N | 11.16 E |
| Chiamussu → Jiamusi | 89 | 46.50 N | 130.21 E |
| Chian → Ji'an | 100 | 27.07 N | 114.58 E |
| Chiana, Val di V | 66 | 43.15 N | 11.50 E |
| Chianciano Terme | 66 | 43.03 N | 11.50 E |
| Chiang Dao | 110 | 19.22 N | 98.58 E |
| Chiange | 152 | 15.45 S | 13.48 E |
| Chiang Kham | 110 | 19.32 N | 100.18 E |
| Chiang Khan | 110 | 17.52 N | 101.36 E |
| Chiang Khian | 110 | 19.37 N | 100.00 E |
| Chiang Mai | 110 | 18.47 N | 98.59 E |
| Chiangmen → Jiangmen | 100 | 22.35 N | 113.05 E |
| Chiang Rai | 110 | 19.54 N | 99.50 E |
| Chiang Saen | 110 | 20.16 N | 100.05 E |
| Chiangtu → Yangzhou | 100 | 32.24 N | 119.26 E |
| Chiangyin → Jiangyin | 106 | 31.55 N | 120.16 E |
| Chiani ≃ | 66 | 42.44 N | 12.07 E |
| Chianni | 66 | 43.29 N | 10.38 E |
| Chianti □[9] | 66 | 43.25 N | 11.20 E |
| Chianti, Monti del ⋏ | 66 | 43.32 N | 11.25 E |
| Chiaohsi | 100 | 24.49 N | 121.46 E |
| Chiaohsien → Jiaoxian | 98 | 36.18 N | 119.58 E |
| Chiaopan | 100 | 24.50 N | 121.21 E |
| Chiaotso → Jiaozuo | 102 | 35.15 N | 113.13 E |
| Chiao-Tung Normal University ʊ[2] | 269b | 31.14 N | 121.24 E |
| Chiapa | 248 | 19.32 S | 69.13 W |
| Chiapa de Corzo | 234 | 16.42 N | 93.00 W |
| Chiapaot'ai | 100 | 24.11 N | 121.00 E |
| Chiapas □[3] | 232 | 16.30 N | 92.30 W |
| Chiaramonte Gulfi | 70 | 37.02 N | 14.42 E |
| Chiaramonti | 71 | 40.45 N | 8.49 E |
| Chiaravalle | 66 | 43.36 N | 13.19 E |
| Chiaravalle Centrale | 68 | 38.41 N | 16.25 E |
| Chiareggio | 64 | 46.19 N | 9.47 E |
| Chiari | 62 | 45.32 N | 9.56 E |
| Chiaromonte | 68 | 40.07 N | 16.13 E |
| Chiasso | 58 | 45.50 N | 9.01 E |
| Chiautla de Tapia | 234 | 18.17 N | 98.36 W |
| Chiavari | 62 | 44.19 N | 9.19 E |
| Chiavenna | 58 | 46.19 N | 9.24 E |
| Chiawelo | 273d | 26.17 S | 27.52 E |
| Chiba | 94 | 35.36 N | 140.07 E |
| Chiba □[5] | 94 | 35.30 N | 140.20 E |
| Chibabava | 156 | 20.19 S | 33.39 E |
| Chiba-kō ϲ | 268 | 35.35 N | 140.06 E |
| Chibakou | 100 | 29.36 N | 113.01 E |
| Chibango | 152 | 13.38 S | 21.56 E |
| Chiba University ʊ[2] | 268 | 35.38 N | 140.06 E |
| Chibemba | 152 | 15.45 S | 14.05 E |
| Chibi | 154 | 20.19 S | 30.30 E |
| Chibia | 152 | 15.11 S | 13.41 E |
| Chibouet ≃ | 206 | 45.47 N | 72.52 W |
| Chibougamau | 176 | 49.55 N | 74.22 W |
| Chibuto | 156 | 24.44 S | 33.33 E |
| Chibuzhangchu Hu ⊜ | 120 | 33.25 N | 90.15 E |
| Chibwe | 154 | 14.12 S | 28.31 E |
| Chicago, Il., U.S. | 216 | 41.51 N | 87.39 W |
| Chicago, Il., U.S. | 278 | 41.51 N | 87.39 W |
| Chicago, North Branch ≃ | 216 | 41.53 N | 87.38 W |
| Chicago, North Branch, West Fork ≃ | 278 | 42.03 N | 87.54 W |
| Chicago, South Branch ≃ | 278 | 41.53 N | 87.38 W |
| Chicago, University of ʊ[2] | 278 | 41.47 N | 87.36 W |
| Chicago Botanic Garden ♦ | 278 | 42.09 N | 87.47 W |
| Chicago Harbor ϲ | 278 | 41.53 N | 87.37 W |
| Chicago Heights | 216 | 41.30 N | 87.38 W |
| Chicago-Hinsdale Airport ⊠ | 278 | 41.46 N | 87.56 W |
| Chicago Lawn ◆[8] | 278 | 41.47 N | 87.41 W |
| Chicago-Midway Airport ⊠ | 216 | 41.47 N | 87.45 W |
| Chicago-O'Hare International Airport ⊠ | 278 | 41.59 N | 87.54 W |
| Chicago Park | 226 | 39.09 N | 120.58 W |
| Chicago Portage National Historic Site ⊥ | 278 | 41.48 N | 87.49 W |
| Chicago Ridge | 216 | 41.42 N | 87.46 W |
| Chicago Sanitary and Ship Canal ≍ | 216 | 41.32 N | 88.05 W |
| Chicago Stadium ♦ | 278 | 41.53 N | 87.40 W |
| Chicama ≃ | 248 | 7.56 S | 79.17 W |
| Chicamacomico ≃ | 208 | 38.26 N | 75.59 W |
| Chicamba, Barragem de ◆[6] | 156 | 19.08 S | 33.00 E |
| Chicapa ≃ | 152 | 6.26 S | 20.47 E |
| Chicayán ≃ | 234 | 21.59 N | 94.06 W |
| Chic-Chocs, Monts ⋏ | 186 | 48.55 N | 66.00 W |
| Chichagof Island I | 180 | 57.30 N | 135.30 W |
| Chichas, Cordillera de ⋏ | 248 | 21.00 S | 66.20 W |
| Chīchāwatni | 123 | 30.32 N | 72.42 E |
| Chiché ≃ | 250 | 8.15 S | 53.30 W |
| Chicheng | 98 | 40.54 N | 115.46 E |
| Chichén Itzá ⊥ | 232 | 20.40 N | 88.35 W |
| Chichester, Eng., U.K. | 42 | 50.50 N | 0.48 W |
| Chichester, N.Y., U.S. | 210 | 42.06 N | 74.19 W |
| Chichester Range ⋏ | 162 | 22.00 S | 118.50 E |
| Chichi | 100 | 23.50 N | 120.47 E |
| Chichibu | 94 | 35.59 N | 139.05 E |
| Chichibu-Tama-kokuritsu-kōen ♦ | 94 | 35.52 N | 139.00 E |
| Chichica | 236 | 8.22 N | 81.40 W |
| Chichicastenango | 236 | 14.56 N | 91.07 W |
| Chichigalpa | 236 | 12.34 N | 87.02 W |
| Chichigapa | 234 | 17.47 N | 94.25 W |
| Ch'ich'ihaerh → Qiqihar | 89 | 47.19 N | 123.55 E |
| Chichihualco | 234 | 17.41 N | 99.39 W |
| Chichijima-rettō II | 14 | 27.06 N | 142.12 E |
| Chichimilá | 232 | 20.37 N | 88.13 W |
| Chichiriviche | 246 | 10.56 N | 68.16 W |
| Chicholi | 124 | 22.01 N | 77.40 E |
| Chichra | 126 | 22.19 N | 86.53 E |
| Chickahominy ≃ | 208 | 37.14 N | 76.53 W |
| Chickaloon | 180 | 61.48 N | 148.28 W |
| Chickamauga | 192 | 34.52 N | 85.17 W |
| Chickamauga Lake ⊜[1] | 192 | 35.22 N | 85.02 W |
| Chickamin ≃ | 182 | 55.47 N | 130.58 W |
| Chickasaw, Al., U.S. | 194 | 30.45 N | 88.04 W |
| Chickasaw, Oh., U.S. | 216 | 40.26 N | 84.30 W |
| Chickasaw Bogue ≃ | 194 | 32.17 N | 87.55 W |
| Chickasawhatchie Creek ≃ | 192 | 31.19 N | 84.29 W |
| Chickasawhay ≃ | 194 | 31.00 N | 88.45 W |
| Chickasaw National Recreation Area ♦ | 196 | 34.25 N | 96.59 W |
| Chickasha | 196 | 35.03 N | 97.56 W |
| Chicken | 180 | 64.04 N | 141.56 W |
| Chicken Brook ≃ | 283 | 42.08 N | 71.25 W |
| Chickerell | 42 | 50.37 N | 2.30 W |
| Chickies Creek ≃ | 208 | 40.03 N | 76.32 W |
| Chiclana de la Frontera | 34 | 36.25 N | 6.08 W |
| Chiclayo | 248 | 6.46 S | 79.51 W |
| Chico, Ca., U.S. | 204 | 39.43 N | 121.50 W |
| Chico, Tx., U.S. | 196 | 33.17 N | 97.47 W |
| Chico, Wa., U.S. | 224 | 47.36 N | 122.42 W |
| Chico ≃, Arg. | 254 | 43.48 S | 66.25 W |
| Chico ≃, Arg. | 254 | 42.25 S | 70.30 W |
| Chico ≃, Arg. | 254 | 49.56 S | 68.32 W |
| Chico ≃, Cuba | 286b | 23.02 N | 82.17 W |
| Chico ≃, Pan. | 236 | 8.20 N | 80.28 W |
| Chico ≃, Pil. | 116 | 17.58 N | 121.36 E |
| Chico ≃, S.A. | 254 | 51.40 S | 69.09 W |
| Chicoasén, Presa ⊜[1] | 234 | 16.55 N | 93.05 W |
| Chicobi, Lac ⊜ | 190 | 48.53 N | 78.30 W |
| Chico Creek ≃ | 198 | 38.15 N | 104.20 W |
| Chicolete Creek ≃ | 222 | 29.05 N | 96.49 W |
| Chicomba | 152 | 14.09 S | 14.57 E |
| Chicomo | 156 | 24.31 S | 34.17 E |
| Chicomuselo | 232 | 15.46 N | 92.16 W |
| Chiconautla, Cerro ʌ | 286a | 19.39 N | 98.58 W |
| Chiconono | 154 | 12.56 S | 35.43 E |
| Chicontepec de Tejeda | 234 | 20.58 N | 98.10 W |
| Chicopee, Ga., U.S. | 192 | 34.15 N | 83.50 W |
| Chicopee, Ma., U.S. | 207 | 42.08 N | 72.36 W |
| Chicopee ≃ | 207 | 42.09 N | 72.37 W |
| Chicora | 214 | 40.56 N | 79.44 W |
| Chicot, Lake ⊜ | 194 | 33.20 N | 91.14 W |
| Chicot, Rivière du ≃ | 275a | 45.35 N | 73.51 W |
| Chicot State Park ♦ | 194 | 30.47 N | 92.19 W |
| Chicoutimi | 186 | 48.26 N | 71.04 W |
| Chicoutimi ≃ | 186 | 48.26 N | 71.05 W |
| Chicoutimi, Réserve ♦ | 186 | 48.30 N | 70.15 W |
| Chicú, Cerro ʌ | 236 | 8.35 N | 80.51 W |
| Chicualoque | 234 | 20.23 N | 97.39 W |
| Chicuma | 152 | 13.23 S | 14.51 E |
| Chicxulub | 232 | 21.08 N | 89.31 W |
| Chidambaram | 122 | 11.24 N | 79.42 E |
| Chiddingfold | 42 | 51.06 N | 0.37 W |
| Chiddingstone Causeway | 260 | 51.12 N | 0.10 E |
| Chidenguele | 156 | 24.54 S | 34.13 E |
| Chidlow | 168a | 31.52 S | 116.14 E |
| Chi-do I | 98 | 35.04 N | 126.13 E |
| Chidralada Palace ʊ | 269a | 13.46 N | 100.32 E |
| Chief | 222 | 32.33 N | 96.10 W |
| Chief Justice William Cushing Memorial State Park ♦ | 283 | 42.10 N | 70.45 W |
| Chiefland | 192 | 29.28 N | 82.51 W |
| Chiefs Point › | 212 | 44.42 N | 81.18 W |
| Chief's Point Indian Reserve ◆[4] | 212 | 44.41 N | 81.17 W |
| Chiehyang → Jieyang | 100 | 23.35 N | 116.21 E |
| Chiemgauer Alpen ⋏ | 64 | 47.40 N | 12.30 E |
| Chiemsee ⊜ | 64 | 47.54 N | 12.29 E |
| Chien, Bayou de ≃ | 194 | 36.35 N | 89.11 W |
| Chienes (Kiens) | 64 | 46.48 N | 11.50 E |
| Chiengi | 154 | 8.39 S | 29.10 E |
| Chiengo | 152 | 13.20 S | 21.55 E |
| Chiens, Rivière aux ≃ | 275a | 45.39 N | 73.46 W |
| Chienti ≃ | 66 | 43.18 N | 13.45 E |
| Chieo Lan Reservoir ⊜[1] | 110 | 9.00 N | 98.45 E |
| Chieri | 62 | 45.01 N | 7.49 E |
| Chiers ≃ | 56 | 49.39 N | 5.00 E |
| Chiesa in Valmalenco | 64 | 46.16 N | 9.51 E |
| Chiese ≃ | 64 | 45.08 N | 10.25 E |
| Chieti | 66 | 42.21 N | 14.10 E |
| Chieti □[4] | 66 | 42.07 N | 14.21 E |
| Chietla | 234 | 18.31 N | 98.35 W |
| Chieuti | 68 | 41.51 N | 15.10 E |
| Chieveley | 42 | 51.27 N | 1.19 W |
| Chièvres | 50 | 50.35 N | 3.48 E |
| Chifeng (Ulanhad) | 98 | 42.18 N | 119.00 E |
| Chigasaki | 94 | 35.19 N | 139.24 E |
| Chiginagak, Mount ʌ | 180 | 57.08 N | 156.59 W |
| Chigmit Mountains ⋏ | 180 | 60.00 N | 153.00 W |
| Chignahuapan | 234 | 19.50 N | 98.02 W |
| Chignall Saint James | 260 | 51.46 N | 0.25 E |
| Chignall Smealy | 260 | 51.47 N | 0.25 E |
| Chignecto, Cape › | 186 | 45.20 N | 64.57 W |
| Chignecto Bay ϲ | 186 | 45.35 N | 64.45 W |
| Chignik | 180 | 56.18 N | 158.23 W |
| Chignik Bay ϲ | 180 | 56.22 N | 158.15 W |
| Chignik Lagoon | 180 | 56.21 N | 158.31 W |
| Chignik Lake | 180 | 56.15 N | 158.45 W |
| Chignolo Po | 62 | 45.09 N | 9.29 E |
| Chigombe ≃ | 156 | 23.26 S | 33.19 E |
| Chigorodó | 246 | 7.41 N | 76.42 W |
| Chigu | 100 | 27.34 N | 114.40 E |
| Chigubo | 156 | 22.50 S | 33.34 E |
| Chigu Co ⊜ | 120 | 28.40 N | 91.45 E |
| Chigwell | 42 | 51.38 N | 0.05 E |
| Chigwell Row | 260 | 51.37 N | 0.07 E |
| Chigyŏng | 98 | 39.51 N | 127.26 E |
| Chihaya-akasaka | 270 | 34.24 N | 135.38 E |
| Chihaya Castle ⊥ | 270 | 34.24 N | 135.40 E |
| Chihe | 100 | 32.32 N | 117.58 E |
| Ch'ihfeng → Chifeng | 98 | 42.18 N | 119.00 E |
| Chihli, Gulf of → Bo Hai ϲ | 98 | 38.30 N | 120.00 E |
| Chihpen | 100 | 22.42 N | 121.02 E |
| Ch'ihshang | 100 | 23.07 N | 121.12 E |
| Chihsi → Jixi | 89 | 45.17 N | 130.59 E |
| Ch'ihsing Shan ʌ, T'aiwan | 100 | 25.10 N | 121.33 E |
| Ch'ihsing Shan ʌ, T'aiwan | 269d | 25.10 N | 121.33 E |
| Ch'ihsing Yen I | 100 | 21.46 N | 120.49 E |
| Chihtungtsun | 100 | 22.44 N | 120.14 E |
| Chihu | 100 | 24.07 N | 117.51 E |
| Chihuahua | 232 | 28.38 N | 106.05 W |
| Chihuahua □[3] | 232 | 28.30 N | 106.00 W |
| Chihuahuan Desert ◆[2] | 16 | 35.00 N | 106.00 W |
| Chii-san ʌ | 98 | 35.20 N | 127.44 E |
| Chii-san Kukrip Kongwŏn ♦ | 98 | 35.20 N | 127.39 E |
| Chiitola | 26 | 61.16 N | 29.38 E |
| Chikaskia ≃ | 196 | 36.37 N | 97.15 W |
| Chik Ballāpur | 122 | 13.28 N | 77.44 E |
| Chikhli | 122 | 20.21 N | 76.15 E |
| Chikindzonot | 232 | 20.20 N | 88.29 W |
| Chikmagalūr | 122 | 13.19 N | 75.47 E |
| Chiknai ≃ | 126 | 24.06 N | 89.17 E |
| Chiknāyakanhalli | 122 | 13.26 N | 76.37 E |
| Chikoa | 154 | 13.24 S | 32.07 E |
| Chikodi | 122 | 16.26 N | 74.36 E |
| Chikou | 100 | 30.44 N | 117.32 E |
| Chikrêng ≃ | 110 | 12.51 N | 104.14 E |
| Ch'iku | 100 | 23.08 N | 120.07 E |



| | | | | |
|---|---|---|---|---|
| ≃ River | Fluß | Río | Rivière | Rio |
| ≍ Canal | Kanal | Canal | Canal | Canal |
| ᒪ Waterfall, Rapids | Wasserfall, Stromschnellen | Cascada, Rápidos | Chute d'eau, Rapides | Cascata, Rápidos |
| ʯ Strait | Meeresstraße | Estrecho | Détroit | Estreito |
| ϲ Bay, Gulf | Bucht, Golf | Bahía, Golfo | Baie, Golfe | Baía, Golfo |
| ⊜ Lake, Lakes | See, Seen | Lago, Lagos | Lac, Lacs | Lago, Lagos |
| ☷ Swamp | Sumpf | Pantano | Marais | Pântano |
| ⍓ Ice Features, Glacier | Eis- und Gletscherformen | Accidentes Glaciales | Formes glaciaires | Acidentes glaciares |
| ⍑ Other Hydrographic Features | Andere Hydrographische Objekte | Otros Elementos Hidrográficos | Autres données hydrographiques | Outros acidentes hidrográficos |
| ✣ Submarine Features | Untermeerische Objekte | Accidentes Submarinos | Formes de relief sous-marin | Acidentes submarinos |
| □ Political Unit | Politische Einheit | Unidad Politica | Entité politique | Unidade política |
| ʊ Cultural Institution | Kulturelle Institution | Institución Cultural | Institution culturelle | Institução cultural |
| ⊥ Historical Site | Historische Stätte | Sitio Histórico | Site historique | Sitio histórico |
| ♦ Recreational Site | Erholungs- und Ferienort | Sitio de Recreo | Centre de loisirs | Area de Lazer |
| ⊠ Airport | Flughafen | Aeropuerto | Aéroport | Aeroporto |
| ■ Military Installation | Militäranlage | Instalación Militar | Installation militaire | Instalação militar |
| ◆ Miscellaneous | Verschiedenes | Misceláneo | Divers | Diversos |

ENGLISH: Name, Page, Lat.°′, Long.°′ — DEUTSCH: Name, Seite, Breite°′, Länge°′ E = Ost


| Name | Page | Lat.°′ | Long.°′ |
|---|---|---|---|
| Chikugo | 96 | 33.12 N | 130.30 E |
| Chikugo ≃ | 92 | 33.09 N | 130.21 E |
| Chikujō-kichi, Kōkū-jieitai- ■ | 96 | 33.41 N | 131.03 E |
| Chikuma ≃ | 94 | 36.59 N | 138.35 E |
| Chikuminuk Lake ⊜ | 180 | 60.14 N | 159.00 W |
| Chikura | 94 | 34.57 N | 139.57 E |
| Chikusa | 96 | 35.09 N | 134.26 E |
| Chikusa ≃ | 96 | 34.44 N | 134.24 E |
| Chikushino | 96 | 33.29 N | 130.31 E |
| Chikwawa | 154 | 16.03 S | 34.48 E |
| Chi-kyaw | 110 | 20.17 N | 93.54 E |
| Chikyu-misaki › | 92a | 42.18 N | 141.00 E |
| Chila | 152 | 12.04 S | 14.29 E |
| Chilacachapa | 234 | 18.17 N | 99.43 W |
| Chilakalūrupet | 122 | 16.05 N | 80.10 E |
| Chilako ≃ | 182 | 53.54 N | 122.59 W |
| Chilam Chauki | 123 | 35.03 N | 75.07 E |
| Chilanga | 154 | 15.34 S | 28.17 E |
| Chilanko Forks | 182 | 52.06 N | 124.10 W |
| Chilapa de Álvarez | 234 | 17.36 N | 99.10 W |
| Chilās | 123 | 35.26 N | 74.05 E |
| Chilaw | 122 | 7.34 N | 79.47 E |
| Chilca, Perú | 248 | 12.32 S | 76.44 W |
| Chilca, Perú | 248 | 12.09 S | 75.11 W |
| Chilca, Punta › | 248 | 12.27 S | 76.48 W |
| Chilchota | 234 | 19.51 N | 102.08 W |
| Chilcotin ≃ | 182 | 51.45 N | 122.24 W |
| Chilcott Island I | 166 | 16.58 S | 149.58 E |
| Childers | 166 | 25.14 S | 152.17 E |
| Childersburg | 194 | 33.16 N | 86.21 W |
| Childer Thornton | 262 | 53.17 N | 2.57 W |
| Childress | 196 | 34.25 N | 100.12 W |
| Childs | 210 | 41.34 N | 75.32 W |
| Chile □[1] | 244 | 30.00 S | 71.00 W |
| Chile, Hipódromo ♦ | 286e | 33.24 S | 70.41 W |
| Chile, Universidad de ✿[2] | 286e | 33.27 S | 70.40 W |
| Chile Basin ✤[1] | 18 | 33.00 S | 80.00 W |
| Chile Chico | 254 | 46.33 S | 71.44 W |
| Chilecito, Arg. | 252 | 29.10 S | 67.30 W |
| Chilecito, Arg. | 252 | 33.53 S | 69.03 W |
| Chilengue, Serra do ⋀ | 152 | 13.10 S | 15.18 E |
| Chileno, Arroyo ≃, Ur. | 258 | 33.55 S | 58.08 W |
| Chileno, Arroyo ≃, Ur. | 288 | 34.22 S | 57.54 W |
| Chile Rise ✤[3] | 18 | 40.00 S | 90.00 W |
| Chilete | 248 | 7.14 S | 78.51 W |
| Chilham | 42 | 51.15 N | 0.57 E |
| Chilhowie | 192 | 36.47 N | 81.40 W |
| Chili | 216 | 40.52 N | 86.02 W |
| Chili → Chile □[1] | 244 | 30.00 S | 71.00 W |
| Chili ≃ | 248 | 16.23 S | 71.46 W |
| Chili, Ouadi V | 146 | 16.44 N | 20.53 E |
| Chilia, Braţul ≃[1] | 78 | 45.18 N | 29.40 E |
| Chili Center | 210 | 43.06 N | 77.44 W |
| Chilika Lake ⊜ | 122 | 19.45 N | 85.25 E |
| Chililabombwe (Bancroft) | 154 | 12.18 S | 27.43 E |
| Chilin → Jilin | 89 | 43.51 N | 126.33 E |
| Chilingchang | 107 | 28.58 N | 105.31 E |
| Chilivani | 71 | 40.36 N | 8.56 E |
| Chilkat Pass )( | 180 | 59.43 N | 136.35 W |
| Chilko ≃ | 182 | 52.08 N | 123.30 W |
| Chilko Lake ⊜ | 182 | 51.20 N | 124.05 W |
| Chilko Lake Indian Reserve ◆[4] | 182 | 51.25 N | 124.07 W |
| Chillagoe | 166 | 17.09 S | 144.32 E |
| Chillán | 252 | 36.36 S | 72.07 W |
| Chillar | 252 | 37.18 S | 59.59 W |
| Chilla Saroda ◆[8] | 272a | 28.36 N | 77.18 E |
| Chillicothe, Il., U.S. | 190 | 40.55 N | 89.29 W |
| Chillicothe, Mo., U.S. | 194 | 39.47 N | 93.33 W |
| Chillicothe, Oh., U.S. | 218 | 39.19 N | 82.58 W |
| Chillicothe, Tx., U.S. | 196 | 34.15 N | 99.30 W |
| Chilliwack | 224 | 49.10 N | 121.57 W |
| Chilliwack ≃ | 224 | 49.05 N | 121.57 W |
| Chilliwack Lake ⊜ | 224 | 49.03 N | 121.25 W |
| Chillón | 286d | 11.55 S | 77.05 W |
| Chillón ≃ | 248 | 11.57 S | 77.09 W |
| Chillon, Château de ⊥ | 58 | 46.25 N | 6.56 E |
| Chillum | 284c | 38.58 N | 76.59 W |
| Chilly-Mazarin | 261 | 48.42 N | 2.19 E |
| Chilmāri | 124 | 25.33 N | 89.43 E |
| Chilmark | 207 | 41.20 N | 70.44 W |
| Chilo | 218 | 38.48 N | 84.08 W |
| Chiloane, Ilha I | 156 | 20.40 S | 34.55 E |
| Chiloé, Isla Grande de I | 254 | 42.30 S | 73.55 W |
| Chilok | 88 | 51.21 N | 110.28 E |
| Chilok ≃ | 88 | 51.19 N | 106.59 E |
| Chilón | 232 | 17.14 N | 92.25 W |
| Chilonga | 154 | 12.03 S | 31.21 E |
| Chilongo | 152 | 13.55 S | 16.35 E |
| Chiloquin | 202 | 42.34 N | 121.51 W |
| Chilovo | 76 | 57.46 N | 29.23 E |
| Chilpancingo de los Bravo | 234 | 17.33 N | 99.30 W |
| Chilpi | 124 | 22.15 N | 81.33 E |
| Chilston Park ♦ | 260 | 51.12 N | 0.42 E |
| Chiltern □[8] | 260 | 51.40 N | 0.37 W |
| Chiltern Hills ⋀[2] | 42 | 51.42 N | 0.48 W |
| Chilton, Eng., U.K. | 44 | 54.39 N | 1.33 W |
| Chilton, Tx., U.S. | 222 | 31.16 N | 97.03 W |
| Chilton, Wi., U.S. | 190 | 44.01 N | 88.09 W |
| Chiluage | 152 | 9.30 S | 21.47 E |
| Chilubula Mission | 154 | 10.09 S | 31.00 E |
| Chilumba | 154 | 10.28 S | 34.12 E |
| Chilung | 100 | 25.08 N | 121.44 E |
| Chilung ≃ | 269d | 25.07 N | 121.27 E |
| Chilung Kang c | 269d | 25.09 N | 121.45 E |
| Chilung Shih □[7] | 269d | 25.08 N | 121.45 E |
| Chiluvya | 154 | 12.18 S | 34.01 E |
| Chilwa, Lake ⊜ | 154 | 15.12 S | 35.50 E |
| Chilwell | 169 | 38.10 S | 144.21 E |
| Chimaco | 152 | 15.12 S | 21.56 E |
| Chimacum | 224 | 48.00 N | 122.46 W |
| Chimacum Creek ≃ | 224 | 48.03 N | 122.45 W |
| Chimakela | 152 | 15.24 S | 16.58 E |
| Chimaltenango | 236 | 14.40 N | 90.49 W |
| Chimaltenango □[5] | 236 | 14.40 N | 90.55 W |
| Chimaltitán | 234 | 21.46 N | 103.50 W |
| Chimán | 246 | 8.42 N | 78.37 W |
| Chimanimani National Park ♦ | 154 | 19.48 S | 33.56 E |
| Chimay | 50 | 50.03 N | 4.19 E |
| Chimayo | 200 | 36.00 N | 105.55 W |
| Chimbarongo | 252 | 34.42 S | 71.03 W |
| Chimbas | 252 | 31.29 S | 68.32 W |
| Chimborazo □[4] | 246 | 2.00 S | 78.40 W |
| Chimborazo ∧ | 236 | 13.05 N | 85.58 W |
| Chimborazo ∧[1] | 246 | 1.28 S | 78.48 W |
| Chimbote | 248 | 9.05 S | 78.36 W |
| Chimbua | 152 | 16.32 S | 15.08 E |
| Ch'imei Yü I | 100 | 23.13 N | 119.26 E |
| Chimichagua | 246 | 9.15 N | 73.49 W |
| Chimkent → Šymkent | 85 | 42.18 N | 69.36 E |
| Chimki | 82 | 55.54 N | 37.26 E |
| Chimki-Chovrino ◆[8] | 265b | 55.51 N | 37.30 E |
| Chimkinskoje vodochranilišče ⊜[1] | 265b | 55.51 N | 37.28 E |
| Chimney Reservoir ⊜[1] | 204 | 41.25 N | 117.10 W |
| Chimney Rock National Historic Site ⊥ | 198 | 41.39 N | 103.20 W |
| Chimoio | 156 | 19.08 S | 33.29 E |
| Chimon Island I | 276 | 41.04 N | 73.23 W |
| Chimpay | 252 | 39.10 S | 66.09 W |
| Chimpembe | 154 | 9.31 S | 29.33 E |
| Chimpôro ≃ | 152 | 17.20 S | 17.17 E |
| Chin □[8] | 110 | 22.00 N | 93.30 E |
| China, Méx. | 232 | 25.42 N | 99.14 W |
| Chinā, Nihon | 174m | 26.24 N | 127.46 E |
| China (Zhongguo) □[1] | 90 | 35.00 N | 105.00 E |
| China, Tanjong › | 271c | 1.14 N | 103.51 E |
| Chinácota | 246 | 7.37 N | 72.36 W |
| China Grove | 192 | 35.34 N | 80.34 W |
| China Lake ⊜ | 204 | 35.46 N | 117.39 W |
| China Lake Naval Weapons Center ■ | 204 | 35.35 N | 117.10 W |
| Chinameca | 236 | 13.30 N | 88.21 W |
| China Meridional, Mar de → South China Sea ⫪[2] | 108 | 10.00 N | 113.00 E |
| Chinan, Taehan | 98 | 35.48 N | 127.25 E |
| Chinan → Jinan, Zhg. | 98 | 36.40 N | 116.57 E |
| Chinandega | 236 | 12.37 N | 87.09 W |
| Chinandega □[5] | 236 | 12.45 N | 87.05 W |
| China Spring | 222 | 31.39 N | 97.18 W |
| Chinati Peak ∧ | 196 | 29.57 N | 104.29 W |
| Chinatown ◆[8] | 282 | 37.48 N | 122.26 W |
| Chincha Alta | 248 | 13.27 S | 76.08 W |
| Chinchaga ≃ | 176 | 58.50 N | 118.20 W |
| Chincheros | 248 | 13.27 S | 73.44 W |
| Chinchiang → Quanzhou | 100 | 24.54 N | 118.35 E |
| Chinchilla, Austl. | 166 | 26.45 S | 150.38 E |
| Chinchilla, Pa., U.S. | 210 | 41.28 N | 75.41 W |
| Chinchilla de Monte-Aragón | 34 | 38.55 N | 1.43 W |
| Chinchiná | 246 | 4.58 N | 75.36 W |
| Chincholi | 272c | 19.10 N | 73.08 E |
| Chinchón, Esp. | 34 | 40.08 N | 3.25 W |
| Chinch'ŏn, Taehan | 98 | 36.52 N | 127.26 E |
| Chinchorro, Banco ✤[4] | 232 | 18.35 N | 87.22 W |
| Chinchou → Jinzhou | 104 | 41.07 N | 121.08 E |
| Chincolco | 252 | 32.13 S | 70.50 W |
| Chincoteague | 208 | 37.55 N | 75.22 W |
| Chincoteague Bay c | 208 | 38.06 N | 75.15 W |
| Chincoteague Inlet c | 208 | 37.53 N | 75.25 W |
| Chinde | 156 | 18.37 S | 36.24 E |
| Chindo | 98 | 34.28 N | 126.15 E |
| Chin-do I | 98 | 34.25 N | 126.15 E |
| Chindong | 98 | 35.07 N | 128.29 E |
| Chindwinn ≃ | 110 | 21.26 N | 95.15 E |
| Chine (la République populaire de) → China □[1], Asia | 90 | 35.00 N | 105.00 E |
| Chine (nationaliste) → Taiwan □[1], Asia | 100 | 23.30 N | 121.00 E |
| Chinen | 174m | 26.09 N | 127.49 E |
| Chineni | 123 | 33.02 N | 75.17 E |
| Chine Orientale, Mer de → East China Sea ⫪[2] | 90 | 30.00 N | 126.00 E |
| Chinese Camp | 226 | 37.52 N | 120.26 W |
| Chinese Cemetery ◆ | 269f | 14.38 N | 120.59 E |
| Chinese University ✿[2] | 271d | 22.26 N | 114.12 E |
| Chingamba | 152 | 12.49 S | 18.20 E |
| Chingansk | 89 | 49.07 N | 131.11 E |
| Chingarora Creek ≃ | 276 | 40.27 N | 74.12 W |
| Ch'ingchiang → Qingjiang | 100 | 33.35 N | 119.02 E |
| Chingford ◆[8] | 260 | 51.38 N | 0.01 E |
| Chingleput | 122 | 12.42 N | 79.59 E |
| Chingmei ◆[8] | 269d | 24.59 N | 121.32 E |
| Chingola | 154 | 12.32 S | 27.52 E |
| Chingoni | 157a | 12.48 S | 45.08 E |
| Chingoroi | 152 | 13.37 S | 14.01 E |
| Chingshih → Jinshi | 102 | 29.39 N | 111.52 E |
| Ch'ingtao → Qingdao | 98 | 36.06 N | 120.19 E |
| Chingtechen → Jingdezhen | 100 | 29.16 N | 117.11 E |
| Ch'ingt'ung | 269d | 25.02 N | 121.43 E |
| Chinguar | 152 | 12.36 S | 16.20 E |
| Chinguetti | 150 | 20.27 N | 12.22 W |
| Chingune | 156 | 20.38 S | 34.55 E |
| Chinhae | 98 | 35.09 N | 128.40 E |
| Chinhae-man c | 98 | 35.01 N | 128.34 E |
| Chin Hills ⋀[2] | 110 | 22.30 N | 93.30 E |
| Chinhoyi | 154 | 17.22 S | 30.12 E |
| Chinhsien → Jinxian | 98 | 39.04 N | 121.40 E |
| Chinhua → Jinhua | 100 | 29.07 N | 119.39 E |
| Ch'inhuangtao → Qinhuangdao | 98 | 39.56 N | 119.36 E |
| Chīni | 120 | 31.32 N | 78.15 E |
| Chiniak, Cape › | 180 | 57.36 N | 152.08 W |
| Chining → Jining, Zhg. | 98 | 35.25 N | 116.36 E |
| Chining → Jining, Zhg. | 102 | 40.57 N | 113.02 E |
| Chiniot | 123 | 31.43 N | 72.59 E |
| Chinīt ≃ | 110 | 12.55 N | 105.35 E |
| Chinitna Point › | 180 | 59.43 N | 153.02 W |
| Chinizíua | 156 | 19.00 S | 35.09 E |
| Chinjan | 120 | 30.34 N | 67.58 E |
| Chinju | 98 | 35.11 N | 128.05 E |
| Chinkiang → Zhenjiang | 106 | 32.13 N | 119.26 E |
| Chinko ≃ | 136 | 4.50 N | 23.53 E |
| Chinkuashih | 100 | 25.07 N | 121.51 E |
| Chin Lakes ⊜ | 182 | 49.37 N | 112.13 W |
| Chinle | 200 | 36.09 N | 109.33 W |
| Chinle Creek ≃ | 200 | 37.12 N | 109.43 W |
| Chinle Wash V | 200 | 36.54 N | 109.45 W |
| Chinley | 262 | 53.20 N | 1.56 W |
| Chinley Churn ∧[2] | 262 | 53.21 N | 1.57 W |
| Chinmen | 100 | 24.27 N | 118.21 E |
| Chinmen Tao I | 100 | 24.27 N | 118.23 E |
| Chinnampo → Namp'o | 98 | 38.45 N | 125.23 E |
| Chinnor | 42 | 51.43 N | 0.56 W |
| Chino, Nihon | 94 | 35.59 N | 138.09 E |
| Chino, Ca., U.S. | 228 | 34.00 N | 117.41 W |
| Chino Airport ⊠ | 280 | 33.59 N | 117.38 W |
| Chino Creek ≃ | 280 | 33.53 N | 117.38 W |
| Chino Hills | 228 | 34.01 N | 117.43 W |
| Chino Hills ⋀[2] | 280 | 33.56 N | 117.45 W |
| Chinon | 50 | 47.10 N | 0.15 E |
| Chinook, Ab., Can. | 184 | 51.27 N | 110.56 W |
| Chinook, Mt., U.S. | 202 | 48.35 N | 109.13 W |
| Chinook, Wa., U.S. | 224 | 46.16 N | 123.56 W |
| Chinook Cove | 182 | 51.14 N | 120.10 W |
| Chino Valley | 200 | 34.45 N | 112.27 W |
| Chinpāi | 126 | 23.50 N | 87.28 E |
| Chinquapin | 192 | 34.49 N | 77.49 W |
| Chinsali | 154 | 10.34 S | 32.03 E |
| Chinshan | 100 | 25.13 N | 121.38 E |
| Chinshui | 100 | 24.36 N | 120.53 E |
| Chintāmani | 122 | 13.24 N | 78.04 E |
| Chintembwe | 154 | 13.25 S | 33.59 E |
| Chintheche | 154 | 11.52 S | 34.09 E |
| Chinú | 246 | 9.06 N | 75.24 W |
| Chinunje | 154 | 11.19 S | 37.19 E |
| Chinwangtao → Qinhuangdao | 98 | 39.56 N | 119.36 E |
| Chiny | 56 | 49.44 N | 5.20 E |
| Chinyama Litapi | 152 | 13.31 S | 22.21 E |
| Chioco | 154 | 16.25 S | 32.50 E |
| Chioggia | 64 | 45.13 N | 12.17 E |
| Chiomonte | 62 | 45.07 N | 6.59 E |
| Chios → Khíos | 38 | 38.22 N | 26.08 E |
| Chios → Khíos I | 38 | 38.22 N | 26.00 E |
| Chipamanu (Xipamanu) ≃ | 248 | 10.43 S | 67.50 W |
| Chipao | 248 | 14.15 S | 73.57 W |
| Chipata (Fort Jameson) | 154 | 13.39 S | 32.40 E |
| Chipei Tao I | 100 | 23.45 N | 119.37 E |
| Chipera | 154 | 15.28 S | 32.30 E |
| Chiperceni | 38 | 47.32 N | 28.50 E |
| Chiperone ∧ | 154 | 16.28 S | 35.12 E |
| Chipili | 154 | 10.44 S | 29.04 E |
| Chiping | 98 | 36.37 N | 116.16 E |
| Chipinge | 154 | 20.12 S | 32.38 E |
| Chip Lake ⊜ | 182 | 53.40 N | 115.20 W |
| Chipley | 194 | 30.46 N | 85.32 W |
| Chiplūn | 122 | 17.32 N | 73.31 E |
| Chipman | 186 | 46.11 N | 65.53 W |
| Chipogolo | 154 | 6.52 S | 36.02 E |
| Chipoka | 154 | 14.00 S | 34.31 E |
| Chipola ≃ | 192 | 30.01 N | 85.05 W |
| Chippawa ◆[8] | 284a | 43.04 N | 79.03 W |
| Chippawa Channel ≃[1] | 284a | 43.04 N | 79.01 W |
| Chippego Lake ⊜ | 212 | 44.34 N | 76.49 W |
| Chippenham | 42 | 51.28 N | 2.07 W |
| Chipperfield | 260 | 51.42 N | 0.29 W |
| Chippewa ≃, Mi., U.S. | 190 | 43.35 N | 84.17 W |
| Chippewa ≃, Mn., U.S. | 198 | 44.56 N | 95.44 W |
| Chippewa ≃, Wi., U.S. | 190 | 44.25 N | 92.10 W |
| Chippewa, East Branch ≃ | 198 | 45.20 N | 95.36 W |
| Chippewa, East Fork ≃ | 190 | 45.53 N | 91.05 W |
| Chippewa, Lake ⊜ | 190 | 45.56 N | 91.13 W |
| Chippewa Bay c | 212 | 44.27 N | 75.47 W |
| Chippewa Creek ≃ | 212 | 44.27 N | 75.46 W |
| Chippewa Falls | 190 | 44.56 N | 91.23 W |
| Chippewa Lake | 214 | 41.04 N | 81.54 W |
| Chippewanuck Creek ≃ | 216 | 41.07 N | 86.12 W |
| Chipping Campden | 42 | 52.03 N | 1.46 W |
| Chipping Norton | 42 | 51.56 N | 1.32 W |
| Chipping Ongar | 42 | 51.43 N | 0.15 E |
| Chipping Sodbury | 42 | 51.33 N | 2.24 W |
| Chippis | 58 | 46.17 N | 7.33 E |
| Chippokes Plantation State Park ♦ | 208 | 37.08 N | 76.44 W |
| Chipps Island I | 282 | 38.03 N | 121.55 W |
| Chipre → Cyprus □[1] | 130 | 35.00 N | 33.00 E |
| Chipstead, Eng., U.K. | 260 | 51.17 N | 0.09 E |
| Chipstead, Eng., U.K. | 260 | 51.18 N | 0.10 W |
| Chipuriro | 154 | 16.39 S | 30.42 E |
| Chiquelequele | 152 | 16.40 S | 19.06 E |
| Chiquián | 248 | 10.09 S | 77.11 W |
| Chiquihuitlán | 234 | 17.59 N | 96.48 W |
| Chiquimula | 236 | 14.48 N | 89.33 W |
| Chiquimula □[5] | 236 | 14.40 N | 89.25 W |
| Chiquimulilla | 236 | 14.05 N | 90.23 W |
| Chiquinquirá | 246 | 5.37 N | 73.50 W |
| Chiquintirca | 248 | 13.09 S | 73.41 W |
| Chiquita | 152 | 8.38 S | 17.05 E |
| Chiquito ≃ | 234 | 18.29 N | 101.07 W |
| Chiquito Creek ≃ | 226 | 37.20 N | 119.20 W |
| Chira ≃ | 246 | 4.54 S | 81.08 W |
| Chira, Isla I | 236 | 10.06 N | 85.09 W |
| Chirad | 272c | 19.09 N | 73.07 E |
| Chiradzulu | 154 | 15.42 S | 35.10 E |
| Chirāgh Delhi ◆[8] | 272a | 28.32 N | 77.14 E |
| Chīrāla | 122 | 15.49 N | 80.21 E |
| Chiramba | 154 | 16.55 S | 34.39 E |
| Chirape | 156 | 21.18 S | 33.33 E |
| Chirāwa | 120 | 28.15 N | 75.38 E |
| Chirchik → Čirčik | 85 | 41.29 N | 69.35 E |
| Chire (Shire) ≃ | 154 | 17.42 S | 35.19 E |
| Chiredzi | 154 | 21.03 S | 31.45 E |
| Chireno | 194 | 31.30 N | 94.21 W |
| Chirens | 62 | 45.25 N | 5.33 E |
| Chirfa | 146 | 20.57 N | 12.21 E |
| Chīrgaon | 124 | 25.35 N | 78.49 E |
| Chiriaco ≃ | 248 | 5.05 S | 78.19 W |
| Chiricahua Mountains ⋀ | 200 | 31.50 N | 109.15 W |
| Chiricahua National Monument ♦ | 200 | 32.02 N | 109.19 W |
| Chiricahua Peak ∧ | 200 | 31.52 N | 109.20 W |
| Chiriguaná | 246 | 9.22 N | 73.36 W |
| Chirikof Island I | 180 | 55.50 N | 155.35 W |
| Chirilagua | 236 | 13.13 N | 88.08 W |
| Chirinos | 248 | 5.16 S | 78.52 W |
| Chiriquí | 236 | 8.24 N | 82.19 W |
| Chiriquí □[4] | 236 | 8.30 N | 82.00 W |
| Chiriquí, Golfo de c | 246 | 8.00 N | 82.20 W |
| Chiriquí, Laguna de c | 236 | 9.03 N | 82.00 W |
| Chiriquí Grande | 236 | 8.57 N | 82.07 W |
| Chiriquí Viejo ≃ | 236 | 8.20 N | 82.41 W |
| Chirk | 42 | 52.56 N | 3.03 W |
| Chirki | 126 | 24.03 N | 86.09 E |
| Chirle | 272c | 18.56 N | 73.02 E |
| Chirmiri | 124 | 23.12 N | 82.21 E |
| Chirnside | 46 | 55.48 N | 2.13 W |
| Chiromo | 154 | 16.33 S | 35.08 E |
| Chirovo | 76 | 58.56 N | 33.24 E |
| Chirripó ≃ | 236 | 10.41 N | 83.41 W |
| Chirripó, Cerro ∧ | 236 | 9.29 N | 83.30 W |
| Chirripó, Parque Nacional ♦ | 236 | 9.30 N | 83.30 W |
| Chirsa | 84 | 41.31 N | 46.06 E |
| Chirundu | 154 | 15.59 S | 28.54 E |
| Chirvosti | 265a | 59.57 N | 30.37 E |
| Chiryū | 94 | 35.00 N | 137.02 E |
| Chisago City | 190 | 45.22 N | 92.53 W |
| Chisamba | 154 | 14.58 S | 28.23 E |
| Chisana | 180 | 62.09 N | 142.10 W |
| Chisasibi | 176 | 53.50 N | 79.00 W |
| Chiscas | 246 | 6.33 N | 72.29 W |
| Chisec | 236 | 15.49 N | 90.17 W |
| Chiseldon | 42 | 51.31 N | 1.44 W |
| Chisenga | 154 | 9.56 S | 33.26 E |
| Chisep'o | 98 | 34.50 N | 128.42 E |
| Ch'ishan | 100 | 22.53 N | 120.28 E |
| Chishanji | 98 | 36.56 N | 122.23 E |
| Chishi | 100 | 27.42 N | 117.58 E |
| Chishisi | 100 | 25.32 N | 113.11 E |
| Chisholm, Al., U.S. | 194 | 32.25 N | 86.15 W |
| Chisholm, Me., U.S. | 188 | 44.28 N | 70.12 W |
| Chisholm, Mn., U.S. | 190 | 47.29 N | 92.53 W |
| Chisholm, Tx., U.S. | 222 | 32.51 N | 96.22 W |
| Chisholm Mills | 182 | 54.55 N | 114.08 W |
| Chishtiān Mandi | 123 | 29.48 N | 72.52 E |
| Chishui | 102 | 28.29 N | 105.38 E |
| Chishui ≃, Zhg. | 102 | 28.53 N | 105.48 E |
| Chishui ≃, Zhg. | 107 | 28.49 N | 105.50 E |
| Chishuihe | 102 | 27.50 N | 105.32 E |
| Chišig-Öndör | 88 | 48.19 N | 103.25 E |
| Chisimaio → Kismaayo | 144 | 0.22 N | 42.32 E |
| Chişinău (Kishinev) | 38 | 47.00 N | 28.50 E |
| Chişineu-Criş | 38 | 46.31 N | 21.31 E |
| Chislaviči | 76 | 54.11 N | 32.10 E |
| Chislehurst ◆[8] | 260 | 51.25 N | 0.04 E |
| Chisone ≃ | 62 | 44.49 N | 7.25 E |
| Chisone, Valle del V | 62 | 45.01 N | 7.07 E |
| Chisos Mountains ⋀ | 196 | 29.15 N | 103.20 W |
| Chisseaux | 50 | 47.20 N | 1.05 E |
| Chissengue | 152 | 9.14 S | 20.42 E |
| Chissilo | 152 | 13.34 S | 16.30 E |
| Chistochina | 180 | 62.34 N | 144.40 W |
| Chistopol → Čistopol' | 80 | 55.21 N | 50.37 E |
| Chiswellgreen | 260 | 51.44 N | 0.22 W |
| Chiswick ◆[8] | 260 | 51.29 N | 0.16 W |
| Chita, Bol. | 248 | 20.06 S | 66.57 W |
| Chita, Col. | 246 | 6.11 N | 72.28 W |
| Chita, Nihon | 94 | 35.00 N | 136.51 E |
| Chita → Čita, Ross. | 88 | 52.03 N | 113.30 E |
| Chitado | 152 | 17.20 S | 13.54 E |
| Chitagá | 246 | 7.09 N | 72.40 W |
| Chita-hantō ›[1] | 94 | 34.50 N | 136.53 E |
| Chitambo | 154 | 12.55 S | 30.39 E |
| Chitanda ≃ | 152 | 16.01 S | 15.12 E |
| Chitarda | 126 | 21.50 N | 86.57 E |
| Chitata | 152 | 13.47 S | 15.43 E |
| Chitato | 152 | 7.20 S | 20.47 E |
| Chita-wan c | 94 | 34.47 N | 136.58 E |
| Chiţcani | 38 | 46.47 N | 29.36 E |
| Chitek ≃ | 184 | 54.06 N | 108.16 W |
| Chitek Lake ⊜, Mb., Can. | 184 | 52.26 N | 99.25 W |
| Chitek Lake ⊜, Sk., Can. | 184 | 53.44 N | 107.47 W |
| Chitembo | 152 | 13.34 S | 16.40 E |
| Chitina | 180 | 61.31 N | 144.27 W |
| Chitina ≃ | 180 | 61.30 N | 144.28 W |
| Chitipa | 154 | 9.43 S | 33.16 E |
| Chitokoloki | 152 | 13.50 S | 23.13 E |
| Chitose | 92a | 42.49 N | 141.39 E |
| Chitose-chūtonchi, Rikujō-jieitai- ■ | 92a | 42.46 N | 141.40 E |
| Chitou Shan I | 100 | 27.40 N | 120.50 E |
| Chitra ≃[1] | 126 | 22.53 N | 89.40 E |
| Chitradurga | 122 | 14.14 N | 76.24 E |
| Chitrakūt Dham | 124 | 25.11 N | 80.52 E |
| Chitrāl | 123 | 35.51 N | 71.47 E |
| Chitrasāli | 272b | 22.52 N | 88.09 E |
| Chitrāvati ≃ | 122 | 14.48 N | 78.14 E |
| Chitré | 236 | 7.58 N | 80.26 W |
| Chittagong | 120 | 22.20 N | 91.50 E |
| Chittagong □[5] | 120 | 23.00 N | 91.00 E |
| Chīttāpur | 122 | 17.07 N | 77.05 E |
| Chittaranjan | 126 | 23.52 N | 86.52 E |
| Chittaurgarh | 120 | 24.53 N | 74.38 E |
| Chittenango | 210 | 43.02 N | 75.52 W |
| Chittenango Creek ≃ | 210 | 43.11 N | 76.00 W |
| Chittenango Falls | 210 | 42.59 N | 75.50 W |
| Chittering | 162 | 31.29 S | 116.06 E |
| Chittoor | 122 | 13.12 N | 79.07 E |
| Chittūr | 122 | 10.42 N | 76.45 E |
| Chitu, Ityo. | 144 | 8.36 N | 37.59 E |
| Ch'itu, T'aiwan | 269d | 25.06 N | 121.43 E |
| Chitungwiza | 154 | 17.45 S | 31.16 E |
| Chiuchiang → Jiujiang | 100 | 29.44 N | 115.59 E |
| Chíuchíu | 252 | 22.21 S | 68.39 W |
| Chiuduno | 62 | 45.40 N | 9.51 E |
| Chiumbe | 152 | 12.29 S | 16.08 E |
| Chiumbe ≃ | 152 | 7.00 S | 21.12 E |
| Chiúme | 152 | 15.03 S | 21.14 E |
| Chiuppano | 64 | 45.46 N | 11.28 E |
| Chiuro | 64 | 46.10 N | 9.59 E |
| Chiusa (Klausen) | 64 | 46.38 N | 11.34 E |
| Chiusa di Pesio | 62 | 44.19 N | 7.40 E |
| Chiusa di San Michele | 62 | 45.06 N | 7.19 E |
| Chiusaforte | 64 | 46.24 N | 13.18 E |
| Chiusa Sclafani | 70 | 37.41 N | 13.16 E |
| Chiusella ≃ | 62 | 45.24 N | 7.55 E |
| Chiusi | 66 | 43.01 N | 11.57 E |
| Chiusi, Lago di ⊜ | 66 | 43.03 N | 11.58 E |
| Chiúta | 154 | 15.34 S | 33.17 E |
| Chiuta, Lake ⊜ | 154 | 14.55 S | 35.50 E |
| Chiv | 84 | 41.46 N | 47.54 E |
| Chiva | 72 | 41.24 N | 60.22 E |
| Chivacoa | 246 | 10.10 N | 68.54 W |
| Chivasso | 62 | 45.11 N | 7.53 E |
| Chivato, Punta › | 232 | 27.05 N | 111.59 W |
| Chivay | 248 | 15.40 S | 71.35 W |
| Chivhu | 154 | 19.01 S | 30.53 E |
| Chivilcoy | 252 | 34.53 S | 60.01 W |
| Chivirira Falls ⌊ | 154 | 21.14 S | 32.20 E |
| Chiwanda | 154 | 11.22 S | 34.54 E |
| Chiwawa ≃ | 224 | 47.47 N | 120.40 W |
| Chixi | 100 | 28.22 N | 116.22 E |
| Chixoy (Salinas) ≃ | 232 | 16.28 N | 90.33 W |
| Chixoy, Embalse ⊜[1] | 236 | 15.15 N | 90.30 W |
| Chiyoda, Nihon | 94 | 36.12 N | 139.26 E |
| Chiyoda, Nihon | 94 | 36.11 N | 140.14 E |
| Chiyoda, Nihon | 96 | 34.41 N | 132.32 E |
| Chiyoda ◆[8] | 268 | 35.41 N | 139.44 E |
| Chizarira National Park ♦ | 154 | 17.45 S | 28.00 E |
| Chizhen | 100 | 31.55 N | 118.12 E |
| Chizizhen | 100 | 32.22 N | 115.11 E |
| Chizu | 96 | 35.16 N | 134.14 E |
| Chjargas | 88 | 49.32 N | 93.48 E |
| Chjargas nuur ⊜ | 88 | 49.12 N | 93.24 E |
| Chkalov → Orenburg | 86 | 51.54 N | 55.06 E |
| Chkalove | 78 | 46.28 N | 34.11 E |
| Chlebnikovo, Ross. | 80 | 56.38 N | 49.56 E |
| Chlebnikovo, Ross. | 265b | 55.58 N | 37.31 E |
| Chlebodarnyj | 80 | 46.41 N | 40.50 E |
| Chlevnoje | 76 | 52.12 N | 39.05 E |
| Chloride | 200 | 35.24 N | 114.11 W |
| Chlum | 60 | 48.52 N | 13.55 E |
| Chlum ∧ | 61 | 48.42 N | 14.04 E |
| Chmelevicy | 80 | 57.45 N | 46.22 E |
| Chmelevo | 82 | 56.09 N | 39.08 E |
| Chmelita | 76 | 55.25 N | 33.53 E |
| Chmel'niki, Ross. | 82 | 56.52 N | 38.13 E |
| Chmel'niki, Ross. | 82 | 56.53 N | 38.39 E |
| Chmielnik | 30 | 50.37 N | 20.46 E |
| Chmost' ≃ | 76 | 54.45 N | 32.34 E |
| Choa Chu Kang | 271c | 1.22 N | 103.41 E |
| Choāli | 272b | 22.24 N | 88.24 E |
| Chŏâm Khsant | 110 | 14.13 N | 104.56 E |
| Choba | 154 | 2.26 N | 38.03 E |
| Chobe □[5] | 156 | 18.30 S | 25.00 E |
| Chobe ≃ | 156 | 17.50 S | 25.05 E |
| Chobeju | 24 | 64.53 N | 60.10 E |
| Chobe National Park ♦ | 156 | 18.45 S | 24.15 E |
| Chobham | 260 | 51.21 N | 0.36 W |
| Chobham Common ♦ | 260 | 51.23 N | 0.37 W |
| Chobi | 84 | 42.21 N | 41.53 E |
| Chocamán | 234 | 18.59 N | 97.01 W |
| Choccolocco Creek ≃ | 194 | 33.33 N | 86.11 W |
| Choceň | 30 | 50.00 N | 16.13 E |
| Chocenice | 60 | 49.33 N | 13.31 E |
| Chochis, Cerro ∧ | 248 | 18.04 S | 60.03 W |
| Choch'iwŏn | 98 | 36.37 N | 127.18 E |
| Chochloma | 80 | 56.58 N | 43.54 E |
| Chöchmor't | 88 | 47.21 N | 94.33 E |
| Chochol'skij | 78 | 51.34 N | 38.45 E |
| Cho Chu | 110 | 21.54 N | 105.39 E |
| Chocianów | 30 | 51.25 N | 15.55 E |
| Chociwel | 30 | 53.28 N | 15.19 E |
| Chocó □[5] | 246 | 6.00 N | 77.00 W |
| Chocolate Bay c | 222 | 29.11 N | 95.09 W |
| Chocolate Bayou ≃ | 222 | 29.13 N | 95.13 W |
| Chocolate Mountains ⋀ | 204 | 33.20 N | 115.15 W |
| Chocontá | 246 | 5.09 N | 73.41 W |
| Chocope | 248 | 7.47 S | 79.13 W |
| Choctawhatchee, East Fork ≃ | 194 | 31.21 N | 85.33 W |
| Choctawhatchee, West Fork ≃ | 194 | 31.21 N | 85.33 W |
| Choctawhatchee Bay c | 194 | 30.25 N | 86.21 W |
| Choctaw Lake ⊜[1] | 218 | 39.58 N | 83.29 W |
| Chodarus | 88 | 52.36 N | 99.19 E |
| Chodavaram | 122 | 17.50 N | 82.57 E |
| Chodecz | 30 | 52.24 N | 19.01 E |
| Ch'o-do I, C.M.I.K. | 98 | 38.32 N | 124.50 E |
| Ch'o-do I, Taehan | 98 | 34.14 N | 127.15 E |
| Chodoi | 114 | 2.50 N | 101.27 E |
| Chodov | 54 | 50.11 N | 12.43 E |
| Chodovaja Griva | 80 | 57.08 N | 50.16 E |
| Chodovaricha | 24 | 68.57 N | 53.40 E |
| Chodz' ≃ | 84 | 44.43 N | 40.45 E |
| Chodžaimetk | 85 | 39.37 N | 69.14 E |
| Chodžakala | 128 | 38.43 N | 56.20 E |
| Chodžejli | 72 | 42.48 N | 59.25 E |
| Chodzież | 30 | 52.59 N | 16.56 E |
| Choele-Choel | 252 | 39.16 S | 65.41 W |
| Chofombo | 154 | 14.35 S | 31.50 E |
| Chōfu | 94 | 35.39 N | 139.33 E |
| Chofu Airport ⊠ | 268 | 35.40 N | 139.32 E |
| Chogo Lungma Glacier ⊓ | 123 | 35.52 N | 75.19 E |
| Chogot | 88 | 53.15 N | 105.52 E |
| Choiceland | 184 | 53.27 N | 104.25 W |
| Choichuff, Laga ≃ | 154 | 1.34 N | 39.24 E |
| Choire, Loch ⊜ | 46 | 58.13 N | 4.21 W |
| Choisel | 261 | 48.41 N | 2.01 E |
| Choiseul | 241f | 13.47 N | 61.03 W |
| Choiseul □[4] | 175e | 6.40 S | 157.15 E |
| Choiseul I | 175e | 7.05 S | 157.00 E |
| Choiseul Sound ʊ | 254 | 51.57 S | 58.35 W |
| Choisy | 58 | 45.59 N | 6.03 E |
| Choisy-le-Roi | 261 | 48.46 N | 2.25 E |
| Choix | 232 | 26.43 N | 108.17 W |
| Chojna | 30 | 52.58 N | 14.28 E |
| Chojnice | 30 | 53.42 N | 17.34 E |
| Chojnów | 30 | 51.17 N | 15.56 E |
| Chōkai-san ∧ | 92 | 39.06 N | 140.03 E |
| Choke ⋀ | 144 | 10.45 N | 37.35 E |
| Choke Canyon Lake ⊜[1] | 196 | 28.30 N | 98.20 W |
| Chokio | 198 | 45.34 N | 96.10 W |
| Chokoloskee | 220 | 25.48 N | 81.21 W |
| Chokwé | 156 | 24.36 S | 33.00 E |
| Cholame | 226 | 35.43 N | 120.17 W |
| Cholame Creek ≃ | 226 | 35.39 N | 120.22 W |
| Cholame Hills ⋀[2] | 226 | 35.45 N | 120.30 W |
| Cholbon | 88 | 51.53 N | 116.15 E |
| Choldarkipčak | 85 | 39.51 N | 68.52 E |
| Cholet | 32 | 47.04 N | 0.53 W |
| Cholila | 254 | 42.31 S | 71.27 W |
| Chŏlla Namdo □[4] | 98 | 34.45 N | 127.00 E |
| Chŏlla Pukdo □[4] | 98 | 35.45 N | 127.15 E |
| Cholm | 76 | 57.09 N | 31.11 E |
| Cholmec | 76 | 56.21 N | 33.21 E |
| Cholmogorovka | 86 | 44.25 N | 78.31 E |
| Cholmogorskaja | 24 | 63.49 N | 40.39 E |
| Cholmogory | 24 | 64.15 N | 41.40 E |
| Cholmsk | 89 | 47.03 N | 142.03 E |
| Cholmskij | 78 | 44.52 N | 38.24 E |
| Cholmy | 82 | 54.56 N | 38.33 E |
| Cholm-Žirkovskij | 76 | 55.31 N | 33.29 E |
| Choloj ≃ | 88 | 53.12 N | 112.47 E |
| Choloma | 236 | 15.34 N | 87.56 W |
| Chölönbujr | 88 | 47.55 N | 112.57 E |
| Ch'ŏlsan | 98 | 39.46 N | 124.40 E |
| Cholsey | 42 | 51.34 N | 1.10 W |
| Choltobino | 82 | 54.11 N | 38.28 E |
| Choltoson | 88 | 50.20 N | 103.20 E |
| Choluj, Ross. | 80 | 56.34 N | 41.53 E |
| Choluj, Ross. | 80 | 56.04 N | 42.08 E |
| Cholula de Rivadabia | 234 | 19.04 N | 98.18 W |
| Choluteca | 236 | 13.18 N | 87.12 W |
| Choluteca □[5] | 236 | 13.20 N | 87.10 W |
| Choluteca ≃ | 236 | 13.07 N | 87.19 W |
| Choma | 154 | 16.48 S | 26.59 E |
| Chomedey ◆[8] | 275a | 45.32 N | 73.44 W |
| Chomen Swamp ⩶ | 144 | 9.25 N | 37.20 E |
| Chomérac | 62 | 44.42 N | 4.39 E |
| Chomičev | 80 | 48.11 N | 45.01 E |
| Chomiomo ∧ | 124 | 28.01 N | 88.31 E |
| Cho Moi, Viet | 110 | 10.33 N | 105.24 E |
| Cho Moi, Viet | 269c | 10.51 N | 106.38 E |
| Chomo Lhāri ∧ | 124 | 27.50 N | 89.15 E |
| Chom Thong | 110 | 18.25 N | 98.41 E |
| Chomūm | 120 | 27.10 N | 75.44 E |
| Chomutov | 54 | 50.28 N | 13.26 E |
| Chomutovka | 78 | 51.56 N | 34.33 E |
| Chomutovka ≃ | 54 | 50.11 N | 13.37 E |
| Chomutovo, Ross. | 76 | 52.51 N | 37.27 E |
| Chomutovo, Ross. | 88 | 52.28 N | 104.25 E |
| Chomutovskaja | 83 | 47.03 N | 40.04 E |
| Chōnan, Nihon | 94 | 35.24 N | 140.14 E |
| Ch'ŏnan, Taehan | 98 | 36.48 N | 127.09 E |
| Chon'atino | 82 | 55.11 N | 38.07 E |
| Chon Buri | 110 | 13.22 N | 100.59 E |
| Chonchi | 254 | 42.38 S | 73.47 W |
| Choncholoj | 88 | 51.08 N | 108.14 E |
| Chon Daen | 110 | 16.11 N | 100.51 E |
| Chone | 246 | 0.41 S | 80.06 W |
| Chone ≃ | 246 | 0.35 S | 80.25 W |
| Chong'an | 100 | 27.45 N | 118.02 E |
| Ch'ŏngch'ŏn-gang ≃ | 98 | 39.35 N | 125.28 E |
| Ch'ŏngdan | 98 | 37.58 N | 125.56 E |
| Chongde | 106 | 30.32 N | 120.26 E |
| Ch'ŏngdo | 98 | 35.38 N | 128.43 E |
| Chonggu | 106 | 31.12 N | 121.10 E |
| Ch'ŏngha | 98 | 36.13 N | 129.20 E |
| Ch'onghak-ni | 271b | 37.43 N | 127.05 E |
| Chonghe | 89 | 44.43 N | 127.45 E |
| Ch'ŏngjin | 98 | 41.47 N | 129.50 E |
| Chŏngju, C.M.I.K. | 98 | 39.41 N | 125.13 E |
| Ch'ŏngju, Taehan | 98 | 36.39 N | 127.31 E |
| Chŏng Kal | 110 | 13.57 N | 103.35 E |
| Chongkanzhen | 107 | 30.09 N | 105.37 E |
| Chongli (Xiwanzi) | 98 | 40.54 N | 115.16 E |
| Chongming | 106 | 31.37 N | 121.24 E |
| Chongming Dao I | 106 | 31.36 N | 121.33 E |
| Chongoene | 156 | 25.00 S | 33.47 E |
| Chongor | 102 | 45.59 N | 112.45 E |
| Chongos Bajo | 248 | 12.07 S | 75.16 W |
| Chongoyape | 248 | 6.39 S | 79.24 W |
| Chong Pang | 271c | 1.26 N | 103.50 E |
| Chŏngp'yŏng-chŏsuji ⊜[1] | 98 | 37.40 N | 127.30 E |
| Chongqing, Zhg. | 107 | 30.39 N | 103.41 E |
| Chongqing (Chungking), Zhg. | 107 | 29.34 N | 106.35 E |
| Chongren, Zhg. | 100 | 29.37 N | 120.43 E |
| Chongren, Zhg. | 100 | 27.46 N | 116.01 E |
| Chongru | 100 | 27.01 N | 120.10 E |
| Ch'ŏngsan | 98 | 36.22 N | 127.46 E |
| Ch'ŏngsan-do I | 98 | 34.11 N | 126.54 E |
| Chongshi | 100 | 25.24 N | 115.28 E |
| Chŏngsŏn | 98 | 37.22 N | 128.38 E |
| Ch'ŏngsong | 98 | 41.47 N | 129.48 E |
| Chŏngŭp | 98 | 35.36 N | 126.51 E |
| Chongwe ≃ | 154 | 15.43 S | 29.20 E |
| Chongwu | 100 | 24.53 N | 118.55 E |
| Chongxi | 98 | 42.07 N | 128.59 E |
| Chongxin | 102 | 35.13 N | 107.29 E |
| Ch'ŏngyang, Taehan | 98 | 36.27 N | 126.48 E |
| Chongyang, Zhg. | 100 | 29.33 N | 114.00 E |
| Chongyang ≃ | 100 | 27.18 N | 118.08 E |
| Chongyi | 100 | 25.44 N | 114.18 E |
| Chongzuo | 102 | 22.21 N | 107.26 E |
| Choni | 84 | 42.20 N | 42.25 E |
| Chŏnju | 98 | 35.49 N | 127.08 E |
| Chonkham | 120 | 27.48 N | 96.02 E |
| Ch'ŏnma | 98 | 40.03 N | 125.01 E |
| Chonobad | 85 | 40.48 N | 72.58 E |
| Chonos, Archipiélago de los II | 254 | 45.00 S | 74.00 W |
| Ch'ŏnsu-ri | 98 | 41.43 N | 128.45 E |
| Chontaleña, Cordillera ⋀ | 236 | 11.50 N | 84.50 W |
| Chontales □[5] | 236 | 12.05 N | 85.10 W |
| Chon Thanh | 110 | 11.24 N | 106.36 E |
| Chŏnŭi | 98 | 36.42 N | 127.11 E |
| Chonuu | 74 | 66.27 N | 143.06 E |
| Chonzie, Ben ∧ | 46 | 56.27 N | 3.59 W |
| Cho Oyu → Chopu ∧ | 124 | 28.06 N | 86.39 E |
| Chop | 78 | 48.26 N | 22.10 E |
| Chopda | 120 | 21.15 N | 75.18 E |
| Cho Phuoc Hai | 110 | 10.26 N | 107.18 E |
| Chopim ≃ | 252 | 25.35 S | 53.05 W |
| Chopinzinho | 252 | 25.51 S | 52.30 W |
| Chopon | 124 | 24.31 N | 83.02 E |
| Chop'or ≃ | 80 | 49.36 N | 42.19 E |
| Chop'orskij zapovednik ◆[4] | 80 | 51.15 N | 41.48 E |
| Chopovychi | 78 | 50.49 N | 27.58 E |
| Choptank ≃ | 208 | 38.38 N | 76.13 W |
| Chopu ∧ | 124 | 28.06 N | 86.39 E |
| Chopwell | 44 | 54.55 N | 1.49 W |
| Chor | 89 | 47.53 N | 134.58 E |
| Chor ≃ | 89 | 47.48 N | 134.43 E |
| Chora Saādatpur | 272a | 28.36 N | 77.21 E |
| Chordil sar'dag ⋀ | 88 | 50.50 N | 99.40 E |
| Chorejver | 24 | 67.25 N | 58.03 E |
| Chorges | 62 | 44.33 N | 6.17 E |
| Chorin ⊥ | 54 | 52.54 N | 13.52 E |
| Chorinsk | 88 | 52.10 N | 109.46 E |
| Chorley | 44 | 53.39 N | 2.39 W |
| Chorley □[8] | 262 | 53.38 N | 2.38 W |
| Chorleywood | 260 | 51.39 N | 0.31 W |
| Chorlovo | 82 | 55.20 N | 38.49 E |
| Chorlton-cum-Hardy ◆[8] | 262 | 53.27 N | 2.17 W |
| Chorna | 78 | 47.37 N | 29.20 E |
| Chornobay | 78 | 49.41 N | 32.19 E |
| Chornobayivka | 78 | 46.42 N | 32.32 E |
| Chornobyl' | 78 | 51.16 N | 30.14 E |
| Chornomors'ke, Ukr. | 78 | 45.30 N | 32.42 E |
| Chornomors'ke, Ukr. | 78 | 45.03 N | 35.58 E |
| Chornukhy | 78 | 50.16 N | 32.57 E |
| Chornukhyne | 83 | 48.19 N | 38.30 E |
| Chornyy Ostriv | 78 | 49.32 N | 26.46 E |
| Chornyy Tashlyk ≃ | 78 | 48.11 N | 30.51 E |
| Chorog | 120 | 37.31 N | 71.33 E |
| Chorol' | 89 | 44.25 N | 132.04 E |
| Chorolque, Cerro ∧ | 248 | 20.56 S | 66.01 W |
| Choros, Isla I | 252 | 29.16 S | 71.33 W |
| Chorošovo | 82 | 55.08 N | 38.47 E |
| Chorošovo ◆[8] | 265b | 55.47 N | 37.28 E |
| Choroszcz | 30 | 53.09 N | 22.59 E |
| Chorreras | 232 | 28.50 N | 105.18 W |
| Chorrillos | 286d | 12.10 S | 77.02 W |
| Chorrochó | 250 | 8.59 S | 39.06 W |
| Chorro Creek ≃ | 226 | 35.20 N | 120.50 W |
| Chort'ak, gora ∧ | 88 | 53.15 N | 110.45 E |
| Chortkiv | 78 | 49.01 N | 25.48 E |
| Chortomlyk | 78 | 47.37 N | 34.09 E |
| Ch'ŏrwŏn | 98 | 38.16 N | 127.12 E |
| Chorzele | 30 | 53.16 N | 20.55 E |
| Ch'osan | 98 | 40.50 N | 125.47 E |
| Chosanch'am | 98 | 40.22 N | 126.11 E |
| Chosedachard | 24 | 67.02 N | 59.22 E |
| Chosen | 220 | 26.42 N | 80.41 W |
| Chošeutovo | 80 | 47.02 N | 47.50 E |
| Chōshi | 94 | 35.44 N | 140.50 E |
| Choshi-ōhashi ◆[5] | 94 | 35.44 N | 140.50 E |
| Chōshi-zuka-kofun ⊥ | 94 | 34.42 N | 137.50 E |
| Choshui ≃ | 100 | 24.03 N | 120.24 E |
| Chosica | 248 | 11.54 S | 76.42 W |
| Chos Malal | 252 | 37.23 S | 70.16 W |
| Chosŏn Minjujuŭi In'min Konghwaguk → Korea, North □[1] | 98 | 40.00 N | 127.00 E |
| Chosrech | 84 | 41.59 N | 47.18 E |
| Chosta | 84 | 43.33 N | 39.53 E |
| Choszczno | 30 | 53.10 N | 15.26 E |
| Chota | 248 | 6.33 S | 78.39 W |
| Chotanāgpur Plateau ⋀[1] | 124 | 23.30 N | 84.30 E |
| Chotča ≃ | 82 | 56.54 N | 37.35 E |
| Choteau | 202 | 47.48 N | 112.10 W |
| Choteau Creek ≃ | 198 | 42.51 N | 98.09 W |
| Chotěboř | 30 | 49.43 N | 15.40 E |
| Chotěšov | 60 | 49.39 N | 13.12 E |
| Chotila | 120 | 22.25 N | 71.11 E |
| Chotilovo | 76 | 57.44 N | 34.05 E |
| Chotisino | 82 | 54.24 N | 36.33 E |
| Chot'kovo, Ross. | 76 | 53.46 N | 35.14 E |
| Chot'kovo, Ross. | 76 | 52.56 N | 35.23 E |
| Chot'kovo, Ross. | 82 | 56.15 N | 38.00 E |
| Chotuš' | 82 | 54.32 N | 37.44 E |
| Chotynec | 76 | 53.08 N | 35.24 E |
| Chotyrboky | 78 | 50.02 N | 27.01 E |
| Chouchiak'ou → Shangshui | 100 | 33.33 N | 114.34 E |
| Chouk'ou → Shangshui | 100 | 33.33 N | 114.34 E |
| Choûm | 148 | 21.18 N | 13.01 W |
| Chouteau | 196 | 36.11 N | 95.20 W |
| Chovaling | 85 | 38.21 N | 69.58 E |
| Chovd, Mong. | 86 | 49.16 N | 90.55 E |
| Chovd, Mong. | 86 | 48.08 N | 91.23 E |
| Chovd, Mong. | 86 | 48.01 N | 91.38 E |
| Chovd, Mong. | 102 | 44.42 N | 102.24 E |
| Chovd □[4] | 86 | 48.00 N | 91.30 E |
| Chovd ≃ | 90 | 48.06 N | 92.11 E |
| Chövsgöl | 102 | 43.36 N | 109.39 E |
| Chövsgöl □[4] | 88 | 50.00 N | 100.00 E |
| Chövsgöl nuur ⊜ | 88 | 51.00 N | 100.30 E |
| Chovu-Aksy | 88 | 51.11 N | 93.53 E |
| Chowan ≃ | 192 | 36.00 N | 76.40 W |
| Chowchilla | 226 | 37.07 N | 120.15 W |
| Chowchilla ≃ | 226 | 37.07 N | 120.32 W |
| Chowchilla, East Fork ≃ | 226 | 37.20 N | 119.50 W |
| Chowchilla, West Fork ≃ | 226 | 37.20 N | 119.50 W |
| Chowkay | 123 | 34.41 N | 70.56 E |
| Chown, Mount ∧ | 182 | 53.24 N | 119.22 W |
| Ch'owŏn-ni | 98 | 39.40 N | 127.17 E |
| Choya | 252 | 28.30 S | 64.52 W |
| Choyak-to I | 98 | 34.22 N | 126.54 E |
| Chr'aščevka | 80 | 53.48 N | 49.06 E |
| Chrást | 60 | 49.48 N | 13.29 E |
| Chrebtovo | 82 | 56.35 N | 38.16 E |
| Chrenovoje | 80 | 51.07 N | 40.17 E |
| Chreščatij | 83 | 49.37 N | 39.42 E |
| Chřibská | 54 | 50.50 N | 14.29 E |
| Chříč | 60 | 49.57 N | 13.39 E |
| Chriesman | 222 | 30.36 N | 96.46 W |
| Chrisman | 194 | 39.48 N | 87.40 W |
| Chrissiesmeer | 158 | 26.16 S | 30.13 E |
| Chrissiesmeer ⊜ | 158 | 26.19 S | 30.13 E |
| Christanshåb (Qasigiannguit) | 176 | 68.50 N | 51.12 W |
| Christchurch, N.Z. | 172 | 43.32 S | 172.38 E |
| Christchurch, Eng., U.K. | 42 | 50.44 N | 1.45 W |
| Christ Church Cathedral ✿[1] | 273a | 6.27 N | 3.23 E |
| Christian □[6] | 219 | 39.33 N | 89.18 W |
| Christian ≃ | 180 | 66.36 N | 145.49 W |
| Christian, Cape › | 176 | 70.31 N | 68.18 W |
| Christian, Point › | 174e | 25.04 S | 130.07 W |
| Christiana, Jam. | 241q | 18.10 N | 77.29 W |
| Christiana, S. Afr. | 158 | 27.52 S | 25.08 E |
| Christiana, De., U.S. | 285 | 39.39 N | 75.39 W |
| Christiana, Pa., U.S. | 208 | 39.57 N | 75.59 W |
| Christiana Creek ≃ | 216 | 41.41 N | 85.59 W |
| Christianburg | 218 | 38.17 N | 85.06 W |
| Christian Channel ʊ | 212 | 44.47 N | 80.08 W |
| Christian Island I | 212 | 44.50 N | 80.13 W |
| Christian Island Indian Reserve ◆[4] | 212 | 44.50 N | 80.10 W |
| Christiansburg, Oh., U.S. | 218 | 40.03 N | 84.01 W |
| Christiansburg, Va., U.S. | 192 | 37.07 N | 80.24 W |
| Christiansfeld | 41 | 55.21 N | 9.29 E |
| Christiansø I | 26 | 55.19 N | 15.12 E |
| Christian Sound ʊ | 180 | 55.56 N | 134.40 W |
| Christiansted | 241n | 17.45 N | 64.42 W |
| Christie, Mount ∧ | 180 | 63.01 N | 129.40 W |
| Christie, Mount ∧[2] | 216 | 42.53 N | 83.20 W |
| Christie Bay c | 176 | 62.32 N | 111.10 W |
| Christie Lake ⊜, Mb., Can. | 184 | 56.54 N | 96.56 W |
| Christie Lake ⊜, On., Can. | 212 | 44.48 N | 76.26 W |
| Christina ≃, Ab., Can. | 184 | 56.40 N | 111.03 W |
| Christina ≃, De., U.S. | 285 | 39.43 N | 75.31 W |
| Christina Lake ⊜, Ab., Can. | 182 | 55.38 N | 110.55 W |
| Christina Lake ⊜, B.C., Can. | 182 | 49.05 N | 118.14 W |
| Christmas | 220 | 28.32 N | 81.01 W |
| Christmas Bay c | 222 | 29.03 N | 95.11 W |
| Christmas Creek | 162 | 18.53 S | 125.55 E |
| Christmas Creek ≃ | 162 | 18.29 S | 125.23 E |
| Christmas Island □[2], Oc. | 108 | 10.30 S | 105.40 E |
| Christmas Island □[2], Oc. | 112 | 10.30 S | 105.40 E |
| Christmas Island → Kiritimati I[1] | 174o | 1.52 N | 157.20 W |
| Christmas Mountain ∧ | 180 | 64.34 N | 160.34 W |
| Christmas Ridge ✤[3] | 14 | 5.00 N | 160.00 W |
| Christoforovo | 24 | 60.53 N | 47.13 E |
| Christ of the Andes → Cristo Redentor ⊥ | 252 | 32.50 S | 70.05 W |


**Symbols** in the index entries represent the broad categories identified in the key at the right. Symbols with superior numbers (⋀[1]) identify subcategories (see complete key on page *I · 1)*.

**Symbole** im Register stellen die rechts im Schlüssel erklärten Kategorien dar. Symbole mit hochgestellten Ziffern (⋀[1]) bezeichnen Unterabteilungen einer Kategorie (vgl. vollständiger Schlüssel auf Seite *I · 1)*.

**Los símbolos** incluídos en el texto del índice representan las grandes categorías identificadas con la clave a la derecha. Los símbolos con numeros en su parte superior (⋀[1]) identifican las subcategorías (véase la clave completa en la página *I · 1)*.

**Les symboles** de l'index représentent les catégories indiquées dans la légende à droite. Les symboles suivis d'un indice (⋀[1]) représentent des sous-catégories (voir légende complète à la page *I · 1)*.

**Os símbolos** incluídos no texto do índice representam as grandes categorias identificadas com a chave à direita. Os símbolos com números em sua parte superior (⋀[1]) identificam as subcategorias (veja-se a chave completa à página *I · 1)*.

| | English | Deutsch | Español | Français | Português |
|---|---|---|---|---|---|
| ∧ | Mountain | Berg | Montaña | Montagne | Montanha |
| ⋀ | Mountains | Gebirge | Montañas | Montagnes | Montanhas |
| )( | Pass | Paß | Paso | Col | Passo |
| V | Valley, Canyon | Tal, Cañon | Valle, Cañón | Vallée, Canyon | Vale, Canhão |
| ≌ | Plain | Ebene | Llano | Plaine | Planície |
| › | Cape | Kap | Cabo | Cap | Cabo |
| I | Island | Insel | Isla | Île | Ilha |
| II | Islands | Inseln | Islas | Îles | Ilhas |
| ⊥ | Other Topographic Features | Andere Topographische Objekte | Otros Elementos Topográficos | Autres données topographiques | Outros acidentes topográficos |

ESPAÑOL — Nombre · Página · Lat.°′ · Long.°′ W = Oeste
FRANÇAIS — Nom · Page · Lat.°′ · Long.°′ W = Ouest
PORTUGUÊS — Nome · Página · Lat.°′ · Long.°′ W = Oeste


Christoph Columbus-Spitze → Cristóbal Colón, Pico ∧ 246 10.50 N 73.41 W
Christopher 194 37.58 N 89.03 W
Christopher, Lake ⊜ 162 24.49 S 127.42 E
Christoval 196 31.12 N 100.30 W
Chroma ≏ 74 71.36 N 144.49 E
Chromtau 86 50.17 N 58.27 E
Chrudim 30 49.57 N 15.48 E
Chrustal'nyj 89 44.24 N 135.06 E
Chrzanów 30 50.09 N 19.24 E
Chu (Xam) ≏, Asia 110 19.53 N 105.45 E
Chu ≏, Zhg. 100 32.08 N 118.43 E
Chu ≏, Zhg. 106 32.15 N 119.03 E
Chuādanga 124 23.38 N 88.51 E
Chualar 226 36.34 N 121.31 W
Chuanbu 106 31.17 N 119.49 E
Chuanchang ≊ 100 33.46 N 119.51 E
Chuanergu 105 39.20 N 117.43 E
Chuan'gang 106 31.57 N 121.04 E
Chuangjiapuzi 104 40.50 N 124.06 E
Chuanliao 100 28.17 N 120.13 E
Chuansha 106 31.12 N 121.42 E
Chuanshan 100 29.53 N 121.57 E
Chuanxindian 104 41.25 N 120.30 E
Chuanyao Gang ⊂ 106 32.12 N 121.25 E
Chuathbaluk 180 61.40 N 159.15 W
Chubbuck 202 42.55 N 112.27 W
Chūbu-Sangaku-kokuritsu-kōen ♠ 94 36.30 N 137.41 E
Chubut □[4] 254 44.00 S 69.00 W
Chubut ≏ 254 43.20 S 65.03 W
Ch'üchiang → Shaoguan 100 24.50 N 113.37 E
Chuchi Lake ⊜ 182 55.10 N 124.33 W
Chuchou → Zhuzhou 100 27.50 N 113.09 E
Chu Chua 182 51.21 N 120.10 W
Chuchuwayha Indian Reserve ◆[4] 182 49.21 N 120.06 W
Chuckatuck 208 36.52 N 76.35 W
Chučni 84 41.57 N 47.55 E
Chucuito 248 15.53 S 69.53 W
Chucun 100 33.04 N 116.32 E
Chucunaque ≏ 246 8.09 N 77.44 W
Chudan ≏ 88 52.08 N 109.40 E
Chudanskij chrebet ⋏ 88 52.00 N 110.00 E
Chudeč 60 49.58 N 13.05 E
Chudleigh 42 50.36 N 3.38 W
Chudniv 78 50.04 N 28.06 E
Chudojelan' 88 54.42 N 99.37 E
Chudžand (Leninabad) 85 40.17 N 69.37 E
Chudžand □[4] 85 39.15 N 69.30 E
Chudzirt 86 47.05 N 91.10 E
Chuen Lung 271d 22.24 N 114.06 E
Chugach Islands II 180 59.06 N 151.42 W
Chugach Mountains ⋏ 180 61.00 N 145.00 W
Chuginadak Island I 180 52.49 N 169.50 W
Chūgoku-sanchi ⋏ 96 34.58 N 132.57 E
Chugwater 200 41.45 N 104.49 W
Chugwater Creek ≏ 198 42.07 N 104.51 W
Chugyn-ri 271b 37.39 N 126.50 E
Chūhar Kāna 123 31.45 N 73.48 E
Chuhe 100 34.03 N 113.35 E
Chuhuichupa 232 29.38 N 108.22 W
Chuhuyiv 78 49.50 N 36.41 E
Chuhynka 83 48.55 N 39.39 E
Chuí 252 33.41 S 53.27 W
Chuius Mountain ∧ 182 54.51 N 124.30 W
Chukai 114 4.15 N 103.25 E
Chukchi Sea ⫪[2] 16 69.00 N 171.00 W
Chuke Hu ⊜ 120 31.40 N 88.00 E
Chukou 100 25.44 N 113.22 E
Chulalongkorn University ʊ[2] 269a 13.44 N 100.33 E
Chula Vista 228 32.38 N 117.05 W
Chuld 102 45.04 N 105.35 E
Chulga ≏ 24 64.20 N 61.00 E
Chullora 274a 33.54 S 151.04 E
Chulmleigh 42 50.55 N 3.52 W
Chulo 84 41.41 N 42.18 E
Chulp'o 98 35.37 N 126.40 E
Chulucanas 248 5.06 S 80.10 W
Chulumani 248 16.24 S 67.31 W
Chuluota 220 28.38 N 81.10 W
Chuma 248 15.24 S 68.56 W
Chumalag 84 43.14 N 44.28 E
Chumbicha 252 28.52 S 66.14 W
Chummi, ozero ⊜ 89 50.18 N 137.17 E
Chum Phae 110 16.32 N 102.06 E
Chumphon 110 10.30 N 99.10 E
Chumphon Buri 110 15.21 N 103.24 E
Chumpi 248 15.06 S 73.46 W
Chum Saeng 110 15.54 N 100.19 E
Chumunjin 98 37.54 N 128.49 E
Chunal 262 53.25 N 1.57 W
Chunan, T'aiwan 100 24.41 N 120.52 E
Chun'an, Zhg. 100 29.35 N 118.58 E
Chunār 124 25.08 N 82.54 E
Chuncheon → Ch'unch'ŏn 98 37.52 N 127.43 E
Chunchi, Ec. 246 2.17 S 78.55 W
Chunchi, Zhg. 100 27.22 N 119.20 E
Ch'unch'ŏn 98 37.52 N 127.43 E
Chunchula 194 30.55 N 88.12 W
Chūnd 123 31.26 N 72.16 E
Chung-ang University ʊ[2] 271b 37.30 N 126.58 E
Chungari ≏ 89 50.04 N 136.55 E
Ch'ungch'ŏng Namdo □[4] 98 36.30 N 127.00 E
Ch'ungch'ŏng Pukdo □[4] 98 36.45 N 128.00 E
Chunggang-ni 98 40.52 N 127.20 E
Chung Hau 271d 22.16 N 114.00 E
Chungho 269d 25.00 N 121.30 E
Chung Hsing Bridge ◆[5] 269d 25.03 N 121.29 E
Chunghwa 98 38.52 N 125.47 E
Ch'ungju 98 36.58 N 127.58 E
Chungking → Chongqing 107 29.34 N 106.35 E
Chungli 100 24.57 N 121.13 E
Chungliao 100 22.41 N 121.28 E
Ch'ungmu 98 34.51 N 128.25 E
Chungp'u 100 23.25 N 120.31 E
Chungp'yŏngjang 98 41.11 N 128.03 E
Chungsam-ni 98 38.34 N 127.09 E
Chŭngsan 98 39.06 N 125.22 E
Chŭngsanha-ri ◆[8] 271b 37.35 N 126.54 E
Chungshan → Zhongshan 100 22.31 N 113.22 E
Chungshan Bridge ◆[5] 269d 25.05 N 121.31 E
Chunguj ≏ 88 48.51 N 93.32 E
Chungyang Shanmo ⋏ 100 23.30 N 121.00 E
Chunheji 100 32.12 N 115.22 E
Chunhua, Zhg. 102 34.50 N 108.31 E
Chunhua, Zhg. 106 31.56 N 118.56 E
Chunhuhux 232 19.12 N 88.55 W
Chūniān 123 30.58 N 73.59 E
Chuntuquí 232 17.31 N 90.09 W
Chünüj ≏ 88 48.48 N 102.00 E
Chunya 154 8.32 S 33.25 E
Ch'unyang, Taehan 98 36.56 N 128.54 E
Chunyang, Zhg. 89 43.43 N 129.28 E
Chunzach 84 42.33 N 46.43 E
Chūō 96 35.00 N 133.58 E
Chūō ◆[8], Nihon 268 35.40 N 139.47 E
Chūō ◆[8], Nihon 270 34.42 N 135.11 E
Chuŏr Phnum Krâvanh ⋏ 110 12.00 N 103.15 E
Chuosijia 102 31.53 N 101.59 E
Chupaca 248 12.04 S 75.19 W
Chupadera Arroyo ⋁ 200 33.47 N 106.37 W
Chupadero, Cerro ∧ 200 31.01 N 111.37 W
Chupakhivka 78 50.23 N 34.36 E
Chupara Point › 241r 10.48 N 61.22 W
Chuquibamba 248 15.50 S 72.39 W
Chuquibambilla 248 14.07 S 72.43 W
Chuquicamata 252 22.19 S 68.56 W
Chuquisaca □[5] 248 20.00 S 64.20 W
Chuquitanta 286d 11.58 S 77.06 W
Chur 58 46.51 N 9.32 E
Churach ≏ 88 48.37 N 110.42 E
Churāchāndpur 120 24.20 N 93.40 E
Churāmankāti 126 23.14 N 89.09 E
Churcampa 248 12.42 S 74.24 W
Church 262 53.45 N 2.24 W
Churchdown 42 51.53 N 2.10 W
Church Hill 192 36.31 N 82.42 W
Churchill, Mb., Can. 176 58.46 N 94.10 W
Churchill, Oh., U.S. 214 41.09 N 80.39 W
Churchill, Pa., U.S. 279b 40.27 N 79.51 W
Churchill, Va., U.S. 284c 38.54 N 77.10 W
Churchill ≏, Can. 176 58.47 N 94.12 W
Churchill ≏, Nf., Can. 176 53.30 N 60.10 W
Churchill, Cape › 176 58.46 N 93.12 W
Churchill, Mount ∧, B.C., Can. 182 49.58 N 123.51 W
Churchill, Mount ∧, Ak., U.S. 180 61.25 N 141.43 W
Churchill Downs ♠ 218 38.12 N 85.46 W
Churchill Falls ∟ 176 53.35 N 64.27 W
Churchill Lake ⊜ 184 55.55 N 108.20 W
Churchill National Park ♠ 169 37.58 S 145.17 E
Church Point 194 30.24 N 92.12 W
Church Rock 200 35.32 N 108.35 W
Church Street 260 51.26 N 0.28 E
Church Stretton 42 52.32 N 2.49 W
Churchton 208 38.48 N 76.32 W
Churchtown, Eng., U.K. 262 53.40 N 2.58 W
Churchtown, Pa., U.S. 208 40.08 N 75.58 W
Church View 208 37.41 N 76.41 W
Churchville, On., Can. 275b 43.38 N 79.45 W
Churchville, Md., U.S. 208 39.33 N 76.14 W
Churchville, N.Y., U.S. 210 43.06 N 77.53 W
Churchville, Pa., U.S. 285 40.11 N 75.01 W
Churdan 198 42.09 N 94.28 W
Churen Himāl ∧ 124 28.44 N 83.12 E
Chure Śringklā ⋏ 124 27.40 N 83.40 E
Churfirsten ⋏ 58 47.08 N 9.17 E
Chürmen 102 43.20 N 104.05 E
Churmuli 89 51.00 N 136.50 E
Churn ≏ 42 51.38 N 1.53 W
Churn Creek ≏ 182 51.30 N 122.17 W
Churnet ≏ 44 52.55 N 1.50 W
Churni ≏[1] 126 23.08 N 88.30 E
Chursdorf 54 50.46 N 12.15 E
Chūru 120 28.18 N 74.57 E
Churubusco, In., U.S. 216 41.13 N 85.19 W
Churubusco, N.Y., U.S. 206 44.57 N 73.56 W
Churuguara 246 10.49 N 69.32 W
Churumuco de Morelos 234 18.37 N 101.38 W
Churwalden 58 46.47 N 9.33 E
Chušenga 88 51.27 N 110.55 E
Chushan 100 23.45 N 120.40 E
Chushul 120 33.36 N 78.39 E
Chuska Mountains ⋏ 200 36.15 N 108.50 W
Chuska Peak ∧ 200 35.53 N 108.50 W
Chusovoy → Čusovoj 86 58.17 N 57.49 E
Chusuut uul ∧ 88 47.45 N 105.45 E
Chūta 174m 26.32 N 127.58 E
Chutag 88 49.23 N 102.43 E
Chutag Uul 102 43.23 N 110.13 E
Chute-à-Blondeau 206 45.35 N 74.29 W
Chute-Panet 206 46.51 N 71.51 W
Chutorskoj 80 46.52 N 42.59 E
Chutove 78 49.43 N 35.10 E
Chutu ≏ 89 49.27 N 140.02 E
Chutung 100 24.44 N 121.05 E
Chuuk (Truk Islands) II 175c 7.25 N 151.47 E
Chuŭl 98 41.33 N 129.34 E
Chuvashia → Čuvašija □[3] 80 55.30 N 47.00 E
Chuwang 98 36.02 N 114.52 E
Chuwang-san Kukrip Kongwŏn ♠ 98 36.26 N 129.10 E
Chuwei 269d 25.08 N 121.27 E
Chuxian 100 32.19 N 118.17 E
Chuxiong 102 25.02 N 101.30 E
Chuy 252 33.41 S 53.27 W
Chuzenji-ko ⊜ 94 36.44 N 139.29 E
Chuzhai 100 33.22 N 113.37 E
Chužir 88 53.11 N 107.20 E
Chūzu 94 35.06 N 136.00 E
Chvalynsk 80 52.30 N 48.07 E
Chvančkara 84 42.34 N 43.01 E
Chvastoviči 76 53.28 N 35.06 E
Chvatovka 80 52.21 N 46.34 E
Chvojnaja 76 58.54 N 34.32 E
Chvorost'anka 80 52.36 N 48.59 E
Chvostovo 92a 46.08 N 142.14 E
Chwefru ≏ 42 52.09 N 3.25 W
Ch'wiya-ri 98 38.03 N 125.32 E
Chychykliya ≏ 78 47.23 N 31.34 E
Chyhyryn 78 49.04 N 32.40 E
Chynadiyeve 78 48.30 N 22.50 E
Chypre → Cyprus □[1] 130 35.00 N 33.00 E
Chystovodivka 83 49.24 N 37.20 E
Ci ≏, Zhg. 98 38.19 N 115.23 E
Ci ≏, Zhg. 100 33.27 N 115.31 E
Ciadâr Lunga 38 46.03 N 28.47 E
Ciago 64 46.12 N 12.46 E
Ciagola, Monte ∧ 68 39.54 N 15.53 E
Ciales 240m 18.20 N 66.28 W
Ciamis 115a 7.20 S 108.21 E
Ciampino 66 41.48 N 12.36 E
Ciampino, Aeroporto di ⊠ 267a 41.48 N 12.36 E
Cianciana 70 37.31 N 13.26 E
Ciandur 115a 6.24 S 105.59 E
Cianjur 115a 6.49 S 107.08 E
Ciano d'Enza 64 44.36 N 10.24 E
Cianorte 255 23.37 S 52.37 W
Çians, Gorges du ⋁ 62 43.57 N 6.59 E
Čiatura 84 42.17 N 43.17 E
Ciavolo 70 37.46 N 12.33 E
Ciawi, Indon. 115a 7.10 S 108.09 E
Ciawi, Indon. 115a 6.40 S 106.50 E
Ciawigebang 115a 6.58 S 108.34 E
Ciba 107 29.07 N 105.55 E
Cibadak 115a 6.53 S 106.46 E
Cibaliung 115a 6.46 S 105.51 E
Čibargata 85 41.08 N 69.48 E
Cibatu 115a 7.06 S 107.59 E
Cibeber 115a 6.56 S 107.07 E
Cibecue 200 34.02 N 110.29 W
Cibiana 64 46.23 N 12.17 E
Cibinong 115a 6.27 S 106.51 E
Čibisovka 78 50.47 N 40.05 E
Čibižek 86 54.27 N 93.40 E
Cibolo Creek ≏, Tx., U.S. 196 28.57 N 97.53 W
Cibolo Creek ≏, Tx., U.S. 196 29.34 N 104.24 W
Cibolo Creek ≏, Tx., U.S. 196 28.27 N 98.54 W
Cibuta 200 31.04 N 110.54 W
Cicagna 62 44.25 N 9.14 E
Cicala 68 39.01 N 16.29 E
Cicalengka 115a 6.59 S 107.50 E
Čićarija ⋏ 36 45.30 N 13.54 E
Čičatka 89 54.03 N 121.18 E
Cicciano 68 40.58 N 14.32 E
Cicero, Il., U.S. 216 41.50 N 87.45 W
Cicero, In., U.S. 218 40.07 N 86.00 W
Cicero, N.Y., U.S. 210 43.10 N 76.07 W
Cicero Creek ≏ 194 40.01 N 86.01 W
Cícero Dantas 250 10.36 S 38.23 W
Čichačovo, Ross. 76 57.17 N 29.54 E
Čichačovo, Ross. 89 51.50 N 141.07 E
Čichareši 84 42.48 N 43.03 E
Ciche, Sgurr na ∧ 46 57.01 N 5.27 W
Cicheng 100 30.00 N 121.22 E
Čičkajul ≏ 86 57.34 N 85.44 E
Cícladas, Islas → Kikládhes II 38 37.30 N 25.00 E
Cicolano ◆[1] 66 42.12 N 13.12 E
Cicurug 115a 6.47 S 106.47 E
Cidacos ≏ 34 42.19 N 1.55 W
Cidade, Rio da ≏ 256 22.25 S 43.09 W
Cidade Universitária ʊ[2], Bra. 287a 22.52 S 43.14 W
Cidade Universitária ʊ[2], Bra. 287b 23.33 S 46.43 W
Cide 130 41.54 N 33.00 E
Cidra 240m 18.11 N 66.10 W
Cidra, Lago de ⊜[1] 240m 18.12 N 66.08 W
Ciechanów 30 52.53 N 20.38 E
Ciechanów □[4] 30 53.00 N 20.20 E
Ciechanowiec 30 52.42 N 22.31 E
Ciechocinek 30 52.52 N 18.49 E
Ciego de Ávila 240p 21.51 N 78.46 W
Ciego de Ávila □[4] 240p 22.00 N 78.40 W
Ciempozuelos 34 40.10 N 3.37 W
Ciénaga 246 11.01 N 74.15 W
Ciénaga de Oro 246 8.53 N 75.37 W
Ciénega de Flores 196 25.57 N 100.11 W
Cienfuegos 240p 22.09 N 80.27 W
Cienfuegos □[4] 240p 22.10 N 80.25 W
Cienfuegos, Bahía de ⊂ 240p 22.07 N 80.29 W
Čierna [nad Tisou] 30 48.25 N 22.05 E
Čierny Balog 30 48.45 N 19.40 E
Cíes, Illas II 34 42.13 N 8.54 W
Cieszanów 30 50.16 N 23.08 E
Cieszyn 30 49.45 N 18.38 E
Cieza 34 38.14 N 1.25 W
Çiftalan ◆[8] 267b 41.15 N 28.54 E
Çiftehan 130 37.31 N 34.46 E
Çifteler 130 39.22 N 31.03 E
Çiftlik 130 38.11 N 34.30 E
Cifuentes, Cuba 240p 22.39 N 80.03 W
Cifuentes, Esp. 34 40.47 N 2.37 W
Čiganak, Kaz. 86 45.06 N 73.58 E
Čiganak, Ross. 80 51.47 N 43.18 E
Čiganaki 80 47.57 N 43.05 E
Cigliano 62 45.18 N 8.01 E
Čigorak 80 51.26 N 42.09 E
Cigou 100 33.51 N 113.35 E
Cigüela ≏ 34 39.08 N 3.44 W
Cihanbeyli 130 38.40 N 32.56 E
Cihara 115a 6.52 S 106.06 E
Cihuatlán 234 19.14 N 104.35 W
Čiili 86 44.10 N 66.45 E
Cijara, Embalse de ⊜[1] 34 39.18 N 4.52 W
Čijen 85 43.08 N 75.55 E
Cijiawu 105 39.48 N 115.59 E
Čijirčik, pereval )( 85 40.15 N 73.20 E
Čijli ≏ 85 40.17 N 72.38 E
Cijulang 115a 7.44 S 108.27 E
Čik 86 55.01 N 82.27 E
Cikajang 115a 7.22 S 107.47 E
Cikalong-kulon 115a 6.42 S 107.12 E
Cikampek 115a 6.24 S 107.27 E
Čikan 88 54.54 N 105.39 E
Cikarang 115a 6.15 S 107.09 E
Cikatomas 115a 7.37 S 108.15 E
Čikišl'ar 128 37.34 N 53.55 E
Čikoj 88 50.16 N 106.54 E
Čikoj ≏ 88 51.02 N 106.39 E
Čikola 84 43.12 N 43.55 E
Cikou 100 29.42 N 114.46 E
Cıksı 130 38.30 N 40.55 E
Cilacap 115a 7.44 S 109.00 E
Cilamaya 115a 6.15 S 107.35 E
Cilavegna 62 45.19 N 8.44 E
Çıldır 84 41.08 N 43.07 E
Çıldır Gölü ⊜ 84 41.04 N 43.15 E
Ciledug 115a 6.54 S 108.44 E
Cilegon 115a 6.01 S 106.03 E
Čilekovo 80 47.50 N 43.30 E
Cilento ◆[1] 68 40.15 N 15.15 E
Čil'gazi 85 40.10 N 70.39 E
Cili 102 29.17 N 111.00 E
Cilicia □[9] 130 36.40 N 34.20 E
Čilik, Kaz. 85 43.36 N 78.15 E
Čilik, Kaz. 86 51.07 N 54.07 E
Čilik ≏, Kaz. 85 43.05 N 78.28 E
Čilik ≏, Kaz. 85 43.50 N 78.06 E
Cililin 115a 6.56 S 107.26 E
Cilimus 115a 6.52 S 108.29 E
Cilincing ◆[8] 269e 6.06 S 106.56 E
Cill Airne → Killarney 48 52.03 N 9.30 W
Cill Chainnigh → Kilkenny 48 52.39 N 7.15 W
Cilleruelo de Bezana 34 42.58 N 3.51 W
Cil'ma ≏ 24 65.27 N 52.06 E
Çilov ada I 84 40.19 N 50.36 E
Cimabanche (Schluderbach) 64 46.37 N 12.11 E
Cima Gogna 64 46.31 N 12.28 E
Cimahi 115a 6.53 S 107.32 E
Cimalaka 115a 6.49 S 107.56 E
Cimalmotto 58 46.17 N 8.29 E
Cimarron, Ks., U.S. 198 37.48 N 100.20 W
Cimarron, N.M., U.S. 200 36.30 N 104.54 W
Cimarron ≏, U.S. 196 36.10 N 96.17 W
Cimarron ≏, N.M., U.S. 196 36.20 N 104.31 W
Cimarron, North Fork ≏ 196 37.25 N 101.13 W
Čimbaj 86 42.57 N 59.47 E
Čimčinej, gora ∧[2] 180 63.37 N 178.04 E
Cimini, Monti ⋏ 66 42.20 N 12.10 E
Ciminna 70 37.54 N 13.34 E
Cimino, Monte ∧ 66 42.24 N 12.12 E
Čimion 85 40.16 N 71.31 E
Cimişlia 38 46.32 N 28.44 E
Cimitile 68 40.56 N 14.31 E
Čimkavičy 76 53.03 N 27.00 E
Čimkent → Šymkent 85 42.18 N 69.36 E
Čimkorgon 85 42.50 N 75.30 E
Ciml̃a ≏ 80 48.01 N 42.24 E
Ciml'ansk 80 47.38 N 42.04 E
Ciml'anskoje vodochranilišče ⊜[1] 80 48.00 N 43.00 E
Cimolais 64 46.17 N 12.26 E
Cimone, Monte ∧ 64 44.12 N 10.42 E
Cimpu 112 3.25 S 120.22 E
Čimtarga, gora ∧ 85 39.12 N 68.10 E
Čina ≏ 88 54.20 N 112.24 E
Cina, Tanjung › 112 5.56 S 104.45 E
Činabad 85 40.52 N 71.58 E
Cinandali 84 41.53 N 45.34 E
Çınar 130 37.44 N 40.25 E
Çınarcık 130 40.39 N 29.06 E
Cinaruco ≏ 246 6.41 N 67.07 W
Činaz 85 40.56 N 68.45 E
Cinca ≏ 34 41.26 N 0.21 E
Cincar ∧ 36 43.54 N 17.04 E
Cincinnati, Ia., U.S. 190 40.37 N 92.55 W
Cincinnati, Oh., U.S. 218 39.09 N 84.27 W
Cincinnatus 210 42.32 N 75.53 W
Cinco, Canal Numero ≊ 252 37.35 S 57.20 W
Cinco Balas, Cayos II 240p 21.06 N 79.20 W
Cinco de Mayo 196 25.46 N 104.19 W
Cinco Pinos 236 13.14 N 86.52 W
Cinco Saltos 252 38.49 S 68.04 W
Cinderella 273d 26.15 S 28.16 E
Cinderella Dam ⊜[1] 273d 26.15 S 28.14 E
Cinderford 42 51.50 N 2.29 W
Cinder Island I 276 40.36 N 73.36 W
Çine 130 37.36 N 28.04 E
Cinebar 224 46.36 N 122.32 W
Cinecittà ʊ[3] 267a 41.51 N 12.34 E
Cinema 182 53.14 N 122.27 W
Ciney 56 50.18 N 5.06 E
Cinfães 34 41.04 N 8.05 W
Čingaly 86 60.13 N 69.45 E
Čingis 86 54.08 N 81.41 E
Cingoli 66 43.22 N 13.13 E
Cinigiano 66 42.53 N 11.24 E
Cinisello Balsamo 62 45.33 N 9.13 E
Cinișeuți 38 47.42 N 28.52 E
Cinisi 70 38.09 N 13.06 E
Činja-Voryk 24 63.13 N 52.38 E
Cinkota ◆[8] 264c 47.31 N 19.14 E
Cinnaminson 285 40.00 N 74.59 W
Cínovec 54 50.43 N 13.45 E
Cinq, Lac des ⊜ 206 46.51 N 72.59 W
Cinq Doigts, Lac ⊜ 206 46.36 N 74.32 W
Cinquefrondi 68 38.25 N 16.06 E
Cinquemiglia, Piano delle ≡ 66 41.50 N 14.00 E
Cinqueterre □[9] 62 44.10 N 9.45 E
Cintalapa 234 16.44 N 93.43 W
Cinto, Monte ∧ 36 42.23 N 8.56 E
Cinto Euganeo 64 45.16 N 11.40 E
Cintra → Sintra 34 38.48 N 9.23 W
Cintra, Golfe de ⊂ 148 23.00 N 16.20 W
Ciocănești 38 44.12 N 27.04 E
Ciociaria ◆[1] 66 41.45 N 13.15 E
Ciomas 115a 6.12 S 106.01 E
Čiovo, Otok I 36 43.30 N 16.20 E
Cipa ≏ 88 55.23 N 115.55 E
Ciparay 115a 7.03 S 107.43 E
Cipatujah 115a 7.45 S 108.00 E
Cipikan 88 54.55 N 113.21 E
Cipikan ≏ 88 55.14 N 113.05 E
Cipó 250 11.06 S 38.31 W
Cipó ≏ 255 18.40 S 43.59 W
Cipolândia 255 20.08 S 55.24 W
Cipolletti 252 38.56 S 67.59 W
Ciqikou 107 29.35 N 106.26 E
Čir 80 48.29 N 43.10 E
Čir ≏ 80 48.35 N 42.51 E
Ciraadhame 144 10.30 N 49.22 E
Čirachčaj ≏ 84 41.40 N 48.11 E
Ciragidzor 84 40.27 N 46.19 E
Ciranjang 115a 6.49 S 107.14 E
Circeo, Monte ∧ 66 41.14 N 13.03 E
Circeo, Parco Nazionale del ♠ 66 41.17 N 13.05 E
Čirčik 85 41.29 N 69.35 E
Čirčik ≏ 85 40.54 N 68.41 E
Çırçır 130 40.04 N 36.48 E
Circle, Ak., U.S. 180 65.50 N 144.04 W
Circle, Mt., U.S. 202 47.20 N 105.35 W
Circle Hot Springs 180 65.28 N 144.39 W
Circleville, N.Y., U.S. 210 41.31 N 75.23 W
Circleville, Oh., U.S. 218 39.36 N 82.56 W
Circleville, Pa., U.S. 279b 40.20 N 79.44 W
Circleville, Ut,. U.S. 200 38.10 N 112.16 W
Circleville Mountain ∧ 200 38.12 N 112.24 W
Circular Reef ✣[2] 164 3.25 S 147.47 E
Circus World ♠ 220 28.14 N 81.38 W
Cirebon 115a 6.44 S 108.34 E
Cireglio 66 43.59 N 10.51 E
Ciremay, Gunung ∧ 115a 6.54 S 108.24 E
Cirencester 42 51.44 N 1.59 W
Cirey-sur-Vezouze 58 48.35 N 6.57 E
Čirgalandy 88 50.36 N 97.20 E
Ciriè 62 45.14 N 7.36 E
Cirigliano 68 40.24 N 16.10 E
Čirikovo 82 55.23 N 37.14 E
Ciriquiri ≏ 248 8.05 S 65.18 W
Cirk, gora ∧ 180 64.33 N 175.25 E
Cirò 68 39.23 N 17.04 E
Cirò Marina 68 39.22 N 17.08 E
Ciro Redondo 240p 22.01 N 78.43 W
Čirpan 38 42.12 N 25.20 E
Ciruas 115a 6.06 S 106.13 E
Cisa, Passo della )( 64 44.28 N 9.55 E
Cisano 64 45.32 N 10.43 E
Cisarua 115a 6.40 S 106.59 E
Cisco, Il., U.S. 219 40.01 N 88.43 W
Cisco, Tx., U.S. 196 32.23 N 98.58 W
Cishan 98 36.37 N 114.07 E
Cishangang 106 30.55 N 119.31 E
Ciskei □[9] 158 32.50 S 27.00 E
Cislago 62 45.39 N 8.58 E
Cisliano 266b 45.27 N 8.59 E
Çismar 54 54.11 N 10.59 E
Čismena 82 56.02 N 36.13 E
Cismon ≏ 64 45.55 N 11.43 E
Cismon del Grappa 64 45.55 N 11.44 E
Čišmy 86 54.35 N 55.20 E
Cisnădie 38 45.43 N 24.09 E
Cisne 194 38.31 N 88.26 W
Cisneros 246 6.33 N 75.04 W
Cisnes ≏ 254 44.45 S 72.42 W
Cisolok 115a 6.57 S 106.26 E
Cison di Valmarino 64 45.58 N 12.10 E
Cispus ≏ 224 46.25 N 122.10 W
Cisse ≏ 50 47.25 N 0.47 E
Cissna Park 216 40.33 N 87.53 W
Čistá, Česká Rep. 54 50.06 N 12.44 E
Čistá, Česká Rep. 60 50.02 N 13.35 E
Cisterna di Latina 66 41.35 N 12.49 E
Cisternino 68 40.44 N 17.25 E
Cistern Point › 238 23.43 N 77.35 W
Cistierna 34 42.48 N 5.07 W
Čistoje 80 56.32 N 43.02 E
Čistooz'ornoje 86 54.43 N 76.33 E
Čistopol' 80 55.21 N 50.37 E
Čistopolje, Kaz. 86 52.34 N 67.15 E
Čistopolje, Ross. 83 47.31 N 39.27 E
Čita 88 52.03 N 113.30 E
Čita ≏ 88 52.00 N 113.30 E
Citac, Nevado ∧ 248 12.48 S 75.14 W
Čita Oblast' □[4] 88 52.00 N 117.00 E
Citaré ≏ 250 1.11 N 54.41 W
Cité Universitaire ʊ[2] 261 48.49 N 2.20 E
Citlaltépetl, Volcán → Orizaba, Pico de ∧[1] 234 19.01 N 97.16 E
Citra 192 29.24 N 82.06 W
Citronelle 194 31.05 N 88.13 W
Citrus □[6] 220 28.52 N 82.28 W
Citrusdal 158 32.36 S 19.00 E
Citrus Heights 226 38.42 N 121.16 W
Citrus Springs 220 29.00 N 82.27 W
Citrus Tower ʊ 220 28.33 N 81.44 W
Cittadella 64 45.39 N 11.47 E
Città della Pieve 66 42.57 N 12.00 E
Città del Vaticano → Vatican City □[1] 66 41.54 N 12.27 E
Città di Castello 66 43.27 N 12.14 E
Cittaducale 66 42.23 N 12.57 E
Cittanova 68 38.21 N 16.05 E
Cittareale 66 42.37 N 13.10 E
Città Sant'Angelo 66 42.31 N 14.03 E
Città Universitaria ʊ[2] 267a 41.55 N 12.31 E
City Beach 168a 31.56 S 115.45 E
City Bell ◆[8] 258 34.52 S 58.05 W
City Island ◆[8] 276 40.51 N 73.47 W
City Mills 283 42.06 N 71.21 W
City of Hope National Medical Center ʊ 280 34.08 N 117.58 W
City Of Industry 280 34.01 N 117.57 W
City of London ◆[8] 260 51.31 N 0.05 W
City of Refuge → Pu'uhonua o Honaunau National Historic Site ⊥ 229d 19.25 N 155.54 W
City of Sunrise 220 26.08 N 80.14 W
City Point 220 28.24 N 80.45 W
City University of New York Brooklyn College ʊ[2] 276 40.38 N 73.57 W
City University of New York City College ʊ[2] 276 40.49 N 73.57 W
City University of New York Queens College ʊ[2] 276 40.44 N 73.49 W
City University of New York York College ʊ[2] 276 40.42 N 73.48 W
Ciucaș, Vârful ∧ 38 45.31 N 25.55 E
Ciuciuleni 38 47.02 N 28.22 E
Ciudad Acuña 232 29.18 N 100.55 W
Ciudad Altamirano 234 18.20 N 100.40 W
Ciudad Barrios 236 13.46 N 88.16 W
Ciudad Bolívar 246 8.08 N 63.33 W
Ciudad Bolivia 246 8.21 N 70.34 W
Ciudad Camargo 232 26.19 N 98.50 W
Ciudad Constitución 232 24.59 N 111.39 W
Ciudad Cortés 236 8.58 N 83.32 W
Ciudad Cuauhtémoc 234 22.28 N 102.20 W
Ciudad Darío 236 12.43 N 86.08 W
Ciudad de Carangas 248 17.53 S 66.11 W
Ciudad de Guayana → Ciudad Guayana 246 8.22 N 62.40 W
Ciudad de la Habana □[4] 240p 23.08 N 82.22 W
Ciudad del Cabo → Cape Town 158 33.55 S 18.22 E
Ciudad del Carmen 232 18.38 N 91.50 W
Ciudad del Este 252 25.30 S 54.36 W
Ciudad del Maíz 234 22.24 N 99.36 W
Ciudad de los Deportes ♠ 286a 19.23 N 99.11 W
Ciudad del Vaticano → Vatican City □[1] 66 41.54 N 12.27 E
Ciudad de México (Mexico City), Méx. 234 19.24 N 99.09 W
Ciudad de México (Mexico City), Méx. 286a 19.24 N 99.09 W
Ciudad de Nutrias 246 8.05 N 69.18 W
Ciudad Deportiva ♠, Cuba 286b 23.07 N 82.22 W
Ciudad Deportiva ♠, Méx. 286a 19.24 N 99.06 W
Ciudadela, Parque de la ♠ 266d 41.23 N 2.11 E
Ciudad General Belgrano 288 34.43 S 58.32 W
Ciudad Guayana 246 8.22 N 62.40 W
Ciudad Guzmán 234 19.41 N 103.29 W
Ciudad Hidalgo, Méx. 234 19.41 N 100.34 W
Ciudad Hidalgo, Méx. 236 14.41 N 92.09 W
Ciudad Juárez 232 31.44 N 106.29 W
Ciudad Lerdo 196 25.32 N 103.32 W
Ciudad Lerdo de Tejada 234 18.37 N 95.31 W
Ciudad Lineal ◆[8] 266a 40.27 N 3.40 W
Ciudad López Mateos 286a 19.33 N 99.15 W
Ciudad Madero 234 22.16 N 97.50 W
Ciudad Mante 234 22.44 N 98.57 W
Ciudad Manuel Doblado 234 20.44 N 101.56 W
Ciudad Mendoza 234 18.48 N 97.11 W
Ciudad Miguel Alemán 232 26.23 N 99.01 W
Ciudad Morelos 232 32.38 N 114.52 W
Ciudad Obregón 232 27.29 N 109.56 W
Ciudad Ojeda (Lagunillas) 246 10.12 N 71.19 W
Ciudad Piar 246 7.27 N 63.19 W
Ciudad Real 34 38.59 N 3.56 W
Ciudad Real □[4] 34 38.50 N 3.45 W
Ciudad Rodrigo 34 40.36 N 6.32 W
Ciudad Sahagún 234 19.47 N 98.33 W
Ciudad Sandino 236 13.43 N 86.08 W
Ciudad Serdán 234 18.59 N 97.27 W
Ciudad Tecún Umán 236 14.40 N 92.09 W
Ciudad Trujillo → Santo Domingo 238 18.28 N 69.54 W
Ciudad Universitaria ◆[8] 266a 40.27 N 3.44 W
Ciudad Universitaria ʊ[2], Esp. 266a 40.27 N 3.43 W
Ciudad Universitaria ʊ[2], Méx. 286a 19.20 N 99.11 W
Ciudad Universitaria ʊ[2], Ven. 286c 10.29 N 66.53 W
Ciudad Valles 234 21.59 N 99.01 W
Ciudad Victoria, Méx. 204 32.20 N 115.06 W
Ciudad Victoria, Méx. 234 23.44 N 99.08 W
Ciudad Vieja 236 14.31 N 90.46 W
Ciuma 152 13.14 S 15.40 E
Ciutadella 34 40.02 N 3.50 E
Civa Burnu › 130 41.22 N 36.35 E
Civate 62 45.50 N 9.21 E
Civenna 58 45.56 N 9.16 E
Civetta, Monte ∧ 64 46.23 N 12.03 E
Civezzano 64 46.05 N 11.11 E
Cividale del Friuli 64 46.06 N 13.25 E
Cividate al Piano 62 45.33 N 9.50 E
Cividate Camuno 64 45.57 N 10.17 E
Civil' ≏ 80 56.08 N 47.35 E
Civil'sk 80 55.53 N 47.29 E
Civita 68 39.49 N 16.18 E
Civitacampomarano 66 41.47 N 14.41 E
Civita Castellana 66 42.17 N 12.25 E
Civita di Bagno 66 42.18 N 13.26 E
Civitanova Alta 66 43.19 N 13.40 E
Civitanova del Sannio 66 41.40 N 14.24 E
Civitanova Marche 66 43.18 N 13.44 E
Civitaquana 66 42.19 N 13.54 E
Civitavecchia 66 42.06 N 11.48 E
Civitella del Tronto 66 42.46 N 13.40 E
Civitella di Romagna 66 44.00 N 11.56 E
Civitella in Val di Chiana 66 43.25 N 11.43 E
Civitella Marittima 66 43.00 N 11.17 E
Civitella Roveto 66 41.54 N 13.25 E
Civray 32 46.09 N 0.18 E
Çivril 130 38.18 N 29.45 E
Ciwidey 115a 7.06 S 107.27 E
Cixerri ≏ 71 39.17 N 8.59 E
Cixi 100 30.11 N 121.15 E
Cixian 98 36.22 N 114.23 E
Ciyutuo 104 41.31 N 122.53 E
Čiža 24 67.06 N 44.19 E
Čižapka ≏ 86 59.01 N 79.36 E
Čiža Vtoraja 80 50.52 N 49.40 E
Cize 58 46.12 N 5.26 E
Cizhuping 107 29.11 N 103.36 E
Čižinskije razlivy ≡ 80 50.25 N 49.40 E
Cizre 130 37.20 N 42.12 E
Cjahcin 76 53.51 N 29.44 E
Cjaluša 76 53.03 N 29.31 E
C.J. Strike Reservoir ⊜[1] 202 42.57 N 115.53 W
Čkalov → Orenburg 86 51.54 N 55.06 E
Čkalovo 86 53.38 N 70.24 E
Čkalovsk, Kaz. 85 41.15 N 68.00 E
Čkalovsk, Ross. 80 56.46 N 43.16 E
Čkalovsk, Taj. 85 40.13 N 69.50 E
Čkalovskij 265b 55.54 N 38.04 E
C K Creek ≏ 202 47.36 N 108.29 W
Čkyně 60 49.07 N 13.49 E
Čl'a, ozero ⊜ 89 53.27 N 140.03 E
Clachan 46 55.45 N 5.34 W
Clackamas 224 45.24 N 122.34 W
Clackamas □[6] 224 45.10 N 122.16 W
Clackamas ≏ 224 45.22 N 122.36 W
Clackamas, Oak Grove Fork ≏ 224 45.05 N 122.03 W
Clackamas Heights 224 45.23 N 122.34 W
Clackline 168a 31.43 S 116.31 E
Clackmannan 46 56.06 N 3.46 W
Clacton-on-Sea 42 51.48 N 1.09 E
Cladich 46 56.21 N 5.05 W
Claerwen ≏ 42 52.16 N 3.35 W
Claerwen Reservoir ⊜[1] 42 52.17 N 3.43 W
Claflin 198 38.31 N 98.32 W
Claiborne 194 31.32 N 87.31 W
Clain ≏ 32 46.47 N 0.32 E
Claire, Lake ⊜ 176 58.35 N 112.05 W
Claire, Pointe › 275a 45.25 N 73.50 W
Clairefontaine-en-Yvelines 50 48.37 N 1.55 E
Clair Engle Lake ⊜[1] 204 40.52 N 122.43 W
Claireville 275b 43.45 N 79.38 W
Claireville Reservoir ⊜[1] 275b 43.44 N 79.39 W
Clairis ≏ 50 48.07 N 2.45 E
Clairmarais 50 50.46 N 2.18 E
Clairmont 182 55.16 N 118.47 W
Clairton 214 40.17 N 79.52 W
Clairvaux-les-Lacs 58 46.34 N 5.45 E
Claix 62 45.07 N 5.40 E
Clallam □[6] 224 48.10 N 123.49 W
Clallam Bay 224 48.15 N 124.15 W
Clam ≏, Mi., U.S. 190 44.05 N 85.00 W
Clam ≏, Wi., U.S. 190 45.57 N 92.33 W
Clam, North Fork ≏ 190 45.46 N 92.18 W
Clamart 261 48.48 N 2.16 E
Clamecy 50 47.27 N 3.31 E
Clam Gulch 180 60.15 N 151.22 W
Clam Lake ⊜ 184 55.19 N 105.43 W
Clampton 162 29.56 S 119.06 E
Clan Alpine Mountains ⋏ 204 39.40 N 117.55 W
Clandonald 182 53.34 N 110.44 W
Clandon Park ♠ 260 51.15 N 0.30 W
Clandulla 170 32.55 S 149.57 E
Clane 48 53.18 N 6.41 W
Clans 62 44.00 N 7.09 E
Clanton 194 32.50 N 86.37 W
Clanwilliam 158 32.11 S 18.54 E
Claonaig 46 55.46 N 5.22 W
Clapham 42 52.09 N 0.29 W
Clapier, Mont ∧ 62 44.07 N 7.25 E
Clapperton Island I 190 46.02 N 82.13 W
Clapp Farm 214 41.24 N 79.32 W
Clàr, Loch nan ⊜ 46 58.17 N 4.08 W
Clara, Arg. 252 31.50 S 58.49 W
Clara, Ire. 48 53.20 N 7.36 W
Clara, Ms., U.S. 194 31.34 N 88.41 W
Clara ≏ 166 18.30 S 141.18 E
Clara City 198 44.57 N 95.21 W
Clara Island I 110 10.54 N 97.55 E
Claraz 252 37.54 S 59.17 W
Clare, Austl. 166 33.25 S 143.55 E
Clare, Austl. 168b 33.50 S 138.36 E
Clare, Eng., U.K. 42 52.05 N 0.35 E
Clare, Mi., U.S. 190 43.49 N 84.46 W
Clare □[6] 48 52.50 N 9.00 W
Clare ≏, On., Can. 212 44.28 N 77.17 W
Clare ≏, Ire. 48 53.20 N 9.03 W
Clarecastle 48 52.49 N 8.57 W
Claregalway 48 53.21 N 8.57 W
Clare Island I 48 53.48 N 10.00 W
Claremont, On., Can. 212 43.58 N 79.07 W
Claremont, Eng., U.K. 260 51.21 N 0.22 W
Claremont, Ca., U.S. 228 34.05 N 117.43 W
Claremont, N.H., U.S. 188 43.22 N 72.20 W
Claremont, S.D., U.S. 198 45.40 N 98.00 W
Claremont, Va., U.S. 208 37.13 N 76.57 W
Claremont ∧ 204 39.53 N 120.57 W
Claremore 196 36.18 N 95.36 W
Claremorris 48 53.44 N 9.00 W
Clarence, N.Z. 172 42.10 S 173.56 E
Clarence, Il., U.S. 216 40.28 N 87.58 W
Clarence, Ia., U.S. 190 41.53 N 91.03 W
Clarence, Mo., U.S. 219 39.44 N 92.15 W
Clarence, N.Y., U.S. 210 42.59 N 78.35 W
Clarence, Pa., U.S. 214 41.03 N 77.56 W
Clarence ≏, Austl. 166 29.25 S 153.22 E
Clarence ≏, N.Z. 172 42.10 S 173.57 E
Clarence, Isla I 254 54.10 S 71.50 W
Clarence, Port ⊂ 180 65.15 N 166.40 W
Clarence Cannon Dam ◆[6] 219 39.31 N 91.39 W
Clarence Center 210 43.00 N 78.35 W
Clarence Creek 206 45.30 N 75.13 W
Clarence Fahnestock Memorial State Park ♠ 210 41.26 N 73.50 W
Clarence Island I 9 61.09 S 54.06 W
Clarence J. Brown Reservoir ⊜[1] 218 39.58 N 83.44 W
Clarence Strait ʮ, Austl. 164 12.00 S 131.00 E
Clarence Strait ʮ, Ak., U.S. 180 55.25 N 132.00 W
Clarence Town, Austl. 170 32.35 S 151.47 E
Clarence Town, Ba. 238 23.06 N 74.59 W
Clarenceville, P.Q., Can. 206 45.04 N 73.15 W
Clarenceville, Mi., U.S. 281 42.27 N 83.19 W
Clarendon, Austl. 168b 35.07 S 138.38 E
Clarendon, Ar., U.S. 194 34.41 N 91.18 W
Clarendon, N.Y., U.S. 210 43.11 N 78.04 W
Clarendon, Pa., U.S. 214 41.46 N 79.05 W
Clarendon, Tx., U.S. 196 34.56 N 100.53 W
Clarendon Hills 278 41.47 N 87.57 W
Clarens 158 28.30 S 28.29 E
Clarenville 186 48.10 N 53.58 W
Claresholm 182 50.02 N 113.35 W
Claret 62 43.52 N 3.54 E
Clarholz 52 51.54 N 8.11 E
Claridge 214 40.21 N 79.37 W
Clarie Coast ⍓[2] 9 66.30 S 133.00 E
Clarin 116 9.58 N 124.01 E
Clarinda 198 40.44 N 95.02 W
Clarines 246 9.56 N 65.10 W
Clarington 214 41.20 N 79.07 W
Clarion, Ia., U.S. 190 42.43 N 93.43 W
Clarion, Pa., U.S. 214 41.12 N 79.23 W
Clarion □[6] 214 41.13 N 79.24 W
Clarion ≏ 214 41.07 N 79.41 W
Clarión, Isla I 232 18.22 N 114.44 W
Clarion, West Branch ≏ 214 41.29 N 78.41 W
Clarion Fracture Zone ✣ 16 18.00 N 122.00 W
Clarissa 198 46.07 N 94.56 W
Clark, N.J., U.S. 276 40.38 N 74.18 W
Clark, Oh., U.S. 214 40.27 N 81.54 W
Clark, S.D., U.S. 198 44.52 N 97.43 W
Clark, Tx., U.S. 222 30.23 N 94.46 W
Clark □[6], In., U.S. 218 38.17 N 85.44 W
Clark □[6], Oh., U.S. 218 39.56 N 83.49 W
Clark □[6], Wa., U.S. 224 45.48 N 122.31 W
Clark, Lake ⊜ 180 60.15 N 154.15 W
Clark, Mount ∧ 180 64.25 N 124.12 W
Clark, Point › 190 44.04 N 81.45 W
Clark Air Base (U.S.) ■ 116 15.11 N 120.32 E
Clark Branch ≏ 285 39.43 N 74.45 W
Clark Canyon Reservoir ⊜[1] 202 44.58 N 112.51 W
Clark Creek ≏ 208 40.22 N 76.58 W
Clarkdale 200 34.46 N 112.03 W
Clarke ≏ 166 19.12 S 145.30 E
Clarke City 186 50.12 N 66.38 W
Clarke Island I 166 40.33 S 148.10 E
Clarke Lake ⊜ 184 54.25 N 106.51 W
Clarke Range ⋏ 166 20.50 S 148.33 E
Clarkesville 192 34.36 N 83.31 W
Clarkfield 198 44.47 N 95.48 W
Clark Fork 202 48.08 N 116.10 W
Clark Fork ≏ 202 48.09 N 116.15 W
Clark Hill 218 38.18 N 83.12 W
Clarklake 216 42.04 N 84.21 W
Clark Lake ⊜ 216 42.07 N 84.19 W
Clark Mills 210 43.06 N 75.22 W
Clark Mountain ∧, Ca., U.S. 204 35.32 N 115.35 W


| Symbol | English | Deutsch | Español | Français | Português |
|---|---|---|---|---|---|
| ≏ | River | Fluß | Río | Rivière | Rio |
| ≊ | Canal | Kanal | Canal | Canal | Canal |
| ∟ | Waterfall, Rapids | Wasserfall, Stromschnellen | Cascada, Rápidos | Chute d'eau, Rapides | Cascata, Rápidos |
| ʮ | Strait | Meeresstraße | Estrecho | Détroit | Estreito |
| ⊂ | Bay, Gulf | Bucht, Golf | Bahía, Golfo | Baie, Golfe | Baía, Golfo |
| ⊜ | Lake, Lakes | See, Seen | Lago, Lagos | Lac, Lacs | Lago, Lagos |
| ≡ | Swamp | Sumpf | Pantano | Marais | Pântano |
| ⍓ | Ice Features, Glacier | Eis- und Gletscherformen | Accidentes Glaciales | Formes glaciaires | Acidentes glaciares |
| ⫪ | Other Hydrographic Features | Andere Hydrographische Objekte | Otros Elementos Hidrográficos | Autres données hydrographiques | Outros acidentes hidrográficos |
| ✣ | Submarine Features | Untermeerische Objekte | Accidentes Submarinos | Formes de relief sous-marin | Acidentes submarinos |
| □ | Political Unit | Politische Einheit | Unidad Politica | Entité politique | Unidade política |
| ʊ | Cultural Institution | Kulturelle Institution | Institución Cultural | Institution culturelle | Institução cultural |
| ⊥ | Historical Site | Historische Stätte | Sitio Histórico | Site historique | Sitio histórico |
| ♠ | Recreational Site | Erholungs- und Ferienort | Sitio de Recreo | Centre de loisirs | Area de Lazer |
| ⊠ | Airport | Flughafen | Aeropuerto | Aéroport | Aeroporto |
| ■ | Military Installation | Militäranlage | Instalación Militar | Installation militaire | Instalação militar |
| ◆ | Miscellaneous | Verschiedenes | Misceláneo | Divers | Diversos |

ENGLISH — Name, Page, Lat.°′, Long.°′ | DEUTSCH — Name, Seite, Breite°′, Länge°′ E = Ost


| Name | Page | Lat.°′ | Long.°′ |
|---|---|---|---|
| Clark Mountain ∧, Wa., U.S. | 224 | 48.03 N | 120.57 W |
| Clarks, La., U.S. | 194 | 32.01 N | 92.08 W |
| Clarks, Ne., U.S. | 198 | 41.12 N | 97.50 W |
| Clarks ≃ | 194 | 37.03 N | 88.33 W |
| Clarks, West Fork ≃ | 194 | 36.59 N | 88.31 W |
| Clarksboro | 285 | 39.47 N | 75.13 W |
| Clarksburg, On., Can. | 212 | 44.43 N | 80.27 W |
| Clarksburg, Ca., U.S. | 226 | 38.25 N | 121.32 W |
| Clarksburg, Il., U.S. | 219 | 39.20 N | 88.44 W |
| Clarksburg, In., U.S. | 218 | 39.26 N | 85.20 W |
| Clarksburg, Md., U.S. | 208 | 39.14 N | 77.16 W |
| Clarksburg, N.J., U.S. | 208 | 40.11 N | 74.26 W |
| Clarksburg, Oh., U.S. | 218 | 39.30 N | 83.09 W |
| Clarksburg, W.V., U.S. | 188 | 39.16 N | 80.20 W |
| Clarksburg State Park ♠ | 207 | 42.43 N | 73.06 W |
| Clarks Creek ≃, Ks., U.S. | 198 | 39.05 N | 96.42 W |
| Clarks Creek ≃, Ky., U.S. | 218 | 38.40 N | 84.44 W |
| Clarksdale | 194 | 34.12 N | 90.34 W |
| Clarks Green | 210 | 41.30 N | 75.42 W |
| Clark's Harbour | 186 | 43.26 N | 65.38 W |
| Clarks Hill | 216 | 40.14 N | 86.43 W |
| Clarks Hill Lake ⊜[1] | 192 | 33.50 N | 82.20 W |
| Clarks Island I | 283 | 42.01 N | 70.38 W |
| Clarks Mills | 214 | 41.24 N | 80.11 W |
| Clarkson, On., Can. | 275b | 43.31 N | 79.37 W |
| Clarkson, Ky., U.S. | 194 | 37.29 N | 86.13 W |
| Clarkson, Ne., U.S. | 198 | 41.43 N | 97.07 W |
| Clarkson, N.Y., U.S. | 210 | 43.14 N | 77.56 W |
| Clarks Point | 180 | 58.51 N | 158.30 W |
| Clarks Summit | 210 | 41.29 N | 75.42 W |
| Clarkston, Mi., U.S. | 216 | 42.44 N | 83.25 W |
| Clarkston, Wa., U.S. | 202 | 46.24 N | 117.02 W |
| Clark's Town | 241q | 18.25 N | 77.34 W |
| Clarksville, Ar., U.S. | 194 | 35.28 N | 93.27 W |
| Clarksville, De., U.S. | 208 | 38.32 N | 75.08 W |
| Clarksville, In., U.S. | 218 | 38.15 N | 85.47 W |
| Clarksville, Ia., U.S. | 190 | 42.47 N | 92.40 W |
| Clarksville, Md., U.S. | 208 | 39.12 N | 76.56 W |
| Clarksville, Mi., U.S. | 216 | 42.50 N | 85.14 W |
| Clarksville, Mo., U.S. | 219 | 39.22 N | 90.54 W |
| Clarksville, N.Y., U.S. | 210 | 42.35 N | 73.58 W |
| Clarksville, Oh., U.S. | 218 | 39.24 N | 83.58 W |
| Clarksville, Tn., U.S. | 194 | 36.31 N | 87.21 W |
| Clarksville, Tx., U.S. | 196 | 33.36 N | 95.03 W |
| Clarksville, Va., U.S. | 192 | 36.37 N | 78.33 W |
| Clarksville City | 222 | 32.32 N | 94.34 W |
| Clarkton, Mo., U.S. | 194 | 36.27 N | 89.58 W |
| Clarkton, N.C., U.S. | 192 | 34.29 N | 78.39 W |
| Claro ≃, Bra. | 248 | 13.25 S | 56.35 W |
| Claro ≃, Bra. | 255 | 15.28 S | 51.43 W |
| Claro ≃, Bra. | 255 | 19.06 S | 47.52 W |
| Claro ≃, Bra. | 255 | 19.08 S | 50.40 W |
| Claro, Arroyo ≃ | 288 | 34.25 S | 58.41 W |
| Claro, Ribeirão ≃ | 287b | 23.40 S | 46.17 W |
| Clary | 50 | 50.05 N | 3.24 E |
| Claryville | 210 | 41.55 N | 74.34 W |
| Clashmore | 48 | 52.00 N | 7.48 W |
| Clatskanie | 224 | 46.06 N | 123.12 W |
| Clatskanie ≃ | 224 | 46.08 N | 123.14 W |
| Clatsop □[6] | 224 | 46.01 N | 123.41 W |
| Clatsop Spit ≻[2] | 224 | 46.13 N | 124.01 W |
| Clatteringshaws Lake ⊜ | 44 | 55.05 N | 4.17 W |
| Claude | 196 | 35.07 N | 101.22 W |
| Claudy | 48 | 54.54 N | 7.09 W |
| Claughton | 44 | 54.06 N | 2.40 W |
| Claussnitz | 54 | 50.56 N | 12.53 E |
| Clausthal-Zellerfeld | 52 | 51.48 N | 10.20 E |
| Claver | 116 | 9.35 N | 125.44 E |
| Claverack | 210 | 42.13 N | 73.44 W |
| Claveria, Pil. | 116 | 18.37 N | 121.05 E |
| Claveria, Pil. | 116 | 8.38 N | 124.55 E |
| Clavet | 184 | 52.00 N | 106.23 W |
| Clavey ≃ | 226 | 37.52 N | 120.07 W |
| Clawit, Mount ∧ | 116 | 16.58 N | 120.58 E |
| Clawson, Mi., U.S. | 281 | 42.32 N | 83.08 W |
| Clawson, Tx., U.S. | 222 | 31.24 N | 94.47 W |
| Claxton | 192 | 32.09 N | 81.54 W |
| Clay, Ky., U.S. | 194 | 37.28 N | 87.49 W |
| Clay, Tx., U.S. | 222 | 30.23 N | 96.21 W |
| Clay, W.V., U.S. | 188 | 38.27 N | 81.05 W |
| Clay □[6] | 219 | 38.45 N | 88.40 W |
| Claybank Creek ≃ | 194 | 31.10 N | 85.44 W |
| Clay Center, Ks., U.S. | 198 | 39.22 N | 97.07 W |
| Clay Center, Ne., U.S. | 198 | 40.31 N | 98.03 W |
| Clay Center, Oh., U.S. | 214 | 41.33 N | 83.21 W |
| Clay City, Il., U.S. | 194 | 38.41 N | 88.21 W |
| Clay City, In., U.S. | 194 | 39.16 N | 87.06 W |
| Clay City, Ky., U.S. | 192 | 37.51 N | 83.55 W |
| Clay Creek ≃ | 198 | 38.06 N | 102.31 W |
| Clay Cross | 44 | 53.10 N | 1.24 W |
| Claydon | 42 | 52.06 N | 1.07 E |
| Claye-Souilly | 50 | 48.57 N | 2.42 E |
| Claygate | 260 | 51.22 N | 0.20 W |
| Claygate Cross | 260 | 51.16 N | 0.19 E |
| Clayhole Wash V | 200 | 36.59 N | 113.17 W |
| Clayhurst | 182 | 56.15 N | 120.01 W |
| Claymont | 208 | 39.48 N | 75.27 W |
| Clayoquot Sound ʉ | 182 | 49.11 N | 126.08 W |
| Claypole | 288 | 34.48 S | 58.20 W |
| Claypool, Az., U.S. | 200 | 33.24 N | 110.50 W |
| Claypool, In., U.S. | 216 | 41.07 N | 85.52 W |
| Claysburg | 214 | 40.17 N | 78.27 W |
| Clay Springs | 200 | 34.21 N | 110.17 W |
| Claysville | 214 | 40.07 N | 80.24 W |
| Clayton, Austl. | 274b | 37.56 S | 145.07 E |
| Clayton, Eng., U.K. | 262 | 53.47 N | 1.50 W |
| Clayton, Al., U.S. | 194 | 31.52 N | 85.26 W |
| Clayton, Ca., U.S. | 282 | 37.57 N | 121.56 W |
| Clayton, De., U.S. | 208 | 39.17 N | 75.38 W |
| Clayton, Ga., U.S. | 192 | 34.52 N | 83.24 W |
| Clayton, Il., U.S. | 219 | 40.01 N | 90.57 W |
| Clayton, In., U.S. | 218 | 39.41 N | 86.31 W |
| Clayton, La., U.S. | 194 | 31.43 N | 91.32 W |
| Clayton, Mi., U.S. | 216 | 41.52 N | 84.14 W |
| Clayton, Mo., U.S. | 219 | 38.38 N | 90.19 W |
| Clayton, N.J., U.S. | 208 | 39.39 N | 75.05 W |
| Clayton, N.M., U.S. | 196 | 36.27 N | 103.11 W |
| Clayton, N.Y., U.S. | 212 | 44.14 N | 76.05 W |
| Clayton, N.C., U.S. | 192 | 35.39 N | 78.27 W |
| Clayton, Ok., U.S. | 196 | 34.35 N | 95.21 W |
| Clayton, Tx., U.S. | 222 | 32.06 N | 94.28 W |
| Clayton, Wa., U.S. | 182 | 48.00 N | 117.33 W |
| Clayton ≃ | 166 | 29.06 S | 138.05 E |
| Claytonia | 214 | 41.00 N | 79.58 W |
| Clayton-le-Moors | 262 | 53.47 N | 2.23 W |
| Clayton-le-Woods | 262 | 53.41 N | 2.38 W |
| Clayton Park ♠ | 285 | 39.52 N | 75.29 W |
| Clayton Valley V | 282 | 37.58 N | 121.58 W |
| Claytonville | 216 | 40.34 N | 87.49 W |
| Clay Village | 218 | 38.11 N | 85.07 W |
| Clayville | 210 | 42.59 N | 75.15 W |
| Clear ≃ | 182 | 56.11 N | 119.42 W |
| Clear, Cape ≻, Ire. | 48 | 51.24 N | 9.30 W |
| Clear, Cape ≻, Ak., U.S. | 180 | 59.48 N | 147.54 W |
| Clear, Lake ⊜ | 212 | 45.26 N | 77.12 W |
| Clear, Mount ∧ | 171b | 35.52 S | 149.04 E |
| Clear Boggy Creek ≃ | 196 | 34.03 N | 95.47 W |
| Clearbrook, B.C., Can. | 224 | 49.08 N | 122.26 W |
| Clearbrook, Mn., U.S. | 198 | 47.41 N | 95.25 W |
| Clear Creek | 218 | 39.07 N | 86.32 W |
| Clear Creek ≃, Al., U.S. | 194 | 34.00 N | 87.19 W |
| Clear Creek ≃, Az., U.S. | 200 | 34.59 N | 110.38 W |
| Clear Creek ≃, Ca., U.S. | 204 | 40.31 N | 122.22 W |
| Clear Creek ≃, Ca., U.S. | 280 | 34.17 N | 118.12 W |
| Clear Creek ≃, Ca., U.S. | 282 | 37.20 N | 122.21 W |
| Clear Creek ≃, Ky., U.S. | 218 | 38.10 N | 85.17 W |
| Clear Creek ≃, Mo., U.S. | 194 | 38.00 N | 93.56 W |
| Clear Creek ≃, Mt., U.S. | 202 | 48.46 N | 109.25 W |
| Clear Creek ≃, Ne., U.S. | 198 | 41.08 N | 99.06 W |
| Clear Creek ≃, Oh., U.S. | 218 | 39.33 N | 84.20 W |
| Clear Creek ≃, Or., U.S. | 224 | 45.09 N | 121.31 W |
| Clear Creek ≃, Or., U.S. | 224 | 45.23 N | 122.29 W |
| Clear Creek ≃, Tn., U.S. | 192 | 36.05 N | 84.42 W |
| Clear Creek ≃, Tx., U.S. | 196 | 33.16 N | 97.03 W |
| Clear Creek ≃, Tx., U.S. | 222 | 29.33 N | 95.05 W |
| Clear Creek ≃, Tx., U.S. | 222 | 29.09 N | 97.23 W |
| Clear Creek ≃, Wa., U.S. | 224 | 46.07 N | 122.00 W |
| Clear Creek ≃, Wy., U.S. | 202 | 44.53 N | 106.04 W |
| Clear Creek State Park ♠ | 214 | 41.20 N | 79.05 W |
| Clearfield, Ia., U.S. | 198 | 40.48 N | 94.28 W |
| Clearfield, Ky., U.S. | 218 | 38.09 N | 83.25 W |
| Clearfield, Pa., U.S. | 214 | 41.01 N | 78.26 W |
| Clearfield, Ut,. U.S. | 200 | 41.06 N | 112.01 W |
| Clearfield □[6] | 214 | 41.02 N | 78.27 W |
| Clearfield Creek ≃ | 214 | 41.02 N | 78.24 W |
| Clear Fork Reservoir ⊜[1] | 214 | 40.42 N | 82.38 W |
| Clearing ◆[8] | 278 | 41.47 N | 87.47 W |
| Clear Island I | 48 | 51.26 N | 9.30 W |
| Clearlake, Ca., U.S. | 226 | 38.57 N | 122.38 W |
| Clear Lake, Ia., U.S. | 190 | 43.08 N | 93.22 W |
| Clear Lake, S.D., U.S. | 198 | 44.44 N | 96.40 W |
| Clearlake, Wa., U.S. | 224 | 48.28 N | 122.14 W |
| Clear Lake, Wi., U.S. | 190 | 45.15 N | 92.16 W |
| Clear Lake ⊜, Mb., Can. | 184 | 50.42 N | 100.00 W |
| Clear Lake ⊜, On., Can. | 212 | 45.14 N | 79.57 W |
| Clear Lake ⊜, On., Can. | 212 | 44.30 N | 78.13 W |
| Clear Lake ⊜, On., Can. | 212 | 44.59 N | 79.33 W |
| Clear Lake ⊜, In., U.S. | 216 | 41.44 N | 84.50 W |
| Clear Lake ⊜[1], Ca., U.S. | 204 | 39.02 N | 122.50 W |
| Clear Lake ⊜[1], La., U.S. | 194 | 31.55 N | 93.05 W |
| Clearlake Oaks | 226 | 39.07 N | 122.40 W |
| Clear Lake Reservoir ⊜[1] | 204 | 41.52 N | 121.08 W |
| Clear Lake Shores | 222 | 29.33 N | 95.02 W |
| Clearmont | 202 | 44.38 N | 106.22 W |
| Clear Run | 214 | 41.08 N | 78.45 W |
| Clear Site | 180 | 64.19 N | 149.11 W |
| Clearview, Oh., U.S. | 214 | 41.25 N | 82.10 W |
| Clearview, Wa., U.S. | 224 | 47.45 N | 122.06 W |
| Clearview, W.V., U.S. | 214 | 40.09 N | 80.41 W |
| Clearview Estates | 279b | 40.34 N | 80.16 W |
| Clearwater, B.C., Can. | 182 | 51.38 N | 120.02 W |
| Clearwater, Mb., Can. | 184 | 49.08 N | 99.01 W |
| Clearwater, Fl., U.S. | 220 | 27.57 N | 82.48 W |
| Clearwater, Ks., U.S. | 198 | 37.30 N | 97.30 W |
| Clearwater, Ne., U.S. | 198 | 42.10 N | 98.11 W |
| Clearwater, S.C., U.S. | 192 | 33.29 N | 81.53 W |
| Clearwater, Wa., U.S. | 224 | 47.34 N | 124.17 W |
| Clearwater ≃, Can. | 184 | 56.44 N | 111.23 W |
| Clearwater ≃, Ab., Can. | 182 | 52.23 N | 114.50 W |
| Clearwater ≃, B.C., Can. | 182 | 51.42 N | 120.00 W |
| Clearwater ≃, Id., U.S. | 202 | 46.25 N | 117.02 W |
| Clearwater ≃, Mn., U.S. | 198 | 47.54 N | 96.16 W |
| Clearwater ≃, Mt., U.S. | 202 | 46.58 N | 113.23 W |
| Clearwater ≃, Wa., U.S. | 224 | 47.33 N | 124.21 W |
| Clearwater, Middle Fork ≃ | 202 | 46.09 N | 115.59 W |
| Clearwater, North Fork ≃ | 202 | 46.30 N | 116.19 W |
| Clearwater, South Fork ≃ | 202 | 46.09 N | 115.59 W |
| Clear Water Bay ⊂ | 271d | 22.17 N | 114.18 E |
| Clearwater Beach Island I | 220 | 27.59 N | 82.49 W |
| Clearwater Lake ⊜, B.C., Can. | 182 | 52.15 N | 120.13 W |
| Clearwater Lake ⊜, Mb., Can. | 184 | 54.05 N | 101.00 W |
| Clearwater Lake Provincial Park ♠ | 184 | 54.03 N | 101.10 W |
| Clearwater Mountains ⋏ | 202 | 46.00 N | 115.30 W |
| Cleator Moor | 44 | 54.31 N | 3.30 W |
| Clebit | 196 | 34.21 N | 94.52 W |
| Cleburne | 222 | 32.20 N | 97.23 W |
| Cleckheaton | 44 | 53.43 N | 1.43 W |
| Cle Elum | 224 | 47.11 N | 120.56 W |
| Cle Elum ≃ | 224 | 47.11 N | 121.01 W |
| Cle Elum Lake ⊜[1] | 224 | 47.18 N | 121.06 W |
| Cleethorpes | 44 | 53.34 N | 0.02 W |
| Cleeve Cloud ∧[2] | 42 | 51.54 N | 2.00 W |
| Clefmont | 58 | 48.06 N | 5.31 E |
| Cleggan | 48 | 53.33 N | 10.09 W |
| Cleland Conservation Park ♠ | 168b | 34.59 S | 138.44 E |
| Cleland Heights | 285 | 39.44 N | 75.34 W |
| Clelles | 62 | 44.50 N | 5.37 E |
| Clementon | 285 | 39.48 N | 74.59 W |
| Clementsport | 186 | 44.40 N | 65.37 W |
| Clemson | 192 | 34.41 N | 82.50 W |
| Clemville | 222 | 29.00 N | 96.08 W |
| Clendenin | 188 | 38.29 N | 81.20 W |
| Clendening Lake ⊜[1] | 214 | 40.16 N | 81.13 W |
| Clenze | 54 | 52.56 N | 10.58 E |
| Cleobury Mortimer | 42 | 52.23 N | 2.29 W |
| Cleona | 208 | 40.20 N | 76.28 W |
| Cléon-d'Andran | 62 | 44.37 N | 4.56 E |
| Cleopatra Needle ∧ | 116 | 10.07 N | 118.58 E |
| Clères | 50 | 49.36 N | 1.07 E |
| Clerke Rocks II[1] | 244 | 55.01 S | 34.41 W |
| Clermont, Austl. | 166 | 22.49 S | 147.39 E |
| Clermont, P.Q., Can. | 186 | 47.41 N | 70.14 W |
| Clermont, Fr. | 50 | 49.23 N | 2.24 E |
| Clermont, Fl., U.S. | 220 | 28.32 N | 81.46 W |
| Clermont, N.J., U.S. | 285 | 39.59 N | 74.48 W |
| Clermont, Pa., U.S. | 214 | 41.41 N | 78.29 W |
| Clermont □[6] | 218 | 39.05 N | 84.11 W |
| Clermont-en-Argonne | 56 | 49.06 N | 5.04 E |
| Clermont-Ferrand | 32 | 45.47 N | 3.05 E |
| Clermont State Park ♠ | 210 | 42.05 N | 73.55 W |
| Clerval | 58 | 47.24 N | 6.30 E |
| Clervaux | 56 | 50.04 N | 6.01 E |
| Cléry-Saint-André | 50 | 47.49 N | 1.45 E |
| Cles | 64 | 46.22 N | 11.02 E |
| Cleve | 166 | 33.42 S | 136.30 E |
| Clevedon | 42 | 51.27 N | 2.51 W |
| Cleveland, Austl. | 171a | 27.32 S | 153.17 E |
| Cleveland, Al., U.S. | 194 | 33.59 N | 86.34 W |
| Cleveland, Fl., U.S. | 220 | 26.57 N | 82.00 W |
| Cleveland, Ga., U.S. | 192 | 34.35 N | 83.45 W |
| Cleveland, Ms., U.S. | 194 | 33.44 N | 90.43 W |
| Cleveland, N.Y., U.S. | 210 | 43.14 N | 75.53 W |
| Cleveland, N.C., U.S. | 192 | 35.43 N | 80.40 W |
| Cleveland, Oh., U.S. | 214 | 41.29 N | 81.41 W |
| Cleveland, Oh., U.S. | 279a | 41.29 N | 81.41 W |
| Cleveland, Ok., U.S. | 196 | 36.18 N | 96.27 W |
| Cleveland, Tn., U.S. | 194 | 35.09 N | 84.52 W |
| Cleveland, Tx., U.S. | 222 | 30.20 N | 95.05 W |
| Cleveland, Va., U.S. | 192 | 36.56 N | 82.09 W |
| Cleveland □[6] | 44 | 54.35 N | 1.15 W |
| Cleveland, Cape ≻ | 166 | 19.11 S | 147.01 E |
| Cleveland, Mount ∧, Austl. | 166 | 41.25 S | 145.23 E |
| Cleveland, Mount ∧, Mt., U.S. | 202 | 48.56 N | 113.51 W |
| Cleveland Heights | 214 | 41.31 N | 81.33 W |
| Cleveland Hills ⋏[2] | 44 | 54.23 N | 1.05 W |
| Cleveland-Hopkins International Airport ⊠ | 279a | 41.25 N | 81.51 W |
| Clevelândia | 252 | 26.24 S | 52.21 W |
| Clevelândia do Norte | 250 | 3.49 N | 51.52 W |
| Cleveland Museum of Art ʊ | 279a | 41.31 N | 81.37 W |
| Cleveland National Forest ♠ | 280 | 33.47 N | 117.38 W |
| Cleveland Park ◆[8] | 284c | 38.56 N | 77.04 W |
| Cleveland Peninsula ≻[1] | 182 | 55.45 N | 132.00 W |
| Cleveland Pond ⊜ | 283 | 42.07 N | 70.58 W |
| Cleveland State University ʊ[2] | 279a | 41.30 N | 81.40 W |
| Cleveland Zoo ♠ | 279a | 41.27 N | 81.43 W |
| Cleveleys | 44 | 53.53 N | 3.03 W |
| Cleversburg | 208 | 40.02 N | 77.28 W |
| Cleves → Kleve, Dtsch. | 52 | 51.48 N | 6.09 E |
| Cleves, Oh., U.S. | 218 | 39.10 N | 84.45 W |
| Clew Bay ⊂ | 48 | 53.50 N | 9.50 W |
| Clewer | 158 | 25.55 S | 29.07 E |
| Clewiston | 220 | 26.45 N | 80.56 W |
| Cley next the Sea | 42 | 52.58 N | 1.03 E |
| Clichy | 50 | 48.54 N | 2.18 E |
| Clichy-sous-Bois | 261 | 48.55 N | 2.33 E |
| Clifden | 48 | 53.29 N | 10.01 W |
| Clifden Bay ⊂ | 48 | 53.28 N | 10.05 W |
| Cliffdale Creek ≃ | 166 | 16.56 S | 138.48 E |
| Cliffdell | 224 | 46.44 N | 120.42 W |
| Cliffe | 42 | 51.28 N | 0.30 E |
| Cliffe Marshes ≋ | 260 | 51.28 N | 0.30 E |
| Cliffe Woods | 260 | 51.26 N | 0.30 E |
| Clifford, On., Can. | 212 | 43.58 N | 80.58 W |
| Clifford, S. Afr. | 158 | 31.04 S | 27.28 E |
| Clifford, In., U.S. | 218 | 39.16 N | 85.52 W |
| Clifford, Pa., U.S. | 210 | 41.39 N | 75.36 W |
| Clifford Park ♠ | 274b | 37.43 S | 145.16 E |
| Cliffside | 210 | 42.31 N | 74.59 W |
| Cliffside Park | 276 | 40.58 N | 73.57 W |
| Cliffwood | 276 | 40.26 N | 74.14 W |
| Cliffwood Beach | 276 | 40.26 N | 74.13 W |
| Clifton, Austl. | 171a | 27.56 S | 151.54 E |
| Clifton, Eng., U.K. | 262 | 53.46 N | 2.49 W |
| Clifton, Az., U.S. | 200 | 33.03 N | 109.17 W |
| Clifton, Il., U.S. | 216 | 40.56 N | 87.56 W |
| Clifton, Ks., U.S. | 198 | 39.34 N | 97.16 W |
| Clifton, N.J., U.S. | 210 | 40.51 N | 74.09 W |
| Clifton, N.Y., U.S. | 210 | 43.03 N | 77.49 W |
| Clifton, Or., U.S. | 224 | 46.12 N | 123.27 W |
| Clifton, Tn., U.S. | 194 | 35.23 N | 87.59 W |
| Clifton, Tx., U.S. | 222 | 31.46 N | 97.34 W |
| Clifton, Lake ⊜ | 168a | 32.49 S | 115.41 E |
| Clifton Court Forebay ⊜[1] | 226 | 37.50 N | 121.35 W |
| Clifton Forge | 192 | 37.48 N | 79.49 W |
| Clifton Gorge V | 42 | 51.28 N | 2.37 W |
| Clifton Heights, N.Y., U.S. | 284a | 42.44 N | 78.56 W |
| Clifton Heights, Pa., U.S. | 285 | 39.55 N | 75.17 W |
| Clifton Hills | 166 | 26.52 S | 138.50 E |
| Clifton Knolls | 210 | 42.52 N | 73.46 W |
| Clifton Park ♠ | 284b | 39.19 N | 76.35 W |
| Clifton Point ≻ | 240b | 25.01 N | 77.34 W |
| Clifton Springs | 210 | 42.57 N | 77.08 W |
| Clifty, Mount ∧ | 224 | 47.07 N | 121.10 W |
| Clifty Creek ≃ | 218 | 39.09 N | 85.54 W |
| Clifty Falls State Park ♠ | 218 | 38.45 N | 85.26 W |
| Clignon ≃ | 50 | 49.07 N | 3.04 E |
| Climax, Sk., Can. | 184 | 49.13 N | 108.23 W |
| Climax, Co., U.S. | 200 | 39.22 N | 106.10 W |
| Climax, Ga., U.S. | 192 | 30.52 N | 84.25 W |
| Climax, Mi., U.S. | 216 | 42.14 N | 85.20 W |
| Climax, Pa., U.S. | 214 | 40.59 N | 79.23 W |
| Clinch ≃ | 192 | 35.53 N | 84.29 W |
| Clinchco | 192 | 37.09 N | 82.21 W |
| Clingen | 54 | 51.14 N | 10.55 E |
| Clingmans Dome ∧ | 192 | 35.35 N | 83.30 W |
| Clinton, B.C., Can. | 182 | 51.05 N | 121.35 W |
| Clinton, On., Can. | 190 | 43.37 N | 81.32 W |
| Clinton, N.Z. | 172 | 46.12 S | 169.22 E |
| Clinton, Al., U.S. | 194 | 32.55 N | 88.00 W |
| Clinton, Ar., U.S. | 194 | 35.35 N | 92.27 W |
| Clinton, Ct., U.S. | 207 | 41.16 N | 72.31 W |
| Clinton, Il., U.S. | 219 | 40.09 N | 88.57 W |
| Clinton, In., U.S. | 194 | 39.39 N | 87.23 W |
| Clinton, Ia., U.S. | 190 | 41.50 N | 90.11 W |
| Clinton, Ky., U.S. | 194 | 36.40 N | 88.59 W |
| Clinton, La., U.S. | 194 | 30.51 N | 91.00 W |
| Clinton, Me., U.S. | 188 | 44.38 N | 69.30 W |
| Clinton, Md., U.S. | 208 | 38.45 N | 76.53 W |
| Clinton, Ma., U.S. | 207 | 42.25 N | 71.41 W |
| Clinton, Mi., U.S. | 216 | 42.04 N | 83.58 W |
| Clinton, Mn., U.S. | 198 | 45.27 N | 96.26 W |
| Clinton, Ms., U.S. | 194 | 32.20 N | 90.19 W |
| Clinton, Mo., U.S. | 194 | 38.22 N | 93.46 W |
| Clinton, N.J., U.S. | 210 | 40.38 N | 74.54 W |
| Clinton, N.Y., U.S. | 210 | 43.02 N | 75.22 W |
| Clinton, N.C., U.S. | 192 | 34.59 N | 78.19 W |
| Clinton, Oh., U.S. | 214 | 40.56 N | 81.42 W |
| Clinton, Ok., U.S. | 196 | 35.30 N | 98.58 W |
| Clinton, Pa., U.S. | 214 | 40.29 N | 80.18 W |
| Clinton, S.C., U.S. | 192 | 34.28 N | 81.52 W |
| Clinton, Tn., U.S. | 192 | 36.06 N | 84.07 W |
| Clinton, Tx., U.S. | 222 | 33.06 N | 96.14 W |
| Clinton, Wa., U.S. | 224 | 47.58 N | 122.21 W |
| Clinton, Wi., U.S. | 216 | 42.33 N | 88.51 W |
| Clinton □[6], Il., U.S. | 219 | 38.37 N | 89.22 W |
| Clinton □[6], In., U.S. | 216 | 40.17 N | 86.31 W |
| Clinton □[6], Mi., U.S. | 216 | 42.56 N | 84.36 W |
| Clinton □[6], N.Y., U.S. | 206 | 44.57 N | 73.42 W |
| Clinton □[6], Oh., U.S. | 218 | 39.27 N | 83.50 W |
| Clinton □[6], Pa., U.S. | 210 | 41.08 N | 71.26 W |
| Clinton ≃ | 214 | 42.36 N | 82.48 W |
| Clinton, Cape ≻ | 166 | 22.32 S | 150.47 E |
| Clinton, Lake ⊜[1] | 194 | 40.10 N | 88.50 W |
| Clinton, Middle Branch ≃ | 281 | 42.36 N | 82.54 W |
| Clinton, North Branch ≃ | 214 | 42.36 N | 82.54 W |
| Clinton-Colden Lake ⊜ | 176 | 63.58 N | 107.27 W |
| Clintondale | 210 | 41.01 N | 77.29 W |
| Clinton Lake ⊜[1] | 198 | 38.55 N | 95.25 W |
| Clinton Park | 210 | 42.36 N | 73.43 W |
| Clinton Reservoir ⊜[1] | 276 | 41.05 N | 74.27 W |
| Clinton Township | 214 | 42.33 N | 82.53 W |
| Clintonville, Mi., U.S. | 281 | 42.43 N | 83.22 W |
| Clintonville, Pa., U.S. | 214 | 41.12 N | 79.53 W |
| Clintonville, Wi., U.S. | 190 | 44.37 N | 88.45 W |
| Clintwood | 192 | 37.09 N | 82.27 W |
| Clio, Al., U.S. | 194 | 31.42 N | 85.36 W |
| Clio, Mi., U.S. | 190 | 43.10 N | 83.44 W |
| Clio, S.C., U.S. | 192 | 34.34 N | 79.32 W |
| Clipperton, Île I[1] | 230 | 10.17 N | 109.13 W |
| Clipperton Fracture Zone ✢ | 16 | 10.00 N | 115.00 W |
| Clisham ∧ | 46 | 57.57 N | 6.49 W |
| Clisson | 32 | 47.05 N | 1.17 W |
| Clitheroe | 44 | 53.53 N | 2.23 W |
| Clitunno ≃ | 66 | 42.56 N | 12.37 E |
| Clive | 172 | 39.35 S | 176.55 E |
| Cloates, Point ≻ | 162 | 22.43 S | 113.40 E |
| Clock Face | 262 | 53.25 N | 2.43 W |
| Clocolan | 158 | 29.00 S | 27.30 E |
| Clodomira | 252 | 27.35 S | 64.08 W |
| Cloe | 214 | 40.56 N | 78.56 W |
| Cloete | 196 | 27.55 N | 101.10 W |
| Cloghan, Ire. | 48 | 54.51 N | 7.56 W |
| Cloghan, Ire. | 48 | 53.13 N | 7.53 W |
| Cloghane | 48 | 52.13 N | 10.12 W |
| Clogheen | 48 | 52.16 N | 8.00 W |
| Clogher | 48 | 54.25 N | 7.12 W |
| Clogher Head ≻ | 48 | 53.48 N | 6.12 W |
| Cloghjordan | 48 | 52.57 N | 8.02 W |
| Clonakilty | 48 | 51.37 N | 8.54 W |
| Clonakilty Bay ⊂ | 48 | 51.35 N | 8.50 W |
| Cloncurry | 166 | 20.42 S | 140.30 E |
| Cloncurry ≃ | 166 | 18.37 S | 140.40 E |
| Clondalkin | 48 | 53.19 N | 6.24 W |
| Clonee | 48 | 53.25 N | 6.26 W |
| Clones | 48 | 54.11 N | 7.15 W |
| Clonfert | 48 | 53.14 N | 8.05 W |
| Clonmacnois ⊥ | 48 | 53.20 N | 7.59 W |
| Clonmany | 48 | 55.14 N | 7.25 W |
| Clonmel | 48 | 52.21 N | 7.42 W |
| Clonroche | 48 | 52.27 N | 6.43 W |
| Clontarf | 274a | 33.48 S | 151.16 E |
| Cloone | 48 | 53.57 N | 7.46 W |
| Clo-oose | 224 | 48.40 N | 124.49 W |
| Cloppenburg | 52 | 52.50 N | 8.02 E |
| Cloquallum Creek ≃ | 224 | 46.58 N | 123.24 W |
| Cloquet | 190 | 46.43 N | 92.27 W |
| Cloquet ≃ | 190 | 46.52 N | 92.35 W |
| Clorinda | 252 | 25.17 S | 57.43 W |
| Closter | 276 | 40.58 N | 73.57 W |
| Cloudcroft | 200 | 32.57 N | 105.44 W |
| Cloud Peak ∧, Ak., U.S. | 180 | 68.24 N | 148.26 W |
| Cloud Peak ∧, Wy., U.S. | 202 | 44.25 N | 107.10 W |
| Cloudy Bay ⊂ | 172 | 41.27 S | 174.10 E |
| Cloudy Mountain ∧ | 180 | 63.11 N | 156.05 W |
| Clough | 48 | 54.18 N | 5.50 W |
| Clough Foot | 262 | 53.43 N | 2.08 W |
| Clova | 46 | 56.50 N | 3.06 W |
| Clova, Glen V | 46 | 56.49 N | 3.04 W |
| Clove Lakes Park ♠ | 276 | 40.37 N | 74.07 W |
| Clovelly, Austl. | 274a | 33.55 S | 151.16 E |
| Clovelly, Eng., U.K. | 42 | 51.00 N | 4.24 W |
| Clover | 192 | 35.06 N | 81.13 W |
| Clover Bank | 210 | 42.45 N | 78.53 W |
| Clover Creek ≃, Id., U.S. | 202 | 43.00 N | 115.11 W |
| Clover Creek ≃, Id., U.S. | 202 | 42.34 N | 115.38 W |
| Cloverdale, B.C., Can. | 224 | 49.06 N | 122.44 W |
| Cloverdale, Al., U.S. | 194 | 34.56 N | 87.46 W |
| Cloverdale, Ca., U.S. | 204 | 38.48 N | 123.00 W |
| Cloverdale, Il., U.S. | 278 | 41.56 N | 88.07 W |
| Cloverdale, In., U.S. | 194 | 39.30 N | 86.47 W |
| Cloverdale, Ky., U.S. | 218 | 38.10 N | 84.53 W |
| Cloverdale, Mi., U.S. | 216 | 42.32 N | 85.23 W |
| Cloverdale, Oh., U.S. | 216 | 41.01 N | 84.18 W |
| Cloverdale, Or., U.S. | 224 | 45.12 N | 123.53 W |
| Cloverdale Mall ◆[9] | 275b | 43.38 N | 79.34 W |
| Cloverdene | 273d | 26.09 S | 28.22 E |
| Cloverleaf | 222 | 29.46 N | 95.10 W |
| Clover Pass | 182 | 55.28 N | 131.47 W |
| Cloverport | 194 | 37.50 N | 86.37 W |
| Cloverville | 216 | 43.11 N | 86.10 W |
| Clovis, Ca., U.S. | 226 | 36.49 N | 119.42 W |
| Clovis, N.M., U.S. | 196 | 34.24 N | 103.12 W |
| Clowbridge Reservoir ⊜[1] | 262 | 53.45 N | 2.16 W |
| Clowne | 44 | 53.18 N | 1.16 W |
| Cloyes-sur-le-Loir | 50 | 48.00 N | 1.14 E |
| Cloyne | 48 | 51.51 N | 8.08 W |
| Cluain Meala → Clonmel | 48 | 52.21 N | 7.42 W |
| Cluanie, Loch ⊜ | 46 | 57.07 N | 5.05 W |
| Cluj □[6] | 38 | 46.45 N | 23.45 E |
| Cluj-Napoca | 38 | 46.47 N | 23.36 E |
| Clun | 42 | 52.26 N | 3.00 W |
| Clun ≃ | 42 | 52.22 N | 2.53 W |
| Clune | 214 | 40.34 N | 79.18 W |
| Clunes | 169 | 37.18 S | 143.47 E |
| Clun Forest ◆[3] | 42 | 52.28 N | 3.07 W |
| Clunie Water ≃ | 46 | 57.00 N | 3.24 W |
| Cluny, Austl. | 166 | 24.31 S | 139.35 E |
| Cluny, Fr. | 58 | 46.26 N | 4.39 E |
| Cluses | 58 | 46.04 N | 6.36 E |
| Clusone | 64 | 45.53 N | 9.57 E |
| Clute | 222 | 29.01 N | 95.23 W |
| Clutha ≃ | 172 | 46.21 S | 169.48 E |
| Clwyd □[6] | 44 | 53.05 N | 3.20 W |
| Clwyd ≃ | 44 | 53.20 N | 3.30 W |
| Clwyd, Vale of V | 44 | 53.12 N | 3.24 W |
| Clwydian Range ⋏ | 44 | 53.10 N | 3.20 W |
| Clydach | 42 | 51.43 N | 3.50 W |
| Clyde, Austl. | 274a | 33.50 S | 151.00 E |
| Clyde, Ab., Can. | 182 | 54.09 N | 113.39 W |
| Clyde, N.Z. | 172 | 45.11 S | 169.19 E |
| Clyde, Ca., U.S. | 226 | 38.02 N | 122.02 W |
| Clyde, Ks., U.S. | 198 | 39.35 N | 97.23 W |
| Clyde, Mi., U.S. | 281 | 42.41 N | 83.37 W |
| Clyde, N.Y., U.S. | 210 | 43.05 N | 76.52 W |
| Clyde, N.C., U.S. | 192 | 35.32 N | 82.54 W |
| Clyde, Oh., U.S. | 214 | 41.18 N | 82.58 W |
| Clyde, Tx., U.S. | 196 | 32.24 N | 99.30 W |
| Clyde ≃, Austl. | 170 | 35.23 S | 150.15 E |
| Clyde ≃, N.S., Can. | 186 | 43.35 N | 65.25 W |
| Clyde ≃, On., Can. | 212 | 44.58 N | 76.22 W |
| Clyde ≃, Scot., U.K. | 46 | 55.44 N | 4.55 W |
| Clyde ≃, N.Y., U.S. | 210 | 43.04 N | 77.00 W |
| Clyde ≃, Vt., U.S. | 188 | 44.56 N | 72.12 W |
| Clyde, Firth of ⊂[1] | 46 | 55.42 N | 5.00 W |
| Clydebank | 46 | 55.54 N | 4.24 W |
| Clydegale Lake ⊜ | 212 | 45.25 N | 78.23 W |
| Clyde Lake ⊜ | 182 | 55.18 N | 111.28 W |
| Clyde No. 3 | 214 | 39.59 N | 80.03 W |
| Clyde Park | 202 | 45.53 N | 110.36 W |
| Clyde Potts Reservoir ⊜[1] | 276 | 40.48 N | 74.35 W |
| Clyde River | 176 | 70.25 N | 68.30 W |
| Clydesdale | 158 | 26.54 S | 27.55 E |
| Clydesdale V | 46 | 55.42 N | 3.50 W |
| Clymer, N.Y., U.S. | 214 | 42.01 N | 79.37 W |
| Clymer, Pa., U.S. | 214 | 40.40 N | 79.00 W |
| Clynnog-fawr | 44 | 53.01 N | 4.23 W |
| Clywedog ≃ | 42 | 52.27 N | 3.32 W |
| Ćmielów | 30 | 50.53 N | 21.31 E |
| Cna ≃, Bela. | 76 | 52.10 N | 27.03 E |
| Cna ≃, Ross. | 76 | 57.33 N | 34.36 E |
| Cna ≃, Ross. | 80 | 54.32 N | 42.05 E |
| Cna ≃, Ross. | 82 | 55.03 N | 39.09 E |
| Cnori | 84 | 41.37 N | 45.59 E |
| Cnossus → Knossós ⊥ | 38 | 35.20 N | 25.10 E |
| Côa ≃ | 34 | 41.05 N | 7.06 W |
| Coacalco | 286a | 19.37 N | 99.05 W |
| Coachella | 204 | 33.40 N | 116.10 W |
| Coachella Canal ≈ | 204 | 33.34 N | 116.00 W |
| Coachford | 48 | 51.53 N | 8.48 W |
| Coacoyole | 232 | 24.31 N | 106.34 W |
| Coacuilco | 234 | 21.07 N | 98.35 W |
| Coahoma | 196 | 32.18 N | 101.18 W |
| Coahuayana | 234 | 18.44 N | 103.41 W |
| Coahuayutla de Guerrero | 234 | 18.19 N | 101.49 W |
| Coahuila | 200 | 32.12 N | 114.59 W |
| Coahuila □[3] | 232 | 27.20 N | 102.00 W |
| Coal ≃ | 180 | 59.39 N | 126.57 W |
| Coalbrook | 158 | 26.51 S | 27.53 E |
| Coalbrookdale | 42 | 52.38 N | 2.30 W |
| Coalburg | 214 | 41.11 N | 80.36 W |
| Coalburn | 46 | 55.36 N | 3.54 W |
| Coal City | 216 | 41.17 N | 88.17 W |
| Coalcomán ≃ | 234 | 18.11 N | 103.08 W |
| Coalcomán de Matamoros | 234 | 18.47 N | 103.09 W |
| Coal Creek | 180 | 65.22 N | 143.10 W |
| Coal Creek ≃, Co., U.S. | 198 | 40.30 N | 104.26 W |
| Coal Creek ≃, In., U.S. | 194 | 39.57 N | 87.25 W |
| Coal Creek ≃, Wa., U.S. | 202 | 47.19 N | 118.36 W |
| Coal Creek Flat | 172 | 45.29 S | 169.18 E |
| Coaldale, Ab., Can. | 182 | 49.43 N | 112.37 W |
| Coaldale, Pa., U.S. | 210 | 40.49 N | 75.54 W |
| Coal Fire Creek ≃ | 194 | 33.15 N | 88.18 W |
| Coal Fork | 188 | 38.19 N | 81.32 W |
| Coalgate, N.Z. | 172 | 43.29 S | 171.58 E |
| Coalgate, Ok., U.S. | 196 | 34.32 N | 96.13 W |
| Coal Grove | 188 | 38.30 N | 82.38 W |
| Coal Harbour | 182 | 50.36 N | 127.35 W |
| Coal Hill | 194 | 35.26 N | 93.40 W |
| Coal Hill Park ♠ | 271a | 39.56 N | 116.23 E |
| Coalhurst | 182 | 49.45 N | 112.56 W |
| Coalinga | 226 | 36.08 N | 120.21 W |
| Coalisland | 48 | 54.33 N | 6.42 W |
| Coal Island I | 172 | 46.07 S | 166.38 E |
| Coalmont | 182 | 49.31 N | 120.41 W |
| Coalpit Heath | 42 | 51.32 N | 2.28 W |
| Coalport | 214 | 40.44 N | 78.32 W |
| Coal River | 180 | 59.45 N | 126.55 W |
| Coal Run ≃ | 279b | 40.21 N | 80.07 W |
| Coalspur | 182 | 53.11 N | 117.01 W |
| Coalton | 219 | 39.17 N | 89.19 W |
| Coaltown | 214 | 41.02 N | 80.20 W |
| Coal Valley V | 204 | 38.00 N | 115.05 W |
| Coalville, S. Afr. | 158 | 26.01 S | 29.10 E |
| Coalville, Eng., U.K. | 42 | 52.44 N | 1.20 W |
| Coalville, Ut,. U.S. | 200 | 40.55 N | 111.23 W |
| Coamo | 240m | 18.05 N | 66.22 W |
| Coamo, Lago ⊜[1] | 240m | 18.01 N | 66.23 W |
| Coapilla | 234 | 17.08 N | 93.10 W |
| Coaraci | 255 | 14.38 S | 39.32 W |
| Coari | 246 | 4.05 S | 63.08 W |
| Coari ≃ | 246 | 4.30 S | 63.33 W |
| Coari, Lago de ⊜ | 246 | 4.15 S | 63.22 W |
| Coarsegold | 226 | 37.16 N | 119.42 W |
| Coast □[4] | 154 | 3.00 S | 39.30 E |
| Coast Mountains ⋏ | 176 | 55.00 N | 129.00 W |
| Coast Ranges ⋏ | 178 | 41.00 N | 123.30 W |
| Coatán ≃ | 236 | 14.48 N | 92.31 W |
| Coatbridge | 46 | 55.52 N | 4.01 W |
| Coatepec | 234 | 19.27 N | 96.58 W |
| Coatepec Harinas | 234 | 18.54 N | 99.43 W |
| Coatepeque | 236 | 14.42 N | 91.52 W |
| Coatepeque, Lago de ⊜ | 236 | 13.52 N | 89.33 W |
| Coates Creek ≃ | 212 | 44.24 N | 79.54 W |
| Coatesville | 208 | 39.58 N | 75.49 W |
| Coaticook | 206 | 45.08 N | 71.48 W |
| Coaticook ≃ | 206 | 45.20 N | 71.53 W |
| Coatsburg | 219 | 40.02 N | 91.10 W |
| Coats Island I | 176 | 62.30 N | 83.00 W |
| Coats Land ◆[1] | 9 | 77.00 S | 28.00 W |
| Coatzacoalcos | 234 | 18.09 N | 94.25 W |
| Coatzacoalcos ≃ | 234 | 18.10 N | 94.27 W |
| Coatzintla | 234 | 20.29 N | 97.27 W |
| Coayllo | 248 | 12.44 S | 76.28 W |
| Coazze | 62 | 45.03 N | 7.18 E |
| Cobá ⊥ | 232 | 20.36 N | 87.35 W |
| Cobadin | 38 | 44.04 N | 28.13 E |
| Coballo Cocha | 246 | 3.54 S | 70.32 W |
| Cobalt, On., Can. | 190 | 47.24 N | 79.41 W |
| Cobalt, Ct., U.S. | 207 | 41.33 N | 72.33 W |
| Cobán | 236 | 15.29 N | 90.19 W |
| Çobanlar | 130 | 38.41 N | 30.47 E |
| Čobar | 166 | 31.30 S | 145.49 E |
| Cobargo | 166 | 36.23 S | 149.53 E |
| Cobb | 226 | 38.49 N | 122.43 W |
| Cobb Creek ≃ | 196 | 35.05 N | 98.25 W |
| Cobberas, Mount ∧ | 166 | 36.52 S | 148.10 E |
| Cobbetts Pond ⊜ | 283 | 42.48 N | 71.17 W |
| Cobbin's Brook ≃ | 260 | 51.41 N | 0.01 W |
| Cobb Island | 208 | 38.16 N | 76.51 W |
| Cobb Island I, Md., U.S. | 208 | 38.16 N | 76.51 W |
| Cobb Island I, Va., U.S. | 208 | 37.20 N | 75.44 W |
| Cobbitty | 274a | 34.01 S | 150.41 E |
| Cobbitty ∧[2] | 274a | 33.59 S | 150.42 E |
| Cobble Hill | 224 | 48.41 N | 123.36 W |
| Cobble Mountain Reservoir ⊜[1] | 207 | 42.08 N | 72.55 W |
| Cobblestone Mountain ∧ | 228 | 34.37 N | 118.52 W |
| Cobb Neck ≻[1] | 208 | 38.20 N | 76.55 W |
| Cobbs Creek ≃ | 285 | 39.54 N | 75.15 W |
| Cobbs Creek Park ♠ | 285 | 39.58 N | 75.16 W |
| Cobb Seamount ✢[3] | 16 | 46.46 N | 130.49 W |
| Cobden, Austl. | 169 | 38.20 S | 143.05 E |
| Cobden, On., Can. | 190 | 45.38 N | 76.53 W |
| Cobden, Il., U.S. | 194 | 37.31 N | 89.15 W |
| Cobeña | 266a | 40.34 N | 3.30 W |
| Cobequid Bay ⊂ | 186 | 45.21 N | 63.45 W |
| Cobequid Mountains ⋏ | 186 | 45.31 N | 64.05 W |
| Cobh | 48 | 51.51 N | 8.17 W |
| Cobham, Eng., U.K. | 42 | 51.20 N | 0.25 W |
| Cobham, Eng., U.K. | 260 | 51.23 N | 0.24 E |
| Cobham ≃ | 184 | 53.15 N | 93.58 W |
| Cobham Hall ⊥ | 260 | 51.23 N | 0.25 E |
| Cobija, Bol. | 248 | 11.02 S | 68.44 W |
| Cobija, Chile | 252 | 22.33 S | 70.16 W |
| Coblenz → Koblenz | 56 | 50.21 N | 7.35 E |
| Cobleskill | 210 | 42.40 N | 74.29 W |
| Cobleskill Creek ≃ | 210 | 42.43 N | 74.20 W |
| Coboconk | 212 | 44.39 N | 78.48 W |
| Cobo Hall ʊ | 281 | 42.19 N | 83.03 W |
| Cobolgo, gora ∧ | 84 | 42.50 N | 46.23 E |
| Çoboto, Cerro ∧ | 200 | 31.29 N | 112.05 W |
| Čoboty | 265b | 55.39 N | 37.21 E |
| Cobourg | 212 | 43.58 N | 78.10 W |
| Cobourg Peninsula ≻[1] | 164 | 11.20 S | 132.15 E |
| Cobquecura | 252 | 36.08 S | 72.47 W |
| Cobram | 166 | 35.55 S | 145.39 E |
| Cobras, Ilha das I | 287a | 22.54 S | 43.10 W |
| Cobras, Ribeirão das ≃ | 256 | 23.08 S | 46.05 W |
| Cobre ≃ | 236 | 8.01 N | 81.18 W |
| Cobre, Barranca del V | 232 | 27.28 N | 107.50 W |
| Cóbuè | 154 | 12.04 S | 34.50 E |
| Coburg, Austl. | 169 | 37.45 S | 144.58 E |
| Coburg, Dtsch. | 56 | 50.15 N | 10.58 E |
| Coburg Island I | 176 | 76.00 N | 79.25 W |
| Coburn | 210 | 40.52 N | 77.28 W |
| Coburn Mountain ∧ | 188 | 45.28 N | 70.06 W |
| Coca ≃ | 246 | 0.29 S | 76.58 W |
| Coca, Laguna ⊜ | 286b | 22.57 N | 82.27 W |
| Coca, Pizzo di ∧ | 64 | 46.04 N | 10.01 E |
| Cocachacra | 248 | 17.06 S | 71.46 W |
| Cocais, Ribeirão dos ≃ | 256 | 21.59 S | 47.15 W |
| Cocal | 250 | 3.28 S | 41.34 W |
| Cocalico Creek ≃ | 208 | 40.07 N | 76.14 W |
| Coccaglio | 64 | 45.34 N | 9.58 E |
| Cocconato | 62 | 45.05 N | 8.02 E |
| Cocentaina | 34 | 38.45 N | 0.26 W |
| Cochabamba | 248 | 17.24 S | 66.09 W |
| Çochabamba □[5] | 248 | 17.30 S | 65.40 W |
| Čochatauri | 84 | 42.01 N | 42.15 E |
| Cochato ≃ | 283 | 42.10 N | 71.01 W |
| Coche, Isla I | 246 | 10.45 N | 63.55 W |
| Cochem | 56 | 50.11 N | 7.09 E |
| Cochesett | 283 | 42.01 N | 71.02 W |
| Cochetopa Creek ≃ | 200 | 38.31 N | 106.47 W |
| Cochichewick, Lake ⊜ | 283 | 42.42 N | 71.06 W |
| Cochin | 122 | 9.58 N | 76.14 E |
| Cochin China → Nam Phan □[9] | 110 | 11.00 N | 107.00 E |
| Cochinos, Bahía de (Bay of Pigs) ⊂ | 240p | 22.07 N | 81.10 W |
| Cochinos, Cayos II | 236 | 15.57 N | 86.33 W |
| Cochise Head ∧ | 200 | 32.03 N | 109.18 W |
| Cochiti Indian Reservation ◆[4] | 200 | 35.37 N | 106.20 W |
| Cochituate | 207 | 42.19 N | 71.21 W |
| Cochituate, Lake ⊜ | 283 | 42.17 N | 71.22 W |
| Cochituate State Park ♠ | 207 | 42.20 N | 71.22 W |
| Cochran | 192 | 32.23 N | 83.21 W |
| Cochrane, Ab., Can. | 182 | 51.11 N | 114.28 W |
| Cochrane, On., Can. | 176 | 49.04 N | 81.01 W |
| Cochrane, Chile | 254 | 47.16 S | 72.33 W |
| Cochrane, Wi., U.S. | 190 | 44.13 N | 91.50 W |
| Cochrane ≃ | 176 | 57.52 N | 101.38 W |
| Cochrane, Cerro (Monte San Lorenzo) ∧ | 254 | 47.37 S | 72.19 W |
| Cochrane, Lago (Lago Pueyrredón) ⊜ | 254 | 47.20 S | 72.00 W |
| Cochranton | 214 | 41.31 N | 80.02 W |
| Cochranville | 208 | 39.53 N | 75.55 W |
| Cochstedt | 54 | 51.53 N | 11.24 E |
| Cockatoo-Inseln → Buccaneer Archipelago II | 160 | 16.17 S | 123.20 E |
| Cock Bridge | 46 | 57.09 N | 3.14 W |
| Cockburn | 166 | 32.05 S | 141.00 E |
| Cockburn, Canal ʉ | 254 | 54.20 S | 71.30 W |
| Cockburn, Cape ≻ | 164 | 11.20 S | 132.52 E |
| Cockburn, Mount ∧ | 162 | 22.46 S | 130.36 E |
| Cockburn Island I | 190 | 45.55 N | 83.22 W |
| Cockburn Sound ʉ | 168a | 32.12 S | 115.42 E |
| Cockburnspath | 46 | 55.56 N | 2.21 W |
| Cock Clarks | 260 | 51.42 N | 0.37 E |
| Cockenoe Island I | 276 | 41.05 N | 73.21 W |
| Cockenzie | 46 | 55.58 N | 2.58 W |
| Cocker ≃ | 44 | 54.39 N | 3.22 W |
| Cockerham | 44 | 53.59 N | 2.50 W |
| Cockermouth | 44 | 54.40 N | 3.21 W |
| Cockeysville | 208 | 39.28 N | 76.38 W |
| Cockfield | 44 | 54.37 N | 1.48 W |
| Cockfosters ◆[8] | 260 | 51.39 N | 0.09 W |
| Cocklebiddy | 162 | 32.02 S | 126.06 E |
| Cockpit Country ◆[1] | 241q | 18.18 N | 77.43 W |
| Cockrell Hill | 222 | 32.44 N | 96.53 W |
| Cockroach Island I | 240m | 18.24 N | 65.04 W |
| Cockscomb Point ≻ | 174u | 14.14 S | 170.40 W |
| Coclé □[4] | 236 | 8.30 N | 80.15 W |
| Coclé del Norte ≃ | 236 | 9.05 N | 80.35 W |
| Coclois | 50 | 48.28 N | 4.20 E |
| Coco ≃ | 236 | 15.00 N | 83.10 W |
| Coco, Cayo I | 240p | 22.30 N | 78.28 W |
| Coco, Isla del I | 230 | 5.32 N | 87.04 W |
| Côco, Rio do ≃ | 250 | 9.27 S | 50.02 W |
| Cocoa | 220 | 28.23 N | 80.44 W |
| Cocoa Beach | 220 | 28.19 N | 80.36 W |
| Cocobeach | 152 | 0.59 N | 9.36 E |
| Coco Channel ʉ | 110 | 13.45 N | 93.00 E |
| Cococi | 250 | 6.25 S | 40.30 W |
| Cocodrie Lake ⊜[1] | 194 | 30.58 N | 92.25 W |
| Coco Islands II | 110 | 14.05 N | 93.18 E |
| Coconino Plateau ⋏[1] | 200 | 35.50 N | 112.30 W |
| Cocorocuma, Cayos ✢[2] | 236 | 15.45 N | 83.00 W |
| Cocos | 255 | 14.10 S | 44.33 W |
| Cocos (Keeling) Islands □[2] | 14 | 12.10 S | 96.55 E |
| Cocos Bay ⊂ | 241r | 10.27 N | 61.00 W |
| Cocos Island I | 174p | 13.14 N | 144.39 E |
| Cocos Lagoon ⊂ | 174p | 13.14 N | 144.38 E |
| Cocos Ridge ✢[3] | 16 | 5.30 N | 86.00 W |
| Cocotá ◆[8] | 287a | 22.49 S | 43.11 W |
| Cocuiza ≃ | 246 | 10.59 N | 71.17 W |
| Cocula, Méx. | 234 | 18.14 N | 99.40 W |
| Cocula, Méx. | 234 | 20.23 N | 103.50 W |
| Cod ≃ | 44 | 54.10 N | 1.22 W |
| Cod, Cape ≻[1] | 207 | 41.42 N | 70.15 W |
| Codăești | 38 | 46.52 N | 27.46 E |
| Codajás | 246 | 3.50 S | 62.05 W |
| Codaruina | 71 | 40.56 N | 8.49 E |
| Coddenham | 42 | 52.09 N | 1.07 E |
| Codera, Cabo ≻ | 246 | 10.35 N | 66.05 W |
| Coderre | 184 | 50.10 N | 106.23 W |
| Coderre, Ruisseau ≃ | 275a | 45.43 N | 73.19 W |
| Codesa | 182 | 55.45 N | 118.04 W |
| Codfish Island I | 172 | 46.47 S | 167.38 E |
| Codigoro | 66 | 44.49 N | 12.08 E |
| Cod Island I | 176 | 57.45 N | 61.50 W |
| Codlea | 38 | 45.42 N | 25.27 E |
| Codnor | 44 | 53.03 N | 1.23 W |
| Codó | 250 | 4.29 S | 43.53 W |
| Codogno | 62 | 45.09 N | 9.42 E |
| Codorus | 208 | 39.48 N | 76.52 W |
| Codorus Creek ≃ | 208 | 40.03 N | 76.38 W |
| Codorus State Park ♠ | 208 | 39.48 N | 76.54 W |
| Codòzinho | 250 | 4.46 S | 44.10 W |
| Codpa | 248 | 18.50 S | 69.44 W |
| Çodrii ⋏[2] | 38 | 47.10 N | 28.25 E |
| Čodro | 86 | 50.50 N | 88.34 E |
| Codroipo | 64 | 45.58 N | 12.59 E |
| Codrongianos | 71 | 40.39 N | 8.41 E |
| Codroy | 186 | 47.53 N | 59.24 W |
| Codroy Pond | 186 | 48.04 N | 58.52 W |
| Codru-Moma, Munții ⋏ | 38 | 46.30 N | 22.20 E |
| Codsall | 42 | 52.38 N | 2.12 W |
| Cody, Ne., U.S. | 198 | 42.56 N | 101.14 W |
| Cody, Wy., U.S. | 202 | 44.31 N | 109.03 W |
| Coeburn | 192 | 36.56 N | 82.27 W |
| Coelemu | 252 | 36.29 S | 72.42 W |
| Coelho da Rocha | 256 | 22.47 S | 43.23 W |
| Coelho Neto | 250 | 4.15 S | 43.00 W |
| Coemba | 152 | 12.08 S | 18.05 E |
| Coen | 164 | 13.56 S | 143.12 E |
| Coen ≃, Austl. | 164 | 13.56 S | 142.02 E |
| Coén ≃, C.R. | 236 | 9.34 N | 82.58 W |
| Coeneo [de la Libertad] | 234 | 19.49 N | 101.35 W |
| Coeroeni ≃ | 250 | 3.21 N | 57.31 W |
| Coesfeld | 52 | 51.56 N | 7.10 E |
| Coetivy Island I | 138 | 7.08 S | 56.16 E |
| Coeur d'Alene | 202 | 47.40 N | 116.46 W |
| Coeur d'Alene ≃ | 202 | 47.28 N | 116.48 W |
| Coeur d'Alene Indian Reservation ◆[4] | 202 | 47.18 N | 116.45 W |
| Coeur d'Alene Lake ⊜ | 202 | 47.32 N | 116.48 W |
| Coeur d'Alene Mountains ⋏ | 202 | 47.50 N | 116.05 W |
| Coevorden | 52 | 52.40 N | 6.45 E |
| Coeymans | 210 | 42.28 N | 73.48 W |
| Coffeen | 219 | 39.05 N | 89.24 W |
| Coffeen Lake ⊜[1] | 219 | 39.03 N | 89.20 W |
| Coffeeville | 194 | 33.58 N | 89.40 W |
| Coffeyville | 198 | 37.02 N | 95.36 W |
| Coffin Bay | 162 | 34.37 S | 135.29 E |
| Coffin Bay ⊂ | 162 | 34.27 S | 135.19 E |
| Coffin Bay Peninsula ≻[1] | 162 | 34.32 S | 135.15 E |
| Coffs Harbour | 166 | 30.18 S | 153.08 E |
| Cofimvaba | 158 | 32.00 S | 27.35 E |
| Cofradía | 236 | 15.24 N | 88.09 W |
| Cofre de Perote, Cerro ∧ | 234 | 19.29 N | 97.08 W |
| Cofre de Perote, Parque Nacional ♠ | 234 | 19.32 N | 97.10 W |
| Cofrents | 34 | 39.14 N | 1.04 W |
| Cogâlnic (Kohyl'nyk) ≃ | 78 | 45.51 N | 29.38 E |
| Coggeshall | 42 | 51.52 N | 0.41 E |
| Coggiola | 62 | 45.41 N | 8.11 E |
| Coggon | 190 | 42.16 N | 91.31 W |
| Coghill, Mount ∧ | 170 | 35.10 S | 149.44 E |
| Coghinas ≃ | 71 | 40.56 N | 8.48 E |
| Coghinas, Lago del ⊜ | 71 | 40.45 N | 9.02 E |
| Coglians, Monte (Hohe Warte) ∧ | 64 | 46.37 N | 12.53 E |
| Cogliate | 266b | 45.39 N | 9.05 E |
| Cognac | 32 | 45.42 N | 0.20 W |
| Cogne | 62 | 45.37 N | 7.21 E |
| Cognin | 62 | 45.34 N | 5.54 E |
| Cogo | 152 | 1.05 N | 9.42 E |


**Symbols** in the index entries represent the broad categories identified in the key at the right. Symbols with superior numbers (⋏[1]) identify subcategories (see complete key on page *I · 1).*

**Symbole** im Register stellen die rechts im Schlüssel erklärten Kategorien dar. Symbole mit hochgestellten Ziffern (⋏[1]) bezeichnen Unterabteilungen einer Kategorie (vgl. vollständiger Schlüssel auf Seite *I · 1).*

**Los símbolos** incluídos en el texto del índice representan las grandes categorías identificadas con la clave a la derecha. Los símbolos con numeros en su parte superior (⋏[1]) identifican las subcategorías (véase la clave completa en la página *I · 1).*

**Les symboles** de l'index représentent les catégories indiquées dans la légende à droite. Les symboles suivis d'un indice (⋏[1]) représentent des sous-catégories (voir légende complète à la page *I · 1).*

**Os símbolos** incluídos no texto do índice representam as grandes categorias identificadas com a chave à direita. Os símbolos com números em sua parte superior (⋏[1]) identificam as subcategorias (veja-se a chave completa à página *I · 1).*

| Symbol | English | Deutsch | Español | Français | Português |
|---|---|---|---|---|---|
| ∧ | Mountain | Berg | Montaña | Montagne | Montanha |
| ⋏ | Mountains | Gebirge | Montañas | Montagnes | Montanhas |
| )( | Pass | Paß | Paso | Col | Passo |
| V | Valley, Canyon | Tal, Cañon | Valle, Cañón | Vallée, Canyon | Vale, Canhão |
| ≚ | Plain | Ebene | Llano | Plaine | Planície |
| ≻ | Cape | Kap | Cabo | Cap | Cabo |
| I | Island | Insel | Isla | Île | Ilha |
| II | Islands | Inseln | Islas | Îles | Ilhas |
| ⊥ | Other Topographic Features | Andere Topographische Objekte | Otros Elementos Topográficos | Autres données topographiques | Outros acidentes topográficos |

Cogoleto 62 44.23 N 8.39 E
Cogolin 62 43.15 N 6.32 E
Cogollo del Cengio 64 45.47 N 11.25 E
Cogolludo 34 40.57 N 3.05 W
Cogolo 64 46.21 N 10.41 E
Cogoon ≃ 166 27.19 S 148.50 E
Čograjuskoje vodochranilišče ⊜¹ 80 45.30 N 44.25 E
Cogswell 198 46.06 N 97.46 W
Cogswell Reservoir ⊜¹ 280 34.14 N 117.58 W
Cogt 102 45.20 N 96.38 E
Cogtoandman' 102 45.50 N 104.28 E
Cogton Bay c 116 9.51 N 124.33 E
Cogt-Ovoo 102 44.25 N 105.20 E
Čoğun 130 39.20 N 34.08 E
Cohansey ≃ 208 39.21 N 75.22 W
Cohasset 207 42.14 N 70.48 W
Cohasset Harbor c 283 42.15 N 70.47 W
Cohengu ≃ 248 10.17 S 73.57 W
Cohoctah 216 42.46 N 83.57 W
Cohocton 210 42.30 N 77.30 W
Cohocton ≃ 210 42.09 N 77.05 W
Cohoe 180 60.23 N 151.18 W
Cohoes 210 42.46 N 73.42 W
Cohoon, Lake ⊜¹ 208 36.45 N 76.38 W
Cohuna 166 35.49 S 144.13 E
Coiba, Isla de I 246 7.27 N 81.45 W
Coig ≃ 254 50.58 S 69.11 W
Coigeach, Rubha ≻ 46 58.06 N 5.26 W
Coignières 261 48.45 N 1.55 E
Coihaique 254 45.34 S 72.04 W
Coils Creek ≃ 204 39.32 N 116.16 W
Coimbatore 122 11.00 N 76.58 E
Coimbra, Bra. 248 19.55 S 57.47 W
Coimbra, Bra. 255 20.52 S 42.48 W
Coimbra, Port. 34 40.12 N 8.25 W
Coín, Esp. 34 36.40 N 4.45 W
Coin, Ia., U.S. 198 40.39 N 95.13 W
Coina ≃ 266c 38.38 N 9.03 W
Coipasa, Lago ⊜ 248 19.12 S 68.07 W
Coipasa, Salar de ≃ 248 19.26 S 68.09 W
Coire — Chur 58 46.51 N 9.32 E
Čojbalsan, Mong. 88 48.25 N 114.52 E
Čojbalsan, Mong. 88 48.04 N 114.30 E
Čojbalsan uul ʌ 88 47.49 N 107.00 E
Cojedes 246 9.37 N 68.55 W
Cojedes ▫³ 246 9.20 N 68.20 W
Cojímar ◆⁸ 286b 23.10 N 82.18 W
Cojímar ≃ 286b 23.10 N 82.17 W
Cojudo Blanco, Cerro ʌ 254 47.05 S 69.20 W
Cojumatlán de Régules 234 20.07 N 102.50 W
Cojutepeque 236 13.43 N 88.56 W
Čokak 130 37.45 N 36.19 E
Čokato 190 45.04 N 94.11 W
Cokeburg 214 40.06 N 80.04 W
Coker 273a 6.29 N 3.20 E
Cokeville 200 42.04 N 110.57 W
Čokpar 85 43.49 N 74.21 E
Čoktal 85 42.36 N 76.44 E
Čokurdach 74 70.38 N 147.55 E
Colâba ◆⁸ 272c 18.54 N 72.48 E
Colâba Point ≻ 272c 18.53 N 72.48 E
Colac 169 38.20 S 143.35 E
Colac, Lake ⊜ 169 38.18 S 143.35 E
Čolakli 130 38.22 N 38.33 E
Colalao del Valle 252 26.22 S 65.57 W
Colapsin Point ≻ 116 6.38 N 125.25 E
Colares, Bra. 250 0.56 S 48.17 W
Colares, Port. 266c 38.48 N 9.27 W
Colares, Ribeira de ≃ 266c 38.49 N 9.28 W
Colatina 255 19.32 S 40.37 W
Cölbe 56 50.51 N 8.48 E
Colbeck, Cape ≻ 9 77.06 S 157.48 W
Colberry Park 281 42.36 N 83.16 W
Colbert 196 33.51 N 96.30 W
Colbinabbin 166 36.35 S 144.49 E
Colbitz 54 52.19 N 11.36 E
Colbitz-Letzlinger Heide ◆³ 54 52.27 N 11.35 E
Colborne, On., Can. 212 42.51 N 80.19 W
Colborne, On., Can. 212 44.00 N 77.53 W
Colbún 252 35.42 S 71.25 W
Colbún, Embalse ⊜¹ 252 35.40 S 71.20 W
Colburn, Eng., U.K. 44 54.23 N 1.41 W
Colburn, In., U.S. 216 40.31 N 86.42 W
Colby, Ks., U.S. 198 39.23 N 101.03 W
Colby, Wi., U.S. 190 44.54 N 90.18 W
Colca 248 12.18 S 75.13 W
Colca ≃ 248 15.51 S 72.26 W
Colcamar 248 6.16 S 77.55 W
Colchester, On., Can. 214 41.59 N 82.56 W
Colchester, Eng., U.K. 42 51.54 N 0.54 E
Colchester, Ct., U.S. 207 41.34 N 72.19 W
Colchester, Il., U.S. 190 40.25 N 90.47 W
Coldbackie 46 58.31 N 4.23 W
Cold Bay 180 55.11 N 162.30 W
Cold Bay c 180 55.13 N 162.33 W
Coldblow ◆⁸ 260 51.26 N 0.10 E
Cold Brook 210 43.15 N 75.03 W
Cold Creek ≃ 212 44.12 N 77.36 W
Colden 210 42.39 N 78.41 W
Cold Fell ʌ 44 54.54 N 2.36 W
Cold Harbor Battlefield ⊥ 208 37.36 N 77.20 W
Coldingham 46 55.53 N 2.10 W
Colditz 54 51.07 N 12.48 E
Cold Lake 184 54.27 N 110.10 W
Cold Lake ⊜ 184 54.33 N 110.05 W
Cold Lake, Canadian Forces Base ■ 184 54.25 N 110.17 W
Cold Lake Indian Reserve ◆⁴ 184 54.33 N 110.10 W
Cold Norton 260 51.40 N 0.40 E
Coldrano 64 46.38 N 10.50 E
Cold Spring, Ky., U.S. 218 39.01 N 84.26 W
Cold Spring, Mn., U.S. 190 45.27 N 94.25 W
Cold Spring, N.J., U.S. 208 38.58 N 74.55 W
Cold Spring, N.Y., U.S. 210 41.25 N 73.57 W
Coldspring, Tx., U.S. 222 30.36 N 95.08 W
Cold Spring Harbor 276 40.52 N 73.27 W
Cold Spring Harbor c 276 40.53 N 73.28 W
Coldsprings, On., Can. 212 44.17 N 78.18 W
Cold Springs, N.Y., U.S. 210 43.08 N 76.15 W
Cold Spring Terrace 276 40.50 N 73.26 W
Coldstream, Austl. 169 37.44 S 145.23 E
Coldstream, Scot., U.K. 46 55.39 N 2.15 W
Cold Stream ≃ 226 39.35 N 120.22 W
Coldwater, On., Can. 212 44.42 N 79.40 W
Coldwater, Ks., U.S. 198 37.16 N 99.19 W
Coldwater, Mi., U.S. 216 41.56 N 85.00 W
Coldwater, Ms., U.S. 194 34.41 N 89.58 W
Coldwater, Oh., U.S. 216 40.28 N 84.37 W
Coldwater ≃, On., Can. 212 44.44 N 79.39 W
Coldwater ≃, Mi., U.S. 216 42.04 N 85.08 W
Coldwater ≃, Ms., U.S. 194 34.11 N 90.13 W
Coldwater Canyon V 280 34.14 N 117.44 W
Coldwater Creek ≃ 196 36.40 N 101.08 W
Coldwater Indian Reserve ◆⁴ 182 50.04 N 120.48 W
Coldwater Lake ⊜ 216 41.49 N 84.58 W
Cole ▫⁶ 219 38.30 N 92.13 W
Cole ≃, Ang. 152 9.07 S 15.50 E
Cole ≃, Eng., U.K. 42 51.42 N 1.42 W
Coleambally 166 34.49 S 145.52 E
Colebrook, N.H., U.S. 188 44.53 N 71.29 W
Colebrook, Oh., U.S. 214 41.32 N 80.46 W
Colebrook River Lake ⊜¹ 207 42.03 N 73.04 W
Cole Camp 194 38.27 N 93.12 W
Coledale 170 34.17 S 150.57 E
Coleen ≃ 180 67.05 N 142.31 W
Coleford, Eng., U.K. 42 51.48 N 2.36 W
Coleford, Eng., U.K. 42 51.14 N 2.27 W
Colégio, Morro do ʌ 287b 23.38 S 46.21 W
Coleman, Ab., Can. 182 49.38 N 114.30 W
Coleman, Fl., U.S. 220 28.47 N 82.04 W
Coleman, Md., U.S. 208 39.20 N 76.04 W
Coleman, Mi., U.S. 190 43.45 N 84.35 W
Coleman, Tx., U.S. 196 31.49 N 99.25 W
Coleman, Wi., U.S. 190 45.03 N 88.02 W
Coleman ≃ 164 15.06 S 141.38 E
Coleman, Lake ⊜¹ 196 32.02 N 99.30 W
Colembert 50 50.45 N 1.50 E
Colen Lakes ⊜ 184 54.33 N 95.25 W
Colenso 158 28.50 S 29.44 E
Colerain 214 40.07 N 80.49 W
Coleraine, Austl. 166 37.36 S 141.42 E
Coleraine, N. Ire., U.K. 48 55.08 N 6.40 W
Coleraine, Mn., U.S. 190 47.17 N 93.25 W
Coleridge 198 42.30 N 97.12 W
Coleridge, Lake ⊜ 172 43.17 S 171.30 E
Coles 194 31.16 N 91.01 W
Coles, Punta ≻ 248 17.42 S 71.23 W
Colesberg 158 30.45 S 25.05 E
Coles Brook ≃ 276 40.55 N 74.02 W
Coleshill, Eng., U.K. 42 52.30 N 1.42 W
Coleshill, Eng., U.K. 260 51.39 N 0.38 W
Coles Point 208 38.09 N 76.38 W
Colesville, Md., U.S. 284c 39.05 N 77.00 W
Colesville, N.J., U.S. 210 41.15 N 74.39 W
Coleto Creek ≃ 196 28.41 N 97.01 W
Coleville, Sk., Can. 184 51.43 N 109.16 W
Coleville, Ca., U.S. 226 38.33 N 119.30 W
Colfax, Ca., U.S. 226 39.06 N 120.57 W
Colfax, Il., U.S. 216 40.34 N 88.36 W
Colfax, In., U.S. 194 40.11 N 86.40 W
Colfax, Ia., U.S. 190 41.40 N 93.14 W
Colfax, La., U.S. 194 31.31 N 92.42 W
Colfax, Wa., U.S. 202 46.52 N 117.21 W
Colfax, Wi., U.S. 190 44.59 N 91.43 W
Colfiorito 66 43.02 N 12.55 E
Colgate 216 43.12 N 88.12 W
Colgate Creek ≃ 284b 39.15 N 76.32 W
Colgong 124 25.16 N 87.13 E
Colgrave Sound ⊔ 46a 60.37 N 0.58 W
Colhué Huapí, Lago ⊜ 254 45.30 S 68.48 W
Coliban ≃ 169 36.56 S 144.33 E
Colibris, Pointe des ≻, Guad. 241o 16.15 N 61.11 W
Colibris, Pointe des ≻, Guad. 241o 16.17 N 61.06 W
Colico 58 46.08 N 9.22 E
Coligny, Fr. 58 46.23 N 5.21 E
Coligny, S. Afr. 158 26.17 S 26.15 E
Colijnsplaat 52 51.36 N 3.51 E
Colima, Méx. 200 32.25 N 115.05 W
Colima, Méx. 234 19.14 N 103.43 W
Colima ▫³ 234 19.10 N 104.00 W
Colima, Nevado de ʌ 234 19.33 N 103.38 W
Colimes ≃ 246 1.32 S 80.00 W
Colin ≃ 50 47.08 N 2.32 E
Colina 252 33.12 S 70.41 W
Colinas, Bra. 250 6.02 S 44.14 W
Colinas, Bra. 255 14.12 S 48.03 W
Colinet 186 47.13 N 53.33 W
Colinton, Austl. 171b 35.51 S 149.09 E
Colinton, Ab., Can. 182 54.37 N 113.15 W
Coliseo — Colosseo ⊥ 267a 41.54 N 12.29 E
Coll I 46 56.38 N 6.34 W
Colla 258 34.04 S 57.21 W
Colla, Arroyo ≃ 258 34.19 S 57.20 W
Collagna 64 44.21 N 10.16 E
Collalbo (Klobenstein) 64 46.32 N 11.28 E
Collalto Sabino 66 42.08 N 13.02 E
Collamer 210 43.06 N 76.04 W
Collarenebri 166 29.33 S 148.35 E
Collarmele 66 42.03 N 13.38 E
Collaroy 274a 33.44 S 151.18 E
Collazzone 66 42.54 N 12.26 E
Colibran 200 39.14 N 107.57 W
Collecchio 64 44.45 N 10.13 E
Collecorvino 66 42.27 N 14.01 E
Colle di Tora 66 42.13 N 12.57 E
Colle di Val d'Elsa 66 43.25 N 11.07 E
Colleen Bawn 154 21.00 S 29.13 E
Colleferro 66 41.44 N 12.59 E
College 180 64.51 N 147.47 W
College City 226 39.00 N 122.00 W
College Corner 218 39.30 N 84.36 W
Collegedale 194 35.04 N 85.03 W
College Meadows 218 39.56 N 86.07 W
College Park, Ga., U.S. 192 33.39 N 84.26 W
College Park, Md., U.S. 208 38.58 N 76.56 W
College Park Airport ⊠ 284c 38.58 N 76.55 W
College Place 202 46.02 N 118.23 W
College Point ◆⁸ 276 40.47 N 73.51 W
College Station, Ar., U.S. 194 34.43 N 92.13 W
College Station, Tx., U.S. 222 30.37 N 96.20 W
Collegeville, In., U.S. 216 40.54 N 87.09 W
Collegeville, Pa., U.S. 208 40.11 N 75.27 W
Collégien 261 48.50 N 2.40 E
Collegno 62 45.05 N 7.34 E
Colle Isarco (Gossensass) 64 46.56 N 11.26 E
Collepardo 66 41.46 N 13.22 E
Collepasso 68 40.04 N 18.10 E
Collepietro 66 42.13 N 13.46 E
Collerina 166 29.41 S 146.38 E
Collesalvetti 66 43.35 N 10.28 E
Colle Sannita 68 41.22 N 14.50 E
Collesano 70 37.55 N 13.56 E
Colletorto 66 41.40 N 14.58 E
Colleymount 182 54.01 N 126.09 W
Colleyville 222 32.52 N 97.09 W
Colliano 68 40.43 N 15.17 E
Colli a Volturno 66 41.36 N 14.06 E
Colli del Tronto 66 42.52 N 13.44 E
Colli di Monte Bove ʌ 66 42.06 N 13.09 E
Collie 168a 33.21 S 116.09 E
Collie ≃ 168a 33.18 S 115.44 E
Collie East ≃ 168a 33.18 S 116.10 E
Collier ▫⁶ 220 26.10 N 81.22 W
Collier Bay c 160 16.10 S 124.15 E
Collier Bridge ◆⁵ 220 26.57 N 82.04 W
Collier City 220 26.14 N 80.09 W
Collier Law ʌ² 44 54.46 N 1.58 W
Collier Range ʌ 162 24.43 S 119.12 E
Collier Range National Park ♦ 162 24.40 S 119.15 E
Collier Row ◆⁸ 260 51.36 N 0.10 E
Colliers 214 40.22 N 80.32 W
Collier-Seminole State Park ♦ 220 25.59 N 81.36 W
Colliersville 210 42.29 N 74.59 W
Collierville 194 35.02 N 89.39 W
Collie South ≃ 168a 33.18 S 116.10 E
Collieston 46 57.21 N 1.56 W
Collifford Lake Reservoir ⊜¹ 42 50.32 N 4.33 W
Colligis-Crandelain 48 52.06 N 7.38 W
Collin ▫⁶ 222 33.07 N 96.35 W
Collingbourne Kingston 42 51.18 N 1.40 W
Collingdale 208 39.54 N 75.16 W
Collingham 44 53.54 N 1.24 W
Collingswood 285 39.55 N 75.04 W
Collingwood, Austl. 274b 37.48 S 145.00 E
Collingwood, On., Can. 212 44.29 N 80.13 W
Collingwood, N.Z. 172 40.40 S 172.41 E
Collingwood Bay c 164 9.20 S 149.30 E
Collins, Ga., U.S. 192 32.10 N 82.06 W
Collins, Ia., U.S. 190 41.54 N 93.18 W
Collins, Ms., U.S. 194 31.38 N 89.33 W
Collins, N.Y., U.S. 210 42.30 N 78.55 W
Collins, Oh., U.S. 214 41.16 N 82.30 W
Collins ≃ 194 35.48 N 85.37 W
Collins, Mount ʌ² 190 47.51 N 80.59 W
Collins Bay 212 44.15 N 76.36 W
Collinsburg 214 40.13 N 79.46 W
Collins Center 210 42.30 N 78.51 W
Collins Lake ⊜ 212 44.22 N 76.27 W
Collins Park 208 39.41 N 75.33 W
Collinston 194 32.41 N 91.52 W
Collinsville, Austl. 166 20.34 S 147.51 E
Collinsville, Al., U.S. 194 34.15 N 85.51 W
Collinsville, Ca., U.S. 282 38.05 N 121.51 W
Collinsville, Ct., U.S. 207 41.48 N 72.55 W
Collinsville, Il., U.S. 219 38.40 N 89.59 W
Collinsville, Ms., U.S. 194 32.29 N 88.50 W
Collinsville, N.J., U.S. 276 40.49 N 74.28 W
Collinsville, Ok., U.S. 196 36.21 N 95.50 W
Collinsville, Tx., U.S. 196 33.32 N 96.54 W
Collinwood 194 35.10 N 87.44 W
Collio 64 45.48 N 10.20 E
Collipulli 252 37.57 S 72.26 W
Collister 202 43.38 N 116.15 W
Collobrières 62 43.14 N 6.18 E
Collombey 58 46.16 N 6.57 E
Collomsville 210 41.09 N 77.09 W
Collon 48 53.47 N 6.29 W
Collonges 58 46.08 N 5.54 E
Collooney 48 54.11 N 8.29 W
Collserola, Serra de ʌ 266d 41.26 N 2.07 E
Colma 226 37.41 N 122.28 W
Colma Creek ≃ 282 37.38 N 122.23 W
Colman 198 43.58 N 96.48 W
Colmar 58 48.05 N 7.22 E
Colmar Manor 284c 38.55 N 76.56 W
Colmars 62 44.11 N 6.38 E
Colmenar 34 36.54 N 4.20 W
Colmenar de Oreja 34 40.06 N 3.23 W
Colmenar Viejo 34 40.40 N 3.46 W
Colmeneros 234 18.06 N 101.40 W
Colmesneil 134 30.54 N 94.25 W
Colmnitz 54 50.54 N 13.31 E
Colmonell 44 55.08 N 4.55 W
Coln ≃ 42 51.42 N 1.42 W
Colnbrook 260 51.29 N 0.31 W
Colne 44 53.52 N 2.09 W
Colne ≃, Eng., U.K. 42 51.48 N 1.01 E
Colne ≃, Eng., U.K. 260 51.26 N 0.30 W
Colney Heath 260 51.44 N 0.15 W
Colney Street 260 51.42 N 0.20 W
Colo 190 42.01 N 93.18 W
Colo ≃ 170 33.26 S 150.53 E
Colobraro 68 40.11 N 16.25 E
Cologna Veneta 64 45.18 N 11.23 E
Cologne — Köln, Dtsch. 56 50.56 N 6.59 E
Cologne, Mn., U.S. 190 44.46 N 93.46 W
Cologne, N.J., U.S. 208 39.30 N 74.36 W
Cologno al Serio 62 45.37 N 9.42 E
Cologno Monzese 266b 45.32 N 9.17 E
Cololo, Nevado ʌ 248 14.53 S 69.06 W
Coloma, Ca., U.S. 226 38.48 N 120.53 W
Coloma, Mi., U.S. 216 42.11 N 86.18 W
Coloma, Wi., U.S. 190 44.02 N 89.31 W
Colomb-Béchar — Béchar 148 31.37 N 2.13 W
Colombes 50 48.55 N 2.15 E
Colombey-les-Belles 58 48.32 N 5.54 E
Colombey-les-Deux-Églises 58 48.13 N 4.53 E
Colombia, Bra. 255 20.30 S 48.37 W
Colombia, Col. 246 3.24 N 74.49 W
Colombia, Cuba 240p 20.59 N 77.25 W
Colombia, Méx. 196 27.42 N 99.45 W
Colombia ▫¹, S.A. 242 4.00 N 72.00 W
Colombia ▫¹, S.A. 246 4.00 N 72.00 W
Colombian Basin ◆⁴ ¹ 16 13.00 N 76.00 W
Colombie — Colombia ▫¹ 246 4.00 N 72.00 W
Colombie-Britannique — British Columbia ▫⁴ 182 54.00 N 125.00 W
Colombier 58 46.58 N 6.52 E
Colombo, Bra. 252 25.17 S 49.14 W
Colombo, S. Lan. 122 6.56 N 79.51 E
Colome 198 43.15 N 99.42 W
Colomiers 32 43.37 N 1.20 E
Colón, Arg. 252 33.53 S 61.07 W
Colón, Arg. 252 32.13 S 58.08 W
Colón, Cuba 240p 22.43 N 80.54 W
Colón, Méx. 234 20.48 N 100.03 W
Colón, Pan. 236 9.22 N 79.54 W
Colón, Mi., U.S. 216 41.57 N 85.19 W
Colón, Ur. 252 33.53 S 54.43 W
Colón, Ur. 258 34.48 S 56.14 W
Colón ▫⁴ 236 15.40 N 80.20 W
Colón ▫⁵ 236 15.40 N 85.30 W
Colón, Archipiélago de (Galapagos Islands) II 246a 0.30 S 90.30 W
Colón, Cementerio ◆ 286b 23.08 N 82.23 W
Colón, Isla I 236 9.24 N 82.17 W
Colón, Montañas de ʌ 236 14.55 N 84.45 W
Colón, Teatro ♦ 288 34.36 S 58.23 W
Colona 162 31.38 S 132.05 E
Colonard-Corubert 50 48.25 N 0.39 E
Colonarie ≃ 241h 13.14 N 61.06 W
Colonel Danforth Park ♦ 275b 43.47 N 79.10 W
Colonelganj 124 27.08 N 81.42 E
Colonești 38 46.34 N 27.18 E
Colonet 204 31.05 N 116.10 W
Colonet, Cabo ≻ 204 30.58 N 116.19 W
Colongulac, Lake ⊜ 169 38.10 S 143.11 E
Colonia — Köln, Dtsch. 56 50.56 N 6.59 E
Colonia, Micron. 174q 9.31 N 138.08 E
Colonia, N.J., U.S. 208 40.34 N 74.18 W
Colonia ▫⁵ 258 34.10 S 57.30 W
Colônia ≃ 255 15.11 S 39.45 W
Colonia, Aeropuerto ⊠ 258 34.28 S 57.49 W
Colonia, Cuchilla de la ʌ² 258 34.15 S 57.35 W
Colonia Alvear 252 35.00 S 67.40 W
Colonia Caroya 252 31.02 S 64.05 W
Colonia del Sacramento 258 34.28 S 57.51 W
Colonia Dora 252 28.36 S 62.57 W
Colonia Elisa 252 26.56 S 59.32 W
Colonia Guadalupe 204 32.04 N 116.37 W
Colonia Hogar Ricardo Gutiérrez 288 34.51 S 58.51 W
Colonia José Mármol 252 26.59 S 60.44 W
Colonia Lavalleja 252 31.06 S 57.01 W
Colonial Beach 208 38.15 N 76.57 W
Colonial Heights 208 37.14 N 77.24 W
Colonia Leopoldina 250 8.57 S 35.39 W
Colonial Heights 208 37.14 N 77.24 W
Colonial Manor 285 39.51 N 75.09 W
Colonial National Historical Park ♦ 208 37.12 N 76.45 W
Colonial Park 208 40.18 N 76.48 W
Colonial Village, N.Y., U.S. 210 43.08 N 78.58 W
Colonial Village, Pa., U.S. 285 40.04 N 75.24 W
Colonial Village Airport ⊠ 284a 43.08 N 78.58 W
Colonial Williamsburg ⊥ 208 37.16 N 76.42 W
Colonia Morelos 200 30.50 N 109.10 W
Colonia Nicolich 258 34.50 S 56.02 W
Colonia Progreso 204 32.35 N 115.37 W
Colonia Providencia 240m 17.59 N 66.00 W
Colonias Unidas 252 26.42 S 59.38 W
Colonia Valdense 258 34.20 S 57.14 W
Colonia Vicente Guerrero 232 30.45 N 116.00 W
Colonia Villafañe 252 26.12 S 59.05 W
Colonie 210 42.43 N 73.50 W
Colon Koret 152 0.34 N 23.28 E
Colonna 267a 41.50 N 12.45 E
Colonna, Capo ≻ 68 39.02 N 17.11 E
Colonnata 64 44.05 N 10.10 E
Colón Ridge ◆⁴ ³ 18 2.00 N 96.00 W
Colonsay 184 51.59 N 105.53 W
Colonsay I 46 56.04 N 6.13 W
Colony 198 38.04 N 95.21 W
Colora 208 39.40 N 76.06 W
Colorada, Laguna ⊜ 254 44.50 S 68.15 W
Colorada, Punta ≻ 288 34.45 S 58.06 W
Colorada Grande, Salina ≃ 252 38.15 S 63.47 W
Coloradas, Lomas ʌ² 254 43.24 S 67.24 W
Colorado, C.R. 236 10.46 N 83.35 W
Colorado, Hond. 236 15.47 N 87.19 W
Colorado, Ak., U.S. 180 63.09 N 149.26 W
Colorado ▫⁶ 222 29.40 N 96.30 W
Colorado ▫³ 178 39.00 N 105.30 W
Colorado ≃, Arg. 244 39.50 S 62.08 W
Colorado ≃, Bra. 248 13.03 S 62.20 W
Colorado ≃, Méx. 234 16.30 N 97.31 W
Colorado ≃, N.A. 200 31.54 N 114.57 W
Colorado ≃, Tx., U.S. 196 28.36 N 95.58 W
Colorado, Canal do ≃ 287a 23.00 S 43.25 W
Colorado, Cerro ʌ, Arg. 254 45.02 S 69.38 W
Colorado, Cerro ʌ, Chile 286e 33.24 S 70.45 W
Colorado, Cerro ʌ, Perú 286d 12.07 S 76.55 W
Colorado, Williams Fork ≃ 200 40.03 N 106.11 W
Colorado City, Az., U.S. 200 36.59 N 112.58 W
Colorado City, Co., U.S. 200 37.56 N 104.50 W
Colorado City, Tx., U.S. 196 32.23 N 100.51 W
Colorado de Abajo 196 26.28 N 99.54 W
Colorado National Monument ♦ 200 39.04 N 108.25 W
Colorado Plateau ʌ¹ 200 36.30 N 108.00 W
Colorado River Aqueduct ≃¹ 204 33.50 N 117.23 W
Colorado River Indian Reservation ◆⁴ 200 34.00 N 114.25 W
Colorados, Archipiélago de los II 240p 22.36 N 84.20 W
Colorado Springs 200 38.50 N 104.49 W
Colorines 234 19.07 N 100.12 W
Colorno 64 44.56 N 10.23 E
Colosimi 68 39.07 N 16.24 E
Colosseo ⊥ 267a 41.54 N 12.29 E
Colotepec ≃ 234 15.47 N 97.03 W
Colotlán 234 22.06 N 103.16 W
Colotlán ≃ 234 22.06 N 103.42 W
Colotlipa 234 17.25 N 99.09 W
Colquiri Vale 170 34.24 S 150.29 E
Čolpon 85 42.12 N 75.28 E
Čolpon-Ata 85 42.40 N 77.06 E
Colpoys Bay c 212 44.47 N 81.05 W
Colquechaca 248 18.40 S 66.01 W
Colquencha 248 17.00 S 68.17 W
Colquiri 248 17.25 S 67.08 W
Colquitt 192 31.10 N 84.44 W
Colsterworth 42 52.48 N 0.37 W
Colstrip 202 45.53 N 106.37 W
Colt 194 35.07 N 90.48 W
Colta 248 15.10 S 73.18 W
Coltauco 252 34.18 S 71.06 W
Coltishall 42 52.44 N 1.22 E
Colton, Austl. 162 33.29 S 134.56 E
Colton, Ca., U.S. 228 34.04 N 117.18 W
Colton, Oh., U.S. 216 41.28 N 83.57 W
Colton, Or., U.S. 224 45.10 N 122.26 W
Colton, S.D., U.S. 198 43.47 N 96.55 W
Coltons Point 208 38.13 N 76.45 W
Colts Neck 208 40.17 N 74.10 W
Coltsville Center 214 41.05 N 80.34 W
Columbia, Al., U.S. 192 31.17 N 85.06 W
Columbia, Ca., U.S. 226 38.02 N 120.24 W
Columbia, Ct., U.S. 207 41.42 N 72.18 W
Columbia, Il., U.S. 219 38.26 N 90.12 W
Columbia, In., U.S. 218 39.35 N 85.12 W
Columbia, Ky., U.S. 194 37.06 N 85.18 W
Columbia, La., U.S. 194 32.06 N 92.04 W
Columbia, Md., U.S. 208 39.14 N 76.50 W
Columbia, Ms., U.S. 194 31.15 N 89.50 W
Columbia, Mo., U.S. 219 38.57 N 92.20 W
Columbia, N.J., U.S. 210 40.55 N 75.05 W
Columbia, N.C., U.S. 192 35.55 N 76.15 W
Columbia, Pa., U.S. 208 40.02 N 76.30 W
Columbia, S.C., U.S. 192 34.00 N 81.02 W
Columbia, Tn., U.S. 194 35.36 N 87.02 W
Columbia ▫⁶, N.Y., U.S. 210 42.15 N 73.47 W
Columbia ▫⁶, Or., U.S. 224 45.57 N 123.03 W
Columbia ▫⁶, Pa., U.S. 210 41.00 N 76.28 W
Columbia ≃ 176 46.15 N 124.05 W
Columbia, Cape ≻ 16 83.08 N 70.35 W
Columbia, Lake ⊜¹ 216 42.05 N 84.18 W
Columbia, Mount ʌ 182 52.09 N 117.25 W
Columbia Airport ⊠ 279a 41.19 N 81.58 W
Columbia Basin ≃¹ 202 46.45 N 119.05 W
Columbia Center 279a 41.19 N 81.56 W
Columbia City, In., U.S. 216 41.09 N 85.29 W
Columbia City, Or., U.S. 224 45.53 N 122.48 W
Columbia Cross Roads 210 41.50 N 76.48 W
Columbia Falls, Me., U.S. 188 44.39 N 67.43 W
Columbia Falls, Mt., U.S. 202 48.22 N 114.10 W
Columbia Heights 284b 39.15 N 76.50 W
Columbia Hills 182 52.10 N 117.30 W
Columbia Icefield ⊠ 182 50.15 N 115.57 W
Columbia Lake ⊜ 182 50.15 N 115.57 W
Columbia Lake Indian Reserve ◆⁴ 182 50.25 N 115.57 W
Columbia Mountains ʌ 182 52.00 N 119.00 W
Columbiana, Al., U.S. 194 33.10 N 86.36 W
Columbiana, Oh., U.S. 214 40.53 N 80.41 W
Columbiana ▫⁶ 214 40.47 N 80.46 W
Columbia Plateau ʌ¹ 202 44.00 N 117.30 W
Columbia Regional Airport ⊠ 219 38.50 N 92.13 W
Columbia Road Reservoir ⊜¹ 198 45.45 N 98.15 W
Columbia State Historical Park ♦ 226 38.02 N 120.25 W
Columbia Station 214 41.20 N 81.57 W
Columbia University ᵾ² 276 40.48 N 73.58 W
Columbiaville, Mi., U.S. 190 43.09 N 83.24 W
Columbiaville, N.Y., U.S. 210 42.19 N 73.45 W
Columbine, Cape ≻ 158 32.47 S 17.52 E
Columbrets, Illes II 34 39.52 N 0.40 E
Columbus, Ga., U.S. 192 32.29 N 84.59 W
Columbus, In., U.S. 218 39.12 N 85.55 W
Columbus, Ks., U.S. 198 37.10 N 94.50 W
Columbus, Ms., U.S. 194 33.29 N 88.25 W
Columbus, Mt., U.S. 202 45.38 N 109.15 W
Columbus, Ne., U.S. 198 41.25 N 97.22 W
Columbus, N.J., U.S. 208 40.04 N 74.43 W
Columbus, N.M., U.S. 200 31.49 N 107.38 W
Columbus, N.C., U.S. 192 35.15 N 82.11 W
Columbus, N.D., U.S. 198 48.54 N 102.46 W
Columbus, Oh., U.S. 214 39.57 N 82.59 W
Columbus, Pa., U.S. 214 41.56 N 79.35 W
Columbus, Tx., U.S. 222 29.42 N 96.32 W
Columbus, Wi., U.S. 190 43.20 N 89.00 W
Columbus Air Force Base ■ 194 33.38 N 88.26 W
Columbus Grove 216 40.55 N 84.03 W
Columbus Junction 190 41.16 N 91.21 W
Columbus Lake ⊜¹ 194 33.35 N 88.24 W
Columbus Park ♦ 278 41.53 N 87.47 W
Columbus Point ≻, Ba. 238 24.08 N 75.16 W
Columbus Point ≻, Trin. 241r 11.08 N 60.48 W
Columbus Salt Marsh ≃ 204 38.04 N 117.58 W
Coluna 255 18.14 S 42.50 W
Colusa 226 39.12 N 122.00 W
Colusa ▫⁶ 226 39.13 N 122.01 W
Colusa Trough ≃ 226 39.02 N 121.59 W
Colver 214 40.32 N 78.47 W
Colville, N.Z. 172 36.38 S 175.28 E
Colville, Wa., U.S. 202 48.32 N 117.54 W
Colville ≃, Ak., U.S. 180 70.25 N 150.30 W
Colville ≃, Wa., U.S. 202 48.37 N 118.05 W
Colville, Cape ≻ 172 36.28 S 175.21 E
Colville Channel ⊔ 172 36.23 S 175.24 E
Colville Indian Reservation ◆⁴ 202 48.15 N 119.00 W
Colville Lake ⊜ 180 67.10 N 126.00 W
Colvin Run 284c 38.58 N 77.18 W
Colwell 44 55.04 N 2.04 W
Colwood 224 48.26 N 123.29 W
Colwyn 285 39.55 N 75.15 W
Colwyn Bay 44 53.18 N 3.43 W
Colyton, Austl. 274a 33.47 S 150.48 E
Colyton, Eng., U.K. 42 50.44 N 3.04 W
Comacchio 64 44.42 N 12.11 E
Comacchio, Valli di c 66 44.38 N 12.06 E
Comal 115a 6.55 S 109.31 E
Comala 234 19.19 N 103.45 W
Comalapa, Guat. 236 14.44 N 90.53 W
Comalapa, Nic. 236 12.17 N 85.31 W
Comalcalco 234 18.16 N 93.13 W
Comallo, Arroyo ≃ 254 40.29 S 70.12 W
Coman, Mount ʌ 9 74.02 S 65.04 W
Comana 38 43.54 N 28.19 E
Comanche, Ok., U.S. 196 34.22 N 97.57 W
Comanche, Tx., U.S. 196 31.53 N 98.36 W
Comanche Creek ≃, Co., U.S. 198 39.53 N 104.19 W
Comanche Creek ≃, Tx., U.S. 196 31.06 N 102.24 W
Comandante Ferraz ᵾ³ 9 62.05 S 58.23 W
Comandante Fontana 252 25.20 S 59.41 W
Comandante Leal 252 30.53 S 65.47 W
Comandante Luis Piedrabuena 254 49.59 S 68.54 W
Comandante Nicanor Otamendi 252 38.07 S 57.51 W
Comănești 38 46.25 N 26.26 E
Comanjá de Corona 234 21.19 N 101.42 W
Comarapa 248 17.54 S 64.29 W
Comar Gambon 144 3.10 N 45.47 E
Comas, Perú 248 11.46 S 75.02 W
Comas, Perú 286d 11.57 S 77.04 W
Comayagua 236 14.25 N 87.37 W
Comayagua ▫⁵ 236 14.30 N 87.40 W
Comayagua, Montañas de ʌ 236 14.23 N 87.26 W
Combahee ≃ 192 32.30 N 80.31 W
Combarbalá 252 31.11 S 71.02 W
Combault 261 48.48 N 2.36 E
Combeaufontaine 58 47.43 N 5.53 E
Combe Bank ◆³ 14 12.32 S 177.35 W
Combe Martin 42 51.13 N 4.02 W
Comber, On., Can. 214 42.14 N 82.33 W
Comber, N. Ire., U.K. 48 54.33 N 5.45 W
Comberbach 262 53.17 N 2.32 W
Combermere Bay c 110 19.37 N 93.34 E
Comberton 42 52.11 N 0.02 E
Combie, Lake ⊜¹ 226 39.01 N 121.02 W
Comblain-au-Pont 56 50.28 N 5.35 E
Combles 50 50.01 N 2.52 E
Combloux 62 45.54 N 6.39 E
Combourg 32 48.25 N 1.45 W
Comboyne 166 31.36 S 152.29 E
Comboyuro Point ≻ 171a 27.04 S 153.24 E
Combres 50 48.19 N 1.04 E
Combrond 32 45.59 N 3.05 E
Combs 262 53.18 N 1.57 W
Combs-la-Ville 50 48.40 N 2.34 E
Combs Reservoir ⊜¹ 262 53.19 N 1.57 W
Comburg ᵾ¹ 56 49.06 N 9.44 E
Comb Wash V 200 37.13 N 109.42 W
Come by Chance 186 47.51 N 53.58 W
Comeglians 64 46.31 N 12.52 E
Comelico Superiore 64 46.35 N 12.30 E
Comendado Levy Gasparain 256 22.01 S 43.12 W
Comendador 238 18.53 N 71.42 W
Comendador Gomes 255 19.41 S 49.05 W
Comer 192 34.03 N 83.07 W
Comercinho 255 16.19 S 41.47 W
Comerío 240m 18.13 N 66.14 W
Comet 166 23.37 S 148.33 E
Comet ≃ 166 23.34 S 148.32 E
Cometela 156 21.51 S 34.29 E
Comfort, N.C., U.S. 192 35.00 N 77.30 W
Comfort, Tx., U.S. 196 29.58 N 98.54 W
Comfort, Cape ≻ 176 65.08 N 83.21 W
Comfort, Point ≻ 276 40.27 N 74.08 W
Comfrey 198 44.06 N 94.54 W
Comilla 124 23.27 N 91.12 E
Comines 50 50.46 N 3.01 E
Comino — Kemmuna I 36 36.00 N 14.20 E
Comino, Capo ≻ 71 40.32 N 9.49 E
Comiskey Park ♦ 278 41.50 N 87.38 W
Comiso 70 36.56 N 14.36 E
Comitan de Domínguez 232 16.15 N 92.08 W
Comitini 70 37.24 N 13.39 E
Comloșu Mare 38 45.54 N 20.38 E
Commack 210 40.50 N 73.17 W
Commagene ▫⁹ 130 37.50 N 38.00 E
Commencement Bay c 224 47.17 N 122.28 W
Commentry 32 46.17 N 2.44 E
Commerce, Ca., U.S. 280 34.00 N 118.09 W
Commerce, Ga., U.S. 192 34.12 N 83.27 W
Commerce, Mi., U.S. 216 42.34 N 83.30 W
Commerce, Ok., U.S. 196 36.56 N 94.52 W
Commerce, Tx., U.S. 196 33.14 N 95.53 W
Commerce City 198 39.49 N 104.56 W
Commerciale Luigi Bocconi, Università ᵾ² 266b 45.26 N 9.11 E
Commercial Point 218 39.46 N 83.04 W
Commercy 56 48.45 N 5.35 E
Commewijne ▫⁵ 250 5.50 N 55.00 W
Commewijne ≃ 250 5.54 N 55.05 W
Commingues ◆¹ 32 43.15 N 0.45 E
Committee Bay c 176 68.30 N 86.30 W
Commodore 214 40.43 N 78.57 W
Commodore Barry Bridge ◆⁵ 285 39.49 N 75.22 W
Commondale 158 27.20 S 30.56 E
Common Edge 262 53.47 N 3.02 W
Commonwealth Bay c 9 66.54 S 142.40 E
Commonwealth Range ʌ 9 84.15 S 172.20 E
Commoron Creek ≃ 166 28.22 S 150.08 E
Como, Austl. 274a 34.00 S 151.04 E
Como, It. 62 45.47 N 9.05 E
Como, Ms., U.S. 194 34.30 N 89.56 W
Como, N.C., U.S. 208 36.30 N 77.00 W
Como, Tx., U.S. 222 33.03 N 95.28 W
Como, Wi., U.S. 216 42.37 N 88.28 W
Como ▫⁴ 58 45.59 N 9.13 E
Como, Lago di ⊜ 58 46.00 N 9.20 E
Como, Lake ⊜ 216 42.36 N 88.29 W
Como, Mount ʌ 226 39.02 N 119.28 W
Comodoro Rivadavia 254 45.52 S 67.30 W
Como Lake ⊜ 190 47.55 N 83.30 W
Comologno 58 46.12 N 8.34 E
Comonfort 234 20.43 N 100.46 W
Comoras — Comoros ▫¹ 157a 12.10 S 44.15 E
Comores — Comoros ▫¹ 157a 12.10 S 44.15 E
Comores, Archipel des II 157a 12.10 S 44.15 E
Comorin, Cape ≻ 122 8.06 N 77.33 E
Comoros (Comores) ▫¹, Afr. 138 12.10 S 44.15 E
Comoros (Comores) ▫¹, Afr. 157a 12.10 S 44.15 E
Comox 182 49.40 N 124.55 W
Comox, Canadian Forces Base ■ 182 49.43 N 124.54 W
Companhia Siderúrgica Nacional ᵾ³ 256 22.31 S 44.07 W
Compans 261 49.00 N 2.40 E
Compatsch 58 46.58 N 10.25 E
Compiègne 50 49.25 N 2.50 E
Compo Cove c 276 41.07 N 73.21 W
Compostela, Méx. 234 21.15 N 104.53 W
Compostela, Pil. 116 7.40 N 126.02 E
Comprida, Ilha I, Bra. 252 24.50 S 47.42 W
Comprida, Ilha I, Bra. 287a 23.02 S 43.12 W
Comps-sur-Artuby 62 43.43 N 6.30 E
Compstall 262 53.25 N 2.03 W
Compton, Eng., U.K. 260 51.13 N 0.38 W
Compton, Ca., U.S. 228 33.53 N 118.13 W
Compton, Il., U.S. 216 41.42 N 89.05 W
Compton ▫⁶ 206 45.20 N 71.25 W
Compton Airport ⊠ 280 33.53 N 118.15 W
Compton Creek ≃, Ca., U.S. 280 33.50 N 118.12 W
Compton Creek ≃, N.J., U.S. 276 40.26 N 74.05 W
Comptonville 273d 26.17 S 27.58 E
Comrat 38 46.18 N 28.40 E
Comrie 46 56.22 N 4.00 W
Comstock, Mi., U.S. 216 42.17 N 85.30 W
Comstock, Ne., U.S. 198 41.33 N 99.15 W
Comstock, Tx., U.S. 196 29.41 N 101.11 W
Comstock Park 216 43.02 N 85.40 W
Comunanza 66 42.57 N 13.25 E
Con ≃, Ross. 76 52.54 N 36.00 E
Con ≃, Viet 110 19.02 N 104.58 E
Čona ≃, Ross. 74 62.54 N 111.06 E
Cona ≃, Scot., U.K. 46 56.46 N 5.14 W
Co Nag ⊜ 120 32.00 N 91.15 E
Conakry 150 9.31 N 13.43 W
Conambo ≃ 246 2.07 S 76.03 W
Conanicut Island I 207 41.32 N 71.21 W
Cona Niyeo 254 41.53 S 67.00 W
Conara Junction 166 41.50 S 147.26 E
Conasauga ≃ 192 34.33 N 84.55 W
Conaskonk Point ≻ 276 40.27 N 74.11 W
Conca ≃ 66 43.58 N 12.43 E
Concarán 252 32.34 S 65.15 W
Concarneau 32 47.52 N 3.55 W
Conceição, Bra. 248 7.24 S 58.05 W
Conceição, Bra. 250 7.33 S 38.31 W
Conceição, Moç. 156 18.45 S 36.10 E
Conceição, Cachoeira ⌊ 248 9.34 S 64.22 W
Conceição, Ilha da I 287a 22.52 S 43.07 W
Conceição da Barra 255 18.35 S 39.45 W
Conceição da Pedra 256 22.09 S 45.27 W
Conceição das Alagoas 255 19.55 S 48.23 W
Conceição de Ipanema 255 19.55 S 41.41 W
Conceição de Jacareí 256 23.02 S 44.09 W
Conceição do Almeida 255 12.48 S 39.12 W
Conceição do Araguaia 250 8.15 S 49.17 W
Conceição do Canindé 250 7.54 S 41.34 W
Conceição do Coité 250 11.33 S 39.16 W
Conceição do Formoso 256 21.25 S 43.21 W
Conceição do Mato Dentro 255 19.01 S 43.25 W
Conceição do Maú 246 3.35 N 59.53 W
Conceição do Norte 255 12.13 S 47.18 W
Conceição do Rio Verde 256 21.53 S 45.05 W
Conceição dos Ouros 256 22.25 S 45.47 W
Concepción, Arg. 252 28.23 S 57.53 W
Concepción, Arg. 252 27.20 S 65.35 W
Concepción, Bol. 248 11.29 S 66.31 W
Concepción, Bol. 248 16.15 S 62.04 W
Concepción, Chile 252 36.50 S 73.03 W
Concepción, Col. 246 6.46 N 72.42 W
Concepción, Para. 252 23.25 S 57.17 W
Concepción, Perú 248 11.55 S 75.17 W
Concepción, Pil. 116 11.13 N 123.06 E
Concepcion, Pil. 116 10.42 N 123.02 E
Concepcion, Pil. 116 12.24 N 122.06 E
Concepcion, Pil. 116 15.19 N 120.39 E
Concepción ▫⁵ 252 23.00 S 57.00 W
Concepción, Bahía c 252 26.39 N 111.48 W
Concepción, Canal ⊔ 254 50.30 S 74.55 W
Concepción, Laguna ⊜ 248 17.29 S 61.25 W
Concepción, Volcán ʌ¹ 236 11.34 N 85.37 W
Concepcion Bay c 116 11.15 N 123.07 E
Concepción de Ataco 236 13.52 N 89.51 W
Concepción de Buenos Aires 234 19.58 N 103.16 W
Concepción de la Sierra 252 27.59 S 55.31 W
Concepción del Oro 232 24.38 N 101.25 W
Concepción del Uruguay 252 32.29 S 58.14 W
Concepción Huista 236 15.37 N 91.41 W
Concepción Quezaltepeque 236 14.06 N 88.58 W
Conception, Point ≻ 204 34.27 N 120.27 W
Conception Bay c, Nf., Can. 186 47.45 N 53.00 W
Conception Bay c, Namibia 156 23.53 S 14.28 E
Concession 154 17.22 S 30.57 E
Conchagua 236 13.19 N 87.52 W
Conchagua, Volcán ʌ¹ 236 13.14 N 87.46 W
Conchal 256 22.20 S 47.10 W
Conchalí 286e 33.24 S 70.39 W
Conchalí, Cerros de ʌ 286e 33.20 S 70.38 W
Conchas ≃ 196 35.23 N 104.18 W
Conchas Dam 196 35.22 N 104.11 W
Conchas Lake ⊜¹ 196 35.25 N 104.14 W
Conche 186 50.53 N 55.54 W
Conches-en-Ouche 50 48.58 N 0.56 E
Conchi 252 22.02 S 68.59 W
Conchillas 258 34.15 S 58.04 W
Conchitas, Arroyo ≃ 288 34.45 S 58.09 W
Concho 200 34.28 N 109.36 W
Concho ≃ 196 31.34 N 99.43 W
Conchos ≃, Méx. 232 29.35 N 104.25 W
Conchos ≃, Méx. 232 24.55 N 97.40 W
Concise 58 46.51 N 6.43 E


≃ River / Fluß / Río / Rivière / Rio
≃ Canal / Kanal / Canal / Canal / Canal
⌊ Waterfall, Rapids / Wasserfall, Stromschnellen / Cascada, Rápidos / Chute d'eau, Rapides / Cascata, Rápidos
⊔ Strait / Meeresstraße / Estrecho / Détroit / Estreito
c Bay, Gulf / Bucht, Golf / Bahía, Golfo / Baie, Golfe / Baía, Golfo
⊜ Lake, Lakes / See, Seen / Lago, Lagos / Lac, Lacs / Lago, Lagos
≡ Swamp / Sumpf / Pantano / Marais / Pântano
⊡ Ice Features, Glacier / Eis- und Gletscherformen / Accidentes Glaciales / Formes glaciaires / Acidentes glaciares
≂ Other Hydrographic Features / Andere Hydrographische Objekte / Otros Elementos Hidrográficos / Autres données hydrographiques / Outros acidentes hidrográficos

◆ Submarine Features / Untermeer'sche Objekte / Accidentes Submarinos / Formes de relief sous-marin / Acidentes submarinos
▫ Political Unit / Politische Einheit / Unidad Política / Entité politique / Unidade política
ᵾ Cultural Institution / Kulturelle Institution / Institución Cultural / Institution culturelle / Instituição cultural
⊥ Historical Site / Historische Stätte / Sitio Histórico / Site historique / Sítio histórico
♦ Recreational Site / Erholungs- und Ferienort / Sitio de Recreo / Centre de loisirs / Área de Lazer
⊠ Airport / Flughafen / Aeropuerto / Aéroport / Aeroporto
■ Military Installation / Militäranlage / Instalación Militar / Installation militaire / Instalação militar
◆ Miscellaneous / Verschiedenes / Misceláneo / Divers / Diversos

| Name | Page | Lat.°′ | Long.°′ |
|---|---|---|---|
| Conco | 64 | 45.48 N | 11.36 E |
| Concón | 252 | 32.55 S | 71.31 W |
| Conconongon Point › | 116 | 12.14 N | 120.13 E |
| Conconully | 182 | 48.33 N | 119.44 W |
| Concord, Austl. | 274a | 33.52 S | 151.06 E |
| Concord, On., Can. | 275b | 43.48 N | 79.29 W |
| Concord, Ca., U.S. | 226 | 37.58 N | 122.01 W |
| Concord, Ga., U.S. | 192 | 33.05 N | 84.26 W |
| Concord, Il., U.S. | 219 | 39.49 N | 90.22 W |
| Concord, Ky., U.S. | 218 | 38.41 N | 83.29 W |
| Concord, Ma., U.S. | 207 | 42.27 N | 71.20 W |
| Concord, Mi., U.S. | 216 | 42.10 N | 84.38 W |
| Concord, Mo., U.S. | 219 | 38.31 N | 90.23 W |
| Concord, N.H., U.S. | 188 | 43.12 N | 71.32 W |
| Concord, N.C., U.S. | 192 | 35.24 N | 80.34 W |
| Concord, Pa., U.S. | 214 | 40.15 N | 77.42 W |
| Concord, Tx., U.S. | 222 | 31.16 N | 96.09 W |
| Concord ≃ | 283 | 42.39 N | 71.18 W |
| Concord Battleground ⊥ | 283 | 42.28 N | 71.21 W |
| Concordia, Arg. | 252 | 31.24 S | 58.02 W |
| Concórdia, Bra. | 246 | 4.35 S | 66.35 W |
| Concórdia, Bra. | 252 | 27.14 S | 52.01 W |
| Concordia, Méx. | 234 | 23.17 N | 106.04 W |
| Concordia, Perú | 246 | 4.30 S | 74.55 W |
| Concordia, Ks., U.S. | 198 | 39.34 N | 97.39 W |
| Concordia, Mo., U.S. | 194 | 38.59 N | 93.34 W |
| Concordia Gardens | 216 | 41.09 N | 85.08 W |
| Concordia Sagittaria ⊥ | 64 | 45.45 N | 12.51 E |
| Concordia sulla Secchia | 64 | 44.55 N | 10.59 E |
| Concord Naval Weapons Station ■ | 282 | 38.03 N | 122.02 W |
| Concordville | 285 | 39.53 N | 75.31 W |
| Concord West | 274a | 33.51 S | 151.05 E |
| Concorezzo | 62 | 45.35 N | 9.20 E |
| Concrete | 224 | 48.32 N | 121.44 W |
| Con Cuong | 110 | 19.02 N | 104.54 E |
| Conda | 152 | 11.06 S | 14.20 E |
| Condamine | 166 | 26.56 S | 150.08 E |
| Condamine ≃ | 166 | 27.07 S | 149.48 E |
| Condé, Ang. | 152 | 10.50 S | 14.37 E |
| Conde, Bra. | 255 | 11.49 S | 37.37 W |
| Condé, Fr. | 32 | 48.51 N | 0.33 W |
| Conde, S.D., U.S. | 198 | 45.09 N | 98.05 W |
| Condécourt | 261 | 49.02 N | 1.57 E |
| Condé-en-Brie | 50 | 49.00 N | 3.33 E |
| Condega | 236 | 13.21 N | 86.24 W |
| Condeixa | 250 | 0.54 S | 48.36 W |
| Condé-sur-l'Escaut | 50 | 50.27 N | 3.35 E |
| Condé-sur-Vesgre | 261 | 48.45 N | 1.40 E |
| Condeúba | 255 | 14.53 S | 41.59 W |
| Condevilla | 286d | 12.02 S | 77.05 W |
| Condino | 64 | 45.53 N | 10.36 E |
| Condobolin | 166 | 33.05 S | 147.09 E |
| Condom | 32 | 43.58 N | 0.22 E |
| Condon | 202 | 45.14 N | 120.11 W |
| Condoto | 246 | 5.06 N | 76.37 W |
| Condove | 62 | 45.07 N | 7.18 E |
| Condrieu | 62 | 45.27 N | 4.46 E |
| Condroz □[9] | 56 | 50.25 N | 5.00 E |
| Cone | 196 | 33.48 N | 101.23 W |
| Conecuh ≃ | 194 | 30.58 N | 87.14 W |
| Conegliano | 64 | 45.53 N | 12.18 E |
| Conejos | 200 | 37.05 N | 106.01 W |
| Conejos ≃ | 200 | 37.18 N | 105.44 W |
| Conemaugh ≃ | 214 | 40.28 N | 79.27 W |
| Conemaugh River Lake ⊜[1] | 214 | 40.28 N | 79.17 W |
| Conembaro, Cerro ∧ | 234 | 18.40 N | 102.06 W |
| Cone Mountain ∧ | 180 | 66.12 N | 156.03 W |
| Conero, Monte ∧ | 66 | 43.33 N | 13.36 E |
| Conestoga | 208 | 39.57 N | 76.21 W |
| Conestoga Creek ≃ | 208 | 39.56 N | 76.23 W |
| Conestogo | 212 | 43.32 N | 80.30 W |
| Conestogo ≃ | 212 | 43.32 N | 80.29 W |
| Conestogo Lake ⊜ | 212 | 43.44 N | 80.44 W |
| Conesus | 210 | 42.43 N | 77.41 W |
| Conesus Lake ⊜ | 210 | 42.47 N | 77.43 W |
| Conesville | 214 | 40.11 N | 81.53 W |
| Conewago Creek ≃ | 208 | 40.07 N | 76.42 W |
| Conewago Lake ⊜ | 208 | 40.06 N | 76.52 W |
| Conewango Creek ≃ | 214 | 41.50 N | 79.09 W |
| Coney Island ◆[8] | 276 | 40.34 N | 74.00 W |
| Confederation Lake ⊜ | 184 | 51.05 N | 92.44 W |
| Configni | 66 | 42.25 N | 12.38 E |
| Conflans-en-Jarnisy | 56 | 49.10 N | 5.51 E |
| Conflans-Sainte-Honorine | 50 | 48.59 N | 2.06 E |
| Conflenti | 68 | 39.04 N | 16.17 E |
| Conflict Group II | 164 | 10.45 S | 151.45 E |
| Confluence | 188 | 39.48 N | 79.21 W |
| Confolens | 32 | 46.01 N | 0.41 E |
| Confraternidad, Parque ♠ | 286d | 12.09 S | 77.02 W |
| Confusion Bay ⊂ | 186 | 49.58 N | 55.47 W |
| Confuso ≃ | 252 | 25.09 S | 57.34 W |
| Cong | 48 | 53.32 N | 9.19 W |
| Congamond | 207 | 42.01 N | 72.46 W |
| Congaree ≃ | 192 | 33.45 N | 80.37 W |
| Congaz | 38 | 46.07 N | 28.33 E |
| Congelin | 168a | 32.50 S | 116.54 E |
| Congers | 210 | 41.09 N | 73.56 W |
| Congers Lake ⊜ | 276 | 41.09 N | 73.57 W |
| Cong Hoa Stadium ♠ | 269c | 10.45 N | 106.40 E |
| Conghua | 100 | 23.32 N | 113.32 E |
| Congjiang | 102 | 25.41 N | 108.47 E |
| Congleton | 44 | 53.10 N | 2.13 W |
| Congo □[1], Afr. | 138 | 1.00 S | 15.00 E |
| Congo □[1], Afr. | 152 | 1.00 S | 15.00 E |
| Congo (Zaire) (Zaïre) ≃ | 138 | 6.04 S | 12.24 E |
| Congo, Democratic Republic of the → Zaire □[1] | 138 | 4.00 S | 25.00 E |
| Congo, République démocratique du → Zaire □[1] | 138 | 4.00 S | 25.00 E |
| Congo, république du → Congo □[1] | 152 | 1.00 S | 15.00 E |
| Congo, Serra do ⋏ | 152 | 6.30 S | 13.43 E |
| Congo Basin ≚[1] | 10 | 0.00 | 20.00 E |
| Congonhal | 256 | 22.09 S | 46.02 W |
| Congonhas, Aeroporto de ⊠ | 256 | 23.38 S | 46.38 W |
| Congost ≃ | 266d | 41.33 N | 2.15 E |
| Congresbury | 42 | 51.23 N | 2.48 W |
| Congress, Sk., Can. | 184 | 49.46 N | 106.00 W |
| Congress, Oh., U.S. | 214 | 40.55 N | 82.03 W |
| Conie ≃ | 50 | 48.06 N | 1.21 E |
| Conigli, Isola dei I | 70a | 35.30 N | 12.33 E |
| Coningsby | 44 | 53.07 N | 0.10 W |
| Conisbrough | 44 | 53.29 N | 1.13 W |
| Coniston, On., Can. | 190 | 46.29 N | 80.51 W |
| Coniston, Eng., U.K. | 44 | 54.22 N | 3.05 W |
| Coniston Water ⊜ | 44 | 54.20 N | 3.04 W |
| Conitaca | 232 | 24.10 N | 106.43 W |
| Conjeeveram → Kānchipuram | 122 | 12.50 N | 79.43 E |
| Conjola | 170 | 35.13 S | 150.27 E |
| Conjola Lake ⊂ | 170 | 35.16 S | 150.27 E |
| Čon-Kemin ≃ | 85 | 42.42 N | 75.54 E |
| Conklin, Ab., Can. | 182 | 55.38 N | 111.05 W |
| Conklin, N.Y., U.S. | 210 | 42.02 N | 75.48 W |
| Conklingville Dam ◆[6] | 210 | 43.17 N | 74.02 W |
| Conklin Point › | 276 | 40.41 N | 73.17 W |
| Conkouati | 152 | 4.00 S | 11.13 E |
| Conliège | 58 | 46.39 N | 5.36 E |
| Conlin, Lake ⊜ | 220 | 28.14 N | 81.07 W |
| Conn, Lough ⊜ | 48 | 54.04 N | 9.20 W |
| Connah's Quay | 44 | 53.13 N | 3.03 W |
| Connaught □[9] | 48 | 53.45 N | 9.00 W |
| Connaughton | 285 | 40.05 N | 75.19 W |
| Connaughton, Mount ∧[2] | 162 | 22.42 S | 122.40 E |
| Connaught Place ♠ | 272a | 28.38 N | 77.12 E |
| Connaux | 62 | 44.05 N | 4.36 E |
| Conneaut | 214 | 41.56 N | 80.33 W |
| Conneaut Creek ≃ | 214 | 41.58 N | 80.33 W |
| Conneaut Lake | 214 | 41.36 N | 80.19 W |
| Conneaut Lake ⊜ | 214 | 41.37 N | 80.18 W |
| Conneaut Outlet ≃ | 214 | 41.33 N | 80.06 W |
| Conneautville | 214 | 41.45 N | 80.22 W |
| Connecticut □[3], U.S. | 178 | 41.45 N | 72.45 W |
| Connecticut □[3], U.S. | 207 | 41.45 N | 72.45 W |
| Connecticut ≃ | 188 | 41.17 N | 72.21 W |
| Connell | 202 | 46.39 N | 118.51 W |
| Connell, Mount ∧ | 182 | 49.18 N | 115.38 W |
| Connellsville | 188 | 40.01 N | 79.35 W |
| Connelly | 210 | 41.55 N | 73.59 W |
| Connel Park | 44 | 55.23 N | 4.12 W |
| Connemara | 166 | 24.13 S | 142.17 E |
| Connemara ◆[1] | 48 | 53.25 N | 9.45 W |
| Conner | 116 | 17.48 N | 121.19 E |
| Conner, Mount ∧ | 162 | 25.23 S | 131.54 E |
| Connerré | 50 | 48.03 N | 0.30 E |
| Connersville, Fl., U.S. | 220 | 27.54 N | 81.47 W |
| Connersville, In., U.S. | 218 | 39.38 N | 85.08 W |
| Connetquot ≃ | 276 | 40.43 N | 73.08 W |
| Connetquot Brook ≃ | 276 | 40.45 N | 73.09 W |
| Connetquot River State Park ♠ | 210 | 40.46 N | 73.09 W |
| Connewarre, Lake ⊜ | 169 | 38.14 S | 144.27 E |
| Conn Island I | 284c | 39.00 N | 77.16 W |
| Conn Lake ⊜ | 176 | 70.34 N | 73.30 W |
| Connoquenessing | 214 | 40.49 N | 80.59 W |
| Connoquenessing Creek ≃ | 214 | 40.51 N | 80.19 W |
| Connors Range ⋏ | 166 | 21.40 S | 149.10 E |
| Conodoguinet Creek ≃ | 208 | 40.17 N | 76.55 W |
| Conon ≃ | 46 | 57.34 N | 4.26 W |
| Cononaco ≃ | 246 | 1.32 S | 75.35 W |
| Cononbridge | 46 | 57.34 N | 4.26 W |
| Conorochite ≃ | 246 | 2.41 N | 67.29 W |
| Conotton Creek ≃ | 214 | 40.34 N | 81.23 W |
| Conover | 192 | 35.42 N | 81.13 W |
| Conowingo | 208 | 39.40 N | 76.09 W |
| Conowingo ◆[6] | 208 | 39.33 N | 76.04 W |
| Conowingo Creek ≃ | 208 | 39.41 N | 76.12 W |
| Conowingo Dam ◆[6] | 208 | 39.39 N | 76.10 W |
| Conquest | 184 | 51.32 N | 107.17 W |
| Conquista | 255 | 19.56 S | 47.33 W |
| Conrad, Ia., U.S. | 190 | 42.13 N | 92.52 W |
| Conrad, Mt., U.S. | 202 | 48.10 N | 111.56 W |
| Conrado | 256 | 22.32 S | 43.33 W |
| Conroe | 222 | 30.18 N | 95.27 W |
| Conroe, Lake ⊜[1] | 222 | 30.25 N | 95.37 W |
| Consandolo | 66 | 44.39 N | 11.46 E |
| Čon-Saryoj | 85 | 42.37 N | 76.53 E |
| Conscience Bay ⊂ | 276 | 40.57 N | 73.07 W |
| Consdorf | 56 | 49.46 N | 6.20 E |
| Consecon | 212 | 44.00 N | 77.31 W |
| Conselheiro Lafaiete | 255 | 20.40 S | 43.48 W |
| Conselheiro Paulino | 256 | 22.13 S | 42.31 W |
| Conselheiro Pena | 255 | 19.10 S | 41.30 W |
| Conselice | 66 | 44.31 N | 11.49 E |
| Conselve | 64 | 45.14 N | 11.52 E |
| Conservatória | 256 | 22.18 S | 43.57 W |
| Consett | 44 | 54.51 N | 1.49 W |
| Conshohocken | 208 | 40.04 N | 75.18 W |
| Consolação | 256 | 22.33 S | 45.55 W |
| Consolação ◆[8] | 287b | 23.33 S | 46.39 W |
| Consolación del Sur | 240p | 22.30 N | 83.31 W |
| Consolidated Main Reef Mines ◆[7] | 273d | 26.11 S | 27.56 E |
| Con Son II | 110 | 8.43 N | 106.36 E |
| Consort | 184 | 52.01 N | 110.46 W |
| Constable | 206 | 44.56 N | 74.18 W |
| Constableville | 212 | 43.34 N | 75.25 W |
| Constance → Konstanz | 58 | 47.40 N | 9.10 E |
| Constance, Lake → Bodensee ⊜ | 58 | 47.35 N | 9.25 E |
| Constance, Mount ∧ | 224 | 47.46 N | 123.08 W |
| Constance Lake ⊜ | 212 | 45.25 N | 75.58 W |
| Constância | 34 | 39.28 N | 8.20 W |
| Constanța | 38 | 44.11 N | 28.39 E |
| Constanța □[6] | 38 | 44.20 N | 28.20 E |
| Constant Creek ≃ | 212 | 45.17 N | 76.46 W |
| Constantia | 210 | 43.14 N | 76.00 W |
| Constantina | 34 | 37.52 N | 5.37 W |
| Constantine → Qacentina, Alg. | 148 | 36.22 N | 6.37 E |
| Constantine, Mi., U.S. | 216 | 41.50 N | 85.40 W |
| Constantine, Cape › | 180 | 58.25 N | 158.50 W |
| Constantinople → İstanbul | 130 | 41.01 N | 28.58 E |
| Constant Lake ⊜ | 212 | 45.24 N | 77.00 W |
| Constitución, Chile | 252 | 35.20 S | 72.25 W |
| Constitución, Ur. | 252 | 31.05 S | 57.50 W |
| Constitución ◆[8] | 288 | 34.37 S | 58.23 W |
| Constitución de 1857, Parque Nacional ♠ | 204 | 32.05 N | 115.55 W |
| Constitution, Mount ∧ | 224 | 48.40 N | 122.50 W |
| Consuegra | 34 | 39.28 N | 3.36 W |
| Consul | 184 | 49.21 N | 109.30 W |
| Consuma | 66 | 43.47 N | 11.35 E |
| Consuma, Passo della )( | 66 | 43.47 N | 11.36 E |
| Contai | 126 | 21.47 N | 87.45 E |
| Contamana | 248 | 7.15 S | 74.54 W |
| Contarina | 64 | 45.00 N | 12.13 E |
| Contas, Rio de ≃ | 255 | 14.17 S | 39.01 W |
| Contee | 208 | 39.05 N | 76.52 W |
| Contendas do Sincorá | 255 | 13.45 S | 41.02 W |
| Contentnea Creek ≃ | 192 | 35.21 N | 77.23 W |
| Contes | 62 | 43.49 N | 7.19 E |
| Contessa Entellina | 70 | 37.44 N | 13.11 E |
| Contigliano | 66 | 42.24 N | 12.46 E |
| Continental | 216 | 41.06 N | 84.15 W |
| Continental Peak ∧ | 200 | 42.16 N | 108.43 W |
| Contoocook Lake ⊜ | 207 | 42.47 N | 72.01 W |
| Contraalmirante Cordero | 252 | 38.44 S | 68.10 W |
| Contra Costa □[6] | 226 | 37.55 N | 121.55 W |
| Contra Costa Canal ≍ | 282 | 38.02 N | 121.58 W |
| Contra Loma Reservoir ⊜[1] | 282 | 37.58 N | 121.49 W |
| Contramaestre | 240p | 20.18 N | 76.15 W |
| Contramaestre ≃ | 240p | 20.31 N | 76.18 W |
| Contratación | 246 | 6.18 N | 73.29 W |
| Contrecoeur | 206 | 45.51 N | 73.14 W |
| Contre Island ›[1] | 276 | 40.54 N | 73.32 W |
| Contreras, Embalse de ⊜[1] | 34 | 39.32 N | 1.30 W |
| Contreras, Isla I | 254 | 51.55 S | 74.55 W |
| Contres | 50 | 47.25 N | 1.26 E |
| Contrexéville | 58 | 48.11 N | 5.54 E |
| Contrisson | 56 | 48.48 N | 4.57 E |
| Controller Bay ⊂ | 180 | 60.07 N | 144.15 W |
| Contumazá | 248 | 7.22 S | 78.49 W |
| Contursi | 68 | 40.39 N | 15.14 E |
| Contwoyto Lake ⊜ | 176 | 65.42 N | 110.50 W |
| Conty | 50 | 49.44 N | 2.09 E |
| Contz-les-Bains | 56 | 49.27 N | 6.21 E |
| Convención | 246 | 8.28 N | 73.21 W |
| Convent | 194 | 30.01 N | 90.49 W |
| Convento | 236 | 9.21 N | 83.30 W |
| Convent Station | 276 | 40.47 N | 74.26 W |
| Conversano | 68 | 40.58 N | 17.08 E |
| Converse | 216 | 40.34 N | 85.52 W |
| Converse Lake ⊜ | 276 | 41.08 N | 73.39 W |
| Converse Pond Brook ≃ | 276 | 41.03 N | 73.40 W |
| Convoy | 216 | 40.55 N | 84.42 W |
| Conway, P.E., Can. | 186 | 46.40 N | 63.59 W |
| Conway, S. Afr. | 158 | 31.43 S | 25.16 E |
| Conway, Ar., U.S. | 194 | 35.05 N | 92.26 W |
| Conway, Fl., U.S. | 220 | 28.30 N | 81.19 W |
| Conway, Ma., U.S. | 207 | 42.30 N | 72.42 W |
| Conway, Mo., U.S. | 194 | 37.30 N | 92.49 W |
| Conway, N.H., U.S. | 188 | 43.58 N | 71.07 W |
| Conway, N.C., U.S. | 192 | 36.26 N | 77.13 W |
| Conway, Pa., U.S. | 214 | 40.39 N | 80.14 W |
| Conway, S.C., U.S. | 192 | 33.50 N | 79.02 W |
| Conway, Wa., U.S. | 224 | 48.21 N | 122.21 W |
| Conway, Cape › | 166 | 20.32 S | 148.56 E |
| Conway, Lake ⊜ | 162 | 28.17 S | 135.35 E |
| Conway, Lake ⊜[1] | 194 | 35.00 N | 92.25 W |
| Conway, Mount ∧ | 162 | 23.45 S | 133.25 E |
| Conway National Park ♠ | 166 | 20.22 S | 148.51 E |
| Conway Springs | 198 | 37.23 N | 97.38 W |
| Conwy | 44 | 53.17 N | 3.50 W |
| Conwy ≃ | 44 | 53.17 N | 3.50 W |
| Conwy, Vale of ∨ | 44 | 53.12 N | 3.48 W |
| Conwy Bay ⊂ | 44 | 53.18 N | 3.55 W |
| Conyers | 192 | 33.40 N | 84.01 W |
| Conyngham | 210 | 40.59 N | 76.03 W |
| Coo | 56 | 50.24 N | 5.52 E |
| Coober Pedy | 162 | 29.01 S | 134.43 E |
| Coogee, Austl. | 168a | 32.07 S | 115.46 E |
| Coogee, Austl. | 274a | 33.55 S | 151.16 E |
| Coogee Bay ⊂ | 274a | 33.55 S | 151.16 E |
| Cook, Austl. | 162 | 30.37 S | 130.25 E |
| Cook, In., U.S. | 216 | 41.22 N | 87.26 W |
| Cook, Mn., U.S. | 190 | 47.51 N | 92.41 W |
| Cook, Ne., U.S. | 198 | 40.30 N | 96.09 W |
| Cook, Wa., U.S. | 224 | 45.43 N | 121.40 W |
| Cook □[6] | 216 | 41.53 N | 87.45 W |
| Cook, Bahía ⊂ | 254 | 55.10 S | 70.10 W |
| Cook, Baie de ⊂ | 174s | 17.29 S | 149.49 W |
| Cook, Cape › | 182 | 50.08 N | 127.55 W |
| Cook, Mount ∧ | 172 | 43.36 S | 170.10 E |
| Cook, Point › | 274b | 37.55 S | 144.48 E |
| Cook, Récif de ✢[2] | 175f | 19.25 S | 163.50 E |
| Cookardinia | 171b | 35.34 S | 147.14 E |
| Cook Bay ⊂ | 212 | 44.15 N | 79.30 W |
| Cook Creek ≃ | 224 | 47.17 N | 124.05 W |
| Cooke, Mount ∧ | 168a | 32.25 S | 116.18 E |
| Cookernup | 168a | 33.00 S | 115.54 E |
| Cookes Peak ∧ | 200 | 32.32 N | 107.44 W |
| Cookeville | 194 | 36.09 N | 85.30 W |
| Cook Forest State Park ♠ | 214 | 41.22 N | 79.12 W |
| Cookham | 42 | 51.34 N | 0.43 W |
| Cookhouse | 158 | 32.45 S | 25.49 E |
| Cook Ice Shelf ⊓ | 9 | 68.40 S | 152.30 E |
| Cooking Lake ⊜ | 182 | 53.25 N | 113.02 W |
| Cook Inlet ⊂ | 180 | 60.30 N | 152.00 W |
| Cook-Inseln → Cook Islands □[2] | 14 | 20.00 S | 158.00 W |
| Cook Island I | 174o | 1.57 N | 157.28 W |
| Cook Islands □[2] | 14 | 20.00 S | 158.00 W |
| Cooks ≃ | 274a | 33.56 S | 151.10 E |
| Cooksburg | 214 | 41.20 N | 79.12 W |
| Cooks Falls | 210 | 41.57 N | 74.59 W |
| Cook's Harbour | 186 | 51.36 N | 55.52 W |
| Cookshire | 206 | 45.25 N | 71.38 W |
| Cooksmill Green | 260 | 51.44 N | 0.22 E |
| Cooks Mills | 284a | 43.00 N | 79.11 W |
| Cookstown, On., Can. | 212 | 44.11 N | 79.42 W |
| Cookstown, N. Ire., U.K. | 48 | 54.39 N | 6.45 W |
| Cook Strait ⊔ | 172 | 41.15 S | 174.30 E |
| Cooksville, Il., U.S. | 216 | 40.33 N | 88.43 W |
| Cooksville, Md., U.S. | 208 | 39.19 N | 77.01 W |
| Cooksville, Wi., U.S. | 216 | 42.50 N | 89.14 W |
| Cooksville Creek ≃ | 275b | 43.34 N | 79.34 W |
| Cooktown | 164 | 15.28 S | 145.15 E |
| Cookville | 222 | 33.11 N | 94.51 W |
| Coolabah | 166 | 31.02 S | 146.43 E |
| Cooladdi | 166 | 26.39 S | 145.28 E |
| Coolah | 166 | 31.50 S | 149.42 E |
| Coolamon | 166 | 34.49 S | 147.12 E |
| Coolaney | 48 | 54.10 N | 8.36 W |
| Coolangatta | 171a | 28.10 S | 153.32 E |
| Coolawanyah | 162 | 21.47 S | 117.48 E |
| Coole ≃ | 50 | 48.56 N | 4.21 E |
| Cooleemee | 192 | 35.48 N | 80.33 W |
| Cooley Lake ⊜ | 281 | 42.37 N | 83.27 W |
| Coolgardie | 162 | 30.57 S | 121.10 E |
| Coolidge, Az., U.S. | 200 | 32.58 N | 111.31 W |
| Coolidge, Ga., U.S. | 192 | 31.00 N | 83.51 W |
| Coolidge, Tx., U.S. | 222 | 31.45 N | 96.38 W |
| Coolidge, Mount ∧ | 198 | 43.44 N | 103.29 W |
| Coolidge Dam ◆[6] | 200 | 33.00 N | 110.20 W |
| Coolidge Point › | 283 | 42.34 N | 70.44 W |
| Coolin | 202 | 48.28 N | 116.50 W |
| Cooling | 260 | 51.27 N | 0.32 E |
| Cooloola National Park ♠ | 166 | 26.05 S | 153.00 E |
| Cooloongup, Lake ⊜ | 168a | 32.18 S | 115.47 E |
| Coolspring | 214 | 41.02 N | 79.05 W |
| Coolumburra Hill ∧ | 170 | 35.01 S | 150.10 E |
| Coolup | 168a | 32.44 S | 115.53 E |
| Cooma | 171b | 36.14 S | 149.08 E |
| Cooma Creek ≃ | 171b | 36.07 S | 149.11 E |
| Coombe Cottage ⊥ | 274b | 37.43 S | 145.23 E |
| Coomberdale | 162 | 30.28 S | 116.02 E |
| Coomera | 171a | 27.52 S | 153.19 E |
| Coomera ≃ | 171a | 27.53 S | 153.24 E |
| Coominya | 171a | 27.23 S | 152.30 E |
| Coonabarabran | 166 | 31.16 S | 149.17 E |
| Coonalpyn | 166 | 35.42 S | 139.51 E |
| Coonamble | 166 | 30.57 S | 148.23 E |
| Coonana | 162 | 31.01 S | 123.07 E |
| Coon Creek ≃, Ca., U.S. | 226 | 38.51 N | 121.34 W |
| Coon Creek ≃, Il., U.S. | 216 | 42.15 N | 88.48 W |
| Coon Creek ≃, Tx., U.S. | 222 | 31.59 N | 95.52 W |
| Coon Creek Lake ⊜[1] | 222 | 32.04 N | 95.52 W |
| Coondambo | 166 | 31.04 S | 135.52 E |
| Coongan ≃ | 162 | 20.53 S | 119.47 E |
| Coonoor | 122 | 11.21 N | 76.49 E |
| Coon Rapids, Ia., U.S. | 198 | 41.52 N | 94.41 W |
| Coon Rapids, Mn., U.S. | 190 | 45.10 N | 93.19 W |
| Coontown | 276 | 40.37 N | 74.31 W |
| Coon Valley | 190 | 43.42 N | 91.00 W |
| Cooper | 196 | 33.22 N | 95.41 W |
| Cooper ≃, N.J., U.S. | 285 | 39.57 N | 75.07 W |
| Cooper ≃, Wa., U.S. | 224 | 47.23 N | 121.23 W |
| Cooper, Mount ∧, Austl. | 162 | 26.11 S | 127.56 E |
| Cooper, Mount ∧, B.C., Can. | 182 | 50.11 N | 117.12 W |
| Cooper, North Branch ≃ | 285 | 39.55 N | 75.02 W |
| Cooper Center | 216 | 42.23 N | 85.37 W |
| Cooper Creek ≃ | 166 | 28.29 S | 137.46 E |
| Cooper Island I | 240m | 18.22 N | 64.30 W |
| Cooper Landing | 180 | 60.29 N | 149.51 W |
| Cooper Mountain ∧ | 180 | 60.23 N | 149.51 W |
| Cooper River Parkway ♠ | 285 | 39.55 N | 75.03 W |
| Cooper Road | 194 | 32.26 N | 93.48 W |
| Coopers | 194 | 32.46 N | 86.33 W |
| Coopersale Common | 260 | 51.42 N | 0.08 E |
| Coopersburg | 208 | 40.30 N | 75.23 W |
| Coopers Plains, Austl. | 171a | 27.34 S | 153.02 E |
| Coopers Plains, N.Y., U.S. | 210 | 42.11 N | 77.08 W |
| Cooperstown, N.Y., U.S. | 210 | 42.42 N | 74.55 W |
| Cooperstown, N.D., U.S. | 198 | 47.26 N | 98.07 W |
| Cooperstown, Pa., U.S. | 214 | 41.30 N | 79.52 W |
| Cooperstown, Pa., U.S. | 214 | 40.43 N | 79.57 W |
| Coopersville | 216 | 43.03 N | 85.56 W |
| Coorabie | 162 | 31.54 S | 132.18 E |
| Cooranbong | 170 | 33.04 S | 151.27 E |
| Coorong National Park ♠ | 166 | 36.01 S | 139.32 E |
| Coorow | 162 | 29.53 S | 116.01 E |
| Cooroy | 166 | 26.25 S | 152.55 E |
| Coorparoo | 171a | 27.30 S | 153.03 E |
| Coos □[6] | 206 | 45.04 N | 71.20 W |
| Coosa ≃ | 194 | 32.30 N | 86.16 W |
| Coosawhatchie ≃ | 192 | 32.32 N | 80.52 W |
| Coos Bay | 202 | 43.22 N | 124.12 W |
| Coos Bay ⊂ | 202 | 43.23 N | 124.16 W |
| Cootamundra | 166 | 34.39 S | 148.02 E |
| Cootehill | 48 | 54.04 N | 7.05 W |
| Cooyar | 171a | 26.59 S | 151.50 E |
| Cooyar Creek ≃ | 171a | 26.50 S | 152.04 E |
| Cooyar Mountain ∧ | 171a | 26.57 S | 151.47 E |
| Copacabana, Arg. | 252 | 28.12 S | 67.29 W |
| Copacabana, Bol. | 248 | 16.10 S | 69.05 W |
| Copacabana, Col. | 246 | 6.20 N | 75.30 W |
| Copacabana ◆[8] | 287a | 22.58 S | 43.11 W |
| Copacabana, Forte de ⊥ | 287a | 22.59 S | 43.11 W |
| Copainalá | 234 | 17.05 N | 93.12 W |
| Copake | 210 | 42.06 N | 73.33 W |
| Copake Falls | 210 | 42.07 N | 73.31 W |
| Copala | 234 | 16.37 N | 98.58 W |
| Copalillo | 234 | 18.02 N | 99.07 W |
| Copalis ≃ | 224 | 47.07 N | 124.13 W |
| Copalis Beach | 224 | 47.06 N | 124.10 W |
| Copalita ≃ | 234 | 15.46 N | 96.03 W |
| Copán, Hond. | 236 | 14.50 N | 89.09 W |
| Copan, Ok., U.S. | 196 | 36.53 N | 95.55 W |
| Copán □[5] | 236 | 14.50 N | 89.00 W |
| Copán ⊥ | 236 | 14.50 N | 89.09 W |
| Copanatoyac | 234 | 17.15 N | 98.45 W |
| Copándaro | 234 | 19.53 N | 101.13 W |
| Copan Lake ⊜[1] | 196 | 36.55 N | 95.56 W |
| Copano Bay ⊂ | 196 | 28.05 N | 97.05 W |
| Copatana | 246 | 2.48 S | 67.04 W |
| Cope | 198 | 39.39 N | 102.51 W |
| Copeá, Paraná ≃[1] | 246 | 3.52 S | 63.20 W |
| Copeau ≃ | 184 | 52.45 N | 103.00 W |
| Copeland | 220 | 25.57 N | 81.21 W |
| Copeland Island I | 48 | 54.41 N | 5.32 W |
| Copenhagen → København, Dan. | 41 | 55.40 N | 12.35 E |
| Copenhagen, N.Y., U.S. | 212 | 43.53 N | 75.40 W |
| Copenhague → København | 41 | 55.40 N | 12.35 E |
| Copenhaver | 284c | 39.04 N | 77.11 W |
| Copertino | 68 | 40.16 N | 18.03 E |
| Copetonas | 252 | 38.43 S | 60.27 W |
| Copeville | 222 | 33.05 N | 96.25 W |
| Copiague | 210 | 40.40 N | 73.24 W |
| Copiague Neck ›[1] | 276 | 40.40 N | 73.22 W |
| Copiapó | 252 | 27.22 S | 70.20 W |
| Copiapó ≃ | 252 | 27.19 S | 70.56 W |
| Copinsay I | 46 | 58.54 N | 2.40 W |
| Coplay | 208 | 40.40 N | 75.29 W |
| Copley, Austl. | 166 | 30.32 S | 138.25 E |
| Copley, Oh., U.S. | 214 | 41.06 N | 81.39 W |
| Copmanthorpe | 44 | 53.55 N | 1.08 W |
| Copoas, Mount ∧ | 116 | 10.48 N | 119.17 E |
| Copolo | 152 | 10.22 S | 14.07 E |
| Copparo | 64 | 44.54 N | 11.49 E |
| Coppell | 222 | 32.57 N | 97.01 W |
| Coppename ≃ | 250 | 5.48 N | 55.55 W |
| Coppenbrügge | 52 | 52.07 N | 9.32 E |
| Copper ≃ | 180 | 60.30 N | 144.50 W |
| Copperas Cove | 196 | 31.07 N | 97.54 W |
| Copperas Mountain ∧ | 276 | 41.02 N | 74.28 W |
| Copperbelt □[4] | 154 | 13.00 S | 28.00 E |
| Copper Butte ∧ | 202 | 48.42 N | 118.28 W |
| Copper Canyon → Cobre, Barranca del ∨ | 232 | 27.28 N | 107.50 W |
| Copper Center | 180 | 61.58 N | 145.19 W |
| Copper Cliff | 190 | 46.28 N | 81.04 W |
| Copper Creek ≃ | 192 | 36.40 N | 82.45 W |
| Copper Harbor | 190 | 47.27 N | 87.53 W |
| Coppermine | 176 | 67.50 N | 115.05 W |
| Coppermine ≃ | 176 | 67.49 N | 115.04 W |
| Copper Mine Point ›, Br. Vir. Is. | 240m | 18.26 N | 64.25 W |
| Coppermine Point ›, On., Can. | 190 | 46.59 N | 84.47 W |
| Copper Mountain | 182 | 49.20 N | 120.33 W |
| Copper Mountain ∧, Ak., U.S. | 182 | 55.14 N | 132.36 W |
| Copper Mountain ∧, Wy., U.S. | 200 | 43.27 N | 107.57 W |
| Copperopolis | 226 | 37.59 N | 120.38 W |
| Coppet | 58 | 46.19 N | 6.12 E |
| Coppin State College ʊ[2] | 284b | 39.19 N | 76.40 W |
| Copplestone | 42 | 50.49 N | 3.45 W |
| Coppull | 262 | 53.37 N | 2.40 W |
| Copster Green | 262 | 53.48 N | 2.30 W |
| Coptic Museum ʊ | 273c | 30.00 N | 31.13 E |
| Copton Creek ≃ | 182 | 54.16 N | 119.15 W |
| Copton Point › | 116 | 10.00 N | 123.22 E |
| Coqên | 120 | 31.20 N | 85.25 E |
| Coquet ≃ | 44 | 55.22 N | 1.37 W |
| Coquet Dale ∨ | 44 | 55.16 N | 1.50 W |
| Coquí | 240m | 17.59 N | 66.14 W |
| Coquilhatville → Mbandaka | 152 | 0.04 N | 18.16 E |
| Coquille | 202 | 43.10 N | 124.11 W |
| Coquille ≃ | 202 | 43.07 N | 124.26 W |
| Coquille, East Fork ≃ | 202 | 43.06 N | 124.04 W |
| Coquille, Middle Fork ≃ | 202 | 43.05 N | 124.09 W |
| Coquille, South Fork ≃ | 202 | 43.02 N | 124.07 W |
| Coquimatlán | 234 | 19.12 N | 103.48 W |
| Coquimbo | 252 | 29.58 S | 71.21 W |
| Coquimbo □[4] | 252 | 30.45 S | 71.00 W |
| Coquina Key I | 220 | 27.44 N | 82.38 W |
| Coquitlam | 224 | 49.14 N | 122.52 W |
| Corabia | 38 | 43.46 N | 24.30 E |
| Coração de Jesus | 255 | 16.42 S | 44.22 W |
| Coração de Maria | 255 | 12.14 S | 38.45 W |
| Corace ≃ | 68 | 38.49 N | 16.37 E |
| Coracora | 248 | 15.02 S | 73.47 W |
| Corail, Mer de → Coral Sea ⊤[2] | 14 | 20.00 S | 158.00 E |
| Coral | 214 | 40.29 N | 79.10 W |
| Coral Bay ⊂, Pil. | 116 | 8.25 N | 117.20 E |
| Coral Bay ⊂, Vir. Is., U.S. | 240m | 18.20 N | 64.41 W |
| Coral Gables | 220 | 25.43 N | 80.16 W |
| Coral Harbour | 176 | 64.08 N | 83.10 W |
| Coral Hills | 284c | 38.52 N | 76.55 W |
| Coralque ≃ | 248 | 16.26 S | 70.45 W |
| Coral Sea ⊤[2] | 14 | 20.00 S | 158.00 E |
| Coral Sea Basin ✢[1] | 14 | 14.00 S | 152.00 E |
| Coral Sea Islands Territory □[8] | 166 | 18.30 S | 152.00 E |
| Coral Springs | 220 | 26.16 N | 80.13 W |
| Coralville | 190 | 41.40 N | 91.34 W |
| Coralville Lake ⊜[1] | 190 | 41.47 N | 91.48 W |
| Coram, Mt., U.S. | 202 | 48.25 N | 114.02 W |
| Coram, N.Y., U.S. | 210 | 40.52 N | 73.00 W |
| Corangamite, Lake ⊜ | 169 | 38.10 S | 143.25 E |
| Corantijn (Corentyne) ≃ | 250 | 5.55 N | 57.05 W |
| Coraopolis | 214 | 40.31 N | 80.10 W |
| Coraopolis Heights | 279b | 40.29 N | 80.10 W |
| Corato | 68 | 41.09 N | 16.25 E |
| Corbara, Lago di ⊜[1] | 66 | 42.43 N | 12.15 E |
| Corbeil-Essonnes | 50 | 48.36 N | 2.29 E |
| Corbenay | 58 | 47.54 N | 6.20 E |
| Corbeny | 50 | 49.28 N | 3.49 E |
| Corbera, Riera de ≃ | 266d | 41.27 N | 1.59 E |
| Corberon | 58 | 47.01 N | 4.59 E |
| Corbett | 210 | 42.03 N | 75.02 W |
| Corbetta | 62 | 45.28 N | 8.55 E |
| Corbett National Park ♠ | 124 | 29.40 N | 78.45 E |
| Corbettsville | 210 | 42.01 N | 75.48 W |
| Corbie | 50 | 49.55 N | 2.30 E |
| Corbière Point › | 43b | 49.11 N | 2.15 W |
| Corbières ⋏ | 32 | 42.55 N | 2.38 E |
| Corbigny | 50 | 47.15 N | 3.40 E |
| Corbin | 192 | 36.56 N | 84.05 W |
| Corbion | 56 | 49.48 N | 5.00 E |
| Corbola | 64 | 45.00 N | 12.05 E |
| Corbones ≃ | 34 | 37.36 N | 5.39 W |
| Corbridge | 44 | 54.58 N | 2.01 W |
| Corbu | 38 | 44.29 N | 24.43 E |
| Corby | 42 | 52.29 N | 0.40 W |
| Corcaigh → Cork | 48 | 51.54 N | 8.28 W |
| Córcega | 240m | 18.19 N | 67.15 W |
| Córcega, Isla de → Corse I | 36 | 42.00 N | 9.00 E |
| Corciano | 66 | 43.08 N | 12.17 E |
| Corcieux | 58 | 48.10 N | 6.53 E |
| Corcolle ◆[8] | 267a | 41.55 N | 12.46 E |
| Corcoran | 226 | 36.05 N | 119.33 W |
| Corcovado, Golfo ⊂ | 254 | 43.30 S | 73.30 W |
| Corcovado, Morro do ∧ | 287a | 22.57 S | 43.13 W |
| Corcovado, Parque Nacional ♠ | 236 | 8.35 N | 83.40 W |
| Corcovado, Volcán ∧[1] | 254 | 43.12 S | 72.48 W |
| Corcubión | 34 | 42.57 N | 9.11 W |
| Cordeaux Reservoir ⊜[1] | 170 | 34.22 S | 150.45 E |
| Cordeiro | 255 | 22.02 S | 42.22 W |
| Cordele, Ga., U.S. | 192 | 31.57 N | 83.46 W |
| Cordele, Tx., U.S. | 222 | 29.08 N | 96.38 W |
| Cordell | 196 | 35.17 N | 98.59 W |
| Cordell Hull Reservoir ⊜[1] | 194 | 36.25 N | 85.40 W |
| Cordenons | 64 | 45.59 N | 12.42 E |
| Corder | 194 | 39.05 N | 93.38 W |
| Cordes | 32 | 44.04 N | 1.57 E |
| Cordevole ≃ | 64 | 46.05 N | 12.04 E |
| Cordignano | 64 | 45.57 N | 12.25 E |
| Cordillera □[5] | 252 | 25.15 S | 57.00 W |
| Cordillera de los Picachos, Parque Nacional ♠ | 246 | 3.00 N | 74.30 W |
| Cordillo Downs | 166 | 26.43 S | 140.38 E |
| Cordisburgo | 255 | 19.07 S | 44.21 W |
| Cordislândia | 256 | 21.48 S | 45.43 W |
| Córdoba, Arg. | 252 | 31.24 S | 64.11 W |
| Córdoba, Esp. | 34 | 37.53 N | 4.46 W |
| Córdoba, Méx. | 234 | 18.53 N | 96.56 W |
| Córdoba □[4], Arg. | 252 | 32.00 S | 64.00 W |
| Córdoba □[4], Esp. | 34 | 38.00 N | 4.50 W |
| Córdoba □[5] | 246 | 8.20 N | 75.40 W |
| Córdoba, Península ›[1] | 254 | 53.20 S | 72.50 W |
| Cordon | 116 | 16.40 N | 121.28 E |
| Cordova → Córdoba, Esp. | 34 | 37.53 N | 4.46 W |
| Córdova, Perú | 248 | 14.04 S | 75.03 W |
| Cordova, Al., U.S. | 194 | 33.45 N | 87.11 W |
| Cordova, Ak., U.S. | 180 | 60.33 N | 145.46 W |
| Cordova, Il., U.S. | 190 | 41.41 N | 90.19 W |
| Cordova, Md., U.S. | 208 | 38.52 N | 75.59 W |
| Cordova Bay ⊂ | 182 | 54.55 N | 132.35 W |
| Cordova Lake ⊜ | 212 | 44.35 N | 77.49 W |
| Cordova Peak ∧ | 180 | 60.51 N | 145.16 W |
| Corea, Estrecho de → Korea Strait ⊔ | 90 | 34.00 N | 129.00 E |
| Corea del Norte → Korea, North □[1] | 98 | 40.00 N | 127.00 E |
| Corea del Sur → Korea, South □[1] | 98 | 36.30 N | 128.00 E |
| Coreaú | 250 | 3.33 S | 40.39 W |
| Coreaú ≃ | 250 | 2.54 S | 40.50 W |
| Core Creek ≃ | 285 | 40.11 N | 74.55 W |
| Corée, Détroit de → Korea Strait ⊔ | 90 | 34.00 N | 129.00 E |
| Coree, Mount ∧ | 171b | 35.18 S | 148.48 E |
| Corée du Nord → Korea, North □[1] | 98 | 40.00 N | 127.00 E |
| Corée du Sud → Korea, South □[1] | 98 | 36.30 N | 128.00 E |
| Coreglia Antelminelli | 64 | 44.04 N | 10.31 E |
| Coreinbob | 171b | 35.13 S | 147.38 E |
| Coremas | 250 | 7.01 S | 37.58 W |
| Corentyne (Corantijn) ≃ | 250 | 5.55 N | 57.05 W |
| Corerepe | 232 | 25.40 N | 108.40 W |
| Corese Terra | 66 | 42.10 N | 12.42 E |
| Corey Lake ⊜ | 216 | 41.55 N | 85.45 W |
| Corfe Castle | 42 | 50.38 N | 2.04 W |
| Corfield | 166 | 21.43 S | 143.22 E |
| Corfu → Kérkira, Ellás | 38 | 39.36 N | 19.56 E |
| Corfu, N.Y., U.S. | 210 | 42.57 N | 78.24 W |
| Corfu → Kérkira I | 38 | 39.40 N | 19.45 E |
| Corhanwarrabul Creek ≃ | 274b | 37.55 S | 145.12 E |
| Cori | 66 | 41.39 N | 12.55 E |
| Coria | 34 | 39.59 N | 6.32 W |
| Coria del Río | 34 | 37.16 N | 6.03 W |
| Coribe | 255 | 13.50 S | 44.28 W |
| Coricudgy, Mount ∧ | 170 | 32.50 S | 150.22 E |
| Corigliano Calabro | 68 | 39.36 N | 16.31 E |
| Corigliano d'Otranto | 68 | 40.09 N | 18.15 E |
| Corinaldo | 66 | 43.39 N | 13.03 E |
| Corinda | 166 | 17.53 S | 138.35 E |
| Corinne, Pa., U.S. | 285 | 39.54 N | 75.40 W |
| Corinne, Ut,. U.S. | 200 | 41.33 N | 112.06 W |
| Corinne, W.V., U.S. | 192 | 37.34 N | 81.21 W |
| Corinth → Kórinthos, Ellás | 38 | 37.56 N | 22.56 E |
| Corinth, Ky., U.S. | 218 | 38.29 N | 84.33 W |
| Corinth, Ms., U.S. | 194 | 34.56 N | 88.31 W |
| Corinth, N.Y., U.S. | 210 | 43.14 N | 73.49 W |
| Corinth, Gulf of → Korinthiakós Kólpos ⊂ | 38 | 38.19 N | 22.04 E |
| Corinth Canal → Korínthou, Dhiórix ≍ | 38 | 37.57 N | 22.56 E |
| Corinto, Bra. | 255 | 18.21 S | 44.27 W |
| Corinto, El Sal. | 236 | 13.49 N | 87.58 W |
| Corinto, Nic. | 236 | 12.29 N | 87.10 W |
| Corio | 169 | 38.04 S | 144.23 E |
| Corio Bay ⊂ | 169 | 38.07 S | 144.24 E |
| Coripata | 248 | 16.18 S | 67.36 W |
| Corire | 248 | 16.14 S | 72.28 W |
| Coris | 248 | 9.50 S | 77.45 W |
| Corisco, Isla de I | 152 | 0.53 N | 9.20 E |
| Corixo Grande (Curiche Grande) ≃ | 248 | 17.43 S | 57.43 W |
| Corjeuți | 38 | 48.13 N | 27.02 E |
| Cork (Corcaigh) | 48 | 51.54 N | 8.28 W |
| Cork □[6] | 48 | 51.58 N | 8.35 W |
| Cork Airport ⊠ | 48 | 51.51 N | 8.29 W |
| Cork Harbour ⊂ | 48 | 51.45 N | 8.15 W |
| Corkscrew | 220 | 26.28 N | 81.33 W |
| Corkscrew Swamp ≡ | 220 | 26.25 N | 81.34 W |
| Čorku | 85 | 39.58 N | 70.33 E |
| Corlay | 32 | 48.19 N | 3.03 W |
| Corleone | 70 | 37.49 N | 13.18 E |
| Corleto Perticara | 68 | 40.23 N | 16.03 E |
| Çorlu | 130 | 41.09 N | 27.48 E |
| Cormainville | 50 | 48.08 N | 1.36 E |
| Cormano | 266b | 45.33 N | 9.10 E |
| Cormatin | 58 | 46.33 N | 4.41 E |
| Cormeilles | 50 | 49.15 N | 0.23 E |
| Cormeilles-en-Parisis | 50 | 48.59 N | 2.12 E |
| Cormery | 50 | 47.16 N | 0.51 E |
| Cormons | 64 | 45.58 N | 13.28 E |
| Cormorant | 184 | 54.14 N | 100.35 W |
| Cormorant Lake ⊜ | 184 | 54.13 N | 100.47 W |
| Corna | 64 | 45.53 N | 10.10 E |
| Čornaja, Ross. | 24 | 68.35 N | 56.30 E |
| Čornaja, Ross. | 82 | 55.45 N | 38.04 E |
| Čornaja ≃, Ross. | 265a | 59.47 N | 30.10 E |
| Čornaja ≃, Ross. | 265a | 59.50 N | 30.00 E |
| Čornaja ≃, Ross. | 265a | 60.01 N | 30.10 E |
| Čornaja ≃, Ross. | 265a | 59.55 N | 30.59 E |
| Čornaja ≃, Ross. | 265b | 55.41 N | 37.58 E |
| Čornaja Cholunica | 86 | 58.51 N | 51.42 E |
| Čornaja Gr'az', Ross. | 82 | 54.31 N | 35.52 E |
| Čornaja Gr'az', Ross. | 82 | 54.58 N | 36.48 E |
| Čornaja Gr'az', Ross. | 265b | 55.58 N | 37.19 E |
| Čornaja Rečka | 265a | 59.56 N | 30.58 E |
| Čornaja rečka ≃, Ross. | 265a | 59.46 N | 30.45 E |
| Čornaja rečka ≃, Ross. | 265a | 59.55 N | 30.22 E |
| Čornaja Sloboda | 24 | 60.48 N | 37.46 E |
| Cornaredo | 266b | 45.30 N | 9.02 E |
| Cornas | 62 | 44.58 N | 4.51 E |
| Cornedo Vicentino | 64 | 45.37 N | 11.20 E |
| Cornelia, S. Afr. | 158 | 27.13 S | 28.52 E |
| Cornelia, Ga., U.S. | 192 | 34.30 N | 83.31 W |
| Cornélio Procópio | 255 | 23.08 S | 50.39 W |
| Cornelius, N.C., U.S. | 192 | 35.29 N | 80.51 W |
| Cornelius, Or., U.S. | 224 | 45.31 N | 123.03 W |
| Cornelius Grinnell Bay ⊂ | 176 | 63.20 N | 64.50 W |
| Cornell, Il., U.S. | 216 | 41.00 N | 88.44 W |
| Cornell, Wi., U.S. | 190 | 45.10 N | 91.08 W |
| Cornellà de Llobregat | 266d | 41.21 N | 2.05 E |
| Corner Brook | 186 | 48.57 N | 57.57 W |
| Corner Inlet ⊂ | 169 | 38.43 S | 146.20 E |
| Corner Store | 285 | 40.07 N | 75.30 W |
| Cornersville | 194 | 35.21 N | 86.50 W |
| Cornes, Lac des ⊜ | 206 | 46.43 N | 75.09 W |
| Cornești | 38 | 47.22 N | 27.59 E |
| Corneta, Punta › | 234 | 15.39 N | 96.34 W |
| Cornforth | 44 | 54.42 N | 1.31 W |
| Cornhill | 46 | 57.36 N | 2.42 W |
| Cornholme | 262 | 53.44 N | 2.08 W |
| Cornia ≃ | 66 | 42.57 N | 10.33 E |
| Corniglia | 62 | 44.07 N | 9.42 E |
| Corniglio | 64 | 44.28 N | 10.05 E |
| Corning, Ar., U.S. | 194 | 36.24 N | 90.34 W |
| Corning, Ca., U.S. | 204 | 39.55 N | 122.10 W |
| Corning, Ia., U.S. | 198 | 40.59 N | 94.44 W |
| Corning, Ks., U.S. | 198 | 39.39 N | 96.01 W |
| Corning, N.Y., U.S. | 210 | 42.08 N | 77.03 W |
| Corning, Oh., U.S. | 188 | 39.36 N | 82.05 W |
| Cornish | 188 | 43.48 N | 70.48 W |
| Cornish, Mount ∧ | 162 | 20.13 S | 126.28 E |
| Cornland | 219 | 39.56 N | 89.24 W |
| Corno ≃ | 66 | 42.49 N | 12.55 E |
| Corno Grande ∧ | 66 | 42.28 N | 13.34 E |
| Čornoje, Kaz. | 86 | 51.44 N | 77.34 E |
| Čornoje, Ross. | 80 | 57.32 N | 46.25 E |
| Čornolesskoje | 84 | 44.42 N | 43.42 E |
| Čornomorskij | 78 | 44.51 N | 38.29 E |
| Čornoreck | 86 | 52.45 N | 76.40 E |
| Cornuda | 64 | 45.50 N | 12.00 E |
| Cornwall, On., Can. | 206 | 45.02 N | 74.44 W |
| Cornwall, N.Y., U.S. | 210 | 41.26 N | 74.01 W |
| Cornwall, Pa., U.S. | 208 | 40.16 N | 76.24 W |
| Cornwall □[6] | 42 | 50.30 N | 4.40 W |
| Cornwall Bridge | 207 | 41.49 N | 73.22 W |
| Cornwallis Island I | 176 | 75.15 N | 94.30 W |
| Cornwall on Hudson | 210 | 41.27 N | 74.00 W |
| Cornwell | 220 | 27.23 N | 81.05 W |
| Čornyj Jar | 80 | 48.04 N | 46.08 E |
| Čornyj Mys, Ross. | 24 | 68.20 N | 38.37 E |
| Čornyj Mys, Ross. | 86 | 55.33 N | 80.04 E |
| Čornyj Otrog | 86 | 51.55 N | 55.59 E |
| Corny Point | 166 | 34.55 S | 137.03 E |
| Coro | 246 | 11.25 N | 69.41 W |
| Coro, Golfete de ⊂ | 241s | 11.30 N | 69.55 W |
| Coroaci | 255 | 18.35 S | 42.17 W |
| Coroa Grande | 256 | 22.54 S | 43.52 W |
| Coroatá | 250 | 4.08 S | 44.08 W |
| Coroca ≃ | 152 | 15.43 S | 11.55 E |
| Čoroch (Çoruh) ≃ | 130 | 41.36 N | 41.35 E |
| Corocoro | 248 | 17.12 S | 68.29 W |
| Corocoro Island I | 246 | 8.30 N | 60.10 W |
| Coroico | 248 | 16.10 S | 67.44 W |
| Coroico ≃ | 248 | 15.27 S | 67.50 W |
| Coromandel, Bra. | 255 | 18.28 S | 47.13 W |
| Coromandel, N.Z. | 172 | 36.46 S | 175.30 E |
| Coromandel Coast ⊥[2] | 122 | 13.30 N | 80.30 E |
| Coromandel Peninsula ›[1] | 172 | 36.50 S | 175.35 E |
| Coromandel Range ⋏ | 172 | 37.00 S | 175.40 E |
| Coron | 116 | 12.00 N | 120.12 E |
| Corona, Ca., U.S. | 228 | 33.52 N | 117.33 W |
| Corona, N.M., U.S. | 200 | 34.15 N | 105.36 W |
| Corona ◆[8] | 276 | 40.45 N | 73.52 W |
| Coronación, Golfo de la → Coronation Gulf ⊂ | 176 | 68.25 N | 110.00 W |
| Coronación, Isla de la → Coronation Island I | 9 | 60.37 S | 45.30 W |
| Corona del Mar ◆[8] | 228 | 33.36 N | 117.52 W |
| Coronado, Méx. | 234 | 22.55 N | 100.56 W |
| Coronado, Ca., U.S. | 228 | 32.41 N | 117.10 W |
| Coronado, Bahía de ⊂ | 236 | 9.00 N | 83.50 W |
| Coronado National Memorial ⊥ | 200 | 31.10 N | 110.29 W |
| Coronado Naval Amphibious Base ■ | 228 | 32.40 N | 117.10 W |
| Coronados, Golfo ⊂ | 254 | 41.40 S | 74.00 W |
| Coronation | 182 | 52.05 N | 111.27 W |
| Coronation Gardens ♠ | 275b | 43.41 N | 79.29 W |
| Coronation Gulf ⊂ | 176 | 68.25 N | 110.00 W |
| Coronation Island I, Ant. | 9 | 60.37 S | 45.30 W |
| Coronation Island I, Ak., U.S. | 180 | 55.52 N | 134.15 W |
| Coronation Park ♠ | 273d | 26.06 S | 27.47 E |
| Coron Bay ⊂ | 116 | 11.54 N | 120.08 E |
| Coronda | 252 | 31.58 S | 60.55 W |
| Coronel | 252 | 37.01 S | 73.08 W |
| Coronel Bogado | 252 | 27.11 S | 56.18 W |
| Coronel Dorrego | 252 | 38.42 S | 61.17 W |
| Coronel Du Graty | 252 | 27.40 S | 60.56 W |
| Coronel Eugenio del Busto | 252 | 38.57 S | 64.15 W |
| Coronel Fabriciano | 255 | 19.31 S | 42.38 W |
| Coronel Moldes, Arg. | 252 | 25.16 S | 65.29 W |
| Coronel Moldes, Arg. | 252 | 33.38 S | 64.36 W |
| Coronel Murta | 255 | 16.37 S | 42.11 W |
| Coronel Oviedo | 252 | 25.25 S | 56.27 W |
| Coronel Pacheco | 256 | 21.35 S | 43.16 W |
| Coronel Ponce | 255 | 15.34 S | 55.01 W |
| Coronel Pringles | 252 | 37.58 S | 61.22 W |
| Coronel Sapucaia | 255 | 23.15 S | 55.31 W |
| Coronel Suárez | 252 | 37.28 S | 61.55 W |
| Coronel Vidal | 252 | 37.27 S | 57.43 W |
| Coronel Vivida | 252 | 25.58 S | 52.34 W |
| Corongo | 248 | 8.35 S | 77.55 W |
| Corongoros | 234 | 19.17 N | 102.48 W |
| Coronie □[5] | 250 | 5.50 N | 56.20 W |
| Coron Island I | 116 | 11.55 N | 120.14 E |
| Coronita | 228 | 33.52 N | 117.36 W |
| Coropuna, Nevado ∧ | 248 | 15.31 S | 72.42 W |
| Çorovodë | 38 | 40.30 N | 20.13 E |
| Corowa | 166 | 36.02 S | 146.23 E |
| Corozal, Belize | 232 | 18.24 N | 88.24 W |
| Corozal, Col. | 246 | 9.19 N | 75.18 W |
| Corozal, Hond. | 236 | 15.48 N | 86.43 W |
| Corozal, P.R. | 240m | 18.21 N | 66.17 W |
| Corps | 62 | 44.49 N | 5.57 E |
| Corpus | 252 | 27.07 S | 55.31 W |
| Corpus Christi | 196 | 27.48 N | 97.23 W |
| Corpus Christi, Lake ⊜[1] | 196 | 28.10 N | 97.53 W |
| Corpus Christi Bay ⊂ | 196 | 27.48 N | 97.20 W |
| Corpus Christi Naval Air Station ■ | 196 | 27.42 N | 97.16 W |
| Corque | 248 | 18.21 S | 67.42 W |
| Corquín | 236 | 14.34 N | 88.52 W |
| Corral | 254 | 39.52 S | 73.26 W |
| Corral de Almaguer | 34 | 39.46 N | 3.11 W |
| Corral de Bustos | 252 | 33.17 S | 62.12 W |
| Corralero, Laguna ⊂ | 234 | 16.12 N | 98.07 W |
| Corralillo | 240p | 22.59 N | 80.35 W |
| Corralito | 252 | 32.03 S | 64.12 W |
| Corralito, Arroyo del ≃ | 258 | 33.39 S | 58.03 W |


**Symbols** in the index entries represent the broad categories identified in the key at the right. Symbols with superior numbers (⋏[1]) identify subcategories (see complete key on page *I* · *1).*

**Symbole** im Register stellen die rechts im Schlüssel erklärten Kategorien dar. Symbole mit hochgestellten Ziffern (⋏[1]) bezeichnen Unterabteilungen einer Kategorie (vgl. vollständiger Schlüssel auf Seite *I* · *1).*

**Los símbolos** incluídos en el texto del índice representan las grandes categorías identificadas con la clave a la derecha. Los símbolos con numeros en su parte superior (⋏[1]) identifican las subcategorías (véase la clave completa en la página *I* · *1).*

**Les symboles** de l'index représentent les catégories indiquées dans la légende à droite. Les symboles suivis d'un indice (⋏[1]) représentent des sous-catégories (voir légende complète à la page *I* · *1).*

**Os símbolos** incluídos no texto do índice representam as grandes categorias identificadas com a chave à direita. Os símbolos com números em sua parte superior (⋏[1]) identificam as subcategorias (veja-se a chave completa à página *I* · *1).*

| Symbol | English | Deutsch | Español | Français | Português |
|---|---|---|---|---|---|
| ∧ | Mountain | Berg | Montaña | Montagne | Montanha |
| ⋏ | Mountains | Gebirge | Montañas | Montagnes | Montanhas |
| )( | Pass | Paß | Paso | Col | Passo |
| ∨ | Valley, Canyon | Tal, Cañon | Valle, Cañón | Vallée, Canyon | Vale, Canhão |
| ≚ | Plain | Ebene | Llano | Plaine | Planície |
| › | Cape | Kap | Cabo | Cap | Cabo |
| I | Island | Insel | Isla | Île | Ilha |
| II | Islands | Inseln | Islas | Îles | Ilhas |
| ⊥ | Other Topographic Features | Andere Topographische Objekte | Otros Elementos Topográficos | Autres données topographiques | Outros acidentes topográficos |

ESPAÑOL · FRANÇAIS · PORTUGUÊS

| Nombre / Nom / Nome | Página / Page | Lat.°′ | Long.°′ W = Oeste / Ouest |
|---|---|---|---|
| Corralito, Cuchilla del ⋏[2] | 258 | 33.40 S | 57.44 W |
| Corralitos, Méx. | 196 | 26.57 N | 104.39 W |
| Corralitos, Ca., U.S. | 226 | 36.59 N | 121.48 W |
| Corran | 46 | 56.43 N | 5.14 W |
| Corraun Peninsula ›[1] | 48 | 53.54 N | 9.53 W |
| Correas, Arroyo ≃ | 288 | 34.24 S | 58.32 W |
| Correboi, Arcu )( | 71 | 40.05 N | 9.21 E |
| Correctionville | 198 | 42.28 N | 95.47 W |
| Corredor | 287b | 23.27 S | 46.19 W |
| Correggio | 64 | 44.46 N | 10.47 E |
| Corregidor Island I | 116 | 14.23 N | 120.35 E |
| Corrego do Bom Jesus | 256 | 22.38 S | 46.02 W |
| Córrego do Ouro | 256 | 21.22 S | 45.47 W |
| Córrego Rico | 255 | 15.14 S | 47.48 W |
| Correia de Almeida | 256 | 21.17 S | 43.38 W |
| Corrente | 250 | 10.27 S | 45.10 W |
| Corrente ≃, Bra. | 255 | 19.19 S | 50.50 W |
| Corrente ≃, Bra. | 255 | 13.08 S | 43.28 W |
| Correntes | 250 | 9.08 S | 36.19 W |
| Correntes ≃ | 248 | 17.21 S | 55.37 W |
| Correntes, Cabo das › | 156 | 24.11 S | 35.34 E |
| Correnti, Isola delle I | 70 | 36.38 N | 15.05 E |
| Correntina | 255 | 13.20 S | 44.39 W |
| Corrèze □[5] | 32 | 45.20 N | 1.50 E |
| Correzzana | 266b | 45.40 N | 9.18 E |
| Corrib, Lough ⊜ | 48 | 53.26 N | 9.14 W |
| Corridonia | 66 | 43.15 N | 13.30 E |
| Corrientes | 252 | 27.28 S | 58.50 W |
| Corrientes □[4] | 252 | 29.00 S | 58.00 W |
| Corrientes ≃, Arg. | 252 | 30.21 S | 59.33 W |
| Corrientes ≃, S.A. | 246 | 3.43 S | 74.35 W |
| Corrientes, Bahía de ⊂ | 240p | 21.51 N | 84.36 W |
| Corrientes, Cabo ›, Arg. | 252 | 38.01 S | 57.32 W |
| Corrientes, Cabo ›, Col. | 246 | 5.30 N | 77.34 W |
| Corrientes, Cabo ›, Cuba | 240p | 21.45 N | 84.31 W |
| Corrientes, Cabo ›, Méx. | 234 | 20.25 N | 105.42 W |
| Corrigan | 222 | 30.59 N | 94.49 W |
| Corrigin | 162 | 32.21 S | 117.52 E |
| Corrimal | 170 | 34.22 S | 150.54 E |
| Corringham | 260 | 51.31 N | 0.28 E |
| Corriverton | 246 | 5.53 N | 57.08 W |
| Corrofin | 48 | 52.56 N | 9.03 W |
| Corroios | 266c | 38.38 N | 9.09 W |
| Corropoli | 66 | 42.49 N | 13.50 E |
| Corrumpa Creek ≃ | 196 | 36.36 N | 102.52 W |
| Corry | 214 | 41.55 N | 79.38 W |
| Corryong | 171b | 36.12 S | 147.54 E |
| Corryong Creek ≃ | 171b | 36.06 S | 147.59 E |
| Corryvreckan, Gulf of ʉ | 46 | 56.09 N | 5.44 W |
| Corsano | 68 | 39.53 N | 18.22 E |
| Corse (Corsica) I | 36 | 42.00 N | 9.00 E |
| Corse, Cap › | 36 | 43.00 N | 9.25 E |
| Corse-du-Sud □[5] | 36 | 41.50 N | 9.00 E |
| Corserine ∧ | 44 | 55.09 N | 4.22 W |
| Corsham | 42 | 51.26 N | 2.11 W |
| Corsica, Pa., U.S. | 214 | 41.10 N | 79.12 W |
| Corsica, S.D., U.S. | 198 | 43.25 N | 98.24 W |
| Corsica → Corse I | 36 | 42.00 N | 9.00 E |
| Corsicana | 222 | 32.05 N | 96.28 W |
| Corsica River ⊂ | 208 | 39.05 N | 76.08 W |
| Corsico | 62 | 45.26 N | 9.07 E |
| Corsock | 44 | 55.04 N | 3.57 W |
| Corson Inlet ⊂ | 208 | 39.12 N | 74.39 W |
| Cortaccia (Kurtatsch) | 64 | 46.19 N | 11.13 E |
| Cortachy | 46 | 56.43 N | 2.58 W |
| Cort Adelaer, Kap › | 176 | 62.00 N | 42.00 W |
| Cortale | 68 | 38.50 N | 16.25 E |
| Cortazar | 234 | 20.29 N | 100.56 W |
| Corte | 36 | 42.18 N | 9.08 E |
| Corte Alto | 254 | 40.57 S | 73.10 W |
| Cortegana | 34 | 37.55 N | 6.49 W |
| Corte Madera | 226 | 37.55 N | 122.31 W |
| Corte Madera Creek ≃ | 282 | 37.23 N | 122.14 W |
| Cortemaggiore | 64 | 44.59 N | 9.56 E |
| Cortemilia | 62 | 44.35 N | 8.12 E |
| Corteno Golgi | 64 | 46.10 N | 10.15 E |
| Cortes | 116 | 9.17 N | 126.11 E |
| Cortés □[5] | 236 | 15.30 N | 88.00 W |
| Cortes ʋ | 266a | 40.25 N | 3.41 W |
| Cortés, Bahía de ⊂ | 240p | 22.05 N | 83.52 W |
| Cortez, Co., U.S. | 200 | 37.20 N | 108.35 W |
| Cortez, Fl., U.S. | 220 | 27.28 N | 82.41 W |
| Cortez, Sea of → California, Golfo de ⊂ | 232 | 28.00 N | 112.00 W |
| Cortez Mountains ⋏ | 204 | 40.20 N | 116.20 W |
| Cortina Creek ≃ | 226 | 39.06 N | 122.02 W |
| Cortina d'Ampezzo | 64 | 46.32 N | 12.08 E |
| Cortines | 258 | 34.34 S | 59.13 W |
| Cortland, Il., U.S. | 216 | 41.55 N | 88.41 W |
| Cortland, In., U.S. | 218 | 38.58 N | 85.58 W |
| Cortland, Ne., U.S. | 198 | 40.30 N | 96.42 W |
| Cortland, N.Y., U.S. | 210 | 42.36 N | 76.10 W |
| Cortland, Oh., U.S. | 214 | 41.19 N | 80.43 W |
| Cortland □[6] | 210 | 42.36 N | 76.11 W |
| Corton | 42 | 52.32 N | 1.44 E |
| Cortona | 66 | 43.16 N | 11.59 E |
| Çorubal (Koliba) ≃ | 150 | 11.57 N | 15.06 W |
| Čoruch-Dajron | 85 | 40.24 N | 69.40 E |
| Coruche | 34 | 38.57 N | 8.31 W |
| Çoruh (Čoroch) ≃ | 130 | 41.36 N | 41.35 E |
| Çorum, Tür. | 130 | 39.14 N | 28.27 E |
| Çorum, Tür. | 130 | 40.33 N | 34.58 E |
| Çorum □[4] | 130 | 40.30 N | 34.40 E |
| Corumbá | 248 | 19.01 S | 57.39 W |
| Corumbá ≃ | 255 | 18.19 S | 48.55 W |
| Corumbá de Goiás | 255 | 15.55 S | 48.48 W |
| Corumbaíba | 255 | 18.09 S | 48.34 W |
| Corumbataí ≃ | 252 | 23.55 S | 51.57 W |
| Corumbaú, Ponta do › | 255 | 16.53 S | 39.06 W |
| Corumbiara ≃ | 248 | 13.13 S | 62.06 W |
| Corumo ≃ | 246 | 6.49 N | 60.52 W |
| Corund | 38 | 46.28 N | 25.11 E |
| Corunna, On., Can. | 214 | 42.53 N | 82.26 W |
| Corunna → La Coruña, Esp. | 34 | 43.22 N | 8.23 W |
| Corunna, In., U.S. | 216 | 41.26 N | 85.08 W |
| Corunna, Mi., U.S. | 216 | 42.58 N | 84.07 W |
| Corunna Downs | 162 | 21.28 S | 119.51 E |
| Coruripe | 250 | 10.08 S | 36.10 W |
| Corvallis, Mt., U.S. | 202 | 46.18 N | 114.06 W |
| Corvallis, Or., U.S. | 202 | 44.33 N | 123.15 W |
| Corvara in Badia | 64 | 46.33 N | 11.52 E |
| Corve Dale V | 42 | 52.30 N | 2.40 W |
| Corvey, Kloster ʋ[1] | 52 | 51.46 N | 9.25 E |
| Corviale -•[8] | 267a | 41.52 N | 12.25 E |
| Corvo I | 148a | 39.42 N | 31.06 W |
| Corwen | 42 | 52.59 N | 3.22 W |
| Corwin, Cape › | 180 | 59.54 N | 165.41 W |
| Corwith | 190 | 42.59 N | 93.57 W |
| Corydon, In., U.S. | 218 | 38.12 N | 86.07 W |
| Corydon, Ia., U.S. | 190 | 40.45 N | 93.19 W |
| Corydon, Ky., U.S. | 194 | 37.44 N | 87.42 W |
| Coryell | 222 | 31.33 N | 97.37 W |
| Coryell □[6] | 222 | 31.25 N | 97.40 W |
| Coryell Creek ≃ | 222 | 31.23 N | 97.35 W |
| Coryton | 260 | 51.31 N | 0.31 E |
| Coryville | 214 | 41.53 N | 78.24 W |
| Corzu | 38 | 44.28 N | 23.10 E |
| Corzuela | 252 | 26.57 S | 60.58 W |
| Cos → Kos I | 38 | 36.50 N | 27.10 E |
| Cosa (Ansedonia) ⊥ | 66 | 42.25 N | 11.18 E |
| Cosamaloapan [de Carpio] | 232 | 18.22 N | 95.48 W |
| Cosapa | 248 | 18.11 S | 68.40 W |
| Coscile ≃ | 68 | 39.42 N | 16.28 E |
| Cos Cob | 276 | 41.02 N | 73.36 W |
| Cos Cob Harbor ⊂ | 276 | 41.01 N | 73.36 W |
| Coscomatepec [de Bravo] | 234 | 19.04 N | 97.02 W |
| Coseley | 42 | 52.33 N | 2.06 W |
| Cosenza | 68 | 39.17 N | 16.15 E |
| Cosenza □[4] | 68 | 39.28 N | 16.25 E |
| Cosgroves Creek ≃ | 274a | 33.50 S | 150.46 E |
| Coshocton | 214 | 40.16 N | 81.51 W |
| Coshocton □[6] | 214 | 40.16 N | 81.51 W |
| Cosigüina, Punta › | 236 | 12.54 N | 87.41 W |
| Cosigüina, Volcán ∧[1] | 236 | 12.59 N | 87.34 W |
| Coslada | 266a | 40.26 N | 3.34 W |
| Cosmo -•[8] | 256 | 22.54 S | 43.37 W |
| Cosmoledo Island I | 138 | 9.43 S | 47.35 E |
| Cosmópolis, Bra. | 256 | 22.38 S | 47.12 W |
| Cosmopolis, Wa., U.S. | 224 | 46.57 N | 123.46 W |
| Cosmos | 198 | 44.56 N | 94.41 W |
| Cosmos -•[8] | 287a | 22.55 S | 44.37 W |
| Cosne-Cours-sur-Loire | 50 | 47.24 N | 2.55 E |
| Cosoleacaque | 234 | 18.00 N | 94.37 W |
| Cospán | 248 | 7.26 S | 78.33 W |
| Cosquín | 252 | 31.15 S | 64.29 W |
| Cossato | 62 | 45.34 N | 8.10 E |
| Cossatot ≃ | 194 | 33.48 N | 94.09 W |
| Cossayuna | 210 | 43.11 N | 73.26 W |
| Cossayuna Lake ⊜ | 210 | 43.12 N | 73.25 W |
| Cossebaude | 54 | 51.05 N | 13.38 E |
| Cossé-le-Vivien | 28 | 47.57 N | 0.55 W |
| Cossoine | 71 | 40.27 N | 8.43 E |
| Cosson ≃ | 50 | 47.30 N | 1.15 E |
| Cossonay | 58 | 46.37 N | 6.31 E |
| Cost | 222 | 29.26 N | 97.32 W |
| Costa, Cayo I | 220 | 26.41 N | 82.15 W |
| Costa, Cordillera de la ⋏ | 286c | 10.33 N | 66.52 W |
| Costa, Sierra de la → Coast Ranges ⋏ | 178 | 41.00 N | 123.30 W |
| Costacciaro | 66 | 43.21 N | 12.42 E |
| Costa de Caparica | 266c | 38.38 N | 9.14 W |
| Costa del Marfil → Cote d'Ivoire □[1] | 150 | 8.00 N | 5.00 W |
| Costa de San José | 258 | 33.51 S | 56.53 W |
| Costa di Rovigo | 64 | 45.03 N | 11.42 E |
| Costa Mesa | 228 | 33.38 N | 117.55 W |
| Costanera, Cadena → Coast Mountains ⋏ | 176 | 55.00 N | 129.00 W |
| Costanera Sur, Parque Natural ♦ | 288 | 34.37 S | 58.21 W |
| Costanero, Canal de ≊ | 288 | 34.28 S | 58.28 W |
| Costa Rica | 232 | 24.32 N | 107.18 W |
| Costa Rica □[1], N.A. | 230 | 10.00 N | 84.00 W |
| Costa Rica □[1], N.A. | 236 | 10.00 N | 84.00 W |
| Costaros | 62 | 44.54 N | 3.50 E |
| Costas | 256 | 22.39 S | 45.56 W |
| Costello | 214 | 41.36 N | 78.03 W |
| Costelloe | 48 | 53.17 N | 9.32 W |
| Costermansville → Bukavu | 154 | 2.30 S | 28.52 E |
| Costessey | 42 | 52.40 N | 1.11 E |
| Costeşti, Mol. | 38 | 46.52 N | 28.44 E |
| Costeşti, Rom. | 38 | 44.40 N | 24.53 E |
| Costiera, Catena ⋏ | 68 | 39.20 N | 16.05 E |
| Costigan Lake ⊜ | 184 | 56.56 N | 105.55 W |
| Costigliole d'Asti | 62 | 44.47 N | 8.11 E |
| Costigliole Saluzzo | 62 | 44.34 N | 7.29 E |
| Costilla | 200 | 36.58 N | 105.31 W |
| Costilla Creek ≃ | 200 | 36.59 N | 105.43 W |
| Cosumnes ≃ | 226 | 38.16 N | 121.26 W |
| Cosumnes, Middle Fork ≃ | 226 | 38.33 N | 120.51 W |
| Cosumnes, North Fork ≃ | 226 | 38.33 N | 120.51 W |
| Cosumnes, South Fork ≃ | 226 | 38.33 N | 120.49 W |
| Coswig, Dtsch. | 54 | 51.07 N | 13.34 E |
| Coswig, Dtsch. | 54 | 51.53 N | 12.26 E |
| Cotabambas | 248 | 13.45 S | 72.21 W |
| Cotabato | 116 | 7.13 N | 124.15 E |
| Cotacajes ≃ | 248 | 16.00 S | 67.01 W |
| Cotagaita | 248 | 20.50 S | 65.41 W |
| Cotagaita ≃ | 248 | 21.01 S | 65.23 W |
| Cotahuasi | 248 | 15.12 S | 72.56 W |
| Cotão ∧[2] | 266c | 38.45 N | 9.18 W |
| Cotati | 226 | 38.20 N | 122.42 W |
| Coteau-Landing | 206 | 45.15 N | 74.13 W |
| Coteau-Station | 206 | 45.17 N | 74.14 W |
| Coteaux | 238 | 18.12 N | 74.02 W |
| Cote d'Ivoire (Ivory Coast) □[1], Afr. | 134 | 8.00 N | 5.00 W |
| Cote d'Ivoire □[1], Afr. | 150 | 8.00 N | 5.00 W |
| Côte-d'Or □[5] | 32 | 47.30 N | 4.50 E |
| Cotegipe | 255 | 12.02 S | 44.15 W |
| Cote Indian Reserve -•[4] | 184 | 51.38 N | 101.53 W |
| Cotentin ›[1] | 32 | 49.30 N | 1.30 W |
| Côte-Saint-Luc | 275a | 45.28 N | 73.40 W |
| Côtes-d'Armor □[5] | 32 | 48.25 N | 2.40 W |
| Côte Visitation -•[8] | 275a | 45.33 N | 73.36 W |
| Cothi ≃ | 42 | 51.52 N | 4.10 W |
| Coti ≃ | 248 | 8.36 S | 65.33 W |
| Cotia | 256 | 23.37 S | 46.56 W |
| Cotia □[7] | 287b | 23.38 S | 46.56 W |
| Cotia ≃ | 256 | 23.31 S | 46.51 W |
| Cotia, Represa de ⊜[1] | 287b | 23.44 S | 46.57 W |
| Cotignac | 62 | 43.32 N | 6.09 E |
| Cotignola | 66 | 44.23 N | 11.56 E |
| Cotija de la Paz | 234 | 19.49 N | 102.43 W |
| Cotingo ≃ | 246 | 3.55 N | 60.30 W |
| Cotis, Laguna ⊜ | 258 | 35.11 S | 59.16 W |
| Cotiujeni | 38 | 47.51 N | 28.36 E |
| Cotmeana ≃ | 38 | 44.24 N | 24.45 E |
| Cotoca | 248 | 17.49 S | 63.03 W |
| Cotonou | 150 | 6.21 N | 2.26 E |
| Cotopaxi □[4] | 246 | 0.55 S | 78.55 W |
| Cotopaxi ∧[1] | 246 | 0.40 S | 78.26 W |
| Cotopaxi, Parque Nacional ♦ | 246 | 0.15 S | 78.25 W |
| Cotorra, Isla I | 241r | 10.02 N | 62.16 W |
| Cotorro -•[8] | 286b | 23.03 N | 82.16 W |
| Cotronei | 68 | 39.09 N | 16.47 E |
| Cotswold Hills ⋏[2] | 42 | 51.45 N | 2.10 W |
| Cottage Grove, In., U.S. | 218 | 39.36 N | 84.52 W |
| Cottage Grove, Or., U.S. | 202 | 43.47 N | 123.03 W |
| Cottage Grove, Wi., U.S. | 216 | 43.05 N | 89.12 W |
| Cottage Hills | 219 | 38.55 N | 90.04 W |
| Cottageville | 192 | 32.56 N | 80.28 W |
| Cottam, On., Can. | 214 | 42.08 N | 82.45 W |
| Cottam, Eng., U.K. | 262 | 53.47 N | 2.46 W |
| Cottanello | 66 | 42.24 N | 12.41 E |
| Cottbus | 54 | 51.45 N | 14.19 E |
| Cottekill | 210 | 41.51 N | 74.06 W |
| Cottel Island I | 186 | 48.51 N | 53.42 W |
| Cottenham | 42 | 52.18 N | 0.09 E |
| Cotter | 194 | 36.16 N | 92.32 W |
| Cotter ≃ | 171b | 35.19 S | 148.57 E |
| Cottesloe | 168a | 31.59 S | 115.45 E |
| Cottiennes, Alpes (Alpi Cozie) ⋏ | 62 | 44.45 N | 7.00 E |
| Cottingham | 44 | 53.47 N | 0.24 W |
| Cottleville | 219 | 38.44 N | 90.39 W |
| Cottondale, Al., U.S. | 194 | 33.11 N | 87.27 W |
| Cottondale, Fl., U.S. | 192 | 30.47 N | 85.22 W |
| Cotton Lake ⊜, Mb., Can. | 184 | 55.05 N | 96.50 W |
| Cotton Lake ⊜, Tx., U.S. | 222 | 29.48 N | 94.48 W |
| Cotton Plant | 194 | 35.00 N | 91.15 W |
| Cottonport | 194 | 30.59 N | 92.03 W |
| Cotton Valley | 194 | 32.49 N | 93.25 W |
| Cottonwood, Az., U.S. | 200 | 34.44 N | 112.00 W |
| Cottonwood, Ca., U.S. | 204 | 40.23 N | 122.16 W |
| Cottonwood, Id., U.S. | 202 | 46.02 N | 116.20 W |
| Cottonwood, Mn., U.S. | 198 | 44.36 N | 95.40 W |
| Cottonwood ≃, Ks., U.S. | 198 | 38.23 N | 96.03 W |
| Cottonwood ≃, Mn. U.S. | 198 | 44.17 N | 94.25 W |
| Cottonwood Creek ≃, Ca., U.S. | 226 | 36.52 N | 120.12 W |
| Cottonwood Creek ≃, Ca., U.S. | 226 | 36.27 N | 119.20 W |
| Cottonwood Creek ≃, Mt., U.S. | 202 | 48.33 N | 107.45 W |
| Cottonwood Creek ≃, N.D., U.S. | 198 | 46.16 N | 98.15 W |
| Cottonwood Creek ≃, Ok., U.S. | 196 | 35.54 N | 97.27 W |
| Cottonwood Creek ≃, Or., U.S. | 202 | 43.53 N | 117.43 W |
| Cottonwood Creek ≃, Tx., U.S. | 196 | 32.48 N | 100.21 W |
| Cottonwood Creek ≃, Tx., U.S. | 196 | 31.23 N | 103.46 W |
| Cottonwood Creek ≃, Ut,. U.S. | 200 | 39.09 N | 110.55 W |
| Cottonwood Creek ≃, Wy., U.S. | 202 | 43.51 N | 108.09 W |
| Cottonwood Creek, Middle Fork ≃ | 204 | 40.23 N | 122.20 W |
| Cottonwood Creek, South Fork ≃ | 204 | 40.23 N | 122.20 W |
| Cottonwood Falls | 198 | 38.22 N | 96.32 W |
| Cottonwood Wash V, Az., U.S. | 200 | 35.00 N | 110.39 W |
| Cottonwood Wash V, Az., U.S. | 200 | 36.19 N | 113.59 W |
| Cotubandê | 287a | 22.51 S | 43.01 W |
| Cotuhé ≃ | 246 | 2.53 S | 69.44 W |
| Cotui | 238 | 19.03 N | 70.09 W |
| Cotuit | 207 | 41.37 N | 70.26 W |
| Cotulla | 196 | 28.26 N | 99.14 W |
| Cotunduba, Ilha de I | 287a | 22.58 S | 43.09 W |
| Coubert | 261 | 48.40 N | 2.42 E |
| Coubre, Pointe de la › | 32 | 45.41 N | 1.13 W |
| Coubron | 261 | 48.55 N | 2.35 E |
| Couches-les-Mines | 58 | 46.52 N | 4.34 E |
| Couchiching, Lake ⊜ | 212 | 44.40 N | 79.23 W |
| Coucouron | 62 | 44.48 N | 3.58 E |
| Coucy-le-Château-Auffrique | 50 | 49.31 N | 3.19 E |
| Coudekerque-Branche | 50 | 51.02 N | 2.24 E |
| Coudersport | 214 | 41.46 N | 78.01 W |
| Coudres, Île aux I | 186 | 47.24 N | 70.23 W |
| Couesnon ≃ | 32 | 48.37 N | 1.31 W |
| Cougar | 224 | 46.03 N | 122.17 W |
| Cougar Reservoir ⊜[1] | 202 | 44.06 N | 122.12 W |
| Couhé | 32 | 46.18 N | 0.11 E |
| Couillet | 50 | 50.23 N | 4.27 E |
| Couilly-Pont-aux-Dames | 261 | 48.53 N | 2.52 E |
| Coulanges-la-Vineuse | 50 | 47.42 N | 3.35 E |
| Coulanges-sur-Yonne | 50 | 47.31 N | 3.32 E |
| Coulee City | 202 | 47.36 N | 119.17 W |
| Coulee Dam | 202 | 47.57 N | 118.58 W |
| Coulee Dam National Recreation Area ♦ | 202 | 48.10 N | 118.15 W |
| Coulihaut | 240d | 15.30 N | 61.29 W |
| Coulman Island I | 9 | 73.27 S | 169.40 E |
| Coulmier-le-Sec | 58 | 47.45 N | 4.29 E |
| Coulogne | 50 | 50.55 N | 1.53 E |
| Coulomby | 50 | 50.42 N | 2.00 E |
| Coulommiers | 50 | 48.49 N | 3.05 E |
| Coulon ≃ | 62 | 43.51 N | 5.00 E |
| Coulonge ≃ | 190 | 45.51 N | 76.46 W |
| Coulonge Est ≃ | 190 | 46.06 N | 76.44 W |
| Coulsdon -•[8] | 260 | 51.19 N | 0.08 W |
| Coulta | 166 | 34.23 S | 135.29 E |
| Coulters | 279b | 40.18 N | 79.48 W |
| Coulterville, Ca., U.S. | 226 | 37.42 N | 120.11 W |
| Coulterville, Il., U.S. | 194 | 38.11 N | 89.36 W |
| Counce | 194 | 35.02 N | 88.16 W |
| Council | 202 | 44.44 N | 116.26 W |
| Council Bluffs | 198 | 41.15 N | 95.51 W |
| Council Grove | 198 | 38.39 N | 96.29 W |
| Council Grove Lake ⊜[1] | 198 | 38.42 N | 96.31 W |
| Coundon | 44 | 54.40 N | 1.39 W |
| Countegany | 171b | 36.11 S | 149.27 E |
| Countesthorpe | 42 | 52.33 N | 1.08 W |
| Country Campus | 222 | 30.49 N | 95.26 W |
| Country Club Estates | 220 | 28.03 N | 81.57 W |
| Country Club Hills | 278 | 41.34 N | 87.43 W |
| Country Club View | 284c | 38.49 N | 77.19 W |
| Country Hills | 279b | 40.19 N | 79.42 W |
| Country Homes | 202 | 47.44 N | 117.24 W |
| Country Ridge Estates | 276 | 41.02 N | 73.41 W |
| Countryside | 278 | 41.46 N | 87.52 W |
| Countryside Lake ⊜ | 278 | 42.15 N | 88.03 W |
| Countryside Manor | 278 | 42.18 N | 87.56 W |
| Coupar Angus | 46 | 56.33 N | 3.17 W |
| Coupeville | 224 | 48.13 N | 122.41 W |
| Coupland | 222 | 30.28 N | 97.24 W |
| Coupon | 214 | 40.32 N | 78.31 W |
| Coupvray | 261 | 48.54 N | 2.48 E |
| Courbevoie | 50 | 48.54 N | 2.15 E |
| Courbons | 62 | 44.06 N | 6.12 E |
| Courçay | 50 | 47.15 N | 0.52 E |
| Courcelle | 261 | 48.42 N | 2.06 E |
| Courcelles, Bel. | 50 | 50.28 N | 4.22 E |
| Courcelles, Fr. | 261 | 49.07 N | 2.18 E |
| Courcelles-Chaussy | 56 | 49.07 N | 6.24 E |
| Courcelles-sur-Nied | 56 | 49.04 N | 6.18 E |
| Courchevel | 62 | 45.25 N | 6.38 E |
| Cour-Cheverny | 50 | 47.30 N | 1.27 E |
| Courcibo ≃ | 250 | 4.53 N | 53.00 W |
| Courçon | 32 | 46.15 N | 0.49 W |
| Courcouronnes | 261 | 48.37 N | 2.24 E |
| Courdimanche | 261 | 49.02 N | 2.00 E |
| Cour-et-Buis | 62 | 45.26 N | 5.00 E |
| Courgent, Fr. | 261 | 48.54 N | 1.40 E |
| Courgent, Fr. | 261 | 49.04 N | 1.35 E |
| Courland → Kurzeme □[9] | 76 | 56.50 N | 22.30 E |
| Courmayeur | 62 | 45.47 N | 6.58 E |
| Couronne, Cap › | 62 | 43.19 N | 5.03 E |
| Couronnement, Île du → Coronation Island I | 9 | 60.37 S | 45.30 W |
| Courpière | 62 | 45.45 N | 3.33 E |
| Courquetaine | 261 | 48.41 N | 2.45 E |
| Course Brook ≃ | 283 | 42.17 N | 71.22 W |
| Courseulles | 28 | 49.20 N | 0.27 W |
| Courson-les-Carrières | 50 | 47.36 N | 3.30 E |
| Court | 58 | 47.14 N | 7.20 E |
| Courtacon | 50 | 48.42 N | 3.17 E |
| Courtalain | 50 | 48.05 N | 1.09 E |
| Courteilles | 50 | 48.58 N | 0.29 E |
| Courtenay, B.C., Can. | 182 | 49.41 N | 125.00 W |
| Courtenay, Fr. | 50 | 48.02 N | 3.03 E |
| Courthézon | 62 | 44.05 N | 4.53 E |
| Courtice | 212 | 43.55 N | 78.46 W |
| Courtisols | 56 | 48.59 N | 4.31 E |
| Courtland, On., Can. | 212 | 42.51 N | 80.38 W |
| Courtland, Al., U.S. | 194 | 34.40 N | 87.18 W |
| Courtland, Ca., U.S. | 226 | 38.20 N | 121.34 W |
| Courtland, Va., U.S. | 208 | 36.42 N | 77.04 W |
| Courtleigh | 284b | 39.22 N | 76.46 W |
| Courtmacsherry | 48 | 51.38 N | 8.43 W |
| Courtmacsherry Bay ⊂ | 48 | 51.35 N | 8.40 W |
| Courtney, Pa., U.S. | 279b | 40.13 N | 79.58 W |
| Courtney, Tx., U.S. | 222 | 30.16 N | 96.04 W |
| Courtney Creek ≃ | 196 | 31.16 N | 102.50 W |
| Courtomer, Fr. | 50 | 48.38 N | 0.22 E |
| Courtomer, Fr. | 261 | 48.39 N | 2.54 E |
| Courtown | 48 | 52.38 N | 6.13 W |
| Courtrai → Kortrijk | 50 | 50.50 N | 3.16 E |
| Courtright | 214 | 42.49 N | 82.28 W |
| Courtry, Fr. | 261 | 48.33 N | 2.46 E |
| Courtry, Fr. | 261 | 48.55 N | 2.36 E |
| Court-Saint-Étienne | 50 | 50.39 N | 4.34 E |
| Courville-sur-Eure | 50 | 48.27 N | 1.15 E |
| Coushatta | 194 | 32.00 N | 93.20 W |
| Cousin ≃ | 50 | 47.32 N | 3.46 E |
| Cousiño Macul, Parque ♦ | 286e | 33.30 S | 70.35 W |
| Cousolre | 50 | 50.15 N | 4.09 E |
| Coussegrey | 50 | 47.57 N | 4.01 E |
| Coussey | 58 | 48.25 N | 5.41 E |
| Coustellet | 62 | 43.53 N | 5.11 E |
| Coutances | 32 | 49.03 N | 1.26 W |
| Coutevroult | 261 | 48.52 N | 2.51 E |
| Couto do Magalhães | 250 | 8.17 S | 49.16 W |
| Couto Magalhães ≃ | 255 | 13.37 S | 53.09 W |
| Coutras | 32 | 45.02 N | 0.08 W |
| Coutts | 182 | 49.00 N | 111.57 W |
| Couture, Lac ⊜ | 176 | 60.07 N | 75.20 W |
| Couture-sur-Loir | 50 | 47.45 N | 0.41 E |
| Couves, Ilha das I | 256 | 23.25 S | 44.52 W |
| Couvet | 58 | 46.56 N | 6.38 E |
| Couvin | 50 | 50.03 N | 4.29 E |
| Cova da Piedade | 266c | 38.40 N | 9.10 W |
| Covane | 156 | 21.22 S | 33.56 E |
| Covasna | 38 | 45.51 N | 26.11 E |
| Covasna □[6] | 38 | 46.00 N | 26.00 E |
| Cove, Scot., U.K. | 46 | 57.51 N | 5.42 W |
| Cove, Or., U.S. | 202 | 45.17 N | 117.48 W |
| Cove Bay | 46 | 57.06 N | 2.04 W |
| Covedale | 218 | 39.07 N | 84.36 W |
| Cove Harbor ⊂ | 276 | 41.03 N | 73.30 W |
| Cove Island I | 190 | 45.17 N | 81.44 W |
| Covelo, Ang. | 152 | 12.06 S | 13.55 E |
| Covelo, Ca., U.S. | 204 | 39.47 N | 123.14 W |
| Cove Neck | 276 | 40.53 N | 73.31 W |
| Cove Neck ›[1] | 276 | 40.53 N | 73.30 W |
| Coventry, Eng., U.K. | 42 | 52.25 N | 1.30 W |
| Coventry, Ct., U.S. | 207 | 41.46 N | 72.18 W |
| Coventry, De., U.S. | 285 | 39.40 N | 75.38 W |
| Coventry, R.I., U.S. | 207 | 41.41 N | 71.34 W |
| Coventry Cathedral ʋ[1] | 42 | 52.25 N | 1.30 W |
| Coventryville | 285 | 40.10 N | 75.41 W |
| Cove Palisades State Park ♦ | 202 | 44.34 N | 121.15 W |
| Cove Point | 208 | 38.22 N | 76.23 W |
| Cove Point › | 208 | 38.23 N | 76.23 W |
| Cover ≃ | 44 | 54.17 N | 1.46 W |
| Covered Wells | 200 | 31.48 N | 111.59 W |
| Covert | 216 | 42.17 N | 86.15 W |
| Covigliaio | 66 | 44.08 N | 11.18 E |
| Covilhã | 34 | 40.17 N | 7.30 W |
| Covina | 228 | 34.05 N | 117.53 W |
| Covington, Ga., U.S. | 192 | 33.35 N | 83.51 W |
| Covington, In., U.S. | 194 | 40.08 N | 87.23 W |
| Covington, Ky., U.S. | 218 | 39.05 N | 84.30 W |
| Covington, La., U.S. | 194 | 30.28 N | 90.06 W |
| Covington, Oh., U.S. | 218 | 40.07 N | 84.21 W |
| Covington, Ok., U.S. | 196 | 36.18 N | 97.35 W |
| Covington, Pa., U.S. | 210 | 41.45 N | 77.05 W |
| Covington, Tn., U.S. | 194 | 35.33 N | 89.38 W |
| Covington, Tx., U.S. | 222 | 32.11 N | 97.16 W |
| Covington, Va., U.S. | 192 | 37.47 N | 79.59 W |
| Covões | 266c | 38.50 N | 9.20 W |
| Covunco, Arroyo ≃ | 252 | 38.29 S | 69.32 W |
| Cow ≃ | 190 | 47.23 N | 83.59 W |
| Cowal ›[1] | 46 | 56.05 N | 5.08 W |
| Cowal, Lake ⊜ | 166 | 33.35 S | 147.25 E |
| Cowan, Ky., U.S. | 218 | 38.24 N | 83.54 W |
| Cowan, Tn., U.S. | 194 | 35.09 N | 86.00 W |
| Cowan, Lake ⊜ | 162 | 31.50 S | 121.50 E |
| Cowan Creek ≃ | 274a | 33.40 S | 151.10 E |
| Cowanesque | 210 | 41.56 N | 77.30 W |
| Cowanesque ≃ | 210 | 42.00 N | 77.07 W |
| Cowan Heights | 280 | 33.47 N | 117.47 W |
| Cowan Lake ⊜, Sk., Can. | 184 | 54.00 N | 107.15 W |
| Cowan Lake ⊜, Oh., U.S. | 218 | 39.23 N | 83.54 W |
| Cowan Lake State Park ♦ | 218 | 39.23 N | 83.53 W |
| Cowansburg | 279b | 40.15 N | 79.46 W |
| Cowanshannock Creek ≃ | 214 | 40.51 N | 79.30 W |
| Cowansville, P.Q., Can. | 206 | 45.12 N | 72.45 W |
| Cowansville, Pa., U.S. | 214 | 40.53 N | 79.36 W |
| Cowaramup | 162 | 33.52 S | 115.05 E |
| Coward | 192 | 33.58 N | 79.44 W |
| Coward Springs | 166 | 29.24 S | 136.49 E |
| Cowarie | 166 | 27.43 S | 138.20 E |
| Cow Bayou ≃ | 222 | 31.19 N | 97.00 W |
| Cowbridge | 42 | 51.28 N | 3.27 W |
| Cowburn Tunnel -•[5] | 262 | 53.21 N | 1.52 W |
| Cow Canyon V | 280 | 34.01 N | 120.06 W |
| Cowcowing Lakes ⊜ | 162 | 31.01 S | 117.18 E |
| Cow Creek ≃, Ks., U.S. | 198 | 38.02 N | 97.56 W |
| Cow Creek ≃, Mt., U.S. | 202 | 47.47 N | 108.56 W |
| Cow Creek ≃, Ok., U.S. | 196 | 34.10 N | 98.00 W |
| Cow Creek ≃, Or., U.S. | 202 | 42.57 N | 123.20 W |
| Cow Creek ≃, Wa., U.S. | 202 | 46.45 N | 118.09 W |
| Cowden, Il., U.S. | 219 | 39.15 N | 88.52 W |
| Cowden, Pa., U.S. | 279b | 40.19 N | 80.13 W |
| Cowdenbeath | 46 | 56.07 N | 3.21 W |
| Coweeman ≃ | 224 | 46.06 N | 122.52 W |
| Cowell | 166 | 33.41 S | 136.55 E |
| Cowen | 188 | 38.24 N | 80.33 W |
| Cowen, Mount ∧ | 202 | 45.23 N | 110.29 W |
| Cowes, Austl. | 169 | 38.27 S | 145.14 E |
| Cowes, Eng., U.K. | 42 | 50.45 N | 1.18 W |
| Cowessess Indian Reserve -•[4] | 184 | 50.31 N | 102.42 W |
| Coweta | 196 | 35.57 N | 95.39 W |
| Cow Green Reservoir ⊜[1] | 44 | 54.40 N | 2.18 W |
| Cow Gulch ≃ | 202 | 46.02 N | 107.52 W |
| Cow Head | 186 | 49.55 N | 57.48 W |
| Cowhouse Creek ≃ | 222 | 31.10 N | 97.35 W |
| Cowichan ≃ | 224 | 48.46 N | 123.38 W |
| Cowichan Bay | 224 | 48.44 N | 123.40 W |
| Cowichan Lake ⊜ | 224 | 48.54 N | 124.20 W |
| Cowiche Creek, North Fork ≃ | 224 | 46.38 N | 120.41 W |
| Cowiche Creek, South Fork ≃ | 224 | 46.38 N | 120.41 W |
| Cowie Water ≃ | 46 | 56.58 N | 2.12 W |
| Cowles Dam ⊜[1] | 273d | 26.13 S | 28.28 E |
| Cowlesville | 210 | 42.51 N | 78.28 W |
| Cowley, Austl. | 166 | 26.54 S | 144.49 E |
| Cowley, Ab., Can. | 182 | 49.34 N | 114.05 W |
| Cowley, Eng., U.K. | 42 | 51.43 N | 1.12 W |
| Cowley, Wy., U.S. | 202 | 44.53 N | 108.28 W |
| Cowley -•[8] | 260 | 51.32 N | 0.29 W |
| Cowley, Mount ∧ | 169 | 38.33 S | 143.52 E |
| Cowlitz □[6] | 224 | 46.07 N | 122.43 W |
| Cowlitz ≃ | 224 | 46.05 N | 122.53 W |
| Cowm Reservoir ⊜[1] | 262 | 53.40 N | 2.11 W |
| Cow Palace ʋ | 282 | 37.42 N | 122.25 W |
| Cowpasture ≃ | 188 | 37.48 N | 79.45 W |
| Cowpens | 192 | 35.01 N | 81.48 W |
| Cowpens National Battlefield ♦ | 192 | 35.06 N | 81.46 W |
| Cowra | 166 | 33.50 S | 148.41 E |
| Cox ≃ | 164 | 15.19 S | 135.25 E |
| Cox, Mount ∧[2] | 162 | 24.55 S | 125.36 E |
| Coxá ≃ | 255 | 14.16 S | 44.11 W |
| Cox Creek ≃ | 212 | 43.35 N | 80.29 W |
| Coxheath | 42 | 51.14 N | 0.30 E |
| Coxim | 255 | 18.30 S | 54.45 W |
| Coxim ≃ | 255 | 18.34 S | 54.46 W |
| Coxipi, Lac ⊜ | 186 | 51.33 N | 58.25 W |
| Coxquihui | 234 | 20.11 N | 97.35 W |
| Cox River Aboriginal Reserve -•[4] | 164 | 15.40 S | 134.45 E |
| Coxs ≃ | 170 | 33.57 S | 150.25 E |
| Coxsackie | 210 | 42.21 N | 73.48 W |
| Cox's Bāzār | 120 | 21.26 N | 91.59 E |
| Cox's Cove | 186 | 49.07 N | 58.05 W |
| Coyaguaima, Cerro ∧ | 252 | 22.55 S | 66.35 W |
| Coyah | 150 | 9.43 N | 13.23 W |
| Coyame | 232 | 29.28 N | 105.06 W |
| Coyanosa Draw V | 196 | 31.18 N | 103.06 W |
| Coya Sur | 252 | 22.25 S | 69.38 W |
| Coyle, Water of ≃ | 44 | 55.28 N | 4.32 W |
| Coyoacán -•[8] | 286a | 19.20 N | 99.10 W |
| Coyote Creek ≃, Ca., U.S. | 204 | 33.13 N | 116.13 W |
| Coyote Creek ≃, Ca., U.S. | 226 | 37.28 N | 122.03 W |
| Coyote Creek ≃, Ca., U.S. | 280 | 33.47 N | 118.05 W |
| Coyote Creek, East Fork ≃ | 226 | 37.10 N | 121.30 W |
| Coyote Creek, Middle Fork ≃ | 226 | 37.10 N | 121.30 W |
| Coyote Hills ⋏[2] | 282 | 37.33 N | 122.05 W |
| Coyote Hills Regional Park ♦ | 282 | 37.33 N | 122.06 W |
| Coyote Lake ⊜ | 204 | 35.04 N | 116.45 W |
| Coyote Lake ⊜[1] | 226 | 37.06 N | 121.32 W |
| Coyotepec | 234 | 19.46 N | 99.12 W |
| Coyote Point › | 282 | 37.35 N | 122.19 W |
| Coyote Wash V, Az., U.S. | 200 | 32.40 N | 114.08 W |
| Coyote Wash V, N.M., U.S. | 200 | 36.11 N | 108.33 W |
| Coy Pond ⊜ | 283 | 42.36 N | 70.49 W |
| Coyuca de Benítez | 234 | 17.02 N | 100.04 W |
| Coyuca de Catalán | 234 | 18.20 N | 100.39 W |
| Coyutla | 234 | 20.15 N | 97.39 W |
| Cozad | 198 | 40.51 N | 99.59 W |
| Cozes | 32 | 45.35 N | 0.50 W |
| Cozie, Alpi (Alpes Cottiennes) ⋏ | 62 | 44.45 N | 7.00 E |
| Cozoyoapan | 234 | 16.46 N | 98.15 W |
| Cozumel | 232 | 20.31 N | 86.55 W |
| Cozumel, Isla I | 232 | 20.25 N | 86.55 W |
| Cozy Lake | 276 | 41.01 N | 74.30 W |
| Crab Alley Bay ⊂ | 208 | 38.55 N | 76.17 W |
| Crab Creek ≃ | 202 | 46.49 N | 119.55 W |
| Crab Meadow ≡ | 276 | 40.55 N | 73.20 W |
| Crab Orchard, Ky., U.S. | 192 | 37.27 N | 84.30 W |
| Crab Orchard, Tn., U.S. | 192 | 35.54 N | 84.52 W |
| Crab Orchard Lake ⊜[1] | 194 | 37.43 N | 89.05 W |
| Crabtree | 214 | 40.21 N | 79.28 W |
| Crabtree Creek ≃ | 279b | 40.21 N | 79.30 W |
| Crabtree Mills | 206 | 45.58 N | 73.28 W |
| Craches | 261 | 48.34 N | 1.49 E |
| Crackenback ≃ | 171b | 36.21 S | 148.36 E |
| Craco | 68 | 40.23 N | 16.26 E |
| Cracovia → Kraków | 30 | 50.03 N | 19.58 E |
| Cracovie → Kraków | 30 | 50.03 N | 19.58 E |
| Cradle Mountain-Lake Saint Clair National Park ♦ | 166 | 42.00 S | 146.00 E |
| Cradock, Austl. | 166 | 32.04 S | 138.30 E |
| Cradock, S. Afr. | 158 | 32.08 S | 25.36 E |
| Cradock Channel ʉ | 172 | 36.11 S | 175.15 E |
| Crafers | 168b | 35.01 S | 138.47 E |
| Crafton | 214 | 40.26 N | 80.03 W |
| Crafts Creek ≃ | 285 | 40.07 N | 74.46 W |
| Cragg Vale | 262 | 53.42 N | 2.00 W |
| Cragsmoor | 210 | 41.40 N | 74.23 W |
| Crai | 42 | 51.55 N | 3.36 W |
| Craig, B.C., Can. | 224 | 49.18 N | 124.15 W |
| Craig, Ak., U.S. | 182 | 55.29 N | 133.09 W |
| Craig, Co., U.S. | 200 | 40.30 N | 107.32 W |
| Craig, Mo., U.S. | 194 | 40.11 N | 95.22 W |
| Craig, Ne., U.S. | 198 | 41.47 N | 96.21 W |
| Craig, Point ∧ | 162 | 26.51 S | 126.19 E |
| Craigavon | 48 | 54.27 N | 6.24 W |
| Craig Beach | 214 | 41.07 N | 81.01 W |
| Craig Creek ≃ | 192 | 37.39 N | 79.49 W |
| Craigellachie | 182 | 50.59 N | 118.43 W |
| Craighall -•[8] | 273d | 26.07 S | 28.02 E |
| Craighall Park -•[8] | 273d | 26.08 S | 28.01 E |
| Craighouse | 46 | 55.51 N | 5.57 W |
| Craigmont | 202 | 46.14 N | 116.27 W |
| Craigmyle | 182 | 51.40 N | 112.15 W |
| Craignish Point › | 46 | 56.07 N | 5.37 W |
| Craignure | 46 | 56.28 N | 5.42 W |
| Craigsville, Pa., U.S. | 214 | 40.51 N | 79.39 W |
| Craigsville, Va., U.S. | 192 | 38.04 N | 79.23 W |
| Craigville | 216 | 40.47 N | 85.06 W |
| Craik | 184 | 51.03 N | 105.49 W |
| Crail | 46 | 56.16 N | 2.38 W |
| Crailsheim | 56 | 49.08 N | 10.04 E |
| Craiova | 38 | 44.19 N | 23.48 E |
| Crake ≃ | 44 | 54.14 N | 3.03 W |
| Craley | 208 | 39.57 N | 76.31 W |
| Cramant | 50 | 48.59 N | 3.59 E |
| Cramlington | 44 | 55.05 N | 1.36 W |
| Cranage | 262 | 53.12 N | 2.22 W |
| Cranberry | 214 | 41.21 N | 79.43 W |
| Cranberry Brook ≃ | 283 | 42.11 N | 71.01 W |
| Cranberry Creek | 210 | 43.09 N | 74.14 W |
| Cranberry Island I | 212 | 44.44 N | 81.18 W |
| Cranberry Lake | 210 | 40.57 N | 74.44 W |
| Cranberry Lake ⊜, On., Can. | 212 | 44.26 N | 76.19 W |
| Cranberry Lake ⊜, On., Can. | 212 | 44.47 N | 75.50 W |
| Cranberry Lake ⊜, N.Y., U.S. | 188 | 44.10 N | 74.50 W |
| Cranberry Lake ⊜, Wa., U.S. | 224 | 47.17 N | 123.05 W |
| Cranberry Mountain ∧ | 182 | 50.42 N | 118.12 W |
| Cranberry Pond ⊜ | 276 | 41.08 N | 74.12 W |
| Cranberry Portage | 184 | 54.35 N | 101.23 W |
| Cranborne Chase -•[3] | 42 | 50.55 N | 2.05 W |
| Cranbourne | 169 | 38.06 S | 145.17 E |
| Cranbrook, Austl. | 162 | 34.18 S | 117.32 E |
| Cranbrook, B.C., Can. | 182 | 49.31 N | 115.46 W |
| Cranbrook, Eng., U.K. | 42 | 51.06 N | 0.33 E |
| Cranbrook Academy of Art ʋ | 281 | 42.34 N | 83.14 W |
| Cranbury | 276 | 40.18 N | 74.30 W |
| Cranbury Brook ≃ | 276 | 40.19 N | 74.37 W |
| Crandall | 222 | 32.37 N | 96.27 W |
| Crandon | 190 | 45.34 N | 88.54 W |
| Crandon Lakes | 210 | 41.07 N | 74.50 W |
| Crane, Az., U.S. | 204 | 32.42 N | 114.40 W |
| Crane, In., U.S. | 194 | 38.53 N | 86.54 W |
| Crane, Mo., U.S. | 194 | 36.54 N | 93.34 W |
| Crane, Tx., U.S. | 196 | 31.23 N | 102.20 W |
| Crane Beach ⊥[2] | 283 | 42.41 N | 70.46 W |
| Cranebrook | 274a | 33.43 S | 150.42 E |
| Crane Creek ≃ | 190 | 43.01 N | 91.58 W |
| Crane Lake ⊜, On., Can. | 212 | 45.13 N | 79.57 W |
| Crane Lake ⊜, Sk., Can. | 184 | 50.06 N | 109.06 W |
| Crane Mountain ∧ | 202 | 42.04 N | 120.13 W |
| Crane Neck Point › | 210 | 40.58 N | 73.10 W |
| Crane River Indian Reserve -•[4] | 184 | 51.30 N | 99.14 W |
| Cranesville | 214 | 41.54 N | 80.21 W |
| Cranfield | 42 | 52.05 N | 0.35 W |
| Cranfills Gap | 222 | 31.46 N | 97.50 W |
| Cranford | 210 | 40.39 N | 74.19 W |
| Crange -•[8] | 263 | 51.32 N | 7.11 E |
| Crângeni | 38 | 44.01 N | 24.47 E |
| Cran-Gévrier | 58 | 45.54 N | 6.0[illegible] E |
| Crank | 262 | 53.29 N | 2.4[illegible] W |
| Cranleigh | 42 | 51.09 N | 0.3[illegible] W |
| Crans | 58 | 46.19 N | 7.2[illegible] E |
| Cranston | 207 | 41.46 N | 71.26 W |
| Cranston Heights | 285 | 39.38 N | 75.38 W |
| Craon | 32 | 47.51 N | 0.57 W |
| Craonne | 50 | 49.26 N | 3.47 E |
| Craponne, Fr. | 62 | 45.44 N | 4.43 E |
| Craponne, Fr. | 62 | 45.20 N | 3.51 E |
| Craponne, Canal de ≊ | 62 | 43.40 N | 4.39 E |
| Craryville | 210 | 42.11 N | 73.35 W |
| Crasna, Rom. | 38 | 46.31 N | 27.51 E |
| Crasna, Rom. | 38 | 45.36 N | 26.08 E |
| Crasna (Kraszna) ≃ | 38 | 48.09 N | 22.20 |
| Crasnoe | 38 | 46.38 N | 29.50 |
| Crassier | 58 | 46.22 N | 6.11 E |
| Crater Lake ⊜ | 202 | 42.56 N | 122.06 W |
| Crater Lake National Park ♦ | 202 | 42.49 N | 122.08 W |
| Crater Mount ∧ | 164 | 6.30 S | 145.10 E |
| Crater Point › | 164 | 5.22 S | 152.09 E |
| Craters of the Moon National Monument ♦ | 202 | 43.20 N | 113.35 W |
| Crateús | 250 | 5.10 S | 40.40 W |
| Crathie | 46 | 57.02 N | 3.12 W |
| Crati ≃ | 68 | 39.43 N | 16.31 E |
| Crato | 250 | 7.14 S | 39.23 W |
| Crau -•[1] | 62 | 43.36 N | 4.50 E |
| Crauford, Cape › | 176 | 73.43 N | 84.50 W |
| Craughwell | 48 | 53.13 N | 8.43 W |
| Cravant | 50 | 47.41 N | 3.41 E |
| Cravari ≃ | 248 | 12.06 S | 58.03 W |
| Cravat | 219 | 38.25 N | 89.06 W |
| Craven | 184 | 50.39 N | 104.50 W |
| Craven Arms | 42 | 52.26 N | 2.50 W |
| Cravensville | 171b | 36.24 S | 147.34 E |
| Cravo Norte | 246 | 6.18 N | 70.12 W |
| Cravo Norte ≃ | 246 | 6.18 N | 70.12 W |
| Cravo Sur ≃ | 246 | 4.42 N | 71.36 W |
| Crawfish ≃ | 216 | 43.00 N | 88.49 W |
| Crawford, Scot., U.K. | 44 | 55.28 N | 3.40 W |
| Crawford, Co., U.S. | 200 | 38.42 N | 107.36 W |
| Crawford, Ms., U.S. | 194 | 33.18 N | 88.36 W |
| Crawford, Ne., U.S. | 198 | 42.40 N | 103.24 W |
| Crawford, Tx., U.S. | 222 | 31.32 N | 97.27 W |
| Crawford □[6], In., U.S. | 218 | 38.20 N | 86.28 W |
| Crawford □[6], Oh., U.S. | 214 | 40.48 N | 82.58 W |
| Crawford □[6], Pa., U.S. | 214 | 41.39 N | 80.10 W |
| Crawford Bay | 182 | 49.42 N | 116.48 W |
| Crawford Countryside | 278 | 41.32 N | 87.43 W |
| Crawford Notch State Park ♦ | 188 | 44.13 N | 71.25 W |
| Crawfordsville, Ar., U.S. | 194 | 35.13 N | 90.19 W |
| Crawfordsville, In., U.S. | 194 | 40.02 N | 86.52 W |
| Crawfordville, Fl., U.S. | 192 | 30.10 N | 84.22 W |
| Crawfordville, Ga., U.S. | 192 | 33.33 N | 82.53 W |
| Crawinkel | 54 | 50.47 N | 10.47 E |
| Crawley | 42 | 51.07 N | 0.12 W |
| Crawshawbooth | 262 | 53.43 N | 2.17 W |
| Crayford -•[8] | 260 | 51.27 N | 0.11 E |
| Crays Hill | 260 | 51.36 N | 0.28 E |
| Crazy Mountains ⋏ | 202 | 46.08 N | 110.20 W |
| Crazy Peak ∧ | 202 | 46.01 N | 110.16 W |
| Crazy Woman Creek ≃ | 202 | 44.29 N | 106.08 W |
| Creagan | 46 | 56.33 N | 5.17 W |
| Creagorry | 46 | 57.26 N | 7.19 W |
| Creal Springs | 194 | 37.37 N | 88.50 W |
| Creamery | 285 | 40.13 N | 75.25 W |
| Crean Lake ⊜ | 184 | 54.05 N | 106.10 W |
| Crêches-sur-Saône | 58 | 46.15 N | 4.47 E |
| Crécy, Forêt de ♦ | 261 | 48.48 N | 2.53 E |
| Crécy-en-Brie | 50 | 48.51 N | 2.55 E |
| Crécy-en-Ponthieu | 50 | 50.15 N | 1.53 E |
| Crécy-sur-Serre | 50 | 49.42 N | 3.37 E |
| Credenhill | 42 | 52.06 N | 2.48 W |
| Credit ≃ | 212 | 43.33 N | 79.35 W |
| Crediton | 42 | 50.47 N | 3.39 W |
| Cree ≃, Sk., Can. | 176 | 59.00 N | 105.47 W |
| Cree ≃, Scot., U.K. | 44 | 54.52 N | 4.20 W |
| Creede | 200 | 37.50 N | 106.55 W |
| Creedmoor | 192 | 36.07 N | 78.41 W |
| Creedmore | 222 | 30.12 N | 97.43 W |
| Creegh | 48 | 52.44 N | 9.26 W |
| Creek Brook ≃ | 283 | 42.47 N | 71.08 W |
| Creek Locks | 210 | 41.52 N | 74.03 W |
| Creekmouth -•[8] | 260 | 51.31 N | 0.06 E |
| Creekside | 214 | 40.40 N | 79.11 W |
| Creekwood | 278 | 41.39 N | 87.59 W |
| Creel | 232 | 27.45 N | 107.38 W |
| Cree Lake ⊜ | 176 | 57.30 N | 106.30 W |
| Creemore | 212 | 44.19 N | 80.06 W |
| Creetown | 44 | 54.54 N | 4.23 W |
| Cregganbaun | 48 | 53.42 N | 9.51 W |
| Creglingen | 56 | 49.28 N | 10.01 E |
| Crégy-lès-Meaux | 261 | 48.58 N | 2.52 E |
| Créhange | 56 | 49.03 N | 6.35 E |
| Creighton, Sk., Can. | 184 | 54.45 N | 101.54 W |
| Creighton, S. Afr. | 158 | 30.01 S | 29.51 E |
| Creighton, Ne., U.S. | 198 | 42.28 N | 97.54 W |
| Creighton, Pa., U.S. | 214 | 40.35 N | 79.46 W |
| Creighton Mine | 190 | 46.28 N | 81.11 W |
| Creightons Creek ≃ | 169 | 36.43 S | 145.22 E |
| Creil, Fr. | 50 | 49.16 N | 2.29 E |
| Creil, Ned. | 52 | 52.45 N | 5.40 E |
| Crema | 62 | 45.22 N | 9.41 E |
| Cremia | 58 | 46.05 N | 9.16 E |
| Crémieu | 62 | 45.43 N | 5.15 E |
| Cremlingen | 54 | 52.15 N | 10.39 E |
| Cremona, Ab., Can. | 182 | 51.33 N | 114.29 W |
| Cremona, It. | 64 | 45.07 N | 10.02 E |
| Cremona □[4] | 64 | 45.12 N | 10.00 E |
| Crenshaw, Ms., U.S. | 194 | 34.30 N | 90.12 W |
| Crenshaw, Pa., U.S. | 214 | 41.15 N | 78.46 W |
| Crep Nudo ∧ | 64 | 46.13 N | 12.24 E |
| Crepori ≃ | 250 | 5.42 S | 57.08 W |
| Crépy-en-Laonnois | 50 | 49.36 N | 3.31 E |
| Crépy-en-Valois | 50 | 49.14 N | 2.54 E |
| Créquy | 50 | 50.29 N | 2.03 E |
| Creran, Loch ⊜ | 46 | 56.31 N | 5.20 W |
| Cres | 36 | 44.58 N | 14.25 E |
| Cres, Otok I | 36 | 44.50 N | 14.25 E |
| Cresaptown | 188 | 39.35 N | 78.50 W |
| Crescent, N.Y., U.S. | 210 | 42.49 N | 73.43 W |
| Crescent, Ok., U.S. | 196 | 35.57 N | 97.35 W |
| Crescent, Or., U.S. | 202 | 43.27 N | 121.41 W |
| Crescent, Lake ⊜ | 224 | 48.05 N | 123.50 W |
| Crescent Beach, B.C., Can. | 224 | 49.04 N | 122.53 W |
| Crescent Beach, Fl., U.S. | 220 | 27.15 N | 82.32 W |
| Crescent City, Ca., U.S. | 204 | 41.45 N | 124.12 W |
| Crescent City, Fl., U.S. | 192 | 29.25 N | 81.30 W |
| Crescent City, Il., U.S. | 216 | 40.46 N | 87.51 W |
| Crescent Ditch ≊ | 226 | 36.29 N | 120.07 W |
| Crescent Heights, N.J., U.S. | 285 | 39.58 N | 74.43 W |
| Crescent Heights, Tx., U.S. | 222 | 32.11 N | 95.56 W |
| Crescent Lake ⊜, Fl., U.S. | 192 | 29.28 N | 81.30 W |
| Crescent Lake ⊜, Or., U.S. | 202 | 43.29 N | 121.59 W |
| Crescent Lake Estates | 281 | 42.38 N | 83.25 W |
| Crescent Spur | 182 | 53.35 N | 120.41 W |

| | English | Deutsch | Español | Français | Português |
|---|---|---|---|---|---|
| ≃ | River | Fluß | Río | Rivière | Rio |
| ≊ | Canal | Kanal | Canal | Canal | Canal |
| ʟ | Waterfall, Rapids | Wasserfall, Stromschnellen | Cascada, Rápidos | Chute d'eau, Rapides | Cascata, Rápidos |
| ʉ | Strait | Meeresstraße | Estrecho | Détroit | Estreito |
| ⊂ | Bay, Gulf | Bucht, Golf | Bahía, Golfo | Baie, Golfe | Baía, Golfo |
| ⊜ | Lake, Lakes | See, Seen | Lago, Lagos | Lac, Lacs | Lago, Lagos |
| ≡ | Swamp | Sumpf | Pantano | Marais | Pântano |
| ⍓ | Ice Features, Glacier | Eis- und Gletscherformen | Accidentes Glaciales | Formes glaciaires | Acidentes glaciares |
| ⍑ | Other Hydrographic Features | Andere Hydrographische Objekte | Otros Elementos Hidrográficos | Autres données hydrographiques | Outros acidentes hidrográficos |
| ✢ | Submarine Features | Untermeerische Objekte | Accidentes Submarinos | Formes de relief sous-marin | Acidentes submarinos |
| □ | Political Unit | Politische Einheit | Unidad Politica | Entité politique | Unidade política |
| ʋ | Cultural Institution | Kulturelle Institution | Institución Cultural | Institution culturelle | Instituição cultural |
| ⊥ | Historical Site | Historische Stätte | Sitio Histórico | Site historique | Sitio histórico |
| ♦ | Recreational Site | Erholungs- und Ferienort | Sitio de Recreo | Centre de loisirs | Area de Lazer |
| ⊠ | Airport | Flughafen | Aeropuerto | Aéroport | Aeroporto |
| ■ | Military Installation | Militäranlage | Instalación Militar | Installation militaire | Instalação militar |
| -• | Miscellaneous | Verschiedenes | Misceláneo | Divers | Diversos |

| ENGLISH | | | | DEUTSCH | | | |
|---|---|---|---|---|---|---|---|
| Name | Page | Lat.°′ | Long.°′ | Name | Seite | Breite°′ | Länge°′ E = Ost |


Crescentville ◆[8] 285 40.02 N 75.05 W
Crescenzago ◆[8] 266b 45.30 N 9.15 E
Cresco, Ia., U.S. 190 43.22 N 92.06 W
Cresco, Pa., U.S. 210 41.09 N 75.17 W
Crespano del Grappa 64 45.49 N 11.50 E
Crespian 62 43.53 N 4.06 E
Crespières 261 48.53 N 1.55 E
Crespin 50 50.25 N 3.39 E
Crespino 64 44.59 N 11.53 E
Crespo 252 32.02 S 60.19 W
Cressbrook Creek ≃ 171a 27.05 S 152.27 E
Cressely 261 48.43 N 2.05 E
Cressey 226 37.25 N 120.40 W
Cresskill 276 40.56 N 73.57 W
Cresskill Brook ≃ 276 40.57 N 73.58 W
Cresson, Pa., U.S. 214 40.27 N 78.35 W
Cresson, Tx., U.S. 222 32.32 N 97.37 W
Cressona 208 40.37 N 76.11 W
Cressy 169 38.02 S 143.38 E
Crest 62 44.44 N 5.02 E
Cresta 58 46.28 N 9.31 E
Crested Butte 200 38.52 N 106.59 W
Cresthaven 220 26.03 N 80.08 W
Crest Hill 216 41.33 N 88.05 W
Crestline, Ca., U.S. 228 34.14 N 117.17 W
Crestline, Oh., U.S. 214 40.47 N 82.44 W
Creston, B.C., Can. 182 49.06 N 116.31 W
Creston, Nf., Can. 186 47.09 N 55.11 W
Creston, Ca., U.S. 226 35.31 N 120.31 W
Creston, Il., U.S. 216 41.56 N 88.58 W
Creston, Ia., U.S. 198 41.03 N 94.21 W
Creston, Oh., U.S. 214 40.59 N 81.53 W
Crestone Peak ∧ 200 37.58 N 105.36 W
Crestview, Fl., U.S. 194 30.45 N 86.34 W
Crestview, Wi., U.S. 216 42.49 N 87.49 W
Crestview Heights 210 42.05 N 76.07 W
Crestwood, Il., U.S. 278 41.39 N 87.45 W
Crestwood, Ky., U.S. 218 38.19 N 85.28 W
Crestwood, Mo., U.S. 219 38.33 N 90.22 W
Crestwood Hills 192 35.56 N 84.05 W
Creswell, Eng., U.K. 44 53.16 N 1.12 W
Creswell, Or., U.S. 202 43.55 N 123.01 W
Creswell Bay ⊂ 176 72.35 N 93.25 W
Creswell Creek ≃ 162 18.10 S 135.11 E
Creswell Downs 162 17.57 S 135.55 E
Creswick 169 37.26 S 143.54 E
Creta → Kríti I 38 35.15 N 25.00 E
Crete, Il., U.S. 216 41.27 N 87.38 W
Crete, Ne., U.S. 198 40.37 N 96.57 W
Crete → Kríti I 38 35.15 N 25.00 E
Crete, Sea of → Kritikón Pélagos ⊤[2] 38 35.46 N 23.54 E
Créteil 50 48.48 N 2.28 E
Crétéville 36 36.40 N 10.20 E
Cretin, Cape ▸ 164 6.40 S 147.52 E
Creus, Cap de ▸ 34 42.19 N 3.19 E
Creuse □[5] 32 46.05 N 2.00 E
Creuse ≃ 32 47.00 N 0.34 E
Creussen 60 49.51 N 11.37 E
Creutzwald 56 49.12 N 6.41 E
Creuzburg 56 51.03 N 10.15 E
Crevacuore 62 45.41 N 8.15 E
Crevalcore 64 44.43 N 11.09 E
Creve Coeur, Il., U.S. 190 40.38 N 89.35 W
Creve Coeur, Mo., U.S. 219 38.39 N 90.25 W
Crèvecœur-en-Auge 50 49.07 N 0.01 E
Crèvecœur-en-Brie 261 48.45 N 2.55 E
Crèvecœur-le-Grand 50 49.36 N 2.05 E
Crevillent 34 38.15 N 0.48 W
Crevoladossola 58 46.09 N 8.18 E
Crewe, Eng., U.K. 44 53.05 N 2.27 W
Crewe, Va., U.S. 192 37.10 N 78.07 W
Crewkerne 42 50.53 N 2.48 W
Crews Lake ⊜ 220 28.23 N 82.31 W
Crewsville 220 27.16 N 81.36 W
Crianlarich 46 56.23 N 4.36 W
Crib Point 169 38.22 S 145.12 E
Cricamola ≃ 236 8.59 N 81.54 W
Cricaré ≃ 255 18.37 S 40.05 W
Criccieth 42 52.55 N 4.14 W
Crichi 68 38.57 N 16.38 E
Criciúma 252 28.40 S 49.23 W
Crick 42 52.21 N 1.07 W
Cricket 192 36.10 N 81.11 W
Crickhowell 42 51.53 N 3.07 W
Cricklade 42 51.39 N 1.51 W
Cridersville 216 40.39 N 84.09 W
Crieff 46 56.23 N 3.52 W
Criel-sur-Mer 50 50.01 N 1.19 E
Criffell ∧ 44 54.57 N 3.38 W
Crikvenica 36 45.11 N 14.42 E
Crillon, Mount ∧ 180 58.40 N 137.10 W
Crimean Peninsula → Kryms'kyy pivostriv ▸[1] 78 45.00 N 34.00 E
Crimmitschau 54 50.49 N 12.23 E
Crimond 46 57.36 N 1.54 W
Crinan 46 56.05 N 5.35 W
Cringila 170 34.28 S 150.53 E
Cripple Creek 200 38.44 N 105.10 W
Criquetot l'Esneval 50 49.39 N 0.16 E
Crirninoso, Monte ∧ 256 21.32 S 43.25 W
Crisenoy 261 48.36 N 2.45 E
Crisfield 208 37.59 N 75.51 W
Crisólia 256 22.15 S 46.25 W
Crisóstomo, Ribeirão ≃ 250 10.19 S 50.26 W
Crispiano 68 40.36 N 17.14 E
Criss Creek 182 51.03 N 120.44 W
Crissiumal 252 27.30 S 54.07 W
Cristal, Monts de ⩘ 152 0.30 N 10.30 E
Cristal, Sierra del ⩘ 240p 20.33 N 75.31 W
Cristalândia 250 10.36 S 49.11 W
Cristália 255 16.43 S 42.52 W
Cristalina 255 16.45 S 47.36 W
Cristalino ≃ 255 12.38 S 50.40 W
Cristallo ∧ 64 46.34 N 12.12 E
Cristianópolis 255 17.13 S 48.45 W
Cristina 256 22.13 S 45.16 W
Cristinápolis 250 11.29 S 37.46 W
Cristino Castro 250 8.49 S 44.13 W
Cristóbal 236 9.21 N 79.55 W
Cristóbal Colón, Pico ∧ 246 10.50 N 73.41 W
Cristóbal Obregón 234 16.20 N 93.30 W
Cristoforo Colombo, Aeroporto di ⊠ 62 44.25 N 8.49 E
Cristo Redentor ⊥ 252 32.50 S 70.05 W
Cristo Redentor, Estatua do ◆[1] 287a 22.57 S 43.13 W
Cristuru Secuiesc 38 46.17 N 25.02 E
Crișul Alb ≃ 38 46.42 N 21.17 E
Crișul Negru ≃ 38 46.42 N 21.16 E
Crișul Repede (Sebes Körös) ≃ 38 46.55 N 20.59 E
Crittenden 218 38.46 N 84.36 W
Criuleni 38 47.13 N 29.09 E
Crivitz, Dtsch. 54 53.35 N 11.38 E
Crivitz, Wi., U.S. 190 45.13 N 88.00 W
Crixalândia 255 15.18 S 47.15 W
Crixás 255 14.27 S 49.58 W
Crixás ≃ 250 11.02 S 48.34 W
Crixás-Açu ≃ 255 13.19 S 50.36 W
Crixás-Mirim ≃ 255 13.30 S 50.30 W
Črna 61 46.28 N 14.51 E
Crna ≃ 38 41.35 N 21.59 E
Crna Gora □[3] 38 42.30 N 19.18 E
Črni vrh ∧ 61 46.29 N 15.14 E
Črnomelj 36 45.34 N 15.11 E
Croachy 46 57.19 N 4.14 W
Croagh Patrick ∧ 48 53.46 N 9.40 W
Croajingolong National Park ♠ 166 37.40 S 149.30 E
Croal ≃ 262 53.33 N 2.23 W
Croatia (Hrvatska) □[1], Europe 38 45.10 N 15.30 E
Croatia (Hrvatska) □[1], Europe 36 45.10 N 15.30 E
Croce dello Scrivano, Passo )( 68 40.34 N 15.50 E
Croce Domini, Passo di )( 64 45.54 N 10.24 E
Crocefieschi 62 44.35 N 9.01 E
Crocetta del Montello 64 45.50 N 12.02 E
Crocheron 208 38.14 N 76.03 W
Crockenhill 260 51.23 N 0.10 E
Crocker 194 37.56 N 92.15 W
Crocker, Banjaran ⩘ 112 5.40 N 116.14 E
Crockery Creek ≃ 216 43.02 N 86.05 W
Crocketford 44 55.02 N 3.50 W
Crockett, Ca., U.S. 226 38.03 N 122.12 W
Crockett, Tx., U.S. 222 31.19 N 95.27 W
Crockham Hill 260 51.14 N 0.04 E
Crocus Hill → The Valley 238 18.13 N 63.04 W
Croft 262 53.26 N 2.33 W
Crofton, B.C., Can. 224 48.52 N 123.38 W
Crofton, Ky., U.S. 194 37.02 N 87.29 W
Crofton, Md., U.S. 208 39.00 N 76.41 W
Crofton, Ne., U.S. 198 42.43 N 97.29 W
Croft State Park ♠ 192 34.49 N 81.52 W
Croggan 46 56.22 N 5.42 W
Croghan 212 43.53 N 75.23 W
Croglin 44 54.49 N 2.39 W
Croick 46 57.53 N 4.35 W
Croil Islands II 206 44.58 N 74.58 W
Croisette, Cap ▸ 62 43.13 N 5.20 E
Croisilles 50 50.12 N 2.53 E
Croissy-Beaubourg 261 48.50 N 2.40 E
Croissy-sur-Seine 261 48.53 N 2.09 E
Croix 50 50.40 N 3.09 E
Croix, Lac à la ⊜ 186 51.16 N 70.13 W
Croix, Lac la ⊜ 190 48.21 N 92.05 W
Croker, Cape ▸, Austl. 164 10.58 S 132.35 E
Croker, Cape ▸, On., Can. 212 44.58 N 80.59 W
Croker Island I 164 11.12 S 132.32 E
Crolles 62 45.17 N 5.53 E
Cromarty 46 57.40 N 4.02 W
Cromarty Firth ⊂[1] 46 57.41 N 4.07 W
Cromby 285 40.09 N 75.32 W
Cromer, Austl. 274a 33.44 S 151.17 E
Cromer, Eng., U.K. 42 52.56 N 1.18 E
Cromford 44 53.06 N 1.34 W
Cromínia 255 17.17 S 49.21 W
Cromore 46 58.09 N 6.29 W
Crompton Point ▸ 240d 15.35 N 61.19 W
Cromwell, N.Z. 172 45.03 S 169.12 E
Cromwell, Al., U.S. 194 32.13 N 88.16 W
Cromwell, Ct., U.S. 207 41.35 N 72.38 W
Cromwell, In., U.S. 216 41.24 N 85.36 W
Cromwell Park ♠ 279a 41.28 N 82.08 W
Cronadun 172 42.02 S 171.52 E
Cronenberg ◆[8] 263 51.12 N 7.08 E
Cronin, Mount ∧ 182 54.54 N 126.52 W
Cronton 262 53.23 N 2.46 W
Cronulla 170 34.03 S 151.09 E
Cronulla Beach ⊥[2] 274a 34.02 S 151.11 E
Croob, Slieve ∧[2] 48 54.20 N 5.58 W
Crook, Eng., U.K. 44 54.43 N 1.44 W
Crook, Co., U.S. 198 40.51 N 102.48 W
Crooked ≃, B.C., Can. 182 54.50 N 122.54 W
Crooked ≃, Mo., U.S. 194 39.13 N 93.49 W
Crooked ≃, Or., U.S. 202 44.34 N 121.16 W
Crooked Creek 180 61.52 N 158.08 W
Crooked Creek ≃, U.S. 196 36.57 N 100.06 W
Crooked Creek ≃, Ar., U.S. 194 36.14 N 92.29 W
Crooked Creek ≃, Il., U.S. 219 38.30 N 89.25 W
Crooked Creek ≃, In., U.S. 216 40.45 N 86.30 W
Crooked Creek ≃, Mo., U.S. 219 39.34 N 91.55 W
Crooked Creek ≃, Pa., U.S. 210 41.55 N 77.08 W
Crooked Creek ≃, Pa., U.S. 214 40.45 N 79.33 W
Crooked Creek Lake ⊜[1] 214 40.42 N 79.30 W
Crooked Island I 238 22.45 N 74.13 W
Crooked Island Passage ⊔ 238 22.55 N 74.35 W
Crooked Lake, In., U.S. 216 41.41 N 85.02 W
Crooked Lake, Mi., U.S. 216 42.29 N 85.25 W
Crooked Lake ⊜, Nf., Can. 186 48.24 N 56.17 W
Crooked Lake ⊜, Sk., Can. 184 50.36 N 102.45 W
Crooked Lake ⊜, N.A. 190 48.13 N 91.50 W
Crooked Lake ⊜, Fl., U.S. 220 27.48 N 81.35 W
Crooked Lake ⊜, In., U.S. 216 41.40 N 85.03 W
Crooked River 184 52.51 N 103.44 W
Crookes Point ▸ 276 40.32 N 74.08 W
Crookham 279b 40.12 N 79.59 W
Crookston 198 47.46 N 96.36 W
Crookstown 48 51.50 N 8.50 W
Crooksville 188 39.46 N 82.05 W
Crookwell 166 34.28 S 149.28 E
Croom 48 52.31 N 8.42 W
Cropalati 68 39.31 N 16.43 E
Cropani 68 38.58 N 16.47 E
Cropper 218 38.18 N 85.06 W
Crosby, Eng., U.K. 44 53.30 N 3.02 W
Crosby, Mn., U.S. 190 46.28 N 93.57 W
Crosby, Ms., U.S. 194 31.17 N 91.03 W
Crosby, N.D., U.S. 198 48.54 N 103.17 W
Crosby, Pa., U.S. 214 41.45 N 78.24 W
Crosby, Tx., U.S. 222 29.55 N 95.04 W
Crosby, Mount ∧ 202 43.53 N 109.20 W
Crosby Lake ⊜ 212 44.45 N 76.26 W
Crosbyton 196 33.39 N 101.14 W
Crosia 68 39.34 N 16.46 E
Crosne 261 48.43 N 2.28 E
Cross ≃ 152 4.42 N 8.21 E
Cross Banks II 283 42.43 N 70.49 W
Cross Bay ⊂ 184 53.15 N 99.25 W
Cross Bay Bridge ◆[5] 276 40.35 N 73.49 W
Crossbost 46 58.08 N 6.23 W
Cross City 192 29.38 N 83.07 W
Cross County Center ◆[9] 276 40.56 N 73.51 W
Cross Creek ≃, Ca., U.S. 226 36.08 N 119.38 W
Cross Creek ≃, Oh., U.S. 214 40.18 N 80.36 W
Crossens 262 53.41 N 2.57 W
Crossett 194 33.07 N 91.57 W
Cross Fell ∧ 44 54.42 N 2.29 W
Crossfield 182 51.26 N 114.02 W
Crossgar 48 54.24 N 5.45 W
Cross Hands 42 51.48 N 4.04 W
Crosshaven 48 51.48 N 8.17 W
Crosshill 44 55.19 N 4.39 W
Crossinsee ⊜ 264a 52.22 N 13.41 E
Cross Island I 272c 18.57 N 72.51 E
Cross Keys 285 39.42 N 75.01 W
Cross Keys Airfield ⊠ 285 39.42 N 75.02 W
Cross Lake 184 54.37 N 97.47 W
Cross Lake ⊜, Mb., Can. 184 54.45 N 97.30 W
Cross Lake ⊜, On., Can. 190 46.53 N 79.57 W
Cross Lake ⊜, N.Y., U.S. 210 43.08 N 76.29 W
Crossley, Mount ∧ 172 42.50 S 172.04 E
Crossmaglen 48 54.05 N 6.37 W
Crossman 168a 32.47 S 116.36 E
Crossman 168a 32.47 S 116.36 E
Crossman Peak ∧ 200 34.32 N 114.07 W
Crossmolina 48 54.06 N 9.20 W
Cross Plains, In., U.S. 218 38.57 N 85.12 W
Cross Plains, Tx., U.S. 196 32.08 N 99.11 W
Cross Plains, Wi., U.S. 190 43.06 N 89.39 W
Cross Roads 222 32.03 N 95.58 W
Cross Sound ⊔ 180 58.10 N 136.30 W
Crossville, Il., U.S. 194 38.09 N 88.03 W
Crossville, Tn., U.S. 194 35.56 N 85.01 W
Crosswicks 285 40.09 N 74.38 W
Crosswicks Creek ≃ 208 40.09 N 74.43 W
Crostolo ≃ 64 44.55 N 10.38 E
Croston 44 53.39 N 2.46 W
Croswell 190 43.16 N 82.37 W
Crotch Lake ⊜ 212 44.55 N 76.48 W
Crotenay 58 46.45 N 5.49 E
Crothersville 218 38.48 N 85.50 W
Croton 214 40.14 N 82.41 W
Crotona Park ♠ 276 40.50 N 73.54 W
Croton Creek ≃ 196 33.18 N 100.25 W
Crotone 68 39.05 N 17.07 E
Crotone □[4] 68 39.10 N 17.00 E
Croton Falls 210 41.21 N 73.40 W
Croton-on-Hudson 210 41.12 N 73.53 W
Croton Point ▸ 276 41.10 N 73.54 W
Crottendorf 54 50.30 N 12.56 E
Crouch ≃ 42 51.37 N 0.57 E
Crouse Run ≃ 279b 40.35 N 79.58 W
Crouy 50 49.24 N 3.22 E
Crow ≃ 190 45.15 N 93.31 W
Crow, North Fork ≃ 190 45.05 N 93.45 W
Crow, South Fork ≃ 190 45.05 N 93.45 W
Crow Agency 202 45.36 N 107.27 W
Crowborough 42 51.03 N 0.09 E
Crow Creek ≃, U.S. 198 40.23 N 104.29 W
Crow Creek ≃, Ca., U.S. 282 37.42 N 122.03 W
Crow Creek ≃, Il., U.S. 194 40.56 N 89.27 W
Crow Creek ≃, Mt., U.S. 198 45.45 N 105.06 W
Crow Creek ≃, Mt., U.S. 202 46.11 N 111.29 W
Crow Creek ≃, S.D., U.S. 198 43.57 N 99.15 W
Crow Creek ≃, Wy., U.S. 202 43.19 N 109.09 W
Crow Creek Indian Reservation ◆[4] 198 44.11 N 99.30 W
Crowder, Ms., U.S. 194 34.10 N 90.08 W
Crowder, Ok., U.S. 196 35.07 N 95.40 W
Crowduck Lake ⊜ 184 50.08 N 95.15 W
Crowdy Head ▸ 166 31.50 S 152.45 E
Crowe ≃ 212 44.22 N 77.46 W
Crowe Lake ⊜ 212 44.29 N 77.46 W
Crowell 196 33.59 N 99.43 W
Crowfoot, Mount ∧ 172 45.33 S 167.03 E
Crow Hill ∧[2] 262 53.42 N 1.58 W
Crowhurst 260 51.12 N 0.01 W
Crow Indian Reservation ◆[4] 202 45.27 N 108.00 W
Crow Lake 184 49.12 N 93.57 W
Crow Lake ⊜ 212 44.43 N 76.37 W
Crowland 42 52.41 N 0.11 W
Crowle 44 53.37 N 0.49 W
Crowley, La., U.S. 194 30.12 N 92.22 W
Crowley, Tx., U.S. 222 32.34 N 97.21 W
Crowley, Lake ⊜[1] 204 37.37 N 118.44 W
Crowleys Ridge ∧ 194 35.45 N 90.45 W
Crowlin Islands II 46 57.20 N 5.44 W
Crown 214 41.23 N 79.16 W
Crown Hill 212 44.26 N 79.39 W
Crown Island I 164 5.05 S 146.55 E
Crown Memorial Beach ♠ 282 37.46 N 122.16 W
Crown Mines ◆[7] 273d 26.13 S 28.00 E
Crown Mountain ∧ 240m 18.21 N 64.58 W
Crown Point, In., U.S. 216 41.25 N 87.21 W
Crownpoint, N.M., U.S. 200 35.40 N 108.09 W
Crown Point, N.Y., U.S. 188 43.57 N 73.26 W
Crown Point State Park ♠ 224 45.32 N 122.15 W
Crown Prince Frederik Island I 176 70.02 N 86.50 W
Crown Village 276 40.40 N 73.27 W
Crow Peak ∧ 202 46.18 N 111.54 W
Crow Rock Creek ≃ 202 47.06 N 106.15 W
Crows Fork Creek ≃ 219 38.47 N 91.52 W
Crows Landing 226 37.24 N 121.04 W
Crows Nest, Austl. 171a 27.16 S 152.03 E
Crows Nest, Austl. 274a 33.50 S 151.12 E
Crowsnest, Ab., Can. 182 49.38 N 114.41 W
Crows Nest Falls National Park ♠ 171a 27.16 S 152.08 E
Crowsnest Pass 182 49.36 N 114.26 W
Crowsnest Pass )( 182 49.39 N 114.45 W
Crows Nest Peak ∧ 198 44.03 N 103.58 W
Crowthorne 42 51.23 N 0.49 W
Crowton 262 53.16 N 2.38 W
Crow Wing ≃ 198 46.19 N 94.20 W
Croxley Green 42 51.39 N 0.27 W
Croxteth Park ♠ 262 53.26 N 2.53 W
Croy 46 57.31 N 4.02 W
Croyde 42 51.07 N 4.13 W
Croydon, Austl. 166 18.12 S 142.14 E
Croydon, Austl. 169 37.48 S 145.17 E
Croydon, Austl. 274a 33.53 S 151.07 E
Croydon, Pa., U.S. 208 40.05 N 74.54 W
Croydon ◆[8] 42 51.23 N 0.06 W
Croydon Park 274a 33.54 S 151.07 E
Croydon Peak ∧ 188 43.28 N 72.13 W
Croydon Station 182 53.05 N 119.44 W
Crozet 192 38.04 N 78.42 W
Crozet, Archipel II 6 46.00 S 52.00 E
Crozet Basin ◆[1] 6 39.00 S 60.00 E
Crozon 32 48.15 N 4.29 W
Cruachan, Ben ∧ 46 56.25 N 5.08 W
Cruas 62 44.39 N 4.46 E
Crucea 38 44.32 N 28.14 E
Crucero 248 14.21 S 70.00 W
Cruces, Cuba 240p 22.21 N 80.16 W
Cruces, Méx. 232 29.26 N 107.24 W
Crucoli 68 39.25 N 17.00 E
Cruden Bay 46 57.25 N 1.50 W
Crudgington 42 52.46 N 2.33 W
Crudine Creek ≃ 170 33.05 S 149.40 E
Cruger 194 33.19 N 90.13 W
Cruillas 232 24.45 N 98.31 W
Crum Creek ≃ 285 39.51 N 75.19 W
Crumhorn Mountain ∧ 210 42.33 N 74.55 W
Crumlin, On., Can. 212 43.01 N 81.09 W
Crumlin, N. Ire., U.K. 48 54.37 N 6.14 W
Crum Lynne 285 39.52 N 75.20 W
Crummock Water ⊜ 44 54.34 N 3.18 W
Crump Lake ⊜ 202 42.17 N 119.50 W
Crumpton 208 39.14 N 75.55 W
Crumstown 216 41.38 N 86.25 W
Crupet 56 50.21 N 4.48 E
Cruseilles 58 46.02 N 6.07 E
Cruser Brook ≃ 276 40.27 N 74.39 W
Crusheen 48 52.58 N 8.54 W
Crusnes 56 49.26 N 5.55 E
Crusnes ≃ 56 49.27 N 5.36 E
Crustepec, Cerro ∧ 234 21.15 N 97.53 W
Cruz, Arroyo de la ≃, Ca., U.S. 226 35.42 N 121.09 W
Cruz, Arroyo de la ≃, Ur. 258 34.00 S 56.08 W
Cruz, Cabo ▸ 240p 19.51 N 77.44 W
Cruz, Cañada de la ≃ 258 34.09 S 58.58 W
Cruz, Cayo I 240p 22.15 N 77.49 W
Cruz, Pico de la ∧ 148 28.44 N 17.52 W
Cruz Alta, Arg. 252 33.01 S 61.49 W
Cruz Alta, Bra. 252 28.39 S 53.36 W
Cruz Bay 240m 18.20 N 64.48 W
Cruz de Elorza 234 23.49 N 100.29 W
Cruz del Eje 252 30.44 S 64.48 W
Cruz del Marquez, Cerro ∧ 286a 19.12 N 99.15 W
Cruzeiro 256 22.34 S 44.58 W
Cruzeiro do Oeste 255 23.46 S 53.04 W
Cruzeiro do Sul 248 7.38 S 72.36 W
Cruzeta 250 6.25 S 36.47 W
Cruz Grande, Chile 252 29.25 S 71.18 W
Cruz Grande, Méx. 234 16.44 N 99.08 W
Cruzília 256 21.50 S 44.48 W
Cruz Machado 252 26.01 S 51.21 W
Cruzy-le-Châtel 50 47.51 N 4.12 E
Crvenka 38 45.39 N 19.28 E
Crymych 42 51.59 N 4.40 W
Crynant 42 51.43 N 3.45 W
Crysler 188 45.13 N 75.09 W
Crystal, Mn., U.S. 190 45.01 N 93.21 W
Crystal, N.D., U.S. 198 48.35 N 97.40 W
Crystal ≃ 200 39.25 N 107.14 W
Crystal Bay 226 39.13 N 120.00 W
Crystal Bay ⊂ 220 28.55 N 82.43 W
Crystal Beach, On., Can. 284a 42.52 N 79.04 W
Crystal Beach, Fl., U.S. 220 28.05 N 82.46 W
Crystal Beach, Tx., U.S. 222 29.27 N 94.38 W
Crystal Brook 166 33.21 S 138.13 E
Crystal Cave ⊥[5] 208 40.32 N 75.51 W
Crystal City, Mb., Can. 184 49.09 N 98.56 W
Crystal City, Mo., U.S. 219 38.13 N 90.22 W
Crystal City, Tx., U.S. 196 28.40 N 99.49 W
Crystal Creek ≃ 278 41.58 N 87.51 W
Crystal Falls 190 46.05 N 88.20 W
Crystal Gardens 216 42.14 N 88.23 W
Crystal Lake, Il., U.S. 216 42.14 N 88.18 W
Crystal Lake, N.Y., U.S. 210 42.31 N 74.12 W
Crystal Lake, N.Y., U.S. 210 42.28 N 78.20 W
Crystal Lake ⊜, On., Can. 212 44.45 N 78.30 W
Crystal Lake ⊜, Ma., U.S. 283 42.29 N 71.05 W
Crystal Lake ⊜, Ma., U.S. 283 42.48 N 71.09 W
Crystal Lake ⊜, Mi., U.S. 190 44.40 N 86.10 W
Crystal Lake ⊜, N.J., U.S. 276 41.02 N 74.15 W
Crystal Lakes 218 39.52 N 84.04 W
Crystal Lawns 216 41.34 N 88.09 W
Crystal Manor 216 42.14 N 88.17 W
Crystal Palace Stadium and Motor Race Track ♠ 260 51.25 N 0.04 W
Crystal River 192 28.54 N 82.35 W
Crystal Spring Lake ⊜ 285 39.43 N 75.01 W
Crystal Springs, Fl., U.S. 220 28.10 N 82.09 W
Crystal Springs, Ms., U.S. 194 31.59 N 90.21 W
Crystal Springs Dam ◆[6] 282 37.32 N 122.22 W
Crystal Vista 216 42.14 N 88.24 W
Csepel ◆[8] 264c 47.24 N 19.14 E
Csepel-sziget I 30 47.15 N 18.57 E
Csepreg 61 47.24 N 16.43 E
Cserhát ⩘ 30 47.55 N 19.30 E
Cserta ≃ 61 46.35 N 16.36 E
Csesznek ⊥ 30 47.16 N 17.53 E
Csesztreg 61 46.43 N 16.31 E
Csobánka 264c 47.38 N 18.58 E
Csomád 264c 47.40 N 19.15 E
Csömodér 61 46.37 N 16.39 E
Csömör 264c 47.33 N 19.14 E
Csömöri-patak ≃ 264c 47.36 N 19.07 E
Csongrád 30 46.43 N 20.09 E
Csongrád □[6] 30 46.25 N 20.15 E
Csorna 30 47.37 N 17.16 E
Csurgó 30 46.16 N 17.06 E
Ču □[4] 85 42.30 N 74.30 E
Ču ≃ 86 45.00 N 67.44 E
Cúa 246 10.10 N 66.54 W
Cuacnopalan 234 18.49 N 97.30 W
Cuácua ≃ 154 17.54 S 36.48 E
Cuajimalpa ◆[8] 286a 19.21 N 99.18 W
Cuajinicuilapa 234 16.28 N 98.25 W
Cuajone 248 17.00 S 70.43 W
Cuále 152 8.06 S 16.03 E
Cua Lo 110 18.49 N 105.43 E
Cuamato 152 17.05 S 15.09 E
Cuamba 154 14.49 S 36.33 E
Cuambog 116 7.20 N 125.52 E
Cuanavale ≃ 152 15.07 S 19.14 E
Cuando 152 16.32 S 22.07 E
Cuando (Kwando) ≃ 152 18.27 S 23.32 E
Cuando Cubango □[5] 152 16.00 S 20.00 E
Cuangar 152 17.36 S 18.39 E
Cuango, Ang. 152 14.30 S 18.59 E
Cuango, Ang. 152 9.10 S 17.58 E
Cuango, Ang. 152 6.17 S 16.41 E
Cuango (Kwango) ≃ 152 3.14 S 17.23 E
Cuanza ≃ 152 9.19 S 13.08 E
Cuanza Norte □[5] 152 8.50 S 14.30 E
Cuanza Sul □[5] 152 10.50 S 14.50 E
Cuao ≃ 246 4.55 N 67.40 W
Cuapiaxtla 234 19.18 N 97.46 W
Cuareim (Quaraí) ≃ 252 30.12 S 57.36 W
Cuaró 252 30.37 S 56.54 W
Cuartillo, Arroyo ≃ 258 33.45 S 59.06 W
Cuarto ≃ 252 33.25 S 62.56 W
Cuatir ≃ 152 17.01 S 18.09 E
Cuatro Caminos 286b 22.54 N 82.23 W
Cuatro Ciénegas [de Carranza] 196 26.59 N 102.05 W
Cuatro Islands II 116 10.31 N 124.39 E
Cuauhtémoc, Méx. 232 28.25 N 106.52 W
Cuauhtémoc, Méx. 234 19.20 N 103.36 W
Cuauhtémoc, Méx. 234 22.38 N 98.08 W
Cuautepec el Alto ◆[8] 286a 19.34 N 99.08 W
Cuautitlán 234 19.26 N 104.23 W
Cuautitlán ≃ 286a 19.41 N 99.13 W
Cuautitlán [de Romero Rubio] 234 19.40 N 99.11 W
Cuautitlán Izcalli 286a 19.39 N 99.13 W
Cuautla, Méx. 234 20.11 N 104.21 W
Cuautla, Méx. 234 18.48 N 98.57 W
Cuautzin, Volcán ∧[1] 286a 19.09 N 99.06 W
Cuba, Port. 34 38.10 N 7.53 W
Cuba, Al., U.S. 194 32.25 N 88.22 W
Cuba, Il., U.S. 190 40.29 N 90.11 W
Cuba, Ks., U.S. 198 39.48 N 97.27 W
Cuba, Mo., U.S. 194 38.03 N 91.24 W
Cuba, N.M., U.S. 200 36.01 N 106.57 W
Cuba, N.Y., U.S. 210 42.13 N 78.16 W
Cuba □[1], N.A. 230 21.30 N 80.00 W
Cuba □[1], N.A. 240p 21.30 N 80.00 W
Cubabi, Cerro ∧ 200 31.42 N 112.46 W
Cubagua, Isla I 246 10.48 N 64.10 W
Cuba Island I 276 40.38 N 73.32 W
Cubal 152 13.02 S 14.19 E
Cubal ≃, Ang. 152 12.42 S 13.56 E
Cubal ≃, Ang. 152 11.19 S 13.48 E
Cuba Lake ⊜ 210 42.15 N 78.18 W
Cubanea 254 41.02 S 70.16 W
Cubango (Okavango) ≃ 138 18.50 S 22.25 E
Cubanguí ≃ 152 14.22 S 19.58 E
Čubaricha 86 57.37 N 68.22 E
Čubarovo 82 55.12 N 36.56 E
Cubatão 256 23.53 S 46.25 W
Cubatão, Serra do ⊥[4] 256 23.52 S 46.28 W
Cubati 250 6.51 S 36.21 W
Cub Hills ⩘[2] 184 54.20 N 104.30 W
Cubia ≃ 152 16.01 S 21.50 E
Čublas 24 64.44 N 45.00 E
Cub Run ≃ 208 38.48 N 77.28 W
Çubuk 130 40.15 N 33.02 E
Cuc ≃ 250 1.22 N 53.33 W
Cucamonga 228 34.06 N 117.35 W
Cucamonga Creek ≃ 280 33.57 N 117.37 W
Cucamonga Peak ∧ 228 34.14 N 117.36 W
Cuccaro Vetere 68 40.09 N 15.18 E
Cucco, Monte ∧ 66 43.22 N 12.45 E
Cucharas ≃ 198 37.55 N 104.32 W
Cucharas, Sierra ⩘ 234 22.20 N 98.55 W
Cuchi 152 14.36 S 16.58 E
Cuchi ≃ 152 15.28 S 17.21 E
Cuchibi ≃ 152 15.00 S 20.45 E
Cuchilla Alta, Cerro ∧ 236 15.10 N 88.12 W
Cuchillo-Có 252 38.20 S 64.37 W
Cuchillo Negro Creek ≃ 200 33.08 N 107.14 W
Cuchivero ≃ 246 7.40 N 65.57 W
Čuchloma 76 58.45 N 42.41 E
Čuchlomskoje, ozero ⊜ 76 58.46 N 42.35 E
Cuchumatanes, Sierra los ⩘ 236 15.35 N 91.25 W
Cuckels Brook ≃ 276 40.33 N 74.33 W
Cuckfield 42 51.00 N 0.09 W
Cuckney 44 53.15 N 1.08 W
Cuckold Point ▸ 284b 39.14 N 76.24 W
Čučkovo, Ross. 76 59.36 N 41.14 E
Čučkovo, Ross. 80 54.17 N 41.26 E
Cucuí 246 1.12 N 66.50 W
Cucumbi 152 10.17 S 19.05 E
Cucuron 62 43.47 N 5.26 E
Cucurpe 232 30.20 N 110.43 W
Cúcuta 246 7.54 N 72.31 W
Cudachar 84 42.21 N 47.11 E
Cudahy, Ca., U.S. 280 33.57 N 118.11 W
Cudahy, Wi., U.S. 216 42.57 N 87.51 W
Cuddalore 122 11.45 N 79.45 E
Cuddapah 122 14.28 N 78.49 E
Cuddeback Lake ⊜ 228 35.18 N 117.28 W
Cuddebackville 210 41.28 N 74.36 W
Cuddia ≃ 70 37.53 N 12.37 E
Cuddington 44 53.14 N 2.36 W
Cuddle Lake ⊜ 184 55.25 N 95.47 W
Cuddy 279b 40.21 N 80.09 W
Cuddy Mountain ∧ 202 44.46 N 116.47 W
Cudgegong 170 32.48 S 149.49 E
Cudgegong ≃ 170 32.37 S 149.43 E
Cudgewa 171b 36.12 S 147.46 E
Cudgewa Creek ≃ 171b 36.03 S 147.55 E
Cudham ◆[8] 260 51.19 N 0.05 E
Cudia Park ♠ 275b 43.43 N 79.13 W
Cudjoe Key I 220 24.40 N 81.30 W
Čudovo 76 59.07 N 31.41 E
Čudskoje ozero (Peipsi järv) ⊜ 76 58.45 N 27.30 E
Cudworth, Sk., Can. 184 52.30 N 105.45 W
Cudworth, Eng., U.K. 44 53.35 N 1.25 W
Čudzin 76 52.44 N 26.59 E
Cue 162 27.25 S 117.54 E
Cuebe ≃ 152 15.48 S 17.30 E
Cueio ≃, Ang. 152 15.27 S 21.21 E
Cueio ≃, Ang. 152 16.17 S 17.46 E
Cuelei ≃ 152 15.33 S 17.21 E
Cuéllar 34 41.24 N 4.19 W
Cuenca, Ec. 246 2.53 S 78.59 W
Cuenca, Esp. 34 40.04 N 2.08 W
Cuenca □[4] 34 39.55 N 2.10 W
Cuencamé [de Ceniceros] 232 24.53 N 103.42 W
Cuerámaro 234 20.37 N 101.43 W
Cuernavaca 234 18.55 N 99.15 W
Cuero 222 29.05 N 97.17 W
Cuers 62 43.14 N 6.04 E
Cuervos 204 32.38 N 114.52 W
Cuesmes 50 50.26 N 3.55 E
Cuesta Pass )( 226 35.21 N 120.38 W
Cueto 240p 20.39 N 75.56 W
Cuetzala del Progreso 234 18.07 N 99.50 W
Cuetzalan del Progreso 234 20.02 N 97.31 W
Cuevas del Almanzora 34 37.18 N 1.53 W
Cuevo 248 20.27 S 63.32 W
Čufarovo 80 54.06 N 47.19 E
Cuffley 42 51.42 N 0.07 W
Cufra → Al-Kufrah ⊤[4] 146 24.20 N 23.15 E
Cufré 258 34.12 S 57.06 W
Cufré, Arroyo ≃ 258 34.27 S 57.09 W
Cuggiono 62 45.31 N 8.49 E
Cugir 38 45.50 N 23.22 E
Cuglieri 71 40.11 N 8.34 E
Cugo ≃ 152 7.18 S 16.39 E
Čugujevka 89 44.08 N 133.53 E
Čugunaš 86 52.52 N 87.46 E
Čuguš, gora ∧ 84 43.47 N 40.16 E
Cuiabá 248 15.35 S 56.05 W
Cuiabá ≃ 248 17.53 S 57.27 W
Cuiari 246 1.30 N 68.11 W
Cuiari ≃ 246 1.30 N 68.11 W
Cuicatlán 234 17.48 N 96.58 W
Cuichapa 234 17.59 N 94.15 W
Cuieiras ≃ 246 2.50 S 60.31 W
Cuigezhuang, Zhg. 105 40.01 N 116.28 E
Cuigezhuang, Zhg. 105 40.02 N 117.54 E
Cuihuangkou 105 39.32 N 117.11 E
Cuijiatun 104 40.57 N 121.09 E
Cuijiazhuang 104 40.57 N 122.44 E
Cuilapa 236 14.17 N 90.18 W
Cuilcagh ∧ 48 54.10 N 7.48 W
Cuilco 236 15.24 N 91.58 W
Cuillin Hills ⩘[2] 46 57.15 N 6.15 W
Cuilo (Kwilu) ≃, Afr. 152 3.22 S 17.22 E
Cuilo ≃, Afr. 152 5.52 S 16.35 E
Cuilo Futa 152 6.25 S 15.44 E
Cuimba 152 6.08 S 14.38 E
Cuio 152 12.58 S 12.58 E
Cuiqiao 98 34.12 N 114.36 E
Cuiseaux 58 46.30 N 5.24 E
Cuisery 58 46.33 N 5.00 E
Cuisy 261 49.01 N 2.46 E
Cuité 250 6.29 S 36.09 W
Cuitláhuac 234 18.49 N 96.43 W
Cuíto ≃ 152 18.01 S 20.48 E
Cuíto-Cuanavale 152 15.10 S 19.10 E
Cuitzeo, Laguna de ⊜ 234 19.55 N 101.05 W
Cuitzeo del Porvenir 234 19.59 N 101.09 W
Cuiuni ≃ 246 0.45 S 63.07 W
Cuivre ≃ 219 38.56 N 90.42 W
Cuivre, North Fork ≃ 219 39.02 N 90.59 W
Cuivre, West Fork ≃ 219 39.02 N 90.59 W
Cuivre River State Park ♠ 219 39.02 N 90.57 W
Čuja 88 59.12 N 112.25 E
Čuja ≃, Ross. 86 50.24 N 86.39 E
Čuja ≃, Ross. 88 59.17 N 112.24 E
Cují 286c 10.28 N 67.02 W
Cukas 112 0.25 S 104.18 E
Čukčagirskoje ozero ⊜ 89 52.00 N 136.36 E
Čukotskij, mys ▸ 180 64.14 N 173.10 W
Čukotskij Avtonomnyj Okrug □[8] 180 66.00 N 178.00 E
Čukotskij poluostrov ▸[1] 180 66.00 N 175.00 W
Çukurca 128 37.15 N 43.37 E
Čukurova 85 41.47 N 71.07 E
Culaba 116 11.40 N 124.32 E
Čulakkurgan 85 43.46 N 69.12 E
Culaman 116 5.58 N 125.40 E
Culari 250 1.27 N 53.42 W
Culasi, Pil. 116 11.26 N 122.03 E
Culasi, Pil. 116 10.43 N 125.43 E
Culasian 116 8.51 N 117.29 E
Culasi Point ▸ 116 11.37 N 122.42 E
Culbertson, Mt., U.S. 198 48.08 N 104.30 W
Culbertson, Ne., U.S. 198 40.13 N 100.50 W
Culbertson Run ≃ 285 40.03 N 75.45 W
Culbin 168a 33.10 S 116.50 E
Culburra 170 34.57 S 150.47 E
Culcairn 166 35.40 S 147.03 E
Culcheth 262 53.27 N 2.32 W
Culdaff 48 55.18 N 7.11 W
Culdaff Bay ⊂ 48 55.17 N 7.10 W
Culebra 240m 18.18 N 65.18 W
Culebra, Isla de I 240m 18.19 N 65.17 W
Culebra, Sierra de la ⩘ 34 41.54 N 6.20 W
Culebra Peak ∧ 200 37.07 N 105.11 W
Culebrinas ≃ 240m 18.24 N 67.11 W
Culebrita, Isla I 240m 18.19 N 65.14 W
Culebro, Arroyo del ≃ 266a 40.19 N 3.34 W
Culemborg 52 51.56 N 5.13 E
Culfa 84 38.58 N 45.38 E
Culgoa ≃ 166 29.56 S 146.20 E
Culham Inlet ⊂ 162 33.55 S 120.04 E
Culiacán, Méx. 232 24.48 N 107.24 W
Culiacán, Méx. 232 24.04 N 107.05 W
Culiacán, Cerro ∧ 234 20.20 N 100.58 W
Culiacancito 232 24.50 N 107.32 W
Culijón, Nevado ∧ 248 14.38 S 69.14 W
Culion 116 11.53 N 120.01 E
Culion Island I 116 11.50 N 119.55 E
Cúllar 34 37.35 N 2.34 W
Cull Creek ≃ 282 37.42 N 122.03 W
Cullen, Scot., U.K. 46 57.41 N 2.49 W
Cullen, La., U.S. 194 32.58 N 93.27 W
Cullen Bullen 170 33.18 S 150.01 E
Cullen Point ▸ 164 11.57 S 141.54 E
Culleoka, Tn., U.S. 194 35.28 N 86.58 W
Culleoka, Tx., U.S. 222 33.08 N 96.29 W
Cullera 34 39.10 N 0.15 W
Cullicudden 46 57.39 N 4.13 W
Cullin, Lough ⊜ 48 53.57 N 9.12 W
Cullinan 158 25.40 S 28.31 E
Cullman 194 34.10 N 86.50 W
Culloden Battlesite ⊥ 46 57.28 N 4.05 W
Cullom 216 40.53 N 88.16 W
Cullompton 42 50.52 N 3.24 W
Cullowhee 192 35.18 N 83.10 W
Cully 58 46.29 N 6.44 E
Cullybackey 48 54.53 N 6.21 W
Culm ≃ 42 50.46 N 3.31 W
Čul'man 74 56.52 N 124.52 E
Cülmen 130 37.19 N 38.48 E
Culmore 284c 38.51 N 77.08 W
Culoz 62 45.51 N 5.47 E
Culpeper 188 38.28 N 77.59 W
Culpina 248 20.50 S 64.58 W
Culrain 46 57.55 N 4.24 W
Cults 46 57.07 N 2.10 W
Cultus Lake 224 49.04 N 121.58 W
Cultus Lake ⊜ 224 49.03 N 121.58 W
Cultus Lake Provincial Park ♠ 224 49.03 N 121.58 W
Culú-Culú, Arroyo ≃ 258 35.19 S 58.57 W
Culú-Culú, Laguna ⊜ 258 35.20 S 58.59 W
Culuene ≃ 255 12.56 S 52.51 W
Čuluunchoroot 88 49.41 N 114.15 E
Čuluut 102 45.48 N 107.05 E
Čuluutyn ≃ 88 49.11 N 100.41 E
Culvain ∧ 46 56.56 N 5.17 W
Culver, In., U.S. 216 41.13 N 86.25 W
Culver, Or., U.S. 202 44.31 N 121.12 W
Culver, Point ▸ 162 32.54 S 124.43 E
Culver City 228 34.01 N 118.23 W
Culverden 172 42.46 S 172.51 E
Culvers Lake 210 41.10 N 74.48 W
Culverstone Green 260 51.20 N 0.21 E
Čulym 86 55.06 N 80.58 E
Čulym ≃, Ross. 86 57.43 N 83.51 E
Čulym ≃, Ross. 86 54.38 N 78.16 E
Čulyšman ≃ 86 51.20 N 87.45 E
Čum 24 67.06 N 63.07 E
Cuma 152 12.52 S 15.05 E
Cuma (Cumae) ⊥ 68 40.50 N 14.06 E
Čumakovo 86 55.41 N 79.02 E
Cumalı 130 36.42 N 27.27 E
Cumaná 246 10.28 N 64.10 W
Cumanacoa 246 10.15 N 63.55 W
Cumanayagua 240p 22.09 N 80.12 W
Cumaovası 130 38.15 N 27.09 E
Cumare, Cerro ∧[2] 246 0.28 N 73.52 W
Cumari 255 18.16 S 48.11 W
Cumbal 246 0.54 N 77.47 W
Cumbal, Nevado ∧ 246 0.57 N 77.52 W
Cumbe 250 10.21 S 37.14 W
Cumbee 220 28.04 N 81.55 W
Cumberland, B.C., Can. 182 49.37 N 125.01 W
Cumberland, Ia., U.S. 198 41.16 N 94.52 W
Cumberland, Ky., U.S. 192 36.58 N 82.59 W
Cumberland, Md., U.S. 188 39.39 N 78.45 W
Cumberland, Va., U.S. 192 37.29 N 78.14 W
Cumberland, Wa., U.S. 224 47.16 N 121.55 W
Cumberland, Wi., U.S. 190 45.31 N 92.01 W
Cumberland □[6], N.J., U.S. 208 39.26 N 75.14 W
Cumberland □[6], Pa., U.S. 208 40.12 N 77.12 W
Cumberland ≃ 178 37.09 N 88.25 W
Cumberland, Lake ⊜[1] 194 36.57 N 84.55 W
Cumberland, South Fork ≃ 192 36.58 N 84.36 W
Cumberland City 194 36.23 N 87.38 W
Cumberland Falls State Resort Park ♠ 192 36.50 N 84.20 W
Cumberland Gap )( 192 36.36 N 83.41 W
Cumberland Gap National Historical Park ♠ 192 36.36 N 83.40 W
Cumberland Hill 207 41.58 N 71.27 W
Cumberland House 184 53.58 N 102.16 W
Cumberland Indian Reserve ◆[4] 184 53.04 N 104.50 W
Cumberland Island National Seashore ♠ 192 30.50 N 81.27 W
Cumberland Islands II 166 20.40 S 149.09 E
Cumberland Lake ⊜ 184 54.02 N 102.17 W
Cumberland Peninsula ▸[1] 176 66.50 N 64.00 W
Cumberland Plateau ⩘[1] 192 36.20 N 84.30 W
Cumberland Sound ⊔ 176 65.10 N 65.30 W
Cumbernauld 46 55.58 N 3.59 W
Cumborah 166 29.44 S 147.46 E
Cumbria □[6] 44 54.30 N 3.00 W
Cumbrian Mountains ∧ 44 54.30 N 3.05 W
Čumbur-Kosa 83 46.57 N 38.53 E
Cumby 222 33.08 N 95.50 W
Cumeral Nuevo 200 30.54 N 110.51 W
Cumiana 62 44.59 N 7.22 E
Čumikan 89 54.42 N 135.19 E
Cuminá → Paru de Oeste ≃ 250 1.30 S 56.00 W
Cuminapanema ≃ 250 1.09 S 54.54 W
Cumnestown 46 57.32 N 2.20 W
Cumming 192 34.12 N 84.08 W
Cummings Mountain ∧ 228 35.03 N 118.34 W
Cummington 207 42.27 N 72.53 W
Cummins 166 34.16 S 135.44 E


**Symbols** in the index entries represent the broad categories identified in the key at the right. Symbols with superior numbers (⩘[1]) identify subcategories (see complete key on page I · 1).

**Symbole** im Register stellen die rechts im Schlüssel erklärten Kategorien dar. Symbole mit hochgestellten Ziffern (⩘[1]) bezeichnen Unterabteilungen einer Kategorie (vgl. vollständiger Schlüssel auf Seite I · 1).

**Los símbolos** incluídos en el texto del índice representan las grandes categorías identificadas con la clave a la derecha. Los símbolos con números en su parte superior (⩘[1]) identifican las subcategorías (véase la clave completa en la página I · 1).

**Les symboles** de l'index représentent les catégories indiquées dans la légende à droite. Les symboles suivis d'un indice (⩘[1]) représentent des sous-catégories (voir légende complète à la page I · 1).

**Os símbolos** incluídos no texto do índice representam as grandes categorias identificadas com a chave à direita. Os símbolos com números em sua parte superior (⩘[1]) identificam as subcategorias (veja-se a chave completa à página I · 1).

| | | | | | | |
|---|---|---|---|---|---|---|
| ∧ Mountain | Berg | Montaña | Montagne | Montanha |
| ⩘ Mountains | Gebirge | Montañas | Montagnes | Montanhas |
| )( Pass | Paß | Paso | Col | Passo |
| ∨ Valley, Canyon | Tal, Cañon | Valle, Cañón | Vallée, Canyon | Vale, Canhão |
| = Plain | Ebene | Llano | Plaine | Planície |
| ▸ Cape | Kap | Cabo | Cap | Cabo |
| I Island | Insel | Isla | Île | Ilha |
| II Islands | Inseln | Islas | Îles | Ilhas |
| ◆ Other Topographic Features | Andere Topographische Objekte | Otros Elementos Topográficos | Autres données topographiques | Outros acidentes topográficos |

ESPAÑOL — FRANÇAIS — PORTUGUÊS


| Nombre / Nom / Nome | Página / Page | Lat.°′ | Long.°′ W = Oeste / W = Ouest |
|---|---|---|---|
| Cummins, Mount ∧ | 182 | 52.03 N | 118.15 W |
| Cummins Creek ≃ | 222 | 29.43 N | 96.31 W |
| Cummins Range ⋏ | 162 | 19.05 S | 127.10 E |
| Cumnock | 44 | 55.27 N | 4.16 W |
| Cumnor | 42 | 51.44 N | 1.20 W |
| Cumpas | 232 | 30.02 N | 109.48 W |
| Çumra | 130 | 37.34 N | 32.48 E |
| Cumshewa Inlet ⊂ | 182 | 53.03 N | 131.45 W |
| Cumuripa | 232 | 28.08 N | 109.53 W |
| Cumwhinton | 44 | 54.52 N | 2.51 W |
| Čumyš ≃ | 86 | 53.31 N | 83.10 E |
| Čun'a ≃, Ross. | 74 | 61.36 N | 96.30 E |
| Čuna ≃, Ross. | 88 | 57.47 N | 95.26 E |
| Cunani | 250 | 2.52 N | 51.06 W |
| Cunauaru ≃ | 246 | 3.10 S | 63.01 W |
| Cunaviche | 246 | 7.22 N | 67.25 W |
| Cunco | 252 | 38.55 S | 72.02 W |
| Cuncumén | 252 | 31.53 S | 70.38 W |
| Cundeelee Reserve ✦[4] | 162 | 30.30 S | 123.25 E |
| Cunderdin | 162 | 31.39 S | 117.15 E |
| Cundinamarca □[5] | 246 | 5.00 N | 74.00 W |
| Cunduacán | 234 | 18.04 N | 93.10 W |
| Čundža | 86 | 43.32 N | 79.28 E |
| Cunene □[5] | 152 | 16.30 S | 15.30 E |
| Cunene (Kunene) ≃ | 152 | 17.20 S | 11.50 E |
| Cuneo | 62 | 44.23 N | 7.32 E |
| Cuneo □[4] | 62 | 44.31 N | 7.34 E |
| Cunewalde | 54 | 51.06 N | 14.30 E |
| Cuney | 222 | 32.02 N | 95.25 W |
| Cung Hau, Cua ≃[1] | 110 | 9.46 N | 106.34 E |
| Cung Son | 110 | 13.02 N | 108.58 E |
| Çüngüş | 130 | 38.13 N | 39.17 E |
| Cunha | 256 | 23.05 S | 44.58 W |
| Cunhambebe | 256 | 23.00 S | 44.20 W |
| Cunha Porã | 252 | 26.54 S | 53.09 W |
| Cunhinga | 152 | 12.11 S | 16.47 E |
| Cunhinga ≃ | 152 | 10.38 S | 16.48 E |
| Cunhuã, Igarapé ≃ | 248 | 5.46 S | 64.36 W |
| Cunlhat | 62 | 45.38 N | 3.35 E |
| Cunliffe | 168b | 34.05 S | 137.45 E |
| Cunnamulla | 166 | 28.04 S | 145.41 E |
| Cunningham, Austl. | 171a | 28.09 S | 151.51 E |
| Cunningham, Ks., U.S. | 198 | 37.38 N | 98.25 W |
| Cunningham, Lake ◎ | 240b | 25.04 N | 77.26 W |
| Cunninghame □[9] | 46 | 55.40 N | 4.30 W |
| Cunningham Falls State Park ♠ | 208 | 39.35 N | 77.27 W |
| Cunningham Park ♠, Ma., U.S. | 283 | 42.15 N | 71.03 W |
| Cunningham Park ♠, N.Y., U.S. | 276 | 40.44 N | 73.46 W |
| Čunojar | 88 | 57.27 N | 97.18 E |
| Cunqian | 100 | 28.30 N | 115.10 E |
| Čunskij, Ross. | 88 | 56.05 N | 99.41 E |
| Čunskij, Ross. | 88 | 57.26 N | 97.31 E |
| Cuntan | 107 | 29.37 N | 106.36 E |
| Cunucunuma ≃ | 246 | 3.13 N | 65.58 W |
| Čuny | 76 | 59.39 N | 36.04 E |
| Čuokkaraš'ša ∧ | 24 | 69.57 N | 24.32 E |
| Cuorgnè | 62 | 45.23 N | 7.39 E |
| Čupa | 24 | 66.16 N | 33.00 E |
| Čupalejka | 80 | 55.11 N | 42.33 E |
| Cupar, Sk., Can. | 184 | 50.57 N | 104.12 W |
| Cupar, Scot., U.K. | 46 | 56.19 N | 3.01 W |
| Cupecê, Ribeirão ≃ | 287b | 23.37 S | 46.42 W |
| Cupello | 66 | 42.04 N | 14.40 E |
| Cuperly | 50 | 49.04 N | 4.26 E |
| Cupertino | 226 | 37.19 N | 122.01 W |
| Cupica, Golfo de ⊂ | 246 | 6.35 N | 77.25 W |
| Cupins | 255 | 19.51 S | 51.03 W |
| Cupra Marittima | 66 | 43.01 N | 13.51 E |
| Cupramontana | 66 | 43.27 N | 13.07 E |
| Ćuprija | 38 | 43.56 N | 21.23 E |
| Čuprovo | 24 | 64.14 N | 46.36 E |
| Cupsaw Lake ◎ | 276 | 41.07 N | 74.15 W |
| Cuqiao | 107 | 30.36 N | 103.59 E |
| Cuquema ≃ | 152 | 12.03 S | 17.40 E |
| Cuquenán ≃ | 246 | 4.45 N | 61.30 W |
| Cuquío | 234 | 20.55 N | 103.02 W |
| Čur | 80 | 57.07 N | 52.58 E |
| Curaçá | 250 | 8.59 S | 39.54 W |
| Curaçao I | 241s | 12.11 N | 69.00 W |
| Curacautín | 252 | 38.26 S | 71.53 W |
| Curacaví | 252 | 33.24 S | 71.09 W |
| Čuračiki | 80 | 55.44 N | 47.26 E |
| Curaglia | 58 | 46.41 N | 8.51 E |
| Cural Novo, Ribeirão ≃ | 256 | 21.17 S | 43.51 W |
| Curanilahue | 252 | 37.28 S | 73.21 W |
| Curanipe | 252 | 35.50 S | 72.38 W |
| Curanja ≃ | 248 | 9.58 S | 70.58 W |
| Čurapča | 74 | 62.00 N | 132.24 E |
| Curapi ≃ | 250 | 1.25 N | 53.49 W |
| Curaray ≃ | 246 | 2.20 S | 74.05 W |
| Čurbek | 85 | 39.59 N | 69.56 E |
| Curcani | 38 | 44.12 N | 26.35 E |
| Curdies ≃ | 169 | 38.30 S | 142.55 E |
| Cure ≃ | 50 | 47.40 N | 3.41 E |
| Curecanti National Recreation Area ♠ | 200 | 38.24 N | 107.25 W |
| Curepipe | 157c | 20.19 S | 57.31 E |
| Curepto | 252 | 35.05 S | 72.01 W |
| Curequetê ≃ | 248 | 8.20 S | 65.40 W |
| Curiapo | 246 | 8.33 N | 61.00 W |
| Curib | 84 | 42.14 N | 46.49 E |
| Curiche Grande (Corixo Grande) ≃ | 248 | 17.43 S | 57.43 W |
| Curicó | 252 | 34.59 S | 71.14 W |
| Curicuriari ≃ | 246 | 0.14 S | 66.48 W |
| Curières, Lac ◎ | 206 | 46.41 N | 74.51 W |
| Curimatá | 250 | 10.02 S | 44.17 W |
| Curimeo | 234 | 20.01 N | 101.42 W |
| Curinga | 68 | 38.49 N | 16.19 E |
| Curious, Mount ∧ | 162 | 27.28 S | 114.20 E |
| Curisevo ≃ | 255 | 12.14 S | 53.17 W |
| Curitiba | 252 | 25.25 S | 49.15 W |
| Curitibanos | 252 | 27.18 S | 50.36 W |
| Curiuaú ≃ | 246 | 1.51 S | 61.14 W |
| Curiúva | 255 | 24.02 S | 50.27 W |
| Curl Curl | 274a | 33.46 S | 151.18 E |
| Curlew | 182 | 48.53 N | 118.35 W |
| Curlewis | 166 | 31.07 S | 150.16 E |
| Curnamona | 166 | 31.39 S | 139.32 E |
| Curoca Norte | 152 | 16.18 S | 12.58 E |
| Curone ≃ | 62 | 45.03 N | 8.54 E |
| Curon Venosta (Graun) | 64 | 46.49 N | 10.32 E |
| Čurovići | 78 | 52.10 N | 32.01 E |
| Currais Novos | 250 | 6.15 S | 36.31 W |
| Curralinho | 250 | 1.48 S | 49.47 W |
| Curramulka | 168b | 34.42 S | 137.42 E |
| Curran | 219 | 39.44 N | 89.46 W |
| Currant Creek ≃, Co., U.S. | 200 | 38.29 N | 105.24 W |
| Currant Creek ≃, Mt., U.S. | 202 | 46.22 N | 108.39 W |
| Currant Mountain ∧ | 204 | 38.55 N | 115.25 W |
| Currarong | 170 | 35.01 S | 150.49 E |
| Currency Creek | 168b | 35.28 S | 138.46 E |
| Current ≃, On., Can. | 190 | 48.27 N | 89.11 W |
| Current ≃, U.S. | 194 | 36.16 N | 90.57 W |
| Current Islands II | 192 | 25.22 N | 76.49 W |
| Currie, Austl. | 166 | 39.56 S | 143.52 E |
| Currie, Scot., U.K. | 46 | 55.54 N | 3.20 W |
| Currie, Mn., U.S. | 198 | 44.04 N | 95.39 W |
| Currituck | 192 | 36.26 N | 76.00 W |
| Currituck □[6] | 208 | 36.28 N | 76.03 W |
| Currituck Seamount ✢[3] | 14 | 30.00 S | 173.30 W |
| Currituck Sound ≍ | 192 | 36.20 N | 75.52 W |
| Curry | 180 | 62.37 N | 150.01 W |
| Curry, Lake ◎[1] | 226 | 38.22 N | 122.08 W |
| Curry Rivel | 42 | 51.02 N | 2.52 W |
| Curryville, Mo., U.S. | 219 | 39.20 N | 91.20 W |
| Curryville, Pa., U.S. | 214 | 40.17 N | 78.20 W |
| Cursi | 68 | 40.09 N | 18.18 E |
| Curslack ✦[8] | 52 | 53.27 N | 10.13 E |
| Curtarolo | 64 | 45.31 N | 11.50 E |
| Curtea de Argeș | 38 | 45.08 N | 24.41 E |
| Curtice | 214 | 41.29 N | 82.49 W |
| Curtina | 252 | 32.09 S | 56.07 W |
| Curtin Springs | 162 | 25.20 S | 131.45 E |
| Curtis, Ar., U.S. | 194 | 33.59 N | 93.06 W |
| Curtis, Ne., U.S. | 198 | 40.37 N | 100.30 W |
| Curtis, Port ⊤[3] | 166 | 24.00 S | 151.30 E |
| Curtis Bay ⊂ | 284b | 39.13 N | 76.35 W |
| Curtis Channel ≍ | 166 | 23.30 S | 151.45 E |
| Curtis Creek ⊂ | 284b | 39.12 N | 76.35 W |
| Curtis Island I, Austl. | 166 | 23.38 S | 151.09 E |
| Curtis Island I, N.Z. | 14 | 30.30 S | 178.34 W |
| Curtis Lake ◎ | 176 | 66.38 N | 89.02 W |
| Curtisville | 214 | 40.38 N | 79.51 W |
| Curu ≃ | 250 | 3.22 S | 39.04 W |
| Curuá ≃, Bra. | 250 | 5.23 S | 54.22 W |
| Curuá ≃, Bra. | 250 | 1.55 S | 55.07 W |
| Curuá ≃, Bra. | 255 | 13.51 S | 51.38 W |
| Curuá, Ilha do I | 250 | 0.48 N | 50.10 W |
| Curuaés ≃ | 250 | 7.30 S | 54.45 W |
| Curuan | 116 | 7.13 N | 122.14 E |
| Curuá-Una ≃ | 250 | 2.24 S | 54.05 W |
| Curubandé | 236 | 10.43 N | 85.26 W |
| Curuçá | 250 | 0.43 S | 47.50 W |
| Curuçá ✦[8] | 287b | 23.30 S | 46.25 W |
| Curuçá ≃ | 246 | 4.27 S | 71.23 W |
| Curuçambaba | 250 | 2.08 S | 49.18 W |
| Curug, Indon. | 115a | 6.15 S | 106.33 E |
| Čurug, Jugo. | 38 | 45.29 N | 20.04 E |
| Curuguaty | 252 | 24.31 S | 55.42 W |
| Curumo | 286c | 10.27 N | 66.52 W |
| Curumu | 250 | 1.01 S | 51.03 W |
| Curunga | 152 | 12.51 S | 21.12 E |
| Curup | 112 | 3.28 S | 102.32 E |
| Curupá | 250 | 9.54 S | 45.54 W |
| Curupayty, Riacho ≃ | 248 | 22.03 S | 58.00 W |
| Cururu ≃, Bra. | 248 | 7.12 S | 58.03 W |
| Cururu ≃, Bra. | 250 | 0.39 S | 50.11 W |
| Cururu-Açu ≃ | 250 | 8.58 S | 57.13 W |
| Cururupu | 250 | 1.50 S | 44.52 W |
| Curuzú Cuatiá | 252 | 29.47 S | 58.03 W |
| Curva Grande | 250 | 2.37 S | 45.27 W |
| Curvelo | 255 | 18.45 S | 44.25 W |
| Curwensville | 214 | 40.58 N | 78.31 W |
| Curwensville Lake ◎[1] | 214 | 40.55 N | 78.37 W |
| Curwensville State Park ♠ | 214 | 40.55 N | 78.34 W |
| Cusago | 266b | 45.27 N | 9.02 E |
| Cusano Milanino | 62 | 45.33 N | 9.11 E |
| Cusano Mutri | 68 | 41.20 N | 14.30 E |
| Cusco | 248 | 13.31 S | 71.59 W |
| Cusco □[5] | 248 | 12.30 S | 72.30 W |
| Cuscuzeiro, Pico do ∧ | 256 | 23.18 S | 44.47 W |
| Cushabatay ≃ | 248 | 7.09 S | 75.08 W |
| Cushendall | 48 | 55.06 N | 6.04 W |
| Cushendun | 48 | 55.07 N | 6.03 W |
| Cushina ≃ | 48 | 53.11 N | 7.05 W |
| Cushing, Ok., U.S. | 196 | 35.59 N | 96.46 W |
| Cushing, Tx., U.S. | 222 | 31.43 N | 94.50 W |
| Cushing Memorial State Park ♠ | 283 | 42.10 N | 70.45 W |
| Cushman | 194 | 35.52 N | 91.45 W |
| Cushman, Lake ◎[1] | 224 | 47.28 N | 123.14 W |
| Cusiana ≃ | 246 | 4.33 N | 71.51 W |
| Cusick | 202 | 48.20 N | 117.17 W |
| Cusihuiriáchic | 232 | 28.14 N | 106.50 W |
| Cusna, Monte ∧ | 64 | 44.17 N | 10.23 E |
| Čusovaja ≃ | 86 | 58.13 N | 56.22 E |
| Čusovoj | 86 | 58.17 N | 57.49 E |
| Cusset | 32 | 46.08 N | 3.28 E |
| Cusseta | 192 | 32.18 N | 84.46 W |
| Cussewago Creek ≃ | 214 | 41.38 N | 80.11 W |
| Cussey-sur-l'Ognon | 58 | 47.20 N | 5.56 E |
| Cusso ≃ | 152 | 14.16 S | 15.36 E |
| Cust, N.Z. | 172 | 43.19 S | 172.22 E |
| Čust, Uzb. | 85 | 41.00 N | 71.15 E |
| Custar | 216 | 41.17 N | 83.51 W |
| Custer, Mi., U.S. | 190 | 43.57 N | 86.13 W |
| Custer, Mt., U.S. | 202 | 46.07 N | 107.33 W |
| Custer, Ok., U.S. | 196 | 35.40 N | 98.53 W |
| Custer, S.D., U.S. | 198 | 43.46 N | 103.35 W |
| Custer, Wa., U.S. | 224 | 48.55 N | 122.38 W |
| Custer City | 214 | 41.54 N | 78.39 W |
| Custer Creek ≃ | 198 | 46.42 N | 105.29 W |
| Custer State Park ♠ | 198 | 43.43 N | 103.23 W |
| Custines | 56 | 48.48 N | 6.09 E |
| Custódia | 250 | 8.07 S | 37.39 W |
| Custonaci | 70 | 38.04 N | 12.41 E |
| Cut, Nuhu I | 164 | 5.35 S | 133.00 E |
| Cut and Shoot | 222 | 30.19 N | 95.25 W |
| Cutato ≃ | 152 | 10.33 S | 16.48 E |
| Cut Bank | 202 | 48.37 N | 112.19 W |
| Cutbank ≃ | 182 | 54.44 N | 118.31 W |
| Cut Bank Creek ≃, N.A. | 198 | 48.35 N | 100.52 W |
| Cut Bank Creek ≃, Mt., U.S. | 202 | 48.29 N | 112.14 W |
| Cut Beaver Lake ◎ | 184 | 53.47 N | 102.38 W |
| Čutejevo | 80 | 55.16 N | 47.47 E |
| Cutervo | 248 | 6.22 S | 78.51 W |
| Cutervo, Parque Nacional ♠ | 248 | 6.10 S | 78.45 W |
| Cuthand Creek ≃ | 194 | 33.23 N | 94.57 W |
| Cuthbert | 192 | 31.46 N | 84.47 W |
| Cut Knife | 184 | 52.44 N | 109.01 W |
| Cutler, Ca., U.S. | 226 | 36.31 N | 119.17 W |
| Cutler, Me., U.S. | 188 | 44.39 N | 67.12 W |
| Cutler Ridge | 220 | 25.34 N | 80.20 W |
| Cutlerville | 216 | 42.50 N | 85.39 W |
| Cutral-Có | 252 | 38.56 S | 69.14 W |
| Cutro | 68 | 39.02 N | 16.59 E |
| Cutrofiano | 68 | 40.07 N | 18.12 E |
| Cuttack | 120 | 20.30 N | 85.50 E |
| Cuttyhunk Island I | 207 | 41.25 N | 70.56 W |
| Čutyr' | 80 | 57.24 N | 53.17 E |
| Cutzamala ≃ | 234 | 18.22 N | 100.39 W |
| Cutzamala de Pinzón | 234 | 18.28 N | 100.34 W |
| Cutzio | 234 | 18.39 N | 100.54 W |
| Čuvašija □[3] | 80 | 55.30 N | 47.00 E |
| Cuvette □[5] | 152 | 0.30 S | 16.00 E |
| Cuvier, Cape > | 162 | 24.05 S | 113.22 E |
| Cuvilly | 50 | 49.33 N | 2.42 E |
| Cuvo ≃ | 152 | 10.50 S | 13.47 E |
| Cuxhaven | 52 | 53.52 N | 8.42 E |
| Cuxton | 260 | 51.22 N | 0.27 E |
| Cuyabá → Cuiabá | 248 | 15.35 S | 56.05 W |
| Cuyaguateje ≃ | 240p | 22.05 N | 83.58 W |
| Cuyahoga □[6] | 214 | 41.30 N | 81.41 W |
| Cuyahoga ≃ | 214 | 41.30 N | 81.42 W |
| Cuyahoga County Airport ⊠ | 279a | 41.34 N | 81.29 W |
| Cuyahoga Falls | 214 | 41.08 N | 81.29 W |
| Cuyahoga Heights | 279a | 41.26 N | 81.39 W |
| Cuyahoga Valley National Recreation Area ♠ | 214 | 41.20 N | 81.35 W |
| Cuyama ≃ | 204 | 34.54 N | 120.18 W |
| Cuyamaca Peak ∧ | 204 | 32.57 N | 116.36 W |
| Cuyamaca Rancho State Park ♠ | 204 | 32.58 N | 116.32 W |
| Cuyamel | 236 | 15.38 N | 88.12 W |
| Cuyapo | 116 | 15.46 N | 120.40 E |
| Cuyk | 52 | 51.44 N | 5.52 E |
| Cuyler | 210 | 42.44 N | 75.57 W |
| Cuylerville | 210 | 42.47 N | 77.52 W |
| Cuyo | 116 | 10.51 N | 121.00 E |
| Cuyo East Pass ≍ | 116 | 11.00 N | 121.28 E |
| Cuyo Island I | 116 | 10.51 N | 121.02 E |
| Cuyo Islands II | 116 | 11.04 N | 120.57 E |
| Cuyo West Pass ≍ | 116 | 11.00 N | 120.30 E |
| Cuyubini ≃ | 246 | 8.20 N | 60.20 W |
| Cuyuni ≃ | 246 | 6.23 N | 58.41 W |
| Cuyuni-Mazaruni □[4] | 246 | 6.00 N | 60.00 W |
| Cuyutlán, Laguna ⊂ | 234 | 19.00 N | 104.10 W |
| Cuzco → Cusco | 248 | 13.31 S | 71.59 W |
| Čuzik ≃ | 86 | 58.03 N | 80.37 E |
| Cuzna ≃ | 34 | 38.04 N | 4.41 W |
| Cuzzago | 58 | 46.00 N | 8.22 E |
| Cvetnogorsk | 86 | 54.14 N | 90.27 E |
| Cvikov | 54 | 50.48 N | 14.40 E |
| Cwmbran | 42 | 51.39 N | 3.00 W |
| Cyangugu | 154 | 2.29 S | 28.54 E |
| Cybinka | 30 | 52.12 N | 14.48 E |
| Cyclades → Kikládhes II | 38 | 37.30 N | 25.00 E |
| Cyclone | 214 | 41.50 N | 78.35 W |
| Cygnet | 216 | 41.14 N | 83.38 W |
| Cygnet Bay ⊂ | 162 | 16.35 S | 123.05 E |
| Cygnet Lake ◎ | 184 | 56.47 N | 94.54 W |
| Cygnet River | 168b | 35.42 S | 137.31 E |
| Cylburn Park ♠ | 284b | 39.21 N | 76.39 W |
| Cynin ≃ | 42 | 51.48 N | 4.29 W |
| Cynthiana, Ky., U.S. | 218 | 38.23 N | 84.17 W |
| Cynthiana, Oh., U.S. | 218 | 39.10 N | 83.21 W |
| Cynwyl Elfed | 42 | 51.55 N | 4.22 W |
| Cypern → Cyprus □[1] | 130 | 35.00 N | 33.00 E |
| Cypress, Ca., U.S. | 280 | 33.49 N | 118.02 W |
| Cypress, La., U.S. | 194 | 31.36 N | 93.02 W |
| Cypress, Tx., U.S. | 222 | 29.58 N | 95.42 W |
| Cypress Bayou ≃ | 194 | 35.03 N | 91.42 W |
| Cypress Creek ≃, Fl., U.S. | 220 | 28.05 N | 82.24 W |
| Cypress Creek ≃, Tx., U.S. | 194 | 30.19 N | 93.45 W |
| Cypress Creek ≃, Tx., U.S. | 222 | 30.02 N | 95.19 W |
| Cypress Gardens ♠ | 220 | 28.00 N | 81.42 W |
| Cypress Hills ⋏[2] | 184 | 49.40 N | 109.30 W |
| Cypress Hills Provincial Park ♠, Ab., Can. | 184 | 49.39 N | 110.10 W |
| Cypress Hills Provincial Park ♠, Sk., Can. | 134 | 49.39 N | 109.30 W |
| Cypress Island I | 224 | 48.35 N | 122.42 W |
| Cypress Lake ◎, Sk., Can. | 184 | 49.28 N | 109.29 W |
| Cypress Lake ◎, Fl., U.S. | 220 | 28.05 N | 81.19 W |
| Cypress Point > | 226 | 36.35 N | 121.59 W |
| Cypress Quarters | 220 | 27.15 N | 80.48 W |
| Cypress River | 184 | 49.34 N | 99.05 W |
| Cypress Swamp ≃ | 208 | 37.02 N | 76.53 W |
| Cypress Swamp ≋ | 208 | 38.30 N | 75.17 W |
| Cyprus □[1], Asia | 22 | 35.00 N | 33.00 E |
| Cyprus □[1], Asia | 130 | 35.00 N | 33.00 E |
| Cyprus, North (Kuzey Kıbrıs) □[1], Asia | 22 | 35.15 N | 33.40 E |
| Cyprus, North (Kuzey Kıbrıs) □[1], Asia | 130 | 35.15 N | 33.40 E |
| Cyrenaica → Barqah □[9] | 146 | 31.00 N | 22.30 E |
| Cyrene | 219 | 39.17 N | 91.06 W |
| Cyrene ⊥ | 146 | 32.49 N | 21.52 E |
| Cyril | 196 | 34.53 N | 98.12 W |
| Cyrildene ✦[8] | 273d | 26.11 S | 28.06 E |
| Cyrus Field Bay ⊂ | 176 | 62.50 N | 64.55 W |
| Čyrvonae, vozero ◎ | 76 | 52.24 N | 27.57 E |
| Cysoing | 50 | 50.34 N | 3.13 E |
| Cythera → Kíthira I | 38 | 36.20 N | 22.58 E |
| Czaplinek | 30 | 53.34 N | 16.14 E |
| Czarna Białostocka | 30 | 53.19 N | 23.16 E |
| Czarna Woda | 30 | 53.51 N | 18.06 E |
| Czarne | 30 | 53.42 N | 16.57 E |
| Czarnków | 30 | 52.55 N | 16.34 E |
| Czech Republic (Česká Republika) □[1], Europe | 22 | 49.40 N | 15.10 E |
| Czech Republic (Česká Republika) □[1], Europe | 30 | 49.40 N | 15.10 E |
| Czempiń | 30 | 52.10 N | 16.47 E |
| Czerniejewo | 30 | 52.26 N | 17.30 E |
| Czernowitz → Chernivtsi | 78 | 48.18 N | 25.56 E |
| Czersk | 30 | 53.48 N | 18.00 E |
| Czerwieńsk | 30 | 52.01 N | 15.25 E |
| Częstochowa | 30 | 50.49 N | 19.06 E |
| Częstochowa □[4] | 30 | 50.40 N | 19.15 E |
| Człopa | 30 | 53.06 N | 16.08 E |
| Człuchów | 30 | 53.41 N | 17.21 E |
| Czudec | 30 | 49.57 N | 21.50 E |
| **D** | | | |
| Da → Black ≃, Asia | 110 | 21.15 N | 105.20 E |
| Da ≃, Zhg. | 100 | 28.10 N | 120.14 E |
| Daaden | 56 | 50.44 N | 7.58 E |
| Da'an, Zhg. | 89 | 45.28 N | 124.18 E |
| Da'an, Zhg. | 100 | 23.05 N | 115.37 E |
| Da'an, Zhg. | 107 | 29.23 N | 106.01 E |
| Da'an, Zhg. | 110 | 23.19 N | 110.34 E |
| Daanbantayan | 116 | 11.14 N | 124.00 E |
| Daba | 104 | 42.06 N | 122.00 E |
| Dabāb, Jabal aḍ- ∧ | 132 | 31.02 N | 35.38 E |
| Dabagou | 104 | 42.27 N | 122.00 E |
| Ḍab'ah, Ra's aḍ- > | 140 | 31.05 N | 28.26 E |
| Dabai | 150 | 11.31 N | 5.11 E |
| Dabaizhuang | 105 | 39.27 N | 117.23 E |
| Dabajuro | 246 | 11.02 N | 70.40 W |
| Dabakala | 150 | 8.22 N | 4.26 W |
| Dabali | 104 | 41.51 N | 120.37 E |
| Daba Ling ∧ | 100 | 24.28 N | 113.17 E |
| Dabancheng | 86 | 43.21 N | 88.19 E |
| Dabangdian | 100 | 31.37 N | 113.41 E |
| Dabaojiagangzi | 104 | 42.09 N | 123.33 E |
| Dabaozhuang | 105 | 40.18 N | 116.58 E |
| Dabaozi | 105 | 40.11 N | 115.10 E |
| Daba Shan ⋏ | 102 | 31.55 N | 109.05 E |
| Dabasi | 107 | 28.55 N | 105.09 E |
| Dabat | 144 | 12.58 N | 37.48 E |
| Dabayingzi | 104 | 42.11 N | 121.35 E |
| Dabbāgh, Jabal ∧ | 128 | 27.52 N | 35.45 E |
| Dabbūriya | 132 | 32.41 N | 35.22 E |
| Dabegabis | 158 | 28.07 S | 18.36 E |
| Dabeiba | 246 | 7.01 N | 76.16 W |
| Dabeiwa | 105 | 40.48 N | 117.31 E |
| Dabeiyingzi | 104 | 42.05 N | 122.08 E |
| Dabendorf | 54 | 52.14 N | 13.26 E |
| Daberas | 156 | 25.38 S | 18.29 E |
| Daberg ✦[8] | 263 | 51.40 N | 7.47 E |
| Dabhoi | 120 | 22.11 N | 73.26 E |
| Dābhol | 122 | 17.36 N | 73.10 E |
| Ḍab'ī, Wādī aḍ- V | 132 | 31.42 N | 36.42 E |
| Dąbie | 30 | 52.06 N | 18.49 E |
| Dąbie ✦[8] | 54 | 53.24 N | 14.40 E |
| Dąbie, Jezioro ◎ | 54 | 53.27 N | 14.40 E |
| Dabie Shan ⋏ | 100 | 31.00 N | 115.40 E |
| Dabilda | 146 | 12.46 N | 14.34 E |
| Dablān | 130 | 34.52 N | 40.34 E |
| Ďáblice ✦[8] | 54 | 50.08 N | 14.29 E |
| Dabnou | 150 | 14.09 N | 5.22 E |
| Dabo | 58 | 48.39 N | 7.14 E |
| Dabob Bay ⊂ | 224 | 47.47 N | 122.50 W |
| Dabobeizhuang | 105 | 39.18 N | 117.59 E |
| Dabola | 150 | 10.45 N | 11.07 W |
| Dabong | 114 | 5.23 N | 102.01 E |
| Daborow | 144 | 6.21 N | 48.43 E |
| Dabou | 150 | 5.19 N | 4.23 W |
| Daboya | 150 | 9.32 N | 1.23 W |
| Dabra | 124 | 25.54 N | 78.20 E |
| Dabraslauka | 76 | 52.24 N | 26.15 E |
| Dābri ✦[8] | 272a | 28.37 N | 77.05 E |
| Dabringhausen | 52 | 51.05 N | 7.11 E |
| Dąbrowa Białostocka | 30 | 53.39 N | 23.20 E |
| Dąbrowa Tarnowska | 30 | 50.11 N | 21.00 E |
| Dabryn' | 78 | 51.46 N | 29.12 E |
| Dabsan Hu ◎ | 102 | 36.58 N | 94.55 E |
| Dabu, Zhg. | 100 | 23.52 N | 116.54 E |
| Dabu, Zhg. | 100 | 24.20 N | 114.35 E |
| Dabu, Zhg. | 100 | 24.19 N | 116.43 E |
| Dabus ≃ | 144 | 10.48 N | 35.10 E |
| Dabusutu-Ula, gora ∧ | 86 | 50.44 N | 92.40 E |
| Dacaitun | 104 | 41.38 N | 121.18 E |
| Dacangzigou | 104 | 40.59 N | 121.01 E |
| Dacaocun | 105 | 40.34 N | 117.07 E |
| Dacca → Dhaka | 126 | 23.43 N | 90.25 E |
| Dachakou | 100 | 29.38 N | 118.18 E |
| Dachang, Zhg. | 105 | 39.53 N | 116.59 E |
| Dachang, Zhg. | 106 | 32.12 N | 118.45 E |
| Dachang, Zhg. | 106 | 31.18 N | 121.25 E |
| Dachang Airport ⊠ | 269b | 31.18 N | 121.25 E |
| Dachangshan Dao I | 98 | 39.10 N | 122.34 E |
| Dachau | 60 | 48.15 N | 11.27 E |
| Dachauer Moos ≋ | 60 | 48.12 N | 11.25 E |
| Dacheng | 100 | 28.34 N | 115.31 E |
| Dachengji | 100 | 33.52 N | 119.26 E |
| Dachenjiabao | 106 | 32.11 N | 120.22 E |
| Dachen Shan I | 106 | 30.21 N | 121.52 E |
| Dachixu | 100 | 25.10 N | 116.46 E |
| Dachongyu | 105 | 40.23 N | 117.41 E |
| Dachsberg ∧[2] | 263 | 51.30 N | 6.30 E |
| Dachsteinhöhlen ⊥[5] | 64 | 47.32 N | 13.43 E |
| Dačice | 61 | 49.05 N | 15.26 E |
| Dac Lac, Cao Nguyen ⋏[1] | 110 | 12.50 N | 108.05 E |
| Dačnoje ✦[8] | 265a | 59.50 N | 30.16 E |
| Dacoma | 196 | 36.39 N | 98.33 W |
| Dacorum □[8] | 260 | 51.45 N | 0.30 W |
| Dac To | 110 | 14.42 N | 107.51 E |
| Dacun, Zhg. | 102 | 27.55 N | 101.08 E |
| Dacun, Zhg. | 106 | 31.12 N | 119.40 E |
| Dadal | 88 | 49.01 N | 111.37 E |
| Dadanawa | 246 | 2.50 N | 59.30 W |
| Dadaolizhuang | 105 | 39.59 N | 116.59 E |
| Dadaotun | 104 | 41.46 N | 122.13 E |
| Dadar ✦[8] | 272c | 19.01 N | 72.50 E |
| Daday | 130 | 41.28 N | 33.28 E |
| Dadayungou | 104 | 41.23 N | 123.25 E |
| Daddys Creek ≃ | 192 | 36.05 N | 84.47 W |
| Dade □[6] | 220 | 25.33 N | 80.32 W |
| Dade Battlefield Historic Memorial ⊥ | 220 | 28.38 N | 82.09 W |
| Dade City | 220 | 28.21 N | 82.11 W |
| Dadeldhurā | 124 | 29.18 N | 80.35 E |
| Dadès, Oued ≃ | 148 | 30.55 N | 6.47 W |
| Dadeville | 194 | 32.49 N | 85.45 W |
| Dādhar | 120 | 29.28 N | 67.39 E |
| Dadian | 100 | 33.36 N | 117.16 E |
| Dadiangas → General Santos | 116 | 6.07 N | 125.11 E |
| Dadianzi | 104 | 42.11 N | 124.02 E |
| Dadingjiawopu | 104 | 41.13 N | 122.16 E |
| D'adino | 88 | 55.44 N | 105.45 E |
| Dadiya | 146 | 9.37 N | 11.26 E |
| Dadle | 144 | 5.20 N | 46.58 E |
| Dadnah | 128 | 25.33 N | 56.21 E |
| Dadonggejiang | 105 | 39.51 N | 116.48 E |
| Dadongzhou | 104 | 41.44 N | 124.00 E |
| Dadou ≃ | 32 | 43.44 N | 1.49 E |
| Dādpur, India | 272b | 22.42 N | 88.33 E |
| Dādpur, India | 272b | 22.54 N | 88.31 E |
| Dādra and Nagar Haveli □[8] | 122 | 20.05 N | 73.00 E |
| Dādu | 120 | 26.44 N | 67.47 E |
| Dadu ≃ | 102 | 29.33 N | 103.45 E |
| Dadugang | 102 | 22.23 N | 100.55 E |
| Dadukou, Zhg. | 100 | 25.44 N | 119.05 E |
| Dadukou, Zhg. | 107 | 28.45 N | 105.13 E |
| Dadukou, Zhg. | 107 | 29.28 N | 106.29 E |
| Daegu → Taegu | 98 | 35.52 N | 128.35 E |
| Daejeon → Taejŏn | 98 | 36.20 N | 127.26 E |
| Daerhanwangfu | 89 | 44.19 N | 122.15 E |
| Da'erhao | 98 | 41.45 N | 116.01 E |
| Daet | 116 | 14.05 N | 122.55 E |
| Daf' | 146 | 28.03 N | 19.57 E |
| Dafan, Zhg. | 100 | 29.41 N | 114.40 E |
| Dafan, Zhg. | 104 | 42.38 N | 122.11 E |
| Dafang | 102 | 27.04 N | 105.31 E |
| Dafangshen, Zhg. | 104 | 42.25 N | 123.14 E |
| Dafangshen, Zhg. | 104 | 42.34 N | 123.28 E |
| Dafangshen, Zhg. | 104 | 42.36 N | 123.04 E |
| Dafanhe | 104 | 42.13 N | 123.43 E |
| Dafanpuzi | 104 | 41.37 N | 122.50 E |
| Dafeng | 100 | 33.12 N | 120.30 E |
| Dafna | 132 | 33.14 N | 35.38 E |
| Dafoe | 184 | 51.46 N | 104.32 W |
| Dafoe ≃ | 184 | 55.55 N | 94.48 W |
| Dafoe Lake ◎ | 184 | 55.43 N | 96.15 W |
| Da Fo Si (Great Buddha Temple) ᵿ[1] | 106 | 30.16 N | 120.09 E |
| Dafoutuo | 105 | 40.24 N | 115.58 E |
| Dafu | 100 | 29.55 N | 118.35 E |
| Dafu ≃ | 100 | 30.52 N | 113.32 E |
| Dāfūr al-Janūbīyah □[4] | 140 | 11.45 N | 25.25 E |
| Dagā ≃ | 110 | 16.56 N | 94.45 E |
| Daga Medo | 144 | 7.59 N | 43.01 E |
| Dagana | 150 | 16.31 N | 15.30 W |
| Dagang, Zhg. | 100 | 33.12 N | 120.07 E |
| Dagang, Zhg. | 100 | 22.49 N | 113.23 E |
| Dagang, Zhg. | 106 | 32.12 N | 119.39 E |
| Dagangtou | 100 | 28.18 N | 119.44 E |
| Daganwangzhai | 104 | 40.49 N | 122.33 E |
| Daganzo de Arriba | 266a | 40.33 N | 3.27 W |
| Dagaokan | 104 | 40.46 N | 122.22 E |
| Dagaolifangcun | 104 | 41.10 N | 122.28 E |
| Dagaolitun | 104 | 42.26 N | 123.53 E |
| Dagaoyang | 106 | 30.35 N | 120.26 E |
| Daga Post | 140 | 9.12 N | 33.58 E |
| Dağardı | 130 | 39.26 N | 29.00 E |
| Dagash | 140 | 19.22 N | 33.24 E |
| Dağbeli | 130 | 37.12 N | 30.31 E |
| Dagcanglhamo | 102 | 34.02 N | 102.30 E |
| Dagda | 76 | 56.06 N | 27.32 E |
| Dageløkke | 41 | 55.04 N | 10.53 E |
| Dagenham ✦[8] | 260 | 51.32 N | 0.10 E |
| Dagestan □[3] | 72 | 43.00 N | 47.00 E |
| Dagestanskije Ogni | 84 | 42.07 N | 48.12 E |
| Daggafontein | 273d | 26.18 S | 28.28 E |
| Daggafontein Mines ✦[7] | 273d | 26.18 S | 28.29 E |
| Daggett | 228 | 34.51 N | 116.53 W |
| Dagg Sound ≍ | 172 | 45.23 S | 166.46 E |
| Daghfalī | 140 | 19.17 N | 32.30 E |
| Dağkızılca | 130 | 38.18 N | 27.24 E |
| Daglung | 120 | 28.54 N | 90.33 E |
| Dagmersellen | 58 | 47.13 N | 7.59 E |
| Dagö → Hiiumaa I | 76 | 58.52 N | 22.40 E |
| Dagomys | 84 | 43.40 N | 39.41 E |
| Dagongtun | 89 | 42.48 N | 121.58 E |
| Dagoretti | 154 | 1.18 S | 36.46 E |
| Dagsboro | 208 | 38.32 N | 75.14 W |
| Dagshai | 123 | 30.53 N | 77.03 E |
| Dagu | 105 | 38.59 N | 117.41 E |
| Dagu ≃ | 98 | 36.15 N | 120.06 E |
| Dagua | 164 | 3.25 S | 143.20 E |
| Daguan, Zhg. | 100 | 31.14 N | 117.01 E |
| Daguan, Zhg. | 102 | 27.44 N | 104.16 E |
| Daguan Hu ◎ | 100 | 30.00 N | 116.24 E |
| Daguao | 240m | 18.14 N | 65.41 W |
| Dagufen'gou | 105 | 40.41 N | 116.20 E |
| D'Aguilar, Cape > | 271d | 22.14 N | 114.15 E |
| D'Aguilar, Mount ∧ | 171a | 27.19 S | 152.47 E |
| D'Aguilar Range ⋏ | 171a | 27.10 S | 152.45 E |
| Dagujia | 98 | 42.22 N | 124.52 E |
| Dagujiazi | 104 | 42.20 N | 123.20 E |
| Da Guokui Shan ∧ | 89 | 45.17 N | 129.30 E |
| Dagupan | 116 | 16.03 N | 120.20 E |
| Daguragu Aboriginal Reserve ✦[4] | 162 | 17.35 S | 130.30 E |
| Dagushan | 104 | 41.03 N | 123.02 E |
| Dagus Mines | 214 | 41.21 N | 78.36 W |
| Dagutang | 100 | 29.38 N | 116.06 E |
| Dagwin | 110 | 18.04 N | 97.41 E |
| Dagzê Co ◎ | 120 | 31.55 N | 87.35 E |
| Dahabān | 144 | 21.55 N | 39.04 E |
| Dahalac National Park ♠ | 144 | 15.40 N | 40.05 E |
| Dahanchang | 105 | 39.29 N | 117.05 E |
| Dahaneh-ye Ghowrī | 120 | 35.54 N | 68.30 E |
| Dahaneh-ye Kāshār | 120 | 35.09 N | 66.14 E |
| Dahan-e Qowmghī | 120 | 34.28 N | 66.31 E |
| Dahantun | 104 | 42.10 N | 122.41 E |
| Dahasah, Wādī V | 142 | 28.08 N | 31.00 E |
| Dahdāh, Tall ∧[2] | 132 | 32.36 N | 36.03 E |
| Dahe | 106 | 31.42 N | 120.37 E |
| Dahebei | 105 | 39.10 N | 117.39 E |
| Dahei | 120 | 21.42 N | 72.35 E |
| Daheiding Shan ∧ | 89 | 47.58 N | 129.07 E |
| Daheiyugou | 104 | 41.21 N | 121.55 E |
| Dahekou | 106 | 32.16 N | 119.05 E |
| Dahengdu | 100 | 29.03 N | 121.30 E |
| Dahenqin Dao I | 100 | 22.06 N | 113.30 E |
| Daheqiao | 100 | 29.25 N | 115.16 E |
| Dahijuri | 126 | 22.31 N | 86.59 E |
| Da Hinggan Ling ⋏ | 90 | 49.00 N | 122.00 E |
| Dahīrpur ✦[8] | 272a | 28.43 N | 77.12 E |
| Dahl | 56 | 51.18 N | 7.31 E |
| Dahlak Archipelago II | 144 | 15.45 N | 40.30 E |
| Dahle | 263 | 51.18 N | 7.45 E |
| Dahlem | 56 | 50.23 N | 6.33 E |
| Dahlem ✦[8] | 264a | 52.28 N | 13.17 E |
| Dahlem, Museum ᵿ | 264a | 52.27 N | 13.18 E |
| Dahlen | 54 | 51.22 N | 12.59 E |
| Dahlenburg | 54 | 53.11 N | 10.44 E |
| Dahlerau | 263 | 51.13 N | 7.19 E |
| Dahlewitz | 54 | 52.19 N | 13.26 E |
| Dahlgren, Il., U.S. | 194 | 38.12 N | 88.41 W |
| Dahlgren, Va., U.S. | 208 | 38.19 N | 77.03 W |
| Dahlia | 154 | 18.35 S | 27.08 E |
| Dahlonega | 192 | 34.31 N | 83.59 W |
| Dahlonega Plateau ⋏[1] | 192 | 34.10 N | 84.20 W |
| Dahlwitz | 264a | 52.30 N | 13.38 E |
| Dahlwitz-Hoppegarten | 54 | 52.30 N | 13.38 E |
| Dahmani | 36 | 35.57 N | 8.50 E |
| Dahmarū | 142 | 28.41 N | 30.49 E |
| Dahme, Dtsch. | 54 | 51.52 N | 13.25 E |
| Dahme, Dtsch. | 54 | 54.13 N | 11.04 E |
| Dahme ≃ | 54 | 52.25 N | 13.35 E |
| Dahn | 56 | 49.09 N | 7.47 E |
| Dāhod | 120 | 22.50 N | 74.16 E |
| Dahomey → Benin □[1] | 150 | 9.30 N | 2.15 E |
| Dahong | 106 | 31.53 N | 121.17 E |
| Dahongmen | 105 | 39.50 N | 116.25 E |
| Dahongqi | 104 | 41.52 N | 122.36 E |
| Dahong Shan ⋏ | 100 | 31.30 N | 113.00 E |
| Dahongtaizi | 104 | 41.41 N | 121.23 E |
| Dahoucun | 105 | 38.51 N | 115.37 E |
| Dahra | 146 | 29.34 N | 17.50 E |
| Dahra ⋏ | 34 | 36.25 N | 1.00 E |
| Dähre | 54 | 52.48 N | 10.54 E |
| Dahsah, Wādī ad- V | 142 | 27.19 N | 31.26 E |
| Dahshūr | 142 | 29.45 N | 31.14 E |
| Dahu, Zhg. | 100 | 26.22 N | 119.06 E |
| Dahu, Zhg. | 100 | 26.04 N | 117.19 E |
| Dahua | 102 | 23.44 N | 107.59 E |
| Dahuan | 100 | 22.33 N | 113.29 E |
| Dahuangdi | 104 | 42.08 N | 122.27 E |
| Dahuangji | 98 | 35.06 N | 115.15 E |
| Dahuangpu | 105 | 39.26 N | 117.16 E |
| Dahuangshanpu | 104 | 41.16 N | 121.23 E |
| Dahuashan | 105 | 40.17 N | 117.04 E |
| Dahuasi | 107 | 30.05 N | 104.08 E |
| Dahujiang | 100 | 26.10 N | 114.57 E |
| Dahūk | 128 | 36.52 N | 43.00 E |
| Dahūk □[4] | 128 | 37.00 N | 43.00 E |
| Dahuni | 164 | 10.31 S | 149.55 E |
| Dahuofang Shuiku ◎[1] | 98 | 41.55 N | 124.15 E |
| Dahushan | 104 | 41.37 N | 122.09 E |
| Daḥy, Nafūd ad- ✦[2] | 118 | 22.20 N | 45.35 E |
| Dai I | 175e | 7.57 S | 160.37 E |
| Dai ≃ | 100 | 26.14 N | 119.40 E |
| Dai, Pulau I | 164 | 7.33 S | 129.41 E |
| Daia | 38 | 44.00 N | 25.59 E |
| Daian | 94 | 35.05 N | 136.33 E |
| Daibosatsu-rei ∧ | 94 | 35.45 N | 138.51 E |
| Daibu, Zhg. | 100 | 32.19 N | 117.12 E |
| Daibu, Zhg. | 106 | 31.18 N | 119.30 E |
| Daibutsu ᵿ[1] | 94 | 35.19 N | 139.32 E |
| Daiei | 96 | 35.29 N | 133.45 E |
| Daifang | 100 | 27.32 N | 115.41 E |
| Daigo | 94 | 36.46 N | 140.21 E |
| Daigo ✦[8] | 270 | 34.57 N | 135.50 E |
| Daiguantun | 105 | 39.57 N | 117.50 E |
| Dai Hai ◎ | 102 | 40.31 N | 112.43 E |
| Daihaiyingzi | 104 | 42.30 N | 121.26 E |
| Daiji | 100 | 33.48 N | 115.03 E |
| Daijiagou | 107 | 30.00 N | 106.33 E |
| Daijiayao | 100 | 32.56 N | 120.19 E |
| Daikanbō ∧ | 96 | 33.00 N | 131.04 E |
| Daik-u | 110 | 17.47 N | 96.40 E |
| Dā'il | 132 | 32.45 N | 36.08 E |
| Dailekh | 124 | 28.50 N | 81.44 E |
| Dailing | 89 | 47.01 N | 129.02 E |
| Dailly | 44 | 55.16 N | 4.43 W |
| Daimanji-san ∧ | 92 | 36.15 N | 133.19 E |
| Daimiel | 34 | 39.04 N | 3.37 W |
| Daimon, Nihon | 94 | 36.44 N | 137.03 E |
| Daimon, Nihon | 268 | 35.53 N | 139.44 E |
| Daimuken-zan ∧ | 94 | 35.15 N | 138.10 E |
| Dainan | 100 | 32.43 N | 120.06 E |
| Daingean | 48 | 53.18 N | 7.17 W |
| Daingerfield | 222 | 33.01 N | 94.43 W |
| Dainhāt | 126 | 23.37 N | 88.04 E |
| Dainichiga-take ∧ | 94 | 36.00 N | 136.50 E |
| Dainkog | 102 | 32.31 N | 97.59 E |
| Daintree | 164 | 16.15 S | 145.19 E |
| Daintree National Park ♠ | 164 | 16.15 S | 145.10 E |
| Daiō-zaki > | 92 | 34.17 N | 136.54 E |
| Dāira Dīn Panāh | 123 | 30.34 N | 70.56 E |
| Dairago | 266b | 45.34 N | 8.52 E |
| Daireaux | 252 | 36.36 S | 61.45 W |
| Dairen → Dalian | 98 | 38.53 N | 121.35 E |
| Dairsie | 46 | 56.20 N | 2.56 W |
| Dairy City → Cypress | 280 | 33.50 N | 118.01 W |
| Dairy Creek, East Fork ≃ | 224 | 45.34 N | 123.09 W |
| Dairy Creek, West Fork ≃ | 224 | 45.34 N | 123.09 W |
| Dairyland → La Palma, Ca., U.S. | 280 | 33.51 N | 118.02 W |
| Dairyland, N.Y., U.S. | 210 | 41.45 N | 74.33 W |
| Dairyland Reservoir ◎[1] | 190 | 45.30 N | 91.00 W |
| Dairy Valley → Cerritos | 280 | 33.51 N | 118.05 W |
| Dai-sen ∧ | 96 | 35.22 N | 133.33 E |
| Daisen-oki-kokuritsu-kōen ♠ | 96 | 35.20 N | 133.35 E |
| Daisen-zan ∧ | 96 | 34.07 N | 133.56 E |
| Daisetsu-zan-kokuritsu-kōen ♠ | 92a | 43.30 N | 142.57 E |
| Daisetta | 222 | 30.06 N | 94.38 W |
| Daishan | 100 | 30.14 N | 122.12 E |
| Daishin | 94 | 37.12 N | 140.15 E |
| Daishōji ≃ | 94 | 36.18 N | 136.15 E |
| Daisizhen | 107 | 29.14 N | 105.09 E |
| Daitō, Nihon | 96 | 34.42 N | 135.38 E |
| Daitō, Nihon | 96 | 35.19 N | 132.58 E |
| Daiwa, Nihon | 96 | 34.32 N | 132.57 E |
| Daiwa, Nihon | 96 | 34.57 N | 132.39 E |
| Daixi | 106 | 30.40 N | 120.01 E |
| Daixian | 102 | 39.08 N | 113.01 E |
| Daixiqiao | 106 | 31.36 N | 120.04 E |
| Daiya ≃ | 94 | 36.45 N | 139.46 E |
| Daiyun Shan ⋏ | 100 | 25.46 N | 118.16 E |
| Dajabón | 238 | 19.33 N | 71.42 W |
| Dājal | 120 | 29.33 N | 70.23 E |
| Da'jānīyah, Jabal ad- ∧ | 132 | 30.34 N | 35.43 E |
| Dajarra | 166 | 21.41 S | 139.31 E |
| Dajian Shan ∧ | 102 | 26.42 N | 103.34 E |
| Dajidian | 105 | 38.50 N | 115.26 E |
| Dajindian | 100 | 34.24 N | 112.58 E |
| Dajing, Zhg. | 100 | 28.24 N | 121.07 E |
| Dajing, Zhg. | 100 | 28.59 N | 113.19 E |
| Dajin Shan II | 106 | 30.41 N | 121.26 E |
| Dajishan | 100 | 24.38 N | 114.26 E |
| Dajitai | 104 | 42.20 N | 121.11 E |
| Dajiuba | 120 | 36.50 N | 89.35 E |
| Daji Yang ≍ | 100 | 30.54 N | 122.18 E |
| Daju | 105 | 39.12 N | 115.31 E |
| Da Juh | 102 | 36.36 N | 94.04 E |
| Dak ◎ | 128 | 32.48 N | 61.14 E |
| Daka ≃ | 150 | 8.19 N | 0.13 W |
| Dakangpu | 104 | 41.32 N | 121.06 E |
| Dakanzi | 104 | 40.52 N | 122.53 E |
| Dakar | 150 | 14.40 N | 17.26 W |
| Dakar □[4] | 150 | 14.45 N | 17.25 W |
| Dākātia ≃[1] | 126 | 22.57 N | 90.42 E |
| Dakeng | 100 | 26.18 N | 115.32 E |
| Dakengkou | 100 | 24.33 N | 113.37 E |
| Daketa ≃ | 144 | 7.16 N | 42.13 E |
| Dak Gle | 110 | 15.11 N | 107.48 E |
| Dakhal, Bi'r ad- ⊤[4] | 142 | 28.40 N | 32.24 E |
| Dakhal, Wādī ad- V | 142 | 28.49 N | 32.45 E |
| Dākhilah, Al-Wāḥāt ad- ⊤[4] | 140 | 25.30 N | 29.05 E |
| Dakhin Shāhbāzpur Island I | 126 | 22.30 N | 90.45 E |
| Dakhla | 148 | 23.43 N | 15.57 W |
| Dakhlet Nouâdhibou □[4] | 148 | 20.40 N | 16.00 W |
| Dakingari | 150 | 11.37 N | 4.01 E |
| Dakka → Dhaka | 124 | 23.43 N | 90.25 E |
| Dākoānk | 110 | 7.02 N | 93.43 E |
| Dakongcheng | 105 | 39.30 N | 117.09 E |
| Dakongwan | 104 | 40.51 N | 122.19 E |
| Dakoro | 150 | 14.31 N | 6.46 E |
| Dakota City, Ia., U.S. | 190 | 42.43 N | 94.12 W |
| Dakota City, Ne., U.S. | 198 | 42.24 N | 96.25 W |
| Dakou | 100 | 34.27 N | 112.44 E |
| Dakoutun | 105 | 39.35 N | 117.14 E |
| Đakovica | 38 | 42.23 N | 20.25 E |
| Đakovo | 38 | 45.19 N | 18.25 E |
| Dakshingram | 126 | 24.03 N | 87.48 E |
| Dakumu | 89 | 48.51 N | 124.18 E |
| Dakunlun | 98 | 36.34 N | 117.52 E |
| Dakwa | 154 | 4.00 N | 26.26 E |
| Dakwah, Tall ad- ∧[2] | 132 | 33.25 N | 36.56 E |
| Dala, Ang. | 152 | 11.03 S | 20.17 E |
| Dala, Ang. | 152 | 8.05 S | 15.50 E |
| Dala, Sol.Is. | 175e | 8.35 S | 160.40 E |
| Dalaas | 58 | 47.07 N | 10.00 E |
| Dalaba | 150 | 10.42 N | 12.15 W |
| Dalabani | 150 | 10.28 N | 9.27 W |
| Dala Cachibo | 152 | 10.28 S | 14.39 E |
| Dalad Qi | 102 | 40.28 N | 110.02 E |
| Dala-Floda | 40 | 60.31 N | 14.47 E |
| Dalaguete | 116 | 9.46 N | 123.32 E |
| Dalahan (Shiqizhan) | 89 | 52.06 N | 125.46 E |
| Dala-Husby | 40 | 60.21 N | 16.00 E |
| Dala-Järna | 26 | 60.33 N | 14.21 E |
| Dalajchöl | 86 | 47.59 N | 90.47 E |
| Dalaji | 89 | 51.38 N | 120.06 E |
| Dalälven ≃ | 40 | 60.38 N | 17.27 E |
| Dalama | 130 | 37.47 N | 28.04 E |
| Dalaman ≃ | 130 | 36.40 N | 28.45 E |
| Dalāmī | 140 | 11.52 N | 30.28 E |
| Dalan | 100 | 23.19 N | 114.47 E |
| Dalan Dzadgad | 102 | 43.37 N | 104.29 E |
| Dalandžargalan | 102 | 45.55 N | 109.05 E |
| Dalane ✦[1] | 26 | 58.35 N | 6.20 E |
| Dalang | 100 | 22.57 N | 113.56 E |
| Dalantuozi | 104 | 41.28 N | 122.47 E |
| Dalao | 150 | 11.29 N | 13.40 W |
| Dalarna □[9] | 26 | 61.01 N | 14.04 E |
| Dalarö | 40 | 59.08 N | 18.24 E |
| Dalat, Malay. | 112 | 2.44 N | 111.56 E |
| Da Lat, Viet | 110 | 11.56 N | 108.25 E |
| Dalayaozi | 105 | 40.49 N | 117.41 E |
| Dālbandin | 128 | 28.53 N | 64.25 E |
| Dalbeattie | 44 | 54.56 N | 3.49 W |
| D'Albertis Dome ∧ | 164 | 5.00 S | 142.05 E |
| Dalbosjön ⊂ | 26 | 58.45 N | 12.48 E |
| Dalby, Austl. | 166 | 27.11 S | 151.16 E |
| Dalby, Sve. | 41 | 55.40 N | 13.20 E |
| Dalby Söderskogs Nationalpark ♠ | 41 | 55.43 N | 13.17 E |
| Dalcahue | 254 | 42.23 S | 73.40 W |
| Dalch ≃ | 42 | 50.52 N | 3.47 W |
| Dale, Nor. | 26 | 60.35 N | 5.49 E |
| Dale, Nor. | 26 | 61.22 N | 5.25 E |
| Dale, Wales, U.K. | 42 | 51.43 N | 5.11 W |
| Dale, In., U.S. | 194 | 38.10 N | 86.59 W |
| Dale, Pa., U.S. | 214 | 40.18 N | 78.54 W |
| Dale, Tx., U.S. | 222 | 29.56 N | 97.34 W |
| Dale ≃ | 168a | 32.10 S | 116.49 E |
| Dale, Mount ∧ | 168a | 32.08 S | 116.18 E |
| Dale Bridge | 168a | 32.05 S | 116.49 E |
| Dalecarlia → Dalarna □[9] | 26 | 61.01 N | 14.04 E |
| Dale City | 208 | 38.38 N | 77.18 W |
| Dale Hollow Lake ◎[1] | 192 | 36.36 N | 85.19 W |
| Dale Lake ◎ | 204 | 34.08 N | 115.42 W |
| Dalen | 26 | 59.27 N | 8.00 E |
| Dalengtu | 98 | 41.11 N | 113.45 E |
| Dalešice, údolní nádrž ◎[1] | 61 | 49.09 N | 16.05 E |
| Daleside | 158 | 26.30 S | 28.04 E |
| Dale South ≃ | 168a | 32.16 S | 116.47 E |
| Dalesville | 206 | 45.42 N | 74.24 W |
| Dalesville ≃ | 206 | 45.40 N | 74.24 W |
| Daleszyce | 30 | 50.48 N | 20.48 E |
| Dalet | 110 | 19.59 N | 93.51 E |
| Daleville, Al., U.S. | 194 | 31.18 N | 85.42 W |
| Daleville, In., U.S. | 218 | 40.07 N | 85.33 W |
| Daleville, Pa., U.S. | 210 | 41.18 N | 75.31 W |
| Dalfsen | 52 | 52.30 N | 6.16 E |
| Dalgaranga | 162 | 27.46 S | 117.02 E |
| Dalgaranger ∧ | 162 | 27.51 S | 117.06 E |
| Dalgety | 171b | 36.30 S | 148.50 E |
| Dalgety Bay | 46 | 56.02 N | 3.20 W |
| Dalgety Brook ≃ | 162 | 25.07 S | 115.47 E |
| Dalgety Downs | 162 | 25.17 S | 116.15 E |
| Dalgomai | 124 | 26.06 N | 90.47 E |
| Dalhalvaig | 46 | 58.28 N | 3.54 W |
| Dalhart | 196 | 36.03 N | 102.30 W |
| Dalhausen | 52 | 51.37 N | 9.17 E |
| Dalhousie, N.B., Can. | 186 | 48.04 N | 66.23 W |
| Dalhousie, India | 123 | 32.32 N | 75.59 E |
| Dalhousie, Cape > | 180 | 70.14 N | 129.42 W |
| Dalhousie Island I | 126 | 21.35 N | 88.45 E |
| Dalhousie Lake ◎ | 212 | 44.58 N | 76.35 W |
| Dalhousie Square ♠ | 272b | 22.33 N | 88.22 E |
| Dali, Zhg. | 102 | 34.47 N | 109.57 E |
| Dali, Zhg. | 102 | 25.38 N | 100.09 E |
| Dalian (Dairen) | 98 | 38.53 N | 121.35 E |
| Dalian Dao I | 100 | 25.40 N | 119.42 E |
| Daliangdi | 98 | 41.54 N | 115.45 E |
| Daliang Shan ⋏ | 102 | 28.00 N | 103.00 E |
| Dalianhe | 104 | 40.57 N | 123.15 E |
| Daliankeng | 105 | 40.54 N | 117.45 E |
| Dalian Wan ⊂ | 98 | 38.57 N | 121.45 E |
| Dalianwukou | 106 | 30.17 N | 119.00 E |
| Daliao ≃ | 104 | 40.42 N | 122.08 E |
| Dalías | 34 | 36.49 N | 2.52 W |
| Dälidağ ∧ | 84 | 39.55 N | 46.02 E |
| Dalikou | 100 | 26.52 N | 118.00 E |
| Dälimämmadli | 84 | 40.42 N | 46.34 E |
| Dalin, Zhg. | 89 | 43.43 N | 122.45 E |
| Dalin, Zhg. | 107 | 30.17 N | 104.07 E |
| Daling | 104 | 41.27 N | 121.15 E |
| Daling ≃ | 98 | 40.56 N | 121.43 E |
| Dalingbeigou | 104 | 40.42 N | 123.08 E |
| Dalipe Point > | 116 | 10.46 N | 121.55 E |
| Daliushugou | 104 | 40.46 N | 122.14 E |
| Daliutai | 104 | 41.25 N | 121.55 E |


| Symbol | English | Deutsch | Español | Français | Português |
|---|---|---|---|---|---|
| ≃ | River | Fluß | Río | Rivière | Rio |
| ⩶ | Canal | Kanal | Canal | Canal | Canal |
| Ⅼ | Waterfall, Rapids | Wasserfall, Stromschnellen | Cascada, Rápidos | Chute d'eau, Rapides | Cascata, Rápidos |
| ≍ | Strait | Meeresstraße | Estrecho | Détroit | Estreito |
| ⊂ | Bay, Gulf | Bucht, Golf | Bahía, Golfo | Baie, Golfe | Baia, Golfo |
| ◎ | Lake, Lakes | See, Seen | Lago, Lagos | Lac, Lacs | Lago, Lagos |
| ≋ | Swamp | Sumpf | Pantano | Marais | Pântano |
| ⍓ | Ice Features, Glacier | Eis- und Gletscherformen | Accidentes Glaciales | Formes glaciaires | Acidentes glaciares |
| ⊤ | Other Hydrographic Features | Andere Hydrographische Objekte | Otros Elementos Hidrográficos | Autres données hydrographiques | Outros acidentes hidrográficos |
| ✢ | Submarine Features | Untermeerische Objekte | Accidentes Submarinos | Formes de relief sous-marin | Acidentes submarinos |
| □ | Political Unit | Politische Einheit | Unidad Politica | Entité politique | Unidade política |
| ᵿ | Cultural Institution | Kulturelle Institution | Institución Cultural | Institution culturelle | Institução cultural |
| ⊥ | Historical Site | Historische Stätte | Sitio Histórico | Site historique | Sitio histórico |
| ♠ | Recreational Site | Erholungs- und Ferienort | Sitio de Recreo | Centre de loisirs | Area de Lazer |
| ⊠ | Airport | Flughafen | Aeropuerto | Aéroport | Aeroporto |
| ■ | Military Installation | Militäranlage | Instalación Militar | Installation militaire | Instalação militar |
| ✦ | Miscellaneous | Verschiedenes | Misceláneo | Divers | Diversos |

| Name | Page | Lat.°′ | Long.°′ |
|---|---|---|---|
| Daliutun | 104 | 42.14 N | 122.46 E |
| Daliuzhen | 105 | 38.51 N | 116.19 E |
| Daliuzhuang | 100 | 33.04 N | 114.03 E |
| Daliyat et Karmil | 132 | 32.42 N | 35.03 E |
| Daliyya | 132 | 32.35 N | 35.04 E |
| Dalizi | 98 | 41.45 N | 126.49 E |
| Dalj | 38 | 45.29 N | 18.59 E |
| Daljā' | 142 | 27.39 N | 30.42 E |
| Dalkarlsberg | 40 | 59.26 N | 14.51 E |
| Dalkeith | 46 | 55.54 N | 3.04 W |
| Dālkola | 124 | 25.52 N | 87.51 E |
| Dall, Mount ∧ | 180 | 62.35 N | 152.18 W |
| Dāllah, 'Ayn ⍑[4] | 140 | 27.19 N | 27.20 E |
| Dallardsville | 222 | 30.38 N | 94.38 W |
| Dallas, Scot., U.K. | 46 | 57.33 N | 3.28 W |
| Dallas, Al., U.S. | 194 | 33.50 N | 86.39 W |
| Dallas, Ga., U.S. | 192 | 33.55 N | 84.50 W |
| Dallas, N.C., U.S. | 192 | 35.18 N | 81.10 W |
| Dallas, Or., U.S. | 202 | 44.55 N | 123.18 W |
| Dallas, Pa., U.S. | 210 | 41.20 N | 75.57 W |
| Dallas, Tx., U.S. | 222 | 32.46 N | 96.47 W |
| Dallas, Wi., U.S. | 190 | 45.15 N | 91.48 W |
| Dallas ▫[6] | 222 | 32.17 N | 96.47 W |
| Dallas Center | 190 | 41.41 N | 93.57 W |
| Dallas City | 190 | 40.38 N | 91.10 W |
| Dallas-Fort Worth Regional Airport ⊠ | 222 | 32.54 N | 97.01 W |
| Dallas Naval Air Station ■ | 222 | 32.44 N | 96.59 W |
| Dallastown | 208 | 39.53 N | 76.38 W |
| Dallgow | 54 | 52.32 N | 13.05 E |
| Dallıbahçe | 130 | 39.09 N | 39.53 E |
| Dalli Rājhara | 122 | 20.35 N | 81.04 E |
| Dall Island I | 182 | 54.50 N | 132.55 W |
| Dall Lake ⊜ | 180 | 60.18 N | 163.35 W |
| Dalmā I | 128 | 24.30 N | 52.20 E |
| Dalmacija ▫[9] | 36 | 43.00 N | 17.00 E |
| Dalmacio Vélez Sarsfield | 252 | 32.36 S | 63.35 W |
| Dalmally | 46 | 56.24 N | 4.58 W |
| Dalmatia | 208 | 40.39 N | 76.54 W |
| Dalmatia → Dalmacija ▫[9] | 36 | 43.00 N | 17.00 E |
| Dalmatovo | 86 | 56.16 N | 62.56 E |
| Dalmau | 124 | 26.04 N | 81.02 E |
| Dalmellington | 44 | 55.19 N | 4.24 W |
| Dalmeny | 184 | 52.20 N | 106.46 W |
| Dalmine | 62 | 45.39 N | 9.36 E |
| Dalmose | 41 | 55.18 N | 11.26 E |
| Dal'n'aja | 89 | 45.56 N | 142.04 E |
| Dal'n'aja Muja | 88 | 54.21 N | 103.37 E |
| Dalnaspidal | 46 | 56.50 N | 4.14 W |
| Dal'negorsk | 89 | 44.35 N | 135.35 E |
| Dal'neje-Konstantinovo | 80 | 55.49 N | 44.06 E |
| Dal'nerečensk | 89 | 45.55 N | 133.43 E |
| Dal'ne-Rusanovo | 82 | 54.15 N | 36.45 E |
| Dal'nyk | 78 | 46.28 N | 30.34 E |
| Daloa | 150 | 6.53 N | 6.27 W |
| Dalongchang | 105 | 39.50 N | 116.06 E |
| Dalonghua | 105 | 39.18 N | 115.18 E |
| Dalongtian | 100 | 24.14 N | 115.44 E |
| Dalovice | 54 | 50.11 N | 12.55 E |
| Dalqū | 140 | 20.07 N | 30.37 E |
| Dalroy | 182 | 51.07 N | 113.39 W |
| Dalry, Scot., U.K. | 44 | 55.07 N | 4.10 W |
| Dalry, Scot., U.K. | 46 | 55.43 N | 4.44 W |
| Dalrymple | 44 | 55.23 N | 4.35 W |
| Dalrymple, Mount ∧ | 166 | 21.02 S | 148.38 E |
| Dalrymple Creek ≃ | 171a | 27.59 S | 151.46 E |
| Dalrymple Lake ⊜ | 212 | 44.38 N | 79.07 W |
| Dalsbruk (Taalintehdas) | 26 | 60.02 N | 22.31 E |
| Dalsingpara | 124 | 26.47 N | 89.22 E |
| Dalsing Sarai | 124 | 25.40 N | 85.50 E |
| Dalsjöfors | 26 | 57.43 N | 13.05 E |
| Dalsland ▫[9] | 26 | 58.30 N | 12.50 E |
| Dals-Långed | 26 | 58.55 N | 12.18 E |
| Dal'stroja | 180 | 68.19 N | 177.39 W |
| Dāltenganj | 124 | 24.02 N | 84.04 E |
| Dalton, S. Afr. | 158 | 29.20 S | 30.40 E |
| Dalton, Eng., U.K. | 262 | 53.34 N | 2.46 W |
| Dalton, Ga., U.S. | 192 | 34.47 N | 84.58 W |
| Dalton, Ma., U.S. | 207 | 42.28 N | 73.10 W |
| Dalton, Ne., U.S. | 198 | 41.24 N | 102.58 W |
| Dalton, N.Y., U.S. | 210 | 42.32 N | 77.57 W |
| Dalton, Oh., U.S. | 214 | 40.47 N | 81.41 W |
| Dalton, Pa., U.S. | 210 | 41.32 N | 75.44 W |
| Dalton City | 219 | 39.43 N | 88.48 W |
| Dalton Gardens | 202 | 47.43 N | 116.46 W |
| Dalton-in-Furness | 44 | 54.09 N | 3.11 W |
| Dalu | 104 | 41.27 N | 123.19 E |
| Dalubeikou | 105 | 38.59 N | 117.12 E |
| Daludalu | 114 | 1.05 N | 100.15 E |
| Dalu Dao I | 98 | 39.44 N | 123.45 E |
| Daluis, Gorges de V | 62 | 44.04 N | 6.49 E |
| Dalum, Dan. | 41 | 55.22 N | 10.22 E |
| Dalum, Dtsch. | 52 | 52.35 N | 7.14 E |
| Daluojiazhuang | 106 | 32.09 N | 120.08 E |
| Daluotaozi | 104 | 41.17 N | 122.52 E |
| Daluoxi | 100 | 25.14 N | 118.36 E |
| Daluping | 100 | 26.11 N | 114.30 E |
| Dalupiri Island I, Pil. | 116 | 19.05 N | 121.14 E |
| Dalupiri Island I, Pil. | 116 | 12.25 N | 124.16 E |
| Daluxi | 100 | 24.28 N | 117.01 E |
| Dalview | 273d | 26.15 S | 28.21 E |
| Dalvík | 24a | 65.59 N | 18.32 W |
| Dalwallinu | 162 | 30.17 S | 116.40 E |
| Dalwhinnie | 46 | 56.56 N | 4.14 W |
| Dalworthington Gardens | 222 | 32.42 N | 97.10 W |
| Daly ≃ | 164 | 13.20 S | 130.19 E |
| Daly Bay ⊂ | 176 | 64.00 N | 89.40 W |
| Daly City | 226 | 37.43 N | 122.31 W |
| Daly Lake ⊜ | 184 | 56.33 N | 105.40 W |
| Daly Point › | 212 | 44.53 N | 80.14 W |
| Daly River | 164 | 13.45 S | 130.50 E |
| Daly River Aboriginal Reserve ◆[4] | 164 | 14.20 S | 130.00 E |
| Daly Waters | 164 | 16.15 S | 133.22 E |
| Dam ≃ | 120 | 33.56 N | 92.41 E |
| Dāmā, Sūrīy. | 132 | 32.57 N | 36.25 E |
| Dama, Zhg. | 100 | 32.03 N | 118.02 E |
| Damačava | 78 | 51.44 N | 23.37 E |
| Damagum | 146 | 11.41 N | 11.20 E |
| Damān | 122 | 20.25 N | 72.51 E |
| Damān ▫[8] | 122 | 20.10 N | 73.00 E |
| Damanhār Shubra | 273c | 30.07 N | 31.14 E |
| Damanhūr | 142 | 31.02 N | 30.28 E |
| Damanling | 105 | 40.36 N | 115.08 E |
| Damaopu | 104 | 41.16 N | 121.07 E |
| Damar | 130 | 41.15 N | 41.34 E |
| Damar, Pulau I, Indon. | 164 | 7.09 S | 128.40 E |
| Damar, Pulau I, Indon. | 164 | 1.00 S | 128.24 E |
| Damara | 152 | 4.58 N | 18.42 E |
| Damaraland ▫[9] | 156 | 22.34 S | 17.06 E |
| Damāṣ, Miṣr | 142 | 30.48 N | 31.20 E |
| Damas → Dimashq, Sūrīy. | 132 | 33.30 N | 36.18 E |
| Damasco → Dimashq | 132 | 33.30 N | 36.18 E |
| Damascus → Dimashq, Sūrīy. | 132 | 33.30 N | 36.18 E |
| Damascus, Ar., U.S. | 194 | 35.22 N | 92.24 W |
| Damascus, Ga., U.S. | 192 | 34.33 N | 84.56 W |
| Damascus, Md., U.S. | 208 | 39.17 N | 77.12 W |
| Damascus, Oh., U.S. | 214 | 40.54 N | 80.58 W |
| Damascus, Pa., U.S. | 210 | 41.42 N | 75.04 W |
| Damascus, Va., U.S. | 192 | 36.38 N | 81.47 W |
| Damascus International Airport ⊠ | 132 | 33.29 N | 36.13 E |
| Damaskus → Dimashq | 132 | 33.30 N | 36.18 E |
| Damāṭ | 142 | 30.57 N | 30.57 E |
| Damaturu | 146 | 11.45 N | 11.58 E |
| Damāvand | 128 | 35.43 N | 52.04 E |
| Damāvand, Qolleh-ye ∧ | 128 | 35.56 N | 52.08 E |
| Damba, Ang. | 152 | 6.41 S | 15.08 E |
| Damba, Kaz. | 80 | 46.57 N | 51.47 E |
| Dambach-la-Ville | 58 | 48.20 N | 7.26 E |
| Dambarta | 150 | 12.26 N | 8.31 E |
| Dambeck | 54 | 52.48 N | 11.09 E |
| Dâmbovița ▫[6] | 38 | 45.00 N | 25.30 E |
| Dâmbovița ≃ | 38 | 44.14 N | 26.27 E |
| Dambuki | 89 | 54.21 N | 127.38 E |
| Dam Doi | 110 | 8.50 N | 105.15 E |
| Damelevières | 58 | 48.33 N | 6.23 E |
| Damen Dao I | 100 | 27.58 N | 121.06 E |
| Damengjialazi | 104 | 41.04 N | 120.53 E |
| Damengzhuang | 105 | 39.32 N | 116.59 E |
| Damergou ◆[1] | 150 | 15.00 N | 8.55 E |
| Damerham | 42 | 50.57 N | 1.52 W |
| Dämeritzsee ⊜ | 264a | 52.25 N | 13.45 E |
| Damery | 50 | 49.04 N | 3.53 E |
| Dames Quarter | 208 | 38.11 N | 75.53 W |
| Dam Gamad | 140 | 13.17 N | 27.28 E |
| Dāmghān | 128 | 36.09 N | 54.22 E |
| Damianópolis | 255 | 14.33 S | 46.10 W |
| Damianzhen | 107 | 30.36 N | 104.10 E |
| Damiao, Zhg. | 98 | 42.26 N | 118.22 E |
| Damiao, Zhg. | 98 | 34.20 N | 117.23 E |
| Damiao, Zhg. | 102 | 37.18 N | 104.39 E |
| Damiao, Zhg. | 104 | 42.33 N | 122.18 E |
| Damiaochang | 107 | 29.39 N | 106.05 E |
| Damiaogou | 104 | 41.06 N | 123.52 E |
| Damiaojiang | 106 | 31.00 N | 120.28 E |
| Damiaoshang | 105 | 39.56 N | 115.12 E |
| Dămienești | 38 | 46.44 N | 26.59 E |
| Damietta → Dumyāṭ | 142 | 31.25 N | 31.48 E |
| Damietta Branch → Dumyāṭ, Far' ≃ | 142 | 31.32 N | 31.51 E |
| Damietta Mouth → Dumyāṭ, Maṣabb ≃[1] | 142 | 31.32 N | 31.51 E |
| Damin | 100 | 28.56 N | 120.29 E |
| Daming | 98 | 36.19 N | 115.06 E |
| Damingzhen | 104 | 42.34 N | 123.36 E |
| Damintun | 104 | 41.52 N | 122.56 E |
| Dāmiyā | 132 | 32.06 N | 35.33 E |
| Damlacık | 130 | 37.56 N | 38.39 E |
| Damm | 263 | 51.40 N | 6.48 E |
| Dammai Island I | 116 | 5.47 N | 120.25 E |
| Dammarie | 50 | 48.21 N | 1.30 E |
| Dammarie-lès-Lys | 50 | 48.31 N | 2.39 E |
| Dammartin-en-Goële | 50 | 49.03 N | 2.41 E |
| Dammartin-en-Serve | 50 | 48.54 N | 1.37 E |
| Dammastock ∧ | 58 | 46.39 N | 8.25 E |
| Damme, Bel. | 50 | 51.15 N | 3.17 E |
| Damme, Dtsch. | 52 | 52.31 N | 8.12 E |
| Damme, Dtsch. | 54 | 53.17 N | 14.01 E |
| Dammer Berge ⩘[2] | 52 | 52.32 N | 8.10 E |
| Dāmodar ≃ | 124 | 22.17 N | 88.05 E |
| Dāmodar Main Canal ≍ | 126 | 23.01 N | 87.53 E |
| Damoh, India | 118 | 23.50 N | 79.27 E |
| Damoh, India | 124 | 23.50 N | 79.27 E |
| Damon | 222 | 29.17 N | 95.45 W |
| Damongo | 150 | 9.05 N | 1.49 W |
| Damotapāda | 272c | 19.03 N | 73.04 E |
| Damous | 34 | 36.33 N | 1.42 E |
| Damozhuang | 105 | 39.53 N | 115.40 E |
| Dampar, Tasek ⊜ | 114 | 3.02 N | 102.43 E |
| Dampelas → Sabang | 112 | 0.11 N | 119.51 E |
| Dampier | 162 | 20.39 S | 116.45 E |
| Dampier, Cape › | 164 | 6.02 S | 151.02 E |
| Dampier, Selat ⊔ | 164 | 0.40 S | 130.40 E |
| Dampier Archipelago II | 162 | 20.35 S | 116.35 E |
| Dampier Land ›[1] | 162 | 17.30 S | 122.55 E |
| Dampierre, Fr. | 50 | 48.42 N | 1.59 E |
| Dampierre, Fr. | 58 | 47.09 N | 5.45 E |
| Dampierre, Château de ⊥ | 261 | 48.42 N | 1.59 E |
| Dampierre-en-Burly | 50 | 47.46 N | 2.31 E |
| Dampierre-sur-Linotte | 58 | 47.31 N | 6.14 E |
| Dampierre-sur-Salon | 58 | 47.33 N | 5.41 E |
| Dampier Strait ⊔ | 164 | 5.36 S | 148.12 E |
| Dampit | 115a | 8.13 S | 112.45 E |
| Dampmart | 261 | 48.53 N | 2.44 E |
| Damprichard | 58 | 47.15 N | 6.53 E |
| Dâmrei, Chuŏr Phnum ⩘ | 110 | 11.00 N | 104.05 E |
| Damují ≃ | 240p | 22.11 N | 80.33 W |
| Damüls | 58 | 47.17 N | 9.53 E |
| Dāmurhuda | 126 | 23.36 N | 88.47 E |
| Damutougou | 98 | 42.28 N | 118.56 E |
| Damville | 50 | 48.52 N | 1.04 E |
| Damvillers | 56 | 49.20 N | 5.24 E |
| Damxung | 120 | 30.31 N | 91.08 E |
| Dan | 132 | 33.14 N | 35.39 E |
| Dan ≃, U.S. | 192 | 36.42 N | 78.45 W |
| Dan ≃, Zhg. | 102 | 33.02 N | 111.20 E |
| Dana, Cam. | 146 | 10.14 N | 15.18 E |
| Dana, In., U.S. | 194 | 39.48 N | 87.29 W |
| Dana, Mount ∧ | 226 | 37.54 N | 119.13 W |
| Dana, Pulau I | 112 | 10.50 S | 121.16 E |
| Danahu | 102 | 42.28 N | 93.32 E |
| Danai | 112 | 0.29 N | 103.26 E |
| Danajon Bank ✦[4] | 116 | 10.16 N | 124.17 E |
| Danakil → Denakil ◆[1] | 144 | 13.00 N | 41.00 E |
| Danakil National Park ♦ | 144 | 10.50 N | 40.45 E |
| Danané | 150 | 7.16 N | 8.09 W |
| Da Nang | 110 | 16.04 N | 108.13 E |
| Danan'gou | 105 | 40.32 N | 117.49 E |
| Danao, Pil. | 116 | 10.32 N | 124.02 E |
| Danao, Pil. | 116 | 12.29 N | 122.39 E |
| Dana Point | 228 | 33.29 N | 117.44 W |
| Dana Point › | 228 | 33.28 N | 117.43 W |
| Dānāpur | 124 | 25.38 N | 85.03 E |
| Danba | 102 | 31.00 N | 101.50 E |
| Danboro | 208 | 40.21 N | 75.08 W |
| Danbury, Eng., U.K. | 42 | 51.44 N | 0.33 E |
| Danbury, Ct., U.S. | 207 | 41.23 N | 73.27 W |
| Danbury, Ia., U.S. | 198 | 42.14 N | 95.43 W |
| Danbury, Ne., U.S. | 198 | 40.02 N | 100.24 W |
| Danbury, N.C., U.S. | 192 | 36.24 N | 80.12 W |
| Danbury, Tx., U.S. | 222 | 29.14 N | 95.21 W |
| Danby Lake ⊜ | 204 | 34.14 N | 115.07 W |
| Dancheng | 100 | 33.39 N | 115.11 E |
| Danchengji | 100 | 33.47 N | 116.17 E |
| Dancug | 144 | 10.58 N | 49.04 E |
| Dand | 120 | 31.37 N | 65.41 E |
| Dandaragan | 162 | 30.40 S | 115.42 E |
| Dande ≃ | 152 | 8.28 S | 13.21 E |
| Dandeli | 122 | 15.15 N | 74.37 E |
| Dandenong | 169 | 37.59 S | 145.12 E |
| Dandenong, Mount ∧ | 274b | 37.50 S | 145.21 E |
| Dandenong Creek ≃ | 274b | 38.01 S | 145.05 E |
| Dandenong Ranges National Park ♦ | 169 | 37.53 S | 145.20 E |
| Danderyd | 40 | 59.25 N | 18.01 E |
| Dandīl | 142 | 29.10 N | 31.02 E |
| Dandong | 98 | 40.08 N | 124.20 E |
| Dandot | 123 | 32.39 N | 72.58 E |
| Dandridge | 192 | 36.00 N | 83.24 W |
| Dan Dume | 150 | 11.27 N | 7.10 E |
| Dane ▫[6] | 216 | 43.04 N | 89.15 W |
| Dane ≃ | 44 | 53.15 N | 2.31 W |
| Dane County Regional Airport-Truax Field ⊠ | 216 | 43.08 N | 89.20 W |
| Dänemark → Denmark ▫[1] | 26 | 56.00 N | 10.00 E |
| Dänemark-Strasse → Denmark Strait ⊔ | 10 | 67.00 N | 25.00 W |
| Danevang | 222 | 29.03 N | 96.13 W |
| Danewitz | 264a | 52.44 N | 13.40 E |
| Danfeng | 102 | 33.40 N | 110.17 E |
| Danfengzhen | 102 | 24.50 N | 103.56 E |
| Danforth, Il., U.S. | 216 | 40.49 N | 87.59 W |
| Danforth, Me., U.S. | 188 | 45.39 N | 67.52 W |
| Danforth Hills ⩘ | 200 | 40.15 N | 108.00 W |
| Dang ≃ | 102 | 40.30 N | 94.42 E |
| Dānga, Bngl. | 126 | 23.54 N | 90.36 E |
| Dānga, India | 272b | 22.47 N | 88.28 E |
| Danga ≃ | 271c | 1.27 N | 103.43 E |
| Dangādiha | 126 | 21.30 N | 86.19 E |
| Dangan Liedao II | 100 | 22.00 N | 114.14 E |
| Dangara, Taj. | 85 | 38.06 N | 69.22 E |
| Dangara, Uzb. | 85 | 40.35 N | 70.54 E |
| Dangba | 98 | 40.46 N | 118.32 E |
| Dangchang | 102 | 34.03 N | 104.23 E |
| Dangcheng | 98 | 38.46 N | 114.34 E |
| Dange, Ang. | 152 | 7.56 S | 15.02 E |
| Dange, Ang. | 152 | 8.09 S | 14.46 E |
| Dange, Nig. | 150 | 12.52 N | 5.21 E |
| Dange-lá-Menha | 152 | 9.32 S | 14.39 E |
| Danger, Point › | 171a | 28.10 S | 153.33 E |
| Danger Point › | 158 | 34.40 S | 19.17 E |
| Danggali Conservation Park ♦ | 166 | 33.20 S | 140.40 E |
| Danghe Nanshan ⩘ | 102 | 38.53 N | 96.11 E |
| Danghui | 105 | 40.03 N | 117.04 E |
| Dangila | 144 | 11.16 N | 36.50 E |
| Dangkou | 106 | 31.32 N | 120.34 E |
| Dango | 140 | 10.00 N | 24.45 E |
| Dan Gora | 150 | 11.30 N | 8.09 E |
| Dāngori | 120 | 27.40 N | 95.32 E |
| Dangriga | 232 | 16.58 N | 88.13 W |
| Dangshan | 98 | 34.26 N | 116.21 E |
| Dangtu | 100 | 31.34 N | 118.30 E |
| Dan Gulbi | 150 | 11.38 N | 6.16 E |
| Dangyang | 102 | 30.50 N | 111.38 E |
| Dangyu | 105 | 40.00 N | 118.01 E |
| Dani | 150 | 13.43 N | 0.10 W |
| Dania | 220 | 26.03 N | 80.08 W |
| Daniel | 200 | 42.51 N | 110.04 W |
| Daniel, Mount ∧ | 224 | 47.34 N | 121.11 W |
| Daniel Boone Home ⊥ | 219 | 38.39 N | 90.52 W |
| Daniel Boone Homestead State Historic Site ⊥ | 208 | 40.21 N | 75.49 W |
| Daniel-Johnson, Barrage ◆[6] | 186 | 50.39 N | 68.44 W |
| Daniels | 284b | 39.26 N | 77.03 W |
| Daniel's Harbour | 186 | 50.14 N | 57.35 W |
| Danielskuil | 158 | 28.11 S | 23.33 E |
| Danielson | 207 | 41.48 N | 71.53 W |
| Daniels Pass )( | 200 | 40.18 N | 111.15 W |
| Daniels Run ≃ | 284c | 38.51 N | 77.17 W |
| Danielsville, Ga., U.S. | 192 | 34.07 N | 83.13 W |
| Danielsville, Pa., U.S. | 208 | 40.48 N | 75.32 W |
| Danilov | 80 | 58.12 N | 40.12 E |
| Danilovka, Kaz. | 86 | 52.23 N | 70.39 E |
| Danilovka, Ross. | 80 | 52.33 N | 45.23 E |
| Danilovka, Ross. | 80 | 50.21 N | 44.06 E |
| Danilovo | 82 | 55.40 N | 38.46 E |
| Danilovskaja vozvyšennosť ⩘[1] | 80 | 58.12 N | 40.16 E |
| Danilovskoje | 82 | 56.48 N | 35.45 E |
| Daning, Zhg. | 102 | 24.39 N | 111.51 E |
| Daning, Zhg. | 102 | 36.33 N | 110.38 E |
| Daningbashi | 85 | 38.45 N | 75.04 E |
| Dänisch Nienhof | 54 | 54.28 N | 10.07 E |
| Daniupucun | 104 | 41.23 N | 122.37 E |
| Dänizkänarı | 84 | 40.13 N | 49.33 E |
| Danja | 150 | 11.21 N | 7.31 E |
| Danjiangkou Shuiku ⊜[1] | 102 | 32.37 N | 111.30 E |
| Danjo-guntō II | 92 | 32.02 N | 128.23 E |
| Danjoutin | 58 | 47.37 N | 6.52 E |
| Dank | 128 | 23.33 N | 56.17 E |
| Dankama | 150 | 13.20 N | 7.44 E |
| Dankersen | 52 | 52.17 N | 8.58 E |
| Danki | 82 | 54.55 N | 37.34 E |
| Dankov | 76 | 53.15 N | 39.08 E |
| Dankova, Pik ∧ | 85 | 41.05 N | 77.38 E |
| Danleng, Zhg. | 102 | 29.58 N | 103.31 E |
| Danleng, Zhg. | 102 | 29.18 N | 103.10 E |
| Danleng, Zhg. | 107 | 30.01 N | 103.30 E |
| Danlí | 236 | 14.00 N | 86.35 W |
| Danmark → Denmark ▫[1] | 26 | 56.00 N | 10.00 E |
| Dannebrog | 198 | 41.07 N | 98.32 W |
| Dannemare | 41 | 54.45 N | 11.12 E |
| Dannemarie | 58 | 47.38 N | 7.08 E |
| Dannemora, Sve. | 40 | 60.11 N | 17.49 E |
| Dannemora, N.Y., U.S. | 188 | 44.43 N | 73.43 W |
| Dannenberg | 54 | 53.06 N | 11.05 E |
| Dannenreich | 264a | 52.19 N | 13.45 E |
| Dannenwalde | 54 | 53.04 N | 13.11 E |
| Dannevirke | 172 | 40.12 S | 176.07 E |
| Dannewerk | 41 | 54.29 N | 9.31 E |
| Dannhauser | 158 | 28.04 S | 30.04 E |
| Dano | 150 | 11.09 N | 3.04 W |
| Danompari | 112 | 0.09 N | 115.02 E |
| Dañoso, Cabo › | 254 | 48.50 S | 67.13 W |
| Dan Ryan Woods ♦ | 278 | 41.45 N | 87.39 W |
| Dan Sai | 110 | 17.17 N | 101.09 E |
| Danshan | 107 | 30.06 N | 104.54 E |
| Danshui | 100 | 22.49 N | 114.27 E |
| Dansville, Mi., U.S. | 216 | 42.34 N | 84.18 W |
| Dansville, N.Y., U.S. | 210 | 42.33 N | 77.41 W |
| Dāntan | 126 | 21.57 N | 87.16 E |
| Dante | 192 | 36.58 N | 82.17 W |
| Dantewāra | 122 | 18.54 N | 81.21 E |
| Dantuzhen | 106 | 32.12 N | 119.31 E |
| Danube ≃ | 22 | 45.20 N | 29.40 E |
| Danube, Mouths of the ≃[1] | 38 | 45.10 N | 29.50 E |
| Danubio → Danube ≃ | 22 | 45.20 N | 29.40 E |
| Danubyu | 110 | 17.15 N | 95.35 E |
| Danvers, Il., U.S. | 190 | 40.31 N | 89.10 W |
| Danvers, Ma., U.S. | 207 | 42.34 N | 70.55 W |
| Danvers ≃ | 283 | 42.32 N | 70.53 W |
| Danville, P.Q., Can. | 206 | 45.47 N | 72.01 W |
| Danville, Ar., U.S. | 194 | 35.03 N | 93.23 W |
| Danville, Ca., U.S. | 226 | 37.49 N | 121.59 W |
| Danville, Ga., U.S. | 192 | 32.36 N | 83.14 W |
| Danville, Il., U.S. | 194 | 40.07 N | 87.37 W |
| Danville, In., U.S. | 218 | 39.45 N | 86.31 W |
| Danville, Ky., U.S. | 194 | 37.42 N | 84.46 W |
| Danville, Mo., U.S. | 219 | 38.54 N | 91.32 W |
| Danville, Oh., U.S. | 214 | 40.26 N | 82.15 W |
| Danville, Pa., U.S. | 210 | 40.57 N | 76.36 W |
| Danville, Vt., U.S. | 188 | 44.25 N | 72.07 W |
| Danville, Va., U.S. | 192 | 36.35 N | 79.23 W |
| Danville, Wa., U.S. | 182 | 48.59 N | 118.30 W |
| Danxian (Nada) | 110 | 19.35 N | 109.17 E |
| Danyang, Zhg. | 100 | 26.22 N | 119.30 E |
| Danyang, Zhg. | 106 | 32.00 N | 119.35 E |
| Danylivka | 83 | 49.08 N | 39.38 E |
| Danzig → Gdańsk | 30 | 54.23 N | 18.40 E |
| Dao | 116 | 10.31 N | 121.57 E |
| Dâo ≃, Port. | 34 | 40.20 N | 8.11 W |
| Dao ≃, Zhg. | 100 | 30.44 N | 114.39 E |
| Daocheng | 102 | 29.06 N | 100.38 E |
| Daodemiao | 89 | 43.41 N | 120.19 E |
| Daodi | 105 | 39.32 N | 118.11 E |
| Daoguanhe | 100 | 30.54 N | 114.57 E |
| Daohu | 100 | 29.42 N | 117.29 E |
| Daolazui | 105 | 40.06 N | 115.06 E |
| Daoliban | 104 | 41.52 N | 121.37 E |
| Daolin | 100 | 27.59 N | 112.42 E |
| Daolinggang | 98 | 34.02 N | 114.34 E |
| Daoliupu | 107 | 30.12 N | 105.09 E |
| Daomaguan | 98 | 39.07 N | 114.38 E |
| Daosa | 124 | 26.53 N | 76.20 E |
| Daoshiwu | 106 | 30.18 N | 118.57 E |
| Daoshuqiao | 106 | 31.51 N | 119.41 E |
| Daotiandi | 89 | 48.53 N | 130.03 E |
| Dao Timmi | 146 | 20.32 N | 13.33 E |
| Daotou | 98 | 37.14 N | 120.20 E |
| Daoukro | 150 | 7.03 N | 3.58 W |
| Daoulas | 32 | 48.22 N | 4.15 W |
| Daoura, Oued V | 148 | 28.15 N | 3.30 W |
| Daoxian | 102 | 25.35 N | 111.27 E |
| Daozhen | 102 | 28.42 N | 107.56 E |
| Daozi | 89 | 45.00 N | 123.43 E |
| Dapa | 116 | 9.46 N | 126.03 E |
| Dapango | 150 | 10.52 N | 0.12 E |
| Dapanzhuang | 98 | 37.20 N | 115.28 E |
| Dapaozi | 89 | 45.27 N | 122.07 E |
| Dapchi | 146 | 12.28 N | 11.32 E |
| Dapdap | 116 | 14.14 N | 122.15 E |
| Dapeng | 100 | 22.34 N | 114.29 E |
| Daphne | 194 | 30.36 N | 87.54 W |
| Dapiak, Mount ∧ | 116 | 8.15 N | 123.28 E |
| Daping, Zhg. | 100 | 23.11 N | 115.49 E |
| Daping, Zhg. | 100 | 24.24 N | 115.58 E |
| Dapingshan | 102 | 25.30 N | 109.39 E |
| Dapishi | 100 | 26.30 N | 112.54 E |
| Dapitan | 116 | 8.39 N | 123.25 E |
| Dapitan ≃ | 116 | 8.38 N | 123.25 E |
| Dapitan Bay ⊂ | 116 | 8.40 N | 123.23 E |
| Dapto | 170 | 34.30 S | 150.47 E |
| Dapu, Zhg. | 98 | 40.34 N | 124.12 E |
| Dapu, Zhg. | 100 | 23.16 N | 113.32 E |
| Dapu, Zhg. | 106 | 31.19 N | 119.56 E |
| Dapujie | 100 | 27.01 N | 112.46 E |
| Da Qaidam | 102 | 37.53 N | 95.07 E |
| Da Qaidam Hu ⊜ | 102 | 37.50 N | 95.00 E |
| Daqian | 106 | 30.55 N | 120.11 E |
| Daqiangmen | 106 | 31.29 N | 120.27 E |
| Daqiangzi | 104 | 42.21 N | 120.29 E |
| Daqiao, Zhg. | 100 | 29.39 N | 121.26 E |
| Daqiao, Zhg. | 100 | 26.38 N | 118.54 E |
| Daqiao, Zhg. | 100 | 28.11 N | 114.16 E |
| Daqiao, Zhg. | 100 | 32.21 N | 119.41 E |
| Daqiao, Zhg. | 100 | 24.56 N | 113.09 E |
| Daqiao, Zhg. | 106 | 30.59 N | 121.14 E |
| Daqiao, Zhg. | 107 | 28.52 N | 105.40 E |
| Daqiaojie | 106 | 30.46 N | 119.14 E |
| Daqiaokou | 100 | 27.06 N | 113.38 E |
| Daqiaotou | 106 | 30.47 N | 120.52 E |
| Daqiaozhai | 102 | 25.21 N | 106.15 E |
| Daqing | 98 | 39.13 N | 118.51 E |
| Daqing ≃ | 105 | 39.04 N | 116.55 E |
| Daqinggou, Zhg. | 98 | 41.16 N | 114.10 E |
| Daqinggou, Zhg. | 98 | 41.12 N | 125.07 E |
| Daqing Shan ∧, Zhg. | 89 | 45.35 N | 127.51 E |
| Daqing Shan ∧, Zhg. | 104 | 42.03 N | 123.45 E |
| Daqing Shan ∧, Zhg. | 104 | 41.47 N | 121.15 E |
| Daqiu | 100 | 25.24 N | 119.39 E |
| Daqqāq | 140 | 12.56 N | 26.58 E |
| Daquan | 102 | 41.21 N | 95.17 E |
| Daquanshan | 98 | 40.14 N | 113.47 E |
| Daquantou | 105 | 39.31 N | 114.46 E |
| Daquanyan | 104 | 42.37 N | 123.32 E |
| Dāqūf | 142 | 28.24 N | 30.38 E |
| Daqu Shan I | 100 | 30.27 N | 122.20 E |
| Dara, Sén. | 150 | 15.21 N | 15.29 W |
| Dar'ā, Sūrīy. | 132 | 32.37 N | 36.06 E |
| Dar'ā ▫[8] | 132 | 33.00 N | 36.10 E |
| Dārāb | 128 | 28.45 N | 54.34 E |
| Darāban | 120 | 31.44 N | 70.20 E |
| Darabani | 38 | 48.11 N | 26.35 E |
| Darāfisah | 140 | 13.23 N | 31.59 E |
| Daraga | 116 | 11.54 N | 123.52 E |
| Daragodleh | 144 | 10.10 N | 44.51 E |
| Daraina | 157b | 13.12 S | 49.40 E |
| Darājīl | 142 | 30.39 N | 30.52 E |
| Daram Island I | 116 | 11.38 N | 124.47 E |
| Dārān | 128 | 32.59 N | 50.24 E |
| Daraoli ◆[8] | 272c | 19.11 N | 72.48 E |
| Darap | 112 | 1.13 S | 112.03 E |
| Dār as-Salām | 273c | 29.59 N | 31.13 E |
| Darasun | 88 | 51.40 N | 114.00 E |
| Daraut-Kurgan | 85 | 39.33 N | 72.13 E |
| Darave | 272c | 19.02 N | 73.01 E |
| Darāw | 140 | 24.25 N | 32.56 E |
| Darawah | 142 | 30.13 N | 31.06 E |
| Dārayyā | 132 | 33.27 N | 36.15 E |
| Darazo | 146 | 11.00 N | 10.24 E |
| Darb Al-Ḥājj | 142 | 30.10 N | 31.33 E |
| Darb al-Ḥajj, Jabal ∧ | 132 | 30.05 N | 35.26 E |
| Darband | 123 | 34.20 N | 72.52 E |
| Darbāsīyah | 130 | 37.04 N | 40.39 E |
| Darbaza | 85 | 41.35 N | 69.02 E |
| Darbėnai | 76 | 56.01 N | 21.15 E |
| Dar-ben-Karriche-el-Bahri | 34 | 35.30 N | 5.20 W |
| Darbhanga | 124 | 26.10 N | 85.54 E |
| Darbod (Taikang) | 89 | 46.52 N | 124.27 E |
| D'Arbonne, Bayou ≃ | 194 | 32.34 N | 92.09 W |
| Darburruk | 144 | 9.44 N | 44.31 E |
| Darby, Mt., U.S. | 202 | 46.01 N | 114.10 W |
| Darby, Pa., U.S. | 208 | 39.55 N | 75.15 W |
| Darby, Cape › | 180 | 64.20 N | 162.22 W |
| Darby Creek ≃ | 285 | 39.52 N | 75.18 W |
| Darbydale | 218 | 39.51 N | 83.11 W |
| Darčeli | 84 | 42.27 N | 41.42 E |
| Darchan | 88 | 49.29 N | 105.55 E |
| D'Archiac, Mount ∧ | 172 | 43.28 S | 170.35 E |
| D'Arcy | 182 | 50.33 N | 122.29 W |
| D'Arcy Island I | 224 | 48.34 N | 123.17 W |
| Darda | 38 | 45.37 N | 18.41 E |
| Dardadine | 168a | 33.14 S | 116.50 E |
| Dardanelle, Ar., U.S. | 194 | 35.13 N | 93.09 W |
| Dardanelle, Ca., U.S. | 226 | 38.20 N | 119.50 W |
| Dardanelle Lake ⊜[1] | 194 | 35.25 N | 93.20 W |
| Dardanelles → Çanakkale Boğazı ⊔ | 130 | 40.15 N | 26.25 E |
| Dardanup | 168a | 33.24 S | 115.45 E |
| Dardara | 34 | 35.08 N | 5.15 W |
| Dardenelles Cone ∧ | 226 | 38.25 N | 119.53 W |
| Dardenne Creek ≃ | 219 | 38.52 N | 90.32 W |
| Dardesheim | 54 | 51.59 N | 10.49 E |
| Dardistān ▫[9] | 123 | 35.30 N | 74.00 E |
| Dare | 208 | 37.10 N | 76.26 W |
| Darebin Creek ≃ | 274b | 37.47 S | 145.02 E |
| Dareda | 154 | 4.13 S | 35.33 E |
| Dar-el-Beida → Casablanca | 148 | 33.39 N | 7.35 W |
| Darende | 130 | 38.34 N | 37.30 E |
| Darent ≃ | 42 | 51.28 N | 0.13 E |
| Daresbury | 262 | 53.21 N | 2.38 W |
| Dar es Salaam | 154 | 6.48 S | 39.17 E |
| Dar es Salaam ▫[4] | 154 | 6.30 S | 39.25 E |
| Daressalam → Dar es Salaam | 154 | 6.48 S | 39.17 E |
| Darfeld | 52 | 52.01 N | 7.16 E |
| Darfo | 64 | 45.53 N | 10.11 E |
| Dārfūr ash-Shamālīyah ▫[4] | 140 | 16.00 N | 25.25 E |
| Dargai | 123 | 34.30 N | 71.54 E |
| Dargan-Ata | 72 | 40.29 N | 62.10 E |
| Dargaville | 172 | 35.56 S | 173.53 E |
| Dargeçit | 130 | 37.33 N | 41.44 E |
| Dargol | 150 | 13.55 N | 1.15 E |
| Dargol ≃ | 150 | 13.53 N | 1.33 E |
| Dargun | 54 | 53.54 N | 12.51 E |
| Darhan Muminggan Lianheqi | 102 | 41.50 N | 110.27 E |
| Dari | 140 | 5.48 N | 30.21 E |
| Dāriāpur | 126 | 23.36 N | 89.27 E |
| Darıca | 130 | 40.45 N | 29.23 E |
| Darie Hills ⩘ | 144 | 8.21 N | 47.16 E |
| Darién, Col. | 246 | 3.56 N | 76.31 W |
| Darien, Ct., U.S. | 207 | 41.04 N | 73.28 W |
| Darien, Ga., U.S. | 192 | 31.22 N | 81.26 W |
| Darien, Il., U.S. | 278 | 41.45 N | 87.58 W |
| Darien, N.Y., U.S. | 210 | 42.54 N | 78.21 W |
| Darien, Wi., U.S. | 216 | 42.36 N | 88.42 W |
| Darien, Parque Nacional ♦ | 246 | 7.40 N | 77.40 W |
| Darién, Serranía del ⩘ | 246 | 8.20 N | 77.22 W |
| Darien Center | 210 | 42.54 N | 78.23 W |
| Darien Lakes State Park ♦ | 210 | 42.55 N | 78.25 W |
| Dariense, Cordillera ⩘ | 236 | 12.55 N | 85.30 W |
| Dariganga | 102 | 45.18 N | 113.52 E |
| Darigayos Point › | 116 | 16.50 N | 120.20 E |
| Dar'inskij | 86 | 49.04 N | 72.56 E |
| Dar'inskoje | 80 | 51.20 N | 51.44 E |
| Dariv | 88 | 46.57 N | 93.38 E |
| Darjevka | 83 | 47.42 N | 39.41 E |
| Dārjiling | 124 | 27.02 N | 88.16 E |
| Darkan | 168a | 33.20 S | 116.44 E |
| Darke ▫[6] | 218 | 40.06 N | 84.38 W |
| Darke Peak | 166 | 33.28 S | 136.12 E |
| Darkhāna | 123 | 30.39 N | 72.11 E |
| Dar Khazīneh | 128 | 31.54 N | 48.59 E |
| Dark Head › | 241h | 13.17 N | 61.16 W |
| Darkin ≃ | 168a | 32.00 S | 116.14 E |
| Darkūsh | 130 | 35.59 N | 36.23 E |
| Darlag | 102 | 33.48 N | 99.52 E |
| Darley Woods | 285 | 39.49 N | 75.28 W |
| Darling, S. Afr. | 158 | 33.23 S | 18.23 E |
| Darling, Ms., U.S. | 194 | 34.21 N | 90.16 W |
| Darling ≃ | 166 | 34.07 S | 141.55 E |
| Darling, Lake ⊜[1] | 198 | 48.35 N | 101.40 W |
| Darling Downs ◆[1] | 166 | 27.30 S | 150.30 E |
| Darlingford | 184 | 49.12 N | 98.22 W |
| Darling Range ⩘ | 162 | 31.25 S | 116.00 E |
| Darlington, Austl. | 169 | 38.00 S | 143.03 E |
| Darlington, Eng., U.K. | 44 | 54.31 N | 1.34 W |
| Darlington, Md., U.S. | 208 | 39.38 N | 76.12 W |
| Darlington, Pa., U.S. | 214 | 40.49 N | 80.26 W |
| Darlington, Pa., U.S. | 285 | 39.54 N | 75.28 W |
| Darlington, S.C., U.S. | 192 | 34.17 N | 79.52 W |
| Darlington, Wi., U.S. | 190 | 42.40 N | 90.07 W |
| Darlington Brook ≃ | 276 | 41.05 N | 74.11 W |
| Darlington Corners | 285 | 39.55 N | 75.34 W |
| Darlington Range ⩘ | 171a | 27.50 S | 153.15 E |
| Darlot, Lake ⊜ | 162 | 27.48 S | 121.35 E |
| Darłowo | 30 | 54.26 N | 16.23 E |
| Darmagī, Kūh-e ∧ | 128 | 26.35 N | 58.54 E |
| Darmstadt | 56 | 49.53 N | 8.40 E |
| Darmstadt ▫[5] | 56 | 49.45 N | 8.40 E |
| Darnah | 146 | 32.46 N | 22.39 E |
| Darnall | 158 | 29.23 S | 31.18 E |
| Darnétal | 50 | 49.27 N | 1.09 E |
| Darney | 58 | 48.05 N | 6.03 E |
| Darnick | 166 | 32.51 S | 143.37 E |
| Darnley, Cape › | 9 | 67.43 S | 69.30 E |
| Darnley Bay ⊂ | 176 | 69.35 N | 123.30 W |
| Daroca | 34 | 41.07 N | 1.25 W |
| Darodih | 126 | 23.14 N | 86.27 E |
| Daror | 144 | 8.14 N | 44.42 E |
| Dar-Ould-Zidouh | 148 | 32.22 N | 6.49 W |
| Darou Mousti | 150 | 15.03 N | 16.03 W |
| Darovoje | 82 | 54.34 N | 38.22 E |
| Darr ≃ | 166 | 23.39 S | 143.50 E |
| Darra | 171a | 27.34 S | 152.58 E |
| Darragh | 279b | 40.16 N | 79.41 W |
| Darrah, Mount ∧ | 182 | 49.28 N | 114.35 W |
| Darregueira | 252 | 37.42 S | 63.10 W |
| Darreh Gaz | 128 | 37.27 N | 59.07 E |
| Darrington | 224 | 48.15 N | 121.36 W |
| Darrouzett | 196 | 36.27 N | 100.20 W |
| Darryl Gardens | 284b | 39.25 N | 76.25 W |
| Dārsana | 126 | 23.32 N | 88.52 E |
| Darscheid | 56 | 50.12 N | 6.53 E |
| Darss ›[1] | 54 | 54.25 N | 12.31 E |
| Darsser Ort › | 54 | 54.29 N | 12.31 E |
| Dart ≃ | 42 | 50.20 N | 3.33 W |
| Dart, Cape › | 9 | 73.06 S | 126.20 W |
| Dār Ta'izzah | 130 | 36.17 N | 36.51 E |
| Dartford | 42 | 51.27 N | 0.14 E |
| Dartford ▫[8] | 260 | 51.26 N | 0.15 E |
| Dartford Tunnel ◆[5] | 260 | 51.28 N | 0.16 E |
| Dartmoor | 166 | 37.55 S | 141.17 E |
| Dartmoor ◆[3] | 42 | 50.35 N | 3.55 W |
| Dartmoor National Park ♦ | 42 | 50.37 N | 3.52 W |
| Dartmouth, N.S., Can. | 186 | 44.40 N | 63.34 W |
| Dartmouth, Eng., U.K. | 42 | 50.21 N | 3.35 W |
| Dartmouth ≃ | 186 | 48.53 N | 64.34 W |
| Dartmouth, Lake ⊜ | 166 | 26.04 S | 145.18 E |
| Dartmouth Woods | 285 | 39.50 N | 75.31 W |
| Darton | 44 | 53.36 N | 1.32 W |
| Daru, Pap. N. Gui. | 164 | 9.04 S | 143.21 E |
| Daru, S.L. | 150 | 7.59 N | 10.50 W |
| Daruvar | 36 | 45.36 N | 17.13 E |
| Darvaza | 128 | 40.11 N | 58.24 E |
| Darvazskij chrebet ⩘ | 85 | 38.30 N | 71.15 E |
| Darvel | 46 | 55.37 N | 4.18 W |
| Darvinskij zapovednik ◆[4] | 76 | 58.50 N | 37.40 E |
| Darwāzahgêy | 120 | 31.48 N | 67.44 E |
| Darwen | 44 | 53.42 N | 2.28 W |
| Darwen ≃ | 262 | 53.45 N | 2.41 W |
| Darwendale | 154 | 17.43 S | 30.33 E |
| Dārwha | 122 | 20.19 N | 77.46 E |
| Darwin, Arg. | 254 | 39.12 S | 65.46 W |
| Darwin, Austl. | 164 | 12.28 S | 130.50 E |
| Darwin, Bahía ⊂ | 254 | 45.27 S | 74.40 W |
| Darwin, Cordillera ⩘ | 254 | 54.40 S | 70.00 W |
| Darwin, Isla I | 246a | 1.39 N | 92.00 W |
| Darwin, Volcán ∧[1] | 246a | 0.10 S | 91.18 W |
| Darwin River | 164 | 12.49 S | 130.58 E |
| Daryābād | 124 | 26.53 N | 81.33 E |
| Darya Khān | 123 | 31.48 N | 71.06 E |
| Daryāpur | 120 | 20.56 N | 77.20 E |
| Darzāb | 120 | 35.58 N | 65.22 E |
| Darzo | 64 | 45.51 N | 10.33 E |
| Dār Zubi | 140 | 13.07 N | 23.40 E |
| Dās | 123 | 35.05 N | 75.05 E |
| Dās I | 128 | 25.09 N | 52.53 E |
| Dasanjiazi | 104 | 42.31 N | 122.54 E |
| Daš Balbar | 88 | 49.31 N | 114.21 E |
| Dasburg | 56 | 50.03 N | 6.07 E |
| Daščhovuze ▫[8] | 128 | 40.15 N | 59.00 E |
| Dase → Dese | 144 | 11.05 N | 39.41 E |
| Dasha ≃ | 98 | 38.20 N | 115.22 E |
| Dashafa | 105 | 39.19 N | 116.19 E |
| Dashalitu | 104 | 42.31 N | 122.30 E |
| Dashan | 98 | 38.02 N | 117.39 E |
| Dashankou | 105 | 40.17 N | 115.49 E |
| Dashanpu | 107 | 29.25 N | 104.49 E |
| Dashaping | 100 | 29.24 N | 113.51 E |
| Dashava | 78 | 49.16 N | 24.01 E |
| Dashengfenchang | 106 | 31.53 N | 121.34 E |
| Dashengpu | 104 | 41.13 N | 121.02 E |
| Dashentang | 105 | 39.13 N | 117.56 E |
| Dashetai | 102 | 40.58 N | 109.19 E |
| Dashi | 107 | 30.39 N | 105.37 E |
| Dashi ≃ | 105 | 39.35 N | 116.05 E |
| Dashields Dam ◆[6] | 214 | 40.33 N | 80.12 W |
| Dashiqiao, Zhg. | 100 | 33.57 N | 113.53 E |
| Dashiqiao, Zhg. | 104 | 41.52 N | 123.17 E |
| Dashiqiao, Zhg. | 107 | 30.07 N | 106.12 E |
| Dashiqiao, Zhg. | 107 | 30.28 N | 106.29 E |
| Dashitou, Zhg. | 89 | 43.19 N | 128.28 E |
| Dashitou, Zhg. | 102 | 42.49 N | 95.19 E |
| Dashiv | 78 | 49.00 N | 29.26 E |
| Dashizhai | 89 | 46.16 N | 121.25 E |
| Dashlūṭ | 142 | 27.34 N | 30.42 E |
| Dash Point | 224 | 47.19 N | 122.26 W |
| Dasht ≃ | 128 | 25.10 N | 61.40 E |
| Dashu | 106 | 31.13 N | 120.56 E |
| Dashun | 100 | 28.06 N | 119.52 E |
| Dashutang | 102 | 23.00 N | 103.55 E |
| Dashuwan | 105 | 40.37 N | 117.19 E |
| Dasi (Huangfansi) | 102 | 38.15 N | 100.22 E |
| Dasiji | 100 | 33.48 N | 115.55 E |
| Dašinčilen | 88 | 47.51 N | 104.03 E |
| Dasing | 60 | 48.23 N | 11.03 E |
| Dasizhan | 89 | 45.53 N | 130.24 E |
| Daska | 123 | 32.20 N | 74.21 E |
| Daşkäsän | 84 | 40.30 N | 46.04 E |
| Daškauka | 76 | 53.44 N | 30.13 E |
| Daskop | 158 | 33.44 S | 22.43 E |
| Dasmina | 126 | 22.17 N | 90.35 E |
| Dasol | 116 | 15.59 N | 119.52 E |
| Dasol Bay ⊂ | 116 | 15.53 N | 119.51 E |
| Dassalan Island I | 116 | 6.45 N | 121.28 E |
| Dassel, Dtsch. | 52 | 51.48 N | 9.41 E |
| Dassel, Mn., U.S. | 190 | 45.04 N | 94.18 W |
| Dasseneiland I | 158 | 33.26 S | 18.04 E |
| Dasserat, Lac ⊜ | 190 | 48.16 N | 79.25 W |
| Dassiefontein | 158 | 31.35 S | 24.25 E |
| Dassow | 54 | 53.50 N | 10.59 E |
| Dastakert | 84 | 39.23 N | 46.02 E |
| Dastgardān | 128 | 34.19 N | 56.51 E |
| Daštidžum | 85 | 38.01 N | 70.12 E |
| Daštioburdon | 85 | 39.24 N | 69.04 E |
| Dastjerd | 128 | 34.33 N | 50.15 E |
| Dasūa | 123 | 31.49 N | 75.38 E |
| Dāsuria | 126 | 24.07 N | 89.08 E |
| Datachang | 107 | 28.55 N | 104.21 E |
| Datagenoyang | 112 | 2.03 N | 115.10 E |
| Datai | 105 | 39.58 N | 115.54 E |
| Dataizi | 104 | 41.17 N | 121.46 E |
| Datan, Zhg. | 98 | 41.35 N | 116.00 E |
| Datan, Zhg. | 98 | 39.31 N | 122.11 E |
| Datang, Zhg. | 100 | 24.47 N | 113.43 E |
| Datang, Zhg. | 100 | 25.17 N | 114.56 E |
| Datang, Zhg. | 102 | 22.23 N | 108.23 E |
| Datang, Zhg. | 102 | 24.11 N | 109.00 E |
| Datça | 130 | 36.45 N | 27.40 E |
| Datchet | 260 | 51.29 N | 0.34 W |
| Datchet Reservoir ⊜[1] | 260 | 51.29 N | 0.33 W |
| Date | 92a | 42.27 N | 140.51 E |
| Date Creek ≃ | 200 | 34.13 N | 113.29 W |
| Datia | 124 | 25.40 N | 78.28 E |
| Datian, Zhg. | 100 | 25.42 N | 117.49 E |
| Datian, Zhg. | 100 | 24.06 N | 116.19 E |
| Datian Ding ∧ | 102 | 22.17 N | 111.13 E |
| Datianwei | 100 | 25.54 N | 115.10 E |
| Dativli | 272c | 19.11 N | 73.03 E |
| D'at'kovo | 76 | 53.36 N | 34.20 E |
| D'atlovo | 82 | 56.14 N | 36.16 E |
| Datong, Zhg. | 89 | 46.03 N | 124.50 E |
| Datong, Zhg. | 100 | 30.48 N | 117.45 E |
| Datong, Zhg. | 100 | 32.50 N | 118.52 E |
| Datong, Zhg. | 102 | 37.03 N | 101.45 E |
| Datong, Zhg. | 102 | 40.05 N | 113.18 E |
| Datong ≃ | 102 | 36.20 N | 102.55 E |
| Datong Shan ⩘ | 102 | 38.00 N | 99.30 E |
| Datongzhen | 106 | 32.12 N | 121.19 E |
| Datoushan | 98 | 41.50 N | 117.08 E |
| Dātra | 272b | 22.58 N | 88.16 E |
| Datta | 89 | 49.18 N | 140.22 E |
| Dattapāra | 126 | 23.01 N | 90.53 E |
| Dattapukur | 126 | 22.45 N | 88.33 E |
| Dattapulia | 126 | 23.14 N | 88.43 E |
| Datteln | 52 | 51.40 N | 7.23 E |
| Datteln-Hamm-Kanal ≍ | 263 | 51.39 N | 7.21 E |
| Dattilo | 70 | 37.58 N | 12.39 E |
| Datu, Tanjung › | 112 | 2.05 N | 109.39 E |
| Datuan | 106 | 30.58 N | 121.44 E |
| Datumakuta | 112 | 2.32 N | 117.51 E |
| Datun, Zhg. | 89 | 43.49 N | 125.12 E |
| Datun, Zhg. | 98 | 40.37 N | 119.57 E |
| Datun, Zhg. | 104 | 40.59 N | 122.55 E |
| Datuopu | 100 | 28.03 N | 112.58 E |
| Datu Piang | 116 | 7.01 N | 124.30 E |
| Daua (Dawa) ≃ | 144 | 4.11 N | 42.06 E |
| Daudkāndi | 126 | 23.32 N | 90.43 E |
| Dāud Khel | 123 | 32.53 N | 71.34 E |
| Daudnagar | 124 | 25.02 N | 84.24 E |
| Daugai | 76 | 54.22 N | 24.20 E |
| Daugård | 41 | 55.44 N | 9.43 E |
| Daugava (Zahodnjaja Dzvina) ≃ | 76 | 57.04 N | 24.03 E |
| Daugavpils | 76 | 55.53 N | 26.32 E |
| Dauhinava | 76 | 54.39 N | 27.29 E |
| Dauin | 116 | 9.12 N | 123.16 E |
| Daulatabad | 126 | 24.08 N | 88.22 E |
| Daulatkhān | 126 | 22.38 N | 90.49 E |
| Daulatpur, Bngl. | 126 | 24.00 N | 88.52 E |
| Daulatpur, Bngl. | 126 | 22.53 N | 89.31 E |
| Daulatpur, Bngl. | 126 | 23.58 N | 89.50 E |
| Daulatpur, India | 272b | 22.26 N | 88.18 E |
| Daulatpur, Pāk. | 120 | 26.30 N | 67.58 E |
| Daulatpur ◆[8] | 272a | 28.44 N | 77.06 E |
| Daule, Ec. | 246 | 0.24 N | 80.00 W |
| Daule, Ec. | 246 | 1.50 S | 79.56 W |
| Daule, India | 272c | 19.10 N | 73.03 E |
| Daule ≃ | 246 | 2.10 S | 79.52 W |
| Daultāla | 123 | 33.12 N | 73.09 E |
| Daulton Creek ≃ | 226 | 37.04 N | 119.59 W |
| Daun | 56 | 50.11 N | 6.50 E |
| Daund | 122 | 18.28 N | 74.36 E |
| Daung Kyun I | 110 | 12.14 N | 98.05 E |
| Dauphin, Mb., Can. | 184 | 51.09 N | 100.03 W |
| Dauphin, Pa., U.S. | 208 | 40.22 N | 76.55 W |
| Dauphin ▫[6] | 208 | 40.15 N | 76.52 W |
| Dauphin ≃ | 184 | 51.58 N | 98.04 W |
| Dauphiné ▫[9] | 62 | 44.50 N | 6.00 E |
| Dauphin Island | 194 | 30.15 N | 88.07 W |
| Dauphin Island I | 194 | 30.14 N | 88.12 W |
| Dauphin Lake ⊜ | 184 | 51.17 N | 99.48 W |
| Daura | 150 | 13.02 N | 8.21 E |
| Daurija | 88 | 49.56 N | 116.52 E |
| Daurskoje | 86 | 55.14 N | 92.05 E |
| Dausenau | 56 | 50.20 N | 7.45 E |
| D'Auteuil, Lac ⊜ | 186 | 50.38 N | 61.17 W |
| Dautphetal | 56 | 50.51 N | 8.32 E |
| Däväçi | 84 | 41.12 N | 48.59 E |
| Dāvangere | 122 | 14.28 N | 75.55 E |
| Davant | 194 | 29.37 N | 89.51 W |
| Davao | 116 | 7.04 N | 125.36 E |
| Davao ▫[4] | 116 | 7.40 N | 125.50 E |
| Davao ≃ | 116 | 7.04 N | 125.37 E |
| Davao del Sur ▫[4] | 116 | 6.50 N | 125.20 E |
| Davao Gulf ⊂ | 116 | 6.40 N | 125.55 E |
| Davao Oriental ▫[4] | 116 | 7.30 N | 126.30 E |
| Dāvar Panāh | 128 | 27.21 N | 62.21 E |
| Dāvarzan | 128 | 36.23 N | 56.50 E |
| Davegoriale | 144 | 8.45 N | 44.50 E |
| Davel | 158 | 26.24 S | 29.40 E |
| Daveluyville | 206 | 46.12 N | 72.08 W |
| Davenda | 88 | 53.33 N | 119.18 E |
| Davenham | 262 | 53.14 N | 2.31 W |
| Davenport, Ca., U.S. | 226 | 37.00 N | 122.11 W |
| Davenport, Fl., U.S. | 220 | 28.09 N | 81.36 W |
| Davenport, Ia., U.S. | 190 | 41.31 N | 90.34 W |
| Davenport, Ne., U.S. | 198 | 40.18 N | 97.48 W |
| Davenport, N.Y., U.S. | 210 | 42.28 N | 74.51 W |
| Davenport, Ok., U.S. | 196 | 35.42 N | 96.45 W |
| Davenport, Wa., U.S. | 202 | 47.39 N | 118.08 W |
| Davenport, Mount ∧ | 162 | 22.23 S | 130.51 E |
| Davenport Downs | 166 | 24.08 S | 141.07 E |
| Davenport Range ⩘ | 162 | 20.47 S | 134.48 E |
| Daventry | 42 | 52.16 N | 1.09 W |
| Davey, Port ⊂ | 166 | 43.19 S | 145.55 E |
| Daveyton | 273d | 26.09 S | 28.25 E |
| David | 236 | 8.26 N | 82.26 W |
| David City | 198 | 41.15 N | 97.07 W |
| Davids Island I | 276 | 40.53 N | 73.46 W |
| Davidson, Sk., Can. | 184 | 51.16 N | 105.59 W |
| Davidson, N.C., U.S. | 192 | 35.29 N | 80.50 W |
| Davidson, Ok., U.S. | 196 | 34.14 N | 99.04 W |
| Davidson, Mount ∧ | 170 | 33.09 S | 150.07 E |
| Davidson Creek ≃ | 222 | 30.21 N | 96.27 W |
| Davidson Heights | 214 | 40.35 N | 80.15 W |
| Davidson Lake ⊜ | 184 | 53.47 N | 99.37 W |
| Davidson Mountains ⩘ | 180 | 68.45 N | 142.10 W |
| Davidson Park ♦ | 274a | 33.45 S | 151.12 E |
| Davidsville | 214 | 40.14 N | 78.56 W |
| Davie | 220 | 26.03 N | 80.13 W |
| Davies, Mount ∧ | 162 | 26.14 S | 129.16 E |
| Davignab | 158 | 27.32 S | 19.48 E |
| Davila | 116 | 18.29 N | 120.35 E |
| Davilla | 222 | 30.47 N | 97.17 W |
| Davington | 44 | 55.18 N | 3.12 W |
| Davin Lake ⊜ | 184 | 56.50 N | 103.40 W |
| Davinópolis | 255 | 15.58 S | 50.08 W |
| Daviot | 46 | 57.25 N | 4.08 W |
| Davis, Ca., U.S. | 226 | 38.32 N | 121.44 W |
| Davis, N.C., U.S. | 192 | 34.47 N | 76.27 W |
| Davis, Ok., U.S. | 196 | 34.30 N | 97.07 W |
| Davis, W.V., U.S. | 188 | 39.07 N | 79.27 W |
| Davis ≃ | 162 | 21.42 S | 121.05 E |
| Davis ʊ[3] | 9 | 68.35 S | 77.58 E |
| Davis, Mount ∧ | 188 | 39.47 N | 79.10 W |
| Davis Bay ⊂ | 9 | 66.08 S | 134.05 E |
| Davisboro | 192 | 32.58 N | 82.36 W |
| Davisburg | 216 | 42.45 N | 83.33 W |
| Davis City | 190 | 40.38 N | 93.48 W |
| Davis Cove | 186 | 47.40 N | 54.18 W |
| Davis Creek ≃, Mi., U.S. | 281 | 42.27 N | 83.43 W |


**Symbols** in the index entries represent the broad categories identified in the key at the right. Symbols with superior numbers (⩘[1]) identify subcategories (see complete key on page *I · 1*).

**Symbole** im Register stellen die rechts im Schlüssel erklärten Kategorien dar. Symbole mit hochgestellten Ziffern (⩘[1]) bezeichnen Unterabteilungen einer Kategorie (vgl. vollständiger Schlüssel auf Seite *I · 1*).

**Los símbolos** incluídos en el texto del índice representan las grandes categorías identificadas con la clave a la derecha. Los símbolos con numeros en su parte superior (⩘[1]) identifican las subcategorías (véase la clave completa en la página *I · 1*).

**Les symboles** de l'index représentent les catégories indiquées dans la légende à droite. Les symboles suivis d'un indice (⩘[1]) représentent des sous-catégories (voir légende complète à la page *I · 1*).

**Os símbolos** incluídos no texto do índice representam as grandes categorias identificadas com a chave à direita. Os símbolos com números em sua parte superior (⩘[1]) identificam as subcategorias (veja-se a chave completa à página *I · 1*).

| | English | Deutsch | Español | Français | Português |
|---|---|---|---|---|---|
| ∧ | Mountain | Berg | Montaña | Montagne | Montanha |
| ⩘ | Mountains | Gebirge | Montañas | Montagnes | Montanhas |
| )( | Pass | Paß | Paso | Col | Passo |
| V | Valley, Canyon | Tal, Cañon | Valle, Cañón | Vallée, Canyon | Vale, Canhão |
| ≚ | Plain | Ebene | Llano | Plaine | Planície |
| › | Cape | Kap | Cabo | Cap | Cabo |
| I | Island | Insel | Isla | Île | Ilha |
| II | Islands | Inseln | Islas | Îles | Ilhas |
| ⊥ | Other Topographic Features | Andere Topographische Objekte | Otros Elementos Topográficos | Autres données topographiques | Outros acidentes topográficos |

ESPAÑOL · FRANÇAIS · PORTUGUÊS


| Nombre / Nom / Nome | Página / Page / Página | Lat.°′ | Long.°′ W = Oeste / W = Ouest / W = Oeste |
|---|---|---|---|
| Davis Creek ≃, Mo., U.S. | 219 | 39.12 N | 91.53 W |
| Davis Dam | 200 | 35.10 N | 114.33 W |
| Davis Dam ◆[6] | 200 | 35.11 N | 114.21 W |
| Davis Island I | 279b | 40.29 N | 80.05 W |
| Davis Lake ⊜ | 278 | 42.16 N | 88.05 W |
| Davis-Monthan Air Force Base ■ | 200 | 32.11 N | 110.53 W |
| Davis Mountains ⋏ | 196 | 30.35 N | 104.00 W |
| Davison | 216 | 43.02 N | 83.31 W |
| Davis Park | 210 | 40.42 N | 72.59 W |
| Davis Point › | 282 | 38.03 N | 122.15 W |
| Davis Sea ⊤[2] | 9 | 66.00 S | 92.00 E |
| Davis Strait ⊔ | 176 | 67.00 N | 57.00 W |
| Davlekanovo | 86 | 54.13 N | 55.03 E |
| Davo ≃ | 150 | 5.00 N | 6.08 W |
| Davoli | 68 | 38.39 N | 16.29 E |
| Davos | 58 | 46.48 N | 9.50 E |
| Davron | 261 | 48.52 N | 1.57 E |
| Davst | 86 | 50.36 N | 92.28 E |
| Davulga | 130 | 38.58 N | 31.23 E |
| Davutlar | 130 | 37.43 N | 27.17 E |
| Davy | 192 | 37.28 N | 81.39 W |
| Davyd-Haradok | 78 | 52.03 N | 27.14 E |
| Davydiv Brid | 78 | 47.14 N | 33.12 E |
| Davydkovo, Ross. | 82 | 56.17 N | 36.49 E |
| Davydkovo, Ross. | 265b | 55.35 N | 37.12 E |
| Davydov, gora ∧ | 88 | 52.34 N | 107.25 E |
| Davydovka | 78 | 51.10 N | 39.25 E |
| Davydovo | 82 | 55.37 N | 38.52 E |
| Davydovskoje | 82 | 55.52 N | 36.48 E |
| Davyhulme | 262 | 53.27 N | 2.22 W |
| Dawa, Zhg. | 104 | 41.00 N | 122.03 E |
| Dawa, Zhg. | 104 | 41.54 N | 123.32 E |
| Dawa (Daua) ≃ | 144 | 4.11 N | 42.06 E |
| Dawaki | 150 | 12.06 N | 8.20 E |
| Dawan | 102 | 23.52 N | 109.29 E |
| Dawang | 98 | 36.58 N | 118.31 E |
| Dawangcun | 106 | 30.45 N | 118.59 E |
| Dawangdian | 105 | 39.04 N | 115.26 E |
| Dawangdong | 105 | 38.53 N | 116.21 E |
| Dawangjia Dao I | 98 | 39.27 N | 123.07 E |
| Dawangsangou | 104 | 41.43 N | 121.36 E |
| Dawangzhai | 269b | 31.22 N | 121.25 E |
| Dawangzhuang, Zhg. | 105 | 39.23 N | 116.28 E |
| Dawangzhuang, Zhg. | 105 | 38.59 N | 115.56 E |
| Dawāsir, Wādī ad- V | 144 | 20.24 N | 46.29 E |
| Dawatun | 104 | 41.05 N | 121.01 E |
| Dawei (Tavoy) | 110 | 14.05 N | 98.12 E |
| Daweizhuang | 105 | 39.34 N | 116.53 E |
| Daweizigou | 104 | 42.38 N | 123.09 E |
| Dawen ≃ | 98 | 35.38 N | 116.24 E |
| Dawenkou | 98 | 35.59 N | 117.07 E |
| Dawera, Pulau I | 164 | 7.44 S | 130.00 E |
| Dawes Park ♠ | 278 | 42.03 N | 87.40 W |
| Dawlan | 110 | 16.44 N | 98.01 E |
| Dawlish | 42 | 50.35 N | 3.28 W |
| Dawn | 208 | 37.50 N | 77.22 W |
| Dawna Range ⋏ | 110 | 16.50 N | 98.15 E |
| Dawqah | 144 | 19.36 N | 40.54 E |
| Dawrah | 140 | 12.22 N | 24.19 E |
| Daws Heath | 260 | 51.34 N | 0.37 E |
| Dawson, Yk., Can. | 180 | 64.04 N | 139.25 W |
| Dawson, Ga., U.S. | 192 | 31.46 N | 84.26 W |
| Dawson, Il., U.S. | 219 | 39.51 N | 89.28 W |
| Dawson, Mn., U.S. | 198 | 44.55 N | 96.03 W |
| Dawson, Ne., U.S. | 198 | 40.07 N | 95.49 W |
| Dawson, Tx., U.S. | 222 | 31.53 N | 96.42 W |
| Dawson ≃ | 166 | 23.38 S | 149.46 E |
| Dawson, Isla I | 254 | 53.55 S | 70.45 W |
| Dawson, Mount ∧ | 182 | 51.09 N | 117.25 W |
| Dawson Bay c | 184 | 52.55 N | 100.50 W |
| Dawson Creek | 182 | 55.46 N | 120.14 W |
| Dawson Inlet c | 176 | 61.50 N | 93.25 W |
| Dawson Range ⋏, Austl. | 166 | 24.20 S | 149.45 E |
| Dawson Range ⋏, Yk., Can. | 180 | 62.40 N | 139.00 W |
| Dawson Ridge | 214 | 40.42 N | 80.22 W |
| Dawson Springs | 194 | 37.10 N | 87.41 W |
| Dawsonville | 192 | 34.25 N | 84.07 W |
| Dawu, Zhg. | 100 | 31.34 N | 114.06 E |
| Dawu, Zhg. | 102 | 31.07 N | 101.08 E |
| Dawudapu | 104 | 41.36 N | 123.03 E |
| Dawuji | 271a | 39.51 N | 116.30 E |
| Dawujiawopeng | 104 | 41.55 N | 122.29 E |
| Dawujiazi | 104 | 42.16 N | 121.52 E |
| Dawulaba | 104 | 42.13 N | 122.23 E |
| Dawulah | 104 | 41.56 N | 121.05 E |
| Dax | 32 | 43.43 N | 1.03 W |
| Daxian | 102 | 31.18 N | 107.30 E |
| Daxin, Zhg. | 100 | 33.54 N | 118.30 E |
| Daxin, Zhg. | 102 | 22.50 N | 107.26 E |
| Daxing, Zhg. | 98 | 39.44 N | 116.20 E |
| Daxing (Huangcun), Zhg. | 105 | 39.44 N | 116.20 E |
| Daxing, Zhg. | 106 | 31.50 N | 121.40 E |
| Daxingchang | 107 | 30.17 N | 103.26 E |
| Daxingcun | 106 | 31.45 N | 121.40 E |
| Daxingzhai | 102 | 23.13 N | 102.21 E |
| Daxinji | 100 | 34.03 N | 119.28 E |
| Daxinzhuang, Zhg. | 105 | 40.23 N | 116.44 E |
| Daxinzhuang, Zhg. | 105 | 39.26 N | 118.20 E |
| Daxiyang | 106 | 30.21 N | 121.58 E |
| Daxu, Zhg. | 100 | 29.32 N | 121.52 E |
| Daxu, Zhg. | 102 | 25.09 N | 110.21 E |
| Daxue Shan ⋏ | 102 | 30.10 N | 101.50 E |
| Daxujia | 98 | 34.18 N | 117.34 E |
| Dayakou | 102 | 22.46 N | 100.18 E |
| Dayanchi | 102 | 27.41 N | 101.55 E |
| Dayang, Zhg. | 98 | 36.04 N | 116.31 E |
| Dayang, Zhg. | 100 | 25.56 N | 118.48 E |
| Dayang ≃ | 98 | 39.54 N | 123.40 E |
| Dayang Bunting, Pulau I | 114 | 6.14 N | 99.48 E |
| Dayangcha | 98 | 42.04 N | 126.43 E |
| Dayanggou | 104 | 41.14 N | 123.51 E |
| Dayang Shan I | 106 | 30.35 N | 122.00 E |
| Dayangshu | 89 | 49.45 N | 124.35 E |
| Dayao, Zhg. | 100 | 27.59 N | 113.42 E |
| Dayao, Zhg. | 102 | 25.43 N | 101.13 E |
| Dayaoshan | 102 | 24.05 N | 110.17 E |
| Daya Wan c | 100 | 22.37 N | 114.40 E |
| Dayboro | 171a | 27.11 S | 152.50 E |
| Daye | 100 | 30.06 N | 114.57 E |
| Dayghar | 272c | 19.09 N | 73.03 E |
| Day Heights | 218 | 39.11 N | 84.14 W |
| Dayi | 107 | 30.37 N | 103.31 E |
| Dayiji | 100 | 32.32 N | 119.14 E |
| Daying, Zhg. | 98 | 34.27 N | 113.59 E |
| Daying, Zhg. | 98 | 37.19 N | 115.43 E |
| Daying, Zhg. | 98 | 39.53 N | 123.07 E |
| Daying, Zhg. | 98 | 39.19 N | 113.46 E |
| Daying, Zhg. | 100 | 33.59 N | 112.51 E |
| Daying, Zhg. | 105 | 39.05 N | 116.06 E |
| Daying (Taping) ≃ | 102 | 24.17 N | 97.14 E |
| Dayingzi, Zhg. | 98 | 41.19 N | 118.19 E |
| Dayingzi, Zhg. | 98 | 41.28 N | 120.21 E |
| Dayingzi, Zhg. | 104 | 41.08 N | 122.50 E |
| Dayiqiao | 106 | 31.44 N | 120.45 E |
| Day Island | 224 | 47.15 N | 122.33 W |
| Day Lake ⊜ | 224 | 48.23 N | 121.58 W |
| Daylesford | 169 | 37.21 S | 144.09 E |
| Daymán ≃ | 252 | 31.30 S | 58.02 W |
| Daym Zubayr | 140 | 7.43 N | 26.13 E |
| Dayong, Zhg. | 100 | 22.28 N | 113.16 E |
| Dayong, Zhg. | 102 | 29.06 N | 110.29 E |
| Dayou | 98 | 34.12 N | 119.52 E |
| Dayr, Jabal ad- ∧ | 140 | 12.27 N | 30.42 E |
| Dayr Abū Sa'īd | 132 | 32.30 N | 35.41 E |
| Dayr al-Balaḥ | 132 | 31.25 N | 34.21 E |
| Dayr al-Ghuṣūn | 132 | 32.21 N | 35.05 E |
| Dayr 'Alī | 132 | 33.17 N | 36.18 E |
| Dayr 'Allā | 132 | 32.12 N | 35.37 E |
| Dayr 'Aṭīyah | 130 | 34.06 N | 36.46 E |
| Dayr az-Zawr | 130 | 35.20 N | 40.09 E |
| Dayr az-Zawr □[8] | 130 | 35.00 N | 40.30 E |
| Dayr Dibwān | 132 | 31.55 N | 35.16 E |
| Dayr Hāfir | 130 | 36.09 N | 37.42 E |
| Dayr Jabal Aṭ-Ṭayr | 142 | 28.17 N | 30.45 E |
| Dayr Mawās | 142 | 27.38 N | 30.51 E |
| Dayr Qānūn | 132 | 33.36 N | 36.08 E |
| Dayr Sharaf | 132 | 32.15 N | 35.11 E |
| Dayrūṭ, Miṣr | 142 | 27.33 N | 30.49 E |
| Dayrūṭ, Miṣr | 142 | 31.13 N | 30.30 E |
| Dayrūṭ ash-Sharīf | 142 | 27.35 N | 30.49 E |
| Days Island I | 284b | 39.24 N | 76.22 W |
| Daysland | 182 | 52.52 N | 112.15 W |
| Day Star Indian Reserve ◆[4] | 184 | 51.43 N | 104.14 W |
| Dayton, Il., U.S. | 216 | 41.23 N | 88.47 W |
| Dayton, In., U.S. | 216 | 40.22 N | 86.46 W |
| Dayton, Ia., U.S. | 190 | 42.15 N | 94.04 W |
| Dayton, Ky., U.S. | 218 | 39.06 N | 84.28 W |
| Dayton, Mi., U.S. | 216 | 41.48 N | 86.26 W |
| Dayton, Nv., U.S. | 226 | 39.14 N | 119.35 W |
| Dayton, N.J., U.S. | 276 | 40.22 N | 74.30 W |
| Dayton, N.Y., U.S. | 210 | 42.25 N | 78.58 W |
| Dayton, Oh., U.S. | 218 | 39.45 N | 84.11 W |
| Dayton, Or., U.S. | 224 | 45.13 N | 123.04 W |
| Dayton, Pa., U.S. | 214 | 40.52 N | 79.14 W |
| Dayton, Tn., U.S. | 194 | 35.29 N | 85.00 W |
| Dayton, Tx., U.S. | 222 | 30.02 N | 94.53 W |
| Dayton, Va., U.S. | 188 | 38.24 N | 78.56 W |
| Dayton, Wa., U.S. | 202 | 46.19 N | 117.58 W |
| Dayton, Wy., U.S. | 202 | 44.52 N | 107.15 W |
| Daytona Beach | 192 | 29.12 N | 81.01 W |
| Dayton Municipal Airport ⊠ | 218 | 39.54 N | 84.13 W |
| Dayu, Indon. | 112 | 1.59 S | 115.04 E |
| Dayu, Zhg. | 100 | 25.24 N | 114.22 E |
| Dayuba | 107 | 29.15 N | 103.34 E |
| Dayu Ling ⋏ | 100 | 25.20 N | 114.16 E |
| Da Yunhe (Grand Canal) ≡ | 90 | 32.12 N | 119.31 E |
| Dayu Shan I, Zhg. | 100 | 26.57 N | 120.21 E |
| Dayu Shan I, Zhg. | 106 | 30.19 N | 121.58 E |
| Dayushupu | 104 | 41.32 N | 121.24 E |
| Dayville, Ct., U.S. | 207 | 41.50 N | 71.53 W |
| Dayville, Or., U.S. | 202 | 44.28 N | 119.32 W |
| Dazaifu ⊥ | 96 | 33.31 N | 130.31 E |
| Dazaoliyingzi | 104 | 42.07 N | 121.20 E |
| Dazaomiao | 106 | 32.06 N | 121.29 E |
| Dazhang ≃ | 100 | 25.56 N | 119.12 E |
| Dazhangzi | 98 | 40.38 N | 118.07 E |
| Dazhaotai | 104 | 41.14 N | 123.03 E |
| Dazhengjiatun | 98 | 39.37 N | 122.52 E |
| Dazhengzhuangzi | 105 | 39.16 N | 116.46 E |
| Dazhi | 100 | 34.29 N | 113.17 E |
| Dazhiba | 102 | 27.09 N | 99.52 E |
| Dazhifang | 104 | 41.21 N | 123.12 E |
| Dazhou | 100 | 28.53 N | 118.58 E |
| Dazhu | 102 | 30.48 N | 107.12 E |
| Dazhuangke | 105 | 40.32 N | 115.42 E |
| Dazhubao | 107 | 28.59 N | 103.38 E |
| Dazhuyuan | 100 | 23.43 N | 115.57 E |
| Dazifangshen | 104 | 42.27 N | 124.12 E |
| Daziling | 104 | 41.21 N | 121.26 E |
| Daziying | 104 | 41.42 N | 123.36 E |
| Dazkırı | 130 | 37.55 N | 29.52 E |
| Dazu | 107 | 29.43 N | 105.42 E |
| Dazui | 100 | 30.16 N | 114.02 E |
| De Aar | 158 | 30.39 S | 24.00 E |
| Dead ≃, Me., U.S. | 188 | 45.20 N | 69.58 W |
| Dead ≃, Mi., U.S. | 190 | 46.34 N | 87.24 W |
| Dead ≃, N.J., U.S. | 276 | 40.39 N | 74.31 W |
| Deadhorse | 180 | 70.11 N | 148.27 W |
| Dead Horse Point State Park ♠ | 200 | 38.28 N | 109.44 W |
| Deadman ≃ | 182 | 50.45 N | 120.55 W |
| Deadman Brook ≃ | 276 | 41.08 N | 73.22 W |
| Deadman Creek ≃ | 226 | 37.12 N | 120.42 W |
| Deadman Hill ∧ | 162 | 23.48 S | 119.25 E |
| Deadman's Cay | 238 | 23.14 N | 75.14 W |
| Deadmans Creek ≃ | 274a | 33.58 S | 151.00 E |
| Deadman's Creek Indian Reserve ◆[4] | 182 | 50.49 N | 121.00 W |
| Dead Run ≃ | 284c | 38.57 N | 77.11 W |
| Dead Sea (Al-Baḥr al-Mayyit) (Yam HaMelaḥ) ⊜ | 132 | 31.30 N | 35.30 E |
| Deadwood | 198 | 44.22 N | 103.43 W |
| Deadwood ≃ | 202 | 44.05 N | 115.40 W |
| Deagan Island I | 116 | 12.15 N | 123.51 E |
| Deakin | 162 | 30.46 S | 128.58 E |
| Deakin, Mount ∧[2] | 162 | 17.38 S | 130.48 E |
| Deakin Bay c | 9 | 68.23 S | 150.10 E |
| Deal, Eng., U.K. | 42 | 51.14 N | 1.24 E |
| Deal, N.J., U.S. | 208 | 40.15 N | 74.00 W |
| Deale | 208 | 38.46 N | 76.33 W |
| Dealesville | 158 | 28.40 S | 25.37 E |
| Deal Island | 208 | 38.09 N | 75.56 W |
| Deal Island I | 208 | 38.09 N | 75.56 W |
| Deam Lake ⊜[1] | 218 | 38.28 N | 85.51 W |
| De'an | 100 | 29.20 N | 115.46 E |
| Dean ≃, B.C., Can. | 182 | 52.50 N | 126.57 W |
| Dean ≃, Eng., U.K. | 262 | 53.20 N | 2.14 W |
| Dean, Forest of ◆[3] | 42 | 51.48 N | 2.30 W |
| Dean Channel ⊔ | 182 | 52.33 N | 127.13 W |
| Deane | 262 | 53.34 N | 2.28 W |
| Deán Funes | 252 | 30.26 S | 64.21 W |
| Dean Row | 262 | 53.20 N | 2.11 W |
| Deans | 276 | 40.24 N | 74.30 W |
| Deansboro | 210 | 43.00 N | 75.26 W |
| Deans Dundas Bay c | 176 | 72.15 N | 118.25 W |
| Deanville | 222 | 30.26 N | 96.46 W |
| Dearborn | 216 | 42.18 N | 83.10 W |
| Dearborn □[6] | 218 | 39.06 N | 84.51 W |
| Dearborn ≃ | 202 | 47.07 N | 111.55 W |
| Dearborn Heights | 216 | 42.20 N | 83.16 W |
| Dearg, Beinn ∧ | 46 | 57.47 N | 4.56 W |
| Dearham | 44 | 54.42 N | 3.26 W |
| Dearne ≃ | 44 | 53.30 N | 1.16 W |
| Dear Reservoir ⊜[1] | 44 | 55.20 N | 3.37 W |
| Dease ≃ | 180 | 59.54 N | 128.30 W |
| Dease Arm c | 180 | 66.52 N | 119.37 W |
| Dease Lake ⊜ | 180 | 58.35 N | 130.02 W |
| Dease Strait ⊔ | 176 | 68.40 N | 108.00 W |
| Death Valley | 204 | 36.18 N | 116.25 W |
| Death Valley V | 204 | 36.30 N | 117.00 W |
| Death Valley National Park ♠ | 204 | 36.30 N | 117.00 W |
| Deatsville | 194 | 32.36 N | 86.23 W |
| Deauville | 50 | 49.22 N | 0.04 E |
| Deba | 146 | 10.20 N | 11.54 E |
| Debagrām | 126 | 23.41 N | 88.18 E |
| Debal'tseve | 83 | 48.20 N | 38.24 E |
| Debānāndapur | 272b | 22.56 N | 88.22 E |
| Debao | 102 | 23.21 N | 106.31 E |
| Debar | 38 | 41.31 N | 20.30 E |
| De Bary | 220 | 28.52 N | 81.18 W |
| Debauch Mountain ∧ | 180 | 64.31 N | 159.52 W |
| Débé | 241r | 10.12 N | 61.27 W |
| Debed ≃ | 84 | 41.22 N | 44.58 E |
| Deben ≃ | 42 | 51.58 N | 1.24 E |
| Debenham | 42 | 52.13 N | 1.11 E |
| De Beque | 200 | 39.20 N | 108.12 W |
| De Berry | 194 | 32.18 N | 94.10 W |
| Debesy | 80 | 57.39 N | 53.49 E |
| Debhāta | 124 | 22.33 N | 88.58 E |
| Dębica | 30 | 50.04 N | 21.24 E |
| De Bilt | 52 | 52.06 N | 5.10 E |
| Debipur | 126 | 24.14 N | 88.38 E |
| Debīr Char | 126 | 22.24 N | 90.41 E |
| Dęblin | 30 | 51.35 N | 21.50 E |
| Dębno | 30 | 52.45 N | 14.40 E |
| Débo, Lac ⊜ | 150 | 15.18 N | 4.09 W |
| Deborah, Mount ∧ | 180 | 63.38 N | 147.15 W |
| Deborah West, Lake ⊜ | 162 | 30.45 S | 119.07 E |
| Deboyne Islands II | 164 | 10.45 S | 152.25 E |
| Debra | 126 | 22.24 N | 87.33 E |
| Debra Sina | 144 | 9.51 N | 39.50 E |
| Debre Birhan | 144 | 9.40 N | 39.33 E |
| Debrecen | 30 | 47.32 N | 21.38 E |
| Debre Markos | 144 | 10.20 N | 37.45 E |
| Debre May | 144 | 11.19 N | 37.30 E |
| Debre Tabor | 144 | 11.50 N | 38.05 E |
| Debre Zebit | 144 | 11.50 N | 38.40 E |
| Debre Zeyit | 144 | 8.45 N | 38.59 E |
| Debrzno | 30 | 53.33 N | 17.14 E |
| Debstedt | 52 | 53.37 N | 8.38 E |
| Decatur, Al., U.S. | 194 | 34.36 N | 86.59 W |
| Decatur, Ga., U.S. | 192 | 33.46 N | 84.17 W |
| Decatur, Il., U.S. | 219 | 39.50 N | 88.57 W |
| Decatur, In., U.S. | 216 | 40.50 N | 84.56 W |
| Decatur, Mi., U.S. | 216 | 42.06 N | 85.58 W |
| Decatur, Ms., U.S. | 194 | 32.26 N | 89.06 W |
| Decatur, Ne., U.S. | 198 | 42.00 N | 96.14 W |
| Decatur, Oh., U.S. | 218 | 38.49 N | 83.42 W |
| Decatur, Tn., U.S. | 192 | 35.30 N | 84.47 W |
| Decatur, Tx., U.S. | 222 | 33.14 N | 97.35 W |
| Decatur □[6] | 218 | 39.20 N | 85.29 W |
| Decatur, Lake ⊜[1] | 219 | 39.51 N | 88.52 W |
| Decatur Island I | 224 | 48.31 N | 122.50 W |
| Decatur Municipal Airport ⊠ | 219 | 39.50 N | 88.52 W |
| Decaturville | 194 | 35.35 N | 88.07 W |
| Decazeville | 32 | 44.34 N | 2.15 E |
| Deccan ⋏[1] | 122 | 17.00 N | 78.00 E |
| Decelles, Réservoir ⊜[1] | 190 | 47.42 N | 78.08 W |
| Deception ≃ | 156 | 21.04 S | 24.25 E |
| Deception, Mount ∧ | 224 | 47.49 N | 123.14 W |
| Deception Bay c | 171a | 27.07 S | 153.05 E |
| Deception Island I | 9 | 62.57 S | 60.38 W |
| Deception Lake ⊜ | 184 | 56.33 N | 104.15 W |
| Deception Pass ≡ | 224 | 48.24 N | 122.38 W |
| Deception Pass State Park ♠ | 224 | 48.24 N | 122.39 W |
| Dechang | 102 | 27.24 N | 102.10 E |
| Dechêne, Lac ⊜ | 186 | 51.15 N | 67.51 W |
| Dechenhöhle ⊥[5] | 263 | 51.22 N | 7.39 E |
| Decherd | 194 | 35.12 N | 86.04 W |
| Dechhu | 120 | 26.47 N | 72.20 E |
| Déchy | 50 | 50.21 N | 3.07 E |
| Decimomannu | 71 | 39.19 N | 8.58 E |
| Decimoputzu | 71 | 39.20 N | 8.55 E |
| Děčín | 54 | 50.48 N | 14.13 E |
| Děčínské stěny ⋏ | 54 | 50.50 N | 14.12 E |
| Decize | 32 | 46.50 N | 3.27 E |
| Decker Lake | 182 | 54.17 N | 125.50 W |
| Deckers Point | 214 | 40.46 N | 78.59 W |
| Deckerville | 190 | 43.31 N | 82.44 W |
| De Cocksdorp | 52 | 53.08 N | 4.52 E |
| Decollatura | 68 | 39.03 N | 16.21 E |
| Decorah | 190 | 43.18 N | 91.47 W |
| Decs | 30 | 46.17 N | 18.46 E |
| Deda | 38 | 46.57 N | 24.53 E |
| Dedaye | 110 | 16.24 N | 95.53 E |
| Deddington | 42 | 51.59 N | 1.19 W |
| Dededo | 174p | 13.31 N | 144.49 E |
| Dedegöl Dağları ⋏ | 130 | 37.47 N | 31.13 E |
| Dedegöl Tepesi ∧ | 130 | 37.39 N | 31.17 E |
| Dedeleben | 54 | 52.02 N | 10.54 E |
| Dedeli | 84 | 39.11 N | 43.05 E |
| Dedelow | 54 | 53.22 N | 13.48 E |
| Dedemsvaart | 52 | 52.36 N | 6.28 E |
| Dedenevo | 82 | 56.15 N | 37.31 E |
| Deder | 144 | 9.22 N | 41.26 E |
| Dedesdorf | 52 | 53.27 N | 8.30 E |
| Dedham | 207 | 42.14 N | 71.10 W |
| Dedilovskije Vyselki | 82 | 54.20 N | 38.03 E |
| Dedinovo | 82 | 55.03 N | 39.07 E |
| Dedo, Cerro ∧ | 254 | 44.49 S | 71.52 W |
| Dedo de Deus, Pico ∧ | 256 | 22.30 S | 43.03 W |
| De Doorns | 158 | 33.28 S | 19.41 E |
| Dedoplis Ckaro | 84 | 41.28 N | 46.07 E |
| Dédougou | 150 | 12.28 N | 3.28 W |
| Dedoviči | 76 | 57.32 N | 29.56 E |
| Dedovsk | 82 | 55.52 N | 37.07 E |
| Dedu | 89 | 48.31 N | 126.14 E |
| Deduru ≃ | 122 | 7.36 N | 79.48 E |
| Dedza | 154 | 14.22 S | 34.20 E |
| Dee ≃, Ire. | 48 | 53.52 N | 6.21 W |
| Dee ≃, U.K. | 44 | 53.20 N | 3.12 W |
| Dee ≃, Eng., U.K. | 44 | 54.18 N | 2.32 W |
| Dee ≃, Scot., U.K. | 44 | 54.50 N | 4.03 W |
| Dee ≃, Scot., U.K. | 46 | 57.09 N | 2.07 W |
| Dee, Loch ⊜ | 44 | 55.05 N | 4.24 W |
| Deedsville | 216 | 40.55 N | 86.06 W |
| De Efteling ♠ | 52 | 51.39 N | 5.02 E |
| Deeg | 124 | 27.28 N | 77.20 E |
| Deelfontein | 158 | 30.59 S | 23.48 E |
| Deelpan | 158 | 26.19 S | 25.36 E |
| Deenwood | 192 | 31.14 N | 82.23 W |
| Deep ≃, In., U.S. | 216 | 41.34 N | 87.17 W |
| Deep ≃, N.C., U.S. | 192 | 35.36 N | 79.03 W |
| Deepavaal Brook ≃ | 276 | 40.53 N | 74.16 W |
| Deep Bay c | 184 | 56.25 N | 103.00 W |
| Deep Brook ≃, Ma., U.S. | 283 | 42.38 N | 71.22 W |
| Deep Brook ≃, N.J., U.S. | 276 | 40.58 N | 74.09 W |
| Deep Creek ≃, Austl. | 169 | 37.37 S | 144.48 E |
| Deep Creek ≃, U.S. | 200 | 41.44 N | 113.00 W |
| Deep Creek ≃, Ca., U.S. | 228 | 34.20 N | 117.14 W |
| Deep Creek ≃, De., U.S. | 208 | 38.38 N | 75.37 W |
| Deep Creek ≃, Id., U.S. | 202 | 42.15 N | 116.40 W |
| Deep Creek ≃, Md., U.S. | 284b | 39.17 N | 76.28 W |
| Deep Creek ≃, Tx., U.S. | 196 | 32.45 N | 99.10 W |
| Deep Creek ≃, Tx., U.S. | 196 | 32.31 N | 100.55 W |
| Deep Creek ≃, Ut,. U.S. | 200 | 40.10 N | 113.50 W |
| Deep Creek Conservation Park ♠ | 168b | 35.39 S | 138.12 E |
| Deep Creek Indian Reserve ◆[4] | 182 | 52.16 N | 122.07 W |
| Deeping Fen ⁝ | 42 | 52.44 N | 0.13 W |
| Deep Red Creek ≃ | 196 | 34.17 N | 98.39 W |
| Deep River, On., Can. | 190 | 46.06 N | 77.30 W |
| Deep River, Ct., U.S. | 207 | 41.23 N | 72.26 W |
| Deep River, Ia., U.S. | 190 | 41.34 N | 92.22 W |
| Deep River, Wa., U.S. | 224 | 46.21 N | 123.41 W |
| Deep Run ≃, Md., U.S. | 284b | 39.13 N | 76.42 W |
| Deep Run ≃, Md., U.S. | 284b | 39.25 N | 76.40 W |
| Deep Run ≃, N.J., U.S. | 276 | 40.26 N | 74.22 W |
| Deep Run ≃, N.J., U.S. | 285 | 39.44 N | 74.41 W |
| Deepwater, Austl. | 166 | 29.27 S | 151.51 E |
| Deepwater, Mo., U.S. | 194 | 38.15 N | 93.46 W |
| Deep Water, N.J., U.S. | 208 | 39.41 N | 75.29 W |
| Deep Well | 162 | 24.25 S | 134.05 E |
| Deer ≃, N.Y., U.S. | 188 | 44.55 N | 74.43 W |
| Deer ≃, N.Y., U.S. | 212 | 43.56 N | 75.34 W |
| Deer Creek, In., U.S. | 216 | 40.37 N | 86.23 W |
| Deer Creek, Mn., U.S. | 198 | 46.23 N | 95.19 W |
| Deer Creek ≃, U.S. | 208 | 39.37 N | 76.09 W |
| Deer Creek ≃, Ca., U.S. | 204 | 39.56 N | 122.04 W |
| Deer Creek ≃, Ca., U.S. | 226 | 39.13 N | 121.17 W |
| Deer Creek ≃, Ca., U.S. | 226 | 35.56 N | 119.28 W |
| Deer Creek ≃, Ca., U.S. | 226 | 38.22 N | 121.21 W |
| Deer Creek ≃, Ca., U.S. | 282 | 37.24 N | 122.09 W |
| Deer Creek ≃, Il., U.S. | 278 | 41.32 N | 87.37 W |
| Deer Creek ≃, In., U.S. | 216 | 40.34 N | 86.41 W |
| Deer Creek ≃, Ks., U.S. | 198 | 39.40 N | 99.06 W |
| Deer Creek ≃, Ms., U.S. | 194 | 32.33 N | 90.47 W |
| Deer Creek ≃, Ne., U.S. | 198 | 40.28 N | 100.00 W |
| Deer Creek ≃, Oh., U.S. | 218 | 39.27 N | 83.00 W |
| Deer Creek ≃, Ok., U.S. | 196 | 35.38 N | 98.28 W |
| Deer Creek ≃, Or., U.S. | 224 | 45.08 N | 123.15 W |
| Deer Creek ≃, Pa., U.S. | 279b | 40.32 N | 79.51 W |
| Deer Creek ≃, Wa., U.S. | 224 | 48.16 N | 121.55 W |
| Deer Creek ≃, Wy., U.S. | 200 | 42.52 N | 105.52 W |
| Deer Creek ≃, Wy., U.S. | 202 | 43.09 N | 107.42 W |
| Deer Creek Indian Reservation ◆[4] | 190 | 47.50 N | 93.25 W |
| Deer Creek Lake ⊜[1] | 218 | 39.40 N | 83.15 W |
| Deerfield, Il., U.S. | 216 | 42.10 N | 87.50 W |
| Deerfield, In., U.S. | 216 | 40.17 N | 84.59 W |
| Deerfield, Ks., U.S. | 198 | 37.58 N | 101.07 W |
| Deerfield, Ma., U.S. | 207 | 42.32 N | 72.36 W |
| Deerfield, Mi., U.S. | 216 | 41.53 N | 83.46 W |
| Deerfield, Oh., U.S. | 214 | 41.01 N | 81.03 W |
| Deerfield, Wi., U.S. | 216 | 43.03 N | 89.04 W |
| Deerfield ≃ | 207 | 42.35 N | 72.35 W |
| Deerfield Beach | 220 | 26.19 N | 80.06 W |
| Deerfield Street | 208 | 39.31 N | 75.14 W |
| Deer Grove ♠ | 278 | 42.09 N | 88.04 W |
| Deer Harbor | 224 | 48.37 N | 123.00 W |
| Deering | 180 | 66.05 N | 162.43 W |
| Deering, Mount ∧[2] | 162 | 24.53 S | 129.04 E |
| Deer Island ›[1] | 283 | 42.21 N | 70.58 W |
| Deer Island I, N.B., Can. | 186 | 45.00 N | 66.57 W |
| Deer Island I, Ak., U.S. | 180 | 54.53 N | 162.25 W |
| Deer Island I, Or., U.S. | 224 | 45.58 N | 122.50 W |
| Deer Isle | 188 | 44.13 N | 68.40 W |
| Deer Lake, Nf., Can. | 186 | 49.10 N | 57.26 W |
| Deer Lake, Pa., U.S. | 208 | 40.37 N | 76.03 W |
| Deer Lake ⊜, Nf., Can. | 186 | 49.07 N | 57.35 W |
| Deer Lake ⊜, On., Can. | 184 | 52.40 N | 94.30 W |
| Deer Lakes Regional Park ♠ | 279b | 40.38 N | 79.49 W |
| Deerlijk | 50 | 50.51 N | 3.21 E |
| Deer Lodge | 202 | 46.23 N | 112.44 W |
| Deer Mountain ∧ | 188 | 45.01 N | 70.56 W |
| Deer Park, Austl. | 274b | 37.47 S | 144.47 E |
| Deer Park, Al., U.S. | 194 | 31.13 N | 88.19 W |
| Deer Park, Ca., U.S. | 226 | 38.32 N | 122.28 W |
| Deer Park, Il., U.S. | 278 | 42.09 N | 88.04 W |
| Deer Park, N.Y., U.S. | 210 | 40.45 N | 73.19 W |
| Deer Park, Oh., U.S. | 218 | 39.12 N | 84.23 W |
| Deer Park, Tx., U.S. | 222 | 29.42 N | 95.07 W |
| Deer Park, Wa., U.S. | 202 | 47.57 N | 117.28 W |
| Deer Park ♠ | 272a | 28.33 N | 77.11 E |
| Deer Park Airport ⊠ | 276 | 40.46 N | 73.19 W |
| Deerpass Bay c | 180 | 65.56 N | 122.25 W |
| Deer Pond ⊜, Nf., Can. | 186 | 48.30 N | 54.45 W |
| Deer Pond ⊜, N.J., U.S. | 276 | 40.57 N | 74.24 W |
| Deer River, Mn., U.S. | 190 | 47.19 N | 93.47 W |
| Deer River, N.Y., U.S. | 212 | 43.56 N | 75.36 W |
| Deer Sound ⊔ | 46 | 58.58 N | 2.48 W |
| Deersville | 214 | 40.19 N | 81.11 W |
| Deer Trail | 198 | 39.36 N | 104.02 W |
| Deerwood | 190 | 46.28 N | 93.53 W |
| Dee Why | 170 | 33.45 S | 151.17 E |
| Dee Why Head › | 274a | 33.46 S | 151.19 E |
| Dee Why Lagoon c | 274a | 33.45 S | 151.18 E |
| Deex Nugaaleed V | 144 | 7.58 N | 49.51 E |
| Defengzhuang | 98 | 41.02 N | 113.16 E |
| Defereggen V | 64 | 46.55 N | 12.25 E |
| Defereggen Alpen ⋏ | 64 | 46.52 N | 12.20 E |
| Deferiet | 212 | 44.02 N | 75.41 W |
| Defiance, Ia., U.S. | 198 | 41.49 N | 95.20 W |
| Defiance, Oh., U.S. | 216 | 41.17 N | 84.21 W |
| Defiance, Pa., U.S. | 214 | 40.10 N | 78.14 W |
| Defiance □[6] | 216 | 41.19 N | 84.30 W |
| Defiance, Mount ∧ | 224 | 45.38 N | 121.43 W |
| Defiance Plateau ⋏[1] | 200 | 36.00 N | 109.15 W |
| De Forest | 190 | 43.14 N | 89.20 W |
| De Forest Lake ⊜ | 276 | 41.08 N | 73.58 W |
| Defu | 271c | 1.21 N | 103.54 E |
| De Funiak Springs | 194 | 30.43 N | 86.06 W |
| Deganga | 126 | 22.40 N | 88.39 E |
| Deganwy | 44 | 53.17 N | 3.50 W |
| Deganya | 132 | 32.42 N | 35.35 E |
| Dêgê | 102 | 31.50 N | 98.40 E |
| Degeberga | 26 | 55.50 N | 14.05 E |
| Degeh Bur | 144 | 8.13 N | 43.34 E |
| Dégelis (Sainte-Rose-du-Dégelis) | 186 | 47.33 N | 68.39 W |
| Degema | 150 | 4.45 N | 6.47 E |
| Degerby | 26 | 60.02 N | 20.23 E |
| Degeres | 85 | 43.14 N | 75.49 E |
| Degerfors | 40 | 59.14 N | 14.26 E |
| Degerhamn | 26 | 56.21 N | 16.24 E |
| Deggendorf | 60 | 48.51 N | 12.59 E |
| Deggenhausertal | 58 | 47.47 N | 9.24 E |
| Deggingen | 56 | 48.36 N | 9.43 E |
| Degh ≃ | 123 | 31.36 N | 74.09 E |
| Değirmendere | 130 | 38.07 N | 27.09 E |
| Değirmenlik | 130 | 35.15 N | 33.29 E |
| Deglunden ⊜ | 40 | 60.05 N | 13.49 E |
| Dego | 62 | 44.27 N | 8.19 E |
| Degollado | 234 | 20.28 N | 102.09 W |
| Degoma | 144 | 12.28 N | 37.37 E |
| Degong | 114 | 4.05 N | 101.08 E |
| De Graafschap ◆[1] | 52 | 52.00 N | 6.30 E |
| De Graff | 216 | 40.18 N | 83.54 W |
| De Gray Lake ⊜[1] | 194 | 34.15 N | 93.15 W |
| De Grey | 162 | 20.10 S | 119.12 E |
| De Grey ≃ | 162 | 20.12 S | 119.11 E |
| Degt'arka ≃ | 265a | 59.57 N | 30.52 E |
| Degunino ◆[8] | 265b | 55.52 N | 37.33 E |
| De Haan | 50 | 51.16 N | 3.02 E |
| Dehak ≃ | 128 | 32.01 N | 58.35 E |
| Dehalak Deset I | 144 | 15.40 N | 40.05 E |
| Deharda | 126 | 21.40 N | 87.25 E |
| De Hart Reservoir ⊜[1] | 208 | 40.28 N | 76.45 W |
| Deh Bālā | 123 | 34.04 N | 70.29 E |
| Deh Bīd | 128 | 30.38 N | 53.13 E |
| Dehdez | 128 | 31.43 N | 50.17 E |
| Deh-e Salm | 128 | 31.12 N | 59.19 E |
| Dehgolān | 128 | 35.17 N | 47.25 E |
| Dehibat | 148 | 32.01 N | 10.42 E |
| Dehiwala-Mount Lavinia | 122 | 6.51 N | 79.52 E |
| Deh Kord | 128 | 33.49 N | 48.53 E |
| Dehlorān | 128 | 32.41 N | 47.16 E |
| De Hoek | 158 | 32.57 S | 18.46 E |
| Dehpehk I | 174r | 6.57 N | 158.18 E |
| Dehra Dūn | 124 | 30.19 N | 78.02 E |
| Dehri | 124 | 24.52 N | 84.11 E |
| Dehrn | 56 | 50.25 N | 8.05 E |
| Dehu | 122 | 18.35 N | 73.51 E |
| Dehua | 100 | 25.32 N | 118.15 E |
| Dehuang | 98 | 35.12 N | 114.25 E |
| Dehui | 89 | 44.34 N | 125.43 E |
| Deidesheim | 56 | 49.24 N | 8.11 E |
| Deilbach ≃ | 263 | 51.23 N | 7.05 E |
| Deilinghofen | 56 | 51.22 N | 7.47 E |
| Deining | 60 | 49.13 N | 11.32 E |
| Deinze | 50 | 50.59 N | 3.32 E |
| Deir el Asad | 132 | 32.56 N | 35.16 E |
| Deisslingen, Dtsch. | 58 | 48.07 N | 8.36 E |
| Deisslingen, Dtsch. | 58 | 48.07 N | 8.36 E |
| Deister ⋏ | 52 | 52.15 N | 9.30 E |
| Deiva Marina | 62 | 44.13 N | 9.30 E |
| Dej | 38 | 47.09 N | 23.52 E |
| Deje | 40 | 59.36 N | 13.28 E |
| Dejima | 94 | 36.05 N | 140.20 E |
| Dejnau | 128 | 39.15 N | 63.11 E |
| De Jongs, Tanjong › | 164 | 6.56 S | 138.32 E |
| Deka ≃ | 154 | 18.04 S | 26.42 E |
| De Kalb, Il., U.S. | 216 | 41.55 N | 88.45 W |
| De Kalb, Ms., U.S. | 194 | 32.46 N | 88.39 W |
| De Kalb, Tx., U.S. | 194 | 33.30 N | 94.36 W |
| De Kalb □[6], Il., U.S. | 216 | 41.59 N | 88.41 W |
| De Kalb □[6], In., U.S. | 216 | 41.22 N | 85.04 W |
| De Kalb Junction | 212 | 44.30 N | 75.16 W |
| Dekan, Hochland von → Deccan ⋏[1] | 122 | 17.00 N | 78.00 E |
| De-Kastri | 89 | 51.28 N | 140.47 E |
| Dekehtik I | 174r | 7.00 N | 158.12 E |
| Dekemhare | 144 | 15.05 N | 39.02 E |
| Dekese | 152 | 3.27 S | 21.24 E |
| Deke Sokehs I | 174r | 6.59 N | 158.11 E |
| Dekhgila Military Base ■ | 142 | 31.08 N | 29.48 E |
| Dekina | 150 | 7.39 N | 7.02 E |
| Dékoa | 152 | 6.19 N | 19.04 E |
| De Koog | 52 | 53.05 N | 4.45 E |
| De Krim | 52 | 52.38 N | 6.38 E |
| De La Blanche, Lac ⊜ | 186 | 50.05 N | 69.29 W |
| Delabole | 42 | 50.37 N | 4.42 W |
| Delafield | 216 | 43.03 N | 88.24 W |
| Del Aire | 280 | 33.55 N | 118.21 W |
| Delamere, Austl. | 164 | 15.45 S | 131.33 E |
| Delamere, Austl. | 168b | 35.35 S | 138.11 E |
| Delamere, Eng., U.K. | 262 | 53.13 N | 2.39 W |
| Delamere Forest ◆[3] | 44 | 53.14 N | 2.38 W |
| Delami Mayal, Jabal ∧ | 140 | 11.38 N | 30.23 E |
| Del Amo Fashion Center ◆[9] | 280 | 33.50 N | 118.21 W |
| De Lancey, N.Y., U.S. | 210 | 42.12 N | 74.58 W |
| De Lancey, Pa., U.S. | 214 | 40.59 N | 78.58 W |
| Delanco | 208 | 40.03 N | 74.57 W |
| De Land | 220 | 29.01 N | 81.18 W |
| Delanggu | 115a | 7.37 S | 110.41 E |
| Delano, Ca., U.S. | 226 | 35.46 N | 119.14 W |
| Delano, Mn., U.S. | 190 | 45.02 N | 93.47 W |
| Delano, Pa., U.S. | 210 | 40.50 N | 76.04 W |
| Delano Peak ∧ | 200 | 38.22 N | 112.23 W |
| Delanson | 210 | 42.44 N | 74.11 W |
| Delaport Point › | 240b | 25.05 N | 77.27 W |
| Delapu | 120 | 31.35 N | 90.35 E |
| Delārām | 128 | 32.11 N | 63.25 E |
| Delareyville | 158 | 26.44 S | 25.29 E |
| Delarof Islands II | 181a | 51.30 N | 178.45 W |
| Delaronde Lake ⊜ | 184 | 54.05 N | 107.05 W |
| Delatite ≃ | 169 | 37.10 S | 146.00 E |
| Delavan, Il., U.S. | 194 | 40.22 N | 89.32 W |
| Delavan, Wi., U.S. | 216 | 42.37 N | 88.38 W |
| Delavan Lake | 216 | 42.35 N | 88.37 W |
| Delavan Lake ⊜ | 216 | 42.37 N | 88.38 W |
| Delaware, On., Can. | 214 | 42.55 N | 81.25 W |
| Delaware, N.J., U.S. | 210 | 40.53 N | 75.03 W |
| Delaware, Oh., U.S. | 214 | 40.17 N | 83.04 W |
| Delaware, Ok., U.S. | 196 | 36.46 N | 95.38 W |
| Delaware □[6], In., U.S. | 216 | 40.18 N | 85.23 W |
| Delaware □[6], N.Y., U.S. | 210 | 42.17 N | 74.55 W |
| Delaware □[6], Oh., U.S. | 214 | 40.18 N | 83.04 W |
| Delaware □[6], Pa., U.S. | 208 | 39.55 N | 75.23 W |
| Delaware □[3], U.S. | 178 | 39.10 N | 75.30 W |
| Delaware □[3], U.S. | 208 | 39.10 N | 75.30 W |
| Delaware ≃, U.S. | 188 | 39.20 N | 75.25 W |
| Delaware ≃, U.S. | 196 | 32.02 N | 104.01 W |
| Delaware ≃, Ks., U.S. | 198 | 39.03 N | 95.24 W |
| Delaware, East Branch ≃ | 210 | 41.55 N | 75.17 W |
| Delaware, University of ʊ[2] | 285 | 39.41 N | 75.45 W |
| Delaware, West Branch ≃ | 210 | 41.56 N | 75.17 W |
| Delaware and Raritan Canal ≡ | 208 | 40.29 N | 74.26 W |
| Delaware Aqueduct ≡[1] | 210 | 42.05 N | 74.54 W |
| Delaware Bay c | 208 | 39.05 N | 75.15 W |
| Delaware City | 208 | 39.34 N | 75.35 W |
| Delaware Lake ⊜[1] | 214 | 40.20 N | 83.00 W |
| Delaware Memorial Bridge ◆[5] | 285 | 40.07 N | 74.50 W |
| Delaware Memorial Bridges ◆[5] | 208 | 39.41 N | 75.31 W |
| Delaware Mountains ⋏ | 196 | 31.35 N | 104.40 W |
| Delaware Museum of Natural History ʊ | 285 | 39.47 N | 75.36 W |
| Delaware Park | 210 | 40.43 N | 75.11 W |
| Delaware Park ♠ | 284a | 42.56 N | 78.52 W |
| Delaware Park Race Track ♠ | 285 | 39.42 N | 75.40 W |
| Delaware Seashore State Park ♠ | 208 | 38.38 N | 75.04 W |
| Delaware State Park ♠ | 214 | 40.23 N | 83.04 W |
| Delaware Water Gap | 210 | 40.59 N | 75.09 W |
| Delaware Water Gap National Recreation Area ♠ | 210 | 41.08 N | 74.55 W |
| Delbrück | 52 | 51.46 N | 8.33 E |
| Delburne | 182 | 52.12 N | 113.14 W |
| Delcambre | 194 | 29.57 N | 91.59 W |
| Del Campillo | 252 | 34.22 S | 64.29 W |
| Del Carril | 258 | 35.31 S | 59.30 W |
| Del City | 196 | 35.26 N | 97.26 W |
| Delcommune, Lac ⊜[1] | 154 | 10.45 S | 25.45 E |
| Del Dios | 228 | 33.04 N | 117.08 W |
| Delegate | 166 | 37.03 S | 148.58 E |
| Délembé | 146 | 9.53 N | 22.37 E |
| Delémont | 58 | 47.22 N | 7.21 E |
| De Leon | 196 | 32.06 N | 98.32 W |
| De Leon Springs | 192 | 29.07 N | 81.21 W |
| Delet ⊔ | 26 | 60.15 N | 20.35 E |
| Delevan | 210 | 42.29 N | 78.28 W |
| Delfim Moreira | 256 | 22.30 S | 45.17 W |
| Delfinópolis | 255 | 20.20 S | 46.51 W |
| Delft | 52 | 52.00 N | 4.21 E |
| Delft Island I | 122 | 9.30 N | 79.42 E |
| Delfzijl | 52 | 53.19 N | 6.46 E |
| Delgada, Punta › | 254 | 42.46 S | 63.38 W |
| Delgado | 236 | 13.43 N | 89.10 W |
| Delgado, Cabo › | 154 | 10.40 S | 40.35 E |
| Del Gallego | 116 | 13.56 N | 122.36 E |
| Delgany | 48 | 53.08 N | 6.05 W |
| Delger ≃ | 88 | 49.17 N | 100.40 E |
| Delger chaan uul ∧ | 88 | 50.00 N | 106.22 E |
| Delgerchangaj | 102 | 45.15 N | 104.50 E |
| Delgerchet | 102 | 45.52 N | 110.26 E |
| Delgercogt | 102 | 46.08 N | 106.23 E |
| Delgerech | 102 | 45.48 N | 111.12 E |
| Del Haven | 208 | 39.03 N | 74.56 W |
| Delhi, On., Can. | 212 | 42.51 N | 80.30 W |
| Delhi, India | 124 | 28.40 N | 77.13 E |
| Delhi, India | 272a | 28.40 N | 77.13 E |
| Delhi, Ca., U.S. | 226 | 37.26 N | 120.46 W |
| Delhi, Il., U.S. | 219 | 39.03 N | 90.15 W |
| Delhi, Ia., U.S. | 190 | 42.25 N | 91.19 W |
| Delhi, La., U.S. | 194 | 32.27 N | 91.29 W |
| Delhi, N.Y., U.S. | 210 | 42.16 N | 74.54 W |
| Delhi □[8] | 124 | 28.37 N | 77.10 E |
| Delhi Cantonment | 272a | 28.36 N | 77.08 E |
| Delhi Hills | 218 | 39.05 N | 84.36 W |
| Delhi Railroad Station ◆[5] | 272a | 28.40 N | 77.13 E |
| Delhi Tail Distributary ≡ | 272a | 28.41 N | 77.10 E |
| Delhi University ʊ[2] | 272a | 28.42 N | 77.13 E |
| Deli, Pulau I | 115a | 7.00 S | 105.32 E |
| Delia, Ab., Can. | 182 | 51.38 N | 112.23 W |
| Delia, It. | 70 | 37.21 N | 13.55 E |
| Delia ≃ | 70 | 37.38 N | 12.37 E |
| Delianuova | 68 | 38.14 N | 15.55 E |
| Deliblato | 38 | 44.50 N | 21.03 E |
| Delice | 130 | 39.58 N | 34.02 E |
| Delice ≃ | 130 | 40.28 N | 34.10 E |
| Delices | 240d | 15.17 N | 61.16 W |
| Deliceto | 68 | 41.13 N | 15.23 E |
| Delicias, Cuba | 240p | 21.11 N | 76.34 W |
| Delicias, Méx. | 232 | 28.13 N | 105.28 W |
| De Lier | 52 | 51.57 N | 4.15 E |
| Delight | 194 | 34.01 N | 93.30 W |
| Delightful | 214 | 41.18 N | 80.57 W |
| Deliilyas | 130 | 39.20 N | 36.48 E |
| Delījān | 128 | 33.59 N | 50.40 E |
| Deliktaş | 130 | 39.21 N | 37.13 E |
| Delingde | 74 | 70.08 N | 114.00 E |
| Delingha | 102 | 37.14 N | 97.11 E |
| Dēliņkalns ∧[2] | 76 | 57.30 N | 26.58 E |
| Déli Pályaudvar ◆[5] | 264c | 47.30 N | 19.01 E |
| Delisle | 184 | 51.55 N | 107.08 W |
| Delisle ≃ | 206 | 45.17 N | 74.11 W |
| Delitua | 114 | 3.30 N | 98.41 E |
| Delitzsch | 54 | 51.31 N | 12.20 E |
| Delkern | 228 | 35.21 N | 119.01 W |
| Dell | 46 | 58.30 N | 6.20 W |
| Dellach | 64 | 46.40 N | 13.05 E |
| Dell City | 200 | 31.56 N | 105.12 W |
| Delle | 58 | 47.30 N | 7.00 E |
| Dellenbaugh, Mount ∧ | 200 | 36.07 N | 113.32 W |
| Dellensjöarna ⊜ | 26 | 61.54 N | 16.41 E |
| Delles | 148 | 36.55 N | 3.55 E |
| Delligsen | 52 | 51.57 N | 9.48 E |
| Dello | 64 | 45.25 N | 10.04 E |
| Dell Rapids | 198 | 43.50 N | 96.43 W |
| Dellroy | 214 | 40.33 N | 81.11 W |
| Dellwig | 263 | 51.29 N | 7.41 E |
| Dellwig ◆[8] | 263 | 51.29 N | 6.56 E |
| Dellwood | 219 | 38.44 N | 90.17 W |
| Dellwood Highlands | 278 | 41.34 N | 88.03 W |
| Del Mar, Ca., U.S. | 228 | 32.57 N | 117.15 W |
| Delmar, De., U.S. | 208 | 38.27 N | 75.34 W |
| Delmar, Ia., U.S. | 190 | 42.00 N | 90.36 W |
| Delmar, Md., U.S. | 208 | 38.27 N | 75.34 W |
| Delmar, N.Y., U.S. | 210 | 42.37 N | 73.49 W |
| Del Mar Hills | 196 | 27.37 N | 99.26 W |
| Delmarva Peninsula ›[1] | 208 | 38.30 N | 75.30 W |
| Del Mar Woods | 278 | 42.12 N | 87.51 W |
| Delmas, Sk., Can. | 184 | 52.55 N | 108.36 W |
| Delmas, S. Afr. | 158 | 26.08 S | 28.43 E |
| Delmas □[5] | 273d | 26.10 S | 28.33 E |
| Delme | 56 | 48.53 N | 6.24 E |
| Delme ≃ | 52 | 53.05 N | 8.40 E |
| Delmenhorst | 52 | 53.03 N | 8.38 E |
| Delmiro Gouveia | 250 | 9.23 S | 37.59 W |
| Delmont, N.J., U.S. | 208 | 39.12 N | 74.57 W |
| Delmont, Pa., U.S. | 214 | 40.25 N | 79.34 W |
| Delmont, S.D., U.S. | 198 | 43.16 N | 98.09 W |
| Del Monte Park | 226 | 36.36 N | 121.56 W |
| Delnice | 36 | 45.24 N | 14.48 E |
| Del Norte | 200 | 37.40 N | 106.21 W |
| Del Norte Coast Redwood State Park ♠ | 204 | 41.38 N | 124.05 W |
| De-Longa, ostrova II | 74 | 76.30 N | 153.00 E |
| De Long Mountains ⋏ | 180 | 68.20 N | 162.00 W |
| De-Long-Strasse → Longa, proliv ⊔ | 74 | 70.20 N | 178.00 E |
| Deloraine, Austl. | 166 | 41.31 S | 146.39 E |
| Deloraine, Mb., Can. | 184 | 49.12 N | 100.29 W |
| Delorme, Lac ⊜ | 176 | 54.31 N | 69.52 W |
| Deloro | 212 | 44.31 N | 77.37 W |
| Delos → Dhílos ⊥ | 38 | 37.26 N | 25.16 E |
| Delph | 44 | 53.34 N | 2.01 W |
| Delphi | 216 | 40.35 N | 86.40 W |
| Delphi → Dhelfoí ⊥ | 38 | 38.30 N | 22.29 E |
| Delphi Falls | 210 | 42.53 N | 75.55 W |
| Delphos, Ks., U.S. | 198 | 39.16 N | 97.46 W |
| Delphos, Oh., U.S. | 216 | 40.50 N | 84.20 W |
| Delph Reservoir ⊜[1] | 262 | 53.38 N | 2.27 W |
| Delportshoop | 158 | 28.22 S | 24.20 E |
| Del Puerto Creek ≃ | 226 | 37.32 N | 121.07 W |
| Delran | 285 | 40.01 N | 74.57 W |
| Delrath | 263 | 51.08 N | 6.47 E |
| Delray ◆[8] | 281 | 42.18 N | 83.08 W |
| Delray Beach | 220 | 26.27 N | 80.04 W |
| Del Rey | 226 | 36.40 N | 119.36 W |
| Del Rey Oaks | 226 | 36.36 N | 121.50 W |
| Del Rio, Fl., U.S. | 220 | 28.03 N | 82.26 W |
| Del Rio, Tx., U.S. | 196 | 29.21 N | 100.53 W |
| Delsbo | 26 | 61.48 N | 16.35 E |
| Delson | 206 | 45.22 N | 73.33 W |
| Delstern ◆[8] | 263 | 51.20 N | 7.31 E |
| Delta, B.C., Can. | 224 | 49.10 N | 122.55 W |
| Delta, On., Can. | 212 | 44.37 N | 76.08 W |
| Delta, Méx. | 200 | 32.22 N | 115.12 W |
| Delta, Co., U.S. | 200 | 38.44 N | 108.04 W |
| Delta, Mo., U.S. | 194 | 37.11 N | 89.44 W |
| Delta, Oh., U.S. | 216 | 41.34 N | 84.00 W |
| Delta, Pa., U.S. | 208 | 39.43 N | 76.19 W |
| Delta, Ut,. U.S. | 200 | 39.21 N | 112.34 W |
| Delta □[9] | 194 | 33.30 N | 90.45 W |
| Delta ≃ | 180 | 64.09 N | 146.18 W |
| Delta Amacuro □[8] | 246 | 8.30 N | 61.30 W |
| Delta Barrage ◆[6] | 142 | 30.11 N | 31.07 E |
| Delta Beach | 184 | 50.11 N | 98.19 W |
| Delta City | 194 | 33.04 N | 90.47 W |
| Delta Downs | 166 | 17.00 S | 141.18 E |
| Delta Junction | 180 | 64.02 N | 145.41 W |
| Delta-Mendota Canal ≡ | 226 | 37.49 N | 121.34 W |
| Delta Peak ∧ | 180 | 56.39 N | 129.34 W |
| Delta Reservoir ⊜[1] | 210 | 43.17 N | 75.26 W |
| Deltaville | 208 | 37.33 N | 76.20 W |
| Delton | 216 | 42.29 N | 85.24 W |
| Deltona | 220 | 28.54 N | 81.15 W |
| Delungra | 166 | 29.39 S | 150.50 E |
| Del'un-Uranskij chrebet ⋏ | 88 | 56.30 N | 114.00 E |
| Delüün | 86 | 47.42 N | 90.59 E |
| De Luz Creek ≃ | 228 | 33.22 N | 117.19 W |
| Del Valle | 222 | 30.12 N | 97.40 W |
| Del Valle, Lake ⊜[1] | 226 | 37.35 N | 121.43 W |
| Del Verme Falls ∟ | 144 | 5.27 N | 40.17 E |
| Delvin | 48 | 53.36 N | 7.05 W |
| Delvinë | 38 | 39.57 N | 20.06 E |
| Del Viso | 258 | 34.27 S | 58.48 W |
| Delyatyn | 78 | 48.32 N | 24.37 E |
| Delyn □[8] | 262 | 53.16 N | 3.11 W |
| Demak | 115a | 6.53 S | 110.38 E |
| Demaki | 80 | 58.26 N | 51.43 E |
| Dem'ansk | 76 | 57.38 N | 32.28 E |
| Demarcation Point › | 180 | 69.40 N | 141.15 W |
| Demarest | 276 | 40.57 N | 73.57 W |
| Demarest Brook ≃ | 276 | 40.57 N | 73.58 W |
| Demavend, Mount → Damāvand, Qolleh-ye ∧ | 128 | 35.56 N | 52.08 E |
| Demba | 152 | 5.30 S | 22.16 E |
| Demba Chio | 152 | 9.41 S | 13.41 E |
| Dembecha | 144 | 10.35 N | 37.30 E |
| Dembéni | 157a | 11.50 S | 43.24 E |
| Dembi | 144 | 8.05 N | 36.27 E |
| Dembia, Centraf. | 154 | 5.07 N | 24.25 E |
| Dembia, Zaïre | 154 | 3.31 N | 25.50 E |
| Dembi Dolo | 144 | 8.32 N | 34.48 E |
| Dembo | 152 | 3.56 S | 12.35 E |
| Dême ≃ | 50 | 47.43 N | 0.29 E |
| Demen | 54 | 53.38 N | 11.46 E |
| Demer ≃ | 56 | 50.58 N | 4.42 E |
| Demerara ≃ | 246 | 6.48 N | 58.10 W |
| Demerara-Mahaica □[4] | 246 | 6.40 N | 58.00 W |
| Demerthin | 54 | 52.58 N | 12.17 E |
| Demidov | 76 | 55.16 N | 31.31 E |
| Demidovo | 76 | 59.17 N | 38.17 E |
| Deming, N.M., U.S. | 200 | 32.16 N | 107.45 W |


| | | | | | |
|---|---|---|---|---|---|
| ≃ | River | Fluß | Río | Rivière | Rio |
| ≡ | Canal | Kanal | Canal | Canal | Canal |
| ∟ | Waterfall, Rapids | Wasserfall, Stromschnellen | Cascada, Rápidos | Chute d'eau, Rapides | Cascata, Rápidos |
| ⊔ | Strait | Meeresstraße | Estrecho | Détroit | Estreito |
| c | Bay, Gulf | Bucht, Golf | Bahía, Golfo | Baie, Golfe | Baía, Golfo |
| ⊜ | Lake, Lakes | See, Seen | Lago, Lagos | Lac, Lacs | Lago, Lagos |
| ⁝ | Swamp | Sumpf | Pantano | Marais | Pântano |
| ✱ | Ice Features, Glacier | Eis- und Gletscherformen | Accidentes Glaciales | Formes glaciaires | Acidentes glaciares |
| ⊤ | Other Hydrographic Features | Andere Hydrographische Objekte | Otros Elementos Hidrográficos | Autres données hydrographiques | Outros acidentes hidrográficos |

| | | | | | |
|---|---|---|---|---|---|
| ◆ | Submarine Features | Untermeerische Objekte | Accidentes Submarinos | Formes de relief sous-marin | Acidentes submarinos |
| □ | Political Unit | Politische Einheit | Unidad Politica | Entité politique | Unidade política |
| ʊ | Cultural Institution | Kulturelle Institution | Institución Cultural | Institution culturelle | Instituição cultural |
| ⊥ | Historical Site | Historische Stätte | Sitio Histórico | Site historique | Sitio histórico |
| ♠ | Recreational Site | Erholungs- und Ferienort | Sitio de Recreo | Centre de loisirs | Area de Lazer |
| ⊠ | Airport | Flughafen | Aeropuerto | Aéroport | Aeroporto |
| ■ | Military Installation | Militäranlage | Instalación Militar | Installation militaire | Instalação militar |
| ◆ | Miscellaneous | Verschiedenes | Misceláneo | Divers | Diversos |

Deming, Wa., U.S. 224 48.49 N 122.12 W
Demini ≃ 246 0.46 S 62.56 W
Demirci 130 39.03 N 28.40 E
Demirköprü Barajı ⊜[1] 130 38.40 N 28.20 E
Demirköy 130 41.49 N 27.45 E
Demirtaş 130 40.16 N 29.06 E
Demitz-Thumitz 54 51.09 N 14.14 E
Demjanka ≃ 86 59.34 N 69.20 E
Demjanovo 24 60.22 N 47.03 E
Demjanskoje 86 59.36 N 69.18 E
Demjas 80 51.13 N 49.08 E
Demmeltrath ◆[8] 263 51.11 N 7.03 E
Demmin 54 53.54 N 13.02 E
Demmitt 182 55.26 N 119.54 W
Demnate 148 31.44 N 6.59 W
Democracy Monument ⊥ 269a 13.45 N 100.30 E
Democrat Point › 276 40.37 N 73.18 W
Demoiselles, Grotte des ⩍[5] 62 43.55 N 3.45 E
Demone, Val ◆[1] 70 37.58 N 14.35 E
Demonte 62 44.19 N 7.17 E
De Montigny, Lac ⊜ 190 48.08 N 77.54 W
Demopolis 194 32.31 N 87.50 W
Demorest 192 34.33 N 83.32 W
De Mossville 218 38.48 N 84.25 W
Demotte 216 41.12 N 87.12 W
Dempo, Gunung ∧ 112 4.02 S 103.09 E
Dempster, Point › 162 33.39 S 123.52 E
Demsa 146 9.32 N 13.14 E
Demta 164 2.20 S 140.08 E
Demuryne 78 48.10 N 36.29 E
Demydivka 78 50.25 N 25.20 E
De Naauwte 158 30.08 S 21.42 E
Denain 50 50.20 N 3.23 E
Denair 226 37.32 N 120.47 W
Denakil ◆[1] 144 13.00 N 41.00 E
Denali 180 63.11 N 147.28 W
Denali National Park 180 63.44 N 148.54 W
Denali National Park ♠ 180 63.15 N 150.30 W
Denan 144 6.30 N 43.30 E
Denare Beach 184 54.40 N 102.05 W
Denau 85 38.16 N 67.54 E
Denbigh, On., Can. 212 45.08 N 77.16 W
Denbigh, Wales, U.K. 44 53.11 N 3.25 W
Denbigh, Cape › 180 64.23 N 161.31 W
Den Burg 52 53.03 N 4.48 E
Denby Dale 44 53.35 N 1.38 W
Den Chai 110 17.59 N 100.04 E
Dendang 112 3.05 S 107.54 E
Dender (Dendre) ≃ 50 51.02 N 4.06 E
Denderleeuw 50 50.53 N 4.04 E
Dendermonde 50 51.02 N 4.07 E
Dendre (Dender) ≃ 50 51.02 N 4.06 E
Dendron, S. Afr. 156 23.25 S 29.11 E
Dendron, Va., U.S. 208 37.02 N 76.56 W
Dendy Park ♠ 274b 37.56 S 145.00 E
Deneba 144 9.50 N 39.09 E
Denekamp 52 52.23 N 7.00 E
Denenchōfu ◆[8] 268 35.35 N 139.41 E
Deneysville 158 26.53 S 28.06 E
Denezhnykove 83 49.02 N 38.57 E
Denežnikovo 82 55.26 N 38.07 E
Dengcheng 100 33.41 N 114.27 E
Deng Deng 152 5.12 N 13.31 E
Denge 154 3.34 N 28.14 E
Denge Marsh ≡ 42 50.57 N 0.55 E
Dengfeng 100 34.29 N 113.04 E
Denggongchang 107 30.24 N 103.49 E
Dengguanzhen 107 29.10 N 104.56 E
Dengkou 102 40.20 N 106.59 E
Denglongshu 98 41.20 N 115.15 E
Dengmingsi 98 37.53 N 116.42 E
Dêngqên 102 31.32 N 95.27 E
Dengshahe 98 39.13 N 122.04 E
Dengta 100 24.01 N 114.49 E
Denguiro 152 5.38 N 23.02 E
Dengxian 102 32.42 N 112.01 E
Dengyoufang 98 41.34 N 114.32 E
Den Haag → 's-Gravenhage 52 52.06 N 4.18 E
Denham, Austl. 162 25.55 S 113.32 E
Denham, Eng., U.K. 260 51.34 N 0.30 W
Denham, In., U.S. 216 41.09 N 86.43 W
Denham, Mount ∧ 241q 18.13 N 77.32 W
Denham Aerodrome ⊠ 260 51.36 N 0.31 W
Denham Island I 166 16.43 S 139.09 E
Denham Place ʋ 260 51.34 N 0.30 W
Denham Range ⩘ 166 21.55 S 147.46 E
Denham Sound Ц 162 25.40 S 113.15 E
Denham Springs 194 30.29 N 90.57 W
Den Helder 52 52.54 N 4.45 E
Denholme 262 53.48 N 1.54 W
Dénia 34 38.51 N 0.07 E
Denial Bay 162 32.06 S 133.32 E
Dénié 150 11.14 N 7.29 W
Deniliquin 166 35.32 S 144.58 E
Deniskoviči 76 52.19 N 31.43 E
Denison, Ia., U.S. 198 42.01 N 95.21 W
Denison, Tx., U.S. 196 33.45 N 96.32 W
Denison, Mount ∧ 180 58.25 N 154.27 W
Denison Dam ◆[6] 196 33.50 N 96.34 W
Denisovka 24 66.14 N 55.20 E
Denisōvo 82 54.28 N 37.51 E
Denisy 261 48.33 N 1.56 E
Denizli 130 37.46 N 29.06 E
Denizli □[4] 130 37.40 N 29.15 E
Denkanikota 122 12.32 N 77.48 E
Denkendorf 60 48.56 N 11.27 E
Denkingen 58 47.53 N 9.19 E
Denklingen 58 47.55 N 10.51 E
Den'kovo 82 56.01 N 36.21 E
Denmark, Austl. 162 34.57 S 117.21 E
Denmark, S.C., U.S. 192 33.19 N 81.08 W
Denmark, Wi., U.S. 190 44.20 N 87.49 W
Denmark (Danmark) □[1], Europe 22 56.00 N 10.00 E
Denmark (Danmark) □[1], Europe 26 56.00 N 10.00 E
Denmark, Lake ⊜ 276 40.58 N 74.31 W
Denmark Bay c 176 70.33 N 103.20 W
Denmark Strait Ц 10 67.00 N 25.00 W
Denmead 42 50.54 N 1.04 W
Dennemont 261 49.01 N 1.42 E
Dennery 241f 13.55 N 60.54 W
Dennis 207 41.44 N 70.11 W
Dennis Head › 46 59.23 N 2.23 W
Dennison 214 40.23 N 81.20 W
Dennis Port 207 41.39 N 70.07 W
Denniston 172 41.44 S 171.48 E
Denniston Creek ≃ 282 37.30 N 122.28 W
Dennisville 208 39.11 N 74.49 W
Denny 46 56.02 N 3.55 W
Den Oever 52 52.56 N 5.02 E
Denouval 261 48.58 N 2.03 E
Denpasar 115b 8.39 S 115.13 E
Denshaw 262 53.35 N 2.02 W
Dent Ditch ≋ 279a 41.18 N 82.08 W
Denton, Eng., U.K. 44 53.27 N 2.07 W
Denton, Md., U.S. 208 38.53 N 75.49 W
Denton, Mi., U.S. 281 42.20 N 83.03 W
Denton, Mt., U.S. 202 47.19 N 109.56 W
Denton, N.C., U.S. 192 35.38 N 80.06 W
Denton, Tx., U.S. 222 33.12 N 97.07 W
Denton □[6] 222 33.07 N 97.10 W
Denton Creek ≃ 196 32.58 N 96.57 W
Dentonia Park ♠ 275b 43.42 N 79.17 W
D'Entrecasteaux, Point › 162 34.50 S 116.00 E
D'Entrecasteaux Islands II 164 9.30 S 150.40 E
D'Entrecasteaux National Park ♠ 162 34.41 S 115.58 E
Dents du Midi ⩘ 58 46.10 N 6.56 E
Denver, Co., U.S. 200 39.44 N 104.59 W
Denver, In., U.S. 216 40.51 N 86.04 W
Denver, Ia., U.S. 190 42.40 N 92.20 W
Denver, Pa., U.S. 208 40.13 N 76.08 W
Denver City 196 32.57 N 102.49 W
Denville 210 40.53 N 74.28 W
Denzlingen 58 48.04 N 7.52 E
Deoband 124 29.42 N 77.41 E
Deocha 126 24.03 N 87.35 E
Deodoro ◆[8] 287a 22.51 S 43.23 W
Deogarh, India 120 25.32 N 73.54 E
Deogarh, India 122 21.32 N 84.44 E
Deogarh, India 124 24.33 N 78.15 E
Deogarh ∧ 124 23.32 N 82.16 E
Deogarh Hills ⩘[2] 124 23.35 N 82.30 E
Deoghar 124 24.29 N 86.42 E
Deogsu Palace ʋ 271b 37.35 N 126.58 E
Deolāli 122 19.57 N 73.50 E
Deoli 126 22.03 N 86.49 E
Deoli ◆[8] 272a 28.30 N 77.14 E
Deongwar, Mount ∧ 171a 27.12 S 152.16 E
Deopāra 126 22.55 N 90.15 E
Deori, India 124 23.08 N 78.41 E
Deori, India 124 23.24 N 79.01 E
Deoria 124 26.31 N 83.47 E
Deosai Mountains ⩘ 123 35.20 N 75.12 E
Deosil 124 23.42 N 82.15 E
Dep ≃ 89 52.54 N 127.45 E
Depāl 126 21.44 N 87.33 E
De Panne 50 51.06 N 2.35 E
Depāra 272b 22.53 N 88.34 E
Departure Bay 224 49.12 N 123.58 W
DePaul University ʋ[2] 278 41.56 N 87.39 W
Depauville 212 44.08 N 76.04 W
Depauw 218 38.20 N 86.13 W
De Peel ≡ 52 51.25 N 6.00 E
De Pere 190 44.26 N 88.03 W
Depew, N.Y., U.S. 210 42.54 N 78.41 W
Depew, Ok., U.S. 196 35.48 N 96.30 W
Deping 98 37.28 N 116.57 E
De Pinte 50 51.00 N 3.39 E
Depoe Bay 202 44.48 N 124.03 W
Depok 115a 6.24 S 106.50 E
Deport 196 33.32 N 95.19 W
Deposit 210 42.03 N 75.25 W
Deptford 285 39.50 N 75.07 W
Deptford ◆[8] 260 51.28 N 0.02 W
Deptford Mall ◆[9] 285 39.50 N 75.06 W
Deptford Terrace 285 39.48 N 75.09 W
Depuch Island I 162 20.38 S 117.43 E
Depue 190 41.19 N 89.18 W
Deputy 218 38.48 N 85.39 W
Dêqên 102 28.38 N 98.52 E
Deqing, Zhg. 102 23.09 N 111.45 E
Deqing, Zhg. 106 30.33 N 120.05 E
De Queen 194 34.02 N 94.20 W
De Quincy 194 30.27 N 93.25 W
Dera ≃ 264c 47.39 N 19.05 E
Dera, Lach (Lak Dera) V 144 0.35 N 41.50 E
Dera Bugti 120 29.02 N 69.09 E
Dera Ghāzi Khān 123 30.03 N 70.38 E
Dera Gopipur 123 31.54 N 76.13 E
Dera Ismāīl Khān 123 31.50 N 70.54 E
Derakht-e Yahyá 120 31.50 N 68.08 E
Dera Nānak 123 32.02 N 75.01 E
Dera Nawāb 123 29.06 N 71.16 E
Derāwar Fort 123 28.46 N 71.20 E
Derazhnya 78 49.16 N 27.26 E
Derbent 84 42.03 N 48.18 E
Derbeškinskij 80 55.52 N 53.30 E
Derbetovka 80 45.48 N 43.05 E
Der Bodden Ц 54 54.16 N 13.12 E
Derby, Austl. 162 17.18 S 123.38 E
Derby, Austl. 166 41.09 S 147.47 E
Derby, S. Afr. 158 25.55 S 27.02 E
Derby, Eng., U.K. 42 52.55 N 1.29 W
Derby, Ct., U.S. 207 41.19 N 73.05 W
Derby, Ks., U.S. 198 37.32 N 97.16 W
Derby, Me., U.S. 188 45.14 N 68.53 W
Derby, N.Y., U.S. 210 42.40 N 78.58 W
Derby, Oh., U.S. 218 39.46 N 83.12 W
Derby, Vt., U.S. 206 44.57 N 72.08 W
Derby Acres 226 35.15 N 119.35 W
Derby Line 206 45.00 N 72.05 W
Derbyshire □[6] 44 53.00 N 1.33 W
Der-Chantecoq, Lac du ⊜[1] 58 48.35 N 4.46 E
Derdepoort 156 24.42 S 26.20 E
Dere 130 39.00 N 39.18 E
Derecske 30 47.21 N 21.34 E
Dereköy, Tür. 130 39.16 N 27.19 E
Dereköy, Tür. 130 40.08 N 37.47 E
Dereköy, Tür. 130 41.56 N 27.21 E
Dereli 130 40.45 N 38.27 E
Derenburg 54 51.52 N 10.54 E
Derendorf ◆[8] 263 51.15 N 6.48 E
Derenwu 105 39.40 N 116.46 E
Dereseki ◆[8] 267b 41.08 N 29.08 E
Derev'anka 24 61.34 N 34.27 E
Derg ≃ 48 54.44 N 7.25 W
Derg, Lough ⊜, Ire. 48 52.57 N 8.19 W
Derg, Lough ⊜, Ire. 48 54.36 N 7.53 W
Dergači 80 51.14 N 48.46 E
Dergaon 120 26.42 N 93.58 E
Der Grabow c 54 54.23 N 12.50 E
Derhachi 78 50.07 N 36.07 E
De Ridder 194 30.50 N 93.17 W
De Rijp 52 52.34 N 4.50 E
Derik 130 37.22 N 40.17 E
Derinkuyu 130 38.23 N 34.45 E
Der Kanal → English Channel Ц 28 50.20 N 1.00 W
Derkul 80 51.16 N 51.18 E
Derkul ≃ 83 48.35 N 39.41 E
Dermbach 56 50.43 N 10.06 E
Dermentobe 86 45.44 N 63.37 E
Dermott 194 33.31 N 91.26 W
Dermulo 64 46.20 N 11.04 E
Derne 263 51.35 N 7.41 E
Derne ◆[8] 263 51.34 N 7.31 E
Dernieres, Isles II 194 29.02 N 90.47 W
Dernoviči 78 51.36 N 29.43 E
Deroche 224 49.11 N 122.04 W
Dero Eri 144 9.01 N 46.43 E
Dêrong 102 28.47 N 99.14 E
Déroute, Passage de la Ц 32 49.25 N 2.00 W
Derrame 196 26.19 N 104.23 W
Derravaragh, Lough ⊜ 48 53.40 N 7.24 W
Derre 154 16.56 S 36.11 E
Derrick City 214 41.58 N 78.34 W
Derrinallum 169 37.57 S 143.13 E
Derry → Londonderry, N. Ire., U.K. 48 54.59 N 7.20 W
Derry, N.H., U.S. 188 42.52 N 71.19 W
Derry, Pa., U.S. 214 40.20 N 79.18 W
Derrybrien 48 53.04 N 8.36 W
Derrykeighan 48 55.08 N 6.29 W
Derryveagh Mountains ⩘ 48 55.00 N 8.05 W
Derry West 275b 43.39 N 79.42 W
Der Sārāi ◆[8] 272a 28.33 N 77.11 E
Dersau 54 54.07 N 10.20 E
Dersingham 42 52.51 N 0.30 E
Derudeb 140 17.32 N 36.06 E
De Rust 158 33.30 S 22.32 E
Deruta 66 42.59 N 12.25 E
De Ruyter 210 42.45 N 75.53 W
DeRuyter Reservoir ⊜[1] 210 42.49 N 75.53 W
Der'uzino 82 56.18 N 38.16 E
Derval 32 47.40 N 1.40 W
Derventa 38 44.58 N 17.55 E
Derwent 182 53.39 N 110.58 W
Derwent ≃, Austl. 166 43.03 S 147.22 E
Derwent ≃, Eng., U.K. 44 54.57 N 1.41 W
Derwent ≃, Eng., U.K. 44 54.38 N 3.34 W
Derwent ≃, Eng., U.K. 44 52.53 N 1.17 W
Derwent ≃, Eng., U.K. 44 53.45 N 0.57 W
Derwent Bridge 166 42.08 S 146.13 E
Derwent Reservoir ⊜[1] 44 54.50 N 2.00 W
Derwent Water ⊜ 44 54.34 N 3.08 W
Deržavino 80 53.13 N 52.22 E
Deržavinsk 86 51.03 N 66.19 E
Desaguadero ≃, Arg. 252 34.13 S 66.47 W
Desaguadero ≃, Bol. 248 18.24 S 67.05 W
Desagüe, Canal de ≋ 286a 19.29 N 99.05 W
Des Allemands 194 29.49 N 90.28 W
Desamparados 236 9.54 N 84.04 W
Désappointement, Îles du II 14 14.10 S 141.20 W
Des Arc 194 34.58 N 91.29 W
Desborough 42 52.27 N 0.49 W
Descabezado Grande, Volcán ∧[1] 252 35.36 S 70.45 W
Descanso, Bra. 252 26.50 S 53.35 W
Descanso, Ca., U.S. 204 32.51 N 116.37 W
Descanso, Punta › 204 32.16 N 117.03 W
Descanso Gardens ♠ 280 34.12 N 118.13 W
Descartes 32 46.58 N 0.42 E
Deschaillons 206 46.32 N 72.07 W
Deschambault 206 46.39 N 71.56 W
Deschambault Lake 184 54.55 N 103.22 W
Deschambault Lake ⊜ 184 54.40 N 103.35 W
Descharme Lake ⊜ 184 57.05 N 109.13 W
Deschênes 212 45.23 N 75.48 W
Deschênes, Lac ⊜ 212 45.22 N 75.51 W
Deschutes ≃, Or., U.S. 202 45.38 N 120.54 W
Deschutes ≃, Wa., U.S. 224 47.02 N 122.54 W
Descoberto 256 21.27 S 42.58 W
Desdunes 238 19.17 N 72.39 W
Dese 144 11.05 N 39.41 E
Deseado ≃ 254 47.45 S 65.54 W
Deseado, Cabo › 254 52.44 S 74.44 W
Desembarco de los 33 Orientales, Monumento ⊥ 258 33.48 S 58.25 W
Desengaño, Punta › 254 49.15 S 67.37 W
Desenzano del Garda 64 45.28 N 10.32 E
Deseret Peak ∧ 200 40.28 N 112.38 W
Deseronto 212 44.12 N 77.03 W
Désert ≃ 190 46.23 N 75.58 W
Désert, Lac ⊜ 190 46.35 N 76.19 W
Desertas, Ilhas II 148 32.30 N 16.30 W
Desert Creek ≃ 226 38.48 N 119.19 W
Desert Hot Springs 204 33.57 N 116.30 W
Desert Lake ⊜, On., Can. 212 44.32 N 76.35 W
Desert Lake ⊜, Nv., U.S. 204 36.58 N 115.05 W
Desert Mountains ⩘ 226 39.16 N 119.00 W
Desert Peak ∧ 200 41.11 N 113.22 W
Desert Valley V 204 41.15 N 118.20 W
Desert View Highlands 228 34.37 N 118.13 W
Desford 42 52.39 N 1.17 W
Desha 194 35.44 N 91.40 W
Deshaies 241o 16.18 N 61.48 W
Desheng 102 24.45 N 108.28 E
Deshengchang 107 29.06 N 105.25 E
Deshengpo 102 26.58 N 103.59 E
Deshengtai 104 42.14 N 123.45 E
Deshengyingzi 104 41.44 N 123.14 E
Deshler, Ne., U.S. 198 40.08 N 97.43 W
Deshler, Oh., U.S. 216 41.12 N 83.53 W
Deshnok 120 27.48 N 73.21 E
Deshon Manor 214 40.52 N 79.57 W
Deshu 128 30.26 N 63.19 E
Deshun 106 31.58 N 120.29 E
Desiderio Tello 252 31.13 S 66.19 W
Desio 62 45.37 N 9.13 E
Des Lacs ≃ 198 48.17 N 101.25 W
Deslinde, Arroyo ≃ 258 33.44 S 58.52 W
Desloge 194 37.52 N 90.31 W
Desmarais 182 55.56 N 113.49 W
De Smet 198 44.23 N 97.33 W
De Smet, Lake ⊜[1] 202 44.29 N 106.45 W
Des Moines, Ia., U.S. 190 41.36 N 93.36 W
Des Moines, N.M., U.S. 196 36.45 N 103.50 W
Des Moines, Wa., U.S. 224 47.24 N 122.19 W
Des Moines ≃ 178 40.22 N 91.26 W
Des Moines, East Fork ≃ 198 42.41 N 94.12 W
Dešná, Česká Rep. 61 48.58 N 15.33 E
Desna, Ukr. 78 50.56 N 30.46 E
Desna ≃, Europe 78 50.33 N 30.32 E
Desna ≃, Ross. 82 55.26 N 37.30 E
Desolación, Isla I 254 53.00 S 74.10 W
Désolation, Cap de la → Disappointment, Cape › 244 54.53 S 36.07 W
Desolation Point › 116 10.28 N 125.39 E
Desor, Mount ∧[2] 190 47.58 N 89.01 W
De Soto, Il., U.S. 194 37.49 N 89.13 W
De Soto, In., U.S. 216 40.15 N 85.17 W
De Soto, Mo., U.S. 194 38.08 N 90.33 W
De Soto, Tx., U.S. 222 32.35 N 96.51 W
De Soto □[6] 220 27.11 N 81.48 W
De Soto City 220 27.26 N 81.24 W
De Soto National Memorial ⊥ 220 27.31 N 82.40 W
De Soto State Park ♠ 194 34.28 N 85.36 W
Despatch 158 33.46 S 25.30 E
Despeñaperros, Desfiladero de )( 34 38.24 N 3.30 W
Des Plaines 216 42.02 N 87.53 W
Des Plaines ≃ 216 41.24 N 88.16 W
Despotovac 38 44.05 N 21.33 E
Despujols 116 12.31 N 122.01 E
Desroches, Île I 138 5.41 S 53.41 E
Desruisseaux 241f 13.47 N 60.56 W
Dessau 54 51.50 N 12.14 E
Dessel 56 51.14 N 5.07 E
Deşt 130 39.10 N 39.22 E
Destacado Island I 116 12.16 N 124.06 E
De Steeg 52 52.02 N 6.04 E
Destek 130 40.51 N 36.12 E
Destelbergen 50 51.03 N 3.48 E
Desterro 250 7.17 S 37.06 W
Destin 194 30.23 N 86.29 W
Destruction, Mount ∧[2] 162 24.35 S 127.59 E
Destruction Bay 180 61.15 N 138.48 W
Destruction Island I 224 47.40 N 124.30 W
Desulo 71 40.01 N 9.14 E
Desvres 50 50.40 N 1.50 E
Deta 38 45.24 N 21.13 E
Detčino 82 54.49 N 36.19 E
Dete 154 18.38 S 26.50 E
Dethlingen 52 52.57 N 10.07 E
Detling 260 51.18 N 0.34 E
Detmold 52 51.56 N 8.52 E
Detmold □[5] 52 52.00 N 8.45 E
Detour, Point › 190 45.36 N 86.37 W
De Tour Village 190 46.00 N 83.54 W
Detrital Wash V 200 36.02 N 114.28 W
Detroit, Il., U.S. 219 39.37 N 90.40 W
Detroit, Mi., U.S. 216 42.20 N 83.03 W
Detroit, Mi., U.S. 281 42.20 N 83.03 W
Detroit, Or., U.S. 202 44.44 N 122.08 W
Detroit, Tx., U.S. 196 33.40 N 95.16 W
Detroit ≃ 214 42.06 N 83.08 W
Detroit Beach 216 41.55 N 83.20 W
Detroit City Airport ⊠ 281 42.25 N 83.01 W
Detroit Institute of Arts ʋ 281 42.22 N 83.04 W
Detroit Lake ⊜[1] 202 44.42 N 122.10 W
Detroit Lakes 198 46.48 N 95.50 W
Detroit Mercy, University Of ʋ[2] 281 42.25 N 83.08 W
Detroit Metropolitan-Wayne County Airport ⊠ 281 42.13 N 83.22 W
Detroit Race Course ♠ 281 42.23 N 83.19 W
Detroit-Windsor Tunnel ◆[5] 281 42.20 N 83.02 W
Detroit Zoological Park ♠ 281 42.29 N 83.09 W
Detskosel'skij 265a 59.44 N 30.28 E
Dettelbach 56 49.48 N 10.09 E
Dettifoss ㄴ 24a 65.50 N 16.20 W
Dettingen an der Erms 56 48.32 N 9.20 E
Dettwiller 56 48.45 N 7.28 E
Det Udom 110 14.54 N 105.05 E
Detva 30 48.31 N 19.28 E
Deua National Park ♠ 166 36.00 S 149.45 E
Deuben 54 51.06 N 12.04 E
Deuels Corners 284a 42.45 N 78.45 W
Deuil-la-Barre 261 48.59 N 2.20 E
Deūlgaon Rāja 122 20.01 N 76.02 E
Deulpur 272b 22.36 N 88.10 E
Deulti 126 22.26 N 87.56 E
Deurne, Bel. 50 51.13 N 4.28 E
Deurne, Ned. 52 51.28 N 5.47 E
Deusen ◆[8] 263 51.33 N 7.26 E
Deutsche Bucht c 30 54.30 N 7.30 E
Deutsch Eylau → Iława 30 53.37 N 19.33 E
Deutschfeistritz 61 47.11 N 15.20 E
Deutschkreutz 61 47.36 N 16.38 E
Deutsch Krone → Wałcz 30 53.17 N 16.28 E
Deutschland → Germany □[1] 30 51.00 N 10.00 E
Deutschlandsberg 61 46.49 N 15.13 E
Deutschneudorf 54 50.38 N 13.27 E
Deutsch Wagram 61 48.18 N 16.34 E
Deutsch Wusterhausen 264a 52.18 N 13.35 E
Deutzen 54 51.06 N 12.26 E
Deux-Montagnes 206 45.32 N 73.53 W
Deux-Montagnes □[6] 206 45.35 N 74.05 W
Deux Montagnes, Lac des ⊜ 206 45.28 N 73.59 W
Deux-Sèvres □[5] 32 46.30 N 0.20 W
Deva 38 45.53 N 22.55 E
Devakottai 122 9.57 N 78.49 E
De Valls Bluff 194 34.47 N 91.27 W
Devaprayāg 124 30.09 N 78.37 E
Dev'atern'a 80 56.12 N 53.24 E
Dev'atiny 24 60.56 N 36.46 E
Devault 285 40.05 N 75.32 W
Dévaványa 30 47.02 N 20.58 E
Devecikonağı 130 39.55 N 28.34 E
Devecser 30 47.06 N 17.26 E
Devedağı Tepesi ∧ 130 40.34 N 41.21 E
Devegeçidi Barajı ⊜[1] 130 38.05 N 39.55 E
Develi 130 38.23 N 35.30 E
Deventer 52 52.15 N 6.10 E
Deveron ≃ 46 57.40 N 2.31 W
Devers 222 30.02 N 94.36 W
Devers Canal, West Branch ≋ 222 29.57 N 94.46 W
Deversoir Military Base ■ 142 30.25 N 32.20 E
Devès, Monts du ⩘ 32 45.00 N 3.45 E
Devgadh Bāriva 120 22.42 N 73.54 E
De View, Bayou ≃ 194 34.48 N 91.18 W
Devīkot 120 26.42 N 71.12 E
Devil Lake ⊜ 212 44.35 N 76.27 W
Deville 56 49.53 N 4.42 E
Déville-lès-Rouen 50 49.28 N 1.02 E
Devil Peak ∧ 226 37.32 N 119.44 W
Devil River Peak ∧ 172 40.58 S 172.39 E
Devils ≃ 196 29.39 N 100.58 W
Devil's Bridge 42 52.23 N 3.51 W
Devils Brook ≃ 276 40.20 N 74.37 W
Devils Canyon V 280 34.16 N 117.58 W
Devil's Den State Park ♠ 194 35.46 N 94.16 W
Devils Hole Rapids ㄴ 284a 43.08 N 79.03 W
Devils Hopyard State Park ♠ 207 41.28 N 72.22 W
Devils Island → Diable, Île du I 250 5.17 N 52.35 W
Devils Lake 198 48.06 N 98.51 W
Devils Lake ⊜, Mi., U.S. 216 41.58 N 84.17 W
Devils Lake ⊜, N.D., U.S. 198 48.01 N 98.52 W
Devils Lake State Park ♠ 190 43.24 N 89.44 W
Devils Marbles ♠ 162 20.30 S 134.14 E
Devils Paw ∧ 180 58.44 N 133.50 W
Devils Postpile National Monument ♠ 226 37.37 N 119.05 W
Devils Tower ∧ 198 44.31 N 104.57 W
Devils Tower National Monument ♠ 198 44.31 N 104.57 W
Devil's Water ≃ 44 54.58 N 2.02 W
Devin 38 41.45 N 24.24 E
Devine, B.C., Can. 182 50.32 N 122.30 W
Devine, Tx., U.S. 196 29.08 N 98.54 W
Devizes 42 51.22 N 1.59 W
Devladove 78 48.07 N 33.45 E
Devli 120 25.45 N 75.23 E
De Voe Lake ⊜ 276 40.23 N 74.23 W
Devoll ≃ 38 40.49 N 19.51 E
Dévoluy ⩘ 62 44.39 N 5.53 E
Devon, Ab., Can. 182 53.22 N 113.44 W
Devon, S. Afr. 158 26.21 S 28.48 E
Devon, Pa., U.S. 285 40.02 N 75.25 W
Devon □[6] 42 50.45 N 3.50 W
Devon ≃, Eng., U.K. 42 53.04 N 0.43 W
Devon ≃, Scot., U.K. 46 56.07 N 3.51 W
Devon Island I 16 75.00 N 87.00 W
Devonport, Austl. 166 41.11 S 146.21 E
Devonport, N.Z. 172 36.49 S 174.48 E
Devonport, Eng., U.K. 42 50.22 N 4.10 W
Devonshire 285 39.49 N 75.32 W
Devonshire Plaza ◆[9] 281 42.17 N 83.00 W
Devore 228 34.13 N 117.25 W
Devoto 252 31.24 S 62.19 W
Devrek 130 41.13 N 31.57 E
Devrekâni 130 41.36 N 33.51 E
Devres ≃ 130 41.06 N 34.25 E
Devure ≃ 154 20.00 S 32.20 E
Dewa, Ujung › 114 2.55 N 95.48 E
Dewakang-lompo, Pulau I 112 5.24 S 118.25 E
Dewar 196 35.27 N 95.56 W
Dewart 210 41.07 N 76.53 W
Dewart Lake ⊜ 216 41.22 N 85.47 W
Dewās 120 22.58 N 76.04 E
Dewa-sanchi ⩘[2] 92 39.05 N 140.10 E
Dewdney 224 49.10 N 122.12 W
Dewetsdorp 158 29.33 S 26.34 E
Dewey, Il., U.S. 216 40.19 N 88.17 W
Dewey, Ok., U.S. 196 36.47 N 95.56 W
Dewey, Wa., U.S. 224 48.25 N 122.37 W
Dewey Beach 208 38.41 N 75.04 W
Deweyville 194 30.18 N 93.45 W
De Witt, Ar., U.S. 194 34.17 N 91.20 W
Dewitt, Il., U.S. 219 40.11 N 88.47 W
De Witt, Ia., U.S. 190 41.49 N 90.32 W
De Witt, Mi., U.S. 216 42.50 N 84.34 W
De Witt, Ne., U.S. 198 40.23 N 96.55 W
De Witt, N.Y., U.S. 210 43.02 N 76.03 W
De Witt □[6], Il., U.S. 216 40.12 N 88.55 W
De Witt □[6], Tx., U.S. 222 29.07 N 97.20 W
Dewittville 214 42.14 N 79.27 W
Dewsbury 44 53.42 N 1.37 W
Dexing 100 28.54 N 117.36 E
Dexingjie 98 39.54 N 122.50 E
Dexter, Me., U.S. 188 45.01 N 69.17 W
Dexter, Mi., U.S. 216 42.20 N 83.53 W
Dexter, Mo., U.S. 194 36.47 N 89.57 W

ENGLISH
Name Page Lat.°′ Long.°′

Dexter, N.M., U.S. 196 33.11 N 104.22 W
Dexter, N.Y., U.S. 212 44.00 N 76.02 W
Dexterity Fiord c[2] 176 71.11 N 73.03 W
Deyang 102 31.14 N 104.22 E
Dey-Dey, Lake ⊜ 162 29.12 S 131.04 E
Deyhūk 128 33.17 N 57.30 E
Deyyer 128 27.50 N 51.55 E
Dez ≃ 128 31.39 N 48.52 E
Dezfūl 128 32.23 N 48.24 E
Dez Gerd 128 30.45 N 51.57 E
Dezhou 98 37.27 N 116.18 E
Dežneva, mys › 180 66.06 N 169.45 W
Dezong 120 32.09 N 90.20 E
Dezzo di Scalve 64 45.59 N 10.05 E
Dgâmcha, Sebkhet te-n- ⊜ 150 18.45 N 15.48 W
Dhabān Singh 123 31.44 N 73.34 E
Dhāding 124 27.52 N 84.55 E
Dhādkā 126 22.47 N 86.30 E
Dháfna ∧ 267c 38.07 N 23.38 E
Dháfni, Ellás 38 37.48 N 22.01 E
Dháfni, Ellás 267c 38.01 N 23.38 E
Dhafníon Monastery ʋ[1] 267c 38.01 N 23.38 E
Dhahab 140 28.29 N 34.32 E
Dhahab, Wādī adh- V 132 32.44 N 35.54 E
Dhahran → Az-Zahrān 128 26.18 N 50.08 E
Dhaka (Dacca), Bngl. 126 23.43 N 90.25 E
Dhāka, India 124 26.41 N 85.10 E
Dhaka □[5] 120 24.15 N 90.15 E
Dhākauli 124 24.45 N 77.51 E
Dhakuria Lake ⊜ 272b 22.31 N 88.22 E
Dhaleswari ≃ 126 23.32 N 90.34 E
Dháli 130 35.01 N 33.25 E
Dhamār 144 14.46 N 44.23 E
Dhāmpur 124 29.19 N 78.31 E
Dhāmrai 126 23.55 N 90.13 E
Dhamtari 122 20.41 N 81.34 E
Dhāmura 126 22.53 N 90.12 E
Dhanaula 123 30.17 N 75.35 E
Dhanaura 124 28.58 N 78.15 E
Dhanbād 126 23.48 N 86.27 E
Dhandhuka 120 22.22 N 71.59 E
Dhanera 126 23.25 N 86.39 E
Dhaneswargāti 126 23.25 N 89.20 E
Dhangadhī 124 28.41 N 80.36 E
Dhaniakhāli 126 22.58 N 88.06 E
D'Hanis 196 29.20 N 99.17 W
Dhankuṭa 124 26.59 N 87.20 E
Dhansar 272c 19.07 N 73.05 E
Dhānyahānā 272b 22.48 N 88.11 E
Dhār 120 22.36 N 75.18 E
Dharampur 122 20.32 N 73.11 E
Dharān 124 26.49 N 87.17 E
Dharangaon 120 21.01 N 75.16 E
Dhārāpuram 122 10.44 N 77.31 E
Dhāri 120 21.20 N 71.01 E
Dhārīwāl 123 31.57 N 75.19 E
Dharmābād 122 18.54 N 77.51 E
Dharmapuri 122 12.08 N 78.10 E
Dharmavaram 122 14.26 N 77.43 E
Dharmjaygarh 124 22.28 N 83.13 E
Dharmkot 123 30.57 N 75.14 E
Dharmshāla 123 32.13 N 76.19 E
Dharoor, Tog V 144 10.20 N 50.30 E
Dharug National Park ♠ 170 33.25 S 151.05 E
Dhasān ≃ 124 25.48 N 79.24 E
Dhātrigrām 126 23.15 N 88.20 E
Dhaulpur 124 26.42 N 77.54 E
Dhawalāgiri □[8] 124 28.30 N 83.30 E
Dhawalāgiri ∧ 124 28.42 N 83.30 E
Dhebar Lake ⊜ 120 24.16 N 74.00 E
Dhelfoí ⊥ 38 38.30 N 22.29 E
Dhenkānāl 120 20.40 N 85.36 E
Dhenoúsa I 38 37.06 N 25.49 E
Dherínia 130 35.03 N 33.57 E
Dhërmiu ʋ[1] 38 40.08 N 19.42 E
Dherue, Loch an ⊜ 46 58.25 N 4.27 W
Dheskáti 38 39.55 N 21.49 E
Dheune ≃ 58 46.54 N 5.00 E
Dhiavolítsion 38 37.18 N 21.58 E
Dhībān 132 31.30 N 35.47 E
Dhidhimótikhon 38 41.21 N 26.30 E
Dhiinsoor 144 2.24 N 42.59 E
Dhíkti ∧ 38 35.08 N 25.30 E
Dhílos ⊥ 38 37.26 N 25.16 E
Dhimitsána 38 37.37 N 22.03 E
Dhiónisos 267c 38.06 N 23.53 E
Dhī Qār □[4] 128 31.00 N 46.15 E
Dhirāsrām 126 23.57 N 90.25 E
Dhirwah, Wādī adh- V 132 31.18 N 36.56 E
Dhodhekánisos (Dodecanese) II 38 36.30 N 27.00 E
Dhodhóni ⊥ 38 39.34 N 20.47 E
Dhofar → Ẓufār ◆[1] 118 17.00 N 54.10 E
Dhokra 272b 22.40 N 88.34 E
Dholka 120 22.43 N 72.28 E
Dhomhnuill, Sgurr ∧ 46 56.45 N 5.27 W
Dhone 122 15.25 N 77.53 E
Dhopākhola 126 23.08 N 89.10 E
Dhorāji 120 21.44 N 70.27 E
Dhosha 126 22.15 N 88.33 E
Dhowa 126 24.03 N 86.54 E
Dhoxáton 38 41.05 N 24.14 E
Dhrāngadhra 120 22.59 N 71.28 E
Dhrapetsóna 267c 37.57 N 23.37 E
Dhrol 120 22.34 N 70.25 E
Dhron ≃ 56 49.52 N 6.54 E
Dhubāb 144 12.56 N 43.25 E
Dhuburi 124 26.01 N 89.59 E
Dhudiāl 123 33.04 N 72.58 E
Dhulāgarh 272b 22.35 N 88.11 E
Dhule 120 20.54 N 74.47 E
Dhulia → Dhule 120 20.54 N 74.47 E
Dhuliān 124 24.41 N 87.58 E
Dhulikhel 124 27.37 N 85.33 E
Dhūlsīrās ◆[8] 272a 28.33 N 77.02 E
Dhünn 56 51.06 N 7.16 E
Dhünn-Stausee ⊜[1] 263 51.05 N 7.16 E
Dhupgāri 124 26.36 N 89.01 E
Dhurbo 144 11.37 N 50.20 E
Dhūri 124 30.22 N 75.52 E
Dhutumkhar ≃ 272c 18.54 N 73.00 E
Dhuudo 144 9.20 N 50.12 E
Dhuudo V 144 9.14 N 50.39 E
Dhuusa Mareeb 144 5.31 N 46.24 E
Dhytikí Ellás □[4] 38 38.00 N 21.30 E
Dhytikí Makedhonía □[4] 38 40.30 N 21.30 E
Día I 38 35.27 N 25.13 E
Diabaig 46 57.34 N 5.40 W
Diabakania 150 10.38 N 10.58 W
Diable, Île du (Devils Island) I 250 5.17 N 52.35 W
Diable, Lac du ⊜ 206 46.31 N 74.20 W
Diable, Pointe du › 240e 14.47 N 60.54 W
Diable, Rivière du ≃ 206 46.03 N 74.38 W
Diables, Morne aux ∧ 240d 15.37 N 61.27 W
Diablo, Ca., U.S. 226 37.50 N 121.58 W
Diablo, Wa., U.S. 224 48.43 N 121.09 W
Diablo, Canyon V 200 35.18 N 110.59 W
Diablo, Isla del → Diable, Île du I 250 5.17 N 52.35 W
Diablo, Mount ∧ 226 37.53 N 121.55 W
Diablo, Pico del ∧ 232 30.59 N 115.45 W
Diablo, Sierra del ⩘ 196 27.20 N 104.05 W
Diablo Lake ⊜[1] 224 48.43 N 121.08 W
Diablo Plateau ⩘[1] 200 31.30 N 105.30 W
Diablo Range ⩘ 226 37.00 N 121.20 W
Diablotins, Morne ∧ 240d 15.30 N 61.24 W
Diabo 150 7.47 N 5.11 W
Diaca 154 11.30 S 39.59 E
Diadema 256 23.42 S 46.37 W
Diadema □[7] 287b 23.42 S 46.36 W
Diafarabé 150 14.09 N 5.01 W

DEUTSCH
Name Seite Breite°′ Länge°′ E = Ost

Diagonal 198 40.48 N 94.20 W
Diaka ≃[1] 150 15.13 N 4.14 W
Dialakoto 150 13.19 N 13.18 W
Dialassagou 150 13.45 N 3.37 W
Diamant, Pointe du › 240e 14.27 N 61.03 W
Diamante, Arg. 252 32.04 S 60.39 W
Diamante, It. 68 39.41 N 15.49 E
Diamante ≃ 252 34.31 S 66.56 W
Diamante, Punta › 234 16.47 N 99.52 W
Diamante de Ubá 256 21.12 S 42.55 W
Diamantina 255 18.15 S 43.36 W
Diamantina ≃ 166 26.45 S 139.10 E
Diamantina Fracture Zone ⊹ 14 36.00 S 105.00 E
Diamantina Lakes 166 23.46 S 141.09 E
Diamantino 248 14.25 S 56.27 W
Diamantino ≃ 255 16.08 S 52.28 W
Diamond, Il., U.S. 216 41.17 N 88.15 W
Diamond, Mo., U.S. 194 37.00 N 94.19 W
Diamond, Oh., U.S. 214 41.06 N 81.01 W
Diamond Bar 228 34.01 N 117.48 W
Diamond Brook ≃ 276 40.56 N 74.08 W
Diamond Creek 274b 37.41 S 145.09 E
Diamond Creek ≃ 169 37.44 S 145.09 E
Diamond Harbour 126 22.12 N 88.12 E
Diamond Head ⩍[6] 229c 21.16 N 157.49 W
Diamond Hill 207 41.59 N 71.24 W
Diamond Hill Reservoir ⊜[1] 283 42.00 N 71.24 W
Diamond Hill State Park ♠ 283 42.00 N 71.26 W
Diamond Islets II 166 17.25 S 150.58 E
Diamond Lake 278 42.15 N 88.00 W
Diamond Lake ⊜, On., Can. 212 45.04 N 78.02 W
Diamond Lake ⊜, Il., U.S. 278 42.15 N 88.00 W
Diamond Lake ⊜, Mi., U.S. 216 41.54 N 85.59 W
Diamond Lake ⊜, Or., U.S. 202 43.10 N 122.09 W
Diamond Peak ∧, Id., U.S. 202 44.09 N 113.05 W
Diamond Peak ∧, Or., U.S. 202 43.33 N 122.09 W
Diamond Peak ∧, Wa., U.S. 202 46.07 N 117.32 W
Diamond Springs 226 38.41 N 120.48 W
Diamondville 200 41.46 N 110.32 W
Diana 222 32.43 N 94.45 W
Diana Bay c 176 60.50 N 69.50 W
Dianalund 41 55.32 N 11.30 E
Dianbai 102 21.30 N 111.01 E
Dian Chi ⊜ 102 24.50 N 102.42 E
Diancun 105 39.55 N 116.14 E
Dianfangba 102 32.54 N 103.35 E
Diangounté Kamara 150 14.33 N 9.31 W
Dianhu 100 33.58 N 119.38 E
Dianji 98 36.32 N 120.27 E
Dianjiang 102 30.21 N 107.23 E
Diano, Vallo di V 68 40.21 N 15.36 E
Diano Marina 62 43.54 N 8.05 E
Dianópolis 250 11.38 S 46.50 W
Dianqianhe 100 30.44 N 116.02 E
Dianra 150 8.45 N 6.14 W
Dianshang 106 31.10 N 118.51 E
Dianshan Hu ⊜ 106 31.08 N 120.55 E
Diantou 100 27.18 N 120.11 E
Dianzi 104 41.37 N 122.05 E
Diaobingshan 104 42.28 N 123.33 E
Diao'ecun 105 40.43 N 115.49 E
Diaohetou 105 39.17 N 116.41 E
Diaopu 100 32.22 N 119.54 E
Diaoshuilouzi 104 40.59 N 122.22 E
Diaotai 100 29.40 N 119.39 E
Diaowo 105 39.30 N 116.04 E
Diapaga 150 12.04 N 1.47 E
Diapangou 150 12.07 N 0.11 E
Diapblo, Puntan › 174n 15.00 N 145.35 E
Dias 256 22.28 S 45.34 W
Diascund Creek Reservoir ⊜[1] 208 37.27 N 76.54 W
Diawala 150 10.07 N 5.28 W
Diaz 194 35.38 N 91.15 W
Diaz Point › 156 26.38 S 15.05 E
Dibai 124 28.13 N 78.15 E
Dibāng ≃ 120 27.50 N 95.32 E
Dibay → Dubayy 128 25.18 N 55.18 E
Dibaya 152 6.30 S 22.57 E
Dibbīn 132 32.26 N 36.34 E
Dibeng 158 27.35 S 22.54 E
D'Iberville 194 30.25 N 88.53 W
Dibete 156 23.45 S 26.26 E
Dibi 144 4.13 N 41.56 E
Dibo 144 6.31 N 41.52 E
Diboll 222 31.11 N 94.46 W
Dibrugarh 120 27.29 N 94.54 E
Dibs 140 12.34 N 24.14 E
Dibs, Bi'r ⊤[4] 140 22.12 N 29.32 E
Dichāon Kalān ◆[8] 272a 28.39 N 76.59 E
Dick, Mount ∧[2] 168a 31.35 S 116.42 E
Dickelsbach ≃ 263 51.24 N 6.45 E
Dickens 196 33.37 N 100.50 W
Dickerson 208 39.13 N 77.25 W
Dickey ≃ 224 47.55 N 124.37 W
Dickey Lake ⊜, On., Can. 212 44.47 N 77.44 W
Dickey Lake ⊜, Wa., U.S. 224 48.06 N 124.31 W
Dickinson, N.D., U.S. 198 46.52 N 102.47 W
Dickinson, Pa., U.S. 208 40.07 N 77.20 W
Dickinson, Tx., U.S. 222 29.27 N 95.03 W
Dickinson Bayou ≃ 222 29.28 N 94.58 W
Dickinson Island I 281 42.37 N 82.38 W
Dickins Seamount ⊹[3] 16 54.30 N 137.00 W
Dicks 158 27.43 S 30.10 E
Dickson, Ok., U.S. 196 34.11 N 96.59 W
Dickson, Tn., U.S. 194 36.04 N 87.23 W
Dickson City 210 41.28 N 75.36 W
Dicle, Tür. 130 37.18 N 42.04 E
Dicle, Tür. 130 38.22 N 40.04 E
Dicle → Tigris ≃ 128 31.00 N 47.25 E
Dicomano 66 43.53 N 11.31 E
Diculom 116 7.54 N 122.14 E
Dicun 100 33.46 N 117.32 E
Didam 52 51.56 N 6.08 E
Didao 89 45.22 N 130.51 E
Didbiran 89 51.58 N 139.20 E
Didcot 42 51.37 N 1.15 W
Didesa ≃ 144 9.56 N 35.45 E
Didiéni 150 13.53 N 8.06 W
Didimbo 152 17.30 S 21.45 E
Didinga Hills ⩘ 154 4.20 N 33.35 E
Didsbury 182 51.40 N 114.08 W
Didsbury ◆[8] 262 53.25 N 2.14 W
Diduyon ≃ 116 16.36 N 121.42 E
Dīdwāna 120 27.24 N 74.34 E
Didy 157b 18.07 S 48.32 E
Die 62 44.45 N 5.22 E
Die Aue ◆[1] 263 51.40 N 6.35 E
Die Berg ∧ 156 25.12 S 30.09 E
Die Boss 158 31.59 S 19.44 E
Diébougou 150 10.58 N 3.15 W
Dieburg 56 49.54 N 8.50 E
Dieciocho de Julio 252 33.41 S 53.33 W
Diecke 150 7.21 N 8.58 W
Diedenhofen → Thionville 56 49.22 N 6.10 E
Diedersdorf 264a 52.20 N 13.21 E
Diedorf 58 48.21 N 10.47 E
Die Erpe ≃ 264a 52.27 N 13.38 E
Diefenbaker, Lake ⊜[1] 184 51.00 N 106.55 W
Diego de Almagro 252 26.23 S 70.03 W
Diego de Almagro, Isla I 254 51.25 S 75.10 W
Diego de Ocampo, Pico ∧ 238 19.35 N 70.45 W
Diego Garcia I 12 7.20 S 72.25 E

**Symbols** in the index entries represent the broad categories identified in the key at the right. Symbols with superior numbers (⩘[1]) identify subcategories (see complete key on page *I · 1).*

**Symbole** im Register stellen die rechts im Schlüssel erklärten Kategorien dar. Symbole mit hochgestellten Ziffern (⩘[1]) bezeichnen Unterabteilungen einer Kategorie (vgl. vollständiger Schlüssel auf Seite *I · 1).*

**Los símbolos** incluídos en el texto del índice representan las grandes categorías identificadas con la clave a la derecha. Los símbolos con numeros en su parte superior (⩘[1]) identifican las subcategorías (véase la clave completa en la página *I · 1).*

**Les symboles** de l'index représentent les catégories indiquées dans la légende à droite. Les symboles suivis d'un indice (⩘[1]) représentent des sous-catégories (voir légende complète à la page *I · 1).*

**Os símbolos** incluídos no texto do índice representam as grandes categorias identificadas com a chave à direita. Os símbolos com números em sua parte superior (⩘[1]) identificam as subcategorias (veja-se a chave completa à página *I · 1).*

| | | | | |
|---|---|---|---|---|
| ∧ Mountain | Berg | Montaña | Montagne | Montanha |
| ⩘ Mountains | Gebirge | Montañas | Montagnes | Montanhas |
| )( Pass | Paß | Paso | Col | Passo |
| V Valley, Canyon | Tal, Cañon | Valle, Cañón | Vallée, Canyon | Vale, Canhão |
| ≚ Plain | Ebene | Llano | Plaine | Planície |
| › Cape | Kap | Cabo | Cap | Cabo |
| I Island | Insel | Isla | Île | Ilha |
| II Islands | Inseln | Islas | Îles | Ilhas |
| ◆ Other Topographic Features | Andere Topographische Objekte | Otros Elementos Topográficos | Autres données topographiques | Outros acidentes topográficos |

ESPAÑOL: Nombre / Página / Lat.°′ / Long.°′ W = Oeste
FRANÇAIS: Nom / Page / Lat.°′ / Long.°′ W = Ouest
PORTUGUÊS: Nome / Página / Lat.°′ / Long.°′ W = Oeste


| Nombre / Nom / Nome | Página / Page | Lat.°′ | Long.°′ |
|---|---|---|---|
| Diego Gaynor | 258 | 34.17 S | 59.14 W |
| Diego Pérez, Cayería de II | 240p | 22.05 N | 81.40 W |
| Diego Ramírez, Islas II | 244 | 56.30 S | 68.44 W |
| Die Haard ⧫ [1] | 263 | 51.41 N | 7.15 E |
| Diekirch | 56 | 49.53 N | 6.10 E |
| Dieksee ⊜ | 54 | 54.10 N | 10.30 E |
| Dieleemu | 86 | 46.22 N | 88.43 E |
| Dielingen | 52 | 52.26 N | 8.20 E |
| Dielsdorf | 58 | 47.29 N | 8.27 E |
| Diéma | 150 | 14.32 N | 9.12 W |
| Diemansputs | 158 | 29.54 S | 21.33 E |
| Diembéring | 150 | 12.28 N | 16.47 W |
| Diemel ≏ | 52 | 51.39 N | 9.27 E |
| Diemelstadt | 52 | 51.29 N | 9.01 E |
| Diemel-Talsperre ⧫ [6] | 56 | 51.22 N | 8.43 E |
| Diemen | 52 | 52.20 N | 4.58 E |
| Diemuchuoke | 120 | 32.42 N | 79.29 E |
| Dien Bien Phu | 110 | 21.23 N | 103.01 E |
| Dien Khanh | 110 | 12.15 N | 109.06 E |
| Diepenau | 52 | 52.25 N | 8.44 E |
| Diepenbeek | 56 | 50.54 N | 5.24 E |
| Diepenheim | 52 | 52.12 N | 6.33 E |
| Diepensee | 264a | 52.22 N | 13.31 E |
| Diepenveen | 52 | 52.18 N | 6.08 E |
| Diepholz | 52 | 52.35 N | 8.21 E |
| Diepoldsau | 58 | 47.23 N | 9.38 E |
| Dieppe, N.B., Can. | 186 | 46.06 N | 64.45 W |
| Dieppe, Fr. | 50 | 49.56 N | 1.05 E |
| Dierbao | 98 | 40.20 N | 114.32 E |
| Dierdorf | 56 | 50.33 N | 7.39 E |
| Dieren | 52 | 52.03 N | 6.06 E |
| Dierks | 194 | 34.07 N | 94.00 W |
| Diersbach | 60 | 48.25 N | 13.34 E |
| Di'er Songhua ≏ | 89 | 45.26 N | 124.39 E |
| Diesdorf | 54 | 52.45 N | 10.52 E |
| Dieskau | 54 | 51.26 N | 12.02 E |
| Diessem ⧫ [8] | 263 | 51.20 N | 6.35 E |
| Diessen | 64 | 47.56 N | 11.06 E |
| Diessenhofen | 58 | 47.41 N | 8.45 E |
| Diest | 56 | 50.59 N | 5.03 E |
| Dietenheim | 58 | 48.12 N | 10.04 E |
| Dietenhofen | 56 | 49.24 N | 10.41 E |
| Dietersburg | 60 | 48.30 N | 12.55 E |
| Dietersdorf | 56 | 50.13 N | 10.49 E |
| Dietfurt | 56 | 48.57 N | 10.56 E |
| Dietfurt an der Altmühl | 60 | 49.02 N | 11.35 E |
| Dietikon | 58 | 47.24 N | 8.24 E |
| Dietmannsried | 58 | 47.49 N | 10.17 E |
| Dietramszell | 64 | 47.51 N | 11.35 E |
| Dietrich | 202 | 42.54 N | 114.15 W |
| Dietzenbach | 56 | 50.01 N | 8.47 E |
| Dietzhölztal | 56 | 50.50 N | 8.19 E |
| Dieue-sur-Meuse | 56 | 49.04 N | 5.25 E |
| Dieulefit | 62 | 44.31 N | 5.04 E |
| Dieulouard | 56 | 48.51 N | 6.04 E |
| Dieuze | 56 | 48.49 N | 6.43 E |
| Dievenišk̇ės | 76 | 54.12 N | 25.37 E |
| Diever | 52 | 52.52 N | 6.19 E |
| Die Ville ⩙ [2] | 56 | 50.40 N | 6.55 E |
| Die Wurzen (Koren) )( | 64 | 46.31 N | 13.45 E |
| Diez | 56 | 50.22 N | 8.01 E |
| Diez de Octubre | 232 | 24.44 N | 104.39 W |
| Dif | 144 | 0.59 N | 40.57 E |
| Difang | 98 | 35.23 N | 117.52 E |
| Diffa | 146 | 13.19 N | 12.37 E |
| Diffa □ [5] | 146 | 16.00 N | 13.30 E |
| Differdange | 56 | 49.32 N | 5.52 E |
| Difficult Run ≏ | 284c | 38.58 N | 77.14 W |
| Diffun | 116 | 16.34 N | 121.33 E |
| Difuri I | 122 | 5.24 N | 73.38 E |
| Digambar Jain Temple ʊ [1] | 272b | 22.36 N | 88.23 E |
| Digambarpur | 126 | 21.57 N | 88.22 E |
| Digba | 154 | 4.24 N | 25.47 E |
| Digboi | 120 | 27.23 N | 95.38 E |
| Digby | 186 | 44.37 N | 65.46 W |
| Digby Neck ≻ [1] | 186 | 44.30 N | 66.10 W |
| Dige | 98 | 34.22 N | 114.28 E |
| Digerberget ∧ [2] | 40 | 60.35 N | 13.25 E |
| Digges Islands II | 176 | 62.35 N | 77.50 W |
| Diggle | 262 | 53.34 N | 1.59 W |
| Dighalia | 126 | 23.07 N | 89.39 E |
| Dighipāra | 126 | 21.58 N | 88.17 E |
| Dighode | 272c | 18.54 N | 73.02 E |
| Dighra | 272b | 22.47 N | 88.32 E |
| Dighton, Ks., U.S. | 198 | 38.28 N | 100.28 W |
| Dighton, Ma., U.S. | 207 | 41.48 N | 71.07 W |
| Di Giorgio | 228 | 35.15 N | 118.51 W |
| Dīglūr | 122 | 18.33 N | 77.36 E |
| Digmoor | 262 | 53.32 N | 2.45 W |
| Dīgnagar | 126 | 23.27 N | 87.41 E |
| Dignano | 64 | 46.05 N | 12.56 E |
| Digne | 62 | 44.06 N | 6.14 E |
| Digoin | 32 | 46.29 N | 3.59 E |
| Digomi | 84 | 41.47 N | 44.44 E |
| Digong | 104 | 42.11 N | 122.03 E |
| Digor | 84 | 40.23 N | 43.24 E |
| Digora | 84 | 43.10 N | 44.09 E |
| Digos | 116 | 6.45 N | 125.20 E |
| Digra | 272b | 22.50 N | 88.20 E |
| Digras | 122 | 20.07 N | 77.43 E |
| Digri | 120 | 25.10 N | 69.07 E |
| Digui | 152 | 5.28 N | 20.50 E |
| Digul ≏ | 164 | 7.07 S | 138.42 E |
| Dihaer | 86 | 42.35 N | 89.49 E |
| Dihtyari | 78 | 50.35 N | 32.45 E |
| Dihun | 144 | 7.18 N | 42.42 E |
| Dijag | 24 | 65.48 N | 57.39 E |
| Dijlah → Tigris ≏ | 128 | 31.00 N | 47.25 E |
| Dijlah, Wādī V | 142 | 29.58 N | 31.18 E |
| Dijle (Dyle) ≏ | 56 | 51.04 N | 4.25 E |
| Dijohan Point ≻ | 116 | 16.19 N | 122.14 E |
| Dijon | 58 | 47.19 N | 5.01 E |
| Dik | 146 | 9.58 N | 17.31 E |
| Dikaja | 76 | 59.15 N | 39.30 E |
| Dikala | 154 | 4.41 N | 31.23 E |
| Dikbıyık | 130 | 41.13 N | 36.38 E |
| Dike | 190 | 42.27 N | 92.37 W |
| Dikhil | 144 | 11.06 N | 42.22 E |
| Dikili | 130 | 39.04 N | 26.53 E |
| Dikirnis | 142 | 31.05 N | 31.35 E |
| Dikli | 76 | 57.35 N | 25.06 E |
| Diklosmta, gora ∧ | 84 | 42.29 N | 45.47 E |
| Dikmen | 130 | 39.53 N | 32.50 E |
| Dikodougou | 150 | 9.04 N | 5.46 W |
| Diksmuide (Dixmude) | 50 | 51.02 N | 2.52 E |
| Dikson | 74 | 73.30 N | 80.35 E |
| Dikwa | 146 | 12.02 N | 13.56 E |
| Dila | 144 | 6.21 N | 38.17 E |
| Dilektepe | 130 | 38.04 N | 41.49 E |
| Dile Point ≻ | 116 | 17.34 N | 120.20 E |
| Dilerpur | 272b | 22.51 N | 88.10 E |
| Dili | 112 | 8.33 S | 125.35 E |
| Dilia V | 146 | 16.53 N | 11.00 E |
| Diligent Strait ʯ | 110 | 12.11 N | 92.57 E |
| Di Linh | 110 | 11.35 N | 108.04 E |
| Diližan | 84 | 40.45 N | 44.52 E |
| Diližanskij zapovednik ♠ | 84 | 40.40 N | 45.00 E |
| Dill ≏ | 56 | 50.33 N | 8.29 E |
| Dill City | 196 | 35.16 N | 99.08 W |
| Dillenburg | 56 | 50.44 N | 8.17 E |
| Diller | 198 | 40.06 N | 96.56 W |
| Dilley, Or., U.S. | 224 | 45.29 N | 123.07 W |
| Dilley, Tx., U.S. | 196 | 28.40 N | 99.10 W |
| Dilling | 140 | 12.03 N | 29.39 E |
| Dillingen | 56 | 49.21 N | 6.44 E |
| Dillingen an der Donau | 56 | 48.34 N | 10.29 E |
| Dillingham | 180 | 59.02 N | 158.29 W |
| Dillon, Co., U.S. | 200 | 39.37 N | 106.02 W |
| Dillon, Mt., U.S. | 202 | 45.12 N | 112.38 W |
| Dillon, S.C., U.S. | 192 | 34.24 N | 79.22 W |
| Dillon ≏ | 184 | 55.56 N | 108.57 W |
| Dillon Cone ∧ | 172 | 42.16 S | 173.13 E |
| Dillon Lake ⊜ | 184 | 55.45 N | 109.30 W |
| Dillon Lake ⊜ [1] | 188 | 40.02 N | 82.10 W |
| Dillon Mountain ∧ | 200 | 33.51 N | 108.48 W |
| Dillon Reservoir ⊜ [1] | 200 | 39.35 N | 106.02 W |
| Dillon State Park ♠ | 188 | 40.03 N | 82.08 W |
| Dillonvale | 214 | 40.11 N | 80.46 W |
| Dillsboro | 218 | 39.01 N | 85.03 W |
| Dillsburg | 208 | 40.06 N | 77.02 W |
| Dilltown | 214 | 40.29 N | 79.00 W |
| Dillwyn | 192 | 37.32 N | 78.27 W |
| Dilly | 150 | 15.01 N | 7.40 W |
| Dilolo | 152 | 10.42 S | 22.20 E |
| Dilsen | 56 | 51.02 N | 5.44 E |
| Dilworth | 198 | 46.52 N | 96.42 W |
| Dilworthtown | 285 | 39.54 N | 75.34 W |
| Dima, Ang. | 152 | 15.27 S | 20.10 E |
| Dima, Indon. | 114 | 1.20 N | 97.20 E |
| Dimāpur | 120 | 25.54 N | 93.44 E |
| Dimaro | 64 | 46.20 N | 10.52 E |
| Dimasalang | 116 | 12.12 N | 123.51 E |
| Dimashq (Damascus) | 132 | 33.30 N | 36.18 E |
| Dimashq □ [8] | 132 | 33.30 N | 37.00 E |
| Dimass, Rass ≻ | 36 | 35.37 N | 11.03 E |
| Dimataling | 116 | 7.32 N | 123.22 E |
| Dimbelenge | 152 | 5.33 S | 23.07 E |
| Dimbokro | 150 | 6.39 N | 4.42 W |
| Dimboola | 166 | 36.27 S | 142.02 E |
| Dimbulah | 166 | 17.09 S | 145.07 E |
| Dime | 144 | 6.16 N | 36.20 E |
| Dime Box | 222 | 30.21 N | 96.50 W |
| Dimitrovgrad, Blg. | 38 | 42.03 N | 25.36 E |
| Dimitrovgrad, Jugo. | 38 | 43.01 N | 22.47 E |
| Dimitrovgrad, Ross. | 80 | 54.14 N | 49.39 E |
| Dimitrovo → Pernik | 38 | 42.36 N | 23.02 E |
| Dimitrovskoje | 85 | 40.16 N | 69.03 E |
| Dimlang ∧ | 146 | 8.24 N | 11.47 E |
| Dimmitt | 196 | 34.33 N | 102.18 W |
| Dimo | 154 | 5.19 N | 29.10 E |
| Dimock | 210 | 41.45 N | 75.32 W |
| Dimona | 132 | 31.04 N | 35.02 E |
| Dimondale | 216 | 42.38 N | 84.38 W |
| Dina | 123 | 33.02 N | 73.36 E |
| Dinach | 144 | 9.15 N | 50.37 E |
| Dinagat | 116 | 9.59 N | 125.35 E |
| Dinagat Island I | 116 | 10.12 N | 125.35 E |
| Dinagat Sound ʯ | 116 | 9.59 N | 125.50 E |
| Dinahican Point ≻ | 116 | 14.42 N | 121.44 E |
| Dinājpur | 124 | 25.38 N | 88.38 E |
| Dinalupihan | 116 | 14.52 N | 120.28 E |
| Dinamarca → Denmark □ [1] | 26 | 56.00 N | 10.00 E |
| Dinamarca, Estrecho de → Denmark Strait ʯ | 10 | 67.00 N | 25.00 W |
| Dinami | 68 | 38.31 N | 16.09 E |
| Dinamita | 196 | 25.43 N | 103.38 W |
| Dinamo | 80 | 50.15 N | 41.38 E |
| Dinan | 32 | 48.27 N | 2.02 W |
| Dīnānagar | 123 | 32.09 N | 75.28 E |
| Dinant | 56 | 50.16 N | 4.55 E |
| Dinar | 130 | 38.04 N | 30.10 E |
| Dinara (Dinaric Alps) ⩙ | 36 | 43.50 N | 16.35 E |
| Dinard | 32 | 48.38 N | 2.04 W |
| Dinaric Alps → Dinara ⩙ | 36 | 43.50 N | 16.35 E |
| Dinarische Alpen → Dinara ⩙ | 36 | 43.50 N | 16.35 E |
| Dinas, Pil. | 116 | 7.38 N | 123.20 E |
| Dinas, Wales, U.K. | 42 | 52.00 N | 4.54 W |
| Dinas Head ≻ | 42 | 52.02 N | 4.55 W |
| Dinas Powys | 42 | 51.26 N | 3.14 W |
| Dindanko | 150 | 14.08 N | 9.30 W |
| Dindar, Nahr ad- (Dinder) ≏ | 140 | 14.06 N | 33.40 E |
| Dīndārpur ⧫ [8] | 272a | 28.36 N | 76.59 E |
| Dinde | 152 | 14.12 S | 13.44 E |
| Dinder (Nahr ad-Dindar) ≏ | 140 | 14.06 N | 33.40 E |
| Dinder National Park ♠ | 140 | 12.40 N | 35.20 E |
| Dindi ≏ | 122 | 16.21 N | 79.13 E |
| Dindigul | 122 | 10.21 N | 77.57 E |
| Dindima | 150 | 10.18 N | 10.12 E |
| Dindori | 124 | 22.57 N | 81.05 E |
| Dineksaray | 130 | 37.23 N | 32.37 E |
| Dinga, Pāk. | 120 | 25.26 N | 67.10 E |
| Dinga, Pāk. | 123 | 32.38 N | 73.43 E |
| Dinga, Zaïre | 152 | 5.19 S | 16.34 E |
| Dingalan Bay c | 116 | 15.18 N | 121.25 E |
| Ding'an | 110 | 19.44 N | 110.21 E |
| Dingba | 154 | 3.24 N | 27.55 E |
| Dingbian | 102 | 37.40 N | 107.41 E |
| Dingbianji | 102 | 36.37 N | 108.41 E |
| Dingbu | 106 | 31.18 N | 119.10 E |
| Dingden | 52 | 51.46 N | 6.37 E |
| Dinge | 152 | 4.58 S | 12.22 E |
| Dingelstädt | 54 | 51.18 N | 10.19 E |
| Dingelstedt | 54 | 51.58 N | 10.58 E |
| Dingeryu | 105 | 39.37 N | 114.55 E |
| Dingfeng | 106 | 31.20 N | 121.45 E |
| Dinggou | 100 | 32.34 N | 119.39 E |
| Dinggyê | 124 | 28.29 N | 88.06 E |
| Dinghai | 100 | 30.02 N | 122.06 E |
| Dingila | 154 | 3.39 N | 26.22 E |
| Dingjia | 107 | 29.24 N | 106.09 E |
| Dingjiagou | 104 | 40.40 N | 122.35 E |
| Dingjiandian | 106 | 32.06 N | 120.52 E |
| Dingjiasuo | 100 | 32.32 N | 120.40 E |
| Dingjiazhuang | 106 | 32.11 N | 120.16 E |
| Dingkouzhen | 102 | 39.55 N | 106.40 E |
| Dingle | 48 | 52.08 N | 10.15 W |
| Dingle ⧫ [8] | 262 | 53.23 N | 2.57 W |
| Dingle Bay c | 48 | 52.05 N | 10.15 W |
| Dingley | 274b | 37.58 S | 145.07 E |
| Dingman Creek ≏ | 212 | 42.55 N | 81.25 W |
| Dingmans Ferry | 210 | 41.14 N | 74.53 W |
| Dingnan | 100 | 24.48 N | 114.59 E |
| Dingnan ≏ | 100 | 24.28 N | 115.26 E |
| Dingo | 166 | 23.39 S | 149.20 E |
| Dingolfing | 60 | 48.38 N | 12.31 E |
| Dingras | 116 | 18.06 N | 120.42 E |
| Dingshuzhen | 106 | 31.17 N | 119.50 E |
| Dingtao | 98 | 35.04 N | 115.34 E |
| Dingtuna | 40 | 59.34 N | 16.22 E |
| Dinguira | 150 | 14.11 N | 11.16 W |
| Dinguiraye | 150 | 11.18 N | 10.43 W |
| Dingwall, N.S., Can. | 186 | 46.54 N | 60.28 W |
| Dingwall, Scot., U.K. | 46 | 57.35 N | 4.29 W |
| Dingxi | 102 | 35.33 N | 104.32 E |
| Dingxian | 98 | 38.32 N | 114.59 E |
| Dingxiang | 102 | 38.30 N | 113.00 E |
| Dingxiao | 102 | 25.13 N | 105.07 E |
| Dingxing | 105 | 39.17 N | 115.46 E |
| Dingyan | 100 | 32.23 N | 120.45 E |
| Dingyuan | 100 | 32.32 N | 117.40 E |
| Dingzhouying | 105 | 40.20 N | 115.43 E |
| Dingzichang | 107 | 28.54 N | 106.08 E |
| Dingzi Gang c | 98 | 36.37 N | 120.50 E |
| Dinh, Mui ≻ | 110 | 11.22 N | 109.01 E |
| Dinhāta | 124 | 26.08 N | 89.28 E |
| Dinh Ca | 110 | 21.45 N | 106.03 E |
| Dinh Lap | 110 | 21.33 N | 107.06 E |
| Dinin ≏ | 48 | 52.43 N | 7.18 W |
| Dinkel ≏ | 52 | 52.30 N | 6.58 E |
| Dinkelsbühl | 56 | 49.04 N | 10.19 E |
| Dinkelscherben | 58 | 48.21 N | 10.35 E |
| Dinkey Creek ≏ | 226 | 36.54 N | 119.07 W |
| Dinklage | 52 | 52.40 N | 8.07 E |
| Dinnebito Wash V | 200 | 35.29 N | 111.14 W |
| Dinner Point ≻ | 220 | 28.28 N | 82.41 W |
| Dinnet | 46 | 57.03 N | 2.54 W |
| Dinnington | 44 | 53.22 N | 1.12 W |
| Dinokwe | 156 | 23.24 S | 26.40 E |
| Dinorwic | 184 | 49.41 N | 92.30 W |
| Dinorwic Lake ⊜ | 184 | 49.37 N | 92.33 W |
| Dinosaur | 200 | 40.14 N | 109.00 W |
| Dinosaur Lake ⊜ [1] | 182 | 55.57 N | 122.07 W |
| Dinosaur National Monument ♠ | 200 | 40.32 N | 108.58 W |
| Dinosaur Provincial Park ♠ | 182 | 50.45 N | 111.30 W |
| Dinskaja | 78 | 45.13 N | 39.14 E |
| Dinslaken | 52 | 51.34 N | 6.44 E |
| Dinslakener Bruch | 263 | 51.35 N | 6.43 E |
| Dinslaken-Schwarze Heide, Flughafen ⊠ | 263 | 51.37 N | 6.51 E |
| Dinsmore | 184 | 51.20 N | 107.26 W |
| Dintel ≏ | 52 | 51.39 N | 4.22 E |
| Dinteloord | 52 | 51.37 N | 4.22 E |
| Dinuba | 226 | 36.32 N | 119.23 W |
| Dinwiddie, S. Afr. | 273d | 26.16 S | 28.10 E |
| Dinwiddie, Va., U.S | 208 | 37.04 N | 77.35 W |
| Dinwiddie □ [6] | 208 | 37.10 N | 77.20 W |
| Dinxperlo | 52 | 51.52 N | 6.29 E |
| Diö | 26 | 56.38 N | 14.13 E |
| Diobo | 152 | 2.16 N | 20.29 E |
| Dioïla | 150 | 12.29 N | 6.48 W |
| Diois ⧫ [1] | 62 | 44.40 N | 5.20 E |
| Diomede | 180 | 65.47 N | 169.00 W |
| Dion ≏ | 150 | 10.12 N | 8.39 W |
| Dionísio | 255 | 19.49 S | 42.45 W |
| Dionísio Cerqueira | 252 | 26.15 S | 53.38 W |
| Dionne, Lac ⊜ | 186 | 49.26 N | 67.55 W |
| Dions | 62 | 43.56 N | 4.19 E |
| Diorama | 255 | 16.21 S | 51.14 W |
| Dios | 175e | 5.33 S | 154.58 E |
| Dios, Cayos de II | 240p | 21.39 N | 81.09 W |
| Diósd | 264c | 47.25 N | 18.57 E |
| Diouloulou | 150 | 13.03 N | 16.36 W |
| Dioumanténé | 150 | 10.32 N | 5.55 W |
| Dioundiou | 150 | 12.37 N | 3.33 E |
| Dioungani | 150 | 14.19 N | 2.44 W |
| Dioura | 150 | 14.50 N | 5.15 W |
| Diourbel | 150 | 14.40 N | 16.15 W |
| Diourbel □ [4] | 150 | 14.45 N | 16.30 W |
| Dipaculao | 116 | 15.51 N | 121.32 E |
| Dipai | 100 | 23.50 N | 114.06 E |
| Dīpālpur | 123 | 30.40 N | 73.39 E |
| Dipignano | 68 | 39.15 N | 16.15 E |
| Dipilo, Pizzo ∧ | 70 | 37.57 N | 13.59 E |
| Dipkarpaz | 130 | 35.36 N | 34.23 E |
| Diplo | 120 | 24.28 N | 69.35 E |
| Dipolog | 116 | 8.35 N | 123.20 E |
| Dippoldiswalde | 54 | 50.54 N | 13.40 E |
| Dipton | 172 | 45.54 S | 168.22 E |
| Dipu | 106 | 30.38 N | 119.41 E |
| Diqiyingzi | 104 | 42.11 N | 121.29 E |
| Dique Florentino Ameghino | 254 | 43.40 S | 66.25 W |
| Dīr | 123 | 35.12 N | 71.53 E |
| Dira, Djebel ∧ | 34 | 36.05 N | 3.38 E |
| Diré | 150 | 16.16 N | 3.24 W |
| Direction, Cape ≻ | 164 | 12.51 S | 143.32 E |
| Dire Dawa | 144 | 9.37 N | 41.52 E |
| Direkli | 130 | 39.43 N | 36.40 E |
| Diriamba | 236 | 11.51 N | 86.14 W |
| Dirico | 152 | 17.58 S | 20.47 E |
| Dirillo, Lago ⊜ | 70 | 37.08 N | 14.42 E |
| Diriomo | 236 | 11.52 N | 86.03 W |
| Dirj | 146 | 30.09 N | 10.26 E |
| Dirk Hartog Island I | 162 | 25.48 S | 113.00 E |
| Dirkiesdorp | 158 | 27.10 S | 30.25 E |
| Dirkou | 146 | 19.01 N | 12.53 E |
| Dirkshorn | 52 | 52.45 N | 4.45 E |
| Dirksland | 52 | 51.44 N | 4.06 E |
| Dirnaich | 60 | 48.27 N | 12.30 E |
| Dirrah | 140 | 13.37 N | 26.06 E |
| Dirranbandi | 166 | 28.35 S | 148.14 E |
| Dirri | 144 | 4.20 N | 46.37 E |
| Dirs | 144 | 18.32 N | 42.05 E |
| Dirschau → Tczew | 30 | 54.06 N | 18.47 E |
| Dirty Devil ≏ | 200 | 37.53 N | 110.24 W |
| Dīsa | 120 | 24.15 N | 72.10 E |
| Dīsah | 140 | 12.02 N | 34.19 E |
| Disappointment, Cape ≻, S. Geor. | 244 | 54.53 S | 36.07 W |
| Disappointment, Cape ≻, Wa., U.S. | 224 | 46.18 N | 124.03 W |
| Disappointment, Lake ⊜ | 162 | 23.30 S | 122.50 E |
| Disappointment, Mount ∧ | 169 | 37.25 S | 145.18 E |
| Disappointment Creek ≏ | 200 | 38.01 N | 108.51 W |
| Disaster Bay c | 166 | 37.17 S | 150.00 E |
| Disautel | 182 | 48.22 N | 119.14 W |
| Disbrow Drain ≊ | 281 | 42.06 N | 83.27 W |
| Disco | 214 | 42.41 N | 83.02 W |
| Discovery | 273d | 26.10 S | 27.54 E |
| Discovery Bay c, Austl. | 166 | 38.12 S | 141.07 E |
| Discovery Bay c, H.K. | 271d | 22.18 N | 114.01 E |
| Discovery Bay c, Wa., U.S. | 224 | 48.05 N | 122.52 W |
| Discovery Island I | 224 | 48.25 N | 123.15 W |
| Discovery Passage ʯ | 182 | 50.00 N | 125.15 W |
| Discovery Tablemount ✣ [3] | 8 | 42.00 S | 0.10 E |
| Disentis | 58 | 46.43 N | 8.51 E |
| Dishāshah | 142 | 28.59 N | 30.51 E |
| Dishergarh | 126 | 23.41 N | 86.50 E |
| Dishman | 202 | 47.39 N | 117.16 W |
| Dishnā | 140 | 26.07 N | 32.28 E |
| Dishna ≏ | 180 | 63.37 N | 157.18 W |
| Disihao | 89 | 50.28 N | 124.35 E |
| Disko | 216 | 41.00 N | 85.57 W |
| Disko I | 176 | 69.50 N | 53.30 W |
| Disko Bugt c | 176 | 69.15 N | 52.00 W |
| Disley | 262 | 53.21 N | 2.02 W |
| Disley Tunnel ⧫ [5] | 262 | 53.22 N | 2.03 W |
| Dismal ≏ | 198 | 41.50 N | 100.05 W |
| Dismal Lakes ⊜ | 176 | 67.26 N | 117.07 W |
| Dismal Swamp Canal ≊ | 208 | 36.45 N | 76.20 W |
| Disney | 196 | 36.28 N | 95.00 W |
| Disneyland ♠ | 228 | 33.48 N | 117.55 W |
| Disneyworld ♠ | 220 | 28.27 N | 81.28 W |
| Diso | 68 | 40.00 N | 18.23 E |
| Dispur | 120 | 26.08 N | 91.47 E |
| Disputanta | 208 | 37.07 N | 77.13 W |
| Disraeli | 206 | 45.54 N | 71.21 W |
| Diss | 42 | 52.23 N | 1.07 E |
| Dissimieux, Lac ⊜ | 186 | 49.51 N | 69.48 W |
| Distant | 214 | 40.58 N | 79.21 W |
| Disteghil Sār ∧ | 123 | 36.19 N | 75.12 E |
| Disteln | 263 | 51.36 N | 7.09 E |
| Distington | 44 | 54.36 N | 3.32 W |
| District Heights | 284c | 38.51 N | 76.53 W |
| District of Columbia □ [3] | 208 | 38.54 N | 77.01 W |
| Distrito Especial □ [5] | 246 | 4.15 N | 74.15 W |
| Distrito Federal □ [5], Arg. | 258 | 34.36 S | 58.26 W |
| Distrito Federal □ [5], Bra. | 255 | 15.45 S | 47.45 W |
| Distrito Federal □ [5], Méx. | 234 | 19.15 N | 99.10 W |
| Distrito Federal □ [5], Ven. | 246 | 10.30 N | 66.55 W |
| Distroff | 56 | 49.20 N | 6.16 E |
| Disūq | 142 | 31.08 N | 30.39 E |
| Ditfurt | 54 | 51.50 N | 11.11 E |
| Dithmarschen ⧫ [1] | 30 | 54.05 N | 9.00 E |
| Dit Island I | 116 | 11.15 N | 120.56 E |
| Dittáino ≏ | 70 | 37.25 N | 15.00 E |
| Dittelbrunn | 56 | 50.05 N | 10.13 E |
| Ditton, Eng., U.K. | 260 | 51.18 N | 0.27 E |
| Ditton, Eng., U.K. | 262 | 53.22 N | 2.45 W |
| Ditton ≏ | 206 | 45.23 N | 71.12 W |
| Ditton Priors | 42 | 52.30 N | 2.35 W |
| Ditzingen | 56 | 48.49 N | 9.03 E |
| Ditzum | 52 | 53.18 N | 7.16 E |
| Diu | 120 | 20.42 N | 70.59 E |
| Diu □ [8] | 120 | 20.42 N | 70.59 E |
| Diuata Mountains ⩙ | 116 | 9.10 N | 125.47 E |
| Diuata Point ≻ | 116 | 9.05 N | 125.12 E |
| Dīva | 272c | 19.09 N | 72.59 E |
| Divalá | 236 | 8.25 N | 82.43 W |
| Dīvāndarreh | 128 | 35.55 N | 47.02 E |
| Dívčice | 61 | 49.06 N | 14.19 E |
| Dive | 272c | 19.11 N | 73.02 E |
| Divejevo | 80 | 55.03 N | 43.15 E |
| Divenié | 152 | 2.41 S | 12.05 E |
| Divenskaja | 76 | 59.12 N | 30.01 E |
| Diveria ≏ | 58 | 46.09 N | 8.19 E |
| Divernon | 219 | 39.33 N | 89.39 W |
| Dives ≏ | 32 | 49.19 N | 0.05 W |
| Dividing Creek | 208 | 39.16 N | 75.06 W |
| Dividing Creek ≏ | 208 | 38.05 N | 75.32 W |
| Dividing Ridge ∧ | 219 | 39.07 N | 90.39 W |
| Divignano | 266b | 45.40 N | 8.36 E |
| Divilacan Bay c | 116 | 17.25 N | 122.19 E |
| Divine Corners | 210 | 41.48 N | 74.40 W |
| Divinhe | 156 | 20.40 S | 34.49 E |
| Divino | 255 | 20.37 S | 42.09 W |
| Divinolândia | 256 | 21.40 S | 46.45 W |
| Divinópolis | 255 | 20.09 S | 44.54 W |
| Divi Point ≻ | 122 | 15.58 N | 81.09 E |
| Divis ∧ [2] | 48 | 54.37 N | 6.01 W |
| Divisa Nova | 256 | 21.31 S | 46.12 W |
| Divisor, Serra do (Cordillera Ultraoriental) ⩙ [1] | 248 | 8.20 S | 73.30 W |
| Divnogorsk | 86 | 55.58 N | 92.22 E |
| Divnoje | 80 | 45.55 N | 43.22 E |
| Divo | 150 | 5.50 N | 5.22 W |
| Divodar | 120 | 24.06 N | 71.47 E |
| Divonne-les-Bains | 58 | 46.22 N | 6.08 E |
| Divriği | 130 | 39.23 N | 38.07 E |
| Dīwāl Qol | 120 | 34.19 N | 67.54 E |
| Dix, Il., U.S. | 219 | 38.27 N | 88.56 W |
| Dix, Ne., U.S. | 198 | 41.14 N | 103.29 W |
| Dix ≏ | 192 | 37.49 N | 84.43 W |
| Dix, Lac des ⊜ | 58 | 46.03 N | 7.24 E |
| Dixboro | 216 | 42.19 N | 83.39 W |
| Dixfield | 188 | 44.32 N | 70.27 W |
| Dix Hills | 276 | 40.49 N | 73.22 W |
| Dixie | 275b | 43.36 N | 79.36 W |
| Dixie Valley V | 204 | 39.50 N | 117.55 W |
| Dix Milles, Lac ⊜ | 190 | 46.46 N | 77.45 W |
| Dixmoor | 278 | 41.38 N | 87.40 W |
| Dixmude → Diksmuide | 50 | 51.02 N | 2.52 E |
| Dixon, Ca., U.S. | 226 | 38.19 N | 121.49 W |
| Dixon, Il., U.S. | 190 | 41.50 N | 89.28 W |
| Dixon, Ky., U.S. | 194 | 37.31 N | 87.41 W |
| Dixon, Mo., U.S. | 194 | 37.59 N | 92.05 W |
| Dixon, N.M., U.S. | 200 | 36.11 N | 105.53 W |
| Dixon, Oh., U.S. | 216 | 40.57 N | 84.48 W |
| Dixon Entrance ʯ | 182 | 54.25 N | 132.30 W |
| Dixons Mills | 194 | 32.04 N | 87.47 W |
| Dixons Pond ⊜ | 276 | 40.56 N | 74.27 W |
| Dixonville | 214 | 40.42 N | 79.00 W |
| Dixville | 206 | 45.04 N | 71.46 W |
| Diyā al-Kawm | 142 | 30.38 N | 31.05 E |
| Diyadin | 84 | 39.33 N | 43.41 E |
| Diyālā □ [4] | 128 | 34.00 N | 45.00 E |
| Diyālā (Sīrvān) ≏ | 128 | 33.14 N | 44.31 E |
| Diyanga | 152 | 1.29 S | 11.52 E |
| Diyarbakır | 130 | 37.55 N | 40.14 E |
| Diyarbakır □ [4] | 130 | 38.05 N | 40.15 E |
| Diyarb Najm | 142 | 30.45 N | 31.26 E |
| Diyu al-Wasta | 142 | 30.54 N | 31.30 E |
| Dizangsi | 104 | 41.26 N | 120.57 E |
| Dizhou | 102 | 23.00 N | 106.20 E |
| Dizy | 50 | 49.04 N | 3.58 E |
| Dizzard Point ≻ | 42 | 50.45 N | 4.38 W |
| Dja ≏ | 152 | 2.02 N | 15.12 E |
| Dja, Réserve du ⧫ [4] | 152 | 3.05 N | 13.00 E |
| Djabalpur → Jabalpur | 124 | 23.10 N | 79.57 E |
| Djabir | 152 | 0.32 N | 24.05 E |
| Djadié ≏ | 152 | 0.46 N | 12.58 E |
| Djado | 146 | 21.01 N | 12.18 E |
| Djado, Plateau du ⩙ [1] | 146 | 21.45 N | 12.50 E |
| Djaipur → Jaipur | 120 | 26.55 N | 75.49 E |
| Djakarta → Jakarta | 269e | 6.10 S | 106.48 E |
| Djakonovo | 82 | 54.34 N | 38.20 E |
| Djakovka | 80 | 50.43 N | 46.46 E |
| Djakovo ⧫ [8] | 265b | 55.39 N | 37.40 E |
| Djamâa | 148 | 33.32 N | 6.00 E |
| Djamba, Ang. | 152 | 16.46 S | 13.59 E |
| Djamba, Zaïre | 152 | 9.49 S | 22.07 E |
| Djambala | 152 | 2.33 S | 14.45 E |
| Djamschedpur → Jamshedpur | 126 | 22.48 N | 86.11 E |
| Djanet | 148 | 24.34 N | 9.29 E |
| Djaouro Mbali | 152 | 5.52 N | 13.29 E |
| Djaret, Oued V | 148 | 26.32 N | 1.30 E |
| Djebobo ∧ | 150 | 8.20 N | 0.35 E |
| Djébrène | 146 | 11.14 N | 19.01 E |
| Djédaa | 146 | 13.31 N | 18.34 E |
| Djedda → Jiddah | 144 | 21.30 N | 39.12 E |
| Djedi, Oued V | 148 | 34.28 N | 6.05 E |
| Djéké Djéké | 146 | 8.25 N | 18.12 E |
| Djelo-Binza | 273b | 4.23 S | 15.16 E |
| Djema | 140 | 6.03 N | 25.19 E |
| Djember → Jember, Indon. | 115a | 8.10 S | 113.42 E |
| Djember, Tchad | 146 | 10.25 N | 17.50 E |
| Djemila ⊥ | 34 | 36.25 N | 5.44 E |
| Djénné | 150 | 13.54 N | 4.33 W |
| Djenoun, Garet el ∧ | 148 | 25.05 N | 5.25 E |
| Djérem ≏ | 152 | 5.20 N | 13.24 E |
| Djibasso | 150 | 13.07 N | 4.10 W |
| Djibo | 150 | 14.06 N | 1.38 W |
| Djibouti | 144 | 11.36 N | 43.09 E |
| Djibouti □ [1], Afr. | 136 | 11.30 N | 43.00 E |
| Djibouti □ [1], Afr. | 144 | 11.30 N | 43.00 E |
| Djibrouïa | 150 | 13.13 N | 11.14 W |
| Djiri | 273b | 4.08 S | 15.19 E |
| Djiri ≏ | 273b | 4.11 S | 15.20 E |
| Djohong | 152 | 6.50 N | 14.42 E |
| Djokjakarta → Yogyakarta | 115a | 7.48 S | 110.22 E |
| Djokoumatombi | 152 | 0.47 N | 15.22 E |
| Djokupunda | 152 | 5.27 S | 20.58 E |
| Djolu | 152 | 0.37 N | 22.21 E |
| Djombo | 152 | 1.21 N | 20.22 E |
| Djoua ≏ | 152 | 1.13 N | 13.12 E |
| Djouari ≏ | 273b | 4.13 S | 15.08 E |
| Djoubissi | 152 | 6.12 N | 20.45 E |
| Djoué ≏ | 273b | 4.19 S | 15.14 E |
| Djougou | 150 | 9.42 N | 1.40 E |
| Djoum | 152 | 2.40 N | 12.40 E |
| Djouna | 146 | 10.27 N | 20.04 E |
| Djourab, Erg du ⊥ [8] | 146 | 16.40 N | 18.50 E |
| Djugu | 154 | 1.55 N | 30.30 E |
| Djúpivogur | 24a | 64.40 N | 14.10 W |
| Djura | 40 | 60.37 N | 15.00 E |
| Djurås | 40 | 60.33 N | 15.08 E |
| Djurmo | 40 | 60.33 N | 15.10 E |
| Djurö | 40 | 59.19 N | 18.41 E |
| Djurö I | 26 | 58.52 N | 13.28 E |
| Djursholm | 40 | 59.24 N | 18.05 E |
| Dlouhá Ves | 60 | 49.12 N | 13.31 E |
| Dmanisi | 84 | 41.22 N | 44.12 E |
| Dmitr'ašovka | 76 | 52.09 N | 39.04 E |
| Dmitrija Lapteva, proliv ʯ | 74 | 73.00 N | 142.00 E |
| Dmitrijevka, Kaz. | 85 | 43.30 N | 77.02 E |
| Dmitrijevka, Ross. | 76 | 52.53 N | 40.47 E |
| Dmitrijevka, Ross. | 86 | 55.10 N | 75.36 E |
| Dmitrijev-L'govskij | 78 | 52.08 N | 35.05 E |
| Dmitrijevskoje, Kaz. | 86 | 49.08 N | 57.50 E |
| Dmitrijevskoje, Ross. | 80 | 45.48 N | 41.54 E |
| Dmitrijevskoje, Ross. | 82 | 54.40 N | 37.38 E |
| Dmitrijev Usad, Ross. | 76 | 54.08 N | 43.08 E |
| Dmitrijev Usad, Ross. | 80 | 54.14 N | 43.18 E |
| Dmitrijevy Gory | 80 | 55.12 N | 41.47 E |
| Dmitrivka | 78 | 45.29 N | 35.04 E |
| Dmitrov | 82 | 56.21 N | 37.31 E |
| Dmitrovcy | 82 | 55.16 N | 38.55 E |
| Dmitrovskij Pogost | 76 | 55.19 N | 39.49 E |
| Dmitrovsk-Orlovskij | 76 | 52.30 N | 35.09 E |
| Dmukhaylivka | 78 | 49.03 N | 34.46 E |
| Dmytrivka, Ukr. | 78 | 46.51 N | 36.35 E |
| Dmytrivka, Ukr. | 78 | 50.56 N | 32.58 E |
| Dmytrivka, Ukr. | 78 | 48.48 N | 32.44 E |
| Dmytrivka, Ukr. | 83 | 48.55 N | 39.10 E |
| Dmytriyivka | 83 | 47.56 N | 38.56 E |
| Dnepropetrovsk → Dnipropetrovs'k | 78 | 48.27 N | 34.59 E |
| Dneprovskoje | 76 | 55.40 N | 33.55 E |
| Dnieper (Dnipro) (Dnjapro) ≏ | 78 | 46.30 N | 32.18 E |
| Dniepropetrovsk → Dnipropetrovs'k | 78 | 48.27 N | 34.59 E |
| Dniester (Dnister) (Nistru) ≏ | 78 | 46.18 N | 30.17 E |
| Dniprodzerzhyns'k | 78 | 48.30 N | 34.37 E |
| Dniprodzerzhyns'ke vodoskhovyshche ⊜ [1] | 78 | 48.45 N | 34.00 E |
| Dnipropetrovs'k | 78 | 48.27 N | 34.59 E |
| Dnipropetrovs'k □ [4] | 78 | 48.30 N | 35.00 E |
| Dniprovka | 78 | 47.26 N | 34.38 E |
| Dniprovs'kyy lyman c [1] | 78 | 46.35 N | 31.55 E |
| Dnipryany | 78 | 46.44 N | 33.16 E |
| Dnistrovs'ke vodoskhovyshche ⊜ [1] | 78 | 48.30 N | 26.45 E |
| Dnistrovs'kyy lyman ⊜ | 78 | 46.15 N | 30.17 E |
| Dnjaprouska Buhski, kanal ≊ | 76 | 52.03 N | 25.35 E |
| Dno | 76 | 57.50 N | 29.59 E |
| Do, Lac ⊜ | 150 | 15.54 N | 2.45 W |
| Doa | 154 | 16.44 S | 34.32 E |
| Do Āb-e Mīkh-e Zarrīn | 120 | 35.16 N | 68.00 E |
| Doaktown | 186 | 46.33 N | 66.08 W |
| Doangdoangan-Besar, Pulau I | 112 | 5.24 S | 117.55 E |
| Doany | 157b | 14.22 S | 49.31 E |
| Doba | 146 | 8.39 N | 16.51 E |
| Dobane | 140 | 6.24 N | 24.42 E |
| Dobbertin | 54 | 53.37 N | 12.04 E |
| Dobbiaco (Toblach) | 64 | 46.44 N | 12.14 E |
| Dobbin | 222 | 30.22 N | 95.46 W |
| Dobbins | 226 | 39.22 N | 121.12 W |
| Dobbins Air Force Base ■ | 192 | 33.54 N | 84.31 W |
| Dobbs Ferry | 210 | 41.00 N | 73.52 W |
| Dobczyce | 30 | 49.54 N | 20.06 E |
| Dobel | 56 | 48.48 N | 8.29 E |
| Dobele | 76 | 56.37 N | 23.16 E |
| Döbeln | 54 | 51.07 N | 13.07 E |
| Doberai, Jazirah (Vogelkop) ≻ [1] | 164 | 1.30 S | 132.30 E |
| Döberitz | 264a | 52.33 N | 13.03 E |
| Doberlug-Kirchhain | 54 | 51.38 N | 13.34 E |
| Döbern | 54 | 51.37 N | 14.36 E |
| Dobiegniew | 30 | 52.59 N | 15.47 E |
| Döbling ⧫ [8] | 264b | 48.15 N | 16.22 E |
| Dobo | 164 | 5.46 S | 134.13 E |
| Doboj | 38 | 44.44 N | 18.06 E |
| Dobra, Pol. | 30 | 51.54 N | 18.37 E |
| Dobra, Pol. | 30 | 53.35 N | 15.18 E |
| Dobra ≏ | 36 | 45.33 N | 15.31 E |
| Dobr'anka | 86 | 58.27 N | 56.24 E |
| Dobřany | 60 | 49.40 N | 13.18 E |
| Dobra Stausee ⊜ [1] | 61 | 48.35 N | 15.20 E |
| Dobre Miasto | 30 | 53.59 N | 20.25 E |
| Döbriach | 64 | 46.47 N | 13.39 E |
| Dobrič | 38 | 43.34 N | 27.50 E |
| Dobrich → Dobrič | 38 | 43.34 N | 27.50 E |
| Dobrinka, Ross. | 80 | 52.09 N | 40.29 E |
| Dobrinka, Ross. | 80 | 48.49 N | 42.58 E |
| Dobrinka, Ross. | 80 | 50.49 N | 41.51 E |
| Dobříš | 30 | 49.47 N | 14.11 E |
| Dobritz | 54 | 52.01 N | 12.13 E |
| Dobrodzień | 30 | 50.44 N | 18.27 E |
| Dobroje, Ross. | 76 | 57.06 N | 32.02 E |
| Dobroje, Ross. | 76 | 52.52 N | 39.48 E |
| Dobroměřice | 54 | 50.23 N | 13.46 E |
| Dobromyl' | 78 | 49.34 N | 22.47 E |
| Dobropillya | 78 | 48.28 N | 37.05 E |
| Dobroteasa | 38 | 44.47 N | 24.23 E |
| Dobrotvir | 78 | 50.14 N | 24.22 E |
| Dobrovelychkivka | 78 | 48.23 N | 31.11 E |
| Dobrovillya | 78 | 48.41 N | 36.37 E |
| Dobrovol'sk | 76 | 54.46 N | 22.31 E |
| Dobrudžansko plato ⩙ [1] | 38 | 43.32 N | 27.50 E |
| Dobruja □ [9] | 38 | 44.00 N | 28.00 E |
| Dobruš | 76 | 52.25 N | 31.19 E |
| Dobruška | 30 | 50.17 N | 16.10 E |
| Dobryanka, Ukr. | 78 | 52.04 N | 31.11 E |
| Dobryanka, Ukr. | 78 | 48.21 N | 30.54 E |
| Dobrzany | 30 | 53.22 N | 15.25 E |
| Dobrzyń nad Wisłą | 30 | 52.38 N | 19.20 E |
| Dobšiná | 30 | 48.49 N | 20.23 E |
| Dobson | 192 | 36.23 N | 80.43 W |
| Dobzha | 120 | 28.28 N | 88.14 E |
| Doce ≏, Bra. | 255 | 19.37 S | 39.49 W |
| Doce ≏, Bra. | 255 | 18.28 S | 51.05 W |
| Doce de Octubre | 196 | 25.38 N | 97.47 W |
| Dochart ≏ | 46 | 56.28 N | 4.20 W |
| Döčin ≏ | 88 | 49.39 N | 114.48 E |
| Docker River | 162 | 24.52 S | 129.05 E |
| Docking | 42 | 52.55 N | 0.38 E |
| Dock Junction | 192 | 31.11 N | 81.31 W |
| Dockton | 224 | 47.22 N | 122.27 W |
| Dockweiler | 56 | 50.15 N | 6.46 E |
| Dockweiler Beach State Park ♠ | 280 | 33.55 N | 118.26 W |
| Doctor Arroyo | 234 | 23.40 N | 100.11 W |
| Doctor Cecilio Báez | 252 | 25.03 S | 56.19 W |
| Doctor Coss | 196 | 25.55 N | 99.11 W |
| Doctor Edmund A. Babler Memorial State Park ♠ | 219 | 38.36 N | 90.43 W |
| Doctor Hicks Range ⩙ | 162 | 28.40 S | 124.20 E |
| Doctor Pedro P. Peña | 252 | 22.26 S | 62.22 W |
| Doctors Creek ≏ | 208 | 40.11 N | 74.41 W |
| Doda | 123 | 33.08 N | 75.34 E |
| Dod Ballāpur | 122 | 13.18 N | 77.32 E |
| Doddinghurst | 42 | 51.40 N | 0.18 E |
| Doddridge | 194 | 33.05 N | 93.54 W |
| Dodds Island I | 219 | 38.35 N | 91.59 W |
| Doddsville | 194 | 33.39 N | 90.31 W |
| Dodecanese → Dhodhekánisos II | 38 | 36.30 N | 27.00 E |
| Dodéo | 152 | 7.29 N | 12.04 E |
| Dodge, Ne., U.S. | 198 | 41.43 N | 96.52 W |
| Dodge, Tx., U.S. | 222 | 30.45 N | 95.24 W |
| Dodge □ [6] | 216 | 43.14 N | 88.40 W |
| Dodge Brothers State Park Number 4♠, Mi., U.S. | 281 | 42.37 N | 83.22 W |
| Dodge Brothers State Park Number 8♠, Mi., U.S. | 281 | 42.36 N | 83.01 W |
| Dodge Center | 190 | 44.01 N | 92.51 W |
| Dodge City | 198 | 37.45 N | 100.01 W |
| Dodge Park | 284c | 38.56 N | 76.53 W |
| Dodger Stadium ♠ | 280 | 34.04 N | 118.14 W |
| Dodgeville | 190 | 42.57 N | 90.07 W |
| Dodman Point ≻ | 42 | 50.13 N | 4.48 W |
| Dodo Goei | 140 | 5.57 N | 29.26 E |
| Dodola | 144 | 7.02 N | 39.07 E |
| Dodoma | 154 | 6.11 S | 35.45 E |
| Dodoma □ [4] | 154 | 6.00 S | 36.00 E |
| Dodori ≏ | 154 | 1.52 S | 41.02 E |
| Dodsland | 184 | 51.48 N | 108.49 W |
| Dodson, La., U.S. | 194 | 32.04 N | 92.39 W |
| Dodson, Mt., U.S. | 202 | 48.23 N | 108.14 W |
| Dodson, Tx., U.S. | 196 | 34.46 N | 100.02 W |
| Dodurga | 130 | 39.48 N | 29.55 E |
| Doe Lake ⊜ | 212 | 45.32 N | 79.25 W |
| Doe River | 182 | 56.00 N | 120.05 W |
| Doerun | 192 | 31.19 N | 83.55 W |
| Doesburg | 52 | 52.01 N | 6.09 E |
| Doetinchem | 52 | 51.58 N | 6.17 E |
| Dog ≏ | 190 | 48.51 N | 89.37 W |
| Dogāchia | 272b | 22.58 N | 88.31 E |
| Dogai Coring ⊜ | 120 | 34.30 N | 89.15 E |
| Dōga-mori ∧ | 96 | 33.09 N | 132.53 E |
| Doğanbey, Tür. | 130 | 37.37 N | 27.11 E |
| Doğanbey, Tür. | 130 | 38.04 N | 26.53 E |
| Doğanbey, Tür. | 130 | 37.48 N | 31.54 E |
| Doğanca | 130 | 37.49 N | 42.20 E |
| Doğançay | 130 | 40.37 N | 30.20 E |
| Doganella | 66 | 41.34 N | 12.56 E |
| Doğanhisar | 130 | 38.09 N | 31.41 E |
| Doğankent, Tür. | 130 | 40.48 N | 38.56 E |
| Doğankent, Tür. | 130 | 36.52 N | 35.18 E |
| Doğanşehir | 130 | 38.06 N | 37.53 E |
| Doğanyol | 130 | 38.19 N | 39.03 E |
| Doğanyurt, Tür. | 130 | 42.00 N | 33.27 E |
| Doğanyurt, Tür. | 130 | 40.41 N | 36.43 E |
| Dog Creek | 182 | 51.35 N | 122.15 W |
| Dog Creek ≏, B.C., Can. | 182 | 51.35 N | 122.17 W |
| Dog Creek ≏, Mt., U.S. | 202 | 47.44 N | 109.36 W |
| Dog Creek ≏, Oh., U.S. | 216 | 41.03 N | 84.23 W |
| Dog Ear Creek ≏ | 198 | 43.42 N | 99.59 W |
| Dog Island I, Anguilla | 238 | 18.17 N | 63.16 W |
| Dog Island I, Fl., U.S. | 192 | 29.48 N | 84.35 W |
| Dog Islands II | 240m | 18.29 N | 64.28 W |
| Dog Lake ⊜, Mb., Can. | 184 | 51.02 N | 98.30 W |
| Dog Lake ⊜, On., Can. | 190 | 48.46 N | 89.32 W |
| Dog Lake ⊜, On., Can. | 190 | 48.18 N | 84.10 W |
| Dog Lake ⊜, On., Can. | 212 | 44.27 N | 76.20 W |
| Dogliani | 62 | 44.32 N | 7.56 E |
| Dogna | 64 | 46.27 N | 13.19 E |
| Dōgo I | 92 | 36.15 N | 133.16 E |
| Do Gonbadān | 128 | 30.21 N | 50.48 E |
| Dogondoutchi | 150 | 13.38 N | 4.02 E |
| Doğonşar | 130 | 40.14 N | 37.33 E |
| Dōgo-yama ∧ | 96 | 35.04 N | 133.14 E |
| Dogpound Creek ≏ | 182 | 51.50 N | 114.24 W |
| Dogs, Isle of I | 260 | 51.29 N | 0.01 W |
| D'ogtevo, Ross. | 78 | 49.10 N | 40.39 E |
| D'ogtevo, Ross. | 80 | 49.11 N | 40.39 E |
| Doğubayazıt | 84 | 39.32 N | 44.08 E |
| Doguéraoua | 150 | 13.58 N | 5.35 E |
| Doğu Karadeniz Dağları ⩙ | 130 | 40.30 N | 40.30 E |
| Dogura | 164 | 10.05 S | 150.05 E |
| Doha → Ad-Dawḥah | 128 | 25.17 N | 51.32 E |
| Dohār | 126 | 23.35 N | 90.09 E |
| Dohhi | 124 | 24.32 N | 84.54 E |
| Dohna | 54 | 50.57 N | 13.51 E |
| Döhren | 52 | 52.26 N | 9.02 E |
| Dohrgaul | 263 | 51.06 N | 7.27 E |
| Dohrīghāt | 124 | 26.16 N | 83.31 E |
| Doi | 96 | 33.57 N | 133.26 E |
| Doi, Kinh ≊ | 269c | 10.43 N | 106.37 E |
| Doilungdêqên | 124 | 29.48 N | 90.47 E |
| Doiran, Lake ⊜ | 38 | 41.13 N | 22.44 E |
| Doiras, Embalse de ⊜ [1] | 34 | 43.10 N | 6.45 W |
| Dois de Novembro, Cachoeira ∟ | 248 | 8.52 S | 62.16 W |
| Dois Irmãos, Pico ∧ | 287a | 22.59 S | 43.14 W |
| Dois Irmãos de Goiás | 250 | 9.16 S | 49.05 W |
| Doi Suthep-Pui National Park ♠ | 110 | 18.50 N | 98.50 E |
| Dōjō | 268 | 35.51 N | 139.37 E |
| Dōjō ⧫ [8] | 270 | 34.52 N | 135.14 E |
| Doka, Indon. | 164 | 6.39 S | 134.15 E |
| Doka, Sūd. | 140 | 13.31 N | 35.46 E |
| Doki ≏ | 96 | 34.18 N | 133.48 E |
| Dokka | 26 | 60.50 N | 10.05 E |
| Dokkum | 52 | 53.19 N | 6.00 E |
| Dökmetepe | 130 | 40.19 N | 36.18 E |
| Dokri | 120 | 27.23 N | 68.06 E |
| Dokská pahorkatina ⩙ [2] | 54 | 50.30 N | 14.45 E |
| Doksy | 54 | 50.35 N | 14.38 E |
| Dokšycy | 76 | 54.54 N | 27.46 E |
| Dokuchayevs'k | 83 | 47.44 N | 37.40 E |
| Dola | 216 | 40.47 N | 83.42 W |
| Dolak ≏ | 164 | 7.48 S | 139.00 E |
| Doland | 198 | 44.53 N | 98.06 W |
| Dolany | 60 | 49.27 N | 13.15 E |
| Dolavon | 254 | 43.18 S | 65.42 W |
| Dolayoba | 267b | 40.54 N | 29.15 E |
| Dolbeau | 176 | 48.53 N | 72.14 W |
| Dolberg | 52 | 51.42 N | 7.55 E |
| Dolceacqua | 62 | 43.51 N | 7.37 E |
| Dolcedorme, Serra ∧ | 68 | 39.53 N | 16.13 E |
| Dol-de-Bretagne | 32 | 48.33 N | 1.45 W |
| Dole | 58 | 47.06 N | 5.30 E |
| Dolega | 236 | 8.34 N | 82.25 W |
| Dolen | 222 | 30.26 N | 94.54 W |
| Dolgaja | 86 | 55.49 N | 64.15 E |
| Dolgaja, kosa ≻ [2] | 78 | 46.43 N | 37.41 E |
| Dolgarrog | 44 | 53.11 N | 3.51 W |
| Dolgelin | 54 | 52.29 N | 14.24 E |
| Dolgellau | 42 | 52.44 N | 3.53 W |
| Dolgeville | 210 | 43.06 N | 74.46 W |
| Dolgij, ostrov I | 24 | 69.15 N | 59.04 E |
| Dolgij Most | 88 | 56.45 N | 96.48 E |
| Dolgoi Island I | 180 | 55.10 N | 161.45 W |
| Dolgoje | 78 | 52.04 N | 37.34 E |
| Dolgoprudnyj | 82 | 55.56 N | 37.31 E |
| Dolgorukovo | 76 | 52.19 N | 38.21 E |
| Dolgoščelje | 24 | 66.03 N | 43.24 E |
| Dolianova | 71 | 39.22 N | 9.10 E |
| Dolinnyj | 80 | 51.16 N | 52.11 E |
| Dolinsk | 89 | 47.21 N | 142.48 E |
| Dolisie | 152 | 4.12 S | 12.41 E |
| Dolj □ [6] | 38 | 44.15 N | 23.45 E |
| Döllach | 64 | 46.58 N | 12.54 E |
| Dollar | 46 | 56.09 N | 3.40 W |
| Dollard c | 52 | 53.17 N | 7.10 E |
| Dollard-des-Ormeaux | 206 | 45.29 N | 73.49 W |
| Dollar Law ∧ | 46 | 55.33 N | 3.17 W |
| Döllbach | 56 | 50.26 N | 9.44 E |
| Dolle | 54 | 52.25 N | 11.37 E |
| Dollern | 52 | 53.32 N | 9.32 E |
| Dollerup | 41 | 54.46 N | 9.40 E |
| Döllnitz | 54 | 51.24 N | 12.01 E |
| Dollnstein | 60 | 48.52 N | 11.04 E |
| Döllstädt | 54 | 51.05 N | 10.49 E |
| Dolmabahce Palace ʊ | 267b | 41.02 N | 29.00 E |
| Dolmativka | 78 | 46.13 N | 32.26 E |
| Dolmatovskij | 80 | 57.29 N | 42.18 E |
| Dolni Dăbnik | 38 | 43.24 N | 24.26 E |
| Dolní Dvořiště | 61 | 48.39 N | 14.27 E |
| Dolní Jiřetín | 54 | 50.35 N | 13.33 E |
| Dolni Lom | 38 | 43.31 N | 22.47 E |
| Dolní Žandov | 60 | 50.02 N | 12.34 E |
| Dolný Kubín | 30 | 49.12 N | 19.17 E |
| Dolo | 64 | 45.25 N | 12.05 E |
| Dolohmwar ∧ | 174r | 6.52 N | 158.14 E |
| Dolokmerawan | 114 | 3.10 N | 99.08 E |
| Dolokparibuan | 114 | 3.01 N | 98.39 E |
| Dolomites → Dolomiti ⩙ | 64 | 46.25 N | 11.50 E |
| Dolomiti (Dolomiten) ⩙ | 64 | 46.25 N | 11.50 E |
| Dolon' | 86 | 50.40 N | 79.18 E |
| Dolon ≏ | 62 | 45.18 N | 4.46 E |
| Dolon, pereval )( | 85 | 41.52 N | 75.45 E |
| Dolores, Arg. | 252 | 36.20 S | 57.40 W |
| Dolores, Col. | 246 | 3.33 N | 74.54 W |


| Symbol | English | Deutsch | Español | Français | Português |
|---|---|---|---|---|---|
| ≏ | River | Fluß | Río | Rivière | Rio |
| ≊ | Canal | Kanal | Canal | Canal | Canal |
| ∟ | Waterfall, Rapids | Wasserfall, Stromschnellen | Cascada, Rápidos | Chute d'eau, Rapides | Cascata, Rápidos |
| ʯ | Strait | Meeresstraße | Estrecho | Détroit | Estreito |
| c | Bay, Gulf | Bucht, Golf | Bahía, Golfo | Baie, Golfe | Baía, Golfo |
| ⊜ | Lake, Lakes | See, Seen | Lago, Lagos | Lac, Lacs | Lago, Lagos |
| ≡ | Swamp | Sumpf | Pantano | Marais | Pântano |
| ⩎ | Ice Features, Glacier | Eis- und Gletscherformen | Accidentes Glaciales | Formes glaciaires | Acidentes glaciares |
| ⍑ | Other Hydrographic Features | Andere Hydrographische Objekte | Otros Elementos Hidrográficos | Autres données hydrographiques | Outros acidentes hidrográficos |
| ✣ | Submarine Features | Untermeerische Objekte | Accidentes Submarinos | Formes de relief sous-marin | Acidentes submarinos |
| □ | Political Unit | Politische Einheit | Unidad Politica | Entité politique | Unidade política |
| ʊ | Cultural Institution | Kulturelle Institution | Institución Cultural | Institution culturelle | Instituição cultural |
| ⊥ | Historical Site | Historische Stätte | Sitio Histórico | Site historique | Sitio histórico |
| ♠ | Recreational Site | Erholungs- und Ferienort | Sitio de Recreo | Centre de loisirs | Area de Lazer |
| ⊠ | Airport | Flughafen | Aeropuerto | Aéroport | Aeroporto |
| ■ | Military Installation | Militäranlage | Instalación Militar | Installation militaire | Instalação militar |
| ⧫ | Miscellaneous | Verschiedenes | Misceláneo | Divers | Diversos |

Dolores, Guat. 232 16.31 N 89.25 W
Dolores, Méx. 196 26.20 N 101.29 W
Dolores, Co., U.S. 200 37.28 N 108.30 W
Dolores, Ur. 252 33.33 S 58.13 W
Dolores, Ven. 246 8.18 N 69.34 W
Dolores ≃, Pil. 116 12.02 N 125.29 E
Dolores ≃, U.S. 200 38.49 N 109.17 W
Dolores, Mission ♁[1] 282 37.46 N 122.26 W
Dolores Hidalgo 234 21.10 N 100.56 W
Dolphin, Cape › 254 51.15 S 58.57 W
Dolphin and Union Strait ⊔ 176 69.05 N 114.45 W
Dolphin Head ∧ 241q 18.22 N 78.10 W
Dölsach 64 46.49 N 12.51 E
Dolsk 30 52.00 N 17.03 E
Dol'skoje 82 54.47 N 36.26 E
Dolton, Eng., U.K. 42 50.53 N 4.01 W
Dolton, Il., U.S. 216 41.38 N 87.36 W
Dolwyddelan 44 53.03 N 3.53 W
Dolyna, Ukr. 78 48.58 N 24.01 E
Dolyna, Ukr. 83 48.59 N 37.27 E
Dolyns'ka 78 48.07 N 32.44 E
Dolžanskaja 78 46.37 N 37.48 E
Dolzhak 78 48.41 N 26.32 E
Dolžicy, Ross. 76 58.00 N 29.51 E
Dolžicy, Ross. 76 58.31 N 29.08 E
Dom ∧ 58 46.06 N 7.50 E
Dom, Gunung ∧ 164 2.40 S 136.53 E
D'oma ≃ 86 54.42 N 55.57 E
Domacha 76 52.28 N 34.58 E
Domadare 144 1.50 N 41.13 E
Domaine, Pointe du › 275a 45.23 N 73.54 W
Domaniči 76 53.02 N 33.25 E
Domanico 68 39.13 N 16.12 E
Domanivka 78 47.37 N 30.58 E
Dom Aquino 255 15.48 S 54.53 W
Domar, Enneri V 146 18.11 N 18.04 E
Domariāganj 124 27.13 N 82.40 E
Domart-en-Ponthieu 50 50.04 N 2.07 E
Domasi 154 15.18 S 35.20 E
Domaška 80 53.00 N 50.47 E
Domaso 58 46.09 N 9.19 E
Domat/Ems 58 46.50 N 9.28 E
Domažlice 60 49.27 N 12.56 E
Dombaj 84 43.17 N 41.37 E
Dombaj-Ul'gen, gora ∧ 84 43.14 N 41.41 E
Dombarovskij 86 50.46 N 59.32 E
Dombås 26 62.05 N 9.08 E
Dombasle-sur-Meurthe 58 48.38 N 6.21 E
Dombe 156 19.59 S 33.25 E
Dombe Grande 152 12.58 S 13.11 E
Dombes ◂[1] 58 46.00 N 5.03 E
Dombóvár 30 46.23 N 18.08 E
Dombrád 30 48.14 N 21.56 E
Dombresson 58 47.04 N 6.58 E
Domburg 52 51.34 N 3.30 E
Dom Cavati 255 19.23 S 42.06 W
Dôme, Puy de ∧ 32 45.47 N 2.58 E
Dome Creek 182 53.44 N 121.01 W
Domegge di Cadore 64 46.27 N 12.25 E
Domène 62 45.12 N 5.50 E
Dome Peak ∧, Pil. 116 5.37 N 125.20 E
Dome Peak ∧, Wa., U.S. 224 48.18 N 121.02 W
Domett 172 42.51 S 173.13 E
Domèvre-en-Haye 56 48.49 N 5.55 E
Domeyko 252 28.57 S 70.54 W
Domeyko, Cordillera ∧∧ 252 24.30 S 69.00 W
Domfront 32 48.36 N 0.39 W
Domiciano Ribeiro 255 16.56 S 47.46 W
Domingo M. Irala 252 25.54 S 54.43 W
Domingos Martins 255 20.22 S 40.40 W
Dominguez 280 33.50 N 118.13 W
Dominguez Channel ⊔ 280 38.47 N 118.15 W
Dominguez Hills ∧∧[2] 280 33.52 N 118.14 W
Dominica □[1], N.A. 230 15.30 N 61.20 W
Dominica □[1], N.A. 240d 15.30 N 61.20 W
Dominicain (république) → Dominican Republic □[1] 238 19.00 N 70.40 W
Dominical 236 9.13 N 83.51 W
Dominicana, República → Dominican Republic □[1] 238 19.00 N 70.40 W
Dominican Republic (República Dominicana) □[1], N.A. 230 19.00 N 70.40 W
Dominican Republic (República Dominicana) □[1], N.A. 238 19.00 N 70.40 W
Dominica Passage ⊔ 238 15.45 N 61.30 W
Dominikanische Republik → Dominican Republic □[1] 238 19.00 N 70.40 W
Dominion 186 46.13 N 60.01 W
Dominion, Cape › 176 66.13 N 74.28 W
Dominion Astrophysical Observatory ♁[3] 224 48.31 N 123.25 W
Dominion City 184 49.08 N 97.09 W
Dominique → Dominica □[1] 240d 15.30 N 61.20 W
Domiongo 152 4.37 S 21.15 E
Domitilla, Catacombe di ⊥ 267a 41.52 N 12.31 E
Dömitz 54 53.08 N 11.14 E
Dom Joaquim 255 18.57 S 43.16 W
Domleschg V 58 46.44 N 9.28 E
Dommartin-lès-Toul 58 48.40 N 5.54 E
Dommartin-Varimont 56 48.58 N 4.46 E
Dommary-Baroncourt 56 49.17 N 5.42 E
Dommel ≃ 52 51.40 N 5.20 E
Dommitzsch 54 51.38 N 12.53 E
Domnarvet 40 60.30 N 15.27 E
Domnești 38 44.25 N 25.56 E
Domnino 82 54.10 N 38.11 E
Dom Noi ≃ 110 15.17 N 105.28 E
Domo 144 7.54 N 46.52 E
Domodedovo 82 55.26 N 37.46 E
Domodossola 58 46.07 N 8.17 E
Domohani 124 26.35 N 88.48 E
Domoni 157a 12.15 S 44.32 E
Domont 261 49.02 N 2.20 E
Dompaire 58 48.13 N 6.13 E
Dom Pedrito 252 30.59 S 54.40 W
Dom Pedro 250 4.29 S 44.27 W
Dom Pedro II, Estação ◂[5] 287a 23.54 S 43.12 W
Dompu 115b 8.32 S 118.28 E
Domremy 184 52.47 N 105.44 W
Domrémy-la-Pucelle 58 48.27 N 5.41 E
Domselaar 258 35.04 S 58.18 W
Dom Silvério 255 20.09 S 42.58 W
Domsjö 26 63.15 N 18.43 E
Domus de Maria 71 38.57 N 8.52 E
Domusnovas 71 39.19 N 8.39 E
Domuyo, Volcán ∧[1] 252 36.38 S 70.26 W
Domvast 50 50.12 N 1.55 E
Dom Viçoso 256 22.13 S 45.09 W
Dom Yai ≃ 110 15.18 N 105.10 E
Domžale 36 46.08 N 14.36 E
Don ≃, On., Can. 212 43.39 N 79.21 W
Don ≃, India 122 16.17 N 76.27 E
Don ≃, Lao 110 15.07 N 105.48 E
Don ≃, Ross. 72 47.04 N 39.18 E
Don ≃, Eng., U.K. 44 53.39 N 0.59 W
Don ≃, Eng., U.K. 262 53.47 N 2.14 W
Don ≃, Scot., U.K. 46 57.08 N 2.05 W
Don, East Branch ≃, On., Can. 212 43.42 N 79.20 W
Don, East Branch ≃, On., Can. 275b 43.43 N 79.20 W
Don, West Branch ≃ 275b 43.43 N 79.20 W
Dona Ana, Moç. 154 17.25 S 35.07 E
Dona Ana, N.M., U.S. 200 32.23 N 106.48 W
Donada 64 45.02 N 12.12 E
Donadeu 252 26.43 S 62.44 W
Dona Euzébia 256 21.18 S 42.48 W
Donaghadee 48 54.39 N 5.33 W
Donaghmore 48 54.32 N 6.49 W
Donahoe Creek ≃ 222 30.49 N 97.12 W
Donald 166 36.22 S 143.00 E
Donalda 182 52.35 N 112.34 W
Donaldson, Ar., U.S. 194 34.14 N 92.55 W
Donaldson, In., U.S. 216 41.22 N 86.27 W
Donaldson, Pa., U.S. 208 40.38 N 76.24 W
Donaldson Crossroads 279b 40.16 N 80.07 W
Donaldson Dam ⊜[1] 273d 26.17 S 27.41 E
Donaldsonville 194 30.06 N 90.59 W
Donalsonville 192 31.02 N 84.52 W
Doñana, Parque Nacional de ♦ 34 37.00 N 6.30 W
Donard, Slieve ∧ 48 54.11 N 5.55 W
Donau → Danube ≃ 22 45.20 N 29.40 E
Donaueschingen 58 47.57 N 8.29 E
Donaufeld ◂[8] 264b 48.15 N 16.25 E
Donaukanal ≅ 264b 48.10 N 16.30 E
Donaumoos ≡, Dtsch. 58 48.30 N 10.15 E
Donaumoos ≡, Dtsch. 60 48.40 N 11.15 E
Donaupark ♦ 264b 48.14 N 16.25 E
Donauried ◂[1] 56 48.35 N 10.40 E
Donaustadt ◂[8] 264b 48.13 N 16.30 E
Donaustauf 60 49.02 N 12.13 E
Donauturm ♁ 264b 48.14 N 16.25 E
Donauwörth 56 48.43 N 10.46 E
Don Benito 34 38.57 N 5.52 W
Dönberg ◂[8] 263 51.18 N 7.10 E
Don Bosco ◂[8] 258 34.42 S 58.18 W
Doncaster, Austl. 274b 37.47 S 145.08 E
Doncaster, On., Can. 275b 43.48 N 79.25 W
Doncaster, Eng., U.K. 44 53.32 N 1.07 W
Doncaster ≃ 206 45.58 N 74.06 W
Doncaster East 274b 37.47 S 145.10 E
Doncaster Indian Reserve ◂[4] 206 46.09 N 74.07 W
Donchéry 56 49.42 N 4.52 E
Dondaicha 120 21.20 N 74.34 E
Dondo, Ang. 152 9.38 S 14.25 E
Dondo, Moç. 156 19.36 S 34.44 E
Dondo, Teluk c 112 0.55 N 120.30 E
Dondra Head › 122 5.55 N 80.35 E
Donduşeni 38 48.15 N 27.37 E
Doneck 83 48.21 N 40.02 E
Donegal, Ire. 48 54.39 N 8.07 W
Donegal, S. Afr. 158 26.10 S 23.58 E
Donegal, Pa., U.S. 214 40.07 N 79.23 W
Donegal □[6] 48 54.50 N 8.00 W
Donegal Bay c 48 54.30 N 8.30 W
Doneraile, Ire. 48 52.13 N 8.35 W
Doneraile, S.C., U.S. 192 34.19 N 79.53 W
Donets'k 83 48.00 N 37.48 E
Donets'k □[4] 78 48.00 N 37.30 E
Donets'kyy ◂[8] 83 48.42 N 38.41 E
Donets'kyy kryazh ∧ 83 48.15 N 38.45 E
Dong ≃, Zhg. 100 23.06 N 114.00 E
Dong ≃, Zhg. 100 25.00 N 118.27 E
Dong ≃, Zhg. 100 23.42 N 117.13 E
Dong ≃, Zhg. 102 42.10 N 101.00 E
Donga ≃ 146 8.19 N 9.58 E
Dong'an, Zhg. 89 47.20 N 134.10 E
Dongan → Mishan, Zhg. 89 45.33 N 131.52 E
Dong'an, Zhg. 100 33.24 N 114.24 E
Dong'an, Zhg. 102 26.17 N 111.07 E
Dong'an, Zhg. 106 30.30 N 118.48 E
Dong'an, Zhg. 106 31.35 N 119.44 E
Dongao 100 29.12 N 121.25 E
Dongara 162 29.15 S 114.56 E
Dongargarh 120 21.12 N 80.44 E
Dongba, Zhg. 105 39.58 N 116.32 E
Dongba, Zhg. 106 31.18 N 119.03 E
Dongbahe 105 39.58 N 116.27 E
Dongbaimiao 105 40.34 N 116.05 E
Dongbei 100 27.15 N 116.06 E
Dongbeicha 98 41.43 N 127.23 E
Dongbeijipo 98 36.06 N 117.08 E
Dongchan 107 30.20 N 105.20 E
Dongchang 106 31.52 N 121.38 E
Dongchangjie 106 32.04 N 119.18 E
Dongcheng 100 28.56 N 121.16 E
Dongchong 100 26.35 N 119.52 E
Dongchuan (Xincun) 102 26.10 N 103.01 E
Dongcun 106 30.57 N 121.46 E
Dongdaoan 98 38.21 N 117.12 E
Dong Dian ≡ 105 39.03 N 116.35 E
Dongduluo 105 39.04 N 115.15 E
Dong'e (Tongcheng) 98 36.14 N 116.16 E
Dongen 52 51.37 N 4.56 E
Dong'ezhen 98 36.11 N 116.16 E
Dongfang (Basuo) 110 19.05 N 108.39 E
Dongfeng, Zhg. 98 42.40 N 125.28 E
Dongfeng, Zhg. 100 27.20 N 118.53 E
Dongfengtai 105 39.34 N 117.45 E
Donggala 112 0.40 S 119.44 E
Donggang 100 22.58 N 115.57 E
Donggangzi 89 45.53 N 129.49 E
Donggi 112 1.33 S 122.15 E
Donggi Cona ⊜ 102 37.10 N 96.55 E
Donggong Shan ∧∧ 100 27.36 N 119.26 E
Donggongsuo 106 32.07 N 121.25 E
Donggou, Zhg. 98 39.54 N 124.09 E
Donggou, Zhg. 100 33.38 N 119.40 E
Donggou, Zhg. 106 32.17 N 118.59 E
Donggu 100 26.46 N 115.22 E
Dongguan, Zhg. 100 27.49 N 116.25 E
Dongguan, Zhg. 100 23.03 N 113.46 E
Dongguan, Zhg. 106 30.22 N 119.28 E
Dongguan, Zhg. 107 30.47 N 106.16 E
Dongguang 98 37.53 N 116.30 E
Dongguanpu 106 31.13 N 120.43 E
Dongguanyingzi 104 41.55 N 120.38 E
Donggugang 105 39.10 N 116.49 E
Dong Hai, Viet 110 12.34 N 109.14 E
Donghai (Niushan), Zhg. 98 34.30 N 118.47 E
Dong Hai → East China Sea ⊤[2] 90 30.00 N 126.00 E
Donghai Dao I 102 21.02 N 110.25 E
Dongheng ≅ 106 31.54 N 120.17 E
Donghezhen 106 31.08 N 120.17 E
Dong Hoi 110 17.29 N 106.36 E
Donghu 100 26.28 N 113.07 E
Dong Hu ⊜ 120 32.10 N 84.40 E
Donghuanggou 104 40.43 N 123.29 E
Dongi 112 2.02 S 121.28 E
Dongio 58 46.27 N 8.58 E
Dongjia 98 37.18 N 118.24 E
Dongjiangkou 102 33.37 N 108.49 E
Dongjie 100 25.53 N 116.22 E
Dongjielang 100 31.03 N 115.57 E
Dongjingcheng 89 44.07 N 129.09 E
Dongjingji 98 40.02 N 114.01 E
Dongjingling 104 41.18 N 123.15 E
Dongjug 120 29.58 N 94.53 E
Dongkaihecheng 104 41.04 N 122.38 E
Dongkalang 112 0.10 N 120.06 E
Dongkeng, Zhg. 100 24.59 N 114.54 E
Dongkeng, Zhg. 100 27.48 N 119.42 E
Dong Khe 110 22.26 N 106.27 E
Dongkou 98 35.29 N 115.20 E
Donglan 102 24.40 N 107.18 E
Donglaohuyu 104 42.28 N 124.17 E
Donglaojunpu 104 41.24 N 121.22 E
Dongli 102 20.50 N 110.20 E
Dongliang 104 42.00 N 121.25 E
Dongliangjia 105 40.52 N 118.17 E
Donglidian 98 36.02 N 118.23 E
Donglinchang 107 29.39 N 104.07 E
Dongling 104 41.50 N 123.35 E
Dongliu, Zhg. 100 30.14 N 116.53 E
Dongliu, Zhg. 106 32.06 N 118.58 E
Dongliujiazi 104 42.21 N 122.44 E
Donglizhuang 105 39.21 N 116.47 E
Donglong 100 23.36 N 116.50 E
Donglucun 89 49.28 N 128.50 E
Dongmen 100 28.29 N 114.02 E
Dongming 98 35.18 N 115.08 E
Dong Nai ≃ 110 10.45 N 106.46 E
Dongnangou 104 41.25 N 122.02 E
Dong Nhien, Rach ≃ 269c 10.49 N 106.46 E
Dongning 89 44.04 N 131.07 E
Dongo, Ang. 152 14.36 S 15.48 E
Dongo, It. 58 46.07 N 9.17 E
Dongo, Zaïre 152 2.43 N 18.24 E
Dongobe 152 4.37 N 23.12 E
Dongobesh 154 4.04 S 35.23 E
Dongola → Dunqulah 140 19.10 N 30.29 E
Dongon Point › 116 12.44 N 120.48 E
Dongou 152 2.02 N 18.04 E
Dongping, Zhg. 98 35.55 N 116.18 E
Dongping, Zhg. 100 27.24 N 118.39 E
Dongping, Zhg. 102 21.43 N 112.15 E
Dongping Hu ⊜ 98 36.00 N 116.12 E
Dongpu 100 30.03 N 120.34 E
Dongqian 106 30.52 N 120.23 E
Dongqiao 100 31.12 N 112.48 E
Dongqing 106 31.49 N 120.03 E
Dongqingduizi 104 41.02 N 122.08 E
Dongsanjiazi 104 41.54 N 122.48 E
Dongsanlintang 106 31.09 N 121.31 E
Dongsanpu 100 33.38 N 117.09 E
Dongsha ≃ 104 41.07 N 121.50 E
Dongshaer 120 28.41 N 89.09 E
Dongshajiao 100 30.19 N 122.09 E
Dongshan, Zhg. 100 23.42 N 117.24 E
Dongshan, Zhg. 102 19.50 N 110.14 E
Dongshan, Zhg. 106 31.04 N 120.24 E
Dongshan Dao I 100 23.40 N 117.25 E
Dongshanqiao 106 31.52 N 118.46 E
Dongshe 106 32.07 N 121.12 E
Dongsheng 102 39.49 N 109.59 E
Dongsheshanzi 104 42.15 N 123.09 E
Dongshi, Zhg. 100 24.42 N 118.27 E
Dongshi, Zhg. 100 24.43 N 115.59 E
Dongshi, Zhg. 271a 39.49 N 116.34 E
Dongshuiyan 105 39.15 N 115.23 E
Dongtai 100 32.51 N 120.20 E
Dongtai Hu c 106 31.05 N 120.30 E
Dongtaipingzhen 89 45.18 N 122.05 E
Dongtangou 105 39.23 N 118.22 E
Dongtianmu Shan ∧ 106 30.22 N 119.31 E
Dongtiao ≃ 106 30.51 N 120.06 E
Dongting 98 38.29 N 115.08 E
Dongtinghu 106 30.53 N 119.30 E
Dongting Hu ⊜ 102 29.20 N 112.54 E
Dongtingxi 102 28.34 N 110.36 E
Dongtou 100 27.50 N 121.09 E
Dongtou Shan I 100 27.50 N 121.08 E
Dong Trieu 110 21.05 N 106.31 E
Dongtuhulu 104 41.55 N 121.33 E
Dongtuoshanzi 104 42.10 N 123.08 E
Dongtuozi 104 41.17 N 121.53 E
Dong Van 110 23.16 N 105.22 E
Dongwangfu 89 44.47 N 120.53 E
Dongwangzhuang 106 32.16 N 120.32 E
Dongwe ≃ 152 13.58 S 23.53 E
Dongwuquan 105 39.20 N 115.43 E
Dongxi, Zhg. 100 28.35 N 120.02 E
Dongxi, Zhg. 102 28.47 N 106.39 E
Dongxi, Zhg. 107 30.24 N 104.33 E
Dongxia 106 31.11 N 119.05 E
Dongxiagaogao 104 42.36 N 122.30 E
Dongxiang 100 28.13 N 116.35 E
Dongxiang Dao I 100 25.36 N 119.48 E
Dongxing 89 46.23 N 127.52 E
Dongxingchang, Zhg. 107 29.16 N 103.55 E
Dongxingchang, Zhg. 107 29.36 N 105.04 E
Dongxinghe 105 39.46 N 114.49 E
Dongxinpu 104 41.00 N 123.18 E
Dongxinzhen 106 31.57 N 121.42 E
Dongyang, Zhg. 89 48.03 N 124.17 E
Dongyang, Zhg. 100 29.16 N 120.14 E
Dongyangqiao 106 30.52 N 120.34 E
Dongyao 98 35.56 N 113.58 E
Dongyian 105 39.22 N 115.46 E
Dongyin ≃ 105 39.09 N 117.43 E
Dongyou 100 27.10 N 118.37 E
Dongyuemiao 106 31.36 N 119.14 E
Dongyuezhen 107 30.24 N 103.32 E
Dongzhang 100 25.44 N 119.17 E
Dongzhaocun 105 40.02 N 116.46 E
Dongzhaozhuang 105 39.57 N 118.24 E
Dongzhenbeng 106 30.59 N 121.01 E
Dongzhi 100 30.07 N 116.59 E
Dongzhizhuang 105 40.25 N 116.50 E
Dongzhuangpu 105 40.34 N 115.42 E
Dongziya 105 38.50 N 116.44 E
Donie 222 31.29 N 96.13 W
Doninga 150 10.37 N 1.26 W
Donington 42 52.55 N 0.12 W
Doniphan, Mo., U.S. 194 36.37 N 90.49 W
Doniphan, Ne., U.S. 198 40.46 N 98.22 W
Don Islands II 116 11.05 N 123.38 E
Donja Stubica 36 45.59 N 15.58 E
Donjek ≃ 180 62.35 N 140.00 W
Donjezk → Donets'k 83 48.00 N 37.48 E
Donji Vakuf 36 44.09 N 17.25 E
Donk 52 51.33 N 5.37 E
Donkerpoort 158 30.32 S 25.30 E
Donkey Creek ≃ 198 44.12 N 104.58 W
Donkey Town 260 51.20 N 0.39 W
Donmānick Islands II 126 22.00 N 90.37 E
Don Martín 196 27.32 N 100.37 W
Don Matías 246 6.30 N 75.22 W
Don Mills ◂[8] 275b 43.44 N 79.20 W
Don Mills Centre ◂[9] 275b 43.44 N 79.21 W
Don Muang Airport ⊠ 269a 13.56 N 100.37 E
Donna 196 26.10 N 98.03 W
Donna, Punta sa ∧ 71 40.35 N 9.25 E
Donna Buang, Mount ∧ 169 37.43 S 145.40 E
Donnacona 206 46.40 N 71.47 W
Donnalucata 70 36.45 N 14.38 E
Donnaz 62 45.36 N 7.46 E
Donnell Lake ⊜[1] 226 38.20 N 119.56 W
Donnellson 219 39.02 N 89.29 W
Donnelly, Ab., Can. 182 55.44 N 117.06 W
Donnelly, Ak., U.S. 180 63.41 N 145.53 W
Donnelly, Id., U.S. 202 44.43 N 116.04 W
Donnellys Crossing 172 35.43 S 173.37 E
Donnemarie-Dontilly 50 48.29 N 3.08 E
Donner 194 29.41 N 90.56 W
Donner Lake ⊜[1] 226 39.20 N 120.16 W
Donner Memorial State Park ♦ 226 39.18 N 120.16 W
Donner Pass )( 226 39.19 N 120.20 W
Donnersberg ∧ 56 49.38 N 7.55 E
Donner und Blitzen ≃ 202 43.17 N 118.49 W
Donnybrook, Austl. 162 33.35 S 115.49 E
Donnybrook, S. Afr. 158 30.00 S 29.48 E
Donora 214 40.10 N 79.51 W
Donostia (San Sebastián) 34 43.19 N 1.59 W
Donovan 216 40.53 N 87.37 W
Don Peninsula ›[1] 182 52.30 N 128.10 W
Donque 152 15.28 S 14.06 E
Donskaja gr'ada ∧∧[2] 80 49.30 N 42.00 E
Dons'ke 83 47.31 N 37.33 E
Donskoj, Ross. 76 53.58 N 38.20 E
Donskoj, Ross. 83 48.49 N 40.06 E
Donskoj, Ross. 83 47.25 N 40.14 E
Donskoje, Ross. 76 52.37 N 39.00 E
Donskoje, Ross. 80 45.21 N 41.59 E
Donskoje belogorje ∧∧[1] 78 50.30 N 39.45 E
Donsol 116 12.54 N 123.36 E
Don Torcuato 288 34.30 S 58.38 W
Don Torcuato, Aeródromo ⊠ 288 34.30 S 58.36 W
Dontsivka 83 49.35 N 39.16 E
Donuzlav, ozero ⊜ 78 45.23 N 33.05 E
Donyztau, čink ∧∧ 86 46.25 N 57.00 E
Donzdorf 56 48.41 N 9.48 E
Donzère 62 44.27 N 4.43 E
Donzy 50 47.22 N 3.08 E
Dooagh 48 53.59 N 10.09 W
Dood nuur ⊜ 88 51.20 N 99.20 E
Doogort 48 54.01 N 10.01 W
Doolow 144 4.10 N 42.05 E
Doomadgee 166 17.56 S 138.49 E
Doomadgee Aboriginal Reserve ◂[4] 166 17.43 S 138.36 E
Doon, On., Can. 212 43.23 N 80.26 W
Doon, Ia., U.S. 198 43.16 N 96.13 W
Doon ≃ 44 55.26 N 4.38 W
Doon, Loch ⊜ 44 55.15 N 4.22 W
Doonbeg 48 52.44 N 9.32 W
Doonbeg ≃ 48 52.44 N 9.34 W
Doon Doon Aboriginal Reserve ◂[4] 164 16.15 S 128.15 E
Doonerak, Mount ∧ 180 67.56 N 150.37 W
Doonside 274a 33.46 S 150.52 E
Dooralong 170 33.12 S 151.22 E
Doorn 52 52.03 N 5.21 E
Doorndam 158 28.03 S 21.03 E
Doornik → Tournai 50 50.36 N 3.23 E
Door Peninsula ›[1] 190 44.55 N 87.20 W
Dopping Brook ≃ 283 42.12 N 71.23 W
Do Qal'eh 128 32.18 N 61.31 E
Dor 132 32.37 N 34.55 E
Dora 194 33.43 N 87.05 W
Dora, Lake ⊜, Austl. 162 22.05 S 122.55 E
Dora, Lake ⊜, Fl., U.S. 220 29.00 N 81.37 W
Dora Baltea ≃ 62 45.11 N 8.05 E
Dora di Rhêmes ≃ 62 45.42 N 7.11 E
Dorado 240m 18.28 N 66.15 W
Dorāha 123 30.49 N 76.01 E
Dorāh Ān )( 123 36.07 N 71.15 E
Dorain, Beinn ∧ 46 56.30 N 4.42 W
Dorândia 256 22.27 S 43.57 W
Dora Riparia ≃ 62 45.05 N 7.44 E
Doraville 192 33.53 N 84.17 W
Dorback Burn ≃ 46 57.31 N 3.40 W
Dorcheat, Bayou ≃ 194 32.30 N 93.21 W
Dorchester, N.B., Can. 186 45.54 N 64.31 W
Dorchester, On., Can. 212 42.59 N 81.04 W
Dorchester, Eng., U.K. 42 50.43 N 2.26 W
Dorchester, Eng., U.K. 42 51.39 N 1.10 W
Dorchester, Il., U.S. 219 39.05 N 89.53 W
Dorchester, Ne., U.S. 198 40.38 N 97.06 W
Dorchester, N.J., U.S. 208 39.16 N 74.58 W
Dorchester, Wi., U.S. 190 45.00 N 90.20 W
Dorchester □[6] 208 38.34 N 76.04 W
Dorchester ◂[8] 283 42.17 N 71.04 W
Dorchester, Cape › 176 65.29 N 77.30 W
Dorchester Bay c 283 42.19 N 71.02 W
Dorchester Crossing 186 46.10 N 64.34 W
Dorchester Estates 284c 38.47 N 76.55 W
Dorchester Heights National Historic Site ⊥ 283 42.20 N 71.03 W
Dorchheim 56 50.30 N 8.04 E
Dordabis 156 22.52 S 17.38 E
Dordives 50 48.09 N 2.46 E
Dordogne □[5] 32 45.10 N 0.45 E
Dordogne ≃ 32 45.02 N 0.35 W
Dordon 42 52.36 N 1.37 W
Dordrecht, Ned. 52 51.49 N 4.40 E
Dordrecht, S. Afr. 158 31.20 S 27.03 E
Doré ≃, Sk., Can. 184 54.56 N 107.45 W
Dore ≃, Fr. 62 45.50 N 3.35 E
Dore ≃, Eng., U.K. 42 51.57 N 2.52 W
Dore, Monts ∧∧ 32 45.30 N 2.45 E
Doreissou 146 10.33 N 15.08 E
Doré Lake 184 54.38 N 107.24 W
Doré Lake ⊜ 184 54.46 N 107.17 W
Dorena 202 43.43 N 122.51 W
Dörentrup 52 52.03 N 8.59 E
Dores 46 57.22 N 4.15 W
Dores do Indaiá 255 19.27 S 45.36 W
Dores do Paraibuna 256 21.31 S 43.39 W
Dorfen 60 48.17 N 12.08 E
Dorfgastein 64 47.15 N 13.06 E
Dorfmark 52 52.54 N 9.46 E
Dorgali 71 40.17 N 9.35 E
Dörgön nuur ⊜ 88 47.40 N 93.30 E
Doring ≃ 158 31.54 S 18.39 E
Doringbaai 158 31.48 S 18.15 E
Doringkop ∧ 273d 26.15 S 27.50 E
Dorino 82 56.28 N 36.09 E
Dorion-Vaudreuil 206 45.23 N 74.01 W
Dorje Lāpka ∧ 124 28.11 N 85.47 E
Dorking 42 51.14 N 0.20 W
Dorloo 210 42.43 N 74.37 W
Dormaa Ahenkro 150 7.17 N 2.53 W
Dormagen 56 51.05 N 6.50 E
Dormans 50 49.04 N 3.38 E
Dormidontovka 89 47.45 N 134.57 E
Dormont 279b 40.23 N 80.02 W
Dornach 58 47.29 N 7.37 E
Dornap ◂[8] 263 51.15 N 7.04 E
Dornbach ◂[8] 264b 48.14 N 16.18 E
Dornbirn 58 47.25 N 9.44 E
Dornburg, Dtsch. 54 51.01 N 11.40 E
Dornburg, Dtsch. 56 50.30 N 8.07 E
Dorndorf 56 50.50 N 10.05 E
Dorndorf-Steudnitz 54 51.00 N 11.40 E
Dornecy 50 47.26 N 3.35 E
Dorney 260 51.30 N 0.40 W
Dornhan 58 48.21 N 8.30 E
Dornie 46 57.17 N 5.31 W
Dorno 62 45.09 N 8.57 E
Dornoch 46 57.52 N 4.02 W
Dornoch Firth c[1] 46 57.53 N 4.00 W
Dornod □[4] 88 48.00 N 115.00 E
Dornogov' □[4] 102 44.30 N 110.00 E
Dornsife 208 40.45 N 76.47 W
Dornstadt 58 48.28 N 9.56 E
Dornstetten 58 48.28 N 8.30 E
Dornumersiel 52 53.40 N 7.28 E
Doro, Indon. 115a 7.02 S 109.41 E
Doro, Mali 150 16.09 N 0.51 W
Dorochovo 82 55.33 N 36.23 E
Dorog 30 47.43 N 18.44 E
Dorogobuž 76 54.55 N 33.18 E
Doroḩ 128 32.17 N 60.30 E
Dorohoi 38 47.57 N 26.24 E
Dorokempo 115b 8.33 S 118.15 E
Doromata 115b 8.46 S 118.13 E
Doromo 154 3.49 N 26.17 E
Dorošata 80 57.21 N 51.08 E
Dorošicha 82 56.52 N 35.50 E
Dorotea 26 64.16 N 16.24 E
Dorothy 208 39.24 N 74.49 W
Dorothy, Lake ⊜ 224 47.34 N 121.22 W
Dorotockeys Run ≃ 276 40.59 N 73.58 W
Dorpat → Tartu 76 58.23 N 26.43 E
Dörpen 52 52.57 N 7.20 E
Dorr 216 42.43 N 85.43 W
Dorrance 198 38.50 N 98.35 W
Dorre Island I 162 25.09 S 113.07 E
Dorrigo 166 30.21 S 152.43 E
Dorris 204 41.58 N 121.55 W
Dorsale ∧∧ 36 36.00 N 9.50 E
Dorset, Oh., U.S. 214 41.41 N 80.40 W
Dorset, Vt., U.S. 210 43.15 N 73.05 W
Dorset □[6] 42 50.47 N 2.20 W
Dorset Peak ∧ 188 43.19 N 73.02 W
Dorsey Run ≃ 284b 39.11 N 76.48 W
Dorseyville 279b 40.35 N 79.53 W


| ENGLISH Name | Page | Lat.°′ | Long.°′ |
|---|---|---|---|


Dorsten 52 51.39 N 6.58 E
Dorstfeld ◂[8] 263 51.31 N 7.25 E
Dort → Dordrecht 52 51.49 N 4.40 E
Dortan 58 46.19 N 5.40 E
Dörtdivan 130 40.43 N 32.04 E
Dortmund, Dtsch. 52 51.31 N 7.28 E
Dortmund, Dtsch. 263 51.31 N 7.28 E
Dortmund-Ems-Kanal ≅ 52 51.32 N 7.27 E
Dortmunder Rieselfelder ◂[1] 263 51.39 N 7.25 E
Dortmund-Wickede, Flughafen ⊠ 263 51.32 N 7.35 E
Dorton 192 37.16 N 82.34 W
Dörtyol 130 36.52 N 36.12 E
Do Rūd 128 33.28 N 49.04 E
Dorum 52 53.41 N 8.34 E
Doruma 154 4.44 N 27.42 E
Dorval 206 45.27 N 73.44 W
Dorval, Île I 275a 45.26 N 73.45 W
Dorval Gardens Centre ◂[9] 275a 45.27 N 73.44 W
Dörverden 52 52.51 N 9.13 E
Dörvöldžin 88 48.08 N 93.58 E
Dörzbach 56 49.23 N 9.42 E
Dos, Canal Numero ≅ 252 36.21 S 56.54 W
Dosara 150 12.32 N 6.09 E
Do Sārī 128 28.25 N 57.59 E
Dos Arroyos 234 17.02 N 99.40 W
Dosatuj 88 50.23 N 118.38 E
Dos Bahías, Cabo › 254 44.55 S 65.32 W
Dos Bocas 240m 18.20 N 66.40 W
Dos Bocas, Lago ⊜[1] 240m 18.19 N 66.40 W
Dosčatoje 80 55.23 N 42.07 E
Döşemealtı 130 37.04 N 30.36 E
Dosewallips ≃ 224 47.42 N 122.53 W
Dos Hermanas 34 37.17 N 5.55 W
Dos Hermanas, Islas II 258 34.05 S 58.17 W
Dōshi 94 35.32 N 139.02 E
Dōshi ≃ 94 35.36 N 139.14 E
Doshisha University ♁[2] 270 35.02 N 135.46 E
Dosi 164 5.56 S 134.34 E
Dösjebro 41 55.49 N 13.01 E
Do Son 110 20.42 N 106.47 E
Dosoris Island ›[1] 276 40.53 N 73.38 W
Dosoris Pond ⊜ 276 40.54 N 73.38 W
Dos Pos 241s 12.15 N 68.20 W
Dos Quebradas 246 4.51 N 75.40 W
Dos Reyes, Punta › 252 24.33 S 70.35 W
Dosse ≃ 54 53.13 N 12.20 E
Dosséo, Bahr ≃ 146 9.01 N 19.38 E
Dossin Great Lakes Museum ♁ 281 42.20 N 82.59 W
Dosso 150 13.03 N 3.12 E
Dosso □[5] 150 13.00 N 3.00 E
Dossor 80 47.32 N 53.01 E
Doster 216 42.27 N 85.33 W
Doswell 208 37.51 N 77.27 W
Dothan 194 31.13 N 85.23 W
Doting Cove 186 49.27 N 53.57 W
Dot Lake 180 63.40 N 144.04 W
Dötlingen 52 52.56 N 8.23 E
Dotnuva 76 55.21 N 23.54 E
Dotson 222 32.01 N 94.31 W
Döttingen 58 47.34 N 8.16 E
Doty 224 46.38 N 123.16 W
Dou ≃ 105 39.13 N 118.03 E
Douai 50 50.22 N 3.04 E
Douala 152 4.03 N 9.42 E
Douala-Edéa, Réserve de ◂[4] 152 4.30 S 9.50 E
Douarnenez 32 48.06 N 4.20 W
Doubabougou 150 14.13 N 7.59 W
Double, Lac ⊜ 186 50.46 N 70.23 W
Doublé, Pointe › 241o 16.20 N 61.00 W
Double Bayou 222 29.41 N 94.39 W
Double Cone ∧ 172 45.04 S 168.48 E
Double Island Point › 166 25.56 S 153.11 E
Double Mountain ∧ 228 35.02 N 118.29 W
Double Point › 166 17.39 S 146.09 E
Double Springs 194 34.08 N 87.24 W
Doubletop Peak ∧ 200 43.21 N 110.17 W
Doubs 58 46.56 N 6.21 E
Doubs □[5] 58 47.10 N 6.25 E
Doubs ≃ 58 46.54 N 5.02 E
Doubs, Saut de ∟ 58 47.05 N 6.43 E
Doubtful Sound ⊔ 172 45.17 S 166.51 E
Doubtless Bay c 172 34.55 S 173.25 E
Douchy 50 47.57 N 3.03 E
Douchy-les-Mines 50 50.18 N 3.23 E
Doudeville 50 49.43 N 0.48 E
Doudian 105 39.39 N 116.03 E
Doué ≃[1] 150 16.38 N 15.02 W
Douentza 150 15.00 N 2.57 W
Dougga ⊥ 36 36.25 N 9.13 E
Doughboy 170 35.15 S 149.39 E
Doughboy Bay c 172 47.02 S 167.41 E
Douglas, Austl. 164 16.29 S 145.28 E
Douglas, Mb., Can. 184 49.53 N 99.42 W
Douglas, On., Can. 212 45.31 N 76.56 W
Douglas, I. of Man 44 54.09 N 4.28 W
Douglas, S. Afr. 158 29.04 S 23.46 E
Douglas, Scot., U.K. 46 55.33 N 3.51 W
Douglas, Ak., U.S. 180 58.16 N 134.22 W
Douglas, Az., U.S. 200 31.20 N 109.32 W
Douglas, Ga., U.S. 192 31.30 N 82.51 W
Douglas, Mi., U.S. 216 42.38 N 86.12 W
Douglas, N.D., U.S. 198 47.51 N 101.30 W
Douglas, Wy., U.S. 200 42.45 N 105.22 W
Douglas □[6] 226 38.55 N 119.39 W
Douglas ≃ 44 53.43 N 2.50 W
Douglas, Cape › 180 58.52 N 153.18 W
Douglas, Mount ∧ 180 58.52 N 153.31 W
Douglas, Mount ∧[2] 162 28.39 S 123.53 E
Douglas Aircraft Company ♁[3] 280 33.50 N 118.09 W
Douglas Channel ⊔ 182 53.30 N 129.12 W
Douglas Creek ≃ 200 40.06 N 108.46 W
Douglas Lake 182 50.10 N 120.12 W
Douglas Lake ⊜[1] 192 36.00 N 83.22 W
Douglas Lake Indian Reserve ◂[4] 182 50.10 N 120.49 W
Douglas Park 170 34.11 S 150.43 E
Douglas Park ♦ 278 41.52 N 87.42 W
Douglass, Ks., U.S. 198 37.31 N 97.01 W
Douglass, Tx., U.S. 222 31.40 N 94.53 W
Douglass Run ≃ 279b 40.15 N 79.48 W
Douglassville 208 40.15 N 75.44 W
Douglasville 192 33.45 N 84.44 W
Douglas Water ≃ 46 55.38 N 3.46 W
Dougouzi, Zhg. 89 49.57 N 127.01 E
Dougouzi, Zhg. 104 41.16 N 122.34 E
Douhutun 98 42.06 N 124.50 E
Douigny 152 3.11 S 10.45 E
Doujiapu 104 41.05 N 122.12 E
Doujiazhuang 105 40.22 N 116.59 E
Doukkane, Djebel ∧ 36 35.23 N 8.00 E
Doulaincourt 58 48.19 N 5.12 E
Doulevant-le-Château 58 48.23 N 4.55 E
Doullens 50 50.09 N 2.21 E
Doumanaba 150 11.40 N 5.56 W
Doumanga 152 2.41 S 12.40 E
Doumba Bélo 152 5.05 N 14.18 E
Doumdégué 152 7.29 N 18.58 E
Doumé, Cam. 152 4.14 N 13.27 E
Doumé, Cam. 152 5.32 N 12.19 E
Doumé ≃ 152 4.06 N 14.34 E
Doumen, Zhg. 100 22.12 N 113.16 E
Doumen, Zhg. 105 39.18 N 115.53 E
Douna 150 14.39 N 1.44 W
Doune 46 56.12 N 4.05 W
Doune Castle ⊥ 46 56.11 N 4.03 W
Dounguila 152 2.53 S 11.58 E
Doupov 54 50.10 N 13.08 E
Doupovské hory ∧∧ 54 50.13 N 13.08 E
Dour 50 50.24 N 3.47 E
Doura 150 13.14 N 5.55 W


| DEUTSCH Name | Seite | Breite°′ | Länge°′ E = Ost |
|---|---|---|---|


Dourada, Serra ∧∧[1] 255 13.10 S 48.45 W
Douradinho 256 21.45 S 45.46 W
Dourado ≃ 256 21.43 S 45.44 W
Dourados 255 22.13 S 54.48 W
Dourados ≃ 255 21.58 S 54.18 W
Dourbali 146 11.49 N 15.52 E
Dourdan 50 48.32 N 2.01 E
Dourdou ≃ 32 44.00 N 2.41 E
Dourges 50 50.26 N 2.59 E
Dourkoulé 146 14.27 N 22.13 E
Douro ≃, Bra. 287a 22.42 S 43.35 W
Douro (Duero) ≃, Europe 34 41.08 N 8.40 W
Doushanhe 100 31.38 N 114.42 E
Dousman 216 43.00 N 88.28 W
Douthat State Park ♦ 192 37.55 N 79.50 W
Douvaine 58 46.19 N 6.18 E
Douvres → Dover 42 51.08 N 1.19 E
Douvres, Falaises de ±[4] 273b 4.06 S 15.25 E
Douvrin 50 50.31 N 2.50 E
Doux ≃ 62 45.04 N 4.50 E
Douy-la-Ramée 261 49.04 N 2.53 E
Douyu 98 37.53 N 114.30 E
Douz 148 33.28 N 9.01 E
Douze ≃ 32 43.54 N 0.30 W
Douzhangzhuang 105 39.23 N 116.55 E
Douzishan 107 29.04 N 104.57 E
Douziyu 105 40.18 N 117.19 E
Douzy 56 49.40 N 5.03 E
Dovadola 66 44.07 N 11.53 E
Dovbysh 78 50.22 N 27.59 E
Dove ≃, Eng., U.K. 44 52.50 N 1.35 W
Dove ≃, Eng., U.K. 44 54.12 N 0.54 W
Dove Creek 200 37.45 N 108.54 W
Dove Creek ≃, Tx., U.S. 196 31.20 N 100.36 W
Dove Creek ≃, Ut., U.S. 200 41.37 N 113.15 W
Dove Holes 262 53.18 N 1.53 W
Dove Holes Tunnel ◂[5] 262 53.18 N 1.53 W
Dover, Austl. 166 43.19 S 147.01 E
Dover, S. Afr. 158 27.02 S 27.46 E
Dover, Eng., U.K. 42 51.08 N 1.19 E
Dover, Ar., U.S. 194 35.24 N 93.06 W
Dover, De., U.S. 208 39.09 N 75.31 W
Dover, Fl., U.S. 220 27.59 N 82.13 W
Dover, Id., U.S. 202 48.15 N 116.36 W
Dover, Ky., U.S. 218 38.45 N 83.52 W
Dover, Ma., U.S. 283 42.14 N 71.17 W
Dover, N.H., U.S. 188 43.11 N 70.52 W
Dover, N.J., U.S. 210 40.53 N 74.34 W
Dover, N.C., U.S. 192 35.12 N 77.26 W
Dover, Oh., U.S. 214 40.31 N 81.28 W
Dover, Ok., U.S. 196 35.58 N 97.54 W
Dover, Pa., U.S. 208 40.00 N 76.51 W
Dover, Tn., U.S. 194 36.29 N 87.50 W
Dover, Point › 162 32.32 S 125.32 E
Dover, Strait of (Pas de Calais) ⊔ 50 51.00 N 1.30 E
Dover Air Force Base ■ 208 39.08 N 75.28 W
Dover-Foxcroft 188 45.11 N 69.13 W
Dover Heights 274a 33.53 S 151.17 E
Dover Hills 276 40.52 N 74.33 W
Dover Plains 210 41.44 N 73.35 W
Dovers Hills ∧∧[2] 162 23.10 S 128.45 E
Dove Stone Reservoir ⊜[1] 262 53.32 N 1.58 W
Doveton 274b 38.00 S 145.14 E
Dovey Valley V 42 52.35 N 3.50 W
Dovhen'ke 83 49.01 N 37.19 E
Dovol'noje 86 54.30 N 79.40 E
Dovre 26 61.59 N 9.15 E
Dovrefjell ∧∧ 26 62.06 N 9.25 E
Dovrefjell Nasjonalpark ♦ 26 62.18 N 9.36 E
Dovsk 76 53.09 N 30.28 E
Dovzhyk 78 50.13 N 35.55 E
Dowa 154 13.40 S 33.58 E
Dowagiac 216 41.59 N 86.06 W
Dowagiac ≃ 216 41.51 N 86.16 W
Dowagiac Creek ≃ 216 41.49 N 86.10 W
Dowally 46 56.36 N 3.37 W
Dow City 198 41.55 N 95.29 W
Dowden Terrace 284c 38.50 N 77.08 W
Dowell 208 38.20 N 76.27 W
Dowerin 162 31.12 S 117.02 E
Dowi, Tanjung › 114 1.31 N 97.25 E
Dowker, Île I 275a 45.24 N 73.54 W
Dowlatābād, Afg. 120 36.59 N 66.50 E
Dowlatābād, Afg. 120 36.26 N 64.55 E
Dowlatābād, Īrān 128 28.18 N 56.40 E
Dowlat Yār 120 34.33 N 65.47 E
Dowling Lake ⊜ 182 51.44 N 112.00 W
Downderry 42 50.22 N 4.22 W
Downe ◂[8] 260 51.20 N 0.03 E
Down East 285 40.03 N 75.32 W
Downers Grove 216 41.48 N 88.00 W
Downey, Ca., U.S. 228 33.56 N 118.07 W
Downey, Id., U.S. 202 42.25 N 112.07 W
Downey Creek ≃ 224 48.16 N 121.14 W
Downham, Eng., U.K. 42 52.26 N 0.15 E
Downham, Eng., U.K. 260 51.38 N 0.30 E
Downham Market 42 52.36 N 0.23 E
Down House ⊥ 260 51.20 N 0.03 E
Downieville 226 39.33 N 120.49 W
Downing 194 40.29 N 92.22 W
Downingtown 208 40.00 N 75.42 W
Downingtown Airport ⊠ 285 39.59 N 75.45 W
Downpatrick 48 54.20 N 5.43 W
Downpatrick Head › 48 54.20 N 9.20 W
Downs, Il., U.S. 216 40.24 N 88.52 W
Downs, Ks., U.S. 198 39.30 N 98.32 W
Downs Mountain ∧ 200 43.18 N 109.40 W
Downsview Dells Park ♦ 275b 43.44 N 79.30 W
Downsville 210 42.04 N 74.59 W
Downsville Dam ◂[6] 210 42.05 N 74.58 W
Downton 42 51.00 N 1.44 W
Downton, Mount ∧ 182 52.42 N 124.51 W
Downton Lake ⊜ 182 50.51 N 123.00 W
Downwind Acres Airfield ⊠ 281 42.09 N 83.34 W
Dows 190 42.39 N 93.30 W
Dowshī 120 35.37 N 68.41 E
Doygaab 144 0.59 N 43.32 E
Doyle 204 40.01 N 120.06 W
Doyles 186 47.50 N 59.12 W
Doylesburg 214 40.13 N 77.42 W
Doylestown, Oh., U.S. 214 40.58 N 81.41 W
Doylestown, Pa., U.S. 208 40.18 N 75.07 W
Doyline 194 32.32 N 93.25 W
Dōzan ≃ 96 33.58 N 133.47 E
Dōzen II 92 36.05 N 133.05 E
Dozier 194 31.29 N 86.21 W
Dozois, Réservoir ⊜[1] 190 47.30 N 77.05 W
Dozza 66 44.22 N 11.37 E
Drâa, Cap › 148 28.44 N 11.08 W
Dra'a, Hamada du ◂[2] 148 29.00 N 6.45 W
Drâa, Oued V 148 28.43 N 11.09 W
Draa el Mizan 34 36.32 N 3.50 E
Drabble → José Enrique Rodó 258 33.41 S 57.34 W
Drabenderhöhe 56 50.57 N 7.27 E
Drabiv 78 49.58 N 32.08 E
Drac ≃ 62 45.13 N 5.41 E
Dracena 255 21.32 S 51.29 W
Drachenfels ⊥ 56 50.40 N 7.12 E
Drachselsried 60 49.06 N 13.01 E
Drachten 52 53.06 N 6.05 E
Dracut 207 42.40 N 71.18 W
Dragalina 38 44.26 N 27.20 E
Drăgănești-Olt 38 44.10 N 24.32 E


**Symbols** in the index entries represent the broad categories identified in the key at the right. Symbols with superior numbers (∧∧[1]) identify subcategories (see complete key on page *I · 1)*.

**Symbole** im Register stellen die rechts im Schlüssel erklärten Kategorien dar. Symbole mit hochgestellten Ziffern (∧∧[1]) bezeichnen Unterabteilungen einer Kategorie (vgl. vollständiger Schlüssel auf Seite *I · 1)*.

**Los símbolos** incluídos en el texto del índice representan las grandes categorías identificadas con la clave a la derecha. Los símbolos con numeros en su parte superior (∧∧[1]) identifican las subcategorías (véase la clave completa en la página *I · 1)*.

**Les symboles** de l'index représentent les catégories indiquées dans la légende à droite. Les symboles suivis d'un indice (∧∧[1]) représentent des sous-catégories (voir légende complète à la page *I · 1)*.

**Os símbolos** incluídos no texto do índice representam as grandes categorias identificadas com a chave à direita. Os símbolos com números em sua parte superior (∧∧[1]) identificam as subcategorias (veja-se a chave completa à página *I · 1)*.

| | English | Deutsch | Español | Français | Português |
|---|---|---|---|---|---|
| ∧ | Mountain | Berg | Montaña | Montagne | Montanha |
| ∧∧ | Mountains | Gebirge | Montañas | Montagnes | Montanhas |
| )( | Pass | Paß | Paso | Col | Passo |
| V | Valley, Canyon | Tal, Cañon | Valle, Cañón | Vallée, Canyon | Vale, Canhão |
| ≍ | Plain | Ebene | Llano | Plaine | Planície |
| › | Cape | Kap | Cabo | Cap | Cabo |
| I | Island | Insel | Isla | Île | Ilha |
| II | Islands | Inseln | Islas | Îles | Ilhas |
| ± | Other Topographic Features | Andere Topographische Objekte | Otros Elementos Topográficos | Autres données topographiques | Outros acidentes topográficos |

ESPAÑOL — Nombre / Página / Lat.°' / Long.°' W = Oeste
FRANÇAIS — Nom / Page / Lat.°' / Long.°' W = Ouest
PORTUGUÊS — Nome / Página / Lat.°' / Long.°' W = Oeste


Drăgănești-Vlașca 38 44.06 N 25.36 E
Drăgășani 38 44.40 N 24.16 E
Drag Lake 212 45.05 N 78.24 W
Dragone 64 44.23 N 10.37 E
Dragonera I 34 39.35 N 2.19 E
Dragoni 68 41.16 N 14.18 E
Dragonja 64 45.28 N 13.37 E
Dragons Mouths 241r 10.45 N 61.46 W
Dragon Swamp 208 37.33 N 76.34 W
Dragoon 200 32.01 N 110.02 W
Drager 41 55.36 N 12.41 E
Draguignan 62 43.32 N 6.28 E
Drahičyn 76 52.11 N 25.09 E
Drain 202 43.39 N 123.19 W
Drake, Mo., U.S. 219 38.28 N 91.28 W
Drake, N.D., U.S. 198 47.55 N 100.22 W
Drakenburg 52 52.41 N 9.13 E
Drakensberg 156 27.00 S 30.00 E
Drake Passage 18 58.00 S 70.00 W
Drake Peak 202 42.19 N 120.07 W
Drakesboro 194 37.13 N 87.02 W
Drakes Branch 192 36.59 N 78.36 W
Drakes Brook 276 40.49 N 74.43 W
Drake Well Museum 214 41.36 N 79.39 W
Drakino 82 54.52 N 37.17 E
Dráma 38 41.09 N 24.08 E
Drammen 26 59.44 N 10.15 E
Dran 110 11.51 N 108.35 E
Drancy 50 48.56 N 2.27 E
Dranda 84 42.53 N 41.09 E
Drang 110 13.19 N 107.21 E
Drangajökull 24a 66.11 N 22.15 W
Drangstedt 52 53.36 N 8.44 E
Dranov, Ostrovul I 38 44.52 N 29.15 E
Dransfeld 52 51.30 N 9.45 E
Dranske 54 54.38 N 13.14 E
Drap 62 43.45 N 7.19 E
Draper, N.C., U.S. 192 36.31 N 79.44 W
Draper, Ut., U.S. 200 40.31 N 111.51 W
Draperstown 48 54.48 N 6.47 W
Drăs 123 34.27 N 75.46 E
Drăs 123 34.37 N 75.59 E
Drau (Drava) (Dráva) 36 45.33 N 18.55 E
Drava (Drau) (Dráva) 36 45.33 N 18.55 E
Draveil 50 48.41 N 2.25 E
Dravinja 36 46.22 N 15.57 E
Dravograd 61 46.35 N 15.02 E
Dravosburg 279b 40.21 N 79.51 W
Drawno 30 53.13 N 15.45 E
Drawsko Pomorskie 30 53.32 N 15.48 E
Drayton, On., Can. 212 43.46 N 80.40 W
Drayton, Eng., U.K. 42 51.38 N 1.18 W
Drayton, N.D., U.S. 198 48.34 N 97.10 W
Drayton, S.C., U.S. 192 34.58 N 81.54 W
Drayton Plains 216 42.41 N 83.22 W
Drayton Valley 182 53.13 N 114.59 W
Draženov 60 49.28 N 12.52 E
Drean 36 36.41 N 7.46 E
Drebkau 54 51.39 N 14.13 E
Dreetz 54 52.48 N 12.28 E
Dreieich 56 50.01 N 8.41 E
Dreifelder Weiher 56 50.36 N 7.49 E
Dreihausen 56 50.43 N 8.50 E
Dreiherrnspitze (Picco dei Tre Signori) 64 47.04 N 12.15 E
Dreikikir 164 3.35 S 142.45 E
Drejø I 41 54.58 N 10.25 E
Dremsel, Mount 164 2.10 S 146.55 E
Drena 64 45.58 N 10.56 E
Drenovec 38 43.42 N 22.59 E
Drensteinfurt 52 51.48 N 7.44 E
Drenthe 52 52.45 N 6.30 E
Dresde → Dresden 54 51.03 N 13.44 E
Dresden, On., Can. 214 42.35 N 82.11 W
Dresden, Dtsch. 54 51.03 N 13.44 E
Dresden, N.Y., U.S. 210 42.41 N 76.58 W
Dresden, Oh., U.S. 214 40.07 N 82.00 W
Dresden, Tn., U.S. 194 36.17 N 88.42 W
Dresher 285 40.08 N 75.10 W
Drëtun' 76 55.41 N 29.13 E
Dreux 50 48.44 N 1.22 E
Drevenack 263 51.40 N 6.45 E
Drew 194 33.48 N 90.31 W
Drewer 263 51.40 N 7.07 E
Drewitz, Dtsch. 54 52.22 N 13.07 E
Drewitz, Dtsch. 54 52.12 N 12.10 E
Drewitz 264a 52.22 N 13.08 E
Drewryville 208 36.42 N 77.18 W
Drews Reservoir 202 42.10 N 120.40 W
Drew University 276 40.46 N 74.25 W
Drexel 218 39.44 N 84.17 W
Drexel Gardens 218 39.44 N 86.15 W
Drexel Hill 285 39.56 N 75.17 W
Drexel University 285 39.57 N 75.11 W
Drezdenko 30 52.51 N 15.50 E
Drezna 82 55.44 N 38.51 E
Driebergen 52 52.03 N 5.16 E
Drienov 30 48.53 N 21.17 E
Drifton 210 41.00 N 75.54 W
Driftpile 182 55.23 N 115.40 W
Drift Pile River Indian Reserve 182 55.18 N 115.45 W
Driftwood, B.C., Can. 182 55.49 N 126.25 W
Driftwood, Pa., U.S. 214 41.20 N 78.08 W
Driftwood, B.C., Can. 182 55.43 N 126.15 W
Driftwood, In., U.S. 218 39.12 N 85.56 W
Driftwood Creek 218 40.11 N 100.39 W
Driggs 202 43.43 N 111.06 W
Drimnin 46 56.36 N 6.00 W
Drimoleague 48 51.38 N 9.14 W
Drin 38 41.45 N 19.34 E
Drina 38 44.53 N 19.21 E
Dringenberg 52 51.40 N 9.02 E
Drini i Zi 38 42.00 N 20.21 E
Drinit, Gjiri i 38 41.45 N 19.28 E
Driorejo 115a 7.21 S 112.37 E
Driscoll 196 27.40 N 97.45 W
Driskill Mountain 194 32.25 N 92.54 W
Driver 208 36.49 N 76.30 W
Drizzle Lake 212 45.20 N 78.10 W
Drjanovo 38 42.58 N 25.27 E
Drmholec 36 48.52 N 16.29 E
Drniš 36 43.51 N 16.09 E
Dro 64 45.58 N 10.54 E
Drøbak 26 59.39 N 10.39 E
Drobeta-Turnu Severin 38 44.38 N 22.39 E
Drobylevo 82 55.44 N 35.53 E
Drobysheve 83 49.02 N 37.44 E
Drobyšovo 86 53.58 N 74.40 E
Drochia 38 48.03 N 27.48 E
Drochtersen 52 53.42 N 9.23 E
Drocourt 261 49.03 N 1.46 E
Droë Harts 158 27.35 S 24.41 E
Drogheda (Droichead Átha) 48 53.43 N 6.21 W
Drohiczyn 30 52.24 N 22.41 E
Drohobych 78 49.21 N 23.30 E
Drohobycz → Drohobych 78 49.21 N 23.30 E
Droichead Átha → Drogheda 48 53.43 N 6.21 W
Droichead Nua 48 53.11 N 6.48 W
Droitwich 42 52.16 N 2.09 W
Drolshagen 56 51.01 N 7.46 E
Dromahair 48 54.14 N 8.19 W
Dromana 169 38.21 S 144.58 E
Dromara 48 54.23 N 6.01 W
Dromcolliher 48 52.20 N 8.54 W
Drôme 62 44.35 N 5.10 E
Drôme 62 44.46 N 4.46 E
Drömling 54 52.29 N 11.04 E
Dromod 48 53.51 N 7.55 W
Dromore, N. Ire., U.K. 48 54.31 N 7.28 W
Dromore, N. Ire., U.K. 48 54.25 N 6.09 W
Dromore West 48 54.15 N 8.53 W
Dronero 62 44.28 N 7.22 E
Dronfield 44 53.19 N 1.27 W
Drongan 44 55.26 N 4.27 W
Drongen 50 51.03 N 3.40 E
Dronne 32 45.02 N 0.09 W
Dronninglund 26 57.09 N 10.18 E
Dronrijp 52 53.11 N 5.38 E
Dröschede 263 51.22 N 7.39 E
Drosendorf Stadt 61 48.52 N 15.37 E
Drosiá 267c 38.07 N 23.52 E
Drösing 61 48.32 N 16.54 E
Droskovo 76 52.31 N 37.05 E
Drottningholm slott 40 59.19 N 17.53 E
Droué 50 48.02 N 1.05 E
Drouë-sur-Drouette 261 48.36 N 1.42 E
Drouette 261 48.37 N 1.37 E
Drouin 169 38.08 S 145.51 E
Drov'anaja 88 51.35 N 113.02 E
Droylsden 262 53.29 N 2.10 W
Droyssig 54 51.02 N 12.01 E
Druc' 76 53.03 N 30.42 E
Druid Hill Park 284b 39.19 N 76.39 W
Druja 76 55.47 N 27.27 E
Drūkšiai 76 55.38 N 26.35 E
Druk-Yul → Bhutan 120 27.30 N 90.30 E
Drulingen 58 48.52 N 7.11 E
Drum, Mount 180 62.07 N 144.35 W
Drumbeg 46 58.14 N 5.12 W
Drumbo 212 43.14 N 80.33 W
Drumcliff 48 54.20 N 8.30 W
Drumheller 182 51.28 N 112.42 W
Drumlish 48 53.48 N 7.46 W
Drummond, N.Z. 172 46.09 S 168.09 E
Drummond, Mt., U.S. 202 46.40 N 113.08 W
Drummond, Wi., U.S. 190 46.20 N 91.15 W
Drummond 206 45.50 N 72.20 W
Drummond, Lake 208 36.36 N 76.28 W
Drummond Island I 190 46.00 N 83.40 W
Drummond Range 166 23.30 S 147.15 E
Drummondville 206 45.53 N 72.29 W
Drummore 44 54.42 N 4.54 W
Drummoyne 274a 33.51 S 151.09 E
Drumquin 48 54.37 N 7.30 W
Drumright 196 35.59 N 96.36 W
Drumshanbo 48 54.02 N 8.02 W
Drunen 52 51.42 N 5.08 E
Druskeninkai 56 48.46 N 7.57 E
Druskininkai 76 54.01 N 23.58 E
Druten 52 51.54 N 5.36 E
Druyes-les-Belles-Fontaines 50 47.33 N 3.25 E
Družba, Kaz. 86 45.15 N 82.26 E
Družba, Ross. 265b 55.53 N 37.45 E
Družba 78 52.03 N 33.56 E
Družkhivka 83 48.37 N 37.33 E
Družina 74 68.14 N 145.18 E
Družnaja Gorka 76 59.17 N 30.08 E
Drvar 36 44.22 N 16.24 E
Drweca 30 53.00 N 18.42 E
Dry 164 14.54 S 132.24 E
Dry Arm 202 47.45 N 106.20 W
Dry Bay 180 59.08 N 138.25 W
Dryberry Lake 184 49.33 N 93.53 W
Drybin 76 54.08 N 31.06 E
Dryburgh Abbey 46 55.34 N 2.40 W
Dry Cimarron 196 36.54 N 102.59 W
Dry Creek, Ca., U.S. 204 38.35 N 122.51 W
Dry Creek, Ca., U.S. 226 38.39 N 121.28 W
Dry Creek, Ca., U.S. 226 38.22 N 122.18 W
Dry Creek, Ca., U.S. 226 38.58 N 121.32 W
Dry Creek, Ca., U.S. 226 39.13 N 121.25 W
Dry Creek, Ca., U.S. 226 38.14 N 121.24 W
Dry Creek, Ca., U.S. 226 36.58 N 120.13 W
Dry Creek, Ca., U.S. 226 36.47 N 119.46 W
Dry Creek, Ca., U.S. 226 37.27 N 120.37 W
Dry Creek, Ca., U.S. 282 37.22 N 122.23 W
Dry Creek, Or., U.S. 202 43.34 N 117.21 W
Dry Creek, Or., U.S. 224 45.30 N 121.03 W
Dry Creek, Tx., U.S. 222 32.46 N 95.28 W
Dry Creek, Wy., U.S. 202 43.13 N 108.54 W
Dry Creek, Wy., U.S. 202 44.30 N 108.03 W
Dry Creek Mountain 204 41.22 N 116.22 W
Dryden, On., Can. 184 49.47 N 92.50 W
Dryden, N.Y., U.S. 210 42.29 N 76.17 W
Dryden, Wa., U.S. 224 47.32 N 120.33 W
Dry Devils, Tx., U.S. 196 30.20 N 100.57 W
Dry Devils, Tx., U.S. 196 29.47 N 100.59 W
Dryfe Water 44 55.08 N 3.26 W
Dry Fork 194 37.58 N 91.31 W
Dry Frio 196 29.17 N 99.39 W
Drygalski Island I 9 65.45 S 92.30 E
Dry Lake 198 48.15 N 98.58 W
Drymen 46 56.04 N 4.27 W
Dry Prong 194 31.34 N 92.31 W
Dry Ridge 218 38.40 N 84.35 W
Dry Run 214 40.10 N 77.45 W
Drysa 76 55.47 N 27.55 E
Drysdale 169 38.11 S 144.34 E
Drysdale 164 13.59 S 126.51 E
Drysdale River National Park 164 15.00 S 127.00 E
Dry Tortugas II 220 24.38 N 82.55 W
Dry Tortugas National Park 220 24.37 N 82.54 W
Drzewica 30 51.27 N 20.28 E
Drzewice 54 52.38 N 14.38 E
Dschang 152 5.27 N 10.04 E
Dschidda → Jiddah 144 21.30 N 39.12 E
Dschuba → Jubba 144 0.15 S 42.38 E
Du 150 10.30 N 0.59 W
Du 102 32.48 N 110.38 E
Duabo 150 5.40 N 8.05 W
Duāigaon 126 24.14 N 90.51 E
Duala → Douala 152 4.03 N 9.42 E
Dualchi 71 40.13 N 8.54 E
Du'an 102 24.06 N 108.10 E
Duancun 105 38.52 N 115.56 E
Duane L. Bliss State Park 226 38.59 N 120.06 W
Duanesburg 210 42.46 N 74.08 W
Duanjialing 105 39.59 N 117.09 E
Duaringa 166 23.43 S 149.40 E
Duarte 280 34.08 N 117.58 W
Duarte, Pico 238 19.02 N 70.59 W
Duartina 255 22.24 S 49.25 W
Duas Barras 256 22.02 S 42.32 W
Duayaw Nkwanta 150 7.10 N 2.06 W
Dubā, Bi'r 128 27.21 N 35.40 E
Dubá, Česká Rep. 54 50.34 N 14.33 E
Dubach 194 32.41 N 92.39 W
Dubai → Dubayy 128 25.18 N 55.18 E
Dubăsari (Dubesar') 38 47.16 N 29.08 E
Dubăsari, Lacul 38 47.35 N 29.00 E
Dubawnt 176 64.33 N 100.06 W
Dubawnt Lake 176 63.08 N 101.30 W
Dubayy 128 25.18 N 55.18 E
Dubbeldam 52 51.47 N 4.42 E
Dubbo 166 32.15 S 148.36 E
Dube 150 5.45 N 8.00 W
Dubele 154 2.54 N 29.33 E
Dübendorf 58 47.25 N 8.38 E
Dübener Heide 54 51.40 N 12.40 E
Dubenskij 86 51.27 N 56.38 E
Dubh Artach II 46 56.08 N 6.40 W
Dubí 54 50.42 N 13.45 E
Dubi Bheri 272b 22.53 N 88.17 E
Dubica 36 45.11 N 16.48 E
Dubie 154 8.33 S 28.32 E
Dubinino 82 56.09 N 37.01 E
Dubino 58 46.09 N 9.27 E
Dubjazy 80 56.08 N 49.13 E
Dubki, Ross. 265a 60.00 N 30.00 E
Dubki, Ross. 265b 55.41 N 37.14 E
Dubki, Ross. 168b 34.27 S 138.21 E
Dublin, Austl. 212 43.31 N 81.17 W
Dublin, On., Can.
Dublin (Baile Átha Cliath), Ire. 48 53.20 N 6.15 W
Dublin, Ca., U.S. 226 37.42 N 121.56 W
Dublin, Ga., U.S. 192 32.32 N 82.54 W
Dublin, In., U.S. 218 39.48 N 85.12 W
Dublin, Md., U.S. 208 39.39 N 76.16 W
Dublin, Oh., U.S. 214 40.06 N 83.07 W
Dublin, Pa., U.S. 208 40.22 N 75.12 W
Dublin, Tx., U.S. 196 32.05 N 98.20 W
Dublin, Va., U.S. 192 37.06 N 80.41 W
Dublin 48 53.20 N 6.15 W
Dublin (Collinstown) Airport 48 53.26 N 6.15 W
Dublin Bay 48 53.20 N 6.06 W
Dublin Canyon 282 37.42 N 121.59 W
Dublon I 175c 7.23 N 151.53 E
Dubna, Ross. 82 54.09 N 36.58 E
Dubna, Ross. 82 56.44 N 37.10 E
Dubna, Lat. 76 56.22 N 26.10 E
Dubna, Ross. 76 56.47 N 37.15 E
Dubňany 30 48.55 N 17.06 E
Dubnevo 82 55.06 N 38.08 E
Dubnica nad Váhom 30 48.58 N 18.09 E
Dubno 78 50.26 N 25.44 E
Dubois, Id., U.S. 202 44.10 N 112.13 W
Dubois, Il., U.S. 219 38.13 N 89.13 W
Dubois, In., U.S. 194 38.26 N 86.48 W
Du Bois, Ne., U.S. 198 40.02 N 96.02 W
Du Bois, Pa., U.S. 214 41.07 N 78.45 W
Dubois, Wy., U.S. 200 43.32 N 109.37 W
Du Bois Reservoir 214 41.06 N 78.38 W
Duboistown 210 41.13 N 77.02 W
Dub'onki 80 54.27 N 46.18 E
Dubovaja Rošča 76 53.11 N 36.04 E
Dubovka, Ross. 78 51.26 N 41.25 E
Dubovka, Ross. 80 49.03 N 44.50 E
Dubovoje 76 53.08 N 40.05 E
Dubovskij 80 56.21 N 46.48 E
Dubovskoje 80 47.25 N 42.46 E
Dubov'yazivka 78 51.08 N 33.22 E
Dubovychi 78 51.38 N 33.35 E
Dubovyj Ovrag 80 48.20 N 44.37 E
Dubovyj Umet 80 52.59 N 50.17 E
Dubovyj Umet
Dubréka 150 9.48 N 13.31 W
Dubrovka 54 51.38 N 40.57 E
...

| | | | |
|---|---|---|---|
| Düppel, Berliner Forst ✦[3] | 264a | 52.25 N | 13.08 E |
| Dupree | 198 | 45.02 N | 101.36 W |
| Duque Bacelar | 250 | 4.09 S | 42.57 W |
| Duque de Caxias | 256 | 22.47 S | 43.18 W |
| Duque de Caxias □[7] | 287a | 22.45 S | 43.16 W |
| Duque de York, Isla I | 254 | 50.40 S | 75.20 W |
| Duquesne | 214 | 40.22 N | 79.51 W |
| Duquesne University ψ[2] | 279b | 40.26 N | 79.59 W |
| DuQuoin | 194 | 37.59 N | 89.15 W |
| Dūrā | 132 | 31.30 N | 35.02 E |
| Durach, Dtsch. | 58 | 47.42 N | 10.20 E |
| Durach, Dtsch. | 64 | 47.42 N | 10.20 E |
| Durack ≃ | 164 | 15.33 S | 127.52 E |
| Durack Ranges ∧∧ | 160 | 17.00 S | 128.00 E |
| Durağan | 130 | 41.25 N | 35.04 E |
| Durak | 130 | 39.42 N | 28.17 E |
| Durak Dağı ∧ | 84 | 39.47 N | 43.42 E |
| Dural | 170 | 33.41 S | 151.02 E |
| Duran | 200 | 34.28 N | 105.23 W |
| Durance ≃ | 62 | 43.55 N | 4.44 E |
| Durand, Il., U.S. | 190 | 42.26 N | 89.19 W |
| Durand, Mi., U.S. | 216 | 42.54 N | 83.59 W |
| Durand, Wi., U.S. | 190 | 44.37 N | 91.57 W |
| Durand Reef ✧[2] | 175f | 22.03 S | 168.39 E |
| Duran Durat I | 271c | 1.15 N | 103.51 E |
| Durango, Esp. | 34 | 43.10 N | 2.37 W |
| Durango, Méx. | 234 | 24.02 N | 104.40 W |
| Durango, Co., U.S. | 200 | 37.16 N | 107.52 W |
| Durango □[3] | 232 | 24.50 N | 104.50 W |
| Duranillin | 168a | 33.31 S | 116.48 E |
| Durant, Ia., U.S. | 190 | 41.35 N | 90.54 W |
| Durant, Ms., U.S. | 194 | 33.04 N | 89.51 W |
| Durant, Ok., U.S. | 196 | 33.59 N | 96.22 W |
| Duras | 32 | 44.41 N | 0.11 E |
| Duratón ≃ | 34 | 41.37 N | 4.07 W |
| Duraur V | 144 | 10.33 N | 49.07 E |
| Durazno | 252 | 33.22 S | 56.31 W |
| Durazzo → Durrës | 38 | 41.19 N | 19.26 E |
| Durbach | 58 | 48.30 N | 8.01 E |
| Durbādānga | 126 | 22.57 N | 89.15 E |
| Durban | 158 | 29.55 S | 30.56 E |
| Durban Roodepoort Deep Gold Mines ✦[7] | 273d | 26.10 S | 27.51 E |
| Durbanville | 158 | 33.50 S | 18.39 E |
| Durbe | 76 | 56.35 N | 21.21 E |
| D'urbel'džin | 85 | 41.16 N | 74.57 E |
| Durbet-Daba, pereval )( | 86 | 49.37 N | 89.25 E |
| Durbin | 188 | 38.32 N | 79.49 W |
| Durbuy | 56 | 50.21 N | 5.28 E |
| Durchholz | 263 | 51.23 N | 7.17 E |
| Durdent ≃ | 50 | 49.51 N | 0.36 E |
| Đurđevac | 36 | 46.03 N | 17.04 E |
| Durdur V | 144 | 10.34 N | 43.58 E |
| Dureji | 120 | 25.53 N | 67.18 E |
| Düren | 56 | 50.48 N | 6.28 E |
| Durg | 120 | 21.11 N | 81.17 E |
| Durgāpur | 126 | 23.29 N | 87.20 E |
| Durham, On., Can. | 212 | 44.10 N | 80.49 W |
| Durham, Eng., U.K. | 44 | 54.47 N | 1.34 W |
| Durham, Ca., U.S. | 204 | 39.38 N | 121.47 W |
| Durham, Ct., U.S. | 207 | 41.28 N | 72.40 W |
| Durham, Mo., U.S. | 219 | 39.58 N | 91.40 W |
| Durham, N.H., U.S. | 188 | 43.08 N | 70.55 W |
| Durham, N.C., U.S. | 192 | 35.59 N | 78.53 W |
| Durham, Or., U.S. | 224 | 45.25 N | 122.46 W |
| Durham □[6], On., Can. | 212 | 43.56 N | 78.53 W |
| Durham □[6], Eng., U.K. | 44 | 54.45 N | 1.45 W |
| Durham Cathedral ψ[1] | 44 | 54.46 N | 1.36 W |
| Durham Downs | 166 | 27.05 S | 141.54 E |
| Durham Heights ∧ | 176 | 71.08 N | 122.56 W |
| Durham Pond ◎ | 276 | 41.00 N | 74.27 W |
| Durhamville | 210 | 43.07 N | 75.40 W |
| Durian ≃ | 115a | 6.01 S | 106.24 E |
| Durian, Selat ⋓ | 114 | 0.42 N | 103.42 E |
| Duriansebatang | 112 | 0.47 S | 109.56 E |
| Durian Tipus | 114 | 3.07 N | 102.13 E |
| D'urinskije razlivy ≡ | 80 | 50.25 N | 50.20 E |
| Durlabhpur | 272b | 22.47 N | 88.29 E |
| Durlești | 38 | 47.02 N | 28.45 E |
| Durmersheim | 56 | 48.56 N | 8.16 E |
| Durmitor ∧ | 38 | 43.08 N | 19.01 E |
| Durness | 46 | 58.33 N | 4.45 W |
| Durness, Kyle of ⊂ | 46 | 58.34 N | 4.49 W |
| Durneva, ostrova II | 80 | 45.25 N | 52.50 E |
| Durnikino | 80 | 51.39 N | 42.49 E |
| Dürnkrut | 61 | 48.28 N | 16.51 E |
| Dürnstein ⊥ | 61 | 48.24 N | 15.32 E |
| Duro ∧ | 144 | 5.31 N | 37.12 E |
| Durón | 34 | 40.38 N | 2.43 W |
| Duross Heights | 285 | 39.40 N | 75.37 W |
| Dürre Liesing ≃ | 264b | 48.08 N | 16.16 E |
| Durrell | 186 | 49.40 N | 54.44 W |
| Dürrenboden | 58 | 46.57 N | 8.50 E |
| Durrës | 38 | 41.19 N | 19.26 E |
| Durrie | 166 | 25.38 S | 140.16 E |
| Durrington | 42 | 51.13 N | 1.45 W |
| Durrow | 48 | 52.50 N | 7.22 W |
| Durrus | 48 | 51.36 N | 9.31 W |
| Dürrwangen | 56 | 49.07 N | 10.23 E |
| Dursey Head > | 48 | 51.35 N | 10.14 W |
| Dursey Island I | 48 | 51.36 N | 10.12 W |
| Dursley | 42 | 51.42 N | 2.21 W |
| Dursunbey | 130 | 39.35 N | 28.38 E |
| D'urt'uli | 86 | 55.29 N | 54.52 E |
| Duru | 154 | 4.14 N | 28.45 E |
| Duru Gölü ◎ | 130 | 41.20 N | 28.35 E |
| Durulova | 130 | 38.17 N | 38.01 E |
| Durunkah | 142 | 27.08 N | 31.10 E |
| Durūz, Jabal ad- ∧∧ | 132 | 32.40 N | 36.44 E |
| D'Urville, Tanjung > | 164 | 1.28 S | 137.54 E |
| D'Urville Island I | 172 | 40.50 S | 173.52 E |
| Duryea | 210 | 41.20 N | 75.44 W |
| Dury Voe ⊂ | 46a | 60.20 N | 1.08 W |
| Dušak | 128 | 37.13 N | 60.02 E |
| Dušanbe | 85 | 38.35 N | 68.48 E |
| Dušekan | 74 | 60.39 N | 109.03 E |
| Dušeti | 84 | 42.06 N | 44.42 E |
| Dusetos | 76 | 55.45 N | 25.51 E |
| Dushan, Zhg. | 100 | 31.36 N | 116.14 E |
| Dushan, Zhg. | 102 | 25.53 N | 107.30 E |
| Du Shan ∧ | 98 | 40.30 N | 118.45 E |
| Dushanbe → Dušanbe | 85 | 38.35 N | 68.48 E |
| Dushan Hu ◎ | 98 | 35.06 N | 116.52 E |
| Dushantou | 106 | 30.46 N | 119.47 E |
| Dushanzi | 86 | 44.20 N | 84.51 E |
| Dusheng | 98 | 38.23 N | 116.33 E |
| Dushichang | 107 | 29.10 N | 106.31 E |
| Dushikou | 98 | 41.17 N | 115.38 E |
| Dushore | 210 | 41.31 N | 76.24 W |
| Düshorn | 52 | 52.49 N | 9.37 E |
| Dushu | 100 | 33.21 N | 113.09 E |
| Dushu Hu ◎ | 106 | 31.17 N | 120.42 E |
| Dusia ◎ | 76 | 54.18 N | 23.42 E |
| Dusky Sound ⋓ | 172 | 45.47 S | 166.28 E |
| Dušocha, gora ∧ | 85 | 39.10 N | 70.01 E |
| Duson | 194 | 30.14 N | 92.11 W |
| Dušonovo | 82 | 56.04 N | 38.18 E |
| Düssel | 263 | 51.16 N | 7.03 E |
| Düssel ≃ | 263 | 51.13 N | 6.45 E |
| Düsseldorf, Dtsch. | 56 | 51.12 N | 6.47 E |
| Düsseldorf, Dtsch. | 263 | 51.12 N | 6.47 E |
| Düsseldorf □[5] | 52 | 51.15 N | 7.00 E |
| Düsseldorf, Flughafen ⊠ | 56 | 51.17 N | 6.47 E |
| Düsseldorf, Universität ψ[2] | 263 | 51.12 N | 6.48 E |
| Dusslingen | 58 | 48.27 N | 9.03 E |
| Dussnang | 58 | 47.26 N | 8.58 E |
| Dustin | 196 | 35.16 N | 96.01 W |
| Dutch Creek ≃, B.C., Can. | 182 | 50.20 N | 115.52 W |
| Dutch Creek ≃, Ar., U.S. | 194 | 35.03 N | 93.24 W |
| Dutchess □[6] | 210 | 41.42 N | 73.56 W |
| Dutch Harbor | 180 | 53.53 N | 166.32 W |
| Dutch John | 200 | 40.55 N | 109.23 W |
| Dutchman Creek ≃ | 226 | 37.11 N | 120.28 W |
| Dutianjie | 102 | 24.38 N | 101.31 E |
| Dutluca | 130 | 39.09 N | 38.37 E |
| Dutlwe | 156 | 23.55 S | 23.47 E |
| Dutoitspiek ∧ | 158 | 33.46 S | 19.12 E |
| Dutou, Zhg. | 100 | 22.54 N | 115.12 E |
| Dutou, Zhg. | 106 | 31.19 N | 120.54 E |
| Dutovlje | 64 | 45.46 N | 13.50 E |
| Dutovo | 24 | 63.47 N | 56.35 E |
| Dutsen Wai | 150 | 10.50 N | 8.12 E |
| Dutton, Austl. | 168b | 34.22 S | 139.08 E |
| Dutton, On., Can. | 214 | 42.39 N | 81.30 W |
| Dutton, Eng., U.K. | 262 | 53.19 N | 2.38 W |
| Dutton, Mi., U.S. | 216 | 42.50 N | 85.35 W |
| Dutton, Mt., U.S. | 202 | 47.50 N | 111.42 W |
| Dutton ≃ | 166 | 20.45 S | 143.12 E |
| Dutton, Mount ∧, Ak., U.S. | 180 | 55.10 N | 162.15 W |
| Dutton, Mount ∧, Ut,. U.S. | 200 | 38.01 N | 112.13 W |
| Dutun | 105 | 39.46 N | 117.02 E |
| Dutzow | 219 | 38.37 N | 90.59 W |
| Duut | 86 | 47.30 N | 91.40 E |
| Duval, Lac ◎ | 190 | 46.19 N | 76.55 W |
| Duvall | 224 | 47.44 N | 121.59 W |
| Duvan | 86 | 55.42 N | 57.54 E |
| Duvanka ≃ | 83 | 49.35 N | 38.10 E |
| Duved | 26 | 63.24 N | 12.52 E |
| Duvernay ✦[8] | 275a | 45.35 N | 73.40 W |
| Duvno | 36 | 43.43 N | 17.14 E |
| Duwamish | 224 | 47.32 N | 122.19 W |
| Duwaydār, Bi'r ad- ⊤[4] | 142 | 30.55 N | 32.31 E |
| Duxbury | 207 | 42.02 N | 70.40 W |
| Duxbury Bay ⊂ | 207 | 42.02 N | 70.39 W |
| Duxbury Beach ±[2] | 283 | 42.03 N | 70.38 W |
| Duxun | 100 | 23.55 N | 117.37 E |
| Duyagan Point > | 116 | 12.36 N | 121.33 E |
| Duyun | 102 | 26.12 N | 107.31 E |
| Düzce | 130 | 40.50 N | 31.10 E |
| Duze | 100 | 29.07 N | 118.56 E |
| Dve Mogili | 38 | 43.36 N | 25.52 E |
| Dvina Occidental → Zapadnaja Dvina ≃ | 76 | 57.04 N | 24.03 E |
| Dvina Septentrional → Severnaja Dvina ≃ | 24 | 64.32 N | 40.30 E |
| Dvinje, ozero ◎ | 76 | 56.08 N | 31.12 E |
| Dvinsk → Daugavpils | 76 | 55.53 N | 26.32 E |
| Dvinskaja guba ⊂ | 24 | 65.00 N | 39.45 E |
| Dvojnovskij | 80 | 51.03 N | 42.27 E |
| Dvorcy | 82 | 54.37 N | 36.00 E |
| Dvorec | 88 | 58.23 N | 99.56 E |
| Dvorichna | 78 | 49.52 N | 37.40 E |
| Dvoriši | 76 | 58.12 N | 35.13 E |
| Dvornikovo | 82 | 55.30 N | 38.38 E |
| Dvuch Cirkov, gora ∧ | 74 | 67.35 N | 168.07 E |
| Dvugorbaja, gora ∧ | 180 | 68.30 N | 179.20 E |
| Dvulučnoje | 78 | 50.02 N | 38.02 E |
| Dvůr Králové [nad Labem] | 30 | 50.26 N | 15.48 E |
| Dwangwa ≃ | 154 | 12.33 S | 34.12 E |
| Dwarbasini | 272b | 22.59 N | 88.14 E |
| Dwārka | 120 | 22.14 N | 68.58 E |
| Dwārka ≃ | 126 | 23.44 N | 88.11 E |
| Dwārkeswar ≃ | 126 | 23.06 N | 87.21 E |
| Dwarli | 272c | 19.12 N | 73.08 E |
| Dwars Kill ≃ | 276 | 40.58 N | 73.58 W |
| Dwellingup | 168a | 32.43 S | 116.02 E |
| D.W. Field Park ♠ | 283 | 42.06 N | 71.03 W |
| Dwight | 216 | 41.05 N | 88.25 W |
| Dwight D. Eisenhower Lock ✦[5] | 206 | 45.00 N | 74.45 W |
| Dwina-Bucht → Dvinskaja guba ⊂ | 24 | 65.00 N | 39.45 E |
| Dwingeloo | 52 | 52.50 N | 6.21 E |
| Dworshak Reservoir ◎[1] | 202 | 46.40 N | 116.00 W |
| Dwyfor ≃ | 44 | 52.55 N | 4.17 W |
| Dwyka | 158 | 33.02 S | 21.30 E |
| Dwyka ≃ | 158 | 33.18 S | 21.39 E |
| Dyakove | 83 | 47.57 N | 39.09 E |
| Dyaul Island I | 164 | 2.56 S | 150.55 E |
| Dybbøl | 41 | 54.55 N | 9.45 E |
| Dyberry Creek ≃ | 210 | 41.35 N | 75.15 W |
| Dyce | 46 | 57.12 N | 2.11 W |
| Dyche Stadium ♠ | 278 | 42.04 N | 87.41 W |
| Dychtau, gora ∧ | 84 | 43.03 N | 43.08 E |
| Dyck, Schloss ⊥ | 263 | 51.09 N | 6.34 E |
| Dyer, In., U.S. | 216 | 41.29 N | 87.31 W |
| Dyer, Tn., U.S. | 194 | 36.04 N | 88.59 W |
| Dyer, Cape > | 176 | 66.37 N | 61.18 W |
| Dyer Bay ⊂ | 212 | 45.10 N | 81.18 W |
| Dyer Island I | 158 | 34.41 S | 19.25 E |
| Dyero | 150 | 12.50 N | 6.30 W |
| Dyersburg | 194 | 36.02 N | 89.23 W |
| Dyersville | 190 | 42.29 N | 91.07 W |
| Dyess Air Force Base ■ | 196 | 32.25 N | 99.51 W |
| Dyfed □[6] | 42 | 52.00 N | 4 30 W |
| Dyfi ≃ | 42 | 52.32 N | 4.03 W |
| Dyje (Thaya) ≃ | 61 | 48.37 N | 16.56 E |
| Dykan'ka | 78 | 49.49 N | 34.32 E |
| Dyke | 46 | 57.36 N | 3.41 W |
| Dyke Ackland Bay ⊂ | 164 | 9.00 S | 148.45 E |
| Dyken Pond ◎ | 210 | 42.43 N | 73.26 W |
| Dykes Pond ◎ | 283 | 42.36 N | 70.44 W |
| Dyle (Dijle) ≃ | 56 | 51.04 N | 4.25 E |
| Dyleň ∧ | 60 | 49.58 N | 12.30 E |
| Dylym | 84 | 43.04 N | 46.38 E |
| Dymchurch | 42 | 51.02 N | 1.00 E |
| Dyment | 184 | 49.37 N | 92.19 W |
| Dymer | 78 | 50.47 N | 30.18 E |
| Dymock | 42 | 51.59 N | 2.26 W |
| Dymytrov | 83 | 48.15 N | 37.18 E |
| Dymytrove | 78 | 48.36 N | 33.01 E |
| Dynamo Stadium ♠ | 265b | 55.48 N | 37.34 E |
| Dynów | 30 | 49.49 N | 22.14 E |
| Dyreborg | 41 | 55.04 N | 10.13 E |
| Dyrnesvågen | 26 | 63.26 N | 7.51 E |
| Dyrotz | 264a | 52.33 N | 12.58 E |
| Dysart, Austl. | 166 | 22.27 S | 148.20 E |
| Dysart, Sk., Can. | 184 | 50.56 N | 104.02 W |
| Dysart, Scot., U.K. | 46 | 56.08 N | 3.08 W |
| Dysart, Ia., U.S. | 190 | 42.10 N | 92.18 W |
| Dysart, Pa., U.S. | 214 | 40.36 N | 78.31 W |
| Dýšina | 60 | 49.46 N | 13.29 E |
| Dysna (Dzisna) ≃ | 76 | 55.34 N | 28.12 E |
| Dysnai ◎ | 76 | 55.29 N | 26.20 E |
| Dysselsdorp | 158 | 33.34 S | 22.28 E |
| Dysynni ≃ | 42 | 52.36 N | 4.05 W |
| Dyviziya | 78 | 45.57 N | 29.59 E |
| Dzaamar | 88 | 48.10 N | 104.50 E |
| Dzaamaryn uul ∧ | 88 | 48.10 N | 104.30 E |
| Džabžur | 84 | 40.54 N | 43.58 E |
| Dzachuj | 102 | 44.59 N | 96.37 E |
| Džagdy, chrebet ∧∧ | 89 | 53.40 N | 131.00 E |
| Džalagaš | 86 | 45.05 N | 64.40 E |
| Džalal-Abad | 85 | 40.56 N | 73.00 E |
| Džalal-Abad □[4] | 85 | 41.30 N | 72.30 E |
| Džalinda | 89 | 53.29 N | 123.54 E |
| Džamantau, gory ∧∧ | 85 | 40.55 N | 74.40 E |
| Džamašuj | 85 | 40.52 N | 71.28 E |
| Džambejty | 80 | 50.16 N | 52.35 E |
| Džambul, Kaz. | 80 | 47.34 N | 50.12 E |
| Džambul → Žambyl, Kaz. | 85 | 42.54 N | 71.22 E |
| Džambul, gora ∧ | 86 | 44.46 N | 73.08 E |
| Džanga | 128 | 40.00 N | 53.03 E |
| Džangi-Džol | 85 | 41.36 N | 72.08 E |
| Džansugurov | 86 | 45.24 N | 79.29 E |
| Džanybek | 80 | 49.25 N | 46.51 E |
| Dzaoudzi | 157a | 12.47 S | 45.17 E |
| Džardžan | 74 | 68.43 N | 124.02 E |
| Džargalant → Chovd, Mong. | 86 | 48.01 N | 91.39 E |
| Džargalant, Mong. | 88 | 48.40 N | 100.43 E |
| Džargalant, Mong. | 88 | 46.57 N | 115.15 E |
| Džargalant, Mong. | 88 | 48.33 N | 99.20 E |
| Džargaltchaan | 88 | 47.28 N | 109.30 E |
| Dzaudzhikau → Vladikavkaz | 84 | 43.03 N | 44.40 E |
| Džaur | 89 | 50.02 N | 138.30 E |
| Džava | 84 | 42.24 N | 43.54 E |
| Dzavchan | 88 | 48.48 N | 93.07 E |
| Dzavchan □[4] | 88 | 48.00 N | 96.00 E |
| Dzavchan ≃ | 88 | 48.54 N | 93.23 E |
| Dzavchan Mandal | 88 | 48.19 N | 95.07 E |
| Džavchlant → Uliastaj | 88 | 47.45 N | 96.49 E |
| Džazator | 86 | 49.45 N | 87.23 E |
| Džbán ∧ | 54 | 50.12 N | 13.45 E |
| Džebel | 128 | 39.38 N | 54.14 E |
| Dzelter ≃ | 88 | 50.30 N | 105.06 E |
| Dzemul | 232 | 21.12 N | 89.18 W |
| Dzeng | 152 | 3.45 N | 12.00 E |
| Dženretlen, mys > | 180 | 67.07 N | 173.45 W |
| Džergetal | 85 | 41.30 N | 75.47 E |
| Džermuk | 84 | 39.51 N | 45.41 E |
| Dzerzhinsk → Dzeržinsk | 80 | 56.15 N | 43.24 E |
| Dzerzhyns'k, Ukr. | 78 | 50.09 N | 27.56 E |
| Dzerzhyns'k, Ukr. | 83 | 48.26 N | 37.50 E |
| Dzeržinsk | 80 | 56.15 N | 43.24 E |
| Dzeržinskij | 82 | 55.38 N | 37.50 E |
| Dzeržinskoje, Kaz. | 86 | 45.50 N | 81.07 E |
| Dzeržinskoje, Ross. | 86 | 56.49 N | 95.18 E |
| Džetim, chrebet ∧∧ | 85 | 41.35 N | 77.05 E |
| Džetygara | 86 | 52.11 N | 61.12 E |
| Džetyoguz | 85 | 42.27 N | 78.14 E |
| Džetyoguzskij zapovednik ♠ | 85 | 42.15 N | 78.20 E |
| Džetysaj | 85 | 40.47 N | 68.16 E |
| Dzhambul → Žambyl | 85 | 42.54 N | 71.22 E |
| Dzhankoy | 78 | 45.43 N | 34.24 E |
| Dzharylhach, ostriv I | 78 | 46.02 N | 32.55 E |
| Dzharylhats'ka zatoka ⊂ | 78 | 46.05 N | 32.50 E |
| Dzhuryn | 78 | 48.41 N | 28.18 E |
| Działdowo | 30 | 53.15 N | 20.10 E |
| Działoszyce | 30 | 50.22 N | 20.21 E |
| Dzibalchén | 232 | 19.31 N | 89.45 W |
| Dzibilchaltun ⊥ | 232 | 21.05 N | 89.36 W |
| Džida ≃ | 88 | 50.37 N | 106.14 E |
| Džidinskij chrebet ∧∧ | 88 | 50.10 N | 102.00 E |
| Dzierzgoń | 30 | 53.56 N | 19.21 E |
| Dzierżoniów (Reichenbach) | 30 | 50.44 N | 16.39 E |
| Dzilam González | 232 | 21.17 N | 88.56 W |
| Džilav | 85 | 39.19 N | 67.45 E |
| Džinst | 102 | 45.24 N | 100.35 E |
| Dzioua | 148 | 33.14 N | 5.14 E |
| Džirgatal' | 85 | 39.13 N | 71.12 E |
| Dzisna | 76 | 55.33 N | 28.10 E |
| Dzisna (Dysna) ≃ | 76 | 55.34 N | 28.12 E |
| Dzitás | 232 | 20.51 N | 88.31 W |
| Dzitbalché | 232 | 20.19 N | 90.03 W |
| Dzivin | 76 | 51.58 N | 24.35 E |
| Dziwna ≃[1] | 54 | 54.01 N | 14.44 E |
| Dziwnów | 30 | 54.03 N | 14.45 E |
| Džizak | 85 | 40.06 N | 67.50 E |
| Džizak □[4] | 85 | 40.30 N | 67.45 E |
| Dzjaniskavičy | 76 | 52.44 N | 26.41 E |
| Dzjarèčyn | 76 | 53.15 N | 24.55 E |
| Dzjaršynskaja, hara ∧[2] | 76 | 53.51 N | 27.03 E |
| Dzjaržynsk | 76 | 53.41 N | 27.08 E |
| Dzjatlava | 76 | 53.28 N | 25.24 E |
| Dzjatlavičy | 76 | 52.20 N | 26.50 E |
| Dzmitravičy | 76 | 53.59 N | 29.06 E |
| Dzodze | 150 | 6.14 N | 1.00 E |
| Džubga | 78 | 44.20 N | 38.43 E |
| Džugdžur, chrebet ∧∧ | 74 | 58.00 N | 136.00 E |
| Džūkste | 76 | 56.47 N | 23.15 E |
| Džumabazar | 85 | 39.31 N | 67.13 E |
| Džumgoltau, chrebet ∧∧ | 85 | 42.18 N | 74.32 E |
| Dzungarian Basin → Junggar Pendi ⊻[1] | 86 | 45.00 N | 88.00 E |
| Dzungarian Gate (Džungarskije vorota) )( | 86 | 45.25 N | 82.25 E |
| Džungarskij Alatau, chrebet ∧∧ | 86 | 45.00 N | 81.00 E |
| Džungarskije vorota → Dzungarian Gate )( | 86 | 45.25 N | 82.25 E |
| Džurak-Sal ≃ | 80 | 47.18 N | 43.36 E |
| Dzürch | 88 | 48.55 N | 100.10 E |
| Džusaly | 86 | 45.28 N | 64.05 E |
| Dzüün Changaj | 88 | 49.17 N | 95.14 E |
| Džüün Charaa | 88 | 48.52 N | 106.28 E |
| Dzüün Gov | 88 | 49.55 N | 93.47 E |
| Dzuunmod | 88 | 47.45 N | 106.55 E |
| Džvari | 84 | 42.43 N | 42.04 E |
| Dzyhivka | 78 | 48.22 N | 28.19 E |
| **E** | | | |
| Eads | 198 | 38.28 N | 102.46 W |
| Eagar | 200 | 34.06 N | 109.17 W |
| Eagle, Ak., U.S. | 180 | 64.46 N | 141.16 W |
| Eagle, Co., U.S. | 200 | 39.39 N | 106.49 W |
| Eagle, N.Y., U.S. | 210 | 42.33 N | 78.18 W |
| Eagle, Wi., U.S. | 216 | 42.52 N | 88.28 W |
| Eagle ≃, Nf., Can. | 176 | 53.35 N | 57.25 W |
| Eagle ≃, Yk., Can. | 180 | 67.20 N | 137.10 W |
| Eagle ≃, Co., U.S. | 200 | 39.39 N | 107.04 W |
| Eagle, Mount ∧[2] | 241n | 17.46 N | 64.49 W |
| Eagle Bay | 182 | 50.56 N | 119.12 W |
| Eagle Bend | 198 | 46.09 N | 95.02 W |
| Eagle Bridge | 210 | 42.57 N | 73.24 W |
| Eagle Butte | 198 | 45.00 N | 101.14 W |
| Eagle Chief Creek ≃ | 196 | 36.22 N | 98.27 W |
| Eagle Creek | 224 | 45.21 N | 122.21 W |
| Eagle Creek ≃, Sk., Can. | 184 | 52.22 N | 107.24 W |
| Eagle Creek ≃, Az., U.S. | 200 | 32.58 N | 109.25 W |
| Eagle Creek ≃, In., U.S. | 218 | 39.43 N | 86.12 W |
| Eagle Creek ≃, Ky., U.S. | 218 | 38.36 N | 85.04 W |
| Eagle Creek ≃, Mt., U.S. | 202 | 48.12 N | 111.11 W |
| Eagle Creek ≃, N.M., U.S. | 196 | 32.47 N | 104.20 W |
| Eagle Creek ≃, Oh., U.S. | 214 | 41.18 N | 80.53 W |
| Eagle Creek ≃, Oh., U.S. | 218 | 38.43 N | 83.51 W |
| Eagle Creek ≃, Or., U.S. | 202 | 44.45 N | 117.10 W |
| Eagle Creek ≃, Or., U.S. | 224 | 45.21 N | 122.23 W |
| Eagle Creek, East Fork ≃ | 218 | 38.47 N | 83.43 W |
| Eagle Creek, West Fork ≃ | 218 | 38.47 N | 83.43 W |
| Eagle Creek Reservoir ◎[1] | 218 | 39.50 N | 86.18 W |
| Eagledale | 224 | 47.37 N | 122.32 W |
| Eagle Grove | 190 | 42.39 N | 93.54 W |
| Eagle Harbor | 210 | 43.15 N | 78.15 W |
| Eaglehawk | 169 | 36.43 S | 144.15 E |
| Eagle Hill ≃ | 283 | 42.42 N | 70.49 W |
| Eagle Key I | 220 | 25.09 N | 80.36 W |
| Eagle Lake, Fl., U.S. | 220 | 27.59 N | 81.45 W |
| Eagle Lake, Me., U.S. | 186 | 47.02 N | 68.35 W |
| Eagle Lake, Mi., U.S. | 216 | 41.48 N | 86.02 W |
| Eagle Lake, Tx., U.S. | 222 | 29.35 N | 96.20 W |
| Eagle Lake ◎, B.C., Can. | 182 | 51.55 N | 124.25 W |
| Eagle Lake ◎, On., Can. | 184 | 50.39 N | 94.54 W |
| Eagle Lake ◎, On., Can. | 184 | 49.42 N | 93.13 W |
| Eagle Lake ◎, On., Can. | 212 | 44.41 N | 76.43 W |
| Eagle Lake ◎, On., Can. | 212 | 45.08 N | 78.29 W |
| Eagle Lake ◎, Ca., U.S. | 204 | 40.39 N | 120.44 W |
| Eagle Lake ◎, Me., U.S. | 186 | 46.20 N | 69.20 W |
| Eagle Lake ◎, Mi., U.S. | 216 | 41.48 N | 86.02 W |
| Eagle Lake ◎, Tx., U.S. | 222 | 29.34 N | 96.21 W |
| Eagle Lake ◎, Wi., U.S. | 216 | 42.42 N | 88.07 W |
| Eagle Mountain, Ca., U.S. | 204 | 33.49 N | 115.27 W |
| Eagle Mountain, Tx., U.S. | 222 | 32.52 N | 97.30 W |
| Eagle Mountain ∧ | 202 | 46.20 N | 115.07 W |
| Eagle Mountain ∧[2] | 190 | 47.54 N | 90.33 W |
| Eagle Mountain Lake ◎[1] | 222 | 32.55 N | 97.30 W |
| Eagle Nest Butte ∧ | 198 | 43.27 N | 101.39 W |
| Eagle Nest Lake ◎ | 222 | 29.13 N | 95.37 W |
| Eagle Pass | 196 | 28.42 N | 100.29 W |
| Eagle Peak ∧, Ca., U.S. | 204 | 41.17 N | 120.12 W |
| Eagle Peak ∧, Ca., U.S. | 228 | 35.15 N | 118.28 W |
| Eagle Peak ∧, Ca., U.S. | 282 | 37.54 N | 121.54 W |
| Eagle River, Mi., U.S. | 190 | 47.24 N | 88.18 W |
| Eagle River, Wi., U.S. | 190 | 45.55 N | 89.14 W |
| Eagle Rock | 192 | 37.38 N | 79.48 W |
| Eagle Rock ✦[8] | 280 | 34.09 N | 118.12 W |
| Eagle Rock Reservation ♠ | 276 | 40.49 N | 74.14 W |
| Eaglesfield | 44 | 55.03 N | 3.12 W |
| Eaglesham, Ab., Can. | 182 | 55.47 N | 117.53 W |
| Eaglesham, Scot., U.K. | 46 | 55.44 N | 4.18 W |
| Eagles Mere | 210 | 41.25 N | 76.35 W |
| Eagleton Village | 192 | 35.46 N | 83.56 W |
| Eagletown | 194 | 34.02 N | 94.34 W |
| Eagle Village | 180 | 64.47 N | 141.07 W |
| Eagleville, Ct., U.S. | 207 | 41.47 N | 72.16 W |
| Eagleville, Pa., U.S. | 285 | 40.10 N | 75.24 W |
| Eagleville, Wi., U.S. | 216 | 42.52 N | 88.26 W |
| Ealing ✦[8] | 42 | 51.31 N | 0.20 W |
| Eamont ≃ | 44 | 54.40 N | 2.39 W |
| Earaheedy | 162 | 25.34 S | 121.39 E |
| Earby | 44 | 53.56 N | 2.08 W |
| Earcroft | 262 | 53.43 N | 2.29 W |
| Eardisley | 42 | 52.08 N | 2.59 W |
| Eardley Lake ◎ | 184 | 52.32 N | 96.05 W |
| Ear Falls | 184 | 50.38 N | 93.13 W |
| Earle | 194 | 35.16 N | 90.28 W |
| Earlestown | 262 | 53.27 N | 2.39 W |
| Earl Grey | 184 | 50.56 N | 104.45 W |
| Earlham | 194 | 41.29 N | 94.07 W |
| Earlimart | 226 | 35.53 N | 119.16 W |
| Earlington | 194 | 37.16 N | 87.30 W |
| Earlish | 46 | 57.34 N | 6.23 W |
| Earl Park | 216 | 40.40 N | 87.24 W |
| Earl Rowe Provincial Park ♠ | 212 | 44.10 N | 79.54 W |
| Earls Barton | 42 | 52.15 N | 0.45 W |
| Earls Colne | 42 | 51.56 N | 0.42 E |
| Earlsferry | 46 | 56.11 N | 2.50 W |
| Earl Shilton | 42 | 52.35 N | 1.20 W |
| Earl Soham | 42 | 52.14 N | 1.16 E |
| Earlston | 46 | 55.39 N | 2.40 W |
| Earlton | 210 | 42.21 N | 73.54 W |
| Earlville, Il., U.S. | 216 | 41.35 N | 88.55 W |
| Earlville, N.Y., U.S. | 210 | 42.44 N | 75.33 W |
| Earlville, Pa., U.S. | 208 | 40.19 N | 75.44 W |
| Earlwood | 274a | 33.56 S | 151.08 E |
| Early, Ia., U.S. | 198 | 42.27 N | 95.09 W |
| Early, Tx., U.S. | 196 | 31.45 N | 98.54 W |
| Early Winters Creek ≃ | 224 | 48.35 N | 120.35 W |
| Earn ≃ | 46 | 56.21 N | 3.19 W |
| Earn, Loch ◎ | 46 | 56.23 N | 4.14 W |
| Earnslaw, Mount ∧ | 172 | 44.37 S | 168.24 E |
| Earth | 196 | 34.14 N | 102.24 W |
| Eas | 175f | 16.22 S | 168.12 E |
| Easington, Eng., U.K. | 44 | 54.47 N | 1.19 W |
| Easington, Eng., U.K. | 44 | 53.40 N | 0.07 E |
| Easingwold | 44 | 54.07 N | 1.11 W |
| Easky | 48 | 54.18 N | 8.58 W |
| Easley | 192 | 34.49 N | 82.36 W |
| East ≃, On., Can. | 190 | 45.20 N | 79.17 W |
| East ≃, Co., U.S. | 200 | 38.40 N | 106.51 W |
| East ≃, N.Y., U.S. | 276 | 40.48 N | 73.48 W |
| East, University of the ψ[2] | 269f | 14.36 N | 120.59 E |
| East Acton | 283 | 42.28 N | 71.24 W |
| East Allen ≃ | 44 | 54.55 N | 2.19 W |
| East Alliance | 214 | 40.55 N | 81.04 W |
| East Alligator ≃ | 164 | 12.08 S | 132.42 E |
| East Alton | 219 | 38.52 N | 90.06 W |
| East Amherst | 210 | 43.01 N | 78.42 W |
| East-Angus | 206 | 45.29 N | 71.40 W |
| East Arlington | 210 | 43.03 N | 73.08 W |
| East Atlantic Beach | 276 | 40.35 N | 73.43 W |
| East Aurora | 210 | 42.46 N | 78.36 W |
| East Avon | 210 | 42.55 N | 77.42 W |
| East Baines ≃ | 164 | 15.38 S | 129.58 E |
| East Bangor | 210 | 40.52 N | 75.11 W |
| East Barming | 260 | 51.16 N | 0.28 E |
| East Barnet ✦[8] | 260 | 51.38 N | 0.09 W |
| East Basin ⊂ | 279a | 41.32 N | 81.40 W |
| East Bay ⊂, Fl., U.S. | 194 | 30.05 N | 85.32 W |
| East Bay ⊂, N.Y., U.S. | 210 | 40.38 N | 73.32 W |
| East Bay ⊂, Tx., U.S. | 222 | 29.30 N | 94.35 W |
| East Bedfont ✦[8] | 260 | 51.27 N | 0.26 W |
| East Bend | 192 | 36.12 N | 80.30 W |
| East Berbice-Corentyne □[4] | 246 | 4.00 N | 58.15 W |
| East Berkshire | 206 | 44.56 N | 72.42 W |
| East Berlin, Ct., U.S. | 207 | 41.37 N | 72.42 W |
| East Berlin, N.J., U.S. | 285 | 39.48 N | 74.55 W |
| East Berlin, Pa., U.S. | 208 | 39.56 N | 76.58 W |
| East Bernard | 222 | 29.32 N | 96.04 W |
| East Bernstadt | 192 | 37.11 N | 84.07 W |
| East Berwick | 210 | 41.03 N | 76.13 W |
| East Bethany | 210 | 42.56 N | 78.06 W |
| East Bhāgīrath Plain ⊻ | 126 | 23.30 N | 88.30 E |
| East Bijou Creek ≃ | 198 | 39.51 N | 104.08 W |
| East Billerica | 283 | 42.34 N | 71.14 W |
| East Blackstone | 207 | 42.02 N | 71.31 W |
| East Bloomfield | 210 | 42.54 N | 77.26 W |
| East Boston ✦[8] | 283 | 42.23 N | 71.02 W |
| Eastbourne, N.Z. | 172 | 41.18 S | 174.54 E |
| Eastbourne, Eng., U.K. | 42 | 50.46 N | 0.17 E |
| East Brady | 214 | 40.59 N | 79.36 W |
| East Braintree | 184 | 49.37 N | 95.38 W |
| East Branch | 210 | 41.59 N | 75.08 W |
| East Branch Lake ◎[1] | 214 | 41.35 N | 78.35 W |
| East Brewster | 207 | 41.46 N | 70.03 W |
| East Brewton | 194 | 31.05 N | 87.03 W |
| East Bridgewater | 207 | 42.02 N | 70.58 W |
| East Brimfield Lake ◎[1] | 207 | 42.06 N | 72.10 W |
| East Brookfield | 207 | 42.13 N | 72.02 W |
| East Brooklyn | 207 | 41.47 N | 71.53 W |
| East Brother I | 271d | 22.20 N | 113.58 E |
| East Brunswick | 208 | 40.25 N | 74.23 W |
| East Bucas Island I | 116 | 9.43 N | 126.02 E |

**ENGLISH**

| Name | Page | Lat.°′ | Long.°′ |
|---|---|---|---|
| East Burwood | 274b | 37.51 S | 145.09 E |
| Eastbury | 260 | 51.37 N | 0.25 W |
| East Butler | 214 | 40.53 N | 79.51 W |
| East Cache Creek ≃ | 196 | 34.08 N | 98.16 W |
| East Caicos I | 238 | 21.41 N | 71.30 W |
| East Calder | 46 | 55.54 N | 3.27 W |
| East Canaan | 207 | 42.00 N | 73.17 W |
| East Canada Creek ≃ | 210 | 43.00 N | 74.45 W |
| East Canton | 214 | 40.47 N | 81.17 W |
| East Cape >, N.Z. | 172 | 37.41 S | 178.33 E |
| East Cape >, Ak., U.S. | 181a | 51.21 N | 179.29 E |
| East Cape >, Fl., U.S. | 220 | 25.07 N | 81.05 W |
| East Carancahua Creek ≃ | 222 | 28.51 N | 96.19 W |
| East Carbon | 200 | 39.32 N | 110.24 W |
| East Carlisle | 214 | 41.19 N | 82.05 W |
| East Caroline Basin ✧[1] | 14 | 4.00 N | 146.45 E |
| East Castor ≃ | 212 | 45.16 N | 75.17 W |
| East Catfish Creek ≃ | 212 | 42.47 N | 81.04 W |
| East Channel ≃[1] | 180 | 69.20 N | 134.00 W |
| East Chatham | 210 | 42.25 N | 73.32 W |
| East Chelmsford | 207 | 42.36 N | 71.18 W |
| Eastchester | 210 | 40.57 N | 73.49 W |
| Eastchester Bay ⊂ | 276 | 40.51 N | 73.48 W |
| East Chicago | 216 | 41.38 N | 87.27 W |
| East Chicago Heights | 278 | 41.30 N | 87.35 W |
| East China Sea ⊤[2] | 90 | 30.00 N | 126.00 E |
| Eastchurch | 42 | 51.25 N | 0.52 E |
| East Clandon | 260 | 51.15 N | 0.29 W |
| East Claridon | 214 | 41.32 N | 81.07 W |
| East Cleddau ≃ | 42 | 51.46 N | 4.52 W |
| East Cleveland | 214 | 41.31 N | 81.34 W |
| East Coast Bays | 172 | 36.45 S | 174.46 E |
| East Concord | 210 | 42.33 N | 78.38 W |
| Eastcote ✦[8] | 260 | 51.35 N | 0.24 W |
| East Cote Blanche Bay ⊂ | 194 | 29.35 N | 91.40 W |
| East Coulee | 182 | 51.20 N | 112.29 W |
| East Creek ≃ | 276 | 40.27 N | 74.09 W |
| East Cross Creek ≃ | 212 | 44.17 N | 78.44 W |
| East Dean | 42 | 50.45 N | 0.12 E |
| East Delaware Aqueduct ≍[1] | 210 | 41.52 N | 74.31 W |
| East Dennis | 207 | 41.44 N | 70.09 W |
| East Dereham | 42 | 52.41 N | 0.56 E |
| East Dismal Swamp ≡ | 192 | 35.45 N | 76.35 W |
| East Ditch ≍ | 276 | 40.56 N | 74.19 W |
| East Douglas | 207 | 42.04 N | 71.42 W |
| East Dublin | 192 | 32.32 N | 82.52 W |
| East Dubuque | 190 | 42.29 N | 90.38 W |
| East Dundee | 216 | 42.06 N | 88.16 W |
| East Durham | 210 | 42.22 N | 74.06 W |
| East Ely | 204 | 39.15 N | 114.53 W |
| Eastend, Sk., Can. | 184 | 49.31 N | 108.48 W |
| East End, Vir. Is., U.S. | 240m | 18.21 N | 64.40 W |
| East End Point > | 240b | 25.03 N | 77.16 W |
| East Enterprise | 218 | 38.52 N | 84.59 W |
| Easter Island → Pascua, Isla de I | 174z | 27.07 S | 109.22 W |
| Easterly | 222 | 31.06 N | 96.23 W |
| Eastern □[4], Ghana | 150 | 6.30 N | 0.30 W |
| Eastern □[4], Kenya | 154 | 0.05 N | 38.00 E |
| Eastern □[4], S.L. | 150 | 8.15 N | 11.00 W |
| Eastern □[4], Zam. | 154 | 13.00 S | 32.15 E |
| Eastern □[5] | 154 | 1.25 N | 33.50 E |
| Eastern Bay ⊂ | 208 | 38.51 N | 76.19 W |
| Eastern Cape □[4] | 158 | 32.30 S | 26.30 E |
| Eastern Channel → Tsushima-kaikyō ⋓ | 92 | 34.00 N | 129.00 E |
| Eastern Cherokee Indian Reservation ✦[4] | 192 | 35.25 N | 83.24 W |
| Eastern Cove ⊂ | 168b | 35.46 S | 137.50 E |
| Eastern Creek ≃, Austl. | 166 | 20.10 S | 141.08 E |
| Eastern Creek ≃, Austl. | 274a | 33.39 S | 150.51 E |
| Eastern Division □[5] | 175g | 19.00 S | 180.00 E |
| Eastern Fields ✧[2] | 164 | 10.20 S | 145.45 E |
| Eastern Ghāts ∧∧ | 122 | 14.00 N | 78.50 E |
| Eastern Highlands □[5] | 164 | 6.30 S | 145.15 E |
| Eastern Island I | 174g | 28.12 N | 177.20 W |
| Eastern Isles II | 42a | 49.57 N | 6.15 W |
| Eastern Michigan University ψ[2] | 281 | 42.15 N | 83.37 W |
| Eastern Neck Island I | 208 | 39.02 N | 76.13 W |
| Eastern Point > | 283 | 42.35 N | 70.40 W |
| Eastern Samar □[4] | 116 | 12.00 N | 125.00 E |
| Eastern Sayans → Vostočnyj Sajan ∧∧ | 88 | 53.00 N | 97.00 E |
| Eastern Shore ✦[1] | 208 | 38.40 N | 75.50 W |
| Eastern Yamuna Canal ≍ | 272a | 28.40 N | 77.15 E |
| East Falkland I | 254 | 51.55 S | 59.00 W |
| East Falls ✦[8] | 285 | 40.01 N | 75.11 W |
| East Falmouth | 207 | 41.34 N | 70.33 W |
| East Farleigh | 260 | 51.15 N | 0.29 E |
| East Farmingdale | 276 | 40.44 N | 73.26 W |
| East Faxon | 210 | 41.15 N | 76.58 W |
| East Fayetteville | 192 | 35.05 N | 78.51 W |
| Eastfield | 44 | 54.14 N | 0.24 W |
| East Flat Rock | 192 | 35.16 N | 82.25 W |
| East Foot Hills | 226 | 37.21 N | 121.49 W |
| Eastford | 207 | 41.54 N | 72.04 W |
| East Foxboro | 283 | 42.03 N | 71.12 W |
| East Freedom | 214 | 40.21 N | 78.26 W |
| East Freetown | 207 | 41.46 N | 70.57 W |
| East Frisian Islands → Ostfriesische Inseln II | 52 | 53.44 N | 7.25 E |
| East Gaffney | 192 | 35.04 N | 81.37 W |
| East Gallatin ≃ | 202 | 45.53 N | 111.20 W |
| Eastgate | 224 | 47.34 N | 122.09 W |
| East Ghor Canal → Ghawr ash-Sharqīyah, Qanāt al- ≍ | 132 | 32.41 N | 35.38 E |
| East Glacier Park | 202 | 48.26 N | 113.13 W |
| East Glenville | 210 | 42.53 N | 73.55 W |
| East Granby | 207 | 41.56 N | 72.43 W |
| East Grand Forks | 198 | 47.55 N | 97.01 W |
| East Grand Rapids | 216 | 42.56 N | 85.36 W |
| East Greenbush | 210 | 42.35 N | 73.42 W |
| East Greenville, Oh., U.S. | 214 | 40.48 N | 81.36 W |
| East Greenville, Pa., U.S. | 208 | 40.24 N | 75.30 W |
| East Greenwich, N.Y., U.S. | 210 | 43.09 N | 73.24 W |
| East Greenwich, R.I., U.S. | 207 | 41.39 N | 71.27 W |
| East Grinstead | 42 | 51.08 N | 0.01 W |
| East Gwillimbury | 212 | 44.08 N | 79.25 W |
| East Haddam | 207 | 41.27 N | 72.27 W |
| East Half Hollow Hills | 276 | 40.57 N | 72.11 W |
| Eastham, Eng., U.K. | 262 | 53.19 N | 2.58 W |
| Eastham, Ma., U.S. | 207 | 41.49 N | 69.58 W |
| East Ham ✦[8] | 260 | 51.32 N | 0.03 E |
| East Hampton, Ct., U.S. | 207 | 41.34 N | 72.30 W |
| Easthampton, Ma., U.S. | 207 | 42.16 N | 72.40 W |
| East Hampton, N.Y., U.S. | 207 | 40.57 N | 72.11 W |
| East Hanningfield | 260 | 51.41 N | 0.34 E |
| East Hanover | 276 | 40.48 N | 74.22 W |
| East Harbor State Park ♠ | 214 | 41.32 N | 82.49 W |
| East Harling | 42 | 52.26 N | 0.55 E |
| East Hartford | 207 | 41.46 N | 72.36 W |
| East Hartland | 207 | 41.59 N | 72.54 W |
| East Harwich | 207 | 41.43 N | 70.02 W |
| East Haven | 207 | 41.16 N | 72.52 W |
| East Hazel Crest | 278 | 41.35 N | 87.39 W |

**DEUTSCH**

| Name | Seite | Breite°′ | Länge°′ E = Ost |
|---|---|---|---|
| East Helena | 202 | 46.35 N | 111.54 W |
| East Hemet | 228 | 33.45 N | 116.57 W |
| East Herkimer | 210 | 43.02 N | 74.58 W |
| East Hertfordshire □[8] | 260 | 51.46 N | 0.02 W |
| East Hickory | 214 | 41.35 N | 79.24 W |
| East Highland Park | 208 | 37.36 N | 77.25 W |
| East Hills, Austl. | 274a | 33.58 S | 150.59 E |
| East Hills, N.Y., U.S. | 276 | 40.47 N | 73.37 W |
| East Hoathly | 42 | 50.55 N | 0.10 E |
| East Horsley | 42 | 51.15 N | 0.26 W |
| East Humber ≃ | 212 | 43.47 N | 79.35 W |
| East Huntington | 276 | 40.52 N | 73.24 W |
| East Ilsley | 42 | 51.32 N | 1.17 W |
| East Irvington | 276 | 41.03 N | 73.51 W |
| East Island >[1] | 276 | 40.54 N | 73.38 W |
| East Islip | 276 | 40.43 N | 73.11 W |
| East Jewett | 210 | 42.14 N | 74.09 W |
| East Jordan | 190 | 45.09 N | 85.07 W |
| East Keansburg | 276 | 40.26 N | 74.07 W |
| East Kelowna | 182 | 49.51 N | 119.25 W |
| East Kilbride | 46 | 55.46 N | 4.10 W |
| East Killingly | 207 | 41.50 N | 71.49 W |
| East Kingston | 210 | 41.57 N | 73.58 W |
| Eastlake, Mi., U.S. | 190 | 44.15 N | 86.18 W |
| Eastlake, Oh., U.S. | 214 | 41.39 N | 81.27 W |
| East Lake ◎, On., Can. | 184 | 53.42 N | 93.10 W |
| East Lake ◎, On., Can. | 212 | 43.55 N | 77.12 W |
| East Lake ◎, N.J., U.S. | 276 | 40.58 N | 74.21 W |
| East Lake Tohopekaliga ◎ | 220 | 28.18 N | 81.17 W |
| East Lamma Channel ⋓ | 271d | 22.14 N | 114.09 E |
| Eastland | 196 | 32.24 N | 98.49 W |
| Eastland Center ✦[9] | 281 | 42.27 N | 82.56 W |
| Eastland Shopping Plaza ✦[9] | 279b | 40.22 N | 79.50 W |
| East Lansdowne | 285 | 39.56 N | 75.16 W |
| East Lansing | 216 | 42.44 N | 84.29 W |
| East Laurinburg | 192 | 34.46 N | 79.26 W |
| East Leake | 42 | 52.49 N | 1.10 W |
| Eastleigh | 42 | 50.58 N | 1.22 W |
| East Lewistown | 214 | 40.57 N | 80.42 W |
| East Liberty | 216 | 40.19 N | 83.34 W |
| East Liberty ✦[8] | 279b | 40.27 N | 79.55 W |
| East Licking Creek ≃ | 208 | 40.32 N | 77.24 W |
| East Lindfield | 274a | 33.46 S | 151.11 E |
| East Linton | 46 | 55.59 N | 2.39 W |
| East Liverpool | 214 | 40.37 N | 80.34 W |
| East London (Oos-Londen) | 158 | 33.00 S | 27.55 E |
| East Longmeadow | 207 | 42.03 N | 72.30 W |
| East Los Angeles | 228 | 34.01 N | 118.10 W |
| East Lyme | 207 | 41.22 N | 72.13 W |
| East Lynn | 216 | 40.28 N | 87.48 W |
| East Lynn Lake ◎[1] | 188 | 38.05 N | 82.20 W |
| Eastmain | 176 | 52.15 N | 78.30 W |
| Eastmain ≃ | 176 | 52.15 N | 78.35 W |
| Eastmain-Opinaca, Réservoir ◎[1] | 176 | 52.25 N | 76.35 W |
| East Malling | 260 | 51.17 N | 0.26 E |
| Eastman, P.Q., Can. | 206 | 45.18 N | 72.19 W |
| Eastman, Ga., U.S. | 192 | 32.11 N | 83.10 W |
| Eastman Lake ◎[1] | 226 | 37.14 N | 119.58 W |
| East Mansfield | 283 | 42.01 N | 71.10 W |
| East Mariana Basin ✧[1] | 14 | 12.00 N | 153.00 E |
| East Marin Island I | 282 | 37.58 N | 122.27 W |
| East Markham | 44 | 53.15 N | 0.54 W |
| East McKeesport | 279b | 40.23 N | 79.48 W |
| East Meadow | 210 | 40.43 N | 73.33 W |
| East Meadow ≃ | 283 | 42.47 N | 71.02 W |
| East Meadow Brook ≃ | 276 | 40.39 N | 73.34 W |
| East Meadowview | 216 | 41.08 N | 87.52 W |
| East Mecca | 214 | 41.24 N | 80.45 W |
| East Meredith | 210 | 42.25 N | 74.53 W |
| East Midlands Airport ⊠ | 42 | 52.50 N | 1.20 W |
| East Millbury | 207 | 42.13 N | 71.44 W |
| East Mill Creek ≃ | 222 | 29.55 N | 96.17 W |
| East Millinocket | 188 | 45.37 N | 68.34 W |
| East Millstone | 276 | 40.30 N | 74.35 W |
| East Missoula | 202 | 46.52 N | 113.58 W |
| East Molesey | 260 | 51.24 N | 0.21 W |
| East Moline | 190 | 41.30 N | 90.26 W |
| East Monongahela | 279b | 40.12 N | 79.55 W |
| East Mountain | 222 | 32.35 N | 94.51 W |
| East Mustang Creek ≃ | 222 | 29.03 N | 96.27 W |
| East Naples | 220 | 26.06 N | 81.44 W |
| East Nassau | 210 | 42.30 N | 73.30 W |
| East Newark | 276 | 40.48 N | 73.59 W |
| East New Britain □[5] | 164 | 6.00 S | 152.00 E |
| East New Market | 208 | 38.35 N | 75.55 W |
| East New York ✦[8] | 276 | 40.40 N | 73.53 W |
| East Nishnabotna ≃ | 198 | 40.39 N | 95.37 W |
| East Nodaway ≃ | 194 | 40.38 N | 95.01 W |
| East Norriton | 208 | 40.09 N | 75.18 W |
| East Northfield | 207 | 42.43 N | 72.27 W |
| East Northport | 210 | 40.52 N | 73.19 W |
| East Norwich | 210 | 40.50 N | 73.32 W |
| East Novaya Zemlya Trough ✧[1] | 12 | 73.30 N | 61.00 E |
| East Olympia | 224 | 46.58 N | 122.50 W |
| Easton, Eng., U.K. | 42 | 50.32 N | 2.26 W |
| Easton, Ca., U.S. | 226 | 36.39 N | 119.47 W |
| Easton, Ct., U.S. | 207 | 41.15 N | 73.17 W |
| Easton, Il., U.S. | 219 | 40.14 N | 89.50 W |
| Easton, Md., U.S. | 208 | 38.46 N | 76.04 W |
| Easton, Ma., U.S. | 283 | 42.02 N | 71.06 W |
| Easton, Pa., U.S. | 208 | 40.41 N | 75.13 W |
| Easton, Tx., U.S. | 222 | 32.23 N | 94.35 W |
| Easton, Wa., U.S. | 224 | 47.14 N | 121.10 W |
| Eastondale | 283 | 42.02 N | 71.04 W |
| Easton Reservoir ◎[1] | 207 | 41.16 N | 73.16 W |
| East Orange | 210 | 40.46 N | 74.12 W |
| East Orleans | 207 | 41.47 N | 69.58 W |
| East Otto | 210 | 42.23 N | 78.45 W |
| Eastover | 192 | 33.52 N | 80.41 W |
| East Pacific Rise ✧[3] | 6 | 20.00 S | 115.00 W |
| East Pakistan → Bangladesh □[1] | 118 | 24.00 N | 90.00 E |
| East Palatka | 192 | 29.39 N | 81.35 W |
| East Palestine | 214 | 40.50 N | 80.32 W |
| East Palo Alto | 226 | 37.28 N | 122.08 W |
| East Park Reservoir ◎[1] | 226 | 39.21 N | 122.30 W |
| East Parkrose | 224 | 45.33 N | 122.32 W |
| East Peak ∧ | 116 | 11.13 N | 119.29 E |
| East Peckham | 42 | 51.15 N | 0.23 E |
| East Pecos | 200 | 35.34 N | 105.39 W |
| East Pembroke, Ma., U.S. | 283 | 42.05 N | 70.46 W |
| East Pembroke, N.Y., U.S. | 210 | 42.59 N | 78.18 W |
| East Peoria | 190 | 40.39 N | 89.34 W |
| East Pepperell | 207 | 42.39 N | 71.34 W |
| East Petersburg | 208 | 40.06 N | 76.21 W |
| East Pharsalia | 210 | 42.34 N | 75.43 W |
| East Pine | 182 | 55.43 N | 121.13 W |
| East Pines | 284c | 38.57 N | 76.55 W |
| East Pittsburgh | 279b | 40.23 N | 79.50 W |
| Eastpoint, Fl., U.S. | 192 | 29.44 N | 84.52 W |
| East Point, Ga., U.S. | 192 | 33.40 N | 84.26 W |
| East Point >, P.E., Can. | 186 | 46.27 N | 61.58 W |
| East Point >, Ma., U.S. | 207 | 42.25 N | 70.54 W |
| East Point >, Vir. Is., U.S. | 241n | 17.45 N | 64.34 W |
| Eastpoint ✦[9] | 284b | 39.18 N | 76.31 W |
| Eastpointe | 214 | 42.28 N | 82.57 W |
| Eastport, Nf., Can. | 186 | 48.39 N | 53.45 W |
| Eastport, Id., U.S. | 202 | 49.00 N | 116.10 W |
| Eastport, Me., U.S. | 188 | 44.54 N | 66.59 W |
| Eastport, N.Y., U.S. | 207 | 40.49 N | 72.44 W |
| East Porterville | 204 | 36.04 N | 118.56 W |
| East Potomac Park ♠ | 284c | 38.52 N | 77.01 W |


**Symbols** in the index entries represent the broad categories identified in the key at the right. Symbols with superior numbers (∧∧[1]) identify subcategories (see complete key on page *I · 1).*

**Symbole** im Register stellen die rechts im Schlüssel erklärten Kategorien dar. Symbole mit hochgestellten Ziffern (∧∧[1]) bezeichnen Unterabteilungen einer Kategorie (vgl. vollständiger Schlüssel auf Seite *I · 1).*

**Los símbolos** incluídos en el texto del índice representan las grandes categorías identificadas con la clave a la derecha. Los símbolos con numeros en su parte superior (∧∧[1]) identifican las subcategorías (véase la clave completa en la página *I · 1).*

**Les symboles** de l'index représentent les catégories indiquées dans la légende à droite. Les symboles suivis d'un indice (∧∧[1]) représentent des souscatégories (voir légende complète à la page *I · 1).*

**Os símbolos** incluídos no texto do índice representam as grandes categorias identificadas com a chave à direita. Os símbolos com números em sua parte superior (∧∧[1]) identificam as subcategorias (vejase a chave completa à página *I · 1).*

| | | | | |
|---|---|---|---|---|
| ∧ Mountain | Berg | Montaña | Montagne | Montanha |
| ∧∧ Mountains | Gebirge | Montañas | Montagnes | Montanhas |
| )( Pass | Paß | Paso | Col | Passo |
| V Valley, Canyon | Tal, Cañon | Valle, Cañón | Vallée, Canyon | Vale, Canhão |
| ⊻ Plain | Ebene | Llano | Plaine | Planície |
| > Cape | Kap | Cabo | Cap | Cabo |
| I Island | Insel | Isla | Île | Ilha |
| II Islands | Inseln | Islas | Îles | Ilhas |
| ± Other Topographic Features | Andere Topographische Objekte | Otros Elementos Topográficos | Autres données topographiques | Outros acidentes topográficos |

ESPAÑOL — Nombre | Página | Lat.°' | Long.°' W = Oeste
FRANÇAIS — Nom | Page | Lat.°' | Long.°' W = Ouest
PORTUGUÊS — Nome | Página | Lat.°' | Long.°' W = Oeste


| | | | |
|---|---|---|---|
| East Prairie | 194 | 36.46 N | 89.23 W |
| East Prairie ≃ | 182 | 55.34 N | 116.25 W |
| East Prospect | 208 | 39.58 N | 76.31 W |
| East Providence | 207 | 41.48 N | 71.22 W |
| East Pryor Mountain ∧ | 202 | 45.11 N | 108.20 W |
| East Quogue | 207 | 40.51 N | 72.35 W |
| East Rājasthān Uplands ⩘[1] | 124 | 26.40 N | 76.35 E |
| East Randolph | 210 | 42.10 N | 78.56 W |
| East Retford | 44 | 53.19 N | 0.56 W |
| East Richmond | 282 | 37.57 N | 122.19 W |
| Eastridge Center ◆[9] | 282 | 37.20 N | 121.49 W |
| East Rigaud ≃ | 206 | 45.27 N | 74.22 W |
| Eastriggs | 44 | 54.59 N | 3.10 W |
| East River c | 208 | 37.24 N | 76.21 W |
| East Rochester, N.Y., U.S. | 210 | 43.06 N | 77.29 W |
| East Rochester, Oh., U.S. | 214 | 40.45 N | 81.02 W |
| East Rockaway | 276 | 40.38 N | 73.40 W |
| East Rockingham | 192 | 34.55 N | 79.45 W |
| East Rockwood | 216 | 42.03 N | 83.13 W |
| East Rosebud Creek ≃ | 202 | 45.29 N | 109.27 W |
| East Rudolf National Park ♠ | 154 | 3.55 N | 36.20 E |
| East Rutherford | 276 | 40.50 N | 74.05 W |
| Eastry | 42 | 51.15 N | 1.18 E |
| East Saint Louis | 219 | 38.38 N | 90.09 W |
| East Salem | 208 | 40.37 N | 77.14 W |
| East Salt Creek ≃ | 200 | 39.13 N | 108.54 W |
| East Sandwich | 207 | 41.44 N | 70.27 W |
| East Sandy Creek ≃ | 214 | 41.22 N | 79.51 W |
| East Schodack | 210 | 42.34 N | 73.38 W |
| East Scotia Basin ✢[1] | 9 | 57.00 S | 35.00 W |
| East Sepik □[5] | 164 | 4.00 S | 143.30 E |
| East Setauket | 210 | 40.57 N | 73.06 W |
| East Shoal Lake ⊜ | 184 | 50.23 N | 97.37 W |
| East Siberian Sea → Vostočno-Sibirskoje more ⊤[2] | 12 | 74.00 N | 166.00 E |
| East Side | 210 | 41.04 N | 75.46 W |
| Eastside Bypass ≊ | 226 | 37.05 N | 120.28 W |
| East Side Canal ≊, Ca., U.S. | 226 | 37.21 N | 120.55 W |
| East Side Canal ≊, Ca., U.S. | 226 | 35.33 N | 119.33 W |
| East Sixteen Mile Creek ≃ | 275b | 43.28 N | 79.48 W |
| East Smethport | 214 | 41.49 N | 78.26 W |
| East Smithfield | 210 | 41.52 N | 76.38 W |
| East Sooke | 224 | 48.22 N | 123.43 W |
| Eastsound | 224 | 48.41 N | 122.54 W |
| East Sound ʊ | 224 | 48.39 N | 122.53 W |
| East Sparta | 214 | 40.40 N | 81.21 W |
| East Spencer | 192 | 35.40 N | 80.25 W |
| East Springbrook | 284c | 39.04 N | 77.00 W |
| East Springfield, Oh., U.S. | 214 | 40.27 N | 80.52 W |
| East Springfield, Pa., U.S. | 214 | 41.57 N | 80.28 W |
| East Stony Creek ≃ | 210 | 43.15 N | 74.12 W |
| East Stour ≃ | 42 | 51.08 N | 0.53 E |
| East Stroudsburg | 210 | 40.59 N | 75.10 W |
| East Sudbury | 283 | 42.24 N | 71.24 W |
| East Sussex □[6] | 42 | 50.55 N | 0.15 E |
| East Syracuse | 210 | 43.04 N | 76.05 W |
| East Tawas | 190 | 44.16 N | 83.29 W |
| East Templeton | 207 | 42.33 N | 72.02 W |
| East Texas | 210 | 40.33 N | 75.33 W |
| East Thompson | 207 | 42.00 N | 71.48 W |
| East Tilbury | 260 | 51.28 N | 0.26 E |
| East Troy | 216 | 42.47 N | 88.24 W |
| East Tustin | 280 | 33.46 N | 117.49 W |
| Eastvale | 214 | 40.46 N | 80.19 W |
| East Vandergrift | 214 | 40.36 N | 79.34 W |
| Eastview | 218 | 40.19 N | 80.38 W |
| Eastville | 208 | 37.21 N | 75.56 W |
| East Walker ≃ | 204 | 38.53 N | 119.10 W |
| East Walpole | 207 | 42.09 N | 71.12 W |
| East Wareham | 207 | 41.45 N | 70.40 W |
| East Washington | 214 | 40.10 N | 80.14 W |
| East Waterford | 208 | 40.22 N | 77.36 W |
| East Wemyss | 46 | 56.09 N | 3.04 W |
| East Wenatchee | 202 | 47.24 N | 120.17 W |
| East Wenonah | 285 | 39.47 N | 75.08 W |
| East White Plains | 276 | 41.03 N | 73.47 W |
| Eastwick ◆[8] | 285 | 39.55 N | 75.14 W |
| East Wickham ◆[8] | 260 | 51.28 N | 0.07 E |
| East Williamson | 210 | 43.14 N | 77.09 W |
| East Williston | 276 | 40.46 N | 73.38 W |
| East Wilmington | 192 | 34.13 N | 77.53 W |
| East Wittering | 42 | 50.41 N | 0.53 W |
| Eastwood, Austl. | 274a | 33.48 S | 151.05 E |
| Eastwood, Eng., U.K. | 44 | 53.01 N | 1.18 W |
| Eastwood, Eng., U.K. | 260 | 51.34 N | 0.40 E |
| Eastwood, Eng., U.K. | 262 | 53.43 N | 2.03 W |
| Eastwood, Mi., U.S. | 216 | 42.18 N | 85.33 W |
| Eastwood, Pa., U.S. | 279b | 40.17 N | 79.31 W |
| East Worcester | 210 | 42.37 N | 74.40 W |
| East Yegua Creek ≃ | 222 | 30.19 N | 96.45 W |
| East Yellow Creek ≃ | 194 | 39.38 N | 93.04 W |
| East York, On., Can. | 212 | 43.41 N | 79.20 W |
| East York, Pa., U.S. | 208 | 39.58 N | 76.43 W |
| Eaton, Austl. | 168a | 33.19 S | 115.43 E |
| Eaton, Co., U.S. | 200 | 40.31 N | 104.42 W |
| Eaton, In., U.S. | 216 | 40.20 N | 85.21 W |
| Eaton, N.Y., U.S. | 210 | 42.51 N | 75.37 W |
| Eaton, Oh., U.S. | 218 | 39.44 N | 84.38 W |
| Eaton ≃ | 206 | 45.28 N | 71.39 W |
| Eaton Estates | 214 | 41.19 N | 82.01 W |
| Eatonia | 184 | 51.13 N | 109.23 W |
| Eaton Nord ≃ | 206 | 45.24 N | 71.35 W |
| Eaton Park | 220 | 28.00 N | 81.54 W |
| Eaton Rapids | 216 | 42.30 N | 84.39 W |
| Eatons Neck | 276 | 40.56 N | 73.24 W |
| Eatons Neck ≻[1] | 276 | 40.57 N | 73.23 W |
| Eatons Neck Point ≻ | 210 | 40.57 N | 73.24 W |
| Eaton Socon | 42 | 52.13 N | 0.18 W |
| Eatonton | 192 | 33.19 N | 83.23 W |
| Eatontown | 208 | 40.17 N | 74.03 W |
| Eatonville | 224 | 46.52 N | 122.15 W |
| Eaton Wash V | 280 | 34.04 N | 118.03 W |
| Eaton Wash Dam ◆[6] | 280 | 34.10 N | 118.06 W |
| Eau ≃ | 44 | 53.31 N | 0.44 W |
| Eaubonne | 261 | 49.00 N | 2.17 E |
| Eau Claire, Mi., U.S. | 216 | 41.59 N | 86.17 W |
| Eau Claire, Pa., U.S. | 214 | 41.08 N | 79.48 W |
| Eau Claire, Wi., U.S. | 190 | 44.48 N | 91.29 W |
| Eau Claire ≃, Wi., U.S. | 190 | 44.49 N | 91.31 W |
| Eau Claire ≃, Wi., U.S. | 190 | 44.55 N | 89.37 W |
| Eau Claire, Lac à l' ⊜, P.Q., Can. | 176 | 56.10 N | 74.25 W |
| Eau Claire, Lac à l' ⊜, P.Q., Can. | 206 | 46.33 N | 73.04 W |
| Eau Galle ≃ | 190 | 44.37 N | 92.00 W |
| Eau Gallie | 220 | 28.08 N | 80.38 W |
| Eaulne ≃ | 50 | 49.54 N | 1.07 E |
| Eauripik I[1] | 108 | 6.42 N | 143.03 E |
| Eauripik Rise ✢[3] | 14 | 3.00 N | 142.00 E |
| Eauze | 32 | 43.52 N | 0.06 E |
| Ebabaka | 152 | 2.30 S | 18.19 E |
| Eban | 150 | 9.44 N | 4.56 E |
| Ebanga | 152 | 12.44 S | 14.44 E |
| Ebangalakata | 152 | 0.29 S | 21.29 E |
| Ebano | 234 | 22.13 N | 98.22 W |
| Ebb and Flow Indian Reserve ◆[4] | 184 | 51.05 N | 99.05 W |
| Ebb and Flow Lake ⊜ | 184 | 51.05 N | 98.56 W |
| Ebbegebirge ⩘ | 56 | 51.08 N | 7.46 E |
| Ebben Creek ≃ | 283 | 42.38 N | 70.45 W |
| Ebberup | 41 | 55.15 N | 9.59 E |
| Ebbetts Pass )( | 226 | 38.33 N | 119.48 W |
| Ebbs | 64 | 47.38 N | 12.13 E |
| Ebbw ≃ | 42 | 51.33 N | 2.59 W |
| Ebbw Vale | 42 | 51.47 N | 3.12 W |
| Ebebiyín | 152 | 2.09 N | 11.20 E |
| Ebeji (El Beïd) ≃ | 146 | 12.32 N | 14.11 E |
| Ebejty, ozero ⊜ | 86 | 54.38 N | 71.44 E |
| Ebeleben | 54 | 51.17 N | 10.43 E |
| Ebeltoft | 41 | 56.12 N | 10.41 E |
| Ebeltoft Vig c | 41 | 56.10 N | 10.36 E |
| Ebenau | 64 | 47.47 N | 13.11 E |
| Ebendorf | 54 | 52.11 N | 11.34 E |
| Ebene Reichenau | 64 | 46.51 N | 13.54 E |
| Ebenezer | 275b | 43.46 N | 79.40 W |
| Ebenezer Ridge ∧ | 218 | 39.06 N | 84.55 W |
| Eben Junction | 190 | 46.21 N | 86.58 W |
| Ebensburg | 214 | 40.29 N | 78.43 W |
| Ebensee | 64 | 47.48 N | 13.46 E |
| Ebensfeld | 56 | 50.04 N | 10.58 E |
| Eberbach | 56 | 49.28 N | 8.59 E |
| Ebergassing | 264b | 48.03 N | 16.31 E |
| Eber Gölü ⊜ | 130 | 38.38 N | 31.12 E |
| Ebergötzen | 52 | 51.34 N | 10.06 E |
| Ebermannstadt | 60 | 49.43 N | 11.13 E |
| Ebern | 56 | 50.05 N | 10.47 E |
| Eberndorf | 61 | 46.35 N | 14.38 E |
| Ebersbach, Dtsch. | 54 | 51.15 N | 13.37 E |
| Ebersbach, Dtsch. | 54 | 51.00 N | 14.35 E |
| Ebersbach, Dtsch. | 56 | 48.43 N | 9.31 E |
| Ebersberg | 60 | 48.05 N | 11.58 E |
| Eberschwang | 60 | 48.09 N | 13.34 E |
| Ebersdorf, Dtsch. | 52 | 53.31 N | 9.03 E |
| Ebersdorf, Dtsch. | 54 | 50.29 N | 11.40 E |
| Ebersdorf bei Coburg | 56 | 50.13 N | 11.04 E |
| Eberstein | 61 | 46.48 N | 14.34 E |
| Eberswalde-Finow | 54 | 52.50 N | 13.49 E |
| Ebetsu | 92a | 43.07 N | 141.34 E |
| Ebian | 102 | 29.10 N | 103.20 E |
| Ebina | 94 | 35.26 N | 139.25 E |
| Ebino | 92 | 32.03 N | 130.50 E |
| Ebinur Hu ⊜ | 86 | 44.55 N | 82.55 E |
| Ebi-Sekigahara-Yōrō-kokutei-kōen ♠ | 94 | 35.30 N | 136.30 E |
| Ebnat | 58 | 47.15 N | 9.08 E |
| Ebo | 152 | 11.02 S | 14.41 E |
| Ebola ≃ | 152 | 3.20 N | 20.57 E |
| Eboli | 68 | 40.37 N | 15.04 E |
| Ebolowa | 152 | 2.54 N | 11.09 E |
| Ebon I[1] | 14 | 4.35 N | 168.44 E |
| Ebonda | 152 | 2.12 N | 22.21 E |
| Ebony | 156 | 22.05 S | 15.15 E |
| Eboshi-yama ∧ | 96 | 35.04 N | 133.04 E |
| Eboué Stadium ♠ | 273b | 4.17 S | 15.18 E |
| Ebrach | 56 | 49.50 N | 10.29 E |
| Ebre, Delta de l' ≚[2] | 34 | 40.43 N | 0.54 E |
| Ebreichsdorf | 61 | 47.58 N | 16.24 E |
| Ébrié, Lagune c | 150 | 5.14 N | 4.26 W |
| Ebro (Ebre) ≃ | 34 | 40.43 N | 0.54 E |
| Ebro, Embalse del ⊜[1] | 34 | 43.00 N | 3.58 W |
| Ebstorf | 52 | 53.01 N | 10.25 E |
| Ebute-Ikorodu | 273a | 6.37 N | 3.30 E |
| Ebute-Metta ◆[8] | 273a | 6.29 N | 3.23 E |
| Ecatepec | 286a | 19.35 N | 99.04 W |
| Écaussinnes-d'Enghen | 50 | 50.34 N | 4.10 E |
| Ecclefechan | 44 | 55.03 N | 3.17 W |
| Eccles, Eng., U.K. | 44 | 53.29 N | 2.21 W |
| Eccles, Eng., U.K. | 260 | 51.19 N | 0.29 E |
| Eccles, W.V., U.S. | 192 | 37.46 N | 81.15 W |
| Eccleshall | 42 | 52.52 N | 2.15 W |
| Eccleston, Eng., U.K. | 44 | 53.38 N | 2.43 W |
| Eccleston, Eng., U.K. | 262 | 53.27 N | 2.47 W |
| Eccleston, Md., U.S. | 284b | 39.24 N | 76.44 W |
| Eceabat | 130 | 40.11 N | 26.21 E |
| Echabi | 89 | 53.30 N | 142.59 E |
| Echague | 116 | 16.42 N | 121.40 E |
| Echallens | 58 | 46.38 N | 6.38 E |
| Echaporã | 255 | 22.26 S | 50.12 W |
| Echarcon | 261 | 48.34 N | 2.24 E |
| Échauffour | 50 | 48.44 N | 0.23 E |
| Ech Cheliff (Orléansville) | 148 | 36.10 N | 1.20 E |
| Echeconnee Creek ≃ | 192 | 32.39 N | 83.36 W |
| Echelon Mall ◆[9] | 285 | 39.51 N | 75.00 W |
| Echeng | 100 | 30.24 N | 114.51 E |
| Échenoz-la-Méline | 58 | 47.36 N | 6.08 E |
| Echi ≃ | 94 | 35.13 N | 136.07 E |
| Echigawa | 94 | 35.10 N | 136.12 E |
| Echigo-sammyaku ⩘ | 92 | 37.50 N | 139.50 E |
| Echimamish ≃ | 184 | 54.20 N | 97.27 W |
| Echizen | 94 | 35.54 N | 136.00 E |
| Echizen-Kaga-kaigan-kokutei-kōen ♠ | 94 | 36.08 N | 136.05 E |
| Echizen-misaki ≻ | 94 | 35.59 N | 135.57 E |
| Echo | 198 | 44.37 N | 95.25 W |
| Echo Bay | 176 | 66.05 N | 118.02 W |
| Echo Bay c | 276 | 40.54 N | 73.46 W |
| Echoing ≃ | 184 | 55.51 N | 92.05 W |
| Echoing Lake ⊜ | 184 | 54.31 N | 92.15 W |
| Echo Lake ⊜, Il., U.S. | 278 | 42.13 N | 88.05 W |
| Echo Lake ⊜, N.J., U.S. | 276 | 41.04 N | 74.25 W |
| Echo Summit ∧ | 226 | 38.50 N | 120.02 W |
| Echouani, Lac ⊜ | 190 | 47.46 N | 75.42 W |
| Echt, Ned. | 52 | 51.06 N | 5.52 E |
| Echt, Scot., U.K. | 46 | 57.08 N | 2.26 W |
| Echternach | 56 | 49.48 N | 6.26 E |
| Echternacherbrück | 56 | 49.49 N | 6.25 E |
| Echuca | 166 | 36.08 S | 144.46 E |
| Echunga | 168b | 35.07 S | 138.48 E |
| Écija | 34 | 37.32 N | 5.05 W |
| Ecilda Paullier | 258 | 34.22 S | 57.04 W |
| Eck, Loch ⊜ | 46 | 56.05 N | 5.00 W |
| Eckartsberga | 54 | 51.07 N | 11.34 E |
| Eckbolsheim | 58 | 48.35 N | 7.41 E |
| Eckental | 60 | 49.35 N | 11.15 E |
| Eckernförde | 41 | 54.28 N | 9.50 E |
| Eckernförder Bucht c | 41 | 54.30 N | 10.02 E |
| Eckerö I | 26 | 60.14 N | 19.35 E |
| Eckersdorf | 60 | 49.56 N | 11.30 E |
| Eckington | 44 | 53.19 N | 1.21 W |
| Eckley | 210 | 40.59 N | 75.51 W |
| Eckville | 182 | 52.21 N | 114.22 W |
| Eckwarderhörne | 52 | 53.31 N | 8.14 E |
| Eclectic | 194 | 32.38 N | 86.02 W |
| Ecleto | 222 | 29.03 N | 97.45 W |
| Ecleto Creek ≃ | 196 | 28.52 N | 97.45 W |
| Eclipse Sound ʊ | 176 | 72.38 N | 79.00 W |
| Ečmiadzin | 84 | 40.10 N | 44.18 E |
| Ecola State Park ♠ | 224 | 45.57 N | 123.58 W |
| École ≃ | 261 | 48.32 N | 2.33 E |
| École Militaire (Saint-Cyr) ■ | 261 | 48.48 N | 2.04 E |
| Écommoy | 50 | 47.50 N | 0.16 E |
| Econfina ≃ | 192 | 30.02 N | 83.55 W |
| Econlockhatchee ≃ | 220 | 28.42 N | 81.02 W |
| Economy, In., U.S. | 218 | 39.58 N | 85.05 W |
| Economy, Pa., U.S. | 214 | 40.39 N | 80.14 W |
| Economy Park ♠ | 279b | 40.37 N | 80.12 W |
| Ecoporanga | 255 | 18.23 S | 40.50 W |
| Écorce, Lac de l' ⊜[1] | 190 | 47.05 N | 76.24 W |
| Écorces, Lac des ⊜ | 206 | 46.00 N | 74.32 W |
| Ecorse | 216 | 42.14 N | 83.08 W |
| Ecorse ≃ | 281 | 42.14 N | 83.09 W |
| Ecorse, South Branch ≃ | 281 | 42.14 N | 83.09 W |
| Écos | 50 | 49.10 N | 1.39 E |
| Écosse → Scotland □[8] | 28 | 57.00 N | 4.00 W |
| Écouen | 50 | 49.01 N | 2.23 E |
| Écouen, Château d' ⊥ | 261 | 49.01 N | 2.23 E |
| Écouis | 50 | 49.19 N | 1.26 E |
| Ecoute, Ru d' ≃ | 261 | 48.39 N | 2.26 E |
| Ecquevilly | 261 | 48.57 N | 1.55 E |
| Écrins, Barre des ∧ | 62 | 44.55 N | 6.22 E |
| Écrins, Massif des ⩘[1] | 62 | 44.55 N | 6.20 E |
| Écrins, Parc National des ♠ | 62 | 44.50 N | 6.15 E |
| Écrosnes | 261 | 48.33 N | 1.44 E |
| Ecru | 194 | 34.21 N | 89.01 W |
| Ecser | 264c | 47.27 N | 19.20 E |
| Ecstall ≃ | 182 | 54.09 N | 129.56 W |
| Ecuador □[1], S.A. | 242 | 2.00 S | 77.30 W |
| Ecuador □[1], S.A. | 246 | 2.00 S | 77.30 W |
| Ecuandureo | 234 | 20.10 N | 102.11 W |
| Écueillé | 32 | 47.05 N | 1.21 E |
| Écuisses | 58 | 46.45 N | 4.32 E |
| Ecum Secum | 186 | 44.58 N | 62.08 W |
| Écury-sur-Coole | 50 | 48.54 N | 4.20 E |
| Ed, Erit. | 144 | 13.52 N | 41.40 E |
| Ed, Sve. | 26 | 58.55 N | 11.55 E |
| Eda ◆[8] | 268 | 35.34 N | 139.34 E |
| Edah | 162 | 28.17 S | 117.10 E |
| Edam, Sk., Can. | 184 | 53.12 N | 108.46 W |
| Edam, Ned. | 52 | 52.31 N | 5.03 E |
| Eday I | 46 | 59.11 N | 2.47 W |
| Edderton | 46 | 57.50 N | 4.10 W |
| Eddington Gardens | 285 | 40.06 N | 74.57 W |
| Eddleston | 46 | 55.43 N | 3.13 W |
| Eddrachillis Bay c | 46 | 58.18 N | 5.15 W |
| Eddy | 222 | 31.18 N | 97.15 W |
| Eddystone | 208 | 39.51 N | 75.20 W |
| Eddystone Point ≻ | 166 | 41.00 S | 148.21 E |
| Eddystone Rocks II[1] | 42 | 50.12 N | 4.15 W |
| Eddyville, Ia., U.S. | 190 | 41.09 N | 92.38 W |
| Eddyville, Ky., U.S. | 194 | 37.05 N | 88.04 W |
| Eddyville, N.Y., U.S. | 210 | 41.54 N | 74.02 W |
| Ede, Ned. | 52 | 52.03 N | 5.40 E |
| Ede, Nig. | 150 | 7.44 N | 4.27 E |
| Edéa | 152 | 3.48 N | 10.08 E |
| Edebäck | 40 | 60.04 N | 13.33 E |
| Edebo | 40 | 60.01 N | 18.34 E |
| Edegem | 52 | 51.09 N | 4.27 E |
| Edehon Lake ⊜ | 176 | 60.25 N | 97.15 W |
| Edéia | 255 | 17.18 S | 49.55 W |
| Edelény | 30 | 48.18 N | 20.44 E |
| Edelsfeld | 60 | 49.34 N | 11.42 E |
| Edelshausen | 60 | 48.37 N | 11.17 E |
| Edelweiss | 273d | 26.16 S | 28.28 E |
| Edelweiss Spitze ∧ | 64 | 47.07 N | 12.50 E |
| Edemissen | 52 | 52.23 N | 10.16 E |
| Eden, Austl. | 166 | 37.04 S | 149.54 E |
| Éden, Bra. | 287a | 22.48 S | 43.24 W |
| Eden, N. Ire., U.K. | 48 | 54.44 N | 5.47 W |
| Eden, Mi., U.S. | 216 | 42.32 N | 84.26 W |
| Eden, Ms., U.S. | 194 | 32.59 N | 90.19 W |
| Eden, N.Y., U.S. | 210 | 42.39 N | 78.53 W |
| Eden, Tx., U.S. | 196 | 31.12 N | 99.50 W |
| Eden, Wy., U.S. | 200 | 42.03 N | 109.26 W |
| Eden ≃, Eng., U.K. | 42 | 51.10 N | 0.11 E |
| Eden ≃, Eng., U.K. | 44 | 54.57 N | 3.01 W |
| Eden ≃, Scot., U.K. | 46 | 56.22 N | 2.50 W |
| Eden ≃, Wales, U.K. | 42 | 52.48 N | 3.53 W |
| Edenbridge | 42 | 51.12 N | 0.04 E |
| Edenburg | 158 | 29.45 S | 25.56 E |
| Eden Canyon V | 282 | 37.42 N | 122.01 W |
| Edendale, N.Z. | 172 | 46.19 S | 168.47 E |
| Edendale, S. Afr. | 158 | 29.39 S | 30.18 E |
| Edendale, S. Afr. | 273d | 26.09 S | 28.09 E |
| Edenderry | 48 | 53.20 N | 7.03 W |
| Edenfield | 262 | 53.40 N | 2.18 W |
| Eden Hill ∧[2] | 207 | 41.20 N | 73.19 W |
| Edenkoben | 56 | 49.17 N | 8.07 E |
| Eden Lake ⊜ | 184 | 56.38 N | 100.15 W |
| Eden Mills | 212 | 43.35 N | 80.09 W |
| Eden Park ◆[8] | 260 | 51.23 N | 0.02 W |
| Edenside V | 44 | 54.40 N | 2.35 W |
| Edenton | 192 | 36.03 N | 76.36 W |
| Edenvale | 273d | 26.08 S | 28.09 E |
| Eden Valley, Austl. | 168b | 34.39 S | 139.06 E |
| Eden Valley, Mn., U.S. | 190 | 45.19 N | 94.32 W |
| Edenville | 158 | 27.37 S | 27.34 E |
| Edeowie | 166 | 31.27 S | 138.27 E |
| Eder ≃ | 56 | 51.13 N | 9.27 E |
| Ederkopf ∧ | 56 | 50.56 N | 8.12 E |
| Ederny | 48 | 54.32 N | 7.39 W |
| Edersee ⊜[1] | 56 | 51.11 N | 9.00 E |
| Eder-Talsperre ◆[6] | 56 | 51.11 N | 9.02 E |
| Edesheim | 56 | 49.16 N | 8.08 E |
| Edessa → Édhessa | 38 | 40.48 N | 22.03 E |
| Edewecht | 52 | 53.07 N | 8.02 E |
| Edfu → Idfū | 140 | 24.58 N | 32.52 E |
| Edgar, Ne., U.S. | 198 | 40.22 N | 97.58 W |
| Edgar, Wi., U.S. | 190 | 44.55 N | 89.57 W |
| Edgard | 194 | 30.03 N | 90.34 W |
| Edgar Ranges ⩘ | 162 | 18.43 S | 123.25 E |
| Edgars Creek ≃ | 274b | 37.44 S | 144.58 E |
| Edgartown | 207 | 41.23 N | 70.30 W |
| Edgartown Harbor c | 207 | 41.24 N | 70.30 W |
| Edgecliff | 222 | 32.39 N | 97.22 W |
| Edgecumbe | 172 | 37.59 S | 176.50 E |
| Edgefield | 192 | 33.47 N | 81.55 W |
| Edge Hill ◆[8] | 262 | 53.24 N | 2.57 W |
| Edge Hill ∧ | 42 | 52.08 N | 1.27 W |
| Edgeley, On., Can. | 275b | 43.48 N | 79.31 W |
| Edgeley, N.D., U.S. | 198 | 46.21 N | 98.42 W |
| Edgely | 285 | 40.07 N | 74.50 W |
| Edgemere | 208 | 39.14 N | 76.26 W |
| Edgemont, Pa., U.S. | 285 | 39.57 N | 75.27 W |
| Edgemont, S.D., U.S. | 198 | 43.18 N | 103.49 W |
| Edgemont Park | 216 | 42.44 N | 84.36 W |
| Edgemoor | 285 | 39.45 N | 75.30 W |
| Edge Mountain ∧ | 180 | 58.12 N | 152.06 W |
| Edgeøya I | 12 | 77.45 N | 22.30 E |
| Edgeroi | 166 | 30.07 S | 149.48 E |
| Edgerton, Ab., Can. | 184 | 52.45 N | 110.27 W |
| Edgerton, In., U.S. | 216 | 41.05 N | 84.49 W |
| Edgerton, Mn., U.S. | 198 | 43.52 N | 96.07 W |
| Edgerton, Oh., U.S. | 216 | 41.26 N | 84.44 W |
| Edgerton, Wi., U.S. | 216 | 42.50 N | 89.04 W |
| Edgerton, Wy., U.S. | 200 | 43.24 N | 106.14 W |
| Edgewater, Al., U.S. | 194 | 33.31 N | 86.57 W |
| Edgewater, Fl., U.S. | 220 | 28.59 N | 80.54 W |
| Edgewater, N.J., U.S. | 276 | 40.50 N | 73.58 W |
| Edgewater Park | 285 | 40.04 N | 74.54 W |
| Edgewater Park ♠ | 279a | 41.29 N | 81.43 W |
| Edgewater Point ≻ | 276 | 40.55 N | 73.44 W |
| Edgewood, B.C., Can. | 182 | 49.47 N | 118.08 W |
| Edgewood, Fl., U.S. | 220 | 28.29 N | 81.22 W |
| Edgewood, Il., U.S. | 219 | 38.55 N | 88.40 W |
| Edgewood, In., U.S. | 218 | 40.06 N | 85.44 W |
| Edgewood, Ia., U.S. | 190 | 42.38 N | 91.24 W |
| Edgewood, Md., U.S. | 208 | 39.25 N | 76.17 W |
| Edgewood, Oh., U.S. | 214 | 41.52 N | 80.46 W |
| Edgewood, Pa., U.S. | 279b | 40.25 N | 79.52 W |
| Edgewood, Tx., U.S. | 222 | 32.42 N | 95.53 W |
| Edgeworth | 214 | 40.33 N | 80.11 W |
| Edgeworthstown → Mostrim | 48 | 53.42 N | 7.36 W |
| Edgware ◆[8] | 260 | 51.37 N | 0.17 W |
| Edgworth | 262 | 53.39 N | 2.24 W |
| Édhessa | 38 | 40.48 N | 22.03 E |
| Ediger-Eller | 56 | 50.06 N | 7.09 E |
| Edimbourg → Edinburgh | 46 | 55.57 N | 3.13 W |
| Edimburgo → Edinburgh | 46 | 55.57 N | 3.13 W |
| Edina, Liber. | 150 | 6.01 N | 10.10 W |
| Edina, Mn., U.S. | 190 | 44.53 N | 93.20 W |
| Edina, Mo., U.S. | 219 | 40.10 N | 92.10 W |
| Edinboro | 214 | 41.52 N | 80.07 W |
| Edinboro Lake ⊜ | 214 | 41.53 N | 80.08 W |
| Edinburg, Il., U.S. | 219 | 39.39 N | 89.23 W |
| Edinburg, In., U.S. | 218 | 39.21 N | 85.58 W |
| Edinburg, Ms., U.S. | 194 | 32.47 N | 89.20 W |
| Edinburg, N.Y., U.S. | 210 | 43.13 N | 74.07 W |
| Edinburg, N.D., U.S. | 198 | 48.29 N | 97.51 W |
| Edinburg, Oh., U.S. | 214 | 41.06 N | 81.09 W |
| Edinburg, Tx., U.S. | 196 | 26.18 N | 98.09 W |
| Edinburg, Va., U.S. | 188 | 38.49 N | 78.33 W |
| Edinburgh | 46 | 55.57 N | 3.13 W |
| Edinburgh (Turnhouse) Airport ⊠ | 46 | 55.57 N | 3.21 W |
| Edinburgh, Arrecife ✢[2] | 236 | 14.50 N | 82.39 W |
| Edinburgh Castle ⊥ | 46 | 55.56 N | 3.14 W |
| Edinburgh Channel ʊ | 236 | 14.45 N | 82.40 W |
| Edinburgh Mountain ∧ | 224 | 48.38 N | 124.24 W |
| Edincik | 130 | 40.20 N | 27.51 E |
| Edineț | 38 | 48.10 N | 27.19 E |
| Edingen → Enghien | 50 | 50.42 N | 4.02 E |
| Edirne | 130 | 41.40 N | 26.34 E |
| Edirne □[4] | 130 | 41.20 N | 26.40 E |
| Edison, Ga., U.S. | 192 | 31.33 N | 84.44 W |
| Edison, N.J., U.S. | 210 | 40.27 N | 74.18 W |
| Edison, Oh., U.S. | 214 | 40.33 N | 82.51 W |
| Edison, Pa., U.S. | 208 | 40.17 N | 75.07 W |
| Edison Bridge ◆[5] | 214 | 41.27 N | 82.49 W |
| Edison National Historic Site ⊥ | 276 | 40.47 N | 74.14 W |
| Edison Park ◆[8] | 278 | 42.01 N | 87.49 W |
| Edisseja | 84 | 44.03 N | 44.33 E |
| Edisto ≃ | 192 | 32.39 N | 80.24 W |
| Edisto, North Fork ≃ | 192 | 33.16 N | 80.53 W |
| Edisto, South Fork ≃ | 192 | 33.16 N | 80.53 W |
| Edisto Island I | 192 | 32.35 N | 80.20 W |
| Edith | 170 | 33.48 S | 149.55 E |
| Edith, Mount ∧ | 202 | 46.26 N | 111.11 W |
| Edithburgh | 168b | 35.06 S | 137.44 E |
| Edith Cavell, Mount ∧ | 182 | 52.40 N | 118.03 W |
| Edith River | 164 | 14.11 S | 132.02 E |
| Edithvale | 274b | 38.02 S | 145.07 E |
| Edith Weston | 42 | 52.37 N | 0.37 W |
| Edjejou, Oued i-n- V | 148 | 22.46 N | 4.05 E |
| Edjeleh | 148 | 27.38 N | 9.50 E |
| Edjerir ≃ | 150 | 18.06 N | 0.50 E |
| Edjudina | 162 | 29.48 S | 122.23 E |
| Edmeston | 210 | 42.41 N | 75.14 W |
| Edmond | 196 | 35.39 N | 97.28 W |
| Edmondbyers | 44 | 54.51 N | 1.58 W |
| Edmonds | 224 | 47.48 N | 122.22 W |
| Edmondson Heights | 284b | 39.18 N | 76.43 W |
| Edmonston | 284c | 38.57 N | 76.56 W |
| Edmonton, Austl. | 166 | 17.01 S | 145.45 E |
| Edmonton, Ab., Can. | 182 | 53.33 N | 113.28 W |
| Edmonton, Ky., U.S. | 194 | 36.58 N | 85.36 W |
| Edmonton ◆[8] | 260 | 51.37 N | 0.04 W |
| Edmore, Mi., U.S. | 190 | 43.24 N | 85.02 W |
| Edmore, N.D., U.S. | 198 | 48.24 N | 98.27 W |
| Edmund | 162 | 23.46 S | 116.02 E |
| Edmund Lake ⊜ | 184 | 54.45 N | 93.15 W |
| Edmundson Acres | 228 | 35.14 N | 118.49 W |
| Edmundston | 186 | 47.22 N | 68.20 W |
| Edna, Ks., U.S. | 198 | 37.03 N | 95.21 W |
| Edna, Pa., U.S. | 279b | 40.19 N | 79.39 W |
| Edna, Tx., U.S. | 222 | 28.58 N | 96.38 W |
| Edna Bay | 180 | 55.57 N | 133.40 W |
| Ednor | 208 | 39.09 N | 76.59 W |
| Edo ≃ | 94 | 35.37 N | 139.53 E |
| Edogawa ◆[8] | 268 | 35.42 N | 139.52 E |
| Edolo | 64 | 46.11 N | 10.20 E |
| Edom | 222 | 32.22 N | 95.37 W |
| Edon | 216 | 41.33 N | 84.46 W |
| Edosaki | 94 | 35.57 N | 140.19 E |
| Edremit | 130 | 39.35 N | 27.01 E |
| Edremit Körfezi c | 130 | 39.30 N | 26.45 E |
| Edrengijn nuruu ⩘ | 102 | 44.15 N | 97.45 E |
| Edsall Park | 284c | 38.48 N | 77.11 W |
| Edsbro | 40 | 59.54 N | 18.29 E |
| Edsbruk | 26 | 58.02 N | 16.28 E |
| Edsbyn | 26 | 61.23 N | 15.49 E |
| Edsgatan | 40 | 59.26 N | 13.33 E |
| Edson | 182 | 53.35 N | 116.26 W |
| Edson Butte ∧ | 202 | 42.52 N | 124.20 W |
| Eduardo Castex | 252 | 35.54 S | 64.18 W |
| Eduardo VII, Península → Edward VII Peninsula ≻[1] | 9 | 77.40 S | 155.00 W |
| Eduni, Mount ∧ | 180 | 64.15 N | 128.04 W |
| Edward ≃, Austl. | 164 | 14.44 S | 141.35 E |
| Edward ≃, Austl. | 166 | 35.33 S | 144.58 E |
| Edward, Lake ⊜ | 154 | 0.25 S | 29.30 E |
| Edward, Mount ∧ | 162 | 23.22 S | 131.55 E |
| Edwardes Park ♠ | 274b | 37.43 S | 145.00 E |
| Edward Island I | 190 | 48.24 N | 88.36 W |
| Edward River Aboriginal Reserve ◆[4] | 164 | 14.30 S | 141.45 E |
| Edwards, Ca., U.S. | 228 | 34.54 N | 117.53 W |
| Edwards, Ms., U.S. | 194 | 32.19 N | 90.36 W |
| Edwards, N.Y., U.S. | 212 | 44.19 N | 75.15 W |
| Edwards ≃ | 190 | 41.09 N | 90.59 W |
| Edwards Air Force Base ■ | 228 | 34.54 N | 117.52 W |
| Edwards Airport ⊠ | 276 | 40.45 N | 73.03 W |
| Edwardsburg | 216 | 41.47 N | 86.04 W |
| Edwards Butte ∧ | 224 | 45.23 N | 123.41 W |
| Edwards Gardens ♠ | 275b | 43.44 N | 79.22 W |
| Edwards Plateau ⩘[1] | 196 | 31.20 N | 101.00 W |
| Edwards Point ≻ | 169 | 38.13 S | 144.42 E |
| Edwards Run ≃ | 285 | 39.48 N | 75.12 W |
| Edwardsville, Il., U.S. | 219 | 38.48 N | 89.57 W |
| Edwardsville, In., U.S. | 218 | 38.16 N | 85.55 W |
| Edwardsville, Pa., U.S. | 210 | 41.16 N | 75.55 W |
| Edward VIII Bay c | 9 | 66.50 S | 57.00 E |
| Edward VII Peninsula ≻[1] | 9 | 77.40 S | 155.00 W |
| Edwinstowe | 44 | 53.12 N | 1.04 W |
| Edzell | 46 | 56.48 N | 2.39 W |
| Edziza, Mount ∧ | 180 | 57.40 N | 130.36 W |
| Eede | 52 | 51.15 N | 3.28 E |
| Eefde | 52 | 52.10 N | 6.14 E |
| Eek | 180 | 60.12 N | 162.15 W |
| Eek ≃ | 180 | 60.12 N | 162.15 W |
| Eeklo | 50 | 51.11 N | 3.34 E |
| Eel ≃, Ca., U.S. | 204 | 40.40 N | 124.20 W |
| Eel ≃, In., U.S. | 194 | 39.07 N | 86.57 W |
| Eel ≃, In., U.S. | 216 | 40.45 N | 86.22 W |
| Eel, Middle Fork ≃ | 204 | 39.42 N | 123.21 W |
| Eel, North Fork ≃ | 204 | 39.57 N | 123.26 W |
| Eel, South Fork ≃ | 204 | 40.22 N | 123.55 W |
| Eel Bay c | 212 | 44.19 N | 76.02 W |
| Eelde | 52 | 53.07 N | 6.35 E |
| Eels Creek ≃ | 212 | 44.35 N | 78.03 W |
| Eels Lake ⊜ | 212 | 44.54 N | 78.08 W |
| Eemskanaal ≊ | 52 | 53.15 N | 6.45 E |
| Eerbeek | 52 | 52.07 N | 6.04 E |
| Eersel | 52 | 51.22 N | 5.19 E |
| Eesti → Estonia □[1] | 22 | 59.00 N | 26.00 E |
| Eexta | 52 | 53.10 N | 6.59 E |
| Efate □[8] | 175l | 17.45 S | 168.20 E |
| Éfaté I | 175l | 17.40 S | 168.25 E |
| Eferding | 61 | 48.18 N | 14.02 E |
| Efes (Ephesus) ⊥ | 130 | 37.55 N | 27.17 E |
| Effigy Mounds National Monument ♠ | 190 | 43.06 N | 91.13 W |
| Effingham, Eng., U.K. | 260 | 51.16 N | 0.24 W |
| Effingham, Il., U.S. | 194 | 39.07 N | 88.32 W |
| Effingham, Ks., U.S. | 198 | 39.31 N | 95.24 W |
| Effingham □[6] | 219 | 39.07 N | 88.33 W |
| Effingham Lake ⊜ | 212 | 44.59 N | 77.22 W |
| Effort | 210 | 40.56 N | 75.26 W |
| Efiduasi | 150 | 6.51 N | 1.24 W |
| Efkere | 130 | 38.47 N | 35.40 E |
| Eflâni | 130 | 41.26 N | 32.57 E |
| Eforie Nord | 38 | 44.06 N | 28.38 E |
| Eforie Sud | 38 | 44.03 N | 28.38 E |
| Efringen-Kirchen | 58 | 47.39 N | 7.34 E |
| Ega ≃ | 34 | 42.19 N | 1.55 W |
| Egadi, Isole II | 70 | 37.58 N | 12.16 E |
| Egan | 222 | 32.28 N | 97.17 W |
| Egaña | 252 | 36.59 S | 59.06 W |
| Egan Range ⩘ | 204 | 39.10 N | 114.55 W |
| Eganville | 190 | 45.32 N | 77.06 W |
| Egau ≃ | 56 | 48.36 N | 10.34 E |
| Egbe, Nig. | 150 | 8.16 N | 5.31 E |
| Egbe, Nig. | 273a | 6.33 N | 3.17 E |
| Egbunda | 154 | 2.44 N | 27.12 E |
| Egedesminde (Aasiaat) | 176 | 68.42 N | 52.45 W |
| Égée, Mer → Aegean Sea ⊤[2] | 38 | 38.30 N | 25.00 E |
| Egegik | 180 | 58.13 N | 157.22 W |
| Egeln | 54 | 51.56 N | 11.25 E |
| Egeo, Mar → Aegean Sea ⊤[2] | 38 | 38.30 N | 25.00 E |
| Eger → Cheb, Česká Rep. | 54 | 50.01 N | 12.25 E |
| Eger, Magy. | 30 | 47.54 N | 20.23 E |
| Eger ≃, Dtsch. | 56 | 48.50 N | 10.37 E |
| Eger (Ohře) ≃, Europe | 54 | 50.32 N | 14.08 E |
| Egeria Mountain ∧ | 182 | 53.55 N | 130.22 W |
| Egernsund | 41 | 54.54 N | 9.37 E |
| Egerpohl | 263 | 51.07 N | 7.27 E |
| Egersund | 26 | 58.27 N | 6.00 E |
| Egerton | 262 | 53.38 N | 2.26 W |
| Egerton, Mount ∧ | 9 | 80.50 S | 158.50 E |
| Egeskov ⊥ | 41 | 55.10 N | 10.30 E |
| Egestorf | 52 | 53.11 N | 10.04 E |
| Egestorf [am Süntel] | 52 | 52.17 N | 9.31 E |
| Egg | 58 | 47.26 N | 9.54 E |
| Egg Creek ≃ | 198 | 48.22 N | 100.47 W |
| Egge ⩘ | 52 | 51.40 N | 8.55 E |
| Eggebek | 41 | 54.37 N | 9.22 E |
| Eggelsberg | 60 | 48.05 N | 13.00 E |
| Eggenberg, Schloss ⊥ | 61 | 47.05 N | 15.25 E |
| Eggenburg | 61 | 48.39 N | 15.50 E |
| Eggenfelden | 60 | 48.25 N | 12.46 E |
| Eggerscheid | 263 | 51.19 N | 6.53 E |
| Eggersdorf | 54 | 52.32 N | 13.49 E |
| Eggesin | 54 | 53.41 N | 14.05 E |
| Egg Harbor City | 208 | 39.31 N | 74.38 W |
| Egg Island Point ≻ | 208 | 39.11 N | 75.08 W |
| Egg Lagoon | 166 | 39.39 S | 143.58 E |
| Egg Lake ⊜, Mb., Can. | 184 | 54.21 N | 101.26 W |
| Egg Lake ⊜, Sk., Can. | 184 | 55.05 N | 105.30 W |
| Egglestone Abbey ʋ[1] | 44 | 54.32 N | 1.54 W |
| Egglham | 60 | 48.32 N | 13.04 E |
| Egglkofen | 60 | 48.24 N | 12.27 E |
| Eggmühl | 60 | 48.51 N | 12.11 E |
| Eggolsheim | 60 | 49.46 N | 11.04 E |
| Egham | 42 | 51.26 N | 0.34 W |
| Egherta | 144 | 2.04 N | 43.11 E |
| Éghezée | 56 | 50.36 N | 4.54 E |
| Egijn ≃ | 88 | 49.24 N | 103.36 E |
| Eğil | 130 | 38.15 N | 40.05 E |
| Egilsay I | 46 | 59.09 N | 2.56 W |
| Egilsstaðir | 24a | 65.16 N | 14.18 W |
| Eging | 60 | 48.43 N | 13.16 E |
| Egipto → Egypt □[1] | 140 | 27.00 N | 30.00 E |
| Égletons | 32 | 45.24 N | 2.03 E |
| Eglin Air Force Base ■ | 194 | 30.29 N | 86.30 W |
| Egling | 64 | 47.56 N | 11.31 E |
| Eglinton | 48 | 55.02 N | 7.11 W |
| Eglisau | 58 | 47.34 N | 8.32 E |
| Egloffstein | 60 | 49.42 N | 11.15 E |
| Egloskerry | 42 | 50.39 N | 4.27 W |
| Égly | 261 | 48.35 N | 2.13 E |
| Egmond aan Zee | 52 | 52.36 N | 4.37 E |
| Egmond-Binnen | 52 | 52.35 N | 4.39 E |
| Egmont, Cape ≻ | 172 | 39.17 S | 173.45 E |
| Egmont, Mount → Taranaki, Mount ∧ | 172 | 39.18 S | 174.04 E |
| Egmont Bay c | 186 | 46.35 N | 64.12 W |
| Egmont Channel ʊ | 220 | 27.36 N | 82.45 W |
| Egmont Key I | 220 | 27.35 N | 82.46 W |
| Egmont National Park ♠ | 172 | 39.15 S | 174.05 E |
| Egna (Neumarkt) | 64 | 46.19 N | 11.16 E |
| Egnach | 58 | 47.33 N | 9.23 E |
| Egnazia ⊥ | 68 | 40.53 N | 17.24 E |
| Egoryevsk → Jegorjevsk | 82 | 55.23 N | 39.02 E |
| Egota ◆[8] | 268 | 35.43 N | 139.40 E |
| Egra | 126 | 21.54 N | 87.32 E |
| Egremont, Ab., Can. | 182 | 54.02 N | 113.08 W |
| Egremont, Eng., U.K. | 44 | 54.29 N | 3.33 W |
| Égreville | 50 | 48.10 N | 2.52 E |
| Eğridir | 130 | 37.52 N | 30.51 E |
| Eğridir Gölü ⊜ | 130 | 38.02 N | 30.53 E |
| Eğriköy | 130 | 38.44 N | 27.21 E |
| Egrisskij chrebet ⩘ | 84 | 42.49 N | 42.24 E |
| Egton | 44 | 54.26 N | 0.45 W |
| Egtved | 41 | 55.37 N | 9.18 E |
| Éguas, Rio das ≃ | 255 | 13.26 S | 44.14 W |
| Éguilles | 62 | 43.34 N | 5.22 E |
| Eguisheim | 58 | 48.03 N | 7.18 E |
| Egum Atoll I[1] | 164 | 9.25 S | 151.55 E |
| Egvekinot | 180 | 66.19 N | 179.10 W |
| Egyházasrádóc | 61 | 47.05 N | 16.37 E |
| Egypt, Ma., U.S. | 207 | 42.12 N | 70.45 W |
| Egypt, Pa., U.S. | 208 | 40.41 N | 75.32 W |
| Egypt, Tx., U.S. | 222 | 29.24 N | 96.14 W |
| Egypt (Mișr) □[1], Afr. | 136 | 27.00 N | 30.00 E |
| Egypt (Mișr) □[1], Afr. | 140 | 27.00 N | 30.00 E |
| Egypt, Lake of ⊜[1] | 194 | 37.35 N | 88.55 W |
| Égypte → Egypt □[1] | 140 | 27.00 N | 30.00 E |
| Egyptian Museum ʋ | 273c | 30.03 N | 31.14 E |
| Eha-Amufu | 150 | 6.40 N | 7.46 E |
| Ehekirchen | 60 | 48.38 N | 11.06 E |
| Ehen ≃ | 44 | 54.25 N | 3.30 W |
| Ehime □[5] | 96 | 33.40 N | 132.50 E |
| Ehingen | 58 | 48.17 N | 9.43 E |
| Ehingen ◆[8] | 263 | 51.22 N | 6.42 E |
| Ehle ≃ | 54 | 52.12 N | 11.44 E |
| Ehlershausen | 52 | 52.31 N | 10.01 E |
| Ehmen | 54 | 52.24 N | 10.41 E |
| Ehra-Lessien | 54 | 52.34 N | 10.46 E |
| Ehrenberg | 200 | 33.36 N | 114.31 W |
| Ehrenberg Range ⩘ | 162 | 23.18 S | 130.20 E |
| Ehrenbreitstein, Feste ⊥ | 56 | 50.21 N | 7.37 E |
| Ehrenburg ⊥ | 56 | 50.12 N | 7.27 E |
| Ehrenfeld | 214 | 40.22 N | 78.46 W |
| Ehrenfriedersdorf | 54 | 50.38 N | 12.58 E |
| Ehrenhausen | 61 | 46.43 N | 15.35 E |
| Ehreshoven | 56 | 50.58 N | 7.20 E |
| Ehrhardt | 192 | 33.05 N | 81.00 W |
| Ehrhorn | 52 | 53.10 N | 9.53 E |
| Ehringhausen | 263 | 51.11 N | 7.33 E |
| Ehringhausen ◆[8] | 263 | 51.09 N | 7.11 E |
| Ehringshausen | 56 | 50.36 N | 8.23 E |
| Ehrwald | 64 | 47.24 N | 10.55 E |
| Ehwa Women's University ʋ[2] | 271b | 37.34 N | 126.56 E |
| Ei | 92 | 31.12 N | 130.30 E |
| Eibar | 34 | 43.11 N | 2.28 W |
| Eibau | 54 | 50.58 N | 14.40 E |
| Eibelstadt | 56 | 49.43 N | 10.00 E |
| Eibenstock | 54 | 50.29 N | 12.35 E |
| Eibergen | 52 | 52.06 N | 6.39 E |
| Eibiswald | 61 | 46.41 N | 15.15 E |
| Eibsee ⊜ | 64 | 47.27 N | 10.58 E |
| Eich | 56 | 49.45 N | 8.24 E |
| Eicha | 54 | 50.21 N | 10.34 E |
| Eich-Berg ∧[2] | 264a | 52.39 N | 13.50 E |
| Eiche, Dtsch. | 264a | 52.34 N | 13.36 E |
| Eiche, Dtsch. | 264a | 52.25 N | 12.58 E |
| Eichenau | 64 | 48.10 N | 11.19 E |
| Eichenbarleben | 54 | 52.10 N | 11.24 E |
| Eichenbrandt | 264a | 52.38 N | 13.51 E |
| Eichendorf | 60 | 48.38 N | 12.51 E |
| Eichenzell | 56 | 50.30 N | 9.41 E |
| Eichgraben | 61 | 48.10 N | 15.59 E |
| Eichigt | 54 | 50.21 N | 12.10 E |
| Eichlinghofen ◆[8] | 263 | 51.29 N | 7.24 E |
| Eichsfeld ◆[1] | 56 | 51.20 N | 10.10 E |
| Eichstädt | 264a | 52.42 N | 13.07 E |
| Eichstätt | 60 | 48.54 N | 11.12 E |
| Eichtersheim | 56 | 49.14 N | 8.46 E |
| Eichwalde | 54 | 52.22 N | 13.37 E |
| Eickelborn | 52 | 51.39 N | 8.13 E |
| Eicken ◆[8] | 263 | 51.13 N | 6.26 E |
| Eickerend | 263 | 51.13 N | 6.34 E |
| Eickerkopf ∧[2] | 263 | 51.21 N | 7.42 E |
| Eicklingen | 52 | 52.33 N | 10.10 E |
| Eide | 26 | 62.55 N | 7.26 E |
| Eidelstedt ◆[8] | 52 | 53.36 N | 9.53 E |
| Eider ≃ | 41 | 54.19 N | 8.58 E |
| Eiderstedt ≻[1] | 41 | 54.22 N | 8.50 E |
| Eidfjord | 26 | 60.28 N | 7.05 E |
| Eidsvåg, Nor. | 26 | 60.27 N | 5.21 E |
| Eidsvåg, Nor. | 26 | 62.47 N | 8.03 E |
| Eidsvold | 166 | 25.22 S | 151.07 E |
| Eidsvoll | 26 | 60.19 N | 11.14 E |
| Eifa | 56 | 50.58 N | 8.34 E |
| Eifel ⩘ | 56 | 50.15 N | 6.45 E |
| Eiffel, Tour ⊥ | 261 | 48.51 N | 2.18 E |
| Eiffel Flats | 154 | 18.15 S | 29.59 E |
| Eifgenbach ≃ | 263 | 51.05 N | 7.09 E |
| Eige, Carn ∧ | 46 | 57.17 N | 5.07 W |
| Eigen ◆[8] | 263 | 51.33 N | 6.57 E |
| Eigenji | 94 | 35.04 N | 136.18 E |
| Eigenrieden | 54 | 51.11 N | 10.22 E |
| Eiger ∧ | 58 | 46.35 N | 8.00 E |
| Eigg I | 46 | 56.54 N | 6.10 W |
| Eigg, Sound of ʊ | 46 | 56.51 N | 6.13 W |
| Eight Degree Channel ʊ | 122 | 8.00 N | 73.00 E |
| Eighteenmile Creek ≃, N.Y., U.S. | 210 | 42.43 N | 78.58 W |
| Eighteenmile Creek ≃, N.Y., U.S. | 210 | 43.21 N | 78.43 W |
| Eight Mile Creek ≃, On., Can. | 284a | 43.14 N | 79.11 W |
| Eightmile Creek ≃, In., U.S. | 216 | 40.57 N | 85.22 W |
| Eightmile Creek ≃, Or., U.S. | 224 | 45.36 N | 121.05 W |
| Eights Coast ±[2] | 9 | 73.30 S | 93.00 W |
| Eighty Four | 279b | 40.11 N | 80.08 W |
| Eighty Mile Beach ±[2] | 162 | 19.45 S | 121.00 E |
| Eiheiji | 94 | 36.05 N | 136.20 E |
| Eijerlandsche Gat c | 52 | 53.12 N | 4.50 E |
| Eijsden | 56 | 50.47 N | 5.43 E |
| Eikeren ⊜ | 26 | 59.38 N | 9.58 E |
| Eikisdalsvatnet ⊜ | 26 | 62.34 N | 8.11 E |
| Eildon | 169 | 37.14 S | 145.56 E |
| Eildon, Lake ⊜[1] | 169 | 37.11 S | 145.55 E |
| Eilean Gowan Island I | 212 | 45.02 N | 79.25 W |
| Eileen | 216 | 41.17 N | 88.15 W |
| Eilenburg | 54 | 51.27 N | 12.37 E |
| Eilsleben | 54 | 52.09 N | 11.13 E |
| Eimbeckhausen | 52 | 52.14 N | 9.25 E |
| Eimke | 52 | 52.58 N | 10.19 E |
| Eina | 26 | 60.38 N | 10.36 E |
| Einasleigh | 166 | 18.31 S | 144.05 E |
| Einasleigh ≃ | 166 | 17.30 S | 142.17 E |
| Einbeck | 52 | 51.49 N | 9.52 E |
| Eindhoven | 52 | 51.26 N | 5.28 E |
| Eine | 50 | 50.52 N | 3.37 E |
| Einme | 110 | 16.54 N | 95.11 E |
| Einöd | 56 | 49.16 N | 7.19 E |
| Einödriegel ∧ | 60 | 48.56 N | 13.02 E |
| Einruhr | 56 | 50.35 N | 6.22 E |
| Einsiedel | 54 | 50.46 N | 12.58 E |
| Einsiedeln | 58 | 47.08 N | 8.45 E |
| Einville-au-Jard | 58 | 48.39 N | 6.30 E |
| Eirauli | 272c | 19.10 N | 72.59 E |
| Éire → Ireland □[1] | 48 | 53.00 N | 8.00 W |
| Eiru ≃ | 248 | 6.42 S | 69.52 W |
| Eirunepé | 248 | 6.40 S | 69.52 W |
| Eisbach ≃ | 56 | 49.38 N | 8.22 E |
| Eisch ≃ | 56 | 49.45 N | 6.07 E |
| Eiseb ≃ | 156 | 20.33 S | 20.59 E |
| Eiselfing | 64 | 48.03 N | 12.14 E |
| Eisenach | 54 | 50.59 N | 10.19 E |
| Eisenberg, Dtsch. | 54 | 50.58 N | 11.53 E |
| Eisenberg, Dtsch. | 56 | 49.38 N | 8.05 E |
| Eisenberg ∧[2] | 61 | 47.12 N | 16.24 E |
| Eisenerz | 61 | 47.33 N | 14.53 E |
| Eisenerzer Alpen ⩘ | 61 | 47.28 N | 14.45 E |
| Eisenhower Center ʋ | 198 | 38.54 N | 97.12 W |
| Eisenhower Memorial Park ♠ | 276 | 40.44 N | 73.34 W |
| Eisenhüttenstadt | 54 | 52.10 N | 14.39 E |
| Eisenkappel | 61 | 46.29 N | 14.35 E |
| Eisenschmitt | 56 | 50.03 N | 6.43 E |
| Eisenstadt | 61 | 47.51 N | 16.32 E |
| Eisfeld | 54 | 50.26 N | 10.54 E |
| Eisgarn | 61 | 48.54 N | 15.06 E |
| Eishken | 46 | 58.01 N | 6.32 W |
| Eishort, Loch c | 46 | 57.10 N | 5.59 W |
| Eišiškės | 76 | 54.10 N | 25.00 E |
| Eisk → Jejsk | 78 | 46.42 N | 38.16 E |
| Eislingen | 56 | 48.42 N | 9.42 E |
| Eisriesenwelt ±[5] | 64 | 47.32 N | 13.10 E |
| Eita | 174t | 1.21 N | 173.05 E |
| Eiterfeld | 56 | 50.46 N | 9.48 E |
| Eitorf | 56 | 50.46 N | 7.26 E |
| Eivissa | 34 | 38.54 N | 1.26 E |
| Eivissa (Ibiza) I | 34 | 39.00 N | 1.25 E |
| Ejasi → Eyasi, Lake ⊜ | 154 | 3.40 S | 35.05 E |
| Ejby, Dan. | 41 | 55.30 N | 12.07 E |
| Ejby, Dan. | 41 | 55.26 N | 9.57 E |
| Ejea de los Caballeros | 34 | 42.08 N | 1.08 W |
| Ejeda | 157b | 24.20 S | 44.31 E |
| Ejército Rebelde, Presa ⊜[1] | 286b | 23.01 N | 82.20 W |
| Ejido | 246 | 8.33 N | 71.14 W |
| Ejido Jaboncillos | 232 | 28.57 N | 102.39 W |
| Ejigbo | 273a | 6.33 N | 3.18 E |
| Ejin Horo Qi | 102 | 39.27 N | 109.40 E |
| Ejin Qi | 102 | 41.50 N | 100.50 E |
| Ejstrup | 41 | 55.59 N | 9.17 E |
| Ejura | 150 | 7.23 N | 1.22 W |
| Ejutla de Crespo | 234 | 16.34 N | 96.44 W |
| Ekalaka | 198 | 45.53 N | 104.33 W |
| Ekáli | 267c | 38.07 N | 23.50 E |
| Ekanga | 152 | 2.23 S | 23.14 E |
| Ekas | 115b | 8.53 S | 116.27 E |
| Ekaterinburg → Jekaterinburg | 86 | 56.51 N | 60.36 E |
| Ekaterinodar → Krasnodar | 78 | 45.02 N | 39.00 E |
| Ekaterinoslav → Dnipropetrovs'k | 78 | 48.27 N | 34.59 E |
| Ekeby | 41 | 56.00 N | 12.58 E |
| Ekenäs (Taamisaari) | 26 | 59.58 N | 23.26 E |
| Ekenässjön | 26 | 57.30 N | 15.00 E |
| Ekerö I | 40 | 59.18 N | 17.43 E |
| Eket, Nig. | 150 | 4.39 N | 7.56 E |
| Eket, Sve. | 41 | 56.15 N | 13.11 E |
| Eketahuna | 172 | 40.39 S | 175.42 E |
| Ekhínos | 38 | 41.17 N | 24.59 E |
| Ekibastuz | 86 | 51.42 N | 75.22 E |
| Ekimčan | 89 | 53.04 N | 132.58 E |
| Ekitykskij chrebet ⩘ | 180 | 67.45 N | 179.00 E |
| Eko → Lagos | 150 | 6.27 N | 3.24 E |
| Ekoli | 152 | 0.23 S | 24.16 E |
| Ekoln ⊜ | 40 | 59.45 N | 17.37 E |
| Ekolsund | 40 | 59.37 N | 17.22 E |
| Ekolsundsviken c | 40 | 59.35 N | 17.24 E |
| Ekombe | 152 | 1.16 N | 21.36 E |
| Ekonda | 74 | 65.47 N | 105.17 E |
| Ekoungounou | 152 | 0.33 S | 15.38 E |
| Ekovamou | 152 | 0.07 N | 16.31 E |
| Ekpoma | 150 | 6.46 N | 6.08 E |
| Eksāra | 272b | 22.38 N | 88.17 E |
| Eksel | 56 | 51.09 N | 5.23 E |
| Eksjö | 26 | 57.40 N | 14.57 E |
| Ekuk | 180 | 58.49 N | 158.34 W |
| Ekuku | 152 | 0.42 S | 21.38 E |
| Ekuta | 152 | 2.59 N | 18.42 E |
| Ekvyvatapskij chrebet ⩘ | 180 | 69.00 N | 178.30 E |
| Ekwan ≃ | 176 | 53.14 N | 82.13 W |
| Ekwata | 152 | 0.13 S | 9.18 E |


| | | | | |
|---|---|---|---|---|
| ≃ River | Fluß | Río | Rivière | Rio |
| ≊ Canal | Kanal | Canal | Canal | Canal |
| ʟ Waterfall, Rapids | Wasserfall, Stromschnellen | Cascada, Rápidos | Chute d'eau, Rapides | Cascata, Rápidos |
| ʊ Strait | Meeresstraße | Estrecho | Détroit | Estreito |
| c Bay, Gulf | Bucht, Golf | Bahía, Golfo | Baie, Golfe | Baía, Golfo |
| ⊜ Lake, Lakes | See, Seen | Lago, Lagos | Lac, Lacs | Lago, Lagos |
| ⩩ Swamp | Sumpf | Pantano | Marais | Pântano |
| ⍓ Ice Features, Glacier | Eis- und Gletscherformen | Accidentes Glaciales | Formes glaciaires | Acidentes glaciares |
| ⊤ Other Hydrographic Features | Andere Hydrographische Objekte | Otros Elementos Hidrográficos | Autres données hydrographiques | Outros acidentes hidrográficos |

| | | | | |
|---|---|---|---|---|
| ✢ Submarine Features | Untermeerische Objekte | Accidentes Submarinos | Formes de relief sous-marin | Acidentes submarinos |
| □ Political Unit | Politische Einheit | Unidad Politica | Entité politique | Unidade política |
| ʋ Cultural Institution | Kulturelle Institution | Institución Cultural | Institution culturelle | Instituição cultural |
| ⊥ Historical Site | Historische Stätte | Sitio Histórico | Site historique | Sitio histórico |
| ♠ Recreational Site | Erholungs- und Ferienort | Sitio de Recreo | Centre de loisirs | Area de Lazer |
| ⊠ Airport | Flughafen | Aeropuerto | Aéroport | Aeroporto |
| ■ Military Installation | Militäranlage | Instalación Militar | Installation militaire | Instalação militar |
| ◆ Miscellaneous | Verschiedenes | Misceláneo | Divers | Diversos |

Ekwendeni 154 11.23 S 33.50 E
Ekwok 180 59.22 N 157.30 W
El-
→ Ad-, Al-, An-, Ar-, As-, Ash-, At-, Az-
Ela 110 19.37 N 96.13 E
El Aaiún (La'youn) 148 27.09 N 13.12 W
El Abiadh Sidi Cheikh 148 32.56 N 0.42 E
El 'Açâba □[4] 150 16.10 N 11.30 W
El 'Açâba ⋏[1] 150 16.00 N 12.00 W
El Adde 144 2.35 N 46.09 E
El Adeb Larache 148 27.22 N 8.52 E
El Adelanto 236 14.10 N 89.50 W
El Affroun 34 36.30 N 2.38 E
El Agreb 148 30.48 N 5.30 E
El Aguacate 286c 10.28 N 66.59 W
El Aguacate ≃ 234 18.16 N 100.40 W
El Aguilar 252 23.12 S 65.42 W
El Agustino 286d 12.03 S 76.59 W
El Agustino, Cerro ∧[2] 286d 12.04 S 77.00 W
Elaine 194 34.18 N 90.51 W
El Alamein
→ Al-'Alamayn 140 30.49 N 28.57 E
El Álamo, Méx. 196 27.32 N 100.52 W
El Álamo, Méx. 196 26.29 N 99.46 W
El Álamo, Méx. 204 31.34 N 116.02 W
El Alia 36 37.10 N 10.03 E
El Alto, Arg. 252 28.18 S 65.22 W
El Alto, Perú 246 4.18 S 81.07 W
Elam 285 39.51 N 75.32 W
Elamanchili 122 17.33 N 82.52 E
El Amparo de Apure 246 7.06 N 70.45 W
Elan ≃, Rom. 38 46.07 N 28.04 E
Elan ≃, Wales, U.K. 42 52.17 N 3.31 W
Élancourt 261 48.47 N 1.58 E
Elands ≃, S. Afr. 156 25.10 S 29.10 E
Elands ≃, S. Afr. 158 25.31 S 26.39 E
Elandsbaai 158 32.19 S 18.21 E
Elandsfontein 273d 26.10 S 28.12 E
Elandsvlei 158 32.19 S 19.33 E
El Angel 246 0.37 N 77.56 W
Elanora Heights 274a 33.42 S 151.17 E
El Aouinet 36 35.52 N 7.54 E
El Arba 34 36.37 N 3.13 E
El Arco 232 28.00 N 113.25 W
El Arenal 234 20.47 N 103.42 W
El Aricha 148 34.09 N 1.10 W
El Aroussa 36 36.22 N 9.28 E
El Arrayán 286e 33.21 S 70.28 W
Elassón 38 39.54 N 22.11 E
El Astillero 34 43.24 N 3.49 W
Elat 132 29.33 N 34.57 E
Elat, Gulf of
→ Aqaba, Gulf of c 128 29.00 N 34.40 E
Elat, Sede Te'ufa ⊠ 132 29.34 N 34.55 E
El Avagi 144 3.36 N 46.57 E
El Ávila, Cerro ∧ 286c 10.33 N 66.52 W
El Ávila, Parque Nacional ♣ 246 10.35 N 66.48 W
Elazığ 130 38.41 N 39.14 E
Elazığ □[4] 130 38.35 N 39.30 E
El Azúcar, Presa de ⊜[1] 196 26.10 N 99.00 W
El Azul, Sierra ⋏ 234 23.25 N 100.30 W
Elba, Al., U.S. 194 31.24 N 86.04 W
Elba, Mi., U.S. 216 43.02 N 83.26 W
Elba, N.Y., U.S. 210 43.04 N 78.11 W
Elba
→ Elbe ≃ 30 53.50 N 9.00 E
Elba, Isola d' I 66 42.46 N 10.17 E
El'ban 89 50.06 N 136.31 E
El Banco 246 9.00 N 73.58 W
El Barco de Ávila 34 40.21 N 5.31 W
El Barreal 200 31.17 N 107.10 W
El Barril 234 23.02 N 102.08 W
Elbasan 38 41.06 N 20.05 E
Elbaşı 130 38.41 N 35.59 E
El Baúl 246 8.57 N 68.17 W
El Baúl, Cerro ∧, Méx. 234 16.36 N 94.13 W
El Baúl, Cerro ∧, Méx. 234 17.38 N 100.19 W
Elbe 224 46.45 N 121.49 W
Elbe (Labe) ≃ 30 53.50 N 9.00 E
Elbe, Île d'
→ Elba, Isola d' I 66 42.46 N 10.17 E
Elbe-Havel-Kanal ≋ 54 52.24 N 12.23 E
El Beïd (Ebeji) ≃ 146 12.32 N 14.11 E
El-Beida
→ Al-Bayḍā' 146 32.46 N 21.43 E
Elbe-Lübeck-Kanal ≋ 54 53.50 N 10.36 E
Elberfeld ✦[8] 263 51.16 N 7.08 E
Elbert 198 39.13 N 104.32 W
Elbert, Mount ∧ 200 39.07 N 106.27 W
Elberta 190 44.37 N 86.13 W
Elberton 192 34.06 N 82.52 W
Elbeuf 50 49.17 N 1.00 E
Elbeyli 130 36.41 N 37.26 E
El Beyyadh 148 33.40 N 1.01 E
Elbing
→ Elbląg 30 54.10 N 19.25 E
Elbingerode 54 51.45 N 10.46 E
Elbistan 130 38.13 N 37.12 E
Elbląg (Elbing) 30 54.10 N 19.25 E
Elbląg □[4] 30 54.00 N 19.30 E
El Bluff 236 11.59 N 83.40 W
El Bolsón 254 41.58 S 71.31 W
El Bonillo 34 38.57 N 2.32 W
El-Borj 34 35.43 N 5.40 W
El-Borouj 148 32.30 N 7.10 W
El Bosque, Chile 286e 33.34 S 70.41 W
El Bosque, Méx. 234 17.04 N 92.44 W
El Boulaïda 148 36.28 N 2.50 E
Elbow 184 51.07 N 106.35 W
Elbow ≃ 182 51.03 N 114.02 W
Elbow Cay I 238 23.57 N 80.29 W
Elbow Lake 198 45.59 N 95.58 W
Elbow Lake ⊜ 184 54.50 N 100.53 W
Elbridge 210 43.02 N 76.27 W
El'brus, gora (Mount Elbrus) ∧ 84 43.21 N 42.26 E
Elbrus, Mount
→ El'brus, gora ∧ 84 43.21 N 42.26 E
El'brusskij 84 43.38 N 42.10 E
Elbsandsteingebirge ⋏ 54 50.50 N 14.20 E
Elburg 52 52.26 N 5.50 E
Elburn 216 41.53 N 88.28 W
Elburz Mountains
→ Alborz, Reshteh-ye Kūhhā-ye ⋏ 128 36.00 N 53.00 E
El'buzd 83 46.53 N 39.41 E
El'buzd ≃ 83 46.53 N 39.43 E
El Cabezo, Arrecífe ✢[2] 234 19.04 N 95.51 W
El Caburé 252 26.01 S 62.22 W
El Caimanero, Laguna c 234 23.00 N 106.07 W
El Cajon 228 32.47 N 116.57 W
El Cajón, Embalse ⊜[1] 236 15.00 N 87.35 W
El Calafate 254 50.20 S 72.18 W
El Callao 246 7.21 N 61.49 W
El Calvario, Col. 246 4.22 N 73.40 W
El Calvario, Ven. 246 8.59 N 67.00 W
El Calvario ✦[8] 286b 23.05 N 82.20 W
El Campamento 240m 18.22 N 66.28 W
El Campamento ✦[8] 266a 40.24 N 3.46 W
El Campo 222 29.11 N 96.16 W
El Capitan ∧, Ca., U.S. 226 37.43 N 119.38 W
El Capitan ∧, Mt., U.S. 202 46.01 N 114.23 W
El Caracol Depósito de Evaporación Solar ʋ[3] 286a 19.35 N 99.00 W
El Caribe 286c 10.37 N 66.50 W
El Carmen, Arg. 252 24.23 S 65.16 W
El Cármen, Bol. 248 18.49 S 58.33 W
El Carmen, Chile 286e 33.21 S 70.43 W
El Carmen, Col. 246 8.30 N 73.27 W
El Carmen, Méx. 234 15.35 N 93.05 W
El Carmen, Perú 248 13.30 S 76.04 W
El Carmen, Ven. 286c 10.24 N 67.01 W
El Carmen, Ven. 286c 10.24 N 66.50 W
El Carmen ≃ 232 30.42 N 106.29 W
El Carmen, Canal ≋ 286e 33.18 S 70.41 W
El Carmen, Laguna c 234 18.17 N 93.48 W
El Carmen de Bolívar 246 9.43 N 75.08 W
El Carricito 232 28.24 N 103.23 W
El Carril 252 25.05 S 65.28 W
El Casco 196 25.34 N 104.35 W
El Castillo de La Concepción 236 11.01 N 84.24 W
El Cedral 236 16.26 N 90.03 W
El Cedrito 232 29.11 N 101.59 W
El Centinela 204 32.38 N 115.40 W
El Centinela, Cerro ∧ 234 19.13 N 104.17 W
El Centro 204 32.47 N 115.33 W
El Cerrito, Col. 246 3.42 N 76.19 W
El Cerrito, Ca., U.S. 226 37.54 N 122.18 W
El Cerrito, Ca., U.S. 228 37.54 N 122.18 W
El Cerro, Bol. 248 17.31 S 61.34 W
El Cerro, Ur. 258 34.00 S 58.15 W
El Cerro Del Aripo ∧ 241r 10.43 N 61.15 W
El Chamal 234 23.56 N 97.54 W
El Chante 234 19.41 N 104.10 W
Elche
→ Elx 34 38.15 N 0.42 W
Elche de la Sierra 34 38.27 N 2.03 W
El Chichonal, Volcán ∧[1] 234 17.22 N 93.14 W
El Chile, Montaña ∧ 236 14.22 N 86.51 W
Elchingen 58 48.27 N 10.07 E
El'chkakvun ≃ 180 68.42 N 171.00 E
Elcho 190 45.26 N 89.11 W
Elcho Island I 164 11.55 S 135.45 E
El Chorrillo 252 33.18 S 66.16 W
El Ciprés 204 31.50 N 116.38 W
El Cobre 240p 20.03 N 75.57 W
El Cocuy 246 6.25 N 72.27 W
El Cojo 286c 10.37 N 66.53 W
El Cojo, Quebrada ≃ 286c 10.37 N 66.53 W
El Colorado 252 26.18 S 59.22 W
El Cóndor, Cerro ∧ 252 26.38 S 68.22 W
El Congo 236 13.54 N 89.30 W
El Corazón 246 1.12 S 79.06 W
El Corcovado 254 43.32 S 71.36 W
El Corozo 286c 10.35 N 66.58 W
El Corpus 236 13.16 N 87.03 W
El Corte ≃ 234 17.03 N 94.54 W
El Corte de Madera Creek ≃ 282 37.19 N 122.20 W
El Cortijo 286e 33.22 S 70.42 W
El Coto 240m 18.28 N 66.44 W
El Coyote 200 30.50 N 112.40 W
El Coyote ≃ 232 30.32 N 113.02 W
El Coyote, Laguna ⊜ 196 27.14 N 103.18 W
El Cozón 232 31.18 N 112.29 W
El Cristo 240p 20.07 N 75.45 W
El Cubo
→ Casigua 246 8.46 N 72.30 W
El Cuco 236 13.10 N 88.07 W
El Cuervo, Laguna ⊜ 232 29.17 N 105.57 W
El Cuidado 234 22.20 N 103.07 W
El Cuy 254 39.56 S 68.20 W
Elda 34 38.29 N 0.47 W
Eldagsen 52 52.10 N 9.40 E
El Dambahaddo 144 3.17 N 46.40 E
El Dátil 232 30.07 N 112.15 W
Elde ≃ 54 53.14 N 11.27 E
Eldekanal ≋ 54 53.24 N 11.36 E
Eldena, Dtsch. 54 53.13 N 11.25 E
Eldena, Dtsch. 54 54.05 N 13.26 E
El Der V 144 8.49 N 47.28 E
El Dere 144 5.07 N 43.10 E
Elder Island I 276 40.38 N 73.23 W
Elder Mills 275b 43.49 N 79.38 W
Eldersville 214 40.21 N 80.29 W
Elderton 214 40.42 N 79.21 W
El Descanso 204 32.12 N 116.55 W
El Desemboque, Méx. 232 29.30 N 112.27 W
El Desemboque, Méx. 232 30.30 N 112.59 W
Eldforsen 40 60.26 N 14.13 E
El'dikan 74 60.48 N 135.11 E
Eldingen 52 52.41 N 10.21 E
Eld Inlet c 224 47.04 N 123.01 W
Eldivan 130 40.32 N 33.31 E
El Diviso 246 1.22 N 78.14 W
El Djazaïr (Algiers) 148 36.47 N 3.03 E
El Djelfa 148 34.40 N 3.15 E
El Doce 234 17.13 N 94.03 W
Eldon, Ia., U.S. 190 40.55 N 92.13 W
Eldon, Mo., U.S. 194 38.20 N 92.34 W
Eldon Hazlet State Park ♣ 219 38.39 N 89.22 W
Eldora, Ia., U.S. 190 42.21 N 93.05 W
Eldora, Pa., U.S. 279b 40.10 N 79.53 W
Eldorado, Arg. 252 26.24 S 54.38 W
Eldorado, Bra. 252 24.32 S 48.06 W
El Dorado, Méx. 232 24.17 N 107.21 W
El Dorado, Ar., U.S. 194 33.12 N 92.39 W
El Dorado, Ca., U.S. 226 38.41 N 120.51 W
Eldorado, Il., U.S. 194 37.48 N 88.26 W
El Dorado, Ks., U.S. 198 37.49 N 96.51 W
Eldorado, Oh., U.S. 218 39.54 N 84.40 W
Eldorado, Ok., U.S. 196 34.28 N 99.38 W
Eldorado, Tx., U.S. 196 30.51 N 100.36 W
El Dorado, Ven. 246 6.44 N 61.38 W
El Dorado □[6] 226 38.43 N 120.48 W
Eldorado Hills 226 38.37 N 120.27 W
Eldoradopark 273d 26.18 S 27.53 E
El Dorado Park ♣ 280 33.49 N 118.05 W
Eldorado Peak ∧ 224 48.32 N 121.08 W
El Dorado Springs 194 37.52 N 94.01 W
Eldoret 154 0.31 N 35.17 E
Eldred, Il., U.S. 219 39.17 N 90.33 W
Eldred, N.Y., U.S. 210 41.32 N 74.53 W
Eldred, Pa., U.S. 214 41.57 N 78.23 W
Eldridge 190 41.39 N 90.35 W
Eldridge, Mount ∧ 180 64.46 N 141.48 W
Eldridges Hill 285 39.40 N 75.18 W
El Dudu 144 2.37 N 41.46 E
El Durazno, Arroyo ≃ 258 34.41 S 58.52 W
Eleanor 188 38.32 N 81.55 W
Eleanor, Lake ⊜[1] 226 37.59 N 119.51 W
Eleasar 158 26.40 S 26.53 E
Electra 196 34.01 N 98.55 W
Electric City 202 47.56 N 119.02 W
Eleele 229b 21.55 N 159.35 W
Elefante, Isla del
→ Elephant Island I 9 61.10 S 55.14 W
Elefantes, Estero c[2] 254 46.10 S 73.41 W
Elefantes, Rio dos (Olifants) ≃ 156 24.10 S 32.40 E
Elegest ≃ 88 51.32 N 94.05 E
El Eglab ✦[2] 148 26.25 N 5.00 W
Elei, Wādī V 140 22.04 N 34.27 E
Eleja 76 56.26 N 23.42 E
Elektrogorsk 82 55.53 N 38.47 E
Elektrostal' 82 55.47 N 38.28 E
Elektrougli 82 55.43 N 38.13 E
Elektrozavod 80 52.34 N 54.01 E
Elele 150 5.07 N 6.48 E
Elena 38 42.56 N 25.53 E
El Encantado 286c 10.27 N 66.47 W
El Encanto, Col. 246 1.37 S 73.14 W
El Encanto, Guat. 232 17.17 N 89.34 W
Elend 54 51.44 N 10.41 E
Elepete 273a 6.41 N 3.28 E
Elephant, Mount ∧[2] 169 37.58 S 143.12 E
Elephanta Caves ⊥[5] 272c 18.58 N 72.56 E
Elephanta Island (Ghārāpuri) I 272c 18.57 N 72.55 E
Elephant Butte Lake State Park ♣ 200 33.11 N 107.14 W
Elephant Butte Reservoir ⊜[1] 200 33.19 N 107.10 W
Elephant Island I 9 61.10 S 55.14 W
Elephant Lake ⊜ 212 45.08 N 78.07 W
Elephant Mountain ∧ 188 44.46 N 70.46 W
Elesbão Veloso 250 6.13 S 42.08 W
Eleşkirt 130 39.48 N 42.42 E
El Espinal 234 16.29 N 95.03 W
El Estor 236 15.32 N 89.21 W
Elets
→ Jelec 76 52.37 N 38.30 E
El Eulma 148 36.08 N 5.40 E
Eleusis
→ Elevsís 38 38.02 N 23.32 E
Eleutério 256 22.19 S 46.43 W
Eleutero ≃ 70 38.06 N 13.29 E
Eleuthera I 238 25.10 N 76.14 W
Eleuthera Point › 238 24.40 N 76.11 W
Eleva 190 44.34 N 91.28 W
Eleven Point ≃ 194 36.09 N 91.05 W
Elevsínos, Kólpos c 267c 38.02 N 23.34 E
Elevsís 38 38.02 N 23.32 E
Elevtheroúpolis 38 40.55 N 24.16 E
El Fahs 36 36.22 N 9.55 E
El Faro 240m 18.00 N 66.47 W
Elfenbeinküste
→ Cote d'Ivoire □[1] 150 8.00 N 5.00 W
Elfers 220 28.13 N 82.43 W
Elfershausen 56 50.09 N 9.58 E
Elfgen 263 51.05 N 6.32 E
Elfin Cove 180 58.12 N 136.20 W
Elfrida 200 31.41 N 109.41 W
Elfros 184 51.43 N 103.52 W
El Fud 144 7.20 N 42.50 E
El Fuerte 232 26.25 N 108.39 W
El Galpón 252 25.23 S 64.38 W
El Ghazawet 148 35.06 N 1.51 W
Elgin, Austl. 168a 33.31 S 115.37 E
Elgin, On., Can. 212 44.36 N 76.13 W
Elgin, Scot., U.K. 46 57.39 N 3.20 W
Elgin, Il., U.S. 216 42.02 N 88.16 W
Elgin, Ia., U.S. 190 42.57 N 91.37 W
Elgin, Mn., U.S. 190 44.07 N 92.15 W
Elgin, Ne., U.S. 198 41.59 N 98.05 W
Elgin, N.D., U.S. 198 46.24 N 101.50 W
Elgin, Oh., U.S. 216 40.44 N 84.28 W
Elgin, Ok., U.S. 196 34.46 N 98.17 W
Elgin, Or., U.S. 202 45.33 N 117.54 W
Elgin, Pa., U.S. 214 41.54 N 79.45 W
Elgin, Tx., U.S. 222 30.20 N 97.22 W
Elgin □[6] 214 42.42 N 81.15 W
Elgin, Lake ⊜ 206 45.45 N 71.20 W
Elgol 46 57.09 N 6.06 W
El Golfete ⊜ 236 15.44 N 88.53 W
El Goloso ✦[8] 266a 40.33 N 3.42 W
Elgon, Mount ∧ 154 1.08 N 34.33 E
Elgoras, gora ∧ 24 68.06 N 31.30 E
El Granada 226 37.30 N 122.28 W
El Grara 148 32.46 N 4.34 E
El Grullo 234 19.48 N 104.13 W
El Guaje 232 27.52 N 103.18 W
El Guaje, Laguna ⊜ 232 28.00 N 103.13 W
El Guamo 246 10.02 N 74.59 W
El Guanábano 286c 10.24 N 67.01 W
El Guapo 246 10.09 N 65.58 W
El Guarapo 286c 10.36 N 66.58 W
El Guayabo de Abajo 232 26.00 N 107.26 W
El Guayaneco, Parque Nacional ♣ 254 48.15 S 75.30 W
El'gygytgyn, ozero ⊜ 180 67.30 N 172.00 E
El Hadjar 36 36.48 N 7.45 E
Elham 42 51.10 N 1.07 E
El Ḥammâmi ✦[1] 148 23.03 N 11.30 W
El Hank ⊥[4] 148 24.30 N 7.00 W
El Haouaria 36 37.03 N 11.02 E
El Hatillo 286c 10.26 N 66.49 W
El Hatillo, Quebrada ≃ 286c 10.27 N 66.47 W
El Havre
→ Le Havre 50 49.30 N 0.08 E
El Higo 234 21.46 N 98.28 W
Elhovo 38 42.10 N 26.34 E
El Huecú 252 37.37 S 70.36 W
El Huisache 234 22.55 N 100.25 W
Eliase 164 8.21 S 130.47 E
Elías Romero 258 34.46 S 58.52 W
Eliasville 196 32.57 N 98.46 W
Elida, N.M., U.S. 196 33.56 N 103.39 W
Elida, Oh., U.S. 216 40.47 N 84.12 W
El Ídolo, Isla I 234 21.25 N 97.27 W
El Idrissia 148 34.30 N 2.37 E
Elila 154 2.43 S 25.53 E
Elila ≃ 154 2.45 S 25.53 E
Elim, Namibia 156 17.48 S 15.31 E
Elim, S. Afr. 158 34.35 S 19.45 E
Elim, Ak., U.S. 180 64.37 N 162.15 W
Elimsport 210 41.08 N 77.02 W
El Infiernillo, Canal ⊔ 232 29.09 N 112.15 W
Elingampangu 152 2.03 S 24.02 E
Elin Pelin 38 42.40 N 23.36 E
Eliot 188 43.09 N 70.48 W
Elipa 152 0.53 S 24.34 E
Elisabeth-Sophien-Koog 41 54.30 N 8.53 E
Élisabethville, Fr. 261 48.58 N 1.51 E
Élisabethville
→ Lubumbashi, Zaïre 154 11.40 S 27.28 E
Elisenvaara 24 61.25 N 29.46 E
Eliseu Martins 250 8.13 S 43.42 W
Elista 80 46.16 N 44.14 E
Elizabeth, Austl. 168b 34.43 S 138.40 E
Elizabeth, Co., U.S. 200 39.21 N 104.35 W
Elizabeth, Il., U.S. 190 42.19 N 90.13 W
Elizabeth, La., U.S. 194 30.52 N 92.47 W
Elizabeth, N.J., U.S. 210 40.39 N 74.12 W
Elizabeth, Pa., U.S. 214 40.16 N 79.53 W
Elizabeth, W.V., U.S. 188 39.03 N 81.23 W
Elizabeth ≃, N.J., U.S. 276 40.38 N 74.12 W
Elizabeth ≃, Va., U.S. 208 36.54 N 76.20 W
Elizabeth, Bahía c 246a 0.38 S 91.27 W
Elizabeth, Cape › 224 47.22 N 124.22 W
Elizabeth, Lake ⊜[1] 282 37.33 N 121.58 W
Elizabeth, West Branch ≃ 276 40.42 N 74.14 W
Elizabeth Bay c 156 27.04 S 15.11 E
Elizabeth City 192 36.18 N 76.13 W
Elizabeth Creek ≃ 222 33.02 N 97.14 W
Elizabeth Islands II 207 41.27 N 70.47 W
Elizabeth Lake ⊜ 281 42.38 N 83.23 W
Elizabeth Lake Estates 281 42.38 N 83.22 W
Elizabeth Park ♣ 281 42.07 N 83.11 W
Elizabeth Reef I[1] 160 29.56 S 159.04 E
Elizabethton 192 36.20 N 82.12 W
Elizabethtown, Il., U.S. 194 37.26 N 88.18 W
Elizabethtown, In., U.S. 218 39.08 N 85.48 W
Elizabethtown, Ky., U.S. 194 37.41 N 85.51 W
Elizabethtown, N.Y., U.S. 188 44.12 N 73.35 W
Elizabethtown, N.C., U.S. 192 34.37 N 78.36 W
Elizabethtown, Pa., U.S. 208 40.09 N 76.36 W
Elizabethville 208 40.32 N 76.48 W
Eliza Howell Park ♣ 281 42.24 N 83.16 W
Elizaville, In., U.S. 218 40.08 N 86.24 W
Elizaville, N.Y., U.S. 210 42.03 N 73.48 W
El-Jadida (Mazagan) 148 33.16 N 8.30 W
El-Jadida □[4] 148 33.00 N 8.40 W
El Jaralito 232 26.07 N 104.10 W
El Jebel 200 39.23 N 107.05 W
El-Jebha 34 35.13 N 4.38 W
El Jem 148 35.18 N 10.43 E
El Jícaro ≃ 236 13.31 N 86.00 W
El Jobean 220 26.58 N 82.13 W
El Juile 234 17.45 N 94.59 W
Ełk 30 53.50 N 22.22 E
Elk □[6] 214 41.26 N 78.43 W
Elk ≃, Ab., Can. 182 52.55 N 115.40 W
Elk ≃, B.C., Can. 182 49.10 N 115.14 W
Ełk ≃, Pol. 30 53.31 N 22.47 E
Elk ≃, U.S. 194 34.46 N 87.16 W
Elk ≃, Co., U.S. 200 40.29 N 106.58 W
Elk ≃, Ks., U.S. 198 37.15 N 95.41 W
Elk ≃, Mn., U.S. 190 45.18 N 93.34 W
Elk ≃, Mo., U.S. 194 36.38 N 94.38 W
Elk ≃, W.V., U.S. 188 38.21 N 81.38 W
Elk ≃, Wi., U.S. 190 45.42 N 90.37 W
Elkader 190 42.51 N 91.24 W
El Kantara 148 33.41 N 10.55 E
El-Karafab 140 18.10 N 31.36 E
Elk Bayou ≃ 226 36.06 N 119.24 W
Elk City 196 35.24 N 99.24 W
Elk City Lake ⊜[1] 198 37.15 N 95.55 W
Elk Creek 204 39.36 N 122.32 W
Elk Creek ≃, Ok., U.S. 196 34.48 N 99.09 W
Elk Creek ≃, Or., U.S. 202 43.38 N 123.34 W
Elk Creek ≃, Pa., U.S. 214 42.01 N 80.22 W
Elk Creek ≃, S.D., U.S. 198 44.15 N 102.22 W
Elk Creek ≃, Wa., U.S. 224 46.38 N 123.17 W
Elkedra ≃ 162 21.08 S 136.22 E
El Kef 148 36.11 N 8.43 E
El-Kelâa-des-Srarhna 148 32.02 N 7.23 W
El-Kelâa-des-Srarhna □[4] 148 32.05 N 7.30 W
El Kere 144 5.51 N 42.06 E
El Kerma 34 35.36 N 0.35 W
Elk Grove 226 38.24 N 121.22 W
Elk Grove Village 278 42.00 N 87.58 W
Elkhart, Il., U.S. 219 40.01 N 89.29 W
Elkhart, In., U.S. 216 41.40 N 85.58 W
Elkhart, Ks., U.S. 198 37.00 N 101.53 W
Elkhart, Tx., U.S. 222 31.38 N 95.35 W
Elkhart □[6] 216 41.35 N 85.50 W
Elkhart ≃ 216 41.41 N 85.58 W
Elkhart Lake 190 43.50 N 88.01 W
El Khatt ⊥[4] 148 22.40 N 10.05 W
Elkhead Creek ≃ 200 40.31 N 107.26 W
Elkhead Mountains ⋏ 200 40.50 N 107.05 W
Elk Hills ⋏[2] 226 35.15 N 119.25 W
El Khnâchîch ⊥[4] 148 21.50 N 3.45 W
Elkhorn, Mb., Can. 184 49.58 N 101.14 W
Elk Horn, Ia., U.S. 198 41.35 N 95.03 W
Elkhorn, Wi., U.S. 216 42.40 N 88.32 W
Elkhorn ≃ 198 41.07 N 96.19 W
Elkhorn City 192 37.18 N 82.21 W
Elkhorn Creek ≃, Ky., U.S. 218 38.19 N 84.52 W
Elkhorn Creek ≃, Mo., U.S. 219 39.05 N 91.20 W
Elkhorn Mountain ∧ 182 49.48 N 125.50 W
Elkin 192 36.14 N 80.50 W
Elkins 188 38.55 N 79.50 W
Elkins Park 208 40.04 N 75.07 W
Elk Island I 184 50.45 N 96.32 W
Elk Island National Park ♣ 182 53.37 N 112.45 W
Elkland 210 41.59 N 77.18 W
Elk Mills 208 39.39 N 75.49 W
Elk Mountain 200 41.41 N 106.24 W
Elk Mountain ∧, Wa., U.S. 224 46.08 N 122.28 W
Elk Mountain ∧, Wy., U.S. 200 41.38 N 106.32 W
Elk Neck ›[1] 208 39.35 N 75.55 W
Elk Neck State Park ♣ 208 39.30 N 75.58 W
Elko, B.C., Can. 182 49.18 N 115.07 W
Elko, Nv., U.S. 204 40.49 N 115.45 W
El Kouif 36 35.29 N 8.19 E
Elk Peak ∧ 202 46.27 N 110.46 W
Elk Plain 224 47.04 N 122.24 W
Elk Point, Ab., Can. 182 53.54 N 110.54 W
Elk Point, S.D., U.S. 198 42.41 N 96.41 W
Elk Rapids 190 44.53 N 85.24 W
El Krib 36 36.19 N 9.09 E
Elkridge 284b 39.12 N 76.42 W
Elk River, Id., U.S. 202 46.47 N 116.10 W
Elk River, Mn., U.S. 190 45.18 N 93.35 W
Elk River c 208 39.31 N 75.55 W
El Kseur 34 36.46 N 4.49 E
Elk State Park ♣ 214 41.38 N 78.34 W
Elkton, Ky., U.S. 194 36.48 N 87.09 W
Elkton, Md., U.S. 208 39.36 N 75.50 W
Elkton, Mi., U.S. 190 43.49 N 83.10 W
Elkton, Oh., U.S. 214 40.46 N 80.42 W
Elkton, S.D., U.S. 198 44.14 N 96.28 W
Elkton, Va., U.S. 188 38.24 N 78.37 W
El Kure 144 5.41 N 42.21 E
Elkville 194 37.54 N 89.14 W
Ell, Lake ⊜ 162 29.13 S 127.46 E
Ellamar 180 60.54 N 146.42 W
Elland 44 53.41 N 1.50 W
Ellard Lake ⊜ 184 54.33 N 91.55 W
Ellás
→ Greece □[1] 38 39.00 N 22.00 E
Ellavalla 162 25.05 S 114.22 E
Ellaville 192 32.14 N 84.18 W
Ellefeld 54 50.29 N 12.23 E
Ellef Ringnes Island I 16 78.30 N 104.00 W
El Leh 144 3.48 N 39.48 E
Elleker 162 35.00 S 117.43 E
Ellemandsbjerg ∧[2] 41 56.07 N 10.32 E
Ellen ≃ 44 54.43 N 3.30 W
Ellen, Mount ∧ 200 38.07 N 110.49 W
Ellen Brook ≃ 168a 31.48 S 116.00 E
Ellendale, Austl. 162 17.56 S 124.48 E
Ellendale, De., U.S. 208 38.48 N 75.25 W
Ellendale, Mn., U.S. 190 43.52 N 93.18 W
Ellendale, N.D., U.S. 198 46.00 N 98.31 W
Ellensburg 202 46.59 N 120.32 W
Ellenton, Fl., U.S. 220 27.31 N 82.31 W
Ellenton, Ga., U.S. 192 31.10 N 83.35 W
Ellenville 210 41.43 N 74.23 W
Eller ✦[8] 263 51.12 N 6.51 E
Ellerau 52 53.45 N 9.55 E
Ellerbe 192 35.04 N 79.46 W
Ellero ≃ 62 44.27 N 7.54 E
Ellerspring ∧[2] 56 49.55 N 7.37 E
Ellès 36 35.57 N 9.06 E
Ellesmere 42 52.54 N 2.54 W
Ellesmere, Lake c 172 43.48 S 172.25 E
Ellesmere Island I 16 81.00 N 80.00 W
Ellesmere Park 262 53.29 N 2.20 W
Ellesmere Port 44 53.17 N 2.54 W
Ellesmere Port □[8] 262 53.18 N 2.47 W
Ellettsville 194 39.14 N 86.37 W
Ellewoutsdijk 52 51.24 N 3.49 E
Ellezelles 50 50.44 N 3.41 E
Ellice ≃ 176 68.02 N 103.26 W
Ellice Islands
→ Tuvalu □[1] 14 8.00 S 178.00 E
Ellichpur
→ Achalpur 120 21.16 N 77.31 E
Ellicott City 208 39.16 N 76.47 W
Ellicott Creek ≃ 210 43.01 N 78.53 W
Ellicott Creek Park ♣ 284a 43.01 N 78.50 W
Ellicottville 210 42.16 N 78.40 W
Ellijay 192 34.41 N 84.28 W
El Limón, Méx. 234 18.05 N 101.59 W
El Limón, Méx. 234 19.49 N 104.11 W
El Limoncito 286c 10.29 N 66.47 W
El Limón de Teachi 232 24.43 N 107.08 W
Ellingen 56 49.04 N 10.58 E
Ellinger 222 29.50 N 96.44 W
Ellinghorst ✦[8] 263 51.34 N 6.57 E
Ellington, Eng., U.K. 44 55.13 N 1.34 W
Ellington, Ct., U.S. 207 41.54 N 72.28 W
Ellington, Mo., U.S. 194 37.14 N 90.58 W
Ellington, N.Y., U.S. 214 42.13 N 79.07 W
Elliniko International Airport ⊠ 267c 37.54 N 23.44 E
Ellinikón 267c 37.53 N 23.44 E
Ellinwood 198 38.21 N 98.34 W
Elliot 158 31.18 S 27.50 E
Elliot, Mount ∧ 166 19.29 S 146.58 E
Elliotdale 158 31.55 S 28.38 E
Elliotganj 126 23.31 N 90.52 E
Elliot Lake 190 46.23 N 82.39 W
Elliot Lake ⊜ 184 52.55 N 95.20 W
Elliott, Austl. 162 17.33 S 133.32 E
Elliott, Il., U.S. 216 40.28 N 88.16 W
Elliott, Ia., U.S. 198 41.09 N 95.10 W
Elliott, Ms., U.S. 194 33.36 N 89.45 W
Elliott □[6] 218 38.13 N 83.10 W
Elliott, Mount ∧ 162 20.29 S 126.37 E
Elliott Bay c 224 47.36 N 122.22 W
Elliott Key I 220 25.27 N 80.11 W
Elliottville 218 38.11 N 83.16 W
Ellis 198 38.56 N 99.33 W
Ellis □[6] 222 32.20 N 96.48 W
Ellisburg 212 43.44 N 76.08 W
Ellis Island I 276 40.42 N 74.02 W
Ellis Mountain ∧ 224 48.10 N 124.19 W
Ellison Creek Reservoir ⊜[1] 222 32.56 N 94.43 W
Ellisport 224 47.25 N 122.26 W
Ellisras 156 23.40 S 27.46 E
Elliston, Austl. 162 33.39 S 134.55 E
Elliston, Nf., Can. 186 48.38 N 53.03 W
Elliston, Mt., U.S. 202 46.33 N 112.25 W
Ellisville, Ms., U.S. 194 31.36 N 89.11 W
Ellisville, Mo., U.S. 219 38.35 N 90.35 W
Ellmau 64 47.31 N 12.18 E
Ellmauer Halt ∧ 64 47.34 N 12.18 E
Ellon 46 57.22 N 2.05 W
Ellora 122 20.01 N 75.10 E
Ellore
→ Elūru 122 16.42 N 81.06 E
Elloree 192 33.31 N 80.34 W
Ellport 214 40.51 N 80.15 W
Ellrich 54 51.35 N 10.40 E
Ellsworth, Il., U.S. 216 40.27 N 88.43 W
Ellsworth, Ks., U.S. 198 38.43 N 98.13 W
Ellsworth, Me., U.S. 188 44.32 N 68.25 W
Ellsworth, Mi., U.S. 190 45.09 N 85.14 W
Ellsworth, Mn., U.S. 198 43.31 N 96.01 W
Ellsworth, Oh., U.S. 214 41.01 N 80.52 W
Ellsworth, Pa., U.S. 214 40.06 N 80.01 W
Ellsworth, Wa., U.S. 224 45.37 N 122.36 W
Ellsworth, Wi., U.S. 190 44.43 N 92.29 W
Ellsworth Air Force Base ■ 198 44.08 N 103.05 W
Ellsworth Land ✦[1] 9 75.30 S 80.00 W
Ellsworth Mountains ⋏ 9 79.00 S 85.00 W
El Lucero 196 25.53 N 103.25 W
Ellwangen 56 48.57 N 10.07 E
Ellwanger Berge ⋏[2] 56 49.00 N 10.01 E
Ellwood City 214 40.51 N 80.17 W
Elm, Dtsch. 52 53.31 N 9.12 E
Elm, Schw. 58 46.55 N 9.11 E
Elm, Eng., U.K. 42 52.38 N 0.10 E
Elm ∧ 64 47.40 N 13.57 E
Elm ⋏[2] 54 52.09 N 10.53 E
Elm ≃, U.S. 198 45.36 N 98.19 W
Elm ≃, Il., U.S. 194 38.24 N 88.14 W
Elm ≃, N.D., U.S. 198 47.15 N 96.50 W
Elma, Ia., U.S. 190 43.14 N 92.26 W
Elma, N.Y., U.S. 210 42.51 N 78.38 W
Elma, Wa., U.S. 224 47.00 N 123.24 W
El Machorro, Punta › 200 31.03 N 114.51 W
Elmadağ (Küçükyozgat) 130 39.55 N 33.15 E
Elmadağ ∧ 130 39.49 N 33.00 E
El Mahia ✦[1] 148 22.30 N 2.30 W
El Maitén 254 42.03 S 71.10 W
El Malah 34 35.24 N 1.05 W
Elmalı 130 36.44 N 29.56 E
Elmalı Bendi ✦[6] 267b 41.04 N 29.06 E
El Maneadero 232 31.45 N 116.35 W
El Manteco 246 7.27 N 62.32 W
El Marsa el Kebir 148 35.45 N 0.43 W
Elmas 71 39.16 N 9.03 E
Elmas, Aeroporto di ⊠ 71 39.14 N 9.03 E
Elmas Burnu › 267b 41.13 N 29.13 E
El Masnou 266d 41.29 N 2.19 E
Elmaton 222 28.53 N 96.09 W
El Mayoco 254 42.39 S 70.59 W
Elmbridge □[8] 260 51.22 N 0.23 W
Elm Brook ≃ 283 42.29 N 71.16 W
Elm City 192 35.48 N 77.51 W
Elm Creek, Mb., Can. 184 49.41 N 98.00 W
Elm Creek, Ne., U.S. 198 40.43 N 99.22 W
Elm Creek ≃, Mn., U.S. 198 43.45 N 94.11 W
Elm Creek ≃, S.D., U.S. 198 44.21 N 102.42 W
Elm Creek ≃, Tx., U.S. 196 28.54 N 100.12 W
Elm Creek ≃, Tx., U.S. 196 32.40 N 99.41 W
Elm Creek ≃, Tx., U.S. 196 33.12 N 98.50 W
Elm Creek ≃, Tx., U.S. 222 29.15 N 97.32 W
El Meco 234 22.35 N 99.20 W
El Médano 232 24.25 N 111.30 W
Elmen 58 47.20 N 10.32 E
El Menia 148 30.30 N 2.50 E
Elmer 208 39.35 N 75.10 W
El Mghayyar 148 33.55 N 5.58 E
Elm Grove 216 43.02 N 88.04 W
Elmhurst, Austl. 169 37.11 S 143.15 E
Elmhurst, Il., U.S. 216 41.53 N 87.56 W
Elmhurst, Pa., U.S. 210 41.22 N 75.32 W
Elmhurst ✦[8] 276 40.44 N 73.53 W
El Mijao 286c 10.23 N 66.48 W
El Milagro 252 31.01 S 65.59 W
El Miliyya 148 36.48 N 6.14 E
El Mimbre 196 25.40 N 102.20 W
Elmina 150 5.05 N 1.21 W
El Minao 240m 18.22 N 66.05 W
Elmira, On., Can. 212 43.36 N 80.33 W
Elmira, P.E., Can. 186 46.27 N 62.04 W
Elmira, Ca., U.S. 226 38.21 N 121.55 W
Elmira, N.Y., U.S. 210 42.05 N 76.48 W
El Mirador ∧ 234 19.25 N 98.42 W
El Mirage 200 33.36 N 112.19 W
El Mirage Lake ⊜ 228 34.38 N 117.35 W
Elmira Heights 210 42.07 N 76.49 W
Elm Mott 222 31.40 N 97.06 W
Elmo, Mt., U.S. 182 47.49 N 114.20 W
Elmo, Tx., U.S. 222 32.43 N 96.10 W
El Mochito 236 14.49 N 88.06 W
El Mohammadia 148 35.33 N 0.03 E
El Molinillo 34 39.28 N 4.13 W
Elmont, N.Y., U.S. 276 40.42 N 73.42 W
Elmont, Va., U.S. 208 37.42 N 77.29 W
El Monte, Chile 252 33.41 S 71.01 W
El Monte, Ca., U.S. 228 34.04 N 118.01 W
El Monte Airport ⊠ 280 34.06 N 118.02 W
Elmora 214 40.36 N 78.45 W
El Moral 196 28.51 N 100.39 W
Elmore, Austl. 166 36.30 S 144.37 E
Elmore, Mn., U.S. 190 43.30 N 94.05 W
Elmore, Oh., U.S. 214 41.28 N 83.17 W
Elmore City 196 34.37 N 97.23 W
El Morro ⊥ 240m 18.28 N 66.07 W
El Morro National Monument ♣ 200 35.05 N 108.22 W
Elm Point › 276 40.49 N 73.46 W
Elmpt 56 51.13 N 6.10 E
El Mreiti ⊤[4] 148 23.29 N 7.52 W
El Mreyyé ✦[1] 150 19.30 N 7.00 W
Elmschenhagen ✦[8] 54 54.18 N 10.12 E
Elmsdale 186 44.58 N 63.30 W
Elmsford 210 41.03 N 73.49 W
Elmshorn 52 53.45 N 9.39 E
Elm Springs 194 36.12 N 94.14 W
Elmsta 26 59.58 N 18.48 E
Elmstein 56 49.21 N 7.56 E
Elmswell 42 52.15 N 0.53 E
El Mulato 196 29.22 N 104.10 W
El Multe 232 17.41 N 91.24 W
Elmvale 212 44.35 N 79.52 W
Elmville 218 38.20 N 84.46 W
Elmwood, On., Can. 212 44.14 N 81.03 W
Elmwood, Il., U.S. 190 40.46 N 89.57 W
Elmwood, Md., U.S. 284b 39.21 N 76.32 W
Elmwood, Ma., U.S. 283 42.00 N 70.57 W
Elmwood, Ne., U.S. 198 40.50 N 96.17 W
Elmwood, Wi., U.S. 190 44.46 N 92.08 W
Elmwood ✦[8] 285 39.56 N 75.14 W
Elmwood Park, Il., U.S. 216 41.55 N 87.48 W
Elmwood Park, N.J., U.S. 276 40.54 N 74.07 W
Elmwood Park, Wi., U.S. 216 42.41 N 87.50 W
Elmwood Park ♣ 285 40.08 N 75.21 W
El Naranjo ≃ 234 18.41 N 103.45 W
El Naranjo de Chila 234 18.55 N 102.28 W
Elne 32 42.36 N 2.58 E
El Negralejo 266a 40.24 N 3.31 W
El Negrito 236 15.16 N 87.41 W
El Nido, Pil. 116 11.11 N 119.23 E
El Nido, Ca., U.S. 226 37.08 N 120.29 W
El Nihuil 252 35.02 S 68.40 W
El Niybo 144 4.32 N 39.59 E
El Nopal, Cerro ∧ 232 28.15 N 107.36 W
Elnora, Ab., Can. 182 51.59 N 113.12 W
Elnora, In., U.S. 194 38.52 N 87.05 W
El Oasis 286c 10.35 N 66.59 W
El-Obeid
→ Al-Ubayyiḍ 140 13.11 N 30.13 E
Elobey, Islas II 152 0.59 N 9.30 E
El Ocote, Cerro ∧ 232 25.58 N 106.08 W
Elogbatindi 152 3.27 N 10.08 E
Eloida, Lake ⊜ 212 44.40 N 75.58 W
Elói Mendes 256 21.37 S 45.34 W
Eloise 220 27.59 N 81.44 W
Elora, On., Can. 212 43.41 N 80.26 W
Elora, Tn., U.S. 194 35.00 N 86.21 W
El Oro □[4] 246 3.30 S 79.50 W
Elortondo 252 33.42 S 61.37 W
Elorza 246 7.03 N 69.31 W
El Otro Lado 286c 10.24 N 66.49 W
Eloy 200 32.45 N 111.33 W
Eloy Alfaro 246 2.12 S 79.50 W
Éloyes 58 48.06 N 6.37 E
El Pacayal 232 15.37 N 92.02 W
El Palmar, Bol. 248 21.54 S 63.39 W
El Palmar, Ven. 246 7.58 N 61.53 W
El Palmar, Ven. 286c 10.38 N 66.52 W
El Palomar 288 34.36 S 58.36 W
El Palomar, Base Aérea Militar ■ 288 34.37 S 58.37 W
El Palqui 252 30.45 S 70.59 W
El Pantanoso, Arroyo ≃ 288 34.47 S 58.40 W
El Pao, Ven. 246 8.01 N 62.38 W
El Pao, Ven. 246 9.38 N 68.08 W
El Papiol 266d 41.26 N 2.01 E
El Paraíso, Hond. 236 13.51 N 86.34 W
El Paraíso, Méx. 234 17.25 N 100.15 W
El Paraíso □[5] 236 14.10 N 86.30 W
El Pardo ✦[8] 266a 40.31 N 3.47 W
El Pardo, Embalse de ⊜[1] 266a 40.33 N 3.48 W
El Pardo, Monte de ⋏[2] 266a 40.33 N 3.48 W
El Paso, Il., U.S. 216 40.44 N 89.00 W
El Paso, Tx., U.S. 200 31.45 N 106.29 W
El Paso Creek ≃ 228 35.02 N 118.51 W
El Paso de Robles
→ Paso Robles 226 35.38 N 120.41 W
El Paso Peaks ⋏ 204 35.28 N 117.43 W
El Paují 286c 10.26 N 66.49 W
El Pedregal ✦[8] 286c 10.30 N 66.51 W
El Peñón Blanco, Cerro ∧ 234 22.31 N 101.40 W
El Peñuelo 232 24.34 N 100.46 W
El Peral 286e 33.35 S 70.34 W
El Perú 246 7.19 N 61.49 W
El Pescadero, Laguna c 234 22.12 N 105.20 W
El Pescado, Arroyo ≃ 258 34.54 S 57.47 W
Elphin 48 53.51 N 8.12 W
Elphinstone 184 50.33 N 100.19 W
El Picacho, Cerro ∧ 234 20.40 N 100.43 W
El Pilar 246 10.32 N 63.09 W
El Pinar, Parque Nacional ♣ 286c 10.29 N 66.56 W
El Piñón 246 10.24 N 74.50 W
El Pintado 252 24.38 S 61.27 W
El Piojo, Arroyo ≃ 288 34.50 S 58.45 W
El Piquete 252 24.13 S 64.39 W
El Pital, Cerro ∧ 236 14.23 N 89.08 W
El Placer 234 23.33 N 106.10 W
El Planchón, Volcán ∧[1] 252 35.13 S 70.34 W
El Plantío ✦[8] 266a 40.28 N 3.49 W
El Plomo 200 31.15 N 112.04 W
El Polvorín 240m 18.26 N 66.17 W
El Pont de Segur 34 42.24 N 0.45 E
El Porcal 266a 40.18 N 3.32 W
El Portal, Ca., U.S. 226 37.40 N 119.46 W
El Portal, Fl., U.S. 220 25.51 N 80.11 W
El Porvenir, Méx. 196 27.33 N 104.57 W
El Porvenir, Méx. 234 15.44 N 93.22 W
El Porvenir, Perú 248 8.05 S 79.00 W
El Potosí, Punta › 234 17.32 N 101.28 W
El Potrero 196 26.23 N 100.27 W
El Prat de Llobregat 34 41.20 N 2.06 E
El Progreso, Ec. 246a 0.54 S 89.33 W
El Progreso, Guat. 236 14.21 N 89.51 W
El Progreso, Hond. 236 15.21 N 87.49 W
El Progreso □[5] 236 14.50 N 90.00 W
El Puerto de Santa María 34 36.36 N 6.13 W
El Puesto 252 27.57 S 67.38 W
El Qala 148 36.50 N 8.30 E
El Qoll 148 37.00 N 6.34 E
El Quebrachal 252 25.17 S 64.04 W
El Quelite 234 23.32 N 106.28 W
Elquera Bushland ♣ 274a 33.42 S 151.04 E
Elqui ≃ 252 29.54 S 71.17 W
Elrama 214 40.15 N 79.55 W
El Ranchito 234 18.40 N 103.41 W
El Rastro 246 9.03 N 67.27 W
El Real de Santa María 246 8.08 N 77.43 W
El Recreo ✦[8] 286c 10.30 N 66.53 W
El Refugio 234 21.57 N 100.02 W
El Remolino 196 28.44 N 101.07 W
El Reno 196 35.31 N 97.57 W
El Rey, Parque Nacional ♣ 252 25.00 S 64.40 W
El Rio 228 34.13 N 119.10 W
El Rito 200 36.20 N 106.11 W
El Rito ≃ 200 36.12 N 106.14 W
El Roba 154 3.57 N 40.01 E
El Roble, Mesa ∧ 232 31.31 N 115.31 W
El Rom 132 33.11 N 35.46 E
El Rosario, Laguna ⊜ 234 17.52 N 93.48 W
El Rosarito 232 28.38 N 114.04 W
Elrose 184 51.13 N 108.01 W
Elroy 190 43.44 N 90.16 W
El Rucio 234 23.23 N 102.05 W
Elsa, Yk., Can. 180 63.55 N 135.28 W
Elsa, Tx., U.S. 196 26.17 N 97.59 W
Elsa ≃ 66 43.43 N 10.52 E
Elsah 219 38.57 N 90.22 W
El Sahuaro 200 31.05 N 112.55 W
El Salado 252 26.25 S 70.19 W
El Salado, Parque Nacional ♣ 246 2.12 S 80.00 W
El Salitre 246 1.50 S 79.48 W
El Salto, Méx. 234 23.47 N 105.22 W
El Salto, Méx. 234 20.32 N 103.11 W


**Symbols** in the index entries represent the broad categories identified in the key at the right. Symbols with superior numbers (⋏[1]) identify subcategories (see complete key on page *I · 1).*

**Symbole** im Register stellen die rechts im Schlüssel erklärten Kategorien dar. Symbole mit hochgestellten Ziffern (⋏[1]) bezeichnen Unterabteilungen einer Kategorie (vgl. vollständiger Schlüssel auf Seite *I · 1).*

**Los símbolos** incluídos en el texto del índice representan las grandes categorías identificadas con la clave a la derecha. Los símbolos con numeros en su parte superior (⋏[1]) identifican las subcategorías (véase la clave completa en la página *I · 1).*

**Les symboles** de l'index représentent les catégories indiquées dans la légende à droite. Les symboles suivis d'un indice (⋏[1]) représentent des sous-catégories (voir légende complète à la page *I · 1).*

**Os símbolos** incluídos no texto do índice representam as grandes categorias identificadas com a chave à direita. Os símbolos com números em sua parte superior (⋏[1]) identificam as subcategorias (veja-se a chave completa à página *I · 1).*

| | | | | |
|---|---|---|---|---|
| ∧ Mountain | Berg | Montaña | Montagne | Montanha |
| ⋏ Mountains | Gebirge | Montañas | Montagnes | Montanhas |
| )( Pass | Paß | Paso | Col | Passo |
| V Valley, Canyon | Tal, Cañon | Valle, Cañón | Vallée, Canyon | Vale, Canhão |
| ≚ Plain | Ebene | Llano | Plaine | Planície |
| › Cape | Kap | Cabo | Cap | Cabo |
| I Island | Insel | Isla | Île | Ilha |
| II Islands | Inseln | Islas | Îles | Ilhas |
| ⊥ Other Topographic Features | Andere Topographische Objekte | Otros Elementos Topográficos | Autres données topographiques | Outros acidentes topográficos |

ESPAÑOL

| Nombre | Página | Lat.°′ | Long.°′ W = Oeste |
|---|---|---|---|
| El Salvador, Chile | 252 | 26.17 S | 69.43 W |
| El Salvador, Pil. | 116 | 8.34 N | 124.32 E |
| El Salvador □[1], N.A. | 230 | 13.50 N | 88.55 W |
| El Salvador □[1], N.A. | 236 | 13.50 N | 88.55 W |
| El Samán de Apure | 246 | 7.55 N | 68.44 W |
| El Santo | 240p | 22.42 N | 79.41 W |
| Elsass → Alsace □[9] | 32 | 48.30 N | 7.30 E |
| El Sauce, Laguna ⊜ | 258 | 35.20 S | 58.16 W |
| El Sauz | 232 | 29.02 N | 106.16 W |
| El Sauzal | 232 | 31.54 N | 116.41 W |
| Elsberry | 219 | 39.10 N | 90.46 W |
| Elsbethen | 64 | 47.45 N | 13.05 E |
| Elsburg | 273d | 26.15 S | 28.12 E |
| Elsdorf, Dtsch. | 52 | 53.14 N | 9.20 E |
| Elsdorf, Dtsch. | 56 | 50.54 N | 6.34 E |
| El Seco, Laguna ⊜ | 258 | 35.31 S | 58.42 W |
| El Segundo | 228 | 33.55 N | 118.24 W |
| El Seibo | 238 | 18.46 N | 69.02 W |
| Elsen | 52 | 51.44 N | 8.39 E |
| Elsenham | 42 | 51.55 N | 0.14 E |
| Elsen Nur ⊜ | 120 | 35.11 N | 92.15 E |
| Elsenz ≃ | 56 | 49.24 N | 8.48 E |
| Elsfleth | 52 | 53.14 N | 8.28 E |
| El Siasgo, Arroyo ≃ | 258 | 35.33 S | 58.33 W |
| Elsie, Mi., U.S. | 216 | 43.05 N | 84.23 W |
| Elsie, Or., U.S. | 224 | 45.52 N | 123.35 W |
| Elsinore → Helsingør, Dan. | 41 | 56.02 N | 12.37 E |
| Elsinore, Ut,. U.S. | 200 | 38.40 N | 112.08 W |
| Elsinore, Lake ⊜[1] | 228 | 33.39 N | 117.21 W |
| El Sitio | 286c | 10.28 N | 66.46 W |
| El'sk | 78 | 51.48 N | 29.09 E |
| Elsmere, De., U.S. | 208 | 39.44 N | 75.35 W |
| Elsmere, Ky., U.S. | 218 | 39.00 N | 84.36 W |
| Elsmere, N.Y., U.S. | 210 | 42.37 N | 73.49 W |
| El Sobrante | 226 | 37.58 N | 122.17 W |
| El Socorro | 246 | 8.59 N | 65.44 W |
| El Sombrero | 246 | 9.23 N | 67.03 W |
| Elspark | 273d | 26.16 S | 28.14 E |
| Elspeet | 52 | 52.17 N | 5.46 E |
| Elst | 52 | 51.55 N | 5.50 E |
| Elstal | 54 | 52.32 N | 12.59 E |
| Elstead | 42 | 51.11 N | 0.43 W |
| Elster | 54 | 51.50 N | 12.49 E |
| Elsterberg | 54 | 50.36 N | 12.10 E |
| Elstergebirge ⩘ | 54 | 50.15 N | 12.20 E |
| Elsterwerda | 54 | 51.28 N | 13.31 E |
| Elston, In., U.S. | 216 | 40.22 N | 86.55 W |
| Elston, Mo., U.S. | 219 | 38.37 N | 92.19 W |
| Elstra | 54 | 51.13 N | 14.08 E |
| Elstree | 42 | 51.39 N | 0.16 W |
| Elstree Aerodrome ⊠ | 260 | 51.39 N | 0.19 W |
| El Sueco | 232 | 29.54 N | 106.24 W |
| El Tagarete, Cerro ∧ | 232 | 26.31 N | 105.56 W |
| El Tajín ⊥ | 234 | 20.27 N | 97.23 W |
| El Tala | 252 | 26.07 S | 65.17 W |
| El Talar | 258 | 34.27 S | 58.39 W |
| El Tamarindo | 236 | 13.11 N | 87.54 W |
| El Tambo, Col. | 246 | 1.26 N | 77.23 W |
| El Tambo, Perú | 248 | 12.04 S | 75.13 W |
| El Tanque | 196 | 26.28 N | 99.38 W |
| El Tapextle | 234 | 23.52 N | 105.33 W |
| El Tarf | 36 | 36.45 N | 8.20 E |
| El Tecuán | 232 | 25.29 N | 107.00 W |
| El Tejocote, Cerro ∧ | 234 | 18.48 N | 103.03 W |
| Elten | 52 | 51.52 N | 6.10 E |
| El Terrero | 234 | 18.58 N | 102.28 W |
| Eltham, Austl. | 169 | 37.44 S | 145.09 E |
| Eltham, N.Z. | 172 | 39.26 S | 174.18 E |
| Eltham ◆[8] | 260 | 51.27 N | 0.04 E |
| Eltham Palace ʊ | 260 | 51.27 N | 0.03 E |
| El Tigre | 246 | 8.55 N | 64.15 W |
| El Tigre, Isla I | 236 | 13.16 N | 87.38 W |
| El Tigrito → San José de Guanipa | 246 | 8.54 N | 64.09 W |
| El Timbiriche | 234 | 18.38 N | 101.31 W |
| Eltmann | 56 | 49.58 N | 10.40 E |
| El Tocuyo | 246 | 9.47 N | 69.48 W |
| El Tofo | 252 | 29.27 S | 71.15 W |
| El'ton, Ross. | 80 | 49.08 N | 46.50 E |
| Elton, Eng., U.K. | 262 | 53.16 N | 2.49 W |
| Elton, La., U.S. | 194 | 30.28 N | 92.41 W |
| Elton, Pa., U.S. | 214 | 40.17 N | 78.48 W |
| El'ton, ozero ⊜ | 80 | 49.16 N | 46.35 E |
| El Toreo ♠ | 286a | 19.27 N | 99.13 W |
| El Toro | 228 | 33.37 N | 117.41 W |
| El Toro ∧ | 240m | 18.16 N | 65.49 W |
| El Toro, Isla I | 234 | 21.26 N | 97.31 W |
| El Toro Marine Corps Air Station ■ | 228 | 33.41 N | 117.44 W |
| El Tránsito, Chile | 252 | 28.52 S | 70.17 W |
| El Tránsito, El Sal. | 236 | 13.22 N | 88.21 W |
| El Trébol | 252 | 32.12 S | 61.42 W |
| El Triunfo, Hond. | 236 | 13.06 N | 87.00 W |
| El Triunfo, Méx. | 232 | 23.47 N | 110.08 W |
| El Triunfo, Cerro ∧ | 234 | 15.40 N | 92.49 W |
| El Triunfo de la Cruz | 236 | 15.46 N | 87.26 W |
| El Tuito | 234 | 20.19 N | 105.22 W |
| El Tulillo | 234 | 22.30 N | 104.05 W |
| El Tunal | 252 | 25.15 S | 64.27 W |
| El Turbio | 254 | 51.41 S | 72.05 W |
| Eltville | 56 | 50.02 N | 8.07 E |
| Eltz, Burg ⊥ | 56 | 50.12 N | 7.20 E |
| El-Uarre | 144 | 3.41 N | 45.20 E |
| Elura → Ellora | 122 | 20.01 N | 75.10 E |
| Elūru | 122 | 16.42 N | 81.06 E |
| Elva | 76 | 58.13 N | 26.25 E |
| El Valle | 236 | 8.36 N | 80.08 W |
| El Valle ◆[8] | 286c | 10.27 N | 66.55 W |
| Elvas | 34 | 38.53 N | 7.10 W |
| Elvas ≃ | 256 | 21.12 S | 44.08 W |
| Elven | 32 | 47.44 N | 2.35 W |
| El Vendrell | 34 | 41.13 N | 1.32 E |
| El Verano | 226 | 38.18 N | 122.29 W |
| El Verde | 234 | 23.21 N | 106.09 W |
| Elverdissen | 52 | 52.05 N | 8.38 E |
| Elverlingsen | 263 | 51.17 N | 7.42 E |
| Elverta | 226 | 38.43 N | 121.28 W |
| Elverum | 26 | 60.53 N | 11.34 E |
| El Viejo | 236 | 12.40 N | 87.10 W |
| El Vigía | 246 | 8.38 N | 71.39 W |
| El Vigía, Cerro ∧ | 234 | 21.19 N | 104.03 W |
| Elvins | 194 | 37.50 N | 90.31 W |
| Elvira | 258 | 35.14 S | 59.29 W |
| Elvo ≃ | 62 | 45.23 N | 8.21 E |
| El Volcán | 252 | 33.49 S | 70.11 W |
| El Wad | 148 | 33.20 N | 6.58 E |
| El Wak | 154 | 2.49 N | 40.56 E |
| El Walamo | 234 | 23.07 N | 106.15 W |
| El Wanza | 148 | 35.57 N | 8.04 E |
| Elwell, Lake ⊜[1] | 202 | 48.22 N | 111.17 W |
| Elwha ≃ | 224 | 48.10 N | 123.35 W |
| Elwood, Austl. | 274b | 37.53 S | 144.59 E |
| Elwood, Il., U.S. | 216 | 41.24 N | 88.07 W |
| Elwood, In., U.S. | 216 | 40.16 N | 85.50 W |
| Elwood, Ks., U.S. | 198 | 39.45 N | 94.52 W |
| Elwood, Ne., U.S. | 198 | 40.35 N | 99.51 W |
| Elwood, N.J., U.S. | 208 | 39.35 N | 74.43 W |
| Elwood, N.Y., U.S. | 207 | 40.50 N | 73.20 W |
| Elwood Park, Fl., U.S. | 220 | 27.28 N | 82.30 W |
| Elwood Park, Pa., U.S. | 279b | 40.10 N | 80.17 W |
| Elwy ≃ | 44 | 53.16 N | 3.26 W |
| Elwyn | 285 | 39.54 N | 75.24 W |
| Elx | 34 | 38.15 N | 0.42 W |
| Elxleben | 54 | 51.02 N | 10.56 E |
| Ely, Eng., U.K. | 42 | 52.24 N | 0.16 E |
| Ely, Mn., U.S. | 190 | 47.54 N | 91.52 W |
| Ely, Mo., U.S. | 219 | 39.41 N | 91.39 W |
| Ely, Nv., U.S. | 204 | 39.14 N | 114.53 W |
| Ely, Isle of ◆[1] | 42 | 52.24 N | 0.10 E |
| El Yagual | 246 | 7.29 N | 68.25 W |
| Ely Cathedral ʊ[1] | 42 | 52.24 N | 0.16 E |
| Elyria | 214 | 41.22 N | 82.06 W |
| Elyria Airport ⊠ | 279a | 41.20 N | 82.06 W |
| Elysburg | 210 | 40.51 N | 76.33 W |

FRANÇAIS

| Nom | Page | Lat.°′ | Long.°′ W = Ouest |
|---|---|---|---|
| Elysian Park ♠ | 280 | 34.05 N | 118.14 W |
| El Yunque ∧ | 240m | 18.19 N | 65.48 W |
| Elywood Park ♠ | 279a | 41.23 N | 82.06 W |
| Elz | 56 | 50.25 N | 8.02 E |
| Elz ≃ | 58 | 48.21 N | 7.45 E |
| Elzach | 58 | 48.10 N | 8.04 E |
| El Zamural | 286c | 10.27 N | 67.00 W |
| El Zapotal | 234 | 15.27 N | 93.10 W |
| Elzbach ≃ | 56 | 50.12 N | 7.22 E |
| Elze, Dtsch. | 52 | 52.35 N | 9.44 E |
| Elze, Dtsch. | 52 | 52.07 N | 9.44 E |
| El Zig-Zag | 286c | 10.33 N | 66.58 W |
| Elztal | 56 | 49.24 N | 9.12 E |
| Émaé I | 175f | 17.04 S | 168.24 E |
| Emajõgi ≃ | 76 | 58.26 N | 27.15 E |
| Emali | 154 | 2.05 S | 37.38 E |
| Emam Khomeyni Mosque ʊ[1] | 267d | 35.40 N | 51.25 E |
| Emāmshahr (Shāhrūd) | 128 | 36.25 N | 55.01 E |
| Emån ≃ | 26 | 57.08 N | 16.30 E |
| Émancé | 261 | 48.35 N | 1.44 E |
| Emas, Parque Nacional das ♠ | 255 | 18.08 S | 52.48 W |
| Emba | 86 | 48.50 N | 58.08 E |
| Emba ≃ | 80 | 46.38 N | 53.14 E |
| Embarcación | 252 | 23.13 S | 64.06 W |
| Embarras ≃, Ab., Can. | 182 | 53.27 N | 116.37 W |
| Embarras ≃, Il., U.S. | 194 | 38.39 N | 87.37 W |
| Embarras, North Fork ≃ | 194 | 38.55 N | 87.59 W |
| Embarrass | 190 | 44.39 N | 88.42 W |
| Embarrass ≃, Mn., U.S. | 190 | 47.24 N | 92.25 W |
| Embarrass ≃, Wi., U.S. | 190 | 44.23 N | 88.45 W |
| Embetsu | 92a | 44.44 N | 141.47 E |
| Embid | 34 | 40.58 N | 1.43 W |
| Embleton | 44 | 55.30 N | 1.37 W |
| Embo | 46 | 57.54 N | 3.59 W |
| Emboabas | 256 | 21.18 S | 44.08 W |
| Embondo | 152 | 0.15 N | 19.38 E |
| Emborcação, Represa ⊜[1] | 255 | 18.30 S | 47.50 W |
| Embrach | 58 | 47.30 N | 8.36 E |
| Embreeville, Pa., U.S. | 285 | 39.56 N | 75.44 W |
| Embreeville, Tn., U.S. | 192 | 36.10 N | 82.27 W |
| Embro | 212 | 43.09 N | 80.54 W |
| Embrun, On., Can. | 212 | 45.16 N | 75.17 W |
| Embrun, Fr. | 62 | 44.34 N | 6.30 E |
| Embry | 50 | 50.29 N | 1.58 E |
| Embsay | 44 | 53.58 N | 1.59 W |
| Embu, Bra. | 256 | 23.39 S | 46.51 W |
| Embu, Kenya | 154 | 0.32 S | 37.27 E |
| Embu □[7] | 287b | 23.40 S | 46.50 W |
| Embu-Guaçu | 256 | 23.49 S | 46.48 W |
| Embu-Guaçu □[7] | 287b | 23.48 S | 46.48 W |
| Embu-mirim ≃ | 287b | 23.39 S | 46.51 W |
| Emden, Dtsch. | 52 | 53.22 N | 7.12 E |
| Emden, Il., U.S. | 194 | 40.18 N | 89.29 W |
| Emden, Mo., U.S. | 219 | 39.48 N | 91.52 W |
| Emei | 107 | 29.36 N | 103.31 E |
| Emeigh | 214 | 40.42 N | 78.47 W |
| Emel' (Emin) ≃ | 86 | 46.20 N | 81.46 E |
| Emelle | 194 | 32.43 N | 88.18 W |
| Emerado | 198 | 47.55 N | 97.21 W |
| Émerainville | 261 | 48.49 N | 2.37 E |
| Emerald, Austl. | 166 | 23.32 S | 148.10 E |
| Emerald, Austl. | 169 | 37.56 S | 145.26 E |
| Emerald Bay State Park ♠ | 226 | 38.57 N | 120.05 W |
| Emerson, Mb., Can. | 184 | 49.00 N | 97.12 W |
| Emerson, Ar., U.S. | 194 | 33.05 N | 93.11 W |
| Emerson, Ga., U.S. | 192 | 34.07 N | 84.45 W |
| Emerson, Ia., U.S. | 198 | 41.01 N | 95.24 W |
| Emerson, Mo., U.S. | 219 | 39.53 N | 91.42 W |
| Emerson, Ne., U.S. | 198 | 42.17 N | 96.44 W |
| Emerson, N.J., U.S. | 276 | 40.58 N | 74.01 W |
| Emery, S.D., U.S. | 198 | 43.36 N | 97.37 W |
| Emery, Ut,. U.S. | 200 | 38.55 N | 111.14 W |
| Emeryville, On., Can. | 214 | 42.18 N | 82.45 W |
| Emeryville, Ca., U.S. | 226 | 37.50 N | 122.17 W |
| Emet | 130 | 39.20 N | 29.15 E |
| Emgayet | 146 | 29.04 N | 12.58 E |
| Emhouse | 222 | 32.09 N | 96.35 W |
| Emi | 88 | 50.36 N | 97.49 E |
| Emigrant Gap | 226 | 39.17 N | 120.40 W |
| Emigrant Gap )( | 226 | 39.18 N | 120.40 W |
| Emigsville | 208 | 40.01 N | 76.44 W |
| Emiliano Mitre, Canal ⊔ | 288 | 34.36 S | 58.18 W |
| Emiliano Zapata, Méx. | 232 | 17.45 N | 91.46 W |
| Emiliano Zapata, Méx. | 234 | 16.10 N | 94.01 W |
| Emiliano Zapata, Bahía ⊂ | 232 | 19.40 N | 87.30 W |
| Emilia-Romagna □[4] | 36 | 44.35 N | 11.00 E |
| Emílio de Carvalho | 152 | 5.55 S | 12.57 E |
| Emily Provincial Park ♠ | 212 | 44.21 N | 78.31 W |
| Emin | 86 | 46.32 N | 83.39 E |
| Emin (Emel') ≃ | 86 | 46.20 N | 81.46 E |
| Eminābād | 123 | 32.02 N | 74.16 E |
| Emine, nos ≻ | 38 | 42.42 N | 27.51 E |
| Eminence, Ky., U.S. | 218 | 38.22 N | 85.10 W |
| Eminence, Mo., U.S. | 194 | 37.09 N | 91.21 W |
| Emiralem | 130 | 38.36 N | 27.09 E |
| Emiratos Arabes Unidos → United Arab Emirates □[1] | 128 | 24.00 N | 54.00 E |
| Emirau Island I | 164 | 1.40 S | 150.00 E |
| Emirdağ | 130 | 39.01 N | 31.10 E |
| Emir Dağları ⩘ | 130 | 38.50 N | 31.15 E |
| Emirhan | 130 | 39.42 N | 37.46 E |
| Emir Pasha Gulf ⊂ | 154 | 2.32 S | 31.52 E |
| Emissi, Tarso ∧ | 146 | 21.13 N | 18.32 E |
| Emita | 166 | 40.00 S | 147.54 E |
| Emlembe ∧ | 158 | 25.57 S | 31.11 E |
| Emlenton | 214 | 41.11 N | 79.43 W |
| Emlichheim | 52 | 52.36 N | 6.50 E |
| Emmaån ≃ | 40 | 58.44 N | 15.35 E |
| Emmaboda | 26 | 56.38 N | 15.32 E |
| Emmaste | 76 | 58.42 N | 22.36 E |
| Emmaus, Ross. | 82 | 56.47 N | 36.07 E |
| Emmaus, Pa., U.S. | 208 | 40.32 N | 75.29 W |
| Emmaville | 166 | 29.26 S | 151.36 E |
| Emme ≃ | 58 | 47.13 N | 7.34 E |
| Emmeline Lake ⊜ | 184 | 55.00 N | 106.22 W |
| Emmeloord | 52 | 52.43 N | 5.45 E |
| Emmen | 52 | 52.47 N | 6.54 E |
| Emmenbrücke | 58 | 47.04 N | 8.17 E |
| Emmendingen | 58 | 48.07 N | 7.50 E |
| Emmental V | 58 | 46.56 N | 7.45 E |
| Emmer ≃ | 52 | 52.03 N | 9.23 E |
| Emmer-Compascuum | 52 | 52.48 N | 7.02 E |
| Emmer-Erfscheidenveen | 52 | 52.48 N | 7.01 E |
| Emmerich | 52 | 51.50 N | 6.15 E |
| Emmerstedt | 54 | 52.15 N | 10.58 E |
| Emmerthal | 52 | 52.03 N | 9.23 E |
| Emmet, Austl. | 166 | 24.40 S | 144.28 E |
| Emmet, Ar., U.S. | 194 | 33.43 N | 93.28 W |
| Emmetsburg | 198 | 43.06 N | 94.40 W |
| Emmett, Id., U.S. | 202 | 43.52 N | 116.29 W |
| Emmett, Mi., U.S. | 214 | 42.59 N | 82.45 W |
| Emmiganūru | 122 | 15.44 N | 77.29 E |
| Emmingen-Liptingen | 58 | 47.56 N | 8.51 E |
| Emmitsburg | 208 | 39.42 N | 77.20 W |
| Emmonak | 180 | 62.46 N | 164.30 W |
| Emneth | 42 | 52.38 N | 0.11 E |
| Emo | 190 | 48.38 N | 93.50 W |
| Emőd | 30 | 47.56 N | 20.49 E |
| Emory | 222 | 32.52 N | 95.46 W |
| Emory ≃ | 192 | 35.56 N | 84.29 W |
| Emory Peak ∧ | 196 | 29.13 N | 103.17 W |
| Empalme | 232 | 27.58 N | 110.51 W |
| Empalme Escobedo | 234 | 20.41 N | 100.44 W |

PORTUGUÊS

| Nome | Página | Lat.°′ | Long.°′ W = Oeste |
|---|---|---|---|
| Empalme Purísima | 234 | 23.55 N | 105.05 W |
| Empalme San Vicente | 258 | 34.58 S | 58.22 W |
| Empangeni | 158 | 28.50 S | 31.48 E |
| Empedrado, Arg. | 252 | 27.57 S | 58.48 W |
| Empedrado, Chile | 252 | 35.36 S | 72.17 W |
| Emperor Jimmu, Tomb of ⊥ | 270 | 34.29 N | 135.47 E |
| Emperor Nintoku, Tomb of ⊥ | 270 | 34.34 N | 135.29 E |
| Emperor Range ⩘ | 175e | 5.45 S | 154.55 E |
| Emperor Seamounts ✢[3] | 6 | 42.00 N | 170.00 E |
| Emperor Tenchi, Tomb of ⊥ | 270 | 34.59 N | 135.48 E |
| Empfingen | 58 | 48.24 N | 8.42 E |
| Empire, Ca., U.S. | 226 | 37.38 N | 120.54 W |
| Empire, La., U.S. | 194 | 29.23 N | 89.35 W |
| Empire, Nv., U.S. | 204 | 40.34 N | 119.20 W |
| Empire, Oh., U.S. | 214 | 40.30 N | 80.37 W |
| Empoli | 66 | 43.43 N | 10.57 E |
| Emporia, Ks., U.S. | 198 | 38.24 N | 96.10 W |
| Emporia, Va., U.S. | 208 | 36.41 N | 77.32 W |
| Emporium | 214 | 41.30 N | 78.14 W |
| Empress | 184 | 50.57 N | 110.00 W |
| Empress Augusta Bay ⊂ | 175e | 6.25 S | 155.05 E |
| Emptinne | 56 | 50.19 N | 5.07 E |
| Empty Quarter → Ar-Rub' al-Khālī ◆[2] | 118 | 20.00 N | 51.00 E |
| Ems ≃ | 52 | 53.20 N | 7.06 E |
| Emsbüren | 52 | 52.24 N | 7.17 E |
| Emscher ≃ | 263 | 51.34 N | 6.42 E |
| Emscherbruch ◆[1] | 263 | 51.34 N | 7.09 E |
| Emsdetten | 52 | 52.10 N | 7.31 E |
| Ems-Jade-Kanal ≅ | 52 | 53.19 N | 7.10 E |
| Emskirchen | 56 | 49.33 N | 10.43 E |
| Emsland ◆[1] | 52 | 52.50 N | 7.20 E |
| Emst ◆[8] | 263 | 51.21 N | 7.30 E |
| Emstek | 52 | 52.50 N | 8.09 E |
| Emsworth, Eng., U.K. | 42 | 50.51 N | 0.56 W |
| Emsworth, Pa., U.S. | 214 | 40.30 N | 80.05 W |
| Emsworth Dam ◆[6] | 279b | 40.30 N | 80.05 W |
| Emu | 89 | 43.45 N | 128.10 E |
| Emu, Mount ∧[2] | 169 | 37.35 S | 143.27 E |
| Emu Creek ≃ | 171a | 26.56 S | 152.19 E |
| Emu Downs | 168b | 33.54 S | 138.59 E |
| Emukae | 92 | 33.18 N | 129.38 E |
| Emu Park | 166 | 23.15 S | 150.50 E |
| Emu Plains | 274a | 33.45 S | 150.41 E |
| Emur ≃ | 89 | 53.24 N | 124.00 E |
| Emuren | 273a | 6.40 N | 3.31 E |
| Emyvale | 48 | 54.20 N | 6.59 W |
| En (Inn) ≃, Europe | 32 | 48.35 N | 13.28 E |
| En ≃, Zhg. | 100 | 27.12 N | 115.08 E |
| Ena | 94 | 35.27 N | 137.25 E |
| Enana | 156 | 17.29 S | 16.19 E |
| Enånger | 26 | 61.32 N | 17.00 E |
| Enard Bay ⊂ | 46 | 58.05 N | 5.20 W |
| Enarotali | 164 | 3.55 S | 136.21 E |
| Ena-san ∧ | 94 | 35.26 N | 137.36 E |
| Ena-san Tunnel ◆[5] | 94 | 35.30 N | 137.40 E |
| Enbacka | 40 | 60.25 N | 15.36 E |
| Enborne ≃ | 42 | 51.24 N | 1.06 W |
| Encampment | 200 | 41.12 N | 106.47 W |
| Encampment ≃ | 200 | 41.18 N | 106.43 W |
| Encantado | 252 | 29.15 S | 51.53 W |
| Encantado ◆[8] | 287a | 22.54 S | 43.18 W |
| Encanto, Cape ≻ | 116 | 15.44 N | 121.37 E |
| Encarnação ◆[8] | 266c | 38.47 N | 9.06 W |
| Encarnación | 252 | 27.20 S | 55.54 W |
| Encarnación de Díaz | 234 | 21.31 N | 102.14 W |
| Encha | 98 | 37.25 N | 115.42 E |
| Enchenberg | 56 | 49.01 N | 7.20 E |
| Enchi | 150 | 5.49 N | 2.49 W |
| Enchilayas | 200 | 30.50 N | 112.50 W |
| Enchovas, Enseada das ⊂ | 256 | 23.57 S | 45.18 W |
| Enciastraia, Monte ∧ | 62 | 44.22 N | 6.53 E |
| Encinal | 196 | 28.02 N | 99.21 W |
| Encinitas | 228 | 33.02 N | 117.17 W |
| Encino, N.M., U.S. | 200 | 34.39 N | 105.27 W |
| Encino, Tx., U.S. | 196 | 26.57 N | 98.08 W |
| Encino ◆[8] | 280 | 34.09 N | 118.30 W |
| Encino Reservoir ⊜[1] | 280 | 34.05 N | 118.31 W |
| Encontrados | 246 | 9.03 N | 72.14 W |
| Encounter Bay ⊂ | 168b | 35.35 S | 138.44 E |
| Encrucijada, Cuba | 240p | 22.37 N | 79.52 W |
| Encrucijada, Méx. | 234 | 18.18 N | 93.29 W |
| Encruzilhada | 255 | 15.31 S | 40.54 W |
| Encruzilhada do Sul | 252 | 30.32 S | 52.31 W |
| Encs | 30 | 48.20 N | 21.08 E |
| Endako | 182 | 54.05 N | 125.02 W |
| Endako ≃ | 182 | 54.05 N | 124.55 W |
| Endau ≃ | 114 | 2.39 N | 103.38 E |
| Ende | 115b | 8.50 S | 121.39 E |
| Ende, Pulau I | 115b | 8.53 S | 121.32 E |
| Ende, Teluk ⊂ | 115b | 8.52 S | 121.30 E |
| Endeavor, Pa., U.S. | 214 | 41.35 N | 79.23 W |
| Endeavor, Wi., U.S. | 190 | 43.42 N | 89.27 W |
| Endeavour | 184 | 52.08 N | 102.40 W |
| Endeavour Strait ⊔ | 164 | 10.50 S | 142.15 E |
| Endelave I | 41 | 55.46 N | 10.17 E |
| Enderbury I[1] | 14 | 3.08 S | 171.05 W |
| Enderby, B.C., Can. | 182 | 50.33 N | 119.08 W |
| Enderby, Eng., U.K. | 42 | 52.36 N | 1.12 W |
| Enderby Land ◆[1] | 9 | 67.30 S | 53.00 E |
| Enderlin | 198 | 46.37 N | 97.36 W |
| Endicott, N.Y., U.S. | 210 | 42.05 N | 76.02 W |
| Endicott, Wa., U.S. | 202 | 46.55 N | 117.40 W |
| Endicott Mountains ⩘ | 180 | 67.50 N | 152.00 W |
| Endimari ≃ | 248 | 8.46 S | 66.07 W |
| Endine | 64 | 45.46 N | 9.59 E |
| Endine Gaiano | 64 | 45.48 N | 9.59 E |
| Endingen | 58 | 48.09 N | 7.42 E |
| Endja, Oued ≃ | 34 | 36.31 N | 6.15 E |
| Endō | 268 | 35.23 N | 139.27 E |
| Endola | 156 | 17.37 S | 15.50 E |
| 'En Dor | 132 | 32.39 N | 35.25 E |
| Endre ≃ | 62 | 43.28 N | 6.36 E |
| Endrick ∧ | 170 | 35.12 S | 150.12 E |
| Endrick ≃ | 170 | 35.01 S | 150.03 E |
| Endwell | 210 | 42.06 N | 76.01 W |
| Ene ≃ | 248 | 11.09 S | 74.19 W |
| Eneabba | 162 | 29.50 S | 115.20 E |
| Enemonzo | 64 | 46.25 N | 12.53 E |
| Enewetak I[1] | 14 | 11.30 N | 162.15 E |
| Enez | 130 | 40.44 N | 26.04 E |
| Enfica | 36 | 36.07 N | 10.23 E |
| Enfield, Austl. | 168b | 34.53 S | 138.35 E |
| Enfield, Austl. | 274a | 33.53 S | 151.06 E |
| Enfield, N.Z. | 172 | 45.03 S | 170.52 E |
| Enfield, Ct., U.S. | 207 | 41.58 N | 72.35 W |
| Enfield, N.H., U.S. | 188 | 43.38 N | 72.08 W |
| Enfield, N.C., U.S. | 192 | 36.10 N | 77.40 W |
| Enfield, Va., U.S. | 208 | 37.43 N | 77.12 W |
| Enfield ◆[8] | 42 | 51.40 N | 0.05 W |
| Enga □[5] | 164 | 5.30 S | 143.30 E |
| Engadine | 170 | 34.04 S | 151.01 E |
| Engaño, Cabo ≻ | 238 | 18.37 N | 68.20 W |
| Engaru | 92a | 44.03 N | 143.31 E |
| Engažimo | 88 | 57.51 N | 114.56 E |
| Engcobo | 158 | 31.37 S | 28.00 E |
| 'En Gedi | 132 | 31.27 N | 35.23 E |
| Engelberg | 58 | 46.49 N | 8.25 E |
| Engelhard | 192 | 35.30 N | 75.59 W |
| Engelhartszell | 60 | 48.31 N | 13.44 E |
| Engel's | 80 | 51.30 N | 46.07 E |
| Engelsdorf | 54 | 51.20 N | 12.29 E |
| Engelskirchen | 56 | 50.59 N | 7.24 E |
| Engelsmanplaat I | 52 | 53.28 N | 6.02 E |
| Engen, B.C., Can. | 182 | 54.02 N | 124.18 W |
| Engen, Dtsch. | 58 | 47.51 N | 8.46 E |
| Engenheiro Navarro | 255 | 17.17 S | 43.57 W |
| Engenheiro Passos | 256 | 22.30 S | 44.41 W |
| Engenheiro Paulo de Frontin | 256 | 22.33 S | 43.41 W |
| Engenho | 248 | 15.10 S | 56.25 W |
| Engenho, Ilha do I | 287a | 22.50 S | 43.07 W |
| Engenho de Dentro ◆[8] | 287a | 22.54 S | 43.18 W |
| Engenho do Mato | 287a | 22.52 S | 43.01 W |
| Engenho Novo | 256 | 21.49 S | 43.00 W |
| Engenho Nôvo ◆[8] | 287a | 22.55 S | 43.17 W |
| Enger | 52 | 52.08 N | 8.34 E |
| Engestofte | 41 | 54.46 N | 11.34 E |
| Engesvang | 41 | 56.10 N | 9.21 E |
| 'En Gev | 132 | 32.47 N | 35.38 E |
| Enggano, Pulau I | 112 | 5.24 S | 102.16 E |
| Enghershatu ∧ | 144 | 16.40 N | 38.20 E |
| Enghien (Edingen) | 50 | 50.42 N | 4.02 E |
| Enghien-les-Bains | 261 | 48.58 N | 2.19 E |
| Enghien-Moisselles, Aéroport d' ⊠ | 261 | 49.02 N | 2.21 E |
| Engiadina Bassa V | 58 | 46.50 N | 10.20 E |
| Engis | 56 | 50.35 N | 5.25 E |
| Engizek Dağı ∧ | 130 | 37.50 N | 37.10 E |
| Engjan | 26 | 63.09 N | 8.32 E |
| England | 194 | 34.32 N | 91.58 W |
| England □[8] | 28 | 52.30 N | 1.30 W |
| England Air Force Base ■ | 194 | 31.20 N | 92.33 W |
| Englebright Lake ⊜[1] | 226 | 39.15 N | 121.15 W |
| Englee | 186 | 50.44 N | 56.06 W |
| Englefield, Cape ≻ | 176 | 69.51 N | 85.39 W |
| Englefield Green | 260 | 51.26 N | 0.35 W |
| Englefontaine | 50 | 50.11 N | 3.39 E |
| Englehart | 190 | 47.49 N | 79.52 W |
| Englehart ≃ | 190 | 47.51 N | 79.50 W |
| Engleside | 208 | 38.43 N | 77.05 W |
| Englewood, B.C., Can. | 182 | 50.33 N | 126.53 W |
| Englewood, Co., U.S. | 200 | 39.38 N | 104.59 W |
| Englewood, Fl., U.S. | 220 | 26.57 N | 82.21 W |
| Englewood, In., U.S. | 218 | 38.50 N | 86.31 W |
| Englewood, Ks., U.S. | 198 | 37.02 N | 99.58 W |
| Englewood, N.J., U.S. | 210 | 40.53 N | 73.58 W |
| Englewood, Oh., U.S. | 218 | 39.52 N | 84.18 W |
| Englewood, Tn., U.S. | 192 | 35.25 N | 84.29 W |
| Englewood ◆[8] | 278 | 41.47 N | 87.39 W |
| Englewood Cliffs | 276 | 40.53 N | 73.57 W |
| Englewood Dam ◆[6] | 218 | 39.52 N | 84.17 W |
| English, In., U.S. | 218 | 38.20 N | 86.27 W |
| English, Ky., U.S. | 218 | 38.37 N | 85.08 W |
| English ≃, On., Can. | 176 | 50.12 N | 95.00 W |
| English (Rivière des Anglais) ≃, N.A. | 206 | 45.13 N | 73.50 W |
| English ≃, Ia., U.S. | 190 | 41.29 N | 91.30 W |
| English Bay | 180 | 59.22 N | 151.55 W |
| English Bāzār → Ingrāj Bāzār | 124 | 25.00 N | 88.09 E |
| English Center | 210 | 41.26 N | 77.17 W |
| English Channel (La Manche) ⊔ | 28 | 50.20 N | 1.00 W |
| English Coast ⊓[2] | 9 | 73.45 S | 73.00 W |
| English Harbour West | 186 | 47.28 N | 55.29 W |
| Englishman ≃ | 224 | 49.22 N | 124.18 W |
| Englishtown | 208 | 40.17 N | 74.21 W |
| Engong | 152 | 0.36 N | 10.06 E |
| Engstingen | 58 | 48.23 N | 9.17 E |
| Engter | 52 | 52.23 N | 8.04 E |
| Énguera | 34 | 38.59 N | 0.41 W |
| Engum | 41 | 55.44 N | 9.40 E |
| Engure | 76 | 57.10 N | 23.13 E |
| Engures ezers ⊜ | 76 | 57.16 N | 23.06 E |
| Engwilen | 58 | 47.37 N | 9.05 E |
| 'En Harod | 132 | 32.33 N | 35.23 E |
| 'En HaShofét | 132 | 32.35 N | 35.06 E |
| Enid | 196 | 36.23 N | 97.52 W |
| Enid Lake ⊜[1] | 194 | 34.10 N | 89.50 W |
| Enilda | 182 | 55.25 N | 116.18 W |
| Eningen unter Achalm | 58 | 48.29 N | 9.16 E |
| Eniwa | 92a | 42.45 N | 141.33 E |
| Eniwetok → Enewetak I[1] | 14 | 11.30 N | 162.15 E |
| eNjesuthi ∧ | 158 | 29.09 S | 29.23 E |
| Enka | 192 | 35.32 N | 82.39 W |
| Enkenbach-Alsenborn | 56 | 49.29 N | 7.54 E |
| Enkhuizen | 52 | 52.42 N | 5.17 E |
| Enkirch | 56 | 49.59 N | 7.07 E |
| Enköping | 40 | 59.38 N | 17.04 E |
| Enle | 102 | 24.00 N | 101.07 E |
| Enmedio | 196 | 29.04 N | 103.29 W |
| Enmedio, Cerro de ∧ | 234 | 19.48 N | 100.36 W |
| Enmelen | 180 | 65.01 N | 175.54 W |
| Enna | 70 | 37.34 N | 14.16 E |
| Enna □[4] | 70 | 37.35 N | 14.26 E |
| Ennadai Lake ⊜ | 176 | 60.53 N | 101.15 W |
| Enné, Ouadi V | 146 | 14.24 N | 18.45 E |
| Ennedi ⩘[1] | 146 | 17.15 N | 22.00 E |
| Ennell, Lough ⊜ | 48 | 53.28 N | 7.24 W |
| Ennenda | 58 | 47.01 N | 9.05 E |
| Ennepe ≃ | 263 | 51.22 N | 7.27 E |
| Ennepestausee ⊜[1] | 263 | 51.14 N | 7.25 E |
| Ennepetal | 56 | 51.18 N | 7.22 E |
| Ennerdale Water ⊜ | 44 | 54.31 N | 3.23 W |
| Ennery | 261 | 49.05 N | 2.06 E |
| Enngonia | 166 | 29.19 S | 145.51 E |
| Enniger | 52 | 51.50 N | 7.56 E |
| Ennigerloh | 52 | 51.50 N | 8.02 E |
| Ennigloh | 52 | 52.12 N | 8.34 E |
| Ennis, Ire. | 48 | 52.50 N | 8.59 W |
| Ennis, Mt., U.S. | 202 | 45.20 N | 111.43 W |
| Ennis, Tx., U.S. | 222 | 32.19 N | 96.37 W |
| Enniscorthy | 48 | 52.30 N | 6.34 W |
| Enniskillen | 48 | 54.21 N | 7.38 W |
| Ennis Lake ⊜[1] | 202 | 45.26 N | 111.41 W |
| Ennistimon | 48 | 52.57 N | 9.15 W |
| Enns | 61 | 48.13 N | 14.29 E |
| Enns ≃ | 61 | 48.14 N | 14.32 E |
| Ennstaler Alpen ⩘ | 61 | 47.37 N | 14.35 E |
| Eno | 26 | 62.48 N | 30.09 E |
| Enø I | 41 | 55.10 N | 11.40 E |
| Eno ≃ | 96 | 34.53 N | 132.41 E |
| Enochs | 196 | 33.52 N | 102.46 W |
| Enogera Military Camp ■ | 171a | 27.25 S | 152.58 E |
| Enola | 208 | 40.17 N | 76.56 W |
| Enon | 218 | 39.53 N | 83.56 W |
| Enontekiö | 24 | 68.23 N | 23.38 E |
| Enon Valley | 214 | 40.51 N | 80.28 W |
| Enoree ≃ | 192 | 34.26 N | 81.25 W |
| Enosburg Falls | 188 | 44.54 N | 72.48 W |
| Eno-shima I | 94 | 35.18 N | 139.29 E |
| Enping | 102 | 22.11 N | 112.17 E |
| Enrekang | 112 | 3.34 S | 119.47 E |
| Enrile | 116 | 17.34 N | 121.42 E |
| Enrique Fynn | 258 | 34.50 S | 59.08 W |
| Enrique Urien | 252 | 27.34 S | 60.32 W |
| Enriquillo | 238 | 17.54 N | 71.14 W |
| Enriquillo, Lago ⊜ | 238 | 18.27 N | 71.39 W |
| Ens | 52 | 52.38 N | 5.50 E |
| Ensay I | 46 | 57.46 N | 7.05 W |
| Enschede | 52 | 52.12 N | 6.53 E |
| Ensdorf | 60 | 49.21 N | 11.56 E |
| Ensenada, Arg. | 258 | 34.51 S | 57.55 W |
| Ensenada, Méx. | 232 | 31.52 N | 116.37 W |
| Ensenada, P.R. | 240m | 17.58 N | 66.56 W |
| Ensenada □[5] | 288 | 34.50 S | 58.00 W |
| Enshi | 102 | 30.17 N | 109.19 E |
| Enshū-nada ⫪[2] | 92 | 34.27 N | 137.38 E |
| Ensisheim | 58 | 47.52 N | 7.21 E |
| Enstaberga | 40 | 58.45 N | 16.51 E |
| Entebbe | 154 | 0.04 N | 32.28 E |
| Entenbühl ∧ | 60 | 49.46 N | 12.24 E |
| Enter | 52 | 52.18 N | 6.34 E |
| Enterprise, Guy. | 246 | 6.56 N | 58.24 W |
| Enterprise, Al., U.S. | 194 | 31.18 N | 85.51 W |
| Enterprise, Ca., U.S. | 204 | 39.32 N | 121.22 W |
| Enterprise, Ks., U.S. | 198 | 38.54 N | 97.07 W |
| Enterprise, Ms., U.S. | 194 | 32.10 N | 88.49 W |
| Enterprise, Or., U.S. | 202 | 45.25 N | 117.16 W |
| Enterprise, Ut,. U.S. | 200 | 37.34 N | 113.43 W |
| Entiat ≃ | 202 | 47.40 N | 120.14 W |
| Entiat, Lake ⊜[1] | 202 | 47.40 N | 120.12 W |
| Entiat Mountains ⩘ | 224 | 48.00 N | 120.42 W |
| Entinas, Punta ≻ | 34 | 36.41 N | 2.46 W |
| Entlebuch | 58 | 47.00 N | 8.04 E |
| Entlebuch V | 58 | 46.58 N | 8.00 E |
| Entracque | 62 | 44.14 N | 7.24 E |
| Entraigues-sur-Sorgue | 62 | 44.00 N | 4.55 E |
| Entrains-sur-Nohain | 50 | 47.27 N | 3.15 E |
| Entrance, Cape ≻ | 164 | 2.21 S | 150.12 E |
| Entraunes | 62 | 44.11 N | 6.45 E |
| Entraygues | 32 | 44.39 N | 2.34 E |
| Entrechaux | 62 | 44.13 N | 5.08 E |
| Entrée, Île d' I | 186 | 47.17 N | 61.42 W |
| Entremont-le-Vieux | 62 | 45.26 N | 5.53 E |
| Entrepeñas, Embalse de ⊜[1] | 34 | 40.34 N | 2.42 W |
| Entre Rios, Bol. | 248 | 21.32 S | 64.12 W |
| Entre Rios, Bra. | 255 | 11.56 S | 38.05 W |
| Entre Ríos □[4] | 252 | 32.00 S | 59.00 W |
| Entre Ríos, Cordillera ⩘ | 236 | 14.05 N | 85.37 W |
| Entre-Rios de Minas | 255 | 20.41 S | 44.04 W |
| Entrevaux | 62 | 43.57 N | 6.49 E |
| Entrèves | 62 | 45.49 N | 6.57 E |
| Entriken | 214 | 40.20 N | 78.12 W |
| Entroncamento | 34 | 39.28 N | 8.28 W |
| Entupido | 256 | 22.30 S | 44.51 W |
| Entwistle | 182 | 53.36 N | 115.00 W |
| Enu, Pulau I | 164 | 7.05 S | 134.30 E |
| Enugu | 150 | 6.27 N | 7.27 E |
| Enumclaw | 224 | 47.12 N | 121.59 W |
| Enurmino | 180 | 66.57 N | 171.49 W |
| Envalira, Port d' )( | 34 | 42.35 N | 1.45 E |
| Envermeu | 50 | 49.54 N | 1.16 E |
| Envies, Rivière des ≃ | 206 | 46.37 N | 72.24 W |
| Envigado | 246 | 6.10 N | 75.35 W |
| Envira | 248 | 7.18 S | 70.13 W |
| Envira ≃ | 248 | 6.42 S | 69.46 W |
| 'En Yahav | 132 | 30.38 N | 35.11 E |
| Enyamba | 154 | 3.40 S | 24.58 E |
| Enyang | 102 | 31.48 N | 106.31 E |
| Enyellé | 152 | 2.49 N | 18.06 E |
| Enys, Mount ∧ | 172 | 43.14 S | 171.38 E |
| Enz ≃ | 56 | 49.01 N | 9.07 E |
| Enza ≃ | 64 | 44.54 N | 10.31 E |
| Enzan | 94 | 35.42 N | 138.44 E |
| Enzbach ≃ | 56 | 49.54 N | 6.25 E |
| Enzenkirchen | 60 | 48.23 N | 13.39 E |
| Enzesfeld | 61 | 47.55 N | 16.10 E |
| Enzklösterle | 56 | 48.40 N | 8.28 E |
| Eo ≃ | 34 | 43.28 N | 7.03 W |
| Eolia | 219 | 39.14 N | 91.00 W |
| Eolie o Lipari, Isole II | 70 | 38.30 N | 14.50 E |
| Epanomí | 38 | 40.26 N | 22.56 E |
| Épars, Bois de l' ♠ | 261 | 48.45 N | 1.45 E |
| Epe, Dtsch. | 52 | 52.11 N | 7.02 E |
| Epe, Ned. | 52 | 52.21 N | 6.00 E |
| Epe, Nig. | 150 | 6.37 N | 3.59 E |
| Epecuén, Lago ⊜ | 252 | 37.10 S | 62.54 W |
| Épéhy | 50 | 50.02 N | 3.10 E |
| Epéna | 152 | 1.22 N | 17.29 E |
| Épernay | 50 | 49.03 N | 3.57 E |
| Épernon | 50 | 48.37 N | 1.41 E |
| Epes | 194 | 32.41 N | 88.07 W |
| Epfendorf | 58 | 48.15 N | 8.36 E |
| Ephesus → Efes ⊥ | 130 | 37.55 N | 27.17 E |
| Ephraim | 200 | 39.21 N | 111.35 W |
| Ephrata, Pa., U.S. | 208 | 40.10 N | 76.10 W |
| Ephrata, Wa., U.S. | 202 | 47.19 N | 119.33 W |
| Ephrata Cloister ⊥ | 208 | 40.12 N | 76.09 W |
| Ephratah | 210 | 43.00 N | 74.32 W |
| Epi □[8] | 175f | 16.42 S | 168.15 E |
| Épi I | 175f | 16.43 S | 168.15 E |
| Épiais-lès-Louvres | 261 | 49.02 N | 2.33 E |
| Épila | 34 | 41.36 N | 1.17 W |
| Épinac-les-Mines | 58 | 46.59 N | 4.31 E |
| Épinal | 58 | 48.11 N | 6.27 E |
| Épinay-sous-Sénart | 261 | 48.42 N | 2.31 E |
| Épinay-sur-Orge | 261 | 48.40 N | 2.20 E |
| Épinay-sur-Seine | 261 | 48.57 N | 2.19 E |
| Epirus → Ípeiros □[9] | 38 | 39.40 N | 20.50 E |
| Episcopia | 68 | 40.04 N | 16.06 E |
| Episkopí | 130 | 34.40 N | 32.54 E |
| Époisses | 50 | 47.30 N | 4.10 E |
| Epokiro | 156 | 21.41 S | 19.08 E |
| Epomeo, Monte ∧ | 68 | 40.44 N | 13.54 E |
| Épône | 261 | 48.57 N | 1.49 E |
| Eport, Loch ⊂ | 46 | 57.33 N | 7.11 W |
| Eppalock, Lake ⊜[1] | 169 | 36.52 S | 144.31 E |
| Eppelborn | 56 | 49.24 N | 6.58 E |
| Eppendorf | 54 | 50.48 N | 13.14 E |
| Eppendorf ◆[8] | 263 | 51.27 N | 7.11 E |
| Eppenhausen ◆[8] | 263 | 51.21 N | 7.31 E |
| Eppeville | 50 | 49.44 N | 3.03 E |
| Epping, Austl. | 169 | 37.39 S | 145.02 E |
| Epping, Austl. | 274a | 33.46 S | 151.05 E |
| Epping, Eng., U.K. | 42 | 51.43 N | 0.07 E |
| Epping, N.H., U.S. | 188 | 43.02 N | 71.04 W |
| Eppingen | 56 | 49.08 N | 8.54 E |
| Epping Forest □[8] | 260 | 51.43 N | 0.10 E |
| Epping Forest ◆[3] | 42 | 51.40 N | 0.03 E |
| Epping Green, Eng., U.K. | 260 | 51.45 N | 0.07 W |
| Epping Green, Eng., U.K. | 260 | 51.44 N | 0.05 E |
| Epping Upland | 260 | 51.43 N | 0.06 E |
| Epsom | 42 | 51.20 N | 0.16 W |
| Epsom and Ewell □[8] | 260 | 51.20 N | 0.16 W |
| Epsom Downs Race Course ♠ | 260 | 51.19 N | 0.15 W |
| Epte ≃ | 50 | 49.04 N | 1.37 E |
| Épuisay | 50 | 47.54 N | 0.56 E |
| Epukiro ≃ | 156 | 20.45 S | 21.05 E |
| Epupa Falls ⌊ | 152 | 16.55 S | 13.10 E |
| Epuyén | 254 | 42.14 S | 71.21 W |
| Epworth | 44 | 53.32 N | 0.49 W |
| Eqlīd | 128 | 30.55 N | 52.39 E |
| Equality | 194 | 37.44 N | 88.20 W |
| Équateur □[4] | 152 | 1.00 N | 20.30 E |
| Équateur → Ecuador □[1] | 246 | 2.00 S | 77.30 W |
| Equatorial Guinea (Guinea Ecuatorial) □[1] | 152 | 2.00 N | 9.00 E |
| Équihen-Plage | 50 | 50.41 N | 1.34 E |
| Equimina ≃ | 152 | 13.11 S | 12.47 E |
| Equinox Mountain ∧ | 210 | 43.10 N | 73.08 W |
| Equinunk | 210 | 41.51 N | 75.14 W |
| Equi Terme | 64 | 44.09 N | 10.10 E |
| Era ≃, It. | 66 | 43.40 N | 10.38 E |
| Era ≃, Pap. N. Gui. | 164 | 7.35 S | 144.41 E |
| Erac Creek ≃ | 166 | 26.56 S | 145.48 E |
| Eraclea | 64 | 45.35 N | 12.40 E |
| Eraclea ⊥ | 68 | 40.13 N | 16.40 E |
| Eraclea Minoa ⊥ | 70 | 37.23 N | 13.17 E |
| Eradu | 162 | 28.41 S | 115.02 E |
| Éragny | 261 | 49.01 N | 2.06 E |
| Eramosa ≃ | 212 | 43.32 N | 80.14 W |
| Eran Bay ⊂ | 116 | 9.06 N | 117.43 E |
| Eranga | 152 | 1.52 S | 18.56 E |
| Erangal ◆[8] | 272c | 19.10 N | 72.47 E |
| Erap | 164 | 6.35 S | 146.40 E |
| Erath | 194 | 29.57 N | 92.02 W |
| Erave | 164 | 6.40 S | 143.50 E |
| Erave ≃ | 164 | 6.40 S | 143.55 E |
| Erba | 62 | 45.48 N | 9.15 E |
| Erba, Jabal ∧, Sūd. | 140 | 19.04 N | 36.46 E |
| Erba, Jabal ∧, Sūd. | 140 | 20.45 N | 36.50 E |
| Erbaa | 130 | 40.42 N | 36.36 E |
| Erbach, Dtsch. | 56 | 49.40 N | 8.59 E |
| Erbach, Dtsch. | 58 | 48.20 N | 9.53 E |
| Erbendorf | 60 | 49.50 N | 12.03 E |
| Erbeskopf ∧ | 56 | 49.44 N | 7.05 E |
| Erchie | 68 | 40.26 N | 17.44 E |
| Erciş | 84 | 39.02 N | 43.22 E |
| Erciyes Dağı ∧ | 130 | 38.32 N | 35.28 E |
| Ercolano | 68 | 40.48 N | 14.21 E |
| Ercolano (Herculaneum) ⊥ | 68 | 40.46 N | 14.20 E |
| Érd | 30 | 47.23 N | 18.56 E |
| Erdao ≃, Zhg. | 98 | 42.39 N | 127.35 E |
| Erdao ≃, Zhg. | 104 | 42.16 N | 122.20 E |
| Erdao Bai ≃ | 98 | 42.34 N | 128.08 E |
| Erdaobaihe | 98 | 42.22 N | 128.07 E |
| Erdaofang, Zhg. | 104 | 41.54 N | 123.57 E |
| Erdaofang, Zhg. | 104 | 41.37 N | 122.34 E |
| Erdaofangshen | 104 | 42.09 N | 123.17 E |
| Erdaogangzi, Zhg. | 104 | 41.57 N | 122.09 E |
| Erdaogangzi, Zhg. | 104 | 42.04 N | 123.06 E |
| Erdaohe | 89 | 43.37 N | 127.35 E |
| Erdaohezi, Zhg. | 89 | 45.07 N | 127.16 E |
| Erdaohezi, Zhg. | 89 | 45.08 N | 129.39 E |
| Erdaojingzi | 104 | 41.49 N | 122.20 E |
| Erdaoliangzi, Zhg. | 98 | 40.50 N | 119.04 E |
| Erdaoliangzi, Zhg. | 105 | 40.31 N | 118.03 E |
| Erdaowan | 89 | 47.58 N | 124.33 E |
| Erdek | 130 | 40.24 N | 27.48 E |
| Erdemli | 130 | 36.37 N | 34.18 E |
| Erdene, Mong. | 88 | 47.48 N | 107.55 E |
| Erdene, Mong. | 102 | 44.15 N | 111.14 E |
| Erdene, Mong. | 102 | 45.08 N | 97.45 E |
| Erdene Bulgan | 88 | 50.07 N | 101.35 E |
| Erdene-Büren | 86 | 48.26 N | 91.27 E |
| Erdenedalaj | 102 | 46.02 N | 104.55 E |
| Erdene Mandal | 88 | 48.30 N | 101.21 E |
| Erdenheim | 285 | 40.05 N | 75.12 W |
| Erdevik | 38 | 45.07 N | 19.25 E |
| Erdiao | 106 | 32.12 N | 121.12 E |
| Erding | 60 | 48.18 N | 11.54 E |
| Erdinger Moos ≋ | 60 | 48.22 N | 11.52 E |
| Erdnijevskij | 80 | 46.52 N | 46.17 E |
| Erebato ≃ | 246 | 5.54 N | 64.16 W |
| Erebus, Mount ∧ | 9 | 77.32 S | 167.09 E |
| Ereğli, Tür. | 130 | 37.31 N | 34.04 E |
| Ereğli, Tür. | 130 | 41.17 N | 31.25 E |
| Eregun | 273a | 6.36 N | 3.22 E |
| Erei, Monti ⩘ | 70 | 37.27 N | 14.19 E |
| Erenas | 116 | 12.25 N | 124.19 E |
| Erenhot | 102 | 43.46 N | 112.05 E |
| Erenköy ◆[8] | 267b | 40.58 N | 29.04 E |
| Erepecuru, Lago do ⊜ | 250 | 1.20 S | 56.35 W |
| Eresma ≃ | 34 | 41.26 N | 4.45 W |
| Eressós | 38 | 39.10 N | 25.56 E |
| Erétria | 38 | 38.24 N | 23.48 E |
| Erexim | 252 | 27.38 S | 52.17 W |
| Erez | 132 | 31.34 N | 34.34 E |
| Érezée | 56 | 50.18 N | 5.33 E |
| Erfa ≃ | 56 | 49.43 N | 9.15 E |
| Erfde | 41 | 54.19 N | 9.19 E |
| Erfelek | 130 | 41.53 N | 34.55 E |
| Erfenisdam ⊜[1] | 158 | 28.33 S | 26.50 E |
| Erfoud | 148 | 31.28 N | 4.10 W |
| Erft ≃ | 56 | 51.11 N | 6.44 E |
| Erftstadt | 56 | 50.48 N | 6.46 E |
| Erfurt | 54 | 50.58 N | 11.01 E |
| Ergak-Targak-Tajga, chrebet ⩘ | 88 | 53.25 N | 95.30 E |
| Ergani | 130 | 38.17 N | 39.46 E |
| Ergene ≃ | 130 | 41.01 N | 26.22 E |
| Ergenzingen | 58 | 48.29 N | 8.48 E |
| Erges (Erjas) ≃ | 34 | 39.40 N | 7.01 W |
| Ērgli | 76 | 56.54 N | 25.38 E |
| Ergolding | 60 | 48.35 N | 12.10 E |
| Ergoldsbach | 60 | 48.41 N | 12.12 E |
| Ergste | 56 | 51.25 N | 7.34 E |
| Erguig, Bahr ≃ | 146 | 11.22 N | 15.24 E |
| Ergun (Argun') ≃ | 74 | 53.20 N | 121.28 E |
| Ergun Youqi | 89 | 50.14 N | 120.10 E |
| Ergun Zuoqi | 89 | 50.47 N | 121.31 E |
| Erguvejem ≃ | 180 | 65.20 N | 176.00 W |
| Er Hai ⊜ | 102 | 25.48 N | 100.11 E |
| Erhlin | 100 | 23.54 N | 120.22 E |
| Erhshui | 100 | 23.49 N | 120.36 E |
| Erhulai | 98 | 41.23 N | 125.08 E |
| Eria ≃ | 34 | 42.03 N | 5.44 W |
| Erial | 208 | 39.46 N | 75.00 W |
| Eriba | 140 | 16.37 N | 36.04 E |
| Eriboll | 46 | 58.28 N | 4.41 W |
| Eriboll, Loch ⊂ | 46 | 58.31 N | 4.41 W |
| Erica, Austl. | 169 | 37.59 S | 146.22 E |
| Erica, Ned. | 52 | 52.43 N | 6.55 E |
| Erice | 70 | 38.02 N | 12.35 E |
| Ericeira | 34 | 38.59 N | 9.25 W |
| Erichsen Lake ⊜ | 176 | 70.38 N | 80.21 W |
| Erichshagen | 52 | 52.40 N | 9.14 E |
| Ericht, Loch ⊜ | 46 | 56.48 N | 4.24 W |
| Erick | 196 | 35.12 N | 99.51 W |
| Erickson, B.C., Can. | 182 | 49.05 N | 116.28 W |
| Erickson, Mb., Can. | 184 | 50.30 N | 99.55 W |
| Ericson | 198 | 41.46 N | 98.40 W |
| Erie, Co., U.S. | 200 | 40.03 N | 105.03 W |
| Erie, Il., U.S. | 190 | 41.39 N | 90.04 W |
| Erie, Ks., U.S. | 198 | 37.34 N | 95.14 W |
| Erie, Mi., U.S. | 216 | 41.47 N | 83.29 W |
| Erie, Pa., U.S. | 214 | 42.07 N | 80.05 W |
| Erie □[6], N.Y., U.S. | 210 | 42.54 N | 78.53 W |
| Erie □[6], Oh., U.S. | 214 | 41.27 N | 82.42 W |
| Erie □[6], Pa., U.S. | 214 | 42.08 N | 80.04 W |
| Erie, Lake ⊜ | 214 | 42.15 N | 81.00 W |
| Erieau | 214 | 42.16 N | 81.56 W |
| Erie Basin ⊂ | 276 | 40.40 N | 74.01 W |
| Erie Beach, On., Can. | 214 | 42.16 N | 82.00 W |
| Erie Beach, On., Can. | 284a | 42.53 N | 78.57 W |
| Erie Canal → New York State Barge Canal ≅ | 210 | 43.05 N | 78.43 W |
| Erie County Fairgrounds ♠ | 284a | 42.45 N | 78.49 W |
| Erie International Airport ⊠ | 214 | 42.05 N | 80.11 W |
| Eriksberg ⊥ | 40 | 58.56 N | 16.22 E |
| Eriksdale | 184 | 50.52 N | 98.06 W |
| Erímanthos ∧ | 38 | 37.59 N | 21.51 E |
| Erimo | 92a | 42.01 N | 143.09 E |
| Erimo-misaki ≻ | 92a | 41.55 N | 143.15 E |
| Erin, On., Can. | 212 | 43.45 N | 80.07 W |
| Erin, N.Y., U.S. | 210 | 42.11 N | 76.40 W |
| Erin, Tn., U.S. | 194 | 36.19 N | 87.41 W |
| Erindale | 275b | 43.32 N | 79.39 W |
| Ering | 60 | 48.18 N | 13.09 E |
| Eriskay I | 46 | 57.04 N | 7.18 W |
| Erisort, Loch ⊂ | 46 | 58.07 N | 6.24 W |
| Eriswil | 58 | 47.05 N | 7.51 E |
| Erith ◆[8] | 260 | 51.29 N | 0.10 E |
| Erithraí | 38 | 38.13 N | 23.19 E |
| Eritrea □[1], Afr. | 136 | 15.20 N | 39.00 E |
| Eritrea □[1], Afr. | 144 | 15.20 N | 39.00 E |
| Erivan → Jerevan | 84 | 40.11 N | 44.30 E |
| Erjas (Erges) ≃ | 34 | 39.40 N | 7.01 W |
| Erjiazhen | 106 | 32.02 N | 121.13 E |
| Erkelenz | 56 | 51.05 N | 6.19 E |
| Erken ⊜ | 40 | 59.51 N | 18.34 E |
| Erken-Jurt | 84 | 44.27 N | 41.54 E |
| Erkheim | 58 | 48.02 N | 10.20 E |
| Erkilet | 130 | 38.49 N | 35.27 E |
| Erkina ≃ | 48 | 52.51 N | 7.23 W |
| Erkner | 54 | 52.25 N | 13.45 E |
| Erkner, Forst ◆[3] | 264a | 52.22 N | 13.47 E |
| Erkowit | 140 | 18.46 N | 37.07 E |
| Erkrath | 56 | 51.13 N | 6.55 E |
| Erl | 64 | 47.41 N | 12.11 E |
| Erlach, Öst. | 61 | 47.43 N | 16.13 E |
| Erlach, Schw. | 58 | 47.03 N | 7.06 E |
| Erlands Point | 224 | 47.36 N | 122.42 W |
| Erlangen | 60 | 49.36 N | 11.01 E |
| Erlanger | 218 | 39.01 N | 84.36 W |
| Erlanghe | 100 | 30.19 N | 116.04 E |
| Erlangmiao | 100 | 33.46 N | 112.23 E |
| Erlau ≃ | 60 | 48.34 N | 13.36 E |
| Erlauf ≃ | 61 | 48.12 N | 15.11 E |
| Erlbach | 54 | 50.18 N | 12.22 E |
| Erldunda | 162 | 25.14 S | 133.12 E |
| Erle ◆[8] | 263 | 51.33 N | 7.05 E |
| Erlenbach | 56 | 49.48 N | 9.10 E |
| Erli | 62 | 44.08 N | 8.06 E |
| Erling | 106 | 31.53 N | 119.36 E |
| Erling, Lake ⊜[1] | 194 | 33.05 N | 93.35 W |


| Symbol | English | Deutsch | Español | Français | Português |
|---|---|---|---|---|---|
| ≃ | River | Fluß | Río | Rivière | Rio |
| ≅ | Canal | Kanal | Canal | Canal | Canal |
| ⌊ | Waterfall, Rapids | Wasserfall, Stromschnellen | Cascada, Rápidos | Chute d'eau, Rapides | Cascata, Rápidos |
| ⊔ | Strait | Meeresstraße | Estrecho | Détroit | Estreito |
| ⊂ | Bay, Gulf | Bucht, Golf | Bahía, Golfo | Baie, Golfe | Baía, Golfo |
| ⊜ | Lake, Lakes | See, Seen | Lago, Lagos | Lac, Lacs | Lago, Lagos |
| ≋ | Swamp | Sumpf | Pantano | Marais | Pântano |
| ⊓ | Ice Features, Glacier | Eis- und Gletscherformen | Accidentes Glaciales | Formes glaciaires | Acidentes glaciares |
| ⫪ | Other Hydrographic Features | Andere Hydrographische Objekte | Otros Elementos Hidrográficos | Autres données hydrographiques | Outros acidentes hidrográficos |

| Symbol | English | Deutsch | Español | Français | Português |
|---|---|---|---|---|---|
| ✢ | Submarine Features | Untermeerische Objekte | Accidentes Submarinos | Formes de relief sous-marin | Acidentes submarinos |
| □ | Political Unit | Politische Einheit | Unidad Politica | Entité politique | Unidade política |
| ʊ | Cultural Institution | Kulturelle Institution | Institución Cultural | Institution culturelle | Instituição cultural |
| ⊥ | Historical Site | Historische Stätte | Sitio Histórico | Site historique | Sitio histórico |
| ♠ | Recreational Site | Erholungs- und Ferienort | Sitio de Recreo | Centre de loisirs | Area de Lazer |
| ⊠ | Airport | Flughafen | Aeropuerto | Aéroport | Aeroporto |
| ■ | Military Installation | Militäranlage | Instalación Militar | Installation militaire | Instalação militar |
| ◆ | Miscellaneous | Verschiedenes | Misceláneo | Divers | Diversos |

Erlistoun 162 28.20 S 122.08 E
Erlongshan, Zhg. 89 47.20 N 132.28 E
Erlongshan, Zhg. 89 50.04 N 126.47 E
Erlongshantun 89 48.28 N 126.31 E
Erlsbach 64 46.55 N 12.15 E
Erma 208 38.58 N 74.54 W
Ermana, chrebet ⩘ 88 50.00 N 113.30 E
Ermatingen 58 47.41 N 9.06 E
Erme ≃ 42 50.18 N 3.56 W
Ermelindo Matarazo ♦[8] 287b 23.29 S 46.29 W
Ermelo, Ned. 52 52.17 N 5.37 E
Ermelo, S. Afr. 158 26.34 S 29.58 E
Ermendegou 104 42.02 N 121.56 E
Ermenek 130 36.38 N 32.54 E
Ermenek ≃ 130 36.35 N 33.23 E
Ermenonville 50 49.08 N 2.42 E
Ermidas 34 38.00 N 8.23 W
Ermil Post 140 13.37 N 27.36 E
Ermineskin Indian Reserve ♦[4] 182 52.52 N 113.30 W
Ermington 274a 33.48 S 151.04 E
Ermita de Guadalupe 234 22.36 N 103.03 W
Ermita de los Correas 234 22.54 N 103.01 W
Ermont 50 48.59 N 2.16 E
Ermoúpolis 38 37.26 N 24.56 E
Ermsleben 54 51.44 N 11.21 E
Ernabella 162 26.17 S 132.07 E
Erndtebrück 56 50.59 N 8.15 E
Erne ≃ 48 54.30 N 8.16 W
Erne, Lower Lough ⊜ 48 54.26 N 7.46 W
Erne, Upper Lough ⊜ 48 54.14 N 7.32 W
Ernée 32 48.18 N 0.56 W
Ernest 214 40.41 N 79.10 W
Ernestina 258 35.16 S 59.34 W
Ernest Sound ⊔ 182 55.52 N 132.10 W
Ernici, Monti ⩘ 66 41.48 N 13.22 E
Ernstbrunn 61 48.32 N 16.22 E
Ernst Thälmann, Pioneerpark ♦ 264a 52.28 N 13.33 E
Ernst-Thälmann-Stadion ♦ 264a 52.23 N 13.05 E
Ernz Blanche ≃ 56 49.52 N 6.16 E
Erode 122 11.21 N 77.44 E
Eromanga 166 26.40 S 143.16 E
Erongo 156 21.44 S 15.53 E
Erongo □4 156 22.00 S 15.00 E
Erongo ⩘ 156 21.45 S 15.37 E
Erota 144 16.14 N 37.55 E
Erp 56 50.46 N 6.43 E
Erpuzi 105 40.29 N 115.33 E
Erquelinnes 50 50.18 N 4.07 E
Err, Piz d' ∧ 58 46.33 N 9.41 E
Errabiddy 162 25.28 S 117.07 E
Er-Rachidia 148 31.58 N 4.25 W
Er-Rachidia □4 148 31.15 N 4.05 W
Errego 154 16.02 S 37.14 E
Errer ≃ 144 7.32 N 42.05 E
Er-Riad → Ar-Riyāḍ 128 24.38 N 46.43 E
Errigal Mountain ∧ 48 55.02 N 8.07 W
Errington 224 49.17 N 124.22 W
Erris Head > 48 54.19 N 10.00 W
Errochty, Loch ⊜ 46 56.45 N 4.12 W
Errogie 46 57.16 N 4.22 W
Errol Heights 224 45.28 N 122.36 W
Erromango I 175f 18.45 S 169.05 E
Ersekë 38 40.20 N 20.41 E
Ershijiazi 104 41.17 N 120.32 E
Ershilipu 105 40.07 N 117.24 E
Ershiqizhan 89 53.23 N 123.16 E
Ershiwuzhan 89 53.22 N 123.55 E
Erskine 198 47.40 N 96.00 W
Erskine, Lake ⊜ 276 41.06 N 74.15 W
Erskine Inlet c 176 76.15 N 102.20 W
Erskine Park 274a 33.49 S 150.47 E
Erstein 58 48.26 N 7.40 E
Erste Wiener Hochquellenleitung ≃[1] 61 48.10 N 16.17 E
Erstfeld 58 46.49 N 8.39 E
Ertai, Zhg. 86 46.07 N 90.06 E
Ertai, Zhg. 86 44.14 N 80.52 E
Ertaizi, Zhg. 104 41.52 N 121.56 E
Ertaizi, Zhg. 104 42.05 N 123.35 E
Ertaizi, Zhg. 104 42.35 N 124.00 E
Ertaizi, Zhg. 104 40.47 N 120.54 E
Ertil' 78 51.51 N 40.49 E
Ertingen 58 48.06 N 9.28 E
Ertix (Irtyš) ≃ 74 61.04 N 68.52 E
Erto 64 46.16 N 12.22 E
Ertuğrul 130 39.34 N 27.43 E
Ertvelde 50 51.11 N 3.45 E
Eruar 126 23.28 N 87.52 E
Erudina 166 31.28 S 139.23 E
Eruh 130 37.46 N 42.11 E
Erundu 156 20.36 S 16.25 E
Erunkan 273a 6.37 N 3.24 E
Erva, Ponta da > 266c 38.50 N 8.58 W
Erval 252 32.02 S 53.24 W
Erval d'Oeste 252 27.13 S 51.34 W
Ervalla 40 59.22 N 15.15 E
Erving 207 42.36 N 72.23 W
Ervy-le-Châtel 50 48.02 N 3.55 E
Erwin, N.C., U.S. 192 35.19 N 78.40 W
Erwin, Tn., U.S. 192 36.08 N 82.25 W
Erwitte 52 51.37 N 8.20 E
Erwood 184 52.50 N 102.10 W
Erxleben 54 52.13 N 11.14 E
Erythrée → Eritrea □1 144 15.20 N 39.00 E
Eryuan 102 26.06 N 99.55 E
Erzaohang 106 31.05 N 121.49 E
Erzberg ♦[7] 61 47.32 N 14.54 E
Erzgebirge (Krušné hory) ⩘ 54 50.30 N 13.10 E
Erzhan 89 43.58 N 128.44 E
Erzhuang 105 39.24 N 117.22 E
Erzin 130 39.44 N 39.29 E
Erzincan 130 39.44 N 39.30 E
Erzincan □4 130 39.40 N 39.30 E
Erzurum 130 39.55 N 41.17 E
Erzurum □4 130 40.00 N 41.30 E
Esa 76 54.53 N 28.40 E
Esa'ala 164 9.44 S 150.49 E
Esambo 152 3.40 S 23.24 E
Esan-misaki > 92a 41.49 N 141.11 E
Esashi, Nihon 92 41.52 N 140.07 E
Esashi, Nihon 92 39.12 N 141.09 E
Esashi, Nihon 92a 44.56 N 142.35 E
Esbiye 130 40.57 N 38.44 E
Esbjerg 26 55.28 N 8.27 E
Esbly 261 48.54 N 2.49 E
Esbo → Espoo 26 60.13 N 24.40 E
Esborn 263 51.23 N 7.20 E
Esca ≃ 34 42.37 N 1.03 W
Escada 250 8.22 S 35.14 W
Escalada 258 34.10 S 59.07 W
Escalante, Pil. 116 10.50 N 123.33 E
Escalante, Ut,. U.S. 200 37.46 N 111.36 W
Escalante ≃, Ut,. U.S. 200 37.17 N 110.53 W
Escalante ≃, Ven. 246 9.15 N 71.50 W
Escalante Desert ♦[2] 200 37.50 N 113.30 W
Escalaplano 71 39.37 N 9.21 E
Escalón, Méx. 232 26.45 N 104.20 W
Escalon, Ca., U.S. 226 37.47 N 120.59 W
Escalona 34 40.10 N 4.24 W
Escambia ≃ 194 30.32 N 87.11 W
Escanaba 190 45.44 N 87.04 W
Escanaba ≃ 190 45.47 N 87.04 W
Escandón, Puerto )( 34 40.17 N 1.00 W
Escárcega 232 18.37 N 90.43 W
Escarpada Point > 116 18.31 N 122.13 E
Escarpado Peak ∧ 116 8.36 N 117.22 E
Escarpment 284a 43.10 N 79.00 W
Escatawpa ≃ 194 30.25 N 88.35 W
Escaudain 50 50.20 N 3.21 E
Escaut (Schelde) ≃ 50 51.22 N 4.15 E
Eschach 58 47.44 N 9.36 E
Eschau, Dtsch. 56 49.49 N 9.15 E
Eschau, Fr. 58 48.29 N 7.43 E
Eschborn 56 50.09 N 8.34 E
Esche ≃ 56 48.54 N 6.04 E
Eschede 52 52.44 N 10.14 E
Eschen 58 47.13 N 9.31 E
Eschenbach 60 49.45 N 11.49 E
Eschenburg 56 50.49 N 8.20 E
Eschenlohe 64 47.36 N 11.11 E
Eschershausen 52 51.56 N 9.38 E
Eschkam 60 49.18 N 12.55 E
Escholzmatt 58 46.55 N 7.56 E
Eschscholtz Bay c 180 66.18 N 161.25 W
Esch-sur-Alzette 56 49.30 N 5.59 E
Esch-sur-Sûre 56 49.55 N 5.55 E
Eschwege 56 51.11 N 10.04 E
Eschweiler 56 50.49 N 6.16 E
Esclave, Grand Lac de l' → Great Slave Lake ⊜ 176 61.30 N 114.00 W
Escobal 236 9.09 N 79.58 W
Escobar □5 288 34.23 S 58.46 W
Escobar, Arroyo ≃ 288 34.21 S 58.44 W
Escobedo, Méx. 196 27.13 N 101.21 W
Escobedo, Méx. 232 29.05 N 102.19 W
Escocesa, Bahía c 238 19.25 N 69.45 W
Escoheag 207 41.36 N 71.45 W
Escondido 228 33.07 N 117.05 W
Escondido ≃, Méx. 196 28.39 N 100.34 W
Escondido ≃, Nic. 236 12.04 N 83.45 W
Escondido Creek ≃ 228 33.01 N 117.15 W
Escorial → San Lorenzo de El Escorial 34 40.35 N 4.09 W
Escoutay ≃ 62 44.29 N 4.42 E
Escravos ≃[1] 150 5.35 N 5.10 E
Escrick 44 53.53 N 1.02 W
Escuadrón 201 ♦[8] 286a 19.22 N 99.06 W
Escudero, Arroyo ≃ 258 34.20 S 57.05 W
Escudo de Veraguas, Isla I 236 9.06 N 81.33 W
Escuinapa de Hidalgo 234 22.51 N 105.48 W
Escuintla, Guat. 236 14.18 N 90.47 W
Escuintla, Méx. 232 15.20 N 92.38 W
Escuintla □5 236 14.10 N 91.00 W
Escuminac, Point > 186 47.04 N 64.46 W
Esebi 154 2.57 N 30.39 E
Eséka 152 3.39 N 10.46 E
Eşen 130 36.27 N 29.16 E
Eşen ≃ 130 36.16 N 29.15 E
Esenler ♦[8] 267b 41.02 N 28.51 E
Esens 52 53.39 N 7.37 E
Esera ≃ 34 42.06 N 0.15 E
Esesi 130 39.49 N 39.19 E
Eṣfahān (Isfahan) 128 32.40 N 51.38 E
Eṣfahān □4 128 33.00 N 52.00 E
Esfandaqeh 128 28.38 N 57.12 E
Esfarāyen 128 37.02 N 57.27 E
Esgueva ≃ 34 41.40 N 4.43 W
Eshan 102 24.11 N 102.22 E
Esher ♦[8] 42 51.23 N 0.22 W
Eshkāshem 123 36.42 N 71.34 E
Eshowe 158 28.58 S 31.29 E
Esh-Sham → Dimashq 132 33.30 N 36.18 E
Eshta'ol 132 31.47 N 35.00 E
Esh Winning 44 54.47 N 1.43 W
Esiama 150 4.56 N 2.21 W
Esigodini 154 20.18 S 28.56 E
Esine 64 45.55 N 10.15 E
Esino ≃ 66 43.39 N 13.22 E
Esira 157b 24.20 S 46.42 E
Esk 171a 27.15 S 152.25 E
Esk ≃, N.Z. 172 43.06 S 171.57 E
Esk ≃, U.K. 44 54.58 N 3.04 W
Esk ≃, Eng., U.K. 44 54.29 N 0.37 W
Esk ≃, Eng., U.K. 44 54.21 N 3.23 W
Esk ≃, Scot., U.K. 46 55.57 N 3.03 W
Eskdale, N.Z. 172 39.24 S 176.50 E
Eskdale, W.V., U.S. 188 38.05 N 81.26 W
Eskdale V 44 55.10 N 3.00 W
Eske, Lough ⊜ 48 54.41 N 8.03 W
Eski Dzhumaya → Tărgovište 38 43.15 N 26.34 E
Eskifjörður 24a 65.04 N 13.59 W
Eskiiban 85 43.12 N 68.31 E
Eskilstrup 41 54.51 N 11.54 E
Eskilstuna 40 59.22 N 16.30 E
Eskimalatya 130 38.26 N 38.23 E
Eskimo Lakes ⊜ 180 69.15 N 132.17 W
Eskimo Point 176 61.07 N 94.03 W
Eskipazar 130 40.58 N 32.33 E
Eskişehir 130 39.46 N 30.32 E
Eskişehir □4 130 39.35 N 31.10 E
Eskridge 198 38.51 N 96.06 W
Esla ≃ 34 41.29 N 6.03 W
Eslāmābād 128 34.06 N 46.31 E
Eslām Qal'eh 128 34.40 N 61.04 E
Eslāmshahr 128 35.40 N 51.10 E
Eslarn 60 49.35 N 12.32 E
Eslohe 56 51.15 N 8.09 E
Eslöv 41 55.50 N 13.20 E
Eşme 130 38.24 N 28.59 E
Esmeralda, Austl. 166 18.50 S 142.34 E
Esmeralda, Cuba 240p 21.51 N 78.07 W
Esmeralda, Méx. 196 25.40 N 103.30 W
Esmeralda, Isla I 254 48.57 S 75.25 W
Esmeraldas 246 0.59 N 79.42 W
Esmeraldas □4 246 0.40 N 79.30 W
Esmeraldas ≃ 246 0.58 N 79.38 W
Esmirna → İzmir 130 38.25 N 27.09 E
Esmond, N.D., U.S. 198 48.02 N 99.45 W
Esmond, R.I., U.S. 207 41.52 N 71.29 W
Esnagi Lake ⊜ 190 48.38 N 84.32 W
Esneux 56 50.32 N 5.34 E
Esong 152 2.09 N 10.58 E
Esopus Creek ≃ 210 42.04 N 73.56 W
Espada, Punta > 246 12.05 N 71.07 W
Espagne → Spain □1 34 40.00 N 4.00 W
Espalion 32 44.31 N 2.46 E
Espaly-Saint-Marcel 62 45.03 N 3.52 E
España → Spain □1 34 40.00 N 4.00 W
Espanola, On., Can. 190 46.15 N 81.46 W
Espanola, N.M., U.S. 200 35.59 N 106.04 W
Española, Isla I 246a 1.25 S 89.42 W
Esparto 226 38.41 N 122.00 W
Esparza 236 9.59 N 84.40 W
Espasingen 58 47.49 N 9.00 E
Espe, Dan. 41 55.12 N 10.25 E
Espe, Kaz. 85 43.52 N 74.10 E
Espejo 34 37.41 N 4.33 W
Espelkamp 52 52.25 N 8.36 E
Espenberg, Cape > 180 66.33 N 163.36 W
Espenhain 54 51.11 N 12.29 E
Espera, Arroyo ≃[1] 288 34.24 S 58.36 W
Espera Feliz 255 20.39 S 41.55 W
Esperança, Bra. 246 4.24 S 69.52 W
Esperança, Bra. 250 7.01 S 35.51 W
Esperance, Austl. 162 33.51 S 121.53 E
Esperance, N.Y., U.S. 210 42.46 N 74.15 W
Esperance Bay c 162 33.51 S 121.53 E
Esperantina 250 3.54 S 42.14 W
Esperantinópolis 250 4.53 S 44.53 W
Esperanza, Arg. 252 31.27 S 60.56 W
Esperanza, Cuba 240p 22.27 N 80.06 W
Esperanza, Méx. 232 27.35 N 109.56 W
Esperanza, Méx. 234 18.52 N 97.24 W
Esperanza, Pil. 116 8.43 N 125.36 E
Esperanza, Pil. 116 11.44 N 124.03 E
Esperanza, P.R. 240m 18.06 N 65.28 W
Esperanza, S. Afr. 158 30.21 S 30.40 E
Esperanza ≃[3] 9 63.24 S 56.59 W
Esperanza Inlet c 182 49.48 N 126.50 W
Espergærde 41 56.00 N 12.34 E
Esperia 66 41.23 N 13.41 E
Esperito, Arroyo ≃[1] 288 34.23 S 58.36 W
Espevær 26 59.36 N 5.10 E
Espichel, Cabo > 34 38.25 N 9.13 W
Espinal 246 4.09 N 74.53 W
Espinazo 196 26.16 N 101.06 W
Espinazo, Sierra del → Espinhaço, Serra do ⩘ 255 17.30 S 43.30 W
Espingarda ≃ 250 10.03 S 47.13 W
Espinhaço, Serra do ⩘ 255 17.30 S 43.30 W
Espinho 34 41.00 N 8.39 W
Espinillo 252 24.58 S 58.34 W
Espinillo, Arroyo ≃ 258 34.59 S 57.36 W
Espinillo, Punta del > 258 34.50 S 56.26 W
Espino 246 8.34 N 66.01 W
Espinosa 255 14.56 S 42.50 W
Espírito Santo → Vila Velha 250 3.13 N 51.13 W
Espírito Santo □3 255 19.30 S 40.30 W
Espírito Santo do Dourado 256 22.03 S 45.58 W
Espiritu Santo I 175f 15.15 S 166.50 E
Espiritu Santo, Isla I 232 24.30 N 110.22 W
Espita 232 21.01 N 88.19 W
Espoir, Bay d' c 186 47.50 N 55.51 W
Espoo (Esbo) 26 60.13 N 24.40 E
Es Port de Pollença 34 39.55 N 3.05 E
Esposende 34 41.32 N 8.47 W
Esposizione Universale di Roma ♦ 267a 41.50 N 12.28 E
Espugues de Llobregat 266d 41.22 N 2.05 E
Espumoso 252 28.44 S 52.51 W
Espungabera 156 20.29 S 32.48 E
Espy 210 41.00 N 76.24 W
Espyville Station 214 41.36 N 80.29 W
Esquatzel Coulee V 202 46.17 N 119.07 W
Esquel 254 42.54 S 71.19 W
Esquimalt 224 48.26 N 123.24 W
Esquina 252 30.01 S 59.32 W
Esquina Negra 258 35.02 S 58.03 W
Esquipulas, Guat. 236 14.34 N 89.21 W
Esquipulas, Nic. 236 12.40 N 85.47 W
Esquiú 252 29.23 S 65.17 W
Esrum Sø ⊜ 41 56.00 N 12.24 E
Essaoui Mellene, Oued V 148 27.26 N 6.40 E
Essaouira (Mogador) 148 31.30 N 9.47 W
Essaouira □4 148 31.25 N 9.30 W
Essarts 261 48.30 N 1.46 E
Essé 152 4.05 N 11.53 E
Esse ≃ 66 43.16 N 11.54 E
Esseg → Osijek 38 45.33 N 18.41 E
Es-Sekhira 148 34.17 N 10.06 E
Essen, Bel. 50 51.28 N 4.28 E
Essen, Dtsch. 52 52.43 N 7.56 E
Essen, Dtsch. 56 51.28 N 7.01 E
Essen, Dtsch. 263 51.28 N 7.01 E
Essenbach 60 48.37 N 12.13 E
Essenberg ♦[8] 263 51.26 N 6.42 E
Essendon, Austl. 169 37.46 S 144.55 E
Essendon, Eng., U.K. 260 51.46 N 0.09 W
Essendon, Mount ∧ 162 24.59 S 120.28 E
Essendon Airport ⊠ 169 37.43 S 144.53 E
Essen-Mülheim, Flughafen ⊠ 263 51.24 N 6.58 E
Essentuki → Jessentuki 84 44.03 N 42.51 E
Essequibo ≃ 246 6.59 N 58.23 W
Essequibo Islands-West Demerara □4 246 6.40 N 58.30 W
Es Sers 36 36.04 N 9.02 E
Essex, On., Can. 214 42.10 N 82.49 W
Essex, Ct., U.S. 207 41.21 N 72.23 W
Essex, Il., U.S. 216 41.11 N 88.11 W
Essex, Ia., U.S. 198 40.50 N 95.18 W
Essex, Md., U.S. 208 39.18 N 76.28 W
Essex, Ma., U.S. 207 42.37 N 70.47 W
Essex, Mo., U.S. 194 36.48 N 89.51 W
Essex, Mt., U.S. 182 48.16 N 113.36 W
Essex □6, On., Can. 214 42.10 N 82.50 W
Essex □6, Eng., U.K. 42 51.48 N 0.40 E
Essex □6, Ma., U.S. 207 42.40 N 70.55 W
Essex □6, N.J., U.S. 210 40.48 N 74.12 W
Essex □6, Vt., U.S. 206 44.57 N 71.43 W
Essex □6, Va., U.S. 208 37.55 N 76.55 W
Essex ≃ 283 42.39 N 70.46 W
Essex Bay c 283 42.39 N 70.44 W
Essex Fells 276 40.49 N 74.17 W
Essex Junction 188 44.29 N 73.06 W
Essex Skypark ⊠ 284b 39.18 N 76.28 W
Essexville 190 43.36 N 83.50 W
Essing 60 48.56 N 11.47 E
Essington 285 39.52 N 75.18 W
Essling ♦[8] 264b 48.13 N 16.32 E
Esslingen 56 48.45 N 9.16 E
Es Smala es Souassi 36 35.21 N 10.33 E
Esson Lake ⊜ 212 45.02 N 78.16 W
Essonne □5 50 48.36 N 2.20 E
Essonne ≃ 50 48.37 N 2.29 E
Essoyes 58 48.04 N 4.32 E
Es-Suki 140 13.20 N 33.54 E
Essvik 26 62.19 N 17.24 E
Est □4 152 4.00 N 14.00 E
Est, Canal de l' ≃ 56 48.45 N 5.35 E
Est, Cap > 157b 15.16 S 50.29 E
Est, Gare ♦[5] 261 48.53 N 2.22 E
Est, Île de l' I 186 47.37 N 61.26 W
Est, Pointe de l' > 186 49.08 N 61.41 W
Estacada 224 45.17 N 122.19 W
Estaca de Bares, Punta da la > 34 43.46 N 7.42 W
Estacado, Llano ≐ 196 33.30 N 102.40 W
Estación La Colorado 234 23.52 N 102.26 W
Estado, Parque do ♦ 287b 23.39 S 46.37 W
Estados, Isla de los (Staten Island) I 254 54.47 S 64.15 W
Estados Unidos → United States □1 178 38.00 N 97.00 W
Eṣṭahbān 128 29.08 N 54.04 E
Estaires 50 50.38 N 2.43 E
Estambul → İstanbul 130 41.01 N 28.58 E
Estância, Bra. 250 11.16 S 37.26 W
Estancia, Pil. 116 11.28 N 123.09 E
Estancia, S. Afr. 158 26.17 S 29.52 E
Estancia, N.M., U.S. 200 34.45 N 106.03 W
Estancia Los López 234 20.53 N 104.31 W
Estanislao del Campo 252 25.03 S 60.06 W
Estanzuelas 236 13.38 N 88.30 W
Estarreja 34 40.45 N 8.34 W
Estats, Pique d' ∧ 34 42.40 N 1.24 E
Estavayer-le-Lac 58 46.51 N 6.50 E
Estcourt 158 29.01 S 29.52 E
Este 64 45.14 N 11.39 E
Este ≃ 52 53.32 N 9.47 E
Este, Parque Nacional del ♦ 286c 10.30 N 66.50 W
Este, Punta > 240m 18.08 N 65.16 W
Esteban Echeverría 258 34.50 S 58.28 W
Esteban Echeverría □5 288 34.51 S 58.32 W
Estefanía, Lago → Stefanie, Lake ⊜ 144 4.40 N 36.50 E
Esteio 252 29.51 S 51.10 W
Estelí 236 13.05 N 86.23 W
Estelí □5 236 13.10 N 86.20 W
Estella 34 42.40 N 2.02 W
Estelline, S.D., U.S. 198 44.34 N 96.54 W
Estelline, Tx., U.S. 196 34.33 N 100.26 W
Estell Manor 208 39.24 N 74.44 W
Estenfeld 56 49.50 N 10.01 E
Estepa 34 37.18 N 4.54 W
Estepas de Kirguises → Kirgizskij chrebet ⩘ 85 42.30 N 74.00 E
Estepona 34 36.26 N 5.08 W
Ester 180 64.51 N 148.01 W
Esterel ⩘ 62 43.30 N 6.50 E
Esterhazy 184 50.40 N 102.08 W
Esterházy, Schloss ⊥ 61 47.51 N 16.32 E
Estérias, Cap > 152 0.37 N 9.20 E
Esternay 50 48.44 N 3.34 E
Estero 220 26.26 N 81.49 W
Estero Bay c, Ca., U.S. 226 35.24 N 120.53 W
Estero Bay c, Fl., U.S. 220 26.25 N 81.52 W
Estero Island I 220 26.26 N 81.56 W
Estéron ≃ 62 43.49 N 7.11 E
Esteros 252 26.37 S 63.39 W
Esterwegen 52 52.59 N 7.38 E
Estes Park 200 40.22 N 105.31 W
Este Sudeste, Cayos del II 236 12.26 N 81.27 W
Estevan 184 49.08 N 102.59 W
Estevan Group II 182 53.05 N 129.40 W
Estevan Point 182 49.23 N 126.33 W
Esther Island I 180 60.50 N 148.05 W
Estherville 198 43.24 N 94.49 W
Estill 192 32.45 N 81.14 W
Estissac 50 48.16 N 3.49 E
Estiva 256 22.28 S 46.02 W
Estiva, Ribeirão da ≃ 287b 23.44 S 46.23 W
Estiva, Rio da ≃ 255 12.23 S 45.05 W
Estling, Lake ⊜ 276 40.53 N 74.30 W
Estocolmo → Stockholm 40 59.20 N 18.03 E
Eston, Sk., Can. 184 51.10 N 108.46 W
Eston, Eng., U.K. 44 54.34 N 1.07 W
Estonia (Eesti) □1, Europe 22 59.00 N 26.00 E
Estonia (Eesti) □1, Europe 76 59.00 N 26.00 E
Estoril 34 38.42 N 9.23 W
Estrasburgo → Strasbourg 58 48.35 N 7.45 E
Estrées-Saint-Denis 50 49.26 N 2.39 E
Estrela 252 29.29 S 51.58 W
Estrela ∧ 34 40.19 N 7.37 W
Estrela ≃ 287a 22.43 S 43.13 W
Estrela, Serra da ⩘ 34 40.20 N 7.38 W
Estrela do Norte 255 13.49 S 49.04 W
Estrela do Sul 255 18.46 S 47.42 W
Estrella ≃ 226 35.45 N 120.41 W
Estremadura □9 34 39.15 N 9.10 W
Estremoz 34 38.51 N 7.35 W
Estribo 234 22.26 N 99.17 W
Estrondo, Serra do ⩘[1] 250 9.00 S 48.45 W
Estuaire □4 152 0.15 N 10.00 E
Estuary 184 50.56 N 109.46 W
Esumba, Île I 152 2.00 N 21.12 E
Eszék → Osijek 38 45.33 N 18.41 E
Esztergom 30 47.48 N 18.45 E
Étables 32 48.38 N 2.50 W
Etadunna 166 28.43 S 138.38 E
Etah, India 124 27.38 N 78.40 E
Etah, Kal. Nun. 16 78.19 N 72.38 W
Étain 56 49.13 N 5.38 E
Etajima 96 34.15 N 132.30 E
Eta-jima I 96 34.15 N 132.28 E
Étalle 56 49.41 N 5.36 E
Étamaniou ≃ 186 50.17 N 59.58 W
Étampes 50 48.26 N 2.09 E
Étamunbanie, Lake ⊜ 166 26.15 S 139.44 E
Étaples 50 50.31 N 1.39 E
États-Unis → United States □1 178 38.00 N 97.00 W
Etāwah 124 26.46 N 79.02 E
Etchemin ≃ 186 46.46 N 71.14 W
Etchojoa 232 26.55 N 109.38 W
Etéké 152 1.29 S 11.35 E
Etembue 152 1.17 N 9.25 E
Étendard, Pic de l' ∧ 62 45.09 N 6.09 E
Ethan 198 43.32 N 97.59 W
Ethel 194 33.07 N 89.27 W
Ethel ≃ 162 24.09 S 118.26 E
Ethel, Mount ∧ 200 40.39 N 106.41 W
Ethelbert 184 51.31 N 100.22 W
Ethel Creek 162 22.54 S 120.09 E
Ethel Lake ⊜ 180 63.21 N 136.00 W
Etherow ≃ 262 53.24 N 2.03 W
Ethiopia (Ityopiya) □1, Afr. 136 9.00 N 39.00 E
Ethiopia (Ityopiya) □1, Afr. 144 9.00 N 39.00 E
Ethiopian Plateau ⩘[1] 144 9.00 N 38.00 E
Ethiopie → Ethiopia □1 144 9.00 N 39.00 E
Ethridge, Mt., U.S. 202 48.33 N 112.07 W
Ethridge, Tn., U.S. 194 35.19 N 87.18 W
Eticoga 150 11.09 N 16.08 W
Eticuera Creek ≃ 226 38.41 N 122.16 W
Etigo-heiya ≐ 92 37.45 N 139.00 E
Etili 130 39.59 N 26.54 E
Étiolles 261 48.38 N 2.29 E
Etiopia → Ethiopia □1 144 9.00 N 39.00 E
Etive, Loch ⊜ 46 56.29 N 5.09 W
Etjo ∧ 156 21.05 S 16.30 E
Etna, Ca., U.S. 204 41.27 N 122.53 W
Etna, N.Y., U.S. 210 42.29 N 76.23 W
Etna, Pa., U.S. 214 40.30 N 79.56 W
Etna, Wy., U.S. 200 43.02 N 111.00 W
Etna, Monte (Mongibello) ∧[1] 70 37.46 N 15.00 E
Etna Green 216 41.17 N 86.03 W
Etne 26 59.40 N 5.56 E
Etobicoke 212 43.42 N 79.32 W
Etobicoke Creek ≃ 212 43.35 N 79.32 W
Etoile 154 11.38 S 27.34 E
Étoile, Chaîne de l' ⩘ 62 43.23 N 5.25 E
Etoka 152 0.10 N 23.23 E
Etolin Island I 180 56.08 N 132.26 W
Etolin Strait ⊔ 180 60.20 N 165.15 W
Etomami ≃ 184 52.48 N 102.33 W
Eton, Austl. 166 21.16 S 148.58 E
Eton, Eng., U.K. 42 51.30 N 0.36 W
Eton College ♦[2] 260 51.30 N 0.36 W
Etondo 152 7.46 S 23.36 E
Etorofu-tō → Iturup, ostrov I 92a 44.54 N 147.30 E
Etosha National Park ♦ 156 19.00 S 15.50 E
Etosha Pan ≐ 156 18.45 S 16.15 E
Etoumbi 152 0.01 S 14.57 E
Etowah 192 35.19 N 84.31 W
Etowah ≃ 192 34.15 N 85.11 W
Étréchy 50 48.30 N 2.12 E
Étrépagny 50 49.18 N 1.37 E
Étretat 50 49.42 N 0.12 E
Etrotroka 157b 22.53 S 47.36 E
Etroubles 62 45.49 N 7.14 E
Etrusca, Necropoli ⊥ 66 42.15 N 11.47 E
Etsch → Adige ≃ 64 45.10 N 12.20 E
Ettal 64 47.34 N 11.05 E
Ettalong 170 33.31 S 151.21 E
Ettelbruck 56 49.52 N 6.05 E
Ettenheim 58 48.15 N 7.49 E
Etten-Leur 52 51.34 N 4.38 E
Etterbeek 56 50.50 N 4.23 E
Etters 208 40.09 N 76.45 W
Et Tîdra I 150 19.44 N 16.24 W
Ettington 42 52.09 N 1.36 W
Ettlingen 56 48.56 N 8.24 E
Ettrema Creek ≃ 170 34.50 S 150.22 E
Ettrick 208 37.14 N 77.25 W
Ettrick Forest ♦[3] 46 55.30 N 3.00 W
Ettrick Pen ∧ 44 55.22 N 3.16 W
Ettrick Water ≃ 46 55.31 N 2.55 W
Ettringen, Dtsch. 56 50.21 N 7.13 E
Ettringen, Dtsch. 58 48.06 N 10.39 E
Etuku 154 3.43 S 25.44 E
Etyka 88 51.00 N 116.50 E
Etzatlán 234 20.46 N 104.05 W
Etzikom Coulee ≃ 184 49.25 N 111.10 W
Etzná ⊥ 232 19.35 N 90.15 W
Eu 50 50.03 N 1.25 E
Eua I 14 21.22 S 174.56 W
Eua Iki I 174w 21.07 S 174.59 W
Eubank Acres 222 30.23 N 97.42 W
Euboea → Évvoia I 38 38.34 N 23.50 E
Euchiniko ≃ 182 53.14 N 123.30 W
Eucla 162 31.43 S 128.52 E
Euclid, Oh., U.S. 214 41.35 N 81.31 W
Euclid, Pa., U.S. 214 41.00 N 79.56 W
Euclid Center 216 42.08 N 86.24 W
Euclid Creek ≃ 279a 41.35 N 81.35 W
Euclid Creek Reservation ♦ 279a 41.33 N 81.32 W
Euclides da Cunha 250 10.31 S 39.01 W
Eucumbene 171b 36.07 S 148.38 E
Eucumbene ≃ 171b 36.21 S 148.38 E
Eucumbene, Lake ⊜[1] 171b 36.05 S 148.45 E
Eudistes, Lac des ⊜ 186 50.30 N 65.15 W
Eudora, Ar., U.S. 194 33.06 N 91.15 W
Eudora, Ks., U.S. 198 38.56 N 95.05 W
Eudunda 168b 34.11 S 139.04 E
Eufaula, Al., U.S. 194 31.53 N 85.08 W
Eufaula, Ok., U.S. 196 35.17 N 95.34 W
Eufaula Lake ⊜[1] 196 35.17 N 95.31 W
Eufrates → Euphrates ≃ 128 31.00 N 47.25 E
Euganei, Colli ⩘[2] 64 45.19 N 11.40 E
Eugendorf 64 47.52 N 13.07 E
Eugene 202 44.03 N 123.05 W
Eugenia, Punta > 232 27.50 N 115.05 W
Eugenia Lake ⊜ 212 44.20 N 80.30 W
Eugenio Bustos 252 33.46 S 69.04 W
Eugênio de Melo 256 23.09 S 45.47 W
Eugmo I 26 63.49 N 22.45 E
Eugowra 166 33.26 S 148.23 E
Euijeongbu → Ŭijŏngbu 98 37.44 N 127.03 E
Euless 222 32.50 N 97.04 W
Eulo 166 28.10 S 145.03 E
Eume ≃ 34 43.25 N 8.08 W
Eumemmerring Creek ≃ 274b 38.03 S 145.10 E
Eumungerie 166 31.57 S 148.37 E
Eunápolis 255 16.22 S 39.35 W
Eungella National Park ♦ 166 21.00 S 148.30 E
Eunice, La., U.S. 194 30.29 N 92.25 W
Eunice, N.M., U.S. 196 32.26 N 103.09 W
Eupen 56 50.38 N 6.02 E
Euphrat → Euphrates ≃ 128 31.00 N 47.25 E
Euphrates (Firat) (Nahr al-Furāt) ≃ 128 31.00 N 47.25 E
Eupora 194 33.32 N 89.16 W
Eure 208 36.25 N 76.51 W
Eure □5 50 49.10 N 1.00 E
Eure ≃ 50 49.18 N 1.12 E
Eure-et-Loir □5 50 48.30 N 1.30 E
Eureka, Ak., U.S. 180 61.56 N 147.10 W
Eureka, Ca., U.S. 204 40.48 N 124.09 W
Eureka, Il., U.S. 190 40.43 N 89.16 W
Eureka, Ks., U.S. 198 37.49 N 96.17 W
Eureka, Mo., U.S. 219 38.30 N 90.37 W
Eureka, Mt., U.S. 202 48.52 N 115.03 W
Eureka, Nv., U.S. 204 39.30 N 115.57 W
Eureka, Pa., U.S. 214 40.15 N 78.46 W
Eureka, S.C., U.S. 192 34.42 N 81.11 W
Eureka, S.D., U.S. 198 45.46 N 99.37 W
Eureka, Tx., U.S. 222 32.01 N 96.18 W
Eureka, Ut., U.S. 200 39.57 N 112.07 W
Eureka, Mount ∧ 162 26.34 S 121.32 E
Eureka Springs 194 36.24 N 93.44 W
Eurialo, Castello ⊥ 70 37.06 N 15.14 E
Eurinilla Creek ≃ 166 30.50 S 140.01 E
Euroa 169 36.45 S 145.35 E
Euro Disney, Parc ♦ 261 48.51 N 2.47 E
Europa, Île I 156 22.20 S 40.22 E
Europabrücke ♦[5] 64 47.11 N 11.23 E
Europa Point > 34 36.10 N 5.22 W
Europe ♦[1] 4 50.00 N 28.00 E
Europe ♦[1] 10 50.00 N 28.00 E
Europoort ♦[5] 52 51.57 N 4.07 E
Eursinge 52 52.46 N 6.28 E
Eurville 58 48.35 N 5.02 E
Euskal Herriko □3 34 43.00 N 2.30 W
Euskirchen 56 50.39 N 6.47 E
Eustace 222 32.18 N 96.01 W
Eustis, Fl., U.S. 220 28.51 N 81.41 W
Eustis, Ne., U.S. 198 40.39 N 100.09 W
Eustis, Lake ⊜ 220 28.50 N 81.44 W
Euston Station ♦[5] 260 51.32 N 0.08 W
Eutaw 194 32.50 N 87.53 W
Eutin 54 54.08 N 10.37 E
Eutsuk Lake ⊜ 182 53.20 N 126.44 W
Eutzsch 54 51.49 N 12.38 E
Euxton 44 53.39 N 2.40 W
Euzet-les-Bains 62 44.03 N 4.13 E
Eva 194 34.20 N 86.46 W
Evadale 194 30.21 N 94.04 W
Eva Downs 162 18.01 S 134.52 E
Evale 152 16.33 S 15.44 E
Evällen ⊜ 40 60.03 N 18.20 E
Evançon ≃ 62 45.40 N 7.41 E
Evandale 166 41.34 S 147.14 E
Evans 200 40.22 N 104.41 W
Evans, Lac ⊜ 176 50.55 N 77.00 W
Evans, Mount ∧ 200 39.35 N 105.38 W
Evansburg, Ab., Can. 182 53.36 N 115.01 W
Evansburg, Pa., U.S. 285 40.11 N 75.26 W
Evans Center 210 42.39 N 79.02 W
Evans City 214 40.46 N 80.03 W
Evans Creek ≃ 202 42.35 N 123.11 W
Evansdale 198 42.28 N 92.16 W
Evans Head > 166 29.07 S 153.26 E
Evans Mills 212 44.05 N 75.48 W
Evansport 216 41.25 N 84.24 W
Evans Strait ⊔ 176 63.15 N 82.00 W
Evanston, Il., U.S. 216 42.02 N 87.41 W
Evanston, Wy., U.S. 200 41.16 N 110.57 W
Evansville, Il., U.S. 194 38.05 N 89.56 W
Evansville, In., U.S. 194 37.58 N 87.33 W
Evansville, Mn., U.S. 198 46.00 N 95.40 W
Evansville, Wi., U.S. 216 42.46 N 89.17 W
Evansville, Wy., U.S. 200 42.51 N 106.16 W
Evant 196 31.29 N 98.09 W
Evanton 46 57.40 N 4.20 W
Eva Perón → La Plata 258 34.55 S 57.57 W
Evart 190 43.54 N 85.15 W
Evarts 192 36.51 N 83.11 W
Evaz 128 27.46 N 53.59 E
Eve 261 49.05 N 2.42 E
Evecquemont 261 49.02 N 1.57 E
Eveking 263 51.14 N 7.44 E
Eveleth 190 47.27 N 92.32 W
Evelyn, Mount ∧[2] 164 13.36 S 132.53 E
Evening Shade 194 36.04 N 91.37 W
Evenkamp 263 51.40 N 7.39 E
Evenlode ≃ 42 51.47 N 1.21 W
Evensk 74 61.57 N 159.14 E
Evenwood 44 54.37 N 1.46 W
Even Yehuda 132 32.16 N 34.53 E
Everard, Lake ⊜ 162 31.25 S 135.05 E
Everard, Mount ∧, Austl. 162 26.16 S 132.04 E
Everard, Mount ∧, B.C., Can. 182 51.05 N 125.45 W
Everard Ranges ⩘ 162 27.05 S 132.28 E
Evercreech 42 51.09 N 2.30 W
Evere 56 50.52 N 4.24 E
Everest 198 39.40 N 95.25 W
Everest, Mount (Qomolangma Feng) ∧ 124 27.59 N 86.56 E
Everett, On., Can. 212 44.11 N 79.57 W
Everett, Ma., U.S. 207 42.24 N 71.03 W
Everett, N.J., U.S. 276 40.21 N 74.09 W
Everett, Pa., U.S. 188 40.00 N 78.22 W
Everett, Wa., U.S. 224 47.58 N 122.12 W
Everett, Mount ∧ 207 42.06 N 73.25 W
Evergem 50 51.07 N 3.42 E
Everglades, The ≋ 220 26.00 N 80.40 W
Everglades City 220 25.52 N 81.23 W
Everglades National Park ♦ 220 25.27 N 80.53 W
Evergreen, Al., U.S. 194 31.26 N 86.57 W
Evergreen, Ca., U.S. 204 35.54 N 120.26 W
Evergreen, Mt., U.S. 202 48.13 N 114.18 W
Evergreen, Tx., U.S. 222 30.33 N 95.14 W
Evergreen Lake ⊜[1] 216 40.40 N 89.02 W
Evergreen Park 216 41.43 N 87.42 W
Evergreen Plaza ♦[9] 278 41.43 N 87.41 W
Everly 198 43.09 N 95.19 W
Everman 222 32.37 N 97.17 W
Everman, Volcán ∧[1] 232 18.48 N 110.59 W
Everöd 26 55.54 N 14.06 E
Eversael 263 51.33 N 6.39 E
Eversen 52 52.45 N 10.02 E
Everson, Pa., U.S. 214 40.05 N 79.35 W
Everson, Wa., U.S. 224 48.55 N 122.20 W
Everswinkel 52 51.55 N 7.50 E
Everton 218 39.34 N 85.05 W
Everton ♦[8] 262 53.25 N 2.58 W
Everton Football Ground ♦ 262 53.26 N 2.58 W
Evesen 52 52.17 N 8.59 E
Evesham, Sk., Can. 184 52.24 N 109.50 W
Evesham, Eng., U.K. 42 52.06 N 1.56 W
Evesham, Vale of V 42 52.06 N 1.50 W
Évian-les-Bains 58 46.23 N 6.35 E
Evijärvi 26 63.22 N 23.29 E
Evinayong 152 1.27 N 10.34 E
Eving ♦[8] 263 51.33 N 7.29 E
Evingsen 263 51.18 N 7.44 E
Evionnaz 58 46.11 N 7.01 E
Evisa 36 42.15 N 8.47 E
Evje 26 58.36 N 7.51 E
Evolène 58 46.07 N 7.30 E
Évora 34 38.34 N 7.54 W
Evoron, ozero ⊜ 89 51.28 N 136.30 E
Evpatoria → Yevpatoriya 78 45.12 N 33.22 E
Évrange 56 49.30 N 6.12 E
Évreux 50 49.01 N 1.09 E
Evrieu 62 45.35 N 5.34 E
'Evron 132 32.59 N 35.06 E
Évros (Marica) (Meriç) ≃ 38 40.52 N 26.12 E
Evrótas ≃ 38 36.48 N 22.40 E
Évry 50 48.38 N 2.27 E
Évry-les-Châteaux 261 48.39 N 2.38 E
E. V. Spence Reservoir ⊜[1] 196 31.55 N 100.35 W
Evungu 154 4.27 S 25.12 E
Évvoia I 38 38.34 N 23.50 E
Évzonos ∧ 267c 37.57 N 23.49 E
Ewa 229c 21.20 N 158.02 W
Ewa Beach 229c 21.18 N 158.00 W
Ewan 285 39.42 N 75.11 W
Ewaninga 162 23.58 S 133.58 E
Ewan Lake ⊜ 285 39.42 N 75.11 W
Ewansville 285 39.59 N 74.44 W
Ewbank 158 26.14 S 23.35 E
Ewbank da Câmara 256 21.31 S 43.33 W
Ewe, Loch c 46 57.48 N 5.40 W
Ewell, Eng., U.K. 260 51.21 N 0.15 W
Ewell, Md., U.S. 208 37.59 N 76.02 W
Ewen 190 46.32 N 89.16 W
Ewenkiku Zizhiqi 89 49.07 N 119.40 E
Ewes Water ≃ 44 55.08 N 3.00 W
Ewing, Ky., U.S. 218 38.25 N 83.51 W
Ewing, Mo., U.S. 219 40.00 N 91.42 W
Ewing, Ne., U.S. 198 42.15 N 98.20 W
Ewing, Va., U.S. 192 36.38 N 83.25 W
Ewingsville 279b 40.24 N 80.06 W
Ewing Township 208 40.16 N 74.46 W
Ewo 152 0.53 S 14.49 E
Ewu 273a 6.33 N 3.19 E
Exaltación 248 13.16 S 65.15 W
Excelda 158 32.16 S 22.08 E
Excello 218 39.29 N 84.25 W
Excelsior 158 28.56 S 27.06 E
Excelsior Mountain ∧ 226 38.02 N 119.18 W
Excelsior Park ♦ 274a 33.45 S 151.01 E
Excelsior Springs 194 39.20 N 94.13 W
Excenevex 58 46.21 N 6.21 E
Exchange 214 41.07 N 76.41 W
Exchange Station ♦[5] 262 53.25 N 2.59 W
Excursion Inlet 180 58.25 N 135.27 W
Exe ≃ 42 50.37 N 3.25 W
Executive Committee Range ⩘ 9 76.50 S 126.00 W
Exeter, Austl. 170 34.38 S 150.19 E
Exeter, On., Can. 190 43.21 N 81.29 W
Exeter, Eng., U.K. 42 50.43 N 3.31 W
Exeter, Ca., U.S. 226 36.17 N 119.08 W
Exeter, Ne., U.S. 198 40.38 N 97.26 W
Exeter, N.H., U.S. 188 42.58 N 70.56 W
Exeter, Pa., U.S. 210 41.19 N 75.49 W
Exeter, R.I., U.S. 207 41.34 N 71.32 W
Exeter ≃ 188 43.02 N 70.55 W
Exeter Sound ⊔ 176 66.14 N 62.00 W
Exford 42 51.08 N 3.38 W
Exhibition of Economic Achievements ♦ 265b 55.50 N 37.37 E
Exhibition Park ♦ 275b 43.38 N 79.25 W
Exhibition Stadium ♦ 275b 43.38 N 79.25 W
Exincourt 58 47.30 N 6.50 E
Exira 198 41.35 N 94.52 W
Exline Slough ≃ 216 41.05 N 87.47 W
Exmes 50 48.45 N 0.11 E
Exminster 42 50.41 N 3.29 W
Exmoor ⩘[1] 42 51.10 N 3.45 W
Exmoor National Park ♦ 42 51.12 N 3.46 W
Exmore 208 37.31 N 75.49 W
Exmouth, Austl. 162 21.56 S 114.07 E
Exmouth, Eng., U.K. 42 50.37 N 3.25 W
Exmouth Gulf c 162 22.00 S 114.20 E
Exmouth Plateau ♦[3] 14 19.00 S 114.00 E
Exning 42 52.16 N 0.21 E
Expedition Range ⩘ 166 24.30 S 149.05 E
Experiment 192 33.15 N 84.16 W
Exploits ≃ 186 49.05 N 55.20 W
Exploits, Bay of c 186 49.24 N 55.00 W
Exploits Dam ♦[6] 186 48.45 N 56.30 W
Expo Memorial Park ♦ 270 34.48 N 135.32 E
Export 214 40.25 N 79.37 W
Exposition Park ♦ 280 34.01 N 118.17 W
Exshaw 182 51.03 N 115.09 W
Extension 224 49.06 N 123.57 W
Exter 52 52.08 N 8.46 E
Externsteine ⊥ 52 51.52 N 8.55 E
Extertal 52 52.04 N 9.07 E
Exton 208 40.02 N 75.37 W
Extoraz ≃ 234 21.06 N 99.23 W
Extrema 256 22.51 S 46.19 W
Extremadura □3 34 39.15 N 6.15 W
Exu 250 7.31 S 39.43 W
Exuma Cays II 238 24.15 N 76.30 W
Exuma Sound ⊔ 238 24.15 N 76.00 W
Eyam 44 53.17 N 1.41 W
Eyasi, Lake ⊜ 154 3.40 S 35.05 E
Eydehavn 26 58.31 N 8.53 E
Eye, Eng., U.K. 42 52.19 N 1.09 E
Eye, Eng., U.K. 42 52.35 N 0.11 W
Eyebrow 184 50.47 N 106.09 W
Eyehill Creek ≃ 184 52.40 N 109.39 W


**Symbols** in the index entries represent the broad categories identified in the key at the right. Symbols with superior numbers (⩘[1]) identify subcategories (see complete key on page *I · 1).*

**Symbole** im Register stellen die rechts im Schlüssel erklärten Kategorien dar. Symbole mit hochgestellten Ziffern (⩘[1]) bezeichnen Unterabteilungen einer Kategorie (vgl. vollständiger Schlüssel auf Seite *I · 1).*

**Los símbolos** incluídos en el texto del índice representan las grandes categorías identificadas con la clave a la derecha. Los símbolos con numeros en su parte superior (⩘[1]) identifican las subcategorías (véase la clave completa en la página *I · 1).*

**Les symboles** de l'index représentent les catégories indiquées dans la légende à droite. Les symboles suivis d'un indice (⩘[1]) représentent des sous-catégories (voir légende complète à la page *I · 1).*

**Os símbolos** incluídos no texto do índice representam as grandes categorias identificadas com a chave à direita. Os símbolos com números em sua parte superior (⩘[1]) identificam as subcategorias (veja-se a chave completa à página *I · 1).*

| | | | | |
|---|---|---|---|---|
| ∧ Mountain | Berg | Montaña | Montagne | Montanha |
| ⩘ Mountains | Gebirge | Montañas | Montagnes | Montanhas |
| )( Pass | Paß | Paso | Col | Passo |
| V Valley, Canyon | Tal, Cañon | Valle, Cañón | Vallée, Canyon | Vale, Canhão |
| ≐ Plain | Ebene | Llano | Plaine | Planície |
| > Cape | Kap | Cabo | Cap | Cabo |
| I Island | Insel | Isla | Île | Ilha |
| II Islands | Inseln | Islas | Îles | Ilhas |
| ♦ Other Topographic Features | Andere Topographische Objekte | Otros Elementos Topográficos | Autres données topographiques | Outros acidentes topográficos |

ESPAÑOL | FRANÇAIS | PORTUGUÊS


| Nombre / Nom / Nome | Página / Page | Lat.°′ | Long.°′ W = Oeste / W = Ouest |
|---|---|---|---|
| Eyemouth | 46 | 55.52 N | 2.06 W |
| Eye Peninsula ≻[1] | 46 | 58.13 N | 6.13 W |
| Eyers Grove | 210 | 41.05 N | 76.31 W |
| Eye Water ≃ | 46 | 55.53 N | 2.06 W |
| Eygalières | 62 | 43.45 N | 4.57 E |
| Eyguières | 62 | 43.42 N | 5.02 E |
| Eyhorne Street | 260 | 51.16 N | 0.38 E |
| Eyjafjördur c[2] | 24a | 65.54 N | 18.15 W |
| Eyl | 144 | 7.59 N | 49.49 E |
| Eylar Mountain ∧ | 204 | 37.28 N | 121.33 W |
| Eymet | 32 | 44.40 N | 0.24 E |
| Eymir | 130 | 40.02 N | 35.14 E |
| Eymoutiers | 32 | 45.44 N | 1.44 E |
| Eynesil | 130 | 41.03 N | 39.08 E |
| Eynhallow Sound ⋓ | 46 | 59.08 N | 3.06 W |
| Eynort, Loch c | 46 | 57.13 N | 7.18 W |
| Eynsford | 260 | 51.22 N | 0.13 E |
| Eynsham | 42 | 51.48 N | 1.22 W |
| Eyota | 190 | 43.59 N | 92.13 W |
| Eyrarbakki | 24a | 63.53 N | 21.05 W |
| Eyre | 162 | 32.15 S | 126.18 E |
| Eyrecourt | 48 | 53.11 N | 8.07 W |
| Eyre Creek ≃ | 166 | 26.40 S | 139.00 E |
| Eyre Mountains ⋏ | 172 | 45.20 S | 168.30 E |
| Eyre North, Lake ⊜ | 166 | 28.40 S | 137.10 E |
| Eyre Peninsula ≻[1] | 162 | 34.00 S | 135.45 E |
| Eyre South, Lake ⊜ | 166 | 29.30 S | 137.20 E |
| Eyrieux ≃ | 62 | 44.48 N | 4.48 E |
| Eystrup | 52 | 52.46 N | 9.13 E |
| Eythorne | 42 | 51.11 N | 1.17 E |
| Eyüp ◆[8] | 267b | 41.03 N | 28.55 E |
| Eyvānekey | 128 | 35.20 N | 52.04 E |
| Eyzaguirre, Canal ≍ | 286e | 33.36 S | 70.41 W |
| Ézanville | 261 | 49.02 N | 2.22 E |
| Ezbekīyah ◆[8] | 273c | 30.03 N | 31.15 E |
| Ezeiza, Aeropuerto Internacional de ⊠ | 288 | 34.49 S | 58.32 W |
| Ezequiel Ramos Mexía, Embalse ⊜[1] | 254 | 39.30 S | 69.00 W |
| Ezere | 76 | 56.26 N | 22.22 E |
| Ežerėlis | 76 | 54.53 N | 23.37 E |
| Ezeriș | 38 | 45.24 N | 21.53 E |
| Ezine | 130 | 39.47 N | 26.20 E |
| Ezinepazarı | 130 | 40.34 N | 36.09 E |
| Ezjaryšča | 76 | 55.50 N | 29.59 E |
| Ezop, chrebet ⋏ | 89 | 52.36 N | 133.37 E |
| Ežva | 24 | 61.47 N | 50.40 E |
| Ézy-sur-Eure | 50 | 48.52 N | 1.25 E |
| Ezzell | 222 | 29.17 N | 96.58 W |
| **F** | | | |
| Faaa Airport ⊠ | 174s | 17.33 S | 149.36 W |
| Faafaxdhuun | 144 | 2.13 N | 41.37 E |
| Faal | 174q | 9.37 N | 138.10 E |
| Faaone | 174s | 17.40 S | 149.18 W |
| Fabala | 150 | 9.44 N | 9.05 W |
| Fabbrico | 64 | 44.52 N | 10.50 E |
| Fabens | 200 | 31.30 N | 106.09 W |
| Fåberg | 26 | 61.10 N | 10.24 E |
| Faber Lake ⊜ | 176 | 63.56 N | 117.15 W |
| Fabert Seamount ✣[3] | 14 | 24.07 S | 158.33 W |
| Fabius | 210 | 42.50 N | 75.59 W |
| Fåborg | 41 | 55.06 N | 10.15 E |
| Fábrega, Cerro ∧ | 236 | 9.07 N | 82.52 W |
| Fabrègues | 62 | 43.33 N | 3.46 E |
| Fabreville ◆[8] | 275a | 45.34 N | 73.50 W |
| Fabriano | 66 | 43.20 N | 12.54 E |
| Fabrica di Roma | 66 | 42.20 N | 12.18 E |
| Fabričnyj | 85 | 43.11 N | 76.24 E |
| Fabrizia | 68 | 38.29 N | 16.18 E |
| Facatativá | 246 | 4.49 N | 74.22 W |
| Facha | 146 | 29.27 N | 17.18 E |
| Faches-Thumesnil | 50 | 50.35 N | 3.04 E |
| Fachi | 146 | 18.06 N | 11.34 E |
| Facpi Point ≻ | 174p | 13.20 N | 144.38 E |
| Factoryville | 210 | 41.34 N | 75.47 W |
| Facundo | 254 | 45.18 S | 69.58 W |
| Fada | 146 | 17.14 N | 21.33 E |
| Fada, Lochan ⊜ | 46 | 57.41 N | 5.18 W |
| Fadalto | 64 | 46.05 N | 12.20 E |
| Fada Ngourma | 150 | 12.04 N | 0.21 E |
| Fadd | 30 | 46.28 N | 18.50 E |
| Faddeja, zaliv c | 74 | 76.40 N | 107.20 E |
| Faddejevskij, ostrov I | 74 | 75.30 N | 144.00 E |
| Faddoi | 140 | 8.07 N | 32.07 E |
| Fadian Point ≻ | 174p | 13.26 N | 144.49 E |
| Fadiffolu Atoll I[1] | 122 | 5.25 N | 73.30 E |
| Fadit | 140 | 9.58 N | 32.13 E |
| Faedis | 64 | 46.10 N | 13.20 E |
| Fænø I | 41 | 55.29 N | 9.42 E |
| Faenza | 66 | 44.17 N | 11.53 E |
| Faeroe Islands □[2] | 22 | 62.00 N | 7.00 W |
| Faeröerne → Faeroe Islands □[2] | 22 | 62.00 N | 7.00 W |
| Faete, Monte ∧ | 267a | 41.45 N | 12.44 E |
| Fafa | 150 | 15.20 N | 0.43 E |
| Fafa ≃ | 152 | 7.18 N | 18.16 E |
| Fafakourou | 150 | 13.04 N | 14.34 W |
| Fafe | 34 | 41.27 N | 8.10 W |
| Fafen ≃ | 144 | 5.59 N | 44.25 E |
| Faga ≃ | 150 | 13.15 N | 0.55 E |
| Fagaitua | 174u | 14.16 S | 170.37 W |
| Fagamalo | 175a | 13.25 S | 172.21 W |
| Făgăraș | 38 | 45.51 N | 24.58 E |
| Făgărașului, Munții ⋏ | 38 | 45.35 N | 25.00 E |
| Fagasa | 174u | 14.17 S | 170.43 W |
| Fagatogo | 174u | 14.17 S | 170.41 W |
| Fagernes | 26 | 60.59 N | 9.15 E |
| Fagersta | 40 | 60.00 N | 15.47 E |
| Fagertärn ◆[4] | 40 | 58.46 N | 14.42 E |
| Fagerviken | 40 | 60.33 N | 17.45 E |
| Făget | 38 | 45.51 N | 22.10 E |
| Faggen Bach ≃ | 64 | 47.05 N | 10.40 E |
| Faggo | 150 | 11.23 N | 9.57 E |
| Fagnano, Lago ⊜ | 254 | 54.35 S | 68.00 W |
| Fagnano Castello | 68 | 39.34 N | 16.03 E |
| Fagnano Olona | 62 | 45.40 N | 8.52 E |
| Fagnières | 50 | 48.58 N | 4.19 E |
| Faguibine, Lac ⊜ | 150 | 16.45 N | 3.54 W |
| Fagundes, Rio do ≃ | 256 | 22.12 S | 43.11 W |
| Fagurhólsmýri | 24a | 63.54 N | 16.38 W |
| Fagwir | 140 | 9.33 N | 30.25 E |
| Fahan | 48 | 55.05 N | 7.28 W |
| Fahl, Oued el V | 148 | 31.15 N | 4.41 E |
| Fahraj | 128 | 28.58 N | 58.52 E |
| Fährdorf | 54 | 53.58 N | 11.28 E |
| Fahrland | 54 | 52.28 N | 13.01 E |
| Fahrlander See ⊜ | 264a | 52.27 N | 13.01 E |
| Fahrnau | 58 | 47.39 N | 7.50 E |
| Fahuaqiao | 106 | 30.52 N | 121.25 E |
| Faial I | 148a | 38.34 N | 28.42 W |
| Faichuk II | 175c | 7.23 N | 151.40 E |
| Fā'id | 142 | 30.19 N | 32.19 E |
| Fā'id Military Base ■ | 142 | 30.20 N | 32.16 E |
| Faido | 58 | 46.29 N | 8.48 E |
| Faillon, Lac ⊜ | 190 | 48.21 N | 76.38 W |
| Failsworth | 44 | 53.31 N | 2.09 W |
| Fains-les-Sources | 56 | 48.47 N | 5.08 E |
| Fairbairn Airport ⊠ | 171b | 35.18 S | 149.15 E |
| Fairbairn Park ♠ | 274b | 37.47 S | 144.55 E |
| Fairbairn Reservoir ⊜[1] | 166 | 23.45 S | 148.00 E |
| Fairbank | 190 | 42.38 N | 92.02 W |
| Fairbanks, Ak., U.S. | 180 | 64.51 N | 147.43 W |
| Fairbanks, La., U.S. | 194 | 30.00 N | 92.02 W |
| Fair Bluff | 192 | 34.18 N | 79.02 W |
| Fairborn | 218 | 39.49 N | 84.01 W |
| Fairbourne | 42 | 52.41 N | 4.03 W |
| Fairburn | 192 | 33.34 N | 84.34 W |
| Fairbury, Il., U.S. | 216 | 40.44 N | 88.30 W |
| Fairbury, Ne., U.S. | 198 | 40.08 N | 97.10 W |
| Fairchance | 188 | 39.49 N | 79.45 W |
| Fairchild | 190 | 44.36 N | 90.57 W |
| Fairchild Air Force Base ■ | 202 | 47.38 N | 117.38 W |
| Fairchild Creek ≃ | 212 | 43.07 N | 80.07 W |
| Fairdale | 216 | 42.06 N | 88.56 W |
| Faire | 116 | 17.53 N | 121.34 E |
| Fairfax, Al., U.S. | 194 | 32.47 N | 85.11 W |
| Fairfax, Ca., U.S. | 226 | 37.59 N | 122.35 W |
| Fairfax, De., U.S. | 285 | 39.47 N | 75.32 W |
| Fairfax, Mn., U.S. | 198 | 44.31 N | 94.43 W |
| Fairfax, Mo., U.S. | 194 | 40.20 N | 95.23 W |
| Fairfax, Ok., U.S. | 196 | 36.34 N | 96.42 W |
| Fairfax, S.C., U.S. | 192 | 32.57 N | 81.14 W |
| Fairfax, S.D., U.S. | 198 | 43.01 N | 98.53 W |
| Fairfax, Vt., U.S. | 188 | 44.39 N | 73.00 W |
| Fairfax, Va., U.S. | 208 | 38.50 N | 77.18 W |
| Fairfax □[6] | 208 | 38.45 N | 77.15 W |
| Fairfax Forest | 284c | 38.52 N | 77.15 W |
| Fairfax Park | 284c | 38.47 N | 77.14 W |
| Fairfax State Recreation Area ♠ | 218 | 39.02 N | 86.29 W |
| Fairfax Station | 284c | 38.48 N | 77.19 W |
| Fairfield, Austl. | 170 | 33.52 S | 150.57 E |
| Fairfield, Al., U.S. | 194 | 33.33 N | 86.47 W |
| Fairfield, Ca., U.S. | 226 | 38.14 N | 122.02 W |
| Fairfield, Ct., U.S. | 210 | 41.08 N | 73.15 W |
| Fairfield, Id., U.S. | 202 | 43.20 N | 114.47 W |
| Fairfield, Il., U.S. | 194 | 38.22 N | 88.21 W |
| Fairfield, Ia., U.S. | 190 | 41.00 N | 91.57 W |
| Fairfield, Me., U.S. | 188 | 44.35 N | 69.35 W |
| Fairfield, Mt., U.S. | 202 | 47.36 N | 111.58 W |
| Fairfield, Ne., U.S. | 198 | 40.25 N | 98.06 W |
| Fairfield, N.J., U.S. | 276 | 40.53 N | 74.16 W |
| Fairfield, N.Y., U.S. | 210 | 43.08 N | 74.55 W |
| Fairfield, Oh., U.S. | 218 | 39.20 N | 84.33 W |
| Fairfield, Pa., U.S. | 214 | 39.47 N | 77.22 W |
| Fairfield, Tx., U.S. | 222 | 31.43 N | 96.09 W |
| Fairfield □[6] | 207 | 41.15 N | 73.20 W |
| Fairfield Lake ⊜[1] | 222 | 31.50 N | 96.05 W |
| Fairfield University ʊ[2] | 276 | 41.09 N | 73.15 W |
| Fairford | 42 | 51.44 N | 1.47 W |
| Fairgrove | 190 | 43.31 N | 83.32 W |
| Fair Harbor | 210 | 40.38 N | 73.11 W |
| Fairhaven, Ma., U.S. | 207 | 41.38 N | 70.54 W |
| Fair Haven, Mi., U.S. | 214 | 42.40 N | 82.39 W |
| Fair Haven, N.J., U.S. | 208 | 40.21 N | 74.02 W |
| Fair Haven, N.Y., U.S. | 210 | 43.18 N | 76.42 W |
| Fairhaven, Oh., U.S. | 218 | 39.38 N | 84.47 W |
| Fair Haven, Vt., U.S. | 188 | 43.35 N | 73.15 W |
| Fair Haven, Va., U.S. | 284c | 38.47 N | 77.05 W |
| Fairhaven Bay ⊜ | 283 | 42.26 N | 71.21 W |
| Fair Haven Beach State Park ♠, N.Y., U.S. | 210 | 43.21 N | 76.41 W |
| Fair Haven Beach State Park ♠, N.Y., U.S. | 212 | 43.21 N | 76.41 W |
| Fair Head ≻ | 48 | 55.13 N | 6.09 W |
| Fairhope, Al., U.S. | 194 | 30.31 N | 87.54 W |
| Fairhope, Oh., U.S. | 214 | 40.51 N | 81.19 W |
| Fairhope, Pa., U.S. | 214 | 40.07 N | 79.50 W |
| Fair Isle I | 46 | 59.32 N | 1.39 W |
| Fairknoll | 284c | 39.05 N | 76.59 W |
| Fairland, In., U.S. | 218 | 39.35 N | 85.51 W |
| Fairland, Md., U.S. | 284c | 39.05 N | 76.58 W |
| Fairland, Ok., U.S. | 196 | 36.45 N | 94.50 W |
| Fairlane Town Center ◆[9] | 281 | 42.19 N | 83.13 W |
| Fair Lawn, N.J., U.S. | 210 | 40.56 N | 74.07 W |
| Fairlawn, Oh., U.S. | 214 | 41.07 N | 81.36 W |
| Fairlee | 284c | 38.52 N | 77.16 W |
| Fairleigh Dickinson University (Teaneck) ʊ[2], N.J., U.S. | 276 | 40.53 N | 74.02 W |
| Fairleigh Dickinson University ʊ[2], N.J., U.S. | 276 | 40.50 N | 74.07 W |
| Fairleigh Dickinson University (Florham-Madison) ʊ[2], N.J., U.S. | 276 | 40.46 N | 74.26 W |
| Fairless Hills | 208 | 40.10 N | 74.51 W |
| Fairlie, N.Z. | 172 | 44.06 S | 170.50 E |
| Fairlie, Scot., U.K. | 46 | 55.46 N | 4.51 W |
| Fairlight | 42 | 50.53 N | 0.40 E |
| Fairmont, Il., U.S. | 216 | 41.33 N | 88.03 W |
| Fairmont, Mn., U.S. | 198 | 43.39 N | 94.27 W |
| Fairmont, Ne., U.S. | 198 | 40.38 N | 97.35 W |
| Fairmont, N.C., U.S. | 192 | 34.29 N | 79.06 W |
| Fairmont, Pa., U.S. | 279b | 40.19 N | 79.43 W |
| Fairmont, Wa., U.S. | 224 | 48.54 N | 122.16 W |
| Fairmont, W.V., U.S. | 188 | 39.29 N | 80.08 W |
| Fairmont City | 219 | 38.40 N | 90.06 W |
| Fairmont Hot Springs | 182 | 50.19 N | 115.53 W |
| Fairmont Reservoir ⊜[1] | 228 | 34.43 N | 118.26 W |
| Fairmont Terrace | 282 | 37.43 N | 122.07 W |
| Fairmount, Ga., U.S. | 192 | 34.26 N | 84.42 W |
| Fairmount, Il., U.S. | 194 | 40.03 N | 87.56 W |
| Fairmount, In., U.S. | 216 | 40.24 N | 85.39 W |
| Fairmount, N.Y., U.S. | 210 | 43.02 N | 76.14 W |
| Fairmount, N.D., U.S. | 198 | 46.03 N | 96.36 W |
| Fairmount City | 214 | 41.01 N | 79.19 W |
| Fairmount Heights | 208 | 38.54 N | 76.54 W |
| Fairmount Park ♠ | 285 | 40.00 N | 75.12 W |
| Fair Ness ≻ | 176 | 63.24 N | 72.05 W |
| Fair Oaks, Ca., U.S. | 226 | 38.38 N | 121.16 W |
| Fair Oaks, Ga., U.S. | 192 | 33.54 N | 84.32 W |
| Fair Oaks, In., U.S. | 216 | 41.05 N | 87.16 W |
| Fairoaks, Pa., U.S. | 279b | 40.34 N | 80.13 W |
| Fairoaks Airport ⊠ | 260 | 51.21 N | 0.32 W |
| Fair Plain | 216 | 42.05 N | 86.27 W |
| Fairplains | 192 | 36.13 N | 81.10 W |
| Fairplay | 200 | 39.13 N | 106.00 W |
| Fairpoint | 214 | 40.07 N | 80.55 W |
| Fairport, On., Can. | 275b | 43.49 N | 79.05 W |
| Fairport, N.Y., U.S. | 210 | 43.05 N | 77.26 W |
| Fairport Beach | 275b | 43.48 N | 79.06 W |
| Fairport Harbor | 214 | 41.44 N | 81.16 W |
| Fairseat | 260 | 51.20 N | 0.20 E |
| Fairton | 208 | 39.22 N | 75.13 W |
| Fairview, Austl. | 164 | 15.33 S | 144.19 E |
| Fairview, Ab., Can. | 182 | 56.04 N | 118.23 W |
| Fairview, Ga., U.S. | 192 | 34.56 N | 85.17 W |
| Fairview, Il., U.S. | 190 | 40.38 N | 90.10 W |
| Fairview, In., U.S. | 216 | 40.18 N | 85.11 W |
| Fairview, Ks., U.S. | 198 | 39.50 N | 95.43 W |
| Fairview, Md., U.S. | 208 | 39.09 N | 76.29 W |
| Fairview, Mi., U.S. | 190 | 44.43 N | 84.03 W |
| Fairview, Mt., U.S. | 198 | 47.51 N | 104.02 W |
| Fairview, N.J., U.S. | 276 | 40.51 N | 73.58 W |
| Fairview, N.Y., U.S. | 210 | 41.43 N | 73.55 W |
| Fairview, Oh., U.S. | 214 | 40.03 N | 81.14 W |
| Fairview, Ok., U.S. | 196 | 36.16 N | 98.28 W |
| Fairview, Pa., U.S. | 214 | 42.01 N | 80.15 W |
| Fairview, Tn., U.S. | 194 | 35.58 N | 87.07 W |
| Fairview, Ut,. U.S. | 200 | 39.37 N | 111.26 W |
| Fairview, W.V., U.S. | 188 | 39.35 N | 80.14 W |
| Fairview Heights | 219 | 38.10 N | 90.00 W |
| Fairview Lanes | 214 | 41.23 N | 82.40 W |
| Fairview Mall ◆[9] | 275b | 43.47 N | 79.21 W |
| Fairview Park, In., U.S. | 194 | 39.40 N | 87.25 W |
| Fairview Park, Oh., U.S. | 214 | 41.26 N | 81.51 W |
| Fairview Park, Pa., U.S. | 210 | 41.10 N | 75.53 W |
| Fairview Peak ∧, Nv., U.S. | 204 | 39.14 N | 118.08 W |
| Fairview Peak ∧, Or., U.S. | 202 | 43.35 N | 122.39 W |
| Fairview Pointe Claire Centre ◆[9] | 275a | 45.28 N | 73.50 W |
| Fairview Shores | 220 | 28.35 N | 81.23 W |
| Fairview Village | 285 | 40.10 N | 75.23 W |
| Fairvilla | 220 | 28.35 N | 81.24 W |
| Fairville | 285 | 39.51 N | 75.38 W |
| Fairweather Mountain ∧ | 180 | 58.54 N | 137.32 W |
| Fairy Lake ⊜ | 212 | 45.20 N | 79.11 W |
| Fairy Meadow | 170 | 34.23 S | 150.54 E |
| Fairy Stone State Park ♠ | 192 | 36.48 N | 80.06 W |
| Fairy Water ≃ | 48 | 54.37 N | 7.20 W |
| Fais I | 108 | 9.46 N | 140.31 E |
| Faisalabad (Lyallpur) | 123 | 31.25 N | 73.05 E |
| Faison | 192 | 35.06 N | 78.08 W |
| Faistós ⊥ | 38 | 35.01 N | 24.48 E |
| Faith | 198 | 45.01 N | 102.02 W |
| Faiyum → Al-Fayyūm | 142 | 29.19 N | 30.50 E |
| Faizābād | 124 | 26.47 N | 82.08 E |
| Fajansovyj | 76 | 54.04 N | 34.24 E |
| Fajardo | 240m | 18.20 N | 65.39 W |
| Fajou, Îlet à I | 241o | 16.21 N | 61.35 W |
| Fajr, Wādī V | 128 | 30.06 N | 38.18 E |
| Fajzabad | 85 | 38.34 N | 69.19 E |
| Fakahatchee Strand ⁘ | 220 | 26.10 N | 81.35 W |
| Fakaofo I[1] | 14 | 9.22 S | 171.14 W |
| Fakarava I[1] | 14 | 16.20 S | 145.37 W |
| Fakejev | 80 | 48.57 N | 49.56 E |
| Fakel | 80 | 57.38 N | 53.02 E |
| Fakenham | 42 | 52.50 N | 0.51 E |
| Fakfak | 164 | 2.55 S | 132.18 E |
| Fakılı | 130 | 39.13 N | 35.00 E |
| Fakīrganj | 124 | 25.58 N | 90.02 E |
| Fakī Ṣādiq | 140 | 12.08 N | 23.55 E |
| Fakrinkotti | 140 | 18.01 N | 31.20 E |
| Fakse | 41 | 55.15 N | 12.08 E |
| Fakse Bugt c | 41 | 55.10 N | 12.15 E |
| Fakse Ladeplads | 41 | 55.13 N | 12.11 E |
| Faku | 104 | 42.30 N | 123.24 E |
| Fal ≃ | 42 | 50.08 N | 5.02 W |
| Falaba | 150 | 9.51 N | 11.19 W |
| Faladyé | 150 | 13.08 N | 8.20 W |
| Falaise | 32 | 48.54 N | 0.12 W |
| Fālākāta | 124 | 26.32 N | 89.12 E |
| Falam | 110 | 22.55 N | 93.40 E |
| Falāvarjān | 128 | 32.33 N | 51.30 E |
| Falcade | 64 | 46.21 N | 11.51 E |
| Falcão | 256 | 22.17 S | 44.16 W |
| Fălciu | 38 | 46.18 N | 28.08 E |
| Falck | 56 | 49.14 N | 6.38 E |
| Falcognana di Sotto ◆[8] | 267a | 41.45 N | 12.33 E |
| Falcón □[3] | 246 | 11.00 N | 69.50 W |
| Falcon, Cap ≻ | 34 | 35.46 N | 0.48 W |
| Falcon, Cape ≻ | 224 | 45.46 N | 123.59 W |
| Falcón, Presa (Falcon Reservoir) ⊜[1] | 196 | 26.37 N | 99.11 W |
| Falconara Albanese | 68 | 39.16 N | 16.05 E |
| Falconara Alta | 66 | 43.37 N | 13.24 E |
| Falconara Marittima | 66 | 43.37 N | 13.24 E |
| Falconbridge | 190 | 46.35 N | 80.48 W |
| Falconcrest | 285 | 39.58 N | 75.33 W |
| Falcone | 70 | 38.07 N | 15.05 E |
| Falcone, Capo del ≻ | 71 | 40.58 N | 8.12 E |
| Falconer | 214 | 42.07 N | 79.11 W |
| Falcon Heights | 202 | 42.08 N | 121.45 W |
| Falcon Reservoir (Presa Falcón) ⊜[1] | 196 | 26.37 N | 99.11 W |
| Falconwood | 210 | 43.00 N | 78.57 W |
| Faldsled | 41 | 55.09 N | 10.09 E |
| Faléa | 150 | 12.16 N | 11.17 W |
| Faleasao | 174y | 14.13 S | 169.32 W |
| Falelatai | 175a | 13.55 S | 171.59 W |
| Falelima | 175a | 13.32 S | 172.41 W |
| Falémé ≃ | 150 | 14.46 N | 12.14 W |
| Falenki | 80 | 58.22 N | 51.35 E |
| Falerii Novi ⊥ | 66 | 42.16 N | 12.20 E |
| Falerna | 68 | 39.00 N | 16.10 E |
| Falerone | 66 | 43.06 N | 13.28 E |
| Fălești | 38 | 47.34 N | 27.43 E |
| Falfurrias | 196 | 27.13 N | 98.08 W |
| Falher | 182 | 55.44 N | 117.12 W |
| Falicon | 62 | 43.45 N | 7.17 E |
| Fálirou, Órmos c | 267c | 37.56 N | 23.40 E |
| Falkenberg, Dtsch. | 54 | 52.48 N | 13.58 E |
| Falkenberg, Dtsch. | 54 | 51.35 N | 13.14 E |
| Falkenberg, Dtsch. | 60 | 49.52 N | 12.14 E |
| Falkenberg, Dtsch. | 60 | 48.28 N | 12.43 E |
| Falkenberg, Sve. | 26 | 56.54 N | 12.28 E |
| Falkenberg ◆[8] | 264a | 52.34 N | 13.33 E |
| Falkenhagen, Dtsch. | 54 | 53.12 N | 12.12 E |
| Falkenhagen, Dtsch. | 54 | 52.26 N | 14.19 E |
| Falkenhagener See ⊜ | 264a | 52.34 N | 13.08 E |
| Falkenhain | 54 | 51.25 N | 12.53 E |
| Falkenrehde | 264a | 52.30 N | 12.56 E |
| Falkensee | 54 | 52.33 N | 13.04 E |
| Falkenstein, Dtsch. | 54 | 50.29 N | 12.22 E |
| Falkenstein, Dtsch. | 60 | 49.06 N | 12.29 E |
| Falkenthal | 54 | 52.54 N | 13.17 E |
| Falkirk | 46 | 56.00 N | 3.48 W |
| Falkland, B.C., Can. | 182 | 50.30 N | 119.33 W |
| Falkland, Scot., U.K. | 46 | 56.15 N | 3.12 W |
| Falkland-Inseln → Falkland Islands □[2] | 254 | 51.45 S | 59.00 W |
| Falkland Islands □[2], S.A. | 244 | 51.45 S | 59.00 W |
| Falkland Islands □[2], S.A. | 254 | 51.45 S | 59.00 W |
| Falkland Plateau ✣[3] | 18 | 51.00 S | 50.00 W |
| Falkland Sound ⋓ | 254 | 51.45 S | 59.25 W |
| Falköping | 26 | 58.10 N | 13.31 E |
| Falkville | 194 | 34.22 N | 86.54 W |
| Fall ≃, On., Can. | 212 | 44.59 N | 76.22 W |
| Fall ≃, Ks., U.S. | 198 | 37.24 N | 95.40 W |
| Fall ≃, Wa., U.S. | 224 | 46.47 N | 123.30 W |
| Falla | 40 | 58.41 N | 15.45 E |
| Fallais | 56 | 50.37 N | 5.10 E |
| Fallbach | 61 | 48.39 N | 16.25 E |
| Fallbrook | 228 | 33.22 N | 117.15 W |
| Fallbrook Square ◆[9] | 280 | 34.12 N | 118.38 W |
| Fall City | 224 | 47.34 N | 121.53 W |
| Fall Creek | 190 | 44.45 N | 91.16 W |
| Fall Creek ≃, In., U.S. | 218 | 39.47 N | 86.11 W |
| Fall Creek ≃, N.Y., U.S. | 210 | 42.28 N | 76.31 W |
| Fall Creek Falls State Park ♠, Tn., U.S. | 192 | 35.39 N | 85.25 W |
| Fall Creek Falls State Park ♠, Tn., U.S. | 194 | 35.39 N | 85.25 W |
| Fallen Jerusalem I | 240m | 18.25 N | 64.27 W |
| Fallen Leaf | 226 | 38.53 N | 120.04 W |
| Fallen Leaf Reservoir ⊜[1] | 226 | 38.54 N | 120.03 W |
| Fallentimber | 214 | 40.41 N | 78.30 W |
| Fallentimber Creek ≃ | 182 | 51.45 N | 114.39 W |
| Fallen Timbers State Memorial ⊥ | 216 | 41.33 N | 83.42 W |
| Fallin | 46 | 56.06 N | 3.52 W |
| Falling ≃ | 192 | 37.01 N | 78.55 W |
| Fallingbostel | 52 | 52.52 N | 9.41 E |
| Falling Creek ≃ | 208 | 37.26 N | 77.26 W |
| Fallon, Mt., U.S. | 198 | 46.50 N | 105.07 W |
| Fallon, Nv., U.S. | 204 | 39.28 N | 118.46 W |
| Fall River, Ks., U.S. | 198 | 37.36 N | 96.01 W |
| Fall River, Ma., U.S. | 207 | 41.42 N | 71.09 W |
| Fall River, Wi., U.S. | 190 | 43.23 N | 89.02 W |
| Fall River Lake ⊜[1] | 198 | 37.42 N | 96.08 W |
| Fall River Mills | 204 | 41.00 N | 121.26 W |
| Falls | 210 | 41.28 N | 75.51 W |
| Falls □[6] | 222 | 31.17 N | 96.55 W |
| Fallsburg | 210 | 41.44 N | 74.36 W |
| Falls Church | 208 | 38.53 N | 77.11 W |
| Falls City, Ne., U.S. | 198 | 40.03 N | 95.36 W |
| Falls City, Or., U.S. | 202 | 44.51 N | 123.26 W |
| Falls Creek, Austl. | 170 | 34.59 S | 150.36 E |
| Falls Creek, Pa., U.S. | 214 | 41.09 N | 78.48 W |
| Falls Creek ≃ | 226 | 37.57 N | 119.46 W |
| Fallsington | 208 | 40.12 N | 74.48 W |
| Falls Lake ⊜[1] | 192 | 36.00 N | 78.45 W |
| Falls Pond ⊜ | 283 | 41.58 N | 71.20 W |
| Falls Run ≃ | 284b | 39.22 N | 76.52 W |
| Fallston | 208 | 39.31 N | 76.25 W |
| Falls Village | 207 | 41.57 N | 73.21 W |
| Falmer | 42 | 50.51 N | 0.04 W |
| Falmey | 150 | 12.36 N | 2.51 E |
| Falmouth, Jam. | 241q | 18.30 N | 77.39 W |
| Falmouth, Eng., U.K. | 42 | 50.08 N | 5.04 W |
| Falmouth, Ky., U.S. | 218 | 38.40 N | 84.19 W |
| Falmouth, Me., U.S. | 188 | 43.43 N | 70.14 W |
| Falmouth, Ma., U.S. | 207 | 41.33 N | 70.36 W |
| Falmouth, Va., U.S. | 208 | 38.19 N | 77.28 W |
| Falmouth Bay c | 42 | 50.05 N | 5.01 W |
| Falmouth Heights | 207 | 41.33 N | 70.36 W |
| False Cape ≻, Fl., U.S. | 220 | 28.35 N | 80.34 W |
| False Cape ≻, Va., U.S. | 208 | 36.39 N | 76.51 W |
| False Divi Point ≻ | 122 | 15.43 N | 80.49 E |
| False Ducks Islands II | 212 | 43.57 N | 76.49 W |
| False Pass | 180 | 54.52 N | 163.24 W |
| Falset | 34 | 41.08 N | 0.49 E |
| Falsino ≃ | 250 | 0.56 N | 51.35 W |
| Fal'šivyj Gelendžik | 78 | 44.31 N | 38.09 E |
| Falso, Cabo ≻, Hond. | 236 | 15.12 N | 83.20 W |
| Falso, Cabo ≻, Rep. Dom. | 238 | 17.47 N | 71.41 W |
| Falso Cabo de Hornos ≻ | 254 | 55.43 S | 68.05 W |
| Falster I | 41 | 54.48 N | 11.58 E |
| Falsterbo | 41 | 55.24 N | 12.50 E |
| Falstone | 44 | 55.11 N | 2.25 W |
| Fălticeni | 38 | 47.28 N | 26.18 E |
| Falun, Sve. | 40 | 60.36 N | 15.38 E |
| Falun, Zhg. | 107 | 29.58 N | 104.29 E |
| Falzarego, Passo di )( | 64 | 46.31 N | 12.00 E |
| Fam, Kepulauan II | 164 | 0.40 S | 130.15 E |
| Fama | 256 | 21.25 S | 46.51 W |
| Fama, Ouadi V | 146 | 15.22 N | 20.34 E |
| Famagusta → Gazimağusa | 130 | 35.07 N | 33.57 E |
| Famaillá | 252 | 27.03 S | 65.24 W |
| Famatina | 252 | 28.55 S | 67.31 W |
| Famatina, Sierra de ⋏ | 252 | 29.00 S | 67.51 W |
| Fameck | 56 | 49.18 N | 6.07 E |
| Famenne ◆[1] | 56 | 50.10 N | 5.15 E |
| Familleureux | 50 | 50.31 N | 4.12 E |
| Family Lake ⊜ | 184 | 51.54 N | 95.30 W |
| Fan ≃ | 104 | 42.16 N | 123.40 E |
| Fana | 150 | 12.47 N | 6.57 W |
| Fanaco, Lago ⊜ | 70 | 37.39 N | 13.33 E |
| Fanad Head ≻ | 48 | 55.16 N | 7.38 W |
| Fanado ≃ | 255 | 17.10 S | 42.40 W |
| Fanambana | 157b | 13.34 S | 50.00 E |
| Fanan I | 175c | 7.11 N | 151.59 E |
| Fanano | 64 | 44.12 N | 10.47 E |
| Fanārah | 142 | 30.17 N | 32.21 E |
| Fanchang | 100 | 31.07 N | 118.12 E |
| Fanch'eng → Xiangfan | 102 | 32.03 N | 112.01 E |
| Fancher, Il., U.S. | 219 | 39.16 N | 88.47 W |
| Fancher, N.Y., U.S. | 210 | 43.15 N | 66.06 W |
| Fanchon, Pointe ≻ | 238 | 18.26 N | 74.29 W |
| Fanchuan | 100 | 32.40 N | 119.42 E |
| Fancy | 241h | 13.22 N | 61.11 W |
| Fancy Creek ≃ | 198 | 39.28 N | 96.45 W |
| Fancy Prairie | 219 | 39.59 N | 89.36 W |
| Fandriana | 157b | 20.14 S | 47.23 E |
| Fane ≃ | 48 | 53.57 N | 6.22 W |
| Fanepura | 123 | 31.29 N | 72.54 E |
| Faneromenis Monastery ʊ[1] | 267c | 37.59 N | 23.26 E |
| Fang | 110 | 19.55 N | 99.13 E |
| Fangaga ∧ | 144 | 17.30 N | 38.01 E |
| Fangak | 140 | 9.04 N | 30.53 E |
| Fangbian | 106 | 31.42 N | 119.06 E |
| Fangcheng, Zhg. | 100 | 33.16 N | 112.59 E |
| Fangcheng, Zhg. | 102 | 21.49 N | 108.22 E |
| Fangcheng, Zhg. | 105 | 39.16 N | 115.28 E |
| Fangcun, Zhg. | 100 | 29.04 N | 118.36 E |
| Fangcun, Zhg. | 100 | 26.50 N | 118.15 E |
| Fangdao | 100 | 27.01 N | 118.06 E |
| Fängersee ⊜ | 264a | 52.35 N | 13.50 E |
| Fangguan | 105 | 39.20 N | 115.58 E |
| Fangji | 100 | 31.54 N | 115.35 E |
| Fangjiachang | 107 | 30.05 N | 104.16 E |
| Fangjiazhuang | 106 | 30.45 N | 119.53 E |
| Fangliao | 100 | 22.22 N | 120.35 E |
| Fangmutun | 98 | 42.34 N | 124.34 E |
| Fangniu | 102 | 27.40 N | 100.25 E |
| Fangshan, T'aiwan | 100 | 22.16 N | 120.39 E |
| Fangshan, Zhg. | 98 | 39.42 N | 115.58 E |
| Fang Shan ∧ | 106 | 31.40 N | 119.16 E |
| Fang Shan ∧[2] | 106 | 31.29 N | 119.09 E |
| Fangshanzhen | 104 | 41.54 N | 122.05 E |
| Fangshen | 104 | 42.02 N | 124.04 E |
| Fangshengpu | 107 | 30.20 N | 104.54 E |
| Fangsi | 98 | 36.56 N | 116.29 E |
| Fangtai | 106 | 31.19 N | 121.12 E |
| Fangxi | 100 | 28.23 N | 114.38 E |
| Fangxian | 102 | 32.02 N | 110.45 E |
| Fangxianzhen | 106 | 32.00 N | 119.44 E |
| Fangzheng | 89 | 45.50 N | 128.50 E |
| Fangzi | 98 | 36.36 N | 119.07 E |
| Fanhões | 266c | 38.53 N | 9.09 W |
| Fanipal' | 76 | 53.45 N | 27.20 E |
| Fanjakana | 157b | 21.10 S | 46.53 E |
| Fanjiadai | 106 | 32.04 N | 120.15 E |
| Fanjiadian | 104 | 41.41 N | 121.50 E |
| Fanjiatun | 89 | 43.43 N | 125.06 E |
| Fanjiazhuang | 105 | 39.12 N | 117.20 E |
| Fannarâki ∧ | 26 | 61.31 N | 7.55 E |
| Fannettsburg | 214 | 40.04 N | 77.50 W |
| Fannich, Loch ⊜ | 46 | 57.38 N | 5.00 W |
| Fannrem | 26 | 63.16 N | 9.50 E |
| Fanny, Mount ∧ | 202 | 45.20 N | 117.41 W |
| Fanny Bay | 182 | 49.30 N | 124.50 W |
| Fano | 66 | 43.50 N | 13.01 E |
| Fanø I | 26 | 55.25 N | 8.25 E |
| Fanqiao | 100 | 28.48 N | 121.10 E |
| Fans, Col des )( | 62 | 44.56 N | 4.47 E |
| Fanshan, Zhg. | 100 | 27.21 N | 120.24 E |
| Fanshan, Zhg. | 105 | 40.13 N | 115.25 E |
| Fanshang | 106 | 31.40 N | 120.01 E |
| Fanshawe Lake ⊜ | 212 | 43.05 N | 81.10 W |
| Fansher Creek ≃ | 214 | 42.37 N | 82.01 W |
| Fanshui | 100 | 33.07 N | 119.25 E |
| Fan Si Pan ∧ | 110 | 22.15 N | 103.46 E |
| Fantasy Island ♠ | 284a | 43.02 N | 78.58 W |
| Fanthyttan | 40 | 59.40 N | 15.06 E |
| Fanwood | 276 | 40.38 N | 74.23 W |
| Fanxian | 98 | 35.57 N | 115.38 E |
| Fanzhen | 98 | 36.14 N | 117.21 E |
| Faoileann, Bàgh nam c | 46 | 57.23 N | 7.17 W |
| Faqīrah, Wādī V | 142 | 28.52 N | 30.57 E |
| Faqqū'ah | 132 | 32.30 N | 35.24 E |
| Fāqūs | 142 | 30.44 N | 31.48 E |
| Farab | 85 | 39.14 N | 67.28 E |
| Faraday ʊ[3] | 9 | 65.15 S | 64.16 W |
| Faraday, Mount ∧ | 172 | 42.02 S | 171.34 E |
| Faradje | 154 | 3.44 N | 29.43 E |
| Faradofay | 157b | 25.02 S | 47.00 E |
| Farafangana | 157b | 22.49 S | 47.50 E |
| Farāfirah, Al-Wāḥat al- ⫪[4] | 140 | 27.15 N | 28.10 E |
| Farāh | 128 | 32.22 N | 62.07 E |
| Farāh □[4] | 128 | 33.00 N | 62.30 E |
| Farāh ≃ | 128 | 31.29 N | 61.24 E |
| Farahābād | 267d | 35.42 N | 51.30 E |
| Farahalana | 157b | 14.26 S | 50.10 E |
| Farā'id, Jabal al- ∧ | 140 | 23.31 N | 35.20 E |
| Fara in Sabina | 66 | 42.12 N | 12.43 E |
| Farallón, Paso del ⋓ | 288 | 34.41 S | 57.57 W |
| Farallon de Medinilla I | 108 | 16.01 N | 146.04 E |
| Farallon de Pajaros I | 108 | 20.32 N | 144.54 E |
| Farallon Islands II | 204 | 37.43 N | 123.03 W |
| Faramana | 150 | 12.03 N | 4.40 W |
| Faranah | 150 | 10.02 N | 10.44 W |
| Farángi Samariás (Samaria Gorge) V | 38 | 35.18 N | 24.00 E |
| Fara Novarese | 62 | 45.33 N | 8.27 E |
| Farasān, Jazā'ir II | 144 | 16.48 N | 41.54 E |
| Farasān al-Kabīr I | 144 | 16.42 N | 42.00 E |
| Faratsiho | 157b | 19.24 S | 46.57 E |
| Faraulep I[1] | 108 | 8.36 N | 144.33 E |
| Farber | 219 | 39.16 N | 91.34 W |
| Farbovane | 78 | 50.09 N | 31.51 E |
| Farcău, Vârful ∧ | 38 | 47.56 N | 24.27 E |
| Farchant | 64 | 47.32 N | 11.06 E |
| Farcy | 261 | 48.31 N | 2.37 E |
| Fardes ≃ | 34 | 37.35 N | 3.00 W |
| Fare ≃ | 50 | 47.39 N | 0.14 E |
| Fareara, Pointe ≻ | 174s | 17.52 S | 149.39 W |
| Fareham | 42 | 50.51 N | 1.10 W |
| Fårevejle | 41 | 55.48 N | 11.27 E |
| Farewell | 180 | 62.31 N | 153.53 W |
| Farewell, Cape ≻ | 172 | 40.30 S | 172.41 E |
| Farewell Spit ≻[2] | 172 | 40.31 S | 172.52 E |
| Färgelanda | 26 | 58.34 N | 11.59 E |
| Fargniers | 50 | 49.39 N | 3.19 E |
| Fargo | 198 | 46.52 N | 96.47 W |
| Far Hills | 276 | 40.41 N | 74.38 W |
| Faria ≃ | 287a | 22.53 S | 43.15 W |
| Fāri'ah, Wādī al- V | 132 | 32.06 N | 35.31 E |
| Faribault | 190 | 44.17 N | 93.16 W |
| Faribault, Lac ⊜ | 176 | 59.00 N | 72.00 W |
| Farīdābad | 124 | 28.26 N | 77.19 E |
| Farīdganj | 126 | 23.08 N | 90.45 E |
| Farīdkot | 123 | 30.40 N | 74.45 E |
| Farīdnagar | 124 | 28.46 N | 77.37 E |
| Farīdpur, Bngl. | 126 | 24.10 N | 89.26 E |
| Farīdpur, Bngl. | 126 | 23.36 N | 89.50 E |
| Farīdpur, India | 124 | 28.13 N | 79.33 E |
| Farié Haoussa | 150 | 13.48 N | 1.38 E |
| Fārigh, Wādī al- V | 146 | 29.59 N | 19.25 E |
| Färila | 26 | 61.48 N | 15.51 E |
| Farilhões II | 34 | 39.28 N | 9.34 W |
| Farim | 150 | 12.27 N | 15.17 W |
| Farīmān | 128 | 35.43 N | 59.53 E |
| Farina | 219 | 38.50 N | 88.46 W |
| Faringdon | 42 | 51.40 N | 1.35 W |
| Farington | 262 | 53.43 N | 2.42 W |
| Farinha ≃ | 250 | 6.51 S | 47.30 W |
| Farini d'Olmo | 62 | 44.43 N | 9.34 E |
| Fariš | 85 | 40.35 N | 66.52 E |
| Fariske | 130 | 36.37 N | 32.38 E |
| Fāriskūr | 142 | 31.20 N | 31.43 E |
| Farit, Amba ∧ | 144 | 10.56 N | 38.58 E |
| Färjestaden | 26 | 56.39 N | 16.27 E |
| Farkwa | 154 | 5.24 S | 35.36 E |
| Farleigh | 260 | 51.19 N | 0.02 W |
| Farley | 190 | 42.26 N | 91.00 W |
| Farley Green | 260 | 51.12 N | 0.29 W |
| Farmahīn | 128 | 34.30 N | 49.41 E |
| Farmer City | 216 | 40.14 N | 88.38 W |
| Farmers Branch | 222 | 32.55 N | 96.53 W |
| Farmersburg | 194 | 39.14 N | 87.22 W |
| Farmers Fork | 208 | 38.02 N | 76.45 W |
| Farmer's Museum ʊ | 210 | 42.42 N | 74.57 W |
| Farmers Retreat | 218 | 38.58 N | 85.06 W |
| Farmersville, Ca., U.S. | 226 | 36.17 N | 119.12 W |
| Farmersville, Il., U.S. | 219 | 39.26 N | 89.39 W |
| Farmersville, Pa., U.S. | 208 | 40.08 N | 76.10 W |
| Farmersville, Tx., U.S. | 222 | 33.09 N | 96.21 W |
| Farmersville Station | 210 | 42.26 N | 78.22 W |
| Farmerville | 194 | 32.46 N | 92.24 W |
| Farmingdale, N.J., U.S. | 208 | 40.11 N | 74.10 W |
| Farmingdale, N.Y., U.S. | 276 | 40.43 N | 73.26 W |
| Farmington, Ca., U.S. | 226 | 37.56 N | 120.59 W |
| Farmington, Ct., U.S. | 207 | 41.43 N | 72.49 W |
| Farmington, De., U.S. | 208 | 38.52 N | 75.34 W |
| Farmington, Il., U.S. | 190 | 40.41 N | 90.00 W |
| Farmington, Ia., U.S. | 190 | 40.38 N | 91.44 W |
| Farmington, Me., U.S. | 188 | 44.40 N | 70.09 W |
| Farmington, Mi., U.S. | 216 | 42.27 N | 83.22 W |
| Farmington, Mn., U.S. | 190 | 44.38 N | 93.08 W |
| Farmington, Mo., U.S. | 194 | 37.47 N | 90.25 W |
| Farmington, Mt., U.S. | 182 | 47.54 N | 112.11 W |
| Farmington, N.H., U.S. | 188 | 43.23 N | 71.03 W |
| Farmington, N.M., U.S. | 200 | 36.43 N | 108.13 W |
| Farmington, Ut,. U.S. | 200 | 40.58 N | 111.53 W |
| Farmington ≃ | 207 | 41.51 N | 72.38 W |
| Farmington, West Branch ≃ | 207 | 41.52 N | 72.57 W |
| Farmington Flood Control Basin ⊜[1] | 226 | 37.55 N | 120.55 W |
| Farmington Hills | 281 | 42.28 N | 83.23 W |
| Farmingville | 210 | 40.49 N | 73.01 W |
| Farmland | 218 | 40.11 N | 85.07 W |
| Far Mountain ∧ | 182 | 52.46 N | 125.17 W |
| Farm Pond ⊜, Ma., U.S. | 283 | 42.17 N | 71.26 W |
| Farm Pond ⊜, Ma., U.S. | 283 | 42.14 N | 71.21 W |
| Farmville, N.C., U.S. | 192 | 35.35 N | 77.35 W |
| Farmville, Va., U.S. | 192 | 37.18 N | 78.23 W |
| Färna | 40 | 59.47 N | 15.51 E |
| Farnam | 198 | 40.42 N | 100.12 W |
| Farnawā | 142 | 30.59 N | 30.39 E |
| Farnborough | 42 | 51.17 N | 0.46 W |
| Farnborough ◆[8] | 260 | 51.21 N | 0.04 E |
| Farncombe | 260 | 51.12 N | 0.36 W |
| Farndon | 44 | 53.05 N | 0.51 W |
| Färnebofjärden ⊜ | 40 | 60.14 N | 16.47 E |
| Farne Islands II | 44 | 55.38 N | 1.38 W |
| Farnham, P.Q., Can. | 206 | 45.17 N | 72.59 W |
| Farnham, Eng., U.K. | 42 | 51.13 N | 0.49 W |
| Farnham, N.Y., U.S. | 214 | 42.36 N | 79.05 W |
| Farnham, Va., U.S. | 208 | 37.53 N | 76.37 W |
| Farnham, Mount ∧ | 182 | 50.29 N | 116.30 W |
| Farnham Common | 260 | 51.33 N | 0.37 W |
| Farnham Royal | 260 | 51.32 N | 0.37 W |
| Farnhamville | 198 | 42.16 N | 94.24 W |
| Farningham | 260 | 51.23 N | 0.13 E |
| Farnworth, Eng., U.K. | 44 | 53.33 N | 2.24 W |
| Farnworth, Eng., U.K. | 262 | 53.23 N | 2.44 W |
| Faro, Bra. | 250 | 2.11 S | 56.44 W |
| Faro, Port. | 34 | 37.01 N | 7.56 W |
| Faro □[5] | 34 | 37.15 N | 8.00 W |
| Faro ≃ | 146 | 9.21 N | 12.55 E |
| Faro, Punta del ≻ | 70 | 38.16 N | 15.39 E |
| Faro, Réserve du ◆[4] | 146 | 8.10 N | 12.35 E |
| Färöer → Faeroe Islands □[2] | 22 | 62.00 N | 7.00 W |
| Fårön I | 26 | 57.56 N | 19.08 E |
| Fårösund | 26 | 57.52 N | 19.03 E |
| Farquhar, Cape ≻ | 162 | 23.37 S | 113.37 E |
| Farquhar Group II | 138 | 10.10 S | 51.10 E |
| Farr | 46 | 57.21 N | 4.12 W |
| Farra d'Isonzo | 64 | 45.56 N | 13.31 E |
| Farragut | 198 | 40.43 N | 95.28 W |
| Farragut State Recreation Area ♠ | 202 | 47.55 N | 116.35 W |
| Farrandsville | 210 | 41.10 N | 77.31 W |
| Farrar ≃ | 46 | 57.24 N | 4.50 W |
| Farrar Pond ⊜ | 283 | 42.25 N | 71.21 W |
| Farrars Creek ≃ | 166 | 25.35 S | 140.43 E |
| Farrāshband | 128 | 28.53 N | 52.06 E |
| Farrell | 214 | 41.12 N | 80.29 W |
| Farrell Flat | 168b | 33.50 S | 138.47 E |
| Farrer Park ♠ | 271c | 1.19 N | 103.51 E |
| Farrington Lake ⊜ | 276 | 40.26 N | 74.28 W |
| Farrington Lake Heights | 276 | 40.26 N | 74.27 W |
| Far Rockaway ◆[8] | 276 | 40.36 N | 73.45 W |
| Farrukhābād | 124 | 27.24 N | 79.34 E |
| Farrukhnagar, India | 124 | 28.27 N | 76.49 E |
| Farrukhnagar, India | 272a | 28.43 N | 77.23 E |
| Fārs □[4] | 128 | 29.00 N | 53.00 E |
| Fársala | 38 | 39.18 N | 22.23 E |
| Farschviller | 56 | 49.06 N | 6.54 E |
| Fārsī | 128 | 33.47 N | 63.15 E |
| Fārsī, Jazīreh-ye I | 128 | 27.58 N | 50.11 E |
| Farsīs | 142 | 30.40 N | 31.14 E |
| Farsø | 26 | 56.47 N | 9.21 E |
| Farsta | 40 | 59.14 N | 18.04 E |
| Farsund | 26 | 58.05 N | 6.48 E |
| Fartak, Ra's ≻ | 118 | 15.38 N | 52.15 E |
| Farukolu I | 122 | 6.12 N | 73.16 E |
| Farum | 41 | 55.48 N | 12.22 E |
| Fårvang | 41 | 56.16 N | 9.44 E |
| Farvel, Kap ≻ | 176 | 59.45 N | 44.00 W |
| Farwell, Mi., U.S. | 190 | 43.50 N | 84.52 W |
| Farwell, Tx., U.S. | 196 | 30.15 N | 103.15 W |
| Fāryāb □[4] | 128 | 36.00 N | 65.00 E |
| Fasā | 128 | 28.56 N | 53.42 E |
| Fasano | 68 | 40.50 N | 17.22 E |
| Fashchivka | 83 | 48.16 N | 38.37 E |
| Fashkhah, 'Ayn ⫪[4] | 132 | 31.43 N | 35.27 E |
| Fåsjön ⊜ | 40 | 59.36 N | 14.58 E |
| Fassa | 150 | 13.26 N | 8.15 W |
| Fassberg | 52 | 52.54 N | 10.10 E |
| Fasterholt | 41 | 56.01 N | 9.07 E |
| Fastiv | 78 | 50.06 N | 29.55 E |
| Fastnet Rock I[2] | 48 | 51.24 N | 9.35 W |
| Fastoveckaja | 78 | 45.56 N | 40.09 E |
| Fatagar Tuting, Tanjung ≻ | 164 | 2.46 S | 131.57 E |
| Fataki | 154 | 4.46 S | 28.11 E |
| Fatala ≃ | 150 | 10.13 N | 14.00 W |
| Fat Deer Key I | 220 | 24.44 N | 81.00 W |
| Fate | 222 | 32.56 N | 96.23 W |
| Fatehābād, India | 123 | 29.31 N | 75.27 E |
| Fatehābād, India | 124 | 27.01 N | 78.19 E |
| Fatehgarh, India | 124 | 27.22 N | 79.38 E |
| Fatehgarh, India | 124 | 24.48 N | 76.53 E |
| Fatehgarh Chūriān | 123 | 31.52 N | 74.58 E |
| Fatehjang | 123 | 33.34 N | 72.39 E |
| Fatehpur, India | 120 | 27.59 N | 74.57 E |
| Fatehpur, India | 124 | 25.56 N | 80.48 E |
| Fatehpur, India | 124 | 27.10 N | 81.13 E |
| Fatehpur, India | 126 | 22.17 N | 88.14 E |
| Fatehpur, India | 126 | 24.05 N | 87.44 E |
| Fatehpur, Pāk. | 123 | 31.09 N | 71.13 E |
| Fatehpur Sīkri | 124 | 27.06 N | 77.40 E |
| Fathai | 140 | 8.05 N | 31.48 E |
| Fathom Five National Marine Park ♠ | 190 | 45.15 N | 81.40 W |
| Fatick | 150 | 14.20 N | 16.25 W |
| Fatick □[4] | 150 | 14.00 N | 16.30 W |
| Fatigue, Mount ∧ | 169 | 38.34 S | 146.18 E |
| Fatima, Arg. | 258 | 34.26 S | 59.00 W |
| Fátima, Port. | 34 | 39.37 N | 8.39 W |
| Fatima do Sol | 255 | 22.16 S | 54.25 W |
| Fatima do Sul | 252 | 22.16 S | 54.22 W |
| Fāṭimah, Wādī V | 144 | 21.27 N | 39.09 E |
| Fatoto | 150 | 13.26 N | 13.52 W |
| Fat'ož | 78 | 52.07 N | 35.52 E |
| Fatsa | 130 | 41.02 N | 37.31 E |
| Fatshan → Foshan | 100 | 23.03 N | 113.09 E |
| Fat Tong Point ≻ | 271d | 22.16 N | 114.15 E |
| Fatu-Berlio | 112 | 8.56 S | 125.52 E |
| Fatulla | 126 | 23.38 N | 90.29 E |
| Fatumu | 174w | 21.13 S | 175.07 W |
| Fatunda | 152 | 4.08 S | 17.13 E |
| Fatwā | 124 | 25.31 N | 85.19 E |
| Fauabu | 175e | 8.34 S | 160.43 E |
| Faucigny | 58 | 46.07 N | 6.22 E |
| Faucille, Col de la )( | 58 | 46.22 N | 6.02 E |
| Faucilles, Monts ⋏ | 58 | 48.07 N | 6.16 E |
| Faucogney | 58 | 47.51 N | 6.34 E |
| Faucon-de-Barcelonnette | 62 | 44.24 N | 6.41 E |
| Fauglia | 66 | 43.34 N | 10.31 E |
| Fauldhouse | 46 | 55.50 N | 3.37 W |
| Faulkton | 198 | 45.02 N | 99.07 W |
| Faulquemont | 56 | 49.03 N | 6.36 E |
| Fauquembergues | 50 | 50.36 N | 2.05 E |
| Fauquier | 182 | 49.53 N | 118.05 W |
| Fauquier □[6] | 208 | 38.35 N | 77.35 W |
| Făurei | 38 | 45.06 N | 27.14 E |
| Faure Island I | 162 | 25.51 S | 113.52 E |
| Fauresmith | 158 | 29.42 S | 25.21 E |
| Fauro Island I | 175e | 6.55 S | 156.04 E |
| Fauske | 24 | 67.15 N | 15.24 E |
| Faust | 182 | 55.19 N | 115.38 W |
| Faustovo | 82 | 55.26 N | 38.29 E |
| Fauville-en-Caux | 50 | 49.39 N | 0.35 E |
| Fauvillers | 56 | 49.51 N | 5.40 E |
| Faux-Cap | 157b | 25.33 S | 45.32 E |
| Fåvang | 26 | 61.27 N | 10.11 E |
| Favara | 70 | 37.19 N | 13.39 E |
| Faverges | 62 | 45.45 N | 6.18 E |
| Faverney | 58 | 47.46 N | 6.06 E |
| Faversham | 42 | 51.20 N | 0.53 E |
| Favières | 261 | 48.46 N | 2.47 E |
| Favignana | 70 | 37.56 N | 12.20 E |
| Favignana, Isola I | 70 | 37.56 N | 12.19 E |
| Favoriten ◆[8] | 264b | 48.11 N | 16.23 E |
| Favourable Lake ⊜ | 184 | 52.53 N | 93.56 W |
| Favrieux | 261 | 48.57 N | 1.39 E |
| Fawcett | 182 | 54.32 N | 114.05 W |
| Fawcett Lake ⊜ | 182 | 55.19 N | 113.57 W |
| Fawkham Green | 260 | 51.22 N | 0.17 E |
| Fawkner | 274b | 37.43 S | 144.58 E |
| Fawkner Park ♠ | 274b | 37.50 S | 144.59 E |
| Fawley | 42 | 50.49 N | 1.20 W |
| Fawn ≃, On., Can. | 176 | 55.22 N | 88.20 W |
| Fawn ≃, U.S. | 216 | 41.51 N | 85.40 W |
| Fawn Grove | 208 | 39.44 N | 76.27 W |
| Fawnie Nose ∧ | 182 | 53.16 N | 125.08 W |
| Fawnie Range ⋏ | 182 | 53.10 N | 125.00 W |
| Fawsett Farms | 284c | 38.59 N | 77.14 W |
| Faxaflói c | 24a | 64.25 N | 23.00 W |
| Faxälven ≃ | 26 | 63.13 N | 17.13 E |
| Faxinal | 255 | 23.59 S | 51.22 W |
| Faxinal do Soturno | 252 | 29.37 S | 53.26 W |
| Faxon | 210 | 41.15 N | 76.58 W |
| Faya-Largeau | 146 | 17.55 N | 19.07 E |
| Fayd | 128 | 27.07 N | 42.27 E |
| Fayence | 62 | 43.37 N | 6.41 E |
| Fayerweather Island I | 276 | 41.08 N | 73.13 W |
| Fayette, Al., U.S. | 194 | 33.41 N | 87.49 W |
| Fayette, Ia., U.S. | 190 | 42.50 N | 91.48 W |
| Fayette, Ms., U.S. | 194 | 31.42 N | 91.03 W |
| Fayette, Mo., U.S. | 194 | 39.08 N | 92.41 W |
| Fayette, N.Y., U.S. | 210 | 42.49 N | 76.49 W |
| Fayette, Oh., U.S. | 216 | 41.40 N | 84.19 W |
| Fayette □[6], Il., U.S. | 219 | 38.58 N | 89.06 W |
| Fayette □[6], In., U.S. | 218 | 39.39 N | 85.08 W |
| Fayette □[6], Ky., U.S. | 218 | 38.07 N | 84.30 W |
| Fayette □[6], Oh., U.S. | 218 | 39.32 N | 83.26 W |
| Fayette □[6], Pa., U.S. | 214 | 40.05 N | 79.39 W |
| Fayette □[6], Tx., U.S. | 222 | 29.50 N | 96.57 W |
| Fayette City | 214 | 40.06 N | 79.50 W |
| Fayetteville, Ar., U.S. | 194 | 36.03 N | 94.09 W |
| Fayetteville, Ga., U.S. | 192 | 33.26 N | 84.27 W |
| Fayetteville, Il., U.S. | 219 | 38.22 N | 89.48 W |
| Fayetteville, N.Y., U.S. | 210 | 43.02 N | 76.00 W |
| Fayetteville, N.C., U.S. | 192 | 35.03 N | 78.52 W |
| Fayetteville, Oh., U.S. | 218 | 39.11 N | 83.55 W |
| Fayetteville, Pa., U.S. | 208 | 39.54 N | 77.33 W |
| Fayetteville, Tn., U.S. | 194 | 35.09 N | 86.34 W |
| Fayetteville, Tx., U.S. | 222 | 29.54 N | 96.41 W |
| Fayetteville, W.V., U.S. | 188 | 38.03 N | 81.06 W |
| Faylakah I | 128 | 29.27 N | 48.20 E |
| Fayl-Billot | 58 | 47.47 N | 5.36 E |
| Fayrā | 144 | 13.17 N | 43.25 E |
| Fay-sur-Lignon | 62 | 44.59 N | 4.14 E |
| Fayville | 207 | 42.17 N | 71.30 W |
| Fayyum → Al-Fayyūm | 142 | 29.19 N | 30.50 E |
| Fažana | 64 | 44.55 N | 13.49 E |
| Fazao | 150 | 8.42 N | 0.46 E |
| Fazao, Parc National du ♠ | 150 | 8.40 N | 0.42 E |
| Fazeley | 42 | 52.37 N | 1.42 W |
| Fazenda de Cima | 248 | 15.56 S | 56.37 W |
| Fazenda Libongo | 152 | 8.24 S | 13.24 E |


| Symbol | English | Deutsch | Español | Français | Português |
|---|---|---|---|---|---|
| ≃ | River | Fluß | Río | Rivière | Rio |
| ≍ | Canal | Kanal | Canal | Canal | Canal |
| ʟ | Waterfall, Rapids | Wasserfall, Stromschnellen | Cascada, Rápidos | Chute d'eau, Rapides | Cascata, Rápidos |
| ⋓ | Strait | Meeresstraße | Estrecho | Détroit | Estreito |
| c | Bay, Gulf | Bucht, Golf | Bahía, Golfo | Baie, Golfe | Baía, Golfo |
| ⊜ | Lake, Lakes | See, Seen | Lago, Lagos | Lac, Lacs | Lago, Lagos |
| ⁘ | Swamp | Sumpf | Pantano | Marais | Pântano |
| ⌗ | Ice Features, Glacier | Eis- und Gletscherformen | Accidentes Glaciales | Formes glaciaires | Acidentes glaciares |
| ⫪ | Other Hydrographic Features | Andere Hydrographische Objekte | Otros Elementos Hidrográficos | Autres données hydrographiques | Outros acidentes hidrográficos |
| ✣ | Submarine Features | Untermeerische Objekte | Accidentes Submarinos | Formes de relief sous-marin | Acidentes submarinos |
| □ | Political Unit | Politische Einheit | Unidad Política | Entité politique | Unidade política |
| ʊ | Cultural Institution | Kulturelle Institution | Institución Cultural | Institution culturelle | Instituição cultural |
| ⊥ | Historical Site | Historische Stätte | Sitio Histórico | Site historique | Sítio histórico |
| ♠ | Recreational Site | Erholungs- und Ferienort | Sitio de Recreo | Centre de loisirs | Area de Lazer |
| ⊠ | Airport | Flughafen | Aeropuerto | Aéroport | Aeroporto |
| ■ | Military Installation | Militäranlage | Instalación Militar | Installation militaire | Instalação militar |
| ◆ | Miscellaneous | Verschiedenes | Misceláneo | Divers | Diversos |

| Name | Page | Lat. | Long. |
|---|---|---|---|
| Fazenda Nova | **255** | 16.11 S | 50.48 W |
| Fāzilka | **123** | 30.24 N | 74.02 E |
| Fāzilpur | **120** | 29.18 N | 70.27 E |
| Fazzān (Fezzan) □[9] | **146** | 26.00 N | 14.00 E |
| Fdérik | **148** | 22.41 N | 12.43 W |
| Feale ≃ | **48** | 52.28 N | 9.40 W |
| Fear, Cape › | **192** | 33.50 N | 77.58 W |
| Fearnhead | **262** | 53.25 N | 2.33 W |
| Feasterville | **208** | 40.08 N | 75.00 W |
| Feather ≃ | **204** | 38.47 N | 121.36 W |
| Feather, Middle Fork ≃ | **204** | 39.34 N | 121.26 W |
| Feather, North Fork ≃ | **204** | 39.34 N | 121.28 W |
| Feather, North Fork, East Branch ≃ | **204** | 40.01 N | 121.13 W |
| Feather, South Fork ≃ | **204** | 39.33 N | 121.28 W |
| Featherbed Top ∧ | **262** | 53.26 N | 1.52 W |
| Featherly Regional Park ♦ | **280** | 33.52 N | 117.42 W |
| Featherston | **172** | 41.07 S | 175.20 E |
| Featherstone, Eng., U.K. | **44** | 53.41 N | 1.21 W |
| Featherstone, Zimb. | **154** | 18.42 S | 30.49 E |
| Feathertop, Mount ∧ | **166** | 36.54 S | 147.08 E |
| Fécamp | **50** | 49.45 N | 0.22 E |
| Fedala → Mohammedia | **148** | 33.44 N | 7.24 W |
| Fedderwardergroden | **52** | 53.35 N | 8.05 E |
| Feddet ›[1] | **41** | 55.09 N | 12.07 E |
| Federación | **252** | 31.00 S | 57.54 W |
| Federal, Arg. | **252** | 30.57 S | 58.48 W |
| Federal, Pa., U.S. | **279b** | 40.23 N | 80.09 W |
| Federalsburg | **208** | 38.41 N | 75.46 W |
| Federal Way | **224** | 47.19 N | 122.18 W |
| Federation Forest State Park ♦ | **224** | 47.09 N | 121.40 W |
| Federsee ⊜ | **58** | 48.05 N | 9.38 E |
| Fedeshk | **128** | 32.45 N | 58.50 E |
| Fedje | **26** | 60.47 N | 4.42 E |
| Fedorino | **82** | 55.08 N | 36.06 E |
| Fedorivka, Ukr. | **78** | 49.23 N | 35.07 E |
| Fedorivka, Ukr. | **78** | 47.33 N | 36.33 E |
| Fedosejevka | **80** | 46.53 N | 44.00 E |
| Fedosejevskaja | **24** | 62.07 N | 40.42 E |
| Fedosicha | **86** | 54.47 N | 81.54 E |
| Fedosjino | **82** | 55.08 N | 38.30 E |
| Fedotovo | **82** | 55.41 N | 39.12 E |
| Feeagh, Lough ⊜ | **48** | 53.55 N | 9.36 W |
| Feeding Hills | **207** | 42.04 N | 72.40 W |
| Feerfeer | **144** | 8.30 N | 47.55 E |
| Feesburg | **218** | 38.52 N | 83.58 W |
| Fefan I | **175c** | 7.21 N | 151.51 E |
| Fehérgyarmat | **30** | 47.58 N | 22.32 E |
| Fehmarn I | **54** | 54.28 N | 11.08 E |
| Fehmarnbelt (Femer Bælt) Ʉ | **41** | 54.35 N | 11.15 E |
| Fehmarnsund Ʉ | **54** | 54.24 N | 11.07 E |
| Fehrbellin | **54** | 52.49 N | 12.46 E |
| Fehring | **61** | 46.56 N | 16.01 E |
| Feia, Lagoa c | **255** | 22.00 S | 41.20 W |
| Feicheng | **98** | 36.15 N | 116.46 E |
| Feichten | **58** | 47.02 N | 10.44 E |
| Feidong | **100** | 31.52 N | 117.29 E |
| Feignies | **50** | 50.18 N | 3.55 E |
| Feigumfossen ˪ | **26** | 61.23 N | 7.26 E |
| Feiheji | **100** | 33.36 N | 115.36 E |
| Fei Huang ≃ | **100** | 33.35 N | 119.02 E |
| Feijó | **248** | 8.09 S | 70.21 W |
| Feiketu | **89** | 45.46 N | 127.09 E |
| Feilding | **172** | 40.13 S | 175.34 E |
| Feiler ∧ | **64** | 47.07 N | 10.52 E |
| Feiliqiao | **106** | 31.05 N | 119.05 E |
| Feilitzsch | **54** | 50.22 N | 11.56 E |
| Feilong, Zhg. | **107** | 30.25 N | 106.20 E |
| Feilong, Zhg. | **107** | 30.36 N | 105.54 E |
| Feilongguan | **107** | 28.57 N | 105.05 E |
| Feiluan | **100** | 26.35 N | 119.35 E |
| Feira | **154** | 15.37 S | 30.25 E |
| Feira de Santana | **255** | 12.15 S | 38.57 W |
| Feistritz ≃ | **61** | 47.01 N | 16.08 E |
| Feistritz an der Gail | **64** | 46.34 N | 13.36 E |
| Feistritzer Spitze ∧ | **61** | 46.31 N | 14.45 E |
| Feixi | **100** | 31.42 N | 117.10 E |
| Feixian | **98** | 35.18 N | 117.57 E |
| Feixiang | **98** | 36.34 N | 114.49 E |
| Feiyun ≃ | **100** | 27.48 N | 120.36 E |
| Fejaj, Chott ≡ | **148** | 33.55 N | 9.10 E |
| Fejér □[6] | **30** | 47.10 N | 18.35 E |
| Fejø I | **41** | 54.57 N | 11.26 E |
| Feke | **130** | 37.53 N | 35.58 E |
| Feklistova, ostrov I | **89** | 55.02 N | 136.55 E |
| Felâhiye | **130** | 39.06 N | 35.35 E |
| Felanitx | **34** | 39.28 N | 3.08 E |
| Felbertauerntunnel -•-[5] | **64** | 47.08 N | 12.31 E |
| Felda | **220** | 26.33 N | 81.26 W |
| Felda ≃, Dtsch. | **56** | 50.42 N | 9.03 E |
| Felda ≃, Dtsch. | **56** | 50.51 N | 10.05 E |
| Feldafing | **64** | 47.57 N | 11.17 E |
| Feldaist ≃ | **61** | 48.19 N | 14.34 E |
| Feld am See | **64** | 46.47 N | 13.45 E |
| Feldbach | **61** | 46.57 N | 15.54 E |
| Feldberg, Dtsch. | **54** | 53.20 N | 13.26 E |
| Feldberg, Dtsch. | **58** | 47.51 N | 8.02 E |
| Feldberg ∧ | **58** | 47.52 N | 8.00 E |
| Felderbach ≃ | **263** | 51.22 N | 7.08 E |
| Feldhausen -•-[8] | **263** | 51.37 N | 6.59 E |
| Feldis | **58** | 46.48 N | 9.26 E |
| Feldkirch | **58** | 47.14 N | 9.36 E |
| Feldkirchen an der Donau | **61** | 48.21 N | 14.03 E |
| Feldkirchen bei Graz | **61** | 47.01 N | 15.27 E |
| Feldkirchen in Kärnten | **61** | 46.43 N | 14.05 E |
| Feldkirchen-Westerham | **64** | 47.54 N | 11.50 E |
| Feldmark | **263** | 51.41 N | 6.38 E |
| Feldstetten | **58** | 48.28 N | 9.37 E |
| Felhit | **144** | 16.43 N | 38.02 E |
| Feliciano, Méx. | **234** | 18.01 N | 101.58 W |
| Feliciano, P.R. | **240m** | 18.28 N | 67.08 W |
| Feliciano, Arroyo ≃ | **252** | 31.06 S | 59.54 W |
| Felicity | **218** | 38.50 N | 84.05 W |
| Felina | **64** | 44.27 N | 10.27 E |
| Felino | **64** | 44.42 N | 10.15 E |
| Felipe Carrillo Puerto, Méx. | **234** | 19.08 N | 102.42 W |
| Felipe Carrillo Puerto, Méx. | **234** | 21.09 N | 104.52 W |
| Felix, Cape › | **176** | 69.54 N | 97.50 W |
| Felix, Rio ≃ | **196** | 33.08 N | 104.19 W |
| Felixburg | **154** | 19.29 S | 30.51 E |
| Felixdorf | **61** | 47.53 N | 16.15 E |
| Felixlândia | **255** | 18.47 S | 44.55 W |
| Felixstowe | **42** | 51.58 N | 1.20 E |
| Felixton | **158** | 28.50 S | 31.53 E |
| Félix U. Gómez | **232** | 29.50 N | 111.30 W |
| Felizzano | **62** | 44.54 N | 8.26 E |
| Fell | **56** | 49.46 N | 6.47 E |
| Fella ≃ | **64** | 46.21 N | 13.07 E |
| Fellbach | **56** | 48.48 N | 9.15 E |
| Felletin | **32** | 45.53 N | 2.10 E |
| Felling | **44** | 54.57 N | 1.33 W |
| Fellingsbro | **40** | 59.26 N | 15.35 E |
| Fellows | **226** | 35.11 N | 119.32 W |
| Fellows Creek ≃ | **281** | 42.17 N | 83.26 W |
| Fellowship | **285** | 39.55 N | 74.58 W |
| Fellsburg | **214** | 40.11 N | 79.49 W |
| Fellsmere | **220** | 27.46 N | 80.36 W |
| Fellwick | **285** | 40.08 N | 75.11 W |
| Felpham | **42** | 50.47 N | 0.39 W |
| Felsberg | **56** | 51.08 N | 9.25 E |
| Felső-Válicka ≃ | **61** | 46.52 N | 16.53 E |
| Feltham -•-[8] | **260** | 51.27 N | 0.24 W |
| Felt Lake ⊜ | **282** | 37.23 N | 122.11 W |
| Felton, Ca., U.S. | **226** | 37.03 N | 122.04 W |
| Felton, De., U.S. | **208** | 39.00 N | 75.34 W |
| Felton, Pa., U.S. | **208** | 39.51 N | 76.34 W |
| Feltre | **64** | 46.01 N | 11.54 E |
| Felts Mills | **212** | 44.01 N | 75.46 W |
| Feltwell | **42** | 52.29 N | 0.32 E |
| Femer Bælt (Fehmarnbelt) Ʉ | **41** | 54.35 N | 11.15 E |
| Femme Osage Creek ≃ | **219** | 38.39 N | 90.44 W |
| Femmøller | **41** | 56.14 N | 10.35 E |
| Femø I | **41** | 54.58 N | 11.33 E |
| Femund ⊜ | **26** | 62.12 N | 11.52 E |
| Femundsenden | **26** | 61.55 N | 11.55 E |
| Femundsmarka Nasjonalpark ♦ | **26** | 62.20 N | 12.07 E |
| Fen ≃ | **102** | 35.36 N | 110.42 E |
| Fena Valley Reservoir ⊜[1] | **174p** | 13.21 N | 144.42 E |
| Fendaozi | **104** | 41.35 N | 120.51 E |
| Fenelon Falls | **212** | 44.32 N | 78.45 W |
| Fenelton | **214** | 40.52 N | 79.44 W |
| Feneppi I | **175c** | 7.07 N | 151.53 E |
| Fener -•-[8] | **267b** | 41.02 N | 28.56 E |
| Fenerbahce Stadium ♦ | **267b** | 40.59 N | 29.02 E |
| Fener Burnu › | **130** | 41.07 N | 39.25 E |
| Fener Tepesi ∧[2] | **267b** | 41.09 N | 28.47 E |
| Fenestrelle | **62** | 45.02 N | 7.03 E |
| Fénétrange | **56** | 48.51 N | 7.01 E |
| Feng ≃ | **105** | 39.25 N | 116.57 E |
| Fengcheng, Zhg. | **98** | 40.27 N | 124.02 E |
| Fengcheng, Zhg. | **100** | 28.10 N | 115.46 E |
| Fengcheng, Zhg. | **102** | 38.32 N | 101.50 E |
| Fengcheng, Zhg. | **106** | 30.55 N | 121.38 E |
| Fengdengwu | **105** | 39.42 N | 117.55 E |
| Fengdian | **107** | 30.41 N | 104.51 E |
| Fengdu | **102** | 29.58 N | 107.41 E |
| Fengfeng | **98** | 36.28 N | 114.14 E |
| Fenggang, Zhg. | **100** | 28.34 N | 116.34 E |
| Fenggang, Zhg. | **102** | 27.58 N | 107.47 E |
| Fenggaopu | **107** | 29.24 N | 105.41 E |
| Fenghua | **100** | 29.40 N | 121.24 E |
| Fenghuang, Zhg. | **100** | 23.58 N | 116.44 E |
| Fenghuang, Zhg. | **102** | 24.25 N | 107.17 E |
| Fenghuang, Zhg. | **102** | 27.58 N | 109.19 E |
| Fenghuang, Zhg. | **106** | 31.21 N | 121.44 E |
| Fenghuangchang | **107** | 29.44 N | 106.19 E |
| Fenghuang Shan ∧ | **107** | 28.54 N | 106.35 E |
| Fenghuanjing | **100** | 31.11 N | 117.49 E |
| Fenghui | **100** | 29.56 N | 120.58 E |
| Fengjia, Zhg. | **98** | 37.03 N | 121.42 E |
| Fengjia, Zhg. | **104** | 42.35 N | 122.30 E |
| Fengjiabao | **102** | 36.12 N | 104.49 E |
| Fengjiakou | **98** | 38.11 N | 116.44 E |
| Fengjianjiao | **106** | 30.41 N | 120.51 E |
| Fengjiatun | **104** | 41.14 N | 122.00 E |
| Fengjiawopeng | **104** | 42.19 N | 123.40 E |
| Fengjiaxiang | **106** | 30.56 N | 121.06 E |
| Fengjie | **102** | 31.03 N | 109.31 E |
| Fengjing | **106** | 30.53 N | 121.01 E |
| Fengkou | **100** | 30.05 N | 113.18 E |
| Fengle, Zhg. | **89** | 45.47 N | 125.26 E |
| Fengle, Zhg. | **100** | 27.13 N | 118.11 E |
| Fenglezhen | **98** | 36.14 N | 114.18 E |
| Fengliang | **100** | 23.59 N | 116.14 E |
| Fenglin, T'aiwan | **100** | 23.45 N | 121.26 E |
| Fenglin, Zhg. | **100** | 28.19 N | 120.46 E |
| Fengling Guan )( | **100** | 28.14 N | 118.29 E |
| Fenglingtou | **100** | 28.26 N | 117.50 E |
| Fengman | **89** | 43.46 N | 126.41 E |
| Fengnan (Xugezhuang) | **105** | 39.34 N | 118.06 E |
| Fengning (Dagezhen) | **98** | 41.12 N | 116.32 E |
| Fengpin | **100** | 23.36 N | 121.31 E |
| Fengpingzi | **102** | 32.46 N | 105.12 E |
| Fengqiao, Zhg. | **100** | 29.46 N | 120.26 E |
| Fengqiao, Zhg. | **106** | 31.19 N | 120.33 E |
| Fengqing | **102** | 24.46 N | 99.52 E |
| Fengqiu | **98** | 35.05 N | 114.25 E |
| Fengrun | **105** | 39.50 N | 118.07 E |
| Fengshan, Zhg. | **89** | 46.22 N | 128.30 E |
| Fengshan, Zhg. | **98** | 41.14 N | 117.05 E |
| Fengshan, Zhg. | **102** | 22.01 N | 109.59 E |
| Fengshi | **100** | 24.42 N | 116.34 E |
| Fengshun | **100** | 23.48 N | 116.11 E |
| Fengtai, Zhg. | **100** | 32.44 N | 116.43 E |
| Fengtai, Zhg. | **105** | 39.51 N | 116.16 E |
| Fengtian, Zhg. | **100** | 27.24 N | 114.43 E |
| Fengtian, Zhg. | **100** | 25.46 N | 115.30 E |
| Fengtien → Shenyang | **104** | 41.48 N | 123.27 E |
| Fengting | **100** | 25.16 N | 118.54 E |
| Fengwan | **100** | 24.48 N | 113.50 E |
| Fengxi | **102** | 31.48 N | 109.50 E |
| Fengxian, Zhg. | **98** | 34.42 N | 116.34 E |
| Fengxian, Zhg. | **102** | 33.57 N | 106.44 E |
| Fengxian, Zhg. | **106** | 30.55 N | 121.27 E |
| Fengxiang | **102** | 34.29 N | 107.29 E |
| Fengxin | **100** | 28.43 N | 115.23 E |
| Fengyang, Zhg. | **100** | 32.52 N | 117.34 E |
| Fengyang, Zhg. | **100** | 24.49 N | 117.53 E |
| Fengyi | **102** | 31.44 N | 103.53 E |
| Fengyu | **100** | 26.31 N | 119.18 E |
| Fengyüan | **100** | 24.15 N | 120.43 E |
| Fengzhen | **102** | 40.24 N | 113.09 E |
| Fengzhou | **100** | 25.41 N | 113.52 E |
| Fengzhuangtou | **106** | 31.00 N | 118.39 E |
| Fenholloway ≃ | **192** | 29.59 N | 83.47 W |
| Fen Hu ⊜ | **106** | 31.00 N | 120.47 E |
| Feni | **124** | 23.00 N | 91.24 E |
| Fenicia Moncata ⊥ | **70** | 37.33 N | 14.57 E |
| Feni Islands II | **14** | 4.05 S | 153.42 E |
| Fenimore Pass Ʉ | **180** | 52.00 N | 175.35 W |
| Fenino | **265b** | 55.44 N | 37.57 E |
| Fenis | **62** | 45.44 N | 7.29 E |
| Feniscowles | **262** | 53.43 N | 2.32 W |
| Fenjie | **106** | 32.17 N | 120.20 E |
| Fennimore | **190** | 42.59 N | 90.39 W |
| Fennville | **216** | 42.35 N | 86.06 W |
| Fenny Compton | **42** | 52.09 N | 1.20 W |
| Fenny Stratford | **42** | 52.00 N | 0.43 W |
| Feno, Capo di ›, Fr. | **36** | 41.57 N | 8.36 E |
| Feno, Capo di ›, Fr. | **71** | 41.23 N | 9.06 E |
| Fenoarivo, Madag. | **157b** | 18.26 S | 46.34 E |
| Fenoarivo, Madag. | **157b** | 21.43 S | 46.24 E |
| Fenoarivo, Madag. | **157b** | 20.52 S | 46.53 E |
| Fenoarivo Atsinanana | **157b** | 17.22 S | 49.25 E |
| Fensfjorden c[2] | **26** | 60.51 N | 4.50 E |
| Fenshui | **104** | 40.41 N | 122.32 E |
| Fenshui ≃ | **100** | 29.49 N | 119.41 E |
| Fenshui'ao | **100** | 25.20 N | 114.43 E |
| Fenshuidunshen | **106** | 31.30 N | 120.01 E |
| Fenshuiling, Zhg. | **107** | 28.51 N | 105.35 E |
| Fenshuiling, Zhg. | **107** | 30.20 N | 105.15 E |
| Fenshuipu | **107** | 30.05 N | 104.05 E |
| Fenshuizhen | **107** | 29.44 N | 103.55 E |
| Fenshuizui | **100** | 30.35 N | 113.38 E |
| Fensmark | **41** | 55.17 N | 11.49 E |
| Fenstanton | **42** | 52.18 N | 0.04 W |
| Fenton, Mi., U.S. | **216** | 42.47 N | 83.42 W |
| Fenton, Mo., U.S. | **219** | 38.32 N | 90.22 W |
| Fenton, Lake ⊜ | **216** | 42.50 N | 83.43 W |
| Fentou | **105** | 38.53 N | 116.32 E |
| Fentress | **222** | 29.45 N | 97.47 W |
| Fenway Park ♦ | **283** | 42.21 N | 71.06 W |
| Fenwick | **188** | 38.13 N | 80.34 W |
| Fenwick Island ›[1] | **208** | 38.25 N | 75.03 W |
| Fenyang | **102** | 37.17 N | 111.48 E |
| Fenyi | **100** | 27.47 N | 114.42 E |
| Feodosiya | **78** | 45.02 N | 35.23 E |
| Feodosiys'ka zatoka c | **78** | 45.05 N | 35.35 E |
| Fépin | **56** | 50.01 N | 4.44 E |
| Fer, Cap de › | **148** | 37.05 N | 7.10 E |
| Ferbane | **48** | 53.15 N | 7.49 W |
| Ferbitz | **264a** | 52.30 N | 13.01 E |
| Ferch | **264a** | 52.19 N | 12.56 E |
| Fercher Berge ∧[2] | **264a** | 52.19 N | 12.57 E |
| Ferchland | **54** | 52.26 N | 12.00 E |
| Ferdig | **182** | 48.45 N | 111.46 W |
| Ferdinand | **194** | 38.13 N | 86.51 W |
| Ferdinandshof | **54** | 53.39 N | 13.53 E |
| Ferdows | **128** | 34.00 N | 58.09 E |
| Fère-Champenoise | **50** | 48.45 N | 3.59 E |
| Fère-en-Tardenois | **50** | 49.12 N | 3.31 E |
| Ferencváros -•-[8] | **264c** | 47.28 N | 19.06 E |
| Ferentillo | **66** | 42.37 N | 12.47 E |
| Ferentino | **66** | 41.42 N | 13.15 E |
| Fergana | **85** | 40.23 N | 71.46 E |
| Fergana □[4] | **85** | 40.30 N | 71.20 E |
| Ferganskaja dolina V | **85** | 40.50 N | 71.30 E |
| Ferganskij chrebet ⋏ | **85** | 41.00 N | 74.00 E |
| Fergus | **212** | 43.42 N | 80.22 W |
| Fergus Falls | **198** | 46.16 N | 96.04 W |
| Ferguson, Austl. | **168a** | 33.26 S | 115.51 E |
| Ferguson, B.C., Can. | **182** | 50.41 N | 117.28 W |
| Ferguson, Ky., U.S. | **192** | 37.04 N | 84.36 W |
| Ferguson, Mo., U.S. | **219** | 38.44 N | 90.18 W |
| Ferguson ≃ | **168a** | 33.21 S | 115.40 E |
| Fergusonville | **285** | 40.07 N | 74.54 W |
| Fergusson Island I | **164** | 9.30 S | 150.40 E |
| Fériana | **148** | 34.57 N | 8.34 E |
| Ferihegyi Airport ⊠ | **264c** | 47.26 N | 19.15 E |
| Ferkéssédougou | **150** | 9.36 N | 5.12 W |
| Ferla | **70** | 37.07 N | 14.56 E |
| Ferlach | **61** | 46.31 N | 14.18 E |
| Ferleiten | **64** | 47.10 N | 12.49 E |
| Ferlo -•-[1] | **150** | 0.15 N | 0.14 W |
| Ferlo, Vallée du V | **150** | 15.42 N | 15.30 W |
| Fermiers, Île aux I | **275a** | 45.40 N | 73.27 W |
| Fermignano | **66** | 43.40 N | 12.39 E |
| Fermin, Point › | **228** | 33.42 N | 118.18 W |
| Fermi National Accelerator Laboratory ʊ[3] | **216** | 41.50 N | 88.15 W |
| Fermo | **66** | 43.09 N | 13.43 E |
| Fermont | **176** | 52.47 N | 67.05 W |
| Fermoselle | **34** | 41.19 N | 6.23 W |
| Fermoy | **48** | 52.08 N | 8.16 W |
| Fernández | **252** | 27.55 S | 63.54 W |
| Fernández Leal | **200** | 30.51 N | 108.17 W |
| Fernandina, Isla I | **246a** | 0.25 S | 91.30 W |
| Fernandina Beach | **192** | 30.40 N | 81.27 W |
| Fernando de la Mora | **252** | 25.19 S | 57.36 W |
| Fernando de Noronha, Ilha I | **250** | 3.51 S | 32.25 W |
| Fernandópolis | **255** | 20.16 S | 50.14 W |
| Fernando Póo → Bioko I | **152** | 3.30 N | 8.40 E |
| Fernán-Núñez | **34** | 37.40 N | 4.43 W |
| Fernão Veloso, Baía de c | **154** | 14.20 S | 40.45 E |
| Ferndale, S. Afr. | **273d** | 26.05 S | 27.59 E |
| Ferndale, Ca., U.S. | **204** | 40.34 N | 124.15 W |
| Ferndale, Fl., U.S. | **220** | 28.37 N | 81.42 W |
| Ferndale, Md., U.S. | **208** | 39.10 N | 76.38 W |
| Ferndale, Mi., U.S. | **216** | 42.27 N | 83.08 W |
| Ferndale, N.Y., U.S. | **210** | 41.46 N | 74.44 W |
| Ferndale, Pa., U.S. | **214** | 40.17 N | 78.54 W |
| Ferndale, Wa., U.S. | **202** | 48.50 N | 122.35 W |
| Ferndale Lake ⊜ | **222** | 32.57 N | 95.05 W |
| Ferndown | **42** | 50.48 N | 1.55 W |
| Ferney-Voltaire | **58** | 46.15 N | 6.07 E |
| Fern Glen | **210** | 40.57 N | 76.10 W |
| Fernhill Heath | **42** | 52.14 N | 2.12 W |
| Fernie | **182** | 49.30 N | 115.03 W |
| Fernilee | **262** | 53.18 N | 1.58 W |
| Fernilee Reservoir ⊜[1] | **262** | 53.17 N | 1.59 W |
| Fernley | **204** | 39.36 N | 119.15 W |
| Ferno | **266b** | 45.37 N | 8.45 E |
| Fernow, Mount ∧ | **224** | 47.45 N | 121.14 W |
| Fern Park | **220** | 28.41 N | 81.20 W |
| Fernpass )( | **58** | 47.22 N | 10.50 E |
| Fern Ridge Lake ⊜[1] | **202** | 44.05 N | 123.18 W |
| Ferns | **48** | 52.35 N | 6.31 W |
| Fernvale | **171a** | 27.27 S | 152.39 E |
| Fernway | **214** | 40.41 N | 80.07 W |
| Fernwood, Id., U.S. | **202** | 47.06 N | 116.23 W |
| Fernwood, N.Y., U.S. | **210** | 43.16 N | 73.40 W |
| Fernwood, Pa., U.S. | **285** | 39.57 N | 75.15 W |
| Ferny Creek | **274b** | 37.53 S | 145.21 E |
| Feroé, Islas → Faeroe Islands □[2] | **22** | 62.00 N | 7.00 W |
| Feroës → Faeroe Islands □[2] | **22** | 62.00 N | 7.00 W |
| Ferokh | **122** | 11.11 N | 75.51 E |
| Feroleto Antico | **68** | 38.58 N | 16.23 E |
| Feroleto della Chiesa | **68** | 38.28 N | 16.04 E |
| Ferolle Point › | **186** | 51.05 N | 57.07 W |
| Ferozepore → Fīrozpur | **123** | 30.55 N | 74.36 E |
| Ferrandina | **68** | 40.29 N | 16.28 E |
| Ferrara | **64** | 44.50 N | 11.35 E |
| Ferrara □[4] | **64** | 44.48 N | 11.50 E |
| Ferrat, Cap › | **34** | 35.54 N | 0.23 W |
| Ferrato, Capo › | **71** | 39.18 N | 9.38 E |
| Ferraz de Vasconcelos | **256** | 23.32 S | 46.22 W |
| Ferraz de Vasconcelos □[7] | **287b** | 23.33 S | 46.21 W |
| Ferrazzano | **66** | 41.32 N | 14.40 E |
| Ferré, Cap › | **240e** | 14.28 N | 60.49 W |
| Ferreira, Ang. | **152** | 12.53 S | 22.48 E |
| Ferreira, S. Afr. | **158** | 29.13 S | 26.10 E |
| Ferreira do Alentejo | **34** | 38.03 N | 8.07 W |
| Ferreira Gomes | **250** | 0.48 N | 51.08 W |
| Ferreiros | **256** | 22.25 S | 43.34 W |
| Ferrell | **285** | 39.41 N | 75.12 W |
| Ferrells Bridge Dam -•-[6] | **222** | 32.45 N | 94.30 W |
| Ferreñafe | **248** | 6.38 S | 79.45 W |
| Ferrera Erbognone | **62** | 45.07 N | 8.52 E |
| Ferret | **58** | 45.55 N | 7.06 E |
| Ferret, Cap › | **32** | 44.37 N | 1.15 W |
| Ferreyra | **252** | 31.28 S | 64.08 W |
| Ferriday | **194** | 31.37 N | 91.33 W |
| Ferriere | **62** | 44.38 N | 9.30 E |
| Ferrière-la-Grande | **50** | 50.15 N | 4.00 E |
| Ferrières | **50** | 48.05 N | 2.47 E |
| Ferrières-en-Brie | **50** | 48.49 N | 2.43 E |
| Ferris | **222** | 32.32 N | 96.39 W |
| Ferritslev | **41** | 55.18 N | 10.36 E |
| Ferro ≃ | **255** | 12.27 S | 54.31 W |
| Ferro, Canale del V | **64** | 46.21 N | 13.07 E |
| Ferrol → El Ferrol del Caudillo, Esp. | **34** | 43.29 N | 8.14 W |
| Ferrol, Esp. | **34** | 43.29 N | 8.14 W |
| Ferrol, Península de ›[1] | **248** | 9.10 S | 78.37 W |
| Ferron | **200** | 39.05 N | 111.08 W |
| Ferron Creek ≃ | **200** | 39.09 N | 110.55 W |
| Ferros | **255** | 19.14 S | 43.02 W |
| Ferru, Monte ∧, It. | **71** | 39.44 N | 9.38 E |
| Ferru, Monte ∧, It. | **71** | 40.08 N | 8.36 E |
| Ferruzzano | **68** | 38.02 N | 16.05 E |
| Ferry, Pointe › | **241o** | 16.17 N | 61.49 W |
| Ferryhill | **44** | 54.41 N | 1.33 W |
| Ferryland | **186** | 47.02 N | 52.53 W |
| Ferry Point Park ♦ | **276** | 40.49 N | 73.50 W |
| Ferrysburg | **216** | 43.05 N | 86.13 W |
| Ferry Village | **284a** | 43.58 N | 78.57 W |
| Ferryville → Menzel Bourguiba | **148** | 37.10 N | 9.48 E |
| Feršampenuaz | **86** | 53.32 N | 59.51 E |
| Fertile | **198** | 47.32 N | 96.16 W |
| Fertilia, Aeroporto di ⊠ | **71** | 40.37 N | 8.15 E |
| Fertő (Neusiedler See) ⊜ | **61** | 47.50 N | 16.45 E |
| Fertőd ⊥ | **61** | 47.37 N | 16.53 E |
| Fertőrákos | **61** | 47.43 N | 16.39 E |
| Fertőújlak | **61** | 47.40 N | 16.51 E |
| Ferulargiu, Monte ∧ | **71** | 40.31 N | 9.34 E |
| Ferzikovo | **82** | 54.32 N | 36.45 E |
| Fès | **148** | 34.05 N | 4.57 W |
| Fès □[4] | **148** | 33.55 N | 4.57 W |
| Feshi | **152** | 6.07 S | 18.10 E |
| Feshie ≃ | **46** | 57.08 N | 3.55 W |
| Fessenden | **198** | 47.38 N | 99.37 W |
| Festus | **219** | 38.13 N | 90.23 W |
| Fetcham | **42** | 51.17 N | 0.22 W |
| Fet Dom, Tanjung › | **164** | 1.53 S | 129.43 E |
| Fété Bowé | **150** | 14.56 N | 13.30 W |
| Fetești | **38** | 44.23 N | 27.50 E |
| Fethaland, Point of › | **46a** | 60.38 N | 1.18 W |
| Fethard | **48** | 52.27 N | 7.41 W |
| Fethiye | **130** | 36.37 N | 29.07 E |
| Fethiye Körfezi c | **130** | 36.40 N | 29.00 E |
| Fetisovo | **72** | 42.46 N | 52.38 E |
| Fetlar I | **46a** | 60.37 N | 0.52 W |
| Fetsund | **26** | 59.56 N | 11.10 E |
| Fetterangus | **46** | 57.33 N | 2.01 W |
| Fettercairn | **46** | 56.51 N | 2.34 W |
| Feucherolles | **261** | 48.52 N | 1.58 E |
| Feucht | **60** | 49.22 N | 11.13 E |
| Feuchtwangen | **56** | 49.10 N | 10.20 E |
| Feudingen | **56** | 50.56 N | 8.19 E |
| Feuerland → Tierra del Fuego, Isla Grande de I | **254** | 54.00 S | 69.00 W |
| Feuet | **146** | 24.57 N | 10.04 E |
| Feuilles, Baie aux c | **176** | 58.55 N | 69.20 W |
| Feuilles, Rivière aux ≃ | **176** | 58.47 N | 70.04 W |
| Feuquières-en-Vimeu | **50** | 50.04 N | 1.36 E |
| Feura Bush | **210** | 42.35 N | 73.53 W |
| Feurs | **62** | 45.45 N | 4.14 E |
| Fevik | **26** | 58.23 N | 8.42 E |
| Fevzipaşa | **130** | 37.07 N | 36.37 E |
| Féy | **56** | 49.02 N | 6.06 E |
| Feyẕābād, Afg. | **120** | 37.06 N | 70.34 E |
| Feyẕābād, Īrān | **128** | 35.01 N | 58.46 E |
| Feyzin | **62** | 45.40 N | 4.51 E |
| Fez → Fès | **148** | 34.05 N | 4.57 W |
| Fezzan → Fazzān □[9] | **146** | 26.00 N | 14.00 E |
| Ffestiniog | **42** | 52.58 N | 3.55 W |
| Fforest Fawr -•-[1] | **42** | 51.52 N | 3.36 W |
| F. Gilbert Hills State Forest ♦ | **283** | 42.03 N | 71.17 W |
| Fhada, Beinn ∧ | **46** | 57.13 N | 5.18 W |
| Fiambalá | **252** | 27.41 S | 67.38 W |
| Fiamignano | **66** | 42.16 N | 13.07 E |
| Fian | **150** | 10.23 N | 2.29 W |
| Fianarantsoa | **157b** | 21.26 S | 47.05 E |
| Fianarantsoa □[4] | **157b** | 22.00 S | 47.00 E |
| Fianga | **146** | 9.55 N | 15.09 E |
| Fiano | **62** | 45.13 N | 7.31 E |
| Fiantsonana | **157b** | 19.09 S | 46.12 E |
| Fiastra, Abbazia di ʊ[1] | **66** | 43.13 N | 13.25 E |
| Fiavè | **64** | 46.00 N | 10.50 E |
| Ficarazzi | **70** | 38.05 N | 13.28 E |
| Ficarolo | **64** | 44.57 N | 11.26 E |
| Ficarra | **70** | 38.06 N | 14.50 E |
| Fiche | **144** | 9.52 N | 38.46 E |
| Fichtelberg | **60** | 50.01 N | 11.51 E |
| Fichtelberg ∧ | **54** | 50.26 N | 12.57 E |
| Fichtelgebirge ⋏ | **30** | 50.00 N | 11.55 E |
| Fichtenau | **264a** | 52.27 N | 13.42 E |
| Ficksburg | **158** | 28.57 S | 27.50 E |
| Ficulle | **66** | 42.50 N | 12.04 E |
| Ficuzza ≃ | **70** | 37.00 N | 14.20 E |
| Fidalgo ≃ | **250** | 7.28 S | 42.32 W |
| Fidalgo Island I | **224** | 48.25 N | 122.35 W |
| Fidān, Wādī al- V | **132** | 30.46 N | 35.18 E |
| Fiddlers Hamlet | **260** | 51.41 N | 0.08 E |
| Fiddletown | **226** | 38.30 N | 120.46 W |
| Fiddyment Creek ≃ | **278** | 41.36 N | 88.03 W |
| Fidelity | **219** | 39.09 N | 90.10 W |
| Fidenza | **64** | 44.52 N | 10.03 E |
| Fidīmīn | **142** | 29.23 N | 30.46 E |
| Fiditi | **150** | 7.45 N | 3.53 E |
| Fidji → Fiji □[1] | **175g** | 18.00 S | 178.00 E |
| Fidler Lake ⊜ | **184** | 57.11 N | 96.57 W |
| Fidschi → Fiji □[1] | **175g** | 18.00 S | 178.00 E |
| Fiè (Völs) | **64** | 46.31 N | 11.30 E |
| Fieberbrunn | **64** | 47.29 N | 12.33 E |
| Field | **182** | 51.24 N | 116.29 W |
| Fieldale | **192** | 36.42 N | 79.56 W |
| Field Museum ʊ | **278** | 41.53 N | 87.37 W |
| Fieldon | **219** | 39.07 N | 90.30 W |
| Fieldsboro | **285** | 40.08 N | 74.43 W |
| Fieldstone | **276** | 40.44 N | 74.33 W |
| Fiemme, Val di V | **64** | 46.20 N | 11.35 E |
| Fiener Bruch ≡ | **54** | 52.19 N | 12.10 E |
| Fienvillers | **50** | 50.07 N | 2.14 E |
| Fier | **38** | 40.43 N | 19.34 E |
| Fier ≃ | **58** | 45.56 N | 5.50 E |
| Fiéra Campionaria ♦ | **266b** | 45.28 N | 9.09 E |
| Fiera di Primiero | **64** | 46.10 N | 11.49 E |
| Fierenana | **157b** | 18.29 S | 48.24 E |
| Fiery Creek ≃, Austl. | **166** | 18.23 S | 139.52 E |
| Fiery Creek ≃, Austl. | **169** | 37.44 S | 142.56 E |
| Fiery Range ⋏ | **171b** | 35.30 S | 148.40 E |
| Fierzës, Liqeni i ⊜[1] | **38** | 42.10 N | 20.15 E |
| Fiesch | **58** | 46.20 N | 8.10 E |
| Fiesole | **66** | 43.48 N | 11.17 E |
| Fiesso d'Artico | **64** | 45.24 N | 12.02 E |
| Fiesso Umbertiano | **64** | 44.56 N | 11.36 E |
| Fife | **224** | 47.14 N | 122.22 W |
| Fife □[4] | **46** | 56.13 N | 3.02 W |
| Fife Lake, Sk., Can. | **184** | 49.12 N | 105.43 W |
| Fife Lake, Mi., U.S. | **190** | 44.34 N | 85.21 W |
| Fife Lake ⊜ | **184** | 49.14 N | 105.53 W |
| Fife Ness › | **46** | 56.17 N | 2.36 W |
| Fifield | **190** | 45.52 N | 90.25 W |
| Fifteenmile Creek ≃, Or., U.S. | **224** | 45.37 N | 121.07 W |
| Fifteenmile Creek ≃, Tx., U.S. | **222** | 28.51 N | 97.14 W |
| Fifteenmile Creek ≃, Wy., U.S. | **202** | 44.01 N | 108.01 W |
| Fifth Cataract → Khāmis, Ash-Shallāl al- ˪ | **140** | 18.23 N | 33.47 E |
| Fifth Depot Lake ⊜ | **212** | 44.36 N | 76.52 W |
| Figeac | **32** | 44.37 N | 2.02 E |
| Figeholm | **26** | 57.22 N | 16.33 E |
| Fig Garden | **226** | 36.48 N | 119.47 W |
| Fighting Island I | **281** | 42.13 N | 83.07 W |
| Figline Valdarno | **66** | 43.37 N | 11.28 E |
| Figtree | **154** | 20.24 S | 28.21 E |
| Figueira → Governador Valadares, Bra. | **255** | 18.51 S | 41.56 W |
| Figueira, Bra. | **287a** | 22.42 S | 43.27 W |
| Figueira, Cachoeira ˪ | **250** | 9.49 S | 58.13 W |
| Figueira da Foz | **34** | 40.09 N | 8.52 W |
| Figueres | **34** | 42.16 N | 2.58 E |
| Figuig | **148** | 32.10 N | 1.15 W |
| Figuig □[4] | **148** | 32.40 N | 2.15 W |
| Fihaonana | **157b** | 18.36 S | 47.12 E |
| Fiherenana ≃ | **157b** | 23.19 S | 43.37 E |
| Fiji □[1], Oc. | **14** | 18.00 S | 178.00 E |
| Fiji □[1], Oc. | **175g** | 18.00 S | 178.00 E |
| Fiji Islands II | **14** | 18.00 S | 178.00 E |
| Fijnaart | **52** | 51.37 N | 4.31 E |
| Fik | **144** | 8.10 N | 42.18 E |
| Fika | **146** | 11.17 N | 11.18 E |
| Fiktūriyā, Bi'r ⊤[4] | **142** | 30.24 N | 30.36 E |
| Filabusi | **154** | 20.34 S | 29.20 E |
| Filadélfia, Bra. | **250** | 7.21 S | 47.30 W |
| Filadelfia, C.R. | **236** | 10.26 N | 85.34 W |
| Filadelfia, It. | **68** | 38.48 N | 16.18 E |
| Filadelfia → Philadelphia, Pa., U.S. | **208** | 39.57 N | 75.07 W |
| Fil'akovo | **30** | 48.17 N | 19.51 E |
| Filandari | **68** | 38.37 N | 16.02 E |
| Filatova Gora | **76** | 57.40 N | 28.10 E |
| Filchner Ice Shelf ⊓ | **9** | 79.00 S | 40.00 W |
| Filderstadt | **56** | 48.41 N | 9.13 E |
| File Lake ⊜ | **184** | 54.53 N | 100.20 W |
| Filettino | **66** | 41.53 N | 13.19 E |
| Filey | **44** | 54.12 N | 0.17 W |
| Filey Bay c | **44** | 54.12 N | 0.16 W |
| Fili -•-[8] | **265b** | 55.45 N | 37.31 E |
| Filí ⊥ | **38** | 38.06 N | 23.40 E |
| Filiano | **68** | 40.49 N | 15.42 E |
| Filiași | **38** | 44.33 N | 23.31 E |
| Filiatrá | **38** | 37.10 N | 21.35 E |
| Filicudi, Isola I | **70** | 38.34 N | 14.34 E |
| Filimonovo | **86** | 56.12 N | 95.28 E |
| Filingué | **150** | 14.21 N | 3.19 E |
| Filipinas → Philippines □[1] | **116** | 13.00 N | 122.00 E |
| Filipinas, Mar de → Philippine Sea ⊤[2] | **14** | 20.00 N | 135.00 E |
| Filipino Cemetery and Memorial -•- | **269f** | 14.31 N | 121.02 E |
| Fílippoi ⊥ | **38** | 41.00 N | 24.16 E |
| Filippovka | **80** | 53.59 N | 49.46 E |
| Filippovo | **80** | 58.18 N | 50.30 E |
| Filippovskoje, Ross. | **82** | 56.06 N | 38.37 E |
| Filippovskoje, Ross. | **82** | 56.48 N | 39.07 E |
| Filipstad | **40** | 59.43 N | 14.10 E |
| Filisola | **234** | 17.50 N | 94.19 W |
| Fillmore, Sk., Can. | **184** | 49.50 N | 103.25 W |
| Fillmore, Ca., U.S. | **228** | 34.23 N | 118.55 W |
| Fillmore, Il., U.S. | **219** | 39.07 N | 89.17 W |
| Fillmore, N.Y., U.S. | **210** | 42.27 N | 78.06 W |
| Fillmore, Ut., U.S. | **200** | 38.58 N | 112.19 W |
| Fillmore Glen State Park ♦ | **210** | 42.42 N | 76.20 W |
| Filogaso | **68** | 38.41 N | 16.14 E |
| Filomeno Mata | **234** | 20.12 N | 97.42 W |
| Filonovskaja | **80** | 50.34 N | 42.46 E |
| Filottrano | **66** | 43.26 N | 13.21 E |
| Fils ≃ | **56** | 48.42 N | 9.25 E |
| Filskov | **41** | 55.48 N | 9.02 E |
| Filton | **42** | 51.31 N | 2.35 W |
| Filtu | **144** | 5.07 N | 40.39 E |
| Filzbach | **58** | 47.07 N | 9.08 E |
| Fimi ≃ | **152** | 3.01 S | 16.58 E |
| Fina, Réserve de -•-[4] | **150** | 12.50 N | 8.30 W |
| Finale Emilia | **64** | 44.50 N | 11.17 E |
| Finale Ligure | **62** | 44.10 N | 8.20 E |
| Finarwa | **144** | 13.06 N | 39.01 E |
| Fincastle | **192** | 37.29 N | 79.52 W |
| Finch | **206** | 45.11 N | 75.07 W |
| Fincham | **42** | 52.37 N | 0.30 E |
| Finchley -•-[8] | **260** | 51.36 N | 0.10 W |
| Finderne | **276** | 40.34 N | 74.35 W |
| Findhorn | **46** | 57.39 N | 3.36 W |
| Findhorn ≃ | **46** | 57.38 N | 3.38 W |
| Fındık | **130** | 37.31 N | 41.58 E |
| Findlay, Il., U.S. | **219** | 39.31 N | 88.45 W |
| Findlay, Oh., U.S. | **216** | 41.02 N | 83.39 W |
| Findlay, Mount ∧ | **182** | 50.04 N | 116.28 W |
| Findley Lake | **214** | 42.07 N | 79.44 W |
| Findley Lake ⊜ | **214** | 42.06 N | 79.43 W |
| Findochty | **46** | 57.41 N | 2.54 W |
| Fine Arts, Museum of ʊ | **283** | 42.20 N | 71.06 W |
| Finedon | **42** | 52.20 N | 0.39 W |
| Finejevo | **82** | 56.02 N | 38.53 E |
| Finesville | **210** | 40.36 N | 75.10 W |
| Fingal, On., Can. | **214** | 42.43 N | 81.19 W |
| Fingal, N.D., U.S. | **198** | 46.45 N | 97.47 W |
| Finger Lake ⊜ | **184** | 53.09 N | 93.30 W |
| Fíngoè | **154** | 15.12 S | 31.50 E |
| Finike | **130** | 36.18 N | 30.09 E |
| Finike Körfezi c | **130** | 36.17 N | 30.16 E |
| Finisk ≃ | **48** | 52.07 N | 7.50 W |
| Finistère □[5] | **32** | 48.20 N | 4.00 W |
| Finisterre | **196** | 25.59 N | 103.15 W |
| Finisterre → Land's End › | **42** | 50.03 N | 5.44 W |
| Finisterre Range ⋏ | **164** | 5.50 S | 146.05 E |
| Finja | **41** | 56.10 N | 13.41 E |
| Finjasjön ⊜ | **41** | 56.08 N | 13.42 E |
| Finke | **162** | 25.34 S | 134.35 E |
| Finke ≃ | **162** | 26.20 S | 136.00 E |
| Finke, Mount ∧[2] | **162** | 30.55 S | 134.02 E |
| Finke Gorge National Park ♦ | **162** | 24.15 S | 132.50 E |
| Finkenkrug | **264a** | 52.34 N | 13.03 E |
| Finkenwerder -•-[8] | **52** | 53.31 N | 9.52 E |
| Finksburg | **208** | 39.29 N | 76.53 W |
| Finland (Suomi) □[1], Europe | **22** | 64.00 N | 26.00 E |
| Finland (Suomi) □[1], Europe | **24** | 64.00 N | 26.00 E |
| Finland, Gulf of (Suomenlahti) (Finskij zaliv) c | **26** | 60.00 N | 27.00 E |
| Finlande → Finland □[1] | **24** | 64.00 N | 26.00 E |
| Finlandia → Finland □[1] | **24** | 64.00 N | 26.00 E |
| Finlandia, Golfo de → Finland, Gulf of c | **26** | 60.00 N | 27.00 E |
| Finland Station -•-[5] | **265a** | 59.57 N | 30.22 E |
| Finlas, Loch ⊜ | **44** | 55.15 N | 4.25 W |
| Finlay ≃ | **176** | 56.54 N | 124.57 W |
| Finley, Austl. | **166** | 35.39 S | 145.35 E |
| Finley, N.D., U.S. | **198** | 47.30 N | 97.50 W |
| Finley Creek ≃ | **194** | 36.58 N | 93.22 W |
| Finleyville, Pa., U.S. | **214** | 40.15 N | 80.00 W |
| Finleyville, Pa., U.S. | **214** | 40.09 N | 78.11 W |
| Finleyville Airport ⊠ | **279b** | 40.15 N | 80.01 W |
| Finmoore | **182** | 53.59 N | 123.37 W |
| Finn ≃ | **48** | 54.50 N | 7.29 W |
| Finne -•-[1] | **54** | 51.13 N | 11.19 E |
| Finnegan | **182** | 51.07 N | 112.04 W |
| Finnentrop | **56** | 51.09 N | 7.58 E |
| Finnerödja | **40** | 58.56 N | 14.26 E |
| Finney Creek ≃ | **224** | 48.31 N | 121.51 W |
| Finnhamn | **40** | 59.28 N | 18.50 E |
| Finnigan, Mount ∧ | **164** | 15.49 S | 145.17 E |
| Finnis, Cape › | **162** | 33.38 S | 134.51 E |
| Finnischer Meerbusen → Finland, Gulf of c | **26** | 60.00 N | 27.00 E |
| Finniss | **168b** | 35.24 S | 138.49 E |
| Finniss ≃ | **168b** | 35.30 S | 138.53 E |
| Finnland → Finland □[1] | **24** | 64.00 N | 26.00 E |
| Finnmark □[6] | **24** | 70.00 N | 25.00 E |
| Finn Mountain ∧ | **180** | 60.37 N | 157.11 W |
| Finno ∧[2] | **154** | 3.27 N | 41.32 E |
| Finnskogen -•-[3] | **26** | 60.40 N | 12.40 E |
| Finnsnes | **24** | 69.14 N | 17.59 E |
| Finocchio -•-[8] | **267a** | 41.53 N | 12.41 E |
| Finow | **54** | 52.50 N | 13.43 E |
| Finowfurt | **54** | 52.51 N | 13.41 E |
| Finowkanal ≖ | **54** | 52.51 N | 13.24 E |
| Fins, Fr. | **50** | 50.02 N | 3.03 E |
| Fins, 'Umān | **128** | 22.56 N | 59.13 E |
| Finsbury | **273d** | 26.13 S | 27.39 E |
| Finschhafen | **164** | 6.35 S | 147.50 E |
| Finse | **26** | 60.36 N | 7.30 E |
| Finskij zaliv → Finland, Gulf of c | **26** | 60.00 N | 27.00 E |
| Finspång | **40** | 58.43 N | 15.47 E |
| Finsta | **40** | 59.44 N | 18.30 E |
| Finsteraarhorn ∧ | **58** | 46.32 N | 8.08 E |
| Finsterwalde | **54** | 51.38 N | 13.42 E |
| Finsterwolde | **52** | 53.12 N | 7.04 E |
| Fintel | **52** | 53.10 N | 9.40 E |
| Fintona | **48** | 54.30 N | 7.19 W |
| Fintown | **48** | 54.52 N | 8.08 W |
| Finvoy | **48** | 55.00 N | 6.30 W |
| Fionn Loch ⊜ | **46** | 57.46 N | 5.29 W |
| Fiora ≃ | **66** | 42.20 N | 11.34 E |
| Fiorano Modenese | **64** | 44.32 N | 10.49 E |
| Fiordland National Park ♦ | **172** | 45.30 S | 167.20 E |
| Fiorenzuola d'Arda | **62** | 44.56 N | 9.55 E |
| Fiorenzuola di Focara | **66** | 43.57 N | 12.48 E |
| Fiorito -•-[8] | **288** | 34.42 S | 58.27 W |
| Fīq | **132** | 32.47 N | 35.42 E |
| Fırat → Euphrates ≃ | **128** | 31.00 N | 47.25 E |
| Firavitoba | **246** | 5.40 N | 73.00 W |
| Fircrest | **224** | 47.14 N | 122.30 W |
| Fire ≃ | **190** | 48.52 N | 83.21 W |
| Firebaugh | **226** | 36.51 N | 120.27 W |
| Firebrick | **218** | 38.41 N | 83.03 W |
| Fire Island I | **210** | 40.42 N | 73.00 W |
| Fire Island Inlet c | **276** | 40.38 N | 73.16 W |
| Fire Island National Seashore ♦ | **188** | 40.38 N | 73.08 W |
| Fire Island Pines | **276** | 40.40 N | 73.04 W |
| Fire Islands II | **276** | 40.40 N | 73.11 W |
| Firenze (Florence) | **66** | 43.46 N | 11.15 E |
| Firenze □[4] | **66** | 43.50 N | 11.20 E |
| Firenzuola | **66** | 44.07 N | 11.23 E |
| Firesteel Creek ≃ | **198** | 43.43 N | 97.58 W |
| Firgrove | **262** | 53.37 N | 2.08 W |
| Firmat | **252** | 33.27 S | 61.29 W |
| Firminópolis | **255** | 16.40 S | 50.19 W |
| Firminy | **62** | 45.23 N | 4.18 E |
| Firmo | **68** | 39.43 N | 16.10 E |
| Firovo | **76** | 57.29 N | 33.40 E |
| Fīrozābād | **124** | 27.09 N | 78.25 E |
| Fīrozpur | **123** | 30.55 N | 74.36 E |
| Fīrozpur Jhirka | **124** | 27.48 N | 76.57 E |
| Firsanovka | **265b** | 55.57 N | 37.15 E |
| Firsovo | **88** | 52.20 N | 118.06 E |
| First Broad ≃ | **192** | 35.11 N | 81.37 W |
| First Cataract → Awwal, Ash-Shallāl al- ˪ | **140** | 24.01 N | 32.52 E |
| First Cliff ⊥[4] | **283** | 42.12 N | 70.43 W |
| First Connecticut Lake ⊜ | **206** | 45.05 N | 71.15 W |
| First Han-gang Bridge -•-[5] | **271b** | 37.32 N | 126.56 E |
| First Herring Brook ≃ | **283** | 42.11 N | 70.45 W |
| First Watchung Mountain ∧ | **276** | 40.55 N | 74.10 W |
| Firth | **198** | 40.31 N | 96.36 W |
| Firth ≃ | **180** | 69.32 N | 139.22 W |
| Fir'uza | **128** | 37.56 N | 58.04 E |
| Fīrūzābād | **128** | 28.50 N | 52.36 E |
| Fīrūz Kūh | **128** | 35.45 N | 52.47 E |
| Fischa ≃ | **61** | 48.07 N | 16.41 E |
| Fischach | **58** | 48.17 N | 10.39 E |
| Fischamend | **61** | 48.07 N | 16.37 E |
| Fischbach, Dtsch. | **56** | 49.44 N | 7.23 E |
| Fischbach, Dtsch. | **60** | 49.25 N | 11.12 E |
| Fischbachau | **64** | 47.43 N | 11.57 E |
| Fischbacher Alpen ⋏ | **61** | 47.28 N | 15.30 E |
| Fischbeck, Dtsch. | **52** | 52.09 N | 9.17 E |
| Fischbeck, Dtsch. | **54** | 52.32 N | 12.01 E |
| Fischeln -•-[8] | **263** | 51.18 N | 6.35 E |
| Fischen | **58** | 47.28 N | 10.16 E |
| Fischhausen → Primorsk | **76** | 54.44 N | 20.01 E |
| Fischland ⊥[2] | **54** | 54.22 N | 12.25 E |
| Fish ≃, Austl. | **170** | 33.29 S | 149.37 E |
| Fish (Vis) ≃, Namibia | **156** | 28.07 S | 17.45 E |
| Fish ≃, Al., U.S. | **194** | 30.25 N | 87.50 W |
| Fish ≃, Me., U.S. | **186** | 47.15 N | 68.36 W |
| Fishbourne | **42** | 50.44 N | 1.12 W |
| Fish Brook ≃, Ma., U.S. | **283** | 42.38 N | 70.58 W |
| Fish Brook ≃, Ma., U.S. | **283** | 42.42 N | 71.13 W |
| Fish Camp | **226** | 37.29 N | 119.38 W |
| Fish Canyon V | **280** | 34.11 N | 117.55 W |
| Fish Creek ≃, On., Can. | **212** | 43.13 N | 81.13 W |
| Fish Creek ≃, U.S. | **216** | 41.28 N | 84.45 W |
| Fish Creek ≃, Mi., U.S. | **190** | 43.04 N | 84.51 W |
| Fish Creek ≃, Mt., U.S. | **202** | 46.17 N | 109.13 W |
| Fish Creek ≃, N.Y., U.S. | **212** | 43.12 N | 75.43 W |
| Fish Creek ≃, Or., U.S. | **224** | 45.09 N | 122.09 W |
| Fish Creek, East Branch ≃ | **212** | 43.16 N | 75.38 W |
| Fish Creek, West Branch ≃ | **212** | 43.16 N | 75.38 W |
| Fish Creek Mountain ∧ | **224** | 45.05 N | 122.08 W |
| Fisheating Creek ≃ | **220** | 26.57 N | 81.07 W |
| Fisher, Austl. | **162** | 30.33 S | 130.58 E |
| Fisher, Ar., U.S. | **194** | 35.29 N | 90.58 W |
| Fisher, Il., U.S. | **216** | 40.18 N | 88.21 W |
| Fisher, La., U.S. | **194** | 31.29 N | 93.27 W |
| Fisher, Pa., U.S. | **214** | 41.16 N | 79.15 W |
| Fisher ≃, Mb., Can. | **184** | 51.26 N | 97.18 W |
| Fisher ≃, Mt., U.S. | **202** | 48.22 N | 115.19 W |
| Fisher Bay c, Mb., Can. | **184** | 51.30 N | 97.16 W |
| Fisher Bay c, Mi., U.S. | **281** | 42.36 N | 82.39 W |
| Fisher Branch | **184** | 51.05 N | 97.37 W |
| Fisher Channel Ʉ | **182** | 52.10 N | 127.42 W |
| Fisher Heights | **279b** | 40.10 N | 79.54 W |
| Fishermans Island I | **208** | 37.06 N | 75.58 W |
| Fisherman's Wharf ⊥ | **282** | 37.48 N | 122.25 W |
| Fisher Peak ∧ | **192** | 36.33 N | 80.50 W |
| Fisher River Indian Reserve -•-[4] | **184** | 51.26 N | 97.20 W |
| Fishers, In., U.S. | **218** | 39.57 N | 86.00 W |
| Fishers, N.Y., U.S. | **210** | 43.00 N | 77.28 W |
| Fishers Island I | **207** | 41.16 N | 72.02 W |
| Fishers Peak ∧ | **196** | 37.06 N | 104.28 W |
| Fisher Strait Ʉ | **176** | 63.15 N | 83.30 W |
| Fishertown | **214** | 40.08 N | 78.35 W |
| Fisherville | **275b** | 43.47 N | 79.28 W |
| Fishguard | **42** | 51.59 N | 4.59 W |
| Fishhook | **219** | 39.48 N | 90.53 W |
| Fish House | **210** | 43.08 N | 74.08 W |
| Fishing Bay c | **208** | 38.18 N | 76.01 W |
| Fishing Creek | **208** | 38.20 N | 76.14 W |
| Fishing Creek ≃, Ky., U.S. | **192** | 37.06 N | 84.41 W |
| Fishing Creek ≃, N.C., U.S. | **192** | 35.57 N | 77.31 W |
| Fishing Creek ≃, Pa., U.S. | **210** | 41.07 N | 77.29 W |
| Fishing Creek ≃, Pa., U.S. | **210** | 40.58 N | 76.28 W |
| Fishing Creek ≃, S.C., U.S. | **192** | 34.36 N | 80.54 W |
| Fishing Islands II | **212** | 44.45 N | 81.20 W |
| Fishing Lake ⊜, Mb., Can. | **184** | 52.07 N | 95.25 W |
| Fishing Lake ⊜, Sk., Can. | **184** | 51.50 N | 103.32 W |
| Fishkill | **210** | 41.32 N | 73.53 W |
| Fishkill Creek ≃ | **210** | 41.29 N | 73.59 W |
| Fish Lake | **216** | 41.34 N | 86.33 W |
| Fish Lake ⊜, On., Can. | **212** | 44.06 N | 77.11 W |
| Fish Lake ⊜, Mi., U.S. | **216** | 42.03 N | 85.52 W |
| Fish Lake ⊜, Wa., U.S. | **224** | 47.50 N | 120.42 W |
| Fishmoor Reservoir ⊜[1] | **262** | 53.44 N | 2.28 W |
| Fish Point › | **214** | 41.43 N | 82.40 W |
| Fishpool | **262** | 53.35 N | 2.17 W |
| Fish River | **166** | 17.55 S | 137.45 E |
| Fishs Eddy | **210** | 41.58 N | 75.10 W |
| Fisk | **194** | 36.46 N | 90.12 W |
| Fiskárdhon | **38** | 38.27 N | 20.35 E |
| Fiskdale | **207** | 42.06 N | 72.06 W |
| Fiskebäckskil | **26** | 58.15 N | 11.27 E |
| Fismes | **50** | 49.18 N | 3.41 E |
| Fišt, gora ∧ | **84** | 43.58 N | 39.54 E |
| Fisterra, Cabo de › | **34** | 42.53 N | 9.16 W |
| Fitchburg, Ma., U.S. | **207** | 42.35 N | 71.48 W |
| Fitchburg, Wi., U.S. | **216** | 42.57 N | 89.28 W |
| Fitchville, Ct., U.S. | **207** | 41.33 N | 72.09 W |
| Fitchville, Oh., U.S. | **214** | 41.06 N | 82.29 W |
| Fitful Head › | **46a** | 59.54 N | 1.23 W |
| Fitiuta | **174y** | 14.13 S | 169.27 W |
| Fito, Mount ∧ | **175a** | 13.55 S | 171.44 W |


**Symbols** in the index entries represent the broad categories identified in the key at the right. Symbols with superior numbers (⋏[1]) identify subcategories (see complete key on page *I · 1).*

**Symbole** im Register stellen die rechts im Schlüssel erklärten Kategorien dar. Symbole mit hochgestellten Ziffern (⋏[1]) bezeichnen Unterabteilungen einer Kategorie (vgl. vollständiger Schlüssel auf Seite *I · 1).*

**Los símbolos** incluídos en el texto del índice representan las grandes categorías identificadas con la clave a la derecha. Los símbolos con numeros en su parte superior (⋏[1]) identifican las subcategorías (véase la clave completa en la página *I · 1).*

**Les symboles** de l'index représentent les catégories indiquées dans la légende à droite. Les symboles suivis d'un indice (⋏[1]) représentent des sous-catégories (voir légende complète à la page *I · 1).*

**Os símbolos** incluídos no texto do índice representam as grandes categorias identificadas com a chave à direita. Os símbolos com números em sua parte superior (⋏[1]) identificam as subcategorias (veja-se a chave completa à página *I · 1).*

| ENGLISH | DEUTSCH | | | |
|---|---|---|---|---|
| ∧ Mountain | Berg | Montaña | Montagne | Montanha |
| ⋏ Mountains | Gebirge | Montañas | Montagnes | Montanhas |
| )( Pass | Paß | Paso | Col | Passo |
| V Valley, Canyon | Tal, Cañon | Valle, Cañón | Vallée, Canyon | Vale, Canhão |
| ≃ Plain | Ebene | Llano | Plaine | Planície |
| › Cape | Kap | Cabo | Cap | Cabo |
| I Island | Insel | Isla | Île | Ilha |
| II Islands | Inseln | Islas | Îles | Ilhas |
| ⊥ Other Topographic Features | Andere Topographische Objekte | Otros Elementos Topográficos | Autres données topographiques | Outros acidentes topográficos |

**ESPAÑOL**

| Nombre | Página | Lat.°′ | Long.°′ W = Oeste |
|---|---|---|---|
| Fitri, Lac ⊜ | 146 | 12.50 N | 17.28 E |
| Fittja | 40 | 59.15 N | 17.52 E |
| Fittleworth | 42 | 50.58 N | 0.35 W |
| Fitzgerald | 192 | 31.42 N | 83.15 W |
| Fitzgerald River National Park ♦ | 162 | 34.00 S | 119.30 E |
| Fitz Henry | 279b | 40.10 N | 79.45 W |
| Fitz Hugh Sound Ʉ | 182 | 51.40 N | 127.57 W |
| Fitzmaurice ≏ | 164 | 14.50 S | 129.44 E |
| Fitz Roy, Arg. | 254 | 47.02 S | 67.15 W |
| Fitzroy, Austl. | 274b | 37.48 S | 144.59 E |
| Fitzroy ≏, Austl. | 162 | 17.31 S | 123.35 E |
| Fitzroy ≏, Austl. | 166 | 23.32 S | 150.52 E |
| Fitzroy, Monte (Cerro Chaltel) ∧ | 254 | 49.17 S | 73.05 W |
| Fitzroy Crossing | 162 | 18.11 S | 125.35 E |
| Fitzroy Falls Reservoir ⊜[1] | 170 | 34.38 S | 150.30 E |
| Fitzroy Island I | 166 | 16.56 S | 146.00 E |
| Fitzwilliam | 207 | 42.46 N | 72.08 W |
| Fitzwilliam Island I | 190 | 45.30 N | 81.45 W |
| Fiuggi | 66 | 41.48 N | 13.13 E |
| Fiumalbo | 64 | 44.11 N | 10.39 E |
| Fiume → Rijeka | 36 | 45.20 N | 14.27 E |
| Fiumedinisi | 70 | 38.02 N | 15.23 E |
| Fiumefreddo Bruzio | 68 | 39.14 N | 16.04 E |
| Fiumefreddo di Sicilia | 70 | 37.47 N | 15.12 E |
| Fiumesino | 66 | 43.38 N | 13.22 E |
| Fiume Veneto | 64 | 45.56 N | 12.44 E |
| Fiumicino ⬥[8] | 66 | 41.46 N | 12.14 E |
| Five Corners | 283 | 42.01 N | 71.07 W |
| Five Cowrie Creek ≏[1] | 273a | 6.27 N | 3.27 E |
| Five Dock | 274a | 33.52 S | 151.08 E |
| Five Forks | 284c | 38.47 N | 77.16 W |
| Five Islands | 186 | 45.25 N | 64.02 W |
| Five Islands Harbour C | 240c | 17.06 N | 61.54 W |
| Fivemile ≏ | 276 | 41.03 N | 73.27 W |
| Fivemile Creek ≏, N.Y., U.S. | 210 | 42.22 N | 77.22 W |
| Fivemile Creek ≏, Or., U.S. | 224 | 45.36 N | 121.05 W |
| Fivemile Creek ≏, Wy., U.S. | 202 | 43.14 N | 108.12 W |
| Fivemile Point | 210 | 42.06 N | 75.48 W |
| Fivemiletown | 48 | 54.23 N | 7.18 W |
| Five Penny Borve | 46 | 58.25 N | 6.25 W |
| Five Points, Ca., U.S. | 226 | 36.26 N | 120.06 W |
| Five Points, In., U.S. | 218 | 39.35 N | 86.20 W |
| Five Points, N.M., U.S. | 200 | 35.03 N | 106.39 W |
| Five Points, Oh., U.S. | 218 | 39.41 N | 83.12 W |
| Five Points, Pa., U.S. | 214 | 40.34 N | 80.15 W |
| Five Points, Pa., U.S. | 285 | 39.50 N | 75.42 W |
| Fivizzano | 64 | 44.14 N | 10.08 E |
| Fiwila Mission | 154 | 13.58 S | 29.36 E |
| Fixin | 58 | 47.15 N | 4.58 E |
| Fix-Saint-Geneys | 62 | 45.08 N | 3.40 E |
| Fizi | 154 | 4.18 S | 28.57 E |
| Fjællebroen | 41 | 55.03 N | 10.24 E |
| Fjærlandsfjorden C[2] | 26 | 61.17 N | 6.40 E |
| Fjällåsen | 24 | 67.29 N | 20.10 E |
| Fjällbacka | 26 | 58.36 N | 11.17 E |
| Fjällsjöälven ≏ | 26 | 63.29 N | 16.50 E |
| Fjärdhundra | 40 | 59.47 N | 16.56 E |
| Fjärdhundra □[9] | 40 | 59.47 N | 16.55 E |
| Fjenneslev | 41 | 55.26 N | 11.40 E |
| Fjerritslev | 26 | 57.05 N | 9.16 E |
| Fjugesta | 40 | 59.10 N | 14.52 E |
| Fkih-Ben-Salah | 148 | 32.32 N | 6.40 W |
| Flacksta | 40 | 59.23 N | 16.27 E |
| Fladnitz im Raabtal | 61 | 46.59 N | 15.47 E |
| Fladså ≏ | 41 | 55.19 N | 8.54 E |
| Fladungen | 56 | 50.31 N | 10.08 E |
| Flag Creek ≏ | 278 | 41.43 N | 87.55 W |
| Flagler | 198 | 39.17 N | 103.04 W |
| Flagler Beach | 192 | 29.28 N | 81.07 W |
| Flagstaff, S. Afr. | 158 | 31.05 S | 29.29 E |
| Flagstaff, Az., U.S. | 200 | 35.11 N | 111.39 W |
| Flagstaff Lake ⊜[1] | 188 | 45.10 N | 70.15 W |
| Flagtown | 276 | 40.31 N | 74.41 W |
| Flaken-See ⊜ | 264a | 52.25 N | 13.46 E |
| Flåm | 26 | 60.50 N | 7.07 E |
| Flambeau ≏ | 190 | 45.18 N | 91.15 W |
| Flambeau, South Fork ≏ | 190 | 45.39 N | 90.48 W |
| Flamborough, On., Can. | 212 | 43.20 N | 79.53 W |
| Flamborough, Eng., U.K. | 44 | 54.06 N | 0.07 W |
| Flamborough Head › | 44 | 54.07 N | 0.04 W |
| Fläming ⬥[1] | 54 | 52.00 N | 12.30 E |
| Flaming Gorge National Recreation Area ♦ | 200 | 41.30 N | 109.30 W |
| Flaming Gorge Reservoir ⊜[1] | 200 | 41.15 N | 109.30 W |
| Flamingo | 220 | 25.09 N | 80.56 W |
| Flamingo, Teluk C | 164 | 5.33 S | 138.00 E |
| Flanagan | 216 | 40.52 N | 88.51 W |
| Flanagan ≏ | 184 | 52.50 N | 93.28 W |
| Flanagan Passage Ʉ | 240m | 18.18 N | 64.39 W |
| Flanders, On., Can. | 190 | 48.44 N | 92.05 W |
| Flanders, N.J., U.S. | 276 | 40.50 N | 74.41 W |
| Flanders, N.Y., U.S. | 207 | 40.49 N | 72.36 W |
| Flanders (Flandre) □[9] | 50 | 51.00 N | 3.00 E |
| Flanders Airport ⊠ | 276 | 40.50 N | 74.41 W |
| Flandes | 246 | 4.18 N | 74.49 W |
| Flandorf | 264b | 48.21 N | 16.23 E |
| Flandre → Flanders □[9] | 50 | 51.00 N | 3.00 E |
| Flandreau | 198 | 44.02 N | 96.35 W |
| Flannan Islands II | 46 | 58.18 N | 7.36 W |
| Flåren ⊜ | 26 | 57.02 N | 14.06 E |
| Flasher | 198 | 46.27 N | 101.13 W |
| Flåsjön ⊜ | 26 | 64.06 N | 15.51 E |
| Flat, Ak., U.S. | 180 | 62.27 N | 158.01 W |
| Flat, Tx., U.S. | 222 | 31.19 N | 97.38 W |
| Flat ≏, N.T., Can. | 180 | 61.33 N | 125.18 W |
| Flat ≏, Mi., U.S. | 190 | 42.56 N | 85.20 W |
| Flat ≏, N.C., U.S. | 192 | 36.05 N | 78.49 W |
| Flat Bay | 186 | 48.24 N | 58.36 W |
| Flat Branch ≏ | 219 | 39.33 N | 89.16 W |
| Flatbush ⬥[8] | 276 | 40.39 N | 73.56 W |
| Flat Creek ≏, Ky., U.S. | 218 | 38.17 N | 83.48 W |
| Flat Creek ≏, Mo., U.S. | 194 | 36.45 N | 93.31 W |
| Flat Creek ≏, Mt., U.S. | 202 | 47.43 N | 109.50 W |
| Flat Creek ≏, N.J., U.S. | 276 | 40.27 N | 74.10 W |
| Flatey | 24a | 65.19 N | 23.07 W |
| Flateyri | 24a | 65.59 N | 23.42 W |
| Flathead ≏ | 202 | 47.22 N | 114.47 W |
| Flathead, Middle Fork ≏ | 202 | 48.28 N | 114.04 W |
| Flathead, North Fork ≏ | 202 | 48.28 N | 114.04 W |
| Flathead, South Fork ≏ | 202 | 48.23 N | 114.04 W |
| Flathead Indian Reservation ⬥[4] | 202 | 47.30 N | 114.25 W |
| Flathead Lake ⊜ | 202 | 47.52 N | 114.08 W |
| Flat Holm I | 42 | 51.23 N | 3.08 W |
| Flat Lake ⊜ | 182 | 54.39 N | 112.55 W |
| Flat Lick | 192 | 36.49 N | 83.46 W |
| Flatonia | 222 | 29.41 N | 97.06 W |
| Flatow | 264a | 52.44 N | 12.57 E |
| Flat River, P.E., Can. | 186 | 46.01 N | 62.52 W |
| Flat River, Mo., U.S. | 194 | 37.51 N | 90.31 W |
| Flat River Reservoir ⊜[1] | 207 | 41.42 N | 71.37 W |
| Flat Rock, Al., U.S. | 194 | 34.46 N | 85.42 W |
| Flat Rock, Il., U.S. | 194 | 38.54 N | 87.40 W |
| Flat Rock, In., U.S. | 218 | 39.22 N | 85.50 W |
| Flat Rock, Mi., U.S. | 216 | 42.05 N | 83.17 W |
| Flat Rock, Oh., U.S. | 214 | 41.14 N | 82.51 W |

**FRANÇAIS**

| Nom | Page | Lat.°′ | Long.°′ W = Ouest |
|---|---|---|---|
| Flatrock ≏ | 218 | 39.12 N | 85.56 W |
| Flatrock Creek ≏ | 216 | 41.10 N | 84.27 W |
| Flatrock Lake ⊜ | 184 | 55.37 N | 100.47 W |
| Flatruet ⋏[2] | 26 | 62.45 N | 12.50 E |
| Flats | 222 | 32.50 N | 95.53 W |
| Flattery, Cape ›, Austl. | 164 | 14.58 S | 145.21 E |
| Flattery, Cape ›, Wa., U.S. | 224 | 48.23 N | 124.43 W |
| Flatts | 240a | 32.19 N | 64.44 W |
| Flatwillow Creek ≏ | 202 | 46.56 N | 107.55 W |
| Flatwood | 194 | 32.27 N | 86.15 W |
| Flatwoods | 188 | 38.31 N | 82.43 W |
| Flaugherty Run ≏ | 279b | 40.33 N | 80.13 W |
| Flaunden | 260 | 51.42 N | 0.32 W |
| Flavigny-sur-Moselle | 58 | 48.34 N | 6.11 E |
| Flavigny-sur-Ozerain | 58 | 47.30 N | 4.32 E |
| Flavy-le-Martel | 50 | 49.43 N | 3.12 E |
| Flawil | 58 | 47.24 N | 9.12 E |
| Flaxcombe | 184 | 51.29 N | 109.36 W |
| Flaxman Island I | 180 | 70.13 N | 146.00 W |
| Flax Pond ⊜, Ma., U.S. | 283 | 42.29 N | 70.57 W |
| Flax Pond ⊜, N.Y., U.S. | 276 | 40.58 N | 73.08 W |
| Flaxton | 198 | 48.53 N | 102.23 W |
| Flaxville | 198 | 48.48 N | 105.10 W |
| Flechas Point › | 116 | 10.22 N | 119.34 E |
| Flechtingen | 54 | 52.20 N | 11.14 E |
| Fleckeby | 41 | 54.29 N | 9.41 E |
| Flecken Zechlin | 54 | 53.09 N | 12.46 E |
| Fleesensee ⊜ | 54 | 53.30 N | 12.29 E |
| Fleet | 42 | 51.16 N | 0.50 W |
| Fleet ≏ | 46 | 57.57 N | 4.05 W |
| Fleetmark | 54 | 52.48 N | 1.23 E |
| Fleets Bay C | 208 | 37.40 N | 76.19 W |
| Fleetville | 210 | 41.36 N | 75.43 W |
| Fleetwing Estates | 285 | 40.07 N | 74.51 W |
| Fleetwood, Eng., U.K. | 44 | 53.56 N | 3.01 W |
| Fleetwood, Pa., U.S. | 208 | 40.27 N | 75.49 W |
| Flehe ⬥[3] | 263 | 51.12 N | 6.47 E |
| Flehingen | 56 | 49.05 N | 8.46 E |
| Fleischmanns | 210 | 42.09 N | 74.31 W |
| Fleischman Village | 284c | 38.51 N | 76.57 W |
| Flekkefjord | 26 | 58.17 N | 6.41 E |
| Fleming, Co., U.S. | 198 | 40.40 N | 102.50 W |
| Fleming, Pa., U.S. | 214 | 40.55 N | 77.52 W |
| Fleming □[6] | 218 | 38.21 N | 83.42 W |
| Fleming Creek ≏, On., Can. | 214 | 42.38 N | 81.47 W |
| Fleming Creek ≏, Ky., U.S. | 218 | 38.22 N | 83.57 W |
| Fleming Creek ≏, Mi., U.S. | 281 | 42.16 N | 83.40 W |
| Fleming-Neon | 192 | 37.11 N | 82.42 W |
| Flemingsburg | 218 | 38.25 N | 83.44 W |
| Flemington, N.J., U.S. | 210 | 40.30 N | 74.51 W |
| Flemington, Pa., U.S. | 210 | 41.07 N | 77.28 W |
| Flemington Racecourse ♦ | 274b | 37.47 S | 144.55 E |
| Flemish Cap ✦[4] | 16 | 47.00 N | 45.00 W |
| Flemsdorf | 54 | 53.02 N | 14.10 E |
| Flen | 40 | 59.04 N | 16.35 E |
| Flensburg | 41 | 54.47 N | 9.26 E |
| Flensburger Förde C | 41 | 54.49 N | 9.45 E |
| Fleres (Boden) | 64 | 46.58 N | 11.21 E |
| Flers | 32 | 48.45 N | 0.34 W |
| Flers-sur-Noye | 50 | 49.44 N | 2.15 E |
| Flesherton | 212 | 44.16 N | 80.33 W |
| Flesko, Tanjung › | 112 | 0.29 N | 124.30 E |
| Flessau | 54 | 52.46 N | 11.40 E |
| Fletcher, On., Can. | 214 | 42.18 N | 82.18 W |
| Fletcher, N.C., U.S. | 192 | 35.25 N | 82.30 W |
| Fletcher, Oh., U.S. | 218 | 40.08 N | 84.06 W |
| Fletcher, Ok., U.S. | 196 | 34.49 N | 98.14 W |
| Fletcher Islands II | 9 | 72.40 S | 94.10 W |
| Fletcher Moss Museum ʊ | 262 | 53.25 N | 2.14 W |
| Fletcher Pond ⊜[1] | 190 | 44.58 N | 83.52 W |
| Fletchers Creek ≏ | 275b | 43.38 N | 79.42 W |
| Fleurance | 32 | 43.50 N | 0.40 E |
| Fleur-de-Lys | 186 | 50.07 N | 56.08 W |
| Fleurier | 58 | 46.54 N | 6.35 E |
| Fleurieu Peninsula ›[1] | 168b | 35.30 S | 138.30 E |
| Fleurus | 56 | 50.29 N | 4.33 E |
| Fleurville | 58 | 46.27 N | 4.53 E |
| Fleury-les-Aubrais | 50 | 47.56 N | 1.55 E |
| Fleury-Mérogis | 261 | 48.38 N | 2.22 E |
| Fleury-sur-Andelle | 50 | 49.22 N | 1.22 E |
| Fleuth ≏ | 263 | 51.32 N | 6.26 E |
| Flevoland □[4] | 52 | 52.30 N | 5.30 E |
| Flexanville | 261 | 48.51 N | 1.44 E |
| Flexenpass )( | 58 | 47.09 N | 10.10 E |
| Fley ⬥[8] | 263 | 51.23 N | 7.30 E |
| Flieden | 56 | 50.25 N | 9.33 E |
| Flierich | 263 | 51.35 N | 7.48 E |
| Flight Locks ʊ[3] | 284a | 43.08 N | 79.12 W |
| Flimby | 44 | 54.41 N | 3.31 W |
| Flims | 58 | 46.50 N | 9.17 E |
| Flinders | 169 | 38.28 S | 145.01 E |
| Flinders ≏ | 166 | 17.36 S | 140.36 E |
| Flinders Bay C | 162 | 34.23 S | 115.19 E |
| Flinders Chase National Park ♦ | 166 | 36.00 S | 136.45 E |
| Flinders Island I, Austl. | 162 | 33.44 S | 134.31 E |
| Flinders Island I, Austl. | 166 | 40.00 S | 148.00 E |
| Flinders Peak ∧ | 171a | 27.49 S | 152.49 E |
| Flinders Peak ∧[2] | 169 | 37.51 S | 144.24 E |
| Flinders Ranges National Park ♦ | 166 | 31.20 S | 138.45 E |
| Flinders Reefs ✦[2] | 166 | 17.37 S | 148.31 E |
| Flinders Street Station ⬥[5] | 274b | 37.49 S | 144.58 E |
| Flinesjön ⊜ | 40 | 60.23 N | 16.06 E |
| Flines-lèz-Râches | 50 | 50.25 N | 3.11 E |
| Flin Flon | 184 | 54.46 N | 101.53 W |
| Flingern ⬥[8] | 263 | 51.14 N | 6.49 E |
| Flins-sur-Seine | 261 | 48.58 N | 1.52 E |
| Flint, Wales, U.K. | 44 | 53.15 N | 3.07 W |
| Flint, Mi., U.S. | 216 | 43.00 N | 83.41 W |
| Flint, Tx., U.S. | 222 | 32.12 N | 95.21 W |
| Flint I | 14 | 11.26 S | 151.48 W |
| Flint ≏, U.S. | 194 | 34.30 N | 86.31 W |
| Flint ≏, Ga., U.S. | 192 | 30.52 N | 84.38 W |
| Flint ≏, Mi., U.S. | 190 | 43.21 N | 84.03 W |
| Flint, South Branch ≏ | 216 | 43.10 N | 83.23 W |
| Flint Castle ⊥ | 262 | 53.16 N | 3.07 W |
| Flint Creek ≏, Al., U.S. | 194 | 34.30 N | 86.57 W |
| Flint Creek ≏, Mt., U.S. | 202 | 46.39 N | 113.08 W |
| Flint Creek ≏, N.Y., U.S. | 210 | 42.57 N | 77.03 W |
| Flint Creek Range ⋏ | 202 | 46.20 N | 113.05 W |
| Flinthill | 219 | 38.53 N | 90.52 W |
| Flint Hills ⋏[2] | 198 | 37.50 N | 96.40 W |
| Flint Lake ⊜, N.T., Can. | 176 | 69.10 N | 74.20 W |
| Flint Lake ⊜, In., U.S. | 216 | 41.31 N | 87.03 W |
| Flinton, Austl. | 166 | 27.54 S | 149.34 E |
| Flinton, Pa., U.S. | 214 | 40.43 N | 78.31 W |
| Flint Peak ∧ | 280 | 34.10 N | 118.12 W |
| Flint Pond ⊜ | 283 | 42.40 N | 71.26 W |
| Flintrännan Ʉ | 41 | 55.34 N | 12.50 E |
| Flintridge | 228 | 34.11 N | 118.11 W |
| Flintsbach | 64 | 47.43 N | 12.08 E |
| Flints Pond ⊜ | 283 | 42.26 N | 71.19 W |
| Flintville | 194 | 35.03 N | 86.25 W |
| Flipper Point › | 174a | 19.18 N | 166.35 E |
| Flippin | 194 | 36.16 N | 92.35 W |
| Flirey | 56 | 48.53 N | 5.50 E |
| Flirsch | 58 | 47.09 N | 10.24 E |
| Flisa | 26 | 60.34 N | 12.06 E |
| Flitwick | 42 | 52.00 N | 0.29 W |
| Flix, Pantà de ⊜[1] | 34 | 41.15 N | 0.25 E |

**PORTUGUÊS**

| Nome | Página | Lat.°′ | Long.°′ W = Oeste |
|---|---|---|---|
| Flixecourt | 50 | 50.01 N | 2.05 E |
| Flize | 56 | 49.42 N | 4.46 E |
| Flobecq (Vloesberg) | 50 | 50.44 N | 3.44 E |
| Floby | 26 | 58.08 N | 13.20 E |
| Floda, Sve. | 26 | 57.48 N | 12.22 E |
| Floda, Sve. | 40 | 59.04 N | 16.21 E |
| Flodden | 44 | 55.38 N | 2.10 W |
| Flodden Field Battlesite ⊥ | 44 | 55.38 N | 2.13 W |
| Flogny | 50 | 47.57 N | 3.52 E |
| Flöha | 54 | 50.51 N | 13.04 E |
| Flöha ≏ | 54 | 50.51 N | 13.04 E |
| Floing | 56 | 49.43 N | 4.56 E |
| Flomaton | 194 | 31.00 N | 87.15 W |
| Flomborn | 56 | 49.41 N | 8.08 E |
| Flomot | 196 | 34.14 N | 100.59 W |
| Floodwood | 190 | 46.55 N | 92.55 W |
| Flora, Il., U.S. | 194 | 38.40 N | 88.29 W |
| Flora, In., U.S. | 216 | 40.32 N | 86.31 W |
| Flora, Ms., U.S. | 194 | 32.32 N | 90.18 W |
| Florac | 32 | 44.19 N | 3.36 E |
| Florala | 194 | 31.00 N | 86.19 W |
| Floral City | 220 | 28.45 N | 82.17 W |
| Floral Park, Mt., U.S. | 202 | 45.57 N | 112.26 W |
| Floral Park, N.Y., U.S. | 210 | 40.43 N | 73.42 W |
| Florange | 56 | 49.20 N | 6.07 E |
| Florânia | 250 | 6.08 S | 36.49 W |
| Flora Vista | 200 | 36.47 N | 108.04 W |
| Flore, Piton ∧ | 241f | 13.58 N | 60.57 W |
| Floreffe | 56 | 50.26 N | 4.45 E |
| Florence → Firenze, It. | 66 | 43.46 N | 11.15 E |
| Florence, Al., U.S. | 194 | 34.47 N | 87.40 W |
| Florence, Az., U.S. | 200 | 33.02 N | 111.23 W |
| Florence, Ca., U.S. | 228 | 33.58 N | 118.14 W |
| Florence, Co., U.S. | 200 | 38.23 N | 105.07 W |
| Florence, Ks., U.S. | 198 | 38.14 N | 96.55 W |
| Florence, Ky., U.S. | 218 | 38.59 N | 84.37 W |
| Florence, N.J., U.S. | 285 | 40.07 N | 74.49 W |
| Florence, Or., U.S. | 202 | 43.58 N | 124.05 W |
| Florence, Pa., U.S. | 214 | 40.26 N | 80.26 W |
| Florence, S.C., U.S. | 192 | 34.11 N | 79.45 W |
| Florence, Tx., U.S. | 222 | 30.51 N | 97.48 W |
| Florence, Wi., U.S. | 190 | 45.55 N | 88.15 W |
| Florencia, Col. | 246 | 1.36 N | 75.36 W |
| Florencia → Firenze, It. | 66 | 43.46 N | 11.15 E |
| Florencio Sánchez | 258 | 33.53 S | 57.24 W |
| Florencio Varela | 258 | 34.49 S | 58.17 W |
| Florencio Varela □[5] | 288 | 34.52 S | 58.15 W |
| Florennes | 56 | 50.15 N | 4.37 E |
| Florentia | 273d | 26.16 S | 28.08 E |
| Florentino Ameghino, Embalse ⊜[1] | 254 | 43.55 S | 66.20 W |
| Florenville | 56 | 49.42 N | 5.18 E |
| Florenz → Firenze | 66 | 43.46 N | 11.15 E |
| Flores | 250 | 7.51 S | 37.59 W |
| Flores □[5] | 258 | 33.48 S | 56.50 W |
| Flores ⬥[8] | 288 | 34.38 S | 58.28 W |
| Flores I, Indon. | 115b | 8.30 S | 121.00 E |
| Flores I, Port. | 148a | 39.26 N | 31.13 W |
| Flores, Laut (Flores Sea) ⍑[2] | 112 | 8.00 S | 120.00 E |
| Flores, Rio das ≏ | 256 | 22.05 S | 43.34 W |
| Flores, Selat Ʉ | 115b | 8.25 S | 122.55 E |
| Flores da Cunha | 252 | 29.02 S | 51.11 W |
| Flores de Goiás | 255 | 14.34 S | 47.04 W |
| Flores Island I | 182 | 49.20 N | 126.10 W |
| Flores Sea → Flores, Laut ⍑[2] | 112 | 8.00 S | 120.00 E |
| Floresta, Bra. | 250 | 8.36 S | 38.34 W |
| Floresta, It. | 70 | 37.59 N | 14.55 E |
| Floresta ⬥[8] | 288 | 34.38 S | 58.29 W |
| Floresta Azul | 255 | 14.51 S | 39.41 W |
| Florestal de Monsanto, Parque ♦ | 266c | 38.43 N | 9.11 W |
| Florești | 38 | 47.53 N | 28.17 E |
| Floresville | 196 | 29.08 N | 98.09 W |
| Florham Park | 210 | 40.47 N | 74.23 W |
| Floriano, Bra. | 250 | 6.47 S | 43.01 W |
| Floriano, Bra. | 256 | 22.27 S | 44.18 W |
| Floriano Peixoto | 248 | 9.03 S | 67.24 W |
| Florianópolis | 252 | 27.35 S | 48.34 W |
| Florida, Col. | 246 | 3.21 N | 76.15 W |
| Florida, Cuba | 240p | 21.32 N | 78.14 W |
| Florida, Hond. | 236 | 15.01 N | 88.50 W |
| Florida, Perú | 248 | 5.50 S | 77.55 W |
| Florida, P.R. | 240m | 18.22 N | 66.34 W |
| Florida, P.R. | 240m | 18.14 N | 65.47 W |
| Florida, S. Afr. | 273d | 26.11 S | 27.55 E |
| Florida, In., U.S. | 218 | 40.10 N | 85.42 W |
| Florida, N.Y., U.S. | 210 | 41.19 N | 74.21 W |
| Florida, Oh., U.S. | 216 | 41.20 N | 84.12 W |
| Florida, Ur. | 258 | 34.06 S | 56.13 W |
| Florida □[5] | 258 | 34.00 S | 56.15 W |
| Florida ⬥[8] | 288 | 34.31 S | 58.30 W |
| Florida □[3], U.S. | 178 | 28.00 N | 82.00 W |
| Florida □[3], U.S. | 192 | 28.00 N | 82.00 W |
| Florida ≏ | 200 | 37.03 N | 107.52 W |
| Florida, Cape › | 220 | 25.40 N | 80.09 W |
| Florida, Straits of Ʉ | 238 | 25.00 N | 79.45 W |
| Florida Bay C | 220 | 25.00 N | 80.45 W |
| Floridablanca | 246 | 7.04 N | 73.06 W |
| Florida Caverns State Park ♦ | 192 | 30.50 N | 85.18 W |
| Florida City | 220 | 25.26 N | 80.28 W |
| Florida Islands II | 175e | 9.00 S | 160.10 E |
| Florida Keys II | 220 | 24.45 N | 81.00 W |
| Florida Lake ⊜[1] | 273d | 26.11 S | 27.54 E |
| Florida Ridge | 220 | 27.35 N | 80.23 W |
| Floridia | 70 | 37.05 N | 15.09 E |
| Florido ≏ | 232 | 27.43 N | 105.10 W |
| Floridsdorf ⬥[8] | 264b | 48.16 N | 16.24 E |
| Floridsdorfer Brücke ⬥[5] | 264b | 48.14 N | 16.23 E |
| Florien | 194 | 31.26 N | 93.27 W |
| Florin | 226 | 38.29 N | 121.24 W |
| Flórina | 38 | 40.47 N | 21.24 E |
| Florisbad | 158 | 28.46 S | 26.06 E |
| Florissant | 219 | 38.47 N | 90.19 W |
| Florissant Fossil Beds National Monument ♦ | 200 | 38.54 N | 105.16 W |
| Floriston | 226 | 39.24 N | 120.01 W |
| Florø | 26 | 61.36 N | 5.00 E |
| Flörsheim | 56 | 50.01 N | 8.26 E |
| Florvåg | 26 | 60.25 N | 5.14 E |
| Flosaille | 62 | 45.39 N | 5.18 E |
| Floss | 60 | 49.44 N | 12.17 E |
| Flossach ≏ | 58 | 48.24 N | 10.25 E |
| Flossenbürg | 60 | 49.44 N | 12.21 E |
| Flossmoor | 216 | 41.32 N | 87.41 W |
| Flotantes, Jardínes ♦ | 286a | 19.16 N | 99.06 W |
| Flöthbach ≏ | 263 | 51.17 N | 6.26 E |
| Flotta I | 46 | 58.50 N | 3.07 W |
| Flotte, Cap de › | 175f | 21.10 S | 167.25 E |
| Flotten Lake ⊜ | 184 | 54.38 N | 108.30 W |
| Flourtown | 285 | 40.06 N | 75.12 W |
| Flower Hill | 276 | 40.48 N | 73.40 W |
| Flower Mound | 222 | 33.02 N | 97.04 W |
| Flower's Cove | 186 | 51.18 N | 56.44 W |
| Flowery Branch | 192 | 34.11 N | 83.55 W |
| Floyd, N.M., U.S. | 196 | 34.13 N | 103.35 W |
| Floyd, Tx., U.S. | 222 | 33.09 N | 96.15 W |
| Floyd, Va., U.S. | 192 | 36.54 N | 80.19 W |
| Floyd □[6] | 218 | 38.18 N | 85.49 W |
| Floyd ≏ | 198 | 42.29 N | 96.23 W |
| Floydada | 196 | 33.59 N | 101.20 W |
| Floyds Fork ≏ | 194 | 38.00 N | 85.41 W |
| Fluchthorn ∧ | 58 | 46.53 N | 10.13 E |
| Flüela Pass )( | 58 | 46.45 N | 9.57 E |
| Flüelen | 58 | 46.54 N | 8.38 E |
| Fluessen ⊜ | 52 | 52.57 N | 5.30 E |
| Flühli | 58 | 46.53 N | 8.01 E |
| Flumen ≏ | 34 | 41.43 N | 0.09 W |
| Flumendosa ≏ | 71 | 39.26 N | 9.37 E |

| | | | |
|---|---|---|---|
| Flumendosa, Lago Alto del ⊜ | 71 | 39.56 N | 9.26 E |
| Flumendosa, Lago del ⊜[1] | 71 | 39.40 N | 9.17 E |
| Flumeri | 68 | 41.05 N | 15.09 E |
| Flumet | 62 | 45.49 N | 6.30 E |
| Fluminimaggiore | 71 | 39.26 N | 8.30 E |
| Flums | 58 | 47.05 N | 9.20 E |
| Flüren | 263 | 51.41 N | 6.33 E |
| Flushing → Vlissingen, Ned. | 52 | 51.26 N | 3.35 E |
| Flushing, Mi., U.S. | 216 | 43.03 N | 83.51 W |
| Flushing, Oh., U.S. | 214 | 40.08 N | 81.03 W |
| Flushing ⬥[8] | 276 | 40.45 N | 73.49 W |
| Flushing Airport ⊠ | 276 | 40.47 N | 73.50 W |
| Flushing Bay C | 276 | 40.47 N | 73.51 W |
| Flushing Meadow-Corona Park ♦ | 276 | 40.45 N | 73.51 W |
| Fluvanna, N.Y., U.S. | 214 | 42.07 N | 79.18 W |
| Fluvanna, Tx., U.S. | 196 | 32.53 N | 101.09 W |
| Fluvià ≏ | 34 | 42.12 N | 3.07 E |
| Fly ≏ | 164 | 8.30 S | 143.41 E |
| Fly Creek | 210 | 42.43 N | 74.59 W |
| Fly Creek ≏ | 202 | 45.59 N | 107.59 W |
| Flyinge | 41 | 55.45 N | 13.21 E |
| Flying Fish Cove | 112 | 10.25 S | 105.43 E |
| Flynn | 222 | 31.09 N | 96.08 W |
| Foam Lake | 184 | 51.39 N | 103.33 W |
| Fobbing | 260 | 51.32 N | 0.29 E |
| Fobello | 62 | 45.53 N | 8.10 E |
| Foča, Bos. | 38 | 43.31 N | 18.46 E |
| Foça, Tür. | 130 | 38.39 N | 26.46 E |
| Focene ⬥[8] | 267a | 41.48 N | 12.14 E |
| Fochabers | 46 | 57.37 N | 3.05 W |
| Fochville | 158 | 26.30 S | 27.30 E |
| Fockbek | 41 | 54.18 N | 9.36 E |
| Focșani | 38 | 45.41 N | 27.11 E |
| Fodda, Oued ≏ | 34 | 36.14 N | 1.33 E |
| Fodé | 152 | 5.29 N | 23.18 E |
| Fodécontea | 150 | 10.50 N | 14.22 W |
| Foding Shan ∧ | 102 | 27.08 N | 108.02 E |
| F'odorovka, Kaz. | 80 | 51.09 N | 51.59 E |
| F'odorovka, Kaz. | 86 | 53.22 N | 76.18 E |
| F'odorovka, Kaz. | 86 | 53.38 N | 62.42 E |
| F'odorovka, Ross. | 80 | 53.28 N | 49.38 E |
| F'odorovka, Ross. | 80 | 52.21 N | 52.55 E |
| F'odorovka, Ross. | 82 | 56.15 N | 37.14 E |
| F'odorovka, Ross. | 83 | 47.20 N | 38.23 E |
| F'odorovka, Ross. | 86 | 53.11 N | 55.11 E |
| F'odorovka, Ross. | 86 | 56.05 N | 78.49 E |
| F'odorovskoje, Ross. | 82 | 56.44 N | 36.58 E |
| F'odorovskoje, Ross. | 82 | 56.08 N | 38.04 E |
| F'odorovskoje, Ross. | 82 | 56.07 N | 38.52 E |
| Foëcy | 50 | 47.10 N | 2.10 E |
| Foelsche ≏ | 164 | 16.03 S | 136.50 E |
| Foeni | 38 | 45.30 N | 20.53 E |
| Fogang (Shijiao) | 100 | 23.52 N | 113.32 E |
| Fogdön ›[1] | 40 | 59.25 N | 16.52 E |
| Fogelevo | 85 | 42.03 N | 69.32 E |
| Fogelsville | 208 | 40.35 N | 75.38 W |
| Foggaret el Arab | 148 | 27.03 N | 2.59 E |
| Foggaret ez Zoua | 148 | 27.20 N | 3.00 E |
| Foggia | 68 | 41.27 N | 15.34 E |
| Foggia □[4] | 68 | 41.30 N | 15.30 E |
| Foggy Island Bay C | 180 | 70.15 N | 147.30 W |
| Foglia ≏ | 66 | 43.55 N | 12.54 E |
| Foglianise | 68 | 41.10 N | 14.40 E |
| Fogliano, Lago di C | 66 | 41.24 N | 12.54 E |
| Foglizzo | 62 | 45.16 N | 7.49 E |
| Fogo | 186 | 49.43 N | 54.17 W |
| Fogo I | 150a | 14.55 N | 24.25 W |
| Fogo, Cape › | 186 | 49.39 N | 54.00 W |
| Fogo Island I | 186 | 49.40 N | 54.13 W |
| Fogolawa | 150 | 12.19 N | 8.41 E |
| Fogueteiro | 266c | 38.37 N | 9.07 W |
| Fohnsdorf | 61 | 47.13 N | 14.41 E |
| Föhr I | 30 | 54.43 N | 8.30 E |
| Föhren | 56 | 49.52 N | 6.46 E |
| Foia ∧ | 34 | 37.19 N | 8.36 W |
| Foiano della Chiana | 66 | 43.15 N | 11.49 E |
| Foiano di Val Fortore | 68 | 41.21 N | 14.59 E |
| Foinaven ∧ | 46 | 58.25 N | 4.53 W |
| Foins, Lac aux ⊜ | 190 | 47.05 N | 78.11 W |
| Foivre ≏ | 56 | 49.30 N | 4.32 E |
| Foix | 32 | 42.58 N | 1.36 E |
| Foix □[9] | 32 | 43.00 N | 1.40 E |
| Fojnica | 36 | 43.58 N | 17.54 E |
| Foki | 80 | 56.42 N | 54.21 E |
| Fokino | 76 | 53.27 N | 34.24 E |
| Fokku | 150 | 11.40 N | 4.31 E |
| Folakara | 157b | 18.20 S | 45.02 E |
| Folamasi | 104 | 41.56 N | 121.27 E |
| Folarskardnuten ∧ | 26 | 60.37 N | 7.45 E |
| Folcroft | 208 | 39.53 N | 75.17 W |
| Folda C[2] | 24 | 67.36 N | 14.50 E |
| Foldingbro | 41 | 55.26 N | 9.01 E |
| Folégandros I | 38 | 36.38 N | 24.54 E |
| Folembray | 50 | 49.33 N | 3.17 E |
| Foley, Al., U.S. | 194 | 30.24 N | 87.41 W |
| Foley, Mn., U.S. | 190 | 45.39 N | 93.54 W |
| Foley, Mo., U.S. | 219 | 39.02 N | 90.44 W |
| Foleyet | 190 | 48.15 N | 82.27 W |
| Foley Island I | 176 | 68.35 N | 75.10 W |
| Folgaria | 64 | 45.55 N | 11.10 E |
| Folgefonni ⩍ | 26 | 60.00 N | 6.20 E |
| Folger Hill ∧[2] | 207 | 41.17 N | 70.01 W |
| Foligno | 66 | 42.57 N | 12.42 E |
| Folk | 219 | 38.26 N | 92.06 W |
| Folkärna | 40 | 60.09 N | 16.19 E |
| Folkestone | 42 | 51.05 N | 1.11 E |
| Folkingham | 42 | 52.54 N | 0.24 W |
| Folkston | 192 | 30.49 N | 82.00 W |
| Folkwangmuseum ʊ | 263 | 51.27 N | 7.00 E |
| Follafoss | 26 | 63.59 N | 11.06 E |
| Follainville-Dennemont | 261 | 49.01 N | 1.43 E |
| Follansbee | 214 | 40.19 N | 80.35 W |
| Folldal | 26 | 62.08 N | 10.03 E |
| Folle Anse, Pointe de › | 241o | 15.57 N | 61.20 W |
| Follebu | 26 | 61.14 N | 10.17 E |
| Follets Island I | 222 | 29.02 N | 95.10 W |
| Follett | 196 | 36.26 N | 100.08 W |
| Follina | 64 | 45.57 N | 12.07 E |
| Föllinge | 26 | 63.40 N | 14.37 E |
| Follonica | 66 | 42.55 N | 10.45 E |
| Follonica, Golfo di C | 66 | 42.54 N | 10.43 E |
| Folly Branch ≏ | 284b | 38.56 N | 76.49 W |
| Folmhusen | 52 | 53.10 N | 7.28 E |
| Folschviller | 56 | 49.04 N | 6.41 E |
| Folsom, Ca., U.S. | 226 | 38.40 N | 121.10 W |
| Folsom, N.J., U.S. | 208 | 39.36 N | 74.50 W |
| Folsom, Pa., U.S. | 285 | 39.53 N | 75.19 W |
| Folsom Lake ⊜[1] | 226 | 38.43 N | 121.08 W |
| Folsom Lake State Recreation Area ♦ | 226 | 38.46 N | 121.06 W |
| Fomboni | 157a | 12.16 S | 43.45 E |
| Fomento, Cuba | 240p | 22.06 N | 79.43 W |
| Fomento, Ur. | 258 | 34.26 S | 57.14 W |
| Fomin | 80 | 46.58 N | 43.38 E |
| Fominiči | 76 | 54.07 N | 34.41 E |
| Fominki | 80 | 55.57 N | 42.22 E |
| Fominskaja | 24 | 61.17 N | 48.40 E |
| Fominskoje, Ross. | 24 | 59.43 N | 42.05 E |
| Fominskoje, Ross. | 76 | 58.59 N | 39.06 E |
| Fomkino | 80 | 54.25 N | 50.30 E |
| Foncine-le-Bas | 58 | 46.38 N | 6.03 E |
| Fonda, Ia., U.S. | 198 | 42.34 N | 94.50 W |
| Fonda, N.Y., U.S. | 210 | 42.57 N | 74.22 W |
| Fondachelli | 70 | 37.58 N | 15.11 E |
| Fond du Lac, Sk., Can. | 176 | 59.19 N | 107.10 W |
| Fond du Lac, Wi., U.S. | 190 | 43.46 N | 88.26 W |
| Fond du Lac ≏ | 176 | 59.17 N | 106.00 W |
| Fond du Lac Indian Reservation ⬥[4] | 190 | 46.45 N | 92.37 W |
| Fondi | 66 | 41.21 N | 13.25 E |
| Fondi, Lago di C | 66 | 41.19 N | 13.20 E |
| Fondo | 64 | 46.26 N | 11.08 E |

| | | | |
|---|---|---|---|
| Fondouk el Aouareb | 36 | 35.34 N | 9.46 E |
| Fongfong | 140 | 12.56 N | 23.14 E |
| Fonni | 71 | 40.07 N | 9.15 E |
| Fonseca | 246 | 10.54 N | 72.51 W |
| Fonseca, Golfo de C | 236 | 13.10 N | 87.40 W |
| Fons-Outre-Gardon | 62 | 43.54 N | 4.11 E |
| Font ≏ | 44 | 55.10 N | 1.44 W |
| Fontaine, Fr. | 58 | 47.40 N | 7.00 E |
| Fontaine, Fr. | 62 | 45.11 N | 5.40 E |
| Fontainebleau, Fr. | 50 | 48.24 N | 2.42 E |
| Fontainebleau, S. Afr. | 273d | 26.07 S | 27.59 E |
| Fontaine-Française | 58 | 47.31 N | 5.22 E |
| Fontaine-le-Dun | 50 | 49.49 N | 0.51 E |
| Fontaine-lès-Dijon | 58 | 47.21 N | 5.01 E |
| Fontaine-lès-Grès | 50 | 48.25 N | 3.54 E |
| Fontaine-lès-Luxeuil | 58 | 47.51 N | 6.20 E |
| Fontaines | 58 | 46.51 N | 4.46 E |
| Fontaines-sur-Saône | 62 | 45.50 N | 4.51 E |
| Fontan | 62 | 44.00 N | 7.33 E |
| Fontana, Arg. | 252 | 27.25 S | 59.02 W |
| Fontana, Ca., U.S. | 228 | 34.05 N | 117.26 W |
| Fontana, Wi., U.S. | 216 | 42.33 N | 88.34 W |
| Fontana, Lago ⊜ | 254 | 44.56 S | 71.30 W |
| Fontanafredda | 64 | 45.58 N | 12.34 E |
| Fontana Lake ⊜[1] | 192 | 35.26 N | 83.38 W |
| Fontanarosa | 68 | 41.01 N | 15.01 E |
| Fontanarossa, Aeroporto di ⊠ | 70 | 37.29 N | 15.03 E |
| Fontanelas | 266c | 38.51 N | 9.26 W |
| Fontanelice | 66 | 44.15 N | 11.33 E |
| Fontanella | 64 | 45.27 N | 9.48 E |
| Fontanellato | 64 | 44.53 N | 10.10 E |
| Fontanelle | 198 | 41.17 N | 94.33 W |
| Fontanetto Po | 62 | 45.12 N | 8.11 E |
| Fontanigorda | 62 | 44.33 N | 9.19 E |
| Fontarabie, Lac ⊜ | 186 | 51.10 N | 66.25 W |
| Fontas ≏ | 176 | 58.20 N | 121.50 W |
| Fonte, Bra. | 287b | 23.25 S | 46.21 W |
| Fonte, It. | 64 | 45.47 N | 11.53 E |
| Fonte, It. | 66 | 41.46 N | 13.13 E |
| Fonte Avellana, Monastero di ʊ[1] | 66 | 43.29 N | 12.45 E |
| Fonte Blanda | 66 | 42.34 N | 11.10 E |
| Fonte Boa | 246 | 2.32 S | 66.01 W |
| Fonte Colombo, Convento di ʊ[1] | 66 | 42.23 N | 12.50 E |
| Fontenay, Abbaye de ʊ[1] | 50 | 47.39 N | 4.24 E |
| Fontenay-aux-Roses | 261 | 48.47 N | 2.17 E |
| Fontenay-en-Parisis | 261 | 49.03 N | 2.27 E |
| Fontenay-le-Comte | 32 | 46.28 N | 0.48 W |
| Fontenay-le-Fleury | 261 | 48.49 N | 2.03 E |
| Fontenay-lès-Briis | 261 | 48.37 N | 2.09 E |
| Fontenay-le-Vicomte | 261 | 48.33 N | 2.24 E |
| Fontenay-Saint-Père | 261 | 49.02 N | 1.45 E |
| Fontenay-sous-Bois | 261 | 48.51 N | 2.29 E |
| Fontenay-Trésigny | 50 | 48.42 N | 2.52 E |
| Fonteneau, Lac ⊜ | 186 | 51.55 N | 61.30 W |
| Fontenelle | 186 | 48.53 N | 64.33 W |
| Fontenelle Creek ≏ | 200 | 42.05 N | 110.08 W |
| Fontenelle Reservoir ⊜[1] | 200 | 42.05 N | 110.06 W |
| Fontespina | 66 | 43.17 N | 13.45 E |
| Fontevivo | 64 | 44.51 N | 10.10 E |
| Font Hill Manor | 284b | 39.17 N | 76.52 W |
| Fonti del Clitunno ⍑[4] | 66 | 42.49 N | 12.46 E |
| Fontoy | 56 | 49.21 N | 6.00 E |
| Fontur › | 24a | 66.23 N | 14.30 W |
| Fontvieille | 62 | 43.43 N | 4.43 E |
| Fonyód | 30 | 46.44 N | 17.34 E |
| Fonzaso | 64 | 46.01 N | 11.48 E |
| Foochow → Fuzhou | 100 | 26.06 N | 119.17 E |
| Foot Creek ≏ | 198 | 45.26 N | 98.29 W |
| Foothill Farms | 226 | 38.40 N | 121.20 W |
| Foothills | 182 | 53.04 N | 116.48 W |
| Footprint Lake ⊜ | 184 | 55.47 N | 98.53 W |
| Footscray | 169 | 37.48 S | 144.54 E |
| Footville | 216 | 42.40 N | 89.12 W |
| Foping | 102 | 33.21 N | 107.59 E |
| Foppolo | 64 | 46.03 N | 9.45 E |
| Fora, Ponta de › | 287a | 22.57 S | 43.07 W |
| Foraker, Mount ∧ | 180 | 62.56 N | 151.26 W |
| Forari | 175f | 17.39 S | 168.32 E |
| Forbach, Dtsch. | 56 | 48.41 N | 8.21 E |
| Forbach, Fr. | 56 | 49.11 N | 6.54 E |
| Forbes | 166 | 33.23 S | 148.01 E |
| Forbes, Lac ⊜ | 206 | 46.31 N | 74.12 W |
| Forbes, Mount ∧ | 182 | 51.52 N | 116.56 W |
| Forbesganj | 124 | 26.18 N | 87.15 E |
| Forbes Reef | 158 | 26.10 S | 31.05 E |
| Forbes Road | 214 | 40.21 N | 79.32 W |
| Forbestown | 226 | 39.31 N | 121.16 W |
| Forcados | 150 | 5.22 N | 5.24 E |
| Forcados ≏[1] | 150 | 5.25 N | 5.19 E |
| Forcalquier | 62 | 43.58 N | 5.47 E |
| Force | 214 | 41.15 N | 78.30 W |
| Forchheim, Dtsch. | 54 | 50.43 N | 13.16 E |
| Forchheim, Dtsch. | 60 | 49.43 N | 11.04 E |
| Forchtenberg | 56 | 49.17 N | 9.34 E |
| Forclaz, Col de la )( | 58 | 46.04 N | 7.00 E |
| Ford, Scot., U.K. | 46 | 56.10 N | 5.26 W |
| Ford, Ks., U.S. | 198 | 37.38 N | 99.45 W |
| Ford □[6] | 216 | 40.27 N | 88.06 W |
| Ford ≏ | 190 | 45.40 N | 87.09 W |
| Ford, Cape › | 164 | 13.26 S | 129.52 E |
| Ford City, Ca., U.S. | 226 | 35.09 N | 119.27 W |
| Ford City, Pa., U.S. | 214 | 40.46 N | 79.31 W |
| Ford City ⬥[9] | 278 | 41.46 N | 87.44 W |
| Ford Cliff | 214 | 40.45 N | 79.32 W |
| Ford Dam ⬥[6] | 281 | 42.13 N | 83.33 W |
| Ford Dry Lake ⊜ | 204 | 33.38 N | 115.00 W |
| Førde, Nor. | 26 | 59.36 N | 5.29 E |
| Førde, Nor. | 26 | 61.27 N | 5.52 E |
| Førdefjorden C[2] | 26 | 61.28 N | 5.39 E |
| Forden | 42 | 52.36 N | 3.08 W |
| Förderstedt | 54 | 51.54 N | 11.38 E |
| Fordham University ʊ[2] | 276 | 40.51 N | 73.53 W |
| Fordingbridge | 42 | 50.56 N | 1.47 W |
| Ford Lake ⊜ | 281 | 42.13 N | 83.36 W |
| Ford Mansion ⊥ | 276 | 40.48 N | 74.28 W |
| Ford Motor Company (River Rouge Plant) ʊ[3] | 281 | 42.18 N | 83.10 W |
| Ford Museum ʊ | 281 | 42.18 N | 83.14 W |
| Fordongianus | 71 | 39.59 N | 8.48 E |
| Ford Ranges ⋏ | 9 | 77.00 S | 145.00 W |
| Fords | 276 | 40.31 N | 74.18 W |
| Fords Bridge | 166 | 29.45 S | 145.26 E |
| Fordsburg ⬥[8] | 273d | 26.13 S | 28.02 E |
| Fords Prairie | 224 | 46.44 N | 122.59 W |
| Fordsville | 194 | 37.38 N | 86.43 W |
| Fordville | 198 | 48.13 N | 97.47 W |
| Fordyce | 194 | 33.48 N | 92.24 W |
| Fordyce Lake ⊜[1] | 226 | 39.23 N | 120.28 W |
| Foré | 150 | 13.08 N | 10.42 W |
| Forécariah | 150 | 9.26 N | 13.06 W |
| Forel, Mont ∧ | 176 | 67.00 N | 37.00 W |
| Foreland Point › | 42 | 51.16 N | 3.47 W |
| Foreman | 194 | 33.43 N | 94.23 W |
| Foremost | 184 | 49.29 N | 111.25 W |
| Forenza | 68 | 40.51 N | 15.51 E |
| Forepaugh Airport ⊠ | 279a | 41.21 N | 81.30 W |
| Foresman | 216 | 40.52 N | 87.18 W |
| Forest, Bel. | 50 | 50.48 N | 4.19 E |
| Forest, On., Can. | 190 | 43.06 N | 82.00 W |
| Forest, In., U.S. | 216 | 40.22 N | 86.19 W |
| Forest, Ms., U.S. | 194 | 32.21 N | 89.28 W |
| Forest, Oh., U.S. | 216 | 40.48 N | 83.30 W |
| Forest □[6] | 214 | 41.29 N | 79.27 W |
| Forest, Middle Branch ≏ | 198 | 48.13 N | 97.48 W |
| Forest Acres | 192 | 34.01 N | 80.59 W |
| Forestburg | 182 | 52.35 N | 112.04 W |
| Forest City, Ia., U.S. | 190 | 43.15 N | 93.38 W |
| Forest City, N.C., U.S. | 192 | 35.20 N | 81.51 W |
| Forest City, Pa., U.S. | 210 | 41.39 N | 75.28 W |
| Forest Creek ≏ | 226 | 38.23 N | 120.28 W |

| | | | |
|---|---|---|---|
| Forest Gate ⬥[8] | 260 | 51.33 N | 0.0[illegible] E |
| Forest Glade | 222 | 31.39 N | 96.3[illegible] W |
| Forest Grove, B.C., Can. | 182 | 51.46 N | 121.0[illegible] W |
| Forest Grove, Or., U.S. | 224 | 45.31 N | 123.0[illegible] W |
| Forest Grove, Pa., U.S. | 279b | 40.18 N | 75.04 W |
| Forest Heights | 284c | 38.49 N | 77.00 W |
| Forest Hill, Austl. | 171a | 27.35 S | 152.22 E |
| Forest Hill, Austl. | 171b | 35.09 S | 147.27 E |
| Forest Hill, Austl. | 274b | 37.50 S | 145.11 E |
| Foresthill, Ca., U.S. | 226 | 39.01 N | 120.49 W |
| Forest Hill, Md., U.S. | 208 | 39.35 N | 76.23 W |
| Forest Hill, Tx., U.S. | 222 | 32.40 N | 97.16 W |
| Forest Hill ⬥[8] | 275b | 43.42 N | 79.24 W |
| Forest Hill Park ♦ | 279a | 41.31 N | 81.35 W |
| Forest Hill Parkway ♦ | 279a | 41.33 N | 81.36 W |
| Forest Hills | 279b | 40.25 N | 79.51 W |
| Forest Hills ⬥[8] | 276 | 40.42 N | 73.51 W |
| Forest Home | 194 | 31.52 N | 86.50 W |
| Forestier Peninsula ›[1] | 166 | 42.57 S | 147.55 E |
| Forest Knolls | 284c | 39.02 N | 77.01 W |
| Forest Lake, Il., U.S. | 216 | 42.13 N | 88.03 W |
| Forest Lake, Mn., U.S. | 190 | 45.16 N | 92.59 W |
| Forest Lake ⊜, Il., U.S. | 278 | 42.13 N | 88.03 W |
| Forest Lake ⊜, Ma., U.S. | 283 | 42.43 N | 71.15 W |
| Forest Lawn Memorial Park ⬥ | 280 | 34.09 N | 118.19 W |
| Forest Manor | 284c | 38.50 N | 76.53 W |
| Forest Park, Ga., U.S. | 192 | 33.37 N | 84.22 W |
| Forest Park, Il., U.S. | 278 | 41.52 N | 87.48 W |
| Forest Park, Oh., U.S. | 218 | 39.16 N | 84.34 W |
| Forest Park ⬥[8] | 284b | 39.19 N | 76.41 W |
| Forest Park ♦ | 276 | 40.42 N | 73.51 W |
| Forest River | 278 | 42.05 N | 87.54 W |
| Forest Row | 42 | 51.06 N | 0.02 E |
| Forest View | 278 | 41.49 N | 87.47 W |
| Forestville, Austl. | 274a | 33.46 S | 151.13 E |
| Forestville, P.Q., Can. | 186 | 48.45 N | 69.06 W |
| Forestville, Md., U.S. | 284c | 38.50 N | 76.52 W |
| Forestville, N.Y., U.S. | 214 | 42.28 N | 79.10 W |
| Forestville, Pa., U.S. | 214 | 41.06 N | 80.00 W |
| Forestville, Wi., U.S. | 190 | 44.41 N | 87.28 W |
| Forêt l'Orient, Lac de la ⊜[1] | 50 | 48.17 N | 4.20 E |
| Forêt-Noire → Schwarzwald ⋏ | 58 | 48.00 N | 8.15 E |
| Forez, Monts du ⋏ | 32 | 45.35 N | 3.48 E |
| Forfar | 46 | 56.38 N | 2.54 W |
| Forfry | 261 | 49.03 N | 2.51 E |
| Forgan | 196 | 36.54 N | 100.32 W |
| Forgaria | 64 | 46.13 N | 12.58 E |
| Forge Acres | 284b | 39.25 N | 76.27 W |
| Forge Heights | 284b | 39.25 N | 76.25 W |
| Forges-les-Bains | 261 | 48.38 N | 2.06 E |
| Forges-les-Eaux | 50 | 49.37 N | 1.33 E |
| Forget, Pointe › | 275a | 45.27 N | 73.58 W |
| Forge Village | 207 | 42.34 N | 71.29 W |
| Forggensee ⊜ | 58 | 47.36 N | 10.44 E |
| Forillon, Parc National de ♦ | 186 | 48.55 N | 64.12 W |
| Forino | 68 | 40.52 N | 14.44 E |
| Foristell | 219 | 38.49 N | 90.57 W |
| Fork | 208 | 39.28 N | 76.27 W |
| Forked Creek ≏ | 216 | 41.19 N | 88.09 W |
| Forked Deer ≏ | 194 | 35.56 N | 89.35 W |
| Forked Deer, Middle Fork ≏ | 194 | 36.01 N | 89.13 W |
| Forked Deer, North Fork ≏ | 194 | 36.00 N | 89.26 W |
| Forked Deer, South Fork ≏ | 194 | 36.00 N | 89.26 W |
| Forked River | 208 | 39.50 N | 74.11 W |
| Forks | 224 | 47.57 N | 124.23 W |
| Forkston | 210 | 41.31 N | 76.07 W |
| Forksville | 210 | 41.29 N | 76.36 W |
| Forleti, Arroyo ≏ | 288 | 34.35 S | 58.41 W |
| Forlì | 66 | 44.13 N | 12.03 E |
| Forlì □[4] | 64 | 44.05 N | 12.02 E |
| Forlimpopoli | 66 | 44.11 N | 12.07 E |
| Forman | 198 | 46.06 N | 97.38 W |
| Formazza | 58 | 46.22 N | 8.26 E |
| Formby | 44 | 53.34 N | 3.05 W |
| Formby Hills ⋏[2] | 262 | 53.34 N | 3.06 W |
| Formby Point › | 44 | 53.33 N | 3.06 W |
| Formentera I | 34 | 38.42 N | 1.28 E |
| Formentor, Cap de › | 34 | 39.58 N | 3.12 E |
| Formerie | 50 | 49.39 N | 1.44 E |
| Formia | 66 | 41.15 N | 13.37 E |
| Formiga | 255 | 20.27 S | 45.25 W |
| Formiga ≏ | 250 | 11.15 S | 48.27 W |
| Formigine | 64 | 44.34 N | 10.51 E |
| Formignana | 64 | 44.50 N | 11.51 E |
| Formosa, Arg. | 252 | 26.11 S | 58.11 W |
| Formosa, Bra. | 255 | 15.32 S | 47.20 W |
| Formosa □[4] | 252 | 25.00 S | 60.00 W |
| Formosa → Taiwan □[1] | 100 | 23.30 N | 121.00 E |
| Formosa, Ilha I | 150 | 11.29 N | 15.58 W |
| Formosa, Serra ⋏[1] | 250 | 12.00 S | 55.00 W |
| Formosa Strait → Taiwan Strait Ʉ | 100 | 24.00 N | 119.00 E |
| Formoso ≏, Bra. | 250 | 10.34 S | 49.56 W |
| Formoso ≏, Bra. | 255 | 13.26 S | 44.14 W |
| Formoso ≏, Bra. | 255 | 18.25 S | 52.28 W |
| Formoso ≏, Bra. | 256 | 21.20 S | 43.10 W |
| Fornæs › | 26 | 56.27 N | 10.58 E |
| Forncelle | 66 | 43.55 N | 11.06 E |
| Fornelli | 71 | 41.00 N | 8.14 E |
| Forney | 222 | 32.44 N | 96.28 W |
| Forni Avoltri | 64 | 46.35 N | 12.46 E |
| Forni di sopra | 64 | 46.25 N | 12.35 E |
| Forni di sotto | 64 | 46.23 N | 12.40 E |
| Forni di Val d'Astico | 64 | 45.51 N | 11.22 E |
| Forno | 64 | 46.21 N | 11.37 E |
| Forno Alpi Graie | 62 | 45.22 N | 7.13 E |
| Forno di Zoldo | 64 | 46.21 N | 12.11 E |
| Fornosovo | 76 | 59.35 N | 30.35 E |
| Fornovo di Taro | 64 | 44.42 N | 10.06 E |
| Foro Romano ⊥ | 267a | 41.54 N | 12.29 E |
| Føroyar → Faeroe Islands □[2] | 22 | 62.00 N | 7.00 W |
| Forpost | 86 | 56.47 N | 72.10 E |
| Forres, Arg. | 252 | 27.53 S | 63.58 W |
| Forres, Scot., U.K. | 46 | 57.37 N | 3.38 W |
| Forrest, Austl. | 162 | 30.51 S | 128.06 E |
| Forrest, Austl. | 169 | 38.31 S | 143.43 E |
| Forrest, Il., U.S. | 216 | 40.45 N | 88.24 W |
| Forrest ≏ | 164 | 15.18 S | 128.04 E |
| Forrest, Mount ∧ | 162 | 24.48 S | 127.45 E |
| Forrestal Research Center ʊ[3] | 276 | 40.21 N | 74.37 W |
| Forrest City | 194 | 35.00 N | 90.47 W |
| Forrester Island I | 182 | 54.48 N | 133.32 W |
| Forrest Lakes ⊜ | 162 | 29.12 S | 128.46 E |
| Forreston, Il., U.S. | 190 | 42.07 N | 89.34 W |
| Forreston, Tx., U.S. | 222 | 32.16 N | 96.52 W |
| Forrest River Aboriginal Reserve ⬥[4] | 164 | 15.00 S | 127.40 E |
| Fors | 40 | 60.13 N | 16.18 E |
| Forsan | 196 | 32.07 N | 101.22 W |
| Forsayth | 166 | 18.35 S | 143.36 E |
| Forsbacka | 40 | 60.37 N | 16.53 E |
| Forsby | 26 | 60.30 N | 25.56 E |
| Forserum | 26 | 57.42 N | 14.28 E |
| Forshaga | 40 | 59.32 N | 13.28 E |
| Forsmark | 40 | 60.22 N | 18.09 E |
| Forssa | 26 | 60.49 N | 23.38 E |
| Forst | 54 | 51.44 N | 14.39 E |
| Förste | 52 | 51.44 N | 10.10 E |
| Forster | 166 | 32.11 S | 152.31 E |


| | | | | | |
|---|---|---|---|---|---|
| ≏ | River | Fluß | Río | Rivière | Rio |
| ≊ | Canal | Kanal | Canal | Canal | Canal |
| ∟ | Waterfall, Rapids | Wasserfall, Stromschnellen | Cascada, Rápidos | Chute d'eau, Rapides | Cascata, Rápidos |
| Ʉ | Strait | Meeresstraße | Estrecho | Détroit | Estreito |
| C | Bay, Gulf | Bucht, Golf | Bahía, Golfo | Baie, Golfe | Baía, Golfo |
| ⊜ | Lake, Lakes | See, Seen | Lago, Lagos | Lac, Lacs | Lago, Lagos |
| ≡ | Swamp | Sumpf | Pantano | Marais | Pântano |
| ⩍ | Ice Features, Glacier | Eis- und Gletscherformen | Accidentes Glaciales | Formes glaciaires | Acidentes glaciares |
| ⍑ | Other Hydrographic Features | Andere Hydrographische Objekte | Otros Elementos Hidrográficos | Autres données hydrographiques | Outros acidentes hidrográficos |
| ✦ | Submarine Features | Untermeerische Objekte | Accidentes Submarinos | Formes de relief sous-marin | Acidentes submarinos |
| □ | Political Unit | Politische Einheit | Unidad Politica | Entité politique | Unidade política |
| ʊ | Cultural Institution | Kulturelle Institution | Institución Cultural | Institution culturelle | Instituição cultural |
| ⊥ | Historical Site | Historische Stätte | Sitio Histórico | Site historique | Sitio histórico |
| ♦ | Recreational Site | Erholungs- und Ferienort | Sitio de Recreo | Centre de loisirs | Area de Lazer |
| ⊠ | Airport | Flughafen | Aeropuerto | Aéroport | Aeroporto |
| ■ | Military Installation | Militäranlage | Instalación Militar | Installation militaire | Instalação militar |
| ⬥ | Miscellaneous | Verschiedenes | Misceláneo | Divers | Diversos |

| Name | Page | Lat.°′ | Long.°′ |
|---|---|---|---|
| Forstwald ◆⁸ | 263 | 51.18 N | 6.30 E |
| Forsyth, Ga., U.S. | 192 | 33.02 N | 83.56 W |
| Forsyth, Il., U.S. | 219 | 39.56 N | 88.57 W |
| Forsyth, Mo., U.S. | 194 | 36.41 N | 93.07 W |
| Forsyth, Mt., U.S. | 202 | 46.15 N | 106.40 W |
| Forsyth Island I | 164 | 16.50 S | 139.06 E |
| Forsyth Range ⋏ | 166 | 22.45 S | 143.15 E |
| Fort ◆⁸ | 272c | 18.56 N | 72.50 E |
| Fort Abbās | 123 | 29.12 N | 72.52 E |
| Fort Adams | 194 | 31.05 N | 91.32 W |
| Fort Albany | 176 | 52.15 N | 81.37 W |
| Fort Alexander Indian Reserve ◆⁴ | 184 | 50.27 N | 96.15 W |
| Fortaleza | 250 | 3.43 S | 38.30 W |
| Fortaleza ≃ | 248 | 10.40 S | 77.52 W |
| Fortaleza de Santa Teresa ⊥ | 252 | 33.59 S | 53.32 W |
| Fortaleza do Ituxi | 248 | 7.29 S | 66.20 W |
| Fortaleza dos Nogueiras | 250 | 6.54 S | 46.09 W |
| Fort Amherst National Historic Park ♦ | 186 | 46.12 N | 63.09 W |
| Fort Ancient State Memorial ⊥ | 218 | 39.24 N | 84.06 W |
| Fort Anne National Historic Park ♦ | 186 | 44.44 N | 65.26 W |
| Fort Apache Indian Reservation ◆⁴ | 200 | 34.01 N | 110.28 W |
| Fort-Archambault → Sarh | 146 | 9.09 N | 18.23 E |
| Fort Assiniboine | 182 | 54.20 N | 114.46 W |
| Fort Atkinson | 216 | 42.55 N | 88.50 W |
| Fort Augusta ⊥ | 210 | 40.53 N | 76.46 W |
| Fort Augustus | 46 | 57.09 N | 4.41 W |
| Fort Baker ■ | 282 | 37.50 N | 122.29 W |
| Fort Battleford National Historic Park ♦ | 184 | 52.42 N | 108.15 W |
| Fort Bayard → Zhanjiang | 102 | 21.16 N | 110.28 E |
| Fort Beaufort | 158 | 32.46 S | 26.40 E |
| Fort Beauséjour National Historic Park ♦ | 186 | 45.51 N | 64.18 W |
| Fort Belknap Agency | 202 | 48.28 N | 108.45 W |
| Fort Belknap Indian Reservation ◆⁴ | 202 | 48.16 N | 108.38 W |
| Fort Belvoir ■ | 208 | 38.44 N | 77.10 W |
| Fort Bend □⁶ | 222 | 29.32 N | 95.47 W |
| Fort Benjamin Harrison ■ | 218 | 39.52 N | 86.01 W |
| Fort Benning ■ | 192 | 32.22 N | 84.50 W |
| Fort Benton | 202 | 47.49 N | 110.40 W |
| Fort Berthold Indian Reservation ◆⁴ | 198 | 47.40 N | 102.25 W |
| Fort Bidwell | 204 | 41.51 N | 120.09 W |
| Fort Bliss ■ | 200 | 32.15 N | 106.00 W |
| Fort Bowie National Historic Site ⊥ | 200 | 32.09 N | 109.24 W |
| Fort Bragg | 204 | 39.26 N | 123.48 W |
| Fort Bragg ■ | 192 | 35.09 N | 78.59 W |
| Fort Branch | 194 | 38.15 N | 87.34 W |
| Fort Bridger | 200 | 41.19 N | 110.23 W |
| Fort Calhoun | 198 | 41.27 N | 96.01 W |
| Fort Campbell ■ | 194 | 36.39 N | 87.29 W |
| Fort Canby State Park ♦ | 224 | 46.17 N | 124.04 W |
| Fort-Carnot | 157b | 21.53 S | 47.28 E |
| Fort Caroline National Memorial ⊥ | 192 | 30.20 N | 81.30 W |
| Fort Carson ■ | 200 | 38.44 N | 104.48 W |
| Fort Casey Historical State Park ♦ | 224 | 48.10 N | 122.40 W |
| Fort Chambly National Historic Park ♦ | 206 | 45.27 N | 73.17 W |
| Fort Chipewyan | 176 | 58.42 N | 111.08 W |
| Fort Churchill Historic State Monument ⊥ | 226 | 39.18 N | 119.17 W |
| Fort Clatsop National Memorial ⊥ | 224 | 46.08 N | 123.54 W |
| Fort Cobb | 196 | 35.05 N | 98.26 W |
| Fort Cobb Reservoir ⊜¹ | 196 | 35.12 N | 98.29 W |
| Fort Collins | 200 | 40.35 N | 105.05 W |
| Fort Columbia Historical State Park ♦ | 224 | 46.15 N | 123.56 W |
| Fort Constantine | 166 | 20.28 S | 140.37 E |
| Fort-Coulonge | 188 | 45.51 N | 76.44 W |
| Fort Covington | 206 | 44.59 N | 74.29 W |
| Fort Custer State Recreation Area ♦ | 216 | 42.18 N | 85.20 W |
| Fort Davis, Al., U.S. | 194 | 32.14 N | 85.42 W |
| Fort Davis, Tx., U.S. | 196 | 30.35 N | 103.53 W |
| Fort Davis National Historic Site ⊥ | 196 | 30.33 N | 103.53 W |
| Fort de Douaumont ⊥ | 56 | 49.13 N | 5.25 E |
| Fort Defiance | 200 | 35.44 N | 109.04 W |
| Fort-de-France | 240e | 14.36 N | 61.05 W |
| Fort-de-France, Baie de ⊂ | 240e | 14.34 N | 61.04 W |
| Fort-de-France-Lamentin, Aérodrome de ⊠ | 240e | 14.35 N | 61.00 W |
| Fort Deposit | 194 | 31.59 N | 86.34 W |
| Fort Detrick ■ | 208 | 39.27 N | 77.26 W |
| Fort de Vaux ⊥ | 56 | 49.12 N | 5.28 E |
| Fort Devens ■ | 207 | 42.32 N | 71.37 W |
| Fort Dix ■ | 208 | 40.00 N | 74.33 W |
| Fort Dodge | 190 | 42.29 N | 94.10 W |
| Fort Donelson National Military Park ♦ | 194 | 36.26 N | 87.49 W |
| Fort Duchesne | 200 | 40.17 N | 109.51 W |
| Fort Dupont Park ♦ | 284c | 38.53 N | 76.57 W |
| Forte, Monte ∧² | 71 | 40.43 N | 8.15 E |
| Forteau | 186 | 51.28 N | 56.58 W |
| Forte dei Marmi | 64 | 43.57 N | 10.10 E |
| Forte de Magoito | 266c | 38.52 N | 9.27 W |
| Fort Edward | 210 | 43.16 N | 73.35 W |
| Forte República | 152 | 7.45 S | 16.23 E |
| Fort Erie | 212 | 42.54 N | 78.56 W |
| Fort Erie Race Track ♦ | 284a | 42.55 N | 78.56 W |
| Fortescue ≃ | 162 | 21.00 S | 116.06 E |
| Fort Eustis ■ | 208 | 37.09 N | 76.35 W |
| Fortevoit | 46 | 56.20 N | 3.32 W |
| Fortezza (Franzensfeste) | 64 | 46.47 N | 11.37 E |
| Fort Fairfield | 186 | 46.46 N | 67.50 W |
| Fort Fitzgerald | 176 | 59.53 N | 111.37 W |
| Fort Foote Village | 284c | 38.46 N | 77.01 W |
| Fort-Foureau | 146 | 12.05 N | 15.02 E |
| Fort Frances | 190 | 48.36 N | 93.24 W |
| Fort Franklin | 180 | 65.11 N | 123.46 W |
| Fort Fraser | 182 | 54.04 N | 124.33 W |
| Fort Frederica National Monument ♦ | 192 | 31.12 N | 81.26 W |
| Fort Gaines | 192 | 31.36 N | 85.02 W |
| Fort Garland | 200 | 37.25 N | 105.26 W |
| Fort Gay | 188 | 38.06 N | 82.35 W |
| Fort George ⊥ | 284a | 43.15 N | 79.04 W |
| Fort George G. Meade ■ | 208 | 39.05 N | 76.50 W |
| Fort Gibson | 196 | 35.47 N | 95.15 W |
| Fort Gibson Lake ⊜¹ | 196 | 36.00 N | 95.18 W |
| Fort Good Hope | 180 | 66.15 N | 128.38 W |
| Fort Gordon ■ | 192 | 33.25 N | 82.11 W |
| Fort-Gouraud → Fdérik | 148 | 22.41 N | 12.43 W |
| Fort Green | 220 | 27.36 N | 81.56 W |
| Forth | 46 | 55.47 N | 3.41 W |
| Forth ≃ | 46 | 56.03 N | 3.44 W |
| Forth, Carse of V | 46 | 56.08 N | 4.05 W |
| Forth, Firth of ⊂ | 46 | 56.10 N | 2.45 W |
| Förtha | 56 | 50.56 N | 10.14 E |
| Fort Hall | 202 | 43.02 N | 112.26 W |
| Fort Hall Indian Reservation ◆⁴ | 202 | 43.10 N | 112.10 W |
| Fort Hamilton ■ | 276 | 40.37 N | 74.02 W |
| Forth Bridge ◆⁵ | 46 | 56.00 N | 3.25 W |
| Fort Hertz → Putao | 102 | 27.21 N | 97.24 E |
| Fort Hill → Chitipa | 154 | 9.43 S | 33.16 E |
| Fort Hill ■ | 188 | 38.04 N | 77.19 W |
| Fort Hill State Memorial ⊥ | 218 | 39.07 N | 83.25 W |
| Fort Hood ■ | 222 | 31.08 N | 97.46 W |
| Fort Howard | 208 | 39.12 N | 76.27 W |
| Fort Huachuca ■ | 200 | 31.33 N | 110.20 W |
| Fort Hunter | 210 | 42.57 N | 74.17 W |
| Fort Hunter Liggett ■ | 226 | 35.55 N | 121.15 W |
| Fortierville | 206 | 46.29 N | 72.02 W |
| Fortín | 234 | 18.54 N | 97.00 W |
| Fortin, Lac ⊜ | 186 | 50.50 N | 67.46 W |
| Fortín Ayacucho | 248 | 19.58 S | 59.47 W |
| Fortín Coroneles Sanchez | 248 | 19.20 S | 59.58 W |
| Fortine | 182 | 48.45 N | 114.54 W |
| Fortín Florida | 248 | 20.45 S | 59.17 W |
| Fortín Garrapatal | 248 | 21.27 S | 61.30 W |
| Fortín Teniente Montanía | 252 | 22.04 S | 59.57 W |
| Fortín Uno | 252 | 38.51 S | 65.17 W |
| Fort Jackson ■ | 192 | 34.01 N | 80.57 W |
| Fort Jameson → Chipata | 154 | 13.39 S | 32.40 E |
| Fort Jennings | 216 | 40.54 N | 84.17 W |
| Fort Jeudy, Point of › | 241k | 12.00 N | 61.42 W |
| Fort Johnson | 210 | 42.57 N | 74.14 W |
| Fort Johnston → Mangochi | 154 | 14.28 S | 35.16 E |
| Fort Jones | 204 | 41.36 N | 122.50 W |
| Fort Kent | 186 | 47.15 N | 68.35 W |
| Fort Klamath | 202 | 42.42 N | 121.59 W |
| Fort Knox ■ | 194 | 37.54 N | 85.57 W |
| Fort-Lamy → N'Djamena | 146 | 12.07 N | 15.03 E |
| Fort Langley | 224 | 49.10 N | 122.35 W |
| Fort Langley National Historic Park ♦ | 224 | 49.10 N | 122.35 W |
| Fort Laramie | 200 | 42.12 N | 104.31 W |
| Fort Laramie National Historic Site ⊥ | 198 | 42.09 N | 104.41 W |
| Fort Larned National Historic Site ⊥ | 198 | 38.10 N | 99.12 W |
| Fort Lauderdale | 220 | 26.07 N | 80.08 W |
| Fort Lauderdale-Hollywood International Airport ⊠ | 220 | 26.04 N | 80.09 W |
| Fort Laurens State Memorial ⊥ | 214 | 40.38 N | 81.27 W |
| Fort Leavenworth ■ | 198 | 39.21 N | 94.55 W |
| Fort Le Boeuf ⊥ | 214 | 41.56 N | 79.59 W |
| Fort Lee | 210 | 40.51 N | 73.58 W |
| Fort Lee ■ | 208 | 37.14 N | 77.20 W |
| Fort Lennox National Historic Park ♦ | 206 | 45.06 N | 73.16 W |
| Fort Leonard Wood ■ | 194 | 37.45 N | 92.07 W |
| Fort Lewis ■ | 224 | 47.05 N | 122.37 W |
| Fort Liard | 176 | 60.15 N | 123.28 W |
| Fort-Liberté | 238 | 19.39 N | 71.49 W |
| Fort Lincoln State Park ♦ | 198 | 46.45 N | 100.52 W |
| Fort Littleton | 214 | 40.04 N | 77.58 W |
| Fort Loramie | 216 | 40.21 N | 84.22 W |
| Fort Loudoun Lake ⊜¹ | 192 | 35.45 N | 84.10 W |
| Fort Lupton | 200 | 40.05 N | 104.48 W |
| Fort Lyon Canal ≍ | 198 | 38.11 N | 102.31 W |
| Fort Macleod | 182 | 49.43 N | 113.25 W |
| Fort Madison | 190 | 40.37 N | 91.18 W |
| Fort-Mahon-Plage | 50 | 50.21 N | 1.34 E |
| Fort Malden National Historic Park ♦ | 281 | 42.06 N | 83.07 W |
| Fort Matanzas National Monument ♦ | 192 | 29.40 N | 81.18 W |
| Fort McClellan ■ | 194 | 33.43 N | 85.47 W |
| Fort McDermitt Indian Reservation ◆⁴ | 202 | 42.00 N | 117.32 W |
| Fort McDowell Indian Reservation ◆⁴ | 200 | 33.38 N | 111.41 W |
| Fort McHenry National Monument and Historic Shrine ♦ | 208 | 39.16 N | 76.35 W |
| Fort Mckinley | 218 | 39.47 N | 84.15 W |
| Fort McMurray | 184 | 56.44 N | 111.23 W |
| Fort McNair ■ | 284c | 38.52 N | 77.04 W |
| Fort McPherson | 180 | 67.27 N | 134.53 W |
| Fort Meade | 220 | 27.45 N | 81.48 W |
| Fort Mill | 192 | 35.00 N | 80.56 W |
| Fort Miller | 210 | 43.10 N | 73.35 W |
| Fort Mitchell, Al., U.S. | 192 | 32.21 N | 85.01 W |
| Fort Mitchell, Ky., U.S. | 218 | 39.03 N | 84.32 W |
| Fort Mojave Indian Reservation ◆⁴ | 200 | 34.55 N | 114.35 W |
| Fort Monmouth ■ | 208 | 40.19 N | 74.02 W |
| Fort Monroe ■ | 208 | 37.00 N | 76.18 W |
| Fort Montgomery | 210 | 41.20 N | 73.59 W |
| Fort Morgan | 198 | 40.15 N | 103.47 W |
| Fort Myer ■ | 284c | 38.53 N | 77.05 W |
| Fort Myers | 220 | 26.38 N | 81.52 W |
| Fort Myers Beach | 220 | 26.27 N | 81.56 W |
| Fort Myers Shores | 220 | 26.43 N | 81.45 W |
| Fort Myers Villas | 220 | 26.34 N | 81.52 W |
| Fort Necessity National Battlefield ⊥ | 188 | 39.47 N | 79.39 W |
| Fort Neck ›¹ | 276 | 40.39 N | 73.28 W |
| Fort Nelson | 176 | 58.49 N | 122.43 W |
| Fort Nelson ≃ | 176 | 59.30 N | 124.00 W |
| Fort Niagara Beach | 284a | 43.16 N | 79.03 W |
| Fort Niagara State Park ♦, N.Y., U.S. | 210 | 43.16 N | 79.03 W |
| Fort Niagara State Park ♦, N.Y., U.S. | 284a | 43.16 N | 79.03 W |
| Fort Nonsense ⊥ | 276 | 40.48 N | 74.29 W |
| Fort Norman | 180 | 64.54 N | 125.34 W |
| Fort Nottingham | 158 | 29.25 S | 29.55 E |
| Fort Ogden | 220 | 27.05 N | 81.57 W |
| Fort Ord ■ | 226 | 36.40 N | 121.48 W |
| Fortore ≃ | 68 | 41.55 N | 15.17 E |
| Fort Parker State Park ♦ | 222 | 31.36 N | 96.33 W |
| Fort Payne | 194 | 34.26 N | 85.43 W |
| Fort Peck | 202 | 48.00 N | 106.26 W |
| Fort Peck Dam ◆⁶ | 202 | 47.52 N | 106.38 W |
| Fort Peck Indian Reservation ◆⁴ | 202 | 48.22 N | 105.40 W |
| Fort Peck Lake ⊜¹ | 202 | 47.45 N | 106.50 W |
| Fort Pierce | 220 | 27.26 N | 80.19 W |
| Fort Pierce Inlet ⊂ | 220 | 27.28 N | 80.18 W |
| Fort Pierre | 198 | 44.21 N | 100.22 W |
| Fort Pitt Tunnels ◆⁵ | 279b | 40.25 N | 80.00 W |
| Fort Plain | 210 | 42.55 N | 74.37 W |
| Fort Point National Historic Site ⊥ | 282 | 37.48 N | 122.28 W |
| Fort Polk ■ | 194 | 31.04 N | 93.11 W |
| Fort Portal | 154 | 0.40 N | 30.17 E |
| Fort Providence | 176 | 61.21 N | 117.39 W |
| Fort Pulaski National Monument ♦ | 192 | 32.01 N | 80.59 W |
| Fort Qu'Appelle | 184 | 50.46 N | 103.48 W |
| Fort Raleigh National Historic Site ⊥ | 192 | 35.55 N | 75.40 W |
| Fort Randall Dam ◆⁶ | 198 | 42.48 N | 98.35 W |
| Fort Recovery | 216 | 40.24 N | 84.46 W |
| Fort Resolution | 176 | 61.10 N | 113.40 W |
| Fortress Mountain ∧ | 202 | 44.20 N | 109.47 W |
| Fortress of Louisbourg National Historic Park ♦ | 186 | 45.56 N | 59.57 W |
| Fort Riley ■ | 198 | 39.04 N | 96.47 W |
| Fort Ritchie ■ | 208 | 39.43 N | 77.30 W |
| Fort Rixon | 154 | 20.01 S | 29.18 E |
| Fort Robinson State Park ♦ | 198 | 42.41 N | 103.30 W |
| Fort Rodd Hill National Historic Park ♦ | 224 | 48.26 N | 123.28 W |
| Fortrose, N.Z. | 172 | 46.34 S | 168.48 E |
| Fortrose, Scot., U.K. | 46 | 57.34 N | 4.09 W |
| Fort Rosebery → Mansa | 154 | 11.12 S | 28.53 E |
| Fort Rucker ■ | 194 | 31.20 N | 85.42 W |
| Fort Saint James | 182 | 54.26 N | 124.15 W |
| Fort Saint John | 182 | 56.15 N | 120.51 W |
| Fort Salonga | 276 | 40.55 N | 73.18 W |
| Fort Sam Houston ■ | 196 | 29.27 N | 98.27 W |
| Fort Saskatchewan | 182 | 53.43 N | 113.13 W |
| Fort Scott | 198 | 37.50 N | 94.42 W |
| Fort Seneca | 214 | 41.13 N | 83.10 W |
| Fort-Ševčenko | 84 | 44.31 N | 50.16 E |
| Fort Severn | 176 | 56.00 N | 87.38 W |
| Fort Shawnee | 216 | 40.41 N | 84.08 W |
| Fort Sheridan ■ | 216 | 42.13 N | 87.48 W |
| Fort Sill ■ | 196 | 34.40 N | 98.25 W |
| Fort Simcoe Historical State Park ♦ | 224 | 46.21 N | 120.50 W |
| Fort Simpson | 176 | 61.52 N | 121.23 W |
| Fort Sisseton State Park ♦ | 198 | 45.39 N | 97.32 W |
| Fort Smith, N.T., Can. | 176 | 60.00 N | 111.53 W |
| Fort Smith, Ar., U.S. | 194 | 35.23 N | 94.23 W |
| Fort Steele | 182 | 49.37 N | 115.38 W |
| Fort Stevens State Park ♦ | 224 | 46.10 N | 124.00 W |
| Fort Stewart ■ | 192 | 31.52 N | 81.37 W |
| Fort Stockton | 196 | 30.53 N | 102.52 W |
| Fort Sumner | 196 | 34.28 N | 104.14 W |
| Fort Sumter National Monument ♦ | 192 | 32.44 N | 79.46 W |
| Fort Supply | 196 | 36.34 N | 99.34 W |
| Fort Tejon State Historical Park ♦ | 228 | 34.52 N | 118.53 W |
| Fort Thomas, Az., U.S. | 200 | 33.02 N | 109.57 W |
| Fort Thomas, Ky., U.S. | 218 | 39.04 N | 84.26 W |
| Fort Thompson | 198 | 44.04 N | 99.26 W |
| Fort Tilden ■ | 276 | 40.33 N | 73.53 W |
| Fort Totten | 198 | 47.58 N | 98.59 W |
| Fort Totten Indian Reservation ◆⁴ | 198 | 47.53 N | 98.50 W |
| Fort Totten Park ♦ | 284c | 38.57 N | 77.00 W |
| Fort Towson | 196 | 34.01 N | 95.15 W |
| Fort-Trinquet → Bîr Mogreïn | 148 | 25.14 N | 11.35 W |
| Fortuna, Arg. | 252 | 35.07 S | 65.23 W |
| Fortuna, C.R. | 236 | 10.30 N | 84.35 W |
| Fortuna, Ca., U.S. | 204 | 40.35 N | 124.09 W |
| Fortuna, Río de la ≃ | 248 | 16.36 S | 58.46 W |
| Fortuna Ledge (Marshall) | 180 | 61.53 N | 162.05 W |
| Fortune | 186 | 47.04 N | 55.50 W |
| Fortune Bay ⊂ | 186 | 47.25 N | 55.25 W |
| Fortune Ditch ≍ | 279a | 41.20 N | 82.03 W |
| Fortune Harbour | 186 | 49.31 N | 55.15 W |
| Fortuneswell | 42 | 50.34 N | 2.27 W |
| Fort Union National Monument ♦ | 200 | 35.55 N | 105.01 W |
| Fort Union Trading Post National Historic Site ⊥ | 198 | 48.00 N | 104.03 W |
| Fort Valley | 192 | 32.33 N | 83.53 W |
| Fort Vancouver National Historic Site ⊥ | 224 | 45.38 N | 122.37 W |
| Fort Vermilion | 176 | 58.24 N | 116.00 W |
| Fortville | 218 | 39.55 N | 85.50 W |
| Fort Walton Beach | 194 | 30.24 N | 86.37 W |
| Fort Washakie | 200 | 43.00 N | 108.52 W |
| Fort Washington | 208 | 40.08 N | 75.12 W |
| Fort Washington Forest | 208 | 38.43 N | 76.59 W |
| Fort Washington State Park ♦ | 285 | 40.07 N | 75.14 W |
| Fort Wayne | 216 | 41.07 N | 85.07 W |
| Fort Wayne Military Museum ʋ | 281 | 42.18 N | 83.06 W |
| Fort Wellington | 246 | 6.24 N | 57.36 W |
| Fort Wellington National Historic Park ♦ | 212 | 44.44 N | 75.31 W |
| Fort White | 192 | 29.55 N | 82.42 W |
| Fort William → Thunder Bay, On., Can. | 190 | 48.23 N | 89.15 W |
| Fort William, Scot., U.K. | 46 | 56.49 N | 5.07 W |
| Fort Worth | 222 | 32.43 N | 97.19 W |
| Fort Yates | 198 | 46.05 N | 100.37 W |
| Forty Foot Drain ≍ | 42 | 52.28 N | 0.05 W |
| Forty Fort | 210 | 41.16 N | 75.52 W |
| Fortymile ≃ | 180 | 64.26 N | 140.32 W |
| Fort Yukon | 180 | 66.34 N | 145.17 W |
| Fort Yuma Indian Reservation ◆⁴ | 204 | 32.48 N | 114.34 W |
| Forum ♦ | 275a | 45.29 N | 73.35 W |
| Forūr, Jazīreh-ye I | 128 | 26.17 N | 54.32 E |
| Forza d'Agrò | 70 | 37.55 N | 15.20 E |
| Foscagno, Passo di )( | 64 | 46.30 N | 10.08 E |
| Fosdinovo | 64 | 44.08 N | 10.01 E |
| Fosforescente, Bahía ⊂ | 240m | 17.59 N | 67.01 W |
| Fosforitnyj | 82 | 55.19 N | 38.54 E |
| Foshan | 100 | 23.03 N | 113.09 E |
| Fosna ›¹, Nor. | 24 | 64.00 N | 10.30 E |
| Fosna ›¹, Nor. | 26 | 63.45 N | 10.25 E |
| Fosnavåg | 26 | 62.21 N | 5.39 E |
| Foso | 150 | 5.42 N | 1.17 W |
| Foss | 46 | 56.41 N | 3.58 W |
| Foss ≃, Eng., U.K. | 44 | 53.57 N | 1.06 W |
| Foss ≃, Wa., U.S. | 224 | 47.43 N | 121.18 W |
| Fossacesia | 66 | 42.15 N | 14.29 E |
| Fossacesia Marina | 66 | 42.15 N | 14.30 E |
| Fossa Eugeniana ≍ | 263 | 51.33 N | 6.36 E |
| Fossano | 62 | 44.33 N | 7.43 E |
| Fossato, Colle di )( | 66 | 43.19 N | 12.47 E |
| Fossé | 56 | 49.27 N | 5.00 E |
| Fosse-Martin | 261 | 49.05 N | 2.54 E |
| Fosses | 261 | 49.06 N | 2.29 E |
| Fosses-la-Ville | 56 | 50.24 N | 4.42 E |
| Fossil | 202 | 44.59 N | 120.12 W |
| Fossil Butte National Monument ♦ | 202 | 41.50 N | 110.40 W |
| Fossil Downs | 162 | 18.08 S | 125.38 E |
| Fossil Lake ⊜ | 202 | 43.18 N | 120.15 W |
| Fossombrone | 66 | 43.41 N | 12.48 E |
| Fosston | 198 | 47.34 N | 95.45 W |
| Fos-sur-Mer | 62 | 43.26 N | 4.57 E |
| Foster, Austl. | 169 | 38.39 S | 146.12 E |
| Foster, Ky., U.S. | 218 | 38.47 N | 84.12 W |
| Foster, R.I., U.S. | 207 | 41.51 N | 71.45 W |
| Foster ≃ | 184 | 55.47 N | 105.49 W |
| Foster, Mount ∧ | 180 | 59.48 N | 135.29 W |
| Foster Brook | 214 | 41.59 N | 78.37 W |
| Foster City | 226 | 37.33 N | 122.16 W |
| Foster Creek ≃ | 198 | 44.34 N | 98.12 W |
| Fosterdale | 210 | 41.42 N | 74.58 W |
| Foster Joseph Sayers Reservoir ⊜¹ | 214 | 41.02 N | 77.40 W |
| Fosters | 194 | 33.05 N | 87.41 W |
| Fosters Pond ⊜ | 283 | 42.37 N | 71.08 W |
| Foster Street | 260 | 51.46 N | 0.09 E |
| Foster Village | 229c | 21.21 N | 157.55 W |
| Fostoria | 214 | 41.09 N | 83.25 W |
| Fót | 264c | 47.37 N | 19.12 E |
| Fotadrevo | 157b | 24.03 S | 45.01 E |
| Fotan | 100 | 24.12 N | 117.53 E |
| Fóti-Somlyó ∧² | 264c | 47.38 N | 19.13 E |
| Foucarmont | 50 | 49.51 N | 1.34 E |
| Fou-Chouen → Fushun | 104 | 41.52 N | 123.53 E |
| Fouesnant | 32 | 47.54 N | 4.01 W |
| Foug | 56 | 48.41 N | 5.47 E |
| Fougamou | 152 | 1.13 S | 10.36 E |
| Fougères | 32 | 48.21 N | 1.12 W |
| Fougères-sur-Bièvre | 50 | 47.27 N | 1.21 E |
| Fougerolles | 58 | 47.53 N | 6.24 E |
| Fouhsin → Fuxin | 104 | 42.03 N | 121.46 E |
| Fouju | 261 | 48.35 N | 2.47 E |
| Fouke | 194 | 33.16 N | 93.53 W |
| Foula I | 46a | 60.08 N | 2.05 W |
| Foulain | 58 | 48.02 N | 5.13 E |
| Foulalaba | 150 | 10.41 N | 7.22 W |
| Foula Mori | 150 | 12.10 N | 13.51 W |
| Foulatari | 146 | 13.41 N | 12.03 E |
| Foul Bay ⊂ | 140 | 23.30 N | 35.39 E |
| Fouling → Fuling | 102 | 29.42 N | 107.21 E |
| Foulness ≃ | 44 | 53.47 N | 0.43 W |
| Foulness Island I | 42 | 51.36 N | 0.55 E |
| Foulness Point › | 42 | 51.38 N | 0.57 E |
| Foulpointe | 157b | 17.41 S | 49.31 E |
| Foulsham | 42 | 52.48 N | 1.01 E |
| Foulwind, Cape › | 172 | 41.45 S | 171.28 E |
| Foumban | 152 | 5.43 N | 10.55 E |
| Foumbot | 152 | 5.30 N | 10.38 E |
| Foumbouni | 157a | 11.50 S | 43.30 E |
| Foum-el-Hisn | 148 | 28.59 N | 8.55 W |
| Foum-Zguid | 148 | 30.04 N | 6.54 W |
| Foundiougne | 150 | 14.08 N | 16.28 W |
| Fountain, Co., U.S. | 198 | 38.40 N | 104.42 W |
| Fountain, Fl., U.S. | 192 | 30.09 N | 85.38 W |
| Fountain □⁶ | 216 | 40.17 N | 87.13 W |
| Fountain City, In., U.S. | 218 | 39.57 N | 84.55 W |
| Fountain City, Wi., U.S. | 190 | 44.07 N | 91.43 W |
| Fountain Creek ≃, Co., U.S. | 198 | 38.15 N | 104.35 W |
| Fountain Creek ≃, Il., U.S. | 219 | 38.20 N | 90.22 W |
| Fountain Green | 200 | 39.37 N | 111.38 W |
| Fountain Hill | 208 | 40.36 N | 75.23 W |
| Fountain Inn | 192 | 34.41 N | 82.11 W |
| Fountain Park | 216 | 41.50 N | 84.32 W |
| Fountain Peak ∧ | 204 | 34.57 N | 115.32 W |
| Fountain Place | 194 | 30.31 N | 91.09 W |
| Fountains Abbey ʋ¹ | 44 | 54.07 N | 1.34 W |
| Fountains Creek ≃ | 208 | 36.33 N | 77.21 W |
| Fountaintown | 218 | 39.41 N | 85.46 W |
| Fountain Valley | 228 | 33.42 N | 117.57 W |
| Fourche LaFave ≃ | 194 | 34.58 N | 92.35 W |
| Fourche Maline ≃ | 194 | 34.55 N | 94.55 W |
| Fourchu | 186 | 45.43 N | 60.15 W |
| Four Corners | 202 | 44.55 N | 122.58 W |
| Four Elms | 260 | 51.13 N | 0.06 E |
| Four Hole Swamp ≃ | 192 | 33.03 N | 80.24 W |
| Fouriesburg | 158 | 28.38 S | 28.14 E |
| Fourmies | 50 | 50.00 N | 4.03 E |
| Four Mile Creek ≃, On., Can. | 284a | 43.15 N | 79.08 W |
| Fourmile Creek ≃, N.Y., U.S. | 284a | 43.17 N | 79.00 W |
| Four Mile Creek ≃, Oh., U.S. | 218 | 39.26 N | 84.32 W |
| Four Mile Creek State Park ♦ | 284a | 43.16 N | 79.00 W |
| Fourmile Draw V | 196 | 32.40 N | 104.18 W |
| Four Mile Lake ⊜ | 212 | 44.40 N | 78.44 W |
| Four Mile Run ≃ | 284c | 38.50 N | 77.02 W |
| Four Mountains, Islands of II | 180 | 52.50 N | 170.00 W |
| Fournaise, Piton de la ∧ | 157c | 21.14 S | 55.43 E |
| Fourneau, Pointe à › | 275a | 45.22 N | 73.51 W |
| Fourneaux, Fr. | 50 | 47.53 N | 1.48 E |
| Fourneaux, Fr. | 62 | 45.11 N | 6.39 E |
| Fournier, Lac ⊜ | 186 | 51.33 N | 65.25 W |
| Fournière, Lac ⊜ | 190 | 48.04 N | 78.03 W |
| Foúrnoi I | 38 | 37.34 N | 26.30 E |
| Four Oaks | 192 | 35.26 N | 78.25 W |
| Fourqueux | 261 | 48.53 N | 2.04 E |
| Fours | 32 | 46.49 N | 3.43 E |
| Fourteenmile Creek ≃ | 218 | 38.26 N | 85.37 W |
| Fourth Cataract → Rābi', Ash-Shallāl ar- ⌊ | 140 | 18.47 N | 32.03 E |
| Fourth Cliff ⊥⁴ | 283 | 42.09 N | 70.42 W |
| Four Towns | 281 | 42.37 N | 83.25 W |
| Fous, Pointe des › | 240d | 15.12 N | 61.20 W |
| Foussard ≃ | 50 | 48.16 N | 1.17 E |
| Fouta Djalon ◆¹ | 150 | 11.30 N | 12.30 W |
| Fou-Tcheou → Fuzhou | 100 | 26.06 N | 119.17 E |
| Foux, Cap à › | 238 | 19.41 N | 73.27 W |
| Fouyang → Fuyang | 100 | 32.54 N | 115.49 E |
| Fouzon ≃ | 50 | 47.16 N | 1.27 E |
| Foveaux Strait ȣ | 172 | 46.35 S | 168.00 E |
| Foveran | 46 | 57.18 N | 2.02 W |
| Fowey | 42 | 50.20 N | 4.38 W |
| Fowler, Ca., U.S. | 226 | 36.37 N | 119.40 W |
| Fowler, Co., U.S. | 198 | 38.07 N | 104.01 W |
| Fowler, In., U.S. | 216 | 40.37 N | 87.19 W |
| Fowler, Ks., U.S. | 198 | 37.23 N | 100.11 W |
| Fowler, Mi., U.S. | 216 | 43.00 N | 84.44 W |
| Fowler, Oh., U.S. | 214 | 41.19 N | 80.40 W |
| Fowler, Lake ⊜ | 168b | 35.06 S | 137.37 E |
| Fowler, Point › | 162 | 32.02 S | 132.29 E |
| Fowler Creek ≃ | 281 | 42.17 N | 83.30 W |
| Fowlers Bay | 162 | 31.59 S | 132.27 E |
| Fowlerton | 196 | 28.28 N | 98.48 W |
| Fowlerville | 216 | 42.39 N | 84.04 W |
| Fowliang → Jingdezhen | 100 | 29.16 N | 117.11 E |
| Fowman | 128 | 37.13 N | 49.19 E |
| Fox | 180 | 64.51 N | 147.46 W |
| Fox ≃, Mb., Can. | 184 | 56.03 N | 93.18 W |
| Fox ≃, U.S. | 194 | 40.18 N | 91.30 W |
| Fox ≃, U.S. | 216 | 41.21 N | 88.50 W |
| Fox ≃, Il., U.S. | 194 | 38.32 N | 88.08 W |
| Fox ≃, Wi., U.S. | 190 | 44.32 N | 88.01 W |
| Fox, Cape › | 182 | 54.47 N | 130.51 W |
| Foxboro, On., Can. | 212 | 44.15 N | 77.26 W |
| Foxboro, Ma., U.S. | 207 | 42.03 N | 71.15 W |
| Foxboro Raceway ♦ | 283 | 42.06 N | 71.16 W |
| Foxboro Stadium ♦ | 283 | 42.05 N | 71.16 W |
| Fox Brook ≃ | 276 | 41.03 N | 74.13 W |
| Foxburg | 214 | 41.09 N | 79.41 W |
| Fox Chapel | 279b | 40.30 N | 79.55 W |
| Fox Chase ◆⁸ | 285 | 40.04 N | 75.05 W |
| Fox Chase Manor | 285 | 40.05 N | 75.06 W |
| Fox Creek ≃, Ky., U.S. | 218 | 38.16 N | 83.41 W |
| Fox Creek ≃, N.Y., U.S. | 210 | 42.41 N | 74.18 W |
| Foxe Basin ⊂ | 176 | 68.25 N | 77.00 W |
| Foxe-Becken → Foxe Basin ⊂ | 176 | 68.25 N | 77.00 W |
| Foxe Channel ȣ | 176 | 64.30 N | 80.00 W |
| Foxen ⊜ | 26 | 59.23 N | 11.52 E |
| Foxe Peninsula ›¹ | 176 | 65.00 N | 76.00 W |
| Foxford | 48 | 53.58 N | 9.08 W |
| Fox Glacier | 172 | 43.28 S | 170.00 E |
| Foxhall | 284c | 39.04 N | 77.03 W |
| Fox Harbour | 186 | 47.19 N | 53.55 W |
| Fox Hills | 284c | 39.02 N | 77.11 W |
| Foxhole | 42 | 50.21 N | 4.52 W |
| Foxholes | 44 | 54.08 N | 0.28 W |
| Fox Hollow Lake ⊜ | 276 | 41.02 N | 74.40 W |


**ENGLISH**


| Name | Page | Lat.°′ | Long.°′ |
|---|---|---|---|
| Fox Island I, On., Can. | 212 | 44.28 N | 78.24 W |
| Fox Island I, Wa., U.S. | 224 | 47.16 N | 122.37 W |
| Fox Islands II | 180 | 53.30 N | 168.00 W |
| Fox Lake, Il., U.S. | 216 | 42.23 N | 88.11 W |
| Fox Lake, Wi., U.S. | 190 | 43.33 N | 88.54 W |
| Fox Lake ⊜ | 216 | 42.25 N | 88.09 W |
| Fox Mountain ∧ | 180 | 61.55 N | 133.22 W |
| Foxpark | 200 | 41.05 N | 106.09 W |
| Fox Point | 216 | 43.09 N | 87.54 W |
| Fox Point › | 276 | 40.54 N | 73.35 W |
| Fox River Estates | 216 | 41.58 N | 88.20 W |
| Fox River Grove | 216 | 42.12 N | 88.12 W |
| Foxton | 172 | 40.28 S | 175.18 E |
| Foxton Beach | 172 | 40.28 S | 175.13 E |
| Foxvale | 283 | 42.02 N | 71.14 W |
| Fox Valley, Austl. | 274a | 33.45 S | 151.06 E |
| Fox Valley, Sk., Can. | 184 | 50.29 N | 109.28 W |
| Foxwells | 208 | 37.38 N | 76.18 W |
| Foxwist Green | 262 | 53.12 N | 2.34 W |
| Foxworth | 194 | 31.14 N | 89.52 W |
| Foyedong | 98 | 40.41 N | 119.12 E |
| Foyers | 46 | 57.14 N | 4.29 W |
| Foyle ≃ | 48 | 54.59 N | 7.18 W |
| Foyle, Lough ⊂ | 48 | 55.06 N | 7.08 W |
| Foynes | 48 | 52.37 N | 9.06 W |
| Foza | 64 | 45.54 N | 11.38 E |
| Foz do Areia, Represa de ⊜¹ | 252 | 26.00 S | 51.35 W |
| Foz do Cunene | 152 | 17.16 S | 11.50 E |
| Foz do Iguaçu | 252 | 25.33 S | 54.35 W |
| Foz do Jordão | 248 | 9.23 S | 71.56 W |
| Foz Giraldo | 34 | 40.00 N | 7.43 W |
| Foziling | 100 | 31.20 N | 116.17 E |
| Frabosa Soprana | 62 | 44.17 N | 7.48 E |
| Frackville | 208 | 40.47 N | 76.13 W |
| Fraction Run ≃ | 278 | 41.34 N | 88.04 W |
| Fraga, Arg. | 252 | 33.30 S | 65.48 W |
| Fraga, Esp. | 34 | 41.31 N | 0.21 E |
| Fragagnano | 68 | 40.26 N | 17.28 E |
| Fragneto Monforte | 68 | 41.15 N | 14.46 E |
| Fragoso, Cayo I | 240p | 22.44 N | 79.30 W |
| Fragrant Hills Park ♦ | 271a | 39.59 N | 116.11 E |
| Fragua, Sierra de la ⋏ | 196 | 26.41 N | 102.13 W |
| Fraile Muerto | 252 | 32.31 S | 54.32 W |
| Fraïn, Chott el ⊜ | 34 | 35.57 N | 5.38 E |
| Fraire | 50 | 50.16 N | 4.30 E |
| Fraisans | 58 | 47.09 N | 5.46 E |
| Fraisse | 62 | 45.23 N | 4.15 E |
| Fraize | 58 | 48.11 N | 7.00 E |
| Fram | 61 | 46.27 N | 15.38 E |
| Frameries | 50 | 50.24 N | 3.54 E |
| Framingham | 207 | 42.16 N | 71.25 W |
| Framingham State College ʋ² | 283 | 42.18 N | 71.26 W |
| Framlingham | 42 | 52.13 N | 1.21 E |
| Frammersbach | 56 | 50.04 N | 9.28 E |
| Framnes Mountains ⋏ | 9 | 67.50 S | 62.35 E |
| Frampol | 30 | 50.41 N | 22.40 E |
| Frampton Cotterell | 42 | 51.32 N | 2.29 W |
| Frampton on Severn | 42 | 51.46 N | 2.22 W |
| França, Bra. | 250 | 11.34 S | 40.36 W |
| Franca, Bra. | 255 | 20.32 S | 47.24 W |
| Franca-Iosifa, Zeml'a (Franz Josef Land) II | 12 | 81.00 N | 55.00 E |
| Français, Récif des ◆² | 175f | 19.40 S | 163.20 E |
| Francavilla al Mare | 66 | 42.25 N | 14.17 E |
| Francavilla Angitola | 68 | 38.46 N | 16.16 E |
| Francavilla d'Ete | 66 | 43.11 N | 13.32 E |
| Francavilla di Sicilia | 70 | 37.54 N | 15.08 E |
| Francavilla Fontana | 68 | 40.31 N | 17.35 E |
| Francavilla in Sinni | 68 | 40.05 N | 16.12 E |
| Francavilla Marittima | 68 | 39.49 N | 16.23 E |
| France □¹, Europe | 22 | 46.00 N | 2.00 E |
| France □¹, Europe | 32 | 46.00 N | 2.00 E |
| Frances ≃ | 180 | 60.12 N | 129.02 W |
| Francés, Cabo ›, Cuba | 240p | 21.54 N | 84.02 W |
| Francés, Cabo ›, Cuba | 240p | 21.38 N | 83.12 W |
| Frances Creek | 164 | 13.35 S | 131.52 E |
| Francês dos Carvalhos | 256 | 22.05 S | 44.29 W |
| Frances Lake ⊜ | 180 | 61.25 N | 129.30 W |
| Francés Viejo, Cabo › | 238 | 19.39 N | 69.55 W |
| Francesville | 216 | 40.59 N | 86.52 W |
| Franceville | 152 | 1.38 S | 13.35 E |
| Francfort-sur-Main → Frankfurt am Main | 56 | 50.07 N | 8.40 E |
| Franche-Comté □⁹ | 58 | 47.00 N | 6.00 E |
| Franchère, Lac ⊜ | 206 | 46.47 N | 74.58 W |
| Franches-Montagnes ⋏ | 58 | 47.12 N | 7.00 E |
| Francia | 252 | 32.33 S | 56.37 W |
| Francia → France □¹ | 32 | 46.00 N | 2.00 E |
| Francia, Estación de ◆⁵ | 266d | 41.23 N | 2.11 E |
| Francis | 184 | 50.05 N | 103.55 W |
| Francis, Lake ⊜ | 206 | 45.02 N | 71.20 W |
| Francis Case, Lake ⊜¹ | 198 | 43.15 N | 99.00 W |
| Francisco A. Berra | 258 | 35.23 S | 58.51 W |
| Francisco Álvarez | 258 | 34.38 S | 58.52 W |
| Francisco Beltrão | 252 | 26.05 S | 53.04 W |
| Francisco I. Madero, Méx. | 232 | 25.45 N | 103.21 W |
| Francisco I. Madero, Méx. | 232 | 24.32 N | 104.22 W |
| Francisco I. Madero, Méx. | 234 | 21.36 N | 104.49 W |
| Francisco José, Tierra → Franca-Iosifa, Zeml'a II | 12 | 81.00 N | 55.00 E |
| Francisco Morato | 256 | 23.16 S | 46.45 W |
| Francisco Morazán □⁵ | 236 | 14.15 N | 87.15 W |
| Francisco Murguía | 234 | 24.00 N | 103.01 W |
| Francisco Perito Moreno, Parque Nacional ♦ | 254 | 47.50 S | 72.08 W |
| Francisco Sá | 255 | 16.28 S | 43.30 W |
| Francisco Zarco | 204 | 32.06 N | 116.30 W |
| Francis E. Warren Air Force Base ■ | 198 | 41.09 N | 104.52 W |
| Francistown | 156 | 21.11 S | 27.32 E |
| Francitas | 222 | 28.52 N | 96.20 W |
| Franco da Rocha | 256 | 23.20 S | 46.43 W |
| Francofonte | 70 | 37.14 N | 14.53 E |
| François | 186 | 47.35 N | 56.45 W |
| François, Lacs à ⊜ | 186 | 51.40 N | 65.49 W |
| François-Joseph, Îles du → Franca-Iosifa, Zeml'a II | 12 | 81.00 N | 55.00 E |
| François Lake | 182 | 54.04 N | 125.44 W |
| François Lake ⊜ | 182 | 54.00 N | 125.40 W |
| Francolise | 68 | 41.11 N | 14.03 E |
| Franconia Notch State Park ♦ | 188 | 44.06 N | 71.43 W |
| Franconville | 261 | 48.59 N | 2.14 E |
| Francs Peak ∧ | 202 | 43.58 N | 109.20 W |
| Francueil | 50 | 47.19 N | 1.05 E |
| Franeker | 52 | 53.11 N | 5.32 E |
| Frangy | 58 | 46.01 N | 5.56 E |
| Frank | 279b | 40.16 N | 79.48 W |
| Frank and Poet Drain ≍ | 281 | 42.06 N | 83.12 W |
| Frankby | 262 | 53.22 N | 3.08 W |
| Frankel City | 196 | 32.23 N | 102.47 W |
| Franken □⁹ | 30 | 50.00 N | 10.00 E |
| Frankenau | 56 | 51.05 N | 8.56 E |
| Frankenberg | 54 | 50.54 N | 13.01 E |
| Frankenberg-Eder | 56 | 51.03 N | 8.48 E |


**DEUTSCH**


| Name | Seite | Breite°′ | Länge°′ E = Ost |
|---|---|---|---|
| Frankenburg | 60 | 48.05 N | 13.30 E |
| Frankenheim | 56 | 50.32 N | 10.04 E |
| Frankenhöhe ⋏ | 56 | 49.15 N | 10.15 E |
| Frankenmarkt | 64 | 47.59 N | 13.25 E |
| Frankenmuth | 190 | 43.19 N | 83.44 W |
| Frankenstein | 56 | 49.26 N | 7.58 E |
| Frankenthal | 56 | 49.32 N | 8.21 E |
| Frankenwald ⋏ | 54 | 50.18 N | 11.36 E |
| Frankfield | 241q | 18.09 N | 77.22 W |
| Frankford, On., Can. | 212 | 44.12 N | 77.36 W |
| Frankford, De., U.S. | 208 | 38.31 N | 75.14 W |
| Frankford, Mo., U.S. | 219 | 39.29 N | 91.19 W |
| Frankford ◆⁸ | 285 | 40.01 N | 75.05 W |
| Frankford Arsenal ■ | 285 | 40.00 N | 75.04 W |
| Frankfort, S. Afr. | 158 | 32.44 S | 27.28 E |
| Frankfort, S. Afr. | 158 | 27.17 S | 28.30 E |
| Frankfort, Il., U.S. | 216 | 41.29 N | 87.50 W |
| Frankfort, In., U.S. | 216 | 40.16 N | 86.30 W |
| Frankfort, Ks., U.S. | 198 | 39.42 N | 96.25 W |
| Frankfort, Ky., U.S. | 218 | 38.12 N | 84.52 W |
| Frankfort, Mi., U.S. | 190 | 44.38 N | 86.14 W |
| Frankfort, N.Y., U.S. | 210 | 43.02 N | 75.04 W |
| Frankfort, Oh., U.S. | 218 | 39.24 N | 83.10 W |
| Frankfort, S.D., U.S. | 198 | 44.52 N | 98.18 W |
| Frankfort Springs | 214 | 40.30 N | 80.25 W |
| Frankfurt | 54 | 52.20 N | 14.33 E |
| Frankfurt am Main | 56 | 50.07 N | 8.40 E |
| Frankfurt am Main, Flughafen ⊠ | 56 | 50.02 N | 8.33 E |
| Frank G. Bonelli Regional County Park ♦ | 280 | 34.05 N | 117.49 W |
| Frank Hann National Park ♦ | 162 | 32.50 S | 120.25 E |
| Fränkische Alb ⋏² | 60 | 49.20 N | 11.30 E |
| Fränkische Rezat ≃ | 56 | 49.11 N | 11.01 E |
| Fränkische Saale ≃ | 56 | 50.03 N | 9.42 E |
| Fränkische Schweiz ◆¹ | 60 | 49.45 N | 11.25 E |
| Frank Key I | 220 | 25.07 N | 80.54 W |
| Frankland ≃ | 162 | 34.58 S | 116.49 E |
| Frankleben | 54 | 51.18 N | 11.56 E |
| Franklin, S. Afr. | 158 | 30.18 S | 29.30 E |
| Franklin, Az., U.S. | 200 | 32.40 N | 109.04 W |
| Franklin, Ga., U.S. | 192 | 33.16 N | 85.05 W |
| Franklin, Id., U.S. | 202 | 42.00 N | 111.48 W |
| Franklin, Il., U.S. | 219 | 39.37 N | 90.03 W |
| Franklin, In., U.S. | 218 | 39.28 N | 86.03 W |
| Franklin, Ky., U.S. | 194 | 36.43 N | 86.34 W |
| Franklin, La., U.S. | 194 | 29.47 N | 91.30 W |
| Franklin, Me., U.S. | 188 | 44.35 N | 68.13 W |
| Franklin, Ma., U.S. | 207 | 42.05 N | 71.23 W |
| Franklin, Mi., U.S. | 281 | 42.31 N | 83.18 W |
| Franklin, Mn., U.S. | 198 | 44.31 N | 94.52 W |
| Franklin, Ne., U.S. | 198 | 40.05 N | 98.57 W |
| Franklin, N.H., U.S. | 188 | 43.26 N | 71.38 W |
| Franklin, N.J., U.S. | 210 | 41.07 N | 74.34 W |
| Franklin, N.Y., U.S. | 210 | 42.20 N | 75.09 W |
| Franklin, N.C., U.S. | 192 | 35.10 N | 83.22 W |
| Franklin, Oh., U.S. | 218 | 39.33 N | 84.18 W |
| Franklin, Pa., U.S. | 214 | 41.24 N | 79.50 W |
| Franklin, Tn., U.S. | 194 | 35.55 N | 86.52 W |
| Franklin, Tx., U.S. | 222 | 31.01 N | 96.29 W |
| Franklin, Vt., U.S. | 206 | 44.58 N | 72.55 W |
| Franklin, Va., U.S. | 208 | 36.40 N | 76.55 W |
| Franklin, W.V., U.S. | 188 | 38.39 N | 79.20 W |
| Franklin, Wi., U.S. | 216 | 42.54 N | 88.03 W |
| Franklin □⁶, In., U.S. | 218 | 39.25 N | 85.01 W |
| Franklin □⁶, Ky., U.S. | 218 | 38.14 N | 84.52 W |
| Franklin □⁶, Ma., U.S. | 207 | 42.36 N | 72.36 W |
| Franklin □⁶, Mo., U.S. | 219 | 38.25 N | 91.03 W |
| Franklin □⁶, N.Y., U.S. | 206 | 44.57 N | 74.18 W |
| Franklin □⁶, Oh., U.S. | 218 | 39.57 N | 83.00 W |
| Franklin □⁶, Pa., U.S. | 208 | 39.56 N | 77.40 W |
| Franklin □⁶, Tx., U.S. | 222 | 33.07 N | 95.13 W |
| Franklin □⁶, Vt., U.S. | 206 | 44.57 N | 72.52 W |
| Franklin, Mount ∧ | 171b | 35.29 S | 148.47 E |
| Franklin, Point › | 180 | 70.54 N | 158.48 W |
| Franklin Bay ⊂ | 176 | 69.45 N | 126.00 W |
| Franklin Canyon Reservoir ⊜¹ | 280 | 34.06 N | 118.25 W |
| Franklin Delano Roosevelt National Historic Site ⊥ | 210 | 41.46 N | 73.56 W |
| Franklin Delano Roosevelt Park ♦ | 285 | 39.54 N | 75.11 W |
| Franklin D. Roosevelt Lake ⊜¹ | 202 | 48.20 N | 118.10 W |
| Franklin Farms | 279b | 40.10 N | 80.16 W |
| Franklin Grove | 190 | 41.50 N | 89.18 W |
| Franklin Harbor ⊂ | 166 | 33.42 S | 136.56 E |
| Franklin Institute ʋ | 285 | 39.57 N | 75.11 W |
| Franklin Island I | 212 | 45.24 N | 80.20 W |
| Franklin Lake ⊜, N.T., Can. | 176 | 66.56 N | 96.03 W |
| Franklin Lake ⊜, Nv., U.S. | 204 | 40.24 N | 115.12 W |
| Franklin Lake ⊜, N.J., U.S. | 276 | 40.59 N | 74.13 W |
| Franklin Lakes | 276 | 41.01 N | 74.12 W |
| Franklin-Lower Gordon Wild Rivers National Park ♦ | 166 | 42.46 S | 145.45 E |
| Franklin Mountains ⋏, N.T., Can. | 180 | 63.00 N | 123.50 W |
| Franklin Mountains ⋏, N.Z. | 172 | 44.55 S | 167.45 E |
| Franklin Park, Il., U.S. | 216 | 41.56 N | 87.51 W |
| Franklin Park, Md., U.S. | 284c | 39.03 N | 77.06 W |
| Franklin Park, N.J., U.S. | 276 | 40.26 N | 74.32 W |
| Franklin Park, N.Y., U.S. | 210 | 43.05 N | 76.05 W |
| Franklin Park, Pa., U.S. | 214 | 40.35 N | 80.06 W |
| Franklin Park, Va., U.S. | 284c | 38.55 N | 77.09 W |
| Franklin Park ♦ | 283 | 42.18 N | 71.06 W |
| Franklin Pond ⊜ | 276 | 41.06 N | 74.35 W |
| Franklin Ridge ∧ | 282 | 38.00 N | 122.10 W |
| Franklin River | 224 | 49.06 N | 124.49 W |
| Franklin Roosevelt Park ◆⁸ | 273d | 26.09 S | 27.59 E |
| Franklin Springs | 210 | 43.02 N | 75.24 W |
| Franklin Square | 210 | 40.42 N | 73.40 W |
| Franklin State Forest ♦ | 283 | 42.04 N | 71.26 W |
| Franklin Strait ȣ | 176 | 72.00 N | 96.00 W |
| Franklinton, La., U.S. | 194 | 30.50 N | 90.09 W |
| Franklinton, N.C., U.S. | 192 | 36.06 N | 78.27 W |
| Franklintown | 208 | 40.05 N | 77.02 W |
| Franklinville, N.J., U.S. | 208 | 39.37 N | 75.04 W |
| Franklinville, N.Y., U.S. | 210 | 42.20 N | 78.27 W |
| Frankreich → France □¹ | 32 | 46.00 N | 2.00 E |
| Frankston, Austl. | 169 | 38.08 S | 145.07 E |
| Frankston, Tx., U.S. | 222 | 32.03 N | 95.30 W |
| Franksville | 216 | 42.45 N | 87.54 W |
| Frankton | 216 | 40.13 N | 85.46 W |
| Frankville | 194 | 31.38 N | 88.08 W |
| Frånö | 26 | 62.54 N | 17.50 E |
| Fr'anovo | 82 | 56.08 N | 38.27 E |
| Franschhoek | 158 | 33.55 S | 19.09 E |
| Fransfontein | 156 | 20.12 S | 15.01 E |
| Fränsta | 26 | 62.30 N | 16.09 E |
| Františkovy Lázně | 54 | 50.04 N | 12.21 E |
| Franvillers | 50 | 49.58 N | 2.30 E |
| Franzburg | 54 | 54.11 N | 12.52 E |
| Franzensburg ⊥ | 264b | 48.04 N | 16.22 E |
| Franzensfeste → Fortezza | 64 | 46.47 N | 11.37 E |
| Franz Josef | 172 | 43.24 S | 170.11 E |
| Franz Josef Land → Franca Iosifa, Zeml'a II | 12 | 81.00 N | 55.00 E |


**Symbols** in the index entries represent the broad categories identified in the key at the right. Symbols with superior numbers (⋏¹) identify subcategories (see complete key on page *I* · *1*).

**Symbole** im Register stellen die rechts im Schlüssel erklärten Kategorien dar. Symbole mit hochgestellten Ziffern (⋏¹) bezeichnen Unterabteilungen einer Kategorie (vgl. vollständiger Schlüssel auf Seite *I* · *1*).

**Los símbolos** incluídos en el texto del índice representan las grandes categorías identificadas con la clave a la derecha. Los símbolos con numeros en su parte superior (⋏¹) identifican las subcategorías (véase la clave completa en la página *I* · *1*).

**Les symboles** de l'index représentent les catégories indiquées dans la légende à droite. Les symboles suivis d'un indice (⋏¹) représentent des sous-catégories (voir légende complète à la page *I* · *1*).

**Os símbolos** incluídos no texto do índice representam as grandes categorias identificadas com a chave à direita. Os símbolos com números em sua parte superior (⋏¹) identificam as subcategorias (veja-se a chave completa à página *I* · *1*).

| | | | | |
|---|---|---|---|---|
| ∧ Mountain | Berg | Montaña | Montagne | Montanha |
| ⋏ Mountains | Gebirge | Montañas | Montagnes | Montanhas |
| )( Pass | Paß | Paso | Col | Passo |
| V Valley, Canyon | Tal, Cañon | Valle, Cañón | Vallée, Canyon | Vale, Canhão |
| ≃ Plain | Ebene | Llano | Plaine | Planície |
| › Cape | Kap | Cabo | Cap | Cabo |
| I Island | Insel | Isla | Île | Ilha |
| II Islands | Inseln | Islas | Îles | Ilhas |
| ⊥ Other Topographic Features | Andere Topographische Objekte | Otros Elementos Topográficos | Autres données topographiques | Outros acidentes topográficos |

ESPAÑOL

| Nombre | Página | Lat.°′ | Long.°′ W = Oeste |
|---|---|---|---|
| Franz-Josefs-Bahnhof ◆[5] | 264b | 48.13 N | 16.21 E |
| Franz-Josefs-Höhe ♦ | 64 | 47.04 N | 12.45 E |
| Französische Süd- und Antarktis-Gebiete → French Southern and Antarctic Ter □[2] | 6 | 49.30 S | 69.30 E |
| Französisch-Polynesien → French Polynesia □[2] | 14 | 15.00 S | 140.00 W |
| Frasca, Capo della ➤ | 71 | 39.46 N | 8.27 E |
| Frascati | 66 | 41.48 N | 12.41 E |
| Frascineto | 68 | 39.50 N | 16.16 E |
| Frasdorf | 64 | 47.48 N | 12.16 E |
| Fraser, Co., U.S. | 200 | 39.56 N | 105.49 W |
| Fraser, Mi., U.S. | 281 | 42.32 N | 82.56 W |
| Fraser ≃, B.C., Can. | 182 | 49.09 N | 123.12 W |
| Fraser ≃, Nf., Can. | 176 | 56.35 N | 61.55 W |
| Fraser ≃, Co., U.S. | 200 | 40.06 N | 105.58 W |
| Fraser, Mount ʌ | 162 | 25.39 S | 118.23 E |
| Fraserburg | 158 | 31.55 S | 21.30 E |
| Fraserburgh | 46 | 57.42 N | 2.00 W |
| Fraser Island I | 166 | 25.15 S | 153.10 E |
| Fraser Lake | 182 | 54.04 N | 124.51 W |
| Fraser Lake @ | 182 | 54.05 N | 124.35 W |
| Fraser National Park ♦ | 169 | 37.10 S | 145.50 E |
| Fraser Plateau ⩤[1] | 182 | 52.00 N | 123.00 W |
| Fraser Range | 162 | 32.03 S | 122.48 E |
| Frasertown | 172 | 38.58 S | 177.24 E |
| Frasne | 58 | 46.51 N | 6.10 E |
| Frasnes-lez-Anvaing | 50 | 50.40 N | 3.36 E |
| Frassine ≃ | 64 | 45.18 N | 11.37 E |
| Frassinoro | 64 | 44.18 N | 10.34 E |
| Frati, Monte dei ʌ | 66 | 43.40 N | 12.10 E |
| Fratres | 61 | 48.59 N | 15.21 E |
| Frattamaggiore | 68 | 40.57 N | 14.16 E |
| Frattócchie | 267a | 41.46 N | 12.37 E |
| Frauenfeld | 58 | 47.34 N | 8.54 E |
| Frauenkirchen | 61 | 47.50 N | 16.56 E |
| Frauenstein | 54 | 50.48 N | 13.32 E |
| Frauental an der Lassnitz | 61 | 46.48 N | 15.14 E |
| Frauenwald | 54 | 50.35 N | 10.51 E |
| Fray Bentos | 252 | 33.08 S | 58.18 W |
| Fray Jorge, Parque Nacional ♦ | 252 | 30.40 S | 71.45 W |
| Fray Luis Beltrán | 252 | 39.19 S | 65.46 W |
| Fray Marcos | 252 | 34.11 S | 55.44 W |
| Frazee | 198 | 46.43 N | 95.42 W |
| Frazer, Mt., U.S. | 202 | 48.03 N | 106.02 W |
| Frazer, Pa., U.S. | 208 | 40.02 N | 75.33 W |
| Frazeysburg | 214 | 40.07 N | 82.07 W |
| Frazier Mountain ʌ | 228 | 34.47 N | 118.58 W |
| Frazier Park | 228 | 34.49 N | 118.56 W |
| Fr'azino | 82 | 55.58 N | 38.04 E |
| Frazzanò | 70 | 38.04 N | 14.44 E |
| Frechen | 56 | 50.54 N | 6.49 E |
| Frechilla | 34 | 42.08 N | 4.50 W |
| Freckenhorst | 52 | 51.55 N | 7.58 E |
| Freckleton | 262 | 53.45 N | 2.52 W |
| Freddo ≃ | 70 | 38.01 N | 12.54 E |
| Fredeburg | 56 | 51.11 N | 8.18 E |
| Fredelsloh | 52 | 51.44 N | 9.47 E |
| Freden | 52 | 51.56 N | 9.54 E |
| Fredenbeck | 52 | 53.32 N | 9.24 E |
| Fredensborg | 41 | 55.58 N | 12.24 E |
| Fredensborg ⊥ | 41 | 55.58 N | 12.23 E |
| Frederic | 190 | 45.39 N | 92.28 W |
| Frederica | 208 | 39.00 N | 75.27 W |
| Fredericia | 41 | 55.35 N | 9.46 E |
| Frederick, Il., U.S. | 219 | 40.04 N | 90.26 W |
| Frederick, Md., U.S. | 208 | 39.24 N | 77.24 W |
| Frederick, Ok., U.S. | 196 | 34.23 N | 99.01 W |
| Frederick, S.D., U.S. | 198 | 45.49 N | 98.30 W |
| Frederick □[6] | 208 | 39.25 N | 77.25 W |
| Frederick Hills ⩤[2] | 164 | 12.41 S | 136.00 E |
| Frederick House ≃ | 190 | 49.06 N | 81.10 W |
| Frederick House Lake @ | 190 | 48.40 N | 80.55 W |
| Frederick Island I | 162 | 34.04 S | 122.00 E |
| Frederick Reef ◆[2] | 166 | 20.58 S | 154.23 E |
| Fredericksburg, In., U.S. | 218 | 38.26 N | 86.11 W |
| Fredericksburg, Ia., U.S. | 190 | 42.57 N | 92.11 W |
| Fredericksburg, Oh., U.S. | 214 | 40.40 N | 81.52 W |
| Fredericksburg, Pa., U.S. | 214 | 40.27 N | 76.26 W |
| Fredericksburg, Tx., U.S. | 196 | 30.16 N | 98.52 W |
| Fredericksburg, Va., U.S. | 208 | 38.18 N | 77.27 W |
| Fredericksburg Battlefield ⊥ | 208 | 38.17 N | 77.28 W |
| Frederick Sound ʁ | 180 | 57.00 N | 133.00 W |
| Fredericktown, Mo., U.S. | 194 | 37.33 N | 90.17 W |
| Fredericktown, Oh., U.S. | 214 | 40.28 N | 82.32 W |
| Frederico Westphalen | 252 | 27.22 S | 53.24 W |
| Fredericton | 186 | 45.58 N | 66.39 W |
| Fredericton Junction | 186 | 45.40 N | 66.37 W |
| Frederik Hendrikeiland → Yos Sudarso, Pulau I | 164 | 7.50 S | 138.30 E |
| Frederiksberg, Dan. | 41 | 55.25 N | 11.34 E |
| Frederiksberg, Dan. | 41 | 55.41 N | 12.32 E |
| Frederiksborg □[6] | 41 | 55.56 N | 12.18 E |
| Frederiksborg ⊥ | 41 | 55.56 N | 12.19 E |
| Frederikshåb (Paamiut) | 176 | 62.00 N | 49.43 W |
| Frederikshavn | 26 | 57.26 N | 10.32 E |
| Frederikssund | 41 | 55.50 N | 12.04 E |
| Frederiksted | 241n | 17.43 N | 64.53 W |
| Frederiksværk | 41 | 55.58 N | 12.02 E |
| Frederik Willem IV Vallen ⊾ | 250 | 3.28 N | 57.37 W |
| Fredersdorf | 54 | 52.31 N | 13.44 E |
| Fredonia, Col. | 246 | 5.55 N | 75.41 W |
| Fredonia, Az., U.S. | 200 | 36.03 N | 112.08 W |
| Fredonia, Ks., U.S. | 198 | 37.32 N | 95.49 W |
| Fredonia, N.Y., U.S. | 214 | 42.26 N | 79.19 W |
| Fredonia, N.D., U.S. | 198 | 46.19 N | 99.05 W |
| Fredonia, Pa., U.S. | 214 | 41.20 N | 80.14 W |
| Fredrika | 26 | 64.05 N | 18.24 E |
| Fredriksberg | 40 | 60.08 N | 14.23 E |
| Fredrikstad | 26 | 59.13 N | 10.57 E |
| Freeburg, Il., U.S. | 219 | 38.25 N | 89.54 W |
| Freeburg, Mo., U.S. | 219 | 38.18 N | 91.55 W |
| Freeburg, Pa., U.S. | 208 | 40.46 N | 76.57 W |
| Freedom, Ca., U.S. | 226 | 36.56 N | 121.46 W |
| Freedom, Pa., U.S. | 214 | 40.40 N | 80.14 W |
| Freehold, N.J., U.S. | 208 | 40.15 N | 74.16 W |
| Freehold, N.Y., U.S. | 210 | 42.22 N | 74.03 W |
| Freeland, Mi., U.S. | 190 | 43.31 N | 84.07 W |
| Freeland, Pa., U.S. | 210 | 41.01 N | 75.53 W |
| Freeland, Wa., U.S. | 224 | 48.01 N | 122.32 W |
| Freeland Park | 216 | 40.37 N | 87.30 W |
| Freeling, Mount ʌ | 162 | 22.35 S | 133.06 E |
| Freel Peak ʌ | 226 | 38.52 N | 119.54 W |
| Freels, Cape ➤, Nf., Can. | 186 | 46.37 N | 53.33 W |
| Freels, Cape ➤, Nf., Can. | 186 | 49.15 N | 53.28 W |
| Freeman | 198 | 43.21 N | 97.26 W |
| Freeman ≃ | 182 | 54.20 N | 114.47 W |
| Freeman, Lake @ | 216 | 40.42 N | 86.45 W |
| Freemansburg | 210 | 40.37 N | 75.20 W |
| Freemount | 48 | 52.16 N | 8.53 W |
| Freeport, Ba. | 238 | 26.30 N | 78.45 W |
| Freeport, N.S., Can. | 186 | 44.17 N | 66.19 W |
| Freeport, On., Can. | 212 | 43.25 N | 80.25 W |
| Freeport, Fl., U.S. | 194 | 30.29 N | 86.08 W |
| Freeport, Il., U.S. | 190 | 42.17 N | 89.37 W |

FRANÇAIS

| Nom | Page | Lat.°′ | Long.°′ W = Ouest |
|---|---|---|---|
| Freeport, Me., U.S. | 188 | 43.51 N | 70.06 W |
| Freeport, Mi., U.S. | 216 | 42.45 N | 85.18 W |
| Freeport, N.Y., U.S. | 210 | 40.39 N | 73.35 W |
| Freeport, Oh., U.S. | 214 | 40.12 N | 81.15 W |
| Freeport, Pa., U.S. | 210 | 40.40 N | 79.41 W |
| Freeport, Tx., U.S. | 222 | 28.57 N | 95.21 W |
| Freer | 196 | 27.52 N | 98.37 W |
| Freest | 54 | 54.08 N | 13.43 E |
| Freeston | 222 | 31.32 N | 96.15 W |
| Freestone | 171a | 28.08 S | 152.08 E |
| Freestone □[6] | 222 | 31.44 N | 96.10 W |
| Freetown, Antig. | 240c | 17.03 N | 61.42 W |
| Freetown, S.L. | 150 | 8.30 N | 13.15 W |
| Freetown, In., U.S. | 218 | 38.58 N | 86.07 W |
| Freetown, N.Y., U.S. | 207 | 40.58 N | 72.11 W |
| Freeville | 210 | 42.30 N | 76.20 W |
| Freewood Acres | 208 | 40.10 N | 74.15 W |
| Freezeout Lake @ | 202 | 47.40 N | 112.03 W |
| Fregenal de la Sierra | 34 | 38.10 N | 6.39 W |
| Fregene ◆[8] | 66 | 41.51 N | 12.12 E |
| Freiamt | 58 | 48.10 N | 7.55 E |
| Freiberg, Dtsch. | 54 | 50.54 N | 13.20 E |
| Freiberg, Dtsch. | 56 | 48.56 N | 9.12 E |
| Freiberger Mulde ≃ | 54 | 51.10 N | 12.48 E |
| Freiburg, Dtsch. | 52 | 53.49 N | 9.17 E |
| Freiburg → Fribourg, Schw. | 58 | 46.48 N | 7.09 E |
| Freiburg □[5] | 58 | 48.00 N | 8.25 E |
| Freiburg im Breisgau | 58 | 47.59 N | 7.51 E |
| Freienbach | 58 | 47.12 N | 8.45 E |
| Freienhufen | 54 | 51.35 N | 13.58 E |
| Freiensteinau | 56 | 50.26 N | 9.24 E |
| Freie Universität v[2] | 264a | 52.26 N | 13.16 E |
| Freigericht | 56 | 50.08 N | 9.07 E |
| Freihung | 60 | 49.37 N | 11.55 E |
| Freiland | 61 | 47.58 N | 15.34 E |
| Freilassing | 64 | 47.50 N | 12.59 E |
| Freilingen | 56 | 50.33 N | 7.50 E |
| Freinberg | 60 | 48.34 N | 13.31 E |
| Freinsheim | 56 | 49.30 N | 8.13 E |
| Freirina | 252 | 28.30 S | 71.06 W |
| Freisen | 56 | 49.33 N | 7.14 E |
| Freisenbruch ◆[8] | 263 | 51.27 N | 7.06 E |
| Freising | 60 | 48.23 N | 11.44 E |
| Freistadt | 61 | 48.31 N | 14.31 E |
| Freital | 54 | 51.00 N | 13.39 E |
| Freiwalde | 54 | 51.58 N | 13.44 E |
| Freixial | 266c | 38.54 N | 9.09 W |
| Fréjus | 62 | 43.26 N | 6.44 E |
| Fréjus, Tunnel du ◆[5] | 62 | 45.08 N | 6.40 E |
| Frémainville | 261 | 49.04 N | 1.52 E |
| Fremantle | 168a | 32.03 S | 115.45 E |
| Fremdingen | 56 | 48.58 N | 10.27 E |
| Fremington | 42 | 51.04 N | 4.07 W |
| Fremont, Ca., U.S. | 226 | 37.32 N | 121.59 W |
| Fremont, In., U.S. | 216 | 41.43 N | 84.55 W |
| Fremont, Ia., U.S. | 190 | 41.12 N | 92.26 W |
| Fremont, Mi., U.S. | 190 | 43.28 N | 85.56 W |
| Fremont, Ne., U.S. | 198 | 41.26 N | 96.29 W |
| Fremont, N.C., U.S. | 192 | 35.32 N | 77.58 W |
| Fremont, Oh., U.S. | 214 | 41.21 N | 83.07 W |
| Fremont, Wi., U.S. | 190 | 44.15 N | 88.51 W |
| Fremont ≃ | 200 | 38.24 N | 110.42 W |
| Fremont Canyon V | 280 | 33.48 N | 117.42 W |
| Fremont Island I | 200 | 41.09 N | 112.20 W |
| Fremont Lake @ | 202 | 42.57 N | 109.49 W |
| Fremont Peak ʌ, Ca., U.S. | 226 | 36.46 N | 121.30 W |
| Fremont Peak ʌ, Ca., U.S. | 228 | 35.12 N | 117.27 W |
| Fremont Valley V | 228 | 35.10 N | 118.00 W |
| French ≃ | 190 | 45.56 N | 80.54 W |
| French Broad ≃ | 192 | 35.57 N | 83.51 W |
| Frenchburg | 192 | 37.57 N | 83.37 W |
| French Camp | 226 | 37.53 N | 121.16 W |
| Frenchcap Cay I | 240m | 18.14 N | 64.51 W |
| French Creek ≃, Mb., Can. | 184 | 57.02 N | 92.12 W |
| French Creek ≃, U.S. | 214 | 41.25 N | 79.50 W |
| French Creek ≃, Oh., U.S. | 279a | 41.27 N | 82.07 W |
| French Creek ≃, Pa., U.S. | 208 | 40.08 N | 75.31 W |
| French Creek ≃, S.D., U.S. | 198 | 43.38 N | 102.55 W |
| French Creek, South Branch ≃, Pa., U.S. | 214 | 41.54 N | 79.54 W |
| French Creek, South Branch ≃, Pa., U.S. | 285 | 40.10 N | 75.42 W |
| French Creek, West Branch ≃ | 214 | 41.58 N | 79.52 W |
| French Creek State Park ♦ | 208 | 40.13 N | 75.47 W |
| French Frigate Shoals ◆[2] | 14 | 23.45 N | 166.10 W |
| French Guiana (Guyane français) □[2], S.A. | 242 | 4.00 N | 53.00 W |
| French Guiana (Guyane français) □[2], S.A. | 250 | 4.00 N | 53.00 W |
| French Island I | 169 | 38.21 S | 145.21 E |
| French Lick | 194 | 38.32 N | 86.37 W |
| Frenchman (Frenchman Creek) ≃ | 202 | 48.24 N | 107.05 W |
| Frenchman Bay c | 188 | 44.25 N | 68.10 W |
| Frenchman Butte | 184 | 53.35 N | 109.38 W |
| Frenchman Creek (Frenchman) ≃, N.A. | 202 | 48.24 N | 107.05 W |
| Frenchman Creek ≃, U.S. | 198 | 40.13 N | 100.50 W |
| Frenchman Lake @ | 204 | 36.48 N | 116.56 W |
| Frenchman Point ➤ | 212 | 44.35 N | 81.18 W |
| Frenchman's Bay c | 275b | 43.49 N | 79.05 W |
| Frenchmans Cap ʌ | 166 | 42.16 S | 145.50 E |
| Frenchman's Creek ≃, On., Can. | 284a | 42.56 N | 78.56 W |
| Frenchmans Creek ≃, Ca., U.S. | 282 | 37.29 N | 122.27 W |
| French Meadows Reservoir @[1] | 226 | 39.07 N | 120.25 W |
| Frenchpark | 48 | 53.52 N | 8.26 W |
| French Pass | 172 | 40.56 S | 173.50 E |
| French Polynesia □[2] | 14 | 15.00 S | 140.00 W |
| Frenchs Forest | 274a | 33.45 S | 151.14 E |
| French Stream ≃ | 283 | 42.07 N | 70.53 W |
| Frenchtown | 210 | 40.31 N | 75.03 W |
| Frenda | 148 | 35.02 N | 1.01 E |
| Freneuse | 261 | 49.03 N | 1.36 E |
| Frensdorferhaar | 52 | 52.25 N | 7.03 E |
| Frenštát pod Radhoštěm | 30 | 49.33 N | 18.14 E |
| Frentani, Monti dei ⩤ | 66 | 41.54 N | 14.37 E |
| Frépillon | 261 | 49.03 N | 2.12 E |
| Frere | 158 | 28.52 S | 29.47 E |
| Freren | 52 | 52.29 N | 7.32 E |
| Fresco | 150 | 5.05 N | 5.34 W |
| Fresco ≃ | 250 | 6.39 S | 51.59 W |
| Freshfield | 262 | 53.34 N | 3.04 W |
| Freshfield, Mount ʌ | 182 | 51.44 N | 116.57 W |
| Freshford | 48 | 52.43 N | 7.24 W |
| Fresh Meadows ◆[8] | 276 | 40.44 N | 73.48 W |
| Fresh Pond @, Ma., U.S. | 283 | 42.23 N | 71.09 W |
| Fresh Pond @, N.Y., U.S. | 276 | 40.55 N | 73.18 W |
| Freshwater | 42 | 50.40 N | 1.30 W |
| Freshwater Creek ≃ | 226 | 39.12 N | 122.04 W |
| Fresia | 254 | 41.09 S | 73.27 W |
| Fresnes | 261 | 48.45 N | 2.19 E |
| Fresne-Saint-Mamès | 58 | 47.33 N | 5.52 E |
| Fresnes-en-Woëvre | 56 | 49.08 N | 5.39 E |
| Fresnes-sur-Escaut | 50 | 50.26 N | 3.35 E |
| Fresnes-sur-Marne | 261 | 48.56 N | 2.45 E |
| Fresnillo | 234 | 23.10 N | 102.53 W |
| Fresno, Col. | 246 | 5.09 N | 75.01 W |

PORTUGUÊS

| Nome | Página | Lat.°′ | Long.°′ W = Oeste |
|---|---|---|---|
| Fresno, Ca., U.S. | 226 | 36.44 N | 119.46 W |
| Fresno, Oh., U.S. | 214 | 40.20 N | 81.44 W |
| Fresno, Tx., U.S. | 222 | 29.32 N | 95.27 W |
| Fresno □[6] | 226 | 36.38 N | 119.45 W |
| Fresno ≃ | 226 | 37.05 N | 120.33 W |
| Fresno, Lewis Fork ≃ | 226 | 37.20 N | 119.39 W |
| Fresno Air Terminal ⊠ | 226 | 36.46 N | 119.43 W |
| Fresno Reservoir @[1] | 202 | 48.41 N | 109.57 W |
| Fresno Slough ≃ | 226 | 36.47 N | 120.22 W |
| Fresnoy-Folny | 50 | 49.53 N | 1.26 E |
| Fresnoy-le-Grand | 50 | 49.57 N | 3.25 E |
| Fressenneville | 50 | 50.04 N | 1.34 E |
| Fressin | 50 | 50.27 N | 2.03 E |
| Freswick | 46 | 58.35 N | 3.05 W |
| Fréteval | 50 | 47.53 N | 1.13 E |
| Frétigney-et-Velloreille | 58 | 47.29 N | 5.56 E |
| Fretin | 50 | 50.33 N | 3.08 E |
| Frettes | 58 | 47.41 N | 5.34 E |
| Freu, Cap des ➤ | 34 | 39.45 N | 3.27 E |
| Freudenberg, Dtsch. | 56 | 49.44 N | 9.19 E |
| Freudenberg, Dtsch. | 56 | 50.54 N | 7.52 E |
| Freudenberg, Dtsch. | 60 | 49.29 N | 11.59 E |
| Freudenberg, Dtsch. | 264a | 52.42 N | 13.49 E |
| Freudenstadt | 58 | 48.28 N | 8.25 E |
| Frévent | 50 | 50.16 N | 2.17 E |
| Frew ≃ | 162 | 20.00 S | 135.38 E |
| Frewena | 162 | 19.25 S | 135.25 E |
| Frewsburg | 214 | 42.03 N | 79.09 W |
| Freyburg | 54 | 51.13 N | 11.46 E |
| Freycinet, Cape ➤ | 162 | 34.06 S | 114.59 E |
| Freycinet Estuary c[1] | 162 | 26.25 S | 113.45 E |
| Freycinet National Park ♦ | 166 | 42.10 S | 148.20 E |
| Freycinet Peninsula ➤[1] | 166 | 42.13 S | 148.18 E |
| Freyenstein | 54 | 53.17 N | 12.20 E |
| Freyming-Merlebach | 56 | 49.09 N | 6.48 E |
| Freyre | 252 | 31.10 S | 62.06 W |
| Freystadt | 60 | 49.12 N | 11.20 E |
| Freyung | 60 | 48.48 N | 13.33 E |
| Fria | 150 | 10.05 N | 13.32 W |
| Fria, Cape ➤ | 152 | 18.30 S | 12.01 E |
| Friant | 226 | 36.59 N | 119.42 W |
| Friant Dam ◆[6] | 226 | 37.00 N | 119.43 W |
| Friant-Kern Canal ≋ | 226 | 35.22 N | 119.06 W |
| Friars Point | 194 | 34.22 N | 90.38 W |
| Frías, Arg. | 252 | 28.39 S | 65.09 W |
| Frías, Perú | 248 | 4.52 S | 79.57 W |
| Fribourg (Freiburg) | 58 | 46.48 N | 7.09 E |
| Fribourg (Freiburg) □[3] | 58 | 46.45 N | 7.05 E |
| Frick | 58 | 47.31 N | 8.01 E |
| Frick Park ♦ | 279b | 40.26 N | 79.54 W |
| Friday | 222 | 31.07 N | 95.15 W |
| Friday Harbor | 224 | 48.32 N | 123.00 W |
| Fridaythorpe | 44 | 54.01 N | 0.40 W |
| Fridingen an der Donau | 58 | 48.01 N | 8.56 E |
| Fridley | 190 | 45.05 N | 93.15 W |
| Fridolfing | 60 | 48.00 N | 12.49 E |
| Fridtjof Nansen, Mount ʌ | 9 | 85.21 S | 167.33 W |
| Friedberg, Dtsch. | 56 | 50.20 N | 8.45 E |
| Friedberg, Dtsch. | 58 | 48.21 N | 10.58 E |
| Friedberg, Öst. | 61 | 47.27 N | 16.03 E |
| Friedeburg [/Saale] | 54 | 51.37 N | 11.44 E |
| Friedenau ◆[8] | 264a | 52.28 N | 13.20 E |
| Friedens | 214 | 40.03 N | 79.00 W |
| Friedensburg | 208 | 40.36 N | 76.14 W |
| Friedersdorf, Dtsch. | 54 | 52.17 N | 13.47 E |
| Friedersdorf, Dtsch. | 54 | 51.01 N | 14.34 E |
| Friedersdorf, Dtsch. | 54 | 51.39 N | 12.21 E |
| Friedesheim | 158 | 27.55 S | 26.43 E |
| Friedland, Dtsch. | 54 | 52.06 N | 14.16 E |
| Friedland, Dtsch. | 54 | 53.40 N | 13.33 E |
| Friedland, Dtsch. | 56 | 51.25 N | 9.55 E |
| Friedrich-Ebert-Brücke ◆[5] | 263 | 51.28 N | 6.43 E |
| Friedrich Krupp-Aktiengesellschaft v[3] | 263 | 51.28 N | 7.00 E |
| Friedrichroda | 54 | 50.52 N | 10.34 E |
| Friedrichsbrunn | 54 | 51.41 N | 11.02 E |
| Friedrichsdorf | 56 | 50.15 N | 8.38 E |
| Friedrichsfeld | 263 | 51.38 N | 6.39 E |
| Friedrichsfelde ◆[8] | 264a | 52.31 N | 13.31 E |
| Friedrichshafen | 58 | 47.39 N | 9.28 E |
| Friedrichshagen ◆[8] | 264a | 52.27 N | 13.38 E |
| Friedrichshain ◆[8] | 264a | 52.31 N | 13.25 E |
| Friedrichshof | 264a | 52.19 N | 13.46 E |
| Friedrichsort ◆[8] | 54 | 54.24 N | 10.11 E |
| Friedrichsruh, Schloss ⊥ | 52 | 53.32 N | 10.20 E |
| Friedrichsruhe | 54 | 53.31 N | 11.45 E |
| Friedrichstadt | 41 | 54.22 N | 9.05 E |
| Friedrichsthal, Dtsch. | 54 | 52.48 N | 13.16 E |
| Friedrichsthal, Dtsch. | 56 | 49.19 N | 7.06 E |
| Friedrichstrasse, Bahnhof ◆[5] | 264a | 52.31 N | 13.24 E |
| Friedrichswalde | 54 | 53.02 N | 13.42 E |
| Frielas | 266c | 38.49 N | 9.09 W |
| Frielendorf | 56 | 50.58 N | 9.19 E |
| Friemersheim ◆[8] | 263 | 51.23 N | 6.42 E |
| Friend, Ne., U.S. | 198 | 40.39 N | 97.17 W |
| Friend, Or., U.S. | 224 | 45.21 N | 121.16 W |
| Friends Colony ◆[8] | 272a | 28.34 N | 77.16 E |
| Friendship, N.Y., U.S. | 210 | 42.12 N | 78.08 W |
| Friendship, Tn., U.S. | 194 | 35.54 N | 89.14 W |
| Friendship, Wi., U.S. | 190 | 43.58 N | 89.49 W |
| Friendship Creek ≃ | 285 | 39.55 N | 74.43 W |
| Friendship Shoal ◆[2] | 112 | 5.58 N | 112.31 E |
| Friends Meeting House State Memorial ⊥ | 214 | 40.09 N | 80.47 W |
| Friendswood | 222 | 29.31 N | 95.12 W |
| Friern Barnet ◆[8] | 260 | 51.37 N | 0.10 W |
| Fries | 192 | 36.42 N | 80.58 W |
| Friesach | 61 | 46.57 N | 14.24 E |
| Friesack | 54 | 52.44 N | 12.34 E |
| Friesenheim | 58 | 48.22 N | 7.53 E |
| Friesenhofen | 58 | 47.45 N | 10.04 E |
| Friesenried | 58 | 47.52 N | 10.31 E |
| Friesland □[4] | 52 | 53.03 N | 5.45 E |
| Friesland □[9] | 30 | 53.00 N | 5.40 E |
| Fries Mills | 285 | 39.39 N | 75.03 W |
| Friesoythe | 52 | 53.01 N | 7.51 E |
| Frigate Point ➤ | 174g | 28.11 N | 177.24 W |
| Frigento | 68 | 41.01 N | 15.06 E |
| Frignano | 68 | 41.00 N | 14.10 E |
| Frignano ◆[1] | 64 | 44.20 N | 10.51 E |
| Friguia | 150 | 12.03 N | 10.56 W |
| Friitala | 26 | 61.26 N | 21.52 E |
| Frillendorf ◆[8] | 263 | 51.28 N | 7.05 E |
| Frindsbury | 260 | 51.24 N | 0.30 E |
| Frinsted | 260 | 51.17 N | 0.43 E |
| Frinton-on-Sea | 42 | 51.50 N | 1.14 E |
| Frintrop ◆[8] | 263 | 51.29 N | 6.55 E |
| Frío ≃, N.A. | 236 | 11.08 N | 84.46 W |
| Frio ≃, Tx., U.S. | 196 | 28.30 N | 98.10 W |
| Frio, Cabo ➤ | 255 | 22.53 S | 42.00 W |
| Friockheim | 46 | 56.38 N | 2.38 W |
| Frio Draw V | 196 | 34.50 N | 102.19 W |
| Friona | 196 | 34.38 N | 102.43 W |
| Frisa, Loch @ | 46 | 56.34 N | 6.05 W |
| Frisange | 56 | 49.32 N | 6.12 E |
| Frisches Haff → Vislinskij zaliv c | 30 | 54.27 N | 19.40 E |
| Frisco, Pa., U.S. | 214 | 40.51 N | 80.16 W |
| Frisco, Tx., U.S. | 222 | 33.09 N | 96.49 W |
| Frisco City | 194 | 31.26 N | 87.24 W |
| Frisco Creek ≃ | 196 | 36.34 N | 101.23 W |
| Frisian Islands II | 30 | 53.35 N | 6.40 E |
| Friskney | 44 | 53.04 N | 0.11 E |
| Fristad | 26 | 57.50 N | 13.01 E |
| Fritch | 196 | 35.38 N | 101.36 W |
| Fritsla | 26 | 57.33 N | 12.47 E |
| Fritzlar | 56 | 51.08 N | 9.16 E |
| Friuli □[9] | 64 | 46.00 N | 13.00 E |
| Friuli-Venezia Giulia □[4] | 64 | 46.00 N | 13.00 E |
| Friza, proliv ʁ | 74 | 45.30 N | 149.10 E |
| Frizington | 44 | 54.32 N | 3.30 W |
| Frobisher | 184 | 49.12 N | 102.26 W |
| Frobisher Bay c | 176 | 62.30 N | 66.00 W |
| Frobisher Lake @ | 184 | 56.25 N | 108.20 W |
| Frodsham, Eng., U.K. | 44 | 53.18 N | 2.44 W |
| Frodsham, Eng., U.K. | 262 | 53.18 N | 2.44 W |
| Frog Lake @ | 184 | 53.55 N | 110.18 W |
| Frohavet ʁ | 24 | 63.52 N | 9.26 E |
| Frohburg | 54 | 51.03 N | 12.33 E |
| Frohlinde ◆[8] | 263 | 51.32 N | 7.21 E |
| Frohnau ◆[8] | 264a | 52.38 N | 13.18 E |
| Frohnhausen | 263 | 51.29 N | 7.48 E |
| Frohnhausen ◆[8] | 263 | 51.27 N | 6.58 E |
| Frohnleiten | 61 | 47.16 N | 15.20 E |
| Froid | 198 | 48.20 N | 104.30 W |
| Froid, Lac @ | 206 | 46.40 N | 74.32 W |
| Froid, Ruisseau ≃ | 206 | 46.23 N | 74.46 W |
| Froidmont-Cohartille | 50 | 49.41 N | 3.42 E |
| Froidos | 56 | 49.03 N | 5.07 E |
| Froissy | 50 | 49.34 N | 2.13 E |
| Froitzheim | 56 | 50.42 N | 6.34 E |
| Frolišči, Ross. | 80 | 56.25 N | 42.39 E |
| Frolišči, Ross. | 82 | 56.18 N | 39.13 E |
| Frolovo | 80 | 49.47 N | 43.39 E |
| Froman Run ≃ | 279b | 40.12 N | 80.00 W |
| Fromberg | 202 | 45.23 N | 108.54 W |
| Frombork | 30 | 54.22 N | 19.41 E |
| Frome | 42 | 51.14 N | 2.20 W |
| Frome ≃, Austl. | 166 | 29.06 S | 137.52 E |
| Frome ≃, Eng., U.K. | 42 | 52.03 N | 2.38 W |
| Frome ≃, Eng., U.K. | 42 | 50.41 N | 2.04 W |
| Frome, Lake @ | 166 | 30.48 S | 139.48 E |
| Frome Downs | 166 | 31.13 S | 139.46 E |
| Fromelennes | 56 | 50.08 N | 4.52 E |
| Fromentières | 50 | 48.54 N | 3.43 E |
| Frömern | 263 | 51.30 N | 7.44 E |
| Frommern | 58 | 48.15 N | 8.52 E |
| Fröndenberg | 56 | 51.28 N | 7.46 E |
| Fronhausen | 56 | 50.42 N | 8.42 E |
| Fronreute | 58 | 47.52 N | 9.35 E |
| Frönsberg | 263 | 51.21 N | 7.46 E |
| Fronteiras | 250 | 7.05 S | 40.37 W |
| Frontenac, Fl., U.S. | 220 | 28.27 N | 80.46 W |
| Frontenac, Ks., U.S. | 198 | 37.27 N | 94.41 W |
| Frontenac □[6], On., Can. | 212 | 44.40 N | 76.45 W |
| Frontenac □[6], P.Q., Can. | 206 | 45.42 N | 71.15 W |
| Frontenard | 58 | 46.55 N | 5.10 E |
| Frontenex-Villard-Rosset | 62 | 45.38 N | 6.19 E |
| Frontenhausen | 60 | 48.33 N | 12.32 E |
| Frontera, Méx. | 232 | 26.56 N | 101.27 W |
| Frontera, Méx. | 234 | 18.32 N | 92.38 W |
| Fronteras | 200 | 30.56 N | 109.31 W |
| Frontier, Sk., Can. | 184 | 49.12 N | 108.34 W |
| Frontier, Mi., U.S. | 216 | 41.47 N | 84.36 W |
| Frontier, Wy., U.S. | 200 | 41.48 N | 110.32 W |
| Frontignan | 62 | 43.27 N | 3.45 E |
| Frontino | 246 | 6.46 N | 76.08 W |
| Frontino, Páramo ʌ | 246 | 6.28 N | 76.04 W |
| Frontón, Isla I | 286d | 12.07 S | 77.11 W |
| Front Range ⩤, Leso. | 158 | 29.05 S | 28.20 E |
| Front Range ⩤, Co., U.S. | 200 | 39.45 N | 105.45 W |
| Front Royal | 188 | 38.55 N | 78.11 W |
| Frose | 54 | 51.48 N | 11.23 E |
| Frosinone | 66 | 41.38 N | 13.19 E |
| Frosinone □[4] | 66 | 41.37 N | 13.27 E |
| Frosolone | 66 | 41.36 N | 14.27 E |
| Frösön | 26 | 63.11 N | 14.32 E |
| Frost | 222 | 32.05 N | 96.48 W |
| Frostavallen | 41 | 55.58 N | 13.30 E |
| Frostburg | 188 | 39.39 N | 78.55 W |
| Frostproof | 220 | 27.44 N | 81.31 W |
| Frotheim | 52 | 52.21 N | 8.40 E |
| Frouard | 56 | 48.46 N | 6.08 E |
| Frövi | 40 | 59.28 N | 15.22 E |
| Frøya I | 24 | 63.43 N | 8.42 E |
| Fruges | 50 | 50.31 N | 2.08 E |
| Fruita | 200 | 39.09 N | 108.43 W |
| Fruitdale, Al., U.S. | 194 | 31.20 N | 88.24 W |
| Fruitdale, Or., U.S. | 202 | 42.24 N | 123.20 W |
| Fruithurst | 194 | 33.43 N | 85.26 W |
| Fruitland, Id., U.S. | 202 | 44.00 N | 116.54 W |
| Fruitland, Md., U.S. | 208 | 38.19 N | 75.37 W |
| Fruitland Park | 220 | 28.51 N | 81.54 W |
| Fruitport | 216 | 43.07 N | 86.09 W |
| Fruitvale, B.C., Can. | 182 | 49.07 N | 117.33 W |
| Fruitvale, Tx., U.S. | 222 | 32.41 N | 95.48 W |
| Fruitvale, Wa., U.S. | 202 | 46.37 N | 120.33 W |
| Fruitville | 192 | 27.19 N | 82.27 W |
| Frumușița | 38 | 45.40 N | 28.04 E |
| Frunze, Kyrg. | 85 | 40.07 N | 71.44 E |
| Frunze → Biškek, Kyrg. | 85 | 42.54 N | 74.36 E |
| Frunze, Ukr. | 78 | 46.16 N | 34.52 E |
| Frunze, Ukr. | 83 | 48.40 N | 38.45 E |
| Frunzivka | 78 | 47.20 N | 29.44 E |
| Frutal | 255 | 20.02 S | 48.55 W |
| Frutigen | 58 | 46.35 N | 7.39 E |
| Frutillar | 254 | 41.07 S | 73.03 W |
| Fryburg | 214 | 41.21 N | 79.26 W |
| Frýdek-Místek | 30 | 49.41 N | 18.22 E |
| Frýdlant | 30 | 50.56 N | 15.05 E |
| Frye | 279b | 40.11 N | 79.56 W |
| Fryeburg | 188 | 44.00 N | 70.58 W |
| Fryerning | 260 | 51.41 N | 0.22 E |
| Fryingpan ≃ | 200 | 39.22 N | 107.02 W |
| Fu ≃, Zhg. | 100 | 29.52 N | 115.28 E |
| Fu ≃, Zhg. | 100 | 28.36 N | 116.04 E |
| Fu ≃, Zhg. | 102 | 29.59 N | 106.16 E |
| Fua'amotu | 174w | 21.16 S | 175.08 W |
| Fua'amotu International Airport ⊠ | 174w | 21.17 S | 175.08 W |
| Fu'an, Zhg. | 100 | 27.08 N | 119.40 E |
| Fu'an, Zhg. | 100 | 32.41 N | 120.41 E |
| Fuanjie | 100 | 25.29 N | 117.53 E |
| Fubao | 107 | 28.47 N | 106.05 E |
| Fubine | 62 | 44.58 N | 8.26 E |
| Fucecchio | 66 | 43.44 N | 10.48 E |
| Fuchang | 100 | 30.06 N | 113.08 E |
| Fucheng | 98 | 37.52 N | 116.07 E |
| Fuchikou | 100 | 29.51 N | 115.27 E |
| Fuchow → Fuzhou | 100 | 28.01 N | 116.20 E |
| Fuchs-Berg ʌ[2] | 264a | 52.27 N | 13.51 E |
| Fuchskaute ʌ | 56 | 50.40 N | 8.06 E |
| Fuchsmühl | 60 | 49.56 N | 12.09 E |
| Füchtorf | 52 | 52.03 N | 8.02 E |
| Fuchū, Nihon | 94 | 35.40 N | 139.29 E |
| Fuchū, Nihon | 94 | 36.39 N | 137.10 E |
| Fuchū, Nihon | 96 | 34.24 N | 132.30 E |
| Fuchū, Nihon | 96 | 34.34 N | 133.14 E |
| Fuchun ≃ | 106 | 30.10 N | 120.09 E |
| Fucine | 64 | 46.18 N | 10.44 E |
| Fucino, Conca del ≋ | 66 | 42.01 N | 13.31 E |
| Fudan University v[2] | 269b | 31.17 N | 121.29 E |
| Fuday I | 46 | 57.03 N | 7.23 W |
| Fuding | 100 | 27.21 N | 120.12 E |
| Fudu ≃ | 107 | 29.52 N | 106.10 E |
| Fuefuki ≃ | 94 | 35.33 N | 138.28 E |
| Fuego, Volcán de ʌ[1] | 236 | 14.29 N | 90.53 W |
| Fuelbeckestausee @[1] | 263 | 51.15 N | 7.40 E |
| Fuencaliente | 34 | 38.24 N | 4.18 W |
| Fuencarral ◆[8] | 266a | 40.30 N | 3.41 W |
| Fuengirola | 34 | 36.32 N | 4.37 W |
| Fuenlabrada | 266a | 40.17 N | 3.48 W |
| Fuensalida | 34 | 40.03 N | 4.12 W |
| Fuensanta, Embalse de @[1] | 34 | 38.23 N | 2.13 W |
| Fuente | 196 | 28.40 N | 100.32 W |
| Fuente de Cantos | 34 | 38.15 N | 6.18 W |
| Fuente de Oro | 246 | 3.28 N | 73.37 W |
| Fuente Obejuna | 34 | 38.16 N | 5.25 W |
| Fuentesaúco | 34 | 41.14 N | 5.30 W |
| Fuentes de Ebro | 34 | 41.31 N | 0.38 W |
| Fuerli | 105 | 39.40 N | 116.41 E |
| Fuerte ≃ | 232 | 25.54 N | 109.22 W |
| Fuerte Olimpo | 248 | 21.02 S | 57.54 W |
| Fuerteventura I | 148 | 28.20 N | 14.00 W |
| Fuerza, Castillo de la ⊥ | 286b | 23.09 N | 82.21 W |
| Fufeng | 102 | 34.20 N | 107.51 E |
| Fuga Island I | 116 | 18.52 N | 121.22 E |
| Fugama, Wādī V | 140 | 14.43 N | 24.36 E |
| Fügen | 64 | 47.21 N | 11.51 E |
| Fuglebjerg | 41 | 55.18 N | 11.34 E |
| Fugløysund ʁ | 24 | 70.12 N | 20.20 E |
| Fugong | 102 | 27.09 N | 98.52 E |
| Fugou | 98 | 34.04 N | 114.24 E |
| Fuhai | 86 | 47.06 N | 87.23 E |
| Fuhe | 100 | 23.22 N | 113.37 E |
| Fuhlenbrock ◆[8] | 263 | 51.32 N | 6.54 E |
| Fuhrberg | 52 | 52.34 N | 9.50 E |
| Fuhse ≃ | 52 | 52.37 N | 10.03 E |
| Fuhsien → Fuxian | 98 | 39.37 N | 122.01 E |
| Fuhu | 100 | 29.11 N | 118.04 E |
| Fuji, Nihon | 94 | 35.09 N | 138.39 E |
| Fuji, Zhg. | 98 | 34.24 N | 114.48 E |
| Fuji, Zhg. | 107 | 29.09 N | 105.23 E |
| Fuji ≃ | 94 | 35.07 N | 138.39 E |
| Fuji, Mount → Fuji-san ʌ[1] | 94 | 35.22 N | 138.44 E |
| Fujiafeng | 105 | 39.11 N | 117.32 E |
| Fujian (Fukien) □[4] | 100 | 26.00 N | 118.00 E |
| Fujiatun | 104 | 41.42 N | 123.44 E |
| Fujiawopu | 104 | 40.58 N | 122.14 E |
| Fujiazhen | 107 | 29.57 N | 104.18 E |
| Fujiazhuangcun | 104 | 41.15 N | 122.20 E |
| Fujie | 106 | 31.09 N | 119.27 E |
| Fujieda | 94 | 34.52 N | 138.16 E |
| Fuji-Hakone-Izu-kokuritsu-kōen ♦ | 94 | 35.21 N | 138.44 E |
| Fujiidera | 96 | 34.34 N | 135.36 E |
| Fujikawa | 94 | 35.08 N | 138.37 E |
| Fujikubo | 268 | 35.50 N | 139.32 E |
| Fujimi, Nihon | 94 | 36.27 N | 139.05 E |
| Fujimi, Nihon | 94 | 35.55 N | 138.15 E |
| Fujimi, Nihon | 94 | 35.51 N | 139.33 E |
| Fujin | 89 | 47.14 N | 132.00 E |
| Fujino | 94 | 35.37 N | 139.10 E |
| Fujinomiya | 94 | 35.12 N | 138.38 E |
| Fujioka, Nihon | 94 | 35.12 N | 137.12 E |
| Fujioka, Nihon | 94 | 36.15 N | 139.05 E |
| Fujioka, Nihon | 94 | 36.15 N | 139.39 E |
| Fuji-san ʌ[1] | 94 | 35.22 N | 138.44 E |
| Fujisawa | 94 | 35.21 N | 139.29 E |
| Fujishiro | 94 | 35.55 N | 140.07 E |
| Fujiwara, Nihon | 94 | 35.09 N | 136.30 E |
| Fujiwara, Nihon | 94 | 36.51 N | 139.44 E |
| Fujiwara-dam ◆[6] | 94 | 36.49 N | 139.02 E |
| Fujiyama → Fuji-san ʌ[1] | 94 | 35.22 N | 138.44 E |
| Fuji-yoshida | 94 | 35.29 N | 138.48 E |
| Fukagawa | 92a | 43.43 N | 142.03 E |
| Fukagawa ◆[8] | 268 | 35.40 N | 139.48 E |
| Fukami | 268 | 35.28 N | 139.28 E |
| Fukane I | 174w | 21.05 S | 175.02 W |
| Fukang | 86 | 44.10 N | 87.59 E |
| Fukasaka-tunnel ◆[5] | 94 | 35.35 N | 136.10 E |
| Fuka Shan ʌ | 89 | 47.55 N | 120.53 E |
| Fukaya | 94 | 36.12 N | 139.17 E |
| Fukiage | 94 | 36.06 N | 139.27 E |
| Fukiai ◆[8] | 270 | 34.42 N | 135.12 E |
| Fukien → Fujian □[4] | 100 | 26.00 N | 118.00 E |
| Fukou, Zhg. | 100 | 25.45 N | 118.28 E |
| Fukou, Zhg. | 100 | 26.28 N | 117.40 E |
| Fukube | 96 | 35.33 N | 134.18 E |
| Fukuchiyama | 96 | 35.18 N | 135.07 E |
| Fukude | 94 | 34.40 N | 137.53 E |
| Fukue | 92 | 32.41 N | 128.50 E |
| Fukuei Chiao ➤ | 100 | 25.18 N | 121.32 E |
| Fukue-jima I | 92 | 32.40 N | 128.45 E |
| Fukui, Nihon | 94 | 36.04 N | 136.13 E |
| Fukui, Nihon | 270 | 34.51 N | 135.34 E |
| Fukui □[5] | 92 | 36.00 N | 136.15 E |
| Fukuma | 96 | 33.46 N | 130.28 E |
| Fukumitsu | 94 | 36.33 N | 136.52 E |
| Fukuno | 94 | 36.35 N | 136.55 E |
| Fukuoka, Nihon | 94 | 35.34 N | 137.27 E |
| Fukuoka, Nihon | 94 | 36.42 N | 136.56 E |
| Fukuoka, Nihon | 96 | 33.35 N | 130.24 E |
| Fukuoka □[5] | 96 | 33.45 N | 130.30 E |
| Fukuoka-chūtonchi, Rikujō-jieitai- ■ | 96 | 33.32 N | 130.28 E |
| Fukuroda-no-taki ⊾ | 94 | 36.46 N | 140.25 E |
| Fukuroi | 94 | 34.45 N | 137.55 E |
| Fukushima, Nihon | 92 | 37.45 N | 140.28 E |
| Fukushima, Nihon | 92a | 41.29 N | 140.15 E |
| Fukushima □[5] | 94 | 37.08 N | 140.00 E |
| Fukushima ◆[8] | 270 | 34.42 N | 135.29 E |
| Fukusumi | 270 | 34.37 N | 135.56 E |
| Fukutani ◆[8] | 270 | 34.43 N | 135.02 E |
| Fukuyama | 96 | 34.29 N | 133.22 E |
| Fukuzaki | 96 | 34.57 N | 134.45 E |
| Fulacunda | 150 | 11.44 N | 15.03 W |
| Fūlādī, Kūh-e ʌ | 120 | 34.38 N | 67.32 E |
| Fūlād Maḩalleh | 128 | 36.02 N | 53.44 E |
| Fulanga Island I | 175g | 19.08 S | 178.20 W |
| Fulanga Passage ʁ | 175g | 19.00 S | 178.40 W |
| Fulbourn | 42 | 52.11 N | 0.13 E |
| Fulda, Dtsch. | 56 | 50.33 N | 9.41 E |
| Fulda, Mn., U.S. | 198 | 43.52 N | 95.36 W |
| Fulda ≃ | 30 | 51.25 N | 9.39 E |
| Fuldatal, Dtsch. | 52 | 51.21 N | 9.32 E |
| Fuldatal, Dtsch. | 56 | 51.22 N | 9.31 E |
| Fuldera | 58 | 46.37 N | 10.22 E |
| Fule | 102 | 25.27 N | 104.19 E |
| Fulerum ◆[8] | 263 | 51.26 N | 6.57 E |
| Fulford Harbour | 224 | 48.46 N | 123.27 W |
| Fulgatore | 70 | 37.57 N | 12.42 E |
| Fulham ◆[8] | 260 | 51.29 N | 0.12 W |
| Fuli | 100 | 23.11 N | 121.14 E |
| Fuliji | 100 | 33.47 N | 116.59 E |
| Fuling | 102 | 29.42 N | 107.22 E |
| Fulitun | 89 | 46.42 N | 131.10 E |
| Fullarton ≃ | 166 | 20.15 S | 141.10 E |
| Fullen @ | 40 | 60.31 N | 16.09 E |
| Fuller Springs | 222 | 31.18 N | 94.41 W |
| Fullerton, Ca., U.S. | 228 | 33.52 N | 117.55 W |
| Fullerton, Ky., U.S. | 218 | 38.43 N | 82.58 W |
| Fullerton, Md., U.S. | 208 | 39.23 N | 76.31 W |
| Fullerton, Ne., U.S. | 198 | 41.21 N | 97.58 W |
| Fullerton, Pa., U.S. | 208 | 40.38 N | 75.28 W |
| Fullerton Municipal Airport ⊠ | 280 | 33.52 N | 117.59 W |
| Fullerton Point ➤ | 240c | 17.06 N | 61.54 W |
| Fulmer | 260 | 51.33 N | 0.34 W |
| Fulong | 107 | 30.29 N | 107.41 E |
| Fulongchang | 107 | 30.03 N | 103.38 E |
| Fulongquan | 89 | 44.22 N | 124.36 E |
| Fulpmes | 64 | 47.10 N | 11.21 E |
| Fulshear | 222 | 29.41 N | 95.54 W |
| Fulton, Al., U.S. | 194 | 31.47 N | 87.43 W |
| Fulton, Ar., U.S. | 194 | 33.36 N | 93.48 W |
| Fulton, Il., U.S. | 190 | 41.52 N | 90.09 W |
| Fulton, In., U.S. | 216 | 40.56 N | 86.15 W |
| Fulton, Ks., U.S. | 198 | 38.00 N | 94.43 W |
| Fulton, Ky., U.S. | 194 | 36.30 N | 88.52 W |
| Fulton, Md., U.S. | 208 | 39.09 N | 76.55 W |
| Fulton, Mi., U.S. | 216 | 47.17 N | 88.21 W |
| Fulton, Ms., U.S. | 194 | 34.16 N | 88.24 W |
| Fulton, Mo., U.S. | 219 | 38.50 N | 91.56 W |
| Fulton, N.Y., U.S. | 210 | 43.19 N | 76.25 W |
| Fulton, Oh., U.S. | 214 | 40.27 N | 82.49 W |
| Fulton, Tx., U.S. | 196 | 28.04 N | 97.02 W |
| Fulton □[6], Il., U.S. | 219 | 40.13 N | 90.17 W |
| Fulton □[6], In., U.S. | 216 | 41.04 N | 86.13 W |
| Fulton □[6], N.Y., U.S. | 210 | 43.00 N | 74.22 W |
| Fulton □[6], Oh., U.S. | 216 | 41.33 N | 84.09 W |
| Fulton □[6], Pa., U.S. | 214 | 40.06 N | 78.04 W |
| Fulton ≃ | 182 | 54.48 N | 126.07 W |
| Fultondale | 194 | 33.36 N | 86.47 W |
| Fultonham | 210 | 42.31 N | 75.03 W |
| Fultonville | 210 | 42.57 N | 74.22 W |
| Fuluchang | 107 | 29.38 N | 106.08 E |
| Fulufjället ʌ | 26 | 61.33 N | 12.43 E |
| Fuluzhen | 107 | 29.18 N | 103.40 E |
| Fulwood | 44 | 53.47 N | 2.41 W |
| Fumaça | 256 | 22.17 S | 44.19 W |
| Fumahashi | 94 | 36.42 N | 137.19 E |
| Fumane | 156 | 24.29 S | 33.58 E |
| Fumay | 56 | 49.59 N | 4.42 E |
| Fumel | 32 | 44.29 N | 0.57 E |
| Fumin, Zhg. | 102 | 25.16 N | 102.26 E |
| Fumin, Zhg. | 106 | 31.54 N | 121.10 E |
| Fumintun | 98 | 42.29 N | 126.22 E |
| Fuminzhen | 106 | 31.37 N | 121.39 E |
| Funa ≃ | 273b | 4.23 S | 15.19 E |
| Funabashi | 94 | 35.42 N | 139.59 E |
| Funafuti I | 14 | 8.31 S | 179.13 E |
| Funagawa → Oga | 92 | 39.53 N | 139.51 E |
| Funakuyā | 175d | 24.30 N | 124.17 E |
| Funan | 100 | 32.39 N | 115.32 E |
| Funan Gaba | 144 | 4.25 N | 37.57 E |
| Funaoka | 96 | 35.23 N | 134.14 E |
| Funasaka | 270 | 34.48 N | 135.17 E |
| Funäsdalen | 26 | 62.32 N | 12.33 E |
| Funchal | 148 | 32.38 N | 16.54 W |
| Funchal □[5] | 148 | 32.40 N | 16.55 W |
| Fundación | 246 | 10.31 N | 74.11 W |
| Fundão | 34 | 40.08 N | 7.30 W |
| Fundão, Ilha do I | 287a | 22.51 S | 43.14 W |
| Funde | 272c | 18.54 N | 72.58 E |
| Fundo ≃ | 250 | 10.12 S | 44.39 W |
| Fundo, Arroio ≃ | 287a | 22.58 S | 43.22 W |
| Fundy, Bay of c | 186 | 45.00 N | 66.00 W |
| Fundy National Park ♦ | 186 | 45.38 N | 65.00 W |
| Fünfkirchen → Pécs | 30 | 46.05 N | 18.13 E |
| Funhalouro | 156 | 23.03 S | 34.25 E |
| Funil, Represa do @[1] | 256 | 22.33 S | 44.35 W |
| Funil, Ribeirão do ≃ | 256 | 22.02 S | 43.46 W |
| Funil, Rio do ≃ | 256 | 22.58 S | 44.34 W |
| Funing, Zhg. | 98 | 39.54 N | 119.14 E |
| Funing, Zhg. | 100 | 33.47 N | 119.48 E |
| Funing, Zhg. | 102 | 23.33 N | 105.35 E |
| Funiuchang | 107 | 29.03 N | 106.33 E |
| Funiu Shan ⩤ | 100 | 33.40 N | 112.30 E |
| Funk Island I | 186 | 49.46 N | 53.10 W |
| Funks Creek ≃ | 226 | 39.19 N | 122.11 W |
| Funkturm v | 264a | 52.31 N | 13.16 E |
| Funne ≃ | 263 | 51.42 N | 7.36 E |
| Funnel Creek ≃ | 166 | 22.18 S | 148.57 E |
| Funnel Hill ʌ[2] | 272c | 18.54 N | 73.07 E |
| Funo | 96 | 34.53 N | 132.47 E |
| Funshinagh, Lough @ | 48 | 53.31 N | 8.07 W |
| Funsi | 150 | 10.17 N | 1.58 W |
| Funtana Coberta ⊥ | 71 | 39.34 N | 9.21 E |
| Funtua | 150 | 11.31 N | 7.17 E |
| Funza | 246 | 4.40 N | 74.09 W |
| Fuorn, Pass dal (Ofenpass) )( | 58 | 46.37 N | 10.15 E |
| Fuping | 102 | 34.47 N | 109.07 E |
| Fuqiao | 106 | 31.36 N | 121.12 E |
| Fuqikou | 100 | 29.44 N | 117.48 E |
| Fuqing | 100 | 25.44 N | 119.22 E |
| Fuquay-Varina | 192 | 35.35 N | 78.48 W |
| Füramoos | 58 | 48.00 N | 9.53 E |
| Furancungo | 154 | 14.55 S | 33.35 E |
| Furano | 92a | 43.21 N | 142.24 E |
| Furāt, Nahr al- → Euphrates ≃ | 128 | 31.00 N | 47.25 E |
| Furci Siculo | 70 | 37.57 N | 15.23 E |
| Furculești | 38 | 43.52 N | 25.09 E |
| Fures | 62 | 45.19 N | 5.30 E |
| Fūrg | 128 | 28.18 N | 55.13 E |
| Furkapass )( | 58 | 46.34 N | 8.25 E |
| Furka-Tunnel ◆[5] | 58 | 46.33 N | 8.26 E |
| Furlong | 208 | 40.18 N | 75.05 W |
| Furmanov | 80 | 57.15 N | 41.07 E |
| Furmanovka | 86 | 44.17 N | 72.57 E |
| Furmanovo | 80 | 49.42 N | 49.28 E |
| Furn, Wādī al- V | 142 | 30.13 N | 31.40 E |
| Furnace | 46 | 56.09 N | 5.10 W |
| Furnace Brook ≃ | 283 | 42.06 N | 70.43 W |
| Furnace Creek ≃ | 284b | 39.11 N | 76.35 W |
| Furnace Pond @ | 283 | 42.03 N | 70.49 W |
| Furnari | 70 | 38.07 N | 15.08 E |
| Furnas, Represa de @[1] | 255 | 20.45 S | 46.00 W |
| Furn ash-Shubbāk | 132 | 33.52 N | 35.31 E |
| Furneaux Group II | 166 | 40.10 S | 148.05 E |
| Furnes → Veurne | 50 | 51.04 N | 2.40 E |
| Furness Abbey v[1] | 44 | 54.07 N | 3.12 W |
| Furness Fells ⩤[2] | 44 | 54.18 N | 3.07 W |
| Furong Shan ʌ | 100 | 27.30 N | 115.52 E |
| Furqlus | 130 | 34.36 N | 37.05 E |
| Fürstenau, Dtsch. | 52 | 51.50 N | 9.19 E |
| Fürstenau, Dtsch. | 52 | 52.31 N | 7.40 E |
| Fürstenberg | 52 | 51.44 N | 9.24 E |
| Fürstenberg/Havel | 54 | 53.11 N | 13.08 E |
| Fürstenfeld | 61 | 47.03 N | 16.05 E |
| Fürstenfeldbruck | 60 | 48.10 N | 11.15 E |
| Fürstenhagen | 56 | 51.12 N | 9.41 E |
| Fürstenstein | 60 | 48.43 N | 13.20 E |
| Fürstenwalde | 54 | 52.21 N | 14.04 E |
| Fürstenwerder | 54 | 53.24 N | 13.34 E |
| Fürstenzell | 60 | 48.32 N | 13.19 E |
| Furtei | 71 | 39.34 N | 8.57 E |
| Fürth, Dtsch. | 56 | 49.28 N | 10.59 E |
| Fürth, Dtsch. | 56 | 49.39 N | 8.47 E |
| Furth, Dtsch. | 60 | 48.35 N | 12.02 E |
| Furth im Wald | 60 | 49.18 N | 12.51 E |
| Furtwangen | 58 | 48.03 N | 8.12 E |
| Furuba ≃ | 256 | 23.21 S | 44.57 W |
| Furubō-san ʌ[2] | 270 | 34.53 N | 135.19 E |
| Furudal | 26 | 61.10 N | 15.08 E |
| Furudono | 94 | 37.05 N | 140.34 E |
| Furukawa, Nihon | 92 | 38.34 N | 140.58 E |
| Furukawa, Nihon | 94 | 36.14 N | 137.11 E |
| Furulund | 41 | 55.46 N | 13.04 E |
| Furusund | 40 | 59.40 N | 18.55 E |
| Furu-tone ≃ | 94 | 35.48 N | 139.51 E |
| Furuvik | 40 | 60.39 N | 17.20 E |
| Furuyakami | 268 | 35.55 N | 139.32 E |
| Fürwiggestausee @[1] | 263 | 51.09 N | 7.41 E |
| Fury and Hecla Strait ʁ | 176 | 69.56 N | 84.00 W |
| Fusagasugá | 246 | 4.21 N | 74.22 W |
| Fusain ≃ | 50 | 48.09 N | 2.44 E |
| Fusan → Pusan | 98 | 35.06 N | 129.03 E |
| Fuscaldo | 68 | 39.25 N | 16.02 E |
| Fusch | 64 | 47.14 N | 12.49 E |
| Fuschl am See | 64 | 47.48 N | 13.18 E |
| Fuschun → Fushun | 104 | 41.52 N | 123.53 E |
| Fuse → Higashiōsaka, Nihon | 96 | 34.39 N | 135.35 E |
| Fuse, Nihon | 268 | 35.53 N | 140.00 E |
| Fushan, Zhg. | 98 | 37.29 N | 121.16 E |
| Fushan, Zhg. | 102 | 35.58 N | 111.51 E |
| Fushan, Zhg. | 106 | 31.49 N | 120.46 E |
| Fushimi ◆[8] | 270 | 34.55 N | 135.46 E |
| Fushino ≃ | 96 | 34.03 N | 131.24 E |
| Fushuigang | 100 | 31.21 N | 113.40 E |
| Fushun (Funan), Zhg. | 104 | 41.52 N | 123.53 E |
| Fushun, Zhg. | 107 | 29.11 N | 105.00 E |
| Fushuncheng | 104 | 41.53 N | 123.51 E |
| Fusignano | 66 | 44.28 N | 11.57 E |
| Fusilier | 184 | 51.51 N | 109.46 W |
| Fusin → Fuxin | 104 | 42.03 N | 121.46 E |
| Fusine in Valromana | 64 | 46.30 N | 13.39 E |
| Fusio | 58 | 46.27 N | 8.40 E |
| Fusō | 94 | 35.21 N | 136.55 E |
| Fusong | 98 | 42.18 N | 127.20 E |
| Fussa | 94 | 35.45 N | 139.20 E |


| | | | | |
|---|---|---|---|---|
| ≃ River | Fluß | Río | Rivière | Rio |
| ≋ Canal | Kanal | Canal | Canal | Canal |
| ⊾ Waterfall, Rapids | Wasserfall, Stromschnellen | Cascada, Rápidos | Chute d'eau, Rapides | Cascata, Rápidos |
| ʁ Strait | Meeresstraße | Estrecho | Détroit | Estreito |
| c Bay, Gulf | Bucht, Golf | Bahía, Golfo | Baie, Golfe | Baía, Golfo |
| @ Lake, Lakes | See, Seen | Lago, Lagos | Lac, Lacs | Lago, Lagos |
| ⩸ Swamp | Sumpf | Pantano | Marais | Pântano |
| Ice Features, Glacier | Eis- und Gletscherformen | Accidentes Glaciales | Formes glaciaires | Acidentes glaciares |
| Other Hydrographic Features | Andere Hydrographische Objekte | Otros Elementos Hidrográficos | Autres données hydrographiques | Outros acidentes hidrográficos |
| ◆ Submarine Features | Untermeerische Objekte | Accidentes Submarinos | Formes de relief sous-marin | Acidentes submarinos |
| □ Political Unit | Politische Einheit | Unidad Politica | Entité politique | Unidade política |
| v Cultural Institution | Kulturelle Institution | Institución Cultural | Institution culturelle | Institução cultural |
| ⊥ Historical Site | Historische Stätte | Sitio Histórico | Site historique | Sitio histórico |
| ♦ Recreational Site | Erholungs- und Ferienort | Sitio de Recreo | Centre de loisirs | Area de Lazer |
| ⊠ Airport | Flughafen | Aeropuerto | Aéroport | Aeroporto |
| ■ Military Installation | Militäranlage | Instalación Militar | Installation militaire | Instalação militar |
| ◆ Miscellaneous | Verschiedenes | Misceláneo | Divers | Diversos |

| Name | Page | Lat.°′ | Long.°′ |
|---|---|---|---|
| Füssen | 64 | 47.34 N | 10.42 E |
| Fuste, Picacho del ∧ | 196 | 27.35 N | 102.47 W |
| Fusui | 102 | 22.32 N | 107.56 E |
| Futa, Passo della )( | 66 | 44.05 N | 11.17 E |
| Futaba | 94 | 35.41 N | 138.30 E |
| Futago-san ∧ | 96 | 33.35 N | 131.36 E |
| Futamata → Tenryū | 94 | 34.52 N | 137.49 E |
| Futamatagawa ◆[8] | 268 | 35.28 N | 139.33 E |
| Futami, Nihon | 94 | 34.30 N | 136.47 E |
| Futami, Nihon | 96 | 33.41 N | 132.38 E |
| Futang, Zhg. | 102 | 24.26 N | 112.09 E |
| Futang, Zhg. | 106 | 30.40 N | 119.35 E |
| Futaoi-jima I | 96 | 34.06 N | 130.47 E |
| Futatabi-yama ∧ | 270 | 34.43 N | 135.11 E |
| Futatsubashi ◆[8] | 268 | 35.28 N | 139.30 E |
| Futatsu-ne I[2] | 174f | 24.46 N | 141.18 E |
| Fu Tau Pun Chau I | 271d | 22.21 N | 114.22 E |
| Futian | 100 | 27.26 N | 114.56 E |
| Futianhe | 100 | 31.30 N | 115.05 E |
| Futianpu | 100 | 27.22 N | 112.47 E |
| Futjāni ≃ | 126 | 24.06 N | 90.09 E |
| Futschou → Fuzhou | 100 | 26.06 N | 119.17 E |
| Futtsu, Nihon | 94 | 35.19 N | 139.49 E |
| Futtsu, Nihon | 94 | 35.13 N | 139.52 E |
| Futtsu-misaki ≻ | 268 | 35.19 N | 139.46 E |
| Futun ≃ | 100 | 26.51 N | 117.46 E |
| Futuna I | 175f | 19.32 S | 170.14 E |
| Futuna, Île I | 14 | 14.15 S | 178.09 W |
| Futuyu | 105 | 39.18 N | 114.50 E |
| Fuveau | 62 | 43.27 N | 5.34 E |
| Fuwah | 142 | 31.12 N | 30.33 E |
| Fuwen | 86 | 47.13 N | 89.39 E |
| Fuxi, Zhg. | 100 | 27.14 N | 119.50 E |
| Fuxi, Zhg. | 100 | 25.14 N | 113.52 E |
| Fuxi ≃ | 107 | 29.09 N | 104.57 E |
| Fuxian (Wafangdian), Zhg. | 98 | 39.37 N | 122.01 E |
| Fuxian, Zhg. | 102 | 36.02 N | 109.13 E |
| Fuxian Hu ⊜ | 102 | 24.30 N | 102.55 E |
| Fuxin, Zhg. | 104 | 42.08 N | 121.45 E |
| Fuxin, Zhg. | 104 | 42.03 N | 121.46 E |
| Fuxing, Zhg. | 107 | 30.27 N | 106.04 E |
| Fuxing, Zhg. | 107 | 30.24 N | 104.53 E |
| Fuxing, Zhg. | 107 | 29.54 N | 105.43 E |
| Fuxingchang | 107 | 29.40 N | 105.13 E |
| Fuxing Dao I | 269b | 31.17 N | 121.23 E |
| Fuxinghao | 104 | 42.35 N | 120.32 E |
| Fuyang, Zhg. | 100 | 32.54 N | 115.49 E |
| Fuyang, Zhg. | 100 | 30.03 N | 119.57 E |
| Fuyang, Zhg. | 100 | 23.36 N | 116.37 E |
| Fuyang ≃ | 98 | 38.14 N | 116.05 E |
| Fuyouertuo Shan ∧ | 89 | 45.52 N | 119.48 E |
| Fuyu, Zhg. | 89 | 47.49 N | 124.27 E |
| Fuyu, Zhg. | 89 | 45.10 N | 124.50 E |
| Fuyuan, Zhg. | 89 | 48.21 N | 134.18 E |
| Fuyuan, Zhg. | 102 | 25.39 N | 104.12 E |
| Fuzhai | 100 | 29.32 N | 120.02 E |
| Fuzhong | 102 | 24.28 N | 111.22 E |
| Fuzhou, Zhg. | 100 | 28.01 N | 116.20 E |
| Fuzhou (Foochow), Zhg. | 100 | 26.06 N | 119.17 E |
| Fuzhoucheng | 98 | 39.45 N | 121.47 E |
| Fuzhuang | 98 | 34.57 N | 118.17 E |
| Fuzhuangyi | 98 | 38.02 N | 116.08 E |
| Füzuli | 84 | 39.37 N | 47.08 E |
| Fyfield | 42 | 51.45 N | 0.16 E |
| Fylde □[8] | 262 | 53.46 N | 2.53 W |
| Fylde ≻[1] | 44 | 53.47 N | 2.56 W |
| Fyn □[6] | 41 | 55.20 N | 10.25 E |
| Fyn I | 41 | 55.20 N | 10.30 E |
| Fyne, Loch c | 46 | 56.00 N | 5.24 W |
| Fyns Hoved ≻ | 41 | 55.37 N | 10.36 E |
| Fyresvatn ⊜ | 26 | 59.06 N | 8.12 E |
| Fyrisån ≃ | 40 | 59.47 N | 17.39 E |
| Fysingen ⊜ | 40 | 59.34 N | 17.55 E |
| Fyvie | 46 | 57.25 N | 2.23 W |
| Fzâra, Gara'et ⊜ | 36 | 36.47 N | 7.30 E |
| **G** | | | |
| Ga | 150 | 9.47 N | 2.30 W |
| Gaaden | 264b | 48.03 N | 16.12 E |
| Gaalkacyo | 144 | 6.47 N | 47.26 E |
| Gaanderen | 52 | 51.56 N | 6.21 E |
| Gabah | 144 | 8.08 N | 50.02 E |
| Gabai | 146 | 11.05 N | 11.39 E |
| Gabaldon | 116 | 15.28 N | 121.19 E |
| Gabare | 38 | 43.19 N | 23.55 E |
| Gabarus | 186 | 45.50 N | 60.09 W |
| Gabarus Bay c | 186 | 45.51 N | 60.07 W |
| Gabas ≃ | 32 | 43.46 N | 0.42 W |
| Gabbs | 204 | 38.52 N | 117.55 W |
| Gabby Heights | 214 | 40.09 N | 80.15 W |
| Gabela | 152 | 10.48 S | 14.20 E |
| Gaberones → Gaborone | 156 | 24.45 S | 25.55 E |
| Gabès | 148 | 33.53 N | 10.07 E |
| Gabès, Golfe de c | 148 | 34.00 N | 10.25 E |
| Gabia | 152 | 4.34 S | 17.07 E |
| Gabiarra | 255 | 16.15 S | 39.41 W |
| Gabicce Mare | 66 | 43.58 N | 12.46 E |
| Gabii ⊥ | 267a | 41.54 N | 12.43 E |
| Gabil | 146 | 11.09 N | 18.12 E |
| Gabilan Creek ≃ | 226 | 36.41 N | 121.38 W |
| Gabilan Range ⩘ | 226 | 36.30 N | 121.15 W |
| Gąbin | 30 | 52.25 N | 19.44 E |
| Gabir | 140 | 8.35 N | 24.40 E |
| Gable Mountain ∧ | 182 | 54.30 N | 121.40 W |
| Gablenz | 54 | 51.41 N | 14.31 E |
| Gablingen | 58 | 48.27 N | 10.49 E |
| Gablitz | 61 | 48.14 N | 16.09 E |
| Gablonz → Jablonec nad Nisou | 30 | 50.44 N | 15.10 E |
| Gabon □[1], Afr. | 138 | 1.00 S | 11.45 E |
| Gabon □[1], Afr. | 152 | 1.00 S | 11.45 E |
| Gabon, Estuaire du c[1] | 152 | 0.25 N | 9.20 E |
| Gaborone | 156 | 24.45 S | 25.55 E |
| Gabras | 140 | 10.16 N | 26.14 E |
| Gabria | 64 | 45.52 N | 13.34 E |
| Gabriel | 250 | 11.14 S | 41.53 W |
| Gabriel Strait ⊔ | 176 | 61.45 N | 65.30 W |
| Gabriel y Galan, Embalse de ⊜[1] | 34 | 40.15 N | 6.15 W |
| Gabriel Zamora | 234 | 19.05 N | 102.05 W |
| Gābrīk | 128 | 25.44 N | 58.28 E |
| Gabriola | 224 | 49.12 N | 123.50 W |
| Gabriola Island I | 224 | 49.10 N | 123.47 W |
| Gabrovo | 38 | 42.52 N | 25.19 E |
| Gabun → Gabon □[1] | 152 | 1.00 S | 11.45 E |
| Gaby | 62 | 45.43 N | 7.53 E |
| Gacé | 50 | 48.48 N | 0.18 E |
| Gachetá | 246 | 4.49 N | 73.36 W |
| Gachpar | 174q | 9.33 N | 138.10 E |
| Gachsārān | 128 | 30.12 N | 50.47 E |
| Gackle | 198 | 46.37 N | 99.08 W |
| Gacko | 38 | 43.10 N | 18.32 E |
| Gädäbäy | 84 | 40.34 N | 45.49 E |
| Gadag | 122 | 15.25 N | 75.37 E |
| Gadamai | 140 | 17.09 N | 36.06 E |
| Gādarwāra | 124 | 22.55 N | 78.47 E |
| Gadbjerg | 41 | 55.46 N | 9.20 E |
| Gäddede | 26 | 64.30 N | 14.09 E |
| Gadderbaum | 52 | 52.00 N | 8.31 E |
| Gade ≃ | 260 | 51.38 N | 0.28 W |
| Gadebusch | 54 | 53.42 N | 11.07 E |
| Gadein | 140 | 8.11 N | 28.44 E |
| Gadera ≃ | 64 | 46.47 N | 11.54 E |
| Gadevang | 41 | 55.58 N | 12.18 E |
| Gadis ≃ | 114 | 1.03 N | 98.55 E |
| Gadmen | 58 | 46.44 N | 8.21 E |
| Gado Bravo, Ilha do I | 250 | 10.54 S | 42.52 W |
| Gádor | 34 | 36.57 N | 2.29 W |
| Gadra | 120 | 25.40 N | 70.37 E |
| Gadsden, Al., U.S. | 194 | 34.00 N | 86.00 W |
| Gadsden, Az., U.S. | 200 | 32.33 N | 114.47 W |
| Gadwāl | 122 | 16.14 N | 77.48 E |
| Gadzi | 152 | 4.47 N | 16.42 E |
| Gaerwen | 44 | 53.13 N | 4.16 W |
| Găești | 38 | 44.43 N | 25.19 E |
| Gaeta | 66 | 41.12 N | 13.35 E |
| Gaeta, Golfo di c | 66 | 41.06 N | 13.30 E |
| Gaferut I | 108 | 9.14 N | 145.23 E |
| Gaffney | 192 | 35.04 N | 81.39 W |
| Gafour | 36 | 36.18 N | 9.19 E |
| Gafsa | 148 | 34.25 N | 8.48 E |
| Gafurov | 85 | 40.14 N | 69.44 E |
| Gag, Pulau I | 164 | 0.27 S | 129.52 E |
| Gagal | 146 | 9.01 N | 15.08 E |
| Gagarawa | 150 | 12.25 N | 9.32 E |
| Gagarin | 76 | 55.33 N | 35.00 E |
| Gage | 196 | 36.18 N | 99.45 W |
| Gägelow | 54 | 53.55 N | 11.25 E |
| Gagere ≃ | 150 | 13.21 N | 6.23 E |
| Gages Lake | 278 | 42.21 N | 87.59 W |
| Gages Lake ⊜ | 278 | 42.21 N | 88.00 W |
| Gagetown | 186 | 45.47 N | 66.09 W |
| Gagetown, Canadian Forces Base ■ | 186 | 45.43 N | 66.15 W |
| Gaggenau | 56 | 48.48 N | 8.19 E |
| Gaggi | 70 | 37.51 N | 15.13 E |
| Gaggiano | 62 | 45.24 N | 9.02 E |
| Gaghamni | 140 | 11.41 N | 28.19 E |
| Gagil Tamil I | 174q | 9.32 N | 138.10 E |
| Gagino | 80 | 55.14 N | 45.02 E |
| Gagliano Castelferrato | 70 | 37.43 N | 14.32 E |
| Gagliano del Capo | 68 | 39.50 N | 18.22 E |
| Gagnef | 40 | 60.35 N | 15.04 E |
| Gagnia | 152 | 1.28 S | 16.02 E |
| Gagnoa | 150 | 6.08 N | 5.56 W |
| Gagnon | 176 | 51.53 N | 68.10 W |
| Gagnon, Lac ⊜ | 206 | 46.07 N | 75.07 W |
| Gagny | 261 | 48.53 N | 2.32 E |
| Gagra | 84 | 43.20 N | 40.15 E |
| Gagret | 123 | 31.40 N | 76.04 E |
| Gahanna | 218 | 40.01 N | 82.52 W |
| Gahlen | 52 | 51.40 N | 6.52 E |
| Gaiarine | 64 | 45.52 N | 12.29 E |
| Gaibandha | 124 | 25.19 N | 89.33 E |
| Gaichtpass )( | 58 | 47.27 N | 10.37 E |
| Gaigalava | 76 | 56.40 N | 27.18 E |
| Gaighāta | 126 | 22.56 N | 88.44 E |
| Gaijiatun | 104 | 40.50 N | 122.37 E |
| Gail | 196 | 32.46 N | 101.27 W |
| Gail ≃ | 64 | 46.36 N | 13.53 E |
| Gailberg Sattel )( | 64 | 46.43 N | 12.58 E |
| Gail Creek ≃ | 222 | 31.07 N | 95.23 W |
| Gaildorf | 56 | 49.00 N | 9.46 E |
| Gaillac | 32 | 43.54 N | 1.55 E |
| Gaillard, Château ⊥ | 50 | 49.13 N | 1.25 E |
| Gaillard, Lac ⊜ | 186 | 50.06 N | 68.47 W |
| Gaillard, Lake ⊜ | 207 | 41.21 N | 72.46 W |
| Gaillefontaine | 50 | 49.39 N | 1.37 E |
| Gaillimh → Galway | 48 | 53.16 N | 9.03 W |
| Gaillon, Fr. | 50 | 49.10 N | 1.20 E |
| Gaillon, Fr. | 261 | 49.02 N | 1.54 E |
| Gailtaler Alpen ⩘ | 64 | 46.42 N | 13.00 E |
| Gaima | 164 | 8.20 S | 142.55 E |
| Gaimán | 254 | 43.17 S | 65.29 W |
| Gaimersheim | 60 | 48.49 N | 11.22 E |
| Gaines, Mi., U.S. | 216 | 42.52 N | 83.54 W |
| Gaines, Pa., U.S. | 210 | 41.45 N | 77.34 W |
| Gainesboro | 194 | 36.21 N | 85.39 W |
| Gainesville, Fl., U.S. | 192 | 29.39 N | 82.19 W |
| Gainesville, Ga., U.S. | 192 | 34.17 N | 83.49 W |
| Gainesville, Mo., U.S. | 194 | 36.36 N | 92.25 W |
| Gainesville, N.Y., U.S. | 210 | 42.38 N | 78.08 W |
| Gainesville, Tx., U.S. | 196 | 33.37 N | 97.07 W |
| Gainford | 44 | 54.32 N | 1.44 W |
| Gainsborough, Sk., Can. | 184 | 49.10 N | 101.26 W |
| Gainsborough, Eng., U.K. | 44 | 53.24 N | 0.46 W |
| Gainsborough Creek ≃ | 184 | 49.10 N | 101.02 W |
| Gaiole in Chianti | 66 | 43.28 N | 11.26 E |
| Gairatganj | 124 | 23.24 N | 78.13 E |
| Gairdner ≃ | 162 | 34.17 S | 119.28 E |
| Gairdner, Lake ⊜ | 162 | 31.35 S | 136.00 E |
| Gairloch | 46 | 57.42 N | 5.40 W |
| Gairloch, Loch c | 46 | 57.44 N | 5.44 W |
| Gairn ≃ | 46 | 57.03 N | 3.05 W |
| Gais, It. | 64 | 46.50 N | 11.57 E |
| Gais, Schw. | 58 | 47.22 N | 9.27 E |
| Gaisberg ∧ | 64 | 47.48 N | 13.07 E |
| Gaisbeuren | 58 | 47.54 N | 9.43 E |
| Gaital, Cerro ∧ | 236 | 8.37 N | 80.07 W |
| Gaither | 208 | 39.21 N | 76.59 W |
| Gaithersburg | 208 | 39.08 N | 77.12 W |
| Gaixian | 98 | 40.24 N | 122.22 E |
| Gaizina Kalns ∧[2] | 76 | 56.52 N | 25.57 E |
| Gaj, Hrv. | 36 | 45.29 N | 17.02 E |
| Gaj, Ross. | 86 | 51.27 N | 58.27 E |
| Gajā | 272b | 22.52 N | 88.10 E |
| Gajahmungkur, Waduk ⊜[1] | 115a | 7.55 S | 110.55 E |
| Gajendragarh | 122 | 15.44 N | 75.59 E |
| Gajiram | 146 | 12.30 N | 13.12 E |
| Gajny | 24 | 60.15 N | 54.15 E |
| Gājol | 124 | 25.13 N | 88.12 E |
| Gajsinghpur | 123 | 29.40 N | 73.27 E |
| Gajuapara ≃ | 250 | 4.17 S | 47.25 W |
| Gajutino | 76 | 58.42 N | 38.32 E |
| Gakarosa ∧ | 158 | 27.54 S | 23.33 E |
| Gakona | 180 | 62.18 N | 145.18 W |
| Gākuch | 123 | 36.10 N | 73.45 E |
| Gakugsa | 24 | 61.34 N | 36.26 E |
| Gāla, Bngl. | 126 | 24.18 N | 89.54 E |
| Gala, Zhg. | 124 | 28.16 N | 89.23 E |
| Galaassija | 128 | 39.52 N | 64.27 E |
| Galāchipa | 126 | 22.10 N | 90.25 E |
| Galahad | 182 | 52.31 N | 111.56 W |
| Galamares | 266c | 38.48 N | 9.25 W |
| Galán, Cerro ∧ | 252 | 25.55 S | 66.52 W |
| Galana ≃ | 154 | 3.09 S | 40.08 E |
| Galangue | 152 | 13.48 S | 16.09 E |
| Galanovo | 80 | 56.09 N | 54.07 E |
| Galanta | 30 | 48.12 N | 17.43 E |
| Galápagos □[4] | 246a | 0.30 S | 90.30 W |
| Galápagos, Parque Nacional de ◆ | 246a | 0.15 S | 90.15 W |
| Galapagos Islands → Colón, Archipiélago de II | 246a | 0.30 S | 90.30 W |
| Galaroza | 34 | 37.55 N | 6.42 W |
| Galas ≃ | 114 | 5.31 N | 102.12 E |
| Galashiels | 46 | 55.37 N | 2.49 W |
| Galata ◆[8] | 267b | 41.01 N | 28.58 E |
| Galata Köprüsü ◆[5] | 267b | 41.00 N | 28.57 E |
| Galata Tower ʋ | 267b | 41.01 N | 28.58 E |
| Galatea | 172 | 38.25 S | 176.45 E |
| Galați | 38 | 45.26 N | 28.03 E |
| Galați □[6] | 38 | 45.45 N | 27.45 E |
| Galatia | 194 | 37.50 N | 88.36 W |
| Galatia □[9] | 130 | 39.30 N | 32.40 E |
| Galatina | 68 | 40.10 N | 18.10 E |
| Galatone | 68 | 40.09 N | 18.04 E |
| Galatro | 68 | 38.28 N | 16.06 E |
| Galátsion | 267c | 38.01 N | 23.45 E |
| Galatz → Galați | 38 | 45.26 N | 28.03 E |
| Galaure ≃ | 62 | 45.11 N | 4.49 E |
| Gala Water ≃ | 46 | 55.37 N | 2.48 W |
| Galax | 192 | 36.39 N | 80.55 W |
| Galaxídhion | 38 | 38.22 N | 22.23 E |
| Galbyn gov' ◆[2] | 102 | 42.30 N | 107.00 E |
| Galdhøpiggen ∧ | 26 | 61.37 N | 8.17 E |
| Gale, Lac ⊜ | 190 | 46.46 N | 76.51 W |
| Galeairy Lake ⊜ | 212 | 45.29 N | 78.17 W |
| Galeana, Méx. | 232 | 30.07 N | 107.38 W |
| Galeana, Méx. | 232 | 24.50 N | 100.04 W |
| Galeão, Aeroporto do ⊠ | 256 | 22.50 S | 43.15 W |
| Galeata | 66 | 44.00 N | 11.55 E |
| Galegu | 140 | 12.36 N | 35.02 E |
| Galeh Dār | 128 | 27.38 N | 52.42 E |
| Galela | 108 | 1.50 N | 127.50 E |
| Galena, Austl. | 162 | 27.50 S | 114.41 E |
| Galena, Ak., U.S. | 180 | 64.44 N | 156.57 W |
| Galena, Il., U.S. | 190 | 42.25 N | 90.25 W |
| Galena, In., U.S. | 218 | 38.21 N | 85.56 W |
| Galena, Ks., U.S. | 198 | 37.04 N | 94.38 W |
| Galena, Md., U.S. | 208 | 39.20 N | 75.52 W |
| Galena, Mo., U.S. | 194 | 36.48 N | 93.27 W |
| Galena, Oh., U.S. | 214 | 40.12 N | 82.52 W |
| Galena Park | 222 | 29.43 N | 95.13 W |
| Galenbecker See ⊜ | 54 | 53.38 N | 13.43 E |
| Galeota Point ≻ | 241r | 10.08 N | 60.59 W |
| Galera ≃ | 248 | 14.25 S | 60.07 W |
| Galera, Punta ≻, Chile | 254 | 39.59 S | 73.43 W |
| Galera, Punta ≻, Ec. | 246 | 0.49 N | 80.03 W |
| Galera, Punta de ≻ | 34 | 39.06 N | 1.31 E |
| Galera Point ≻ | 241r | 10.49 N | 60.55 W |
| Galeras, Volcán ∧[1] | 246 | 1.13 N | 77.22 W |
| Galeria ⊥ | 267a | 42.02 N | 12.18 E |
| Galeria, Fosso la ≃ | 267a | 41.48 N | 12.21 E |
| Galesburg, Il., U.S. | 190 | 40.56 N | 90.22 W |
| Galesburg, Mi., U.S. | 216 | 42.17 N | 85.25 W |
| Gales Creek | 224 | 45.35 N | 123.12 W |
| Gales Creek ≃ | 224 | 45.29 N | 123.06 W |
| Gales Ferry | 207 | 41.25 N | 72.04 W |
| Gales Point ≻ | 283 | 42.33 N | 70.47 W |
| Galesville, Md., U.S. | 208 | 38.50 N | 76.32 W |
| Galesville, Wi., U.S. | 190 | 44.04 N | 91.20 W |
| Galeton | 214 | 41.43 N | 77.38 W |
| Galeville | 210 | 43.05 N | 76.10 W |
| Galgasc | 144 | 0.11 N | 41.38 E |
| Galgate | 44 | 54.00 N | 2.47 W |
| Galguduud □[4] | 144 | 5.00 N | 46.30 E |
| Galheiros | 255 | 13.18 S | 46.25 W |
| Gali | 84 | 42.38 N | 41.44 E |
| Gali, Torrente de ≃ | 266d | 41.28 N | 2.00 E |
| Galiano | 224 | 48.52 N | 123.21 W |
| Galiano Island I | 224 | 48.56 N | 123.29 W |
| Galibier, Col du )( | 62 | 45.04 N | 6.24 E |
| Galič | 80 | 58.23 N | 42.21 E |
| Galicia □[3] | 34 | 42.45 N | 8.00 W |
| Galicia □[9] | 22 | 49.00 N | 22.00 E |
| Galičskaja vozvyšennost' ⩘[2] | 24 | 58.25 N | 42.20 E |
| Galičskoje, ozero ⊜ | 80 | 58.24 N | 42.18 E |
| Galien | 216 | 41.47 N | 86.29 W |
| Galien ≃ | 216 | 41.48 N | 86.45 W |
| Galilee | 207 | 41.22 N | 71.30 W |
| Galilee → HaGalil □[9] | 132 | 32.54 N | 35.20 E |
| Galilee, Lake ⊜ | 166 | 22.21 S | 145.48 E |
| Galilee, Sea of → Kinneret, Yam ⊜ | 132 | 32.48 N | 35.35 E |
| Galiléia | 255 | 19.00 S | 41.33 W |
| Galim | 152 | 7.06 N | 12.29 E |
| Galina Point ≻ | 241q | 18.24 N | 76.53 W |
| Galindo Creek ≃ | 282 | 37.58 N | 122.02 W |
| Galion | 214 | 40.44 N | 82.47 W |
| Galion, Baie du c | 240e | 14.44 N | 60.57 W |
| Galis | 115a | 7.08 S | 113.33 E |
| Galisteo Creek ≃ | 200 | 35.31 N | 106.22 W |
| Galite, Canal de la ⊔ | 36 | 37.20 N | 9.00 E |
| Galiuro Mountains ⩘ | 200 | 32.40 N | 110.20 W |
| Galiwinku | 164 | 12.02 S | 135.34 E |
| Galižana | 64 | 44.56 N | 13.52 E |
| Galka'yo | 144 | 6.47 N | 47.26 E |
| Galkhausen | 263 | 51.05 N | 6.58 E |
| Galkino, Kaz. | 86 | 52.14 N | 78.20 E |
| Galkino, Ross. | 82 | 54.46 N | 35.49 E |
| Galkino, Ross. | 86 | 55.36 N | 62.55 E |
| Gall'aaral | 85 | 40.02 N | 67.35 E |
| Gallan Head ≻ | 46 | 58.14 N | 7.03 W |
| Gallarate | 62 | 45.40 N | 8.47 E |
| Gallardon | 50 | 48.32 N | 1.42 E |
| Gallatin, Mo., U.S. | 194 | 39.54 N | 93.57 W |
| Gallatin, Pa., U.S. | 279b | 40.12 N | 79.53 W |
| Gallatin, Tn., U.S. | 194 | 36.23 N | 86.26 W |
| Gallatin, Tx., U.S. | 222 | 31.54 N | 95.09 W |
| Gallatin □[6] | 218 | 38.45 N | 84.51 W |
| Gallatin ≃ | 202 | 45.56 N | 111.29 W |
| Gallatin Range ⩘ | 202 | 45.15 N | 111.05 W |
| Galle | 122 | 6.02 N | 80.13 E |
| Gállego ≃ | 34 | 41.39 N | 0.51 W |
| Gallegos ≃ | 254 | 51.36 S | 68.59 W |
| Galles → Wales □[8] | 28 | 52.30 N | 3.30 W |
| Galleyend | 260 | 51.42 N | 0.29 E |
| Galley Head ≻ | 48 | 51.30 N | 8.57 W |
| Galleywood | 260 | 51.42 N | 0.28 E |
| Galliano | 194 | 29.26 N | 90.17 W |
| Galliate | 62 | 45.29 N | 8.42 E |
| Gallicano | 64 | 44.04 N | 10.26 E |
| Gallicano nel Lazio | 267a | 41.52 N | 12.49 E |
| Gallicchio | 68 | 40.17 N | 16.08 E |
| Gallico | 68 | 38.10 N | 15.41 E |
| Galliera Veneta | 64 | 45.39 N | 11.49 E |
| Gallinara I | 62 | 44.02 N | 8.14 E |
| Gallinas ≃ | 196 | 35.10 N | 104.55 W |
| Gallinas, Punta ≻ | 246 | 12.28 N | 71.40 W |
| Gallinas Creek ≃ | 282 | 38.01 N | 122.30 W |
| Gallinas Peak ∧ | 200 | 34.13 N | 105.45 W |
| Gallio | 64 | 45.53 N | 11.33 E |
| Gallipoli, Austl. | 166 | 19.10 S | 137.55 E |
| Gallipoli, It. | 68 | 40.03 N | 17.58 E |
| Gallipoli → Gelibolu, Tür. | 130 | 40.24 N | 26.40 E |
| Gallipoli Peninsula → Gelibolu Yarımadası ≻[1] | 130 | 40.20 N | 26.30 E |
| Gallipolis | 188 | 38.48 N | 82.12 W |
| Gallitzin | 214 | 40.28 N | 78.33 W |
| Gallivaggio | 58 | 46.21 N | 9.21 E |
| Gällivare | 24 | 67.07 N | 20.45 E |
| Gallneukirchen | 61 | 48.21 N | 14.25 E |
| Gällö | 26 | 62.55 N | 15.14 E |
| Gallo, Capo ≻ | 70 | 38.13 N | 13.19 E |
| Gallo, Laguna ⊜ | 258 | 35.30 S | 58.28 W |
| Gallo Arroyo V | 200 | 33.55 N | 105.00 W |
| Galloo Island I | 212 | 43.54 N | 76.25 W |
| Galloupes Point ≻ | 283 | 42.28 N | 70.53 W |
| Galloway □[9] | 44 | 55.00 N | 4.25 W |
| Galloway, Mull of ≻ | 44 | 54.38 N | 4.50 W |
| Galloway Creek ≃, Md., U.S. | 284b | 39.18 N | 76.23 W |
| Galloway Creek ≃, Mi., U.S. | 281 | 42.39 N | 83.12 W |
| Galluis | 261 | 48.48 N | 1.48 E |
| Gallup | 200 | 35.31 N | 108.44 W |
| Gallupville | 210 | 42.40 N | 74.14 W |
| Gallur | 34 | 41.52 N | 1.19 W |
| Gallura ◆[1] | 71 | 41.00 N | 9.13 E |
| Gally, Ru de ≃ | 261 | 48.53 N | 1.53 E |
| Gälnan ⊔ | 40 | 59.31 N | 18.45 E |
| Gålö I | 40 | 59.05 N | 18.17 E |
| Galop Island I | 212 | 44.46 N | 75.24 W |
| Galoppo, Ippodromo del ◆ | 266b | 45.28 N | 9.07 E |
| Galougo | 150 | 13.50 N | 11.04 W |
| Galsi | 126 | 23.20 N | 87.42 E |
| Galston | 46 | 55.36 N | 4.24 W |
| Galt, Mong. | 88 | 48.46 N | 99.53 E |
| Galt, Ca., U.S. | 226 | 38.15 N | 121.17 W |
| Gal Tardo | 144 | 3.34 N | 45.58 E |
| Galtat Zemmour | 148 | 25.15 N | 12.20 W |
| Galtelli | 71 | 40.23 N | 9.37 E |
| Galten | 41 | 56.09 N | 9.55 E |
| Galten c | 40 | 59.27 N | 16.09 E |
| Galtür | 58 | 46.58 N | 10.11 E |
| Galtymore Mountain ∧ | 48 | 52.22 N | 8.10 W |
| Galty Mountains ⩘ | 48 | 52.25 N | 8.10 W |
| Galūgāh-e Āsīyeh | 128 | 34.01 N | 59.55 E |
| Galugur | 114 | 2.34 N | 99.39 E |
| Galula | 154 | 8.36 S | 33.02 E |
| Galunggung, Gunung ∧ | 115a | 7.15 S | 108.03 E |
| Galuut | 88 | 48.33 N | 113.12 E |
| Galva, Il., U.S. | 190 | 41.10 N | 90.02 W |
| Galva, Ia., U.S. | 198 | 42.30 N | 95.25 W |
| Galva, Ks., U.S. | 198 | 38.22 N | 97.32 W |
| Galvarino | 252 | 38.24 S | 72.47 W |
| Galveston, In., U.S. | 216 | 40.34 N | 86.11 W |
| Galveston, Tx., U.S. | 222 | 29.17 N | 94.47 W |
| Galveston □[6] | 222 | 29.20 N | 94.53 W |
| Galveston Bay c | 222 | 29.36 N | 94.57 W |
| Galveston Island I | 222 | 29.13 N | 94.55 W |
| Gálvez | 252 | 32.02 S | 61.13 W |
| Gálvez ≃ | 248 | 5.12 S | 72.53 W |
| Galvin, Austl. | 274b | 37.51 S | 144.49 E |
| Galvin, Wa., U.S. | 224 | 46.44 N | 123.01 W |
| Galway (Gaillimh), Ire. | 48 | 53.16 N | 9.03 W |
| Galway, N.Y., U.S. | 210 | 43.01 N | 74.02 W |
| Galway □[6] | 48 | 53.20 N | 9.00 W |
| Galway Bay c | 48 | 53.10 N | 9.15 W |
| Gam (Jin) ≃ | 110 | 21.55 N | 105.12 E |
| Gam, Pulau I | 164 | 0.27 S | 130.36 E |
| Gama, Isla I | 254 | 40.29 S | 62.12 W |
| Gamaches | 50 | 49.59 N | 1.33 E |
| Gamagōri | 94 | 34.50 N | 137.14 E |
| Gamalejevka | 80 | 52.16 N | 53.26 E |
| Gamaliel | 194 | 36.38 N | 85.47 W |
| Ga-Mankoeng | 156 | 23.57 S | 29.42 E |
| Gamare, Lake ⊜ | 144 | 11.30 N | 41.40 E |
| Gamarra | 246 | 8.20 N | 73.45 W |
| Gamawa | 146 | 12.08 N | 10.32 E |
| Gamay | 116 | 12.23 N | 125.18 E |
| Gamay Bay c | 116 | 12.21 N | 125.21 E |
| Gamba | 120 | 28.17 N | 88.32 E |
| Gambach | 56 | 50.28 N | 8.44 E |
| Gambaga | 150 | 10.32 N | 0.26 W |
| Gambais | 261 | 48.46 N | 1.40 E |
| Gambaiseuil | 261 | 48.45 N | 1.44 E |
| Gambang | 114 | 3.43 N | 103.06 E |
| Gambara, It. | 64 | 45.15 N | 10.18 E |
| Gámbara, Méx. | 234 | 18.55 N | 102.05 W |
| Gambarie | 68 | 38.10 N | 15.50 E |
| Gambassi | 66 | 43.32 N | 10.57 E |
| Gambatesa | 66 | 41.30 N | 14.54 E |
| Gambela | 144 | 8.18 N | 34.37 E |
| Gambell | 180 | 63.46 N | 171.46 W |
| Gambellara | 64 | 45.28 N | 11.20 E |
| Gamber | 208 | 39.27 N | 76.56 W |
| Gambia □[1], Afr. | 134 | 13.30 N | 15.30 W |
| Gambia □[1], Afr. | 150 | 13.30 N | 15.30 W |
| Gambia (Gambie) ≃ | 150 | 13.28 N | 16.34 W |
| Gambi Aṭrash | 140 | 10.03 N | 33.47 E |
| Gambie → Gambia □[1] | 150 | 13.30 N | 15.30 W |
| Gambie (Gambia) ≃ | 150 | 13.28 N | 16.34 W |
| Gambier | 214 | 40.22 N | 82.23 W |
| Gambier, Îles II | 6 | 21.20 S | 136.30 W |
| Gamble Mansion State Historic Site ⊥ | 220 | 27.32 N | 82.32 W |
| Gambo, Nf., Can. | 186 | 48.46 N | 54.14 W |
| Gambo, Centraf. | 152 | 4.39 N | 22.16 E |
| Gamboa | 236 | 9.07 N | 79.42 W |
| Gamboli | 120 | 29.50 N | 68.26 E |
| Gambolò | 62 | 45.15 N | 8.51 E |
| Gamboma | 152 | 1.53 S | 15.51 E |
| Gamboula | 152 | 4.08 N | 15.09 E |
| Gambrill State Park ◆ | 208 | 39.30 N | 77.30 W |
| Gamchab ≃ | 156 | 28.15 S | 17.26 E |
| Gamé | 150 | 6.44 N | 1.11 E |
| Game Creek ≃ | 285 | 39.41 N | 75.28 W |
| Gamensee ⊜ | 264a | 52.40 N | 13.51 E |
| Gaming | 61 | 47.56 N | 15.06 E |
| Gamış dağ ∧ | 84 | 40.18 N | 46.23 E |
| Gamka ≃ | 158 | 33.18 S | 21.39 E |
| Gamlakarleby → Kokkola | 26 | 63.50 N | 23.07 E |
| Gamla Uppsala | 40 | 59.54 N | 17.38 E |
| Gamleby | 26 | 57.54 N | 16.24 E |
| Gamlitz | 61 | 46.43 N | 15.33 E |
| Gammel Estrup ⊥ | 26 | 56.26 N | 10.21 E |
| Gammelstad ʋ[1] | 26 | 65.38 N | 22.01 E |
| Gammertingen | 58 | 48.15 N | 9.13 E |
| Gammon ≃ | 184 | 51.07 N | 95.09 W |
| Gammon, Point ≻ | 207 | 41.36 N | 70.16 W |
| Gammon Ranges National Park ◆ | 166 | 30.29 S | 139.10 E |
| Gamō, Nihon | 94 | 35.03 N | 136.11 E |
| Gamō, Nihon | 268 | 35.52 N | 139.48 E |
| Gamoep | 158 | 29.55 S | 18.25 E |
| Ga-Mogara ≃ | 158 | 27.07 S | 22.57 E |
| Gamo Gofa □[4] | 144 | 5.45 N | 37.00 E |
| Gamon | 150 | 13.20 N | 12.55 W |
| Gamova, mys ≻ | 89 | 42.35 N | 131.12 E |
| Gamph, Slieve ⩘ | 48 | 54.05 N | 9.00 W |
| Gampoko | 273b | 4.16 S | 15.10 E |
| Gampola | 122 | 7.10 N | 80.34 E |
| Gampongbatak | 114 | 4.48 N | 97.39 E |
| Gampoui | 273b | 4.08 S | 15.22 E |
| Gams | 58 | 47.12 N | 9.28 E |
| Gamsfeld ∧ | 64 | 47.37 N | 13.29 E |
| Gamtoos ≃ | 158 | 33.58 S | 25.01 E |
| Gamud ∧ | 144 | 4.05 N | 38.03 E |
| Gan ≃, Zhg. | 89 | 49.12 N | 125.14 E |
| Gan ≃, Zhg. | 100 | 29.12 N | 116.00 E |
| Ganado, Az., U.S. | 200 | 35.42 N | 109.32 W |
| Ganado, Tx., U.S. | 222 | 29.02 N | 96.31 W |
| Ganano ≃ | 116 | 16.45 N | 121.44 E |
| Gananoque | 212 | 44.20 N | 76.10 W |
| Gananoque ≃ | 212 | 44.19 N | 76.09 W |
| Gananoque Lake ⊜ | 212 | 44.27 N | 76.09 W |
| Ganaraska ≃ | 212 | 43.57 N | 78.18 W |
| Ganargua Creek ≃ | 210 | 43.04 N | 77.00 W |
| Ganassi | 116 | 7.49 N | 124.06 E |
| Ganāveh | 128 | 29.34 N | 50.31 E |
| Gäncä | 84 | 40.40 N | 46.22 E |
| Gäncäçay ≃ | 84 | 40.54 N | 46.28 E |
| Ganchangba | 107 | 28.52 N | 103.41 E |
| Ganči | 85 | 39.58 N | 69.08 E |
| Gand → Gent | 50 | 51.03 N | 3.43 E |
| Ganda, Ang. | 152 | 13.02 S | 14.40 E |
| Ganda, Zaïre | 152 | 4.05 N | 23.32 E |
| Gandadiwata, Bulu ∧ | 112 | 2.42 S | 119.27 E |
| Gandajika | 152 | 6.45 S | 23.57 E |
| Gandak (Nārāyaṇi) ≃ | 124 | 25.39 N | 85.13 E |
| Gaṇḍakī □[8] | 124 | 28.15 N | 84.15 E |
| Gandara, Arg. | 258 | 35.26 S | 58.06 W |
| Gándara, Esp. | 34 | 43.32 N | 8.10 W |
| Ganda Singhwāla | 123 | 31.02 N | 74.31 E |
| Gandāva | 120 | 28.37 N | 67.29 E |
| Gandavaroyi Falls ⌞ | 154 | 17.17 S | 29.07 E |
| Gānde | 126 | 24.10 N | 86.26 E |
| Gander | 186 | 48.57 N | 54.37 W |
| Gander ≃ | 186 | 49.15 N | 54.30 W |
| Gander Bay | 186 | 49.18 N | 54.29 W |
| Gander Bay c | 186 | 49.25 N | 54.28 W |
| Ganderkesee | 52 | 53.02 N | 8.32 E |
| Gander Lake ⊜ | 186 | 48.55 N | 54.40 W |
| Gandesa | 34 | 41.03 N | 0.26 E |
| Gândești | 38 | 47.53 N | 28.23 E |
| Gandevi | 120 | 20.49 N | 72.59 E |
| Gāndhinagar | 120 | 23.12 N | 72.40 E |
| Gāndhi Sāgar ⊜[1] | 120 | 24.18 N | 75.21 E |
| Gandi | 150 | 12.55 N | 5.49 E |
| Gandi, Wādī V | 140 | 11.23 N | 24.31 E |
| Gandia | 34 | 38.58 N | 0.11 W |
| Gandino | 62 | 45.49 N | 9.54 E |
| Gando | 152 | 12.30 S | 17.25 E |
| Gandole | 146 | 8.26 N | 11.34 E |
| Gandou | 152 | 2.24 N | 17.27 E |
| Gandrange | 56 | 49.16 N | 6.08 E |
| Gandria | 58 | 46.01 N | 9.00 E |
| Gandu | 255 | 13.45 S | 39.30 W |
| Gandy Bridge ◆[5] | 220 | 27.53 N | 82.34 W |
| Ganfang | 100 | 28.40 N | 114.51 E |
| Ganfosi | 107 | 29.36 N | 104.03 E |
| Ganga → Ganges ≃ | 124 | 23.22 N | 90.32 E |
| Gangādharpur | 272b | 22.36 N | 88.11 E |
| Gangafani | 150 | 14.23 N | 2.24 W |
| Gangājalghāti | 126 | 23.25 N | 87.07 E |
| Gangala-Na-Bodio | 154 | 3.41 N | 29.08 E |



| ENGLISH Name | Page | Lat.°′ | Long.°′ |
|---|---|---|---|
| Gangalingolo | 273b | 4.20 S | 15.09 E |
| Gan Gan | 254 | 42.30 S | 68.16 W |
| Gangānagar | 123 | 29.55 N | 73.53 E |
| Gangāpur, India | 120 | 25.13 N | 74.16 E |
| Gangāpur, India | 122 | 19.41 N | 75.01 E |
| Gangāpur, India | 124 | 26.29 N | 76.43 E |
| Gangara, Niger | 150 | 14.36 N | 8.30 E |
| Gangara, Niger | 150 | 13.33 N | 7.14 E |
| Gāngārāmpur | 124 | 25.24 N | 88.31 E |
| Ganga Sāgar | 126 | 21.38 N | 88.05 E |
| Gangaw | 110 | 22.11 N | 94.07 E |
| Gangāwati | 122 | 15.26 N | 76.32 E |
| Gangaw Range ⩘ | 110 | 24.50 N | 96.40 E |
| Ganga-Yamuna Doāb ⩘[1] | 124 | 26.40 N | 79.30 E |
| Gangcheng | 98 | 35.52 N | 116.52 E |
| Gangdaba, Tchabal ∧ | 152 | 7.44 N | 12.45 E |
| Gangdhār | 120 | 23.57 N | 75.37 E |
| Gangdisê Shan ⩘ | 120 | 31.00 N | 82.00 E |
| Gangelt | 56 | 50.59 N | 5.59 E |
| Ganges, B.C., Can. | 224 | 48.51 N | 123.30 W |
| Ganges, Fr. | 62 | 43.56 N | 3.42 E |
| Ganges (Ganga) (Padma) ≃ | 124 | 23.22 N | 90.32 E |
| Ganges, Mouths of the ≃[1] | 120 | 22.00 N | 89.00 E |
| Ganges Delta ≚[2] | 124 | 23.00 N | 89.00 E |
| Ganghu | 120 | 32.05 N | 86.45 E |
| Gangi | 70 | 37.49 N | 14.13 E |
| Gangkofen | 60 | 48.26 N | 12.34 E |
| Gangkou, Zhg. | 100 | 29.12 N | 113.19 E |
| Gangkou, Zhg. | 100 | 29.45 N | 115.44 E |
| Gangkou, Zhg. | 100 | 29.21 N | 117.58 E |
| Gangkou, Zhg. | 100 | 22.38 N | 113.22 E |
| Gangkou, Zhg. | 100 | 22.36 N | 114.54 E |
| Gangkou, Zhg. | 106 | 30.44 N | 118.54 E |
| Gangkouzhen | 106 | 31.45 N | 120.40 E |
| Gangmar Co ⊜ | 120 | 33.46 N | 84.15 E |
| Gang Mills | 210 | 42.08 N | 77.06 W |
| Gāngnāpur | 126 | 23.09 N | 88.38 E |
| Gangneung → Kangnŭng | 98 | 37.45 N | 128.54 E |
| Gango ≃ | 152 | 9.48 S | 15.40 E |
| Gangoa | 102 | 37.15 N | 100.28 E |
| Gangoh | 124 | 29.46 N | 77.15 E |
| Gangotri, India | 120 | 30.56 N | 79.02 E |
| Gangotri, India | 120 | 31.01 N | 78.27 E |
| Gangou | 98 | 40.30 N | 119.27 E |
| Gangoumen | 98 | 41.40 N | 116.35 E |
| Gangouyi | 102 | 36.01 N | 105.03 E |
| Gangqiao | 107 | 30.13 N | 105.22 E |
| Gang Ranch | 182 | 51.33 N | 122.20 W |
| Gangshangji | 100 | 28.06 N | 116.30 E |
| Gangtok | 124 | 27.20 N | 88.37 E |
| Gangtou | 98 | 38.04 N | 113.56 E |
| Gangtouli | 106 | 31.42 N | 119.02 E |
| Gangu | 102 | 34.45 N | 105.20 E |
| Gangwa, Zaïre | 152 | 3.30 S | 20.55 E |
| Gangwa, Zhg. | 105 | 39.48 N | 116.10 E |
| Gangwei | 100 | 24.20 N | 118.01 E |
| Ganhezi | 86 | 44.08 N | 88.32 E |
| Ganhu | 102 | 44.33 N | 94.09 E |
| Gani | 164 | 0.47 S | 128.13 E |
| Ganišob | 85 | 39.03 N | 70.47 E |
| Ganj Dundwara | 124 | 27.44 N | 78.57 E |
| Ganjiang | 107 | 29.42 N | 103.38 E |
| Ganlan Shan ∧ | 124 | 29.54 N | 90.02 E |
| Ganlu | 106 | 31.32 N | 120.35 E |
| Ganluchang | 107 | 29.54 N | 104.47 E |
| Ganluo | 102 | 29.03 N | 102.59 E |
| Gannahoek | 158 | 26.44 S | 24.08 E |
| Gannan | 89 | 47.54 N | 123.30 E |
| Gannano, Lago di ⊜ | 68 | 40.19 N | 16.26 E |
| Gannapan | 158 | 30.23 S | 22.12 E |
| Gannat | 32 | 46.06 N | 3.12 E |
| Gannett Peak ∧ | 200 | 43.11 N | 109.39 W |
| Gannvalley | 198 | 44.02 N | 98.59 W |
| Ganpingsi | 102 | 35.13 N | 102.30 E |
| Ganpu | 106 | 30.24 N | 120.53 E |
| Ganq | 120 | 37.25 N | 92.15 E |
| Ganquan | 102 | 36.25 N | 109.16 E |
| Gansbaai | 158 | 34.35 S | 19.22 E |
| Gänsbrunnen | 58 | 47.16 N | 7.28 E |
| Gänserndorf | 61 | 48.20 N | 16.43 E |
| Gansevoort | 210 | 43.12 N | 73.39 W |
| Ganshoren | 56 | 50.52 N | 4.18 E |
| Ganspan | 158 | 27.57 S | 24.47 E |
| Gansu (Kansu) □[4] | 102 | 37.00 N | 103.00 E |
| Ganta | 150 | 7.15 N | 8.59 W |
| Gantan | 100 | 29.37 N | 119.34 E |
| Gantang, Zhg. | 100 | 26.56 N | 119.40 E |
| Gantang, Zhg. | 102 | 22.58 N | 109.00 E |
| Gantao ≃ | 98 | 38.01 N | 114.07 E |
| Gante → Gent | 50 | 51.03 N | 3.43 E |
| Gantheaume, Cape ≻ | 166 | 36.05 S | 137.27 E |
| Gantheaume Bay c | 162 | 27.44 S | 114.07 E |
| Gantheaume Point ≻ | 162 | 17.59 S | 122.10 E |
| Gantiadi | 84 | 43.24 N | 40.06 E |
| Gantian | 100 | 27.30 N | 113.10 E |
| Gantt | 194 | 31.24 N | 86.29 W |
| Gantung | 112 | 2.58 S | 108.09 E |
| Gantung, Mount ∧ | 116 | 8.57 N | 117.48 E |
| Gan'uškino | 80 | 46.36 N | 49.16 E |
| Ganwo | 150 | 11.13 N | 4.42 E |
| Ganxi, Zhg. | 100 | 28.08 N | 118.06 E |
| Ganxi, Zhg. | 102 | 29.02 N | 109.32 E |
| Ganyanchi | 102 | 36.39 N | 105.18 E |
| Ganyesa | 158 | 26.35 S | 24.10 E |
| Ganyu (Qing Kou) | 98 | 34.52 N | 119.10 E |
| Ganzê | 102 | 31.40 N | 100.01 E |
| Ganzhenyi | 100 | 30.33 N | 113.21 E |
| Ganzhou, Zhg. | 100 | 25.54 N | 114.55 E |
| Ganzhou, Zhg. | 100 | 28.49 N | 115.25 E |
| Ganzhou → Zhangye, Zhg. | 102 | 38.56 N | 100.27 E |
| Ganzhuermiao | 88 | 48.24 N | 118.08 E |
| Ganzlin | 54 | 53.23 N | 12.15 E |
| Ganzo Azul | 248 | 8.51 S | 74.44 W |
| Gao | 150 | 16.16 N | 0.03 W |
| Gao □[4] | 150 | 18.00 N | 1.30 E |
| Gao'an | 100 | 28.25 N | 115.22 E |
| Gaobaita | 271a | 39.53 N | 116.30 E |
| Gaobei | 100 | 26.37 N | 114.38 E |
| Gaobeidian | 271a | 39.54 N | 116.33 E |
| Gaobu | 100 | 27.48 N | 117.01 E |
| Gaochang | 107 | 28.49 N | 104.24 E |
| Gaocheng, Zhg. | 98 | 38.04 N | 114.49 E |
| Gaocheng, Zhg. | 100 | 31.57 N | 113.25 E |
| Gaocheng, Zhg. | 106 | 31.28 N | 119.48 E |
| Gaochengzhai | 104 | 41.24 N | 123.43 E |
| Gaochun | 106 | 31.20 N | 118.52 E |
| Gaocun | 98 | 37.05 N | 122.12 E |
| Gaodianzi | 102 | 30.40 N | 110.01 E |
| Gao Feng ∧ | 106 | 30.34 N | 118.40 E |
| Gaogongmiao | 100 | 33.25 N | 115.53 E |
| Gaogou | 100 | 34.03 N | 119.15 E |
| Gaohe | 100 | 22.47 N | 112.57 E |
| Gaohebu | 100 | 30.44 N | 116.50 E |
| Gaoil, Sliabh ∧ | 46 | 55.55 N | 5.28 W |
| Gaojiabu | 102 | 38.30 N | 110.11 E |
| Gaojiadi | 98 | 41.33 N | 114.58 E |
| Gaojiadian | 98 | 42.40 N | 124.28 E |
| Gaojian | 100 | 29.04 N | 121.14 E |
| Gaojiapuzi | 104 | 41.22 N | 123.36 E |
| Gaojiaqiao | 106 | 30.43 N | 120.38 E |
| Gaojiatun | 104 | 41.06 N | 121.19 E |
| Gaojiawopeng | 104 | 41.28 N | 122.10 E |
| Gaojiawopu | 104 | 41.50 N | 122.47 E |
| Gaojiazhai | 269b | 31.23 N | 121.33 E |
| Gaojiazhen | 102 | 30.05 N | 107.51 E |
| Gaokan | 104 | 40.46 N | 122.23 E |
| Gaokeng | 100 | 27.40 N | 113.58 E |
| Gaolan | 102 | 36.25 N | 103.56 E |
| Gaolan Dao I | 100 | 21.55 N | 113.15 E |
| Gaolao | 104 | 41.54 N | 120.59 E |
| Gaoli | 105 | 39.17 N | 115.38 E |
| Gaoliang | 107 | 29.45 N | 105.15 E |
| Gaoliban | 104 | 41.39 N | 121.58 E |
| Gaolifangshen | 104 | 42.27 N | 123.21 E |
| Gaolimen | 98 | 40.22 N | 124.02 E |



| DEUTSCH Name | Seite | Breite°′ | Länge°′ E = Ost |
|---|---|---|---|
| Gaoling | 105 | 40.32 N | 117.01 E |
| Gaolinying | 105 | 39.06 N | 115.38 E |
| Gaoliying | 105 | 40.10 N | 116.29 E |
| Gaoliyingzi | 104 | 41.56 N | 124.17 E |
| Gaolong | 100 | 26.56 N | 113.45 E |
| Gaolou | 105 | 39.59 N | 116.50 E |
| Gaolouchang, Zhg. | 107 | 29.51 N | 104.41 E |
| Gaolouchang, Zhg. | 107 | 30.03 N | 105.58 E |
| Gaoluo | 98 | 37.27 N | 113.55 E |
| Gaomi | 98 | 36.23 N | 119.44 E |
| Gaona | 252 | 25.12 S | 64.05 W |
| Gaopi | 100 | 24.14 N | 116.39 E |
| Gaoping, Zhg. | 102 | 35.48 N | 112.52 E |
| Gaoping, Zhg. | 107 | 30.28 N | 105.45 E |
| Gaopingba | 107 | 30.47 N | 106.06 E |
| Gaoqiao, Zhg. | 100 | 30.08 N | 119.56 E |
| Gaoqiao, Zhg. | 100 | 26.36 N | 117.46 E |
| Gaoqiao, Zhg. | 102 | 28.06 N | 106.36 E |
| Gaoqiao, Zhg. | 106 | 32.14 N | 119.38 E |
| Gaoqiao, Zhg. | 106 | 31.21 N | 121.34 E |
| Gaoqiaomen | 106 | 32.01 N | 118.51 E |
| Gaoqiaozhen | 104 | 40.55 N | 121.00 E |
| Gaoqing (Tianzhen) | 98 | 37.11 N | 117.47 E |
| Gaoqipu | 104 | 41.32 N | 121.40 E |
| Gaosha | 100 | 26.27 N | 117.56 E |
| Gaoshaling | 105 | 38.51 N | 117.36 E |
| Gaoshan, Zhg. | 100 | 25.29 N | 119.34 E |
| Gaoshan, Zhg. | 107 | 29.26 N | 104.28 E |
| Gaoshanbao | 105 | 40.40 N | 117.29 E |
| Gaoshangbao | 98 | 39.11 N | 118.30 E |
| Gaoshanpu | 102 | 27.10 N | 105.14 E |
| Gaoshantai | 104 | 42.22 N | 122.28 E |
| Gaoshanzi | 104 | 41.34 N | 122.02 E |
| Gaoshengchang | 107 | 29.59 N | 105.31 E |
| Gaoshengzhen | 104 | 41.20 N | 122.12 E |
| Gaoshi | 107 | 29.36 N | 104.44 E |
| Gaoshikan | 107 | 29.12 N | 105.04 E |
| Gaosichang | 107 | 30.17 N | 104.52 E |
| Gaotai | 102 | 39.20 N | 99.58 E |
| Gaotaishan | 104 | 42.02 N | 122.52 E |
| Gaotan, Zhg. | 100 | 30.23 N | 117.23 E |
| Gaotan, Zhg. | 100 | 23.12 N | 115.22 E |
| Gaotan, Zhg. | 102 | 32.22 N | 108.36 E |
| Gaotang | 98 | 36.54 N | 116.14 E |
| Gaotangji | 100 | 32.24 N | 116.01 E |
| Gaotingsi | 100 | 26.05 N | 112.53 E |
| Gaotuozi | 104 | 41.08 N | 122.40 E |
| Gaoua | 150 | 10.20 N | 3.11 W |
| Gaoual | 150 | 11.45 N | 13.12 W |
| Gaoxian | 102 | 28.20 N | 104.38 E |
| Gaoxingru | 100 | 26.28 N | 115.14 E |
| Gaoxinji | 98 | 34.11 N | 115.33 E |
| Gaoya | 98 | 36.22 N | 118.49 E |
| Gaoyang | 98 | 34.30 N | 114.40 E |
| Gaoyapu | 107 | 29.14 N | 106.19 E |
| Gaoyi | 98 | 37.36 N | 114.36 E |
| Gaoyou, Zhg. | 100 | 32.47 N | 119.27 E |
| Gaoyou, Zhg. | 100 | 28.25 N | 115.31 E |
| Gaoyou Hu ⊜ | 100 | 32.50 N | 119.20 E |
| Gaozhangjia | 102 | 36.06 N | 107.18 E |
| Gaozhou | 102 | 21.55 N | 110.50 E |
| Gaozi | 106 | 32.11 N | 119.18 E |
| Gaoziba | 107 | 29.01 N | 106.00 E |
| Gaozuo | 100 | 33.57 N | 118.03 E |
| Gap, Fr. | 62 | 44.34 N | 6.05 E |
| Gap, Pa., U.S. | 208 | 39.59 N | 76.01 W |
| Gapālnagar | 272b | 22.49 N | 88.08 E |
| Gapan | 116 | 15.19 N | 120.57 E |
| Gapeau ≃ | 62 | 43.07 N | 6.11 E |
| Gapern ⊜ | 40 | 59.31 N | 13.40 E |
| Gar | 120 | 32.11 N | 79.59 E |
| Gar ≃ | 120 | 32.28 N | 79.44 E |
| Gara, Lough ⊜ | 48 | 53.55 N | 8.25 W |
| Garacad | 144 | 6.57 N | 49.19 E |
| Garachiné | 246 | 8.04 N | 78.22 W |
| Garadag | 144 | 9.26 N | 46.52 E |
| Gārādāha | 126 | 24.14 N | 89.34 E |
| Garagoa | 246 | 5.05 N | 73.21 W |
| Garaguso | 68 | 40.33 N | 16.14 E |
| Garah | 166 | 29.04 S | 149.38 E |
| Garai ≃[1] | 126 | 23.32 N | 89.31 E |
| Garaina | 164 | 7.50 S | 147.10 E |
| Gārākhola Madhukhāli | 126 | 23.33 N | 89.38 E |
| Garamba ≃ | 154 | 3.53 N | 29.12 E |
| Garamba, Parc National de la ◆ | 154 | 4.10 N | 29.30 E |
| Gara Muleta ∧ | 144 | 9.17 N | 41.47 E |
| Garānberia | 272b | 22.24 N | 88.34 E |
| Garancières | 261 | 48.49 N | 1.46 E |
| Garango | 150 | 11.48 N | 0.34 W |
| Garanhuns | 250 | 8.54 S | 36.29 W |
| Garapan | 174n | 15.12 N | 145.43 E |
| Garara | 164 | 8.37 S | 148.17 E |
| Garautha | 124 | 25.34 N | 79.18 E |
| Garba | 146 | 9.12 N | 20.30 E |
| Garbagna | 266b | 45.23 N | 8.39 E |
| Garbagnate Milanese | 266b | 45.35 N | 9.05 E |
| Garbahaarrey | 144 | 3.19 N | 42.13 E |
| Garbatella ◆[8] | 267a | 41.52 N | 12.29 E |
| Garba Tula | 154 | 0.32 N | 38.31 E |
| Garber | 196 | 36.26 N | 97.35 W |
| Garberville | 204 | 40.06 N | 123.47 W |
| Garbokaraj | 88 | 54.09 N | 99.52 E |
| Garboldisham | 42 | 52.24 N | 0.56 E |
| Gârbova | 38 | 46.50 N | 29.21 E |
| Gârbovu | 38 | 44.44 N | 23.21 E |
| Garbsen | 52 | 52.25 N | 9.34 E |
| Garça | 255 | 22.14 S | 49.37 W |
| Garças, Rio das ≃ | 255 | 15.54 S | 52.16 W |
| Garcevo | 76 | 52.45 N | 32.59 E |
| Garches | 261 | 48.51 N | 2.11 E |
| Garching | 60 | 48.15 N | 11.39 E |
| Garching an der Alz | 60 | 48.08 N | 12.34 E |
| Garchitorena | 116 | 13.52 N | 123.40 E |
| García | 232 | 29.59 N | 108.20 W |
| García, Laguna ⊜ | 288 | 34.58 S | 58.09 W |
| García de la Cadena | 234 | 21.09 N | 103.28 W |
| García de Sola, Embalse de ⊜[1] | 34 | 39.15 N | 5.05 W |
| Garcia Hernandez | 116 | 9.37 N | 124.18 E |
| Garcias | 255 | 20.34 S | 52.13 W |
| Garcitas Creek ≃ | 222 | 28.51 N | 96.46 W |
| Gard □[5] | 32 | 44.00 N | 4.00 E |
| Gard ≃ | 62 | 43.51 N | 4.37 E |
| Gard, Pont du ◆[5] | 62 | 43.56 N | 4.36 E |
| Garda | 64 | 45.34 N | 10.42 E |
| Garda, Lago di ⊜ | 64 | 45.40 N | 10.41 E |
| Gardabani | 84 | 41.28 N | 45.06 E |
| Gardanne | 62 | 43.27 N | 5.28 E |
| Garde, Lac la ⊜ | 190 | 46.46 N | 78.14 W |
| Gardelegen | 54 | 52.31 N | 11.23 E |
| Garden ≃ | 190 | 46.32 N | 84.09 W |
| Gardena | 228 | 33.53 N | 118.18 W |
| Gardena, Val V | 64 | 46.35 N | 11.35 E |
| Garden Acres | 226 | 37.58 N | 121.13 W |
| Garden City, Ga., U.S. | 192 | 32.06 N | 81.09 W |
| Garden City, Ks., U.S. | 198 | 37.58 N | 100.52 W |
| Garden City, Mi., U.S. | 216 | 42.19 N | 83.19 W |
| Garden City, Mo., U.S. | 194 | 38.33 N | 94.11 W |
| Garden City, N.Y., U.S. | 210 | 40.43 N | 73.38 W |
| Garden City, Tx., U.S. | 196 | 31.52 N | 101.29 W |
| Garden City → Qasr al-Dubārā ◆[8] | 273c | 30.02 N | 31.14 E |
| Garden City Park | 276 | 40.44 N | 73.39 W |
| Garden City Raceway ◆ | 284a | 43.09 N | 79.11 W |
| Gardendale | 194 | 33.39 N | 86.48 W |
| Garden Farms | 226 | 35.24 N | 120.07 W |
| Garden Gate Village | 282 | 37.20 N | 122.02 W |
| Garden Grove, Ca., U.S. | 228 | 33.46 N | 117.56 W |
| Garden Grove, Ia., U.S. | 190 | 40.50 N | 93.36 W |


**Symbols** in the index entries represent the broad categories identified in the key at the right. Symbols with superior numbers (⩘[1]) identify subcategories (see complete key on page *I · 1).*

**Symbole** im Register stellen die rechts im Schlüssel erklärten Kategorien dar. Symbole mit hochgestellten Ziffern (⩘[1]) bezeichnen Unterabteilungen einer Kategorie (vgl. vollständiger Schlüssel auf Seite *I · 1).*

**Los símbolos** incluídos en el texto del índice representan las grandes categorías identificadas con la clave a la derecha. Los símbolos con numeros en su parte superior (⩘[1]) identifican las subcategorías (véase la clave completa en la página *I · 1).*

**Les symboles** de l'index représentent les catégories indiquées dans la légende à droite. Les symboles suivis d'un indice (⩘[1]) représentent des sous-catégories (voir légende complète à la page *I · 1).*

**Os símbolos** incluídos no texto do índice representam as grandes categorias identificadas com a chave à direita. Os símbolos com números em sua parte superior (⩘[1]) identificam as subcategorias (veja-se a chave completa à página *I · 1).*

| Symbol | English | Deutsch | Español | Français | Português |
|---|---|---|---|---|---|
| ∧ | Mountain | Berg | Montaña | Montagne | Montanha |
| ⩘ | Mountains | Gebirge | Montañas | Montagnes | Montanhas |
| )( | Pass | Paß | Paso | Col | Passo |
| V | Valley, Canyon | Tal, Cañon | Valle, Cañón | Vallée, Canyon | Vale, Canhão |
| ≚ | Plain | Ebene | Llano | Plaine | Planície |
| ≻ | Cape | Kap | Cabo | Cap | Cabo |
| I | Island | Insel | Isla | Île | Ilha |
| II | Islands | Inseln | Islas | Îles | Ilhas |
| ⊥ | Other Topographic Features | Andere Topographische Objekte | Otros Elementos Topográficos | Autres données topographiques | Outros acidentes topográficos |

ESPAÑOL

| Nombre | Página | Lat.°′ | Long.°′ W = Oeste |
|---|---|---|---|
| Garden Home | 224 | 45.27 N | 122.45 W |
| Garden Island I, Austl. | 168a | 32.13 S | 115.41 E |
| Garden Island I, Mi., U.S. | 190 | 45.49 N | 85.30 W |
| Garden Lakes | 192 | 34.17 N | 85.16 W |
| Garden Peninsula ›[1] | 190 | 45.45 N | 86.35 W |
| Garden Plain | 198 | 37.39 N | 97.41 W |
| Garden Prairie | 216 | 42.15 N | 88.44 W |
| Garden Reach | 126 | 22.33 N | 88.17 E |
| Gardenside | 218 | 38.03 N | 84.33 W |
| Garden State Arts Center ʋ | 276 | 40.24 N | 74.11 W |
| Garden State Park Race Track ♦, N.J., U.S. | 285 | 39.55 N | 75.02 W |
| Garden State Park Race Track ♦, Pa., U.S. | 285 | 39.55 N | 75.02 W |
| Garden State Plaza ✤[9] | 276 | 40.55 N | 74.05 W |
| Gardenton | 184 | 49.05 N | 96.40 W |
| Garden Valley | 226 | 38.51 N | 120.51 W |
| Garden View | 210 | 41.16 N | 77.03 W |
| Gardenville | 208 | 40.22 N | 75.07 W |
| Gardermoen | 26 | 60.13 N | 11.06 E |
| Gardey | 252 | 37.17 S | 59.21 W |
| Gardeyz | 120 | 33.37 N | 69.07 E |
| Gardinas → Hrodna | 76 | 53.41 N | 23.50 E |
| Gardiner, Me., U.S. | 188 | 44.13 N | 69.46 W |
| Gardiner, Mt., U.S. | 202 | 45.01 N | 110.42 W |
| Gardiner, N.Y., U.S. | 210 | 41.41 N | 74.09 W |
| Gardiner, Or., U.S. | 202 | 43.43 N | 124.06 W |
| Gardiner, Wa., U.S. | 224 | 48.03 N | 122.55 W |
| Gardiner Dam ✤[6] | 184 | 51.17 N | 106.51 W |
| Gardiner Range ⋏ | 162 | 23.50 S | 131.46 E |
| Gardiners Bay c | 207 | 41.08 N | 72.10 W |
| Gardiners Creek ≃ | 274b | 37.50 S | 145.02 E |
| Gardiners Island I | 207 | 41.05 N | 72.07 W |
| Garding | 41 | 54.20 N | 8.46 E |
| Gardner, Il., U.S. | 216 | 41.11 N | 88.18 W |
| Gardner, Ks., U.S. | 198 | 38.48 N | 94.55 W |
| Gardner, Ma., U.S. | 207 | 42.34 N | 71.59 W |
| Gardner Canal c | 182 | 53.28 N | 128.15 W |
| Gardner Lake ⊜ | 207 | 41.31 N | 72.13 W |
| Gardner Pinnacles II[1] | 14 | 25.00 N | 167.55 W |
| Gardnersville | 218 | 38.46 N | 84.30 W |
| Gardnertown | 210 | 41.32 N | 74.04 W |
| Gardnerville | 226 | 38.56 N | 119.44 W |
| Gardno | 54 | 53.15 N | 14.38 E |
| Gardolo | 64 | 46.07 N | 11.05 E |
| Gardon d'Alès ≃ | 62 | 44.02 N | 4.08 E |
| Gardon d'Anduze ≃ | 62 | 44.02 N | 4.08 E |
| Gardone Riviera | 64 | 45.37 N | 10.34 E |
| Gardone Val Trompia | 64 | 45.41 N | 10.11 E |
| Gårdsjö | 40 | 58.52 N | 14.19 E |
| Gårdskär | 40 | 60.37 N | 17.35 E |
| Gare Loch c | 46 | 56.01 N | 4.48 W |
| Garelochhead | 46 | 56.05 N | 4.50 W |
| Gareloi Island I | 181a | 51.47 N | 178.48 W |
| Garenfeld ✤[8] | 263 | 51.24 N | 7.31 E |
| Garenin | 46 | 58.21 N | 6.50 W |
| Gare Simon | 273b | 4.15 S | 15.11 E |
| Garešnica | 36 | 45.35 N | 16.56 E |
| Garessio | 62 | 44.12 N | 8.02 E |
| Garet, Mont ∧[1] | 175f | 14.16 S | 167.30 E |
| Garfield, Ks., U.S. | 198 | 38.04 N | 99.14 W |
| Garfield, N.J., U.S. | 210 | 40.52 N | 74.06 W |
| Garfield, N.M., U.S. | 200 | 32.45 N | 107.15 W |
| Garfield, Wa., U.S. | 202 | 47.00 N | 117.08 W |
| Garfield Heights | 214 | 41.25 N | 81.36 W |
| Garfield Mountain ∧ | 202 | 44.31 N | 112.37 W |
| Garfield Park | 285 | 39.42 N | 75.33 W |
| Garfield Park ♦, Il., U.S. | 278 | 41.53 N | 87.43 W |
| Garfield Park ♦, Oh., U.S. | 279a | 41.26 N | 81.36 W |
| Garfield Peak ∧ | 200 | 42.47 N | 107.18 W |
| Garforth | 44 | 53.48 N | 1.22 W |
| Garga | 88 | 54.26 N | 110.33 E |
| Gargaliánoi | 38 | 37.04 N | 21.39 E |
| Gargano, Promontorio del › | 68 | 41.50 N | 16.00 E |
| Gargano, Testa del › | 68 | 41.49 N | 16.12 E |
| Gargantua, Cape › | 190 | 47.36 N | 85.02 W |
| Garga Sarali | 152 | 5.11 N | 14.00 E |
| Gargazzone (Gargazon) | 64 | 46.35 N | 11.12 E |
| Gargellen | 58 | 46.58 N | 9.56 E |
| Gargenville | 261 | 49.00 N | 1.49 E |
| Garges-lès-Gonesse | 261 | 48.58 N | 2.25 E |
| Gargnano | 64 | 45.41 N | 10.40 E |
| Gargouna | 150 | 15.56 N | 0.13 E |
| Gargrave | 44 | 53.59 N | 2.06 W |
| Gargždai | 76 | 55.43 N | 21.24 E |
| Garhākota | 124 | 23.46 N | 79.09 E |
| Garhbeta | 126 | 22.51 N | 87.19 E |
| Garhdīwāla | 123 | 31.44 N | 75.45 E |
| Garhi Habībullāh Khān | 123 | 34.24 N | 73.23 E |
| Garhi Jasaya | 272a | 28.46 N | 77.16 E |
| Garhi Katiya | 272a | 28.45 N | 77.16 E |
| Garhi Khairo | 120 | 28.04 N | 67.59 E |
| Garhi Malehra | 124 | 25.02 N | 79.40 E |
| Garhjāt Hills ⋏[2] | 126 | 21.47 N | 86.20 E |
| Garhmuktesar | 124 | 28.48 N | 78.06 E |
| Garhshankar | 123 | 31.13 N | 76.08 E |
| Garhwa | 124 | 24.11 N | 83.49 E |
| Gari | 86 | 59.26 N | 62.21 E |
| Garibaldi, Bra. | 252 | 29.15 S | 51.32 W |
| Garibaldi, B.C., Can. | 182 | 49.58 N | 123.09 W |
| Garibaldi, Or., U.S. | 224 | 45.34 N | 123.55 W |
| Garibaldi, Casa di ⊥ | 71 | 41.13 N | 9.27 E |
| Garibaldi, Mount ∧ | 182 | 49.51 N | 123.01 W |
| Garibaldi Provincial Park ♦ | 182 | 50.00 N | 122.50 W |
| Garies | 158 | 30.30 S | 18.00 E |
| Garigliano ≃ | 66 | 41.13 N | 13.45 E |
| Gariglione, Monte ∧ | 68 | 39.09 N | 16.41 E |
| Garín | 258 | 34.26 S | 58.44 W |
| Garín, Arroyo ≃ | 288 | 34.23 S | 58.43 W |
| Garin Regional Park ♦ | 282 | 37.38 N | 122.03 W |
| Garipçe Burnu › | 267b | 41.13 N | 29.07 E |
| Garissa | 154 | 0.28 S | 39.38 E |
| Garita Palmera | 236 | 13.44 N | 90.05 W |
| Gariya | 272b | 22.28 N | 88.23 E |
| Gārji | 272b | 22.51 N | 88.19 E |
| Garkida | 146 | 10.25 N | 12.36 E |
| Garko | 150 | 11.38 N | 8.48 E |
| Garland, Al., U.S. | 194 | 31.33 N | 86.49 W |
| Garland, Md., U.S. | 284b | 39.11 N | 76.39 W |
| Garland, Pa., U.S. | 214 | 41.49 N | 79.27 W |
| Garland, Tx., U.S. | 222 | 32.54 N | 96.38 W |
| Garland, Ut,. U.S. | 200 | 41.44 N | 112.09 W |
| Garland Park ♦ | 275b | 43.44 N | 79.35 W |
| Garland Peak ∧ | 224 | 48.01 N | 120.43 W |
| Garlasco | 62 | 45.12 N | 8.55 E |
| Garlate | 62 | 45.49 N | 9.23 E |
| Garlate, Lago di ⊜ | 58 | 45.49 N | 9.24 E |
| Garliava | 76 | 54.49 N | 23.52 E |
| Garlieston | 44 | 54.48 N | 4.22 W |
| Garlin | 32 | 43.34 N | 0.15 W |
| Garm | 85 | 39.02 N | 70.22 E |
| Garm Āb | 120 | 32.14 N | 65.01 E |
| Garmal | 144 | 8.35 N | 50.19 E |
| Gärmersdorf | 60 | 49.26 N | 11.54 E |
| Garmī | 128 | 39.01 N | 48.03 E |
| Garmisch-Partenkirchen | 64 | 47.29 N | 11.05 E |
| Garmouth | 46 | 57.40 N | 3.07 W |
| Garmsār | 128 | 35.20 N | 52.13 E |
| Garnavillo | 190 | 42.52 N | 91.14 W |
| Garne | 261 | 48.41 N | 1.58 E |
| Garner, Ia., U.S. | 190 | 43.06 N | 93.36 W |
| Garner, N.C., U.S. | 192 | 35.42 N | 78.36 W |
| Garnet Range ⋏ | 202 | 46.45 N | 113.15 W |
| Garnett | 198 | 38.16 N | 95.14 W |

FRANÇAIS

| Nom | Page | Lat.°′ | Long.°′ W = Ouest |
|---|---|---|---|
| Garnijskij zapovednik ♦ | 84 | 40.00 N | 44.55 E |
| Garnish | 186 | 47.14 N | 55.22 W |
| Garnock ≃ | 46 | 55.38 N | 4.42 W |
| Garnpung, Lake ⊜ | 166 | 33.30 S | 143.12 E |
| Gāro Hills ⋏[2] | 124 | 25.30 N | 90.30 E |
| Garona → Garonne ≃ | 32 | 45.02 N | 0.36 W |
| Garonne ≃ | 32 | 45.02 N | 0.36 W |
| Garoowe | 144 | 8.24 N | 48.29 E |
| Garou, Lac ⊜ | 150 | 16.04 N | 2.45 W |
| Garoua, Cam. | 146 | 9.18 N | 13.24 E |
| Garoua, Niger | 146 | 13.53 N | 13.11 E |
| Garoua Boulaï | 152 | 5.53 N | 14.33 E |
| Garove Island I | 164 | 4.40 S | 149.30 E |
| Garpenberg | 40 | 60.19 N | 16.12 E |
| Garphyttan | 40 | 59.19 N | 14.56 E |
| Garphyttans Nationalpark ♦ | 40 | 59.17 N | 14.51 E |
| Garqu Yan, Zhg. | 118 | 34.29 N | 92.35 E |
| Garqu Yan, Zhg. | 120 | 33.50 N | 92.28 E |
| Garraf, Costa de ⊥[2] | 266d | 41.16 N | 2.02 E |
| Garrattsville | 210 | 42.39 N | 75.10 W |
| Garrel | 52 | 52.57 N | 8.01 E |
| Garret Mountain Reservation ♦ | 276 | 40.54 N | 74.11 W |
| Garretson | 198 | 43.43 N | 96.30 W |
| Garrett, In., U.S. | 216 | 41.20 N | 85.08 W |
| Garrett, Ky., U.S. | 192 | 37.28 N | 82.49 W |
| Garrett Creek ≃ | 222 | 32.57 N | 95.44 W |
| Garrett Park | 208 | 39.02 N | 77.05 W |
| Garrett Park Estates | 284c | 39.02 N | 77.06 W |
| Garrettsville | 214 | 41.17 N | 81.06 W |
| Garrison, N. Ire., U.K. | 48 | 54.25 N | 8.05 W |
| Garrison, Ky., U.S. | 218 | 38.36 N | 83.10 W |
| Garrison, Md., U.S. | 208 | 39.24 N | 76.45 W |
| Garrison, Mt., U.S. | 202 | 46.31 N | 112.48 W |
| Garrison, N.Y., U.S. | 210 | 41.23 N | 73.56 W |
| Garrison, N.D., U.S. | 198 | 47.39 N | 101.24 W |
| Garrison, Tx., U.S. | 222 | 31.49 N | 94.30 W |
| Garrison Dam ✤[6] | 198 | 47.22 N | 101.25 W |
| Garron Point › | 48 | 55.03 N | 5.57 W |
| Garros | 46 | 57.37 N | 6.11 W |
| Garrovillas | 34 | 39.43 N | 6.33 W |
| Garry ≃ | 46 | 56.43 N | 3.47 W |
| Garry, Loch ⊜ | 206 | 45.15 N | 74.43 W |
| Garry Bay c | 176 | 68.55 N | 85.05 W |
| Garry Lake ⊜ | 176 | 66.00 N | 100.00 W |
| Gars am Kamp | 61 | 48.36 N | 15.40 E |
| Garsdale Head | 44 | 54.19 N | 2.20 W |
| Garsen | 154 | 2.16 S | 40.07 E |
| Garskolk | 158 | 30.41 S | 22.02 E |
| Gårslev | 41 | 55.38 N | 9.43 E |
| Garson | 190 | 46.34 N | 80.52 W |
| Garson Lake ⊜ | 184 | 56.19 N | 110.02 W |
| Garstang | 44 | 53.55 N | 2.47 W |
| Garstedt | 52 | 53.41 N | 9.58 E |
| Garstedterheide ✤[3] | 52 | 53.17 N | 8.43 E |
| Garsten | 61 | 48.01 N | 14.24 E |
| Garston | 260 | 51.41 N | 0.23 W |
| Garston ✤[8] | 262 | 53.21 N | 2.53 W |
| Garswood | 262 | 53.29 N | 2.40 W |
| Gartempe ≃ | 32 | 46.48 N | 0.50 E |
| Gartenstadt ✤[8] | 263 | 51.30 N | 7.26 E |
| Garthby Station (Beaulac) | 206 | 45.50 N | 71.23 W |
| Gartow | 54 | 53.02 N | 11.29 E |
| Gärtringen | 58 | 48.39 N | 8.54 E |
| Gartrop-Bühl | 263 | 51.40 N | 6.49 E |
| Gartz | 54 | 53.12 N | 14.23 E |
| Garu | 150 | 10.51 N | 0.11 W |
| Garub | 156 | 26.33 S | 16.00 E |
| Garubhāsa | 124 | 26.33 N | 90.22 E |
| Gārulia | 126 | 22.49 N | 88.22 E |
| Garut | 115a | 7.13 S | 107.54 E |
| Garve | 46 | 57.37 N | 4.42 W |
| Garvellachs II | 46 | 56.14 N | 5.47 W |
| Garvey Reservoir ⊜[1] | 280 | 34.13 N | 118.07 W |
| Garvie Mountains ⋏ | 172 | 45.30 S | 168.50 E |
| Garwin | 190 | 42.05 N | 92.40 W |
| Garwolin | 30 | 51.54 N | 21.37 E |
| Garwood, N.J., U.S. | 276 | 40.39 N | 74.19 W |
| Garwood, Tx., U.S. | 222 | 29.27 N | 96.24 W |
| Gary, In., U.S. | 216 | 41.35 N | 87.20 W |
| Gary, S.D., U.S. | 198 | 44.47 N | 96.27 W |
| Gary, Tx., U.S. | 194 | 32.07 N | 94.22 W |
| Gary, W.V., U.S. | 192 | 37.21 N | 81.33 W |
| Garyarsa | 120 | 31.44 N | 80.21 E |
| Gary Harbor c | 278 | 41.38 N | 87.20 W |
| Garyi | 102 | 30.54 N | 98.56 E |
| Gary Municipal Airport ⊠ | 278 | 41.37 N | 87.25 W |
| Garysburg | 208 | 36.27 N | 77.33 W |
| Garz | 54 | 54.19 N | 13.20 E |
| Garza | 252 | 28.09 S | 63.32 W |
| Garza Ayala | 196 | 26.29 N | 100.02 W |
| Garza García | 196 | 25.40 N | 100.24 W |
| Garzas Creek ≃ | 226 | 37.13 N | 120.57 W |
| Garzeno | 58 | 46.08 N | 9.15 E |
| Garzón, Col. | 246 | 2.12 N | 75.38 W |
| Garzón, Ur. | 252 | 34.36 S | 54.33 W |
| Gas | 261 | 48.34 N | 1.40 E |
| Gasan | 116 | 13.19 N | 121.51 E |
| Gasan-Kuli | 128 | 37.27 N | 53.59 E |
| Gas City | 216 | 40.29 N | 85.36 W |
| Gascogne □[9] | 32 | 44.00 N | 0.05 E |
| Gascogne, Golfe de → Biscay, Bay of c | 32 | 44.00 N | 4.00 W |
| Gasconade | 219 | 38.40 N | 91.33 W |
| Gasconade □[6] | 219 | 38.27 N | 91.30 W |
| Gasconade ≃ | 194 | 38.40 N | 91.33 W |
| Gasconade, Osage Fork ≃ | 194 | 37.45 N | 92.26 W |
| Gascoyne ≃ | 162 | 24.52 S | 113.37 E |
| Gascoyne, Mount ∧ | 162 | 24.58 S | 116.38 E |
| Gascoyne Junction | 162 | 25.03 S | 115.12 E |
| Gash (Nahr al-Qāsh) ≃ | 140 | 16.48 N | 35.51 E |
| Gashaka | 146 | 7.21 N | 11.27 E |
| Gasherbrum I ∧ | 123 | 35.43 N | 76.43 E |
| Gas Hu ⊜ | 120 | 38.10 N | 90.42 E |
| Gashua | 146 | 12.54 N | 11.00 E |
| Gasline | 284a | 42.53 N | 79.11 W |
| Gasny | 50 | 49.05 N | 1.36 E |
| Gaspar | 252 | 26.56 S | 48.58 W |
| Gaspard Creek ≃ | 182 | 51.34 N | 122.17 W |
| Gasparilla Island I | 220 | 26.46 N | 82.16 W |
| Gasparilla Sound ⋓ | 220 | 26.48 N | 82.15 W |
| Gaspé | 186 | 48.50 N | 64.29 W |
| Gaspé, Baie de c | 186 | 48.46 N | 64.17 W |
| Gaspé, Cap › | 186 | 48.45 N | 64.10 W |
| Gaspé Peninsula → Gaspésie, Péninsule de la ›[1] | 186 | 48.30 N | 65.00 W |
| Gaspereau Lake ⊜ | 186 | 44.57 N | 64.34 W |
| Gasperina | 68 | 38.44 N | 16.30 E |
| Gaspésie, Parc Provincial de la ♦ | 186 | 48.55 N | 66.00 W |
| Gaspésie, Péninsule de la ›[1] | 186 | 48.30 N | 65.00 W |
| Gaspoltshofen | 60 | 48.08 N | 13.46 E |
| Gasport | 210 | 43.11 N | 78.34 W |
| Gassan | 150 | 12.49 N | 3.12 W |
| Gas-san ∧ | 92 | 38.32 N | 140.01 E |
| Gassaway | 188 | 38.40 N | 80.46 W |
| Gasse | 64 | 47.23 N | 11.09 E |
| Gasselte | 52 | 52.57 N | 6.46 E |
| Gassin | 62 | 43.13 N | 6.35 E |
| Gassino Torinese | 62 | 45.08 N | 7.49 E |
| Gassol | 146 | 8.32 N | 10.28 E |
| Gastein → Badgastein | 64 | 47.07 N | 13.08 E |
| Gasteiner Tal V | 64 | 47.11 N | 13.06 E |
| Gasteiz → Vitoria | 34 | 42.51 N | 2.40 W |
| Gastello | 89 | 49.07 N | 142.58 E |
| Gaston, In., U.S. | 216 | 40.18 N | 85.30 W |
| Gaston, N.C., U.S. | 192 | 36.30 N | 77.38 W |
| Gaston, Or., U.S. | 224 | 45.26 N | 123.08 W |

PORTUGUÊS

| Nome | Página | Lat.°′ | Long.°′ W = Oeste |
|---|---|---|---|
| Gaston, Lake ⊜[1] | 192 | 36.35 N | 78.00 W |
| Gastonia, N.C., U.S. | 192 | 35.15 N | 81.11 W |
| Gastonia, Tx., U.S. | 222 | 32.37 N | 96.24 W |
| Gastonville | 279b | 40.15 N | 79.59 W |
| Gastoúni | 38 | 37.51 N | 21.16 E |
| Gastre | 254 | 42.17 S | 69.14 W |
| Gästrikland □[9] | 40 | 60.30 N | 16.27 E |
| Gat | 132 | 31.37 N | 34.47 E |
| Gata, Cabo de › | 34 | 36.43 N | 2.12 W |
| Gata, Sierra de ⋏ | 34 | 40.14 N | 6.45 W |
| Gătaia | 38 | 45.26 N | 21.26 E |
| Gátas, Akrotírion › | 130 | 34.34 N | 33.02 E |
| Gatčina | 76 | 59.34 N | 30.08 E |
| Gate | 196 | 36.51 N | 100.03 W |
| Gateacre ✤[8] | 262 | 53.23 N | 2.51 W |
| Gate City | 192 | 36.38 N | 82.34 W |
| Gatehouse of Fleet | 44 | 54.53 N | 4.11 W |
| Gatersleben | 54 | 51.49 N | 11.17 E |
| Gates, N.Y., U.S. | 210 | 43.09 N | 77.41 W |
| Gates, N.C., U.S. | 208 | 36.30 N | 76.46 W |
| Gates □[6] | 208 | 36.28 N | 76.43 W |
| Gateshead | 44 | 54.58 N | 1.37 W |
| Gateshead Island I | 176 | 70.22 N | 100.27 W |
| Gates Mills | 279a | 41.31 N | 81.24 W |
| Gates of the Arctic National Park ♦ | 180 | 67.45 N | 153.30 W |
| Gatesville, N.C., U.S. | 192 | 36.24 N | 76.45 W |
| Gatesville, Tx., U.S. | 222 | 31.26 N | 97.44 W |
| Gateway | 200 | 38.40 N | 108.58 W |
| Gateway Arch ʋ | 219 | 38.37 N | 90.12 W |
| Gateway National Recreation Area ♦ | 276 | 40.34 N | 74.06 W |
| Gateway of India ⊥ | 272c | 18.55 N | 72.50 E |
| Gateway Stadium ♦ | 279a | 41.30 N | 81.41 W |
| Gaths Mine | 154 | 20.00 S | 30.31 E |
| Gathurst | 262 | 53.34 N | 2.42 W |
| Gatié Loumo | 150 | 15.28 N | 4.37 W |
| Gatineau | 212 | 45.29 N | 75.38 W |
| Gatineau □[6] | 212 | 45.25 N | 75.45 W |
| Gatineau ≃ | 176 | 45.27 N | 75.40 W |
| Gatineau, Parc de la ♦ | 188 | 45.30 N | 76.05 W |
| Gatley | 262 | 53.23 N | 2.14 W |
| Gatlinburg | 192 | 35.42 N | 83.30 W |
| Gato, Arroyo del ≃, Arg. | 288 | 34.51 S | 57.56 W |
| Gato, Arroyo del ≃, Arg. | 288 | 34.55 S | 58.37 W |
| Ga'ton | 132 | 33.00 N | 35.13 E |
| Gato Negro | 286c | 10.33 N | 66.57 W |
| Gatow ✤[8] | 54 | 52.29 N | 13.11 E |
| Gatow, Flugplatz ⊠ | 264a | 52.28 N | 13.08 E |
| Gattendorf | 61 | 48.01 N | 16.59 E |
| Gattières | 62 | 43.46 N | 7.11 E |
| Gattinara | 62 | 45.37 N | 8.22 E |
| Gatton | 171a | 27.33 S | 152.17 E |
| Gattorna | 62 | 44.26 N | 9.11 E |
| Gatún, Esclusas de ✤[5] | 236 | 9.16 N | 79.55 W |
| Gatún, Lago ⊜[1] | 236 | 9.12 N | 79.55 W |
| Gatvand | 128 | 32.15 N | 48.50 E |
| Gau-Algesheim | 56 | 49.57 N | 8.01 E |
| Gauchy | 50 | 49.49 N | 3.16 E |
| Gaucín | 34 | 36.31 N | 5.19 W |
| Gauer Lake ⊜ | 184 | 57.00 N | 97.50 W |
| Gauguin, Musée ʋ | 174s | 17.45 S | 149.23 W |
| Gauja ≃ | 76 | 57.09 N | 24.16 E |
| Gaujiena | 76 | 57.30 N | 26.40 E |
| Gaukler Point › | 281 | 42.27 N | 82.52 W |
| Gaula ≃ | 26 | 63.21 N | 10.14 E |
| Gauley ≃ | 188 | 38.10 N | 81.12 W |
| Gauley Bridge | 188 | 38.10 N | 81.11 W |
| Gaultois | 186 | 47.36 N | 55.54 W |
| Gaunless ≃ | 44 | 54.40 N | 1.41 W |
| Gau-Odernheim | 56 | 49.47 N | 8.11 E |
| Gaur | 124 | 26.46 N | 85.17 E |
| Gaurain-Ramecroix | 50 | 50.35 N | 3.29 E |
| Gaurambha | 126 | 22.39 N | 89.34 E |
| Gaurela | 124 | 22.45 N | 81.54 E |
| Gaurhāti | 126 | 22.46 N | 87.48 E |
| Gauribaradia | 126 | 23.45 N | 89.52 E |
| Gauribidanūr | 122 | 13.37 N | 77.31 E |
| Gauri Phānta | 124 | 28.41 N | 80.33 E |
| Gauripur | 124 | 26.05 N | 89.58 E |
| Gaurīśaṅkar ∧ | 124 | 27.57 N | 86.21 E |
| Gaurnadi | 126 | 22.58 N | 90.14 E |
| Gause | 222 | 30.47 N | 96.43 W |
| Gausta ∧ | 26 | 59.50 N | 8.35 E |
| Gauteng □[4] | 156 | 26.00 S | 28.15 E |
| Gauthiot, Chutes ʟ | 146 | 9.43 N | 14.34 E |
| Gauting | 60 | 48.04 N | 11.23 E |
| Gavà | 34 | 41.18 N | 2.01 E |
| Gāvanpāda | 272c | 18.57 N | 73.01 E |
| Gavardo | 64 | 45.35 N | 10.26 E |
| Gávdhos I | 38 | 34.50 N | 24.06 E |
| Gávea ✤[8] | 287a | 22.58 S | 43.14 W |
| Gávea, Hipódromo da ♦ | 287a | 22.58 S | 43.13 W |
| Gávea, Pedra da ∧ | 287a | 23.00 S | 43.17 W |
| Gavel-Långsjön ⊜ | 40 | 59.50 N | 18.18 E |
| Gavello | 64 | 45.01 N | 11.55 E |
| Gavet | 62 | 45.04 N | 5.52 E |
| Gavi | 62 | 44.41 N | 8.49 E |
| Gavia, Arroyo de la ≃ | 266a | 40.21 N | 3.40 W |
| Gavião ≃ | 255 | 14.06 S | 41.01 W |
| Gavião, Pico do ∧ | 256 | 21.37 S | 44.50 W |
| Gavien | 164 | 3.54 S | 144.07 E |
| Gavilán | 286c | 10.24 N | 66.51 W |
| Gavinana | 66 | 44.05 N | 10.45 E |
| Gavins Point Dam ✤[6] | 198 | 42.48 N | 97.40 W |
| Gaviões | 256 | 22.34 S | 42.33 W |
| Gavirate | 62 | 45.50 N | 8.43 E |
| Gāv Khūnī, Bāṭlāq-e ≡ | 128 | 32.10 N | 52.50 E |
| Gävle | 40 | 60.40 N | 17.10 E |
| Gävleborgs Län □[6] | 26 | 61.30 N | 16.15 E |
| Gävlebukten c | 40 | 60.42 N | 17.20 E |
| Gavnø | 41 | 55.11 N | 11.44 E |
| Gavoi | 71 | 40.10 N | 9.12 E |
| Gavorrano | 66 | 42.55 N | 10.54 E |
| Gavrilov-Jam | 80 | 57.18 N | 39.51 E |
| Gavrilovka Vtoraja | 80 | 52.53 N | 42.46 E |
| Gavrilov Posad | 80 | 56.33 N | 40.07 E |
| Gávrion | 38 | 37.52 N | 24.46 E |
| Gavry | 76 | 56.55 N | 27.53 E |
| Gawachab | 156 | 27.03 S | 17.50 E |
| Gāwān | 124 | 24.37 N | 85.55 E |
| Gaweinstal | 61 | 48.28 N | 16.35 E |
| Gāwīlgarh Hills ⋏[2] | 122 | 21.20 N | 77.00 E |
| Gawler | 168b | 34.37 S | 138.44 E |
| Gawler ≃ | 168b | 34.41 S | 138.27 E |
| Gawler Ranges ⋏ | 162 | 32.30 S | 136.00 E |
| Gawso | 150 | 6.48 N | 2.31 W |
| Gawsworth | 262 | 53.13 N | 2.10 W |
| Gawthorpe Hall ⊥ | 262 | 53.48 N | 2.18 W |
| Gaxun Nur (Juyanhai) ⊜ | 102 | 42.22 N | 100.34 E |
| Gaya, India | 124 | 24.47 N | 85.00 E |
| Gaya, Niger | 150 | 11.53 N | 3.27 E |
| Gaya, Nig. | 150 | 11.53 N | 9.02 E |
| Gay City State Park ♦ | 207 | 41.42 N | 72.28 W |
| Gayéri | 150 | 12.39 N | 0.29 E |
| Gay Head | 207 | 41.20 N | 70.48 W |
| Gay Hill | 222 | 30.16 N | 96.30 W |
| Gaylord, Mi., U.S. | 190 | 45.01 N | 84.40 W |
| Gaylord, Mn., U.S. | 190 | 44.33 N | 94.13 W |
| Gaylordsville | 207 | 41.38 N | 73.29 W |
| Gayndah | 166 | 25.37 S | 151.36 E |
| Gays Mills | 190 | 43.19 N | 90.50 W |
| Gayton, Eng., U.K. | 42 | 52.45 N | 0.34 E |
| Gayton, Eng., U.K. | 262 | 53.19 N | 3.06 W |
| Gaza → Ghazzah | 132 | 31.30 N | 34.28 E |
| Gaza □[5] | 156 | 23.30 S | 32.45 E |
| Gazalkent | 85 | 41.33 N | 69.47 E |
| Gazaoua | 150 | 13.32 N | 7.55 E |
| Gaza Strip □[9] | 132 | 31.25 N | 34.20 E |
| Gazelle Channel ⋓ | 164 | 2.50 S | 150.55 E |
| Gazelle Peninsula ›[1] | 164 | 4.40 S | 152.00 E |
| Gazeran | 261 | 48.38 N | 1.46 E |
| Gazeran, Bois de ♦ | 261 | 48.40 N | 1.45 E |
| Gazi, Kenya | 154 | 4.25 S | 39.30 E |
| Gazi, Zaïre | 154 | 1.04 N | 24.31 E |
| Gaziantep | 130 | 37.05 N | 37.22 E |
| Gaziantep □[4] | 130 | 37.00 N | 37.20 E |
| Gazimağusa (Famagusta) | 130 | 35.07 N | 33.57 E |
| Gazimağusa Körfezi c | 130 | 35.15 N | 34.10 E |
| Gazimur ≃ | 88 | 52.57 N | 120.22 E |
| Gazimurskij Zavod | 88 | 51.33 N | 118.22 E |
| Gazipaşa | 130 | 36.17 N | 32.20 E |
| Gazira Sporting Club ♦ | 273c | 30.04 N | 31.13 E |
| Gazivoda Jezero ⊜[1] | 38 | 42.55 N | 20.40 E |
| Gaznau | 85 | 40.10 N | 71.02 E |
| Gazoldo degli Ippoliti | 64 | 45.12 N | 10.35 E |
| Gazos Creek ≃ | 226 | 37.10 N | 122.22 W |
| Gazzada | 62 | 45.47 N | 8.51 E |
| Gazzaniga | 62 | 45.48 N | 9.50 E |
| Gazzuolo | 64 | 45.04 N | 10.35 E |
| Gbangbatok | 150 | 7.48 N | 12.23 W |
| Gbanhala ≃ | 150 | 10.14 N | 8.38 W |
| Gbaoui Bodanga | 152 | 5.33 N | 16.45 E |
| Gbarnga | 150 | 7.00 N | 9.29 W |
| Gbogbo | 273a | 6.36 N | 3.31 E |
| Gboko | 150 | 7.20 N | 8.57 E |
| Gbon | 150 | 9.50 N | 6.27 W |
| Gbwado | 152 | 3.54 N | 20.46 E |
| Gcoverega | 156 | 19.08 S | 24.15 E |
| Gdańsk (Danzig) | 30 | 54.23 N | 18.40 E |
| Gdańsk □[4] | 30 | 54.15 N | 18.25 E |
| Gdansk, Gulf of c | 30 | 54.40 N | 19.15 E |
| Gdov | 76 | 58.44 N | 27.48 E |
| Gdyel | 34 | 35.48 N | 0.26 W |
| Gdynia | 30 | 54.32 N | 18.33 E |
| Gearhart | 224 | 46.01 N | 123.54 W |
| Gearhart Mountain ∧ | 202 | 42.30 N | 120.53 W |
| Gearhartville | 214 | 40.53 N | 78.15 W |
| Geary, N.B., Can. | 186 | 45.46 N | 66.29 W |
| Geary, Ok., U.S. | 196 | 35.43 N | 98.22 W |
| Geauga □[6] | 214 | 41.35 N | 81.12 W |
| Geauga Lake Park ♦ | 279a | 41.21 N | 81.23 W |
| Geba ≃ | 150 | 11.46 N | 15.36 W |
| Gebaberg ∧ | 56 | 50.36 N | 10.16 E |
| Gebe, Pulau I | 164 | 0.05 S | 129.20 E |
| Gebeit Mine | 140 | 21.03 N | 36.19 E |
| Gebenbach | 60 | 49.32 N | 11.53 E |
| Gebesee | 54 | 51.07 N | 10.56 E |
| Gebi | 84 | 42.46 N | 43.30 E |
| Gebilu | 144 | 10.35 N | 41.28 E |
| Gebiz | 130 | 37.06 N | 30.56 E |
| Gebra | 54 | 51.24 N | 10.35 E |
| Gebweiler → Guebwiller | 58 | 47.55 N | 7.12 E |
| Gebze | 130 | 40.48 N | 29.25 E |
| Gecha | 144 | 7.31 N | 35.22 E |
| Gechang | 106 | 31.05 N | 119.27 E |
| Geçitkale | 130 | 35.15 N | 33.45 E |
| Gecun | 106 | 32.10 N | 119.37 E |
| Geddes, Mi., U.S. | 281 | 42.16 N | 83.40 W |
| Geddes, S.D., U.S. | 198 | 43.15 N | 98.41 W |
| Gede, Gunung ∧ | 115a | 6.47 S | 106.59 E |
| Gedera | 132 | 31.49 N | 34.46 E |
| Gedern | 56 | 50.25 N | 9.12 E |
| Gedian | 100 | 30.32 N | 114.38 E |
| Gedikler | 130 | 39.06 N | 38.49 E |
| Gediksaray | 130 | 40.27 N | 35.38 E |
| Gedi National Monument ♦ | 154 | 3.19 S | 40.03 E |
| Gedinne | 56 | 49.59 N | 4.56 E |
| Gediz | 130 | 39.02 N | 29.25 E |
| Gediz ≃ | 130 | 38.35 N | 26.48 E |
| Gedlegube | 144 | 6.52 N | 45.02 E |
| Gedo | 144 | 8.58 N | 37.27 E |
| Gedo □[4] | 144 | 3.00 N | 42.00 E |
| Gedongdalem | 112 | 5.04 S | 105.25 E |
| Gedongtataan | 115a | 5.23 S | 105.05 E |
| Gedser | 41 | 54.35 N | 11.57 E |
| Gedser Odde › | 41 | 54.34 N | 11.59 E |
| Geduld | 273d | 26.15 S | 28.25 E |
| Gedun | 100 | 27.39 N | 118.26 E |
| Geebung | 171a | 27.22 S | 153.03 E |
| Gee Cross | 262 | 53.26 N | 2.04 W |
| Geehi | 171b | 36.24 S | 148.11 E |
| Geehi ≃ | 171b | 36.11 S | 148.02 E |
| Geel | 56 | 51.10 N | 5.00 E |
| Geelong | 169 | 38.08 S | 144.21 E |
| Geelong West | 169 | 38.08 S | 144.20 E |
| Geelvink Channel ⋓ | 162 | 28.30 S | 114.10 E |
| Geer ≃ | 56 | 50.51 N | 5.42 E |
| Geeste | 52 | 52.36 N | 7.16 E |
| Geeste ≃ | 52 | 53.32 N | 8.35 E |
| Geesthacht | 52 | 53.26 N | 10.22 E |
| Geeveston | 166 | 43.10 S | 146.55 E |
| Gefell | 54 | 50.26 N | 11.52 E |
| Gefle → Gävle | 40 | 60.40 N | 17.10 E |
| Gefrees | 54 | 50.06 N | 11.44 E |
| Gegang | 100 | 30.04 N | 117.38 E |
| Gegenmiao | 89 | 45.58 N | 122.15 E |
| Gegong | 100 | 30.05 N | 117.11 E |
| Gegou | 98 | 35.24 N | 118.32 E |
| Gegu | 105 | 38.59 N | 117.30 E |
| Gehackte Berge ⋏[2] | 264a | 52.41 N | 13.30 E |
| Gehrden | 52 | 52.18 N | 9.36 E |
| Gehren | 54 | 50.39 N | 10.59 E |
| Gehu | 100 | 27.46 N | 119.16 E |
| Ge Hu ⊜ | 106 | 31.36 N | 119.51 E |
| Gehua | 164 | 10.20 S | 150.25 E |
| Geidam | 146 | 12.57 N | 11.57 E |
| Geiger | 194 | 32.52 N | 88.18 W |
| Geigertown | 208 | 40.13 N | 75.50 W |
| Geihoku | 96 | 34.44 N | 132.17 E |
| Geikie ≃ | 176 | 57.45 N | 103.52 W |
| Geilenkirchen | 56 | 50.57 N | 6.07 E |
| Geilo | 26 | 60.31 N | 8.12 E |
| Geinō | 94 | 34.48 N | 136.25 E |
| Geiranger | 26 | 62.06 N | 7.12 E |
| Geisa | 56 | 50.43 N | 9.57 E |
| Geisberg ∧ | 60 | 49.53 N | 11.03 E |
| Geisecke | 263 | 51.27 N | 7.37 E |
| Geisei | 96 | 33.31 N | 133.49 E |
| Geiselhöring | 60 | 48.50 N | 12.23 E |
| Geiselwind | 56 | 49.46 N | 10.28 E |
| Geisenfeld | 60 | 48.41 N | 11.37 E |
| Geisenhausen | 60 | 48.28 N | 12.15 E |
| Geisenheim | 56 | 49.59 N | 7.58 E |
| Geising | 54 | 50.46 N | 13.47 E |
| Geisingen | 58 | 47.55 N | 8.38 E |
| Geislingen | 58 | 48.17 N | 8.49 E |
| Geislingen an der Steige | 56 | 48.36 N | 9.50 E |
| Geismar | 52 | 51.31 N | 9.57 E |
| Geispolsheim | 58 | 48.31 N | 7.39 E |
| Geisstein ∧ | 64 | 47.20 N | 12.30 E |
| Geistenbeck ✤[8] | 263 | 51.09 N | 6.27 E |
| Geistown | 214 | 40.17 N | 78.52 W |
| Geist Reservoir ⊜[1], In., U.S. | 218 | 39.56 N | 85.56 W |
| Geist Reservoir ⊜[1], Pa., U.S. | 285 | 39.57 N | 75.24 W |
| Geisweid | 56 | 50.55 N | 8.01 E |
| Geita | 154 | 2.52 S | 32.10 E |
| Geithain | 54 | 51.03 N | 12.41 E |
| Geiyō-shotō II | 96 | 34.10 N | 132.45 E |
| Gejah | 272a | 28.31 N | 77.23 E |
| Gejiatun | 98 | 40.27 N | 119.55 E |
| Gejiu (Kokiu) | 102 | 23.22 N | 103.06 E |
| Geka, mys › | 180 | 64.26 N | 178.10 E |
| Gela | 70 | 37.04 N | 14.15 E |
| Gela ≃ | 70 | 37.03 N | 14.15 E |
| Gela, Golfo di c | 70 | 37.03 N | 14.10 E |
| Geladandong ∧ | 120 | 33.16 N | 91.27 E |
| Geladi | 144 | 6.57 N | 46.25 E |
| Gelai ∧[1] | 154 | 2.33 S | 36.05 E |
| Gelan | 102 | 30.03 N | 107.04 E |
| Gelang, Tanjong › | 114 | 3.58 N | 103.26 E |
| Gelaochang | 107 | 29.36 N | 103.39 E |
| Gelasa, Selat ⋓ | 112 | 2.40 S | 107.15 E |
| Gelbensande | 54 | 54.12 N | 12.18 E |
| Gelber Fluss → Huang ≃ | 90 | 37.32 N | 118.19 E |
| Gelbes Meer → Yellow Sea ⊤[2] | 90 | 36.00 N | 123.00 E |
| Gelderland □[4] | 52 | 52.10 N | 5.50 E |
| Geldermalsen | 52 | 51.53 N | 5.17 E |
| Geldern | 52 | 51.31 N | 6.20 E |
| Geldrop | 52 | 51.25 N | 5.33 E |
| Geleen | 56 | 50.58 N | 5.52 E |
| Gelembe | 130 | 39.10 N | 27.50 E |
| Gelemso | 144 | 8.48 N | 40.35 E |
| Gelenau | 54 | 50.42 N | 12.58 E |
| Gelendost | 130 | 38.07 N | 31.01 E |
| Gelendžik | 78 | 44.33 N | 38.06 E |
| Gelfingen | 58 | 47.13 N | 8.16 E |
| Gelgaudiškis | 76 | 55.05 N | 23.00 E |
| Gelib → Jilib | 144 | 0.29 N | 42.46 E |
| Gelibolu | 130 | 40.24 N | 26.40 E |
| Gelibolu Yarımadası (Gallipoli Peninsula) ›[1] | 130 | 40.20 N | 26.30 E |
| Gelibolu Yarımadası Milli Parkı ♦ | 130 | 40.05 N | 26.10 E |
| Gelinden | 56 | 50.46 N | 5.15 E |
| Gélise ≃ | 32 | 44.11 N | 0.17 E |
| Geliting | 115b | 8.39 S | 122.18 E |
| Geliting, Teluk c | 115b | 8.36 S | 122.17 E |
| Gellénháza | 61 | 46.46 N | 16.47 E |
| Gellenstrom ⋓ | 54 | 54.28 N | 13.03 E |
| Gellep-Stratum ✤[8] | 263 | 51.20 N | 6.41 E |
| Gellibrand ≃ | 169 | 38.41 S | 143.09 E |
| Gellibrand, Mount ∧[2] | 169 | 38.14 S | 143.48 E |
| Gellibrand, Point › | 274b | 37.52 S | 144.54 E |
| Gellibrand River | 169 | 38.32 S | 143.32 E |
| Gellingen → Ghislenghien | 50 | 50.39 N | 3.52 E |
| Gellinsoor | 144 | 6.26 N | 46.42 E |
| Gelnhausen | 56 | 50.11 N | 9.11 E |
| Gelså ≃ | 41 | 55.19 N | 8.54 E |
| Gelsdorf | 56 | 50.35 N | 7.02 E |
| Gelsenkirchen | 52 | 51.31 N | 7.07 E |
| Gelsenkirchen-Horst, Galopprennbahn ♦ | 263 | 51.32 N | 7.02 E |
| Gelsted | 41 | 55.24 N | 9.59 E |
| Gelt ≃ | 44 | 54.56 N | 2.47 W |
| Gelterkinden | 58 | 47.28 N | 7.51 E |
| Gelting | 41 | 54.45 N | 9.53 E |
| Geltow | 54 | 52.22 N | 12.58 E |
| Geltsa | 144 | 6.14 N | 37.05 E |
| Geluji | 98 | 37.08 N | 121.50 E |
| Geluksburg | 158 | 28.30 S | 29.33 E |
| Geluwe | 50 | 50.48 N | 3.04 E |
| Gemas | 114 | 2.35 N | 102.37 E |
| Gembloux | 56 | 50.34 N | 4.41 E |
| Gembrook | 169 | 37.57 S | 145.33 E |
| Gemen | 52 | 51.51 N | 6.52 E |
| Gemena | 152 | 3.15 N | 19.46 E |
| Gémenos | 62 | 43.18 N | 5.38 E |
| Gemerek | 130 | 39.11 N | 36.05 E |
| Gemert | 52 | 51.34 N | 5.40 E |
| Gemla | 26 | 56.52 N | 14.38 E |
| Gemlik | 130 | 40.26 N | 29.09 E |
| Gemlik Körfezi c | 130 | 40.25 N | 28.55 E |
| Gemolong | 115a | 7.24 S | 110.50 E |
| Gemona del Friuli | 64 | 46.16 N | 13.09 E |
| Gemonio | 62 | 45.53 N | 8.40 E |
| Gemsbok National Park ♦ | 156 | 25.15 S | 21.10 E |
| Gemünd | 56 | 50.34 N | 6.30 E |
| Gemünden, Dtsch. | 56 | 50.03 N | 9.41 E |
| Gemünden, Dtsch. | 56 | 50.58 N | 8.58 E |
| Gemünden, Dtsch. | 56 | 49.54 N | 7.28 E |
| Gen ≃ | 89 | 50.16 N | 119.22 E |
| Genadendal | 158 | 34.02 S | 19.33 E |
| Genaibashi | 268 | 35.21 N | 140.04 E |
| Genale (Jubba) ≃ | 144 | 0.15 S | 42.38 E |
| Genappe | 50 | 50.36 N | 4.27 E |
| Genarp | 41 | 55.36 N | 13.23 E |
| Genazzano | 66 | 41.50 N | 12.58 E |
| Genç | 130 | 38.46 N | 40.35 E |
| Gençay | 32 | 46.23 N | 0.24 E |
| Gencek | 130 | 37.27 N | 31.33 E |
| Gencsapáti | 61 | 47.17 N | 16.36 E |
| Gending | 115a | 7.48 S | 113.18 E |
| Gendrey | 58 | 47.12 N | 5.41 E |
| Gendringen | 52 | 51.52 N | 6.22 E |
| Gendt | 52 | 51.53 N | 5.59 E |
| Genegantslet Creek ≃ | 210 | 42.18 N | 75.48 W |
| Genemuiden | 52 | 52.37 N | 6.07 E |
| General ≃ | 236 | 8.59 N | 83.11 W |
| General Acha | 252 | 37.23 S | 64.36 W |
| General Alvear, Arg. | 252 | 36.03 S | 60.01 W |
| General Alvear, Arg. | 252 | 34.58 S | 67.42 W |
| General Aquino | 252 | 24.26 S | 56.42 W |
| General Arenales | 252 | 34.18 S | 61.18 W |
| General Belgrano | 252 | 35.46 S | 58.30 W |
| General Bernardo O'Higgins ʋ[3] | 9 | 63.19 S | 57.54 W |
| General Bravo | 232 | 25.48 N | 99.10 W |
| General Butler State Resort Park ♦ | 218 | 38.40 N | 85.10 W |
| General Cabrera | 252 | 32.48 S | 63.52 W |
| General Campos | 252 | 31.32 S | 58.24 W |
| General Carneiro | 255 | 15.42 S | 52.45 W |
| General Carrera, Lago (Lago Buenos Aires) ⊜ | 254 | 46.35 S | 72.00 W |
| General Cepeda | 232 | 25.23 N | 101.27 W |
| General Conesa, Arg. | 252 | 36.30 S | 57.20 W |
| General Conesa, Arg. | 254 | 40.06 S | 64.26 W |
| General Daniel Cerri | 252 | 38.42 S | 62.24 W |
| General del Sur, Cementerio ✤ | 286c | 10.28 N | 66.55 W |
| General Elizardo Aquino | 252 | 26.53 S | 56.17 W |
| General Enrique Martínez | 252 | 33.12 S | 53.48 W |
| General Enrique Mosconi | 252 | 22.36 S | 63.49 W |
| General Escobedo, Méx. | 196 | 25.49 N | 100.20 W |
| General Escobedo, Méx. | 232 | 25.30 N | 105.15 W |
| General Eugenio A. Garay, Para. | 248 | 20.31 S | 62.08 W |
| General Eugenio A. Garay, Para. | 252 | 25.55 S | 56.11 W |
| General Galarza | 252 | 32.43 S | 59.24 W |
| General Güemes | 252 | 24.40 S | 65.03 W |
| General Guido | 252 | 36.40 S | 57.46 W |
| General Hornos | 258 | 34.53 S | 58.56 W |
| General Island I | 116 | 9.25 N | 126.00 E |
| General José de San Martín | 252 | 26.33 S | 59.21 W |
| General Juan José Ríos | 232 | 25.40 N | 108.40 W |
| General Juan Madariaga | 252 | 37.00 S | 57.09 W |
| General La Madrid | 252 | 37.16 S | 61.17 W |
| General Las Heras | 258 | 34.56 S | 58.57 W |
| General Las Heras □[5] | 288 | 34.56 S | 58.51 W |
| General Lavalle | 252 | 36.24 S | 56.58 W |
| General Leonidas Plaza Gutiérrez | 246 | 2.58 S | 78.25 W |
| General Levalle | 252 | 34.01 S | 63.56 W |
| General Lorenzo Vintter | 254 | 40.44 S | 64.29 W |
| General Luna | 116 | 9.47 N | 126.09 E |
| General MacArthur (Pambuhan Sur) | 116 | 11.15 N | 125.32 E |
| General Mansilla (Bartolomé Bavio) | 258 | 35.05 S | 57.45 W |
| General Manuel Belgrano, Cerro ∧ | 252 | 29.01 S | 67.49 W |
| General Mitchell Field ⊠ | 216 | 42.57 N | 87.54 W |
| General Motors Corporation (Pontiac Division) ʋ[3] | 281 | 42.49 N | 83.17 W |
| General Motors Proving Grounds ʋ[3] | 281 | 42.35 N | 83.41 W |
| General Motors Technical Center ʋ[3] | 281 | 42.31 N | 83.02 W |
| General'nyj ≃ | 265a | 60.00 N | 30.32 E |
| General O'Brien | 252 | 34.54 S | 60.45 W |
| General Pacheco | 288 | 34.28 S | 58.38 W |
| General Pánfilo Natera | 234 | 22.40 N | 102.06 W |
| General Paz | 258 | 35.31 S | 58.19 W |
| General Pico | 252 | 35.40 S | 63.44 W |
| General Pinedo | 252 | 27.19 S | 61.17 W |
| General Pinto | 252 | 34.46 S | 61.53 W |
| General Pizarro | 252 | 24.13 S | 64.01 W |
| General Roca | 252 | 39.02 S | 67.35 W |
| General Rodríguez | 258 | 34.36 S | 58.57 W |
| General San Martín, Arg. | 252 | 37.59 S | 63.34 W |
| General San Martín, Arg. | 258 | 34.34 S | 58.32 W |
| General San Martín □[5] | 288 | 34.34 S | 58.34 W |
| General Santos (Dadiangas) | 116 | 6.07 N | 125.11 E |
| General Sarmiento | 258 | 34.33 S | 58.43 W |
| General Sarmiento □[5] | 288 | 34.32 S | 58.43 W |
| General'skoje | 83 | 47.28 N | 39.35 E |
| General Terán | 232 | 25.16 N | 99.41 W |
| General Tinio | 116 | 15.21 N | 121.03 E |
| General Toševo | 38 | 43.42 N | 28.02 E |
| General Treviño | 196 | 26.14 N | 99.29 W |
| General Viamonte (Los Toldos) | 252 | 35.01 S | 61.01 W |
| General Villegas | 252 | 35.02 S | 63.01 W |
| General Vintter, Lago (Lago Palena) ⊜ | 254 | 43.55 S | 71.40 W |
| General Warren Village | 285 | 40.02 N | 75.32 W |
| General Zuazua | 196 | 25.54 N | 100.07 W |
| Gênes → Genova | 62 | 44.25 N | 8.57 E |
| Genesee, Id., U.S. | 202 | 46.33 N | 116.55 W |
| Genesee, Pa., U.S. | 214 | 41.59 N | 77.52 W |
| Genesee, Wi., U.S. | 216 | 42.58 N | 88.21 W |
| Genesee □[6], Mi., U.S. | 216 | 42.56 N | 83.41 W |
| Genesee □[6], N.Y., U.S. | 210 | 43.00 N | 78.11 W |
| Genesee ≃ | 210 | 43.16 N | 77.36 W |
| Geneseo, Il., U.S. | 190 | 41.26 N | 90.09 W |
| Geneseo, Ks., U.S. | 198 | 38.30 N | 98.09 W |
| Geneseo, N.Y., U.S. | 210 | 42.47 N | 77.49 W |
| Geneva → Genève, Schw. | 58 | 46.12 N | 6.09 E |
| Geneva, S. Afr. | 158 | 27.50 S | 27.08 E |
| Geneva, Al., U.S. | 194 | 31.01 N | 85.51 W |
| Geneva, Fl., U.S. | 220 | 28.44 N | 81 07 W |
| Geneva, Il., U.S. | 216 | 41.53 N | 88.18 W |
| Geneva, In., U.S. | 216 | 40.35 N | 84.57 W |
| Geneva, Ne., U.S. | 198 | 40.31 N | 97.35 W |
| Geneva, N.Y., U.S. | 210 | 42.52 N | 77.00 W |
| Geneva, Oh., U.S. | 214 | 41.48 N | 80.56 W |
| Geneva, Pa., U.S. | 214 | 41.35 N | 80.14 W |
| Geneva, Wa., U.S. | 224 | 48.45 N | 122.24 W |
| Geneva, Lake (Lac Léman) (Lac de Gèneve) ⊜, Europe | 58 | 46.25 N | 6.30 E |
| Geneva, Lake ⊜, Wi., U.S. | 216 | 42.34 N | 88.30 W |
| Geneva-on-the-Lake | 214 | 41.52 N | 80.57 W |
| Genève (Geneva) | 58 | 46.12 N | 6.09 E |
| Genève □[3] | 58 | 46.15 N | 6.10 E |
| Genève, Lac de → Geneva, Lake ⊜ | 58 | 46.25 N | 6.30 E |
| Genève-Cointrin, Aéroport ⊠ | 58 | 46.14 N | 6.06 E |
| Genevois ✤[1] | 58 | 46.03 N | 6.14 E |
| Genévriers, Île des I | 186 | 51.15 N | 58.26 W |
| Genf → Genève | 58 | 46.12 N | 6.09 E |
| Genga | 66 | 43.26 N | 12.56 E |
| Gengenbach | 58 | 48.24 N | 8.01 E |
| Genghis Khan, Wall of ⊥, Asia | 88 | 49.00 N | 115.00 E |
| Genghis Khan, Wall of ⊥, Mong. | 88 | 49.00 N | 116.00 E |
| Gengji | 100 | 33.47 N | 112.47 E |
| Gengma | 102 | 23.34 N | 99.06 E |
| Gengputou | 106 | 31.12 N | 119.55 E |
| Gengzhuang | 104 | 40.59 N | 122.42 E |
| Génicourt | 261 | 49.05 N | 2.04 E |
| Génicourt-sur-Meuse | 56 | 49.02 N | 5.26 E |
| Genil ≃ | 34 | 37.42 N | 5.19 W |
| Génissiat | 58 | 46.03 N | 5.47 E |
| Genk | 56 | 50.58 N | 5.30 E |
| Genkai | 96 | 33.51 N | 130.30 E |
| Genkai-kokutei-kōen ♦ | 96 | 33.54 N | 130.31 E |
| Genkai-nada ⊤[2] | 92 | 34.00 N | 130.00 E |
| Genkanyj, chrebet ⋏ | 180 | 66.15 N | 172.20 W |
| Genlis | 58 | 47.14 N | 5.13 E |
| Gennach ≃ | 58 | 48.10 N | 10.43 E |
| Gennargentu, Monti del ⋏ | 71 | 40.01 N | 9.19 E |
| Gennebreck | 263 | 51.19 N | 7.12 E |
| Gennep | 52 | 51.42 N | 5.58 E |
| Genner | 41 | 55.07 N | 9.26 E |
| Gennes | 32 | 47.20 N | 0.14 W |
| Gennevilliers | 261 | 48.56 N | 2.18 E |
| Genoa, Austl. | 166 | 37.29 S | 149.35 E |
| Genoa → Genova, It. | 62 | 44.25 N | 8.57 E |
| Genoa, Il., U.S. | 216 | 42.05 N | 88.41 W |
| Genoa, Ne., U.S. | 198 | 41.26 N | 97.43 W |
| Genoa, Nv., U.S. | 226 | 39.00 N | 119.50 W |
| Genoa, N.Y., U.S. | 210 | 42.40 N | 76.32 W |
| Genoa, Oh., U.S. | 214 | 41.31 N | 83.21 W |
| Genoa, Wi., U.S. | 190 | 43.34 N | 91.13 W |
| Genoa, Arroyo ≃ | 254 | 44.58 S | 70.06 W |
| Genoa City | 216 | 42.29 N | 88.19 W |
| Genoa Peak ∧ | 226 | 39.03 N | 119.53 W |
| Genola | 62 | 44.35 N | 7.39 E |
| Génolhac | 62 | 44.21 N | 3.57 E |
| Genova (Genoa) | 62 | 44.25 N | 8.57 E |
| Genova □[4] | 62 | 44.30 N | 9.04 E |
| Genova, Golfo di c | 62 | 44.10 N | 8.55 E |
| Genova, Val V | 64 | 46.11 N | 10.40 E |
| Genovesa, Isla I | 246a | 0.20 N | 89.58 W |
| Genrijetty, ostrov I | 74 | 77.06 N | 156.30 E |
| Gensan → Wŏnsan | 98 | 39.09 N | 127.25 E |
| Gens de Terre ≃ | 190 | 46.53 N | 76.00 W |
| Genshagen | 264a | 52.19 N | 13.19 E |
| Genshagener Heide ✤[3] | 264a | 52.20 N | 13.18 E |
| Genshiryoku-kenkyūsho ʋ[3] | 94 | 36.27 N | 140.36 E |
| Gensingen | 56 | 49.53 N | 7.55 E |
| Gensungen | 56 | 51.08 N | 9.26 E |
| Gent (Gand) | 50 | 51.03 N | 3.43 E |
| Gentbrugge | 50 | 51.03 N | 3.45 E |
| Gent-Brugge, Kanaal ≅ | 50 | 51.03 N | 3.43 E |
| Genteng | 115a | 8.22 S | 114.09 E |
| Genteng, Gili I | 115a | 7.12 S | 113.54 E |
| Genteng, Tanjung › | 115a | 7.23 S | 106.24 E |
| Genthin | 54 | 52.24 N | 12.09 E |
| Gentilly | 261 | 48.49 N | 2.21 E |
| Gentilly ≃ | 206 | 46.24 N | 72.21 W |
| Genting | 114 | 3.42 N | 98.10 E |
| Gentio do Ouro | 250 | 11.25 S | 42.30 W |
| Gentioux | 32 | 45.47 N | 1.59 E |


| | | | | | |
|---|---|---|---|---|---|
| ≃ River | Fluß | Río | Rivière | Rio | |
| ≅ Canal | Kanal | Canal | Canal | Canal | |
| ʟ Waterfall, Rapids | Wasserfall, Stromschnellen | Cascada, Rápidos | Chute d'eau, Rapides | Cascata, Rápidos | |
| ⋓ Strait | Meeresstraße | Estrecho | Détroit | Estreito | |
| c Bay, Gulf | Bucht, Golf | Bahía, Golfo | Baie, Golfe | Baía, Golfo | |
| ⊜ Lake, Lakes | See, Seen | Lago, Lagos | Lac, Lacs | Lago, Lagos | |
| ≡ Swamp | Sumpf | Pantano | Marais | Pântano | |
| ⍓ Ice Features, Glacier | Eis- und Gletscherformen | Accidentes Glaciales | Formes glaciaires | Acidentes glaciares | |
| ⊤ Other Hydrographic Features | Andere Hydrographische Objekte | Otros Elementos Hidrográficos | Autres données hydrographiques | Outros acidentes hidrográficos | |

| | | | | | |
|---|---|---|---|---|---|
| ✢ Submarine Features | Untermeerische Objekte | Accidentes Submarinos | Formes de relief sous-marin | Acidentes submarinos | |
| □ Political Unit | Politische Einheit | Unidad Politica | Entité politique | Unidade política | |
| ʋ Cultural Institution | Kulturelle Institution | Institución Cultural | Institution culturelle | Institução cultural | |
| ⊥ Historical Site | Historische Stätte | Sitio Histórico | Site historique | Sitio histórico | |
| ♦ Recreational Site | Erholungs- und Ferienort | Sitio de Recreo | Centre de loisirs | Area de Lazer | |
| ⊠ Airport | Flughafen | Aeropuerto | Aéroport | Aeroporto | |
| ■ Military Installation | Militäranlage | Instalación Militar | Installation militaire | Instalação militar | |
| ✤ Miscellaneous | Verschiedenes | Misceláneo | Divers | Diversos | |

| Name | Page | Lat.°′ | Long.°′ |
|---|---|---|---|
| Gentofte | 41 | 55.45 N | 12.33 E |
| Gentry | 194 | 36.16 N | 94.29 W |
| Gentry, Lake ⊜ | 220 | 28.08 N | 81.15 W |
| Genua → Genova | 62 | 44.25 N | 8.57 E |
| Genuang | 114 | 2.29 N | 102.53 E |
| Genval | 50 | 50.43 N | 4.29 E |
| Genyem | 164 | 2.46 S | 140.12 E |
| Genzano di Lucania | 68 | 40.51 N | 16.02 E |
| Genzano di Roma | 66 | 41.42 N | 12.41 E |
| Geographe Bay c | 162 | 33.35 S | 115.15 E |
| Geographe Channel Ʉ | 162 | 24.40 S | 113.20 E |
| Geok-Tepe | 128 | 38.09 N | 57.58 E |
| Geonkhāli | 126 | 22.12 N | 88.03 E |
| George, S. Afr. | 158 | 33.58 S | 22.24 E |
| George, Ia., U.S. | 198 | 43.20 N | 96.00 W |
| George, Tx., U.S. | 222 | 30.59 N | 96.07 W |
| George ≃, Austl. | 162 | 20.50 S | 117.28 E |
| George ≃, P.Q., Can. | 176 | 58.49 N | 66.10 W |
| George, Cape › | 186 | 45.53 N | 61.53 W |
| George, Lake ⊜, Austl. | 162 | 22.37 S | 123.38 E |
| George, Lake ⊜, Austl. | 166 | 35.05 S | 149.25 E |
| George, Lake ⊜, N.A. | 190 | 46.28 N | 84.10 W |
| George, Lake ⊜, Ug. | 154 | 0.02 N | 30.12 E |
| George, Lake ⊜, U.S. | 216 | 41.45 N | 85.00 W |
| George, Lake ⊜, Fl., U.S. | 192 | 29.17 N | 81.36 W |
| George, Lake ⊜, In., U.S. | 216 | 41.40 N | 87.30 W |
| George, Lake ⊜, N.Y., U.S. | 188 | 43.35 N | 73.35 W |
| George Air Force Base ■ | 228 | 34.35 N | 117.22 W |
| George B. Stevenson Dam ◆[6] | 214 | 41.25 N | 78.01 W |
| George Gill Range ⋀ | 162 | 24.15 S | 131.36 E |
| George H. Crosby Manitou State Park ♠ | 190 | 47.29 N | 91.10 W |
| George Island I | 254 | 52.19 S | 59.45 W |
| George Mason University ʋ[2] | 284c | 38.50 N | 77.17 W |
| Georgensgmünd | 56 | 49.11 N | 11.00 E |
| Georgenthal | 54 | 50.49 N | 10.40 E |
| Georges ≃ | 170 | 33.57 S | 150.58 E |
| Georges Bank ✢[4] | 16 | 41.15 N | 67.30 W |
| Georges Island I | 283 | 42.19 N | 70.56 W |
| George Sound Ʉ | 172 | 44.50 S | 167.23 E |
| Georges River Bridge ◆[5] | 274a | 34.00 S | 151.07 E |
| Georges Run | 214 | 40.21 N | 80.37 W |
| Georges Run ≃ | 279b | 40.23 N | 80.06 W |
| Georgetown, Austl. | 166 | 18.18 S | 143.33 E |
| George Town, Austl. | 166 | 41.06 S | 146.50 E |
| Georgetown → Halton Hills, On., Can. | 190 | 43.37 N | 79.56 W |
| Georgetown, P.E., Can. | 186 | 46.11 N | 62.32 W |
| George Town, Cay. Is. | 238 | 19.18 N | 81.23 W |
| Georgetown, Gam. | 150 | 13.30 N | 14.47 W |
| Georgetown, Guy. | 246 | 6.48 N | 58.10 W |
| George Town (Pinang), Malay. | 114 | 5.25 N | 100.20 E |
| Georgetown, St. Vin. | 241h | 13.16 N | 61.08 W |
| Georgetown, Ca., U.S. | 226 | 38.54 N | 120.50 W |
| Georgetown, Co., U.S. | 200 | 39.42 N | 105.41 W |
| Georgetown, Ct., U.S. | 207 | 41.15 N | 73.26 W |
| Georgetown, De., U.S. | 208 | 38.41 N | 75.23 W |
| Georgetown, Fl., U.S. | 192 | 29.23 N | 81.38 W |
| Georgetown, Ga., U.S. | 192 | 31.53 N | 85.06 W |
| Georgetown, Id., U.S. | 202 | 42.29 N | 111.22 W |
| Georgetown, Il., U.S. | 194 | 39.58 N | 87.38 W |
| Georgetown, In., U.S. | 218 | 38.17 N | 85.58 W |
| Georgetown, Ky., U.S. | 218 | 38.12 N | 84.33 W |
| Georgetown, Ma., U.S. | 207 | 42.43 N | 70.59 W |
| Georgetown, Ms., U.S. | 194 | 31.52 N | 90.09 W |
| Georgetown, N.J., U.S. | 285 | 40.04 N | 74.39 W |
| Georgetown, N.Y., U.S. | 210 | 42.46 N | 75.44 W |
| Georgetown, Oh., U.S. | 218 | 38.51 N | 83.54 W |
| Georgetown, Pa., U.S. | 214 | 40.39 N | 80.30 W |
| Georgetown, S.C., U.S. | 192 | 33.22 N | 79.17 W |
| Georgetown, Tx., U.S. | 222 | 30.37 N | 97.40 W |
| Georgetown ◆[8] | 284c | 38.54 N | 77.03 W |
| Georgetown, Lake ⊜[1] | 222 | 30.40 N | 97.45 W |
| Georgetown Lake ⊜ | 202 | 46.11 N | 113.17 W |
| Georgetown Rowley State Forest ♠ | 283 | 42.42 N | 70.58 W |
| Georgetown University ʋ[2] | 284c | 38.54 N | 77.04 W |
| George V Coast ⊥[2] | 9 | 68.30 S | 147.30 E |
| George VI Sound Ʉ | 9 | 71.00 S | 68.00 W |
| George Washington Birthplace National Monument ♠ | 208 | 38.11 N | 76.56 W |
| George Washington Bridge ◆[5] | 276 | 40.51 N | 73.57 W |
| George Washington Carver National Monument ♠ | 194 | 37.00 N | 94.19 W |
| George West | 196 | 28.19 N | 98.07 W |
| Georg Forster ʋ[3] | 9 | 70.47 S | 11.51 E |
| Georgia □[1], Asia | 72 | 42.00 N | 44.00 E |
| Georgia □[1], Asia | 84 | 42.00 N | 44.00 E |
| Georgia □[3], U.S. | 178 | 32.50 N | 83.15 W |
| Georgia □[3], U.S. | 192 | 32.50 N | 83.15 W |
| Georgia, Strait of Ʉ | 182 | 49.20 N | 124.00 W |
| Georgia del Sur, Isla de → South Georgia I | 244 | 54.15 S | 36.45 W |
| Georgiana | 194 | 31.38 N | 86.44 W |
| Georgian Bay c | 190 | 45.15 N | 80.50 W |
| Georgian Bay Islands National Park ♠ | 190 | 44.54 N | 79.52 W |
| Géorgie du Sud → South Georgia I | 244 | 54.15 S | 36.45 W |
| Georgijevka, Kaz. | 85 | 43.03 N | 74.43 E |
| Georgijevka, Kaz. | 85 | 42.11 N | 70.00 E |
| Georgijevka, Kaz. | 86 | 49.19 N | 81.35 E |
| Georgijevka, Ross. | 80 | 53.18 N | 51.01 E |
| Georgijevsk | 84 | 44.09 N | 43.28 E |
| Georgina ≃ | 166 | 23.30 S | 139.47 E |
| Georgina Island I | 212 | 44.23 N | 79.17 W |
| Georgina Island Indian Reserve ◆[4] | 212 | 44.22 N | 79.19 W |
| Georgsmarienhütte | 52 | 52.12 N | 8.02 E |
| Gera | 54 | 50.52 N | 12.04 E |
| Gera ≃ | 54 | 51.08 N | 10.56 E |
| Geraardsbergen | 50 | 50.46 N | 3.52 E |
| Geraberg | 54 | 50.43 N | 10.50 E |
| Gerabronn | 56 | 49.15 N | 9.55 E |
| Gerace | 68 | 38.16 N | 16.13 E |
| Geraci Siculo | 70 | 37.51 N | 14.09 E |
| Geral, Serra ⊥[4], Bra. | 250 | 11.15 S | 46.30 W |
| Geral, Serra ⊥[4], Bra. | 252 | 26.30 S | 50.30 W |
| Gerald | 219 | 38.23 N | 91.19 W |
| Geral de Goiás, Serra ⊥[4] | 242 | 13.00 S | 46.15 W |
| Geraldine, N.Z. | 172 | 44.05 S | 171.14 E |
| Geraldine, Mt., U.S. | 202 | 47.36 N | 110.15 W |
| Geraldton, Austl. | 162 | 28.46 S | 114.36 E |
| Geraldton, On., Can. | 176 | 49.44 N | 86.57 W |
| Gerar, Naḥal V | 132 | 31.24 N | 34.26 E |
| Gerard, Lake ⊜ | 276 | 41.06 N | 74.33 W |
| Gerard, Mount ∧ | 162 | 27.13 S | 122.41 E |
| Gérardmer | 58 | 48.04 N | 6.53 E |
| Geras | 61 | 48.48 N | 15.40 E |
| Gerasa ⊥ | 132 | 32.17 N | 35.53 E |
| Gerasdorf | 61 | 48.18 N | 16.28 E |
| Gerasimovka | 86 | 58.37 N | 71.53 E |
| Gerber | 204 | 40.03 N | 122.08 W |
| Gerber Reservoir ⊜[1] | 202 | 42.12 N | 121.06 W |
| Gerbéviller | 58 | 48.30 N | 6.31 E |
| Gerblingerode | 52 | 51.29 N | 10.15 E |
| Gerbstedt | 54 | 51.38 N | 11.37 E |
| Gerchsheim | 56 | 49.42 N | 9.47 E |
| Gercüş | 130 | 37.34 N | 41.23 E |
| Gerdau | 158 | 26.28 S | 26.06 E |
| Gerdine, Mount ∧ | 180 | 61.35 N | 152.26 W |
| Gerdview | 273d | 26.10 S | 28.11 E |
| Gère ≃ | 62 | 45.32 N | 4.54 E |
| Gerede | 130 | 40.48 N | 32.12 E |
| Gereja Cathedral ʋ[1] | 269e | 6.10 S | 106.49 E |
| Gerenzano | 266b | 45.38 N | 9.00 E |
| Gereshk | 120 | 31.48 N | 64.34 E |
| Geretsried | 64 | 47.51 N | 11.28 E |
| Gérgal | 34 | 37.07 N | 2.33 W |
| Gerge'bil | 84 | 42.31 N | 47.05 E |
| Gerger | 130 | 37.57 N | 39.01 E |
| Geria Nij | 126 | 23.56 N | 86.55 E |
| Gerik | 114 | 5.25 N | 101.08 E |
| Gering | 198 | 41.49 N | 103.39 W |
| Geringswalde | 54 | 51.04 N | 12.54 E |
| Geriş | 130 | 36.58 N | 31.44 E |
| Gerlachovský štít ∧ | 30 | 49.12 N | 20.08 E |
| Gerlafingen | 58 | 47.10 N | 7.34 E |
| Gerli ◆[8] | 288 | 34.41 S | 58.23 W |
| Gerlingen | 56 | 48.48 N | 9.03 E |
| Gerlos | 64 | 47.14 N | 12.02 E |
| Gerlospass )( | 64 | 47.14 N | 12.08 E |
| Gerlova Hut' | 60 | 49.10 N | 13.17 E |
| Germa (Jarmah) ⊥ | 146 | 26.33 N | 13.04 E |
| Germagnano | 62 | 45.15 N | 7.28 E |
| Germain, Grand lac ⊜ | 186 | 51.12 N | 66.41 W |
| Germania | 214 | 41.39 N | 77.40 W |
| Germano | 214 | 40.25 N | 80.57 W |
| Germansen, Mount ∧ | 182 | 55.37 N | 124.50 W |
| Germansen Lake ⊜ | 182 | 55.41 N | 124.53 W |
| Germansen Landing | 182 | 55.47 N | 124.43 W |
| Germansville | 208 | 40.42 N | 75.42 W |
| Germantown, Il., U.S. | 219 | 38.33 N | 89.32 W |
| Germantown, Ky., U.S. | 218 | 38.39 N | 83.57 W |
| Germantown, N.Y., U.S. | 210 | 42.08 N | 73.54 W |
| Germantown, Oh., U.S. | 218 | 39.37 N | 84.22 W |
| Germantown, Tn., U.S. | 194 | 35.05 N | 89.48 W |
| Germantown, Wi., U.S. | 216 | 43.13 N | 88.06 W |
| Germantown ◆[8] | 285 | 40.03 N | 75.11 W |
| Germantown Dam ◆[6] | 218 | 39.38 N | 84.24 W |
| Germany (Deutschland) □[1], Europe | 22 | 51.00 N | 10.00 E |
| Germany (Deutschland) □[1], Europe | 30 | 51.00 N | 10.00 E |
| Germany Flats ≚ | 276 | 41.05 N | 74.39 W |
| Germaringen | 58 | 47.56 N | 10.40 E |
| Germay | 58 | 48.25 N | 5.21 E |
| Germencik | 130 | 37.51 N | 27.37 E |
| Germendorf | 54 | 52.45 N | 13.10 E |
| Germering | 60 | 48.08 N | 11.22 E |
| Germersheim | 56 | 49.13 N | 8.22 E |
| Germfask | 190 | 46.14 N | 85.55 W |
| Germiston | 158 | 26.13 S | 28.11 E |
| Germiston □[5] | 273d | 26.15 S | 28.10 E |
| Germiston South | 273d | 26.15 S | 28.10 E |
| Gernikao (Guernica) | 34 | 43.19 N | 2.41 W |
| Gernrode | 54 | 51.43 N | 11.08 E |
| Gernsbach | 56 | 48.46 N | 8.19 E |
| Gernsheim | 56 | 49.44 N | 8.29 E |
| Gero | 94 | 35.48 N | 137.14 E |
| Geroda | 56 | 50.17 N | 9.53 E |
| Gerola Alta | 58 | 46.03 N | 9.32 E |
| Geroldsgrün | 54 | 50.20 N | 11.35 E |
| Geroldstein | 56 | 50.06 N | 7.56 E |
| Gerolsbach | 60 | 48.30 N | 11.22 E |
| Gerolstein | 56 | 50.13 N | 6.40 E |
| Gerolzhofen | 56 | 49.54 N | 10.21 E |
| Gerona → Girona, Esp. | 34 | 41.59 N | 2.49 E |
| Gerona, Pil. | 116 | 15.36 N | 120.36 E |
| Geronimo | 196 | 34.28 N | 98.22 W |
| Gerpinnes | 50 | 50.20 N | 4.31 E |
| Gerrards Cross | 260 | 51.35 N | 0.34 W |
| Gerrei ◆[1] | 71 | 39.28 N | 9.17 E |
| Gerresheim ◆[8] | 263 | 51.14 N | 6.52 E |
| Gerringong | 170 | 34.45 S | 150.50 E |
| Gerry | 214 | 42.12 N | 79.15 W |
| Gers □[5] | 32 | 43.40 N | 0.30 E |
| Gers ≃ | 32 | 44.09 N | 0.39 E |
| Gersau | 58 | 47.00 N | 8.32 E |
| Gersdorf | 54 | 50.45 N | 12.42 E |
| Gersfeld | 56 | 50.27 N | 9.55 E |
| Gershøj | 41 | 55.43 N | 11.59 E |
| Gersprenz ≃ | 56 | 49.59 N | 9.04 E |
| Gerstetten | 56 | 48.37 N | 10.01 E |
| Gersthofen | 58 | 48.25 N | 10.53 E |
| Gerstungen | 56 | 50.58 N | 10.04 E |
| Gerswalde | 54 | 53.10 N | 13.46 E |
| Gertak Sanggul, Tanjong › | 114 | 5.15 N | 100.11 E |
| Gerthe ◆[8] | 263 | 51.31 N | 7.17 E |
| Gerufa | 156 | 19.17 S | 26.02 E |
| Gervais | 224 | 45.06 N | 122.53 W |
| Gerwisch | 54 | 52.10 N | 11.44 E |
| Gerza | 142 | 29.26 N | 31.11 E |
| Gerze, Tür. | 130 | 41.48 N | 35.12 E |
| Gêrzê, Zhg. | 120 | 32.16 N | 84.12 E |
| Gerzen | 60 | 48.31 N | 12.25 E |
| Gerzensee | 58 | 46.51 N | 7.33 E |
| Gescher | 52 | 51.57 N | 6.59 E |
| Geschriebenstein (Írottkő) ∧ | 61 | 47.21 N | 16.26 E |
| Geschwenda | 54 | 50.44 N | 10.49 E |
| Gesees | 60 | 49.54 N | 11.32 E |
| Geseke | 52 | 51.38 N | 8.31 E |
| Geser | 164 | 3.53 S | 130.54 E |
| Gesher HaZiw | 132 | 33.02 N | 35.06 E |
| Gesi | 115a | 7.20 S | 111.01 E |
| Gesoa | 164 | 8.25 S | 143.35 E |
| Gespunsart | 56 | 49.49 N | 4.50 E |
| Gessertshausen | 58 | 48.20 N | 10.44 E |
| Gesso ≃ | 62 | 44.24 N | 7.33 E |
| Gessopalena | 66 | 42.03 N | 14.16 E |
| Gesten | 41 | 55.31 N | 9.12 E |
| Gesualdo | 68 | 41.00 N | 15.04 E |
| Geta | 26 | 60.23 N | 19.50 E |
| Getafe | 34 | 40.18 N | 3.43 W |
| Getafe, Aeropuerto ⊠ | 266a | 40.18 N | 3.43 W |
| Gete ≃ | 56 | 50.57 N | 5.07 E |
| Gethaoli | 272c | 19.08 N | 73.01 E |
| Geti | 154 | 1.13 N | 30.12 E |
| Getinge | 26 | 56.49 N | 12.44 E |
| Gettorf | 41 | 54.24 N | 9.58 E |
| Gettysburg, Oh., U.S. | 218 | 40.06 N | 84.29 W |
| Gettysburg, Pa., U.S. | 208 | 39.49 N | 77.13 W |
| Gettysburg, S.D., U.S. | 198 | 45.00 N | 99.57 W |
| Gettysburg National Military Park ♠ | 208 | 39.49 N | 77.15 W |
| Getulândia | 256 | 22.40 S | 44.06 W |
| Getulina | 255 | 21.49 S | 49.55 W |
| Getulio | 116 | 10.45 N | 122.40 E |
| Getúlio Vargas | 252 | 27.50 S | 52.16 W |
| Getz Ice Shelf ⊓ | 9 | 75.00 S | 129.00 W |
| Getzville | 210 | 43.01 N | 78.46 W |
| Geumpang | 114 | 4.48 N | 96.09 E |
| Geureudong, Gunung ∧ | 114 | 4.48 N | 96.48 E |
| Gevān | 128 | 26.03 N | 57.17 E |
| Gevaş | 128 | 38.16 N | 43.07 E |
| Gevelsberg | 56 | 51.19 N | 7.20 E |
| Gevgelija | 38 | 41.08 N | 22.30 E |
| Gévora ≃ | 34 | 38.53 N | 6.57 W |
| Gevrey-Chambertin | 58 | 47.14 N | 4.57 E |
| Gewane | 144 | 10.10 N | 40.39 E |
| Geweke ◆[8] | 263 | 51.22 N | 7.25 E |
| Gex | 58 | 46.20 N | 6.04 E |
| Geyer | 54 | 50.37 N | 12.55 E |
| Geyer Ditch ≚ | 216 | 41.36 N | 86.25 W |
| Geyikli | 130 | 39.48 N | 26.12 E |
| Geysdorp | 158 | 26.32 S | 25.18 E |
| Geyser | 202 | 47.15 N | 110.29 W |
| Geyserville | 204 | 38.42 N | 122.54 W |
| Geyshtasar, Kūh-e ∧ | 84 | 38.51 N | 47.14 E |
| Geyuan | 100 | 28.31 N | 117.44 E |
| Geyve | 130 | 40.30 N | 30.18 E |
| Gézenti | 146 | 21.41 N | 18.18 E |
| Gezer | 132 | 31.52 N | 34.55 E |
| Gföhl | 61 | 48.31 N | 15.30 E |
| Ghaapplato ⋀[1] | 158 | 27.30 S | 24.00 E |
| Ghabāghib | 132 | 33.10 N | 36.13 E |
| Ghābat al-ʿArab | 140 | 9.02 N | 29.29 E |
| Ghadaf, Wādī al- V | 132 | 31.46 N | 36.50 E |
| Ghadāmis | 146 | 30.08 N | 9.30 E |
| Ghaddūwah | 146 | 26.26 N | 14.18 E |
| Ghafe | 272c | 19.05 N | 73.07 E |
| Ghagghar ≃ | 123 | 29.30 N | 74.53 E |
| Ghāghara ≃ | 124 | 25.47 N | 84.37 E |
| Ghaghar Reservoir ⊜[1] | 124 | 24.38 N | 83.11 E |
| Ghāghra | 124 | 23.17 N | 84.33 E |
| Ghakhar | 123 | 32.18 N | 74.09 E |
| Ghallah, Wādī al- V | 140 | 10.25 N | 27.32 E |
| Ghammāzah al-Kubrā | 142 | 29.43 N | 31.18 E |
| Ghamrīn | 142 | 30.30 N | 30.55 E |
| Ghana □[1], Afr. | 134 | 8.00 N | 1.00 W |
| Ghana □[1], Afr. | 150 | 8.00 N | 1.00 W |
| Ghansoli | 272c | 19.08 N | 72.59 E |
| Ghanzi | 156 | 21.38 S | 21.45 E |
| Ghanzi □[5] | 156 | 22.00 S | 23.00 E |
| Ghārāpuri | 272c | 18.54 N | 72.56 E |
| Gharaunda | 124 | 29.33 N | 76.58 E |
| Gharbah, Wādī V | 142 | 29.40 N | 31.58 E |
| Gharbi, Chott ⊜ | 148 | 33.50 N | 1.30 W |
| Gharbi, Oued el V | 148 | 31.50 N | 0.51 E |
| Gharbīyah, Aṣ-Ṣaḥrā' al- (Western Desert) ◆[2] | 140 | 27.00 N | 27.00 E |
| Ghardaïa | 148 | 32.31 N | 3.37 E |
| Ghardimaou | 36 | 36.26 N | 8.27 E |
| Gharghoda | 124 | 22.10 N | 83.21 E |
| Gharībwāl | 123 | 32.41 N | 73.10 E |
| Gharīfah | 132 | 33.38 N | 35.33 E |
| Gharig | 140 | 10.47 N | 27.33 E |
| Ghārīyat al-Gharbīyah | 132 | 32.41 N | 36.13 E |
| Ghārīyat ash-Sharqīyah | 132 | 32.40 N | 36.16 E |
| Gharo | 120 | 24.44 N | 67.35 E |
| Gharrāf, Shaṭṭ al- ≃ | 128 | 32.30 N | 45.48 E |
| Gharroli ◆[8] | 272a | 28.37 N | 77.20 E |
| Gharsa, Chott el ⊜ | 148 | 34.06 N | 7.50 E |
| Gharw, Jazīrat I | 142 | 31.21 N | 30.06 E |
| Gharyān | 146 | 32.10 N | 13.01 E |
| Ghaṣm | 132 | 32.33 N | 36.22 E |
| Ghāt | 146 | 24.58 N | 10.11 E |
| Ghātāl | 126 | 22.40 N | 87.43 E |
| Ghatampur | 272b | 22.54 N | 88.10 E |
| Ghatere, Mount ∧ | 175e | 7.49 S | 158.54 E |
| Ghates Occidentales → Western Ghāts ⋀ | 122 | 14.00 N | 75.00 E |
| Ghates Orientales → Eastern Ghāts ⋀ | 122 | 14.00 N | 78.50 E |
| Ghātkopar ◆[8] | 272c | 19.05 N | 72.54 E |
| Ghātprabha ≃ | 122 | 16.20 N | 75.48 E |
| Ghātsīla | 126 | 22.36 N | 86.29 E |
| Għawdex (Gozo) I | 36 | 36.03 N | 14.15 E |
| Ghawr ash-Sharqīyah, Qanāt al- (East Ghor Canal) ≚ | 132 | 32.41 N | 35.38 E |
| Ghaylah ∧[1] | 132 | 33.11 N | 37.05 E |
| Ghayl Bā Wazīr | 144 | 14.48 N | 49.21 E |
| Ghayl Bin Yumayn ⊤[4] | 144 | 15.33 N | 49.23 E |
| Ghayth, Wādī V | 132 | 30.59 N | 36.00 E |
| Ghazāl, Baḥr al- ≃ | 140 | 9.31 N | 30.25 E |
| Ghazal, Bahr el V | 146 | 13.01 N | 15.28 E |
| Ghazālat al-Khīs | 142 | 30.34 N | 31.34 E |
| Ghāziābād | 123 | 28.40 N | 77.26 E |
| Ghāzīpur, India | 124 | 25.35 N | 83.34 E |
| Ghazipur, India | 272b | 22.36 N | 88.34 E |
| Ghāzipur ◆[8] | 272a | 28.38 N | 77.19 E |
| Ghazīr | 130 | 34.01 N | 35.40 E |
| Ghazlūna | 120 | 31.24 N | 67.49 E |
| Ghaznī | 120 | 33.33 N | 68.26 E |
| Ghaznī □[4] | 120 | 33.15 N | 67.45 E |
| Ghaznī ≃ | 120 | 32.35 N | 67.58 E |
| Ghazni Khel | 123 | 32.33 N | 70.44 E |
| Ghazzah (Gaza), Gaza | 132 | 31.30 N | 34.28 E |
| Ghazzah, Lubnān | 132 | 33.40 N | 35.49 E |
| Gheā ≃ | 272b | 22.52 N | 88.19 E |
| Ghedi | 64 | 45.24 N | 10.16 E |
| Ghemme | 62 | 45.37 N | 8.25 E |
| Ghennes Heights | 279b | 40.09 N | 79.56 W |
| Ghent → Gent, Bel. | 50 | 51.03 N | 3.43 E |
| Ghent, Ky., U.S. | 218 | 38.44 N | 85.03 W |
| Ghent, N.Y., U.S. | 210 | 42.19 N | 73.36 W |
| Ghent, Oh., U.S. | 214 | 41.09 N | 81.38 W |
| Gheora ◆[8] | 272a | 28.42 N | 77.01 E |
| Gheorgheni | 38 | 46.43 N | 25.36 E |
| Gherla | 38 | 47.02 N | 23.55 E |
| Ghesar | 272c | 19.09 N | 73.05 E |
| Ghigo | 62 | 44.53 N | 7.03 E |
| Ghilarza | 71 | 40.07 N | 8.50 E |
| Ghilizane | 148 | 35.44 N | 0.30 E |
| Ghīn, Tall ∧ | 132 | 32.39 N | 36.43 E |
| Ghior | 126 | 23.54 N | 89.53 E |
| Ghislenghien (Gellingen) | 50 | 50.39 N | 3.52 E |
| Ghisonaccia | 36 | 42.00 N | 9.25 E |
| Ghizar ≃ | 123 | 36.15 N | 73.25 E |
| Ghizunabeana Islands II | 175e | 7.31 S | 158.42 E |
| Ghlin | 50 | 50.28 N | 3.53 E |
| Ghlò, Beinn a' ∧ | 46 | 56.50 N | 3.43 W |
| Ghogha | 120 | 21.41 N | 72.17 E |
| Gholson | 222 | 31.43 N | 97.12 W |
| Ghonda ◆[8] | 272a | 28.41 N | 77.16 E |
| Ghondi ◆[8] | 272a | 28.42 N | 77.16 E |
| Ghorāsahan | 124 | 26.50 N | 85.08 E |
| Ghoshpur, Bngl. | 126 | 23.27 N | 89.39 E |
| Ghoshpur, India | 272b | 22.23 N | 88.29 E |
| Ghotki | 120 | 28.01 N | 69.19 E |
| Ghowr □[4] | 128 | 34.00 N | 65.00 E |
| Ghubaysh | 140 | 12.09 N | 27.21 E |
| Ghudāf, Wādī al- V | 128 | 32.56 N | 43.30 E |
| Ghulayfiqah | 144 | 14.27 N | 43.02 E |
| Ghunthur | 130 | 34.23 N | 37.09 E |
| Ghurāb, Jabal ∧[2] | 142 | 28.58 N | 31.16 E |
| Ghurayrah | 144 | 18.37 N | 42.41 E |
| Ghūrīān | 128 | 34.21 N | 61.30 E |
| Ghushuri | 272b | 22.37 N | 88.22 E |
| Ghuwaybah, Wādī V | 142 | 29.36 N | 32.20 E |
| Ghuwayr, ʿAyn al- ⊤[4] | 132 | 31.37 N | 35.25 E |
| Ghuzzayil, Sabkhat ⊜ | 146 | 29.50 N | 19.35 E |
| Giaginskaja | 78 | 44.53 N | 40.05 E |
| Gianh ≃ | 110 | 17.40 N | 106.30 E |
| Giannutri, Isola di I | 66 | 42.15 N | 11.06 E |
| Giano, Monte ∧ | 66 | 42.25 N | 13.06 E |
| Giano dell'Umbria | 66 | 42.50 N | 12.35 E |
| Giant City State Park ♠ | 194 | 37.39 N | 89.12 W |
| Giant Mountain ∧ | 188 | 44.10 N | 73.44 W |
| Giant's Castle ∧ | 158 | 29.21 S | 29.27 E |
| Giant's Castle Game Reserve ◆[4] | 158 | 29.16 S | 29.30 E |
| Giant's Causeway ♠ | 48 | 55.14 N | 6.30 W |
| Giants Neck | 207 | 41.18 N | 72.13 W |
| Giants Stadium ♠ | 276 | 40.49 N | 74.05 W |
| Giants Tomb Island I | 212 | 44.55 N | 80.00 W |
| Gianyar | 115b | 8.32 S | 115.20 E |
| Gia Rai | 110 | 9.14 N | 105.28 E |
| Giardinello | 70 | 38.05 N | 13.09 E |
| Giardinetto | 68 | 41.19 N | 15.24 E |
| Giardini | 70 | 37.50 N | 15.17 E |
| Giarratana | 70 | 37.03 N | 14.48 E |
| Giarre | 70 | 37.43 N | 15.11 E |
| Giaveno | 62 | 45.02 N | 7.21 E |
| Giazza | 64 | 45.39 N | 11.07 E |
| Giba | 71 | 39.04 N | 8.38 E |
| Gibara | 240p | 21.07 N | 76.08 W |
| Gibbon, Mn., U.S. | 190 | 44.32 N | 94.31 W |
| Gibbon, Ne., U.S. | 198 | 40.44 N | 98.50 W |
| Gibbons | 182 | 53.50 N | 113.20 W |
| Gibbons Creek Lake ⊜[1] | 222 | 30.38 N | 96.04 W |
| Gibbonsville | 202 | 45.33 N | 113.55 W |
| Gibb River | 164 | 16.25 S | 126.22 E |
| Gibbs, Mount ∧ | 162 | 32.55 S | 120.00 E |
| Gibbsboro | 285 | 39.50 N | 74.58 W |
| Gibbstown | 208 | 39.49 N | 75.17 W |
| Gibellina | 70 | 37.47 N | 12.58 E |
| Gibeon | 156 | 25.09 S | 17.43 E |
| Gibilmanna, Santuario di ʋ[1] | 70 | 37.59 N | 14.02 E |
| Gibraleón | 34 | 37.23 N | 6.58 W |
| Gibraltar, Gib. | 34 | 36.08 N | 5.21 W |
| Gibraltar, Mi., U.S. | 216 | 42.06 N | 83.12 W |
| Gibraltar, Pa., U.S. | 208 | 40.17 N | 75.52 W |
| Gibraltar □[2], Europe | 22 | 36.08 N | 5.21 W |
| Gibraltar □[2], Europe | 34 | 36.08 N | 5.21 W |
| Gibraltar, Strait of (Estrecho de Gibraltar) Ʉ | 34 | 35.57 N | 5.36 W |
| Gibraltar Point ›, On., Can. | 275b | 43.36 N | 79.23 W |
| Gibraltar Point ›, Eng., U.K. | 44 | 53.05 N | 0.19 E |
| Gibsland | 194 | 32.32 N | 93.03 W |
| Gibson, Austl. | 162 | 33.39 S | 121.48 E |
| Gibson, Ga., U.S. | 192 | 33.14 N | 82.35 W |
| Gibson, N.Y., U.S. | 210 | 42.08 N | 76.59 W |
| Gibson, Pa., U.S. | 210 | 41.44 N | 75.38 W |
| Gibson ≃ | 212 | 44.58 N | 79.51 W |
| Gibson, Lake ⊜[1] | 284a | 43.06 N | 79.14 W |
| Gibsonburg | 214 | 41.23 N | 83.19 W |
| Gibson City | 216 | 40.27 N | 88.22 W |
| Gibson Desert ◆[2] | 162 | 24.30 S | 126.00 E |
| Gibson Hill ∧[2] | 214 | 41.51 N | 80.10 W |
| Gibsonia, Fl., U.S. | 220 | 28.06 N | 81.58 W |
| Gibsonia, Pa., U.S. | 214 | 40.38 N | 79.59 W |
| Gibson Indian Reserve ◆[4] | 212 | 45.01 N | 79.44 W |
| Gibson Island I | 208 | 39.05 N | 76.26 W |
| Gibsons | 182 | 49.24 N | 123.30 W |
| Gibsonton | 220 | 27.51 N | 82.22 W |
| Gicäki dağ ∧ | 84 | 40.25 N | 49.01 E |
| Gidajevo | 24 | 59.57 N | 52.22 E |
| Gidami | 144 | 9.58 N | 34.37 E |
| Gidda | 144 | 9.34 N | 35.23 E |
| Giddalūr | 122 | 15.21 N | 78.55 E |
| Giddarbāha | 123 | 30.12 N | 74.40 E |
| Giddings | 222 | 30.10 N | 96.56 W |
| Gideälven ≃ | 26 | 63.20 N | 19.08 E |
| Gidea Park ◆[8] | 260 | 51.35 N | 0.12 E |
| Gideåvallen | 26 | 63.29 N | 18.58 E |
| Gideon | 194 | 36.27 N | 89.55 W |
| Gidgee | 162 | 27.16 S | 119.22 E |
| Gidgi, Lake ⊜ | 162 | 29.16 S | 126.03 E |
| Gidhni | 126 | 22.29 N | 86.51 E |
| Gidole | 144 | 5.38 N | 37.30 E |
| Gidrotorf | 80 | 56.28 N | 43.33 E |
| Giebelstadt | 56 | 49.39 N | 9.56 E |
| Gieboldehausen | 52 | 51.36 N | 10.13 E |
| Giedraičiai | 76 | 55.05 N | 25.15 E |
| Gielow | 54 | 53.42 N | 12.44 E |
| Gielsdorf | 264a | 52.36 N | 13.52 E |
| Gien | 50 | 47.42 N | 2.38 E |
| Giengen | 56 | 48.37 N | 10.14 E |
| Giens | 62 | 43.02 N | 6.08 E |
| Gier ≃ | 62 | 45.35 N | 4.46 E |
| Gierath | 263 | 51.07 N | 6.33 E |
| Gierle | 56 | 51.16 N | 4.51 E |
| Gieselwerder | 52 | 51.36 N | 9.33 E |
| Giesen | 52 | 52.12 N | 9.54 E |
| Giesenkirchen ◆[8] | 263 | 51.09 N | 6.30 E |
| Giessbachfälle L | 58 | 46.42 N | 8.03 E |
| Giessen | 56 | 50.35 N | 8.40 E |
| Giessen □[5] | 56 | 50.40 N | 8.40 E |
| Gieten | 52 | 53.00 N | 6.46 E |
| Giethoorn | 52 | 52.43 N | 6.05 E |
| Gièvres | 50 | 47.16 N | 1.40 E |
| Giez | 62 | 45.45 N | 6.15 E |
| Giffone | 68 | 38.27 N | 16.10 E |
| Gifford, Scot., U.K. | 46 | 55.54 N | 2.45 W |
| Gifford, Fl., U.S. | 220 | 27.40 N | 80.24 W |
| Gifford, Il., U.S. | 216 | 40.18 N | 88.01 W |
| Gifford, In., U.S. | 216 | 41.06 N | 87.01 W |
| Gifford, Pa., U.S. | 214 | 41.51 N | 78.36 W |
| Gifford ≃ | 176 | 70.21 N | 83.05 W |
| Gifford Creek | 162 | 24.05 S | 116.11 E |
| Gifford Pinchot State Park ♠ | 208 | 40.04 N | 76.53 W |
| Giffre ≃ | 58 | 46.05 N | 6.30 E |
| Gifhorn | 52 | 52.29 N | 10.33 E |
| Giflitz | 56 | 51.09 N | 9.07 E |
| Gif-sur-Yvette | 261 | 48.42 N | 2.08 E |
| Gifu | 94 | 35.25 N | 136.45 E |
| Gifu □[5] | 94 | 35.45 N | 137.00 E |
| Gigant | 80 | 46.30 N | 41.20 E |
| Giganta, Sierra de la ⋀ | 232 | 26.00 N | 111.30 W |
| Gigante | 246 | 2.23 N | 75.33 W |
| Gigante Islands II | 116 | 11.36 N | 123.20 E |
| Gigen | 38 | 43.42 N | 24.29 E |
| Gigena → Alcira | 252 | 32.45 S | 64.20 W |
| Giggleswick | 44 | 54.04 N | 2.17 W |
| Gigha, Sound of Ʉ | 46 | 55.41 N | 5.42 W |
| Gigha Island I | 46 | 55.41 N | 5.46 W |
| Gig Harbor | 224 | 47.19 N | 122.34 W |
| Giglio, Isola del I | 66 | 42.21 N | 10.54 E |
| Giglio Castello | 66 | 42.22 N | 10.54 E |
| Gigliola | 66 | 44.51 N | 12.14 E |
| Giglio Porto | 66 | 42.22 N | 10.55 E |
| Gigmoto | 116 | 13.47 N | 124.23 E |
| Gignod | 62 | 45.46 N | 7.17 E |
| Gihu → Gifu | 94 | 35.25 N | 136.45 E |
| Gijón | 34 | 43.32 N | 5.40 W |
| Gikongoro | 154 | 2.29 S | 29.34 E |
| Gila ≃ | 200 | 32.43 N | 114.33 W |
| Gila, Middle Fork ≃ | 200 | 33.14 N | 108.14 W |
| Gila Bend | 200 | 32.56 N | 112.42 W |
| Gila Bend Indian Reservation ◆[4] | 200 | 33.00 N | 112.46 W |
| Gila Bend Mountains ⋀ | 200 | 33.10 N | 113.10 W |
| Gila Cliff Dwellings National Monument ♠ | 200 | 33.02 N | 108.16 W |
| Gila Mountains ⋀ | 200 | 33.05 N | 109.50 W |
| Gīlān □[4] | 128 | 37.15 N | 49.30 E |
| Gīlān-e Gharb | 128 | 34.08 N | 45.55 E |
| Gila River Indian Reservation ◆[4] | 200 | 33.12 N | 112.00 W |
| Gilātala | 126 | 22.36 N | 89.41 E |
| Giläzi Dili burnu › | 84 | 40.50 N | 49.33 E |
| Gilberdyke | 44 | 53.45 N | 0.44 W |
| Gilbert, La., U.S. | 194 | 32.02 N | 91.39 W |
| Gilbert, Mn., U.S. | 190 | 47.29 N | 92.27 W |
| Gilbert ≃, Austl. | 166 | 16.35 S | 141.15 E |
| Gilbert ≃, Austl. | 168b | 34.22 S | 138.40 E |
| Gilbert, Mount ∧ | 182 | 50.51 N | 124.20 W |
| Gilbert Airport ⊠ | 279a | 41.22 N | 81.58 W |
| Gilbert Island I | 219 | 39.35 N | 91.11 W |
| Gilbert Islands → Kiribati □[1] | 14 | 5.00 S | 170.00 W |
| Gilbert Lake ⊜ | 281 | 42.34 N | 83.17 W |
| Gilbert Lake State Park ♠ | 210 | 42.36 N | 75.08 W |
| Gilberton | 210 | 40.48 N | 76.13 W |
| Gilbertown | 194 | 31.52 N | 88.19 W |
| Gilbert Peak ∧ | 224 | 46.30 N | 121.25 W |
| Gilbert Plains | 184 | 51.09 N | 100.29 W |
| Gilbert River | 166 | 18.09 S | 142.52 E |
| Gilbert Seamount ✢[3] | 16 | 52.50 N | 150.10 W |
| Gilbertsville, N.Y., U.S. | 210 | 42.28 N | 75.19 W |
| Gilbertsville, Pa., U.S. | 208 | 40.19 N | 75.37 W |
| Gilbertville | 207 | 42.18 N | 72.12 W |
| Gilbjerg Hoved › | 41 | 56.08 N | 12.17 E |
| Gilboa | 216 | 41.01 N | 83.55 W |
| Gilboaʿ, Haré ⋀[2] | 132 | 32.30 N | 35.23 E |
| Gilbués | 250 | 9.50 S | 45.21 W |
| Gilching | 60 | 48.07 N | 11.17 E |
| Gildehaus | 52 | 52.18 N | 7.06 E |
| Gildford | 202 | 48.34 N | 110.17 W |
| Gilead | 216 | 41.48 N | 85.09 W |
| Giles, Arroyo de ≃ | 258 | 34.20 S | 59.23 W |
| Giles Meteorological Station ʋ[3] | 162 | 25.02 S | 128.18 E |
| Giles Point › | 168b | 35.03 S | 137.45 E |
| Gilette | 62 | 43.51 N | 7.10 E |
| Gilford | 48 | 54.23 N | 6.22 W |
| Gilford Island I | 182 | 50.45 N | 126.25 W |
| Gilford Park | 208 | 39.58 N | 74.08 W |
| Gilgai | 162 | 31.15 S | 119.56 E |
| Gilgandra | 166 | 31.42 S | 148.39 E |
| Gilgil | 154 | 0.30 S | 36.19 E |
| Gil Gil Creek ≃ | 166 | 29.10 S | 148.51 E |
| Gilgit | 123 | 35.55 N | 74.18 E |
| Gilgit ≃ | 123 | 35.44 N | 74.38 E |
| Gilgo Island I | 276 | 40.38 N | 73.25 W |
| Gilgo State Park ♠ | 276 | 40.38 N | 73.22 W |
| Gilima | 154 | 3.55 N | 28.22 E |
| Gilimanuk | 115a | 8.10 S | 114.26 E |
| Gilirang | 112 | 3.55 S | 120.09 E |
| Gil Island I | 182 | 53.13 N | 129.15 W |
| Gill, Lough ⊜ | 48 | 54.16 N | 8.24 W |
| Gillam | 184 | 56.21 N | 94.43 W |
| Gilleland Creek ≃ | 222 | 30.13 N | 97.32 W |
| Gilleleje | 41 | 56.07 N | 12.19 E |
| Gillen, Lake ⊜ | 162 | 26.11 S | 124.38 E |
| Gilles, Lake ⊜ | 166 | 32.50 S | 136.45 E |
| Gillespie | 219 | 39.07 N | 89.49 W |
| Gillespies Point › | 172 | 43.24 S | 169.50 E |
| Gillett, Ar., U.S. | 194 | 34.07 N | 91.22 W |
| Gillett, Pa., U.S. | 210 | 41.57 N | 76.48 W |
| Gillett, Wi., U.S. | 190 | 44.53 N | 88.18 W |
| Gillette, N.J., U.S. | 276 | 40.41 N | 74.28 W |
| Gillette, Wy., U.S. | 198 | 44.17 N | 105.30 W |
| Gillette Castle State Park ♠ | 207 | 41.26 N | 72.25 W |
| Gillian, Lake ⊜ | 176 | 69.32 N | 75.23 W |
| Gillingham, Eng., U.K. | 42 | 51.24 N | 0.33 E |
| Gillingham, Eng., U.K. | 42 | 51.02 N | 2.17 W |
| Gillingham □[8] | 260 | 51.22 N | 0.35 E |
| Gills Rock | 190 | 45.17 N | 87.01 W |
| Gilman, Ct., U.S. | 207 | 41.34 N | 72.11 W |
| Gilman, Il., U.S. | 216 | 40.46 N | 87.59 W |
| Gilman, Ia., U.S. | 190 | 41.52 N | 92.47 W |
| Gilman, Wi., U.S. | 190 | 45.10 N | 90.48 W |
| Gilman Hot Springs | 228 | 33.50 N | 116.59 W |
| Gilman Lake | 285 | 39.41 N | 75.11 W |
| Gilmer, Il., U.S. | 278 | 42.14 N | 88.02 W |
| Gilmer, Tx., U.S. | 222 | 32.43 N | 94.56 W |
| Gilmer Park | 216 | 41.36 N | 86.15 W |
| Gilmore | 171b | 35.20 S | 148.11 E |
| Gilmore City | 198 | 42.44 N | 94.27 W |
| Gilmore Creek ≃ | 171b | 35.18 S | 148.13 E |
| Gilo ≃ | 144 | 8.10 N | 33.15 E |
| Gilroy | 226 | 37.00 N | 121.34 W |
| Gilserberg | 56 | 50.57 N | 9.04 E |
| Gilsizer Slough ≃ | 226 | 38.58 N | 121.44 W |
| Gilston Park ♠ | 260 | 51.48 N | 0.04 E |
| Giltner | 198 | 40.46 N | 98.09 W |
| Gil'uj ≃ | 89 | 53.58 N | 127.30 E |
| Giluwe, Mount ∧ | 164 | 6.05 S | 143.50 E |
| Gilwern | 42 | 51.51 N | 3.06 W |
| Gilze | 52 | 51.33 N | 4.57 E |
| Gimån ≃ | 26 | 62.28 N | 16.20 E |
| Gimbi | 144 | 9.10 N | 35.42 E |
| Gimborn | 52 | 51.03 N | 7.28 E |
| Gimcheon → Kimch'ŏn | 98 | 36.07 N | 128.05 E |
| Gimie, Mount ∧ | 241f | 13.52 N | 61.01 W |
| Gimigliano | 68 | 38.58 N | 16.32 E |
| Gimlet | 218 | 38.13 N | 83.09 W |
| Gimli | 184 | 50.38 N | 96.59 W |
| Gimo | 40 | 60.11 N | 18.11 E |
| Gimoly | 24 | 63.03 N | 32.19 E |
| Gimone ≃ | 32 | 44.00 N | 1.06 E |
| Gimont | 32 | 43.38 N | 0.53 E |
| Gimpu | 112 | 1.36 S | 120.02 E |
| Ginderich | 263 | 51.39 N | 6.32 E |
| Ginebra → Genève | 58 | 46.12 N | 6.09 E |
| Gineste, Col de la )( | 62 | 43.15 N | 5.27 E |
| Gingell | 216 | 42.43 N | 83.17 W |
| Gingera, Mount ∧ | 171b | 35.35 S | 148.47 E |
| Ginger Hill | 279b | 40.12 N | 80.00 W |
| Ginger Island I | 240m | 18.24 N | 64.28 W |
| Gingin, Austl. | 162 | 31.21 S | 115.42 E |
| Gin Gin, Austl. | 166 | 25.00 S | 151.58 E |
| Gingindlovu | 158 | 29.02 S | 31.30 E |
| Gingoog | 116 | 8.50 N | 125.07 E |
| Gingoog Bay c | 116 | 8.59 N | 125.05 E |
| Gingst | 54 | 54.27 N | 13.16 E |
| Ginir | 144 | 7.07 N | 40.46 E |
| Ginkakuji Temple ʋ[1] | 270 | 35.03 N | 135.47 E |
| Ginkgo State Park ♠ | 202 | 46.59 N | 120.01 W |
| Ginnosar | 132 | 32.51 N | 35.31 E |
| Ginosa | 68 | 40.35 N | 16.46 E |
| Ginostra | 70 | 38.47 N | 15.11 E |
| Ginowan | 174m | 26.17 N | 127.46 E |
| Ginoza | 174m | 26.28 N | 127.57 E |
| Ginter | 214 | 40.46 N | 78.23 W |
| Ginza ◆[8] | 268 | 35.40 N | 139.47 E |
| Gioi | 68 | 40.17 N | 15.13 E |
| Gioia, Golfo di c | 68 | 38.30 N | 15.45 E |
| Gioia dei Marsi | 66 | 41.57 N | 13.42 E |
| Gioia del Colle | 68 | 40.48 N | 16.56 E |
| Gioia Tauro | 68 | 38.26 N | 15.54 E |
| Gioia Vecchio | 66 | 41.54 N | 13.44 E |
| Gioiosa Ionica | 68 | 38.20 N | 16.18 E |
| Gioiosa Marea | 70 | 38.10 N | 14.54 E |
| Giong Rieng | 110 | 9.55 N | 105.19 E |
| Giornico | 58 | 46.24 N | 8.52 E |
| Giovi, Passo dei )( | 62 | 44.33 N | 8.57 E |
| Giovinazzo | 68 | 41.11 N | 16.40 E |
| Giporlos | 116 | 11.07 N | 125.27 E |
| Gipping ≃ | 42 | 52.04 N | 1.10 E |
| Gipsy | 214 | 40.48 N | 78.53 W |
| Gipuzkoako □[4] | 34 | 43.10 N | 2.10 W |
| Giraglia, Île de la I | 62 | 43.02 N | 9.24 E |
| Giralia | 162 | 22.41 S | 114.21 E |
| Giraltovce | 30 | 49.07 N | 21.31 E |
| Girard, Il., U.S. | 219 | 39.26 N | 89.46 W |
| Girard, Ks., U.S. | 198 | 37.30 N | 94.50 W |
| Girard, Mi., U.S. | 216 | 42.02 N | 85.00 W |
| Girard, Oh., U.S. | 214 | 41.09 N | 80.42 W |
| Girard, Pa., U.S. | 214 | 42.00 N | 80.19 W |
| Girard, Tx., U.S. | 196 | 33.22 N | 100.40 W |
| Girardot | 246 | 4.18 N | 74.48 W |
| Girardville | 208 | 40.47 N | 76.17 W |
| Giraud, Pointe › | 240d | 15.19 N | 61.15 W |
| Giraul ≃ | 152 | 15.04 S | 12.08 E |
| Giraumont | 56 | 49.10 N | 5.55 E |
| Girdletree | 208 | 38.05 N | 75.23 W |
| Giresun | 130 | 40.55 N | 38.24 E |
| Giresun □[4] | 130 | 40.30 N | 38.30 E |
| Giresun Dağları ⋀ | 130 | 40.30 N | 39.00 E |
| Girgarre | 166 | 36.24 S | 144.59 E |
| Girgaum ◆[8] | 272c | 18.57 N | 72.48 E |
| Girgenti → Agrigento | 70 | 37.18 N | 13.35 E |
| Girgir, Cape › | 164 | 3.50 S | 144.34 E |
| Giri ≃ | 152 | 0.28 N | 17.59 E |
| Girīdīh | 126 | 24.11 N | 86.18 E |
| Girifalco | 68 | 38.49 N | 16.25 E |
| Girilambone | 166 | 31.15 S | 146.54 E |
| Girmeli | 130 | 37.07 N | 41.26 E |
| Girna ≃ | 122 | 21.08 N | 75.19 E |
| Gir National Park ♠ | 120 | 21.00 N | 70.50 E |
| Girne (Kyrenia) | 130 | 35.20 N | 33.19 E |
| Giro, Nig. | 150 | 11.06 N | 4.46 E |
| Giro, Zaïre | 154 | 3.08 N | 29.15 E |
| Giromagny | 58 | 47.45 N | 6.50 E |
| Girón, Ec. | 246 | 3.10 S | 79.08 W |
| Giron, Fr. | 58 | 46.14 N | 5.46 E |
| Girona | 34 | 41.59 N | 2.49 E |
| Girona □[4] | 34 | 42.00 N | 2.40 E |
| Gironde □[5] | 32 | 44.45 N | 0.35 W |
| Gironde c[1] | 32 | 45.20 N | 0.45 W |
| Gironville-sous-les-Côtes | 56 | 48.48 N | 5.40 E |
| Girou ≃ | 32 | 43.46 N | 1.23 E |
| Girouxville | 182 | 55.45 N | 117.20 W |
| Gīr Range ⋀ | 120 | 21.18 N | 71.00 E |
| Girton | 42 | 52.14 N | 0.05 E |
| Girtys Run ≃ | 279b | 40.28 N | 79.58 W |
| Giru | 166 | 19.31 S | 147.06 E |
| Giruá | 252 | 28.02 S | 54.21 W |
| Girvan | 44 | 55.15 N | 4.51 W |
| Girvan, Water of ≃ | 44 | 55.15 N | 4.51 W |
| Girvas | 24 | 62.30 N | 33.40 E |
| Gisborne, Austl. | 169 | 37.29 S | 144.35 E |
| Gisborne, N.Z. | 172 | 38.40 S | 178.01 E |
| Gisborne Lake ⊜ | 186 | 47.48 N | 54.50 W |
| Giscome | 182 | 54.04 N | 122.22 W |
| Gisenyi | 154 | 1.42 S | 29.15 E |
| Gishyita | 154 | 2.11 S | 29.18 E |
| Gislaved | 26 | 57.18 N | 13.32 E |
| Gislev | 41 | 55.13 N | 10.37 E |
| Gislinge | 41 | 55.44 N | 11.33 E |
| Gislövs läge | 41 | 55.21 N | 13.14 E |
| Gisors | 50 | 49.17 N | 1.47 E |
| Gissar | 85 | 38.33 N | 68.35 E |
| Gissarskij chrebet ⋀ | 85 | 39.00 N | 68.40 E |
| Gisselfeld | 41 | 55.18 N | 11.59 E |
| Gissi | 66 | 42.01 N | 14.33 E |
| Gisslarbo | 40 | 59.38 N | 15.49 E |
| Gistel | 50 | 51.10 N | 2.57 E |
| Giswil | 58 | 46.50 N | 8.11 E |
| Gitambo | 154 | 4.21 N | 24.45 E |
| Gitarama | 154 | 2.07 S | 29.45 E |
| Gitega | 154 | 3.26 S | 29.56 E |
| Gittelde | 52 | 51.48 N | 10.10 E |
| Giuba, Isole II | 144 | 0.45 S | 42.19 E |
| Giudicarie, Valli V | 64 | 45.58 N | 10.45 E |
| Giugliano in Campania | 68 | 40.56 N | 14.12 E |
| Giuliana | 70 | 37.40 N | 13.14 E |
| Giulianova | 66 | 42.45 N | 13.57 E |
| Giulie, Alpi → Julian Alps ⋀ | 36 | 46.00 N | 14.00 E |
| Giumbo → Jumboo | 144 | 0.15 S | 42.38 E |
| Giurgiu | 38 | 43.53 N | 25.57 E |
| Giurgiu □[6] | 38 | 44.10 N | 26.00 E |
| Giussano | 62 | 45.42 N | 9.14 E |
| Giuvala, Pasul )( | 38 | 45.26 N | 25.17 E |
| Givʿatayim | 132 | 32.04 N | 34.48 E |
| Givʿat Brenner | 132 | 31.52 N | 34.48 E |
| Give | 41 | 55.51 N | 9.15 E |
| Giverny | 50 | 49.04 N | 1.32 E |
| Givet | 56 | 50.08 N | 4.50 E |
| Givors | 62 | 45.35 N | 4.46 E |
| Givrine, Col de la )( | 58 | 46.27 N | 6.05 E |
| Givry | 58 | 46.47 N | 4.45 E |
| Givry-en-Argonne | 56 | 48.57 N | 4.53 E |
| Giyon | 144 | 8.30 N | 38.00 E |
| Giza → Al-Jīzah | 142 | 30.01 N | 31.13 E |
| Gīzāb | 120 | 33.23 N | 66.16 E |
| Gižduvan | 128 | 40.06 N | 64.41 E |
| Gizen | 140 | 10.49 N | 34.48 E |
| Gizeux | 50 | 47.24 N | 0.12 E |
| Gižiga | 74 | 62.03 N | 160.30 E |
| Gižiginskaja guba c | 74 | 61.30 N | 158.00 E |
| Gizo | 175e | 8.06 S | 156.51 E |
| Gizo Island I | 175e | 8.04 S | 156.48 E |
| Giżycko | 30 | 54.03 N | 21.47 E |
| Gizzeria | 68 | 38.59 N | 16.12 E |
| Gjedved | 41 | 55.56 N | 9.51 E |
| Gjern | 41 | 56.14 N | 9.45 E |
| Gjirokastër | 38 | 40.05 N | 20.10 E |
| Gjoa Haven | 176 | 68.38 N | 95.57 W |
| Gjøvik | 26 | 60.48 N | 10.42 E |
| Gjuesevo | 38 | 42.14 N | 22.28 E |
| Gjuhëzës, Kep i › | 38 | 40.25 N | 19.18 E |
| Glace Bay | 186 | 46.12 N | 59.57 W |
| Glacier, B.C., Can. | 182 | 51.16 N | 117.31 W |
| Glacier, Wa., U.S. | 224 | 48.53 N | 121.56 W |
| Glacier Bay c | 180 | 58.40 N | 136.00 W |
| Glacier Bay National Park ♠ | 180 | 58.45 N | 136.30 W |
| Glacier Hills | 276 | 40.51 N | 74.28 W |
| Glacier National Park ♠, B.C., Can. | 182 | 51.15 N | 117.35 W |
| Glacier National Park ♠, Mt., U.S. | 202 | 48.35 N | 113.40 W |
| Glacier Peak ∧ | 224 | 48.07 N | 121.07 W |
| Glad' | 76 | 59.07 N | 32.06 E |
| Gl'ad'anskoje | 86 | 54.54 N | 65.06 E |
| Gladbach → Mönchengladbach | 56 | 51.12 N | 6.28 E |
| Gladbeck | 52 | 51.34 N | 6.59 E |
| Gladbrook | 190 | 42.11 N | 92.42 W |
| Gladden | 279b | 40.21 N | 80.11 W |
| Gladden Heights | 279b | 40.22 N | 80.15 W |
| Glade Creek ≃ | 202 | 45.54 N | 119.42 W |
| Gladenbach | 56 | 50.46 N | 8.34 E |
| Glades □[6] | 220 | 26.59 N | 81.12 W |
| Glade Spring | 192 | 36.47 N | 81.46 W |
| Gladesville | 274a | 33.50 S | 151.08 E |
| Gladewater | 222 | 32.32 N | 94.56 W |
| Gladewater, Lake ⊜[1] | 222 | 32.35 N | 94.57 W |
| Gladsakse | 41 | 55.44 N | 12.29 E |
| Gladstone, Austl. | 166 | 23.51 S | 151.16 E |
| Gladstone, Austl. | 166 | 33.17 S | 138.22 E |
| Gladstone, Mb., Can. | 184 | 50.13 N | 98.57 W |
| Gladstone, Mi., U.S. | 190 | 45.51 N | 87.01 W |
| Gladstone, Mo., U.S. | 194 | 39.12 N | 94.33 W |
| Gladstone, N.J., U.S. | 210 | 40.43 N | 74.39 W |
| Gladstone, Or., U.S. | 224 | 45.22 N | 122.35 W |
| Gladstone Brook ≃ | 276 | 40.43 N | 74.40 W |
| Gladwin | 190 | 43.58 N | 84.29 W |
| Gladwyne | 285 | 40.02 N | 75.17 W |
| Gladys Lake ⊜ | 180 | 59.55 N | 132.55 W |
| Glænø I | 41 | 55.12 N | 11.28 E |
| Glafsfjorden ⊜ | 26 | 59.34 N | 12.37 E |
| Glåma ≃ | 26 | 59.12 N | 10.57 E |
| Glamis | 46 | 56.36 N | 3.00 W |
| Glamis Castle ⊥ | 46 | 56.37 N | 3.00 W |
| Glamoč | 36 | 44.03 N | 16.51 E |
| Glamor Lake ⊜ | 212 | 44.58 N | 78.23 W |
| Glamsbjerg | 41 | 55.16 N | 10.07 E |
| Glan | 116 | 5.49 N | 125.10 E |
| Glan ⊜ | 40 | 58.37 N | 15.58 E |
| Glan ≃, Dtsch. | 56 | 49.47 N | 7.43 E |
| Glan ≃, Öst. | 61 | 46.36 N | 14.25 E |
| Glan ≃, Pil. | 116 | 5.50 N | 125.12 E |
| Glanamman | 42 | 51.48 N | 3.54 W |
| Gland | 58 | 46.26 N | 6.16 E |
| Gland ≃ | 50 | 49.55 N | 4.05 E |
| Glandon, Col du )( | 62 | 45.14 N | 6.11 E |
| Glandorf, Dtsch. | 52 | 52.05 N | 7.59 E |
| Glandorf, Oh., U.S. | 216 | 41.01 N | 84.04 W |
| Glâne ≃ | 58 | 46.47 N | 7.08 E |
| Glanegg | 61 | 46.44 N | 14.11 E |
| Glanerbrug | 52 | 52.13 N | 6.58 E |
| Glanmire | 48 | 51.55 N | 8.24 W |
| Glanshammar | 40 | 59.19 N | 15.24 E |


**Symbols** in the index entries represent the broad categories identified in the key at the right. Symbols with superior numbers (⋀[1]) identify subcategories (see complete key on page *I · 1).*

**Symbole** im Register stellen die rechts im Schlüssel erklärten Kategorien dar. Symbole mit hochgestellten Ziffern (⋀[1]) bezeichnen Unterabteilungen einer Kategorie (vgl. vollständiger Schlüssel auf Seite *I · 1).*

**Los símbolos** incluídos en el texto del índice representan las grandes categorías identificadas con la clave a la derecha. Los símbolos con numeros en su parte superior (⋀[1]) identifican las subcategorías (véase la clave completa en la página *I · 1).*

**Les symboles** de l'index représentent les catégories indiquées dans la légende à droite. Les symboles suivis d'un indice (⋀[1]) représentent des sous-catégories (voir légende complète à la page *I · 1).*

**Os símbolos** incluídos no texto do índice representam as grandes categorias identificadas com a chave à direita. Os símbolos com números em sua parte superior (⋀[1]) identificam as subcategorias (veja-se a chave completa à página *I · 1).*

| | | | | | |
|---|---|---|---|---|---|
| ∧ Mountain | Berg | Montaña | Montagne | Montanha |
| ⋀ Mountains | Gebirge | Montañas | Montagnes | Montanhas |
| )( Pass | Paß | Paso | Col | Passo |
| V Valley, Canyon | Tal, Cañon | Valle, Cañón | Vallée, Canyon | Vale, Canhão |
| ≚ Plain | Ebene | Llano | Plaine | Planície |
| › Cape | Kap | Cabo | Cap | Cabo |
| I Island | Insel | Isla | Île | Ilha |
| II Islands | Inseln | Islas | Îles | Ilhas |
| ⊥ Other Topographic Features | Andere Topographische Objekte | Otros Elementos Topográficos | Autres données topographiques | Outros acidentes topográficos |

ESPAÑOL — Nombre, Página, Lat.°′, Long.°′ W = Oeste
FRANÇAIS — Nom, Page, Lat.°′, Long.°′ W = Ouest
PORTUGUÊS — Nome, Página, Lat.°′, Long.°′ W = Oeste


| Nombre | Página | Lat.°′ | Long.°′ W = Oeste |
|---|---|---|---|
| Glanum ⊥ | 62 | 43.49 N | 4.47 E |
| Glan-y-Don | 262 | 53.19 N | 3.15 W |
| Glaris → Glarus | 58 | 47.02 N | 9.04 E |
| Glarner Alpen ⋏ | 58 | 46.55 N | 9.00 E |
| Glärnisch ⋏ | 58 | 47.00 N | 9.00 E |
| Glarus | 58 | 47.02 N | 9.04 E |
| Glarus □3 | 58 | 47.00 N | 9.03 E |
| Glascarnoch, Loch ◎ | 46 | 57.40 N | 4.50 W |
| Glasco, Ks., U.S. | 198 | 39.21 N | 97.50 W |
| Glasco, N.Y., U.S. | 210 | 42.02 N | 73.56 W |
| Glasgow, Scot., U.K. | 46 | 55.53 N | 4.15 W |
| Glasgow, Il., U.S. | 219 | 39.33 N | 90.29 W |
| Glasgow, Ky., U.S. | 194 | 36.59 N | 85.54 W |
| Glasgow, Mo., U.S. | 194 | 39.13 N | 92.50 W |
| Glasgow, Mt., U.S. | 202 | 48.11 N | 106.38 W |
| Glasgow, Pa., U.S. | 214 | 40.42 N | 78.27 W |
| Glasgow, Va., U.S. | 192 | 37.38 N | 79.27 W |
| Glasgow (Abbotsinch) Airport ✈ | 46 | 55.52 N | 4.26 W |
| Glashütte ◆8 | 263 | 51.13 N | 6.52 E |
| Glaslyn | 184 | 53.21 N | 108.22 W |
| Glaslyn ≐ | 44 | 52.56 N | 4.06 W |
| Glas Maol ∧ | 46 | 56.52 N | 3.22 W |
| Glasow | 54 | 52.20 N | 13.28 E |
| Glass, Loch ◎ | 46 | 57.43 N | 4.30 W |
| Glassan | 48 | 53.28 N | 7.52 W |
| Glassboro | 208 | 39.42 N | 75.06 W |
| Glassboro State College ᵾ2 | 285 | 39.42 N | 75.07 W |
| Glass House Mountains | 171a | 26.53 S | 152.58 E |
| Glassmanor | 284c | 38.49 N | 76.59 W |
| Glass Mountains ⋏ | 196 | 30.25 N | 103.15 W |
| Glassport | 214 | 40.19 N | 79.53 W |
| Glastonbury, Eng., U.K. | 42 | 51.06 N | 2.43 W |
| Glastonbury, Ct., U.S. | 207 | 41.42 N | 72.36 W |
| Glatt ≐ | 58 | 47.34 N | 8.28 E |
| Glatten | 58 | 48.26 N | 8.31 E |
| Glattfelden | 58 | 47.33 N | 8.30 E |
| Glatz → Kłodzko | 30 | 50.27 N | 16.39 E |
| Glaubitz | 54 | 51.19 N | 13.22 E |
| Glauchau | 54 | 50.49 N | 12.32 E |
| Glaven ≐ | 42 | 52.58 N | 1.03 E |
| Glaze Brook ≐ | 262 | 53.25 N | 2.27 W |
| Glazebury | 262 | 53.28 N | 2.30 W |
| Glaževo | 76 | 59.41 N | 32.05 E |
| Glazok | 80 | 53.06 N | 40.42 E |
| Glazov | 80 | 58.09 N | 52.40 E |
| Glazovo, Ross. | 82 | 54.47 N | 37.34 E |
| Glazovo, Ross. | 82 | 55.38 N | 35.46 E |
| Glazovo, Ross. | 82 | 54.57 N | 37.22 E |
| Glazunovka | 76 | 52.30 N | 36.19 E |
| Glazunovskaja | 80 | 49.50 N | 42.51 E |
| Gleason | 194 | 36.12 N | 88.36 W |
| Glebovka | 78 | 46.38 N | 39.59 E |
| Glebovo, Ross. | 82 | 56.54 N | 37.43 E |
| Glebovo, Ross. | 82 | 56.39 N | 38.42 E |
| Gleed | 224 | 46.40 N | 120.37 W |
| Glehn | 263 | 51.10 N | 6.35 E |
| Gleichen | 182 | 50.52 N | 113.03 W |
| Gleidingen | 52 | 52.16 N | 9.50 E |
| Gleinalpe ⋏ | 61 | 47.15 N | 15.03 E |
| Gleisdorf | 61 | 47.06 N | 15.44 E |
| Gleiwitz → Gliwice | 30 | 50.17 N | 18.40 E |
| Glejbjerg | 41 | 55.33 N | 8.50 E |
| Glemsford | 42 | 52.06 N | 0.41 E |
| Glen ≐, Ire. | 48 | 54.38 N | 8.40 W |
| Glen ≐, Eng., U.K. | 42 | 52.51 N | 0.06 W |
| Glen Acres | 285 | 39.58 N | 75.34 W |
| Glen Afton | 172 | 37.37 S | 175.02 E |
| Glen Alice | 170 | 33.02 S | 150.13 E |
| Glen Allen | 208 | 37.39 N | 77.30 W |
| Glen Alpine | 192 | 35.43 N | 81.46 W |
| Glenamoy | 48 | 54.14 N | 9.42 W |
| Glenarchy | 275b | 43.29 N | 79.46 W |
| Glenarden | 208 | 38.56 N | 76.52 W |
| Glenarm, N. Ire., U.K. | 48 | 54.58 N | 5.57 W |
| Glen Arm, Md., U.S. | 284b | 39.27 N | 76.30 W |
| Glen Ashton Farms | 285 | 40.06 N | 74.55 W |
| Glen Aubrey | 210 | 42.15 N | 76.01 W |
| Glenavon, Sk., Can. | 184 | 50.10 N | 103.10 W |
| Glen Avon, S. Afr. | 158 | 31.43 S | 26.12 E |
| Glen Avon, Ca., U.S. | 228 | 34.01 N | 117.29 W |
| Glenavy, N.Z. | 172 | 44.55 S | 171.06 E |
| Glenavy, N. Ire., U.K. | 48 | 54.36 N | 6.13 W |
| Glenboro | 184 | 49.32 N | 99.15 W |
| Glenbrook | 170 | 33.46 S | 150.37 E |
| Glenbrook Heights | 226 | 39.15 N | 121.02 W |
| Glenburn, N.D., U.S. | 198 | 48.30 N | 101.13 W |
| Glenburn, Pa., U.S. | 210 | 41.31 N | 75.44 W |
| Glen Burnie | 208 | 39.09 N | 76.37 W |
| Glen Burnie Park | 208 | 39.09 N | 76.38 W |
| Glen Campbell | 214 | 40.49 N | 78.50 W |
| Glen Canyon V | 200 | 37.10 N | 110.50 W |
| Glen Canyon Dam ◆6 | 200 | 36.48 N | 111.13 W |
| Glen Canyon National Recreation Area ♦ | 200 | 37.00 N | 111.20 W |
| Glen Carbon | 219 | 38.44 N | 89.58 W |
| Glencoe, Austl. | 166 | 37.42 S | 140.37 E |
| Glencoe, On., Can. | 214 | 42.45 N | 81.43 W |
| Glencoe, S. Afr. | 158 | 28.12 S | 30.07 E |
| Glencoe, Al., U.S. | 194 | 33.57 N | 85.55 W |
| Glencoe, Il., U.S. | 216 | 42.08 N | 87.45 W |
| Glencoe, Ky., U.S. | 218 | 38.42 N | 84.49 W |
| Glencoe, Md., U.S. | 208 | 39.32 N | 76.38 W |
| Glencoe, Mn., U.S. | 190 | 44.46 N | 94.09 W |
| Glencolumbkille | 48 | 54.43 N | 8.45 W |
| Glencoul, Loch c | 46 | 58.14 N | 4.58 W |
| Glencova | 154 | 19.59 S | 31.26 E |
| Glen Cove | 210 | 40.51 N | 73.38 W |
| Glendale, Az., U.S. | 200 | 33.32 N | 112.11 W |
| Glendale, Ca., U.S. | 228 | 34.08 N | 118.15 W |
| Glendale, Ma., U.S. | 207 | 42.17 N | 73.20 W |
| Glendale, Ms., U.S. | 194 | 31.21 N | 89.18 W |
| Glendale, Mo., U.S. | 219 | 38.35 N | 90.22 W |
| Glendale, Or., U.S. | 202 | 42.44 N | 123.25 W |
| Glendale, R.I., U.S. | 207 | 41.58 N | 71.37 W |
| Glendale, Tx., U.S. | 222 | 31.01 N | 95.18 W |
| Glendale, Ut,. U.S. | 200 | 37.19 N | 112.35 W |
| Glendale, Wi., U.S. | 216 | 43.08 N | 87.56 W |
| Glendale, Zimb. | 154 | 17.21 S | 31.04 E |
| Glendale Heights, Il., U.S. | 278 | 41.54 N | 88.04 W |
| Glendale Heights, Md., U.S. | 284c | 38.59 N | 76.49 W |
| Glendale Lake ◎ | 214 | 40.41 N | 78.32 W |
| Glendalough ⊥ | 48 | 53.01 N | 6.26 W |
| Glen Davis | 170 | 33.08 S | 150.17 E |
| Glendive | 198 | 47.06 N | 104.42 W |
| Glendo | 200 | 42.30 N | 105.01 W |
| Glendoe Forest ◆3 | 46 | 57.06 N | 4.37 W |
| Glendon, Ab., Can. | 182 | 54.15 N | 111.10 W |
| Glendon, Pa., U.S. | 208 | 40.40 N | 75.14 W |
| Glendora, Ca., U.S. | 228 | 34.08 N | 117.51 W |
| Glendora, N.J., U.S. | 285 | 39.50 N | 75.04 W |
| Glendo Reservoir ◎1 | 198 | 42.31 N | 104.58 W |
| Glendo State Park ♦ | 198 | 42.33 N | 104.58 W |
| Glendowan | 48 | 54.58 N | 7.57 W |
| Glen Eagle, Austl. | 168a | 32.17 S | 116.11 E |
| Gleneagle, Austl. | 171a | 27.57 S | 152.59 E |
| Glen Echo | 284c | 38.58 N | 77.08 W |
| Glen Echo Amusement Park ♦ | 284c | 38.58 N | 77.08 W |
| Glen Echo Heights | 284c | 38.58 N | 77.08 W |
| Gleneden Beach | 202 | 44.53 N | 124.02 W |
| Glen Elder | 198 | 39.29 N | 98.18 W |
| Glenelg, Austl. | 168b | 34.59 S | 138.31 E |
| Glenelg, Scot., U.K. | 46 | 57.13 N | 5.38 W |
| Glenelg ≐ | 166 | 38.03 S | 141.00 E |
| Glen Ellen | 226 | 38.22 N | 122.31 W |
| Glenelly ≐ | 48 | 54.44 N | 7.18 W |
| Glen Ellyn | 278 | 41.52 N | 88.04 W |
| Glen Ellyn Countryside | 278 | 41.55 N | 88.04 W |
| Glenfarg | 46 | 56.16 N | 3.24 W |
| Glenfarne | 48 | 54.17 N | 7.59 W |
| Glenfield, Austl. | 274a | 33.58 S | 150.54 E |
| Glenfield, Eng., U.K. | 42 | 52.39 N | 1.12 W |
| Glenfield, N.Y., U.S. | 212 | 43.43 N | 75.24 W |
| Glenfield, Pa., U.S. | 279b | 40.31 N | 80.08 W |
| Glenfinnan | 46 | 56.52 N | 5.27 W |
| Glen Flora | 222 | 29.21 N | 96.12 W |
| Glen Florrie | 162 | 22.55 S | 115.59 E |
| Glenford | 210 | 42.00 N | 74.07 W |
| Glen Forest | 168a | 31.54 S | 116.06 E |
| Glengallan Creek ≐ | 171a | 28.09 S | 151.53 E |
| Glen Gardner | 210 | 40.41 N | 74.56 W |
| Glengarriff | 48 | 51.45 N | 9.33 W |
| Glengarry Range ⋏ | 162 | 26.13 S | 118.59 E |
| Glengyle | 166 | 24.48 S | 139.37 E |
| Glenham | 210 | 41.31 N | 73.55 W |
| Glenhaven | 274a | 33.42 S | 151.00 E |
| Glen Head | 276 | 40.50 N | 73.37 W |
| Glen Helen | 162 | 23.43 S | 132.40 E |
| Glen Hills | 208 | 39.04 N | 77.12 W |
| Glenhope | 172 | 41.39 S | 172.39 E |
| Glenhuntly | 274b | 37.54 S | 145.03 E |
| Glen Innes | 166 | 29.44 S | 151.44 E |
| Glen Island I | 276 | 40.53 N | 73.47 W |
| Glen Lake | 224 | 48.26 N | 123.31 W |
| Glenluce | 44 | 54.53 N | 4.49 W |
| Glenluce Abbey ᵾ1 | 44 | 54.53 N | 4.50 W |
| Glen Lyon | 210 | 41.10 N | 76.04 W |
| Glen Miller | 212 | 44.08 N | 77.35 W |
| Glen Mills | 285 | 39.55 N | 75.30 W |
| Glenmont, N.Y., U.S. | 210 | 42.36 N | 73.46 W |
| Glenmont, Oh., U.S. | 214 | 40.31 N | 82.06 W |
| Glenmoor | 214 | 40.40 N | 80.37 W |
| Glenmoore, Pa., U.S. | 208 | 40.05 N | 75.46 W |
| Glen Moore, Pa., U.S. | 208 | 40.03 N | 76.18 W |
| Glenmora | 194 | 30.58 N | 92.35 W |
| Glenmore | 284b | 39.11 N | 76.36 W |
| Glenmorgan | 166 | 27.15 S | 149.41 E |
| Glenn, Ca., U.S. | 226 | 39.31 N | 122.01 W |
| Glenn, Mi., U.S. | 216 | 42.31 N | 86.13 W |
| Glenn □6 | 226 | 39.29 N | 122.18 W |
| Glennallen | 180 | 62.07 N | 145.33 W |
| Glennamaddy | 48 | 53.37 N | 8.35 W |
| Glenn-Colusa Canal ≋ | 226 | 39.07 N | 122.08 W |
| Glenn Dale | 284c | 38.59 N | 76.49 W |
| Glenns Creek ≐ | 218 | 38.09 N | 84.52 W |
| Glenns Ferry | 202 | 42.57 N | 115.18 W |
| Glenn Shoals, Lake ◎1 | 219 | 39.13 N | 89.28 W |
| Glennville | 192 | 31.56 N | 81.55 W |
| Glen Oak | 278 | 41.53 N | 88.02 W |
| Glenolden | 285 | 39.54 N | 75.17 W |
| Glenoma | 224 | 46.30 N | 122.09 W |
| Glenorchy | 172 | 44.51 S | 168.23 E |
| Glenore Grove | 171a | 27.32 S | 152.24 E |
| Glenorie | 170 | 33.33 S | 151.00 E |
| Glenormiston | 166 | 22.55 S | 138.43 E |
| Glen Park | 212 | 44.00 N | 75.57 W |
| Glenreagh | 166 | 30.03 S | 152.59 E |
| Glen Richey | 214 | 40.57 N | 78.29 W |
| Glen Riddle | 285 | 39.54 N | 75.26 W |
| Glenridge, Ma., U.S. | 283 | 42.14 N | 71.19 W |
| Glen Ridge, N.J., U.S. | 276 | 40.48 N | 74.12 W |
| Glen Robertson | 206 | 45.21 N | 74.30 W |
| Glen Rock, N.J., U.S. | 276 | 40.57 N | 74.08 W |
| Glen Rock, Pa., U.S. | 208 | 39.47 N | 76.43 W |
| Glenrock, Wy., U.S. | 200 | 42.52 N | 105.52 W |
| Glen Rose | 222 | 32.14 N | 97.45 W |
| Glen Ross | 212 | 44.16 N | 77.36 W |
| Glenrothes | 46 | 56.12 N | 3.10 W |
| Glenroy, Austl. | 162 | 21.46 S | 114.49 E |
| Glenroy, Austl. | 162 | 17.22 S | 126.06 E |
| Glenroy, Austl. | 274b | 37.42 S | 144.55 E |
| Glenroy ≐ | 172 | 42.00 S | 172.20 E |
| Glens Falls | 210 | 43.18 N | 73.38 W |
| Glenshaw | 279b | 40.31 N | 79.58 W |
| Glenshee V | 46 | 56.48 N | 3.30 W |
| Glenside, S. Afr. | 158 | 29.25 S | 30.47 E |
| Glenside, N.J., U.S. | 208 | 39.40 N | 75.29 W |
| Glenside, Pa., U.S. | 208 | 40.06 N | 75.09 W |
| Glen Spey | 210 | 41.29 N | 74.49 W |
| Glen Stewart Park ♦ | 275b | 43.41 N | 79.18 W |
| Glenties | 48 | 54.47 N | 8.17 W |
| Glen Ullin | 198 | 46.48 N | 101.49 W |
| Glenview | 216 | 42.04 N | 87.47 W |
| Glenview Countryside | 278 | 42.04 N | 87.50 W |
| Glenview Naval Air Station ■ | 216 | 42.05 N | 87.50 W |
| Glenville, Ire. | 48 | 52.03 N | 8.26 W |
| Glenville, Mn., U.S. | 190 | 43.34 N | 93.16 W |
| Glenville, N.Y., U.S. | 276 | 41.04 N | 73.50 W |
| Glenville, W.V., U.S. | 188 | 38.56 N | 80.50 W |
| Glenvista | 273d | 26.17 S | 28.13 E |
| Glen Waverley | 274b | 37.53 S | 145.10 E |
| Glen White | 192 | 37.43 N | 81.16 W |
| Glen Wild | 210 | 41.29 N | 74.49 W |
| Glen Wild Lake ◎ | 276 | 41.02 N | 74.20 W |
| Glenwillard | 214 | 40.34 N | 80.13 W |
| Glen Williams | 212 | 43.40 N | 79.55 W |
| Glenwillow | 214 | 41.22 N | 81.28 W |
| Glenwood, Ab., Can. | 182 | 49.22 N | 113.31 W |
| Glenwood, Nf., Can. | 186 | 48.59 N | 54.52 W |
| Glenwood, Al., U.S. | 194 | 31.39 N | 86.10 W |
| Glenwood, Ar., U.S. | 194 | 34.19 N | 93.33 W |
| Glenwood, Ga., U.S. | 192 | 32.10 N | 82.40 W |
| Glenwood, Il., U.S. | 278 | 41.32 N | 87.36 W |
| Glenwood, In., U.S. | 218 | 39.37 N | 85.18 W |
| Glenwood, Ia., U.S. | 198 | 41.02 N | 95.44 W |
| Glenwood, Mn., U.S. | 198 | 45.39 N | 95.23 W |
| Glenwood, N.J., U.S. | 210 | 41.15 N | 74.29 W |
| Glenwood, N.M., U.S. | 200 | 33.19 N | 108.52 W |
| Glenwood, N.Y., U.S. | 210 | 42.37 N | 78.39 W |
| Glenwood, Or., U.S. | 224 | 45.38 N | 123.16 W |
| Glenwood, Tx., U.S. | 222 | 32.39 N | 94.51 W |
| Glenwood, Ut,. U.S. | 200 | 38.45 N | 111.59 W |
| Glenwood, Va., U.S. | 192 | 36.35 N | 79.21 W |
| Glenwood, Wa., U.S. | 224 | 46.01 N | 121.17 W |
| Glenwood City | 190 | 45.03 N | 92.10 W |
| Glenwood Landing | 276 | 40.50 N | 73.39 W |
| Glenwood Park | 284c | 38.58 N | 76.50 W |
| Glenwood Springs | 200 | 39.33 N | 107.19 W |
| Gleschendorf | 54 | 54.02 N | 10.40 E |
| Glesien | 54 | 51.27 N | 12.13 E |
| Gletsch | 58 | 46.34 N | 8.22 E |
| Gleussen | 54 | 50.08 N | 10.53 E |
| Glew | 258 | 34.53 S | 58.23 W |
| Glidden, Ia., U.S. | 198 | 42.03 N | 94.43 W |
| Glidden, Tx., U.S. | 222 | 29.42 N | 96.35 W |
| Glidden, Wi., U.S. | 190 | 46.08 N | 90.34 W |
| Glide | 202 | 43.18 N | 123.06 W |
| Gliener Berg ∧2 | 264a | 52.42 N | 13.00 E |
| Glienicke, Dtsch. | 54 | 52.13 N | 14.05 E |
| Glienicke, Dtsch. | 54 | 52.37 N | 13.19 E |
| Glífa | 38 | 38.57 N | 22.58 E |
| Glifádha | 267c | 37.52 N | 23.45 E |
| Glimåkra | 26 | 56.18 N | 14.08 E |
| Glimmingehus | 26 | 55.30 N | 14.13 E |
| Glin | 48 | 52.34 N | 9.17 W |
| Glina | 36 | 45.20 N | 16.06 E |
| Glina ≐ | 36 | 45.26 N | 16.07 E |
| Glinde | 52 | 53.32 N | 10.13 E |
| Glindow | 54 | 52.21 N | 12.54 E |
| Glindowsee ◎ | 264a | 52.21 N | 12.56 E |
| Glinka | 76 | 54.39 N | 32.52 E |
| Glinkovo | 85 | 42.55 N | 69.40 E |
| Glittertinden ∧ | 26 | 61.39 N | 8.33 E |
| Gliwice (Gleiwitz) | 30 | 50.17 N | 18.40 E |
| G. L. Martin State Airport ✈ | 284b | 39.20 N | 76.25 W |
| Globe, Az., U.S. | 200 | 33.23 N | 110.47 W |
| Globe, Ky., U.S. | 218 | 38.17 N | 83.14 W |
| Glodeanu-Siliştea | 38 | 44.50 N | 26.48 E |
| Glodeni | 38 | 47.47 N | 27.31 E |
| Glodok ◆8 | 269e | 6.08 S | 106.48 E |
| Glogau → Głogów | 30 | 51.40 N | 16.05 E |
| Gloggnitz | 61 | 47.40 N | 15.57 E |
| Glogn ≐ | 58 | 46.46 N | 9.12 E |
| Głogów, Pol. | 30 | 51.40 N | 16.05 E |
| Głogów, Pol. | 30 | 50.10 N | 21.58 E |
| Głogówek | 30 | 50.22 N | 17.51 E |
| Glommersträsk | 26 | 65.16 N | 19.38 E |
| Glonn | 64 | 47.59 N | 11.52 E |
| Glonn ≐ | 60 | 48.26 N | 11.36 E |
| Glorenza (Glurns) | 64 | 46.40 N | 10.33 E |
| Glória | 250 | 9.11 S | 38.18 W |
| Gloria, Bahía de la c | 240p | 21.50 N | 77.40 W |
| Glória de Dourados | 255 | 22.21 S | 54.13 W |
| Gloria Glens Park | 214 | 41.03 N | 81.54 W |
| Glorieta | 200 | 35.34 N | 105.46 W |
| Glorieuses, Îles II | 138 | 11.30 S | 47.20 E |
| Glörstausee ◎1 | 263 | 51.14 N | 7.29 E |
| Glos-la-Ferrière | 50 | 48.51 N | 0.36 E |
| Glossop | 44 | 53.27 N | 1.57 W |
| Glossopteris, Mount ∧ | 9 | 84.44 S | 113.51 W |
| Gloster | 194 | 31.11 N | 91.01 W |
| Glostrup | 41 | 55.40 N | 12.24 E |
| Glotovka | 80 | 53.57 N | 46.42 E |
| Glotovo | 24 | 63.30 N | 49.23 E |
| Gloucester, Austl. | 166 | 31.59 S | 151.58 E |
| Gloucester, On., Can. | 212 | 45.22 N | 75.35 W |
| Gloucester, Eng., U.K. | 42 | 51.53 N | 2.14 W |
| Gloucester, Ma., U.S. | 207 | 42.36 N | 70.39 W |
| Gloucester, Va., U.S. | 208 | 37.24 N | 76.31 W |
| Gloucester □6, N.J., U.S. | 208 | 39.50 N | 75.10 W |
| Gloucester □6, Va., U.S. | 208 | 37.25 N | 76.30 W |
| Gloucester, Cape › | 164 | 5.27 S | 148.25 E |
| Gloucester, Vale of V | 42 | 51.55 N | 2.10 W |
| Gloucester City | 285 | 39.53 N | 75.07 W |
| Gloucester Fisherman ⊥ | 283 | 42.36 N | 70.40 W |
| Gloucester Harbor c | 207 | 42.36 N | 70.40 W |
| Gloucester Island I | 166 | 20.01 S | 148.27 E |
| Gloucester Point | 208 | 37.15 N | 76.29 W |
| Gloucester Pool ◎ | 212 | 44.51 N | 79.43 W |
| Gloucestershire □6 | 42 | 51.47 N | 2.15 W |
| Glouster | 188 | 39.30 N | 82.05 W |
| Glover-Archbold Park ♦ | 284c | 38.55 N | 77.05 W |
| Glover Creek ≐ | 194 | 34.02 N | 94.56 W |
| Glover Island I | 186 | 48.44 N | 57.45 W |
| Glovers Reef ✛2 | 232 | 16.49 N | 87.48 W |
| Gloversville | 210 | 43.03 N | 74.20 W |
| Glovertown | 186 | 48.41 N | 54.02 W |
| Glowe | 54 | 54.35 N | 13.28 E |
| Glöwen | 54 | 52.55 N | 12.05 E |
| Głowno | 30 | 51.58 N | 19.44 E |
| Głubczyce | 30 | 50.13 N | 17.49 E |
| Glubokij, Ross. | 78 | 48.31 N | 40.19 E |
| Glubokij, Ross. | 80 | 47.01 N | 42.47 E |
| Glubokij, Ross. | 89 | 52.53 N | 129.44 E |
| Glubokoje, Kaz. | 86 | 50.06 N | 82.19 E |
| Glubokoje, Ross. | 82 | 54.32 N | 38.32 E |
| Głuchołazy | 30 | 50.20 N | 17.22 E |
| Gluchovo | 265b | 55.46 N | 37.16 E |
| Glückauf-Kampfbahn ♦ | 263 | 51.32 N | 7.05 E |
| Glücksburg | 41 | 54.50 N | 9.33 E |
| Glückstadt, Dtsch. | 52 | 53.47 N | 9.25 E |
| Gluckstadt, S. Afr. | 158 | 27.57 S | 31.02 E |
| Glucomanka, gora ∧ | 89 | 45.10 N | 135.48 E |
| Glud | 41 | 55.49 N | 10.00 E |
| Glumslöv | 41 | 55.56 N | 12.48 E |
| Glumsø | 41 | 55.21 N | 11.42 E |
| Glusburn | 44 | 53.54 N | 1.59 W |
| Gluškovo | 78 | 51.22 N | 34.38 E |
| Glyde ≐, Austl. | 164 | 12.15 S | 135.03 E |
| Glyde ≐, Ire. | 48 | 53.52 N | 6.21 W |
| Glyder Fawr ∧ | 44 | 53.06 N | 4.01 W |
| Glyme ≐ | 42 | 51.49 N | 1.22 W |
| Glyndebourne | 42 | 50.52 N | 0.04 E |
| Glyndon, Md., U.S. | 208 | 39.28 N | 76.48 W |
| Glyndon, Mn., U.S. | 198 | 46.52 N | 96.34 W |
| Glyngøre | 26 | 56.46 N | 8.52 E |
| Glyn-Neath | 42 | 51.46 N | 3.38 W |
| Gmelinka | 80 | 50.24 N | 46.54 E |
| Gmünd, Öst. | 61 | 48.47 N | 15.00 E |
| Gmünd, Öst. | 64 | 46.54 N | 13.32 E |
| Gmund am Tegernsee | 64 | 47.45 N | 11.44 E |
| Gmunden | 64 | 47.55 N | 13.48 E |
| Gnadenhutten | 214 | 40.21 N | 81.26 W |
| Gnadenhutten Monument ⊥ | 214 | 40.21 N | 81.25 W |
| Gnalta | 166 | 31.03 S | 142.20 E |
| Gnaraloo | 162 | 23.51 S | 113.31 E |
| Gnarp | 26 | 62.03 N | 17.16 E |
| Gnarpurt, Lake ◎ | 169 | 38.03 S | 143.24 E |
| Gnarrenburg | 52 | 53.22 N | 9.00 E |
| Gnaw Bone | 218 | 39.12 N | 86.09 W |
| Gneisenaustadt Schildau | 54 | 51.27 N | 12.56 E |
| Gnesen → Gniezno | 30 | 52.31 N | 17.37 E |
| Gnesta | 40 | 59.03 N | 17.18 E |
| Gnezdovo | 76 | 54.47 N | 31.47 E |
| Gniben › | 41 | 56.01 N | 11.18 E |
| Gniew | 30 | 53.51 N | 18.49 E |
| Gniewkowo | 30 | 52.54 N | 18.25 E |
| Gniezno | 30 | 52.31 N | 17.37 E |
| Gnilec | 76 | 52.22 N | 36.01 E |
| Gnjilane | 38 | 42.28 N | 21.29 E |
| Gnoien | 54 | 53.58 N | 12.42 E |
| Gnosall | 42 | 52.47 N | 2.15 W |
| Gnosjö | 26 | 57.22 N | 13.44 E |
| Gnowangerup | 162 | 33.56 S | 117.59 E |
| Gō ≐ | 96 | 35.02 N | 132.13 E |
| Goa | 116 | 13.42 N | 123.29 E |
| Goa □3 | 122 | 15.20 N | 74.00 E |
| Goageb | 156 | 26.44 S | 17.15 E |
| Goalen Head › | 166 | 36.40 S | 150.05 E |
| Goāliar ≐ | 126 | 24.07 N | 90.18 E |
| Goālpāra | 124 | 26.11 N | 90.37 E |
| Goāltor | 126 | 22.43 N | 87.10 E |
| Goan | 150 | 13.14 N | 5.09 W |
| Goascorán | 236 | 13.36 N | 87.45 W |
| Goascorán ≐ | 236 | 13.25 N | 87.48 W |
| Goat Fell ∧ | 46 | 55.38 N | 5.12 W |
| Goathland | 44 | 54.23 N | 0.44 W |
| Goat Island I | 284a | 43.05 N | 79.04 W |
| Goat Mountain ∧ | 202 | 47.21 N | 113.21 W |
| Goat Peak ∧ | 224 | 46.56 N | 121.16 W |
| Goba, Ityo. | 144 | 7.02 N | 40.00 E |
| Goba, Moç. | 156 | 26.12 S | 32.08 E |
| Gobabis | 156 | 22.30 S | 18.58 E |
| Gobai ≐ | 126 | 23.37 N | 86.28 E |
| Gobardānga | 126 | 22.53 N | 88.45 E |
| Göbel | 130 | 40.00 N | 28.09 E |
| Gobernador Andonaegui | 258 | 34.10 S | 59.19 W |
| Gobernador Costa | 254 | 44.04 S | 70.35 W |
| Gobernador Gregores | 254 | 48.46 S | 70.15 W |
| Gobernador Ingeniero Valentín Virasoro | 252 | 28.03 S | 56.02 W |
| Gobernador Juan E. Martínez | 252 | 28.55 S | 58.56 W |
| Gobernador Monteverde | 288 | 34.48 S | 58.16 W |
| Gobernador Racedo | 252 | 31.34 S | 60.04 W |
| Gobernador Udaondo | 258 | 35.18 S | 58.36 W |
| Gobi ◆2 | 102 | 43.00 N | 105.00 E |
| Gobindapur, India | 126 | 23.16 N | 87.58 E |
| Gobindapur, India | 272b | 22.23 N | 88.25 E |
| Gobindapur, India | 272b | 22.55 N | 88.12 E |
| Gobindgarh | 123 | 30.41 N | 76.18 E |
| Gobindpur | 126 | 23.50 N | 86.31 E |
| Göblberg ∧ | 60 | 48.06 N | 13.32 E |
| Gobles | 216 | 42.21 N | 85.52 W |
| Gobō | 96 | 33.53 N | 135.10 E |
| Gobowen | 42 | 52.53 N | 3.02 W |
| Gobra | 126 | 23.45 N | 89.12 E |
| Gobur | 154 | 4.20 N | 31.04 E |
| Gobza ≐ | 76 | 55.16 N | 31.31 E |
| Göçbeyli | 130 | 39.13 N | 27.25 E |
| Goceano, Catena del ⋏ | 71 | 40.28 N | 9.02 E |
| Goce Delčev | 38 | 41.34 N | 23.44 E |
| Goch | 52 | 51.41 N | 6.10 E |
| Gochas | 156 | 24.55 S | 18.55 E |
| Gochsheim | 56 | 50.01 N | 10.16 E |
| Go Cong | 269c | 10.50 N | 106.50 E |
| Göcsej ⋏2 | 61 | 46.43 N | 16.42 E |
| Goðafoss ʟ | 24a | 65.40 N | 17.30 W |
| Godalming | 42 | 51.11 N | 0.37 W |
| Godalo | 144 | 4.28 N | 43.24 E |
| Godar | 128 | 28.10 N | 63.14 E |
| Godāvari ≐ | 122 | 17.00 N | 81.45 E |
| Godāvari, Mouths of the ≐1 | 122 | 16.25 N | 82.00 E |
| Godbout | 186 | 49.19 N | 67.37 W |
| Godbout ≐ | 186 | 49.19 N | 67.36 W |
| Godda | 124 | 24.50 N | 87.13 E |
| Goddard | 218 | 38.22 N | 83.37 W |
| Goddard Space Flight Center ᵾ | 284c | 39.00 N | 76.52 W |
| Godeffroy | 210 | 41.27 N | 74.37 W |
| Godega di Sant'Urbano | 64 | 45.56 N | 12.24 E |
| Godegård | 40 | 58.44 N | 15.09 E |
| Godelheim | 52 | 51.44 N | 9.22 E |
| Godere | 144 | 5.05 N | 43.50 E |
| Goderich | 190 | 43.45 N | 81.43 W |
| Goderville | 50 | 49.39 N | 0.22 E |
| Godfrey | 219 | 38.57 N | 90.11 W |
| Godhavn (Qeqertarsuaq) | 176 | 69.15 N | 53.33 W |
| Godhra | 120 | 22.45 N | 73.38 E |
| Godinlabe | 144 | 5.54 N | 46.38 E |
| Godinne | 56 | 50.21 N | 4.52 E |
| Godley | 222 | 32.27 N | 97.32 W |
| Godmanchester | 42 | 52.19 N | 0.11 W |
| Godo, Indon. | 115b | 8.33 S | 118.40 E |
| Gōdo, Nihon | 94 | 35.25 N | 136.36 E |
| Gōdo, Nihon | 268 | 35.51 N | 139.44 E |
| Gödöllő | 264c | 47.36 N | 19.22 E |
| Gödöllői Dombság ⋏2 | 264c | 47.37 N | 19.16 E |
| Godong | 115a | 7.02 S | 110.46 E |
| Godoy Cruz | 252 | 32.55 S | 68.50 W |
| Godramstein | 56 | 49.12 N | 8.05 E |
| Godrano | 70 | 37.54 N | 13.26 E |
| Gods ≐ | 184 | 56.22 N | 92.51 W |
| Godshill | 42 | 50.38 N | 1.14 W |
| Godshorn | 52 | 52.26 N | 9.43 E |
| Gods Lake | 184 | 54.40 N | 94.09 W |
| Gods Lake ◎ | 184 | 54.40 N | 94.20 W |
| Gods Mercy, Bay of c | 176 | 63.30 N | 86.10 W |
| Godstone | 42 | 51.15 N | 0.04 W |
| Godthåb (Nuuk) | 176 | 64.11 N | 51.44 W |
| Godunovo | 82 | 56.29 N | 39.02 E |
| Godwin Austen → K2 ∧ | 123 | 35.53 N | 76.30 E |
| Goéland, Lac au ◎ | 176 | 49.47 N | 76.48 W |
| Goélands, Lac aux ◎ | 176 | 55.27 N | 64.17 W |
| Goeree I | 52 | 51.50 N | 3.55 E |
| Goes | 52 | 51.30 N | 3.54 E |
| Goetzenbruck | 56 | 48.59 N | 7.23 E |
| Goff, Som. | 144 | 2.39 N | 41.00 E |
| Goff, Ks., U.S. | 198 | 39.39 N | 95.55 W |
| Goff Creek ≐ | 196 | 36.43 N | 101.29 W |
| Goffle Brook ≐ | 276 | 40.56 N | 74.08 W |
| Goff's Oak | 260 | 51.43 N | 0.05 W |
| Goffstown | 188 | 43.01 N | 71.36 W |
| Gogama | 190 | 47.40 N | 81.43 W |
| Gogebic, Lake ◎ | 190 | 46.30 N | 89.35 W |
| Gogebic Range ⋏2 | 190 | 46.30 N | 90.10 W |
| Göggingen | 58 | 48.20 N | 10.52 E |
| Gogland, ostrov I | 76 | 60.04 N | 27.00 E |
| Goglio | 58 | 46.18 N | 8.16 E |
| Gogoi | 156 | 20.17 S | 33.08 E |
| Gogonou | 150 | 10.50 N | 2.50 E |
| Gogo-shima I | 96 | 33.54 N | 132.41 E |
| Gogrial | 140 | 8.32 N | 28.07 E |
| Gohad | 124 | 26.26 N | 78.27 E |
| Gohāla | 126 | 23.15 N | 89.59 E |
| Gohāla ≐ | 126 | 24.08 N | 89.35 E |
| Gohāna | 124 | 29.08 N | 76.42 E |
| Gohfeld | 52 | 52.12 N | 8.45 E |
| Gohitafla | 150 | 7.30 N | 5.53 W |
| Göhl | 54 | 54.17 N | 10.56 E |
| Gohoku | 96 | 33.39 N | 133.21 E |
| Go Home Lake ◎ | 212 | 45.00 N | 79.51 W |
| Gohpur | 120 | 26.53 N | 93.38 E |
| Gohr | 263 | 51.06 N | 6.43 E |
| Göhrde | 54 | 53.08 N | 10.52 E |
| Göhren | 54 | 54.20 N | 13.44 E |
| Goiana, Bra. | 250 | 7.33 S | 34.59 W |
| Goianá, Bra. | 256 | 21.32 S | 43.12 W |
| Goianápolis | 255 | 16.30 S | 49.01 W |
| Goiandira | 255 | 18.08 S | 48.06 W |
| Goianésia | 255 | 15.18 S | 49.07 W |
| Goiânia | 255 | 16.40 S | 49.16 W |
| Goianinha | 250 | 6.16 S | 35.12 W |
| Goiás | 255 | 15.56 S | 50.08 W |
| Goiás □3 | 255 | 16.00 S | 50.00 W |
| Goiatuba | 255 | 18.01 S | 49.22 W |
| Goichran | 120 | 31.04 N | 78.07 E |
| Goil, Loch c | 46 | 56.08 N | 4.52 W |
| Goio-Erê | 252 | 24.12 S | 53.01 W |
| Gôio-Erê ≐ | 252 | 24.14 S | 53.21 W |
| Goirle | 52 | 51.32 N | 5.04 E |
| Góis | 34 | 40.09 N | 8.07 W |
| Goito | 64 | 45.15 N | 10.40 E |
| Gojam □4 | 144 | 11.00 N | 37.00 E |
| Gojeb ≐ | 144 | 7.20 N | 37.21 E |
| Gojō | 96 | 34.21 N | 135.42 E |
| Gojōme | 92 | 39.56 N | 140.07 E |
| Gojra | 123 | 31.09 N | 72.41 E |
| Gojtchskij, pereval )( | 84 | 44.18 N | 39.18 E |
| Gök ≐ | 130 | 41.24 N | 35.08 E |
| Gokāk | 122 | 16.10 N | 74.50 E |
| Gokarna | 126 | 24.03 N | 88.07 E |
| Gokase ≐ | 92 | 32.35 N | 131.42 E |
| Gökçeada I | 130 | 40.10 N | 25.50 E |
| Gökçebey | 130 | 41.19 N | 32.08 E |
| Gökçedağ | 130 | 39.33 N | 28.56 E |
| Gökçekent | 130 | 40.19 N | 38.07 E |
| Gökçeli | 130 | 40.35 N | 36.44 E |
| Gökçen | 130 | 38.07 N | 27.53 E |
| Gökçesu | 130 | 40.54 N | 31.58 E |
| Gökdere, Tür. | 130 | 40.29 N | 36.47 E |
| Gökdere, Tür. | 130 | 38.44 N | 40.13 E |
| Gōkōmutsumi | 268 | 35.48 N | 139.59 E |
| Gökova Körfezi c | 130 | 36.50 N | 28.00 E |
| Göksholm | 40 | 59.16 N | 15.33 E |
| Göksu ≐, Tür. | 84 | 39.19 N | 42.17 E |
| Göksu ≐, Tür. | 130 | 36.19 N | 34.02 E |
| Göksu ≐, Tür. | 130 | 37.37 N | 35.35 E |
| Göksu ≐, Tür. | 267b | 41.06 N | 29.03 E |
| Göksun | 130 | 38.03 N | 36.30 E |
| Göktaş | 130 | 41.17 N | 41.46 E |
| Göktepe | 130 | 37.15 N | 28.36 E |
| Göktürk ◆8 | 267b | 41.11 N | 28.53 E |
| Gokwe | 154 | 18.07 S | 28.58 E |
| Gol | 26 | 60.42 N | 8.57 E |
| Gol, Khawr V | 140 | 6.55 N | 30.16 E |
| Golabāri | 272b | 22.36 N | 88.20 E |
| Golāghāt | 120 | 26.31 N | 93.58 E |
| Gola Gokarannāth | 124 | 28.05 N | 80.28 E |
| Gola Island I | 48 | 55.05 N | 8.22 W |
| Gołańcz | 30 | 52.57 N | 17.18 E |
| Golan Heights ⋏4 | 132 | 32.55 N | 35.42 E |
| Golāshkerd | 128 | 27.59 N | 57.16 E |
| Golbāf | 128 | 29.51 N | 57.44 E |
| Gölbası, Tür. | 130 | 37.50 N | 37.40 E |
| Gölbaşı, Tür. | 130 | 39.48 N | 32.49 E |
| Golborne | 262 | 53.29 N | 2.36 W |
| Golcar | 262 | 53.39 N | 1.51 W |
| Gol'čicha | 74 | 71.43 N | 83.36 E |
| Golconda, Il., U.S. | 194 | 37.22 N | 88.29 W |
| Golconda, Nv., U.S. | 204 | 40.57 N | 117.29 W |
| Gölcük, Tür. | 130 | 39.18 N | 27.59 E |
| Gölcük, Tür. | 130 | 40.44 N | 29.48 E |
| Golczewo | 54 | 53.49 N | 14.59 E |
| Gołdap | 30 | 54.19 N | 22.19 E |
| Goldau | 58 | 47.03 N | 8.33 E |
| Goldbach | 56 | 50.00 N | 9.11 E |
| Gold Bar | 224 | 47.51 N | 121.41 W |
| Gold Beach | 202 | 42.24 N | 124.25 W |
| Goldbeck | 54 | 52.43 N | 11.52 E |
| Goldberg | 54 | 53.35 N | 12.05 E |
| Goldberger See ◎ | 54 | 53.36 N | 12.07 E |
| Goldbergtunnel ◆5 | 263 | 51.21 N | 7.28 E |
| Goldbey | 58 | 48.12 N | 6.26 E |
| Goldboro | 186 | 45.11 N | 61.39 W |
| Gold Bridge | 182 | 50.51 N | 122.50 W |
| Gold Coast → Southport | 171a | 27.58 S | 153.25 E |
| Gold Coast ⊥2 | 150 | 5.20 N | 0.45 W |
| Gold Creek | 180 | 62.46 N | 149.41 W |
| Gold Creek ≐ | 182 | 49.04 N | 115.12 W |
| Golden, B.C., Can. | 182 | 51.18 N | 116.58 W |
| Golden, Ire. | 48 | 52.29 N | 7.58 W |
| Golden, Co., U.S. | 200 | 39.45 N | 105.13 W |
| Golden, Il., U.S. | 219 | 40.07 N | 91.01 W |
| Golden Bay c | 172 | 40.40 S | 172.50 E |
| Golden Beach | 220 | 25.57 N | 80.07 W |
| Golden Brook ≐ | 283 | 42.44 N | 71.19 W |
| Golden City | 194 | 37.23 N | 94.05 W |
| Goldendale | 224 | 45.49 N | 120.49 W |
| Golden Ears Provincial Park ♦ | 182 | 49.30 N | 122.25 W |
| Goldene Aue V | 54 | 51.25 N | 11.00 E |
| Golden Gate | 220 | 26.09 N | 81.43 W |
| Golden Gate ⋈ | 226 | 37.49 N | 122.29 W |
| Golden Gate Bridge ◆5 | 282 | 37.49 N | 122.28 W |
| Golden Gate Fields Race Track ♦ | 282 | 37.53 N | 122.19 W |
| Golden Gate Highlands National Park ♦ | 158 | 28.30 S | 28.40 E |
| Golden Gate National Recreation Area ♦ | 282 | 37.49 N | 122.31 W |
| Golden Gate Park ♦ | 282 | 37.46 N | 122.28 W |
| Golden Green | 260 | 51.12 N | 0.21 E |
| Golden Hill Creek ≐ | 210 | 43.22 N | 78.28 W |
| Golden Hinde ∧ | 182 | 49.40 N | 125.45 W |
| Golden Horn → Haliç c | 267b | 41.02 N | 28.58 E |
| Golden Lake ◎ | 190 | 45.35 N | 77.20 W |
| Golden Meadow | 194 | 29.22 N | 90.15 W |
| Golden Prairie | 184 | 50.14 N | 109.38 W |
| Golden Ring Mall ◆9 | 284b | 39.20 N | 76.29 W |
| Golden Rock | 122 | 10.48 N | 78.44 E |
| Goldenrod | 220 | 28.37 N | 81.18 W |
| Golden Spike National Historic Site ⊥ | 202 | 41.38 N | 112.35 W |
| Goldenstedt | 52 | 52.48 N | 8.25 E |
| Golden Valley V | 42 | 52.02 N | 2.56 W |
| Golders Green ◆8 | 260 | 51.35 N | 0.12 W |
| Goldfield, Ia., U.S. | 190 | 42.44 N | 93.55 W |
| Goldfield, Nv., U.S. | 204 | 37.42 N | 117.14 W |
| Goldkronach | 60 | 50.01 N | 11.41 E |
| Gold Lake ◎ | 212 | 44.43 N | 78.17 W |
| Goldlauter | 54 | 50.38 N | 10.44 E |
| Gold Mountain ∧ | 204 | 37.15 N | 117.18 W |
| Goldney | 258 | 34.37 S | 59.18 W |
| Goldonna | 194 | 32.01 N | 92.54 W |
| Goldpan Peak ∧ | 180 | 61.12 N | 153.22 W |
| Gold River | 182 | 49.41 N | 126.08 W |
| Gold Rock | 184 | 49.27 N | 92.43 W |
| Gold Run | 226 | 39.10 N | 120.52 W |
| Goldsand Lake ◎ | 184 | 57.02 N | 101.08 W |
| Goldsboro, Md., U.S. | 208 | 39.02 N | 75.47 W |
| Goldsboro, N.C., U.S. | 192 | 35.23 N | 77.59 W |
| Goldsmith, In., U.S. | 216 | 40.17 N | 86.08 W |
| Goldsmith, Tx., U.S. | 196 | 31.58 N | 102.36 W |
| Goldsmith, Lake ◎ | 169 | 37.32 S | 143.21 E |
| Goldston | 192 | 35.35 N | 79.19 W |
| Goldstone Lake ◎ | 228 | 35.22 N | 116.54 W |
| Goldstream Provincial Park ♦ | 224 | 48.29 N | 123.33 W |
| Goldsworthy | 162 | 20.20 S | 119.30 E |
| Goldsworthy, Mount ∧2 | 162 | 20.21 S | 119.32 E |
| Goldthwaite | 196 | 31.26 N | 98.34 W |
| Göle | 130 | 40.48 N | 42.36 E |
| Golec, gora ∧ | 88 | 58.39 N | 94.10 E |
| Goleen | 48 | 51.28 N | 9.43 W |
| Golela | 158 | 27.20 S | 31.55 E |
| Goleniów | 30 | 53.36 N | 14.50 E |
| Golestan Palace ᵾ | 267d | 35.41 N | 51.25 E |
| Goleta | 204 | 34.26 N | 119.49 W |
| Golf, Fl., U.S. | 220 | 26.31 N | 80.06 W |
| Golf, Il., U.S. | 278 | 42.03 N | 87.48 W |
| Golfcrest | 216 | 41.57 N | 83.22 W |
| Golfe-Juan | 62 | 43.34 N | 7.05 E |
| Golfito | 236 | 8.38 N | 83.11 W |
| Golf Manor | 285 | 39.42 N | 75.28 W |
| Golf Mill ◆9 | 278 | 42.03 N | 87.50 W |
| Golfo Aranci | 71 | 40.59 N | 9.38 E |
| Golfo de Santa Clara | 232 | 31.42 N | 114.30 W |
| Golfside | 281 | 42.15 N | 83.41 W |
| Golf View | 208 | 39.43 N | 75.28 W |
| Golfview Hills | 278 | 41.47 N | 87.56 W |
| Gölhisar | 130 | 37.10 N | 29.30 E |
| Goliad | 196 | 28.40 N | 97.23 W |
| Goliad □6 | 222 | 28.52 N | 97.22 W |
| Golicyno, Ross. | 80 | 53.38 N | 44.07 E |
| Golicyno, Ross. | 80 | 55.58 N | 40.26 E |
| Golicyno, Ross. | 82 | 55.37 N | 36.59 E |
| Golina | 30 | 52.16 N | 18.05 E |
| Golin Baixing | 89 | 44.53 N | 121.58 E |
| Golinda | 222 | 31.25 N | 97.05 W |
| Goljama Kamčija ≐ | 38 | 43.03 N | 27.29 E |
| Goljam Perelik ∧ | 38 | 41.36 N | 24.34 E |
| Goljanovo ◆8 | 265b | 55.49 N | 37.48 E |
| Goljevo | 265b | 55.48 N | 37.19 E |
| Gölköy | 130 | 40.42 N | 37.38 E |
| Gollach ≐ | 56 | 49.31 N | 10.00 E |
| Göllersbach ≐ | 61 | 48.22 N | 16.11 E |
| Göllet | 130 | 40.45 N | 42.18 E |
| Göllheim | 56 | 49.36 N | 8.03 E |
| Golling an der Salzach | 64 | 47.36 N | 13.10 E |
| Golm | 264a | 52.24 N | 12.58 E |
| Gölmarmara | 130 | 38.42 N | 27.56 E |
| Golmberg ∧2 | 54 | 52.01 N | 13.21 E |
| Golmud | 102 | 36.22 N | 94.55 E |
| Golmud ≐ | 102 | 36.54 N | 95.11 E |
| Golo ≐ | 36 | 42.31 N | 9.32 E |
| Golodnaja Guba, ozero ◎ | 24 | 67.52 N | 52.48 E |
| Golo Island I | 116 | 13.40 N | 120.22 E |
| Golok (Kolok) ≐ | 114 | 6.15 N | 102.05 E |
| Golongoso | 146 | 9.00 N | 19.09 E |
| Gölören | 130 | 37.48 N | 33.52 E |
| Gölova | 130 | 40.04 N | 38.37 E |
| Golovačovka | 85 | 42.52 N | 71.13 E |
| Golovanovo | 80 | 54.55 N | 40.27 E |
| Golovčino | 78 | 50.32 N | 35.47 E |
| Golovin | 180 | 64.33 N | 163.02 W |
| Golovinka | 84 | 43.48 N | 39.28 E |
| Golovino, Ross. | 76 | 55.58 N | 40.26 E |
| Golovino, Ross. | 82 | 56.01 N | 39.11 E |
| Golovinščino | 80 | 53.18 N | 43.59 E |
| Golovinskaja | 88 | 53.26 N | 102.43 E |
| Golovnino | 82 | 54.23 N | 36.10 E |
| Golovskoje | 88 | 55.30 N | 105.32 E |
| Golpāyegān | 128 | 33.27 N | 50.18 E |
| Gölpazarı | 130 | 40.15 N | 30.19 E |
| Golra | 123 | 33.42 N | 72.58 E |
| Golrān | 128 | 35.06 N | 61.41 E |
| Gols | 61 | 47.54 N | 16.55 E |
| Golspie, Austl. | 170 | 34.17 S | 149.40 E |
| Golspie, Scot., U.K. | 46 | 57.58 N | 3.58 W |
| Golssen | 54 | 51.58 N | 13.36 E |
| Gol't'ajevo | 82 | 55.13 N | 36.02 E |
| Gol't'avino | 88 | 58.26 N | 98.27 E |
| Golub-Dobrzyń | 30 | 53.08 N | 19.02 E |
| Golubi | 76 | 59.28 N | 41.39 E |
| Golubinskij | 80 | 48.52 N | 43.34 E |
| Golubovka | 86 | 53.09 N | 74.12 E |
| Golumet' | 88 | 53.03 N | 102.21 E |
| Golungo Alto | 152 | 9.08 S | 14.46 E |
| Golva | 198 | 46.44 N | 103.59 W |
| Golweyn | 144 | 1.40 N | 44.35 E |
| Gölyaka | 130 | 40.47 N | 30.59 E |
| Golynki | 76 | 54.52 N | 31.23 E |
| Golyšmanovo, Ross. | 86 | 56.23 N | 68.23 E |
| Golyšmanovo, Ross. | 86 | 56.28 N | 68.38 E |
| Golzheim ◆8 | 263 | 51.15 N | 6.46 E |
| Golzow, Dtsch. | 54 | 52.34 N | 14.29 E |
| Golzow, Dtsch. | 54 | 52.16 N | 12.36 E |
| Goma | 154 | 1.41 S | 29.14 E |
| Gomadan-zan ∧ | 96 | 34.03 N | 135.34 E |
| Gomagoi | 64 | 46.35 N | 10.32 E |
| Gomang Co ◎ | 120 | 31.15 N | 89.15 E |
| Gomaringen | 58 | 48.27 N | 9.05 E |
| Gomas, Sierra de ⋏ | 196 | 26.23 N | 100.32 W |
| Gomati ≐ | 124 | 25.32 N | 83.10 E |
| Gomati Plain ≚ | 124 | 26.30 N | 81.10 E |
| Goma Tsétsé | 273b | 4.14 S | 15.08 E |
| Gombari | 154 | 2.43 N | 29.04 E |
| Gombe, Nig. | 146 | 10.19 N | 11.02 E |
| Gombe, Zaïre | 152 | 0.42 S | 17.35 E |
| Gombe Stream National Park ♦ | 154 | 4.30 S | 29.42 E |
| Gombi | 146 | 10.10 N | 12.45 E |
| Gomboro | 150 | 13.29 N | 2.46 W |
| Gomel' → Homel' | 76 | 52.25 N | 31.00 E |
| Gomer | 216 | 40.51 N | 84.11 W |
| Gomera I | 148 | 28.06 N | 17.08 W |
| Gometra I | 46 | 56.29 N | 6.17 W |
| Gometz-la-Ville | 261 | 48.40 N | 2.08 E |
| Gometz-le-Châtel | 261 | 48.41 N | 2.08 E |
| Gomez | 220 | 27.06 N | 80.09 W |
| Gómez Farías, Méx. | 232 | 29.18 N | 107.40 W |
| Gómez Farías, Méx. | 234 | 19.47 N | 103.29 W |
| Gómez Palacio | 232 | 25.34 N | 103.30 W |
| Gómez Plata | 246 | 6.41 N | 75.12 W |
| Gomīshān | 128 | 37.04 N | 54.06 E |
| Gommécourt | 261 | 49.05 N | 1.36 E |
| Gommern | 54 | 52.04 N | 11.50 E |
| Gomo Co ◎ | 120 | 33.47 N | 85.30 E |
| Gomogomo | 164 | 6.40 S | 134.43 E |
| Gomoh | 126 | 23.52 N | 86.10 E |
| Gompa | 123 | 35.02 N | 77.20 E |
| Goms V | 58 | 46.27 N | 8.15 E |
| Gomshall | 260 | 51.13 N | 0.27 W |
| Gomumu, Pulau I | 164 | 1.49 S | 127.38 E |
| Gonābād | 128 | 34.20 N | 58.42 E |
| Gonaïves | 238 | 19.27 N | 72.41 W |
| Gonaka | 152 | 2.56 S | 13.14 E |
| Gonam | 74 | 57.21 N | 131.12 E |
| Gonam ≐ | 74 | 57.21 N | 131.14 E |
| Gonarezhou National Park ♦ | 154 | 21.30 S | 32.00 E |
| Gonars | 64 | 45.53 N | 13.13 E |
| Gonäs | 40 | 60.09 N | 15.06 E |
| Gonâve, Golfe de la c | 238 | 19.00 N | 73.30 W |
| Gonâve, Île de la I | 238 | 18.51 N | 73.03 W |
| Gonbad-e Qābūs | 128 | 37.17 N | 55.17 E |
| Gonçalves | 256 | 22.40 S | 45.51 W |
| Gonçalves Dias | 250 | 4.57 S | 44.14 W |
| Gončarovka | 78 | 50.32 N | 39.28 E |
| Goncelin | 62 | 45.20 N | 5.59 E |
| Gonda | 124 | 27.08 N | 81.56 E |
| Gondal | 120 | 21.58 N | 70.48 E |
| Gondang | 115a | 7.24 S | 111.06 E |
| Gondar → Gonder | 144 | 12.40 N | 37.30 E |
| Gondarbal | 123 | 34.14 N | 74.47 E |
| Gonder | 144 | 12.40 N | 37.30 E |
| Gonder □4 | 144 | 13.10 N | 37.00 E |
| Gondey | 146 | 9.09 N | 19.19 E |
| Gondia | 120 | 21.27 N | 80.12 E |
| Gondola | 156 | 19.10 S | 33.40 E |
| Gondomar | 34 | 41.09 N | 8.32 W |
| Gondrecourt-le-Château | 58 | 48.31 N | 5.30 E |
| Gondreville | 58 | 48.42 N | 5.58 E |
| Gondrexange, Étang de ◎ | 56 | 48.42 N | 6.54 E |
| Goneāna | 123 | 30.19 N | 74.54 E |
| Gönen, Tür. | 130 | 40.06 N | 27.39 E |
| Gonén, Yis. | 132 | 33.08 N | 35.39 E |
| Gonesse | 50 | 48.59 N | 2.27 E |
| Gonfaron | 62 | 43.19 N | 6.17 E |
| Gong ≐ | 100 | 26.00 N | 115.22 E |
| Gong'an | 102 | 30.02 N | 112.04 E |
| Gonganbao | 86 | 44.59 N | 86.18 E |
| Gonganpucun | 104 | 41.19 N | 123.27 E |
| Gongbuchang | 105 | 40.17 N | 116.15 E |
| Gongchangling | 104 | 41.06 N | 123.30 E |
| Gongcheng | 102 | 24.49 N | 110.46 E |
| Gongchenqiao | 106 | 30.20 N | 120.08 E |
| Gongchuan, Zhg. | 100 | 26.06 N | 117.24 E |
| Gongchuan, Zhg. | 102 | 23.40 N | 107.50 E |
| Gongcun | 105 | 39.28 N | 116.10 E |
| Gongdaoqiao | 100 | 32.36 N | 119.22 E |
| Gongdian | 100 | 28.06 N | 116.56 E |
| Gongen-yama ∧ | 94 | 35.40 N | 139.01 E |
| Gongfang | 100 | 27.36 N | 115.34 E |
| Gonggar | 120 | 29.17 N | 90.46 E |
| Gongga Shan (Minya Konka) ∧ | 102 | 29.35 N | 101.51 E |
| Gonghe | 102 | 36.20 N | 100.48 E |
| Gonghui | 98 | 41.12 N | 114.37 E |
| Gongjialu | 106 | 31.17 N | 121.40 E |
| Gongjiatun | 104 | 40.55 N | 120.37 E |
| Gongjiazhai | 104 | 41.57 N | 124.01 E |
| Gongjing | 107 | 29.21 N | 104.43 E |
| Gongjingying | 105 | 39.12 N | 116.11 E |
| Gongkou | 98 | 35.38 N | 119.47 E |
| Gongli | 98 | 35.55 N | 117.24 E |
| Gongling | 100 | 26.18 N | 119.40 E |
| Gongliu | 86 | 43.30 N | 82.15 E |
| Gonglu Shan ∧ | 106 | 30.39 N | 119.18 E |
| Gongo | 146 | 9.00 N | 18.56 E |
| Gongola ≐ | 146 | 9.30 N | 12.04 E |
| Gongoué | 152 | 0.32 S | 9.12 E |
| Gongo-Yembe | 152 | 1.58 S | 18.40 E |
| Gongpengzi | 89 | 45.09 N | 125.39 E |
| Gongping | 100 | 23.05 N | 115.24 E |
| Gongpingxu | 100 | 26.12 N | 112.51 E |
| Gongshan | 102 | 25.50 N | 103.13 E |
| Gongshiya | 120 | 31.25 N | 84.37 E |
| Gongsizhen | 106 | 31.41 N | 121.48 E |
| Gongtangtou | 106 | 31.48 N | 118.42 E |
| Gongxi | 100 | 27.38 N | 115.52 E |
| Gongxian | 102 | 34.48 N | 113.03 E |
| Gongyefu | 98 | 42.16 N | 118.32 E |
| Gongyemiao | 89 | 43.40 N | 121.06 E |
| Gongyingzi | 98 | 40.54 N | 119.41 E |
| Gongzhutun | 104 | 42.10 N | 123.00 E |
| Gongzui | 107 | 29.19 N | 103.28 E |
| Goni, It. | 71 | 39.34 N | 9.17 E |
| Goñi, Ur. | 252 | 33.31 S | 56.24 W |
| Goniądz | 30 | 53.30 N | 22.45 E |
| Gonini ≐ | 250 | 4.10 N | 54.24 W |
| Goniri | 146 | 11.30 N | 12.20 E |
| Gonjo | 102 | 30.43 N | 98.19 E |
| Gonnesa | 71 | 39.16 N | 8.28 E |
| Gonnesa, Golfo di c | 71 | 39.17 N | 8.23 E |
| Gonnosfanadiga | 71 | 39.29 N | 8.39 E |
| Gonnostramatza | 71 | 39.41 N | 8.50 E |
| Gonochovo | 86 | 52.57 N | 81.20 E |
| Gōnoura | 92 | 33.45 N | 129.41 E |
| Gonubie Mouth | 158 | 32.57 S | 28.01 E |
| Gonža | 89 | 53.36 N | 125.19 E |
| Gonzaga, It. | 64 | 44.57 N | 10.49 E |
| Gonzaga, Pil. | 116 | 18.16 N | 122.00 E |
| Gonzales, Ca., U.S. | 226 | 36.30 N | 121.26 W |
| Gonzales, La., U.S. | 194 | 30.14 N | 90.55 W |
| Gonzales, Tx., U.S. | 222 | 29.30 N | 97.27 W |
| Gonzales □6 | 222 | 29.28 N | 97.30 W |


| Symbol | English | Deutsch | Español | Français | Português |
|---|---|---|---|---|---|
| ≐ | River | Fluß | Río | Rivière | Rio |
| ≋ | Canal | Kanal | Canal | Canal | Canal |
| ʟ | Waterfall, Rapids | Wasserfall, Stromschnellen | Cascada, Rápidos | Chute d'eau, Rapides | Cascata, Rápidos |
| ⋈ | Strait | Meeresstraße | Estrecho | Détroit | Estreito |
| c | Bay, Gulf | Bucht, Golf | Bahía, Golfo | Baie, Golfe | Baía, Golfo |
| ◎ | Lake, Lakes | See, Seen | Lago, Lagos | Lac, Lacs | Lago, Lagos |
| ≚ | Swamp | Sumpf | Pantano | Marais | Pântano |
| ❄ | Ice Features, Glacier | Eis- und Gletscherformen | Accidentes Glaciales | Formes glaciaires | Acidentes glaciares |
| ⊤ | Other Hydrographic Features | Andere Hydrographische Objekte | Otros Elementos Hidrográficos | Autres données hydrographiques | Outros acidentes hidrográficos |
| ✛ | Submarine Features | Untermeerische Objekte | Accidentes Submarinos | Formes de relief sous-marin | Acidentes submarinos |
| □ | Political Unit | Politische Einheit | Unidad Política | Entité politique | Unidade política |
| ᵾ | Cultural Institution | Kulturelle Institution | Institución Cultural | Institution culturelle | Instituição cultural |
| ⊥ | Historical Site | Historische Stätte | Sitio Histórico | Site historique | Sítio histórico |
| ♦ | Recreational Site | Erholungs- und Ferienort | Sitio de Recreo | Centre de loisirs | Área de Lazer |
| ✈ | Airport | Flughafen | Aeropuerto | Aéroport | Aeroporto |
| ■ | Military Installation | Militäranlage | Instalación Militar | Installation militaire | Instalação militar |
| ◆ | Miscellaneous | Verschiedenes | Misceláneo | Divers | Diversos |

ENGLISH / DEUTSCH


| Name | Page | Lat.°′ | Long.°′ |
|---|---|---|---|
| González, Méx. | 234 | 22.50 N | 98.27 W |
| González, Ur. | 258 | 34.14 S | 56.52 W |
| González, Riacho ≃ | 252 | 22.48 S | 57.54 W |
| González Catán | 258 | 34.46 S | 58.39 W |
| González Chaves | 252 | 38.02 S | 60.06 W |
| González Moreno | 252 | 35.33 S | 63.22 W |
| González Ortega, Méx. | 204 | 32.40 N | 115.23 W |
| González Ortega, Méx. | 234 | 23.11 N | 102.29 W |
| González Ortega, Méx. | 234 | 23.59 N | 103.27 W |
| González Risos | 258 | 34.52 S | 59.13 W |
| Gonzanamá | 246 | 4.15 S | 79.27 W |
| Goobarragandra ≃ | 171b | 35.20 S | 148.15 E |
| Goochland | 192 | 37.41 N | 77.53 W |
| Good Easter | 260 | 51.47 N | 0.21 E |
| Goodells | 214 | 42.59 N | 82.40 W |
| Goode Mountain ∧ | 224 | 48.29 N | 120.55 W |
| Goodenough, Mount ∧ | 180 | 67.56 N | 135.31 W |
| Goodenough Bay c | 164 | 9.55 S | 150.00 E |
| Goodenough Island I | 164 | 9.20 S | 150.15 E |
| Gooderham | 212 | 44.54 N | 78.23 W |
| Goodeve | 184 | 51.04 N | 103.10 W |
| Goodfellow Air Force Base ■ | 196 | 31.26 N | 100.25 W |
| Good Hope, S. Afr. | 158 | 31.51 S | 21.55 E |
| Good Hope, Oh., U.S. | 218 | 39.26 N | 83.21 W |
| Good Hope, Cape of (Kaap die Gooie Hoop) › | 158 | 34.24 S | 18.30 E |
| Goodhope Bay c | 180 | 66.10 N | 163.45 W |
| Good Hope Mountain ∧ | 182 | 51.09 N | 124.10 W |
| Goodhouse | 158 | 28.57 S | 18.13 E |
| Goodhue | 190 | 44.24 N | 92.37 W |
| Gooding | 202 | 42.56 N | 114.42 W |
| Goodison | 214 | 42.44 N | 83.10 W |
| Goodland, Fl., U.S. | 220 | 25.55 N | 81.38 W |
| Goodland, In., U.S. | 216 | 40.45 N | 87.17 W |
| Goodland, Ks., U.S. | 198 | 39.21 N | 101.42 W |
| Goodlands | 184 | 49.05 N | 100.35 W |
| Goodlow Park | 222 | 32.07 N | 96.14 W |
| Goodman, Ms., U.S. | 194 | 32.58 N | 89.54 W |
| Goodman, Wi., U.S. | 190 | 45.37 N | 88.21 W |
| Goodna | 171a | 27.37 S | 152.54 E |
| Goodnews Bay | 180 | 59.07 N | 161.35 W |
| Goodnight | 200 | 38.14 N | 104.43 W |
| Goodooga | 166 | 29.07 S | 147.27 E |
| Goodradigbee ≃ | 171b | 35.08 S | 148.41 E |
| Goodrich, Mi., U.S. | 216 | 42.55 N | 83.30 W |
| Goodrich, N.D., U.S. | 198 | 47.28 N | 100.07 W |
| Goodrich, Tx., U.S. | 222 | 30.36 N | 94.57 W |
| Good Spirit Lake ⊜ | 184 | 51.34 N | 102.40 W |
| Good Spirit Lake Provincial Park ♦ | 184 | 51.36 N | 102.45 W |
| Good Thunder | 190 | 44.00 N | 94.03 W |
| Goodview | 190 | 44.03 N | 91.41 W |
| Goodville | 208 | 40.08 N | 76.00 W |
| Goodwater | 194 | 33.03 N | 86.03 W |
| Goodwell | 196 | 36.35 N | 101.38 W |
| Goodwick | 42 | 52.00 N | 5.00 W |
| Goodwin, Lake ⊜ | 224 | 48.08 N | 122.18 W |
| Goodwives ≃ | 276 | 41.04 N | 73.28 W |
| Goodwood | 212 | 44.02 N | 79.12 W |
| Goodyear | 200 | 33.26 N | 112.21 W |
| Goof, Webi ≃ | 144 | 1.10 N | 43.43 E |
| Googong Reservoir ⊜[1] | 171b | 35.27 S | 149.16 E |
| Gooie Hoop, Kaap die → Good Hope, Cape of › | 158 | 34.24 S | 18.30 E |
| Goole | 44 | 53.42 N | 0.52 W |
| Goolgowi | 166 | 33.59 S | 145.42 E |
| Goolwa | 168b | 35.31 S | 138.47 E |
| Goomalling | 162 | 31.19 S | 116.49 E |
| Goombalie | 166 | 29.59 S | 145.23 E |
| Goombungee | 171a | 27.18 S | 151.51 E |
| Goomburra | 171a | 28.03 S | 152.07 E |
| Goonda | 156 | 19.51 S | 34.00 E |
| Goondiwindi | 166 | 28.32 S | 150.19 E |
| Goongarrie | 162 | 30.03 S | 121.09 E |
| Goongarrie National Park ♦ | 162 | 29.58 S | 121.34 E |
| Goonyella | 166 | 21.45 S | 147.55 E |
| Goor | 52 | 52.14 N | 6.35 E |
| Goose ≃, Ab., Can. | 182 | 54.58 N | 117.11 W |
| Goose ≃, N.D., U.S. | 198 | 47.28 N | 96.52 W |
| Goose Bay → Happy Valley-Goose Bay | 176 | 53.20 N | 60.25 W |
| Goose Bay c | 281 | 42.35 N | 82.41 W |
| Gooseberry Creek ≃ | 202 | 43.55 N | 108.04 W |
| Goose Creek | 192 | 32.58 N | 80.01 W |
| Goose Creek ≃, U.S. | 202 | 42.33 N | 113.46 W |
| Goose Creek ≃, Ne., U.S. | 198 | 42.02 N | 100.03 W |
| Goose Creek ≃, N.Y., U.S. | 214 | 42.06 N | 79.22 W |
| Goose Creek ≃, Va., U.S. | 208 | 39.06 N | 77.29 W |
| Goose Island I | 182 | 51.55 N | 128.25 W |
| Goose Lake ⊜, Mb., Can. | 184 | 54.26 N | 101.30 W |
| Goose Lake ⊜, On., Can. | 184 | 51.46 N | 93.00 W |
| Goose Lake ⊜, On., Can. | 212 | 44.25 N | 78.52 W |
| Goose Lake ⊜, On., Can. | 214 | 42.31 N | 82.31 W |
| Goose Lake ⊜, Sk., Can. | 184 | 51.45 N | 107.23 W |
| Goose Lake ⊜, U.S. | 204 | 41.57 N | 120.25 W |
| Goose Lake Canal ≅ | 226 | 35.50 N | 119.37 W |
| Goose Lake Prairie State Park ♦ | 216 | 41.21 N | 88.18 W |
| Gooseprairie | 224 | 46.54 N | 121.15 W |
| Goostrey | 262 | 53.13 N | 2.20 W |
| Gooty | 122 | 15.07 N | 77.38 E |
| Gopālganj, Bngl. | 124 | 23.01 N | 89.50 E |
| Gopālganj, India | 124 | 26.28 N | 84.26 E |
| Gopālnagar, India | 126 | 23.03 N | 88.45 E |
| Gopālnagar, India | 272b | 22.50 N | 88.14 E |
| Gopālpur, Bngl. | 124 | 24.33 N | 89.56 E |
| Gopālpur, India | 272b | 22.38 N | 88.27 E |
| Gopeng | 114 | 4.28 N | 101.10 E |
| Göpfritz an der Wild | 61 | 48.43 N | 15.24 E |
| Gopiballabhpur | 126 | 22.13 N | 86.54 E |
| Gopichettipālaiyam | 122 | 11.28 N | 77.27 E |
| Gopinagar | 272b | 22.50 N | 88.07 E |
| Goppenstein | 58 | 46.22 N | 7.45 E |
| Göppingen | 56 | 48.42 N | 9.40 E |
| Goqên | 102 | 29.15 N | 96.59 E |
| Go Quao | 110 | 9.43 N | 105.17 E |
| Gor | 123 | 35.32 N | 74.31 E |
| Góra, Pol. | 30 | 51.40 N | 16.33 E |
| Gora, Ross. | 76 | 60.02 N | 41.43 E |
| Gor'ačegorsk | 86 | 55.24 N | 88.55 E |
| Gor'ačij Kl'uč | 84 | 44.37 N | 39.07 E |
| Gor'ačinsk | 88 | 52.59 N | 108.18 E |
| Goradit | 144 | 11.25 N | 38.25 E |
| Góra Kalwaria | 30 | 51.59 N | 21.12 E |
| Gorakhpur | 124 | 26.45 N | 83.22 E |
| Goranboy | 84 | 40.36 N | 46.47 E |
| Goras | 124 | 25.32 N | 76.56 E |
| Goražde | 38 | 43.40 N | 18.56 E |
| Gorbatov | 80 | 56.08 N | 43.04 E |
| Gorbatovka | 80 | 56.15 N | 43.45 E |
| Gorbica | 88 | 53.06 N | 119.13 E |
| Gorčucha | 80 | 57.43 N | 43.43 E |
| Gorda, Punta ›, Chile | 248 | 19.18 S | 70.18 W |
| Gorda, Punta ›, Cuba | 240p | 22.24 N | 82.10 W |
| Gorda, Punta ›, Nic. | 236 | 11.26 N | 83.48 W |
| Gorda, Punta ›, Nic. | 236 | 14.21 N | 83.12 W |
| Gorda, Punta ›, Ca., U.S. | 204 | 40.16 N | 124.22 W |
| Gordejevka | 76 | 52.59 N | 31.58 E |
| Gordes, Fr. | 62 | 43.54 N | 5.12 E |
| Gördes, Tür. | 130 | 38.54 N | 28.18 E |
| Gordil | 146 | 9.44 N | 21.35 E |
| Gørding | 41 | 55.29 N | 8.48 E |
| Gordion ⊥ | 130 | 39.41 N | 32.01 E |
| Gordo | 194 | 33.19 N | 87.54 W |
| Gordo, Cerro ∧ | 234 | 20.46 N | 102.35 W |
| Gordola | 58 | 46.11 N | 8.52 E |
| Gordon, Scot., U.K. | 46 | 55.41 N | 2.34 W |
| Gordon, Ga., U.S. | 192 | 32.52 N | 83.19 W |
| Gordon, Ne., U.S. | 198 | 42.48 N | 102.12 W |
| Gordon, Oh., U.S. | 218 | 39.56 N | 84.31 W |
| Gordon, Pa., U.S. | 208 | 40.45 N | 76.21 W |
| Gordon, Wi., U.S. | 190 | 46.14 N | 91.47 W |
| Gordon ≃ | 224 | 48.35 N | 124.24 W |
| Gordon, Isla I | 254 | 54.58 S | 69.35 W |
| Gordon, Lake ⊜[1] | 166 | 42.42 S | 146.12 E |
| Gordon Creek ≃ | 198 | 42.49 N | 100.40 W |
| Gordon Downs | 162 | 18.44 S | 128.35 E |
| Gordon Heights | 207 | 40.51 N | 72.58 W |
| Gordon Horne Peak ∧ | 182 | 51.46 N | 118.50 W |
| Gordon Indian Reserve ♦[4] | 184 | 51.16 N | 104.16 W |
| Gordon Lake ⊜, Ab., Can. | 184 | 56.30 N | 110.25 W |
| Gordon Lake ⊜, Sk., Can. | 184 | 55.50 N | 106.26 W |
| Gordon Lakes | 276 | 41.03 N | 74.22 W |
| Gordon Pass c | 220 | 26.06 N | 81.48 W |
| Gordon River | 224 | 48.47 N | 124.21 W |
| Gordon's Bay | 158 | 34.10 S | 18.52 E |
| Gordonsville | 188 | 38.08 N | 78.11 W |
| Gordonton | 172 | 37.40 S | 175.18 E |
| Gordonvale | 166 | 17.05 S | 145.47 E |
| Gordonville | 220 | 27.57 N | 81.49 W |
| Gore, Austl. | 166 | 28.17 S | 151.29 E |
| Gore, N.S., Can. | 186 | 45.07 N | 63.43 W |
| Gore, Ityo. | 144 | 8.08 N | 35.33 E |
| Gore, N.Z. | 172 | 46.06 S | 168.58 E |
| Goré, Tchad | 146 | 7.53 N | 16.40 E |
| Gore Bay | 190 | 45.55 N | 82.28 W |
| Gorebridge | 46 | 55.51 N | 3.02 W |
| Goreda | 164 | 3.39 S | 134.58 E |
| Goree | 196 | 33.28 N | 99.31 W |
| Gore Hill | 274a | 33.49 S | 151.11 E |
| Görele | 130 | 41.02 N | 39.00 E |
| Gorelki | 82 | 54.15 N | 37.37 E |
| Goreloje | 80 | 52.57 N | 41.28 E |
| Gorelovo | 265a | 59.47 N | 30.08 E |
| Gorelovo Airport ⊠ | 265a | 59.47 N | 30.05 E |
| Gorelyj ≃ | 265a | 59.58 N | 30.28 E |
| Göreme Milli Parkı ♦ | 130 | 38.26 N | 34.54 E |
| Gore Mountain ∧ | 188 | 44.55 N | 71.48 W |
| Gorenki | 265b | 55.48 N | 37.55 E |
| Gore Point ›, Austl. | 166 | 17.38 S | 139.56 E |
| Gore Point ›, Ak., U.S. | 180 | 59.12 N | 151.00 W |
| Gore Range ⩘ | 200 | 40.00 N | 106.30 W |
| Goretovka ≃ | 265b | 55.56 N | 37.20 E |
| Goreville | 194 | 37.33 N | 88.58 W |
| Gorey, Ire. | 48 | 52.40 N | 6.18 W |
| Gorey, Jersey | 43b | 49.12 N | 2.02 W |
| Gorfoundurei | 144 | 4.30 N | 46.41 E |
| Gorgān | 128 | 36.50 N | 54.29 E |
| Gorgān ≃ | 128 | 36.59 N | 54.00 E |
| Gorge Lake ⊜[1] | 224 | 48.42 N | 121.13 W |
| Görgeshausen | 56 | 50.24 N | 7.56 E |
| Gorgoglione | 68 | 40.23 N | 16.09 E |
| Gorgol □[4] | 150 | 16.00 N | 13.00 W |
| Gorgol el Abiod ≃ | 150 | 16.14 N | 12.58 W |
| Gorgol el Akhdar ≃ | 150 | 16.13 N | 12.58 W |
| Gorgona, Isla I | 246 | 2.59 N | 78.12 W |
| Gorgona, Isola di I | 36 | 43.26 N | 9.54 E |
| Gorgonzola | 62 | 45.32 N | 9.24 E |
| Gorgor | 248 | 10.35 S | 77.02 W |
| Gorgora | 144 | 12.13 N | 37.16 E |
| Gorgoram | 146 | 12.38 N | 10.43 E |
| Gorgota | 38 | 44.47 N | 26.05 E |
| Gorgova | 38 | 45.11 N | 29.10 E |
| Gorham, Me., U.S. | 188 | 43.40 N | 70.26 W |
| Gorham, N.H., U.S. | 188 | 44.23 N | 71.10 W |
| Gorham, N.Y., U.S. | 210 | 42.47 N | 77.07 W |
| Gorhambury House ⊥ | 260 | 51.47 N | 0.24 W |
| Gori | 84 | 41.58 N | 44.07 E |
| Goria | 272b | 22.24 N | 88.29 E |
| Gorica → Gorizia | 64 | 45.57 N | 13.38 E |
| Goričan | 61 | 46.23 N | 16.41 E |
| Goricy | 76 | 57.09 N | 36.44 E |
| Gorinchem | 52 | 51.50 N | 5.00 E |
| Goring | 42 | 51.32 N | 1.09 W |
| Goring-by-Sea | 42 | 50.49 N | 0.25 W |
| Goring Gap V | 42 | 51.32 N | 1.08 W |
| Goris | 84 | 39.31 N | 46.23 E |
| Göritz | 54 | 53.24 N | 13.54 E |
| Göritzhain | 54 | 50.58 N | 12.47 E |
| Gorizia | 64 | 45.57 N | 13.38 E |
| Gorizia □[4] | 64 | 45.55 N | 13.30 E |
| Gorj □[6] | 38 | 45.00 N | 23.20 E |
| Gorjan | 38 | 45.24 N | 18.21 E |
| Gor'kaja Balka | 84 | 44.17 N | 43.59 E |
| Gor'kaja balka ≃ | 84 | 44.38 N | 45.00 E |
| Görke | 54 | 53.51 N | 13.38 E |
| Gorkhā | 124 | 28.00 N | 84.37 E |
| Gorki, Ross. | 80 | 57.38 N | 45.05 E |
| Gorki → Nižnij Novgorod, Ross. | 80 | 56.20 N | 44.00 E |
| Gorki, Ross. | 82 | 54.18 N | 36.08 E |
| Gorki, Ross. | 82 | 55.32 N | 37.45 E |
| Gorki, Ross. | 82 | 56.54 N | 38.51 E |
| Gorki, Ross. | 265b | 55.57 N | 37.55 E |
| Gor'kij → Nižnij Novgorod | 80 | 56.20 N | 44.00 E |
| Gorki Vtoryje | 265b | 55.44 N | 37.11 E |
| Gor'koje, ozero ⊜ | 86 | 52.30 N | 81.20 E |
| Gor'ko-Solenoje, ozero ⊜ | 80 | 49.20 N | 46.05 E |
| Gor'kovskoje | 86 | 55.22 N | 74.24 E |
| Gor'kovskoje vodochranilišče ⊜[1] | 80 | 57.00 N | 43.10 E |
| Gorky → Nižnij Novgorod | 80 | 56.20 N | 44.00 E |
| Gorky Park ♦ | 265b | 55.44 N | 37.36 E |
| Gorlago | 62 | 45.40 N | 9.49 E |
| Gorla Maggiore | 266b | 45.40 N | 8.53 E |
| Gorla Minore | 266b | 45.39 N | 8.54 E |
| Gorleston on Sea | 42 | 52.36 N | 1.43 E |
| Gørlev | 41 | 55.32 N | 11.14 E |
| Gorlice | 30 | 49.40 N | 21.10 E |
| Görlitz | 54 | 51.09 N | 14.59 E |
| Gorlosen | 54 | 53.11 N | 11.27 E |
| Gorlovka, Sak. | 84 | 41.14 N | 43.42 E |
| Gorlovka → Horlivka, Ukr. | 83 | 48.18 N | 38.03 E |
| Gorlovo | 76 | 53.50 N | 39.02 E |
| Gorm, Loch ⊜ | 46 | 55.48 N | 6.25 W |
| Gorman, Ca., U.S. | 228 | 34.48 N | 118.51 W |
| Gorman, Tx., U.S. | 196 | 32.12 N | 98.40 W |
| Gorman Creek ≃ | 228 | 34.38 N | 118.45 W |
| Görmin | 54 | 53.59 N | 13.16 E |
| Gorn'ackij, Ross. | 24 | 67.32 N | 64.03 E |
| Gorn'ackij, Ross. | 78 | 48.17 N | 40.55 E |
| Gorna Dzhumaya → Blagoevgrad | 38 | 42.01 N | 23.06 E |
| Gornaja Prolejka | 80 | 49.24 N | 44.59 E |
| Gorn'ak, Ross. | 76 | 53.36 N | 39.29 E |
| Gorn'ak, Ross. | 86 | 51.00 N | 81.29 E |
| Gornalunga ≃ | 70 | 37.24 N | 15.03 E |
| Gorna Orjahovica | 38 | 43.07 N | 25.41 E |
| Gornergrat ♦ | 58 | 45.59 N | 7.47 E |
| Gornja Radgona | 36 | 46.41 N | 16.00 E |
| Gornji Grad | 36 | 46.18 N | 14.49 E |
| Gornji Milanovac | 38 | 44.01 N | 20.27 E |
| Gornji Vakuf | 36 | 43.56 N | 17.35 E |
| Gorno-Altajsk | 86 | 51.58 N | 85.58 E |
| Gorno-Altay → Altaj □[3] | 86 | 51.00 N | 86.00 E |
| Gorno-Badachšanskaja Avtonomnaja Respublika □[3] | 85 | 38.30 N | 73.00 E |
| Gornoje | 86 | 48.29 N | 85.00 E |
| Gorno-Lesnoj zapovednik ♦ | 85 | 41.10 N | 69.55 E |
| Gornopravdinsk | 86 | 60.07 N | 69.54 E |
| Gorno-Vod'anoje | 80 | 49.16 N | 44.56 E |
| Gornovodnoje | 89 | 43.42 N | 134.44 E |
| Gornozavodsk, Ross. | 86 | 58.20 N | 58.32 E |
| Gornozavodsk, Ross. | 89 | 46.34 N | 141.49 E |
| Gornyj, Ross. | 80 | 51.46 N | 48.34 E |
| Gornyj, Ross. | 89 | 50.48 N | 136.29 E |
| Gornyj, Ross. | 89 | 44.57 N | 133.59 E |
| Gornyj Balyklej | 80 | 49.34 N | 45.04 E |
| Gornyje Kl'uči | 89 | 45.12 N | 133.31 E |
| Goro, Ityo. | 144 | 6.56 N | 40.32 E |
| Goro, N. Cal. | 175f | 22.16 S | 167.02 E |
| Gorochan ∧ | 144 | 9.22 N | 37.04 E |
| Gorochovec | 80 | 56.12 N | 42.40 E |
| Gorochovje | 76 | 56.31 N | 30.29 E |
| Gorodec, Ross. | 76 | 58.32 N | 29.47 E |
| Gorodec, Ross. | 80 | 56.38 N | 43.30 E |
| Gorodišče, Ross. | 76 | 59.38 N | 32.08 E |
| Gorodišče, Ross. | 78 | 51.09 N | 38.04 E |
| Gorodišče, Ross. | 80 | 53.17 N | 45.42 E |
| Gorodišče, Ross. | 80 | 48.48 N | 44.29 E |
| Gorodišče, Ross. | 82 | 54.53 N | 38.13 E |
| Gorodišče, Ross. | 82 | 56.47 N | 38.52 E |
| Gorodišči | 82 | 55.52 N | 39.05 E |
| Gorodn'a, Ross. | 82 | 54.57 N | 38.49 E |
| Gorodn'a, Ross. | 82 | 56.43 N | 36.19 E |
| Gorodn'a ≃ | 265b | 55.38 N | 37.48 E |
| Gorodno | 76 | 57.32 N | 29.35 E |
| Goroka | 164 | 6.05 S | 145.25 E |
| Gorokan | 170 | 33.16 S | 151.30 E |
| Gorom-Gorom | 150 | 14.26 N | 0.14 W |
| Gorong, Pulau I | 164 | 3.59 S | 131.25 E |
| Gorongosa, Parque Nacional da ♦ | 156 | 18.45 S | 34.15 E |
| Gorongosa, Serra da ∧ | 154 | 18.30 S | 34.03 E |
| Gorongose ≃ | 156 | 20.30 S | 34.40 E |
| Gorontalo | 112 | 0.33 N | 123.03 E |
| Goronyo | 150 | 13.29 N | 5.39 E |
| Goroubi ≃ | 150 | 12.54 N | 2.23 E |
| Gorouol ≃ | 150 | 14.42 N | 0.53 E |
| Górowo Iławeckie | 30 | 54.17 N | 20.30 E |
| Gorple Reservoirs ⊜[1] | 262 | 53.47 N | 2.06 W |
| Gorran ⊜ | 40 | 59.43 N | 17.32 E |
| Gorredijk | 52 | 53.00 N | 6.05 E |
| Gorron | 28 | 48.25 N | 0.49 W |
| Görsdorf | 54 | 51.54 N | 13.29 E |
| Goršečnoje | 78 | 51.32 N | 38.02 E |
| Gorsedd | 262 | 53.17 N | 3.16 W |
| Gorseinon | 42 | 51.40 N | 4.02 W |
| Gorskaja | 265a | 60.03 N | 29.59 E |
| Gorškovo | 82 | 54.26 N | 37.59 E |
| Gorst | 224 | 47.32 N | 122.42 W |
| Gort | 48 | 53.04 N | 8.50 W |
| Gortahork | 48 | 55.08 N | 8.09 W |
| Gorton ♦[8] | 262 | 53.27 N | 2.10 W |
| Görtschitz ≃ | 61 | 46.45 N | 14.32 E |
| Goru, Vârful ∧ | 38 | 45.48 N | 26.25 E |
| Görükle | 130 | 40.14 N | 28.50 E |
| Gorumna Island I | 48 | 53.14 N | 9.40 W |
| Gor'un ≃ | 89 | 50.45 N | 137.50 E |
| Gorutuba ≃ | 255 | 14.57 S | 43.33 W |
| Görwihl | 58 | 47.39 N | 8.04 E |
| Gory, Bela. | 76 | 54.16 N | 31.13 E |
| Gory, Kaz. | 80 | 48.38 N | 51.46 E |
| Görz → Gorizia | 64 | 45.57 N | 13.38 E |
| Gorzano, Monte ∧ | 66 | 42.37 N | 13.24 E |
| Gorze | 56 | 49.03 N | 6.00 E |
| Görzig | 54 | 51.40 N | 12.00 E |
| Görzke | 54 | 52.10 N | 12.22 E |
| Górzno | 30 | 53.13 N | 19.38 E |
| Gorzów Śląski | 30 | 51.02 N | 18.24 E |
| Gorzów Wielkopolski (Landsberg an der Warthe) | 30 | 52.44 N | 15.15 E |
| Gorzów Wielkopolski □[4] | 30 | 52.45 N | 15.20 E |
| Górzyca | 54 | 52.29 N | 14.40 E |
| Gosāba | 126 | 22.10 N | 88.48 E |
| Gosairhāt | 126 | 23.05 N | 90.26 E |
| Gosaldo | 64 | 46.13 N | 11.58 E |
| Gosau | 64 | 47.34 N | 13.31 E |
| Gosauseen ⊜ | 64 | 47.32 N | 13.31 E |
| Gosberton | 42 | 52.51 N | 0.09 W |
| Göschenen | 58 | 46.40 N | 8.35 E |
| Goschen Strait ⋃ | 164 | 10.09 S | 150.56 E |
| Gose | 96 | 34.27 N | 135.44 E |
| Gosen, Dtsch. | 264a | 52.24 N | 13.43 E |
| Gosen, Nihon | 92 | 37.44 N | 139.11 E |
| Gosford | 170 | 33.26 S | 151.21 E |
| Gosforth, Eng., U.K. | 44 | 55.01 N | 1.37 W |
| Gosforth, Eng., U.K. | 44 | 54.26 N | 3.27 W |
| Gosforth Park ♦ | 273d | 26.14 S | 28.10 E |
| Gosforth Park Race Course ♦ | 273d | 26.14 S | 28.08 E |
| Goshabi | 140 | 17.58 N | 31.06 E |
| Goshen, N.S., Can. | 186 | 45.23 N | 61.59 W |
| Goshen, Ca., U.S. | 226 | 36.21 N | 119.25 W |
| Goshen, Ct., U.S. | 207 | 41.49 N | 73.13 W |
| Goshen, In., U.S. | 216 | 41.34 N | 85.50 W |
| Goshen, Ma., U.S. | 207 | 42.26 N | 72.48 W |
| Goshen, N.J., U.S. | 208 | 39.08 N | 74.51 W |
| Goshen, N.Y., U.S. | 210 | 41.24 N | 74.19 W |
| Goshen, Oh., U.S. | 218 | 39.14 N | 84.10 W |
| Goshiki | 96 | 34.24 N | 134.47 E |
| Goshogawara | 92 | 40.48 N | 140.27 E |
| Goshute Indian Reservation ♦[4] | 200 | 39.53 N | 114.08 W |
| Goshute Lake ⊜ | 204 | 40.08 N | 114.38 W |
| Goshute Valley V | 204 | 40.40 N | 114.30 W |
| Goslar | 52 | 51.54 N | 10.25 E |
| Gosnells | 168a | 32.04 S | 116.00 E |
| Gospić | 36 | 44.33 N | 15.23 E |
| Gosport, Eng., U.K. | 42 | 50.48 N | 1.08 W |
| Gosport, In., U.S. | 194 | 39.21 N | 86.40 W |
| Gossa | 54 | 51.40 N | 12.26 E |
| Gossas | 150 | 14.30 N | 16.04 W |
| Gossau | 58 | 47.25 N | 9.15 E |
| Gosse ♦[8] | 263 | 51.08 N | 7.01 E |
| Gosse Bluff ∧ | 162 | 23.49 S | 132.19 E |
| Gosselies | 56 | 50.28 N | 4.25 E |
| Gössenheim | 56 | 50.01 N | 9.46 E |
| Gossensass → Colle Isarco | 64 | 46.56 N | 11.26 E |
| Gosser Hill | 279b | 40.37 N | 79.37 W |
| Gossi | 150 | 15.49 N | 1.17 W |
| Gossinga | 140 | 8.39 N | 25.59 E |
| Gössnitz | 54 | 50.53 N | 12.26 E |
| Gossolengo | 62 | 44.59 N | 9.37 E |
| Gössweinstein | 60 | 49.46 N | 11.20 E |
| Gostagajevskaja | 78 | 45.01 N | 37.30 E |
| Gostilovo | 82 | 55.18 N | 38.36 E |
| Gostiščevo | 78 | 50.47 N | 36.39 E |
| Gostivar | 38 | 41.47 N | 20.54 E |
| Göstling an der Ybbs | 61 | 47.48 N | 14.55 E |
| Gostyń | 30 | 51.53 N | 17.00 E |
| Gostynin | 30 | 52.26 N | 19.29 E |
| Göta älv ≃ | 26 | 57.42 N | 11.52 E |
| Göta kanal ≅ | 40 | 58.50 N | 13.58 E |
| Gotchen Creek ≃ | 224 | 46.00 N | 121.30 W |
| Got Creek ≃ | 284a | 43.03 N | 78.42 W |
| Gotebo | 196 | 35.04 N | 98.52 W |
| Göteborg (Gothenburg) | 26 | 57.43 N | 11.58 E |
| Göteborgs och Bohus län □[6] | 26 | 58.30 N | 11.30 E |
| Gotel Mountains ⩘ | 152 | 6.55 N | 11.15 E |
| Gotemba | 94 | 35.18 N | 138.56 E |
| Götene | 26 | 58.32 N | 13.29 E |
| Gotești | 38 | 46.09 N | 28.10 E |
| Gotha, Dtsch. | 54 | 50.57 N | 10.41 E |
| Gotha, Fl., U.S. | 220 | 28.32 N | 81.31 W |
| Gothem | 26 | 57.35 N | 18.43 E |
| Gothenburg → Göteborg, Sve. | 26 | 57.43 N | 11.58 E |
| Gothenburg, Ne., U.S. | 198 | 40.55 N | 100.09 W |
| Gothèye | 150 | 13.52 N | 1.34 E |
| Gotland I | 26 | 57.30 N | 18.33 E |
| Gotlands Län □[6] | 26 | 57.30 N | 18.30 E |
| Gotoputovo | 86 | 56.46 N | 70.10 E |
| Gotō-rettō II | 92 | 32.50 N | 129.00 E |
| Gotska Sandön I | 26 | 58.23 N | 19.16 E |
| Gōtsu | 96 | 35.00 N | 132.14 E |
| Gottenheim | 58 | 48.03 N | 7.44 E |
| Götterswickerhamm | 263 | 51.35 N | 6.40 E |
| Gottesbrücke | 264a | 52.25 N | 13.49 E |
| Gotthard Tunnel ♦[5] | 58 | 46.35 N | 8.35 E |
| Göttin | 264a | 52.27 N | 12.54 E |
| Göttingen, Dtsch. | 52 | 51.32 N | 9.55 E |
| Göttingen, Dtsch. | 56 | 50.52 N | 8.46 E |
| Göttin See ⊜ | 264a | 52.28 N | 12.54 E |
| Gottmadingen | 58 | 47.44 N | 8.47 E |
| Gottolengo | 64 | 45.17 N | 10.16 E |
| Gottorf, Schloss ⊥ | 41 | 54.30 N | 9.32 E |
| Gottsbüren | 52 | 51.35 N | 9.30 E |
| Gottvaterkapelle ♦[1] | 60 | 49.42 N | 11.41 E |
| Götzendorf | 264b | 48.01 N | 16.35 E |
| Götzis | 58 | 47.20 N | 9.38 E |
| Gouarec | 32 | 48.13 N | 3.11 W |
| Goubangzi | 104 | 41.22 N | 121.46 E |
| Goubone | 146 | 20.43 N | 17.08 E |
| Gouda, Ned. | 52 | 52.01 N | 4.43 E |
| Gouda, S. Afr. | 158 | 33.19 S | 19.04 E |
| Goudet | 62 | 44.53 N | 3.55 E |
| Goudge | 252 | 34.40 S | 68.08 W |
| Goudhurst | 42 | 51.07 N | 0.28 E |
| Goudiry | 150 | 14.11 N | 12.43 W |
| Goudoumaria | 146 | 13.42 N | 11.10 E |
| Goudswaard | 52 | 51.47 N | 4.16 E |
| Gouéké | 150 | 8.02 N | 8.43 W |
| Goûfi, Djebel el ∧ | 34 | 36.57 N | 6.27 E |
| Gougezhuang | 105 | 38.53 N | 116.11 E |
| Gough Island I | 10 | 40.20 S | 10.00 W |
| Gough Lake ⊜ | 182 | 52.02 N | 112.28 W |
| Gouin, Réservoir ⊜[1] | 176 | 48.38 N | 74.54 W |
| Goujiaozhen | 107 | 30.36 N | 106.33 E |
| Goukou | 89 | 48.39 N | 122.06 E |
| Goulais ≃ | 190 | 46.43 N | 84.27 W |
| Goulburn | 170 | 34.45 S | 149.43 E |
| Goulburn ≃ | 169 | 36.41 S | 145.12 E |
| Goulburn Islands II | 164 | 11.33 S | 133.26 E |
| Goulburn Weir ⊜[1] | 169 | 36.45 S | 145.08 E |
| Gould | 194 | 33.59 N | 91.33 W |
| Gould City | 190 | 46.05 N | 85.41 W |
| Gould Park | 214 | 40.04 N | 82.53 W |
| Goulds | 220 | 25.33 N | 80.22 W |
| Gouldsboro | 210 | 41.44 N | 75.28 W |
| Gouldsboro State Park ♦ | 210 | 41.13 N | 75.28 W |
| Goulet Lake ⊜ | 184 | 55.23 N | 96.18 W |
| Goulia | 150 | 10.01 N | 7.11 W |
| Goulicun | 106 | 31.40 N | 120.00 E |
| Goulimime | 148 | 28.56 N | 10.04 W |
| Goulimine □[4] | 148 | 28.30 N | 9.45 W |
| Goulmima | 148 | 31.02 N | 5.00 W |
| Goumbati ∧[2] | 150 | 13.08 N | 12.06 W |
| Goumbou | 150 | 14.59 N | 7.27 W |
| Gouménissa | 38 | 40.57 N | 22.27 E |
| Goumois | 58 | 47.16 N | 6.57 E |
| Gouna | 146 | 8.32 N | 13.34 E |
| Gounda ≃ | 146 | 9.25 N | 20.57 E |
| Goundam | 150 | 16.25 N | 3.40 W |
| Goundi | 146 | 9.22 N | 17.22 E |
| Gounou-Gaya | 146 | 9.38 N | 15.31 E |
| Gouougang, Mount ∧ | 170 | 33.53 S | 150.07 E |
| Goupillières | 261 | 48.53 N | 1.46 E |
| Gouraya | 34 | 36.34 N | 1.55 E |
| Gourbassi | 150 | 13.24 N | 11.38 W |
| Gourbeyre | 241o | 16.00 N | 61.42 W |
| Gourcy | 150 | 13.13 N | 2.21 W |
| Gourdhead Run ≃ | 279b | 40.33 N | 79.57 W |
| Gourdon, Fr. | 32 | 44.44 N | 1.23 E |
| Gourdon, Fr. | 62 | 43.43 N | 6.59 E |
| Gouré | 150 | 13.58 N | 10.18 E |
| Gouri ⊥ | 124 | 24.53 N | 88.07 E |
| Gourin | 32 | 48.08 N | 3.36 W |
| Gouripur | 124 | 24.46 N | 90.34 E |
| Gourits ≃ | 158 | 34.21 S | 21.52 E |
| Gourlay Lake ⊜ | 190 | 48.52 N | 84.54 W |
| Gourma Rharous | 150 | 16.53 N | 1.55 W |
| Gournay-en-Bray | 50 | 49.29 N | 1.44 E |
| Gournay-sur-Marne | 261 | 48.52 N | 2.34 E |
| Gouro | 146 | 19.33 N | 19.33 E |
| Gourock | 46 | 55.58 N | 4.49 W |
| Goussainville | 50 | 49.01 N | 2.28 E |
| Goussonville | 261 | 48.55 N | 1.46 E |
| Goutou | 105 | 39.49 N | 117.11 E |
| Gouveia, Bra. | 255 | 18.27 S | 43.44 W |
| Gouveia, Port. | 266c | 38.50 N | 9.26 W |
| Gouverneur | 212 | 44.20 N | 75.27 W |
| Gouyadong | 100 | 25.10 N | 112.55 E |
| Gouyave | 241k | 12.10 N | 61.44 W |
| Gov'altaj □[4] | 102 | 45.30 N | 96.00 E |
| Govan | 184 | 51.18 N | 105.00 W |
| Go Vap | 269c | 10.49 N | 106.41 E |
| Govardhan | 124 | 27.30 N | 77.28 E |
| Gove | 198 | 38.57 N | 100.29 W |
| Govea ≃ | 286b | 22.56 N | 82.30 W |
| Govena, mys › | 74 | 59.48 N | 166.06 E |
| Govenlock | 184 | 49.15 N | 109.48 W |
| Gove Peninsula ›[1] | 164 | 12.20 S | 136.50 E |
| Governador, Ilha do I | 287a | 22.48 S | 43.12 W |
| Governador Portela | 256 | 22.29 S | 43.30 W |
| Governador Valadares | 255 | 18.51 S | 41.56 W |
| Government Camp | 224 | 45.18 N | 121.45 W |
| Governor Bond Lake ⊜[1] | 219 | 38.56 N | 89.23 W |
| Governor Dodge State Park ♦ | 190 | 43.00 N | 90.07 W |
| Governor Generoso | 116 | 6.39 N | 126.05 E |
| Governor Head › | 170 | 35.07 S | 150.46 E |
| Governor Nice Memorial Bridge ♦[5] | 208 | 38.22 N | 77.00 W |
| Governor Printz Park ♦ | 285 | 39.52 N | 75.18 W |
| Governor's Harbour | 238 | 25.10 N | 76.14 W |
| Governors Island I | 276 | 40.41 N | 74.01 W |
| Govind Ballabh Pant Sāgar ⊜[1] | 124 | 24.05 N | 82.50 E |
| Govindgarh | 124 | 24.23 N | 81.18 E |
| Govind Sāgar ⊜[1] | 123 | 31.20 N | 76.45 E |
| Gov'-Ugtaal | 102 | 46.04 N | 107.30 E |
| Gowan ≃ | 184 | 55.49 N | 94.08 W |
| Gowanda | 210 | 42.27 N | 78.56 W |
| Gowan Range ⩘ | 166 | 25.00 S | 145.00 E |
| Gowen City | 208 | 40.45 N | 76.32 W |
| Gower | 194 | 39.36 N | 94.35 W |
| Gower ›[1] | 42 | 51.36 N | 4.10 W |
| Gowerton | 42 | 51.39 N | 4.01 W |
| Gowienica ≃ | 54 | 53.40 N | 14.38 E |
| Gowmal (Gumal) ≃ | 120 | 31.56 N | 70.22 E |
| Gowmal Kalay | 120 | 32.29 N | 68.55 E |
| Gowna, Lough ⊜ | 48 | 53.51 N | 7.34 W |
| Gowrie | 198 | 42.16 N | 94.17 W |
| Gowy ≃ | 44 | 53.17 N | 2.51 W |
| Goya | 252 | 29.08 S | 59.16 W |
| Goyania → Goiânia | 255 | 16.40 S | 49.16 W |
| Goyatz-Guhlen | 54 | 52.01 N | 14.09 E |
| Goyave | 241o | 16.08 N | 61.34 W |
| Goyaves, Grande Rivière à ≃ | 241o | 16.18 N | 61.37 W |
| Goyaves, Îlets à II | 241o | 16.10 N | 61.48 W |
| Göyçay | 84 | 40.39 N | 47.44 E |
| Göyçay ≃ | 84 | 40.39 N | 47.45 E |
| Goyder ≃ | 164 | 12.38 S | 135.11 E |
| Goyder Creek ≃ | 162 | 25.39 S | 134.47 E |
| Goyelle, Lac ⊜ | 186 | 50.47 N | 60.45 W |
| Goyeneche | 258 | 35.20 S | 58.43 W |
| Goyer, Île I | 275a | 45.29 N | 73.17 W |
| Goyerkāta | 124 | 26.42 N | 89.02 E |
| Göynücek | 130 | 40.24 N | 35.32 E |
| Göynük, Tür. | 130 | 39.08 N | 40.53 E |
| Göynük, Tür. | 130 | 40.24 N | 30.47 E |
| Göynük ≃, Tür. | 130 | 40.20 N | 30.05 E |
| Göynük ≃, Tür. | 130 | 38.53 N | 40.34 E |
| Goyt ≃ | 262 | 53.24 N | 2.09 W |
| Göytäpä | 84 | 39.08 N | 48.36 E |
| Goz-Beïda | 146 | 12.13 N | 21.25 E |
| Gozdnica | 30 | 51.26 N | 15.06 E |
| Gozdowice | 54 | 52.45 N | 14.18 E |
| Göze Dağı ∧ | 130 | 41.24 N | 42.30 E |
| Gözeli | 130 | 38.25 N | 39.04 E |
| Gozen-yama | 94 | 36.32 N | 140.20 E |
| Gozha Co ⊜ | 120 | 34.59 N | 81.06 E |
| Gözne | 130 | 36.59 N | 34.34 E |
| Gozo → Għawdex I | 36 | 36.03 N | 14.15 E |
| Göz Tepe ∧[2] | 267b | 41.06 N | 29.06 E |
| Gozzano | 62 | 45.45 N | 8.26 E |
| Graaff-Reinet | 158 | 32.14 S | 24.32 E |
| Graafwater | 158 | 32.00 S | 18.37 E |
| Graauw | 52 | 51.20 N | 4.05 E |
| Grabc'ovo | 82 | 54.34 N | 36.22 E |
| Graben-Neudorf | 56 | 49.09 N | 8.29 E |
| Grabenstätt | 64 | 47.51 N | 12.32 E |
| Grabill | 216 | 41.12 N | 84.58 W |
| Grabo | 150 | 4.55 N | 7.30 W |
| Grabouw | 158 | 34.09 S | 19.02 E |
| Grabovo | 86 | 53.07 N | 74.52 E |
| Grabow | 54 | 53.16 N | 11.34 E |
| Grabowhöfe | 54 | 53.34 N | 12.36 E |
| Grabowiec | 30 | 50.50 N | 23.33 E |
| Grabów nad Prosną | 30 | 51.31 N | 18.06 E |
| Gračac | 36 | 44.18 N | 15.51 E |
| Gračanica | 38 | 44.42 N | 18.19 E |
| Gračanica, Manastir ♦[1] | 38 | 42.36 N | 21.09 E |
| Graçay | 50 | 47.08 N | 1.51 E |
| Grace | 202 | 42.34 N | 111.43 W |
| Gracefield | 188 | 46.06 N | 76.03 W |
| Graceham | 208 | 39.36 N | 77.22 W |
| Graceton | 214 | 40.30 N | 79.10 W |
| Graceville, Fl., U.S. | 192 | 30.57 N | 85.31 W |
| Graceville, Mn., U.S. | 198 | 45.34 N | 96.26 W |
| Gračevka | 82 | 55.06 N | 36.49 E |
| Grächen | 58 | 46.12 N | 7.50 E |
| Grachovo | 80 | 56.04 N | 51.58 E |
| Grači | 80 | 49.49 N | 43.33 E |
| Gracia ♦[8] | 266d | 41.23 N | 2.09 E |
| Gracias | 236 | 14.35 N | 88.35 W |
| Gracias a Dios □[5] | 236 | 15.10 N | 84.20 W |
| Gracias a Dios, Cabo › | 236 | 15.00 N | 83.10 W |
| Gračiki ≃ | 83 | 48.30 N | 39.52 E |
| Graciosa I | 148a | 39.04 N | 28.00 W |
| Graciosa, Isla I | 148 | 29.15 N | 13.30 W |
| Gračov | 80 | 49.26 N | 41.32 E |
| Gračovka, Ross. | 80 | 52.07 N | 40.01 E |
| Gračovka, Ross. | 80 | 52.57 N | 52.52 E |
| Gračov Kust | 80 | 51.59 N | 49.50 E |
| Gradačac | 38 | 44.53 N | 18.26 E |
| Gradara | 66 | 43.57 N | 12.46 E |
| Gradaús | 250 | 7.43 S | 51.11 W |
| Gr'adcy | 76 | 56.24 N | 31.55 E |
| Gräddö | 40 | 59.46 N | 19.02 E |
| Gradisca d'Isonzo | 64 | 45.53 N | 13.30 E |
| Grado, Esp. | 34 | 43.23 N | 6.04 W |
| Grado, It. | 64 | 45.40 N | 13.23 E |
| Grado, Laguna di c | 64 | 45.43 N | 13.20 E |
| Gradoli | 66 | 42.39 N | 11.51 E |
| Grad Sofija □[4] | 38 | 42.41 N | 23.19 E |
| Grady, Ar., U.S. | 194 | 34.04 N | 91.42 W |
| Grady, N.M., U.S. | 196 | 34.49 N | 103.19 W |
| Gradyville | 285 | 39.57 N | 75.28 W |
| Graemsay I | 46 | 58.56 N | 3.17 W |
| Græsted | 41 | 56.04 N | 12.17 E |
| Graettinger | 198 | 43.14 N | 94.45 W |
| Gräfelfing | 60 | 48.07 N | 11.25 E |
| Grafenau | 60 | 48.52 N | 13.25 E |
| Gräfenberg | 60 | 49.39 N | 11.15 E |
| Grafenberg ♦[8] | 263 | 51.14 N | 6.50 E |
| Gräfenhainichen | 54 | 51.44 N | 12.27 E |
| Gräfenroda | 54 | 50.45 N | 10.48 E |
| Gräfenthal | 54 | 50.31 N | 11.18 E |
| Gräfentonna | 54 | 51.05 N | 10.44 E |
| Grafenwöhr | 60 | 49.43 N | 11.54 E |
| Graffignano | 66 | 42.34 N | 12.12 E |
| Grafham Water ⊜ | 42 | 52.17 N | 0.20 W |
| Gräfinau-Angstedt | 54 | 50.42 N | 11.01 E |
| Grafing bei München | 60 | 48.02 N | 11.59 E |
| Gråfjell ∧ | 26 | 60.16 N | 9.29 E |
| Grafling | 60 | 48.54 N | 12.59 E |
| Graford | 196 | 32.56 N | 98.14 W |
| Grafrath | 64 | 48.07 N | 11.10 E |
| Gräfrath ♦[8] | 263 | 51.13 N | 7.04 E |
| Grafschaft Bentheim □[9] | 52 | 52.30 N | 7.00 E |
| Grafton, Austl. | 166 | 29.41 S | 152.56 E |
| Grafton, On., Can. | 212 | 44.00 N | 78.01 W |
| Grafton, Il., U.S. | 219 | 38.58 N | 90.25 W |
| Grafton, Ma., U.S. | 207 | 42.12 N | 71.41 W |
| Grafton, N.Y., U.S. | 210 | 42.46 N | 73.27 W |
| Grafton, N.D., U.S. | 198 | 48.24 N | 97.24 W |
| Grafton, Oh., U.S. | 214 | 41.16 N | 82.03 W |
| Grafton, W.V., U.S. | 188 | 39.20 N | 80.01 W |
| Grafton, Wi., U.S. | 190 | 43.19 N | 87.57 W |
| Grafton, Cape › | 164 | 16.52 S | 145.55 E |
| Grafton Lakes State Park ♦ | 210 | 42.48 N | 73.28 W |
| Grafty Green | 260 | 51.12 N | 0.41 E |
| Graglia | 62 | 45.33 N | 7.59 E |
| Gragnano | 68 | 40.41 N | 14.31 E |
| Gragnano Trebbiense | 62 | 45.01 N | 9.34 E |
| Graham, Ca., U.S. | 280 | 34.15 N | 118.31 W |
| Graham, N.C., U.S. | 192 | 36.04 N | 79.24 W |
| Graham, Tx., U.S. | 196 | 33.06 N | 98.35 W |
| Graham, Wa., U.S. | 224 | 47.03 N | 122.17 W |
| Graham, Mount ∧ | 200 | 32.42 N | 109.52 W |
| Graham Cave State Park ♦ | 219 | 38.55 N | 91.32 W |
| Graham Creek ≃ | 218 | 38.49 N | 85.39 W |
| Graham Hill County Park ♦ | 276 | 41.07 N | 73.48 W |
| Graham Island I | 182 | 53.40 N | 132.30 W |
| Graham Lake ⊜, On., Can. | 212 | 44.34 N | 75.53 W |
| Graham Lake ⊜, Me., U.S. | 188 | 44.40 N | 68.25 W |
| Graham Land ♦[1] | 9 | 66.00 S | 63.30 W |
| Graham Memorial Park ♦ | 284b | 39.25 N | 76.30 W |
| Graham Moore, Cape › | 176 | 72.52 N | 76.04 W |
| Graham Moore Bay c | 176 | 75.26 N | 101.25 W |
| Grahamstad → Grahamstown | 158 | 33.19 S | 26.31 E |
| Grahamstown | 158 | 33.19 S | 26.31 E |
| Grahamsville | 210 | 41.51 N | 74.33 W |
| Grahn | 218 | 38.17 N | 83.04 W |
| Graie, Alpi (Alpes Grées) ⩘ | 62 | 45.30 N | 7.10 E |
| Graiguenarmanagh | 48 | 52.32 N | 6.57 W |
| Grain | 42 | 51.28 N | 0.43 E |
| Grain, Isle of I | 42 | 51.27 N | 0.41 E |
| Grain Coast ⊥[2] | 150 | 5.00 N | 9.00 W |
| Grainfield | 198 | 39.06 N | 100.27 W |
| Grajagan | 115a | 8.35 S | 114.13 E |
| Grajagan, Teluk c | 115a | 8.40 S | 114.18 E |
| Grajaú | 250 | 5.49 S | 46.08 W |
| Grajaú ≃ | 250 | 3.41 S | 44.48 W |
| Grajewo | 30 | 53.39 N | 22.27 E |
| Grajvoron | 78 | 50.28 N | 35.39 E |
| Gram | 41 | 55.17 N | 9.04 E |
| Gramacho | 287a | 22.44 S | 43.18 W |
| Gramada | 38 | 43.50 N | 22.39 E |
| Gramado | 252 | 29.24 S | 50.54 W |
| Gramalote | 246 | 7.53 N | 72.48 W |
| Gramastetten | 61 | 48.23 N | 14.12 E |
| Gramat | 32 | 44.47 N | 1.43 E |
| Gramatneusiedl | 264b | 48.02 N | 16.29 E |
| Grambling | 194 | 32.31 N | 92.42 W |
| Grambow | 54 | 53.25 N | 14.20 E |
| Gramilla | 252 | 27.18 S | 64.37 W |
| Gramínea | 256 | 22.10 S | 46.38 W |
| Graminha, Reprêsa ⊜[1] | 256 | 21.40 S | 46.35 W |
| Grammer | 218 | 39.09 N | 85.43 W |
| Grammichele | 70 | 37.13 N | 14.38 E |
| Grammont → Geraardsbergen | 50 | 50.46 N | 3.52 E |
| Gramoteino | 86 | 54.31 N | 86.22 E |
| Grampian | 214 | 40.57 N | 78.36 W |
| Grampian □[4] | 46 | 57.15 N | 2.45 W |
| Grampian Mountains ⩘ | 46 | 56.55 N | 4.00 W |
| Grampians National Park ♦ | 166 | 37.20 S | 142.30 E |
| Gramschatz | 56 | 49.56 N | 9.58 E |
| Gramsh | 38 | 40.52 N | 20.11 E |
| Gramzow | 54 | 53.12 N | 14.00 E |
| Gran → Esztergom | 30 | 47.48 N | 18.45 E |
| Grana ≃ | 62 | 44.25 N | 7.27 E |
| Granaatboskolk | 158 | 30.02 S | 19.51 E |
| Granada, Col. | 246 | 3.34 N | 73.45 W |
| Granada, Esp. | 34 | 37.13 N | 3.41 W |
| Granada, Nic. | 236 | 11.56 N | 85.57 W |
| Granada, Pil. | 116 | 10.40 N | 123.02 E |
| Granada, Co., U.S. | 198 | 38.03 N | 102.18 W |
| Granada, Mn., U.S. | 190 | 43.41 N | 94.20 W |
| Granada □[4] | 34 | 37.15 N | 3.15 W |
| Granada □[5] | 236 | 11.50 N | 86.00 W |
| Granada → Grenada □[1] | 241k | 12.07 N | 61.40 W |
| Granada Hills ♦[8] | 280 | 34.16 N | 118.31 W |
| Granado | 286d | 12.04 S | 76.57 W |
| Granaglione | 66 | 44.07 N | 10.58 E |
| Gran Altiplanicie Central ⩘[1] | 254 | 48.55 S | 69.45 W |
| Granard | 48 | 53.47 N | 7.30 W |
| Granarolo dell'Emilia | 64 | 44.33 N | 11.27 E |
| Granatello | 70 | 37.53 N | 12.32 E |
| Gran Bahía Australiana → Great Australian Bight c[3] | 162 | 35.00 S | 135.00 E |
| Gran Bajo de San Julián V | 254 | 49.30 S | 68.30 W |
| Gran Barrera de Arrecifes → Great Barrier Reef ♦[2] | 160 | 18.00 S | 145.50 E |
| Granbergsdal | 40 | 59.24 N | 14.35 E |
| Granbury | 222 | 32.26 N | 97.47 W |
| Granbury, Lake ⊜[1] | 222 | 32.25 N | 97.45 W |
| Granby, P.Q., Can. | 206 | 45.24 N | 72.44 W |
| Granby, Co., U.S. | 200 | 40.05 N | 105.56 W |
| Granby, Ct., U.S. | 207 | 41.57 N | 72.47 W |
| Granby, Ma., U.S. | 207 | 42.15 N | 72.31 W |
| Granby, Mo., U.S. | 194 | 36.55 N | 94.15 W |
| Granby ≃ | 182 | 49.03 N | 118.25 W |
| Granby, Lake ⊜[1] | 200 | 40.09 N | 105.50 W |
| Gran Canaria I | 148 | 28.00 N | 15.36 W |
| Grancey-le-Château | 58 | 47.40 N | 5.02 E |
| Gran Chaco ♦[1] | 18 | 23.00 S | 60.00 W |
| Grand | 58 | 48.23 N | 5.29 E |
| Grand ≃, On., Can. | 212 | 42.51 N | 79.34 W |
| Grand ≃, U.S. | 194 | 39.23 N | 93.06 W |
| Grand ≃, Mi., U.S. | 216 | 43.04 N | 86.15 W |
| Grand ≃, Oh., U.S. | 214 | 41.46 N | 81.17 W |
| Grand ≃, S.D., U.S. | 198 | 45.40 N | 100.32 W |
| Grand ≃, Wi., U.S. | 190 | 43.45 N | 89.16 W |
| Grand, East Fork ≃ | 194 | 40.12 N | 94.21 W |
| Grand, Lac ⊜ | 190 | 47.10 N | 76.57 W |
| Grand, North Fork ≃ | 198 | 45.47 N | 102.16 W |
| Grand, South Fork ≃ | 198 | 45.43 N | 102.17 W |
| Grandas | 34 | 43.13 N | 6.52 W |
| Grand Bahama I | 238 | 26.38 N | 78.25 W |
| Grand Ballon ∧ | 58 | 47.55 N | 7.08 E |
| Grand Bank | 186 | 47.06 N | 55.46 W |
| Grand Banks of Newfoundland ♦[4] | 16 | 45.00 N | 53.00 W |
| Grand-Bassam | 150 | 5.12 N | 3.44 W |
| Grand Bay, N.B., Can. | 186 | 45.18 N | 66.12 W |
| Grand Bay, Al., U.S. | 194 | 30.28 N | 88.20 W |
| Grand Beach | 184 | 50.35 N | 96.40 W |
| Grand Bend | 190 | 43.15 N | 81.45 W |
| Grand Béréby | 150 | 4.38 N | 6.55 W |
| Grand Blanc | 216 | 42.55 N | 83.37 W |
| Grand-Bourg | 241o | 15.53 N | 61.19 W |
| Grand Bruit | 186 | 47.41 N | 58.13 W |
| Grand Caille Point › | 241f | 13.52 N | 61.05 W |
| Grand Calumet ≃ | 278 | 41.38 N | 87.34 W |
| Grand Calumet, Île du I | 190 | 45.44 N | 76.41 W |
| Grand Canal ≅, Ire. | 48 | 53.21 N | 6.14 W |
| Grand Canal → Da Yunhe ≅, Zhg. | 90 | 32.12 N | 119.31 E |
| Grand Cane | 194 | 32.05 N | 93.48 W |
| Grand Cañon du Verdon ♦ | 62 | 43.47 N | 6.27 E |
| Grand Canyon | 200 | 36.03 N | 112.08 W |
| Grand Canyon V | 200 | 36.10 N | 112.45 W |
| Grand Canyon National Park ♦ | 200 | 36.15 N | 112.58 W |
| Grand Canyon of Pennsylvania ♦ | 210 | 41.43 N | 77.28 W |
| Grand Cayman I | 238 | 19.20 N | 81.15 W |
| Grand Central Terminal ♦[5] | 276 | 40.45 N | 73.59 W |
| Grand Centre | 184 | 54.25 N | 110.13 W |
| Grand Cess | 150 | 4.36 N | 8.10 W |
| Grandchamp, Fr. | 58 | 47.43 N | 5.27 E |
| Grandchamp, Fr. | 261 | 48.43 N | 1.37 E |
| Grand-Charmont | 58 | 47.32 N | 6.50 E |
| Grand Chenier | 194 | 29.46 N | 92.58 W |
| Grand Combin ∧ | 58 | 45.56 N | 7.18 E |
| Grand Coulee | 202 | 47.56 N | 119.00 W |
| Grand Coulee V | 202 | 47.45 N | 119.15 W |
| Grand Coulee Dam ♦[6] | 202 | 47.57 N | 118.59 W |
| Grand-Couronne | 50 | 49.21 N | 1.00 E |
| Grand Cul-de-Sac Marin c | 241o | 16.20 N | 61.35 W |
| Grande ≃, Arg. | 252 | 36.52 S | 69.45 W |
| Grande ≃, Arg. | 252 | 24.12 S | 64.42 W |
| Grande ≃, Bol. | 248 | 15.51 S | 64.39 W |
| Grande ≃, Bra. | 242 | 11.05 S | 43.09 W |
| Grande ≃, Bra. | 255 | 20.06 S | 51.04 W |
| Grande ≃, Bra. | 287a | 22.55 S | 43.25 W |
| Grande ≃, Bra. | 287b | 23.45 S | 46.22 W |
| Grande ≃, Chile | 252 | 30.35 S | 71.11 W |
| Grande ≃, Esp. | 34 | 39.07 N | 0.44 W |
| Grande ≃, It. | 70 | 37.55 N | 13.13 E |
| Grande ≃, Méx. | 234 | 17.43 N | 96.56 W |
| Grande ≃, Méx. | 234 | 18.50 N | 102.05 W |
| Grande ≃, Nic. | 236 | 12.28 N | 86.21 W |
| Grande ≃, Pan. | 236 | 8.18 N | 80.24 W |
| Grande ≃, Perú | 248 | 14.59 S | 75.29 W |
| Grande ≃, S.A. | 254 | 53.48 S | 67.40 W |
| Grande ≃, Ven. | 246 | 8.39 N | 60.59 W |
| Grande, Arroyo ≃, Arg. | 258 | 34.37 S | 59.25 W |
| Grande, Arroyo ≃, Arg. | 288 | 34.45 S | 58.08 W |
| Grande, Arroyo ≃, Méx. | 234 | 23.55 N | 98.44 W |
| Grande, Arroyo ≃, Ur. | 252 | 33.08 S | 57.09 W |
| Grande, Arroyo ≃, Ur. | 258 | 33.37 S | 57.09 W |
| Grande, Bahía c[3] | 254 | 50.45 S | 68.45 W |
| Grande, Boca c | 220 | 26.43 N | 82.16 W |
| Grande, Boca ≃[1] | 246 | 8.38 N | 60.30 W |
| Grande, Cañada ≃, Arg. | 258 | 35.19 S | 57.48 W |
| Grande, Cañada ≃, Arg. | 258 | 35.15 S | 59.23 W |
| Grande, Cayo I | 240p | 20.59 N | 79.09 W |


**Symbols** in the index entries represent the broad categories identified in the key at the right. Symbols with superior numbers (⩘[1]) identify subcategories (see complete key on page *I · 1*).

**Symbole** im Register stellen die rechts im Schlüssel erklärten Kategorien dar. Symbole mit hochgestellten Ziffern (⩘[1]) bezeichnen Unterabteilungen einer Kategorie (vgl. vollständiger Schlüssel auf Seite *I · 1*).

**Los símbolos** incluídos en el texto del índice representan las grandes categorías identificadas con la clave a la derecha. Los símbolos con numeros en su parte superior (⩘[1]) identifican las subcategorías (véase la clave completa en la página *I · 1*).

**Les symboles** de l'index représentent les catégories indiquées dans la légende à droite. Les symboles suivis d'un indice (⩘[1]) représentent des sous-catégories (voir légende complète à la page *I · 1*).

**Os símbolos** incluídos no texto do índice representam as grandes categorias identificadas com a chave à direita. Os símbolos com números em sua parte superior (⩘[1]) identificam as subcategorias (veja-se a chave completa à página *I · 1*).

| | English | Deutsch | Español | Français | Português |
|---|---|---|---|---|---|
| ∧ | Mountain | Berg | Montaña | Montagne | Montanha |
| ⩘ | Mountains | Gebirge | Montañas | Montagnes | Montanhas |
| )( | Pass | Paß | Paso | Col | Passo |
| V | Valley, Canyon | Tal, Cañon | Valle, Cañón | Vallée, Canyon | Vale, Canhão |
| ≃ | Plain | Ebene | Llano | Plaine | Planície |
| › | Cape | Kap | Cabo | Cap | Cabo |
| I | Island | Insel | Isla | Île | Ilha |
| II | Islands | Inseln | Islas | Îles | Ilhas |
| ⊥ | Other Topographic Features | Andere Topographische Objekte | Otros Elementos Topográficos | Autres données topographiques | Outros acidentes topográficos |

## ESPAÑOL

| Nombre | Página | Lat.°′ | Long.°′ W = Oeste |
|---|---|---|---|
| Grande, Cerro ∧, Méx. | 232 | 28.46 N | 107.32 W |
| Grande, Cerro ∧, Méx. | 234 | 23.22 N | 103.35 W |
| Grande, Cerro ∧, Méx. | 234 | 21.45 N | 103.05 W |
| Grande, Cerro ∧, Méx. | 234 | 20.43 N | 101.12 W |
| Grande, Cerro ∧, Méx. | 234 | 23.39 N | 100.51 W |
| Grande, Corixa (Curiche Grande) ≡ | 248 | 17.10 S | 58.20 W |
| Grande, Cuchilla ∧ | 252 | 33.15 S | 55.07 W |
| Grande, Curiche (Corixa Grande) ≃ | 248 | 17.10 S | 58.20 W |
| Grande, Igarapé ≃ | 250 | 3.37 S | 48.53 W |
| Grande, Ilha I, Bra. | 252 | 23.45 S | 54.03 W |
| Grande, Ilha I, Bra. | 256 | 23.09 S | 44.14 W |
| Grande, Isola I | 70 | 37.53 N | 12.26 E |
| Grande, Lago ⊜, Arg. | 254 | 47.44 S | 68.04 W |
| Grande, Lago ⊜, Bra. | 250 | 2.16 S | 54.17 W |
| Grande, Laguna ⊜, Arg. | 258 | 34.14 S | 58.53 W |
| Grande, Laguna ⊜, Méx. | 234 | 20.06 N | 96.40 W |
| Grande, Mare c | 68 | 40.27 N | 17.12 E |
| Grande, Naviglio ≍ | 266b | 45.35 N | 8.42 E |
| Grande, Ponta › | 255 | 16.22 S | 39.01 W |
| Grande, Praia ⩦[2] | 256 | 24.05 S | 46.30 W |
| Grande, Punta › | 252 | 21.54 S | 70.12 W |
| Grande, Ribeirão ≃ | 256 | 21.24 S | 44.29 W |
| Grande, Rio (Bravo del Norte) ≃ | 178 | 25.55 N | 97.09 W |
| Grande, Salina ≡ | 68 | 40.26 N | 17.18 E |
| Grande, Serra ⩕ | 250 | 6.00 S | 40.52 W |
| Grande, Sierra ⩕ | 196 | 29.40 N | 104.55 W |
| Grande-Anse | 186 | 47.48 N | 65.11 W |
| Grande Anse, La c | 275a | 45.23 N | 73.53 W |
| Grande Anse Bay c | 241k | 12.02 N | 61.45 W |
| Grande Baie, La c | 275a | 45.29 N | 74.00 W |
| Grande Cache | 182 | 53.53 N | 119.08 W |
| Grande Casse, Pointe de la ∧ | 62 | 45.24 N | 6.50 E |
| Grande Cayemite I | 238 | 18.37 N | 73.45 W |
| Grande Chartreuse, Couvent de la ʋ[1] | 62 | 45.22 N | 5.50 E |
| Grande de Añasco ≃ | 240m | 18.16 N | 67.11 W |
| Grande de Arecibo ≃ | 240m | 18.29 N | 66.42 W |
| Grande de Jutaí, Ilha I | 250 | 3.15 S | 49.37 W |
| Grande de Lipez ≃ | 248 | 20.47 S | 67.14 W |
| Grande de Loíza ≃ | 240m | 18.27 N | 65.53 W |
| Grande de Manacapuru, Lago ⊜ | 246 | 3.04 S | 61.25 W |
| Grande de Manatí ≃ | 240m | 18.29 N | 66.32 W |
| Grande de Matagalpa ≃ | 236 | 12.54 N | 83.32 W |
| Grande de Santiago ≃ | 234 | 21.36 N | 105.26 W |
| Grande de Tarija ≃ | 248 | 22.53 S | 64.21 W |
| Grande de Térraba ≃ | 236 | 8.59 N | 83.37 W |
| Grande do Curuaí, Lago ⊜ | 250 | 2.15 S | 55.20 W |
| Grande do Gurupá, Ilha I | 250 | 1.00 S | 51.30 W |
| Grande do Tapará, Ilha I | 250 | 2.14 S | 54.39 W |
| Grande Île de Criques I | 273b | 4.20 S | 15.25 E |
| Grande Inferior, Cuchilla ⩕[2] | 258 | 33.50 S | 56.27 W |
| Grand-Entrée | 186 | 47.33 N | 61.34 W |
| Grande-Prairie | 182 | 55.10 N | 118.48 W |
| Grand Erg de Bilma ◆[2] | 146 | 18.30 N | 14.00 E |
| Grand Erg Occidental ◆[2] | 148 | 30.30 N | 0.30 E |
| Grand Erg Oriental ◆[2] | 148 | 30.30 N | 7.00 E |
| Grande-Rivière | 186 | 48.24 N | 64.30 W |
| Grande Rivière, La ≃ | 176 | 53.50 N | 79.00 W |
| Grande Ronde ≃ | 202 | 46.05 N | 116.59 W |
| Grandes, Salinas ≚, Arg. | 252 | 23.43 S | 66.00 W |
| Grandes, Salinas ≚, Arg. | 252 | 30.05 S | 65.05 W |
| Grandes Antillas, Islas → Greater Antilles II | 238 | 20.00 N | 74.00 W |
| Grandes Antilles, Îles → Greater Antilles II | 238 | 20.00 N | 74.00 W |
| Grande Sassière, Aiguille de la ∧ | 62 | 45.30 N | 7.00 E |
| Grande Sauldre ≃ | 50 | 47.26 N | 2.05 E |
| Gran Desierto de Arena → Great Sandy Desert ◆[2] | 162 | 21.30 S | 125.00 E |
| Gran Desierto Victoria → Great Victoria Desert ◆[2] | 162 | 28.30 S | 127.45 E |
| Grandes-Piles | 206 | 46.41 N | 72.44 W |
| Grande-Synthe | 50 | 51.01 N | 2.19 E |
| Grand-Étang | 186 | 46.33 N | 61.02 W |
| Grande-Terre I | 241o | 16.20 N | 61.25 W |
| Grande Vigie, Pointe de la › | 241o | 16.31 N | 61.28 W |
| Grand Eyvia ≃ | 62 | 45.42 N | 7.14 E |
| Grand Falls, N.B., Can. | 186 | 47.03 N | 67.44 W |
| Grand Falls, Nf., Can. | 186 | 48.56 N | 55.40 W |
| Grandfalls, Tx., U.S. | 196 | 31.20 N | 102.51 W |
| Grandfather Mountain ∧ | 192 | 36.07 N | 81.48 W |
| Grandfield | 196 | 34.13 N | 98.41 W |
| Grand Forks, B.C., Can. | 182 | 49.02 N | 118.27 W |
| Grand Forks, N.D., U.S. | 198 | 47.55 N | 97.01 W |
| Grand Forks Air Force Base ■ | 198 | 47.57 N | 97.25 W |
| Grand-Fort-Philippe | 50 | 51.00 N | 2.06 E |
| Grand-Fougeray | 32 | 47.44 N | 1.44 W |
| Grand-Gallargues | 62 | 43.43 N | 4.10 E |
| Grand Gorge | 210 | 42.21 N | 74.29 W |
| Grand-Halleux | 56 | 50.19 N | 5.54 E |
| Grand Haven | 216 | 43.03 N | 86.13 W |
| Grand Haven State Park ♠ | 216 | 43.02 N | 86.13 W |
| Grand Hers ≃ | 32 | 43.47 N | 1.20 E |
| Grandin, Lac ⊜ | 176 | 63.59 N | 119.00 W |
| Grandioznyj, pik ∧ | 88 | 53.50 N | 96.11 E |
| Grand Island, Fl., U.S. | 220 | 28.53 N | 81.44 W |
| Grand Island, Ne., U.S. | 198 | 40.55 N | 98.20 W |
| Grand Island, N.Y., U.S. | 212 | 43.01 N | 78.58 W |
| Grand Island I, On., Can. | 212 | 44.34 N | 78.50 W |
| Grand Island I, Mi., U.S. | 190 | 46.30 N | 86.40 W |
| Grand Island I, N.Y., U.S. | 210 | 43.02 N | 78.58 W |
| Grand Isle | 194 | 29.14 N | 89.59 W |
| Grand Isle □[6] | 206 | 44.57 N | 73.17 W |
| Grand Junction, Co., U.S. | 200 | 39.03 N | 108.33 W |
| Grand Junction, Ia., U.S. | 198 | 42.01 N | 94.14 W |
| Grand Junction, Mi., U.S. | 216 | 42.24 N | 86.04 W |
| Grand Junction, Tn., U.S. | 194 | 35.02 N | 89.11 W |

## FRANÇAIS

| Nom | Page | Lat.°′ | Long.°′ W = Ouest |
|---|---|---|---|
| Grand Lac Salé → Great Salt Lake ⊜ | 200 | 41.10 N | 112.30 W |
| Grand lac Victoria ⊜ | 190 | 47.31 N | 77.30 W |
| Grand-Lahou | 150 | 5.08 N | 5.01 W |
| Grand Lake | 200 | 40.15 N | 105.49 W |
| Grand Lake ⊜, N.B., Can. | 186 | 45.55 N | 66.05 W |
| Grand Lake ⊜, Nf., Can. | 186 | 49.00 N | 57.25 W |
| Grand Lake ⊜, N.A. | 186 | 45.43 N | 67.50 W |
| Grand Lake ⊜, La., U.S. | 194 | 29.55 N | 91.25 W |
| Grand Lake ⊜, La., U.S. | 194 | 29.55 N | 92.47 W |
| Grand Lake ⊜, Mi., U.S. | 190 | 45.18 N | 83.30 W |
| Grand Lake ⊜, Oh., U.S. | 216 | 40.30 N | 84.32 W |
| Grand Lake Saint Marys State Park ♠ | 216 | 40.33 N | 84.27 W |
| Grand Ledge | 216 | 42.45 N | 84.44 W |
| Grand Lieu, Lac de ⊜ | 32 | 47.06 N | 1.40 W |
| Grand'Maison, Barrage de ◆[6] | 62 | 45.12 N | 6.07 E |
| Grand Manan Channel ʯ | 186 | 44.45 N | 66.52 W |
| Grand Manan Island I | 186 | 44.40 N | 66.50 W |
| Grand Marais, Mi., U.S. | 190 | 46.40 N | 85.59 W |
| Grand Marais, Mn., U.S. | 190 | 47.45 N | 90.20 W |
| Grand Meadow | 190 | 43.42 N | 92.34 W |
| Grand-Mère | 206 | 46.37 N | 72.41 W |
| Grand Mesa ∧ | 200 | 39.00 N | 108.00 W |
| Grandmesnil, Lac ⊜ | 186 | 51.19 N | 67.33 W |
| Grand Morin ≃ | 50 | 48.54 N | 2.50 E |
| Grand Muveran ∧ | 58 | 46.14 N | 7.08 E |
| Grandola, It. | 58 | 46.02 N | 9.13 E |
| Grândola, Port. | 34 | 38.10 N | 8.34 W |
| Grand Pabos, Rivière du ≃ | 186 | 48.21 N | 64.43 W |
| Grand Palace ʋ | 269a | 13.45 N | 100.30 E |
| Grand Passage ʯ | 175f | 18.45 S | 163.10 E |
| Grand-Popo | 150 | 6.17 N | 1.50 E |
| Grand Portage | 190 | 47.57 N | 89.41 W |
| Grand Portage Indian Reservation ◆[4] | 190 | 47.55 N | 89.45 W |
| Grand Portage National Monument ♠ | 190 | 48.02 N | 89.38 W |
| Grand Prairie | 222 | 32.44 N | 96.59 W |
| Grandpré | 56 | 49.20 N | 4.52 E |
| Grand Pré National Historic Park ♠ | 186 | 45.08 N | 64.18 W |
| Grand Prix Airport ⊠ | 281 | 42.33 N | 83.11 W |
| Grand Rapids, Mb., Can. | 184 | 53.08 N | 99.20 W |
| Grand Rapids, Mi., U.S. | 216 | 42.58 N | 85.40 W |
| Grand Rapids, Mn., U.S. | 190 | 47.14 N | 93.31 W |
| Grand Rapids, Oh., U.S. | 216 | 41.24 N | 83.51 W |
| Grand Rhône ≃ | 62 | 43.20 N | 4.50 E |
| Grand Ridge | 216 | 41.14 N | 88.50 W |
| Grandrieu, Bel. | 50 | 50.12 N | 4.10 E |
| Grandrieu, Fr. | 62 | 44.47 N | 3.38 E |
| Grand River | 214 | 41.44 N | 81.17 W |
| Grand' Rivière | 240e | 14.52 N | 61.11 W |
| Grand Ronde | 224 | 45.03 N | 123.36 W |
| Grand Roy | 241k | 12.08 N | 61.45 W |
| Grand Ruisseau, Le ≃ | 275a | 45.39 N | 73.12 W |
| Grand-Saint-Bernard, Col du )( | 58 | 45.50 N | 7.10 E |
| Grand-Saint-Bernard, Tunnel du ◆[5] | 58 | 45.51 N | 7.11 E |
| Grand Saline | 222 | 32.40 N | 95.42 W |
| Grand Saline Creek ≃ | 222 | 32.41 N | 95.36 W |
| Grand-Santi | 250 | 4.19 N | 54.24 W |
| Grandson | 58 | 46.49 N | 6.38 E |
| Grand Terrace | 228 | 34.02 N | 117.18 W |
| Grand Teton ∧ | 202 | 43.44 N | 110.48 W |
| Grand Teton National Park ♠ | 202 | 43.30 N | 110.45 W |
| Grand Tower | 194 | 37.37 N | 89.29 W |
| Grand Traverse Bay c | 190 | 45.02 N | 85.30 W |
| Grand Traverse Bay, East Arm c | 190 | 44.52 N | 85.28 W |
| Grand Traverse Bay, West Arm c | 190 | 44.52 N | 85.35 W |
| Grandtully | 46 | 56.39 N | 3.46 W |
| Grand Turk | 238 | 21.28 N | 71.08 W |
| Grand Union Canal ≍ | 260 | 51.30 N | 0.02 W |
| Grand Valley, On., Can. | 212 | 43.54 N | 80.19 W |
| Grand Valley, Pa., U.S. | 214 | 41.43 N | 79.32 W |
| Grandview, Mb., Can. | 184 | 51.10 N | 100.42 W |
| Grandview, Il., U.S. | 219 | 39.48 N | 89.37 W |
| Grandview, Mo., U.S. | 194 | 38.53 N | 94.31 W |
| Grandview, Pa., U.S. | 279b | 40.10 N | 79.52 W |
| Grandview, Tx., U.S. | 222 | 32.16 N | 97.11 W |
| Grandview, Wa., U.S. | 202 | 46.15 N | 119.54 W |
| Grand View, Wi., U.S. | 190 | 46.22 N | 91.06 W |
| Grandview Beach | 216 | 41.50 N | 83.24 W |
| Grandview Heights, Oh., U.S. | 218 | 39.58 N | 83.02 W |
| Grandview Heights, Pa., U.S. | 208 | 40.03 N | 76.17 W |
| Grandview Homes | 216 | 40.44 N | 84.04 W |
| Grand View-on-Hudson | 276 | 41.44 N | 73.55 W |
| Grandvillars | 58 | 47.33 N | 6.58 E |
| Grandville | 216 | 42.54 N | 85.45 W |
| Grandvilliers | 50 | 49.40 N | 1.56 E |
| Grand Wash Cliffs ⩦[4] | 200 | 35.40 N | 113.50 W |
| Grandyle Village | 210 | 43.00 N | 78.57 W |
| Grâne | 62 | 44.44 N | 4.55 E |
| Grañén | 34 | 41.56 N | 0.22 W |
| Graneros | 252 | 34.04 S | 70.44 W |
| Graney, Lough ⊜ | 48 | 52.59 N | 8.40 W |
| Grangärde | 40 | 60.16 N | 14.59 E |
| Grange, Austl. | 168b | 34.54 S | 138.30 E |
| Grange, Eng., U.K. | 262 | 53.23 N | 3.09 W |
| Grange, Bois de la ♠ | 261 | 48.45 N | 2.30 E |
| Grange-Bléneau, Château de la ⊥ | 50 | 48.41 N | 2.55 E |
| Grange Hill | 260 | 51.37 N | 0.05 E |
| Grangemouth | 46 | 56.02 N | 3.45 W |
| Grängen ⊜ | 40 | 59.45 N | 14.47 E |
| Grangent, Lac de ⊜[1] | 62 | 45.25 N | 4.15 E |
| Grange-over-Sands | 44 | 54.12 N | 2.55 W |
| Granger, In., U.S. | 216 | 41.45 N | 86.06 W |
| Granger, Tx., U.S. | 222 | 30.43 N | 97.26 W |
| Granger, Wa., U.S. | 202 | 46.20 N | 120.11 W |
| Granger, Wy., U.S. | 200 | 41.35 N | 109.58 W |
| Granger Draw ∨ | 196 | 30.20 N | 100.57 W |
| Granger Lake ⊜[1] | 222 | 30.42 N | 97.22 W |
| Granges → Grenchen | 58 | 47.11 N | 7.24 E |
| Grängesberg | 40 | 60.05 N | 14.59 E |
| Granges-sur-Vologne | 58 | 48.09 N | 6.47 E |
| Grangeville, Id., U.S. | 202 | 45.55 N | 116.07 W |
| Grangeville, Pa., U.S. | 208 | 39.47 N | 76.58 W |
| Grangousier Hill ∧[2] | 190 | 47.35 N | 84.56 W |
| Gran Guardia | 252 | 25.52 S | 58.53 W |
| Granite, Md., U.S. | 284b | 39.21 N | 76.51 W |
| Granite, Ok., U.S. | 196 | 34.57 N | 99.22 W |
| Granite City | 219 | 38.42 N | 90.08 W |
| Granite Creek ≃ | 224 | 48.43 N | 120.55 W |
| Granite Dome ∧ | 226 | 38.13 N | 119.44 W |
| Granite Downs | 162 | 26.57 S | 133.30 E |
| Granite Falls, Mn., U.S. | 198 | 44.48 N | 95.32 W |

## PORTUGUÊS

| Nome | Página | Lat.°′ | Long.°′ W = Oeste |
|---|---|---|---|
| Granite Falls, N.C., U.S. | 192 | 35.47 N | 81.25 W |
| Granite Falls, Wa., U.S. | 224 | 48.05 N | 121.58 W |
| Granite Lake ⊜[1] | 186 | 48.08 N | 57.05 W |
| Granite Mountain ∧, Austl. | 171b | 35.44 S | 148.13 E |
| Granite Mountain ∧, Ak., U.S. | 180 | 65.26 N | 161.14 W |
| Granite Mountain ∧, Ak., U.S. | 182 | 55.30 N | 132.35 W |
| Granite Mountains ⩕ | 202 | 42.35 N | 107.30 W |
| Granite Pass )( | 202 | 44.38 N | 107.30 W |
| Granite Peak | 162 | 25.38 S | 121.21 E |
| Granite Peak ∧, Mt., U.S. | 202 | 45.10 N | 109.48 W |
| Granite Peak ∧, Mt., U.S. | 202 | 45.34 N | 112.02 W |
| Granite Peak ∧, Nv., U.S. | 204 | 41.40 N | 117.35 W |
| Granite Peak ∧, Nv., U.S. | 204 | 40.48 N | 119.25 W |
| Granite Range ⩕ | 204 | 41.00 N | 119.35 W |
| Graniteville, Ma., U.S. | 207 | 42.35 N | 71.27 W |
| Graniteville, S.C., U.S. | 192 | 33.33 N | 81.48 W |
| Graniteville, Vt., U.S. | 188 | 44.09 N | 72.29 W |
| Graniti | 70 | 37.53 N | 15.14 E |
| Granitogorsk | 85 | 42.44 N | 73.27 E |
| Granitola, Capo › | 70 | 37.34 N | 12.41 E |
| Granitola Torretta | 70 | 37.34 N | 12.40 E |
| Granity | 172 | 41.38 S | 171.51 E |
| Granitzenbach ≃ | 61 | 47.11 N | 14.46 E |
| Granja, Bra. | 250 | 3.06 S | 40.50 W |
| Granja, Port. | 266c | 38.51 N | 9.06 W |
| Gran Khingan → Da Hinggan Ling ⩕ | 90 | 49.00 N | 122.00 E |
| Granki | 76 | 54.51 N | 31.27 E |
| Grankulla (Kauniainen) | 26 | 60.13 N | 24.45 E |
| Gran Lago Salado → Great Salt Lake ⊜ | 200 | 41.10 N | 112.30 W |
| Gran Laguna Salada ⊜ | 254 | 44.24 S | 67.23 W |
| Granma □[4] | 240p | 21.20 N | 76.50 W |
| Gränna | 26 | 58.01 N | 14.28 E |
| Grannoch, Loch ⊜ | 44 | 55.00 N | 4.17 W |
| Granollers | 34 | 41.37 N | 2.18 E |
| Granön | 26 | 64.15 N | 19.19 E |
| Gran Pajonal ⩕ | 248 | 10.45 S | 74.30 W |
| Gran Paradiso ∧ | 62 | 45.32 N | 7.16 E |
| Gran Paradiso, Parco Nazionale del ♠ | 62 | 45.34 N | 7.18 E |
| Gran Pilastro (Hochfeiler) ∧ | 64 | 46.58 N | 11.44 E |
| Gran Rio ≃ | 250 | 4.01 N | 55.31 W |
| Gran Sasso d'Italia ⩕ | 66 | 42.27 N | 13.42 E |
| Gransee | 54 | 53.00 N | 13.09 E |
| Grant, Fl., U.S. | 220 | 27.55 N | 80.31 W |
| Grant, Mi., U.S. | 190 | 43.20 N | 85.48 W |
| Grant, Ne., U.S. | 198 | 40.50 N | 101.43 W |
| Grant □[6], In., U.S. | 216 | 40.33 N | 85.40 W |
| Grant □[6], Ky., U.S. | 218 | 38.39 N | 84.39 W |
| Grant ≃ | 190 | 42.40 N | 90.45 W |
| Grant, Lake ⊜ | 218 | 39.00 N | 83.53 W |
| Grant, Mount ∧ | 204 | 38.34 N | 118.48 W |
| Grant, Point › | 169 | 38.31 S | 145.07 E |
| Granta ≃ | 42 | 52.10 N | 0.06 E |
| Grant Birthplace ⊥ | 218 | 38.54 N | 84.14 W |
| Grant City | 194 | 40.29 N | 94.24 W |
| Grantham, Austl. | 171a | 27.34 S | 152.12 E |
| Grantham, Eng., U.K. | 42 | 52.55 N | 0.39 W |
| Grantham, Pa., U.S. | 208 | 40.09 N | 77.00 W |
| Grant-Kohrs Ranch National Historic Site ⊥ | 202 | 46.25 N | 112.40 W |
| Grant Lake ⊜[1] | 226 | 37.50 N | 119.07 W |
| Grantley Adams International Airport ⊠ | 241g | 13.04 N | 59.29 W |
| Grant Mills | 283 | 41.57 N | 71.26 W |
| Granton | 46 | 55.59 N | 3.14 W |
| Grantorto | 64 | 45.36 N | 11.43 E |
| Grantown-on-Spey | 46 | 57.19 N | 3.37 W |
| Grant Park | 216 | 41.14 N | 87.39 W |
| Grant Park ♠ | 278 | 41.52 N | 87.37 W |
| Grant Point › | 176 | 68.19 N | 98.53 W |
| Grant Range ⩕ | 204 | 38.25 N | 115.30 W |
| Grants | 200 | 35.09 N | 107.50 W |
| Grantsburg, In., U.S. | 218 | 38.17 N | 86.28 W |
| Grantsburg, Wi., U.S. | 190 | 45.46 N | 92.40 W |
| Grantshouse | 46 | 55.53 N | 2.19 W |
| Grants Pass | 202 | 42.26 N | 123.19 W |
| Grants Patch | 162 | 30.27 S | 121.07 E |
| Grant-Suttie Bay c | 176 | 69.47 N | 77.15 W |
| Grantsville, Ut., U.S. | 200 | 40.36 N | 112.27 W |
| Grantsville, W.V., U.S. | 188 | 38.55 N | 81.05 W |
| Grantville, Ga., U.S. | 192 | 33.14 N | 84.50 W |
| Grantville, Pa., U.S. | 208 | 40.23 N | 76.39 W |
| Granum | 182 | 49.52 N | 113.30 W |
| Granville, Austl. | 274a | 33.50 S | 151.01 E |
| Granville, Fr. | 32 | 48.50 N | 1.36 W |
| Granville, Il., U.S. | 190 | 41.15 N | 89.13 W |
| Granville, Ma., U.S. | 207 | 42.04 N | 72.51 W |
| Granville, Mo., U.S. | 219 | 39.34 N | 92.06 W |
| Granville, N.Y., U.S. | 188 | 43.24 N | 73.15 W |
| Granville, N.D., U.S. | 198 | 48.16 N | 100.50 W |
| Granville, Oh., U.S. | 214 | 40.04 N | 82.31 W |
| Granville, Pa., U.S. | 208 | 40.33 N | 77.38 W |
| Granville, W.V., U.S. | 188 | 39.38 N | 79.59 W |
| Granville Lake ⊜ | 184 | 56.18 N | 100.30 W |
| Granvin | 26 | 60.33 N | 6.43 E |
| Granzin, Dtsch. | 54 | 53.25 N | 12.53 E |
| Granzin, Dtsch. | 54 | 53.30 N | 11.56 E |
| Grão Mogol | 255 | 16.34 S | 42.54 W |
| Grão-Mogol ≃ | 256 | 21.46 S | 43.40 W |
| Grape Creek ≃ | 200 | 38.26 N | 105.16 W |
| Grape Island I | 283 | 42.16 N | 70.55 W |
| Grapeland | 222 | 31.29 N | 95.28 W |
| Grapeview | 224 | 47.19 N | 122.50 W |
| Grapeville | 214 | 40.19 N | 79.36 W |
| Grapevine | 222 | 32.56 N | 97.04 W |
| Grapevine Lake ⊜[1] | 222 | 32.59 N | 97.06 W |
| Grapevine Peak ∧ | 204 | 36.57 N | 117.09 W |
| Grappa, Monte ∧ | 64 | 45.52 N | 11.48 E |
| Grappenhall | 262 | 53.22 N | 2.32 W |
| Grarem | 34 | 36.31 N | 6.19 E |
| Gras, Lac de ⊜ | 176 | 64.30 N | 110.30 W |
| Grasberg | 52 | 53.11 N | 8.59 E |
| Grasbult | 158 | 30.52 S | 21.47 E |
| Graskop | 156 | 24.58 S | 30.49 E |
| Grasleben | 54 | 52.18 N | 11.01 E |
| Grasmere, S. Afr. | 158 | 26.26 S | 27.52 E |
| Grasmere, Eng., U.K. | 44 | 54.28 N | 3.02 W |
| Grasmere Lake ⊜ | 276 | 40.36 N | 74.05 W |
| Gräsö | 40 | 60.21 N | 18.28 E |
| Gräsö I | 40 | 60.24 N | 18.25 E |
| Grasonville | 208 | 38.57 N | 76.12 W |
| Grass ≃, Mb., Can. | 184 | 56.03 N | 96.33 W |
| Grass ≃, N.Y., U.S. | 188 | 44.59 N | 74.46 W |
| Grass, North Branch ≃ | 188 | 44.25 N | 75.06 W |
| Grass, South Branch ≃ | 188 | 44.22 N | 75.05 W |
| Grassano | 68 | 40.38 N | 16.18 E |
| Grassau | 64 | 47.47 N | 12.27 E |
| Grass Creek | 202 | 43.56 N | 108.39 W |
| Grass Creek ≃ | 202 | 43.52 N | 108.22 W |
| Grasscroft | 262 | 53.32 N | 2.02 W |
| Grasse | 62 | 43.40 N | 6.55 E |
| Grassendale ◆[8] | 262 | 53.21 N | 2.54 W |
| Grassflat | 214 | 41.00 N | 78.07 W |
| Grass Hassock Channel ʯ | 276 | 40.36 N | 73.48 W |
| Grasshopper Creek ≃ | 202 | 45.06 N | 112.47 W |
| Grassington | 44 | 54.04 N | 2.00 W |
| Grass Island I | 276 | 40.39 N | 73.18 W |
| Grässjön ⊜ | 40 | 59.52 N | 13.43 E |
| Grass Lake | 216 | 42.15 N | 84.13 W |
| Grass Lake ⊜ | 216 | 42.27 N | 88.10 W |
| Grassmere, Lake ⊜ | 172 | 41.44 S | 174.10 E |
| Grass Patch | 162 | 33.14 S | 121.43 E |
| Grass Range | 202 | 47.01 N | 108.48 W |
| Grassridge Dam ⊜[1] | 158 | 31.45 S | 25.29 E |
| Grass River Provincial Park ♠ | 184 | 54.40 N | 100.50 W |
| Grass Valley, Austl. | 168a | 31.38 S | 116.48 E |
| Grass Valley, Ca., U.S. | 226 | 39.13 N | 121.03 W |
| Grass Valley, Or., U.S. | 224 | 45.21 N | 120.47 W |
| Grassy | 166 | 40.03 S | 144.04 E |
| Grassy ≃ | 190 | 48.22 N | 81.27 W |
| Grassy Bay c | 276 | 40.38 N | 73.48 W |
| Grassy Brook ≃ | 284a | 43.03 N | 79.07 W |
| Grassy Creek ≃, In., U.S. | 216 | 40.55 N | 86.30 W |
| Grassy Creek ≃, Mo., U.S. | 219 | 39.54 N | 91.37 W |
| Grassy Hill ∧ | 271d | 22.25 N | 114.09 E |
| Grassy Island I | 276 | 41.04 N | 73.23 W |
| Grassy Island Lake ⊜ | 184 | 51.50 N | 110.20 W |
| Grassy Key I | 220 | 24.46 N | 80.57 W |
| Grassy Lake | 182 | 49.49 N | 111.43 W |
| Grassy Lake ⊜ | 220 | 27.13 N | 81.20 W |
| Grassy Plains | 182 | 53.57 N | 125.54 W |
| Grassy Sprain Reservoir ⊜[1] | 276 | 40.58 N | 73.51 W |
| Gråsten | 41 | 54.55 N | 9.36 E |
| Grästorp | 26 | 58.20 N | 12.40 E |
| Graterford | 285 | 40.13 N | 75.27 W |
| Graterford State Correctional Institution ʋ | 285 | 40.14 N | 75.26 W |
| Grates Point › | 186 | 48.10 N | 52.57 W |
| Gratis | 218 | 39.38 N | 84.31 W |
| Gratitunon | 115a | 7.43 S | 113.00 E |
| Gratkorn | 61 | 47.08 N | 15.21 E |
| Gratwein | 61 | 47.07 N | 15.19 E |
| Gratz, Ky., U.S. | 218 | 38.28 N | 84.57 W |
| Gratz, Pa., U.S. | 208 | 40.37 N | 76.43 W |
| Gratztown | 279b | 40.14 N | 79.47 W |
| Graubünden (Grischun) □[3] | 58 | 46.45 N | 9.30 E |
| Graudenz → Grudziądz | 30 | 53.29 N | 18.45 E |
| Graue Hörner ∧ | 58 | 46.57 N | 9.23 E |
| Graukogel ∧ | 64 | 47.06 N | 13.10 E |
| Graulhet | 32 | 43.46 N | 2.00 E |
| Graulinster | 56 | 49.45 N | 6.18 E |
| Graun → Curon Venosta | 64 | 46.49 N | 10.32 E |
| Graupa | 54 | 51.00 N | 13.54 E |
| Gravatá | 250 | 8.12 S | 35.34 W |
| Gravatá ≃ | 255 | 16.53 S | 42.10 W |
| Grave | 52 | 51.45 N | 5.44 E |
| Grave Creek ≃ | 202 | 42.39 N | 123.35 W |
| Gravedona | 58 | 46.09 N | 9.18 E |
| Gravelbourg | 184 | 49.53 N | 106.34 W |
| Gravelines | 50 | 50.59 N | 2.07 E |
| Gravellona-Toce | 58 | 45.55 N | 8.26 E |
| Gravell Point › | 176 | 67.10 N | 76.43 W |
| Gravelly Bay c | 284a | 42.52 N | 79.15 W |
| Gravelly Brook ≃ | 276 | 40.25 N | 74.13 W |
| Gravelly Pond ⊜ | 283 | 42.36 N | 70.48 W |
| Gravelotte, Fr. | 56 | 49.07 N | 6.01 E |
| Gravelotte, S. Afr. | 156 | 23.56 S | 30.34 E |
| Gravenhurst | 212 | 44.55 N | 79.22 W |
| Grävenwiesbach | 56 | 50.23 N | 8.27 E |
| Grave Peak ∧ | 202 | 46.24 N | 114.44 W |
| Gravesend, Austl. | 166 | 29.35 S | 150.19 E |
| Gravesend, Eng., U.K. | 42 | 51.27 N | 0.24 E |
| Gravesend Bay c | 276 | 40.36 N | 74.01 W |
| Gravesham □[8] | 260 | 51.25 N | 0.24 E |
| Gravette | 194 | 36.25 N | 94.27 W |
| Gravigny | 50 | 49.03 N | 1.10 E |
| Gravina | 70 | 37.34 N | 15.03 E |
| Gravina di Matera ≃ | 68 | 40.29 N | 16.43 E |
| Gravina in Puglia | 68 | 40.49 N | 16.25 E |
| Gravina Island I | 182 | 55.17 N | 131.45 W |
| Gray, Fr. | 58 | 47.27 N | 5.35 E |
| Gray, Ga., U.S. | 192 | 33.00 N | 83.32 W |
| Gray, Ky., U.S. | 192 | 36.56 N | 84.00 W |
| Gray, Pa., U.S. | 214 | 40.08 N | 79.05 W |
| Grayback Mountain ∧, Ak., U.S. | 180 | 57.08 N | 153.54 W |
| Grayback Mountain ∧, Or., U.S. | 202 | 42.07 N | 123.18 W |
| Grayland | 224 | 46.48 N | 124.05 W |
| Grayling, Ak., U.S. | 180 | 62.57 N | 160.03 W |
| Grayling, Mi., U.S. | 190 | 44.39 N | 84.42 W |
| Graylyn Crest | 285 | 39.48 N | 75.31 W |
| Grays | 42 | 51.29 N | 0.20 E |
| Grays ≃ | 224 | 46.18 N | 123.41 W |
| Grays Harbor □[6] | 224 | 47.09 N | 123.45 W |
| Grays Harbor c | 224 | 46.56 N | 124.05 W |
| Grayshott | 42 | 51.11 N | 0.45 W |
| Grayslake | 216 | 42.21 N | 88.03 W |
| Grays Lake ⊜ | 278 | 42.21 N | 88.03 W |
| Grays Lake ≡ | 202 | 43.04 N | 111.26 W |
| Grays Lake Outlet ≃ | 202 | 43.22 N | 111.46 W |
| Grayson, Sk., Can. | 184 | 50.44 N | 102.40 W |
| Grayson, Al., U.S. | 194 | 34.16 N | 87.19 W |
| Grayson, Ca., U.S. | 226 | 37.33 N | 121.10 W |
| Grayson, Ky., U.S. | 218 | 38.19 N | 82.56 W |
| Grayson, La., U.S. | 194 | 32.02 N | 92.06 W |
| Grayson Lake ⊜[1] | 218 | 38.13 N | 83.00 W |
| Grayson Lake State Park ♠ | 218 | 38.13 N | 83.02 W |
| Grays Peak ∧ | 200 | 39.37 N | 105.45 W |
| Grays Point | 274a | 34.04 S | 151.05 E |
| Grays River | 224 | 46.21 N | 123.36 W |
| Gray Summit | 219 | 38.29 N | 90.49 W |
| Graysville | 194 | 35.26 N | 85.05 W |
| Graytown | 214 | 41.33 N | 83.16 W |
| Grayville | 194 | 37.57 N | 88.10 W |
| Gray Wolf ≃ | 224 | 47.55 N | 123.07 W |
| Graz | 61 | 47.05 N | 15.27 E |
| Grazalema | 34 | 36.46 N | 5.22 W |
| Graždanka ◆[8] | 265a | 60.00 N | 30.24 E |
| Gr'azeva ≃ | 265b | 55.51 N | 37.08 E |
| Gr'azi | 80 | 52.29 N | 39.57 E |
| Grazierville | 214 | 40.40 N | 78.16 W |
| Gr'aznoje | 82 | 54.02 N | 39.07 E |
| Gr'aznovo, Ross. | 82 | 54.18 N | 36.49 E |
| Gr'aznovo, Ross. | 265b | 55.57 N | 37.34 E |
| Gr'aznyj Irtek | 80 | 51.56 N | 53.11 E |
| Gr'azovec | 76 | 58.53 N | 40.14 E |
| Grdelica | 38 | 42.54 N | 22.04 E |
| Greåker | 26 | 59.16 N | 11.02 E |
| Greasby | 262 | 53.23 N | 3.07 W |
| Great ≃ | 241k | 12.08 N | 61.36 W |
| Great Adventure ♠ | 208 | 40.09 N | 74.27 W |
| Great Altcar | 262 | 53.33 N | 3.01 W |
| Great America ♠ | 282 | 37.24 N | 121.59 W |
| Great Amwell | 260 | 51.48 N | 0.01 W |
| Great Artesian Basin ≚[1] | 166 | 25.00 S | 143.00 E |
| Great Australian Bight c[3] | 162 | 35.00 S | 130.00 E |
| Great Ayton | 44 | 54.30 N | 1.08 W |
| Great Baddow | 42 | 51.43 N | 0.29 E |
| Great Bahama Bank ✢[4] | 238 | 23.15 N | 78.00 W |
| Great Barford | 42 | 52.09 N | 0.21 W |
| Great Barrier Island I | 172 | 36.10 S | 175.25 E |
| Great Barrier Reef ✢[2] | 160 | 18.00 S | 146.50 E |
| Great Barrier Reef Marine Park ♠ | 166 | 21.00 S | 151.00 E |
| Great Barrington | 207 | 42.11 N | 73.21 W |
| Great Barrow | 262 | 53.12 N | 2.48 W |
| Great Basin ≚[1] | 178 | 40.00 N | 117.00 W |
| Great Basin National Park ♠ | 204 | 38.55 N | 114.14 W |
| Great Bay c | 208 | 39.30 N | 74.23 W |
| Great Bear ≃ | 180 | 64.54 N | 125.35 W |
| Great Bear Lake ⊜ | 176 | 66.00 N | 120.00 W |
| Great Beaver Lake ⊜ | 182 | 54.25 N | 123.45 W |
| Great Belt → Storebælt ʯ | 41 | 55.30 N | 11.00 E |
| Great Bend, Ks., U.S. | 198 | 38.21 N | 98.45 W |
| Great Bend, N.Y., U.S. | 212 | 44.02 N | 75.43 W |
| Great Bend, Pa., U.S. | 210 | 41.58 N | 75.44 W |
| Great Bernera I | 46 | 58.13 N | 6.49 W |
| Great Bitter Lake → Murrah al-Kubrā, Al-Buḥayrah al- ⊜ | 142 | 30.20 N | 32.23 E |
| Great Blasket Island I | 48 | 52.05 N | 10.32 W |
| Great Blue Hill ∧[2] | 207 | 42.13 N | 71.07 W |
| Great Bookham | 260 | 51.16 N | 0.22 W |
| Great Braxted | 260 | 51.48 N | 0.42 E |
| Great Brewster Island I | 283 | 42.20 N | 70.53 W |
| Great Britain I | 22 | 54.00 N | 2.00 W |
| Great Brook ≃ | 276 | 40.42 N | 74.31 W |
| Great Buddha ʋ[1] | 268 | 35.19 N | 139.32 E |
| Great Budworth | 262 | 53.18 N | 2.30 W |
| Great Burnt Lake ⊜ | 186 | 48.20 N | 56.13 W |
| Great Burstead | 260 | 51.36 N | 0.25 E |
| Great Camanoe I | 240m | 18.29 N | 64.32 W |
| Great Captain Island I | 276 | 40.59 N | 73.38 W |
| Great Central | 182 | 49.19 N | 124.59 W |
| Great Central Lake ⊜ | 182 | 49.27 N | 125.12 W |
| Great Channel ʯ | 110 | 6.25 N | 94.20 E |
| Great Chazy ≃ | 188 | 44.56 N | 73.23 W |
| Great Clifton | 44 | 54.39 N | 3.29 W |
| Great Coco Island I | 110 | 14.05 N | 93.24 E |
| Great Coharie Creek ≃ | 192 | 34.50 N | 78.22 W |
| Great Cove c | 276 | 40.43 N | 73.14 W |
| Great Crosby | 262 | 53.29 N | 3.01 W |
| Great Crossing | 218 | 38.08 N | 84.38 W |
| Great Cumbrae Island I | 46 | 55.46 N | 4.55 W |
| Great Dismal Swamp ≡ | 192 | 36.30 N | 76.30 W |
| Great Ditch ≍ | 276 | 40.24 N | 74.31 W |
| Great Divide Basin ≚[1] | 202 | 42.00 N | 108.10 W |
| Great Dividing Range ⩕ | 160 | 25.00 S | 147.00 E |
| Great Driffield | 44 | 54.00 N | 0.27 W |
| Great Duck Island I | 190 | 45.40 N | 82.58 W |
| Great Dunmow | 42 | 51.53 N | 0.22 E |
| Great Eau ≃ | 44 | 53.25 N | 0.13 E |
| Great Egg Harbor ≃ | 208 | 39.18 N | 74.40 W |
| Great Egg Harbor Bay c | 208 | 39.18 N | 74.37 W |
| Great Egg Harbor Inlet c | 208 | 39.20 N | 74.34 W |
| Greater Antilles II | 238 | 20.00 N | 74.00 W |
| Greater Buffalo International Airport ⊠ | 210 | 42.56 N | 78.44 W |
| Greater Cincinnati Airport ⊠ | 218 | 39.03 N | 84.40 W |
| Greater Khingan Range → Da Hinggan Ling ⩕ | 90 | 49.00 N | 122.00 E |
| Greater London □[6] | 42 | 51.30 N | 0.10 W |
| Greater Manchester □[6] | 44 | 53.30 N | 2.20 W |
| Greater Pittsburgh International Airport ⊠ | 214 | 40.29 N | 80.14 W |
| Greater Sunda Islands II | 108 | 2.00 S | 110.00 E |
| Greater Wilmington Airport ⊠ | 208 | 39.41 N | 75.36 W |
| Greater Wollongong → Wollongong | 170 | 34.25 S | 150.54 E |
| Great Escape ♠ | 210 | 43.22 N | 73.42 W |
| Great Exuma I | 238 | 23.32 N | 75.50 W |
| Great Falls, Mb., Can. | 184 | 50.27 N | 96.02 W |
| Great Falls, Mt., U.S. | 202 | 47.30 N | 111.17 W |
| Great Falls, S.C., U.S. | 192 | 34.34 N | 80.54 W |
| Great Falls, Va., U.S. | 284c | 39.00 N | 77.17 W |
| Great Falls ʟ | 284c | 39.00 N | 77.16 W |
| Great Falls Park ♠ | 284c | 39.00 N | 77.15 W |
| Great Fish Point › | 158 | 33.30 S | 27.10 E |
| Great Gable ∧ | 44 | 54.28 N | 3.12 W |
| Great Gaddesden | 260 | 51.47 N | 0.30 W |
| Great Grimsby → Grimsby | 44 | 53.35 N | 0.05 W |
| Great Guana Cay I | 238 | 24.00 N | 76.20 W |
| Great Hameldon ∧[2] | 262 | 53.45 N | 2.19 W |
| Great Harwood | 44 | 53.48 N | 2.24 W |
| Great Haywood | 42 | 52.48 N | 2.00 W |
| Great Himalaya Range ⩕ | 120 | 29.00 N | 83.00 E |
| Greathouse Peak ∧ | 202 | 46.46 N | 109.21 W |
| Great Inagua I | 238 | 21.05 N | 73.18 W |
| Great Indian Desert (Thar Desert) ◆[2] | 120 | 27.00 N | 71.00 E |
| Great Island I, Ire. | 48 | 51.52 N | 8.17 W |
| Great Island I, N.Y., U.S. | 276 | 40.38 N | 73.30 W |
| Great Island I, N.Y., U.S. | 276 | 41.05 N | 73.44 W |
| Great Karroo (Groot Karroo) ⩕[1] | 158 | 32.25 S | 22.40 E |
| Great Kills ◆[8] | 276 | 40.33 N | 74.10 W |
| Great Kills Harbor c | 276 | 40.32 N | 74.08 W |
| Great Kills Park ♠ | 276 | 40.33 N | 74.08 W |
| Great La Cloche Island I | 190 | 46.01 N | 81.52 W |
| Great Lake ⊜ | 166 | 41.52 S | 146.45 E |
| Great Lakes Naval Training Center ■ | 216 | 42.18 N | 87.50 W |
| Great Lakes Steel Works ʋ[3] | 281 | 42.15 N | 83.08 W |
| Great Machipongo Inlet c | 208 | 37.22 N | 75.43 W |
| Great Malvern | 42 | 52.07 N | 2.19 W |
| Great Marsh ≡ | 208 | 36.32 N | 75.57 W |
| Great Marton | 262 | 53.48 N | 3.02 W |
| Great Massingham | 42 | 52.46 N | 0.40 E |
| Great Meadows | 210 | 40.52 N | 74.54 W |
| Great Meadows National Wildlife Refuge ◆[4] | 283 | 42.29 N | 71.20 W |
| Great Mercury Island I | 172 | 36.37 S | 175.48 E |
| Great Meteor Tablemount ✢[3] | 18 | 30.00 N | 28.30 W |
| Great Miami ≃ | 188 | 39.06 N | 84.49 W |
| Great Mills | 208 | 38.14 N | 76.30 W |
| Great Misery Island I | 283 | 42.33 N | 70.48 W |
| Great Missenden | 42 | 51.43 N | 0.43 W |
| Great Mis Tor ∧ | 42 | 50.34 N | 4.01 W |
| Great Mosque ʋ[1] | 146 | 32.46 N | 22.40 E |
| Great Namaqualand □[9] | 156 | 25.00 S | 17.00 E |
| Great Neck | 276 | 40.48 N | 73.43 W |
| Great Neck ›[1], Ma., U.S. | 283 | 42.42 N | 70.48 W |
| Great Neck ›[1], N.Y., U.S. | 276 | 40.50 N | 73.45 W |
| Great Neck Estates | 276 | 40.47 N | 73.44 W |
| Great Nicobar I | 110 | 7.00 N | 93.50 E |
| Great North East Channel ʯ | 164 | 9.30 S | 143.25 E |
| Great Notch Reservoir ⊜[1] | 276 | 40.53 N | 74.12 W |
| Great Ormes Head › | 44 | 53.21 N | 3.52 W |
| Great Ouse ≃ | 42 | 52.47 N | 0.22 E |
| Great Oxney Green | 260 | 51.44 N | 0.25 E |
| Great Palm Island I | 166 | 18.43 S | 146.37 E |
| Great Parndon | 260 | 51.45 N | 0.05 E |
| Great Patchogue Lake ⊜ | 276 | 40.46 N | 73.01 W |
| Great Peconic Bay c | 207 | 40.56 N | 72.30 W |
| Great Pee Dee ≃ | 192 | 33.21 N | 79.16 W |
| Great Piece Meadows ≡ | 276 | 40.54 N | 74.19 W |
| Great Plain of the Koukdjuak ≚ | 176 | 66.00 N | 73.00 W |
| Great Plains ≚ | 16 | 42.00 N | 100.00 W |
| Great Point › | 207 | 41.23 N | 70.03 W |
| Great Pubnico Lake ⊜ | 186 | 43.42 N | 65.43 W |
| Great Quittacas Pond ⊜ | 207 | 41.48 N | 70.54 W |
| Great River | 276 | 40.45 N | 73.10 W |
| Great Ruaha ≃ | 154 | 7.56 S | 37.52 E |
| Great Sacandaga Lake ⊜ | 210 | 43.08 N | 74.10 W |
| Great Saint Bernard Pass → Grand-Saint-Bernard, Col du )( | 58 | 45.50 N | 7.10 E |
| Great Sale Cay I | 192 | 27.00 N | 78.12 W |
| Great Salt Lake ⊜ | 200 | 41.10 N | 112.30 W |
| Great Salt Lake Desert ◆[2] | 200 | 40.40 N | 113.30 W |
| Great Salt Plains Lake ⊜[1] | 196 | 36.44 N | 98.12 W |
| Great Sand Dunes National Monument ♠ | 200 | 37.43 N | 105.36 W |
| Great Sand Hills ⩕[2] | 184 | 50.35 N | 109.05 W |
| Great Sandy Desert ◆[2] | 162 | 21.30 S | 125.00 E |
| Great Sandy National Park ♠ | 166 | 24.59 S | 153.17 E |
| Great Sankey | 44 | 53.23 N | 2.37 W |
| Great Santa Cruz Island I | 116 | 6.52 N | 122.03 E |
| Great Scarcies (Kolenté) ≃ | 150 | 8.55 N | 13.08 W |
| Great Sea Reef ✢[2] | 175g | 16.15 S | 179.00 E |
| Great Seneca Creek ≃ | 208 | 39.08 N | 77.20 W |
| Great Shelford | 42 | 52.09 N | 0.09 E |
| Great Sitkin Island I | 180 | 52.03 N | 176.07 W |
| Great Slave Lake ⊜ | 176 | 61.30 N | 114.00 W |
| Great Smoky Mountains ⩕ | 192 | 35.35 N | 83.30 W |
| Great Smoky Mountains National Park ♠ | 192 | 35.39 N | 83.30 W |
| Great Sound ʯ, Ber. | 240a | 32.17 N | 64.51 W |
| Great Sound ʯ, N.J., U.S. | 208 | 39.06 N | 74.47 W |
| Great South Bay c | 210 | 40.40 N | 73.17 W |
| Great Stour ≃ | 42 | 51.19 N | 1.15 E |
| Great Sutton | 262 | 53.17 N | 2.56 W |
| Great Swamp ≡ | 276 | 40.43 N | 74.28 W |
| Great Swamp National Wildlife Refuge ◆[4] | 276 | 40.43 N | 74.28 W |
| Great Tenasserim ≃ | 110 | 12.24 N | 98.37 E |
| Great Tobago I | 240m | 18.27 N | 64.48 W |
| Great Torrington | 42 | 50.57 N | 4.08 W |
| Great Totham | 260 | 51.47 N | 0.43 E |
| Great Usutu (Maputo) (Lusutfu) ≃ | 158 | 26.11 S | 32.42 E |
| Great Valley | 210 | 42.13 N | 78.38 W |
| Great Victoria Desert ◆[2] | 162 | 28.30 S | 127.45 E |
| Great Wall ʋ[3] | 9 | 62.13 S | 58.58 W |
| Great Wall → Chang Cheng ⊥ | 98 | 40.30 N | 116.30 E |
| Great Waltham | 260 | 51.48 N | 0.28 E |
| Great Warley | 260 | 51.35 N | 0.17 E |
| Great Western Forum ♠ | 280 | 33.57 N | 118.20 W |
| Great Whernside ∧ | 44 | 54.09 N | 1.59 W |
| Great Wicomico ≃ | 208 | 37.48 N | 76.18 W |
| Great Wyrley | 42 | 52.41 N | 2.01 W |
| Great Yarmouth | 42 | 52.37 N | 1.44 E |
| Great Zab (Büyükzap) (Az-Zāb al-Kabīr) ≃ | 128 | 36.00 N | 43.21 E |
| Great Zimbabwe Ruins National Park ♠ | 154 | 20.17 S | 30.57 E |
| Grebbestad | 26 | 58.42 N | 11.15 E |
| Grebenau | 56 | 50.45 N | 9.28 E |
| Grebenhain | 56 | 50.29 N | 9.19 E |
| Grebenstein | 56 | 51.26 N | 9.24 E |
| Grebnevo | 265b | 55.58 N | 38.05 E |
| Gréboun ∧ | 150 | 20.00 N | 8.35 E |
| Grèce → Greece □[1] | 38 | 39.00 N | 22.00 E |
| Grecia | 236 | 10.05 N | 84.18 W |
| Grecia → Greece □[1] | 38 | 39.00 N | 22.00 E |
| Grecken ⊜ | 40 | 59.35 N | 14.44 E |
| Greco | 252 | 32.48 S | 57.03 W |
| Greco ◆[8] | 266b | 45.30 N | 9.13 E |
| Greco, Monte ∧ | 66 | 41.48 N | 14.00 E |
| Greco Island I | 282 | 37.31 N | 122.11 W |
| Greding | 60 | 49.03 N | 11.21 E |
| Gredos, Sierra de ⩕ | 34 | 40.18 N | 5.05 W |
| Gredstedbro | 41 | 55.24 N | 8.45 E |
| Greece | 210 | 43.12 N | 77.41 W |
| Greece (Ellás) □[1], Europe | 22 | 39.00 N | 22.00 E |
| Greece (Ellás) □[1], Europe | 38 | 39.00 N | 22.00 E |
| Greeley, Co., U.S. | 200 | 40.25 N | 104.42 W |
| Greeley, Ks., U.S. | 198 | 38.19 N | 95.26 W |
| Greeley, Ne., U.S. | 198 | 41.33 N | 98.32 W |
| Greeley, Pa., U.S. | 210 | 41.25 N | 75.00 W |
| Greeleyville | 192 | 33.34 N | 79.59 W |
| Green □[6] | 216 | 42.48 N | 89.25 W |
| Green ≃, N.B., Can. | 186 | 47.18 N | 68.09 W |
| Green ≃, U.S. | 200 | 38.11 N | 109.53 W |
| Green ≃, U.S. | 207 | 42.10 N | 73.22 W |
| Green ≃, U.S. | 207 | 42.35 N | 72.36 W |
| Green ≃, Il., U.S. | 190 | 41.28 N | 90.23 W |
| Green ≃, Il., U.S. | 216 | 41.46 N | 89.10 W |
| Green ≃, Ky., U.S. | 194 | 37.55 N | 87.30 W |
| Green ≃, N.D., U.S. | 198 | 46.52 N | 102.35 W |
| Green ≃, Vt., U.S. | 210 | 43.06 N | 73.13 W |
| Green ≃, Wa., U.S. | 224 | 47.33 N | 122.20 W |
| Green ≃, Wa., U.S. | 224 | 46.20 N | 122.34 W |
| Greenacres, Ca., U.S. | 226 | 35.23 N | 119.07 W |
| Green Acres, De., U.S. | 285 | 39.47 N | 75.30 W |
| Greenacres, Wa., U.S. | 202 | 47.39 N | 117.06 W |
| Green Acres ◆[9] | 276 | 40.40 N | 73.43 W |
| Greenacres City | 220 | 26.37 N | 80.07 W |
| Greenbackville | 208 | 38.00 N | 75.23 W |
| Greenbank | 224 | 48.06 N | 122.34 W |
| Green Bay | 190 | 44.31 N | 88.01 W |
| Green Bay c, Nf., Can. | 186 | 49.43 N | 55.58 W |
| Green Bay c, On., Can. | 212 | 44.38 N | 76.36 W |
| Green Bay c, U.S. | 190 | 45.00 N | 87.30 W |
| Greenbelt | 284c | 39.00 N | 76.52 W |
| Greenbelt Park ♠ | 284c | 38.59 N | 76.54 W |
| Greenbo Lake ⊜ | 218 | 38.29 N | 82.54 W |
| Greenbo Lake State Resort Park ♠ | 218 | 38.29 N | 82.54 W |
| Greenbooth Reservoir ⊜[1] | 262 | 53.38 N | 2.13 W |
| Greenbrae | 226 | 37.57 N | 122.31 W |
| Greenbrier, Ar., U.S. | 194 | 35.14 N | 92.23 W |
| Green Brier, Tn., U.S. | 194 | 36.25 N | 86.48 W |
| Greenbrier ≃ | 192 | 37.39 N | 80.53 W |
| Greenbrier State Park ♠ | 208 | 39.33 N | 77.38 W |
| Green Brook | 276 | 40.36 N | 74.27 W |
| Green Brook ≃ | 276 | 40.33 N | 74.32 W |


| | | | | | |
|---|---|---|---|---|---|
| ≃ | River | Fluß | Río | Rivière | Rio |
| ≍ | Canal | Kanal | Canal | Canal | Canal |
| ʟ | Waterfall, Rapids | Wasserfall, Stromschnellen | Cascada, Rápidos | Chute d'eau, Rapides | Cascata, Rápidos |
| ʯ | Strait | Meeresstraße | Estrecho | Détroit | Estreito |
| c | Bay, Gulf | Bucht, Golf | Bahía, Golfo | Baie, Golfe | Baía, Golfo |
| ⊜ | Lake, Lakes | See, Seen | Lago, Lagos | Lac, Lacs | Lago, Lagos |
| ≡ | Swamp | Sumpf | Pantano | Marais | Pântano |
| ⊓ | Ice Features, Glacier | Eis- und Gletscherformen | Accidentes Glaciales | Formes glaciaires | Acidentes glaciares |
| ⊤ | Other Hydrographic Features | Andere Hydrographische Objekte | Otros Elementos Hidrográficos | Autres données hydrographiques | Outros acidentes hidrográficos |

| | | | | | |
|---|---|---|---|---|---|
| ✢ | Submarine Features | Untermeerische Objekte | Accidentes Submarinos | Formes de relief sous-marin | Acidentes submarinos |
| □ | Political Unit | Politische Einheit | Unidad Politica | Entité politique | Unidade política |
| ʋ | Cultural Institution | Kulturelle Institution | Institución Cultural | Institution culturelle | Institução cultural |
| ⊥ | Historical Site | Historische Stätte | Sitio Histórico | Site historique | Sitio histórico |
| ♠ | Recreational Site | Erholungs- und Ferienort | Sitio de Recreo | Centre de loisirs | Area de Lazer |
| ⊠ | Airport | Flughafen | Aeropuerto | Aéroport | Aeroporto |
| ■ | Military Installation | Militäranlage | Instalación Militar | Installation militaire | Instalação militar |
| ◆ | Miscellaneous | Verschiedenes | Misceláneo | Divers | Diversos |

ENGLISH

| Name | Page | Lat.°′ | Long.°′ |
|---|---|---|---|
| Greenburg | **194** | 30.51 N | 90.40 W |
| Greenbush, Ma., U.S. | **207** | 42.11 N | 70.45 W |
| Greenbush, Mn., U.S. | **198** | 48.42 N | 96.10 W |
| Greenbush, Va., U.S. | **208** | 37.45 N | 75.41 W |
| Greenbushes | **162** | 33.51 S | 116.03 E |
| Green Camp | **214** | 40.31 N | 83.12 W |
| Green Cape ≻ | **166** | 37.15 S | 150.03 E |
| Greencastle, Ire. | **48** | 55.12 N | 6.59 W |
| Greencastle, In., U.S. | **194** | 39.38 N | 86.51 W |
| Greencastle, Pa., U.S. | **188** | 39.47 N | 77.43 W |
| Green City | **194** | 40.16 N | 92.57 W |
| Green Cove Springs | **192** | 29.59 N | 81.40 W |
| Green Creek | **208** | 39.02 N | 74.54 W |
| Green Creek ≃, Oh., U.S. | **214** | 41.26 N | 83.01 W |
| Green Creek ≃, Pa., U.S. | **285** | 39.53 N | 75.28 W |
| Greencrest Park | **214** | 41.23 N | 80.24 W |
| Greendale, Austl. | **274a** | 33.55 S | 150.39 E |
| Greendale, In., U.S. | **218** | 39.06 N | 84.51 W |
| Greendale, Wi., U.S. | **216** | 42.56 N | 87.59 W |
| Greene, Dtsch. | **52** | 51.52 N | 9.56 E |
| Greene, Ia., U.S. | **190** | 42.53 N | 92.48 W |
| Greene, N.Y., U.S. | **210** | 42.19 N | 75.46 W |
| Greene, R.I., U.S. | **207** | 41.41 N | 71.44 W |
| Greene □[6], Il., U.S. | **219** | 39.18 N | 90.24 W |
| Greene □[6], N.Y., U.S. | **210** | 42.13 N | 73.52 W |
| Greene □[6], Oh., U.S. | **218** | 39.41 N | 83.56 W |
| Greeneville | **192** | 36.06 N | 82.42 W |
| Greenfield, Eng., U.K. | **262** | 53.32 N | 2.01 W |
| Greenfield, Wales, U.K. | **44** | 53.18 N | 3.13 W |
| Greenfield, Ca., U.S. | **226** | 36.19 N | 121.14 W |
| Greenfield, Il., U.S. | **219** | 39.20 N | 90.12 W |
| Greenfield, In., U.S. | **218** | 39.47 N | 85.46 W |
| Greenfield, Ia., U.S. | **198** | 41.18 N | 94.27 W |
| Greenfield, Ma., U.S. | **207** | 42.35 N | 72.36 W |
| Greenfield, Mo., U.S. | **194** | 37.24 N | 93.50 W |
| Greenfield, Oh., U.S. | **218** | 39.21 N | 83.22 W |
| Greenfield, Tn., U.S. | **194** | 36.09 N | 88.48 W |
| Greenfield, Wi., U.S. | **216** | 42.58 N | 88.02 W |
| Greenfield-Park, P.Q., Can. | **275a** | 45.29 N | 73.29 W |
| Greenfield Park, N.Y., U.S. | **210** | 41.44 N | 74.29 W |
| Greenfields Village | **285** | 75.10 N | 39.49 W |
| Greenfield Village ⊥ | **281** | 42.18 N | 83.14 W |
| Greenford ◆[8] | **260** | 51.32 N | 0.21 W |
| Green Forest | **194** | 36.20 N | 93.26 W |
| Green Harbor | **207** | 42.04 N | 70.39 W |
| Green Harbor ≃ | **283** | 42.05 N | 70.39 W |
| Green Head ≻ | **162** | 30.05 S | 114.58 E |
| Green Hill | **285** | 39.59 N | 75.36 W |
| Greenhill ◆[8] | **260** | 51.35 N | 0.20 W |
| Greenhills, S. Afr. | **273d** | 26.10 S | 27.40 E |
| Greenhills, Oh., U.S. | **218** | 39.16 N | 84.31 W |
| Greenhithe | **260** | 51.27 N | 0.17 E |
| Greenhorn Creek ≃ | **198** | 38.08 N | 104.38 W |
| Greenhurst | **214** | 42.07 N | 79.19 W |
| Green Hut Park | **276** | 40.50 N | 74.39 W |
| Green Island, N.Z. | **172** | 45.54 S | 170.26 E |
| Greenisland, N. Ire., U.K. | **48** | 54.42 N | 5.52 W |
| Green Island, N.Y., U.S. | **210** | 42.44 N | 73.41 W |
| Green Island I | **241k** | 12.14 N | 61.35 W |
| Green Island Bay c | **116** | 10.12 N | 119.22 E |
| Green Islands II | **14** | 4.30 S | 154.10 E |
| Green Knoll | **276** | 40.36 N | 74.36 W |
| Green Lake, Sk., Can. | **184** | 54.17 N | 107.47 W |
| Green Lake, Wi., U.S. | **190** | 43.50 N | 88.57 W |
| Green Lake ⊜, B.C., Can. | **182** | 51.24 N | 121.15 W |
| Green Lake ⊜, Sk., Can. | **184** | 54.10 N | 107.43 W |
| Green Lake ⊜, Mi., U.S. | **281** | 42.36 N | 83.25 W |
| Green Lake ⊜, N.Y., U.S. | **284a** | 42.45 N | 78.45 W |
| Green Lake ⊜, Wi., U.S. | **190** | 43.41 N | 88.57 W |
| Green Lakes State Park ♦ | **212** | 43.03 N | 75.58 W |
| Greenlal (Saint-Grégoire-de-Greenlay) | **206** | 45.34 N | 72.01 W |
| Greenland, Ar., U.S. | **194** | 35.59 N | 94.10 W |
| Greenland, Mi., U.S. | **190** | 46.46 N | 89.06 W |
| Greenland (Kalaallit Nunaat) □[2] | **16** | 70.00 N | 40.00 W |
| Greenland Basin ✢[1] | **16** | 73.30 N | 5.00 W |
| Greenland-Iceland Rise ✢[3] | **10** | 67.00 N | 27.00 W |
| Greenlands | **158** | 27.07 S | 27.40 E |
| Greenland Sea ᴛ[2] | **16** | 77.00 N | 1.00 W |
| Green Lane | **208** | 40.20 N | 75.28 W |
| Green Lane Reservoir ⊜[1] | **208** | 40.22 N | 75.29 W |
| Greenlaw | **46** | 55.43 N | 2.28 W |
| Greenlawn | **276** | 40.52 N | 73.21 W |
| Greenlawn Park | **285** | 40.07 N | 74.51 W |
| Greenleaf | **198** | 39.43 N | 96.58 W |
| Green Lookout Mountain ʌ | **224** | 45.52 N | 122.08 W |
| Green Manorville | **207** | 42.00 N | 72.32 W |
| Green Meadows | **284c** | 38.58 N | 76.57 W |
| Greenmount, Austl. | **171a** | 27.47 S | 151.54 E |
| Greenmount, Eng., U.K. | **262** | 53.37 N | 2.20 W |
| Greenmount, Md., U.S. | **208** | 39.37 N | 76.51 W |
| Green Mountains ⋏ | **188** | 43.45 N | 72.45 W |
| Green Oak Lake ⊜ | **281** | 42.27 N | 83.43 W |
| Green Oaks | **278** | 42.18 N | 87.55 W |
| Greenock, Austl. | **168b** | 34.27 S | 138.55 E |
| Greenock, Scot., U.K. | **46** | 55.57 N | 4.45 W |
| Greenock, Pa., U.S. | **279b** | 40.19 N | 79.48 W |
| Greenodd | **44** | 54.14 N | 3.04 W |
| Greenore Point ≻ | **48** | 52.15 N | 6.18 W |
| Greenough | **162** | 28.57 S | 114.44 E |
| Greenough ≃ | **162** | 28.51 S | 114.38 E |
| Greenough, Mount ʌ | **180** | 69.10 N | 141.35 W |
| Green Park | **208** | 40.23 N | 77.19 W |
| Green Peter Lake ⊜[1] | **202** | 44.28 N | 122.30 W |
| Green Point ≻ | **276** | 40.43 N | 73.06 W |
| Green Pond, Al., U.S. | **194** | 33.13 N | 87.07 W |
| Green Pond, N.J., U.S. | **276** | 41.01 N | 74.29 W |
| Green Pond ⊜ | **276** | 41.00 N | 74.30 W |
| Green Pond Brook ≃ | **276** | 40.53 N | 74.34 W |
| Greenport | **207** | 41.06 N | 72.21 W |
| Green Ridge | **285** | 39.51 N | 75.25 W |
| Green River, Pap. N. Gui. | **164** | 3.55 S | 141.10 E |
| Green River, Ut,. U.S. | **200** | 38.59 N | 110.09 W |
| Green River, Wy., U.S. | **200** | 41.31 N | 109.27 W |
| Green River Lake ⊜[1] | **194** | 37.15 N | 85.15 W |
| Greensboro, Al., U.S. | **194** | 32.42 N | 87.35 W |
| Greensboro, Fl., U.S. | **192** | 30.34 N | 84.44 W |
| Greensboro, Ga., U.S. | **192** | 33.34 N | 83.10 W |
| Greensboro, Md., U.S. | **208** | 38.58 N | 75.48 W |
| Greensboro, N.C., U.S. | **192** | 36.04 N | 79.47 W |
| Greensborough | **274b** | 37.42 S | 145.06 E |
| Greensburg, In., U.S. | **218** | 39.20 N | 85.29 W |
| Greensburg, Ks., U.S. | **198** | 37.36 N | 99.17 W |
| Greensburg, Ky., U.S. | **194** | 37.15 N | 85.29 W |
| Greensburg, Oh., U.S. | **214** | 40.56 N | 81.28 W |
| Greensburg, Pa., U.S. | **214** | 40.18 N | 79.32 W |
| Greens Farms | **276** | 41.07 N | 73.19 W |
| Greens Fork | **218** | 39.53 N | 85.02 W |
| Greens Fork ≃ | **218** | 39.45 N | 85.07 W |
| Greenside ◆[8] | **273d** | 26.09 S | 28.01 E |
| Greens Lake c | **222** | 29.16 N | 94.59 W |
| Greens Peak ʌ | **200** | 34.07 N | 109.35 W |
| Greenspond | **186** | 49.04 N | 53.34 W |
| Green Springs | **214** | 41.15 N | 83.03 W |
| Greenstead | **260** | 51.42 N | 0.14 E |
| Greenstone | **208** | 39.45 N | 77.27 W |
| Greenstone Point ≻ | **46** | 57.55 N | 5.38 W |
| Green Street | **260** | 51.40 N | 0.16 W |
| Green Street Green ◆[8] | **260** | 51.21 N | 0.04 E |
| Greensville □[6] | **208** | 36.40 N | 77.30 W |
| Green Swamp ≡, Fl., U.S. | **220** | 28.20 N | 81.48 W |
| Green Swamp ≡, N.C., U.S. | **192** | 34.10 N | 78.20 W |
| Greentown, In., U.S. | **216** | 40.28 N | 85.58 W |
| Greentown, Oh., U.S. | **214** | 40.56 N | 81.28 W |
| Greentown, Pa., U.S. | **210** | 41.19 N | 75.18 W |
| Green Tree | **279b** | 40.24 N | 80.02 W |
| Greenup, Il., U.S. | **194** | 39.14 N | 88.09 W |
| Greenup, Ky., U.S. | **218** | 38.34 N | 82.49 W |
| Greenup □[6] | **218** | 38.33 N | 83.00 W |
| Greenup Dam ◆[6] | **218** | 38.39 N | 82.52 W |
| Greenvale, Austl. | **166** | 18.59 S | 145.07 E |
| Greenvale, N.Y., U.S. | **276** | 40.49 N | 73.38 W |
| Green Valley, On., Can. | **206** | 45.16 N | 74.36 W |
| Green Valley, Az., U.S. | **200** | 31.52 N | 110.59 W |
| Green Valley, Il., U.S. | **190** | 40.24 N | 89.38 W |
| Green Valley Creek ≃ | **226** | 38.13 N | 122.08 W |
| Greenview | **219** | 40.04 N | 89.44 W |
| Green Village, N.J., U.S. | **276** | 40.44 N | 74.27 W |
| Greenvillage, Pa., U.S. | **208** | 40.00 N | 77.36 W |
| Greenville, Liber. | **150** | 5.01 N | 9.03 W |
| Greenville, Al., U.S. | **194** | 31.49 N | 86.37 W |
| Greenville, Ca., U.S. | **204** | 40.08 N | 120.57 W |
| Greenville, Fl., U.S. | **192** | 30.28 N | 83.37 W |
| Greenville, Ga., U.S. | **192** | 33.01 N | 84.42 W |
| Greenville, Il., U.S. | **219** | 38.53 N | 89.24 W |
| Greenville, In., U.S. | **218** | 38.22 N | 85.59 W |
| Greenville, Ky., U.S. | **194** | 37.12 N | 87.10 W |
| Greenville, Me., U.S. | **188** | 45.28 N | 69.35 W |
| Greenville, Mi., U.S. | **190** | 43.10 N | 85.15 W |
| Greenville, Ms., U.S. | **194** | 33.24 N | 91.03 W |
| Greenville, Mo., U.S. | **194** | 37.08 N | 90.27 W |
| Greenville, N.H., U.S. | **207** | 42.46 N | 71.48 W |
| Greenville, N.Y., U.S. | **210** | 40.59 N | 73.49 W |
| Greenville, N.Y., U.S. | **276** | 40.59 N | 73.49 W |
| Greenville, N.C., U.S. | **192** | 35.36 N | 77.22 W |
| Greenville, Oh., U.S. | **218** | 40.06 N | 84.37 W |
| Greenville, Pa., U.S. | **214** | 41.24 N | 80.23 W |
| Greenville, R.I., U.S. | **207** | 41.52 N | 71.33 W |
| Greenville, S.C., U.S. | **192** | 34.51 N | 82.23 W |
| Greenville, Tx., U.S. | **222** | 33.08 N | 96.06 W |
| Greenville Creek ≃ | **218** | 40.07 N | 84.22 W |
| Greenville Place | **285** | 39.46 N | 75.36 W |
| Greenwater ≃ | **224** | 47.09 N | 121.39 W |
| Greenwater Lake ⊜ | **190** | 48.34 N | 90.26 W |
| Greenwater Lake Provincial Park ♦ | **184** | 52.33 N | 103.33 W |
| Greenwell Point | **170** | 34.55 S | 150.44 E |
| Greenwich, Austl. | **274a** | 33.50 S | 151.11 E |
| Greenwich, Ct., U.S. | **207** | 41.01 N | 73.37 W |
| Greenwich, N.J., U.S. | **208** | 39.23 N | 75.20 W |
| Greenwich, N.Y., U.S. | **210** | 43.05 N | 73.29 W |
| Greenwich, Oh., U.S. | **214** | 41.01 N | 82.30 W |
| Greenwich ◆[8] | **42** | 51.28 N | 0.02 E |
| Greenwich Cove c | **276** | 41.01 N | 73.35 W |
| Greenwich Creek ≃ | **276** | 41.02 N | 73.37 W |
| Greenwich Observatory ʊ[3] | **260** | 51.28 N | 0.00 |
| Greenwich Point ≻ | **276** | 41.00 N | 73.34 W |
| Greenwich Village ◆[8] | **276** | 40.44 N | 74.00 W |
| Greenwood, B.C., Can. | **182** | 49.05 N | 118.41 W |
| Greenwood, Ar., U.S. | **194** | 35.12 N | 94.15 W |
| Greenwood, Ca., U.S. | **226** | 38.54 N | 120.55 W |
| Greenwood, De., U.S. | **208** | 38.48 N | 75.35 W |
| Greenwood, In., U.S. | **218** | 39.36 N | 86.06 W |
| Greenwood, Ma., U.S. | **283** | 42.29 N | 71.04 W |
| Greenwood, Ms., U.S. | **194** | 33.30 N | 90.10 W |
| Greenwood, Ne., U.S. | **198** | 40.57 N | 96.26 W |
| Greenwood, N.Y., U.S. | **210** | 42.08 N | 77.38 W |
| Greenwood, Pa., U.S. | **214** | 40.32 N | 78.21 W |
| Greenwood, S.C., U.S. | **192** | 34.11 N | 82.09 W |
| Greenwood, Wi., U.S. | **190** | 44.46 N | 90.35 W |
| Greenwood, Lake ⊜[1] | **192** | 34.15 N | 82.02 W |
| Greenwood Cemetery ◆ | **276** | 40.39 N | 73.59 W |
| Greenwood Lake | **210** | 41.13 N | 74.17 W |
| Greenwood Lake ⊜, U.S. | **210** | 41.11 N | 74.19 W |
| Greenwood Lake ⊜, Ma., U.S. | **283** | 42.00 N | 71.17 W |
| Greenwood Race Track ♦ | **275b** | 43.40 N | 79.19 W |
| Greer, Oh., U.S. | **214** | 40.31 N | 82.13 W |
| Greer, S.C., U.S. | **192** | 34.56 N | 82.13 W |
| Greers Ferry Lake ⊜[1] | **194** | 35.30 N | 92.10 W |
| Greerton | **172** | 37.43 S | 176.08 E |
| Grées, Alpes (Alpi Graie) ⋏ | **62** | 45.30 N | 7.10 E |
| Greeson, Lake ⊜[1] | **194** | 34.10 N | 93.45 W |
| Greet ≃ | **44** | 53.03 N | 0.53 W |
| Greetland | **262** | 53.41 N | 1.52 W |
| Greetsiel | **52** | 53.30 N | 7.05 E |
| Greffiers | **261** | 48.37 N | 1.51 E |
| Grefrath, Dtsch. | **56** | 51.20 N | 6.20 E |
| Grefrath, Dtsch. | **263** | 51.10 N | 6.38 E |
| Gregadoo | **171b** | 35.14 S | 147.27 E |
| Gregbe | **150** | 6.48 N | 6.43 W |
| Gregg | **279b** | 40.24 N | 80.10 W |
| Gregg □[6] | **222** | 32.30 N | 94.50 W |
| Greggio | **62** | 45.27 N | 8.23 E |
| Greg Greg | **171b** | 36.03 S | 148.02 E |
| Gregoire Lake Indian Reserve ◆[4] | **184** | 56.28 N | 111.10 W |
| Gregório ≃ | **248** | 6.50 S | 70.46 W |
| Gregory, Mi., U.S. | **216** | 42.27 N | 84.05 W |
| Gregory, S.D., U.S. | **198** | 43.13 N | 99.25 W |
| Gregory, Tx., U.S. | **196** | 27.55 N | 97.17 W |
| Gregory ≃ | **166** | 17.53 S | 139.17 E |
| Gregory, Lake ⊜, Austl. | **162** | 25.38 S | 119.58 E |
| Gregory, Lake ⊜, Austl. | **162** | 20.10 S | 127.20 E |
| Gregory, Lake ⊜, Austl. | **166** | 28.55 S | 139.00 E |
| Gregory National Park ♦ | **164** | 16.30 S | 130.30 E |
| Gregory Range ⋏ | **166** | 19.00 S | 143.05 E |
| Grégy-sur-Yerre | **261** | 48.40 N | 2.37 E |
| Greifenburg | **64** | 46.45 N | 13.11 E |
| Greifendorf | **54** | 51.01 N | 13.06 E |
| Greifensee | **58** | 47.22 N | 8.41 E |
| Greifensee ⊜ | **58** | 47.21 N | 8.41 E |
| Greifenstein, Dtsch. | **56** | 50.37 N | 8.18 E |
| Greifenstein, Öst. | **264b** | 48.21 N | 16.15 E |
| Greiffenberg | **54** | 53.05 N | 13.58 E |
| Greiffenburg ⊥ | **263** | 51.20 N | 6.38 E |
| Greifswald | **54** | 54.05 N | 13.23 E |
| Greifswalder Bodden c | **54** | 54.15 N | 13.35 E |
| Greifswalder Oie I | **54** | 54.14 N | 13.55 E |
| Greim ʌ | **61** | 47.15 N | 14.09 E |
| Grein | **61** | 48.14 N | 14.51 E |
| Greiz | **54** | 50.39 N | 12.12 E |
| Grejdernoje | **80** | 46.53 N | 45.01 E |
| Grejsdal | **41** | 55.45 N | 9.32 E |
| Grekov | **80** | 47.24 N | 43.41 E |
| Grekovo | **83** | 48.54 N | 40.14 E |
| Grem'ačevo | **82** | 54.14 N | 36.15 E |
| Grem'ačij | **88** | 57.01 N | 108.12 E |
| Grem'ačinsk, Ross. | **86** | 58.34 N | 57.51 E |
| Grem'ačinsk, Ross. | **88** | 52.48 N | 107.57 E |
| Grem'ačje | **78** | 51.29 N | 39.00 E |
| Gremersdorf | **54** | 54.20 N | 10.55 E |
| Gremicha | **24** | 68.03 N | 39.27 E |
| Grenå | **26** | 56.25 N | 10.53 E |
| Grenada | **194** | 33.46 N | 89.48 W |
| Grenada □[1], N.A. | **230** | 12.07 N | 61.40 W |
| Grenada □[1], N.A. | **241k** | 12.07 N | 61.40 W |
| Grenada Lake ⊜[1] | **194** | 33.50 N | 89.40 W |
| Grenade → Grenada □[1] | **241k** | 12.07 N | 61.40 W |
| Grenadier Island I | **212** | 44.03 N | 76.22 W |
| Grenadier Pond ⊜ | **275b** | 43.38 N | 79.28 W |
| Grenadines II | **238** | 12.40 N | 61.15 W |
| Grenagh | **48** | 52.00 N | 8.37 W |
| Grenay | **50** | 50.27 N | 2.44 E |
| Grenchen | **58** | 47.11 N | 7.24 E |
| Grenell | **212** | 44.16 N | 76.04 W |
| Grenen ≻[2] | **26** | 57.44 N | 10.40 E |
| Grenfell, Austl. | **166** | 33.54 S | 148.10 E |
| Grenfell, Sk., Can. | **184** | 50.25 N | 102.56 W |
| Grenloch | **285** | 39.47 N | 75.03 W |
| Grenoble | **62** | 45.10 N | 5.43 E |
| Grenola | **198** | 37.20 N | 96.27 W |
| Grenora | **198** | 48.37 N | 103.56 W |
| Grenville, P.Q., Can. | **206** | 45.37 N | 74.36 W |
| Grenville, Gren. | **241k** | 12.07 N | 61.37 W |
| Grenville, Cape ≻ | **164** | 11.58 S | 143.14 E |
| Grenville, Point ≻ | **224** | 47.18 N | 124.17 W |
| Grenville Bay | **206** | 45.38 N | 74.36 W |
| Grenville Bay c | **241k** | 12.07 N | 61.36 W |
| Grenville Channel ʮ | **182** | 53.40 N | 129.40 W |
| Grenzaa ≃ | **52** | 52.39 N | 6.45 E |
| Grenzach-Wyhlen | **58** | 47.33 N | 7.41 E |
| Grenz-Berge ʌ[2] | **264a** | 52.27 N | 13.44 E |
| Grenzlandring ♦ | **56** | 51.11 N | 6.17 E |
| Gréolières | **62** | 43.48 N | 6.57 E |
| Gréoux-les-Bains | **62** | 43.45 N | 5.53 E |
| Greppin | **54** | 51.39 N | 12.18 E |
| Gresenhorst | **54** | 54.09 N | 12.26 E |
| Gresham | **224** | 45.29 N | 122.25 W |
| Gresham Park | **192** | 33.42 N | 84.19 W |
| Gresik, Indon. | **112** | 2.18 S | 103.57 E |
| Gresik, Indon. | **115a** | 7.09 S | 112.38 E |
| Gressåmoen Nasjonalpark ♦ | **26** | 64.15 N | 13.08 E |
| Gresse-en-Vercors | **62** | 44.54 N | 5.34 E |
| Gressey | **261** | 48.50 N | 1.37 E |
| Gressitt | **208** | 37.29 N | 76.43 W |
| Gressoney, Val di V | **62** | 45.47 N | 7.49 E |
| Gressoney-la-Trinité | **62** | 45.50 N | 7.49 E |
| Gressoney-Saint-Jean | **62** | 45.47 N | 7.49 E |
| Gressy | **261** | 48.58 N | 2.41 E |
| Gresten | **61** | 48.00 N | 15.02 E |
| Grésy-sur-Aix | **62** | 45.43 N | 5.57 E |
| Grésy-sur-Isère | **62** | 45.36 N | 6.15 E |
| Greta | **170** | 32.41 S | 151.24 E |
| Greta ≃, Eng., U.K. | **44** | 54.09 N | 2.36 W |
| Greta ≃, Eng., U.K. | **44** | 54.32 N | 1.53 W |
| Greta ≃, Eng., U.K. | **44** | 54.36 N | 3.10 W |
| Gretna, Mb., Can. | **184** | 49.02 N | 97.35 W |
| Gretna, Scot., U.K. | **44** | 54.59 N | 3.04 W |
| Gretna, La., U.S. | **194** | 29.54 N | 90.03 W |
| Gretna, Va., U.S. | **192** | 36.57 N | 79.21 W |
| Gretz-Armainvilliers | **50** | 48.44 N | 2.44 E |
| Greussen | **54** | 51.14 N | 10.57 E |
| Greve, Dan. | **41** | 55.36 N | 12.15 E |
| Greve, It. | **66** | 43.35 N | 11.19 E |
| Greve ≃ | **66** | 43.46 N | 11.13 E |
| Grevel ◆[8] | **263** | 51.34 N | 7.33 E |
| Grevelingen ʮ | **52** | 51.45 N | 4.00 E |
| Grevelingendam ◆[5] | **52** | 51.40 N | 4.10 E |
| Greven | **52** | 52.05 N | 7.36 E |
| Grevená | **38** | 40.05 N | 21.25 E |
| Grevenbroich | **56** | 51.05 N | 6.35 E |
| Greven-Granzin | **54** | 53.29 N | 10.48 E |
| Grevenmacher | **56** | 49.42 N | 6.20 E |
| Grevesmühlen | **54** | 53.51 N | 11.10 E |
| Greve Strand | **41** | 55.35 N | 12.14 E |
| Greville Bay c | **186** | 45.22 N | 64.38 W |
| Grevinge | **41** | 55.48 N | 11.34 E |
| Grey □[6] | **212** | 44.20 N | 80.45 W |
| Grey ≃, Nf., Can. | **186** | 47.38 N | 57.05 W |
| Grey ≃, N.Z. | **172** | 42.27 S | 171.12 E |
| Grey, Cape ≻ | **164** | 13.00 S | 136.40 E |
| Grey, Point ≻, Austl. | **169** | 38.34 S | 143.59 E |
| Grey, Point ≻, B.C., Can. | **224** | 49.16 N | 123.16 W |
| Greyabbey | **48** | 54.32 N | 5.33 W |
| Greybull | **202** | 44.29 N | 108.03 W |
| Greybull ≃ | **202** | 44.28 N | 108.03 W |
| Grey Eagle | **190** | 45.49 N | 94.44 W |
| Grey Islands II | **186** | 50.50 N | 55.37 W |
| Greylingstad | **158** | 26.44 S | 28.45 E |
| Greylock, Mount ʌ | **207** | 42.38 N | 73.10 W |
| Greymouth | **172** | 42.28 S | 171.12 E |
| Grey Range ⋏ | **166** | 27.00 S | 143.35 E |
| Grey River | **186** | 47.35 N | 57.06 W |
| Greys ≃ | **202** | 43.10 N | 111.00 W |
| Greystanes | **274a** | 33.49 S | 150.55 E |
| Greystoke | **44** | 54.40 N | 2.52 W |
| Greystones | **48** | 53.09 N | 6.04 W |
| Greyton | **158** | 34.04 S | 19.38 E |
| Greytown, N.Z. | **172** | 41.05 S | 175.27 E |
| Greytown → San Juan del Norte, Nic. | **236** | 10.55 N | 83.42 W |
| Greytown, S. Afr. | **158** | 29.07 S | 30.30 E |
| Grez-Doiceau | **56** | 50.44 N | 4.42 E |
| Grez-sur-Loing | **50** | 48.19 N | 2.42 E |
| Grezzana | **64** | 45.31 N | 11.01 E |
| Gribanovskij | **80** | 51.27 N | 41.58 E |
| Gribbel Island I | **182** | 53.25 N | 129.00 W |
| Gribbin Head ≻ | **42** | 50.19 N | 4.40 W |
| Gribingui □[5] | **152** | 7.00 N | 19.15 E |
| Gribingui ≃ | **146** | 8.33 N | 19.05 E |
| Gribingui-Bamingui, Réserve de Faune du ◆[4] | **146** | 8.00 N | 19.10 E |
| Gribovka | **82** | 54.19 N | 38.27 E |
| Gridley, Ca., U.S. | **226** | 39.21 N | 121.41 W |
| Gridley, Il., U.S. | **216** | 40.44 N | 88.52 W |
| Grieben | **54** | 52.26 N | 11.58 E |
| Griebnitz See ⊜ | **264a** | 52.24 N | 13.06 E |
| Griechenland → Greece □[1] | **38** | 39.00 N | 22.00 E |
| Griekwastad | **158** | 28.49 S | 23.15 E |
| Grier City | **210** | 40.50 N | 76.04 W |
| Gries am Brenner | **64** | 47.03 N | 11.29 E |
| Griesbach im Rottal | **60** | 48.28 N | 13.11 E |
| Griesen | **64** | 47.29 N | 10.56 E |
| Griesheim | **56** | 49.50 N | 8.34 E |
| Gries im Sellrain | **64** | 47.12 N | 11.09 E |
| Grieskirchen | **60** | 48.14 N | 13.50 E |
| Griessem | **52** | 52.00 N | 9.12 E |
| Griesspitzen ʌ | **64** | 47.22 N | 10.58 E |
| Griffen | **61** | 46.42 N | 14.44 E |
| Griffin, Sk., Can. | **184** | 49.40 N | 103.26 W |
| Griffin, Ga., U.S. | **192** | 33.14 N | 84.15 W |
| Griffin, Lake ⊜ | **220** | 28.52 N | 81.51 W |
| Griffin Bay c | **224** | 48.30 N | 122.58 W |
| Griffiss Air Force Base ■ | **210** | 43.14 N | 75.26 W |
| Griffith, Austl. | **166** | 34.17 S | 146.03 E |
| Griffith, In., U.S. | **216** | 41.31 N | 87.25 W |
| Griffith Airport ⊠ | **278** | 41.31 N | 87.23 W |
| Griffith Island I, N.T., Can. | **176** | 74.35 N | 95.30 W |
| Griffith Island I, On., Can. | **212** | 44.51 N | 80.54 W |
| Griffith Park ♦ | **280** | 34.09 N | 118.17 W |
| Grifton | **192** | 35.22 N | 77.26 W |
| Griggs Drain ≋ | **281** | 42.11 N | 83.26 W |
| Griggs Reservoir ⊜[1] | **214** | 40.03 N | 83.06 W |
| Griggstown | **276** | 40.26 N | 74.36 W |
| Griggsville | **219** | 39.42 N | 90.43 W |
| Grignan | **62** | 44.25 N | 4.54 E |
| Grignano | **64** | 45.42 N | 13.43 E |
| Grignasco | **62** | 45.41 N | 8.20 E |
| Grigno | **64** | 46.01 N | 11.38 E |
| Grignols | **32** | 44.23 N | 0.03 W |
| Grignon | **261** | 48.51 N | 1.57 E |
| Grigny, Fr. | **62** | 45.37 N | 4.47 E |
| Grigny, Fr. | **261** | 48.40 N | 2.24 E |
| Grigoriopol | **38** | 47.10 N | 29.18 E |
| Grigorjevka, Kyrg. | **85** | 42.43 N | 77.30 E |
| Grigorjevka, Ross. | **83** | 47.27 N | 38.23 E |
| Grigorjevskoje, Ross. | **82** | 54.49 N | 37.59 E |
| Grigorjevskoje, Ross. | **82** | 54.48 N | 39.15 E |
| Grigorovka | **82** | 54.38 N | 36.20 E |
| Grigorovo | **82** | 56.42 N | 37.35 E |
| Grigorovskoje | **82** | 54.17 N | 36.21 E |
| Grijalva ≃, Méx. | **232** | 18.36 N | 92.39 W |
| Grijalva (Cuilco) ≃, N.A. | **232** | 17.01 N | 93.22 W |
| Grijpskerk | **52** | 53.15 N | 6.18 E |
| Grillby | **40** | 59.37 N | 17.15 E |
| Grim, Cape ≻ | **166** | 40.41 S | 144.41 E |
| Grima | **152** | 3.59 N | 17.06 E |
| Grimaldi | **68** | 39.08 N | 16.14 E |
| Grimari | **152** | 5.44 N | 20.03 E |
| Grimaud | **62** | 43.16 N | 6.31 E |
| Grimbergen | **50** | 50.56 N | 4.23 E |
| Grimeford Village | **262** | 53.36 N | 2.34 W |
| Grimes | **226** | 39.04 N | 121.54 W |
| Grimes □[6] | **222** | 30.35 N | 96.00 W |
| Grimlinghausen | **263** | 51.10 N | 6.44 E |
| Grimma | **54** | 51.14 N | 12.43 E |
| Grimmen | **54** | 54.07 N | 13.02 E |
| Grimmenstein | **61** | 47.38 N | 16.06 E |
| Grimmialp | **58** | 46.34 N | 7.29 E |
| Grimnitzsee ⊜ | **54** | 52.58 N | 13.47 E |
| Grimsargh | **262** | 53.48 N | 2.38 W |
| Grimsby, On., Can. | **212** | 43.12 N | 79.34 W |
| Grimsby, Eng., U.K. | **44** | 53.35 N | 0.05 W |
| Grimselpass )( | **58** | 46.34 N | 8.21 E |
| Grimselsee ⊜ | **58** | 46.34 N | 8.18 E |
| Grímsey I | **24a** | 66.34 N | 18.00 W |
| Grimshaw | **182** | 56.11 N | 117.36 W |
| Grímsstaðir | **24a** | 65.40 N | 16.01 W |
| Grimstad | **26** | 58.20 N | 8.36 E |
| Grimstead | **208** | 37.30 N | 76.18 W |
| Grímsvötn ʌ | **24a** | 64.24 N | 17.22 W |
| Grindavík | **24a** | 63.52 N | 22.27 W |
| Grindelwald | **58** | 46.37 N | 8.02 E |
| Grindsted | **41** | 55.45 N | 8.56 E |
| Grindstone Island → Cap-aux-Meules | **186** | 47.23 N | 61.52 W |
| Grindstone Island I | **212** | 44.16 N | 76.07 W |
| Grinnell | **190** | 41.44 N | 92.43 W |
| Grinnell, Lake ⊜ | **276** | 41.06 N | 74.38 W |
| Grinnell Peninsula ≻[1] | **176** | 76.40 N | 95.00 W |
| Grin'ovo | **76** | 52.35 N | 33.04 E |
| Grintavec ʌ | **61** | 46.21 N | 14.32 E |
| Grinzing ◆[8] | **264b** | 48.15 N | 16.21 E |
| Grip | **26** | 63.14 N | 7.37 E |
| Gripsholm slott ⊥ | **40** | 59.15 N | 17.13 E |
| Gripsholmsviken c | **40** | 59.17 N | 17.20 E |
| Griqualand East □[9] | **158** | 30.30 S | 29.00 E |
| Griqualand West □[9] | **158** | 28.20 S | 23.30 E |
| Grisdale | **224** | 47.22 N | 123.37 W |
| Grisee → Gresik | **115a** | 7.09 S | 112.38 E |
| Grišino | **82** | 56.13 N | 37.40 E |
| Gris-Nez, Cap ≻ | **50** | 50.52 N | 1.35 E |
| Grisolia | **68** | 39.43 N | 15.51 E |
| Grisons → Graubünden □[3] | **58** | 46.45 N | 9.30 E |
| Grisslehamn | **40** | 60.06 N | 18.50 E |
| Grissom Air Force Base ■ | **216** | 40.40 N | 86.08 W |
| Gristow | **54** | 54.10 N | 13.20 E |
| Griswold, Mb., Can. | **184** | 49.45 N | 100.25 W |
| Griswold, Ia., U.S. | **198** | 41.14 N | 95.08 W |
| Griswold Creek ≃ | **279a** | 41.27 N | 81.23 W |
| Griswoldville | **207** | 42.39 N | 72.42 W |
| Grisy-Suisnes | **261** | 48.41 N | 2.40 E |
| Grivaï Pamia | **152** | 7.03 N | 19.26 E |
| Grivenskaja | **78** | 45.38 N | 38.09 E |
| Grizzana | **64** | 44.15 N | 11.09 E |
| Grizzly Bay c | **226** | 38.07 N | 122.01 W |
| Grizzly Bear Mountain ʌ | **176** | 65.22 N | 121.00 W |
| Grizzly Bear's Head and Lead Man Indian Reserve ◆[4] | **184** | 52.33 N | 108.16 W |
| Grizzly Creek ≃ | **282** | 37.52 N | 122.06 W |
| Grizzly Flats | **226** | 38.38 N | 120.31 W |
| Grizzly Island I | **282** | 38.08 N | 121.58 W |
| Grizzly Mountain ʌ, Id., U.S. | **202** | 47.43 N | 116.06 W |
| Grizzly Mountain ʌ, Or., U.S. | **202** | 44.26 N | 120.57 W |
| Grizzly Mountain ʌ, Wa., U.S. | **202** | 48.25 N | 118.30 W |
| Grizzly Slough ≃ | **282** | 38.06 N | 121.53 W |
| Grmeč ⋏ | **36** | 44.40 N | 16.30 E |
| Groaíras | **250** | 3.53 S | 40.23 W |
| Groais Island I | **186** | 50.57 N | 55.35 W |
| Grobbendonk | **56** | 51.12 N | 4.43 E |
| Gröben | **264a** | 52.17 N | 13.10 E |
| Gröbener-See ⊜ | **264a** | 52.17 N | 13.11 E |
| Gröbenzell | **60** | 48.11 N | 11.22 E |
| Gröbers | **54** | 51.26 N | 12.07 E |
| Grobiņa | **76** | 56.33 N | 21.10 E |
| Groblersdal | **156** | 25.15 S | 29.25 E |
| Groblershoop | **158** | 28.55 S | 20.59 E |
| Gröbming | **64** | 47.26 N | 13.54 E |
| Grobogan | **115a** | 7.01 S | 110.55 E |
| Gröbzig | **54** | 51.41 N | 11.52 E |
| Grödig | **64** | 47.44 N | 13.02 E |
| Grodikovo | **85** | 42.49 N | 71.29 E |
| Gröditsch | **54** | 52.03 N | 13.59 E |
| Gröditz | **54** | 51.24 N | 13.27 E |
| Grodków | **30** | 50.43 N | 17.22 E |
| Grodno → Hrodna | **76** | 53.41 N | 23.50 E |
| Grodzisk Mazowiecki | **30** | 52.07 N | 20.37 E |
| Grodzisk [Wielkopolski] | **30** | 52.14 N | 16.22 E |
| Groede | **52** | 51.23 N | 3.30 E |
| Groen ≃, S. Afr. | **158** | 30.40 S | 23.17 E |
| Groen ≃, S. Afr. | **158** | 29.00 S | 22.10 E |
| Groënland → Greenland □[2] | **16** | 70.00 N | 40.00 W |
| Groenlandia → Greenland □[2] | **16** | 70.00 N | 40.00 W |
| Groenlo | **52** | 52.03 N | 6.38 E |
| Groenvlei | **158** | 27.27 S | 30.13 E |
| Groesbeck, Oh., U.S. | **218** | 39.13 N | 84.35 W |
| Groesbeck, Tx., U.S. | **222** | 31.31 N | 96.32 W |
| Groesbeek | **52** | 51.47 N | 5.55 E |
| Grofa, hora ʌ | **78** | 48.37 N | 23.56 E |
| Grogol, Kali ≃ | **269e** | 6.10 S | 106.47 E |
| Grogol-hilir ◆[8] | **269e** | 6.13 S | 106.47 E |
| Grohnde | **52** | 52.01 N | 9.25 E |
| Groitzsch | **54** | 51.09 N | 12.16 E |
| Groix | **32** | 47.38 N | 3.28 W |
| Groix, Île de I | **32** | 47.38 N | 3.27 W |
| Grójec | **30** | 51.52 N | 20.52 E |
| Grokgak | **115a** | 8.11 S | 114.47 E |
| Grolley | **58** | 46.50 N | 7.05 E |
| Grombalia | **148** | 36.36 N | 10.30 E |
| Grömitz | **54** | 54.09 N | 10.58 E |
| Gromo | **64** | 45.58 N | 9.56 E |
| Gromoslavka | **80** | 48.12 N | 43.37 E |
| Gronau, Dtsch. | **52** | 52.13 N | 7.00 E |
| Gronau, Dtsch. | **52** | 52.05 N | 9.46 E |
| Grondines (Saint-Charles-des-Grondines) | **206** | 46.36 N | 72.03 W |
| Grondneus | **158** | 28.06 S | 20.48 E |
| Grone | **52** | 51.32 N | 9.53 E |
| Grönenbach | **58** | 47.52 N | 10.13 E |
| Grong | **24** | 64.28 N | 12.18 E |
| Gröningen, Dtsch. | **54** | 51.56 N | 11.13 E |
| Groningen, Ned. | **52** | 53.13 N | 6.33 E |
| Groningen, Sur. | **250** | 5.48 N | 55.28 W |
| Groningen □[4] | **52** | 53.15 N | 6.45 E |
| Grønland → Greenland □[2] | **16** | 70.00 N | 40.00 W |
| Gronlid | **184** | 53.06 N | 104.28 W |
| Grønsund ʮ | **41** | 54.53 N | 12.08 E |
| Grönwohld | **52** | 53.39 N | 10.25 E |
| Groom | **196** | 35.12 N | 101.06 W |
| Groom Lake ⊜ | **204** | 37.15 N | 115.48 W |
| Groot ≃, S. Afr. | **158** | 33.54 S | 21.39 E |
| Groot ≃, S. Afr. | **158** | 33.45 S | 24.36 E |
| Groot-Berg ≃ | **158** | 32.47 S | 18.08 E |
| Groot-Brakrivier | **158** | 34.02 S | 22.14 E |
| Grootdraaidam ⊜[1] | **158** | 26.56 S | 29.20 E |
| Grootebroek | **52** | 52.43 N | 5.13 E |
| Groote Eylandt I | **164** | 14.00 S | 136.40 E |
| Groote Eylandt Aboriginal Reserve ◆[4] | **164** | 14.00 S | 136.40 E |
| Grootfontein | **156** | 19.32 S | 18.05 E |
| Groot Karasberge ⋏ | **158** | 27.20 S | 18.40 E |
| Groot Karroo → Great Karroo ⋏[1] | **158** | 32.25 S | 22.40 E |
| Groot-Kei ≃ | **158** | 32.41 S | 28.22 E |
| Groot Laagte ≃ | **156** | 20.37 S | 21.37 E |
| Groot-Letaba ≃ | **156** | 23.58 S | 31.50 E |
| Groot-Marico | **156** | 25.37 S | 26.26 E |
| Grootpan | **158** | 25.58 S | 26.33 E |
| Groot-Swartberge ⋏ | **158** | 33.22 S | 22.20 E |
| Groot-Vis ≃ | **158** | 33.30 S | 27.08 E |
| Grootvlei | **158** | 26.44 S | 28.32 E |
| Grootvloer ≚ | **158** | 30.00 S | 20.40 E |
| Gröpelingen ◆[8] | **52** | 53.07 N | 8.46 E |
| Gropello Cairoli | **62** | 45.11 N | 9.00 E |
| Gropeni | **38** | 45.04 N | 27.53 E |
| Grosbliederstroff | **56** | 49.09 N | 7.01 E |
| Gros Bois, Parc de ♦ | **261** | 48.44 N | 2.32 E |
| Groscavallo | **62** | 45.22 N | 7.15 E |
| Grose ≃ | **170** | 33.36 S | 150.41 E |
| Grosio | **64** | 46.18 N | 10.16 E |
| Gros Islet | **241f** | 14.05 N | 60.58 W |
| Groslay | **261** | 48.59 N | 2.21 E |
| Gros Mécatina, Cap du ≻ | **186** | 50.45 N | 59.00 W |
| Gros-Morne | **240e** | 14.43 N | 61.01 W |
| Gros Morne ʌ | **186** | 49.36 N | 57.48 W |
| Gros Morne National Park ♦ | **186** | 49.40 N | 57.45 W |
| Grosne ≃ | **58** | 46.42 N | 4.56 E |
| Grosnez Point ≻ | **43b** | 49.16 N | 2.15 W |
| Grosotto | **64** | 46.17 N | 10.15 E |
| Gros Piton ʌ | **241f** | 13.49 N | 61.04 W |
| Grosrouvre | **261** | 48.47 N | 1.46 E |
| Grossa, Ponta ≻, Bra. | **256** | 23.35 S | 45.13 W |
| Grossa, Ponta ≻, Bra. | **287a** | 22.47 S | 43.11 W |
| Grossache (Tiroler Ache) ≃ | **60** | 47.51 N | 12.30 E |
| Grossaitingen | **58** | 48.14 N | 10.47 E |
| Grossalmerode | **56** | 51.15 N | 9.46 E |
| Grossalsleben | **54** | 51.59 N | 11.13 E |
| Gross Ammensleben | **54** | 52.14 N | 11.31 E |
| Grossarl | **64** | 47.14 N | 13.12 E |
| Gross-Beeren | **54** | 52.21 N | 13.18 E |
| Gross Berkel | **52** | 52.04 N | 9.19 E |
| Grossbodungen | **54** | 51.28 N | 10.28 E |
| Gross Börnecke | **54** | 51.50 N | 11.29 E |
| Grossbothen | **54** | 51.11 N | 12.44 E |
| Grossbottwar | **56** | 49.00 N | 9.17 E |
| Grossbreitenbach | **54** | 50.35 N | 11.02 E |
| Grossdeuben | **54** | 51.14 N | 12.23 E |
| Grossdubrau | **54** | 51.15 N | 14.28 E |
| Gross Düngen | **52** | 52.06 N | 10.01 E |
| Grosse Antillen → Greater Antilles II | **238** | 20.00 N | 74.00 W |
| Grosse Aue ≃ | **52** | 52.37 N | 9.10 E |
| Grosse Australische Bucht → Great Australian Bight c[3] | **162** | 35.00 S | 135.00 E |
| Grossebersdorf | **54** | 50.47 N | 11.57 E |
| Grosse Ebene → Great Plains ≚ | **16** | 42.00 N | 100.00 W |
| Grossefehn | **52** | 53.24 N | 7.36 E |
| Grosse Herrenwiese ≡ | **264a** | 52.17 N | 13.20 E |
| Grosse Ile | **216** | 42.08 N | 83.09 W |
| Grosse Ile I | **216** | 42.08 N | 83.09 W |
| Grosse Île, La I | **186** | 47.37 N | 61.31 W |
| Grosse Laber ≃ | **60** | 48.56 N | 12.30 E |
| Grosse Mühl ≃ | **61** | 48.25 N | 13.59 E |
| Grossenbaum ◆[8] | **263** | 51.22 N | 6.47 E |
| Grossenbrode | **54** | 54.22 N | 11.05 E |
| Grossenehrich, Dtsch. | **54** | 51.15 N | 10.50 E |
| Grossenehrich, Dtsch. | **56** | 51.15 N | 10.52 E |
| Grossengottern | **54** | 51.09 N | 10.34 E |
| Grossenhain | **54** | 51.17 N | 13.31 E |
| Grossenkneten | **52** | 52.56 N | 8.16 E |
| Grossenlüder | **56** | 50.35 N | 9.32 E |
| Grossenwiehe | **41** | 54.43 N | 9.15 E |
| Gross-Enzersdorf | **61** | 48.12 N | 16.33 E |
| Grosse Pointe | **214** | 42.23 N | 82.54 W |
| Grosse Pointe ≻ | **241o** | 16.01 N | 61.16 W |
| Grosse Pointe Farms | **214** | 42.25 N | 82.53 W |
| Grosse Pointe Park | **214** | 42.22 N | 82.56 W |
| Grosse Pointe Shores | **214** | 42.26 N | 82.53 W |
| Grosse Pointe Woods | **214** | 42.26 N | 82.54 W |
| Grosser Arber ʌ | **60** | 49.07 N | 13.07 E |
| Grosser Bären-See → Great Bear Lake ⊜ | **176** | 66.00 N | 120.00 W |
| Grosser Beerberg ʌ | **54** | 50.37 N | 10.44 E |
| Grosser Bösenstein ʌ | **61** | 47.26 N | 14.24 E |
| Grosser Buchstein ʌ | **61** | 47.36 N | 14.35 E |
| Grosser Chingan → Da Hinggan Ling ⋏ | **90** | 49.00 N | 122.00 E |
| Grosser Feldberg ʌ | **56** | 50.14 N | 8.26 E |
| Grosser Galtenberg ʌ | **64** | 47.20 N | 11.58 E |
| Grosser Gleichberg ʌ | **54** | 50.23 N | 10.35 E |
| Grosser Heuberg ⋏[1] | **58** | 48.06 N | 8.55 E |
| Grosser Inselsberg ʌ | **54** | 50.52 N | 10.28 E |
| Grosser Jasmunder Bodden c | **54** | 54.31 N | 13.29 E |
| Grosser Knallstein ʌ | **61** | 47.19 N | 13.58 E |
| Grosser Königstuhl ʌ | **64** | 46.57 N | 13.47 E |
| Grosser Müggelsee ⊜ | **54** | 52.26 N | 13.39 E |
| Grosse Röder ≃ | **54** | 51.30 N | 13.25 E |
| Grosser oder Kaiser-Kanal → Da Yunhe ≋ | **90** | 32.12 N | 119.31 E |
| Grosse Rodl ≃ | **61** | 48.20 N | 14.09 E |
| Grosser Peilstein ʌ | **61** | 48.18 N | 15.06 E |
| Grosser Plessower See ⊜ | **264a** | 52.23 N | 12.54 E |
| Grosser Plöner See ⊜ | **54** | 54.06 N | 10.25 E |
| Grosser Priel ʌ | **61** | 47.43 N | 14.04 E |
| Grosser Rachel ʌ | **60** | 48.59 N | 13.24 E |
| Grosser Ravens-Berg ʌ[2] | **264a** | 52.21 N | 13.04 E |
| Grosser Salz-See → Great Salt Lake ⊜ | **200** | 41.10 N | 112.30 W |
| Grosser Seddiner See ⊜ | **264a** | 52.17 N | 13.02 E |
| Grosser Selchower See ⊜ | **54** | 52.14 N | 13.53 E |
| Grosser Sklaven-See → Great Slave Lake ⊜ | **176** | 61.30 N | 114.00 W |
| Grosser Speikkogel ʌ | **61** | 46.47 N | 14.58 E |

DEUTSCH

| Name | Seite | Breite°′ | Länge°′ E = Ost |
|---|---|---|---|
| Grosser Walfisch-Fluss → Baleine, Grande rivière de la ≃ | **176** | 55.16 N | 77.47 W |
| Grosser Wannsee ⊜ | **264a** | 52.26 N | 13.11 E |
| Grosser Winterberg ʌ[2] | **54** | 50.54 N | 14.16 E |
| Grosser Zern-See ⊜ | **264a** | 52.24 N | 12.56 E |
| Grosse Sandspitze ʌ | **64** | 46.46 N | 12.49 E |
| Grosse Sandwüste → Great Sandy Desert ◆[2] | **162** | 21.30 S | 125.00 E |
| Grosses Barrier-Riff → Great Barrier Reef ✢[2] | **160** | 18.00 S | 145.50 E |
| Grosses Meer ⊜ | **52** | 53.25 N | 7.17 E |
| Grosses Moor ◆[3], Dtsch. | **52** | 52.35 N | 8.45 E |
| Grosses Moor ◆[3], Dtsch. | **52** | 52.40 N | 8.20 E |
| Grosses Schulerloch ♦ | **60** | 48.55 N | 11.48 E |
| Grosse Sundainseln → Greater Sunda Islands II | **108** | 2.00 S | 110.00 E |
| Grosses Walsertal V | **58** | 47.14 N | 9.56 E |
| Grosse Syrte → Surt, Khalīj c | **146** | 31.30 N | 18.00 E |
| Grosseto | **66** | 42.46 N | 11.08 E |
| Grosseto □[4] | **66** | 42.50 N | 11.15 E |
| Grosseto, Formiche di I | **66** | 42.39 N | 10.53 E |
| Grosse Tulln ≃ | **61** | 48.20 N | 16.02 E |
| Grossevići | **89** | 47.59 N | 139.30 E |
| Grosse Windgällen ʌ | **58** | 46.49 N | 8.44 E |
| Gross-Gerau | **56** | 49.55 N | 8.29 E |
| Gross-Gerungs | **61** | 48.34 N | 14.57 E |
| Gross Gleidingen | **54** | 52.14 N | 10.25 E |
| Gross Glienicke | **264a** | 52.28 N | 13.07 E |
| Gross-Glienicker See ⊜ | **264a** | 52.28 N | 13.06 E |
| Grossglockner ʌ | **64** | 47.04 N | 12.42 E |
| Grossgmain | **64** | 47.43 N | 12.55 E |
| Grossgörschen | **54** | 51.13 N | 12.11 E |
| Gross Grönau | **54** | 53.46 N | 10.44 E |
| Grosshansdorf | **52** | 53.40 N | 10.17 E |
| Grosshartmannsdorf | **54** | 50.48 N | 13.19 E |
| Gross-Hehlen | **52** | 52.39 N | 10.03 E |
| Grossheide | **52** | 53.35 N | 7.20 E |
| Grosshennersdorf | **54** | 50.59 N | 14.47 E |
| Grosshöchstetten | **58** | 46.55 N | 7.38 E |
| Grossjedlersdorf ◆[8] | **264b** | 48.17 N | 16.25 E |
| Grosskarolinenfeld, Dtsch. | **64** | 47.53 N | 12.05 E |
| Grosskarolinenfeld, Dtsch. | **64** | 47.53 N | 12.05 E |
| Grosskayna | **54** | 51.17 N | 11.56 E |
| Gross Kienitz | **264a** | 52.19 N | 13.28 E |
| Gross Kiesow | **54** | 54.01 N | 13.29 E |
| Gross-Kollmar | **52** | 53.44 N | 9.30 E |
| Grosskorbetha | **54** | 51.16 N | 12.01 E |
| Gross Kreutz | **54** | 52.24 N | 12.46 E |
| Grosskrut | **61** | 48.38 N | 16.43 E |
| Grosslehna | **54** | 51.18 N | 12.10 E |
| Gross Leine | **54** | 52.00 N | 14.03 E |
| Gross Leuthen, Dtsch. | **54** | 52.05 N | 14.05 E |
| Gross Leuthen, Dtsch. | **54** | 52.05 N | 14.05 E |
| Grosslittgen | **56** | 50.02 N | 6.47 E |
| Gross-Machnow | **264a** | 52.16 N | 13.28 E |
| Grossmehring | **60** | 48.46 N | 11.32 E |
| Gross Miltzow, Dtsch. | **54** | 53.32 N | 13.36 E |
| Gross Miltzow, Dtsch. | **54** | 53.32 N | 13.36 E |
| Grossmont | **228** | 32.47 N | 116.59 W |
| Gross Muckrow | **54** | 52.04 N | 14.26 E |
| Gross Nemerow, Dtsch. | **54** | 53.28 N | 13.14 E |
| Gross Nemerow, Dtsch. | **54** | 53.28 N | 13.14 E |
| Gross Oesingen | **52** | 52.38 N | 10.29 E |
| Grossörner | **54** | 51.37 N | 11.29 E |
| Grossos | **250** | 4.59 S | 37.09 W |
| Grossostheim | **56** | 49.55 N | 9.04 E |
| Grosspetersdorf | **61** | 47.14 N | 16.19 E |
| Grosspostwitz | **54** | 51.07 N | 14.26 E |
| Grossquenstedt | **54** | 51.56 N | 11.07 E |
| Grossraming | **61** | 47.53 N | 14.33 E |
| Grossräschen | **54** | 51.35 N | 14.00 E |
| Grossrinderfeld | **56** | 49.39 N | 9.44 E |
| Gross Rodensleben | **54** | 52.08 N | 11.25 E |
| Grossröhrsdorf | **54** | 51.08 N | 14.01 E |
| Gross Rosenburg | **54** | 51.55 N | 11.53 E |
| Grossrückerswalde | **54** | 50.38 N | 13.07 E |
| Grossrudestedt | **54** | 51.05 N | 11.06 E |
| Gross Sankt Florian | **61** | 46.49 N | 15.19 E |
| Gross-Sarau | **54** | 53.45 N | 10.44 E |
| Gross Schacksdorf, Dtsch. | **54** | 51.42 N | 14.38 E |
| Gross Schacksdorf, Dtsch. | **54** | 51.42 N | 14.38 E |
| Grossschirma | **54** | 50.58 N | 13.17 E |
| Grossschönau | **54** | 50.54 N | 14.40 E |
| Gross Schönebeck | **54** | 52.54 N | 13.32 E |
| Gross-Schulzendorf | **264a** | 52.16 N | 13.21 E |
| Gross-Siegharts | **61** | 48.48 N | 15.24 E |
| Grosssölk | **64** | 47.25 N | 13.58 E |
| Gross Stieten, Dtsch. | **54** | 53.49 N | 11.27 E |
| Gross Stieten, Dtsch. | **54** | 53.49 N | 11.27 E |
| Gross-Umstadt | **56** | 49.52 N | 8.55 E |
| Grossvenediger ʌ | **64** | 47.06 N | 12.21 E |
| Grosswardein → Oradea | **38** | 47.03 N | 21.57 E |
| Grossweil | **64** | 47.41 N | 11.18 E |
| Grossweissenbach | **61** | 48.33 N | 15.10 E |
| Gross Wittensee | **41** | 54.24 N | 9.46 E |
| Gross Ziethen, Dtsch. | **264a** | 52.24 N | 13.27 E |
| Gross Ziethen, Dtsch. | **264a** | 52.44 N | 13.01 E |
| Gross-Zimmern | **56** | 49.52 N | 8.50 E |
| Grostenquin | **56** | 48.59 N | 6.44 E |
| Grosvenor, Lake ⊜ | **180** | 58.40 N | 155.15 W |
| Grosvenor Dale | **207** | 41.58 N | 71.53 W |
| Gros Ventre ≃ | **202** | 43.33 N | 110.46 W |
| Groswater Bay c | **176** | 54.20 N | 57.30 W |
| Grote Nete ≃ | **56** | 51.07 N | 4.34 E |
| Groton, Ct., U.S. | **207** | 41.21 N | 72.04 W |
| Groton, Ma., U.S. | **207** | 42.36 N | 71.34 W |
| Groton, N.Y., U.S. | **210** | 42.35 N | 76.22 W |
| Groton, S.D., U.S. | **198** | 45.26 N | 98.05 W |
| Grottaferrata | **66** | 41.47 N | 12.40 E |
| Grottaglie | **68** | 40.32 N | 17.26 E |
| Grottaminarda | **68** | 41.04 N | 15.02 E |
| Grottammare | **66** | 42.59 N | 13.52 E |
| Grotte | **70** | 37.24 N | 13.42 E |
| Grotte di Castro | **66** | 42.40 N | 11.52 E |
| Grotteria | **68** | 38.22 N | 16.17 E |
| Grottoes | **188** | 38.16 N | 78.49 W |
| Grottole | **68** | 40.36 N | 16.23 E |
| Grou, Oued V | **148** | 33.56 N | 6.45 W |
| Grouard Mission | **182** | 55.31 N | 116.09 W |
| Groundbirch | **182** | 55.47 N | 120.55 W |
| Groundhog ≃ | **176** | 49.43 N | 81.58 W |
| Grouse Creek ≃, Ks., U.S. | **198** | 37.00 N | 96.55 W |
| Grouse Creek ≃, Ut,. U.S. | **200** | 41.22 N | 113.55 W |
| Grouse Creek Mountain ʌ | **202** | 44.22 N | 113.54 W |
| Grouw | **52** | 53.05 N | 5.45 E |
| Grove, Eng., U.K. | **42** | 51.36 N | 1.25 W |
| Grove, Ok., U.S. | **196** | 36.35 N | 94.46 W |
| Grove, Pa., U.S. | **285** | 40.01 N | 75.38 W |
| Grove City, Fl., U.S. | **220** | 26.54 N | 82.19 W |
| Grove City, Mn., U.S. | **198** | 45.09 N | 94.40 W |
| Grove City, Oh., U.S. | **218** | 39.52 N | 83.05 W |
| Grove City, Pa., U.S. | **214** | 41.09 N | 80.05 W |
| Grove Hill | **194** | 31.42 N | 87.46 W |


**Symbols** in the index entries represent the broad categories identified in the key at the right. Symbols with superior numbers (⋏[1]) identify subcategories (see complete key on page *I · 1).*

**Symbole** im Register stellen die rechts im Schlüssel erklärten Kategorien dar. Symbole mit hochgestellten Ziffern (⋏[1]) bezeichnen Unterabteilungen einer Kategorie (vgl. vollständiger Schlüssel auf Seite *I · 1).*

**Los símbolos** incluídos en el texto del índice representan las grandes categorías identificadas con la clave a la derecha. Los símbolos con numeros en su parte superior (⋏[1]) identifican las subcategorías (véase la clave completa en la página *I · 1).*

**Les symboles** de l'index représentent les catégories indiquées dans la légende à droite. Les symboles suivis d'un indice (⋏[1]) représentent des sous-catégories (voir légende complète à la page *I · 1).*

**Os símbolos** incluídos no texto do índice representam as grandes categorias identificadas com a chave à direita. Os símbolos com números em sua parte superior (⋏[1]) identificam as subcategorias (veja-se a chave completa à página *I · 1).*

| | | | | |
|---|---|---|---|---|
| ʌ Mountain | Berg | Montaña | Montagne | Montanha |
| ⋏ Mountains | Gebirge | Montañas | Montagnes | Montanhas |
| )( Pass | Paß | Paso | Col | Passo |
| V Valley, Canyon | Tal, Cañon | Valle, Cañón | Vallée, Canyon | Vale, Canhão |
| ≚ Plain | Ebene | Llano | Plaine | Planície |
| ≻ Cape | Kap | Cabo | Cap | Cabo |
| I Island | Insel | Isla | Île | Ilha |
| II Islands | Inseln | Islas | Îles | Ilhas |
| ⏏ Other Topographic Features | Andere Topographische Objekte | Otros Elementos Topográficos | Autres données topographiques | Outros acidentes topográficos |

| ESPAÑOL Nombre | Página | Lat.°′ | Long.°′ W = Oeste |
|---|---|---|---|
| Groveland, Ca., U.S. | 226 | 37.50 N | 120.13 W |
| Groveland, Fl., U.S. | 220 | 28.33 N | 81.51 W |
| Groveland, Ma., U.S. | 207 | 42.45 N | 71.01 W |
| Groveland, N.Y., U.S. | 210 | 42.39 N | 77.46 W |
| Grovely Ridge ∧ | 42 | 51.08 N | 2.04 W |
| Grove Mountains ⋏ | 9 | 72.53 S | 74.53 E |
| Grove Park ◆[8] | 260 | 51.26 N | 0.01 E |
| Groveport | 218 | 39.52 N | 82.53 W |
| Grover | 210 | 41.37 N | 76.52 W |
| Grover City | 204 | 35.07 N | 120.37 W |
| Grover Cleveland Birthplace ⊥ | 276 | 40.50 N | 74.16 W |
| Grover Cleveland Park ♦ | 284a | 42.57 N | 78.49 W |
| Grover Hill | 216 | 41.01 N | 84.28 W |
| Grovers Mills | 276 | 40.19 N | 74.37 W |
| Groves | 194 | 29.56 N | 93.55 W |
| Groveton, N.H., U.S. | 188 | 44.35 N | 71.30 W |
| Groveton, Pa., U.S. | 279b | 40.30 N | 80.06 W |
| Groveton, Tx., U.S. | 222 | 31.03 N | 95.07 W |
| Groveton, Va., U.S. | 284c | 38.46 N | 77.05 W |
| Grovetown | 192 | 33.27 N | 82.11 W |
| Groveville | 208 | 40.10 N | 74.40 W |
| Growa Point › | 150 | 4.21 N | 7.37 W |
| Growler Peak ∧ | 200 | 32.24 N | 113.07 W |
| Growler Wash V | 200 | 32.35 N | 113.30 W |
| Groznoje | 85 | 42.36 N | 71.12 E |
| Groznyj | 84 | 43.20 N | 45.42 E |
| Groznyy → Groznyj | 84 | 43.20 N | 45.42 E |
| Grube, Dtsch. | 54 | 54.14 N | 11.01 E |
| Grube, Dtsch. | 264a | 52.26 N | 12.57 E |
| Grubišno Polje | 36 | 45.42 N | 17.10 E |
| Grudziądz | 30 | 53.29 N | 18.45 E |
| Gruesa, Punta › | 248 | 20.22 S | 70.11 W |
| Gruetli-Laager | 194 | 35.22 N | 85.40 W |
| Grugapark ♦ | 263 | 51.26 N | 7.00 E |
| Grugliasco | 62 | 45.04 N | 7.35 E |
| Gruia | 38 | 44.16 N | 22.42 E |
| Gruinard Bay c | 46 | 57.53 N | 5.31 W |
| Gruinart, Loch c | 46 | 55.52 N | 6.20 W |
| Gruiten | 56 | 51.14 N | 7.01 E |
| Gruitrode | 56 | 51.05 N | 5.35 E |
| Grulla | 196 | 26.16 N | 98.39 W |
| Grumello del Monte | 62 | 45.38 N | 9.52 E |
| Grumento Nova | 68 | 40.17 N | 15.53 E |
| Grumentum ⊥ | 68 | 40.17 N | 15.55 E |
| Grumman-Bethpage Airport ⊠ | 276 | 40.45 N | 73.29 W |
| Grumman Corporation ʋ[3] | 276 | 40.45 N | 73.30 W |
| Grumme ◆[8] | 263 | 51.30 N | 7.14 E |
| Grumo Appula | 68 | 41.01 N | 16.42 E |
| Grums | 26 | 59.21 N | 13.06 E |
| Grüna | 54 | 50.49 N | 12.47 E |
| Grünau | 156 | 27.44 S | 18.23 E |
| Grünau ◆[8] | 264a | 52.25 N | 13.34 E |
| Grünau im Almtal | 64 | 47.51 N | 13.57 E |
| Grunavat, Loch ⊜ | 46 | 58.10 N | 6.55 W |
| Grünbach | 54 | 50.26 N | 12.22 E |
| Grünberg, Dtsch. | 56 | 50.35 N | 8.58 E |
| Grünberg → Zielona Góra, Pol. | 30 | 51.56 N | 15.31 E |
| Grünburg | 61 | 47.57 N | 14.15 E |
| Grundlsee ⊜ | 64 | 47.38 N | 13.52 E |
| Grundy | 192 | 37.16 N | 82.05 W |
| Grundy □[6] | 216 | 41.22 N | 88.26 W |
| Grundy Center | 190 | 42.21 N | 92.46 W |
| Grundy Lake Provincial Park ♦ | 190 | 45.48 N | 80.34 W |
| Grüneberg | 54 | 52.52 N | 13.14 E |
| Grünefeld | 264a | 52.41 N | 12.58 E |
| Grünenplan | 52 | 51.57 N | 9.44 E |
| Grünewald, Dtsch. | 54 | 51.24 N | 14.00 E |
| Grünewald, Dtsch. | 263 | 51.13 N | 7.37 E |
| Grunewald ◆[8] | 264a | 52.30 N | 13.17 E |
| Grunewald, Berliner Forst ◆[3] | 264a | 52.28 N | 13.13 E |
| Grunewald, Jagdschloss ⊥ | 264a | 52.28 N | 13.16 E |
| Grünhain | 54 | 50.35 N | 12.48 E |
| Grünhainichen | 54 | 50.46 N | 13.08 E |
| Grünheide | 54 | 52.25 N | 13.49 E |
| Grünsfeld | 56 | 49.36 N | 9.44 E |
| Grünstadt | 56 | 49.34 N | 8.10 E |
| Grüntal | 264a | 52.45 N | 13.44 E |
| Grunthal | 184 | 49.25 N | 96.52 W |
| Grünwald | 60 | 48.02 N | 11.31 E |
| Gruševka | 78 | 47.55 N | 40.40 E |
| Gruševka ≃ | 83 | 47.26 N | 40.00 E |
| Gruševskaja | 83 | 47.26 N | 39.57 E |
| Grušino | 76 | 59.27 N | 44.09 E |
| Gruting | 46a | 60.14 N | 1.30 W |
| Gruver | 196 | 36.16 N | 101.24 W |
| Gruyère, Lac de la ⊜ | 58 | 46.38 N | 7.06 E |
| Gruyères | 58 | 46.35 N | 7.05 E |
| Gruzdžiai | 76 | 56.06 N | 23.16 E |
| Gruzija → Georgia □[1] | 72 | 42.00 N | 44.00 E |
| Gruziya → Georgia □[1] | 72 | 42.00 N | 44.00 E |
| Gruznovka | 88 | 55.09 N | 105.12 E |
| Gruzskaja Balka | 78 | 46.25 N | 40.19 E |
| Grybów | 30 | 49.38 N | 20.56 E |
| Grycken ⊜ | 40 | 60.27 N | 16.13 E |
| Gryfice | 30 | 53.56 N | 15.12 E |
| Gryfino | 30 | 53.12 N | 14.30 E |
| Grytgöl | 40 | 58.48 N | 15.33 E |
| Grythyttan | 40 | 59.42 N | 14.32 E |
| Gschnitz | 64 | 47.03 N | 11.22 E |
| Gschütt, Pass )( | 64 | 47.35 N | 13.30 E |
| Gschwend | 56 | 48.56 N | 9.44 E |
| Gstaad | 58 | 46.28 N | 7.17 E |
| Gsteig | 58 | 46.23 N | 7.16 E |
| Gu ≃ | 100 | 27.02 N | 115.03 E |
| Gua | 124 | 22.12 N | 85.23 E |
| Guabaria ≃[1] | 126 | 22.10 N | 90.30 E |
| Guabito | 236 | 9.30 N | 82.37 W |
| Guabu | 106 | 32.16 N | 118.53 E |
| Guacanayabo, Golfo de c | 240p | 20.28 N | 77.30 W |
| Guacara | 246 | 10.14 N | 67.53 W |
| Guacarí | 246 | 3.46 N | 76.20 W |
| Gu Achi | 200 | 32.19 N | 112.02 W |
| Guachinango | 234 | 20.32 N | 104.24 W |
| Guachiría ≃ | 246 | 5.27 N | 70.36 W |
| Guachochi | 232 | 26.51 N | 107.05 W |
| Guaçuí | 255 | 20.46 S | 41.41 W |
| Guadajoz ≃ | 34 | 37.50 N | 4.51 W |
| Guadalajara, Esp. | 34 | 40.38 N | 3.10 W |
| Guadalajara, Méx. | 234 | 20.40 N | 103.20 W |
| Guadalajara □[4] | 34 | 40.50 N | 2.30 W |
| Guadalaviar ≃ | 34 | 40.21 N | 1.08 W |
| Guadalcanal | 34 | 38.06 N | 5.49 W |
| Guadalcanal □[4] | 175e | 9.50 S | 160.00 E |
| Guadalcanal I | 175e | 9.32 S | 160.12 E |
| Guadalcázar | 234 | 22.37 N | 100.24 W |
| Guadalén ≃ | 34 | 38.05 N | 3.32 W |
| Guadalén, Embalse de ⊜[1] | 34 | 38.25 N | 3.15 W |
| Guadalentin ≃ | 34 | 37.59 N | 1.04 W |
| Guadalete ≃ | 34 | 36.35 N | 6.13 W |
| Guadalhorce ≃ | 34 | 36.41 N | 4.27 W |
| Guadalimar ≃ | 34 | 38.01 N | 3.45 W |
| Guadalmena ≃ | 34 | 38.19 N | 2.56 W |
| Guadalmez ≃ | 34 | 38.46 N | 5.04 W |
| Guadalope ≃ | 34 | 41.15 N | 0.03 W |
| Guadalquivir ≃ | 34 | 36.47 N | 6.22 W |
| Guadalupe, Bol. | 248 | 18.33 S | 64.05 W |
| Guadalupe, Col. | 246 | 2.01 N | 75.45 W |
| Guadalupe, C.R. | 236 | 9.57 N | 84.03 W |
| Guadalupe, Méx. | 196 | 28.09 N | 100.36 W |
| Guadalupe, Méx. | 232 | 25.41 N | 100.15 W |
| Guadalupe, Méx. | 234 | 22.45 N | 102.31 W |
| Guadalupe, Perú | 248 | 7.15 S | 79.29 W |
| Guadalupe, Ca., U.S. | 204 | 34.58 N | 120.34 W |
| Guadalupe □[6] | 222 | 29.37 N | 97.45 W |
| Guadalupe ◆[8] | 287a | 22.50 S | 43.23 W |

| FRANÇAIS Nom | Page | Lat.°′ | Long.°′ W = Ouest |
|---|---|---|---|
| Guadalupe → Guadeloupe □[2] | 241o | 16.15 N | 61.35 W |
| Guadalupe ≃, Méx. | 204 | 32.05 N | 116.53 W |
| Guadalupe ≃, Ca., U.S. | 282 | 37.25 N | 121.58 W |
| Guadalupe ≃, Tx., U.S. | 196 | 28.30 N | 96.53 W |
| Guadalupe, Basílica de ʋ[1] | 286a | 19.29 N | 99.07 W |
| Guadalupe, Isla I | 178 | 29.00 N | 118.16 W |
| Guadalupe, Presa de ⊜[1] | 286a | 19.37 N | 99.16 W |
| Guadalupe, Sierra de ⋏, Esp. | 34 | 39.26 N | 5.25 W |
| Guadalupe, Sierra de ⋏, Méx. | 286a | 19.35 N | 99.08 W |
| Guadalupe [Bravos] | 232 | 31.23 N | 106.07 W |
| Guadalupe del Norte ≅ | 286a | 19.34 N | 99.01 W |
| Guadalupe de Ramírez | 234 | 17.45 N | 98.10 W |
| Guadalupe Mountains ⋏ | 196 | 32.20 N | 105.00 W |
| Guadalupe Mountains National Park ♦ | 196 | 31.55 N | 104.55 W |
| Guadalupe Peak ∧ | 196 | 31.50 N | 104.52 W |
| Guadalupe Seamount ⊹[3] | 14 | 27.50 N | 168.45 E |
| Guadalupe Slough ≃ | 282 | 37.27 N | 122.02 W |
| Guadalupe Victoria, Méx. | 196 | 27.47 N | 101.04 W |
| Guadalupe Victoria, Méx. | 232 | 24.27 N | 104.07 W |
| Guadalupe Victoria, Méx. | 234 | 19.17 N | 97.21 W |
| Guadalupe Victoria, Presa ⊜[1] | 234 | 23.50 N | 104.46 W |
| Guadalupita | 200 | 36.08 N | 105.14 W |
| Guadarrama, Puerto de )( | 34 | 40.43 N | 4.10 W |
| Guadarrama, Sierra de ⋏ | 34 | 40.55 N | 4.00 W |
| Guadazaón ≃ | 34 | 39.42 N | 1.36 W |
| Guadeloupe □[2], N.A. | 230 | 16.15 N | 61.35 W |
| Guadeloupe □[2], N.A. | 241o | 16.15 N | 61.35 W |
| Guadeloupe Passage ⊍ | 238 | 16.45 N | 61.30 W |
| Guadiana ≃ | 34 | 37.14 N | 7.22 W |
| Guadiana, Bahía de c | 240p | 22.05 N | 84.24 W |
| Guadiana Menor ≃ | 34 | 37.56 N | 3.15 W |
| Guadiaro ≃ | 34 | 36.17 N | 5.17 W |
| Guadiato ≃ | 34 | 37.48 N | 5.03 W |
| Guadiela ≃ | 34 | 40.22 N | 2.49 W |
| Guadix | 34 | 37.18 N | 3.08 W |
| Guafo, Isla I | 254 | 43.36 S | 74.43 W |
| Guagnano | 68 | 40.24 N | 17.57 E |
| Guagua | 116 | 14.58 N | 120.38 E |
| Guahe | 105 | 39.12 N | 115.00 E |
| Guaianases ◆[8] | 287b | 23.33 S | 46.25 W |
| Guaíba | 252 | 30.06 S | 51.19 W |
| Guaíba c[1] | 252 | 30.15 S | 51.12 W |
| Guaicaipuro □[5] | 286c | 10.25 N | 66.57 W |
| Guaihe | 100 | 33.28 N | 112.59 E |
| Guaimaca | 236 | 14.32 N | 86.51 W |
| Guáimaro | 240p | 21.03 N | 77.21 W |
| Guaimoreto, Laguna de c | 236 | 15.58 N | 85.55 W |
| Guaimozi | 98 | 41.31 N | 125.26 E |
| Guainía □[5] | 246 | 2.30 N | 69.00 W |
| Guainía ≃ | 246 | 2.01 N | 67.07 W |
| Guaió ≃ | 287b | 23.31 S | 46.19 W |
| Guaipava | 256 | 21.40 S | 45.43 W |
| Guaiquinima, Cerro ∧ | 246 | 5.49 N | 63.40 W |
| Guaíra, Bra. | 252 | 24.04 S | 54.15 W |
| Guaíra, Bra. | 255 | 20.19 S | 48.18 W |
| Guairá □[5] | 252 | 25.45 S | 56.30 W |
| Guaire ≃ | 286c | 10.25 N | 66.46 W |
| Guáitara ≃ | 246 | 1.34 N | 77.27 W |
| Guaitecas, Archipiélago de las II | 254 | 43.57 S | 73.50 W |
| Guajaba, Cayo I | 240p | 21.50 N | 77.30 W |
| Guajará ≃ | 250 | 1.48 S | 53.02 W |
| Guajará-Açu | 250 | 1.38 S | 48.07 W |
| Guajará-Miri | 250 | 1.29 S | 48.17 W |
| Guajará-Mirim | 248 | 10.48 S | 65.22 W |
| Guajataca ≃ | 240m | 18.29 N | 66.57 W |
| Guajataca, Lago de ⊜[1] | 240m | 18.23 N | 66.55 W |
| Guajiasi | 104 | 41.15 N | 120.54 E |
| Gualaca | 236 | 8.32 N | 82.18 W |
| Gualaceo | 246 | 2.54 S | 78.47 W |
| Gualala | 204 | 38.45 N | 123.31 W |
| Gualán | 236 | 15.08 N | 89.22 W |
| Gualaquiza | 246 | 3.24 S | 78.33 W |
| Gualdo Tadino | 66 | 43.14 N | 12.47 E |
| Gualeguay | 252 | 33.09 S | 59.20 W |
| Gualeguay ≃ | 252 | 33.19 S | 59.39 W |
| Gualeguaychú | 252 | 33.01 S | 58.31 W |
| Gualicho, Salina del ≡ | 254 | 40.24 S | 65.15 W |
| Gualjaina | 254 | 42.42 S | 70.30 W |
| Gualtieri | 64 | 44.54 N | 10.38 E |
| Guam □[2], Oc. | 14 | 13.28 N | 144.47 E |
| Guam □[2], Oc. | 174p | 13.28 N | 144.47 E |
| Guamá ≃, Bra. | 250 | 1.29 S | 48.30 W |
| Guamá ≃, Cuba | 240p | 22.11 N | 83.41 W |
| Guamal, Col. | 246 | 9.09 N | 74.14 W |
| Guamal, Col. | 246 | 3.52 N | 73.44 W |
| Guamal, Quebrada ≃ | 286c | 10.31 N | 66.59 W |
| Guamblín, Isla I | 254 | 44.51 S | 75.05 W |
| Guaminí | 252 | 37.02 S | 62.25 W |
| Guam International Airport ⊠ | 174p | 13.29 N | 144.48 E |
| Guamo | 246 | 4.02 N | 74.58 W |
| Guamo Embarcadero | 240p | 20.37 N | 76.58 W |
| Guamote | 246 | 1.56 S | 78.43 W |
| Guamúchil, Méx. | 232 | 25.28 N | 108.06 W |
| Guamúchil, Méx. | 234 | 25.28 N | 108.06 W |
| Guamués ≃ | 246 | 0.32 N | 76.33 W |
| Gua Musang | 114 | 4.53 N | 101.58 E |
| Gu'an | 105 | 39.26 N | 116.18 E |
| Guan ≃, Zhg. | 100 | 34.29 N | 119.49 E |
| Guan ≃, Zhg. | 100 | 32.16 N | 115.42 E |
| Guanábana | 240m | 18.01 N | 67.07 W |
| Guanabara, Baía de c | 287a | 22.50 S | 43.10 W |
| Guanabara, Palácio ʋ | 287a | 22.56 S | 43.11 W |
| Guanacaste □[4] | 236 | 10.30 N | 85.15 W |
| Guanacaste, Cordillera de ⋏ | 236 | 10.45 N | 85.05 W |
| Guanacaste, Parque Nacional ♦ | 236 | 10.50 N | 85.30 W |
| Guanacaure, Cerro ∧ | 236 | 13.14 N | 87.07 W |
| Guanaceví | 232 | 25.56 N | 105.57 W |
| Guanache ≃ | 248 | 5.53 S | 74.21 W |
| Guanahacabibes, Golfo de c | 240p | 22.08 N | 84.35 W |
| Guanahacabibes, Península de ›[1] | 240p | 21.57 N | 84.35 W |
| Guana Island I | 240m | 18.29 N | 64.34 W |
| Guanaja | 236 | 16.27 N | 85.54 W |
| Guanaja, Isla de I | 236 | 16.30 N | 85.55 W |
| Guanajay | 240p | 22.55 N | 82.42 W |
| Guanajibo ≃ | 240m | 18.10 N | 67.11 W |
| Guanajibo, Punta › | 240m | 18.10 N | 67.11 W |
| Guanajuato | 234 | 21.01 N | 101.15 W |
| Guanajuato □[3] | 234 | 21.00 N | 101.00 W |
| Guanambi | 255 | 14.13 S | 42.47 W |
| Guanaparo, Caño ≃ | 246 | 8.19 N | 68.10 W |
| Guañape, Islas II | 248 | 8.33 S | 78.57 W |
| Guanare | 246 | 9.03 N | 69.45 W |
| Guanare ≃ | 246 | 8.13 N | 67.46 W |
| Guanarito | 246 | 8.42 N | 69.12 W |
| Guanay | 248 | 15.28 S | 67.52 W |
| Guanay, Cerro ∧ | 246 | 5.51 N | 66.18 W |
| Guanay, Cerro ∧[2] | 286d | 12.07 S | 77.13 W |
| Guanbuqiao | 100 | 29.56 N | 114.21 E |
| Guanchao | 100 | 26.41 N | 114.58 E |
| Guancheng, Zhg. | 100 | 30.11 N | 121.25 E |

| PORTUGUÊS Nome | Página | Lat.°′ | Long.°′ W = Oeste |
|---|---|---|---|
| Guancheng, Zhg. | 107 | 30.01 N | 103.54 E |
| Guancun | 106 | 31.30 N | 119.43 E |
| Guandacol | 252 | 29.31 S | 68.32 W |
| Guandanghu | 100 | 30.06 N | 113.37 E |
| Guandi, Zhg. | 98 | 41.48 N | 116.52 E |
| Guandi, Zhg. | 98 | 42.37 N | 118.27 E |
| Guandian | 100 | 32.40 N | 118.04 E |
| Guandu, Zhg. | 100 | 24.17 N | 113.53 E |
| Guandu, Zhg. | 107 | 30.04 N | 106.25 E |
| Guane | 240p | 22.12 N | 84.05 W |
| Guang'an | 107 | 30.28 N | 106.39 E |
| Guang'anmen Station ◆[5] | 271a | 39.53 N | 116.20 E |
| Guangchang | 100 | 26.50 N | 116.14 E |
| Guangde | 106 | 30.54 N | 119.26 E |
| Guangdong (Kwangtung) □[4] | 90 | 23.00 N | 113.00 E |
| Guangfeng | 100 | 28.25 N | 118.11 E |
| Guangfu, Zhg. | 106 | 31.18 N | 120.23 E |
| Guangfu, Zhg. | 107 | 30.13 N | 104.41 E |
| Guangfu, Zhg. | 269b | 31.21 N | 121.19 E |
| Guangfuyingzi | 104 | 42.14 N | 120.58 E |
| Guanghua | 102 | 32.25 N | 111.36 E |
| Guangji | 100 | 29.52 N | 115.34 E |
| Guangling, Zhg. | 98 | 39.47 N | 114.17 E |
| Guangling, Zhg. | 106 | 32.06 N | 120.13 E |
| Guanglu Dao I | 98 | 39.09 N | 122.21 E |
| Guangmao Shan ∧ | 102 | 27.02 N | 100.58 E |
| Guangming Ding ∧ | 100 | 30.07 N | 118.10 E |
| Guangnan | 102 | 24.10 N | 105.06 E |
| Guangningsi, Zhg. | 98 | 39.08 N | 121.45 E |
| Guangningsi, Zhg. | 98 | 40.27 N | 118.31 E |
| Guangping | 98 | 36.30 N | 114.57 E |
| Guangrao | 98 | 37.02 N | 118.25 E |
| Guangshunchang | 107 | 29.22 N | 105.31 E |
| Guangshan | 100 | 32.02 N | 114.52 E |
| Guangshui | 100 | 31.40 N | 114.00 E |
| Guangxing | 107 | 29.04 N | 106.33 E |
| Guangxi Zhuangzu Zizhiqu (Kwangsi Chuang) □[4] | 102 | 24.00 N | 109.00 E |
| Guangyuan | 102 | 32.26 N | 105.52 E |
| Guangyuanzhen | 107 | 30.37 N | 104.47 E |
| Guangze | 100 | 27.32 N | 117.20 E |
| Guangzhen | 106 | 30.45 N | 121.07 E |
| Guangzhou (Canton) | 100 | 23.06 N | 113.16 E |
| Guangzong | 98 | 37.06 N | 115.08 E |
| Guanhães | 255 | 18.46 S | 42.53 W |
| Guanhu | 98 | 34.26 N | 117.59 E |
| Guánica | 240m | 17.58 N | 66.55 W |
| Guánica, Laguna de ⊜ | 240m | 18.00 N | 66.56 W |
| Guaniguanico, Cordillera de ⋏ | 240p | 22.35 N | 83.45 W |
| Guanipa ≃ | 246 | 9.56 N | 62.26 W |
| Guanjian | 107 | 29.59 N | 105.59 E |
| Guanjian ≃ | 107 | 30.00 N | 106.01 E |
| Guankou, Zhg. | 100 | 30.35 N | 115.20 E |
| Guankou, Zhg. | 107 | 30.39 N | 103.26 E |
| Guanlin | 106 | 31.32 N | 119.42 E |
| Guanling | 102 | 25.57 N | 105.29 E |
| Guanlipu | 104 | 41.37 N | 123.18 E |
| Guanmenshan | 89 | 47.23 N | 122.20 E |
| Guannan (Xin'anzhen) | 98 | 34.07 N | 119.23 E |
| Guano | 246 | 1.35 S | 78.38 W |
| Guano Creek ≃ | 202 | 42.12 N | 119.31 W |
| Guanputou | 105 | 38.58 N | 117.04 E |
| Guanqian, Zhg. | 100 | 30.42 N | 117.39 E |
| Guanqian, Zhg. | 100 | 27.48 N | 118.31 E |
| Guanqian, Zhg. | 100 | 25.57 N | 116.33 E |
| Guanqian, Zhg. | 100 | 26.12 N | 117.57 E |
| Guanqiao, Zhg. | 98 | 34.58 N | 117.14 E |
| Guanqiao, Zhg. | 100 | 25.03 N | 118.06 E |
| Guanqiaopu | 100 | 31.08 N | 112.54 E |
| Guanshanchang | 107 | 28.46 N | 103.42 E |
| Guanshi | 100 | 26.43 N | 112.53 E |
| Guanshui | 98 | 40.55 N | 124.33 E |
| Guanta | 246 | 10.14 N | 64.36 W |
| Guantánamo | 240p | 20.08 N | 75.12 W |
| Guantánamo □[4] | 240p | 20.20 N | 75.00 W |
| Guantánamo ≃ | 240p | 19.55 N | 75.12 W |
| Guantánamo, Bahía de c | 240p | 20.00 N | 75.08 W |
| Guantanamo Bay Naval Station ■ | 240p | 19.55 N | 75.10 W |
| Guantang | 106 | 31.37 N | 119.06 E |
| Guantangqiao | 106 | 32.09 N | 119.27 E |
| Guantao (Nanguantao) | 98 | 36.35 N | 115.19 E |
| Guanting, Zhg. | 100 | 34.19 N | 113.47 E |
| Guanting, Zhg. | 105 | 40.13 N | 115.37 E |
| Guanting Shuiku ⊜[1] | 105 | 40.20 N | 115.38 E |
| Guantou, Zhg. | 100 | 28.03 N | 120.41 E |
| Guantou, Zhg. | 100 | 26.08 N | 119.33 E |
| Guantunpu | 98 | 40.28 N | 113.24 E |
| Guanxian, Zhg. | 98 | 36.30 N | 115.27 E |
| Guanxian, Zhg. | 102 | 31.00 N | 103.40 E |
| Guanxun | 100 | 24.19 N | 117.45 E |
| Guanyin | 107 | 30.16 N | 103.51 E |
| Guanyinchang, Zhg. | 107 | 29.15 N | 104.02 E |
| Guanyinchang, Zhg. | 107 | 30.28 N | 105.16 E |
| Guanyingzicun | 104 | 41.52 N | 121.53 E |
| Guanyinpu | 107 | 28.58 N | 104.53 E |
| Guanyinqiao, Zhg. | 107 | 29.05 N | 104.46 E |
| Guanyinqiao, Zhg. | 107 | 29.46 N | 104.12 E |
| Guanyinshan | 106 | 32.01 N | 120.58 E |
| Guanyinsi | 106 | 31.48 N | 118.57 E |
| Guanyintan | 107 | 29.35 N | 105.14 E |
| Guanyintang, Zhg. | 100 | 31.01 N | 112.35 E |
| Guanyintang, Zhg. | 105 | 39.52 N | 116.31 E |
| Guanyintang, Zhg. | 106 | 32.09 N | 121.09 E |
| Guanyinzhen | 107 | 29.06 N | 104.24 E |
| Guanyinzhou | 100 | 29.30 N | 113.09 E |
| Guanyun (Dayishan) | 98 | 34.20 N | 119.17 E |
| Guanzhuang, Zhg. | 98 | 37.12 N | 114.30 E |
| Guanzhuang, Zhg. | 100 | 32.49 N | 114.16 E |
| Guanzhuang, Zhg. | 100 | 28.58 N | 117.24 E |
| Guapí | 246 | 2.36 N | 77.54 W |
| Guapiaçu ≃ | 256 | 22.40 S | 42.55 W |
| Guapiara | 255 | 24.10 S | 48.32 W |
| Guápiles | 236 | 10.13 N | 83.46 W |
| Guapimirim | 256 | 22.32 S | 42.59 W |
| Guapimirim ≃ | 256 | 22.40 S | 42.58 W |
| Guapo Bay c | 241r | 10.12 N | 61.40 W |
| Guaporé | 252 | 28.51 S | 51.54 W |
| Guaporé (Itenes) ≃ | 248 | 11.54 S | 65.01 W |
| Guaqui | 248 | 16.35 S | 68.51 W |
| Guará ≃ | 255 | 12.59 S | 44.49 W |
| Guarabira | 250 | 6.51 S | 35.29 W |
| Guaraçaí | 255 | 21.02 S | 51.11 W |
| Guaracarumbo | 286c | 10.34 N | 66.59 W |
| Guaraci | 255 | 20.29 S | 48.57 W |
| Guaraciaba do Norte | 250 | 4.10 S | 40.46 W |
| Guaraciana | 255 | 17.03 S | 43.41 W |
| Guaraguara, Punta › | 241r | 10.31 N | 62.19 W |
| Guaraí ≃ | 287a | 22.42 S | 43.02 W |
| Guaramirim | 252 | 26.27 S | 49.00 W |
| Guaranda | 246 | 1.36 S | 79.00 W |
| Guaranésia | 256 | 21.18 S | 46.48 W |
| Guarani | 256 | 21.22 S | 43.03 W |
| Guaraniaçu | 252 | 25.06 S | 52.52 W |
| Guarani das Missões | 252 | 28.08 S | 54.34 W |
| Guarani de Goiás | 255 | 13.59 S | 46.31 W |
| Guarapari | 255 | 20.40 S | 40.30 W |
| Guarapiranga, Represa ⊜[1] | 256 | 23.44 S | 46.44 W |
| Guarapuava | 252 | 25.23 S | 51.27 W |
| Guaraqueçaba | 252 | 25.17 S | 48.21 W |
| Guarará | 256 | 21.43 S | 43.02 W |
| Guarará ≃ | 287b | 23.39 S | 46.30 W |
| Guararé | 246 | 7.49 N | 80.17 W |
| Guararema | 256 | 23.25 S | 46.02 W |
| Guaratiba, Morro de ∧ | 287a | 23.04 S | 43.33 W |
| Guaratinga | 255 | 16.34 S | 39.34 W |
| Guaratinguetá | 256 | 22.49 S | 45.13 W |
| Guaratinguetá ≃ | 256 | 22.49 S | 45.13 W |
| Guaratuba | 252 | 25.54 S | 48.34 W |
| Guar Chempedak | 114 | 5.52 N | 100.28 E |
| Guarcino | 66 | 41.48 N | 13.19 E |

| | | | |
|---|---|---|---|
| Guarda | 34 | 40.32 N | 7.16 W |
| Guardado de Abajo | 196 | 26.22 N | 98.57 W |
| Guardafui, Cape → Gwardafuy, Gees › | 144 | 11.49 N | 51.15 E |
| Guardavalle | 68 | 38.30 N | 16.30 E |
| Guardea | 66 | 42.37 N | 12.18 E |
| Guardia Escolta | 252 | 28.59 S | 62.08 W |
| Guardiagrele | 66 | 42.11 N | 14.13 E |
| Guardia Lombardi | 68 | 40.57 N | 15.12 E |
| Guardia Mitre | 254 | 40.26 S | 63.41 W |
| Guardia Sanframondi | 68 | 41.15 N | 14.36 E |
| Guardo | 34 | 42.47 N | 4.50 W |
| Guareña | 34 | 38.51 N | 6.06 W |
| Guareña ≃ | 34 | 41.29 N | 5.23 W |
| Guarenas | 246 | 10.28 N | 66.37 W |
| Guarenas ≃ | 286c | 10.30 N | 66.45 W |
| Guariba ≃ | 248 | 7.41 S | 60.18 W |
| Guarico | 246 | 9.32 N | 69.48 W |
| Guárico □[3] | 246 | 8.40 N | 66.35 W |
| Guárico ≃ | 246 | 7.55 N | 67.23 W |
| Guárico, Embalse del ⊜[1] | 246 | 9.05 N | 67.25 W |
| Guarico, Punta › | 240p | 20.37 N | 74.44 W |
| Guariquito ≃ | 246 | 7.40 N | 66.18 W |
| Guarizama | 236 | 14.55 N | 86.20 W |
| Guarujá | 256 | 24.00 S | 46.16 W |
| Guarulhos | 256 | 23.28 S | 46.32 W |
| Guarulhos □[7] | 287b | 23.26 S | 46.29 W |
| Guasare ≃ | 246 | 11.03 N | 72.02 W |
| Guasave | 232 | 25.34 N | 108.27 W |
| Guasdualito | 246 | 7.15 N | 70.44 W |
| Guasila | 71 | 39.34 N | 9.03 E |
| Guasipati | 246 | 7.28 N | 61.54 W |
| Guastalla | 64 | 44.55 N | 10.39 E |
| Guastatoya | 236 | 14.51 N | 90.04 W |
| Guāsuba ≃[1] | 126 | 21.38 N | 88.53 E |
| Guatajiagua | 236 | 13.40 N | 88.13 W |
| Guatemala, Cuba | 240p | 20.46 N | 75.39 W |
| Guatemala, Guat. | 236 | 14.38 N | 90.31 W |
| Guatemala □[5] | 236 | 14.40 N | 90.30 W |
| Guatemala □[1], N.A. | 230 | 15.30 N | 90.15 W |
| Guatemala □[1], N.A. | 236 | 15.30 N | 90.15 W |
| Guatemala Basin ⊹[1] | 16 | 11.00 N | 95.00 W |
| Guateque | 246 | 5.00 N | 73.28 W |
| Guatimozín | 252 | 33.27 S | 62.27 W |
| Guatopo, Parque Nacional ♦ | 246 | 10.05 N | 66.25 W |
| Guatraché | 252 | 37.40 S | 63.32 W |
| Guatuaro Point › | 241r | 10.20 N | 60.59 W |
| Guaugurina | 164 | 10.37 S | 150.28 E |
| Guavi ≃ | 164 | 7.49 S | 143.15 E |
| Guaviare □[8] | 246 | 2.00 N | 72.00 W |
| Guaviare ≃ | 246 | 4.03 N | 67.44 W |
| Guaxindiba ≃ | 287a | 22.44 S | 43.02 W |
| Guaxupé | 256 | 21.18 S | 46.42 W |
| Guayabal, Cuba | 240p | 20.42 N | 77.36 W |
| Guayabal, Ven. | 246 | 8.00 N | 67.24 W |
| Guayabal, Lago ⊜[1] | 240m | 18.06 N | 66.30 W |
| Guayabero ≃ | 246 | 2.36 N | 72.47 W |
| Guayacán | 252 | 29.58 S | 71.22 W |
| Guayaguayare | 241r | 10.08 N | 61.02 W |
| Guayalejo ≃ | 234 | 22.27 N | 98.29 W |
| Guayama | 240m | 17.59 N | 66.07 W |
| Guayambre ≃ | 236 | 14.26 N | 86.02 W |
| Guayameo | 234 | 18.12 N | 101.19 W |
| Guayana → Ciudad Guayana | 246 | 8.22 N | 62.40 W |
| Guayana → Guyana □[1] | 246 | 5.00 N | 59.00 W |
| Guayaneco, Archipiélago II | 254 | 47.45 S | 75.10 W |
| Guayanés, Punta › | 240m | 18.04 N | 65.48 W |
| Guayanilla | 240m | 18.01 N | 66.47 W |
| Guayanilla, Bahía de c | 240m | 18.00 N | 66.46 W |
| Guayape | 236 | 14.45 N | 86.52 W |
| Guayape ≃ | 236 | 14.26 N | 85.58 W |
| Guayapo ≃ | 246 | 4.30 N | 67.35 W |
| Guayaquil | 246 | 2.10 S | 79.50 W |
| Guayaquil, Golfo de c | 246 | 3.00 S | 80.30 W |
| Guayaramerín | 248 | 10.48 S | 65.23 W |
| Guayas □[4] | 246 | 2.00 S | 80.00 W |
| Guayas ≃, Col. | 246 | 1.23 N | 74.50 W |
| Guayas ≃, Ec. | 246 | 2.36 S | 79.52 W |
| Guayatayoc, Laguna de ⊜ | 252 | 23.25 S | 65.51 W |
| Guaycora | 232 | 28.50 N | 109.21 W |
| Guaycurú, Arroyo ≃ | 258 | 34.00 S | 56.50 W |
| Guaymas | 232 | 27.56 N | 110.54 W |
| Guaynabo | 240m | 18.22 N | 66.07 W |
| Guayquiraró ≃ | 252 | 30.10 S | 58.34 W |
| Guayuriba ≃ | 246 | 3.55 N | 73.05 W |
| Guazacapán | 236 | 14.04 N | 90.25 W |
| Guazapares | 232 | 27.22 N | 108.15 W |
| Guazárachi | 232 | 25.57 N | 106.43 W |
| Guazhou | 106 | 32.15 N | 119.23 E |
| Guazunamby, Arroyo ≃ | 288 | 34.24 S | 58.38 W |
| Guba, Ityo. | 144 | 10.16 N | 35.17 E |
| Guba, Zaïre | 154 | 10.40 S | 26.26 E |
| Gubacha | 86 | 58.52 N | 57.36 E |
| Gubam | 164 | 8.40 S | 141.55 E |
| Gubany | 76 | 56.37 N | 30.40 E |
| Gubari | 80 | 51.32 N | 42.33 E |
| Gubat | 116 | 12.55 N | 124.07 E |
| Gubavica ∟ | 36 | 43.26 N | 16.54 E |
| Gubbi | 122 | 13.19 N | 76.56 E |
| Gubbio | 66 | 43.21 N | 12.35 E |
| Gubeikou | 105 | 40.42 N | 117.09 E |
| Guben | 54 | 51.57 N | 14.43 E |
| Gubentaoligai | 104 | 42.16 N | 122.13 E |
| Gubin | 30 | 51.56 N | 14.45 E |
| Gubino, Ross. | 80 | 53.19 N | 48.44 E |
| Gubino, Ross. | 82 | 55.42 N | 39.07 E |
| Gubio | 146 | 12.29 N | 12.48 E |
| Gubkin | 78 | 51.18 N | 37.32 E |
| Gubug | 115a | 7.03 S | 110.40 E |
| Gucheng (Zhengjiakou), Zhg. | 98 | 37.22 N | 115.56 E |
| Gucheng, Zhg. | 100 | 33.59 N | 117.29 E |
| Gucheng, Zhg. | 100 | 25.53 N | 116.11 E |
| Gucheng, Zhg. | 100 | 32.46 N | 118.32 E |
| Gucheng, Zhg. | 102 | 32.18 N | 111.35 E |
| Gucheng, Zhg. | 105 | 40.32 N | 116.02 E |
| Gucheng, Zhg. | 105 | 39.08 N | 115.42 E |
| Gucheng, Zhg. | 106 | 30.29 N | 119.46 E |
| Guchengcang | 100 | 32.34 N | 115.20 E |
| Gucheng Hu ⊜ | 106 | 31.17 N | 118.54 E |
| Guchengzi, Zhg. | 104 | 42.33 N | 123.45 E |
| Guchengzi, Zhg. | 104 | 40.58 N | 122.36 E |
| Guchengzi, Zhg. | 104 | 40.40 N | 120.31 E |
| Guchengzi, Zhg. | 104 | 41.44 N | 123.35 E |
| Gučin-Us | 102 | 45.27 N | 102.25 E |
| Gücük | 130 | 38.12 N | 37.29 E |
| Gūdalūr | 122 | 9.41 N | 77.16 E |
| Gúdar, Sierra de ⋏ | 34 | 40.27 N | 0.42 W |
| Gudauta | 84 | 43.06 N | 40.37 E |
| Gudbrandsdalen V | 26 | 61.30 N | 10.00 E |
| Gudenå ≃ | 26 | 56.29 N | 10.13 E |
| Gudensberg | 56 | 51.10 N | 9.22 E |
| Gudermes | 84 | 43.20 N | 46.08 E |
| Guderup | 41 | 54.59 N | 9.53 E |
| Gudgenby ≃ | 171b | 35.39 S | 149.04 E |
| Gudhjem | 26 | 55.13 N | 14.59 E |
| Gudianzi | 100 | 31.49 N | 116.05 E |
| Gudivāda | 122 | 16.27 N | 80.59 E |
| Gudiyāttam | 122 | 12.57 N | 78.52 E |
| Gudme | 41 | 55.09 N | 10.43 E |
| Gudow | 54 | 53.33 N | 10.46 E |
| Güdül | 130 | 40.13 N | 32.15 E |
| Gūdūr | 122 | 14.08 N | 79.51 E |
| Gudvangen | 26 | 60.52 N | 6.50 E |
| Guebwiller (Gebweiler) | 58 | 47.55 N | 7.12 E |
| Guéckédou | 150 | 8.33 N | 10.09 W |
| Gué-de-Longroi | 261 | 48.30 N | 1.43 E |
| Gué-d'Hossus | 50 | 49.57 N | 4.32 E |
| Guédi, Mont ∧ | 146 | 12.14 N | 18.58 E |

| | | | |
|---|---|---|---|
| Guéguen, Lac ⊜ | 190 | 48.06 N | 77.13 W |
| Guéherville | 261 | 48.32 N | 1.53 E |
| Güejar ≃ | 246 | 2.55 N | 73.14 W |
| Guélendeng | 146 | 10.56 N | 15.32 E |
| Guelma | 148 | 36.28 N | 7.26 E |
| Guelph | 212 | 43.33 N | 80.15 W |
| Guéméné-sur-Scorff | 32 | 48.04 N | 3.12 W |
| Güemes | 234 | 23.56 N | 99.00 W |
| Guemes Island I | 224 | 48.33 N | 122.37 W |
| Guené | 150 | 11.44 N | 3.13 E |
| Guenguel ≃ | 254 | 45.41 S | 70.20 W |
| Guer | 32 | 47.54 N | 2.07 W |
| Guéra □[5] | 146 | 11.30 N | 18.30 E |
| Guéra, Massif de ∧ | 146 | 11.55 N | 18.12 E |
| Guérande | 32 | 47.20 N | 2.26 W |
| Guercif | 148 | 34.15 N | 3.21 W |
| Guerdjoumane, Djebel ∧ | 34 | 36.25 N | 2.51 E |
| Güere ≃ | 246 | 9.50 N | 65.08 W |
| Guéréda | 146 | 14.31 N | 22.05 E |
| Guéret | 32 | 46.10 N | 1.52 E |
| Guérin Kouka | 150 | 9.41 N | 0.37 E |
| Guerla Mandata Shan ∧ | 120 | 30.26 N | 81.20 E |
| Guermantes | 261 | 48.51 N | 2.42 E |
| Guerne | 214 | 40.46 N | 81.54 W |
| Guernes | 261 | 49.01 N | 1.38 E |
| Guerneville | 204 | 38.30 N | 123.00 W |
| Guernica, Arg. | 258 | 34.56 S | 58.25 W |
| Guernica → Gernika, Esp. | 34 | 43.19 N | 2.41 W |
| Guernsey | 200 | 42.16 N | 104.44 W |
| Guernsey □[6] | 214 | 40.08 N | 81.30 W |
| Guernsey □[2], Europe | 22 | 49.28 N | 2.35 W |
| Guernsey □[2], Europe | 43b | 49.28 N | 2.35 W |
| Guernsey Reservoir ⊜[1] | 198 | 42.19 N | 104.48 W |
| Guernsey State Park ♦ | 198 | 42.20 N | 104.50 W |
| Guerrero, Méx. | 196 | 28.20 N | 100.23 W |
| Guerrero, Méx. | 232 | 28.33 N | 107.30 W |
| Guerrero □[3] | 234 | 17.40 N | 100.00 W |
| Guerrero Negro | 232 | 27.56 N | 114.08 W |
| Guerville | 261 | 48.57 N | 1.44 E |
| Guerzim | 148 | 29.45 N | 1.47 W |
| Guesle ≃ | 261 | 48.36 N | 1.40 E |
| Guessou-Sud | 150 | 10.03 N | 2.38 E |
| Guest Peninsula ›[1] | 9 | 76.18 S | 148.00 W |
| Gueydan | 194 | 30.01 N | 92.30 W |
| Guéyo | 150 | 5.49 N | 6.36 W |
| Gufang | 100 | 29.04 N | 119.32 E |
| Guffin Bay c | 212 | 44.01 N | 76.09 W |
| Guga | 89 | 52.43 N | 137.35 E |
| Gugang | 100 | 28.17 N | 113.46 E |
| Guge ∧ | 144 | 6.10 N | 37.26 E |
| Gugera | 123 | 30.58 N | 73.19 E |
| Gugging | 264b | 48.19 N | 16.15 E |
| Güglia, Pass dal )( | 58 | 46.28 N | 9.44 E |
| Güglingen | 56 | 49.04 N | 9.00 E |
| Guglionesi | 66 | 41.55 N | 14.55 E |
| Gugu ∧ | 144 | 8.12 N | 39.58 E |
| Guguan | 102 | 40.27 N | 99.13 E |
| Guguan I | 108 | 17.19 N | 145.51 E |
| Guhe | 100 | 31.54 N | 117.58 E |
| Gui ≃ | 102 | 23.28 N | 111.18 E |
| Guia | 248 | 15.22 S | 56.14 W |
| Guia de Pacobaíba | 256 | 22.43 S | 43.10 W |
| Guia Lopes da Laguna | 248 | 21.26 S | 56.07 W |
| Guiana Basin ⊹[1] | 18 | 11.00 N | 52.00 W |
| Guiana Island I | 240c | 17.07 N | 61.44 W |
| Guibéroua | 150 | 6.14 N | 6.10 W |
| Guibes | 156 | 26.41 S | 16.42 E |
| Güicán | 246 | 6.28 N | 72.25 W |
| Guichen | 32 | 47.58 N | 1.48 W |
| Guichi | 100 | 30.40 N | 117.28 E |
| Guichón | 252 | 32.21 S | 57.12 W |
| Guicun | 100 | 33.37 N | 114.11 E |
| Guidan Roumji | 150 | 13.40 N | 6.42 E |
| Guidari | 146 | 9.17 N | 16.40 E |
| Guide | 102 | 36.03 N | 101.28 E |
| Guide, Mount ∧[2] | 162 | 22.36 S | 136.54 E |
| Guide Post | 44 | 55.10 N | 1.35 W |
| Guider | 146 | 9.56 N | 13.57 E |
| Guide Rock | 198 | 40.04 N | 98.19 W |
| Guidexiang | 107 | 29.51 N | 104.47 E |
| Guidigri | 146 | 13.40 N | 9.51 E |
| Guidimaka □[4] | 150 | 15.30 N | 12.10 W |
| Guidimouni | 150 | 13.42 N | 9.30 E |
| Guiding | 102 | 26.34 N | 107.14 E |
| Guidizzolo | 64 | 45.19 N | 10.35 E |
| Guidong | 100 | 26.05 N | 113.57 E |
| Guidonia | 66 | 42.01 N | 12.45 E |
| Guidouma | 152 | 1.37 S | 10.41 E |
| Guiers ≃ | 62 | 45.37 N | 5.37 E |
| Guiers, Lac de ⊜ | 150 | 16.12 N | 15.50 W |
| Guifujie | 100 | 27.20 N | 120.01 E |
| Guiglia | 64 | 44.26 N | 10.58 E |
| Guiglo | 150 | 6.33 N | 7.29 W |
| Guignes-Rabutin | 50 | 48.38 N | 2.48 E |
| Guihuayuan | 107 | 30.37 N | 105.25 E |
| Guihulngan | 116 | 10.07 N | 123.16 E |
| Güija, Lago de ⊜ | 236 | 14.17 N | 89.31 W |
| Guijalo | 116 | 13.44 N | 123.52 E |
| Guiji | 100 | 32.51 N | 116.33 E |
| Guijingqiao | 106 | 31.21 N | 119.40 E |
| Guijuelo | 34 | 40.33 N | 5.40 W |
| Guil ≃ | 62 | 44.40 N | 6.36 E |
| Guilarte, Monte ∧ | 240m | 18.09 N | 66.46 W |
| Guilderland | 210 | 42.42 N | 73.54 W |
| Guildford, Austl. | 274a | 33.51 S | 150.59 E |
| Guildford, Eng., U.K. | 42 | 51.14 N | 0.35 W |
| Guildford □[8] | 260 | 51.16 N | 0.32 W |
| Guildford Cathedral ʋ[1] | 260 | 51.14 N | 0.35 W |
| Guildhall | 188 | 44.33 N | 71.33 W |
| Guildtown | 46 | 56.28 N | 3.24 W |
| Guiler | 89 | 46.11 N | 121.45 E |
| Guilford, Ct., U.S. | 207 | 41.17 N | 72.40 W |
| Guilford, In., U.S. | 218 | 39.10 N | 84.55 W |
| Guilford, Me., U.S. | 188 | 45.10 N | 69.23 W |
| Guilford, N.Y., U.S. | 210 | 42.24 N | 75.29 W |
| Guilford Courthouse National Military Park ♦ | 192 | 36.01 N | 79.45 W |
| Guilherand | 62 | 44.56 N | 4.52 E |
| Guilin (Kweilin) | 102 | 25.17 N | 110.17 E |
| Guilinchang | 107 | 30.13 N | 105.50 E |
| Guilinzhen | 107 | 30.15 N | 104.53 E |
| Guillaume-Delisle, Lac ⊜ | 176 | 56.15 N | 76.17 W |
| Guillaumes | 62 | 44.05 N | 6.51 E |
| Guillermo E. Hudson | 288 | 34.47 S | 58.10 W |
| Guillestre | 62 | 44.40 N | 6.39 E |
| Guillon | 50 | 47.31 N | 4.06 E |
| Guilsfield | 42 | 52.42 N | 3.09 W |
| Guilvinec | 32 | 47.47 N | 4.17 W |
| Guimarães, Bra. | 250 | 2.08 S | 44.36 W |
| Guimarães, Port. | 34 | 41.27 N | 8.18 W |
| Guimaras Island I | 116 | 10.35 N | 122.37 E |
| Guimaras Strait ⊍ | 116 | 10.30 N | 122.44 E |
| Guimba | 116 | 15.40 N | 120.46 E |
| Guimbal | 116 | 10.40 N | 122.19 E |
| Guimeishan | 100 | 24.44 N | 114.52 E |
| Guimu Zhang ∧ | 100 | 24.40 N | 116.48 E |
| Guin | 194 | 33.57 N | 87.54 W |
| Guinan | 102 | 35.24 N | 100.57 E |
| Guinayang | 269f | 14.42 N | 121.08 E |
| Guinayangan | 116 | 13.54 N | 122.27 E |
| Guinda | 226 | 38.50 N | 122.12 W |
| Guindulman | 116 | 9.46 N | 124.29 E |
| Guindulman Bay c | 116 | 9.44 N | 124.29 E |
| Guiné → Guinea-Bissau □[1] | 150 | 12.00 N | 15.00 W |
| Guinea | 208 | 38.08 N | 77.26 W |
| Guinea (Guinée) □[1], Afr. | 134 | 11.00 N | 10.00 W |
| Guinea (Guinée) □[1], Afr. | 150 | 11.00 N | 10.00 W |

| | | | |
|---|---|---|---|
| Guinea, Gulf of c | 10 | 2.00 N | 2.30 E |
| Guinea Basin ⊹[1] | 10 | 0.00 | 5.00 W |
| Guinea-Bissau (Guiné-Bissau) □[1], Afr. | 134 | 12.00 N | 15.00 W |
| Guinea-Bissau (Guiné-Bissau) □[1], Afr. | 150 | 12.00 N | 15.00 W |
| Guineacor Creek ≃ | 170 | 34.21 S | 150.05 E |
| Guinea Ecuatorial → Equatorial Guinea □[1] | 152 | 2.00 N | 9.00 E |
| Guinea Rise ⊹[3] | 10 | 8.00 S | 0.00 |
| Guiné-Bissau → Guinea-Bissau □[1] | 150 | 12.00 N | 15.00 W |
| Guinecourt, Lac ⊜ | 186 | 50.55 N | 69.16 W |
| Guinée → Guinea □[1] | 150 | 11.00 N | 10.00 W |
| Guinée-Bissau → Guinea-Bissau □[1] | 150 | 12.00 N | 15.00 W |
| Guinée équitoriale → Equatorial Guinea □[1] | 152 | 2.00 N | 9.00 E |
| Güines, Cuba | 240p | 22.50 N | 82.02 W |
| Guînes, Fr. | 50 | 50.52 N | 1.52 E |
| Guingamp | 32 | 48.33 N | 3.11 W |
| Guinguinéo | 150 | 14.16 N | 15.57 W |
| Guinobatan | 116 | 13.11 N | 123.36 E |
| Güinope | 236 | 13.51 N | 86.55 W |
| Guintacan Island I | 116 | 11.19 N | 123.54 E |
| Guintinguintin, Mount ∧ | 116 | 12.25 N | 122.24 E |
| Guintinua Island I | 116 | 14.26 N | 122.51 E |
| Guiones, Punta › | 236 | 9.54 N | 85.41 W |
| Guiong | 116 | 6.25 N | 122.01 E |
| Guiperreux | 261 | 48.40 N | 1.42 E |
| Guiperreux, Étang de ⊜ | 261 | 48.40 N | 1.43 E |
| Guiping | 102 | 23.20 N | 110.09 E |
| Guir, Hammada du ◆[2] | 148 | 30.45 N | 3.15 W |
| Guir, Oued V | 148 | 30.29 N | 2.17 W |
| Güira de Melena | 240p | 22.48 N | 82.30 W |
| Guiraí ≃ | 255 | 22.40 S | 53.34 W |
| Guiratinga | 255 | 16.21 S | 53.45 W |
| Guiren | 100 | 33.42 N | 118.12 E |
| Güiria | 246 | 10.34 N | 62.18 W |
| Guiricema | 255 | 21.00 S | 42.43 W |
| Guisachan Forest ◆[3] | 46 | 57.17 N | 4.55 W |
| Guisanbourg | 250 | 4.25 N | 51.56 W |
| Guisborough | 44 | 54.32 N | 1.04 W |
| Guiscard | 50 | 49.39 N | 3.03 E |
| Guise | 50 | 49.54 N | 3.38 E |
| Guiseley | 44 | 53.53 N | 1.42 W |
| Guisijan | 116 | 11.05 N | 122.03 E |
| Güisisil ∧ | 236 | 12.37 N | 86.13 W |
| Guist Creek ≃ | 218 | 38.09 N | 85.13 W |
| Guitiriz | 34 | 43.11 N | 7.54 W |
| Guitou | 100 | 24.58 N | 113.25 E |
| Guitrancourt | 261 | 49.01 N | 1.47 E |
| Guîtres | 32 | 45.03 N | 0.11 W |
| Guitry | 150 | 5.31 N | 5.14 W |
| Guiuan | 116 | 11.02 N | 125.43 E |
| Guixi | 100 | 28.16 N | 117.10 E |
| Guixian | 102 | 23.06 N | 109.39 E |
| Guiyang, Zhg. | 100 | 25.46 N | 112.43 E |
| Guiyang (Kweiyang), Zhg. | 102 | 26.35 N | 106.43 E |
| Güiza ≃ | 246 | 1.22 N | 78.36 W |
| Guizhou (Kweichow) □[4] | 102 | 27.00 N | 107.00 E |
| Gujarāt □[3] | 118 | 22.00 N | 72.00 E |
| Gūjar Khān | 123 | 33.16 N | 73.19 E |
| Gujba | 146 | 11.30 N | 11.55 E |
| Gujiabeng | 106 | 30.45 N | 120.59 E |
| Gujiang | 100 | 27.11 N | 114.49 E |
| Gujiatun | 104 | 40.39 N | 124.08 E |
| Gujiatuo | 107 | 29.14 N | 106.12 E |
| Gujiazhai | 269b | 31.22 N | 121.28 E |
| Gujiazi, Zhg. | 104 | 42.02 N | 123.01 E |
| Gujiazi, Zhg. | 104 | 41.44 N | 124.11 E |
| Gujrānwāla | 123 | 32.09 N | 74.11 E |
| Gujrāt | 123 | 32.34 N | 74.05 E |
| Gukas'an | 84 | 41.03 N | 43.52 E |
| Gukou | 100 | 26.27 N | 118.38 E |
| Gukovo | 83 | 48.03 N | 39.56 E |
| Gul, Tanjong › | 271c | 1.17 N | 103.39 E |
| Gul'a | 88 | 54.41 N | 121.01 E |
| Gul'aj-Borisovka | 78 | 46.38 N | 40.13 E |
| Gul'ajevskije Koški, ostrova II | 24 | 68.55 N | 55.10 E |
| Gulang | 102 | 37.36 N | 102.58 E |
| Gulaothi | 124 | 28.36 N | 77.47 E |
| Gulargambone | 166 | 31.20 S | 148.28 E |
| Gulbarga | 122 | 17.20 N | 76.50 E |
| Gulbene | 76 | 57.11 N | 26.45 E |
| Gul'ča | 85 | 40.19 N | 73.26 E |
| Gul'ča ≃ | 85 | 40.20 N | 73.26 E |
| Guldasteh | 267d | 35.36 N | 51.16 E |
| Guldborg | 41 | 54.52 N | 11.45 E |
| Guldborg Sund ⊍ | 41 | 54.48 N | 11.48 E |
| Guldsmedshyttan | 40 | 59.42 N | 15.06 E |
| Güldüzü | 130 | 36.52 N | 37.07 E |
| Gülebağdı | 130 | 39.52 N | 39.50 E |
| Guledagudda | 122 | 16.03 N | 75.48 E |
| Guleitou | 100 | 23.47 N | 117.36 E |
| Gülek Boğazı )( | 130 | 37.16 N | 34.48 E |
| Gulf □[5] | 164 | 7.00 S | 145.00 E |
| Gulf Gate Estates | 220 | 27.15 N | 82.31 W |
| Gulf Hammock | 192 | 29.15 N | 82.43 W |
| Gulf Harbors | 220 | 28.14 N | 82.45 W |
| Gulf Islands National Seashore ♦ | 194 | 30.14 N | 88.42 W |
| Gulf of Alaska Seamount Province ⊹ | 16 | 56.00 N | 147.00 W |
| Gulfport, Fl., U.S. | 220 | 27.45 N | 82.40 W |
| Gulfport, Ms., U.S. | 194 | 30.22 N | 89.05 W |
| Gulf Shores | 194 | 30.14 N | 87.42 W |
| Gulf State Park ♦ | 194 | 30.16 N | 87.40 W |
| Gulf Stream ≃ | 212 | 43.51 N | 75.56 W |
| Gulgong | 166 | 32.22 S | 149.32 E |
| Guli | 106 | 31.38 N | 120.50 E |
| Gulian | 89 | 52.55 N | 122.19 E |
| Gulicun | 106 | 31.52 N | 118.41 E |
| Gul Imām | 123 | 32.16 N | 70.32 E |
| Gulistān, Pāk. | 120 | 30.36 N | 66.35 E |
| Gulistan, Uzb. | 85 | 40.30 N | 68.46 E |
| Guliya Shan ∧ | 89 | 49.48 N | 122.25 E |
| Guljanci | 38 | 43.38 N | 24.42 E |
| Gulkana | 180 | 62.16 N | 145.23 W |
| Gull ≃ | 212 | 44.37 N | 78.49 W |
| Gulland Rock II[1] | 42 | 50.34 N | 4.59 W |
| Gullane | 46 | 56.02 N | 2.50 W |
| Gullfoss ∟ | 24a | 64.24 N | 20.08 W |
| Gullholmen | 26 | 58.11 N | 11.24 E |
| Gullion, Slieve ∧[2] | 48 | 54.08 N | 6.27 W |
| Gull Island I | 281 | 42.32 N | 82.41 W |
| Gullivan Bay c | 220 | 25.52 N | 81.38 W |
| Gull Lake | 184 | 50.08 N | 108.27 W |
| Gull Lake ⊜, Ab., Can. | 182 | 52.35 N | 114.00 W |
| Gull Lake ⊜, On., Can. | 184 | 51.18 N | 91.58 W |
| Gull Lake ⊜, On., Can. | 212 | 44.51 N | 78.47 W |
| Gull Lake ⊜, Mi., U.S. | 216 | 42.24 N | 85.25 W |
| Gull Lake ⊜, Mn., U.S. | 190 | 46.25 N | 94.20 W |
| Gullrock Lake ⊜ | 184 | 50.58 N | 93.40 W |
| Gullspång | 40 | 58.59 N | 14.06 E |
| Güllük | 130 | 37.14 N | 27.36 E |
| Güllük Körfezi c | 130 | 37.12 N | 27.20 E |
| Gulmarg | 123 | 34.03 N | 74.23 E |
| Gulnam | 140 | 6.55 N | 29.30 E |
| Gülnar | 130 | 36.20 N | 33.25 E |
| Gulong | 89 | 45.51 N | 124.14 E |
| Gulpen | 56 | 50.48 N | 5.54 E |

| | | | | |
|---|---|---|---|---|
| ≃ River | Fluß | Río | Rivière | Rio |
| ≊ Canal | Kanal | Canal | Canal | Canal |
| ∟ Waterfall, Rapids | Wasserfall, Stromschnellen | Cascada, Rápidos | Chute d'eau, Rapides | Cascata, Rápidos |
| ⊍ Strait | Meeresstraße | Estrecho | Détroit | Estreito |
| c Bay, Gulf | Bucht, Golf | Bahía, Golfo | Baie, Golfe | Baía, Golfo |
| ⊜ Lake, Lakes | See, Seen | Lago, Lagos | Lac, Lacs | Lago, Lagos |
| ≡ Swamp | Sumpf | Pantano | Marais | Pântano |
| ⊓ Ice Features, Glacier | Eis- und Gletscherformen | Accidentes Glaciales | Formes glaciaires | Acidentes glaciares |
| ⊤ Other Hydrographic Features | Andere Hydrographische Objekte | Otros Elementos Hidrográficos | Autres données hydrographiques | Outros acidentes hidrográficos |

| | | | | |
|---|---|---|---|---|
| ⊹ Submarine Features | Untermeerische Objekte | Accidentes Submarinos | Formes de relief sous-marin | Acidentes submarinos |
| □ Political Unit | Politische Einheit | Unidad Politica | Entité politique | Unidade política |
| ʋ Cultural Institution | Kulturelle Institution | Institución Cultural | Institution culturelle | Instituição cultural |
| ⊥ Historical Site | Historische Stätte | Sitio Histórico | Site historique | Sítio histórico |
| ♦ Recreational Site | Erholungs- und Ferienort | Sitio de Recreo | Centre de loisirs | Area de Lazer |
| ⊠ Airport | Flughafen | Aeropuerto | Aéroport | Aeroporto |
| ■ Military Installation | Militäranlage | Instalación Militar | Installation militaire | Instalação militar |
| ◆ Miscellaneous | Verschiedenes | Misceláneo | Divers | Diversos |

| Name | Page | Lat.°′ | Long.°′ |
|---|---|---|---|
| Gülper See ⊜ | 54 | 52.44 N | 12.14 E |
| Gulph Mills | 285 | 40.04 N | 75.21 W |
| Gülpınar | 130 | 39.32 N | 26.07 E |
| Gul'ripš | 84 | 42.57 N | 41.06 E |
| Gul'šad | 86 | 46.39 N | 74.24 E |
| Gülşehir | 130 | 38.45 N | 34.38 E |
| Gulshan | 126 | 23.49 N | 90.27 E |
| Gulsvik | 26 | 60.23 N | 9.35 E |
| Gulu, Ug. | 154 | 2.47 N | 32.18 E |
| Gulu, Zhg. | 120 | 28.06 N | 89.17 E |
| Gulukguluk | 115a | 7.04 S | 113.40 E |
| Guluogongba | 120 | 34.20 N | 84.50 E |
| Guluy | 144 | 14.44 N | 36.43 E |
| Gulwe | 154 | 6.30 S | 36.29 E |
| Gumaca | 116 | 13.55 N | 122.06 E |
| Gumahang | 116 | 12.35 N | 123.16 E |
| Gumal (Gowmal) ≃ | 120 | 31.56 N | 70.22 E |
| Gumare | 156 | 19.21 S | 22.12 E |
| Gumba, Ang. | 152 | 11.40 S | 16.34 E |
| Gumba, Zaïre | 152 | 2.57 N | 21.26 E |
| Gumbinnen → Gusev | 76 | 54.36 N | 22.12 E |
| Gumbiro | 154 | 10.16 S | 35.39 E |
| Gumel | 150 | 12.39 N | 9.22 E |
| Gumeracha | 168b | 34.49 S | 138.53 E |
| Gumiao | 100 | 32.26 N | 113.16 E |
| Gumieńce ◆[8] | 54 | 53.25 N | 14.30 E |
| Gumistskij zapovednik ♠ | 84 | 43.15 N | 41.05 E |
| Gumla | 124 | 23.03 N | 84.33 E |
| Gumma □[5] | 94 | 36.30 N | 139.00 E |
| Gummersbach | 56 | 51.02 N | 7.34 E |
| Gummi | 150 | 12.09 N | 5.09 E |
| Gumpas Pond ⊜ | 283 | 42.44 N | 71.22 W |
| Gumpas Pond Brook ≃ | 283 | 42.42 N | 71.21 W |
| Gumpoldskirchen | 264b | 48.03 N | 16.17 E |
| Gum Swamp Creek ≃ | 192 | 32.08 N | 82.55 W |
| Gumti ≃ | 126 | 23.32 N | 90.43 E |
| Gümüşçay | 130 | 40.16 N | 27.17 E |
| Gümüşhacıköy | 130 | 40.53 N | 35.14 E |
| Gümüşhane | 130 | 40.27 N | 39.29 E |
| Gümüşhane □[4] | 130 | 40.15 N | 39.45 E |
| Gümüşkent | 130 | 38.50 N | 34.32 E |
| Gümüşköy ◆[8] | 267b | 41.14 N | 28.58 E |
| Gümüşova | 130 | 40.51 N | 30.57 E |
| Gümüşsü | 130 | 38.14 N | 30.01 E |
| Gun ≃ | 216 | 42.28 N | 85.40 W |
| Guna, India | 124 | 24.39 N | 77.19 E |
| Guna, Ityo. | 144 | 8.19 N | 39.51 E |
| Guna ∧ | 144 | 11.42 N | 38.12 E |
| Gunbar | 166 | 34.01 S | 145.25 E |
| Gun Barrel City | 222 | 32.20 N | 96.10 W |
| Gun Creek ≃ | 284a | 43.03 N | 78.55 W |
| Gunda | 88 | 52.47 N | 111.44 E |
| Gundagai | 166 | 35.04 S | 148.07 E |
| Gundelfingen | 56 | 48.33 N | 10.22 E |
| Gundelsheim | 56 | 49.17 N | 9.09 E |
| Gundik | 115a | 7.12 S | 110.54 E |
| Gundji | 152 | 2.05 N | 21.27 E |
| Gundlakamma ≃ | 122 | 15.32 N | 80.14 E |
| Gundlupet | 122 | 11.48 N | 76.41 E |
| Gündoğdu | 130 | 40.15 N | 27.07 E |
| Gündoğmuş | 130 | 36.48 N | 32.01 E |
| Guneh Ghar ∧ | 123 | 35.19 N | 71.47 E |
| Güney | 130 | 38.09 N | 29.05 E |
| Gungartan ∧ | 171b | 36.18 S | 148.24 E |
| Gungi | 152 | 6.21 S | 19.15 E |
| Gungo | 152 | 11.48 S | 14.08 E |
| Güngören ◆[8] | 267b | 41.01 N | 28.53 E |
| Gungu | 152 | 5.44 S | 19.19 E |
| Gunib | 84 | 42.25 N | 46.57 E |
| Gunisao ≃ | 184 | 53.54 N | 97.58 W |
| Gunisao Lake ⊜ | 184 | 53.33 N | 96.15 W |
| Gunjrauliya | 124 | 26.35 N | 84.34 E |
| Gun Lake ⊜ | 216 | 42.37 N | 85.32 W |
| Gunma | 94 | 36.24 N | 139.00 E |
| Gunnar | 176 | 59.23 N | 108.53 W |
| Günnarijn | 102 | 45.38 N | 102.01 E |
| Gunnarn | 26 | 65.00 N | 17.40 E |
| Gunnbjørn Fjeld ∧ | 16 | 68.55 N | 29.53 W |
| Gunnebo | 26 | 57.43 N | 16.32 E |
| Gunnedah | 166 | 30.59 S | 150.15 E |
| Gunning Island I | 276 | 40.22 N | 73.59 W |
| Gunnislake | 42 | 50.31 N | 4.12 W |
| Gunnison, Co., U.S. | 200 | 38.32 N | 106.55 W |
| Gunnison, Ut,. U.S. | 200 | 39.09 N | 111.49 W |
| Gunnison ≃ | 200 | 39.03 N | 108.35 W |
| Gunnison, Lake Fork ≃ | 200 | 38.28 N | 107.19 W |
| Gunnison, North Fork ≃ | 200 | 38.47 N | 107.50 W |
| Gunn Peak ∧ | 224 | 47.49 N | 121.27 W |
| Gunong Mulu National Park ♠ | 112 | 4.10 N | 114.55 E |
| Gunpowder Creek ≃, Austl. | 166 | 19.14 S | 139.58 E |
| Gunpowder Creek ≃, Ky., U.S. | 218 | 38.53 N | 84.47 W |
| Gunpowder Falls ≃ | 208 | 39.24 N | 76.22 W |
| Gunpowder Falls State Park ♠ | 208 | 39.37 N | 76.40 W |
| Gunpowder River ⊂ | 208 | 39.22 N | 76.22 W |
| Gunsan → Kunsan | 98 | 35.58 N | 126.41 E |
| Gunskirchen | 60 | 48.08 N | 13.57 E |
| Gunston Cove ⊂ | 208 | 38.40 N | 77.09 W |
| Guntakal | 122 | 15.10 N | 77.23 E |
| Güntersberge | 54 | 51.38 N | 10.59 E |
| Guntersblum | 56 | 49.47 N | 8.21 E |
| Guntersdorf | 61 | 48.39 N | 16.03 E |
| Guntersville | 194 | 34.21 N | 86.17 W |
| Guntersville Dam ◆[6] | 194 | 34.13 N | 86.23 W |
| Guntersville Lake ⊜[1] | 194 | 34.45 N | 86.03 W |
| Guntingsaga | 114 | 2.33 N | 99.39 E |
| Guntramsdorf | 61 | 48.03 N | 16.19 E |
| Guntung | 114 | 1.38 N | 101.34 E |
| Guntūr | 122 | 16.18 N | 80.27 E |
| Gunungkencana | 115a | 6.34 S | 106.04 E |
| Gunungmegang | 112 | 3.27 S | 103.52 E |
| Gunungsahilan | 112 | 0.06 N | 101.18 E |
| Gunungsitoli | 114 | 1.17 N | 97.37 E |
| Gunungtua | 114 | 1.30 N | 99.37 E |
| Gunupur | 122 | 19.05 N | 83.49 E |
| Gunyidi | 162 | 30.08 S | 116.04 E |
| Günyüzü | 130 | 39.24 N | 31.50 E |
| Günz ≃ | 58 | 48.27 N | 10.16 E |
| Gunza ≃ | 152 | 11.10 S | 13.50 E |
| Günzburg | 58 | 48.27 N | 10.16 E |
| Gunzenhausen | 56 | 49.07 N | 10.45 E |
| Gunzigou | 104 | 41.31 N | 123.58 E |
| Guo ≃ | 100 | 32.57 N | 117.14 E |
| Guobei | 107 | 29.33 N | 105.08 E |
| Guodian | 106 | 30.27 N | 120.33 E |
| Guoji | 100 | 32.59 N | 113.06 E |
| Guojiadian | 104 | 41.51 N | 121.30 E |
| Guojiajiang | 106 | 32.17 N | 120.50 E |
| Guojiatun, Zhg. | 98 | 41.31 N | 117.02 E |
| Guojiatun, Zhg. | 104 | 42.00 N | 122.51 E |
| Guojiatun, Zhg. | 104 | 40.52 N | 122.04 E |
| Guojiawopeng | 104 | 42.03 N | 122.46 E |
| Guojiayao | 105 | 40.37 N | 115.39 E |
| Guojiayuan | 106 | 32.10 N | 120.35 E |
| Guojiga | 86 | 43.47 N | 80.48 E |
| Guoleizhuang | 98 | 40.44 N | 114.36 E |
| Guolutan | 100 | 32.04 N | 115.40 E |
| Guosu | 98 | 38.24 N | 114.00 E |
| Guoyang | 100 | 33.32 N | 116.12 E |
| Guoyangzhen | 102 | 38.54 N | 112.50 E |
| Guozhuang | 98 | 35.25 N | 117.10 E |
| Guozhuangmiao | 106 | 31.49 N | 119.01 E |
| Gupei | 98 | 34.09 N | 117.54 E |
| Gupis | 123 | 36.14 N | 73.26 E |
| Gura | 80 | 57.18 N | 51.25 E |
| Gura, Wādī V | 140 | 17.28 N | 35.10 E |
| Gurabo | 240m | 18.16 N | 65.58 W |
| Guraferda | 144 | 6.51 N | 35.04 E |
| Gura Galbehei | 38 | 46.43 N | 28.42 E |
| Gurage ∧ | 144 | 8.24 N | 38.24 E |
| Gurahonț | 38 | 46.16 N | 22.21 E |
| Gura Humorului | 38 | 47.33 N | 25.54 E |
| Gurais | 123 | 34.38 N | 74.50 E |
| Guran | 88 | 54.46 N | 100.38 E |
| Gurara ≃ | 150 | 8.12 N | 6.41 E |
| Gurban Anggir | 102 | 37.45 N | 97.30 E |
| Gurban Obo | 102 | 43.14 N | 112.28 E |
| Gurdāspur | 123 | 32.02 N | 75.31 E |
| Gurdon | 194 | 33.55 N | 93.09 W |
| Gurdžaani | 84 | 41.43 N | 45.48 E |
| Güre | 130 | 38.39 N | 29.10 E |
| Gurejev | 80 | 47.21 N | 43.16 E |
| Gürgan | 84 | 40.23 N | 50.19 E |
| Gurgaon | 124 | 28.28 N | 77.02 E |
| Gurgei, Jabal ∧ | 140 | 13.50 N | 24.19 E |
| Gurghiului, Munții ⩕ | 38 | 46.41 N | 25.12 E |
| Gurgó ∧[2] | 61 | 46.31 N | 16.50 E |
| Gurgueia ≃ | 250 | 6.50 S | 43.24 W |
| Gurgur | 144 | 7.48 N | 41.32 E |
| Gurha | 120 | 25.11 N | 71.40 E |
| Guri | 144 | 7.27 N | 40.36 E |
| Guri, Embalse de ⊜[1] | 246 | 7.30 N | 62.50 W |
| Gurig National Park ♠ | 164 | 11.25 S | 132.15 E |
| Gurjevo | 82 | 54.42 N | 36.28 E |
| Gurjevsk, Ross. | 76 | 54.47 N | 20.38 E |
| Gurjevsk, Ross. | 86 | 54.17 N | 85.56 E |
| Gurk | 61 | 46.52 N | 14.18 E |
| Gurk ≃ | 61 | 46.36 N | 14.31 E |
| Gurk ʋ[1] | 61 | 46.52 N | 14.15 E |
| Gurktaler Alpen ⩕ | 64 | 46.55 N | 14.00 E |
| Gūr Kūh ∧ | 128 | 26.06 N | 58.28 E |
| Gurla Mandhata → Guerla Mandata Shan ∧ | 120 | 30.26 N | 81.20 E |
| Gurlevo | 76 | 59.28 N | 28.54 E |
| Gurnee | 216 | 42.22 N | 87.54 W |
| Gurnet Point › | 283 | 42.01 N | 70.34 W |
| Gürpınar | 128 | 38.18 N | 43.25 E |
| Gurror | 174q | 9.27 N | 138.04 E |
| Gursarai | 124 | 25.37 N | 79.11 E |
| Gurskoje | 89 | 50.21 N | 138.12 E |
| Gurskøy I | 26 | 62.15 N | 5.41 E |
| Gürsu | 130 | 40.13 N | 29.12 E |
| Gurué | 154 | 15.25 S | 36.58 E |
| Guru Har Sahāi | 123 | 30.43 N | 74.25 E |
| Gurumeti ≃ | 154 | 2.05 S | 33.57 E |
| Gurun, Malay. | 114 | 5.49 N | 100.29 E |
| Gürün, Tür. | 130 | 38.43 N | 37.17 E |
| Gurupá | 250 | 1.25 S | 51.39 W |
| Gurupi | 250 | 11.43 S | 49.04 W |
| Gurupi ≃ | 250 | 1.13 S | 46.06 W |
| Guru Sikhar ∧ | 120 | 24.39 N | 72.46 E |
| Gurvanbulag | 88 | 47.38 N | 103.31 E |
| Gurvansajchan | 102 | 45.32 N | 107.00 E |
| Gurvan Sajchan uul ⩕ | 102 | 43.50 N | 103.30 E |
| Gurvantes | 102 | 43.26 N | 101.36 E |
| Gus' ≃ | 80 | 55.00 N | 41.11 E |
| Gusar | 85 | 39.28 N | 67.50 E |
| Gušari | 85 | 38.55 N | 68.51 E |
| Gusau | 150 | 12.12 N | 6.40 E |
| Gus'-Chrustal'nyj | 80 | 55.37 N | 40.40 E |
| Guselka | 80 | 50.27 N | 45.09 E |
| Güsen | 54 | 52.21 N | 11.59 E |
| Gusen ≃ | 61 | 48.15 N | 14.30 E |
| Gusev, Ross. | 76 | 54.36 N | 22.12 E |
| Gusev, Ross. | 78 | 48.27 N | 40.32 E |
| Gusevo | 76 | 56.06 N | 33.21 E |
| Gusevskij | 80 | 55.40 N | 40.34 E |
| Gushan, Zhg. | 98 | 39.53 N | 123.36 E |
| Gushan, Zhg. | 98 | 36.30 N | 116.53 E |
| Gushan, Zhg. | 106 | 31.44 N | 120.33 E |
| Gu Shan ∧, Zhg. | 100 | 26.05 N | 119.22 E |
| Gu Shan ∧, Zhg. | 104 | 41.18 N | 120.35 E |
| Gushanbeizifu | 104 | 42.10 N | 120.30 E |
| Gushankou | 105 | 39.38 N | 115.49 E |
| Gushantun | 89 | 48.18 N | 123.47 E |
| Gushanzi, Zhg. | 98 | 40.22 N | 120.03 E |
| Gushanzi, Zhg. | 104 | 41.03 N | 123.03 E |
| Gushi, Zhg. | 100 | 28.34 N | 119.24 E |
| Gushi, Zhg. | 100 | 32.12 N | 115.41 E |
| Gushiago | 150 | 9.55 N | 0.12 W |
| Gushikami | 174m | 26.07 N | 127.45 E |
| Gushikawa | 174m | 26.21 N | 127.52 E |
| Gushu, Zhg. | 104 | 42.36 N | 123.26 E |
| Gushu, Zhg. | 105 | 39.55 N | 117.35 E |
| Gushuji | 98 | 34.15 N | 115.48 E |
| Gusi | 112 | 6.07 N | 117.08 E |
| Gusino | 76 | 54.44 N | 31.22 E |
| Gusinoje, ozero ⊜ | 88 | 51.12 N | 106.24 E |
| Gusinoje Ozero | 88 | 51.09 N | 106.10 E |
| Gusinoozersk | 88 | 51.17 N | 106.30 E |
| Guskef | 85 | 39.02 N | 69.20 E |
| Guskhara | 126 | 23.30 N | 87.45 E |
| Gus'-Khrustal'nyy → Gus'-Chrustal'nyj | 80 | 55.37 N | 40.40 E |
| Guskube | 175d | 24.45 N | 125.26 E |
| Gusong | 102 | 28.18 N | 105.14 E |
| Gusow | 54 | 52.34 N | 14.21 E |
| Guspini | 71 | 39.32 N | 8.37 E |
| Gussago | 64 | 45.35 N | 10.09 E |
| Gusselby | 40 | 59.39 N | 15.14 E |
| Güssing | 61 | 47.04 N | 16.20 E |
| Gussola | 64 | 45.00 N | 10.20 E |
| Gusswerk | 61 | 47.45 N | 15.18 E |
| Gustav Holm, Kap › | 176 | 67.00 N | 34.00 W |
| Gustavo A. Madero ◆[8] | 286a | 19.29 N | 99.07 W |
| Gustavo Díaz Ordaz | 234 | 17.44 N | 94.23 W |
| Gustavsberg | 40 | 59.19 N | 18.23 E |
| Gustavus | 180 | 58.25 N | 135.44 W |
| Güsten | 54 | 51.49 N | 11.35 E |
| Gustia | 272b | 22.59 N | 88.26 E |
| Gustine, Ca., U.S. | 226 | 37.15 N | 120.59 W |
| Gustine, Tx., U.S. | 196 | 31.51 N | 98.24 W |
| Gustorf | 56 | 51.04 N | 6.34 E |
| Güstrow | 54 | 53.48 N | 12.10 E |
| Gusum | 26 | 58.16 N | 16.29 E |
| Gus'-Železnyj | 80 | 55.03 N | 41.10 E |
| Gutach | 58 | 48.15 N | 8.13 E |
| Gutaj | 88 | 49.59 N | 108.12 E |
| Gutanggou | 104 | 42.02 N | 124.10 E |
| Gutara ≃ | 88 | 54.50 N | 97.23 E |
| Gutarskij chrebet ⩕ | 88 | 54.30 N | 97.40 E |
| Gutau | 61 | 48.25 N | 14.37 E |
| Gutcher | 46a | 60.40 N | 1.00 W |
| Gutenfels, Burg ⊥ | 56 | 50.07 N | 7.46 E |
| Guten Hoffnung, Kap der → Good Hope, Cape of › | 158 | 34.24 S | 18.30 E |
| Güterfelde | 264a | 52.22 N | 13.12 E |
| Gütersloh | 52 | 51.54 N | 8.23 E |
| Guthrie, In., U.S. | 218 | 38.59 N | 86.31 W |
| Guthrie, Ky., U.S. | 194 | 36.38 N | 87.09 W |
| Guthrie, Ok., U.S. | 196 | 35.52 N | 97.25 W |
| Guthrie, Tx., U.S. | 196 | 33.37 N | 100.19 W |
| Guthrie Center | 198 | 41.40 N | 94.30 W |
| Guthrie Lake ⊜ | 184 | 55.17 N | 100.38 W |
| Gutian, Zhg. | 100 | 26.36 N | 118.46 E |
| Gutian, Zhg. | 100 | 25.15 N | 116.46 E |
| Gutian, Zhg. | 100 | 25.43 N | 116.57 E |
| Gutian ≃ | 100 | 26.22 N | 118.42 E |
| Gutierrez | 248 | 19.25 S | 63.34 W |
| Gutiérrez Zamora | 234 | 20.27 N | 97.05 W |
| Gutland ◆[1] | 56 | 49.40 N | 6.10 E |
| Gutob Bay ⊂ | 116 | 12.09 N | 119.54 E |
| Guton, gora ∧ | 84 | 41.51 N | 46.45 E |
| Gutorfölde | 61 | 46.39 N | 16.44 E |
| Guttannen | 58 | 46.39 N | 8.18 E |
| Guttau | 54 | 51.15 N | 14.34 E |
| Guttenberg, Ia., U.S. | 190 | 42.47 N | 91.05 W |
| Guttenberg, N.J., U.S. | 276 | 40.47 N | 74.00 W |
| Gutu | 154 | 19.38 S | 31.10 E |
| Gutujevskij, ostrov I | 265a | 59.54 N | 30.14 E |
| Gutulia Nasjonalpark ♠ | 26 | 62.02 N | 12.12 E |
| Gützkow | 54 | 53.56 N | 13.24 E |
| Güvem | 130 | 40.36 N | 32.40 E |
| Guwāhāti | 120 | 26.10 N | 91.45 E |
| Guxhagen | 56 | 51.12 N | 9.28 E |
| Guxi | 107 | 30.18 N | 105.52 E |
| Guxian, Zhg. | 98 | 37.35 N | 121.09 E |
| Guxian, Zhg. | 100 | 32.26 N | 113.37 E |
| Guxian, Zhg. | 100 | 27.09 N | 115.31 E |
| Guxiandu | 100 | 29.06 N | 116.50 E |
| Guxiansi | 100 | 32.01 N | 116.20 E |
| Guxiong | 106 | 31.55 N | 118.38 E |
| Guy | 222 | 29.21 N | 95.47 W |
| Guyana □[1], S.A. | 242 | 5.00 N | 59.00 W |
| Guyana □[1], S.A. | 246 | 5.00 N | 59.00 W |
| Guyancourt | 261 | 48.46 N | 2.04 E |
| Guyancourt, Aéroport de ⊠ | 261 | 48.45 N | 2.05 E |
| Guyandotte ≃ | 188 | 38.26 N | 82.23 W |
| Guyane → Guyana □[1] | 246 | 5.00 N | 59.00 W |
| Guyane française → French Guiana □[2] | 250 | 4.00 N | 53.00 W |
| Guyang, Zhg. | 98 | 34.58 N | 114.58 E |
| Guyang, Zhg. | 102 | 41.03 N | 110.03 E |
| Guye | 105 | 39.44 N | 118.25 E |
| Guy Fawkes River National Park ♠ | 166 | 30.02 S | 152.18 E |
| Guyi, Zhg. | 100 | 25.38 N | 118.47 E |
| Guyi, Zhg. | 107 | 30.22 N | 103.33 E |
| Guyin | 102 | 23.58 N | 105.47 E |
| Guymon | 196 | 36.40 N | 101.28 W |
| Guyonne, Ruisseau la ≃ | 261 | 48.49 N | 1.52 E |
| Guyot, Mount ∧ | 192 | 35.42 N | 83.15 W |
| Guyra | 166 | 30.14 S | 151.40 E |
| Guysborough | 186 | 45.23 N | 61.30 W |
| Guys Mills | 214 | 41.38 N | 79.59 W |
| Guyton | 192 | 32.20 N | 81.23 W |
| Guyuan (Pingdingbu), Zhg. | 98 | 41.40 N | 115.41 E |
| Guyuan, Zhg. | 102 | 36.01 N | 106.17 E |
| Guzar | 72 | 38.36 N | 66.15 E |
| Güzel ≃ | 84 | 39.44 N | 43.01 E |
| Güzelbahçe | 130 | 38.21 N | 26.54 E |
| Güzelsu | 130 | 36.54 N | 31.53 E |
| Güzelyurt, Kıbrıs | 130 | 35.12 N | 32.59 E |
| Güzelyurt, Tür. | 130 | 38.17 N | 34.23 E |
| Güzelyurt Körfezi ⊂ | 130 | 35.10 N | 32.50 E |
| Guzhang | 102 | 28.31 N | 109.57 E |
| Guzhen, Zhg. | 100 | 22.37 N | 113.11 E |
| Guzhen, Zhg. | 100 | 33.19 N | 117.21 E |
| Guzhu | 100 | 26.58 N | 116.16 E |
| Guzmán, Méx. | 232 | 31.13 N | 107.27 W |
| Guzmán → Ciudad Guzmán, Méx. | 234 | 19.41 N | 103.29 W |
| Guzmán, Laguna de ⊜ | 200 | 31.20 N | 107.30 W |
| Gvardejsk | 76 | 54.39 N | 21.05 E |
| Gvazda | 78 | 50.44 N | 40.30 E |
| Gwa | 110 | 17.36 N | 94.35 E |
| Gwabegar | 166 | 30.36 S | 148.58 E |
| Gwadabawa | 150 | 13.20 N | 5.15 E |
| Gwādar | 128 | 25.07 N | 62.19 E |
| Gwagwada | 150 | 10.14 N | 7.14 E |
| Gwai | 154 | 19.15 S | 27.42 E |
| Gwai ≃ | 154 | 17.59 S | 26.52 E |
| Gwalangu | 152 | 2.19 N | 18.11 E |
| Gwalchmai | 44 | 53.15 N | 4.25 W |
| Gwāl Haidarzai | 120 | 30.44 N | 68.48 E |
| Gwalia | 162 | 28.55 S | 121.20 E |
| Gwalior | 124 | 26.13 N | 78.10 E |
| Gwambygine | 168a | 31.59 S | 116.48 E |
| Gwanda | 154 | 20.57 S | 29.01 E |
| Gwandu | 150 | 12.30 N | 4.41 E |
| Gwane | 154 | 4.43 N | 25.50 E |
| Gwangjang Bridge ◆[5] | 271b | 37.33 N | 127.05 E |
| Gwangju → Kwangju | 98 | 35.09 N | 126.54 E |
| Gwardafuy, Gees › | 144 | 11.49 N | 51.15 E |
| Gwarzo | 150 | 11.56 N | 7.56 E |
| Gwasero | 150 | 9.29 N | 3.30 E |
| Gwash ≃ | 42 | 52.39 N | 0.27 W |
| Gwātar Bay ⊂ | 128 | 25.04 N | 61.36 E |
| Gwatt | 58 | 46.43 N | 7.38 E |
| Gwaun ≃ | 42 | 52.00 N | 4.58 W |
| Gwda ≃ | 30 | 53.04 N | 16.44 E |
| Gweebarra ≃ | 48 | 54.50 N | 8.20 W |
| Gweebarra Bay ⊂ | 48 | 54.52 N | 8.20 W |
| Gweedore | 48 | 55.03 N | 8.14 W |
| Gweesalia | 48 | 54.07 N | 9.54 W |
| Gwelo ≃ | 154 | 18.45 S | 28.36 E |
| Gwembe | 154 | 16.30 S | 27.35 E |
| Gwendraeth Fâch ≃ | 42 | 51.44 N | 4.18 W |
| Gwendraeth Fawr ≃ | 42 | 51.43 N | 4.18 W |
| Gwent □[6] | 42 | 51.43 N | 2.57 W |
| Gweru | 154 | 19.27 S | 29.49 E |
| Gweta | 156 | 20.10 S | 25.18 E |
| Gwinhurst | 285 | 39.47 N | 75.29 W |
| Gwinn | 190 | 46.16 N | 87.26 W |
| Gwinner | 198 | 46.13 N | 97.39 W |
| Gwobu | 154 | 2.37 N | 26.13 E |
| Gwongorella National Park ♠ | 171a | 28.10 S | 153.17 E |
| Gwydir ≃ | 166 | 29.27 S | 149.48 E |
| Gwynedd | 285 | 40.12 N | 75.15 W |
| Gwynedd □[6] | 28 | 53.00 N | 4.00 W |
| Gwynedd Square | 285 | 40.13 N | 75.18 W |
| Gwynedd Valley | 285 | 40.11 N | 75.15 W |
| Gwynn | 208 | 37.30 N | 76.17 W |
| Gwynneville | 218 | 39.39 N | 85.38 W |
| Gwynn Island I | 208 | 37.30 N | 76.17 W |
| Gwynns Falls ≃ | 284b | 39.16 N | 76.37 W |
| Gwynns Falls Park ♠ | 284b | 39.18 N | 76.41 W |
| Gy | 58 | 47.24 N | 5.49 E |
| Gyál | 264c | 47.23 N | 19.14 E |
| Gya La )( | 124 | 28.44 N | 84.40 E |
| Gyáli-patak ≃ | 264c | 47.24 N | 19.07 E |
| Gyangtse → Gyangzê | 120 | 28.57 N | 89.35 E |
| Gyangzê | 120 | 28.57 N | 89.35 E |
| Gyaring Co ⊜ | 120 | 31.10 N | 88.15 E |
| Gyaring Hu ⊜ | 102 | 34.53 N | 97.58 E |
| Gybdan | 80 | 56.33 N | 51.39 E |
| Gyda | 74 | 70.52 N | 78.30 E |
| Gydanskaja guba ⊂ | 74 | 71.20 N | 76.30 E |
| Gydanskij poluostrov ›[1] | 74 | 70.50 N | 79.00 E |
| Gyebu | 164 | 3.03 S | 133.51 E |
| Gyemo Chen ∧ | 124 | 27.20 N | 88.52 E |
| Gyeongbog Palace ʋ | 271b | 37.36 N | 126.57 E |
| Gyeongju → Kyŏngju | 98 | 35.51 N | 129.14 E |
| Gyhum | 52 | 53.13 N | 9.19 E |
| Gyirong, Zhg. | 120 | 28.29 N | 85.20 E |
| Gyirong, Zhg. | 120 | 28.57 N | 85.15 E |
| Gyldenløves Fjord ⊂[2] | 176 | 64.30 N | 41.30 W |
| Gyldenløveshøj ∧[2] | 41 | 55.33 N | 11.52 E |
| Gylling | 41 | 55.53 N | 10.11 E |
| Gymea Bay | 274a | 34.02 S | 151.05 E |
| Gym Peak ∧ | 200 | 32.04 N | 107.35 W |
| Gympie | 166 | 26.11 S | 152.40 E |
| Gyobingauk | 110 | 18.13 N | 95.39 E |
| Gyōda | 94 | 36.08 N | 139.28 E |
| Gyoma | 30 | 46.56 N | 20.50 E |
| Gyöngyös | 30 | 47.47 N | 19.56 E |
| Gyöngyös ≃ | 61 | 47.14 N | 16.55 E |
| Győr | 30 | 47.42 N | 17.38 E |
| Győr-Moson-Sopron □[6] | 30 | 47.35 N | 17.15 E |
| Gypsey Race ≃ | 44 | 54.05 N | 0.12 W |
| Gypsum, Co., U.S. | 200 | 39.38 N | 106.57 W |
| Gypsum, Ks., U.S. | 198 | 38.42 N | 97.25 W |
| Gypsum, Oh., U.S. | 214 | 41.29 N | 82.52 W |
| Gypsum Creek ≃, U.S. | 200 | 37.09 N | 109.52 W |
| Gypsum Creek ≃, Ks., U.S. | 198 | 38.51 N | 97.25 W |
| Gypsum Hills ⩕[2] | 196 | 36.25 N | 99.20 W |
| Gypsum Point › | 176 | 61.53 N | 114.35 W |
| Gypsumville | 184 | 51.45 N | 98.35 W |
| Gysinge | 40 | 60.17 N | 16.53 E |
| Gyttorp | 40 | 59.31 N | 14.58 E |
| Gyula | 30 | 46.39 N | 21.17 E |
| Gyulafehérvár → Alba Iulia | 38 | 46.04 N | 23.35 E |
| Gžat' ≃ | 76 | 55.56 N | 34.33 E |
| Gžatsk | 86 | 55.42 N | 78.11 E |
| Gžel' | 82 | 55.36 N | 38.24 E |
| Gzhatsk → Gagarin | 76 | 55.33 N | 35.00 E |


## H


| Name | Page | Lat.°′ | Long.°′ |
|---|---|---|---|
| Haag → 's-Gravenhage, Ned. | 52 | 52.06 N | 4.18 E |
| Haag, Öst. | 61 | 48.07 N | 14.34 E |
| Haag am Hausruck | 60 | 48.11 N | 13.38 E |
| Haagen | 58 | 47.38 N | 7.40 E |
| Haag in Oberbayern | 60 | 48.10 N | 12.11 E |
| Haaksbergen | 52 | 52.09 N | 6.44 E |
| Haalenberg | 156 | 26.52 S | 15.30 E |
| Haaltert | 50 | 50.54 N | 4.00 E |
| Haamstede | 52 | 51.43 N | 3.45 E |
| Haan | 56 | 51.11 N | 7.00 E |
| Haapajärvi | 26 | 63.45 N | 25.20 E |
| Haapajärvi ⊜ | 26 | 63.33 N | 27.00 E |
| Haapamäki | 26 | 62.15 N | 24.28 E |
| Haapavesi | 26 | 64.08 N | 25.22 E |
| Haapiti | 174s | 17.34 S | 149.52 W |
| Haapsalu | 76 | 58.56 N | 23.33 E |
| Haar | 60 | 48.06 N | 11.44 E |
| Haar ◆[8] | 263 | 51.26 N | 7.13 E |
| Ha'Arava (Wādī al-'Arabah) V, Asia | 132 | 30.10 N | 35.10 E |
| Ha'Arava (Wādī al-Jayb) V, Asia | 132 | 30.58 N | 35.24 E |
| Haarbach | 60 | 48.30 N | 13.09 E |
| Haardt ⩕ | 56 | 49.15 N | 8.00 E |
| Haaren, Dtsch. | 52 | 51.34 N | 8.44 E |
| Haaren, Ned. | 52 | 51.36 N | 5.12 E |
| Haarlem, Ned. | 52 | 52.23 N | 4.38 E |
| Haarlem, S. Afr. | 158 | 33.44 S | 23.20 E |
| Haarlemmermeer ◆[1] | 52 | 52.15 N | 4.38 E |
| Haarstrang ∧ | 52 | 51.35 N | 8.10 E |
| Haarzopf ◆[8] | 263 | 51.25 N | 6.58 E |
| Haast | 172 | 43.53 S | 169.03 E |
| Haast ≃ | 172 | 43.50 S | 169.02 E |
| Haast Bluff | 162 | 23.30 S | 131.50 E |
| Haast Pass )( | 172 | 44.06 S | 169.21 E |
| Haasts Bluff Reserve ◆[4] | 162 | 23.30 S | 130.30 E |
| Haatinao, Pointe › | 174x | 9.47 S | 138.51 W |
| Haava, Canal ⩌ | 174x | 9.53 S | 139.04 W |
| Hab ≃ | 120 | 24.53 N | 66.41 E |
| Habahe | 86 | 47.53 N | 86.12 E |
| Habana, Bahía de la ⊂ | 286b | 23.08 N | 82.20 W |
| Habaqi, Zhg. | 104 | 42.38 N | 122.02 E |
| Habaqi, Zhg. | 104 | 42.36 N | 122.52 E |
| Habaqila | 102 | 42.01 N | 106.02 E |
| Habartov | 54 | 50.08 N | 12.33 E |
| Habashīyah, Jabal ⩕ | 144 | 16.40 N | 49.40 E |
| Habaswein | 154 | 1.01 N | 39.29 E |
| Habawnah, Wādī V | 144 | 17.51 N | 44.59 E |
| Habay-la-Neuve | 56 | 49.44 N | 5.39 E |
| Habbān | 144 | 14.21 N | 47.05 E |
| Habbānīyah, Hawr al- ⊜ | 128 | 33.17 N | 43.29 E |
| Habbūsh | 132 | 33.24 N | 35.29 E |
| Hab Chauki | 120 | 25.01 N | 66.53 E |
| Habère-Poche | 58 | 46.15 N | 6.29 E |
| Haberfield | 274a | 33.53 S | 151.08 E |
| Haberli | 130 | 37.19 N | 41.38 E |
| Habermehl Peak ∧ | 9 | 71.49 S | 6.38 E |
| Ḥabīb, Wādī V | 142 | 27.20 N | 31.30 E |
| Habiganj | 120 | 24.23 N | 91.25 E |
| Habikino | 96 | 34.33 N | 135.37 E |
| Habīlah | 140 | 12.41 N | 22.33 E |
| Habinghorst | 263 | 51.35 N | 7.18 E |
| Habo | 26 | 57.55 N | 14.04 E |
| Habob, Wādī V | 140 | 18.07 N | 35.01 E |
| Habomai-shotō → Malaja Kuril'skaja Gr'ada II | 92a | 43.30 N | 146.10 E |
| Haboro | 92a | 44.22 N | 141.42 E |
| Hābra | 126 | 22.50 N | 88.38 E |
| Habsburg ⊥ | 58 | 47.28 N | 8.13 E |
| Habsheim | 58 | 47.44 N | 7.25 E |
| Habu | 270 | 34.27 N | 135.24 E |
| Habur (Nahr al-Khābūr) ≃ | 130 | 35.08 N | 40.26 E |
| Habutaki | 270 | 34.25 N | 135.26 E |
| Hache, Lac la ⊜ | 182 | 51.50 N | 121.30 W |
| Hachen | 56 | 51.22 N | 7.59 E |
| Hachenburg | 56 | 50.39 N | 7.50 E |
| Hachi | 120 | 27.46 N | 94.01 E |
| Hachijō | 270 | 34.37 N | 135.48 E |
| Hachijō-jima I | 90 | 33.05 N | 139.48 E |
| Hachiman → Ōmi-hachiman, Nihon | 94 | 35.08 N | 136.06 E |
| Hachiman, Nihon | 94 | 35.45 N | 136.57 E |
| Hachiman-misaki › | 94 | 35.08 N | 140.19 E |
| Hachinohe | 92 | 40.30 N | 141.29 E |
| Hachiōji | 94 | 35.39 N | 139.20 E |
| Hachmühlen | 52 | 52.10 N | 9.28 E |
| Hacıbektaş | 130 | 38.57 N | 34.35 E |
| Hacienda Heights | 228 | 34.00 N | 117.57 W |
| Hacienda Miravalles | 236 | 10.41 N | 85.14 W |
| Hacienda Murciélago | 236 | 10.55 N | 85.44 W |
| Hacıhamza | 130 | 41.05 N | 34.28 E |
| Hacıkänd | 84 | 40.31 N | 46.21 E |
| Hacılar | 130 | 38.39 N | 35.27 E |
| Hacı Zeynalabdin | 84 | 40.37 N | 49.34 E |
| Hack, Mount ∧ | 166 | 30.46 S | 138.48 E |
| Hackås | 26 | 62.55 N | 14.31 E |
| Hackberry, Az., U.S. | 200 | 35.22 N | 113.43 W |
| Hackberry, La., U.S. | 194 | 29.59 N | 93.20 W |
| Hackberry Creek ≃, Ks., U.S. | 198 | 38.48 N | 100.03 W |
| Hackberry Creek ≃, Tx., U.S. | 222 | 31.53 N | 97.12 W |
| Hackensack | 210 | 40.53 N | 74.02 W |
| Hackensack ≃ | 276 | 40.43 N | 74.06 W |
| Hacketstown | 48 | 52.52 N | 6.33 W |
| Hackett, Ar., U.S. | 194 | 35.11 N | 94.24 W |
| Hackett, Pa., U.S. | 279b | 40.15 N | 80.01 W |
| Hacketts | 260 | 51.45 N | 0.05 W |
| Hackettstown | 210 | 40.52 N | 74.48 W |
| Hacking ≃ | 274a | 34.04 S | 151.06 E |
| Hacking, Port ⊂ | 274a | 34.05 S | 151.09 E |
| Hackleburg | 194 | 34.16 N | 87.49 W |
| Hackney ◆[8] | 260 | 51.33 N | 0.03 W |
| Hack Point | 208 | 39.27 N | 75.52 W |
| Håckren ⊜ | 26 | 63.11 N | 13.35 E |
| Haco | 152 | 10.12 S | 15.44 E |
| Hacreş Dağları ⩕ | 130 | 38.38 N | 41.37 E |
| Hadāli | 123 | 32.18 N | 72.12 E |
| Hadalīya | 140 | 16.10 N | 36.06 E |
| Hadamar | 56 | 50.27 N | 8.02 E |
| Ḥadan, Ḥarrat ⫠[9] | 144 | 21.30 N | 41.23 E |
| Hadano | 94 | 35.22 N | 139.14 E |
| Ḥadāribah, Ra's al- › | 140 | 22.04 N | 36.54 E |
| HaDarom □[5] | 132 | 30.40 N | 34.50 E |
| Hadat | 89 | 49.40 N | 119.40 E |
| Hadayingzi | 104 | 42.22 N | 121.40 E |
| Ḥadd, Ra's al- › | 118 | 22.32 N | 59.48 E |
| Haddad, Ouadi V | 146 | 14.40 N | 18.46 E |
| Ḥaddādīn, Qārat al- ∧[2] | 142 | 30.04 N | 30.58 E |
| Haddam, Ct., U.S. | 207 | 41.28 N | 72.30 W |
| Haddam, Ks., U.S. | 198 | 39.51 N | 97.18 W |
| Haddenham, Eng., U.K. | 42 | 51.46 N | 0.56 W |
| Haddenham, Eng., U.K. | 42 | 52.22 N | 0.09 E |
| Haddington | 46 | 55.58 N | 2.47 W |
| Haddock | 192 | 33.01 N | 83.25 W |
| Haddon Downs | 166 | 26.21 S | 140.50 E |
| Haddonfield | 208 | 39.53 N | 75.02 W |
| Haddon Heights | 208 | 39.52 N | 75.03 W |
| Haddon Hills | 285 | 39.54 N | 75.03 W |
| Hadejia | 150 | 12.30 N | 9.59 E |
| Hadejia ≃ | 134 | 12.50 N | 10.51 E |
| Hadeln, Land ◆[1] | 52 | 53.45 N | 8.45 E |
| Haden | 171a | 27.14 S | 151.53 E |
| Ḥadera | 132 | 32.26 N | 34.55 E |
| Ḥadera ≃ | 132 | 32.27 N | 34.53 E |
| Hadersdorf ◆[8] | 264b | 48.13 N | 16.14 E |
| Hadersfeld | 264b | 48.20 N | 16.15 E |
| Haderslev | 41 | 55.15 N | 9.30 E |
| Haderslev Fjord ⊂ | 41 | 55.17 N | 9.40 E |
| Hadfield, Austl. | 274b | 37.42 S | 144.56 E |
| Hadfield, Eng., U.K. | 262 | 53.28 N | 1.58 W |
| Hadībū | 118 | 12.38 N | 54.02 E |
| Ḥadīd, Jabal ∧[2] | 142 | 30.20 N | 30.06 E |
| Ḥadīd, Jabal al- ∧[2] | 142 | 28.47 N | 31.04 E |
| Hadım | 130 | 36.59 N | 32.28 E |
| Hadjout | 34 | 36.31 N | 2.25 E |
| Hadleigh, Eng., U.K. | 42 | 52.03 N | 0.58 E |
| Hadleigh, Eng., U.K. | 260 | 51.33 N | 0.37 E |
| Hadleigh Castle ⊥ | 260 | 51.33 N | 0.36 E |
| Hadley, Eng., U.K. | 42 | 52.42 N | 2.29 W |
| Hadley, Ma., U.S. | 207 | 42.20 N | 72.35 W |
| Hadley, Mi., U.S. | 216 | 42.57 N | 83.24 W |
| Hadley, N.Y., U.S. | 210 | 43.19 N | 73.50 W |
| Hadley, Pa., U.S. | 214 | 41.25 N | 80.14 W |
| Hadley Bay ⊂ | 176 | 72.30 N | 107.45 W |
| Hadley Creek ≃ | 219 | 39.37 N | 91.12 W |
| Hadlock | 224 | 48.01 N | 122.45 W |
| Hadlow | 42 | 51.14 N | 0.20 E |
| Hadlyme | 207 | 41.25 N | 72.24 W |
| Hadmersleben | 54 | 51.59 N | 11.18 E |
| Hadong, Taehan | 98 | 35.05 N | 127.44 E |
| Ha Dong, Viet | 110 | 20.58 N | 105.46 E |
| Ḥaḍramawt ◆[1] | 144 | 15.00 N | 50.00 E |
| Hadrian's Wall ⊥ | 44 | 54.59 N | 2.26 W |
| Hadrut | 84 | 39.32 N | 47.02 E |
| Hadsten | 41 | 56.20 N | 10.03 E |
| Hadsund | 26 | 56.43 N | 10.07 E |
| Hadyach | 78 | 50.22 N | 34.00 E |
| Hadyai → Hat Yai | 110 | 7.01 N | 100.28 E |
| Hadzilavičy | 76 | 53.05 N | 30.16 E |
| Haeju | 98 | 38.02 N | 125.42 E |
| Haemgon-ni ◆[8] | 271b | 37.35 N | 126.49 E |
| Haena | 229b | 22.14 N | 159.34 W |
| Haenam | 98 | 34.34 N | 126.35 E |
| Haena Point › | 229b | 22.14 N | 159.34 W |
| Haenertsburg | 156 | 24.00 S | 29.50 E |
| Haengyŏng-ni | 98 | 42.33 N | 129.56 E |
| Haernao | 104 | 41.46 N | 120.28 E |
| Hafeïra, Oued el V | 148 | 25.18 N | 10.48 W |
| Hafelekarspitze ∧ | 64 | 47.19 N | 11.23 E |
| Haffen-Mehr | 52 | 51.44 N | 6.28 E |
| Hafford | 184 | 52.43 N | 107.21 W |
| Haffouz | 36 | 35.38 N | 9.41 E |
| Hafik | 130 | 39.52 N | 37.24 E |
| Ḥafīra, Qā' al- ≚ | 132 | 31.06 N | 36.14 E |
| Ḥafīrat al-'Ayda | 128 | 26.26 N | 39.10 E |
| Ḥafīt, Jabal ∧ | 128 | 24.03 N | 55.46 E |
| Ḥāfiẓ, Bi'r ⊤[4] | 142 | 30.51 N | 29.40 E |
| Hāfizābād | 123 | 32.04 N | 73.41 E |
| Hāflong | 120 | 25.11 N | 93.02 E |
| Hafnarfjörður | 24a | 64.03 N | 21.56 W |
| Haft Gel | 128 | 31.27 N | 49.27 E |
| Haga, Nihon | 94 | 36.32 N | 140.04 E |
| Haga, Nihon | 96 | 35.09 N | 134.33 E |
| Hagachi-zaki › | 94 | 34.41 N | 138.45 E |
| HaGadol, HaMakhtésh ⫠[7] | 132 | 30.56 N | 34.59 E |
| Haga-Haga | 158 | 32.46 S | 28.14 E |
| Hagal | 98 | 40.23 N | 127.15 E |
| HaGalil (Galilee) □[9] | 132 | 32.54 N | 35.20 E |
| Hagaman | 210 | 42.59 N | 74.09 W |
| Hagan | 192 | 32.09 N | 81.56 W |
| Hagari ≃ | 122 | 15.45 N | 76.56 E |
| Hagar Shores | 216 | 42.13 N | 86.22 W |
| Hagarstown | 219 | 38.57 N | 89.10 W |
| Hage | 52 | 53.36 N | 7.17 E |
| Hagelberg ∧[2] | 54 | 52.08 N | 12.32 E |
| Hagemeister Island I | 180 | 58.40 N | 161.00 W |
| Hagen, Dtsch. | 52 | 52.34 N | 9.26 E |
| Hagen, Dtsch. | 52 | 52.12 N | 7.59 E |
| Hagen, Dtsch. | 56 | 51.22 N | 7.28 E |
| Hagenbach | 56 | 49.01 N | 8.15 E |
| Hagenbrunn | 264b | 48.20 N | 16.25 E |
| Hagengebirge ⩕ | 64 | 47.32 N | 13.07 E |
| Hagenow | 54 | 53.26 N | 11.11 E |
| Hagensborg | 182 | 52.23 N | 126.33 W |
| Hagenwerder | 54 | 51.04 N | 14.58 E |
| Hagere Hiywet | 144 | 8.59 N | 37.51 E |
| Hagere Selam | 144 | 6.29 N | 38.31 E |
| Hagerman, Id., U.S. | 202 | 42.48 N | 114.53 W |
| Hagerman, N.M., U.S. | 196 | 33.06 N | 104.19 W |
| Hagerman Corners | 275b | 43.50 N | 79.18 W |
| Hagerstown, In., U.S. | 218 | 39.54 N | 85.09 W |
| Hagerstown, Md., U.S. | 188 | 39.38 N | 77.43 W |
| Hagersville | 212 | 42.58 N | 80.03 W |
| Hagetmau | 32 | 43.40 N | 0.35 W |
| Hagfors | 40 | 60.02 N | 13.42 E |
| Haggen ⊜ | 40 | 60.06 N | 15.13 E |
| Haggetts Pond ⊜ | 283 | 42.39 N | 71.12 W |
| Haggin, Mount ∧ | 202 | 46.05 N | 113.05 W |
| Hagi | 96 | 34.24 N | 131.25 E |
| Ha Giang | 110 | 22.50 N | 104.59 E |
| Hagitani | 270 | 34.54 N | 135.35 E |
| Hagiwara | 94 | 35.52 N | 137.12 E |
| Hagley | 42 | 52.26 N | 2.08 W |
| Hagley Museum ʋ | 285 | 39.46 N | 75.35 W |
| Hagondange | 56 | 49.15 N | 6.10 E |
| HaGosherim | 132 | 33.13 N | 35.37 E |
| Hags Head › | 48 | 52.57 N | 9.30 W |
| Hague, Sk., Can. | 184 | 52.30 N | 106.25 W |
| Hague, N.D., U.S. | 198 | 46.01 N | 99.59 W |
| Hague, Cap de la › | 32 | 49.43 N | 1.57 W |
| Haguenau | 56 | 48.49 N | 7.47 E |
| Hagues Peak ∧ | 200 | 40.29 N | 105.38 W |
| Hahaïa | 157a | 11.33 S | 43.17 E |
| Hahajima-rettō II | 14 | 26.37 N | 142.10 E |
| Haharro, Uebi ≃ | 144 | 1.37 N | 44.13 E |
| Hāhipur | 272b | 22.47 N | 88.10 E |
| Hahira | 192 | 30.59 N | 83.22 W |
| Hahlen | 52 | 52.18 N | 8.50 E |
| Hahn am See | 56 | 50.31 N | 7.53 E |
| Hahnbach | 60 | 49.32 N | 11.48 E |
| Hahndorf | 168b | 35.03 S | 138.49 E |
| Hahnenberg | 263 | 51.12 N | 7.24 E |
| Hahnenkamm ∧ | 64 | 47.25 N | 12.22 E |
| Hahnenklee-Bockswiese | 52 | 51.51 N | 10.20 E |
| Hahnerberg ◆[8] | 263 | 51.13 N | 7.09 E |
| Hahnstätten | 56 | 50.18 N | 8.04 E |
| Hahntown | 279b | 40.19 N | 79.44 W |
| Haho ≃ | 150 | 6.17 N | 1.23 E |
| Hahyŏn-ni | 98 | 38.33 N | 127.57 E |
| Hai ≃ | 105 | 39.00 N | 117.43 E |
| Hai'an | 100 | 32.34 N | 120.28 E |
| Haian Shanmo ⩕ | 100 | 23.25 N | 121.25 E |
| Haibara, Nihon | 94 | 34.32 N | 135.57 E |
| Haibara, Nihon | 94 | 34.44 N | 138.13 E |
| Haibatpur | 272a | 28.37 N | 77.26 E |
| Haibei | 89 | 47.39 N | 126.51 E |
| Haicheng, Zhg. | 100 | 24.25 N | 117.51 E |
| Haicheng, Zhg. | 104 | 40.52 N | 122.45 E |
| Haicheng ≃ | 104 | 40.56 N | 122.21 E |
| Haidargarh | 124 | 26.37 N | 81.22 E |
| Haidārpur ◆[8] | 272a | 28.43 N | 77.09 E |
| Haidenaab ≃ | 60 | 49.36 N | 12.08 E |
| Haiderabad → Hyderābād, India | 122 | 17.23 N | 78.29 E |
| Haiderabad → Hyderābād, Pāk. | 120 | 25.22 N | 68.22 E |
| Haidershofen | 61 | 48.05 N | 14.28 E |
| Haidian | 105 | 39.59 N | 116.18 E |
| Haiding | 60 | 48.13 N | 13.58 E |
| Haidmühle | 60 | 48.50 N | 13.46 E |
| Haïdra | 36 | 35.34 N | 8.27 E |
| Haidstein ∧ | 60 | 49.13 N | 12.48 E |
| Haidun | 100 | 29.36 N | 121.49 E |
| Hai Duong | 110 | 20.56 N | 106.19 E |
| Haifa → Ḥefa | 132 | 32.50 N | 35.00 E |
| Haifa, Bay of → Ḥefa, Mifraẕ ⊂ | 132 | 32.52 N | 35.03 E |
| Haifeng | 100 | 22.59 N | 115.21 E |
| Haifengzheng | 106 | 31.53 N | 121.46 E |
| Haifuzhen | 106 | 31.59 N | 121.42 E |
| Haig | 162 | 31.01 S | 126.05 E |
| Haig, Mount ∧ | 182 | 49.17 N | 114.29 W |
| Haiger | 56 | 50.44 N | 8.13 E |
| Haigerloch | 58 | 48.22 N | 8.48 E |
| Haigh | 262 | 53.35 N | 2.36 W |
| Haigler | 198 | 40.00 N | 101.56 W |
| Haihezhen | 100 | 33.44 N | 120.02 E |
| Haijima | 268 | 35.42 N | 139.21 E |
| Haikang | 102 | 20.56 N | 110.04 E |
| Haikou, Zhg. | 100 | 28.20 N | 120.06 E |
| Haikou, Zhg. | 100 | 25.43 N | 119.28 E |
| Haikou, Zhg. | 100 | 29.04 N | 117.46 E |
| Haikou, Zhg. | 102 | 20.03 N | 110.19 E |
| Haiku | 229a | 20.55 N | 156.19 W |
| Ḥā'il | 128 | 27.33 N | 41.42 E |
| Hailākāndi | 120 | 24.41 N | 92.34 E |
| Hailar | 89 | 49.12 N | 119.42 E |
| Hailar ≃ | 90 | 49.35 N | 117.55 E |
| Hailasen | 89 | 46.13 N | 121.00 E |
| Hailesboro | 212 | 44.18 N | 75.27 W |
| Hailey, Eng., U.K. | 260 | 51.46 N | 0.01 W |
| Hailey, Id., U.S. | 202 | 43.31 N | 114.18 W |
| Haileybury | 190 | 47.27 N | 79.38 W |
| Haileyville | 196 | 34.51 N | 95.34 W |
| Hailin | 89 | 44.35 N | 129.22 E |
| Hailing Dao I | 102 | 21.37 N | 111.55 E |
| Haillicourt | 50 | 50.28 N | 2.35 E |
| Hailong (Meihekou) | 98 | 42.32 N | 125.38 E |
| Hailsham | 42 | 50.52 N | 0.16 E |
| Hailun | 89 | 47.28 N | 126.58 E |
| Hailuoto | 26 | 65.00 N | 24.43 E |
| Hailuoto I | 26 | 65.02 N | 24.42 E |
| Haiman Tepesi ∧[2] | 267b | 41.12 N | 29.15 E |
| Haimen, Zhg. | 100 | 28.41 N | 121.27 E |
| Haimen, Zhg. | 100 | 23.14 N | 116.38 E |
| Haimen, Zhg. | 106 | 31.55 N | 121.10 E |
| Haimen Wan ⊂ | 100 | 23.09 N | 116.34 E |
| Haimhausen | 60 | 48.19 N | 11.34 E |
| Haimiao | 98 | 37.13 N | 119.51 E |
| Haiming | 64 | 47.15 N | 10.53 E |
| Haina | 56 | 51.02 N | 8.58 E |
| Hainan □[4] | 110 | 19.00 N | 109.30 E |
| Hainan → Hainan Dao I | 110 | 19.00 N | 109.30 E |
| Hainan Dao I | 110 | 19.00 N | 109.30 E |
| Hainault ◆[8] | 260 | 51.36 N | 0.06 E |
| Hainaut □[4] | 50 | 50.30 N | 3.50 E |
| Hainaut □[9] | 50 | 50.15 N | 3.45 E |
| Hainburg an der Donau | 61 | 48.09 N | 16.57 E |
| Hainchen | 56 | 50.51 N | 8.12 E |
| Haines, Ak., U.S. | 180 | 59.14 N | 135.27 W |
| Haines, Or., U.S. | 202 | 44.54 N | 117.56 W |
| Haines City | 220 | 28.06 N | 81.37 W |
| Haines Falls | 210 | 42.11 N | 74.05 W |
| Haines Junction | 180 | 60.45 N | 137.30 W |
| Hainesport | 208 | 39.59 N | 74.49 W |
| Hainesville | 278 | 42.21 N | 88.04 W |
| Hainewalde | 54 | 50.54 N | 14.41 E |
| Hainfeld | 61 | 48.02 N | 15.46 E |
| Hainich ⩕ | 54 | 51.05 N | 10.27 E |
| Hainichen | 54 | 50.58 N | 13.07 E |
| Haining (Xiashi) | 106 | 30.32 N | 120.41 E |
| Hainleite ⩕ | 54 | 51.20 N | 10.48 E |
| Hainzenberg | 64 | 47.13 N | 11.54 E |
| Hai Phong | 110 | 20.52 N | 106.41 E |
| Haiqiao | 106 | 31.47 N | 121.19 E |
| Haiqing | 89 | 47.53 N | 134.40 E |
| Haitangxi | 107 | 29.33 N | 106.35 E |
| Haitan Xia ⩌ | 100 | 25.27 N | 119.38 E |
| Haiterbach | 58 | 48.32 N | 8.39 E |
| Haiti (Haïti) □[1], N.A. | 230 | 19.00 N | 72.25 W |
| Haiti (Haïti) □[1], N.A. | 238 | 19.00 N | 72.25 W |
| Haitou, Zhg. | 98 | 34.56 N | 119.10 E |
| Haitou, Zhg. | 110 | 19.34 N | 108.58 E |
| Haitouji | 98 | 35.23 N | 115.19 E |
| Haitun | 102 | 38.50 N | 96.41 E |
| Haiwee Reservoirs ⊜[1] | 204 | 36.10 N | 117.57 W |
| Haiyan, Zhg. | 102 | 36.54 N | 101.12 E |
| Haiyan, Zhg. | 106 | 30.31 N | 120.57 E |
| Haiyang (Dongcun) | 98 | 36.46 N | 121.10 E |
| Haiyang Dao I | 98 | 39.02 N | 123.14 E |
| Haiyuan | 102 | 36.35 N | 105.40 E |
| Haizhou, Zhg. | 98 | 34.34 N | 119.11 E |
| Haizhou, Zhg. | 100 | 22.40 N | 113.10 E |
| Haizhoumiao | 104 | 42.00 N | 121.39 E |
| Haizhou Wan ⊂ | 98 | 35.00 N | 119.30 E |
| Haizhouyingzi | 104 | 42.07 N | 121.46 E |
| Ḥajar, Tall al- ∧[2] | 132 | 33.21 N | 37.03 E |
| Hajar Banga | 140 | 11.30 N | 23.00 E |
| Hajdú-Bihar □[6] | 30 | 47.25 N | 21.30 E |
| Hajdúböszörmény | 30 | 47.41 N | 21.30 E |
| Hajdúnánás | 30 | 47.51 N | 21.26 E |
| Hajdúszoboszló | 30 | 47.27 N | 21.24 E |
| Hajeb el Ayoun | 36 | 35.24 N | 9.33 E |
| Hajiadian | 98 | 41.32 N | 117.10 E |
| Hājīganj | 126 | 23.15 N | 90.50 E |
| Hajiki-saki › | 92 | 38.19 N | 138.31 E |
| Haji Langar | 120 | 35.52 N | 79.21 E |
| Hājīpur, India | 124 | 25.41 N | 85.13 E |
| Hājīpur, India | 126 | 22.49 N | 87.38 E |
| Hajipur, India | 272b | 22.57 N | 88.19 E |
| Ḥājj, Wādī al- V | 142 | 30.03 N | 32.45 E |
| Hajnówka | 30 | 52.45 N | 23.36 E |
| Hajo-do I | 98 | 34.17 N | 126.03 E |
| Ḥajr, Wādī V | 144 | 14.04 N | 48.40 E |
| Ḥajūl, Wādī V | 142 | 29.42 N | 32.22 E |
| Häkäri ≃ | 84 | 39.09 N | 46.51 E |
| Hakata | 96 | 34.12 N | 133.07 E |
| Hakata-jima I | 96 | 34.13 N | 133.05 E |
| Hakataramea ≃ | 172 | 44.44 S | 170.29 E |
| Hakendover | 56 | 50.48 N | 4.59 E |
| Hakha | 110 | 22.39 N | 93.37 E |
| Haki | 96 | 33.20 N | 130.50 E |
| Ḥakīm, Abyār al- ⊤[4] | 146 | 31.36 N | 23.29 E |
| Hakkâri | 128 | 37.34 N | 43.45 E |
| Hakkâri □[4] | 128 | 37.20 N | 43.45 E |
| Hakken-san ∧ | 92 | 34.10 N | 135.54 E |
| Hakkōda-san ∧ | 92 | 40.40 N | 140.53 E |
| Hako-dake ∧ | 92a | 44.40 N | 142.25 E |
| Hakodate | 92a | 41.45 N | 140.43 E |
| Hakone | 94 | 35.12 N | 139.06 E |
| Hakone-no-seki-ato ⊥ | 94 | 35.10 N | 139.02 E |
| Hakone-tōge )( | 94 | 35.11 N | 139.01 E |
| Hakone-yama ∧ | 94 | 35.14 N | 139.02 E |
| Håksberg | 40 | 60.11 N | 15.12 E |
| Hakskeenpan ≚ | 158 | 26.48 S | 20.12 E |
| Haktanır | 130 | 36.51 N | 38.50 E |
| Hakuba | 94 | 36.42 N | 137.52 E |
| Hakui | 94 | 36.53 N | 136.47 E |
| Hakupu | 174v | 19.06 S | 169.50 W |
| Hakusan | 94 | 34.38 N | 136.21 E |
| Haku-san ∧ | 94 | 36.09 N | 136.46 E |
| Haku-san-kokuritsu-kōen ♠ | 94 | 36.12 N | 136.47 E |
| Hakushū | 94 | 35.48 N | 138.20 E |
| Hakuta | 96 | 35.21 N | 133.17 E |
| Hakuta ≃ | 96 | 35.26 N | 133.15 E |
| Hāla | 120 | 25.49 N | 68.25 E |
| Halaaobao | 102 | 42.11 N | 107.20 E |
| Halab (Aleppo) | 130 | 36.12 N | 37.10 E |
| Ḥalab □[8] | 130 | 36.00 N | 37.30 E |
| Ḥalabjah | 128 | 35.10 N | 45.59 E |
| Halachó | 232 | 20.29 N | 90.05 W |
| Halaerjige | 104 | 42.24 N | 122.11 E |
| Halagetu | 104 | 42.34 N | 122.40 E |
| Halahai | 89 | 44.39 N | 125.07 E |
| Halahushao | 104 | 42.11 N | 121.44 E |


**Symbols** in the index entries represent the broad categories identified in the key at the right. Symbols with superior numbers (⩕[1]) identify subcategories (see complete key on page *I · 1).*

**Symbole** im Register stellen die rechts im Schlüssel erklärten Kategorien dar. Symbole mit hochgestellten Ziffern (⩕[1]) bezeichnen Unterabteilungen einer Kategorie (vgl. vollständiger Schlüssel auf Seite *I · 1).*

**Los símbolos** incluídos en el texto del índice representan las grandes categorías identificadas con la clave a la derecha. Los símbolos con numeros en su parte superior (⩕[1]) identifican las subcategorías (véase la clave completa en la página *I · 1).*

**Les symboles** de l'index représentent les catégories indiquées dans la légende à droite. Les symboles suivis d'un indice (⩕[1]) représentent des sous-catégories (voir légende complète à la page *I · 1).*

**Os símbolos** incluídos no texto do índice representam as grandes categorias identificadas com a chave à direita. Os símbolos com números em sua parte superior (⩕[1]) identificam as subcategorias (veja-se a chave completa à página *I · 1).*

| | English | Deutsch | Español | Français | Português |
|---|---|---|---|---|---|
| ∧ | Mountain | Berg | Montaña | Montagne | Montanha |
| ⩕ | Mountains | Gebirge | Montañas | Montagnes | Montanhas |
| )( | Pass | Paß | Paso | Col | Passo |
| V | Valley, Canyon | Tal, Cañon | Valle, Cañón | Vallée, Canyon | Vale, Canhão |
| ≚ | Plain | Ebene | Llano | Plaine | Planície |
| › | Cape | Kap | Cabo | Cap | Cabo |
| I | Island | Insel | Isla | Île | Ilha |
| II | Islands | Inseln | Islas | Îles | Ilhas |
| ⫠ | Other Topographic Features | Andere Topographische Objekte | Otros Elementos Topográficos | Autres données topographiques | Outros acidentes topográficos |

ESPAÑOL — Nombre / Página / Lat.°′ / Long.°′ W = Oeste
FRANÇAIS — Nom / Page / Lat.°′ / Long.°′ W = Ouest
PORTUGUÊS — Nome / Página / Lat.°′ / Long.°′ W = Oeste


Halā'ib 140 22.13 N 36.38 E
Halalii Lake ⊜ 229b 21.52 N 160.11 W
Halamutai 86 46.10 N 84.52 E
Halangingie Point › 174v 19.03 S 169.57 W
Halasa 140 14.26 N 30.39 E
Halas-patak ≃ 264c 47.24 N 19.20 E
Halataojie 104 42.30 N 122.06 E
Halatieke Shan ⋏ 85 40.30 N 77.05 E
Halaula 229d 20.14 N 155.48 W
Hålaveden ⋏[2] 26 58.05 N 14.45 E
Halawa, Cape › 229a 21.10 N 156.43 W
Halawa Bay c 229a 21.10 N 156.44 W
Halawa Heights 229c 21.22 N 157.55 W
Halawotelake 120 37.17 N 90.20 E
Halbach ◆[8] 263 51.12 N 7.12 E
Halba Deset I 144 12.56 N 42.55 E
Halbe 54 52.06 N 13.42 E
Halberstadt 54 51.54 N 11.02 E
Halbert, Lake ⊜[1] 222 32.04 N 96.25 W
Halberton 42 50.55 N 3.25 W
Halblech, Dtsch. 58 47.38 N 10.49 E
Halblech, Dtsch. 64 47.38 N 10.49 E
Halbrite 184 49.30 N 103.33 W
Ḥalbūn 132 33.40 N 36.15 E
Halbury 168b 34.05 S 138.31 E
Halcombe 172 40.09 S 175.30 E
Halcon, Mount ʌ 116 13.16 N 121.00 E
Halcottsville 210 42.12 N 74.36 W
Haldeman 218 38.15 N 83.19 W
Halden 26 59.09 N 11.23 E
Halden ◆[8] 263 51.23 N 7.31 E
Haldensleben 54 52.18 N 11.26 E
Haldern 52 51.46 N 6.27 E
Haldī 126 22.03 N 88.05 E
Haldī ≃ 126 22.01 N 88.03 E
Haldībāri 124 26.20 N 88.46 E
Haldībunia 126 22.26 N 89.38 E
Haldimand 212 43.00 N 79.50 W
Haldimand-Norfolk □[6] 212 42.48 N 80.10 W
Haldwāni 124 29.13 N 79.31 E
Hale, Eng., U.K. 44 53.23 N 2.21 W
Hale, Eng., U.K. 262 53.20 N 2.48 W
Hale, Mo., U.S. 194 39.36 N 93.20 W
Hale ≃ 162 24.56 S 135.53 E
Haleakala Crater ♟[6] 229a 20.43 N 156.13 W
Haleakala National Park ♠ 229a 20.44 N 156.13 W
Haleb → Ḥalab 130 36.12 N 37.10 E
Halebarns 262 53.22 N 2.19 W
Hale Center 196 34.03 N 101.50 W
Hale Creek ≃ 282 37.23 N 122.06 W
Haledon 276 40.56 N 74.11 W
Haledon Reservoir ⊜[1] 276 40.59 N 74.12 W
Hale Eddy 210 42.00 N 75.23 W
Hale Head › 262 53.19 N 2.48 W
Haleiwa 229c 21.35 N 158.06 W
Halekii-Pihana Heiaus State Monument ⊥ 229a 20.54 N 156.29 W
Halenkov 30 49.19 N 18.08 E
Hales Corners 216 42.56 N 88.02 W
Halesite 207 40.52 N 73.25 W
Halesowen 42 52.26 N 2.05 W
Hale Street 260 51.13 N 0.24 E
Halesworth 42 52.21 N 1.30 E
Halewood 262 53.22 N 2.49 W
Haleyville 194 34.13 N 87.37 W
Half Assini 150 5.03 N 2.53 W
Ḥalfāyah, Naqb al- (Halfaya Pass) )( 140 31.30 N 25.11 E
Halfaya Pass → Ḥalfāyah, Naqb al- )( 140 31.30 N 25.11 E
Half Day 278 42.12 N 87.56 W
Halfeti 130 37.15 N 37.52 E
Half Hollow Hills 276 40.48 N 73.21 W
Halfing 64 47.57 N 12.16 E
Halfmoon Bay, B.C., Can. 182 49.31 N 123.54 W
Halfmoon Bay, N.Z. 172 46.54 S 168.08 E
Half Moon Bay, Ca., U.S. 226 37.27 N 122.25 W
Halfmoon Bay c, Austl. 274b 37.58 S 145.00 E
Half Moon Bay c, Ca., U.S. 282 37.29 N 122.28 W
Half Moon Bay Airport ⊠ 282 37.31 N 122.30 W
Half Moon Bay State Beach ♠ 282 37.29 N 122.27 W
Halfway, Md., U.S. 188 39.37 N 77.45 W
Halfway, Or., U.S. 202 44.52 N 117.06 W
Halfway ≃ 176 56.10 N 121.35 W
Halfway Lake ⊜ 184 55.03 N 98.24 W
Halgån ≃ 40 60.16 N 13.27 E
Ḥalḥūl 132 31.35 N 35.07 E
Ḥalī ⊤[4] 144 18.42 N 41.20 E
Haliburton 212 45.03 N 78.31 W
Haliburton □[6] 212 44.10 N 78.30 W
Haliburton Lake ⊜ 212 45.12 N 78.24 W
Halibut Point › 283 42.42 N 70.38 W
Haliç (Golden Horn) c 267b 41.02 N 28.58 E
Halicarnassus ⊥ 130 37.03 N 27.23 E
Halifax, Austl. 166 18.35 S 146.18 E
Halifax, N.S., Can. 186 44.39 N 63.36 W
Halifax, Eng., U.K. 44 53.44 N 1.52 W
Halifax, Ma., U.S. 207 41.59 N 70.51 W
Halifax, N.C., U.S. 192 36.19 N 77.35 W
Halifax, Pa., U.S. 208 40.28 N 76.55 W
Halifax, Va., U.S. 192 36.45 N 78.55 W
Halifax, Canadian Forces Base ■ 186 44.43 N 63.38 W
Halifax Bay c 166 18.50 S 146.30 E
Halifax Citadel National Historic Park ♠ 186 44.36 N 63.39 W
Halifax Harbour c 186 44.35 N 63.31 W
Haliimaile 229a 20.52 N 156.20 W
Halīl ≃ 128 27.28 N 58.44 E
Halimatazi 104 42.37 N 122.35 E
Halim Perdanakusuma Airport ■ 269e 6.16 S 106.54 E
Halimun, Gunung ʌ 115a 6.42 S 106.26 E
Halingen 263 51.27 N 7.44 E
Hālisahar 126 22.56 N 88.25 E
Haliyāl 122 15.20 N 74.46 E
Haljala 76 59.26 N 26.16 E
Halkalı ◆[8] 267b 41.02 N 28.47 E
Halkapınar 130 37.25 N 34.13 E
Halkett, Cape › 180 70.49 N 152.12 W
Halkirk 46 58.30 N 3.30 W
Halkyn 262 53.14 N 3.11 W
Halkyn Mountain ʌ 262 53.14 N 3.13 W
Hall, Austl. 171b 35.10 S 149.04 E
Hall, In., U.S. 218 39.33 N 86.32 W
Hall, N.Y., U.S. 210 42.48 N 77.04 W
Hällabrottet 40 59.07 N 15.12 E
Halladale ≃ 46 58.33 N 3.55 W
Hallam 274b 38.01 S 145.06 E
Hallam Peak ʌ 182 52.11 N 118.46 W
Halland □[9] 26 57.00 N 12.40 E
Hallandale 220 25.58 N 80.08 W
Hallands Län □[6] 26 56.45 N 13.00 E
Hallands Väderö I 26 56.26 N 12.33 E
Halla-san ʌ 90 33.22 N 126.32 E
Hallau 58 47.42 N 8.27 E
Hällberga 40 59.19 N 16.36 E
Hallbergmoos 60 48.20 N 11.45 E
Hällbybrunn 40 59.24 N 16.25 E
Hällbymagasinet ⊜[1] 26 63.56 N 17.13 E
Halle, Bel. 50 50.44 N 4.13 E
Halle, Dtsch. 52 52.04 N 8.22 E
Halle, Dtsch. 52 51.59 N 9.33 E
Halle, Dtsch. 54 51.29 N 11.58 E
Halleberg ʌ[2] 26 58.23 N 12.27 E
Hällefors 40 59.47 N 14.30 E
Hälleforsnäs 40 59.10 N 16.30 E
Hallein 64 47.41 N 13.06 E
Hällekis 26 58.38 N 13.25 E
Hallen 26 63.11 N 14.05 E
Hallenberg 56 51.06 N 8.37 E
Hallencourt 50 49.59 N 1.53 E
Halle-Neustadt 54 51.29 N 11.56 E
Hallertau ◆[1] 60 48.35 N 11.45 E
Hällestad 40 58.44 N 15.34 E
Hallett, Cape › 9 72.19 S 170.18 E
Hallettsville 222 29.26 N 96.56 W
Halley ʋ[3], Ant. 9 75.35 S 26.15 W
Halley ʋ[3], Ant. 9 75.36 S 26.46 W
Halliday 198 47.21 N 102.20 W
Halligen II 30 54.35 N 8.35 E
Halling 260 51.21 N 0.27 E
Hallingdalselvi ≃ 26 60.24 N 9.35 E
Hällingsåfallet ʟ 26 64.20 N 14.20 E
Hall in Tirol 64 47.17 N 11.31 E
Hall Island I 180 60.40 N 173.05 W
Hall Islands II 14 8.37 N 152.00 E
Halliste ≃ 76 58.31 N 25.03 E
Hall-i'-th'-Wood ♠ 262 53.36 N 2.26 W
Hall Lake ⊜ 176 68.41 N 82.17 W
Hall Meadow Brook Reservoir ⊜[1] 207 41.52 N 73.10 W
Hall Mountain ʌ 202 48.49 N 117.15 W
Hällnäs 26 64.19 N 19.38 E
Hallock 198 48.46 N 96.56 W
Hallowell 188 44.17 N 69.47 W
Hall Peninsula ›[1] 176 63.30 N 66.00 W
Halls 194 35.52 N 89.23 W
Halls Bayou ≃ 222 29.12 N 95.07 W
Hallsberg 40 59.04 N 15.07 E
Halls Brook ≃ 283 42.00 N 70.43 W
Halls Creek 162 18.16 S 127.46 E
Halls Creek ≃ 200 37.18 N 110.45 W
Halls Gap 166 37.08 S 142.31 E
Halls Lake ⊜ 212 45.07 N 78.45 W
Halls Stream ≃ 206 45.01 N 71.30 W
Hållsta 40 59.18 N 16.27 E
Hallstadt 56 49.55 N 10.52 E
Hallstahammar 40 59.37 N 16.13 E
Hallstatt 64 47.33 N 13.39 E
Hallstätter See ⊜ 64 47.35 N 13.39 E
Hallstavik 40 60.03 N 18.36 E
Hallstead 210 41.57 N 75.44 W
Hallsville, Mo., U.S. 219 39.07 N 92.13 W
Hallsville, Tx., U.S. 222 32.30 N 94.34 W
Halluin 50 50.47 N 3.08 E
Hallwiler See ⊜ 58 47.18 N 8.13 E
Hallwood 208 37.52 N 75.35 W
Halma 56 50.05 N 5.08 E
Halmahera I 108 1.00 N 128.00 E
Halmahera, Laut (Halmahera Sea) ⊤[2] 108 1.00 S 129.00 E
Halmstad 26 56.39 N 12.50 E
Ḫalopeničy 76 54.31 N 28.58 E
Haloučyn 76 54.04 N 29.55 E
Halpine Village 284c 39.04 N 77.07 W
Hals 26 57.00 N 10.19 E
Halsafjorden c[2] 26 63.03 N 8.11 E
Halsall 262 53.35 N 2.57 W
Hal'šany 76 54.15 N 26.01 E
Halsbrücke 54 50.57 N 13.21 E
Halsey, Ne., U.S. 198 41.54 N 100.16 W
Halsey, Or., U.S. 202 44.23 N 123.06 W
Halsey Harbor c 116 11.45 N 119.56 E
Halsey Valley 210 42.08 N 76.27 W
Hälsingborg → Helsingborg 41 56.03 N 12.42 E
Hälsingland □[9] 26 61.30 N 17.00 E
Halstad 198 47.21 N 96.49 W
Halstead, Eng., U.K. 42 51.57 N 0.38 E
Halstead, Eng., U.K. 260 51.20 N 0.08 E
Halstead, Ks., U.S. 198 38.00 N 97.30 W
Halstenbek 52 53.38 N 9.50 E
Halsteren 52 51.32 N 4.16 E
Halstow Marshes ≡ 260 51.29 N 0.33 E
Haltang ≃ 102 39.00 N 94.40 E
Haltern 52 51.46 N 7.10 E
Haltiatunturi ʌ 24 69.18 N 21.16 E
Haltom City 222 32.47 N 97.16 W
Halton, Eng., U.K. 44 54.05 N 2.46 W
Halton, Eng., U.K. 262 53.20 N 2.42 W
Halton □[6] 212 43.30 N 79.53 W
Halton □[8] 262 53.20 N 2.44 W
Halton Hills 212 43.39 N 79.55 W
Haltwhistle 44 54.58 N 2.27 W
Halura, Pulau I 115b 10.19 S 120.11 E
Ḫaluza, Ḫolot ♟[8] 132 31.05 N 34.28 E
Halūzonī, Wādī al- V 273c 30.05 N 31.24 E
Halvarsgårdarna 40 60.24 N 15.23 E
Halvarsnoren ⊜ 40 59.35 N 14.36 E
Halver 56 51.11 N 7.30 E
Halvorson, Mount ʌ 182 53.15 N 120.33 W
Halwell 42 50.22 N 3.43 W
Halych 78 49.08 N 24.43 E
Ham, Fr. 50 49.45 N 3.04 E
Ham, Tchad 146 10.00 N 15.41 E
Ham ◆[8] 260 51.26 N 0.19 W
Ham ≃ 158 28.32 S 19.34 E
Ham, Oued el ≃ 34 35.42 N 4.52 E
Hamad 140 15.19 N 33.43 E
Hamada 96 34.53 N 132.05 E
Hamadān 128 34.48 N 48.30 E
Hamadān □[4] 128 35.00 N 48.40 E
Ḥamāh 130 35.08 N 36.45 E
Ḥamāh □[8] 130 35.10 N 37.00 E
Hamahika-jima I 174m 26.19 N 127.57 E
Hamakeza 89 47.05 N 120.52 E
Hamakita 94 34.48 N 137.47 E
Hamale 150 10.59 N 2.44 W
Hamamatsu 94 34.42 N 137.44 E
Hamamatsukita-kichi, Kōkū-jieitai- ■ 94 34.45 N 137.42 E
Hamamözü 130 40.48 N 35.02 E
Haman 98 35.15 N 128.24 E
Hamanaka 92a 43.05 N 145.10 E
Hamana-ko ⊜ 94 34.45 N 137.34 E
Hamano 268 35.33 N 140.08 E
Hamaoka 94 34.39 N 138.08 E
Hamar 26 60.48 N 11.06 E
Hamasaka 96 35.37 N 134.27 E
Ḥamāṭah, Jabal ʌ 140 24.12 N 35.00 E
Hamatang 98 40.12 N 124.20 E
Hama-tombetsu 92a 45.07 N 142.23 E
Hambach 56 49.04 N 7.02 E
Hambaek-san ʌ 98 37.09 N 128.55 E
Hambantota 122 6.07 N 81.07 E
Hambergen 52 53.18 N 8.49 E
Hamber Provincial Park ♠ 182 52.25 N 117.40 W
Hamble 42 50.52 N 1.19 W
Hambledon 42 50.56 N 1.04 W
Hambleton 44 53.52 N 2.57 W
Hambleton Hills ⋏[2] 44 54.16 N 1.12 W
Hamborn ◆[8] 263 51.29 N 6.46 E
Hambourg → Hamburg 52 53.33 N 9.59 E
Hambühren 52 52.38 N 9.59 E
Hamburg, Dtsch. 52 53.33 N 9.59 E
Hamburg, S. Afr. 158 33.17 S 27.28 E
Hamburg, Ar., U.S. 194 33.13 N 91.47 W
Hamburg, Ct., U.S. 207 41.23 N 72.21 W
Hamburg, Il., U.S. 219 39.14 N 90.43 W
Hamburg, Ia., U.S. 198 40.36 N 95.39 W
Hamburg, Mi., U.S. 216 42.27 N 83.48 W
Hamburg, N.J., U.S. 210 41.09 N 74.34 W
Hamburg, N.Y., U.S. 210 42.42 N 78.49 W
Hamburg, Pa., U.S. 208 40.33 N 75.58 W
Hamburg □[3] 52 53.35 N 10.00 E
Hamburg, Flughafen ⊠ 52 53.38 N 10.00 E
Hamburg Airport ⊠ 284a 42.42 N 78.55 W
Hamburg Ditch ≍ 208 36.31 N 76.33 W
Hamburger Hallig ›[1] 41 54.36 N 8.49 E
Hamburg Mountains ⋏ 276 41.08 N 74.32 W
Hamburgo → Hamburg 52 53.33 N 9.59 E
Hamburgsund 26 58.33 N 11.16 E
Ḥamḍ, Wādī al- V 128 25.54 N 36.38 E
Ḥamdah 144 19.02 N 43.36 E
Hamdallay Timbou 150 12.03 N 10.37 W
Hamdam Āb, Dasht-e ≍ 128 34.45 N 61.30 E
Ḥamdānah 144 19.58 N 40.35 E
Hamden, Ct., U.S. 207 41.23 N 72.53 W
Hamden, N.Y., U.S. 210 42.12 N 75.00 W
Hamden, Oh., U.S. 188 39.09 N 82.31 W
Hamdibey 130 39.50 N 27.15 E
Häme ◆[1] 26 61.45 N 25.10 E
Hämeenkangas ◆[3] 26 61.45 N 22.40 E
Hämeenkylä 26 60.16 N 24.47 E
Hämeen lääni □[4] 26 61.30 N 24.30 E
Hämeenlinna 26 61.00 N 24.27 E
Hamel 168a 32.52 S 115.55 E
HaMelah, Yam → Dead Sea ⊜ 132 31.30 N 35.30 E
Hämelerwald 52 52.22 N 10.05 E
Hamelin 162 26.26 S 114.11 E
Hamelin Pool c 162 26.15 S 114.05 E
Hameln 52 52.06 N 9.21 E
HaMerkaz □[5] 132 32.05 N 34.55 E
Hamer Koke 144 5.12 N 36.45 E
Hamero Hadad 144 7.34 N 42.18 E
Hamersleben 54 52.04 N 11.05 E
Hamersley Range ⋏ 162 21.53 S 116.46 E
Hamersley Range National Park ♠ 162 22.40 S 118.15 E
Hamersville 218 38.55 N 83.59 W
Hames Creek ≃ 226 35.53 N 120.50 W
Hamgyŏng Namdo □[4] 98 40.00 N 127.30 E
Hamgyŏng Pukdo □[4] 98 41.45 N 129.50 E
Hamgyŏng-sanmaek ⋏ 98 41.00 N 128.30 E
Ham House ⊥ 260 51.27 N 0.19 W
Hamhŭng 98 39.54 N 127.32 E
Hami (Kumul) 102 42.48 N 93.27 E
Hamidiye 130 41.09 N 26.40 E
Hamiguitan, Mount ʌ 116 6.44 N 126.11 E
Hamilton, Austl. 166 37.45 S 142.02 E
Hamilton, Ber. 240a 32.17 N 64.46 W
Hamilton, On., Can. 212 43.15 N 79.51 W
Hamilton, N.Z. 172 37.47 S 175.17 E
Hamilton, Scot., U.K. 46 55.47 N 4.03 W
Hamilton, Al., U.S. 194 34.08 N 87.59 W
Hamilton, Ak., U.S. 180 62.54 N 163.53 W
Hamilton, Ga., U.S. 192 32.45 N 84.52 W
Hamilton, Il., U.S. 190 40.23 N 91.20 W
Hamilton, In., U.S. 216 41.32 N 84.54 W
Hamilton, Ks., U.S. 198 37.58 N 96.09 W
Hamilton, Ma., U.S. 207 42.37 N 70.52 W
Hamilton, Mi., U.S. 216 42.40 N 86.00 W
Hamilton, Mo., U.S. 194 39.44 N 93.59 W
Hamilton, Mt., U.S. 202 46.14 N 114.09 W
Hamilton, N.Y., U.S. 210 42.49 N 75.32 W
Hamilton, N.C., U.S. 192 35.56 N 77.12 W
Hamilton, Oh., U.S. 218 39.23 N 84.33 W
Hamilton, R.I., U.S. 207 41.32 N 71.26 W
Hamilton, Tx., U.S. 196 31.42 N 98.07 W
Hamilton, Wa., U.S. 224 48.31 N 121.59 W
Hamilton □[6], In., U.S. 218 40.03 N 86.01 W
Hamilton □[6], N.Y., U.S. 210 43.24 N 74.25 W
Hamilton □[6], Oh., U.S. 218 39.06 N 84.31 W
Hamilton ◆[8] 284b 39.21 N 76.33 W
Hamilton ≃ 166 23.30 S 139.47 E
Hamilton, Lake ⊜ 220 28.03 N 81.39 W
Hamilton, Lake ⊜[1] 194 34.30 N 93.05 W
Hamilton, Mount ʌ, Ak., U.S. 180 61.10 N 159.46 W
Hamilton, Mount ʌ, Ca., U.S. 226 37.21 N 121.38 W
Hamilton, Mount ʌ, Nv., U.S. 204 39.14 N 115.32 W
Hamilton Acres 180 64.51 N 147.40 W
Hamilton Air Force Base ■ 282 38.03 N 122.31 W
Hamilton City 204 39.44 N 122.00 W
Hamilton Creek ≃ 162 26.40 S 135.19 E
Hamilton Creek Indian Reserve ◆[4] 182 50.11 N 120.30 W
Hamilton Dome 200 43.46 N 108.34 W
Hamilton Harbour c 212 43.17 N 79.50 W
Hamilton Hill 168a 32.05 S 115.46 E
Hamilton Hotel 166 22.50 S 140.35 E
Hamilton Inlet c 176 54.00 N 57.30 W
Hamilton Island I 166 20.22 S 148.57 E
Hamilton Lake ⊜ 216 41.33 N 84.55 W
Hamilton Mountain ʌ 188 43.25 N 74.22 W
Hamilton Park, In., U.S. 216 40.17 N 85.19 W
Hamilton Park, Pa., U.S. 208 40.02 N 76.20 W
Hamilton Sound ʊ 186 49.30 N 54.30 W
Hamilton Square 285 40.13 N 74.39 W
Hamilton-Wentworth □[6] 212 43.15 N 80.00 W
Ḥamīm, Wādī al- V 146 30.10 N 21.32 E
Hamina 26 60.34 N 27.12 E
Hamiota 184 50.11 N 100.36 W
Ḥāmir, Wādī V 128 31.37 N 42.12 E
Hamīrpur, India 123 31.41 N 76.31 E
Hamīrpur, India 124 25.57 N 80.09 E
Hamjong-ni 98 38.59 N 125.17 E
Hamler 216 41.13 N 84.02 W
Hamlet, In., U.S. 216 41.32 N 86.34 W
Hamlet, N.C., U.S. 192 34.53 N 79.41 W
Hamlet, Oh., U.S. 218 39.01 N 84.12 W
Hamlet, Mount ʌ 180 68.47 N 165.57 W
Hamley Bridge 168b 34.21 S 138.41 E
Hamlin, N.Y., U.S. 210 43.18 N 77.55 W
Hamlin, Pa., U.S. 210 41.24 N 75.24 W
Hamlin, Tx., U.S. 196 32.53 N 100.08 W
Hamlin, W.V., U.S. 188 38.16 N 82.06 W
Hamlin Beach State Park ♠ 210 43.22 N 77.58 W
Hamlin Lake ⊜ 190 44.03 N 86.27 W
Hamlin Valley Wash V 200 33.53 N 114.01 W
Hamm 52 51.41 N 7.49 E
Hamm ◆[8], Dtsch. 263 51.12 N 6.44 E
Hamm ◆[8], Dtsch. 263 51.23 N 7.03 E
Ḥammād, Wādī V 142 29.45 N 32.24 E
Hamma Hamma ≃ 224 47.33 N 123.03 W
Håmmålfjell ʌ 26 62.27 N 11.17 E
Ḥammām at-Turkumān 130 36.32 N 39.03 E
Hammamet, Alg. 36 35.27 N 7.58 E
Hammamet, Tun. 148 36.24 N 10.37 E
Hammamet, Golfe de c 36 36.05 N 10.40 E
Hammam Lif 148 36.44 N 10.20 E
Ḥammānā 132 33.49 N 35.44 E
Hammar 40 58.49 N 14.57 E
Ḥammār, Hawr al- ⊜ 128 30.50 N 47.10 E
Hammarby 40 60.33 N 16.34 E
Hammarn 40 59.45 N 14.30 E
Hammarö 40 59.20 N 13.31 E
Hammarön I 40 59.19 N 13.31 E
Hammarstrand 26 63.06 N 16.21 E
Hamme 50 51.06 N 4.08 E
Hamme ≃ 52 53.10 N 8.44 E
Hammel 41 56.15 N 9.52 E
Hammelburg 56 50.07 N 9.53 E
Hamme-Mille 56 50.47 N 4.43 E
Hammerdal 26 63.36 N 15.21 E
Hammerfest 24 70.40 N 23.42 E
Hämmern 263 51.08 N 7.21 E
Hammershus ⊥ 26 55.16 N 14.45 E
Hammersley Inlet c 224 47.12 N 123.00 W
Hammersmith ◆[8] 260 51.30 N 0.14 W
Hammerum 41 56.08 N 9.04 E
Hamminkeln 52 51.44 N 6.35 E
Hammon 196 35.37 N 99.22 W
Hammonasset ≃ 207 41.16 N 72.33 W
Hammond, In., U.S. 216 41.35 N 87.30 W
Hammond, La., U.S. 194 30.30 N 90.27 W
Hammond, N.Y., U.S. 212 44.26 N 75.41 W
Hammond, Or., U.S. 224 46.12 N 123.57 W
Hammond, Wi., U.S. 190 44.58 N 92.26 W
Hammond Island I, Austl. 164 10.35 S 142.13 E
Hammond Island I, Ca., U.S. 282 38.06 N 121.57 W
Hammond Pond Park ♠ 283 42.19 N 71.11 W
Hammondsport 210 42.24 N 77.13 W
Hammondsville 214 40.33 N 80.43 W
Hammondville 274a 33.57 S 150.57 E
Hammonia 158 28.43 S 27.49 E
Hammonton 208 39.38 N 74.48 W
Hamningberg 24 70.31 N 30.37 E
Ham-Nord 206 45.54 N 71.39 W
Hamoir 56 50.26 N 5.32 E
Hamont 56 51.15 N 5.33 E
HaMore, Giv'at ʌ 132 32.37 N 35.21 E
Hamorton 285 39.52 N 75.39 W
Hamoyet, Jabal ʌ 144 17.33 N 38.02 E
Hampden, Austl. 168b 34.09 S 139.03 E
Hampden, Nf., Can. 186 49.33 N 56.51 W
Hampden, N.Z. 172 45.19 S 170.49 E
Hampden, Me., U.S. 188 44.44 N 68.50 W
Hampden, Ma., U.S. 207 42.03 N 72.24 W
Hampden, N.D., U.S. 198 48.32 N 98.39 W
Hampden □[6] 207 42.07 N 72.36 W
Hampden Sydney 192 37.15 N 78.29 W
Hampetorp 40 59.09 N 15.40 E
Hampi 122 15.24 N 76.37 E
Hampshire 216 42.05 N 88.31 W
Hampshire □[6], Eng., U.K. 42 51.05 N 1.15 W
Hampshire □[6], Ma., U.S. 207 42.19 N 72.38 W
Hampshire Downs ⋏[1] 42 51.15 N 1.17 W
Hampshire Heights 279b 40.20 N 79.33 W
Hampstead, P.Q., Can. 275a 45.29 N 73.38 W
Hampstead, Md., U.S. 208 39.36 N 76.51 W
Hampstead, N.C., U.S. 192 34.22 N 77.42 W
Hampstead ◆[8] 260 51.33 N 0.11 W
Hampstead Heath ♠ 260 51.34 N 0.10 W
Hampton, Austl. 274b 37.56 S 145.00 E
Hampton, N.B., Can. 186 45.32 N 65.51 W
Hampton, On., Can. 212 43.58 N 78.45 W
Hampton, Ar., U.S. 194 33.32 N 92.28 W
Hampton, Ct., U.S. 207 41.47 N 72.03 W
Hampton, Fl., U.S. 192 29.51 N 82.07 W
Hampton, Ga., U.S. 192 33.23 N 84.16 W
Hampton, Ia., U.S. 190 42.44 N 93.12 W
Hampton, Ne., U.S. 198 40.52 N 97.53 W
Hampton, N.H., U.S. 188 42.56 N 70.50 W
Hampton, N.J., U.S. 210 40.42 N 74.57 W
Hampton, Pa., U.S. 208 39.56 N 77.04 W
Hampton, S.C., U.S. 192 32.52 N 81.06 W
Hampton, Tn., U.S. 192 36.17 N 82.10 W
Hampton, Va., U.S. 208 37.01 N 76.20 W
Hampton ◆[8] 260 51.25 N 0.22 W
Hampton, Mount ʌ 9 76.29 S 125.48 W
Hampton Bays 207 40.52 N 72.31 W
Hampton Butte ʌ 202 43.46 N 120.17 W
Hampton Court Palace ʋ 42 51.24 N 0.20 W
Hampton Harbour c 162 20.40 S 116.30 E
Hampton National Historic Site ⊥ 284b 39.25 N 76.35 W
Hampton Park 274b 38.02 S 145.15 E
Hampton Roads ⊤[3] 208 36.58 N 76.20 W
Hampton Roads Bridge-Tunnel ◆[5] 208 37.00 N 76.18 W
Hampton Tableland ⋏[1] 162 32.10 S 126.10 E
Hamp'yŏng 98 35.05 N 126.30 E
Hamr 54 50.35 N 13.35 E
Hamra 26 61.39 N 15.00 E
Ḥamrā', Al-Ḥamādah al- ◆[2] 146 30.00 N 12.00 E
Hamra, As Saquia al V 148 27.15 N 13.21 W
Hamra, Ouadi V 146 12.52 N 21.15 E
Ḥamrah, Jabal al- ʌ 132 29.39 N 34.47 E
Ḥamran, Har ʌ 132 30.41 N 34.34 E
Hamra Nationalpark ♠ 26 61.45 N 14.55 E
Ḥamrat ash-Shaykh 140 14.35 N 27.58 E
Hams Bluff ♟[4] 241n 17.46 N 64.52 W
Hams Fork ≃ 200 41.35 N 109.59 W
Hamstreet 42 51.04 N 0.51 E
Ham-Sud 206 45.46 N 71.36 W
Ham Tan 110 10.40 N 107.46 E
Hamtramck 216 42.23 N 83.02 W
Hāmūn, Daryācheh-ye ⊜ 128 30.50 N 61.07 E
Hamur 84 39.36 N 42.59 E
Hamura 94 35.45 N 139.19 E
Hamyang 98 35.32 N 127.42 E
Hamzalı 130 38.19 N 41.09 E
Han 150 10.41 N 2.27 W
Han ≃, Zhg. 100 23.41 N 116.38 E
Han ≃, Zhg. 102 30.35 N 114.17 E
Han, Grottes de ♟[5] 56 50.08 N 5.15 E
Han, Nong ⊜ 110 17.12 N 104.11 E
Hana 229a 20.45 N 155.59 W
Hanábana ≃ 240p 22.23 N 80.58 W
Hanahan 192 32.55 N 80.01 W
Hanailike 85 39.16 N 76.26 E
Ḥanak 128 25.33 N 36.56 E
Hanakaoo Point › 229a 20.55 N 156.42 W
Hanalei 229b 22.12 N 159.30 W
Hanalei Bay c 229b 22.13 N 159.31 W
Hanamaki 92 39.23 N 141.07 E
Hanamaulu 229b 21.59 N 159.21 W
Hanamenu, Baie c 174x 9.46 S 139.08 W
Hanam-ni 98 38.23 N 126.43 E
Hanang ʌ 154 4.26 S 35.24 E
Hanapepe 229b 21.54 N 159.35 W
Hānār Char 126 23.08 N 90.38 E
Hanataka-sen ʌ 96 35.24 N 132.45 E
Hanateio 174x 9.59 S 139.06 W
Hanatetena 174x 9.58 S 139.04 W
Hanau 56 50.08 N 8.55 E
Hanaui 174x 9.45 S 139.05 W
Hanawa, Nihon 94 36.57 N 140.25 E
Hanawa, Nihon 268 35.13 N 139.53 E
Hanbury ≃ 176 63.37 N 104.33 W
Hancavičy 76 52.45 N 26.26 E
Hâncești 38 46.49 N 28.34 E
Hanceville, B.C., Can. 182 51.55 N 123.03 W
Hanceville, Al., U.S. 194 34.03 N 86.46 W
Hanchang 107 30.26 N 103.43 E
Hancheng, Zhg. 102 35.28 N 110.29 E
Hancheng, Zhg. 105 39.39 N 118.02 E
Hanches 261 48.36 N 1.39 E
Hanchō 270 34.49 N 135.27 E
Han-ch'ŏn ≃ 271b 37.33 N 127.02 E
Hanchuan 100 30.39 N 113.48 E
Hanchung → Hanzhong 102 33.08 N 107.02 E
Hancock, Md., U.S. 188 39.41 N 78.10 W
Hancock, Mi., U.S. 190 47.07 N 88.34 W
Hancock, Mn., U.S. 198 45.29 N 95.47 W
Hancock, N.Y., U.S. 210 41.57 N 75.17 W
Hancock, Wi., U.S. 190 44.08 N 89.31 W
Hancock □[6], Il., U.S. 219 40.13 N 91.15 W
Hancock □[6], In., U.S. 218 39.47 N 85.46 W
Hancock □[6], Oh., U.S. 216 41.02 N 83.39 W
Hancock □[6], W.V., U.S. 214 40.30 N 80.33 W
Hancock, Lake ⊜ 220 27.58 N 81.50 W
Hancocks Bridge 208 39.30 N 75.27 W
Hancun 105 39.24 N 116.36 E
Handa, Nihon 94 34.53 N 136.56 E
Handa, Nihon 96 34.02 N 134.02 E
Handa, Som. 144 10.40 N 51.07 E
Handa I 46 58.22 N 5.12 W
Handan 98 36.37 N 114.29 E
Handaokou 98 34.16 N 116.24 E
Handawor 123 34.24 N 74.17 E
Handen 40 59.10 N 18.08 E
Handeni 154 5.26 S 38.01 E
Handforth 262 53.21 N 2.13 W
Handlová 30 48.44 N 18.46 E
Handöl 26 63.16 N 12.26 E
Handorf 52 51.59 N 7.41 E
Handsworth 184 49.48 N 103.00 W
Handub 140 19.14 N 37.16 E
Handzame 50 51.02 N 3.00 E
Haneda Airport ⊠ 268 35.33 N 139.46 E
HaNegev (Negev Desert) ◆[1] 132 30.30 N 34.55 E
Hane-yama ʌ 96 33.14 N 131.08 E
Hane-zaki › 96 33.22 N 134.02 E
Hanford 226 36.19 N 119.38 W
Hanford Site ʋ[3] 202 46.35 N 119.30 W
Han'gang 98 34.39 N 114.38 E
Han-gang ≃ 98 37.45 N 126.11 E
Hanga Roa 174z 27.09 S 109.26 W
Hangatiki 172 38.15 S 175.10 E
Hangbu 100 28.53 N 118.49 E
Hangchow → Hangzhou 106 30.15 N 120.10 E
Hangchow Bay → Hangzhou Wan c 100 30.25 N 121.00 E
Hanger ≃ 144 9.35 N 36.02 E
Hanggai 106 30.35 N 119.23 E
Hanggin Houqi 102 40.55 N 107.15 E
Hanggin Qi 102 39.56 N 108.54 E
Hang Hau Town 271d 22.19 N 114.16 E
Hanging Gardens ♠ 272c 18.58 N 72.48 E
Hanging Rock State Park ♠ 192 36.25 N 80.15 W
Hangingstone Hill ʌ[2] 42 50.39 N 3.57 W
Hanging Woman Creek ≃ 202 45.19 N 106.31 W
Hangklip, Kaap › 158 34.26 S 18.48 E
Hangkou 100 29.03 N 114.27 E
Hangman Creek ≃ 202 47.38 N 117.27 W
Hangö (Hanko) 26 59.50 N 22.57 E
Hangou 105 39.18 N 117.07 E
Hang-Tcheou → Hangzhou 106 30.15 N 120.10 E
Hangtou 106 31.01 N 121.35 E
Hangtschou → Hangzhou 106 30.15 N 120.10 E
Hangu, Pāk. 123 33.32 N 71.04 E
Hangu, Zhg. 105 39.15 N 117.47 E
Hangu, Zhg. 107 28.58 N 104.30 E
Hanguang 100 24.16 N 113.08 E
Hanguchang 107 29.32 N 106.21 E
Hangugang 105 39.15 N 116.56 E
Hangzhou (Hangchow) 106 30.15 N 120.10 E
Hangzhou Wan (Hangchow Bay) c 100 30.25 N 121.00 E
Hani 130 38.24 N 40.24 E
Hänigsen 52 52.29 N 10.05 E
Hanimadu I 122 6.45 N 73.09 E
Ḥanīsh II 144 13.45 N 42.45 E
Ḥanīsh al-Kabīr, Jazīrat al- I 144 13.43 N 42.45 E
Ḥanita 132 33.05 N 35.10 E
Hanjalipan 112 2.15 S 112.47 E
Hanjiagou 104 40.42 N 120.47 E
Hanjiang 100 25.30 N 119.06 E
Hanjiapuzi 104 40.48 N 123.14 E
Hanjiashu 105 39.11 N 117.04 E
Hanjiawa 106 31.16 N 119.18 E
Hankamer 222 29.51 N 94.38 W
Hankasalmi 26 62.23 N 26.26 E
Hanke 26 59.12 N 10.47 E
Hankendi 130 38.35 N 39.04 E
Hankensbüttel 54 52.44 N 10.36 E
Hankey 158 33.50 S 24.53 E
Hankins 210 41.49 N 75.05 W
Hankinson 198 46.04 N 96.54 W
Hanko → Hangö 26 59.50 N 22.57 E
Hankow → Wuhan 100 30.36 N 114.17 E
Hanks Pond ⊜ 276 41.05 N 74.26 W
Hanku → Hangu 105 39.15 N 117.47 E
Hānle 120 32.48 N 79.00 E
Hanley 184 51.37 N 106.27 W
Hanmer 190 46.39 N 80.56 W
Hanmer Springs 172 42.31 S 172.49 E
Hanmiao 89 44.33 N 119.59 E
Hann ≃ 164 17.10 S 126.10 E
Hann, Mount ʌ 164 15.51 S 125.48 E
Hanna, Ab., Can. 182 51.38 N 111.54 W
Hanna, In., U.S. 216 41.24 N 86.46 W
Hanna, Ok., U.S. 196 35.12 N 95.53 W
Hanna, Wy., U.S. 200 41.52 N 106.33 W
Hanna City 190 40.41 N 89.47 W
Hannaford 198 47.18 N 98.11 W
Hannah 198 48.58 N 98.41 W
Hannah Bay c 176 51.05 N 79.45 W
Hannastown 214 40.21 N 79.30 W
Hannibal, Mo., U.S. 219 39.42 N 91.21 W
Hannibal, N.Y., U.S. 210 43.19 N 76.34 W
Hanningfield Reservoir ⊜[1] 260 51.39 N 0.31 E
Hannō 94 35.51 N 139.19 E
Hannover 52 52.24 N 9.44 E
Hannover □[5] 52 52.30 N 9.15 E
Hannover, Flughafen ⊠ 52 52.27 N 9.42 E
Hannut 56 50.40 N 5.05 E
Hanö I 26 56.00 N 14.50 E
Hanobası 130 38.35 N 33.50 E
Hanöbukten c 26 55.45 N 14.30 E
Ha Noi 110 21.02 N 105.51 E
Hanönü 130 41.38 N 34.28 E
Hanoura 96 33.57 N 134.38 E
Hanover, On., Can. 212 44.09 N 81.02 W
Hanover → Hannover, Dtsch. 52 52.24 N 9.44 E
Hanover, S. Afr. 158 31.04 S 24.29 E
Hanover, Ct., U.S. 207 41.38 N 72.03 W
Hanover, Il., U.S. 190 42.15 N 90.16 W
Hanover, In., U.S. 218 38.42 N 85.28 W
Hanover, Ks., U.S. 198 39.53 N 96.52 W
Hanover, Ma., U.S. 207 42.06 N 70.48 W
Hanover, Mi., U.S. 216 42.06 N 84.33 W
Hanover, N.H., U.S. 188 43.42 N 72.17 W
Hanover, N.M., U.S. 200 32.48 N 108.05 W
Hanover, Oh., U.S. 214 40.04 N 82.15 W
Hanover, Pa., U.S. 208 39.48 N 76.59 W
Hanover, Va., U.S. 208 37.45 N 77.22 W
Hanover, Wi., U.S. 216 42.38 N 89.10 W
Hanover □[6] 208 37.42 N 77.20 W
Hanover, Isla I 254 51.00 S 74.40 W
Hanover Airport ⊠ 276 40.50 N 74.21 W
Hanover Center 283 42.07 N 70.50 W
Hanover Park 216 42.00 N 88.09 W
Hanover Road 158 30.58 S 24.33 E
Hanoverton 214 40.45 N 80.56 W
Hanovre → Hannover 52 52.24 N 9.44 E
Hanpan, Cape › 175e 5.01 S 154.37 E
Hanryeosudo Kukrip Kongwŏn ♠ 98 34.46 N 128.30 E
Hansanjiazi 104 41.44 N 122.57 E
Hansard 182 54.05 N 121.52 W
Hanscom Air Force Base ■ 207 42.28 N 71.17 W
Hans Creek ≃ 210 43.06 N 74.08 W
Hansdiha 124 24.36 N 87.05 E
Hansen Dam ◆[6] 280 34.16 N 118.23 W
Hansen Flood Control Basin ≍[1] 228 34.16 N 118.23 W
Hanshan 100 31.44 N 118.08 E
Hansharo ⊥ 94 35.02 N 138.56 E
Hansi, India 120 32.27 N 77.50 E
Hānsi, India 123 29.06 N 75.58 E
Hansia 272b 22.48 N 88.24 E
Hanska 198 44.08 N 94.29 W
Hānskhāli 126 23.21 N 88.37 E
Hans Lollik Island I 240m 18.24 N 64.55 W
Hanslope 42 52.06 N 0.49 W
Hans Meyer Range ⋏ 164 4.20 S 152.55 E
Hanson 207 42.04 N 70.52 W
Hanson ≃ 162 20.15 S 133.25 E
Hanson Lake ⊜ 184 54.42 N 102.49 W
Hanstedt 52 53.16 N 10.01 E
Hanstholm 26 57.07 N 8.38 E
Han-sur-Lesse 56 50.08 N 5.11 E
Han-sur-Nied 56 48.59 N 6.26 E
Hansville 224 47.55 N 122.33 W
Hansweert 52 51.26 N 4.00 E
Hantaj 88 49.31 N 103.13 E
Hāntālbunia 126 22.44 N 89.31 E
Hantamsberg ⋏ 158 31.22 S 19.45 E
Hantan → Handan 98 36.37 N 114.29 E
Hantes ≃ 50 50.19 N 4.11 E
Hant's Harbour 186 48.01 N 53.16 W
Hantsport 186 45.04 N 64.11 W
Hantu, Pulau I 271c 1.14 N 103.45 E
Hantu, Tanjong › 114 4.18 N 100.34 E
Hantzsch ≃ 176 67.32 N 72.25 W
Hanumangarh 123 29.35 N 74.19 E
Hanumān Nagar 124 26.30 N 86.51 E
Hanušovce nad Topl'ou 30 49.02 N 21.30 E
Hanušovice 30 50.05 N 16.55 E
Hanveden ⋏[2] 40 59.07 N 18.00 E
Hanwood 166 34.20 S 146.03 E
Hanworth ◆[8] 260 51.26 N 0.23 W
Hanxinzhuang 105 40.16 N 116.44 E
Hanyang 107 29.44 N 103.44 E
Hanyangping 102 32.41 N 108.34 E
Hanyin 102 32.42 N 108.50 E
Hanyū 94 36.10 N 139.32 E
Hanyuan 102 29.22 N 102.38 E
Hanyuangai 102 29.30 N 102.31 E
Hanzan 96 34.16 N 133.51 E
Hanzhong 102 33.08 N 107.02 E
Hanzhuang 98 34.38 N 117.24 E
Hao I[1] 14 18.15 S 140.54 W
Hao ≃ 100 28.27 N 119.56 E
Haohekou 100 28.38 N 112.49 E
Haojiadian 100 31.47 N 113.44 E
Haoli → Hegang 89 47.24 N 130.17 E
Haoluqi 106 30.38 N 119.34 E
HaOn 132 32.43 N 35.38 E
Hāora 126 22.35 N 88.20 E
Hāora Bridge ◆[5] 272b 22.35 N 88.21 E
Hāora Railroad Station ◆[5] 272b 22.35 N 88.21 E
Haouach, Ouadi V 146 16.45 N 19.35 E
Haoxue 102 30.00 N 112.20 E
Haozhikou 107 29.36 N 105.02 E
Haparanda 26 65.50 N 24.10 E
Hapatoni, Baie c 174x 9.58 S 139.07 W
Hapert 52 51.23 N 5.15 E
Hapeville 192 33.39 N 84.24 W
Happ'o-ri 98 40.40 N 127.49 E
Happy 196 34.45 N 101.52 W
Happy Camp 204 41.47 N 123.22 W
Happy Jack 200 34.45 N 111.11 W
Happy Valley-Goose Bay 176 53.20 N 60.25 W
Happy Valley Race Course ♠ 271d 22.16 N 114.10 E
Hapsford 262 53.16 N 2.48 W
Hapsu 98 41.13 N 128.51 E
Hapton 262 53.47 N 2.19 W
Hāpur 124 28.43 N 77.47 E
Ḥaql 128 29.18 N 34.57 E
Haquira 248 14.13 S 72.11 W
Har 164 5.20 S 133.10 E
Har, Laga ≃ 154 1.40 N 39.36 E
Hara, Nihon 94 35.58 N 138.14 E
Hara, Nihon 268 35.50 N 139.46 E
Ḥaraḍ, Ar. Su. 128 24.08 N 49.05 E
Hārad, Sve. 40 59.23 N 16.55 E
Ḥaraḍ, Yaman 144 16.28 N 43.04 E
Ḥarad, Jabal al- ʌ 132 29.40 N 35.49 E
Haradok 76 55.28 N 29.59 E
Haradzec, Bela. 76 53.33 N 30.02 E
Haradzec, Bela. 76 52.12 N 24.40 E
Haradzec, Bela. 76 52.58 N 30.21 E
Haradzeja 76 53.19 N 26.32 E
Haradzišča 76 53.19 N 26.00 E
Haraiki I[1] 14 17.28 S 143.27 W
Harajuku 268 35.54 N 139.21 E
Haraldsted 41 55.30 N 11.47 E
Haramachi 92 37.38 N 140.58 E
Haramachida 268 35.33 N 139.27 E
Haramosh ʌ 123 35.50 N 74.54 E
Haramosh Range ⋏ 123 35.40 N 75.22 E
Harany 76 55.25 N 29.02 E
Harappa 123 30.38 N 72.52 E
Harappa Road 123 30.36 N 72.55 E
Harar → Harer 144 9.18 N 42.08 E
Harare (Salisbury) 154 17.50 S 31.03 E
Ḥarash, Bi'r al- ⊤[4] 146 25.30 N 22.12 E
Ḥarastā al-Baṣal 132 33.34 N 36.22 E
Hārāt 272b 22.53 N 88.11 E
Haraz-Djombo 146 13.57 N 19.26 E
Haraze-Mangueigne 146 9.55 N 20.48 E
Harbāti 272b 22.55 N 88.33 E
Harbavičy 76 53.49 N 30.41 E
Harbert 216 41.52 N 86.38 W
Harbeson 208 38.43 N 75.17 W
Harbin 89 45.45 N 126.41 E
Harbiye 130 36.11 N 36.05 E
Harbke 54 52.12 N 11.03 E
Harbo 40 60.06 N 17.12 E
Harbonnières 50 49.51 N 2.40 E
Harboør 26 56.37 N 8.12 E
Harbor 202 42.03 N 124.15 W
Harbor Beach 190 43.50 N 82.39 W
Harbor City ◆[8] 280 33.48 N 118.17 W
Harborcreek 214 42.10 N 79.57 W
Harbord 170 33.47 S 151.17 E
Harbor Isle 276 40.36 N 73.40 W
Harbor Side 228 32.37 N 117.05 W
Harbor Springs 190 45.25 N 84.59 W
Harborton 208 37.39 N 75.49 W
Harbor Tunnel ◆[5] 284b 39.15 N 76.34 W
Harbor View 214 41.42 N 83.27 W
Harbour Breton 186 47.29 N 55.48 W
Harbour Buffett 186 47.31 N 54.05 W
Harbour Deep 186 50.22 N 56.31 W
Harbour Grace 186 47.42 N 53.13 W
Harbours, Bay of c 254 52.15 S 59.15 W
Harbourville 186 45.09 N 64.49 W
Harburg 56 48.47 N 10.41 E
Harburg ◆[8] 52 53.28 N 9.59 E
Hårby 41 55.13 N 10.07 E
Harchies 50 50.29 N 3.41 E
Harcourt, Austl. 169 37.00 S 144.15 E
Harcourt, Fr. 50 49.10 N 0.48 E
Harcuvar Mountains ⋏ 200 34.00 N 113.30 W
Hard 58 47.29 N 9.41 E
Harda 124 22.20 N 77.06 E
Hardangerfjorden c[2] 26 60.10 N 6.00 E
Hardangerjøkulen ⊓ 26 60.33 N 7.26 E
Hardangervidda ⋏[1] 26 60.20 N 7.30 E
Hardangervidda Nasjonalpark ♠ 26 60.15 N 7.05 E
Hardap □[4] 156 24.30 S 17.00 E
Hardapdam ⊜[1] 156 24.28 S 17.48 E
Hardee □[6] 220 27.29 N 81.48 W
Hardeeville 192 32.17 N 81.04 W
Hardegarijp 52 53.13 N 5.56 E
Hardegsen 52 51.39 N 9.49 E
Hardelot-Plage 50 50.38 N 1.35 E
Hardenberg 52 52.34 N 6.37 E


≃ River — Fluß — Río — Rivière — Rio
≍ Canal — Kanal — Canal — Canal — Canal
ʟ Waterfall, Rapids — Wasserfall, Stromschnellen — Cascada, Rápidos — Chute d'eau, Rapides — Cascata, Rápidos
ʊ Strait — Meeresstraße — Estrecho — Détroit — Estreito
c Bay, Gulf — Bucht, Golf — Bahía, Golfo — Baie, Golfe — Baía, Golfo
⊜ Lake, Lakes — See, Seen — Lago, Lagos — Lac, Lacs — Lago, Lagos
≡ Swamp — Sumpf — Pantano — Marais — Pântano
⊓ Ice Features, Glacier — Eis- und Gletscherformen — Accidentes Glaciales — Formes glaciaires — Acidentes glaciares
⊤ Other Hydrographic Features — Andere Hydrographische Objekte — Otros Elementos Hidrográficos — Autres données hydrographiques — Outros acidentes hidrográficos

✢ Submarine Features — Untermeerische Objekte — Accidentes Submarinos — Formes de relief sous-marin — Acidentes submarinos
□ Political Unit — Politische Einheit — Unidad Politica — Entité politique — Unidade política
ʋ Cultural Institution — Kulturelle Institution — Institución Cultural — Institution culturelle — Instituição cultural
⊥ Historical Site — Historische Stätte — Sitio Histórico — Site historique — Sitio histórico
♠ Recreational Site — Erholungs- und Ferienort — Sitio de Recreo — Centre de loisirs — Area de Lazer
⊠ Airport — Flughafen — Aeropuerto — Aéroport — Aeroporto
■ Military Installation — Militäranlage — Instalación Militar — Installation militaire — Instalação militar
◆ Miscellaneous — Verschiedenes — Misceláneo — Divers — Diversos

ENGLISH — Name, Page, Lat.°′, Long.°′
DEUTSCH — Name, Seite, Breite°′, Länge°′ E = Ost


| Name | Page | Lat. | Long. |
|---|---|---|---|
| Harderwijk | 52 | 52.21 N | 5.36 E |
| Hardesty | 196 | 36.36 N | 101.11 W |
| Hardey ≃ | 162 | 22.45 S | 116.07 E |
| Hardgrave, Mount ∧[2] | 171a | 27.30 S | 153.29 E |
| Hardheim | 56 | 49.36 N | 9.28 E |
| Hardin, Il., U.S. | 219 | 39.09 N | 90.37 W |
| Hardin, Mt., U.S. | 202 | 45.43 N | 107.36 W |
| Hardin, Tx., U.S. | 222 | 30.09 N | 94.44 W |
| Hardin □[6], Oh., U.S. | 216 | 40.39 N | 83.36 W |
| Hardin □[6], Tx., U.S. | 222 | 30.20 N | 94.35 W |
| Harding, S. Afr. | 158 | 30.34 S | 29.58 E |
| Harding, Il., U.S. | 216 | 41.31 N | 88.51 W |
| Harding, Ma., U.S. | 283 | 42.12 N | 71.27 W |
| Harding, Lake ⊜[1] | 192 | 32.40 N | 85.06 W |
| Harding Lake ⊜ | 184 | 56.13 N | 98.23 W |
| Harding Lakes | 208 | 39.27 N | 74.45 W |
| Hardinsburg, In., U.S. | 218 | 38.27 N | 86.16 W |
| Hardinsburg, Ky., U.S. | 194 | 37.46 N | 86.27 W |
| Hardisty | 182 | 52.40 N | 111.18 W |
| Hardisty Lake ⊜ | 176 | 64.30 N | 117.45 W |
| Hardoi | 124 | 27.25 N | 80.07 E |
| Hardoi Branch ≍ | 124 | 28.41 N | 80.08 E |
| Hardricourt | 261 | 49.01 N | 1.54 E |
| Hardscrabble Wash ∨ | 200 | 34.39 N | 109.28 W |
| Hardt | 263 | 51.07 N | 6.58 E |
| Hardtner | 198 | 37.00 N | 98.38 W |
| Hardwick, Ga., U.S. | 192 | 33.04 N | 83.13 W |
| Hardwick, Ma., U.S. | 207 | 42.21 N | 72.12 W |
| Hardwick, Vt., U.S. | 188 | 44.30 N | 72.22 W |
| Hardwood | 194 | 30.49 N | 91.23 W |
| Hardwood Ridge ∧ | 210 | 41.15 N | 75.23 W |
| Hardy, Ar., U.S. | 194 | 36.18 N | 91.28 W |
| Hardy, Ne., U.S. | 198 | 40.00 N | 97.55 W |
| Hardy, Península ≻[1] | 254 | 55.25 S | 68.30 W |
| Hardy Bay ⊂ | 176 | 75.02 N | 115.16 W |
| Hardy Creek ≃ | 214 | 42.52 N | 81.52 W |
| Hardy Lake ⊜[1] | 218 | 38.47 N | 85.42 W |
| Hardy Lake State Recreation Area ♦ | 218 | 38.44 N | 86.26 W |
| Hardys Pond ⊜ | 283 | 42.25 N | 71.15 W |
| Hare, Mount ∧ | 180 | 66.38 N | 136.12 W |
| Hare Bay | 186 | 48.51 N | 54.01 W |
| Hare Bay ⊂ | 186 | 51.18 N | 55.50 W |
| Harefield ⊕[8] | 260 | 51.36 N | 0.29 W |
| Hareid | 26 | 62.22 N | 6.02 E |
| Hare Indian ≃ | 180 | 66.18 N | 128.38 W |
| Harelbeke | 50 | 50.51 N | 3.18 E |
| Haren, Dtsch. | 52 | 52.47 N | 7.14 E |
| Haren, Ned. | 52 | 53.10 N | 6.35 E |
| Hareøen ı | 176 | 70.25 N | 54.50 W |
| Harer | 144 | 9.18 N | 42.08 E |
| Harerge □[4] | 144 | 8.00 N | 43.00 E |
| Hareskov | 41 | 55.46 N | 12.25 E |
| Hareto | 144 | 9.20 N | 37.06 E |
| Harewa | 144 | 9.55 N | 41.59 E |
| Harewood | 172 | 43.29 S | 172.35 E |
| Harewood Park | 284b | 39.23 N | 76.22 W |
| Harfaz | 130 | 38.01 N | 41.19 E |
| Harfleur | 50 | 49.30 N | 0.12 E |
| Harford, N.Y., U.S. | 210 | 42.26 N | 76.14 W |
| Harford, Pa., U.S. | 210 | 41.47 N | 75.42 W |
| Harford □[6] | 208 | 39.32 N | 76.21 W |
| Harford Heights | 279b | 40.22 N | 79.46 W |
| Harford Mills | 210 | 42.25 N | 76.12 W |
| Harg, Sve. | 40 | 59.49 N | 18.57 E |
| Harg, Sve. | 40 | 60.11 N | 18.24 E |
| Hargele | 144 | 5.20 N | 42.05 E |
| Hargeville | 261 | 48.53 N | 1.45 E |
| Hargeysa | 144 | 9.35 N | 44.04 E |
| Harghita □[6] | 38 | 46.35 N | 25.30 E |
| Harghita, Munții ⋀ | 38 | 46.15 N | 25.45 E |
| Hargrave ≃ | 184 | 54.24 N | 98.48 W |
| Hargrave Lake ⊜ | 184 | 54.29 N | 99.40 W |
| Hargshamn | 40 | 60.10 N | 18.28 E |
| Har Hu (Heihai) ⊜ | 102 | 38.15 N | 97.40 E |
| Hāriabhānga ≃[1] | 126 | 21.43 N | 89.05 E |
| Hariāna | 123 | 31.38 N | 75.51 E |
| Hariarapitu | 114 | 2.33 N | 98.35 E |
| Harīb | 144 | 14.57 N | 45.30 E |
| Haribes | 156 | 24.20 S | 17.40 E |
| Ḥaricha, Ḥamâda el ⊕[2] | 148 | 22.36 N | 3.31 W |
| Haridwār | 124 | 29.58 N | 78.10 E |
| Harigabessho | 270 | 34.37 N | 135.58 E |
| Harihar | 122 | 14.31 N | 75.48 E |
| Harihari | 172 | 43.09 S | 170.33 E |
| Hariharpāra | 126 | 24.02 N | 88.27 E |
| Harīke | 123 | 31.10 N | 74.57 E |
| Ḥārim | 130 | 36.12 N | 36.31 E |
| Ḥarim, Jabal al- ∧ | 128 | 25.58 N | 56.14 E |
| Harima | 96 | 34.42 N | 134.53 E |
| Harima-nada ⫧[2] | 96 | 34.29 N | 134.35 E |
| Harinagar | 124 | 27.09 N | 84.19 E |
| Harinākunda | 126 | 23.39 N | 89.03 E |
| Haringey ⊕[8] | 42 | 51.35 N | 0.07 W |
| Hāringhāta ≃[1] | 126 | 21.54 N | 89.57 E |
| Haringvliet ʮ | 52 | 51.47 N | 4.10 E |
| Haringvlietbrug ⊕[5] | 52 | 51.43 N | 4.20 E |
| Haringvlietdam ⊕[5] | 52 | 51.50 N | 4.03 E |
| Haripāl | 272b | 22.49 N | 88.07 E |
| Haripur, India | 126 | 24.18 N | 87.05 E |
| Haripur, India | 272b | 22.56 N | 88.14 E |
| Harīpur, Pāk. | 123 | 33.59 N | 72.56 E |
| Harirāmpur | 126 | 23.42 N | 89.57 E |
| Harīrūd (Tedžen) ≃ | 128 | 37.24 N | 60.38 E |
| Harischandra Range ⋀ | 122 | 19.15 N | 74.05 E |
| Ḥārithān | 130 | 36.16 N | 37.05 E |
| Hariyo | 144 | 5.00 N | 47.23 E |
| Harjavalta | 26 | 61.19 N | 22.08 E |
| Härjedalen □[9] | 26 | 62.20 N | 13.00 E |
| Harkaway | 274b | 38.00 S | 145.21 E |
| Härkeberga | 40 | 59.42 N | 17.11 E |
| Harkema-Opeinde | 52 | 53.11 N | 6.08 E |
| Harker Heights | 222 | 31.05 N | 97.40 W |
| Harkers Island | 192 | 34.41 N | 76.33 W |
| Harker Village | 285 | 39.51 N | 75.09 W |
| Harkness Memorial State Park ♦ | 207 | 41.18 N | 72.07 W |
| Harkortsee ⊜ | 263 | 51.24 N | 7.25 E |
| Harlan, In., U.S. | 216 | 41.11 N | 84.55 W |
| Harlan, Ia., U.S. | 198 | 41.39 N | 95.19 W |
| Harlan, Ky., U.S. | 192 | 36.50 N | 83.19 W |
| Harlan County Lake ⊜[1] | 198 | 40.04 N | 99.16 W |
| Hârlău | 38 | 47.25 N | 26.54 E |
| Harlech | 42 | 52.52 N | 4.07 W |
| Harlem, Fl., U.S. | 220 | 26.44 N | 80.57 W |
| Harlem, Ga., U.S. | 192 | 33.24 N | 82.18 W |
| Harlem, Mt., U.S. | 202 | 48.32 N | 108.47 W |
| Harlem ⊕[8] | 276 | 40.49 N | 73.56 W |
| Harlem River ʮ | 276 | 40.48 N | 73.54 W |
| Harlem Springs | 214 | 40.31 N | 81.02 W |
| Harlesden ⊕[8] | 260 | 51.32 N | 0.15 W |
| Harlesiel | 52 | 53.43 N | 7.49 E |
| Harleston | 42 | 52.24 N | 1.18 E |
| Harleton | 222 | 32.41 N | 94.35 W |
| Hårlev | 41 | 55.21 N | 12.15 E |
| Harleysville | 208 | 40.17 N | 75.23 W |
| Harlin | 171a | 26.59 S | 152.22 E |
| Harlingen, Ned. | 52 | 53.10 N | 5.24 E |
| Harlingen, Tx., U.S. | 196 | 26.11 N | 97.41 W |
| Harlinger Land ⊕[1] | 52 | 53.40 N | 7.30 E |
| Harlingerode | 54 | 51.54 N | 10.31 E |
| Harlington ⊕[8] | 260 | 51.29 N | 0.26 W |
| Harlösa | 41 | 55.43 N | 13.32 E |
| Harlow | 42 | 51.47 N | 0.08 E |
| Harlow □[8] | 260 | 51.44 N | 0.07 E |
| Harlowton | 202 | 46.26 N | 109.50 W |
| Harlpur | 272b | 22.42 N | 88.10 E |
| Harman | 188 | 38.55 N | 79.31 W |
| Harmancık | 130 | 39.41 N | 29.10 E |
| Harmånger | 26 | 61.56 N | 17.13 E |
| Harmanli, Blg. | 38 | 41.56 N | 25.54 E |
| Harmanlı, Tür. | 130 | 37.51 N | 37.45 E |
| Harmanschlag | 61 | 48.39 N | 14.47 E |
| Harmar Heights | 279b | 40.33 N | 79.49 W |
| Harmarville | 279b | 40.32 N | 79.51 W |
| Hármashatár-hegy ∧ | 264c | 47.33 N | 19.00 E |
| Harmelen | 52 | 52.05 N | 4.58 E |
| Harmil ı | 144 | 16.31 N | 40.09 E |
| Harmonsburg | 214 | 41.40 N | 80.19 W |
| Harmonville | 285 | 40.06 N | 75.17 W |
| Harmony, Ca., U.S. | 226 | 35.35 N | 121.01 W |
| Harmony, In., U.S. | 194 | 39.32 N | 87.06 W |
| Harmony, Mn., U.S. | 190 | 43.33 N | 92.00 W |
| Harmony, N.J., U.S. | 210 | 40.44 N | 75.08 W |
| Harmony, Pa., U.S. | 214 | 40.48 N | 80.07 W |
| Harmony, R.I., U.S. | 207 | 41.53 N | 71.35 W |
| Harmony Brook ≃ | 276 | 40.48 N | 74.34 W |
| Harmony Heights | 220 | 27.29 N | 80.21 W |
| Harmony Hills | 285 | 39.42 N | 75.41 W |
| Harmonyville | 285 | 40.11 N | 75.43 W |
| Harnai, India | 122 | 17.48 N | 73.06 E |
| Harnai, Pāk. | 120 | 30.06 N | 67.56 E |
| Harnäs | 40 | 60.39 N | 17.22 E |
| Harnātānr | 124 | 27.19 N | 84.01 E |
| Harndrup | 41 | 55.28 N | 10.02 E |
| Harnes | 50 | 50.27 N | 2.54 E |
| Härnevi | 40 | 59.44 N | 17.05 E |
| Harney ≃ | 220 | 25.25 N | 81.10 W |
| Harney, Lake ⊜ | 220 | 28.45 N | 81.03 W |
| Harney Basin ⌣[1] | 202 | 43.15 N | 119.00 W |
| Harney Lake ⊜ | 202 | 43.14 N | 119.07 W |
| Harney Peak ∧ | 198 | 43.51 N | 103.31 W |
| Harney Pond Canal ≍ | 220 | 27.00 N | 81.04 W |
| Härnösand | 26 | 62.38 N | 17.56 E |
| Haro, Esp. | 34 | 42.35 N | 2.51 W |
| Haro, Ityo. | 144 | 8.28 N | 38.37 E |
| Haro, Cabo ≻ | 232 | 27.52 N | 110.54 W |
| Ḥarod ≃ | 132 | 32.31 N | 35.33 E |
| Harola | 272a | 28.36 N | 77.19 E |
| Harold Hill ⊕[8] | 260 | 51.36 N | 0.13 E |
| Harold Parker State Forest ♦ | 283 | 42.37 N | 71.05 W |
| Haroldswick | 46a | 60.41 N | 0.50 W |
| Harold Wood ⊕[8] | 260 | 51.36 N | 0.14 E |
| Haro Strait ʮ | 224 | 48.30 N | 123.15 W |
| Haroué | 58 | 48.28 N | 6.11 E |
| Harpālpur | 124 | 25.17 N | 79.20 E |
| Harpanahalli | 122 | 14.48 N | 75.59 E |
| Harpen ⊕[8] | 263 | 51.29 N | 7.16 E |
| Harpenden | 42 | 51.49 N | 0.22 W |
| Harper, Liber. | 150 | 4.25 N | 7.43 W |
| Harper, Ks., U.S. | 198 | 37.17 N | 98.01 W |
| Harper, Tx., U.S. | 196 | 30.18 N | 99.15 W |
| Harper, Wa., U.S. | 224 | 47.31 N | 122.31 W |
| Harper, Mount ∧ | 180 | 64.14 N | 143.50 W |
| Harper Lake ⊜ | 228 | 35.02 N | 117.17 W |
| Harpers Ferry National Historical Park ♦ | 188 | 39.13 N | 77.45 W |
| Harpersfield | 210 | 42.26 N | 74.41 W |
| Harper Town | 44 | 54.55 N | 2.31 W |
| Harper Woods | 214 | 42.25 N | 82.55 W |
| Harpille ∧ | 62 | 43.50 N | 6.48 E |
| Harpstedt | 52 | 52.54 N | 8.35 E |
| Harpster | 214 | 40.44 N | 83.15 W |
| Harpsund ʋ | 40 | 59.06 N | 16.29 E |
| Harpurhey ⊕[8] | 262 | 53.31 N | 2.13 W |
| Harpur Hill | 262 | 53.14 N | 1.54 W |
| Harpursville | 210 | 42.11 N | 75.38 W |
| Harqin | 98 | 41.08 N | 119.38 E |
| Harqin Qi (Jinshan) | 98 | 41.56 N | 118.36 E |
| Harquahala Mountain ∧ | 200 | 33.49 N | 113.21 W |
| Ḥarrah | 144 | 14.57 N | 50.19 E |
| Ḥārrah, Jabal al- ∧ | 132 | 33.04 N | 35.59 E |
| Harrai | 124 | 22.37 N | 79.13 E |
| Harran | 130 | 36.51 N | 39.00 E |
| Ḥarrān al-ʿAwāmīd | 132 | 33.27 N | 36.34 E |
| Harray, Loch of ⊜ | 46 | 59.01 N | 3.13 W |
| Harrell | 194 | 33.30 N | 92.23 W |
| Harricana ≃ | 176 | 51.15 N | 79.45 W |
| Harrietfield | 46 | 56.25 N | 3.39 W |
| Harrietsham | 42 | 51.15 N | 0.41 E |
| Harriman, N.Y., U.S. | 210 | 41.18 N | 74.09 W |
| Harriman, Tn., U.S. | 192 | 35.56 N | 84.33 W |
| Harriman Reservoir ⊜[1] | 207 | 42.50 N | 72.53 W |
| Harriman State Park ♦ | 210 | 41.14 N | 74.09 W |
| Harrington, Eng., U.K. | 44 | 54.37 N | 3.34 W |
| Harrington, De., U.S. | 208 | 38.55 N | 75.34 W |
| Harrington, Me., U.S. | 188 | 44.37 N | 67.48 W |
| Harrington, Wa., U.S. | 202 | 47.28 N | 118.15 W |
| Harrington Creek ≃ | 282 | 37.19 N | 122.18 W |
| Harrington Drain ≍ | 281 | 42.36 N | 82.54 W |
| Harrington Park | 276 | 40.59 N | 73.58 W |
| Harris, Sk., Can. | 184 | 51.44 N | 107.35 W |
| Harris, Scot., U.K. | 46 | 56.59 N | 6.20 W |
| Harris, Mn., U.S. | 190 | 45.35 N | 92.58 W |
| Harris, N.Y., U.S. | 210 | 41.43 N | 74.44 W |
| Harris, R.I., U.S. | 207 | 41.43 N | 71.31 W |
| Harris □[6] | 222 | 29.50 N | 95.22 W |
| Harris ≃ | 168a | 33.18 S | 116.09 E |
| Harris ⊕[1] | 46 | 57.55 N | 6.50 W |
| Harris, Lake ⊜, Austl. | 162 | 31.08 S | 135.14 E |
| Harris, Lake ⊜, Fl., U.S. | 220 | 28.46 N | 81.49 W |
| Harris, Sound of ʮ | 46 | 57.45 N | 7.10 W |
| Harris Bay ⊂ | 212 | 45.23 N | 77.50 W |
| Harris Brook ≃ | 283 | 42.44 N | 71.13 W |
| Harrisburg, Ar., U.S. | 194 | 35.33 N | 90.43 W |
| Harrisburg, Il., U.S. | 194 | 37.44 N | 88.32 W |
| Harrisburg, In., U.S. | 218 | 39.41 N | 85.11 W |
| Harrisburg, Ne., U.S. | 198 | 41.33 N | 103.44 W |
| Harrisburg, Oh., U.S. | 214 | 40.53 N | 81.13 W |
| Harrisburg, Or., U.S. | 202 | 44.16 N | 123.10 W |
| Harrisburg, Pa., U.S. | 208 | 40.16 N | 76.53 W |
| Harrisburg International Airport ⊠ | 208 | 40.12 N | 76.45 W |
| Harris Creek ⊂ | 208 | 38.45 N | 76.18 W |
| Harris Creek ≃, Austl. | 274a | 33.57 S | 150.57 E |
| Harris Creek ≃, Tx., U.S. | 222 | 32.33 N | 95.08 W |
| Harrisfield | 274b | 37.57 S | 145.11 E |
| Harris Hill | 210 | 42.58 N | 78.40 W |
| Harrislee | 41 | 54.48 N | 9.22 E |
| Harrismith, Austl. | 162 | 32.56 S | 117.52 E |
| Harrismith, S. Afr. | 158 | 28.18 S | 29.03 E |
| Harrison, Ar., U.S. | 194 | 36.13 N | 93.06 W |
| Harrison, Id., U.S. | 202 | 47.27 N | 116.47 W |
| Harrison, Il., U.S. | 216 | 42.25 N | 89.11 W |
| Harrison, Mi., U.S. | 190 | 44.01 N | 84.47 W |
| Harrison, Ne., U.S. | 198 | 42.41 N | 103.53 W |
| Harrison, N.J., U.S. | 276 | 40.44 N | 74.09 W |
| Harrison, N.Y., U.S. | 210 | 40.58 N | 73.43 W |
| Harrison, Oh., U.S. | 218 | 39.15 N | 84.49 W |
| Harrison □[6], In., U.S. | 218 | 38.17 N | 86.07 W |
| Harrison □[6], Ky., U.S. | 218 | 38.25 N | 84.19 W |
| Harrison □[6], Oh., U.S. | 214 | 40.16 N | 81.05 W |
| Harrison □[6], Tx., U.S. | 222 | 32.35 N | 94.35 W |
| Harrison ≃ | 224 | 49.14 N | 121.57 W |
| Harrison, Cape ≻ | 176 | 54.55 N | 57.55 W |
| Harrison Bay ⊂ | 180 | 70.30 N | 151.30 W |
| Harrisonburg, La., U.S. | 194 | 31.46 N | 91.49 W |
| Harrisonburg, Va., U.S. | 188 | 38.26 N | 78.52 W |
| Harrison City | 279b | 40.21 N | 79.39 W |
| Harrison Hot Springs | 224 | 49.18 N | 121.47 W |
| Harrison Islands ıı | 176 | 69.13 N | 90.30 W |
| Harrison Lake ⊜ | 182 | 49.30 N | 121.50 W |
| Harrison Mills | 224 | 49.14 N | 121.57 W |
| Harrisons Brook ≃ | 276 | 40.38 N | 74.34 W |
| Harrison Tomb State Memorial ⊥ | 218 | 39.09 N | 84.46 W |
| Harrison Valley | 214 | 41.57 N | 77.39 W |
| Harrisonville, Md., U.S. | 284b | 39.23 N | 77.50 W |
| Harrisonville, Mo., U.S. | 194 | 38.39 N | 94.20 W |
| Harrisonville, N.J., U.S. | 285 | 39.41 N | 75.15 W |
| Harris Park | 274a | 33.49 S | 151.01 E |
| Harris Pond ⊜ | 283 | 42.45 N | 71.16 W |
| Harris Reservoir ⊜[1] | 222 | 29.14 N | 95.33 W |
| Harriston, On., Can. | 212 | 43.54 N | 80.53 W |
| Harriston, Ms., U.S. | 194 | 31.43 N | 91.01 W |
| Harristown | 219 | 39.51 N | 89.05 W |
| Harrisville, Austl. | 171a | 27.49 S | 152.40 E |
| Harrisville, Mi., U.S. | 190 | 44.39 N | 83.17 W |
| Harrisville, N.Y., U.S. | 212 | 44.09 N | 75.19 W |
| Harrisville, Oh., U.S. | 214 | 40.11 N | 80.53 W |
| Harrisville, Pa., U.S. | 214 | 41.08 N | 80.00 W |
| Harrisville, R.I., U.S. | 207 | 41.57 N | 71.40 W |
| Harrisville, W.V., U.S. | 188 | 39.12 N | 81.03 W |
| Harrod | 216 | 40.42 N | 83.55 W |
| Harrodsburg | 194 | 37.45 N | 84.50 W |
| Harrods Creek ≃ | 218 | 38.20 N | 85.38 W |
| Harrogate | 44 | 54.00 N | 1.33 W |
| Harrold | 196 | 34.05 N | 99.02 W |
| Harrop Lake ⊜ | 184 | 52.38 N | 95.58 W |
| Harrow | 214 | 42.02 N | 82.55 W |
| Harrow ⊕[8] | 42 | 51.35 N | 0.21 W |
| Harrow on the Hill ⊕[8] | 260 | 51.34 N | 0.20 W |
| Harrow School ʋ[2] | 260 | 51.34 N | 0.20 W |
| Harrowsmith | 212 | 44.24 N | 76.40 W |
| Harry S. Truman Airport ⊠ | 240m | 18.21 N | 64.59 W |
| Harry S. Truman Reservoir ⊜[1] | 194 | 38.10 N | 93.45 W |
| Har Sai Shan ∧ | 102 | 35.28 N | 97.55 E |
| Harsefeld | 52 | 53.27 N | 9.30 E |
| Harsens Island | 214 | 42.34 N | 82.34 W |
| Harsens Island ı | 281 | 42.35 N | 82.38 W |
| Harsewinkel | 52 | 51.58 N | 8.13 E |
| Harsīn | 128 | 34.16 N | 47.35 E |
| Harşit ≃ | 130 | 41.01 N | 38.52 E |
| Harskamp | 52 | 52.07 N | 5.45 E |
| Harsleben | 54 | 51.52 N | 11.05 E |
| Hârșova | 38 | 44.41 N | 27.57 E |
| Harstad | 24 | 68.46 N | 16.30 E |
| Harstena | 26 | 58.16 N | 17.01 E |
| Har Su | 89 | 48.09 N | 122.25 E |
| Harsūd | 124 | 22.06 N | 76.44 E |
| Harsum | 52 | 52.12 N | 9.57 E |
| Hart, Mi., U.S. | 190 | 43.41 N | 86.21 W |
| Hart, Tx., U.S. | 196 | 34.23 N | 102.07 W |
| Hart ≃ | 180 | 65.51 N | 136.22 W |
| Hart, Lake ⊜, Austl. | 166 | 31.08 S | 136.24 E |
| Hart, Lake ⊜, Fl., U.S. | 220 | 28.22 N | 81.13 W |
| Ḥartā | 132 | 32.42 N | 35.51 E |
| Hartbees ≃ | 158 | 28.45 S | 20.32 E |
| Hartbeesfontein | 158 | 26.42 S | 26.26 E |
| Hartbeespoort | 158 | 25.44 S | 27.52 E |
| Hartberg | 61 | 47.17 N | 15.59 E |
| Hartenholm | 52 | 53.54 N | 10.03 E |
| Hartenstein | 54 | 50.39 N | 12.40 E |
| Hart Fell ∧ | 44 | 55.25 N | 3.25 W |
| Hartfield | 208 | 37.34 N | 76.30 W |
| Hartford, Eng., U.K. | 262 | 53.15 N | 2.33 W |
| Hartford, Al., U.S. | 194 | 31.06 N | 85.41 W |
| Hartford, Ar., U.S. | 194 | 35.01 N | 94.22 W |
| Hartford, Ct., U.S. | 207 | 41.46 N | 72.41 W |
| Hartford, Il., U.S. | 219 | 38.50 N | 90.05 W |
| Hartford, In., U.S. | 218 | 38.59 N | 84.57 W |
| Hartford, Ks., U.S. | 198 | 38.18 N | 95.57 W |
| Hartford, Ky., U.S. | 194 | 37.27 N | 86.54 W |
| Hartford, Mi., U.S. | 216 | 42.12 N | 86.10 W |
| Hartford, N.J., U.S. | 285 | 39.58 N | 74.53 W |
| Hartford, N.Y., U.S. | 210 | 43.21 N | 73.22 W |
| Hartford, Oh., U.S. | 214 | 41.19 N | 80.34 W |
| Hartford, S.D., U.S. | 198 | 43.37 N | 96.56 W |
| Hartford, Wi., U.S. | 190 | 43.19 N | 88.22 W |
| Hartford □[6] | 207 | 41.46 N | 72.41 W |
| Hartford City | 216 | 40.27 N | 85.22 W |
| Hartha | 54 | 51.05 N | 12.58 E |
| Hartington | 198 | 42.37 N | 97.15 W |
| Hart Island ı | 276 | 40.51 N | 73.46 W |
| Hart Lake ⊜ | 202 | 42.24 N | 119.51 W |
| Hartland, N.B., Can. | 186 | 46.18 N | 67.32 W |
| Hartland, Eng., U.K. | 42 | 50.59 N | 4.29 W |
| Hartland, Il., U.S. | 216 | 42.22 N | 88.31 W |
| Hartland, Me., U.S. | 188 | 44.53 N | 69.26 W |
| Hartland, Mi., U.S. | 216 | 42.39 N | 83.45 W |
| Hartland, N.Y., U.S. | 210 | 43.14 N | 78.35 W |
| Hartland, Wi., U.S. | 216 | 43.06 N | 88.20 W |
| Hartland Point ≻ | 42 | 51.02 N | 4.31 W |
| Hartlepool | 44 | 54.42 N | 1.11 W |
| Hartleton | 210 | 40.54 N | 77.10 W |
| Hartley, Austl. | 170 | 33.33 S | 150.11 E |
| Hartley, Eng., U.K. | 260 | 51.23 N | 0.19 E |
| Hartley, Ia., U.S. | 198 | 43.10 N | 95.28 W |
| Hartley, Tx., U.S. | 196 | 35.53 N | 102.24 W |
| Hartley Bay | 182 | 53.25 N | 129.15 W |
| Hartlip | 260 | 51.21 N | 0.39 E |
| Hart Lot | 210 | 43.01 N | 76.28 W |
| Hartly | 208 | 39.10 N | 75.42 W |
| Hartmannsdorf | 54 | 50.53 N | 12.48 E |
| Hartmannshain | 56 | 50.28 N | 9.16 E |
| Hart-Miller Island ı | 208 | 39.15 N | 76.23 W |
| Hart Mountain ∧ | 184 | 52.29 N | 101.25 W |
| Hartney | 184 | 49.28 N | 100.30 W |
| Hartola | 26 | 61.35 N | 26.01 E |
| Harts ≃ | 158 | 28.24 S | 24.17 E |
| Hartsburg | 219 | 38.41 N | 92.18 W |
| Hartsdale | 210 | 41.01 N | 73.47 W |
| Hartselle | 194 | 34.26 N | 86.56 W |
| Härtsfeld ⊕[1] | 56 | 48.50 N | 10.15 E |
| Hartshill | 42 | 52.32 N | 1.32 W |
| Hartshorne | 196 | 34.50 N | 95.33 W |
| Harts Range | 162 | 23.00 S | 134.55 E |
| Hartstene Island ı | 224 | 47.14 N | 122.53 W |
| Hartstown | 214 | 41.33 N | 80.23 W |
| Hartsville, In., U.S. | 218 | 39.16 N | 85.41 W |
| Hartsville, Pa., U.S. | 285 | 40.14 N | 75.05 W |
| Hartsville, S.C., U.S. | 192 | 34.22 N | 80.04 W |
| Hartsville, Tn., U.S. | 194 | 36.23 N | 86.10 W |
| Hartswater | 158 | 27.34 S | 24.43 E |
| Hartville, Mo., U.S. | 194 | 37.15 N | 92.30 W |
| Hartville, Oh., U.S. | 214 | 40.57 N | 81.19 W |
| Hartwell | 192 | 34.21 N | 82.55 W |
| Hartwell Lake ⊜[1] | 192 | 34.30 N | 82.55 W |
| Hartwick | 210 | 42.39 N | 75.02 W |
| Hartwick Pines State Park ♦ | 190 | 44.47 N | 84.41 W |
| Hartz Mountains National Park ♦ | 166 | 43.15 S | 146.50 E |
| Harue | 94 | 36.08 N | 136.14 E |
| Haruki | 270 | 34.29 N | 135.23 E |
| Haruku, Pulau ı | 164 | 3.34 S | 128.29 E |
| Hārūn | 140 | 11.20 N | 25.43 E |
| Haruna | 94 | 36.23 N | 138.53 E |
| Hārūnābād | 123 | 29.37 N | 73.08 E |
| Haruna-san ∧ | 94 | 36.28 N | 138.52 E |
| Haruniye | 130 | 37.17 N | 36.27 E |
| Haruno, Nihon | 94 | 34.57 N | 137.53 E |
| Haruno, Nihon | 96 | 33.30 N | 133.30 E |
| Harūr | 122 | 12.04 N | 78.30 E |
| Hārūt ≃ | 128 | 31.35 N | 61.18 E |
| Harvard, Il., U.S. | 216 | 42.25 N | 88.36 W |
| Harvard, Ma., U.S. | 207 | 42.30 N | 71.35 W |
| Harvard, Ne., U.S. | 198 | 40.37 N | 98.05 W |
| Harvard University ʋ[2] | 283 | 42.22 N | 71.07 W |
| Harvel, Eng., U.K. | 260 | 51.21 N | 0.22 E |
| Harvel, Il., U.S. | 219 | 39.21 N | 89.32 W |
| Harvest, Mount ∧[2] | 162 | 25.54 S | 126.28 E |
| Harvey, Austl. | 168a | 33.05 S | 115.54 E |
| Harvey, N.B., Can. | 186 | 45.43 N | 64.43 W |
| Harvey, Il., U.S. | 216 | 41.36 N | 87.38 W |
| Harvey, N.D., U.S. | 198 | 47.46 N | 99.56 W |
| Harvey ≃ | 168a | 32.46 S | 115.43 E |
| Harvey Estuary ⊂[1] | 168a | 32.43 S | 115.42 E |
| Harvey Mountain ∧ | 207 | 42.18 N | 73.25 W |
| Harvey Reservoir ⊜[1] | 168a | 33.05 S | 115.58 E |
| Harveysburg | 218 | 39.30 N | 84.00 W |
| Harveys Lake | 210 | 41.23 N | 76.02 W |
| Harwell | 42 | 51.37 N | 1.18 W |
| Harwich, Eng., U.K. | 42 | 51.57 N | 1.17 E |
| Harwich, Ma., U.S. | 207 | 41.41 N | 70.04 W |
| Harwich Port | 207 | 41.40 N | 70.04 W |
| Harwick | 279b | 40.34 N | 79.48 W |
| Harwinton | 207 | 41.46 N | 73.03 W |
| Harwood, Eng., U.K. | 262 | 53.35 N | 2.23 W |
| Harwood, Tx., U.S. | 222 | 29.40 N | 97.30 W |
| Harwood Heights | 278 | 41.58 N | 87.48 W |
| Harwood Mines | 210 | 40.57 N | 76.01 W |
| Harwood Park | 284b | 39.12 N | 76.44 W |
| Haryāna □[3] | 120 | 29.20 N | 76.20 E |
| Haryn' (Horyn') ≃ | 78 | 52.08 N | 27.17 E |
| Harz ⋀ | 54 | 51.45 N | 10.30 E |
| Harzgerode | 54 | 51.38 N | 11.08 E |
| Ḥaṣā, Biʾr al- ⫧[4] | 140 | 22.58 N | 35.40 E |
| Ḥasā, Wādī al- ∨ | 132 | 31.05 N | 35.27 E |
| Hasafen | 86 | 45.14 N | 90.20 E |
| Ḥaṣāh, Wādī al- ∨ | 132 | 30.38 N | 37.09 E |
| Hasaki | 94 | 35.44 N | 140.50 E |
| Hasalbag | 120 | 37.54 N | 76.44 E |
| Ḥasanābād | 267d | 35.44 N | 51.19 E |
| Ḥasanābād-e Khāleṣeh | 267d | 35.37 N | 51.12 E |
| Hasan Abdāl | 123 | 33.49 N | 72.41 E |
| Hasançelebi | 130 | 38.58 N | 37.54 E |
| Hasan Dağı ∧ | 130 | 38.08 N | 34.12 E |
| Hasankale → Pasinler | 130 | 39.59 N | 41.41 E |
| Hasankeyf | 130 | 37.43 N | 41.25 E |
| Ḥasan Kīādeh | 128 | 37.24 N | 49.58 E |
| Hasanpur | 124 | 28.43 N | 78.17 E |
| Hasayaz | 130 | 40.15 N | 33.20 E |
| Ḥāṣbānī, Nahr al- ≃ | 132 | 33.11 N | 35.37 E |
| Ḥāṣbayyā | 132 | 33.24 N | 35.41 E |
| Hasbek | 130 | 39.33 N | 35.33 E |
| Hasbergen, Dtsch. | 52 | 52.14 N | 7.57 E |
| Hasbergen, Dtsch. | 52 | 53.05 N | 8.40 E |
| Hasbrouck Heights | 276 | 40.51 N | 74.04 W |
| Hascosay ı | 46a | 60.37 N | 0.59 W |
| Hasdo ≃ | 120 | 21.44 N | 82.44 E |
| Hasdo-Rāmpur Basin ⌣[1] | 124 | 22.50 N | 82.35 E |
| Hase, Nihon | 94 | 35.47 N | 138.06 E |
| Hase, Nihon | 270 | 34.32 N | 135.54 E |
| Hase ≃, Dtsch. | 52 | 52.41 N | 7.18 E |
| Hase ≃, Nihon | 270 | 34.34 N | 135.38 E |
| Hasel ≃ | 54 | 50.32 N | 10.27 E |
| Häselgehr | 58 | 47.19 N | 10.30 E |
| Haselhorst ⊕[8] | 264a | 52.33 N | 13.15 E |
| Haselünne | 52 | 52.40 N | 7.29 E |
| Hasenkamp | 252 | 31.31 S | 59.51 W |
| Ḥashāʾ, Jabal al- ∧ | 144 | 13.45 N | 44.30 E |
| HaShefela ⊕[1] | 132 | 31.40 N | 34.55 E |
| Hashima | 94 | 35.19 N | 136.42 E |
| Hashimoto, Nihon | 96 | 34.19 N | 135.37 E |
| Hashimoto, Nihon | 270 | 34.26 N | 135.23 E |
| Hashira-jima ı | 96 | 34.01 N | 132.25 E |
| Hashiri-jima ı | 96 | 34.21 N | 133.27 E |
| Hashitai | 89 | 49.24 N | 125.18 E |
| Hasht Sāl ⊕[8] | 272a | 28.38 N | 77.03 E |
| Hasil, Pulau ı | 164 | 1.06 S | 128.24 E |
| Hāsilpur | 123 | 29.43 N | 72.33 E |
| Ḥāsīn-e Bozorg | 84 | 39.23 N | 44.42 E |
| Haskayne | 262 | 53.34 N | 2.58 W |
| Haskeir Islands ıı | 46 | 57.42 N | 7.41 W |
| Haskell, Ok., U.S. | 196 | 35.49 N | 95.40 W |
| Haskell, Tx., U.S. | 196 | 33.09 N | 99.44 W |
| Haskell Pond ⊜ | 283 | 42.37 N | 70.44 W |
| Hasketh Bank | 262 | 53.43 N | 2.51 W |
| Haskins | 216 | 41.27 N | 83.42 W |
| Haskovo | 38 | 41.56 N | 25.33 E |
| Haskovo □[4], Blg. | 38 | 42.02 N | 25.50 E |
| Haskovo □[4], Blg. | 130 | 41.50 N | 25.50 E |
| Hasköy, Tür. | 130 | 40.59 N | 42.52 E |
| Hasköy, Tür. | 130 | 41.38 N | 26.41 E |
| Hasköy ⊕[8] | 267b | 41.02 N | 28.58 E |
| Haslach im Kinzigtal | 58 | 48.16 N | 8.06 E |
| Hasle, Dan. | 41 | 55.10 N | 10.10 E |
| Hasle, Schw. | 58 | 47.01 N | 7.39 E |
| Haslemere | 42 | 51.06 N | 0.43 W |
| Haslett | 216 | 42.44 N | 84.24 W |
| Haslev | 41 | 55.20 N | 11.58 E |
| Haslingden | 44 | 53.43 N | 2.18 W |
| Haslingden Grane | 262 | 53.42 N | 2.21 W |
| Haslington | 44 | 53.06 N | 2.24 W |
| Haslital ∨ | 58 | 46.42 N | 8.10 E |
| Haslum | 26 | 59.50 N | 10.22 E |
| Hasmark | 41 | 55.33 N | 10.28 E |
| Ḥasmat ʿUmar, Biʾr ⫧[4] | 140 | 21.46 N | 34.00 E |
| Hāsnābād | 126 | 22.35 N | 88.55 E |
| Hasnācha | 272b | 22.26 N | 88.09 E |
| Haspe ⊕[8] | 263 | 51.21 N | 7.26 E |
| Hasperos Canyon ∨ | 200 | 33.50 N | 105.02 W |
| Hasper-Stausee ⊜[1] | 263 | 51.18 N | 7.25 E |
| Haspra | 78 | 44.27 N | 34.07 E |
| Haspres | 50 | 50.15 N | 3.25 E |
| Ḥaṣṣ, Jabal al- ⋀[2] | 130 | 35.52 N | 37.22 E |
| Hassa | 130 | 36.50 N | 36.29 E |
| Hassan | 122 | 13.00 N | 76.05 E |
| Hassard | 219 | 39.39 N | 91.40 W |
| Hassayampa ≃ | 200 | 33.20 N | 112.43 W |
| Hassberge ⋀[2] | 56 | 50.12 N | 10.29 E |
| Hassbergen | 52 | 52.44 N | 9.13 E |
| Hassel, Dtsch. | 52 | 52.48 N | 9.11 E |
| Hassel, Dtsch. | 263 | 51.39 N | 7.30 E |
| Hassel ⊕[8] | 263 | 51.36 N | 7.03 E |
| Hasselbeck-Schwarzbach | 263 | 51.16 N | 6.53 E |
| Hasselfelde | 54 | 51.41 N | 10.51 E |
| Hasselfors | 40 | 59.05 N | 14.39 E |
| Hassels ⊕[8] | 263 | 51.10 N | 6.53 E |
| Hasselt, Bel. | 56 | 50.56 N | 5.20 E |
| Hasselt, Ned. | 52 | 52.35 N | 6.05 E |
| Hassfurt | 56 | 50.02 N | 10.31 E |
| Hassi Bel Guebbour | 148 | 28.46 N | 6.27 E |
| Hassi el Ghella | 34 | 35.28 N | 1.03 W |
| Hassi Mameche | 34 | 35.52 N | 0.04 E |
| Hassi Messaoud | 148 | 31.43 N | 5.59 E |
| Hassi Zehana | 34 | 35.01 N | 0.53 W |
| Hassleben | 54 | 53.13 N | 13.41 E |
| Hässleholm | 41 | 56.09 N | 13.46 E |
| Hasslinghausen | 56 | 51.20 N | 7.17 E |
| Hassloch | 56 | 49.22 N | 8.16 E |
| Hasson Heights | 214 | 41.26 N | 79.41 W |
| Hästbo | 40 | 60.27 N | 16.27 E |
| Hasten ⊕[8], Dtsch. | 263 | 51.12 N | 7.09 E |
| Hästen ⊕[8], Dtsch. | 263 | 51.09 N | 7.06 E |
| Hastière-Lavaux | 56 | 50.13 N | 4.50 E |
| Hastings, Austl. | 169 | 38.18 S | 145.11 E |
| Hastings, Barb. | 241g | 13.04 N | 59.35 W |
| Hastings, On., Can. | 212 | 44.18 N | 77.57 W |
| Hastings, N.Z. | 172 | 39.38 S | 176.51 E |
| Hastings, Eng., U.K. | 42 | 50.51 N | 0.36 E |
| Hastings, Fl., U.S. | 192 | 29.43 N | 81.30 W |
| Hastings, Il., U.S. | 278 | 41.41 N | 87.58 W |
| Hastings, Mi., U.S. | 216 | 42.39 N | 85.17 W |
| Hastings, Mn., U.S. | 190 | 44.44 N | 92.51 W |
| Hastings, Ne., U.S. | 198 | 40.35 N | 98.23 W |
| Hastings, N.Y., U.S. | 210 | 43.22 N | 76.09 W |
| Hastings, Pa., U.S. | 214 | 40.39 N | 78.42 W |
| Hastings □[6] | 212 | 44.45 N | 77.40 W |
| Hastings Battlesite ⊥ | 42 | 50.53 N | 0.31 E |
| Hastings-on-Hudson | 276 | 40.59 N | 73.52 W |
| Hastingwood | 260 | 51.45 N | 0.09 E |
| Hastrup | 41 | 55.26 N | 12.11 E |
| Hasty | 198 | 38.06 N | 102.57 W |
| Hasuda | 94 | 35.59 N | 139.40 E |
| Hasumi | 96 | 34.52 N | 132.37 E |
| Haswell | 198 | 38.27 N | 103.09 W |
| Hata | 94 | 36.11 N | 137.51 E |
| Hatʾae-do ı | 98 | 34.32 N | 126.03 E |
| Ha Tan | 110 | 18.30 N | 105.20 E |
| Hatanagi-dam ⊕[6] | 94 | 35.18 N | 138.12 E |
| Hatashō | 94 | 35.10 N | 136.15 E |
| Hatay (Antioch) | 130 | 36.14 N | 36.07 E |
| Hatay □[4] | 130 | 36.30 N | 36.15 E |
| Hatboro | 208 | 40.10 N | 75.06 W |
| Hatch, N.M., U.S. | 200 | 32.39 N | 107.09 W |
| Hatch, Ut,. U.S. | 200 | 37.38 N | 112.26 W |
| Hat Chao Mai National Park ♦ | 110 | 7.40 N | 99.35 E |
| Hatches Creek | 162 | 20.56 S | 135.12 E |
| Hatchet Creek ≃ | 194 | 32.52 N | 86.20 W |
| Hatchet Lake | 186 | 44.35 N | 63.40 W |
| Hatchie ≃ | 194 | 35.35 N | 89.53 W |
| Hatchineha, Lake ⊜ | 220 | 28.02 N | 81.25 W |
| Hatchlands ⊥ | 260 | 51.15 N | 0.28 W |
| Hatchmere | 262 | 53.15 N | 2.40 W |
| Hatchville | 207 | 41.37 N | 70.33 W |
| Hatch Wash ∨ | 200 | 38.32 N | 109.36 W |
| Hat Creek ≃, U.S. | 198 | 43.16 N | 103.36 W |
| Hat Creek ≃, Ca., U.S. | 204 | 40.59 N | 121.33 W |
| Haţeg | 38 | 45.37 N | 22.57 E |
| Hateruma-shima ı | 175d | 24.03 N | 123.47 E |
| Hatfield, Austl. | 166 | 33.52 S | 143.45 E |
| Hatfield, Eng., U.K. | 42 | 51.46 N | 0.13 W |
| Hatfield, Eng., U.K. | 44 | 53.34 N | 1.00 W |
| Hatfield, Ar., U.S. | 194 | 34.29 N | 94.22 W |
| Hatfield, Ma., U.S. | 207 | 42.22 N | 72.35 W |
| Hatfield Aerodrome ⊠ | 260 | 51.46 N | 0.16 W |
| Hatfield House ⊥ | 260 | 51.46 N | 0.13 W |
| Hatfield Peverel | 42 | 51.47 N | 0.35 E |
| Hatfield Swamp ≡ | 276 | 40.50 N | 74.20 W |
| Hathāla | 123 | 32.03 N | 70.34 E |
| Hathaway Pines | 226 | 38.07 N | 120.28 W |
| Hatherleigh | 42 | 50.49 N | 4.04 W |
| Hathersage | 44 | 53.19 N | 1.38 W |
| Hāthras | 124 | 27.36 N | 78.03 E |
| Hātia ʮ | 124 | 22.30 N | 91.15 E |
| Ḥāṭibah, Raʾs ≻ | 144 | 21.55 N | 38.58 E |
| Ha Tien | 110 | 10.23 N | 104.29 E |
| Hatillo | 240m | 18.29 N | 66.49 W |
| Ha Tinh | 110 | 18.20 N | 105.54 E |
| Hatinoe → Hachinohe | 92 | 40.30 N | 141.29 E |
| Hatiozi → Hachiōji | 94 | 35.39 N | 139.20 E |
| Hatip | 130 | 37.46 N | 32.25 E |
| Hātisāla | 272b | 22.33 N | 88.32 E |
| Hato, Bocht van ⊂ | 241s | 12.13 N | 68.58 W |
| Hatogaya | 94 | 35.50 N | 139.44 E |
| Hato Mayor [del Rey] | 238 | 18.46 N | 69.15 W |
| Hato Rey | 240m | 18.25 N | 66.03 W |
| Hatounja | 76 | 53.17 N | 30.32 E |
| Hatoyama | 94 | 35.59 N | 139.20 E |
| Hāt Pīplia | 124 | 22.46 N | 76.18 E |
| Hatsukaichi | 96 | 34.21 N | 132.20 E |
| Hatsu-shima ı | 94 | 35.02 N | 139.10 E |
| Hatsutomi | 268 | 35.46 N | 140.01 E |
| Hatta | 124 | 24.07 N | 79.36 E |
| Hattab, Oued el ∨ | 36 | 35.23 N | 9.32 E |
| Hattah-Kulkyne National Park ♦ | 166 | 34.40 S | 142.30 E |
| Hattem | 52 | 52.28 N | 6.04 E |
| Hatten, Dtsch. | 52 | 53.02 N | 8.22 E |
| Hatten, Fr. | 56 | 48.54 N | 7.59 E |
| Hattenhofen | 60 | 48.13 N | 11.07 E |
| Hatteras | 192 | 35.13 N | 75.41 W |
| Hatteras, Cape ≻ | 192 | 35.13 N | 75.32 W |
| Hatteras Island ı | 192 | 35.25 N | 75.30 W |
| Hattiesburg | 194 | 31.19 N | 89.17 W |
| Hatting | 41 | 55.51 N | 9.46 E |
| Hattingen | 56 | 51.23 N | 7.10 E |
| Hattingspruit | 158 | 28.09 S | 30.11 E |
| Hatton, Eng., U.K. | 262 | 53.20 N | 2.36 W |
| Hatton, Scot., U.K. | 46 | 57.25 N | 1.54 W |
| Hatton, Al., U.S. | 194 | 34.33 N | 87.24 W |
| Hatton, N.D., U.S. | 198 | 47.38 N | 97.27 W |
| Hatton ⊕[8] | 260 | 51.28 N | 0.25 W |
| Hatton Fields | 226 | 36.33 N | 121.54 W |
| Hattorf [am Harz] | 52 | 51.39 N | 10.14 E |
| Hattori, Nihon | 270 | 34.46 N | 135.27 E |
| Hattori, Nihon | 270 | 34.52 N | 135.36 E |
| Hattstatt | 58 | 48.01 N | 7.17 E |
| Hattstedt | 41 | 54.31 N | 9.01 E |
| Hatunsaray | 130 | 37.35 N | 32.21 E |
| Hatvan | 30 | 47.40 N | 19.41 E |
| Hat Yai | 110 | 7.01 N | 100.28 E |
| Hatyničy | 76 | 52.38 N | 26.18 E |
| Hatzfeld | 56 | 51.00 N | 8.33 E |
| Hatzfeld ⊕[8] | 263 | 51.17 N | 7.11 E |
| Hatzic | 224 | 49.09 N | 122.15 W |
| Hatzic Lake ⊜ | 224 | 49.10 N | 122.14 W |
| Haubstadt | 194 | 38.12 N | 87.34 W |
| Hāudullāpur | 272b | 22.25 N | 88.33 E |
| Hauge | 26 | 58.18 N | 6.15 E |
| Haugesund | 26 | 59.25 N | 5.18 E |
| Haugh of Urr | 44 | 54.58 N | 3.52 W |
| Haughton Green | 262 | 53.27 N | 2.06 W |
| Haugsdorf | 61 | 48.42 N | 16.05 E |
| Hau Hoi Wan ⊂ | 100 | 22.28 N | 113.56 E |
| Hauhungaroa Range ⋀ | 172 | 38.50 S | 175.34 E |
| Hauja ≃ | 76 | 53.49 N | 25.35 E |
| Haukeligrend | 26 | 59.45 N | 7.31 E |
| Haukipudas | 26 | 65.11 N | 25.21 E |
| Haukivesi ⊜ | 26 | 62.06 N | 28.28 E |
| Haukivuori | 26 | 62.01 N | 27.13 E |
| Hauldres, Ru des ≃ | 261 | 48.37 N | 2.28 E |
| Haulerwijk | 52 | 53.04 N | 6.20 E |
| Haultain ≃ | 184 | 55.51 N | 106.46 W |
| Haune ≃ | 56 | 50.52 N | 9.43 E |
| Haunersdorf | 60 | 48.36 N | 12.43 E |
| Haunstetten | 58 | 48.18 N | 10.54 E |
| Haunts Creek ʮ | 276 | 40.37 N | 73.31 W |
| Hauppauge | 210 | 40.49 N | 73.12 W |
| Hauptsrus | 158 | 26.33 S | 26.18 E |
| Hauraki Gulf ⊂ | 172 | 36.20 S | 175.05 E |
| Hauroko, Lake ⊜ | 172 | 46.00 S | 167.20 E |
| Hauru, Pointe ≻ | 174s | 17.29 S | 149.55 W |
| Haus | 64 | 47.25 N | 13.49 E |
| Hausa | 273a | 6.37 N | 3.21 E |
| Hausach | 58 | 48.17 N | 8.10 E |
| Hausham | 64 | 47.45 N | 11.50 E |
| Hausruck ⋀ | 60 | 48.07 N | 13.35 E |
| Haussee ⊜ | 264a | 52.38 N | 13.41 E |
| Haussömmern | 54 | 51.11 N | 10.49 E |
| Haut, Isle au ı | 188 | 44.03 N | 68.38 W |
| Haut Atlas ⋀ | 148 | 31.30 N | 6.00 W |
| Haut-Bout | 261 | 48.32 N | 1.55 E |
| Haute Colme, Canal de la ≍ | 50 | 50.50 N | 2.12 E |
| Hautecombe, Abbaye de ʋ[1] | 62 | 45.45 N | 5.50 E |
| Haute-Corse □[5] | 36 | 42.30 N | 9.00 E |
| Haute-Garonne □[5] | 32 | 43.25 N | 1.30 E |
| Haute-Kotto □[5] | 152 | 7.00 N | 23.00 E |
| Haute-Loire □[5] | 32 | 45.05 N | 3.50 E |
| Hauteluce | 62 | 45.45 N | 6.35 E |
| Haute-Marne □[5] | 58 | 48.05 N | 5.10 E |
| Hauterive | 186 | 49.12 N | 68.16 W |
| Hauterives | 62 | 45.15 N | 5.02 E |
| Hautes-Alpes □[5] | 62 | 44.40 N | 6.30 E |
| Haute-Sangha □[5] | 152 | 4.30 N | 16.00 E |
| Haute-Saône □[5] | 58 | 47.40 N | 6.10 E |
| Haute-Savoie □[5] | 32 | 46.00 N | 6.20 E |
| Haute Seine, Canal de la ≍ | 50 | 48.34 N | 3.43 E |
| Hautes Fagnes ⋀ | 56 | 50.30 N | 6.05 E |
| Hautes-Pyrénées □[5] | 32 | 43.00 N | 0.10 E |
| Haute Sûre, Lac de la ⊜[1] | 56 | 49.52 N | 5.52 E |
| Haute-Vienne □[5] | 32 | 45.50 N | 1.15 E |
| Hauteville-Lompnes | 58 | 45.58 N | 5.36 E |
| Haute Volta → Burkina Faso □[1] | 150 | 13.00 N | 1.30 W |
| Haut-Folin ∧ | 32 | 47.00 N | 4.02 E |
| Haut-Kœnigsbourg, Château du ⊥ | 58 | 48.14 N | 7.22 E |
| Haut-Mbomou □[5] | 140 | 6.00 N | 26.00 E |
| Hautmont | 50 | 50.15 N | 3.56 E |
| Haut-Ogooué □[4] | 152 | 1.00 S | 13.50 E |
| Haut-Rhin □[5] | 58 | 47.53 N | 7.13 E |
| Hauts-de-Seine □[5] | 261 | 48.50 N | 2.11 E |
| Hautvillers | 50 | 49.05 N | 3.57 E |
| Haut-Zaïre □[4] | 154 | 2.20 N | 27.00 E |
| Hauula | 229c | 21.36 N | 157.54 W |
| Hauzenberg | 60 | 48.39 N | 13.38 E |
| Hauz Rāni ⊕[8] | 272a | 28.32 N | 77.13 E |
| Havana → La Habana, Cuba | 240p | 23.08 N | 82.22 W |
| Havana, Ar., U.S. | 194 | 35.06 N | 93.31 W |
| Havana, Fl., U.S. | 192 | 30.37 N | 84.24 W |
| Havana, Il., U.S. | 194 | 40.18 N | 90.03 W |
| Havana, N.D., U.S. | 198 | 45.57 N | 97.37 W |
| Havane, La → La Habana | 240p | 23.08 N | 82.22 W |
| Havannah, Canal de la ʮ | 175f | 22.22 S | 167.01 E |
| Havant | 42 | 50.51 N | 0.59 W |
| Havasu, Lake ⊜[1] | 200 | 34.30 N | 114.20 W |
| Havasu Creek ≃ | 200 | 36.19 N | 112.46 W |
| Havasupai Indian Reservation ⊕[4] | 200 | 36.13 N | 112.40 W |
| Havdrup | 41 | 55.32 N | 12.08 E |
| Havel ≃ | 54 | 52.53 N | 11.58 E |
| Havelange | 56 | 50.23 N | 5.14 E |
| Havelberg | 54 | 52.50 N | 12.04 E |
| Havelberg ∧[2] | 264a | 52.28 N | 13.12 E |
| Haveli | 123 | 30.27 N | 73.42 E |
| Haveliān | 123 | 34.03 N | 73.10 E |
| Havel-Kanal ≍ | 264a | 52.36 N | 13.12 E |
| Havelland ⊕[1] | 54 | 52.25 N | 12.45 E |
| Havelländischer Grosser Hauptkanal ≍ | 264a | 52.37 N | 13.03 E |
| Havelländisches Luch ≡ | 54 | 52.40 N | 12.40 E |
| Havelock, On., Can. | 212 | 44.26 N | 77.53 W |
| Havelock, N.Z. | 172 | 41.17 S | 173.46 E |
| Havelock, N.C., U.S. | 192 | 34.52 N | 76.54 W |
| Havelock Island ı | 110 | 11.58 N | 93.00 E |
| Havelock North | 172 | 39.40 S | 176.53 E |
| Haven | 198 | 37.53 N | 97.46 W |
| Haverford | 285 | 40.00 N | 75.17 W |
| Haverford College ʋ[2] | 285 | 40.00 N | 75.18 W |
| Haverfordwest | 42 | 51.49 N | 4.58 W |
| Haverhill, Eng., U.K. | 42 | 52.05 N | 0.26 E |
| Haverhill, Ma., U.S. | 207 | 42.46 N | 71.04 W |
| Haverhill Airport ⊠ | 283 | 42.48 N | 71.04 W |
| Haverhill-Riverside Airport ⊠ | 283 | 42.46 N | 71.02 W |
| Hāveri | 122 | 14.48 N | 75.24 E |
| Haverigg | 44 | 54.11 N | 3.17 W |
| Havering ⊕[8] | 42 | 51.34 N | 0.14 E |
| Havering-atte-Bower ⊕[8] | 260 | 51.37 N | 0.11 E |
| Havering's Grove | 260 | 51.38 N | 0.23 E |
| Havern ⊜ | 26 | 62.17 N | 15.07 E |
| Haverö | 26 | 62.24 N | 15.05 E |
| Haverstraw | 210 | 41.11 N | 73.57 W |
| Havertown | 208 | 39.58 N | 75.18 W |
| Haviland, Ks., U.S. | 198 | 37.37 N | 99.06 W |
| Haviland, Oh., U.S. | 216 | 41.01 N | 84.35 W |
| Haviland Brook ≃ | 276 | 41.07 N | 73.33 W |
| Ḥavīq | 128 | 38.10 N | 48.54 E |
| Havířov | 30 | 49.47 N | 18.27 E |
| Havixbeck | 52 | 51.58 N | 7.25 E |
| Hävla | 40 | 58.55 N | 15.52 E |
| Havlíčkův Brod | 30 | 49.36 N | 15.35 E |
| Havnbjerg | 41 | 55.02 N | 9.48 E |
| Havnsø | 41 | 55.45 N | 11.20 E |
| Havran | 130 | 39.33 N | 27.06 E |
| Havré, Bel. | 50 | 50.28 N | 4.02 E |
| Havre → Le Havre, Fr. | 50 | 49.30 N | 0.08 E |
| Havre, Mt., U.S. | 202 | 48.32 N | 109.40 W |
| Havre-Aubert | 186 | 47.14 N | 61.51 W |
| Havre Aubert, Île du ı | 186 | 47.14 N | 61.57 W |
| Havre aux Maisons, Île du ı | 186 | 47.25 N | 61.47 W |
| Havre de Grace | 208 | 39.32 N | 76.05 W |
| Havre de Grace Heights | 208 | 39.35 N | 76.07 W |
| Havre North | 202 | 48.36 N | 109.41 W |
| Havre-Saint-Pierre | 186 | 50.14 N | 63.36 W |
| Havsa | 130 | 41.33 N | 26.49 E |
| Havza | 130 | 40.58 N | 35.41 E |
| Haw ≃ | 192 | 35.36 N | 79.03 W |
| Hawaii □[3] | 229d | 20.00 N | 157.45 W |
| Hawaii ı | 229d | 19.30 N | 155.30 W |
| Hawaiian Gardens | 280 | 33.49 N | 118.04 W |
| Hawaiian Islands ıı | 229d | 20.30 N | 157.30 W |
| Hawaiian Ridge ✢[3] | 14 | 24.00 N | 165.00 W |
| Hawaii Volcanoes National Park ♦ | 229d | 19.23 N | 155.17 W |
| Hawal ≃ | 146 | 10.00 N | 12.05 E |
| Hawarden, Sk., Can. | 184 | 51.23 N | 106.36 W |
| Hawarden, N.Z. | 172 | 42.56 S | 172.38 E |
| Hawarden, Wales, U.K. | 44 | 53.11 N | 3.02 W |
| Hawarden, Ia., U.S. | 198 | 42.59 N | 96.29 W |
| Ḥawashīyah, Wādī ∨ | 140 | 28.31 N | 32.58 E |
| Haw Creek ≃ | 218 | 39.11 N | 85.55 W |
| Hawea, Lake ⊜ | 172 | 44.30 S | 169.17 E |
| Hawera | 172 | 39.35 S | 174.17 E |
| Hawes | 44 | 54.18 N | 2.12 W |
| Hawesville | 194 | 37.54 N | 86.45 W |
| Haweswater Reservoir ⊜ | 44 | 54.32 N | 2.48 W |
| Ḥawf, Jabal ⋀[2] | 273c | 29.55 N | 31.21 E |
| Ḥawf, Wādī ∨ | 142 | 29.53 N | 31.18 E |
| Hawi | 229d | 20.14 N | 155.50 W |
| Hawick | 44 | 55.25 N | 2.47 W |
| Hawk Creek ≃ | 198 | 44.44 N | 95.25 W |
| Hawkdun Range ⋀ | 172 | 44.46 S | 170.00 E |
| Hawke, Cape ≻ | 166 | 32.13 S | 152.34 E |
| Hawke Bay ⊂ | 172 | 39.20 S | 177.30 E |
| Hawker | 166 | 31.53 S | 138.25 E |
| Hawkes, Mount ∧ | 9 | 83.56 S | 55.45 W |
| Hawkes Brook ≃ | 283 | 42.45 N | 71.08 W |
| Hawkesbury | 206 | 45.36 N | 74.37 W |
| Hawkesbury ≃ | 170 | 33.30 S | 151.10 E |
| Hawkesbury Island ı | 182 | 53.38 N | 129.00 W |
| Hawkes Pond ⊜ | 283 | 42.30 N | 71.02 W |
| Hawkeye | 190 | 42.56 N | 91.57 W |
| Hawkhurst | 42 | 51.02 N | 0.30 E |
| Hawking | 42 | 51.06 N | 1.10 E |
| Hawkins, Tx., U.S. | 222 | 32.35 N | 95.12 W |
| Hawkins, Wi., U.S. | 190 | 45.30 N | 90.43 W |
| Hawkins, Lake ⊜[1] | 222 | 32.38 N | 95.15 W |
| Hawkins Island ı | 180 | 60.30 N | 146.00 W |
| Hawkinsville | 192 | 32.17 N | 83.28 W |
| Hawk Junction | 190 | 48.05 N | 84.34 W |
| Hawk Lake | 184 | 49.48 N | 93.59 W |
| Haw Knob ∧ | 192 | 35.19 N | 84.02 W |
| Hawk Point | 219 | 38.58 N | 91.07 W |
| Hawk Run | 214 | 40.55 N | 78.12 W |
| Hawksbill ∧ | 188 | 38.33 N | 78.23 W |
| Hawksbill Creek ⊂ | 192 | 26.32 N | 78.43 W |
| Hawks Nest Point ≻ | 238 | 24.09 N | 75.32 W |
| Hawkwell | 260 | 51.36 N | 0.40 E |
| Hawkwood | 166 | 25.47 S | 150.50 E |
| Hawley, Eng., U.K. | 260 | 51.25 N | 0.14 E |
| Hawley, Mn., U.S. | 198 | 46.52 N | 96.18 W |
| Hawley, Pa., U.S. | 210 | 41.28 N | 75.10 W |
| Hawleyton | 210 | 42.01 N | 75.55 W |
| Hawleyville | 207 | 41.25 N | 73.21 W |
| Haworth, Eng., U.K. | 44 | 53.49 N | 1.57 W |
| Haworth, N.J., U.S. | 276 | 40.57 N | 73.59 W |
| Haw Par Villa ʋ | 271c | 1.16 N | 103.47 E |
| Hawr | 142 | 27.52 N | 30.44 E |
| Ḥawrān, Wādī ∨ | 128 | 33.58 N | 42.34 E |
| Ḥawsh ʿĪsā | 142 | 30.55 N | 30.17 E |
| Hawthorn, Austl. | 274b | 37.49 S | 145.02 E |
| Hawthorn, Pa., U.S. | 214 | 41.01 N | 79.17 W |
| Hawthorne, Ca., U.S. | 228 | 33.54 N | 118.21 W |
| Hawthorne, Fl., U.S. | 192 | 29.35 N | 82.05 W |
| Hawthorne, Nv., U.S. | 204 | 38.31 N | 118.37 W |
| Hawthorne, N.J., U.S. | 210 | 40.56 N | 74.09 W |
| Hawthorne, N.Y., U.S. | 210 | 41.06 N | 73.47 W |
| Hawthorne Lake ⊜ | 276 | 41.03 N | 74.35 W |
| Hawthorne Municipal Airport ⊠ | 280 | 33.55 N | 118.20 W |
| Hawthorne Race Course ♦ | 278 | 41.50 N | 87.45 W |
| Hawthorn Woods | 278 | 42.13 N | 88.03 W |
| Ḥawwārah | 132 | 32.32 N | 35.54 E |
| Ḥawwārat ʿAdlān | 142 | 29.12 N | 30.58 E |
| Ḥawwārat al-Maqṭaʿ | 142 | 29.15 N | 30.54 E |
| Hawza | 148 | 27.06 N | 10.55 W |
| Hawzen | 144 | 13.56 N | 39.28 E |
| Haxby | 44 | 54.01 N | 1.04 W |


**Symbols** in the index entries represent the broad categories identified in the key at the right. Symbols with superior numbers (⋀[1]) identify subcategories (see complete key on page *I · 1).*

**Symbole** im Register stellen die rechts im Schlüssel erklärten Kategorien dar. Symbole mit hochgestellten Ziffern (⋀[1]) bezeichnen Unterabteilungen einer Kategorie (vgl. vollständiger Schlüssel auf Seite *I · 1).*

**Los símbolos** incluídos en el texto del índice representan las grandes categorías identificadas con la clave a la derecha. Los símbolos con numeros en su parte superior (⋀[1]) identifican las subcategorías (véase la clave completa en la página *I · 1).*

**Les symboles** de l'index représentent les catégories indiquées dans la légende à droite. Les symboles suivis d'un indice (⋀[1]) représentent des sous-catégories (voir légende complète à la page *I · 1).*

**Os símbolos** incluídos no texto do índice representam as grandes categorias identificadas com a chave à direita. Os símbolos com números em sua parte superior (⋀[1]) identificam as subcategorias (veja-se a chave completa à página *I · 1).*

| | | | | |
|---|---|---|---|---|
| ∧ Mountain | Berg | Montaña | Montagne | Montanha |
| ⋀ Mountains | Gebirge | Montañas | Montagnes | Montanhas |
| )( Pass | Paß | Paso | Col | Passo |
| ∨ Valley, Canyon | Tal, Cañon | Valle, Cañón | Vallée, Canyon | Vale, Canhão |
| ⌣ Plain | Ebene | Llano | Plaine | Planície |
| ≻ Cape | Kap | Cabo | Cap | Cabo |
| ı Island | Insel | Isla | Île | Ilha |
| ıı Islands | Inseln | Islas | Îles | Ilhas |
| ⊥ Other Topographic Features | Andere Topographische Objekte | Otros Elementos Topográficos | Autres données topographiques | Outros acidentes topográficos |

## ESPAÑOL

| Nombre | Página | Lat.°′ | Long.°′ W = Oeste |
|---|---|---|---|
| Haxey | 44 | 53.29 N | 0.50 W |
| Haxtun | 198 | 40.38 N | 102.37 W |
| Hay | 166 | 34.30 S | 144.51 E |
| Hay ≃, Austl. | 166 | 25.14 S | 138.00 E |
| Hay ≃, Can. | 176 | 60.52 N | 115.44 W |
| Hay ≃, Wi., U.S. | 190 | 44.59 N | 91.51 W |
| Hay, Cape ≻ | 176 | 74.25 N | 113.00 W |
| Hay, Mount ∧, Austl. | 162 | 23.28 S | 133.05 E |
| Hay, Mount ∧, Austl. | 170 | 33.37 S | 150.26 E |
| Hay, Mount ∧, N.A. | 180 | 59.15 N | 137.37 W |
| Hay, South Fork ≃ | 190 | 45.03 N | 91.57 W |
| Haya | 164 | 3.27 S | 129.33 E |
| Haya ≃, Nihon | 94 | 35.14 N | 139.09 E |
| Haya ≃, Nihon | 94 | 35.25 N | 138.27 E |
| Hayachine-san ∧ | 92 | 39.34 N | 141.29 E |
| Hayakawa | 94 | 35.25 N | 138.22 E |
| Hayama, Nihon | 94 | 35.16 N | 139.35 E |
| Hayama, Nihon | 96 | 33.26 N | 133.13 E |
| Hayang | 98 | 35.55 N | 128.47 E |
| Hayange | 56 | 49.20 N | 6.03 E |
| Hayashima | 96 | 34.36 N | 133.50 E |
| Hayastan → Armenia □[1] | 22 | 40.00 N | 45.00 E |
| Hayasui-seto ʯ | 96 | 33.18 N | 131.59 E |
| Haybān | 140 | 11.13 N | 30.31 E |
| Haybān, Jabal ∧ | 140 | 11.15 N | 30.31 E |
| Hay Bay C | 212 | 44.10 N | 76.55 W |
| Haybes | 56 | 50.00 N | 4.43 E |
| Haychur ≃ | 78 | 47.57 N | 36.11 E |
| Haydān, Wādī al- V | 132 | 31.27 N | 35.36 E |
| Haydarlı | 130 | 38.16 N | 30.23 E |
| Hayden, Az., U.S. | 200 | 33.00 N | 110.47 W |
| Hayden, Co., U.S. | 200 | 40.29 N | 107.15 W |
| Hayden, In., U.S. | 218 | 38.58 N | 85.44 W |
| Hayden Peak ∧ | 202 | 42.59 N | 116.39 W |
| Haydenville, Ma., U.S. | 207 | 42.22 N | 72.42 W |
| Haydenville, Oh., U.S. | 188 | 39.28 N | 82.19 W |
| Haydock | 44 | 53.28 N | 2.39 W |
| Haydock Park Race Course ♦ | 262 | 53.29 N | 2.37 W |
| Haydon Bridge | 44 | 54.58 N | 2.14 W |
| Haye, La → 's-Gravenhage | 52 | 52.06 N | 4.18 E |
| Hayes | 194 | 30.06 N | 92.55 W |
| Hayes ◆[8], Eng., U.K. | 260 | 51.31 N | 0.25 W |
| Hayes ◆[8], Eng., U.K. | 260 | 51.23 N | 0.01 E |
| Hayes ≃, Mb., Can. | 184 | 57.03 N | 92.09 W |
| Hayes ≃, N.T., Can. | 176 | 67.18 N | 95.02 W |
| Hayes, Mount ∧ | 180 | 63.37 N | 146.43 W |
| Hayes Center | 198 | 40.30 N | 101.01 W |
| Hayes State Memorial ⊥ | 214 | 41.21 N | 83.08 W |
| Hayesville, N.C., U.S. | 192 | 35.02 N | 83.49 W |
| Hayesville, Oh., U.S. | 214 | 40.46 N | 82.15 W |
| Hayesville, Or., U.S. | 224 | 44.59 N | 122.58 W |
| Hayfield, Eng., U.K. | 262 | 53.23 N | 1.57 W |
| Hayfield, Mn., U.S. | 190 | 43.53 N | 92.50 W |
| Hayford Peak ∧ | 204 | 36.40 N | 115.11 W |
| Hayfork | 204 | 40.33 N | 123.10 W |
| Hayfork Bally ∧ | 204 | 40.39 N | 123.13 W |
| Hayfork Creek ≃ | 204 | 40.37 N | 123.26 W |
| Hayingen | 58 | 48.17 N | 9.29 E |
| Hay Island I | 212 | 44.53 N | 80.58 W |
| Hayk, Lake ⊜ | 144 | 11.21 N | 39.43 E |
| Haykota | 144 | 15.10 N | 37.03 E |
| Hay Lake ⊜ | 212 | 45.23 N | 78.11 W |
| Hay Lakes | 182 | 53.13 N | 113.03 W |
| Hayle | 42 | 50.11 N | 5.23 W |
| Haymakers Run ≃ | 279b | 40.25 N | 79.43 W |
| Haymana | 130 | 39.27 N | 32.30 E |
| Haynes | 194 | 34.53 N | 90.47 W |
| Haynes Creek ≃ | 285 | 39.53 N | 74.50 W |
| Haynesville, La., U.S. | 194 | 32.57 N | 93.08 W |
| Haynesville, Va., U.S. | 208 | 37.57 N | 76.40 W |
| Hayneville | 194 | 32.11 N | 86.34 W |
| Haynin | 144 | 15.50 N | 48.19 E |
| Hay-on-Wye | 42 | 52.04 N | 3.07 W |
| Hay Point ≻ | 166 | 21.17 S | 149.18 E |
| Hayrabolu | 130 | 41.12 N | 27.06 E |
| Hay River | 176 | 60.51 N | 115.40 W |
| Hays, Ab., Can. | 182 | 50.06 N | 111.48 W |
| Hays, Ks., U.S. | 198 | 38.52 N | 99.19 W |
| Hays, Mt., U.S. | 202 | 47.59 N | 108.41 W |
| Hays □[6] | 222 | 30.02 N | 97.45 W |
| Hays ◆[8] | 279b | 40.23 N | 79.56 W |
| Hayshah, Sabkhat al- ≡ | 146 | 31.45 N | 15.20 E |
| Hays Mill Creek ≃ | 285 | 39.44 N | 74.50 W |
| Hay Springs | 198 | 42.41 N | 102.41 W |
| Haystack Mountain ∧ | 204 | 41.39 N | 115.38 W |
| Haysville, Ks., U.S. | 198 | 37.33 N | 97.21 W |
| Haysville, Pa., U.S. | 279b | 40.32 N | 80.09 W |
| Haysyn | 78 | 48.48 N | 29.24 E |
| Hayti, Mo., U.S. | 194 | 36.14 N | 89.44 W |
| Hayti, Pa., U.S. | 208 | 39.59 N | 75.51 W |
| Hayti, S.D., U.S. | 198 | 44.39 N | 97.12 W |
| Hayvoron | 78 | 48.22 N | 29.52 E |
| Hayward, Ca., U.S. | 226 | 37.40 N | 122.04 W |
| Hayward, Wi., U.S. | 190 | 46.00 N | 91.29 W |
| Hayward Brook ≃ | 283 | 42.22 N | 71.20 W |
| Hayward Municipal Airport ⊠ | 282 | 37.40 N | 122.08 W |
| Haywards Heath | 42 | 51.00 N | 0.06 W |
| Haywood | 184 | 49.40 N | 98.12 W |
| Ḥayy, Jabal al- ∧ | 142 | 29.43 N | 31.35 E |
| HaẒafon □[5] | 132 | 32.50 N | 35.20 E |
| Hazār, Kūh-e ∧ | 128 | 29.30 N | 57.18 E |
| Hazard | 192 | 37.14 N | 83.11 W |
| Hazardville | 207 | 41.59 N | 72.32 W |
| Hazar Gölü ⊜ | 130 | 38.30 N | 39.25 E |
| Hazārībāg | 124 | 23.59 N | 85.21 E |
| Hazārībāg Plateau ⋀[1] | 124 | 24.00 N | 85.10 E |
| Haze, Cape ≻ | 220 | 26.46 N | 82.10 W |
| Hazebrouck | 50 | 50.43 N | 2.32 E |
| Hazel ≃ | 188 | 38.33 N | 77.51 W |
| Hazelbrook | 170 | 33.44 S | 150.27 E |
| Hazel Crest | 278 | 41.34 N | 87.41 W |
| Hazel Dell | 224 | 45.40 N | 122.39 W |
| Hazel Green | 190 | 42.31 N | 90.26 W |
| Hazelgrove, Austl. | 170 | 33.40 S | 149.52 E |
| Hazel Grove, Eng., U.K. | 44 | 53.23 N | 2.08 W |
| Hazel Hurst | 214 | 41.42 N | 78.35 W |
| Hazel Kirk | 279b | 40.11 N | 79.57 W |
| Hazel Park | 216 | 42.27 N | 83.06 W |
| Hazel Park Raceway ♦ | 281 | 42.29 N | 83.05 W |
| Hazelton, B.C., Can. | 182 | 55.15 N | 127.40 W |
| Hazelton, Id., U.S. | 202 | 42.35 N | 114.08 W |
| Hazelton, N.D., U.S. | 198 | 46.29 N | 100.16 W |
| Hazelton Mountains ⋀ | 182 | 54.30 N | 128.20 W |
| Hazelton Peak ∧ | 202 | 44.06 N | 107.03 W |
| Hazelwood, Mo., U.S. | 219 | 38.46 N | 90.22 W |
| Hazelwood, N.C., U.S. | 192 | 35.28 N | 83.00 W |
| Hazelwood ◆[8] | 279b | 40.25 N | 79.56 W |
| Hazen, Ar., U.S. | 194 | 34.46 N | 91.34 W |
| Hazen, Nv., U.S. | 226 | 39.33 N | 119.02 W |
| Hazen, N.D., U.S. | 198 | 47.17 N | 101.37 W |
| Hazen, Pa., U.S. | 214 | 41.12 N | 78.58 W |
| Hazen Bay C | 180 | 61.00 N | 165.10 W |
| Ḥazerim | 132 | 31.14 N | 34.43 E |
| Hazlehurst, Ga., U.S. | 192 | 31.52 N | 82.35 W |
| Hazlehurst, Ms., U.S. | 194 | 31.51 N | 90.23 W |
| Hazlet, Sk., Can. | 184 | 50.25 N | 108.36 W |
| Hazlet, N.J., U.S. | 208 | 40.26 N | 74.13 W |
| Hazleton, Ia., U.S. | 190 | 42.37 N | 91.54 W |
| Hazleton, Pa., U.S. | 210 | 40.57 N | 75.58 W |
| Hazlett, Lake ⊜ | 162 | 21.30 S | 128.48 E |
| Ḥazor HaGelilit | 132 | 32.59 N | 35.33 E |
| Hazro, Pāk. | 123 | 33.54 N | 72.29 E |
| Hazro, Tür. | 130 | 38.15 N | 40.47 E |
| Hazu | 94 | 34.47 N | 137.08 E |
| He ≃, Zhg. | 100 | 27.05 N | 114.59 E |
| He ≃, Zhg. | 102 | 23.26 N | 111.30 E |

## FRANÇAIS

| Nom | Page | Lat.°′ | Long.°′ W = Ouest |
|---|---|---|---|
| Heacham | 42 | 52.55 N | 0.30 E |
| Head ≃ | 212 | 44.44 N | 79.15 W |
| Head Bay d'Espoir | 186 | 47.56 N | 55.45 W |
| Headcorn | 42 | 51.11 N | 0.37 E |
| Headford | 48 | 53.28 N | 9.05 W |
| Head Lake ⊜ | 212 | 44.45 N | 78.55 W |
| Headland | 194 | 31.21 N | 85.20 W |
| Headlands | 154 | 18.14 S | 32.03 E |
| Headley, Eng., U.K. | 42 | 51.07 N | 0.50 W |
| Headley, Eng., U.K. | 260 | 51.17 N | 0.16 W |
| Headley, Mount ∧ | 202 | 47.44 N | 115.15 W |
| Head of the Harbor | 276 | 40.54 N | 73.10 W |
| Heald Green | 262 | 53.22 N | 2.14 W |
| Heald Moor ◆[3] | 262 | 53.44 N | 2.10 W |
| Healdsburg | 204 | 38.36 N | 122.52 W |
| Healdton | 196 | 34.13 N | 97.29 W |
| Healesville | 169 | 37.40 S | 145.31 E |
| Healing | 44 | 53.34 N | 0.10 W |
| Healy, Ak., U.S. | 180 | 63.52 N | 148.58 W |
| Healy, Ks., U.S. | 198 | 38.36 N | 100.37 W |
| Healy, Mount ∧ | 180 | 63.46 N | 149.01 W |
| Healy Lake ⊜ | 212 | 45.10 N | 79.55 W |
| Heani, Mont ∧ | 174x | 9.47 S | 139.04 W |
| Heanna | 174m | 26.19 N | 127.54 E |
| Heanor | 44 | 53.01 N | 1.22 W |
| Heany Junction | 154 | 20.06 S | 28.54 E |
| Heard Island I | 6 | 53.06 S | 73.30 E |
| Heard Pond ⊜ | 283 | 42.21 N | 71.22 W |
| Hearne | 222 | 30.52 N | 96.35 W |
| Hearst | 176 | 49.41 N | 83.40 W |
| Hearst Island I | 9 | 69.25 S | 62.10 W |
| Hearst San Simeon State Historical Park ♦ | 226 | 35.42 N | 121.10 W |
| Heart ≃, Ab., Can. | 182 | 56.14 N | 117.17 W |
| Heart ≃, N.D., U.S. | 198 | 46.47 N | 100.51 W |
| Heart Lake ⊜, Ab., Can. | 182 | 55.02 N | 111.30 W |
| Heart Lake ⊜, On., Can. | 275b | 43.44 N | 79.48 W |
| Heart Lake Indian Reserve ◆[4] | 182 | 55.02 N | 111.30 W |
| Heart Pond ⊜ | 283 | 42.34 N | 71.23 W |
| Heart's Content | 186 | 47.53 N | 53.22 W |
| Heath, Ma., U.S. | 207 | 42.40 N | 72.49 W |
| Heath, Oh., U.S. | 214 | 40.02 N | 82.28 W |
| Heath, Tx., U.S. | 222 | 32.50 N | 96.29 W |
| Heath ≃ | 248 | 12.31 S | 68.38 W |
| Heath, Pointe ≻ | 186 | 49.05 N | 61.42 W |
| Heathcote, Austl. | 169 | 36.55 S | 144.42 E |
| Heathcote, Austl. | 274a | 34.05 S | 151.01 E |
| Heathcote Brook ≃ | 276 | 40.23 N | 74.37 W |
| Heath End | 42 | 51.22 N | 1.09 W |
| Heatherton | 274b | 37.58 S | 145.06 E |
| Heathfield | 42 | 50.59 N | 0.17 E |
| Heathmont | 274b | 37.49 S | 145.15 E |
| Heath Springs | 192 | 34.35 N | 80.40 W |
| Heathsville | 208 | 37.55 N | 76.28 W |
| Heatley | 262 | 53.24 N | 2.27 W |
| Heaton Hall ⊥ | 262 | 53.32 N | 2.15 W |
| Heaton Moor | 262 | 53.25 N | 2.11 W |
| Heaven, Temple of ⊍[1] | 271a | 39.53 N | 116.25 E |
| Heavener | 194 | 34.53 N | 94.36 W |
| Heaverham | 260 | 51.18 N | 0.15 E |
| Heaviley | 262 | 53.24 N | 2.09 W |
| Hebaochang | 107 | 29.33 N | 105.32 E |
| Hebao Dao I | 100 | 21.52 N | 113.09 E |
| Hebbronville | 196 | 27.18 N | 98.40 W |
| Hebburn | 44 | 54.59 N | 1.30 W |
| Hebbville | 284b | 39.20 N | 77.46 W |
| Hebden Bridge | 44 | 53.45 N | 2.00 W |
| Hebden Water ≃ | 262 | 53.44 N | 2.00 W |
| Hebei, Zhg. | 104 | 40.43 N | 122.12 E |
| Hebei, Zhg. | 104 | 41.01 N | 123.51 E |
| Hebei (Hopeh) □[4] | 98 | 38.00 N | 116.00 E |
| Hebeitun | 105 | 39.35 N | 117.07 E |
| Hebel | 166 | 28.59 S | 147.48 E |
| Heber, Az., U.S. | 200 | 34.25 N | 110.35 W |
| Heber, Ca., U.S. | 204 | 32.44 N | 115.32 W |
| Heber City | 200 | 40.30 N | 111.24 W |
| Heber Springs | 194 | 35.29 N | 92.01 W |
| Hebertsfelden | 60 | 48.24 N | 12.49 E |
| Hebgen Lake ⊜[1] | 202 | 44.47 N | 111.14 W |
| Hebi | 98 | 35.59 N | 114.11 E |
| Hebian | 107 | 30.29 N | 105.08 E |
| Hebo, Or., U.S. | 224 | 45.13 N | 123.51 W |
| Hebo, Zhg. | 102 | 31.29 N | 98.58 E |
| Hebo, Mount ∧ | 224 | 45.12 N | 123.45 W |
| Hébridas, Islas → Hebrides II | 46 | 57.00 N | 6.30 W |
| Hebrides II | 22 | 57.00 N | 6.30 W |
| Hebrides, Sea of the ⊤[2] | 46 | 57.07 N | 6.55 W |
| Hebron, Nf., Can. | 176 | 58.12 N | 62.38 W |
| Hebron, Ct., U.S. | 207 | 41.39 N | 72.21 W |
| Hebron, Il., U.S. | 216 | 42.28 N | 88.25 W |
| Hebron, In., U.S. | 216 | 41.19 N | 87.12 W |
| Hebron, Ky., U.S. | 218 | 39.03 N | 84.42 W |
| Hebron, Md., U.S. | 208 | 38.25 N | 75.41 W |
| Hebron, Ne., U.S. | 198 | 40.09 N | 97.35 W |
| Hebron, N.D., U.S. | 198 | 46.54 N | 102.02 W |
| Hebron, Pa., U.S. | 208 | 40.21 N | 76.24 W |
| Hebron, Tx., U.S. | 222 | 33.01 N | 96.52 W |
| Hebron, Wi., U.S. | 216 | 42.56 N | 88.42 W |
| Hebron → Al-Khalīl, W.B. | 132 | 31.32 N | 35.06 E |
| Hebu | 100 | 27.50 N | 115.22 E |
| Hebutu | 104 | 42.19 N | 122.20 E |
| Heby | 40 | 59.56 N | 16.53 E |
| Hecao | 105 | 40.21 N | 116.47 E |
| Hecate Strait ʯ | 182 | 53.00 N | 131.00 W |
| Hecelchakán | 232 | 20.10 N | 90.08 W |
| Heceta Island I | 180 | 55.45 N | 133.35 W |
| Hechi | 102 | 24.42 N | 108.02 E |
| Hechiceros | 196 | 28.33 N | 103.38 W |
| Hechingen | 58 | 48.21 N | 8.58 E |
| Hechtel | 56 | 51.08 N | 5.21 E |
| Hechthausen | 52 | 53.38 N | 9.14 E |
| Hechuan | 107 | 30.00 N | 106.16 E |
| Heckelberg | 54 | 52.44 N | 13.50 E |
| Hecker | 219 | 38.18 N | 90.00 W |
| Heckington | 42 | 52.59 N | 0.18 W |
| Hecklingen | 54 | 51.51 N | 11.32 E |
| Heckscher State Park ♦ | 210 | 40.43 N | 73.10 W |
| Hecla, Mb., Can. | 184 | 51.08 N | 96.40 W |
| Hecla, S.D., U.S. | 198 | 45.52 N | 98.09 W |
| Hecla Island I | 184 | 51.08 N | 96.45 W |
| Hecla Provincial Park ♦ | 184 | 51.12 N | 96.35 W |
| Hectanooga | 186 | 44.06 N | 66.02 W |
| Hector, N.Z. | 172 | 41.36 S | 171.53 E |
| Hector, Mn., U.S. | 198 | 44.44 N | 94.42 W |
| Hector, Mount ∧ | 172 | 40.57 S | 175.17 E |
| Heda | 94 | 34.58 N | 138.46 E |
| Hedal | 26 | 60.37 N | 9.42 E |
| Hedaru | 154 | 4.30 S | 37.54 E |
| Heddal ⊍[1] | 26 | 59.35 N | 9.11 E |
| Hedding | 285 | 40.06 N | 74.44 W |
| Hédé, Fr. | 32 | 48.18 N | 1.48 W |
| Hede, Sve. | 26 | 62.25 N | 13.30 E |
| Hedehusene | 41 | 55.39 N | 12.12 E |
| Hedel | 52 | 51.45 N | 5.15 E |
| Hedemora | 40 | 60.17 N | 15.59 E |
| Hedemünden | 56 | 51.23 N | 9.46 E |
| Hedensted | 41 | 55.46 N | 9.42 E |
| Hedersleben | 54 | 51.51 N | 11.15 E |
| Hedesunda | 40 | 60.24 N | 16.59 E |
| Hedesundafjärdarna ⊜ | 40 | 60.20 N | 17.00 E |
| He Devil ∧ | 202 | 45.21 N | 116.33 W |
| Hedge End | 42 | 50.54 N | 1.18 W |
| Hedgerley | 260 | 51.35 N | 0.36 W |
| Hedian | 100 | 32.45 N | 114.18 E |
| Hedley, B.C., Can. | 182 | 49.21 N | 120.04 W |
| Hedley, Tx., U.S. | 196 | 34.52 N | 100.39 W |
| Hedmark □[6] | 26 | 61.30 N | 11.45 E |
| Hednesford | 42 | 52.43 N | 2.00 W |
| Hedo | 174m | 26.51 N | 128.16 E |

## PORTUGUÊS

| Nome | Página | Lat.°′ | Long.°′ W = Oeste |
|---|---|---|---|
| Hedo-misaki ≻ | 174m | 26.52 N | 128.16 E |
| Hedon | 44 | 53.44 N | 0.12 W |
| Hedrick | 190 | 41.10 N | 92.18 W |
| Hedströmmen ≃ | 40 | 59.28 N | 16.04 E |
| Hedutne | 272c | 19.10 N | 73.06 E |
| Hedwig Village | 222 | 29.47 N | 95.27 W |
| Heek | 52 | 52.07 N | 7.06 E |
| Heel | 52 | 51.11 N | 5.53 E |
| Heel Point ≻ | 174a | 19.19 N | 166.37 E |
| Heemskerk | 52 | 52.31 N | 4.40 E |
| Heemstede | 52 | 52.21 N | 4.37 E |
| Heepen | 52 | 52.01 N | 8.35 E |
| Heer, Bel. | 56 | 50.10 N | 4.50 E |
| Heer, Ned. | 56 | 50.50 N | 5.44 E |
| Heerde | 52 | 52.23 N | 6.03 E |
| Heerdt ◆[8] | 263 | 51.13 N | 6.43 E |
| Heerenveen | 52 | 52.57 N | 5.55 E |
| Heeren-Werve | 52 | 51.35 N | 7.43 E |
| Heerhugowaard | 52 | 52.40 N | 4.50 E |
| Heerkan | 107 | 29.32 N | 103.56 E |
| Heerlen | 56 | 50.54 N | 5.59 E |
| Heesch | 52 | 51.44 N | 5.32 E |
| Heeslingen | 52 | 53.19 N | 9.20 E |
| Heessen | 52 | 51.42 N | 7.50 E |
| Heeze | 52 | 51.24 N | 5.35 E |
| Ḥefa (Haifa) | 132 | 32.50 N | 35.00 E |
| Ḥefa □[5] | 132 | 32.35 N | 35.00 E |
| Ḥefa, Mifraẕ C | 132 | 32.52 N | 35.03 E |
| Ḥefa, Sede-Te'ufa ⊠ | 132 | 32.49 N | 35.02 E |
| Hefei | 100 | 31.51 N | 117.17 E |
| Hefengchang | 107 | 30.26 N | 104.43 E |
| Heffron Park ♦ | 274a | 33.57 S | 151.15 E |
| Heflin | 194 | 33.38 N | 85.35 W |
| Hegang | 89 | 47.24 N | 130.22 E |
| Hegau ◆[1] | 58 | 47.50 N | 8.45 E |
| Hégenheim | 58 | 47.34 N | 7.32 E |
| Hegewisch ◆[8] | 278 | 41.40 N | 87.33 W |
| Hegins | 208 | 40.39 N | 76.29 W |
| Hegra | 26 | 63.28 N | 11.07 E |
| Hegura-jima I | 92 | 37.51 N | 136.55 E |
| Heguri | 270 | 34.38 N | 135.42 E |
| Hegyeshalom | 61 | 47.55 N | 17.10 E |
| Heha, Mont ∧ | 154 | 3.38 S | 29.30 E |
| Hehlen | 52 | 51.59 N | 9.28 E |
| Heho | 110 | 20.43 N | 96.49 E |
| Hehou | 100 | 28.40 N | 114.28 E |
| Hei ≃, Zhg. | 102 | 40.18 N | 99.26 E |
| Hei ≃, Zhg. | 105 | 40.44 N | 116.27 E |
| Heicheng (Karakhoto) ⊥ | 102 | 41.47 N | 101.03 E |
| Heichengzhen | 102 | 36.16 N | 106.06 E |
| Heichengzi | 104 | 42.10 N | 121.01 E |
| Heidayingzi | 98 | 40.52 N | 116.12 E |
| Heidberg ∧[2] | 263 | 51.15 N | 7.21 E |
| Heide | 30 | 54.12 N | 9.06 E |
| Heide ◆[8], Dtsch. | 263 | 51.26 N | 7.01 E |
| Heide ◆[8], Dtsch. | 263 | 51.31 N | 6.52 E |
| Heideck | 60 | 49.08 N | 11.07 E |
| Heidelberg, Austl. | 169 | 37.45 S | 145.04 E |
| Heidelberg, On., Can. | 212 | 43.31 N | 80.37 W |
| Heidelberg, Dtsch. | 56 | 49.25 N | 8.43 E |
| Heidelberg, S. Afr. | 158 | 34.06 S | 20.59 E |
| Heidelberg, S. Afr. | 158 | 26.32 S | 28.18 E |
| Heidelberg, Ms., U.S. | 194 | 31.53 N | 88.59 W |
| Heidelberg, Pa., U.S. | 279b | 40.23 N | 80.05 W |
| Heidelberg □[5] | 273d | 26.19 S | 28.16 E |
| Heidelberg, Schloss ⊥ | 56 | 49.24 N | 8.42 E |
| Heidelsheim | 56 | 49.06 N | 8.38 E |
| Heiden, Dtsch. | 52 | 51.50 N | 6.56 E |
| Heiden, Dtsch. | 52 | 51.59 N | 8.50 E |
| Heiden, Schw. | 58 | 47.27 N | 9.33 E |
| Heiden, Port C | 180 | 56.55 N | 158.45 W |
| Heidenau, Dtsch. | 52 | 53.19 N | 9.39 E |
| Heidenau, Dtsch. | 54 | 50.59 N | 13.52 E |
| Heidenheim | 56 | 49.01 N | 10.44 E |
| Heidenheim an der Brenz | 56 | 48.40 N | 10.08 E |
| Heidenheimer | 222 | 31.01 N | 97.18 W |
| Heidenoldendorf | 52 | 51.57 N | 8.50 E |
| Heidenreichstein | 61 | 48.52 N | 15.07 E |
| Heider Ditch ≊ | 279a | 41.31 N | 82.01 W |
| Heiderscheid | 56 | 49.53 N | 5.54 E |
| Heidhausen ◆[8] | 263 | 51.23 N | 7.01 E |
| Heidhof ◆[8] | 263 | 51.11 N | 7.11 E |
| Heidlersburg | 208 | 39.57 N | 77.09 W |
| Heidouwo | 105 | 39.42 N | 117.15 E |
| Heigenbrücken | 56 | 50.02 N | 9.23 E |
| Heigoutaicun | 104 | 41.30 N | 123.01 E |
| Heigun-tō I | 96 | 33.47 N | 132.14 E |
| Heihai → Har Hu ⊜ | 102 | 38.15 N | 97.40 E |
| Heihe → Aihui | 89 | 50.16 N | 127.28 E |
| Heijō → P'yŏngyang | 98 | 39.01 N | 125.45 E |
| Heikega-dake ∧ | 96 | 34.19 N | 131.54 E |
| Heikendorf | 54 | 54.22 N | 10.12 E |
| Heil | 263 | 51.38 N | 7.35 E |
| Heilangkou | 105 | 39.37 N | 117.24 E |
| Heilbad Heiligenstadt | 56 | 51.23 N | 10.09 E |
| Heilbron | 158 | 27.21 S | 27.58 E |
| Heilbronn | 56 | 49.08 N | 9.13 E |
| Heilenbecker-Stausee ⊜[1] | 263 | 51.15 N | 7.22 E |
| Heiligenberg | 58 | 47.49 N | 9.19 E |
| Heiligenblut | 64 | 47.02 N | 12.50 E |
| Heiligendamm | 54 | 54.08 N | 11.50 E |
| Heiligenhafen | 54 | 54.22 N | 10.58 E |
| Heiligenhaus | 56 | 51.19 N | 6.59 E |
| Heiligensee ◆[8] | 264a | 52.36 N | 13.13 E |
| Heiligenstadt | 60 | 49.51 N | 11.10 E |
| Heilin | 98 | 35.01 N | 118.58 E |
| Hei Ling Chau I | 271d | 22.15 N | 114.02 E |
| Heilong (Amur) ≃ | 89 | 52.56 N | 141.10 E |
| Heilongguan | 102 | 36.19 N | 111.11 E |
| Heilongjiang □[4] | 89 | 48.00 N | 128.00 E |
| Heilongtan, Zhg. | 105 | 40.44 N | 116.31 E |
| Heilongtan, Zhg. | 105 | 40.02 N | 116.11 E |
| Heilongtan Shuiku ⊜[1] | 107 | 30.03 N | 104.02 E |
| Heiloo | 52 | 52.36 N | 4.43 E |
| Heilsbronn | 56 | 49.20 N | 10.47 E |
| Heiltz-le-Maurupt | 56 | 48.48 N | 4.49 E |
| Heilungkiang → Heilongjiang □[4] | 89 | 48.00 N | 128.00 E |
| Heilwood | 214 | 40.37 N | 78.54 W |
| Heimaey I | 24a | 63.26 N | 20.17 W |
| Heimbach | 56 | 50.38 N | 6.28 E |
| Heimbuchenthal | 56 | 49.53 N | 9.17 E |
| Heimburg | 54 | 51.49 N | 10.54 E |
| Heimdal | 26 | 63.21 N | 10.22 E |
| Heimenkirch | 58 | 47.37 N | 9.53 E |
| Heimsheim | 56 | 48.48 N | 8.51 E |
| Heinävesi | 26 | 62.26 N | 28.36 E |
| Heinersdorf, Dtsch. | 54 | 52.27 N | 14.13 E |
| Heinersdorf, Dtsch. | 264a | 52.23 N | 13.20 E |
| Heinersdorf ◆[8] | 264a | 52.34 N | 13.27 E |
| Heiniuyingzi | 98 | 41.07 N | 120.19 E |
| Heino | 52 | 52.26 N | 6.14 E |
| Heinola | 26 | 61.13 N | 26.02 E |
| Heinsberg | 56 | 51.03 N | 6.05 E |
| Heiquan | 102 | 39.32 N | 99.42 E |
| Heirnkut | 110 | 25.14 N | 94.45 E |
| Heisfelde | 52 | 53.15 N | 7.26 E |
| Heishan | 104 | 41.41 N | 122.07 E |
| Heishanguan | 98 | 38.33 N | 113.41 E |
| Heishantou, Zhg. | 89 | 50.13 N | 119.28 E |
| Heishantou, Zhg. | 98 | 42.28 N | 125.33 E |
| Heishui | 98 | 42.09 N | 119.28 E |
| Heishuisi | 102 | 36.08 N | 108.42 E |
| Heisingen ◆[8] | 263 | 51.25 N | 7.04 E |
| Heisler | 182 | 52.41 N | 112.13 W |
| Heislerville | 208 | 39.13 N | 74.59 W |
| Heissen ◆[8] | 263 | 51.26 N | 6.56 E |
| Heist-aan-Zee | 50 | 51.21 N | 3.15 E |
| Heist-op-den-Berg | 56 | 51.05 N | 4.43 E |
| Heitang | 102 | 26.29 N | 105.09 E |
| Heitersheim | 58 | 47.53 N | 7.40 E |
| Heiwa | 94 | 35.12 N | 136.44 E |
| Heiyanghebao | 105 | 39.07 N | 118.15 E |
| Heiyantang | 102 | 27.28 N | 101.11 E |

| Nome | Página | Lat.°′ | Long.°′ |
|---|---|---|---|
| Heiyanzi | 105 | 39.13 N | 118.08 E |
| Hejaz → Al-Ḥijāz ◆[1] | 118 | 24.30 N | 38.30 E |
| Hejiachang | 107 | 29.24 N | 104.56 E |
| Hejian, Zhg. | 98 | 38.26 N | 116.05 E |
| Hejian, Zhg. | 105 | 39.25 N | 116.25 E |
| Hejiang | 107 | 28.49 N | 105.50 E |
| Hejiangzhen | 107 | 29.16 N | 104.16 E |
| Hejiaqiao | 100 | 27.24 N | 113.21 E |
| Hejiawopeng | 104 | 41.32 N | 122.07 E |
| Hejiaying | 105 | 39.55 N | 118.19 E |
| Hejiazhen | 107 | 29.52 N | 104.26 E |
| Hejin | 102 | 35.39 N | 110.40 E |
| Hejlsminde | 41 | 55.22 N | 9.37 E |
| Hejnsvig | 41 | 55.41 N | 8.59 E |
| Hekelgem | 50 | 50.54 N | 4.06 E |
| Hekili Point ≻ | 229a | 20.48 N | 156.37 W |
| Hekimhan | 130 | 38.49 N | 37.56 E |
| Hekinan | 94 | 34.51 N | 136.58 E |
| Hekla ∧[1] | 24a | 64.00 N | 19.39 W |
| Hekou, Zhg. | 100 | 31.22 N | 114.26 E |
| Hekou, Zhg. | 102 | 36.09 N | 103.22 E |
| Hekou, Zhg. | 102 | 28.22 N | 108.14 E |
| Hekou, Zhg. | 102 | 29.57 N | 111.04 E |
| Hekou, Zhg. | 102 | 22.38 N | 103.56 E |
| Hekouchang | 107 | 29.21 N | 104.21 E |
| Hekouji | 100 | 32.09 N | 116.04 E |
| Hekoujie | 102 | 26.31 N | 100.39 E |
| Hekpoort | 158 | 25.55 S | 27.38 E |
| Hel | 30 | 54.37 N | 18.48 E |
| Helagsfjället ∧ | 26 | 62.55 N | 12.27 E |
| Helaluo | 102 | 33.56 N | 102.10 E |
| Helangou | 104 | 41.00 N | 123.25 E |
| Helan Shan ⋀ | 102 | 38.40 N | 105.57 E |
| Helbe ≃ | 54 | 51.13 N | 11.06 E |
| Helbra | 54 | 51.33 N | 11.29 E |
| Helchteren | 56 | 51.03 N | 5.22 E |
| Heldburg | 54 | 50.17 N | 10.44 E |
| Helden | 56 | 51.07 N | 7.56 E |
| Heldra | 56 | 51.07 N | 10.11 E |
| Heldrungen | 54 | 51.18 N | 11.13 E |
| Helechos, Cañada de los ≃ | 286a | 19.22 N | 99.12 W |
| Helemano Stream ≃ | 229c | 21.35 N | 158.06 W |
| Helen, Mount ∧ | 166 | 21.34 S | 141.13 E |
| Helena, Ar., U.S. | 194 | 34.31 N | 90.35 W |
| Helena, Mt., U.S. | 202 | 46.35 N | 112.02 W |
| Helena, N.Y., U.S. | 206 | 44.55 N | 74.44 W |
| Helena, Oh., U.S. | 214 | 41.21 N | 83.18 W |
| Helena, Ok., U.S. | 196 | 36.32 N | 98.16 W |
| Helena ≃ | 168a | 31.54 S | 116.00 E |
| Helena River Reservoir ⊜[1] | 168a | 31.59 S | 116.13 E |
| Helendale | 228 | 34.45 N | 117.18 W |
| Helenenberg | 56 | 49.51 N | 6.32 E |
| Helenental V | 264b | 48.01 N | 16.11 E |
| Helen Island I | 108 | 2.58 N | 131.49 E |
| Helensburgh, Austl. | 170 | 34.11 S | 150.59 E |
| Helensburgh, Scot., U.K. | 46 | 56.01 N | 4.44 W |
| Helen Springs | 162 | 18.26 S | 133.52 E |
| Helensville | 172 | 36.40 S | 174.28 E |
| Helenville | 216 | 43.01 N | 88.41 W |
| Helenwood | 192 | 36.25 N | 84.32 W |
| Ḥeleẕ | 132 | 31.35 N | 34.40 E |
| Helfenberg | 61 | 48.32 N | 14.08 E |
| Helfenstein | 208 | 40.45 N | 76.27 W |
| Helgaå ≃ | 26 | 55.53 N | 14.08 E |
| Helgenæs ≻[1] | 41 | 56.08 N | 10.32 E |
| Helgoland I | 30 | 54.12 N | 7.53 E |
| Helgoländer Bucht C | 30 | 54.10 N | 8.04 E |
| Heli | 89 | 47.05 N | 130.16 E |
| Helicoide ◆[9] | 285c | 10.29 N | 66.55 W |
| Helidon | 171a | 27.33 S | 152.08 E |
| Heliodora | 256 | 22.04 S | 45.32 W |
| Heliópolis | 287a | 22.45 S | 43.25 W |
| Heliopolis → Miṣr al-Jadīdah ◆[8] | 273c | 30.06 N | 31.20 E |
| Heliopolis ⊥ | 142 | 30.08 N | 31.17 E |
| Heliopolis Aerodrome ⊠ | 273c | 30.04 N | 31.19 E |
| Heliopolis Racing Club ♦ | 273c | 30.06 N | 31.19 E |
| Heliuji | 100 | 33.02 N | 116.57 E |
| Helixi | 106 | 30.40 N | 118.59 E |
| Hell | 26 | 63.26 N | 10.54 E |
| Hellam | 208 | 40.00 N | 76.36 W |
| Hellbrunn, Schloss ⊥ | 64 | 47.46 N | 13.04 E |
| Hellebæk | 41 | 56.04 N | 12.34 E |
| Ḥelleh ≃ | 128 | 29.10 N | 50.40 E |
| Hellen Blazes, Lake ⊜ | 220 | 28.01 N | 80.47 W |
| Hellendoorn | 52 | 52.24 N | 6.26 E |
| Hellenthal | 56 | 50.29 N | 6.26 E |
| Hellern | 52 | 52.15 N | 7.58 E |
| Hellersen | 263 | 51.12 N | 7.39 E |
| Hellertown | 208 | 40.34 N | 75.20 W |
| Hellesylt | 26 | 62.05 N | 6.54 E |
| Hellevad | 41 | 55.05 N | 9.13 E |
| Hellevoetsluis | 52 | 51.49 N | 4.08 E |
| Hell Gate ʯ | 276 | 40.47 N | 73.56 W |
| Hell Hole Reservoir ⊜[1] | 226 | 39.04 N | 120.22 W |
| Hellifield | 44 | 54.01 N | 2.12 W |
| Hellín | 34 | 38.31 N | 1.41 W |
| Helli Ness ≻ | 46a | 60.02 N | 1.10 W |
| Hellmonsödt | 61 | 48.26 N | 14.18 E |
| Hell Point ≻ | 186 | 44.16 N | 64.15 W |
| Hells Canyon V | 202 | 45.20 N | 116.45 W |
| Hellsee ⊜ | 264a | 52.45 N | 13.35 E |
| Hells Gate V | 182 | 49.47 N | 121.27 W |
| Hell-Ville | 157b | 13.25 S | 48.16 E |
| Hellweg ◆[1] | 52 | 51.36 N | 8.32 E |
| Helm | 226 | 36.31 N | 120.05 W |
| Helmand □[4] | 128 | 31.00 N | 64.00 E |
| Helmand ≃ | 128 | 31.12 N | 61.34 E |
| Helmbrechts | 54 | 50.14 N | 11.43 E |
| Helmcken Falls ↳ | 182 | 51.57 N | 120.11 W |
| Helme ≃ | 54 | 51.20 N | 11.20 E |
| Helmeringhausen | 156 | 25.54 S | 16.57 E |
| Helmetta | 276 | 40.22 N | 74.25 W |
| Helmetta Pond ⊜ | 276 | 40.23 N | 74.26 W |
| Helmond | 52 | 51.29 N | 5.40 E |
| Helmsburg | 218 | 39.16 N | 86.18 W |
| Helmsdale | 46 | 58.07 N | 3.40 W |
| Helmsdale ≃ | 46 | 58.07 N | 3.40 W |
| Helmshore | 262 | 53.41 N | 2.20 W |
| Helmsley | 44 | 54.14 N | 1.04 W |
| Helmstedt | 54 | 52.13 N | 11.00 E |
| Hel'myaziv | 78 | 49.49 N | 31.49 E |
| Helnæs I | 41 | 55.08 N | 10.02 E |
| Helong | 98 | 42.32 N | 128.59 E |
| Helper | 200 | 39.41 N | 110.51 W |
| Helpmekaar | 158 | 28.29 S | 30.29 E |
| Helpter Berg ∧[2] | 54 | 53.30 N | 13.36 E |
| Helsby | 44 | 53.16 N | 2.46 W |
| Helsby Hill ∧[2] | 262 | 53.16 N | 2.46 W |
| Helsingborg | 41 | 56.03 N | 12.42 E |
| Helsinge | 41 | 56.01 N | 12.12 E |
| Helsingfors → Helsinki | 26 | 60.10 N | 24.58 E |
| Helsingør (Elsinore) | 41 | 56.02 N | 12.37 E |
| Helsinki (Helsingfors) | 26 | 60.10 N | 24.58 E |
| Helska, Mierzeja ≻[2] | 30 | 54.45 N | 18.39 E |
| Helston | 42 | 50.05 N | 5.16 W |
| Heltonville | 218 | 38.55 N | 86.22 W |
| Helvecia | 252 | 31.06 S | 60.05 W |
| Helvellyn ∧ | 44 | 54.31 N | 3.01 W |
| Helvick Head ≻ | 48 | 52.03 N | 7.33 W |
| Helvoirt | 52 | 51.38 N | 5.13 E |
| Hem ≃ | 50 | 50.51 N | 2.06 E |
| Ḥemar, Naḥal V | 132 | 31.08 N | 35.22 E |
| Hemau | 60 | 49.03 N | 11.47 E |
| Hemāvati ≃ | 122 | 12.31 N | 76.27 E |
| Hembe | 152 | 1.54 N | 22.42 E |
| Hemel Hempstead | 42 | 51.46 N | 0.28 W |
| Hemelingen ◆[8] | 52 | 53.03 N | 8.53 E |
| Hemeln | 52 | 51.30 N | 9.36 E |
| Hemer | 56 | 51.23 N | 7.46 E |

| Nome | Página | Lat.°′ | Long.°′ |
|---|---|---|---|
| Hemet | 228 | 33.44 N | 116.58 W |
| Hemfjärden C | 40 | 59.17 N | 15.20 E |
| Hemford | 186 | 44.30 N | 64.47 W |
| Hemfurth-Edersee | 56 | 51.10 N | 9.02 E |
| Hemiksem | 50 | 51.09 N | 4.21 E |
| Héming | 58 | 48.42 N | 6.57 E |
| Hemingford | 198 | 42.19 N | 103.04 W |
| Hemingway | 192 | 33.45 N | 79.26 W |
| Hemlock, In., U.S. | 216 | 40.25 N | 86.03 W |
| Hemlock, N.Y., U.S. | 210 | 42.47 N | 77.36 W |
| Hemlock Lake ⊜ | 210 | 42.43 N | 77.37 W |
| Hemmerde | 52 | 51.33 N | 7.48 E |
| Hemmerden | 263 | 51.07 N | 6.36 E |
| Hemmingen | 52 | 52.19 N | 9.45 E |
| Hemmoor | 52 | 53.41 N | 9.08 E |
| Hemphill | 194 | 31.20 N | 93.50 W |
| Hempnall | 42 | 52.30 N | 1.19 E |
| Hempstead, N.Y., U.S. | 210 | 40.42 N | 73.37 W |
| Hempstead, Tx., U.S. | 222 | 30.05 N | 96.04 W |
| Hempstead Harbor C | 276 | 40.50 N | 73.39 W |
| Hempstead Lake ⊜ | 276 | 40.41 N | 73.38 W |
| Hempstead Lake State Park ♦ | 276 | 40.41 N | 73.38 W |
| Hemsbach | 56 | 49.36 N | 8.40 E |
| Hemsby | 42 | 52.41 N | 1.42 E |
| Hemse | 26 | 57.14 N | 18.22 E |
| Hemsedal | 26 | 60.52 N | 8.34 E |
| Hemslingen | 52 | 53.05 N | 9.36 E |
| Hemsön I | 26 | 62.43 N | 18.05 E |
| Hemstreet Park | 210 | 42.54 N | 73.41 W |
| Hemsworth | 44 | 53.38 N | 1.21 W |
| Hemujing | 98 | 37.54 N | 115.22 E |
| Henan | 102 | 34.35 N | 101.34 E |
| Henan (Honan) □[4] | 90 | 34.00 N | 114.00 E |
| Hen and Chickens II | 172 | 35.55 S | 174.45 E |
| Henares ≃ | 34 | 40.24 N | 3.30 W |
| Henbury, Austl. | 162 | 24.35 S | 133.15 E |
| Henbury, Eng., U.K. | 262 | 53.15 N | 2.11 W |
| Hendek | 130 | 40.48 N | 30.45 E |
| Henderson, Arg. | 252 | 36.18 S | 61.43 W |
| Henderson, In., U.S. | 218 | 39.40 N | 85.31 W |
| Henderson, Ky., U.S. | 194 | 37.50 N | 87.35 W |
| Henderson, Mn., U.S. | 190 | 44.31 N | 93.54 W |
| Henderson, Ne., U.S. | 198 | 40.46 N | 97.48 W |
| Henderson, Nv., U.S. | 204 | 36.02 N | 114.58 W |
| Henderson, N.Y., U.S. | 212 | 43.51 N | 76.11 W |
| Henderson, N.C., U.S. | 192 | 36.19 N | 78.23 W |
| Henderson, Tn., U.S. | 194 | 35.26 N | 88.38 W |
| Henderson, Tx., U.S. | 222 | 32.09 N | 94.47 W |
| Henderson □[6] | 222 | 32.13 N | 95.50 W |
| Henderson Bay C, N.Y., U.S. | 212 | 43.54 N | 76.10 W |
| Henderson Bay C, Wa., U.S. | 224 | 47.18 N | 122.42 W |
| Henderson Creek ≃ | 190 | 40.52 N | 91.02 W |
| Henderson Island I | 6 | 24.22 S | 128.19 W |
| Hendersonville, N.C., U.S. | 192 | 35.19 N | 82.27 W |
| Hendersonville, Pa., U.S. | 214 | 40.18 N | 80.09 W |
| Hendersonville, Tn., U.S. | 194 | 36.18 N | 86.37 W |
| Hendījān | 128 | 30.14 N | 49.43 E |
| Hendon ◆[8] | 260 | 51.35 N | 0.14 W |
| Hendorābī, Jazīreh-ye I | 128 | 26.40 N | 53.37 E |
| Hendricks, Mn., U.S. | 198 | 44.30 N | 96.25 W |
| Hendricks, W.V., U.S. | 188 | 39.04 N | 79.37 W |
| Hendricks □[6] | 218 | 39.46 N | 86.26 W |
| Hendrina | 158 | 26.11 S | 29.45 E |
| Hendry □[6] | 220 | 26.36 N | 81.13 W |
| Hendrysburg | 214 | 40.04 N | 81.10 W |
| Hendy | 42 | 51.43 N | 4.04 W |
| Henefer | 200 | 41.01 N | 111.29 W |
| Henfield | 42 | 50.56 N | 0.17 W |
| Heng ≃, Zhg. | 102 | 28.40 N | 104.25 E |
| Heng ≃, Zhg. | 107 | 28.57 N | 105.22 E |
| Hengām, Jazīreh-ye I | 128 | 26.39 N | 55.53 E |
| Henganofi | 164 | 6.15 S | 145.35 E |
| Hengchow → Hengyang | 102 | 26.54 N | 112.36 E |
| Hengdaochuan | 98 | 41.15 N | 125.31 E |
| Hengdaohe | 104 | 42.02 N | 123.51 E |
| Hengdaohezi | 89 | 43.13 N | 126.44 E |
| Hengdaozi | 89 | 43.18 N | 127.18 E |
| Hengdong | 100 | 27.03 N | 112.57 E |
| Hengelo | 52 | 52.15 N | 6.45 E |
| Hengersberg | 60 | 48.47 N | 13.03 E |
| Hengfan | 106 | 30.20 N | 119.45 E |
| Hengfeng | 100 | 28.24 N | 117.34 E |
| Henggang | 100 | 29.32 N | 115.27 E |
| Henggouzi | 89 | 43.12 N | 124.47 E |
| Henghutou | 104 | 42.05 N | 124.00 E |
| Hengjie | 106 | 31.13 N | 119.30 E |
| Hengjing | 106 | 31.11 N | 120.32 E |
| Hengjinghong | 106 | 30.34 N | 120.59 E |
| Hengli | 100 | 23.12 N | 114.37 E |
| Henglin | 106 | 31.42 N | 120.06 E |
| Henglu | 98 | 41.26 N | 126.04 E |
| Henglutou | 106 | 30.19 N | 119.19 E |
| Hengmian | 106 | 31.09 N | 121.38 E |
| Hengoed | 42 | 51.39 N | 3.10 W |
| Hengsen | 263 | 51.29 N | 7.38 E |
| Heng Sha I | 106 | 31.20 N | 121.50 E |
| Hengshan, Zhg. | 100 | 27.15 N | 112.51 E |
| Hengshan, Zhg. | 102 | 37.56 N | 108.53 E |
| Hengshan, Zhg. | 106 | 31.01 N | 120.32 E |
| Heng Shan ∧ | 100 | 27.16 N | 112.35 E |
| Heng Shan ⋀ | 102 | 39.30 N | 113.45 E |
| Hengshanchang | 107 | 30.33 N | 105.24 E |
| Hengshanqiao | 106 | 31.46 N | 120.07 E |
| Hengshanxia | 106 | 30.18 N | 118.44 E |
| Hengshi, Zhg. | 100 | 26.05 N | 114.38 E |
| Hengshi, Zhg. | 100 | 23.52 N | 113.15 E |
| Hengshi, Zhg. | 100 | 29.32 N | 114.41 E |
| Hengshui | 98 | 37.43 N | 115.40 E |
| Hengsteysee ⊜[1] | 263 | 51.25 N | 7.28 E |
| Hengtangshi | 106 | 31.41 N | 121.02 E |
| Hengtianchi | 107 | 29.07 N | 105.01 E |
| Hengtianxi | 107 | 29.05 N | 105.03 E |
| Hengxi, Zhg. | 100 | 29.42 N | 121.35 E |
| Hengxi, Zhg. | 100 | 28.46 N | 120.29 E |
| Hengxi, Zhg. | 106 | 31.43 N | 118.46 E |
| Hengxian | 102 | 22.42 N | 109.13 E |
| Hengxiang | 106 | 32.12 N | 120.15 E |
| Hengxikou | 100 | 29.26 N | 121.26 E |
| Hengyang | 102 | 26.54 N | 112.36 E |
| Heniches'k | 78 | 46.11 N | 34.48 E |
| Hénin-Beaumont | 50 | 50.25 N | 2.56 E |
| Henley Beach | 168b | 34.55 S | 138.30 E |
| Henley-in-Arden | 42 | 52.17 N | 1.46 W |
| Henley-on-Thames | 42 | 51.32 N | 0.56 W |
| Henlopen, Cape ≻ | 208 | 38.48 N | 75.05 W |
| Henlow | 42 | 52.02 N | 0.18 W |
| Hennan ⊜ | 26 | 62.06 N | 15.46 E |
| Hennaya | 34 | 34.58 N | 1.22 W |
| Henneberg | 54 | 50.29 N | 10.21 E |
| Hennebont | 32 | 47.48 N | 3.17 W |
| Hennef | 56 | 50.46 N | 7.16 E |
| Hennen | 56 | 51.27 N | 7.39 E |
| Hennenman | 158 | 27.59 S | 27.01 E |
| Hennepin | 190 | 41.15 N | 89.21 W |
| Hennepin, Point ≻ | 281 | 42.12 N | 83.09 W |
| Hennersdorf | 264b | 48.07 N | 16.22 E |
| Hennessey | 196 | 36.06 N | 97.53 W |
| Hennessey, Lake ⊜[1] | 226 | 38.29 N | 122.22 W |
| Hennickendorf | 54 | 52.30 N | 13.51 E |
| Henniez | 58 | 46.44 N | 6.54 E |
| Hennigsdorf | 54 | 52.38 N | 13.12 E |
| Henniker | 188 | 43.10 N | 71.49 W |
| Henning, Il., U.S. | 216 | 40.18 N | 87.42 W |
| Henning, Mn., U.S. | 198 | 46.19 N | 95.26 W |
| Henning, Tn., U.S. | 194 | 35.40 N | 89.34 W |
| Henri ≃ | 206 | 46.30 N | 71.47 W |
| Henri, Cap ≻ | 186 | 49.48 N | 64.23 W |
| Henri-Chapelle | 56 | 50.40 N | 5.56 E |
| Henrichemont | 50 | 47.18 N | 2.32 E |

| Nome | Página | Lat.°′ | Long.°′ |
|---|---|---|---|
| Henrichenburg | 263 | 51.35 N | 7.19 E |
| Henrico □[6] | 208 | 37.30 N | 77.20 W |
| Henrietta, N.Y., U.S. | 210 | 43.03 N | 77.36 W |
| Henrietta, N.C., U.S. | 192 | 35.15 N | 81.47 W |
| Henrietta, Tx., U.S. | 196 | 33.49 N | 98.11 W |
| Henrietta Maria, Cape ≻ | 176 | 55.09 N | 82.20 W |
| Henri Pittier, Parque Nacional ♦ | 246 | 10.25 N | 67.43 W |
| Henry, Il., U.S. | 190 | 41.06 N | 89.21 W |
| Henry, S.D., U.S. | 198 | 44.52 N | 97.27 W |
| Henry □[6], In., U.S. | 218 | 39.55 N | 85.22 W |
| Henry □[6], Ky., U.S. | 218 | 38.26 N | 85.09 W |
| Henry □[6], Oh., U.S. | 216 | 41.20 N | 84.04 W |
| Henry ≃ | 162 | 22.40 S | 115.40 E |
| Henry, Cape ≻ | 208 | 36.55 N | 76.01 W |
| Henry, Mount ∧ | 202 | 48.53 N | 115.31 W |
| Henry, Mount ∧[2] | 274a | 33.50 S | 150.38 E |
| Henry, Point ≻ | 162 | 34.29 S | 119.23 E |
| Henry Cowell Redwoods State Park ♦ | 226 | 37.02 N | 122.03 W |
| Henryetta | 196 | 35.26 N | 95.58 W |
| Henry Hagg Lake ⊜[1] | 224 | 45.29 N | 123.13 E |
| Henry Island I | 224 | 48.35 N | 123.11 W |
| Henry Kater, Cape ≻ | 176 | 69.05 N | 66.44 W |
| Henry Mountains ⋀ | 200 | 38.00 N | 110.50 W |
| Henrys Bend | 214 | 41.28 N | 79.37 W |
| Henrys Fork ≃, U.S. | 200 | 41.00 N | 109.39 W |
| Henrys Fork ≃, Id., U.S. | 202 | 43.45 N | 111.56 W |
| Henryville, P.Q., Can. | 206 | 45.08 N | 73.11 W |
| Henryville, In., U.S. | 218 | 38.32 N | 85.46 W |
| Henry W. Coe State Park ♦ | 226 | 37.12 N | 121.30 W |
| Hensall | 190 | 43.26 N | 81.30 W |
| Henshaw, Lake ⊜[1] | 204 | 33.15 N | 116.45 W |
| Hensley | 194 | 34.30 N | 92.12 W |
| Hensley Lake ⊜[1] | 226 | 37.07 N | 119.53 W |
| Henslow, Cape ≻ | 175e | 9.56 S | 160.38 E |
| Henson Creek ≃ | 284b | 38.46 N | 77.00 W |
| Hensonville | 210 | 42.17 N | 74.13 W |
| Henstedt-Ulzburg | 52 | 53.47 N | 9.58 E |
| Henstridge | 42 | 50.59 N | 2.24 W |
| Hentiesbaai | 156 | 22.08 S | 14.18 E |
| Henty | 166 | 35.31 S | 147.02 E |
| Henzada | 110 | 17.38 N | 95.28 E |
| Heorhiyivka | 83 | 48.26 N | 39.17 E |
| Hepburn | 184 | 52.31 N | 106.43 W |
| Hepburn Springs | 169 | 37.19 S | 144.09 E |
| Hephzibah | 192 | 33.18 N | 82.05 W |
| Heping, Zhg. | 100 | 27.10 N | 117.18 E |
| Heping, Zhg. | 100 | 22.01 N | 112.59 E |
| Heping, Zhg. | 100 | 23.17 N | 116.29 E |
| Heping, Zhg. | 100 | 24.28 N | 114.58 E |
| Heping, Zhg. | 106 | 30.50 N | 119.54 E |
| Heppenheim | 56 | 49.39 N | 8.38 E |
| Heppner | 202 | 45.21 N | 119.33 W |
| Heptonstall | 262 | 53.45 N | 2.01 W |
| Heptonstall Moor ≃ | 262 | 53.46 N | 2.05 W |
| Hepu (Lianzhou) | 102 | 21.39 N | 109.11 E |
| Hepworth | 212 | 44.37 N | 81.09 W |
| Heqiao, Zhg. | 100 | 32.55 N | 118.22 E |
| Heqiao, Zhg. | 106 | 31.30 N | 119.53 E |
| Heqing | 102 | 26.34 N | 100.12 E |
| Hequ | 102 | 39.26 N | 111.08 E |
| Héraðsflói C | 24a | 65.45 N | 14.10 W |
| Hera Lacinia, Tempio di ⊥ | 68 | 39.01 N | 17.13 E |
| Herāt | 128 | 34.20 N | 62.12 E |
| Herāt □[4] | 128 | 34.30 N | 62.00 E |
| Hérault □[5] | 32 | 43.40 N | 3.30 E |
| Hérault ≃ | 32 | 43.17 N | 3.26 E |
| Herbasse ≃ | 62 | 45.02 N | 4.57 E |
| Herbault | 50 | 47.36 N | 1.08 E |
| Herbede | 56 | 51.25 N | 7.16 E |
| Herbern | 52 | 51.44 N | 7.39 E |
| Herbert, Sk., Can. | 184 | 50.26 N | 107.12 W |
| Herbert, N.Z. | 172 | 45.14 S | 170.47 E |
| Herbert ≃ | 166 | 18.32 S | 146.17 E |
| Herbert, Mount ∧ | 172 | 43.41 S | 172.44 E |
| Herbertabad | 110 | 11.43 N | 92.37 E |
| Herbert Hoover National Historic Site ⊥ | 190 | 41.38 N | 91.23 W |
| Herbertingen | 58 | 48.04 N | 9.26 E |
| Herbert Island I | 180 | 52.45 N | 170.10 W |
| Herberton | 166 | 17.23 S | 145.23 E |
| Herbertsdale | 158 | 34.01 S | 21.46 E |
| Herbeumont | 56 | 49.47 N | 5.14 E |
| Herbignac | 32 | 47.27 N | 2.19 W |
| Herb Lake | 184 | 54.47 N | 99.47 W |
| Herblay | 50 | 49.00 N | 2.10 E |
| Herblet Lake ⊜ | 184 | 54.56 N | 99.54 W |
| Herbolzheim | 58 | 48.13 N | 7.47 E |
| Herborn | 56 | 50.40 N | 8.17 E |
| Herbrechtingen | 56 | 48.37 N | 10.10 E |
| Herbringhauser-Stausee ⊜[1] | 263 | 51.14 N | 7.16 E |
| Herbsleben | 54 | 51.07 N | 10.50 E |
| Herbstein | 56 | 50.34 N | 9.20 E |
| Herceg-Novi | 38 | 42.27 N | 18.32 E |
| Hercegovina □[9] | 36 | 43.15 N | 17.50 E |
| Herculaneum | 219 | 38.16 N | 90.22 W |
| Hércules, Méx. | 232 | 28.02 N | 103.48 W |
| Hercules, Ca., U.S. | 282 | 38.01 N | 122.17 W |
| Herdecke | 56 | 51.24 N | 7.26 E |
| Herdorf | 56 | 50.46 N | 7.56 E |
| Herdringen | 52 | 51.25 N | 7.58 E |
| Herðubreið ∧ | 24a | 65.13 N | 16.18 W |
| Herdwangen-Schönach | 58 | 47.52 N | 9.10 E |
| Heredia | 236 | 10.00 N | 84.07 W |
| Heredia □[4] | 236 | 10.30 N | 84.00 W |
| Hereford, Eng., U.K. | 42 | 52.04 N | 2.43 W |
| Hereford, Az., U.S. | 200 | 31.26 N | 110.05 W |
| Hereford, Md., U.S. | 208 | 39.35 N | 76.39 W |
| Hereford, Tx., U.S. | 196 | 34.48 N | 102.23 W |
| Hereford and Worcester □[6] | 42 | 52.10 N | 2.30 W |
| Hereford Cathedral ⊍[1] | 42 | 52.04 N | 2.43 W |
| Hereford Mountain ∧ | 206 | 45.05 N | 71.36 W |
| Hereke | 130 | 40.48 N | 29.39 E |
| Herekino | 172 | 35.15 S | 173.13 E |
| Herencia | 34 | 39.21 N | 3.22 W |
| Herent | 56 | 50.54 N | 4.40 E |
| Herentals | 56 | 51.11 N | 4.50 E |
| Herfølge | 41 | 55.25 N | 12.10 E |
| Herford | 52 | 52.06 N | 8.40 E |
| Hergatz | 58 | 47.39 N | 9.50 E |
| Hergisdorf | 54 | 51.32 N | 11.28 E |
| Hergla | 36 | 36.02 N | 10.31 E |
| Herhahn | 56 | 50.33 N | 6.26 E |
| Héricourt | 58 | 47.35 N | 6.45 E |
| Hérimoncourt | 58 | 47.26 N | 6.53 E |
| Heringen, Dtsch. | 54 | 51.27 N | 10.52 E |
| Heringen, Dtsch. | 56 | 50.53 N | 10.00 E |
| Heringsdorf, Dtsch. | 54 | 54.18 N | 11.00 E |
| Heringsdorf, Dtsch. | 54 | 53.56 N | 14.08 E |
| Herington | 198 | 38.40 N | 96.56 W |
| Heriot | 172 | 45.50 S | 169.16 E |
| Herisau | 58 | 47.23 N | 9.17 E |
| Heritage Range ⋀ | 9 | 79.30 S | 84.00 W |
| Herk ≃ | 56 | 50.58 N | 5.07 E |
| Herk-de-Stad | 56 | 50.56 N | 5.10 E |
| Herkimer | 210 | 43.01 N | 74.59 W |
| Herkimer □[6] | 210 | 43.02 N | 74.59 W |
| Herlen → Kerulen ≃ | 90 | 48.48 N | 117.00 E |
| Herleshausen | 56 | 51.00 N | 10.09 E |
| Herlev | 41 | 55.43 N | 12.27 E |
| Herlong | 204 | 40.09 N | 120.08 W |
| Herlufmagle | 41 | 55.19 N | 11.46 E |
| Herlufsholm | 41 | 55.15 N | 11.46 E |
| Hermagor | 64 | 46.37 N | 13.22 E |
| Herman, Mn., U.S. | 198 | 45.48 N | 96.08 W |
| Herman, Ne., U.S. | 198 | 41.40 N | 96.12 W |
| Herman, Pa., U.S. | 214 | 40.50 N | 79.49 W |
| Herman, Lake ⊜ | 282 | 38.05 N | 122.09 W |

| | | | | | |
|---|---|---|---|---|---|
| ≃ | River | Fluß | Río | Rivière | Rio |
| ≊ | Canal | Kanal | Canal | Canal | Canal |
| ↳ | Waterfall, Rapids | Wasserfall, Stromschnellen | Cascada, Rápidos | Chute d'eau, Rapides | Cascata, Rápidos |
| ʯ | Strait | Meeresstraße | Estrecho | Détroit | Estreito |
| C | Bay, Gulf | Bucht, Golf | Bahía, Golfo | Baie, Golfe | Baía, Golfo |
| ⊜ | Lake, Lakes | See, Seen | Lago, Lagos | Lac, Lacs | Lago, Lagos |
| ≡ | Swamp | Sumpf | Pantano | Marais | Pântano |
| ⊓ | Ice Features, Glacier | Eis- und Gletscherformen | Accidentes Glaciales | Formes glaciaires | Acidentes glaciares |
| ⊤ | Other Hydrographic Features | Andere Hydrographische Objekte | Otros Elementos Hidrográficos | Autres données hydrographiques | Outros acidentes hidrográficos |

| | | | | | |
|---|---|---|---|---|---|
| ◆ | Submarine Features | Untermeerische Objekte | Accidentes Submarinos | Formes de relief sous-marin | Acidentes submarinos |
| □ | Political Unit | Politische Einheit | Unidad Politica | Entité politique | Unidade política |
| ⊍ | Cultural Institution | Kulturelle Institution | Institución Cultural | Institution culturelle | Instituição cultural |
| ⊥ | Historical Site | Historische Stätte | Sitio Histórico | Site historique | Sitio histórico |
| ♦ | Recreational Site | Erholungs- und Feriencrt | Sitio de Recreo | Centre de loisirs | Area de Lazer |
| ⊠ | Airport | Flughafen | Aeropuerto | Aéroport | Aeroporto |
| ■ | Military Installation | Militäranlage | Instalación Militar | Installation militaire | Instalação militar |
| ◆ | Miscellaneous | Verschiedenes | Misceláneo | Divers | Diversos |

| Name | Page | Lat.°′ | Long.°′ |
|---|---|---|---|
| Hermana Mayor Island I | 116 | 15.48 N | 119.48 E |
| Hermanas | 196 | 27.13 N | 101.14 W |
| Hermanavičy | 76 | 55.25 N | 27.44 E |
| Herman Eksteen Park ♦ | 273d | 26.10 S | 28.02 E |
| Herma Ness › | 46a | 60.50 N | 0.55 W |
| Hermann | 219 | 38.42 N | 91.26 W |
| Hermannsburg, Austl. | 162 | 23.57 S | 132.45 E |
| Hermannsburg, Dtsch. | 52 | 52.50 N | 10.05 E |
| Hermannsburg Aboriginal Reserve •[4] | 162 | 24.00 S | 132.45 E |
| Hermanns-Denkmal ⊥ | 52 | 51.55 N | 8.50 E |
| Hermannskogel ∧ | 264b | 48.16 N | 16.18 E |
| Hermannstadt → Sibiu | 38 | 45.48 N | 24.09 E |
| Hermano Peak ∧ | 200 | 37.13 N | 108.48 W |
| Hermansverk | 26 | 61.11 N | 6.51 E |
| Hermansville | 190 | 45.42 N | 87.36 W |
| Hermanus | 158 | 34.25 S | 19.16 E |
| Hermanville | 194 | 31.57 N | 90.50 W |
| Hermeray | 261 | 48.38 N | 1.41 E |
| Hermes | 50 | 49.22 N | 2.15 E |
| Hermeskeil | 56 | 49.39 N | 6.56 E |
| Hermidale | 166 | 31.33 S | 146.43 E |
| Hermies | 50 | 50.07 N | 3.02 E |
| Herminie | 214 | 40.15 N | 79.43 W |
| Hermiston | 202 | 45.50 N | 119.17 W |
| Hermitage, Nf., Can. | 186 | 47.33 N | 55.56 W |
| Hermitage, Eng., U.K. | 42 | 51.27 N | 1.16 W |
| Hermitage, Ar., U.S. | 194 | 33.26 N | 92.10 W |
| Hermitage, Mo., U.S. | 194 | 37.56 N | 93.18 W |
| Hermitage Bay ⊂ | 186 | 47.35 N | 56.05 W |
| Hermitage Park | 284c | 39.05 N | 77.04 W |
| Hermite, Isla I | 254 | 55.52 S | 67.20 W |
| Hermit Islands II | 164 | 1.30 S | 145.05 E |
| Hermleigh | 196 | 32.38 N | 100.46 W |
| Hermon, S. Afr. | 158 | 33.27 S | 18.59 E |
| Hermon, N.Y., U.S. | 212 | 44.28 N | 75.13 W |
| Hermon, Mount → Shaykh, Jabal ash- ∧ | 132 | 33.26 N | 35.51 E |
| Hermosa Beach | 280 | 33.51 N | 118.23 W |
| Hermosillo, Méx. | 200 | 32.30 N | 114.59 W |
| Hermosillo, Méx. | 232 | 29.04 N | 110.58 W |
| Hermoso, Cerro ∧ | 246 | 1.10 S | 78.12 W |
| Hermsdorf | 54 | 50.54 N | 11.52 E |
| Hermsdorf •[8] | 54 | 52.37 N | 13.18 E |
| Hermyingyi | 110 | 14.15 N | 98.21 E |
| Hernád ≃ | 30 | 47.56 N | 21.08 E |
| Hernals •[8] | 264b | 48.13 N | 16.20 E |
| Hernandarias | 252 | 25.22 S | 54.45 W |
| Hernández | 234 | 23.01 N | 102.01 W |
| Hernandez Reservoir ⊜[1] | 226 | 36.22 N | 120.49 W |
| Hernando, Arg. | 252 | 32.25 S | 63.44 W |
| Hernando, Fl., U.S. | 220 | 28.54 N | 82.22 W |
| Hernando, Ms., U.S. | 194 | 34.49 N | 89.59 W |
| Hernando □[6] | 220 | 28.34 N | 82.22 W |
| Hernando de Magallanes, Parque Nacional ♦ | 254 | 54.15 S | 72.00 W |
| Hernani | 116 | 11.20 N | 125.37 E |
| Herndon, Ca., U.S. | 226 | 36.49 N | 119.54 W |
| Herndon, Ks., U.S. | 198 | 39.54 N | 100.47 W |
| Herndon, Pa., U.S. | 210 | 40.42 N | 76.50 W |
| Herndon, Va., U.S. | 208 | 38.58 N | 77.23 W |
| Herndon Canal ≋ | 226 | 36.46 N | 119.46 W |
| Herne | 52 | 51.32 N | 7.13 E |
| Herne Bay | 42 | 51.23 N | 1.08 E |
| Herne Hill | 168a | 31.50 S | 116.01 E |
| Herning | 41 | 56.08 N | 8.59 E |
| Hernwood Heights | 284b | 39.22 N | 77.50 W |
| Heroica Zitácuaro | 234 | 19.24 N | 100.22 W |
| Heroldsbach | 60 | 49.42 N | 11.00 E |
| Herongate | 260 | 51.36 N | 0.21 E |
| Herongen | 56 | 51.24 N | 6.15 E |
| Heron Island I | 166 | 23.26 S | 151.55 E |
| Heron Lake | 198 | 43.47 N | 95.19 W |
| Hérons, Île aux I | 275a | 45.25 N | 73.35 W |
| Heronsgate | 260 | 51.38 N | 0.31 W |
| Hérouville | 261 | 49.06 N | 2.08 E |
| Hérouville-Saint-Clair | 32 | 49.12 N | 0.21 W |
| Herpf | 54 | 50.34 N | 10.20 E |
| Herradura | 252 | 26.29 S | 58.18 W |
| Herräng | 40 | 60.08 N | 18.39 E |
| Herreid | 198 | 45.50 N | 100.04 W |
| Herrenberg | 56 | 48.35 N | 8.52 E |
| Herrenchiemsee, Schloss ⊥ | 64 | 47.52 N | 12.23 E |
| Herrera | 252 | 28.29 S | 63.04 W |
| Herrera □[4] | 236 | 7.54 N | 80.38 W |
| Herrera del Duque | 34 | 39.10 N | 5.03 W |
| Herrera de Pisuerga | 34 | 42.36 N | 4.20 W |
| Herrick, Austl. | 166 | 41.06 S | 147.52 E |
| Herrick, Il., U.S. | 219 | 39.13 N | 88.59 W |
| Herrick Creek ≃ | 182 | 54.20 N | 121.30 W |
| Herrick Grove | 212 | 44.04 N | 76.12 W |
| Herricks | 276 | 40.45 N | 73.40 W |
| Herrieden | 56 | 49.14 N | 10.30 E |
| Herrin | 194 | 37.48 N | 89.01 W |
| Herring Bay ⊂ | 208 | 38.44 N | 76.33 W |
| Herring Brook ≃ | 283 | 42.10 N | 70.44 W |
| Herring Cove, N.S., Can. | 186 | 44.34 N | 63.34 W |
| Herring Cove, Ak., U.S. | 182 | 55.21 N | 131.41 W |
| Herring Creek ≃ | 208 | 37.49 N | 77.07 W |
| Herringen | 52 | 51.40 N | 7.44 E |
| Herring Run ≃ | 284b | 39.18 N | 76.31 W |
| Herring Run Park ♦ | 284b | 39.19 N | 76.33 W |
| Herritslev | 41 | 54.42 N | 11.41 E |
| Herrljunga | 26 | 58.05 N | 13.02 E |
| Herrnburg | 54 | 53.47 N | 10.45 E |
| Herrnhut | 54 | 51.01 N | 14.44 E |
| Herrsching am Ammersee | 60 | 48.00 N | 11.10 E |
| Herrs Island I | 279b | 40.28 N | 79.58 W |
| Herrskogen | 40 | 59.32 N | 16.15 E |
| Herry | 50 | 47.13 N | 2.57 E |
| Hersbruck | 60 | 49.30 N | 11.26 E |
| Herschbach | 56 | 50.34 N | 7.44 E |
| Herscheid | 56 | 51.10 N | 7.44 E |
| Herschel, Sk., Can. | 184 | 51.38 N | 108.21 W |
| Herschel, S. Afr. | 158 | 30.37 S | 27.12 E |
| Herschel Island I | 180 | 69.35 N | 139.05 W |
| Herscher | 216 | 41.03 N | 88.06 W |
| Herselt | 56 | 51.03 N | 4.53 E |
| Herserange | 56 | 49.31 N | 5.47 E |
| Hersham | 260 | 51.22 N | 0.23 W |
| Hershey, Ne., U.S. | 198 | 41.09 N | 101.00 W |
| Hershey, Pa., U.S. | 208 | 40.17 N | 76.39 W |
| Hersman | 219 | 39.57 N | 90.44 W |
| Herstadberg | 40 | 58.38 N | 16.10 E |
| Herstal | 56 | 50.40 N | 5.38 E |
| Herstmonceux | 42 | 50.53 N | 0.20 E |
| Herten | 52 | 51.35 N | 7.07 E |
| Hertford, Eng., U.K. | 42 | 51.48 N | 0.05 W |
| Hertford, N.C., U.S. | 192 | 36.11 N | 76.27 W |
| Hertford □[6] | 208 | 36.28 N | 77.01 W |
| Hertfordshire □[6] | 42 | 51.50 N | 0.10 W |
| Hertingfordbury | 260 | 51.48 N | 0.06 W |
| Hertsa | 78 | 48.09 N | 26.16 E |
| Hertsmere □[8] | 260 | 51.41 N | 0.17 W |
| Hertzogville | 158 | 28.08 S | 25.33 E |
| Heruncun | 104 | 40.58 N | 123.27 E |
| Hervás | 34 | 40.16 N | 5.51 W |
| Herve | 56 | 50.38 N | 5.48 E |
| Hervest | 263 | 51.40 N | 7.01 E |
| Hervey Bay ⊂ | 166 | 25.00 S | 153.00 E |
| Herxheim | 56 | 49.09 N | 8.13 E |
| Héry, Fr. | 50 | 47.54 N | 3.38 E |
| Héry, Fr. | 62 | 45.46 N | 6.28 E |
| Herzberg, Dtsch. | 54 | 52.54 N | 12.58 E |
| Herzberg, Dtsch. | 54 | 51.41 N | 13.14 E |
| Herzberg am Harz | 52 | 51.39 N | 10.20 E |
| Herzebrock | 52 | 51.53 N | 8.14 E |
| Herzfelde | 54 | 52.29 N | 13.50 E |
| Herzhausen | 56 | 51.11 N | 8.53 E |
| Herzlake | 52 | 52.41 N | 7.36 E |
| Herzliyya | 132 | 32.10 N | 34.51 E |
| Herznach | 58 | 47.28 N | 8.03 E |
| Herzogenaurach | 56 | 49.34 N | 10.53 E |
| Herzogenbuchsee | 58 | 47.12 N | 7.41 E |
| Herzogenburg | 61 | 48.17 N | 15.42 E |
| Herzogenrath | 56 | 50.52 N | 6.06 E |
| Herzsprung | 54 | 53.04 N | 12.28 E |
| Ḥeṣār, Kūh-e ⋀ | 120 | 34.50 N | 66.30 E |
| Hesarak | 267d | 35.47 N | 51.19 E |
| Hesdin | 50 | 50.22 N | 2.02 E |
| Hesel | 52 | 53.18 N | 7.35 E |
| Hesepe | 52 | 52.26 N | 7.58 E |
| Heshachang | 107 | 30.37 N | 105.40 E |
| Heshan | 110 | 23.52 N | 108.52 E |
| Heshangqiao | 100 | 34.15 N | 113.47 E |
| Heshengqiao | 100 | 30.00 N | 114.22 E |
| Heshi, Zhg. | 100 | 25.04 N | 118.37 E |
| Heshi, Zhg. | 107 | 29.10 N | 104.22 E |
| Heshui, Zhg. | 100 | 24.24 N | 114.56 E |
| Heshui, Zhg. | 102 | 22.48 N | 112.29 E |
| Heshuijian | 100 | 30.33 N | 116.05 E |
| Heshun, Zhg. | 100 | 27.30 N | 117.24 E |
| Heshun, Zhg. | 102 | 37.21 N | 113.35 E |
| Heshuo | 86 | 42.15 N | 86.53 E |
| Hesketh Bank | 262 | 53.42 N | 2.51 W |
| Hesketh Out Marsh ≡ | 262 | 53.43 N | 2.55 W |
| Heskin Green | 262 | 53.38 N | 2.42 W |
| Hesler | 218 | 38.28 N | 84.47 W |
| Hesperange | 56 | 49.34 N | 6.09 E |
| Hesperia, Ca., U.S. | 228 | 34.25 N | 117.18 W |
| Hesperia, Mi., U.S. | 190 | 43.34 N | 86.02 W |
| Hesperus Mountain ∧ | 200 | 37.27 N | 108.05 W |
| Hess ≃ | 180 | 63.34 N | 133.57 W |
| Hesselager | 41 | 55.10 N | 10.45 E |
| Hesselberg ∧ | 56 | 49.04 N | 10.32 E |
| Hesselø I | 41 | 56.12 N | 11.43 E |
| Hesselte | 52 | 52.25 N | 7.22 E |
| Hessen | 54 | 52.01 N | 10.47 E |
| Hessen □[3] | 30 | 50.30 N | 9.15 E |
| Hessen Cassal | 216 | 41.00 N | 85.05 W |
| Hessenthal | 56 | 49.55 N | 9.17 E |
| Hessisch Lichtenau | 56 | 51.12 N | 9.43 E |
| Hessisch Oldendorf | 52 | 52.10 N | 9.15 E |
| Hessle | 44 | 53.44 N | 0.26 W |
| Hesso | 166 | 32.08 S | 137.27 E |
| Hess Tablemount ✢[3] | 14 | 17.50 N | 174.15 W |
| Hesston, Ks., U.S. | 198 | 38.08 N | 97.25 W |
| Hesston, Pa., U.S. | 214 | 40.26 N | 78.07 W |
| Heston •[8] | 260 | 51.29 N | 0.22 W |
| Heswall | 44 | 53.20 N | 3.06 W |
| Het ≃ | 110 | 20.49 N | 104.01 E |
| Hetai | 102 | 23.22 N | 112.19 E |
| Hetanbu | 100 | 28.21 N | 117.11 E |
| Hetang, Zhg. | 100 | 26.40 N | 119.09 E |
| Hetang, Zhg. | 106 | 31.43 N | 120.27 E |
| Hetang, Zhg. | 107 | 28.58 N | 106.03 E |
| Heṭauḍā | 124 | 27.26 N | 85.02 E |
| Hetch Hetchy Aqueduct ≋[1] | 226 | 37.29 N | 122.19 W |
| Hetch Hetchy Reservoir ⊜[1] | 226 | 37.57 N | 119.43 W |
| Hethersett | 42 | 52.36 N | 1.11 E |
| Hetian, Zhg. | 100 | 25.41 N | 116.26 E |
| Hetian, Zhg. | 100 | 23.19 N | 115.38 E |
| Het Loo, Paleis ʊ | 52 | 52.14 N | 5.56 E |
| Hetou | 100 | 24.18 N | 113.29 E |
| Hetoudian | 98 | 37.02 N | 120.35 E |
| Hettange-Grande | 56 | 49.24 N | 6.09 E |
| Hettenleidelheim | 56 | 49.32 N | 8.04 E |
| Hettick | 219 | 39.21 N | 90.02 W |
| Hettingen | 58 | 48.13 N | 9.14 E |
| Hettinger | 198 | 46.00 N | 102.38 W |
| Hetton-le-Hole | 44 | 54.50 N | 1.27 W |
| Hettstedt | 54 | 51.38 N | 11.30 E |
| Hetupu | 100 | 30.50 N | 116.03 E |
| Hetzendorf •[8] | 264b | 48.10 N | 16.18 E |
| Hetzerath | 56 | 49.52 N | 6.49 E |
| Het Zoute | 50 | 51.21 N | 3.18 E |
| Heubach | 56 | 48.48 N | 9.56 E |
| Heuchin | 50 | 50.28 N | 2.16 E |
| Heudeber | 54 | 51.54 N | 10.50 E |
| Heule | 50 | 50.50 N | 3.14 E |
| Heuningspruit | 158 | 27.26 S | 27.28 E |
| Heure, Eau d' ≃ | 56 | 50.18 N | 4.24 E |
| Heusden, Bel. | 50 | 51.02 N | 3.48 E |
| Heusden, Bel. | 56 | 51.02 N | 5.16 E |
| Heustreu | 56 | 50.21 N | 10.15 E |
| Heusweiler | 56 | 49.20 N | 6.55 E |
| Heuvelton | 212 | 44.37 N | 75.24 W |
| Hève, Cap de la › | 50 | 49.31 N | 0.04 E |
| Heven | 263 | 51.26 N | 7.17 E |
| Heverlee | 56 | 50.52 N | 4.42 E |
| Heves | 30 | 47.36 N | 20.17 E |
| Heves □[6] | 30 | 47.50 N | 20.15 E |
| Hevlín | 61 | 48.45 N | 16.23 E |
| Ḥevron, Naḥal V | 132 | 31.15 N | 34.50 E |
| Hewanorra International Airport ⊠ | 241f | 13.45 N | 60.56 W |
| Hewitt, N.J., U.S. | 210 | 41.08 N | 74.18 W |
| Hewitt, Tx., U.S. | 222 | 31.27 N | 97.11 W |
| Hewittsville | 219 | 39.32 N | 89.19 W |
| Hewlett, N.Y., U.S. | 276 | 40.38 N | 73.41 W |
| Hewlett, Va., U.S. | 208 | 37.55 N | 77.35 W |
| Hewlett Bay Park | 276 | 40.38 N | 73.42 W |
| Hewlett Harbor | 276 | 40.38 N | 73.41 W |
| Hewlett Neck | 276 | 40.37 N | 73.42 W |
| Hewlett Point › | 276 | 40.50 N | 73.45 W |
| Hewopu | 104 | 41.14 N | 122.24 E |
| Hewu | 100 | 26.41 N | 113.40 E |
| Hexenkopf ∧ | 58 | 47.01 N | 10.28 E |
| Hexham | 44 | 54.58 N | 2.06 W |
| Hexi, Zhg. | 100 | 24.52 N | 117.15 E |
| Hexi, Zhg. | 102 | 24.09 N | 102.39 E |
| Hexi, Zhg. | 106 | 31.03 N | 119.49 E |
| Hexian, Zhg. | 100 | 31.43 N | 118.22 E |
| Hexian, Zhg. | 102 | 24.15 N | 111.43 E |
| Hexibao | 102 | 38.34 N | 102.11 E |
| Hexingchang | 107 | 30.05 N | 104.35 E |
| Hexingjie | 106 | 31.55 N | 120.36 E |
| Hexiwu | 105 | 39.38 N | 116.58 E |
| Hex Rivierberge ⋀ | 158 | 33.25 S | 19.37 E |
| Hextable | 260 | 51.25 N | 0.11 E |
| Hexton | 172 | 38.37 S | 177.58 E |
| Heyan | 104 | 42.30 N | 120.29 E |
| Heyang, Zhg. | 98 | 35.27 N | 118.33 E |
| Heyang, Zhg. | 102 | 35.15 N | 110.06 E |
| Heybeli •[8] | 267b | 40.53 N | 29.05 E |
| Heybeli Ada I | 267b | 40.53 N | 29.05 E |
| Heybridge, Eng., U.K. | 260 | 51.44 N | 0.41 E |
| Heybridge, Eng., U.K. | 260 | 51.40 N | 0.22 E |
| Heyburn | 202 | 42.33 N | 113.45 W |
| Heyerode | 54 | 51.10 N | 10.25 E |
| Heyrieux | 62 | 45.38 N | 5.03 E |
| Heysham | 44 | 54.02 N | 2.54 W |
| Heyuan | 100 | 23.44 N | 114.41 E |
| Heywood, Austl. | 166 | 38.08 S | 141.38 E |
| Heywood, Eng., U.K. | 44 | 53.36 N | 2.13 W |
| Heyworth | 216 | 40.18 N | 88.58 W |
| Heze (Caozhou) | 98 | 35.17 N | 115.27 E |
| Hezhang | 102 | 27.00 N | 104.37 E |
| Hezhao | 98 | 37.08 N | 115.17 E |
| Hezhen | 100 | 29.56 N | 120.10 E |
| Hezheng | 102 | 35.25 N | 103.10 E |
| Hezijian | 105 | 40.13 N | 116.03 E |
| Hezixu | 100 | 24.54 N | 115.14 E |
| Hezuo | 102 | 34.58 N | 102.57 E |
| Hiale | 110 | 15.55 N | 107.34 E |
| Hialeah | 220 | 25.51 N | 80.16 W |
| Hialeah Park Race Track ♦ | 220 | 25.51 N | 80.17 W |
| Hiaohexi | 100 | 31.21 N | 114.02 E |
| Hiawassee | 192 | 34.56 N | 83.45 W |
| Hiawatha, Ks., U.S. | 198 | 39.51 N | 95.32 W |
| Hiawatha, Ut,. U.S. | 200 | 39.29 N | 111.00 W |
| Hiba-Dōgo-Taishaku-kokutei-kōen ♦ | 96 | 35.07 N | 133.08 E |
| Hibaldstow | 44 | 53.31 N | 0.32 W |
| Hibbing | 190 | 47.25 N | 92.56 W |
| Hibbs, Point › | 166 | 42.38 S | 145.15 E |
| Hibernia | 276 | 40.57 N | 74.30 W |
| Hibernia Reef ✢[2] | 160 | 12.00 S | 123.23 E |
| Hibiki-nada ⊤[2] | 96 | 34.00 N | 130.30 E |
| Hiburi-shima I | 96 | 33.10 N | 132.17 E |
| Hibuson Island I | 116 | 10.27 N | 125.29 E |
| Hickam Air Force Base ■ | 229c | 21.20 N | 157.57 W |
| Hickey, Mount ∧ | 169 | 37.22 S | 145.19 E |
| Hickman, Ca., U.S. | 226 | 37.37 N | 120.45 W |
| Hickman, Ky., U.S. | 194 | 36.34 N | 89.11 W |
| Hickman, Ne., U.S. | 198 | 40.37 N | 96.37 W |
| Hickman, Pa., U.S. | 279b | 40.23 N | 80.09 W |
| Hickman's Harbour | 186 | 48.06 N | 53.44 W |
| Hickory, Ms., U.S. | 194 | 32.19 N | 89.01 W |
| Hickory, N.C., U.S. | 192 | 35.43 N | 81.20 W |
| Hickory, Pa., U.S. | 214 | 40.18 N | 80.18 W |
| Hickory Corners | 216 | 42.26 N | 85.22 W |
| Hickory Creek ≃, Il., U.S. | 278 | 41.30 N | 88.06 W |
| Hickory Creek ≃, Mi., U.S. | 216 | 42.05 N | 86.29 W |
| Hickory Creek ≃, Tx., U.S. | 222 | 31.29 N | 95.07 W |
| Hickory Flat | 194 | 34.36 N | 89.11 W |
| Hickory Hills | 216 | 41.43 N | 87.49 W |
| Hickory Run State Park ♦ | 210 | 41.02 N | 75.41 W |
| Hickory Township | 214 | 41.15 N | 80.27 W |
| Hicks, Point › | 166 | 37.48 S | 149.17 E |
| Hicks Bay | 172 | 37.36 S | 178.18 E |
| Hickson Lake ⊜ | 184 | 56.17 N | 104.25 W |
| Hicksville, N.Y., U.S. | 210 | 40.46 N | 73.31 W |
| Hicksville, Oh., U.S. | 216 | 41.17 N | 84.45 W |
| Hico | 196 | 31.58 N | 98.02 W |
| Hicpochee, Lake ⊜ | 220 | 26.50 N | 81.10 W |
| Hida → Hita | 96 | 33.19 N | 130.56 E |
| Hida ≃ | 94 | 35.26 N | 137.03 E |
| Hidaka, Nihon | 94 | 35.54 N | 139.21 E |
| Hidaka, Nihon | 96 | 35.28 N | 134.47 E |
| Hidaka, Nihon | 96 | 33.55 N | 135.09 E |
| Hidaka ≃ | 96 | 33.52 N | 135.09 E |
| Hidaka-sammyaku ⋀ | 92a | 42.35 N | 142.45 E |
| Hida-Kiso-gawa-kokutei-kōen ♦ | 94 | 35.37 N | 137.15 E |
| Hida-kōchi ⋀[1] | 94 | 36.16 N | 137.05 E |
| Hidalgo, Méx. | 232 | 27.47 N | 99.52 W |
| Hidalgo, Méx. | 232 | 25.59 N | 100.27 W |
| Hidalgo, Méx. | 232 | 24.15 N | 99.26 W |
| Hidalgo □[3] | 234 | 20.30 N | 99.00 W |
| Hidalgo del Parral | 232 | 26.56 N | 105.40 W |
| Hida-sammyaku ⋀ | 94 | 36.25 N | 137.40 E |
| Hiddenhausen | 52 | 52.08 N | 8.38 E |
| Hidden Hills | 228 | 34.09 N | 118.43 W |
| Hiddensee | 54 | 54.33 N | 13.05 E |
| Hiddensee I | 54 | 54.33 N | 13.07 E |
| Hidden Valley, Ca., U.S. | 226 | 38.46 N | 121.09 W |
| Hidden Valley, Tx., U.S. | 222 | 29.54 N | 95.25 W |
| Hiddesen | 52 | 51.55 N | 8.50 E |
| Hiddinghausen | 263 | 51.22 N | 7.17 E |
| Hıdırbaba | 130 | 38.47 N | 39.00 E |
| Hidrolândia | 255 | 16.58 S | 49.14 W |
| Hidrolina | 255 | 14.37 S | 49.25 W |
| Hieflau | 61 | 47.36 N | 14.44 E |
| Hienghène | 175f | 20.41 S | 164.56 E |
| Hierapolis → Pamukkale ⊥ | 130 | 37.58 N | 29.19 E |
| Hierges | 56 | 50.06 N | 4.44 E |
| Hierro (Ferro) I | 148 | 27.45 N | 18.00 W |
| Hiesfeld | 263 | 51.33 N | 6.46 E |
| Hietzing •[8] | 264b | 48.11 N | 16.18 E |
| Higashi | 174m | 26.38 N | 128.09 E |
| Higashi •[8] | 270 | 34.41 N | 135.31 E |
| Higashibetsuin | 270 | 34.56 N | 135.34 E |
| Higashifuji-enshūjō ■ | 94 | 35.17 N | 138.51 E |
| Higashīhiroshima | 96 | 34.26 N | 132.42 E |
| Higashiichiki | 92 | 31.40 N | 130.20 E |
| Higashiiyayama | 96 | 33.52 N | 133.54 E |
| Higashiizu | 94 | 34.48 N | 139.04 E |
| Higashi-jima I | 174f | 24.47 N | 141.23 E |
| Higashikurume | 268 | 35.45 N | 139.32 E |
| Higashimatsuyama | 94 | 36.02 N | 139.24 E |
| Higashimonzen | 268 | 35.56 N | 139.40 E |
| Higashimurayama | 94 | 35.46 N | 139.29 E |
| Higashinada •[8] | 270 | 34.43 N | 135.16 E |
| Higashinakano | 268 | 35.38 N | 139.25 E |
| Higashinari •[8] | 270 | 34.40 N | 135.33 E |
| Higashine | 92 | 38.26 N | 140.24 E |
| Higashinose | 270 | 34.55 N | 135.30 E |
| Higashiōizumi •[8] | 268 | 35.45 N | 139.36 E |
| Higashiōsaka | 96 | 34.39 N | 135.35 E |
| Higashishirakawa | 94 | 35.39 N | 137.19 E |
| Higashisumiyoshi •[8] | 270 | 34.37 N | 135.32 E |
| Higashitokonoo-san ∧ | 96 | 35.25 N | 134.55 E |
| Higashitsuno | 96 | 33.23 N | 133.02 E |
| Higashiura, Nihon | 94 | 34.59 N | 136.58 E |
| Higashiura, Nihon | 270 | 34.33 N | 135.00 E |
| Higashiyama •[8] | 270 | 35.00 N | 135.48 E |
| Higashiyamato | 268 | 35.44 N | 139.26 E |
| Higashiyodogawa •[8] | 270 | 34.44 N | 135.31 E |
| Higashiyoshino | 94 | 34.24 N | 135.58 E |
| Higbee | 194 | 39.18 N | 92.30 W |
| Higganum | 207 | 41.29 N | 72.33 W |
| Higgins | 196 | 36.07 N | 100.02 W |
| Higgins, Mount ∧ | 224 | 48.19 N | 121.45 W |
| Higgins Lake ⊜ | 190 | 44.30 N | 84.45 W |
| Higginsport | 218 | 38.47 N | 83.58 W |
| Higginsville, Austl. | 162 | 31.45 S | 121.43 E |
| Higginsville, Mo., U.S. | 194 | 39.04 N | 93.43 W |
| Higgs' Hope | 158 | 29.19 S | 23.16 E |
| Higham Ferrers | 42 | 52.18 N | 0.36 W |
| Higham Upshire | 260 | 51.26 N | 0.28 E |
| Highbank | 222 | 31.10 N | 96.50 W |
| High Bank Creek ≃ | 216 | 42.37 N | 85.11 W |
| High Bar Indian Reserve •[4] | 182 | 51.06 N | 122.00 W |
| High Beach | 260 | 51.39 N | 0.02 E |
| High Bentham | 44 | 54.08 N | 2.30 W |
| High Bluff Island I | 212 | 43.58 N | 77.45 W |
| Highbridge, Eng., U.K. | 42 | 51.13 N | 2.49 W |
| High Bridge, N.J., U.S. | 210 | 40.40 N | 74.53 W |
| Highbury | 164 | 16.25 S | 143.09 E |
| Highcliff | 279b | 40.32 N | 80.03 W |
| Higher Ballam | 262 | 53.46 N | 2.59 W |
| Higher Broughton •[8] | 262 | 53.30 N | 2.15 W |
| Higher Hogshead ∧[2] | 262 | 53.42 N | 2.09 W |
| Higher Penwortham | 262 | 53.45 N | 2.44 W |
| Higher Walton, Eng., U.K. | 44 | 53.44 N | 2.39 W |
| Higher Walton, Eng., U.K. | 262 | 53.22 N | 2.37 W |
| Higher Whitley | 262 | 53.19 N | 2.35 W |
| Highett | 274b | 37.57 S | 145.03 E |
| High Falls | 210 | 41.50 N | 74.08 W |
| High Falls ᒪ | 212 | 43.56 N | 75.23 W |
| High Force ᒪ | 44 | 54.38 N | 2.13 W |
| Highgate | 214 | 42.30 N | 81.49 W |
| Highgate Center | 206 | 44.56 N | 73.02 W |
| Highgate Springs | 206 | 44.58 N | 73.06 W |
| Highgrove | 228 | 34.01 N | 117.20 W |
| High Halstow | 260 | 51.27 N | 0.34 E |
| High Hesket | 44 | 54.48 N | 2.48 W |
| High Hill | 219 | 38.52 N | 91.23 W |
| High Hill ∧[2] | 276 | 40.49 N | 73.25 W |
| High Hill ≃, Can. | 184 | 56.45 N | 110.30 W |
| High Hill ≃, Mb., Can. | 184 | 55.52 N | 94.42 W |
| High Hill Lake ⊜ | 184 | 55.34 N | 95.40 W |
| High Island I, H.K. | 271d | 22.22 N | 114.21 E |
| High Island I, Mi., U.S. | 190 | 45.42 N | 85.40 W |
| High Island Creek ≃ | 190 | 44.35 N | 93.54 W |
| High Island Reservoir ⊜[1] | 271d | 22.23 N | 114.21 W |
| Highland, Ca., U.S. | 228 | 34.07 N | 117.12 W |
| Highland, Il., U.S. | 219 | 38.44 N | 89.40 W |
| Highland, In., U.S. | 216 | 41.33 N | 87.27 W |
| Highland, Ks., U.S. | 198 | 39.51 N | 95.16 W |
| Highland, Md., U.S. | 208 | 39.11 N | 76.57 W |
| Highland, Mi., U.S. | 281 | 42.38 N | 83.37 W |
| Highland, N.Y., U.S. | 210 | 41.43 N | 73.57 W |
| Highland, Oh., U.S. | 218 | 39.21 N | 83.36 W |
| Highland, Pa., U.S. | 279b | 40.33 N | 80.04 W |
| Highland □[4] | 46 | 57.40 N | 5.00 W |
| Highland □[6] | 218 | 39.12 N | 83.37 W |
| Highland Beach | 220 | 26.25 N | 80.04 W |
| Highland City | 220 | 27.58 N | 81.53 W |
| Highland Creek ≃, On., Can. | 275b | 43.46 N | 79.08 W |
| Highland Creek ≃, Ca., U.S. | 226 | 38.24 N | 121.14 W |
| Highland Falls | 210 | 41.22 N | 73.58 W |
| Highland Heights, Ky., U.S. | 218 | 39.04 N | 84.27 W |
| Highland Heights, Oh., U.S. | 214 | 41.33 N | 81.28 W |
| Highland Hills | 278 | 41.52 N | 88.01 W |
| Highland Home | 194 | 31.57 N | 86.18 W |
| Highland Lake, Il., U.S. | 278 | 42.21 N | 88.04 W |
| Highland Lake, Ma., U.S. | 283 | 42.41 N | 72.37 W |
| Highland Lake, N.Y., U.S. | 210 | 41.32 N | 74.51 W |
| Highland Lake ⊜, Ct., U.S. | 207 | 41.54 N | 73.06 W |
| Highland Lake ⊜, Il., U.S. | 278 | 42.22 N | 88.04 W |
| Highland Lake ⊜, N.J., U.S. | 276 | 41.10 N | 74.28 W |
| Highland Lakes | 210 | 41.10 N | 74.28 W |
| Highland-on-the-Lake | 284a | 42.42 N | 79.59 W |
| Highland Park, Il., U.S. | 216 | 42.10 N | 87.48 W |
| Highland Park, Md., U.S. | 284c | 38.54 N | 76.54 W |
| Highland Park, Mi., U.S. | 216 | 42.24 N | 83.05 W |
| Highland Park, N.J., U.S. | 210 | 40.29 N | 74.25 W |
| Highland Park, Pa., U.S. | 210 | 40.38 N | 77.35 W |
| Highland Park, Tx., U.S. | 222 | 32.50 N | 96.48 W |
| Highland Park •[8] | 280 | 34.07 N | 118.13 W |
| Highland Park ♦, Ma., U.S. | 283 | 42.30 N | 70.55 W |
| Highland Park ♦, Pa., U.S. | 279b | 40.29 N | 79.55 W |
| Highland Peak ∧ | 226 | 38.33 N | 119.45 W |
| Highland Point › | 220 | 25.30 N | 81.12 W |
| Highlands, N.J., U.S. | 208 | 40.24 N | 73.59 W |
| Highlands, N.C., U.S. | 192 | 35.03 N | 83.11 W |
| Highlands, Tx., U.S. | 222 | 29.49 N | 95.03 W |
| Highlands □[6] | 220 | 27.20 N | 81.16 W |
| Highlands Hammock State Park ♦ | 220 | 27.28 N | 81.33 W |
| Highland Silver Lake ⊜[1] | 219 | 38.47 N | 89.39 W |
| Highlands North •[8] | 273d | 26.09 S | 28.05 E |
| Highland Springs | 208 | 37.32 N | 77.19 W |
| Highlands Reservoir ⊜[1] | 222 | 29.50 N | 95.02 W |
| Highland State Recreation Area ♦ | 216 | 42.39 N | 83.33 W |
| Highlandtown •[8] | 284b | 39.17 N | 76.33 W |
| High Laver | 260 | 51.45 N | 0.13 E |
| High Legh | 262 | 53.21 N | 2.27 W |
| Highley | 42 | 52.27 N | 2.23 W |
| Highmore | 198 | 44.31 N | 99.26 W |
| High Ongar | 260 | 51.43 N | 0.16 E |
| High Park ♦ | 275b | 43.39 N | 79.28 W |
| High Peak □[8] | 262 | 53.23 N | 1.55 W |
| High Peak ∧, Pil. | 116 | 15.29 N | 120.07 E |
| High Peak ∧, N.Y., U.S. | 210 | 42.09 N | 74.05 W |
| High Peak •[1] | 44 | 53.22 N | 1.50 W |
| High Point, Fl., U.S. | 220 | 27.55 N | 82.42 W |
| High Point, N.C., U.S. | 192 | 35.57 N | 80.00 W |
| Highpoint, Oh., U.S. | 218 | 39.14 N | 84.24 W |
| High Point ∧, N.J., U.S. | 210 | 41.19 N | 74.40 W |
| High Point ∧, Wy., U.S. | 202 | 41.37 N | 107.47 W |
| High Point State Park ♦ | 210 | 41.18 N | 74.41 W |
| High Prairie | 182 | 55.26 N | 116.29 W |
| High Ridge | 219 | 38.27 N | 90.32 W |
| High River | 182 | 50.35 N | 113.52 W |
| High Rock | 192 | 26.36 N | 76.18 W |
| High Rock ∧ | 188 | 39.33 N | 79.06 W |
| Highrock Indian Reserve •[4] | 184 | 55.54 N | 100.30 W |
| Highrock Lake ⊜, Mb., Can. | 184 | 55.45 N | 100.30 W |
| Highrock Lake ⊜, Sk., Can. | 184 | 57.04 N | 105.30 W |
| High Rock Lake ⊜[1] | 192 | 35.40 N | 80.17 W |
| High Seat ∧ | 44 | 54.24 N | 2.18 W |
| High Spire | 208 | 40.12 N | 76.47 W |
| High Springs | 192 | 29.49 N | 82.35 W |
| High Street ∧ | 44 | 54.29 N | 2.52 W |
| Hightown | 44 | 53.31 N | 3.03 W |
| Hightstown | 208 | 40.16 N | 74.31 W |
| High View | 210 | 41.33 N | 74.27 W |
| Highwater | 206 | 45.01 N | 72.26 W |
| Highway City | 226 | 36.49 N | 119.54 W |
| High Willhays ∧ | 42 | 50.41 N | 3.59 W |
| Highwood, Il., U.S. | 216 | 42.11 N | 87.48 W |
| Highwood, Mt., U.S. | 202 | 47.35 N | 110.47 W |
| Highwood ≃ | 182 | 50.49 N | 113.47 W |
| Highwood Baldy ∧ | 202 | 47.27 N | 110.37 W |
| Highwood Creek ≃ | 202 | 47.40 N | 111.00 W |
| Highwood Mountains ⋀ | 202 | 47.25 N | 110.30 W |
| Highworth | 42 | 51.38 N | 1.43 W |
| High Wycombe | 42 | 51.38 N | 0.46 W |
| Higlet | 154 | 1.04 S | 40.19 E |
| Higuera Blanca | 234 | 19.42 N | 105.10 W |
| Higuera de Abuya | 232 | 24.16 N | 107.04 W |
| Higuera de Zaragoza | 232 | 25.59 N | 109.16 W |
| Higueras | 196 | 25.58 N | 100.01 W |
| Higüero, Punta › | 240m | 18.22 N | 67.16 W |
| Higüey | 238 | 18.37 N | 68.42 W |
| Higuito ≃ | 236 | 14.43 N | 88.40 W |
| Hihétro | 150 | 7.32 N | 1.06 E |
| Hihyā | 142 | 30.40 N | 31.36 E |
| Hii ≃ | 96 | 35.26 N | 132.54 E |
| Hiidenportin kansallispuisto ♦ | 26 | 63.50 N | 28.59 E |
| Hiiraan □[4] | 144 | 4.00 N | 45.30 E |
| Hiiumaa I | 76 | 58.52 N | 22.40 E |
| Hījānah, Buḥayrat al- ⊜ | 132 | 33.18 N | 36.36 E |
| Híjar | 34 | 41.10 N | 0.27 W |
| Hiji | 96 | 33.22 N | 131.32 E |
| Hiji ≃ | 96 | 33.36 N | 132.29 E |
| Hijikawa | 96 | 33.27 N | 132.41 E |
| Hijiri-dake ∧ | 94 | 35.26 N | 138.10 E |
| Hikami | 96 | 35.10 N | 135.02 E |
| Hikari, Nihon | 94 | 35.39 N | 140.30 E |
| Hikari, Nihon | 96 | 33.58 N | 131.56 E |
| Hikarigaoka | 268 | 35.50 N | 139.58 E |
| Hikawa | 96 | 35.25 N | 132.50 E |
| Hikawa Shrine ʊ[1] | 268 | 35.54 N | 139.38 E |
| Hiketa | 96 | 34.13 N | 134.24 E |
| Hiki ≃ | 96 | 33.33 N | 135.27 E |
| Hikigawa | 96 | 33.34 N | 135.27 E |
| Hikimi | 96 | 34.34 N | 132.01 E |
| Hikimi ≃ | 96 | 34.37 N | 131.48 E |
| Hikiura | 270 | 34.33 N | 134.58 E |
| Hikone | 94 | 35.15 N | 136.15 E |
| Hikone-jō ⊥ | 94 | 35.15 N | 136.14 E |
| Hiko-san ∧ | 96 | 33.27 N | 130.54 E |
| Hikueru I[1] | 14 | 17.36 S | 142.37 W |
| Hikurangi | 172 | 35.36 S | 174.18 E |
| Hikurangi ∧ | 172 | 37.55 S | 178.04 E |
| Hikutaia | 172 | 37.17 S | 175.39 E |
| Hikutivake | 174v | 18.56 S | 169.53 W |
| Hila | 112 | 7.35 S | 127.24 E |
| Hilaban Island I | 116 | 12.03 N | 125.34 E |
| Hilāl, Jabal ⋀ | 132 | 30.40 N | 34.00 E |
| Hilāl, Ra's al- › | 146 | 32.57 N | 22.10 E |
| Hilbersdorf | 54 | 50.55 N | 13.23 E |
| Hilbert | 190 | 44.08 N | 88.09 W |
| Hilbre Islands II | 262 | 53.23 N | 3.13 W |
| Hilbre Point › | 262 | 53.23 N | 3.12 W |
| Hilchenbach | 56 | 51.00 N | 8.06 E |
| Hilda | 184 | 50.28 N | 110.03 W |
| Hildburghausen | 54 | 50.25 N | 10.44 E |
| Hilden | 56 | 51.10 N | 6.56 E |
| Hildenborough | 260 | 51.13 N | 0.15 E |
| Hilders | 56 | 50.34 N | 10.00 E |
| Hildesheim | 52 | 52.09 N | 9.57 E |
| Hildreth | 198 | 40.20 N | 99.02 W |
| Hilgen | 263 | 51.06 N | 7.09 E |
| Hilialawa | 114 | 0.41 N | 97.53 E |
| Hiligeo | 114 | 1.22 N | 97.10 E |
| Hiliotaluwa | 114 | 0.44 N | 97.53 E |
| Hill □[6] | 222 | 32.02 N | 97.10 W |
| Hillaby, Mount ∧ | 241g | 13.12 N | 59.35 W |
| Hill Air Force Base ■ | 202 | 41.05 N | 111.58 W |
| Hillandale, S. Afr. | 158 | 33.06 S | 20.36 E |
| Hillandale, Md., U.S. | 284c | 39.01 N | 76.58 W |
| Hillandale Heights | 284c | 39.01 N | 76.59 W |
| Hill Bank | 232 | 17.35 N | 88.42 W |
| Hillburn | 210 | 41.08 N | 74.10 W |
| Hill City, Ks., U.S. | 198 | 39.21 N | 99.50 W |
| Hill City, Mn., U.S. | 190 | 46.59 N | 93.35 W |
| Hill City, S.D., U.S. | 198 | 43.55 N | 103.34 W |
| Hill Creek ≃ | 200 | 39.55 N | 109.40 W |
| Hillcrest, Il., U.S. | 216 | 41.57 N | 89.04 W |
| Hillcrest, N.Y., U.S. | 210 | 41.07 N | 74.02 W |
| Hillcrest, N.Y., U.S. | 210 | 42.09 N | 75.53 W |
| Hillcrest Heights | 284c | 38.49 N | 76.57 W |
| Hillcrest Mines | 182 | 49.34 N | 114.23 W |
| Hillcrest Orchard | 216 | 41.51 N | 83.29 W |
| Hillcrest Park | 282 | 38.07 N | 122.16 W |
| Hill Cumorah ⊥ | 210 | 43.01 N | 77.15 W |
| Hille, Dtsch. | 52 | 52.20 N | 8.44 E |
| Hille, Sve. | 40 | 60.44 N | 17.11 E |
| Hillegom | 52 | 52.18 N | 4.35 E |
| Hillegossen | 52 | 51.59 N | 8.37 E |
| Hillerød | 41 | 55.56 N | 12.19 E |
| Hillers Creek ≃ | 219 | 38.38 N | 91.54 W |
| Hillesheim | 56 | 50.18 N | 6.38 E |
| Hilli | 124 | 25.17 N | 89.01 E |
| Hilliard, Fl., U.S. | 192 | 30.41 N | 81.55 W |
| Hilliard, Oh., U.S. | 218 | 40.02 N | 83.09 W |
| Hilliards | 214 | 41.05 N | 79.50 W |
| Hillingdon •[8] | 42 | 51.32 N | 0.27 W |
| Hillisburg | 216 | 40.17 N | 86.20 W |
| Hill Island Lake ⊜ | 176 | 60.29 N | 109.50 W |
| Hillister | 194 | 30.40 N | 94.23 W |
| Hillman | 190 | 45.03 N | 83.54 W |
| Hillman ≃ | 168a | 33.26 S | 116.48 E |
| Hillmersdorf | 54 | 51.42 N | 13.29 E |
| Hill of Fearn | 46 | 57.45 N | 3.56 W |
| Hills | 198 | 43.31 N | 96.21 W |
| Hills and Dales | 214 | 39.42 N | 84.13 W |
| Hillsboro, Il., U.S. | 219 | 39.09 N | 89.29 W |
| Hillsboro, Ks., U.S. | 198 | 38.21 N | 97.12 W |
| Hillsboro, Ky., U.S. | 218 | 38.18 N | 83.40 W |
| Hillsboro, Md., U.S. | 208 | 38.55 N | 75.56 W |
| Hillsboro, Mo., U.S. | 219 | 38.13 N | 90.33 W |
| Hillsboro, N.H., U.S. | 188 | 43.06 N | 71.53 W |
| Hillsboro, N.M., U.S. | 200 | 32.55 N | 107.33 W |
| Hillsboro, N.D., U.S. | 198 | 47.24 N | 97.03 W |
| Hillsboro, Oh., U.S. | 218 | 39.12 N | 83.36 W |
| Hillsboro, Or., U.S. | 224 | 45.31 N | 122.59 W |
| Hillsboro, Tx., U.S. | 222 | 32.00 N | 97.07 W |
| Hillsboro, Wi., U.S. | 190 | 43.39 N | 90.20 W |
| Hillsboro Beach | 220 | 26.18 N | 80.05 W |
| Hillsboro Canal ≋ | 220 | 26.19 N | 80.05 W |
| Hillsborough, N.B., Can. | 186 | 45.56 N | 64.39 W |
| Hillsborough, N. Ire., U.K. | 48 | 54.28 N | 6.05 W |
| Hillsborough, Ca., U.S. | 226 | 37.34 N | 122.22 W |
| Hillsborough, N.C., U.S. | 192 | 36.04 N | 79.06 W |
| Hillsborough □[6], Fl., U.S. | 220 | 27.55 N | 82.15 W |
| Hillsborough □[6], N.H., U.S. | 207 | 42.49 N | 71.41 W |
| Hillsborough ≃ | 220 | 27.56 N | 82.27 W |
| Hillsborough, Cape › | 166 | 20.54 S | 149.03 E |
| Hillsborough Bay ⊂, P.E., Can. | 186 | 46.10 N | 63.05 W |
| Hillsborough Bay ⊂, Fl., U.S. | 220 | 27.52 N | 82.27 W |
| Hillsborough River State Park ♦ | 220 | 28.09 N | 82.14 W |
| Hillsburgh | 212 | 43.47 N | 80.09 W |
| Hills Creek Lake ⊜[1] | 202 | 43.40 N | 122.26 W |
| Hillsdale, Mi., U.S. | 216 | 41.55 N | 84.37 W |
| Hillsdale, N.J., U.S. | 276 | 41.00 N | 74.02 W |
| Hillsdale, N.Y., U.S. | 210 | 42.10 N | 73.31 W |
| Hillsdale, Pa., U.S. | 214 | 40.45 N | 78.53 W |
| Hillsdale □[6] | 216 | 41.53 N | 84.36 W |
| Hillsdale •[9] | 282 | 37.32 N | 122.18 W |
| Hillsdale Lake ⊜[1] | 198 | 38.40 N | 94.55 W |
| Hills Flat | 226 | 39.14 N | 121.03 W |
| Hillsgrove | 210 | 41.27 N | 76.42 W |
| Hillside, Austl. | 162 | 21.44 S | 119.23 E |
| Hillside, Scot., U.K. | 46 | 56.44 N | 2.29 W |
| Hillside, Il., U.S. | 278 | 41.52 N | 87.54 W |
| Hillside, N.J., U.S. | 276 | 40.42 N | 74.13 W |
| Hillside •[8] | 276 | 40.42 N | 73.47 W |
| Hillside Gardens | 216 | 42.16 N | 84.27 W |
| Hillside Heights | 285 | 39.41 N | 75.41 W |
| Hillside Lake | 210 | 41.36 N | 73.50 W |
| Hillston | 166 | 33.29 S | 145.32 E |
| Hillsville, Pa., U.S. | 214 | 41.00 N | 80.29 W |
| Hillsville, Va., U.S. | 192 | 36.45 N | 80.44 W |
| Hillswick | 46a | 60.28 N | 1.30 W |
| Hilltop | 208 | 39.49 N | 75.04 W |
| Hilltop Center •[9] | 282 | 37.59 N | 122.19 W |
| Hilltown, N. Ire., U.K. | 48 | 54.12 N | 6.09 W |
| Hilltown, Pa., U.S. | 208 | 40.20 N | 75.14 W |
| Hillview | 219 | 39.27 N | 90.33 W |
| Hillview Reservoir ⊜[1] | 276 | 40.55 N | 73.52 W |
| Hillwood | 284c | 38.52 N | 77.10 W |
| Hilmar | 226 | 37.25 N | 120.51 W |
| Hilo | 229d | 19.43 N | 155.05 W |
| Hilo Bay ⊂ | 229d | 19.44 N | 155.05 W |
| Hilonghilong, Mount ∧ | 116 | 9.06 N | 125.44 E |
| Hilongos | 116 | 10.23 N | 124.45 E |
| Hilpotstein | 60 | 49.12 N | 11.12 E |
| Hilpsford Point › | 44 | 54.03 N | 3.12 W |
| Hils ∧ | 52 | 51.55 N | 9.40 E |
| Hilshire Village | 222 | 29.49 N | 95.26 W |
| Hiltaba, Mount ∧ | 162 | 32.09 S | 135.03 E |
| Hilter | 52 | 52.08 N | 8.08 E |
| Hilton, N.Y., U.S. | 210 | 43.17 N | 77.47 W |
| Hilton, Pa., U.S. | 208 | 40.00 N | 76.49 W |
| Hilton Head Island I | 192 | 32.12 N | 80.45 W |
| Hiltpoltstein | 60 | 49.40 N | 11.19 E |
| Hiltrop •[8] | 263 | 51.30 N | 7.15 E |
| Hiltrup | 52 | 51.54 N | 7.38 E |
| Hilvan | 130 | 37.35 N | 38.57 E |
| Hilvarenbeek | 52 | 51.29 N | 5.09 E |
| Hilversum | 52 | 52.14 N | 5.10 E |
| Hima | 192 | 37.07 N | 83.46 W |
| Himāchal Pradesh □[3] | 120 | 32.00 N | 77.00 E |
| Himalayas ⋀ | 120 | 28.00 N | 84.00 E |
| Himāl Chulī ∧ | 124 | 28.25 N | 84.39 E |
| Himamaylan | 116 | 10.06 N | 122.52 E |
| Himanka | 26 | 64.04 N | 23.39 E |
| Himarë | 38 | 40.07 N | 19.44 E |
| Himatnagar | 120 | 23.36 N | 72.57 E |
| Himberg | 61 | 48.05 N | 16.26 E |
| Hime ≃ | 94 | 37.02 N | 137.49 E |
| Himeji | 96 | 34.49 N | 134.42 E |
| Hime-shima I | 96 | 33.43 N | 131.40 E |
| Himeville | 158 | 29.44 S | 29.31 E |
| Himi | 94 | 36.51 N | 136.59 E |
| Himmelbjerget ∧[2] | 41 | 56.06 N | 9.42 E |
| Himmelgeist •[8] | 263 | 51.10 N | 6.49 E |
| Himmelpforten | 52 | 53.36 N | 9.18 E |
| Himmerfjärden ⊂[2] | 40 | 59.00 N | 17.43 E |
| Himmerland •[1] | 26 | 56.50 N | 9.45 E |
| Himmetdede | 130 | 38.55 N | 35.07 E |
| Himrod | 210 | 42.35 N | 76.57 W |
| Ḥimṣ (Homs) | 130 | 34.44 N | 36.43 E |
| Ḥimṣ □[8] | 130 | 34.15 N | 38.00 E |
| Hinabangan | 116 | 11.42 N | 125.04 E |
| Hīnah | 132 | 33.21 N | 35.56 E |
| Hinako, Kepulauan II | 114 | 0.52 N | 97.21 E |
| Hinase | 96 | 34.44 N | 134.16 E |
| Hinatuan | 116 | 8.23 N | 126.20 E |
| Hinatuan Island I | 116 | 9.47 N | 125.43 E |
| Hinatuan Passage ⊔ | 116 | 9.45 N | 125.47 E |
| Hinche | 238 | 19.09 N | 72.01 W |
| Hinchinbrook Entrance ⊔ | 180 | 60.25 N | 146.50 W |
| Hinchinbrook Island I, Austl. | 166 | 18.23 S | 146.17 E |
| Hinchinbrook Island I, Ak., U.S. | 180 | 60.22 N | 146.30 W |
| Hinchinbrook Island National Park ♦ | 166 | 18.20 S | 146.20 E |
| Hinckley, Eng., U.K. | 42 | 52.33 N | 1.21 W |
| Hinckley, Il., U.S. | 216 | 41.46 N | 88.38 W |
| Hinckley, Mn., U.S. | 190 | 46.00 N | 92.56 W |
| Hinckley, Oh., U.S. | 214 | 41.14 N | 81.45 W |
| Hinckley, Ut,. U.S. | 200 | 39.19 N | 112.40 W |
| Hinckley Reservoir ⊜[1] | 210 | 43.20 N | 75.05 W |
| Hindan ≃ | 272a | 28.30 N | 77.27 E |
| Hindang | 116 | 10.26 N | 124.44 E |
| Hindaun | 124 | 26.43 N | 77.01 E |
| Hindelang | 58 | 47.30 N | 10.22 E |
| Hindelbank | 58 | 47.03 N | 7.32 E |
| Hindeloopen | 52 | 52.56 N | 5.24 E |
| Hindenburg → Zabrze | 30 | 50.18 N | 18.46 E |
| Hindhead | 42 | 51.07 N | 0.44 W |
| Hindley | 44 | 53.32 N | 2.35 W |
| Hindley Green | 262 | 53.31 N | 2.32 W |
| Hindman | 192 | 37.20 N | 82.58 W |
| Hindmarsh, Lake ⊜ | 166 | 36.03 S | 141.55 E |
| Hindmarsh Island I | 168b | 35.32 S | 138.52 E |
| Hindmarsh Valley | 168b | 35.30 S | 138.38 E |
| Hindon | 42 | 51.06 N | 2.08 W |
| Hinds | 172 | 44.00 S | 171.34 E |
| Hindsholm ›[1] | 41 | 55.33 N | 10.40 E |
| Hinds Lake ⊜ | 186 | 48.57 N | 57.00 W |
| Hindu Kush ⋀ | 120 | 36.00 N | 71.30 E |
| Hindūmalkot | 123 | 30.09 N | 73.55 E |
| Hindupur | 122 | 13.49 N | 77.29 E |
| Hi-Nella | 285 | 39.50 N | 75.01 W |
| Hines | 202 | 43.33 N | 119.04 W |
| Hines Creek | 182 | 56.15 N | 118.36 W |
| Hines Creek ≃ | 182 | 55.54 N | 118.37 W |
| Hines Peak ∧ | 228 | 34.31 N | 119.05 W |
| Hinesville | 192 | 31.50 N | 81.35 W |
| Hinganghāt | 122 | 20.34 N | 78.50 E |
| Hingatungan | 116 | 10.35 N | 125.11 E |
| Hingham, Eng., U.K. | 42 | 52.35 N | 0.59 E |
| Hingham, Ma., U.S. | 207 | 42.14 N | 70.53 W |
| Hingham Bay ⊂ | 207 | 42.17 N | 70.55 W |
| Hingham Harbor ⊂ | 283 | 42.15 N | 70.53 W |
| Hingol ≃ | 128 | 25.23 N | 65.28 E |
| Hingoli | 122 | 19.43 N | 77.09 E |
| Hinigaran | 116 | 10.17 N | 122.51 E |
| Hınıs | 130 | 39.22 N | 41.44 E |
| Hınıs ≃ | 130 | 39.18 N | 42.12 E |
| Hinkley | 228 | 34.56 N | 117.11 W |
| Hinkson Creek ≃ | 219 | 38.56 N | 92.23 W |
| Hinkston Creek ≃ | 188 | 38.18 N | 84.14 W |
| Hinnerjoki | 26 | 61.00 N | 22.00 E |
| Hinnerup | 41 | 56.16 N | 10.04 E |
| Hinnøya I | 24 | 68.30 N | 16.00 E |
| Hino, Nihon | 94 | 35.00 N | 136.15 E |
| Hino, Nihon | 94 | 35.41 N | 139.24 E |
| Hino, Nihon | 96 | 35.14 N | 133.27 E |
| Hino ≃, Nihon | 94 | 35.09 N | 136.02 E |
| Hino ≃, Nihon | 94 | 36.04 N | 136.11 E |
| Hino ≃, Nihon | 96 | 35.27 N | 133.23 E |
| Hinoba-an | 116 | 9.35 N | 122.28 E |
| Hinode | 94 | 35.45 N | 139.14 E |
| Hinoemata | 94 | 37.01 N | 139.23 E |
| Hinohara | 94 | 35.43 N | 139.09 E |
| Hinojosa del Duque | 34 | 38.30 N | 5.09 W |
| Hinokage | 92 | 32.39 N | 131.24 E |
| Hinomi-saki ›, Nihon | 96 | 33.53 N | 135.04 E |
| Hinomi-saki ›, Nihon | 96 | 35.26 N | 132.38 E |
| Hinsbeck | 56 | 51.21 N | 6.17 E |
| Hinsdale, Il., U.S. | 216 | 41.48 N | 87.56 W |
| Hinsdale, Ma., U.S. | 207 | 42.26 N | 73.07 W |
| Hinsdale, Mt., U.S. | 202 | 48.23 N | 107.05 W |
| Hinsdale, N.H., U.S. | 207 | 42.47 N | 72.29 W |
| Hinsdale, N.Y., U.S. | 210 | 42.10 N | 78.23 W |
| Hinsel •[8] | 263 | 51.26 N | 7.05 E |
| Hinsen ⊜ | 40 | 60.39 N | 16.05 E |
| Hinte | 52 | 53.25 N | 7.11 E |
| Hinterbichl | 64 | 47.01 N | 12.20 E |
| Hinterbrühl | 61 | 48.05 N | 16.15 E |
| Hinterhermsdorf | 54 | 50.55 N | 14.22 E |
| Hinterrhein | 58 | 46.32 N | 9.12 E |
| Hinterrhein ≃ | 58 | 46.49 N | 9.25 E |
| Hintersdorf | 264b | 48.18 N | 16.13 E |
| Hintersee | 54 | 53.37 N | 14.16 E |
| Hinterstoder | 61 | 47.41 N | 14.09 E |
| Hintertux | 64 | 47.07 N | 11.41 E |
| Hinterweidenthal | 56 | 49.12 N | 7.45 E |
| Hinterzarten | 58 | 47.54 N | 8.06 E |
| Hinton, Ab., Can. | 182 | 53.25 N | 117.34 W |
| Hinton, Mo., U.S. | 219 | 39.03 N | 92.21 W |
| Hinton, Ok., U.S. | 196 | 35.28 N | 98.21 W |
| Hinton, W.V., U.S. | 192 | 37.40 N | 80.53 W |
| Hi-numa ⊜ | 94 | 36.16 N | 140.30 E |
| Hinuma ≃ | 94 | 36.16 N | 140.28 E |
| Hinundayan | 116 | 10.21 N | 125.15 E |
| Hinwil | 58 | 47.18 N | 8.51 E |
| Hinzik | 84 | 40.08 N | 40.58 E |
| Hípico, Club ♦ | 286e | 33.28 S | 70.41 W |
| Hipólito | 232 | 25.41 N | 101.26 W |
| Hipólito Yrigoyen | 252 | 32.55 S | 66.20 W |
| Hippolytushoef | 52 | 52.54 N | 4.57 E |
| Hirado | 92 | 33.22 N | 129.33 E |
| Hirado-shima I | 92 | 33.20 N | 129.30 E |
| Hiraiwa-hana › | 174f | 24.48 N | 141.18 E |
| Hiraizumi | 92 | 38.59 N | 141.07 E |
| Hirakata, Nihon | 96 | 34.48 N | 135.38 E |
| Hirakata, Nihon | 268 | 35.56 N | 139.33 E |
| Hirakawa | 270 | 34.52 N | 135.47 E |
| Hīrākud | 122 | 21.31 N | 83.57 E |
| Hīrākud Reservoir ⊜[1] | 120 | 21.35 N | 83.50 E |
| Hiram, Me., U.S. | 188 | 43.52 N | 70.48 W |
| Hiram, Oh., U.S. | 214 | 41.18 N | 81.08 W |
| Hiraman ≃ | 154 | 1.07 S | 39.55 E |
| Hirano | 175d | 24.35 N | 124.19 E |
| Hirano •[8] | 270 | 34.36 N | 135.34 E |
| Hirao | 96 | 33.56 N | 132.04 E |
| Hirao-dai ♦ | 96 | 33.45 N | 130.52 E |
| Hiraoka → Higashiōsaka | 96 | 34.39 N | 135.35 E |
| Hīrāpur | 124 | 24.22 N | 79.13 E |
| Hirara | 175d | 24.48 N | 125.17 E |
| Hirata, Nihon | 94 | 35.15 N | 136.38 E |
| Hirata, Nihon | 96 | 35.26 N | 132.49 E |
| Hiratsuka | 94 | 35.19 N | 139.21 E |
| Hiraya | 94 | 35.19 N | 137.37 E |
| Hirfanlı Barajı ⊜[1] | 130 | 39.10 N | 33.35 E |
| Hirhafok | 148 | 23.49 N | 5.45 E |
| Hiriyūr | 122 | 13.58 N | 76.36 E |
| Ḥirjillah | 132 | 33.22 N | 36.18 E |
| Hirnyk, Ukr. | 78 | 50.20 N | 24.10 E |
| Hirnyk, Ukr. | 83 | 48.04 N | 37.24 E |
| Hirnyts'ke | 78 | 47.42 N | 34.08 E |
| Hirokawa, Nihon | 96 | 33.15 N | 130.32 E |
| Hirokawa, Nihon | 96 | 34.01 N | 135.11 E |
| Hirok Sāmi | 128 | 26.02 N | 63.25 E |
| Hiromi | 96 | 33.15 N | 132.41 E |


**Symbols** in the index entries represent the broad categories identified in the key at the right. Symbols with superior numbers (⋀[1]) identify subcategories (see complete key on page *I · 1)*.

**Symbole** im Register stellen die rechts im Schlüssel erklärten Kategorien dar. Symbole mit hochgestellten Ziffern (⋀[1]) bezeichnen Unterabteilungen einer Kategorie (vgl. vollständiger Schlüssel auf Seite *I · 1)*.

**Los símbolos** incluídos en el texto del índice representan las grandes categorías identificadas con la clave a la derecha. Los símbolos con numeros en su parte superior (⋀[1]) identifican las subcategorías (véase la clave completa en la página *I · 1)*.

**Les symboles** de l'index représentent les catégories indiquées dans la légende à droite. Les symboles suivis d'un indice (⋀[1]) représentent des sous-catégories (voir légende complète à la page *I · 1)*.

**Os símbolos** incluídos no texto do índice representam as grandes categorias identificadas com a chave à direita. Os símbolos com números em sua parte superior (⋀[1]) identificam as subcategorias (veja-se a chave completa à página *I · 1)*.

| | English | Deutsch | Español | Français | Português |
|---|---|---|---|---|---|
| ∧ | Mountain | Berg | Montaña | Montagne | Montanha |
| ⋀ | Mountains | Gebirge | Montañas | Montagnes | Montanhas |
| )( | Pass | Paß | Paso | Col | Passo |
| V | Valley, Canyon | Tal, Cañon | Valle, Cañón | Vallée, Canyon | Vale, Canhão |
| ≚ | Plain | Ebene | Llano | Plaine | Planície |
| › | Cape | Kap | Cabo | Cap | Cabo |
| I | Island | Insel | Isla | Île | Ilha |
| II | Islands | Inseln | Islas | Îles | Ilhas |
| ⊥ | Other Topographic Features | Andere Topographische Objekte | Otros Elementos Topográficos | Autres données topographiques | Outros acidentes topográficos |

ESPAÑOL · FRANÇAIS · PORTUGUÊS


| Nombre / Nom / Nome | Página / Page | Lat.°′ | Long.°′ W = Oeste / W = Ouest |
|---|---|---|---|
| Hiroo | 92a | 42.17 N | 143.19 E |
| Hirooka | 268 | 35.15 N | 140.04 E |
| Hirosaki | 92 | 40.35 N | 140.28 E |
| Hiroschima → Hiroshima | 96 | 34.24 N | 132.27 E |
| Hirose | 96 | 35.22 N | 133.10 E |
| Hiroshima | 96 | 34.24 N | 132.27 E |
| Hiroshima □[5] | 96 | 34.30 N | 133.00 E |
| Hiro-shima I | 96 | 34.22 N | 133.43 E |
| Hiroshima-wan c | 96 | 34.06 N | 132.20 E |
| Hirosima → Hiroshima | 96 | 34.24 N | 132.27 E |
| Hirota | 270 | 34.45 N | 135.21 E |
| Hirsau | 56 | 48.44 N | 8.44 E |
| Hirschaid | 56 | 49.49 N | 10.59 E |
| Hirschau | 60 | 49.33 N | 11.57 E |
| Hirschbach | 54 | 50.33 N | 10.44 E |
| Hirschberg, Dtsch. | 54 | 50.24 N | 11.49 E |
| Hirschberg → Jelenia Góra, Pol. | 30 | 50.55 N | 15.46 E |
| Hirschfeld | 54 | 51.23 N | 13.37 E |
| Hirschfelde, Dtsch. | 54 | 50.57 N | 14.53 E |
| Hirschfelde, Dtsch. | 264a | 52.38 N | 13.48 E |
| Hirschhorn | 56 | 49.27 N | 8.53 E |
| Hirschstetten ◈[8] | 264b | 48.14 N | 16.29 E |
| Hirshfeld Brook ≃ | 276 | 40.57 N | 74.02 W |
| Hirsingue | 58 | 47.35 N | 7.15 E |
| Hirs'ke | 83 | 48.46 N | 38.30 E |
| Hirs'kyy Tikych ≃ | 78 | 48.47 N | 30.53 E |
| Hirson | 50 | 49.55 N | 4.05 E |
| Hirsts Hill ∧ | 171a | 27.13 S | 152.06 E |
| Hirtshals | 26 | 57.35 N | 9.58 E |
| Hirtzfelden | 58 | 47.55 N | 7.27 E |
| Hirukawa | 94 | 35.31 N | 137.23 E |
| Hiru-zen ∧ | 96 | 35.19 N | 133.40 E |
| Hirwaun | 42 | 51.45 N | 3.30 W |
| Hisābpur | 272b | 22.51 N | 88.32 E |
| Hisai, Nihon | 94 | 34.40 N | 136.28 E |
| Hisai, Nihon | 270 | 34.25 N | 135.28 E |
| Hisār | 123 | 29.10 N | 75.43 E |
| Hisarönü | 130 | 41.33 N | 32.02 E |
| Hisbān | 132 | 31.48 N | 35.48 E |
| Hisiu | 164 | 9.05 S | 146.45 E |
| Hisn al-'Abr | 144 | 16.05 N | 47.22 E |
| Ḥiṣn al-Qarn | 144 | 15.11 N | 49.05 E |
| Hispaniola I | 238 | 19.00 N | 71.00 W |
| Hispar Glacier ⊓ | 123 | 36.05 N | 75.20 E |
| Histon | 42 | 52.15 N | 0.06 E |
| Hisua | 124 | 24.50 N | 85.25 E |
| Ḥisyah | 130 | 34.24 N | 36.45 E |
| Hīt | 128 | 33.38 N | 42.49 E |
| Hita | 96 | 33.19 N | 130.56 E |
| Hitachi | 94 | 36.36 N | 140.39 E |
| Hitachi-ōta | 94 | 36.32 N | 140.31 E |
| Hitati → Hitachi | 94 | 36.36 N | 140.39 E |
| Hitchcock | 222 | 29.20 N | 95.00 W |
| Hitchin | 42 | 51.57 N | 0.17 W |
| Hitchins | 218 | 38.16 N | 82.55 W |
| Hither Green ◈[8] | 260 | 51.27 N | 0.01 W |
| Hither Hills State Park ♠ | 207 | 41.01 N | 72.01 W |
| Hitiaa | 174s | 17.36 S | 149.18 W |
| Hitokura | 270 | 34.55 N | 135.25 E |
| Hitotsubashi University ɤ[2] | 268 | 35.42 N | 139.27 E |
| Hitoyoshi | 92 | 32.13 N | 130.45 E |
| Hitra I | 26 | 63.33 N | 8.45 E |
| Hittarp | 41 | 56.06 N | 12.38 E |
| Hittisau | 58 | 47.27 N | 9.57 E |
| Hitzacker | 54 | 53.09 N | 11.02 E |
| Hitze-Berge ∧[2] | 264a | 52.35 N | 13.07 E |
| Hiu I | 175f | 13.10 S | 166.35 E |
| Hiuchiga-take ∧ | 94 | 36.57 N | 139.17 E |
| Hiuchi-nada ⊤[2] | 96 | 34.05 N | 133.20 E |
| Hiūnchuli Pātan ∧ | 124 | 28.50 N | 82.37 E |
| Hiva Oa I | 174x | 9.45 S | 139.00 W |
| Hi Vista | 228 | 34.44 N | 117.47 W |
| Hiwa | 96 | 34.59 N | 132.59 E |
| Hiwannee | 194 | 31.48 N | 88.41 W |
| Hiwasa | 96 | 33.44 N | 134.32 E |
| Hiwassee ≃ | 192 | 35.19 N | 84.47 W |
| Hiwassee Lake ⊜[1] | 192 | 35.10 N | 84.05 W |
| Hixon | 182 | 53.27 N | 122.36 W |
| Hixson | 192 | 35.09 N | 85.14 W |
| Hiyoshi, Nihon | 94 | 35.53 N | 137.45 E |
| Hiyoshi, Nihon | 96 | 33.20 N | 132.48 E |
| Hiyoshi, Nihon | 96 | 35.09 N | 135.31 E |
| Hiyoshi ◈[8] | 268 | 35.33 N | 139.39 E |
| Ḥiyyon, Naḥal V | 132 | 30.12 N | 35.07 E |
| Hizaonna | 174m | 26.24 N | 127.50 E |
| Hjälmare kanal ≊ | 40 | 59.24 N | 15.56 E |
| Hjälmaren ⊜ | 40 | 59.15 N | 15.45 E |
| Hjälmaresund Ʉ | 40 | 59.15 N | 16.06 E |
| Hjarnø I | 41 | 55.50 N | 10.05 E |
| Hjelm I | 41 | 56.08 N | 10.48 E |
| Hjelmelandsvågen | 26 | 59.14 N | 6.11 E |
| Hjeltefjorden c[2] | 26 | 60.40 N | 4.55 E |
| Hjembæk | 41 | 55.42 N | 11.25 E |
| Hjo | 26 | 58.18 N | 14.17 E |
| Hjøllund | 41 | 56.05 N | 9.25 E |
| Hjordkær | 41 | 55.01 N | 9.19 E |
| Hjørring | 26 | 57.28 N | 9.59 E |
| Hjortkvarn | 40 | 58.53 N | 15.25 E |
| Hjørundfjorden c[2] | 26 | 62.21 N | 6.23 E |
| Hkakabo Razi ∧ | 102 | 28.20 N | 97.32 E |
| Hkok (Kok) ≃ | 110 | 20.14 N | 100.09 E |
| Hlabisa | 158 | 28.08 S | 31.52 E |
| Hladkivka | 78 | 46.23 N | 32.36 E |
| Hlaingbwe | 110 | 17.08 N | 97.50 E |
| Hlatikulu | 158 | 27.00 S | 31.25 E |
| Hlegu | 110 | 17.06 N | 96.14 E |
| Hlinsko | 30 | 49.45 N | 15.55 E |
| Hlobane | 158 | 27.42 S | 31.00 E |
| Hlobyne | 78 | 49.23 N | 33.17 E |
| Hlohovec | 30 | 48.25 N | 17.47 E |
| Hluboká ⊥ | 61 | 49.05 N | 14.25 E |
| Hluboká nad Vltavou | 61 | 49.03 N | 14.27 E |
| Hluboš | 60 | 49.45 N | 14.02 E |
| Hlučín | 30 | 49.54 N | 18.12 E |
| Hluhluwe | 158 | 28.01 S | 32.15 E |
| Hluhluwe Game Reserve ◈[4] | 158 | 28.05 S | 32.04 E |
| Hlukhiv | 78 | 51.41 N | 33.53 E |
| Hluša | 76 | 53.05 N | 28.52 E |
| Hlusk | 76 | 52.54 N | 28.41 E |
| Hluškavičy | 78 | 51.34 N | 27.47 E |
| Hluti | 158 | 27.13 S | 31.35 E |
| Hlyboka | 78 | 48.07 N | 25.56 E |
| Hlybokae | 76 | 55.08 N | 27.41 E |
| Hlynyany | 78 | 49.49 N | 24.30 E |
| Hmawbi | 110 | 17.06 N | 96.02 E |
| H. Neely Henry Lake ⊜[1] | 194 | 33.55 N | 86.05 W |
| Hnivan' | 78 | 49.06 N | 28.20 E |
| Hnyla Lypa ≃ | 78 | 49.07 N | 24.44 E |
| Hnylyy Tikych ≃ | 78 | 48.47 N | 30.53 E |
| Hnylyy Yalanets' ≃ | 78 | 47.20 N | 31.44 E |
| Ho | 150 | 6.35 N | 0.30 E |
| Hoa Binh | 110 | 20.50 N | 105.20 E |
| Hoa Da | 110 | 11.11 N | 108.33 E |
| Hoagland | 216 | 40.56 N | 84.59 W |
| Hoagland Ditch ≊ | 216 | 40.48 N | 86.48 W |
| Hoanib ≃ | 156 | 19.27 S | 12.46 E |
| Hoare Bay c | 176 | 65.20 N | 62.30 W |
| Hoarusib ≃ | 156 | 19.03 S | 12.36 E |
| Hoa Thoi | 269c | 10.44 N | 106.35 E |
| Hoback ≃ | 202 | 43.19 N | 110.44 W |
| Hobart, Austl. | 166 | 42.53 S | 147.19 E |
| Hobart, In., U.S. | 216 | 41.31 N | 87.15 W |
| Hobart, N.Y., U.S. | 210 | 42.22 N | 74.40 W |
| Hobart, Ok., U.S. | 196 | 35.01 N | 99.05 W |
| Hobart, Wa., U.S. | 224 | 47.25 N | 121.58 W |
| Hobbs, In., U.S. | 216 | 40.17 N | 85.57 W |
| Hobbs, N.M., U.S. | 196 | 32.42 N | 103.08 W |
| Hobbs Coast ≗[2] | 9 | 74.45 S | 131.00 W |
| Hobe Sound | 220 | 27.03 N | 80.08 W |
| Hobgood | 192 | 36.01 N | 77.23 W |
| Hobhole Drain ≊ | 44 | 52.59 N | 0.02 E |
| Hobhouse | 158 | 29.31 S | 27.08 E |
| Hobo | 246 | 2.35 N | 75.27 W |
| Hoboken, Bel. | 50 | 51.10 N | 4.21 E |
| Hoboken, N.J., U.S. | 210 | 40.44 N | 74.01 W |
| Hoboksar | 86 | 46.47 N | 85.43 E |
| Hobq Shamo ◈[2] | 102 | 40.30 N | 107.55 E |
| Hobro | 26 | 56.38 N | 9.48 E |
| Hobson | 202 | 47.00 N | 109.52 W |
| Hobson Lake ⊜ | 182 | 52.30 N | 120.20 W |
| Hobsons Bay c | 274b | 37.51 S | 144.56 E |
| Hoburgen ≻ | 26 | 56.55 N | 18.07 E |
| Hobyo | 144 | 5.21 N | 48.32 E |
| Hocaköy | 130 | 41.03 N | 30.17 E |
| Hocalar | 130 | 38.34 N | 30.00 E |
| Hocalı | 130 | 38.41 N | 27.41 E |
| Hochalmspitze ∧ | 64 | 47.01 N | 13.19 E |
| Hochandochtla Mountain ∧ | 180 | 65.32 N | 154.50 W |
| Höchberg | 56 | 49.49 N | 9.51 E |
| Hochburg | 60 | 48.07 N | 12.52 E |
| Hochdahl | 56 | 51.13 N | 6.56 E |
| Hochdorf | 58 | 47.10 N | 8.17 E |
| Höchenschwand | 58 | 47.44 N | 8.10 E |
| Hochfeiler (Gran Pilastro) ∧ | 64 | 46.58 N | 11.44 E |
| Hochfeld | 156 | 21.28 S | 17.58 E |
| Hochfeld ◈[8] | 263 | 51.25 N | 6.46 E |
| Hochfelden | 56 | 48.45 N | 7.34 E |
| Hochfilzen | 64 | 47.28 N | 12.37 E |
| Hochfinstermünz | 58 | 46.56 N | 10.29 E |
| Hochgern ∧ | 64 | 47.45 N | 12.30 E |
| Hochgolling ∧ | 64 | 47.16 N | 13.45 E |
| Hochheide ◈[8] | 263 | 51.27 N | 6.41 E |
| Hochheim, Dtsch. | 56 | 50.01 N | 8.20 E |
| Hochheim, Tx., U.S. | 222 | 29.19 N | 97.17 W |
| Ho Chi Minh City → Thanh Pho Ho Chi Minh | 110 | 10.45 N | 106.40 E |
| Hochiss ∧ | 64 | 47.27 N | 11.46 E |
| Hochkirch | 54 | 51.09 N | 14.34 E |
| Hochkönig ∧ | 64 | 47.25 N | 13.04 E |
| Hochkreuz ∧ | 64 | 46.49 N | 13.04 E |
| Hochlantsch ∧ | 61 | 47.21 N | 15.25 E |
| Hochlar | 263 | 51.36 N | 7.10 E |
| Hochneukirch | 56 | 51.06 N | 6.26 E |
| Hochobir ∧ | 61 | 46.30 N | 14.29 E |
| Hochreichhart ∧ | 61 | 47.22 N | 14.41 E |
| Hochries ∧ | 64 | 47.45 N | 12.14 E |
| Hochschwab ∧ | 61 | 47.37 N | 15.09 E |
| Hochschwab ⋏ | 61 | 47.36 N | 15.05 E |
| Hochsimmer ∧ | 56 | 50.21 N | 7.12 E |
| Hochspeyer | 56 | 49.26 N | 7.54 E |
| Höchst, Dtsch. | 56 | 49.48 N | 8.59 E |
| Höchst, Öst. | 58 | 47.28 N | 9.38 E |
| Höchstadt an der Aisch | 56 | 49.42 N | 10.44 E |
| Höchstädt an der Donau | 56 | 48.36 N | 10.34 E |
| Höchsten ◈[8] | 263 | 51.27 N | 7.29 E |
| Höchstenbach | 56 | 50.38 N | 7.44 E |
| Hochstuhl (Veliki Stol) ∧ | 61 | 46.26 N | 14.10 E |
| Hochtor )( | 64 | 47.05 N | 12.51 E |
| Hoch'uan → Hechuan | 107 | 30.00 N | 106.16 E |
| Ho Chung | 271d | 22.22 N | 114.14 E |
| Hochvogel ∧ | 58 | 47.23 N | 10.26 E |
| Hochwildstelle ∧ | 64 | 47.20 N | 13.50 E |
| Hocimsk | 76 | 53.26 N | 32.35 E |
| Hockenheim | 56 | 49.19 N | 8.33 E |
| Hockeroda | 54 | 50.35 N | 11.26 E |
| Hockessin | 285 | 39.47 N | 75.41 W |
| Hocking ≃ | 188 | 39.12 N | 81.45 W |
| Hocking Hills State Park ♠ | 188 | 39.30 N | 82.32 W |
| Hockley, Eng., U.K. | 42 | 51.37 N | 0.40 E |
| Hockley, Tx., U.S. | 222 | 30.02 N | 95.51 W |
| Hockomock Swamp ≡ | 283 | 41.59 N | 71.05 W |
| Hôd ◈[1] | 150 | 16.10 N | 8.40 W |
| Hodal | 124 | 27.54 N | 77.22 E |
| Hodasy | 76 | 53.56 N | 31.29 E |
| Hōdatsu-zan ∧ | 94 | 36.47 N | 136.49 E |
| Hodder ≃ | 44 | 53.50 N | 2.25 W |
| Hoddesdon | 42 | 51.46 N | 0.01 W |
| Hoddlesden | 262 | 53.42 N | 2.26 W |
| Hodeida → Al-Ḥudaydah | 144 | 14.48 N | 42.57 E |
| Hodenhagen | 52 | 52.46 N | 9.35 E |
| Hodge | 194 | 32.16 N | 92.43 W |
| Hodgenville | 194 | 37.34 N | 85.44 W |
| Hodges, Lake ⊜[1] | 228 | 33.03 N | 117.05 W |
| Hodges Brook ≃ | 283 | 41.58 N | 71.14 W |
| Hodges Hill ∧[2] | 186 | 49.04 N | 55.53 W |
| Hodgeville | 184 | 50.08 N | 106.58 W |
| Hodgkins | 278 | 41.46 N | 87.51 W |
| Hodgson | 184 | 51.13 N | 97.34 W |
| Hodgson ≃ | 164 | 14.48 S | 134.35 E |
| Hodgson, Mount ∧[2] | 162 | 22.26 S | 121.10 E |
| Hod HaSharon | 132 | 32.09 N | 34.53 E |
| Hodh ech Chargui □[4] | 150 | 18.10 N | 7.15 W |
| Hodh el Gharbi □[4] | 150 | 16.30 N | 10.00 W |
| Hódmezővásárhely | 30 | 46.25 N | 20.20 E |
| Hodmo V | 144 | 10.41 N | 46.13 E |
| Hodna, Chott el ⊜ | 148 | 35.25 N | 4.45 E |
| Hodna, Monts du ⋏ | 34 | 35.50 N | 4.50 E |
| Hodna, Plaine du ≚ | 34 | 35.38 N | 4.30 E |
| Hodnet | 42 | 52.51 N | 2.35 W |
| Hodogaya ◈[8] | 268 | 35.27 N | 139.36 E |
| Hodogaya Baseball Ground ♠ | 268 | 35.27 N | 139.35 E |
| Hodonín | 30 | 48.51 N | 17.08 E |
| Hodoš | 61 | 46.50 N | 16.20 E |
| Hodzana ≃ | 180 | 66.15 N | 147.48 W |
| Hoed | 41 | 56.19 N | 10.49 E |
| Hoedekenskerke | 52 | 51.25 N | 3.55 E |
| Hoehne | 198 | 37.16 N | 104.22 W |
| Hoeksche Waard I | 52 | 51.45 N | 4.30 E |
| Hoek van Holland | 52 | 51.59 N | 4.09 E |
| Hoeningen | 263 | 51.05 N | 6.41 E |
| Hoensbroek | 56 | 50.55 N | 5.55 E |
| Hœrdt | 58 | 48.42 N | 7.47 E |
| Hoerstgen | 263 | 51.30 N | 6.27 E |
| Hoeryŏng | 98 | 42.27 N | 129.44 E |
| Hoeyang | 98 | 38.43 N | 127.36 E |
| Hof, Dtsch. | 54 | 50.18 N | 11.55 E |
| Hof, Ísland | 24a | 64.34 N | 14.39 W |
| Hofbieber | 56 | 50.35 N | 9.50 E |
| Hofburg ɤ | 264b | 48.12 N | 16.22 E |
| Höfðakaupstaður | 24a | 65.50 N | 20.19 W |
| Hofei → Hefei | 100 | 31.51 N | 117.17 E |
| Höfen | 56 | 50.32 N | 6.15 E |
| Hoffman, Il., U.S. | 219 | 38.32 N | 89.16 W |
| Hoffman, Mn., U.S. | 198 | 45.49 N | 95.47 W |
| Hoffman Estates | 216 | 42.02 N | 88.04 W |
| Hoffman Island I | 276 | 40.35 N | 74.03 W |
| Hoffmans | 210 | 42.54 N | 74.05 W |
| Hoffman Station | 284a | 43.04 N | 78.50 W |
| Hoffnung | 263 | 51.07 N | 7.13 E |
| Hofgeismar | 52 | 51.30 N | 9.22 E |
| Hofheim | 56 | 50.07 N | 8.26 E |
| Hofheim in Unterfranken | 56 | 50.08 N | 10.31 E |
| Hofkirchen | 60 | 48.41 N | 13.07 E |
| Hofkirchen an der Trattnach | 60 | 48.13 N | 13.44 E |
| Höflein an der Donau | 264b | 48.21 N | 16.17 E |
| Hofmeyr | 158 | 31.39 S | 25.50 E |
| Höfn | 24a | 64.17 N | 15.10 W |
| Hofors | 40 | 60.33 N | 16.17 E |
| Hofsjökull ⊓ | 24a | 64.48 N | 18.50 W |
| Hofstade | 50 | 50.58 N | 4.02 E |
| Hofstede ◈[8] | 263 | 51.30 N | 7.12 E |
| Hofstra University ɤ[2] | 276 | 40.43 N | 73.36 W |
| Hōfu | 96 | 34.03 N | 131.34 E |
| Hofuf → Al-Hufūf | 128 | 25.22 N | 49.34 E |
| Hog, Tanjong ≻ | 116 | 5.18 N | 119.16 E |
| Hogalbāria | 126 | 23.53 N | 88.51 E |
| Höganäs | 41 | 56.12 N | 12.33 E |
| Hogan Lake ⊜ | 190 | 45.52 N | 78.30 W |
| Hogansburg | 206 | 44.58 N | 74.39 W |
| Hogansville | 192 | 33.10 N | 84.54 W |
| Hogatza ≃ | 180 | 66.00 N | 155.29 W |
| Hogback Mountain ∧, U.S. | 207 | 42.43 N | 72.25 W |
| Hogback Mountain ∧, Mt., U.S. | 202 | 44.54 N | 112.07 W |
| Hogback Mountain ∧, Ne., U.S. | 198 | 41.40 N | 103.44 W |
| Hogback Mountain ∧, S.C., U.S. | 192 | 35.10 N | 82.17 W |
| Högbo | 40 | 60.40 N | 16.48 E |
| Hog Canyon V | 226 | 35.42 N | 120.35 W |
| Hog Creek ≃ | 222 | 31.32 N | 97.18 W |
| Hoge Veluwe, Nationale Park de ♠ | 52 | 52.02 N | 5.55 E |
| Högfors | 40 | 59.59 N | 15.01 E |
| Hoggar → Ahaggar ⋏ | 148 | 23.00 N | 6.30 E |
| Hoghton | 262 | 53.44 N | 2.35 W |
| Hoghton Tower ⊥ | 262 | 53.44 N | 2.34 W |
| Hog Island I, Ma., U.S. | 283 | 42.40 N | 70.46 W |
| Hog Island I, Mi., U.S. | 190 | 45.48 N | 85.22 W |
| Hog Island I, Vt., U.S. | 206 | 44.57 N | 73.13 W |
| Hog Island I, Va., U.S. | 208 | 37.25 N | 75.41 W |
| Hog Island Bay c | 208 | 37.27 N | 75.46 W |
| Hogoro | 154 | 5.57 S | 36.27 E |
| Hog Point ≻ | 208 | 37.12 N | 76.41 W |
| Hogs Back ≗[4] | 42 | 51.13 N | 0.40 W |
| Högsby | 26 | 57.10 N | 16.02 E |
| Högsjö | 40 | 59.02 N | 15.41 E |
| Hoh ≃ | 224 | 47.45 N | 124.29 W |
| Hoh, South Fork ≃ | 224 | 47.46 N | 124.01 W |
| Hohberg | 58 | 48.25 N | 7.55 E |
| Hohe Acht ∧ | 56 | 50.23 N | 7.00 E |
| Hohebach | 56 | 49.22 N | 9.44 E |
| Hohe Eifel ⋏ | 56 | 50.15 N | 6.45 E |
| Hohegeiss | 54 | 51.40 N | 10.40 E |
| Hohenahr | 56 | 50.41 N | 8.32 E |
| Hohenau | 252 | 27.05 S | 55.45 W |
| Hohenau an der March | 61 | 48.36 N | 16.55 E |
| Höhenberg | 61 | 48.46 N | 14.53 E |
| Hohenbrunn | 60 | 48.03 N | 11.42 E |
| Hohenbucko | 54 | 51.46 N | 13.28 E |
| Hohenbudberg ◈[8] | 263 | 51.23 N | 6.40 E |
| Hohenburg | 60 | 49.18 N | 11.48 E |
| Hohendorf | 54 | 54.01 N | 13.44 E |
| Hohenebra | 54 | 51.18 N | 10.49 E |
| Hohenems | 58 | 47.22 N | 9.41 E |
| Hohenfels | 60 | 49.12 N | 11.51 E |
| Hohenfurch | 58 | 47.51 N | 10.54 E |
| Hohengüstow | 54 | 53.14 N | 13.59 E |
| Hohenhameln | 52 | 52.15 N | 10.03 E |
| Hohenheide | 263 | 51.29 N | 7.47 E |
| Hohenkammer | 60 | 48.25 N | 11.32 E |
| Hohenkirchen, Dtsch. | 52 | 53.39 N | 7.55 E |
| Hohenkirchen, Dtsch. | 54 | 50.51 N | 10.41 E |
| Hohenkirchen, Dtsch. | 54 | 53.51 N | 11.17 E |
| Hohenkirchen, Dtsch. | 56 | 51.23 N | 9.29 E |
| Hohenleipisch | 54 | 51.30 N | 13.34 E |
| Hohenleuben | 54 | 50.43 N | 12.03 E |
| Hohenlimburg | 56 | 51.21 N | 7.35 E |
| Hohenlimburg, Schloss ⊥ | 263 | 51.21 N | 7.34 E |
| Hohenlinden | 60 | 48.09 N | 12.00 E |
| Hohenlockstedt | 52 | 53.58 N | 9.38 E |
| Hohenmölsen | 54 | 51.09 N | 12.06 E |
| Hohen Neuendorf | 54 | 52.40 N | 13.16 E |
| Hohenpolding | 60 | 48.23 N | 12.08 E |
| Hohensalza → Inowrocław | 30 | 52.48 N | 18.15 E |
| Hohenschönhausen ◈[8] | 264a | 52.33 N | 13.30 E |
| Hohenseeden | 54 | 52.19 N | 12.01 E |
| Hohenseefeld | 54 | 51.53 N | 13.18 E |
| Hohenstaufen | 56 | 48.44 N | 9.43 E |
| Hohenstein-Ernstthal | 54 | 50.48 N | 12.42 E |
| Hohensyburg ⊥ | 56 | 51.25 N | 7.29 E |
| Hohentauern | 61 | 47.26 N | 14.29 E |
| Hohentengen | 58 | 48.02 N | 9.23 E |
| Hohenthurm | 54 | 51.31 N | 12.05 E |
| Hohenthurn | 64 | 46.33 N | 13.40 E |
| Hohentwiel ∧ | 58 | 47.46 N | 8.49 E |
| Hohenwald | 194 | 35.32 N | 87.33 W |
| Hohenwart | 60 | 48.36 N | 11.23 E |
| Hohenwarte-Stausee ⊜[1] | 54 | 50.32 N | 11.30 E |
| Hohenwarthe | 54 | 52.13 N | 11.42 E |
| Hohenwutzen | 54 | 52.51 N | 14.07 E |
| Hohenzethen | 54 | 53.03 N | 10.49 E |
| Hohenzollern, Burg ⊥ | 58 | 48.19 N | 8.58 E |
| Hohenzollernkanal ≊ | 264a | 52.32 N | 13.20 E |
| Hoher Bogen ∧ | 60 | 49.15 N | 12.55 E |
| Hoher Dachstein ∧ | 64 | 47.28 N | 13.35 E |
| Hoher Freschen ∧ | 58 | 47.18 N | 9.46 E |
| Hohe Rhön ⋏ | 56 | 50.30 N | 10.00 E |
| Hoher Ifen ∧ | 58 | 47.21 N | 10.05 E |
| Hoherlehme | 264a | 52.19 N | 13.37 E |
| Hoher Mechtin ∧[2] | 54 | 53.03 N | 10.55 E |
| Hoher Riffler ∧ | 58 | 47.07 N | 10.22 E |
| Hoher Sonnblick ∧ | 64 | 47.03 N | 12.57 E |
| Hoher Zinken ∧ | 64 | 47.40 N | 13.20 E |
| Hohe Tauern ⋏ | 64 | 47.10 N | 12.45 E |
| Hohe Warte (Monte Coglians) ∧ | 64 | 46.37 N | 12.53 E |
| Hoh Head ≻ | 224 | 47.46 N | 124.29 W |
| Hohhot | 102 | 40.51 N | 111.40 E |
| Höhn | 56 | 50.37 N | 8.00 E |
| Hohndorf | 54 | 50.45 N | 12.40 E |
| Hohne | 52 | 52.35 N | 10.22 E |
| Hohneck, Le ∧ | 58 | 48.02 N | 7.01 E |
| Hohnstein | 54 | 50.59 N | 14.10 E |
| Hohoe | 150 | 7.09 N | 0.28 E |
| Hōhoku | 96 | 34.17 N | 130.57 E |
| Ho-Ho-Kus | 276 | 40.59 N | 74.06 W |
| Hohokus Brook ≃ | 276 | 40.57 N | 74.06 W |
| Hoholeve | 78 | 49.56 N | 33.48 E |
| Hoholitna ≃ | 180 | 61.31 N | 157.00 W |
| Hoh Sai Hu ⊜ | 120 | 35.43 N | 92.45 E |
| Höhscheid ◈[8] | 263 | 51.09 N | 7.04 E |
| Hohultslätt | 26 | 56.58 N | 15.39 E |
| Hohwacht | 54 | 54.19 N | 10.41 E |
| Hohwachter Bucht c | 54 | 54.20 N | 10.45 E |
| Hoh Xil Hu ⊜ | 120 | 35.35 N | 91.06 E |
| Hoh Xil Shan ⋏ | 120 | 35.20 N | 90.00 E |
| Hoi An | 110 | 15.52 N | 108.19 E |
| Hoihow → Haikou | 102 | 20.03 N | 110.19 E |
| Hoima | 154 | 1.26 N | 31.21 E |
| Hoisdorf | 52 | 53.39 N | 10.20 E |
| Hoisington | 198 | 38.31 N | 98.46 W |
| Hoisten | 263 | 51.08 N | 6.42 E |
| Hoi Xuan | 110 | 20.22 N | 105.07 E |
| Hojāi | 120 | 26.00 N | 92.51 E |
| Højby, Dan. | 41 | 55.55 N | 11.37 E |
| Højby, Dan. | 41 | 55.20 N | 10.27 E |
| Höje | 40 | 59.54 N | 13.33 E |
| Højer | 26 | 54.58 N | 8.43 E |
| Højerup | 41 | 55.17 N | 12.27 E |
| Hojniki | 78 | 51.53 N | 29.56 E |
| Hōjō, Nihon | 96 | 34.54 N | 134.56 E |
| Hōjō, Nihon | 96 | 33.58 N | 132.46 E |
| Hōjō → Kasai, Nihon | 96 | 34.56 N | 134.50 E |
| Hokah | 190 | 43.45 N | 91.20 W |
| Hokang → Hegang | 89 | 47.24 N | 130.17 E |
| Hökåsen | 40 | 59.40 N | 16.35 E |
| Hokendauqua | 208 | 40.39 N | 75.29 W |
| Hökensås ⋏[2] | 26 | 58.11 N | 14.08 E |
| Hokes Bluff | 194 | 33.59 N | 85.51 W |
| Hōki ≃ | 94 | 36.47 N | 140.08 E |
| Hokianga Harbour c | 172 | 35.32 S | 173.22 E |
| Hokitika | 172 | 42.43 S | 170.58 E |
| Hokkaidō □[5] | 92a | 44.00 N | 143.00 E |
| Hokkaidō I | 92a | 44.00 N | 143.00 E |
| Hokksund | 26 | 59.47 N | 9.59 E |
| Hoko ≃ | 224 | 48.17 N | 124.22 W |
| Hōkōji | 270 | 34.52 N | 135.07 E |
| Hököpinge | 41 | 55.30 N | 13.00 E |
| Hokota | 94 | 36.09 N | 140.31 E |
| Hok So Wan | 271d | 22.13 N | 114.14 E |
| Hokubo | 96 | 34.57 N | 133.38 E |
| Hokudan | 96 | 34.32 N | 134.56 E |
| Hokura ≃ | 94 | 37.10 N | 138.16 E |
| Hokuriku-tunnel ◈[5] | 94 | 35.42 N | 136.10 E |
| Hokusei | 94 | 35.09 N | 136.31 E |
| Hola | 154 | 1.29 S | 40.02 E |
| Holalkere | 122 | 14.02 N | 76.11 E |
| Holanda → Netherlands □[1] | 30 | 52.15 N | 5.30 E |
| Hola Prystan' | 78 | 46.31 N | 32.31 E |
| Holbæk | 41 | 55.43 N | 11.43 E |
| Holbeach | 42 | 52.49 N | 0.01 E |
| Holbeach Marsh ≡ | 42 | 52.52 N | 0.05 E |
| Holberg | 182 | 50.39 N | 128.00 W |
| Holborn ◈[8] | 260 | 51.31 N | 0.07 W |
| Holbrook, Austl. | 171b | 35.44 S | 147.19 E |
| Holbrook, Az., U.S. | 200 | 34.54 N | 110.09 W |
| Holbrook, Il., U.S. | 278 | 41.32 N | 87.38 W |
| Holbrook, Md., U.S. | 284b | 39.24 N | 76.51 W |
| Holbrook, Ma., U.S. | 207 | 42.09 N | 71.00 W |
| Holbrook, Ne., U.S. | 198 | 40.18 N | 100.00 W |
| Holbrook, N.Y., U.S. | 210 | 40.48 N | 73.04 W |
| Holbrook, Lake ⊜[1] | 222 | 32.42 N | 95.33 W |
| Holbrook Mountain ∧[2] | 212 | 44.25 N | 77.51 W |
| Holckenhavn | 41 | 55.17 N | 10.47 E |
| Holcomb, Il., U.S. | 216 | 42.04 N | 89.06 W |
| Holcomb, N.Y., U.S. | 210 | 42.54 N | 77.25 W |
| Holcomb Creek ≃ | 228 | 34.17 N | 117.08 W |
| Holden, Ab., Can. | 182 | 53.14 N | 112.14 W |
| Holden, Ma., U.S. | 207 | 42.21 N | 71.51 W |
| Holden, Mo., U.S. | 194 | 38.42 N | 93.59 W |
| Holden, Ut., U.S. | 200 | 39.05 N | 112.16 W |
| Holden, W.V., U.S. | 188 | 37.49 N | 82.03 W |
| Holden, Mount ∧[2] | 216 | 41.40 N | 87.03 W |
| Holdenstedt | 52 | 52.55 N | 10.31 E |
| Holden Village | 224 | 48.12 N | 120.47 W |
| Holdenville | 196 | 35.04 N | 96.23 W |
| Holder | 220 | 28.58 N | 82.25 W |
| Holderness ≻[1] | 44 | 53.47 N | 0.10 W |
| Holdfast | 184 | 50.58 N | 105.25 W |
| Holdich | 254 | 45.57 S | 68.13 W |
| Holdingford | 190 | 45.43 N | 94.28 W |
| Holdorf | 52 | 52.35 N | 8.07 E |
| Holdrege | 198 | 40.26 N | 99.22 W |
| Holeby | 41 | 54.43 N | 11.28 E |
| Hole in the Mountain Peak ∧ | 204 | 40.55 N | 115.05 W |
| Hole Narsipur | 122 | 12.47 N | 76.15 E |
| Holešov | 30 | 49.20 N | 17.35 E |
| Holetown | 241g | 13.11 N | 59.39 W |
| Holgate, S. Afr. | 158 | 33.59 S | 22.21 E |
| Holgate, Oh., U.S. | 216 | 41.14 N | 84.07 W |
| Holguín | 240p | 20.53 N | 76.15 W |
| Holguín □[4] | 240p | 20.55 N | 75.50 W |
| Hol-Hol | 144 | 11.19 N | 42.57 E |
| Holíč | 30 | 48.49 N | 17.10 E |
| Holiday Beach Provincial Park ♠ | 214 | 42.02 N | 83.05 W |
| Holiday Hills | 216 | 42.18 N | 88.13 W |
| Holiday Lake Amusement Park ♠ | 285 | 40.02 N | 74.56 W |
| Holiday Shores | 219 | 38.55 N | 89.56 W |
| Holitna ≃ | 180 | 61.40 N | 157.12 W |
| Höljes | 26 | 60.54 N | 12.36 E |
| Hollabrunn | 61 | 48.34 N | 16.05 E |
| Holladay | 200 | 40.40 N | 111.49 W |
| Holland, Mb., Can. | 184 | 49.36 N | 98.53 W |
| Holland, Mi., U.S. | 216 | 42.47 N | 86.06 W |
| Holland, N.Y., U.S. | 210 | 42.38 N | 78.32 W |
| Holland, Oh., U.S. | 216 | 41.37 N | 83.42 W |
| Holland, Pa., U.S. | 285 | 40.10 N | 74.59 W |
| Holland, Tx., U.S. | 222 | 30.53 N | 97.24 W |
| Holland, Va., U.S. | 208 | 36.41 N | 76.47 W |
| Holland □[9] | 52 | 52.20 N | 4.45 E |
| Holland → Netherlands □[1] | 30 | 52.15 N | 5.30 E |
| Holland ≃ | 212 | 44.12 N | 79.31 W |
| Holland, Mount ∧[2] | 162 | 32.12 S | 119.44 E |
| Hollandale | 194 | 33.10 N | 90.51 W |
| Holland Creek ≃ | 169 | 36.43 S | 146.06 E |
| Hollande, Étangs de ⊜ | 261 | 48.44 N | 1.48 E |
| Holland Fen ≡ | 44 | 53.00 N | 0.10 W |
| Hollandia → Jayapura | 164 | 2.32 S | 140.42 E |
| Holland Landing | 212 | 44.06 N | 79.29 W |
| Holland Park | 171a | 27.31 S | 153.03 E |
| Holland Patent | 210 | 43.14 N | 75.15 W |
| Holland Point ≻ | 208 | 38.43 N | 76.32 W |
| Holland Pond State Park ♠ | 207 | 42.04 N | 72.09 W |
| Hollandsbird Island I | 156 | 24.45 S | 14.34 E |
| Hollandsch Diep Ʉ | 52 | 51.42 N | 4.30 E |
| Hollandstoun | 46 | 59.21 N | 2.26 W |
| Holland Straits Ʉ | 208 | 38.08 N | 76.02 W |
| Holland Tunnel ◈[5] | 276 | 40.44 N | 74.02 W |
| Hollansburg | 218 | 39.59 N | 84.47 W |
| Holle | 52 | 52.05 N | 10.10 E |
| Holleben | 54 | 51.26 N | 11.53 E |
| Hollenfels, Château ⊥ | 56 | 49.43 N | 6.03 E |
| Höllengebirge ⋏ | 64 | 47.48 N | 13.39 E |
| Hollenstedt | 52 | 53.22 N | 9.43 E |
| Hollenstein an der Ybbs | 61 | 47.48 N | 14.46 E |
| Höllensteinberg ∧ | 264b | 48.06 N | 16.11 E |
| Höllental V | 61 | 47.45 N | 15.47 E |
| Hollern | 52 | 53.36 N | 9.32 E |
| Holleton | 162 | 31.57 S | 119.02 E |
| Holley | 210 | 43.13 N | 78.01 W |
| Hollfeld | 60 | 49.56 N | 11.18 E |
| Hollick-Kenyon Plateau ⋏[1] | 9 | 79.00 S | 97.00 W |
| Holliday, Mo., U.S. | 219 | 39.29 N | 92.07 W |
| Holliday, Tx., U.S. | 196 | 33.49 N | 98.42 W |
| Holliday Creek ≃ | 196 | 33.55 N | 98.28 W |
| Holliday Park ♠ | 281 | 42.21 N | 83.24 W |
| Hollidaysburg | 214 | 40.25 N | 78.23 W |
| Hollingbourne | 260 | 51.16 N | 0.38 E |
| Hollingstedt | 41 | 54.27 N | 9.19 E |
| Hollingworth | 262 | 53.28 N | 1.59 W |
| Hollingworth Lake ⊜ | 262 | 53.38 N | 2.06 W |
| Hollins, Eng., U.K. | 262 | 53.34 N | 2.17 W |
| Hollins, Va., U.S. | 192 | 37.20 N | 79.56 W |
| Hollins Green | 262 | 53.25 N | 2.27 W |
| Hollinswood | 284c | 38.55 N | 77.13 W |
| Hollis, N.H., U.S. | 207 | 42.44 N | 71.35 W |
| Hollis, Ok., U.S. | 196 | 34.41 N | 99.54 W |
| Hollis ◈[8] | 276 | 40.43 N | 73.46 W |
| Hollister | 226 | 36.51 N | 121.24 W |
| Hollister, Mount ∧[2] | 162 | 22.08 S | 114.01 E |
| Holliston | 207 | 42.12 N | 71.25 W |
| Hollman, Cape ≻ | 164 | 4.59 S | 150.06 E |
| Holloman Air Force Base ■ | 200 | 32.51 N | 106.05 W |
| Holloway | 214 | 40.10 N | 81.08 W |
| Holloway Terrace | 285 | 39.42 N | 75.32 W |
| Hollow Rock | 194 | 36.02 N | 88.16 W |
| Hollowville | 210 | 42.12 N | 73.42 W |
| Hollsopple | 214 | 40.13 N | 78.56 W |
| Hollum | 52 | 53.26 N | 5.37 E |
| Höllviken c | 41 | 55.26 N | 12.54 E |
| Höllviksnäs | 41 | 55.25 N | 12.57 E |
| Holly, Co., U.S. | 198 | 38.03 N | 102.07 W |
| Holly, Mi., U.S. | 216 | 42.47 N | 83.37 W |
| Holly, Wa., U.S. | 224 | 47.34 N | 122.58 W |
| Holly, Mount ∧[2] | 285 | 40.00 N | 74.47 W |
| Holly Brook | 285 | 39.59 N | 74.48 W |
| Holly Grove | 194 | 34.35 N | 91.11 W |
| Holly Hill, Fl., U.S. | 192 | 29.14 N | 81.02 W |
| Holly Hill, S.C., U.S. | 192 | 33.19 N | 80.24 W |
| Holly Park, N.J., U.S. | 208 | 39.53 N | 74.10 W |
| Holly Park, Va., U.S. | 284c | 38.50 N | 77.17 W |
| Holly Pond ⊜ | 276 | 41.03 N | 73.30 W |
| Holly River State Park ♠ | 188 | 38.40 N | 80.21 W |
| Holly Run ≃ | 285 | 39.47 N | 75.03 W |
| Holly Springs | 194 | 34.46 N | 89.26 W |
| Holly State Recreation Area ♠ | 216 | 42.49 N | 83.32 W |
| Hollywood, Ire. | 48 | 53.06 N | 6.35 W |
| Hollywood, Fl., U.S. | 220 | 26.00 N | 80.08 W |
| Hollywood, Md., U.S. | 208 | 38.20 N | 76.34 W |
| Hollywood, Pa., U.S. | 285 | 40.05 N | 75.06 W |
| Hollywood ◈[8] | 228 | 34.06 N | 118.21 W |
| Hollywood, Mount ∧ | 280 | 34.08 N | 118.18 W |
| Hollywood Bowl ♠ | 280 | 34.07 N | 118.20 W |
| Hollywood-Burbank Airport ⊠ | 228 | 34.12 N | 118.21 W |
| Hollywood Heights | 219 | 38.39 N | 89.59 W |
| Hollywood Indian Reservation ◈[4] | 220 | 26.02 N | 80.13 W |
| Hollywood Park Race Track ♠ | 280 | 33.57 N | 118.20 W |
| Hollywood Reservoir ⊜[1] | 280 | 34.07 N | 118.20 W |
| Holman | 176 | 70.43 N | 117.43 W |
| Hólmavík | 24a | 65.43 N | 21.43 W |
| Holmdel | 208 | 40.20 N | 74.11 W |
| Holme, Dan. | 41 | 56.07 N | 10.11 E |
| Holme, Eng., U.K. | 262 | 53.33 N | 1.50 W |
| Holme ≃ | 44 | 53.41 N | 1.43 W |
| Holme Chapel | 262 | 53.45 N | 2.11 W |
| Holmen, Nor. | 26 | 60.40 N | 10.22 E |
| Holmen, Wi., U.S. | 190 | 43.57 N | 91.15 W |
| Holme-on-Spaulding-Moor | 44 | 53.50 N | 0.46 W |
| Holmes, N.Y., U.S. | 210 | 41.31 N | 73.39 W |
| Holmes, Pa., U.S. | 285 | 39.54 N | 75.19 W |
| Holmes □[6] | 214 | 40.33 N | 81.55 W |
| Holmes, Mount ∧ | 202 | 44.49 N | 110.51 W |
| Holmes Beach | 220 | 27.31 N | 82.43 W |
| Holmesburg ◈[8] | 285 | 40.02 N | 75.03 W |
| Holmes Chapel | 44 | 53.12 N | 2.22 W |
| Holmes Creek ≃ | 194 | 30.30 N | 85.47 W |
| Holmesglen | 274b | 37.53 S | 145.06 E |
| Holmes Harbor c | 224 | 48.04 N | 122.32 W |
| Holmes Lake ⊜ | 184 | 57.05 N | 96.45 W |
| Holmes Reef ✣[2] | 164 | 16.27 S | 148.00 E |
| Holmes Run ≃ | 284c | 38.48 N | 77.07 W |
| Holmes Run Acres | 284c | 38.51 N | 77.13 W |
| Holmestrand | 26 | 59.29 N | 10.18 E |
| Holmesville, N.Y., U.S. | 210 | 42.31 N | 75.24 W |
| Holmesville, Oh., U.S. | 214 | 40.37 N | 81.55 W |
| Holmeswood | 262 | 53.39 N | 2.52 W |
| Holmfirth | 44 | 53.35 N | 1.46 W |
| Holmia | 246 | 4.58 N | 59.35 W |
| Holmivs'kyy | 83 | 48.25 N | 38.05 E |
| Holmön I | 26 | 63.47 N | 20.53 E |
| Holmsbu | 26 | 59.33 N | 10.27 E |
| Holmsjön ⊜, Sve. | 26 | 62.41 N | 16.33 E |
| Holmsjön ⊜, Sve. | 26 | 62.25 N | 15.20 E |
| Holmsund | 26 | 63.42 N | 20.21 E |
| Hölö | 40 | 59.01 N | 17.35 E |
| Holoby | 78 | 51.06 N | 24.59 E |
| Holod | 38 | 46.47 N | 22.08 E |
| Holohory ⋏ | 78 | 49.45 N | 24.35 E |
| Holoit, Punta ≻ | 232 | 21.37 N | 88.08 W |
| Ḥolon | 132 | 32.01 N | 34.46 E |
| Holoog | 156 | 27.22 S | 17.55 E |
| Holopaw | 220 | 28.08 N | 81.04 W |
| Holovanivs'k | 78 | 48.23 N | 30.28 E |
| Holovne | 78 | 51.21 N | 24.04 E |
| Holroyd | 274a | 33.50 S | 150.58 E |
| Holroyd ≃ | 164 | 14.10 S | 141.36 E |
| Holsloot | 52 | 52.44 N | 6.48 E |
| Holstebro | 26 | 56.21 N | 8.38 E |
| Holsted | 41 | 55.30 N | 8.55 E |
| Holstein | 198 | 42.29 N | 95.32 W |
| Holsteinborg ⊥ | 41 | 55.13 N | 11.28 E |
| Holsteinische Schweiz ◈[1] | 54 | 54.11 N | 10.36 E |
| Holsteinsborg (Sisimiut) | 176 | 66.55 N | 53.40 W |
| Holsterhausen | 263 | 51.41 N | 6.57 E |
| Holston ≃ | 192 | 35.57 N | 83.51 W |
| Holston, North Fork ≃ | 192 | 36.33 N | 82.36 W |
| Holston High Knob ∧ | 192 | 36.27 N | 82.05 W |
| Holsworthy | 42 | 50.49 N | 4.21 W |
| Holt, Eng., U.K. | 42 | 52.55 N | 1.05 E |
| Holt, Wales, U.K. | 44 | 53.05 N | 2.53 W |
| Holt, Al., U.S. | 194 | 33.14 N | 87.29 W |
| Holt, Ca., U.S. | 226 | 37.56 N | 121.26 W |
| Holt, Fl., U.S. | 194 | 30.42 N | 86.44 W |
| Holt, Mi., U.S. | 216 | 42.38 N | 84.30 W |
| Holt Creek ≃ | 198 | 42.28 N | 98.50 W |
| Holte | 41 | 55.49 N | 12.28 E |
| Holtemme ≃ | 54 | 51.57 N | 11.10 E |
| Holten | 52 | 52.17 N | 6.25 E |
| Holten ◈[8] | 263 | 51.31 N | 6.48 E |
| Holtenau ◈[8] | 54 | 54.22 N | 10.08 E |
| Holter Lake ⊜[1] | 202 | 46.55 N | 111.57 W |
| Holthausen, Dtsch. | 52 | 52.33 N | 7.17 E |
| Holthausen, Dtsch. | 263 | 51.23 N | 7.13 E |
| Holthausen, Dtsch. | 263 | 51.12 N | 7.01 E |
| Holthausen ◈[8] | 263 | 51.34 N | 7.26 E |
| Holthusen | 52 | 53.08 N | 7.18 E |
| Holton, In., U.S. | 218 | 39.04 N | 85.23 W |
| Holton, Ks., U.S. | 198 | 39.27 N | 95.44 W |
| Holtorf | 52 | 52.40 N | 9.13 E |
| Holts Summit | 219 | 38.39 N | 92.07 W |
| Holtsville | 210 | 40.49 N | 73.02 W |
| Holtug | 41 | 55.21 N | 12.25 E |
| Holtville | 204 | 32.48 N | 115.22 W |
| Holtwick | 52 | 52.00 N | 7.05 E |
| Holtwood | 208 | 39.50 N | 76.19 W |
| Holubivka | 78 | 48.53 N | 35.19 E |
| Holwerd | 52 | 53.22 N | 5.54 E |
| Holycross, Ire. | 48 | 52.38 N | 7.52 W |
| Holy Cross, Ak., U.S. | 180 | 62.12 N | 159.47 W |
| Holy Cross Mountain ∧ | 182 | 53.47 N | 120.47 W |
| Holyhead | 44 | 53.19 N | 4.38 W |
| Holyhead Bay c | 44 | 53.23 N | 4.37 W |
| Holy Island I, Eng., U.K. | 44 | 55.41 N | 1.48 W |
| Holy Island I, Scot., U.K. | 46 | 55.32 N | 5.04 W |
| Holy Island I, Wales, U.K. | 44 | 53.18 N | 4.37 W |
| Holy Island I, Ma., U.S. | 283 | 42.43 N | 70.50 W |
| Holyoke, Co., U.S. | 198 | 40.35 N | 102.18 W |
| Holyoke, Ma., U.S. | 207 | 42.12 N | 72.37 W |
| Holyrood | 198 | 38.35 N | 98.24 W |
| Holyrood Palace ɤ | 46 | 55.56 N | 3.12 W |
| Holýšov | 60 | 49.36 N | 13.05 E |
| Holywell | 44 | 53.17 N | 3.13 W |
| Holywell Green | 262 | 53.41 N | 1.52 W |
| Holywood | 48 | 54.38 N | 5.50 W |
| Holzbüttgen | 263 | 51.12 N | 6.37 E |
| Holzdorf | 54 | 51.46 N | 13.08 E |
| Holzen | 56 | 51.26 N | 7.31 E |
| Holzgau | 58 | 47.16 N | 10.21 E |
| Holzgerlingen | 56 | 48.38 N | 9.00 E |
| Holzhausen, Dtsch. | 52 | 52.17 N | 8.32 E |
| Holzhausen, Dtsch. | 52 | 52.13 N | 8.01 E |
| Holzhausen, Dtsch. | 52 | 52.01 N | 8.44 E |
| Holzhausen, Dtsch. | 54 | 51.18 N | 12.28 E |
| Holzhausen an der Haide | 56 | 50.13 N | 7.55 E |
| Holzheim | 56 | 51.09 N | 6.39 E |
| Holzkirchen | 64 | 47.52 N | 11.42 E |
| Holzminden | 52 | 51.50 N | 9.27 E |
| Holzweissig | 54 | 51.36 N | 12.18 E |
| Holzwickede | 52 | 51.30 N | 7.36 E |
| Hom ≃ | 158 | 28.51 S | 18.37 E |
| Homa Bay | 154 | 0.31 S | 34.27 E |
| Homalin | 110 | 24.52 N | 94.[illegible] E |
| Homathko ≃ | 182 | 50.55 N | 124.[illegible] W |
| Homathko Icefield ⊓ | 182 | 51.05 N | 124.[illegible] W |
| Homberg, Dtsch. | 56 | 50.43 N | 8.[illegible] E |
| Homberg, Dtsch. | 56 | 51.02 N | 9.[illegible] E |
| Homberg, Dtsch. | 56 | 51.28 N | 6.[illegible] E |
| Homberg, Dtsch. | 263 | 51.18 N | 6.5[illegible] E |
| Hombori | 150 | 15.17 N | 1.4[illegible] W |
| Hombori Tondo ∧ | 150 | 15.16 N | 1.4[illegible] W |
| Hombourg-Haut | 56 | 49.08 N | 6.4[illegible] E |
| Hombre Muerto, Salar del ≚ | 252 | 25.23 S | 67.0[illegible] W |
| Hombruch ◈[8] | 263 | 51.29 N | 7.2[illegible] E |
| Homburg, Dtsch. | 56 | 49.19 N | 7.2[illegible] E |
| Homburg → Bad Homburg vor der Höhe, Dtsch. | 56 | 50.13 N | 8.37 E |
| Home, Pa., U.S. | 214 | 40.44 N | 79.06 W |
| Home, Wa., U.S. | 224 | 47.17 N | 122.46 W |
| Homeacre | 214 | 40.51 N | 79.55 W |
| Home Bay c, N.T., Can. | 176 | 68.45 N | 67.10 W |
| Home Bay c, Kiribati | 174d | 0.53 S | 169.35 E |
| Homebush Bay c | 274a | 33.50 S | 151.05 E |
| Home Corner | 216 | 40.31 N | 85.38 W |
| Homécourt | 56 | 49.14 N | 5.59 E |
| Home Creek ≃ | 196 | 31.29 N | 99.14 W |
| Homedale, Id., U.S. | 202 | 43.37 N | 116.55 W |
| Homedale, Oh., U.S. | 214 | 40.04 N | 83.02 W |
| Home Gardens | 228 | 33.52 N | 117.31 W |
| Home Hill | 166 | 19.40 S | 147.25 [illegible] |
| Homel' | 76 | 52.25 N | 31.00 [illegible] |
| Homel' □[8] | 76 | 52.30 N | 30.00 [illegible] |
| Homeland, Ca., U.S. | 228 | 33.44 N | 117.07 W |
| Homeland, Fl., U.S. | 220 | 27.49 N | 81.49 W |
| Homeland Canal ≊ | 226 | 35.57 N | 119.27 W |
| Homeland Park | 192 | 34.27 N | 82.41 W |
| Home Place | 218 | 39.56 N | 86.08 W |
| Homer, Ak., U.S. | 180 | 59.39 N | 151.33 W |
| Homer, Ga., U.S. | 192 | 34.20 N | 83.29 W |
| Homer, La., U.S. | 194 | 32.47 N | 93.03 W |
| Homer, Mi., U.S. | 216 | 42.08 N | 84.48 W |
| Homer, Ne., U.S. | 198 | 42.19 N | 96.29 W |
| Homer, N.Y., U.S. | 210 | 42.38 N | 76.10 W |
| Homer, Oh., U.S. | 214 | 40.15 N | 82.31 W |
| Homer, Tx., U.S. | 222 | 31.18 N | 94.36 W |
| Homer City | 214 | 40.32 N | 79.09 W |
| Homert ∧[2] | 263 | 51.11 N | 7.39 E |
| Homer Tunnel ◈[5] | 172 | 44.45 S | 168.00 E |
| Homerville, Ga., U.S. | 192 | 31.02 N | 82.44 W |
| Homerville, Oh., U.S. | 214 | 41.02 N | 82.08 W |
| Homer Wash V | 204 | 34.20 N | 115.02 W |
| Homer Youngs Peak ∧ | 202 | 45.19 N | 113.41 W |
| Home Seamount ✣[3] | 14 | 12.55 S | 175.37 W |
| Homestead, Austl. | 166 | 20.22 S | 145.39 E |
| Homestead, Fl., U.S. | 220 | 25.28 N | 80.28 W |
| Homestead, Pa., U.S. | 279b | 40.24 N | 79.54 W |
| Homestead Air Force Base ■ | 220 | 25.29 N | 80.23 W |
| Homestead National Monument of America ♠ | 198 | 40.14 N | 96.54 W |
| Homestead Valley | 282 | 37.54 N | 122.32 W |
| Hometown, Il., U.S. | 278 | 41.44 N | 87.43 W |
| Hometown, Pa., U.S. | 210 | 40.49 N | 75.59 W |
| Homewood, Al., U.S. | 194 | 33.28 N | 86.48 W |
| Homewood, Ca., U.S. | 226 | 39.05 N | 120.09 W |
| Homewood, Il., U.S. | 216 | 41.33 N | 87.39 W |
| Homewood, Oh., U.S. | 218 | 39.23 N | 84.33 W |
| Homewood ◈[8] | 279b | 40.27 N | 79.54 W |
| Homewood Acres | 278 | 41.34 N | 87.43 W |
| Homeworth | 214 | 40.50 N | 81.03 W |
| Hominy | 196 | 36.24 N | 96.23 W |
| Hominy Creek ≃ | 196 | 36.20 N | 96.00 W |
| Hommersåk | 26 | 58.58 N | 5.42 E |
| Hommura | 92 | 34.22 N | 139.15 E |
| Homnābād | 122 | 17.46 N | 77.08 E |
| Homochitto ≃ | 194 | 31.09 N | 91.31 W |
| Homoíne | 156 | 23.52 S | 35.09 E |
| Homonhon Island I | 116 | 10.44 N | 125.43 E |
| Homosassa | 220 | 28.46 N | 82.36 W |
| Homosassa Bay c | 220 | 28.45 N | 82.43 W |
| Homosassa Springs | 220 | 28.48 N | 82.35 W |
| Homs → Al-Khums, Lībiyā | 146 | 32.39 N | 14.16 E |
| Homs → Ḥimṣ, Sūrīy. | 130 | 34.44 N | 36.43 E |
| Honai | 96 | 33.30 N | 132.25 E |
| Honaker | 192 | 37.00 N | 81.58 W |
| Honami | 96 | 33.36 N | 130.42 E |
| Honan → Luoyang | 102 | 34.41 N | 112.28 E |
| Honan → Henan □[4] | 90 | 34.00 N | 114.00 E |
| Honāvar | 122 | 14.17 N | 74.27 E |
| Honaz | 130 | 37.45 N | 29.17 E |
| Honbetsu | 92a | 43.07 N | 143.37 E |
| Hon Chong | 110 | 10.10 N | 104.37 E |
| Honda | 246 | 5.12 N | 74.45 W |
| Honda, Bahía c, Col. | 246 | 12.21 N | 71.47 W |
| Honda, Bahía c, Cuba | 240p | 22.57 N | 83.10 W |
| Honda, Cañada ≃ | 258 | 33.57 S | 59.21 W |
| Honda Bay c | 116 | 9.53 N | 118.49 E |
| Honddu ≃, U.K. | 42 | 51.54 N | 2.58 W |
| Honddu ≃, Wales, U.K. | 42 | 51.57 N | 3.23 W |
| Hondeklipbaai | 156 | 30.20 S | 17.18 E |
| Honderfontein | 158 | 32.12 S | 21.22 E |
| Hon Dien, Nui ∧ | 110 | 11.33 N | 108.38 E |
| Hondo, Ab., Can. | 182 | 55.04 N | 114.02 W |
| Hondo, Nihon | 92 | 32.27 N | 130.12 E |
| Hondo, N.M., U.S. | 200 | 33.23 N | 105.16 W |
| Hondo, Tx., U.S. | 196 | 29.20 N | 99.08 W |
| Hondo ≃, Méx. | 286a | 19.26 N | 99.15 W |
| Hondo ≃, N.A. | 232 | 18.29 N | 88.19 W |
| Hondo, Arroyo ≃ | 226 | 37.28 N | 121.47 W |
| Hondo, Rio ≃, Ca., U.S. | 280 | 33.55 N | 118.10 W |
| Hondo, Rio ≃, N.M., U.S. | 196 | 33.22 N | 104.24 W |
| Hondo Creek ≃ | 196 | 28.45 N | 99.11 W |
| Hondoji Temple ɤ[1] | 268 | 35.51 N | 139.56 E |
| Hondschoote | 50 | 50.59 N | 2.35 E |
| Hondsrug ⋏[2] | 52 | 52.55 N | 6.50 E |
| Honduras □[1], N.A. | 230 | 15.00 N | 86.30 W |
| Honduras □[1], N.A. | 236 | 15.00 N | 86.30 W |
| Honduras, Cabo de ≻ | 236 | 16.01 N | 86.02 W |
| Honduras, Gulf of c | 230 | 16.10 N | 87.50 W |
| Honduras, Port c | 236 | 16.13 N | 88.41 W |
| Honea Path | 192 | 34.26 N | 82.23 W |
| Hönebach | 56 | 50.56 N | 9.56 E |
| Hønefoss | 26 | 60.10 N | 10.18 E |
| Honeoye | 210 | 42.47 N | 77.31 W |
| Honeoye Creek ≃ | 210 | 42.58 N | 77.43 W |
| Honeoye Falls | 210 | 42.57 N | 77.35 W |
| Honeoye Lake ⊜ | 210 | 42.45 N | 77.31 W |
| Honesdale | 210 | 41.34 N | 75.15 W |
| Honey Brook | 208 | 40.05 N | 75.54 W |
| Honey Creek | 216 | 42.44 N | 88.18 W |
| Honey Creek ≃, Ia., U.S. | 190 | 42.09 N | 93.03 W |
| Honey Creek ≃, Mo., U.S. | 194 | 39.53 N | 93.34 W |
| Honey Creek ≃, Oh., U.S. | 214 | 41.05 N | 83.12 W |
| Honey Creek ≃, Pa., U.S. | 208 | 40.36 N | 77.35 W |
| Honey Creek ≃, Wi., U.S. | 216 | 42.41 N | 88.17 W |
| Honeydew | 273d | 26.05 S | 27.55 E |
| Honeygo Run ≃ | 284b | 39.22 N | 76.25 W |
| Honey Grove | 196 | 33.35 N | 95.54 W |
| Honey Lake ⊜ | 204 | 40.16 N | 120.19 W |
| Honeymoon Bay | 224 | 48.49 N | 124.10 W |


| | | | | | |
|---|---|---|---|---|---|
| ≃ | River | Fluß | Río | Rivière | Rio |
| ≊ | Canal | Kanal | Canal | Canal | Canal |
| ᒐ | Waterfall, Rapids | Wasserfall, Stromschnellen | Cascada, Rápidos | Chute d'eau, Rapides | Cascata, Rápidos |
| Ʉ | Strait | Meeresstraße | Estrecho | Détroit | Estreito |
| c | Bay, Gulf | Bucht, Golf | Bahía, Golfo | Baie, Golfe | Baía, Golfo |
| ⊜ | Lake, Lakes | See, Seen | Lago, Lagos | Lac, Lacs | Lago, Lagos |
| ≡ | Swamp | Sumpf | Pantano | Marais | Pântano |
| ⊓ | Ice Features, Glacier | Eis- und Gletscherformen | Accidentes Glaciales | Formes glaciaires | Acidentes glaciares |
| ⊤ | Other Hydrographic Features | Andere Hydrographische Objekte | Otros Elementos Hidrográficos | Autres données hydrographiques | Outros acidentes hidrográficos |
| ✣ | Submarine Features | Untermeerische Objekte | Accidentes Submarinos | Formes de relief sous-marin | Acidentes submarinos |
| □ | Political Unit | Politische Einheit | Unidad Politica | Entité politique | Unidade política |
| ɤ | Cultural Institution | Kulturelle Institution | Institución Cultural | Institution culturelle | Institução cultural |
| ⊥ | Historical Site | Historische Stätte | Sitio Histórico | Site historique | Sitio histórico |
| ♠ | Recreational Site | Erholungs- und Ferienort | Sitio de Recreo | Centre de loisirs | Area de Lazer |
| ⊠ | Airport | Flughafen | Aeropuerto | Aéroport | Aeroporto |
| ■ | Military Installation | Militäranlage | Instalación Militar | Installation militaire | Instalação militar |
| ◈ | Miscellaneous | Verschiedenes | Misceláneo | Divers | Diversos |

| Name | Page | Lat.°′ | Long.°′ |
|---|---|---|---|
| Honeyville | 200 | 41.38 N | 112.04 W |
| Honfleur | 50 | 49.25 N | 0.14 E |
| Høng | 41 | 55.31 N | 11.18 E |
| Hong → Red ≃, Asia | 110 | 20.17 N | 106.34 E |
| Hong ≃, Zhg. | 100 | 32.25 N | 115.35 E |
| Honga | 152 | 15.09 S | 15.12 E |
| Hon Gai | 110 | 20.57 N | 107.05 E |
| Hong'an | 100 | 31.18 N | 114.37 E |
| Honga River c | 208 | 38.19 N | 76.10 W |
| Hongawa | 96 | 33.43 N | 133.19 E |
| Hongchang | 100 | 34.05 N | 113.20 E |
| Hongch'ŏn | 98 | 37.42 N | 127.52 E |
| Hongchoudai | 100 | 29.03 N | 121.11 E |
| Hongcun, Zhg. | 100 | 27.10 N | 116.48 E |
| Hongcun, Zhg. | 106 | 31.01 N | 119.15 E |
| Höngen | 56 | 51.02 N | 5.56 E |
| Honggun | 98 | 40.46 N | 128.27 E |
| Honghai Wan c | 100 | 22.40 N | 115.10 E |
| Honghe | 102 | 23.23 N | 102.35 E |
| Honghu | 100 | 29.48 N | 113.27 E |
| Hong Hu ⊜ | 100 | 29.52 N | 113.23 E |
| Honghuaerji | 89 | 48.15 N | 120.01 E |
| Honghuaji | 100 | 33.52 N | 114.26 E |
| Honghualiangzi | 89 | 48.06 N | 123.12 E |
| Honghuamu | 89 | 48.33 N | 125.39 E |
| Hongjiang, Zhg. | 100 | 26.49 N | 120.03 E |
| Hongjiang, Zhg. | 102 | 27.07 N | 109.56 E |
| Hong Kong → Victoria | 271d | 22.17 N | 114.09 E |
| Hong Kong □[2], Asia | 90 | 22.15 N | 114.10 E |
| Hong Kong □[2], Asia | 100 | 22.15 N | 114.10 E |
| Hong Kong I | 271d | 22.15 N | 114.11 E |
| Hong Kong, University of ᵾ[2] | 271d | 22.17 N | 114.08 E |
| Hongkou Park ◆ | 269b | 31.16 N | 121.28 E |
| Honglai | 100 | 25.08 N | 118.32 E |
| Honglanbu | 106 | 31.37 N | 118.57 E |
| Honglinqiao | 106 | 30.59 N | 118.59 E |
| Hongliutai | 85 | 39.48 N | 77.26 E |
| Hongliuyuan | 102 | 41.04 N | 95.26 E |
| Honglongdian | 106 | 30.30 N | 119.00 E |
| Honglongtang | 105 | 40.41 N | 117.37 E |
| Honglu | 100 | 25.44 N | 119.20 E |
| Hongluan | 100 | 28.31 N | 117.01 E |
| Hongluo Shan ∧ | 104 | 40.56 N | 120.42 E |
| Hongluoxian | 104 | 41.01 N | 120.53 E |
| Hongmeichang | 105 | 39.50 N | 115.51 E |
| Hongmendu | 102 | 26.10 N | 102.37 E |
| Hongmenkou | 102 | 27.22 N | 100.30 E |
| Hongmenpu | 107 | 30.37 N | 104.08 E |
| Hongmiaozi | 107 | 28.47 N | 104.02 E |
| Hong Ngu | 110 | 10.48 N | 105.21 E |
| Hongō, Nihon | 96 | 34.24 N | 132.59 E |
| Hongō, Nihon | 96 | 34.17 N | 132.02 E |
| Hongō ◆[8] | 268 | 35.42 N | 139.47 E |
| Hongpailou | 107 | 30.38 N | 104.01 E |
| Hongqi | 89 | 44.23 N | 126.32 E |
| Hongqiao, Zhg. | 100 | 28.14 N | 121.01 E |
| Hongqiao, Zhg. | 105 | 39.50 N | 117.44 E |
| Hongqiao, Zhg. | 106 | 31.29 N | 121.49 E |
| Hongqiao, Zhg. | 269b | 31.12 N | 121.22 E |
| Hongqiao Ji Chang ⊠ | 106 | 31.12 N | 121.20 E |
| Hongrie → Hungary □[1] | 30 | 47.00 N | 20.00 E |
| Hongshan, Zhg. | 89 | 48.02 N | 129.00 E |
| Hongshan, Zhg. | 98 | 36.37 N | 118.00 E |
| Hongshanzi | 98 | 42.34 N | 117.14 E |
| Hongshi, Zhg. | 89 | 43.00 N | 127.04 E |
| Hongshi, Zhg. | 98 | 41.21 N | 119.32 E |
| Hongshidou | 104 | 41.52 N | 122.11 E |
| Hongshili | 98 | 40.41 N | 125.03 E |
| Hongshui | 102 | 37.24 N | 104.00 E |
| Hongshui ≃ | 102 | 23.45 N | 109.30 E |
| Hongshuichuan | 105 | 40.06 N | 117.55 E |
| Hongshuyangzi | 105 | 40.36 N | 116.36 E |
| Hongsŏng | 98 | 36.36 N | 126.39 E |
| Hongtang | 100 | 26.06 N | 119.14 E |
| Hongtian | 100 | 25.52 N | 117.15 E |
| Hongtong | 102 | 36.19 N | 111.39 E |
| Hongtuwan | 98 | 41.03 N | 113.39 E |
| Hongtu Zhang ∧ | 100 | 23.46 N | 115.56 E |
| Honguedo, Détroit d' ꭒ | 186 | 49.15 N | 64.00 W |
| Hongwŏn | 98 | 40.02 N | 127.57 E |
| Hongxin | 100 | 32.43 N | 117.47 E |
| Hongxing | 105 | 39.48 N | 116.27 E |
| Hongxingqiao | 106 | 30.55 N | 119.52 E |
| Hongyang, Zhg. | 100 | 26.32 N | 119.27 E |
| Hongyang, Zhg. | 100 | 23.28 N | 116.13 E |
| Hongyanzi | 104 | 40.38 N | 120.31 E |
| Hongyōtoku | 268 | 35.41 N | 139.55 E |
| Hongze | 100 | 33.19 N | 118.53 E |
| Hongze Hu ⊜ | 100 | 33.16 N | 118.34 E |
| Honiara | 175e | 9.26 S | 159.57 E |
| Honiton | 42 | 50.48 N | 3.13 W |
| Hon-jima I | 96 | 34.23 N | 133.47 E |
| Honjō, Nihon | 92 | 39.23 N | 140.03 E |
| Honjō, Nihon | 94 | 36.24 N | 138.01 E |
| Honjō, Nihon | 94 | 36.14 N | 139.11 E |
| Honkamäki ∧[2] | 26 | 62.58 N | 27.05 E |
| Hon-kawane | 94 | 35.07 N | 138.09 E |
| Honker Bay c | 282 | 38.04 N | 121.56 W |
| Hönne ≃ | 263 | 51.28 N | 7.46 E |
| Honnecourt-sur-Escaut | 50 | 50.02 N | 3.12 E |
| Honningsvåg | 24 | 70.59 N | 25.59 E |
| Hönö | 26 | 57.42 N | 11.39 E |
| Honokaa | 229d | 20.04 N | 155.28 W |
| Honokahua | 229a | 21.00 N | 156.39 W |
| Honokawai | 229a | 20.57 N | 156.41 W |
| Honolulu | 229c | 21.18 N | 157.51 W |
| Honolulu □[6] | 229c | 21.19 N | 157.52 W |
| Honolulu International Airport ⊠ | 229c | 21.20 N | 157.55 W |
| Honomu | 229d | 19.52 N | 155.07 W |
| Honouliuli | 229c | 21.22 N | 158.02 W |
| Hönow | 54 | 52.32 N | 13.38 E |
| Hon Quan | 110 | 11.39 N | 106.36 E |
| Honshū I | 92 | 36.00 N | 138.00 E |
| Hontoon Island State Park ◆ | 220 | 28.59 N | 81.22 W |
| Höntrop ◆[8] | 263 | 51.27 N | 7.08 E |
| Honuapo Bay c | 229d | 19.05 N | 155.33 W |
| Hoo | 260 | 51.25 N | 0.34 E |
| Hood | 226 | 38.22 N | 121.31 W |
| Hood □[6] | 222 | 32.25 N | 97.45 W |
| Hood ≃, N.T., Can. | 176 | 67.26 N | 108.53 W |
| Hood ≃, Or., U.S. | 224 | 45.42 N | 121.30 W |
| Hood, East Fork ≃ | 224 | 45.36 N | 121.38 W |
| Hood, Mount ∧ | 224 | 45.23 N | 121.41 W |
| Hood, West Fork ≃ | 224 | 45.36 N | 121.38 W |
| Hood Canal c | 224 | 47.35 N | 123.00 W |
| Hood Canal Floating Bridge ◆[5] | 224 | 47.52 N | 122.38 W |
| Hoodoo Peak ∧ | 202 | 48.15 N | 120.19 W |
| Hood Point >, Austl. | 162 | 34.23 S | 119.34 E |
| Hood Point >, Pap. N. Gui. | 164 | 10.05 S | 147.45 E |
| Hood Pond ⊜ | 283 | 42.40 N | 70.57 W |
| Hood River | 224 | 45.42 N | 121.31 W |
| Hoodsport | 224 | 47.24 N | 123.08 W |
| Hoods Range ⩘ | 166 | 28.35 S | 144.30 E |
| Hoof | 56 | 51.17 N | 9.20 E |
| Hoogerheide | 52 | 51.25 N | 4.20 E |
| Hoogeveen | 52 | 52.43 N | 6.29 E |
| Hoogeveense Vaart ⩦ | 52 | 52.42 N | 6.11 E |
| Hoogezand-Sappemeer | 52 | 53.09 N | 6.47 E |
| Hoogkerk | 52 | 53.13 N | 6.30 E |
| Hooglede | 50 | 50.59 N | 3.05 E |
| Hoogstede | 52 | 52.34 N | 6.56 E |
| Hoogstraten | 56 | 51.24 N | 4.46 E |
| Hoogte | 158 | 27.28 S | 28.03 E |
| Hoogvliet | 52 | 51.52 N | 4.21 E |
| Hook | 42 | 51.17 N | 0.58 W |
| Hook ◆[8] | 260 | 51.22 N | 0.18 W |
| Hooker | 196 | 36.51 N | 101.12 W |
| Hooker, Bi'r ᴛ[4] | 142 | 30.23 N | 30.20 E |
| Hooker Creek | 162 | 18.20 S | 130.40 E |
| Hooker Creek Aboriginal Reserve ◆[4] | 162 | 18.10 S | 130.25 E |
| Hook Head > | 48 | 52.07 N | 6.55 W |
| Hookina | 166 | 31.45 S | 138.20 E |
| Hook Island I | 166 | 20.08 S | 148.55 E |
| Hook Mountain State Park ◆ | 276 | 41.09 N | 73.55 W |
| Hook Norton | 42 | 51.59 N | 1.29 W |
| Hook Point > | 166 | 25.48 S | 153.05 E |
| Hooks | 194 | 33.28 N | 94.15 W |
| Hooksiel | 52 | 53.38 N | 8.01 E |
| Hoolehua | 229a | 21.10 N | 157.04 W |
| Hoonah | 180 | 58.07 N | 135.26 W |
| Hoopa | 204 | 41.03 N | 123.40 W |
| Hoopa Valley Indian Reservation ◆[4] | 204 | 41.08 N | 123.40 W |
| Hooper | 198 | 41.36 N | 96.32 W |
| Hooper Bay | 180 | 61.31 N | 166.06 W |
| Hooper Islands II | 208 | 38.20 N | 76.13 W |
| Hooper Strait ꭒ | 208 | 38.12 N | 76.03 W |
| Hoopersville | 208 | 38.15 N | 76.10 W |
| Hoopes Reservoir ⊜[1] | 285 | 39.47 N | 75.37 W |
| Hoopeston | 216 | 40.28 N | 87.40 W |
| Hooping Harbour | 186 | 50.37 N | 56.17 W |
| Hoople | 198 | 48.32 N | 97.38 W |
| Hoopstad | 158 | 27.54 S | 25.58 E |
| Hoopstick Brook ≃ | 276 | 40.39 N | 74.41 W |
| Höör | 41 | 55.56 N | 13.32 E |
| Hoorn | 52 | 52.38 N | 5.04 E |
| Hoorn, Kap → Hornos, Cabo de > | 254 | 55.59 S | 67.16 W |
| Hoosac Range ⩘ | 207 | 42.45 N | 73.02 W |
| Hoosac Tunnel ◆[5] | 207 | 42.41 N | 73.03 W |
| Hoosic ≃ | 210 | 42.54 N | 73.39 W |
| Hoosick | 210 | 42.52 N | 73.20 W |
| Hoosick Falls | 210 | 42.54 N | 73.21 W |
| Hooton | 262 | 53.18 N | 2.57 W |
| Hoot Owl Estates | 285 | 39.53 N | 74.50 W |
| Hoover Dam ◆[6] | 200 | 36.00 N | 114.27 W |
| Hoover Reservoir ⊜[1] | 214 | 40.08 N | 82.53 W |
| Hooversville | 214 | 40.08 N | 78.54 W |
| Hopa | 130 | 41.25 N | 41.24 E |
| Hopatcong | 210 | 40.55 N | 74.39 W |
| Hopatcong, Lake ⊜ | 210 | 40.57 N | 74.38 W |
| Hopatcong State Park ◆ | 276 | 40.55 N | 74.40 W |
| Hop Bottom | 210 | 41.42 N | 75.46 W |
| Hop Brook ≃ | 276 | 40.19 N | 74.08 W |
| Hope, B.C., Can. | 182 | 49.23 N | 121.26 W |
| Hope, Ak., U.S. | 180 | 60.55 N | 149.38 W |
| Hope, Ar., U.S. | 194 | 33.40 N | 93.35 W |
| Hope, In., U.S. | 218 | 39.18 N | 85.46 W |
| Hope, N.J., U.S. | 210 | 40.54 N | 74.58 W |
| Hope, N.D., U.S. | 198 | 47.19 N | 97.43 W |
| Hope, R.I., U.S. | 207 | 41.44 N | 71.33 W |
| Hope, Ben ∧ | 46 | 58.24 N | 4.37 W |
| Hope, Loch ⊜ | 46 | 58.27 N | 4.39 W |
| Hope, Point > | 180 | 68.21 N | 166.50 W |
| Hope Bay c | 212 | 44.55 N | 81.08 W |
| Hopedale, Nf., Can. | 176 | 55.28 N | 60.13 W |
| Hopedale, Il., U.S. | 194 | 40.25 N | 89.24 W |
| Hopedale, La., U.S. | 194 | 29.49 N | 89.39 W |
| Hopedale, Ma., U.S. | 207 | 42.07 N | 71.32 W |
| Hopedale, Oh., U.S. | 214 | 40.19 N | 80.54 W |
| Hope Farm | 210 | 41.44 N | 73.40 W |
| Hopefield | 158 | 33.04 S | 18.22 E |
| Hopeh → Hebei □[4] | 98 | 38.00 N | 116.00 E |
| Hope Island I, B.C., Can. | 182 | 50.55 N | 127.53 W |
| Hope Island I, On., Can. | 212 | 44.55 N | 80.12 W |
| Hopeland | 208 | 40.14 N | 76.16 W |
| Hopelawn | 276 | 40.31 N | 74.17 W |
| Hopelchén | 232 | 19.46 N | 89.51 W |
| Hopeman | 46 | 57.42 N | 3.25 W |
| Hope Mills | 192 | 34.58 N | 78.56 W |
| Hopes Advance, Cap > | 176 | 61.04 N | 69.34 W |
| Hopetoun, Austl. | 162 | 33.57 S | 120.07 E |
| Hopetoun, Austl. | 166 | 35.44 S | 142.22 E |
| Hopetown | 158 | 29.34 S | 24.03 E |
| Hope Vale Aboriginal Reserve ◆[4] | 164 | 15.10 S | 145.15 E |
| Hope Valley, Austl. | 168b | 34.50 S | 138.44 E |
| Hope Valley, R.I., U.S. | 207 | 41.30 N | 71.43 W |
| Hopewell, N.J., U.S. | 208 | 40.23 N | 74.45 W |
| Hopewell, Pa., U.S. | 214 | 40.08 N | 78.16 W |
| Hopewell, Va., U.S. | 208 | 37.18 N | 77.17 W |
| Hopewell Islands II | 176 | 58.25 N | 78.00 W |
| Hopewell Junction | 210 | 41.35 N | 73.48 W |
| Hopewell Village National Historic Site ⊥ | 208 | 40.12 N | 75.46 W |
| Hopfgarten | 64 | 47.27 N | 12.10 E |
| Hopfgarten in Defereggen | 64 | 46.55 N | 12.31 E |
| Hopi → Hebi | 98 | 35.59 N | 114.11 E |
| Hopi Buttes ∧ | 200 | 35.20 N | 110.15 W |
| Hopi Indian Reservation ◆[4] | 200 | 35.45 N | 110.35 W |
| Hopkins, Mi., U.S. | 216 | 42.37 N | 85.45 W |
| Hopkins, Mo., U.S. | 194 | 40.33 N | 94.49 W |
| Hopkins □[6] | 222 | 33.07 N | 95.35 W |
| Hopkins ≃ | 166 | 38.24 S | 142.31 E |
| Hopkins, Lake ⊜ | 162 | 24.15 S | 128.50 E |
| Hopkins Creek ≃ | 284a | 43.17 N | 78.46 W |
| Hopkinsville | 194 | 36.51 N | 87.29 W |
| Hopkinton, Ia., U.S. | 190 | 42.20 N | 91.14 W |
| Hopkinton, Ma., U.S. | 207 | 42.13 N | 71.31 W |
| Hopkinton, R.I., U.S. | 207 | 41.27 N | 71.46 W |
| Hopland | 204 | 38.58 N | 123.06 W |
| Hopólito Bouchard | 252 | 34.43 S | 63.31 W |
| Hoppegarten | 264a | 52.31 N | 13.40 E |
| Hoppenrade | 264a | 52.32 N | 12.56 E |
| Hoppo → Hepu | 102 | 21.39 N | 109.11 E |
| Hopsten | 52 | 52.23 N | 7.36 E |
| Hoptrup | 41 | 55.11 N | 9.28 E |
| Ho Pui | 271d | 22.25 N | 114.03 E |
| Hopwood, Mount ∧ | 166 | 21.49 S | 144.26 E |
| Hoque | 152 | 14.39 S | 13.54 E |
| Hoquiam | 224 | 46.58 N | 123.53 W |
| Hoquiam, East Fork ≃ | 224 | 46.58 N | 123.54 W |
| Hora Califo | 144 | 8.49 N | 43.07 E |
| Horace Mountain ∧ | 180 | 67.40 N | 149.06 W |
| Horadiz | 84 | 39.27 N | 47.20 E |
| Horado | 94 | 35.36 N | 136.50 E |
| Hōrai | 94 | 34.56 N | 137.34 E |
| Horancia | 144 | 6.31 N | 38.44 E |
| Horasan | 130 | 40.03 N | 42.11 E |
| Horatio | 194 | 33.56 N | 94.21 W |
| Horatio Gardens | 278 | 42.10 N | 87.57 W |
| Horažďovice | 60 | 49.20 N | 13.43 E |
| Horbachevo-Mykhaylivka | 83 | 47.50 N | 38.00 E |
| Horb am Neckar | 58 | 48.26 N | 8.41 E |
| Horbelev | 41 | 54.49 N | 12.04 E |
| Horbourg | 58 | 48.05 N | 7.23 E |
| Hörby | 41 | 55.51 N | 13.39 E |
| Horconcitos | 236 | 8.19 N | 82.10 W |
| Hordaland □[6] | 26 | 60.15 N | 6.30 E |
| Hörde ◆[8] | 263 | 51.29 N | 7.30 E |
| Horden | 44 | 54.46 N | 1.18 W |
| Horedzu ≃ | 164 | 3.50 S | 141.25 E |
| Horgen | 58 | 47.15 N | 8.36 E |
| Horgenzell | 58 | 47.48 N | 9.30 E |
| Horhany ⩘ | 78 | 48.30 N | 24.00 E |
| Hořice | 60 | 50.22 N | 15.38 E |
| Horicon | 190 | 43.27 N | 88.37 W |
| Horigane | 268 | 35.50 N | 139.27 E |
| Horine | 219 | 38.16 N | 90.25 W |
| Horinger | 102 | 40.23 N | 111.53 E |
| Horinouchi | 94 | 37.14 N | 138.56 E |
| Horinouchi ◆[8] | 268 | 35.41 N | 139.40 E |
| Horizon Tablemount ◆[3] | 14 | 19.40 N | 168.30 W |
| Horizontina | 252 | 27.37 S | 54.19 W |
| Horka | 54 | 51.16 N | 14.56 E |
| Hörken | 40 | 60.02 N | 14.56 E |
| Horki | 76 | 54.17 N | 30.59 E |
| Horley | 42 | 51.11 N | 0.11 W |
| Horlick Mountains ⩘ | 9 | 85.23 S | 121.00 W |
| Horlivka | 83 | 48.18 N | 38.03 E |
| Horloff ≃ | 56 | 50.20 N | 8.52 E |
| Hormigueros | 240m | 18.09 N | 67.08 W |
| Hormoz, Jazīreh-ye I | 128 | 27.04 N | 56.28 E |
| Hormozgān □[4] | 128 | 27.50 N | 56.00 E |
| Hormuz, Strait of ꭒ | 128 | 26.34 N | 56.15 E |
| Horn, Dtsch. | 52 | 51.52 N | 8.56 E |
| Horn, Öst. | 61 | 48.40 N | 15.40 E |
| Horn > | 24a | 66.28 N | 22.28 W |
| Horn ≃, N.T., Can. | 176 | 61.30 N | 118.01 W |
| Horn ≃, Europe | 56 | 49.15 N | 7.20 E |
| Horn, Ben ∧[2] | 46 | 58.01 N | 4.02 W |
| Horn, Cape → Hornos, Cabo de > | 254 | 55.59 S | 67.16 W |
| Hornaday ≃ | 180 | 69.22 N | 123.50 W |
| Hornafjördur c | 24a | 64.17 N | 15.16 W |
| Hornavan ⊜ | 24 | 66.10 N | 17.30 E |
| Hornbach | 56 | 49.11 N | 7.22 E |
| Hornbæk | 41 | 56.05 N | 12.28 E |
| Hornbeak | 194 | 36.19 N | 89.17 W |
| Hornbeck | 194 | 31.19 N | 93.23 W |
| Hornberg | 58 | 48.13 N | 8.13 E |
| Hornbrook | 204 | 41.55 N | 122.33 W |
| Hornburg | 54 | 52.01 N | 10.36 E |
| Hornby, On., Can. | 275b | 43.34 N | 79.50 W |
| Hornby, N.Z. | 172 | 43.33 S | 172.32 E |
| Hornby Bay c | 176 | 66.35 N | 117.50 W |
| Horncastle | 44 | 53.13 N | 0.07 W |
| Hornchurch ◆[8] | 260 | 51.34 N | 0.12 E |
| Horndal | 40 | 60.18 N | 16.25 E |
| Horndean | 42 | 50.55 N | 1.00 W |
| Horndon on the Hill | 260 | 51.31 N | 0.25 E |
| Horne | 41 | 55.06 N | 10.11 E |
| Hornebach ≃ | 263 | 51.39 N | 7.38 E |
| Horneburg, Dtsch. | 52 | 53.30 N | 9.34 E |
| Horneburg, Dtsch. | 263 | 51.38 N | 7.18 E |
| Hörnefors | 26 | 63.38 N | 19.54 E |
| Hornell | 210 | 42.19 N | 77.39 W |
| Hornepayne | 176 | 49.13 N | 84.47 W |
| Hornerstown | 208 | 40.06 N | 74.30 W |
| Hornhausen | 54 | 52.02 N | 11.10 E |
| Horn Head > | 48 | 55.14 N | 7.59 W |
| Horn Hill | 260 | 51.37 N | 0.32 W |
| Horní Jiřetín | 54 | 50.35 N | 13.32 E |
| Hornindal | 26 | 61.58 N | 6.31 E |
| Hornindalsvatnet ⊜ | 26 | 61.56 N | 6.22 E |
| Hørning | 41 | 56.05 N | 10.03 E |
| Hörningsholm | 40 | 59.03 N | 17.40 E |
| Horní Počernice | 54 | 50.06 N | 14.38 E |
| Hornisgrinde ∧ | 56 | 48.36 N | 8.12 E |
| Horn Island I, Austl. | 164 | 10.37 S | 142.17 E |
| Horn Island I, Ms., U.S. | 194 | 30.13 N | 88.38 W |
| Horní Slavkov | 54 | 50.07 N | 12.46 E |
| Horní Stropnice | 61 | 48.46 N | 14.44 E |
| Hornito, Cerro ∧ | 236 | 8.39 N | 82.09 W |
| Hornitos | 226 | 37.30 N | 120.14 W |
| Horní Vltavice | 60 | 48.57 N | 13.46 E |
| Horn Lake | 194 | 34.58 N | 90.02 W |
| Horn Lake ⊜ | 212 | 45.24 N | 79.36 W |
| Hornos, Cabo de (Cape Horn) > | 254 | 55.59 S | 67.16 W |
| Hornos, Isla I | 254 | 55.57 S | 67.17 W |
| Hornos, Islas de II | 288 | 34.25 S | 57.55 W |
| Hornostayivka | 78 | 47.01 N | 33.44 E |
| Hornow | 54 | 51.38 N | 14.31 E |
| Hornoy | 50 | 49.51 N | 1.54 E |
| Horn Plateau ⩘[1] | 176 | 62.15 N | 119.15 W |
| Horn Pond ⊜ | 283 | 42.28 N | 71.09 W |
| Hornsby, Austl. | 170 | 33.42 S | 151.06 E |
| Hornsby, Il., U.S. | 219 | 39.10 N | 89.45 W |
| Hornsbyville | 208 | 37.11 N | 76.28 W |
| Hornsea | 44 | 53.55 N | 0.10 W |
| Hornsey ◆[8] | 260 | 51.35 N | 0.07 W |
| Hornslet | 41 | 56.19 N | 10.20 E |
| Hornstorf | 54 | 53.54 N | 11.32 E |
| Hornsyld | 41 | 55.45 N | 9.51 E |
| Horntown | 208 | 37.58 N | 75.28 W |
| Hornu | 50 | 50.26 N | 3.49 E |
| Horodenka, Ukr. | 38 | 48.41 N | 25.29 E |
| Horodenka, Ukr. | 78 | 48.41 N | 25.29 E |
| Horodets' | 78 | 51.17 N | 26.19 E |
| Horodkivka | 78 | 48.23 N | 28.42 E |
| Horodne | 78 | 45.53 N | 28.50 E |
| Horodnya | 78 | 51.53 N | 31.36 E |
| Horodnytsya | 78 | 50.48 N | 27.20 E |
| Horodok, Ukr. | 78 | 49.10 N | 26.34 E |
| Horodok, Ukr. | 78 | 49.47 N | 23.39 E |
| Horodyshche, Ukr. | 78 | 49.17 N | 31.27 E |
| Horodyshche, Ukr. | 83 | 48.19 N | 38.39 E |
| Horodyshche, Ukr. | 83 | 49.03 N | 39.38 E |
| Horokhiv | 78 | 50.30 N | 24.45 E |
| Horokhuvatka | 83 | 49.21 N | 37.31 E |
| Horoshiri-dake ∧ | 92a | 42.43 N | 142.41 E |
| Horotiu | 172 | 37.43 S | 175.12 E |
| Hořovice | 60 | 49.50 N | 13.54 E |
| Horqin Youyi Qianqi (Ulan Hot) | 89 | 46.05 N | 122.05 E |
| Horqin Youyi Zhongqi | 89 | 45.09 N | 121.24 E |
| Horqin Zuoyi Houqi | 89 | 42.58 N | 122.20 E |
| Horqin Zuoyi Zhongqi | 89 | 44.07 N | 123.18 E |
| Horqueta | 252 | 23.24 S | 56.53 W |
| Horrabridge | 42 | 50.31 N | 4.05 W |
| Horrelville | 172 | 43.20 S | 172.20 E |
| Horrem | 263 | 51.06 N | 6.48 E |
| Hörsching | 61 | 48.14 N | 14.11 E |
| Horse ≃ | 184 | 56.43 N | 111.23 W |
| Horseback Knob ∧[2] | 218 | 39.14 N | 83.06 W |
| Horse Cave | 194 | 37.10 N | 85.54 W |
| Horse Creek | 200 | 41.25 N | 105.11 W |
| Horse Creek ≃, U.S. | 198 | 41.57 N | 103.58 W |
| Horse Creek ≃, Co., U.S. | 198 | 38.05 N | 103.19 W |
| Horse Creek ≃, Fl., U.S. | 220 | 27.06 N | 81.58 W |
| Horse Creek ≃, Il., U.S. | 219 | 39.45 N | 89.34 W |
| Horse Creek ≃, Mo., U.S. | 194 | 37.46 N | 93.53 W |
| Horsefly | 182 | 52.20 N | 121.24 W |
| Horsefly Lake ⊜ | 182 | 52.25 N | 121.00 W |
| Horsehead Creek ≃ | 198 | 43.17 N | 103.22 W |
| Horsehead Lake ⊜ | 198 | 47.02 N | 99.47 W |
| Horseheads | 210 | 42.10 N | 76.49 W |
| Horse Islands II | 186 | 50.13 N | 55.45 W |
| Horsell | 260 | 51.19 N | 0.34 W |
| Horseneck Brook ≃ | 276 | 41.01 N | 73.38 W |
| Horsens | 41 | 55.52 N | 9.52 E |
| Horsens Fjord c | 41 | 55.50 N | 10.05 E |
| Horseshoe Bend, Ar., U.S. | 194 | 36.15 N | 91.43 W |
| Horseshoe Bend, Id., U.S. | 202 | 43.55 N | 116.12 W |
| Horseshoe Bend National Military Park ◆ | 194 | 33.00 N | 85.46 W |
| Horseshoe Cove c | 276 | 40.27 N | 74.00 W |
| Horseshoe Creek ≃ | 198 | 42.27 N | 104.58 W |
| Horseshoe Falls ᒪ | 284a | 43.05 N | 79.04 W |
| Horseshoe Lake ⊜, Mb., Can. | 184 | 52.12 N | 95.50 W |
| Horseshoe Lake ⊜, Mi., U.S. | 281 | 42.24 N | 83.45 W |
| Horseshoe Lake ⊜, N.J., U.S. | 276 | 40.52 N | 74.38 W |
| Horse Shoe Reef ◆[2] | 240m | 18.40 N | 64.12 W |
| Horsfjärden c | 40 | 59.04 N | 18.09 E |
| Horsford | 42 | 52.41 N | 1.15 E |
| Horsforth | 44 | 53.51 N | 1.39 W |
| Horsham, Austl. | 166 | 36.43 S | 142.13 E |
| Horsham, Eng., U.K. | 42 | 51.04 N | 0.21 W |
| Horsham, Pa., U.S. | 208 | 40.10 N | 75.07 W |
| Hørsholm | 41 | 55.53 N | 12.30 E |
| Hörsingen | 54 | 52.16 N | 11.09 E |
| Horsley | 274a | 33.51 S | 150.51 E |
| Horslunde | 41 | 54.54 N | 11.14 E |
| Horšovský Týn | 60 | 49.32 N | 12.56 E |
| Horst, Dtsch. | 52 | 53.48 N | 9.37 E |
| Horst, Dtsch. | 54 | 53.22 N | 10.37 E |
| Horst, Ned. | 52 | 51.27 N | 6.04 E |
| Horst ◆[8] | 263 | 51.32 N | 7.02 E |
| Horsted Keynes | 42 | 51.02 N | 0.01 W |
| Hörstel | 52 | 52.18 N | 7.35 E |
| Horstmar, Dtsch. | 52 | 52.05 N | 7.17 E |
| Horstmar, Dtsch. | 263 | 51.36 N | 7.33 E |
| Horsunlu | 130 | 37.55 N | 28.36 E |
| Horta | 148a | 38.32 N | 28.38 W |
| Horta □[5] | 148a | 38.30 N | 29.00 W |
| Horta ◆[8] | 266d | 41.26 N | 2.00 E |
| Hortaleza ◆[8] | 266a | 40.28 N | 3.39 W |
| Horten | 26 | 59.25 N | 10.30 E |
| Hortobágy ◆[1] | 30 | 47.35 N | 21.00 E |
| Hortobágyi Nemzeti Park ◆ | 30 | 47.30 N | 21.10 E |
| Horton, Eng., U.K. | 260 | 51.28 N | 0.32 W |
| Horton, In., U.S. | 218 | 40.05 N | 86.09 W |
| Horton, Ks., U.S. | 198 | 39.39 N | 95.31 W |
| Horton, Mi., U.S. | 216 | 42.09 N | 84.31 W |
| Horton ≃ | 180 | 70.00 N | 126.53 W |
| Horton in Ribblesdale | 44 | 54.09 N | 2.17 W |
| Horton Kirby | 260 | 51.23 N | 0.15 E |
| Horton Lake ⊜ | 180 | 67.29 N | 122.31 W |
| Hortonville, N.Y., U.S. | 210 | 41.46 N | 75.02 W |
| Hortonville, Wi., U.S. | 190 | 44.20 N | 88.38 W |
| Horumersiel | 52 | 53.41 N | 8.00 E |
| Hørup | 41 | 54.56 N | 9.55 E |
| Hørve | 41 | 55.45 N | 11.28 E |
| Horw | 58 | 47.01 N | 8.18 E |
| Horwich | 44 | 53.37 N | 2.33 W |
| Horwood Lake ⊜ | 190 | 48.03 N | 82.20 W |
| Hory | 76 | 54.16 N | 31.34 E |
| Hory Matky Boží | 60 | 49.16 N | 13.27 E |
| Horyn' (Haryn') ≃ | 78 | 52.08 N | 27.17 E |
| Hōryūji Temple ᵾ[1] | 270 | 34.36 N | 135.44 E |
| Hosaina | 144 | 7.38 N | 37.52 E |
| Hösbach | 56 | 50.00 N | 9.12 E |
| Hosei University ᵾ[2] | 268 | 35.42 N | 139.44 E |
| Hösel | 56 | 51.19 N | 6.54 E |
| Hosena | 54 | 51.27 N | 14.01 E |
| Hoséré Vokré ∧ | 146 | 8.20 N | 13.15 E |
| Ḥoseynābād | 128 | 35.33 N | 47.08 E |
| Ḥoseynīyeh-ye Khodā-Dād | 128 | 32.42 N | 48.14 E |
| Hosford | 192 | 30.23 N | 84.47 W |
| Hoshāb | 128 | 26.01 N | 63.56 E |
| Hoshangābād | 124 | 22.45 N | 77.43 E |
| Hoshangābād Plain ≚ | 124 | 22.35 N | 77.25 E |
| Hoshcha | 78 | 50.36 N | 26.41 E |
| Hoshiārpur, India | 123 | 31.32 N | 75.54 E |
| Hoshiarpur, India | 272a | 28.35 N | 77.22 E |
| Hoshigajō ∧ | 96 | 34.31 N | 134.19 E |
| Hosingen | 56 | 50.01 N | 6.05 E |
| Hosjö | 40 | 60.35 N | 15.46 E |
| Hoskins | 164 | 5.27 S | 150.30 E |
| Hosmer, B.C., Can. | 182 | 49.35 N | 114.57 W |
| Hosmer, S.D., U.S. | 198 | 45.34 N | 99.28 W |
| Hosoe | 94 | 34.49 N | 137.39 E |
| Hospental | 58 | 46.37 N | 8.34 E |
| Hospers | 198 | 43.04 N | 95.54 W |
| Hospet | 122 | 15.16 N | 76.24 E |
| Hospital | 48 | 52.29 N | 8.25 W |
| Hospital de Orbigo | 34 | 42.28 N | 5.53 W |
| Hossegor | 32 | 43.40 N | 1.27 W |
| Hosston | 194 | 32.53 N | 93.52 W |
| Hosta Butte ∧ | 200 | 35.35 N | 108.12 W |
| Hoste, Isla I | 254 | 55.15 S | 69.00 W |
| Hostěradice | 61 | 48.57 N | 16.15 E |
| Hostetter | 214 | 40.16 N | 79.24 W |
| Hostigrām | 272b | 22.26 N | 88.31 E |
| Hostivař ◆[8] | 54 | 50.01 N | 14.32 E |
| Hostivice | 54 | 50.04 N | 14.15 E |
| Hošt'ka | 54 | 50.30 N | 14.20 E |
| Hostomice | 54 | 50.35 N | 13.46 E |
| Hostotipaquillo | 234 | 21.04 N | 104.04 W |
| Hostouň | 60 | 49.34 N | 12.46 E |
| Hosūr | 122 | 12.43 N | 77.49 E |
| Hot | 110 | 18.06 N | 98.36 E |
| Hota | 268 | 35.08 N | 139.51 E |
| Hotagen | 26 | 63.59 N | 14.15 E |
| Hotagen ⊜ | 26 | 63.53 N | 14.29 E |
| Hotagsfjällen ∧ | 26 | 64.20 N | 14.30 E |
| Hotaka | 94 | 36.20 N | 137.53 E |
| Hotaka-dake ∧ | 94 | 36.17 N | 137.39 E |
| Hotamış | 130 | 37.36 N | 33.13 E |
| Hotan | 120 | 37.08 N | 79.54 E |
| Hotan ≃ | 90 | 40.30 N | 80.45 E |
| Hotarele | 38 | 44.10 N | 26.22 E |
| Hotazel | 158 | 27.15 S | 23.00 E |
| Hotchkiss | 200 | 38.47 N | 107.43 W |
| Hotchkissville | 207 | 41.34 N | 73.13 W |
| Hot Creek Range ⩘ | 204 | 38.30 N | 116.25 W |
| Hötensleben | 54 | 52.08 N | 11.01 E |
| Hotevilla | 200 | 35.55 N | 110.40 W |
| Hotham ≃ | 168a | 32.58 S | 116.22 E |
| Hotham Inlet c | 180 | 66.45 N | 162.00 W |
| Hotham Peak ∧ | 180 | 66.48 N | 160.42 W |
| Hoting | 26 | 64.07 N | 16.10 E |
| Hot Springs, Mt., U.S. | 202 | 47.36 N | 114.40 W |
| Hot Springs → Truth or Consequences, N.M., U.S. | 200 | 33.08 N | 107.15 W |
| Hot Springs, N.C., U.S. | 192 | 35.53 N | 82.49 W |
| Hot Springs, S.D., U.S. | 198 | 43.25 N | 103.28 W |
| Hot Springs, Va., U.S. | 192 | 37.59 N | 79.49 W |
| Hot Springs National Park | 194 | 34.30 N | 93.04 W |
| Hot Springs Peak ∧, Ca., U.S. | 204 | 40.22 N | 120.07 W |
| Hot Springs Peak ∧, Nv., U.S. | 204 | 41.22 N | 117.26 W |
| Hot Springs State Park ◆ | 202 | 43.40 N | 108.10 W |
| Hot Sulphur Springs | 200 | 40.04 N | 106.06 W |
| Hottah Lake ⊜ | 176 | 65.04 N | 118.29 W |
| Hottentotbaai c | 156 | 26.05 S | 14.58 E |
| Hottentotskloof | 158 | 33.15 S | 19.40 E |
| Hotton | 56 | 50.16 N | 5.27 E |
| Hötzum | 54 | 52.13 N | 10.37 E |
| Houaïlou | 175f | 21.17 S | 165.38 E |
| Houamuang | 110 | 20.09 N | 103.38 E |
| Houbaishu | 106 | 31.49 N | 119.10 E |
| Houbao | 98 | 41.54 N | 125.14 E |
| Houcheng | 106 | 31.55 N | 120.26 E |
| Houdahepao | 104 | 41.49 N | 123.01 E |
| Houdain | 50 | 50.27 N | 2.32 E |
| Houdan | 50 | 48.47 N | 1.36 E |
| Houdelaincourt | 58 | 48.33 N | 5.28 E |
| Houdeng-Aimeries | 50 | 50.29 N | 4.08 E |
| Houeillès | 32 | 44.12 N | 0.02 E |
| Houffalize | 56 | 50.08 N | 5.47 E |
| Hougang | 271c | 1.22 N | 103.54 E |
| Hough Green | 262 | 53.23 N | 2.47 W |
| Houghton, Mi., U.S. | 190 | 47.07 N | 88.34 W |
| Houghton, N.Y., U.S. | 210 | 42.25 N | 78.09 W |
| Houghton, Wa., U.S. | 224 | 47.40 N | 122.12 W |
| Houghton Estates ◆[8] | 273d | 26.10 S | 28.04 E |
| Houghton Green | 262 | 53.25 N | 2.34 W |
| Houghton Lake | 190 | 44.18 N | 84.45 W |
| Houghton Lake ⊜, Sk., Can. | 184 | 52.23 N | 105.08 W |
| Houghton Lake ⊜, Mi., U.S. | 190 | 44.20 N | 84.45 W |
| Houghton-le-Spring | 44 | 54.51 N | 1.28 W |
| Houghton Regis | 42 | 51.55 N | 0.31 W |
| Houguangzhengtai | 104 | 41.13 N | 122.07 E |
| Hougujiazi | 104 | 42.21 N | 123.22 E |
| Houhuangtukan | 104 | 41.02 N | 122.29 E |


ENGLISH


| Name | Page | Lat.°′ | Long.°′ |
|---|---|---|---|
| Houille ≃ | 56 | 50.08 N | 4.49 E |
| Houillères de la Sarre, Canal des ⩦ | 56 | 48.42 N | 6.55 E |
| Houilles | 261 | 48.56 N | 2.11 E |
| Houjiangfushan | 105 | 40.03 N | 117.09 E |
| Houjiaping | 107 | 30.02 N | 104.38 E |
| Houjiaying | 105 | 39.51 N | 117.15 E |
| Houjie | 100 | 22.58 N | 113.39 E |
| Houjiumen | 104 | 42.38 N | 123.18 E |
| Houkou | 98 | 37.34 N | 115.09 E |
| Houliujia | 104 | 40.47 N | 122.19 E |
| Houlka | 194 | 34.02 N | 89.01 W |
| Houlton | 188 | 46.07 N | 67.50 W |
| Houluan | 105 | 39.13 N | 116.32 E |
| Houma, Tonga | 174w | 21.09 S | 175.19 W |
| Houma, La., U.S. | 194 | 29.35 N | 90.43 W |
| Houma, Zhg. | 102 | 35.36 N | 111.21 E |
| Houmanzhoutun | 104 | 42.29 N | 123.14 E |
| Houmen | 100 | 22.51 N | 115.09 E |
| Houmet Essouq | 148 | 33.59 N | 10.51 E |
| Houmont Park | 222 | 29.50 N | 95.13 W |
| Hound Creek ≃ | 202 | 47.13 N | 111.23 W |
| Houndé | 150 | 11.30 N | 3.31 W |
| Hounslow ◆[8] | 42 | 51.29 N | 0.22 W |
| Houplines | 50 | 50.42 N | 2.55 E |
| Houqianjiayu | 104 | 40.50 N | 120.41 E |
| Houqiao | 105 | 40.04 N | 116.39 E |
| Hourn, Loch c | 46 | 57.08 N | 5.36 W |
| Housatonic | 207 | 42.15 N | 73.22 W |
| Housatonic ≃ | 207 | 41.10 N | 73.07 W |
| House | 196 | 34.38 N | 103.54 W |
| House ≃ | 184 | 56.13 N | 112.31 W |
| House of Seven Gables ⊥ | 283 | 42.32 N | 70.53 W |
| Houserville | 214 | 40.50 N | 77.50 W |
| House Springs | 219 | 38.24 N | 90.34 W |
| Houshan | 106 | 31.03 N | 120.21 E |
| Houston, B.C., Can. | 182 | 54.24 N | 126.38 W |
| Houston, De., U.S. | 208 | 38.55 N | 75.30 W |
| Houston, Mn., U.S. | 190 | 43.45 N | 91.34 W |
| Houston, Ms., U.S. | 194 | 33.53 N | 88.59 W |
| Houston, Mo., U.S. | 194 | 37.19 N | 91.57 W |
| Houston, Oh., U.S. | 216 | 40.15 N | 84.20 W |
| Houston, Pa., U.S. | 214 | 40.14 N | 80.12 W |
| Houston, Tx., U.S. | 222 | 29.45 N | 95.21 W |
| Houston □[6] | 222 | 31.20 N | 95.20 W |
| Houston ≃ | 194 | 30.16 N | 93.13 W |
| Houston, Lake ⊜[1] | 222 | 29.58 N | 95.07 W |
| Houston County Lake ⊜[1] | 222 | 31.25 N | 95.35 W |
| Houston Creek ≃ | 218 | 38.13 N | 84.15 W |
| Houston Intercontinental Airport ⊠ | 222 | 29.59 N | 95.27 W |
| Houston Ship Channel ⩦ | 222 | 29.21 N | 94.47 W |
| Hout ≃ | 156 | 23.04 S | 29.36 E |
| Houtbaai | 158 | 34.03 S | 18.21 E |
| Houthalen | 56 | 51.02 N | 5.22 E |
| Houthulst | 50 | 50.59 N | 2.57 E |
| Houtkop | 158 | 26.36 S | 27.52 E |
| Houtkraal | 158 | 30.23 S | 24.05 E |
| Houtman Abrolhos II | 162 | 28.43 S | 113.48 E |
| Houtskär I | 26 | 60.12 N | 21.22 E |
| Houtzdale | 214 | 40.49 N | 78.21 W |
| Houwuliangdian | 104 | 41.31 N | 121.55 E |
| Houwutaigou | 104 | 41.46 N | 121.42 E |
| Houx | 261 | 48.34 N | 1.37 E |
| Houxijie | 100 | 28.46 N | 118.49 E |
| Houxinlitun | 104 | 41.05 N | 122.33 E |
| Houxinqiu | 104 | 42.34 N | 122.43 E |
| Houyatai | 104 | 41.26 N | 121.49 E |
| Houying | 105 | 39.42 N | 118.18 E |
| Houyingzi | 98 | 40.24 N | 123.50 E |
| Houzhangcun | 105 | 40.08 N | 116.11 E |
| Houzhou | 106 | 31.35 N | 119.22 E |
| Houzitun | 104 | 41.04 N | 121.18 E |
| Hov | 41 | 55.55 N | 10.16 E |
| Hova | 40 | 58.52 N | 14.13 E |
| Hovborg | 41 | 55.36 N | 8.57 E |
| Høve, Dan. | 41 | 55.50 N | 11.30 E |
| Hove, Eng., U.K. | 42 | 50.49 N | 0.10 W |
| Hovedgård | 41 | 55.57 N | 9.58 E |
| Hövelhof | 52 | 51.49 N | 8.40 E |
| Hoven, Dan. | 41 | 55.51 N | 8.46 E |
| Hoven, S.D., U.S. | 198 | 45.14 N | 99.46 W |
| Hovenweep National Monument ◆ | 200 | 37.25 N | 109.04 W |
| Hoverla, hora ∧ | 78 | 48.10 N | 24.32 E |
| Hovmantorp | 26 | 56.47 N | 15.08 E |
| Hovran ⊜ | 40 | 60.16 N | 16.03 E |
| Hovsta | 40 | 59.21 N | 15.13 E |
| Howa, Ouadi (Wādī Howar) V | 140 | 17.30 N | 27.08 E |
| Howakil I | 144 | 15.10 N | 40.16 E |
| Howar, Wādī (Ouadi Howa) V | 140 | 17.30 N | 27.08 E |
| Howard, Austl. | 166 | 25.19 S | 152.34 E |
| Howard, Ks., U.S. | 198 | 37.28 N | 96.15 W |
| Howard, Oh., U.S. | 214 | 40.24 N | 82.19 W |
| Howard, Pa., U.S. | 214 | 41.00 N | 77.39 W |
| Howard, S.D., U.S. | 198 | 44.00 N | 97.31 W |
| Howard, Wi., U.S. | 190 | 44.32 N | 88.05 W |
| Howard □[6], In., U.S. | 216 | 40.29 N | 86.08 W |
| Howard □[6], Md., U.S. | 208 | 39.16 N | 76.48 W |
| Howard Beach ◆[8] | 276 | 40.40 N | 73.51 W |
| Howard City | 190 | 43.23 N | 85.28 W |
| Howard Draw V | 196 | 30.08 N | 101.35 W |
| Howard Hanson Reservoir ⊜[1] | 224 | 47.15 N | 121.45 W |
| Howard Heights | 284b | 39.17 N | 76.50 W |
| Howardian Hills ⩘[2] | 44 | 54.07 N | 1.00 W |
| Howard Island I | 164 | 12.10 S | 135.24 E |
| Howard Lake | 190 | 45.03 N | 94.04 W |
| Howard Prairie Lake ⊜[1] | 202 | 42.15 N | 122.20 W |
| Howard University ᵾ[2] | 284c | 38.55 N | 77.01 W |
| Howden | 44 | 53.45 N | 0.52 W |
| Howe, In., U.S. | 216 | 41.43 N | 85.25 W |
| Howe, Tx., U.S. | 196 | 33.30 N | 96.37 W |
| Howe, Cape > | 166 | 37.31 S | 149.59 E |
| Howe Caverns ◆[5] | 210 | 42.42 N | 74.25 W |
| Howe Green | 260 | 51.42 N | 0.32 E |
| Howe Island I | 212 | 44.17 N | 76.15 W |
| Howeke | 150 | 4.50 N | 7.45 W |
| Howell | 216 | 42.36 N | 83.55 W |
| Howell Airport ⊠ | 278 | 41.39 N | 87.45 W |
| Howell Island I | 219 | 38.40 N | 90.42 W |
| Howells | 198 | 41.43 N | 97.00 W |
| Howells Pond ⊜ | 276 | 41.03 N | 74.42 W |
| Howes Cave | 210 | 42.41 N | 74.23 W |
| Howe Sound ꭒ | 182 | 49.22 N | 123.18 W |
| Howe's Range ⩘ | 170 | 33.08 S | 150.47 E |
| Howes Valley | 170 | 32.50 S | 150.51 E |
| Howey In The Hills | 220 | 28.43 N | 81.47 W |
| Howick, P.Q., Can. | 206 | 45.11 N | 73.51 W |
| Howick, S. Afr. | 158 | 29.28 S | 30.14 E |
| Howitt, Mount ∧ | 166 | 37.10 S | 146.40 E |
| Howland | 188 | 45.14 N | 68.39 W |
| Howland Island I | 14 | 0.48 N | 176.38 W |
| Howley | 186 | 49.10 N | 57.07 W |
| Howley, Mount ∧ | 186 | 48.17 N | 58.26 W |
| Howmore | 46 | 57.18 N | 7.23 W |
| Howqua ≃ | 169 | 37.14 S | 146.08 E |
| Howrah → Hāora | 126 | 22.35 N | 88.20 E |
| Howse Peak ∧ | 182 | 51.49 N | 116.41 W |
| Howser | 182 | 50.18 N | 116.57 W |
| Howson Peak ∧ | 182 | 54.25 N | 127.44 W |
| Howth | 48 | 53.23 N | 6.04 W |
| Howth Head > | 48 | 53.22 N | 6.03 W |
| Ho Xa | 110 | 17.04 N | 107.02 E |
| Hoxie, Ar., U.S. | 194 | 36.03 N | 90.58 W |
| Hoxie, Ks., U.S. | 198 | 39.21 N | 100.26 W |
| Höxter | 52 | 51.46 N | 9.23 E |
| Hoxtolgay | 86 | 46.35 N | 86.01 E |
| Hoxton Park | 274a | 33.55 S | 150.51 E |
| Hoxton Park Aerodrome ⊠ | 274a | 33.54 S | 150.50 E |
| Hoy I | 46 | 58.51 N | 3.18 W |
| Hoya, Dtsch. | 52 | 52.48 N | 9.08 E |


DEUTSCH


| Name | Seite | Breite°′ | Länge°′ E = Ost |
|---|---|---|---|
| Hōya, Nihon | 94 | 35.43 N | 139.34 E |
| Høyanger | 26 | 61.13 N | 6.05 E |
| Hoyerswerda | 54 | 51.26 N | 14.14 E |
| Hoylake | 44 | 53.23 N | 3.11 W |
| Hoyleton, Austl. | 168b | 34.01 S | 138.33 E |
| Hoyleton, Il., U.S. | 219 | 38.27 N | 89.16 W |
| Hoym | 54 | 51.47 N | 11.19 E |
| Hoyos | 34 | 40.10 N | 6.43 W |
| Hōyo-shotō II | 96 | 33.52 N | 132.18 E |
| Höytiäinen ⊜ | 26 | 62.48 N | 29.39 E |
| Hoyt Lakes | 190 | 47.31 N | 92.08 W |
| Hoytville, Mi., U.S. | 216 | 42.45 N | 84.53 W |
| Hoytville, Oh., U.S. | 216 | 41.11 N | 83.47 W |
| Hozain ≃ | 50 | 48.16 N | 4.06 E |
| Hozat | 130 | 39.07 N | 39.14 E |
| Hozumi | 94 | 35.24 N | 136.41 E |
| Hpru-so | 110 | 19.25 N | 97.08 E |
| Hracholusky, údolní nádrž ⊜[1] | 60 | 49.47 N | 13.07 E |
| Hradec Králové | 30 | 50.12 N | 15.50 E |
| Hrádek | 61 | 48.46 N | 16.16 E |
| Hrádek nad Nisou | 54 | 50.48 N | 14.51 E |
| Hradiště ∧ | 54 | 50.13 N | 13.08 E |
| Hradyz'k | 78 | 49.13 N | 33.07 E |
| Hradzjanka | 76 | 53.33 N | 28.45 E |
| Hrandzičy | 76 | 53.43 N | 23.49 E |
| Hranice, Česká Rep. | 30 | 49.33 N | 17.44 E |
| Hranice, Česká Rep. | 54 | 50.15 N | 12.10 E |
| Hranitne | 83 | 47.27 N | 37.52 E |
| Hraniv | 78 | 48.52 N | 29.34 E |
| Hrdlovka | 54 | 50.36 N | 13.40 E |
| Hrebinka | 78 | 50.07 N | 32.25 E |
| Hrebinky | 78 | 49.57 N | 30.12 E |
| Hrechyshkyne | 83 | 48.52 N | 38.54 E |
| Hřensko | 54 | 50.50 N | 14.14 E |
| Hrèsk | 76 | 53.10 N | 27.29 E |
| Hriňová | 30 | 48.36 N | 19.31 E |
| Hrob | 54 | 50.39 N | 13.44 E |
| Hrodivka | 83 | 48.15 N | 37.23 E |
| Hrodna | 76 | 53.41 N | 23.50 E |
| Hrodna □[8] | 76 | 53.30 N | 25.00 E |
| Hromivka | 78 | 46.19 N | 34.06 E |
| Hromokliya ≃ | 78 | 47.21 N | 32.14 E |
| Hron ≃ | 30 | 47.49 N | 18.45 E |
| Hronov | 30 | 50.29 N | 16.12 E |
| Hrotovice | 61 | 49.06 N | 16.07 E |
| Hrubieszów | 30 | 50.49 N | 23.55 E |
| Hrubý Jeseník ⩘ | 30 | 50.00 N | 17.20 E |
| Hrun' | 78 | 50.16 N | 34.36 E |
| Hrušovany | 61 | 48.50 N | 16.23 E |
| Hruzs'kyy Yalanchyk ≃ | 83 | 47.07 N | 38.04 E |
| Hrvatska → Croatia □[1] | 36 | 45.10 N | 15.30 E |
| Hrybova Balka, lis ◆ | 83 | 48.09 N | 38.37 E |
| Hryhorivka, Ukr. | 78 | 46.17 N | 33.44 E |
| Hryhorivka, Ukr. | 78 | 51.03 N | 32.51 E |
| Hryhorivka, Ukr. | 78 | 50.05 N | 30.39 E |
| Hrymayliv | 78 | 49.20 N | 26.01 E |
| Hrynyava | 78 | 47.59 N | 24.49 E |
| Hryshkivtsi | 78 | 49.56 N | 28.36 E |
| Hrytsiv | 78 | 49.58 N | 27.14 E |
| Hsenwi | 110 | 23.18 N | 97.58 E |
| Hsiakuan → Xiaguan | 102 | 25.34 N | 100.14 E |
| Hsiamen → Xiamen | 100 | 24.28 N | 118.07 E |
| Hsian → Xi'an | 102 | 34.15 N | 108.52 E |
| Hsiangt'an → Xiangtan | 100 | 27.51 N | 112.54 E |
| Hsiangyang → Xiangfan | 102 | 32.03 N | 112.01 E |
| Hsiaohungt'ou Yü I | 100 | 21.57 N | 121.36 E |
| Hsichih | 269d | 25.04 N | 121.39 E |
| Hsichi Yü I | 100 | 23.15 N | 119.37 E |
| Hsich'üan Tao I | 100 | 25.59 N | 119.56 E |
| Hsientung | 269d | 25.09 N | 121.44 E |
| Hsienyang → Xianyang | 102 | 34.22 N | 108.42 E |
| Hsi-hseng | 110 | 20.09 N | 97.15 E |
| Hsihu | 100 | 23.58 N | 120.28 E |
| Hsilo | 100 | 23.48 N | 120.27 E |
| Hsilo ≃ | 100 | 23.50 N | 120.15 E |
| Hsim ≃ | 110 | 20.48 N | 98.31 E |
| Hsinch'eng | 100 | 24.08 N | 121.39 E |
| Hsinchu | 100 | 24.48 N | 120.58 E |
| Hsinchuang | 100 | 25.02 N | 121.27 E |
| Hsinghua → Xinghua | 100 | 32.57 N | 119.50 E |
| Hsingt'ai → Xingtai | 98 | 37.04 N | 114.29 E |
| Hsinhailien → Lianyungang | 98 | 34.39 N | 119.16 E |
| Hsinhsiang → Xinxiang | 98 | 35.20 N | 113.51 E |
| Hsinhua | 100 | 23.02 N | 120.18 E |
| Hsining → Xining | 102 | 36.38 N | 101.55 E |
| Hsinking → Changchun | 89 | 43.53 N | 125.19 E |
| Hsinpeit'ou ◆[8] | 269d | 25.09 N | 121.30 E |
| Hsinp'u → Lianyungang | 98 | 34.39 N | 119.16 E |
| Hsinshih | 100 | 23.05 N | 120.17 E |
| Hsintien | 100 | 24.57 N | 121.32 E |
| Hsintien ≃ | 269d | 25.02 N | 121.29 E |
| Hsinyang → Xinyang | 100 | 32.08 N | 114.04 E |
| Hsipaw | 110 | 22.37 N | 97.18 E |
| Hsiukuluan ≃ | 100 | 23.28 N | 121.30 E |
| Hsiyü | 100 | 23.36 N | 119.30 E |
| Hsüanhua → Xuanhua | 105 | 40.37 N | 115.03 E |
| Hsüch'ang → Xuchang | 100 | 34.03 N | 113.49 E |
| Hsüchou → Xuzhou | 98 | 34.16 N | 117.11 E |
| Hsüehchia | 100 | 23.14 N | 120.10 E |
| Hsüeh Shan ∧ | 100 | 24.23 N | 121.13 E |
| Hsuphāng | 110 | 20.18 N | 98.42 E |
| Hua'an | 100 | 25.02 N | 117.34 E |
| Huab ≃ | 156 | 20.52 S | 13.25 E |
| Huabu | 100 | 29.00 N | 118.20 E |
| Huacaña | 248 | 14.02 S | 74.02 W |
| Huacao | 269b | 31.14 N | 121.19 E |
| Huacaraje | 248 | 13.33 S | 63.45 W |
| Huachacalla | 248 | 18.45 S | 68.17 W |
| Huacheng | 100 | 24.04 N | 115.38 E |
| Huachi | 102 | 36.43 N | 107.52 E |
| Huachi, Laguna ⊜ | 248 | 14.11 S | 63.30 W |
| Huachipa | 286d | 12.00 S | 76.56 W |
| Huacho | 248 | 11.07 S | 77.37 W |
| Huachón | 248 | 10.40 S | 75.57 W |
| Huachos | 248 | 13.12 S | 75.31 W |
| Huachuca City | 200 | 31.37 N | 110.20 W |
| Huaco | 252 | 30.09 S | 68.31 W |
| Huacrachuco | 248 | 8.39 S | 77.05 W |
| Huade | 98 | 41.46 N | 114.16 E |
| Huadian | 89 | 42.58 N | 126.43 E |
| Huading Shan ∧ | 100 | 29.15 N | 121.05 E |
| Huafeng | 106 | 32.14 N | 121.16 E |
| Huagutang | 106 | 30.55 N | 119.18 E |
| Hua Hin | 110 | 12.34 N | 99.58 E |
| Huai ≃, Zhg. | 98 | 37.28 N | 114.55 E |
| Huai ≃, Zhg. | 100 | 32.58 N | 118.17 E |
| Huaiá-Miçu ≃ | 250 | 10.52 S | 53.15 W |
| Huai'an (Chaigoubu), Zhg. | 98 | 40.39 N | 114.27 E |
| Huai'an, Zhg. | 100 | 33.32 N | 119.10 E |
| Huaibin | 100 | 32.28 N | 115.24 E |
| Huaide | 89 | 43.32 N | 124.50 E |
| Huaidezhen, Zhg. | 89 | 43.54 N | 124.47 E |
| Huaidezhen, Zhg. | 107 | 28.59 N | 105.15 E |
| Huaihuazhenshi | 106 | 31.05 N | 119.41 E |
| Huaiji | 102 | 24.01 N | 112.18 E |
| Huailai (Shacheng) | 105 | 40.23 N | 115.33 E |
| Huailin | 100 | 31.26 N | 117.36 E |
| Huaillati | 248 | 14.05 S | 72.31 W |
| Huainan | 100 | 32.40 N | 117.00 E |
| Huaining | 100 | 30.25 N | 116.38 E |


**Symbols** in the index entries represent the broad categories identified in the key at the right. Symbols with superior numbers (⩘[1]) identify subcategories (see complete key on page I · 1).

**Symbole** im Register stellen die rechts im Schlüssel erklärten Kategorien dar. Symbole mit hochgestellten Ziffern (⩘[1]) bezeichnen Unterabteilungen einer Kategorie (vgl. vollständiger Schlüssel auf Seite I · 1).

**Los símbolos** incluídos en el texto del índice representan las grandes categorías identificadas con la clave a la derecha. Los símbolos con numeros en su parte superior (⩘[1]) identifican las subcategorías (véase la clave completa en la página I · 1).

**Les symboles** de l'index représentent les catégories indiquées dans la légende à droite. Les symboles suivis d'un indice (⩘[1]) représentent des sous-catégories (voir légende complète à la page I · 1).

**Os símbolos** incluídos no texto do índice representam as grandes categorias identificadas com a chave à direita. Os símbolos com números em sua parte superior (⩘[1]) identificam as subcategorias (veja-se a chave completa à página I · 1).

| | | | | |
|---|---|---|---|---|
| ∧ Mountain | Berg | Montaña | Montagne | Montanha |
| ⩘ Mountains | Gebirge | Montañas | Montagnes | Montanhas |
| ꭒ Pass | Paß | Paso | Col | Passo |
| V Valley, Canyon | Tal, Cañon | Valle, Cañón | Vallée, Canyon | Vale, Canhão |
| ≚ Plain | Ebene | Llano | Plaine | Planície |
| > Cape | Kap | Cabo | Cap | Cabo |
| I Island | Insel | Isla | Île | Ilha |
| II Islands | Inseln | Islas | Îles | Ilhas |
| ◆ Other Topographic Features | Andere Topographische Objekte | Otros Elementos Topográficos | Autres données topographiques | Outros acidentes topográficos |

ESPAÑOL · FRANÇAIS · PORTUGUÊS


| Nombre / Nom / Nome | Página / Page | Lat.°′ | Long.°′ W = Oeste / W = Ouest |
| --- | --- | --- | --- |
| Huairou | 105 | 40.19 N | 116.37 E |
| Huaite → Huaide | 89 | 43.32 N | 124.50 E |
| Huaitunas, Lagunas ⊜ | 248 | 13.06 S | 66.00 W |
| Huaiyang | 100 | 33.44 N | 114.53 E |
| Huai Yot | 110 | 7.45 N | 99.37 E |
| Huaiyuan | 100 | 32.57 N | 117.12 E |
| Huaiyu Shan ⋏ | 100 | 28.50 N | 117.50 E |
| Huaji | 100 | 32.46 N | 115.20 E |
| Huajiang | 102 | 25.50 N | 110.21 E |
| Huajianzi | 104 | 40.48 N | 122.12 E |
| Huajiapuzi | 104 | 40.52 N | 123.14 E |
| Huajiayingzi | 104 | 42.20 N | 121.00 E |
| Huajimic | 234 | 21.42 N | 104.20 W |
| Huajintepec | 234 | 16.36 N | 98.14 W |
| Huajuapan de León | 234 | 17.48 N | 97.46 W |
| Huakou | 100 | 25.13 N | 117.35 E |
| Hualahuises | 232 | 24.53 N | 99.41 W |
| Hualalai ∧[1] | 229d | 19.42 N | 155.52 W |
| Hualañé | 252 | 34.59 S | 71.49 W |
| Hualapai Indian Reservation ◆[4] | 200 | 35.38 N | 113.30 W |
| Hualapai Mountains ⋏ | 200 | 34.50 N | 113.55 W |
| Hualapai Peak ∧ | 200 | 35.04 N | 113.54 W |
| Hualfín | 252 | 27.14 S | 66.50 W |
| Hualgayoc | 248 | 6.46 S | 78.37 W |
| Hualien | 100 | 23.59 N | 121.36 E |
| Hualien ≃ | 100 | 23.57 N | 121.36 E |
| Hualingpuzi | 104 | 41.31 N | 123.54 E |
| Huallaga ≃ | 248 | 5.10 S | 75.32 W |
| Huallamarca, Museo ❦ | 286d | 12.05 S | 77.02 W |
| Huallanca, Perú | 248 | 8.49 S | 77.52 W |
| Huallanca, Perú | 248 | 9.51 S | 76.56 W |
| Huallayabamba ≃ | 248 | 7.04 S | 77.10 W |
| Hualmay | 248 | 11.06 S | 77.38 W |
| Hualong | 102 | 36.05 N | 102.36 E |
| Huamanquiquia | 248 | 13.44 S | 74.15 W |
| Huamantla | 234 | 19.19 N | 97.56 W |
| Huambo (Nova Lisboa) | 152 | 12.44 S | 15.47 E |
| Huambo □[5] | 152 | 12.30 S | 15.40 E |
| Huambos | 248 | 6.28 S | 78.58 W |
| Huameiao | 100 | 26.32 N | 115.47 E |
| Huamei Shan ∧ | 100 | 25.28 N | 113.58 E |
| Huamuxtitlán | 234 | 17.49 N | 98.34 W |
| Huan ≃ | 100 | 30.40 N | 114.05 E |
| Huanan | 89 | 46.13 N | 130.32 E |
| Huancabamba, Perú | 248 | 10.21 S | 75.32 W |
| Huancabamba, Perú | 248 | 5.14 S | 79.28 W |
| Huancané | 248 | 15.12 S | 69.46 W |
| Huancapi | 248 | 13.41 S | 74.04 W |
| Huancarama | 248 | 13.39 S | 73.05 W |
| Huancarqui | 248 | 16.06 S | 72.29 W |
| Huancavelica | 248 | 12.46 S | 75.02 W |
| Huancavelica □[5] | 248 | 13.00 S | 75.00 W |
| Huancaybamba | 248 | 9.05 S | 76.50 W |
| Huancayo | 248 | 12.04 S | 75.14 W |
| Huanchaca | 248 | 20.20 S | 66.39 W |
| Huanchaca, Serranía de ⋏ | 248 | 14.30 S | 60.39 W |
| Huandacareo | 234 | 19.59 N | 101.17 W |
| Huando | 248 | 12.29 S | 74.58 W |
| Huang ≃, Asia | 110 | 17.49 N | 101.33 E |
| Huang ≃, T'aiwan | 269d | 25.14 N | 121.37 E |
| Huang (Yellow) ≃, Zhg. | 90 | 37.32 N | 118.19 E |
| Huang'aicun | 106 | 31.43 N | 118.40 E |
| Huang'an | 98 | 35.28 N | 115.42 E |
| Huang'anshi | 100 | 29.06 N | 113.34 E |
| Huangbai | 98 | 41.17 N | 126.21 E |
| Huangbaozi | 102 | 39.54 N | 99.26 E |
| Huangbeipu | 104 | 42.21 N | 123.25 E |
| Huangcaoping | 100 | 25.42 N | 113.27 E |
| Huangchong | 100 | 22.18 N | 113.03 E |
| Huangchuan | 100 | 32.09 N | 115.03 E |
| Huangcun | 105 | 39.56 N | 116.11 E |
| Huangdaizhen | 106 | 31.26 N | 120.33 E |
| Huangdan | 107 | 29.10 N | 103.44 E |
| Huangda Yang ɥ | 100 | 30.03 N | 122.26 E |
| Huangdi, Zhg. | 98 | 40.14 N | 120.15 E |
| Huangdi, Zhg. | 105 | 40.57 N | 118.24 E |
| Huangdu, Zhg. | 106 | 30.47 N | 118.51 E |
| Huangdu, Zhg. | 106 | 31.16 N | 121.13 E |
| Huangduqiao | 100 | 29.18 N | 120.55 E |
| Huanggai Hu ⊜ | 100 | 29.44 N | 113.23 E |
| Huanggang | 100 | 30.27 N | 114.52 E |
| Huanggangji | 98 | 34.39 N | 116.03 E |
| Huanggangkou | 100 | 28.32 N | 114.33 E |
| Huanggang Shan ∧ | 100 | 27.50 N | 117.45 E |
| Huanggangshi | 100 | 33.09 N | 115.55 E |
| Huangguayingzi | 104 | 41.46 N | 120.46 E |
| Huangguoshu | 102 | 26.02 N | 105.32 E |
| Huang Hai → Yellow Sea ⍑[2] | 90 | 36.00 N | 123.00 E |
| Huanghe Kou ≃[1] | 98 | 37.54 N | 118.48 E |
| Huangho → Huang ≃ | 90 | 37.32 N | 118.19 E |
| Huanghu | 106 | 30.27 N | 119.48 E |
| Huanghua | 98 | 38.22 N | 117.21 E |
| Huanghuadianzi | 104 | 41.44 N | 122.48 E |
| Huanghuashi | 100 | 28.14 N | 113.14 E |
| Huangjialing | 104 | 42.12 N | 122.55 E |
| Huangjialu | 106 | 31.00 N | 121.45 E |
| Huangjiatun | 104 | 41.11 N | 122.54 E |
| Huangjiazhai | 106 | 32.01 N | 121.36 E |
| Huangjinbu | 100 | 28.27 N | 116.47 E |
| Huangjing | 106 | 31.39 N | 121.06 E |
| Huangjinggou | 107 | 29.37 N | 104.35 E |
| Huangjinjing | 107 | 29.44 N | 104.38 E |
| Huangjinzi | 89 | 50.02 N | 127.20 E |
| Huangjuezhen | 107 | 29.50 N | 106.27 E |
| Huangkan | 105 | 40.22 N | 116.28 E |
| Huangkeng | 100 | 27.35 N | 117.39 E |
| Huangkou | 102 | 42.46 N | 93.58 E |
| Huanglaomen | 100 | 29.30 N | 115.49 E |
| Huangli | 106 | 31.39 N | 119.42 E |
| Huanglian | 107 | 29.17 N | 106.18 E |
| Huangling | 102 | 35.41 N | 109.09 E |
| Huanglingji | 100 | 30.25 N | 114.03 E |
| Huanglong, Zhg. | 100 | 31.58 N | 112.28 E |
| Huanglong, Zhg. | 102 | 35.45 N | 109.42 E |
| Huanglongxi | 107 | 30.19 N | 103.58 E |
| Huangmao | 100 | 28.07 N | 114.04 E |
| Huangmapi | 100 | 23.30 N | 114.33 E |
| Huangmei | 100 | 30.04 N | 115.56 E |
| Huangnihe, Zhg. | 89 | 43.32 N | 127.59 E |
| Huangnihe, Zhg. | 100 | 31.06 N | 117.22 E |
| Huangpi, Zhg. | 100 | 30.53 N | 114.22 E |
| Huangpi, Zhg. | 100 | 26.39 N | 115.51 E |
| Huangpu ≃ | 106 | 31.24 N | 121.31 E |
| Huangqi | 100 | 26.21 N | 119.54 E |
| Huangqiao | 106 | 32.15 N | 120.13 E |
| Huangqiao ≃ | 106 | 32.00 N | 120.20 E |
| Huangshahe | 102 | 26.03 N | 110.58 E |
| Huangshajie | 100 | 29.03 N | 113.08 E |
| Huangshan | 98 | 36.57 N | 122.18 E |
| Huangshanguan | 98 | 37.32 N | 120.16 E |
| Huangshapu, Zhg. | 100 | 26.50 N | 113.26 E |
| Huangshapu, Zhg. | 100 | 25.08 N | 112.44 E |
| Huangshaqiao | 100 | 28.56 N | 114.40 E |
| Huangshatuo | 104 | 41.12 N | 122.31 E |
| Huangshi, Zhg. | 100 | 25.23 N | 119.04 E |
| Huangshi, Zhg. | 100 | 30.13 N | 115.05 E |
| Huangshi, Zhg. | 102 | 29.00 N | 111.02 E |
| Huangshidu | 100 | 27.44 N | 116.44 E |
| Huangshiguan | 100 | 26.15 N | 115.54 E |
| Huangshui | 107 | 30.32 N | 103.55 E |
| Huangtan, Zhg. | 100 | 27.44 N | 119.58 E |
| Huangtan, Zhg. | 100 | 26.41 N | 117.17 E |
| Huangtan ≃ | 100 | 24.48 N | 116.31 E |
| Huangtang, Zhg. | 100 | 23.44 N | 114.58 E |
| Huangtang, Zhg. | 106 | 31.47 N | 119.40 E |
| Huangtang, Zhg. | 106 | 31.46 N | 120.21 E |
| Huangtang Hu ⊜ | 100 | 30.00 N | 114.12 E |
| Huangtankou | 100 | 28.50 N | 118.53 E |
| Huangtantuan | 100 | 30.53 N | 113.33 E |
| Huangtian | 100 | 23.52 N | 114.58 E |
| Huangtianfan | 100 | 29.10 N | 120.08 E |
| Huangtu, Zhg. | 100 | 27.36 N | 118.00 E |
| Huangtu, Zhg. | 106 | 31.52 N | 120.03 E |
| Huangtuchang | 107 | 30.41 N | 104.18 E |
| Huangtugang | 100 | 31.25 N | 115.05 E |
| Huangtukan | 104 | 41.21 N | 122.45 E |
| Huangtuliangzi | 98 | 41.14 N | 118.39 E |
| Huangtuling | 100 | 27.18 N | 113.30 E |
| Huangtupo | 105 | 39.47 N | 116.16 E |
| Huanguelén | 252 | 37.02 S | 61.57 W |
| Huangwan | 106 | 30.22 N | 120.48 E |
| Huangxian | 98 | 37.38 N | 120.29 E |
| Huangxu | 106 | 32.06 N | 119.37 E |
| Huangyaguan | 105 | 40.14 N | 117.26 E |
| Huangyan | 100 | 28.39 N | 121.15 E |
| Huangyang Shan ⋏ | 105 | 40.20 N | 115.00 E |
| Huangyanzhuang | 105 | 40.01 N | 118.21 E |
| Huangyuan | 102 | 36.40 N | 101.12 E |
| Huangyuzeng | 104 | 42.05 N | 124.11 E |
| Huangze | 100 | 29.35 N | 120.55 E |
| Huangze Yang ɥ | 100 | 30.36 N | 122.28 E |
| Huangzhai | 100 | 29.27 N | 120.00 E |
| Huangzhong | 102 | 36.31 N | 101.40 E |
| Huangzhu | 110 | 19.29 N | 110.24 E |
| Huangzhuang, Zhg. | 100 | 34.05 N | 112.15 E |
| Huangzhuang, Zhg. | 105 | 39.29 N | 117.31 E |
| Huangzhuang, Zhg. | 105 | 39.53 N | 117.05 E |
| Huangzhuang Wa ⊜ | 105 | 39.33 N | 117.33 E |
| Huaning | 102 | 24.14 N | 102.56 E |
| Huaniugouzi | 104 | 41.34 N | 122.35 E |
| Huaniupuzi | 104 | 41.23 N | 123.31 E |
| Huanjiang | 102 | 24.54 N | 108.21 E |
| Huanren | 98 | 41.14 N | 125.21 E |
| Huanta | 248 | 12.56 S | 74.15 W |
| Huantai (Suozhen) | 98 | 36.59 N | 118.06 E |
| Huantan | 100 | 31.49 N | 113.04 E |
| Huántar | 248 | 9.26 S | 77.15 W |
| Huánuco | 248 | 9.55 S | 76.14 W |
| Huánuco □[5] | 248 | 9.30 S | 75.50 W |
| Huanuni | 248 | 18.16 S | 66.51 W |
| Huanxi | 100 | 26.34 N | 113.36 E |
| Huanxian | 102 | 36.39 N | 107.18 E |
| Huanxiang ≃ | 105 | 39.34 N | 117.45 E |
| Huanxiling | 104 | 41.17 N | 123.54 E |
| Huanzo, Cordillera de ⋏ | 248 | 14.30 S | 73.20 W |
| Huapango, Presa ⊜[1] | 234 | 20.00 N | 99.40 W |
| Huapí, Serranías ⋏ | 236 | 12.30 N | 85.00 W |
| Huap'ing Yü I | 100 | 25.26 N | 121.56 E |
| Huaqiao, Zhg. | 100 | 28.56 N | 121.27 E |
| Huaqiao, Zhg. | 100 | 29.32 N | 117.11 E |
| Huaqiao, Zhg. | 102 | 27.28 N | 110.02 E |
| Huaqiao, Zhg. | 107 | 30.28 N | 103.52 E |
| Huaqiaozhen | 107 | 30.47 N | 106.41 E |
| Huaqiying | 106 | 32.10 N | 118.38 E |
| Huara | 248 | 19.59 S | 69.47 W |
| Huaral | 248 | 11.30 S | 77.12 W |
| Huaráz | 248 | 9.32 S | 77.32 W |
| Huari | 248 | 9.20 S | 77.14 W |
| Huariaca | 248 | 10.27 S | 76.07 W |
| Huaribamba | 248 | 12.16 S | 74.57 W |
| Huarina | 248 | 16.12 S | 68.38 W |
| Huarmey | 248 | 10.04 S | 78.10 W |
| Huarochirí | 248 | 12.09 S | 76.14 W |
| Huarocondo | 248 | 13.25 S | 72.13 W |
| Huarong | 100 | 29.30 N | 112.34 E |
| Huasaga ≃ | 246 | 3.42 S | 76.26 W |
| Hua Sai | 110 | 8.02 N | 100.18 E |
| Huascarán, Nevado ∧ | 248 | 9.07 S | 77.37 W |
| Huasco | 252 | 28.28 S | 71.14 W |
| Huasco ≃ | 252 | 28.27 S | 71.13 W |
| Huashan | 98 | 34.39 N | 116.44 E |
| Huashaoying | 98 | 40.12 N | 114.36 E |
| Huashi | 106 | 31.50 N | 120.28 E |
| Huatabampo | 232 | 26.50 N | 109.38 W |
| Huatangpu | 100 | 25.48 N | 112.52 E |
| Huating | 102 | 35.09 N | 106.38 E |
| Huatong, Zhg. | 98 | 40.03 N | 121.56 E |
| Huatong, Zhg. | 102 | 23.01 N | 106.36 E |
| Huatusco | 234 | 19.09 N | 96.57 W |
| Huauchinango | 234 | 20.11 N | 98.03 W |
| Huaura | 248 | 11.04 S | 77.36 W |
| Huaura ≃ | 248 | 11.06 S | 77.39 W |
| Huautla, Méx. | 234 | 21.02 N | 98.17 W |
| Huautla, Méx. | 234 | 18.08 N | 96.51 W |
| Huaxian (Daokou), Zhg. | 98 | 35.37 N | 114.32 E |
| Huaxian, Zhg. | 100 | 23.22 N | 113.12 E |
| Huaxian, Zhg. | 102 | 34.30 N | 109.40 E |
| Huayan | 107 | 30.01 N | 105.02 E |
| Huayang | 107 | 30.32 N | 104.04 E |
| Huayangzhen | 102 | 33.25 N | 107.44 E |
| Huaying Shan ∧ | 107 | 30.10 N | 106.42 E |
| Huayingtai | 104 | 40.43 N | 122.19 E |
| Huayllay | 248 | 11.01 S | 76.21 W |
| Huayna Potosí, Nevado ∧ | 248 | 16.16 S | 68.11 W |
| Huaytará | 248 | 13.36 S | 75.22 W |
| Hua Yü I | 100 | 23.24 N | 119.19 E |
| Huayuan, Zhg. | 98 | 42.17 N | 127.07 E |
| Huayuan, Zhg. | 100 | 31.16 N | 113.58 E |
| Huayuan, Zhg. | 102 | 28.34 N | 109.13 E |
| Huayuanzui | 100 | 33.00 N | 118.16 E |
| Huayunca, Nevado ∧ | 248 | 14.39 S | 72.28 W |
| Huayuri, Pampa de ≚ | 248 | 14.30 S | 75.30 W |
| Huazhou | 102 | 21.40 N | 110.33 E |
| Huazi | 104 | 41.25 N | 123.29 E |
| Huazigou | 104 | 41.50 N | 121.01 E |
| Huazikou | 106 | 32.13 N | 118.57 E |
| Ḥubārah, Wādī ∨ | 142 | 27.21 N | 31.39 E |
| Ḥubayṭah, Bi'r ⍑[4] | 142 | 30.27 N | 32.27 E |
| Hubbard, Ia., U.S. | 190 | 42.18 N | 93.18 W |
| Hubbard, Oh., U.S. | 214 | 41.09 N | 80.34 W |
| Hubbard, Or., U.S. | 224 | 45.10 N | 122.48 W |
| Hubbard, Tx., U.S. | 222 | 31.50 N | 96.47 W |
| Hubbard Creek ≃ | 196 | 32.54 N | 98.53 W |
| Hubbard Creek Reservoir ⊜[1] | 196 | 32.45 N | 99.00 W |
| Hubbard Lake ⊜ | 190 | 44.49 N | 83.34 W |
| Hubbards | 186 | 44.38 N | 64.04 W |
| Hubbardston | 207 | 42.28 N | 72.00 W |
| Hubbell | 190 | 47.10 N | 88.25 W |
| Hubbell Trading Post National Historic Site ⊥ | 200 | 35.43 N | 109.33 W |
| Hubbelrath ◆[8] | 263 | 51.16 N | 6.55 E |
| Hubei (Hupeh) □[4] | 90 | 31.00 N | 112.00 E |
| Huben, Öst. | 64 | 47.03 N | 10.58 E |
| Huben, Öst. | 64 | 46.56 N | 12.34 E |
| Huberdeau | 206 | 45.58 N | 74.38 W |
| Huber Heights | 218 | 39.50 N | 84.07 W |
| Hublersburg | 210 | 40.58 N | 77.37 W |
| Hubli-Dhārwār | 122 | 15.21 N | 75.10 E |
| Hubuleng | 102 | 41.19 N | 111.08 E |
| Hubynykha | 78 | 48.48 N | 35.15 E |
| Hucaogang | 106 | 32.00 N | 120.29 E |
| Hucclecote | 42 | 51.51 N | 2.11 W |
| Huch'ang | 98 | 41.25 N | 127.03 E |
| Hucheng | 100 | 25.26 N | 118.27 E |
| Huchi | 100 | 31.08 N | 117.40 E |
| Huchow → Huzhou | 106 | 30.52 N | 120.06 E |
| Huckarde ◆[8] | 263 | 51.32 N | 7.24 E |
| Hückelhoven | 56 | 51.03 N | 6.13 E |
| Hückeswagen | 56 | 51.08 N | 7.20 E |
| Hucking | 260 | 51.18 N | 0.39 E |
| Huckingen ◆[8] | 263 | 51.22 N | 6.43 E |
| Huckitta Creek ≃ | 162 | 22.38 S | 135.30 E |
| Huckleberry Island I | 276 | 40.53 N | 73.45 W |
| Huckleberry Mountain ∧ | 202 | 43.51 N | 122.19 W |
| Huckleberry Mountain ∧[2] | 212 | 44.28 N | 75.28 W |
| Hucknall | 42 | 53.02 N | 1.11 W |
| Hucqueliers | 50 | 50.34 N | 1.54 E |
| Hucun | 105 | 39.02 N | 115.56 E |
| Hudangtou | 106 | 30.48 N | 121.22 E |
| Huddart Park ♦ | 282 | 37.26 N | 122.19 W |
| Hudderfield Narrow Canal ≖ | 262 | 53.29 N | 2.06 W |
| Huddersfield | 44 | 53.39 N | 1.47 W |
| Huddinge | 40 | 59.14 N | 17.59 E |
| Huddle Park Municipal Golf Course ♦ | 273d | 26.09 S | 28.07 E |
| Huddunge | 40 | 60.03 N | 16.59 E |
| Hude | 52 | 53.07 N | 8.27 E |
| Huder | 89 | 50.00 N | 121.37 E |
| Hudgin Creek ≃ | 194 | 33.40 N | 91.59 W |
| Hūdī | 140 | 17.42 N | 34.17 E |
| Hudiksvall | 26 | 61.44 N | 17.07 E |
| Hudong | 100 | 22.51 N | 115.56 E |
| Hudson, P.Q., Can. | 206 | 45.27 N | 74.09 W |
| Hudson, Il., U.S. | 216 | 40.36 N | 88.59 W |
| Hudson, In., U.S. | 216 | 41.31 N | 85.04 W |
| Hudson, Ia., U.S. | 190 | 42.24 N | 92.27 W |
| Hudson, Md., U.S. | 208 | 38.35 N | 76.15 W |
| Hudson, Ma., U.S. | 207 | 42.23 N | 71.34 W |
| Hudson, Mi., U.S. | 216 | 41.51 N | 84.21 W |
| Hudson, N.H., U.S. | 207 | 42.45 N | 71.26 W |
| Hudson, N.Y., U.S. | 210 | 42.15 N | 73.47 W |
| Hudson, N.C., U.S. | 192 | 35.50 N | 81.29 W |
| Hudson, Oh., U.S. | 214 | 41.14 N | 81.26 W |
| Hudson, S.D., U.S. | 198 | 43.07 N | 96.27 W |
| Hudson, Tx., U.S. | 222 | 31.19 N | 94.50 W |
| Hudson, Wi., U.S. | 190 | 44.58 N | 92.45 W |
| Hudson, Wy., U.S. | 200 | 42.54 N | 108.34 W |
| Hudson □[6] | 276 | 40.44 N | 74.02 W |
| Hudson ≃, U.S. | 188 | 40.42 N | 74.02 W |
| Hudson ≃, Ga., U.S. | 192 | 34.14 N | 83.10 W |
| Hudson, Cerro ∧ | 254 | 46.04 S | 73.10 W |
| Hudson, Lake ⊜[1] | 194 | 36.20 N | 95.05 W |
| Hudson Bay | 184 | 52.52 N | 102.25 W |
| Hudson Bay ⊂ | 176 | 60.00 N | 86.00 W |
| Hudson-Bayonet Point | 220 | 28.21 N | 82.41 W |
| Hudson Falls | 210 | 43.18 N | 73.35 W |
| Hudson Highlands State Park ♦ | 210 | 41.26 N | 73.58 W |
| Hudson Hope | 182 | 56.02 N | 121.55 W |
| Hudson Lake | 216 | 41.42 N | 86.32 W |
| Hudson Mountains ⋏ | 9 | 74.32 S | 99.20 W |
| Hudsons Peak ∧ | 171b | 36.26 S | 149.10 E |
| Hudson Strait ɥ | 176 | 62.30 N | 72.00 W |
| Hudsonville | 216 | 42.52 N | 85.51 W |
| Hudwin Lake ⊜ | 184 | 53.12 N | 95.42 W |
| Hue | 110 | 16.28 N | 107.36 E |
| Huebra ≃ | 34 | 41.02 N | 6.48 W |
| Huechucuicui, Punta ≻ | 254 | 41.47 S | 74.02 W |
| Huechulafquen, Lago ⊜ | 254 | 39.46 S | 71.28 W |
| Huechuraba | 286e | 33.21 S | 70.40 W |
| Huedin | 38 | 46.52 N | 23.02 E |
| Huehuetán | 236 | 15.01 N | 92.22 W |
| Huehuetenango | 236 | 15.20 N | 91.28 W |
| Huehuetenango □[5] | 236 | 15.40 N | 91.35 W |
| Huehuetlán El Chico | 234 | 18.21 N | 98.42 W |
| Huejúcar | 234 | 22.21 N | 103.13 W |
| Huejuquilla El Alto | 234 | 22.36 N | 103.52 W |
| Huejutla de Reyes | 234 | 21.08 N | 98.25 W |
| Huelgoat | 32 | 48.22 N | 3.45 W |
| Huelma | 34 | 37.39 N | 3.27 W |
| Huelva | 34 | 37.16 N | 6.57 W |
| Huelva □[4] | 34 | 37.30 N | 6.55 W |
| Huelva, Río de ≃ | 34 | 37.27 N | 6.00 W |
| Huenque ≃ | 248 | 16.12 S | 69.44 W |
| Huentelauquén | 252 | 31.35 S | 71.32 W |
| Huércal-Overa | 34 | 37.23 N | 1.57 W |
| Huerfano ≃ | 198 | 38.14 N | 104.15 W |
| Huerfano Mountain ∧ | 200 | 36.26 N | 107.51 W |
| Huerhuero Creek ≃ | 226 | 35.40 N | 120.42 W |
| Huerlumada | 120 | 32.45 N | 90.00 E |
| Huerva ≃ | 34 | 41.39 N | 0.52 W |
| Huesca | 34 | 42.08 N | 0.25 W |
| Huesca □[4] | 34 | 42.05 N | 0.10 W |
| Huéscar | 34 | 37.49 N | 2.32 W |
| Hueston Woods State Park ♦ | 218 | 39.34 N | 84.44 W |
| Huetamo de Núñez | 234 | 18.35 N | 100.53 W |
| Huete | 34 | 40.08 N | 2.41 W |
| Huey | 219 | 38.36 N | 89.17 W |
| Hueyapan de Ocampo | 234 | 18.07 N | 95.09 W |
| Hueytown | 194 | 33.27 N | 86.59 W |
| Hufengzhen | 107 | 29.43 N | 106.07 E |
| Hüffenhardt | 56 | 49.18 N | 9.04 E |
| Huffman | 222 | 30.01 N | 95.05 W |
| Huffman Dam ◆[6] | 218 | 39.48 N | 84.05 W |
| Hüfingen | 58 | 47.55 N | 8.29 E |
| Ḥufrat an-Naḥās | 140 | 9.45 N | 24.19 E |
| Hufu | 106 | 31.16 N | 119.47 E |
| Hügel, Villa ❦ | 263 | 51.25 N | 7.01 E |
| Huggins, Mount ∧ | 9 | 78.17 S | 162.28 E |
| Hugh ≃ | 162 | 25.01 S | 134.01 E |
| Hugh Butler Lake ⊜[1] | 198 | 40.22 N | 100.42 W |
| Hughenden | 166 | 20.51 S | 144.12 E |
| Hughes, Austl. | 162 | 30.42 S | 129.31 E |
| Hughes, Ak., U.S. | 180 | 66.03 N | 154.16 W |
| Hughes, Ar., U.S. | 194 | 34.56 N | 90.28 W |
| Hughes ≃ | 184 | 56.46 N | 100.01 W |
| Hughes, South Fork ≃ | 188 | 39.08 N | 81.20 W |
| Hughes Airport ⊠ | 280 | 33.58 N | 118.25 W |
| Hughes Creek ≃ | 169 | 36.53 S | 145.08 E |
| Hughes Springs | 222 | 33.05 N | 94.38 W |
| Hughesville, Md., U.S. | 208 | 38.31 N | 76.47 W |
| Hughesville, Pa., U.S. | 210 | 41.14 N | 76.43 W |
| Hugh Keenleyside Dam ◆[6] | 182 | 49.20 N | 117.49 W |
| Hughson | 226 | 37.36 N | 120.52 W |
| Hughsonville | 210 | 41.35 N | 73.56 W |
| Hugh Town | 42a | 49.55 N | 6.17 W |
| Hugli ≃ | 126 | 21.55 N | 88.05 E |
| Hugli-Chinsurah | 126 | 22.54 N | 88.24 E |
| Hugo, Co., U.S. | 198 | 39.08 N | 103.28 W |
| Hugo, Ok., U.S. | 196 | 34.00 N | 95.30 W |
| Hugo Lake ⊜[1] | 196 | 34.05 N | 95.25 W |
| Hugoton | 198 | 37.10 N | 101.20 W |
| Hugou | 100 | 33.23 N | 117.08 E |
| Huguenot | 210 | 41.25 N | 74.38 W |
| Huguenot Lake ⊜ | 276 | 40.56 N | 73.47 W |
| Huhehot → Hohhot | 102 | 40.51 N | 111.40 E |
| Huhsi | 100 | 23.35 N | 119.39 E |
| Hui'an, Zhg. | 100 | 25.04 N | 118.47 E |
| Huian, Zhg. | 106 | 31.47 N | 121.45 E |
| Huiarau Range ⋏ | 172 | 38.45 S | 177.00 E |
| Huib-Hoch Plateau ⋏[1] | 156 | 27.00 S | 16.45 E |
| Huibie Yang ɥ | 100 | 30.08 N | 121.44 E |
| Huibu | 100 | 28.18 N | 115.15 E |
| Huichang, Zhg. | 100 | 25.34 N | 115.49 E |
| Huichang, Zhg. | 105 | 39.04 N | 115.04 E |
| Huichapan | 234 | 20.23 N | 99.39 W |
| Hŭich'ŏn | 98 | 40.10 N | 126.17 E |
| Huichou → Huizhou | 100 | 23.05 N | 114.24 E |
| Huichuan | 102 | 35.11 N | 104.02 E |
| Huicungo | 248 | 7.17 S | 76.48 W |
| Huidong | 102 | 26.41 N | 102.36 E |
| Huidui | 105 | 39.04 N | 117.16 E |
| Huihe, Zhg. | 89 | 48.12 N | 119.17 E |
| Huihe, Zhg. | 106 | 31.45 N | 121.43 E |
| Huiji ≃ | 100 | 33.53 N | 115.36 E |
| Huíla | 152 | 15.04 S | 13.32 E |
| Huíla □[5], Ang. | 152 | 15.00 S | 15.00 E |
| Huila □[5], Col. | 246 | 2.30 N | 75.45 W |
| Huila, Nevado del ∧ | 246 | 3.00 N | 76.00 W |
| Huilai | 100 | 23.04 N | 116.18 E |
| Huili | 102 | 26.43 N | 102.10 E |
| Huiliuji | 100 | 32.50 N | 115.58 E |
| Huillapima | 252 | 28.44 S | 65.59 W |
| Huilong, Zhg. | 100 | 27.30 N | 118.24 E |
| Huilong, Zhg. | 100 | 25.22 N | 116.24 E |
| Huilong, Zhg. | 100 | 24.09 N | 113.58 E |
| Huilong, Zhg. | 107 | 30.28 N | 105.26 E |
| Huilong, Zhg. | 107 | 30.35 N | 105.49 E |
| Huilongchang, Zhg. | 107 | 29.41 N | 104.17 E |
| Huilongchang, Zhg. | 107 | 30.18 N | 103.39 E |
| Huilongchang, Zhg. | 107 | 30.41 N | 106.34 E |
| Huilongchang, Zhg. | 107 | 29.17 N | 105.01 E |
| Huimanguillo | 234 | 17.51 N | 93.23 W |
| Huimin | 98 | 37.29 N | 117.29 E |
| Huinan (Chaoyang) | 98 | 42.40 N | 126.00 E |
| Huínaymarca, Lago ⊜ | 248 | 16.20 S | 68.50 W |
| Huinca Renancó | 252 | 34.50 S | 64.23 W |
| Hüinghausen | 263 | 51.11 N | 7.48 E |
| Huining | 102 | 35.41 N | 105.08 E |
| Huisachal | 196 | 26.47 N | 101.07 W |
| Huisduinen | 52 | 52.56 N | 4.44 E |
| Huishan | 106 | 31.35 N | 120.16 E |
| Huishui | 102 | 26.07 N | 106.24 E |
| Huismes | 50 | 47.14 N | 0.15 E |
| Huisne ≃ | 50 | 47.59 N | 0.11 E |
| Huissen | 52 | 51.57 N | 5.56 E |
| Huistepec | 234 | 16.39 N | 98.20 W |
| Huiten Nur ⊜ | 120 | 35.30 N | 92.00 E |
| Huiting | 98 | 34.05 N | 116.04 E |
| Huitiupan | 234 | 17.13 N | 92.39 W |
| Huitong | 102 | 26.54 N | 109.31 E |
| Huitongqiao | 102 | 24.43 N | 98.56 E |
| Huittinen (Lauttakylä) | 26 | 61.11 N | 22.42 E |
| Huitzilán | 234 | 19.58 N | 97.41 W |
| Huitzo | 234 | 17.15 N | 96.52 W |
| Huitzuco de los Figueroa | 234 | 18.18 N | 99.21 W |
| Huixian | 102 | 33.47 N | 106.16 E |
| Huixtla | 232 | 15.09 N | 92.28 W |
| Huiyang → Huizhou | 100 | 23.05 N | 114.24 E |
| Huiyao | 100 | 27.16 N | 118.05 E |
| Huize | 102 | 26.27 N | 103.09 E |
| Huizen | 52 | 52.17 N | 5.14 E |
| Huizhou | 100 | 23.05 N | 114.24 E |
| Hujia, Zhg. | 104 | 41.20 N | 121.52 E |
| Hujia, Zhg. | 106 | 31.25 N | 121.37 E |
| Hujiadian | 107 | 29.41 N | 104.07 E |
| Hujiajie | 104 | 41.06 N | 122.10 E |
| Hujiasi | 107 | 29.16 N | 105.13 E |
| Hujiawopu | 104 | 42.34 N | 122.11 E |
| Hujiayu | 105 | 39.28 N | 115.27 E |
| Hujiazhuang, Zhg. | 105 | 39.51 N | 117.07 E |
| Hujiazhuang, Zhg. | 269b | 31.21 N | 121.25 E |
| Hujie | 102 | 24.56 N | 100.32 E |
| Hukeng | 100 | 27.29 N | 114.18 E |
| Hukou | 100 | 29.45 N | 116.13 E |
| Hŭksan-chedo II | 98 | 34.30 N | 125.20 E |
| Hukui → Fukui | 94 | 36.04 N | 136.13 E |
| Ḥukūmah | 140 | 13.52 N | 36.07 E |
| Hukuntsi | 156 | 24.02 S | 21.48 E |
| Hukuoka → Fukuoka | 96 | 33.35 N | 130.24 E |
| Hukusima → Fukushima | 92 | 37.45 N | 140.28 E |
| Hukuyama → Fukuyama | 96 | 34.29 N | 133.22 E |
| Ḥula, 'Émeq ≚[1] | 132 | 33.08 N | 35.37 E |
| Hulahula ≃ | 180 | 70.00 N | 144.01 W |
| Hulan | 89 | 46.00 N | 126.38 E |
| Hulan ≃ | 89 | 45.55 N | 126.41 E |
| Hulan Ergi | 89 | 47.13 N | 123.39 E |
| Hulbert, Mi., U.S. | 190 | 46.21 N | 85.09 W |
| Hulbert, Ok., U.S. | 194 | 35.55 N | 95.08 W |
| Hulberton | 210 | 43.15 N | 78.04 W |
| Ḥulda | 132 | 31.50 N | 34.53 E |
| Huldrefossen ∟ | 26 | 61.28 N | 5.58 E |
| Hulei | 100 | 24.50 N | 116.48 E |
| Huleia Stream ≃ | 229b | 21.57 N | 159.22 W |
| Hulett | 198 | 44.40 N | 104.36 W |
| Hulín, Česká Rep. | 30 | 49.19 N | 17.28 E |
| Hulin, Zhg. | 89 | 45.46 N | 132.59 E |
| Hulin ≃, Zhg. | 89 | 45.19 N | 124.06 E |
| Hulin ≃, Zhg. | 89 | 44.55 N | 122.35 E |
| Huliu ≃ | 98 | 40.10 N | 114.33 E |
| Hull, P.Q., Can. | 212 | 45.26 N | 75.43 W |
| Hull → Kingston upon Hull, Eng., U.K. | 44 | 53.45 N | 0.20 W |
| Hull, Il., U.S. | 219 | 39.43 N | 91.13 W |
| Hull, Ia., U.S. | 198 | 43.11 N | 96.08 W |
| Hull, Ma., U.S. | 207 | 42.18 N | 70.54 W |
| Hull, Tx., U.S. | 222 | 30.09 N | 94.39 W |
| Hull □[6] | 212 | 45.40 N | 75.35 W |
| Hull ≃ | 44 | 53.44 N | 0.19 W |
| Hullavington | 42 | 51.33 N | 2.09 W |
| Hull Bay ⊂ | 283 | 42.18 N | 70.53 W |
| Hullbridge | 42 | 51.37 N | 0.38 E |
| Hullo | 76 | 59.00 N | 23.14 E |
| Hulmeville | 285 | 40.08 N | 74.55 W |
| Hüls, Dtsch. | 56 | 51.22 N | 6.30 E |
| Hüls, Dtsch. | 263 | 51.40 N | 7.08 E |
| Hülscheid | 56 | 51.16 N | 7.34 E |
| Hülser Berg ◆[8] | 263 | 51.24 N | 6.31 E |
| Hülser Berg ∧[2] | 263 | 51.23 N | 6.33 E |
| Hulst | 52 | 51.17 N | 4.03 E |
| Hult | 40 | 58.40 N | 16.07 E |
| Hultsfred | 26 | 57.29 N | 15.50 E |
| Huludao | 104 | 40.43 N | 121.00 E |
| Hulufa | 105 | 39.42 N | 116.12 E |
| Hulun → Hailar | 89 | 49.12 N | 119.42 E |
| Hulun Nur ⊜ | 88 | 49.01 N | 117.32 E |
| Huluyu | 105 | 40.14 N | 116.53 E |
| Ḥulwān | 142 | 29.51 N | 31.20 E |
| Ḥulwān Observatory ❦[3] | 142 | 29.52 N | 31.21 E |
| Hulyaypole | 78 | 47.38 N | 36.16 E |
| Huma, Tonga | 174w | 21.19 S | 174.57 E |
| Huma, Zhg. | 89 | 51.43 N | 126.38 E |
| Huma ≃ | 89 | 51.40 N | 126.44 E |
| Humacao | 240m | 18.09 N | 65.50 W |
| Humahuaca | 252 | 23.12 S | 65.21 W |
| Humaitá, Bra. | 248 | 7.31 S | 63.02 W |
| Humaitá, Para. | 252 | 27.03 S | 58.33 W |
| Humaitá ≃ | 248 | 8.16 S | 72.44 W |
| Humansdorp | 158 | 34.02 S | 24.46 E |
| Humansville | 194 | 37.47 N | 93.34 W |
| Humara, Jabal al- ∧ | 140 | 16.16 N | 30.59 E |
| Humarock | 283 | 42.08 N | 70.41 W |
| Ḥumaydah | 140 | 14.22 N | 22.31 E |
| Humayingzi | 98 | 41.06 N | 116.48 E |
| Humayun's Tomb ⊥ | 272a | 28.36 N | 77.15 E |
| Humbe | 152 | 16.40 S | 14.55 E |
| Humbe, Serra do ⋏ | 152 | 12.13 S | 15.25 E |
| Humbeek | 50 | 50.58 N | 4.23 E |
| Humber ≃, On., Can. | 212 | 43.38 N | 79.28 W |
| Humber ≃, Eng., U.K. | 44 | 53.40 N | 0.10 W |
| Humber, Mouth of the ≃[1] | 44 | 53.32 N | 0.08 E |
| Humber Bay ⊂ | 275b | 43.38 N | 79.29 W |
| Humber Bridge ◆[5] | 44 | 53.42 N | 0.27 W |
| Humberside □[6] | 44 | 53.55 N | 0.40 W |
| Humberston | 44 | 53.32 N | 0.02 W |
| Humberto de Campos | 250 | 2.37 S | 43.27 W |
| Humber Valley Park ♦ | 275b | 43.39 N | 79.30 W |
| Humbird | 190 | 44.31 N | 90.53 W |
| Humble, Dan. | 41 | 54.50 N | 10.42 E |
| Humble, Tx., U.S. | 222 | 29.59 N | 95.15 W |
| Humboldt, Sk., Can. | 184 | 52.12 N | 105.07 W |
| Humboldt, Az., U.S. | 200 | 34.30 N | 112.14 W |
| Humboldt, Il., U.S. | 194 | 39.36 N | 88.19 W |
| Humboldt, Ia., U.S. | 198 | 42.43 N | 94.12 W |
| Humboldt, Ks., U.S. | 198 | 37.48 N | 95.26 W |
| Humboldt, Ne., U.S. | 198 | 40.09 N | 95.56 W |
| Humboldt, S.D., U.S. | 198 | 43.38 N | 97.04 W |
| Humboldt, Tn., U.S. | 194 | 35.49 N | 88.54 W |
| Humboldt ∧ | 175f | 21.53 S | 166.25 E |
| Humboldt ≃ | 204 | 40.02 N | 118.31 W |
| Humboldt, North Fork ≃ | 204 | 40.56 N | 115.32 W |
| Humboldt, Planetario ❦ | 286c | 10.30 N | 66.50 W |
| Humboldt, South Fork ≃ | 204 | 40.47 N | 115.53 W |
| Humboldt Bay ⊂ | 204 | 40.47 N | 124.11 W |
| Humboldt Lake ⊜ | 204 | 39.58 N | 118.38 W |
| Humboldt Mountains ⋏ | 9 | 71.45 S | 11.30 E |
| Humboldt Park ♦ | 278 | 41.54 N | 87.42 W |
| Humboldt Redwoods State Park ♦ | 204 | 40.19 N | 124.00 W |
| Humboldt Salt Marsh ≡ | 204 | 39.50 N | 117.55 W |
| Hume, Ca., U.S. | 204 | 36.47 N | 118.55 W |
| Hume, N.Y., U.S. | 210 | 42.29 N | 78.08 W |
| Hume, Lake ⊜[1] | 166 | 36.06 S | 147.05 E |
| Hume and Hovell Lookout ♦ | 169 | 37.15 S | 144.59 E |
| Humeburn | 166 | 27.24 S | 145.14 E |
| Hūmedān | 128 | 25.24 N | 59.39 E |
| Hu Men ⊂[1] | 100 | 22.44 N | 113.40 E |
| Humenné | 30 | 48.56 N | 21.55 E |
| Húmera | 266a | 40.26 N | 3.47 W |
| Humeston | 190 | 40.51 N | 93.29 W |
| Humlā Karṇālī ≃ | 124 | 29.38 N | 81.52 E |
| Humlebæk | 41 | 55.58 N | 12.33 E |
| Hummelo | 52 | 52.00 N | 6.14 E |
| Hummelstown | 208 | 40.16 N | 76.43 W |
| Hummels Wharf | 210 | 40.49 N | 76.50 W |
| Hümmling ⋏ | 52 | 52.52 N | 7.31 E |
| Humos, Isla I | 254 | 45.38 S | 73.59 W |
| Humpata | 152 | 15.02 S | 13.24 E |
| Hümpfershausen | 56 | 50.40 N | 10.13 E |
| Humphrey, Ar., U.S. | 194 | 34.25 N | 91.42 W |
| Humphrey, Ne., U.S. | 198 | 41.41 N | 97.29 W |
| Humphreys, Mount ∧ | 204 | 37.17 N | 118.40 W |
| Humphreys Peak ∧ | 200 | 35.20 N | 111.40 W |
| Humpolec | 30 | 49.32 N | 15.22 E |
| Humppila | 26 | 60.56 N | 23.22 E |
| Humptulips | 224 | 47.13 N | 123.57 W |
| Humptulips ≃ | 224 | 47.03 N | 124.03 W |
| Humptulips, East Fork ≃ | 224 | 47.15 N | 123.54 W |
| Humptulips, West Fork ≃ | 224 | 47.15 N | 123.54 W |
| Humptulips Ridge ∧ | 224 | 47.20 N | 123.45 W |
| Humpty Doo | 164 | 12.38 S | 131.15 E |
| Humula | 171b | 35.29 S | 147.45 E |
| Humuya ≃ | 236 | 15.01 N | 87.44 W |
| Hūn | 146 | 29.07 N | 15.56 E |
| Hun ≃, Zhg. | 98 | 41.01 N | 122.27 E |
| Hun ≃, Zhg. | 98 | 40.52 N | 125.42 E |
| Hunabasi → Funabashi | 94 | 35.42 N | 139.59 E |
| Húnaflói ⊂ | 24a | 65.50 N | 20.50 W |
| Hunan □[4] | 102 | 28.00 N | 111.00 E |
| Ḥunayshāt, Ghurd al- ⩡[8] | 142 | 30.07 N | 29.47 E |
| Hunchun | 98 | 42.54 N | 130.22 E |
| Huncoat | 262 | 53.46 N | 2.20 W |
| Hundeluft | 54 | 51.58 N | 12.20 E |
| Hundested | 41 | 55.58 N | 11.52 E |
| Hundewāli | 123 | 31.55 N | 72.38 E |
| Hundorp | 26 | 61.33 N | 9.54 E |
| Hundred | 188 | 39.41 N | 80.27 W |
| Hundred End | 262 | 53.42 N | 2.53 W |
| Hundslund | 41 | 55.55 N | 10.04 E |
| Hundstein ∧ | 64 | 47.20 N | 12.54 E |
| Hundwil | 58 | 47.22 N | 9.19 E |
| Hunedoara | 38 | 45.45 N | 22.54 E |
| Hunedoara □[6] | 38 | 45.45 N | 23.00 E |
| Hünfeld | 56 | 50.40 N | 9.46 E |
| Hungary (Magyarország) □[1], Europe | 22 | 47.00 N | 20.00 E |
| Hungary (Magyarország) □[1], Europe | 30 | 47.00 N | 20.00 E |
| Hungchiang → Hongjiang | 102 | 27.07 N | 109.56 E |
| Hungen | 56 | 50.28 N | 8.54 E |
| Hungerford, Austl. | 166 | 29.00 S | 144.25 E |
| Hungerford, Eng., U.K. | 42 | 51.26 N | 1.30 W |
| Hungerford, Tx., U.S. | 222 | 29.24 N | 96.05 W |
| Hŭngho-ri | 98 | 37.14 N | 127.44 E |
| Hŭngin-ni | 98 | 39.03 N | 126.26 E |
| Hung Long | 269c | 10.40 N | 106.39 E |
| Hungmao | 100 | 24.55 N | 120.58 E |
| Hŭngnam | 98 | 39.50 N | 127.38 E |
| Hungría → Hungary □[1] | 30 | 47.00 N | 20.00 E |
| Hungry Hill ∧ | 48 | 51.41 N | 9.48 W |
| Hungry Horse | 202 | 48.23 N | 114.03 W |
| Hungry Horse Dam ◆[6] | 202 | 48.14 N | 114.04 W |
| Hungry Horse Reservoir ⊜[1] | 202 | 48.15 N | 113.50 W |
| Hungry Lake ⊜ | 212 | 44.48 N | 76.53 W |
| Hungry Law ∧[2] | 44 | 55.21 N | 2.24 W |
| Hung Yen | 110 | 20.39 N | 106.04 E |
| Hunhe | 104 | 41.43 N | 123.22 E |
| Huningue | 58 | 47.36 N | 7.35 E |
| Hunish, Rubha ≻ | 46 | 57.41 N | 6.21 W |
| Huni Valley | 150 | 5.28 N | 1.55 W |
| Hunjiang (Badaojiang) | 98 | 41.56 N | 126.29 E |
| Hunker | 279b | 40.12 N | 79.38 W |
| Ḥunkurāb, Ra's ≻ | 140 | 24.34 N | 35.10 E |
| Hunlen Falls ∟ | 182 | 52.17 N | 125.47 W |
| Hunmanby | 44 | 54.10 N | 0.19 W |
| Hunn ⊜ | 40 | 58.51 N | 15.57 E |
| Hunneberg ∧[2] | 26 | 58.20 N | 12.27 E |
| Hunnebostrand | 26 | 58.27 N | 11.18 E |
| Hunnewell | 219 | 39.40 N | 91.51 W |
| Hunnewell Lake ⊜ | 219 | 39.42 N | 91.52 W |
| Hunsberge ⋏ | 156 | 27.45 S | 17.12 E |
| Hunseby | 41 | 54.48 N | 11.32 E |
| Hunspach | 56 | 48.57 N | 7.57 E |
| Hunsrück ⋏ | 56 | 49.50 N | 6.40 E |
| Hunstanton | 42 | 52.57 N | 0.30 E |
| Hunstein Range ⋏ | 164 | 4.30 S | 142.40 E |
| Hunsūr | 122 | 12.18 N | 76.17 E |
| Hunswinkel | 263 | 51.05 N | 7.48 E |
| Hunt □[6] | 222 | 33.03 N | 96.05 W |
| Hunte ≃ | 52 | 53.15 N | 8.29 E |
| Hunter, N.Y., U.S. | 210 | 42.13 N | 74.13 W |
| Hunter, N.D., U.S. | 198 | 47.11 N | 97.13 W |
| Hunter ≃, Austl. | 170 | 32.50 S | 151.42 E |
| Hunter ≃, N.Z. | 172 | 44.22 S | 169.25 E |
| Hunter, Île I | 14 | 22.24 S | 172.03 E |
| Hunter, Mount ∧ | 180 | 62.57 N | 151.05 W |
| Hunter, Port ⊂ | 170 | 32.55 S | 151.48 E |
| Hunterdon □[6] | 208 | 40.31 N | 74.52 W |
| Hunter Island I, Austl. | 166 | 40.32 S | 144.45 E |
| Hunter Island I, B.C., Can. | 182 | 51.55 N | 128.05 W |
| Hunter Island I, N.Y., U.S. | 276 | 40.53 N | 73.47 W |
| Hunter Mountain ∧ | 210 | 42.10 N | 74.14 W |
| Hunter Mountains ⋏ | 172 | 45.42 S | 167.25 E |
| Hunter Range ⋏ | 170 | 32.50 S | 150.50 E |
| Hunter Ridge ⊸[3] | 14 | 21.30 S | 174.30 E |
| Hunter River | 186 | 46.21 N | 63.21 W |
| Hunters | 182 | 48.07 N | 118.12 W |
| Hunters Bay ⊂ | 110 | 19.57 N | 93.19 E |
| Hunters Creek Village | 222 | 29.46 N | 95.24 W |
| Huntersfield Mountain ∧ | 210 | 42.21 N | 74.21 W |
| Hunters Hill | 274a | 33.50 S | 151.09 E |
| Hunters Point ≻ | 282 | 37.43 N | 122.22 W |
| Hunter's Quay | 46 | 55.58 N | 4.55 W |
| Hunters Road | 154 | 19.09 S | 29.48 E |
| Hunters Run | 208 | 40.05 N | 77.11 W |
| Huntersville | 192 | 35.25 N | 80.50 W |
| Huntertown | 216 | 41.13 N | 85.10 W |
| Hunterville | 172 | 39.56 S | 175.34 E |
| Hunter Wash ∨ | 200 | 36.17 N | 108.34 W |
| Huntingburg | 194 | 38.17 N | 86.57 W |
| Huntingdon, B.C., Can. | 224 | 49.00 N | 122.16 W |
| Huntingdon, P.Q., Can. | 206 | 45.05 N | 74.10 W |
| Huntingdon, Eng., U.K. | 42 | 52.20 N | 0.12 W |
| Huntingdon, Pa., U.S. | 214 | 40.29 N | 78.00 W |
| Huntingdon, Tn., U.S. | 194 | 36.00 N | 88.25 W |
| Huntingdon □[6], P.Q., Can. | 206 | 45.05 N | 74.0[illegible] W |
| Huntingdon □[6], Pa., U.S. | 214 | 40.29 N | 78.0[illegible] W |
| Huntingdon Valley | 285 | 40.07 N | 75.0[illegible] W |
| Huntingdon Valley Creek ≃ | 285 | 40.07 N | 75.0[illegible] W |
| Hunting Island State Park ♦ | 192 | 32.20 N | 80.30 W |
| Hunting Ridge | 284c | 38.55 N | 77.12 W |
| Huntington, Eng., U.K. | 44 | 54.01 N | 1.04 W |
| Huntington, In., U.S. | 216 | 40.52 N | 85.29 W |
| Huntington, Ma., U.S. | 207 | 42.14 N | 72.52 W |
| Huntington, N.Y., U.S. | 210 | 40.51 N | 73.25 W |
| Huntington, Or., U.S. | 202 | 44.21 N | 117.15 W |
| Huntington, Tx., U.S. | 222 | 31.16 N | 94.34 W |
| Huntington, Ut,. U.S. | 200 | 39.19 N | 110.57 W |
| Huntington, Va., U.S. | 284c | 38.48 N | 77.15 W |
| Huntington, W.V., U.S. | 188 | 38.25 N | 82.26 W |
| Huntington □[6] | 216 | 40.53 N | 85.30 W |
| Huntington Bay | 276 | 40.53 N | 73.24 W |
| Huntington Bay ⊂ | 276 | 40.55 N | 73.25 W |
| Huntington Beach, Ca., U.S. | 228 | 33.39 N | 117.59 W |
| Huntington Beach, N.Y., U.S. | 276 | 40.54 N | 73.23 W |
| Huntington Creek ≃, Nv., U.S. | 204 | 40.37 N | 115.43 W |
| Huntington Creek ≃, Pa., U.S. | 210 | 41.06 N | 76.22 W |
| Huntington Creek ≃, Ut,. U.S. | 200 | 39.09 N | 110.55 W |
| Huntington Harbor ⊂ | 276 | 40.54 N | 73.26 W |
| Huntington Lake | 226 | 37.15 N | 119.14 W |
| Huntington Lake ⊜[1], Ca., U.S. | 226 | 37.14 N | 119.12 W |
| Huntington Lake ⊜[1], In., U.S. | 216 | 40.50 N | 85.25 W |
| Huntington Library ❦[3] | 280 | 34.08 N | 118.07 W |
| Huntington Mills | 210 | 41.11 N | 76.14 W |
| Huntington Park | 228 | 33.58 N | 118.13 W |
| Huntington Park ♦ | 279a | 41.29 N | 81.56 W |
| Huntington Station | 210 | 40.51 N | 73.24 W |
| Huntington Woods | 281 | 42.28 N | 83.10 W |
| Huntingtown | 208 | 38.36 N | 76.36 W |
| Hunting Valley | 279a | 41.31 N | 81.23 W |
| Huntingville | 206 | 45.20 N | 71.51 W |
| Huntland | 194 | 35.03 N | 86.16 W |
| Huntley, Il., U.S. | 216 | 42.10 N | 88.25 W |
| Huntley, Mt., U.S. | 202 | 45.53 N | 108.18 W |
| Huntly, N.Z. | 172 | 37.33 S | 175.10 E |
| Huntly, Scot., U.K. | 46 | 57.27 N | 2.47 W |
| Hunt Mountain ∧ | 202 | 44.44 N | 107.45 W |
| Hunton | 260 | 51.13 N | 0.28 E |
| Huntsburg | 214 | 41.32 N | 81.03 W |
| Hunt's Cross ◆[8] | 262 | 53.21 N | 2.51 W |
| Hunts Point | 224 | 47.39 N | 122.14 W |
| Huntsville, On., Can. | 212 | 45.20 N | 79.13 W |
| Huntsville, Al., U.S. | 194 | 34.43 N | 86.35 W |
| Huntsville, Ar., U.S. | 194 | 36.05 N | 93.44 W |
| Huntsville, Il., U.S. | 219 | 40.11 N | 90.52 W |
| Huntsville, In., U.S. | 218 | 40.00 N | 85.43 W |
| Huntsville, Mo., U.S. | 194 | 39.26 N | 92.33 W |
| Huntsville, Oh., U.S. | 216 | 40.26 N | 83.49 W |
| Huntsville, Tn., U.S. | 192 | 36.24 N | 84.29 W |
| Huntsville, Tx., U.S. | 222 | 30.43 N | 95.33 W |
| Huntsville, Ut,. U.S. | 200 | 41.15 N | 111.46 W |
| Huntsville State Park ♦ | 222 | 30.37 N | 95.32 W |
| Hunū, Kathīb al- ⩡[8] | 142 | 30.37 N | 32.49 E |
| Hunucmá | 232 | 21.01 N | 89.52 W |
| Hunut | 130 | 40.39 N | 41.09 E |
| Hünxe | 52 | 51.38 N | 6.46 E |
| Hünxerwald ♦ | 263 | 51.40 N | 6.50 E |
| Hunyani ≃ | 154 | 15.37 S | 30.39 E |
| Hunyuan | 98 | 39.48 N | 113.41 E |
| Hun-yung | 98 | 42.53 N | 130.12 E |
| Hunza □[9] | 123 | 36.30 N | 75.00 E |
| Hunza ≃ | 123 | 35.55 N | 74.22 E |
| Huocheng | 86 | 44.12 N | 80.26 E |
| Huoergeluo | 89 | 45.35 N | 120.56 E |
| Huokou | 100 | 26.28 N | 119.16 E |
| Huolong | 106 | 32.04 N | 121.17 E |
| Huolongmen | 89 | 49.48 N | 125.47 E |
| Huolu | 98 | 38.05 N | 114.18 E |
| Huong Hoa | 110 | 16.37 N | 106.45 E |
| Huong Khe | 110 | 18.13 N | 105.41 E |
| Huong Thuy | 110 | 16.25 N | 107.40 E |
| Huon Gulf ⊂ | 164 | 7.10 S | 147.25 E |
| Huon Peninsula ≻[1] | 164 | 6.25 S | 147.25 E |
| Huonville | 166 | 43.01 S | 147.02 E |
| Huoqiu | 100 | 32.20 N | 116.16 E |
| Huorili | 89 | 49.00 N | 124.41 E |
| Huoshan | 100 | 31.25 N | 116.20 E |
| Huo Shan ∧ | 100 | 31.06 N | 116.12 E |
| Huoshaoliao | 100 | 25.00 N | 121.45 E |
| Huotong | 100 | 26.53 N | 119.25 E |
| Huotong ≃ | 100 | 26.50 N | 119.32 E |
| Huotuolaihuduke | 102 | 40.19 N | 104.18 E |
| Huoxian, Zhg. | 102 | 36.37 N | 111.40 E |
| Huoxian, Zhg. | 105 | 39.46 N | 116.46 E |
| Huoyan | 100 | 33.42 N | 113.40 E |
| Hupeh → Hubei □[4] | 90 | 31.00 N | 112.00 E |
| Huqiao | 106 | 31.25 N | 119.24 E |
| Hura | 126 | 23.18 N | 86.39 E |
| Hūrand | 84 | 38.51 N | 47.22 E |
| Hurāsāgar ≃ | 126 | 24.04 N | 89.40 E |
| Ḥuraydīn, Wādī ∨ | 132 | 30.59 N | 33.53 E |
| Ḥuraymilā | 128 | 25.08 N | 46.08 E |
| Hūrayn | 142 | 30.39 N | 31.08 E |
| Hurd, Cape ≻ | 190 | 45.13 N | 81.44 W |
| Hurdalssjøen ⊜ | 26 | 60.20 N | 11.05 E |
| Hurdiyo | 144 | 10.33 N | 51.08 E |
| Hurdland | 219 | 40.09 N | 92.18 W |
| Hurdsfield | 262 | 53.16 N | 2.06 W |
| Hurepoix ◆[1] | 261 | 48.37 N | 2.07 E |
| Hure Qi | 98 | 42.44 N | 121.40 E |
| Hurffville | 285 | 39.46 N | 75.07 W |
| Huri ∧[2] | 154 | 3.41 N | 37.51 E |
| Huriel | 32 | 46.23 N | 2.29 E |
| Hurleg Hu ⊜ | 102 | 37.20 N | 96.54 E |
| Hurley, Ms., U.S. | 194 | 30.39 N | 88.29 W |
| Hurley, N.M., U.S. | 200 | 32.41 N | 108.07 W |
| Hurley, N.Y., U.S. | 210 | 41.55 N | 74.03 W |
| Hurley, S.D., U.S. | 198 | 43.16 N | 97.05 W |
| Hurley, Wi., U.S. | 190 | 46.26 N | 90.11 W |
| Hurleyville | 210 | 41.44 N | 74.40 W |
| Hurlford | 46 | 55.36 N | 4.28 W |
| Hurliness | 46 | 58.47 N | 3.15 W |
| Hurlingham | 258 | 34.36 S | 58.38 W |
| Hurlock | 208 | 38.37 N | 75.51 W |
| Hurmāgai | 128 | 28.18 N | 64.26 E |
| Huron, Ca., U.S. | 226 | 36.12 N | 120.06 W |
| Huron, Oh., U.S. | 214 | 41.22 N | 82.33 W |
| Huron, S.D., U.S. | 198 | 44.21 N | 98.12 W |
| Huron □[6], On., Can. | 212 | 43.45 N | 81.10 W |
| Huron □[6], Oh., U.S. | 214 | 41.15 N | 82.37 W |
| Huron ≃, Mi., U.S. | 216 | 42.03 N | 83.14 W |
| Huron ≃, Oh., U.S. | 214 | 41.23 N | 82.33 W |
| Huron, East Branch ≃ | 214 | 41.17 N | 82.38 W |
| Huron, Lake ⊜ | 190 | 44.30 N | 82.15 W |
| Huron, Point ≻ | 214 | 42.34 N | 82.47 W |
| Huron, West Branch ≃ | 214 | 41.17 N | 82.38 W |
| Huron Gardens | 216 | 42.38 N | 83.20 W |
| Huron Mountains ⋏[2] | 190 | 46.50 N | 87.55 W |
| Hurons, Rivière des ≃ | 206 | 45.28 N | 73.16 W |
| Hurricane, Ak., U.S. | 180 | 62.59 N | 149.38 W |
| Hurricane, Ut,. U.S. | 200 | 37.10 N | 113.17 W |
| Hurricane, W.V., U.S. | 188 | 38.25 N | 82.01 W |
| Hurricane Bayou ≃ | 222 | 31.21 N | 95.35 W |
| Hurricane Cliffs ⩡[4] | 200 | 37.20 N | 113.10 W |
| Hurricane Creek ≃, Ar., U.S. | 194 | 34.05 N | 92.23 W |


| | | | | | |
| --- | --- | --- | --- | --- | --- |
| ≃ River | Fluß | Río | Rivière | Rio | |
| ≖ Canal | Kanal | Canal | Canal | Canal | |
| ∟ Waterfall, Rapids | Wasserfall, Stromschnellen | Cascada, Rápidos | Chute d'eau, Rapides | Cascata, Rápidos | |
| ɥ Strait | Meeresstraße | Estrecho | Détroit | Estreito | |
| ⊂ Bay, Gulf | Bucht, Golf | Bahía, Golfo | Baie, Golfe | Baía, Golfo | |
| ⊜ Lake, Lakes | See, Seen | Lago, Lagos | Lac, Lacs | Lago, Lagos | |
| ≡ Swamp | Sumpf | Pantano | Marais | Pântano | |
| ⍓ Ice Features, Glacier | Eis- und Gletscherformen | Accidentes Glaciales | Formes glaciaires | Acidentes glaciares | |
| ⍑ Other Hydrographic Features | Andere Hydrographische Objekte | Otros Elementos Hidrográficos | Autres données hydrographiques | Outros acidentes hidrográficos | |
| ⊸ Submarine Features | Untermeerische Objekte | Accidentes Submarinos | Formes de relief sous-marin | Acidentes submarinos | |
| □ Political Unit | Politische Einheit | Unidad Política | Entité politique | Unidade política | |
| ❦ Cultural Institution | Kulturelle Institution | Institución Cultural | Institution culturelle | Instituição cultural | |
| ⊥ Historical Site | Historische Stätte | Sitio Histórico | Site historique | Sitio histórico | |
| ♦ Recreational Site | Erholungs- und Ferienort | Sitio de Recreo | Centre de loisirs | Area de Lazer | |
| ⊠ Airport | Flughafen | Aeropuerto | Aéroport | Aeroporto | |
| ■ Military Installation | Militäranlage | Instalación Militar | Installation militaire | Instalação militar | |
| ◆ Miscellaneous | Verschiedenes | Misceláneo | Divers | Diversos | |

ENGLISH / DEUTSCH


| Name | Page | Lat.°′ | Long.°′ |
|---|---|---|---|
| Hurricane Creek ≃, Ga., U.S. | 192 | 31.23 N | 82.19 W |
| Hurricane Creek ≃, Il., U.S. | 219 | 38.53 N | 89.13 W |
| Hurricane Lake ⊜ | 198 | 48.25 N | 99.30 W |
| Hurricane Wash V | 200 | 37.00 N | 113.23 W |
| Hurshi | 126 | 24.17 N | 88.28 E |
| Hursley | 42 | 51.02 N | 1.24 W |
| Hurso | 144 | 9.38 N | 41.38 E |
| Hurst | 222 | 32.49 N | 97.10 W |
| Hurstbourne Tarrant | 42 | 51.17 N | 1.23 W |
| Hurstbridge | 169 | 37.38 S | 145.12 E |
| Hurst Green | 260 | 51.15 N | 0.01 E |
| Hurstpierpoint | 42 | 50.56 N | 0.11 W |
| Hurstville | 170 | 33.58 S | 151.06 E |
| Hurstwood Reservoir ⊜[1] | 262 | 53.47 N | 2.10 W |
| Hurt | 192 | 37.05 N | 79.17 W |
| Hurtado ≃ | 252 | 30.35 S | 71.11 W |
| Hurtaut ≃ | 50 | 49.42 N | 4.01 E |
| Hürth | 56 | 50.52 N | 6.51 E |
| Hurtsboro | 194 | 32.14 N | 85.24 W |
| Hurunui ≃ | 172 | 42.55 S | 173.17 E |
| Hurup | 26 | 56.45 N | 8.25 E |
| Hurworth-on-Tees | 44 | 54.29 N | 1.31 W |
| Hurzuf | 78 | 44.33 N | 34.17 E |
| Husainābād | 124 | 24.32 N | 84.01 E |
| Husainīwāla | 123 | 30.59 N | 74.34 E |
| Husainpur | 124 | 24.25 N | 90.40 E |
| Husarka | 78 | 47.23 N | 36.31 E |
| Húsavík | 24a | 66.04 N | 17.18 W |
| Husby-Långhundra | 40 | 59.45 N | 18.01 E |
| Huse → Higashiōsaka | 96 | 34.39 N | 135.35 E |
| Husen ◆[8] | 263 | 51.33 N | 7.36 E |
| Hushan, Zhg. | 89 | 45.35 N | 130.35 E |
| Hushan, Zhg. | 100 | 28.36 N | 118.59 E |
| Hushan, Zhg. | 100 | 22.09 N | 113.10 E |
| Husheib | 140 | 14.54 N | 35.07 E |
| Hushi | 107 | 28.57 N | 105.22 E |
| Hushiha | 98 | 40.52 N | 116.59 E |
| Hushitai | 104 | 41.57 N | 123.30 E |
| Hushu, Zhg. | 106 | 31.52 N | 118.59 E |
| Hushu, Zhg. | 106 | 30.18 N | 120.08 E |
| Huşi | 38 | 46.40 N | 28.04 E |
| Husinec | 60 | 49.03 N | 13.58 E |
| Huskisson | 170 | 35.02 S | 150.40 E |
| Huskvarna | 26 | 57.48 N | 14.16 E |
| Huslia | 180 | 65.42 N | 156.25 W |
| Hussar | 182 | 51.03 N | 112.41 W |
| Hussigny-Godbrange | 56 | 49.29 N | 5.52 E |
| Hustisford | 190 | 43.21 N | 88.36 W |
| Huston ≃ | 220 | 25.42 N | 81.17 W |
| Hustontown | 214 | 40.03 N | 78.02 W |
| Hustopeče | 61 | 48.57 N | 16.44 E |
| Husum, Dtsch. | 41 | 54.28 N | 9.03 E |
| Husum, Sve. | 26 | 63.20 N | 19.10 E |
| Husum, Wa., U.S. | 224 | 45.47 N | 121.29 W |
| Husyatyn | 78 | 49.05 N | 26.11 E |
| Hutaimbaru | 114 | 1.34 N | 99.44 E |
| Hutangqiao | 106 | 31.46 N | 119.57 E |
| Hutan Melintang | 114 | 3.53 N | 100.56 E |
| Hutanopan | 114 | 0.41 N | 99.42 E |
| Hutaym, Ḩarrat ⊥[9] | 128 | 26.15 N | 40.20 E |
| Hutberg ∧[2] | 54 | 52.09 N | 14.33 E |
| Hutchins | 222 | 32.39 N | 96.43 W |
| Hutchinson, S. Afr. | 158 | 31.30 S | 23.09 E |
| Hutchinson, Ks., U.S. | 198 | 38.03 N | 97.55 W |
| Hutchinson, Mn., U.S. | 190 | 44.53 N | 94.22 W |
| Hutchinson, Pa., U.S. | 214 | 40.13 N | 79.44 W |
| Hutchinson ≃ | 276 | 40.52 N | 73.50 W |
| Hutchinson Island I | 220 | 27.25 N | 80.17 W |
| Hutch Mountain ∧ | 200 | 34.47 N | 111.22 W |
| Huti | 78 | 50.08 N | 35.21 E |
| Hutou, Zhg. | 100 | 25.15 N | 118.03 E |
| Hutou, Zhg. | 100 | 26.04 N | 118.46 E |
| Hutou, Zhg. | 106 | 31.37 N | 119.37 E |
| Hutou, Zhg. | 106 | 32.14 N | 120.17 E |
| Hutouya | 98 | 37.13 N | 119.46 E |
| Hutsonville | 194 | 39.06 N | 87.39 W |
| Hüttau | 64 | 47.25 N | 13.18 E |
| Hütteldorf ◆[8] | 264b | 48.12 N | 16.16 E |
| Hüttener Berge ⋀[2] | 41 | 54.26 N | 9.40 E |
| Hüttenheim ◆[8] | 263 | 51.22 N | 6.43 E |
| Hüttental | 56 | 50.54 N | 8.02 E |
| Hutte Sauvage, Lac de la ⊜ | 176 | 56.15 N | 64.45 W |
| Hutthurm | 60 | 48.40 N | 13.28 E |
| Huttig | 194 | 33.02 N | 92.10 W |
| Hütting | 60 | 48.48 N | 11.07 E |
| Hüttlingen | 56 | 48.54 N | 10.06 E |
| Hutto | 222 | 30.33 N | 97.33 W |
| Hutton, Eng., U.K. | 260 | 51.38 N | 0.22 E |
| Hutton, Eng., U.K. | 262 | 53.44 N | 2.46 W |
| Hutton, Mount ∧ | 166 | 25.51 S | 148.20 E |
| Hutton Rudby | 44 | 54.27 N | 1.17 W |
| Huttonsville | 212 | 43.38 N | 79.48 W |
| Huttrop ◆[8] | 263 | 51.27 N | 7.03 E |
| Hüttschlag | 64 | 47.10 N | 13.14 E |
| Huttwil | 58 | 47.07 N | 7.51 E |
| Hutubi | 86 | 44.07 N | 86.57 E |
| Hutuo ≃ | 98 | 38.14 N | 116.05 E |
| Hutwisch ∧ | 61 | 47.28 N | 16.13 E |
| Huu | 115b | 8.48 S | 118.25 E |
| Huvalu Forest ◆[3] | 174v | 19.03 S | 169.51 W |
| Huveaune ≃ | 62 | 43.15 N | 5.23 E |
| Huvudskär I | 40 | 58.57 N | 18.34 E |
| Huwan | 100 | 31.41 N | 114.53 E |
| Huwei | 100 | 23.43 N | 120.26 E |
| Huwun | 144 | 4.23 N | 40.08 E |
| Ḩuwwārah | 132 | 32.09 N | 35.15 E |
| Huxford | 194 | 31.13 N | 87.28 W |
| Huxi | 100 | 26.12 N | 114.44 E |
| Huxian | 102 | 34.09 N | 108.32 E |
| Huxley | 182 | 51.56 N | 113.14 W |
| Huy | 56 | 50.31 N | 5.14 E |
| Huy ∧ | 54 | 51.57 N | 10.57 E |
| Huyangzhen | 100 | 32.25 N | 112.45 E |
| Huyton-with-Roby | 262 | 53.25 N | 2.52 W |
| Huyuesi | 106 | 30.23 N | 118.45 E |
| Hüyük | 130 | 37.57 N | 31.37 E |
| Huyutou | 100 | 26.44 N | 119.49 E |
| Hūzgān | 128 | 31.27 N | 48.04 E |
| Huzhen | 100 | 28.50 N | 120.15 E |
| Huzhou | 106 | 30.52 N | 120.06 E |
| Huzhu | 102 | 37.00 N | 102.00 E |
| Huzhuangtun | 104 | 40.43 N | 122.33 E |
| Huzi | 100 | 30.56 N | 113.42 E |
| Huzisawa → Fujisawa | 94 | 35.21 N | 139.29 E |
| Hvalsø | 41 | 55.36 N | 11.50 E |
| Hvannadalshnúkur ∧ | 24a | 64.01 N | 16.41 W |
| Hvar | 36 | 43.10 N | 16.27 E |
| Hvar, Otok I | 36 | 43.09 N | 16.45 E |
| Hvardiys'ke, Ukr. | 78 | 45.07 N | 34.01 E |
| Hvardiys'ke, Ukr. | 78 | 48.44 N | 35.19 E |
| Hvardiys'ke, Ukr. | 78 | 49.20 N | 26.42 E |
| Hvarski Kanal ⋃ | 36 | 43.15 N | 16.37 E |
| Hveragerði | 24a | 64.03 N | 21.10 W |
| Hvide Sande | 26 | 55.59 N | 8.08 E |
| Hvidovre | 41 | 55.39 N | 12.29 E |
| Hvittingfoss | 26 | 59.29 N | 10.01 E |
| Hvizdets' | 78 | 48.34 N | 25.17 E |
| Hvolsvöllur | 24a | 63.45 N | 20.10 W |
| Hwach'ŏn | 98 | 38.06 N | 127.41 E |
| Hwach'ŏn-chŏsuji ⊜[1] | 98 | 38.07 N | 127.52 E |
| Hwach'ŏn-ni | 98 | 39.01 N | 126.02 E |
| Hwainan → Huainan | 100 | 32.40 N | 117.00 E |
| Hwaining → Anqing | 100 | 30.31 N | 117.02 E |
| Hwange | 154 | 18.22 S | 26.29 E |
| Hwange National Park ♠ | 154 | 19.00 S | 26.35 E |
| Hwanggong-ni | 98 | 40.03 N | 129.27 E |
| Hwanghae Namdo □[4] | 98 | 38.15 N | 125.30 E |
| Hwanghae Pukdo □[4] | 98 | 38.30 N | 126.25 E |
| Hwang Ho → Huang ≃ | 90 | 37.32 N | 118.19 E |
| Hwangju | 98 | 38.42 N | 125.46 E |
| Hwangshih → Huangshi | 100 | 30.13 N | 115.05 E |
| Hyak | 224 | 47.23 N | 121.23 W |
| Hyakuna | 174m | 26.08 N | 127.48 E |
| Hyakuri-ga-dake ∧ | 94 | 35.23 N | 135.49 E |
| Hyakuri-kichi, Kōkū-jieitai- ■ | 94 | 36.11 N | 140.25 E |
| Hyannis, Ma., U.S. | 207 | 41.39 N | 70.17 W |
| Hyannis, Ne., U.S. | 198 | 42.00 N | 101.45 W |
| Hyannis Port | 207 | 41.38 N | 70.18 W |
| Hyattsville | 208 | 38.57 N | 76.56 W |
| Hyattville | 202 | 44.14 N | 107.36 W |
| Hybla Valley | 208 | 38.44 N | 77.05 W |
| Hyco ≃ | 192 | 36.40 N | 78.45 W |
| Hyco Lake ⊜[1] | 192 | 36.30 N | 79.05 W |
| Hydaburg | 182 | 55.12 N | 132.49 W |
| Hyde, N.Z. | 172 | 45.18 S | 170.15 E |
| Hyde, Eng., U.K. | 44 | 53.27 N | 2.04 W |
| Hyde, Pa., U.S. | 214 | 41.00 N | 78.28 W |
| Hyden, Austl. | 162 | 32.27 S | 118.53 E |
| Hyden, Ky., U.S. | 192 | 37.10 N | 83.22 W |
| Hyde Park, Guy. | 246 | 6.30 N | 58.16 W |
| Hyde Park, N.Y., U.S. | 210 | 41.47 N | 73.56 W |
| Hyde Park, Vt., U.S. | 188 | 44.35 N | 72.37 W |
| Hyde Park ◆[8], Il., U.S. | 278 | 41.48 N | 87.36 W |
| Hyde Park ◆[8], Ma., U.S. | 283 | 42.15 N | 71.08 W |
| Hyde Park ♠, Austl. | 274a | 33.53 S | 151.13 E |
| Hyde Park ♠, Eng., U.K. | 260 | 51.30 N | 0.10 W |
| Hyde Park ♠, N.Y., U.S. | 284a | 43.06 N | 79.01 W |
| Hyder | 182 | 55.55 N | 130.01 W |
| Hyderābād, India | 122 | 17.23 N | 78.29 E |
| Hyderābād, Pāk. | 120 | 25.22 N | 68.22 E |
| Hydetown | 214 | 41.40 N | 79.44 W |
| Hydra → Ídhra I | 38 | 37.20 N | 23.32 E |
| Hydraulic | 182 | 52.36 N | 121.42 W |
| Hydro | 196 | 35.21 N | 98.22 W |
| Hydrographers Passage ⋃ | 166 | 20.45 S | 150.15 E |
| Hyen ⊜ | 40 | 60.36 N | 16.12 E |
| Hyères | 62 | 43.07 N | 6.07 E |
| Hyères, Îles d' II | 62 | 43.00 N | 6.20 E |
| Hyères-Plage | 62 | 43.06 N | 6.10 E |
| Hyesan | 98 | 41.23 N | 128.12 E |
| Hyland ≃ | 180 | 59.50 N | 128.10 W |
| Hylestad | 26 | 59.05 N | 7.32 E |
| Hyllekrog I | 41 | 54.36 N | 11.30 E |
| Hyllinge, Dan. | 41 | 55.16 N | 11.37 E |
| Hyllinge, Sve. | 41 | 56.06 N | 12.51 E |
| Hyllstofta | 41 | 56.08 N | 13.16 E |
| Hyltebruk | 26 | 57.00 N | 13.14 E |
| Hymaya ≃ | 232 | 24.31 N | 107.41 W |
| Hymera | 194 | 39.11 N | 87.18 W |
| Hyndburn □[8] | 262 | 53.45 N | 2.23 W |
| Hyndman | 188 | 39.49 N | 78.43 W |
| Hyndman Peak ∧ | 202 | 43.45 N | 114.08 W |
| Hynish Bay C | 46 | 56.28 N | 6.50 W |
| Hyōgo □[5] | 96 | 35.00 N | 135.00 E |
| Hyōgo ◆[8] | 270 | 34.39 N | 135.10 E |
| Hyŏn-ni | 98 | 37.57 N | 128.20 E |
| Hyōno-sen ∧ | 96 | 35.21 N | 134.31 E |
| Hyōnosen-Ushiroyama-Nagisan-kokutei-kōen ♠ | 96 | 35.15 N | 134.30 E |
| Hyŏpch'ŏn | 98 | 35.35 N | 128.08 E |
| Hyrum | 200 | 41.38 N | 111.51 W |
| Hyrynsalmi | 26 | 64.40 N | 28.32 E |
| Hysham | 202 | 46.17 N | 107.14 W |
| Hythe, Ab., Can. | 182 | 55.20 N | 119.33 W |
| Hythe, Eng., U.K. | 42 | 51.05 N | 1.05 E |
| Hythe, Eng., U.K. | 42 | 50.51 N | 1.24 W |
| Hythe End | 260 | 51.27 N | 0.32 W |
| Hyūga | 92 | 32.25 N | 131.38 E |
| Hyūga-nada ⊤[2] | 92 | 32.00 N | 131.35 E |
| Hyvinge → Hyvinkää | 26 | 60.38 N | 24.52 E |
| Hyvinkää | 26 | 60.38 N | 24.52 E |
| **I** | | | |
| Iacanga | 255 | 21.54 S | 49.01 W |
| Iaciara | 255 | 14.09 S | 46.40 W |
| Iaco (Yaco) ≃ | 248 | 9.03 S | 68.34 W |
| Iaçu | 255 | 12.45 S | 40.13 W |
| Iaeger | 192 | 37.27 N | 81.48 W |
| Iago | 222 | 29.17 N | 95.58 W |
| Iakora | 157b | 23.06 S | 46.40 E |
| Ialomiţa □[6] | 38 | 44.40 N | 27.20 E |
| Ialomiţa ≃ | 38 | 44.42 N | 27.51 E |
| Ialomiţei, Balta ≋ | 38 | 44.30 N | 28.00 E |
| Ialpug ≃ | 78 | 45.41 N | 28.35 E |
| Iamonia, Lake ⊜ | 192 | 30.38 N | 84.14 W |
| Ianaivo ≃ | 157b | 22.56 S | 46.54 E |
| Ianakafy | 157b | 23.21 S | 45.28 E |
| Ĭanga | 146 | 9.07 N | 18.11 E |
| Iango | 152 | 9.11 S | 17.39 E |
| Iano, Monte ∧ | 267a | 41.46 N | 12.44 E |
| Iapó ≃ | 252 | 24.30 S | 50.24 W |
| Iapu | 255 | 19.26 S | 42.13 W |
| Iargara | 38 | 46.27 N | 28.27 E |
| Iaşi | 38 | 47.10 N | 27.35 E |
| Iaşi □[6] | 38 | 47.15 N | 27.15 E |
| Iato | 70 | 37.58 N | 13.07 E |
| Iato ≃ | 70 | 38.04 N | 13.02 E |
| Iatt, Lake ⊜[1] | 194 | 31.35 N | 92.40 W |
| Iauaretê | 246 | 0.36 N | 69.12 W |
| Iazu | 38 | 44.44 N | 27.25 E |
| Ib ≃ | 120 | 21.34 N | 83.48 E |
| Iba, Pil. | 116 | 15.20 N | 119.58 E |
| Iba, Zaïre | 152 | 3.05 S | 17.38 E |
| 'Ibādah, Wādī V | 142 | 27.49 N | 30.54 E |
| Ibadan | 150 | 7.17 N | 3.30 E |
| Ibagué | 246 | 4.27 N | 75.14 W |
| Ibaiti | 255 | 23.50 S | 50.10 W |
| Ibajay | 116 | 11.49 N | 122.10 E |
| Ibajay ≃ | 116 | 11.49 N | 122.10 E |
| Ibaka | 152 | 4.16 S | 23.12 E |
| Ibambi | 154 | 2.22 N | 27.37 E |
| Ibanda | 154 | 0.08 S | 30.29 E |
| Ibăneşti | 38 | 48.04 N | 26.22 E |
| Ibans, Laguna de C | 236 | 15.53 N | 84.52 W |
| Ibanshe | 152 | 4.58 S | 21.30 E |
| Ibapah Peak ∧ | 200 | 39.50 N | 113.55 W |
| Ibar ≃ | 38 | 43.44 N | 20.45 E |
| Ibara | 96 | 34.36 N | 133.28 E |
| Ibaraki, Nihon | 94 | 36.17 N | 140.26 E |
| Ibaraki, Nihon | 96 | 34.49 N | 135.34 E |
| Ibaraki □[5] | 94 | 36.30 N | 140.30 E |
| Ibarra | 246 | 0.21 N | 78.07 W |
| Ibarreta | 252 | 25.13 S | 59.51 W |
| Ibb | 144 | 14.01 N | 44.10 E |
| Ibba | 154 | 4.48 N | 29.06 E |
| Ibba ≃ | 140 | 7.09 N | 28.41 E |
| Ibbenbüren | 52 | 52.16 N | 7.43 E |
| Ibeke Gembo | 152 | 1.24 S | 18.51 E |
| Ibembo | 152 | 2.38 N | 23.37 E |
| Ibenga ≃ | 152 | 2.20 N | 18.08 E |
| Iberá, Esteros del ≋ | 252 | 28.05 S | 57.05 W |
| Iberia, Mo., U.S. | 194 | 38.05 N | 92.17 W |
| Iberia, Oh., U.S. | 214 | 40.40 N | 82.51 W |
| Ibérica, Península >[1] | 10 | 40.00 N | 5.00 W |
| Ibérico, Sistema ⋀ | 34 | 41.00 N | 2.30 W |
| Ibertioga | 256 | 21.25 S | 43.58 W |
| Iberville | 206 | 45.18 N | 73.14 W |
| Iberville □[6] | 206 | 45.15 N | 73.10 W |
| Iberville, Mont d' (Mount Caubvick) ∧ | 176 | 58.53 N | 63.43 W |
| Ibese | 273a | 6.33 N | 3.29 E |
| Ibeto | 150 | 10.29 N | 5.09 E |
| Ibi | 150 | 8.12 N | 9.45 E |
| Ibi ≃ | 94 | 35.03 N | 136.42 E |
| Ibiá | 255 | 19.29 S | 46.32 W |
| Ibiapina | 250 | 3.55 S | 40.54 W |
| Ibicaraí | 255 | 14.51 S | 39.36 W |
| Ibicuí | 255 | 14.51 S | 39.59 W |
| Ibicuí ≃ | 252 | 29.25 S | 56.47 W |
| Ibicuicito, Arroyo ≃ | 258 | 33.49 S | 58.49 W |
| Ibicuy | 258 | 33.44 S | 59.10 W |
| Ibicuy ≃[1] | 258 | 33.48 S | 59.10 W |
| Ibigawa | 94 | 35.29 N | 136.34 E |
| Ibipira | 250 | 6.31 S | 44.38 W |
| Ibiquera | 255 | 12.38 S | 40.57 W |
| Ibiraci | 255 | 20.28 S | 47.08 W |
| Ibiraçu | 255 | 19.50 S | 40.22 W |
| Ibirama | 252 | 27.04 S | 49.31 W |
| Ibirapuã | 255 | 17.39 S | 40.07 W |
| Ibirapuera ◆[8] | 287b | 23.37 S | 46.40 W |
| Ibirapuera, Parque ♠ | 287b | 23.35 S | 46.39 W |
| Ibirapuitã ≃ | 252 | 29.22 S | 55.57 W |
| Ibirataia | 255 | 14.04 S | 39.38 W |
| Ibiri | 154 | 4.56 S | 32.33 E |
| Ibirubá | 252 | 28.38 S | 53.06 W |
| Ibitiara | 255 | 12.39 S | 42.13 W |
| Ibitinga | 255 | 21.45 S | 48.49 W |
| Ibitiúra De Minas | 256 | 22.04 S | 46.26 W |
| Ibiúna | 256 | 23.39 S | 47.13 W |
| Ibiza → Eivissa I | 34 | 39.00 N | 1.25 E |
| Iblei, Monti ⋀ | 70 | 37.10 N | 14.50 E |
| Ibnahs | 142 | 30.34 N | 31.07 E |
| Ibn Hāni', Ra's > | 130 | 35.35 N | 35.43 E |
| Ibn Sarrār, Bi'r ⊤[4] | 144 | 19.30 N | 42.41 E |
| Ibo | 154 | 12.20 S | 40.35 E |
| Ibo ≃ | 96 | 34.46 N | 134.35 E |
| Ibondo | 154 | 2.38 S | 32.40 E |
| Ibonma | 164 | 3.28 S | 133.28 E |
| Ibor ≃ | 34 | 39.49 N | 5.33 W |
| Ibotirama | 255 | 12.11 S | 43.13 W |
| Iboundji, Mont ∧ | 152 | 1.08 S | 11.48 E |
| Ibrah, Wādī V | 140 | 10.36 N | 24.58 E |
| Ibrāhīmīyah, Qārah al- ≋ | 142 | 29.10 N | 31.10 E |
| Ibresi | 80 | 55.18 N | 47.03 E |
| 'Ibrī | 128 | 23.14 N | 56.30 E |
| İbriktepe | 130 | 41.00 N | 26.30 E |
| Ibshān | 142 | 31.10 N | 31.10 E |
| Ibshawāy | 142 | 29.22 N | 30.41 E |
| Ibstock | 42 | 52.42 N | 1.23 W |
| Ibta' | 132 | 32.47 N | 36.09 E |
| Ibu | 174m | 26.45 N | 128.19 E |
| Ibuki | 94 | 35.24 N | 136.23 E |
| Ibuki-jima I | 96 | 34.08 N | 133.32 E |
| Ibuki-sanchi ⋀ | 94 | 35.35 N | 136.18 E |
| Ibuki-yama ∧ | 94 | 35.25 N | 136.24 E |
| Ibusuki | 92 | 31.16 N | 130.39 E |
| Ibwe Munyama | 154 | 16.09 S | 28.34 E |
| Ibychen, gora ∧ | 88 | 51.36 N | 109.45 E |
| Ica | 248 | 14.04 S | 75.42 W |
| Ica □[5] | 248 | 14.20 S | 75.30 W |
| Ič̌a ≃, Lat. | 76 | 56.52 N | 26.59 E |
| Ica ≃, Perú | 248 | 14.54 S | 75.34 W |
| Ič̌a ≃, Ross. | 86 | 55.30 N | 77.13 E |
| Içá (Putumayo) ≃, S.A. | 246 | 3.07 S | 67.58 W |
| Icabarú ≃ | 246 | 4.45 N | 62.15 W |
| Icacos Point > | 241r | 10.03 N | 61.56 W |
| Icadambanauan Island I | 116 | 10.49 N | 119.38 E |
| Icamaquã ≃ | 252 | 28.34 S | 56.00 W |
| Icamole | 196 | 25.55 N | 100.43 W |
| Içana | 246 | 0.21 N | 67.19 W |
| Içana (Isana) ≃ | 246 | 0.26 N | 67.19 W |
| Icaño, Arg. | 252 | 28.54 S | 65.19 W |
| Icaño, Arg. | 252 | 28.41 S | 62.54 W |
| Icatu | 250 | 2.46 S | 44.04 W |
| Iceberg Pass )( | 200 | 40.25 N | 105.45 W |
| Ice House Reservoir ⊜[1] | 226 | 38.49 N | 120.23 W |
| İçel (Mersin) | 130 | 36.48 N | 34.38 E |
| İçel □[4] | 130 | 36.45 N | 34.00 E |
| Iceland (Ísland) □[1], Europe | 22 | 65.00 N | 18.00 W |
| Iceland (Ísland) □[1], Europe | 24a | 65.00 N | 18.00 W |
| Iceland Basin ◆[1] | 10 | 59.00 N | 23.00 W |
| Icém | 255 | 20.21 S | 49.12 W |
| Ice Mountain ∧ | 182 | 54.25 N | 121.08 W |
| Ičera | 88 | 58.32 N | 109.47 E |
| Ichaikaronji | 122 | 16.42 N | 74.28 E |
| Ichāmati ≃, Asia | 126 | 22.35 N | 88.57 E |
| Ichāmati ≃, Bngl. | 126 | 24.00 N | 89.15 E |
| Ichang → Yichang | 102 | 30.42 N | 111.17 E |
| Ichawaynochaway Creek ≃ | 192 | 31.10 N | 84.28 W |
| Ich Bajan Ajrag uul ∧ | 88 | 47.55 N | 95.02 E |
| Ichbulag | 102 | 45.21 N | 113.10 E |
| Ich Buural uul ∧ | 88 | 48.00 N | 94.30 E |
| Ichchāpuram | 122 | 19.07 N | 84.42 E |
| Ichdžargalan | 102 | 45.31 N | 108.48 E |
| Ichenhausen | 58 | 48.22 N | 10.18 E |
| Ichenheim | 58 | 48.26 N | 7.49 E |
| Ichhapur | 126 | 22.50 N | 88.24 E |
| Ichhāwar | 124 | 23.01 N | 77.01 E |
| Ichi ≃ | 96 | 34.46 N | 134.41 E |
| Ichiba | 96 | 34.05 N | 134.17 E |
| Ichihara | 94 | 35.31 N | 140.05 E |
| Ichikai | 94 | 36.32 N | 140.06 E |
| Ichikawa, Nihon | 94 | 35.44 N | 139.55 E |
| Ichikawa, Nihon | 96 | 34.59 N | 134.46 E |
| Ichikawa-daimon | 94 | 35.34 N | 138.30 E |
| Ichilo ≃ | 248 | 15.57 S | 64.42 W |
| Ichinohe | 92 | 40.13 N | 141.17 E |
| Ichinomiya, Nihon | 94 | 35.18 N | 136.48 E |
| Ichinomiya, Nihon | 94 | 35.22 N | 140.22 E |
| Ichinomiya, Nihon | 94 | 35.39 N | 138.41 E |
| Ichinomiya, Nihon | 94 | 34.41 N | 137.26 E |
| Ichinomiya, Nihon | 96 | 34.28 N | 134.51 E |
| Ichinomiya, Nihon | 96 | 32.57 N | 131.07 E |
| Ichinomiya, Nihon | 96 | 35.07 N | 134.34 E |
| Ichinomoto | 270 | 34.37 N | 135.50 E |
| Ichinose | 270 | 34.53 N | 135.10 E |
| Ichinoseki | 92 | 38.55 N | 141.08 E |
| Ichino-tani ⊥ | 96 | 34.39 N | 135.07 E |
| Ichiu | 96 | 33.57 N | 134.04 E |
| Ichkeul, Lac ⊜ | 36 | 37.10 N | 9.40 E |
| Ichnya | 78 | 50.52 N | 32.24 E |
| Ichoa ≃ | 248 | 15.44 S | 65.15 W |
| Ichoca | 248 | 17.12 S | 67.17 W |
| Ich'on, C.M.I.K. | 98 | 38.30 N | 126.50 E |
| Ich'ŏn, Taehan | 98 | 37.17 N | 127.27 E |
| Ich Ovoo uul ∧ | 90 | 44.40 N | 95.08 E |
| Ichtamir | 88 | 47.30 N | 100.52 E |
| Ichtegem | 50 | 51.06 N | 3.00 E |
| Ichtershausen | 54 | 50.52 N | 10.58 E |
| Ich'un → Yichun | 90 | 47.42 N | 128.55 E |
| Ich Uul, Mong. | 88 | 48.33 N | 98.40 E |
| Ich Uul, Mong. | 88 | 49.27 N | 101.27 E |
| Icicle Creek ≃ | 224 | 47.34 N | 120.40 W |
| Ičinskaja Sopka, vulkan ∧[1] | 74 | 55.42 N | 157.35 E |
| Ička, gora ∧[2] | 80 | 51.13 N | 50.15 E |
| Ickenham ◆[8] | 260 | 51.34 N | 0.27 W |
| Ickern | 263 | 51.36 N | 7.21 E |
| Ickesburg | 208 | 40.27 N | 77.21 W |
| Icking | 64 | 47.57 N | 11.25 E |
| İçme | 130 | 38.37 N | 39.34 E |
| Icó | 250 | 6.24 S | 38.51 W |
| Icoca | 152 | 6.11 S | 16.19 E |
| Iconha | 255 | 20.48 S | 40.48 W |
| Icy Bay C | 180 | 60.00 N | 141.15 W |
| Icy Cape > | 180 | 70.20 N | 161.52 W |
| Icy Strait ⋃ | 180 | 58.18 N | 135.30 W |
| Ida | 216 | 41.54 N | 83.34 W |
| Ida, Mount ∧, Austl. | 162 | 29.14 S | 120.25 E |
| Ida, Mount ∧, Jam. | 241q | 17.58 N | 77.43 W |
| Idabel | 194 | 33.53 N | 94.49 W |
| Idaga Hamus | 144 | 14.12 N | 39.48 E |
| Ida Grove | 198 | 42.20 N | 95.28 W |
| Idah | 150 | 7.07 N | 6.43 E |
| Idaho □[3], U.S. | 178 | 45.00 N | 115.00 W |
| Idaho □[3], U.S. | 202 | 45.00 N | 115.00 W |
| Idaho City | 202 | 43.49 N | 115.50 W |
| Idaho Falls | 202 | 43.28 N | 112.02 W |
| Idaho National Engineering Laboratory ⊻[3] | 202 | 43.40 N | 112.45 W |
| Idaho Springs | 200 | 39.44 N | 105.00 W |
| Idalou | 196 | 33.39 N | 101.40 W |
| Idanha-a-Nova | 34 | 39.55 N | 7.14 W |
| Idāppādi | 122 | 11.35 N | 77.51 E |
| Idar | 120 | 23.50 N | 73.00 E |
| Idarkopf ∧ | 56 | 49.51 N | 7.16 E |
| Idar-Oberstein | 56 | 49.42 N | 7.19 E |
| Idarwald ◆[3] | 56 | 49.49 N | 7.12 E |
| Idaville, In., U.S. | 216 | 40.45 N | 86.38 W |
| Idaville, Or., U.S. | 224 | 45.30 N | 123.51 W |
| Iddo ◆[8] | 273a | 6.28 N | 3.23 E |
| Ide | 96 | 34.47 N | 135.49 E |
| Idel' | 24 | 64.08 N | 34.14 E |
| Idelès | 148 | 23.58 N | 5.53 E |
| Idemba | 152 | 2.38 S | 11.38 E |
| Iden | 54 | 52.46 N | 11.55 E |
| Ider | 88 | 48.13 N | 97.23 E |
| Iderijn ≃ | 88 | 49.16 N | 100.41 E |
| Idermeg | 88 | 47.40 N | 111.05 E |
| Idfīnā | 142 | 31.18 N | 30.31 E |
| Idfū | 140 | 24.58 N | 32.52 E |
| Ídhi Óros ∧ | 38 | 35.18 N | 24.43 E |
| Ídhra | 38 | 37.20 N | 23.29 E |
| Ídhra (Hydra) I | 38 | 37.20 N | 23.32 E |
| Idi | 114 | 4.57 N | 97.46 E |
| Idice ≃ | 64 | 44.35 N | 11.49 E |
| Idi-cut | 114 | 4.59 N | 97.42 E |
| Ididole | 144 | 5.53 N | 43.36 E |
| Idifina Barrage ◆[6] | 142 | 31.17 N | 30.31 E |
| Idil | 130 | 37.21 N | 41.54 E |
| Idimu | 273a | 6.35 N | 3.17 E |
| Idio | 116 | 11.37 N | 122.06 E |
| Idiofa | 152 | 5.02 S | 19.36 E |
| Iditarod ≃ | 180 | 63.02 N | 158.58 W |
| Idjwi, Île I | 154 | 2.09 S | 29.04 E |
| Idkerberget | 40 | 60.23 N | 15.14 E |
| Idkū | 142 | 31.18 N | 30.18 E |
| Idkū, Buḩayrat ⊜ | 142 | 31.16 N | 30.17 E |
| Idle ≃ | 44 | 53.27 N | 0.49 W |
| Idle Hill | 260 | 51.15 N | 0.08 E |
| Idlib | 130 | 35.55 N | 36.38 E |
| Idlib □[8] | 130 | 35.50 N | 36.40 E |
| Idmū | 142 | 28.09 N | 30.41 E |
| Idnah | 132 | 31.34 N | 34.59 E |
| Idodi | 154 | 7.47 S | 35.11 E |
| Idomogu | 273a | 6.43 N | 3.30 E |
| Idoûkâl-n-Taghès ∧ | 150 | 17.43 N | 8.45 E |
| Idracowra | 162 | 25.00 S | 133.47 E |
| Idre | 26 | 61.52 N | 12.43 E |
| Idrica | 76 | 56.21 N | 28.53 E |
| Idrigill Point > | 46 | 57.20 N | 6.35 W |
| Idrija | 36 | 46.00 N | 14.01 E |
| Idrijca ≃ | 64 | 46.09 N | 13.45 E |
| Idrinskoje | 86 | 54.21 N | 92.07 E |
| Idro | 64 | 45.44 N | 10.29 E |
| Idro, Lago d' ⊜ | 64 | 45.47 N | 10.30 E |
| Idroscalo ⊜ | 266b | 45.28 N | 9.18 E |
| Idstedt | 41 | 54.35 N | 9.31 E |
| Idstein | 56 | 50.13 N | 8.16 E |
| Idutywa | 158 | 32.02 S | 28.16 E |
| Idyllwild | 204 | 33.45 N | 116.43 W |
| Idylwood | 284c | 38.54 N | 77.12 W |
| Idževan | 84 | 40.53 N | 45.07 E |
| Ie | 174m | 26.42 N | 127.48 E |
| Iecava | 76 | 56.36 N | 24.12 E |
| Iecava ≃ | 76 | 56.41 N | 23.42 E |
| Ielsi | 66 | 41.30 N | 14.48 E |
| Ienne | 66 | 41.53 N | 13.10 E |
| Iepê | 255 | 22.40 S | 51.05 W |
| Ieper (Ypres) | 50 | 50.51 N | 2.53 E |
| Ierápetra | 38 | 35.00 N | 25.45 E |
| Ierisós | 38 | 40.24 N | 23.52 E |
| Ierzu | 71 | 39.47 N | 9.31 E |
| Ieshima | 96 | 34.40 N | 134.32 E |
| Ie-shima I | 174m | 26.43 N | 127.47 E |
| Ieshima-shotō II | 96 | 34.40 N | 134.32 E |
| Iesolo | 64 | 45.32 N | 12.38 E |
| Ie-suidō ⋃ | 174m | 26.42 N | 127.51 E |
| If, Château d' ⊥ | 62 | 43.17 N | 5.19 E |
| Ifakara | 154 | 8.08 S | 36.41 E |
| Ifako | 273a | 6.39 N | 3.20 E |
| Ifalik I[1] | 108 | 7.15 N | 144.27 E |
| Ifanadiana | 157b | 21.19 S | 47.39 E |
| Ife | 150 | 7.30 N | 4.30 E |
| Iferouâne | 150 | 19.04 N | 8.24 E |
| Iferten → Yverdon | 58 | 46.47 N | 6.39 E |
| Iffezheim | 56 | 48.49 N | 8.08 E |
| Ifni □[9] | 148 | 29.15 N | 10.08 W |
| Ifôghas, Adrar des ⋀ | 150 | 20.00 N | 2.00 E |
| Ifon | 150 | 6.58 N | 5.45 E |
| Ifould Lake ⊜ | 162 | 30.53 S | 132.09 E |
| Ifrane | 148 | 33.32 N | 5.06 W |
| Ifrane □[4] | 148 | 33.15 N | 5.05 W |
| Ifta | 56 | 51.04 N | 10.11 E |
| Ifugao □[4] | 116 | 16.45 N | 121.15 E |
| Iga | 94 | 34.49 N | 136.13 E |
| Iga ≃ | 94 | 34.45 N | 136.01 E |
| Igal | 30 | 46.31 N | 17.55 E |
| Igalula, Tan. | 154 | 5.14 S | 33.00 E |
| Igalula, Tan. | 154 | 5.38 S | 32.38 E |
| Igan | 112 | 2.49 N | 111.43 E |
| Igan ≃ | 112 | 2.51 N | 111.39 E |
| Iganga | 154 | 0.37 N | 33.29 E |
| Iganmu ◆[8] | 273a | 6.29 N | 3.22 E |
| Iganna | 150 | 7.59 N | 3.14 E |
| Igaporã | 255 | 13.46 S | 42.43 W |
| Igara | 250 | 10.24 S | 40.07 W |
| Igaraí | 256 | 21.25 S | 46.49 W |
| Igara Paraná ≃ | 246 | 2.09 S | 71.47 W |
| Igarapé-Açu | 250 | 1.07 S | 47.37 W |
| Igarapé Grande | 250 | 4.41 S | 44.58 W |
| Igarapé-Miri | 250 | 1.59 S | 48.58 W |
| Igaratá | 256 | 23.12 S | 46.07 W |
| Igarka | 74 | 67.28 N | 86.35 E |
| Igarra | 150 | 7.18 N | 6.07 E |
| Igarukiro | 154 | 3.08 S | 33.31 E |
| Igatpuri | 122 | 19.42 N | 73.33 E |
| Igaun | 273a | 6.42 N | 3.23 E |
| Igawa | 154 | 8.35 S | 34.28 E |
| Igbaja | 150 | 8.23 N | 4.52 E |
| Igbobi | 273a | 6.32 N | 3.22 E |
| Igboho | 150 | 8.51 N | 3.45 E |
| Igbologun | 273a | 6.25 N | 3.20 E |
| Igbo-Ora | 150 | 7.26 N | 3.17 E |
| Igbor | 150 | 7.27 N | 8.34 E |
| Igdir, Īrān | 84 | 39.20 N | 47.30 E |
| Iğdır, Tür. | 84 | 39.55 N | 44.02 E |
| Iğdır, Tür. | 130 | 41.14 N | 33.07 E |
| Iğdır, Tür. | 130 | 40.16 N | 35.38 E |
| Igdy | 128 | 39.54 N | 56.54 E |
| Igea Marina | 66 | 44.08 N | 12.29 E |
| Igel | 56 | 49.42 N | 6.32 E |
| Igelfors | 40 | 58.51 N | 15.41 E |
| Igel'vejem ≃ | 180 | 65.40 N | 172.50 W |
| Igersheim | 56 | 49.29 N | 9.49 E |
| Iggensbach | 60 | 48.44 N | 13.08 E |
| Iggesund | 26 | 61.38 N | 17.04 E |
| Igharghar, Oued V, Afr. | 148 | 20.25 N | 6.10 E |
| Igharghar, Oued V, Alg. | 148 | 28.03 N | 6.15 E |
| Ightham | 260 | 51.17 N | 0.17 E |
| Ightham Mote ⊥ | 260 | 51.15 N | 0.16 E |
| Igikpak, Mount ∧ | 180 | 67.25 N | 154.58 W |
| Igirma | 88 | 56.59 N | 103.37 E |
| Igiugig | 180 | 59.20 N | 155.55 W |
| Iglau → Jihlava | 30 | 49.24 N | 15.36 E |
| Iglesia | 252 | 30.24 S | 69.13 W |
| Iglesias | 71 | 39.19 N | 8.32 E |
| Iglesiente ◆[1] | 71 | 39.18 N | 8.40 E |
| Igli | 148 | 30.25 N | 2.12 W |
| Iglino | 86 | 54.50 N | 56.26 E |
| Igloolik | 176 | 69.24 N | 81.49 W |
| Iglovo | 82 | 55.47 N | 36.40 E |
| Igls | 64 | 47.14 N | 11.25 E |
| Ignacio, Ca., U.S. | 226 | 38.05 N | 122.32 W |
| Ignacio, Co., U.S. | 200 | 37.06 N | 107.37 W |
| Ignacio de la Llave | 234 | 18.43 N | 95.59 W |
| Ignacio Zaragoza, Méx. | 232 | 29.35 N | 107.30 W |
| Ignacio Zaragoza, Méx. | 234 | 23.15 N | 98.50 W |
| Ignacio Zaragoza, Méx. | 234 | 23.55 N | 103.42 W |
| Ignalina | 76 | 55.21 N | 26.10 E |
| Ignaţei | 38 | 47.41 N | 28.40 E |
| Ignatjevcy | 80 | 57.32 N | 51.39 E |
| Ignatovka | 80 | 53.57 N | 47.38 E |
| Ignatovo | 82 | 56.10 N | 37.32 E |
| İğneada | 130 | 41.52 N | 27.58 E |
| İğneada Burnu > | 130 | 41.54 N | 28.03 E |
| Igney | 58 | 48.17 N | 6.24 E |
| Ignon ≃ | 58 | 47.31 N | 5.10 E |
| Igny | 261 | 48.45 N | 2.14 E |
| Igodovo | 80 | 58.01 N | 42.21 E |
| Igombe ≃ | 154 | 4.38 S | 31.40 E |
| Igoumenítsa | 38 | 39.30 N | 20.16 E |
| Igra | 80 | 57.33 N | 53.04 E |
| Igreja Nova | 250 | 10.07 S | 36.39 W |
| Iguaçu ≃, Bra. | 256 | 22.45 S | 43.14 W |
| Iguaçu ≃, S.A. | 252 | 25.36 S | 54.36 W |
| Iguaçu, Cataratas do (Iguassu Falls) L | 252 | 25.41 S | 54.26 W |
| Iguaçu, Parque Nacional do ♠ | 252 | 25.30 S | 53.50 W |
| Iguaí | 255 | 14.45 S | 40.04 W |
| Iguala | 234 | 18.21 N | 99.32 W |
| Igualada | 34 | 41.35 N | 1.38 E |
| Iguana ≃ | 246 | 7.54 N | 65.46 W |
| Iguape | 252 | 24.43 S | 47.33 W |
| Iguará ≃ | 250 | 3.28 S | 43.55 W |
| Iguassu Falls → Iguaçu, Cataratas 99do L | 252 | 25.41 S | 54.26 W |
| Iguatemi | 255 | 23.40 S | 54.34 W |
| Iguatemi ≃ | 255 | 23.55 S | 54.10 W |
| Iguatu | 250 | 6.22 S | 39.18 W |
| Iguazú, Parque Nacional ♠ | 252 | 25.35 S | 54.20 W |
| Iguéla | 152 | 1.55 S | 9.19 E |
| Iguéla, Lagune C | 152 | 1.55 S | 9.25 E |
| Iguetti, Sebkhet ≚ | 148 | 25.05 N | 9.50 W |
| Iguîdi, 'Erg ⊥[8] | 148 | 26.35 N | 5.40 W |
| Iguig | 116 | 17.45 N | 121.44 E |
| Igumale | 150 | 6.49 N | 7.59 E |
| Igumnovo | 82 | 55.37 N | 38.18 E |
| Igvak, Cape > | 180 | 57.26 N | 156.00 W |
| Igžej | 88 | 53.59 N | 103.10 E |
| Ihavandiffulu Atoll I[1] | 122 | 7.00 N | 72.55 E |
| Iheya-shima I | 93b | 27.04 N | 127.58 E |
| Ihiala | 150 | 5.51 N | 6.51 E |
| Ihirène, Oued V | 148 | 20.25 N | 4.35 E |
| Ihle ≃ | 54 | 52.17 N | 11.52 E |
| Ihlienworth | 52 | 53.44 N | 8.55 E |
| Ihlow | 52 | 53.25 N | 7.27 E |
| Ihmert | 56 | 51.20 N | 7.44 E |
| Ihnāsiyat al-Madīnah | 142 | 29.05 N | 30.56 E |
| Ihorombe | 157b | 23.00 S | 47.33 E |
| Ihosy | 157b | 22.24 S | 46.08 E |
| Ihosy ≃ | 157b | 21.44 S | 45.53 E |
| Ihotry, Lac ⊜ | 157b | 21.56 S | 43.41 E |
| Ihringen | 58 | 48.02 N | 7.39 E |
| Ihrlerstein | 60 | 48.56 N | 11.52 E |
| İhsangazi | 130 | 41.11 N | 33.33 E |
| Ih Tal | 89 | 43.13 N | 122.15 E |
| Ihtiman | 38 | 42.26 N | 23.49 E |
| Ihu | 164 | 7.55 S | 145.25 E |
| Ihugh | 150 | 7.02 N | 9.00 E |
| Ihwah | 142 | 29.03 N | 31.00 E |
| Iida | 94 | 35.31 N | 137.50 E |
| Iidaan | 144 | 6.06 N | 48.59 E |
| Iijima | 94 | 35.40 N | 137.56 E |
| Iijoki ≃ | 24 | 65.20 N | 25.17 E |
| Iiktu, gora ∧ | 86 | 49.51 N | 87.40 E |
| Iinan | 94 | 34.27 N | 136.24 E |
| Iinashi ≃ | 96 | 35.27 N | 133.13 E |
| Iioka | 94 | 35.42 N | 140.43 E |
| Iisaku | 76 | 59.06 N | 27.19 E |
| Iisalmi | 26 | 63.34 N | 27.11 E |
| Iisvesi | 26 | 62.40 N | 27.02 E |
| Iitaka | 94 | 34.26 N | 136.21 E |
| Iittala | 26 | 61.04 N | 24.10 E |
| Iiyama | 94 | 36.51 N | 138.22 E |
| Iizuka | 96 | 33.38 N | 130.41 E |
| Ij ≃ | 88 | 52.34 N | 96.10 E |
| Ija ≃ | 88 | 55.05 N | 101.05 E |
| Ijâfene ◆[2] | 134 | 20.30 N | 8.00 W |
| Ijaiye | 273a | 6.40 N | 3.18 E |
| Ijaji | 144 | 8.59 N | 37.13 E |
| Ijara | 154 | 1.36 S | 40.31 E |
| Ijebu-Igbo | 150 | 6.56 N | 4.01 E |
| Ijebu-Ode | 150 | 6.50 N | 3.56 E |
| Ijesa-Tedo | 273a | 6.30 N | 3.19 E |
| Ijin | 98 | 42.05 N | 130.08 E |
| Ijira | 94 | 35.31 N | 136.44 E |
| IJmuiden | 52 | 52.27 N | 4.36 E |
| Ijse ≃ | 56 | 50.49 N | 4.38 E |
| IJssel ≃ | 52 | 52.35 N | 5.50 E |
| IJsselmeer (Zuiderzee) ⊤[2] | 52 | 52.45 N | 5.25 E |
| IJsselmuiden | 52 | 52.34 N | 5.56 E |
| IJsselstein | 52 | 52.02 N | 5.03 E |
| Ijuí | 252 | 28.23 S | 53.55 W |
| Ijuí ≃ | 252 | 27.58 S | 55.20 W |
| Iju Junction | 273a | 6.40 N | 3.19 E |
| Ijuw | 174b | 0.30 S | 166.57 E |
| Iju Water Works ⊻[3] | 273a | 6.40 N | 3.20 E |
| IJzendijke | 52 | 51.19 N | 3.38 E |
| IJzer (Yser) ≃ | 50 | 51.09 N | 2.43 E |
| Ik ≃ | 80 | 55.55 N | 52.36 E |
| Ika | 88 | 59.18 N | 106.12 E |
| Ikaalinen | 26 | 61.46 N | 23.03 E |
| Ikaho | 94 | 36.30 N | 138.55 E |
| Ikalamavony | 157b | 21.09 S | 46.35 E |
| Ikali | 152 | 2.02 S | 21.02 E |
| Ikalou | 152 | 4.03 S | 11.48 E |
| Ikamatua | 172 | 42.16 S | 171.41 E |
| Ikamba | 273b | 4.22 S | 15.16 E |
| Ikang | 150 | 4.50 N | 8.32 E |
| Ikara | 150 | 11.12 N | 8.15 E |
| Ikare | 150 | 7.32 N | 5.45 E |
| Ikaría I | 38 | 37.41 N | 26.20 E |
| Ikari-dam ◆[6] | 94 | 36.52 N | 139.42 E |
| Ikari-ko ⊜ | 94 | 36.56 N | 139.41 E |
| Ikaruga | 96 | 34.36 N | 135.44 E |
| Ikast | 41 | 56.08 N | 9.10 E |
| Ikatan | 180 | 54.45 N | 163.19 W |
| Ikatskij chrebet ⋀ | 88 | 54.00 N | 111.00 E |
| Ikawa | 94 | 35.13 N | 138.15 E |
| Ikawa-dam ◆[6] | 94 | 35.12 N | 138.13 E |
| Ikawhenua Range ⋀ | 172 | 38.20 S | 176.56 E |
| Ikazaki | 96 | 33.32 N | 132.39 E |
| Ikeda, Nihon | 92a | 42.55 N | 143.27 E |
| Ikeda, Nihon | 94 | 35.53 N | 136.21 E |
| Ikeda, Nihon | 94 | 35.26 N | 136.34 E |
| Ikeda, Nihon | 94 | 36.25 N | 137.53 E |
| Ikeda, Nihon | 96 | 34.49 N | 135.25 E |
| Ikeda, Nihon | 96 | 34.01 N | 133.48 E |
| Ikegawa | 96 | 33.36 N | 133.11 E |
| Ikej | 88 | 54.12 N | 100.04 E |
| Ikeja | 150 | 6.36 N | 3.21 E |
| Ikela | 152 | 1.11 S | 23.16 E |
| Ikélemba | 152 | 1.14 S | 16.31 E |
| Ikelemba ≃ | 152 | 0.07 N | 18.17 E |
| Ikema-jima I | 175d | 24.56 N | 125.16 E |
| Ikerre | 150 | 7.31 N | 5.14 E |
| Ike-shima I | 174m | 26.23 N | 128.00 E |
| Ikeura | 270 | 34.30 N | 135.25 E |
| Iki I | 92 | 33.47 N | 129.43 E |
| Iki-Burul | 80 | 45.49 N | 44.39 E |
| Ikimba, Lake ⊜ | 154 | 1.28 S | 31.30 E |
| Īkinjī Maryūt | 142 | 31.00 N | 29.45 E |
| Ikire | 150 | 7.23 N | 4.12 E |
| Ikirun | 150 | 7.55 N | 4.41 E |
| İkizce | 130 | 39.36 N | 32.40 E |
| İkizdere | 130 | 40.47 N | 40.33 E |
| Iko | 152 | 0.35 S | 16.01 E |
| Ikole | 150 | 7.49 N | 5.30 E |
| Ikolik, Cape > | 180 | 57.17 N | 154.48 W |
| Ikom | 150 | 5.58 N | 8.42 E |
| Ikoma, Nihon | 96 | 34.41 N | 135.42 E |
| Ikoma, Tan. | 154 | 2.04 S | 34.37 E |
| Ikoma-sanchi ⋀ | 270 | 34.40 N | 135.40 E |
| Ikoma-tunnel ◆[5] | 270 | 34.41 N | 135.41 E |
| Ikoma-yama ∧ | 270 | 34.40 N | 135.41 E |
| Ikon-Chal' | 84 | 44.18 N | 41.55 E |
| Ikopa ≃ | 157b | 17.01 S | 46.45 E |
| Ikorec ≃ | 78 | 50.58 N | 39.45 E |
| Ikorodu | 150 | 6.37 N | 3.31 E |
| Ikot Ekpene | 150 | 5.12 N | 7.40 E |
| Ikoy ≃ | 152 | 0.53 S | 10.36 E |
| Ikoyi ◆[8] | 273a | 6.27 N | 3.26 E |
| Ikoyi Island I | 273a | 6.27 N | 3.26 E |
| Ikoyi Prison ⊻ | 273a | 6.25 N | 3.25 E |
| Ikozi | 154 | 2.32 S | 27.37 E |
| Ikpikpuk ≃ | 180 | 70.50 N | 154.25 W |
| Ikra | 126 | 23.42 N | 87.07 E |
| Ikr'anoje | 80 | 46.06 N | 47.45 E |
| Ikrāsh | 142 | 30.45 N | 31.30 E |
| Ikša | 82 | 56.10 N | 37.31 E |
| Iksa ≃ | 86 | 57.48 N | 82.36 E |
| Ikti, Cape > | 180 | 56.00 N | 158.30 W |
| Ikuata | 273a | 6.25 N | 3.22 E |
| Ikuchi-shima I | 96 | 34.17 N | 133.07 E |
| Ikuji-hana > | 94 | 36.54 N | 137.25 E |
| Ikuktlitlig Mountain ∧ | 180 | 59.16 N | 161.27 W |
| Ikungu | 154 | 1.34 S | 33.40 E |
| Ikuno | 96 | 35.10 N | 134.48 E |
| Ikuno ◆[8] | 270 | 34.39 N | 135.34 E |
| Ikurangi, Mount ∧[2] | 174k | 21.13 S | 159.45 W |
| Ikusaka | 94 | 36.25 N | 137.56 E |
| Ikusu ≃ | 273b | 4.24 S | 15.14 E |
| Ikuta | 268 | 35.36 N | 139.32 E |
| Ikva ≃, Magy. | 61 | 47.42 N | 16.58 E |
| Ikva ≃, Ukr. | 78 | 50.33 N | 25.24 E |
| Ikwah | 142 | 30.41 N | 31.28 E |
| Ila, Nig. | 150 | 8.01 N | 4.55 E |
| Ila, Zaïre | 152 | 2.53 S | 21.05 E |
| Ilabaya | 248 | 17.25 S | 70.31 W |
| Ilacaon Point > | 116 | 11.00 N | 123.12 E |
| Ilagala | 154 | 5.12 S | 29.50 E |
| Ilagan | 116 | 17.10 N | 121.54 E |
| Ilagan ≃ | 116 | 17.09 N | 121.54 E |
| Ilaiyānkudi | 122 | 9.38 N | 78.38 E |
| Ilaka, Madag. | 157b | 19.33 S | 48.52 E |
| Ilaka, Madag. | 157b | 20.20 S | 47.09 E |
| Īlām, Īrān | 128 | 33.38 N | 46.26 E |
| Ilām, Nepāl | 124 | 26.55 N | 87.56 E |
| Īlām □[4] | 128 | 33.15 N | 46.45 E |
| Ilam → Sri Lanka □[1] | 122 | 7.00 N | 81.00 E |
| Ilām Bāzār | 126 | 23.38 N | 87.32 E |
| Ilan | 100 | 24.46 N | 121.45 E |
| Ilan ≃ | 100 | 24.43 N | 121.49 E |
| Ilanskij | 88 | 56.14 N | 96.03 E |
| Ilanz | 58 | 46.46 N | 9.12 E |
| Ilara | 273a | 6.42 N | 3.27 E |
| Ilarionove | 78 | 48.25 N | 35.16 E |
| Ilaro | 150 | 6.53 N | 3.03 E |
| Ilasco | 219 | 39.40 N | 91.18 W |
| Ilave | 248 | 16.06 S | 69.41 W |
| Iława | 30 | 53.37 N | 19.33 E |
| Ilawe-Ekiti | 150 | 7.37 N | 5.06 E |
| Ilay | 58 | 46.37 N | 5.53 E |
| Ilbenge | 74 | 62.49 N | 124.24 E |
| Ilberstedt | 54 | 51.48 N | 11.40 E |
| Il Catalano I | 71 | 39.53 N | 8.17 E |
| Ilchester, Eng., U.K. | 42 | 51.01 N | 2.41 W |
| Ilchester, Md., U.S. | 284b | 39.15 N | 76.45 W |
| Ildefonso, Islas II | 254 | 55.44 S | 69.26 W |
| Île-à-la-Crosse | 184 | 55.27 N | 107.53 W |
| Île-à-la-Crosse, Lac ⊜ | 184 | 55.40 N | 107.45 W |
| Ilebo (Port-Francqui) | 152 | 4.19 S | 20.35 E |
| Île-Cadieux | 275a | 45.25 N | 74.01 W |
| Île-de-France □[9] | 50 | 49.00 N | 2.20 E |
| Île-de-Montréal □[6] | 206 | 45.30 N | 73.40 W |
| Île-Jésus □[6] | 206 | 45.35 N | 73.45 W |
| Ilek | 80 | 51.30 N | 53.22 E |
| Ilek ≃ | 72 | 51.30 N | 53.20 E |
| Ilen ≃ | 48 | 51.33 N | 9.19 W |
| Île-Perrot | 206 | 45.23 N | 73.57 W |
| Ileret | 154 | 4.19 N | 36.13 E |
| Îles, Grand lac des ⊜ | 206 | 46.43 N | 73.30 W |
| Îles, Lac des ⊜, P.Q., Can. | 206 | 46.06 N | 74.02 W |
| Îles, Lac des ⊜, Sk., Can. | 184 | 54.26 N | 109.25 W |
| Ilesha | 150 | 7.38 N | 4.45 E |
| Ilesha Ibarida | 150 | 8.56 N | 3.25 E |
| Îles Loyauté □[4] | 175f | 21.00 S | 167.00 E |
| Ilet' ≃ | 80 | 55.56 N | 48.14 E |
| Ilevskij Pogost | 24 | 60.41 N | 43.46 E |
| Ileza | 24 | 60.43 N | 43.54 E |
| Ilfeld | 54 | 51.34 N | 10.47 E |
| Ilford, Austl. | 170 | 32.58 S | 149.51 E |
| Ilford, Mb., Can. | 184 | 56.04 N | 95.35 W |
| Ilford ◆[8] | 260 | 51.33 N | 0.05 E |
| Ilfracombe, Austl. | 166 | 23.30 S | 144.30 E |
| Ilfracombe, Eng., U.K. | 42 | 51.13 N | 4.08 W |
| Il Fuorn | 58 | 46.40 N | 10.12 E |
| Ilga ≃ | 88 | 55.00 N | 105.04 E |
| Ilgaz | 130 | 40.56 N | 33.38 E |
| Ilgaz Dağları ⋀ | 130 | 41.00 N | 33.35 E |
| Ilgın | 130 | 38.17 N | 31.55 E |
| Ilha ◆[8] | 256 | 23.00 S | 43.33 W |
| Ilhabela | 256 | 23.47 S | 45.21 W |
| Ilha das Flores | 250 | 10.27 S | 36.33 W |
| Ilha Grande, Baía da C | 256 | 23.09 S | 44.30 W |
| Ilhas, Cachoeira das L | 250 | 1.03 S | 57.33 W |
| Ilha Solteira, Reprêsa de ⊜[1] | 255 | 20.20 S | 51.20 W |
| Ilhavo | 34 | 40.36 N | 8.40 W |
| Ilhea Point > | 156 | 23.25 S | 14.27 E |
| Ilhéos → Ilhéus | 255 | 14.49 S | 39.02 W |
| Ilhéus | 255 | 14.49 S | 39.02 W |
| Ili ≃ | 86 | 45.24 N | 74.02 E |
| Ilia | 38 | 45.56 N | 22.39 E |
| Iliamna | 180 | 59.45 N | 154.54 W |
| Iliamna Lake ⊜ | 180 | 59.30 N | 155.00 W |
| Ilian, Mount ∧ | 116 | 10.26 N | 119.33 E |
| Iliatenco | 234 | 16.58 N | 98.40 W |
| Il'ič, Kaz. | 85 | 40.50 N | 68.27 E |
| İliç, Tür. | 130 | 39.28 N | 38.34 E |
| Ilıca, Tür. | 130 | 39.52 N | 27.46 E |
| Ilıca, Tür. | 130 | 39.57 N | 41.07 E |
| Ilicínia | 255 | 20.56 S | 45.50 W |
| Iliff | 198 | 40.45 N | 103.03 W |
| Iliff, Lake ⊜ | 276 | 41.02 N | 74.43 W |
| Iligan | 116 | 8.14 N | 124.14 E |
| Iligan Bay C | 116 | 8.25 N | 124.05 E |
| Ilijan | 116 | 13.38 N | 121.04 E |
| Ilijsk | 85 | 43.53 N | 77.10 E |
| Ilim ≃ | 88 | 57.38 N | 102.34 E |
| Ilimsk | 88 | 56.46 N | 103.52 E |
| Ilin | 116 | 12.15 N | 121.02 E |
| Ilinge | 158 | 31.59 S | 27.02 E |
| Ilin Island I | 116 | 12.14 N | 121.05 E |
| Ilinka | 82 | 54.04 N | 38.12 E |
| Ilinza ∧ | 246 | 0.40 S | 78.42 W |
| Ilion | 210 | 43.00 N | 75.02 W |
| Ilio Point > | 229a | 21.13 N | 157.15 W |
| Ilioúpolis | 267c | 37.56 N | 23.45 E |
| Ilir | 88 | 55.13 N | 100.40 E |
| Ilirska Bistrica | 36 | 45.34 N | 14.15 E |
| Ilisós ≃ | 267c | 37.57 N | 23.41 E |
| Ilizi | 148 | 26.29 N | 8.28 E |
| Il'ja | 76 | 54.25 N | 27.18 E |
| Iljak | 86 | 60.11 N | 77.59 E |
| Iljinka | 80 | 48.32 N | 41.05 E |
| Iljino | 76 | 55.57 N | 31.40 E |
| Iljinskij, Ross. | 24 | 61.02 N | 32.41 E |


**Symbols** in the index entries represent the broad categories identified in the key at the right. Symbols with superior numbers (⋀[1]) identify subcategories (see complete key on page *I · 1)*.

**Symbole** im Register stellen die rechts im Schlüssel erklärten Kategorien dar. Symbole mit hochgestellten Ziffern (⋀[1]) bezeichnen Unterabteilungen einer Kategorie (vgl. vollständiger Schlüssel auf Seite *I · 1)*.

**Los símbolos** incluídos en el texto del índice representan las grandes categorías identificadas con la clave a la derecha. Los símbolos con numeros en su parte superior (⋀[1]) identifican las subcategorías (véase la clave completa en la página *I · 1)*.

**Les symboles** de l'index représentent les catégories indiquées dans la légende à droite. Les symboles suivis d'un indice (⋀[1]) représentent des sous-catégories (voir légende complète à la page *I · 1)*.

**Os símbolos** incluídos no texto do índice representam as grandes categorias identificadas com a chave à direita. Os símbolos com números em sua parte superior (⋀[1]) identificam as subcategorias (veja-se a chave completa à página *I · 1)*.

| | English | Deutsch | Español | Français | Português |
|---|---|---|---|---|---|
| ∧ | Mountain | Berg | Montaña | Montagne | Montanha |
| ⋀ | Mountains | Gebirge | Montañas | Montagnes | Montanhas |
| )( | Pass | Paß | Paso | Col | Passo |
| V | Valley, Canyon | Tal, Cañon | Valle, Cañón | Vallée, Canyon | Vale, Canhão |
| ≚ | Plain | Ebene | Llano | Plaine | Planície |
| > | Cape | Kap | Cabo | Cap | Cabo |
| I | Island | Insel | Isla | Île | Ilha |
| II | Islands | Inseln | Islas | Îles | Ilhas |
| ⊥ | Other Topographic Features | Andere Topographische Objekte | Otros Elementos Topográficos | Autres données topographiques | Outros acidentes topográficos |

| Nombre | Página | Lat.°' | Long.°' W = Oeste |
|---|---|---|---|
| Iljinskij, Ross. | 86 | 58.35 N | 55.41 E |
| Iljinskij, Ross. | 88 | 52.05 N | 114.10 E |
| Iljinskij, Ross. | 89 | 47.58 N | 142.12 E |
| Iljinskij, Ross. | 265b | 55.37 N | 38.06 E |
| Iljinskij Pogost | 82 | 55.28 N | 38.54 E |
| Iljinskoje, Ross. | 76 | 56.58 N | 37.11 E |
| Iljinskoje, Ross. | 76 | 58.47 N | 44.36 E |
| Iljinskoje, Ross. | 76 | 53.14 N | 35.26 E |
| Iljinskoje, Ross. | 76 | 57.19 N | 38.32 E |
| Iljinskoje, Ross. | 80 | 56.29 N | 52.49 E |
| Iljinskoje, Ross. | 82 | 54.59 N | 36.11 E |
| Iljinskoje, Ross. | 82 | 56.34 N | 35.57 E |
| Iljinskoje, Ross. | 265b | 55.46 N | 37.15 E |
| Iljinskoje-Chovanskoje | 80 | 56.58 N | 39.46 E |
| Iljinsko-Podomskoje | 24 | 61.08 N | 47.56 E |
| Iljinsko-Zaborskoje | 80 | 57.16 N | 44.23 E |
| Iljiny gory ⩘[2] | 76 | 56.34 N | 34.12 E |
| Il'ka | 88 | 51.43 N | 108.32 E |
| Ilkal | 122 | 15.58 N | 76.08 E |
| Ilkeston | 42 | 52.59 N | 1.18 W |
| Il'kino | 80 | 55.13 N | 41.36 E |
| Ilkley | 44 | 53.55 N | 1.50 W |
| Ill ≃, Fr. | 58 | 48.40 N | 7.53 E |
| Ill ≃, Öst. | 58 | 47.17 N | 9.33 E |
| Illabot Creek ≃ | 224 | 48.29 N | 121.30 W |
| Illampu, Nevado ∧ | 248 | 15.50 S | 68.34 W |
| Illana Bay ⊂ | 116 | 7.25 N | 123.45 E |
| Illapel | 252 | 31.38 S | 71.10 W |
| Illasi | 64 | 45.28 N | 11.10 E |
| Illawarra, Lake ⊂ | 170 | 34.32 S | 150.50 E |
| Illbillee, Mount ∧ | 162 | 27.02 S | 132.30 E |
| Ille-et-Vilaine □[5] | 32 | 48.10 N | 1.30 W |
| Illéla | 150 | 14.28 N | 5.15 E |
| Iller ≃ | 58 | 48.23 N | 9.58 E |
| Illerkirchberg | 58 | 48.20 N | 10.00 E |
| Illertissen | 58 | 48.13 N | 10.06 E |
| Illescas, Esp. | 34 | 40.07 N | 3.50 W |
| Illescas, Méx. | 234 | 23.13 N | 102.07 W |
| Illfurth | 58 | 47.40 N | 7.16 E |
| Illhaeusern | 58 | 48.11 N | 7.26 E |
| Illi, Ba ≃ | 146 | 10.44 N | 15.21 E |
| Illichivs'k | 78 | 46.18 N | 30.39 E |
| Illiers | 50 | 48.18 N | 1.15 E |
| Illimani, Nevado ∧ | 248 | 16.50 S | 67.54 W |
| Illimo | 248 | 6.28 S | 79.51 W |
| Illingen, Dtsch. | 56 | 48.57 N | 8.55 E |
| Illingen, Dtsch. | 56 | 49.23 N | 7.03 E |
| Illingworth | 262 | 53.45 N | 1.54 W |
| Illinois □[3], U.S. | 178 | 40.00 N | 89.00 W |
| Illinois □[3], U.S. | 194 | 40.00 N | 89.00 W |
| Illinois ≃, U.S. | 194 | 35.30 N | 95.06 W |
| Illinois ≃, Co., U.S. | 200 | 40.45 N | 106.18 W |
| Illinois ≃, Il., U.S. | 194 | 38.58 N | 90.27 W |
| Illinois ≃, Or., U.S. | 202 | 42.33 N | 124.03 W |
| Illinois and Michigan Canal ≍ | 278 | 41.32 N | 88.05 W |
| Illinois at Chicago, University of ʋ[2] | 278 | 41.52 N | 87.39 W |
| Illinois Beach State Park ♦ | 216 | 42.26 N | 87.48 W |
| Illinois Institute of Technology ʋ[2] | 278 | 41.50 N | 87.38 W |
| Illinois Peak ∧ | 202 | 47.02 N | 115.04 W |
| Illintsi | 78 | 49.07 N | 29.12 E |
| Illiopolis | 219 | 39.51 N | 89.14 W |
| Illkirch-Graffenstaden | 58 | 48.32 N | 7.43 E |
| Illminster | 42 | 50.56 N | 2.55 W |
| Illo | 150 | 11.33 N | 3.42 E |
| Illovo, S. Afr. | 158 | 30.05 S | 30.50 E |
| Illovo, S. Afr. | 273d | 26.08 S | 28.03 E |
| Illzach | 58 | 47.47 N | 7.20 E |
| Ilm ≃, Dtsch. | 54 | 51.07 N | 11.40 E |
| Ilm ≃, Dtsch. | 60 | 48.49 N | 11.45 E |
| Ilmajoki | 26 | 62.44 N | 22.34 E |
| Il'men', ozero ⊜ | 76 | 58.17 N | 31.20 E |
| Ilmenau | 54 | 50.41 N | 10.55 E |
| Ilmenau ≃ | 54 | 53.23 N | 10.10 E |
| Il'menskij zapovednik ♦ | 86 | 55.16 N | 60.17 E |
| Il'mino | 80 | 53.47 N | 45.40 E |
| Ilo | 248 | 17.38 S | 71.20 W |
| Ilobasco | 236 | 13.51 N | 88.51 W |
| Ilobu | 150 | 7.51 N | 4.30 E |
| Iloc Island I | 116 | 11.18 N | 119.41 E |
| Ilocos Norte □[4] | 116 | 18.10 N | 120.45 E |
| Ilocos Sur □[4] | 116 | 17.05 N | 120.35 E |
| Iloilo | 116 | 10.42 N | 122.34 E |
| Iloilo □[4] | 116 | 11.00 N | 122.35 E |
| Iloilo Strait ʮ | 116 | 10.43 N | 122.36 E |
| Ilomantsi | 24 | 62.40 N | 30.55 E |
| Ilondola Mission | 154 | 10.42 S | 31.47 E |
| Ilongero | 154 | 4.40 S | 34.52 E |
| Ilop | 164 | 2.54 S | 141.13 E |
| Ilopango, Lago de ⊜ | 236 | 13.40 N | 89.03 W |
| Ilora | 150 | 7.45 N | 3.50 E |
| Ilorin | 150 | 8.30 N | 4.32 E |
| Ilovatka | 80 | 50.31 N | 45.55 E |
| Ilovays'k | 83 | 47.56 N | 38.13 E |
| Ilovka | 78 | 50.43 N | 38.38 E |
| Ilovl'a | 80 | 49.18 N | 43.59 E |
| Ilovl'a ≃ | 80 | 49.14 N | 43.54 E |
| Iłowa | 30 | 51.30 N | 15.12 E |
| Il Palone ∧ | 64 | 46.02 N | 11.04 E |
| Il'pyrskij | 74 | 59.56 N | 164.10 E |
| Ilsan-ni | 271b | 37.41 N | 126.46 E |
| Ilse ≃ | 54 | 52.06 N | 10.35 E |
| Ilsenburg | 54 | 51.52 N | 10.41 E |
| Ilshofen | 56 | 49.10 N | 9.55 E |
| Il'skij | 78 | 44.51 N | 38.35 E |
| Ilskov | 41 | 56.14 N | 9.06 E |
| Il Telegrafo ∧ | 66 | 42.22 N | 11.10 E |
| Ilten | 52 | 52.21 N | 9.55 E |
| Ilu | 152 | 4.12 N | 23.02 E |
| Ilubabor □[4] | 144 | 7.50 N | 35.00 E |
| Iluhār | 126 | 22.48 N | 90.06 E |
| Ilūkste | 76 | 55.58 N | 26.18 E |
| Ilverich | 263 | 51.17 N | 6.42 E |
| Ilwaco | 224 | 46.19 N | 124.03 W |
| Ilwaki | 112 | 7.56 S | 126.26 E |
| Ilwŏl-san ∧ | 98 | 36.50 N | 129.06 E |
| Ilyasbey | 130 | 40.13 N | 29.52 E |
| Ilz | 61 | 47.05 N | 15.55 E |
| Ilz ≃ | 60 | 48.35 N | 13.29 E |
| Iłża | 30 | 51.11 N | 21.14 E |
| Ima | 88 | 55.13 N | 115.55 E |
| Ima ≃ | 96 | 33.45 N | 131.01 E |
| Imabari | 96 | 34.03 N | 133.00 E |
| Imabu ≃ | 250 | 0.44 S | 57.22 W |
| Imadomi | 268 | 35.28 N | 140.06 E |
| Imaichi | 94 | 36.43 N | 139.41 E |
| Imajō | 94 | 35.46 N | 136.12 E |
| Imajuku | 268 | 35.58 N | 139.21 E |
| Imajuku ◆[8] | 268 | 35.29 N | 139.32 E |
| Imaki | 270 | 34.24 N | 135.46 E |
| Imaloto ≃ | 157b | 23.27 S | 45.13 E |
| Imambara ʋ[1] | 272b | 22.54 N | 88.25 E |
| Imanbaj ⊥ | 86 | 43.13 N | 60.25 E |
| Imandan-Makit, gora ∧ | 88 | 54.07 N | 117.43 E |
| Imandra, ozero ⊜ | 24 | 67.30 N | 33.00 E |
| Imanombo | 157b | 24.26 S | 45.49 E |
| Imantau | 86 | 52.58 N | 68.22 E |
| Imari | 92 | 33.16 N | 129.53 E |
| Imaruí | 252 | 28.21 S | 48.49 W |
| Imaruí, Lagoa do ⊂ | 252 | 28.21 S | 48.52 W |
| Imasa | 140 | 18.01 N | 36.12 E |
| Imatra | 26 | 61.10 N | 28.46 E |
| Imavere | 76 | 58.44 N | 25.48 E |
| Imazu | 94 | 35.24 N | 136.02 E |
| Imbābah ◆[8] | 142 | 30.04 N | 31.13 E |
| Imbabura □[4] | 246 | 0.22 N | 78.25 W |
| Imba-numa ⊜ | 94 | 35.45 N | 140.12 E |
| Imbariê | 256 | 22.39 S | 43.13 W |
| Imbituba | 252 | 28.14 S | 48.40 W |
| Imbituva | 252 | 25.12 S | 50.35 W |
| Imboaçu, Canal ≍ | 287a | 22.48 S | 43.04 W |
| Imboden | 194 | 36.12 N | 91.10 W |
| Imbonga | 152 | 0.43 S | 19.46 E |
| Imbundi | 152 | 5.44 S | 16.16 E |
| Ime, Beinn ∧ | 46 | 56.14 N | 4.49 W |
| Imeni Babuškina | 76 | 59.45 N | 43.07 E |
| Imeni Čapajeva | 85 | 43.28 N | 76.50 E |
| Imeni C'urupy | 82 | 55.30 N | 38.39 E |
| Imeni Džambula, Kaz. | 86 | 45.26 N | 74.24 E |
| Imeni Džambula, Kaz. | 86 | 47.43 N | 74.09 E |
| Imeni Frunze | 86 | 46.23 N | 77.20 E |
| Imeni Il-Go Okt'abr'a | 88 | 55.54 N | 119.36 E |
| Imeni Kalinina, Kaz. | 85 | 43.16 N | 74.03 E |
| Imeni Kalinina, Kyrg. | 85 | 41.28 N | 76.22 E |
| Imeni Kalinina, Ross. | 80 | 51.51 N | 52.43 E |
| Imeni Kalinina, Uzb. | 86 | 43.40 N | 59.07 E |
| Imeni Karla Libknechta | 78 | 51.37 N | 35.27 E |
| Imeni Kirova, Kaz. | 86 | 46.27 N | 77.13 E |
| Imeni Kirova, Ross. | 74 | 59.42 N | 128.12 E |
| Imeni Leninskogo Komsomola | 86 | 50.45 N | 66.44 E |
| Imeni Marta | 86 | 46.57 N | 58.58 E |
| Imeni Michajla Ivanoviča Kalinina | 80 | 57.59 N | 45.07 E |
| Imeni Panfilova | 85 | 43.23 N | 77.07 E |
| Imeni Poliny Osipenko | 89 | 52.25 N | 136.28 E |
| Imeni Sardarova Karachana | 85 | 38.26 N | 68.46 E |
| Imeni Şeredy | 83 | 46.52 N | 40.03 E |
| Imeni Ševčenko | 86 | 45.58 N | 61.04 E |
| Imeni Stepana Razina | 80 | 54.54 N | 44.18 E |
| Imeni Tel'mana | 89 | 48.36 N | 134.59 E |
| Imeni Vladimira Iljiča Lenina | 80 | 53.36 N | 46.58 E |
| Imeni Vorovskogo, Ross. | 80 | 55.43 N | 41.06 E |
| Imeni Vorovskogo, Ross. | 82 | 55.43 N | 38.20 E |
| Imeni XXI Partsjezda | 86 | 50.43 N | 67.50 E |
| Imeni Žel'abova | 76 | 58.57 N | 36.36 E |
| Imera ⊥ | 70 | 37.59 N | 13.49 E |
| Imerimandroso | 157b | 17.23 S | 48.38 E |
| Imese | 152 | 2.07 N | 18.06 E |
| Imgenbroich | 56 | 50.34 N | 6.16 E |
| Imi | 144 | 6.28 N | 42.18 E |
| Imías | 240p | 20.04 N | 74.38 W |
| Imilac | 252 | 24.14 S | 68.53 W |
| Imilili ⫪[4] | 148 | 23.18 N | 15.54 W |
| Imi-n'Tanout | 148 | 31.10 N | 8.50 W |
| İmişli | 84 | 39.52 N | 48.04 E |
| Imittós | 267c | 37.57 N | 23.45 E |
| Imittós Óros ⩘ | 267c | 37.55 N | 23.47 E |
| Imja-do I | 98 | 35.05 N | 126.05 E |
| Imjin-gang ≃ | 98 | 37.47 N | 126.40 E |
| Imlay | 204 | 40.39 N | 118.08 W |
| Imlay City | 190 | 43.01 N | 83.04 W |
| Imlaystown | 208 | 40.10 N | 74.31 W |
| Imler | 214 | 40.12 N | 78.31 W |
| Immarna | 162 | 30.30 S | 132.09 E |
| Immendingen | 58 | 47.56 N | 8.44 E |
| Immenhausen | 56 | 51.25 N | 9.28 E |
| Immensen | 52 | 52.23 N | 10.04 E |
| Immenstaad | 58 | 47.40 N | 9.22 E |
| Immenstadt | 58 | 47.33 N | 10.13 E |
| Immigrath | 263 | 51.06 N | 6.57 E |
| Immingham | 44 | 53.36 N | 0.13 W |
| Immokalee | 220 | 26.25 N | 81.25 W |
| Imnaha ≃ | 202 | 45.49 N | 116.46 W |
| Imo ≃ | 150 | 4.36 N | 7.35 E |
| Imogiri | 115a | 7.55 S | 110.23 E |
| Imokt'an | 98 | 38.50 N | 126.41 E |
| Imola | 66 | 44.21 N | 11.42 E |
| Imonda | 164 | 3.20 S | 141.10 E |
| Imore | 273a | 6.26 N | 3.17 E |
| Imoro | 273a | 6.43 N | 3.30 E |
| Im Ostholz ◆[8] | 263 | 51.26 N | 7.12 E |
| Imotski | 36 | 43.27 N | 17.13 E |
| Imp'a | 98 | 35.59 N | 126.49 E |
| Impasugong | 116 | 8.19 N | 125.00 E |
| Impe | 152 | 2.44 S | 15.17 E |
| Impendle | 158 | 29.37 S | 29.55 E |
| Imperatore, Campo ⊓ | 66 | 42.25 N | 13.40 E |
| Imperatriz | 250 | 5.32 S | 47.29 W |
| Imperia | 62 | 43.53 N | 8.03 E |
| Imperia □[4] | 62 | 43.58 N | 7.47 E |
| Imperial, Sk., Can. | 184 | 51.22 N | 105.27 W |
| Imperial, Perú | 248 | 13.04 S | 76.21 W |
| Imperial, Ca., U.S. | 204 | 32.50 N | 115.34 W |
| Imperial, Mo., U.S. | 219 | 38.22 N | 90.22 W |
| Imperial, Ne., U.S. | 198 | 40.31 N | 101.38 W |
| Imperial, Pa., U.S. | 214 | 40.26 N | 80.14 W |
| Imperial, Tx., U.S. | 196 | 31.16 N | 102.41 W |
| Imperial ≃ | 254 | 38.48 S | 73.24 W |
| Imperial Beach | 228 | 32.35 N | 117.06 W |
| Imperial Dam ◆[6] | 204 | 32.55 N | 114.30 W |
| Imperial de Aragón, Canal ≍ | 34 | 42.02 N | 1.33 W |
| Imperiale | 68 | 40.07 N | 16.35 E |
| Imperial Mills | 182 | 55.00 N | 111.44 W |
| Imperial Palace ʋ | 268 | 35.41 N | 139.45 E |
| Imperial Valley V | 204 | 32.50 N | 115.30 W |
| Impflingen | 56 | 49.10 N | 8.07 E |
| Impfondo | 152 | 1.37 N | 18.04 E |
| Imphāl | 120 | 24.49 N | 93.57 E |
| Impilachti | 24 | 61.40 N | 31.04 E |
| Impruneta | 66 | 43.41 N | 11.15 E |
| Impulo | 152 | 13.53 S | 13.39 E |
| İmralı Adası I | 130 | 40.32 N | 28.32 E |
| İmranlı | 130 | 39.54 N | 38.07 E |
| Imroz | 130 | 40.11 N | 25.55 E |
| Imsil | 98 | 35.37 N | 127.15 E |
| Imst | 64 | 47.14 N | 10.44 E |
| Imtān | 132 | 32.24 N | 36.49 E |
| Imuris | 232 | 30.47 N | 110.52 W |
| Imuruan Bay ⊂ | 116 | 10.40 N | 119.16 E |
| Imuruk Basin ⊜ | 180 | 65.06 N | 165.36 W |
| Imuruk Lake ⊜ | 180 | 65.36 N | 163.10 W |
| Imute | 273a | 6.42 N | 3.29 E |
| Imwŏn-ni | 98 | 37.15 N | 129.20 E |
| Ina, Nihon | 94 | 37.10 N | 139.32 E |
| Ina, Nihon | 94 | 35.59 N | 140.03 E |
| Ina, Nihon | 94 | 35.50 N | 137.57 E |
| Ina, Nihon | 268 | 35.59 N | 139.38 E |
| In'a, Ross. | 74 | 59.24 N | 144.48 E |
| In'a, Ross. | 86 | 53.31 N | 82.40 E |
| In'a, Ross. | 86 | 50.48 N | 86.37 E |
| Ina, Il., U.S. | 194 | 38.09 N | 88.54 W |
| Ina ≃, Nihon | 94 | 37.16 N | 139.33 E |
| Ina ≃, Nihon | 96 | 34.43 N | 135.28 E |
| Ina ≃, Pol. | 54 | 53.32 N | 14.38 E |
| In'a ≃, Ross. | 74 | 59.23 N | 144.54 E |
| In'a ≃, Ross. | 86 | 54.59 N | 82.59 E |
| Inaba | 270 | 34.26 N | 135.27 E |
| Inabe | 94 | 35.07 N | 136.33 E |
| Ina-bonchi ⊓[1] | 94 | 35.45 N | 137.57 E |
| Inabu | 94 | 35.13 N | 137.30 E |
| Inaccessible Island I | 10 | 37.17 S | 12.45 W |
| Inada | 270 | 34.54 N | 135.08 E |
| Inagawa | 96 | 34.53 N | 135.22 E |
| Inagawan | 116 | 9.33 N | 118.39 E |
| Inage | 268 | 35.38 N | 140.05 E |
| Inagi | 94 | 35.38 N | 139.30 E |
| Inajá | 250 | 8.54 S | 37.49 W |
| Inajá ≃ | 250 | 8.53 S | 49.44 W |
| In'akino | 80 | 54.26 N | 41.07 E |
| Inakona | 175e | 9.49 S | 160.02 E |
| Inala | 171a | 27.35 S | 152.58 E |
| Inamangando ≃ | 152 | 14.03 S | 12.23 E |
| Inambari ≃ | 248 | 12.41 S | 69.44 W |
| In Amguel | 148 | 23.40 N | 5.10 E |
| Inami, Nihon | 94 | 36.33 N | 136.58 E |
| Inami, Nihon | 96 | 34.45 N | 134.54 E |
| Inami, Nihon | 96 | 33.48 N | 135.13 E |
| In Amnas | 148 | 28.05 N | 9.30 E |
| Inampulugan Island I | 116 | 10.28 N | 122.42 E |
| Inamuragasaki Point ⊥ | 268 | 35.18 N | 139.32 E |
| Inanda | 273d | 26.07 S | 28.03 E |
| Inangahua Junction | 172 | 41.51 S | 171.57 E |
| Inanwatan | 164 | 2.08 S | 132.10 E |
| Iñapari | 248 | 10.57 S | 69.35 W |
| Inaporok | 164 | 8.15 S | 141.55 E |
| In'aptuk, gora ∧ | 88 | 56.22 N | 110.11 E |
| Inari | 24 | 68.54 N | 27.01 E |
| Inarigda | 74 | 63.14 N | 107.27 E |
| Inarijärvi ⊜ | 24 | 69.00 N | 28.00 E |
| Inas, Gunong ∧ | 114 | 5.15 N | 100.56 E |
| Inasa | 94 | 34.50 N | 137.40 E |
| Inatsuki | 96 | 33.36 N | 130.43 E |
| Inauini ≃ | 248 | 8.30 S | 67.24 W |
| Inawaia | 164 | 8.40 S | 146.35 E |
| Inawashiro-ko ⊜ | 92 | 37.29 N | 140.06 E |
| I-n-Azaoua ⫪[4] | 148 | 20.49 N | 7.30 E |
| Inazawa | 94 | 35.15 N | 136.47 E |
| Inba | 94 | 35.46 N | 140.14 E |
| Inba-numa ⊜ | 94 | 35.46 N | 140.12 E |
| In Belbel | 148 | 27.54 N | 1.10 E |
| Inca | 34 | 39.43 N | 2.54 E |
| Inca de Oro | 252 | 26.45 S | 69.54 W |
| Incaguasi | 252 | 29.13 S | 71.03 W |
| Incahuasi, Nevado de ∧ | 252 | 27.02 S | 68.18 W |
| Ince | 262 | 53.17 N | 2.49 W |
| Ince Blundell | 262 | 53.31 N | 3.02 W |
| İnce Burun › | 130 | 42.06 N | 34.56 E |
| Ince-in-Makerfield | 262 | 53.32 N | 2.37 W |
| İncekum Burnu › | 130 | 36.13 N | 33.58 E |
| İncesu | 130 | 38.38 N | 35.11 E |
| Inch | 48 | 52.08 N | 9.59 W |
| I-n-Chaouag ≃ | 150 | 16.23 N | 0.10 E |
| Inchard, Loch ⊂ | 46 | 58.27 N | 5.04 W |
| Inchas Military Base ■ | 142 | 30.20 N | 31.27 E |
| Inchbare | 46 | 56.47 N | 2.38 W |
| Inchcape I[2] | 46 | 56.26 N | 2.23 W |
| Inchelium | 182 | 48.17 N | 118.11 W |
| Inchiri □[4] | 150 | 19.50 N | 15.00 W |
| Inchmarnock I | 46 | 55.47 N | 5.09 W |
| Inchnadamph | 46 | 58.09 N | 4.59 W |
| Inch'ŏn | 98 | 37.28 N | 126.38 E |
| Inch'ŏn □[4] | 98 | 37.28 N | 126.38 E |
| Inchture | 46 | 56.26 N | 3.10 W |
| Inchwagh Lake ⊜ | 281 | 42.27 N | 83.41 W |
| İncirliova | 130 | 37.50 N | 27.43 E |
| Incisa in Val d'Arno | 66 | 43.40 N | 11.27 E |
| Incline Village | 226 | 39.16 N | 119.56 W |
| Incomáti (Komati) ≃ | 156 | 25.46 S | 32.43 E |
| Inconfidência | 256 | 22.16 S | 43.13 W |
| Inconfidentes | 256 | 22.20 S | 46.20 W |
| Inčoun | 180 | 66.18 N | 170.17 W |
| Incudine | 64 | 46.14 N | 10.22 E |
| Incudine, Monte ∧ | 36 | 41.51 N | 9.12 E |
| Incy | 24 | 65.48 N | 40.26 E |
| Indaal, Loch ⊂ | 46 | 55.45 N | 6.21 W |
| Indaiá ≃ | 255 | 18.27 S | 45.22 W |
| Indaiatuba | 256 | 23.05 S | 47.14 W |
| Indalsälven ≃ | 26 | 62.31 N | 17.27 E |
| Indanan | 116 | 5.58 N | 120.59 E |
| Indaparapeo | 234 | 19.47 N | 100.58 W |
| Inda Silase | 144 | 14.05 N | 38.20 E |
| Indaw | 110 | 23.40 N | 94.46 E |
| Indawgyi Lake ⊜ | 110 | 25.10 N | 96.19 E |
| Indé | 232 | 25.54 N | 105.13 W |
| Inde → India □[1] | 118 | 20.00 N | 77.00 E |
| Inde ≃ | 56 | 50.54 N | 6.21 E |
| Indemini | 58 | 46.06 N | 8.50 E |
| Inden | 56 | 50.52 N | 6.21 E |
| Independence, Ca., U.S. | 204 | 36.48 N | 118.11 W |
| Independence, In., U.S. | 216 | 40.20 N | 87.10 W |
| Independence, Ia., U.S. | 190 | 42.28 N | 91.53 W |
| Independence, Ks., U.S. | 198 | 37.13 N | 95.42 W |
| Independence, Ky., U.S. | 218 | 38.56 N | 84.32 W |
| Independence, La., U.S. | 194 | 30.38 N | 90.30 W |
| Independence, Mo., U.S. | 194 | 39.05 N | 94.24 W |
| Independence, Oh., U.S. | 279a | 41.23 N | 81.38 W |
| Independence, Or., U.S. | 202 | 44.51 N | 123.11 W |
| Independence, Pa., U.S. | 214 | 40.15 N | 80.31 W |
| Independence, Tx., U.S. | 222 | 30.19 N | 96.21 W |
| Independence, Va., U.S. | 192 | 36.37 N | 81.09 W |
| Independence, Wi., U.S. | 190 | 44.21 N | 91.25 W |
| Independence ≃ | 188 | 43.45 N | 75.20 W |
| Independence Creek ≃ | 196 | 30.27 N | 101.44 W |
| Independence Hall ⊥ | 285 | 39.57 N | 75.09 W |
| Independence Lake ⊜[1] | 226 | 39.26 N | 120.18 W |
| Independence Mountains ⩘ | 204 | 41.15 N | 115.55 W |
| Independencia, Bol. | 248 | 17.07 S | 66.53 W |
| Independência, Bra. | 250 | 5.23 S | 40.19 W |
| Independencia, Chile | 286e | 33.23 S | 70.40 W |
| Independencia, Perú | 286d | 11.59 S | 77.02 W |
| Independencia, Isla I | 248 | 14.15 S | 76.12 W |
| Independenţa | 38 | 43.58 N | 28.05 E |
| Inder, ozero ⊜ | 80 | 48.27 N | 51.54 E |
| Inderborskij | 80 | 48.33 N | 51.44 E |
| In der Bredde | 263 | 51.20 N | 7.23 E |
| İnderesi | 130 | 37.50 N | 35.40 E |
| Index | 224 | 47.49 N | 121.33 W |
| Index, Mount ∧ | 224 | 47.46 N | 121.35 W |
| Indi | 122 | 17.10 N | 75.58 E |
| India (Bhārat) □[1] | 118 | 20.00 N | 77.00 E |
| India Brook ≃ | 276 | 40.47 N | 74.37 W |
| India Gate ⊥ | 272a | 28.37 N | 77.18 E |
| Indialantic | 220 | 28.05 N | 80.34 W |
| Indian ≃, On., Can. | 212 | 45.16 N | 76.14 W |
| Indian ≃, On., Can. | 212 | 44.13 N | 78.08 W |
| Indian ≃, De., U.S. | 208 | 38.36 N | 75.10 W |
| Indian ≃, Ma., U.S. | 283 | 42.47 N | 70.58 W |
| Indian ≃, Mi., U.S. | 190 | 45.59 N | 86.15 W |
| Indian ≃, N.Y., U.S. | 212 | 44.24 N | 75.39 W |
| Indiana | 214 | 40.37 N | 79.09 W |
| Indiana □[6] | 214 | 40.37 N | 79.09 W |
| Indiana □[3], U.S. | 178 | 40.00 N | 86.15 W |
| Indiana □[3], U.S. | 194 | 40.00 N | 86.15 W |
| Indiana Dunes National Lakeshore ♦ | 216 | 41.40 N | 87.00 W |
| Indiana Dunes State Park ♦ | 216 | 41.40 N | 87.02 W |
| Indian Agricultural Research Institute ʋ[3] | 272a | 28.38 N | 77.10 E |
| Indiana Harbor ⊂ | 278 | 41.40 N | 87.27 W |
| Indiana Harbor Canal ≍ | 278 | 41.40 N | 87.27 W |
| Indianapolis | 218 | 39.46 N | 86.09 W |
| Indianapolis International Airport ⊠ | 218 | 39.43 N | 86.16 W |
| Indianapolis Motor Speedway ♦ | 218 | 39.48 N | 86.14 W |
| Indian Bayou ≃ | 194 | 34.14 N | 91.52 W |
| Indian Brook | 186 | 46.23 N | 60.32 W |
| Indian Caverns ⍊[5] | 214 | 40.38 N | 78.05 W |
| Indian Church | 232 | 17.45 N | 88.40 W |
| Indian Creek | 278 | 42.14 N | 87.59 W |
| Indian Creek ≃, U.S. | 218 | 39.19 N | 84.38 W |
| Indian Creek ≃, Ca., U.S. | 228 | 35.18 N | 118.26 W |
| Indian Creek ≃, Il., U.S. | 216 | 41.26 N | 88.46 W |
| Indian Creek ≃, Il., U.S. | 219 | 39.56 N | 90.32 W |
| Indian Creek ≃, Il., U.S. | 278 | 42.11 N | 87.55 W |
| Indian Creek ≃, In., U.S. | 216 | 40.55 N | 86.42 W |
| Indian Creek ≃, In., U.S. | 218 | 39.23 N | 86.29 W |
| Indian Creek ≃, In., U.S. | 218 | 38.10 N | 86.14 W |
| Indian Creek ≃, In., U.S. | 218 | 38.43 N | 85.06 W |
| Indian Creek ≃, Md., U.S. | 284c | 38.59 N | 76.55 W |
| Indian Creek ≃, Mo., U.S. | 194 | 36.33 N | 94.29 W |
| Indian Creek ≃, Mo., U.S. | 219 | 39.10 N | 91.11 W |
| Indian Creek ≃, N.M., U.S. | 200 | 36.11 N | 108.23 W |
| Indian Creek ≃, N.Y., U.S. | 276 | 40.43 N | 73.06 W |
| Indian Creek ≃, Oh., U.S. | 218 | 39.19 N | 84.38 W |
| Indian Creek ≃, Oh., U.S. | 279a | 41.17 N | 81.31 W |
| Indian Creek ≃, S.D., U.S. | 198 | 44.39 N | 103.19 W |
| Indian Creek ≃, Tn., U.S. | 194 | 35.13 N | 88.08 W |
| Indian Creek Lake ⊜[1] | 222 | 31.44 N | 95.58 W |
| Indianford | 216 | 42.49 N | 88.35 W |
| Indian Grave Mountain ∧[2] | 192 | 32.59 N | 84.21 W |
| Indian Harbor Beach | 220 | 28.08 N | 80.35 W |
| Indian Head, Sk., Can. | 184 | 50.32 N | 103.40 W |
| Indian Head, Md., U.S. | 208 | 38.36 N | 77.09 W |
| Indian Head ≃ | 283 | 42.04 N | 70.52 W |
| Indian Head Park | 278 | 41.47 N | 87.54 W |
| Indian Head Pond ⊜ | 283 | 42.03 N | 70.51 W |
| Indian Heights | 216 | 40.25 N | 86.07 W |
| Indian Island I | 224 | 48.04 N | 122.43 W |
| Indian Kentuck Creek ≃ | 218 | 38.43 N | 85.16 W |
| Indian Lake, Mi., U.S. | 216 | 41.59 N | 86.12 W |
| Indian Lake, N.Y., U.S. | 188 | 43.46 N | 74.16 W |
| Indian Lake ⊜, On., Can. | 190 | 47.08 N | 82.08 W |
| Indian Lake ⊜, Mi., U.S. | 190 | 45.59 N | 86.20 W |
| Indian Lake ⊜, Mi., U.S. | 216 | 42.09 N | 85.29 W |
| Indian Lake ⊜, Mi., U.S. | 216 | 42.00 N | 86.13 W |
| Indian Lake ⊜, N.J., U.S. | 276 | 40.53 N | 74.29 W |
| Indian Lake ⊜, Oh., U.S. | 216 | 40.29 N | 83.53 W |
| Indian Lake Estates | 220 | 27.48 N | 81.19 W |
| Indian Lakes ⊜ | 216 | 41.33 N | 85.25 W |
| Indian Lake State Park ♦ | 216 | 40.29 N | 83.52 W |
| Indian Mills Brook ≃ | 285 | 39.47 N | 74.44 W |
| Indian Mills Lake ⊜ | 285 | 39.48 N | 74.44 W |
| Indian Neck | 207 | 41.15 N | 72.48 W |
| Indian Ocean ⫪[1] | 4 | 10.00 S | 70.00 E |
| Indian Ocean ⫪[1] | 6 | 10.00 S | 70.00 E |
| Indianola, Ia., U.S. | 190 | 41.21 N | 93.33 W |
| Indianola, Ms., U.S. | 194 | 33.27 N | 90.39 W |
| Indianola, Ne., U.S. | 198 | 40.14 N | 100.25 W |
| Indianola, Pa., U.S. | 279b | 40.34 N | 79.51 W |
| Indianola, Wa., U.S. | 224 | 47.45 N | 122.31 W |
| Indianópolis | 255 | 19.02 S | 47.55 W |
| Indianópolis ◆[8] | 287b | 23.36 S | 46.38 W |
| Indian Peak ∧, Ut., U.S. | 200 | 38.16 N | 113.53 W |
| Indian Peak ∧, Wy., U.S. | 202 | 44.47 N | 109.51 W |
| Indian Point › | 212 | 44.37 N | 78.49 W |
| Indian Prairie Canal ≍ | 220 | 27.02 N | 80.57 W |
| Indian Queen Estates | 284c | 38.46 N | 77.02 W |
| Indian River | 190 | 45.24 N | 84.36 W |
| Indian River □[6] | 220 | 27.43 N | 80.36 W |
| Indian River ⊂ | 220 | 28.00 N | 80.30 W |
| Indian River Bay ⊂ | 208 | 38.36 N | 75.05 W |
| Indian River Inlet ⊂ | 208 | 38.37 N | 75.03 W |
| Indian Rock ∧ | 224 | 45.59 N | 120.49 W |
| Indian Rock Dam ◆[6] | 208 | 39.57 N | 76.45 W |
| Indian Rock Paintings ⊥ | 224 | 46.38 N | 120.31 W |
| Indian Rocks Beach | 220 | 27.52 N | 82.51 W |
| Indian Springs, Nv., U.S. | 204 | 36.34 N | 115.40 W |
| Indian Springs, Va., U.S. | 284c | 38.49 N | 77.10 W |
| Indian Stream ≃ | 206 | 45.03 N | 71.26 W |
| Indiantown | 220 | 27.01 N | 80.29 W |
| Indian Town Point › | 240c | 17.06 N | 61.40 W |
| Indian Valley Reservoir ⊜[1] | 226 | 39.07 N | 122.32 W |
| Indian Village, In., U.S. | 218 | 40.10 N | 85.22 W |
| Indian Village, N.Y., U.S. | 210 | 42.57 N | 76.10 W |
| Indiaporã | 255 | 19.57 S | 50.17 W |
| Indiaroba | 250 | 11.32 S | 37.31 W |
| Indibir | 144 | 8.05 N | 37.58 E |
| Indico, Océano → Indian Ocean ⫪[1] | 6 | 10.00 S | 70.00 E |
| Indien → India □[1] | 118 | 20.00 N | 77.00 E |
| Indien, Océan → Indian Ocean ⫪[1] | 6 | 10.00 S | 70.00 E |
| Indien, territoires britanniques de l'Ocean → British Indian Ocean Territory □[2] | 12 | 7.00 S | 72.00 E |
| Indiera Alta | 240m | 18.09 N | 66.53 W |
| Indiga | 24 | 67.41 N | 49.00 E |
| Indigirka ≃ | 74 | 70.48 N | 148.54 E |
| Inđija | 38 | 45.03 N | 20.05 E |
| Indin | 120 | 20.16 N | 92.57 E |
| Indio | 204 | 33.43 N | 116.12 W |
| Indio ≃, Nic. | 236 | 10.57 N | 83.44 W |
| Indio ≃, Pan. | 236 | 9.12 N | 80.11 W |
| Indio, Punta › | 258 | 35.16 S | 57.13 W |
| Indios, Canal de los ʮ | 240p | 21.56 N | 83.16 W |
| Indira Gandhi Canal ≍ | 120 | 31.10 N | 75.00 E |
| Indira Gandhi International Airport ⊠ | 272a | 28.35 N | 77.07 E |
| Indischer Ozean → Indian Ocean ⫪[1] | 6 | 10.00 S | 70.00 E |
| Indispensable Reefs ✢[2] | 160 | 12.40 S | 160.25 E |
| Indispensable Strait ʮ | 175e | 9.00 S | 160.30 E |
| Indo → Indus ≃ | 120 | 24.20 N | 67.47 E |
| Indochina ◆[1] | 108 | 16.00 N | 107.00 E |
| Indom | 24 | 64.36 N | 55.22 E |
| Indonesia □[1] | 108 | 5.00 S | 120.00 E |
| Indonesia, University of ʋ[2] | 269e | 6.12 S | 106.51 E |
| Indonesia in Miniature ♦ | 269e | 6.08 S | 106.49 E |
| Indonesian Culture, Museum of ʋ[3] | 269e | 6.09 N | 106.49 E |
| Indonésie → Indonesia □[1] | 108 | 5.00 S | 120.00 E |
| Indonesien → Indonesia □[1] | 108 | 5.00 S | 120.00 E |
| Indooroopilly | 171a | 27.30 S | 152.58 E |
| Indore | 120 | 22.43 N | 75.50 E |
| Indpur | 126 | 23.10 N | 86.56 E |
| Indragiri ≃ | 112 | 0.22 S | 103.26 E |
| Indramayu | 115a | 6.20 S | 108.19 E |
| Indramayu, Ujung › | 115a | 6.14 S | 108.17 E |
| Indrapuri | 114 | 5.26 N | 95.27 E |
| Indrāvati ≃ | 122 | 18.44 N | 80.16 E |
| Indre □[5] | 32 | 46.45 N | 1.30 E |
| Indre ≃ | 32 | 47.16 N | 0.19 E |
| Indre-et-Loire □[5] | 32 | 47.15 N | 0.45 E |
| Indrois ≃ | 50 | 47.13 N | 0.56 E |
| Indungo | 152 | 14.48 S | 16.17 E |
| Induno Olona | 62 | 45.52 N | 8.51 E |
| Indur → Indore | 120 | 22.43 N | 75.50 E |
| Indura | 76 | 53.27 N | 23.53 E |
| Indus ≃ | 120 | 24.20 N | 67.47 E |
| Industry, Il., U.S. | 194 | 40.20 N | 90.36 W |
| Industry, Pa., U.S. | 214 | 40.39 N | 80.25 W |
| Industry, Tx., U.S. | 222 | 29.58 N | 96.30 W |
| Indwe | 158 | 31.27 S | 27.23 E |
| Indwe ≃ | 158 | 32.01 S | 27.21 E |
| Ine | 96 | 35.39 N | 135.17 E |
| İnebolu | 130 | 41.58 N | 33.46 E |
| İnece | 130 | 41.41 N | 27.04 E |
| İnecik | 130 | 40.56 N | 27.16 E |
| In Ecker | 148 | 24.09 N | 5.03 E |
| İnegöl | 130 | 40.05 N | 29.31 E |
| Inerie, Gunung ∧ | 115b | 8.52 S | 120.56 E |
| Inés, Monte ∧ | 254 | 48.29 S | 69.40 W |
| Ineu | 38 | 46.26 N | 21.49 E |
| Inez, Ky., U.S. | 192 | 37.51 N | 82.32 W |
| Inez, Tx., U.S. | 222 | 28.54 N | 96.47 W |
| Inez, Lake ⊜ | 276 | 41.01 N | 74.17 W |
| Infanta, Pil. | 116 | 15.50 N | 119.55 E |
| Infanta, Pil. | 116 | 14.45 N | 121.39 E |
| Infante, Kaap › | 158 | 34.29 S | 20.51 E |
| Inferior, Laguna ⊂ | 234 | 16.20 N | 94.40 W |
| Inferno, Cachoeira do ᒪ | 250 | 1.00 S | 56.04 W |
| Infiernillo, Presa del ⊜[1] | 234 | 18.35 N | 101.45 W |
| Infiesto | 34 | 43.21 N | 5.22 W |
| Infreschi, Ponta degli › | 68 | 39.59 N | 15.25 E |
| Ing ≃ | 110 | 20.13 N | 100.27 E |
| Ingá | 250 | 7.17 S | 35.36 W |
| Ingabu | 110 | 17.49 N | 95.16 E |
| Ingaí | 256 | 21.24 S | 44.55 W |
| Ingaí ≃ | 256 | 21.23 S | 44.52 W |
| Ingal | 150 | 16.47 N | 6.56 E |
| Ingalls | 218 | 39.57 N | 85.48 W |
| Ingalls Creek ≃ | 224 | 47.28 N | 120.39 W |
| Ingalls Park | 216 | 41.32 N | 88.03 W |
| Inganda | 152 | 0.05 S | 20.57 E |
| Inganno ≃ | 70 | 38.04 N | 14.37 E |
| Ingarö I | 40 | 59.16 N | 18.28 E |
| Ingatestone | 42 | 51.41 N | 0.22 E |
| Ingatestone Hall ⊥ | 260 | 51.39 N | 0.23 E |
| Ingelfingen | 56 | 49.18 N | 9.39 E |
| Ingelheim | 56 | 49.59 N | 8.05 E |
| Ingelmunster | 50 | 50.55 N | 3.15 E |
| Ingelstad | 26 | 56.45 N | 14.55 E |
| Ingende | 152 | 0.15 S | 18.57 E |
| Ingeniería, Universidad Nacional de ʋ[2] | 286d | 12.02 S | 77.02 W |
| Ingeniero Budge ◆[8] | 288 | 34.43 S | 58.28 W |
| Ingeniero Jacobacci | 254 | 41.18 S | 69.35 W |
| Ingeniero Juan Allan | 258 | 34.53 S | 58.11 W |
| Ingeniero Luiggi | 252 | 35.25 S | 64.29 W |
| Ingeniero Luis A. Huergo | 252 | 39.05 S | 67.14 W |
| Ingeniero Maschwitz | 258 | 34.23 S | 58.44 W |
| Ingeniero Romulo Otamendi | 258 | 34.13 S | 58.54 W |
| Ingeniero White | 252 | 38.47 S | 62.16 W |
| Ingeniero Williams | 258 | 34.54 S | 59.22 W |
| Ingenio La Esperanza | 252 | 24.13 S | 64.51 W |
| Ingenio Santa Ana | 252 | 27.28 S | 65.41 W |
| Ingeringbach ≃ | 61 | 47.12 N | 14.49 E |
| Ingersheim | 58 | 48.06 N | 7.18 E |
| Ingersoll | 212 | 43.02 N | 80.53 W |
| Ingham | 166 | 18.39 S | 146.10 E |
| Ingham □[6] | 216 | 42.37 N | 84.22 W |
| Ingička | 85 | 39.52 N | 67.20 E |
| Ingleborough ∧ | 44 | 54.11 N | 2.23 W |
| Ingleburn | 170 | 34.00 S | 150.52 E |
| Inglesa, Costa → English Coast ⍊[2] | 9 | 73.45 S | 73.00 W |
| Ingleside, Austl. | 274a | 33.41 S | 151.13 E |
| Ingleside, On., Can. | 206 | 45.00 N | 75.00 W |
| Ingleside, Il., U.S. | 216 | 42.23 N | 88.09 W |
| Ingleside, Tx., U.S. | 196 | 27.52 N | 97.12 W |
| Ingleside ◆[8] | 282 | 37.43 N | 122.28 W |
| Ingleton | 44 | 54.10 N | 2.27 W |
| Inglewood, Austl. | 166 | 28.25 S | 151.05 E |
| Inglewood, Austl. | 166 | 36.34 S | 143.52 E |
| Inglewood, On., Can. | 212 | 43.47 N | 79.56 W |
| Inglewood, N.Z. | 172 | 39.09 S | 174.12 E |
| Inglewood, Ca., U.S. | 228 | 33.57 N | 118.21 W |
| Inglewood, Wa., U.S. | 224 | 47.44 N | 122.15 W |
| Inglewood Forest ◆[3] | 44 | 54.45 N | 2.50 W |
| Inglis, Mb., Can. | 184 | 50.57 N | 101.15 W |
| Inglis, Fl., U.S. | 220 | 29.02 N | 82.40 W |
| Inglis Lock ◆[5] | 220 | 29.02 N | 82.37 W |
| Ingoda ≃ | 88 | 51.42 N | 115.48 E |
| Ingogo | 158 | 27.32 S | 29.56 E |
| Ingoldmells | 44 | 53.11 N | 0.20 E |
| Ingolstadt | 60 | 48.46 N | 11.27 E |
| Ingomar | 279b | 40.35 N | 80.05 W |
| Ingonish | 186 | 46.42 N | 60.22 W |
| Ingornachoix Bay ⊂ | 186 | 50.38 N | 57.20 W |
| Ingraham, Lake ⊜ | 220 | 25.09 N | 81.08 W |
| Ingrāj Bāzār | 124 | 25.00 N | 88.09 E |
| Ingram, Pa., U.S. | 279b | 40.26 N | 80.04 W |
| Ingram, Tx., U.S. | 196 | 30.04 N | 99.14 W |
| Ingram Bay ⊂ | 208 | 37.48 N | 76.17 W |
| Ingrave | 260 | 51.36 N | 0.21 E |
| Ingrid Christensen Coast ⍊[2] | 9 | 69.30 S | 76.00 E |
| In Guezzam | 150 | 19.32 N | 5.42 E |
| Inguri ≃ | 84 | 42.24 N | 41.33 E |
| Ingushetia → Čečnja-Ingušetija □[3] | 84 | 43.15 N | 45.40 E |
| Inguzet | 86 | 58.50 N | 83.52 E |
| Ingvallsbenning | 40 | 60.15 N | 15.53 E |
| Ingwavuma | 158 | 27.09 S | 32.00 E |
| Ingwe | 154 | 13.02 S | 26.25 E |
| Ingwiller | 56 | 48.52 N | 7.29 E |
| Inhaca, Ilha da I | 158 | 26.03 S | 32.57 E |
| Inhafenga | 156 | 20.35 S | 33.53 E |
| Inhambane | 156 | 23.51 S | 35.29 E |
| Inhambane □[5] | 156 | 23.00 S | 34.30 E |
| Inhambane, Baía de ⊂ | 156 | 23.58 S | 35.51 E |
| Inhambupe | 255 | 11.47 S | 38.21 W |
| Inhaminga | 156 | 18.24 S | 35.00 E |
| Inhanduí ≃ | 255 | 21.37 S | 52.59 W |
| Inhapim | 255 | 19.33 S | 42.07 W |
| Inharrime | 156 | 24.29 S | 35.01 E |
| Inharrime ≃ | 156 | 24.29 S | 35.01 E |
| Inhassoro | 156 | 21.33 S | 35.11 E |
| Inhaúma | 255 | 19.29 S | 44.22 W |
| Inhaúma ◆[8] | 287a | 22.52 S | 43.17 W |
| İnhisar | 130 | 40.03 N | 30.23 E |
| Inhoaíba ◆[8] | 256 | 22.54 S | 43.36 W |
| Inhomirim | 256 | 22.35 S | 43.10 W |
| Inhomirim ≃ | 287a | 22.41 S | 43.13 W |
| Inhul ≃ | 78 | 47.00 N | 31.59 E |
| Inhulets' | 78 | 47.43 N | 33.14 E |
| Inhulets' ≃ | 78 | 46.41 N | 32.48 E |
| Inhulo-Kam'yanka | 78 | 48.17 N | 32.30 E |
| Inhuma | 250 | 6.40 S | 41.42 W |
| Inhumas | 255 | 16.22 S | 49.30 W |
| Ini ≃ | 146 | 9.30 N | 12.20 E |
| Iniesta | 34 | 39.26 N | 1.45 W |
| Inimutaba | 255 | 18.45 S | 44.22 W |
| Ining → Yining | 86 | 43.54 N | 81.21 E |
| Inírida ≃ | 246 | 3.55 N | 67.52 W |
| Inisa | 150 | 7.52 N | 4.20 E |
| Inishbofin I, Ire. | 48 | 53.37 N | 10.15 W |
| Inishbofin I, Ire. | 48 | 55.09 N | 8.1[illegible] W |
| Inishcrone | 48 | 54.12 N | 9.[illegible] W |
| Inisheer I | 48 | 53.02 N | 9.2[illegible] W |
| Inishkea North I | 48 | 54.08 N | 10.1[illegible] W |
| Inishkea South I | 48 | 54.07 N | 10.1[illegible] W |
| Inishmaan I | 48 | 53.05 N | 9.3[illegible] W |
| Inishmore I | 48 | 53.07 N | 9.4[illegible] W |
| Inishmurray I | 48 | 54.26 N | 8.4[illegible] W |
| Inishowen ›[1] | 48 | 55.12 N | 7.2[illegible] W |
| Inishowen Head › | 48 | 55.14 N | 6.5[illegible] W |
| Inishshark I | 48 | 53.37 N | 10.18 W |
| Inishtrahull I | 48 | 55.26 N | 7.14 W |
| Inishturk I | 48 | 53.43 N | 10.08 W |
| Inistioge | 48 | 52.29 N | 7.04 W |
| Initao | 116 | 8.30 N | 124.18 E |
| Inje | 98 | 38.05 N | 128.09 E |
| Injibara | 144 | 11.00 N | 36.59 E |
| Injune | 166 | 25.51 S | 148.34 E |
| Inkeroinen | 26 | 60.42 N | 26.51 |
| Inketete | 152 | 2.37 S | 21.53 |
| Inkisi (Zadi) ≃ | 152 | 4.46 S | 14.52 E |
| Inkom | 202 | 42.47 N | 112.15 W |
| Inkster, Mi., U.S. | 216 | 42.17 N | 83.18 W |
| Inkster, N.D., U.S. | 198 | 48.09 N | 97.38 W |
| Inland Kaikoura Range ⩘ | 172 | 42.00 S | 173.40 E |
| Inland Lake ⊜, Mb., Can. | 184 | 52.17 N | 99.42 W |
| Inland Lake ⊜, Ak., U.S. | 180 | 66.27 N | 159.47 W |
| Inland Sea → Seto-naikai ⫪[2] | 96 | 34.20 N | 133.30 E |
| Inle Lake ⊜ | 110 | 20.32 N | 96.55 E |
| Inman, Ks., U.S. | 198 | 38.13 N | 97.46 W |
| Inman, S.C., U.S. | 192 | 35.02 N | 82.05 W |
| Inman Mills | 192 | 35.02 N | 82.06 W |
| Inman Valley | 168b | 35.30 S | 138.28 E |
| Inn (En) ≃ | 32 | 48.35 N | 13.28 E |
| Innamincka | 166 | 27.45 S | 140.44 E |
| Innbach ≃ | 61 | 48.18 N | 14.07 E |
| Innellan | 46 | 55.54 N | 4.57 W |
| Inner Bay ⊂ | 214 | 42.37 N | 80.24 W |
| Innerbraz | 58 | 47.09 N | 9.55 E |
| Inner Channel ʮ | 232 | 16.35 N | 88.17 W |
| Innerferrera | 58 | 46.31 N | 9.28 E |
| Innerfragant | 64 | 46.58 N | 13.04 E |
| Inner Harbor ⊂ | 276 | 40.52 N | 73.28 W |
| Inner Hebrides II | 46 | 56.30 N | 6.00 W |
| Innerkip | 212 | 43.13 N | 80.42 W |
| Innerleithen | 46 | 55.38 N | 3.05 W |
| Inner Mongolia → Nei Monggol Zizhiqu □[4] | 90 | 43.00 N | 115.00 E |
| Inner Sister Island I | 166 | 39.42 S | 147.55 E |
| Inner Sound ʮ | 46 | 57.25 N | 5.56 W |
| Innerste ≃ | 52 | 52.15 N | 9.50 E |
| Innerstetalsperre ◆[6] | 52 | 51.55 N | 10.17 E |
| Innerthal | 58 | 47.06 N | 8.56 E |
| Innertkirchen | 58 | 46.42 N | 8.14 E |
| Innervillgraten | 64 | 46.48 N | 12.23 E |
| Innichen → San Candido | 64 | 46.44 N | 12.17 E |
| Inning | 60 | 48.05 N | 11.09 E |
| Innisfail, Austl. | 166 | 17.32 S | 146.02 E |
| Innisfail, Ab., Can. | 182 | 52.02 N | 113.57 W |
| Innisfil Creek ≃ | 212 | 44.08 N | 79.49 W |
| Innisfree | 182 | 53.22 N | 111.32 W |
| Innisplain | 171a | 28.10 S | 152.55 E |
| Innokentjevka | 89 | 49.42 N | 136.57 E |
| Innokentjevskij | 89 | 48.37 N | 140.10 E |
| Innoko ≃ | 180 | 62.14 N | 159.45 W |
| Innolovo | 265a | 59.47 N | 29.59 E |
| Innoshima | 96 | 34.17 N | 133.11 E |
| Inno-shima I | 96 | 34.19 N | 133.10 E |
| Innsbruck | 64 | 47.16 N | 11.24 E |
| Innviertel ◆[1] | 60 | 48.10 N | 13.15 E |
| Inny ≃, Ire. | 48 | 53.33 N | 7.48 W |
| Inny ≃, Eng., U.K. | 42 | 50.35 N | 4.17 W |
| Ino, Nihon | 96 | 33.33 N | 133.26 E |
| Ino, Va., U.S. | 208 | 37.46 N | 76.48 W |
| Inoã | 256 | 22.55 S | 42.57 W |
| Inobonto | 112 | 0.52 N | 123.57 E |
| Inocência | 255 | 19.47 S | 51.48 W |
| Inokashira Park ♦ | 268 | 35.42 N | 139.34 E |
| Inokovka | 80 | 52.33 N | 42.34 E |
| Inola | 196 | 36.09 N | 95.30 W |
| Ino-misaki › | 96 | 33.01 N | 133.06 E |
| Inongo | 152 | 1.57 S | 18.16 E |
| Inoni | 152 | 3.04 S | 15.39 E |
| İnönü | 130 | 39.48 N | 30.09 E |
| Inoue | 270 | 34.48 N | 135.03 E |
| Inowrocław | 30 | 52.48 N | 18.15 E |
| Inozemcevo | 84 | 44.06 N | 43.06 E |
| Inp'ung-dong | 98 | 41.25 N | 126.34 E |
| Inrath ◆[8] | 263 | 51.21 N | 6.32 E |
| In Rhar | 148 | 27.10 N | 1.59 E |
| Ins | 58 | 47.00 N | 7.06 E |
| In Salah | 148 | 27.12 N | 2.28 E |
| Insan-ni | 98 | 41.01 N | 127.21 E |
| Insar | 80 | 53.52 N | 44.21 E |
| Insar ≃ | 80 | 54.43 N | 45.18 E |
| Insch | 46 | 57.21 N | 2.37 W |
| Inscription, Cape › | 162 | 25.29 S | 112.59 E |
| Inscription Point › | 274a | 34.00 S | 151.13 E |
| Insel Man → Isle of Man □[2] | 44 | 54.15 N | 4.30 W |
| Inshar | 150 | 8.49 N | 9.40 E |
| Inshāş ar-Raml | 142 | 30.23 N | 31.27 E |
| Insjön | 26 | 60.41 N | 15.05 E |
| Ińsko | 30 | 53.27 N | 15.33 E |
| In Sokki, Oued V | 148 | 29.37 N | 4.13 E |
| Inspiration | 200 | 33.24 N | 110.52 W |
| Insterburg → Čern'achovsk | 76 | 54.38 N | 21.49 E |
| Instow | 184 | 49.44 N | 108.16 W |
| Insurgente José María Morelos, Parque Nacional ♦ | 234 | 19.35 N | 100.55 W |
| Inta | 24 | 66.02 N | 60.08 E |
| Intendente Alvear | 252 | 35.14 S | 63.35 W |
| İntepe | 130 | 40.00 N | 26.20 E |
| Intercession City | 220 | 28.15 N | 81.30 W |
| Intercourse | 208 | 40.02 N | 76.06 W |
| Interlagos ◆[8] | 287b | 23.42 S | 46.42 W |
| Interlaken, Schw. | 58 | 46.41 N | 7.51 E |
| Interlaken, Ma., U.S. | 210 | 42.18 N | 73.19 W |
| Interlaken, N.J., U.S. | 208 | 40.14 N | 74.01 W |
| Interlaken, N.Y., U.S. | 210 | 42.37 N | 76.43 W |
| Interlândia | 255 | 16.12 S | 49.02 W |
| Internacional (Guarulhos), Aeroporto ⊠ | 287b | 23.29 S | 46.28 W |
| International Amphitheatre ʋ | 278 | 41.49 N | 87.39 W |
| International Falls | 190 | 48.36 N | 93.24 W |
| International Peace Garden ♦ | 198 | 49.00 N | 100.04 W |
| International Trade Fair ♦ | 267d | 35.47 N | 51.24 E |
| Interstate State Park ♦ | 190 | 45.23 N | 92.40 W |
| Inthanon, Doi ∧ | 110 | 18.35 N | 98.29 E |
| Intibucá | 236 | 14.16 N | 88.10 W |
| Intibucá □[5] | 236 | 14.20 N | 88.15 W |
| Intipucá | 236 | 13.12 N | 88.04 W |
| Intiyaco | 252 | 28.39 S | 60.05 W |
| Intracoastal Waterway ≍, U.S. | 192 | 24.33 N | 81.46 W |
| Intracoastal Waterway ≍, U.S. | 196 | 26.04 N | 97.12 W |
| Intragna | 58 | 46.10 N | 8.42 E |
| Intrånget | 40 | 60.20 N | 16.09 E |
| Introbio | 58 | 45.57 N | 9.27 E |
| Introdacqua | 66 | 42.00 N | 13.54 E |
| Intschön → Inch'ŏn | 98 | 37.28 N | 126.38 E |
| Intu | 112 | 0.15 S | 115.21 E |
| Intuto | 246 | 3.39 S | 74.44 W |
| Inubō-saki › | 94 | 35.42 N | 140.53 E |
| Inukai | 96 | 33.04 N | 131.38 E |


| | | | | |
|---|---|---|---|---|
| ≃ River | Fluß | Río | Rivière | Rio |
| ≍ Canal | Kanal | Canal | Canal | Canal |
| ᒪ Waterfall, Rapids | Wasserfall, Stromschnellen | Cascada, Rápidos | Chute d'eau, Rapides | Cascata, Rápidos |
| ʮ Strait | Meeresstraße | Estrecho | Détroit | Estreito |
| ⊂ Bay, Gulf | Bucht, Golf | Bahía, Golfo | Baie, Golfe | Baía, Golfo |
| ⊜ Lake, Lakes | See, Seen | Lago, Lagos | Lac, Lacs | Lago, Lagos |
| ≡ Swamp | Sumpf | Pantano | Marais | Pântano |
| ⊓ Ice Features, Glacier | Eis- und Gletscherformen | Accidentes Glaciales | Formes glaciaires | Acidentes glaciares |
| ⫪ Other Hydrographic Features | Andere Hydrographische Objekte | Otros Elementos Hidrográficos | Autres données hydrographiques | Outros acidentes hidrográficos |
| ✢ Submarine Features | Untermeerische Objekte | Accidentes Submarinos | Formes de relief sous-marin | Acidentes submarinos |
| □ Political Unit | Politische Einheit | Unidad Politica | Entité politique | Unidade política |
| ʋ Cultural Institution | Kulturelle Institution | Institución Cultural | Institution culturelle | Instituição cultural |
| ⊥ Historical Site | Historische Stätte | Sitio Histórico | Site historique | Sitio histórico |
| ♦ Recreational Site | Erholungs- und Ferienort | Sitio de Recreo | Centre de loisirs | Area de Lazer |
| ⊠ Airport | Flughafen | Aeropuerto | Aéroport | Aeroporto |
| ■ Military Installation | Militäranlage | Instalación Militar | Installation militaire | Instalação militar |
| ◆ Miscellaneous | Verschiedenes | Misceláneo | Divers | Diversos |

Inukjuak 176 58.27 N 78.06 W
Inútil, Bahía c 254 53.30 S 69.50 W
Inuvik 180 68.25 N 133.30 W
Inuya ≃ 248 10.41 S 73.30 W
Inuyama 94 35.23 N 136.56 E
In'va ≃ 86 58.59 N 55.40 E
Inver 46 57.49 N 3.55 W
Inverallochy 46 57.40 N 1.55 W
Inveralochy 170 34.57 S 149.39 E
Inveraray 46 56.13 N 5.05 W
Inverarish 46 57.21 N 6.04 W
Inverarity 46 56.35 N 2.53 W
Inverbervie 46 56.51 N 2.17 W
Invercargill 172 46.24 S 168.21 E
Inverdruie 46 57.10 N 3.48 W
Inverell 166 29.47 S 151.07 E
Invergarry 46 57.02 N 4.47 W
Invergordon 46 57.42 N 4.10 W
Inverkeilor 46 56.38 N 2.32 W
Inverkeithing 46 56.02 N 3.25 W
Inverkeithny 46 57.30 N 2.37 W
Inverleigh 169 38.06 S 144.03 E
Inverloch 169 38.38 S 145.43 E
Invermay 184 51.48 N 103.09 W
Invermere 182 50.30 N 116.02 W
Invermoriston 46 57.13 N 4.38 W
Inverness, N.S., Can. 186 46.14 N 61.18 W
Inverness, P.Q., Can. 206 46.15 N 71.31 W
Inverness, Scot., U.K. 46 57.27 N 4.15 W
Inverness, Ca., U.S. 204 38.06 N 122.51 W
Inverness, Fl., U.S. 220 28.50 N 82.19 W
Inverness, Il., U.S. 216 42.07 N 88.05 W
Inverness, Ms., U.S. 194 33.21 N 90.35 W
Inveruglas 46 56.15 N 4.43 W
Inveruno 62 45.31 N 8.51 E
Inverurie 46 57.17 N 2.23 W
Inverway 162 17.50 S 129.38 E
Investigator Group II 162 33.45 S 134.30 E
Investigator Shoal ⊹[2] 108 8.09 N 114.44 E
Investigator Strait ʯ 166 35.25 S 137.10 E
Inwood, Mb., Can. 184 50.30 N 97.30 W
Inwood, On., Can. 214 42.49 N 81.59 W
Inwood, Fl., U.S. 220 28.02 N 81.45 W
Inwood, In., U.S. 216 41.19 N 86.12 W
Inwood, Ia., U.S. 198 43.18 N 96.25 W
Inwood, N.Y., U.S. 276 40.37 N 73.44 W
Inwood Hill Park ♠ 276 40.52 N 73.56 W
Inyanga 154 18.13 S 32.46 E
Inyanga Mountains ∧∧ 154 18.00 S 33.00 E
Inyangani ∧ 154 18.20 S 32.50 E
Inyan Kara Mountain ∧ 198 44.13 N 104.21 W
Inyantue 154 18.32 S 26.41 E
Inyati 154 19.39 S 28.54 E
Inyo, Mount ∧ 204 36.44 N 117.59 W
Inyokern 204 35.38 N 117.48 W
Inyo Mountains ∧∧ 204 36.40 N 118.10 W
Inyonga 154 6.43 S 32.04 E
Inywa 110 23.56 N 96.17 E
Inza 80 53.51 N 46.21 E
Inza ≃ 80 53.54 N 45.44 E
Inzago 62 45.32 N 9.29 E
Inzai 94 35.50 N 140.09 E
Inzana Lake ◎ 182 54.58 N 124.40 W
Inžavino 80 52.19 N 42.30 E
Inzell 64 47.46 N 12.44 E
Inzer 86 54.14 N 57.34 E
Inzer ≃ 86 54.30 N 56.28 E
Inzersdorf ◆[8] 264b 48.09 N 16.21 E
Inzia ≃ 152 3.45 S 17.57 E
Ioanna, gora ∧ 180 64.50 N 178.08 E
Ioánnina 38 39.40 N 20.50 E
Ioco 224 49.18 N 122.52 W
Iō-jima (Iwo Jima) I 174f 24.47 N 141.20 E
Iokanga ≃ 24 68.00 N 39.43 E
Iola, Ks., U.S. 198 37.55 N 95.23 W
Iola, Pa., U.S. 210 45.08 N 76.32 W
Iola, Tx., U.S. 222 30.46 N 96.05 W
Iola, Wi., U.S. 190 44.30 N 89.07 W
Iolgo, chrebet ∧∧ 86 51.30 N 86.25 E
Iolotan' 72 37.18 N 62.21 E
Ioma 164 8.20 S 147.50 E
Iôna, Ang. 152 16.50 S 12.20 E
Iona, N.S., Can. 186 45.58 N 60.48 W
Iona, Id., U.S. 202 43.31 N 111.55 W
Iona I 46 56.19 N 6.25 W
Iôna, Parque Nacional do ♠ 152 16.30 S 12.00 E
Iona, Sound of ʯ 46 56.19 N 6.24 W
Iona College ⚜[2] 276 40.56 N 73.47 W
Ione, Ca., U.S. 226 38.21 N 120.55 W
Ione, Or., U.S. 202 45.30 N 119.50 W
Ione, Wa., U.S. 202 48.44 N 117.24 W
Ionia, Mi., U.S. 216 42.59 N 85.04 W
Ionia, N.Y., U.S. 210 42.56 N 77.30 W
Ionia □[6] 216 42.56 N 85.04 W
Ionian Islands → Iónioi Nísoi II 38 38.30 N 20.30 E
Ionian Sea ⊹[2] 22 39.00 N 19.00 E
Ionia State Recreation Area ♠ 216 42.58 N 85.36 W
Ionico, Mare → Ionian Sea ⊹[2] 22 39.00 N 19.00 E
Ionienne, Mer → Ionian Sea ⊹[2] 22 39.00 N 19.00 E
Iónioi Nísoi □[4] 38 38.15 N 20.30 E
Iónioi Nísoi II 38 38.30 N 20.30 E
Ionische Inseln → Iónioi Nísoi II 38 38.30 N 20.30 E
Ionisches Meer → Ionian Sea ⊹[2] 22 39.00 N 19.00 E
Ionivejem ≃ 180 66.12 N 174.00 W
Iony, ostrov I 74 56.26 N 143.25 E
Ioppolo 68 38.35 N 15.53 E
Ioppolo Giancaxio 70 37.23 N 13.33 E
Iordan 85 39.58 N 71.46 E
Iori (Qabırrı) ≃ 84 41.03 N 46.17 E
Iorskoje ploskogorje ∧∧[1] 84 41.20 N 46.00 E
Iory 85 39.30 N 67.53 E
Íos 38 36.44 N 25.17 E
Íos I 38 36.42 N 25.24 E
Ioscoe, Lake ◎ 276 41.02 N 74.19 W
Iosegun ≃ 182 54.44 N 117.11 W
Iosegun Lake 182 54.29 N 116.50 W
Iō-shima I 93b 30.48 N 130.18 E
Iota 194 30.19 N 92.29 W
Iovlevo 82 56.10 N 38.20 E
Iowa 194 30.14 N 93.00 W
Iowa □[3] 178 42.15 N 93.15 W
Iowa ≃ 190 41.10 N 91.02 W
Iowa, South Fork ≃ 190 42.18 N 93.04 W
Iowa City 190 41.39 N 91.31 W
Iowa Falls 190 42.31 N 93.15 W
Iowa Park 196 33.57 N 98.40 W
Iō-zen ∧ 94 36.31 N 136.48 E
Ipa ≃ 76 52.13 N 29.08 E
Ipala 154 4.30 S 32.53 E
Ipameri 255 17.43 S 48.09 W
Ipanema ◆[8] 256 22.59 S 43.12 W
Ipanema ≃ 250 9.53 S 37.15 W
Ipanguaçu 250 5.30 S 36.52 W
Ipat 24 66.13 N 56.33 E
Ipatinga 255 19.30 S 42.32 W
Ipatovo 80 45.43 N 42.53 E
Ipaumirim 250 6.47 S 38.43 W
Ipava 194 40.21 N 90.19 W
Ípeiros □[9] 38 39.40 N 20.50 E
Ipel' (Ipoly) ≃ 30 47.49 N 18.52 E
Iperu 150 6.52 N 3.38 E
Iphigenia Bay c 180 55.40 N 133.55 W
Iphofen 56 49.42 N 10.15 E
Ipiabas 256 22.23 S 43.53 W
Ipiales 246 0.50 N 77.37 W
Ipiaú 255 14.08 S 39.44 W
Ipiíba 256 22.52 S 42.57 W
Ipil 116 7.47 N 122.35 E
Ipin → Yibin 107 28.47 N 104.38 E
Ipirá 255 12.10 S 39.44 W
Ipiranga, Bra. 252 25.01 S 50.35 W
Ipiranga, Bra. 287a 22.43 S 43.12 W
Ipiranga ◆[8] 287b 23.36 S 46.35 W
Ipiranga ≃, Bra. 256 23.21 S 45.10 W
Ipiranga ≃, Bra. 287a 22.48 S 43.37 W
Ipiranga, Canal ⌆ 287a 22.46 S 43.37 W
Ipiranga, Museu do ⚜ 287b 23.35 S 46.36 W
Ípiros □[4] 38 39.30 N 20.30 E
Ipis I 175c 6.59 N 151.59 E
Ipita 248 19.20 S 63.32 W
Ipitinga ≃ 250 0.02 N 53.01 W
Ipixuna 250 4.22 S 44.34 W
Ipixuna ≃, Bra. 248 7.11 S 71.51 W
Ipixuna ≃, Bra. 248 5.45 S 63.02 W
Ipixuna ≃, Bra. 248 6.16 S 61.52 W
Ipixuna, Igarapé ≃ 250 4.32 S 52.40 W
Ipoh 114 4.35 N 101.05 E
Ipojuca ≃ 250 8.25 S 34.58 W
Ipokera 154 8.03 S 35.41 E
Ipole 154 5.47 S 32.44 E
Ipoly (Ipel') ≃ 30 47.49 N 18.52 E
Iporá, Bra. 255 16.28 S 51.07 W
Iporã, Bra. 255 23.59 S 53.37 W
Ipota 175f 18.48 S 169.16 E
Ippari ≃ 70 36.52 N 14.26 E
Ippinghausen 56 51.17 N 9.08 E
Ipplepen 42 50.29 N 3.38 W
Ippy 152 6.15 N 21.12 E
Ipsala 130 40.55 N 26.23 E
Ipswich, Austl. 171a 27.36 S 152.46 E
Ipswich, Eng., U.K. 42 52.04 N 1.10 E
Ipswich, Ma., U.S. 207 42.40 N 70.50 W
Ipswich, S.D., U.S. 198 45.26 N 99.01 W
Ipswich ≃ 207 42.42 N 70.48 W
Ipswich Bay c 207 42.41 N 70.42 W
Ipu 250 4.20 S 40.42 W
Ipubi 250 7.39 S 40.07 W
Ipueiras 250 4.33 S 40.43 W
Ipuh 112 3.00 S 101.30 E
Ipuiúna 256 22.06 S 46.11 W
Ipun, Isla I 254 44.37 S 74.46 W
Ipupiara 255 11.49 S 42.37 W
Iput' ≃ 76 52.26 N 31.02 E
Iqaluit 176 63.44 N 68.28 W
Iqe ≃ 102 38.14 N 94.18 E
Iqfahṣ 142 28.47 N 30.49 E
Iquique 248 20.13 S 70.10 W
Iquitos 246 3.46 S 73.15 W
Ira 196 32.35 N 101.00 W
Iraan, Pil. 116 9.04 N 117.42 E
Iraan, Tx., U.S. 196 30.54 N 101.53 W
Ira Banda 152 5.57 N 22.04 E
Irabu 175d 24.50 N 125.09 E
Irabu-jima I 175d 24.50 N 125.10 E
Iracajá, Cachoeira do ⊥ 248 10.29 S 64.05 W
Iracema 250 5.48 S 38.18 W
Iracoubo 250 5.29 N 53.13 W
Irago-misaki › 94 34.35 N 137.01 E
Irago-suidō ʯ 94 34.35 N 137.00 E
Iraí 252 27.11 S 53.15 W
Irajá ◆[8] 287a 22.51 S 43.19 W
Irajá ≃ 287a 22.49 S 43.17 W
Irajol' 24 64.27 N 55.08 E
Irak → Iraq □[1] 128 33.00 N 44.00 E
Iráklia I 38 36.50 N 25.26 E
Iráklion, Ellás 38 35.20 N 25.09 E
Iráklion, Ellás 267c 38.04 N 23.46 E
Iran (Īrān) □[1], Asia 118 32.00 N 53.00 E
Iran (Īrān) □[1], Asia 128 32.00 N 53.00 E
Iran, Pegunungan ∧∧ 112 2.05 N 114.55 E
Iran National Arts Museum ⚜ 267d 35.41 N 51.27 E
Īrānshahr 128 27.13 N 60.41 E
Irapa 246 10.34 N 62.35 W
Irapuato 234 20.41 N 101.21 W
Iraq (Al-'Irāq) □[1], Asia 118 33.00 N 44.00 E
Iraq (Al-'Irāq) □[1], Asia 128 33.00 N 44.00 E
Irará 255 12.02 S 38.46 W
Iratapuru ≃ 250 0.36 S 52.35 W
Irati 252 25.27 S 50.39 W
Irati ≃ 34 42.35 N 1.16 W
Irauçuba 250 3.45 S 39.47 W
Irazú, Volcán ∧[1] 236 9.58 N 83.53 W
Irba 88 58.07 N 99.00 E
Irbejskoje 88 55.39 N 95.28 E
Irbeni väin (Irbes jūras šaurums) ʯ 76 57.48 N 22.05 E
Irbes jūras šaurums (Irbeni väin) ʯ 76 57.48 N 22.05 E
Irbid 132 32.33 N 35.51 E
Irbid □[8] 132 32.30 N 35.45 E
Irbīl 128 36.11 N 44.01 E
Irbīl □[4] 128 36.10 N 44.00 E
Irbit 86 57.41 N 63.03 E
Irby 262 53.21 N 3.07 W
Irchester 42 52.16 N 0.38 W
Irdning 61 47.33 N 14.01 E
Irdyn' 78 49.23 N 31.44 E
Ire, Mount ∧ 175e 9.10 S 161.05 E
Irebu 152 0.37 S 17.45 E
Irecê 250 11.18 S 41.52 W
Iregua ≃ 34 42.27 N 2.24 W
Ireland (Éire) □[1], Europe 22 53.00 N 8.00 W
Ireland (Éire) □[1], Europe 48 53.00 N 8.00 W
Ireland Brook ≃ 276 40.25 N 74.29 W
Iren' ≃ 86 57.27 N 56.56 E
Irene, S. Afr. 158 25.53 S 28.13 E
Irene, S.D., U.S. 198 43.05 N 97.10 W
Irene, Tx., U.S. 222 31.59 N 96.52 W
Irene, Mount ∧ 172 45.10 S 167.22 E
Ireng (Maú) ≃ 246 3.33 N 59.51 W
Iresick Brook ≃ 276 40.24 N 74.22 W
Ireton 198 42.58 N 96.19 W
Irfon ≃ 42 52.09 N 3.24 W
Irgakly 84 44.22 N 44.45 E
Irgiz 86 48.37 N 61.16 E
Irgiz ≃ 86 48.13 N 62.08 E
Iri 98 35.56 N 126.57 E
Irian Jaya □[4] 164 5.00 S 138.00 E
Iriba 146 15.07 N 22.15 E
Irié 150 8.17 N 9.11 W
Iriga 116 13.25 N 123.25 E
Irigny 62 45.40 N 4.49 E
Irîgui ◆[1] 150 16.43 N 5.30 W
Iriklinskij 86 51.39 N 58.38 E
Iringa 154 7.46 S 35.42 E
Iringa □[4] 154 9.00 S 35.00 E
Irinjālakuda 122 10.20 N 76.14 E
Iriomote-jima I 175d 24.20 N 123.50 E
Iriona 236 15.57 N 85.11 W
Iriri ≃, Bra. 250 3.52 S 52.37 W
Iriri ≃, Bra. 287a 22.41 S 43.05 W
Iriri Novo ≃ 250 8.46 S 53.22 W
Irische See → Irish Sea ⊹[2] 28 53.30 N 5.20 W
Irish, Mount ∧ 204 37.38 N 115.24 W
Irish Sea ⊹[2] 28 53.30 N 5.20 W
Irishtown 166 40.55 S 145.08 E
Irituia 250 1.46 S 47.26 W
Iriyamazu 268 35.16 N 139.39 E
Irkās, Wādī V 142 28.57 N 32.00 E
Irkeštam 85 39.41 N 73.55 E
Irkinejeva ≃ 88 58.30 N 96.48 E
Irkinejevo 88 58.30 N 96.49 E
Irklijevskaja 78 45.51 N 39.39 E
Irkliyiv 78 49.32 N 32.18 E
Irkoutsk → Irkutsk 88 52.16 N 104.20 E
Irkut ≃ 88 52.18 N 104.15 E
Irkutsk 88 52.16 N 104.20 E
Irkutsk Oblast' □[4] 88 56.00 N 106.00 E
Irlam 44 53.28 N 2.25 W
Irland → Ireland □[1] 48 53.00 N 8.00 W
Irlanda, Mar de → Irish Sea ⊹[2] 28 53.30 N 5.20 W
Irlande → Ireland □[1] 48 53.00 N 8.00 W
Irlande, Mer d' → Irish Sea ⊹[2] 28 53.30 N 5.20 W
Irma 182 52.55 N 111.14 W
Irmauw 164 7.25 S 131.42 E
Irminger Basin ⊹[1] 10 61.00 N 35.00 W
Irminio ≃ 70 36.46 N 14.36 E
Irnijärvi ◎ 26 65.36 N 29.05 E
Irnsum 52 53.05 N 5.47 E
Iro, Lac ◎ 146 10.06 N 19.25 E
Iroise c 32 48.15 N 4.55 W
Iron Baron 166 32.59 S 137.09 E
Iron Belt 190 46.24 N 90.19 W
Iron Bottom Sound ʯ 175e 9.15 S 160.00 E
Iron Bridge, On., Can. 190 46.17 N 83.14 W
Iron Bridge, Eng., U.K. 42 52.38 N 2.29 W
Iron Bridge Dam ◆[6] 222 32.50 N 95.54 W
Iron City 194 35.01 N 87.34 W
Iron Cove c 274a 33.52 S 151.10 E
Iron Creek ≃ 182 52.43 N 111.14 W
Irondale, Al., U.S. 194 33.32 N 86.42 W
Irondale, Mo., U.S. 194 37.49 N 90.40 W
Irondale, Oh., U.S. 214 40.34 N 80.43 W
Irondale ≃ 212 44.49 N 78.37 W
Irondequoit 210 43.12 N 77.36 W
Irondequoit Bay c 210 43.12 N 77.32 W
Iron Gate V 38 44.41 N 22.31 E
Iron Gate Reservoir ◎[1] 38 44.30 N 22.00 E
Ironia 276 40.49 N 74.37 W
Iron Knob 166 32.44 S 137.08 E
Iron Mountain 190 45.49 N 88.03 W
Iron Mountain ∧, Az., U.S. 200 33.27 N 111.10 W
Iron Mountain ∧, Ca., U.S. 280 34.17 N 117.43 W
Iron Mountains ∧∧ 192 36.30 N 81.50 W
Iron Range 164 12.42 S 143.18 E
Iron Range National Park ♠ 164 12.44 S 143.16 E
Iron River, Mi., U.S. 190 46.05 N 88.38 W
Iron River, Wi., U.S. 190 46.33 N 91.24 W
Iron Springs 208 39.46 N 77.25 W
Ironton, Mn., U.S. 190 46.28 N 93.58 W
Ironton, Mo., U.S. 194 37.35 N 90.37 W
Ironton, Oh., U.S. 188 38.32 N 82.40 W
Ironwood 190 46.27 N 90.10 W
Ironworks Creek ≃ 285 40.10 N 74.59 W
Iroquois, On., Can. 212 44.51 N 75.19 W
Iroquois, Il., U.S. 216 40.50 N 87.35 W
Iroquois, S.D., U.S. 198 44.22 N 97.51 W
Iroquois □[6] 216 40.47 N 87.44 W
Iroquois ≃ 216 41.05 N 87.49 W
Iroquois Falls 190 48.46 N 80.41 W
Iroquois Lock and Dam ◆[5] 212 44.45 N 75.23 W
Irosin 116 12.42 N 124.02 E
Írottkő (Geschriebenstein) ∧ 61 47.21 N 16.26 E
Irō-zaki › 94 34.36 N 138.51 E
Irpin' 78 50.31 N 30.15 E
Irpin' ≃ 78 50.34 N 30.16 E
Irrawaddy → Ayeyarwady ≃ 110 20.32 N 96.55 E
Irrawaddy, Mouths of the ≃[1] 110 15.45 N 94.50 E
Irregully Creek ≃ 162 23.06 S 116.21 E
Irrel 56 49.51 N 6.28 E
Irricana 182 51.19 N 113.37 W
Irrigon 202 45.53 N 119.29 W
Irschenberg 64 47.50 N 11.55 E
Irsee 58 47.54 N 10.34 E
Irsha ≃ 78 50.45 N 29.30 E
Irshava 78 48.20 N 23.03 E
Irsina 68 40.45 N 16.15 E
Irt ≃ 44 54.22 N 3.26 W
Irtek ≃ 80 51.28 N 52.39 E
Irthing ≃ 44 54.55 N 2.50 W
Irthlingborough 42 52.20 N 0.37 W
Irtyš 86 54.29 N 74.22 E
Irtysh (Irtyš) (Ertix) ≃ 74 61.04 N 68.52 E
Irtyšsk 86 53.21 N 75.27 E
Irubaj 80 50.11 N 51.21 E
Iruma 94 35.50 N 139.24 E
Iruma ≃ 94 35.57 N 139.30 E
Iruma Air Base ■ 268 35.50 N 139.24 E
Iruma-kichi, Kaijō-jieitai- ■ 94 35.50 N 139.24 E
Irumu 154 1.27 N 29.52 E
Irún 34 43.21 N 1.47 W
Irupana 248 16.28 S 67.28 W
Irurzun 34 42.55 N 1.50 W
Irú Tepuy ∧ 246 5.25 N 61.02 W
Irvine, Ab., Can. 184 49.57 N 110.16 W
Irvine, Scot., U.K. 46 55.37 N 4.40 W
Irvine, Ca., U.S. 228 33.40 N 117.49 W
Irvine, Ky., U.S. 192 37.42 N 83.58 W
Irvine, Pa., U.S. 214 41.50 N 79.17 W
Irvine ≃ 46 55.37 N 4.41 W
Irvine, Mount ∧ 210 42.03 N 78.40 W
Irvine Creek ≃ 212 43.41 N 80.25 W
Irvine Park ♠ 280 33.48 N 117.45 W
Irvines Landing 182 49.38 N 124.03 W
Irvinestown 48 54.28 N 7.38 W
Irving, Il., U.S. 219 39.12 N 89.24 W
Irving, N.Y., U.S. 214 42.34 N 79.07 W
Irving, Tx., U.S. 222 32.48 N 96.56 W
Irving Park ◆[8] 278 41.57 N 87.43 W
Irvington, Il., U.S. 219 38.26 N 89.10 W
Irvington, Ky., U.S. 194 37.52 N 86.17 W
Irvington, N.J., U.S. 210 40.43 N 74.13 W
Irvington, N.Y., U.S. 210 41.02 N 73.51 W
Irvington, Oh., U.S. 218 39.51 N 84.15 W
Irvington, Va., U.S. 208 37.39 N 76.25 W
Irvington ◆[8] 284b 39.17 N 76.41 W
Irvona 214 40.46 N 78.33 W
Irwell ≃ 44 53.27 N 2.17 W
Irwin, Austl. 162 29.12 S 115.04 E
Irwin, Oh., U.S. 218 40.07 N 83.29 W
Irwin, Pa., U.S. 279b 40.19 N 79.42 W
Irwin ≃ 162 29.15 S 114.56 E
Irwin, Point › 162 35.04 S 116.56 E
Irwindale 280 34.06 N 117.56 W
Irwinton 192 32.48 N 83.10 W
Is 86 58.48 N 59.43 E
Is, Jabal ∧ 140 21.49 N 35.39 E
Isa 150 13.14 N 6.24 E
'Īsā, Ra's › 144 15.11 N 42.39 E
Isaac ≃ 166 22.52 S 149.20 E
Isaac Lake ◎, B.C., Can. 182 53.10 N 120.50 W
Isaac Lake ◎, On., Can. 212 44.47 N 81.14 W
Isaba 34 42.52 N 0.55 W
Isabel, Pil. 116 10.56 N 124.26 E
Isabel, S.D., U.S. 198 45.23 N 101.25 W
Isabel □[4] 175e 7.55 S 159.10 E
Isabela, Pil. 116 10.12 N 122.59 E
Isabela (Basilan), Pil. 116 6.42 N 121.58 E
Isabela, P.R. 240m 18.30 N 67.01 W
Isabela □[4] 116 17.00 N 122.00 E
Isabela, Cabo › 238 19.56 N 71.01 W
Isabela, Canal ʯ 246a 0.20 S 90.55 W
Isabela, Isla I, Ec. 246a 0.30 S 91.06 W
Isabela, Isla I, Méx. 234 21.51 N 105.55 W
Isabela de Sagua 240p 22.57 N 80.01 W
Isabelia, Cordillera ∧∧ 236 13.45 N 85.15 W
Isabella Indian Reservation ◆[4] 190 43.41 N 84.48 W
Isabella Lake ◎ 212 45.24 N 79.49 W
Isabella Lake ◎[1] 204 35.40 N 118.26 W
Isabelle ≃ 190 47.50 N 91.41 W
Isábena ≃ 34 42.11 N 0.21 E
Isaccea 38 45.16 N 28.28 E
Ísafjarðardjúp c[2] 24a 66.10 N 23.00 W
Ísafjörður 24a 66.08 N 23.13 W
Isāgarh 124 24.50 N 77.53 E
Isagatedo 273a 6.32 N 3.20 E
Isahaya 92 32.50 N 130.03 E
Isak 114 4.28 N 96.55 E
Isaka, Tan. 154 3.54 S 32.56 E
Isaka, Zaïre 152 2.35 S 18.48 E
Isaka-Buku 152 3.55 S 22.03 E
Īsa Khel 123 32.41 N 71.17 E
Isakly 80 54.08 N 51.32 E
Isakovka 86 55.45 N 74.24 E
Isakovo, Ross. 76 55.11 N 34.40 E
Isakovo, Ross. 76 60.30 N 41.13 E
Isakovo, Ross. 82 54.36 N 37.02 E
Isakovo, Ross. 265b 55.59 N 37.23 E
Işalniţa 38 44.24 N 23.44 E
Isalo, Massif de l' ∧∧ 157b 22.45 S 45.15 E
Isalo, Parc National de l' ♠ 157b 22.45 S 45.15 E
Isana (Içana) ≃ 246 0.26 N 67.19 W
Īsānagar 124 27.54 N 81.13 E
Isandhlwana ⊥ 158 28.21 S 30.39 E
Isandja Etat 152 2.59 S 22.00 E
Isando 273d 26.09 S 28.12 E
Isanga 152 1.26 S 22.18 E
Isangano National Park ♠ 154 11.10 S 30.40 E
Isangel 175f 19.32 S 169.16 E
Isangi 152 0.46 N 24.15 E
Is'angulovo 86 52.12 N 56.36 E
Isanlu Makutu 150 8.17 N 5.46 E
Isan-ni 98 40.46 N 128.55 E
Isanti 190 45.29 N 93.14 W
Isar ≃ 60 48.49 N 12.58 E
Isara 150 6.59 N 3.41 E
Isarco (Eisack) ≃ 64 46.27 N 11.18 E
Isarco, Valle V 64 46.45 N 11.37 E
Isarog, Mount ∧ 116 13.39 N 123.23 E
Isasi 273a 6.40 N 3.23 E
Isawa 94 35.39 N 138.38 E
Isbergues 50 50.37 N 2.27 E
Isbister 46a 60.36 N 1.19 W
İscehisar 130 38.51 N 30.45 E
Išč̌eino 76 52.57 N 38.50 E
Iščerskaja 84 43.43 N 45.08 E
Ischgl 58 47.01 N 10.17 E
Ischia 68 40.44 N 13.57 E
Ischia, Isola d' I 68 40.43 N 13.54 E
Ischia di Castro 66 42.33 N 11.45 E
Ischim → Išim ≃ 86 57.45 N 71.12 E
Ischitella 68 41.54 N 15.54 E
Ischma → Ižma ≃ 24 65.19 N 52.54 E
Ischodnaja, gora ∧ 180 64.50 N 173.26 W
Ischua 210 42.15 N 78.24 W
Ischua Creek ≃ 210 42.10 N 78.23 W
Iscuandé ≃ 246 2.38 N 78.04 W
Isdell ≃ 162 16.27 S 124.51 E
Isdes 50 47.40 N 2.15 E
Ise (Uji-yamada) 94 34.29 N 136.42 E
Ise ≃ 54 52.30 N 10.33 E
Isefjord c 41 55.52 N 11.49 E
Isehara 94 35.24 N 139.18 E
Išejevka 80 54.25 N 48.16 E
Iseke 154 6.25 S 35.01 E
Isel ≃ 64 46.50 N 12.47 E
Iselin, N.J., U.S. 210 40.34 N 74.19 W
Iselin, Pa., U.S. 214 40.33 N 79.23 W
Iselle 58 46.12 N 8.12 E
Iseltwald 58 46.43 N 7.58 E
Isen 60 48.13 N 12.04 E
Isen ≃ 60 48.15 N 12.40 E
Isenbajevo 80 56.03 N 53.25 E
Isenbüttel 52 52.26 N 10.34 E
Isenyela 154 8.36 S 33.30 E
Iseo 64 45.39 N 10.03 E
Iseo, Lago d' ◎ 64 45.43 N 10.04 E
Iseramagazi 154 4.40 S 32.09 E
Iseran, Col de l' )( 62 45.25 N 7.02 E
Isère □[5] 62 45.10 N 5.50 E
Isère ≃ 62 44.59 N 4.51 E
Iseri 273a 6.39 N 3.23 E
Iseri-Oke 273a 6.38 N 3.23 E
Iseri-Osun 273a 6.31 N 3.17 E
Iserlohn 56 51.22 N 7.41 E
Isernhagen 52 52.26 N 9.51 E
Isernia 66 41.36 N 14.14 E
Isernia □[4] 66 41.40 N 14.15 E
Isesaki 94 36.19 N 139.12 E
Ise-Shima-kokuritsu-kōen ♠ 92 34.23 N 136.48 E
Iset' ≃ 86 56.36 N 66.24 E
Isetskoje 86 56.29 N 65.21 E
Ise-wan c 94 34.43 N 136.43 E
Iseyin 150 7.58 N 3.36 E
Isezaki → Isesaki 92 36.19 N 139.12 E
Isfahan → Eṣfahān 128 32.40 N 51.38 E
Isfana 85 39.50 N 69.31 E
Isfana ≃ 85 40.13 N 69.26 E
Isfara 85 40.07 N 70.38 E
'Isfiyā 132 32.43 N 35.04 E
Ishenga Oswe 152 3.46 S 22.34 E
Isheri-Olofin 273a 6.35 N 3.17 E
Isherton 246 2.19 N 59.22 W
Ishi ≃ 270 34.35 N 135.38 E
Ishibashi 94 36.26 N 139.52 E
Ishibe 94 35.00 N 136.04 E
Ishigaki 175d 24.20 N 124.09 E
Ishigaki-shima I 175d 24.24 N 124.12 E
Ishige 94 36.07 N 139.58 E
Ishii 96 34.04 N 134.26 E
Ishikari ≃ 92a 43.15 N 141.23 E
Ishikari-dake ∧ 92a 43.33 N 143.02 E
Ishikari-heiya ⊻ 92a 43.15 N 141.23 E
Ishikari-sanchi ∧∧ 92a 43.35 N 143.00 E
Ishikari-wan c 92a 43.25 N 141.01 E
Ishikawa, Nihon 94 37.09 N 140.27 E
Ishikawa, Nihon 174m 26.25 N 127.50 E
Ishikawa □[5] 94 36.45 N 136.45 E
Ishiki 94 34.48 N 137.01 E
Ishikiri 270 34.41 N 135.39 E
I-shima I 96 33.51 N 134.49 E
Ishinomaki 92 38.25 N 141.18 E
Ishinomaki-wan c 92 38.18 N 141.18 E
Ishioka 94 36.11 N 140.16 E
Ishiyama 270 34.58 N 135.55 E
Ishizuchi-san ∧ 96 33.46 N 133.07 E
Ishkumān 123 36.32 N 73.49 E
Ishmant 142 29.12 N 31.11 E
Ishpeming 190 46.29 N 87.40 W
Ishuizu ≃ 270 34.33 N 135.27 E
Ishurdi 124 24.08 N 89.05 E
Isidro Casanova 288 34.42 S 58.35 W
Isigny 32 49.19 N 1.06 W
Işık Dağı ∧ 130 38.21 N 36.32 E
Işıklı 130 38.19 N 29.51 E
Işıklı Burnu › 267b 41.14 N 29.15 E
Isili 71 39.44 N 9.06 E
Isil'kul' 86 54.55 N 71.16 E
Išim 86 56.09 N 69.27 E
Išim ≃ 86 57.45 N 71.12 E
Išimbaj 86 53.28 N 56.02 E
Išimskaja step' ⊻ 86 55.00 N 70.00 E
Išimskoje 86 51.24 N 67.08 E
Isimu 112 0.40 N 122.51 E
Isinga 88 52.55 N 112.00 E
Isiolo 154 0.21 N 37.35 E
Isiolo Game Reserve ◆[4] 154 0.32 N 37.34 E
Isipingo 158 29.59 S 30.56 E
Isipingo Beach 158 29.59 S 30.57 E
Isiro (Paulis) 154 2.47 N 27.37 E
Isis 166 25.12 S 152.13 E
Isisford 166 24.16 S 144.26 E
Iskandar 85 41.36 N 69.43 E
Iskăr ≃ 38 43.44 N 24.27 E
Iskăr, Jazovir ◎[1] 38 42.28 N 23.35 E
Iškašim 123 36.44 N 71.37 E


| ENGLISH | | | | DEUTSCH | | | |
| --- | --- | --- | --- | --- | --- | --- | --- |
| Name | Page | Lat.°' | Long.°' | Name | Seite | Breite°' | Länge°' E = Ost |


Iskaten', chrebet ∧∧ 180 66.30 N 179.00 W
Iškejevo 80 55.51 N 50.56 E
İskele 130 35.17 N 33.52 E
İskenderun 130 36.37 N 36.07 E
İskenderun Körfezi (Gulf of Alexandretta) c 130 36.30 N 35.40 E
Iske-R'az'ap 80 54.36 N 49.42 E
İskilip 130 40.45 N 34.29 E
Iski-Naukat 85 40.16 N 72.36 E
Iskininskij 80 47.13 N 52.41 E
Iskitim 86 54.38 N 83.18 E
Iskona ≃ 82 55.34 N 36.05 E
Iskushuban 144 10.17 N 50.14 E
Iskut ≃ 180 56.42 N 131.45 W
Isla 234 18.01 N 95.30 W
Isla ≃ 46 57.30 N 2.47 W
Isla, Salar de la ⊻ 252 25.49 S 68.53 W
Islač ≃ 76 53.55 N 26.13 E
Isla Cristina 34 37.12 N 7.19 W
Isla de Maipo 252 33.45 S 70.54 W
İslâhiye 130 37.03 N 36.36 E
Islāmābād → Anantnāg, India 123 33.44 N 75.09 E
Islāmābād, Pāk. 123 33.42 N 73.10 E
Isla Mala 258 34.12 S 56.21 W
Islāmkot 120 24.42 N 70.11 E
Islamorada 220 24.55 N 80.37 W
Islāmpur, India 122 17.03 N 74.16 E
Islāmpur, India 124 25.09 N 85.12 E
Islāmpur, India 124 26.16 N 88.12 E
Islāmpur, India 126 24.09 N 88.28 E
Islāmpur, India 126 21.43 N 87.39 E
Isla Mujeres 232 21.12 N 86.43 W
Island 194 37.26 N 87.08 W
Island □[6] 224 48.07 N 122.36 W
Island → Iceland □[1] 24a 65.00 N 18.00 W
Island ≃ 262 53.44 N 2.51 W
Island Bay c 116 9.06 N 118.10 E
Island Beach State Park ♠ 208 39.50 N 74.06 W
Island Bend 171b 36.19 S 148.29 E
Island Creek 283 42.00 N 70.43 W
Island Falls, Sk., Can. 184 55.32 N 102.21 W
Island Falls, Me., U.S. 188 46.00 N 68.16 W
Island Heights 208 39.56 N 74.09 W
Islandia → Iceland □[1] 24a 65.00 N 18.00 W
Island Lagoon ◎ 166 31.30 S 136.40 E
Island Lake, Mb., Can. 184 53.58 N 94.47 W
Island Lake, Il., U.S. 216 42.17 N 88.12 W
Island Lake, Mi., U.S. 281 42.31 N 83.44 W
Island Lake ◎ 184 53.47 N 94.25 W
Island Lake State Recreation Area ♠ 216 42.30 N 83.43 W
Island Park, Id., U.S. 202 44.24 N 111.19 W
Island Park, N.Y., U.S. 276 40.36 N 73.39 W
Island Park, R.I., U.S. 207 41.37 N 71.13 W
Island Park Reservoir ◎[1] 202 44.25 N 111.29 W
Island Point › 162 30.20 S 115.02 E
Island Pond 188 44.48 N 71.52 W
Island Pond ◎ 186 48.25 N 56.23 W
Islands, Bay of c, Nf., Can. 186 49.10 N 58.15 W
Islands, Bay of c, N.Z. 172 35.12 S 174.10 E
Island View 216 40.31 N 83.53 W
Isla Patrulla 252 32.59 S 54.35 W
Islas de la Bahía □[5] 236 16.20 N 86.30 W
Islas Malvinas → Falkland Islands □[2] 254 51.45 S 59.00 W
Isla Verde 252 33.14 S 62.24 W
Isla Vista 204 34.25 N 119.50 W
Islay I 46 55.46 N 6.10 W
Islay, Punta › 248 17.01 S 72.07 W
Islay, Rhinns of ›[1] 46 55.45 N 6.25 W
Islay, Sound of ʯ 46 55.50 N 6.06 W
Isle 190 46.08 N 93.28 W
Isle ≃, Fr. 32 44.55 N 0.15 W
Isle ≃, Eng., U.K. 42 50.59 N 2.53 W
Isle-Adam, Forêt de l' ♠ 261 49.05 N 2.15 E
Isle-aux-Morts 186 47.35 N 58.59 W
Isle of Hope 192 31.58 N 81.05 W
Isle of Man □[2], Europe 22 54.15 N 4.30 W
Isle of Man □[2], Europe 44 54.15 N 4.30 W
Isle of Man (Ronaldsway) Airport ⊠ 44 54.06 N 4.36 W
Isle of Palms 192 32.47 N 79.48 W
Isle of Wight 208 36.54 N 76.42 W
Isle of Wight □[6], Eng., U.K. 42 50.40 N 1.20 W
Isle of Wight □[6], Va., U.S. 208 36.50 N 76.42 W
Isle of Wight Bay c 208 38.22 N 75.06 W
Isle Royale National Park ♠ 190 48.00 N 89.00 W
Isles, Lake of the ◎ 212 44.19 N 75.59 W
Isle Saint George 214 41.43 N 82.49 W
Islesboro Island I 188 44.20 N 68.53 W
Isleta 200 34.54 N 106.41 W
Isleta Indian Reservation ◆[4] 200 34.55 N 106.45 W
Isleton 226 38.09 N 121.36 W
Islets-Caribou 186 49.30 N 67.14 W
Isleworth ◆[8] 260 51.28 N 0.20 W
Islington 207 42.13 N 71.11 W
Islington ◆[8], On., Can. 275b 43.39 N 79.32 W
Islington ◆[8], Eng., U.K. 42 51.34 N 0.06 W
Islip, Eng., U.K. 42 51.50 N 1.14 W
Islip, N.Y., U.S. 276 40.43 N 73.12 W
Islip Terrace 276 40.44 N 73.11 W
Islivig 46 58.05 N 7.11 W
Islón 252 29.54 S 71.12 W
Isluga, Volcán ∧[1] 248 19.10 S 68.51 W
Ismael Cortinas (Arroyo Grande) 258 33.58 S 57.06 W
Ismailia → Al-Ismā'īlīyah 142 30.35 N 32.16 E
Ismā'īlīyah ◆[8] 273c 30.03 N 31.14 E
Ismā'īlīyah, Tur'at al- ⌆ 142 30.04 N 31.16 E
İsmailli 130 38.56 N 27.13 E
Ismailovo 80 55.34 N 54.39 E
Ismaning 60 48.14 N 11.41 E
İsmayıllı 84 40.47 N 48.09 E
Isnā 140 25.18 N 32.33 E
Isny 58 47.41 N 10.02 E
Isoanala 157b 23.50 S 45.44 E
Isobe 94 34.22 N 136.49 E
Isogo ◆[8] 268 35.23 N 139.37 E
Isojoki 26 62.07 N 21.58 E
Isoka 154 10.10 S 32.35 E
Isokyrö 26 63.00 N 22.19 E
Isola, Fr. 62 44.11 N 7.03 E
Isola, Ms., U.S. 194 33.15 N 90.35 W
Isola, Monte ∧ 64 45.42 N 10.05 E
Isola d'Asti 62 44.50 N 8.11 E
Isola del Cantone 62 44.39 N 8.57 E
Isola del Gran Sasso d'Italia 66 42.30 N 13.40 E
Isola della Scala 64 45.16 N 11.00 E
Isola del Liri 66 41.41 N 13.34 E
Isola di Capo Rizzuto 68 38.58 N 17.06 E
Isola Dovarese 64 45.10 N 10.18 E
Isola Farnese ◆[8] 66 42.01 N 12.23 E
Isola Vicentina 64 45.38 N 11.25 E
Isoletta 66 41.30 N 13.34 E
Isolillock Peak ∧ 224 49.18 N 121.27 W
Isolo 273a 6.32 N 3.19 E
Isone 58 46.08 N 8.59 E
Isonzo (Soča) ≃ 64 45.47 N 13.32 E
Isorella 64 45.18 N 10.19 E
Iso-Syöte ∧[2] 26 65.37 N 27.35 E
Iso-zaki › 94 36.23 N 140.38 E
Ispani 68 40.08 N 15.34 E
Isparta 130 37.46 N 30.33 E
Isparta □[4] 130 38.00 N 31.00 E
Isperih 38 43.43 N 26.50 E
Ispica 70 36.47 N 14.55 E
Ispica, Cava d' ⊥[5] 70 36.51 N 14.51 E
Ispikān 128 26.14 N 62.12 E
İspir 130 40.29 N 41.00 E
Ispra 62 45.49 N 8.37 E
Ispringen 56 48.55 N 8.40 E
Israel (Yisra'el) □[1], Asia 118 31.30 N 35.00 E
Israel (Yisra'el) □[1], Asia 132 31.30 N 35.00 E
Israel ≃ 188 44.29 N 71.35 W
Issa 80 53.52 N 44.51 E
Issa ≃ 76 56.58 N 28.47 E
Issano 246 5.49 N 59.25 W
Issaquah 224 47.31 N 122.01 W
Issaran, Ra's › 142 28.48 N 32.47 E
Issel (Oude IJssel) ≃ 52 52.00 N 6.10 E
Isselburg 52 51.51 N 6.28 E
Isselhorst 52 51.57 N 8.24 E
Isser, Oued ≃, Alg. 34 36.52 N 3.48 E
Isser, Oued ≃, Alg. 34 35.08 N 1.28 W
Issia 150 6.29 N 6.35 W
Issigeac 32 44.44 N 0.36 E
Issime 62 45.41 N 7.51 E
Issogne 62 45.39 N 7.41 E
Issoire 32 45.33 N 3.15 E
Issole ≃ 62 43.27 N 6.12 E
Issou 261 48.59 N 1.48 E
Issoudun 32 46.57 N 2.00 E
Issum 52 51.32 N 6.25 E
Issuna 154 5.23 S 34.46 E
Is-sur-Tille 58 47.31 N 5.06 E
Issy 50 48.49 N 2.17 E
Issyk-Kul' (Rybačje) 85 42.26 N 76.12 E
Issyk-Kul' □[4] 85 42.15 N 77.15 E
Issyk-Kul', ozero ◎ 85 42.25 N 77.15 E
Īstādeh-ye Moqor, Āb-e ◎ 120 32.32 N 67.57 E
Istana Presidential Palace ⚜ 269e 6.10 S 106.49 E
İstanbul, Tür. 130 41.01 N 28.58 E
İstanbul, Tür. 267b 41.01 N 28.58 E
İstanbul □[4] 130 41.10 N 28.45 E
Istanbul (Yeşilköy) International Airport ⊠ 267b 40.58 N 28.49 E
İstanbul Boğazı (Bosporus) ʯ 130 41.06 N 29.04 E
Istanbul University ⚜[2] 267b 41.00 N 28.58 E
Iṣṭanhā 142 30.28 N 31.07 E
Istead Rise 260 51.24 N 0.22 E
Isteren ◎ 26 61.58 N 11.48 E
Isthmus Bay c 212 45.00 N 81.15 W
Istiaía 38 38.57 N 23.09 E
İstinye ◆[8] 267b 41.06 N 29.03 E
İstisu 84 39.57 N 45.59 E
Istmina 246 5.10 N 76.39 W
Isto, Mount ∧ 180 69.12 N 143.48 W
Istobensk 80 58.25 N 48.48 E
Istobnoje, Ross. 78 51.08 N 37.21 E
Istobnoje, Ross. 78 51.16 N 38.39 E
Istok 38 42.47 N 20.29 E
Istokpoga, Lake ◎ 220 27.22 N 81.17 W
Istra 82 55.55 N 36.52 E
Istra ›[1] 36 45.15 N 14.00 E
Istra ≃ 82 55.44 N 37.08 E
Istrana 64 45.41 N 12.07 E
Istres 62 43.31 N 4.59 E
Istria → Istra ›[1] 36 45.15 N 14.00 E
Istrinskoje vodochranilišče ◎[1] 82 56.04 N 36.49 E
Isulan 116 6.34 N 124.37 E
Isumi 94 35.17 N 140.19 E
Isumi ≃ 94 35.18 N 140.25 E
Isumrud Strait ʯ 164 4.45 S 145.50 E
Isunba 273a 6.27 N 3.17 E
Iswarīpur 126 22.19 N 89.07 E
Iswepe 158 26.50 S 30.31 E
Itá 252 25.29 S 57.21 W
Itabaiana, Bra. 250 7.20 S 35.20 W
Itabaiana, Bra. 250 10.41 S 37.26 W
Itabaiana, Bra. 250 11.16 S 37.47 W
Itabapoana 255 21.18 S 40.58 W
Itabashi ◆[8] 268 35.45 N 139.43 E
Itaberá 255 23.51 S 49.09 W
Itaberaba 255 12.32 S 40.18 W
Itaberaí 255 16.02 S 49.48 W
Itabi 250 10.08 S 37.06 W
Itabira 255 19.37 S 43.13 W
Itaboca 256 22.03 S 44.05 W
Itaboraí 256 22.45 S 42.52 W
Itaboraí □[7] 287a 22.43 S 43.00 W
Itabuna 255 14.48 S 39.16 W
Itacaiuna ≃ 250 5.21 S 49.08 W
Itacajá 250 8.19 S 47.46 W
Itacambiruçu ≃ 255 16.44 S 42.45 W
Itacaré 255 14.18 S 39.00 W
Itacoatiara 250 3.08 S 58.25 W
Itacoatiara, Ponta de › 287a 22.59 S 43.02 W
Itacurubí del Rosario 252 24.29 S 56.41 W
Itacurussá 256 22.55 S 43.55 W
Itacurussá, Ilha de I 256 22.56 S 43.53 W
Itaeté 255 12.59 S 40.58 W
Itagacaba ≃ 256 22.34 S 44.56 W
Itagi 255 14.10 S 40.01 W
Itaguaçu 255 19.48 S 40.51 W
Itaguaí 256 22.52 S 43.47 W
Itaguajé 255 22.37 S 51.59 W
Itaguara 255 20.23 S 44.29 W
Itaguaré, Pico do ∧ 256 22.30 S 45.10 W
Itaguari ≃ 255 14.11 S 44.40 W
Itaguaru 255 15.44 S 49.37 W
Itaguatins 250 5.47 S 47.29 W
Itagüí 246 6.10 N 75.36 W
Itaí 255 23.24 S 49.06 W
Itá-Ibaté 252 27.26 S 57.20 W
Itaiçaba 250 4.40 S 37.51 W
Itaim 256 22.24 S 45.53 W
Itaim ≃, Bra. 250 7.02 S 42.02 W
Itaim ≃, Bra. 256 23.07 S 45.08 W
Itaim ≃, Bra. 256 22.19 S 45.51 W
Itainópolis 250 7.24 S 41.31 W
Itaiópolis 252 26.20 S 49.56 W
Itaipava 256 22.23 S 43.08 W
Itaipu, Bra. 256 22.58 S 43.02 W
Itaipu, Bra. 287a 22.44 S 43.26 W
Itaipu, Lagoa de c 287a 22.58 S 43.02 W
Itaipu, Ponta de › 287a 22.59 S 43.03 W
Itaipu, Represa de ◎[1] 252 25.00 S 54.30 W
Itäisen Suomenlahden kansallispuisto ♠ 26 60.15 N 27.00 E
Itaituba 250 4.17 S 55.59 W
Itajá 255 19.07 S 51.37 W
Itajaí 252 26.53 S 48.39 W
Itajaí do Sul ≃ 252 27.12 S 49.39 W
Itajipora 256 22.19 S 46.28 W
Itajubá 256 22.26 S 45.27 W
Itaju do Colônia 255 15.09 S 39.44 W
Itajuípe 255 14.41 S 39.22 W
Itaka, Ross. 88 53.53 N 118.42 E
Itaka, Tan. 154 8.52 S 32.47 E
Itaki 273a 6.43 N 3.17 E
Itako 94 35.56 N 140.33 E
Itakura, Nihon 94 36.13 N 139.36 E
Itakura, Nihon 94 37.03 N 138.18 E
Itala Game Reserve ◆[4] 158 27.31 S 31.19 E


**Symbols** in the index entries represent the broad categories identified in the key at the right. Symbols with superior numbers (∧∧[1]) identify subcategories (see complete key on page *I · 1).*

**Symbole** im Register stellen die rechts im Schlüssel erklärten Kategorien dar. Symbole mit hochgestellten Ziffern (∧∧[1]) bezeichnen Unterabteilungen einer Kategorie (vgl. vollständiger Schlüssel auf Seite *I · 1).*

**Los símbolos** incluídos en el texto del índice representan las grandes categorías identificadas con la clave a la derecha. Los símbolos con numeros en su parte superior (∧∧[1]) identifican las subcategorías (véase la clave completa en la página *I · 1).*

**Les symboles** de l'index représentent les catégories indiquées dans la légende à droite. Les symboles suivis d'un indice (∧∧[1]) représentent des sous-catégories (voir légende complète à la page *I · 1).*

**Os símbolos** incluídos no texto do índice representam as grandes categorias identificadas com a chave à direita. Os símbolos com números em sua parte superior (∧∧[1]) identificam as subcategorias (veja-se a chave completa à página *I · 1).*

| | | | | |
| --- | --- | --- | --- | --- |
| ∧ Mountain | Berg | Montaña | Montagne | Montanha |
| ∧∧ Mountains | Gebirge | Montañas | Montagnes | Montanhas |
| )( Pass | Paß | Paso | Col | Passo |
| V Valley, Canyon | Tal, Cañon | Valle, Cañón | Vallée, Canyon | Vale, Canhão |
| ⊻ Plain | Ebene | Llano | Plaine | Planície |
| › Cape | Kap | Cabo | Cap | Cabo |
| I Island | Insel | Isla | Île | Ilha |
| II Islands | Inseln | Islas | Îles | Ilhas |
| ⊥ Other Topographic Features | Andere Topographische Objekte | Otros Elementos Topográficos | Autres données topographiques | Outros acidentes topográficos |

## ESPAÑOL

| Nombre | Página | Lat.°′ | Long.°′ W = Oeste |
|---|---|---|---|
| Italia → Italy □[1] | 36 | 42.50 N | 12.50 E |
| Itálica ⊥ | 34 | 37.30 N | 6.05 W |
| Italie → Italy □[1] | 36 | 42.50 N | 12.50 E |
| Italien → Italy □[1] | 36 | 42.50 N | 12.50 E |
| Italy | 222 | 32.11 N | 96.53 W |
| Italy (Italia) □[1], Europe | 22 | 42.50 N | 12.50 E |
| Italy (Italia) □[1], Europe | 36 | 42.50 N | 12.50 E |
| Itamaraju | 255 | 17.05 S | 39.31 W |
| Itamarandiba | 255 | 17.51 S | 42.51 W |
| Itamarandiba ≃ | 255 | 17.18 S | 42.48 W |
| Itamarati de Minas | 256 | 21.25 S | 42.49 W |
| Itamari | 255 | 13.47 S | 39.37 W |
| Itamataré | 250 | 2.16 S | 46.24 W |
| Itambacuri | 255 | 18.01 S | 41.42 W |
| Itambé | 255 | 15.15 S | 40.37 W |
| Itambi | 256 | 22.44 S | 42.58 W |
| Itami | 96 | 34.46 N | 135.25 E |
| Itami, Camp ■ | 270 | 34.47 N | 135.24 E |
| Itamonte | 256 | 22.17 S | 44.53 W |
| Itampolo | 157b | 24.41 S | 43.57 E |
| Itānagar | 120 | 27.09 N | 93.33 E |
| Itandéua, Lago ⊜ | 250 | 2.01 S | 55.10 W |
| Itandrano | 157b | 21.47 S | 45.17 E |
| Itanhaém | 255 | 24.11 S | 46.47 W |
| Itanhandu | 256 | 22.18 S | 44.57 W |
| Itanhauã ≃ | 248 | 4.45 S | 63.48 W |
| Itanhém | 255 | 17.09 S | 40.20 W |
| Itanhomi | 255 | 19.10 S | 41.52 W |
| Itano | 96 | 34.07 N | 134.28 E |
| Itaobim | 255 | 16.34 S | 41.30 W |
| Itaocaia | 287a | 22.58 S | 43.01 W |
| Itapaci | 255 | 14.57 S | 49.34 W |
| Itapagipe | 255 | 19.54 S | 49.22 W |
| Itapajé | 250 | 3.41 S | 39.34 W |
| Itapanhaú ≃ | 256 | 23.51 S | 46.10 W |
| Itaparaná ≃ | 248 | 5.47 S | 63.03 W |
| Itaparica, Ilha de I | 255 | 13.00 S | 38.42 W |
| Itaparica, Reprêsa de ⊜[1] | 250 | 8.50 S | 38.40 W |
| Itapaya | 248 | 17.34 S | 66.21 W |
| Itapé | 255 | 14.54 S | 39.26 W |
| Itapebi | 255 | 15.56 S | 39.32 W |
| Itapecerica | 255 | 20.28 S | 45.07 W |
| Itapecerica da Serra | 256 | 23.43 S | 46.50 W |
| Itapecerica da Serra □[7] | 287b | 23.44 S | 46.52 W |
| Itapecuru-Mirim | 250 | 3.24 S | 44.20 W |
| Itapemirim | 255 | 21.01 S | 40.50 W |
| Itapera | 250 | 2.32 S | 43.47 W |
| Itaperina, Pointe › | 157b | 24.59 S | 47.06 E |
| Itaperuna | 255 | 21.12 S | 41.54 W |
| Itapetim | 250 | 7.22 S | 37.11 W |
| Itapetinga | 255 | 15.15 S | 40.15 W |
| Itapetininga | 255 | 23.36 S | 48.03 W |
| Itapetininga ≃ | 255 | 23.35 S | 48.27 W |
| Itapeva, Bra. | 255 | 23.58 S | 48.52 W |
| Itapeva, Bra. | 256 | 22.46 S | 46.13 W |
| Itapevi | 256 | 23.33 S | 46.56 W |
| Itapevi □[7] | 287b | 23.31 S | 46.55 W |
| Itapicuru | 250 | 11.19 S | 38.15 W |
| Itapicuru ≃, Bra. | 250 | 2.52 S | 44.12 W |
| Itapicuru ≃, Bra. | 250 | 11.47 S | 37.32 W |
| Itapipoca | 250 | 3.30 S | 39.35 W |
| Itapira | 256 | 22.26 S | 46.50 W |
| Itapiranga, Bra. | 250 | 2.45 S | 58.01 W |
| Itapiranga, Bra. | 252 | 27.08 S | 53.43 W |
| Itapirapuã | 255 | 15.52 S | 50.36 W |
| Itapitanga | 255 | 14.26 S | 39.34 W |
| Itapiúna | 250 | 4.33 S | 38.57 W |
| Itápolis | 255 | 21.35 S | 48.46 W |
| Itaporã | 255 | 22.01 S | 54.54 W |
| Itaporã de Goiás | 250 | 8.02 S | 48.39 W |
| Itaporanga, Bra. | 250 | 7.18 S | 38.10 W |
| Itaporanga, Bra. | 255 | 23.42 S | 49.29 W |
| Itaporanga d'Ajuda | 250 | 10.59 S | 37.18 W |
| Itapúa □[5] | 252 | 26.50 S | 55.50 W |
| Itapuranga | 255 | 15.35 S | 49.59 W |
| Itaquaí ≃ | 246 | 4.20 S | 70.12 W |
| Itaquaquecetuba | 256 | 23.29 S | 46.21 W |
| Itaquaquecetuba □[7] | 287b | 23.28 S | 46.20 W |
| Itaquara | 255 | 13.27 S | 39.57 W |
| Itaquari | 255 | 20.20 S | 40.22 W |
| Itaquaxiara | 287b | 23.47 S | 46.51 W |
| Itaquaxiara, Ribeirão ≃ | 287b | 23.44 S | 46.47 W |
| Itaquera ◆[8] | 256 | 23.32 S | 46.27 W |
| Itaquera, Ribeirão ≃ | 287b | 23.28 S | 46.26 W |
| Itaqui | 252 | 29.08 S | 56.33 W |
| Itaquyry | 252 | 24.56 S | 55.13 W |
| Itarantim | 255 | 15.39 S | 40.03 W |
| Itararé | 255 | 24.07 S | 49.20 W |
| Itārsi | 124 | 22.37 N | 77.45 E |
| Itarumã | 255 | 18.42 S | 51.25 W |
| Itasca, Il., U.S. | 278 | 41.58 N | 88.00 W |
| Itasca, Tx., U.S. | 222 | 32.09 N | 97.08 W |
| Itasca, Lake ⊜ | 198 | 47.11 N | 95.12 W |
| Itasca State Park ♠ | 198 | 47.18 N | 95.18 W |
| Itata ≃ | 252 | 36.23 S | 72.52 W |
| Itatí | 252 | 27.16 S | 58.15 W |
| Itatiaia | 256 | 22.30 S | 44.34 W |
| Itatiaia, Parque Nacional do ♠ | 256 | 22.28 S | 44.37 W |
| Itatiba | 256 | 23.00 S | 46.51 W |
| Itatinga | 255 | 23.07 S | 48.36 W |
| Itatira | 250 | 4.30 S | 39.37 W |
| Itatka | 86 | 56.49 N | 85.37 E |
| Itatolo | 273b | 4.09 S | 15.15 E |
| Itatskij | 86 | 56.04 N | 89.05 E |
| Itatupã | 250 | 0.37 S | 51.12 W |
| Itaú | 250 | 5.50 S | 37.59 W |
| Itaueira | 250 | 7.36 S | 43.02 W |
| Itaueira ≃ | 250 | 6.41 S | 42.55 W |
| Itaúna | 255 | 20.04 S | 44.34 W |
| Itaúna, Morro do ∧[2] | 287a | 22.46 S | 43.02 W |
| Itāwa | 124 | 25.32 N | 76.22 E |
| Itazuke-kūkō ⊠ | 96 | 33.35 N | 130.28 E |
| Itbayat Island I | 108 | 20.46 N | 121.50 E |
| Itéa | 38 | 38.26 N | 22.24 E |
| Itenes (Guaporé) ≃ | 248 | 11.54 S | 65.01 W |
| Ith ∧ | 52 | 52.05 N | 9.35 E |
| Ithaca, Mi., U.S. | 190 | 43.17 N | 84.36 W |
| Ithaca, N.Y., U.S. | 210 | 42.26 N | 76.29 W |
| Itháki | 38 | 38.23 N | 20.42 E |
| Itháki I | 38 | 38.24 N | 20.42 E |
| Ithan Creek ≃ | 285 | 40.00 N | 75.21 W |
| Ithnayn | 142 | 30.41 N | 32.21 E |
| Ithon ≃ | 42 | 52.12 N | 3.27 W |
| Itigi | 154 | 5.42 S | 34.29 E |
| Itikawa → Ichikawa | 94 | 35.44 N | 139.55 E |
| Itimādpur | 124 | 27.15 N | 78.12 E |
| Itimbiri ≃ | 152 | 2.02 N | 22.44 E |
| Itinga | 255 | 16.36 S | 41.47 W |
| Itinga ≃ | 255 | 16.35 S | 41.45 W |
| Itinomiya → Ichinomiya | 94 | 35.18 N | 136.48 E |
| Itipo | 152 | 0.50 S | 18.35 E |
| Itiquira | 255 | 17.12 S | 54.07 W |
| Itiquira ≃ | 248 | 17.21 S | 55.37 W |
| Itirapina | 255 | 22.15 S | 47.49 W |
| Itire | 273a | 6.31 N | 3.21 E |
| Itiruçu | 255 | 13.31 S | 40.09 W |
| Itiúba | 250 | 10.43 S | 39.51 W |
| Itkillik ≃ | 180 | 70.08 N | 150.57 W |
| Itlar' | 82 | 56.51 N | 39.17 E |
| Itlīdim | 142 | 27.52 N | 30.48 E |
| Itmīdah | 142 | 30.46 N | 31.20 E |
| Itmuryn, ozero ⊜ | 80 | 49.30 N | 52.22 E |
| Itō | 94 | 34.58 N | 139.05 E |
| Itobi | 256 | 21.44 S | 46.58 W |
| Itobo | 154 | 4.10 S | 33.01 E |
| Itoculo | 154 | 14.42 S | 40.18 E |
| Itoigawa | 94 | 37.02 N | 137.51 E |
| Itoko | 152 | 1.00 S | 21.45 E |
| Itomamo, Lac ⊜ | 186 | 49.11 N | 70.28 W |

## FRANÇAIS

| Nom | Page | Lat.°′ | Long.°′ W = Ouest |
|---|---|---|---|
| Itoman | 174m | 26.08 N | 127.40 E |
| Iton ≃ | 50 | 49.09 N | 1.12 E |
| Itonamas ≃ | 248 | 12.28 S | 64.24 W |
| Itororó | 255 | 15.07 S | 40.06 W |
| Itri | 66 | 41.17 N | 13.32 E |
| Iṭsā | 142 | 29.15 N | 30.48 E |
| Itsukaichi, Nihon | 94 | 35.44 N | 139.13 E |
| Itsukaichi, Nihon | 96 | 34.24 N | 132.22 E |
| Itsuki | 92 | 32.24 N | 130.50 E |
| Itsuku-shima I | 96 | 34.16 N | 132.19 E |
| Itsuwa | 92 | 32.30 N | 130.10 E |
| Itta Bena | 194 | 33.29 N | 90.19 W |
| Ittel, Oued V | 148 | 34.19 N | 6.01 E |
| Itter ≃ | 263 | 51.09 N | 6.52 E |
| Ittersum | 52 | 52.28 N | 6.07 E |
| Itteville | 261 | 48.31 N | 2.21 E |
| Ittiri | 71 | 40.36 N | 8.34 E |
| Itú | 255 | 23.16 S | 47.19 W |
| Itu ≃ | 252 | 29.25 S | 55.51 W |
| Ituaçu | 255 | 13.49 S | 41.18 W |
| Ituango | 246 | 7.04 N | 75.45 W |
| Ituberá | 255 | 13.44 S | 39.09 W |
| Itucumã ≃ | 248 | 6.59 S | 69.48 W |
| Itueta | 255 | 19.23 S | 41.11 W |
| Ituí | 256 | 21.32 S | 42.55 W |
| Ituí ≃ | 246 | 4.38 S | 70.19 W |
| Ituim ≃ | 252 | 28.35 S | 51.20 W |
| Ituiutaba | 255 | 18.58 S | 49.28 W |
| Itula | 154 | 3.29 S | 27.52 E |
| Itumbiara | 255 | 18.25 S | 49.13 W |
| Itumirim | 256 | 21.19 S | 44.53 W |
| Itum-Kale | 84 | 42.43 N | 45.35 E |
| Ituna | 184 | 51.10 N | 103.30 W |
| Itungi Port | 154 | 9.35 S | 33.56 E |
| Ituni | 246 | 5.30 N | 58.14 W |
| Itupararanga, Reprêsa de ⊜[1] | 256 | 23.37 S | 47.16 W |
| Itupeva | 256 | 23.09 S | 47.04 W |
| Itupeva, Rio da ≃ | 256 | 22.03 S | 47.15 W |
| Itupiranga | 250 | 5.09 S | 49.20 W |
| Ituporanga | 252 | 27.25 S | 49.36 W |
| Iturama | 255 | 19.44 S | 50.11 W |
| Iturbe | 252 | 26.01 S | 56.30 W |
| Iturbide | 232 | 19.40 N | 89.37 W |
| Ituri ≃ | 154 | 1.40 N | 27.01 E |
| Iturup, ostrov (Etorofu-tō) I | 92a | 44.35 N | 147.10 E |
| Itutinga | 256 | 21.18 S | 44.40 W |
| Ituverava | 255 | 20.20 S | 47.47 W |
| Ituxi ≃ | 248 | 7.18 S | 64.51 W |
| Ituzaingó, Arg. | 252 | 27.36 S | 56.41 W |
| Ituzaingó, Arg. | 258 | 34.40 S | 58.40 W |
| Ituzaingó, Ur. | 258 | 34.25 S | 56.26 W |
| Itwa | 124 | 27.20 N | 82.42 E |
| Ityāy al-Bārūd | 142 | 30.53 N | 30.40 E |
| Ityopiya → Ethiopia □[1] | 144 | 9.00 N | 39.00 E |
| Itz ≃ | 56 | 49.58 N | 10.52 E |
| Itzehoe | 52 | 53.55 N | 9.31 E |
| Iubundha ≃ | 126 | 24.06 N | 90.20 E |
| Iue | 76 | 53.56 N | 25.46 E |
| Iuka, Il., U.S. | 219 | 38.37 N | 88.47 W |
| Iuka, Ms., U.S. | 194 | 34.48 N | 88.11 W |
| Iul'tin | 180 | 67.50 N | 178.48 W |
| Iul'tin, gora ∧ | 180 | 67.50 N | 178.25 W |
| Iúna | 255 | 20.21 S | 41.32 W |
| Iupeba | 256 | 23.41 S | 46.22 W |
| Iva | 192 | 34.18 N | 82.39 W |
| Ivacèvičy | 76 | 52.43 N | 25.21 E |
| Ivačovo | 76 | 60.32 N | 36.22 E |
| Ivahona | 157b | 23.27 S | 46.10 E |
| Ivaí ≃ | 255 | 23.18 S | 53.42 W |
| Ivaiporã | 252 | 24.15 S | 51.45 W |
| Ivajlovgrad | 38 | 41.32 N | 26.08 E |
| Ivakoany, Massif de l' ⋏ | 157b | 23.50 S | 46.25 E |
| Ivalo | 24 | 68.42 N | 27.30 E |
| Ivalojoki ≃ | 24 | 68.43 N | 27.36 E |
| Ivanava | 76 | 52.09 N | 25.32 E |
| Ivancevo | 82 | 55.58 N | 36.07 E |
| Ivančice | 61 | 49.06 N | 16.23 E |
| Ivancovo | 82 | 56.39 N | 35.50 E |
| Ivanec | 36 | 46.13 N | 16.08 E |
| Ivane-Puste | 78 | 48.39 N | 26.11 E |
| Ivangorod | 76 | 59.24 N | 28.10 E |
| Ivangrad | 38 | 42.50 N | 19.52 E |
| Ivanhoe, Austl. | 166 | 32.54 S | 144.18 E |
| Ivanhoe, Austl. | 274b | 37.46 S | 145.03 E |
| Ivanhoe, Ca., U.S. | 226 | 36.23 N | 119.13 W |
| Ivanhoe, Il., U.S. | 278 | 42.17 N | 88.02 W |
| Ivanhoe, Mn., U.S. | 198 | 44.27 N | 96.14 W |
| Ivanhoe, Va., U.S. | 192 | 36.50 N | 80.58 W |
| Ivanhoe ≃ | 190 | 48.40 N | 82.11 W |
| Ivanhoe Lake ⊜ | 190 | 48.05 N | 82.38 W |
| Ivanić Grad | 36 | 45.42 N | 16.24 E |
| Ivanišči, Ross. | 76 | 56.36 N | 35.13 E |
| Ivanišči, Ross. | 80 | 55.46 N | 40.26 E |
| Ivaniv | 78 | 49.28 N | 28.21 E |
| Ivanivka, Ukr. | 78 | 46.58 N | 30.28 E |
| Ivanivka, Ukr. | 78 | 46.43 N | 34.33 E |
| Ivanivka, Ukr. | 83 | 48.14 N | 38.58 E |
| Ivanivka, Ukr. | 83 | 47.35 N | 37.19 E |
| Ivanjci | 61 | 46.38 N | 15.54 E |
| Ivanjica | 38 | 43.35 N | 20.14 E |
| Ivankov | 78 | 50.56 N | 29.54 E |
| Ivankovcy | 89 | 49.06 N | 134.28 E |
| Ivan'kovo | 82 | 54.44 N | 37.57 E |
| Ivan'kovskij | 80 | 56.39 N | 40.05 E |
| Ivan'kovskoje vodochranilišče ⊜[1] | 82 | 56.37 N | 36.32 E |
| Ivanof Bay | 180 | 55.54 N | 159.29 W |
| Ivano-Frankivs'k | 78 | 48.55 N | 24.43 E |
| Ivano-Frankivs'k □[4] | 78 | 48.45 N | 24.30 E |
| Ivano-Frankove | 78 | 49.55 N | 23.43 E |
| Ivanopil' | 78 | 49.52 N | 28.12 E |
| Ivano-Šamševo | 83 | 46.52 N | 39.54 E |
| Ivanovka, Kyrg. | 85 | 42.54 N | 75.05 E |
| Ivanovka, Ross. | 80 | 52.51 N | 53.48 E |
| Ivanovka, Ross. | 80 | 51.54 N | 43.46 E |
| Ivanovka, Ross. | 80 | 52.15 N | 41.35 E |
| Ivanovka, Ross. | 89 | 50.22 N | 128.02 E |
| Ivanovka, Ross. | 89 | 43.58 N | 132.30 E |
| Ivanovo | 80 | 57.00 N | 40.59 E |
| Ivanovo Oblast' □[4] | 76 | 57.00 N | 41.00 E |
| Ivanovo-Voznesensk → Ivanovo | 80 | 57.00 N | 40.59 E |
| Ivanovskaja, Ross. | 24 | 60.48 N | 55.52 E |
| Ivanovskaja, Ross. | 78 | 45.17 N | 38.29 E |
| Ivanovskoje, Ross. | 76 | 59.17 N | 28.49 E |
| Ivanovskoje, Ross. | 78 | 51.37 N | 34.57 E |
| Ivanovskoje, Ross. | 82 | 55.05 N | 37.50 E |
| Ivanovskoje, Ross. | 82 | 54.55 N | 36.50 E |
| Ivanovskoje, Ross. | 82 | 55.52 N | 36.55 E |
| Ivanovskoje, Ross. | 82 | 56.23 N | 37.07 E |
| Ivanovskoje, Ross. | 265a | 59.46 N | 30.47 E |
| Ivan-Ozero | 82 | 54.04 N | 38.20 E |
| Ivan-Ozero, ozero ⊜ | 82 | 54.07 N | 38.17 E |
| Ivanpah Lake ⊜ | 204 | 35.35 N | 115.25 W |
| Ivantejevka, Ross. | 80 | 52.16 N | 49.07 E |
| Ivantejevka, Ross. | 82 | 55.58 N | 37.55 E |
| Ivantejevo | 76 | 57.48 N | 33.09 E |
| Ivanychi | 78 | 50.39 N | 24.20 E |
| Ivanytsya | 78 | 50.47 N | 32.36 E |
| Ivato | 157b | 20.37 S | 47.12 E |
| Ivatuba | 255 | 23.37 S | 52.13 W |
| Ivdel' | 72 | 60.42 N | 60.24 E |
| Ivel ≃ | 42 | 52.10 N | 0.18 W |
| Iver | 260 | 51.31 N | 0.30 W |
| Iver Heath | 260 | 51.32 N | 0.31 W |
| Iverny | 261 | 49.00 N | 2.47 E |
| Ivigtut | 176 | 61.12 N | 48.10 W |
| Ivindo ≃ | 152 | 0.09 S | 12.09 E |
| Ivinghoe | 42 | 51.50 N | 0.37 W |
| Ivinheima ≃ | 255 | 23.14 S | 53.42 W |
| Ivjanec | 76 | 53.53 N | 26.45 E |
| Ivn'a | 76 | 51.08 N | 36.07 E |
| Ivnytsya | 78 | 50.09 N | 29.03 E |
| Ivohibe | 157b | 22.29 S | 46.52 E |
| Ivolginsk | 88 | 51.45 N | 107.14 E |
| Ivón | 248 | 11.06 S | 66.08 W |

## PORTUGUÊS

| Nome | Página | Lat.°′ | Long.°′ W = Oeste |
|---|---|---|---|
| Ivondro | 157b | 24.47 S | 46.52 E |
| Ivor | 208 | 36.54 N | 76.54 W |
| Ivorogbo | 150 | 5.30 N | 6.21 E |
| Ivory Coast → Cote d'Ivoire □[1] | 150 | 8.00 N | 5.00 W |
| Ivory Coast ±[2] | 150 | 5.10 N | 5.00 W |
| Ivoryton | 207 | 41.20 N | 72.26 W |
| Ivösjön ⊜ | 26 | 56.06 N | 14.27 E |
| Ivot, Ross. | 76 | 53.42 N | 34.12 E |
| Ivot, Ukr. | 78 | 51.58 N | 33.28 E |
| Ivotka ≃ | 78 | 51.57 N | 33.22 E |
| Ivrea | 62 | 45.28 N | 7.52 E |
| İvrindi | 130 | 39.34 N | 27.29 E |
| Ivry-la-Bataille | 50 | 48.53 N | 1.28 E |
| Ivry [-sur-Seine] | 50 | 48.49 N | 2.23 E |
| Ivujivik | 176 | 62.24 N | 77.55 W |
| Ivybridge | 42 | 50.23 N | 3.56 W |
| Ivy Hatch | 260 | 51.16 N | 0.16 E |
| Ivyland | 285 | 40.12 N | 75.04 W |
| Iwade | 96 | 34.15 N | 135.19 E |
| Iwafune, Nihon | 94 | 36.19 N | 139.40 E |
| Iwafune, Nihon | 270 | 34.44 N | 135.54 E |
| Iwagi | 96 | 34.15 N | 133.09 E |
| Iwai | 94 | 36.03 N | 139.54 E |
| Iwai-shima I | 96 | 33.47 N | 131.58 E |
| Iwaizumi | 92 | 39.50 N | 141.48 E |
| Iwaki (Taira) | 94 | 37.03 N | 140.55 E |
| Iwaki ≃ | 92 | 41.01 N | 140.22 E |
| Iwaki-san ∧ | 92 | 40.39 N | 140.18 E |
| Iwakuni | 96 | 34.09 N | 132.11 E |
| Iwakuni Marine Corps Air Station ■ | 96 | 34.08 N | 132.14 E |
| Iwakura | 94 | 35.17 N | 136.52 E |
| Iwama | 94 | 36.18 N | 140.16 E |
| Iwami, Nihon | 96 | 34.53 N | 132.26 E |
| Iwami, Nihon | 96 | 35.35 N | 134.20 E |
| Iwami-kōgen ⋏[1] | 96 | 35.00 N | 132.30 E |
| Iwami-kokubun-ji ʋ[1] | 96 | 34.56 N | 132.08 E |
| Iwamizawa | 92a | 43.12 N | 141.46 E |
| Iwamura | 94 | 35.22 N | 137.26 E |
| Iwanai | 92a | 42.58 N | 140.30 E |
| Iwanowo → Ivanovo | 80 | 57.00 N | 40.59 E |
| Iwanuma | 92 | 38.06 N | 140.52 E |
| Iwaoka ◆[8] | 270 | 34.44 N | 134.58 E |
| Iwase, Nihon | 94 | 36.21 N | 140.06 E |
| Iwase, Nihon | 268 | 35.17 N | 139.52 E |
| Iwata | 94 | 34.42 N | 137.48 E |
| Iwataki | 96 | 35.34 N | 135.09 E |
| Iwate □[5] | 92 | 39.37 N | 141.22 E |
| Iwate-san ∧ | 92 | 39.51 N | 141.00 E |
| Iwatsuki | 94 | 35.57 N | 139.42 E |
| Iwaya → Awaji, Nihon | 96 | 34.35 N | 135.01 E |
| Iwaya, Nihon | 270 | 34.35 N | 135.02 E |
| Iwayama | 270 | 34.52 N | 135.52 E |
| Iwazono | 270 | 34.45 N | 135.19 E |
| Iwo | 150 | 7.38 N | 4.11 E |
| Iwo Jima → Iō-jima I | 174f | 24.47 N | 141.20 E |
| Iwŏn | 98 | 40.19 N | 128.39 E |
| Iwuy | 50 | 50.14 N | 3.19 E |
| Ixcán ≃ | 236 | 16.07 N | 91.05 W |
| Ixchiguán | 236 | 15.12 N | 91.53 W |
| Ixelles | 56 | 50.50 N | 4.22 E |
| Ixhuatlán | 234 | 19.04 N | 96.59 W |
| Ixiamas | 248 | 13.45 S | 68.09 W |
| Iximché ⊥ | 236 | 14.44 N | 90.59 W |
| Ixmiquilpan | 234 | 20.29 N | 99.14 W |
| Ixonia | 216 | 43.09 N | 88.36 W |
| Ixopo | 158 | 30.08 S | 30.00 E |
| Ixtahuacán | 236 | 15.25 N | 91.46 W |
| Ixtapa | 234 | 17.39 N | 101.36 W |
| Ixtapa, Punta › | 234 | 17.39 N | 101.40 W |
| Ixtapan de la Sal | 234 | 18.50 N | 99.41 W |
| Ixtepec | 234 | 16.34 N | 95.06 W |
| Ixtlahuacán del Río | 234 | 20.52 N | 103.15 W |
| Ixtlán | 234 | 20.11 N | 102.24 W |
| Ixtlán de Juárez | 234 | 17.20 N | 96.29 W |
| Ixtlán del Río | 234 | 21.02 N | 104.22 W |
| Ixworth | 42 | 52.18 N | 0.50 E |
| Iya ≃ | 96 | 33.58 N | 133.47 E |
| 'Iyādh | 144 | 14.59 N | 46.51 E |
| 'Iyāl Bakhīt | 140 | 13.25 N | 28.41 E |
| Iyang, Taehan | 98 | 34.53 N | 127.01 E |
| Iyang → Yiyang, Zhg. | 102 | 28.36 N | 112.20 E |
| Iyang, Gili I | 115a | 6.59 S | 114.10 E |
| Iyo | 96 | 33.46 N | 132.42 E |
| Iyo-mishima | 96 | 33.58 N | 133.33 E |
| Iyo-nada ⊤[2] | 96 | 33.40 N | 132.20 E |
| Iž ≃ | 80 | 55.58 N | 52.38 E |
| Izabal | 236 | 15.24 N | 89.08 W |
| Izabal □[5] | 236 | 15.30 N | 89.00 W |
| Izabal, Lago de ⊜ | 236 | 15.30 N | 89.10 W |
| 'Izab al-Baṣāriṭah | 142 | 31.23 N | 31.47 E |
| Īzad Khvāst | 128 | 31.31 N | 52.07 E |
| Izalco | 236 | 13.45 N | 89.40 W |
| 'Izam, Jabal al- ∧ | 132 | 30.51 N | 35.46 E |
| Izamal | 232 | 20.56 N | 89.01 W |
| Izapa ⊥ | 232 | 14.55 N | 92.10 W |
| 'Izbat Abū Ṣuql | 132 | 31.09 N | 33.49 E |
| Izberbaš | 84 | 42.33 N | 47.52 E |
| Izbica, Pol. | 30 | 54.42 N | 17.26 E |
| Izbica, Pol. | 30 | 50.54 N | 23.09 E |
| Izd'oškovo | 76 | 55.08 N | 33.37 E |
| Izegem | 50 | 50.55 N | 3.12 E |
| Īzeh | 128 | 31.50 N | 49.50 E |
| Izena-shima I | 174m | 26.56 N | 127.56 E |
| Izendy | 86 | 45.48 N | 59.28 E |
| Izernore | 58 | 46.13 N | 5.33 E |
| Iževsk | 80 | 56.51 N | 53.14 E |
| Iževskoje | 80 | 54.34 N | 40.53 E |
| Izkī | 128 | 22.56 N | 57.46 E |
| Ižma | 24 | 65.02 N | 53.55 E |
| Ižma ≃ | 24 | 65.19 N | 52.54 E |
| Izmajlovo | 80 | 53.43 N | 47.14 E |
| Izmajlovo ◆[8] | 265b | 55.48 N | 37.46 E |
| Izmajlovo Park ♠ | 265b | 55.46 N | 37.47 E |
| Izmalkovo | 76 | 52.41 N | 37.58 E |
| Izmayil | 78 | 45.21 N | 28.50 E |
| İzmir | 130 | 38.25 N | 27.09 E |
| İzmir □[4] | 130 | 38.30 N | 27.15 E |
| İzmir Körfezi c | 130 | 38.30 N | 26.50 E |
| İzmit (Kocaeli) | 130 | 40.46 N | 29.55 E |
| İzmit Körfezi c | 130 | 40.45 N | 29.35 E |
| Ižmorskij | 86 | 56.11 N | 86.38 E |
| Iznájar, Embalse de ⊜[1] | 34 | 37.15 N | 4.30 W |
| Iznalloz | 34 | 37.23 N | 3.31 W |
| İznik | 130 | 40.26 N | 29.43 E |
| İznik Gölü ⊜ | 130 | 40.26 N | 29.30 E |
| Iznoski | 76 | 54.59 N | 35.19 E |
| Izola | 64 | 45.32 N | 13.40 E |
| Izoplit | 82 | 56.38 N | 36.12 E |
| Izopo, Punta › | 236 | 15.48 N | 87.23 W |
| Ižora ≃ | 265a | 59.48 N | 30.36 E |
| Izozog, Bañados del ≡ | 248 | 18.48 S | 62.10 W |
| Izra' | 132 | 32.51 N | 36.15 E |
| Izsák | 30 | 46.48 N | 19.22 E |
| Iztacalco ◆[8] | 286a | 19.23 N | 99.07 W |
| Iztaccíhuatl, Volcán ∧[1] | 234 | 19.11 N | 98.39 W |
| Iztaccíhuatl y Popocatéptl, Parques Nacionales ♠ | 234 | 19.10 N | 98.38 W |
| Iztapa | 236 | 13.56 N | 90.43 W |
| Iztapalapa ◆[8] | 286a | 19.21 N | 99.06 W |
| Izucar de Matamoros | 234 | 18.36 N | 98.28 W |
| Izu-hantō ›[1] | 94 | 34.45 N | 139.00 E |
| Izuhara | 92 | 34.12 N | 129.17 E |
| Izumi, Nihon | 92 | 32.05 N | 130.22 E |
| Izumi, Nihon | 92 | 38.20 N | 140.53 E |
| Izumi, Nihon | 96 | 34.55 N | 134.55 E |
| Izumi, Nihon | 96 | 34.29 N | 135.26 E |
| Izumi, Nihon | 268 | 35.22 N | 139.29 E |
| Izumi-ōtsu | 96 | 34.30 N | 135.24 E |
| Izumi-sano | 96 | 34.25 N | 135.19 E |
| Izumizaki | 94 | 37.09 N | 140.17 E |
| Izumo | 96 | 35.22 N | 132.46 E |
| Izumo ≃ | 94 | 34.38 N | 136.33 E |
| Izumo-kokubun-ji ʋ[1] | 96 | 35.26 N | 133.06 E |
| Izumrud | 86 | 57.05 N | 61.23 E |
| Izu-nagaoka | 94 | 35.02 N | 138.56 E |
| Izushi | 96 | 35.28 N | 134.52 E |
| Izu-shotō II | 6 | 32.00 N | 140.00 E |
| Izu Trench ✢[1] | 6 | 31.00 N | 142.00 E |
| Izuwara | 270 | 34.53 N | 135.32 E |
| Izvaryne | 83 | 48.17 N | 39.52 E |
| Izvestij CIK, ostrova II | 74 | 75.55 N | 82.30 E |
| Izvestkovyj | 89 | 48.59 N | 131.33 E |
| Izvorul Muntelui, Lacul ⊜[1] | 38 | 47.00 N | 26.00 E |
| Izyaslav | 78 | 50.07 N | 26.51 E |
| Izynžul' | 86 | 52.24 N | 90.13 E |
| Izyum | 83 | 49.12 N | 37.19 E |

## J

| Nome | Página | Lat.°′ | Long.°′ W = Oeste |
|---|---|---|---|
| Ja'ār, Birkat al- ⊜ | 142 | 30.28 N | 30.10 E |
| Jääsjärvi ⊜ | 26 | 61.36 N | 26.07 E |
| Jaba, Ityo. | 144 | 6.17 N | 35.12 E |
| Jaba, Pap. N. Gui. | 175e | 6.32 S | 155.12 E |
| Jabā, Sūrīy. | 132 | 33.10 N | 35.56 E |
| Jabal, Baḥr al- → Mountain Nile ≃ | 136 | 9.30 N | 30.30 E |
| Jabal Abyad Plateau ⋏[1] | 140 | 19.00 N | 29.00 E |
| Jabal al-Awliyā' | 140 | 15.14 N | 32.30 E |
| Jabal al-Awliyā', Khazzān (White Nile Dam) ◆[6] | 140 | 15.14 N | 32.29 E |
| Jabalambre ∧ | 34 | 40.06 N | 1.03 W |
| Jabal an-Nūr | 142 | 28.57 N | 31.02 E |
| Jabal Aṭ-Ṭayr | 142 | 28.14 N | 30.45 E |
| Jabal Dūd | 140 | 13.25 N | 33.09 E |
| Jabal Lubnān □[4] | 132 | 33.50 N | 35.40 E |
| Jabalón ≃ | 34 | 38.53 N | 4.05 W |
| Jabal os Sarāj | 120 | 35.07 N | 69.14 E |
| Jabalpur | 124 | 23.10 N | 79.57 E |
| Jabal Qerri | 140 | 16.15 N | 32.48 E |
| Jabal 'Uwaybid | 142 | 30.09 N | 32.12 E |
| Jabālyah | 132 | 31.32 N | 34.29 E |
| Jabal Zuqar, Jazīrat I | 144 | 14.00 N | 42.45 E |
| Jabbān, Arḍ al- ◆[1] | 132 | 32.08 N | 36.35 E |
| Jabbeke | 50 | 51.11 N | 3.05 E |
| Jabbi | 123 | 32.24 N | 72.06 E |
| Jabbū, Qā' ≚ | 132 | 29.35 N | 36.13 E |
| Jabbūl, Sabkhat al- ⊜ | 130 | 36.03 N | 37.39 E |
| Jabel | 54 | 53.32 N | 12.32 E |
| Jabi | 114 | 2.32 N | 102.48 E |
| Jabiru | 164 | 12.40 S | 132.53 E |
| Jabjabah, Wādī V | 140 | 22.37 N | 33.17 E |
| Jablah | 130 | 35.21 N | 35.55 E |
| Jablanac | 36 | 44.42 N | 14.54 E |
| Jablanica | 36 | 43.39 N | 17.45 E |
| Jablanica ≃ | 38 | 43.07 N | 21.57 E |
| Jablaničko Jezero ⊜[1] | 36 | 43.40 N | 17.50 E |
| Jablines | 261 | 48.55 N | 2.46 E |
| Jabločnyj | 89 | 47.10 N | 142.04 E |
| Jablonec nad Nisou | 30 | 50.44 N | 15.10 E |
| Jablonica | 30 | 48.37 N | 17.25 E |
| Jabłonka | 30 | 49.29 N | 19.41 E |
| Jablonné v Podještědí | 54 | 50.48 N | 14.47 E |
| Jablonoj → Jablonovyj chrebet ⋏ | 88 | 53.30 N | 115.00 E |
| Jablonovo | 88 | 51.51 N | 112.49 E |
| Jablonovyj chrebet ⋏ | 88 | 53.30 N | 115.00 E |
| Jabłonowo | 30 | 53.24 N | 19.09 E |
| Jablonowy-Gebirge → Jablonovyj chrebet ⋏ | 88 | 53.30 N | 115.00 E |
| Jablunkov | 30 | 49.35 N | 18.47 E |
| Jaboatão | 250 | 8.07 S | 35.01 W |
| Jaboncillos Creek ≃ | 196 | 27.23 N | 97.45 W |
| Jabonga | 116 | 9.20 N | 125.32 E |
| Jaborandi | 255 | 20.40 S | 48.25 W |
| Jaboticabal | 255 | 21.16 S | 48.19 W |
| Jabrat Sa'īd ⊤[4] | 140 | 16.06 N | 31.50 E |
| Jabron ≃ | 62 | 44.33 N | 4.45 E |
| Jabron, Torrent le ≃ | 62 | 44.09 N | 5.57 E |
| Jabung | 115a | 5.29 S | 105.40 E |
| Jabung, Tanjung › | 112 | 1.01 S | 104.22 E |
| Jaca | 34 | 42.34 N | 0.33 W |
| Jacala | 234 | 21.01 N | 99.11 W |
| Jacaleapa | 236 | 14.00 N | 86.40 W |
| Jacaltenango | 236 | 15.40 N | 91.44 W |
| Jacana | 274b | 37.42 S | 144.55 E |
| Jacaraci | 255 | 14.51 S | 42.26 W |
| Jacaré ≃, Bra. | 248 | 5.49 S | 63.35 W |
| Jacaré ≃, Bra. | 250 | 10.10 S | 41.58 W |
| Jacaré ≃, Bra. | 255 | 13.50 S | 40.42 W |
| Jacareí | 256 | 23.19 S | 45.58 W |
| Jacarepaguá ◆[8] | 256 | 22.56 S | 43.20 W |
| Jacarepaguá, Lagoa de c | 256 | 22.59 S | 43.24 W |
| Jacarezinho | 255 | 23.09 S | 49.59 W |
| Jaceel V | 144 | 10.25 N | 51.01 E |
| Jaceruba | 256 | 22.35 S | 43.34 W |
| Jáchal ≃ | 252 | 30.44 S | 68.08 W |
| Jachenau | 64 | 47.36 N | 11.25 E |
| Jachroma | 82 | 56.17 N | 37.30 E |
| Jachroma ≃ | 82 | 56.31 N | 37.07 E |
| Jáchymov | 54 | 50.20 N | 12.55 E |
| Jaciara | 255 | 15.59 S | 54.57 W |
| Jacinto | 255 | 16.10 S | 40.17 W |
| Jacinto Aráuz | 252 | 38.04 S | 63.26 W |
| Jacinto City | 222 | 29.46 N | 95.14 W |
| Jacinto Machado | 252 | 29.00 S | 49.46 W |
| Jaciparaná | 248 | 9.15 S | 64.23 W |
| Jaciparaná ≃ | 248 | 9.22 S | 64.22 W |
| Jackass Creek ≃ | 226 | 37.22 N | 119.23 W |
| Jack Creek ≃ | 202 | 42.59 N | 121.32 W |
| Jackfish Lake ⊜ | 184 | 53.05 N | 108.25 W |
| Jackhead Harbour | 184 | 51.52 N | 97.16 W |
| Jack Lake ⊜ | 212 | 44.42 N | 78.03 W |
| Jack London State Historical Park ♠ | 226 | 38.21 N | 122.32 W |
| Jackman | 188 | 45.38 N | 70.15 W |
| Jackman Creek ≃ | 224 | 48.30 N | 121.43 W |
| Jack Mountain ∧, Mt., U.S. | 202 | 46.21 N | 112.18 W |
| Jack Mountain ∧, Wa., U.S. | 224 | 48.47 N | 120.57 W |
| Jackpot | 204 | 41.59 N | 114.40 W |
| Jacksboro, Tn., U.S. | 192 | 36.19 N | 84.11 W |
| Jacksboro, Tx., U.S. | 196 | 33.13 N | 98.09 W |
| Jacks Creek ≃ | 208 | 40.35 N | 77.33 W |
| Jacks Fork ≃ | 194 | 37.12 N | 91.17 W |
| Jacks Island I | 279b | 40.37 N | 79.43 W |
| Jacks Mountain ∧ | 210 | 40.45 N | 77.30 W |
| Jackson, Al., U.S. | 194 | 31.30 N | 87.53 W |
| Jackson, Ca., U.S. | 226 | 38.20 N | 120.46 W |
| Jackson, Ga., U.S. | 192 | 33.17 N | 83.57 W |
| Jackson, Ky., U.S. | 192 | 37.33 N | 83.23 W |
| Jackson, La., U.S. | 194 | 30.50 N | 91.13 W |
| Jackson, Mi., U.S. | 216 | 42.14 N | 84.24 W |
| Jackson, Mn., U.S. | 198 | 43.37 N | 94.59 W |
| Jackson, Ms., U.S. | 194 | 32.17 N | 90.11 W |
| Jackson, Mo., U.S. | 194 | 37.22 N | 89.39 W |
| Jackson, N.J., U.S. | 208 | 40.08 N | 74.19 W |
| Jackson, N.C., U.S. | 192 | 36.23 N | 77.25 W |
| Jackson, Oh., U.S. | 188 | 39.03 N | 82.38 W |
| Jackson, Pa., U.S. | 210 | 41.50 N | 75.36 W |
| Jackson, S.C., U.S. | 192 | 33.19 N | 81.47 W |
| Jackson, Tn., U.S. | 194 | 35.36 N | 88.48 W |
| Jackson, Wy., U.S. | 200 | 43.28 N | 110.45 W |
| Jackson □[6], Mi., U.S. | 216 | 42.15 N | 84.24 W |
| Jackson □[6], Tx., U.S. | 218 | 33.10 N | 98.30 W |
| Jackson, Cape › | 172 | 41.00 S | 174.18 E |
| Jackson, Lake ⊜, Fl., U.S. | 192 | 30.30 N | 84.17 W |
| Jackson, Lake ⊜, Fl., U.S. | 220 | 27.55 N | 81.10 W |
| Jackson, Lake ⊜, Fl., U.S. | 220 | 27.29 N | 81.28 W |
| Jackson, Mount ∧, Ant. | 9 | 71.23 S | 63.22 W |
| Jackson, Mount ∧, Austl. | 162 | 30.15 S | 119.16 E |
| Jackson, Port c | 170 | 33.50 S | 151.16 E |
| Jackson Bay c | 172 | 43.58 S | 168.42 E |
| Jackson Brook ≃ | 276 | 40.53 N | 74.34 W |
| Jackson Butte ∧ | 226 | 38.20 N | 120.43 W |
| Jackson Center, Oh., U.S. | 216 | 40.27 N | 84.02 W |
| Jackson Center, Pa., U.S. | 214 | 41.16 N | 80.09 W |
| Jackson Creek ≃, Can. | 184 | 49.18 N | 100.50 W |
| Jackson Creek ≃, Ca., U.S. | 226 | 38.18 N | 121.01 W |
| Jackson Creek ≃, Il., U.S. | 216 | 41.26 N | 88.10 W |
| Jackson Head › | 172 | 43.58 S | 168.37 E |
| Jackson Heights ◆[8] | 276 | 40.45 N | 73.53 W |
| Jackson Lake ⊜ | 202 | 43.55 N | 110.40 W |
| Jackson Lake ⊜[1] | 192 | 33.22 N | 83.52 W |
| Jackson Meadows Reservoir ⊜[1] | 226 | 39.29 N | 120.32 W |
| Jackson Mountain ∧ | 188 | 44.46 N | 70.32 W |
| Jackson Park ♠, On., Can. | 281 | 42.17 N | 83.01 W |
| Jackson Park ♠, Il., U.S. | 278 | 41.47 N | 87.35 W |
| Jackson's Arm | 186 | 49.52 N | 56.47 W |
| Jacksons Creek ≃ | 169 | 37.40 S | 144.48 E |
| Jacksonville, Al., U.S. | 194 | 33.48 N | 85.45 W |
| Jacksonville, Ar., U.S. | 194 | 34.51 N | 92.06 W |
| Jacksonville, Fl., U.S. | 192 | 30.19 N | 81.39 W |
| Jacksonville, Il., U.S. | 219 | 39.44 N | 90.13 W |
| Jacksonville, N.J., U.S. | 285 | 40.03 N | 74.46 W |
| Jacksonville, N.Y., U.S. | 210 | 42.31 N | 76.37 W |
| Jacksonville, N.C., U.S. | 192 | 34.45 N | 77.25 W |
| Jacksonville, Or., U.S. | 202 | 42.18 N | 122.57 W |
| Jacksonville, Tx., U.S. | 222 | 31.57 N | 95.16 W |
| Jacksonville, Vt., U.S. | 207 | 42.47 N | 72.49 W |
| Jacksonville, Lake ⊜[1] | 222 | 31.55 N | 95.17 W |
| Jacksonville Beach | 192 | 30.17 N | 81.23 W |
| Jacksonville Naval Air Station ■ | 192 | 30.14 N | 81.41 W |
| Jacks Reef | 210 | 43.06 N | 76.25 W |
| Jacks Run ≃ | 279b | 40.13 N | 79.35 W |
| Jacktown Acres | 279b | 40.19 N | 79.45 W |
| Jacmel | 238 | 18.14 N | 72.32 W |
| Jaco | 232 | 27.50 N | 104.00 W |
| Jacob, Morne ∧ | 240e | 14.46 N | 61.06 W |
| Jacobābād | 120 | 28.17 N | 68.26 E |
| Jacobina | 250 | 11.11 S | 40.31 W |
| Jacob Island I | 212 | 44.28 N | 78.28 W |
| Jacob Riis Park ♠ | 276 | 40.34 N | 73.52 W |
| Jacobs Creek ≃ | 214 | 40.07 N | 79.44 W |
| Jacobsdal | 158 | 29.13 S | 24.41 E |
| Jacobus | 208 | 39.53 N | 76.43 W |
| Jacona de Plancarte | 234 | 19.57 N | 102.16 W |
| Jacques, Lac à ⊜ | 180 | 66.10 N | 127.25 W |
| Jacques-Cartier | 275a | 45.31 N | 73.29 W |
| Jacques-Cartier ≃ | 206 | 46.40 N | 71.45 W |
| Jacques-Cartier, Détroit de ⊔ | 186 | 50.00 N | 63.30 W |
| Jacques-Cartier, Mont ∧ | 186 | 48.59 N | 65.57 W |
| Jacques-Cartier, Pont ◆[5] | 275a | 45.31 N | 73.32 W |
| Jacquet River | 186 | 47.55 N | 66.00 W |
| Jacqueville | 150 | 5.12 N | 4.25 W |
| Jacquinot Bay c | 164 | 5.35 S | 151.30 E |
| Jacu ≃, Bra. | 250 | 6.13 S | 35.09 W |
| Jacú ≃, Bra. | 256 | 23.05 S | 45.08 W |
| Jacu, Rio do ≃ | 287b | 23.29 S | 46.27 W |
| Jacuba ≃ | 255 | 18.25 S | 52.28 W |
| Jacuecanga | 256 | 23.01 S | 44.13 W |
| Jacuí ≃ | 252 | 30.02 S | 51.15 W |
| Jacuípe ≃ | 255 | 12.30 S | 39.05 W |
| Jacumba | 204 | 32.37 N | 116.11 W |
| Jacundá | 250 | 4.33 S | 49.28 W |
| Jacundá ≃ | 250 | 1.57 S | 50.26 W |
| Jacupiranga | 252 | 24.42 S | 48.00 W |
| Jacuriaí ≃ | 250 | 10.57 S | 39.35 W |
| Jacutinga | 256 | 22.17 S | 46.37 W |
| Jada | 146 | 8.46 N | 12.09 E |
| Jada'ah, Jabal ∧[2] | 142 | 29.58 N | 30.40 E |
| Jādabpur | 126 | 22.29 N | 88.23 E |
| Jaddi, Rās › | 128 | 25.14 N | 63.31 E |
| Jade | 52 | 53.20 N | 8.14 E |
| Jade Buddha, Temple of the ʋ[1] | 269b | 31.14 N | 121.26 E |
| Jadebusen c | 52 | 53.30 N | 8.10 E |
| Jäder | 40 | 59.25 N | 16.41 E |
| Jäderfors | 40 | 60.41 N | 16.40 E |
| Jade Run ≃ | 285 | 39.56 N | 74.45 W |
| Jadīdah | 128 | 34.01 N | 42.28 E |
| Jadito Wash V | 200 | 35.22 N | 110.50 W |
| J.A.D. Jensens Nunatakker ∧ | 176 | 62.45 N | 48.00 W |
| Jadotville → Likasi | 154 | 10.59 S | 26.44 E |
| Jadraque | 34 | 40.55 N | 2.55 W |
| Jadrin | 80 | 55.56 N | 46.12 E |
| Jadromino | 82 | 55.57 N | 36.36 E |
| Jādū | 146 | 31.57 N | 12.01 E |
| Jægerspris | 41 | 55.51 N | 11.59 E |
| Jaeger Summit ∧ | 154 | 2.52 S | 35.47 E |
| Jaén, Esp. | 34 | 37.46 N | 3.47 W |
| Jaén, Perú | 248 | 5.42 S | 78.47 W |
| Jaén □[4] | 34 | 38.00 N | 3.30 W |
| Jæren ◆[1] | 26 | 58.45 N | 5.45 E |
| Jāfarābād, India | 120 | 20.52 N | 71.22 E |
| Ja'farābād, Īrān | 128 | 35.43 N | 50.43 E |
| Jāfarpur | 126 | 22.29 N | 89.06 E |
| Jāfarpur ◆[8] | 272a | 28.40 N | 77.01 E |
| Jaffa, Cape › | 166 | 36.58 S | 139.40 E |
| Jaffa, Tel Aviv- → Tel Aviv-Yafo | 132 | 32.04 N | 34.46 E |
| Jaffna | 122 | 9.40 N | 80.00 E |
| Jaffna Lagoon c | 122 | 9.35 N | 80.15 E |
| Jaffrey | 207 | 42.48 N | 72.01 W |
| Jafr, Qā' al- ±[7] | 132 | 30.17 N | 36.20 E |
| Jagādhri | 124 | 30.10 N | 77.18 E |
| Jägala ≃ | 76 | 59.29 N | 25.09 E |
| Jagalūr | 122 | 14.32 N | 76.21 E |
| Jāgan | 120 | 28.05 N | 68.30 E |
| Jagannāthganj Ghāt | 124 | 24.45 N | 89.49 E |
| Jagannāthpūr | 272b | 22.43 N | 88.19 E |
| Jagati | 126 | 23.54 N | 89.06 E |
| Jagatnagar | 272b | 22.47 N | 88.13 E |
| Jagatpur ◆[8] | 272a | 28.44 N | 77.14 E |
| Jagatsingpur | 120 | 20.16 N | 86.10 E |
| Jagdalpur | 122 | 19.04 N | 82.02 E |
| Jagdīspur | 124 | 25.29 N | 84.25 E |
| Jagel | 41 | 54.27 N | 9.32 E |
| Jagel'urta, gora ∧[2] | 24 | 67.33 N | 38.02 E |
| Jagenbach | 61 | 48.38 N | 15.02 E |
| Jägerndorf → Krnov | 30 | 50.05 N | 17.41 E |
| Jagersfontein | 158 | 29.44 S | 25.29 E |
| Jaggayyapeta | 122 | 16.54 N | 80.06 E |
| Jagged Mountain ∧ | 180 | 58.38 N | 162.02 W |
| Jagīn ≃ | 128 | 25.35 N | 58.18 E |
| Jagnob ≃ | 85 | 39.15 N | 68.35 E |
| Jagny-sous-Bois | 261 | 49.05 N | 2.27 E |
| Jagodnoje, Ross. | 74 | 62.33 N | 149.40 E |
| Jagodnoje, Ross. | 80 | 53.36 N | 49.04 E |
| Jagodnyj | 86 | 59.44 N | 65.04 E |
| Jagraon | 123 | 30.47 N | 75.29 E |
| Jagst ≃ | 56 | 49.14 N | 9.11 E |
| Jagstzell | 56 | 49.02 N | 10.05 E |
| Jagtiāl | 122 | 18.48 N | 78.56 E |
| Jaguaquara | 255 | 13.32 S | 39.58 W |
| Jaguarão | 252 | 32.34 S | 53.23 W |
| Jaguarão (Yaguarón) ≃ | 252 | 32.39 S | 53.12 W |
| Jaguarari | 250 | 10.16 S | 40.12 W |
| Jaguaretama | 250 | 5.37 S | 38.46 W |
| Jaguari | 252 | 29.30 S | 54.41 W |
| Jaguari ≃, Bra. | 256 | 22.41 S | 47.17 W |
| Jaguari ≃, Bra. | 256 | 23.10 S | 45.55 W |
| Jaguariaíva | 252 | 24.15 S | 49.42 W |
| Jaguaribara | 250 | 5.40 S | 38.37 W |
| Jaguaribe | 250 | 5.53 S | 38.37 W |
| Jaguaribe ≃ | 250 | 4.25 S | 37.45 W |
| Jaguari-Mirim ≃ | 256 | 21.59 S | 47.17 W |
| Jaguaripe | 255 | 13.06 S | 38.53 W |
| Jaguariúna | 256 | 22.41 S | 46.59 W |
| Jaguaruna | 252 | 28.36 S | 49.02 W |
| Jagüé | 252 | 28.38 S | 68.24 W |
| Jagüey Grande | 240p | 22.32 N | 81.08 W |
| Jāguli | 126 | 22.56 N | 88.32 E |
| Jāgulia | 272b | 22.44 N | 88.32 E |
| Jagungal, Mount ∧ | 171b | 36.09 S | 148.23 E |
| Jagunovskij | 86 | 55.17 N | 85.59 E |
| Jahānābād, India | 124 | 25.13 N | 84.59 E |
| Jahānābād, Pāk. | 123 | 32.11 N | 72.29 E |
| Jahāngīra | 123 | 33.58 N | 72.13 E |
| Jahāngīrābād | 124 | 28.25 N | 78.06 E |
| Jahangirpur ◆[8] | 272a | 28.44 N | 77.13 E |
| Jahānia | 123 | 30.02 N | 71.49 E |
| Jahannam, Qārat ∧[2] | 142 | 29.19 N | 30.09 E |
| Jahdānīyah, Wādī al- V | 132 | 30.12 N | 36.22 E |
| Jahnsdorf | 54 | 50.44 N | 12.51 E |
| Jahrom | 128 | 28.31 N | 53.33 E |
| Jahú → Jaú | 255 | 22.18 S | 48.33 W |
| Jaicós | 250 | 7.21 S | 41.08 W |
| Jaidak | 120 | 31.58 N | 66.43 E |
| Jaihti ≃ | 126 | 24.08 N | 86.48 E |
| Jaijon | 123 | 31.21 N | 76.09 E |
| Jailolo | 108 | 1.05 N | 127.30 E |
| Jaimanitas ≃ | 286b | 23.05 N | 82.29 W |
| Jainca | 102 | 35.59 N | 102.02 E |
| Jainti | 124 | 26.42 N | 89.36 E |
| Jaintiāpur | 120 | 25.08 N | 92.07 E |
| Jaipur | 120 | 26.55 N | 75.49 E |
| Jaipur Hāt | 124 | 25.06 N | 89.01 E |
| Jais | 124 | 26.15 N | 81.32 E |
| Jaisalmer | 120 | 26.55 N | 70.54 E |
| Jaito | 123 | 30.28 N | 74.53 E |
| Jaja | 86 | 56.12 N | 86.26 E |
| Jaja ≃ | 86 | 56.58 N | 86.23 E |
| Jājapur | 120 | 20.51 N | 86.20 E |
| Jājarkoṭ | 124 | 28.42 N | 82.12 E |
| Jājarm | 128 | 36.58 N | 56.27 E |
| Jajce | 36 | 44.21 N | 17.16 E |
| Jajichi | 174m | 26.47 N | 128.13 E |
| Jajjha | 123 | 28.45 N | 70.34 E |
| Jajl'u | 86 | 51.48 N | 87.36 E |
| Jajpan | 85 | 40.23 N | 70.48 E |
| Jajsan | 86 | 50.51 N | 56.14 E |
| Jajva | 86 | 59.20 N | 57.15 E |
| Jajva ≃ | 86 | 59.13 N | 56.40 E |
| Ják | 61 | 47.08 N | 16.35 E |
| Jakarta, Indon. | 115a | 6.10 S | 106.48 E |
| Jakarta, Indon. | 269e | 6.10 S | 106.48 E |
| Jakarta, Teluk c | 115a | 6.05 S | 106.48 E |
| Jakarta Kota Station ◆[5] | 269e | 6.08 S | 106.49 E |
| Jakarta Raya □[4] | 115a | 6.10 S | 106.45 E |
| Jakaulevičy | 76 | 54.20 N | 30.31 E |
| Jakdūl ⊜ | 140 | 17.39 N | 32.59 E |
| Jake Creek Mountain ∧ | 204 | 41.13 N | 116.54 W |
| Jakenan | 115a | 6.45 S | 111.11 E |
| Jākhal | 123 | 29.48 N | 75.50 E |
| Jakhāu | 120 | 23.13 N | 68.43 E |
| Jakkonen | 24 | 66.33 N | 29.52 E |
| Jakobsberg | 40 | 59.26 N | 17.50 E |
| Jakobsdalsberget ∧[2] | 40 | 58.41 N | 16.07 E |
| Jakobshavn (Ilulissat) | 176 | 69.13 N | 51.06 W |
| Jakobstad (Pietarsaari) | 26 | 63.40 N | 22.42 E |
| Jakovlevka | 89 | 44.26 N | 133.28 E |
| Jakovlevo, Ross. | 78 | 50.51 N | 36.27 E |
| Jakovlevo, Ross. | 82 | 54.48 N | 37.26 E |
| Jakša | 24 | 61.48 N | 56.49 E |
| Jakšanga | 80 | 58.23 N | 45.56 E |
| Jakšur-Bodja | 80 | 57.11 N | 53.09 E |
| Jakupica ⋏ | 38 | 41.43 N | 21.26 E |
| Jakutija □[3] | 74 | 67.00 N | 125.00 E |
| Jakutsk | 74 | 62.00 N | 129.40 E |
| Jal | 196 | 32.06 N | 103.11 W |
| Jalacingo | 234 | 19.48 N | 97.18 W |
| Jalaid Qi | 89 | 46.40 N | 122.55 E |
| Jalājil | 128 | 25.41 N | 45.28 E |
| Jalālābād, Afg. | 120 | 34.26 N | 70.28 E |
| Jalālābād, India | 123 | 30.37 N | 74.15 E |
| Jalālābād, India | 124 | 27.43 N | 79.40 E |
| Jalālah al-Baḥrīyah, Jabal ⋏[1] | 142 | 29.20 N | 32.00 E |
| Jalālat al-Qiblīyah, Jabal al- ⋏ | 142 | 28.42 N | 32.22 E |
| Jalālpur, India | 124 | 26.19 N | 82.44 E |
| Jalālpur, Pāk. | 123 | 32.38 N | 74.12 E |
| Jalālpur Pīrwāla | 123 | 29.30 N | 71.13 E |
| Jalan' | 86 | 58.21 N | 91.53 E |
| Jalán ≃ | 236 | 14.39 N | 86.12 W |
| Jalan Besar Stadium ♠ | 271c | 1.18 N | 103.52 E |
| Jalandhar | 123 | 31.19 N | 75.34 E |
| Jalangi | 126 | 24.08 N | 88.42 E |
| Jalangi ≃ | 126 | 23.25 N | 88.22 E |
| Jalan Kayu | 271c | 1.24 N | 103.52 E |
| Jalapa, Guat. | 236 | 14.38 N | 89.59 W |
| Jalapa, Méx. | 234 | 17.43 N | 92.49 W |
| Jalapa, Nic. | 236 | 13.55 N | 86.08 W |
| Jalapa □[5] | 236 | 14.35 N | 89.55 W |
| Jalasjärvi | 26 | 62.30 N | 22.45 E |
| Jalaud ≃ | 116 | 10.45 N | 122.40 E |
| Jālaun | 124 | 26.09 N | 79.21 E |
| Jal'čiki | 80 | 55.09 N | 48.01 E |
| Jalcocotán | 234 | 21.28 N | 105.07 W |
| Jalda | 126 | 21.56 N | 87.30 E |
| Jaleaca de Catalán | 234 | 17.26 N | 99.51 W |
| Jalesar | 124 | 27.29 N | 78.19 E |
| Jaleshwar | 126 | 21.49 N | 87.13 E |
| Jaleśwar | 124 | 26.38 N | 85.48 E |
| Jālgaon, India | 122 | 21.01 N | 75.34 E |
| Jālgaon, India | 122 | 21.03 N | 76.32 E |
| Jal'gelevo | 265a | 59.44 N | 29.57 E |
| Jalhay | 56 | 50.34 N | 5.58 E |
| Jalingo | 146 | 8.53 N | 11.22 E |
| Jalirpār | 126 | 23.13 N | 89.58 E |
| Jalisco □[3] | 234 | 20.20 N | 103.40 W |
| Jalizava | 76 | 53.24 N | 29.01 E |
| Jālna | 122 | 19.50 N | 75.53 E |
| Jalón ≃ | 34 | 41.47 N | 1.04 W |
| Jālor | 120 | 25.21 N | 72.37 E |
| Jalostotitlán | 234 | 21.12 N | 102.28 W |
| Jalpa | 234 | 21.38 N | 102.58 W |
| Jalpa de Méndez | 234 | 18.08 N | 93.05 W |
| Jalpāiguri | 124 | 26.31 N | 88.44 E |
| Jalpan de Serra | 234 | 21.14 N | 99.29 W |
| Jaltepec ≃ | 234 | 17.26 N | 94.59 W |
| Jáltipan de Morelos | 234 | 17.58 N | 94.42 W |
| Jaluit I[1] | 14 | 6.00 N | 169.35 E |
| Jalūlā' | 128 | 34.16 N | 45.10 E |
| Jalutorovsk | 86 | 56.40 N | 66.18 E |
| Jam, Ross. | 82 | 55.29 N | 37.45 E |
| Jam, Uzb. | 85 | 40.07 N | 68.11 E |
| Jām ≃ | 128 | 35.10 N | 61.06 E |
| Jamaame (Margherita) | 144 | 0.04 N | 42.45 E |
| Jamaare ≃ | 146 | 12.06 N | 10.14 E |
| Jāmābāti | 272b | 22.51 N | 88.04 E |


| | | | | | |
|---|---|---|---|---|---|
| ≃ | River | Fluß | Río | Rivière | Rio |
| | Canal | Kanal | Canal | Canal | Canal |
| | Waterfall, Rapids | Wasserfall, Stromschnellen | Cascada, Rápidos | Chute d'eau, Rapides | Cascata, Rápidos |
| ⊔ | Strait | Meeresstraße | Estrecho | Détroit | Estreito |
| c | Bay, Gulf | Bucht, Golf | Bahía, Golfo | Baie, Golfe | Baía, Golfo |
| ⊜ | Lake, Lakes | See, Seen | Lago, Lagos | Lac, Lacs | Lago, Lagos |
| ≡ | Swamp | Sumpf | Pantano | Marais | Pântano |
| | Ice Features, Glacier | Eis- und Gletscherformen | Accidentes Glaciales | Formes glaciaires | Acidentes glaciares |
| ⊤ | Other Hydrographic Features | Andere Hydrographische Objekte | Otros Elementos Hidrográficos | Autres données hydrographiques | Outros acidentes hidrográficos |

| | | | | | |
|---|---|---|---|---|---|
| ✢ | Submarine Features | Untermeerische Objekte | Accidentes Submarinos | Formes de relief sous-marin | Acidentes submarinos |
| □ | Political Unit | Politische Einheit | Unidad Política | Entité politique | Unidade política |
| ʋ | Cultural Institution | Kulturelle Institution | Institución Cultural | Institution culturelle | Instituição cultural |
| ⊥ | Historical Site | Historische Stätte | Sitio Histórico | Site historique | Sitio histórico |
| ♠ | Recreational Site | Erholungs- und Ferienort | Sitio de Recreo | Centre de loisirs | Area de Lazer |
| ⊠ | Airport | Flughafen | Aeropuerto | Aéroport | Aeroporto |
| ■ | Military Installation | Militäranlage | Instalación Militar | Installation militaire | Instalação militar |
| ◆ | Miscellaneous | Verschiedenes | Misceláneo | Divers | Diversos |

| | | | |
|---|---|---|---|
| Jamaica | **240p** | 20.12 N | 75.09 W |
| Jamaica ●[8] | **276** | 40.42 N | 73.47 W |
| Jamaica □[1], N.A. | **230** | 18.15 N | 77.30 W |
| Jamaica □[1], N.A. | **241q** | 18.15 N | 77.30 W |
| Jamaica Bay c | **210** | 40.36 N | 73.51 W |
| Jamaica Channel ʊ | **238** | 18.00 N | 75.30 W |
| Jamaica Plain ●[8] | **283** | 42.19 N | 71.06 W |
| Jamaica Pond ⊜ | **283** | 42.19 N | 71.07 W |
| Jamaika → Jamaica □[1] | **241q** | 18.15 N | 77.30 W |
| Jamaïque → Jamaica □[1] | **241q** | 18.15 N | 77.30 W |
| Jamal, poluostrov ›[1] | **74** | 70.00 N | 70.00 E |
| Jam-Alin', chrebet ⋏ | **89** | 53.00 N | 134.36 E |
| Jamālīyah ●[8] | **273c** | 30.03 N | 31.16 E |
| Jamālpur, Bngl. | **124** | 24.55 N | 89.56 E |
| Jamālpur, India | **124** | 25.18 N | 86.30 E |
| Jamālpurganj | **126** | 23.04 N | 87.59 E |
| Jamanchalinka | **80** | 47.40 N | 51.35 E |
| Jamanota ∧[2] | **241s** | 12.29 N | 69.57 W |
| Jamantau, gora ∧ | **86** | 54.15 N | 58.06 E |
| Jamanxim ≃ | **250** | 4.43 S | 56.18 W |
| Jamapará | **256** | 21.55 S | 42.43 W |
| Jamari ≃ | **248** | 8.27 S | 63.30 W |
| Jamarovka | **88** | 50.38 N | 110.16 E |
| Jamašurma | **80** | 55.58 N | 49.36 E |
| Jamay | **234** | 20.18 N | 102.43 W |
| Jamba | **152** | 13.50 S | 15.30 E |
| Jāmbād | **126** | 22.42 N | 86.35 E |
| Jambeiro | **256** | 23.16 S | 45.41 W |
| Jambeiro, Serra do ⋏[2] | **256** | 23.13 S | 45.38 W |
| Jambelí, Canal de ʊ | **246** | 3.00 S | 80.00 W |
| Jamberoo | **170** | 34.39 S | 150.47 E |
| Jambes | **56** | 50.28 N | 4.52 E |
| Jambi | **112** | 1.36 S | 103.37 E |
| Jambi □[4] | **112** | 1.30 S | 103.00 E |
| Jambin | **166** | 24.12 S | 150.22 E |
| Jamboaye ≃ | **114** | 5.16 N | 97.29 E |
| Jambol | **38** | 42.29 N | 26.30 E |
| Jambongan, Pulau I | **116** | 6.40 N | 117.27 E |
| Jambuair, Tanjung › | **114** | 5.16 N | 97.30 E |
| Jambusar | **120** | 22.03 N | 72.48 E |
| James ≃, Austl. | **166** | 20.36 S | 137.41 E |
| James ≃, Ab., Can. | **182** | 51.55 N | 114.34 W |
| James ≃, U.S. | **198** | 42.52 N | 97.18 W |
| James ≃, Mo., U.S. | **194** | 36.45 N | 93.30 W |
| James ≃, Va., U.S. | **192** | 36.57 N | 76.26 W |
| James, Isla I | **254** | 44.57 S | 74.07 W |
| James, Lake ⊜ | **216** | 41.42 N | 85.02 W |
| James, Lake ⊜[1] | **192** | 35.45 N | 81.55 W |
| James Bay c | **176** | 53.30 N | 80.30 W |
| Jamesburg | **208** | 40.21 N | 74.26 W |
| James Bypass ≊ | **226** | 36.41 N | 120.16 W |
| James City, N.C., U.S. | **192** | 35.05 N | 77.02 W |
| James City, Pa., U.S. | **214** | 41.37 N | 78.50 W |
| James City □[6] | **208** | 37.17 N | 76.48 W |
| James Craik | **252** | 32.09 S | 63.28 W |
| James Creek | **214** | 40.23 N | 78.10 W |
| James Gardens ♦ | **275b** | 43.40 N | 79.31 W |
| James Island, B.C., Can. | **224** | 48.37 N | 123.22 W |
| James Island, S.C., U.S. | **192** | 32.44 N | 79.57 W |
| James Island I | **208** | 38.31 N | 76.20 W |
| Jameson Raid Memorial ⊥ | **273d** | 26.11 S | 27.49 E |
| James Point › | **192** | 25.21 N | 76.24 W |
| Jamesport | **194** | 39.58 N | 93.48 W |
| James Price Point › | **162** | 17.30 S | 122.08 E |
| James Ranges ⋏ | **162** | 24.06 S | 132.30 E |
| James River Bridge ●[5] | **208** | 37.00 N | 76.30 W |
| James Ross, Cape › | **176** | 74.40 N | 114.25 W |
| James Ross Island I | **9** | 64.15 S | 57.45 W |
| James Ross Strait ʊ | **176** | 69.40 N | 95.30 W |
| James Smith Indian Reserve ●[4] | **184** | 53.08 N | 104.52 W |
| Jamestown, Austl. | **166** | 33.12 S | 138.36 E |
| Jamestown, Ire. | **48** | 53.55 N | 8.02 W |
| Jamestown, S. Afr. | **158** | 31.06 S | 26.45 E |
| Jamestown, Ca., U.S. | **226** | 37.57 N | 120.25 W |
| Jamestown, Ks., U.S. | **198** | 39.35 N | 97.51 W |
| Jamestown, Ky., U.S. | **194** | 36.59 N | 85.03 W |
| Jamestown, Mi., U.S. | **216** | 42.50 N | 85.51 W |
| Jamestown, N.Y., U.S. | **214** | 42.05 N | 79.14 W |
| Jamestown, N.C., U.S. | **192** | 35.59 N | 79.56 W |
| Jamestown, N.D., U.S. | **198** | 46.54 N | 98.42 W |
| Jamestown, Oh., U.S. | **218** | 39.39 N | 83.44 W |
| Jamestown, Pa., U.S. | **214** | 41.29 N | 80.26 W |
| Jamestown, R.I., U.S. | **207** | 41.29 N | 71.22 W |
| Jamestown, Tn., U.S. | **194** | 36.25 N | 84.55 W |
| Jamestown ⊥ | **208** | 37.12 N | 76.46 W |
| Jamestown Festival Park ♦ | **208** | 37.14 N | 76.48 W |
| Jamestown Island I | **208** | 37.12 N | 76.46 W |
| Jamestown Reservoir ⊜[1] | **198** | 47.15 N | 98.40 W |
| Jamesville, N.Y., U.S. | **210** | 42.59 N | 76.04 W |
| Jamesville, Va., U.S. | **208** | 37.30 N | 75.55 W |
| Jamet, Lac ⊜ | **206** | 46.34 N | 74.30 W |
| Jametz | **56** | 49.26 N | 5.23 E |
| Jamieson ≃ | **169** | 37.18 S | 146.08 E |
| Jaminauá ≃ | **248** | 9.20 S | 70.59 W |
| Jaminskij | **80** | 50.21 N | 42.14 E |
| Jāmira ≃ | **126** | 21.45 N | 87.02 E |
| Jamira ≃[1] | **126** | 21.35 N | 88.28 E |
| Jamison | **208** | 40.16 N | 75.05 W |
| Jamison City | **210** | 41.18 N | 76.22 W |
| Jamison Town | **274a** | 33.46 S | 150.41 E |
| Jam-Ižora | **265a** | 59.42 N | 30.36 E |
| Jām Jodhpur | **120** | 21.54 N | 70.01 E |
| Jamkhandi | **122** | 16.31 N | 75.18 E |
| Jamki | **86** | 59.33 N | 66.47 E |
| Jamkino | **82** | 55.55 N | 38.24 E |
| Jamm | **76** | 58.26 N | 28.03 E |
| Jammalamadugu | **122** | 14.50 N | 78.24 E |
| Jammerbugten c | **26** | 57.20 N | 9.30 E |
| Jammerland Bugt c | **41** | 55.35 N | 11.05 E |
| Jammu | **123** | 32.42 N | 74.52 E |
| Jammu Airport ⊠ | **123** | 32.42 N | 74.51 E |
| Jammu and Kashmīr □[2] | **120** | 34.00 N | 76.00 E |
| Jamnagar | **120** | 22.28 N | 70.04 E |
| Jamoigne | **56** | 49.42 N | 5.25 E |
| Jamor ≃ | **266c** | 38.42 N | 9.15 W |
| Jampang-kulon | **115a** | 7.16 S | 106.37 E |
| Jāmpur, India | **272b** | 22.56 N | 88.12 E |
| Jāmpur, Pāk. | **123** | 29.39 N | 70.36 E |
| Jämsä | **26** | 61.52 N | 25.12 E |
| Jamsah | **140** | 27.38 N | 33.35 E |
| Jämsänkoski | **26** | 61.55 N | 25.11 E |
| Jamshedpur | **126** | 22.48 N | 86.11 E |
| Jamsk | **74** | 59.35 N | 154.10 E |
| Jamskaja Sloboda | **82** | 55.29 N | 36.01 E |
| Jāmtāra | **126** | 23.57 N | 86.48 E |
| Jämtland □[9] | **26** | 63.30 N | 14.00 E |
| Jämtlands Län □[6] | **24** | 63.00 N | 14.40 E |
| Jamuāni | **126** | 21.57 N | 86.14 E |
| Jamuga | **82** | 56.24 N | 36.40 E |
| Jamūi | **124** | 24.55 N | 86.13 E |
| Jamuna ≃, Bngl. | **124** | 23.51 N | 89.45 E |
| Jamuna ≃, India | **272b** | 22.57 N | 88.35 E |
| Jamundí | **246** | 3.15 N | 76.32 W |
| Jāmuria | **126** | 23.44 N | 87.02 E |
| Jāmurki | **126** | 24.09 N | 90.02 E |
| Jana ≃ | **74** | 71.31 N | 136.32 E |
| Janāi | **272b** | 22.43 N | 88.16 E |
| Janāj | **142** | 31.00 N | 30.46 E |
| Janajkino | **80** | 50.43 N | 51.06 E |
| Janakpur | **124** | 26.39 N | 85.55 E |
| Janakpur □[8] | **124** | 27.15 N | 86.00 E |
| Janas | **266c** | 38.49 N | 9.26 W |
| Janauacá, Lago ⊜ | **246** | 3.28 S | 60.17 W |
| Janaúba | **255** | 15.48 S | 43.19 W |
| Janaucu, Ilha I | **250** | 0.30 N | 50.10 W |
| Janaul | **86** | 56.16 N | 54.56 E |
| Janavičy | **76** | 55.17 N | 30.42 E |
| Jand | **123** | 33.26 N | 72.01 E |
| Jandaia | **255** | 17.06 S | 50.07 W |
| Jandaia do Sul | **255** | 23.36 S | 51.39 W |
| Jandaíra | **250** | 11.34 S | 37.47 W |
| Jandalī, Wādī al- V | **142** | 30.05 N | 31.52 E |
| Jandaq | **128** | 34.02 N | 54.26 E |
| Jandelsbrunn | **60** | 48.44 N | 13.42 E |
| Jandiāla | **123** | 31.36 N | 75.03 E |
| Jandiatuba ≃ | **246** | 3.28 S | 68.42 W |
| Jandira | **256** | 23.31 S | 46.54 W |
| Jandira □[7] | **287b** | 23.32 S | 46.54 W |
| Jandowae | **166** | 26.47 S | 151.06 E |
| Jandrakinot | **180** | 64.54 N | 172.32 W |
| Jándula ≃ | **34** | 38.03 N | 4.06 W |
| Jándula, Embalse de ⊜[1] | **34** | 38.30 N | 4.00 W |
| Janeiro, Rio de ≃ | **250** | 11.51 S | 45.09 W |
| Jane Peak ∧ | **172** | 45.20 S | 168.19 E |
| Janes Island I | **208** | 38.00 N | 75.52 W |
| Janes Island State Park ♦ | **208** | 38.00 N | 75.52 W |
| Janesville, Ca., U.S. | **204** | 40.17 N | 120.31 W |
| Janesville, Mn., U.S. | **190** | 44.06 N | 93.42 W |
| Janesville, Wi., U.S. | **216** | 42.40 N | 89.01 W |
| Jangal Bādhāl | **126** | 23.07 N | 89.21 E |
| Jangamo | **156** | 24.06 S | 35.21 E |
| Jangany | **157b** | 23.14 S | 45.27 E |
| Jangarej | **24** | 68.46 N | 61.25 E |
| Jangel'skij | **86** | 53.08 N | 58.59 E |
| Jangeru | **112** | 2.20 S | 116.29 E |
| Jangiabad | **85** | 41.08 N | 70.05 E |
| Jangi-Bazar | **85** | 41.40 N | 70.53 E |
| Jangijer | **85** | 40.17 N | 68.50 E |
| Jangijul' | **85** | 41.07 N | 69.03 E |
| Jangikišlak | **85** | 40.25 N | 67.10 E |
| Jangikurgan, Uzb. | **85** | 40.34 N | 71.09 E |
| Jangikurgan, Uzb. | **85** | 41.12 N | 71.44 E |
| Jangipāra | **126** | 22.45 N | 88.04 E |
| Jangīpur | **124** | 24.28 N | 88.04 E |
| Jangong | **114** | 4.23 N | 96.48 E |
| Jangoon | **122** | 17.43 N | 79.11 E |
| Jangulovo | **80** | 56.26 N | 50.25 E |
| Janikowo | **30** | 52.45 N | 18.07 E |
| Janīn | **132** | 32.28 N | 35.18 E |
| Janina → Ioánnina | **38** | 39.40 N | 20.50 E |
| Janino | **265a** | 59.56 N | 30.36 E |
| Janisjarvi, ozero ⊜ | **24** | 61.59 N | 30.57 E |
| Janiuay | **116** | 10.58 N | 122.30 E |
| Janja | **38** | 44.40 N | 19.15 E |
| Janjina, Hrv. | **36** | 42.56 N | 17.26 E |
| Janjina, Madag. | **157b** | 20.30 S | 45.50 E |
| Janka | **126** | 21.52 N | 87.56 E |
| Jankan, chrebet ⋏ | **88** | 55.45 N | 118.00 E |
| Jankāpur | **126** | 21.54 N | 87.23 E |
| Jan Kempdorp (Andalusia) | **158** | 27.55 S | 24.51 E |
| Jan Lake ⊜ | **184** | 54.55 N | 102.55 W |
| Janlohong | **112** | 2.15 N | 117.03 E |
| Jan Mayen I, Nor. | **10** | 71.00 N | 8.20 W |
| Jan Mayen I, Nor. | **12** | 71.00 N | 8.20 W |
| Jan Mayen Ridge ✦[3] | **10** | 69.00 N | 8.00 W |
| Jannaale | **144** | 1.48 N | 44.42 E |
| Jannali | **274a** | 34.01 S | 151.04 E |
| Jannali Park ♦ | **274a** | 34.01 S | 151.03 E |
| Janos | **232** | 30.54 N | 108.10 W |
| Jánoshalma | **30** | 46.18 N | 19.20 E |
| Jánosháza | **30** | 47.08 N | 17.10 E |
| János-hegy ∧ | **264c** | 47.31 N | 18.58 E |
| Jánossomorja | **61** | 47.47 N | 17.08 E |
| Janowiec Wielkopolski | **30** | 52.46 N | 17.31 E |
| Janów Lubelski | **30** | 50.43 N | 22.24 E |
| Jānsath | **124** | 29.20 N | 77.51 E |
| Jänschwalde | **54** | 51.48 N | 14.31 E |
| Jansen | **184** | 51.47 N | 104.43 W |
| Jansenville | **158** | 32.56 S | 24.40 E |
| Janskij | **74** | 68.28 N | 134.48 E |
| Janskij zaliv c | **74** | 71.50 N | 136.00 E |
| Jantarnyj | **76** | 54.52 N | 19.57 E |
| Jantetelco | **234** | 18.42 N | 98.46 W |
| Jantikovo | **80** | 55.32 N | 47.48 E |
| Jantra ≃ | **38** | 43.38 N | 25.34 E |
| Januária | **255** | 15.29 S | 44.22 W |
| Januário Cicco | **250** | 6.09 S | 35.35 W |
| Jan Van Riebeeck Park ♦ | **273d** | 26.10 S | 27.59 E |
| Janvarcevo | **80** | 51.26 N | 52.15 E |
| Janville | **50** | 48.12 N | 1.53 E |
| Janville-sur-Juine | **261** | 48.31 N | 2.16 E |
| Janvry | **261** | 48.39 N | 2.09 E |
| Janzé | **32** | 47.58 N | 1.30 W |
| Janzūr | **142** | 30.41 N | 31.02 E |
| Jaora | **120** | 23.38 N | 75.08 E |
| Japan (Nihon) □[1], Asia | **90** | 36.00 N | 138.00 E |
| Japan (Nihon) □[1], Asia | **92** | 36.00 N | 138.00 E |
| Japan, Sea of ⊤[2] | **90** | 40.00 N | 135.00 E |
| Japan Basin ✦[1] | **12** | 40.00 N | 135.00 E |
| Japanisches Meer → Japan, Sea of ⊤[2] | **90** | 40.00 N | 135.00 E |
| Japan Trench ✦[1] | **6** | 37.00 N | 143.00 E |
| Japaratinga | **250** | 9.05 S | 35.15 W |
| Japaratuba | **250** | 10.35 S | 36.57 W |
| Japeri | **256** | 22.39 S | 43.40 W |
| Japi | **250** | 6.27 S | 35.56 W |
| Japim | **248** | 7.37 S | 72.54 W |
| Japla | **124** | 24.33 N | 84.01 E |
| Japoatã | **250** | 10.20 S | 36.48 W |
| Japon → Japan □[1] | **92** | 36.00 N | 138.00 E |
| Japón, Mar del → Japan, Sea of ⊤[2] | **90** | 40.00 N | 135.00 E |
| Japtiksal'a | **74** | 69.21 N | 72.32 E |
| Japuíba | **256** | 22.35 S | 42.42 W |
| Japurá | **246** | 1.48 S | 66.30 W |
| Japurá (Caquetá) ≃ | **246** | 3.08 S | 64.46 W |
| Jaqué | **246** | 7.31 N | 78.10 W |
| Jaqueri-mirim ≃ | **287b** | 23.31 S | 46.51 W |
| Jaquí | **248** | 15.30 S | 74.26 W |
| Jar | **80** | 58.15 N | 52.06 E |
| Jār, Jabal ∧ | **128** | 24.34 N | 38.18 E |
| Jarābulus | **130** | 36.49 N | 38.01 E |
| Jarad | **144** | 18.59 N | 41.24 E |
| Jaradū | **142** | 29.18 N | 30.42 E |
| Jaraguá | **255** | 15.45 S | 49.20 W |
| Jaraguá ●[8] | **287b** | 23.27 S | 46.44 W |
| Jaraguá, Pico do ∧ | **287b** | 23.26 S | 46.46 W |
| Jaraguá do Sul | **252** | 26.29 S | 49.04 W |
| Jaraicejo | **34** | 39.40 N | 5.49 W |
| Jaraíz de la Vera | **34** | 40.04 N | 5.45 W |
| Jaral del Progreso | **234** | 20.22 N | 101.04 W |
| Jarales | **200** | 34.36 N | 106.45 W |
| Jarama ≃ | **34** | 40.02 N | 3.39 W |
| Jarama, Canal del ≊ | **266a** | 40.18 N | 3.32 W |
| Jaramānah | **132** | 33.29 N | 36.21 E |
| Jaramillo | **254** | 47.11 S | 67.09 W |
| Jaramor | **80** | 56.07 N | 48.44 E |
| Jaran' ≃ | **80** | 57.35 N | 48.14 E |
| Jarandilla | **34** | 40.08 N | 5.39 W |
| Jaraniyo | **144** | 10.42 N | 39.55 E |
| Jaransk | **80** | 57.19 N | 47.54 E |
| Jarānwāla | **123** | 31.20 N | 73.26 E |
| Jarash | **132** | 32.17 N | 35.54 E |
| Jaraucu ≃ | **250** | 1.48 S | 52.22 W |
| Jarawī, Wādī V | **142** | 29.47 N | 31.19 E |
| Jarbah, Jabal al- ∧ | **142** | 30.16 N | 32.03 E |
| Jarbah, Wāḥat ⊤[4] | **140** | 29.21 N | 25.20 E |
| Jarbidge ≃ | **202** | 42.19 N | 115.39 W |
| Järbo | **40** | 60.43 N | 16.36 E |
| Jarcevo | **76** | 55.04 N | 32.41 E |
| Jardas al-'Abīd | **146** | 32.19 N | 20.56 E |
| Jardim, Bra. | **248** | 21.28 S | 56.09 W |
| Jardim, Bra. | **250** | 7.35 S | 39.16 W |
| Jardim América ●[8] | **287b** | 23.34 S | 46.41 W |
| Jardim de Piranhas | **250** | 6.22 S | 37.20 W |
| Jardim do Seridó | **250** | 6.35 S | 36.46 W |
| Jardim Paraiso | **256** | 22.48 S | 43.35 W |
| Jardim Paulista ●[8] | **287b** | 23.35 S | 46.40 W |
| Jardín América | **252** | 27.03 S | 55.14 W |
| Jardine ≃ | **164** | 10.55 S | 142.13 E |
| Jardine River National Park ♦ | **164** | 11.20 S | 142.40 E |
| Jardines de la Reina, Archipiélago de los II | **240p** | 20.50 N | 78.55 W |
| Jardinópolis | **255** | 21.02 S | 47.46 W |
| Jaredi | **150** | 12.46 N | 5.05 E |
| Jaren'ga, Ross. | **24** | 63.27 N | 53.26 E |
| Jarenga, Ross. | **24** | 62.43 N | 49.30 E |
| Jarensk | **24** | 62.11 N | 49.02 E |
| Järfälla | **40** | 59.24 N | 17.50 E |
| Jargalang | **89** | 43.06 N | 122.54 E |
| Jargeau | **50** | 47.52 N | 2.07 E |
| Jari ≃, Bra. | **248** | 5.07 S | 62.21 W |
| Jari ≃, Bra. | **250** | 1.09 S | 51.54 W |
| Jari, Lago ⊜ | **246** | 5.00 S | 62.19 W |
| Jāria Jhānjail | **124** | 25.02 N | 90.39 E |
| Jaridih | **124** | 23.38 N | 86.04 E |
| Jarinu | **256** | 23.06 S | 46.44 W |
| Jarīr, Wādī al- V | **128** | 25.38 N | 42.30 E |
| Jarkino | **88** | 59.08 N | 99.23 E |
| Jarkovo | **86** | 57.24 N | 67.05 E |
| Jarkul'-Mat'uškino | **86** | 55.51 N | 76.06 E |
| Järlåsa | **40** | 59.53 N | 17.12 E |
| Jarmen | **54** | 53.55 N | 13.20 E |
| Järna | **40** | 59.06 N | 17.34 E |
| Jarnac | **32** | 45.41 N | 0.10 W |
| Jarny | **56** | 49.09 N | 5.53 E |
| Jaro | **116** | 11.11 N | 124.47 E |
| Jarochta | **88** | 58.58 N | 98.58 E |
| Jarocin | **30** | 51.59 N | 17.31 E |
| Jaroměř | **30** | 50.21 N | 15.55 E |
| Jaroměřice | **61** | 49.05 N | 15.53 E |
| Jaropolec | **82** | 56.08 N | 35.49 E |
| Jaroslavl' | **80** | 57.37 N | 39.52 E |
| Jaroslavl' Oblast' □[4] | **76** | 57.45 N | 39.00 E |
| Jaroslavl' Station ●[5] | **265b** | 55.47 N | 37.39 E |
| Jaroslavskaja | **84** | 44.36 N | 40.27 E |
| Jaroslavskij | **89** | 44.10 N | 132.13 E |
| Jarosław | **30** | 50.02 N | 22.42 E |
| Järpen | **26** | 63.21 N | 13.29 E |
| Jarrahdale | **168a** | 32.21 S | 116.04 E |
| Jarratt | **208** | 36.48 N | 77.28 W |
| Jarreau | **194** | 30.39 N | 91.29 W |
| Jarrell | **222** | 30.49 N | 97.36 W |
| Jarrettsville | **208** | 39.36 N | 76.28 W |
| Jarrīs | **142** | 27.55 N | 30.46 E |
| Jarrow | **44** | 54.59 N | 1.29 W |
| Jarry, Parc ♦ | **275a** | 45.32 N | 73.38 W |
| Jar-Sale | **74** | 66.50 N | 70.50 E |
| Jarsomovy | **86** | 60.15 N | 73.38 E |
| Jartai Yanchi ⊜ | **102** | 39.43 N | 105.41 E |
| Jaru | **248** | 10.26 S | 62.27 W |
| Jaru ≃ | **248** | 10.05 S | 61.59 W |
| Jarud Qi | **89** | 44.37 N | 120.58 E |
| Jaruu | **88** | 48.08 N | 96.45 E |
| Järva-Jaani | **76** | 59.02 N | 25.53 E |
| Järvakandi | **76** | 58.47 N | 24.49 E |
| Järvelä | **26** | 60.52 N | 25.17 E |
| Järvenpää | **26** | 60.28 N | 25.06 E |
| Jarvie | **182** | 54.27 N | 113.59 W |
| Jarville-la-Malgrange | **58** | 48.40 N | 6.13 E |
| Jarvis | **212** | 42.53 N | 80.06 W |
| Jarvisburg | **192** | 36.12 N | 75.52 W |
| Jarvis Island I | **14** | 0.23 S | 160.02 W |
| Järvsö | **26** | 61.43 N | 16.10 E |
| Jarwa | **124** | 27.39 N | 82.31 E |
| Jasaan | **116** | 8.39 N | 124.45 E |
| Jasai | **272c** | 18.56 N | 73.01 E |
| Jašalta | **80** | 46.20 N | 42.17 E |
| Jasašnaja Tašla | **80** | 53.55 N | 48.16 E |
| Jaša Tomić | **38** | 45.27 N | 20.51 E |
| Jasdan | **120** | 22.02 N | 71.12 E |
| Jasel'da ≃ | **76** | 52.07 N | 26.28 E |
| Jasenevo ●[8] | **265b** | 55.36 N | 37.33 E |
| Jasenki | **78** | 51.32 N | 38.12 E |
| Jasenovoje | **82** | 54.10 N | 36.47 E |
| Jasenskaja | **78** | 46.22 N | 38.16 E |
| Jashpurnagar | **124** | 22.54 N | 84.09 E |
| Jāshpur Pāts ●[1] | **124** | 22.55 N | 84.00 E |
| Jasidih | **124** | 24.31 N | 86.39 E |
| Jasień | **30** | 51.46 N | 15.01 E |
| Jasienica | **54** | 53.37 N | 14.32 E |
| Jasikan | **150** | 7.24 N | 0.28 E |
| Jašil'kul', ozero ⊜ | **120** | 37.45 N | 72.55 E |
| Jasin | **114** | 2.19 N | 102.26 E |
| Jasinga | **115a** | 6.29 S | 106.27 E |
| Jāsk | **128** | 25.38 N | 57.46 E |
| Jaskhar | **272c** | 18.54 N | 72.59 E |
| Jaškino, Ross. | **80** | 52.41 N | 53.26 E |
| Jaškino, Ross. | **86** | 55.54 N | 85.26 E |
| Jaskino, Ross. | **265b** | 55.40 N | 37.16 E |
| Jaškul' | **80** | 46.11 N | 45.21 E |
| Jaškul' ≃ | **80** | 46.15 N | 45.05 E |
| Jasło | **30** | 49.45 N | 21.29 E |
| Jasmine Estates | **220** | 28.17 N | 82.42 W |
| Jasmund ›[1] | **54** | 54.32 N | 13.35 E |
| Jasnaja Pol'ana ⊥ | **82** | 54.05 N | 37.32 E |
| Jasnogorsk | **82** | 54.29 N | 37.42 E |
| Jasnomorskij | **89** | 46.45 N | 141.54 E |
| Jasnyj, Ross. | **86** | 51.04 N | 59.58 E |
| Jasnyj, Ross. | **89** | 53.17 N | 127.59 E |
| Jason Islands II | **254** | 51.05 S | 61.00 W |
| Jason Peninsula ›[1] | **9** | 66.10 S | 61.00 W |
| Jasonville | **194** | 39.09 N | 87.11 W |
| Jasper, Ab., Can. | **182** | 52.53 N | 118.05 W |
| Jasper, Al., U.S. | **194** | 33.49 N | 87.16 W |
| Jasper, Ar., U.S. | **194** | 36.00 N | 93.11 W |
| Jasper, Fl., U.S. | **192** | 30.31 N | 82.56 W |
| Jasper, Ga., U.S. | **192** | 34.28 N | 84.25 W |
| Jasper, In., U.S. | **194** | 38.23 N | 86.55 W |
| Jasper, Mi., U.S. | **216** | 41.48 N | 84.02 W |
| Jasper, Mn., U.S. | **198** | 43.51 N | 96.23 W |
| Jasper, Mo., U.S. | **194** | 37.20 N | 94.18 W |
| Jasper, N.Y., U.S. | **210** | 42.07 N | 77.30 W |
| Jasper, Tn., U.S. | **194** | 35.04 N | 85.37 W |
| Jasper, Tx., U.S. | **194** | 30.55 N | 93.59 W |
| Jasper □[6] | **216** | 40.57 N | 87.09 W |
| Jasper Lake ⊜ | **182** | 53.07 N | 118.00 W |
| Jasper National Park ♦ | **182** | 52.53 N | 118.03 W |
| Jaspur | **124** | 29.17 N | 78.49 E |
| Jasra | **124** | 25.17 N | 81.48 E |
| Jassans-Riottier | **58** | 45.59 N | 4.45 E |
| Jassar | **123** | 32.06 N | 74.57 E |
| Jassy → Iași | **38** | 47.10 N | 27.35 E |
| Jassy ≃ | **85** | 40.46 N | 73.05 E |
| Jastarnia | **30** | 54.43 N | 18.40 E |
| Jastrebarsko | **36** | 45.40 N | 15.39 E |
| Jastrebovka, Ross. | **78** | 51.27 N | 37.32 E |
| Jastrebovka, Ross. | **82** | 54.36 N | 36.24 E |
| Jastrowie | **30** | 53.26 N | 16.49 E |
| Jaswantnagar | **124** | 26.53 N | 78.55 E |
| Jászapáti | **30** | 47.31 N | 20.09 E |
| Jászberény | **30** | 47.30 N | 19.55 E |
| Jász-Nagykun-Szolnok □[6] | **30** | 47.12 N | 20.11 E |
| Jataí | **255** | 17.53 S | 51.43 W |
| Jatapu ≃ | **246** | 2.13 S | 58.17 W |
| Jataté ≃ | **232** | 16.15 N | 91.17 W |
| Jati, Bra. | **250** | 7.41 S | 39.01 W |
| Jāti, Pāk. | **120** | 24.21 N | 68.16 E |
| Jatibarang | **115a** | 6.28 S | 108.17 E |
| Jatibonico | **240p** | 21.56 N | 79.10 W |
| Jatibonico del Sur ≃ | **240p** | 21.33 N | 79.09 W |
| Jatilawang | **115a** | 7.32 S | 109.06 E |
| Jatiluhur, Waduk ⊜[1] | **115a** | 6.35 S | 107.20 E |
| Jatinegara ●[8] | **269e** | 6.13 S | 106.52 E |
| Jatiroto | **115a** | 8.07 S | 113.21 E |
| Jatisrono | **115a** | 7.49 S | 111.07 E |
| Jatiwangi | **115a** | 6.44 S | 108.15 E |
| Jatni | **120** | 20.10 N | 85.42 E |
| Jatniel | **273d** | 26.07 S | 28.19 E |
| Jatobá ≃ | **255** | 12.23 S | 54.07 W |
| Jatobá, Ribeirão ≃ | **256** | 21.28 S | 42.49 W |
| Jatoi Janūbi | **123** | 29.31 N | 70.51 E |
| Jātrāpur | **126** | 22.44 N | 89.45 E |
| Jatt (Tel Gat) | **132** | 32.24 N | 35.02 E |
| Jatznick | **54** | 53.35 N | 13.56 E |
| Jáu, Ang. | **152** | 15.12 S | 13.31 E |
| Jaú, Bra. | **255** | 22.18 S | 48.33 W |
| Jaú ≃ | **246** | 1.54 S | 61.26 W |
| Jaú, Parque Nacional do ♦ | **246** | 2.30 S | 63.00 W |
| Jauaperi ≃ | **246** | 1.26 S | 61.35 W |
| Jauerling ∧ | **61** | 48.20 N | 15.20 E |
| Jaugrām | **126** | 23.06 N | 88.05 E |
| Jauja | **248** | 11.48 S | 75.30 W |
| Jauli | **272a** | 28.44 N | 77.21 E |
| Jaumave | **234** | 23.25 N | 99.23 W |
| Jaunde → Yaoundé | **152** | 3.52 N | 11.31 E |
| Jaune, Mer → Yellow Sea ⊤[2] | **90** | 36.00 N | 123.00 E |
| Jaungulbene | **76** | 57.04 N | 26.36 E |
| Jaunjelgava | **76** | 56.37 N | 25.05 E |
| Jaunpass )( | **58** | 46.36 N | 7.20 E |
| Jaunpiebalga | **76** | 57.11 N | 26.03 E |
| Jaunpils | **76** | 56.44 N | 23.01 E |
| Jaunpur | **124** | 25.44 N | 82.41 E |
| Jaupaci | **255** | 16.18 S | 50.54 W |
| Jauquara ≃ | **248** | 15.06 S | 57.06 W |
| Jáuregui | **258** | 34.36 S | 59.10 W |
| Jauru | **250** | 11.06 S | 57.30 W |
| Jauru ≃, Bra. | **248** | 16.22 S | 57.46 W |
| Jauru ≃, Bra. | **255** | 18.40 S | 54.36 W |
| Jausiers | **62** | 44.25 N | 6.44 E |
| Jauza ≃, Ross. | **82** | 56.25 N | 36.05 E |
| Jauza ≃, Ross. | **265b** | 55.45 N | 37.38 E |
| Java | **198** | 45.30 N | 99.53 W |
| Java → Jawa I | **115a** | 7.30 S | 110.00 E |
| Java Center | **210** | 42.39 N | 78.23 W |
| Javādi Hills ⋏[2] | **122** | 12.35 N | 78.50 E |
| Javan | **85** | 38.19 N | 69.02 E |
| Javari (Yavarí) ≃ | **242** | 4.21 S | 70.02 W |
| Javas | **80** | 54.26 N | 42.51 E |
| Java Sea → Jawa, Laut ⊤[2] | **112** | 5.00 S | 110.00 E |
| Java Trench ✦[1] | **12** | 10.30 S | 110.00 E |
| Java Village | **210** | 42.40 N | 78.26 W |
| Jävenitz | **54** | 52.31 N | 11.30 E |
| Javier, Isla I | **254** | 47.06 S | 74.24 W |
| Javlenka | **86** | 54.21 N | 68.27 E |
| Javor ⋏ | **38** | 44.05 N | 18.55 E |
| Javořice ∧ | **61** | 49.14 N | 15.20 E |
| Javorie ∧ | **30** | 48.27 N | 19.18 E |
| Javorná | **60** | 49.13 N | 13.18 E |
| Javorník | **30** | 50.23 N | 17.00 E |
| Javorová skála ∧ | **30** | 49.31 N | 14.30 E |
| Javr ≃ | **24** | 68.09 N | 30.06 E |
| Jävre | **26** | 65.09 N | 21.59 E |
| Jawa (Java) I | **115a** | 7.30 S | 110.00 E |
| Jawa, Laut (Java Sea) ⊤[2] | **112** | 5.00 S | 110.00 E |
| Jawa Barat □[4] | **115a** | 7.00 S | 107.00 E |
| Jaw'āīyāt, Jabal al- ∧ | **132** | 31.26 N | 36.26 E |
| Jawāla Mukhi | **123** | 31.53 N | 76.19 E |
| Jawa Tengah □[4] | **115a** | 7.30 S | 110.00 E |
| Jawa Timur □[4] | **115a** | 8.00 S | 113.00 E |
| Jawbar | **132** | 33.31 N | 36.19 E |
| Jawf, Wādī V | **144** | 15.50 N | 45.30 E |
| Jawi | **112** | 0.48 S | 109.16 E |
| Jawor | **30** | 51.03 N | 16.11 E |
| Jaworzno | **30** | 50.13 N | 19.15 E |
| Jay, Fl., U.S. | **194** | 30.57 N | 87.09 W |
| Jay, Ok., U.S. | **196** | 36.25 N | 94.47 W |
| Jay □[6] | **216** | 40.26 N | 84.59 W |
| Jaya, Puncak ∧ | **164** | 4.05 S | 137.11 E |
| Jayanca | **248** | 6.24 S | 79.50 W |
| Jayapura (Sukarnapura) | **164** | 2.32 S | 140.42 E |
| Jayb, Wādī al- (Ha'Arava) V | **132** | 30.58 N | 35.24 E |
| Jay Cooke State Park ♦ | **190** | 46.41 N | 92.23 W |
| Jay Creek Aboriginal Reserve ●[4] | **162** | 23.45 S | 133.35 E |
| Jaydebpur | **124** | 24.00 N | 90.26 E |
| Jaynagar | **126** | 22.36 N | 90.42 E |
| Jaynagar Majilpur | **126** | 22.11 N | 88.25 E |
| Jaynes | **200** | 32.16 N | 111.01 W |
| Jay Peak ∧ | **188** | 44.55 N | 72.32 W |
| Jaypur, India | **122** | 18.51 N | 82.35 E |
| Jaypur, India | **126** | 23.03 N | 87.27 E |
| Jayrūd | **130** | 33.49 N | 36.44 E |
| Jayton | **196** | 33.15 N | 100.34 W |
| Jayuya | **240m** | 18.13 N | 66.36 W |
| Jaywick | **42** | 51.47 N | 1.08 E |
| Jaz | **80** | 54.54 N | 45.13 E |
| Jaželbicy | **76** | 58.02 N | 32.58 E |
| Jazevec | **24** | 65.43 N | 46.30 E |
| Jazgulem ≃ | **85** | 38.12 N | 71.21 E |
| Jazīrat Muḥammad | **273c** | 30.07 N | 31.12 E |
| Jazjavan | **85** | 40.39 N | 71.44 E |
| Jažma | **24** | 66.56 N | 44.29 E |
| Jaz Mūrīān, Hāmūn-e ⊜ | **128** | 27.20 N | 58.55 E |
| Jazovaja | **86** | 49.27 N | 85.20 E |
| Jazykovo | **80** | 54.18 N | 47.24 E |
| Jazzīn | **132** | 33.32 N | 35.34 E |
| Jbā' | **132** | 33.29 N | 35.31 E |
| J.B. Thomas, Lake ⊜[1] | **196** | 32.35 N | 101.10 W |
| J. C. Murphey Lake ⊜ | **216** | 40.58 N | 87.30 W |
| Jdiouia | **34** | 35.57 N | 0.50 E |
| Jeanerette | **194** | 29.54 N | 91.39 W |
| Jeanesville | **210** | 40.56 N | 75.58 W |
| Jeannette | **214** | 40.19 N | 79.36 W |
| Jebba | **150** | 9.08 N | 4.50 E |
| Jebel | **38** | 45.33 N | 21.14 E |
| Jebeniana | **148** | 35.02 N | 10.55 E |
| Jeber-Bergfrieden | **54** | 51.59 N | 12.20 E |
| Jeberos | **248** | 5.17 S | 76.13 W |
| Jebri | **120** | 27.18 N | 65.44 E |
| Jebus | **112** | 1.44 S | 105.29 E |
| Jechegnadzor | **84** | 39.46 N | 45.21 E |
| Jéci, Serra ∧ | **154** | 12.48 S | 35.12 E |
| Jedane, Oued ti-n- V | **148** | 24.55 N | 6.30 E |
| Jedarma | **88** | 58.44 N | 102.36 E |
| Jedburgh | **44** | 55.29 N | 2.34 W |
| Jedburgh Abbey v[1] | **44** | 55.27 N | 2.34 W |
| Jeddah → Jiddah | **144** | 21.30 N | 39.12 E |
| Jeddore Lake ⊜[1] | **186** | 48.03 N | 55.55 W |
| Jedelevo | **80** | 53.24 N | 47.45 E |
| Jedepo | **150** | 5.16 N | 8.20 W |
| Jedisa | **84** | 42.31 N | 44.16 E |
| Jedlesee ●[8] | **264b** | 48.16 N | 16.23 E |
| Jednevo | **82** | 56.06 N | 36.14 E |
| Jedogon | **88** | 54.15 N | 100.15 E |
| Jedrovo | **76** | 57.55 N | 33.38 E |
| Jędrzejów | **30** | 50.39 N | 20.18 E |
| Jedwabne | **30** | 53.17 N | 22.19 E |
| Jed Water ≃ | **46** | 55.32 N | 2.33 W |
| Jeetzel (Jeetze) ≃ | **54** | 53.09 N | 11.04 E |
| Jefawa | **140** | 10.57 N | 23.48 E |
| Jeffara (Al-Jifārah) ≚ | **146** | 32.30 N | 11.45 E |
| Jeffers | **198** | 44.03 N | 95.11 W |
| Jefferson, Ga., U.S. | **192** | 34.07 N | 83.34 W |
| Jefferson, In., U.S. | **216** | 40.17 N | 86.36 W |
| Jefferson, Ia., U.S. | **198** | 42.00 N | 94.22 W |
| Jefferson, Md., U.S. | **208** | 39.21 N | 77.31 W |
| Jefferson, Ma., U.S. | **207** | 42.21 N | 71.52 W |
| Jefferson, N.J., U.S. | **285** | 39.45 N | 75.13 W |
| Jefferson, N.Y., U.S. | **210** | 42.14 N | 73.54 W |
| Jefferson, N.Y., U.S. | **210** | 42.29 N | 74.37 W |
| Jefferson, N.C., U.S. | **192** | 36.25 N | 81.28 W |
| Jefferson, Oh., U.S. | **214** | 41.44 N | 80.46 W |
| Jefferson, Or., U.S. | **202** | 44.43 N | 123.00 W |
| Jefferson, Pa., U.S. | **279b** | 40.18 N | 80.03 W |
| Jefferson, S.C., U.S. | **192** | 34.39 N | 80.23 W |


### ENGLISH


| Name | Page | Lat.°' | Long.°' |
|---|---|---|---|
| Jefferson, S.D., U.S. | **198** | 42.36 N | 96.33 W |
| Jefferson, Tx., U.S. | **194** | 32.45 N | 94.20 W |
| Jefferson, Wi., U.S. | **216** | 43.00 N | 88.48 W |
| Jefferson □[6], Il., U.S. | **219** | 38.19 N | 88.55 W |
| Jefferson □[6], In., U.S. | **218** | 38.44 N | 85.23 W |
| Jefferson □[6], Ky., U.S. | **218** | 38.14 N | 85.10 W |
| Jefferson □[6], Mo., U.S. | **219** | 38.20 N | 90.34 W |
| Jefferson □[6], N.Y., U.S. | **212** | 43.59 N | 75.55 W |
| Jefferson □[6], Oh., U.S. | **214** | 40.22 N | 80.37 W |
| Jefferson □[6], Pa., U.S. | **214** | 41.09 N | 79.05 W |
| Jefferson □[6], Wa., U.S. | **224** | 47.50 N | 122.36 W |
| Jefferson □[6], Wi., U.S. | **216** | 43.02 N | 88.46 W |
| Jefferson ≃ | **202** | 45.56 N | 111.30 W |
| Jefferson, Mount ∧, U.S. | **202** | 44.34 N | 111.30 W |
| Jefferson, Mount ∧, Nv., U.S. | **204** | 38.46 N | 116.55 W |
| Jefferson, Mount ∧, Or., U.S. | **202** | 44.40 N | 121.47 W |
| Jefferson City, Mo., U.S. | **219** | 38.34 N | 92.10 W |
| Jefferson City, Tn., U.S. | **192** | 36.07 N | 83.29 W |
| Jefferson Farms | **285** | 39.40 N | 75.34 W |
| Jefferson Manor | **284c** | 38.47 N | 77.04 W |
| Jefferson Park ●[8] | **278** | 41.59 N | 87.46 W |
| Jefferson Proving Ground ■ | **218** | 38.50 N | 85.25 W |
| Jeffersonton | **188** | 38.38 N | 77.55 W |
| Jeffersontown | **218** | 38.11 N | 85.33 W |
| Jefferson Village | **284c** | 38.52 N | 77.10 W |
| Jeffersonville, Ga., U.S. | **192** | 32.41 N | 83.20 W |
| Jeffersonville, In., U.S. | **218** | 38.16 N | 85.44 W |
| Jeffersonville, N.Y., U.S. | **210** | 41.46 N | 74.56 W |
| Jeffersonville, Oh., U.S. | **218** | 39.39 N | 83.33 W |
| Jeffrey City | **200** | 42.29 N | 107.49 W |
| Jeffreys Bay | **158** | 34.02 S | 24.54 E |
| Jeffries Creek ≃ | **192** | 34.05 N | 79.32 W |
| Jefimovka | **80** | 52.13 N | 52.03 E |
| Jefimovskij | **76** | 59.30 N | 34.40 E |
| Jefremov | **76** | 53.09 N | 38.07 E |
| Jefremova | **82** | 56.13 N | 38.59 E |
| Jefremovka | **83** | 47.19 N | 38.29 E |
| Jefremovo-Stepanovka | **78** | 48.43 N | 40.50 E |
| Jefremovskaja | **82** | 55.25 N | 38.59 E |
| Jega | **150** | 12.15 N | 4.23 E |
| Jegenstorf | **58** | 47.03 N | 7.30 E |
| Jegindybulak, Kaz. | **86** | 49.45 N | 76.23 E |
| Jegindybulak, Kaz. | **86** | 48.42 N | 81.48 E |
| Jegizkara, gora ∧ | **86** | 46.24 N | 64.09 E |
| Jegorjevka | **89** | 50.42 N | 127.42 E |
| Jegorjevsk | **82** | 55.23 N | 39.02 E |
| Jegorlyk ≃ | **80** | 46.33 N | 41.52 E |
| Jehol → Chengde | **105** | 40.58 N | 117.53 E |
| Jeja ≃ | **78** | 46.41 N | 38.36 E |
| Jejsk | **78** | 46.42 N | 38.16 E |
| Jejskij liman c | **78** | 46.42 N | 38.25 E |
| Jeju → Cheju | **90** | 33.31 N | 126.32 E |
| Jejur | **272b** | 22.53 N | 88.08 E |
| Jēkabpils | **76** | 56.29 N | 25.51 E |
| Jekaterinburg (Sverdlovsk) | **86** | 56.51 N | 60.36 E |
| Jekaterinburg Oblast' □[4] | **86** | 58.00 N | 62.00 E |
| Jekaterinino | **76** | 55.49 N | 33.58 E |
| Jekaterininskoje | **86** | 56.53 N | 74.34 E |
| Jekaterinoslav → Dnipropetrovs'k | **78** | 48.27 N | 34.59 E |
| Jekaterinoslavka | **89** | 50.23 N | 129.08 E |
| Jekaterinovka, Kaz. | **86** | 54.36 N | 70.58 E |
| Jekaterinovka, Ross. | **78** | 46.42 N | 38.46 E |
| Jekaterinovka, Ross. | **80** | 53.04 N | 49.28 E |
| Jekaterinovka, Ross. | **80** | 46.32 N | 41.42 E |
| Jekaterinovka, Ross. | **80** | 52.03 N | 44.21 E |
| Jekaterinovka, Ross. | **83** | 47.33 N | 38.23 E |
| Jekaterinovka ●[8] | **265b** | 55.46 N | 37.23 E |
| Jekaterinovskaja | **78** | 46.20 N | 39.58 E |
| Jekateriny, proliv ʊ, Ross. | **74** | 44.30 N | 146.45 E |
| Jekateriny, proliv ʊ, Ross. | **92a** | 44.25 N | 146.40 E |
| Jekimoviči | **76** | 54.07 N | 33.18 E |
| Jekpindykurylys | **80** | 47.49 N | 47.17 E |
| Jekyll Island I | **192** | 31.04 N | 81.25 W |
| Jekyll Island State Park ♦ | **192** | 31.02 N | 81.25 W |
| Jelabuga | **80** | 55.47 N | 52.04 E |
| Jelai ≃, Indon. | **112** | 2.59 S | 110.45 E |
| Jelai ≃, Malay. | **114** | 4.04 N | 102.20 E |
| Jelan', Ross. | **80** | 52.13 N | 44.11 E |
| Jelan', Ross. | **80** | 50.57 N | 43.44 E |
| Jelan', Ross. | **83** | 48.41 N | 39.47 E |
| Jelan', Ross. | **86** | 57.39 N | 63.42 E |
| Jelan' ≃, Ross. | **78** | 51.07 N | 41.25 E |
| Jelan' ≃, Ross. | **80** | 50.57 N | 43.44 E |
| Jelan' ≃, Ross. | **80** | 51.07 N | 41.26 E |
| Jelancy | **88** | 52.49 N | 106.25 E |
| Jelanka | **86** | 55.37 N | 75.18 E |
| Jelan'-Koleno | **78** | 51.09 N | 41.14 E |
| Jelan'-Kolenovskij | **78** | 51.10 N | 41.10 E |
| Jelat'ma | **80** | 54.58 N | 41.45 E |
| Jelaur, Ross. | **80** | 54.34 N | 50.21 E |
| Jelaur, Ross. | **80** | 53.50 N | 48.48 E |
| Jelchovka | **80** | 53.51 N | 50.18 E |
| Jel'covka | **86** | 53.15 N | 86.15 E |
| Jel'cy, Ross. | **76** | 56.40 N | 33.51 E |
| Jel'cy, Ross. | **82** | 56.11 N | 38.46 E |
| Jelec | **76** | 52.37 N | 38.30 E |
| Jeleckij | **24** | 67.03 N | 64.10 E |
| Jelenia Góra (Hirschberg) | **30** | 50.55 N | 15.46 E |
| Jelenia Góra □[4] | **30** | 51.10 N | 15.30 E |
| Jelenskij | **76** | 53.29 N | 35.23 E |
| Jelep La Pass )( | **124** | 27.23 N | 88.51 E |
| Jelgava | **76** | 56.39 N | 23.42 E |
| Jelgavkrasti | **76** | 57.28 N | 24.26 E |
| Jelizarovo | **80** | 58.33 N | 44.50 E |
| Jelizavetinka | **86** | 51.28 N | 71.12 E |
| Jelizavetopol'skoje | **86** | 52.51 N | 60.36 E |
| Jelizavetovka | **78** | 46.39 N | 38.53 E |
| Jelizavety, mys › | **89** | 54.26 N | 142.42 E |
| Jelli | **154** | 5.22 N | 31.48 E |
| Jellico | **192** | 36.35 N | 84.07 W |
| Jelling | **41** | 55.45 N | 9.26 E |
| Jelloway | **214** | 40.33 N | 82.18 W |
| Jelm Mountain ∧ | **200** | 41.06 N | 105.58 W |
| Jel'n'a | **76** | 54.35 N | 33.11 E |
| Jelnat' | **80** | 57.20 N | 42.49 E |
| Jel'niki | **80** | 54.37 N | 43.53 E |
| Jeloguj ≃ | **74** | 63.13 N | 87.45 E |
| Jelošnoje | **86** | 55.27 N | 66.44 E |
| Jelovo | **80** | 57.03 N | 54.54 E |
| Jels | **41** | 55.21 N | 9.12 E |
| Jelšanka, Ross. | **80** | 51.49 N | 46.23 E |
| Jelšanka, Ross. | **80** | 52.35 N | 47.59 E |
| Jelšanka Pervaja | **80** | 52.53 N | 52.02 E |
| Jelšava | **30** | 48.39 N | 20.14 E |
| Jema ≃ | **144** | 10.09 N | 38.20 E |
| Jemaa | **150** | 9.27 N | 8.23 E |
| Jemaja, Pulau I | **112** | 2.55 N | 105.45 E |
| Jemaluang | **114** | 2.17 N | 103.52 E |
| Jemantajevo | **80** | 53.34 N | 53.50 E |
| Jemanželinsk | **86** | 54.45 N | 61.20 E |
| Jember | **115a** | 8.10 S | 113.42 E |
| Jemca | **24** | 63.04 N | 40.20 E |
| Jemca ≃ | **24** | 63.15 N | 41.20 E |


### DEUTSCH


| Name | Seite | Breite°' | Länge°' E = Ost |
|---|---|---|---|
| Jemeljanovo | **86** | 56.11 N | 92.40 E |
| Jemel'stan | **24** | 61.13 N | 52.29 E |
| Jemen → Yemen □[1] | **144** | 15.00 N | 47.00 E |
| Jemen, Volksrepublik → Yemen □[1] | **144** | 15.00 N | 47.00 E |
| Jemez ≃ | **200** | 35.22 N | 106.31 W |
| Jemez Canyon Reservoir ⊜[1] | **200** | 35.28 N | 106.39 W |
| Jemez Indian Reservation ●[4] | **200** | 35.35 N | 106.45 W |
| Jemez Springs | **200** | 35.46 N | 106.41 W |
| Jemgum | **52** | 53.16 N | 7.23 E |
| Jeminary | **86** | 47.32 N | 85.38 E |
| Jemmal | **148** | 35.38 N | 10.46 E |
| Jemnice | **61** | 49.01 N | 15.35 E |
| Jempang, Kenohan ⊜ | **112** | 0.26 S | 116.12 E |
| Jena, Dtsch. | **54** | 50.56 N | 11.35 E |
| Jena, La., U.S. | **194** | 31.40 N | 92.08 W |
| Jenašimskij Polkan, gora ∧ | **74** | 59.50 N | 92.52 E |
| Jenaz | **58** | 46.55 N | 9.45 E |
| Jenbach | **64** | 47.24 N | 11.47 E |
| Jenbek | **86** | 48.53 N | 77.12 E |
| Jendarata | **114** | 3.55 N | 100.57 E |
| Jendongin | **88** | 53.27 N | 113.01 E |
| Jendouba (Souk el Arba) | **148** | 36.30 N | 8.47 E |
| Jeneponto | **112** | 5.41 S | 119.42 E |
| Jenera | **216** | 40.54 N | 83.44 W |
| Jeniang | **114** | 5.49 N | 100.38 E |
| Jenisej (Yenisey) ≃ | **72** | 71.50 N | 82.40 E |
| Jenisejsk | **86** | 58.27 N | 92.10 E |
| Jenisejskij kr'až ⋏ | **74** | 59.00 N | 93.00 E |
| Jenisejskij zaliv c | **74** | 72.30 N | 80.00 E |
| Jenison | **216** | 42.54 N | 85.47 W |
| Jenkins, Ky., U.S. | **192** | 37.10 N | 82.37 W |
| Jenkins, Tx., U.S. | **222** | 32.59 N | 94.44 W |
| Jenkins, Mount ∧ | **162** | 25.36 S | 129.41 E |
| Jenkinson Lake ⊜[1] | **226** | 38.44 N | 120.33 W |
| Jenkinsville | **192** | 34.16 N | 81.17 W |
| Jenkintown | **208** | 40.05 N | 75.07 W |
| Jenks | **196** | 36.01 N | 95.58 W |
| Jenli | **100** | 23.15 N | 120.08 E |
| Jenners | **214** | 40.08 N | 79.02 W |
| Jennersdorf | **61** | 46.57 N | 16.08 E |
| Jennerstown | **214** | 40.10 N | 79.04 W |
| Jennifer Branch ≃ | **284b** | 39.25 N | 76.30 W |
| Jennings, Fl., U.S. | **192** | 30.36 N | 83.05 W |
| Jennings, La., U.S. | **194** | 30.13 N | 92.39 W |
| Jennings, Mo., U.S. | **219** | 38.43 N | 90.15 W |
| Jennings □[6] | **218** | 38.59 N | 85.36 W |
| Jennings Creek ≃ | **216** | 40.53 N | 84.17 W |
| Jennings Lodge | **224** | 45.23 N | 122.36 W |
| Jenotajevka | **80** | 47.15 N | 47.03 E |
| Jenpeg Dam ●[6] | **184** | 54.33 N | 98.02 W |
| Jensen | **200** | 40.22 N | 109.20 W |
| Jensen Beach | **220** | 27.15 N | 80.13 W |
| Jens Munk Island I | **176** | 69.42 N | 79.30 W |
| Jens Munks Ø I | **176** | 64.40 N | 40.30 W |
| Jenu | **112** | 0.36 S | 109.52 E |
| Jen'uka | **88** | 57.58 N | 121.42 E |
| Jeonju → Chŏnju | **98** | 35.49 N | 127.08 E |
| Jepač | **24** | 66.58 N | 61.22 E |
| Jepara | **115a** | 6.35 S | 110.39 E |
| Jeparit | **166** | 36.09 S | 141.59 E |
| Jepelacio | **248** | 6.07 S | 76.57 W |
| Jepichin | **80** | 48.16 N | 45.14 E |
| Jepifan' | **76** | 53.49 N | 38.33 E |
| Jeppener | **258** | 35.17 S | 58.12 W |
| Jeptha Knob ∧[2] | **218** | 38.11 N | 85.07 W |
| Jepua (Jeppo) | **26** | 63.24 N | 22.37 E |
| Jequeri | **255** | 20.27 S | 42.40 W |
| Jequetepeque ≃ | **248** | 7.21 S | 79.36 W |
| Jequié | **255** | 13.51 S | 40.05 W |
| Jequitaí | **255** | 17.15 S | 44.28 W |
| Jequitinhonha | **255** | 16.26 S | 41.00 W |
| Jequitinhonha ≃ | **255** | 15.51 S | 38.53 W |
| Jerachtur | **80** | 54.43 N | 41.09 E |
| Jerada | **148** | 34.17 N | 2.13 W |
| Jeradou | **36** | 36.15 N | 10.23 E |
| Jerangle | **171b** | 35.52 S | 149.22 E |
| Jeransang | **114** | 3.52 N | 102.22 E |
| Jerantut | **114** | 3.56 N | 102.22 E |
| Jerba, Île de I | **148** | 33.48 N | 10.54 E |
| Jerbar | **140** | 5.39 N | 31.05 E |
| Jerbent | **128** | 39.19 N | 58.36 E |
| Jerbogačon | **74** | 61.16 N | 108.00 E |
| Jercevo | **24** | 60.48 N | 40.05 E |
| Jerdenevo | **82** | 54.55 N | 36.27 E |
| Jerécuaro | **234** | 20.09 N | 100.31 W |
| Jeremejevka | **83** | 46.58 N | 39.33 E |
| Jeremejevo | **82** | 55.57 N | 37.01 E |
| Jérémie | **238** | 18.39 N | 74.07 W |
| Jeremino | **82** | 56.27 N | 37.58 E |
| Jeremoabo | **250** | 10.04 S | 38.21 W |
| Jeremy Hill ∧[2] | **207** | 42.45 N | 71.21 W |
| Jeremy Point › | **207** | 41.53 N | 70.04 W |
| Jerevan | **84** | 40.11 N | 44.30 E |
| Jerez ≃ | **234** | 22.15 N | 103.11 W |
| Jerez de García Salinas | **234** | 22.39 N | 103.00 W |
| Jerez de la Frontera | **34** | 36.41 N | 6.08 W |
| Jerez de los Caballeros | **34** | 38.19 N | 6.46 W |
| Jergač | **86** | 57.28 N | 56.39 E |
| Jergeni ⋏[2] | **80** | 47.00 N | 44.00 E |
| Jergeninskij | **80** | 47.07 N | 44.28 E |
| Jericho → Arīḥā, Ariha | **132** | 31.52 N | 35.27 E |
| Jericho, Austl. | **166** | 23.36 S | 146.08 E |
| Jericho, N.J., U.S. | **285** | 39.48 N | 75.09 W |
| Jericho, N.Y., U.S. | **210** | 40.47 N | 73.32 W |
| Jericho Area □[8] | **132** | 31.50 N | 35.25 E |
| Jericho Dam ⊜[1] | **158** | 26.39 S | 30.28 E |
| Jerichow | **54** | 52.30 N | 12.01 E |
| Jericó, Bra. | **250** | 6.33 S | 37.48 W |
| Jericó, Col. | **246** | 5.47 N | 75.47 W |
| Jericoacoara, Ponta de › | **250** | 2.48 S | 40.29 W |
| Jerid, Chott ≡ | **148** | 33.42 N | 8.26 E |
| Jerilderie | **166** | 35.22 S | 145.44 E |
| Jerimoth Hill ∧[2] | **207** | 41.52 N | 71.47 W |
| Jermak | **86** | 52.02 N | 76.55 E |
| Jermakovo | **80** | 53.11 N | 49.38 E |
| Jermakovskaja | **80** | 48.03 N | 41.17 E |
| Jermakovskoje | **86** | 53.16 N | 92.24 E |
| Jermekejevo | **80** | 54.05 N | 53.40 E |
| Jermentau | **86** | 51.38 N | 73.10 E |
| Jermentau ⋏ | **86** | 51.10 N | 73.10 E |
| Jermica | **24** | 66.56 N | 52.15 E |
| Jermilovka | **86** | 57.40 N | 72.55 E |
| Jermiš' | **80** | 54.46 N | 42.16 E |
| Jermolajevo, Ross. | **86** | 55.13 N | 92.10 E |
| Jermolajevo, Ross. | **86** | 52.46 N | 55.47 E |
| Jermolino, Ross. | **82** | 55.12 N | 36.36 E |
| Jermolino, Ross. | **82** | 55.57 N | 36.54 E |
| Jermolino, Ross. | **82** | 56.48 N | 37.49 E |
| Jermolino, Ross. | **86** | 57.20 N | 64.43 E |
| Jermyn | **210** | 41.31 N | 75.32 W |
| Jernhatten ∧[2] | **41** | 56.15 N | 10.48 E |
| Jernih | **114** | 4.25 N | 97.43 E |
| Jeroaquara | **255** | 15.23 S | 50.25 W |
| Jerofej Pavlovič | **89** | 53.58 N | 122.01 E |
| Jerome, Az., U.S. | **200** | 34.44 N | 112.06 W |
| Jerome, Id., U.S. | **202** | 42.43 N | 114.31 W |
| Jerome, Il., U.S. | **219** | 39.46 N | 89.41 W |
| Jerome, Mi., U.S. | **216** | 42.01 N | 84.28 W |
| Jerome, Pa., U.S. | **214** | 40.12 N | 78.59 W |
| Jeromesville | **214** | 40.48 N | 82.11 W |
| Jer'omino | **86** | 58.35 N | 79.25 E |
| Jerónimos, Mosteiro dos v[1] | **266c** | 38.42 N | 9.12 W |
| Jeröö | **88** | 49.45 N | 106.40 E |
| Jeröö ≃ | **88** | 49.54 N | 106.08 E |
| Jeropol | **74** | 65.15 N | 168.40 E |
| Jerpoint Abbey ⊥ | **48** | 52.29 N | 7.08 W |
| Jerry City | **216** | 41.15 N | 83.36 W |
| Jerry Slough ≃ | **226** | 35.33 N | 119.31 W |
| Jersey | **214** | 40.03 N | 82.46 W |


**Symbols** in the index entries represent the broad categories identified in the key at the right. Symbols with superior numbers (⋏[1]) identify subcategories (see complete key on page *I · 1).*

**Symbole** im Register stellen die rechts im Schlüssel erklärten Kategorien dar. Symbole mit hochgestellten Ziffern (⋏[1]) bezeichnen Unterabteilungen einer Kategorie (vgl. vollständiger Schlüssel auf Seite *I · 1).*

**Los símbolos** incluídos en el texto del índice representan las grandes categorías identificadas con la clave a la derecha. Los símbolos con numeros en su parte superior (⋏[1]) identifican las subcategorías (véase la clave completa en la página *I · 1).*

**Les symboles** de l'index représentent les catégories indiquées dans la légende à droite. Les symboles suivis d'un indice (⋏[1]) représentent des sous-catégories (voir légende complète à la page *I · 1).*

**Os símbolos** incluídos no texto do índice representam as grandes categorias identificadas com a chave à direita. Os símbolos com números em sua parte superior (⋏[1]) identificam as subcategorias (veja-se a chave completa à página *I · 1).*

| | | | | |
|---|---|---|---|---|
| ∧ Mountain | Berg | Montaña | Montagne | Montanha |
| ⋏ Mountains | Gebirge | Montañas | Montagnes | Montanhas |
| )( Pass | Paß | Paso | Col | Passo |
| V Valley, Canyon | Tal, Cañon | Valle, Cañón | Vallée, Canyon | Vale, Canhão |
| ≚ Plain | Ebene | Llano | Plaine | Planície |
| › Cape | Kap | Cabo | Cap | Cabo |
| I Island | Insel | Isla | Île | Ilha |
| II Islands | Inseln | Islas | Îles | Ilhas |
| ♦ Other Topographic Features | Andere Topographische Objekte | Otros Elementos Topográficos | Autres données topographiques | Outros acidentes topográficos |

**ESPAÑOL**

| Nombre | Página | Lat.°′ | Long.°′ W = Oeste |
|---|---|---|---|
| Jersey □[6] | 219 | 39.07 N | 90.20 W |
| Jersey □[2], Europe | 22 | 49.15 N | 2.10 W |
| Jersey □[2], Europe | 43b | 49.15 N | 2.10 W |
| Jersey City | 210 | 40.43 N | 74.04 W |
| Jersey City State College ʊ[2] | 276 | 40.43 N | 74.05 W |
| Jersey Mountain ʌ | 202 | 45.29 N | 115.34 W |
| Jersey Shore | 210 | 41.12 N | 77.16 W |
| Jersey Village | 222 | 29.52 N | 95.35 W |
| Jerseyville | 219 | 39.07 N | 90.19 W |
| Jerši | 76 | 54.24 N | 34.12 E |
| Jeršiči | 76 | 53.40 N | 32.44 E |
| Jeršov | 80 | 51.20 N | 48.17 E |
| Jeršovka | 86 | 54.07 N | 64.59 E |
| Jeršovo | 82 | 55.46 N | 36.52 E |
| Jeršovskij | 86 | 52.29 N | 59.08 E |
| Jertarskij | 86 | 56.47 N | 64.18 E |
| Jerte ≃ | 34 | 39.58 N | 6.17 W |
| Jerteh | 114 | 5.45 N | 102.30 E |
| Jertoma | 24 | 63.32 N | 47.48 E |
| Jerumenha | 250 | 7.05 S | 43.30 W |
| Jerusalem → Yerushalayim | 132 | 31.46 N | 35.14 E |
| Jerusalem Airport ⊠ | 132 | 31.52 N | 35.12 E |
| Jerusalim (Talusan) | 116 | 7.26 N | 122.49 E |
| Jeruslan ≃ | 80 | 50.15 N | 45.42 E |
| Jervaulx Abbey ʊ[1] | 44 | 54.16 N | 1.43 W |
| Jervis, Cape ≻ | 168b | 35.38 S | 138.06 E |
| Jervis Bay | 170 | 35.08 S | 150.42 E |
| Jervis Bay c | 170 | 35.05 S | 150.44 E |
| Jervis Bay Territory □[8] | 170 | 35.05 S | 150.44 E |
| Jervis Inlet c | 182 | 49.46 N | 124.10 W |
| Jervois Range ʌ | 162 | 22.38 S | 136.05 E |
| Jerxheim | 54 | 52.05 N | 10.54 E |
| Jerykly | 80 | 55.11 N | 51.26 E |
| Jerzens | 58 | 47.10 N | 10.45 E |
| Jesenankaty ≃ | 80 | 50.32 N | 51.47 E |
| Jesenice, Česká Rep. | 54 | 50.04 N | 13.29 E |
| Jesenice, Slvn. | 61 | 46.27 N | 14.04 E |
| Jesenice, údolní nádrž ⊜[1] | 60 | 50.04 N | 12.27 E |
| Jeseník | 30 | 50.14 N | 17.13 E |
| Jesenoviči | 76 | 57.17 N | 34.14 E |
| Jesensaj | 80 | 49.54 N | 51.28 E |
| Ješera | 84 | 43.04 N | 40.55 E |
| Jeserig bei Wiesenburg | 54 | 52.05 N | 12.27 E |
| Jesi | 66 | 43.31 N | 13.14 E |
| Jesik | 85 | 43.22 N | 77.28 E |
| Jesil' | 86 | 51.58 N | 66.24 E |
| Jes'ki | 76 | 57.56 N | 36.23 E |
| Jesönbulag → Altaj | 90 | 46.20 N | 96.18 E |
| Jessej | 74 | 68.29 N | 102.10 E |
| Jesselton → Kota Kinabalu | 112 | 5.59 N | 116.04 E |
| Jessen | 54 | 51.47 N | 12.58 E |
| Jessentuki | 84 | 44.03 N | 42.51 E |
| Jesser Point ≻ | 158 | 27.32 S | 32.40 E |
| Jessheim | 26 | 60.09 N | 11.11 E |
| Jessnitz | 54 | 51.41 N | 12.17 E |
| Jessore | 124 | 23.10 N | 89.13 E |
| Jessup, Md., U.S. | 208 | 39.08 N | 76.46 W |
| Jessup, Pa., U.S. | 210 | 41.28 N | 75.33 W |
| Jessup Park ♦ | 280 | 34.15 N | 118.24 W |
| Jestetten | 58 | 47.39 N | 8.34 E |
| Jestřebí | 54 | 50.38 N | 14.36 E |
| Jésuite, Lac du ⊜ | 206 | 46.53 N | 72.36 W |
| Jesup, Ga., U.S. | 192 | 31.36 N | 81.53 W |
| Jesup, Ia., U.S. | 190 | 42.28 N | 92.03 W |
| Jesup, Lake ⊜ | 220 | 28.43 N | 81.14 W |
| Jesús | 252 | 27.03 S | 55.47 W |
| Jésus, Île I | 206 | 45.35 N | 73.45 W |
| Jesús Carranza | 234 | 17.26 N | 95.02 W |
| Jesús de Otoro | 236 | 14.26 N | 87.59 W |
| Jesús María, Arg. | 252 | 30.59 S | 64.06 W |
| Jesús María, Méx. | 232 | 25.06 N | 107.28 W |
| Jesús María, Méx. | 234 | 21.58 N | 102.21 W |
| Jesús María, Perú | 286d | 12.04 S | 77.04 W |
| Jesús María ≃ | 234 | 21.51 N | 104.42 W |
| Jesús María, Punta ≻ | 258 | 34.39 S | 56.55 W |
| Jesús Menéndez | 240p | 21.10 N | 76.29 W |
| Jet | 196 | 36.39 N | 98.10 W |
| Jeta, Ilha de I | 150 | 11.53 N | 16.15 W |
| Jetafe | 116 | 10.09 N | 124.09 E |
| Jetmore | 198 | 38.05 N | 99.53 W |
| Jet Propulsion Laboratory ʊ[3] | 280 | 34.12 N | 118.11 W |
| Jetpur | 120 | 21.44 N | 70.37 E |
| Jetřichovice | 54 | 50.49 N | 14.25 E |
| Jett | 218 | 38.11 N | 84.49 W |
| Jette | 50 | 50.52 N | 4.20 E |
| Jettingen, Dtsch. | 58 | 48.35 N | 8.46 E |
| Jettingen, Dtsch. | 58 | 48.23 N | 10.26 E |
| Jeumont | 50 | 50.18 N | 4.06 E |
| Jeune Landing | 182 | 50.27 N | 127.30 W |
| Jeunieb | 114 | 5.10 N | 96.29 E |
| Jeuram | 114 | 4.14 N | 96.18 E |
| Jever | 52 | 53.34 N | 7.54 E |
| Jeverland •[1] | 52 | 53.35 N | 8.00 E |
| Jevgaščino | 86 | 56.26 N | 74.41 E |
| Jevgenjevka | 85 | 43.31 N | 77.40 E |
| Jevíčko | 30 | 49.38 N | 16.43 E |
| Jevišovice | 61 | 48.59 N | 16.00 E |
| Jevišovka ≃ | 61 | 48.49 N | 16.28 E |
| Jevlaš'ovo | 80 | 53.07 N | 46.51 E |
| Jevnaker | 26 | 60.15 N | 10.28 E |
| Jevra | 86 | 59.56 N | 64.27 E |
| Jevrej □[3] | 89 | 48.30 N | 132.00 E |
| Jewel Cave National Monument ♦ | 198 | 43.42 N | 103.50 W |
| Jewell, Ia., U.S. | 190 | 42.18 N | 93.38 W |
| Jewell, Ks., U.S. | 198 | 39.40 N | 98.09 W |
| Jewell, N.Y., U.S. | 210 | 43.13 N | 75.48 W |
| Jewell, Oh., U.S. | 216 | 41.20 N | 84.17 W |
| Jewell, Or., U.S. | 224 | 45.56 N | 123.30 W |
| Jewell Ridge | 192 | 37.11 N | 81.47 W |
| Jewell Village | 218 | 39.10 N | 85.51 W |
| Jewett, Il., U.S. | 194 | 39.13 N | 88.15 W |
| Jewett, Oh., U.S. | 214 | 40.22 N | 81.00 W |
| Jewett, Tx., U.S. | 222 | 31.22 N | 96.09 W |
| Jewett City | 207 | 41.36 N | 71.58 W |
| Jewett Creek ≃ | 212 | 44.22 N | 75.45 W |
| Jewett Lake ⊜ | 184 | 56.09 N | 104.40 W |
| Jewettville | 284a | 42.43 N | 78.52 W |
| Jey •[8] | 267d | 35.41 N | 51.21 E |
| Jeyretān | 120 | 37.10 N | 67.20 E |
| Jezerce ʌ | 38 | 42.26 N | 19.49 E |
| Jezerní hora ʌ | 60 | 49.10 N | 13.11 E |
| Ježicha | 80 | 58.06 N | 47.40 E |
| Jeziorany | 30 | 53.58 N | 20.46 E |
| Ježovo | 80 | 58.02 N | 52.14 E |
| Jezreel, Valley of → Yizre'el, 'Émeq ≚ | 132 | 32.36 N | 35.14 E |
| J. G. Strijdomdam ⊜[1] | 158 | 27.25 S | 32.05 E |
| Jhābua | 120 | 22.46 N | 74.36 E |
| Jhāhtipahāri | 126 | 23.22 N | 86.54 E |
| Jha Jha | 124 | 24.46 N | 86.22 E |
| Jhajjar | 124 | 28.37 N | 76.39 E |
| Jhal | 120 | 28.17 N | 67.27 E |
| Jhālakāti | 124 | 22.39 N | 90.12 E |
| Jhālārāpātan | 124 | 24.33 N | 76.10 E |
| Jhālāwār | 124 | 24.36 N | 76.09 E |
| Jhalida | 124 | 23.22 N | 85.58 E |
| Jhal Jhao | 120 | 26.18 N | 65.35 E |
| Jhālod | 120 | 23.06 N | 74.09 E |
| Jhang Sadar | 123 | 31.16 N | 72.19 E |
| Jhānsi | 124 | 25.26 N | 78.35 E |
| Jhānsi Post | 123 | 33.52 N | 71.24 E |
| Jhāpā | 124 | 26.29 N | 87.51 E |
| Jhārgrām | 126 | 22.27 N | 86.59 E |
| Jharia | 126 | 23.45 N | 86.24 E |
| Jhārpokhariā | 126 | 22.10 N | 86.38 E |
| Jhārsuguda | 120 | 21.51 N | 84.02 E |
| Jhawāriān | 123 | 32.22 N | 72.38 E |
| Jhelum | 123 | 32.56 N | 73.44 E |
| Jhelum ≃ | 123 | 31.12 N | 72.08 E |
| Jhenida | 124 | 23.33 N | 89.10 E |

**FRANÇAIS**

| Nom | Page | Lat.°′ | Long.°′ W = Ouest |
|---|---|---|---|
| Jhenkāri | 272b | 22.46 N | 88.18 E |
| Jhikergacha | 126 | 23.07 N | 89.07 E |
| Jhikra | 126 | 22.37 N | 87.55 E |
| Jhilimili | 126 | 22.49 N | 86.37 E |
| Jhil Kuranga •[8] | 272a | 28.40 N | 77.17 E |
| Jhilla ≃[1] | 126 | 21.58 N | 88.56 E |
| Jhinkpāni | 124 | 22.25 N | 85.47 E |
| Jhok Rind | 120 | 31.27 N | 70.26 E |
| Jhumra | 123 | 31.34 N | 73.11 E |
| Jhunjhunūn | 120 | 28.08 N | 75.24 E |
| Jiaban, Zhg. | 102 | 25.10 N | 107.03 E |
| Jiaban, Zhg. | 102 | 25.38 N | 107.07 E |
| Jiabong | 116 | 11.46 N | 124.57 E |
| Jiacha | 120 | 29.11 N | 92.44 E |
| Jiading | 106 | 31.23 N | 121.15 E |
| Jiāganj | 126 | 24.14 N | 88.16 E |
| Jiagedan | 89 | 51.35 N | 120.55 E |
| Jiahashitai | 89 | 46.25 N | 122.17 E |
| Jiahe | 102 | 25.43 N | 112.05 E |
| Jiajiachang, Zhg. | 107 | 29.44 N | 105.06 E |
| Jiajiachang, Zhg. | 107 | 30.26 N | 104.21 E |
| Jiajiagou, Zhg. | 104 | 41.44 N | 120.58 E |
| Jiajiagou, Zhg. | 104 | 42.20 N | 121.46 E |
| Jiajiang | 107 | 29.45 N | 103.34 E |
| Jiajiayuan | 106 | 32.18 N | 120.55 E |
| Jiakou | 100 | 30.10 N | 119.03 E |
| Jiakou Wa ≋ | 105 | 38.58 N | 116.50 E |
| Jiali | 120 | 30.47 N | 93.24 E |
| Jialing ≃ | 102 | 29.34 N | 106.35 E |
| Jialou | 100 | 32.54 N | 113.26 E |
| Jialu | 106 | 30.26 N | 118.50 E |
| Jialu ≃ | 100 | 33.38 N | 114.36 E |
| Jiamingzhen | 107 | 29.16 N | 105.20 E |
| Jiamusi (Kiamusze) | 89 | 46.50 N | 130.21 E |
| Jiamuyingzi | 104 | 41.56 N | 121.43 E |
| Ji'an, Zhg. | 98 | 41.06 N | 126.08 E |
| Ji'an, Zhg. | 100 | 27.07 N | 114.58 E |
| Jian ≃, Zhg. | 100 | 26.38 N | 118.12 E |
| Jian ≃, Zhg. | 104 | 40.59 N | 121.51 E |
| Jian'an | 89 | 43.04 N | 125.03 E |
| Jianba | 106 | 31.59 N | 120.35 E |
| Jianbi | 106 | 32.11 N | 119.35 E |
| Jianchang, Zhg. | 98 | 40.51 N | 119.46 E |
| Jianchang, Zhg. | 98 | 39.58 N | 122.35 E |
| Jianchang, Zhg. | 98 | 41.16 N | 124.29 E |
| Ji'anchang, Zhg. | 107 | 30.31 N | 106.02 E |
| Jianchangying | 98 | 40.06 N | 118.49 E |
| Jianchapu | 105 | 39.06 N | 116.31 E |
| Jianchaxi, Zhg. | 102 | 28.08 N | 108.04 E |
| Jianchaxi, Zhg. | 107 | 30.22 N | 104.03 E |
| Jianchuan | 102 | 26.34 N | 99.53 E |
| Jiande | 100 | 29.29 N | 119.16 E |
| Jiang'an | 107 | 28.44 N | 105.05 E |
| Jiangba | 100 | 33.08 N | 118.45 E |
| Jiangbei (Lianglukou) | 107 | 29.44 N | 106.38 E |
| Jiangbeixu | 100 | 26.20 N | 115.26 E |
| Jiangbian | 102 | 24.03 N | 103.37 E |
| Jiangbianzhai | 102 | 23.49 N | 100.11 E |
| Jiangcheng, Zhg. | 102 | 22.40 N | 101.48 E |
| Jiangcheng, Zhg. | 105 | 38.52 N | 115.22 E |
| Jiangcun | 100 | 28.17 N | 117.49 E |
| Jiangdi | 102 | 25.08 N | 104.45 E |
| Jiangdihe | 102 | 25.55 N | 101.31 E |
| Jiangdu | 100 | 32.26 N | 119.34 E |
| Jiangduo | 100 | 32.22 N | 120.15 E |
| Jiange | 102 | 32.06 N | 105.29 E |
| Jianggezhuang | 98 | 39.27 N | 119.09 E |
| Jianghua (Shuikou) | 102 | 24.58 N | 111.38 E |
| Jianghuaqiao | 106 | 32.05 N | 120.00 E |
| Jiangji | 100 | 32.19 N | 115.44 E |
| Jiangjia, Zhg. | 106 | 31.40 N | 121.09 E |
| Jiangjia, Zhg. | 106 | 31.58 N | 121.28 E |
| Jiangjiadian | 104 | 41.41 N | 121.03 E |
| Jiangjiagou | 104 | 41.44 N | 121.44 E |
| Jiangjiaji | 100 | 31.59 N | 115.16 E |
| Jiangjiatun, Zhg. | 104 | 41.42 N | 122.02 E |
| Jiangjiatun, Zhg. | 104 | 41.42 N | 122.25 E |
| Jiangjin | 107 | 29.17 N | 106.15 E |
| Jiangjing | 100 | 25.34 N | 119.25 E |
| Jiangjunmiao | 86 | 44.43 N | 90.05 E |
| Jiangjunqiao | 102 | 31.18 N | 100.55 E |
| Jiangkou, Zhg. | 100 | 29.43 N | 121.25 E |
| Jiangkou, Zhg. | 100 | 27.27 N | 118.03 E |
| Jiangkou, Zhg. | 100 | 25.29 N | 119.12 E |
| Jiangkou, Zhg. | 100 | 27.21 N | 115.31 E |
| Jiangkou, Zhg. | 100 | 27.44 N | 114.49 E |
| Jiangkou, Zhg. | 102 | 23.31 N | 110.17 E |
| Jiangkou, Zhg. | 102 | 27.37 N | 108.48 E |
| Jiangkou, Zhg. | 102 | 30.26 N | 111.42 E |
| Jiangkou, Zhg. | 102 | 33.39 N | 107.12 E |
| Jiangkou, Zhg. | 102 | 29.38 N | 110.20 E |
| Jiangkou, Zhg. | 107 | 30.14 N | 103.55 E |
| Jiangkouji | 100 | 32.50 N | 116.16 E |
| Jiangkoutang | 100 | 27.30 N | 112.44 E |
| Jiangle | 100 | 26.42 N | 117.25 E |
| Jiangliadian | 98 | 42.33 N | 117.27 E |
| Jiangling | 102 | 30.20 N | 112.06 E |
| Jianglingxi | 102 | 31.28 N | 107.13 E |
| Jiangmen | 100 | 22.35 N | 113.05 E |
| Jiangmifeng | 89 | 43.58 N | 126.45 E |
| Jiangning | 106 | 31.58 N | 118.50 E |
| Jiangpu | 100 | 32.04 N | 118.37 E |
| Jiangqiao | 89 | 46.48 N | 123.45 E |
| Jiangqiaotou | 106 | 30.37 N | 120.38 E |
| Jiangshan | 100 | 28.45 N | 118.37 E |
| Jiangshan ≃ | 100 | 28.57 N | 118.50 E |
| Jiangshe | 106 | 31.34 N | 120.08 E |
| Jiangshui | 98 | 37.13 N | 113.59 E |
| Jiangsu (Kiangsu) □[4] | 90 | 33.00 N | 120.00 E |
| Jiangtian | 100 | 25.52 N | 119.34 E |
| Jiangtun, Zhg. | 102 | 23.41 N | 112.37 E |
| Jiangtun, Zhg. | 104 | 41.37 N | 122.22 E |
| Jiangwakou | 105 | 39.31 N | 117.42 E |
| Jiangwan, Zhg. | 100 | 29.25 N | 118.02 E |
| Jiangwan, Zhg. | 106 | 31.18 N | 121.29 E |
| Jiangwan Airport ⊠ | 269b | 31.20 N | 121.30 E |
| Jiangxi | 102 | 22.51 N | 101.50 E |
| Jiangxi (Kiangsi) □[4] | 100 | 28.00 N | 116.00 E |
| Jiangxiacun | 106 | 31.44 N | 121.50 E |
| Jiangxiang | 100 | 32.16 N | 117.37 E |
| Jiangxikou | 100 | 27.36 N | 118.23 E |
| Jiangya | 102 | 29.17 N | 110.39 E |
| Jiangyi | 100 | 29.12 N | 115.46 E |
| Jiangyin | 106 | 31.55 N | 120.16 E |
| Jiangyou | 102 | 31.47 N | 104.45 E |
| Jiangyu, Zhg. | 98 | 36.16 N | 118.40 E |
| Jiangyu, Zhg. | 100 | 27.50 N | 112.46 E |
| Jiangyuanzhen | 107 | 30.35 N | 103.48 E |
| Jiangzaogang | 106 | 32.01 N | 121.03 E |
| Jiangzhasiji | 120 | 30.28 N | 88.55 E |
| Jiangzhong | 120 | 29.10 N | 93.32 E |
| Jianhe, Zhg. | 102 | 26.27 N | 108.33 E |
| Jianhe, Zhg. | 105 | 39.14 N | 118.03 E |
| Jianhu | 100 | 33.28 N | 119.50 E |
| Jianli | 100 | 29.49 N | 112.53 E |
| Jianling | 100 | 32.45 N | 113.12 E |
| Jianning | 100 | 26.50 N | 116.49 E |
| Jian'ou | 100 | 27.03 N | 118.19 E |
| Jianping (Yebaishou) | 98 | 41.24 N | 119.37 E |
| Jianqiao | 106 | 30.20 N | 120.12 E |
| Jianqigou | 104 | 40.54 N | 123.17 E |
| Jianshan, Zhg. | 100 | 29.14 N | 120.44 E |
| Jianshan, Zhg. | 100 | 29.58 N | 120.16 E |
| Jian Shan ʌ | 104 | 41.49 N | 121.44 E |
| Jianshi | 102 | 30.36 N | 109.38 E |
| Jianshui | 102 | 23.38 N | 102.49 E |
| Jiantiao | 100 | 29.04 N | 121.36 E |
| Jiantou | 105 | 39.26 N | 115.41 E |
| Jiantouji | 98 | 34.35 N | 117.34 E |
| Jianyang, Zhg. | 100 | 27.22 N | 118.04 E |
| Jianyang, Zhg. | 100 | 33.27 N | 119.40 E |
| Jianyang, Zhg. | 107 | 30.24 N | 104.32 E |
| Jiao ≃ | 100 | 26.48 N | 119.42 E |
| Jiaocheng | 102 | 37.33 N | 112.02 E |
| Jiaodao | 105 | 39.39 N | 116.06 E |
| Jiaodianzi | 104 | 41.32 N | 121.49 E |
| Jiaodonggou | 104 | 40.50 N | 123.58 E |
| Jiaohe, Zhg. | 89 | 43.42 N | 127.19 E |
| Jiaohe, Zhg. | 98 | 38.01 N | 116.17 E |
| Jiaojiapuzi | 104 | 40.47 N | 123.48 E |

**PORTUGUÊS**

| Nome | Página | Lat.°′ | Long.°′ W = Oeste |
|---|---|---|---|
| Jiaolai ≃, Zhg. | 89 | 43.43 N | 123.05 E |
| Jiaolai ≃, Zhg. | 98 | 42.47 N | 120.44 E |
| Jiaolai ≃, Zhg. | 98 | 37.07 N | 119.35 E |
| Jiaoling | 100 | 24.41 N | 116.10 E |
| Jiaomei | 100 | 24.32 N | 117.54 E |
| Jiaonan (Wanggezhuang) | 98 | 35.51 N | 119.59 E |
| Jiao Shan I | 106 | 31.21 N | 120.06 E |
| Jiaoshanhe | 100 | 29.38 N | 112.33 E |
| Jiaoxi | 106 | 31.49 N | 120.10 E |
| Jiaoxian | 98 | 36.18 N | 119.58 E |
| Jiaoyang | 100 | 27.56 N | 119.16 E |
| Jiaozhou Wan c | 98 | 36.10 N | 120.15 E |
| Jiaozhuang | 100 | 33.14 N | 114.02 E |
| Jiaozuo | 102 | 35.15 N | 113.13 E |
| Jiapu | 106 | 31.06 N | 119.56 E |
| Jiashan, Zhg. | 100 | 32.47 N | 118.00 E |
| Jiashan, Zhg. | 106 | 30.51 N | 120.54 E |
| Jiashi | 85 | 39.28 N | 76.45 E |
| Jiashun Hu ⊜ | 120 | 34.35 N | 86.05 E |
| Jiasi | 107 | 29.06 N | 106.24 E |
| Jiatan | 107 | 30.12 N | 106.29 E |
| Jiatanchang | 107 | 29.09 N | 106.16 E |
| Jiawang | 98 | 34.27 N | 117.27 E |
| Jiaxian, Zhg. | 100 | 33.58 N | 113.13 E |
| Jiaxian, Zhg. | 102 | 38.01 N | 110.31 E |
| Jiaxiang | 98 | 35.25 N | 116.21 E |
| Jiaxing | 106 | 30.46 N | 120.45 E |
| Jiayin | 89 | 48.53 N | 130.24 E |
| Jiayu | 100 | 29.58 N | 113.55 E |
| Jiayun Hu ⊜ | 120 | 35.02 N | 85.40 E |
| Jiaze | 106 | 31.42 N | 119.47 E |
| Jiazhai | 98 | 34.33 N | 115.48 E |
| Jiazhuang | 105 | 39.19 N | 117.22 E |
| Jiazi | 100 | 22.55 N | 116.04 E |
| Jiazier | 85 | 38.40 N | 76.33 E |
| Jibacoa ≃ | 240p | 20.15 N | 77.12 W |
| Jibagalle | 144 | 8.04 N | 48.39 E |
| Jibalei | 144 | 10.09 N | 50.53 E |
| Jibannagar | 126 | 23.25 N | 88.50 E |
| Jíbaro ≃ | 286b | 23.03 N | 82.23 W |
| Jibat ʌ | 144 | 8.45 N | 37.29 E |
| Jibiya | 150 | 13.05 N | 7.12 E |
| Jiboa ≃ | 236 | 13.22 N | 89.04 W |
| Jibóia, Ilha da I | 256 | 23.03 S | 44.22 W |
| Jibuti → Djibouti | 144 | 11.36 N | 43.09 E |
| Jicamarca, Quebrada V | 286d | 12.02 S | 76.57 W |
| Jicarilla Apache Indian Reservation •[4] | 200 | 36.40 N | 107.00 W |
| Jicarón, Isla I | 246 | 7.16 N | 81.47 W |
| Jicatuyo ≃ | 236 | 14.59 N | 88.16 W |
| Jicheng | 105 | 39.23 N | 116.17 E |
| Jičín | 30 | 50.26 N | 15.21 E |
| Jicotea ≃ | 286b | 23.01 N | 82.14 W |
| Jidād | 140 | 11.05 N | 24.44 E |
| Jiddah (Jeddah) | 144 | 21.30 N | 39.12 E |
| Jidingxilin | 120 | 32.52 N | 92.21 E |
| Jidy, Wādī al- V | 142 | 30.13 N | 32.46 E |
| Jiebu | 100 | 28.15 N | 115.02 E |
| Jiedong | 100 | 26.02 N | 113.00 E |
| Jiegou | 100 | 33.21 N | 117.55 E |
| Jiehe | 98 | 35.16 N | 117.04 E |
| Jieji | 100 | 33.33 N | 118.24 E |
| Jiejiang | 106 | 31.58 N | 120.43 E |
| Jiejinkou | 89 | 47.57 N | 132.50 E |
| Jielingkou | 98 | 40.09 N | 119.15 E |
| Jielongchang | 107 | 29.13 N | 106.32 E |
| Jiemian | 100 | 25.56 N | 118.02 E |
| Jiepai, Zhg. | 100 | 26.41 N | 112.46 E |
| Jiepai, Zhg. | 100 | 29.34 N | 115.06 E |
| Jiepai, Zhg. | 106 | 30.55 N | 119.32 E |
| Jiepai, Zhg. | 107 | 29.28 N | 104.43 E |
| Jiepaiji | 100 | 32.15 N | 117.50 E |
| Jiesheng | 100 | 22.45 N | 115.25 E |
| Jieshi, Zhg. | 100 | 22.51 N | 115.49 E |
| Jieshi, Zhg. | 107 | 29.27 N | 105.17 E |
| Jieshi Wan c | 100 | 22.46 N | 115.40 E |
| Jieshou, Zhg. | 100 | 33.18 N | 115.20 E |
| Jieshou, Zhg. | 100 | 27.22 N | 117.40 E |
| Jieshou, Zhg. | 100 | 33.00 N | 119.27 E |
| Jiexi | 100 | 23.28 N | 115.56 E |
| Jiexiu | 102 | 37.05 N | 111.51 E |
| Jieyang | 100 | 23.35 N | 116.21 E |
| Jiezhongdian | 100 | 32.41 N | 112.29 E |
| Jieznas | 76 | 54.36 N | 24.10 E |
| Jifjāfah, Bi'r ⊤[4] | 140 | 30.27 N | 33.11 E |
| Jiftūn, Jazā'ir II | 140 | 27.13 N | 33.56 E |
| Jiggalong | 162 | 23.25 S | 120.47 E |
| Jiggalong Creek ≃ | 162 | 22.53 S | 120.14 E |
| Jigongying | 102 | 26.18 N | 104.48 E |
| Jigongzhen | 98 | 34.02 N | 115.32 E |
| Jiguaní | 240p | 20.22 N | 76.26 W |
| Jiguanshan, Zhg. | 98 | 40.32 N | 123.55 E |
| Jiguanshan, Zhg. | 104 | 41.18 N | 123.36 E |
| Jiguanshan, Zhg. | 104 | 42.08 N | 124.15 E |
| Jigüey, Bahía de c | 240p | 22.08 N | 78.05 W |
| Jigzhi | 102 | 33.28 N | 101.29 E |
| Jihe | 100 | 32.15 N | 112.48 E |
| Jiheier | 85 | 38.11 N | 75.46 E |
| Jihlava | 30 | 49.24 N | 15.36 E |
| Jihlava ≃ | 61 | 48.55 N | 16.37 E |
| Jihočeský Kraj □[4] | 30 | 49.05 N | 14.30 E |
| Jihomoravský Kraj □[4] | 30 | 49.10 N | 16.40 E |
| Jiiqley | 144 | 4.25 N | 45.22 E |
| Jijel | 148 | 36.48 N | 5.46 E |
| Jijia ≃ | 38 | 46.54 N | 28.05 E |
| Jijiadianzi | 98 | 35.31 N | 118.59 E |
| Jijiamiao | 107 | 29.18 N | 104.06 E |
| Jijiapuzi | 104 | 41.16 N | 124.12 E |
| Jijiashi | 106 | 32.08 N | 120.18 E |
| Jijiaying | 105 | 40.20 N | 115.24 E |
| Jijiga | 144 | 9.22 N | 42.47 E |
| Jikawo | 144 | 8.22 N | 33.46 E |
| Jikawo ≃ | 144 | 8.22 N | 33.47 E |
| Jike | 102 | 31.00 N | 99.41 E |
| Jilalin | 89 | 51.19 N | 119.55 E |
| Jilantai | 102 | 39.47 N | 105.45 E |
| Jilbānah, Bi'r al- ⊤[4] | 142 | 30.55 N | 32.29 E |
| Jilemutu | 89 | 52.14 N | 120.47 E |
| Jilib | 144 | 0.29 N | 42.46 E |
| Jilibulake | 120 | 33.05 N | 93.10 E |
| Jili Hu ⊜ | 86 | 46.57 N | 87.27 E |
| Jilin (Kirin) | 89 | 43.51 N | 126.33 E |
| Jilin (Kirin) □[4] | 90 | 44.00 N | 126.00 E |
| Jiliu ≃ | 89 | 52.04 N | 120.48 E |
| Jill, Kediet ej ʌ | 148 | 22.38 N | 12.33 W |
| Jill, Sebkhet ej ⊜ | 148 | 22.47 N | 12.53 W |
| Jiloca ≃ | 34 | 41.21 N | 1.39 W |
| Jilotepec de Abasolo | 234 | 19.58 N | 99.32 W |
| Jilotlán de los Dolores | 234 | 19.14 N | 102.59 W |
| Jílové | 54 | 50.46 N | 14.07 E |
| Jima | 144 | 7.36 N | 36.50 E |
| Jimbaran | 115b | 8.46 S | 115.11 E |
| Jimbolia | 38 | 45.47 N | 20.43 E |
| Jimboomba | 171a | 27.50 S | 153.02 E |
| Jimei | 100 | 24.37 N | 118.07 E |
| Jimena de la Frontera | 34 | 36.26 N | 5.27 W |
| Jiménez, Méx. | 232 | 29.02 N | 100.41 W |
| Jiménez, Méx. | 232 | 27.08 N | 104.55 W |
| Jimenez, Pil. | 116 | 8.20 N | 123.50 E |
| Jiménez, Arroyo ≃ | 288 | 34.44 S | 58.13 W |
| Jiménez, Laguna de ⊜ | 258 | 35.26 S | 59.01 W |
| Jiménez del Téul | 234 | 23.10 N | 104.05 W |
| Jimeta | 146 | 9.16 N | 12.27 E |
| Jimi ≃ | 164 | 5.20 S | 144.20 E |
| Jimingcun | 105 | 39.19 N | 116.09 E |
| Jiminghe | 100 | 30.36 N | 115.32 E |
| Jim Ned Creek ≃ | 196 | 31.50 N | 99.07 W |
| Jimo | 98 | 36.23 N | 120.27 E |
| Jimsar | 86 | 44.00 N | 89.04 E |
| Jim Thorpe | 210 | 40.52 N | 75.43 W |
| Jimuganayaji | 85 | 38.36 N | 75.39 E |
| Jin (Gam) ≃, Asia | 110 | 21.55 N | 105.12 E |
| Jin ≃, Zhg. | 100 | 24.54 N | 118.35 E |
| Jin ≃, Zhg. | 100 | 28.24 N | 115.49 E |

| | | | |
|---|---|---|---|
| Jin ≃, Zhg. | 100 | 26.51 N | 117.46 E |
| Jināḩ | 140 | 25.20 N | 30.31 E |
| Jinan (Tsinan), Zhg. | 98 | 36.40 N | 116.57 E |
| Jin'an, Zhg. | 100 | 28.38 N | 119.18 E |
| Jinbang | 100 | 25.01 N | 118.01 E |
| Jinbo ≃ | 107 | 28.54 N | 103.40 E |
| Jincang | 89 | 43.20 N | 130.30 E |
| Jince | 60 | 49.47 N | 13.59 E |
| Jinchanggouliang | 98 | 41.56 N | 120.19 E |
| Jincheng, Zhg. | 102 | 35.30 N | 112.50 E |
| Jincheng, Zhg. | 104 | 41.12 N | 121.25 E |
| Jinchengshai | 102 | 26.43 N | 111.00 E |
| Jincheng Shan ʌ | 107 | 30.47 N | 106.32 E |
| Jinchuan | 102 | 31.25 N | 102.08 E |
| Jinchuanqiao | 102 | 27.18 N | 101.48 E |
| Jincun | 106 | 31.08 N | 119.49 E |
| Jīnd | 123 | 29.19 N | 76.19 E |
| Jindabyne | 171b | 36.25 S | 148.38 E |
| Jindabyne, Lake ⊜[1] | 171b | 36.22 S | 148.37 E |
| Jindaichang | 107 | 29.43 N | 104.49 E |
| Jindālī, Bi'r ⊤[4] | 142 | 29.55 N | 31.40 E |
| Jindřichovice | 54 | 50.15 N | 12.37 E |
| Jindřichův Hradec | 30 | 49.09 N | 15.00 E |
| Jinfeng | 100 | 26.01 N | 119.36 E |
| Jinfosi | 102 | 39.29 N | 99.00 E |
| Jing ≃, Zhg. | 86 | 44.52 N | 82.50 E |
| Jing ≃, Zhg. | 102 | 34.28 N | 109.00 E |
| Jing'an | 100 | 28.52 N | 115.20 E |
| Jin'gangpo | 107 | 29.38 N | 106.25 E |
| Jingangtou | 100 | 27.54 N | 113.40 E |
| Jingangtuo | 107 | 29.10 N | 106.07 E |
| Jing'anji | 98 | 34.30 N | 116.55 E |
| Jingbian | 102 | 37.25 N | 108.21 E |
| Jingbohu ⊜ | 89 | 43.54 N | 128.54 E |
| Jingcheng | 100 | 24.36 N | 117.30 E |
| Jingde | 100 | 30.19 N | 118.31 E |
| Jingdezhen (Kingtechen) | 100 | 29.16 N | 117.11 E |
| Jingdong | 102 | 24.28 N | 100.52 E |
| Jingellic | 171b | 35.56 S | 147.42 E |
| Jingeryu | 105 | 39.43 N | 115.36 E |
| Jinggang | 100 | 28.28 N | 112.46 E |
| Jinggangshan (Ciping) | 100 | 26.36 N | 114.05 E |
| Jinggongqiao | 100 | 29.45 N | 117.11 E |
| Jinggu | 102 | 23.32 N | 100.41 E |
| Jingguanzhen | 107 | 29.55 N | 106.33 E |
| Jinghai, Zhg. | 100 | 23.03 N | 116.31 E |
| Jinghai, Zhg. | 105 | 38.56 N | 116.55 E |
| Jinghaiwei | 98 | 36.52 N | 122.13 E |
| Jinghe | 86 | 44.39 N | 82.50 E |
| Jinghong | 102 | 22.01 N | 100.49 E |
| Jinghuiling | 105 | 40.22 N | 117.27 E |
| Jingjiang, Zhg. | 102 | 26.19 N | 100.33 E |
| Jingjiang, Zhg. | 106 | 32.01 N | 120.15 E |
| Jingjiayu | 104 | 41.40 N | 123.51 E |
| Jingle | 102 | 38.24 N | 111.54 E |
| Jinglou | 100 | 32.39 N | 112.56 E |
| Jingmen | 102 | 31.00 N | 112.09 E |
| Jingning, Zhg. | 100 | 27.59 N | 119.38 E |
| Jingning, Zhg. | 102 | 35.25 N | 105.56 E |
| Jingou | 104 | 41.38 N | 120.35 E |
| Jingoutun | 98 | 41.03 N | 117.27 E |
| Jingshan | 100 | 31.02 N | 113.05 E |
| Jingtai | 102 | 37.17 N | 104.09 E |
| Jingu | 100 | 25.13 N | 118.07 E |
| Jingxi | 102 | 23.08 N | 106.29 E |
| Jingxian, Zhg. | 98 | 37.42 N | 116.16 E |
| Jingxian, Zhg. | 100 | 30.42 N | 118.24 E |
| Jingxian, Zhg. | 102 | 26.40 N | 109.25 E |
| Jingxin | 100 | 24.14 N | 115.56 E |
| Jingxing, Zhg. | 89 | 47.04 N | 123.01 E |
| Jingxing, Zhg. | 98 | 38.02 N | 114.08 E |
| Jingyan | 107 | 29.40 N | 104.04 E |
| Jingyu | 98 | 42.22 N | 126.50 E |
| Jingyuan, Zhg. | 102 | 36.38 N | 104.37 E |
| Jingyuan, Zhg. | 102 | 35.30 N | 106.48 E |
| Jingzhi | 98 | 36.19 N | 119.23 E |
| Jingzichang | 107 | 29.00 N | 104.41 E |
| Jinhae → Chinhae | 98 | 35.09 N | 128.40 E |
| Jinhu | 100 | 33.00 N | 119.02 E |
| Jinhua | 100 | 29.07 N | 119.39 E |
| Jinhua ≃ | 100 | 29.06 N | 119.39 E |
| Jinhui | 106 | 30.59 N | 121.29 E |
| Jining, Zhg. | 98 | 35.25 N | 116.36 E |
| Jining, Zhg. | 102 | 40.57 N | 113.02 E |
| Jinja | 154 | 0.26 N | 33.12 E |
| Jinjiadian | 98 | 41.39 N | 118.18 E |
| Jinjiang, Zhg. | 100 | 24.50 N | 118.35 E |
| Jinjiang, Zhg. | 110 | 26.19 N | 100.33 E |
| Jinjiawopeng | 104 | 41.38 N | 122.16 E |
| Jinjiawopu | 104 | 42.32 N | 122.10 E |
| Jinjiazhen | 89 | 42.49 N | 123.40 E |
| Jinjing, Zhg. | 100 | 24.37 N | 118.36 E |
| Jinjing, Zhg. | 100 | 28.31 N | 113.25 E |
| Jinjini | 150 | 7.26 N | 2.39 W |
| Jinju → Chinju | 98 | 35.11 N | 128.05 E |
| Jinkeng | 100 | 27.15 N | 117.14 E |
| Jinkichi-mori ʌ | 96 | 33.41 N | 134.07 E |
| Jinkou, Zhg. | 98 | 36.35 N | 120.46 E |
| Jinkou, Zhg. | 100 | 30.22 N | 114.10 E |
| Jinkou, Zhg. | 100 | 29.18 N | 115.15 E |
| Jinkuang | 102 | 28.20 N | 101.54 E |
| Jinlijing | 107 | 29.48 N | 104.45 E |
| Jinlingsi | 104 | 41.42 N | 120.49 E |
| Jinlingyu | 105 | 40.06 N | 117.32 E |
| Jinlingzhen | 98 | 36.49 N | 118.11 E |
| Jinlonggou | 89 | 51.45 N | 125.51 E |
| Jinmachi-chūtonchi, Rikujō-jieitai- ■ | 92 | 38.25 N | 140.27 E |
| Jinmu Jiao ≻ | 110 | 18.09 N | 109.34 E |
| Jinnah Barrage •[6] | 123 | 32.57 N | 71.30 E |
| Jinning | 102 | 24.41 N | 102.35 E |
| Jinniu, Zhg. | 100 | 31.24 N | 117.12 E |
| Jinniu, Zhg. | 100 | 29.59 N | 114.38 E |
| Jinotega | 236 | 13.06 N | 86.00 W |
| Jinotega □[5] | 236 | 14.00 N | 85.25 W |
| Jinotepe | 236 | 11.51 N | 86.12 W |
| Jinping, Zhg. | 102 | 26.38 N | 109.03 E |
| Jinping, Zhg. | 102 | 22.50 N | 103.10 E |
| Jinpingchang | 107 | 28.54 N | 104.43 E |
| Jinpo | 105 | 39.18 N | 115.15 E |
| Jinqian ≃ | 102 | 32.52 N | 110.01 E |
| Jinqiao | 100 | 31.46 N | 116.50 E |
| Jinrui | 100 | 27.57 N | 114.12 E |
| Jinseki | 96 | 34.48 N | 133.11 E |
| Jinsen → Inch'ŏn | 98 | 37.28 N | 126.38 E |
| Jinsha, Zhg. | 100 | 26.12 N | 118.39 E |
| Jinsha, Zhg. | 102 | 27.18 N | 106.10 E |
| Jinsha, Zhg. | 106 | 32.06 N | 121.05 E |
| Jinsha (Yangtze) ≃ | 102 | 28.50 N | 104.36 E |
| Jinshan, Zhg. | 89 | 51.51 N | 126.30 E |
| Jinshan, Zhg. | 106 | 30.54 N | 121.09 E |
| Jinshanwei | 106 | 30.44 N | 121.19 E |
| Jinshanxiang | 107 | 30.35 N | 104.52 E |
| Jinshanzui | 106 | 30.44 N | 121.22 E |
| Jinshi | 102 | 29.39 N | 111.52 E |
| Jinshijing | 107 | 29.23 N | 104.08 E |
| Jinshuzhen | 106 | 31.23 N | 120.24 E |
| Jinsiniangqiao | 106 | 30.43 N | 121.15 E |
| Jinta | 102 | 40.03 N | 98.53 E |
| Jintan | 106 | 31.45 N | 119.34 E |
| Jintang, Zhg. | 102 | 30.54 N | 104.19 E |
| Jintang, Zhg. | 102 | 30.19 N | 102.19 E |
| Jintian | 100 | 27.10 N | 114.27 E |
| Jintotolo Channel ɰ | 116 | 11.48 N | 123.05 E |
| Jintotolo Island I | 116 | 11.51 N | 123.08 E |
| Jinxi, Zhg. | 100 | 27.54 N | 116.43 E |
| Jinxi, Zhg. | 104 | 40.45 N | 120.50 E |
| Jinxian, Zhg. | 98 | 38.02 N | 115.02 E |
| Jinxian, Zhg. | 98 | 39.04 N | 121.40 E |
| Jinxian, Zhg. | 100 | 28.22 N | 116.14 E |
| Jinxian (Dalinghe), Zhg. | 104 | 41.11 N | 121.22 E |
| Jinxiang, Zhg. | 98 | 35.05 N | 116.18 E |
| Jinxiang, Zhg. | 100 | 27.26 N | 120.35 E |
| Jin-ya ⊥ | 94 | 36.06 N | 137.15 E |

| | | | |
|---|---|---|---|
| Jinyun | 100 | 28.40 N | 120.03 E |
| Jinz, Qā' al- ≚ | 132 | 30.45 N | 36.04 E |
| Jinze | 106 | 31.02 N | 120.56 E |
| Jinzhai | 100 | 31.44 N | 115.54 E |
| Jinzhaizhen | 100 | 31.32 N | 115.46 E |
| Jinzhen | 100 | 33.39 N | 118.17 E |
| Jinzhong ≃ | 105 | 39.08 N | 117.42 E |
| Jinzhou (Chinchou) | 104 | 41.07 N | 121.08 E |
| Jinzisi | 107 | 29.09 N | 106.22 E |
| Jinzū ≃ | 94 | 36.46 N | 137.13 E |
| Jiō | 270 | 34.58 N | 135.28 E |
| Ji-Paraná | 248 | 10.52 S | 61.57 W |
| Jipijapa | 246 | 1.20 S | 80.35 W |
| Jipioca, Ilha I | 250 | 1.53 N | 50.12 W |
| Jiquí ≃ | 240p | 21.22 N | 78.32 W |
| Jiquilisco | 236 | 13.19 N | 88.35 W |
| Jiquilisco, Bahía de c | 236 | 13.10 N | 88.28 W |
| Jiquilpan de Juárez | 234 | 19.59 N | 102.43 W |
| Jiquipilas | 234 | 16.40 N | 93.39 W |
| Jiquipilco | 234 | 19.32 N | 99.36 W |
| Jiquiriçá ≃ | 255 | 13.12 S | 38.57 W |
| Jirāfī, Wādī al- (Naḩal Paran) V | 132 | 30.24 N | 35.10 E |
| Jirbān | 140 | 11.03 N | 30.36 E |
| Jiřetín | 54 | 50.50 N | 14.35 E |
| Jiri ≃ | 120 | 24.42 N | 93.06 E |
| Jiřikov | 54 | 50.59 N | 14.35 E |
| Jirjā | 140 | 26.20 N | 31.53 E |
| Jirkov | 54 | 50.30 N | 13.27 E |
| Jīroft | 128 | 28.40 N | 57.46 E |
| Jīsh (Gush Ḩalav) | 132 | 33.02 N | 35.27 E |
| Jishou | 102 | 28.17 N | 109.29 E |
| Jishui, Zhg. | 100 | 27.14 N | 115.06 E |
| Jishui, Zhg. | 100 | 33.46 N | 115.24 E |
| Jisr ash-Shughūr | 130 | 35.48 N | 36.19 E |
| Jitan | 100 | 24.56 N | 115.43 E |
| Jitarning | 162 | 32.48 S | 117.59 E |
| Jitaúna | 255 | 14.01 S | 39.57 W |
| Jitianzhen | 107 | 30.19 N | 104.01 E |
| Jitotol | 234 | 17.02 N | 92.52 W |
| Jitra | 114 | 6.16 N | 100.25 E |
| Jituo | 120 | 34.15 N | 82.05 E |
| Jiu ≃ | 38 | 43.47 N | 23.48 E |
| Jiubao | 100 | 25.57 N | 115.48 E |
| Jiubingtai | 104 | 41.39 N | 124.07 E |
| Jiucheng, Zhg. | 98 | 38.12 N | 117.18 E |
| Jiucheng, Zhg. | 105 | 39.23 N | 116.44 E |
| Jiuchuchang | 107 | 29.55 N | 104.38 E |
| Jiudaoliang | 102 | 31.35 N | 110.12 E |
| Jiudhara | 126 | 22.24 N | 89.44 E |
| Jiudian | 106 | 32.10 N | 120.57 E |
| Jiudongle | 102 | 38.49 N | 101.05 E |
| Jiudu | 106 | 30.31 N | 119.53 E |
| Jiufanxian | 98 | 35.51 N | 115.41 E |
| Jiufeng, Zhg. | 100 | 24.20 N | 117.02 E |
| Jiufeng, Zhg. | 100 | 25.33 N | 119.08 E |
| Jiugang | 105 | 39.03 N | 116.12 E |
| Jiugongan | 102 | 29.52 N | 112.00 E |
| Jiugongkou | 105 | 39.50 N | 114.43 E |
| Jiugong Shan ʌ | 100 | 29.26 N | 114.42 E |
| Jiuguan, Zhg. | 98 | 37.26 N | 121.53 E |
| Jiuguan, Zhg. | 106 | 30.51 N | 120.16 E |
| Jiuguantao | 98 | 36.40 N | 115.25 E |
| Jiuhe | 100 | 23.32 N | 115.04 E |
| Jiuhongshui | 102 | 37.14 N | 103.57 E |
| Jiuhu | 98 | 37.03 N | 117.36 E |
| Jiuhuai'an | 98 | 40.24 N | 114.31 E |
| Jiuhuajie | 100 | 30.25 N | 117.51 E |
| Jiuhuaxian | 100 | 23.30 N | 113.16 E |
| Jiuhuinan | 98 | 42.37 N | 126.14 E |
| Jiujiang, Zhg. | 100 | 29.44 N | 115.59 E |
| Jiujiang, Zhg. | 100 | 22.51 N | 113.02 E |
| Jiujiang, Zhg. | 100 | 29.36 N | 115.52 E |
| Jiujiawopeng | 104 | 40.59 N | 121.22 E |
| Jiujiji | 98 | 35.09 N | 114.48 E |
| Jiujing | 107 | 29.05 N | 103.54 E |
| Jiukou | 100 | 30.52 N | 112.38 E |
| Jiuli | 107 | 29.32 N | 103.32 E |
| Jiulian Shan ʌ | 100 | 24.40 N | 114.46 E |
| Jiuliguan | 100 | 31.50 N | 114.14 E |
| Jiuling Shan ʌ | 100 | 28.46 N | 114.45 E |
| Jiulong → Kowloon, H.K. | 271d | 22.18 N | 114.10 E |
| Jiulong, Zhg. | 100 | 24.08 N | 112.55 E |
| Jiulong, Zhg. | 102 | 29.00 N | 101.50 E |
| Jiulong ≃, Zhg. | 100 | 24.28 N | 117.48 E |
| Jiulong ≃, Zhg. | 100 | 25.59 N | 117.18 E |
| Jiulongchang | 107 | 29.32 N | 106.05 E |
| Jiulonggang | 100 | 32.38 N | 117.03 E |
| Jiulongpo | 107 | 29.29 N | 106.32 E |
| Jiulongzhen | 106 | 31.54 N | 121.34 E |
| Jiumen | 98 | 40.42 N | 120.27 E |
| Jiumianyang | 100 | 30.16 N | 113.13 E |
| Jiumiao | 104 | 42.24 N | 121.36 E |
| Jiumu | 100 | 28.11 N | 118.27 E |
| Jiuninghe | 105 | 39.28 N | 117.46 E |
| Jiuningyang | 100 | 25.38 N | 117.21 E |
| Jiupu, Zhg. | 100 | 32.50 N | 118.45 E |
| Jiupu, Zhg. | 105 | 40.21 N | 115.18 E |
| Jiuquan (Suzhou) | 102 | 39.45 N | 98.34 E |
| Jiurongcheng | 98 | 37.21 N | 122.32 E |
| Jiushangshui | 100 | 33.32 N | 114.32 E |
| Jiushan Liedao II | 100 | 29.26 N | 122.12 E |
| Jiushenqiu | 100 | 33.11 N | 115.08 E |
| Jiusiyang | 100 | 33.41 N | 118.39 E |
| Jiusongyu | 105 | 40.27 N | 116.58 E |
| Jiutai | 89 | 44.08 N | 125.50 E |
| Jiuwuqing | 105 | 39.31 N | 116.52 E |
| Jiuxian, Zhg. | 98 | 37.53 N | 117.06 E |
| Jiuxian, Zhg. | 100 | 31.11 N | 118.04 E |
| Jiuxian, Zhg. | 100 | 33.15 N | 115.35 E |
| Jiuxian, Zhg. | 100 | 25.14 N | 116.31 E |
| Jiuxian, Zhg. | 100 | 33.32 N | 113.17 E |
| Jiuxian, Zhg. | 100 | 25.54 N | 113.22 E |
| Jiuxian, Zhg. | 107 | 30.27 N | 103.51 E |
| Jiuxian, Zhg. | 107 | 29.51 N | 106.13 E |
| Jiuxian ≃ | 100 | 25.07 N | 116.24 E |
| Jiuxiangcheng | 100 | 33.13 N | 114.49 E |
| Jiuyingkou | 105 | 39.42 N | 114.44 E |
| Jiuyingzi | 104 | 42.03 N | 121.38 E |
| Jiuyuanqu | 102 | 35.09 N | 111.51 E |
| Jiuyuhang | 106 | 30.17 N | 119.56 E |
| Jiuyunjie | 86 | 44.12 N | 88.05 E |
| Jiuzhan | 89 | 43.57 N | 126.29 E |
| Jiuzhen | 100 | 24.05 N | 117.42 E |
| Jiuzhou | 105 | 39.30 N | 116.33 E |
| Jiuzhuangwo | 105 | 40.11 N | 115.36 E |
| Jiwangmiao | 269b | 31.14 N | 121.17 E |
| Jiwangtun | 104 | 41.02 N | 122.58 E |
| Jīwani | 128 | 25.03 N | 61.45 E |
| Jiwen | 89 | 50.32 N | 123.15 E |
| Jixi, Zhg. | 89 | 45.17 N | 130.59 E |
| Jixi, Zhg. | 100 | 30.06 N | 118.35 E |
| Jixian, Zhg. | 98 | 35.26 N | 114.05 E |
| Jixian, Zhg. | 98 | 37.36 N | 115.31 E |
| Jixian, Zhg. | 105 | 40.03 N | 117.24 E |
| Jixiangsi | 107 | 30.39 N | 105.32 E |
| Jixiashi | 100 | 28.22 N | 118.44 E |
| Jixingji | 100 | 32.55 N | 116.46 E |
| Jiyang, Zhg. | 98 | 36.59 N | 117.11 E |
| Jiyang, Zhg. | 100 | 27.10 N | 118.07 E |
| Jiyang, Zhg. | 105 | 39.38 N | 115.59 E |
| Jiyi | 102 | 35.50 N | 110.23 E |
| Jiyuan | 102 | 35.08 N | 112.35 E |
| Jiyun ≃ | 105 | 39.07 N | 117.43 E |
| Jiz', Wādī al- V | 144 | 16.19 N | 52.00 E |
| Jīzah, Ahrāmāt al- (Pyramids of Giza) ⊥ | 142 | 29.59 N | 31.08 E |
| Jīzah, Tur'at al- ≊ | 273c | 29.50 N | 31.16 E |
| Jīzān | 144 | 16.54 N | 42.29 E |
| Jizayy | 142 | 30.28 N | 30.51 E |
| Jize | 98 | 36.54 N | 114.52 E |
| Jizera ≃ | 54 | 50.10 N | 14.43 E |
| Jizl, Wādī al- V | 128 | 25.38 N | 38.21 E |
| Jizō-dake ʌ | 94 | 36.36 N | 139.28 E |
| Jizō-zaki ≻ | 96 | 35.34 N | 133.20 E |
| Joaçaba | 252 | 27.10 S | 51.30 W |

| | | | |
|---|---|---|---|
| Joachimsthal → Jáchymov, Česká Rep. | 54 | 50.20 N | 12.55 E |
| Joachimsthal, Dtsch. | 54 | 52.58 N | 13.44 E |
| Joaíma | 255 | 16.39 S | 41.02 W |
| Joal Fadiout | 150 | 14.10 N | 16.51 W |
| Joana Coeli | 250 | 1.58 S | 49.23 W |
| Joana Peres | 250 | 3.18 S | 49.42 W |
| Joanes | 250 | 0.51 S | 48.31 W |
| Joanicó | 258 | 34.36 S | 56.15 W |
| Joanna | 192 | 34.24 N | 81.48 W |
| Joanópolis | 256 | 22.56 S | 46.17 W |
| João Câmara | 250 | 5.32 S | 35.48 W |
| João Mendes ≃ | 287a | 22.57 S | 43.03 W |
| João Neiva | 255 | 19.45 S | 40.24 W |
| João Pessoa | 250 | 7.07 S | 34.52 W |
| João Pinheiro | 255 | 17.45 S | 46.10 W |
| Joaquim Egídio | 256 | 22.53 S | 46.59 W |
| Joaquim Távora | 255 | 23.30 S | 49.58 W |
| Joaquin | 194 | 31.58 N | 94.03 W |
| Joaquin Miller Park ♦ | 282 | 37.49 N | 122.11 W |
| Joaquín Suárez | 258 | 34.44 S | 56.02 W |
| Joaquín V. González | 252 | 25.05 S | 64.11 W |
| Job | 62 | 45.37 N | 3.45 E |
| Jobabo | 240p | 20.54 N | 77.17 W |
| Jobat | 120 | 22.25 N | 74.34 E |
| Jobo Point ≻ | 116 | 8.42 N | 126.15 E |
| Jobos | 240m | 17.58 N | 66.10 W |
| Jobos, Bahía de c | 240m | 17.56 N | 66.13 W |
| Job Peak ʌ | 204 | 39.35 N | 118.14 W |
| Jobstown | 285 | 40.02 N | 74.41 W |
| Jochberg | 64 | 47.23 N | 12.24 E |
| Jock ≃ | 212 | 45.16 N | 75.43 W |
| Jocketa | 54 | 50.33 N | 12.10 E |
| Jockgrim | 56 | 49.06 N | 8.17 E |
| Jocko ≃ | 202 | 47.20 N | 114.17 W |
| Jocolí | 252 | 32.35 S | 68.41 W |
| Jo Co Marsh ≋ | 276 | 40.37 N | 73.47 W |
| Jocón | 236 | 15.17 N | 86.58 W |
| Jocoro | 236 | 13.37 N | 88.01 W |
| Jocotán | 236 | 14.49 N | 89.23 W |
| Jocotepec | 234 | 20.18 N | 103.26 W |
| Jocotitlán | 234 | 19.42 N | 99.48 W |
| Jódar | 34 | 37.50 N | 3.21 W |
| Jodhpur | 120 | 26.17 N | 73.02 E |
| Jodiya | 120 | 22.42 N | 70.18 E |
| Jodoigne | 56 | 50.43 N | 4.52 E |
| Jodrell Bank Radio Telescope ʊ[3] | 262 | 53.14 N | 2.18 W |
| Joe ≃ | 220 | 25.17 N | 81.05 W |
| Joe Batt's Arm | 186 | 49.44 N | 54.10 W |
| Joel | 158 | 28.42 S | 28.21 E |
| Joensuu | 26 | 62.36 N | 29.46 E |
| Joe Pool Lake ⊜[1] | 222 | 32.36 N | 97.01 W |
| Joetsu | 94 | 37.06 N | 138.15 E |
| Jœuf | 56 | 49.14 N | 6.01 E |
| Jofane | 156 | 21.17 S | 34.16 E |
| Joffre, Mount ʌ | 182 | 50.32 N | 115.13 W |
| Jōganzi ≃ | 94 | 36.46 N | 137.18 E |
| Jōga-shima I | 94 | 35.08 N | 139.37 E |
| Jōgawara | 268 | 35.42 N | 139.22 E |
| Jōge | 96 | 34.42 N | 133.07 E |
| Jogeshvari •[8] | 272c | 19.08 N | 72.51 E |
| Jogeshvari Cave •[5] | 272c | 19.08 N | 72.51 E |
| Jõgeva | 76 | 58.45 N | 26.24 E |
| Jog Falls ʟ | 122 | 14.13 N | 74.45 E |
| Joggins | 186 | 45.42 N | 64.27 W |
| Joghatāy | 128 | 36.36 N | 57.01 E |
| Jogindarnagar | 123 | 31.59 N | 76.46 E |
| Jogjakarta → Yogyakarta | 115a | 7.48 S | 110.22 E |
| Jogui ≃ | 255 | 23.45 S | 54.40 W |
| Jōhana | 94 | 36.31 N | 136.54 E |
| Johannesburg, S. Afr. | 158 | 26.12 S | 28.05 E |
| Johannesburg, S. Afr. | 273d | 26.12 S | 28.05 E |
| Johannesburg, Ca., U.S. | 228 | 35.22 N | 117.38 W |
| Johannesburg □[5] | 273d | 26.13 S | 28.02 E |
| Johannesburg (Jan Smuts) Airport ⊠ | 273d | 26.08 S | 28.14 E |
| Johanngeorgenstadt | 54 | 50.26 N | 12.43 E |
| Johanniskreuz | 56 | 49.20 N | 7.49 E |
| Johannisthal •[8] | 264a | 52.26 N | 13.30 E |
| Jōhen | 92 | 32.57 N | 132.35 E |
| Johi | 120 | 26.41 N | 67.37 E |
| Johilla ≃ | 124 | 23.37 N | 81.14 E |
| John ≃ | 180 | 66.55 N | 151.35 W |
| John Boyd Thacher State Park ♦ | 210 | 42.38 N | 74.01 W |
| John Carroll University ʊ[2] | 279a | 41.29 N | 81.32 W |
| John Day | 202 | 44.24 N | 118.57 W |
| John Day ≃ | 202 | 45.44 N | 120.39 W |
| John Day, Middle Fork ≃ | 202 | 44.55 N | 119.18 W |
| John Day, North Fork ≃ | 202 | 44.45 N | 119.38 W |
| John Day, South Fork ≃ | 202 | 44.28 N | 119.31 W |
| John Day Dam •[6] | 224 | 45.43 N | 120.41 W |
| John Day Fossil Beds National Monument ♦ | 202 | 44.34 N | 119.39 W |
| John F. Kennedy International Airport ⊠ | 210 | 40.38 N | 73.47 W |
| John F. Kennedy National Historic Site ⊥ | 283 | 42.21 N | 71.08 W |
| John F. Kennedy Space Center ʊ[3] | 220 | 28.40 N | 80.40 W |
| John Forrest National Park ♦ | 168a | 31.53 S | 116.06 E |
| John Hancock Center ʊ | 278 | 41.55 N | 87.37 W |
| John H. Kerr Reservoir ⊜[1] | 192 | 36.35 N | 78.35 W |
| John J. Duffy Preserve ♦ | 278 | 41.39 N | 87.55 W |
| John Martin Reservoir ⊜[1] | 198 | 38.05 N | 103.02 W |
| John McLaren Park ♦ | 282 | 37.43 N | 122.25 W |
| John Muir National Historic Site ⊥ | 282 | 37.59 N | 122.08 W |
| Johnny Run ≃ | 216 | 41.17 N | 88.21 W |
| John o' Groats | 46 | 58.38 N | 3.05 W |
| John Pennekamp Coral Reef State Park ♦ | 220 | 25.11 N | 80.15 W |
| John Redmond Reservoir ⊜[1] | 198 | 38.18 N | 95.55 W |
| Johns ≃ | 224 | 46.54 N | 124.01 W |
| Johns Creek ≃ | 192 | 37.30 N | 80.06 W |
| Johnshaven | 46 | 56.47 N | 2.20 W |
| Johns Hopkins University ʊ[2] | 284b | 39.20 N | 76.37 W |
| Johns Island I | 192 | 32.40 N | 80.05 W |
| Johnson, Ar., U.S. | 194 | 36.07 N | 94.09 W |
| Johnson, Ks., U.S. | 198 | 37.34 N | 101.45 W |
| Johnson, Ne., U.S. | 198 | 40.24 N | 95.59 W |
| Johnson, N.Y., U.S. | 210 | 41.22 N | 74.30 W |
| Johnson, Vt., U.S. | 188 | 44.38 N | 72.40 W |
| Johnson □[6], In., U.S. | 218 | 39.29 N | 86.03 W |
| Johnson □[6], Tx., U.S. | 222 | 32.20 N | 97.20 W |
| Johnson, Mount ʌ | 226 | 36.37 N | 121.19 W |
| Johnson Bay c | 208 | 38.03 N | 75.20 W |
| Johnsonburg, N.J., U.S. | 210 | 40.58 N | 74.53 W |
| Johnsonburg, N.Y., U.S. | 210 | 42.44 N | 78.18 W |
| Johnsonburg, Pa., U.S. | 214 | 41.29 N | 78.40 W |
| Johnson City, N.Y., U.S. | 210 | 42.06 N | 75.57 W |
| Johnson City, Tn., U.S. | 192 | 36.18 N | 82.21 W |


| | | | | | |
|---|---|---|---|---|---|
| ≃ | River | Fluß | Río | Rivière | Rio |
| ≊ | Canal | Kanal | Canal | Canal | Canal |
| ʟ | Waterfall, Rapids | Wasserfall, Stromschnellen | Cascada, Rápidos | Chute d'eau, Rapides | Cascata, Rápidos |
| ɰ | Strait | Meeresstraße | Estrecho | Détroit | Estreito |
| c | Bay, Gulf | Bucht, Golf | Bahía, Golfo | Baie, Golfe | Baía, Golfo |
| ⊜ | Lake, Lakes | See, Seen | Lago, Lagos | Lac, Lacs | Lago, Lagos |
| ≋ | Swamp | Sumpf | Pantano | Marais | Pântano |
| ≚ | Ice Features, Glacier | Eis- und Gletscherformen | Accidentes Glaciales | Formes glaciaires | Acidentes glaciares |
| ⊤ | Other Hydrographic Features | Andere Hydrographische Objekte | Otros Elementos Hidrográficos | Autres données hydrographiques | Outros acidentes hidrográficos |
| ✣ | Submarine Features | Untermeerische Objekte | Accidentes Submarinos | Formes de relief sous-marin | Acidentes submarinos |
| □ | Political Unit | Politische Einheit | Unidad Politica | Entité politique | Unidade política |
| ʊ | Cultural Institution | Kulturelle Institution | Institución Cultural | Institution culturelle | Institução cultural |
| ⊥ | Historical Site | Historische Stätte | Sitio Histórico | Site historique | Sitio histórico |
| ♦ | Recreational Site | Erholungs- und Ferienort | Sitio de Recreo | Centre de loisirs | Area de Lazer |
| ⊠ | Airport | Flughafen | Aeropuerto | Aéroport | Aeroporto |
| ■ | Military Installation | Militäranlage | Instalación Militar | Installation militaire | Instalação militar |
| • | Miscellaneous | Verschiedenes | Misceláneo | Divers | Diversos |

ENGLISH — DEUTSCH


| Name | Page | Lat.°′ | Long.°′ |
|---|---|---|---|
| Johnson City, Tx., U.S. | **196** | 30.16 N | 98.24 W |
| Johnson Creek, N.Y., U.S. | **210** | 43.15 N | 78.31 W |
| Johnson Creek, Wi., U.S. | **216** | 43.04 N | 88.46 W |
| Johnson Creek ≃, Id., U.S. | **202** | 44.58 N | 115.30 W |
| Johnson Creek ≃, Ky., U.S. | **218** | 38.27 N | 84.04 W |
| Johnson Creek ≃, N.Y., U.S. | **210** | 43.22 N | 78.16 W |
| Johnson Creek ≃, Tx., U.S. | **222** | 32.02 N | 94.59 W |
| Johnson Creek ≃, Wa., U.S. | **224** | 46.35 N | 121.42 W |
| Johnsondale | **204** | 35.58 N | 118.32 W |
| Johnson Drain ≊ | **281** | 42.26 N | 83.28 W |
| Johnson Draw V, Tx., U.S. | **196** | 31.58 N | 101.41 W |
| Johnson Draw V, Tx., U.S. | **196** | 30.08 N | 101.07 W |
| Johnson Hall State Historic Site ⊥ | **210** | 43.01 N | 74.23 W |
| Johnson Park ♦ | **276** | 40.30 N | 74.27 W |
| Johnson Point › | **241h** | 13.07 N | 61.12 W |
| Johnsons Crossing | **180** | 60.29 N | 133.16 W |
| Johnsons Point › | **240c** | 17.02 N | 61.53 W |
| Johnsons Pond ⊜ | **283** | 42.44 N | 71.03 W |
| Johnsons Station | **222** | 32.42 N | 97.08 W |
| Johnsonville, N.Z. | **172** | 41.14 S | 174.47 E |
| Johnsonville, N.Y., U.S. | **210** | 42.55 N | 73.31 W |
| Johnsonville, S.C., U.S. | **192** | 33.49 N | 79.26 W |
| Johnston, Wales, U.K. | **42** | 51.46 N | 5.00 W |
| Johnston, Ia., U.S. | **190** | 41.40 N | 93.41 W |
| Johnston, R.I., U.S. | **207** | 41.46 N | 71.21 W |
| Johnston, S.C., U.S. | **192** | 33.49 N | 81.48 W |
| Johnston, Lake ⊜ | **162** | 32.25 S | 120.30 E |
| Johnston Atoll I[1] | **14** | 16.45 N | 169.32 W |
| Johnston City | **194** | 37.49 N | 88.55 W |
| Johnstone | **46** | 55.50 N | 4.31 W |
| Johnstone Peak ∧ | **280** | 34.10 N | 117.48 W |
| Johnstone Strait U | **182** | 50.25 N | 126.00 W |
| Johnston Falls L | **154** | 10.35 S | 28.40 E |
| Johnstown, Co., U.S. | **200** | 40.20 N | 104.54 W |
| Johnstown, N.Y., U.S. | **210** | 43.00 N | 74.22 W |
| Johnstown, Oh., U.S. | **214** | 40.09 N | 82.41 W |
| Johnstown, Pa., U.S. | **214** | 40.19 N | 78.55 W |
| Johnstown Center | **216** | 42.42 N | 88.50 W |
| Johnstown Flood National Memorial ⊥ | **214** | 40.21 N | 78.47 W |
| John Tyler Arboretum ♦ | **285** | 39.56 N | 75.26 W |
| Jōhoku | **94** | 36.28 N | 140.22 E |
| Johol | **114** | 2.36 N | 102.16 E |
| Johor □[3] | **114** | 2.00 N | 103.30 E |
| Johor ≃ | **114** | 1.27 N | 104.02 E |
| Johor, Selat U | **271c** | 1.28 N | 103.48 E |
| Johor Baharu | **114** | 1.28 N | 103.45 E |
| Jöhstadt | **54** | 50.30 N | 13.05 E |
| Joice Island I | **282** | 38.08 N | 122.02 W |
| Joigny | **50** | 47.59 N | 3.24 E |
| Joiner | **194** | 35.30 N | 90.08 W |
| Joinerville | **222** | 32.11 N | 94.55 W |
| Joinvile | **252** | 26.18 S | 48.50 W |
| Joinville | **58** | 48.27 N | 5.08 E |
| Joinville, Lac ⊜ | **206** | 46.18 N | 75.12 W |
| Joinville Island I | **9** | 63.15 S | 55.45 W |
| Joinville-le-Pont | **261** | 48.49 N | 2.28 E |
| Jōjima | **96** | 33.15 N | 130.26 E |
| Jojogan | **115a** | 6.58 S | 111.46 E |
| Jojutla | **234** | 18.37 N | 99.11 W |
| Joka | **272b** | 22.27 N | 88.18 E |
| Jokau | **140** | 8.24 N | 33.49 E |
| Jokioinen | **26** | 60.49 N | 23.28 E |
| Jokkmokk | **24** | 66.37 N | 19.50 E |
| Jökulsá á Brú ≃ | **24a** | 65.41 N | 14.13 W |
| Jökulsárgljúfur National Park ♦ | **24a** | 66.00 N | 16.20 W |
| Jolārpettai | **122** | 12.34 N | 78.35 E |
| Jolfā | **128** | 38.57 N | 45.38 E |
| Joliet, Il., U.S. | **216** | 41.31 N | 88.04 W |
| Joliet, Mt., U.S. | **202** | 45.29 N | 108.58 W |
| Joliet Correctional Center Ʊ | **278** | 41.33 N | 88.04 W |
| Joliett | **208** | 40.37 N | 76.27 W |
| Joliette | **206** | 46.01 N | 73.27 W |
| Joliette □[6] | **206** | 46.25 N | 74.00 W |
| Jolietville | **218** | 40.03 N | 86.15 W |
| Jollyville | **222** | 30.27 N | 97.47 W |
| Jolo | **116** | 6.03 N | 121.00 E |
| Jolo Group II | **116** | 6.00 N | 121.09 E |
| Jolo Island I | **116** | 5.58 N | 121.06 E |
| Jølstravatnet ⊜ | **26** | 61.32 N | 6.13 E |
| Jomalig Island I | **116** | 14.42 N | 122.22 E |
| Jomba | **102** | 31.27 N | 98.15 E |
| Jombang | **115a** | 7.33 S | 112.14 E |
| Jombo ≃ | **152** | 10.36 S | 17.32 E |
| Jona | **58** | 47.14 N | 8.52 E |
| Jonacatepec | **234** | 18.41 N | 98.48 W |
| Jonah | **222** | 30.38 N | 97.32 W |
| Jönåker | **40** | 58.44 N | 16.40 E |
| Jonathan Dickinson State Park ♦ | **220** | 27.01 N | 80.08 W |
| Jonava | **76** | 55.05 N | 24.17 E |
| Jones, Pil. | **116** | 16.33 N | 121.42 E |
| Jones, Mi., U.S. | **216** | 41.54 N | 85.48 W |
| Jones, Ok., U.S. | **196** | 35.33 N | 97.17 W |
| Jones ≃ | **283** | 42.00 N | 70.42 W |
| Jones and Laughlin Steel Corporation Ʊ[3], Pa., U.S. | **279b** | 40.26 N | 79.58 W |
| Jones and Laughlin Steel Corporation Ʊ[3], Pa., U.S. | **279b** | 40.37 N | 80.14 W |
| Jones Beach State Park ♦ | **210** | 40.35 N | 73.31 W |
| Jonesboro, Ar., U.S. | **194** | 35.50 N | 90.42 W |
| Jonesboro, Ga., U.S. | **192** | 33.31 N | 84.21 W |
| Jonesboro, Il., U.S. | **194** | 37.27 N | 89.16 W |
| Jonesboro, In., U.S. | **216** | 40.28 N | 85.37 W |
| Jonesboro, La., U.S. | **194** | 32.14 N | 92.42 W |
| Jonesboro, Tn., U.S. | **192** | 36.17 N | 82.28 W |
| Jonesburg | **219** | 38.51 N | 91.18 W |
| Jones Creek | **222** | 28.58 N | 95.27 W |
| Jones Creek ≃, On., Can. | **212** | 44.30 N | 75.49 W |
| Jones Creek ≃, Tx., U.S. | **222** | 29.08 N | 96.03 W |
| Jones Falls ≃ | **284b** | 39.18 N | 76.37 W |
| Jones Falls, North Branch ≃ | **284b** | 39.25 N | 76.42 W |
| Jones Inlet ⊂ | **210** | 40.35 N | 73.34 W |
| Jones Mill | **194** | 34.27 N | 92.50 W |
| Jones Mountains ⋀ | **9** | 73.32 S | 94.00 W |
| Jonesport | **188** | 44.31 N | 67.35 W |
| Jones Sound U | **176** | 76.00 N | 85.00 W |
| Jonestown | **194** | 34.19 N | 90.27 W |
| Jonesville, In., U.S. | **218** | 39.04 N | 85.53 W |
| Jonesville, La., U.S. | **194** | 31.37 N | 91.49 W |
| Jonesville, Mi., U.S. | **216** | 41.59 N | 84.40 W |
| Jonesville, N.Y., U.S. | **210** | 42.55 N | 73.49 W |
| Jonesville, N.C., U.S. | **192** | 36.14 N | 80.50 W |
| Jonesville, S.C., U.S. | **192** | 34.50 N | 81.40 W |
| Jonesville, Va., U.S. | **192** | 36.41 N | 83.06 W |
| Jong ≃ | **150** | 7.32 N | 12.23 W |
| Jonglei Canal ≊ | **136** | 9.21 N | 31.32 E |
| Jongunjärvi ⊜ | **26** | 65.17 N | 27.15 E |
| Jónico, Mar → Ionian Sea ⊤[2] | **22** | 39.00 N | 19.00 E |
| Joniškėlis | **76** | 56.02 N | 24.10 E |
| Joniškis | **76** | 56.14 N | 23.37 E |
| Jonkersberg | **158** | 33.55 S | 22.15 E |
| Jönköping | **26** | 57.47 N | 14.11 E |
| Jönköpings Län □[6] | **26** | 57.30 N | 14.30 E |
| Jonquière | **186** | 48.24 N | 71.15 W |
| Jonquières | **62** | 44.07 N | 4.54 E |
| Jonsdorf | **54** | 50.51 N | 14.43 E |
| Jonstorp | **41** | 56.14 N | 12.40 E |
| Jonuta | **232** | 18.05 N | 92.08 W |
| Jonvilliers | **261** | 48.34 N | 1.42 E |
| Jonzac | **32** | 45.27 N | 0.26 W |
| Joondalup, Lake ⊜ | **168a** | 31.45 S | 115.47 E |
| Joplin, Mo., U.S. | **194** | 37.05 N | 94.30 W |
| Joplin, Mt., U.S. | **202** | 48.33 N | 110.46 W |
| Joppa, Il., U.S. | **194** | 37.12 N | 88.50 W |
| Joppa, Md., U.S. | **208** | 39.26 N | 76.21 W |
| Jóquei Clube ♦ | **287b** | 23.35 S | 46.41 W |
| Joquicingo | **234** | 19.03 N | 99.33 W |
| Jora | **124** | 26.20 N | 77.49 E |
| Jordan, Pil. | **116** | 10.40 N | 122.35 E |
| Jordan, Mn., U.S. | **190** | 44.40 N | 93.37 W |
| Jordan, Mt., U.S. | **202** | 47.19 N | 106.54 W |
| Jordan, N.Y., U.S. | **210** | 43.03 N | 76.28 W |
| Jordan (Al-Urdun) □[1], Asia | **118** | 31.00 N | 36.00 E |
| Jordan (Al-Urdun) □[1], Asia | **128** | 31.00 N | 36.00 E |
| Jordan (Nahr al-Urdun) (HaYarden) ≃, Asia | **132** | 31.46 N | 35.33 E |
| Jordan ≃, B.C., Can. | **224** | 48.26 N | 124.08 W |
| Jordan ≃, Ut,. U.S. | **200** | 40.49 N | 112.08 W |
| Jordan Creek ≃ | **202** | 42.52 N | 117.38 W |
| Jordânia | **255** | 15.54 S | 40.11 W |
| Jordania → Jordan □[1] | **128** | 31.00 N | 36.00 E |
| Jordanie → Jordan □[1] | **128** | 31.00 N | 36.00 E |
| Jordanien → Jordan □[1] | **128** | 31.00 N | 36.00 E |
| Jordan Lake ⊜ | **216** | 42.46 N | 85.09 W |
| Jordanów | **30** | 49.40 N | 19.50 E |
| Jordans | **260** | 51.37 N | 0.36 W |
| Jordan Valley | **202** | 42.58 N | 117.03 W |
| Jordanville | **210** | 42.55 N | 74.57 W |
| Jordão ≃ | **252** | 25.46 S | 52.07 W |
| Jordbro | **40** | 59.09 N | 18.07 E |
| Jördenstorf | **54** | 53.52 N | 12.37 E |
| Jordet | **26** | 61.25 N | 12.09 E |
| Jorge Chávez, Aeropuerto Internacional ⊠ | **286d** | 12.02 S | 77.07 W |
| Jorge Grego, Ilha I | **256** | 23.13 S | 44.09 W |
| Jorge Montt, Isla I | **254** | 51.20 S | 74.45 W |
| Jorge V, Costade → George V Coast ±[2] | **9** | 68.30 S | 147.30 E |
| Jorge VI, Estrecho de → George VI Sound U | **9** | 71.00 S | 68.00 W |
| Jorhāt | **120** | 26.46 N | 94.13 E |
| Jork | **52** | 53.32 N | 9.41 E |
| Jorm | **120** | 36.52 N | 70.51 E |
| Jörn | **26** | 65.04 N | 20.02 E |
| Jornado del Muerto •[2] | **200** | 33.20 N | 106.50 W |
| Joroinen | **26** | 62.11 N | 27.50 E |
| Jorong | **112** | 3.58 S | 114.56 E |
| Jørpeland | **26** | 59.01 N | 6.03 E |
| J'orzovka | **80** | 48.56 N | 44.38 E |
| Jos | **150** | 9.55 N | 8.53 E |
| Jose Abad Santos | **116** | 5.38 N | 125.27 E |
| José Batlle y Ordóñez | **252** | 33.28 S | 55.07 W |
| José Bonifácio | **255** | 21.03 S | 49.41 W |
| José Cardel | **234** | 19.22 N | 96.22 W |
| José C. Paz | **258** | 34.30 S | 58.45 W |
| José de Freitas | **250** | 4.45 S | 42.35 W |
| José de San Martín | **254** | 44.02 S | 70.29 W |
| José Enrique Rodó (Drabble) | **258** | 33.41 S | 57.34 W |
| José Francisco Vergara | **252** | 22.28 S | 69.38 W |
| Joselândia | **248** | 16.32 S | 56.12 W |
| José Martí, Aeropuerto Internacional ⊠ | **286b** | 23.00 N | 82.24 W |
| Jose Panganiban | **116** | 14.17 N | 122.41 E |
| José Pedro Varela | **252** | 33.27 S | 54.32 W |
| Joseph | **202** | 45.21 N | 117.13 W |
| Joseph, Lac ⊜ | **176** | 52.45 N | 65.15 W |
| Joseph, Lake ⊜ | **212** | 45.10 N | 79.44 W |
| Joseph Bonaparte Gulf ⊂ | **164** | 14.15 S | 128.30 E |
| Joseph City | **200** | 34.57 N | 110.20 W |
| Joseph Creek ≃ | **202** | 46.03 N | 117.01 W |
| Joseph Davis State Park ♦ | **284a** | 43.13 N | 79.03 W |
| Josephine, Pa., U.S. | **214** | 40.29 N | 79.11 W |
| Josephine, Tx., U.S. | **222** | 33.04 N | 96.19 W |
| Josephine, Lake ⊜ | **220** | 27.24 N | 81.26 W |
| Josephine Peak ∧ | **280** | 34.17 N | 118.09 W |
| Josephstaal | **164** | 4.44 S | 145.01 E |
| José Santos Arévalo | **258** | 35.10 S | 59.14 W |
| Joshīmath | **120** | 30.34 N | 79.34 E |
| Jōshin-Etsu-kōgen-kokuritsu-kōen ♦ | **94** | 36.46 N | 138.40 E |
| Joshua | **222** | 32.28 N | 97.23 W |
| Joshuas Creek ≃ | **275b** | 43.29 N | 79.37 W |
| Joshua Tree | **204** | 34.08 N | 116.18 W |
| Joshua Tree National Park ♦ | **204** | 33.55 N | 116.00 W |
| Joshua Trees State Park ♦ | **228** | 34.41 N | 117.47 W |
| Joškar-Ola | **80** | 56.38 N | 47.52 E |
| Jos Plateau ⋀[1] | **150** | 9.30 N | 9.00 E |
| Jossa | **56** | 50.14 N | 9.35 E |
| Josselin | **32** | 47.57 N | 2.33 W |
| Jossigny | **50** | 48.50 N | 2.45 E |
| Jostedalsbreen ⊓ | **26** | 61.40 N | 7.00 E |
| Jost Van Dyke I | **240m** | 18.28 N | 64.45 W |
| Jōtō •[8] | **270** | 34.42 N | 135.34 E |
| Jotunheimen ⋀ | **26** | 61.38 N | 8.18 E |
| Jotunheimen Nasjonalpark ♦ | **26** | 61.35 N | 8.30 E |
| Jouarre | **50** | 48.56 N | 3.08 E |
| Jouars-Pontchartrain | **261** | 48.47 N | 1.54 E |
| Joubertina | **158** | 33.50 S | 23.51 E |
| Joué-lès-Tours | **50** | 47.21 N | 0.40 E |
| Jougne | **58** | 46.46 N | 6.24 E |
| Jouques | **62** | 43.38 N | 5.38 E |
| Jourdanton | **196** | 28.55 N | 98.32 W |
| Joure | **52** | 52.57 N | 5.47 E |
| Joutsa | **26** | 61.44 N | 26.07 E |
| Joutseno | **26** | 61.06 N | 28.30 E |
| Joutsijärvi | **24** | 66.40 N | 28.00 E |
| Joux, Lac de ⊜ | **58** | 46.38 N | 6.18 E |
| Joux, Vallée de V | **58** | 46.35 N | 6.15 E |
| Jouy | **50** | 48.31 N | 1.33 E |
| Jouy-en-Josas | **261** | 48.46 N | 2.10 E |
| Jouy-le-Moutier | **261** | 49.01 N | 2.03 E |
| Jouy-le-Potier | **50** | 47.45 N | 1.49 E |
| Jovellanos | **240p** | 22.48 N | 81.12 W |
| Jovellar | **116** | 13.04 N | 123.36 E |
| Jovet, Mont ∧ | **62** | 45.30 N | 6.39 E |
| Joveyn ≃ | **128** | 36.48 N | 56.28 E |
| Joviânia | **255** | 17.49 S | 49.30 W |
| Jowai | **120** | 25.27 N | 92.12 E |
| Jowhar | **144** | 2.46 N | 45.31 E |
| Jowlaenga, Mount ∧ | **162** | 17.21 S | 122.56 E |
| Jowzjān □[4] | **120** | 36.30 N | 66.00 E |
| Joy | **190** | 41.12 N | 90.55 W |
| Joy, Mount ∧ | **180** | 63.46 N | 132.55 W |
| Joyce | **194** | 31.56 N | 92.35 W |
| Joyeuse | **62** | 44.29 N | 4.14 E |
| Jōyō | **96** | 34.51 N | 135.47 E |
| Joyous Pavilion Park ♦ | **271a** | 39.52 N | 116.22 E |
| Joyuda | **240m** | 18.07 N | 67.11 W |
| Józefów | **30** | 52.09 N | 21.12 E |
| J. Percy Priest Lake ⊜[1] | **194** | 36.05 N | 86.30 W |
| Ju ≃, Zhg. | **100** | 30.38 N | 114.51 E |
| Ju ≃, Zhg. | **105** | 39.45 N | 117.35 E |
| Juaba | **250** | 2.23 S | 49.33 W |
| Juagdan | **116** | 10.00 N | 124.35 E |
| Juami ≃ | **246** | 1.45 S | 67.30 W |
| Juanacatlán | **234** | 20.31 N | 103.10 W |
| Juana Díaz | **240m** | 18.03 N | 66.31 W |
| Juan Aldama | **232** | 24.19 N | 103.21 W |
| Juan Anchorena •[8] | **288** | 34.29 S | 58.30 W |
| Juan Atucha | **258** | 35.32 S | 59.21 W |
| Juan B. Arruabarrena | **252** | 30.20 S | 58.19 W |
| Juan Bautista Alberdi | **252** | 27.35 S | 65.37 W |
| Juan Blanco, Arroyo ≃ | **258** | 35.05 S | 57.26 W |
| Juancheng | **98** | 35.35 N | 115.29 E |
| Juan de Fuca, Strait of U | **224** | 48.18 N | 124.00 W |
| Juan de Garay | **254** | 38.52 S | 64.34 W |
| Juan de Mena | **252** | 24.55 S | 56.44 W |
| Juan de Nova, Île I | **138** | 17.03 S | 42.45 E |
| Juan Díaz Covarrubias | **234** | 18.07 N | 95.09 W |
| Juan E. Barra | **252** | 37.48 S | 60.29 W |
| Juan Eugenio | **232** | 25.10 N | 103.20 W |
| Juan Fernández, Archipiélago II | **244** | 33.00 S | 80.00 W |
| Juan González Grande, Arroyo ≃ | **258** | 34.00 S | 58.14 W |
| Juan González Romero •[8] | **286a** | 19.30 N | 99.04 W |
| Juangriego | **246** | 11.05 N | 63.57 W |
| Juan Gualberto Gómez | **240p** | 22.52 N | 81.33 W |
| Juan Guerra | **248** | 6.35 S | 76.21 W |
| Juan Jorba | **252** | 33.37 S | 65.16 W |
| Juan José Castelli | **252** | 25.57 S | 60.37 W |
| Juán José Perez | **248** | 15.14 S | 68.58 W |
| Juanjuí | **248** | 7.11 S | 76.45 W |
| Juankoski | **26** | 63.04 N | 28.21 E |
| Juan-les-Pins | **62** | 43.34 N | 7.06 E |
| Juan L. Lacaze | **258** | 34.26 S | 57.27 W |
| Juan N. Fernández | **252** | 38.00 S | 59.16 W |
| Juan Perez Sound U | **182** | 52.30 N | 131.18 W |
| Juan Ramírez, Isla I | **234** | 21.50 N | 97.40 W |
| Juan Rodríguez Clara | **234** | 18.00 N | 95.25 W |
| Juan Tronconi | **258** | 35.30 S | 59.15 W |
| Juan Viñas | **236** | 9.54 N | 83.45 W |
| Juárez, Méx. | **232** | 27.37 N | 100.44 W |
| Juárez, Méx. | **232** | 30.19 N | 108.05 W |
| Juárez → Ciudad Juárez, Méx. | **232** | 31.44 N | 106.29 W |
| Juárez, Méx. | **234** | 17.39 N | 93.10 W |
| Juárez, Cerro ∧ | **234** | 20.37 N | 99.17 W |
| Juárez, Sierra ⋀ | **234** | 17.30 N | 96.30 W |
| Juárez, Sierra de ⋀ | **232** | 32.00 N | 115.50 W |
| Juarzon | **150** | 5.20 N | 8.52 W |
| Juatinga, Ponta de › | **256** | 23.17 S | 44.30 W |
| Juazeirinho | **250** | 7.04 S | 36.35 W |
| Juàzeiro | **250** | 9.25 S | 40.30 W |
| Juazeiro do Norte | **250** | 7.12 S | 39.20 W |
| Jūbā | **154** | 4.51 N | 31.37 E |
| Juba ≃ | **248** | 14.59 S | 57.44 W |
| Jubachstausee ⊜[1] | **263** | 51.10 N | 7.37 E |
| Jūbāl, Maḍīq U | **140** | 27.40 N | 33.55 E |
| Jubal, Strait of → Jūbāl, Maḍīq U | **140** | 27.40 N | 33.55 E |
| Jubayl (Byblos) | **130** | 34.07 N | 35.39 E |
| Jubaysho | **144** | 5.48 N | 37.22 E |
| Jubayt | **140** | 18.57 N | 36.50 E |
| Jubba (Genale) ≃ | **144** | 0.15 S | 42.38 E |
| Jubbada Dhexe □[4] | **144** | 1.00 N | 43.00 E |
| Jubbada Hoose □[4] | **144** | 0.00 | 42.00 E |
| Jubbah | **128** | 28.02 N | 40.56 E |
| Jubb al-Jarrāḥ | **130** | 34.49 N | 37.19 E |
| Jubbātā al-Khashab | **132** | 33.13 N | 35.49 E |
| Jubb Jannīn | **132** | 33.37 N | 35.47 E |
| Jubbulpore → Jabalpur | **124** | 23.10 N | 79.57 E |
| Jubilee Downs | **162** | 18.22 S | 125.17 E |
| Jubilee Lake ⊜, Austl. | **162** | 29.12 S | 126.38 E |
| Jubilee Lake ⊜, Nf., Can. | **186** | 48.04 N | 55.11 W |
| Jubones ≃ | **246** | 3.13 S | 79.57 W |
| Jūbu-san ∧ | **270** | 34.50 N | 135.55 E |
| Juby, Cap › | **148** | 27.58 N | 12.55 W |
| Júcar (Xúquer) ≃ | **34** | 39.09 N | 0.14 W |
| Juçara | **255** | 15.53 S | 50.51 W |
| Júcaro | **240p** | 21.37 N | 78.51 W |
| Jucás | **250** | 6.32 S | 39.32 W |
| Jüchen | **56** | 51.06 N | 6.30 E |
| Juchipila | **234** | 21.25 N | 103.07 W |
| Juchipila ≃ | **234** | 21.03 N | 103.25 W |
| Juchitán de Zaragoza | **234** | 16.26 N | 95.01 W |
| Juchitepec | **234** | 19.06 N | 98.53 W |
| Juchitlán | **234** | 20.05 N | 104.07 W |
| Juchnov | **76** | 54.45 N | 35.14 E |
| Jüchsen | **54** | 50.29 N | 10.29 E |
| Jucuapa | **236** | 13.31 N | 88.24 W |
| Jucurucu ≃ | **255** | 17.21 S | 39.13 W |
| Jucurutu | **250** | 6.02 S | 37.01 W |
| Judaea □[9] | **132** | 31.35 N | 35.00 E |
| Judas, Punta › | **236** | 9.31 N | 84.32 W |
| Judaydat al-Khās | **132** | 33.24 N | 36.33 E |
| Judaydat ʿArṭūz | **132** | 33.26 N | 36.10 E |
| Juddah → Jiddah | **144** | 21.30 N | 39.12 E |
| Jude Island I | **186** | 47.15 N | 54.49 W |
| Judenau | **61** | 48.17 N | 16.00 E |
| Judenburg | **61** | 47.10 N | 14.40 E |
| Judges Hill ∧[2] | **283** | 42.12 N | 70.49 W |
| Judian | **102** | 27.20 N | 99.36 E |
| Judinki, Ross. | **82** | 54.37 N | 37.17 E |
| Judinki, Ross. | **82** | 55.27 N | 35.48 E |
| Judino, Ross. | **76** | 58.43 N | 39.17 E |
| Judino, Ross. | **80** | 55.51 N | 48.55 E |
| Judino, Ross. | **82** | 54.09 N | 38.19 E |
| Judino, Ross. | **265b** | 55.40 N | 37.12 E |
| Judío, Rambla del ≃ | **34** | 38.15 N | 1.27 W |
| Judique | **186** | 45.52 N | 61.30 W |
| Judith ≃ | **202** | 47.44 N | 109.38 W |
| Judith, Point › | **207** | 41.22 N | 71.29 W |
| Judith Gap | **202** | 46.40 N | 109.45 W |
| Judith Mountains ⋀ | **202** | 47.12 N | 109.15 W |
| Judith Peak ∧ | **202** | 47.13 N | 109.13 W |
| Judoma ≃ | **74** | 59.08 N | 135.06 E |
| Judson, S.C., U.S. | **192** | 34.50 N | 82.27 W |
| Judson, Tx., U.S. | **222** | 32.35 N | 94.45 W |
| Judsonia | **194** | 35.16 N | 91.38 W |
| Jue ≃ | **100** | 31.42 N | 113.20 E |
| Juehedian | **105** | 39.26 N | 117.06 E |
| Juelsminde | **41** | 55.43 N | 10.01 E |
| Juexi | **100** | 29.27 N | 121.57 E |
| Juexizhen | **107** | 28.55 N | 104.16 E |
| Jufari ≃ | **246** | 1.13 S | 62.00 W |
| Jufayr, Bi'r al- ⊤[4] | **142** | 30.49 N | 32.40 E |
| Jufrah, Wādī al- V | **142** | 30.24 N | 31.35 E |
| Jug | **86** | 57.43 N | 56.10 E |
| Jug ≃ | **24** | 60.45 N | 46.20 E |
| Jughna | **140** | 12.24 N | 25.06 E |
| Jugo-Kamskij | **86** | 57.42 N | 55.35 E |
| Jugon | **32** | 48.25 N | 2.20 W |
| Jugo-Osetija (South Ossetia) □[9] | **84** | 42.20 N | 44.00 E |
| Jugoslavija → Yugoslavia □[1] | **22** | 44.00 N | 21.00 E |
| Jugoslawien → Yugoslavia □[1] | **22** | 44.00 N | 21.00 E |
| Jugo-Zapad •[8] | **265b** | 55.40 N | 37.32 E |
| Juḥā | **144** | 16.41 N | 42.54 E |
| Juḥavičy | **76** | 56.02 N | 28.39 E |
| Jühnsdorf | **264a** | 52.18 N | 13.23 E |
| Jühnsdorfer Heide •[3] | **264a** | 52.19 N | 13.24 E |
| Juhu •[8] | **272c** | 19.07 N | 72.49 E |
| Juhua Dao I | **98** | 40.29 N | 120.47 E |
| Juhu Airport ⊠ | **272c** | 19.06 N | 72.50 E |
| Jui | **272c** | 19.01 N | 73.05 E |
| Juidongshan | **100** | 23.46 N | 117.31 E |
| Juigalpa | **236** | 12.05 N | 85.24 W |
| Juillac | **32** | 45.19 N | 1.19 E |
| Juilly | **261** | 49.01 N | 2.42 E |
| Juína ≃ | **248** | 12.36 S | 58.57 W |
| Juine ≃ | **50** | 48.32 N | 2.23 E |
| Juist | **52** | 53.40 N | 6.59 E |
| Juist I | **52** | 53.40 N | 7.00 E |
| Juisui | **100** | 23.30 N | 121.21 E |
| Juiz de Fora | **256** | 21.45 S | 43.20 W |
| Jūjō Base ■ | **268** | 35.45 N | 139.43 E |
| Jujurieux | **58** | 46.02 N | 5.25 E |
| Jujuy → San Salvador de Jujuy | **252** | 24.11 S | 65.18 W |
| Jujuy □[4] | **252** | 23.00 S | 66.00 W |
| Jukagirskoje ploskogorje ⋀[1] | **74** | 66.00 N | 155.00 E |
| Jukamenskoje | **80** | 57.53 N | 52.15 E |
| Jukonda ≃ | **86** | 59.38 N | 67.26 E |
| Juksa | **86** | 56.55 N | 85.10 E |
| Juksejevo | **24** | 59.52 N | 54.19 E |
| Jukskei ≃ | **273d** | 26.06 S | 28.06 E |
| Jukta | **74** | 63.23 N | 105.41 E |
| Jula ≃ | **24** | 63.49 N | 44.44 E |
| Julāna | **124** | 29.08 N | 76.25 E |
| Julayfah, Bi'r al- ⊤[4] | **142** | 30.43 N | 29.35 E |
| Julbach | **60** | 48.40 N | 13.52 E |
| Juldybajevo | **86** | 52.20 N | 57.52 E |
| Julebu | **98** | 40.09 N | 113.36 E |
| Julesburg | **198** | 40.59 N | 102.15 W |
| Juli | **248** | 16.13 S | 69.27 W |
| Juliaca | **248** | 15.30 S | 70.08 W |
| Julia Creek | **166** | 20.39 S | 141.45 E |
| Julia Creek ≃ | **166** | 20.00 S | 141.11 E |
| Julian | **214** | 40.52 N | 77.56 W |
| Juliana, Lake ⊜ | **220** | 28.07 N | 81.48 W |
| Julianakanaal ≊ | **56** | 51.05 N | 5.50 E |
| Julian Alps ⋀ | **36** | 46.00 N | 14.00 E |
| Juliana Top ∧ | **250** | 3.41 N | 56.32 W |
| Julianehåb (Qaqortoq) | **176** | 60.43 N | 46.01 W |
| Julia Pfeiffer Burns State Park ♦ | **226** | 36.10 N | 120.40 W |
| Jülich | **56** | 50.55 N | 6.21 E |
| Juliénas | **58** | 46.14 N | 4.43 E |
| Juliette, Lake ⊜[1] | **192** | 33.05 N | 83.50 W |
| Julijske Alpe → Julian Alps ⋀ | **36** | 46.00 N | 14.00 E |
| Julimes | **232** | 28.25 N | 105.27 W |
| Júlio de Castilhos | **252** | 29.14 S | 53.41 W |
| Julio Prestes, Estação •[5] | **287b** | 23.32 S | 46.38 W |
| Julita Ʊ | **40** | 59.09 N | 16.02 E |
| Juliuhe | **104** | 42.03 N | 122.55 E |
| Juliustown | **285** | 40.00 N | 74.40 W |
| Julu | **98** | 37.13 N | 115.01 E |
| Juma | **24** | 65.07 N | 33.16 E |
| Juma ≃ | **98** | 39.34 N | 115.42 E |
| Jumaguzino | **86** | 52.54 N | 56.23 E |
| Jumapolo | **115a** | 7.42 S | 111.00 E |
| Jumaševo | **80** | 54.59 N | 54.25 E |
| Jumay, Volcán ∧[1] | **236** | 14.41 N | 89.59 W |
| Jumbilla | **248** | 5.54 S | 77.45 W |
| Jumbo | **154** | 17.28 S | 30.55 E |
| Jumbo, Raas › | **144** | 1.39 S | 41.36 E |
| Jumboo | **144** | 0.15 S | 42.38 E |
| Jumbo Peak ∧ | **204** | 36.12 N | 114.11 W |
| Jumeauville | **261** | 48.55 N | 1.47 E |
| Jumentos Cays II | **238** | 22.42 N | 75.55 W |
| Jumet | **50** | 50.26 N | 4.25 E |
| Jumièges | **50** | 49.26 N | 0.49 E |
| Jumilla | **34** | 38.29 N | 1.17 W |
| Jumlā | **124** | 29.17 N | 82.10 E |
| Jummayzat Banī ʿAmr | **142** | 30.48 N | 31.32 E |
| Jump ≃ | **190** | 45.17 N | 91.05 W |
| Jump, North Fork ≃ | **190** | 45.25 N | 90.40 W |
| Jump, South Fork ≃ | **190** | 45.25 N | 90.40 W |
| Jumt uul ∧ | **102** | 44.29 N | 97.10 E |
| Jūn | **132** | 33.35 N | 35.27 E |
| Jun ≃ | **100** | 25.57 N | 118.03 E |
| Jūnāgadh | **120** | 21.31 N | 70.28 E |
| Junan (Shizilu) | **98** | 35.11 N | 118.51 E |
| Junayfah | **142** | 30.12 N | 32.25 E |
| Junaynah, Ra's al- ∧ | **140** | 29.01 N | 33.58 E |
| Juncal, Isla I | **258** | 33.58 S | 58.24 W |
| Juncal do Norte ≡ | **266c** | 38.52 N | 8.59 W |
| Juncal do Sul ≡ | **266c** | 38.51 N | 8.58 W |
| Juncheng | **98** | 38.57 N | 114.41 E |
| Juncos | **240m** | 18.14 N | 65.55 W |
| Junction, Tx., U.S. | **196** | 30.29 N | 99.46 W |
| Junction, Ut,. U.S. | **200** | 38.14 N | 112.13 W |
| Junction City, Ar., U.S. | **194** | 33.00 N | 92.43 W |
| Junction City, Il., U.S. | **219** | 38.34 N | 89.07 W |
| Junction City, Ks., U.S. | **198** | 39.01 N | 96.49 W |
| Junction City, Ky., U.S. | **194** | 37.35 N | 84.47 W |
| Junction City, Or., U.S. | **202** | 44.13 N | 123.12 W |
| Junction City, Wa., U.S. | **224** | 46.58 N | 123.46 W |
| Jundah | **166** | 24.50 S | 143.04 E |
| Jundiaí | **256** | 23.11 S | 46.52 W |
| Jundiaí ≃, Bra. | **256** | 23.32 S | 46.15 W |
| Jundiaí ≃, Bra. | **256** | 23.11 S | 47.16 W |
| Jundiaí do Sul | **255** | 23.27 S | 50.17 W |
| Jundiaí-mirim ≃ | **256** | 23.10 S | 46.56 W |
| Jundiapeba | **256** | 23.33 S | 46.15 W |
| Jundu Shan ⋀ | **105** | 40.30 N | 116.05 E |
| Juneau, Ak., U.S. | **180** | 58.20 N | 134.27 W |
| Juneau, Wi., U.S. | **190** | 43.24 N | 88.42 W |
| Junee | **166** | 34.52 S | 147.35 E |
| June in Winter, Lake ⊜ | **220** | 27.18 N | 81.24 W |
| June Lake | **226** | 37.46 N | 119.04 W |
| June Park | **220** | 28.04 N | 80.41 W |
| Jungapeo de Juárez | **234** | 19.27 N | 100.29 W |
| Jungar Qi | **102** | 39.49 N | 111.10 E |
| Jungbluth Ditch ≊ | **279a** | 41.27 N | 82.07 W |
| Jungfernheide •[3] | **264a** | 52.34 N | 13.17 E |
| Jungfernheide, Volkspark ♦ | **264a** | 52.33 N | 13.16 E |
| Jungfern-Inseln → Virgin Islands □[2] | **240m** | 18.20 N | 64.50 W |
| Jungfern-See ⊜ | **264a** | 52.25 N | 13.05 E |
| Jungfrau ∧ | **58** | 46.32 N | 7.58 E |
| Jungfraujoch • | **58** | 46.33 N | 7.58 E |
| Junggar Pendi (Dzungarian Basin) ≚[1] | **86** | 45.00 N | 88.00 E |
| Jungle Habitat ♦ | **276** | 41.08 N | 74.21 W |
| Junglinster | **56** | 49.43 N | 6.15 E |
| Jungshāhi | **120** | 24.51 N | 67.46 E |
| Juniata | **198** | 40.35 N | 98.30 W |
| Juniata □[6] | **208** | 40.34 N | 77.24 W |
| Juniata •[8] | **285** | 40.01 N | 75.07 W |
| Juniata ≃ | **188** | 40.24 N | 77.01 W |
| Juniata, Frankstown Branch ≃ | **214** | 40.34 N | 78.03 W |
| Juniata, Raystown Branch ≃ | **214** | 40.25 N | 77.58 W |
| Juniata Gap | **214** | 40.33 N | 78.26 W |
| Juniata Terrace | **208** | 40.35 N | 77.34 W |
| Junín, Arg. | **252** | 34.35 S | 60.57 W |
| Junín, Ec. | **246** | 0.56 S | 80.13 W |
| Junín, Perú | **248** | 11.10 S | 76.00 W |
| Junín □[5] | **248** | 11.30 S | 75.00 W |
| Junín, Lago de ⊜ | **248** | 11.02 S | 76.06 W |
| Junín de los Andes | **254** | 39.56 S | 71.05 W |
| Junior | **188** | 38.59 N | 79.57 W |
| Juniper | **186** | 46.33 N | 67.13 W |
| Junipero Serra Peak ∧ | **226** | 36.08 N | 121.25 W |
| Juniville | **50** | 49.24 N | 4.23 E |
| Jūniyah | **130** | 33.59 N | 35.38 E |
| Junk Bay ⊂ | **271d** | 22.17 N | 114.15 E |
| Jun Kharchanai | **123** | 36.52 N | 75.01 E |
| Junk Island I | **271d** | 22.17 N | 114.16 E |
| Junkou | **100** | 26.42 N | 116.49 E |
| Junlian | **102** | 28.08 N | 104.35 E |
| Junliangcheng | **105** | 39.04 N | 117.27 E |
| Junling | **100** | 28.17 N | 116.28 E |
| Junnar | **122** | 19.12 N | 73.53 E |
| Juno Beach | **220** | 26.52 N | 80.04 W |
| Junqalī □[4] | **140** | 7.30 N | 32.20 E |
| Junqueiro | **250** | 9.56 S | 36.29 W |
| Junqueirópolis | **255** | 21.32 S | 51.26 W |
| Junsele | **26** | 63.41 N | 16.54 E |
| Juntas | **236** | 10.16 N | 85.00 W |
| Jun Ul Shan ⋀ | **102** | 37.30 N | 97.00 E |
| Junxian | **102** | 32.31 N | 111.30 E |
| Jūō | **94** | 36.40 N | 140.41 E |
| Juodkrantė | **76** | 55.33 N | 21.08 E |
| Juodupė | **76** | 56.05 N | 25.37 E |
| Juojärvi ⊜ | **26** | 62.43 N | 28.33 E |
| Juozapinės kalnas ∧[2] | **76** | 54.32 N | 25.37 E |
| Juparanã, Lagoa ⊜ | **255** | 19.35 S | 40.18 W |
| Jupilingo ≃ | **236** | 14.48 N | 89.14 W |
| Jupille | **56** | 50.39 N | 5.38 E |
| Jupiter | **220** | 26.56 N | 80.05 W |
| Jupiter ≃ | **186** | 49.29 N | 63.37 W |
| Jupiter Inlet ⊂ | **220** | 26.57 N | 80.04 W |
| Jupiter Island I | **220** | 27.04 N | 80.07 W |
| Juqueri ≃ | **256** | 23.24 S | 46.52 W |
| Juqueri, Reservatório do ⊜[1] | **256** | 23.20 S | 46.38 W |
| Juqueriquerê, Serra do ⋀ | **256** | 23.43 S | 45.37 W |
| Juquiá | **252** | 24.19 S | 47.38 W |
| Juquiá ≃ | **256** | 23.56 S | 47.09 W |
| Juquiá, Ponta do › | **252** | 24.25 S | 47.00 W |
| Juquiá-guaçu ≃ | **256** | 24.00 S | 47.16 W |
| Juquitiba | **256** | 23.57 S | 47.03 W |
| Jur | **74** | 59.52 N | 137.39 E |
| Jur ≃ | **140** | 8.39 N | 29.18 E |
| Jura | **38** | 47.31 N | 29.04 E |
| Jura □[3] | **58** | 47.20 N | 7.15 E |
| Jura □[5] | **58** | 46.50 N | 5.50 E |
| Jura ⋀ | **58** | 46.45 N | 6.30 E |
| Jura I | **46** | 56.00 N | 5.50 W |
| Jūra ≃ | **76** | 55.03 N | 22.09 E |
| Jura, Sound of U | **46** | 55.57 N | 5.48 W |
| Juraciški | **76** | 54.02 N | 25.54 E |
| Juramento | **255** | 16.50 S | 43.35 W |
| Jurayrah, Jabal al- ∧ | **128** | 24.06 N | 39.16 E |
| Jurays wa ʿIzbatuhā | **142** | 30.19 N | 30.55 E |
| Jurbarkas | **76** | 55.05 N | 22.48 E |
| Jurcevo | **76** | 60.02 N | 32.36 E |
| Juréia | **256** | 21.17 S | 46.22 W |
| Jurenino | **76** | 59.24 N | 42.47 E |
| Jurf ad-Darāwīsh | **132** | 30.42 N | 35.52 E |
| Jurga | **86** | 55.42 N | 84.51 E |
| Jurgamyš | **86** | 55.21 N | 64.28 E |
| Jurgenson Woods ♦ | **278** | 41.34 N | 87.36 W |
| Jurien | **162** | 30.19 S | 115.02 E |
| Juriesfontein | **158** | 31.40 S | 22.08 E |
| Juring | **164** | 6.26 S | 134.20 E |
| Jurino | **80** | 56.18 N | 46.18 E |
| Jurja | **24** | 59.03 N | 49.14 E |
| Jurjev → Tartu | **76** | 58.23 N | 26.43 E |
| Jurjevec | **80** | 57.18 N | 43.06 E |
| Jurjev-Pol'skij | **80** | 56.30 N | 39.41 E |
| Jurjevskoje | **82** | 55.05 N | 36.13 E |
| Jurla | **86** | 59.17 N | 54.19 E |
| Jurlovo, Ross. | **82** | 55.54 N | 37.16 E |
| Jurlovo, Ross. | **82** | 55.19 N | 35.52 E |
| Jūrmala | **76** | 56.58 N | 23.42 E |
| Jurong, Sing. | **271c** | 1.19 N | 103.43 E |
| Jurong, Zhg. | **106** | 31.57 N | 119.10 E |
| Jurong ≃ | **271c** | 1.18 N | 103.44 E |
| Jurong, Selat U | **271c** | 1.18 N | 103.42 E |
| Jurovo, Ross. | **80** | 57.30 N | 43.50 E |
| Jurovo, Ross. | **82** | 55.30 N | 38.22 E |
| Jurovskoje | **86** | 59.29 N | 69.02 E |
| Jursla | **40** | 58.40 N | 16.11 E |
| Jurty | **88** | 56.03 N | 97.37 E |
| Juruá | **246** | 3.27 S | 66.03 W |
| Juruá ≃ | **242** | 2.37 S | 65.44 W |
| Juruaia | **256** | 21.15 S | 46.35 W |
| Juruá-mirim ≃ | **248** | 8.08 S | 72.48 W |
| Juruena ≃ | **248** | 7.20 S | 58.03 W |
| Jurujuba, Enseada de ⊂ | **287a** | 22.56 S | 43.07 W |
| Jurumirim, Represa ⊜[1] | **255** | 23.20 S | 49.15 W |
| Jurumkuvejem ≃ | **180** | 66.14 N | 173.35 E |
| Jurupari ≃ | **248** | 7.45 S | 70.10 W |
| Jurupari, Arquipélago II | **250** | 0.07 N | 50.30 W |
| Jurupari, Ilha de I | **250** | 0.20 N | 50.07 W |
| Juruti | **250** | 2.09 S | 56.04 W |
| Jur'uzan' | **86** | 54.52 N | 58.26 E |
| Jur'uzan' ≃ | **86** | 55.42 N | 57.00 E |
| Jurva | **26** | 62.41 N | 21.59 E |
| Jušala | **86** | 57.04 N | 64.17 E |
| Juscelândia | **255** | 15.20 S | 51.19 W |
| Jusepín | **246** | 9.45 N | 63.31 W |
| Jushiguan | **102** | 24.47 N | 97.38 E |
| Jūshiyama | **94** | 35.06 N | 136.46 E |
| Juskatla | **182** | 53.37 N | 132.18 W |
| Jus'ki | **80** | 56.39 N | 53.05 E |
| Juškovo | **76** | 59.46 N | 45.11 E |
| Juškozero | **24** | 64.44 N | 32.06 E |
| Jūsō •[8] | **270** | 34.43 N | 135.28 E |
| Jussey | **58** | 47.49 N | 5.54 E |
| Justa | **80** | 47.07 N | 46.18 E |
| Justice | **278** | 41.44 N | 87.50 W |
| Justin | **222** | 33.05 N | 97.18 W |
| Justineberg ∧[2] | **40** | 58.43 N | 15.04 E |
| Justiniano Posse | **252** | 32.53 S | 62.40 W |
| Justo Daract | **252** | 33.52 S | 65.11 W |
| Justus | **214** | 40.42 N | 81.35 W |
| Jušut ≃ | **80** | 56.12 N | 48.23 E |
| Jus'va | **24** | 58.56 N | 54.57 E |
| Jutaí | **248** | 5.11 S | 68.54 W |
| Jutaí ≃ | **242** | 2.43 S | 66.57 W |
| Jutaza | **80** | 54.35 N | 53.16 E |
| Jütchendorf | **264a** | 52.16 N | 13.10 E |
| Jüterbog | **54** | 51.59 N | 13.04 E |
| Juththah, Jabal al- ∧ | **132** | 30.12 N | 35.36 E |
| Juti | **255** | 22.52 S | 54.37 W |
| Jutiapa | **236** | 14.17 N | 89.54 W |
| Jutiapa □[5] | **236** | 14.10 N | 89.50 W |
| Juticalpa | **236** | 14.42 N | 86.15 W |
| Jutiquile | **236** | 14.45 N | 86.08 W |
| Jutland → Jylland •[1] | **26** | 56.00 N | 9.15 E |
| Jutogh | **123** | 31.06 N | 77.07 E |
| Jutrosin | **30** | 51.40 N | 17.10 E |
| Juupajoki | **26** | 61.47 N | 24.27 E |
| Juuru | **76** | 59.04 N | 24.59 E |
| Juva | **26** | 61.54 N | 27.51 E |
| Juventud, Isla de la (Isla de Pinos) I | **240p** | 21.40 N | 82.50 W |
| Juvisy-sur-Orge | **50** | 48.41 N | 2.23 E |
| Juvuln ⊜ | **26** | 63.43 N | 13.09 E |
| Juwana | **115a** | 6.42 S | 111.09 E |
| Juwangi | **115a** | 7.10 S | 110.45 E |
| Juxi | **100** | 27.30 N | 119.08 E |
| Juxian | **98** | 35.37 N | 118.54 E |
| Juxing | **106** | 31.56 N | 121.33 E |
| Juyanhai → Gaxun Nur ⊜ | **102** | 42.22 N | 100.34 E |
| Juye | **98** | 35.23 N | 116.06 E |
| Jūyom | **128** | 28.34 N | 53.56 E |
| Juyongguan | **105** | 40.18 N | 116.04 E |
| Juža | **80** | 56.35 N | 42.01 E |
| Juzennecourt | **58** | 48.11 N | 4.59 E |
| Juzi ≃ | **98** | 40.18 N | 123.35 E |
| Juziers | **261** | 49.00 N | 1.51 E |
| Južna Morava ≃ | **38** | 43.41 N | 21.24 E |
| Južno-Aleksandrovka | **88** | 55.51 N | 96.10 E |
| Južno-Aličurskij chrebet ⋀ | **120** | 37.30 N | 73.20 E |
| Južno-Golodnostepskij kanal ≊ | **85** | 40.15 N | 69.08 E |
| Južno-Jenisejskij | **86** | 58.48 N | 94.39 E |
| Južno-Kazachstan □[4] | **85** | 42.30 N | 68.30 E |
| Južno-Mujskij chrebet ⋀ | **88** | 55.40 N | 114.00 E |
| Južno-Sachalinsk | **89** | 46.58 N | 142.42 E |
| Južno-Suchokumsk | **84** | 44.37 N | 45.34 E |
| Južno-Ural'sk | **86** | 54.26 N | 61.15 E |
| Južnyj, Kaz. | **86** | 49.21 N | 73.01 E |
| Južnyj, Ross. | **80** | 56.08 N | 44.09 E |
| Južnyj, Ross. | **80** | 47.20 N | 41.51 E |
| Južnyj, Ross. | **86** | 53.14 N | 83.42 E |
| Južnyj, Ross. | **86** | 53.33 N | 60.02 E |
| Južnyj, mys › | **74** | 57.45 N | 156.45 E |
| Južnyj-Alamyšik | **85** | 40.46 N | 72.38 E |
| Južnyj Prijut | **84** | 43.12 N | 41.55 E |
| Južnyj Ural ⋀ | **86** | 54.00 N | 58.30 E |
| Juzovka → Donets'k | **83** | 48.00 N | 37.48 E |
| Jwālahari •[8] | **272a** | 28.40 N | 77.06 E |
| Jwayyā | **132** | 33.14 N | 35.19 E |
| Jyderup | **41** | 55.40 N | 11.26 E |
| Jylland (Jutland) •[1] | **26** | 56.00 N | 9.15 E |
| Jyllinge | **41** | 55.45 N | 12.07 E |
| Jyväskylä | **26** | 62.14 N | 25.44 E |
| **K** | | | |
| K2 (Qogir Feng) ∧ | **123** | 35.53 N | 76.30 E |
| Ka ≃ | **150** | 11.40 N | 4.10 E |
| Kaaawa | **229c** | 21.33 N | 157.51 W |
| Kaabong | **154** | 3.31 N | 34.08 E |
| Kaachka | **128** | 37.21 N | 59.36 E |
| Kaala ∧ | **229c** | 21.31 N | 158.09 W |
| Kaalaea | **229c** | 21.28 N | 157.51 W |
| Kaala-Gomén | **175f** | 20.40 S | 164.25 E |
| Kaalspruit | **158** | 29.15 S | 26.10 E |
| Kaapahu Bay ⊂ | **229a** | 20.39 N | 156.05 W |
| Kaapmuiden | **156** | 25.33 S | 31.20 E |
| Kaappunt › | **158** | 34.21 S | 18.30 E |
| Kaapstad → Cape Town | **158** | 33.55 S | 18.22 E |
| Kaarli | **76** | 59.24 N | 26.27 E |
| Kaarssen | **54** | 53.12 N | 11.02 E |
| Kaarst | **56** | 51.14 N | 6.37 E |
| Kaaterskill Creek ≃ | **210** | 42.13 N | 73.53 W |
| Kaatoan, Mount ∧ | **116** | 8.07 N | 124.55 E |
| Kaatsheuvel | **52** | 51.40 N | 5.02 E |
| Kaavi | **26** | 62.59 N | 28.30 E |
| Kaba | **150** | 10.09 N | 11.40 W |
| Kaba ≃ | **86** | 47.53 N | 86.12 E |
| Kaba, Goulbin V | **150** | 13.42 N | 6.19 E |
| Kabacan | **116** | 7.08 N | 124.49 E |
| Kabacan ≃ | **116** | 7.08 N | 124.50 E |
| Kabadak | **126** | 22.13 N | 89.19 E |
| Kabadak ≃[1] | **126** | 22.13 N | 89.18 E |
| Kabadüz | **130** | 40.53 N | 37.56 E |
| Kabaena, Pulau I | **112** | 5.15 S | 121.55 E |
| Kabaena, Selat U | **112** | 5.00 S | 122.00 E |
| Kabah ⊥ | **232** | 20.07 N | 89.29 W |
| Kabala | **150** | 9.35 N | 11.33 W |
| Kabale | **154** | 1.15 S | 29.59 E |
| Kabalebo ≃ | **250** | 5.02 N | 57.21 W |
| Kabalega Falls L | **154** | 2.17 N | 31.41 E |
| Kabalega Falls National Park ♦ | **154** | 2.15 N | 31.50 E |
| Kabali, Indon. | **112** | 1.42 S | 121.54 E |
| Kabalı, Tür. | **130** | 41.52 N | 35.05 E |
| Kabalo | **154** | 6.03 S | 26.55 E |
| Kabambare | **154** | 4.42 S | 27.43 E |
| Kaban' | **86** | 54.39 N | 66.28 E |
| Kabanbaj | **86** | 45.50 N | 80.35 E |
| Kabangu Kuta | **154** | 14.00 S | 24.03 E |
| Kabanjahe | **114** | 3.06 N | 98.30 E |
| Kabankalan | **116** | 9.59 N | 122.49 E |
| Kabanovka | **80** | 53.39 N | 51.18 E |
| Kabanovo | **86** | 55.20 N | 70.52 E |
| Kabansk | **88** | 52.03 N | 106.39 E |
| Kabardinka | **78** | 44.39 N | 37.57 E |
| Kabardino-Balkarija □[3], Ross. | **72** | 43.30 N | 43.30 E |
| Kabardino-Balkarija □[3], Ross. | **84** | 43.30 N | 43.30 E |
| Kabasalan | **116** | 7.48 N | 122.45 E |
| Kabayan | **116** | 16.37 N | 120.51 E |
| Kabba | **150** | 7.50 N | 6.03 E |
| Kabbani ≃ | **122** | 12.13 N | 76.54 E |
| Kåbdalis | **24** | 66.10 N | 20.00 E |
| Kabd aṣ-Ṣārim •[1] | **130** | 34.34 N | 39.33 E |
| Kabd Warqah •[1] | **130** | 34.20 N | 39.37 E |
| Kabel •[8] | **263** | 51.24 N | 7.29 E |
| Kabenung Lake ⊜ | **190** | 48.16 N | 85.00 W |
| Kabetogama Lake ⊜ | **190** | 48.28 N | 92.59 W |
| Kabeya | **154** | 5.40 S | 27.58 E |
| Kab-hegy ∧ | **30** | 47.03 N | 17.39 E |
| Kabia ≃ | **146** | 9.54 N | 15.10 E |
| Kabid, Wādī V | **132** | 30.08 N | 36.31 E |
| Kabinakagami Lake ⊜ | **190** | 48.54 N | 84.25 W |
| Kabin Buri | **110** | 13.59 N | 101.43 E |
| Kabinda | **152** | 6.08 S | 24.29 E |
| Kabinu | **112** | 4.00 N | 116.05 E |
| Kabir | **112** | 8.17 S | 124.13 E |
| Kabira | **175d** | 24.27 N | 124.08 E |
| Kabīr Kili | **123** | 33.11 N | 71.19 E |
| Kabīr Kūh ⋀ | **128** | 33.25 N | 46.45 E |
| Kabīrwāla | **123** | 30.24 N | 71.52 E |
| Kabkābīyah | **140** | 13.39 N | 24.05 E |
| Kablow | **264a** | 52.18 N | 13.44 E |
| Kablower Ziegelei | **264a** | 52.19 N | 13.43 E |
| Kablukovo, Ross. | **82** | 56.50 N | 36.12 E |
| Kablukovo, Ross. | **82** | 56.02 N | 38.10 E |
| Kablumgu, Cape › | **164** | 6.20 S | 150.00 E |
| Kabna | **140** | 19.10 N | 32.41 E |
| Kabo | **152** | 7.39 N | 18.37 E |
| Kabobo | **154** | 5.07 S | 29.03 E |
| Kaboe ≃ | **158** | 28.55 S | 19.17 E |
| Kābol | **120** | 34.31 N | 69.12 E |
| Kābol □[4] | **120** | 34.30 N | 69.15 E |
| Kābol ≃ | **120** | 33.55 N | 72.14 E |
| Kabompo | **154** | 13.36 S | 24.12 E |
| Kabompo ≃ | **138** | 14.10 S | 23.11 E |
| Kabondo-Dianda | **154** | 8.53 S | 25.40 E |
| Kabongo, Zaïre | **154** | 7.19 S | 25.35 E |
| Kabongo, Zaïre | **154** | 8.43 S | 28.11 E |
| Kabongo-Lunda, Chutes L | **152** | 7.34 S | 17.17 E |
| Kaboro | **152** | 6.59 N | 17.33 E |
| Kabot | **150** | 10.48 N | 14.57 W |
| Kabotshome | **154** | 3.46 S | 26.54 E |
| Kabou, Centraf. | **152** | 5.20 N | 21.43 E |
| Kabou, Togo | **150** | 9.27 N | 0.49 E |
| Kaboudia, Rass › | **148** | 35.14 N | 11.10 E |
| Kaboul → Kābol | **120** | 34.31 N | 69.12 E |
| Kabr | **140** | 10.54 N | 26.50 E |
| Kabri | **132** | 33.01 N | 35.09 E |
| Kabūdarāhang | **128** | 35.12 N | 48.44 E |
| Kabūd Gonbad | **128** | 37.00 N | 59.45 E |
| Kābul → Kābol | **120** | 34.30 N | 69.11 E |
| Kabunda | **154** | 12.25 S | 29.22 E |
| Kabunga | **154** | 1.42 S | 28.08 E |
| Kabura ≃ | **94** | 36.17 N | 139.04 E |
| Kaburuang, Pulau I | **108** | 3.48 N | 126.48 E |
| Kabūshīyah | **140** | 16.53 N | 33.42 E |
| Kabwanga | **152** | 7.01 S | 22.37 E |
| Kabwe (Broken Hill) | **154** | 14.27 S | 28.27 E |
| Kabwe-Katanda | **152** | 7.59 S | 24.29 E |
| Kabychivka | **83** | 49.28 N | 39.45 E |
| Kabylie •[1] | **34** | 36.30 N | 4.30 E |
| Kačalinskaja | **80** | 49.07 N | 44.03 E |
| Kačanik | **38** | 42.13 N | 21.14 E |
| Kačanovo | **76** | 57.28 N | 27.46 E |
| Kacbachskij | **86** | 52.58 N | 59.40 E |
| Kačerginė | **76** | 54.56 N | 23.44 E |
| Kacha | **78** | 44.47 N | 33.32 E |
| Kacha ≃[1] | **126** | 22.23 N | 89.54 E |
| Kachagalau ∧ | **154** | 2.19 N | 35.03 E |
| Kach'ang-ni | **98** | 38.24 N | 126.11 E |
| Kachati | **84** | 42.30 N | 41.46 E |
| Kachchh, Gulf of ⊂ | **120** | 22.36 N | 69.30 E |
| Kachemak Bay ⊂ | **180** | 59.35 N | 151.30 W |
| Kachess Lake ⊜[1] | **224** | 47.20 N | 121.14 W |
| Kachhwa | **124** | 25.13 N | 82.43 E |
| Kachia | **150** | 9.53 N | 7.58 E |


**Symbols** in the index entries represent the broad categories identified in the key at the right. Symbols with superior numbers (⋀[1]) identify subcategories (see complete key on page *I · 1).*

**Symbole** im Register stellen die rechts im Schlüssel erklärten Kategorien dar. Symbole mit hochgestellten Ziffern (⋀[1]) bezeichnen Unterabteilungen einer Kategorie (vgl. vollständiger Schlüssel auf Seite *I · 1).*

**Los símbolos** incluídos en el texto del índice representan las grandes categorías identificadas con la clave a la derecha. Los símbolos con numeros en su parte superior (⋀[1]) identifican las subcategorías (véase la clave completa en la página *I · 1).*

**Les symboles** de l'index représentent les catégories indiquées dans la légende à droite. Les symboles suivis d'un indice (⋀[1]) représentent des sous-catégories (voir légende complète à la page *I · 1).*

**Os símbolos** incluídos no texto do índice representam as grandes categorias identificadas com a chave à direita. Os símbolos com números em sua parte superior (⋀[1]) identificam as subcategorias (veja-se a chave completa à página *I · 1).*

| | | | | |
|---|---|---|---|---|
| ∧ Mountain | Berg | Montaña | Montagne | Montanha |
| ⋀ Mountains | Gebirge | Montañas | Montagnes | Montanhas |
| )( Pass | Paß | Paso | Col | Passo |
| V Valley, Canyon | Tal, Cañon | Valle, Cañón | Vallée, Canyon | Vale, Canhão |
| ≚ Plain | Ebene | Llano | Plaine | Planície |
| › Cape | Kap | Cabo | Cap | Cabo |
| I Island | Insel | Isla | Île | Ilha |
| II Islands | Inseln | Islas | Îles | Ilhas |
| ± Other Topographic Features | Andere Topographische Objekte | Otros Elementos Topográficos | Autres données topographiques | Outros acidentes topográficos |

Kachib 84 42.25 N 46.36 E
Kachin □³ 102 26.00 N 97.30 E
Kach'i-ri 98 34.27 N 126.08 E
Kachisi 144 9.39 N 37.50 E
Kachkarivka 78 47.06 N 33.44 E
Kachowka-Stausee
— Kakhovs'ke vodoskhovyshche ⊚¹ 78 47.25 N 34.10 E
K'achta 88 50.26 N 106.25 E
Kachua, Bngl. 126 22.39 N 89.53 E
Kachua, Bngl. 126 23.21 N 90.54 E
Kačiry 86 53.05 N 76.07 E
Kačkanar 86 58.42 N 59.38 E
Kačkanar, gora ∧ 86 58.47 N 59.23 E
Kaçkar Dağı ∧ 130 40.50 N 41.10 E
Kačug 88 53.58 N 105.52 E
Kada ≃ 88 55.03 N 102.04 E
Kadada ≃ 80 53.09 N 46.01 E
Kadaingti 110 17.37 N 97.32 E
Kadaiyanallūr 122 9.05 N 77.21 E
Kadamatt Island I 122 11.14 N 72.47 E
Kadaň 54 50.20 N 13.15 E
Kadanai (Kadaney) ≃ 120 31.02 N 66.09 E
Kadaney (Kadanai) ≃ 120 31.02 N 66.09 E
Kadan Kyun I 110 12.30 N 98.22 E
Kadapongan, Pulau I 112 4.43 S 115.44 E
Kadassa ≃ 115b 9.24 S 120.02 E
Kaddam ⊚¹ 122 19.07 N 78.46 E
Kade 150 6.05 N 0.50 W
Kadéï ≃ 152 3.31 N 16.05 E
Kadena 174m 26.22 N 127.45 E
Kadena Airfield ✈ 174m 26.22 N 127.45 E
Kadeshiki 80 58.08 N 49.11 E
Kadetrenden (Kadet Rinne) ␥ 41 54.30 N 12.15 E
Kadet Rinne (Kadetrenden) ␥ 41 54.30 N 12.15 E
Kadgo, Lake ⊚ 162 26.42 S 127.18 E
Kadī 120 23.18 N 72.20 E
Kadiana 150 10.45 N 6.30 W
Kadıköy 130 40.46 N 26.46 E
Kadina 168b 33.58 S 137.43 E
Kadingir 110 18.19 N 104.00 E
Kadınhanı 130 38.15 N 32.14 E
Kadiolo 150 10.33 N 5.46 W
Kadipaten 115a 6.46 S 108.10 E
Kādīpur 124 26.10 N 82.23 E
Kadiri 122 14.07 N 78.10 E
Kadirli 130 37.23 N 36.05 E
Kadışehri 130 40.00 N 35.49 E
Kadiyevka
— Stakhanov 83 48.34 N 38.40 E
Kadja, Ouadi (Wādī Kaja) V 146 12.02 N 22.28 E
Kadkan 128 35.35 N 58.50 E
Kadnikov 76 59.30 N 40.20 E
Kadnikovskij 76 60.19 N 40.15 E
Kado 150 7.39 N 9.44 E
Ka-do I 98 39.33 N 124.40 E
Kadodo 140 11.04 N 29.31 E
Kadogawa 92 32.28 N 131.39 E
Kadoka 198 43.50 N 101.30 W
Kadom 80 54.34 N 42.30 E
Kadoma, Nihon 270 34.44 N 135.35 E
Kadoma, Zimb. 154 18.21 S 29.55 E
Kadoškino 80 54.01 N 44.25 E
Kadov 60 49.24 N 13.47 E
Kaduj 76 59.12 N 37.09 E
Kadumbul ≃ 115b 9.42 S 120.32 E
Kaduna 150 10.33 N 7.27 E
Kaduna ≃ 150 8.45 N 5.45 E
Kāduqlī 140 11.01 N 29.43 E
Kadūr 122 13.34 N 76.01 E
Kadyj 80 57.47 N 43.11 E
Kadykčan 74 63.02 N 146.50 E
Kadyšovo 80 54.20 N 46.45 E
Kadžerom 24 64.41 N 55.54 E
Kadži-Saj 85 42.08 N 77.10 E
Kaech'ŏn 98 39.42 N 125.53 E
Kaédi 150 16.09 N 13.30 W
Kaedo-ri 98 34.35 N 127.39 E
Kaegudeck Lake ⊚ 186 48.07 N 55.11 W
Kaélé 146 10.07 N 14.27 E
Kaena Point ▸ 229c 21.35 N 158.17 W
Kaeo 172 35.06 S 173.47 E
Kaesŏng 98 37.59 N 126.33 E
Kāf 128 31.24 N 37.24 E
Kafakumba 152 9.41 S 23.44 E
Kafan 84 39.13 N 46.24 E
Kafanchan 150 9.36 N 8.17 E
Kaffraria □⁹ 158 31.30 S 28.30 E
Kaffrine 150 14.06 N 15.33 W
Kafia Kingi 140 9.16 N 24.25 E
Kafin 150 9.30 N 7.04 E
Kafinda 154 12.39 S 30.20 E
Kafin Madaki 150 10.41 N 9.46 E
Kafirévs, Ákra ▸ 38 38.09 N 24.36 E
Kafirnigan ≃ 120 36.58 N 68.02 E
Kafo ≃ 154 1.08 N 31.05 E
Kafr ad-Dawwār 142 31.08 N 30.07 E
Kafr ad-Difrāwī 142 31.03 N 30.40 E
Kafr al-'Āʼid 142 30.27 N 31.35 E
Kafr al-Baṭṭīkh 142 31.24 N 31.44 E
Kafr al-Jarā'idah 142 31.13 N 31.16 E
Kafr ash-Shaykh 142 31.07 N 30.56 E
Kafr ash-Shaykh □⁴ 142 31.15 N 30.50 E
Kafrat Ṭā'iī Mūsā 142 30.53 N 29.44 E
Kafr at-Tamīmī 142 30.37 N 31.21 E
Kafr az-Zayyāt 142 30.49 N 30.49 E
Kafr Diyamā 142 30.48 N 30.52 E
Kafr el-Zaiyat
— Kafr az-Zayyāt 142 30.49 N 30.49 E
Kafr Hakīm 273c 30.05 N 31.07 E
Kafr Hūnah 132 33.29 N 35.35 E
Kafr Kanna 132 32.45 N 35.20 E
Kafr Kilā al-Bāb 142 30.41 N 31.09 E
Kafr Nabrakh 132 33.42 N 35.38 E
Kafr Naffākh 132 33.04 N 35.44 E
Kafr Nāsij 132 33.09 N 36.03 E
Kafr Rabī' 142 30.42 N 30.50 E
Kafr Sa'd 142 31.19 N 31.39 E
Kafr Salīm 142 31.09 N 30.06 E
Kafr Saqr 142 30.48 N 31.37 E
Kafr Shanawān 142 30.30 N 31.01 E
Kafr Shibīn 142 30.18 N 31.18 E
Kafr Shīmā 132 33.49 N 35.32 E
Kafr Shukr 142 30.33 N 31.16 E
Kafr Sūsah 132 33.29 N 36.18 E
Kafr Takhārīm 130 36.07 N 36.31 E
Kafr Tarkhān al-Gharbī 142 29.29 N 31.13 E
Kafr Yasif 132 32.57 N 35.10 E
Kafue 154 15.47 S 28.11 E
Kafue ≃ 154 15.56 S 28.55 E
Kafue Flats ≋ 154 15.40 S 27.25 E
Kafue Gorge V 154 15.54 S 28.34 E
Kafue National Park ♦ 154 15.00 S 25.45 E
Kafulwe Mission 154 9.00 S 29.02 E
Kafumba 152 5.23 S 18.55 E
Kafwira 154 12.10 S 27.33 E
Kaga 94 36.18 N 136.18 E
Kaga Bandoro 152 6.59 N 19.11 E
Kagalaska Island I 180 51.47 N 176.23 W
Kagal'nickaja 83 46.53 N 40.09 E
Kagal'nik 83 47.05 N 39.19 E
Kagal'nik ≃ 83 47.04 N 39.18 E
Kagami 96 33.37 N 133.26 E
Kagamigahara 94 35.24 N 136.54 E
Kagamil Island I 180 53.00 N 169.43 W
Kagamino 96 35.05 N 133.56 E
Kāgān, Pāk. 123 34.47 N 73.32 E
Kagan, Uzb. 128 39.43 N 64.33 E
Kagan Valley V 123 34.25 N 73.17 E
Kagarko 150 9.29 N 7.41 E
Kagawa 96 34.15 N 134.02 E
Kagawa □⁵ 96 34.15 N 134.00 E
Kagawong, Lake ⊚ 190 45.49 N 82.18 W
Kagaznagar 122 19.18 N 79.50 E
Kåge 26 64.50 N 20.59 E
Kagelike 120 37.20 N 67.02 E
Kagera (Akagera) ≃ 154 0.57 S 31.47 E
Kågeröd 41 56.01 N 13.06 E
Kåghet ◆¹ 148 24.00 N 7.30 W
Kāgithane ◆⁸ 267b 41.04 N 28.58 E
Kagitumba 154 1.04 S 30.27 E
Kağızman 84 40.09 N 43.08 E
Kāglan ⁂² 40 59.23 N 15.31 E
Kagmar 140 14.24 N 30.25 E
Kagopal 146 8.17 N 16.27 E
Kagoshima 92 31.36 N 130.33 E
Kagoshima □⁵ 93b 29.00 N 129.30 E
Kagoshima-wan c 92 31.25 N 130.38 E
Kagran ◆⁸ 264b 48.15 N 16.27 E
Kagulu 154 1.15 N 33.18 E
Kagyo-ri 98 34.25 N 126.48 E
Kahaliya, Jabal ∧ 142 29.55 N 32.09 E
Kahaluu 229c 21.27 N 157.50 W
Kahama 154 3.50 S 32.36 E
Kahana Bay c 229c 21.34 N 157.52 W
Kahanavičy 76 55.52 N 28.08 E
Kaharlyk 78 49.51 N 30.50 E
Kahayan ≃ 112 3.20 S 114.04 E
Kahe 154 3.30 S 37.26 E
Kahemba 152 7.17 S 19.00 E
Kahia 154 6.21 S 28.24 E
Kahiu Point ▸ 229a 21.13 N 156.58 W
Kahk 142 29.25 N 30.58 E
Kahl ≃ 56 50.04 N 9.00 E
Kahla 54 50.48 N 11.35 E
Kahl am Main 56 50.04 N 9.00 E
Kahlenberg ∧² 264b 48.16 N 16.21 E
Kahler Asten ∧ 56 51.11 N 8.29 E
Kahlersberg ∧ 64 47.32 N 13.02 E
Kāhna 123 31.22 N 74.22 E
Kahnūj 128 27.58 N 57.45 E
Kahoka 194 40.25 N 91.43 W
Kahoku, Nihon 96 33.39 N 133.47 E
Kahoku, Nihon 96 33.06 N 130.41 E
Kahoku-gata ⊚ 94 36.40 N 136.41 E
Kahoolawe I 229a 20.33 N 156.37 W
Kahouanne, Îlet à I 241o 16.22 N 61.47 W
Kahoué, Mont ∧ 150 7.06 N 7.15 W
Kahramanmaraş 130 37.36 N 36.55 E
Kahraman Maraş □⁴ 130 38.00 N 37.05 E
Kahror Pakka 123 29.37 N 71.55 E
Kahshe Lake ⊚ 212 44.52 N 79.16 W
Kâhta 130 37.46 N 38.36 E
Kahuku 229c 21.40 N 157.57 W
Kahuku Point ▸ 229c 21.43 N 157.59 W
Kahului 229a 20.54 N 156.28 W
Kahului Airport ✈ 229a 20.54 N 156.26 W
Kahului Bay c 229a 20.54 N 156.28 W
Kahurangi Point ▸ 172 40.47 S 172.13 E
Kahūta 123 33.35 N 73.23 E
Kahuzi-Biega, Parc National de ♦ 154 1.50 N 28.40 E
Kahyŏn-bong ∧ 271b 37.38 N 126.39 E
Kahyŏn-ni 271b 37.32 N 126.44 E
Kai 164 2.15 S 136.32 E
Kai, Kepulauan II 164 5.35 S 132.45 E
Kai, Tanjung ▸ 112 2.52 S 118.45 E
Kaia, Wādī V 140 11.31 N 24.15 E
Kaiai, Jabal ∧ 140 19.54 N 36.48 E
Kaiama 150 9.37 N 3.58 E
Kaiapit 164 6.15 S 146.15 E
Kaiapoi 172 43.23 S 172.40 E
Kaibab Indian Reservation ◆⁴ 200 36.55 N 112.40 W
Kaibab Plateau ⁂¹ 200 36.30 N 112.15 W
Kaibara 96 35.08 N 135.05 E
Kai Beab 164 7.29 S 139.40 E
Kaibing 61 47.12 N 15.50 E
Kaibito Plateau ⁂¹ 200 36.40 N 111.20 W
Kaichengqiao 100 31.18 N 117.44 E
Kaida 94 35.56 N 137.36 E
Kaidori 268 35.37 N 139.27 E
Kaidu ≃ 90 41.55 N 86.38 E
Kaiedin 140 9.45 N 32.11 E
Kaieteur Fall ␣ 246 5.10 N 59.28 W
Kaieteur National Park ♦ 246 5.10 N 59.45 W
Kaifeng 98 34.51 N 114.21 E
Kaifu 96 33.35 N 134.21 E
Kaifu ≃ 96 33.35 N 134.22 E
Kaihe 98 35.42 N 116.20 E
Kaihu 172 35.46 S 173.42 E
Kaihua 100 29.09 N 118.23 E
Kai Iwi 172 39.51 S 174.56 E
Kaijian 102 29.42 N 111.48 E
Kaijiang 102 31.05 N 107.55 E
Kaijo
— Kaesŏng 98 37.59 N 126.33 E
Kai Kecil I 164 5.45 S 132.40 E
Kaikohe 172 35.25 S 173.48 E
Kaikoura 172 42.25 S 173.41 E
Kaikoura Peninsula ⁂¹ 172 42.26 S 173.42 E
Kaikukang 89 53.07 N 124.46 E
Kailahun 150 8.17 N 10.34 W
Kailas
— Kangrinboqê Feng ∧ 120 31.04 N 81.18 E
Kailāshahar 120 24.20 N 92.01 E
Kaili 102 26.35 N 107.55 E
Kailu 89 43.36 N 121.14 E
Kailua 229c 21.24 N 157.44 W
Kailua Bay c 229c 21.25 N 157.44 W
Kailua Kona 229d 19.22 N 155.59 W
Kaim ≃ 164 6.40 S 141.45 E
Kaimai Range ∧ 172 37.45 S 175.55 E
Kaimaktsalán ∧ 38 40.58 N 21.48 E
Kaimana 164 3.39 S 133.45 E
Kaimanawa Mountains ∧ 172 39.15 S 175.54 E
Kaiman-Inseln
— Cayman Islands □² 238 19.30 N 80.40 W
Kaimenshan 104 41.03 N 123.08 E
Kaimganj 124 27.33 N 79.20 E
Kaimon-dake ∧ 92 31.11 N 130.32 E
Kain 50 50.38 N 3.22 E
Kaina 76 58.50 N 22.45 E
Kainab ≃ 158 28.31 S 19.35 E
Kainach ≃ 61 46.54 N 15.31 E
Kainan, Nihon 96 33.36 N 134.22 E
Kainan, Nihon 96 34.09 N 135.12 E
Kainantu 164 6.15 S 145.55 E
Kainda 85 42.50 N 73.41 E
Kai-Ndunda 152 5.42 S 12.42 E
Kaingan ≃ 115a 7.44 S 107.54 E
Kainji Lake ⊚¹ 150 10.30 N 4.35 E
Kaioba 112 5.20 S 122.37 E
Kaipara Harbour c 172 36.25 S 174.13 E
Kaiparowits Plateau ⁂¹ 200 37.20 N 111.15 W
Kaiping, Zhg. 102 22.23 N 112.35 E
Kaiping, Zhg. 105 39.41 N 118.16 E
Kaipuri, Pulau I 164 1.51 S 137.01 E
Kairābani 126 24.08 N 87.02 E
Kairaku-en ♦ 94 36.22 N 140.27 E
Kairāna 124 29.24 N 77.12 E
Kairatu 164 3.21 S 128.22 E
Kairiru Island I 164 3.20 S 143.35 E
Kairo
— Al-Qāhirah 142 30.03 N 31.15 E
Kairouan 148 35.41 N 10.07 E
Kaisarganj 124 27.15 N 81.32 E
Kaisariani 267c 37.58 N 23.47 E
Kaisariani Monastery ♥¹ 267c 37.58 N 23.47 E
Kaisergebirge ∧ 64 47.36 N 12.20 E
Kaisermühlen ◆⁸ 264b 48.14 N 16.26 E
Kaiser Pass ✕ 226 37.17 N 119.06 W
Kaiserslautern 56 50.14 N 7.08 E
Kaiserslautern 56 49.26 N 7.46 E
Kaiserstuhl ∧ 58 48.06 N 7.40 E
Kaiserswerth ◆⁸ 263 51.18 N 6.44 E
Kaiser-Wilhelm-Museum ♥ 263 51.20 N 6.34 E
Kaishantun 98 42.43 N 129.43 E
Kaisheim 56 48.46 N 10.48 E
Kaišiadorys 76 54.52 N 24.27 E
Kait, Tanjung ▸ 112 3.14 S 106.05 E
Kaita 96 34.20 N 132.32 E
Kaitaia 172 35.07 S 173.16 E
Kaitaichi-chūtonchi, Rikujō-jieitai- ▪ 96 34.21 N 132.32 E
Kai Tak Airport ✈ 271d 22.20 N 114.12 E
Kaitangata 172 46.18 S 169.51 E
Kaitersberg ⁂ 60 49.11 N 12.57 E
Kaithal 124 29.48 N 76.23 E
Kaituma ≃ 246 8.11 N 59.41 W
Kaiwaka 172 36.10 S 174.27 E
Kaiwatu 164 8.07 S 127.49 E
Kaiwi Channel ␥ 229b 21.15 N 157.30 W
Kaixian 102 31.13 N 108.25 E
Kaiyang 102 26.58 N 106.40 E
Kaiyuan, Zhg. 102 23.44 N 103.11 E
Kaiyuan, Zhg. 104 42.32 N 124.01 E
Kaiyuancheng 98 42.37 N 124.04 E
Kaiyuh Mountains ∧ 180 64.00 N 158.00 W
Kaizhou 104 41.22 N 121.19 E
Kaizu 94 35.13 N 136.38 E
Kaizuka 96 34.27 N 135.21 E
Kaja, Wādī (Ouadi Kadja) V 146 12.02 N 22.28 E
Kajaani 26 64.14 N 27.41 E
Kajabbi 166 20.02 S 140.02 E
Kajakī, Band-e ⊚¹ 128 32.22 N 65.16 E
Kajang, Indon. 112 5.20 S 120.21 E
Kajang, Malay. 114 2.59 N 101.47 E
Kajang, Gunong ∧ 114 2.46 N 104.09 E
Kajasan 86 55.12 N 62.16 E
Kajasula 84 44.19 N 44.59 E
Kajen 115a 7.02 S 109.34 E
Kajga 86 50.55 N 64.43 E
Kajiado 154 1.51 S 36.47 E
Kajikazawa 94 35.33 N 138.27 E
Kajiki 92 31.44 N 130.40 E
Kājīgarh 126 22.07 N 87.47 E
Kajmanačicha 86 53.32 N 75.11 E
Kajmonovo 88 56.50 N 104.54 E
Kajmysovy 86 59.48 N 76.31 E
Kajnar 86 49.12 N 77.25 E
Kajo Kaji 154 3.53 N 31.40 E
Kajrakkum 85 40.16 N 69.49 E
Kajrakkumskoje vodochranilišče ⊚¹ 85 40.20 N 70.10 E
Kajrakty 86 48.31 N 73.14 E
Kajsackoje 80 49.44 N 46.51 E
Kājū ≃ 128 25.34 N 61.13 E
Kajulia 126 23.01 N 89.57 E
Kajuru 150 10.21 N 7.40 E
Kaka, Centraf. 140 6.31 N 26.30 E
Kākā, Sūd. 140 10.36 N 32.11 E
Kaka, Lae c ▸ 229a 20.31 N 156.33 W
Kakabeka Falls ␣ 190 48.24 N 89.37 W
Kakabia, Pulau I 112 6.54 S 122.13 E
Kakadu National Park ♦ 164 13.00 S 132.45 E
Kakagi Lake ⊚ 184 49.13 N 93.52 W
Kakamas 158 28.45 S 20.33 E
Kakamega 154 0.17 N 34.45 E
Kakamigahara 94 35.24 N 136.54 E
Kakana 110 9.07 N 92.49 E
Kakanui Mountains ∧ 172 45.03 S 170.26 E
Kakapa Point 172 46.23 S 169.47 E
Kakaramea 172 39.43 S 174.27 E
Kakasa 164 9.20 S 148.45 E
Kakata 150 6.35 N 10.19 W
Kakatahi 172 39.41 S 175.20 E
Kakdwīp 126 21.53 N 88.11 E
Kake, Nihon 96 34.36 N 132.19 E
Kake, Ak., U.S. 180 56.58 N 133.56 W
Kakegawa 94 34.46 N 138.01 E
Kakehashi ≃ 94 36.25 N 136.25 E
Kakelwe 154 4.49 S 29.00 E
Kakenge 152 4.51 S 21.55 E
Kakerbeck 54 52.40 N 11.17 E
Kakeroma-jima I 93b 28.08 N 129.14 E
Kakeya 96 35.11 N 132.49 E
Kakhonak 180 59.26 N 154.51 W
Kakhovka 78 46.47 N 33.30 E
Kakhovs'ke vodoskhovyshche ⊚¹ 78 47.25 N 34.10 E
Kakhra 126 21.38 N 87.27 E
Kakī 128 28.19 N 51.34 E
Kākināda 122 16.56 N 82.13 E
Kakino 80 55.12 N 44.53 E
Kakinoki 96 34.26 N 131.52 E
Kakisa Lake ⊚ 176 60.55 N 117.40 W
Kakizaki 94 37.15 N 138.25 E
Kako ≃, Guy. 246 5.46 N 60.35 W
Kako ≃, Nihon 96 34.44 N 134.49 E
Kakoa 156 18.40 S 24.22 E
Kakogawa 96 34.46 N 134.51 E
Kakrāla 272a 28.33 N 77.25 E
Kāksa 126 23.28 N 87.28 E
Kaktovik 180 70.08 N 143.37 W
Kakuda 94 37.58 N 140.47 E
Kakui-shima I 96 34.43 N 134.19 E
Kakuma 154 3.43 N 34.52 E
Kakunodate 92 39.35 N 140.34 E
Kakus ≃ 112 2.46 N 113.01 E
Kakwa ≃ 182 54.36 N 118.28 W
Kala 146 12.05 N 14.27 E
Kala ≃ 122 8.18 N 79.50 E
Kalaa Kebira 148 35.52 N 10.32 E
Kalaallit Nunaat
— Greenland □² 16 70.00 N 40.00 W
Kalaa Sghira 36 35.49 N 10.33 E
Kālābāgh 123 32.58 N 71.34 E
Kalabahi 112 8.13 S 124.31 E
Kalabaka 38 39.42 N 21.43 E
Kalabakan 112 4.25 N 117.29 E
Kalabo 152 14.57 S 22.40 E
Kalabula 86 43.24 N 83.06 E
Kalabura 78 50.26 N 41.00 E
Kalačinsk 86 55.03 N 74.34 E
Kalač-Kurtlak 80 49.00 N 42.06 E
Kalač-na-Donu 80 48.43 N 43.31 E
Kalačskaja
vozvyšennost' ⁂¹ 80 50.30 N 41.30 E
Kaladan ≃ 110 20.09 N 92.57 E
Kaladar 212 44.39 N 77.07 W
Kalae 229a 21.10 N 157.00 W
Ka Lae ▸ 229d 18.55 N 155.41 W
Kalaena ≃ 112 2.43 S 120.53 E
Kalagan 89 50.30 N 119.55 E
Kalahari Desert ♦² 156 22.31 S 21.30 E
Kalahari Gemsbok National Park ♦ 156 24.00 S 21.30 E
Kalaheo 229b 21.55 N 159.31 W
Kalaia 164 8.01 S 146.14 E
Kalai-Chumb 85 38.28 N 70.46 E
Kalai-Mor 128 35.39 N 62.33 E
Kalais 80 52.38 N 42.38 E
Kalaiyā 126 27.02 N 85.00 E
Kalajoki 26 64.15 N 23.57 E
Kalajoki ≃ 26 64.17 N 23.55 E
Kalakamate 156 20.39 S 27.21 E
Kalakan 88 55.08 N 116.45 E
Kalakan ≃ 88 55.07 N 116.46 E
Kalakepen 114 2.45 N 97.50 E
Kalakh 130 36.06 N 43.23 E
Kalama, Wa., U.S. 224 46.00 N 122.50 W
Kalama, Zaïre 154 2.55 S 28.33 E
Kalama ≃ 224 46.02 N 122.52 W
Kalamáki 38 37.58 N 23.52 E
Kalamai 38 37.04 N 22.07 E
Kalámai, Pulau I 112 3.15 N 125.28 E
Kalamákion 267c 37.55 N 23.43 E
Kalamalka Lake ⊚ 182 50.09 N 119.22 W
Kalamariá 38 40.35 N 22.57 E
Kalamazoo □⁶ 216 42.14 N 85.32 W
Kalamazoo 216 42.40 N 86.10 W
Kalamazoo, North Branch ≃ 216 42.14 N 84.44 W
Kalamazoo, South Branch ≃ 216 42.14 N 84.44 W
Kalamazoo Lake c 216 42.39 N 86.13 W
Kalamb 122 19.03 N 73.57 E
Kalamba 152 0.26 S 18.17 E
Kalambau, Pulau I 112 4.55 S 115.39 E
Kalambo Falls ␣ 154 8.36 S 31.14 E
Kalamboli 272c 19.01 N 73.06 E
Kalamits'ka zatoka c 78 45.05 N 33.23 E
Kalamo 216 42.32 N 85.01 W
Kalampising 112 3.44 N 116.42 E
Kalamunda 168a 31.57 S 116.03 E
Kalamunda National Park ♦ 168a 31.59 S 116.04 E
Kalana 150 10.47 N 8.12 W
Kalanchak 78 46.16 N 33.17 E
Kalandula 152 9.06 S 15.57 E
Kalange-Bushimaie ≃ 152 7.55 S 23.11 E
Kalanguj 88 51.01 N 116.31 E
Kalankalan 150 10.07 N 8.54 W
Kalannie 162 30.21 S 117.04 E
Kalanshiyū ar-Ramlī al-Kabīr, Sarīr ♦⁸ 146 28.00 N 23.00 E
Kālānwāli 123 29.51 N 74.57 E
Kalao, Pulau I 112 7.18 S 120.58 E
Kalaong 116 6.04 N 124.28 E
Kalaotoa, Pulau I 112 7.22 S 121.47 E
Kalapana 229d 19.21 N 154.58 W
Kalāpāra 126 21.59 N 90.14 E
Kalar ≃ 88 55.23 N 116.18 E
Kalār, Kūh-e ∧ 128 31.50 N 50.53 E
Kalarne 26 62.59 N 16.05 E
Kalāroa 126 22.52 N 89.02 E
Kalasan 84 39.11 N 48.03 E
Kalasi 86 48.43 N 86.59 E
Kalasin, Indon. 112 0.12 N 114.16 E
Kalasin, Thai 110 16.29 N 103.30 E
Kalašnikovo 76 57.17 N 35.13 E
Kalāt 120 29.02 N 66.35 E
Kalatungan Mountain ∧ 116 7.58 N 124.47 E
Kalaupapa 229a 21.11 N 156.59 W
Kalaupapa National Historical Park ♦ 229a 21.12 N 156.58 W
Kalaupapa Peninsula ▸¹ 229a 21.13 N 156.58 W
Kalauri 84 41.49 N 45.42 E
Kalaus ≃ 80 45.43 N 44.07 E
Kalavárdha 38 36.20 N 27.57 E
Kalávrita 38 38.01 N 22.06 E
Kalaw 110 20.38 N 96.34 E
Kalawao □⁶ 229a 21.12 N 156.58 W
Kal'azin 76 57.15 N 37.52 E
Kalb, Nahr al- ≃ 132 33.57 N 35.35 E
Kalb, Ra's al- ▸ 144 14.02 N 48.41 E
Kalbā' 128 25.03 N 56.21 E
Kālbācār 84 40.07 N 46.02 E
Kalbar 171a 27.56 S 152.37 E
Kalbarri 162 27.42 S 114.09 E
Kalbarri National Park ♦ 162 27.45 S 114.25 E
Kalbe 54 52.40 N 11.25 E
Kalbinskij chrebet ∧ 86 49.10 N 83.00 E
Kalchās 120 29.21 N 69.42 E
Kal'chyk ≃ 83 47.07 N 37.36 E
Kaldınım ≃ 267b 41.10 N 29.12 E
Kaldygajty ≃ 80 49.20 N 52.38 E
Kale, Tür. 130 40.23 N 39.39 E
Kale, Tür. 130 37.26 N 28.51 E
Kale, Tür. 130 36.14 N 29.59 E
Kalecik, Tür. 130 40.06 N 33.25 E
Kalecik, Tür. 130 37.17 N 39.02 E
Kaleden 182 49.23 N 119.35 W
Kaledupa, Pulau I 112 5.32 S 123.47 E
Kalefeld 52 51.48 N 10.02 E
Kalegauk Island I 110 15.32 N 97.40 E
Kalehe 154 2.06 S 28.55 E
Kaleindaung ≃ 110 18.50 N 94.00 E
Kalema, Tan. 154 1.12 S 31.50 E
Kalema, Zaïre 154 4.08 S 25.44 E
Kalemie (Albertville) 154 5.56 S 29.12 E
Kalemyo 120 23.12 N 94.10 E
Kalene Hill 152 11.11 S 24.10 E
Kaleščatovka 83 49.35 N 39.55 E
Kaletwa 110 21.45 N 92.48 E
Kalety 30 50.34 N 18.54 E
Kalevala 24 65.13 N 31.09 E
Kalewa 110 23.12 N 94.18 E
Kale Water ≃ 46 55.32 N 2.28 W
Kaleybar 128 38.47 N 47.02 E
Kalfafell 24a 63.58 N 17.40 W
Kalga 88 50.57 N 118.48 E
Kalgačicha 24 63.20 N 36.44 E
Kalgan, Austl. 162 34.53 S 118.01 E
Kalgan
— Zhangjiakou, Zhg. 105 40.50 N 114.53 E
Kalgin Island I 180 60.28 N 151.55 W
Kalgoorlie-Boulder 162 30.45 S 121.28 E
Kalhe 272c 18.52 N 73.06 E
Kali 150 12.10 N 11.29 W
Kali ≃¹ 126 23.40 N 89.12 E
Kālia 126 23.03 N 89.38 E
Kāliāganj 124 25.38 N 88.19 E
Kaliakair 126 22.10 N 87.50 E
Kaliakra, nos ▸ 38 43.21 N 28.27 E
Kalianda 115a 5.45 S 105.38 E
Kalianget 115a 7.03 S 113.56 E
Kalibek, ozero ⊚ 86 53.52 N 70.40 E
Kalibrit Hills ∧² 146 13.37 N 26.47 E
Kalibo 116 11.43 N 122.22 E
Kalida 216 40.59 N 84.12 W
Kalifornien, Golf von
— California, Golfo de c 232 28.00 N 112.00 W
Kālī Gandakī ≃ 124 27.42 N 84.25 E
Kāliganga ≃ 126 23.21 N 89.38 E
Kāliganj, Bngl. 126 23.55 N 90.34 E
Kāliganj, Bngl. 126 23.25 N 89.08 E
Kāliganj, Bngl. 126 22.28 N 89.02 E
Kāliganj, India 126 22.44 N 88.14 E
Kalihiwai ≃ 229b 22.13 N 159.26 W
Kalijati 115a 6.32 S 107.40 E
Kālikāpur, Bngl. 126 22.43 N 89.26 E
Kālikāpur, Bngl. 126 23.46 N 89.04 E
Kālikāpur, India 126 22.37 N 86.17 E
Kālikāpur, India 272b 22.29 N 88.32 E
Kalikino, Ross. 76 52.57 N 39.40 E
Kalikino, Ross. 80 52.55 N 54.05 E
Kalima, Zaïre 154 2.34 S 26.37 E
Kalima, Zhg. 104 41.32 N 122.40 E
Kalimantan
— Borneo I 112 0.30 N 114.00 E
Kalimantan Barat □⁴ 112 0.30 N 110.00 E
Kalimantan Selatan □⁴ 112 2.30 S 115.30 E
Kalimantan Tengah □⁴ 112 2.00 S 113.30 E
Kalimantan Timur □⁴ 112 1.30 N 116.30 E
Kálimnos 38 36.57 N 26.59 E
Kálimnos I 38 37.00 N 27.00 E
Kālimpang 124 27.04 N 88.29 E
Kalina, Pointe de ▸ 273b 4.18 S 15.16 E
Kālīnadi ≃ 122 14.50 N 74.08 E
Kalinagar 126 22.26 N 88.51 E
Kalinga-Apayao □⁴ 116 17.50 N 121.10 E
Kalinga Bil ⊚ 272b 22.33 N 88.23 E
Kalinin, Ross. 80 47.11 N 42.18 E
Kalinin
— Tver', Ross. 82 56.52 N 35.55 E
Kalininabad 85 37.45 N 69.08 E
Kaliningrad 76 54.43 N 20.30 E
Kaliningrad (Königsberg), Ross. 82 55.55 N 37.49 E
Kaliningrad, Ross. 75 48.45 N 21.15 E
Kaliningrad Oblast' □⁴ 78 45.07 N 39.00 E
Kalinino, Ross. 78 45.07 N 39.00 E
Kalinino, Ross. 80 46.21 N 48.53 E
Kalinino, Ross. 86 57.20 N 56.20 E
Kalinino, Ross. 89 49.24 N 129.20 E
Kalininsk, Kyrg. 85 42.29 N 72.06 E
Kalininsk, Ross. 80 51.30 N 44.28 E
Kalininskaja, Ross. 78 45.29 N 38.40 E
Kalininskaja, Ross. 80 47.52 N 42.15 E
Kalinins'ke 78 47.07 N 32.59 E
Kalininskoje 85 42.50 N 73.52 E
Kalinkavičy 76 52.08 N 29.21 E
Kalinku 154 11.12 S 33.12 E
Kalinovik 38 43.31 N 18.26 E
Kalinovka, Kaz. 86 49.58 N 55.22 E
Kalinovka, Ross. 78 51.54 N 34.28 E
Kalinovo 82 54.54 N 37.17 E
Kālīpur 272b 22.41 N 88.17 E
Kaliro 154 0.54 N 33.30 E
Kalis 144 8.23 N 49.05 E
Kalisat 115a 8.08 S 113.48 E
Kalisch
— Kalisz 30 51.46 N 18.06 E
Kāli Sindh ≃ 124 25.32 N 76.17 E
Kalispell 202 48.11 N 114.18 W
Kalistratícha 86 52.59 N 83.35 E
Kalisz 30 51.46 N 18.06 E
Kalisz □⁴ 30 51.40 N 17.45 E
Kalisz Pomorski 30 53.19 N 15.54 E
Kalitva ≃ 78 48.10 N 40.46 E
Kaliua 154 5.04 S 31.48 E
Kaliveli Tank ⊚¹ 122 12.05 N 79.50 E
Kaliwiro 115a 7.27 S 109.51 E
Kaliwungu 115a 6.57 S 110.14 E
Kalix 26 65.51 N 23.08 E
Kalixälven ≃ 24 65.50 N 23.11 E
Kālka 123 30.50 N 76.56 E
Kālkāji ◆⁸ 272a 28.33 N 77.16 E
Kalkaman 86 51.58 N 76.02 E
Kalkan 130 36.15 N 29.24 E
Kalkar 52 51.44 N 6.18 E
Kalkaska 190 44.44 N 85.10 W
Kalkfeld 156 20.53 S 16.11 E
Kalkfontein 156 22.08 S 20.53 E
Kalkfonteindam ⊚¹ 158 29.30 S 25.15 E
Kalkhorst 54 53.58 N 11.02 E
Kalkim 130 39.48 N 27.13 E
Kālkini 126 23.06 N 90.16 E
Kalkmond 158 28.40 S 20.26 E
Kalkrand 156 24.03 S 17.33 E
Kalksburg ◆⁸ 264b 48.08 N 16.15 E
Kalk-See ⊚ 264a 52.26 N 13.46 E
Kalkstasie 158 30.00 S 18.55 E
Kalkum ◆⁸ 263 51.18 N 6.46 E
Kalkutta
— Calcutta 126 22.32 N 88.22 E
Kalkwerf 158 28.39 S 21.43 E
Kall 56 50.32 N 6.32 E
Kallakkurichchi 122 11.44 N 78.58 E
Kallakoopah Creek ≃ 166 27.29 S 138.15 E
Kållandsö I 26 58.40 N 13.09 E
Kallang ≃ 271c 1.19 N 103.52 E
Kallar Kahār 123 32.47 N 72.42 E
Kallaste 76 58.39 N 27.09 E
Kallavesi ⊚ 26 62.50 N 27.45 E
Kalletal 52 52.06 N 8.56 E
Källfallet 40 59.50 N 15.31 E
Källhäll 40 59.27 N 17.48 E
Kalliecahoolie Lake ⊚ 184 54.14 N 95.29 W
Kallinge 26 56.14 N 15.17 E
Kallista 274b 37.53 S 145.22 E
Kallithéa 267c 37.57 N 23.42 E
Kallmünz 60 49.09 N 11.58 E
Kallnach 58 47.01 N 7.14 E
Kallsjön ⊚ 26 63.37 N 13.00 E
Kalmakkora 44 44.03 N 76.64 E
Kalmakkyrgan ≃ 86 46.58 N 64.30 E
Kalmar 26 56.40 N 16.22 E
Kalmar Län □⁶ 26 57.20 N 16.00 E
Kalmarsund ␥ 26 56.40 N 16.25 E
Kalmit ∧ 56 49.19 N 8.05 E
Kal'mius ≃ 83 47.05 N 37.34 E
Kalmthout 50 51.23 N 4.28 E
Kalmunai 122 7.25 N 81.50 E
Kalmyckije Mysy 86 51.53 N 82.16 E
Kalmykia
— Kalmykija □³ 72 46.30 N 45.30 E
Kalmykija □³ 72 46.30 N 45.30 E
Kalmykivka, Ukr. 83 49.17 N 38.39 E
Kalmykivka, Ukr. 83 49.17 N 39.52 E
Kalmykov 80 49.01 N 42.49 E
Kalmykovo 80 49.02 N 51.52 E
Kalna 126 23.13 N 88.22 E
Kalnciems 76 56.50 N 23.37 E
Kalnibolotskaja 78 46.01 N 40.28 E
Kalničko Gorje ∧ 36 46.10 N 16.30 E
Kal'nyboloto 78 48.44 N 31.00 E
Kalo 164 10.00 S 147.45 E
Kálócfa 61 46.45 N 16.34 E
Kalocsa 30 46.32 N 18.59 E
Kalofer 38 42.37 N 24.59 E
Kalohi Channel ␥ 229a 21.00 N 156.56 W
Kaloko 154 6.47 S 25.48 E
Kalol, India 120 22.36 N 73.27 E
Kalol, India 120 23.15 N 72.29 E
Kalole 154 3.42 S 27.22 E
Kalolio 112 0.11 S 121.28 E
Kaloli Point ▸ 229d 19.38 N 154.57 W
Kalomo 154 17.02 S 26.30 E
Kalomo ≃ 154 17.57 S 26.24 E
Kalona 190 41.28 N 91.42 W
Kalonda 152 4.48 S 17.33 E
Kalone Peak ∧ 182 52.38 N 126.37 W
Kalonga 154 9.10 S 27.25 E
Kalorama 274b 37.49 S 145.23 E
Kalosa 115a 7.15 S 110.15 E
Kalø Vig c 41 56.15 N 10.25 E
Kalpáki 38 39.53 N 20.38 E
Kalpeni Island I 122 10.05 N 73.38 E
Kālpi 124 26.07 N 79.44 E
Kal Qal'eh 128 32.38 N 62.32 E
Kalri 123 31.39 N 72.33 E
Kalsdorf bei Graz 61 46.57 N 15.29 E
Kalskag 180 61.30 N 160.23 W
Kalsūbai ∧ 122 19.36 N 73.43 E
Kaltag 180 64.20 N 158.44 W
Kaltan 86 53.30 N 87.17 E
Kaltbrunn 58 47.12 N 9.02 E
Kalte Herberge ∧ 56 50.03 N 7.59 E
Kaltenberg ∧ 58 47.05 N 10.08 E
Kaltenhouse 56 48.48 N 7.50 E
Kaltenkirchen 52 53.50 N 9.58 E
Kaltenleutgeben 264b 48.07 N 16.12 E
Kaltensundheim 56 50.36 N 10.10 E
Kalter Gang ≃ 264b 48.02 N 16.25 E
Kalthof 263 51.20 N 7.40 E
Kaltohu 265a 59.58 N 30.40 E
Kal'tungo 146 9.50 N 11.19 E
Kaluga 82 54.31 N 36.16 E
Kaluga Oblast' □⁴ 76 54.30 N 35.30 E
Kalugino 82 54.59 N 37.11 E
Kalukalukuang, Pulau I 112 5.14 S 117.38 E
Kālu Khuhar 120 25.08 N 67.46 E
Kalulushi 154 12.50 S 28.03 E
Kalumba, Mount ∧ 166 31.49 S 146.22 E
Kalumburu 164 14.18 S 126.38 E
Kalumburu Aboriginal Reserve ◆⁴ 164 14.15 S 126.50 E
Kalundborg 41 55.41 N 11.06 E
Kalundborg Fjord c 41 55.41 N 11.00 E
Kalundu 272c 18.59 N 73.08 E
Kalundu, Zaïre 154 3.26 S 29.08 E
Kalundu, Zam. 154 10.16 S 28.54 E
Kalungwishi ≃ 154 9.01 S 28.57 E
Kalūr Kot 123 32.09 N 71.16 E
Kalush 78 49.03 N 24.23 E
Kałuszyn 30 52.13 N 21.49 E
Kalutara 122 6.35 N 79.58 E
Kalvåg 26 61.46 N 4.53 E
Kalvarija 76 54.24 N 23.14 E
Kälvåz 84 38.39 N 48.18 E
Kalvehave 41 55.00 N 12.10 E
Kälviä 26 63.52 N 23.26 E
Kalwa 272c 19.12 N 72.59 E
Kalwang 61 47.26 N 14.46 E
Kalwaria
Zebrzydowska 30 49.52 N 19.41 E
Kalyān 122 19.15 N 73.09 E
Kalyāndurg 122 14.33 N 77.06 E
Kalynivka, Ukr. 78 50.14 N 30.14 E
Kalynivka, Ukr. 78 49.27 N 28.32 E
Kalynove 83 48.34 N 38.31 E
Kam ≃ 146 8.15 N 11.00 E
Kama, Mya. 110 19.02 N 95.06 E
Kama, Ross. 80 56.19 N 54.06 E
Kama, Ross. 86 60.08 N 62.10 E
Kama, Zaïre 154 3.32 S 27.07 E
Kama ≃, Ross. 72 55.45 N 52.00 E
Kama ≃, Ross. 86 55.35 N 76.54 E
Kamachumu 154 1.35 S 31.37 E
Kamado-zaki ▸ 96 33.04 N 132.02 E
Kamae 92 32.48 N 131.56 E
Kamagaya 94 35.45 N 140.01 E
Kamaiki Point ▸ 229a 20.46 N 156.50 W
Kamaishi 92 39.16 N 141.53 E
Kama-iwa I 174f 24.47 N 141.17 E
Kamajai 76 55.49 N 25.30 E
Kamakou ∧ 229a 21.07 N 156.52 W
Kamakura 94 35.19 N 139.33 E
Kamakwie 150 9.30 N 12.14 W
Kamal 115a 7.10 S 112.42 E
Kamālia 123 30.44 N 72.39 E
Kamamaung 110 17.21 N 97.40 E
Kāman, India 124 27.39 N 77.16 E
Kaman, Tür. 130 39.22 N 33.44 E
Kaman ≃ 110 14.48 N 106.51 E
Kamana 154 5.59 S 24.56 E
Kamanashi ≃ 94 35.33 N 138.28 E
Kamango 154 0.39 N 29.53 E
Kamaniskeg Lake ⊚ 212 45.25 N 77.42 W
Kamanjab 156 19.35 S 14.51 E
Kamapanda 152 12.00 S 24.10 E
Kamara Forest ♦ 264c 47.26 N 19.00 E
Kamarān I 144 15.21 N 42.35 E
Kamaran, Hadjer ∧ 146 12.41 N 21.46 E
Kamarang ≃ 246 5.53 N 60.35 W
Kāmāreddi 122 18.19 N 78.21 E
Kāmārhāti 272b 22.40 N 88.22 E
Kamarik 130 39.37 N 39.18 E
Kāmārkhāli Ghāt 126 23.32 N 89.33 E
Kāmārkunda 272b 22.59 N 88.13 E
Kamaryn 78 51.26 N 30.31 E
Kamas 200 40.38 N 111.16 W
Kamata ◆⁸ 268 35.33 N 139.43 E
Kamatsi Lake ⊚ 184 56.10 N 102.15 W
Kamay 196 33.51 N 98.48 W
Kamba 150 11.53 N 3.36 E
Kamba Kota 152 7.10 N 17.54 E
Kambalda 162 31.12 S 121.40 E
Kambam 122 9.44 N 77.18 E
Kambang 112 1.42 S 100.42 E
Kambangan 152 13.23 S 23.03 E
Kambar 120 27.36 N 68.00 E
Kambara 94 35.07 N 138.36 E
Kambara Island I 175g 18.57 S 178.57 W
Kambara-tunnel ◆⁵ 94 35.02 N 138.31 E
Kambarka 80 56.17 N 54.12 E
Kambia 150 9.07 N 12.55 W
Kambja 76 58.14 N 26.42 E
Kambolé 150 8.45 N 1.36 E
Kambole Mission 154 8.46 S 30.46 E
Kambove 154 10.52 S 26.38 E
Kambu 115b 8.23 S 118.20 E
Kambuye 152 7.18 S 22.50 E
Kamčatka ≃ 74 56.15 N 162.30 E
Kamčatka, poluostrov (Kamchatka) ▸¹ 74 56.00 N 160.00 E
Kamčatskij poluostrov ▸¹ 74 56.15 N 163.00 E
Kamčatskij zaliv c 74 55.35 N 162.21 E
Kamchatka
— Kamčatka, poluostrov ▸¹ 74 56.00 N 160.00 E
Kâmchay Méa 110 11.35 N 105.40 E
Kamčija ≃ 38 43.02 N 27.53 E
Kāmdebpur, India 272b 22.47 N 88.30 E
Kāmdebpur, India 272b 22.54 N 88.20 E
Kāmdeysh 123 35.24 N 71.20 E
Kameari ◆⁸ 268 35.46 N 139.51 E
Kameda 92 37.52 N 139.07 E
Kameel 158 26.38 S 24.58 E
Kamegamori ∧ 96 33.47 N 133.12 E
Kameido ◆⁸ 268 35.42 N 139.50 E
Kamelik ≃ 80 52.06 N 49.30 E
Kamen', Bela. 76 55.01 N 28.53 E
Kamen, Dtsch. 52 51.35 N 7.40 E
Kamen', gora ∧ 74 69.06 N 94.48 E
Kamenda 152 6.28 S 24.33 E
Kameng ≃ 120 26.38 N 92.54 E
Kamenický Šenov 54 50.45 N 14.29 E
Kamenjak, Rt ▸ 36 44.46 N 13.55 E
Kamenka, Kaz. 80 51.07 N 50.19 E
Kamenka, Kaz. 85 42.55 N 72.50 E
Kamenka, Kaz. 86 52.22 N 69.04 E
Kamenka, Ross. 24 65.54 N 44.05 E
Kamenka, Ross. 80 56.11 N 45.35 E
Kamenka, Ross. 80 57.23 N 41.49 E
Kamenka, Ross. 80 53.13 N 44.03 E
Kamenka, Ross. 80 52.04 N 41.49 E
Kamenka, Ross. 82 54.43 N 38.19 E
Kamenka, Ross. 82 56.11 N 37.58 E
Kamenka, Ross. 82 55.13 N 36.59 E
Kamenka, Ross. 86 58.33 N 95.51 E
Kamenka, Ross. 89 44.28 N 136.01 E
Kamenka, Ross. 265a 59.59 N 30.53 E
Kamenka ◆⁸ 265a 60.03 N 30.11 E
Kamenka ≃, Ross. 83 47.30 N 38.54 E
Kamenka ≃, Ross. 88 58.33 N 95.51 E
Kamenka ≃, Ross. 265a 60.01 N 30.12 E
Kamen'-na-Obi 86 53.47 N 81.20 E
Kamennogorsk 24 60.58 N 29.07 E
Kamennomostskij 84 44.18 N 40.12 E
Kamennyj Brod 83 47.26 N 39.51 E
Kamennyj Jar 80 48.58 N 45.55 E
Kamenolomni 83 47.40 N 40.13 E
Kamen'-Rybolov 89 44.46 N 132.02 E
Kamensk 86 51.59 N 106.36 E
Kamenskij 80 50.53 N 45.29 E
Kamenskoje, Ross. 74 62.30 N 166.12 E
Kamenskoje, Ross. 82 55.16 N 36.50 E
Kamensk-Šachtinskij 83 48.19 N 40.16 E
Kamensk-Ural'skij 86 56.28 N 61.54 E
Kamenz 54 51.16 N 14.06 E
Kameoka 96 35.00 N 135.35 E
Kamerik 80 52.06 N 4.54 E
Kamern 54 52.45 N 12.07 E
Kamerun
— Cameroon □¹ 134 6.00 N 12.00 E
Kamerunberg
— Cameroon Mountain ∧ 152 4.12 N 9.11 E
Kames 46 55.54 N 5.15 W
Kameškovo 80 56.21 N 41.00 E
Kāmet ∧ 120 30.54 N 79.37 E
Kameur, Bahr ≃ 146 9.26 N 20.50 E
Kameyama 94 34.51 N 136.27 E
Kami, Nihon 94 35.31 N 137.42 E
Kami, Nihon 96 35.05 N 134.53 E
Kamiah 202 46.13 N 116.01 W
Kamiak Butte ∧ 202 46.52 N 117.10 W
Kamiakotani 270 34.56 N 135.23 E
Kamiasō 268 35.35 N 139.30 E
Kamień Krajeński 30 53.32 N 17.32 E
Kamienna ≃ 30 51.06 N 21.47 E
Kamienna Góra 30 50.47 N 16.01 E
Kamień Pomorski 30 53.58 N 14.46 E
Kamieskroon 156 30.09 S 17.56 E
Kamifukuoka 94 35.52 N 139.32 E
Kamigōri 96 34.52 N 134.22 E


≃ River | Fluß | Río | Rivière | Rio
≅ Canal | Kanal | Canal | Canal | Canal
␣ Waterfall, Rapids | Wasserfall, Stromschnellen | Cascada, Rápidos | Chute d'eau, Rapides | Cascata, Rápidos
␥ Strait | Meeresstraße | Estrecho | Détroit | Estreito
c Bay, Gulf | Bucht, Golf | Bahía, Golfo | Baie, Golfe | Baía, Golfo
⊚ Lake, Lakes | See, Seen | Lago, Lagos | Lac, Lacs | Lago, Lagos
≋ Swamp | Sumpf | Pantano | Marais | Pântano
❄ Ice Features, Glacier | Eis- und Gletscherformen | Accidentes Glaciales | Formes glaciaires | Acidentes glaciares
∓ Other Hydrographic Features | Andere Hydrographische Objekte | Otros Elementos Hidrográficos | Autres données hydrographiques | Outros acidentes hidrográficos

◆ Submarine Features | Untermeerische Objekte | Accidentes Submarinos | Formes de relief sous-marin | Acidentes submarinos
□ Political Unit | Politische Einheit | Unidad Política | Entité politique | Unidade política
♥ Cultural Institution | Kulturelle Institution | Institución Cultural | Institution culturelle | Instituição cultural
♦ Historical Site | Historische Stätte | Sitio Histórico | Site historique | Sítio histórico
♦ Recreational Site | Erholungs- und Ferienort | Sitio de Recreo | Centre de loisirs | Area de Lazer
✈ Airport | Flughafen | Aeropuerto | Aéroport | Aeroporto
▪ Military Installation | Militäranlage | Instalación Militar | Installation militaire | Instalação militar
◆ Miscellaneous | Verschiedenes | Misceláneo | Divers | Diversos

ENGLISH / DEUTSCH


| Name | Page / Seite | Lat.°′ / Breite°′ | Long.°′ / Länge°′ E = Ost |
|---|---|---|---|
| Kamigyō ◆[8] | 270 | 35.02 N | 135.45 E |
| Kamiichi | 94 | 36.42 N | 137.22 E |
| Kamiishihara | 268 | 35.39 N | 139.32 E |
| Kamiiso | 92a | 41.49 N | 140.39 E |
| Kamiita | 96 | 34.07 N | 134.24 E |
| Kami-jima I | 94 | 34.33 N | 136.59 E |
| Kamikamagari-jima I | 96 | 34.11 N | 132.44 E |
| Kamikatsu | 96 | 33.53 N | 134.24 E |
| Kamikawa, Nihon | 92a | 43.51 N | 142.46 E |
| Kamikawa, Nihon | 94 | 36.13 N | 139.07 E |
| Kamikitazawa ◆[8] | 268 | 35.40 N | 139.38 E |
| Kamikume | 270 | 34.55 N | 135.03 E |
| Kâmil | 130 | 41.07 N | 34.47 E |
| Kamilukuak Lake ⊜ | 176 | 62.22 N | 101.40 W |
| Kamimaki | 270 | 34.34 N | 135.43 E |
| Kamimizo | 268 | 35.33 N | 139.22 E |
| Kamina | 154 | 8.44 S | 25.00 E |
| Kaminaka, Nihon | 94 | 35.28 N | 135.51 E |
| Kaminaka, Nihon | 96 | 33.48 N | 134.22 E |
| Kaminak Lake ⊜ | 176 | 62.10 N | 95.00 W |
| Kaminaljuyú ⊥ | 236 | 14.38 N | 90.33 W |
| Kaminka | 83 | 49.38 N | 39.22 E |
| Kamin'-Kashyrs'kyy | 78 | 51.38 N | 24.58 E |
| Kaminoho | 94 | 35.37 N | 137.03 E |
| Kaminokawa | 94 | 36.26 N | 139.55 E |
| Kaminokuni | 92a | 41.48 N | 140.06 E |
| Kaminoseki | 96 | 33.49 N | 132.07 E |
| Kaminoyama | 92 | 38.09 N | 140.17 E |
| Kaminskij | 80 | 57.10 N | 41.28 E |
| Kaminuriak Lake ⊜ | 176 | 63.00 N | 95.40 W |
| Kamioka | 94 | 36.16 N | 137.18 E |
| Kamiotawa | 270 | 34.54 N | 135.31 E |
| Kamioyamada | 268 | 35.35 N | 139.24 E |
| Kámiros ⊥ | 38 | 36.19 N | 27.57 E |
| Kamisato | 94 | 36.15 N | 139.09 E |
| Kamishak Bay c | 180 | 59.15 N | 153.45 W |
| Kamishii | 94 | 36.04 N | 136.24 E |
| Kamishinden | 270 | 34.49 N | 135.30 E |
| Kamisunagawa | 92a | 43.30 N | 142.00 E |
| Kamitaira | 94 | 36.24 N | 136.54 E |
| Kamitakara | 94 | 36.17 N | 137.22 E |
| Kamitakino | 270 | 34.57 N | 134.59 E |
| Kamitomi | 268 | 35.49 N | 139.31 E |
| Kamitonda | 96 | 33.43 N | 135.27 E |
| Kamitsuruma | 268 | 35.31 N | 139.25 E |
| Kamitsushima | 92 | 34.50 N | 129.28 E |
| Kamituga | 154 | 3.04 S | 28.11 E |
| Kamiura | 96 | 33.03 N | 131.55 E |
| Kamiyahagi | 94 | 35.18 N | 137.29 E |
| Kamiyama | 96 | 33.58 N | 134.23 E |
| Kamiyamada | 94 | 36.28 N | 138.09 E |
| Kamiyama-jima I | 174m | 26.15 N | 127.35 E |
| Kamiyugi | 268 | 35.37 N | 139.23 E |
| Kamīzgān | 84 | 38.58 N | 47.44 E |
| Kamjanec | 76 | 52.24 N | 23.49 E |
| Kamkhat Muḥaywir ∧[2] | 132 | 31.08 N | 36.30 E |
| Kamku | 120 | 27.30 N | 96.30 E |
| Kamla (Kamlā) ≃ | 124 | 25.37 N | 86.40 E |
| Kamlach ≃ | 58 | 48.30 N | 10.22 E |
| Kamloops | 182 | 50.40 N | 120.20 W |
| Kamloops Indian Reserve ◆[4] | 182 | 50.42 N | 120.20 W |
| Kamloops Lake ⊜ | 182 | 50.43 N | 120.33 W |
| Kammon-kaikyō Ʉ | 96 | 33.56 N | 130.56 E |
| Kammon-kyō ◆[5] | 96 | 33.56 N | 130.55 E |
| Kammuri-yama ∧ | 96 | 34.28 N | 132.05 E |
| Kamnik | 36 | 46.13 N | 14.37 E |
| Kamniokan | 88 | 56.17 N | 111.57 E |
| Kamo, Haya. | 84 | 40.22 N | 45.08 E |
| Kamo, N.Z. | 172 | 35.41 S | 174.19 E |
| Kamo, Nihon | 92 | 37.39 N | 139.03 E |
| Kamo, Nihon | 94 | 34.50 N | 138.46 E |
| Kamo, Nihon | 96 | 34.45 N | 135.52 E |
| Kamo, Nihon | 96 | 35.10 N | 134.04 E |
| Kamo, Nihon | 96 | 35.20 N | 132.55 E |
| Kamo, Nihon | 270 | 34.55 N | 135.13 E |
| Kamo ≃, Nihon | 94 | 35.06 N | 140.06 E |
| Kamo ≃, Nihon | 96 | 33.56 N | 133.09 E |
| Kamo ≃, Nihon | 270 | 34.56 N | 135.44 E |
| Kamoa Mountains ⋏ | 246 | 1.37 N | 59.00 W |
| Kamoda-misaki › | 96 | 33.50 N | 134.45 E |
| Kamogata | 96 | 34.32 N | 133.35 E |
| Kamogawa, Nihon | 94 | 35.06 N | 140.06 E |
| Kamogawa, Nihon | 96 | 34.51 N | 133.49 E |
| Kamohio Bay c | 229a | 20.31 N | 156.36 W |
| Kamojima | 96 | 34.04 N | 134.21 E |
| Kāmoke | 123 | 31.58 N | 74.13 E |
| Kamoshida ◆[8] | 268 | 35.34 N | 139.30 E |
| Kamoto | 96 | 33.00 N | 130.45 E |
| Kamp ≃ | 61 | 48.23 N | 15.48 E |
| Kāmpa | 272b | 22.56 N | 88.28 E |
| Kampala | 154 | 0.19 N | 32.25 E |
| Kampar | 114 | 4.18 N | 101.09 E |
| Kampar ≃ | 112 | 0.32 N | 103.08 E |
| Kamparkalns ∧[2] | 76 | 57.18 N | 22.47 E |
| Kampar Kanan ≃ | 112 | 0.16 N | 101.41 E |
| Kampen | 52 | 52.33 N | 5.54 E |
| Kampene | 154 | 3.36 S | 26.40 E |
| Kampfe, Lake ⊜ | 276 | 41.02 N | 74.21 W |
| Kamphaeng, Khao ∧ | 110 | 14.37 N | 99.18 E |
| Kamphaeng Phet | 110 | 16.28 N | 99.30 E |
| Kampil | 124 | 27.37 N | 79.17 E |
| Kampinoski Park Narodowy ♠ | 30 | 52.20 N | 20.35 E |
| Kampire Dior ∧ | 123 | 36.38 N | 74.23 E |
| Kamp-Lintfort | 52 | 51.30 N | 6.31 E |
| Kamp'o | 98 | 35.48 N | 129.29 E |
| Kampolombo, Lake ⊜ | 154 | 11.37 S | 29.42 E |
| Kampong Ayer Puteh | 114 | 4.16 N | 103.12 E |
| Kampong Baharu | 114 | 3.43 N | 103.17 E |
| Kampong Benta | 114 | 3.32 N | 103.22 E |
| Kampong Buloh | 114 | 5.32 N | 102.45 E |
| Kâmpóng Cham | 110 | 12.00 N | 105.27 E |
| Kampong Chenor | 114 | 3.29 N | 102.36 E |
| Kâmpóng Chhnăng | 110 | 12.15 N | 104.40 E |
| Kampong Dong | 114 | 3.54 N | 101.54 E |
| Kampong Guchil | 114 | 5.33 N | 102.14 E |
| Kampong Jabor | 114 | 3.57 N | 103.20 E |
| Kampong Jerangau | 114 | 4.51 N | 103.12 E |
| Kampong Kandang | 114 | 2.11 N | 102.18 E |
| Kâmpóng Kântuŏt | 110 | 11.26 N | 104.49 E |
| Kampong Kenyam | 114 | 4.31 N | 102.28 E |
| Kampong Kuala Kemaman | 114 | 4.14 N | 103.27 E |
| Kampong Lamir | 114 | 3.36 N | 103.21 E |
| Kampong Lawa | 114 | 5.40 N | 101.42 E |
| Kampong Mengkarak | 114 | 3.19 N | 102.27 E |
| Kampong Merang | 114 | 5.32 N | 102.57 E |
| Kampong Nuri | 114 | 5.02 N | 102.23 E |
| Kampong Penarek | 114 | 5.37 N | 102.48 E |
| Kampong Raja | 114 | 5.48 N | 102.35 E |
| Kampong Renggong | 114 | 4.33 N | 102.35 E |
| Kâmpóng Saôm | 110 | 10.38 N | 103.30 E |
| Kâmpóng Saôm, Chhâk c | 110 | 10.50 N | 103.32 E |
| Kampong Sebuyau | 112 | 1.31 N | 110.56 E |
| Kampong Sekendi | 114 | 3.43 N | 100.56 E |
| Kampong Surau | 114 | 5.49 N | 100.54 E |
| Kampong Tanjong Batu | 114 | 3.12 N | 103.27 E |
| Kampong Tebing Runtoh | 271c | 1.26 N | 103.40 E |
| Kâmpóng Thum | 110 | 12.42 N | 104.54 E |
| Kâmpóng Trâlach | 110 | 11.54 N | 104.47 E |
| Kampong Ulu | 110 | 10.03 N | 98.33 E |
| Kampong Ulu Chalok | 114 | 5.26 N | 102.50 E |
| Kâmpôt | 110 | 10.37 N | 104.11 E |
| Kampsville | 194 | 39.18 N | 90.37 W |
| Kampti | 150 | 10.08 N | 3.27 W |
| Kâmpŭchéa → Cambodia □[1] | 110 | 13.00 N | 105.00 E |
| Kampung ≃ | 164 | 5.44 S | 138.24 E |
| Kampungbaru | 112 | 1.12 S | 102.57 E |
| Kampville | 219 | 38.51 N | 90.33 W |
| Kāmrānga | 126 | 23.14 N | 90.47 E |
| Kamrau, Teluk c | 164 | 3.32 S | 133.37 E |
| Kamsack | 184 | 51.34 N | 101.54 W |
| Kamsdorf | 54 | 50.38 N | 11.28 E |
| Kamskij | 24 | 60.04 N | 53.13 E |
| Kamskoje Ustje | 80 | 55.13 N | 49.16 E |
| Kamskoje vodochranilišče ⊜[1] | 86 | 58.52 N | 56.15 E |
| Kamslybas, ozero ⊜ | 86 | 46.12 N | 61.48 E |
| Kamsu-ri | 98 | 38.03 N | 125.54 E |
| Kamsuuma | 144 | 0.15 N | 42.47 E |
| Kāmthi | 120 | 21.14 N | 79.12 E |
| Kam Tin | 271d | 22.27 N | 114.03 E |
| Kamuchawie Lake ⊜ | 184 | 56.18 N | 101.59 W |
| Kamudilo | 154 | 7.42 S | 27.18 E |
| Kamuela (Waimea) | 229d | 20.01 N | 155.48 W |
| Kamui-misaki › | 92a | 43.20 N | 140.21 E |
| Kámuk, Cerro ∧ | 236 | 9.17 N | 83.04 W |
| Kamuli | 154 | 0.57 N | 33.07 E |
| Kamundan ≃ | 164 | 2.17 S | 132.39 E |
| Kamutambaie ≃ | 152 | 7.17 S | 23.41 E |
| Kamwandu | 152 | 6.04 S | 22.42 E |
| Kam'yane, Ukr. | 78 | 51.31 N | 27.38 E |
| Kam'yane, Ukr. | 78 | 47.53 N | 35.25 E |
| Kam'yanets'-Podil's'kyy | 78 | 48.41 N | 26.36 E |
| Kam'yanka, Ukr. | 78 | 49.02 N | 32.06 E |
| Kam'yanka, Ukr. | 83 | 49.07 N | 37.18 E |
| Kam'yanka ≃, Ukr. | 78 | 49.47 N | 30.01 E |
| Kam'yanka ≃, Ukr. | 78 | 47.39 N | 34.02 E |
| Kam'yanka ≃, Ukr. | 83 | 49.35 N | 39.05 E |
| Kam'yanka-Buz'ka | 78 | 50.07 N | 24.20 E |
| Kam'yanka-Dniprovs'ka | 78 | 47.29 N | 34.25 E |
| Kam'yans'ke | 78 | 45.49 N | 29.16 E |
| Kam'yanyy Brid | 78 | 50.25 N | 27.49 E |
| Kamyšet | 88 | 55.12 N | 98.42 E |
| Kamyšev, Ross. | 80 | 46.39 N | 42.38 E |
| Kamyšev, Ross. | 80 | 46.53 N | 42.31 E |
| Kamyševatskaja | 78 | 46.25 N | 37.57 E |
| Kamyševskaja | 80 | 47.37 N | 41.49 E |
| Kamyshna (Kamyšnaja) ≃ | 83 | 48.55 N | 39.55 E |
| Kamyšin | 80 | 50.06 N | 45.24 E |
| Kamyškurgon | 85 | 40.34 N | 70.24 E |
| Kamyšla | 80 | 54.07 N | 52.10 E |
| Kamyšlov | 86 | 56.52 N | 62.43 E |
| Kamyšlybaš | 86 | 46.11 N | 61.57 E |
| Kamyšnaja (Kamyshna) ≃ | 83 | 48.55 N | 39.55 E |
| Kamyšnoje | 86 | 51.58 N | 61.47 E |
| Kamyšovyj | 80 | 46.26 N | 45.12 E |
| Kamyš-Samarskich Ozer, razlivy ≡ | 80 | 48.50 N | 50.50 E |
| Kamyz'ak | 80 | 46.07 N | 48.05 E |
| Kamyz'ak ≃ | 80 | 46.00 N | 48.06 E |
| Kan, Īrān | 128 | 35.45 N | 51.16 E |
| Kan, Sūd. | 140 | 9.01 N | 31.47 E |
| Kan ≃ | 86 | 56.31 N | 93.47 E |
| Kana ≃ | 154 | 18.30 S | 27.22 E |
| Kanaaupscow ≃ | 176 | 53.39 N | 77.09 W |
| Kanab | 200 | 37.02 N | 112.31 W |
| Kanab Creek ≃ | 200 | 36.24 N | 112.38 W |
| Kanab Plateau ⋏[1] | 200 | 36.40 N | 112.45 W |
| Kanada | 96 | 33.41 N | 130.47 E |
| Kanada → Canada □[1] | 176 | 60.00 N | 95.00 W |
| Kanadej | 80 | 53.10 N | 47.30 E |
| Kanae | 94 | 35.30 N | 137.49 E |
| Kanafis | 140 | 9.48 N | 25.40 E |
| Kanaga Island I | 180 | 51.45 N | 177.10 W |
| Kanaga Volcano ∧[1] | 180 | 51.50 N | 177.09 W |
| Kanagawa □[5] | 94 | 35.30 N | 139.30 E |
| Kanagawa ◆[8] | 268 | 35.28 N | 139.38 E |
| Kanagi | 96 | 34.53 N | 132.11 E |
| Kanai | 268 | 35.35 N | 139.28 E |
| Kānāipur | 126 | 23.33 N | 89.47 E |
| Kanairiktok ≃ | 176 | 55.05 N | 60.20 W |
| Kanā'is, Ra's al- › | 140 | 31.15 N | 27.51 E |
| Kanajevka, Ross. | 80 | 53.07 N | 45.35 E |
| Kanajevka, Ross. | 80 | 52.12 N | 49.40 E |
| Kanaka Creek ≃ | 226 | 39.25 N | 120.57 W |
| Kanakapura | 122 | 12.33 N | 77.25 E |
| Kanakeswar | 126 | 23.09 N | 90.25 E |
| Kanākir | 132 | 33.15 N | 36.05 E |
| Kanal | 64 | 46.05 N | 13.38 E |
| Kanal-Inseln → Channel Islands II | 28 | 49.20 N | 2.20 W |
| Kanam | 164 | 3.25 S | 152.10 E |
| Kanamachi ◆[8] | 268 | 35.46 N | 139.53 E |
| Kanamori | 268 | 35.32 N | 139.28 E |
| Kanan | 270 | 34.29 N | 135.38 E |
| Kananaskis ≃ | 182 | 51.05 N | 115.03 W |
| Kananga (Luluabourg) | 152 | 5.54 S | 22.25 E |
| Kananggar | 115b | 10.03 S | 120.22 E |
| Kanangra-Boyd National Park ♠ | 170 | 34.00 S | 150.06 E |
| Kananikol'skoje | 86 | 52.47 N | 57.29 E |
| Kanaoka | 270 | 34.33 N | 135.32 E |
| Kanapou Bay c | 229a | 20.33 N | 156.33 W |
| Kanarase-yama ∧ | 96 | 33.26 N | 131.15 E |
| Kanarraville | 200 | 37.32 N | 113.10 W |
| Kanaš | 80 | 55.31 N | 47.30 E |
| Kanasagō | 94 | 36.33 N | 140.28 E |
| Kanata | 212 | 45.19 N | 75.54 W |
| Kanaudi | 124 | 23.36 N | 81.23 E |
| Kanava, Ross. | 24 | 61.07 N | 54.58 E |
| Kanava, Ross. | 80 | 47.13 N | 45.24 E |
| Kanavka | 80 | 50.19 N | 48.33 E |
| Kanawha | 190 | 42.56 N | 93.47 W |
| Kanawha ≃ | 188 | 38.50 N | 82.08 W |
| Kanaya, Nihon | 94 | 34.49 N | 138.08 E |
| Kanaya, Nihon | 96 | 34.04 N | 135.15 E |
| Kanaya, Nihon | 268 | 35.10 N | 139.50 E |
| Kanayama | 94 | 35.39 N | 137.09 E |
| Kanazawa | 94 | 36.34 N | 136.39 E |
| Kanazawa ◆[8] | 268 | 35.20 N | 139.38 E |
| Kanazu | 94 | 36.13 N | 136.14 E |
| Kanbalu | 110 | 23.12 N | 95.31 E |
| Kanbauk | 110 | 14.36 N | 98.02 E |
| Kančalan ≃ | 180 | 65.08 N | 176.25 E |
| Kanchanaburi | 110 | 14.01 N | 99.32 E |
| Kanchanadit | 110 | 9.10 N | 99.28 E |
| Kānchenjunga (Kaṅchanjanggā) ∧ | 124 | 27.42 N | 88.08 E |
| Kānchipuram | 122 | 12.50 N | 79.43 E |
| Kanchow → Ganzhou | 100 | 25.54 N | 114.55 E |
| Kānchrāpāra | 126 | 22.57 N | 88.28 E |
| Kańczuga | 30 | 49.59 N | 22.24 E |
| Kanda | 96 | 33.47 N | 130.59 E |
| Kanda ◆[8] | 268 | 35.42 N | 139.46 E |
| Kandabulak | 80 | 53.58 N | 50.44 E |
| Kandāghāt | 123 | 30.59 N | 77.07 E |
| Kandahar | 184 | 51.46 N | 104.21 W |
| Kandāhu | 120 | 27.33 N | 69.24 E |
| Kanda-Kanda | 152 | 6.56 S | 23.36 E |
| Kandala | 152 | 6.02 S | 19.24 E |
| Kandalakša | 24 | 67.09 N | 32.21 E |
| Kandalakšskaja guba c | 24 | 66.55 N | 32.45 E |
| Kandalakšskij zapovednik ♠ | 24 | 68.50 N | 37.30 E |
| Kandang | 114 | 3.03 N | 97.20 E |
| Kandangan | 112 | 2.47 S | 115.16 E |
| Kandanghaur | 115a | 6.21 S | 108.06 E |
| Kandat | 86 | 57.08 N | 89.02 E |
| Kandava | 76 | 57.05 N | 22.49 E |
| Kandavu Island I | 175g | 19.03 S | 178.13 E |
| Kandavu Passage Ʉ | 175g | 18.45 S | 178.00 E |
| Kandé | 150 | 9.57 N | 1.03 E |
| Kandel | 56 | 49.05 N | 8.11 E |
| Kandel ∧ | 58 | 48.04 N | 8.01 E |
| Kander ≃ | 58 | 46.43 N | 7.38 E |
| Kandern | 58 | 47.43 N | 7.40 E |
| Kandersteg | 58 | 46.30 N | 7.40 E |
| Kandhkot | 120 | 28.14 N | 69.11 E |
| Kāndhla | 124 | 29.19 N | 77.16 E |
| Kandi, Bénin | 150 | 11.08 N | 2.56 E |
| Kandi, India | 126 | 23.57 N | 88.02 E |
| Kandi, Tanjung › | 112 | 1.19 N | 121.28 E |
| Kandia ≃ | 123 | 35.28 N | 73.18 E |
| Kandiāro | 120 | 27.04 N | 68.13 E |
| Kandik ≃ | 180 | 65.24 N | 142.34 W |
| Kandilli ◆[8] | 267b | 41.04 N | 29.03 E |
| Kandıra | 130 | 41.04 N | 30.09 E |
| Kandivli ◆[8] | 272c | 19.12 N | 72.51 E |
| Kandla | 120 | 23.02 N | 70.14 E |
| Kando ≃ | 96 | 35.22 N | 132.40 E |
| Kandor, Ouadi V | 146 | 17.13 N | 20.52 E |
| Kandos | 170 | 32.52 S | 149.58 E |
| Kāndra | 126 | 23.44 N | 87.58 E |
| Kandrāch | 120 | 25.29 N | 65.29 E |
| Kandreho | 157b | 17.29 S | 46.06 E |
| Kandrian | 164 | 6.15 S | 149.35 E |
| Kandry | 80 | 54.34 N | 54.07 E |
| Kandufuri I | 122 | 7.05 N | 72.48 E |
| Kandute I | 122 | 6.20 N | 72.57 E |
| Kandy | 122 | 7.18 N | 80.38 E |
| Kane, Il., U.S. | 219 | 39.11 N | 90.21 W |
| Kane, Pa., U.S. | 214 | 41.39 N | 78.48 W |
| Kane □[6] | 216 | 41.53 N | 88.18 W |
| Kaneda | 268 | 35.28 N | 139.22 E |
| Kaneilio Point › | 229c | 21.27 N | 158.12 W |
| Kanektok ≃ | 180 | 59.45 N | 161.55 W |
| Kanem □[5] | 146 | 15.00 N | 16.00 E |
| Kanemi | 116 | 6.55 N | 123.58 E |
| Kaneohe | 229c | 21.25 N | 157.48 W |
| Kaneohe Bay c | 229c | 21.28 N | 157.49 W |
| Kaneohe Bay Marine Corps Air Station ■ | 229c | 21.27 N | 157.46 W |
| Kaneville | 216 | 41.50 N | 88.31 W |
| Kanevskaja | 78 | 46.05 N | 38.57 E |
| Kaneyama | 94 | 35.28 N | 137.06 E |
| Kanfanar | 64 | 45.07 N | 13.51 E |
| Kang | 156 | 23.41 S | 22.50 E |
| Kangaba | 150 | 11.56 N | 8.25 W |
| Kangal | 130 | 39.15 N | 37.24 E |
| Kangalassy | 74 | 62.23 N | 129.59 E |
| Kangān | 128 | 27.50 N | 52.03 E |
| Kānganheri ◆[8] | 272a | 28.33 N | 76.59 E |
| Kanganpur | 123 | 30.46 N | 74.08 E |
| Kangar | 114 | 6.26 N | 100.12 E |
| Kangaré | 150 | 11.35 N | 8.10 W |
| Kangarilla | 168b | 35.09 S | 138.40 E |
| Kangaroo ≃ | 170 | 34.46 S | 150.18 E |
| Kangaroo Creek Reservoir ⊜[1] | 168b | 34.52 S | 138.46 E |
| Kangaroo Flat | 168b | 34.33 S | 138.40 E |
| Kangaroo Ground | 274b | 37.41 S | 145.13 E |
| Kangaroo Island I | 166 | 35.50 S | 137.06 E |
| Kangaroo Valley | 170 | 34.44 S | 150.32 E |
| Kangasala | 26 | 61.28 N | 24.05 E |
| Kangasniemi | 26 | 61.59 N | 26.38 E |
| Kangāvar | 128 | 34.30 N | 47.58 E |
| Kangbao | 98 | 41.53 N | 114.40 E |
| Kangding | 102 | 30.03 N | 102.02 E |
| Kangdong | 98 | 39.09 N | 126.05 E |
| Kangdu | 100 | 27.00 N | 116.36 E |
| Kangean, Kepulauan II | 112 | 6.55 S | 115.30 E |
| Kangean, Pulau I | 112 | 6.54 S | 115.20 E |
| Kangen ≃ | 140 | 6.47 N | 33.09 E |
| Kanggezhuang | 105 | 40.26 N | 116.44 E |
| Kanggup'o | 98 | 41.07 N | 127.31 E |
| Kanggye | 98 | 40.58 N | 126.34 E |
| Kanggyŏng | 98 | 36.10 N | 127.00 E |
| Kanghwa | 98 | 37.45 N | 126.30 E |
| Kanghwa-do I | 98 | 37.40 N | 126.27 E |
| Kanghwa-man c | 98 | 37.20 N | 126.35 E |
| Kangil | 88 | 52.15 N | 116.20 E |
| Kangiqsualujjuaq | 176 | 58.41 N | 65.57 W |
| Kangiqsujuaq | 176 | 61.36 N | 71.58 W |
| Kangirsuk | 176 | 60.01 N | 70.01 W |
| Kangjin | 98 | 34.39 N | 126.45 E |
| Kangjinjing | 89 | 46.12 N | 126.48 E |
| Kangkar Lenggor | 114 | 2.16 N | 103.44 E |
| Kangkar Teberau | 114 | 1.32 N | 103.45 E |
| Kangley | 216 | 41.09 N | 88.53 W |
| Kangly | 85 | 40.07 N | 67.54 E |
| Kangmaer | 124 | 30.45 N | 85.34 E |
| Kangmar | 120 | 28.34 N | 89.51 E |
| Kangnam ◆[8] | 271b | 37.30 N | 127.01 E |
| Kangnam-sanmaek ⋏ | 98 | 40.30 N | 125.30 E |
| Kangnichumike | 120 | 33.10 N | 80.59 E |
| Kangnŭng | 98 | 37.45 N | 128.54 E |
| Kango | 152 | 0.09 N | 10.08 E |
| Kangoku-iwa I | 174f | 24.48 N | 141.17 E |
| Kangombe | 152 | 14.03 S | 23.40 E |
| Kangongo | 152 | 17.57 S | 21.02 E |
| Kangowa | 152 | 9.55 S | 22.48 E |
| Kangping | 98 | 42.44 N | 123.21 E |
| Kāngpokpi | 120 | 25.08 N | 93.58 E |
| Kangpu | 102 | 27.43 N | 99.00 E |
| Kāngra | 123 | 32.06 N | 76.16 E |
| Kangrinboqê Feng ∧ | 120 | 31.04 N | 81.18 E |
| Kangshan | 100 | 22.48 N | 120.17 E |
| Kangsŏ | 98 | 38.58 N | 125.26 E |
| Kangsŏ-ri | 98 | 38.06 N | 126.58 E |
| Kangto ∧ | 120 | 27.52 N | 92.30 E |
| Kangtuyingzi | 104 | 41.47 N | 121.31 E |
| Känguruh-Insel → Kangaroo Island I | 166 | 35.50 S | 137.06 E |
| Kangwŏn Do □[4], C.M.I.K. | 98 | 38.45 N | 127.35 E |
| Kangwŏn Do □[4], Taehan | 98 | 37.45 N | 128.15 E |
| Kangxianzhuang | 105 | 39.06 N | 116.27 E |
| Kangyidaung | 110 | 16.56 N | 94.54 E |
| Kangzhuang | 105 | 40.23 N | 115.53 E |
| Kanhar ≃ | 124 | 24.28 N | 83.08 E |
| Kanheri Caves ⊥[5] | 272c | 19.13 N | 72.52 E |
| Kanholmsfjärden Ʉ | 40 | 59.20 N | 18.47 E |
| Kanhsien → Ganzhou | 100 | 25.54 N | 114.55 E |
| Kani, C. Iv. | 150 | 8.29 N | 6.36 W |
| Kani, Mya. | 110 | 22.26 N | 94.50 E |
| Kani, Nihon | 94 | 35.22 N | 137.04 E |
| Kaniama | 152 | 7.31 S | 24.11 E |
| Kaniamba | 154 | 7.27 S | 26.57 E |
| Kanibadam | 85 | 40.17 N | 70.25 E |
| Kanie | 94 | 35.08 N | 136.48 E |
| Kaniepa | 154 | 9.00 S | 27.21 E |
| Kaniere | 172 | 42.45 S | 171.00 E |
| Kaniere, Lake ⊜ | 172 | 42.50 S | 171.09 E |
| Kaniet Islands II | 164 | 0.53 S | 145.30 E |
| Kanifay | 174q | 9.32 N | 138.06 E |
| Kanigiri | 122 | 15.24 N | 79.31 E |
| Kanihāula ◆[8] | 272a | 28.44 N | 77.01 E |
| Kanin | 54 | 52.17 N | 12.50 E |
| Kanin, poluostrov ›[1] | 24 | 68.00 N | 45.00 E |
| Kanina | 124 | 28.20 N | 76.19 E |
| Kaningo | 154 | 0.49 S | 38.32 E |
| Kanin-Kamen' ∧ | 24 | 68.18 N | 45.00 E |
| Kanin Nos | 24 | 68.39 N | 43.14 E |
| Kanin Nos, mys › | 24 | 68.39 N | 43.16 E |
| Kaniv | 78 | 49.44 N | 31.28 E |
| Kaniva | 166 | 36.23 S | 141.15 E |
| Kanivs'ke vodoskhovyshche ⊜[1] | 78 | 50.00 N | 31.20 E |
| Kanjiža | 38 | 46.04 N | 20.04 E |
| Kānjur ◆[8] | 272c | 19.08 N | 72.56 E |
| Kanjut Sār ∧ | 123 | 36.14 N | 75.22 E |
| Kankaanpää | 26 | 61.48 N | 22.25 E |
| Kankakee | 216 | 41.07 N | 87.51 W |
| Kankakee □[6] | 216 | 41.07 N | 87.52 W |
| Kankakee ≃ | 216 | 41.23 N | 88.16 W |
| Kankakee River State Park ♠ | 216 | 41.12 N | 87.59 W |
| Kankan | 150 | 10.23 N | 9.18 W |
| Kankar ◆[8] | 272a | 28.46 N | 77.06 E |
| Kankéla | 150 | 10.50 N | 6.40 W |
| Kānker | 122 | 20.17 N | 81.29 E |
| Kankō → Hamhŭng | 98 | 39.54 N | 127.32 E |
| Kankossa | 150 | 15.56 N | 11.31 W |
| Kankunskij | 74 | 57.37 N | 126.08 E |
| Kanlıavşar | 130 | 37.13 N | 38.16 E |
| Kanlıca ◆[8] | 267b | 41.06 N | 29.04 E |
| Kanmaw Kyun I | 110 | 11.40 N | 98.28 E |
| Kanmen | 100 | 28.06 N | 121.16 E |
| Kanmuri-jima I | 96 | 35.41 N | 135.25 E |
| Kanmuri-yama ∧ | 92 | 34.28 N | 132.05 E |
| Kanna ≃ | 94 | 36.17 N | 139.09 E |
| Kannabe | 96 | 34.32 N | 133.23 E |
| Kannabi-san ∧[2] | 270 | 34.48 N | 135.44 E |
| Kannack | 110 | 14.07 N | 108.37 E |
| Kannad | 122 | 20.16 N | 75.08 E |
| Kanna-kō c | 174m | 26.28 N | 127.58 E |
| Kannami | 94 | 35.05 N | 138.57 E |
| Kannapolis | 192 | 35.29 N | 80.37 W |
| Kannauj | 124 | 27.04 N | 79.55 E |
| Kanniyākumari | 122 | 8.05 N | 77.34 E |
| Kannod | 124 | 22.40 N | 76.44 E |
| Kannonkoski | 26 | 62.58 N | 25.15 E |
| Kannon-zaki › | 268 | 35.15 N | 139.45 E |
| Kannose ≃ | 96 | 34.54 N | 132.49 E |
| Kannus | 26 | 63.54 N | 23.54 E |
| Kano, Nig. | 150 | 12.00 N | 8.30 E |
| Kano, Nihon | 96 | 34.14 N | 131.49 E |
| Kano ≃, Nig. | 150 | 11.50 N | 8.31 E |
| Kano ≃, Nihon | 94 | 35.05 N | 138.52 E |
| Kanona | 210 | 42.22 N | 77.22 W |
| Kanoneiland | 158 | 28.39 S | 21.05 E |
| Kanonerskij, ostrov I | 265a | 59.54 N | 30.13 E |
| Kanonji | 96 | 34.07 N | 133.39 E |
| Kanopolis | 198 | 38.42 N | 98.09 W |
| Kanopolis Lake ⊜[1] | 198 | 38.38 N | 98.00 W |
| Kanorado | 198 | 39.19 N | 102.02 W |
| Kanosh | 200 | 38.48 N | 112.26 W |
| Kanouse Brook ≃ | 276 | 41.02 N | 74.26 W |
| Kanouse Mountain ∧ | 276 | 41.04 N | 74.25 W |
| Kan'ovka | 24 | 67.08 N | 39.40 E |
| Kanovlei | 156 | 19.10 S | 19.23 E |
| Kanowit | 112 | 2.06 N | 112.09 E |
| Kanoya | 92 | 31.23 N | 130.51 E |
| Kanō-zan ∧[2] | 268 | 35.15 N | 139.57 E |
| Kanpetlet | 110 | 21.12 N | 94.02 E |
| Kanpoli | 272c | 19.04 N | 73.09 E |
| Kānpur | 124 | 26.28 N | 80.21 E |
| Kanra | 94 | 36.13 N | 138.55 E |
| Kansa ≃ | 94 | 34.55 N | 137.34 E |
| Kansaj | 85 | 40.30 N | 69.41 E |
| Kansanshi | 154 | 12.05 S | 26.26 E |
| Kānsāripāra | 272b | 22.56 N | 88.14 E |
| Kansas, Il., U.S. | 194 | 39.33 N | 87.56 W |
| Kansas, Oh., U.S. | 214 | 41.14 N | 83.17 W |
| Kansas □[3], U.S. | 178 | 38.45 N | 98.15 W |
| Kansas □[3], U.S. | 198 | 38.45 N | 98.15 W |
| Kansas ≃ | 198 | 39.07 N | 94.36 W |
| Kansas City, Ks., U.S. | 198 | 39.06 N | 94.37 W |
| Kansas City, Mo., U.S. | 194 | 39.05 N | 94.34 W |
| Kansau | 110 | 23.50 N | 93.35 E |
| Kansei Gakuin University ᵾ[2] | 270 | 34.46 N | 135.21 E |
| Kansei University ᵾ[2] | 270 | 34.46 N | 135.31 E |
| Kansenia | 154 | 10.19 S | 26.02 E |
| Kanshan | 106 | 30.12 N | 120.25 E |
| Kanshi | 100 | 24.56 N | 116.54 E |
| Kansk | 86 | 56.13 N | 95.41 E |
| Kansŏng | 98 | 38.22 N | 128.29 E |
| Kansu | 85 | 39.45 N | 75.02 E |
| Kansu → Gansu □[4] | 102 | 37.00 N | 103.00 E |
| Kansyat | 164 | 2.15 S | 138.51 E |
| Kant | 85 | 42.55 N | 74.55 E |
| Kantabrisches Gebirge → Cantábrica, Cordillera ⋏ | 34 | 43.00 N | 5.00 W |
| Kantalvi | 272c | 18.54 N | 73.03 E |
| Kantang | 110 | 7.25 N | 99.31 E |
| Kāntāphor | 124 | 22.35 N | 76.34 E |
| Kantchari | 150 | 12.29 N | 1.31 E |
| Kantché | 150 | 13.33 N | 8.28 E |
| Kantemirovka, Kaz. | 85 | 42.51 N | 70.20 E |
| Kantemirovka, Ross. | 83 | 49.41 N | 39.51 E |
| Kānth | 124 | 29.04 N | 78.38 E |
| Kantharalak | 110 | 14.39 N | 104.39 E |
| Kānthi Coastal Plain ≚ | 126 | 21.45 N | 87.45 E |
| Kantishna ≃ | 180 | 64.45 N | 149.58 W |
| Kantner | 214 | 40.06 N | 78.56 W |
| Kantō-heiya ≚ | 94 | 36.00 N | 139.30 E |
| Kanton → Guangzhou | 100 | 23.06 N | 113.16 E |
| Kanton (Canton) I | 174h | 2.50 S | 171.40 W |
| Kantorp | 40 | 59.01 N | 16.28 E |
| Kantō-sanchi ⋏, Nihon | 92 | 35.50 N | 138.50 E |
| Kantō-sanchi ⋏, Nihon | 94 | 35.59 N | 138.43 E |
| Kantuanji | 100 | 32.59 N | 116.19 E |
| Kantubek | 86 | 45.07 N | 59.16 E |
| Kantu-long | 110 | 19.57 N | 97.36 E |
| Kantunilkin | 232 | 21.06 N | 87.29 W |
| Kanturk | 48 | 52.10 N | 8.55 W |
| Kanuku Mountains ⋏ | 246 | 3.12 N | 59.30 W |
| Kanuma | 94 | 36.33 N | 139.44 E |
| Kanus | 156 | 27.54 S | 18.40 E |
| Kanuti ≃ | 180 | 66.26 N | 153.02 W |
| Kan'utino | 76 | 55.33 N | 33.14 E |
| Kanye | 156 | 24.59 S | 25.19 E |
| Kanygtokynmangkyn, laguna c | 180 | 69.20 N | 178.45 E |
| Kanyu | 156 | 20.05 S | 24.39 E |
| Kanyutkwin | 110 | 18.21 N | 96.30 E |
| Kanzaki ≃ | 270 | 34.42 N | 135.25 E |
| Kanzanavolok | 24 | 62.23 N | 36.58 E |
| Kanzenze | 154 | 10.31 S | 25.12 E |
| Kanzi | 98 | 39.34 N | 122.39 E |
| Kaohiung → Kaohsiung | 100 | 22.38 N | 120.17 E |
| Kaohsiung | 100 | 22.38 N | 120.17 E |
| Kaohsiunghsien | 100 | 22.38 N | 120.21 E |
| Kaoje | 150 | 11.14 N | 4.07 E |
| Kaoka Bay c | 175e | 9.42 S | 160.40 E |
| Kaoko Otavi | 156 | 18.14 S | 13.40 E |
| Kaoko Veld ⋏[1] | 156 | 20.00 S | 14.00 E |
| Kaolack | 150 | 14.09 N | 16.04 W |
| Kaolack □[4] | 150 | 14.00 N | 15.30 W |
| Kaolin | 285 | 39.48 N | 75.43 W |
| Kaolun → Kowloon | 271d | 22.18 N | 114.10 E |
| Kaoma | 154 | 14.47 S | 24.48 E |
| Kaongweshi ≃ | 152 | 7.53 S | 22.20 E |
| Kaoping → Changzhi | 102 | 36.11 N | 113.08 E |
| Kaoshanji | 105 | 40.11 N | 117.17 E |
| Kaoshanpu | 100 | 30.54 N | 114.32 E |
| Kaouadja ≃ | 140 | 6.45 N | 24.15 E |
| Kaouar ◆[1] | 146 | 19.00 N | 12.40 E |
| Kao Valley V | 158 | 28.54 S | 18.06 E |
| Kapaa | 229b | 22.04 N | 159.19 W |
| Kapadvanj | 120 | 23.01 N | 73.04 E |
| Kapahiang | 112 | 3.39 S | 102.34 E |
| Kapal | 86 | 45.08 N | 79.03 E |
| Kapalong | 116 | 7.35 N | 125.42 E |
| Kapan | 112 | 9.44 S | 124.17 E |
| Kapanga, Zaïre | 152 | 8.21 S | 22.35 E |
| Kapanga, Zaïre | 152 | 5.04 S | 16.58 E |
| Kapangan | 116 | 16.35 N | 120.35 E |
| Kapaonik ⋏ | 38 | 43.20 N | 20.50 E |
| Kāpāsia | 126 | 24.07 N | 90.32 E |
| Kapatagan | 116 | 7.52 N | 123.44 E |
| Kapatkevičy | 76 | 52.19 N | 28.49 E |
| Kapatu | 154 | 9.43 S | 30.42 E |
| Kapčagaj | 85 | 43.53 N | 77.12 E |
| Kapčagajskoje vodochranilišče ⊜[1] | 86 | 43.50 N | 78.00 E |
| Kapcèvičy | 76 | 52.14 N | 28.19 E |
| Kapchorwa | 154 | 1.24 N | 34.27 E |
| Kapedo | 154 | 1.10 N | 36.06 E |
| Kapelle | 52 | 51.28 N | 3.58 E |
| Kapellen, Bel. | 50 | 51.19 N | 4.26 E |
| Kapellen, Dtsch. | 56 | 51.25 N | 6.35 E |
| Kapellen, Dtsch. | 263 | 51.08 N | 6.38 E |
| Kapellen, Öst. | 61 | 47.38 N | 15.37 E |
| Kapelle-op-den-Bos | 50 | 51.01 N | 4.22 E |
| Kapellerfeld | 264b | 48.19 N | 16.30 E |
| Kapelln | 61 | 48.15 N | 15.45 E |
| Kapellskär | 40 | 59.43 N | 19.04 E |
| Kapema | 154 | 10.42 S | 28.24 E |
| Kapenguria | 154 | 1.04 N | 35.07 E |
| Kapfenberg | 61 | 47.26 N | 15.18 E |
| Kapia | 152 | 4.17 S | 19.46 E |
| Kapıdağ Yarımadası ›[1] | 130 | 40.28 N | 27.50 E |
| Kapikik Lake ⊜ | 184 | 51.32 N | 91.57 W |
| Kapikog Lake ⊜ | 212 | 45.09 N | 79.53 W |
| Kapilmuni | 126 | 22.42 N | 89.20 E |
| Kapingamarangi I[1] | 14 | 1.04 N | 154.46 E |
| Kapiri Mposhi | 154 | 13.58 S | 28.41 E |
| Kāpīsā □[4] | 120 | 34.45 N | 69.30 E |
| Kapiskau ≃ | 176 | 52.47 N | 81.55 W |
| Kapit | 112 | 2.01 N | 112.56 E |
| Kapitanivka | 78 | 48.54 N | 31.42 E |
| Kapiti Island I | 172 | 40.52 S | 174.54 E |
| Kapiura ≃ | 164 | 5.45 S | 150.35 E |
| Kapka, Massif du ⋏ | 146 | 15.07 N | 21.45 E |
| Kapkataš | 85 | 40.23 N | 74.20 E |
| Kapkatas, chrebet ⋏ | 85 | 41.50 N | 76.10 E |
| Kapkinka | 80 | 48.08 N | 43.51 E |
| Kaplan | 194 | 29.59 N | 92.17 W |
| Kaplice | 61 | 48.45 N | 14.30 E |
| Kapoe | 110 | 9.35 N | 98.40 E |
| Kapoeta | 154 | 4.47 N | 33.35 E |
| Kapona | 154 | 7.11 S | 29.09 E |
| Kaponga | 172 | 39.26 S | 174.09 E |
| Kaporskoje | 265a | 59.45 N | 29.58 E |
| Kapos ≃ | 30 | 46.44 N | 18.30 E |
| Kaposvár | 30 | 46.22 N | 17.47 E |
| Kaposvar Creek ≃ | 184 | 50.31 N | 101.55 W |
| Kapotn'a ◆[8] | 265b | 55.38 N | 37.48 E |
| Kapowsin | 224 | 46.59 N | 122.13 W |
| Kapowsin, Lake ⊜ | 224 | 46.58 N | 122.13 W |
| Kapp | 26 | 60.42 N | 10.52 E |
| Kappar | 128 | 25.19 N | 62.42 E |
| Kappel | 56 | 50.00 N | 7.21 E |
| Kappeln | 41 | 54.40 N | 9.56 E |
| Kappelrodeck | 58 | 48.36 N | 8.07 E |
| Kappelshamn | 26 | 57.51 N | 18.47 E |
| Kapps | 156 | 22.22 S | 17.52 E |
| Kapralicha | 86 | 56.11 N | 67.15 E |
| Kaprijke | 50 | 51.13 N | 3.36 E |
| Kaprun | 64 | 47.16 N | 12.46 E |
| Kapsabet | 154 | 0.12 N | 35.06 E |
| Kapsan | 98 | 41.04 N | 128.19 E |
| Kapstadt → Cape Town | 158 | 33.55 S | 18.22 E |
| Kaptai | 120 | 22.21 N | 92.17 E |
| Kaptipada | 126 | 21.31 N | 86.32 E |
| Kaptol | 36 | 45.26 N | 17.44 E |
| Kapuas ≃, Indon. | 112 | 0.25 S | 109.40 E |
| Kapuas ≃, Indon. | 112 | 3.01 S | 114.20 E |
| Kapuas Hulu, Pegunungan ⋏ | 112 | 1.15 N | 113.30 E |
| Kapulo | 154 | 8.18 S | 29.15 E |
| Kapunda | 168b | 34.21 S | 138.54 E |
| Kapūrthala | 123 | 31.23 N | 75.23 E |
| Kapur Utara, Pegunungan ⋏ | 115a | 6.52 S | 111.30 E |
| Kapuskasing | 176 | 49.25 N | 82.26 W |
| Kapuskasing ≃ | 176 | 49.49 N | 82.00 W |
| Kapuskasing Lake ⊜ | 190 | 48.30 N | 82.55 W |
| Kapustin Jar | 80 | 48.36 N | 45.45 E |
| Kapustyane | 78 | 48.57 N | 31.14 E |
| Kapuvár | 30 | 47.36 N | 17.02 E |
| Kap Verde → Cape Verde □[1] | 150a | 16.00 N | 24.00 W |
| Kapyl' | 76 | 53.09 N | 27.05 E |
| Kapyrevščina | 76 | 55.15 N | 32.53 E |
| Kara | 74 | 69.14 N | 65.00 E |
| Kara ≃ | 150 | 10.01 N | 0.25 E |
| Karaali | 130 | 39.40 N | 32.57 E |
| Karababa Dağı ∧ | 130 | 39.31 N | 36.10 E |
| Kara-Balta | 85 | 42.50 N | 73.52 E |
| Karabanovo | 82 | 56.19 N | 38.42 E |
| Karabaš, Ross. | 80 | 54.42 N | 52.36 E |
| Karabaš, Ross. | 86 | 55.29 N | 60.14 E |
| Karabau | 80 | 48.26 N | 52.54 E |
| Karabekaul | 128 | 38.30 N | 64.08 E |
| Karabiğa | 130 | 40.24 N | 27.18 E |
| Karabil', vozvyšennost' ⋏[1] | 128 | 36.25 N | 64.00 E |
| Kara-Bogaz-Gol, zaliv c | 72 | 41.00 N | 53.15 E |
| Karabudachkent | 84 | 42.41 N | 47.34 E |
| Karabük | 130 | 41.12 N | 32.37 E |
| Karabula | 88 | 58.08 N | 97.23 E |
| Karabula ≃ | 88 | 58.22 N | 97.02 E |
| Karabulak, Kaz. | 85 | 42.32 N | 69.46 E |
| Karabulak, Kaz. | 86 | 44.54 N | 78.30 E |
| Karabulak, Kaz. | 86 | 47.34 N | 84.41 E |
| Karabulak, Kyrg. | 85 | 39.51 N | 69.38 E |
| Karabulduk | 130 | 40.50 N | 38.34 E |
| Karaburun | 130 | 38.37 N | 26.31 E |
| Karabutak | 86 | 49.59 N | 60.10 E |
| Karacabey | 130 | 40.13 N | 28.21 E |
| Karacadağ, Tür. | 130 | 41.57 N | 27.40 E |
| Karacadağ, Tür. | 130 | 37.43 N | 39.37 E |
| Karaca Dağ ∧ | 130 | 37.40 N | 39.50 E |
| Karačajevo-Čerkesija □[3], Ross. | 72 | 44.00 N | 42.00 E |
| Karačajevo-Čerkesija □[3], Ross. | 84 | 44.00 N | 42.00 E |
| Karačajevsk | 84 | 43.45 N | 41.54 E |
| Karacaköy | 130 | 41.24 N | 28.22 E |
| Karacaoğlan | 130 | 41.31 N | 27.07 E |
| Karacasu | 130 | 37.43 N | 28.37 E |
| Karacaviran | 130 | 39.44 N | 38.08 E |
| Karaçay | 130 | 36.10 N | 36.02 E |
| Karaçayır | 130 | 39.55 N | 37.01 E |
| Karačev | 76 | 53.07 N | 35.00 E |
| Karachay → Karačajevo-Čerkesija □[3] | 84 | 44.00 N | 42.00 E |
| Karāchi | 120 | 24.52 N | 67.03 E |
| Karachtaj | 85 | 40.55 N | 69.46 E |
| Karači | 80 | 57.59 N | 50.28 E |
| Karād | 122 | 17.17 N | 74.12 E |
| Kara Dağ ∧ | 130 | 40.22 N | 39.05 E |
| Karadarja ≃ | 85 | 40.54 N | 71.45 E |
| Karadeniz → Black Sea ∓[2] | 22 | 43.00 N | 35.00 E |
| Karadere | 130 | 40.40 N | 30.50 E |
| Karadirek | 130 | 38.34 N | 30.11 E |
| Karaftit | 88 | 54.12 N | 111.54 E |
| Karagaj, Kaz. | 80 | 48.39 N | 47.38 E |
| Karagaj, Ross. | 80 | 58.16 N | 54.56 E |
| Karagajly | 86 | 49.20 N | 75.48 E |
| Karaganda | 86 | 49.50 N | 73.10 E |
| Karaganda □[8] | 86 | 50.00 N | 74.00 E |
| Karagel | 128 | 39.23 N | 53.11 E |
| Karagičevskij | 80 | 50.11 N | 42.55 E |
| Karaginskij, ostrov I | 74 | 58.50 N | 164.00 E |
| Karaginskij zaliv c | 74 | 58.50 N | 164.00 E |
| Karagola Road | 124 | 25.29 N | 87.23 E |
| Karagöl Dağı ∧ | 130 | 40.32 N | 38.10 E |
| Kara Gölü ⊜ | 130 | 36.42 N | 29.50 E |
| Karagoš, gora ∧ | 86 | 51.44 N | 89.24 E |
| Karagužicha | 86 | 50.47 N | 83.00 E |
| Karahallı | 130 | 38.20 N | 29.32 E |
| Karaia | 124 | 25.54 N | 78.01 E |
| Karaičev | 80 | 48.37 N | 42.13 E |
| Karaidel' | 86 | 55.50 N | 56.53 E |
| Karaidel'skij | 86 | 55.49 N | 57.05 E |
| Kāraikāl | 122 | 10.55 N | 79.50 E |
| Kāraikkudi | 122 | 10.04 N | 78.47 E |
| Karaisalı | 130 | 37.16 N | 35.03 E |
| Karaitivu I | 122 | 8.23 N | 79.47 E |
| Karaj | 128 | 35.48 N | 50.59 E |
| Karaj ≃ | 267d | 35.35 N | 51.11 E |
| Karajantak | 85 | 40.03 N | 67.54 E |
| Karak | 114 | 3.24 N | 102.02 E |
| Karakabak | 86 | 50.33 N | 75.09 E |
| Karakain | 85 | 41.26 N | 74.19 E |
| Kara-Kala | 128 | 38.26 N | 56.18 E |
| Karakalpak Respublika □[3] | 86 | 43.00 N | 59.00 E |
| Karakaralong, Pulau II | 112 | 4.30 N | 125.30 E |
| Karakastek | 85 | 43.08 N | 76.06 E |
| Karakavak | 85 | 39.41 N | 72.43 E |
| Karakax ≃ | 120 | 37.00 N | 79.45 E |
| Karakaya Barajı ⊜[1] | 130 | 38.25 N | 38.45 E |
| Karakeçı | 130 | 37.26 N | 39.26 E |
| Karakeçili | 130 | 39.36 N | 33.23 E |
| Karakelong, Pulau I | 108 | 4.15 N | 126.48 E |
| Karakemer | 85 | 42.55 N | 75.20 E |
| Karakendža | 85 | 39.14 N | 71.31 E |
| Karakitang, Pulau I | 112 | 3.11 N | 125.32 E |
| Karakojsu ≃ | 84 | 42.33 N | 46.58 E |
| Karakojun ≃ | 85 | 41.10 N | 75.45 E |
| Karakojyn, ozero ⊜ | 86 | 46.10 N | 68.45 E |
| Karakol (Prževal'sk) | 85 | 42.29 N | 78.24 E |
| Karakolka | 85 | 41.32 N | 77.23 E |
| Karakoram Pass )( | 120 | 35.30 N | 77.50 E |
| Karakoram Range ⋏ | 120 | 35.30 N | 77.00 E |
| Karakoro ≃ | 150 | 14.43 N | 12.03 W |
| Karaksar | 88 | 51.16 N | 115.58 E |
| Karakudžur ≃ | 85 | 41.59 N | 75.42 E |
| Karakul', Ross. | 86 | 57.26 N | 70.51 E |
| Karakul', Taj. | 85 | 39.02 N | 73.33 E |
| Karakul', Uzb. | 128 | 39.32 N | 63.50 E |
| Karakul', ozero ⊜ | 85 | 39.05 N | 73.25 E |
| Karakulak | 130 | 39.59 N | 40.01 E |
| Kara-Kul'dža | 85 | 40.37 N | 73.35 E |
| Karakul'dža ≃ | 85 | 40.39 N | 73.26 E |
| Karakulino | 80 | 56.01 N | 53.43 E |
| Karakul'skoje | 86 | 54.04 N | 62.26 E |
| Karakum | 86 | 46.49 N | 79.33 E |
| Karakumskij kanal ≡ | 128 | 37.35 N | 61.50 E |
| Karakumy ◆[2] | 72 | 39.00 N | 60.00 E |
| Karakuni | 270 | 34.28 N | 135.28 E |
| Karakurt | 130 | 40.10 N | 42.36 E |
| Karala ◆[8] | 272a | 28.44 N | 77.02 E |
| Karalat | 80 | 45.55 N | 48.18 E |
| Karalon | 88 | 57.02 N | 115.52 E |
| Karalundi | 162 | 26.07 S | 118.41 E |
| Karam | 88 | 55.09 N | 107.37 E |
| Karama ≃ | 112 | 2.18 S | 119.06 E |
| Karamağara | 130 | 39.42 N | 35.31 E |
| Karamai → Karamay | 86 | 45.30 N | 84.55 E |
| Karaman | 130 | 37.11 N | 33.14 E |
| Karaman □[4] | 130 | 37.00 N | 33.00 E |
| Karamanlı | 130 | 37.22 N | 29.49 E |
| Karamay | 86 | 45.30 N | 84.55 E |
| Karambu | 112 | 3.51 S | 116.04 E |
| Karamea | 172 | 41.15 S | 172.07 E |
| Karamea ≃ | 172 | 41.16 S | 172.06 E |
| Karamea Bight c[3] | 172 | 41.30 S | 171.40 E |
| Karamıkbataklığı ≡ | 130 | 38.25 N | 30.50 E |
| Karamnisa Nāla ⊜[1] | 124 | 25.42 N | 83.25 E |
| Karamoja □[5] | 154 | 2.50 N | 34.15 E |
| Karamola, gora ∧ | 86 | 47.58 N | 66.35 E |
| Karamürsel | 130 | 40.42 N | 29.36 E |
| Karamurt | 85 | 42.19 N | 69.58 E |
| Karamyš ≃ | 80 | 51.20 N | 45.00 E |
| Karamyševo, Ross. | 76 | 57.45 N | 28.45 E |
| Karamyševo, Ross. | 82 | 54.46 N | 36.07 E |
| Karamyševo, Ross. | 88 | 57.34 N | 100.55 E |
| Karamzino | 76 | 56.00 N | 34.33 E |
| Karang, Gunung ∧ | 115a | 6.16 S | 106.03 E |
| Karang, Tanjung › | 112 | 0.38 S | 119.44 E |
| Karangagung | 112 | 2.22 S | 104.27 E |
| Karangampel | 115a | 6.28 S | 108.27 E |
| Karangana | 150 | 12.13 N | 5.02 W |
| Karangasem | 115b | 8.27 S | 115.37 E |
| Karangbinangun | 115a | 7.01 S | 112.30 E |
| Karangbolang, Ujung › | 115a | 7.46 S | 109.02 E |
| Karangbolong | 115a | 7.45 S | 109.28 E |
| Karanggede | 115a | 7.22 S | 110.37 E |
| Karangkates, Waduk ⊜[1] | 115a | 8.11 S | 112.34 E |
| Karangkobar | 115a | 7.16 S | 109.44 E |
| Karangnunggal | 115a | 7.38 S | 108.06 E |
| Karangpandan | 115a | 7.37 S | 111.04 E |
| Karangsembung | 115a | 6.51 S | 108.39 E |
| Kāranja | 122 | 20.29 N | 77.29 E |
| Karanjia | 120 | 21.47 N | 85.58 E |
| Karanpura | 123 | 29.50 N | 73.27 E |
| Karaoba, Kaz. | 86 | 53.17 N | 65.06 E |
| Karaoba, Kaz. | 86 | 47.03 N | 56.20 E |
| Karaoğlan | 130 | 39.14 N | 39.13 E |
| Karaoj | 86 | 45.54 N | 74.45 E |
| Karaozek, Kaz. | 85 | 43.43 N | 77.23 E |
| Karaozek, Kaz. | 86 | 45.03 N | 65.18 E |
| Karaozek, Uzb. | 86 | 43.16 N | 58.40 E |
| Karapınar, Tür. | 130 | 37.43 N | 33.33 E |
| Karapınar, Tür. | 130 | 41.30 N | 32.12 E |
| Karapyshi | 78 | 49.38 N | 30.47 E |
| Karaš | 80 | 56.54 N | 39.24 E |
| Karas □[4] | 156 | 27.00 S | 17.00 E |
| Karas, Pulau I | 164 | 3.27 S | 132.40 E |
| Karasaj | 85 | 41.34 N | 77.49 E |
| Kara-Sal ≃ | 80 | 47.22 N | 43.38 E |
| Karaşar | 130 | 40.20 N | 32.00 E |
| Karasay | 120 | 36.47 N | 83.48 E |
| Karasburg | 156 | 28.00 S | 18.43 E |
| Kara Sea → Karskoje more ∓[2] | 72 | 76.00 N | 80.00 E |
| Karašengel' | 86 | 47.29 N | 75.35 E |
| Karašjåkka ≃ | 24 | 69.26 N | 25.49 E |
| Karasjok | 24 | 69.27 N | 25.30 E |
| Karaskan | 85 | 41.03 N | 71.49 E |
| Karasor, ozero ⊜, Kaz. | 86 | 49.54 N | 75.32 E |
| Karasor, ozero ⊜, Kaz. | 86 | 51.57 N | 75.45 E |
| Karasu, Kaz. | 86 | 52.40 N | 65.28 E |
| Karasu, Kaz. | 86 | 51.20 N | 62.21 E |
| Karasu, Kyrg. | 85 | 43.03 N | 73.57 E |
| Kara-Su, Kyrg. | 85 | 40.44 N | 72.53 E |
| Karasu, Nihon | 94 | 34.39 N | 136.32 E |
| Karasu, Tür. | 130 | 41.06 N | 30.41 E |
| Karasu ≃, Nihon | 94 | 36.15 N | 139.17 E |
| Karasu ≃, Tür. | 130 | 39.07 N | 38.44 E |
| Karasuk | 86 | 53.44 N | 78.02 E |
| Karasuk ≃ | 86 | 53.35 N | 77.30 E |
| Karasuyama | 94 | 36.39 N | 140.09 E |
| Karata | 84 | 42.35 N | 46.21 E |
| Karatal, Kaz. | 86 | 47.36 N | 85.12 E |
| Karatal, Kaz. | 86 | 45.07 N | 77.54 E |
| Karatal ≃ | 86 | 46.26 N | 77.10 E |
| Karataş, Tür. | 130 | 36.36 N | 35.21 E |
| Karataş, Tür. | 130 | 38.34 N | 28.17 E |
| Karataş Burun › | 130 | 36.35 N | 35.22 E |
| Karatau | 85 | 43.10 N | 70.28 E |
| Karatau, chrebet ⋏, Kaz. | 72 | 43.50 N | 68.30 E |
| Karatau, chrebet ⋏, Taj. | 85 | 38.10 N | 69.00 E |
| Karateginskij chrebet ⋏ | 85 | 38.50 N | 69.40 E |
| Karatepe Milli Parkı ♠ | 130 | 37.17 N | 36.13 E |
| Karatia | 126 | 24.14 N | 89.58 E |
| Karatobe | 80 | 49.41 N | 53.31 E |
| Karatogaj | 86 | 48.42 N | 59.40 E |
| Karaton | 86 | 46.25 N | 53.30 E |
| Karatoya ≃ | 124 | 24.13 N | 89.36 E |
| Karatschi → Karāchi | 120 | 24.52 N | 67.03 E |
| Karatsu | 92 | 33.26 N | 129.58 E |
| Karaturyk | 85 | 43.33 N | 77.59 E |
| Karatuzskoje | 86 | 53.36 N | 92.53 E |
| Karau | 164 | 3.45 S | 144.20 E |
| Karaul, Kaz. | 86 | 48.57 N | 79.15 E |
| Karaul, Ross. | 74 | 70.06 N | 83.08 E |
| Karauli | 124 | 26.30 N | 77.01 E |
| Karault'ob'o | 85 | 40.33 N | 75.57 E |
| Karaunk'ur ≃ | 85 | 40.54 N | 72.20 E |
| Karaurğan | 130 | 40.15 N | 42.17 E |
| Karauzak | 86 | 42.59 N | 60.02 E |
| Karauzek | 80 | 47.15 N | 48.25 E |
| Karavan | 85 | 41.30 N | 71.45 E |
| Karavannoje, Ross. | 80 | 45.59 N | 47.08 E |
| Karavannoje, Ross. | 80 | 57.47 N | 47.41 E |
| Karave | 272c | 19.01 N | 73.01 E |
| Karawa | 152 | 3.20 N | 20.18 E |
| Karawang | 115a | 6.19 S | 107.17 E |
| Karawang, Tanjung › | 115a | 5.56 S | 107.00 E |


**Symbols** in the index entries represent the broad categories identified in the key at the right. Symbols with superior numbers (⋏[1]) identify subcategories (see complete key on page I · 1).

**Symbole** im Register stellen die rechts im Schlüssel erklärten Kategorien dar. Symbole mit hochgestellten Ziffern (⋏[1]) bezeichnen Unterabteilungen einer Kategorie (vgl. vollständiger Schlüssel auf Seite I · 1).

**Los símbolos** incluídos en el texto del índice representan las grandes categorías identificadas con la clave a la derecha. Los símbolos con numeros en su parte superior (⋏[1]) identifican las subcategorías (véase la clave completa en la página I · 1).

**Les symboles** de l'index représentent les catégories indiquées dans la légende à droite. Les symboles suivis d'un indice (⋏[1]) représentent des sous-catégories (voir légende complète à la page I · 1).

**Os símbolos** incluídos no texto do índice representam as grandes categorias identificadas com a chave à direita. Os símbolos com números em sua parte superior (⋏[1]) identificam as subcategorias (veja-se a chave completa à página I · 1).

| Symbol | English | Deutsch | Español | Français | Português |
|---|---|---|---|---|---|
| ∧ | Mountain | Berg | Montaña | Montagne | Montanha |
| ⋏ | Mountains | Gebirge | Montañas | Montagnes | Montanhas |
| )( | Pass | Paß | Paso | Col | Passo |
| V | Valley, Canyon | Tal, Cañon | Valle, Cañón | Vallée, Canyon | Vale, Canhão |
| ≚ | Plain | Ebene | Llano | Plaine | Planície |
| › | Cape | Kap | Cabo | Cap | Cabo |
| I | Island | Insel | Isla | Île | Ilha |
| II | Islands | Inseln | Islas | Îles | Ilhas |
| ⊥ | Other Topographic Features | Andere Topographische Objekte | Otros Elementos Topográficos | Autres données topographiques | Outros acidentes topográficos |

ESPAÑOL: Nombre · Página · Lat.°′ · Long.°′ W = Oeste
FRANÇAIS: Nom · Page · Lat.°′ · Long.°′ W = Ouest
PORTUGUÊS: Nome · Página · Lat.°′ · Long.°′ W = Oeste


| Nombre / Nom / Nome | Página / Page | Lat.°′ | Long.°′ |
|---|---|---|---|
| Karawanken ⛰ | 36 | 46.30 N | 14.25 E |
| Karayaka | 130 | 40.45 N | 36.37 E |
| Karayashnyk | 83 | 49.22 N | 39.10 E |
| Karayazı | 130 | 39.41 N | 42.08 E |
| Karaye | 150 | 11.48 N | 8.02 E |
| Karayün | 130 | 39.41 N | 37.19 E |
| Karažal | 86 | 48.02 N | 70.49 E |
| Karbalā' | 128 | 32.36 N | 44.02 E |
| Karbalā' ▫4 | 128 | 32.00 N | 42.15 E |
| Karbenning | 40 | 60.02 N | 16.04 E |
| Kårberg | 40 | 58.58 N | 14.57 E |
| Karbeyaz | 130 | 36.02 N | 36.12 E |
| Kårböle | 26 | 61.59 N | 15.19 E |
| Karby | 40 | 59.34 N | 18.13 E |
| Karcag | 30 | 47.19 N | 20.56 E |
| Karczew | 30 | 52.06 N | 21.15 E |
| Kardail ≃ | 80 | 50.43 N | 42.54 E |
| Kardašova Řečice | 61 | 49.11 N | 14.53 E |
| Kardeljevo | 36 | 43.04 N | 17.26 E |
| Kardhámaina | 38 | 36.47 N | 27.09 E |
| Kardhámila | 38 | 38.32 N | 26.05 E |
| Kardhítsa | 38 | 39.21 N | 21.55 E |
| Kärdla | 76 | 59.00 N | 22.45 E |
| Kardymovo | 76 | 54.54 N | 32.26 E |
| Kărdžali | 38 | 41.39 N | 25.22 E |
| Kardžin | 84 | 43.16 N | 44.16 E |
| Karea | 272b | 22.42 N | 88.33 E |
| Kareeberge ⛰ | 158 | 30.53 S | 21.57 E |
| Kareedouw | 158 | 33.57 S | 24.18 E |
| Kareli | 84 | 42.01 N | 43.54 E |
| Karelia → Karelija ▫3 | 24 | 64.00 N | 32.30 E |
| Karelia ▫9 | 24 | 63.00 N | 32.00 E |
| Karèličy | 76 | 53.34 N | 26.08 E |
| Karelija ▫3, Ross. | 24 | 64.00 N | 32.30 E |
| Karelija ▫3, Ross. | 72 | 64.00 N | 32.30 E |
| Karel'skij Gorodok | 76 | 58.04 N | 36.30 E |
| Karema, Pap. N. Gui. | 164 | 9.12 S | 147.14 E |
| Karema, Tan. | 154 | 6.49 S | 30.26 E |
| Karen | 110 | 12.51 N | 92.53 E |
| Karenga ≃ | 88 | 54.28 N | 116.32 E |
| Karepino | 24 | 61.02 N | 57.02 E |
| Karera | 272a | 28.41 N | 77.23 E |
| Karesuando | 24 | 68.25 N | 22.30 E |
| Kärevere | 76 | 58.26 N | 26.29 E |
| Kāreyz-e Elyās | 128 | 35.25 N | 61.20 E |
| Kargali | 80 | 55.12 N | 50.54 E |
| Kargalinskaja | 84 | 43.44 N | 46.30 E |
| Karganaj | 180 | 65.21 N | 175.25 E |
| Kargapazarı Dağları ⛰ | 130 | 40.07 N | 41.35 E |
| Kargapolje | 86 | 55.57 N | 64.27 E |
| Kargasok | 86 | 59.07 N | 80.53 E |
| Kargat | 86 | 55.10 N | 80.17 E |
| Kargat ≃ | 86 | 54.37 N | 78.12 E |
| Kargı | 130 | 41.08 N | 34.30 E |
| Kargil | 123 | 34.34 N | 76.06 E |
| Karginskaja | 80 | 49.21 N | 41.38 E |
| Karginskij ≃ | 265a | 59.50 N | 30.01 E |
| Kargopol' | 24 | 61.30 N | 38.58 E |
| Karguéri | 146 | 13.27 N | 10.25 E |
| Karhal | 124 | 27.01 N | 78.57 E |
| Karhijärvi ⊜ | 26 | 61.35 N | 22.30 E |
| Karhula | 26 | 60.31 N | 26.57 E |
| Kari | 146 | 11.14 N | 10.34 E |
| Karia-ba-Mohammed | 148 | 34.19 N | 5.10 W |
| Kariaí | 38 | 40.16 N | 24.15 E |
| Karianga | 157b | 22.22 S | 47.26 E |
| Kariba | 154 | 16.30 S | 28.45 E |
| Kariba, Lake ⊜1 | 154 | 17.00 S | 28.00 E |
| Karibib | 156 | 21.58 S | 15.51 E |
| Karibisches Meer → Caribbean Sea ▾2 | 230 | 15.00 N | 73.00 W |
| Karibumba | 154 | 0.22 N | 29.22 E |
| Kariega ≃ | 158 | 33.03 S | 23.28 E |
| Karigasniemi | 24 | 69.24 N | 25.50 E |
| Karikari, Cape > | 172 | 34.47 S | 173.24 E |
| Karimata | 175d | 24.54 N | 125.17 E |
| Karimata, Kepulauan II | 112 | 1.25 S | 109.05 E |
| Karimata, Pulau I | 112 | 1.36 S | 108.55 E |
| Karimata, Selat (Karimata Strait) ⨆ | 112 | 2.05 S | 108.40 E |
| Karīmganj | 120 | 24.52 N | 92.21 E |
| Karīmnagar | 122 | 18.26 N | 79.09 E |
| Karīmpur | 126 | 23.58 N | 88.37 E |
| Karimun, Pulau I | 114 | 1.03 N | 103.22 E |
| Karimunjawa, Kepulauan II | 115a | 5.50 S | 110.25 E |
| Karimunjawa, Pulau I | 115a | 5.51 S | 110.27 E |
| Karin, Som. | 144 | 10.59 N | 49.13 E |
| Karin, Som. | 144 | 10.51 N | 45.47 E |
| Karino | 82 | 54.42 N | 38.56 E |
| Karin Seamount ✦3 | 14 | 17.55 N | 168.58 W |
| Karinskoje | 82 | 55.42 N | 36.41 E |
| Karintorf | 80 | 58.33 N | 50.11 E |
| Karis (Karjaa) | 26 | 60.05 N | 23.40 E |
| Karise | 41 | 55.18 N | 12.13 E |
| Karisimbi, Volcan ∧1 | 154 | 1.30 S | 29.27 E |
| Káristos | 38 | 38.00 N | 24.24 E |
| Kariya | 94 | 34.59 N | 136.59 E |
| Kariye Museum ⅴ1 | 267b | 41.01 N | 28.55 E |
| Kārīz | 128 | 34.49 N | 60.47 E |
| Karjaa → Karis | 26 | 60.05 N | 23.40 E |
| Karjepolje | 24 | 65.34 N | 43.40 E |
| Kārkal | 122 | 13.12 N | 74.59 E |
| Karkalaj | 80 | 57.00 N | 52.24 E |
| Karkaralinsk | 86 | 49.23 N | 75.21 E |
| Karkar Dūmān ◆8 | 272a | 28.39 N | 77.18 E |
| Karkar Island I | 164 | 4.40 S | 146.00 E |
| Karkas, Kūh-e ∧ | 128 | 33.29 N | 51.50 E |
| Karkheh ≃ | 128 | 31.46 N | 47.55 E |
| Karkīndar | 128 | 25.47 N | 59.15 E |
| Karkinits'ka zatoka ⊂ | 78 | 45.55 N | 33.00 E |
| Karkkila | 26 | 60.32 N | 24.11 E |
| Karkku | 26 | 61.25 N | 23.01 E |
| Karkom, Har ∧ | 132 | 30.17 N | 34.44 E |
| Karkonoski Park Narodowy ♦ | 30 | 50.45 N | 15.35 E |
| Kärla | 76 | 58.20 N | 22.15 E |
| Karlholmsbruk | 40 | 60.31 N | 17.35 E |
| Karlik Shan ∧ | 102 | 43.08 N | 94.20 E |
| Karlino | 30 | 54.03 N | 15.51 E |
| Karlıova | 130 | 39.18 N | 41.01 E |
| Karlivka | 78 | 49.27 N | 35.08 E |
| Karl-Marx-Stadt → Chemnitz | 54 | 50.50 N | 12.55 E |
| Karlobag | 36 | 44.32 N | 15.05 E |
| Karlo-Marksove | 83 | 48.16 N | 38.09 E |
| Karloske ≃ | 184 | 55.41 N | 93.56 W |
| Karlovac | 36 | 45.29 N | 15.34 E |
| Karlovo | 38 | 42.38 N | 24.48 E |
| Karlovy Vary (Carlsbad) | 54 | 50.11 N | 12.52 E |
| Karlsbad → Karlovy Vary, Česká Rep. | 54 | 50.11 N | 12.52 E |
| Karlsbad, Dtsch. | 56 | 48.55 N | 8.30 E |
| Karlsborg, Sve. | 26 | 58.32 N | 14.31 E |
| Karlsborg, Sve. | 26 | 65.48 N | 23.17 E |
| Karlsburg, Dtsch. | 54 | 53.58 N | 13.37 E |
| Karlsburg → Alba Iulia, Rom. | 38 | 46.04 N | 23.35 E |
| Karlsby | 40 | 58.38 N | 15.08 E |
| Karlsfeld | 60 | 48.13 N | 11.28 E |
| Karlshagen | 54 | 54.07 N | 13.50 E |
| Karlshamn | 26 | 56.10 N | 14.51 E |
| Karlshorst ◆8 | 264a | 52.29 N | 13.32 E |
| Karlshorst, Trabrennbahn ♦ | 264a | 52.29 N | 13.31 E |
| Karlshuld | 60 | 48.41 N | 11.18 E |
| Karlskoga | 40 | 59.20 N | 14.31 E |
| Karlskron | 60 | 48.41 N | 11.25 E |
| Karlskrona | 26 | 56.10 N | 15.35 E |
| Karlslunde Strand | 41 | 55.34 N | 12.14 E |
| Karlsöarna II | 26 | 57.17 N | 17.58 E |
| Karlsruhe | 56 | 49.03 N | 8.24 E |
| Karlsruhe ▫5, Dtsch. | 56 | 49.20 N | 8.45 E |
| Karlsruhe ▫5, Dtsch. | 58 | 48.30 N | 8.30 E |
| Karlstad, Sve. | 40 | 59.22 N | 13.30 E |
| Karlstad, Mn., U.S. | 198 | 48.34 N | 96.31 W |
| Karlstadt | 56 | 49.57 N | 9.45 E |
| Karlstift | 61 | 48.35 N | 14.45 E |
| Karluk, Ross. | 88 | 53.27 N | 105.58 E |
| Karluk, Ak., U.S. | 180 | 57.34 N | 154.28 W |
| Karl'uk, Uzb. | 85 | 38.12 N | 67.42 E |
| Karma, Bela. | 76 | 53.08 N | 30.48 E |
| Karma, Bela. | 76 | 52.21 N | 31.31 E |
| Karma, Niger | 150 | 13.40 N | 1.49 E |
| Karma, Ouadi V | 146 | 15.38 N | 20.01 E |
| Karmah | 140 | 19.38 N | 30.25 E |
| Karmāla | 122 | 18.25 N | 75.12 E |
| Karmanovka | 80 | 49.24 N | 50.22 E |
| Karmanovo | 76 | 55.52 N | 34.52 E |
| Karmansbo | 40 | 59.42 N | 15.44 E |
| Karmatānr | 126 | 24.05 N | 86.42 E |
| Karmel, Har (Mount Carmel) ∧ | 132 | 32.44 N | 35.02 E |
| Karmi'el | 132 | 32.55 N | 35.18 E |
| Karmiyya | 132 | 31.36 N | 34.33 E |
| Karmøy I | 26 | 59.15 N | 5.15 E |
| Karnack | 194 | 32.40 N | 94.10 W |
| Karnak → Al-Karnak, Mișr | 140 | 25.43 N | 32.39 E |
| Karnak, Il., U.S. | 194 | 37.17 N | 88.58 W |
| Karnāl | 124 | 29.41 N | 76.59 E |
| Karnāla Fort ⊥ | 272c | 18.53 N | 73.07 E |
| Karnālī ▫8 | 124 | 29.30 N | 82.30 E |
| Karnālī ≃ | 124 | 28.15 N | 81.05 E |
| Karnap ◆8 | 263 | 51.31 N | 7.01 E |
| Karnaphuli Reservoir ⊜1 | 120 | 22.42 N | 92.12 E |
| Karnātaka ▫3 | 122 | 14.00 N | 76.00 E |
| Karnaukhivka | 78 | 48.28 N | 34.44 E |
| Karnes ▫6 | 222 | 29.00 N | 97.47 W |
| Karnes City | 196 | 28.53 N | 97.54 W |
| Karni | 150 | 10.40 N | 2.37 W |
| Karniki | 82 | 54.12 N | 38.05 E |
| Karnische Alpen (Alpi Carniche) ⛰ | 64 | 46.40 N | 13.00 E |
| Karnobat | 38 | 42.39 N | 26.59 E |
| Karns City | 214 | 41.00 N | 79.44 W |
| Kärnten ▫3 | 30 | 46.50 N | 13.50 E |
| Karnzow | 54 | 52.59 N | 12.26 E |
| Karoi | 154 | 16.50 S | 29.40 E |
| Karokh | 128 | 34.28 N | 62.35 E |
| Karoli | 124 | 22.55 N | 79.04 E |
| Karolinenhof ◆8 | 264a | 52.23 N | 13.38 E |
| Karomatan | 116 | 7.46 N | 123.44 E |
| Karompa Lompo, Pulau I | 112 | 7.15 S | 121.45 E |
| Karon | 126 | 24.07 N | 86.44 E |
| Karonga | 154 | 9.56 S | 33.56 E |
| Karonie | 162 | 30.58 S | 122.32 E |
| Karoonda | 166 | 35.06 S | 139.54 E |
| Karor | 123 | 31.13 N | 70.57 E |
| Karora | 140 | 17.42 N | 38.22 E |
| Karos | 158 | 28.24 S | 21.35 E |
| Káros I | 38 | 36.53 N | 25.39 E |
| Karosa | 112 | 1.48 S | 119.20 E |
| Karoso, Tanjung > | 115b | 9.33 S | 118.50 E |
| Karotho Post | 154 | 5.11 N | 35.50 E |
| Karou | 150 | 15.07 N | 0.39 E |
| Karow, Dtsch. | 54 | 52.20 N | 12.15 E |
| Karow, Dtsch. | 54 | 53.32 N | 12.15 E |
| Karow ◆8 | 264a | 52.37 N | 13.29 E |
| Karpathen → Carpathian Mountains ⛰ | 22 | 48.00 N | 24.00 E |
| Kárpathos, Ellás | 38 | 35.30 N | 27.14 E |
| Kárpathos, Ellás | 130 | 35.31 N | 27.12 E |
| Kárpathos I | 38 | 35.40 N | 27.10 E |
| Karpats'kyy Pryrodnyy Natsional'nyy Park ♦ | 78 | 48.25 N | 24.30 E |
| Karpenísion | 38 | 38.55 N | 21.40 E |
| Karpinsk | 86 | 59.45 N | 60.01 E |
| Karpivka | 83 | 49.10 N | 37.43 E |
| Karpogory | 24 | 64.00 N | 44.24 E |
| Karpovo, Ross. | 76 | 60.02 N | 36.43 E |
| Karpovo, Ross. | 82 | 55.35 N | 38.34 E |
| Karpunicha | 80 | 57.42 N | 45.20 E |
| Karpuninskij | 86 | 58.43 N | 61.50 E |
| Karpuzlu | 130 | 37.33 N | 27.50 E |
| Karratha | 162 | 20.44 S | 116.51 E |
| Karrats Fjord ⊂2 | 176 | 71.20 N | 54.00 W |
| Karrebæksminde | 41 | 55.11 N | 11.40 E |
| Karres | 58 | 47.13 N | 10.47 E |
| Kärrgruvan | 40 | 60.05 N | 15.56 E |
| Karridale | 162 | 34.13 S | 115.05 E |
| Kars | 84 | 40.36 N | 43.05 E |
| Kars ▫4 | 84 | 40.35 N | 43.00 E |
| Kars ≃ | 84 | 40.37 N | 43.41 E |
| Karša | 80 | 49.48 N | 51.27 E |
| Karsakpaj | 86 | 47.49 N | 66.41 E |
| Karsakuwigamak Lake ⊜ | 184 | 56.22 N | 99.30 W |
| Kärsämäki | 26 | 63.58 N | 25.46 E |
| Karsantı | 130 | 37.33 N | 35.24 E |
| Kārsava | 76 | 56.47 N | 27.40 E |
| Karsdorf | 54 | 51.17 N | 11.39 E |
| Karši | 128 | 38.53 N | 65.48 E |
| Karsin | 30 | 53.54 N | 17.56 E |
| Karšinskaja step' ⌣ | 128 | 39.10 N | 65.00 E |
| Karskije Vorota, proliv ⨆ | 72 | 70.30 N | 58.00 E |
| Karskoje more (Kara Sea) ▾2 | 72 | 76.00 N | 80.00 E |
| Karsovaj | 80 | 58.14 N | 53.11 E |
| Karst → Kras ⛰1 | 64 | 45.48 N | 14.00 E |
| Kårsta, Sve. | 40 | 59.39 N | 18.14 E |
| Kärsta, Sve. | 40 | 59.40 N | 16.49 E |
| Karstädt | 54 | 53.09 N | 11.44 E |
| Karstula | 26 | 62.52 N | 24.47 E |
| Karsun | 80 | 54.11 N | 46.59 E |
| Kartajol' | 24 | 64.32 N | 53.14 E |
| Kartala ∧ | 157a | 11.45 S | 43.22 E |
| Kartaly | 86 | 53.03 N | 60.40 E |
| Kartārpur | 123 | 31.27 N | 75.30 E |
| Karthaus | 214 | 41.07 N | 78.07 W |
| Kartlijskij chrebet ⛰ | 84 | 42.10 N | 44.55 E |
| Kartosuro | 115a | 7.33 S | 110.44 E |
| Karttula | 26 | 62.53 N | 26.58 E |
| Kartuzy | 30 | 54.20 N | 18.12 E |
| Kartzow | 54 | 52.29 N | 12.58 E |
| Käru | 76 | 58.50 N | 25.11 E |
| Karuah ≃ | 170 | 32.39 S | 151.58 E |
| Karufa | 164 | 3.50 S | 133.27 E |
| Karuizawa | 94 | 36.21 N | 138.38 E |
| Karukuwisa | 156 | 18.56 S | 19.40 E |
| Karumai | 92 | 40.19 N | 141.28 E |
| Karumba | 166 | 17.29 S | 140.50 E |
| Kārūn ≃ | 128 | 30.26 N | 48.10 E |
| Karungi | 26 | 66.03 N | 23.57 E |
| Karungu | 154 | 0.51 S | 34.09 E |
| Karuni | 115b | 9.26 S | 119.19 E |
| Karunjie | 164 | 16.18 S | 127.12 E |
| Karunki | 26 | 66.02 N | 24.01 E |
| Karup | 41 | 56.18 N | 9.10 E |
| Karup ≃ | 41 | 56.18 N | 9.10 E |
| Karūr | 122 | 10.57 N | 78.05 E |
| Karuscia, Punta > | 70 | 36.49 N | 11.59 E |
| Karvala | 265a | 59.41 N | 30.09 E |
| Karviná | 30 | 49.50 N | 18.30 E |
| Kārwār | 122 | 14.48 N | 74.08 E |
| Karwendel ⛰ | 64 | 47.27 N | 11.20 E |
| Karwi | 124 | 25.12 N | 80.54 E |
| Karym | 86 | 60.07 N | 66.41 E |
| Karymskoje, Ross. | 88 | 51.37 N | 114.21 E |
| Karymskoje, Ross. | 88 | 54.07 N | 101.49 E |
| Karza | 86 | 58.35 N | 80.50 E |
| Karzachi | 84 | 41.15 N | 43.16 E |
| Kas, Sūd. | 140 | 12.30 N | 24.17 E |
| Kaş, Tür. | 130 | 36.12 N | 29.38 E |
| Kas ≃ | 86 | 59.40 N | 90.00 E |
| Kasaan | 182 | 55.32 N | 132.24 W |
| Kasabi | 152 | 14.48 S | 23.42 E |
| Kasach ≃ | 84 | 40.03 N | 43.52 E |
| Kasadi ≃ | 272c | 19.01 N | 73.03 E |
| Kasa-do I | 98 | 34.28 N | 126.03 E |
| Kasado-shima I | 96 | 33.57 N | 131.51 E |
| Kasagi | 94 | 34.45 N | 135.56 E |
| Kasagi-sanchi ⛰ | 270 | 34.37 N | 135.56 E |
| Kasagi-yama ∧ | 94 | 35.31 N | 137.21 E |
| Kasahara | 94 | 35.17 N | 137.09 E |
| Kasahata | 268 | 35.54 N | 139.25 E |
| Kasai | 96 | 34.56 N | 134.50 E |
| Kasai ◆8 | 268 | 35.39 N | 139.53 E |
| Kasai (Cassai) ≃, Afr. | 152 | 3.02 S | 16.57 E |
| Kāsai ≃, India | 124 | 22.09 N | 87.50 E |
| Kasai-Occidental ▫4 | 152 | 5.30 S | 21.40 E |
| Kasai-Oriental ▫4 | 152 | 4.00 S | 23.30 E |
| Kasaji | 152 | 10.22 S | 23.27 E |
| Kasakake | 94 | 36.23 N | 139.17 E |
| Kasama, Nihon | 94 | 36.23 N | 140.16 E |
| Kasama, Zam. | 154 | 10.13 S | 31.12 E |
| Kasamatsu | 94 | 35.22 N | 136.46 E |
| Kasan → Kazan', Ross. | 80 | 55.49 N | 49.08 E |
| Kasan, Uzb. | 128 | 39.02 N | 65.35 E |
| Kasan-dong | 98 | 41.18 N | 126.55 E |
| Kasane | 156 | 17.50 S | 25.05 E |
| Kasanga | 154 | 8.28 S | 31.09 E |
| Kasangale | 152 | 6.20 S | 22.42 E |
| Kasangeshi ≃ | 152 | 8.24 S | 21.56 E |
| Kasangulu | 152 | 4.36 S | 15.10 E |
| Kasanka National Park ♦ | 154 | 12.35 S | 30.12 E |
| Kasano-misaki > | 94 | 36.21 N | 136.18 E |
| Kasansaj | 85 | 41.15 N | 71.32 E |
| Kasansaj ≃ | 85 | 40.57 N | 71.30 E |
| Kasaoka | 96 | 34.30 N | 133.30 E |
| Kāsaragod | 122 | 12.30 N | 75.00 E |
| Kasari ≃ | 76 | 58.45 N | 23.49 E |
| Kašary | 78 | 49.03 N | 41.00 E |
| Kasatori-yama ∧, Nihon | 94 | 34.44 N | 136.18 E |
| Kasatori-yama ∧, Nihon | 96 | 33.33 N | 132.55 E |
| Kasauli | 123 | 30.55 N | 76.57 E |
| Kasba | 124 | 25.51 N | 87.33 E |
| Kasbagoas | 126 | 24.11 N | 88.30 E |
| Kasba Kamarda | 126 | 21.46 N | 87.21 E |
| Kasba Lake ⊜ | 176 | 60.18 N | 102.07 W |
| Kasba Mirgoda | 126 | 21.42 N | 87.28 E |
| Kasba Nārāyangarh | 126 | 22.10 N | 87.23 E |
| Kasba Patāspur | 126 | 22.02 N | 87.32 E |
| Kasba-Tadla | 148 | 32.34 N | 6.18 W |
| Kaschau → Košice | 30 | 48.43 N | 21.15 E |
| Kascjukouka | 76 | 52.32 N | 30.56 E |
| Kascjukovičy | 76 | 53.20 N | 32.03 E |
| Kåseberga | 26 | 55.23 N | 14.04 E |
| Kaseda | 92 | 31.25 N | 130.19 E |
| Kasempa | 154 | 13.27 S | 25.50 E |
| Kasenga | 154 | 10.22 S | 28.38 E |
| Kasenyi | 154 | 1.24 N | 30.26 E |
| Kasese, Ug. | 154 | 0.10 N | 30.05 E |
| Kasese, Zaïre | 154 | 1.38 S | 27.07 E |
| Kaset Sombun | 110 | 16.17 N | 101.57 E |
| Kasfareet Military Base ▪ | 142 | 30.15 N | 32.24 E |
| Kāsganj | 124 | 27.49 N | 78.39 E |
| Kashabowie Lake ⊜ | 190 | 48.42 N | 90.25 W |
| Kashaf ≃ | 128 | 35.58 N | 61.07 E |
| Kashagawigamog Lake ⊜ | 212 | 44.59 N | 78.37 W |
| Kāshān | 128 | 33.59 N | 51.29 E |
| Kashasha | 154 | 1.44 S | 31.37 E |
| Kashegelok | 180 | 60.50 N | 157.50 W |
| Kashgar → Kashi | 85 | 39.29 N | 75.59 E |
| Kashi | 85 | 39.29 N | 75.59 E |
| Kashiba | 96 | 34.33 N | 135.42 E |
| Kashihara | 96 | 34.30 N | 135.46 E |
| Kashiji Plain ⌣ | 152 | 13.20 S | 22.30 E |
| Kashileshi ≃ | 152 | 9.46 S | 23.05 E |
| Kashima, Nihon | 92 | 33.07 N | 130.06 E |
| Kashima, Nihon | 94 | 35.58 N | 140.38 E |
| Kashima, Nihon | 94 | 36.58 N | 136.55 E |
| Kashima, Nihon | 96 | 35.30 N | 133.01 E |
| Kashima-jingū ⅴ1 | 94 | 35.59 N | 140.40 E |
| Kashima-nada ▾2 | 94 | 36.15 N | 140.45 E |
| Kashima-Yariga-take ∧ | 94 | 36.37 N | 137.45 E |
| Kashimo | 94 | 35.43 N | 137.23 E |
| Kāshināthpur | 126 | 23.58 N | 89.37 E |
| Kashing → Jiaxing | 106 | 30.46 N | 120.45 E |
| Kashio ◆8 | 268 | 35.25 N | 139.33 E |
| Kāshīpur, India | 124 | 29.13 N | 78.57 E |
| Kāshipur, India | 126 | 23.26 N | 86.40 E |
| Kashitu | 154 | 13.42 S | 28.40 E |
| Kashiwa | 94 | 35.52 N | 139.59 E |
| Kashiwara | 96 | 34.35 N | 135.37 E |
| Kashiwazaki, Nihon | 92 | 37.22 N | 138.33 E |
| Kashiwazaki, Nihon | 268 | 35.56 N | 139.42 E |
| Kashlahach ≃ | 83 | 47.45 N | 37.16 E |
| Kāshmar | 128 | 35.12 N | 58.27 E |
| Kashmir → Jammu and Kashmīr ▫2 | 120 | 34.00 N | 76.00 E |
| Kashmir, Vale of V | 123 | 34.00 N | 75.00 E |
| Kashmor | 120 | 28.26 N | 69.35 E |
| Kashmūnd Ghar ⛰ | 123 | 34.42 N | 70.31 E |
| Kashperivka | 78 | 49.26 N | 29.41 E |
| Kashunuk ≃ | 180 | 61.18 N | 165.36 W |
| Kashwakamak Lake ⊜ | 212 | 44.50 N | 77.04 W |
| Kasia | 124 | 26.45 N | 83.55 E |
| Kāsiāni | 126 | 23.14 N | 89.45 E |
| Kasiāri | 126 | 22.08 N | 87.14 E |
| Kasidiji ≃ | 152 | 7.57 S | 23.12 E |
| Kasigau ∧ | 154 | 3.50 S | 38.40 E |
| Kasigluk | 180 | 60.52 N | 162.32 W |
| Kasilof | 180 | 60.24 N | 151.18 W |
| Kasilovo | 78 | 50.38 N | 35.37 E |
| Kasimbar | 112 | 0.09 S | 120.00 E |
| Kasimov | 80 | 54.56 N | 41.24 E |
| Kāsimpur, Bngl. | 126 | 23.59 N | 90.19 E |
| Kāsimpur, India | 272b | 22.46 N | 88.31 E |
| Kašin | 76 | 57.21 N | 37.37 E |
| Kāsināthpur | 272b | 22.35 N | 88.31 E |
| Kasinge | 154 | 6.20 S | 26.59 E |
| Kasinka | 156 | 18.13 S | 24.22 E |
| Kāsipur | 272b | 22.25 N | 88.10 E |
| Kašira | 82 | 54.51 N | 38.10 E |
| Kaširka ≃ | 82 | 54.52 N | 38.13 E |
| Kasiruta, Pulau I | 108 | 0.25 S | 127.12 E |
| Kasiui, Pulau I | 164 | 4.30 S | 131.40 E |
| Kasiwa → Kashiwa | 94 | 35.52 N | 139.59 E |
| Kaskabulak | 86 | 49.34 N | 79.52 E |
| Kaškadarja ▫8 | 128 | 39.00 N | 66.00 E |
| Kaskaden-Kette → Cascade Range ⛰ | 202 | 45.00 N | 121.30 W |
| Kaskana | 85 | 40.45 N | 69.36 E |
| Kaskaskia ≃ | 194 | 37.59 N | 89.56 W |
| Kaskaskia, East Fork ≃ | 219 | 38.43 N | 89.09 W |
| Kaskaskia, North Fork ≃ | 219 | 38.46 N | 89.09 W |
| Kaskattama ≃ | 176 | 57.03 N | 90.07 W |
| Kaskelen | 85 | 43.12 N | 76.37 E |
| Kaskelen ≃ | 85 | 43.53 N | 77.08 E |
| Kaskinen → Kaskö | 26 | 62.23 N | 21.13 E |
| Kaskö (Kaskinen) | 26 | 62.23 N | 21.13 E |
| Kaslātu ∧ | 124 | 23.58 N | 84.54 E |
| Kasli | 86 | 55.53 N | 60.46 E |
| Kaslo | 182 | 49.55 N | 116.55 W |
| Kasn'a | 76 | 55.24 N | 34.20 E |
| Kasn'a ≃ | 76 | 55.51 N | 34.25 E |
| Kaso ≃ | 115a | 7.25 S | 106.40 E |
| Kasongo | 154 | 4.27 S | 26.40 E |
| Kasongo-Lunda | 152 | 6.28 S | 16.49 E |
| Kásos I | 38 | 35.22 N | 26.56 E |
| Kasota | 190 | 44.18 N | 93.57 W |
| Kaspi | 84 | 41.57 N | 44.25 E |
| Kaspijsk | 84 | 42.52 N | 47.38 E |
| Kaspijskij | 22 | 45.22 N | 47.24 E |
| Kaspijskoje more → Caspian Sea ▾2 | 72 | 42.00 N | 50.30 E |
| Kaspische Senke → Prikaspijskaja nizmennost' ⌣ | 80 | 48.00 N | 52.00 E |
| Kaspisches Meer → Caspian Sea ▾2 | 72 | 42.00 N | 50.30 E |
| Kaspl'a | 76 | 55.00 N | 31.38 E |
| Kaspl'a ≃ | 76 | 55.24 N | 30.43 E |
| Kasr, Ra's > | 140 | 18.02 N | 38.35 E |
| Kasrik | 130 | 38.13 N | 41.54 E |
| Kassa → Košice | 30 | 48.43 N | 21.15 E |
| Kassab | 130 | 35.56 N | 35.59 E |
| Kassai → Cassai (Kasai) ≃ | 152 | 3.02 S | 16.57 E |
| Kassalā | 140 | 15.28 N | 36.24 E |
| Kassalā ▫4 | 140 | 15.00 N | 35.00 E |
| Kassándra >1 | 38 | 40.06 N | 23.22 E |
| Kassándras, Kólpos ⊂ | 38 | 40.06 N | 23.30 E |
| Kassel | 56 | 51.19 N | 9.29 E |
| Kassel ▫5 | 56 | 51.10 N | 9.20 E |
| Kasserine | 148 | 35.11 N | 8.48 E |
| Kasshabog Lake ⊜ | 212 | 44.38 N | 77.58 W |
| Kassikaityu ≃ | 246 | 1.49 N | 58.32 W |
| Kassinger | 140 | 18.45 N | 31.54 E |
| Kassîr, Sabkhat al- ⊜ | 130 | 35.03 N | 41.07 E |
| Kasslerfeld ◆8 | 263 | 51.26 N | 6.45 E |
| Kasson | 190 | 44.01 N | 92.45 W |
| Kassou | 150 | 11.35 N | 2.03 W |
| Kassoum | 150 | 13.05 N | 3.18 W |
| Kastamonu | 130 | 41.22 N | 33.47 E |
| Kastamonu ▫4 | 130 | 41.40 N | 33.45 E |
| Kastanéai | 38 | 41.38 N | 26.28 E |
| Kastelholm | 26 | 60.14 N | 20.04 E |
| Kastellaun | 56 | 50.04 N | 7.26 E |
| Kasterlee | 56 | 51.15 N | 4.57 E |
| Kastiyu, Puntan > | 174n | 14.57 N | 145.40 E |
| Kastl, Dtsch. | 60 | 49.50 N | 11.54 E |
| Kastl, Dtsch. | 60 | 49.22 N | 11.42 E |
| Kastorf | 52 | 53.44 N | 10.34 E |
| Kastoría | 38 | 40.31 N | 21.15 E |
| Kastorías, Límni ⊜ | 38 | 40.30 N | 21.17 E |
| Kastornoje | 78 | 51.50 N | 38.06 E |
| Kastrávion, Tekhnití Límni ⊜1 | 38 | 38.50 N | 21.20 E |
| Kastrup Lufthavn ✈ | 41 | 55.38 N | 12.39 E |
| Kasuga, Nihon | 94 | 35.28 N | 136.29 E |
| Kasuga, Nihon | 96 | 33.32 N | 130.27 E |
| Kasuga, Nihon | 96 | 35.10 N | 135.06 E |
| Kasugai, Nihon | 94 | 35.14 N | 136.58 E |
| Kasugai, Nihon | 94 | 35.39 N | 138.39 E |
| Kasuga-kōkūkichi, Kaijō-jieitai- ▪ | 96 | 33.31 N | 130.28 E |
| Kasuga Shrine ⅴ1 | 270 | 34.41 N | 135.51 E |
| Kasuka | 158 | 33.40 S | 26.41 E |
| Kasukabe | 94 | 35.58 N | 139.45 E |
| Kasukawa | 94 | 36.24 N | 139.13 E |
| Kasulu | 154 | 4.34 S | 30.06 E |
| Kasumi | 96 | 35.38 N | 134.38 E |
| Kasumiga-ura ⊜ | 94 | 36.00 N | 140.25 E |
| Kasumkent | 84 | 41.41 N | 48.07 E |
| Kasungan | 112 | 1.58 S | 113.24 E |
| Kasungu | 154 | 13.01 S | 33.30 E |
| Kasungu National Park ♦ | 154 | 12.55 S | 33.15 E |
| Kasupe | 154 | 15.10 S | 35.15 E |
| Kasūr | 123 | 31.07 N | 74.27 E |
| Kaszuby ◆1 | 30 | 54.10 N | 18.15 E |
| Kata | 88 | 58.46 N | 102.40 E |
| Kataba | 154 | 16.05 S | 25.10 E |
| Kataeregi | 150 | 9.22 N | 6.17 E |
| Katagum | 146 | 12.17 N | 10.21 E |
| Katahdin, Mount ∧ | 188 | 45.55 N | 68.55 W |
| Katai | 272c | 19.10 N | 73.05 E |
| Katajevo | 88 | 50.57 N | 108.41 E |
| Katajsk | 86 | 56.18 N | 62.35 E |
| Katako-Kombe | 152 | 3.24 S | 24.25 E |
| Katakura | 270 | 34.29 N | 135.31 E |
| Katakwi | 154 | 1.55 N | 33.57 E |
| Katale | 154 | 4.59 S | 31.03 E |
| Katalla | 180 | 60.12 N | 144.31 W |
| Katanda | 154 | 0.50 S | 29.22 E |
| Katanga ▫9 | 138 | 10.00 S | 26.00 E |
| Katanga ≃ | 74 | 60.08 N | 102.13 E |
| Katangi | 124 | 23.27 N | 79.47 E |
| Katanglad Mountains ⛰ | 116 | 8.06 N | 124.54 E |
| Katangli | 89 | 51.42 N | 143.14 E |
| Katanimara | 126 | 22.17 N | 87.11 E |
| Katanning | 162 | 33.42 S | 117.33 E |
| Katano | 270 | 34.47 N | 135.40 E |
| Katano-hana > | 174f | 24.49 N | 141.20 E |
| Katanti | 154 | 2.18 S | 27.08 E |
| Kataoka | 270 | 35.03 N | 135.58 E |
| Katapakishi | 152 | 8.15 S | 22.49 E |
| Katar → Qatar ▫1 | 128 | 25.00 N | 51.10 E |
| Katara, Depresión de → Qaṭṭārah, Munkhafaḍ al- ⌣7 | 140 | 30.00 N | 27.30 E |
| Katârniān Ghāt | 124 | 28.20 N | 81.09 E |
| Katase | 268 | 35.19 N | 139.29 E |
| Katashina | 94 | 36.46 N | 139.14 E |
| Katašin | 76 | 52.36 N | 32.10 E |
| Katav-Ivanovsk | 86 | 54.45 N | 58.12 E |
| Katayama | 268 | 35.46 N | 139.34 E |
| Katchall Island I | 110 | 7.57 N | 93.22 E |
| Katchewanooka Lake ⊜ | 212 | 44.27 N | 78.16 W |
| Katchin-wan ⊂ | 174m | 26.18 N | 127.53 E |
| Katchirga | 150 | 14.03 N | 0.06 E |
| Katchiungo | 152 | 12.35 S | 16.13 E |
| Kateel ≃ | 180 | 65.28 N | 157.35 W |
| Katélé | 150 | 10.38 N | 5.37 W |
| Katena-wan ⊂ | 174m | 26.50 N | 128.05 E |
| Katepwa Beach | 184 | 50.42 N | 103.38 W |
| Katerbow | 54 | 52.59 N | 12.39 E |
| Kateríni | 38 | 40.16 N | 22.30 E |
| Katerloch ⌣5 | 61 | 47.16 N | 15.32 E |
| Katernberg ◆8, Dtsch. | 263 | 51.16 N | 7.06 E |
| Katernberg ◆8, Dtsch. | 263 | 51.29 N | 7.04 E |
| Katerynopil' | 78 | 48.56 N | 30.59 E |
| Katesbridge | 48 | 54.18 N | 6.08 W |
| Kates Needle ∧ | 180 | 57.03 N | 132.03 W |
| Katešovo | 82 | 54.08 N | 37.00 E |
| Katete, Malawi | 154 | 12.17 S | 33.39 E |
| Katete, Zam. | 154 | 14.05 S | 32.07 E |
| Katex | 84 | 41.39 N | 46.34 E |
| Katghora | 124 | 22.30 N | 82.33 E |
| Katha | 110 | 24.11 N | 96.21 E |
| Kathangor, Jabal ∧ | 140 | 5.45 N | 33.59 E |
| Katherine | 164 | 14.28 S | 132.16 E |
| Katherine ≃ | 164 | 14.39 S | 131.42 E |
| Katherine Creek ≃ | 166 | 23.48 S | 143.42 E |
| Katherine Gorge National Park ♦ | 164 | 14.10 S | 132.30 E |
| Kāthgodām | 124 | 29.16 N | 79.32 E |
| Kāthiāwār Peninsula >1 | 120 | 22.00 N | 71.00 E |
| Kathīb, Ra's > | 144 | 14.55 N | 42.53 E |
| Kathla | 123 | 31.59 N | 76.47 E |
| Kathleen | 220 | 28.07 N | 82.01 W |
| Kathleen Valley | 162 | 27.23 S | 120.38 E |
| Kathlow | 54 | 51.43 N | 14.29 E |
| Kāṭhmāṇḍau | 124 | 27.43 N | 85.19 E |
| Kathmandu → Kāṭhmāṇḍau | 124 | 27.43 N | 85.19 E |
| Kathor | 120 | 21.18 N | 72.56 E |
| Kathrabbā | 132 | 31.08 N | 35.37 E |
| Kathua | 123 | 32.22 N | 75.31 E |
| Kāthuli | 126 | 23.52 N | 88.40 E |
| Kati | 150 | 12.44 N | 8.04 W |
| Kātiādi | 126 | 24.15 N | 90.48 E |
| Katibas ≃ | 112 | 2.01 N | 112.33 E |
| Katihār | 124 | 25.32 N | 87.35 E |
| Katikati | 172 | 37.33 S | 175.55 E |
| Katima Mulilo | 152 | 17.30 S | 24.16 E |
| Katimik Lake ⊜ | 184 | 52.54 N | 99.22 W |
| Katiola | 150 | 8.08 N | 5.06 W |
| Katipunan | 116 | 8.31 N | 123.17 E |
| Katiti Aboriginal Land Reserve ◆4 | 162 | 25.10 S | 131.15 E |
| Kātlang | 123 | 34.22 N | 72.05 E |
| Katlehong | 273d | 26.19 S | 28.09 E |
| Katlenburg-Duhm | 52 | 51.41 N | 10.06 E |
| Katmai, Mount ∧ | 180 | 58.17 N | 154.56 W |
| Katmai National Park ♦ | 180 | 58.30 N | 155.00 W |
| Katmandu → Kāṭhmāṇḍau | 124 | 27.43 N | 85.19 E |
| Katni → Murwāra, India | 124 | 23.51 N | 80.24 E |
| Katni, Ross. | 80 | 57.59 N | 47.46 E |
| Káto Akhaïa | 38 | 38.09 N | 21.32 E |
| Kātol | 120 | 21.16 N | 78.35 E |
| Katompi | 154 | 6.11 S | 26.20 E |
| Katonah | 210 | 41.16 N | 73.41 W |
| Katonga ≃ | 154 | 0.34 N | 31.50 E |
| Katon-Karagaj | 86 | 49.11 N | 85.37 E |
| Katoomba | 170 | 33.42 S | 150.18 E |
| Katopa | 154 | 2.45 S | 25.06 E |
| Katori-jingū ⅴ1 | 94 | 35.52 N | 140.30 E |
| Katoúna | 38 | 38.47 N | 21.07 E |
| Katovice | 60 | 49.16 N | 13.49 E |
| Katowice | 30 | 50.16 N | 19.00 E |
| Katowice ▫4 | 30 | 50.15 N | 19.00 E |
| Katra | 123 | 32.59 N | 74.57 E |
| Kātrās | 126 | 23.48 N | 86.17 E |
| Katričev | 80 | 49.23 N | 45.33 E |
| Kātrīnā, Jabal ∧ | 140 | 28.31 N | 33.57 E |
| Katrine, Loch ⊜ | 46 | 56.15 N | 4.31 W |
| Katrineholm | 40 | 59.00 N | 16.12 E |
| Katsch, Golf von → Kachchh, Gulf of ⊂ | 120 | 22.36 N | 69.30 E |
| Katschbach ≃ | 61 | 47.08 N | 14.17 E |
| Katschberg )( | 64 | 47.03 N | 13.37 E |
| Katsepe | 157b | 15.45 S | 46.15 E |
| Katshungu | 154 | 2.27 S | 27.23 E |
| Katsina | 150 | 13.00 N | 7.32 E |
| Katsina Ala | 150 | 7.10 N | 9.17 E |
| Katsina Ala ≃ | 152 | 7.48 N | 8.52 E |
| Katsunuma | 94 | 35.39 N | 138.44 E |
| Katsura ◆8 | 270 | 34.59 N | 135.42 E |
| Katsura ≃, Nihon | 94 | 35.36 N | 139.15 E |
| Katsura ≃, Nihon | 94 | 34.53 N | 135.42 E |
| Katsura ≃, Nihon | 96 | 34.02 N | 134.35 E |
| Katsura ≃, Nihon | 270 | 34.53 N | 135.42 E |
| Katsuragi | 96 | 34.15 N | 135.30 E |
| Katsuragi-san ∧ | 96 | 34.20 N | 135.27 E |
| Katsushika ◆8 | 268 | 35.43 N | 139.51 E |
| Katsuta, Nihon | 94 | 36.24 N | 140.30 E |
| Katsuta, Nihon | 96 | 35.04 N | 134.11 E |
| Katsuura, Nihon | 94 | 35.08 N | 140.18 E |
| Katsuura, Nihon | 96 | 33.56 N | 134.30 E |
| Katsuyama, Nihon | 94 | 36.03 N | 136.30 E |
| Katsuyama, Nihon | 96 | 35.05 N | 133.41 E |
| Kattakurgan | 72 | 39.55 N | 66.15 E |
| Kattara-Senke → Qaṭṭārah, Munkhafaḍ al- ⌣7 | 140 | 30.00 N | 27.30 E |
| Kattarp | 41 | 56.09 N | 12.46 E |
| Katta-Taldyk | 85 | 40.19 N | 73.12 E |
| Kattaviá | 38 | 35.57 N | 27.46 E |
| Kattegat ⨆ | 26 | 57.00 N | 11.00 E |
| Katternberg ◆8 | 263 | 51.09 N | 7.02 E |
| Katthammarsvik | 26 | 57.26 N | 18.50 E |
| Kattowitz → Katowice | 30 | 50.16 N | 19.00 E |
| Kattrup | 41 | 55.57 N | 9.56 E |
| Kāttuputtūr | 122 | 10.59 N | 78.14 E |
| Katul, Jabal ∧ | 140 | 14.16 N | 29.23 E |
| Katuma | 154 | 6.10 S | 30.34 E |
| Katumba | 154 | 7.45 S | 25.18 E |
| Katun' ≃ | 86 | 52.25 N | 85.05 E |
| Katunino | 80 | 58.01 N | 45.39 E |
| Katunki | 80 | 56.50 N | 43.14 E |
| Kātūria | 124 | 24.44 N | 86.43 E |
| Katu Shan ∧ | 86 | 45.40 N | 82.55 E |
| Katusice | 54 | 50.26 N | 14.50 E |
| Kātwa | 126 | 23.39 N | 88.08 E |
| Katwijk aan de Rijn | 52 | 52.11 N | 4.26 E |
| Katwijk aan Zee | 52 | 52.13 N | 4.24 E |
| Katy | 222 | 29.47 N | 95.49 W |
| Katyn | 76 | 54.47 N | 31.44 E |
| Kąty Wrocławskie | 30 | 51.02 N | 16.46 E |
| Katzenbuckel ∧ | 56 | 49.28 N | 9.02 E |
| Katzenelnbogen | 56 | 50.17 N | 7.59 E |
| Katzhütte | 54 | 50.33 N | 11.03 E |
| Kaua ≃ | 156 | 19.24 S | 22.03 E |
| Kauai ▫6 | 229b | 21.59 N | 159.22 W |
| Kauai I | 229b | 22.00 N | 159.30 W |
| Kauai Channel ⨆ | 229b | 21.45 N | 158.50 W |
| Kaub | 56 | 50.05 N | 7.46 E |
| Kau Desert ◆2 | 229d | 19.21 N | 155.19 W |
| Kaufbeuren | 58 | 47.53 N | 10.37 E |
| Kaufering | 58 | 48.05 N | 10.52 E |
| Kaufman | 222 | 32.35 N | 96.18 W |
| Kaufman ▫6 | 222 | 32.38 N | 96.18 W |
| Kaufungen | 56 | 51.17 N | 9.38 E |
| Kaugama | 150 | 12.28 N | 9.44 E |
| Kauhajoki | 26 | 62.26 N | 22.11 E |
| Kauhanevan-Pohjankankaan kansallispuisto ♦ | 26 | 62.08 N | 22.25 E |
| Kauhava | 26 | 63.06 N | 23.05 E |
| Kauiki Head > | 229a | 20.45 N | 155.59 W |
| Kaukapakapa | 172 | 36.37 S | 174.30 E |
| Kaukasus → Caucasus ⛰ | 84 | 42.30 N | 45.00 E |
| Kaukauna | 190 | 44.16 N | 88.16 W |
| Kaukau Veld ⛰1 | 156 | 19.30 S | 20.30 E |
| Kaukhāli | 126 | 22.38 N | 90.04 E |
| Kaukura I1 | 14 | 15.45 S | 146.42 W |
| Kaula I | 229d | 21.45 N | 160.30 W |
| Kaulakahi Channel ⨆ | 229b | 22.00 N | 159.53 W |
| Kaulille | 56 | 51.11 N | 5.31 E |
| Kauliranta | 24 | 66.27 N | 23.41 E |
| Kaŭl-li | 98 | 37.58 N | 124.37 E |
| Kaulsdorf | 54 | 50.37 N | 11.26 E |
| Kaulsdorf ◆8 | 264a | 52.31 N | 13.33 E |
| Kaulsdorf-Süd ◆8 | 264a | 52.29 N | 13.34 E |
| Kaumakani | 229b | 21.55 N | 159.37 W |
| Kaumalapau | 229a | 20.47 N | 156.59 W |
| Kaunakakai | 229a | 21.05 N | 157.01 W |
| Kaunas | 76 | 54.54 N | 23.54 E |
| Kauneonga Lake | 210 | 41.41 N | 74.50 W |
| Kauner Tal V | 64 | 47.01 N | 10.44 E |
| Kaunghein | 110 | 25.40 N | 95.26 E |
| Kauniainen → Grankulla | 26 | 60.13 N | 24.45 E |
| Kaunuunui > | 229b | 21.56 N | 160.10 W |
| Kaup | 164 | 3.50 S | 144.00 E |
| Kaupanger | 26 | 61.11 N | 7.14 E |
| Kaura Namoda | 150 | 12.35 N | 6.35 E |
| Kauriyāla Ghāt | 124 | 28.23 N | 81.02 E |
| Kauru | 150 | 10.33 N | 8.12 E |
| Kausa | 272c | 19.10 N | 73.02 E |
| Kau Sai Chau I | 271d | 22.22 N | 114.18 E |
| Kausala | 26 | 60.54 N | 26.22 E |
| Kaustinen | 26 | 63.32 N | 23.42 E |
| Kauswagan | 116 | 8.11 N | 124.05 E |
| Kautokeino | 24 | 69.00 N | 23.02 E |
| Kauttua | 26 | 61.06 N | 22.10 E |
| Kau-ye Kyun I | 110 | 11.01 N | 98.32 E |
| Kavača | 74 | 60.16 N | 169.51 E |
| Kavacık | 130 | 39.40 N | 28.30 E |
| Kavadarci | 38 | 41.26 N | 22.00 E |
| Kavajë | 38 | 41.11 N | 19.33 E |
| Kavak, Tür. | 130 | 38.24 N | 39.26 E |
| Kavak, Tür. | 130 | 41.05 N | 36.03 E |
| Kavak, Tür. | 130 | 39.18 N | 37.30 E |
| Kavakbaşı | 130 | 38.29 N | 41.49 E |
| Kavaklıdere | 130 | 37.26 N | 28.22 E |
| Kavála | 38 | 40.56 N | 24.25 E |
| Kavalerovo | 89 | 44.15 N | 135.04 E |
| Kāvali | 122 | 14.55 N | 79.59 E |
| Kavaratti | 122 | 10.34 N | 72.39 E |
| Kavaratti Island I | 122 | 10.33 N | 72.38 E |
| Kavarna | 38 | 43.25 N | 28.20 E |
| Kavendou, Mont ∧ | 150 | 10.41 N | 12.12 W |
| Kāveri ≃ | 122 | 11.09 N | 79.52 E |
| Kāveri Falls ∟ | 122 | 12.18 N | 77.17 E |
| Kaverino, Ross. | 80 | 54.10 N | 41.47 E |
| Kaverino, Ross. | 82 | 56.11 N | 36.15 E |
| Kavieng | 164 | 2.35 S | 150.50 E |
| Kavimba | 156 | 18.02 S | 24.38 E |
| Kavīr, Dasht-e ◆2 | 128 | 34.40 N | 54.30 E |
| Kavkazskij zapovednik ♦ | 84 | 43.55 N | 40.30 E |
| Kävlinge | 41 | 55.48 N | 13.06 E |
| Kävlingeån ≃ | 41 | 55.47 N | 13.06 E |
| Kavungo | 152 | 11.31 S | 23.03 E |
| Kavuu ≃ | 154 | 7.40 S | 31.46 E |
| Kavykuči-Gazimurskije | 88 | 51.22 N | 118.10 E |
| Kaw, Guy. fr. | 250 | 4.29 N | 52.02 W |
| Kaw, Ok., U.S. | 196 | 36.46 N | 96.50 W |
| Kawa | 110 | 17.05 N | 96.28 E |
| Kawaba | 94 | 36.41 N | 139.07 E |
| Kawabe, Nihon | 94 | 35.29 N | 137.04 E |
| Kawabe, Nihon | 96 | 33.55 N | 135.11 E |
| Kawachi, Nihon | 94 | 35.53 N | 140.15 E |
| Kawachi, Nihon | 94 | 36.24 N | 136.38 E |
| Kawachi, Nihon | 94 | 36.37 N | 139.56 E |
| Kawachi-nagano | 96 | 34.27 N | 135.34 E |
| Kawagama Lake ⊜ | 212 | 45.18 N | 78.45 W |
| Kawage | 94 | 34.47 N | 136.33 E |
| Kawagoe | 94 | 35.55 N | 139.29 E |
| Kawaguchi | 94 | 35.48 N | 139.43 E |
| Kawaguchiko | 94 | 35.30 N | 138.46 E |
| Kawaguchi-ko ⊜ | 94 | 35.31 N | 138.45 E |
| Kawahara | 96 | 35.24 N | 134.12 E |
| Kawai, Nihon | 94 | 36.18 N | 137.07 E |
| Kawai, Nihon | 270 | 34.35 N | 135.45 E |
| Kawaihae Bay ⊂ | 229d | 20.02 N | 155.50 W |
| Kawaihoa > | 229b | 21.47 N | 160.12 W |
| Kawaikini ∧ | 229b | 22.05 N | 159.29 W |
| Kawailoa | 229c | 21.36 N | 158.05 W |
| Kawailoa Beach | 229c | 21.37 N | 158.04 W |
| Kawajiri | 96 | 34.14 N | 132.42 E |
| Kawakami, Nihon | 94 | 35.58 N | 138.35 E |
| Kawakami, Nihon | 96 | 34.44 N | 133.29 E |
| Kawakami, Nihon | 96 | 35.17 N | 133.39 E |
| Kawakawa | 172 | 35.23 S | 174.04 E |
| Kawakubo | 270 | 34.54 N | 135.38 E |
| Kawali | 115a | 7.11 S | 108.22 E |
| Kawama Mission | 154 | 10.04 S | 28.37 E |
| Kawamata | 92 | 37.39 N | 140.36 E |
| Kawambwa | 154 | 9.47 S | 29.05 E |
| Kawamoto, Nihon | 94 | 36.09 N | 139.17 E |
| Kawamoto, Nihon | 96 | 34.59 N | 132.30 E |
| Kawane | 94 | 34.57 N | 138.05 E |
| Kawanishi, Nihon | 94 | 37.09 N | 138.45 E |
| Kawanishi, Nihon | 96 | 34.49 N | 135.24 E |
| Kawanishi, Nihon | 270 | 34.35 N | 135.47 E |
| Kawanoe | 96 | 34.01 N | 133.34 E |
| Kawara, Nihon | 96 | 33.40 N | 130.51 E |
| Kawara, Nihon | 270 | 34.59 N | 135.18 E |
| Kawara Débé | 150 | 12.20 N | 3.26 E |
| Kawarai | 268 | 35.25 N | 140.05 E |
| Kawardha | 124 | 22.01 N | 81.15 E |
| Kawartha Park | 212 | 44.32 N | 78.12 W |
| Kawasaki, Nihon | 94 | 35.32 N | 139.43 E |
| Kawasaki, Nihon | 96 | 33.35 N | 130.49 E |
| Kawasaki-kō ⊂ | 268 | 35.30 N | 139.47 E |
| Kawasaki Stadium ♦ | 268 | 35.32 N | 139.43 E |
| Kawashima, Nihon | 94 | 35.21 N | 136.50 E |
| Kawashima, Nihon | 94 | 35.59 N | 139.30 E |
| Kawashima, Nihon | 96 | 34.04 N | 134.19 E |
| Kawashima ◆8 | 268 | 35.28 N | 139.35 E |
| Kawashiri-misaki > | 96 | 34.26 N | 130.58 E |
| Kawatana | 92 | 33.04 N | 129.52 E |
| Kawauchi | 96 | 33.48 N | 132.55 E |
| Kawau Island I | 172 | 36.25 S | 174.51 E |
| Kawawa ◆8 | 268 | 35.31 N | 139.33 E |
| Kawayan | 116 | 11.41 N | 124.21 E |
| Kawazu | 94 | 34.44 N | 138.59 E |
| Kawbein | 110 | 16.33 N | 97.52 E |
| Kawdut | 110 | 15.31 N | 97.47 E |
| Kawe | 164 | 7.50 S | 138.14 E |
| Kawe, Pulau I | 164 | 0.03 S | 130.07 E |
| Kaweenakumik Lake ⊜ | 184 | 52.52 N | 99.30 W |
| Kaweka ∧ | 172 | 39.17 S | 176.23 E |
| Kaweka Range ⛰ | 172 | 39.15 S | 176.20 E |
| Kawerau | 172 | 38.03 S | 176.43 E |
| Kawhia | 172 | 38.04 S | 174.49 E |
| Kawhia Harbour ⊂ | 172 | 38.05 S | 174.50 E |
| Kawich Peak ∧ | 204 | 37.58 N | 116.27 W |
| Kawich Range ⛰ | 204 | 37.40 N | 116.30 W |
| Kawin | 164 | 2.45 S | 150.45 E |
| Kawinda | 115b | 8.07 S | 118.04 E |
| Kawit | 269f | 14.27 N | 120.54 E |
| Kawkabān | 144 | 15.40 N | 43.52 E |
| Kawkareik | 110 | 16.33 N | 98.14 E |
| Kaw Lake ⊜1 | 196 | 36.55 N | 96.57 W |
| Kawludo | 110 | 18.29 N | 97.19 E |
| Kawm | 140 | 13.31 N | 22.50 E |
| Kawm al-Farā'in (Buto) ⊥ | 142 | 31.11 N | 30.45 E |
| Kawm ar-Rāhib | 142 | 28.20 N | 30.37 E |
| Kawm Birah | 273c | 30.05 N | 31.08 E |
| Kawm Dafanah (Daphnæ) ⊥ | 142 | 30.52 N | 32.11 E |
| Kawm Ḥamādah | 142 | 30.46 N | 30.42 E |
| Kawm Ishfīn | 273c | 30.11 N | 31.15 E |
| Kawm Ishū | 142 | 31.07 N | 30.00 E |
| Kawm Ju'ayf (Naucratis) ⊥ | 142 | 30.54 N | 30.36 E |
| Kawm Umbū | 140 | 24.28 N | 32.57 E |
| Kawnglanghpu | 102 | 27.04 N | 98.21 E |
| Kawnipi Lake ⊜ | 190 | 48.24 N | 91.14 W |
| Kawthaung | 110 | 9.59 N | 98.33 E |
| Kax ≃ | 86 | 43.40 N | 81.45 E |
| Kaxgar ≃ | 85 | 39.40 N | 78.00 E |
| Kaya, Burkina | 150 | 13.05 N | 1.05 W |
| Kaya, Nihon | 96 | 35.30 N | 135.06 E |
| Kayaapu | 112 | 5.26 S | 102.24 E |
| Kayadibi, Tür. | 130 | 39.29 N | 36.43 E |
| Kayadibi, Tür. | 130 | 39.55 N | 34.15 E |
| Kayah ▫3 | 110 | 19.15 N | 97.30 E |
| Kayak Island I | 180 | 59.52 N | 144.30 W |
| Kāyalpattinam | 122 | 8.34 N | 78.07 E |
| Kāyamba | 272b | 22.41 N | 88.32 E |
| Kayambi | 154 | 9.27 S | 31.58 E |
| Kayan | 110 | 16.54 N | 96.34 E |
| Kayan ≃ | 112 | 2.55 N | 117.35 E |
| Kayangel Islands II | 108 | 8.04 N | 134.43 E |
| Kayang-san ∧2 | 271b | 37.33 N | 126.43 E |
| Kāyankulam | 122 | 9.11 N | 76.30 E |
| Kayapa | 116 | 16.22 N | 120.53 E |
| Kayapınar | 130 | 37.34 N | 41.10 E |
| Kayaş | 130 | 39.56 N | 32.58 E |
| Kaya-san ∧ | 98 | 35.49 N | 128.07 E |
| Kaya-san Kukrip Kongwŏn ♦ | 98 | 35.47 N | 128.06 E |
| Kaycee | 200 | 43.42 N | 106.38 W |
| Kayeli | 164 | 3.23 S | 127.06 E |
| Kayembe-Mukulu | 152 | 9.03 S | 23.57 E |
| Kayen | 115a | 6.54 S | 110.59 E |
| Kayenta | 200 | 36.43 N | 110.15 W |
| Kayes, Congo | 152 | 4.25 S | 11.41 E |
| Kayes, Mali | 150 | 14.27 N | 11.26 W |
| Kayes ▫4 | 150 | 14.00 N | 11.00 W |
| Kay Gardens | 285 | 39.45 N | 75.25 W |
| Kayima | 150 | 8.53 N | 11.10 W |
| Kayin ▫3 | 110 | 17.30 N | 97.45 E |
| Kayiry | 78 | 46.57 N | 33.43 E |
| Kayış Dağı ∧ | 267b | 40.59 N | 29.10 E |


| Symbol | English | Deutsch | Español | Français | Português |
|---|---|---|---|---|---|
| ≃ | River | Fluß | Río | Rivière | Rio |
| ≍ | Canal | Kanal | Canal | Canal | Canal |
| ∟ | Waterfall, Rapids | Wasserfall, Stromschnellen | Cascada, Rápidos | Chute d'eau, Rapides | Cascata, Rápidos |
| ⨆ | Strait | Meeresstraße | Estrecho | Détroit | Estreito |
| ⊂ | Bay, Gulf | Bucht, Golf | Bahía, Golfo | Baie, Golfe | Baía, Golfo |
| ⊜ | Lake, Lakes | See, Seen | Lago, Lagos | Lac, Lacs | Lago, Lagos |
| ≚ | Swamp | Sumpf | Pantano | Marais | Pântano |
| ⌘ | Ice Features, Glacier | Eis- und Gletscherformen | Accidentes Glaciales | Formes glaciaires | Acidentes glaciares |
| ▾ | Other Hydrographic Features | Andere Hydrographische Objekte | Otros Elementos Hidrográficos | Autres données hydrographiques | Outros acidentes hidrográficos |
| ✦ | Submarine Features | Untermeerische Objekte | Accidentes Submarinos | Formes de relief sous-marin | Acidentes submarinos |
| ▫ | Political Unit | Politische Einheit | Unidad Politica | Entité politique | Unidade política |
| ⅴ | Cultural Institution | Kulturelle Institution | Institución Cultural | Institution culturelle | Instituição cultural |
| ⊥ | Historical Site | Historische Stätte | Sitio Histórico | Site historique | Sitio histórico |
| ♦ | Recreational Site | Erholungs- und Ferienort | Sitio de Recreo | Centre de loisirs | Area de Lazer |
| ✈ | Airport | Flughafen | Aeropuerto | Aéroport | Aeroporto |
| ▪ | Military Installation | Militäranlage | Instalación Militar | Installation militaire | Instalação militar |
| ◆ | Miscellaneous | Verschiedenes | Misceláneo | Divers | Diversos |

Kaymakçı 130 38.10 N 28.08 E
Kaymaz, Tür. 130 39.31 N 31.11 E
Kaymaz, Tür. 130 40.55 N 30.18 E
Kayna 54 50.59 N 12.14 E
Kaynar 130 38.55 N 36.28 E
Kayō, Nihon 96 34.51 N 133.42 E
Kayō, Nihon 174m 26.33 N 128.07 E
Kayoa, Pulau I 164 0.05 S 127.25 E
Kayombo 154 9.36 S 25.37 E
Kaypak 130 37.08 N 36.27 E
Kay Point › 180 69.18 N 138.22 W
Kayser Gebergte ⋏ 250 3.03 N 56.35 W
Kayseri 130 38.43 N 35.30 E
Kayseri □[4] 130 38.30 N 35.55 E
Kaysersberg 58 48.08 N 7.15 E
Kaysville 200 41.02 N 111.56 W
Kayuadi, Pulau I 112 6.49 S 120.47 E
Kayuagung 112 3.24 S 104.50 E
Kayumas 115a 7.50 S 114.08 E
Kayuta Lake ⊜ 210 43.25 N 75.12 W
Kayuyu 154 3.39 S 26.21 E
Kazachskij melkosopočnik ⋏[2] 86 49.00 N 72.00 E
Kazachstan → Kazakhstan □[1] 72 48.00 N 68.00 E
Kazačij 83 46.58 N 40.03 E
Kazačinskoje, Ross. 86 57.49 N 93.17 E
Kazačinskoje, Ross. 88 56.16 N 107.36 E
Kazačje 74 70.44 N 136.13 E
Kazačka 80 51.28 N 43.56 E
Kazackij 86 49.20 N 58.31 E
Kazakdarja 86 43.27 N 59.46 E
Kazakevičevo 89 48.17 N 134.46 E
Kazakhstan □[1], Asia 72 48.00 N 68.00 E
Kazakhstan (Kazachstan) □[1], Asia 86 47.00 N 76.00 E
Kazaki 76 52.38 N 38.16 E
Kazakstan → Kazakhstan □[1] 72 48.00 N 68.00 E
Kazal'cevo 86 59.18 N 80.30 E
Kazalinsk 86 45.46 N 62.07 E
Kazan' 80 55.49 N 49.08 E
Kazan ≃ 176 64.02 N 95.30 W
Kazancı 130 36.30 N 32.53 E
Kazandžik 128 39.16 N 55.32 E
Kazanka, Kaz. 86 53.20 N 67.27 E
Kazanka, Ukr. 78 47.50 N 32.49 E
Kazanka ≃ 80 55.48 N 49.01 E
Kazanlăk 38 42.38 N 25.21 E
Kazan Lake ⊜ 184 55.33 N 108.21 W
Kazanlı 130 36.50 N 34.45 E
Kazanovka 76 53.46 N 38.34 E
Kazan-rettō (Volcano Islands) II 14 25.00 N 141.00 E
Kazanskaja 78 49.48 N 41.09 E
Kazanskoje, Ross. 82 54.59 N 37.39 E
Kazanskoje, Ross. 86 55.38 N 69.14 E
Kazan' Station ⊕[5] 265b 55.46 N 37.40 E
Kazantyp, mys › 78 45.28 N 35.51 E
Kazarman 85 41.24 N 74.03 E
Kazatkul' 86 55.02 N 76.03 E
Kazbegi 84 42.39 N 44.39 E
Kazbek, gora ∧ 84 42.42 N 44.31 E
Kaz Dağı ∧ 130 39.42 N 26.50 E
Kazembe 154 12.11 S 32.37 E
Kazenyy Torets' ≃ 83 48.54 N 37.46 E
Kāzerūn 128 29.37 N 51.38 E
Kazgorodok, Kaz. 86 52.53 N 70.42 E
Kazgorodok, Kaz. 86 49.56 N 71.36 E
Kažim 24 60.20 N 51.30 E
Kazimierza Wielka 30 50.16 N 20.30 E
Kazimierz Dolny 30 51.20 N 21.58 E
Kazincbarcika 30 48.16 N 20.37 E
Kazinka, Ross. 76 52.32 N 39.42 E
Kazinka, Ross. 78 50.14 N 37.50 E
Kāzipāra 272b 22.43 N 88.31 E
Kāzīr Char 126 22.46 N 90.33 E
Kaziza 152 10.42 S 23.52 E
Kaz'jany 76 55.18 N 26.52 E
Kazloŭščyna 76 53.19 N 25.18 E
Kazlų Rūda 76 54.46 N 23.30 E
Kaz'minskoje 84 44.35 N 41.41 E
Kaznačejevo 82 54.31 N 37.16 E
Kazo 94 36.07 N 139.36 E
Kaztalovka 80 49.46 N 48.42 E
Kazuma Pan National Park ♦ 154 18.15 S 25.33 E
Kazumba 152 6.25 S 22.02 E
Kazungula 154 17.45 S 25.20 E
Kazuno 92 40.11 N 140.47 E
Kazvin → Qazvīn 128 36.16 N 50.00 E
Kazy 128 39.13 N 57.30 E
Kazym 74 63.40 N 67.14 E
Kazym ≃ 74 63.54 N 65.50 E
Kazyr ≃ 86 53.47 N 92.53 E
Kbal Dâmrei 110 14.07 N 105.21 E
Kbelnice 60 49.18 N 13.59 E
Kbely ⊕[8] 54 50.07 N 14.32 E
Kcynia 30 53.00 N 17.30 E
Kdyně 60 49.23 N 13.02 E
Kéa 38 37.38 N 24.21 E
Kéa I 38 37.34 N 24.22 E
Keaau 229d 19.37 N 155.02 W
Keady 48 54.15 N 6.42 W
Keahole Point › 229d 19.44 N 156.03 W
Keal, Loch na ⊂ 46 56.28 N 6.04 W
Kealaikahiki, Lae o › 229a 20.32 N 156.42 W
Kealaikahiki Channel ʊ 229a 20.37 N 156.50 W
Kealakekua Bay ⊂ 229d 19.28 N 155.56 W
Kealia 229b 22.06 N 159.18 W
Keams Canyon 200 35.48 N 110.11 W
Keanae 229a 20.51 N 156.09 W
Keanapapa Point › 229a 20.54 N 157.04 W
Kean College of New Jersey ⊍[2] 276 40.41 N 74.14 W
Keansburg 208 40.25 N 74.12 W
Kearney, Mo., U.S. 194 39.22 N 94.21 W
Kearney, Ne., U.S. 198 40.41 N 99.04 W
Kearney, Pa., U.S. 214 40.08 N 78.12 W
Kearns 200 40.39 N 111.59 W
Kearny, Az., U.S. 200 33.03 N 110.54 W
Kearny, N.J., U.S. 210 40.46 N 74.08 W
Kearsley 262 53.32 N 2.23 W
Kearsley Creek ≃ 216 43.04 N 83.40 W
Keasbey 276 40.31 N 74.19 W
Keb' ≃ 76 57.44 N 28.28 E
Kebajoran ⊕[8] 269e 6.13 S 106.46 E
Keban 130 38.48 N 38.45 E
Keban Barajı ⊜[1] 130 38.50 N 39.20 E
Kebanyartimur 115a 7.09 S 112.52 E
Kébara 152 2.27 S 14.25 E
Kebbi 150 12.08 N 4.44 E
Kebeiti 120 36.47 N 79.29 E
Kébémer 150 15.22 N 16.27 W
Kébi, Mayo ≃ 146 9.18 N 13.33 E
Kebili 148 33.42 N 8.58 E
Kebîr, Oued el ≃ 34 36.50 N 6.07 E
Kebnekaise ∧ 24 67.53 N 18.33 E
Kebock Head › 46 58.01 N 6.20 W
Kebri Dehar 144 6.47 N 44.17 E
Kebumen 115a 7.40 S 109.39 E
Keb'uty 80 45.50 N 44.14 E
Keče 85 43.14 N 71.22 E
Kecel 30 46.32 N 19.16 E
Kech ≃ 128 26.00 N 62.44 E
Kechika ≃ 176 59.36 N 127.05 W
Keçiborlu 130 37.57 N 30.18 E
Kecksburg 214 40.11 N 79.28 W
Kecskemét 30 46.54 N 19.42 E
Kedah □[3] 114 6.00 N 100.40 E
Kėdainiai 76 55.17 N 24.00 E
Kédange-sur-Canner 56 49.19 N 6.20 E
Kedārnāth 124 30.44 N 79.04 E
Kedārpur 126 23.18 N 90.27 E
Kedges Straits ʊ 208 38.03 N 76.02 W
Kedgwick 186 47.39 N 67.21 W
Kedgwick ≃ 186 47.40 N 67.29 W
Kédhron 38 39.13 N 22.03 E
Kedian 100 31.23 N 112.51 E
Kediri 115a 7.49 S 112.01 E
Kedjebi 150 8.12 N 0.25 E
Kedon 74 64.08 N 159.14 E
Kedong 89 48.02 N 126.15 E
Kédougou 150 12.33 N 12.11 W
Kedrasju 24 64.36 N 60.24 E
Kedrikí Makedhonía □[4] 38 40.30 N 23.00 E
Kedrovka 86 55.32 N 86.03 E
Kedu 102 26.33 N 104.21 E
Kedungdung 115a 7.06 S 113.15 E
Kedungjati 115a 7.10 S 110.37 E
Kedungwuni 115a 6.58 S 109.39 E
Kedvavom 24 64.15 N 53.27 E
Kędzierzyn Kozle 30 50.20 N 18.12 E
Keecheus Lake ⊜ 224 47.22 N 121.22 W
Keefer 218 38.32 N 84.38 W
Keefers 182 50.02 N 121.33 W
Keego Harbor 216 42.36 N 83.20 W
Keelby 44 53.34 N 0.15 W
Keele 42 53.00 N 2.17 W
Keele ≃ 180 64.24 N 124.50 W
Keele Peak ∧ 180 63.26 N 130.19 W
Keeley Lake ⊜ 184 54.54 N 108.08 W
Keeling Islands → Cocos Islands □[2] 12 12.10 S 96.55 E
Keels 186 48.36 N 53.24 W
Keelung → Chilung 100 25.08 N 121.44 E
Keen, Mount ∧ 46 56.58 N 2.54 W
Keene, On., Can. 212 44.15 N 78.10 W
Keene, Ca., U.S. 228 35.13 N 118.33 W
Keene, Ky., U.S. 192 37.56 N 84.38 W
Keene, N.H., U.S. 188 42.56 N 72.16 W
Keene, Oh., U.S. 214 40.21 N 81.52 W
Keene, Tx., U.S. 222 32.23 N 97.19 W
Keenesburg 200 40.06 N 104.31 W
Keeney Knob ∧ 192 37.47 N 80.42 W
Keeneyville 278 41.59 N 88.07 W
Keep River National Park ♦ 164 15.48 S 129.03 E
Keerbergen 56 51.00 N 4.37 E
Keer-Weer, Cape › 164 13.58 S 141.30 E
Keeseg ∧ 64 46.58 N 12.14 E
Keeseville 188 44.30 N 73.28 W
Keesler Air Force Base ■ 194 30.26 N 88.55 W
Keetmanshoop 156 26.36 S 18.08 E
Keewatin, On., Can. 184 49.46 N 94.34 W
Keewatin, Mn., U.S. 190 47.23 N 93.04 W
Kefa □[4] 144 6.50 N 36.00 E
Kefallinía I 38 38.15 N 20.35 E
Kéfalos 38 36.45 N 27.00 E
Kefamenanu 112 9.27 S 124.29 E
Kefar ʿAzza 132 31.29 N 34.32 E
Kefar Blum 132 33.10 N 35.36 E
Kefar ʿEẕyon 132 31.39 N 35.08 E
Kefar Naḥum (Capernaum) ⊥ 132 32.53 N 35.34 E
Kefar Sava 132 32.10 N 34.54 E
Kefar Shammay 132 32.57 N 35.27 E
Kefar Szold 132 33.11 N 35.39 E
Kefar Vitkin 132 32.23 N 34.53 E
Kefar Warburg 132 31.43 N 34.44 E
Kefar Yona 132 32.19 N 34.55 E
Kefermarkt 61 48.26 N 14.32 E
Keffi 150 8.51 N 7.52 E
Keffin Hausa 150 12.15 N 9.58 E
Keflavík 24a 64.02 N 22.36 W
Keftya 144 13.54 N 37.07 E
Kega 24 65.10 N 36.54 E
Ke Ga, Mui ›, Viet 110 12.53 N 109.28 E
Ke Ga, Mui ›, Viet 110 10.42 N 107.58 E
Kegalla 122 7.15 N 80.21 E
Kégashka 186 50.12 N 61.17 W
Kégashka, Lac ⊜ 186 50.20 N 61.25 W
Kegejli 86 42.45 N 59.35 E
Kegnæs ›[1] 41 54.52 N 9.59 E
Kegon-no-taki ∟ 94 36.44 N 139.31 E
Kegonsa, Lake ⊜ 216 42.58 N 89.15 W
Kegonzhake 120 33.00 N 87.53 E
Keg River 176 57.48 N 117.52 W
Kegums 76 56.46 N 24.45 E
Kegworth 42 52.50 N 1.16 W
Kehdingen, Land ⊕[1] 52 53.45 N 9.15 E
Kehiwin Indian Reserve ⊕[4] 182 54.07 N 110.48 W
Kehl 56 48.35 N 7.50 E
Kehlen 58 47.41 N 9.33 E
Kehoe 218 38.28 N 83.03 W
Kehra 76 59.20 N 25.20 E
Kehrigk 54 52.09 N 13.55 E
Ke-hsi Mānsām 110 21.56 N 97.50 E
Kehychivka 78 49.17 N 35.46 E
Keig 46 57.15 N 2.39 W
Keighley 44 53.52 N 1.54 W
Keihoku 96 35.09 N 135.38 E
Keijō → Sŏul 98 37.33 N 126.58 E
Keila 76 59.18 N 24.25 E
Keilor 169 37.43 S 144.50 E
Keimoes 158 28.41 S 21.00 E
Kei Mouth 158 32.41 S 28.22 E
Keio University ⊍[2] 268 35.38 N 139.45 E
Kei Road 158 32.42 S 27.32 E
Keiser 194 35.40 N 90.05 W
Keiskammahoek 158 32.41 S 27.09 E
Keiskammapunt › 158 32.40 S 27.10 E
Keïta 150 14.46 N 5.46 E
Kéita, Bahr ≃ 146 9.14 N 18.21 E
Keitele 26 63.11 N 26.22 E
Keitele ⊜ 26 62.55 N 26.00 E
Keith, Austl. 166 36.06 S 140.21 E
Keith, Scot., U.K. 46 57.32 N 2.57 W
Keith Arm ⊂ 176 65.20 N 122.15 W
Keithley Creek 182 52.45 N 121.24 W
Keithsburg 190 41.05 N 90.56 W
Keiyasi 175g 17.54 S 177.45 E
Keizer 224 44.59 N 123.01 W
Kejaman 112 2.39 N 113.45 E
Kejimkujik National Park ♦ 186 44.21 N 65.18 W
Kejngypil'gyn, laguna ⊂ 180 63.30 N 178.50 E
Kejni, gora ∧ 180 64.30 N 174.54 W
Kejvy ⋏ 24 67.35 N 38.00 E
Kekaha 229b 21.58 N 159.42 W
Kekek ≃ 190 48.24 N 75.48 W
Kekerengu 172 42.00 S 174.01 E
Kékes ∧ 30 47.55 N 20.02 E
Kekeyaer 85 38.02 N 75.05 E
Kek Lok Si ⊍[1] 114 5.23 N 100.14 E
Kekpāra 126 22.27 N 86.35 E
Kekri 120 25.58 N 75.09 E
Kekurnoi, Cape › 180 57.44 N 155.15 W
Kelafo 144 5.40 N 44.20 E
Kelai ≃ 112 2.10 N 117.29 E
Kelan 102 38.43 N 111.32 E
Kelanang 114 2.48 N 101.26 E
Kelang 114 3.02 N 101.27 E
Kelang, Pulau I, Indon. 164 3.12 S 127.44 E
Kelang, Pulau I, Malay. 114 3.00 N 101.18 E
Kelani ≃ 122 6.58 N 79.52 E
Kelantan 114 0.51 N 101.40 E
Kelantan □[3] 114 5.20 N 102.00 E
Kelantan ≃ 114 6.11 N 102.15 E
Kelapa 112 1.52 S 105.42 E
Kelasuri 84 43.08 N 41.13 E
Kelat 218 38.32 N 84.19 W
Kelayres 210 40.54 N 76.00 W
Kelb, Ouadi V 146 15.19 N 18.51 E
Kelberg 56 50.17 N 6.55 E
Kelbia, Sebkhet ⊜ 36 35.51 N 10.16 E
Kelbra 54 51.26 N 11.02 E
Keld Ula ∧ 86 43.20 N 85.25 E
Kel'd'ušovo 80 55.01 N 44.59 E
Keleft 128 37.21 N 66.15 E
Kelegou 98 41.57 N 118.11 E
Kélékélé 273b 4.20 S 15.08 E
Kelem 144 4.48 N 35.58 E
Kelenföld ⊕[8] 264c 47.28 N 19.03 E
Kelenken, gora ∧ 180 66.07 N 170.52 W
Keles, Tür. 130 39.55 N 29.14 E
Keles, Uzb. 85 41.24 N 69.12 E
Keles ≃ 85 41.02 N 68.37 E
Keleti-főcsatorna ≊ 30 48.01 N 21.20 E
Keleti Pályaudvar ⊕[5] 264c 47.30 N 19.06 E
Kelheim 60 48.55 N 11.52 E
Kelibia 148 36.51 N 11.06 E
Kelkheim 56 50.08 N 8.26 E
Kelkit 130 40.08 N 39.27 E
Kelkit ≃ 130 40.46 N 36.32 E
Kell, Dtsch. 56 49.38 N 6.50 E
Kell, Il., U.S. 219 38.30 N 88.54 W
Kellé 152 0.06 S 14.33 E
Kellen 52 51.48 N 6.10 E
Kellenhusen 54 54.11 N 11.03 E
Keller, Tx., U.S. 222 32.56 N 97.15 W
Keller, Va., U.S. 208 37.37 N 75.45 W
Keller, Wa., U.S. 182 48.04 N 118.41 W
Kellerberg 64 46.40 N 13.42 E
Kellerberrin 162 31.38 S 117.43 E
Kellerjoch ∧ 64 47.19 N 11.46 E
Keller Lake ⊜, N.T., Can. 176 64.00 N 121.30 W
Keller Lake ⊜, Sk., Can. 184 56.04 N 106.46 W
Kellerovka 86 53.50 N 69.17 E
Keller Peak ∧ 228 34.12 N 117.03 W
Kellett, Cape › 176 71.59 N 125.34 W
Kellettville 214 41.33 N 79.16 W
Kelleys Island 214 41.36 N 82.42 W
Kelleys Island I 214 41.36 N 82.42 W
Kelliher 184 51.15 N 103.44 W
Kellinghusen 52 53.57 N 9.43 E
Kellmünz 58 48.07 N 10.08 E
Kelloe 44 54.43 N 1.28 W
Kellogg, Id., U.S. 202 47.32 N 116.07 W
Kellogg, Ia., U.S. 190 41.43 N 92.54 W
Kellogg, Mn., U.S. 190 44.18 N 91.59 W
Kellogg Marsh 224 48.05 N 122.07 W
Kelloggsville 214 41.52 N 80.36 W
Kellojärvi ⊜ 26 64.16 N 29.03 E
Kelloselkä 24 66.56 N 28.50 E
Kells → Ceanannus Mór, Ire. 48 53.44 N 6.53 W
Kells, N. Ire., U.K. 48 54.48 N 6.13 W
Kelly Air Force Base ■ 196 29.24 N 98.35 W
Kelly Lake ⊜ 180 65.30 N 126.10 W
Kelly Run ≃, Pa., U.S. 279b 40.15 N 79.55 W
Kelly Run ≃, Pa., U.S. 279b 40.13 N 79.45 W
Kellyville, Austl. 274a 33.43 S 150.57 E
Kellyville, Ok., U.S. 196 35.56 N 96.12 W
Kelmė 76 55.38 N 22.56 E
Kel'mentsi 78 48.27 N 26.50 E
Kelmet 144 16.04 N 38.55 E
Kelmscott 168a 32.07 S 116.01 E
Kelo 146 9.19 N 15.48 E
Kelolokan 112 1.08 N 117.54 E
Kelottijärvi 24 68.31 N 22.04 E
Kelowna 182 49.53 N 119.29 W
Kelsall 44 53.13 N 2.43 W
Kelsey Bay 182 50.24 N 125.57 W
Kelsey Head › 42 50.24 N 5.08 W
Kelsey Lake ⊜ 184 53.37 N 101.02 W
Kelseyville 204 38.58 N 122.50 W
Kelso, Scot., U.K. 46 55.36 N 2.25 W
Kelso, Wa., U.S. 224 46.08 N 122.54 W
Kelsterbach 56 50.04 N 8.32 E
Kel'temašat 85 42.30 N 70.17 E
Kelty 46 56.08 N 3.23 W
Keluang 114 2.02 N 103.19 E
Keluang, Tanjung › 112 3.02 S 110.39 E
Kelud, Gunung ∧ 115a 7.56 S 112.18 E
Keluo ≃ 89 49.22 N 125.15 E
Keluotun 89 49.16 N 125.44 E
Kelvedon 42 51.51 N 0.42 E
Kelvedon Hatch 260 51.40 N 0.16 E
Kelvington 184 52.10 N 103.30 W
Kelvin Seamount ✣[3] 16 38.50 N 64.00 W
Kelyexeed 144 8.46 N 49.12 E
Kelzenberg 263 51.07 N 6.30 E
Kem' 24 64.57 N 34.36 E
Kem' ≃, Ross. 24 64.57 N 34.41 E
Kem' ≃, Ross. 86 58.31 N 92.04 E
Kema 112 1.23 N 125.04 E
Kema ≃, Ross. 76 60.16 N 37.20 E
Kema ≃, Ross. 76 59.21 N 44.29 E
Ké Macina 150 13.58 N 5.22 W
Kémah, Congo 273b 4.11 S 15.13 E
Kemah, Tür. 130 39.36 N 39.02 E
Kemah, Tx., U.S. 222 29.32 N 95.01 W
Kemaliye 130 39.16 N 38.29 E
Kemalpaşa, Tür. 130 41.30 N 41.30 E
Kemalpaşa, Tür. 130 38.25 N 27.26 E
Kemano 182 53.34 N 127.56 W
Kemasik 114 4.25 N 103.27 E
Kemayan 114 3.08 N 102.22 E
Kemayoran Airport ⊠ 269e 6.09 S 106.51 E
Kembani 112 1.34 S 122.54 E
Kembé 152 4.36 N 21.54 E
Kemberg 54 51.46 N 12.38 E
Kemblesville 208 39.45 N 75.50 W
Kembolcha 144 11.02 N 39.43 E
Kembs 58 47.41 N 7.30 E
Kembul 164 5.55 S 150.40 E
Kemčug ≃ 86 57.14 N 90.31 E
Kemena ≃ 112 3.10 N 113.03 E
Kemeneshát ⋏[2] 61 46.58 N 16.40 E
Kemer, Tür. 130 36.38 N 29.21 E
Kemer, Tür. 130 36.36 N 30.34 E
Kemer, Tür. 130 37.21 N 30.04 E
Kemer ≃ 267b 41.04 N 29.07 E
Kemer Barajı ⊜[1] 130 37.34 N 28.31 E
Kemerburgaz ⊕[8] 267b 41.09 N 28.54 E
Kemerhisar 130 37.49 N 34.36 E
Kemerovo 86 55.20 N 86.05 E
Kemerovo Oblast' □[4] 86 55.00 N 87.00 E
Kemi 26 65.49 N 24.32 E
Kemie 26 62.14 N 30.20 E
Kemijärvi 24 66.40 N 27.25 E
Kemijärvi ⊜ 24 66.36 N 27.24 E
Kemijoki ≃ 24 65.47 N 24.30 E
Kemiö → Kimito 26 60.10 N 22.45 E
Keml'a 80 54.42 N 45.15 E
Kemmel 50 50.47 N 2.49 E
Kemmelberg ∧[2] 50 50.47 N 2.50 E
Kemmerer 200 41.47 N 110.32 W
Kemminghausen ⊕[8] 263 51.34 N 7.29 E
Kemmuna (Comino) I 36 36.00 N 14.20 E
Kemnader See ⊜ 263 51.25 N 7.15 E
Kemnath 60 49.52 N 11.54 E
Kemnay 46 57.14 N 2.27 W
Kemnitz 54 54.04 N 13.31 E
Kémo-Gribingui □[5] 152 6.00 N 19.00 E
Kemp 222 32.26 N 96.13 W
Kemp, Lake ⊜[1] 196 33.45 N 99.13 W
Kemparana 150 12.50 N 4.56 W
Kemp Coast ⊥[2] 9 67.10 S 58.00 E
Kempele 26 64.55 N 25.30 E
Kempen 56 51.22 N 6.25 E
Kempen ⊕[1] 56 51.10 N 5.20 E
Kempener Land ⊕[1] 263 51.19 N 6.29 E
Kempenfelt Bay ⊂ 212 44.23 N 79.36 W
Kempenich 56 50.25 N 7.07 E
Kempens Kanaal ≊ 56 51.10 N 4.49 E
Kemper → Quimper 32 48.00 N 4.06 W
Kemp Mill 284c 39.02 N 77.01 W
Kempner 196 31.05 N 98.00 W
Kemp Peninsula ›[1] 9 73.08 S 60.15 W
Kemps Bay 238 24.02 N 77.33 W
Kemps Creek ≃ 274a 33.51 S 150.46 E
Kempsey, Austl. 166 31.05 S 152.50 E
Kempsey, Eng., U.K. 42 52.08 N 2.12 W
Kempston 42 52.07 N 0.30 W
Kempt, Lac ⊜ 176 47.25 N 74.22 W
Kempten (Allgäu) 58 47.43 N 10.19 E
Kempton, Il., U.S. 216 40.56 N 88.14 W
Kempton, In., U.S. 216 40.17 N 86.13 W
Kempton Park 158 26.06 S 28.14 E
Kempton Park □[5] 273d 26.06 S 28.14 E
Kempton Park Race Course ♦ 260 51.25 N 0.23 W
Kemptville 212 45.01 N 75.38 W
Kemptville Creek ≃ 212 45.03 N 75.39 W
Kemsing 260 51.18 N 0.14 E
Kemubu 114 5.18 N 102.01 E
Kemujan, Pulau I 115a 5.48 S 110.28 E
Kemul, Kong ∧ 112 1.52 N 116.11 E
Ken ≃ 124 25.46 N 80.31 E
Ken, Loch ⊜ 44 55.02 N 4.02 W
Ken, Water of ≃ 44 55.04 N 4.08 W
Kena ≃ 24 62.05 N 39.06 E
Kenai 180 60.33 N 151.15 W
Kenai Fjords National Park ♦ 180 59.45 N 150.00 W
Kenai Mountains ⋏ 180 60.00 N 150.00 W
Kenai Peninsula ›[1] 180 60.10 N 150.00 W
Kenamuke Swamp ≋ 140 6.15 N 33.48 E
Kenansville, Fl., U.S. 220 27.52 N 80.59 W
Kenansville, N.C., U.S. 192 34.57 N 77.57 W
Kenaral 85 42.32 N 72.08 E
Kenašči 80 50.32 N 53.20 E
Kenashiga-sen ∧ 96 35.14 N 133.31 E
Kenaston 184 51.30 N 106.18 W
Kenberma 283 42.17 N 70.52 W
Kenbridge 192 36.57 N 78.07 W
Kenda 126 23.12 N 86.32 E
Kendai 124 22.45 N 82.37 E
Kendal, Sk., Can. 184 50.15 N 103.37 W
Kendal, Indon. 115a 6.55 S 110.12 E
Kendal, S. Afr. 158 26.04 S 28.58 E
Kendal, Eng., U.K. 44 54.20 N 2.45 W
Kendall, Austl. 166 31.38 S 152.43 E
Kendall, Fl., U.S. 220 25.40 N 80.19 W
Kendall, Mi., U.S. 216 42.22 N 85.49 W
Kendall, N.Y., U.S. 210 43.20 N 78.02 W
Kendall, Wi., U.S. 190 43.47 N 90.22 W
Kendall □[6] 216 41.38 N 88.27 W
Kendall, Cape › 176 63.36 N 87.09 W
Kendall, Mount ∧ 172 41.22 S 172.24 E
Kendall Park 208 40.31 N 74.24 W
Kendallville 216 41.26 N 85.15 W
Kendari 112 3.57 S 122.35 E
Kendari, Teluk ⊂ 112 3.57 S 122.38 E
Kendawangan 112 2.32 S 110.12 E
Kende 150 11.30 N 4.12 E
Kendenup 162 34.29 S 117.39 E
Kendghāta 126 24.05 N 87.10 E
Kendikolu I 122 5.57 N 73.24 E
Kendiktas ⋏ 85 43.35 N 74.45 E
Kendleton 222 29.27 N 96.00 W
Kendrāparha 120 20.30 N 86.25 E
Kendrew 158 32.31 S 24.30 E
Kendrick, Fl., U.S. 192 29.22 N 82.12 W
Kendrick, Id., U.S. 202 46.36 N 116.38 W
Kendrick Creek ≃ 226 38.00 N 119.50 W
Kendua 272b 22.34 N 88.10 E
Kendu Bay 154 0.22 S 34.39 E
Kendujhargarh 120 21.38 N 85.35 E
Kendyrlik 86 47.30 N 85.12 E
Kenedy 196 28.49 N 97.50 W
Kenefick 222 30.07 N 94.51 W
Kenema 150 7.52 N 11.12 W
Kenes, Kaz. 85 43.41 N 67.49 E
Kenes, Kaz. 85 43.59 N 73.35 E
Kenesaw 198 40.37 N 98.39 W
Kenga 86 57.27 N 80.57 E
Kenga ≃ 86 58.05 N 80.37 E
Kenge 152 4.52 S 16.59 E
Kengeja 154 5.25 S 39.44 E
Kēng Hkam, Mya. 110 21.01 N 98.29 E
Keng Hkam, Mya. 110 21.27 N 97.03 E
Kengkou, Zhg. 100 29.48 N 117.22 E
Kengkou, Zhg. 100 28.27 N 120.26 E
Kengtian 100 25.54 N 119.26 E
Kēng Tung 110 21.17 N 99.36 E
Kengun-chūtonchi, Rikujō-jieitai- ■ 92 32.46 N 130.45 E
Kenhardt 158 29.19 S 21.12 E
Kenhorst 208 40.18 N 75.57 W
Kenia 152 2.43 S 17.04 E
Kenia → Kenya □[1] 154 1.00 N 38.00 E
Kenia → Kirinyaga ∧ 154 0.10 S 37.20 E
Kéniéba 150 12.50 N 11.14 W
Kenilworth, Eng., U.K. 42 52.21 N 1.34 W
Kenilworth, Il., U.S. 278 42.05 N 87.43 W
Kenilworth, N.J., U.S. 276 40.40 N 74.17 W
Kenilworth, Pa., U.S. 208 40.14 N 75.38 W
Kenilworth, Ut,. U.S. 200 39.41 N 110.48 W
Kenilworth Castle ⊥ 42 52.21 N 1.34 W
Keningau 112 5.20 N 116.10 E
Kenitra 148 34.16 N 6.40 W
Kenitra □[4] 148 34.30 N 6.00 W
Kenley ⊕[8] 260 51.19 N 0.06 W
Kenli (Xishuanghe) 98 37.40 N 118.35 E
Kenly 192 35.35 N 78.07 W
Kenmare, Ire. 48 51.53 N 9.35 W
Kenmare, N.D., U.S. 198 48.40 N 102.04 W
Kenmare River ≃ 48 51.45 N 10.00 W
Kenmawr 279b 40.28 N 80.06 W
Kenmore, Scot., U.K. 46 56.34 N 3.59 W
Kenmore, N.Y., U.S. 210 42.57 N 78.52 W
Kenmore, Wa., U.S. 224 47.45 N 122.14 W
Kenn 56 49.48 N 6.44 E
Kennard, In., U.S. 218 39.54 N 85.31 W
Kennard, Pa., U.S. 214 41.28 N 80.20 W
Kennard, Tx., U.S. 222 31.22 N 95.11 W
Kennebec 198 43.54 N 99.51 W
Kennebec ≃ 188 44.00 N 69.50 W
Kennebecasis Bay ⊂ 186 45.25 N 66.00 W
Kennebec Lake ⊜ 212 44.43 N 77.00 W
Kennebunk 188 43.23 N 70.32 W
Kennedale 222 32.38 N 97.13 W
Kennedy, Al., U.S. 194 33.35 N 87.59 W
Kennedy, N.Y., U.S. 214 42.09 N 79.06 W
Kennedy, Zimb. 154 18.52 S 27.10 E
Kennedy, Cape → Canaveral, Cape › 220 28.27 N 80.32 W
Kennedy, Mount ∧, B.C., Can. 182 50.49 N 125.33 W
Kennedy, Mount ∧, Yk., Can. 180 60.30 N 139.00 W
Kennedy Entrance ʊ 180 59.00 N 152.00 W
Kennedy Lake ⊜ 182 49.05 N 125.40 W
Kennedy Peak ∧ 110 23.19 N 93.45 E
Kennedy Range ⋏ 162 24.30 S 115.00 E
Kennedyville 208 39.18 N 75.59 W
Kennemerduinen, Nationale Park de ♦ 52 52.25 N 4.35 E
Kenner 194 29.59 N 90.14 W
Kennerdell 214 41.16 N 79.51 W
Kennet ≃ 42 51.28 N 0.57 W
Kennetcook 186 45.11 N 63.44 W
Kenneth City 220 27.49 N 82.44 W
Kennett 194 36.14 N 90.03 W
Kennett ≃ 42 52.26 N 0.28 E
Kennett Square 208 39.50 N 75.42 W
Kennewick 202 46.12 N 119.08 W
Kenney 219 40.06 N 89.05 W
Kenney Dam ⊕[6] 182 53.37 N 124.58 W
Kennington, Eng., U.K. 42 51.10 N 0.54 E
Kennington, Eng., U.K. 42 51.43 N 1.15 W
Kennisis Lake ⊜ 212 45.13 N 78.39 W
Kenn Reef ✣[2] 160 21.12 S 155.46 E
Kenny 222 30.03 N 96.20 W
Kennydale 224 47.31 N 122.12 W
Kennywood Park ♦ 279b 40.23 N 79.52 W
Kénogami 186 48.26 N 71.14 W
Kenogami ≃ 176 51.06 N 84.28 W
Kénogami, Lac ⊜ 186 48.20 N 71.23 W
Kenogamissi Lake ⊜ 190 48.15 N 81.31 W
Keno Hill 180 63.55 N 135.18 W
Kenora 184 49.47 N 94.29 W
Kenosha 216 42.35 N 87.49 W
Kenosha □[6] 216 42.35 N 88.03 W
Kenova 188 38.23 N 82.34 W
Kenoza Lake 210 41.44 N 74.57 W
Kenoza Lake ⊜ 283 42.47 N 71.03 W
Kenozero, ozero ⊜ 24 62.03 N 38.14 E
Ken Rock 216 42.15 N 89.03 W
Kensal 198 47.18 N 98.43 W
Kensett 194 35.13 N 91.40 W
Kensico Lake ⊜ 276 41.07 N 73.45 W
Kensico Reservoir ⊜[1] 210 41.05 N 73.46 W
Kensington, Austl. 274a 33.55 S 151.14 E
Kensington, P.E., Can. 186 46.26 N 63.38 W
Kensington, Ca., U.S. 226 37.54 N 122.16 W
Kensington, Ct., U.S. 207 41.38 N 72.46 W
Kensington, Ks., U.S. 198 39.46 N 99.01 W
Kensington, Md., U.S. 284c 39.01 N 77.04 W
Kensington, Oh., U.S. 214 40.44 N 80.57 W
Kensington ⊕[8], S. Afr. 273d 26.12 S 28.06 E
Kensington ⊕[8], N.Y., U.S. 276 40.39 N 73.58 W
Kensington ⊕[8], Pa., U.S. 285 39.58 N 75.08 W
Kensington and Chelsea ⊕[8] 260 51.29 N 0.11 W
Kensington Estates 284c 39.02 N 77.05 W
Kensington Metropolitan Park ♦ 281 42.32 N 83.39 W
Kensington Park 220 27.22 N 82.31 W
Kent, S.L. 150 8.10 N 13.10 W
Kent, Ct., U.S. 207 41.43 N 73.28 W
Kent, N.Y., U.S. 210 43.20 N 78.08 W
Kent, Oh., U.S. 214 41.09 N 81.21 W
Kent, Or., U.S. 224 45.11 N 120.41 W
Kent, Wa., U.S. 224 47.22 N 122.14 W
Kent □[6], On., Can. 214 42.25 N 82.10 W
Kent □[6], Eng., U.K. 42 51.15 N 0.40 E
Kent □[6], De., U.S. 208 39.10 N 75.32 W
Kent □[6], Md., U.S. 208 39.13 N 76.04 W
Kent □[6], Mi., U.S. 216 42.56 N 85.33 W
Kent □[6], R.I., U.S. 207 41.40 N 71.38 W
Kent ≃ 44 54.15 N 2.48 W
Kent, Vale of V 42 51.10 N 0.30 E
Kent Acres 208 39.07 N 75.31 W
Kentallen 46 56.39 N 5.15 W
Kentani 158 32.31 S 28.19 E
Kentau 85 43.36 N 68.36 E
Kent Bridge 214 42.31 N 82.04 W
Kent County Airport ⊠ 216 42.54 N 85.39 W
Kentfield 282 37.57 N 122.33 W
Kent Group II 166 39.27 S 147.20 E
Kenthurst 274a 33.40 S 151.00 E
Kent Island I 208 38.55 N 76.20 W
Kent Lake ⊜ 216 42.32 N 83.40 W
Kentland, In., U.S. 216 40.46 N 87.26 W
Kentland, Md., U.S. 284c 38.55 N 76.53 W
Kenton, Eng., U.K. 42 50.38 N 3.28 W
Kenton, De., U.S. 208 39.13 N 75.39 W
Kenton, Mi., U.S. 190 46.29 N 88.53 W
Kenton, Oh., U.S. 216 40.38 N 83.36 W
Kenton, Tn., U.S. 194 36.12 N 89.00 W
Kenton □[6] 218 38.56 N 84.33 W
Kent Park 283 42.06 N 70.41 W
Kent Park ♦ 273d 26.08 S 28.04 E
Kent Peninsula ›[1] 176 68.30 N 107.00 W
Kent Point › 208 38.50 N 76.22 W
Kentucky □[3] 178 37.30 N 85.15 W
Kentucky ≃ 218 38.41 N 85.11 W
Kentucky, Middle Fork ≃ 192 37.35 N 83.40 W
Kentucky, North Fork ≃ 192 37.34 N 83.42 W
Kentucky, South Fork ≃ 192 37.34 N 83.42 W
Kentucky Horse Park ♦ 218 38.08 N 84.31 W
Kentucky Lake ⊜[1] 194 36.25 N 88.05 W
Kent Village 284c 38.55 N 76.53 W
Kentville 186 45.05 N 64.30 W
Kentwood, La., U.S. 194 30.56 N 90.30 W
Kentwood, Mi., U.S. 216 42.52 N 85.38 W
Kent Woodlands 282 37.57 N 122.34 W
Kenvil 276 40.52 N 74.37 W
Kenwick 168a 32.02 S 115.58 E
Kenwood, Ca., U.S. 226 38.25 N 122.33 W
Kenwood, Md., U.S. 284b 39.21 N 76.31 W
Kenwood, Oh., U.S. 218 39.12 N 84.22 W
Kenwood ⊕[8] 278 41.49 N 87.36 W
Kenwood ⊥ 260 51.34 N 0.10 W
Kenya □[1] 154 1.00 N 38.00 E
Kenya, Mount → Kirinyaga ∧ 154 0.10 S 37.20 E
Kenyon, Eng., U.K. 262 53.27 N 2.34 W
Kenyon, Mn., U.S. 190 44.16 N 92.59 W
Kenyon, R.I., U.S. 207 41.26 N 71.37 W
Ken-zaki › 268 35.08 N 139.41 E
Kenzingen 58 48.11 N 7.46 E
Kenzou 152 4.10 N 15.02 E
Keokea 229a 20.42 N 156.21 W
Keokuk 190 40.23 N 91.23 W
Keoladeo National Park ♦ 124 27.10 N 77.20 E
Keonchi 124 22.38 N 81.47 E
Keo Neua, Col de )( 110 18.23 N 105.09 E
Keon Park 274b 37.42 S 145.01 E
Keosauqua 190 40.43 N 91.57 W
Keota, Ia., U.S. 190 41.21 N 91.57 W
Keota, Ok., U.S. 196 35.15 N 94.55 W
Keowee, Lake ⊜[1] 192 34.45 N 82.55 W
Kepa (Mittagskogel) ∧ 61 46.31 N 13.57 E
Kepala Batas 114 5.31 N 100.26 E
Kepanjen 115a 8.07 S 112.34 E
Kepi 164 6.32 S 139.19 E
Kępice 30 54.15 N 16.52 E
Kepina 24 65.24 N 41.50 E
Keping Shan ⋏ 85 40.00 N 77.10 E
Kępno 30 51.17 N 17.59 E
Kepo 112 2.56 S 106.33 E
Keppel Bay ⊂ 166 23.21 S 150.55 E
Keppel Harbour ⊂ 271c 1.16 N 103.50 E
Kepsut 130 39.41 N 28.09 E
Keptown 219 39.05 N 88.40 W
Kequan 98 36.04 N 114.00 E
Kerala □[3] 122 10.00 N 76.30 E
Keram ≃ 164 4.07 S 144.07 E
Keramian, Pulau I 112 5.04 S 114.36 E
Kerandin 112 0.12 S 104.46 E
Kerang 166 35.44 S 143.55 E
Keranyo 144 5.04 N 38.18 E
Keratéa 38 37.48 N 23.59 E
Keratsínion 267c 37.58 N 23.37 E
Keraudren, Cape › 162 19.57 S 119.45 E
Kerava 26 60.24 N 25.07 E
Keravat 164 4.19 S 152.01 E
Kerbat ≃ 114 5.01 N 102.51 E
Kerbela → Karbalā' 128 32.36 N 44.02 E
Kerbi ≃ 89 52.28 N 136.25 E
Kerby 202 42.11 N 123.39 W
Kerčel' 86 59.18 N 64.46 E
Kerčemja 24 61.28 N 53.50 E
Kerčenskij proliv (Kerchens'ka protoka) ʊ 78 45.22 N 36.38 E
Kerčevskij 24 59.55 N 56.17 E
Kerch 78 45.22 N 36.27 E
Kerchens'ka protoka (Kerčenskij proliv) ʊ 78 45.22 N 36.38 E
Kerchens'kyy pivostriv ›[1] 78 45.15 N 36.00 E
Kerckhoff Lake ⊜[1] 226 37.09 N 119.31 W
Kéré 154 5.16 N 26.11 E
Kéré ≃ 140 5.19 N 25.40 E
Kerec, mys › 24 65.20 N 39.40 E
Kerej, ozero ⊜ 86 50.08 N 68.45 E
Kerema 164 8.00 S 145.45 E
Keremeos 182 49.12 N 119.50 W
Kerem Maharal 132 32.39 N 34.59 E
Kerempe Burnu › 130 42.01 N 33.21 E
Keren 144 15.46 N 38.28 E
Kerend 128 34.16 N 46.15 E
Kerens 222 32.07 N 96.13 W
Kerepes 264c 47.34 N 19.18 E
Keret' 24 66.16 N 33.34 E
Keret', ozero ⊜ 24 65.55 N 32.56 E
Kerewan 150 13.29 N 16.10 W
Kerga 24 62.39 N 46.00 E
Kerguélen, Îles II 6 49.15 S 69.10 E
Kerguelen Plateau ✣[3] 6 55.00 S 75.00 E
Kerhonkson 210 41.46 N 74.17 W
Kerian ≃ 114 5.10 N 100.26 E
Kericho 154 0.22 S 35.17 E
Keri Kera 140 12.21 N 32.46 E
Kerikeri 172 35.13 S 173.58 E
Kerimäki 26 61.55 N 29.17 E
Kerinci, Gunung ∧ 112 1.42 S 101.16 E
Kerio ≃ 154 2.59 N 36.07 E
Keríon 38 37.40 N 20.48 E
Keritang 112 0.51 S 102.39 E
Keriya ≃ 120 38.30 N 8?.10 E
Kerka ≃ 61 46.28 N 16.36 E
Kerkafalva 61 46.46 N 16.30 E
Kerkdriel 52 51.46 N 5.20 E
Kerkebet 144 16.18 N 37.24 E
Kerken 56 51.27 N 6.22 E
Kerkenna, Îles II 148 34.44 N 11.12 E
Kerkhove 50 50.48 N 3.30 E
Kerkhoven 198 45.11 N 95.19 W
Kerki, Ross. 24 63.43 N 54.05 E
Kerki, Turk. 128 37.50 N 65.12 E
Kérkira (Corfu) 38 39.36 N 19.56 E
Kérkira (Corfu) I 38 39.40 N 19.45 E
Kerkrade [-Holz] 56 50.52 N 6.04 E
Kerling 114 3.35 N 101.36 E
Kermadec Islands II 14 29.16 S 177.55 W
Kermadec Ridge ✣[3] 14 30.30 S 178.30 W
Kermadec Trench ✣[1] 14 30.00 S 177.00 W
Kermajärvi ⊜ 26 62.28 N 28.40 E
Kermān, Īrān 128 30.17 N 57.05 E
Kerman, Ca., U.S. 226 36.43 N 120.04 W
Kermān □[4] 128 29.00 N 57.30 E
Kermit 196 31.51 N 103.05 W
Kermit Roosevelt Seamount ✣[3] 16 39.35 N 146.00 W
Kermode, Mount ∧ 182 52.57 N 131.51 W
Kern □[6] 228 35.20 N 118.55 W
Kern ≃ 204 35.13 N 119.17 W
Kern, South Fork ≃ 204 35.40 N 118.27 W
Kernersville 192 36.07 N 80.04 W
Kernforschungszentrum ⊍[3] 56 49.07 N 8.26 E
Kernhof 61 47.49 N 15.32 E
Kern Island Canal ≊ 228 35.22 N 119.01 W
Kern Lake Bed ⊜ 228 35.10 N 119.05 W
Kern River Channel ≃[1] 226 35.49 N 119.40 W
Kernville 204 35.45 N 118.25 W
Keroh 114 5.43 N 101.00 E
Keros 24 60.44 N 52.50 E
Kérou 150 10.50 N 2.06 E
Kérouané 150 9.16 N 9.01 W
Kerowagi 164 5.50 S 144.50 E
Kerpen 56 50.52 N 6.41 E
Kerr 214 41.03 N 78.25 W
Kerrera I 46 56.23 N 5.34 W
Kerridge 262 53.17 N 2.06 W
Kerridge Hill ∧[2] 262 53.17 N 2.06 W
Kerrobert 184 51.55 N 109.08 W
Kerrtown 214 41.38 N 80.10 W
Kerruish Park ♦ 279a 41.26 N 81.34 W
Kerrville 196 30.02 N 99.08 W
Kerry 42 52.30 N 3.16 W
Kerry □[6] 48 52.10 N 9.30 W
Kerry Head › 48 52.25 N 9.57 W
Kersa 144 9.28 N 41.53 E
Kersbrook 168b 34.47 S 138.51 E
Kersey 214 41.21 N 78.35 W
Kershaw 192 34.33 N 80.35 W
Kersinyane 150 15.24 N 10.10 W
Kersley 182 52.49 N 122.25 W
Kerspestausee ⊜[1] 263 51.08 N 7.30 E
Kerstenhausen 56 51.04 N 9.13 E
Kert, Oued ≃ 34 35.15 N 3.15 W
Kertamulia 112 0.23 S 109.09 E
Kerteh 114 4.31 N 103.27 E
Kerteminde 41 55.27 N 10.40 E
Kertosono 115a 7.35 S 112.06 E
Kerulen (Cherlen) (Herlen) ≃ 90 48.48 N 117.00 E
Kerva 80 55.37 N 39.35 E
Kerzaz 148 29.30 N 1.37 W
Kerzendorf 264a 52.16 N 13.17 E
Kerženec 80 56.28 N 44.26 E
Kerženec ≃ 80 56.05 N 45.03 E
Kerzers 58 46.58 N 7.12 E
Kesabpur 126 22.55 N 89.13 E
Ke Sach 110 9.46 N 105.59 E
Kesagami Lake ⊜ 176 50.23 N 80.15 W
Kesälahti 26 61.54 N 29.50 E
Keşan 130 40.51 N 26.37 E
Keşap 130 40.55 N 38.31 E
Kesbern 263 51.20 N 7.42 E
Kesch, Piz ∧ 58 46.38 N 9.52 E
Kesem ≃ 144 9.14 N 40.06 E
Kesennuma 92 38.54 N 141.35 E
Kesh 48 54.32 N 7.43 W
Keshan 89 48.02 N 125.51 E
Keshena 190 44.53 N 88.38 W
Keshendeh 120 36.05 N 66.51 E
Keshequa Creek ≃ 210 42.43 N 77.50 W
Keshod 120 21.18 N 70.15 E
Keşiş Dağları ⋏ 130 39.50 N 39.45 E
Keskastel 56 48.58 N 7.02 E
Keskin 130 39.41 N 33.37 E
Keski-Suomen lääni □[4] 26 62.30 N 25.30 E
Keskozero 24 61.24 N 33.12 E
Keskuvejem, gora ∧ 180 66.12 N 177.40 W
Kes'ma 76 58.27 N 37.04 E
Kesova Gora 76 57.35 N 37.17 E
Kespur 126 22.35 N 87.29 E
Kesra 36 35.49 N 9.22 E
Kessebüren 263 51.31 N 7.43 E
Kessel 56 51.08 N 4.37 E
Kesselsdorf 54 51.02 N 13.35 E
Kessingland 42 52.25 N 1.42 E
Kesswil 58 47.36 N 9.20 E
Kestel Gölü ⊜ 130 37.24 N 30.28 E
Kestell 158 28.19 S 28.38 E
Kesten'ga 24 65.55 N 31.47 E
Kestilä 26 64.21 N 26.17 E
Keston ⊕[8] 260 51.22 N 0.02 E
Keswick, On., Can. 212 44.15 N 79.28 W
Keswick, Eng., U.K. 44 54.37 N 3.08 W
Keszthely 30 46.46 N 17.15 E
Ket' ≃ 86 58.55 N 81.32 E
Keta 150 5.55 N 1.00 E
Keta ≃ 94 34.56 N 137.50 E
Keta, ozero ⊜ 74 68.44 N 90.00 E
Ketaka 96 35.30 N 134.03 E
Keta Lagoon ⊂ 150 5.54 N 0.56 E
Ketam, Pulau I 271c 1.24 N 103.57 E
Ketama 34 34.50 N 4.37 W
Ketang 100 22.58 N 115.28 E
Ketapang, Indon. 112 1.52 S 109.59 E


**Symbols** in the index entries represent the broad categories identified in the key at the right. Symbols with superior numbers (⋏[1]) identify subcategories (see complete key on page *I · 1).*

**Symbole** im Register stellen die rechts im Schlüssel erklärten Kategorien dar. Symbole mit hochgestellten Ziffern (⋏[1]) bezeichnen Unterabteilungen einer Kategorie (vgl. vollständiger Schlüssel auf Seite *I · 1).*

**Los símbolos** incluídos en el texto del índice representan las grandes categorías identificadas con la clave a la derecha. Los símbolos con numeros en su parte superior (⋏[1]) identifican las subcategorías (véase la clave completa en la página *I · 1).*

**Les symboles** de l'index représentent les catégories indiquées dans la légende à droite. Les symboles suivis d'un indice (⋏[1]) représentent des sous-catégories (voir légende complète à la page *I · 1).*

**Os símbolos** incluídos no texto do índice representam as grandes categorias identificadas com a chave à direita. Os símbolos com números em sua parte superior (⋏[1]) identificam as subcategorias (veja-se a chave completa à página *I · 1).*

| | English | Deutsch | Español | Français | Português |
|---|---|---|---|---|---|
| ∧ | Mountain | Berg | Montaña | Montagne | Montanha |
| ⋏ | Mountains | Gebirge | Montañas | Montagnes | Montanhas |
| )( | Pass | Paß | Paso | Col | Passo |
| V | Valley, Canyon | Tal, Cañon | Valle, Cañón | Vallée, Canyon | Vale, Canhão |
| ≐ | Plain | Ebene | Llano | Plaine | Planície |
| › | Cape | Kap | Cabo | Cap | Cabo |
| I | Island | Insel | Isla | Île | Ilha |
| II | Islands | Inseln | Islas | Îles | Ilhas |
| ⊥ | Other Topographic Features | Andere Topographische Objekte | Otros Elementos Topográficos | Autres données topographiques | Outros acidentes topográficos |

ESPAÑOL / FRANÇAIS / PORTUGUÊS


| Nombre / Nom / Nome | Página / Page | Lat.°′ | Long.°′ W = Oeste / Ouest |
|---|---|---|---|
| Ketapang, Indon. | 115a | 6.54 S | 113.17 E |
| Ketapang, Indon. | 115a | 5.44 S | 105.48 E |
| Ketaun | 112 | 3.23 S | 101.49 E |
| Ketčenery | 80 | 47.18 N | 44.31 E |
| Ketchikan | 182 | 55.21 N | 131.35 W |
| Ketchum | 202 | 43.40 N | 114.21 W |
| Kete Krachi | 150 | 7.46 N | 0.03 W |
| Ketelmeer ⊜ | 52 | 52.35 N | 5.45 E |
| Keti Bandar | 120 | 24.08 N | 67.27 E |
| Ketingwan ∧ | 154 | 0.40 N | 35.50 E |
| Ketoj, ostrov ▮ | 74 | 47.20 N | 152.28 E |
| Kétou | 150 | 7.22 N | 2.36 E |
| Ketovo | 86 | 55.21 N | 65.18 E |
| Kętrzyn (Rastenburg) | 30 | 54.06 N | 21.23 E |
| Ketsch | 56 | 49.22 N | 8.31 E |
| Ketta | 152 | 1.28 N | 15.56 E |
| Kettering, Eng., U.K. | 42 | 52.24 N | 0.44 W |
| Kettering, Md., U.S. | 284c | 38.53 N | 76.49 W |
| Kettering, Oh., U.S. | 218 | 39.41 N | 84.10 W |
| Kettinge | 41 | 54.42 N | 11.45 E |
| Kettle ≃, Mb., Can. | 184 | 56.23 N | 94.34 W |
| Kettle ≃, N.A. | 182 | 48.42 N | 118.07 W |
| Kettle ≃, Mn., U.S. | 190 | 45.52 N | 92.45 W |
| Kettle Creek ≃, On., Can. | 212 | 42.40 N | 81.13 W |
| Kettle Creek ≃, Pa., U.S. | 210 | 41.18 N | 77.51 W |
| Kettle Creek State Park ♦ | 214 | 41.23 N | 77.56 W |
| Kettle Falls | 202 | 48.36 N | 118.03 W |
| Kettleman City | 226 | 36.00 N | 119.57 W |
| Kettleman Hills ⋌[2] | 226 | 36.00 N | 120.00 W |
| Kettle Rapids Dam ◆[6] | 184 | 56.23 N | 94.38 W |
| Kettlersville | 216 | 40.22 N | 84.16 W |
| Kettleshulme | 262 | 53.19 N | 2.01 W |
| Kettlewell | 44 | 54.09 N | 2.02 W |
| Kettwig | 56 | 51.22 N | 6.56 E |
| Kęty | 30 | 49.53 N | 19.13 E |
| Ketzin | 54 | 52.28 N | 12.50 E |
| Keudemane | 114 | 5.15 N | 96.55 E |
| Keudepasi | 114 | 4.18 N | 95.56 E |
| Keudeteunom | 114 | 4.27 N | 95.48 E |
| Keudeunga | 114 | 5.01 N | 95.22 E |
| Keuka Lake ⊜ | 210 | 42.27 N | 77.10 W |
| Keuka Lake, West Branch ⊂ | 210 | 42.33 N | 77.09 W |
| Keuka Park | 210 | 42.37 N | 77.06 W |
| Keukenhof ♦ | 52 | 52.16 N | 4.33 E |
| Keul' | 88 | 58.25 N | 102.49 E |
| Keula | 54 | 51.20 N | 10.31 E |
| Keum ≃ | 86 | 59.32 N | 70.35 E |
| Keurboomsrivier | 158 | 34.00 S | 23.24 E |
| Keurusselkä ⊜ | 26 | 62.10 N | 24.40 E |
| Keuruu | 26 | 62.16 N | 24.42 E |
| Kevdo-Mel'sitovo | 80 | 53.09 N | 43.54 E |
| Kevelaer | 52 | 51.35 N | 6.15 E |
| Kevin | 202 | 48.44 N | 111.57 W |
| Kevsala | 80 | 45.48 N | 42.41 E |
| Kew, Austl. | 169 | 37.49 S | 145.02 E |
| Kew, T./C. Is. | 238 | 21.54 N | 72.02 W |
| Kewanee | 190 | 41.14 N | 89.55 W |
| Kewanna | 216 | 41.01 N | 86.25 W |
| Kewaunee | 190 | 44.27 N | 87.30 W |
| Keweenaw Bay ⊂ | 190 | 46.56 N | 88.23 W |
| Keweenaw Peninsula ›[1] | 190 | 47.12 N | 88.25 W |
| Keweenaw Point › | 190 | 47.30 N | 87.50 W |
| Kew Gardens ♦, On., Can. | 275b | 43.40 N | 79.18 W |
| Kew Gardens ♦, Eng., U.K. | 260 | 51.28 N | 0.18 W |
| Key, Lough ⊜ | 48 | 54.00 N | 8.15 W |
| Keyala | 154 | 4.27 N | 32.52 E |
| Keyangkeer Shan ∧ | 120 | 31.20 N | 87.13 E |
| Keya Paha ≃ | 198 | 42.54 N | 99.00 W |
| Key Biscayne | 220 | 25.42 N | 80.10 W |
| Keyes, Ca., U.S. | 226 | 37.33 N | 120.54 W |
| Keyes, Ok., U.S. | 196 | 36.48 N | 102.15 W |
| Keyesport | 219 | 38.44 N | 89.17 W |
| Keyhole Reservoir ⊜[1] | 198 | 44.21 N | 104.51 W |
| Keyhole State Park ♦ | 198 | 44.19 N | 104.48 W |
| Keyihe | 89 | 50.40 N | 122.27 E |
| Keyingham | 44 | 53.42 N | 0.07 W |
| Key Largo | 220 | 25.04 N | 80.28 W |
| Key Largo ▮ | 220 | 25.16 N | 80.19 W |
| Keymer | 42 | 50.55 N | 0.08 W |
| Keynes Hill ∧[2] | 168b | 34.37 S | 139.06 E |
| Keyneton | 168b | 34.34 S | 139.08 E |
| Keynsham | 42 | 51.26 N | 2.30 W |
| Keynshamburg | 154 | 19.15 S | 29.39 E |
| Keyport, N.J., U.S. | 276 | 40.25 N | 74.12 W |
| Keyport, Wa., U.S. | 224 | 47.42 N | 122.38 W |
| Keyport Harbor ⊂ | 276 | 40.26 N | 74.12 W |
| Keysborough | 274b | 38.00 S | 145.10 E |
| Keysbrook | 168a | 32.26 S | 115.59 E |
| Keyser | 188 | 39.26 N | 78.58 W |
| Keystone, In., U.S. | 216 | 40.36 N | 85.16 W |
| Keystone, Ia., U.S. | 190 | 41.59 N | 92.11 W |
| Keystone, S.D., U.S. | 198 | 43.53 N | 103.25 W |
| Keystone, W.V., U.S. | 192 | 37.24 N | 81.27 W |
| Keystone Lake ⊜[1], Ok., U.S. | 196 | 36.15 N | 96.25 W |
| Keystone Lake ⊜[1], Pa., U.S. | 214 | 40.45 N | 79.15 W |
| Keystone Peak ∧ | 200 | 31.53 N | 111.13 W |
| Keystone State Park ♦ | 214 | 40.23 N | 79.24 W |
| Keysville, Fl., U.S. | 220 | 27.52 N | 82.06 W |
| Keysville, Va., U.S. | 192 | 37.02 N | 78.29 W |
| Keytesville | 194 | 39.26 N | 92.56 W |
| Key West | 220 | 24.33 N | 81.46 W |
| Key West Island ▮ | 220 | 24.33 N | 81.47 W |
| Key West Naval Air Station ■ | 220 | 24.34 N | 81.41 W |
| Keyworth | 42 | 52.52 N | 1.05 W |
| Kez | 80 | 57.53 N | 53.43 E |
| Kezi | 154 | 20.58 S | 28.32 E |
| Kezilesu Zizhizhou □[8] | 85 | 40.00 N | 75.30 E |
| Kežma | 88 | 58.59 N | 101.09 E |
| Kežmarok | 30 | 49.08 N | 20.25 E |
| Kgalagadi □[5] | 156 | 25.00 S | 22.00 E |
| Kgatleng □[5] | 156 | 24.28 S | 26.05 E |
| Kgokgole ≃ | 158 | 26.44 S | 22.28 E |
| Kgun Lake ⊜ | 180 | 61.32 N | 163.45 W |
| Khaanziir, Ras › | 144 | 10.55 N | 45.47 E |
| Khabab | 132 | 33.00 N | 36.16 E |
| Khabīr, Kūh-e ∧ | 128 | 28.48 N | 56.26 E |
| Khābūr, Nahr al- (Habur) ≃ | 130 | 35.08 N | 40.26 E |
| Khādar | 272a | 28.33 N | 77.22 E |
| Khadari, Wādī al- ∨ | 140 | 10.29 N | 26.15 E |
| Khadaungnge Taung ∧ | 110 | 18.57 N | 94.37 E |
| Khadki (Kirkee) | 122 | 18.34 N | 73.52 E |
| Khadra | 34 | 36.15 N | 0.35 E |
| Khadzhybeys'kyy lyman ⊜ | 78 | 46.39 N | 30.33 E |
| Khafūrī, Wādī ∨ | 142 | 29.37 N | 32.04 E |
| Khagaria | 124 | 25.30 N | 86.29 E |
| Khagdon ≃[1] | 126 | 22.09 N | 90.05 E |
| Khāgrāmuri | 272b | 22.26 N | 88.14 E |
| Khaïdhárion | 267c | 38.01 N | 23.38 E |
| Khair | 124 | 27.57 N | 77.50 E |
| Khairābād | 124 | 27.32 N | 80.45 E |
| Khairāgarh | 120 | 21.25 N | 80.58 E |
| Khairbani | 126 | 24.14 N | 87.05 E |
| Khairna | 272c | 19.06 N | 73.01 E |
| Khairpur, Pāk. | 120 | 27.32 N | 68.46 E |
| Khairpur, Pāk. | 123 | 29.35 N | 72.14 E |
| Khairwāra | 120 | 23.59 N | 73.35 E |
| Khajrāho | 120 | 24.50 N | 79.58 E |
| Khajuri | 126 | 21.52 N | 87.58 E |
| Khajuri ◆[8] | 272a | 28.43 N | 77.16 E |
| Khakassia → Chakasija □[3] | 86 | 53.00 N | 90.00 E |
| Kha Khaeng ≃ | 110 | 14.55 N | 99.07 E |
| Khakhea | 156 | 24.51 S | 23.20 E |
| Khalándrion | 267c | 38.01 N | 23.48 E |
| Khalatse | 123 | 34.20 N | 76.49 E |
| Khālidī, Khirbat al- ⊥ | 132 | 29.39 N | 35.14 E |
| Khalkhāl | 128 | 37.37 N | 48.32 E |
| Khalkhalah | 132 | 33.04 N | 36.32 E |
| Khálki ▮ | 38 | 36.17 N | 27.35 E |
| Khalkidhikí □[9] | 38 | 40.25 N | 23.27 E |
| Khalkís | 38 | 38.28 N | 23.36 E |
| Khālsar | 120 | 34.31 N | 77.41 E |
| Khalturyne | 78 | 49.31 N | 35.17 E |
| Khambhāliya | 120 | 22.12 N | 69.39 E |
| Khambhāt | 120 | 22.18 N | 72.37 E |
| Khambhāt, Gulf of ⊂ | 122 | 21.00 N | 72.30 E |
| Khāmgaon | 122 | 20.41 N | 76.34 E |
| Khamir | 144 | 16.05 N | 43.55 E |
| Khāmis, Ash-Shallāl al- (Fifth Cataract) ⌊ | 140 | 18.23 N | 33.47 E |
| Khamīs Mushayṭ | 144 | 18.18 N | 42.44 E |
| Khamkeut | 110 | 18.15 N | 104.43 E |
| Khamma | 70 | 36.47 N | 12.02 E |
| Khammam | 122 | 17.15 N | 80.09 E |
| Khamsah | 142 | 30.25 N | 32.23 E |
| Khan ≃, Lao | 110 | 19.54 N | 102.09 E |
| Khan ≃, Namibia | 156 | 22.37 S | 14.56 E |
| Khāna | 126 | 23.20 N | 87.44 E |
| Khānābād | 120 | 36.41 N | 69.07 E |
| Khān Abū Shāmāt | 132 | 33.40 N | 36.54 E |
| Khānākul | 126 | 22.43 N | 87.51 E |
| Khān al-Baghdādī | 128 | 33.51 N | 42.33 E |
| Khānaqīn | 128 | 34.21 N | 45.22 E |
| Khān Arnabah | 132 | 33.11 N | 35.53 E |
| Khancoban | 171b | 36.12 S | 148.05 E |
| Khandaghosh | 126 | 23.13 N | 87.41 E |
| Khandela | 120 | 27.36 N | 75.30 E |
| Khandwa | 124 | 21.50 N | 76.20 E |
| Khān-e Chahār Bāgh, Afg. | 120 | 35.58 N | 69.38 E |
| Khān-e Chahār Bāgh, Afg. | 128 | 37.00 N | 65.14 E |
| Khāneh Khvodī | 128 | 36.02 N | 55.59 E |
| Khānewāl | 123 | 30.18 N | 71.56 E |
| Khāngāh Dogrān | 123 | 31.50 N | 73.37 E |
| Khāngarh, Pāk. | 120 | 28.22 N | 71.43 E |
| Khāngarh, Pāk. | 123 | 29.55 N | 71.10 E |
| Khangkhai | 110 | 19.28 N | 103.15 E |
| Khaniá | 38 | 35.31 N | 24.02 E |
| Khaníon, Kólpos ⊂ | 38 | 35.34 N | 23.48 E |
| Khānkurda | 126 | 22.00 N | 87.25 E |
| Khanna | 123 | 30.42 N | 76.13 E |
| Khannā, Qā' ≃ | 132 | 32.04 N | 36.26 E |
| Khānozai | 120 | 30.37 N | 67.19 E |
| Khānpur, India | 272b | 22.40 N | 88.16 E |
| Khānpur, Pāk. | 123 | 28.39 N | 70.39 E |
| Khānpur ◆[8], India | 272a | 28.34 N | 77.01 E |
| Khānpur ◆[8], India | 272a | 28.31 N | 77.14 E |
| Khān Shaykhūn | 130 | 35.26 N | 36.38 E |
| Khanty-Mansiysk → Chanty-Mansijsk | 74 | 61.00 N | 69.06 E |
| Khān Yūnus | 132 | 31.21 N | 34.19 E |
| Khao Laem Reservoir ⊜[1] | 110 | 14.50 N | 98.30 E |
| Khao Saming | 110 | 12.21 N | 102.27 E |
| Khao Sok National Park ♦ | 110 | 8.55 N | 98.35 E |
| Khao Yoi | 110 | 13.14 N | 99.50 E |
| Khapalu | 123 | 35.10 N | 76.20 E |
| Khaptad National Park ♦ | 124 | 29.28 N | 81.10 E |
| Kharab, Ghoubet al ⊂ | 144 | 11.30 N | 42.35 E |
| Kharabā | 132 | 32.34 N | 36.27 E |
| Kharagdiha | 124 | 24.25 N | 86.10 E |
| Kharagpur, India | 124 | 25.07 N | 86.33 E |
| Kharagpur, India | 126 | 22.20 N | 87.20 E |
| Kharak | 123 | 33.07 N | 71.06 E |
| Khārān | 120 | 28.35 N | 65.25 E |
| Kharānoq | 128 | 32.20 N | 54.39 E |
| Kharar, India | 123 | 30.45 N | 76.39 E |
| Kharar, India | 126 | 22.42 N | 87.41 E |
| Khāravli ∧[2] | 272c | 18.54 N | 72.55 E |
| Kharāyij, Sabkhat al- ⊜ | 130 | 35.40 N | 37.20 E |
| Kharaz, Jabal ∧ | 144 | 12.44 N | 44.09 E |
| Kharbatā | 132 | 31.57 N | 35.04 E |
| Kharbine → Harbin | 89 | 45.45 N | 126.41 E |
| Khardaha | 126 | 22.44 N | 88.22 E |
| Khārghar | 272c | 19.03 N | 73.04 E |
| Kharg Island → Khārk, Jazīreh-ye ▮ | 128 | 29.15 N | 50.20 E |
| Khargon | 120 | 21.49 N | 75.36 E |
| Khāriān Cantonment | 123 | 32.49 N | 73.52 E |
| Khariār Road | 122 | 20.54 N | 82.31 E |
| Khārijah, Al-Wāḥāt al- ⍑[4] | 140 | 25.20 N | 30.35 E |
| Kharīm, Jabal ∧ | 132 | 30.17 N | 33.58 E |
| Kharīṭ, Wādī al- ∨ | 140 | 24.26 N | 33.03 E |
| Khārk, Jazīreh-ye (Kharg Island) ▮ | 128 | 29.15 N | 50.20 E |
| Kharkiv (Kharkov) | 78 | 50.00 N | 36.15 E |
| Kharkiv □[4] | 78 | 49.30 N | 36.30 E |
| Kharkov → Kharkiv | 78 | 50.00 N | 36.15 E |
| Kharmān, Kūh-e ∧ | 128 | 29.13 N | 53.35 E |
| Kharri | 272b | 22.55 N | 88.14 E |
| Kharsāwān | 124 | 22.48 N | 85.50 E |
| Kharsia | 124 | 21.58 N | 83.07 E |
| Khartoum → Al-Kharṭūm | 140 | 15.36 N | 32.32 E |
| Khartoum North → Al-Kharṭūm Baḥrī | 140 | 15.38 N | 32.33 E |
| Khartsyz'k | 83 | 48.02 N | 38.09 E |
| Khartum → Al-Kharṭūm | 140 | 15.36 N | 32.32 E |
| Kharumwa | 154 | 3.12 S | 32.39 E |
| Khāsbāti | 272b | 22.55 N | 88.25 E |
| Khasebake | 156 | 20.41 S | 24.29 E |
| Khāsh, Afg. | 128 | 31.31 N | 62.52 E |
| Khāsh, Īrān | 128 | 28.14 N | 61.14 E |
| Khāsh ≃ | 128 | 31.11 N | 62.05 E |
| Khāsh, Dasht-e ◆[2] | 128 | 31.50 N | 62.30 E |
| Khashab, Jabal al- ∧[2] | 142 | 29.56 N | 31.01 E |
| Khashm al-Qirbah | 140 | 14.58 N | 35.55 E |
| Khashm al-Qirbah, Khazzān ⊜[1] | 140 | 14.40 N | 35.55 E |
| Khashshab, Tur'at al- ≍ | 273c | 29.53 N | 31.17 E |
| Khashum | 140 | 12.27 N | 28.02 E |
| Khāş Konar | 120 | 34.39 N | 70.54 E |
| Khaskovo → Haskovo | 38 | 41.56 N | 25.33 E |
| Khatauli | 124 | 29.17 N | 77.43 E |
| Khātegaon | 124 | 22.36 N | 76.55 E |
| Khātra | 126 | 22.59 N | 86.51 E |
| Khatt, Oued al ∨ | 148 | 26.45 N | 13.03 W |
| Khaur | 123 | 33.16 N | 72.28 E |
| Khāvda | 120 | 23.51 N | 69.43 E |
| Khawrah | 144 | 14.26 N | 46.09 E |
| Khawsa | 110 | 15.03 N | 97.50 E |
| Khayāla ◆[8] | 272a | 28.40 N | 77.06 E |
| Khaybar, Ḥarrat ⩡[9] | 128 | 25.30 N | 39.45 E |
| Khayerpur | 272b | 22.35 N | 88.33 E |
| Khayl, Kathīb al- ⩡[8] | 142 | 30.33 N | 32.28 E |
| Khayra Bil ⊜ | 272b | 22.52 N | 88.29 E |
| Khayrasole | 126 | 23.48 N | 87.16 E |
| Khayung ≃ | 110 | 15.07 N | 104.42 E |
| Kheardaha | 272b | 22.29 N | 88.28 E |
| Khe Bo | 110 | 19.08 N | 104.41 E |
| Khed | 122 | 17.43 N | 73.23 E |
| Khefapur | 272a | 28.30 N | 77.05 E |
| Khejurdaha | 272b | 22.59 N | 88.10 E |
| Khemis | 148 | 36.16 N | 2.13 E |
| Khemis el Khechna | 34 | 36.39 N | 3.20 E |
| Khemisset | 148 | 33.50 N | 6.03 W |
| Khemisset □[4] | 148 | 33.50 N | 6.05 W |
| Khem Karan | 123 | 31.09 N | 74.34 E |
| Khemmarat | 110 | 16.03 N | 105.13 E |
| Khenchla | 148 | 35.28 N | 7.11 E |
| Khenifra | 148 | 33.00 N | 5.40 W |
| Khenifra □[4] | 148 | 32.35 N | 5.10 W |
| Khenjān | 120 | 35.36 N | 70.59 E |
| Khenyen | 272b | 22.59 N | 88.19 E |
| Khera ◆[8] | 272a | 28.46 N | 77.08 E |
| Kheri | 124 | 27.54 N | 80.48 E |
| Kheri Branch ≍ | 124 | 28.11 N | 80.25 E |
| Kherli | 124 | 27.12 N | 77.02 E |
| Kherrata | 148 | 36.31 N | 5.26 E |
| Khersān ≃ | 128 | 31.33 N | 50.22 E |
| Kherson | 78 | 46.38 N | 32.35 E |
| Kherson □[4] | 78 | 46.45 N | 33.30 E |
| Khersones, mys › | 78 | 44.35 N | 33.23 E |
| Khetia | 120 | 21.40 N | 74.35 E |
| Khevāj | 120 | 38.13 N | 71.02 E |
| Khewāri | 120 | 26.36 N | 68.52 E |
| Khewra | 123 | 32.39 N | 73.01 E |
| Kheyr Khāneh | 128 | 34.57 N | 63.37 E |
| Khichīwāra Plateau ⋌[1] | 124 | 24.25 N | 77.30 E |
| Khichripur ◆[8] | 272a | 28.37 N | 77.19 E |
| Khilchipur | 124 | 24.02 N | 76.34 E |
| Khilkāpur | 272b | 22.46 N | 88.29 E |
| Khimki → Chimki | 82 | 55.54 N | 37.26 E |
| Khíos | 38 | 38.22 N | 26.08 E |
| Khíos (Chios) ▮ | 38 | 38.22 N | 26.00 E |
| Khipro | 120 | 25.50 N | 69.22 E |
| Khirbat al-Ghazālah | 132 | 32.44 N | 36.12 E |
| Khirbat 'Awwād | 132 | 32.19 N | 36.43 E |
| Khirbat Qanāfār | 132 | 33.38 N | 35.43 E |
| Khirbat Umm as-Surab | 132 | 32.26 N | 36.19 E |
| Khirbitā | 142 | 30.45 N | 30.40 E |
| Khiri Mat | 110 | 16.50 N | 99.48 E |
| Khirpai | 126 | 22.42 N | 87.37 E |
| Khirr, Wādī al- ∨ | 128 | 31.51 N | 44.29 E |
| Khisfīn | 132 | 32.51 N | 35.49 E |
| Khiuri Khala ∧ | 124 | 29.58 N | 81.18 E |
| Khiva → Chiva | 72 | 41.24 N | 60.22 E |
| Khlibodarivka | 83 | 47.29 N | 37.23 E |
| Khlong Khlung | 110 | 16.12 N | 99.43 E |
| Khlong Thom | 110 | 7.56 N | 99.09 E |
| Khlong Yai | 110 | 11.46 N | 102.54 E |
| Khlung | 110 | 12.27 N | 102.14 E |
| Khmel'nyts'kyy | 78 | 49.25 N | 27.00 E |
| Khmel'nyts'kyy □[4] | 78 | 49.30 N | 27.00 E |
| Khmel'ove | 78 | 48.34 N | 31.24 E |
| Khmil'nyk | 78 | 49.33 N | 27.57 E |
| Khoai, Hon ▮ | 110 | 8.26 N | 104.50 E |
| Khodoriv | 78 | 49.24 N | 24.17 E |
| Khogali | 140 | 6.08 N | 27.47 E |
| Khojāng ∧ | 124 | 28.41 N | 85.09 E |
| Khok Kloi | 110 | 8.17 N | 98.19 E |
| Khok Pho | 110 | 6.43 N | 101.06 E |
| Khoksa | 126 | 23.48 N | 89.17 E |
| Khok Samrong | 110 | 15.04 N | 100.44 E |
| Kholargós | 267c | 38.00 N | 23.48 E |
| Kholm | 120 | 36.42 N | 67.41 E |
| Kholmy | 78 | 51.52 N | 32.36 E |
| Kholombidzo Falls ⌊ | 154 | 15.54 S | 34.44 E |
| Khomām | 128 | 37.22 N | 49.40 E |
| Khomas □[4] | 156 | 23.00 S | 17.00 E |
| Khomas Hochland ⋌[1] | 156 | 22.30 S | 16.30 E |
| Khomeyn | 128 | 33.38 N | 50.04 E |
| Khomeynīshahr | 128 | 32.41 N | 51.31 E |
| Khomodimo | 156 | 22.46 S | 23.52 E |
| Khomutets' | 78 | 50.06 N | 33.44 E |
| Khondmāl Hills ⋌[2] | 122 | 20.20 N | 84.00 E |
| Khong → Mekong ≃ | 12 | 10.33 N | 105.24 E |
| Khoni | 272c | 19.10 N | 73.07 E |
| Khon Kaen | 110 | 16.26 N | 102.50 E |
| Khóra | 38 | 37.04 N | 21.43 E |
| Khorāsān □[4] | 128 | 35.00 N | 58.00 E |
| Khóra Sfakíon | 38 | 35.12 N | 24.09 E |
| Khordha | 120 | 20.11 N | 85.37 E |
| Khorel | 272b | 22.42 N | 88.19 E |
| Khorol | 78 | 49.47 N | 33.17 E |
| Khorol ≃ | 78 | 49.28 N | 33.47 E |
| Khorostkiv | 78 | 49.13 N | 25.55 E |
| Khorramābād | 128 | 33.30 N | 48.20 E |
| Khorram Daraq | 128 | 36.26 N | 48.36 E |
| Khorramshahr | 128 | 30.25 N | 48.11 E |
| Khoru | 272b | 22.51 N | 88.31 E |
| Khoryna ≃ | 83 | 49.23 N | 38.13 E |
| Khossanto | 150 | 13.08 N | 11.58 W |
| Khoteshiv | 78 | 51.43 N | 24.47 E |
| Khotin' | 78 | 51.07 N | 34.46 E |
| Khotyn | 78 | 48.29 N | 26.30 E |
| Khouribga | 148 | 32.54 N | 6.57 W |
| Khouribga □[4] | 148 | 32.50 N | 6.30 W |
| Khowai | 120 | 24.06 N | 91.38 E |
| Khowāng | 120 | 27.16 N | 94.53 E |
| Khowst | 120 | 33.22 N | 69.57 E |
| Khrestyshche | 83 | 48.55 N | 37.30 E |
| Khrisokhoús, Kólpos ⊂ | 130 | 35.06 N | 32.25 E |
| Khrisoúpolis | 38 | 40.58 N | 24.42 E |
| Khrystoforivka | 78 | 47.59 N | 33.05 E |
| Khrystynivka | 78 | 48.49 N | 29.58 E |
| Khudiān | 123 | 30.59 N | 74.17 E |
| Khuff | 128 | 24.57 N | 44.42 E |
| Khugaung | 110 | 26.07 N | 98.18 E |
| Khūgīānī Sānī | 120 | 31.31 N | 66.12 E |
| Khuis | 156 | 26.37 S | 21.45 E |
| Khuīyāla | 120 | 27.14 N | 70.30 E |
| Khu Khan | 110 | 14.42 N | 104.12 E |
| Khukhra | 78 | 50.13 N | 34.49 E |
| Khulna | 124 | 22.48 N | 89.33 E |
| Khulna □[5] | 126 | 22.45 N | 89.30 E |
| Khŭm Bathéay | 110 | 11.59 N | 104.57 E |
| Khumbur Khūlē Ghar ∧ | 120 | 32.49 N | 68.47 E |
| Khungdugang ∧ | 124 | 27.31 N | 89.02 E |
| Khūnjerāb Pass )( | 123 | 36.52 N | 75.27 E |
| Khun Tan, Doi ∧ | 110 | 18.30 N | 99.20 E |
| Khunti | 124 | 23.05 N | 85.17 E |
| Khūr | 128 | 32.57 N | 58.26 E |
| Khurai | 124 | 24.03 N | 78.19 E |
| Khuralji Khās ◆[8] | 272a | 28.39 N | 77.17 E |
| Khuria Tank ⊜[1] | 124 | 22.25 N | 81.36 E |
| Khurigāchi | 272b | 22.49 N | 88.20 E |
| Khurīyā Murīyā, Jazā'ir ▮▮ | 118 | 17.30 N | 56.00 E |
| Khurja | 124 | 28.15 N | 77.51 E |
| Khurli | 120 | 28.59 N | 65.52 E |
| Khurramshahr → Khorramshahr | 128 | 30.25 N | 48.11 E |
| Khūsf | 128 | 32.46 N | 58.53 E |
| Khushāb | 123 | 32.18 N | 72.21 E |
| Khushālgarh | 123 | 33.30 N | 71.54 E |
| Khushk Khurd ◆[8] | 272a | 28.46 N | 77.10 E |
| Khust | 78 | 48.10 N | 23.18 E |
| Khutubi ≃ | 86 | 44.45 N | 86.25 E |
| Khuwayy | 140 | 13.05 N | 29.14 E |
| Khuzdār | 120 | 27.48 N | 66.37 E |
| Khūzestān □[4] | 128 | 31.00 N | 49.00 E |
| Khvāf | 128 | 34.33 N | 60.08 E |
| Khvājeh Moḥammad, Kūh-e ⋌ | 120 | 36.22 N | 70.17 E |
| Khvājeh Ra'ūf | 120 | 33.19 N | 64.43 E |
| Khvor | 128 | 33.47 N | 55.03 E |
| Khvormūj | 128 | 28.39 N | 51.23 E |
| Khvoy | 128 | 38.33 N | 44.58 E |
| Khwae Noi ≃ | 110 | 14.01 N | 99.32 E |
| Khyber Pass )( | 123 | 34.05 N | 71.10 E |
| Khyriv | 78 | 49.33 N | 22.49 E |
| Kia | 175e | 7.33 S | 158.26 E |
| Kialwe | 154 | 9.22 S | 27.08 E |
| Kiama, Austl. | 170 | 34.41 S | 150.51 E |
| Kiama, Zaïre | 152 | 7.15 S | 17.44 E |
| Kiamba | 116 | 5.59 N | 124.37 E |
| Kiambi | 154 | 7.20 S | 28.01 E |
| Kiamboni, Kap → Jumbo, Raas › | 144 | 1.39 S | 41.36 E |
| Kiambu | 154 | 1.10 S | 36.50 E |
| Kiamesha Lake | 210 | 41.41 N | 74.40 W |
| Kiamichi ≃ | 194 | 33.57 N | 95.14 W |
| Kiamika ≃ | 206 | 46.38 N | 75.15 W |
| Kiamika, Barrage ◆[6] | 206 | 46.37 N | 75.08 W |
| Kiamika, Réservoir ⊜[1] | 206 | 46.40 N | 75.05 W |
| Kiamusze → Jiamusi | 89 | 46.50 N | 130.21 E |
| Kian → Ji'an | 100 | 27.07 N | 114.58 E |
| Kiana | 180 | 66.59 N | 160.25 W |
| Kiandra | 171b | 35.53 S | 148.30 E |
| Kiangara | 157b | 17.58 S | 47.02 E |
| Kiangarow, Mount ∧ | 166 | 26.49 S | 151.33 E |
| Kiangsi → Jiangxi □[4] | 100 | 28.00 N | 116.00 E |
| Kiangsu → Jiangsu □[4] | 90 | 33.00 N | 120.00 E |
| Kiantajärvi ⊜ | 26 | 65.03 N | 29.07 E |
| Kiaohsien → Jiaoxian | 98 | 36.18 N | 119.58 E |
| Kibæk | 41 | 56.02 N | 8.51 E |
| Kibaha | 154 | 6.46 S | 38.55 E |
| Kibali ≃ | 154 | 3.37 N | 28.34 E |
| Kibali-Sturi Game Reserve ◆[4] | 154 | 2.45 N | 29.33 E |
| Kibamba | 154 | 4.53 S | 26.33 E |
| Kibanga Port | 154 | 0.11 N | 32.52 E |
| Kibangou | 152 | 3.27 S | 12.21 E |
| Kibanseke | 273b | 4.26 S | 15.23 E |
| Kibar | 120 | 32.20 N | 78.01 E |
| Kibara | 154 | 2.09 S | 33.27 E |
| Kibāsī | 128 | 30.34 N | 47.50 E |
| Kibau Iyayi | 154 | 8.52 S | 34.32 E |
| Kibawe | 116 | 7.34 N | 125.00 E |
| Kibaya | 154 | 5.18 S | 36.34 E |
| Kibenga | 152 | 7.55 S | 17.35 E |
| Kibeni | 164 | 7.25 S | 143.48 E |
| Kiberashi | 154 | 5.23 S | 37.26 E |
| Kiberege | 154 | 7.57 S | 36.52 E |
| Kibi | 150 | 6.10 N | 0.33 W |
| Kibi-kōgen ⋌[1] | 96 | 34.45 N | 133.15 E |
| Kibila | 154 | 8.14 S | 26.23 E |
| Kibiti | 154 | 7.44 S | 38.57 E |
| Kibler Park | 273d | 26.18 S | 28.00 E |
| Kiboga | 154 | 1.02 N | 30.58 E |
| Kiboko | 154 | 2.15 S | 37.42 E |
| Kibombo | 154 | 3.54 S | 25.55 E |
| Kibondo | 154 | 3.35 S | 30.42 E |
| Kibouendé, Congo | 273b | 4.19 S | 15.11 E |
| Kibouendé, Congo | 273b | 4.17 S | 15.09 E |
| Kibouendé I | 273b | 4.11 S | 15.09 E |
| Kibouendé II | 273b | 4.12 S | 15.09 E |
| Kibre Mengist | 144 | 5.52 N | 39.00 E |
| Kıbrıs → Cyprus □[1] | 130 | 35.00 N | 33.00 E |
| Kıbrısçık | 130 | 40.25 N | 31.51 E |
| Kibumbu | 154 | 3.32 S | 29.45 E |
| Kibungo | 154 | 2.10 S | 30.32 E |
| Kibuye, Bdi. | 154 | 3.40 S | 29.59 E |
| Kibuye, Rw. | 154 | 2.03 S | 29.21 E |
| Kibwesa | 154 | 6.28 S | 29.57 E |
| Kibwezi | 154 | 2.25 S | 37.58 E |
| Kibworth Harcourt | 42 | 52.32 N | 0.59 W |
| Kičevo | 38 | 41.31 N | 20.57 E |
| Kichčik | 74 | 53.24 N | 156.03 E |
| Kichijōji | 268 | 35.42 N | 139.35 E |
| Kickapoo ≃ | 190 | 43.05 N | 90.53 W |
| Kickapoo Creek ≃, Il., U.S. | 194 | 40.08 N | 89.27 W |
| Kickapoo Creek ≃, Il., U.S. | 219 | 40.08 N | 89.27 W |
| Kickapoo Creek ≃, Tx., U.S. | 196 | 31.31 N | 99.58 W |
| Kickapoo Creek ≃, Tx., U.S. | 222 | 30.47 N | 95.08 W |
| Kickapoo Creek ≃, Tx., U.S. | 222 | 32.16 N | 95.28 W |
| Kicking Horse Pass )( | 182 | 51.27 N | 116.18 W |
| Kičkino | 80 | 47.05 N | 44.02 E |
| Kičma | 80 | 57.12 N | 48.55 E |
| Kičmengskij Gorodok | 24 | 59.59 N | 45.48 E |
| Kičuj ≃ | 80 | 55.13 N | 51.16 E |
| Kidal | 150 | 18.26 N | 1.24 E |
| Kidapawan | 116 | 7.01 N | 125.03 E |
| Kidatu | 154 | 7.42 S | 36.57 E |
| Kidbrooke ◆[8] | 260 | 51.28 N | 0.02 E |
| Kidderminster | 42 | 52.23 N | 2.14 W |
| Kidderpore ◆[8] | 272b | 22.31 N | 88.19 E |
| Kidderpore Docks ◆[5] | 272b | 22.33 N | 88.19 E |
| Kidd's Beach | 158 | 33.09 S | 27.42 E |
| Kidepo National Park ♦ | 154 | 3.50 N | 33.40 E |
| Kidete, Tan. | 154 | 6.25 S | 37.16 E |
| Kidete, Tan. | 154 | 6.39 S | 36.42 E |
| Kidira | 150 | 14.28 N | 12.13 W |
| Kidlington | 42 | 51.50 N | 1.17 W |
| Kidnappers, Cape › | 172 | 39.39 S | 177.07 E |
| Kido | 164 | 9.15 S | 146.55 E |
| Kidričevo | 61 | 46.24 N | 15.47 E |
| Kidron | 214 | 40.44 N | 81.45 W |
| Kidsgrove | 44 | 53.06 N | 2.15 W |
| Kidston | 166 | 18.53 S | 144.10 E |
| Kidugallo | 154 | 6.47 S | 38.12 E |
| Kidul, Pegunungan ⋌ | 115a | 8.13 S | 111.30 E |
| Kidwelly | 42 | 51.45 N | 4.18 W |
| Kiefersfelden | 64 | 47.37 N | 12.11 E |
| Kiekebusch | 264a | 52.21 N | 13.33 E |
| Kiel, Dtsch. | 41 | 54.20 N | 10.08 E |
| Kiel, Wi., U.S. | 190 | 43.54 N | 88.02 W |
| Kiel Canal → Nord-Ostsee-Kanal ≍ | 30 | 53.53 N | 9.08 E |
| Kielce | 30 | 50.52 N | 20.37 E |
| Kielce □[4] | 30 | 50.30 N | 20.30 E |
| Kielder | 44 | 55.14 N | 2.35 W |
| Kielder Reservoir ⊜[1] | 44 | 55.11 N | 2.30 W |
| Kieler Bucht (Kiel Bay) ⊂ | 41 | 54.35 N | 10.35 E |
| Kieler Förde ⊂ | 41 | 54.24 N | 10.12 E |
| Kiembara | 150 | 13.15 N | 2.44 W |
| Kienberg | 264a | 52.40 N | 12.54 E |
| Kienge | 154 | 10.34 S | 27.33 E |
| Kienitz | 54 | 52.40 N | 14.26 E |
| Kiens → Chienes | 64 | 46.48 N | 11.50 E |
| Kiental | 58 | 46.35 N | 7.43 E |
| Kierling | 264b | 48.19 N | 16.17 E |
| Kierspe | 56 | 51.08 N | 7.35 E |
| Kierspe-Bahnhof | 263 | 51.08 N | 7.37 E |
| Kiester | 190 | 43.32 N | 93.42 W |
| Kieta | 175e | 6.13 S | 155.38 E |
| Kietrz | 30 | 50.05 N | 18.01 E |
| Kietz | 54 | 52.34 N | 14.36 E |
| Kiev → Kyyiv | 78 | 50.26 N | 30.31 E |
| Kiev Station ◆[5] | 265b | 55.45 N | 37.34 E |
| Kiew → Kyyiv | 78 | 50.26 N | 30.31 E |
| Kifaya | 150 | 12.10 N | 13.04 W |
| Kiffa | 150 | 16.37 N | 11.24 W |
| Kifisiá | 38 | 38.04 N | 23.48 E |
| Kifisós ≃, Ellás | 38 | 38.26 N | 23.15 E |
| Kifisós ≃, Ellás | 267c | 37.57 N | 23.40 E |
| Kifrī | 128 | 34.42 N | 44.58 E |
| Kifrī, Jabal ∧ | 142 | 27.48 N | 32.50 E |
| Kigač ≃ | 80 | 46.28 N | 49.12 E |
| Kigali | 154 | 1.57 S | 30.04 E |
| Kiği | 130 | 39.19 N | 40.21 E |
| Kigille | 140 | 8.40 N | 34.02 E |
| Kigoma | 154 | 4.52 S | 29.38 E |
| Kigoma □[4] | 154 | 4.30 S | 30.30 E |
| Kigun, Cape › | 180 | 52.00 N | 175.21 W |
| Kigwa | 154 | 5.10 S | 33.08 E |
| Kihei | 229a | 20.47 N | 156.27 W |
| Kihikihi | 172 | 38.02 S | 175.21 E |
| Kihniö | 26 | 62.12 N | 23.11 E |
| Kihnu ▮ | 76 | 58.08 N | 24.00 E |
| Kiholo Bay ⊂ | 229d | 19.52 N | 155.56 W |
| Kihundo | 154 | 9.25 S | 38.59 E |
| Kihurio | 154 | 4.28 S | 38.04 E |
| Kii-hantō ›[1] | 92 | 34.00 N | 135.45 E |
| Kiik | 86 | 47.31 N | 72.55 E |
| Kiikkaškan | 86 | 49.28 N | 77.04 E |
| Kiiminginjoki ≃ | 26 | 65.12 N | 25.18 E |
| Kii-nagashima | 92 | 34.12 N | 136.20 E |
| Kiirun → Chilung | 100 | 25.08 N | 121.44 E |
| Kii-sanchi ⋌ | 92 | 34.00 N | 135.50 E |
| Kii-suidō ⊻ | 96 | 33.55 N | 134.55 E |
| Kija ≃ | 86 | 56.52 N | 86.39 E |
| Kijabe | 154 | 0.56 S | 36.34 E |
| Kijakty, ozero ⊜ | 86 | 50.00 N | 69.15 E |
| Kijal | 114 | 4.21 N | 103.29 E |
| Kijaly | 86 | 54.17 N | 69.41 E |
| Kijasovo | 80 | 56.21 N | 53.07 E |
| Kijevka, Kaz. | 86 | 50.16 N | 71.34 E |
| Kijevka, Ross. | 80 | 46.05 N | 42.57 E |
| Kijevka, Ross. | 80 | 50.46 N | 48.28 E |
| Kijevskoje | 78 | 45.03 N | 37.52 E |
| Kijima-chosuichi ⊜ | 96 | 35.04 N | 132.44 E |
| Kijimadaira | 94 | 36.51 N | 138.24 E |
| Kijima-dam ◆[6] | 96 | 35.05 N | 132.44 E |
| Kijma | 86 | 51.35 N | 67.34 E |
| Kijoka | 174m | 26.42 N | 128.09 E |
| Kikagati | 154 | 1.02 S | 30.40 E |
| Kikai-shima ▮ | 93b | 28.19 N | 129.59 E |
| Kikale | 154 | 7.50 S | 39.12 E |
| Kikati ≃ | 152 | 14.48 S | 12.28 E |
| Kikenka ≃ | 265a | 59.52 N | 30.04 E |
| Kikerino | 76 | 59.28 N | 29.35 E |
| Kikerk Lake ⊜ | 176 | 67.20 N | 113.20 W |
| Kikimi | 273b | 4.26 S | 15.25 E |
| Kikimorka | 80 | 58.10 N | 49.27 E |
| Kikinda | 38 | 45.50 N | 20.28 E |
| Kikládhes (Cyclades) ▮▮ | 38 | 37.30 N | 25.00 E |
| Kiklah | 146 | 32.05 N | 12.41 E |
| Kiknur | 80 | 57.19 N | 47.14 E |
| Kikombo, Zaïre | 152 | 5.59 S | 18.09 E |
| Kikombo, Zaïre | 152 | 5.40 S | 18.48 E |
| Kikongo | 152 | 4.16 S | 17.11 E |
| Kikori | 164 | 7.25 S | 144.15 E |
| Kikori ≃ | 164 | 7.10 S | 144.05 E |
| Kikorze | 54 | 53.39 N | 15.01 E |
| Kiku ≃ | 94 | 34.39 N | 138.04 E |
| Kikuchi | 96 | 32.59 N | 130.49 E |
| Kikuchi ≃ | 96 | 32.56 N | 130.35 E |
| Kikugawa, Nihon | 94 | 34.45 N | 138.05 E |
| Kikugawa, Nihon | 96 | 34.07 N | 131.02 E |
| Kikuka | 96 | 33.02 N | 130.46 E |
| Kikuma | 96 | 34.03 N | 132.53 E |
| Kikuna | 268 | 35.10 N | 139.40 E |
| Kikusui | 96 | 32.58 N | 130.36 E |
| Kikvidze, Ross. | 80 | 50.53 N | 42.46 E |
| Kikvidze, Ross. | 80 | 50.44 N | 43.03 E |
| Kikvorsberg ⋌ | 158 | 31.17 S | 25.20 E |
| Kikwit | 152 | 5.02 S | 18.49 E |
| Kil | 26 | 59.30 N | 13.19 E |
| Kilaån ≃ | 40 | 58.44 N | 17.01 E |
| Kilafors | 26 | 61.14 N | 16.34 E |
| Kila Kila | 164 | 9.30 S | 147.10 E |
| Kīlakkarai | 122 | 9.14 N | 78.47 E |
| Kilambé, Cerro ∧ | 236 | 13.34 N | 85.42 W |
| Kilauea | 229b | 22.12 N | 159.24 W |
| Kilauea Crater ⩡[6] | 229d | 19.25 N | 155.17 W |
| Kilauea Point › | 229b | 22.14 N | 159.24 W |
| Kilb | 61 | 48.06 N | 15.24 E |
| Kilbaha | 48 | 52.33 N | 9.52 W |
| Kilbarchan | 46 | 55.50 N | 4.33 W |
| Kılbasan | 130 | 37.20 N | 33.12 E |
| Kilbeggan | 48 | 53.22 N | 7.29 W |
| Kilbirnie | 46 | 55.46 N | 4.41 W |
| Kilbourne, Il., U.S. | 219 | 40.09 N | 90.01 W |
| Kilbourne, Oh., U.S. | 214 | 40.20 N | 82.58 W |
| Kilbrannan Sound ⊻ | 46 | 55.40 N | 5.25 W |
| Kilbride | 46 | 57.05 N | 7.27 W |
| Kilbuck Mountains ⋌ | 180 | 60.50 N | 159.45 W |
| Kilbuck Run ≃ | 279b | 40.31 N | 80.08 W |
| Kilcar | 48 | 54.38 N | 8.35 W |
| Kilchberg | 58 | 47.19 N | 8.33 E |
| Kilchis ≃ | 224 | 45.30 N | 123.52 W |
| Kilchoan | 46 | 56.42 N | 6.06 W |
| Kilchreest | 48 | 53.10 N | 8.38 W |
| Kilchrenan | 46 | 56.21 N | 5.11 W |
| Kilchu | 98 | 40.58 N | 129.20 E |
| Kilcock | 48 | 53.24 N | 6.40 W |
| Kilcolgan | 48 | 53.13 N | 8.52 W |
| Kilconnell | 48 | 53.20 N | 8.25 W |
| Kilcoole | 48 | 53.06 N | 6.04 W |
| Kilcormac | 48 | 53.10 N | 7.43 W |
| Kilcoy | 171a | 26.57 S | 152.33 E |
| Kilcreggan | 46 | 55.59 N | 4.50 W |
| Kilcullen | 48 | 53.08 N | 6.45 W |
| Kildare (Saint-Ambroise-de-Kildare), P.Q., Can. | 206 | 46.05 N | 73.32 W |
| Kildare, Ire. | 48 | 53.10 N | 6.55 W |
| Kildare □[6] | 48 | 53.15 N | 6.45 W |
| Kildare, Cape › | 186 | 46.52 N | 63.58 W |
| Kildeer | 278 | 42.10 N | 88.03 W |
| Kil'din, ostrov ▮ | 24 | 69.22 N | 34.12 E |
| Kil'dinstroj | 24 | 68.48 N | 33.06 E |
| Kildonan, B.C., Can. | 182 | 49.00 N | 125.00 W |
| Kildonan, Scot., U.K. | 46 | 58.10 N | 3.51 W |
| Kildonan, Zimb. | 154 | 17.21 S | 30.37 E |
| Kildonan, Strath of ∨ | 46 | 58.09 N | 3.51 W |
| Kildorrery | 48 | 52.14 N | 8.26 W |
| Kildrummy Castle ⊥ | 46 | 57.14 N | 2.52 W |
| Kildurk | 164 | 16.26 S | 129.37 E |
| Kilemary | 80 | 56.47 N | 46.52 E |
| Kilembe, Ug. | 154 | 0.12 N | 30.00 E |
| Kilembe, Zaïre | 152 | 5.42 S | 19.55 E |
| Kilfenora | 48 | 52.59 N | 9.13 W |
| Kilfinnane | 48 | 52.21 N | 8.28 W |
| Kilgard | 224 | 49.03 N | 122.12 W |
| Kilgarvan | 48 | 51.54 N | 9.27 W |
| Kilgore, Oh., U.S. | 214 | 40.28 N | 81.00 W |
| Kilgore, Tx., U.S. | 222 | 32.23 N | 94.52 W |
| Kilham | 44 | 54.04 N | 0.23 W |
| Kili ▮ | 14 | 5.39 N | 169.04 E |
| Kilian Island ▮ | 176 | 73.35 N | 107.53 W |
| Kilibo | 150 | 8.34 N | 2.36 E |
| Kılıç | 130 | 40.38 N | 29.23 E |
| Kilifi | 154 | 3.38 S | 39.51 E |
| Kilikollūr | 122 | 8.54 N | 76.39 E |
| Kilima | 154 | 0.59 S | 29.12 E |
| Kilimanjaro □[4] | 154 | 3.45 S | 37.45 E |
| Kilimanjaro ∧ | 154 | 3.04 S | 37.22 E |
| Kilimanjaro Game Reserve ◆[4] | 154 | 3.05 S | 37.20 E |
| Kilimatinde | 154 | 5.51 S | 34.57 E |
| Kilimavony | 157b | 23.48 S | 43.41 E |
| Kilimli | 130 | 41.28 N | 31.50 E |
| Kilindoni | 154 | 7.55 S | 39.39 E |
| Kilingi-Nõmme | 76 | 58.09 N | 24.58 E |
| Kilis | 130 | 36.44 N | 37.05 E |
| Kiliya | 78 | 45.27 N | 29.16 E |
| Kilkare Woods | 282 | 37.38 N | 121.55 W |
| Kilkee | 48 | 52.41 N | 9.38 W |
| Kilkeel | 48 | 54.04 N | 6.00 W |
| Kilkelly | 48 | 53.53 N | 8.51 W |
| Kilkenny (Cill Chainnigh) | 48 | 52.39 N | 7.15 W |
| Kilkenny □[6] | 48 | 52.40 N | 7.20 W |
| Kilkerrin | 48 | 53.33 N | 8.34 W |
| Kilkhampton | 42 | 50.53 N | 4.29 W |
| Kilkieran | 48 | 53.19 N | 9.43 W |
| Kilkieran Bay ⊂ | 48 | 53.15 N | 9.45 W |
| Kilkís | 38 | 41.00 N | 22.53 E |
| Killadoon | 48 | 53.42 N | 9.56 W |
| Killadysert | 48 | 52.41 N | 9.06 W |
| Killala | 48 | 54.13 N | 9.13 W |
| Killala Bay ⊂ | 48 | 54.15 N | 9.10 W |
| Killaloe | 48 | 52.48 N | 8.27 W |
| Killaloe Station | 190 | 45.33 N | 77.25 W |
| Killam | 182 | 52.47 N | 111.51 W |
| Killara | 274a | 33.46 S | 151.09 E |
| Killarney, Austl. | 166 | 28.20 S | 152.18 E |
| Killarney, Mb., Can. | 184 | 49.12 N | 99.42 W |
| Killarney, On., Can. | 190 | 45.58 N | 81.31 W |
| Killarney, Ire. | 48 | 52.03 N | 9.30 W |
| Killarney, Lake ⊜ | 240b | 25.03 N | 77.27 W |
| Killarney, Lakes of ⊜ | 48 | 52.01 N | 9.30 W |
| Killarney Heights | 274a | 33.46 S | 151.13 E |
| Killarney Provincial Park ♦ | 190 | 46.05 N | 81.30 W |
| Killashandra | 48 | 54.00 N | 7.32 W |
| Killavally | 48 | 53.45 N | 9.23 W |
| Killawog | 210 | 42.24 N | 76.01 W |
| Killbear Provincial Park ♦ | 212 | 45.21 N | 80.12 W |
| Kill Buck, N.Y., U.S. | 210 | 42.10 N | 78.41 W |
| Killbuck, Oh., U.S. | 214 | 40.29 N | 81.59 W |
| Killbuck Creek ≃, Il., U.S. | 216 | 42.10 N | 89.06 W |
| Killbuck Creek ≃, In., U.S. | 218 | 40.07 N | 85.41 W |
| Killbuck Creek ≃, Oh., U.S. | 214 | 40.20 N | 81.57 W |
| Killdeer | 198 | 47.22 N | 102.45 W |
| Killean | 46 | 55.39 N | 5.40 W |
| Killearn | 46 | 56.03 N | 4.22 W |
| Killeen | 222 | 31.07 N | 97.43 W |
| Killen | 194 | 34.51 N | 87.32 W |
| Killenaule | 48 | 52.34 N | 7.40 W |
| Killeter | 48 | 54.40 N | 7.41 W |
| Kıllıdağ ∧ | 130 | 40.21 N | 42.10 E |
| Killik ≃ | 180 | 69.00 N | 153.58 W |
| Killilan | 46 | 57.19 N | 5.25 W |
| Killimor | 48 | 53.10 N | 8.17 W |
| Killin | 46 | 56.28 N | 4.19 W |
| Killington Peak ∧ | 188 | 43.36 N | 72.49 W |
| Killingworth | 207 | 41.21 N | 72.33 W |
| Killíni | 38 | 37.55 N | 21.09 E |
| Killíni ∧ | 38 | 37.57 N | 22.23 E |
| Killiniq Island ▮ | 176 | 60.24 N | 64.40 W |
| Killinkoski | 26 | 62.24 N | 23.52 E |
| Killorglin | 48 | 52.06 N | 9.47 W |
| Killough | 48 | 54.16 N | 5.39 W |
| Killpecker Creek ≃ | 202 | 41.35 N | 109.14 W |
| Killucan | 48 | 53.31 N | 7.07 W |
| Kill Van Kull ⊻ | 276 | 40.39 N | 74.05 W |
| Killybegs | 48 | 54.38 N | 8.27 W |
| Killyleagh | 48 | 54.24 N | 5.39 W |
| Kilmacolm | 46 | 55.54 N | 4.38 W |
| Kilmacthomas | 48 | 52.12 N | 7.25 W |
| Kilmaine | 48 | 53.34 N | 9.09 W |
| Kilmallock | 48 | 52.23 N | 8.34 W |
| Kilmaluag | 46 | 57.41 N | 6.17 W |
| Kilmarnock, Scot., U.K. | 46 | 55.36 N | 4.30 W |
| Kilmarnock, Va., U.S. | 208 | 37.42 N | 76.22 W |
| Kilmartin | 46 | 56.07 N | 5.29 W |
| Kilmar Tor ∧[2] | 42 | 50.33 N | 4.28 W |
| Kilmaurs | 46 | 55.39 N | 4.32 W |
| Kilmelford | 46 | 56.16 N | 5.29 W |
| Kil'mez', Ross. | 80 | 56.57 N | 51.04 E |
| Kil'mez', Ross. | 80 | 57.04 N | 51.21 E |
| Kil'mez' ≃ | 80 | 56.58 N | 50.28 E |
| Kilmichael | 194 | 33.26 N | 89.34 W |
| Kilmichael Point › | 48 | 52.44 N | 6.10 W |
| Kilmore | 169 | 37.18 S | 144.57 E |
| Kilmore Creek ≃ | 216 | 40.20 N | 86.38 W |
| Kilmory | 46 | 57.03 N | 6.22 W |
| Kilnaleck | 48 | 53.52 N | 7.19 W |
| Kilninver | 46 | 56.20 N | 5.31 W |
| Kilo | 115b | 8.21 S | 118.24 E |
| Kilokri ◆[8] | 272a | 28.35 N | 77.16 E |
| Kiloli | 154 | 6.50 S | 33.23 E |
| Kilombero ≃ | 154 | 8.31 S | 37.22 E |
| Kilomines | 154 | 1.48 N | 30.14 E |
| Kilondo | 154 | 9.46 S | 34.21 E |
| Kilosa | 154 | 6.50 S | 36.59 E |
| Kilpisjärvi | 24 | 69.03 N | 20.48 E |
| Kilrea | 48 | 54.58 N | 6.35 W |
| Kilrenny | 46 | 56.14 N | 2.41 W |
| Kilrush | 48 | 52.39 N | 9.30 W |
| Kilsbergen ⋌[2] | 40 | 59.20 N | 14.47 E |
| Kilsmo | 40 | 59.04 N | 15.31 E |
| Kilsyth, Austl. | 274b | 37.48 S | 145.19 E |
| Kilsyth, Scot., U.K. | 46 | 55.59 N | 4.04 W |
| Kiltealy | 48 | 52.34 N | 6.45 W |
| Kiltimagh | 48 | 53.51 N | 9.01 W |
| Kiltoom | 48 | 53.28 N | 8.01 W |
| Kilttān Island ▮ | 122 | 11.29 N | 73.00 E |
| Kiltu-ri | 98 | 34.35 N | 127.20 E |
| Kilwa | 154 | 9.18 S | 28.25 E |
| Kilwa Island ▮ | 154 | 9.20 S | 28.33 E |
| Kilwa Kivinje | 154 | 8.45 S | 39.24 E |
| Kilwa Masoko | 154 | 8.56 S | 39.31 E |
| Kilwinning | 46 | 55.40 N | 4.42 W |
| Kim | 198 | 37.14 N | 103.21 W |
| Kim ≃ | 152 | 5.28 N | 11.07 E |
| Kima | 154 | 1.26 S | 26.43 E |
| Kimaam | 164 | 7.58 S | 138.53 E |
| Kimamba | 154 | 6.47 S | 37.08 E |
| Kimande | 154 | 7.22 S | 35.30 E |
| Kīmān Fāris (Crocodilopolis) (Arsinoe) ⊥ | 142 | 29.19 N | 30.50 E |
| Kimba | 166 | 33.09 S | 136.25 E |
| Kimball, Mn., U.S. | 190 | 45.19 N | 94.18 W |
| Kimball, Ne., U.S. | 198 | 41.14 N | 103.39 W |
| Kimball, S.D., U.S. | 198 | 43.44 N | 98.57 W |
| Kimball, Mount ∧ | 180 | 63.14 N | 144.39 W |
| Kimbanda | 152 | 4.07 S | 17.59 E |
| Kimbe | 164 | 5.31 S | 150.10 E |
| Kimbe Bay ⊂ | 164 | 5.30 S | 150.30 E |
| Kimberley, B.C., Can. | 182 | 49.41 N | 115.59 W |
| Kimberley, S. Afr. | 158 | 28.43 S | 24.46 E |
| Kimberley, Eng., U.K. | 44 | 52.59 N | 1.16 W |
| Kimberley Downs | 162 | 17.24 S | 124.22 E |
| Kimberley Plateau ⋌[1] | 160 | 17.00 S | 127.00 E |
| Kimberling City | 194 | 36.38 N | 93.28 W |
| Kimberly, Id., U.S. | 202 | 42.32 N | 114.21 W |
| Kimberly, Wi., U.S. | 190 | 44.16 N | 88.20 W |
| Kimberton | 208 | 40.08 N | 75.34 W |
| Kimbolton, N.Z. | 172 | 40.03 S | 175.47 E |
| Kimbolton, Eng., U.K. | 42 | 52.18 N | 0.24 W |
| Kimbolton, Oh., U.S. | 214 | 40.09 N | 81.34 W |
| Kimbongo | 152 | 6.08 S | 18.01 E |
| Kimbwala | 273b | 4.22 S | 15.12 E |
| Kimch'aek (Sŏngjin) | 98 | 40.41 N | 129.12 E |
| Kimch'ŏn | 98 | 36.07 N | 128.05 E |
| Kimerka ≃ | 82 | 56.52 N | 37.22 E |
| Kimhae | 98 | 35.14 N | 128.52 E |
| Kimhwa | 98 | 38.26 N | 127.36 E |
| Kími | 38 | 38.37 N | 24.06 E |
| Kimil'tej | 88 | 54.08 N | 101.59 E |
| Kimito (Kemiö) | 26 | 60.10 N | 22.45 E |
| Kimito ▮ | 26 | 60.07 N | 22.40 E |
| Kimi-tōge ∧[2] | 270 | 34.43 N | 135.06 E |
| Kimi-tōge )( | 96 | 34.23 N | 135.37 E |
| Kimitsu | 94 | 35.20 N | 139.54 E |
| Kimiwan Lake ⊜ | 182 | 55.45 N | 116.54 W |
| Kimje | 98 | 35.48 N | 126.52 E |
| Kim Kim ≃ | 271c | 1.26 N | 103.58 E |
| Kimmell | 216 | 41.23 N | 85.32 W |
| Kim-me-ni-oli Wash ∨ | 200 | 36.07 N | 108.11 W |
| Kímolos ▮ | 38 | 36.48 N | 24.34 E |
| Kimongo | 152 | 4.29 S | 12.58 E |
| Kimovsk | 76 | 53.58 N | 38.32 E |
| Kimpangu | 152 | 5.51 S | 15.01 E |
| Kim Plan | 279b | 40.20 N | 79.44 W |
| Kimp'o | 271b | 37.37 N | 126.43 E |
| Kimp'o Airport ⊠ | 271b | 37.33 N | 126.48 E |
| Kimpombo | 273b | 4.17 S | 15.10 E |
| Kimpō-zan ∧ | 94 | 35.53 N | 138.38 E |
| Kimry | 82 | 56.52 N | 37.21 E |
| Kimsquit | 182 | 52.49 N | 126.58 W |
| Kimstad | 40 | 58.32 N | 15.58 E |
| Kimu ≃ | 268 | 35.56 N | 139.57 E |
| Kimuenza | 273b | 4.27 S | 15.17 E |
| Kimvula | 152 | 5.44 S | 15.58 E |
| Kimwanga | 154 | 7.08 S | 28.42 E |
| Kin | 174m | 26.26 N | 127.55 E |
| Kinabalian, Mount ∧ | 116 | 8.14 N | 125.25 E |
| Kinabalu, Gunong ∧ | 112 | 6.05 N | 116.33 E |
| Kinabalu National Park ♦ | 112 | 6.05 N | 116.33 E |


| | | | | |
|---|---|---|---|---|
| ≃ River | Fluß | Río | Rivière | Rio |
| ≍ Canal | Kanal | Canal | Canal | Canal |
| ⌊ Waterfall, Rapids | Wasserfall, Stromschnellen | Cascada, Rápidos | Chute d'eau, Rapides | Cascata, Rápidos |
| ⊻ Strait | Meeresstraße | Estrecho | Détroit | Estreito |
| ⊂ Bay, Gulf | Bucht, Golf | Bahía, Golfo | Baie, Golfe | Baía, Golfo |
| ⊜ Lake, Lakes | See, Seen | Lago, Lagos | Lac, Lacs | Lago, Lagos |
| ⩸ Swamp | Sumpf | Pantano | Marais | Pântano |
| ⍓ Ice Features, Glacier | Eis- und Gletscherformen | Accidentes Glaciales | Formes glaciaires | Acidentes glaciares |
| ⍑ Other Hydrographic Features | Andere Hydrographische Objekte | Otros Elementos Hidrográficos | Autres données hydrographiques | Outros acidentes hidrográficos |

| | | | | |
|---|---|---|---|---|
| ✤ Submarine Features | Untermeerische Objekte | Accidentes Submarinos | Formes de relief sous-marin | Acidentes submarinos |
| □ Political Unit | Politische Einheit | Unidad Politica | Entité politique | Unidade política |
| ✝ Cultural Institution | Kulturelle Institution | Institución Cultural | Institution culturelle | Institução cultural |
| ⊥ Historical Site | Historische Stätte | Sitio Histórico | Site historique | Sitio histórico |
| ♦ Recreational Site | Erholungs- und Ferienort | Sitio de Recreo | Centre de loisirs | Area de Lazer |
| ⊠ Airport | Flughafen | Aeropuerto | Aéroport | Aeroporto |
| ■ Military Installation | Militäranlage | Instalación Militar | Installation militaire | Instalação militar |
| ◆ Miscellaneous | Verschiedenes | Misceláneo | Divers | Diversos |

ENGLISH / DEUTSCH


| Name | Page | Lat.°′ | Long.°′ |
|---|---|---|---|
| Kinabatangan ≃ | 112 | 5.42 N | 118.23 E |
| Kınalı ◆[8] | 267b | 40.55 N | 29.03 E |
| Kınalı Ada I | 267b | 40.55 N | 29.03 E |
| Kinangaly ∧ | 157b | 19.12 S | 45.40 E |
| Kinango | 154 | 4.08 S | 39.19 E |
| Kinapusan Island I | 116 | 5.13 N | 120.40 E |
| Kinara | 164 | 2.16 S | 132.44 E |
| Kinasa | 94 | 36.42 N | 138.01 E |
| Kinaūni | 272a | 28.39 N | 77.23 E |
| Kinbasket Lake ⊜[1] | 182 | 51.58 N | 118.03 W |
| Kinbrace | 46 | 58.15 N | 3.56 W |
| Kinbuck | 46 | 56.13 N | 3.57 W |
| Kincaid, Sk., Can. | 184 | 49.39 N | 107.00 W |
| Kincaid, Il., U.S. | 219 | 39.35 N | 89.24 W |
| Kincardine, On., Can. | 190 | 44.11 N | 81.38 W |
| Kincardine, Scot., U.K. | 46 | 56.04 N | 3.44 W |
| Kinchafoonee Creek ≃ | 192 | 31.38 N | 84.10 W |
| Kinchang | 110 | 26.32 N | 98.02 E |
| Kinchara | 272b | 22.53 N | 88.32 E |
| Kinchega National Park ♠ | 166 | 32.30 S | 142.20 E |
| Kincheloe Air Force Base ■ | 190 | 46.15 N | 84.28 W |
| Kincolith | 182 | 55.00 N | 129.57 W |
| Kincraig | 46 | 57.08 N | 3.55 W |
| Kinda, Zaïre | 152 | 4.47 S | 21.48 E |
| Kinda, Zaïre | 154 | 9.18 S | 25.04 E |
| Kindadal | 112 | 1.35 S | 123.11 E |
| Kindanba | 152 | 3.44 S | 14.31 E |
| Kindarun Mountain ∧ | 170 | 32.49 S | 150.41 E |
| Kindberg | 61 | 47.31 N | 15.27 E |
| Kinde | 190 | 43.56 N | 82.59 W |
| Kindeje | 152 | 7.07 S | 13.44 E |
| Kindel'a | 80 | 51.36 N | 52.58 E |
| Kindel'a ≃ | 80 | 51.30 N | 52.45 E |
| Kindelbrück | 54 | 51.16 N | 11.05 E |
| Kindele | 152 | 8.39 S | 24.11 E |
| Kinder | 194 | 30.29 N | 92.51 W |
| Kinderhook, Il., U.S. | 219 | 39.42 N | 91.09 W |
| Kinderhook, Mi., U.S. | 216 | 41.48 N | 85.00 W |
| Kinderhook, N.Y., U.S. | 210 | 42.23 N | 73.41 W |
| Kinderhook Creek ≃ | 210 | 42.19 N | 73.45 W |
| Kinder Reservoir ⊜[1] | 262 | 53.23 N | 1.55 W |
| Kinder Scout ∧ | 44 | 53.23 N | 1.52 W |
| Kindersley | 184 | 51.27 N | 109.10 W |
| Kindia | 150 | 10.04 N | 12.51 W |
| Kindikan | 88 | 56.02 N | 115.15 E |
| Kinding | 60 | 49.00 N | 11.23 E |
| Kindley Field ⊠ | 240a | 32.22 N | 64.40 W |
| Kindred | 198 | 46.38 N | 97.01 W |
| Kindu | 154 | 2.57 S | 25.56 E |
| Kindykty, ozero ⊜ | 86 | 51.15 N | 62.14 E |
| Kinel' | 80 | 53.14 N | 50.39 E |
| Kinel'-Čerkasy | 80 | 53.29 N | 51.29 E |
| Kinel'skije jary ⋀[1] | 80 | 53.42 N | 52.00 E |
| Kineo, Mount ∧ | 188 | 45.42 N | 69.44 W |
| Kinesi | 154 | 1.28 S | 33.52 E |
| Kinešma | 80 | 57.26 N | 42.09 E |
| Kineton | 42 | 52.10 N | 1.30 W |
| Kinfauns | 46 | 56.22 N | 3.21 W |
| King | 192 | 36.16 N | 80.21 W |
| King □[6] | 224 | 47.26 N | 121.48 W |
| King ≃, Austl. | 164 | 14.41 S | 131.59 E |
| King ≃, Austl. | 169 | 36.41 S | 146.25 E |
| King, Lake ⊜ | 162 | 25.38 S | 120.06 E |
| King, Mont ∧ | 212 | 45.29 N | 75.52 W |
| King, Mount ∧ | 166 | 25.10 S | 147.31 E |
| Kingabwa ◆[8] | 273b | 4.19 S | 15.20 E |
| King and Queen □[6] | 208 | 37.42 N | 76.50 W |
| King and Queen Court House | 208 | 37.40 N | 76.52 W |
| Kingaroy | 166 | 26.33 S | 151.50 E |
| Kingarth | 46 | 55.46 N | 5.03 W |
| King City, On., Can. | 212 | 43.56 N | 79.32 W |
| King City, Ca., U.S. | 226 | 36.12 N | 121.07 W |
| King City, Mo., U.S. | 194 | 40.03 N | 94.31 W |
| King Cove | 180 | 55.04 N | 162.19 W |
| Kingdom City | 219 | 38.58 N | 91.56 W |
| King Edward ≃ | 164 | 14.14 S | 126.35 E |
| Kingersheim | 58 | 47.48 N | 7.20 E |
| King Ferry | 210 | 42.39 N | 76.37 W |
| Kingfield | 188 | 44.57 N | 70.09 W |
| Kingfisher | 196 | 35.51 N | 97.55 W |
| King George | 208 | 38.16 N | 77.11 W |
| King George □[6] | 208 | 38.15 N | 77.10 W |
| King George, Mount ∧ | 182 | 50.35 N | 115.24 W |
| King George Bay c | 254 | 51.33 S | 60.37 W |
| King George Island I | 9 | 62.00 S | 58.15 W |
| King George Islands II | 176 | 57.20 N | 78.25 W |
| King George's Dock ◆[5] | 272b | 22.32 N | 88.18 E |
| King George Sound ʮ | 162 | 35.03 S | 117.57 E |
| King George's Reservoir ⊜[1] | 260 | 51.39 N | 0.01 W |
| King George VI Reservoir ⊜[1] | 260 | 51.27 N | 0.32 W |
| King Hill | 202 | 43.00 N | 115.12 W |
| Kinghorn | 46 | 56.04 N | 3.10 W |
| Kingie ≃ | 46 | 57.04 N | 5.08 W |
| Kingisepp | 76 | 59.22 N | 28.36 E |
| King Island I, Austl. | 166 | 39.50 S | 144.00 E |
| King Island I, B.C., Can. | 182 | 52.12 N | 127.42 W |
| King Island I, Ak., U.S. | 180 | 64.58 N | 168.05 W |
| Kinglake National Park ♠ | 169 | 37.35 S | 145.25 E |
| King Lear Peak ∧ | 204 | 41.12 N | 118.34 W |
| King Leopold Ranges ⋀ | 160 | 17.30 S | 125.45 E |
| Kingman, Az., U.S. | 200 | 35.11 N | 114.03 W |
| Kingman, Ks., U.S. | 198 | 37.38 N | 98.06 W |
| Kingman Reef ✧[2] | 14 | 6.24 N | 162.22 W |
| King Mountain ∧, B.C., Can. | 180 | 58.17 N | 128.54 W |
| King Mountain ∧, Ok., U.S. | 196 | 34.52 N | 99.17 W |
| King Mountain ∧, Or., U.S. | 202 | 42.42 N | 123.14 W |
| King Mountain ∧, Or., U.S. | 202 | 43.49 N | 118.52 W |
| King of Prussia | 208 | 40.05 N | 75.23 W |
| King of Prussia Plaza ◆[9] | 285 | 40.05 N | 75.25 W |
| Kingoma | 152 | 5.11 S | 13.34 E |
| Kingoma-Ngoma | 152 | 5.50 S | 16.49 E |
| Kingombe, Zaïre | 154 | 3.56 S | 26.35 E |
| Kingombe, Zaïre | 154 | 7.24 S | 26.11 E |
| Kingoonya | 162 | 30.54 S | 135.18 E |
| Kingoué | 152 | 3.43 S | 14.09 E |
| King Peak ∧ | 204 | 40.10 N | 124.08 W |
| King Peninsula ≻[1] | 9 | 73.12 S | 101.00 W |
| Kingri | 120 | 30.27 N | 69.49 E |
| Kings, Il., U.S. | 216 | 42.00 N | 89.06 W |
| Kings, Ms., U.S. | 194 | 32.23 N | 90.51 W |
| Kings □[6], Ca., U.S. | 226 | 36.20 N | 119.39 W |
| Kings □[6], N.Y., U.S. | 210 | 40.42 N | 74.00 W |
| Kings ≃, Ar., U.S. | 194 | 36.29 N | 93.35 W |
| Kings ≃, Ca., U.S. | 226 | 36.03 N | 119.49 W |
| Kings ≃, Nv., U.S. | 204 | 41.31 N | 118.08 W |
| Kings, Middle Fork ≃ | 204 | 36.50 N | 118.52 W |
| Kings, North Fork ≃, Ca., U.S. | 204 | 36.52 N | 119.08 W |
| Kings, North Fork ≃, Ca., U.S. | 226 | 36.18 N | 119.52 W |
| Kings, South Fork ≃ | 226 | 36.18 N | 119.52 W |
| King Salmon | 180 | 58.41 N | 156.39 W |
| King Salmon ≃ | 180 | 58.15 N | 157.30 W |
| Kingsbarns | 46 | 56.18 N | 2.39 W |
| Kings Beach | 226 | 39.14 N | 120.01 W |
| Kingsbridge | 42 | 50.17 N | 3.46 W |
| Kingsburg | 226 | 36.30 N | 119.33 W |
| Kingsbury, Eng., U.K. | 42 | 52.35 N | 1.40 W |
| Kingsbury, In., U.S. | 216 | 41.31 N | 86.42 W |
| Kingsbury ◆[8] | 260 | 51.35 N | 0.17 W |
| Kings Canyon National Park ♠ | 204 | 36.48 N | 118.30 W |
| Kingsclere | 42 | 51.20 N | 1.14 W |
| Kingscote | 168b | 35.40 S | 137.38 E |
| Kingscourt | 48 | 53.53 N | 6.48 W |
| Kings Creek | 218 | 40.10 N | 83.44 W |
| Kings Creek ≃, Austl. | 171a | 27.57 S | 151.42 E |
| Kings Creek ≃, Tx., U.S. | 222 | 32.25 N | 96.15 W |
| King's Cross Station ◆[5] | 260 | 51.32 N | 0.07 W |
| Kings Dominion ♠ | 208 | 37.51 N | 77.27 W |
| Kingsdown, Eng., U.K. | 42 | 51.11 N | 1.25 E |
| Kingsdown, Eng., U.K. | 260 | 51.21 N | 0.17 E |
| Kings Falls ↲ | 212 | 43.55 N | 75.38 W |
| Kingsford, Austl. | 274a | 33.56 S | 151.14 E |
| Kingsford, Mi., U.S. | 190 | 45.47 N | 88.04 W |
| Kingsford Heights | 216 | 41.29 N | 86.42 W |
| Kingsford Smith Airport ⊠ | 170 | 33.57 S | 151.11 E |
| Kingsgate | 182 | 49.00 N | 116.11 W |
| Kingsgrove | 274a | 33.57 S | 151.06 E |
| Kingshill | 241n | 17.44 N | 64.48 W |
| Kingshouse | 46 | 56.21 N | 4.19 W |
| Kings Island ♠ | 218 | 39.21 N | 84.16 W |
| Kingskerswell | 42 | 50.30 N | 3.33 W |
| Kingsland, Eng., U.K. | 42 | 52.15 N | 2.47 W |
| Kingsland, Ar., U.S. | 194 | 33.51 N | 92.17 W |
| Kingsland, Ga., U.S. | 192 | 30.47 N | 81.41 W |
| Kingsland, Tx., U.S. | 196 | 30.40 N | 98.26 W |
| Kingsland, Va., U.S. | 208 | 37.24 N | 77.26 W |
| Kings Langley | 42 | 51.43 N | 0.28 W |
| Kingsley, S. Afr. | 158 | 27.55 S | 30.33 E |
| Kingsley, Eng., U.K. | 42 | 53.01 N | 1.59 W |
| Kingsley, Eng., U.K. | 262 | 53.16 N | 2.40 W |
| Kingsley, Ia., U.S. | 198 | 42.35 N | 95.58 W |
| Kingsley, Mi., U.S. | 190 | 44.35 N | 85.32 W |
| Kingsley, Pa., U.S. | 210 | 41.46 N | 75.45 W |
| Kingsley Dam ◆[6] | 198 | 41.11 N | 101.39 W |
| King's Lynn | 42 | 52.45 N | 0.24 E |
| Kings Manor | 285 | 40.05 N | 75.21 W |
| Kingsmere Lake ⊜ | 184 | 54.06 N | 106.27 W |
| Kings Mills | 218 | 39.21 N | 84.14 W |
| Kings Mountain | 192 | 35.14 N | 81.20 W |
| Kings Mountain National Military Park ♠ | 192 | 35.07 N | 81.33 W |
| King Solomon's Mines → Mikhrot Shelomo Hamelekh ⊥ | 132 | 29.45 N | 34.56 E |
| King Sound ʮ | 162 | 17.00 S | 123.30 E |
| Kings Park, N.Y., U.S. | 210 | 40.53 N | 73.16 W |
| Kings Park, Va., U.S. | 284c | 38.48 N | 77.14 W |
| Kings Park ♠ | 168a | 31.57 S | 115.49 E |
| Kings Peak ∧ | 200 | 40.46 N | 110.22 W |
| Kings Plaza ◆[9] | 276 | 40.37 N | 73.55 W |
| King's Point, Nf., Can. | 186 | 49.35 N | 56.11 W |
| Kings Point, N.Y., U.S. | 210 | 40.49 N | 73.44 W |
| Kingsport | 192 | 36.32 N | 82.33 W |
| King's Sutton | 42 | 52.01 N | 1.16 W |
| Kingsteignton | 42 | 50.33 N | 3.35 W |
| King Sterndale | 262 | 53.15 N | 1.52 W |
| Kingsthorpe | 171a | 27.29 S | 151.49 E |
| Kingston, Austl. | 171a | 27.40 S | 153.07 E |
| Kingston, N.S., Can. | 186 | 44.59 N | 64.57 W |
| Kingston, On., Can. | 212 | 44.14 N | 76.30 W |
| Kingston, Jam. | 241q | 18.00 N | 76.48 W |
| Kingston, N.Z. | 172 | 45.20 S | 168.42 E |
| Kingston, Norf. I. | 174c | 29.03 S | 167.58 E |
| Kingston, Ga., U.S. | 192 | 34.14 N | 84.56 W |
| Kingston, Il., U.S. | 216 | 42.06 N | 88.46 W |
| Kingston, Ma., U.S. | 207 | 41.59 N | 70.43 W |
| Kingston, Mo., U.S. | 194 | 39.38 N | 94.02 W |
| Kingston, N.J., U.S. | 276 | 40.22 N | 74.36 W |
| Kingston, N.Y., U.S. | 210 | 41.55 N | 73.59 W |
| Kingston, Oh., U.S. | 218 | 39.28 N | 82.54 W |
| Kingston, Ok., U.S. | 196 | 33.59 N | 96.43 W |
| Kingston, Pa., U.S. | 210 | 41.15 N | 75.53 W |
| Kingston, R.I., U.S. | 207 | 41.29 N | 71.31 W |
| Kingston, Tn., U.S. | 192 | 35.52 N | 84.30 W |
| Kingston, Wa., U.S. | 224 | 47.48 N | 122.30 W |
| Kingston Bay c | 283 | 42.00 N | 70.42 W |
| Kingston Mills | 212 | 44.17 N | 76.27 W |
| Kingston Southeast | 166 | 36.50 S | 139.51 E |
| Kingston upon Hull | 44 | 53.45 N | 0.20 W |
| Kingston [upon Thames] | 28 | 51.25 N | 0.19 W |
| Kingston [upon Thames] ◆[8] | 42 | 51.25 N | 0.19 W |
| Kingstown → Dún Laoghaire, Ire. | 48 | 53.17 N | 6.08 W |
| Kingstown, St. Vin. | 241h | 13.09 N | 61.14 W |
| Kingstree | 192 | 33.40 N | 79.49 W |
| Kingsville, Austl. | 274b | 37.49 S | 144.52 E |
| Kingsville, On., Can. | 214 | 42.02 N | 82.45 W |
| Kingsville, Md., U.S. | 284b | 39.26 N | 76.25 W |
| Kingsville, Oh., U.S. | 214 | 41.53 N | 80.41 W |
| Kingsville, Tx., U.S. | 196 | 27.30 N | 97.51 W |
| Kingsville Naval Air Station ■ | 196 | 27.31 N | 97.47 W |
| Kingswear | 42 | 50.21 N | 3.34 W |
| Kingswinford | 42 | 52.29 N | 2.10 W |
| Kingswood, Austl. | 274a | 33.46 S | 150.43 E |
| Kingswood, S. Afr. | 158 | 27.29 S | 25.46 E |
| Kingswood, Eng., U.K. | 42 | 51.27 N | 2.22 W |
| Kingswood, Eng., U.K. | 260 | 51.17 N | 0.13 W |
| Kingswood Park | 285 | 40.07 N | 74.51 W |
| King's Worthy | 42 | 51.06 N | 1.18 W |
| Kingtechen → Jingdezhen | 100 | 29.16 N | 117.11 E |
| Kington | 42 | 52.12 N | 3.01 W |
| Kingunda | 152 | 6.34 S | 16.58 E |
| Kingungi | 152 | 5.24 S | 17.56 E |
| Kingussie | 46 | 57.05 N | 4.03 W |
| King William | 208 | 37.41 N | 77.00 W |
| King William □[6] | 208 | 37.42 N | 77.05 W |
| King William Island I | 176 | 69.00 N | 97.30 W |
| King William's Town | 158 | 32.51 S | 27.22 E |
| Kingwood, Tx., U.S. | 222 | 29.54 N | 95.18 W |
| Kingwood, W.V., U.S. | 188 | 39.28 N | 79.41 W |
| Kinh Duc | 110 | 11.49 N | 107.58 E |
| Kinhwa → Jinhua | 100 | 29.07 N | 119.39 E |
| Kınık | 130 | 39.05 N | 27.23 E |
| Kinira ≃ | 158 | 31.12 S | 29.17 E |
| Kinistino | 184 | 52.57 N | 105.00 W |
| Kinjar Khās | 123 | 29.55 N | 70.58 E |
| Kinkala | 152 | 4.22 S | 14.46 E |
| Kinker Creek ≃ | 282 | 38.02 N | 121.52 W |
| Kinkony, Lac ⊜ | 157b | 16.08 S | 45.50 E |
| Kinkora | 285 | 40.07 N | 74.45 W |
| Kinleith | 172 | 38.16 S | 175.54 E |
| Kinloch | 46 | 57.01 N | 6.17 W |
| Kinlochbervie | 46 | 58.28 N | 5.03 W |
| Kinlocheil | 46 | 56.51 N | 5.20 W |
| Kinlochewe | 46 | 57.36 N | 5.20 W |
| Kinloch Hourn | 46 | 57.06 N | 5.22 W |
| Kinlochleven | 46 | 56.42 N | 4.58 W |
| Kinloch Rannoch | 46 | 56.42 N | 4.11 W |
| Kinloss | 46 | 57.37 N | 3.34 W |
| Kinmount | 212 | 44.47 N | 78.39 W |
| Kinmundy | 219 | 38.46 N | 88.50 W |
| Kinn | 26 | 61.36 N | 4.45 E |
| Kinna | 26 | 57.30 N | 12.41 E |
| Kinnaird | 182 | 49.17 N | 117.39 W |
| Kinnaird Head ≻ | 46 | 57.42 N | 2.00 W |
| Kinnegad | 48 | 53.26 N | 7.05 W |
| Kinnekulle ∧[2] | 26 | 58.35 N | 13.23 E |
| Kinnelon | 210 | 40.59 N | 74.23 W |
| Kinnel Water ≃ | 44 | 55.08 N | 3.25 W |
| Kinneret | 132 | 32.43 N | 35.33 E |
| Kinneret, Yam (Sea of Galilee) ⊜ | 132 | 32.48 N | 35.35 E |
| Kinneret-Negev Conduit ≚[1] | 132 | 32.52 N | 35.32 E |
| Kinnerley | 42 | 52.47 N | 2.59 W |
| Kinniconick Creek ≃ | 218 | 38.37 N | 83.09 W |
| Kinnula | 26 | 63.22 N | 24.58 E |
| Kino ≃ | 96 | 34.13 N | 135.09 E |
| Kinoe | 96 | 34.14 N | 132.55 E |
| Kinogitan | 116 | 9.00 N | 124.48 E |
| Kinojévis ≃ | 190 | 48.23 N | 78.21 W |
| Kinomoto | 94 | 35.30 N | 136.13 E |
| Kinonge ≃ | 206 | 45.39 N | 74.55 W |
| Kinoni | 154 | 0.39 S | 30.27 E |
| Kinosaki | 96 | 35.37 N | 134.49 E |
| Kinpoku-san ∧ | 92 | 38.05 N | 138.22 E |
| Kinrola | 166 | 23.46 S | 148.45 E |
| Kinross, S. Afr. | 158 | 26.22 S | 29.03 E |
| Kinross, Scot., U.K. | 46 | 56.13 N | 3.27 W |
| Kin-saki ≻ | 174m | 26.26 N | 127.57 E |
| Kinsale, Ire. | 48 | 51.42 N | 8.32 W |
| Kinsale, Va., U.S. | 208 | 38.01 N | 76.34 W |
| Kinsale, Old Head of ≻ | 48 | 51.36 N | 8.32 W |
| Kinsale Harbour c | 48 | 51.41 N | 8.30 W |
| Kinsarvik | 26 | 60.23 N | 6.43 E |
| Kinschasa → Kinshasa | 152 | 4.18 S | 15.18 E |
| Kinshasa (Léopoldville), Zaïre | 152 | 4.18 S | 15.18 E |
| Kinshasa (Léopoldville), Zaïre | 273b | 4.18 S | 15.18 E |
| Kinshasa □[4] | 152 | 4.18 S | 15.18 E |
| Kinshasa (Ndjili) Airport ⊠, Zaïre | 273b | 4.23 S | 15.27 E |
| Kinshasa (Ndolo) Airport ⊠, Zaïre | 273b | 4.20 S | 15.19 E |
| Kinshasa-Est ◆[8] | 273b | 4.18 S | 15.18 E |
| Kinshasa-Ouest ◆[8] | 273b | 4.20 S | 15.15 E |
| Kins'ka ≃ | 78 | 47.40 N | 35.22 E |
| Kinsley | 198 | 37.55 N | 99.24 W |
| Kinsman, Il., U.S. | 216 | 41.11 N | 88.34 W |
| Kinsman, Oh., U.S. | 214 | 41.27 N | 80.36 W |
| Kinston, Al., U.S. | 194 | 31.12 N | 86.10 W |
| Kinston, N.C., U.S. | 192 | 35.15 N | 77.34 W |
| Kintamani | 115b | 8.14 S | 115.19 E |
| Kintamo, Rapides de ↲ | 273b | 4.19 S | 15.15 E |
| Kintampo | 150 | 8.03 N | 1.43 W |
| Kintap | 112 | 3.51 S | 115.13 E |
| Kintari, Mont ∧[2] | 273b | 4.08 S | 15.23 E |
| Kintélé | 273b | 4.09 S | 15.21 E |
| Kintinian | 150 | 11.36 N | 9.23 W |
| Kintinku | 154 | 5.53 S | 35.14 E |
| Kintobongo-Bunge | 154 | 8.54 S | 26.23 E |
| Kintore | 46 | 57.13 N | 2.21 W |
| Kintore, Mount ∧ | 162 | 26.34 S | 130.30 E |
| Kintore Range ⋀ | 162 | 23.25 S | 129.20 E |
| Kintsana | 273b | 4.19 S | 15.10 E |
| Kintus | 86 | 60.09 N | 71.25 E |
| Kintyre ≻[1] | 46 | 55.32 N | 5.35 W |
| Kintyre, Mull of ≻ | 46 | 55.17 N | 5.55 W |
| Kinu ≃ | 94 | 35.56 N | 139.57 E |
| Kinuseo Falls ↲ | 182 | 54.47 N | 121.12 W |
| Kinuso | 182 | 55.20 N | 115.25 W |
| Kinvarra | 48 | 53.08 N | 8.55 W |
| Kinver | 42 | 52.27 N | 2.14 W |
| Kin-wan c | 174m | 26.25 N | 127.54 E |
| Kinyangiri | 154 | 4.27 S | 34.37 E |
| Kinyeti ∧ | 154 | 3.57 N | 32.54 E |
| Kinzia | 152 | 3.36 S | 18.26 E |
| Kinzig ≃, Dtsch. | 56 | 50.08 N | 8.54 E |
| Kinzig ≃, Dtsch. | 58 | 48.37 N | 7.49 E |
| Kinzua | 202 | 44.59 N | 120.03 W |
| Kinzua Creek ≃ | 214 | 41.47 N | 78.50 W |
| Kinzua Dam ◆[6] | 214 | 41.50 N | 79.01 W |
| Kioga-See → Kyoga, Lake ⊜ | 154 | 1.30 N | 33.00 E |
| Kioshkokwi Lake ⊜ | 190 | 46.05 N | 78.52 W |
| Kioto → Kyōto | 94 | 35.00 N | 135.45 E |
| Kiowa, Co., U.S. | 198 | 39.20 N | 104.27 W |
| Kiowa, Ks., U.S. | 198 | 37.01 N | 98.29 W |
| Kiowa, Ok., U.S. | 196 | 34.43 N | 95.53 W |
| Kiowa Creek ≃, U.S. | 196 | 36.46 N | 99.55 W |
| Kiowa Creek ≃, Co., U.S. | 198 | 40.20 N | 104.05 W |
| Kipahigan Lake ⊜ | 184 | 55.20 N | 101.55 W |
| Kipandi | 152 | 5.19 S | 16.46 E |
| Kipanga | 154 | 6.14 S | 35.21 E |
| Kiparissía | 38 | 37.14 N | 21.40 E |
| Kiparissiakós Kólpos c | 38 | 37.37 N | 21.24 E |
| Kipatimu | 154 | 8.29 S | 38.56 E |
| Kipawa ≃ | 190 | 47.03 N | 79.23 W |
| Kipawa, Lac ⊜ | 190 | 46.55 N | 79.00 W |
| Kipawa, Réserve ♠ | 190 | 47.15 N | 78.15 W |
| Kipembawe | 154 | 7.39 S | 33.24 E |
| Kipengere Range ⋀ | 154 | 9.10 S | 34.15 E |
| Kipfenberg | 60 | 48.57 N | 11.24 E |
| Kipijevo | 24 | 65.40 N | 54.30 E |
| Kipili | 154 | 7.26 S | 30.36 E |
| Kipini | 154 | 2.32 S | 40.31 E |
| Kipling | 184 | 50.10 N | 102.38 W |
| Kipnuk | 180 | 59.56 N | 164.03 W |
| Kippax | 44 | 53.46 N | 1.22 W |
| Kippen | 46 | 56.08 N | 4.11 W |
| Kippenheim | 58 | 48.17 N | 7.49 E |
| Kippure ∧ | 48 | 53.10 N | 6.20 W |
| Kípros → Cyprus □[1] | 130 | 35.00 N | 33.00 E |
| Kipsdorf | 54 | 50.47 N | 13.32 E |
| Kipton | 214 | 41.16 N | 82.18 W |
| Kipushi | 154 | 11.46 S | 27.14 E |
| Kipushia, Zaïre | 154 | 6.10 S | 25.12 E |
| Kipushia, Zaïre | 154 | 12.58 S | 29.30 E |
| Kira, Nihon | 94 | 34.49 N | 137.05 E |
| Kir'a, Ross. | 80 | 55.04 N | 46.53 E |
| Kirakira | 175e | 10.27 S | 161.55 E |
| Kirandul | 122 | 18.40 N | 81.16 E |
| Kirane | 150 | 15.25 N | 10.14 W |
| Kiranlık | 130 | 39.07 N | 41.41 E |
| Kiranomena | 157b | 18.17 S | 46.03 E |
| Kīratpur | 124 | 29.31 N | 78.12 E |
| Kirau̡ | 78 | 51.29 N | 29.24 E |
| Kirau̡sk | 76 | 53.16 N | 29.29 E |
| Kiraz | 130 | 38.13 N | 28.13 E |
| Kirazlı | 130 | 40.02 N | 26.41 E |
| Kırbaçbayırı ∧ | 267b | 40.56 N | 29.10 E |
| Kırbaşı | 130 | 40.01 N | 31.50 E |
| Kirbla | 76 | 58.44 N | 23.57 E |
| Kirby Muxloe | 42 | 52.38 N | 1.13 W |
| Kirbys Creek ≃ | 208 | 36.28 N | 77.06 W |
| Kirbyville | 194 | 30.39 N | 93.53 W |
| Kırçal | 130 | 41.39 N | 35.16 E |
| Kırcasalih | 130 | 41.23 N | 26.48 E |
| Kirchanschöring | 64 | 47.57 N | 12.50 E |
| Kirchardt | 56 | 49.12 N | 8.59 E |
| Kirchbach in Steiermark | 61 | 46.54 N | 15.44 E |
| Kirchberg, Dtsch. | 54 | 50.37 N | 12.32 E |
| Kirchberg, Dtsch. | 56 | 49.12 N | 9.58 E |
| Kirchberg, Dtsch. | 56 | 49.56 N | 7.24 E |
| Kirchberg, Dtsch. | 60 | 48.54 N | 13.11 E |
| Kirchberg, Schw. | 58 | 47.25 N | 9.03 E |
| Kirchberg, Schw. | 58 | 47.05 N | 7.35 E |
| Kirch-Berg ∧[2] | 264a | 52.27 N | 13.02 E |
| Kirchberg am Wagram | 61 | 48.26 N | 15.53 E |
| Kirchberg an der Pielach | 61 | 48.02 N | 15.26 E |
| Kirchberg in Tirol | 64 | 47.27 N | 12.19 E |
| Kirchbichl | 64 | 47.31 N | 12.05 E |
| Kirchderne ◆[8] | 263 | 51.33 N | 7.30 E |
| Kirchdorf, Dtsch. | 52 | 52.36 N | 8.49 E |
| Kirchdorf, Dtsch. | 54 | 54.00 N | 11.26 E |
| Kirchdorf an der Krems | 61 | 47.56 N | 14.07 E |
| Kirchdorf im Wald | 60 | 48.55 N | 13.16 E |
| Kirchen | 56 | 50.48 N | 7.53 E |
| Kirchende | 263 | 51.25 N | 7.26 E |
| Kirchenlamitz | 54 | 50.09 N | 11.56 E |
| Kirchenthumbach | 60 | 49.45 N | 11.43 E |
| Kirchhain | 56 | 50.49 N | 8.55 E |
| Kirchheilingen | 54 | 51.11 N | 10.42 E |
| Kirchheim, Dtsch. | 56 | 50.50 N | 9.35 E |
| Kirchheim, Dtsch. | 64 | 48.11 N | 11.45 E |
| Kirchheimbolanden | 56 | 49.40 N | 8.00 E |
| Kirchheim in Schwaben | 58 | 48.10 N | 10.30 E |
| Kirchheim unter Teck | 56 | 48.39 N | 9.27 E |
| Kirchhellen | 52 | 51.36 N | 6.55 E |
| Kirchhellen Heide ◆[3] | 263 | 51.36 N | 6.53 E |
| Kirchhofen | 264a | 52.22 N | 13.53 E |
| Kirchhörde ◆[8] | 263 | 51.27 N | 7.27 E |
| Kirchhundem | 56 | 51.05 N | 8.05 E |
| Kirchlengern | 52 | 52.12 N | 8.35 E |
| Kirchlinde ◆[8] | 263 | 51.32 N | 7.22 E |
| Kirchlinteln | 52 | 52.56 N | 9.19 E |
| Kirchmöser | 54 | 52.22 N | 12.25 E |
| Kirchroth | 60 | 48.57 N | 12.33 E |
| Kirchschlag in der Buckligen Welt | 61 | 47.31 N | 16.18 E |
| Kirchseeon | 64 | 48.04 N | 11.53 E |
| Kirchveischede | 56 | 51.05 N | 7.59 E |
| Kirchwalsede | 52 | 53.01 N | 9.23 E |
| Kirchwerder ◆[8] | 52 | 53.25 N | 10.11 E |
| Kirchzarten | 58 | 47.58 N | 7.56 E |
| Kircubbin | 48 | 54.29 N | 5.32 W |
| Kirda | 85 | 41.06 N | 69.00 E |
| Kirdāsah | 142 | 30.02 N | 31.07 E |
| Kireç | 130 | 39.33 N | 28.22 E |
| Kirej ≃ | 88 | 54.12 N | 100.40 E |
| Kirejevo | 80 | 50.01 N | 44.29 E |
| Kirejevsk | 76 | 53.56 N | 37.56 E |
| Kirejkovo | 76 | 53.38 N | 35.49 E |
| Kirenga ≃ | 88 | 57.47 N | 108.07 E |
| Kirensk | 88 | 57.46 N | 108.08 E |
| Kirghizia → Kyrgyzstan □[1] | 72 | 41.30 N | 75.00 E |
| Kirgili | 85 | 40.24 N | 71.43 E |
| Kirgizija → Kyrgyzstan □[1] | 72 | 41.30 N | 75.00 E |
| Kirgiziya → Kyrgyzstan □[1] | 72 | 41.30 N | 75.00 E |
| Kirgiz-Mijaki | 86 | 53.38 N | 54.47 E |
| Kirgizskij chrebet ⋀ | 85 | 42.30 N | 74.00 E |
| Kiri | 152 | 1.27 S | 19.00 E |
| Kiribati □[1] | 14 | 5.00 S | 170.00 W |
| Kiribati II | 14 | 0.30 S | 174.00 E |
| Kiries West | 158 | 26.34 S | 19.00 E |
| Kiriga-mine ∧ | 94 | 36.06 N | 138.12 E |
| Kırıkhan, Tür. | 130 | 39.32 N | 41.20 E |
| Kırıkhan, Tür. | 130 | 36.32 N | 36.19 E |
| Kirikiri Prisons ʊ | 273a | 6.27 N | 3.19 E |
| Kırıkkale | 130 | 39.50 N | 33.31 E |
| Kırıkkale □[4] | 130 | 40.00 N | 33.45 E |
| Kirillov | 76 | 59.52 N | 38.23 E |
| Kirillovka | 265b | 55.57 N | 37.20 E |
| Kirillovo, Ross. | 80 | 57.07 N | 45.27 E |
| Kirillovo, Ross. | 80 | 53.47 N | 42.40 E |
| Kirillovskoje | 76 | 60.28 N | 29.17 E |
| Kirin → Jilin | 89 | 43.51 N | 126.33 E |
| Kirin → Jilin □[4] | 90 | 44.00 N | 126.00 E |
| Kirinyaga (Mount Kenya) ∧ | 154 | 0.10 S | 37.20 E |
| Kirishima-Yaku-kokuritsu-kōen ♠ | 92 | 31.55 N | 130.51 E |
| Kirishima-yama ∧ | 92 | 31.56 N | 130.52 E |
| Kiriši | 76 | 59.27 N | 32.02 E |
| Kiritimati (Christmas Island) I[1] | 174o | 1.52 N | 157.20 W |
| Kiriwina Island I | 164 | 8.35 S | 151.05 E |
| Kiriwina Islands II | 164 | 8.35 S | 151.05 E |
| Kirizume-tōge ∧[2] | 270 | 34.56 N | 135.16 E |
| Kirjanovskaja Kontora | 88 | 58.18 N | 104.13 E |
| Kırka | 130 | 39.17 N | 30.33 E |
| Kirkabister | 46a | 60.07 N | 1.08 W |
| Kırkağaç | 130 | 39.06 N | 27.40 E |
| Kirkbride | 44 | 54.54 N | 3.12 W |
| Kirkburton | 44 | 53.37 N | 1.42 W |
| Kirkby | 44 | 53.29 N | 2.54 W |
| Kirkby in Ashfield | 44 | 53.06 N | 1.15 W |
| Kirkby Lonsdale | 44 | 54.13 N | 2.36 W |
| Kirkby Malzeard | 44 | 54.11 N | 1.38 W |
| Kirkbymoorside | 44 | 54.16 N | 0.55 W |
| Kirkby Stephen | 44 | 54.28 N | 2.20 W |
| Kirkcaldy | 46 | 56.07 N | 3.10 W |
| Kirkcolm | 44 | 54.58 N | 5.05 W |
| Kirkconnel | 44 | 55.23 N | 4.00 W |
| Kirkcudbright | 44 | 54.50 N | 4.03 W |
| Kirkcudbright Bay c | 44 | 54.48 N | 4.04 W |
| Kirkdale ◆[8] | 262 | 53.26 N | 2.59 W |
| Kirkeby | 41 | 56.09 N | 9.27 E |
| Kirkee → Khadki | 122 | 18.34 N | 73.52 E |
| Kirkel | 56 | 49.17 N | 7.13 E |
| Kirkenær | 26 | 60.28 N | 12.03 E |
| Kirkenes | 24 | 69.40 N | 30.03 E |
| Kirke Stillinge | 41 | 55.26 N | 11.15 E |
| Kirkham | 44 | 53.47 N | 2.53 W |
| Kirkhill | 46 | 57.28 N | 4.26 W |
| Kirkintilloch | 46 | 55.57 N | 4.10 W |
| Kirkjubæjarklaustur | 24a | 63.47 N | 18.04 W |
| Kirkkonummi → Kyrkslätt | 26 | 60.07 N | 24.26 E |
| Kirkland, P.Q., Can. | 275a | 45.27 N | 73.52 W |
| Kirkland, Il., U.S. | 216 | 42.05 N | 88.51 W |
| Kirkland, Tx., U.S. | 196 | 34.23 N | 100.04 W |
| Kirkland, Wa., U.S. | 224 | 47.40 N | 122.12 W |
| Kirkland Creek ≃ | 200 | 34.32 N | 113.00 W |
| Kirkland Lake | 190 | 48.09 N | 80.02 W |
| Kırklar Dağı ∧ | 130 | 40.32 N | 40.35 E |
| Kırklareli | 130 | 41.44 N | 27.12 E |
| Kırklareli □[4] | 130 | 41.40 N | 27.30 E |
| Kirklees □[8] | 262 | 53.36 N | 1.52 W |
| Kirkleydtich | 262 | 53.18 N | 2.12 W |
| Kirklin | 194 | 40.11 N | 86.21 W |
| Kirkliston | 46 | 55.58 N | 3.25 W |
| Kirk Michael, I. of Man | 44 | 54.17 N | 4.35 W |
| Kirkmichael, Scot., U.K. | 46 | 56.43 N | 3.29 W |
| Kirkmuirhill | 46 | 55.40 N | 3.55 W |
| Kirkness Lake ⊜ | 184 | 51.32 N | 93.56 W |
| Kirkpatrick, Mount ∧ | 9 | 84.20 S | 166.19 E |
| Kirkpatrick Lake ⊜ | 182 | 51.52 N | 111.18 W |
| Kirk Sandall | 44 | 53.33 N | 1.04 W |
| Kirksville, Il., U.S. | 219 | 39.34 N | 88.40 W |
| Kirksville, Mo., U.S. | 194 | 40.11 N | 92.34 W |
| Kirkton | 46 | 56.13 N | 2.55 W |
| Kirkton of Culsalmond | 46 | 57.23 N | 2.34 W |
| Kirkton of Glenisla | 46 | 56.44 N | 3.17 W |
| Kirktown of Auchterless | 46 | 57.27 N | 2.28 W |
| Kirkūk | 128 | 35.28 N | 44.28 E |
| Kirkville | 210 | 43.05 N | 75.57 W |
| Kirkwall | 46 | 58.59 N | 2.58 W |
| Kirkwood, S. Afr. | 158 | 33.24 S | 25.26 E |
| Kirkwood, De., U.S. | 208 | 39.34 N | 75.41 W |
| Kirkwood, Il., U.S. | 190 | 40.51 N | 90.44 W |
| Kirkwood, Mo., U.S. | 219 | 38.35 N | 90.24 W |
| Kirkwood, N.J., U.S. | 285 | 39.50 N | 75.01 W |
| Kirkwood, N.Y., U.S. | 210 | 42.02 N | 75.48 W |
| Kirmir ≃ | 130 | 40.07 N | 31.43 E |
| Kirn | 56 | 49.47 N | 7.28 E |
| Kirnāhar | 126 | 23.45 N | 87.52 E |
| Kirotshe | 154 | 1.37 S | 29.02 E |
| Kirov, Ross. | 76 | 54.05 N | 34.20 E |
| Kirov, Ross. | 80 | 58.38 N | 49.42 E |
| Kirovabad → Gäncä | 84 | 40.40 N | 46.22 E |
| Kirovakan | 84 | 40.48 N | 44.30 E |
| Kirove, Ukr. | 78 | 47.41 N | 35.46 E |
| Kirove, Ukr. | 83 | 48.23 N | 37.55 E |
| Kirovgrad | 86 | 57.26 N | 60.04 E |
| Kirovka | 86 | 47.07 N | 82.00 E |
| Kirovo, Ross. | 86 | 55.33 N | 63.46 E |
| Kirovo, Uzb. | 85 | 40.26 N | 70.34 E |
| Kirov Oblast' □[4] | 24 | 59.00 N | 50.00 E |
| Kirovo-Čepeck | 80 | 58.33 N | 50.01 E |
| Kirovohrad | 78 | 48.30 N | 32.18 E |
| Kirovohrad □[4] | 78 | 48.30 N | 32.00 E |
| Kirovsk, Ross. | 24 | 67.37 N | 33.35 E |
| Kirovsk, Ross. | 265a | 59.52 N | 31.00 E |
| Kirovsk, Turk. | 128 | 37.42 N | 60.23 E |
| Kirovs'k, Ukr. | 83 | 49.01 N | 37.56 E |
| Kirovs'k, Ukr. | 83 | 48.38 N | 38.39 E |
| Kirovs'ke, Ukr. | 78 | 48.33 N | 34.53 E |
| Kirovs'ke, Ukr. | 78 | 45.14 N | 35.13 E |
| Kirovs'ke, Ukr. | 83 | 48.09 N | 38.21 E |
| Kirovskij, Kaz. | 86 | 44.52 N | 78.12 E |
| Kirovskij, Ross. | 74 | 54.18 N | 155.47 E |
| Kirovskij, Ross. | 80 | 45.51 N | 48.07 E |
| Kirovskij, Ross. | 89 | 54.26 N | 126.55 E |
| Kirovskij, Ross. | 89 | 45.07 N | 133.30 E |
| Kirovskije ostrova II | 265a | 59.58 N | 30.15 E |
| Kirovskoje | 85 | 42.39 N | 71.35 E |
| Kirov Stadium ♠ | 265a | 59.58 N | 30.14 E |
| Kirov Theatre ʊ | 265a | 59.55 N | 30.18 E |
| Kirpičnyj Zavod | 265a | 60.01 N | 30.48 E |
| Kirpil'skaja | 78 | 45.23 N | 39.43 E |
| Kirriemuir | 46 | 56.41 N | 3.01 W |
| Kirs | 86 | 59.21 N | 52.14 E |
| Kirsanov | 80 | 52.38 N | 42.43 E |
| Kirsanovka | 80 | 52.30 N | 52.53 E |
| Kirschau | 54 | 51.04 N | 14.27 E |
| Kırşehir | 130 | 39.09 N | 34.10 E |
| Kırşehir □[4] | 130 | 39.20 N | 34.10 E |
| Kīrthar National Park ♠ | 120 | 25.50 N | 67.40 E |
| Kīrthar Range ⋀ | 120 | 27.00 N | 67.10 E |
| Kirtland, N.M., U.S. | 200 | 36.44 N | 108.21 W |
| Kirtland, Oh., U.S. | 214 | 41.37 N | 81.21 W |
| Kirtland Air Force Base ■ | 200 | 35.02 N | 106.37 W |
| Kirtland Hills | 214 | 41.37 N | 81.24 W |
| Kirtle Water ≃ | 44 | 54.58 N | 3.05 W |
| Kirton | 42 | 52.56 N | 0.04 W |
| Kirton in Lindsey | 44 | 53.28 N | 0.36 W |
| Kirtorf | 56 | 50.46 N | 9.06 E |
| Kiruna | 24 | 67.51 N | 20.16 E |
| Kirundu | 154 | 0.44 S | 25.32 E |
| Kirurumo | 154 | 5.53 S | 34.11 E |
| Kirvin | 222 | 31.46 N | 96.20 W |
| Kirwan Heights | 279b | 40.22 N | 80.06 W |
| Kirwee | 172 | 43.30 S | 172.13 E |
| Kirwin | 198 | 39.40 N | 99.07 W |
| Kirwin Reservoir ⊜[1] | 198 | 39.39 N | 99.10 W |
| Kiryandongo | 154 | 1.53 N | 32.03 E |
| Kiryū | 94 | 36.24 N | 139.20 E |
| Kirza | 86 | 54.14 N | 81.40 E |
| Kiržač | 82 | 56.09 N | 38.52 E |
| Kiržač ≃ | 82 | 55.52 N | 39.04 E |
| Kisa, Nihon | 96 | 34.43 N | 132.59 E |
| Kisa, Sve. | 26 | 57.59 N | 15.37 E |
| Kisai | 94 | 36.06 N | 139.35 E |
| Kisaichi | 270 | 34.46 N | 135.42 E |
| Kisakata | 92 | 39.13 N | 139.54 E |
| Kisaki | 154 | 7.28 S | 37.36 E |
| Kis Alföld ≍ | 61 | 47.35 N | 17.00 E |
| Kišaly | 76 | 54.23 N | 43.12 E |
| Kisambo | 152 | 6.25 S | 18.14 E |
| Kisanga | 154 | 2.29 N | 26.35 E |
| Kisangani (Stanleyville) | 154 | 0.30 N | 25.12 E |
| Kisantu | 152 | 5.07 S | 15.05 E |
| Kisar, Pulau I | 112 | 8.05 S | 127.10 E |
| Kisaralik ≃ | 180 | 60.51 N | 161.16 W |
| Kisaran | 114 | 2.59 N | 99.37 E |
| Kisarawe | 154 | 6.54 S | 39.04 E |
| Kisarazu | 94 | 35.23 N | 139.55 E |
| Kisarazu-Kichi, Kōkū-jieitai ■ | 94 | 35.24 N | 139.55 E |
| Kisawa | 96 | 33.49 N | 134.18 E |
| K.I. Sawyer Air Force Base ■ | 190 | 46.21 N | 87.25 W |
| Kisbér | 30 | 47.30 N | 18.02 E |
| Kisbey | 184 | 49.38 N | 102.41 W |
| Kise ≃ | 94 | 35.06 N | 138.53 E |
| Kiselevsk → Kisel'ovsk | 86 | 54.00 N | 86.39 E |
| Kisel'ovka | 80 | 47.18 N | 44.07 E |
| Kisel'ovsk | 86 | 54.00 N | 86.39 E |
| Kisengwa | 154 | 6.00 S | 25.50 E |
| Kisen-yama ∧[2] | 270 | 34.54 N | 135.51 E |
| Kiser Lake ⊜ | 218 | 40.11 N | 83.58 W |
| Kīsh, Jazīreh-ye I | 128 | 26.32 N | 53.56 E |
| Kishanda | 154 | 1.42 S | 31.34 E |
| Kishanganga ≃ | 123 | 34.22 N | 73.30 E |
| Kishanganj | 124 | 26.07 N | 87.56 E |
| Kishangarh | 120 | 27.52 N | 70.34 E |
| Kishangarh ◆[8] | 272a | 28.31 N | 77.08 E |
| Kishangarh Bās | 120 | 26.34 N | 74.52 E |
| Kishb, Harrat al- ⊥[9] | 144 | 23.00 N | 41.25 E |
| Kishi, Nig. | 150 | 9.05 N | 3.52 E |
| Kishi, Zaïre | 154 | 10.04 S | 26.26 E |
| Kishida ≃ | 96 | 35.38 N | 134.27 E |
| Kishigawa | 96 | 34.13 N | 135.20 E |
| Kishikas ≃ | 184 | 52.45 N | 91.43 W |
| Kishimoto | 96 | 35.23 N | 133.25 E |
| Kishinev → Chişinău | 38 | 47.00 N | 28.50 E |
| Kishiwada | 96 | 34.28 N | 135.22 E |
| Kishorganj | 124 | 24.26 N | 90.46 E |
| Kishorn, Loch c | 46 | 57.21 N | 5.41 W |
| Kishtwār | 123 | 33.19 N | 75.46 E |
| Kishwaukee ≃ | 216 | 42.11 N | 89.08 W |
| Kishwaukee, South Branch ≃ | 216 | 42.12 N | 88.59 W |
| Kisia | 152 | 4.35 S | 18.22 E |
| Kisigo ≃ | 154 | 7.03 S | 35.50 E |
| Kisii | 154 | 0.41 S | 34.46 E |
| Kisiju | 154 | 7.24 S | 39.20 E |
| Kiši-Karoj, ozero ⊜ | 86 | 54.03 N | 71.20 E |
| Kisika-zaki ≻ | 93b | 30.50 N | 131.04 E |
| Kısıklı ◆[8] | 267b | 41.01 N | 29.03 E |
| Kısır Dağı ∧ | 84 | 40.58 N | 43.04 E |
| Kısırkaya ◆[8] | 267b | 41.14 N | 28.58 E |
| Kısırmandıra ◆[8] | 267b | 41.14 N | 28.49 E |
| Kisiwada → Kishiwada | 96 | 34.28 N | 135.22 E |
| Kisiwani | 154 | 4.08 S | 37.57 E |
| Kisizi | 154 | 1.00 S | 29.56 E |
| Kiska Island I | 181a | 52.00 N | 177.30 E |
| Kiskatinaw ≃ | 182 | 56.06 N | 120.08 W |
| Kiska Volcano ∧[1] | 181a | 52.07 N | 177.36 E |
| Kis-Kevély ∧[2] | 264c | 47.38 N | 18.59 E |
| Kiski Lake ⊜ | 184 | 54.46 N | 98.55 W |
| Kiskimere | 279b | 40.37 N | 79.35 W |
| Kiskiminetas ≃ | 214 | 40.41 N | 79.40 W |
| Kiskittogisu Lake ⊜ | 184 | 54.13 N | 98.20 W |
| Kiskitto Lake ⊜ | 184 | 54.16 N | 98.34 W |
| Kiskörei-viztároló ⊜[1] | 30 | 47.35 N | 20.40 E |
| Kiskőrös | 30 | 46.38 N | 19.17 E |
| Kiskunfélegyháza | 30 | 46.43 N | 19.52 E |
| Kiskunhalas | 30 | 46.26 N | 19.30 E |
| Kiskunmajsa | 30 | 46.30 N | 19.45 E |
| Kiskunsági Nemzeti Park ♠ | 30 | 46.40 N | 19.25 E |
| Kisl'akovskaja | 78 | 46.27 N | 39.40 E |
| Kislovo | 80 | 49.54 N | 45.25 E |
| Kislovodsk | 84 | 43.55 N | 42.44 E |
| Kismaayo | 144 | 0.22 S | 42.32 E |
| Kismet | 276 | 40.38 N | 73.12 W |
| Kisnema | 76 | 60.20 N | 37.39 E |
| Kiso, Nihon | 94 | 35.56 N | 137.47 E |
| Kiso, Nihon | 268 | 35.34 N | 139.26 E |
| Kiso ≃ | 94 | 35.02 N | 136.45 E |
| Kisofukushima | 94 | 35.51 N | 137.42 E |
| Kisogawa | 94 | 35.20 N | 136.47 E |
| Kisoripur | 126 | 22.05 N | 88.34 E |
| Kisoro | 154 | 1.17 S | 29.41 E |
| Kiso-sammyaku ⋀ | 94 | 35.43 N | 137.50 E |
| Kisozaki | 94 | 35.04 N | 136.44 E |
| Kispest ◆[8] | 264c | 47.27 N | 19.08 E |
| Kispiox | 182 | 55.21 N | 127.41 W |
| Kispiox ≃ | 182 | 55.16 N | 127.41 W |
| Kispiox Mountain ∧ | 182 | 55.25 N | 127.57 W |
| Kissamos | 38 | 35.30 N | 23.38 E |
| Kissena Park ♠ | 276 | 40.45 N | 73.49 W |
| Kisseynew Lake ⊜ | 184 | 54.58 N | 101.35 W |
| Kissidougou | 150 | 9.11 N | 10.06 W |
| Kissimmee | 220 | 28.17 N | 81.24 W |
| Kissimmee ≃ | 220 | 27.10 N | 80.53 W |
| Kissimmee, Lake ⊜ | 220 | 27.55 N | 81.16 W |
| Kissing | 60 | 48.18 N | 10.59 E |
| Kississing | 184 | 55.07 N | 101.07 W |
| Kississing Lake ⊜ | 184 | 55.10 N | 101.20 W |
| Kisslegg | 58 | 47.47 N | 9.53 E |
| Kissū, Jabal ∧ | 140 | 21.35 N | 25.09 E |
| Kista | 80 | 46.05 N | 43.06 E |
| Kistanje | 36 | 43.59 N | 15.58 E |
| Kistarcsa | 264c | 47.33 N | 19.16 E |
| Kistendej | 80 | 52.08 N | 43.39 E |
| Kistigan Lake ⊜ | 184 | 54.38 N | 92.37 W |
| Kistler | 214 | 40.22 N | 77.51 W |
| Kisújszállás | 30 | 47.13 N | 20.46 E |
| Kisuki | 96 | 35.17 N | 132.54 E |
| Kisumu | 154 | 0.06 S | 34.45 E |
| Kisvárda | 30 | 48.13 N | 22.05 E |
| Kiswere | 154 | 9.26 S | 39.33 E |
| Kita | 150 | 13.03 N | 9.29 W |
| Kita ◆[8], Nihon | 268 | 35.45 N | 139.44 E |
| Kita ◆[8], Nihon | 270 | 34.45 N | 135.08 E |
| Kita ◆[8], Nihon | 270 | 34.42 N | 135.30 E |
| Kita ◆[8], Nihon | 270 | 35.03 N | 135.45 E |
| Kitaaiki | 94 | 36.04 N | 138.34 E |
| Kita-Daitō-jima I | 90 | 25.57 N | 131.18 E |
| Kitafuji-enshūjō ■ | 94 | 35.25 N | 138.48 E |
| Kitagata | 94 | 35.26 N | 136.41 E |
| Kitagawa | 96 | 33.27 N | 134.03 E |
| Kitagi-shima I | 96 | 34.23 N | 133.32 E |
| Kitaibaraki | 94 | 36.48 N | 140.45 E |
| Kitain Temple ʊ[1] | 268 | 35.54 N | 139.30 E |
| Kita-Iō-jima I | 14 | 25.26 N | 141.17 E |
| Kitairiso | 268 | 35.50 N | 139.26 E |
| Kitajima | 96 | 34.05 N | 134.35 E |
| Kitakami | 92 | 39.18 N | 141.07 E |
| Kitakami ≃ | 92 | 38.25 N | 141.19 E |
| Kitakami-kōchi ⋀ | 92 | 39.30 N | 141.30 E |
| Kitakata | 92 | 37.39 N | 139.52 E |
| Kitakyuschu → Kitakyūshū | 96 | 33.53 N | 130.50 E |
| Kitakyūshū | 96 | 33.53 N | 130.50 E |
| Kitakyushu-kokutei-kōen ♠ | 96 | 33.45 N | 130.50 E |
| Kitale | 154 | 1.01 N | 35.00 E |
| Kitamachi ◆[8] | 268 | 35.46 N | 139.39 E |
| Kitamba ◆[8] | 273b | 4.19 S | 15.14 E |
| Kitami | 92a | 43.48 N | 143.54 E |
| Kitami-sanchi ⋀ | 92a | 44.22 N | 142.43 E |
| Kitamoto | 94 | 36.02 N | 139.32 E |
| Kita-Nagato-kaigan-kokutei-kōen ♠ | 96 | 34.24 N | 131.16 E |
| Kitanakagusuku | 174m | 26.21 N | 127.51 E |
| Kitanda, Zaïre | 154 | 6.36 S | 26.27 E |
| Kitanda, Zaïre | 154 | 9.59 S | 27.28 E |
| Kitangari | 154 | 10.39 S | 39.20 E |
| Kitangiri, Lake ⊜ | 154 | 4.05 S | 34.19 E |
| Kitangua | 152 | 6.17 S | 20.22 E |
| Kitano, Nihon | 96 | 33.20 N | 130.35 E |
| Kitano, Nihon | 268 | 35.47 N | 139.26 E |
| Kitanoshinden | 268 | 35.48 N | 139.26 E |
| Kitatachibana | 94 | 36.29 N | 139.03 E |
| Kitatajima | 268 | 35.56 N | 139.30 E |
| Kitatawara | 270 | 34.44 N | 135.42 E |
| Kitaura | 94 | 36.04 N | 140.32 E |
| Kita-ura ⊜ | 94 | 36.00 N | 140.34 E |
| Kitava Island I | 164 | 8.40 S | 151.20 E |
| Kitaya | 154 | 10.39 S | 40.10 E |
| Kit Carson, Ca., U.S. | 226 | 38.41 N | 120.07 W |
| Kit Carson, Co., U.S. | 198 | 38.45 N | 102.47 W |
| Kitchener, Austl. | 162 | 31.02 S | 124.11 E |
| Kitchener, On., Can. | 212 | 43.27 N | 80.29 W |
| Kitee | 26 | 62.06 N | 30.09 E |
| Kitega → Gitega | 154 | 3.26 S | 29.56 E |
| Kiteiyab | 140 | 17.12 N | 33.43 E |
| Kitenda | 152 | 6.53 S | 17.21 E |
| Kitenevo | 82 | 56.21 N | 36.13 E |
| Kitengo | 152 | 7.26 S | 24.08 E |
| Kitéssa | 154 | 5.20 N | 25.20 E |
| Kitgum | 154 | 3.18 N | 32.53 E |
| Kíthira | 38 | 36.09 N | 23.00 E |
| Kíthira I | 38 | 36.20 N | 22.58 E |
| Kíthnos | 38 | 37.26 N | 24.26 E |
| Kíthnos I | 38 | 37.25 N | 24.28 E |
| Kitimat | 182 | 54.03 N | 128.33 W |
| Kitimat ≃ | 182 | 54.06 N | 128.38 W |
| Kitimat Ranges ⋀ | 182 | 53.30 N | 128.50 W |
| Kitinen ≃ | 24 | 67.08 N | 27.29 E |
| Kitíou, Akrotírion ≻ | 130 | 34.48 N | 33.36 E |
| Kitlope ≃ | 182 | 53.10 N | 127.45 W |
| Kitlope Lake ⊜ | 182 | 53.07 N | 127.47 W |
| Kitō, Nihon | 94 | 34.42 N | 138.03 E |
| Kitō, Nihon | 96 | 33.46 N | 134.12 E |
| Kitoj ≃ | 88 | 52.39 N | 103.56 E |
| Kitridge Point ≻ | 241g | 13.09 N | 59.25 W |
| Kitsap □[6] | 224 | 47.41 N | 122.44 W |
| Kitscoty | 184 | 53.20 N | 110.20 W |
| Kit's Coty House ʊ | 260 | 51.19 N | 0.30 E |
| Kitshua-Nseke | 152 | 4.26 S | 19.36 E |
| Kitsman' | 78 | 48.27 N | 25.44 E |
| Kitsuki | 92 | 33.25 N | 131.37 E |
| Kitsuregawa | 94 | 36.43 N | 140.01 E |
| Kittanning | 214 | 40.48 N | 79.31 W |
| Kittatinny Mountain ∧ | 210 | 41.10 N | 74.55 W |
| Kittatinny Tunnel ◆[5] | 214 | 40.09 N | 77.41 W |
| Kittendorf | 54 | 53.37 N | 12.54 E |
| Kittery | 188 | 43.05 N | 70.44 W |
| Kitt Green | 262 | 53.33 N | 2.41 W |
| Kittilä | 24 | 67.40 N | 24.54 E |
| Kittitas | 202 | 46.59 N | 120.24 W |
| Kittitas □[6] | 224 | 47.13 N | 121.01 W |
| Kitt Peak National Observatory ʊ[3] | 200 | 31.58 N | 111.36 W |
| Kittsee | 61 | 48.05 N | 17.04 E |
| Kitu | 154 | 7.38 S | 27.42 E |
| Kitui | 154 | 1.22 S | 38.01 E |
| Kitumbeine ∧[1] | 154 | 2.44 S | 36.16 E |
| Kitunda | 154 | 6.48 S | 33.13 E |
| Kitutu | 154 | 3.17 S | 28.05 E |
| Kitwanga | 182 | 55.06 N | 128.03 W |
| Kitwangar Indian Reserve ◆[4] | 182 | 55.06 N | 128.04 W |
| Kitwe | 154 | 12.49 S | 28.13 E |
| Kitwitwi | 156 | 17.25 S | 18.25 E |
| Kityang → Jieyang | 100 | 23.35 N | 116.21 E |
| Kitzbühel | 64 | 47.27 N | 12.23 E |
| Kitzbüheler Alpen ⋀ | 64 | 47.20 N | 12.20 E |
| Kitzingen | 56 | 49.44 N | 10.09 E |
| Kitzscher | 54 | 51.09 N | 12.33 E |
| Kiukiang → Jiujiang | 100 | 29.44 N | 115.59 E |
| Kiukiu, Pointe ≻ | 174x | 9.47 S | 139.09 W |
| Kiul | 124 | 25.09 N | 86.06 E |
| Kiunga, Kenya | 154 | 1.45 S | 41.29 E |
| Kiunga, Pap. N. Gui. | 164 | 6.10 S | 141.15 E |
| Kiuruvesi | 26 | 63.39 N | 26.37 E |
| Kiuschu → Kyūshū I | 92 | 33.00 N | 131.00 E |
| Kivak | 180 | 64.16 N | 172.57 W |
| Kivalina | 180 | 67.44 N | 164.33 W |
| Kiveriči | 76 | 57.22 N | 36.36 E |
| Kivertsi | 78 | 50.50 N | 25.27 E |
| Kivijärvi | 26 | 63.04 N | 25.03 E |
| Kivijärvi ⊜ | 26 | 63.10 N | 25.09 E |
| Kivik | 26 | 55.41 N | 14.15 E |
| Kiviõli | 76 | 59.21 N | 26.57 E |
| Kivshyvata | 78 | 49.29 N | 30.38 E |
| Kivu, Lac ⊜ | 154 | 2.00 S | 29.10 E |
| Kiwaba N'zogi | 152 | 8.57 S | 16.32 E |
| Kiwai Island I | 164 | 8.30 S | 143.25 E |
| Kiwalik | 180 | 66.02 N | 161.50 W |
| Kiwanis Lake | 214 | 41.28 N | 81.09 W |
| Kiyama | 96 | 33.25 N | 130.32 E |
| Kīyāmakī Dāgh ∧ | 84 | 38.47 N | 45.51 E |
| Kiyan | 174m | 26.05 N | 127.40 E |


**Symbols** in the index entries represent the broad categories identified in the key at the right. Symbols with superior numbers (⋀[1]) identify subcategories (see complete key on page *I · 1).*

**Symbole** im Register stellen die rechts im Schlüssel erklärten Kategorien dar. Symbole mit hochgestellten Ziffern (⋀[1]) bezeichnen Unterabteilungen einer Kategorie (vgl. vollständiger Schlüssel auf Seite *I · 1).*

**Los símbolos** incluídos en el texto del índice representan las grandes categorías identificadas con la clave a la derecha. Los símbolos con numeros en su parte superior (⋀[1]) identifican las subcategorías (véase la clave completa en la página *I · 1).*

**Les symboles** de l'index représentent les catégories indiquées dans la légende à droite. Les symboles suivis d'un indice (⋀[1]) représentent des sous-catégories (voir légende complète à la page *I · 1).*

**Os símbolos** incluídos no texto do índice representam as grandes categorias identificadas com a chave à direita. Os símbolos com números em sua parte superior (⋀[1]) identificam as subcategorias (veja-se a chave completa à página *I · 1).*

| | | | | | |
|---|---|---|---|---|---|
| ∧ Mountain | Berg | Montaña | Montagne | Montanha |
| ⋀ Mountains | Gebirge | Montañas | Montagnes | Montanhas |
| )( Pass | Paß | Paso | Col | Passo |
| ∨ Valley, Canyon | Tal, Cañon | Valle, Cañón | Vallée, Canyon | Vale, Canhão |
| ≍ Plain | Ebene | Llano | Plaine | Planície |
| ≻ Cape | Kap | Cabo | Cap | Cabo |
| I Island | Insel | Isla | Île | Ilha |
| II Islands | Inseln | Islas | Îles | Ilhas |
| ⊥ Other Topographic Features | Andere Topographische Objekte | Otros Elementos Topográficos | Autres données topographiques | Outros acidentes topográficos |

**ESPAÑOL**

| Nombre | Página | Lat.°′ | Long.°′ W = Oeste |
|---|---|---|---|
| Kiyan-zaki › | 174m | 26.05 N | 127.39 E |
| Kıyıköy | 130 | 41.38 N | 28.05 E |
| Kiyiu Lake ⊜ | 184 | 51.38 N | 108.55 W |
| Kiyl ≃ | 86 | 49.25 N | 54.50 E |
| Kiyokawa | 94 | 35.29 N | 139.17 E |
| Kiyomi | 94 | 36.07 N | 137.11 E |
| Kiyosawa | 94 | 35.03 N | 138.15 E |
| Kiyose | 94 | 35.47 N | 139.32 E |
| Kiyosu | 94 | 35.13 N | 136.50 E |
| Kiyosumi-yama ∧ | 94 | 35.09 N | 140.09 E |
| Kiyotani | 270 | 34.52 N | 134.59 E |
| Kiyotsu ≃ | 94 | 37.03 N | 138.41 E |
| Kizel | 86 | 59.03 N | 57.40 E |
| Kizevatovo | 80 | 53.13 N | 45.18 E |
| Kızıl ≃ | 130 | 41.44 N | 35.58 E |
| Kızıl Adalar II | 130 | 40.52 N | 29.05 E |
| Kızılcabölük | 130 | 37.37 N | 29.01 E |
| Kızılcadağ | 130 | 37.01 N | 29.58 E |
| Kızılcahamam | 130 | 40.28 N | 32.39 E |
| Kızılçakçak | 84 | 40.46 N | 43.37 E |
| Kızıldağ Milli Parkı ♠ | 130 | 37.58 N | 31.28 E |
| Kızıldikme | 130 | 39.05 N | 37.01 E |
| Kızılhisar | 130 | 37.33 N | 29.18 E |
| Kızılırmak | 130 | 40.21 N | 33.59 E |
| Kızılören | 130 | 37.52 N | 32.07 E |
| Kizil'skoje | 86 | 52.44 N | 58.54 E |
| Kızılsu | 130 | 37.28 N | 42.13 E |
| Kiziltašskij liman ⊂ | 78 | 45.07 N | 37.05 E |
| Kızıltepe | 130 | 37.12 N | 40.36 E |
| Kızıltoprak ◆ [8] | 267b | 40.58 N | 29.03 E |
| Kizil'urt | 84 | 43.12 N | 46.53 E |
| Kızılyaka | 130 | 37.09 N | 32.54 E |
| Kižimiz, gora ∧ | 24 | 63.12 N | 58.48 E |
| Kizimkazi | 154 | 6.27 S | 39.28 E |
| Kižinga | 88 | 51.51 N | 109.55 E |
| Kizir ≃ | 86 | 53.51 N | 93.06 E |
| Kızkalesi ⊥ | 130 | 36.28 N | 34.04 E |
| Kızkulesi ◆ [5] | 267b | 41.01 N | 29.00 E |
| Kizl'ar | 84 | 43.50 N | 46.40 E |
| Kizl'arskij zaliv ⊂ | 84 | 44.33 N | 46.55 E |
| Kizner | 80 | 56.17 N | 51.31 E |
| Kiz'oma | 24 | 61.08 N | 44.50 E |
| Kizu | 96 | 34.44 N | 135.49 E |
| Kizu ≃ | 94 | 34.53 N | 135.42 E |
| Kizuki | 268 | 35.34 N | 139.40 E |
| Kizuri | 270 | 34.39 N | 135.34 E |
| Kizyl-Ajak | 128 | 37.40 N | 65.23 E |
| Kizyl-Arvat | 128 | 38.58 N | 56.15 E |
| Kizyl-Atrek | 128 | 37.36 N | 54.46 E |
| Kizyl-Su | 128 | 39.48 N | 53.01 E |
| Kjellerup | 41 | 56.17 N | 9.26 E |
| Kjøbenhavn → København | 41 | 55.40 N | 12.35 E |
| Kjustendil | 38 | 42.17 N | 22.41 E |
| Klaarstroom | 158 | 33.20 S | 22.32 E |
| Klaaswaal | 52 | 51.46 N | 4.26 E |
| Klabat, Gunung ∧ | 112 | 1.28 N | 125.02 E |
| Kladanj | 38 | 44.13 N | 18.41 E |
| Kladbišči | 80 | 55.32 N | 45.33 E |
| Kläden | 54 | 52.38 N | 11.39 E |
| Kladkovo | 82 | 55.24 N | 38.51 E |
| Kladno | 54 | 50.08 N | 14.05 E |
| Kladovo | 38 | 44.37 N | 22.37 E |
| Kladow ◆ [8] | 54 | 52.27 N | 13.09 E |
| Kladruby | 60 | 49.43 N | 12.59 E |
| Klaeng | 110 | 12.47 N | 101.39 E |
| Klagan | 112 | 5.58 N | 117.27 E |
| Klagenfurt | 61 | 46.37 N | 14.18 E |
| Klågerup | 41 | 55.36 N | 13.15 E |
| Klagshamn | 41 | 55.32 N | 12.55 E |
| Klagstorp | 41 | 55.24 N | 13.22 E |
| Klahoose Indian Reserve ◆ [4] | 182 | 50.31 N | 124.19 W |
| Klaipėda (Memel) | 76 | 55.43 N | 21.07 E |
| Klakah | 115a | 7.59 S | 113.15 E |
| Klamath | 204 | 41.31 N | 124.02 W |
| Klamath ≃ | 204 | 41.33 N | 124.04 W |
| Klamath Falls | 202 | 42.13 N | 121.46 W |
| Klamath Marsh ≡ | 202 | 42.54 N | 121.44 W |
| Klamath Mountains ⋏ | 204 | 41.40 N | 123.20 W |
| K. Lamido | 146 | 9.21 N | 11.12 E |
| Klämmingen ⊜ | 40 | 59.07 N | 17.15 E |
| Klammpass )( | 64 | 47.17 N | 13.05 E |
| Klamono | 164 | 1.08 S | 131.30 E |
| Klang → Kelang | 114 | 3.02 N | 101.27 E |
| Klangenan | 115a | 6.42 S | 108.26 E |
| Klangpi | 110 | 22.59 N | 93.20 E |
| Klarälven (Trysilelva) ≃ | 26 | 59.23 N | 13.32 E |
| Kl'as'ma | 265b | 55.59 N | 37.50 E |
| Klášterec | 54 | 50.24 N | 13.10 E |
| Klaten | 115a | 7.42 S | 110.35 E |
| Klatovy | 60 | 49.24 N | 13.18 E |
| Klausdorf, Dtsch. | 54 | 54.18 N | 10.15 E |
| Klausdorf, Dtsch. | 54 | 54.20 N | 13.01 E |
| Klausenburg → Cluj-Napoca | 38 | 46.47 N | 23.36 E |
| Klausenpass )( | 58 | 46.52 N | 8.51 E |
| Kl'avlino | 80 | 54.17 N | 52.01 E |
| Klawer | 158 | 31.44 S | 18.36 E |
| Klawock | 182 | 55.33 N | 133.06 W |
| Klazienaveen | 52 | 52.44 N | 7.00 E |
| Kl'az'ma | 82 | 55.58 N | 37.27 E |
| Kl'az'ma ≃ | 80 | 56.10 N | 42.58 E |
| Kl'az'minskoje vodochranilišče ⊜ [1] | 265b | 55.59 N | 37.35 E |
| Kleck | 76 | 53.04 N | 26.38 E |
| Klecko | 30 | 52.38 N | 17.26 E |
| Kleczew | 30 | 52.23 N | 18.10 E |
| Kledering ◆ [8] | 264b | 48.08 N | 16.26 E |
| Kleef | 263 | 51.11 N | 6.56 E |
| Kleena Kleene | 182 | 51.57 N | 124.50 W |
| Kleinasien → Asia Minor □ [9] | 22 | 39.00 N | 32.00 E |
| Kleinbegin | 158 | 28.50 S | 21.36 E |
| Klein-Blesbokspruit ≃ | 273d | 26.16 S | 28.29 E |
| Kleinbodungen | 54 | 51.28 N | 10.32 E |
| Klein Bonaire I | 241s | 12.10 N | 68.18 W |
| Klein Bünzow | 54 | 53.53 N | 13.48 E |
| Kleinburg | 275b | 43.50 N | 79.38 W |
| Klein Curaçao I | 241s | 12.00 N | 68.40 W |
| Kleine Elster ≃ | 54 | 51.32 N | 13.23 E |
| Kleine Emme ≃ | 58 | 47.04 N | 8.17 E |
| Kleine Emscher ≃ | 263 | 51.31 N | 6.43 E |
| Kleine Erlauf ≃ | 61 | 48.07 N | 15.08 E |
| Kleineichen | 263 | 51.08 N | 7.21 E |
| Kleine Laber ≃ | 60 | 48.55 N | 12.31 E |
| Kleinenberg | 52 | 51.35 N | 8.58 E |
| Kleinenbroich | 263 | 51.12 N | 6.35 E |
| Kleiner Jasmunder Bodden ⊂ | 54 | 54.28 N | 13.32 E |
| Kleiner Ravens-Berg ∧ [2] | 264a | 52.22 N | 13.04 E |
| Kleiner Wannsee ⊜ | 264a | 52.25 N | 13.10 E |
| Kleiner Zern-See ⊜ | 264a | 52.26 N | 12.55 E |
| Kleine Spree ≃ | 54 | 51.31 N | 14.24 E |
| Kleines Walsertal V | 64 | 47.23 N | 10.12 E |
| Kleinfeltersville | 208 | 40.18 N | 76.15 W |
| Kleinglödnitz | 61 | 46.51 N | 14.08 E |
| Kleinhammer | 263 | 51.14 N | 7.46 E |
| Klein-Jukskei ≃ | 273d | 26.08 S | 27.56 E |
| Klein-Karas | 156 | 27.32 S | 18.06 E |
| Klein Karroo → Little Karroo ⋏ [1] | 158 | 33.45 S | 21.30 E |
| Klein Kienitz | 264a | 52.18 N | 13.29 E |
| Kleinlützel | 58 | 47.26 N | 7.25 E |
| Kleinmachnow | 54 | 52.24 N | 13.15 E |
| Klein Marzehns | 54 | 52.01 N | 12.37 E |
| Kleinmond | 158 | 34.21 S | 19.03 E |
| Klein-Olifants ≃ | 158 | 25.41 S | 29.19 E |
| Kleinschönebeck | 264a | 52.29 N | 13.43 E |
| Klein-Soutpan | 158 | 30.26 S | 22.26 E |
| Klein-Vis ≃ | 158 | 33.05 S | 26.00 E |
| Klein Wanzleben | 54 | 52.04 N | 11.21 E |
| Klein Ziethen | 264a | 52.23 N | 13.27 E |
| Klein Ziethener-Berge ∧ [2] | 264a | 52.22 N | 13.26 E |
| Klekovača ∧ | 36 | 44.26 N | 16.31 E |
| Klementjevka | 86 | 50.16 N | 80.56 E |

**FRANÇAIS**

| Nom | Page | Lat.°′ | Long.°′ W = Ouest |
|---|---|---|---|
| Klementjevo | 82 | 55.38 N | 36.01 E |
| Klemme | 190 | 43.00 N | 93.36 W |
| Klemtu | 182 | 52.36 N | 128.31 W |
| Klenovka | 80 | 57.45 N | 54.19 E |
| Klenovo | 82 | 55.19 N | 37.21 E |
| Klerksdorp | 158 | 26.58 S | 26.39 E |
| Klerkskraal | 158 | 26.15 S | 27.10 E |
| Klesiv | 78 | 51.19 N | 26.54 E |
| Klésso | 150 | 10.57 N | 3.59 W |
| Klet' ∧ | 61 | 48.52 N | 14.17 E |
| Kletn'a | 76 | 53.23 N | 33.12 E |
| Kletskij | 80 | 49.19 N | 43.04 E |
| Kletsko-Počtovskij | 80 | 49.36 N | 43.03 E |
| Klettgau ◆ [1] | 58 | 47.40 N | 8.25 E |
| Klettwitz | 54 | 51.32 N | 13.53 E |
| Klevan' | 78 | 50.44 N | 26.02 E |
| Kleve | 52 | 51.48 N | 6.09 E |
| Klevenka | 80 | 52.07 N | 49.33 E |
| Kley ◆ [8] | 263 | 51.30 N | 7.22 E |
| Klibreck, Ben ∧ | 46 | 58.14 N | 4.22 W |
| Kličau | 76 | 53.29 N | 29.21 E |
| Klička | 88 | 50.26 N | 118.00 E |
| Klickitat | 224 | 45.49 N | 121.09 W |
| Klickitat □ [6] | 224 | 45.50 N | 121.07 W |
| Klickitat ≃ | 224 | 45.42 N | 121.17 W |
| Kliedbruch ◆ [1] | 263 | 51.22 N | 6.33 E |
| Klieken | 54 | 51.53 N | 12.22 E |
| Klietz | 54 | 52.40 N | 12.04 E |
| Klimavičy | 76 | 53.37 N | 31.58 E |
| Klimino | 88 | 58.39 N | 98.42 E |
| Klimovo, Ross. | 76 | 52.23 N | 32.11 E |
| Klimovo, Ross. | 82 | 55.22 N | 38.52 E |
| Klimovsk | 82 | 55.22 N | 37.32 E |
| Klimovskoje | 82 | 54.42 N | 37.48 E |
| Klimov Zavod | 76 | 54.50 N | 34.55 E |
| Klimpfjäll | 24 | 65.04 N | 14.52 E |
| Klin, Ross. | 82 | 56.20 N | 36.44 E |
| Klin, Ross. | 82 | 55.19 N | 36.20 E |
| Klinaklini ≃ | 182 | 51.05 N | 125.36 W |
| Klin-Bel'din | 82 | 54.45 N | 39.13 E |
| Klincovka | 80 | 51.41 N | 49.11 E |
| Klincy | 76 | 52.47 N | 32.14 E |
| Kline Ditch ≊ | 279a | 41.28 N | 82.04 W |
| Kling | 116 | 5.58 N | 124.42 E |
| Klingbach ≃ | 56 | 49.10 N | 8.20 E |
| Klingenberg | 54 | 50.55 N | 13.31 E |
| Klingenberg am Main | 56 | 49.47 N | 9.11 E |
| Klingenmünster | 56 | 49.08 N | 8.01 E |
| Klingenthal | 54 | 50.21 N | 12.28 E |
| Klinger Lake ⊜ | 216 | 41.47 N | 85.33 W |
| Klingerstown | 208 | 40.40 N | 76.41 W |
| Klinghardtberge ∧ | 156 | 27.18 S | 15.48 E |
| Klingnau | 58 | 47.35 N | 8.15 E |
| Klink | 54 | 53.29 N | 12.37 E |
| Klínovec ∧ | 54 | 50.24 N | 12.58 E |
| Klinsko-Dmitrovskaja gr'ada ∧ | 82 | 56.15 N | 37.30 E |
| Klintehamn | 26 | 57.24 N | 18.12 E |
| Klintsy → Klincy | 76 | 52.47 N | 32.14 E |
| Klip ≃, S. Afr. | 158 | 27.03 S | 29.03 E |
| Klip ≃, S. Afr. | 273d | 26.19 S | 27.53 E |
| Klipbakken | 158 | 28.50 S | 21.21 E |
| Klipdale | 158 | 34.19 S | 19.57 E |
| Klipdam | 158 | 27.35 S | 19.56 E |
| Kliplev | 41 | 54.56 N | 9.25 E |
| Klippan | 41 | 56.08 N | 13.06 E |
| Klipplaat | 158 | 33.02 S | 24.21 E |
| Klippoortjie | 273d | 26.13 S | 28.10 E |
| Klipriviersberg ⋏ | 273d | 26.17 S | 28.02 E |
| Kliptown | 273d | 26.17 S | 27.53 E |
| Klipwerf | 158 | 31.09 S | 19.52 E |
| Klishkivtsi | 78 | 48.26 N | 26.15 E |
| Klisura | 38 | 42.42 N | 24.27 E |
| Klitmøller | 26 | 57.02 N | 8.31 E |
| Klitten | 54 | 51.20 N | 14.36 E |
| Klixbüll | 41 | 54.48 N | 8.53 E |
| Kljascicy | 76 | 55.53 N | 28.36 E |
| Ključ | 36 | 44.32 N | 16.47 E |
| Klobbicke | 264a | 52.46 N | 13.48 E |
| Klobouky | 61 | 49.00 N | 16.52 E |
| Kłobuck | 30 | 50.55 N | 18.57 E |
| Klobuticy | 76 | 58.35 N | 29.35 E |
| Kłodawa | 30 | 52.16 N | 18.55 E |
| Kłodzko | 30 | 50.27 N | 16.39 E |
| Kløfta | 26 | 60.04 N | 11.09 E |
| Kłomnice | 30 | 50.56 N | 19.21 E |
| Klondike | 216 | 40.28 N | 86.57 W |
| Klondike □ [9] | 180 | 63.30 N | 139.00 W |
| Klondike ≃ | 180 | 64.05 N | 139.26 W |
| Klöntaler See ⊜ | 58 | 47.02 N | 8.58 E |
| Klooga | 76 | 59.19 N | 24.16 E |
| Kloosterveen | 52 | 52.59 N | 6.33 E |
| Kloosterzande | 52 | 51.22 N | 4.02 E |
| Kloster | 54 | 54.35 N | 13.06 E |
| Klosterfelde | 54 | 52.48 N | 13.28 E |
| Klosterhardt ◆ [8] | 263 | 51.31 N | 6.53 E |
| Klösterle | 58 | 47.08 N | 10.05 E |
| Klostermansfeld | 54 | 51.35 N | 11.29 E |
| Klosterneuburg | 61 | 48.18 N | 16.20 E |
| Kloster Oesede | 52 | 52.12 N | 8.07 E |
| Klosters | 58 | 46.54 N | 9.53 E |
| Klostertal V | 58 | 47.08 N | 9.59 E |
| Kloster Zinna | 54 | 52.01 N | 13.07 E |
| Kloten, Schw. | 58 | 47.27 N | 8.35 E |
| Kloten, Sve. | 40 | 59.54 N | 15.17 E |
| Klotz, Lac ⊜ | 176 | 60.32 N | 73.40 W |
| Klötze | 54 | 52.38 N | 11.10 E |
| Kloulklubed | 175b | 7.02 N | 134.15 E |
| Klouto | 150 | 6.57 N | 0.34 E |
| Kluane ≃ | 180 | 61.53 N | 139.43 W |
| Kluane Lake ⊜ | 180 | 61.15 N | 138.40 W |
| Kluane National Park ♠ | 180 | 60.45 N | 139.30 W |
| Kluang | 112 | 2.41 S | 103.54 E |
| Kl'učevaja | 24 | 65.16 N | 41.32 E |
| Kl'učevskaja Sopka, vulkan ∧ [1] | 74 | 56.04 N | 160.38 E |
| Kl'učevskij | 88 | 53.33 N | 119.26 E |
| Kluchorskij, pereval )( | 84 | 43.15 N | 41.54 E |
| Kl'uči, Ross. | 74 | 56.18 N | 160.51 E |
| Kl'uči, Ross. | 80 | 51.59 N | 46.31 E |
| Kl'uči, Ross. | 80 | 51.26 N | 45.11 E |
| Kl'uči, Ross. | 86 | 52.16 N | 79.10 E |
| Kl'učovka, Kyrg. | 85 | 42.34 N | 71.48 E |
| Kl'učovka, Ross. | 86 | 51.22 N | 55.48 E |
| Kluczbork | 30 | 50.59 N | 18.13 E |
| Kluess | 54 | 53.46 N | 12.14 E |
| Kluet ≃ | 114 | 3.04 N | 97.20 E |
| Kl'ukvenka | 86 | 58.34 N | 85.55 E |
| Klukwan | 180 | 59.24 N | 135.54 W |
| Klundert | 52 | 51.40 N | 4.32 E |
| Klungkung | 115b | 8.32 S | 115.24 E |
| Klüppelberg | 56 | 51.06 N | 7.28 E |
| Klüterthöhle ✦ [5] | 52 | 51.18 N | 7.21 E |
| Klutina Lake ⊜ | 180 | 61.37 N | 146.55 W |
| Klütz | 54 | 53.58 N | 11.10 E |
| Klynkyne | 83 | 47.17 N | 38.15 E |
| Knaben gruver | 26 | 58.39 N | 7.04 E |
| Knaddah | 130 | 35.45 N | 36.12 E |
| Kn'aginino | 80 | 55.49 N | 45.03 E |
| Knaik ≃ | 46 | 56.14 N | 3.52 W |
| Knapdaar | 158 | 30.43 S | 26.09 E |
| Knapdale ◆ [1] | 46 | 55.55 N | 5.30 W |
| Knaphill | 260 | 51.19 N | 0.37 W |
| Knapp | 190 | 44.57 N | 92.04 W |
| Knapp Creek | 210 | 42.00 N | 78.30 W |
| Knappenberg | 61 | 46.56 N | 14.35 E |
| Knäred | 26 | 56.32 N | 13.19 E |
| Knaresborough | 44 | 54.00 N | 1.27 W |
| Knargram | 126 | 24.01 N | 87.59 E |
| Knauertown | 285 | 40.10 N | 75.44 W |
| Kn'ažaja Bajgora | 76 | 52.23 N | 40.02 E |
| Kn'azevka | 86 | 57.35 N | 74.10 E |
| Kn'ažji Gory | 76 | 56.05 N | 35.14 E |
| Kn'ažovo | 76 | 59.40 N | 43.54 E |
| Knebel | 41 | 56.13 N | 10.30 E |
| Knebworth | 42 | 51.52 N | 0.12 W |
| Kneehills Creek ≃ | 182 | 51.30 N | 112.50 W |

**PORTUGUÊS**

| Nome | Página | Lat.°′ | Long.°′ W = Oeste |
|---|---|---|---|
| Knee Lake ⊜, Mb., Can. | 184 | 55.03 N | 94.40 W |
| Knee Lake ⊜, Sk., Can. | 184 | 55.51 N | 107.00 W |
| Knesebeck | 54 | 52.41 N | 10.42 E |
| Knesselare | 50 | 51.08 N | 3.25 E |
| Knetzgau | 56 | 50.00 N | 10.33 E |
| Knevicy | 76 | 57.56 N | 32.14 E |
| Kneža | 38 | 43.30 N | 24.05 E |
| Knić | 38 | 43.55 N | 20.43 E |
| Knickerbocker | 196 | 31.16 N | 100.38 W |
| Kniebis | 58 | 48.28 N | 8.17 E |
| Knife ≃ | 198 | 47.20 N | 101.23 W |
| Knife Lake ⊜ | 184 | 53.47 N | 91.20 W |
| Knife River Indian Villages National Historic Site ⊥ | 198 | 47.21 N | 101.23 W |
| Knight Inlet ⊂ | 182 | 50.41 N | 125.40 W |
| Knight Island I | 180 | 60.20 N | 147.45 W |
| Knighton | 42 | 52.21 N | 3.03 W |
| Knightsen | 226 | 37.58 N | 121.40 W |
| Knights Landing | 226 | 38.47 N | 121.43 W |
| Knightstown | 218 | 39.47 N | 85.31 W |
| Knightville Dam ◆ [6] | 207 | 42.17 N | 72.52 W |
| Knik Arm ⊂ | 180 | 61.25 N | 149.45 W |
| Knin | 36 | 44.02 N | 16.12 E |
| Knippa | 196 | 29.18 N | 99.38 W |
| Knislinge | 26 | 56.11 N | 14.05 E |
| Knittelfeld | 61 | 47.14 N | 14.50 E |
| Knittlingen | 56 | 49.01 N | 8.45 E |
| Knivsbjerg ∧ [2] | 41 | 55.08 N | 9.27 E |
| Knivsta | 40 | 59.43 N | 17.48 E |
| Knjaževac | 38 | 43.34 N | 22.16 E |
| Knob, Cape › | 162 | 34.32 S | 119.16 E |
| Knobby Head › | 162 | 29.40 S | 114.58 E |
| Knob Noster | 194 | 38.45 N | 93.33 W |
| Knob Peak ∧ | 116 | 12.28 N | 121.21 E |
| Knoc | 48 | 52.38 N | 9.20 W |
| Knock | 46 | 57.33 N | 2.45 W |
| Knockholt | 260 | 51.18 N | 0.06 E |
| Knockholt Pound | 260 | 51.19 N | 0.08 E |
| Knocklayd ∧ | 48 | 55.09 N | 6.15 W |
| Knocklong | 48 | 52.26 N | 8.24 W |
| Knockmealdown Mountains ⋏ | 48 | 52.10 N | 8.00 W |
| Knokke | 50 | 51.21 N | 3.17 E |
| Knole ⊥ | 260 | 51.16 N | 0.12 E |
| Knolls Green | 262 | 53.19 N | 2.18 W |
| Knollwood, Ct., U.S. | 207 | 41.16 N | 72.23 W |
| Knollwood, Il., U.S. | 278 | 42.17 N | 87.53 W |
| Knollwood, Md., U.S. | 284c | 39.02 N | 76.58 W |
| Knollwood Park | 216 | 42.14 N | 84.22 W |
| Knon ⊜ | 40 | 60.12 N | 13.40 E |
| Knossós ⊥ | 38 | 35.20 N | 25.10 E |
| Knottingley | 44 | 53.43 N | 1.14 W |
| Knott's Berry Farm ♠ | 280 | 33.50 N | 118.00 W |
| Knotts Island | 208 | 36.31 N | 75.56 W |
| Knotty Ash ◆ [8] | 262 | 53.25 N | 2.54 W |
| Knotty Green | 260 | 51.37 N | 0.39 W |
| Knowland State Arboretum and Park ♠ | 282 | 37.45 N | 122.09 W |
| Knowle | 42 | 52.23 N | 1.43 W |
| Knowlesville | 210 | 43.14 N | 78.19 W |
| Knowlton Lake ⊜ | 212 | 44.28 N | 76.41 W |
| Knowltonwood | 285 | 39.53 N | 75.24 W |
| Knowsley | 262 | 53.27 N | 2.51 W |
| Knowsley □ [8] | 262 | 53.27 N | 2.50 W |
| Knowsley Hall ʊ | 262 | 53.26 N | 2.50 W |
| Knowsley Park ♠ | 262 | 53.27 N | 2.49 W |
| Knox, In., U.S. | 216 | 41.17 N | 86.37 W |
| Knox, N.Y., U.S. | 210 | 42.40 N | 74.07 W |
| Knox, Pa., U.S. | 214 | 41.14 N | 79.32 W |
| Knox □ [6], Mo., U.S. | 219 | 40.08 N | 92.09 W |
| Knox □ [6], Oh., U.S. | 214 | 40.23 N | 82.29 W |
| Knox, Cape › | 182 | 54.11 N | 133.04 W |
| Knoxboro | 210 | 42.58 N | 75.36 W |
| Knox City, Mo., U.S. | 219 | 40.08 N | 92.00 W |
| Knox City, Tx., U.S. | 196 | 33.25 N | 99.49 W |
| Knox Coast ✦ [2] | 9 | 66.30 S | 105.00 E |
| Knox Dale | 214 | 41.05 N | 79.02 W |
| Knoxfield | 274b | 37.53 S | 145.15 E |
| Knox Lake ⊜ [1] | 214 | 40.31 N | 82.30 W |
| Knoxville, Ga., U.S. | 192 | 32.43 N | 83.59 W |
| Knoxville, Il., U.S. | 190 | 40.54 N | 90.17 W |
| Knoxville, Ia., U.S. | 190 | 41.19 N | 93.06 W |
| Knoxville, Pa., U.S. | 210 | 41.57 N | 77.26 W |
| Knoxville, Tn., U.S. | 192 | 35.57 N | 83.55 W |
| Knuckles ∧ | 122 | 7.24 N | 80.48 E |
| Knudshoved Odde › [1] | 41 | 55.03 N | 11.45 E |
| Knüll ∧ | 56 | 50.53 N | 9.24 E |
| Knutby | 40 | 59.55 N | 18.15 E |
| Knuthenborg | 41 | 54.50 N | 11.30 E |
| Knutsford | 44 | 53.19 N | 2.22 W |
| Knysna | 158 | 34.02 S | 23.02 E |
| Knyszyn | 30 | 53.19 N | 22.55 E |
| Koala Sanctuary ◆ [4] | 274a | 33.40 S | 151.10 E |
| Koani | 154 | 6.08 S | 39.17 E |
| Kob' | 88 | 55.25 N | 101.24 E |
| Koba | 112 | 2.29 S | 106.24 E |
| Kob'aj | 74 | 63.34 N | 126.30 E |
| Kőbánya ◆ [8] | 264c | 47.29 N | 19.10 E |
| Kobarid | 36 | 46.15 N | 13.35 E |
| Kobar Sink ✦ [7] | 144 | 13.35 N | 40.50 E |
| Kobayashi | 92 | 31.59 N | 130.59 E |
| Kōbe, Nihon | 96 | 34.41 N | 135.10 E |
| Kōbe, Nihon | 270 | 34.41 N | 135.10 E |
| Kōbe-kō ⊂ | 270 | 34.40 N | 135.12 E |
| Kobelyaky | 78 | 49.09 N | 34.12 E |
| København (Copenhagen) | 41 | 55.40 N | 12.35 E |
| København □ [6] | 41 | 55.45 N | 12.25 E |
| Kōbe University ʊ [2] | 270 | 34.43 N | 135.14 E |
| Kobi | 84 | 42.33 N | 44.32 E |
| Koblenz, Dtsch. | 56 | 50.21 N | 7.35 E |
| Koblenz, Schw. | 58 | 47.37 N | 8.14 E |
| Koblenz □ [5] | 56 | 50.10 N | 7.30 E |
| Kobo, Ityo. | 144 | 12.11 N | 39.33 E |
| Kobo, Zaïre | 152 | 4.54 S | 17.09 E |
| Ko-boke ♠ | 96 | 33.50 N | 133.46 E |
| Koboko | 154 | 3.25 N | 30.58 E |
| Koboldo | 89 | 52.58 N | 132.42 E |
| Kobona | 76 | 60.01 N | 31.36 E |
| Kobou ≃ | 152 | 6.13 N | 23.19 E |
| Kobowen Swamp ≡ | 144 | 5.38 N | 33.54 E |
| Koboža | 76 | 58.49 N | 35.01 E |
| Koboža ≃ | 76 | 58.52 N | 36.17 E |
| Kobra | 24 | 60.03 N | 50.44 E |
| Kobrinskoje | 76 | 59.25 N | 30.07 E |
| Kobroor, Pulau I | 164 | 6.12 S | 134.32 E |
| Kobryn | 76 | 52.13 N | 24.21 E |
| Kobuchizawa | 94 | 35.52 N | 138.19 E |
| Kobuga-hara ♠ | 94 | 36.40 N | 139.35 E |
| Kobuk | 180 | 66.54 N | 156.52 W |
| Kobuk ≃ | 180 | 66.45 N | 161.00 W |
| Kobuk Valley National Park ♠ | 180 | 67.20 N | 159.00 W |
| Kobuleti | 84 | 41.50 N | 41.47 E |
| Kobushiga-take ∧ | 94 | 35.54 N | 138.44 E |
| Kobylanka | 54 | 53.19 N | 14.50 E |
| Kobylin | 30 | 51.43 N | 17.13 E |
| Kobyzhcha | 78 | 50.49 N | 31.30 E |
| Kocaali | 130 | 41.03 N | 30.52 E |
| Kocaaliler | 130 | 37.19 N | 30.44 E |
| Kocaavşar ≃ | 130 | 40.08 N | 27.57 E |
| Kocaeli → İzmit | 130 | 40.46 N | 29.55 E |
| Kocaeli □ [4] | 130 | 40.55 N | 29.55 E |
| Koçali | 130 | 37.55 N | 38.15 E |
| Kočani | 38 | 41.55 N | 22.25 E |
| Koçarlı | 130 | 37.45 N | 27.42 E |
| Kocasinan ◆ [8] | 267b | 41.01 N | 28.50 E |
| Koçbaş Tepe ∧ | 84 | 39.25 N | 43.21 E |
| Kočečum ≃ | 74 | 64.17 N | 101.10 E |
| Kočelajevo | 80 | 54.01 N | 44.02 E |
| Kočemary | 80 | 54.50 N | 40.58 E |
| Kočen'ajevka | 80 | 53.52 N | 46.59 E |
| Kočen'ga, Ross. | 76 | 60.09 N | 43.33 E |
| Kočenga, Ross. | 88 | 55.55 N | 104.06 E |
| Kočenga ≃ | 88 | 55.55 N | 104.06 E |
| Kočerdyk | 86 | 54.35 N | 62.58 E |
| Kočerga | 88 | 55.15 N | 103.46 E |
| Kočetovka, Ross. | 80 | 55.16 N | 46.07 E |
| Kočetovka, Ross. | 80 | 52.58 N | 40.29 E |
| Kočevar | 76 | 60.26 N | 42.11 E |
| Kočevje | 36 | 45.38 N | 14.52 E |
| Kočevo | 86 | 59.36 N | 54.18 E |
| Koch'am-ni | 98 | 41.06 N | 129.23 E |
| Kŏch'ang, Taehan | 98 | 35.26 N | 126.42 E |
| Kŏch'ang, Taehan | 98 | 35.41 N | 127.55 E |
| Koch Bihār | 124 | 26.19 N | 89.26 E |
| Kochel | 64 | 47.39 N | 11.22 E |
| Kochelsee ⊜ | 64 | 47.38 N | 11.20 E |
| Kochena | 158 | 27.00 S | 18.50 E |
| Kocher ≃ | 56 | 49.14 N | 9.12 E |
| Kocheriv | 78 | 50.21 N | 29.21 E |
| Kōchi, Nihon | 96 | 33.33 N | 133.33 E |
| Kōchi, Nihon | 96 | 34.28 N | 132.53 E |
| Kōchi □ [5] | 96 | 33.40 N | 133.30 E |
| Kōchi-dani ♠ | 94 | 34.34 N | 136.10 E |
| Kochinda | 174m | 26.08 N | 127.43 E |
| Koch Island I | 176 | 69.38 N | 78.15 W |
| Kochiu → Gejiu | 90 | 23.22 N | 103.06 E |
| Kochma | 80 | 56.56 N | 41.06 E |
| Koch Peak ∧ | 202 | 45.02 N | 111.28 W |
| Kochugaon | 124 | 26.34 N | 90.04 E |
| Kock | 30 | 51.39 N | 22.27 E |
| Kočki, Ross. | 86 | 52.24 N | 80.40 E |
| Kočki, Ross. | 86 | 54.20 N | 80.29 E |
| Kočkor-Ata | 85 | 41.04 N | 72.29 E |
| Kočkorka | 85 | 42.14 N | 75.45 E |
| Kocksoord | 273d | 26.13 S | 27.39 E |
| Kočkurovo | 80 | 54.02 N | 45.26 E |
| Kočmes | 24 | 66.12 N | 60.44 E |
| Kočon'ovo | 86 | 55.02 N | 82.12 E |
| Kočov | 60 | 49.49 N | 12.44 E |
| Kočubej | 84 | 44.24 N | 46.33 E |
| Kočubejevskoje | 84 | 44.41 N | 41.41 E |
| Kōda, Nihon | 94 | 34.52 N | 137.10 E |
| Kōda, Nihon | 96 | 34.42 N | 132.45 E |
| Kodačdikost | 24 | 63.11 N | 55.49 E |
| Kodaikānal | 122 | 10.14 N | 77.29 E |
| Kodaira | 94 | 35.44 N | 139.29 E |
| Kodama | 94 | 36.11 N | 139.08 E |
| Kodar, chrebet ⋏ | 88 | 57.15 N | 118.10 E |
| Kodāri | 124 | 27.56 N | 85.56 E |
| Kodarma | 124 | 24.28 N | 85.36 E |
| Kodera ◆ [8] | 270 | 34.41 N | 135.04 E |
| Kodersdorf | 54 | 51.15 N | 14.53 E |
| Kodi | 152 | 3.34 S | 22.12 E |
| Kodiak | 180 | 57.48 N | 152.23 W |
| Kodiak Island I | 180 | 57.30 N | 153.30 W |
| Kodiang | 114 | 6.24 N | 100.18 E |
| Kodinār | 120 | 20.47 N | 70.42 E |
| Kodino | 24 | 63.43 N | 39.41 E |
| Kodo ≃ | 152 | 7.05 N | 19.10 E |
| Kodo, Jabal ∧ | 140 | 12.26 N | 23.38 E |
| Kodok | 140 | 9.53 N | 32.07 E |
| Kodori ≃ | 84 | 42.47 N | 41.10 E |
| Kodorskij chrebet ⋏ | 84 | 43.00 N | 42.00 E |
| Kodra | 78 | 50.36 N | 29.34 E |
| Kodyma | 78 | 48.07 N | 29.07 E |
| Kodyma ≃ | 78 | 48.01 N | 30.48 E |
| Kodžori | 84 | 41.40 N | 44.41 E |
| Koegas | 158 | 29.16 S | 22.20 E |
| Koehn Lake ⊜ | 228 | 35.20 N | 117.53 W |
| Koekelare | 50 | 51.05 N | 2.58 E |
| Koekenaap | 158 | 31.30 S | 18.18 E |
| Koeltztown | 219 | 38.19 N | 92.03 W |
| Koenigsmacker | 56 | 49.24 N | 6.17 E |
| Koersel | 56 | 51.04 N | 5.16 E |
| Koes | 156 | 25.59 S | 19.08 E |
| Kofa Mountains ⋏ | 200 | 33.20 N | 114.00 W |
| Kofçaz | 130 | 41.58 N | 27.12 E |
| Köfering | 60 | 48.56 N | 12.12 E |
| Koffiefontein | 158 | 29.30 S | 25.00 E |
| Kofiau, Pulau I | 164 | 1.11 S | 129.50 E |
| Köflach | 61 | 47.04 N | 15.05 E |
| Koforidua | 150 | 6.03 N | 0.17 W |
| Kōfu, Nihon | 94 | 35.39 N | 138.35 E |
| Kōfu, Nihon | 96 | 35.17 N | 133.30 E |
| Koga, Nihon | 94 | 36.11 N | 139.43 E |
| Koga, Nihon | 96 | 33.40 N | 130.30 E |
| Koga, Tan. | 154 | 6.14 S | 32.25 E |
| Kogaluc ≃ | 176 | 59.40 N | 77.35 W |
| Kogaluc, Baie ⊂ | 176 | 59.20 N | 77.50 W |
| Kogaluk ≃ | 176 | 56.12 N | 61.44 W |
| Kogan | 166 | 27.03 S | 150.46 E |
| Kogane | 268 | 35.50 N | 139.56 E |
| Koganei | 94 | 35.42 N | 139.32 E |
| Kogarah | 274a | 33.58 S | 151.08 E |
| Kogarah Bay ⊂ | 274a | 33.59 S | 151.07 E |
| Køge, Dan. | 41 | 55.27 N | 12.11 E |
| Kōge, Nihon | 96 | 35.24 N | 134.15 E |
| Køge Bugt ⊂, Dan. | 41 | 55.30 N | 12.20 E |
| Køge Bugt ⊂, Kal. Nun. | 176 | 65.00 N | 40.30 W |
| Kogin Baba | 146 | 7.55 N | 11.30 E |
| Koglhof | 61 | 47.19 N | 15.40 E |
| Kogon ≃ | 150 | 11.09 N | 14.42 W |
| Kogoni | 150 | 14.44 N | 6.02 W |
| Kŏgŭm-do I | 98 | 34.27 N | 127.11 E |
| Kohak | 128 | 25.44 N | 62.33 E |
| Kohala Mountains ⋏ | 229d | 20.05 N | 155.45 W |
| Kohama-shima I | 175d | 24.19 N | 123.59 E |
| Kohanava | 76 | 54.28 N | 30.01 E |
| Kohāt | 123 | 33.35 N | 71.26 E |
| Kohāt ≃ | 123 | 33.24 N | 71.48 E |
| Kohatk Wash V | 200 | 32.38 N | 111.55 W |
| Kohila | 76 | 59.10 N | 24.45 E |
| Kohīma | 120 | 25.40 N | 94.07 E |
| Kohistān □ [9] | 123 | 35.03 N | 72.52 W |
| Kohlberg ∧ [2] | 263 | 51.18 N | 7.46 E |
| Kohler | 190 | 43.44 N | 87.46 W |
| Kohlstädt | 52 | 51.50 N | 8.52 E |
| Kohoku | 94 | 35.26 N | 136.15 E |
| Kōhoku ◆ [8] | 268 | 35.31 N | 139.38 E |
| Kohren-Sahlis | 54 | 51.01 N | 12.36 E |
| Kohsān | 128 | 34.39 N | 61.12 E |
| Kohtla-Järve | 76 | 59.24 N | 27.15 E |
| Kohu → Kōfu | 94 | 35.39 N | 138.35 E |
| Kohukohu | 172 | 35.21 S | 173.32 E |
| Kohŭng | 98 | 34.37 N | 127.16 E |
| Kohunlich ⊥ | 232 | 18.27 N | 89.01 W |
| Kohuratahi | 172 | 39.06 S | 174.46 E |
| Kohyl'nyk (Cogâlnic) ≃ | 78 | 45.51 N | 29.38 E |
| Koide | 94 | 37.13 N | 138.57 E |
| Koidern | 180 | 61.58 N | 140.25 W |
| Koidu | 150 | 8.38 N | 10.59 W |
| Koigi | 76 | 58.50 N | 25.45 E |
| Koihoa | 110 | 8.12 N | 93.29 E |
| Koil-Aligarh → Alīgarh | 124 | 27.53 N | 78.05 E |
| Koimbani | 157a | 11.37 S | 43.23 E |
| Koindu | 150 | 8.26 N | 10.19 W |
| Koin-ni | 98 | 40.28 N | 126.22 E |
| Koito ≃ | 94 | 35.21 N | 139.52 E |
| Kojandy | 86 | 49.51 N | 75.40 E |
| Kojda | 24 | 66.23 N | 42.31 E |
| Kŏje-do I | 98 | 34.52 N | 128.37 E |
| Kojetin | 30 | 49.21 N | 17.18 E |
| Kojgorodok | 24 | 60.26 N | 50.58 E |
| Ko-jima I | 92a | 41.22 N | 139.48 E |
| Kojima-ko ⊜ [1] | 96 | 34.37 N | 134.00 E |
| Kojŏ | 98 | 38.57 N | 127.51 E |
| Kojonup | 162 | 33.50 S | 117.09 E |
| Kojsary | 85 | 42.33 N | 78.10 E |
| Kojsug | 83 | 47.07 N | 39.41 E |
| Kojtas, Kaz. | 86 | 51.32 N | 76.15 E |
| Kojtaš, Uzb. | 85 | 40.11 N | 67.19 E |
| Kok (Hkok) ≃ | 110 | 20.14 N | 100.09 E |
| Kōka | 94 | 34.54 N | 136.13 E |
| Koka, Lake ⊜ [1] | 144 | 8.23 N | 39.05 E |
| Kokai ≃ | 94 | 35.52 N | 140.08 E |
| K'okajgyr | 85 | 40.43 N | 75.37 E |
| Kokalaat | 86 | 49.47 N | 64.15 E |
| Kokand | 85 | 40.33 N | 70.57 E |
| Kokanee Glacier Provincial Park ♠ | 182 | 49.47 N | 117.10 W |
| Kokankišlak | 85 | 40.56 N | 72.30 E |
| Kökar I | 26 | 59.56 N | 20.55 E |
| Kokas | 164 | 2.42 S | 132.26 E |
| Kokašice | 60 | 49.53 N | 12.57 E |
| Kokava nad Rimavicou | 30 | 48.34 N | 19.50 E |
| Kokawa | 96 | 34.16 N | 135.24 E |
| K'okbel' | 85 | 40.17 N | 72.55 E |
| Kokčetav | 86 | 53.17 N | 69.25 E |
| Kokčetav □ [8] | 86 | 53.30 N | 70.00 E |
| Kokčetavskaja vozvyšennost' ⋏ [1] | 86 | 52.50 N | 69.00 E |
| Kokee State Park ♠ | 229b | 22.08 N | 159.40 W |
| Kokemäenjoki ≃ | 26 | 61.33 N | 21.42 E |
| Kokemäki | 26 | 61.15 N | 22.21 E |
| Kokenau | 164 | 4.43 S | 136.26 E |
| Ko Kha | 110 | 18.11 N | 99.24 E |
| Kokhav HaYarden (Belvoir) ⊥ | 132 | 32.36 N | 35.31 E |
| Kókhi, Ákra › | 267c | 37.53 N | 23.27 E |
| Koki | 150 | 15.30 N | 15.59 W |
| Kokinu | 268 | 35.59 N | 139.59 E |
| Kokiu → Gejiu | 102 | 23.22 N | 103.06 E |
| Kok-Jangak | 85 | 41.02 N | 73.12 E |
| Kokka | 140 | 20.00 N | 30.35 E |
| Kokkilai Lagoon ⊂ | 122 | 9.00 N | 80.56 E |
| Kokkola (Karleby) | 26 | 63.50 N | 23.07 E |
| Kokku | 98 | 40.22 N | 128.44 E |
| Koknese | 76 | 56.39 N | 25.29 E |
| Koko | 150 | 11.26 N | 4.32 E |
| Kokoda | 164 | 8.52 S | 147.45 E |
| Koko Head › | 229c | 21.16 N | 157.42 W |
| Kokola | 154 | 0.47 N | 29.36 E |
| Kokole Point › | 229b | 21.59 N | 159.46 W |
| Kokolik ≃ | 180 | 69.46 N | 163.00 W |
| Kokolopozo | 150 | 5.08 N | 6.05 W |
| K'ok'omeren ≃ | 85 | 41.43 N | 73.54 E |
| Kokomo, Hi., U.S. | 229a | 20.52 N | 156.18 W |
| Kokomo, In., U.S. | 216 | 40.29 N | 86.08 W |
| Kokomo, Ms., U.S. | 194 | 31.11 N | 90.00 W |
| Kokong | 156 | 24.27 S | 23.03 E |
| Kokonoe | 96 | 33.10 N | 131.10 E |
| Koko Nor → Qinghai Hu ⊜ | 102 | 36.50 N | 100.20 E |
| Kokopo | 164 | 4.20 S | 152.15 E |
| Kokorevka | 76 | 52.35 N | 34.16 E |
| Kokosing ≃ | 214 | 40.22 N | 82.12 W |
| Kokos-Inseln → Cocos (Keeling) Islands □ [2] | 14 | 12.10 S | 96.55 E |
| Kokoškino | 265b | 55.38 N | 37.11 E |
| Kokpāra Narsinghgarh | 126 | 22.31 N | 86.33 E |
| Kokpaš | 86 | 51.12 N | 87.45 E |
| Kokpekti | 86 | 48.45 N | 82.24 E |
| Kokrājhār | 124 | 26.24 N | 90.16 E |
| Kokrines | 180 | 64.56 N | 154.42 W |
| Kokrines Hills ⋏ [2] | 180 | 65.15 N | 154.00 W |
| Koksa ≃ | 86 | 50.16 N | 85.36 E |
| Kokšaalatau, chrebet ⋏ | 72 | 41.00 N | 78.00 E |
| Koksan | 98 | 38.46 N | 126.40 E |
| Koksaraj | 85 | 42.40 N | 68.08 E |
| Kokšekol', ozero ⊜ | 86 | 46.05 N | 62.00 E |
| Koksijde | 50 | 51.07 N | 2.38 E |
| Koksilah | 224 | 48.40 N | 123.38 W |
| Koksilah ≃ | 224 | 48.45 N | 123.39 W |
| Koksoak ≃ | 176 | 58.32 N | 68.10 W |
| Koksŏng | 98 | 35.17 N | 127.17 E |
| Koksovyj | 78 | 48.12 N | 40.39 E |
| Kokstad | 158 | 30.32 S | 29.29 E |
| Koksu, Kaz. | 85 | 41.27 N | 68.01 E |
| Koksu, Kaz. | 86 | 44.59 N | 77.56 E |
| Koktal | 86 | 44.09 N | 79.48 E |
| Koktas, Kaz. | 86 | 47.33 N | 70.55 E |
| Koktas, Kaz. | 86 | 45.59 N | 73.32 E |
| Kok-Taš, Kyrg. | 85 | 41.12 N | 72.25 E |
| Kokterek | 80 | 49.25 N | 49.15 E |
| Koktubek | 86 | 48.07 N | 56.51 E |
| Kokubu, Nihon | 92 | 31.44 N | 130.46 E |
| Kokubu, Nihon | 96 | 34.56 N | 132.07 E |
| Kokubunji, Nihon | 94 | 36.22 N | 139.51 E |
| Kokubunji, Nihon | 96 | 34.18 N | 133.58 E |
| Kokubunji, Nihon | 268 | 35.42 N | 139.29 E |
| Kokubunji Temple ʊ [1] | 268 | 35.44 N | 139.55 E |
| Kokufu | 96 | 35.28 N | 134.16 E |
| Kokuj | 88 | 52.13 N | 117.33 E |
| Kokujbel' ≃ | 85 | 38.21 N | 72.46 E |
| Kokžar | 86 | 49.01 N | 60.10 E |
| Kol ≃ | 128 | 26.59 N | 55.47 E |
| Kola, Indon. | 164 | 5.26 S | 134.29 E |
| Kola, Ross. | 24 | 68.53 N | 33.01 E |
| Kola ≃ | 24 | 68.53 N | 33.02 E |
| Kolachel | 122 | 8.10 N | 77.15 E |
| Kolāchi ≃ | 120 | 27.08 N | 67.02 E |
| Kolageran | 84 | 40.58 N | 44.37 E |
| Kolahun | 150 | 8.24 N | 10.02 W |
| Kolaka | 112 | 4.03 S | 121.36 E |
| Kolambo | 152 | 7.34 S | 21.58 E |
| Kolambugan | 116 | 8.07 N | 123.55 E |
| Kolangār | 120 | 34.02 N | 69.01 E |
| Kola Peninsula → Kol'skij poluostrov › [1] | 24 | 67.30 N | 37.00 E |
| Kolār | 122 | 13.08 N | 78.08 E |
| Kolāras | 124 | 25.14 N | 77.36 E |
| Kolār Gold Fields | 122 | 12.55 N | 78.17 E |
| Kolari | 24 | 67.20 N | 23.48 E |
| Kolarovgrad → Šumen | 38 | 43.16 N | 26.55 E |
| Kolárovo | 30 | 47.52 N | 18.02 E |
| Kolašin | 38 | 42.49 N | 19.31 E |
| Kolāyat | 120 | 27.50 N | 72.57 E |
| Kolbači | 89 | 54.22 N | 123.02 E |
| Kolbäck | 40 | 59.34 N | 16.15 E |
| Kolbäcksån ≃ | 40 | 59.32 N | 16.16 E |
| Kol'baj, gora ∧ [2] | 86 | 43.43 N | 53.57 E |
| Kolbano | 112 | 10.02 S | 124.31 E |
| Kolberg → Kołobrzeg | 30 | 54.12 N | 15.33 E |
| Kolbermoor | 64 | 47.51 N | 12.04 E |
| Kolbio | 144 | 1.10 S | 41.15 E |
| Kolbnitz | 64 | 46.52 N | 13.19 E |
| Kolbotn | 26 | 59.49 N | 10.48 E |
| Kolbuszowa | 30 | 50.15 N | 21.47 E |
| Kolby Kås | 41 | 55.48 N | 10.33 E |
| Kolchida ≃ | 84 | 42.15 N | 42.00 E |
| Kolchozabad | 120 | 37.27 N | 68.31 E |
| Kol'covo | 82 | 54.27 N | 36.40 E |
| Kol'čuga | 82 | 55.43 N | 37.12 E |
| Kol'čugino | 80 | 56.18 N | 39.23 E |
| Kołczewo | 54 | 53.58 N | 14.38 E |
| Kolda | 150 | 12.53 N | 14.57 W |
| Kolda □ [4] | 150 | 12.50 N | 14.50 W |
| Kolding | 41 | 55.31 N | 9.29 E |
| Kolding Fjord ⊂ | 41 | 55.30 N | 9.35 E |
| Kole, Zaïre | 152 | 3.27 S | 22.29 E |
| Kole, Zaïre | 154 | 2.07 N | 25.26 E |
| Kolea | 34 | 36.38 N | 2.46 E |
| Kolebīra | 124 | 22.43 N | 84.42 E |
| Kole Kalyan ◆ [8] | 272c | 19.06 N | 72.51 E |
| Kolenfeld | 52 | 52.24 N | 9.27 E |
| Koleno | 80 | 51.52 N | 44.07 E |
| Kolenté | 150 | 10.06 N | 12.37 W |
| Kolenté (Great Scarcies) ≃ | 150 | 8.55 N | 13.08 W |
| Kolga | 76 | 59.32 N | 25.42 E |
| Kolgujev, ostrov I | 24 | 69.05 N | 49.15 E |
| Kolhāpur, India | 122 | 16.06 N | 78.16 E |
| Kolhāpur, India | 122 | 16.42 N | 74.13 E |
| Kolho | 26 | 62.08 N | 24.31 E |
| Koli | 76 | 59.30 N | 34.30 E |
| Koli ∧ [2] | 26 | 63.06 N | 29.48 E |
| Koli, Jabal ∧ | 140 | 14.05 N | 25.31 E |
| Kolia | 150 | 9.46 N | 6.28 W |
| Koliba (Corubal) ≃ | 150 | 11.57 N | 15.06 W |
| Koliganek | 180 | 59.48 N | 157.25 W |
| Kolima ⊜ | 26 | 63.16 N | 25.50 E |
| Kolimbine ≃ | 150 | 14.26 N | 11.23 W |
| Kolín | 30 | 50.01 N | 15.13 E |
| Kolisne | 78 | 46.02 N | 29.56 E |
| Kolitzheim | 56 | 49.55 N | 10.14 E |
| Kolka | 76 | 57.45 N | 22.35 E |
| Kølkær | 41 | 56.04 N | 9.06 E |
| Kolkasrags › | 76 | 57.47 N | 22.36 E |
| Kolkwitz | 54 | 51.45 N | 14.15 E |
| Kolky, Ukr. | 78 | 51.07 N | 25.41 E |
| Kolky, Ukr. | 78 | 51.37 N | 26.37 E |
| Kollbach ≃ | 60 | 48.36 N | 12.58 E |
| Kölleda | 54 | 51.11 N | 11.15 E |
| Kollegāl | 122 | 12.09 N | 77.07 E |
| Kolleru Lake ⊜ | 122 | 16.39 N | 81.13 E |
| Kollum | 52 | 53.16 N | 6.09 E |
| Kollund | 41 | 54.51 N | 9.27 E |
| Kolmanskop | 156 | 26.40 S | 15.12 E |
| Kolmården | 40 | 58.40 N | 16.23 E |
| Kolmården ⋏ [2] | 40 | 58.41 N | 16.35 E |
| Kolmårdens Djurpark ♠ | 40 | 58.40 N | 16.29 E |
| Kolmogorovo | 86 | 59.15 N | 91.20 E |
| Köln (Cologne) | 56 | 50.56 N | 6.59 E |
| Köln □ [5] | 56 | 50.55 N | 6.40 E |
| Köln-Bonn, Flughafen ⊠ | 56 | 50.50 N | 7.10 E |
| Kolno | 30 | 53.25 N | 21.56 E |
| Kolo, Niger | 150 | 13.14 N | 2.20 E |
| Koło, Pol. | 30 | 52.12 N | 18.38 E |
| Kolo, Tan. | 154 | 4.44 S | 35.50 E |
| Koloa | 229b | 21.54 N | 159.28 W |
| Kolobovo | 80 | 56.42 N | 41.21 E |
| Kołobrzeg | 30 | 54.12 N | 15.33 E |
| Koloč' ≃ | 82 | 55.34 N | 35.52 E |
| Kolochau | 54 | 51.44 N | 13.16 E |
| Kolodn'a | 76 | 54.48 N | 32.09 E |
| Kologriv | 76 | 58.51 N | 44.17 E |
| Kologrivovka | 80 | 51.44 N | 45.20 E |
| Kolojar | 80 | 52.34 N | 46.58 E |
| Kolok (Golok) ≃ | 114 | 6.15 N | 102.05 E |
| Kolokani | 150 | 13.35 N | 8.02 W |
| Koloko | 150 | 11.05 N | 5.19 W |
| Kolokol'covka, Ross. | 80 | 52.36 N | 49.48 E |
| Kolokol'covka, Ross. | 80 | 51.12 N | 44.36 E |
| Kololo | 144 | 7.29 N | 41.58 E |
| Kolom'agi ◆ [8] | 265a | 60.00 N | 30.17 E |
| Kolom'agi Airport ⊠ | 265a | 60.01 N | 30.17 E |
| Kolomak | 78 | 49.50 N | 35.18 E |
| Kolombangara Island I | 175e | 8.00 S | 157.05 E |
| Kolomea → Kolomyya | 78 | 48.32 N | 25.04 E |
| Kolomenka ≃ | 82 | 55.06 N | 38.46 E |
| Kolomenskaja Sloboda | 82 | 54.22 N | 38.15 E |
| Kolomenskoje ◆ [8] | 265b | 55.40 N | 37.41 E |
| Kolomna | 82 | 55.05 N | 38.49 E |
| Kolomyya | 78 | 48.32 N | 25.04 E |
| Kolondiéba | 150 | 11.05 N | 6.54 W |
| Kolonga | 174w | 21.08 S | 175.04 W |
| Kolonia | 174r | 6.58 N | 158.13 E |
| Kolonie Stolp | 264a | 52.28 N | 13.46 E |
| Kolono | 112 | 4.18 S | 122.41 E |
| Kolonodale | 112 | 2.00 S | 121.19 E |
| Kolora | 272b | 22.55 N | 88.22 E |
| Kolosib | 120 | 24.14 N | 92.42 E |
| Kolosovka | 86 | 56.28 N | 73.36 E |
| Kolovai | 174w | 21.06 S | 175.20 W |
| Kolovertnoje | 80 | 50.36 N | 51.06 E |
| Kolowana Watobo, Teluk ⊂ | 112 | 5.00 S | 123.06 E |
| Kolozsvár → Cluj-Napoca | 38 | 46.47 N | 23.36 E |
| Kolp' ≃ | 76 | 59.20 N | 36.49 E |
| Kolpaševo | 86 | 58.20 N | 82.50 E |
| Kolpino | 76 | 59.45 N | 30.36 E |
| Kölpinsee ⊜ | 54 | 53.30 N | 12.34 E |
| Kolpny | 76 | 52.15 N | 37.02 E |
| Kölsa | 54 | 51.28 N | 12.13 E |
| Kol'skij poluostrov (Kola Peninsula) › [1] | 24 | 67.30 N | 37.00 E |
| Kolsnaren ⊜ | 40 | 59.02 N | 16.01 E |
| Kolsva | 40 | 59.36 N | 15.50 E |
| Kol'togan | 85 | 43.51 N | 67.25 E |
| Koltovskaja | 80 | 52.47 N | 44.16 E |
| Koltubanovskij | 80 | 52.57 N | 52.02 E |
| Koltuši | 265a | 59.56 N | 30.40 E |
| Kol'ubakino | 82 | 55.40 N | 36.32 E |
| Kolubara ≃ | 38 | 44.40 N | 20.15 E |
| Kol'učinskaja guba ⊂ | 180 | 66.40 N | 174.30 W |
| Koluel Kayke | 254 | 46.43 S | 68.14 W |
| Kolumbien → Colombia □ [1] | 246 | 4.00 N | 72.00 W |
| Kol'upanovo | 82 | 54.26 N | 36.14 E |
| Koluškino | 78 | 48.39 N | 40.56 E |
| Koluszki | 30 | 51.44 N | 19.49 E |
| Koluton | 86 | 51.43 N | 69.25 E |
| Koluton ≃ | 86 | 51.42 N | 69.10 E |
| Kolva ≃ | 24 | 65.55 N | 57.15 E |
| Kolvereid | 24 | 64.51 N | 11.32 E |
| Kølvrå | 41 | 56.18 N | 9.08 E |
| Kolwezi | 154 | 10.43 S | 25.28 E |
| Kolyadivka | 83 | 49.05 N | 39.12 E |
| Kolyberovo | 82 | 55.16 N | 38.44 E |
| Kolyčevo | 82 | 55.30 N | 37.52 E |
| Kolyma ≃ | 74 | 69.30 N | 161.00 E |
| Kolymskaja | 74 | 68.44 N | 158.44 E |
| Kolymskaja nizmennost' ≃ | 74 | 68.30 N | 154.00 E |
| Kolyšlej | 80 | 52.42 N | 44.32 E |
| Kolyšovo | 82 | 54.54 N | 36.57 E |
| Kolyvan', Ross. | 86 | 51.18 N | 82.34 E |
| Kolyvan', Ross. | 86 | 55.18 N | 82.45 E |
| Kom → Qom | 128 | 34.39 N | 50.54 E |
| Kom ∧ | 38 | 43.10 N | 23.03 E |
| Kom ≃ | 152 | 2.18 N | 11.40 E |
| Koma, Ityo. | 144 | 8.27 N | 36.52 E |
| Koma, Mya. | 110 | 15.39 N | 98.12 E |
| Koma, Ross. | 86 | 55.02 N | 91.19 E |
| Koma ≃ | 94 | 35.59 N | 139.26 E |
| Komadougou Yobé (Komadugu Yobe) ≃ | 146 | 13.43 N | 13.20 E |
| Komadugu Gana ≃ | 146 | 13.05 N | 12.24 E |
| Komadugu Yobe (Komadougou Yobé) ≃ | 146 | 13.43 N | 13.20 E |
| Komae | 94 | 35.38 N | 139.35 E |
| Komagane | 94 | 35.43 N | 137.55 E |
| Komaga-take ∧, Nihon | 92a | 42.04 N | 140.41 E |
| Komaga-take ∧, Nihon | 94 | 35.45 N | 138.14 E |
| Komaga-take ∧, Nihon | 94 | 35.47 N | 137.48 E |
| Komagome ◆ [8] | 268 | 35.44 N | 139.45 E |
| Komaki | 94 | 35.17 N | 136.55 E |
| Komandorskije ostrova II | 74 | 55.00 N | 167.00 E |
| Komandorski Village | 282 | 37.43 N | 121.54 W |
| Komariči | 76 | 52.27 N | 34.47 E |
| Komarivka | 78 | 51.14 N | 32.07 E |
| Komárno, Slvk. | 30 | 47.45 N | 18.09 E |
| Komarno, Ukr. | 78 | 49.38 N | 23.42 E |
| Komarnyky | 78 | 49.00 N | 23.04 E |
| Komárom | 30 | 47.44 N | 18.08 E |
| Komárom-Esztergom □ [6] | 30 | 47.40 N | 18.15 E |
| Komarovo | 76 | 58.39 N | 33.26 E |
| Komarovy | 86 | 60.26 N | 75.50 E |
| Komati (Incomáti) ≃ | 156 | 25.46 S | 32.43 E |
| Komatipoort | 156 | 25.25 S | 31.55 E |
| Komatsu, Nihon | 94 | 36.24 N | 136.27 E |
| Komatsu, Nihon | 96 | 33.53 N | 133.07 E |
| Komatsu-kūkō ⊠ | 94 | 36.24 N | 136.26 E |
| Komatsushima | 96 | 34.00 N | 134.35 E |
| Kombissiri | 150 | 12.04 N | 1.20 W |
| Kombone | 152 | 4.37 N | 9.19 E |


| | | | | | |
|---|---|---|---|---|---|
| ≃ River | Fluß | Río | Rivière | Rio | |
| ≊ Canal | Kanal | Canal | Canal | Canal | |
| ∟ Waterfall, Rapids | Wasserfall, Stromschnellen | Cascada, Rápidos | Chute d'eau, Rapides | Cascata, Rápidos | |
| ʯ Strait | Meeresstraße | Estrecho | Détroit | Estreito | |
| ⊂ Bay, Gulf | Bucht, Golf | Bahía, Golfo | Baie, Golfe | Baía, Golfo | |
| ⊜ Lake, Lakes | See, Seen | Lago, Lagos | Lac, Lacs | Lago, Lagos | |
| ≡ Swamp | Sumpf | Pantano | Marais | Pântano | |
| ⊓ Ice Features, Glacier | Eis- und Gletscherformen | Accidentes Glaciales | Formes glaciaires | Acidentes glaciares | |
| ⊤ Other Hydrographic Features | Andere Hydrographische Objekte | Otros Elementos Hidrográficos | Autres données hydrographiques | Outros acidentes hidrográficos | |
| ✦ Submarine Features | Untermeerische Objekte | Accidentes Submarinos | Formes de relief sous-marin | Acidentes submarinos | |
| □ Political Unit | Politische Einheit | Unidad Politica | Entité politique | Unidade política | |
| ʊ Cultural Institution | Kulturelle Institution | Institución Cultural | Institution culturelle | Instituição cultural | |
| ⊥ Historical Site | Historische Stätte | Sitio Histórico | Site historique | Sitio histórico | |
| ♠ Recreational Site | Erholungs- und Ferienort | Sitio de Recreo | Centre de loisirs | Area de Lazer | |
| ⊠ Airport | Flughafen | Aeropuerto | Aéroport | Aeroporto | |
| ■ Military Installation | Militäranlage | Instalación Militar | Installation militaire | Instalação militar | |
| ◆ Miscellaneous | Verschiedenes | Misceláneo | Divers | Diversos | |

ENGLISH — DEUTSCH


| Name | Page | Lat.°′ | Long.°′ |
|---|---|---|---|
| Komdhārā | 272b | 22.53 N | 88.14 E |
| Kome Island I | 154 | 0.06 S | 32.45 E |
| Komen | 64 | 45.49 N | 13.44 E |
| Komenda | 150 | 5.03 N | 1.29 W |
| Komenoi | 268 | 35.55 N | 140.01 E |
| Komering ≃ | 112 | 2.59 S | 104.50 E |
| Komeshia | 154 | 8.01 S | 27.07 E |
| Komfane | 164 | 5.39 S | 134.44 E |
| Komga | 158 | 32.35 S | 27.55 E |
| Komi □[3] | 72 | 64.00 N | 54.00 E |
| Kominato → Amatsu-kominato | 94 | 35.07 N | 140.10 E |
| Kominternivs'ke | 78 | 46.49 N | 30.56 E |
| Komin Yanga | 150 | 11.42 N | 0.08 E |
| Komi-Perm'ackij Avtonomnyj Okrug □[8] | 24 | 60.00 N | 54.30 E |
| Komissarovka | 83 | 48.07 N | 40.09 E |
| Komissarovo | 89 | 44.59 N | 131.46 E |
| Komissarovskij | 80 | 47.29 N | 42.59 E |
| Komkans | 158 | 31.16 S | 18.09 E |
| Komló | 30 | 46.12 N | 18.16 E |
| Kommadagga | 158 | 33.09 S | 25.55 E |
| Kommandodrif | 158 | 27.30 S | 26.14 E |
| Kommandokraal | 158 | 33.06 S | 22.51 E |
| Kommetjie | 158 | 34.08 S | 18.21 E |
| Kommunal'naja | 88 | 52.03 N | 115.06 E |
| Kommunar, Ross. | 80 | 58.10 N | 43.33 E |
| Kommunar, Ross. | 86 | 54.20 N | 89.18 E |
| Kommunarka | 265b | 55.34 N | 37.29 E |
| Kommunary | 26 | 60.54 N | 29.47 E |
| Kommunizma, pik ʌ | 85 | 38.57 N | 72.01 E |
| Komo ≃ | 152 | 0.09 N | 9.50 E |
| Komodo | 115b | 8.35 S | 119.30 E |
| Komodo, Pulau I | 115b | 8.36 S | 119.30 E |
| Komoé ≃ | 150 | 5.12 N | 3.44 W |
| Komoé, Parc National de la ♦ | 150 | 9.00 N | 3.30 W |
| Komoka | 214 | 42.57 N | 81.26 W |
| Komono, Congo | 152 | 3.15 S | 13.14 E |
| Komono, Nihon | 94 | 35.00 N | 136.31 E |
| Komoran, Pulau I | 164 | 8.18 S | 138.45 E |
| Komoren → Comoros □[1] | 157a | 12.10 S | 44.10 E |
| Komorin, Kap → Comorin, Cape › | 122 | 8.04 N | 77.34 E |
| Komorn → Komárno | 30 | 47.45 N | 18.09 E |
| Komoro | 94 | 36.19 N | 138.26 E |
| Komotau → Chomutov | 54 | 50.28 N | 13.26 E |
| Komotiní | 38 | 41.08 N | 25.25 E |
| Kompaniyivka | 78 | 48.15 N | 32.12 E |
| Kompasberg ʌ | 158 | 31.45 S | 24.32 E |
| Kompiam | 164 | 5.20 S | 143.55 E |
| Kompot | 112 | 0.24 N | 124.10 E |
| Komsomolabad | 85 | 38.52 N | 69.57 E |
| Komsomolec | 86 | 53.45 N | 62.02 E |
| Komsomolec, ostrov I | 74 | 80.30 N | 95.00 E |
| Komsomolec, zaliv ⊂ | 72 | 45.30 N | 52.45 E |
| Komsomol'sk, Ross. | 80 | 57.02 N | 40.21 E |
| Komsomol'sk, Ross. | 86 | 55.38 N | 88.11 E |
| Komsomol'sk, Ross. | 86 | 57.27 N | 86.02 E |
| Komsomol'sk, Turk. | 128 | 39.02 N | 63.36 E |
| Komsomol's'ke, Ukr. | 78 | 49.35 N | 36.30 E |
| Komsomol's'ke, Ukr. | 78 | 49.43 N | 28.40 E |
| Komsomol's'ke, Ukr. | 83 | 47.40 N | 38.05 E |
| Komsomol'skij, Kaz. | 86 | 51.40 N | 66.39 E |
| Komsomol'skij, Kaz. | 86 | 47.20 N | 53.42 E |
| Komsomol'skij, Ross. | 80 | 54.27 N | 45.49 E |
| Komsomol'skij, Ross. | 89 | 50.22 N | 142.10 E |
| Komsomol'sk-na-Amure | 89 | 50.35 N | 137.02 E |
| Komsomol'sk-na-Ust'urte | 86 | 44.03 N | 58.20 E |
| Komsomol'skoje, Ross. | 80 | 55.16 N | 47.33 E |
| Komsomol'skoje, Ross. | 80 | 50.46 N | 47.03 E |
| Komsomol'skoje, Ross. | 88 | 52.29 N | 111.06 E |
| Komsomol'skoj Pravdy, ostrova II | 74 | 77.20 N | 107.40 E |
| Komsomol's'kyy | 83 | 47.40 N | 37.26 E |
| Kŏmun-do I | 98 | 34.02 N | 127.19 E |
| Kömürcüpınar ⊕[8] | 267b | 41.15 N | 28.51 E |
| Komusan | 98 | 42.08 N | 129.41 E |
| Komyshnya | 78 | 50.12 N | 33.41 E |
| Komyshuvakha, Ukr. | 78 | 47.43 N | 35.32 E |
| Komyshuvakha, Ukr. | 83 | 48.42 N | 38.23 E |
| Kona, India | 272b | 22.37 N | 88.18 E |
| Kona, Mali | 150 | 14.57 N | 3.53 W |
| Kona Coast ⫠[2] | 229d | 19.25 N | 155.55 W |
| Konakovo | 82 | 56.42 N | 36.46 E |
| Konakpınar, Tür. | 130 | 38.53 N | 37.22 E |
| Konakpınar, Tür. | 130 | 39.26 N | 27.53 E |
| Konan → Hŭngnam, C.M.I.K. | 98 | 39.50 N | 127.38 E |
| Konan, C. Iv. | 150 | 8.21 N | 8.00 W |
| Kōnan, Nihon | 94 | 35.20 N | 136.53 E |
| Kōnan, Nihon | 94 | 34.56 N | 136.11 E |
| Kōnan ⊕[8] | 268 | 35.22 N | 139.35 E |
| Konar (Kunar) ≃ | 123 | 34.25 N | 70.32 E |
| Konārak | 120 | 19.54 N | 86.07 E |
| Konār Dam ⊕[6] | 124 | 23.58 N | 85.45 E |
| Konarhā □[4] | 120 | 35.15 N | 71.00 E |
| Konawa | 196 | 34.57 N | 96.45 W |
| Končanskoje-Suvorovskoje | 76 | 58.39 N | 34.04 E |
| Konch | 124 | 25.59 N | 79.09 E |
| Konda | 74 | 61.20 N | 63.58 E |
| Konda ≃, Ross. | 86 | 60.40 N | 69.46 E |
| Konda ≃, Ross. | 88 | 53.30 N | 113.32 E |
| Kondagaon | 122 | 19.36 N | 81.40 E |
| Konde | 154 | 4.57 S | 39.45 E |
| Kondega | 76 | 60.14 N | 33.30 E |
| Kondiaronk, Lac ⊜ | 190 | 46.56 N | 76.45 W |
| Kondinin | 162 | 32.30 S | 118.16 E |
| Kondinskoje | 86 | 59.40 N | 67.22 E |
| Kondli ⊕[8] | 272a | 28.37 N | 77.19 E |
| Kondoa | 154 | 4.54 S | 35.47 E |
| Kondol' | 80 | 52.49 N | 45.03 E |
| Kondolole | 154 | 1.20 N | 25.58 E |
| Kondopoga | 24 | 62.12 N | 34.17 E |
| Kondorfa | 61 | 46.54 N | 16.24 E |
| Kondratjevo, Ross. | 76 | 60.38 N | 28.08 E |
| Kondratjevo, Ross. | 88 | 57.21 N | 98.11 E |
| Kondrovka | 80 | 54.36 N | 43.17 E |
| Kondrovo | 82 | 54.48 N | 35.56 E |
| Kondr'učja ≃ | 80 | 47.43 N | 40.55 E |
| Konduga | 146 | 11.39 N | 13.24 E |
| Kondukūr | 122 | 15.13 N | 79.55 E |
| Kondurča ≃ | 80 | 53.31 N | 50.24 E |
| Kondūz | 120 | 37.45 N | 68.51 E |
| Kondūz □[4] | 120 | 36.45 N | 68.30 E |
| Koné | 175f | 21.04 S | 164.52 E |
| Konecbor | 24 | 64.52 N | 57.44 E |
| Konergino | 180 | 65.54 N | 178.50 W |
| Konfara | 150 | 11.55 N | 8.50 W |
| Kong, C. Iv. | 150 | 9.09 N | 4.37 W |
| Køng, Dan. | 41 | 55.07 N | 11.50 E |
| Kông ≃ | 110 | 13.32 N | 105.58 E |
| Kŏng, Kaôh I | 110 | 11.20 N | 103.00 E |
| Kongakut ≃ | 180 | 69.48 N | 141.50 W |
| Kongbo | 152 | 4.44 N | 21.23 E |
| Kongcheng | 100 | 31.02 N | 117.05 E |
| Kongeå ≃ | 41 | 55.23 N | 8.40 E |
| Kongens Lyngby | 41 | 55.46 N | 12.31 E |
| Kongfang | 100 | 27.58 N | 116.53 E |
| Kongiganak | 180 | 59.58 N | 162.45 W |
| Konginkangas | 26 | 62.46 N | 25.48 E |
| Kongjiamatou | 105 | 39.07 N | 116.10 E |
| Kongjiatun | 104 | 40.42 N | 124.04 E |
| Kongjiawopeng | 89 | 43.58 N | 122.41 E |
| Kongjiazhuang | 105 | 40.47 N | 114.48 E |
| Kongju | 98 | 36.27 N | 127.07 E |
| Konglong | 100 | 29.56 N | 115.54 E |
| Konglongshan | 105 | 40.33 N | 117.17 E |
| Konglu | 102 | 27.16 N | 97.56 E |
| Kongmoon → Jiangmen | 100 | 22.35 N | 113.05 E |
| Kongo → Congo ≃ | 138 | 6.04 S | 12.24 E |
| Kongo, Republik → Zaire □[1] | 138 | 4.00 S | 25.00 E |
| Kongō-Ikoma-kokutei-kōen ♦ | 96 | 34.28 N | 135.40 E |
| Kongolo, Zaïre | 154 | 5.26 S | 24.49 E |
| Kongolo, Zaïre | 154 | 5.23 S | 27.00 E |
| Kongor | 140 | 7.10 N | 31.21 E |
| Kongō-sanchi ⩘ | 270 | 34.27 N | 135.41 E |
| Kongoussi | 150 | 13.19 N | 1.32 W |
| Kongō-zan ʌ | 96 | 34.25 N | 135.41 E |
| Kongsberg | 26 | 59.39 N | 9.39 E |
| Kongsvinger | 26 | 60.12 N | 12.00 E |
| Kongsvoll | 26 | 62.18 N | 9.37 E |
| Kongtan | 107 | 29.10 N | 104.42 E |
| Kongur Shan ʌ | 85 | 38.37 N | 75.20 E |
| Kongwa | 154 | 6.12 S | 36.25 E |
| Kongyangcun | 106 | 31.23 N | 118.54 E |
| Kongzhen | 106 | 31.29 N | 119.00 E |
| Koni | 154 | 10.42 S | 27.15 E |
| Koni ≃ | 150 | 13.05 N | 5.37 W |
| Koniakari | 150 | 14.34 N | 10.54 W |
| Konice | 30 | 49.35 N | 16.53 E |
| Koniecpol | 30 | 50.48 N | 19.41 E |
| Königgrätz → Hradec Králové | 30 | 50.12 N | 15.50 E |
| Königheim | 56 | 49.37 N | 9.35 E |
| Königin Alexandra-Kette → Queen Alexandra Range ⩘ | 9 | 84.00 S | 168.00 E |
| Königin Fabiola-Gebirge → Queen Fabiola Mountains ⩘ | 9 | 71.30 S | 35.40 E |
| Königin Mary-Küste → Queen Mary Coast ⫠[2] | 9 | 67.00 S | 96.00 E |
| Königin Maud-Land → Queen Maud Land ⊕[1] | 9 | 72.30 S | 12.00 E |
| König-Otto-Höhle ⫠[5] | 60 | 49.15 N | 11.42 E |
| Königsbach | 56 | 48.58 N | 8.36 E |
| Königsberg, Dtsch. | 56 | 50.05 N | 10.34 E |
| Königsberg → Kaliningrad, Ross. | 76 | 54.43 N | 20.30 E |
| Königsborn | 263 | 51.33 N | 7.41 E |
| Königsbrück | 54 | 51.16 N | 13.54 E |
| Königsbrunn, Dtsch. | 58 | 48.16 N | 10.53 E |
| Königsbrunn, Öst. | 264b | 48.21 N | 16.25 E |
| Königsdorf | 64 | 47.49 N | 11.28 E |
| Königsee | 54 | 50.39 N | 11.05 E |
| Königsfelden ɤ[1] | 58 | 47.29 N | 8.14 E |
| Königsfeld im Schwarzwald | 58 | 48.08 N | 8.25 E |
| Königshain | 54 | 51.11 N | 14.52 E |
| Königshardt ⊕[8] | 263 | 51.33 N | 6.51 E |
| Königsheim | 58 | 48.06 N | 8.51 E |
| Königslutter | 54 | 52.15 N | 10.49 E |
| Königsmoor ⊕[3] | 52 | 53.15 N | 9.40 E |
| Königssee | 64 | 47.33 N | 12.58 E |
| Königssee ⊜ | 64 | 47.36 N | 12.59 E |
| Königsstuhl ⫠[4] | 54 | 54.34 N | 13.40 E |
| Königstein, Dtsch. | 54 | 50.55 N | 14.04 E |
| Königstein, Dtsch. | 56 | 50.11 N | 8.29 E |
| Königstein, Dtsch. | 60 | 49.37 N | 11.38 E |
| Königstetten | 264b | 48.18 N | 16.09 E |
| Königswalde | 54 | 50.33 N | 13.02 E |
| Königswartha | 54 | 51.18 N | 14.20 E |
| Königswiesen | 61 | 48.24 N | 14.50 E |
| Königswinter | 56 | 50.40 N | 7.11 E |
| Königs Wusterhausen | 54 | 52.18 N | 13.37 E |
| Konin | 30 | 52.13 N | 18.16 E |
| Konin □[4] | 30 | 52.20 N | 18.20 E |
| Konispol | 38 | 39.39 N | 20.10 E |
| Kónitsa | 38 | 40.02 N | 20.45 E |
| Köniz | 58 | 46.56 N | 7.25 E |
| Konjic | 38 | 43.39 N | 17.57 E |
| Könkämäälven ≃ | 24 | 68.29 N | 22.17 E |
| Konkapot ≃ | 210 | 42.03 N | 73.20 W |
| Konkiep ≃ | 156 | 28.03 S | 17.21 E |
| Konkō | 96 | 34.32 N | 133.37 E |
| Kon'-Kolodez' | 76 | 52.08 N | 39.11 E |
| Konkouré ≃ | 150 | 9.58 N | 13.42 W |
| Kon'kove | 83 | 47.20 N | 38.10 E |
| Konkudera | 88 | 57.33 N | 112.30 E |
| Konkug University ɤ[2] | 271b | 37.32 N | 127.05 E |
| Konnagar | 126 | 22.42 N | 88.22 E |
| Könnern | 54 | 51.40 N | 11.46 E |
| Konnevesi ⊜ | 26 | 62.40 N | 26.35 E |
| Konnur | 122 | 16.12 N | 74.45 E |
| Kōno | 94 | 35.49 N | 136.04 E |
| Konobejevo | 82 | 55.24 N | 38.40 E |
| Konohana ⊕[8] | 270 | 34.41 N | 135.26 E |
| Kōnoike | 270 | 34.42 N | 135.37 E |
| Konolfingen | 58 | 46.53 N | 7.38 E |
| Konongo | 150 | 6.37 N | 1.11 W |
| Konoša | 24 | 60.58 N | 40.15 E |
| Kōno-shima I | 96 | 34.28 N | 133.31 E |
| Kōnosu | 94 | 36.03 N | 139.31 E |
| Konotop | 78 | 51.14 N | 33.12 E |
| Konovalovka | 80 | 53.06 N | 51.34 E |
| Kon'ovo, Ross. | 24 | 62.08 N | 39.16 E |
| Kon'ovo, Ross. | 86 | 56.18 N | 70.43 E |
| Konqi ≃ | 90 | 40.40 N | 90.10 E |
| Konradshöhe ⊕[8] | 264a | 52.35 N | 13.14 E |
| Konradsreuth | 54 | 50.16 N | 11.50 E |
| Konsankoro | 150 | 9.02 N | 9.00 W |
| Konsen-daichi ⩘[1] | 92a | 43.25 N | 144.52 E |
| Końskie | 30 | 51.12 N | 20.26 E |
| Konsomol's'kyy | 83 | 48.07 N | 39.39 E |
| Konstabel | 158 | 33.16 S | 20.17 E |
| Konstantinopel → İstanbul | 130 | 41.01 N | 28.58 E |
| Konstantinovka, Ross. | 80 | 56.41 N | 50.53 E |
| Konstantinovka, Ross. | 265a | 59.47 N | 30.08 E |
| Konstantinovka, Ukr. | 83 | 47.52 N | 37.24 E |
| Konstantinovo | 82 | 56.33 N | 38.02 E |
| Konstantinovsk | 80 | 47.35 N | 41.06 E |
| Konstantinovskij | 76 | 57.50 N | 39.36 E |
| Konstantinovskije Porogi | 76 | 60.34 N | 37.04 E |
| Konstantynów Łódzki | 30 | 51.45 N | 19.20 E |
| Konstanz | 58 | 47.40 N | 9.10 E |
| Kontagora | 150 | 10.24 N | 5.28 E |
| Kontcha | 152 | 7.58 N | 12.14 E |
| Kontejevo | 80 | 58.26 N | 41.21 E |
| Kontha | 110 | 19.30 N | 96.03 E |
| Kontich | 50 | 51.08 N | 4.27 E |
| Kontiolahti | 26 | 62.46 N | 29.51 E |
| Kontiomäki | 26 | 64.21 N | 28.09 E |
| Kontseba | 78 | 48.07 N | 29.56 E |
| Kon Tum | 110 | 14.21 N | 108.00 E |
| Kontum, Plateau du ⩘[1] | 110 | 13.55 N | 108.05 E |
| Kōnu | 96 | 34.42 N | 133.05 E |
| Kon'uchovo | 86 | 55.08 N | 70.38 E |
| Konus, gora ʌ | 180 | 67.34 N | 178.10 E |
| Konya | 130 | 37.52 N | 32.31 E |
| Konya □[4] | 130 | 38.00 N | 33.00 E |
| Konyr | 80 | 50.25 N | 53.25 E |
| Konyrat | 80 | 49.36 N | 47.01 E |
| Konyrolen | 86 | 44.16 N | 79.19 E |
| Konyševka | 78 | 51.51 N | 35.18 E |
| Konystanu | 80 | 48.51 N | 53.20 E |
| Konz | 56 | 49.42 N | 6.34 E |
| Konza | 154 | 1.45 S | 37.07 E |
| Konžakovskij Kamen', gora ʌ | 86 | 59.38 N | 59.08 E |
| Konzell | 60 | 49.04 N | 12.43 E |
| Koocanusa, Lake ⊜[1] | 202 | 49.00 N | 115.10 W |
| Koog [aan de Zaan] | 52 | 52.27 N | 4.49 E |
| Kookynie | 162 | 29.20 S | 121.29 E |
| Koolamarra | 166 | 20.12 S | 140.14 E |
| Koolatah | 164 | 15.53 S | 142.27 E |
| Koolau Range ⩘ | 229c | 21.35 N | 158.00 W |
| Kooloonong | 166 | 34.53 S | 143.09 E |
| Koolskamp | 50 | 51.00 N | 3.12 E |
| Koolyanobbing | 162 | 30.50 S | 119.35 E |
| Koolywurtie | 168b | 34.38 S | 137.37 E |
| Koombana Bay ⊂ | 168a | 33.18 S | 115.36 E |
| Koonap ≃ | 158 | 33.03 S | 26.39 E |
| Koondrook | 166 | 35.39 S | 144.08 E |
| Koonga | 76 | 58.35 N | 24.12 E |
| Koonibba | 162 | 31.58 S | 133.27 E |
| Koontz Lake | 216 | 41.25 N | 86.29 W |
| Koontz Lake ⊜ | 216 | 41.25 N | 86.28 W |
| Koopan-Noord | 158 | 26.53 S | 20.41 E |
| Koopan-Suid | 158 | 27.15 S | 20.22 E |
| Koopmansfontein | 158 | 28.14 S | 24.01 E |
| Koorawatha | 166 | 34.02 S | 148.33 E |
| Koorda | 162 | 30.50 S | 117.29 E |
| Koosa | 76 | 58.33 N | 27.07 E |
| Koosfontein | 158 | 27.22 S | 25.27 E |
| Koosharem | 200 | 38.30 N | 111.52 W |
| Kooskia | 202 | 46.08 N | 115.58 W |
| Koossa | 150 | 9.32 N | 8.32 W |
| Kootenai (Kootenay) ≃ | 182 | 49.15 N | 117.39 W |
| Kootenay (Kootenai) ≃ | 182 | 49.15 N | 117.39 W |
| Kootenay Indian Reserve ⊕[4] | 182 | 49.37 N | 115.45 W |
| Kootenay Lake ⊜ | 182 | 49.35 N | 116.50 W |
| Kootenay National Park ♦ | 182 | 51.00 N | 116.00 W |
| Kootjieskolk | 158 | 31.15 S | 20.21 E |
| Kootwijk | 52 | 52.12 N | 5.45 E |
| Koo-wee-rup | 169 | 38.12 S | 145.30 E |
| Kopa | 85 | 43.32 N | 75.50 E |
| Kopa ≃ | 85 | 43.40 N | 76.15 E |
| Kopāganj | 124 | 26.01 N | 83.34 E |
| Kopāi ≃ | 126 | 23.48 N | 87.47 E |
| Kopanbulak | 86 | 48.56 N | 80.52 E |
| Kopang | 115b | 8.39 S | 116.21 E |
| Kopanovka | 80 | 47.27 N | 46.48 E |
| Kopanskaja | 78 | 46.17 N | 38.29 E |
| Kopapan | 80 | 50.20 N | 50.26 E |
| Kopargaon | 122 | 19.53 N | 74.29 E |
| Koparkhairna | 272c | 19.06 N | 72.59 E |
| Koparpāda | 272c | 19.02 N | 73.04 E |
| Kópasker | 24a | 66.20 N | 16.24 W |
| Kópavogur | 24a | 64.06 N | 21.50 W |
| Kopayhorod | 78 | 48.51 N | 27.48 E |
| Kopé, Mont ʌ[2] | 150 | 4.59 N | 7.27 W |
| Kopejsk | 86 | 55.07 N | 61.37 E |
| Kopenhagen → København | 41 | 55.40 N | 12.35 E |
| Köpenick ⊕[8] | 54 | 52.27 N | 13.34 E |
| Köpenick, Schloss ɤ | 264a | 52.27 N | 13.34 E |
| Koper | 36 | 45.33 N | 13.44 E |
| Köpernitz | 54 | 53.04 N | 12.56 E |
| Kopervik | 26 | 59.17 N | 5.18 E |
| Kopetdag, chrebet ⩘ | 128 | 37.50 N | 58.00 E |
| Kopeysk → Kopejsk | 86 | 55.07 N | 61.37 E |
| Kop Geçidi )( | 130 | 40.03 N | 40.33 E |
| Kopice | 54 | 53.44 N | 14.32 E |
| Köping | 40 | 59.31 N | 16.00 E |
| Kopisty | 54 | 50.34 N | 13.35 E |
| Kopjevo | 86 | 55.03 N | 89.50 E |
| Koplik | 38 | 42.13 N | 19.26 E |
| Köpmanholmen | 26 | 63.10 N | 18.34 E |
| Kopnino | 82 | 56.53 N | 38.29 E |
| Kopondei, Tanjung › | 115b | 8.04 S | 122.52 E |
| Koporje | 76 | 59.44 N | 29.01 E |
| Koporskaja guba ⊂ | 76 | 59.52 N | 28.55 E |
| Koppal | 122 | 15.21 N | 76.09 E |
| Koppang | 26 | 61.34 N | 11.04 E |
| Koppány ≃ | 30 | 46.35 N | 18.26 E |
| Kopparberg | 40 | 59.52 N | 14.59 E |
| Kopparbergs Län □[6] | 26 | 61.00 N | 14.30 E |
| Koppel | 214 | 40.50 N | 80.19 W |
| Kopperå | 26 | 63.24 N | 11.51 E |
| Kopperby | 41 | 54.38 N | 9.56 E |
| Kopperl | 222 | 32.04 N | 97.30 W |
| Koppi | 89 | 48.32 N | 140.07 E |
| Koppi ≃ | 89 | 48.33 N | 140.08 E |
| Koppies | 158 | 27.20 S | 27.30 E |
| Koppom | 26 | 59.43 N | 12.09 E |
| Kopri | 272c | 19.11 N | 72.58 E |
| Koprivnica | 36 | 46.10 N | 16.50 E |
| Köprü ≃ | 130 | 36.50 N | 31.10 E |
| Köprülü Kanyon Milli Parkı ♦ | 130 | 37.20 N | 31.18 E |
| Köprüören | 130 | 39.30 N | 29.47 E |
| Kopt'ovo | 80 | 56.43 N | 40.31 E |
| Kopychyntsi | 78 | 49.06 N | 25.55 E |
| Kopylovka | 86 | 58.40 N | 82.22 E |
| Kopylovo, Ross. | 24 | 60.35 N | 45.02 E |
| Kopylovo, Ross. | 82 | 56.26 N | 36.25 E |
| Kopys' | 76 | 54.19 N | 30.18 E |
| Kor ≃ | 128 | 29.36 N | 53.18 E |
| Kōra | 94 | 35.12 N | 136.15 E |
| Koraa Shiir | 144 | 3.18 N | 46.16 E |
| Korab (Maja e Korabit) ʌ | 38 | 41.47 N | 20.34 E |
| Kor Aban | 144 | 3.58 N | 42.44 E |
| Korabit, Maja e (Korab) ʌ | 38 | 41.47 N | 20.34 E |
| Korablino | 80 | 53.55 N | 40.01 E |
| Korahe | 144 | 6.35 N | 44.23 E |
| Kor'akovka | 86 | 52.24 N | 77.08 E |
| Kor'akskaja Sopka, vulkan ʌ[1] | 74 | 53.20 N | 158.43 E |
| Kor'akskoje nagorje ⩘ | 74 | 62.30 N | 172.00 E |
| Kōrakuen ♦ | 96 | 34.38 N | 133.53 E |
| Korakuen Stadium ♦ | 268 | 35.43 N | 139.45 E |
| Korallenmeer → Coral Sea ⊤[2] | 14 | 20.00 S | 158.00 E |
| Koralpe ⩘ | 61 | 46.50 N | 14.58 E |
| Korannaberg ⩘ | 158 | 27.25 S | 22.32 E |
| Korapun | 164 | 5.25 S | 152.00 E |
| Korāput | 122 | 18.49 N | 82.43 E |
| Korarou, Lac ⊜ | 150 | 15.15 N | 3.16 W |
| Korat → Nakhon Ratchasima | 110 | 14.58 N | 102.07 E |
| Koratla | 122 | 18.49 N | 78.43 E |
| Kor'ažma | 24 | 61.18 N | 47.06 E |
| Korba, India | 124 | 22.21 N | 82.41 E |
| Korba, Tun. | 36 | 36.35 N | 10.52 E |
| Korbach | 56 | 51.16 N | 8.52 E |
| Korbeta | 144 | 13.03 N | 39.43 E |
| Korbol | 146 | 10.01 N | 17.43 E |
| Korbous | 36 | 36.49 N | 10.35 E |
| Korbu, Gunong ʌ | 114 | 4.43 N | 101.17 E |
| Korçë | 38 | 40.37 N | 20.46 E |
| Korcovo | 76 | 58.52 N | 42.13 E |
| Korčula | 36 | 42.58 N | 17.08 E |
| Korčula, Otok I | 36 | 42.57 N | 16.50 E |
| Korčulanski Kanal ʮ | 36 | 43.03 N | 16.40 E |
| Kordestān □[4] | 128 | 35.30 N | 47.00 E |
| Kord Kūy | 128 | 36.48 N | 54.07 E |
| Kordovo | 86 | 54.06 N | 93.17 E |
| Korea, North □[1], Asia | 90 | 40.00 N | 127.00 E |
| Korea, North □[1], Asia | 98 | 40.00 N | 127.00 E |
| Korea, South □[1], Asia | 90 | 36.30 N | 128.00 E |
| Korea, South □[1], Asia | 98 | 36.30 N | 128.00 E |
| Korea Bay ⊂ | 98 | 39.00 N | 124.00 E |
| Korea Strait ʮ | 90 | 34.00 N | 129.00 E |
| Korea University ɤ[2] | 271b | 37.36 N | 127.02 E |
| Korekozevo | 82 | 54.20 N | 36.11 E |
| Korelakša | 24 | 65.33 N | 32.22 E |
| Korem | 144 | 12.30 N | 39.30 E |
| Koré Mayroua | 150 | 13.18 N | 3.55 E |
| Koren (Die Wurzen) )( | 64 | 46.31 N | 13.45 E |
| Korenkovo | 78 | 45.07 N | 36.24 E |
| Koren'ovo, Ross. | 78 | 51.25 N | 34.55 E |
| Koren'ovo, Ross. | 265b | 55.40 N | 38.00 E |
| Korenovsk | 78 | 45.29 N | 39.28 E |
| Korets', Ukr. | 78 | 50.37 N | 27.09 E |
| Korets', Ukr. | 78 | 50.35 N | 27.01 E |
| Korf | 74 | 60.19 N | 165.50 E |
| Korfovskij | 89 | 48.13 N | 135.03 E |
| Korga | 158 | 30.12 S | 20.28 E |
| Korgan | 130 | 40.44 N | 37.13 E |
| Korgašino | 82 | 54.45 N | 37.41 E |
| Korgasyn | 86 | 49.15 N | 66.43 E |
| Kõrgessaare | 76 | 58.59 N | 22.28 E |
| Korgonskij chrebet ⩘ | 86 | 50.45 N | 84.30 E |
| Korgöz | 84 | 40.18 N | 49.38 E |
| Korgus | 140 | 19.13 N | 33.29 E |
| Korhogo | 150 | 9.27 N | 5.38 W |
| Kōri | 270 | 34.47 N | 135.39 E |
| Koridhallós | 267c | 37.59 N | 23.39 E |
| Korido | 164 | 0.50 S | 135.35 E |
| Koriella | 169 | 37.10 S | 145.39 E |
| Korienzé | 150 | 15.24 N | 3.47 W |
| Korim | 164 | 0.54 S | 136.02 E |
| Korima, Oued el V | 148 | 33.51 N | 0.23 W |
| Koringberg | 158 | 33.01 S | 18.40 E |
| Koringplaas | 158 | 32.48 S | 20.58 E |
| Korinth | 41 | 55.08 N | 10.21 E |
| Korinthiakós Kólpos (Gulf of Corinth) ⊂ | 38 | 38.19 N | 22.04 E |
| Kórinthos (Corinth) | 38 | 37.56 N | 22.56 E |
| Korínthou, Dhiórix ⋍ | 38 | 37.57 N | 22.56 E |
| Kőris-hegy ʌ | 30 | 47.18 N | 17.45 E |
| Koritsa → Korçë | 38 | 40.37 N | 20.46 E |
| Köritz | 54 | 52.51 N | 12.27 E |
| Kōriyama, Nihon | 92 | 37.24 N | 140.23 E |
| Kōriyama → Yamato-kōriyama, Nihon | 96 | 34.38 N | 135.47 E |
| Korizo, Passe de )( | 146 | 22.28 N | 15.27 E |
| Korkino, Ross. | 86 | 54.54 N | 61.23 E |
| Korkino, Ross. | 88 | 54.23 N | 105.14 E |
| Korkinskoje, ozero ⊜ | 265a | 59.55 N | 30.44 E |
| Korkuteli | 130 | 37.04 N | 30.13 E |
| Korla | 90 | 41.44 N | 86.09 E |
| Korl'aki | 80 | 57.06 N | 46.57 E |
| Korliki | 74 | 61.31 N | 82.22 E |
| Körmend | 30 | 47.01 N | 16.37 E |
| Kormilovka | 86 | 55.00 N | 74.06 E |
| Kormovoje | 80 | 46.17 N | 43.30 E |
| Kornat, Otok I | 36 | 43.50 N | 15.16 E |
| Körnebach ≃ | 263 | 51.35 N | 7.38 E |
| Kornejevka, Kaz. | 86 | 54.01 N | 68.27 E |
| Kornejevka, Kaz. | 86 | 50.12 N | 74.19 E |
| Kornejevka, Ross. | 80 | 51.45 N | 48.46 E |
| Kornelimünster | 56 | 50.43 N | 6.11 E |
| Körner, Dtsch. | 54 | 51.13 N | 10.35 E |
| Korner, Mt., U.S. | 182 | 48.59 N | 112.15 W |
| Korneuburg | 61 | 48.21 N | 16.20 E |
| Kórnik | 30 | 52.17 N | 17.04 E |
| Kornilovo | 86 | 53.32 N | 81.05 E |
| Kornouchovo | 80 | 55.33 N | 49.53 E |
| Korn'ovo | 265a | 60.03 N | 30.45 E |
| Kornsjø | 26 | 58.57 N | 11.39 E |
| Korntal-Münchingen | 56 | 48.50 N | 9.07 E |
| Kornwestheim | 56 | 48.52 N | 9.11 E |
| Kornyn | 78 | 50.06 N | 29.32 E |
| Koro, C. Iv. | 150 | 8.34 N | 7.28 W |
| Koro, Mali | 150 | 14.04 N | 3.05 W |
| Koro I | 175g | 17.19 S | 179.23 E |
| Koroba | 164 | 5.40 S | 142.45 E |
| Koroča | 78 | 50.48 N | 37.11 E |
| Korodougou Markala | 150 | 12.26 N | 6.17 W |
| Köroğlu Tepesi ʌ | 130 | 40.31 N | 31.53 E |
| Korogwe | 154 | 5.09 S | 38.29 E |
| Koroit | 166 | 38.17 S | 142.22 E |
| Korolenko, gora ʌ | 88 | 58.15 N | 115.01 E |
| Koroleve | 78 | 48.09 N | 23.08 E |
| Korolevskij Belok, gora ʌ | 86 | 51.00 N | 83.43 E |
| Korol'ovščina | 76 | 55.49 N | 31.45 E |
| Korom, Bahr ≃ | 146 | 10.35 N | 19.45 E |
| Koromba ʌ | 175g | 17.53 S | 177.34 E |
| Koromiri I | 174k | 21.15 S | 159.43 W |
| Koromo → Toyota | 94 | 35.05 N | 137.09 E |
| Koronadal | 116 | 6.30 N | 124.51 E |
| Koróni | 38 | 36.48 N | 21.56 E |
| Korónia, Límni ⊜ | 38 | 40.41 N | 23.05 E |
| Koronowo | 30 | 53.19 N | 17.57 E |
| Korop | 78 | 51.34 N | 32.56 E |
| Koropélé | 152 | 4.44 N | 17.11 E |
| Koropíon | 38 | 37.54 N | 23.53 E |
| Koror | 175b | 7.20 N | 134.29 E |
| Koror I | 175b | 7.20 N | 134.30 E |
| Kororoit Creek ≃ | 274b | 37.52 S | 144.52 E |
| Körös ≃ | 30 | 46.43 N | 20.12 E |
| Koro Sea ⊤[2] | 175g | 18.00 S | 179.50 E |
| Korosten' | 78 | 50.57 N | 28.39 E |
| Korostyshiv | 78 | 50.19 N | 29.03 E |
| Korotkova | 88 | 56.43 N | 107.55 E |
| Korotojak | 78 | 50.59 N | 39.10 E |
| Koro Toro | 146 | 16.05 N | 18.30 E |
| Korotovo | 76 | 58.57 N | 37.28 E |
| Korotyš | 76 | 52.22 N | 37.27 E |
| Korovin Island I | 180 | 55.25 N | 160.15 W |
| Korovino, Ross. | 78 | 51.25 N | 36.45 E |
| Korovino, Ross. | 80 | 53.49 N | 53.03 E |
| Korovin Volcano ʌ[1] | 180 | 52.22 N | 174.10 W |
| Korovou | 175g | 17.57 S | 178.21 E |
| Korovyntsi | 78 | 50.48 N | 33.45 E |
| Koroyanitu ʌ | 175g | 17.40 S | 177.35 E |
| Korožečna ≃ | 76 | 57.32 N | 38.18 E |
| Korpilahti | 26 | 62.01 N | 25.33 E |
| Korpo (Korppoo) | 26 | 60.10 N | 21.34 E |
| Korså | 40 | 60.38 N | 16.08 E |
| Korsakov | 89 | 46.38 N | 142.46 E |
| Korsakovo | 76 | 53.16 N | 37.21 E |
| Korschenbroich | 56 | 51.11 N | 6.31 E |
| Korselbränna | 26 | 64.27 N | 15.35 E |
| Korševo | 78 | 51.11 N | 40.07 E |
| Korsika → Corse I | 36 | 42.00 N | 9.00 E |
| Korsnäs, Suomi | 26 | 62.47 N | 21.12 E |
| Korsnäs, Sve. | 40 | 60.35 N | 15.43 E |
| Korsør | 41 | 55.20 N | 11.09 E |
| Korsør Nor ⊂ | 41 | 55.20 N | 11.11 E |
| Koršunovo | 88 | 58.37 N | 110.10 E |
| Korsun'-Shevchenkivs'kyy | 78 | 49.26 N | 31.16 E |
| Korsze | 30 | 54.10 N | 21.09 E |
| Kortelisy | 78 | 51.51 N | 24.25 E |
| Kortgene | 52 | 51.34 N | 3.48 E |
| Kortkeros | 24 | 61.49 N | 51.28 E |
| Kortrijk (Courtrai) | 50 | 50.50 N | 3.16 E |
| Kortuz, gora ʌ | 86 | 54.33 N | 91.56 E |
| Koruçam Burnu › | 130 | 35.24 N | 32.56 E |
| Korucu | 130 | 39.28 N | 27.22 E |
| Korumburra | 169 | 38.26 S | 145.49 E |
| Korwai | 124 | 24.08 N | 78.03 E |
| Kōryō | 96 | 34.33 N | 135.45 E |
| Koryŏng | 98 | 35.44 N | 128.15 E |
| Koryta | 60 | 49.24 N | 13.13 E |
| Koryukivka | 78 | 51.46 N | 32.14 E |
| Korženevskoj, pik ʌ | 85 | 39.04 N | 72.00 E |
| Korževka | 80 | 54.12 N | 46.22 E |
| Kos | 38 | 36.53 N | 27.18 E |
| Kos (Cos) I | 38 | 36.50 N | 27.10 E |
| Kosa, Ityo. | 144 | 7.51 N | 36.51 E |
| Kosa, Ross. | 24 | 59.56 N | 54.55 E |
| Kosa, Ross. | 88 | 54.47 N | 108.52 E |
| Kosa ≃, Ross. | 24 | 60.11 N | 55.10 E |
| Kosa ≃, Ross. | 80 | 58.26 N | 51.15 E |
| Kosa ⊥ | 150 | 15.50 N | 7.00 W |
| Kosa Arabats'ka strilka ›[2] | 78 | 45.40 N | 35.00 E |
| Koš-Agač | 86 | 50.00 N | 88.40 E |
| Kosai | 94 | 34.43 N | 137.33 E |
| Kosaja, šivera ∟ | 88 | 58.24 N | 97.48 E |
| Kosaja Gora | 82 | 54.07 N | 37.33 E |
| Kosaka | 92 | 40.19 N | 140.44 E |
| Kosan | 98 | 38.52 N | 127.24 E |
| Košankol' | 80 | 49.56 N | 48.11 E |
| Kosava | 76 | 52.45 N | 25.09 E |
| Koščagyl | 86 | 46.51 N | 53.48 E |
| Kösching | 60 | 48.49 N | 11.30 E |
| Kościan | 30 | 52.06 N | 16.38 E |
| Kościerzyna | 30 | 54.08 N | 18.00 E |
| Kosciusko | 194 | 33.03 N | 89.35 W |
| Kosciusko □[6] | 216 | 41.14 N | 85.51 W |
| Kosciusko, Mount ʌ | 171b | 36.27 S | 148.16 E |
| Kosciusko National Park ♦ | 166 | 36.10 S | 148.15 E |
| Kös Dağı ʌ | 130 | 40.59 N | 34.25 E |
| Kosdaulet, peski ⊕[2] | 80 | 47.45 N | 49.30 E |
| Kose, Eesti | 76 | 59.11 N | 25.10 E |
| Kose, Nihon | 270 | 34.25 N | 135.46 E |
| Köse, Tür. | 130 | 40.13 N | 39.39 E |
| Kösedağı ʌ | 130 | 39.54 N | 42.39 E |
| Kösefakılı | 130 | 39.36 N | 34.09 E |
| Koševlevka | 82 | 55.09 N | 38.05 E |
| Košelicha | 80 | 55.02 N | 43.33 E |
| Koševrovo | 82 | 55.38 N | 38.22 E |
| Koserow | 54 | 54.03 N | 13.59 E |
| Kosha | 140 | 20.49 N | 30.32 E |
| Koshien Stadium ♦ | 270 | 34.42 N | 135.22 E |
| Koshigaya | 94 | 35.54 N | 139.48 E |
| Koshigoe | 268 | 35.18 N | 139.30 E |
| Koshikijima-rettō II | 92 | 31.45 N | 129.49 E |
| Koshino | 94 | 36.02 N | 136.01 E |
| Koshk-e Kohneh | 128 | 34.52 N | 62.31 E |
| Koshkonong | 194 | 36.35 N | 91.38 W |
| Koshkonong, Lake ⊜ | 216 | 42.52 N | 88.58 W |
| Koshkonong Creek ≃ | 216 | 42.53 N | 88.59 W |
| Koshlong Lake ⊜ | 212 | 44.58 N | 78.29 W |
| Kōshoku | 94 | 36.32 N | 138.06 E |
| Koshu → Kwangju | 98 | 35.09 N | 126.54 E |
| Kosī □[8] | 124 | 27.15 N | 87.15 E |
| Kosi ≃ | 124 | 25.26 N | 87.22 E |
| Košice | 30 | 48.43 N | 21.15 E |
| Kosigi | 122 | 15.51 N | 77.16 E |
| Kosi Kalan | 124 | 27.48 N | 77.26 E |
| Kosikovo | 76 | 59.52 N | 43.23 E |
| Kosimeer ⊜ | 158 | 26.55 S | 32.52 E |
| Kosino, Ross. | 80 | 58.23 N | 51.17 E |
| Kosino, Ross. | 82 | 55.43 N | 37.52 E |
| Kosiv | 78 | 48.19 N | 25.05 E |
| Kosju | 24 | 65.38 N | 59.03 E |
| Kosju ≃ | 24 | 66.18 N | 59.53 E |
| Kosjuvom | 24 | 66.17 N | 59.50 E |
| Köşk | 130 | 37.51 N | 28.03 E |
| Koskaecodde Lake ⊜ | 186 | 48.00 N | 55.20 W |
| Koškar | 80 | 47.27 N | 53.29 E |
| Koški, Ross. | 80 | 54.12 N | 50.28 E |
| Koski, Suomi | 26 | 60.39 N | 23.09 E |
| Koškino | 80 | 56.20 N | 50.49 E |
| Koskol' | 86 | 49.31 N | 67.05 E |
| Koskuduk | 86 | 44.06 N | 77.22 E |
| Koskullskulle | 24 | 67.12 N | 20.50 E |
| Koslan | 24 | 63.28 N | 48.52 E |
| Köslin → Koszalin | 30 | 54.12 N | 16.09 E |
| Kosmonosy | 54 | 50.26 N | 15.00 E |
| Kosmynino | 80 | 57.35 N | 40.46 E |
| Kosoba, gora ʌ | 86 | 48.15 N | 79.40 E |
| Kosogor | 80 | 57.07 N | 47.34 E |
| Kosoj, porog ∟, Ross. | 86 | 57.30 N | 95.30 E |
| Kosoj, porog ∟, Ross. | 88 | 57.44 N | 96.20 E |
| Kosolapovo | 80 | 56.57 N | 49.37 E |
| Kosŏng, C.M.I.K. | 98 | 38.40 N | 128.19 E |
| Kosŏng, Taehan | 98 | 34.58 N | 128.18 E |
| Kosovo-Metohija □[4] | 38 | 42.35 N | 21.00 E |
| Kosovska Mitrovica | 38 | 42.53 N | 20.52 E |
| Kosový potok ≃ | 60 | 49.46 N | 12.48 E |
| Kosrae I | 14 | 5.19 N | 162.59 E |
| Kösreli | 130 | 37.11 N | 35.59 E |
| Kossdorf | 54 | 51.29 N | 13.14 E |
| Kosse | 222 | 31.18 N | 96.38 W |
| Kössen | 64 | 47.40 N | 12.24 E |
| Kossindi | 152 | 3.51 N | 16.19 E |
| Kösslarn | 60 | 48.22 N | 13.07 E |
| Kossou, Lac de ⊜[1] | 150 | 7.25 N | 5.45 W |
| Kossuth | 214 | 41.17 N | 79.35 W |
| Kosta | 26 | 56.51 N | 15.23 E |
| Kostajnica | 36 | 45.14 N | 16.33 E |
| Košt'any | 54 | 50.39 N | 13.45 E |
| Koš-Tegirmen | 85 | 42.47 N | 73.53 E |
| Kostelec nad Labem | 54 | 50.11 N | 14.35 E |
| Kostenec | 38 | 42.16 N | 23.49 E |
| Koster | 158 | 25.57 S | 26.42 E |
| Kosterevo | 80 | 55.56 N | 39.37 E |
| Kosteröarna I | 26 | 58.54 N | 11.02 E |
| Koštice | 54 | 50.24 N | 13.55 E |
| Kostino, Ross. | 80 | 52.11 N | 51.20 E |
| Kostino, Ross. | 80 | 52.24 N | 51.39 E |
| Kostino, Ross. | 82 | 56.18 N | 37.43 E |
| Kostino, Ross. | 265b | 55.55 N | 37.51 E |
| Kostino-Otdelec | 78 | 51.33 N | 41.26 E |
| Kost'kovo | 76 | 60.02 N | 33.14 E |
| Košt'ob'o | 85 | 41.06 N | 74.15 E |
| Kostomukša | 24 | 64.41 N | 30.49 E |
| Kostonjärvi ⊜ | 26 | 65.47 N | 28.27 E |
| Kostopil' | 78 | 50.53 N | 26.26 E |
| Kostroma | 76 | 57.46 N | 40.55 E |
| Kostroma ≃ | 24 | 57.47 N | 40.55 E |
| Kostroma Oblast' □[4] | 24 | 58.30 N | 44.00 E |
| Kostrovo | 82 | 55.53 N | 36.42 E |
| Kostryzhivka | 78 | 48.38 N | 25.41 E |
| Kostrzyn | 30 | 52.37 N | 14.39 E |
| Kostyantynivka, Ukr. | 78 | 49.57 N | 35.07 E |
| Kostyantynivka, Ukr. | 78 | 47.51 N | 31.09 E |
| Kostyantynivka, Ukr. | 83 | 48.32 N | 37.43 E |
| Kosugaya ⊕[8] | 268 | 35.22 N | 139.33 E |
| Kosuge | 94 | 35.45 N | 138.57 E |
| Kosugi | 94 | 36.43 N | 137.06 E |
| Kosum Phisai | 110 | 16.13 N | 103.01 E |
| Koszalin (Köslin) | 30 | 54.12 N | 16.09 E |
| Koszalin □[4] | 30 | 54.00 N | 16.00 E |
| Kőszeg | 30 | 47.23 N | 16.33 E |
| Koszyce | 30 | 50.11 N | 20.35 E |
| Kota, India | 120 | 25.11 N | 75.50 E |
| Kota, India | 124 | 22.18 N | 82.02 E |
| Kota, Malay. | 114 | 2.31 N | 102.10 E |
| Kota, Malay. | 114 | 5.35 N | 100.23 E |
| Kotaagung | 112 | 5.30 S | 104.38 E |
| Kotabaharu, Indon. | 112 | 0.48 S | 111.33 E |
| Kota Baharu, Malay. | 114 | 6.08 N | 102.15 E |
| Kotabangun | 112 | 0.16 S | 116.35 E |
| Kotabaru, Indon. | 112 | 3.14 S | 116.13 E |
| Kotabaru, Indon. | 112 | 1.08 S | 101.43 E |
| Kotabaru → Jayapura, Indon. | 164 | 2.32 S | 140.42 E |
| Kota Belud | 112 | 6.25 N | 116.31 E |
| Kotabumi | 112 | 4.50 S | 104.54 E |
| Kotabunan | 112 | 0.49 N | 124.38 E |
| Kotadabok | 112 | 0.30 S | 104.33 E |
| Kot Addu | 123 | 30.28 N | 70.58 E |
| Kotagiri | 122 | 11.26 N | 76.53 E |
| Kot'ajevka | 80 | 46.33 N | 48.46 E |
| Kotake | 96 | 33.41 N | 130.43 E |
| Kota Kinabalu (Jesselton) | 112 | 5.59 N | 116.04 E |
| Kota Kota → Nkhotakota | 154 | 12.57 S | 34.17 E |
| Kotālpur | 126 | 23.02 N | 87.36 E |
| Kotamobagu | 112 | 0.46 N | 124.19 E |
| Kotanemel', gora ʌ | 86 | 47.43 N | 77.18 E |
| Kotapinang | 114 | 1.53 N | 100.05 E |
| Kotari ⩘ | 36 | 44.05 N | 15.30 E |
| Kotaringin | 114 | 0.53 N | 102.03 E |
| Kota Sarang Semut | 114 | 5.59 N | 100.24 E |
| Kotatengah | 114 | 1.05 N | 100.33 E |
| Kota Tinggi | 114 | 1.44 N | 103.54 E |
| Kotawaringin | 112 | 2.29 S | 111.25 E |
| Kotchāndpur | 124 | 23.24 N | 89.01 E |
| Kotcho Lake ⊜ | 176 | 59.05 N | 121.10 W |
| Kot Chutta | 123 | 29.53 N | 70.39 E |
| Kotdwāra | 124 | 29.45 N | 78.32 E |
| Kotel | 38 | 42.53 N | 26.27 E |
| Kotel'nič | 80 | 58.18 N | 48.20 E |
| Kotel'niki | 82 | 55.39 N | 37.52 E |
| Kotel'nikovo | 80 | 47.38 N | 43.09 E |
| Kotel'nyj, ostrov I | 74 | 75.45 N | 138.44 E |
| Kotel'va | 78 | 50.05 N | 34.45 E |
| Kot Fateh | 123 | 30.07 N | 75.05 E |
| Köthen | 54 | 51.45 N | 11.58 E |
| Koti → Kōchi | 96 | 33.33 N | 133.33 E |
| Kotido | 154 | 3.00 N | 34.06 E |
| Kotikovo | 89 | 49.08 N | 144.13 E |
| Kotivka | 78 | 49.08 N | 34.57 E |
| Kotka | 26 | 60.28 N | 26.55 E |
| Kot Kapūra | 123 | 30.35 N | 74.54 E |
| Kotkino | 24 | 67.02 N | 51.03 E |
| Kotla | 123 | 32.15 N | 76.02 E |
| Kotl'akovo | 82 | 56.17 N | 35.49 E |
| Kotlas | 24 | 61.16 N | 46.35 E |
| Kotli | 123 | 33.31 N | 73.55 E |
| Kotlik | 180 | 63.02 N | 163.33 W |
| Kotlin, ostrov I | 76 | 60.00 N | 29.46 E |
| Kotly | 76 | 59.36 N | 28.45 E |
| Kot Mūmin | 123 | 32.11 N | 73.02 E |
| Kotō | 94 | 35.08 N | 136.14 E |
| Kōtō ⊕[8] | 268 | 35.41 N | 139.48 E |
| Koto ≃, Nihon | 96 | 33.58 N | 131.13 E |
| Kotō ≃, Nihon | 96 | 34.21 N | 134.02 E |
| Kotobiki-san ʌ | 96 | 35.03 N | 132.47 E |
| Kotohira | 96 | 34.11 N | 133.49 E |
| Kotohira-gu ɤ[1] | 96 | 34.11 N | 133.49 E |
| Kotohira-yama ʌ | 96 | 34.11 N | 133.48 E |
| Kôtomo, Île I | 175f | 22.40 S | 167.33 E |
| Kotonami | 96 | 34.10 N | 133.56 E |
| Koton-Karifi | 150 | 8.08 N | 6.48 E |
| Kotonkoro | 150 | 11.02 N | 5.58 E |
| Kotor | 38 | 42.25 N | 18.46 E |
| Kotoriba | 36 | 46.21 N | 16.49 E |
| Kotorovo | 80 | 54.54 N | 41.35 E |
| Kotor Varoš | 36 | 44.37 N | 17.23 E |
| Kotouba | 150 | 8.41 N | 3.12 W |
| Kotovo | 80 | 50.18 N | 44.50 E |
| Kotovsk, Ross. | 80 | 52.36 N | 41.32 E |
| Kotovs'k, Ukr. | 78 | 47.45 N | 29.33 E |
| Kot Pūtli | 124 | 27.43 N | 76.12 E |
| Kotra, India | 120 | 24.22 N | 73.10 E |
| Kotra, India | 272b | 22.46 N | 88.34 E |
| Kot Rādha Kishan | 123 | 31.10 N | 74.06 E |
| Kotri | 120 | 25.22 N | 68.18 E |
| Kotri Allāhrakhio | 120 | 24.24 N | 67.50 E |
| Kotrung → Uttarpara-Kotrung | 272b | 22.40 N | 88.21 E |
| Kötschach [-Mauthen] | 64 | 46.40 N | 13.00 E |
| Kot Sultān | 123 | 30.46 N | 70.56 E |
| Kōtsu-zan ʌ | 96 | 34.01 N | 134.12 E |
| Kottagūdem | 122 | 17.33 N | 80.38 E |
| Kottas Mountains ⩘ | 9 | 74.20 S | 12.00 W |
| Kottayam | 122 | 9.35 N | 76.31 E |
| Kotte → Sri Jayawardenepura | 122 | 6.54 N | 79.54 E |
| Kottingbrunn | 61 | 47.57 N | 16.14 E |
| Kotto ≃ | 136 | 4.14 N | 22.02 E |
| Kotton | 144 | 9.35 N | 50.28 E |
| Kottūru | 122 | 14.49 N | 76.13 E |
| Kotuj ≃ | 74 | 71.55 N | 102.05 E |
| Kotwālīpāra | 126 | 22.59 N | 89.59 E |
| Kötz | 58 | 48.25 N | 10.17 E |
| Kotzebue | 180 | 66.53 N | 162.39 W |
| Kotzebue Sound ʮ | 180 | 66.20 N | 163.00 W |
| Kötzting | 60 | 49.11 N | 12.52 E |
| Koualé | 150 | 11.24 N | 7.01 W |
| Kou'an | 106 | 32.19 N | 119.52 E |
| Kouandé | 150 | 10.20 N | 1.42 E |
| Kouango | 152 | 4.58 N | 19.59 E |
| Kouassi-Datékro | 150 | 7.49 N | 3.31 W |
| Koubansaki | 273b | 4.22 S | 15.09 E |
| Koubča | 76 | 53.39 N | 29.14 E |
| Koubia | 150 | 11.35 N | 11.54 W |
| Kouchibouguac National Park ♦ | 186 | 46.50 N | 65.00 W |
| Koudougou | 150 | 12.15 N | 2.22 W |
| Kouéré | 150 | 10.27 N | 3.59 W |
| Kouffo ≃ | 150 | 6.35 N | 1.59 E |
| Kouga | 146 | 9.56 N | 21.03 E |
| Kouga ≃ | 158 | 33.37 S | 22.14 E |
| Kougaberge ⩘ | 158 | 33.40 S | 23.50 E |
| Kougarok Mountain ʌ | 180 | 65.41 N | 165.13 W |
| K'ouhu | 100 | 23.35 N | 120.11 E |
| Kouilou □[5] | 152 | 4.30 S | 12.00 E |
| Kouilou ≃ | 152 | 4.28 S | 11.41 E |
| Koukdjuak ≃ | 176 | 66.45 N | 73.09 W |
| Kouki | 152 | 7.10 N | 17.18 E |
| Koúklia | 130 | 34.42 N | 32.34 E |
| Koukourou ≃ | 152 | 7.32 N | 19.42 E |
| Koukourou-Bamingui, Réserve de Faune du ⊕[4] | 152 | 7.20 N | 20.00 E |
| Koula ≃ | 229b | 21.54 N | 159.36 W |
| Koulamoutou | 152 | 1.08 S | 12.29 E |
| Koulikoro | 150 | 12.53 N | 7.33 W |
| Koulikoro □[4] | 150 | 13.00 N | 8.00 W |
| Koulouguidi | 150 | 13.27 N | 11.03 W |
| Koulountou ≃ | 150 | 13.15 N | 13.37 W |
| Koumac | 175f | 20.33 S | 164.17 E |
| Koumac, Grand Récif de ✣[2] | 175f | 20.32 S | 164.04 E |
| Koumala | 166 | 21.37 S | 149.15 E |
| Koumaméyong | 152 | 0.11 N | 11.51 E |
| Koumankou | 150 | 12.06 N | 6.08 W |
| Koumbakara | 150 | 12.42 N | 14.29 W |
| Koumbal | 146 | 9.26 N | 22.39 E |
| Koumbala ≃ | 146 | 9.14 N | 20.42 E |
| Koumbia, Burkina | 150 | 11.14 N | 3.42 W |
| Koumbia, Guinée | 150 | 11.48 N | 13.30 W |
| Koumbisaleh ⊥ | 150 | 15.46 N | 7.59 W |
| Koumbouma | 150 | 10.24 N | 12.56 W |
| Koumi | 94 | 36.05 N | 138.29 E |
| Koumpentoum | 150 | 13.59 N | 14.34 W |
| Koumra | 146 | 8.55 N | 17.33 E |
| Koundara | 150 | 12.29 N | 13.18 W |
| Koundé | 152 | 6.07 N | 14.38 E |
| Koundian ⊥ | 150 | 13.10 N | 10.41 W |
| Koundougou | 150 | 11.44 N | 4.31 W |
| Koun-Fao | 150 | 7.29 N | 3.15 W |
| Koungheul | 150 | 13.59 N | 14.48 W |
| Koungoulou | 152 | 3.32 S | 13.20 E |
| Kouniohou | 150 | 7.40 N | 0.48 E |
| Kounradskij | 86 | 46.59 N | 75.00 E |
| Kountze | 194 | 30.22 N | 94.18 W |
| Koupé, Mont ʌ | 152 | 4.47 N | 9.43 E |
| Koupéla | 150 | 12.11 N | 0.21 W |
| Kouragué | 150 | 12.18 N | 10.02 W |
| Kourak | 86 | 54.50 N | 84.40 E |
| Kouriles, Détroit des → Pervyj Kuril'skij proliv ʮ | 74 | 50.50 N | 156.36 E |
| Kouri-shima I | 174m | 26.42 N | 128.01 E |
| Kourou | 250 | 5.09 N | 52.39 W |
| Kouroukoto | 150 | 12.35 N | 10.05 W |
| Kourouma | 150 | 11.37 N | 4.48 W |
| Kourouninkoto | 150 | 13.52 N | 9.35 W |
| Kouroussa | 150 | 10.39 N | 9.53 W |
| Koury | 150 | 12.11 N | 4.48 W |
| Koussanar | 150 | 13.52 N | 14.05 W |
| Koussané, Mali | 150 | 14.53 N | 11.14 W |
| Koussane, Sén. | 150 | 14.08 N | 12.26 W |
| Kousser, Massif de ʌ | 148 | 32.02 N | 5.59 W |
| Koussi, Emi ʌ | 146 | 19.50 N | 18.30 E |
| Koussili | 150 | 13.30 N | 11.38 W |
| Koutia Ba | 150 | 14.11 N | 14.28 W |
| Koutiala | 150 | 12.23 N | 5.28 W |
| Kouto | 150 | 9.53 N | 6.25 W |
| Koutou | 98 | 38.35 N | 114.24 E |
| Kouts | 216 | 41.19 N | 87.01 W |
| Kouvola | 26 | 60.52 N | 26.42 E |
| Kouya ≃ | 150 | 10.09 N | 9.45 W |
| Kouyou ≃ | 152 | 0.45 S | 16.38 E |
| Kova | 88 | 58.18 N | 100.21 E |
| Kova ≃ | 88 | 58.18 N | 100.18 E |
| Kovada Milli Parkı ♦ | 130 | 37.32 N | 30.53 E |
| Kovaksa | 80 | 55.31 N | 43.30 E |
| Kovalivka | 78 | 47.16 N | 31.43 E |


**Symbols** in the index entries represent the broad categories identified in the key at the right. Symbols with superior numbers (⩘[1]) identify subcategories (see complete key on page I · 1).

**Symbole** im Register stellen die rechts im Schlüssel erklärten Kategorien dar. Symbole mit hochgestellten Ziffern (⩘[1]) bezeichnen Unterabteilungen einer Kategorie (vgl. vollständiger Schlüssel auf Seite I · 1).

**Los símbolos** incluídos en el texto del índice representan las grandes categorías identificadas con la clave a la derecha. Los símbolos con numeros en su parte superior (⩘[1]) identifican las subcategorías (véase la clave completa en la página I · 1).

**Les symboles** de l'index représentent les catégories indiquées dans la légende à droite. Les symboles suivis d'un indice (⩘[1]) représentent des sous-catégories (voir légende complète à la page I · 1).

**Os símbolos** incluídos no texto do índice representam as grandes categorias identificadas com a chave à direita. Os símbolos com números em sua parte superior (⩘[1]) identificam as subcategorias (veja-se a chave completa à página I · 1).

| | | | | |
|---|---|---|---|---|
| ʌ Mountain | Berg | Montaña | Montagne | Montanha |
| ⩘ Mountains | Gebirge | Montañas | Montagnes | Montanhas |
| )( Pass | Paß | Paso | Col | Passo |
| V Valley, Canyon | Tal, Cañon | Valle, Cañón | Vallée, Canyon | Vale, Canhão |
| ⋍ Plain | Ebene | Llano | Plaine | Planície |
| › Cape | Kap | Cabo | Cap | Cabo |
| I Island | Insel | Isla | Île | Ilha |
| II Islands | Inseln | Islas | Îles | Ilhas |
| ⫠ Other Topographic Features | Andere Topographische Objekte | Otros Elementos Topográficos | Autres données topographiques | Outros acidentes topográficos |

ESPAÑOL — Nombre | Página | Lat.°′ | Long.°′ W = Oeste
FRANÇAIS — Nom | Page | Lat.°′ | Long.°′ W = Ouest
PORTUGUÊS — Nome | Página | Lat.°′ | Long.°′ W = Oeste


| Nombre | Página | Lat.°′ | Long.°′ W = Oeste |
|---|---|---|---|
| Kovarskas | 76 | 55.26 N | 24.55 E |
| Kovarzino | 76 | 60.09 N | 38.33 E |
| Kovdor | 24 | 67.34 N | 30.22 E |
| Kovdozero, ozero ◎ | 24 | 66.47 N | 32.00 E |
| Kovel' | 78 | 51.14 N | 24.41 E |
| Kovernino | 80 | 57.07 N | 43.49 E |
| Kovilpatti | 122 | 9.10 N | 77.52 E |
| Kovin | 38 | 44.45 N | 20.59 E |
| Kovno → Kaunas | 76 | 54.54 N | 23.54 E |
| Kovrina Vtoraja | 80 | 47.01 N | 41.44 E |
| Kovrov | 80 | 56.22 N | 41.18 E |
| Kovsuh ≃ | 83 | 48.48 N | 39.17 E |
| Kovūr | 122 | 14.29 N | 79.59 E |
| Kovvur | 122 | 17.01 N | 81.44 E |
| Kovylkin | 80 | 48.16 N | 41.28 E |
| Kovylkino | 80 | 54.02 N | 43.56 E |
| Kovža | 24 | 61.09 N | 38.58 E |
| Kovžinskij Zavod | 76 | 60.24 N | 37.04 E |
| Kowal | 30 | 52.32 N | 19.09 E |
| Kowalewo Pomorskie | 30 | 53.10 N | 18.53 E |
| Kowangge | 115b | 8.16 S | 118.32 E |
| Kowanyama | 164 | 15.28 S | 141.44 E |
| Kowanyama Aboriginal Reserve ◆[4] | 164 | 15.15 S | 141.45 E |
| Kowār | 126 | 24.13 N | 86.11 E |
| Koweït → Kuwait □[1] | 128 | 29.30 N | 47.45 E |
| Kowel → Kovel' | 78 | 51.14 N | 24.41 E |
| Kowghān ≃ | 128 | 34.15 N | 62.57 E |
| Kowhitirangi | 172 | 42.52 S | 171.01 E |
| Kowie → Port Alfred | 158 | 33.36 S | 26.55 E |
| Kowkcheh ≃ | 120 | 37.10 N | 69.23 E |
| Kowloon City | 271d | 22.19 N | 114.11 E |
| Kowloon Peak ∧ | 271d | 22.21 N | 114.13 E |
| Kowmung ≃ | 170 | 33.52 S | 150.16 E |
| Kowŏn | 98 | 39.26 N | 127.14 E |
| Kowt-e 'Ashrow | 120 | 34.27 N | 68.48 E |
| Koxtag | 120 | 37.23 N | 78.05 E |
| Kōya | 96 | 34.12 N | 135.35 E |
| Koyadaira | 96 | 33.56 N | 134.13 E |
| Kōyaguchi | 96 | 34.18 N | 135.33 E |
| Koyama ◆[8] | 268 | 35.37 N | 139.43 E |
| Koyama-ike ◎ | 96 | 35.30 N | 134.09 E |
| Kōyama-misaki › | 96 | 34.40 N | 131.36 E |
| Koyambattur → Coimbatore | 122 | 11.00 N | 76.58 E |
| Koyang-ni | 98 | 37.42 N | 126.56 E |
| Kōya-Ryūjin-kokutei-kōen ♠ | 96 | 34.10 N | 135.35 E |
| Köyceğiz | 130 | 36.57 N | 28.41 E |
| Köyceğiz Gölü ◎ | 130 | 36.55 N | 28.40 E |
| Koyna Reservoir ◎[1] | 122 | 17.25 N | 73.45 E |
| Koyra ≃[1] | 126 | 22.27 N | 89.16 E |
| Koyuk | 180 | 64.56 N | 161.08 W |
| Koyuk ≃ | 180 | 64.55 N | 161.12 W |
| Koyukuk | 180 | 64.53 N | 157.43 W |
| Koyukuk ≃ | 180 | 64.56 N | 157.30 W |
| Koyukuk, Middle Fork ≃ | 180 | 67.03 N | 151.04 W |
| Koyukuk, North Fork ≃ | 180 | 67.03 N | 151.04 W |
| Koyukuk, South Fork ≃ | 180 | 66.35 N | 151.57 W |
| Koyulhisar | 130 | 40.18 N | 37.51 E |
| Koža | 80 | 57.47 N | 48.57 E |
| Kozacha Lopan' | 78 | 50.21 N | 36.11 E |
| Kozachi Laheri | 78 | 46.42 N | 32.59 E |
| Kozakai | 94 | 34.48 N | 137.22 E |
| Kōzaki | 94 | 35.54 N | 140.24 E |
| Kō-zaki › | 92 | 34.05 N | 129.13 E |
| Kozaklı | 130 | 39.14 N | 34.49 E |
| Kōzan, Nihon | 96 | 34.35 N | 133.03 E |
| Kozan, Tür. | 130 | 37.27 N | 35.49 E |
| Kozáni | 38 | 40.18 N | 21.47 E |
| Kožany | 76 | 52.48 N | 31.44 E |
| Kozara ⋏ | 36 | 45.00 N | 16.50 E |
| Kozarac | 36 | 44.58 N | 16.51 E |
| Kozats'ke | 78 | 51.18 N | 33.29 E |
| Kozdinga | 24 | 63.43 N | 47.32 E |
| Kozelets' | 78 | 50.55 N | 31.08 E |
| Kozel'shchyna | 78 | 49.13 N | 33.51 E |
| Kozel'sk | 82 | 54.02 N | 35.48 E |
| Koževnikovo | 86 | 56.16 N | 84.00 E |
| Kozhanka | 78 | 49.58 N | 29.46 E |
| Kozhikode → Calicut | 122 | 11.15 N | 75.46 E |
| Koziegłowy | 30 | 50.36 N | 19.09 E |
| Kozienice | 30 | 51.35 N | 21.33 E |
| Kožim | 24 | 65.48 N | 59.28 E |
| Kozino | 265b | 55.54 N | 37.11 E |
| Kozjak (Possruck) ⋏ | 61 | 46.37 N | 15.28 E |
| Kozliv | 78 | 49.33 N | 25.20 E |
| Kozlov Bereg | 76 | 58.57 N | 27.44 E |
| Kozlovka, Ross. | 78 | 51.39 N | 41.16 E |
| Kozlovka, Ross. | 78 | 50.52 N | 40.27 E |
| Kozlovka, Ross. | 80 | 55.52 N | 48.14 E |
| Kozlovka, Ross. | 80 | 52.33 N | 45.41 E |
| Kozlovo, Ross. | 76 | 57.34 N | 35.29 E |
| Kozlovo, Ross. | 82 | 56.31 N | 36.16 E |
| Kozlu, Tür. | 130 | 41.26 N | 31.46 E |
| Kozlu, Tür. | 130 | 40.37 N | 36.30 E |
| Kozluk | 130 | 38.11 N | 41.29 E |
| Koźmin | 30 | 51.50 N | 17.28 E |
| Koz'mino | 24 | 61.56 N | 48.19 E |
| Koz'modemjansk | 80 | 56.20 N | 46.36 E |
| Koz'mogorodskoje | 24 | 65.32 N | 44.55 E |
| Kozova | 78 | 49.26 N | 25.09 E |
| Kožpos'olok | 24 | 63.10 N | 38.06 E |
| Kožuchovo | 265b | 55.43 N | 37.54 E |
| Kożuchów | 30 | 51.45 N | 15.35 E |
| Kozuka | 268 | 35.09 N | 139.57 E |
| Kōzuki | 96 | 34.59 N | 134.20 E |
| Kozukue ◆[8] | 268 | 35.30 N | 139.36 E |
| Kozul'ka | 86 | 56.10 N | 91.24 E |
| Kožurla | 86 | 55.21 N | 79.02 E |
| Kōzu-shima I | 92 | 34.13 N | 139.10 E |
| Kozuya | 270 | 34.52 N | 135.45 E |
| Kozyatyn | 78 | 49.43 N | 28.50 E |
| Kozyn | 78 | 50.14 N | 30.39 E |
| Kpandae | 150 | 8.28 N | 0.01 W |
| Kpandu | 150 | 7.00 N | 0.18 E |
| Kpong | 150 | 6.09 N | 0.04 E |
| Kpo Range ⋏ | 150 | 7.15 N | 10.15 W |
| Kra, Isthmus of ⊥[3] | 110 | 10.20 N | 99.00 E |
| Kraai ≃ | 158 | 30.40 S | 26.45 E |
| Kraaifontein | 158 | 33.50 S | 18.43 E |
| Kraal | 158 | 26.34 S | 28.26 E |
| Kraankuil | 158 | 29.52 S | 24.10 E |
| Krabbendijke | 52 | 51.26 N | 4.07 E |
| Krabi | 110 | 8.04 N | 98.55 E |
| Krâchéh | 110 | 12.29 N | 106.01 E |
| Krackow | 54 | 53.20 N | 14.16 E |
| Kraftsdorf | 54 | 50.52 N | 11.55 E |
| Kragan | 115a | 6.42 S | 111.37 E |
| Kragenæs | 41 | 54.55 N | 11.22 E |
| Kragerø | 26 | 58.52 N | 9.25 E |
| Kraghave | 41 | 54.48 N | 11.53 E |
| Kragujevac | 38 | 44.01 N | 20.55 E |
| Krahenhöhe ◆[8] | 263 | 51.10 N | 7.06 E |
| Kraiburg | 60 | 48.10 N | 12.26 E |
| Kraichgau ◆[1] | 56 | 49.10 N | 8.50 E |
| Krailling | 64 | 48.06 N | 11.25 E |
| Krainburg → Kranj | 36 | 46.15 N | 14.21 E |
| Krainka | 82 | 54.07 N | 36.21 E |
| Krai-Russkije | 80 | 57.23 N | 46.50 E |
| Krajčikovo | 86 | 56.16 N | 73.20 E |
| Krajenka | 30 | 53.19 N | 17.00 E |
| Krajeva | 89 | 44.54 N | 131.08 E |
| Krajina □[9] | 36 | 45.00 N | 15.40 E |
| Krajneje | 80 | 47.29 N | 46.01 E |
| Krajnik Dolny | 54 | 53.05 N | 14.25 E |
| Krajnovka | 84 | 43.57 N | 47.24 E |
| Krakatau ∧[1] | 115a | 6.07 S | 105.24 E |
| Krakatoa → Krakatau ∧[1] | 115a | 6.07 S | 105.24 E |
| Krakau → Kraków | 30 | 50.03 N | 19.58 E |
| Krâkôr | 110 | 12.32 N | 104.12 E |
| Krakovets' | 78 | 49.57 N | 23.07 E |
| Krakovo | 80 | 53.36 N | 50.51 E |
| Krakow, Dtsch. | 54 | 53.39 N | 12.16 E |
| Kraków, Pol. | 30 | 50.03 N | 19.58 E |
| Kraków □[4] | 30 | 49.50 N | 20.00 E |
| Krakower See ◎ | 54 | 53.37 N | 12.17 E |
| Kraksaan | 115a | 7.46 S | 113.25 E |
| Kraksdorf | 54 | 54.18 N | 11.04 E |
| Kralendijk | 241s | 12.10 N | 68.17 W |
| Kralice | 61 | 49.11 N | 16.12 E |
| Kraljevica | 36 | 45.16 N | 14.34 E |
| Kraljevo | 38 | 43.43 N | 20.41 E |
| Kralovice | 60 | 49.59 N | 13.29 E |
| Královské Vinohrady ◆[8] | 54 | 50.01 N | 14.29 E |
| Kralupy nad Vltavou | 54 | 50.11 N | 14.18 E |
| Kralupy u Chomutova | 54 | 50.25 N | 13.20 E |
| Králův Dvůr | 60 | 49.56 N | 14.02 E |
| Kramators'k | 83 | 48.43 N | 37.32 E |
| Kramer | 216 | 40.20 N | 87.17 W |
| Kramfors | 26 | 62.56 N | 17.47 E |
| Krammer ⋓ | 52 | 51.38 N | 4.15 E |
| Krampen | 61 | 47.40 N | 15.32 E |
| Krampnitz | 264a | 52.28 N | 13.04 E |
| Krampnitzsee ◎ | 264a | 52.27 N | 13.03 E |
| Kramsach | 64 | 47.27 N | 11.52 E |
| Kranebitten, Flughafen ⊠ | 64 | 47.16 N | 11.20 E |
| Kranenburg | 52 | 51.47 N | 6.03 E |
| Krångede | 26 | 63.09 N | 16.05 E |
| Kranichfeld | 54 | 50.51 N | 11.12 E |
| Kranídhion | 38 | 37.22 N | 23.10 E |
| Kranj | 36 | 46.15 N | 14.21 E |
| Kranji, Sing. | 271c | 1.26 N | 103.46 E |
| Kranji, Sing. | 271c | 1.26 N | 103.45 E |
| Kranji ≃ | 271c | 1.26 N | 103.45 E |
| Kranji Reservoir ◎[1] | 271c | 1.26 N | 103.45 E |
| Kranji War Memorial ⊥ | 271c | 1.26 N | 103.45 E |
| Kranjska Gora | 64 | 46.29 N | 13.47 E |
| Kransaja Pol'ana | 84 | 43.41 N | 40.13 E |
| Kranskop | 158 | 29.00 S | 30.47 E |
| Kranskop ∧ | 158 | 27.43 S | 29.41 E |
| Kranzberg, Dtsch. | 60 | 48.24 N | 11.37 E |
| Kranzberg, Namibia | 156 | 21.55 S | 15.43 E |
| Krapina | 36 | 46.10 N | 15.52 E |
| Krapivinskij | 86 | 55.00 N | 86.49 E |
| Krapivna | 76 | 53.38 N | 35.31 E |
| Krapkowice | 30 | 50.29 N | 17.56 E |
| Krapperup | 41 | 56.16 N | 12.31 E |
| Krapuh | 114 | 3.39 N | 98.10 E |
| Kras (Karst) ⋏[1] | 64 | 45.48 N | 14.00 E |
| Krasavino | 24 | 60.58 N | 46.26 E |
| Krasavka | 80 | 51.11 N | 43.24 E |
| Krasieo ≃ | 110 | 14.49 N | 100.05 E |
| Krasino | 72 | 70.45 N | 54.27 E |
| Krasivaja Meča ≃ | 76 | 52.55 N | 39.03 E |
| Krasivka | 80 | 52.16 N | 42.31 E |
| Krasivoje | 86 | 51.54 N | 66.46 E |
| Kraskino | 89 | 42.44 N | 130.48 E |
| Kraskovo | 265b | 55.39 N | 37.59 E |
| Krāslava | 76 | 55.54 N | 27.10 E |
| Kraslice | 54 | 50.18 N | 12.31 E |
| Krasna ≃ | 83 | 49.01 N | 38.15 E |
| Krasnae | 76 | 54.14 N | 27.05 E |
| Krasnaja Gora, Ross. | 76 | 53.01 N | 31.37 E |
| Krasnaja Gora, Ross. | 76 | 60.16 N | 35.42 E |
| Krasnaja Gorbatka | 80 | 55.52 N | 41.46 E |
| Krasnaja Gorka | 80 | 56.12 N | 43.04 E |
| Krasnaja Jaranga | 180 | 65.40 N | 172.50 W |
| Krasnaja Jaruga | 78 | 50.48 N | 35.39 E |
| Krasnaja Pachra | 82 | 55.27 N | 37.17 E |
| Krasnaja Pol'ana, Ross. | 80 | 56.15 N | 51.09 E |
| Krasnaja Pol'ana, Ross. | 80 | 52.13 N | 53.38 E |
| Krasnaja Pol'ana, Ross. | 80 | 46.06 N | 41.30 E |
| Krasnaja Slabada | 76 | 52.51 N | 27.10 E |
| Krasnaja Sloboda | 84 | 41.24 N | 48.31 E |
| Krasnaja Zar'a | 76 | 52.47 N | 37.41 E |
| Krásná Lípa | 54 | 50.54 N | 14.31 E |
| Krasnaluki | 76 | 54.37 N | 28.50 E |
| Krasn'anka | 80 | 51.04 N | 47.56 E |
| Krasnapolle | 76 | 53.20 N | 31.24 E |
| Krasna Polyana | 78 | 47.33 N | 37.05 E |
| Krasne | 83 | 48.23 N | 39.31 E |
| Krasneno | 180 | 64.38 N | 174.48 E |
| Kraśnik | 30 | 50.56 N | 22.13 E |
| Krasni Okny | 78 | 47.32 N | 29.27 E |
| Krasnivka | 83 | 47.24 N | 37.26 E |
| Krasnoarmejsk, Kaz. | 86 | 53.50 N | 69.42 E |
| Krasnoarmejsk, Ross. | 80 | 51.02 N | 45.42 E |
| Krasnoarmejsk, Ross. | 82 | 56.08 N | 38.08 E |
| Krasnoarmejskaja | 78 | 45.23 N | 38.12 E |
| Krasnoarmejskij, Ross. | 74 | 69.35 N | 172.00 E |
| Krasnoarmejskij, Ross. | 80 | 47.01 N | 42.12 E |
| Krasnoarmejskoje, Ross. | 80 | 55.46 N | 47.11 E |
| Krasnoarmejskoje, Ross. | 80 | 52.44 N | 50.02 E |
| Krasnoarmiys'k | 83 | 48.17 N | 37.11 E |
| Krasnoarmiys'ke | 83 | 47.14 N | 37.56 E |
| Krasnoborsk, Ross. | 24 | 61.34 N | 45.53 E |
| Krasnoborsk, Ross. | 80 | 53.46 N | 48.04 E |
| Krasnobród | 30 | 50.33 N | 23.13 E |
| Krasnobrodskij | 86 | 54.10 N | 86.28 E |
| Krasnodar | 78 | 45.02 N | 39.00 E |
| Krasnodar Kraj □[8] | 78 | 45.30 N | 39.00 E |
| Krasnodarskoje vodochranilišče ◎[1] | 78 | 45.06 N | 39.31 E |
| Krasnodon, Ukr. | 83 | 48.18 N | 39.37 E |
| Krasnodon, Ukr. | 83 | 48.17 N | 39.48 E |
| Krasnofarfornyj | 76 | 59.08 N | 31.51 E |
| Krasnoflotskoje | 80 | 50.04 N | 41.14 E |
| Krasnogorka | 85 | 43.15 N | 75.10 E |
| Krasnogorodskoje | 76 | 56.50 N | 28.17 E |
| Krasnogorsk, Ross. | 82 | 55.50 N | 37.20 E |
| Krasnogorsk, Ross. | 89 | 48.24 N | 142.06 E |
| Krasnogorskij, Ross. | 80 | 56.09 N | 48.20 E |
| Krasnogorskij, Ross. | 86 | 54.36 N | 61.15 E |
| Krasnogorskij, Uzb. | 85 | 41.09 N | 69.39 E |
| Krasnogorskoje, Ross. | 80 | 57.42 N | 52.30 E |
| Krasnogorskoje, Ross. | 86 | 52.18 N | 86.12 E |
| Krasnogovardejskij | 86 | 57.22 N | 62.20 E |
| Krasnogvardejsk | 85 | 39.46 N | 67.16 E |
| Krasnogvardejskij | 82 | 54.04 N | 37.46 E |
| Krasnogvardejskoje, Kaz. | 86 | 51.24 N | 69.18 E |
| Krasnogvardejskoje, Ross. | 78 | 50.39 N | 38.24 E |
| Krasnogvardejskoje, Ross. | 80 | 45.51 N | 41.31 E |
| Krasnohorivka | 83 | 48.00 N | 37.31 E |
| Krasnohrad | 78 | 49.22 N | 35.27 E |
| Krasnohvardiys'ke | 78 | 45.29 N | 34.17 E |
| Krasnojar | 80 | 48.54 N | 51.46 E |
| Krasnojarka, Ross. | 86 | 55.20 N | 73.04 E |
| Krasnojarka, Ross. | 86 | 59.26 N | 60.30 E |
| Krasnoj Armii, proliv ⋓ | 74 | 80.00 N | 94.35 E |
| Krasnojarovo | 89 | 51.27 N | 128.28 E |
| Krasnojarsk | 86 | 56.01 N | 92.50 E |
| Krasnojarskij | 86 | 51.58 N | 59.55 E |
| Krasnojarsk Kraj □[8] | 86 | 56.00 N | 92.22 E |
| Krasnojarskoje vodochranilišče ◎[1] | 86 | 55.00 N | 92.00 E |
| Krasnoje, Ross. | 24 | 59.12 N | 47.49 E |
| Krasnoje, Ross. | 76 | 53.06 N | 33.55 E |
| Krasnoje, Ross. | 76 | 52.51 N | 38.47 E |
| Krasnoje, Ross. | 78 | 50.56 N | 38.41 E |
| Krasnoje, Ross. | 78 | 50.21 N | 38.50 E |
| Krasnoje, Ross. | 78 | 46.44 N | 39.34 E |
| Krasnoje, Ross. | 82 | 54.26 N | 38.38 E |
| Krasnoje, Ross. | 86 | 54.37 N | 85.23 E |
| Krasnoje, ozero ◎ | 74 | 64.30 N | 174.24 E |
| Krasnoje Echo | 80 | 55.48 N | 40.42 E |
| Krasnoje Gorodišče | 82 | 54.04 N | 38.44 E |
| Krasnoje-na-Volge | 80 | 57.31 N | 41.14 E |
| Krasnoje Selo, Ross. | 80 | 48.02 N | 45.13 E |
| Krasnoje Selo, Ross. | 80 | 48.46 N | 42.20 E |
| Krasnoje Selo, Ross. | 265a | 59.44 N | 30.05 E |
| Krasnoje Znam'a, Ross. | 76 | 57.26 N | 35.13 E |
| Krasnoje Znam'a, Turk. | 128 | 36.58 N | 62.30 E |
| Krasnokamsk | 86 | 58.04 N | 55.48 E |
| Krasnokutsk, Kaz. | 86 | 53.01 N | 75.59 E |
| Krasnokuts'k, Ukr. | 78 | 50.06 N | 35.09 E |
| Krasnolesje | 76 | 54.24 N | 22.23 E |
| Krasnolesnyj | 78 | 51.53 N | 39.35 E |
| Krasnomajskij | 76 | 57.37 N | 34.22 E |
| Krasnookt'abr'skij, Kyrg. | 85 | 42.50 N | 74.18 E |
| Krasnookt'abr'skij, Ross. | 80 | 56.40 N | 47.45 E |
| Krasnookt'abr'skij, Ross. | 80 | 48.53 N | 44.45 E |
| Krasnoostrovskij | 76 | 60.18 N | 28.40 E |
| Krasnopavlivka | 78 | 49.08 N | 36.19 E |
| Krasnoperekops'k | 78 | 45.57 N | 33.47 E |
| Krasnopillya | 78 | 50.46 N | 35.16 E |
| Krasnorečenskij | 89 | 44.41 N | 135.14 E |
| Krasnorichens'ke | 83 | 49.11 N | 38.24 E |
| Krasnoščelje | 24 | 67.21 N | 37.02 E |
| Krasnoščokovo | 86 | 51.40 N | 82.45 E |
| Krasnosel'kup | 74 | 65.41 N | 82.28 E |
| Krasnosielc | 30 | 53.03 N | 21.10 E |
| Krasnosil's'ke | 78 | 45.25 N | 32.42 E |
| Krasnoslobodsk, Ross. | 80 | 54.26 N | 43.48 E |
| Krasnoslobodsk, Ross. | 80 | 48.42 N | 44.34 E |
| Krasnotorka | 83 | 48.41 N | 37.31 E |
| Krasnoturansk | 86 | 54.16 N | 91.29 E |
| Krasnoturjinsk | 86 | 59.46 N | 60.12 E |
| Krasnoufimsk | 86 | 56.37 N | 57.46 E |
| Krasnoural'sk | 86 | 58.21 N | 60.03 E |
| Krasnousol'skij | 86 | 53.54 N | 56.27 E |
| Krasnovidovo | 80 | 55.21 N | 49.04 E |
| Krasnovišersk | 24 | 60.23 N | 56.59 E |
| Krasnovka | 83 | 48.47 N | 40.07 E |
| Krasnovodsk | 128 | 40.00 N | 53.00 E |
| Krasnovodskij poluostrov ›[1] | 128 | 40.30 N | 53.15 E |
| Krasnovodskij zaliv ⊂ | 128 | 39.55 N | 53.15 E |
| Krasnoyarsk → Krasnojarsk | 86 | 56.01 N | 92.50 E |
| Krasnoyil's'k | 78 | 48.01 N | 25.34 E |
| Krasnozatonskij | 24 | 61.41 N | 50.58 E |
| Krasnozavodsk | 82 | 56.27 N | 38.13 E |
| Krasnoznamensk | 76 | 54.57 N | 22.30 E |
| Krasnoznamenskoje | 86 | 51.03 N | 69.30 E |
| Krasnoz'orskoje | 86 | 53.59 N | 79.14 E |
| Krásný Dvůr | 54 | 50.10 N | 13.24 E |
| Krasnyj, Ross. | 76 | 54.34 N | 31.26 E |
| Krasnyj, Ross. | 92a | 46.15 N | 141.15 E |
| Krasnyj Aul | 86 | 51.03 N | 81.02 E |
| Krasnyj Bogatyr' | 80 | 56.02 N | 41.08 E |
| Krasnyj Bor, Ross. | 80 | 55.17 N | 43.59 E |
| Krasnyj Bor, Ross. | 80 | 55.53 N | 53.06 E |
| Krasnyj Bor, Ross. | 265a | 59.41 N | 30.41 E |
| Krasnyj Cholm, Ross. | 76 | 58.03 N | 37.07 E |
| Krasnyj Cholm, Ross. | 80 | 54 11 N | 40.42 E |
| Krasnyj Cholm, Ross. | 86 | 51.35 N | 54.09 E |
| Krasnyj Chuduk | 80 | 46.18 N | 46.56 E |
| Krasnyj Čikoj | 88 | 50.22 N | 108.15 E |
| Krasnyje Baki | 80 | 57.08 N | 45.10 E |
| Krasnyje Barrikady | 80 | 46.14 N | 47.53 E |
| Krasnyje Četai | 80 | 55.42 N | 46.09 E |
| Krasnyje Gory | 76 | 58.57 N | 29.29 E |
| Krasnyje Tkači | 80 | 57.30 N | 39.45 E |
| Krasnyj Gorodok | 76 | 57.11 N | 33.44 E |
| Krasnyj Gul'aj | 80 | 54.01 N | 48.22 E |
| Krasnyj Jar, Kaz. | 86 | 53.20 N | 69.14 E |
| Krasnyj Jar, Ross. | 80 | 46.33 N | 48.21 E |
| Krasnyj Jar, Ross. | 80 | 53.30 N | 50.22 E |
| Krasnyj Jar, Ross. | 80 | 51.38 N | 46.25 E |
| Krasnyj Jar, Ross. | 80 | 50.37 N | 45.47 E |
| Krasnyj Jar, Ross. | 80 | 50.42 N | 44.46 E |
| Krasnyj Jar, Ross. | 86 | 55.54 N | 86.57 E |
| Krasnyj Jar, Ross. | 86 | 55.14 N | 72.56 E |
| Krasnyj Jar, Ross. | 86 | 57.07 N | 84.33 E |
| Krasnyj Kl'uč | 86 | 55.26 N | 56.12 E |
| Krasnyj Kut | 80 | 50.57 N | 46.58 E |
| Krasnyj Liman | 78 | 51.32 N | 39.50 E |
| Krasnyj Log | 78 | 51.23 N | 39.46 E |
| Krasnyj Luč | 76 | 57.04 N | 30.05 E |
| Krasnyj Majak | 80 | 56.03 N | 41.23 E |
| Krasnyj Manyč, Ross. | 80 | 46.33 N | 42.10 E |
| Krasnyj Manyč, Ross. | 80 | 45.31 N | 44.42 E |
| Krasnyj Manyč, Ross. | 80 | 46.59 N | 41.07 E |
| Krasnyj Meliorator | 80 | 50 02 N | 46.06 E |
| Krasnyj Okt'abr', Kaz. | 86 | 46.50 N | 75.59 E |
| Krasnyj Okt'abr', Ross. | 80 | 51.33 N | 45.42 E |
| Krasnyj Okt'abr', Ross. | 80 | 56.06 N | 41.23 E |
| Krasnyj Okt'abr', Ross. | 82 | 56.07 N | 38.53 E |
| Krasnyj Okt'abr', Ross. | 82 | 55.37 N | 36.30 E |
| Krasnyj Okt'abr', Ross. | 86 | 55.37 N | 64.48 E |
| Krasnyj Partizan | 80 | 46.20 N | 43.10 E |
| Krasnyj Profintern | 80 | 57.45 N | 40.27 E |
| Krasnyj Rog | 76 | 52.57 N | 33.45 E |
| Krasnyj Steklovar | 80 | 56.13 N | 48.47 E |
| Krasnyj Stroitel' ◆[8] | 265b | 55.35 N | 37.37 E |
| Krasnyj Sulin | 83 | 47.54 N | 40.03 E |
| Krasnyj Tekstil'ščik | 80 | 51.23 N | 45.50 E |
| Krasnyj Tkač | 82 | 55.28 N | 39.05 E |
| Krasnystaw | 30 | 50.59 N | 23.10 E |
| Krasnyy Kut | 83 | 48.12 N | 38.48 E |
| Krasnyy Luch | 83 | 48.08 N | 38.56 E |
| Krasnyy Lyman | 83 | 48.59 N | 37.49 E |
| Krasnyy Perekop | 78 | 46.41 N | 33.46 E |
| Krasucha | 76 | 57.23 N | 33.12 E |
| Kras'ukovskaja | 83 | 47.31 N | 40.06 E |
| Krasyliv | 78 | 49.39 N | 26.59 E |
| Kraszna (Crasna) ≃ | 38 | 48.09 N | 22.20 E |
| Kratovo | 38 | 42.05 N | 22.11 E |
| Krauchenwies | 58 | 48.01 N | 9.14 E |
| Kraul Mountains ⋏ | 9 | 73.10 S | 14.10 W |
| Krauschwitz | 54 | 51.31 N | 14.41 E |
| Krautheim | 56 | 49.23 N | 9.38 E |
| Kravaře, Česká Rep. | 30 | 49.56 N | 18.01 E |
| Kravaře, Česká Rep. | 54 | 50.38 N | 14.23 E |
| Kray ◆[8] | 263 | 51.28 N | 7.05 E |
| Kražiai | 76 | 55.36 N | 22.40 E |
| Krbava ◆[1] | 36 | 44.40 N | 15.35 E |
| Kreamer Island I | 220 | 26.46 N | 80.44 W |
| Kreba-Neudorf | 54 | 51.20 N | 14.40 E |
| Krebs | 196 | 34.55 N | 95.42 W |
| Krečetovo | 24 | 60.56 N | 38.30 E |
| Krečevicy | 76 | 58.37 N | 31.21 E |
| Krefeld | 56 | 51.20 N | 6.34 E |
| Kregme | 41 | 55.57 N | 12.04 E |
| Kreiensen | 52 | 51.51 N | 9.58 E |
| Kreischa | 54 | 50.56 N | 13.45 E |
| Kremastón, Tekhnití Límni ◎[1] | 38 | 38.55 N | 21.30 E |
| Kremenchuk | 78 | 49.04 N | 33 25 E |
| Kremenchuts'ke vodoskhovyshche ◎[1] | 78 | 49.20 N | 32.30 E |
| Kremenets' | 78 | 50.07 N | 25.45 E |
| Kremenivka | 83 | 47.20 N | 37.29 E |
| Kremenskoj | 80 | 47.49 N | 41.08 E |
| Kremenskoje | 82 | 55.06 N | 35.57 E |
| Kreminna | 83 | 49.03 N | 38.14 E |
| Kremlin ⛫ | 265b | 55.45 N | 37.37 E |
| Kremmen | 54 | 52.45 N | 13.01 E |
| Kremmling | 200 | 40.03 N | 106.23 W |
| Kremnica | 30 | 48.43 N | 18.54 E |
| Krempe | 52 | 53.50 N | 9.29 E |
| Krems ≃, Öst. | 61 | 48.14 N | 14.19 E |
| Krems ≃, Öst. | 61 | 48.25 N | 15.36 E |
| Krems an der Donau | 61 | 48.25 N | 15.36 E |
| Kremsbrücke | 64 | 46.57 N | 13.37 E |
| Kremsmünster | 61 | 48.03 N | 14.08 E |
| Krenitzin Islands I | 180 | 54.08 N | 166.00 W |
| Krensitz | 54 | 51.29 N | 12.27 E |
| Krepkaja ≃ | 83 | 47.35 N | 39.23 E |
| Krepoljin | 38 | 44.16 N | 21.37 E |
| Krešchonka | 86 | 55.52 N | 80.06 E |
| Kresgeville | 210 | 40.54 N | 75.30 W |
| Kress | 196 | 34.22 N | 101.45 W |
| Kressbronn | 58 | 47.35 N | 9.36 E |
| Kressey Lake ◎ | 285 | 39.44 N | 75.07 W |
| Kresta, zaliv ⊂ | 180 | 66.00 N | 179.15 W |
| Krestcy, Ross. | 76 | 58.15 N | 32.31 E |
| Krestcy, Ross. | 76 | 58.23 N | 39.00 E |
| Krestjanskij | 85 | 40.32 N | 69.02 E |
| Krestjanskoje | 80 | 45.34 N | 42.56 E |
| Krest-Major | 74 | 67.37 N | 144.45 E |
| Krestovaja Guba | 72 | 74.07 N | 55.33 E |
| Krestovo-Gorodišče | 80 | 54.10 N | 48.36 E |
| Krestovyj, pereval )( | 84 | 42.32 N | 44.28 E |
| Kresty | 82 | 55.16 N | 37.06 E |
| Kreta → Kríti I | 38 | 35.15 N | 25.00 E |
| Kretek | 115a | 7.59 S | 110.19 E |
| Kretinga | 76 | 55.53 N | 21.13 E |
| Kreuth | 64 | 47.38 N | 11.44 E |
| Kreuzau | 56 | 50.45 N | 6.29 E |
| Kreuzberg | 263 | 51.09 N | 7.27 E |
| Kreuzberg ◆[8] | 264a | 52.30 N | 13.23 E |
| Kreuzberg ∧ | 56 | 50.22 N | 9.58 E |
| Kreuzeck-Gruppe ⋏ | 64 | 46.51 N | 13.06 E |
| Kreuzen | 64 | 46.40 N | 13.35 E |
| Kreuzlingen | 58 | 47.39 N | 9.11 E |
| Kreuznach → Bad Kreuznach | 56 | 49.52 N | 7.51 E |
| Kreuztal | 56 | 50.58 N | 7.59 E |
| Kreuzwertheim | 56 | 49.46 N | 9.31 E |
| Krėva | 76 | 54.19 N | 26.17 E |
| Kreyenhagen | 54 | 52.55 N | 10.52 E |
| Krian | 115a | 7.24 S | 112.35 E |
| Kría Vrísi | 38 | 40.41 N | 22.18 E |
| Kribi | 152 | 2.57 N | 9.55 E |
| Kriebstein, Burg ⊥ | 54 | 51.02 N | 13.00 E |
| Krieglach | 61 | 47.33 N | 15.34 E |
| Kriel | 158 | 26.16 S | 29.14 E |
| Krien | 54 | 53.50 N | 13.27 E |
| Kriens | 58 | 47.02 N | 8.17 E |
| Krigujgun, mys › | 180 | 65.30 N | 171.05 W |
| Kriljon, mys › | 89 | 45.53 N | 142.05 E |
| Krim → Kryms'kyy pivostriv ›[1] | 78 | 45.00 N | 34.00 E |
| Křimice | 60 | 49.46 N | 13.15 E |
| Krim-Krim | 146 | 8.58 N | 15.48 E |
| Krimmler Wasserfälle ∟ | 64 | 47.12 N | 12.10 E |
| Krimnicksee ◎ | 264a | 52.18 N | 13.39 E |
| Krimpen aan de IJssel | 52 | 51.54 N | 4.35 E |
| Krimskij | 80 | 47.39 N | 40.44 E |
| Kriničćno-Lugskoje | 83 | 47.45 N | 39.12 E |
| Kripens'kyy | 83 | 48.06 N | 39.03 E |
| Krishna ≃ | 122 | 15.57 N | 80.59 E |
| Krishna, Mouths of the ≃[1] | 122 | 15.43 N | 80.55 E |
| Krishnachaadrapur | 126 | 21.50 N | 86.49 E |
| Krishnagiri | 122 | 12.32 N | 78.14 E |
| Krishnamāti | 272b | 22.40 N | 88.32 E |
| Krishnanagar, India | 126 | 23.24 N | 88.30 E |
| Krishnanagar, India | 126 | 23.13 N | 87.33 E |
| Krishnapur, Bngl. | 126 | 23.30 N | 89.56 E |
| Krishnapur, India | 272b | 22.36 N | 88.26 E |
| Krishnarāja Sāgara ◎[1] | 122 | 12.30 N | 76.26 E |
| Krishnarājpet | 122 | 12.40 N | 76.30 E |
| Krishnarāmpur | 126 | 22.43 N | 88.14 E |
| Kristdala | 26 | 57.24 N | 16.11 E |
| Kristiania → Oslo | 26 | 59.55 N | 10.45 E |
| Kristianopel | 26 | 56.15 N | 16.02 E |
| Kristiansand | 26 | 58.10 N | 8.00 E |
| Kristianstad | 26 | 56.02 N | 14.08 E |
| Kristianstads Län □[6] | 26 | 56.15 N | 14.00 E |
| Kristiansund | 26 | 63.07 N | 7.45 E |
| Kristiinankaupunki → Kristinestad | 26 | 62.17 N | 21.23 E |
| Kristineberg | 26 | 65.04 N | 18.35 E |
| Kristinehamn | 40 | 59.20 N | 14.07 E |
| Kristinestad (Kristiinankaupunki) | 26 | 62.17 N | 21.23 E |
| Kríti □[4] | 38 | 35.15 N | 25.00 E |
| Kríti (Crete) I | 38 | 35.29 N | 24.42 E |
| Kritikón Pélagos (Sea of Crete) ⊤[2] | 38 | 35.46 N | 23.54 E |
| Kritzendorf | 264b | 48.20 N | 16.18 E |
| Kriuša | 82 | 54.28 N | 36.24 E |
| Kriv'ačka | 80 | 58.40 N | 45.27 E |
| Krivaja ≃ | 38 | 44.27 N | 18.09 E |
| Kriv'anskaja | 83 | 47.24 N | 40.10 E |
| Kriva Palanka | 38 | 42.12 N | 22.20 E |
| Krivcy | 82 | 55.28 N | 38.12 E |
| Krivinka | 86 | 51.08 N | 78.10 E |
| Krivodol | 38 | 43.23 N | 23.29 E |
| Krivoj Buzan | 80 | 46.31 N | 48.33 E |
| Křivoklát | 60 | 50.02 N | 13.54 E |
| Krivonosovo | 78 | 49.55 N | 39.16 E |
| Krivorožje | 78 | 48.51 N | 40.45 E |
| Krivošeino | 86 | 57.20 N | 83.57 E |
| Krivoy Rog → Kryvyy Rih | 78 | 47.55 N | 33.21 E |
| Kriwoi-Rog → Kryvyy Rih | 78 | 47.55 N | 33.21 E |
| Križevci | 36 | 46.02 N | 16.33 E |
| Krk, Otok I | 36 | 45.05 N | 14.35 E |
| Krkonošský národní park ♠ | 30 | 50.45 N | 15.35 E |
| Krn ∧ | 64 | 46.16 N | 13.40 E |
| Krnov | 30 | 50.05 N | 17.41 E |
| Krobia | 30 | 51.47 N | 16.58 E |
| Krøderen ◎ | 26 | 60.15 N | 9.38 E |
| Krogager | 41 | 55.42 N | 8.51 E |
| Krögis | 54 | 51.07 N | 13.22 E |
| Krokek | 40 | 58.40 N | 16.24 E |
| Kroken | 24 | 65 22 N | 14.20 E |
| Krokodil ≃, S. Afr. | 156 | 25.26 S | 31.58 E |
| Krokodil ≃, S. Afr. | 156 | 24.12 S | 26.52 E |
| Krokom | 26 | 63.19 N | 14.30 E |
| Krokowa | 30 | 54.48 N | 18.11 E |
| Krolevets' | 78 | 51.33 N | 33.23 E |
| Kröller-Müller, Rijksmuseum ⛫ | 52 | 52.05 N | 5.50 E |
| Krölpa | 54 | 50.41 N | 11.32 E |
| Krom ≃ | 158 | 30.53 S | 19.01 E |
| Krombi Pits | 156 | 19.30 S | 25.02 E |
| Kroměříž | 30 | 49.18 N | 17.24 E |
| Krommenie | 52 | 52.29 N | 4.45 E |
| Krompachy | 30 | 48.56 N | 20.52 E |
| Kromy | 76 | 52.43 N | 35.46 E |
| Kronach | 54 | 50.14 N | 11.20 E |
| Kronberg | 56 | 50.10 N | 8.30 E |
| Kronborg ⊥ | 41 | 56.02 N | 12.38 E |
| Krone | 263 | 51.27 N | 7.20 E |
| Krong Ana ◎[1] | 110 | 12.30 N | 108.00 E |
| Krŏng Kaôh Kŏng | 110 | 11.37 N | 102.59 E |
| Krŏng Kêb | 110 | 10.29 N | 104.19 E |
| Kronobergs Län □[6] | 26 | 56.40 N | 14.40 E |
| Kronoby (Kruunupyy) | 26 | 63.43 N | 23.02 E |
| Kronockaja Sopka, vulkan ∧[1] | 74 | 54.44 N | 160.31 E |
| Kronockij zaliv ⊂ | 74 | 54.12 N | 160.36 E |
| Kronoki | 74 | 54.36 N | 161.10 E |
| Kronshagen | 41 | 54.20 N | 10.05 E |
| Kronstadt → Brașov, Rom. | 38 | 45.39 N | 25.37 E |
| Kronštadt, Ross. | 76 | 59.59 N | 29.45 E |
| Kronwa | 110 | 15.25 N | 98.26 E |
| Kroondal | 158 | 25.45 S | 27.19 E |
| Kroonstad | 158 | 27.46 S | 27.12 E |
| Kröpelin | 54 | 54.04 N | 11.48 E |
| Kropotkin, Ross. | 72 | 45.26 N | 40.34 E |
| Kropotkin, Ross. | 88 | 58.30 N | 115.17 E |
| Kropotkina, gora ∧ | 88 | 53.43 N | 117.32 E |
| Kropp | 41 | 54.24 N | 9.31 E |
| Kroppefjäll ∧[2] | 26 | 58.40 N | 12.13 E |
| Kroppenstedt | 54 | 51.56 N | 11.18 E |
| Kropstädt | 54 | 51.58 N | 12.44 E |
| Kropufino | 76 | 60.23 N | 39.10 E |
| Krościenko | 30 | 49.27 N | 20.26 E |
| Kroshna | 78 | 50.18 N | 28.39 E |
| Kröslin | 54 | 54.07 N | 13.45 E |
| Krośniewice | 30 | 52.16 N | 19.10 E |
| Krosno | 30 | 49.42 N | 21.46 E |
| Krosno □[4] | 30 | 49.30 N | 22.00 E |
| Krosno Odrzańskie | 30 | 52.04 N | 15.05 E |
| Krossen, Dtsch. | 54 | 50.58 N | 11.59 E |
| Krossen, Dtsch. | 54 | 50.58 N | 11.59 E |
| Krostitz | 54 | 51.28 N | 12.27 E |
| Krotoszyn | 30 | 51.42 N | 17.26 E |
| Krotovka | 80 | 53.18 N | 51.12 E |
| Krotovo | 86 | 56.57 N | 69.20 E |
| Krotz Springs | 194 | 30.32 N | 91.45 W |
| Kröv | 56 | 49.59 N | 7.05 E |
| Kroya | 115a | 7.38 S | 109.14 E |
| Krško | 36 | 45.58 N | 15.29 E |
| Krsy | 60 | 49.54 N | 13.03 E |
| Kr'učkov | 80 | 48.01 N | 45.40 E |
| Kr'učkovo | 76 | 57.03 N | 35.34 E |
| Kruckow | 54 | 53.54 N | 13.14 E |
| Krudenburg | 263 | 51.39 N | 6.45 E |
| Kruenggeukueh | 114 | 5.15 N | 97.02 E |
| Kruengluak | 114 | 2.50 N | 97.45 E |
| Kruft | 56 | 50.23 N | 7.20 E |
| Kruger National Park ♠ | 156 | 24.00 S | 31.40 E |
| Krugersdorp | 158 | 26.05 S | 27.35 E |
| Krugersdorp □[5] | 273d | 26.05 S | 27.35 E |
| Krugersdorp Race Course ♠ | 273d | 26.08 S | 27.45 E |
| Krugersdorp West | 273d | 26.06 S | 27.45 E |
| Krugloje | 83 | 47.01 N | 39.15 E |
| Kruglooz'ornoje, Kaz. | 80 | 51.06 N | 51.17 E |
| Kruglooz'ornoje, Ross. | 86 | 55.13 N | 79.01 E |
| Kruglyži | 80 | 58.31 N | 47.42 E |
| Krugzell | 58 | 47.47 N | 10.16 E |
| Kruhlae | 76 | 54.15 N | 29.48 E |
| Krui | 112 | 5.11 S | 103.56 E |
| Kruidfontein | 158 | 32.51 S | 21.57 E |
| Kruiningen | 52 | 51.27 N | 4.02 E |
| Kruis, Kaap › | 156 | 21.49 S | 13.57 E |
| Kruisfontein | 158 | 34.00 S | 24.43 E |
| Kruishoutem | 50 | 50.54 N | 3.31 E |
| Kruisland | 52 | 51.34 N | 4.24 E |
| Kruisrivier | 158 | 33.26 S | 21.55 E |
| Kruisvallei | 158 | 33.53 S | 23.10 E |
| Krujë | 38 | 41.30 N | 19.48 E |
| Krukira, Laguna de ⊂ | 236 | 13.56 N | 83.30 W |
| Kr'ukov | 80 | 47.24 N | 42.28 E |
| Kr'ukovo, Ross. | 74 | 66.30 N | 159.31 E |
| Kr'ukovo, Ross. | 82 | 55.59 N | 37.10 E |
| Kr'ukovo, Ross. | 82 | 55.28 N | 36.32 E |
| Kr'ukovo, Ross. | 83 | 47.40 N | 39.13 E |
| Krukut, Kali ≃ | 269e | 6.12 S | 106.48 E |
| Kruleuščyna | 76 | 55.02 N | 27.45 E |
| Krumasye | 164 | 1.40 S | 133.09 E |
| Krumbach, Dtsch. | 58 | 47.58 N | 9.02 E |
| Krumbach, Dtsch. | 58 | 48.14 N | 10.22 E |
| Krumme Lanke ◎ | 264a | 52.27 N | 13.14 E |
| Krummendammer Heide ◆[3] | 264a | 52.28 N | 13.39 E |
| Krummensee | 264a | 52.36 N | 13.42 E |
| Krumme Steyrling ≃ | 61 | 47.54 N | 14.14 E |
| Krummhörn | 52 | 53.26 N | 7.06 E |
| Krummhörn ◆[1] | 52 | 53.25 N | 7.10 E |
| Krumovgrad | 38 | 41.28 N | 25.39 E |
| Krumroy | 214 | 39.58 N | 81.24 W |
| Krün | 64 | 47.30 N | 11.16 E |
| Krung Thep (Bangkok), Thai | 110 | 13.45 N | 100.31 E |
| Krung Thep (Bangkok), Thai | 269a | 13.45 N | 100.31 E |
| Krung Thep Mahanakhon □[4] | 269a | 13.47 N | 100.43 E |
| Krung Thon Bridge ◆[5] | 269a | 13.47 N | 100.30 E |
| Krupá | 54 | 50.08 N | 13.41 E |
| Krupec | 78 | 51.38 N | 34.21 E |
| Krüpel-See ◎ | 264a | 52.18 N | 13.42 E |
| Krupka | 54 | 50.43 N | 13.46 E |
| Krupki | 76 | 54.19 N | 29.08 E |
| Kruså | 41 | 54.50 N | 9.25 E |
| Kruščica jezero ◎[1] | 36 | 44.39 N | 15.19 E |
| Krusenstern, Cape › | 180 | 67.07 N | 163.43 W |
| Kruševac | 38 | 43.35 N | 21.20 E |
| Kruševo | 38 | 41.22 N | 21.14 E |
| Krušinovka | 76 | 53.14 N | 29.50 E |
| Krušné hory (Erzgebirge) ⋏, Europe | 30 | 50.30 N | 13.10 E |
| Krušné hory (Erzgebirge) ⋏, Europe | 54 | 50.30 N | 13.15 E |
| Kruszwica | 30 | 52.41 N | 18.19 E |
| Krutaja, Ross. | 24 | 63.02 N | 54.38 E |
| Krutaja, Ross. | 86 | 57.24 N | 76.27 E |
| Krutaja Gorka | 86 | 55.25 N | 73.15 E |
| Krutcy | 76 | 57.10 N | 29.23 E |
| Krutec, Ross. | 76 | 60.17 N | 39.25 E |
| Krutec, Ross. | 82 | 56.10 N | 38.33 E |
| Kruticha, Ross. | 86 | 53.58 N | 81.14 E |
| Kruticha, Ross. | 86 | 56.49 N | 77.10 E |
| Krutinka | 86 | 56.01 N | 71.31 E |
| Krutoje | 76 | 52.26 N | 37.28 E |
| Krutoj Log | 86 | 57.53 N | 58.14 E |
| Krutoj Majdan | 80 | 55.35 N | 44.04 E |
| Krutyje Verchi | 82 | 54.19 N | 36.26 E |
| Kruunupyy → Kronoby | 26 | 63.43 N | 23.02 E |
| Kruzenšterna, proliv ⋓ | 74 | 48.30 N | 153.50 E |
| Kruzof Island I | 180 | 57.10 N | 135.40 W |
| Kryčau | 76 | 53.42 N | 31.43 E |
| Krydor | 184 | 52.47 N | 107.03 W |
| Krylatskoje ◆[8] | 265b | 55.45 N | 37.26 E |
| Krylbo | 40 | 60.08 N | 16.13 E |
| Krylovskaja | 78 | 46.07 N | 39.19 E |
| Krym | 83 | 47.19 N | 39.31 E |
| Krym, Respublika □[3] | 78 | 45.00 N | 34.00 E |
| Krymsk | 78 | 44.56 N | 37.59 E |
| Kryms'ke | 83 | 48.45 N | 38.48 E |
| Kryms'ki hory ⋏ | 78 | 44.45 N | 34.25 E |
| Krymskij | 78 | 47.40 N | 40.46 E |
| Kryms'kyy pivostriv (Crimean Peninsula) ›[1] | 78 | 45.00 N | 34.00 E |
| Krynica | 30 | 49.25 N | 20.56 E |
| Krynka ≃ | 83 | 47.36 N | 38.47 E |
| Krynychky | 78 | 48.22 N | 34.27 E |
| Krynychne | 78 | 45.32 N | 28.40 E |
| Kryva kosa ›[2] | 83 | 47.02 N | 38.06 E |
| Kryva Ruda | 78 | 49.31 N | 32.59 E |
| Kryve Ozero | 78 | 47.56 N | 30.21 E |
| Kryvičy | 76 | 54.43 N | 27.17 E |
| Kryvošyn | 76 | 52.52 N | 26.08 E |
| Kryvyy Rih | 78 | 47.55 N | 33.21 E |
| Kryvyy Torets' ≃ | 83 | 48.39 N | 37.32 E |
| Kryzhopil' | 78 | 48.23 N | 28.52 E |
| Kryžina, chrebet ⋏ | 88 | 54.00 N | 95.00 E |
| Kryzs'ke | 83 | 49.28 N | 39.38 E |
| Krzepice | 30 | 50.58 N | 18.44 E |
| Krzeszowice | 30 | 50.09 N | 19.39 E |
| Krzeszyce | 54 | 52.36 N | 15.01 E |
| Krzna ≃ | 30 | 52.08 N | 23.31 E |
| Krzywiń | 30 | 51.58 N | 16.49 E |
| Krzyż | 30 | 52.54 N | 16.01 E |
| Ksar Chellala | 148 | 35.13 N | 2.18 E |
| Ksar el Barka | 150 | 18.24 N | 12.13 W |
| Ksar-el-Kebir | 148 | 35.01 N | 5.54 W |
| Ksar-el-Seghir | 34 | 35.50 N | 5.32 W |
| Ksar Hellal | 36 | 35.39 N | 10.54 E |
| Ksaverivka | 78 | 50.03 N | 30.12 E |
| Ksel, Djebel ∧ | 148 | 33.44 N | 1.10 E |
| Kšen' ≃ | 76 | 52.23 N | 37.44 E |
| Ksenjevka | 88 | 53.34 N | 118.44 E |
| Ksenofontova | 24 | 60.58 N | 56.12 E |
| Kšenskij | 78 | 51.52 N | 37.43 E |
| Książ Wielkopolski | 30 | 52.05 N | 17.14 E |
| Ksob, Oued ≃ | 36 | 35.46 N | 4.34 E |
| Ksour, Monts des ⋏ | 148 | 32.45 N | 0.30 W |
| Ksour Essaf | 148 | 35.25 N | 11.00 E |
| Kstovo | 80 | 56.11 N | 44.11 E |
| Kū', Wādī al- V | 140 | 13.37 N | 25.15 E |
| Kuah | 114 | 6.19 N | 99.51 E |
| Kuai ≃ | 100 | 33.09 N | 117.32 E |
| Kuala, Indon. | 112 | 2.55 N | 105.48 E |
| Kuala, Indon. | 114 | 3.32 N | 98.24 E |
| Kualabee | 114 | 4.24 N | 96.03 E |
| Kuala Berang | 114 | 5.04 N | 103.01 E |
| Kualacenako | 112 | 0.28 S | 102.40 E |
| Kuala Kangsar | 114 | 4.46 N | 100.56 E |
| Kualakapuas | 112 | 3.01 S | 114.21 E |
| Kuala Kedah | 114 | 6.06 N | 100.18 E |
| Kuala Kelawang | 114 | 2.56 N | 102.05 E |
| Kuala Kerai | 114 | 5.32 N | 102.12 E |
| Kuala Kerau | 114 | 3.43 N | 102.22 E |
| Kualakeriau | 112 | 0.50 N | 113.20 E |
| Kuala Ketil | 114 | 5.36 N | 100.39 E |
| Kuala Kubu Baharu | 114 | 3.34 N | 101.39 E |
| Kuala Kurau | 114 | 5.01 N | 100.26 E |
| Kualakurun | 112 | 1.07 S | 113.53 E |
| Kualalangsa | 114 | 4.32 N | 98.01 E |
| Kuala Lipis | 114 | 4.11 N | 102.03 E |
| Kuala Lumpur | 114 | 3.10 N | 101.42 E |
| Kuala Lumpur □[3] | 114 | 3.10 N | 101.42 E |
| Kualamanjual | 112 | 1.25 S | 112.00 E |
| Kuala Nerang | 114 | 6.15 N | 100.36 E |
| Kualapesaguan | 112 | 2.01 S | 110.08 E |
| Kuala Pilah | 114 | 2.44 N | 102.15 E |
| Kualapuu | 229a | 21.09 N | 157.02 W |
| Kuala Selangor | 114 | 3.21 N | 101.15 E |
| Kualasimpang | 114 | 4.17 N | 98.03 E |
| Kuala Terengganu | 114 | 5.20 N | 103.08 E |
| Kualu ≃ | 114 | 2.45 N | 100.00 E |
| Kuamut | 112 | 5.13 N | 117.30 E |
| Kuamut ≃ | 112 | 5.13 N | 117.32 E |
| Kuanbang | 98 | 40.29 N | 120.04 E |
| Kuancheng, Zhg. | 98 | 40.37 N | 118.31 E |
| Kuancheng, Zhg. | 105 | 40.38 N | 118.27 E |
| Kuandang | 112 | 0.52 N | 122.55 E |
| Kuandian | 98 | 40.43 N | 124.44 E |
| Kuando → Cuando ≃ | 152 | 18.27 S | 23.32 E |
| Kuanhsi | 100 | 24.48 N | 121.10 E |
| Kuanmiao | 100 | 22.58 N | 120.19 E |
| Kuanshan | 100 | 23.03 N | 121.09 E |
| Kuan Shan ∧ | 100 | 23.14 N | 120.54 E |
| Kuantan | 114 | 3.48 N | 103.20 E |
| Kuantan ≃ | 114 | 3.50 N | 103.17 E |
| Kuanyin | 100 | 25.02 N | 121.04 E |
| Kuanyün → Guanyun | 98 | 34.20 N | 119.17 E |
| Kuanza → Cuanza ≃ | 152 | 9.19 S | 13.08 E |
| Kuba → Cuba □[1] | 240p | 21.30 N | 80.00 W |
| Kuban' ≃ | 72 | 45.20 N | 37.30 E |
| Kubbī | 140 | 11.08 N | 25.14 E |
| Kubbum | 140 | 11.47 N | 23.47 E |
| Kubena ≃ | 76 | 59.36 N | 39.39 E |
| Kubenskoje | 76 | 59.26 N | 39.40 E |
| Kubenskoje, ozero ◎ | 76 | 59.40 N | 39.25 E |
| Kubiki | 94 | 37.11 N | 138.20 E |
| Kubinka | 82 | 55.35 N | 36.43 E |
| Kubitzer Bodden ⊂ | 54 | 54.24 N | 13.12 E |
| Küblis | 58 | 46.55 N | 9.47 E |
| Kubn'a ≃ | 80 | 55.31 N | 48.27 E |
| Kubokawa | 96 | 33.12 N | 133.08 E |
| Kubor, Mount ∧ | 164 | 6.05 S | 144.45 E |
| Kubr' ≃ | 82 | 56.52 N | 38.17 E |
| Kubrat | 38 | 43.48 N | 26.30 E |
| Kubu | 115b | 8.16 S | 115.35 E |
| Kubuchaj | 88 | 50.30 N | 114.48 E |
| Kubu Gajah | 114 | 5.10 N | 100.41 E |
| Kubumesaai | 112 | 1.31 N | 115.06 E |
| Kubutambahan | 115b | 8.05 S | 115.10 E |
| Kučema | 24 | 65.37 N | 42.28 E |
| Kučen'ajevo | 80 | 54.44 N | 46.24 E |
| Kučevo | 38 | 44.27 N | 21.44 E |
| Kuchaiburi | 126 | 22.16 N | 86.10 E |
| Kuchāman | 120 | 27.09 N | 74.52 E |
| Kuch'ang-ni | 98 | 40.09 N | 124.46 E |
| Kuchelebai | 154 | 1.29 N | 35.01 E |
| Kuchen | 58 | 48.38 N | 9.48 E |
| Kuchenspitze ∧ | 58 | 47.03 N | 10.14 E |
| Kuchinarai | 110 | 16.32 N | 104.04 E |
| Kuching | 112 | 1.33 N | 110.20 E |
| Kuchinoerabu-jima I | 93b | 30.28 N | 130.12 E |
| Kuchino-shima I | 93b | 29.57 N | 129.57 E |
| Kuchiwa | 96 | 34.53 N | 132.55 E |
| Kuchl | 64 | 47.37 N | 13.09 E |
| Kūchnay Darweyshān | 128 | 30.59 N | 64.11 E |
| Kuchterin Lug | 89 | 52.25 N | 128.05 E |
| Kuchtinka | 82 | 54.29 N | 38.10 E |
| Kuchurhan ≃ | 78 | 46.43 N | 29.53 E |
| Kučino | 265b | 55.45 N | 37.58 E |
| Kučkak | 85 | 40.15 N | 70.20 E |
| Kučki | 80 | 53.01 N | 44.29 E |
| Kuçovë | 38 | 40.48 N | 19.54 E |
| Küçük Ağrı Dağı ∧ | 84 | 39.40 N | 44.25 E |
| Küçükbahçe | 130 | 38.33 N | 26.24 E |
| Küçükbakkal ◆[8] | 267b | 40.58 N | 29.06 E |
| Küçükçekmece ◆[8] | 267b | 40.59 N | 28.46 E |
| Küçükçekmece Gölü ◎ | 267b | 41.00 N | 28.46 E |
| Küçükköy ◆[8] | 267b | 41.04 N | 28.54 E |
| Küçükkuyu | 130 | 39.32 N | 26.36 E |
| Kučukskoje, ozero ◎ | 86 | 52.42 N | 79.46 E |
| Kucur, Tanjung › | 115a | 8.39 S | 114.34 E |
| Kūd | 123 | 33.05 N | 75.17 E |
| Kuda ≃ | 88 | 52.25 N | 104.08 E |
| Kudaka-jima I | 174m | 26.09 N | 127.54 E |
| Kudamatsu | 96 | 34.00 N | 131.52 E |
| Kudanggou | 104 | 41.06 N | 124.00 E |
| Kudap | 114 | 1.17 N | 102.26 E |
| Kudara, Ross. | 88 | 52.13 N | 106.39 E |
| Kudara, Taj. | 85 | 38.25 N | 72.41 E |
| Kudara ≃ | 85 | 38.19 N | 72.28 E |
| Kudara-Somon | 88 | 50.10 N | 107.25 E |
| Kudat | 112 | 6.53 N | 116.50 E |
| Kudejevskij | 86 | 54.52 N | 56.46 E |
| Kudene | 164 | 6.14 S | 134.39 E |
| Kudever' | 76 | 56.47 N | 29.23 E |
| Kudinovo | 82 | 55.45 N | 38.12 E |
| Kudirkos Naumiestis | 76 | 54.46 N | 22.53 E |
| Kudongho | 98 | 35.31 N | 126.29 E |
| Kudoyama | 96 | 34.17 N | 135.34 E |
| Kudremukh ∧ | 122 | 13.08 N | 75.16 E |
| Kudrovo | 265a | 59.54 N | 30.31 E |
| Kudus | 115a | 6.48 S | 110.50 E |
| Kudyat al-Islām | 142 | 27.32 N | 30.45 E |
| Kudymkar | 86 | 59.01 N | 54.37 E |
| Kuee Ruins ⊥ | 229d | 19.21 N | 155.23 W |
| Kueishan Tao I | 100 | 24.51 N | 121.57 E |
| Kueisui → Hohhot | 102 | 40.51 N | 111.40 E |
| Kueiyang → Guiyang | 102 | 26.35 N | 106.43 E |


| Symbol | English | Deutsch | Español | Français | Português |
|---|---|---|---|---|---|
| ≃ | River | Fluß | Río | Rivière | Rio |
| ≊ | Canal | Kanal | Canal | Canal | Canal |
| ∟ | Waterfall, Rapids | Wasserfall, Stromschnellen | Cascada, Rápidos | Chute d'eau, Rapides | Cascata, Rápidos |
| ⋓ | Strait | Meeresstraße | Estrecho | Détroit | Estreito |
| ⊂ | Bay, Gulf | Bucht, Golf | Bahía, Golfo | Baie, Golfe | Baía, Golfo |
| ◎ | Lake, Lakes | See, Seen | Lago, Lagos | Lac, Lacs | Lago, Lagos |
| ≡ | Swamp | Sumpf | Pantano | Marais | Pântano |
| ⊓ | Ice Features, Glacier | Eis- und Gletscherformen | Accidentes Glaciales | Formes glaciaires | Acidentes glaciares |
| ⊤ | Other Hydrographic Features | Andere Hydrographische Objekte | Otros Elementos Hidrográficos | Autres données hydrographiques | Outros acidentes hidrográficos |

| Symbol | English | Deutsch | Español | Français | Português |
|---|---|---|---|---|---|
| ✣ | Submarine Features | Untermeerische Objekte | Accidentes Submarinos | Formes de relief sous-marin | Acidentes submarinos |
| □ | Political Unit | Politische Einheit | Unidad Politica | Entité politique | Unidade política |
| ⛫ | Cultural Institution | Kulturelle Institution | Institución Cultural | Institution culturelle | Instituição cultural |
| ⊥ | Historical Site | Historische Stätte | Sitio Histórico | Site historique | Sitio histórico |
| ♠ | Recreational Site | Erholungs- und Ferienort | Sitio de Recreo | Centre de loisirs | Area de Lazer |
| ⊠ | Airport | Flughafen | Aeropuerto | Aéroport | Aeroporto |
| ■ | Military Installation | Militäranlage | Instalación Militar | Installation militaire | Instalação militar |
| ◆ | Miscellaneous | Verschiedenes | Misceláneo | Divers | Diversos |

Kuekvun' ≃ 180 69.14 N 179.25 E
Kuënlun → Kunlun Shan ⋏ 120 36.30 N 88.00 E
Kuerbin 89 49.25 N 128.59 E
K'uerhlo → Korla 90 41.44 N 86.09 E
Kufayr az-Zayt 132 33.26 N 35.44 E
Kufayr Yābūs 132 33.42 N 36.01 E
Kufrinjah 132 32.18 N 35.42 E
Kufstein 64 47.35 N 12.10 E
Kufūr Bilshāy 142 30.51 N 30.48 E
Kufūr Najm 142 30.44 N 31.35 E
Kuga, Nihon 96 34.05 N 132.05 E
Kuga, Nihon 96 33.56 N 132.16 E
Kugaluk ≃ 180 69.10 N 131.00 W
Kugaly 86 44.29 N 78.40 E
Kugarčino 80 55.33 N 50.29 E
Kugart ≃ 85 40.52 N 72.53 E
Kugas 85 38.21 N 70.48 E
Kugej 83 46.53 N 39.19 E
Kugesi 80 56.02 N 47.18 E
Kugmallit Bay ⊂ 180 69.33 N 133.25 W
Kugojeja ≃ 78 46.34 N 39.38 E
Kuguno 94 36.03 N 137.16 E
Kuhaylī 140 19.25 N 32.50 E
Kühbach 60 48.29 N 11.11 E
Kūhdasht 128 33.32 N 47.36 E
Kūh Lab, Ra's-e ≻ 128 25.17 N 60.28 E
Kuhlīyah, Wādī V 142 30.05 N 31.58 E
Kühlungsborn 54 54.09 N 11.43 E
Kuhmo 26 64.08 N 29.31 E
Kuhmoinen 26 61.34 N 25.11 E
Kühnhausen 54 51.02 N 10.58 E
Kühnsdorf 61 46.37 N 14.37 E
Kūhpāyeh 128 32.43 N 52.26 E
Kühren 54 51.20 N 12.50 E
Kuhstedt 52 53.23 N 8.58 E
Kui 164 7.30 S 147.15 E
Kuibyschew → Samara 80 53.12 N 50.09 E
Kuidesu 98 41.46 N 119.29 E
Kuidou 100 25.10 N 118.11 E
Kuikkol', ozero ⊜ 86 50.57 N 64.30 E
Kuikui, Lae o ≻ 229a 20.36 N 156.35 W
Kuilāpāl 126 22.50 N 86.38 E
Kuinre 52 52.47 N 5.50 E
Kuiseb ≃ 156 22.59 S 14.31 E
Kuishi-yama ∧, Nihon 96 33.51 N 133.35 E
Kuishi-yama ∧, Nihon 96 33.40 N 133.31 E
Kuitan 100 23.05 N 115.58 E
Kuito 152 12.22 S 16.56 E
Kuiu Island I 180 56.45 N 134.10 W
Kuivaniemi 26 65.35 N 25.11 E
Kuivastu 76 58.35 N 23.22 E
Kuja, Ross. 24 67.46 N 53.10 E
Kuja, Ross. 24 65.05 N 40.06 E
Kujang 98 39.52 N 126.01 E
Kujani Game Reserve ◆[4] 150 7.10 N 0.50 W
Kujawy ◆[1] 30 52.45 N 18.30 E
Kujbyšev → Samara, Ross. 80 53.12 N 50.09 E
Kujbyšev, Ross. 86 55.27 N 78.19 E
Kujbyševo, Ross. 83 47.49 N 38.55 E
Kujbyševo, Uzb. 85 40.22 N 71.17 E
Kujbyševskij, Kaz. 86 53.15 N 66.51 E
Kujbyševskij, Uzb. 72 37.52 N 68.44 E
Kujbyševskij Zaton 80 55.09 N 49.12 E
Kujbyševskoje vodochranilišče ⊜[1] 80 54.30 N 48.30 E
Kujeda 86 56.26 N 55.35 E
Kujgan 86 45.25 N 74.10 E
Kujgenkol' 80 49.17 N 47.59 E
Kuji 92 40.11 N 141.46 E
Kuji ≃ 94 36.29 N 140.37 E
Kujirai 268 35.56 N 139.27 E
Kujl'uk 85 41.15 N 69.20 E
Kujman' 76 52.52 N 39.16 E
Kujŏng-ni 98 37.53 N 125.54 E
Kujten-Uul ∧ 86 49.08 N 87.49 E
Kujtun 88 54.21 N 101.29 E
Kujū 96 33.01 N 131.18 E
Kujūkuri 94 35.32 N 140.25 E
Kujūkuri-hama ⊥[2] 94 35.35 N 140.30 E
Kujū-san ∧ 96 33.05 N 131.15 E
Kuk ∧ 64 46.16 N 13.45 E
Kuk ≃ 180 70.36 N 160.00 W
Kukaklek Lake ⊜ 180 59.09 N 155.20 W
Kukalaya ≃ 236 13.39 N 83.37 W
Kukan 89 49.12 N 133.28 E
Kukarino 82 55.31 N 35.59 E
Kukawa 146 12.56 N 13.35 E
Kukerin 162 33.11 S 118.05 E
Kukës 38 42.05 N 20.24 E
Kuke Shan ⋏ 85 40.00 N 75.00 E
Kuki 94 36.04 N 139.40 E
Kukipi 164 8.10 S 146.05 E
Kukkola 26 65.59 N 24.04 E
Kukmirn 61 47.04 N 16.13 E
Kukmor 80 56.13 N 50.54 E
Kukoboj 76 58.42 N 39.54 E
Kukol' 76 59.52 N 32.35 E
Kükong → Shaoguan 100 24.50 N 113.37 E
Kukpowruk ≃ 180 69.35 N 163.00 W
Kukpuk ≃ 180 68.23 N 166.20 W
Kukshi 120 22.12 N 74.45 E
Kukuj 76 59.21 N 32.33 E
Kuku-Nor → Qinghai Hu ⊜ 102 36.50 N 100.20 E
Kukup 114 1.19 N 103.27 E
Kuku Point ≻ 174a 19.18 N 166.34 E
Kukuri Mukuri Char I 126 21.56 N 90.39 E
Kukuštan 86 57.38 N 56.30 E
Kula, Blg. 38 43.53 N 22.31 E
Kula, Jugo. 38 45.36 N 19.32 E
Kula, Tür. 130 38.32 N 28.40 E
Kula, Hi., U.S. 229a 20.52 N 156.40 W
Kul'ab 120 37.55 N 69.46 E
Kul'ab □[4] 85 38.15 N 69.45 E
Kulāchi 123 31.56 N 70.27 E
Kulagi 76 52.56 N 32.24 E
Kulagino 80 48.22 N 51.33 E
Kula Gulf ⊔ 175e 8.05 S 157.18 E
Kulai 114 1.40 N 103.36 E
Kulaj 86 57.42 N 75.15 E
Kula Kangri ∧ 124 28.03 N 90.27 E
Kulākh 144 21.18 N 40.41 E
Kulakovo, Ross. 82 55.06 N 37.28 E
Kulakovo, Ross. 86 58.06 N 93.57 E
Kulakši 86 47.12 N 55.24 E
Kulal, Mount ∧ 154 2.43 N 36.56 E
Kulanak 85 41.22 N 75.31 E
Kulandy 86 46.08 N 59.31 E
Kulanotpes ≃ 86 50.21 N 69.08 E
Kular 74 70.41 N 134.22 E
Kulassein Island I 116 6.25 N 120.41 E
Kulaura 120 24.32 N 92.03 E
Kulautuva 76 54.58 N 23.38 E
Kulaykilī 140 11.21 N 25.36 E
Kul'či 89 53.33 N 139.36 E
Kuldīga 76 56.58 N 21.59 E
Kuldja → Yining 86 43.54 N 81.21 E
Kul'dur 89 49.13 N 131.38 E
Kule 156 23.05 S 20.05 E
Kulebaki 80 55.24 N 42.32 E
Kulejevo 86 59.40 N 80.59 E
Kulen Vakuf 36 44.34 N 16.06 E
Kulešovka 83 47.05 N 39.33 E
Kulevčinskij 86 53.12 N 61.26 E
Kulgām 123 33.39 N 75.01 E
Kulgera 162 25.50 S 133.18 E
Kulgunino 86 53.35 N 56.56 E
Kuligi 80 58.11 N 53.46 E
Kulikovka 80 52.14 N 47.36 E
Kulikovo 76 52.14 N 39.35 E
Kulikovskij 80 50.51 N 42.34 E
Kulim 114 5.22 N 100.34 E
Kulin 162 32.40 S 118.10 E
Kuliushucun 105 40.07 N 116.34 E
Kulju 26 61.23 N 23.46 E
Kulkyne Creek ≃ 166 30.16 S 144.12 E
Kullaberg ⋏[2] 41 56.18 N 12.30 E
Kullamaa 76 58.53 N 24.05 E
Küllenhahn ◆[8] 263 51.14 N 7.08 E
Küllstedt 56 51.16 N 10.17 E
Kullu 123 31.58 N 77.06 E
Kulm 198 46.18 N 98.57 W
Kulmbach 54 50.06 N 11.27 E
Kulnura 170 33.14 S 151.13 E
Kuloj, Ross. 24 64.58 N 43.28 E
Kuloj, Ross. 24 61.02 N 42.29 E
Kuloj ≃, Ross. 24 66.03 N 43.22 E
Kuloj ≃, Ross. 76 60.25 N 42.30 E
Kuloli 85 39.22 N 68.03 E
Kulongshan 98 41.43 N 116.54 E
Kulongshanpuzi 104 41.16 N 123.59 E
Kulotino 76 58.27 N 33.21 E
Kulp 130 38.30 N 41.02 E
Kulpahar 124 25.19 N 79.39 E
Kulpara 168b 34.04 S 138.02 E
Kulpawn ≃ 150 10.21 N 1.05 W
Kulpi 126 22.06 N 88.15 E
Kul'pino 82 56.18 N 37.09 E
Kulpmont 208 40.47 N 76.28 W
Kulpsville 285 40.15 N 75.20 W
Kul'sary 86 46.59 N 54.01 E
Kulsbjerge ⋏[2] 41 55.01 N 12.01 E
Külsheim 56 49.40 N 9.31 E
Kültepe ⊥ 130 38.44 N 35.34 E
Kulti 126 23.44 N 86.51 E
Kultikri 126 22.10 N 87.09 E
Kultuk 88 51.44 N 103.42 E
Kulu 130 39.06 N 33.05 E
Kuluha, Jabal ∧ 140 15.31 N 23.25 E
Kulumadau 164 9.03 S 152.43 E
Kulunda 86 52.35 N 78.57 E
Kulunda ≃ 86 52.59 N 79.48 E
Kulundinskaja step' ⩧ 86 53.00 N 79.00 E
Kulundinskoje, ozero ⊜ 86 53.00 N 79.36 E
Kuluqi 89 50.23 N 124.13 E
Kulwin 166 35.02 S 142.33 E
Kulykiv 78 49.58 N 24.04 E
Kulykivka 78 51.23 N 31.37 E
Kum ≃ 130 38.38 N 27.32 E
Kuma 96 33.39 N 132.54 E
Kuma ≃, Nihon 92 32.30 N 130.34 E
Kuma ≃, Ross. 72 44.56 N 47.00 E
Kuma ≃, Ross. 86 59.32 N 66.45 E
Kumagaya 94 36.08 N 139.23 E
Kumai, Indon. 112 3.23 S 112.33 E
Kumai, Indon. 112 2.44 S 111.43 E
Kumai, Teluk ⊂ 112 3.00 S 111.43 E
Kumaishi 92a 42.08 N 139.59 E
Kumajri 84 40.48 N 43.50 E
Kumakanda 88 52.44 N 116.55 E
Kumalarang 116 7.44 N 123.08 E
Kumamba, Kepulauan II 164 1.36 S 138.45 E
Kumamoto 92 32.48 N 130.43 E
Kumamoto □[5] 96 32.58 N 130.55 E
Kumano, Nihon 92 33.54 N 136.05 E
Kumano, Nihon 96 34.20 N 132.34 E
Kumano ≃ 92 33.44 N 136.01 E
Kumano-nada ⊤[2] 92 33.47 N 136.20 E
Kumanovo 38 42.08 N 21.43 E
Kumār ≃[1], Bngl. 126 23.11 N 90.10 E
Kumār ≃[1], Bngl. 126 23.31 N 89.28 E
Kumara, N.Z. 172 42.38 S 171.11 E
Kumara, Ross. 89 51.37 N 126.47 E
Kumārapālaiyam 122 11.28 N 77.43 E
Kumardhubi 126 23.48 N 86.43 E
Kumarganj 126 22.59 N 87.44 E
Kumārghāt 120 24.04 N 92.04 E
Kumārgrām 124 26.37 N 89.50 E
Kumāri ≃ 126 22.57 N 86.48 E
Kumārkhāli 124 23.51 N 89.15 E
Kumarl 162 32.47 S 121.33 E
Kumasi 150 6.41 N 1.35 W
Kumatori 270 34.24 N 135.22 E
Kumawa, Pegunungan ⋏ 164 3.50 S 132.50 E
Kumba 152 4.38 N 9.25 E
Kumbakonam 122 10.58 N 79.23 E
Kumba Pits 156 18.45 S 24.45 E
Kumbar 140 12.03 N 30.16 E
Kumbarilla 166 27.19 S 150.53 E
Kumbe 164 8.21 S 140.13 E
Kumbel' 85 42.30 N 73.11 E
Kümch'ŏn 98 38.10 N 126.29 E
Kum-Dag 128 39.16 N 54.35 E
Kumdah ⊤[4] 144 20.23 N 45.05 E
Kumdan ∧ 123 35.09 N 77.35 E
Kumdanlı 130 38.19 N 30.59 E
Kume 96 35.03 N 133.54 E
Kume-jima I 93b 26.20 N 126.47 E
Kumenan 96 34.56 N 133.58 E
Kumeny 80 58.07 N 49.56 E
Kŭm-gang ≃ 98 36.00 N 126.40 E
Kŭmgang-san ∧ 98 38.35 N 128.10 E
Kumhausen 60 48.30 N 12.10 E
Kŭmhwa 98 38.17 N 127.28 E
Kumi 154 1.29 N 33.56 E
Kumihama 96 35.36 N 134.55 E
Kuminovskoje 86 57.48 N 64.07 E
Kuminskij 86 58.40 N 66.04 E
Kumiyama 270 34.53 N 135.45 E
Kumizawa ◆[8] 268 35.23 N 139.31 E
Kumköy ◆[8] 267b 41.15 N 29.02 E
Kumla 40 59.08 N 15.08 E
Kumli 84 43.58 N 46.04 E
Kumlinge I 26 60.16 N 20.47 E
Kumluca, Tür. 130 36.22 N 30.18 E
Kumluca, Tür. 130 41.27 N 32.28 E
Kummelnäs 40 59.21 N 18.17 E
Kummerow 54 54.17 N 12.53 E
Kummerower See ⊜ 54 53.49 N 12.52 E
Kümmersbruck 60 49.25 N 11.53 E
Kumo 146 10.03 N 11.13 E
Kŭmŏ-do I 98 34.31 N 127.45 E
Kumon Range ⋏ 102 26.30 N 97.15 E
Kumora 88 55.53 N 111.13 E
Kumosō-yama ∧ 96 33.54 N 134.18 E
Kumotori-yama ∧ 94 35.51 N 138.57 E
Kumphawapi 110 17.07 N 103.01 E
Kumrābād 126 24.10 N 87.16 E
Kumru 130 40.53 N 37.17 E
Kŭmsan 98 36.07 N 127.30 E
Kŭmsan-ni 98 37.55 N 125.41 E
Kumsenga 154 3.47 S 30.25 E
Kumta 122 14.25 N 74.24 E
Kumu 154 3.04 N 25.09 E
Kumu ≃ 114 1.24 N 100.43 E
Kumuch 84 42.11 N 47.07 E
Kumukahi, Cape ≻ 229d 19.31 N 154.49 W
Kumukuli 120 37.33 N 88.50 E
Kumusi ≃ 164 8.35 S 148.00 E
Kümüx 86 42.14 N 88.11 E
Kumzār 128 26.20 N 56.25 E
Kuna 202 43.29 N 116.25 W
Kunar (Konar) ≃ 123 34.25 N 70.32 E
Kunašak 86 55.43 N 61.36 E
Kunashiri-tō → Kunašir, ostrov I 92a 44.10 N 146.00 E
Kunašir, ostrov (Kunashiri-tō) I 92a 44.10 N 146.00 E
Kun'batar 84 44.17 N 45.34 E
Kuncheng Hu ⊜ 106 31.35 N 120.45 E
Kunchhā 124 28.08 N 84.20 E
Kunc'ovo ◆[8] 265b 55.44 N 37.26 E
Kunda, Eesti 76 59.29 N 26.32 E
Kunda, Zaïre 154 3.57 S 26.35 E
Kunda Hills ⋏[2] 122 11.10 N 76.30 E
Kundahit 126 23.58 N 87.10 E
Kundam 124 23.13 N 80.21 E
Kundāpura 122 13.38 N 74.42 E
Kundar ≃ 120 31.56 N 69.19 E
Kundat 86 55.14 N 87.51 E
Kundelungu, Parc National de ♦ 154 10.30 S 27.45 E
Kunderu ≃ 122 14.38 N 78.42 E
Kundi 154 1.08 S 40.41 E
Kundiān 123 32.27 N 71.28 E
Kundiawa 164 6.00 S 145.00 E
Kundima 164 4.14 S 143.52 E
Kundl 64 47.28 N 11.59 E
Kundla 120 21.20 N 71.18 E
Kundr'učje ≃ 83 47.52 N 40.15 E
Kundur, Pulau I 112 0.45 N 103.26 E
Kunene □[4] 156 19.00 S 14.00 E
Kunene (Cunene) ≃ 152 17.20 S 11.50 E
Kunersdorf, Forst ◆[3] 264a 52.17 N 12.59 E
Kunes 24 70.21 N 26.31 E
Künes ≃ 86 43.55 N 80.55 E
Kunga ≃[1] 126 21.45 N 89.30 E
Kungälv 26 57.52 N 11.58 E
Kungana 146 7.50 N 10.42 E
Kungchuling → Huaide 89 43.32 N 124.50 E
K'ungej-Ala-Too, chrebet ⋏ 85 42.50 N 77.00 E
Kunggyü Yumco ⊜ 124 30.35 N 82.09 E
Kunghit Island I 182 52.06 N 131.04 W
Kunghsi 100 24.37 N 121.16 E
Kung-pei-tien 269d 25.06 N 121.38 E
Kungrad 86 43.06 N 58.54 E
Kungsängen 40 59.29 N 17.45 E
Kungsängen flygplats ⊠ 40 58.36 N 16.15 E
Kungsbacka 26 57.29 N 12.04 E
Kungsgården 40 60.36 N 16.37 E
Kungshamn 26 58.22 N 11.15 E
Kungsör 40 59.25 N 16.05 E
Kungu 152 2.47 N 19.12 E
Kungur 86 57.25 N 56.57 E
Kunhār ≃ 123 34.17 N 73.29 E
Kunhegyes 30 47.22 N 20.38 E
Kunhing 110 21.18 N 98.26 E
Kuni 94 36.35 N 138.38 E
Kunia 229c 21.29 N 158.07 W
Kunigami 174m 26.45 N 128.10 E
Kunimi 96 33.41 N 131.36 E
Kuningan 115a 6.59 S 108.29 E
Kunisaki 96 33.33 N 131.45 E
Kunisaki-hantō ≻[1] 96 33.30 N 131.40 E
Kunitachi 268 35.41 N 139.26 E
Kuni Vyselki 82 54.18 N 38.41 E
Kunja 76 56.18 N 30.59 E
Kunja ≃, Ross. 76 57.09 N 31.10 E
Kunja ≃, Ross. 82 56.31 N 38.12 E
Kunjāh 123 32.32 N 73.59 E
Kunkle 216 41.38 N 84.30 W
Kunkletown 210 40.51 N 75.27 W
Kunkuri 124 22.45 N 83.57 E
Kunlong 110 23.25 N 98.39 E
Kunlun Shan ⋏ 120 36.30 N 88.00 E
Kunming 102 25.05 N 102.40 E
Kunming Hu ⊜ 271a 39.59 N 116.15 E
Kunmunya Aboriginal Reserve ◆[4] 164 15.45 S 124.45 E
Kunnamkulam 122 10.39 N 76.05 E
Kunost' 76 60.01 N 37.38 E
Kunovice 30 49.03 N 17.29 E
Kunow 54 53.00 N 12.07 E
Kunowice 54 52.20 N 14.50 E
Kunrau 54 52.35 N 11.01 E
Kunsan 98 35.58 N 126.41 E
Kunshan 106 31.23 N 120.57 E
Kunszentmárton 30 46.51 N 20.18 E
Kuntair 150 13.32 N 16.13 W
Kuntaur 150 13.40 N 14.48 W
Kuntiki 86 58.29 N 76.24 E
Kunting 100 29.48 N 121.56 E
Kuntshankoie 152 3.20 S 23.34 E
Kuntuolun 102 45.13 N 115.21 E
Kununurra 164 15.47 S 128.44 E
Kunwi 98 36.15 N 128.34 E
Kunya 150 12.14 N 8.34 E
Kun'ye 83 49.23 N 37.15 E
Kunyo 144 6.17 N 42.33 E
Kunžak 61 49.07 N 15.11 E
Künzell 56 50.33 N 9.42 E
Künzelsau 56 49.16 N 9.41 E
Künzing 60 48.40 N 13.05 E
Kunzulu 152 3.29 S 16.09 E
Kuocang Shan ⋏ 100 28.36 N 120.30 E
Kuohsing 100 24.02 N 120.51 E
Kuokegan 120 37.30 N 89.55 E
Kuolajarvi 24 66.58 N 29.12 E
Kuopio 26 62.54 N 27.41 E
Kuopion lääni □[4] 26 63.00 N 27.30 E
Kuortane 26 62.48 N 23.30 E
Kupa ≃ 36 45.28 N 16.24 E
Kup'abal 271b 37.37 N 126.54 E
Kupang 112 10.10 S 123.35 E
Kupang, Teluk ⊂ 112 10.04 S 123.40 E
Kupanskoje 82 56.51 N 38.43 E
Kuparuk ≃ 180 70.25 N 148.55 W
Kupava 80 51.07 N 42.57 E
Kupavna 265b 55.45 N 38.08 E
Kuper Island I 224 48.58 N 123.39 W
Kupferberg 263 51.09 N 7.27 E
Kupferdreh ◆[8] 263 51.23 N 7.05 E
Kupfermühle 41 54.50 N 9.24 E
Kupferzell 56 49.14 N 9.41 E
Kupiano 164 10.05 S 148.11 E
Kupino 86 54.22 N 77.18 E
Kupiškis 76 55.50 N 24.58 E
Küplü, Tür. 130 41.07 N 26.21 E
Küplü, Tür. 130 40.06 N 30.00 E
Kupol, gora ∧ 180 68.38 N 174.45 E
Kuppenheim 56 48.49 N 8.15 E
Kupper Airport ⊠ 276 40.31 N 74.36 W
Kupreanof 180 56.49 N 132.57 W
Kupreanof Island I 180 56.50 N 133.30 W
Kupreanof Point ≻ 180 55.34 N 159.35 W
Kupres 36 44.00 N 17.17 E
Küps 54 50.11 N 11.16 E
Kupuri 89 54.44 N 130.30 E
Kup'yans'k 83 49.42 N 37.38 E
Kup'yans'k-Vuzlovyy 83 49.39 N 37.39 E
Kupychiv 78 51.00 N 24.44 E
Kuqa 90 41.43 N 82.54 E
Kür (Kura) ≃, Asia 84 39.24 N 49.19 E
Kur ≃, Ross. 89 48.44 N 134.14 E
Kur, Pulau I 164 5.20 S 132.00 E
Kura (Kür) ≃, Asia 84 39.24 N 49.19 E
Kura ≃, Ross. 84 44.06 N 44.57 E
Kurabuchi 94 36.25 N 138.48 E
Kurach 84 41.36 N 47.46 E
Kurach ≃ 84 41.40 N 48.11 E
Kuragaty 85 43.06 N 72.59 E
Kuragaty ≃ 85 43.57 N 73.34 E
Kuragino 86 53.53 N 92.40 E
Kurahashi 96 34.06 N 132.30 E
Kurahashi-jima I 96 34.08 N 132.31 E
Kuraj 86 56.42 N 95.29 E
Kurajlysaj 80 50.07 N 51.51 E
Kurakaki 270 34.59 N 135.28 E
Kurakhivka 83 48.02 N 37.23 E
Kurakhove 83 47.59 N 37.16 E
Kurakino, Ross. 80 52.33 N 44.03 E
Kurakino, Ross. 82 54.30 N 35.48 E
Kurakovo 82 54.05 N 37.14 E
Kūrāli 123 30.50 N 76.35 E
Kuram 85 43.33 N 78.08 E
Kuramā', Ḩarrat ⊥[9] 128 24.30 N 40.15 E
Kurama-yama ∧ 96 35.07 N 135.46 E
Kuraminskij chrebet ⋏ 85 40.45 N 70.10 E
Kuramo Waters ⊂ 273a 6.26 N 3.26 E
Kuranami 268 35.27 N 140.00 E
Kuranec 76 54.33 N 26.57 E
Kuraon 124 24.59 N 82.05 E
Kurar ◆[8] 272c 19.11 N 72.52 E
Kurašasaj 86 50.18 N 56.55 E
Kurashiki 96 34.35 N 133.46 E
Kurasiki → Kurashiki 96 34.35 N 133.46 E
Kurate 96 33.47 N 130.41 E
Kurauli 124 27.24 N 78.59 E
Kuraymah 140 18.33 N 31.51 E
Kurayoshi 96 35.26 N 133.49 E
Kurayyimah 132 32.16 N 35.36 E
Kurba 80 57.34 N 39.32 E
Kurba ≃ 88 52.02 N 108.30 E
Kurbağa Gölü ⊜ 130 38.21 N 35.17 E
Kurbağalı ≃ 267b 40.59 N 29.02 E
Kurbatovo 86 55.34 N 91.10 E
Kurbulik 88 53.45 N 108.57 E
Kurčaloj 84 43.12 N 46.05 E
Kurchatov 78 51.39 N 35.36 E
Kurčum 86 48.37 N 83.40 E
Kurdaj 85 43.21 N 74.59 E
Kürdämir 84 40.21 N 48.08 E
Kurdgelauri 84 41.58 N 45.32 E
Kür dili ≻[2] 84 39.03 N 49.13 E
Kurdistan □[9] 128 37.00 N 45.00 E
Kurdufān al-Janūbīyah □[4] 140 11.00 N 30.00 E
Kurdufān ash-Shamālīyah □[4] 140 14.00 N 29.45 E
Kurduvādi 122 18.05 N 75.26 E
Kurdyumivka 83 48.28 N 37.59 E
Kure, Austl. 164 15.27 S 124.33 E
Kure, Nihon 96 34.14 N 132.34 E
Küre, Tür. 130 41.48 N 33.43 E
Kure Atoll I[1] 14 28.25 N 178.25 W
Küre Dağları ⋏ 130 41.45 N 34.00 E
Kurejka ≃ 74 66.30 N 87.12 E
Kurejskaja 88 58.56 N 111.20 E
Kurenalus 26 65.21 N 26.59 E
Kuresaare 76 58.15 N 22.28 E
Kurgal'džinskij 86 50.36 N 70.01 E
Kurgan 86 55.26 N 65.18 E
Kurgan Oblast' □[4] 86 55.30 N 64.30 E
Kurgan-T'ube 120 37.50 N 68.48 E
Kurgan T'ube □[4] 85 38.15 N 68.50 E
Kurgatej 88 54.23 N 99.27 E
Kurgolovo 76 59.46 N 28.06 E
Kurhan-Mechetnyy, hora ∧[2] 83 48.06 N 39.21 E
Kuria I 14 0.14 N 173.25 E
Kuria Muria Islands → Khurīyā Murīyā, Jazā'ir II 118 17.30 N 56.00 E
Kuriasol 126 22.06 N 86.39 E
Kuridala 166 21.17 S 140.30 E
Kurīgrām 124 25.49 N 89.39 E
Kurihama 268 35.13 N 139.43 E
Kurihashi 94 36.08 N 139.42 E
Kurikka 26 62.37 N 22.25 E
Kurilen → Kuril'skije ostrova II 74 46.10 N 152.00 E
Kurilen-Strasse → Pervyj Kuril'skij proliv ⊔ 74 50.50 N 156.36 E
Kuriles, Islas → Kuril'skije ostrova II 74 46.10 N 152.00 E
Kuril Islands → Kuril'skije ostrova II 74 46.10 N 152.00 E
Kurilovka 80 50.44 N 48.02 E
Kuril'sk 74 45.14 N 147.53 E
Kuril'skije ostrova (Kuril Islands) II 74 46.10 N 152.00 E
Kuril Strait → Pervyj Kuril'skij proliv ⊔ 74 50.50 N 156.36 E
Kuril Trench ◆[1] 6 47.00 N 155.00 E
Kuřim 30 49.18 N 16.32 E
Kurimoto 94 35.49 N 140.30 E
Kurin' 78 51.09 N 32.44 E
Ku-Ring-Gai Chase National Park ♦ 170 33.38 S 151.15 E
Kurinjippadi 122 11.34 N 79.36 E
Kurinwás ≃ 236 12.49 N 83.41 W
Kuripapango 172 39.23 S 176.21 E
Kuriyama, Nihon 92a 43.03 N 141.47 E
Kuriyama, Nihon 94 36.52 N 139.37 E
Kurja, Ross. 24 61.42 N 57.09 E
Kurja, Ross. 86 51.36 N 82.19 E
Kurjanovskaja 76 60.19 N 41.33 E
Kurkijoki 26 61.18 N 29.54 E
Kurkino, Ross. 76 53.26 N 38.40 E
Kurkino, Ross. 265b 55.53 N 37.23 E
Kurkliai 76 55.25 N 25.03 E
Kurl ◆[8] 263 51.35 N 7.35 E
Kurla ◆[8] 272c 19.05 N 72.53 E
Kurlackoje 83 47.21 N 39.03 E
Kurleja 88 52.11 N 119.11 E
Kurlin 80 51.48 N 51.00 E
Kurlovskij 80 55.27 N 40.36 E
Kurmanajevka 80 52.31 N 52.06 E
Kurmani 126 22.47 N 89.53 E
Kurmankol' 80 49.09 N 48.27 E
Kurmenty 85 42.48 N 78.15 E
Kurmuk 140 10.33 N 34.17 E
Kurnell 274a 34.01 S 151.13 E
Kurnell Peninsula ≻[1] 274a 34.02 S 15.11 E
Kurnool 122 15.50 N 78.03 E
Kurobane 94 36.51 N 140.07 E
Kurobe 94 36.51 N 137.26 E
Kurobe ≃ 94 36.55 N 137.25 E
Kurobe-dam ◆[6] 94 36.36 N 137.38 E
Kurodashō 96 35.01 N 135.00 E
Kurogi 96 33.12 N 130.40 E
Kurohone 94 36.30 N 139.17 E
Kuroishi 92 40.38 N 140.36 E
Kuroiso 94 36.58 N 140.03 E
Kuroo-tōge )( 96 35.11 N 134.12 E
Kuropatkino, Ross. 80 46.32 N 45.20 E
Kuropatkino, Uzb. 85 39.57 N 67.27 E
Kurort-Darasun 88 51.12 N 113.44 E
Kurort Hartha 54 50.59 N 13.33 E
Kurort Schmalkalden 54 50.43 N 10.26 E
Kurort Steinbach-Hallenberg 54 50.42 N 10.34 E
Kurort Stolberg 54 51.34 N 10.57 E
Kurort Wippra 54 51.34 N 11.16 E
Kurose 96 34.19 N 132.40 E
Kurose ≃ 96 34.13 N 132.36 E
Kuro-shima I, Nihon 93b 30.50 N 129.57 E
Kuro-shima I, Nihon 175d 24.19 N 124.05 E
Kurosu 268 35.51 N 139.23 E
Kurovo 82 55.49 N 36.00 E
Kurovskoje 82 55.34 N 38.55 E
Kurow 172 44.44 S 170.28 E
Kuroya 268 35.55 N 139.44 E
Kurrajong 170 33.33 S 150.40 E
Kurram 120 30.06 N 66.31 E
Kurram ≃ 123 32.36 N 71.20 E
Kurri Kurri 170 32.49 S 151.29 E
Kuršab ≃ 85 40.46 N 73.06 E
Kursavka 84 44.28 N 42.31 E
Kursela 124 25.27 N 87.15 E
Kuršėnai 76 56.00 N 22.56 E
Kurseong 120 26.53 N 88.17 E
Kuršių marios (Kurššskij zaliv) ⊂ 76 55.00 N 21.00 E
Kursk 78 51.42 N 36.12 E
Kurskaja 84 44.03 N 44.27 E
Kursk Oblast' □[4] 78 51.40 N 36.00 E
Kursk Station ◆[5] 265b 55.46 N 37.40 E
Kurššskaja kosa ≻[2] 76 55.18 N 21.00 E
Kurššskij zaliv (Kuršių marios) ⊂ 76 55.00 N 21.00 E
Kuršumlija 38 43.08 N 21.17 E
Kurşunlu, Tür. 130 40.51 N 33.16 E
Kurşunlu, Tür. 130 38.40 N 37.51 E
Kurtalan 130 37.57 N 41.42 E
Kurtamyš 86 54.55 N 64.27 E
Kurtatsch → Cortaccia 64 46.19 N 11.13 E
Kürten, Dtsch. 56 51.03 N 7.16 E
Kurten, Tx., U.S. 222 30.47 N 96.16 W
Kurthasanlı 130 38.20 N 32.11 E
Kurth Lake ⊜ 222 31.26 N 94.42 W
Kürtī 140 18.07 N 31.33 E
Kurtino 82 54.59 N 38.17 E
Kurtistown 229d 19.36 N 155.03 W
Kurtoğlu Burnu ≻ 130 36.35 N 28.50 E
Kurttinskoje vodochranilišče ⊜[1] 85 43.50 N 76.20 E
Kurtty ≃ 85 44.05 N 76.20 E
Kurtušibinskij chrebet ⋏ 88 52.10 N 93.30 E
Kurtz 218 38.58 N 86.12 W
Kuru, Sūd. 140 7.43 N 26.31 E
Kuru, Suomi 26 61.52 N 23.44 E
Kuru ≃ 140 9.08 N 26.57 E
Kurucaşile 130 41.50 N 32.43 E
Kuruçay 130 39.39 N 38.29 E
Kuruçeşme ◆[8] 267b 41.03 N 29.02 E
Kuruktag ⋏ 90 41.30 N 90.00 E
Kurum 164 4.45 S 145.55 E
Kuruman 158 27.28 S 23.28 E
Kuruman ≃ 158 26.56 S 20.39 E
Kurumanheuwels ⋏[2] 158 27.40 S 23.25 E
Kurumdy, gora ∧ 85 39.28 N 73.32 E
Kurume 96 33.19 N 130.31 E
Kurumkan 88 54.18 N 110.18 E
Kurun ≃ 144 5.30 N 34.17 E
Kurunegala 122 7.29 N 80.22 E
Kurungbaja, Tanjung ≻ 115b 8.15 S 120.35 E
Kurung Tank ⊜[1] 124 22.19 N 82.14 E
Kurunzulaj 88 51.00 N 117.10 E
Kuruqi 89 48.58 N 123.50 E
Kurur, Jabal ∧ 140 20.31 N 31.32 E
Kurusaj 85 40.35 N 69.24 E
Kurushima-kaikyo ⊔ 96 34.07 N 133.00 E
Kuruson-zan ∧ 96 34.12 N 130.58 E
Kuryachivka, Ukr. 83 49.39 N 38.42 E
Kuryachivka, Ukr. 83 49.22 N 39.36 E
Kurylys 86 48.38 N 60.47 E
Kuryongp'o 98 35.59 N 129.32 E
Kurzeme □[9] 76 56.50 N 22.30 E
Kusa 86 55.20 N 59.29 E
Kusabe 270 34.31 N 135.29 E
Kuşadası 130 37.51 N 27.15 E
Kuşadası Körfezi ⊂ 130 37.50 N 27.08 E
Kusak ≃ 86 47.50 N 75.45 E
Kušalino 76 57.07 N 36.05 E
Kusan-ni, Taehan 98 37.43 N 128.49 E
Kusan-ni, Taehan 271b 37.29 N 126.45 E
Kusatsu, Nihon 94 36.37 N 138.36 E
Kusatsu, Nihon 94 35.00 N 135.57 E
Kusawa Lake ⊜ 180 60.20 N 136.15 W
Kusaybah, Bi'r ⊤[4] 140 22.41 N 29.55 E
Kuščovskaja 78 46.33 N 39.37 E
Kuse 96 35.04 N 133.45 E
Kusel 56 49.32 N 7.24 E
Kusey 54 52.36 N 11.05 E
Kuş Gölü ⊜ 130 40.10 N 27.57 E
Kuş Gölü Milli Parkı ♦ 130 40.15 N 27.55 E
Kushaka 150 10.32 N 6.48 E
Kushālgarh 120 23.10 N 74.27 E
Kusheriki 150 10.33 N 6.28 E
Kushi 174m 26.33 N 128.06 E
Kushida ≃ 94 34.36 N 136.34 E
Kushigata 94 35.36 N 138.28 E
Kushihiki 268 35.55 N 139.36 E
Kushikino 92 31.44 N 130.16 E
Kushima 92 31.29 N 131.14 E
Kushimoto 92 33.28 N 135.47 E
Kushira 270 34.28 N 135.43 E
Kushiro 92a 42.58 N 144.23 E
Kushnytsya 78 48.27 N 23.14 E
Kushog Lake ⊜ 212 45.05 N 78.48 W
Kushtia 124 23.55 N 89.07 E
Kushuhum 78 47.42 N 35.14 E
Kushui 102 42.11 N 94.25 E
Kusiro → Kushiro 92a 42.58 N 144.23 E
Kusiyāra ≃ 120 24.36 N 91.44 E
Kuška 128 35.16 N 62.20 E
Kuška ≃ 128 36.00 N 62.40 E
Kuskokwim ≃ 180 60.17 N 162.27 W
Kuskokwim, North Fork ≃ 180 63.06 N 154.37 W
Kuskokwim, South Fork ≃ 180 63.06 N 154.37 W
Kuskokwim Bay ⊂ 180 59.45 N 162.25 W
Kuskokwim Mountains ⋏ 180 62.30 N 156.00 W
Kuskovo ◆[8] 265b 55.44 N 37.49 E
Kuškušara 24 64.58 N 40.21 E
Kuśmā 124 28.14 N 83.41 E
Kušmurun 86 52.27 N 64.36 E
Kušmurun, ozero ⊜ 86 52.40 N 64.48 E
Küsnacht 58 47.19 N 8.35 E
Kušnarenkovo 86 55.06 N 55.22 E
Kusŏng 98 39.59 N 125.15 E
Kusria 272b 22.58 N 88.14 E
Kussharo-ko ⊜ 92a 43.38 N 144.21 E
Küssnacht am Rigi 58 47.05 N 8.27 E
Kustanaj 86 53.10 N 63.35 E
Kustanaj □[8] 86 53.00 N 63.00 E
Kustar'ovka 80 54.16 N 42.16 E
Küsten-Gebirge → Coast Mountains ⋏ 176 55.00 N 129.00 W
Küstenkanal ≊ 52 52.57 N 7.18 E
Küsten-Ketten → Coast Ranges ⋏ 178 41.00 N 123.30 W
Kusthalia 126 23.29 N 87.03 E
Kūstī 140 13.10 N 32.40 E
Kusu, Nihon 94 34.55 N 136.38 E
Kusu, Nihon 96 33.16 N 131.09 E
Kušum ≃ 80 48.54 N 50.32 E
Kusumba 272b 22.27 N 88.24 E
Kusumbāni ∧ 126 21.57 N 86.26 E
Kušumskij 80 51.38 N 48.21 E
Kusung 98 36.18 N 128.55 E
Kusunoki 96 34.03 N 131.15 E
K'us'ur 74 70.39 N 127.15 E
Kušva 86 58.18 N 59.45 E
Kut, Ko I 110 11.40 N 102.35 E
Kuta 150 9.52 N 6.43 E
Kuta ≃ 88 56.46 N 105.40 E
Kutabaru 112 0.44 S 102.56 E
Kutabuloh 114 3.28 N 97.04 E
Kutacane 114 3.30 N 97.48 E
Kütahya 130 39.25 N 29.59 E
Kütahya □[4] 130 39.20 N 29.30 E
Kutais 78 44.32 N 39.18 E
Kutaisi 84 42.15 N 42.40 E
Kutāmat al-Ghābah 142 30.55 N 30.54 E
Kutanibong 114 3.53 N 96.22 E
Kutaradja → Banda Aceh 114 5.34 N 95.20 E
Kutarere 172 38.03 S 177.09 E
Kutasawang 114 5.08 N 96.54 E
Kutch, Rann of (Rann of Kachchh) ◆[1] 120 24.05 N 70.10 E
Kutchan 92a 42.54 N 140.45 E
Kutcharo-ko ⊜ 92a 45.09 N 142.19 E
Kutejnikovo 83 47.34 N 39.46 E
Kutenholz 52 53.29 N 9.19 E
Kuteynykove 83 47.49 N 38.18 E
Kutima 88 57.10 N 108.16 E
Kutima ≃ 88 57.08 N 108.14 E
Kutina 36 45.29 N 16.46 E
Kutiyāna 120 21.38 N 69.59 E
Kutkai 110 23.27 N 97.56 E
Kutluškino 80 55.14 N 50.24 E
Kutná Hora 30 49.57 N 15.16 E
Kutno 30 52.15 N 19.23 E
Kutoarjo 115a 7.43 S 109.54 E
Kutomara 88 51.06 N 118.49 E
Kutse Game Reserve ◆[4] 156 23.30 S 24.05 E
Kutsuki 94 35.21 N 135.55 E
Küttigen 58 47.25 N 8.03 E
Kuttura 24 68.24 N 26.28 E
Kuttusoja 24 67.46 N 28.50 E
Kuttuzi 265a 59.45 N 30.04 E
Kutu 152 2.44 S 18.09 E
Kutubdia Island I 120 21.50 N 91.52 E
Kutubu, Lake ⊜ 164 6.23 S 143.18 E
Kutukovo 80 54.26 N 40.31 E
Kutulik 88 53.21 N 102.48 E
Kutulo, Lagh ≃ 154 2.08 N 40.56 E
Kutuluk ≃ 80 53.19 N 51.09 E
Kutum 140 14.12 N 24.40 E
Kutu-Moke 152 3.12 S 17.21 E
Kúty, Slvk. 30 48.40 N 17.03 E
Kuty, Ukr. 78 48.16 N 25.10 E
Kutztown 210 40.31 N 75.46 W
Kuujjuaq 176 58.06 N 68.25 W
Kuuli-Majak 128 40.14 N 52.42 E
Kuurne 50 50.51 N 3.17 E
Kuusamo 26 65.58 N 29.11 E
Kuusankoski 26 60.54 N 26.38 E
Kuva 85 40.32 N 72.05 E
Kuvak-Nikol'skoje 80 53.37 N 43.30 E
Kuvandyk 86 51.28 N 57.21 E
Kuvango 152 14.28 S 16.20 E
Kuvasaj 85 40.18 N 71.58 E
Kuvet ≃ 180 69.14 N 175.00 E
Kuvšinovo 76 57.02 N 34.10 E
Kuwabara 270 34.53 N 135.15 E
Kuwait → Al-Kuwayt 128 29.20 N 47.59 E
Kuwait (Al-Kuwayt) □[1], Asia 118 29.30 N 47.45 E
Kuwait (Al-Kuwayt) □[1], Asia 128 29.30 N 47.45 E
Kuwait Bay → Kuwayt, Jūn al- ⊂ 128 29.30 N 48.00 E
Kuwana 94 35.04 N 136.42 E
Kuwayt, Jūn al- (Kuwait Bay) ⊂ 128 29.30 N 48.00 E
Kuyāli 126 22.31 N 86.11 E
Kuyal'nyts'kyy lyman ⊜ 78 46.40 N 30.42 E
Kuybyshev → Samara 80 53.12 N 50.09 E
Kuybysheve, Ukr. 78 44.38 N 33.52 E
Kuybysheve, Ukr. 78 47.22 N 36.39 E
Kuybyshevka 78 47.37 N 31.42 E
Kuye ≃ 102 38.30 N 110.44 E
Kūysanjaq 128 36.05 N 44.38 E
Kuyucak, Tür. 130 37.51 N 38.21 E
Kuyucak, Tür. 130 37.55 N 28.28 E
Kuyuwini ≃ 246 2.16 N 58.16 W
Kuyuyukak, Cape ≻ 180 56.54 N 156.50 W
Kuzaranda 24 62.22 N 35.37 E
Kuze 94 35.33 N 136.30 E
Kuze ◆[8] 270 34.57 N 135.43 E
Kuzedejevo 86 53.20 N 87.10 E
Kuzemivka 83 49.31 N 37.59 E
Kuzemyn 78 50.09 N 34.39 E
Kužener 80 56.48 N 48.56 E
Kuženkino 76 57.44 N 33.59 E
Kuzitrin ≃ 180 65.10 N 165.28 W
Kuzkejevo 80 55.46 N 52.48 E
Kuz'miniči 76 54.16 N 33.42 E
Kuz'minka ≃ 265a 59.48 N 30.31 E
Kuz'minki ◆[8] 265b 55.42 N 37.48 E
Kuz'mino, Ross. 82 55.09 N 37.53 E
Kuz'mino, Ross. 82 56.36 N 37.55 E
Kuzmiščevo 82 54.46 N 37.12 E
Kuz'movka 74 62.19 N 92.02 E
Kuznečicha 80 54.43 N 49.38 E
Kuznečikovo 82 56.13 N 36.35 E
Kuzneck, Ross. 80 53.07 N 46.36 E
Kuzneck → Novokuzneck, Ross. 86 53.45 N 87.06 E
Kuzneckij Alatau ⋏ 86 54.45 N 88.00 E
Kuznečnoje 26 61.09 N 29.52 E
Kuznecova 89 46.16 N 138.03 E
Kuznecovka 76 56.18 N 28.33 E
Kuznecovo, Ross. 82 55.30 N 38.21 E
Kuznecovo, Ross. 82 55.27 N 36.57 E
Kuznecovo, Ross. 86 59.15 N 63.28 E
Kuznecovskij 80 47.25 N 40.57 E
Kuznecy 82 55.51 N 38.40 E
Kuznetsk → Kuzneck 80 53.07 N 46.36 E
Kuznetsovo-Mykhaylivka 83 47.27 N 38.13 E
Kuznetsovs'k 78 51.22 N 25.53 E
Kuzomen', Ross. 24 64.17 N 42.53 E
Kuzomen', Ross. 24 66.17 N 36.54 E
Kuzovatovo 80 53.33 N 47.41 E
Kuzucubelen 130 36.51 N 34.27 E
Kuzuha 270 34.52 N 135.41 E
Kuzuryū ≃ 94 36.13 N 136.08 E
Kuzuu 94 36.24 N 139.37 E
Kuzyaka 130 41.14 N 33.44 E
Kvænangen ⊂[2] 24 70.05 N 21.13 E
Kværndrup 41 55.10 N 10.32 E
Kvaisi 84 42.31 N 43.40 E
Kvaløy I 24 69.40 N 18.30 E
Kvaløya I 24 70.37 N 23.52 E
Kvam 26 61.40 N 9.42 E
Kvanløse 41 55.39 N 11.41 E
Kvanndal 26 60.29 N 6.36 E
Kvareli 84 41.56 N 45.54 E
Kvarner ⊂ 36 44.45 N 14.15 E
Kvarnerić ⊔ 36 44.45 N 14.35 E
Kvarnsveden 40 60.31 N 15.24 E
Kvarntorp 40 59.08 N 15.15 E
Kvarsa 80 56.58 N 53.57 E
Kvarsebo 40 58.39 N 16.39 E
Kvašenki 82 56.48 N 37.33 E
Kvenna ≃ 26 60.01 N 7.56 E
Kverkfjöll ∧ 24a 64.43 N 16.38 W
Kvichak Bay ⊂ 180 58.48 N 157.30 W
Kvicksund 40 59.27 N 16.19 E
Kvidinge 41 56.08 N 13.04 E
Kvien ⊜ 40 60.24 N 13.48 E
Kvikkjokk 24 66.55 N 17.50 E
Kvilda 60 49.01 N 13.35 E
Kvina ≃ 26 58.17 N 6.56 E
Kvismare kanal ≊ 40 59.12 N 15.11 E
Kvissleby 26 62.17 N 17.21 E
Kvistbro 40 59.09 N 14.49 E
Kvistgård 41 55.59 N 12.30 E
Kvitok 88 56.03 N 98.30 E
Kwa ≃ 152 3.10 S 16.11 E
Kwachaga 154 5.38 S 38.08 E
Kwada 164 6.09 S 141.53 E
Kwahae-ri ◆[8] 271b 37.33 N 126.50 E
Kwahu Plateau ⋏[1] 150 6.30 N 0.30 W
Kwai → Khwae Noi ≃ 110 14.00 N 99.33 E
Kwajalein I[1] 14 9.05 N 167.20 E
Kwajok 140 8.19 N 28.00 E
Kwakoegron 250 5.15 N 55.20 W
Kwale, Kenya 154 4.11 S 39.27 E
Kwale, Nig. 150 5.46 N 6.26 E
Kwambilo ≃ 273b 4.26 S 15.20 E
Kwa-Mbonambi 158 28.36 S 32.05 E
Kwamisa ∧ 150 7.08 N 1.53 W
Kwamouth 152 3.10 S 16.12 E
Kwa Mtoro 154 5.14 S 35.26 E
Kwanak-san ∧ 271b 37.27 N 126.58 E
Kwando (Cuando) ≃ 152 18.27 S 23.32 E
Kwangchow → Guangzhou 100 23.06 N 113.16 E
Kwangju 98 35.09 N 126.54 E
Kwangju □[4] 98 35.09 N 126.55 E
Kwango (Cuango) ≃ 152 3.14 S 17.23 E
Kwangsi Chuang Autonomous Region → Guangxi Zhuangzu Zizhiqu □[4] 102 24.00 N 109.00 E
Kwangtung → Guangdong □[4] 90 23.00 N 113.00 E
Kwangwazi 154 7.47 S 38.15 E
Kwangyang 98 34.59 N 127.34 E
Kwania, Lake ⊜ 154 1.45 N 32.45 E
Kwanmo-bong ∧ 98 41.42 N 129.13 E
Kwansan-ni 271b 37.43 N 126.51 E


**Symbols** in the index entries represent the broad categories identified in the key at the right. Symbols with superior numbers (⋏[1]) identify subcategories (see complete key on page I · 1).

**Symbole** im Register stellen die rechts im Schlüssel erklärten Kategorien dar. Symbole mit hochgestellten Ziffern (⋏[1]) bezeichnen Unterabteilungen einer Kategorie (vgl. vollständiger Schlüssel auf Seite I · 1).

**Los símbolos** incluídos en el texto del índice representan las grandes categorías identificadas con la clave a la derecha. Los símbolos con numeros en su parte superior (⋏[1]) identifican las subcategorías (véase la clave completa en la página I · 1).

**Les symboles** de l'index représentent les catégories indiquées dans la légende à droite. Les symboles suivis d'un indice (⋏[1]) représentent des sous-catégories (voir légende complète à la page I · 1).

**Os símbolos** incluídos no texto do índice representam as grandes categorias identificadas com a chave à direita. Os símbolos com números em sua parte superior (⋏[1]) identificam as subcategorias (veja-se a chave completa à página I · 1).

| ENGLISH | DEUTSCH | ESPAÑOL | FRANÇAIS | PORTUGUÊS |
|---|---|---|---|---|
| ∧ Mountain | Berg | Montaña | Montagne | Montanha |
| ⋏ Mountains | Gebirge | Montañas | Montagnes | Montanhas |
| )( Pass | Paß | Paso | Col | Passo |
| V Valley, Canyon | Tal, Cañon | Valle, Cañón | Vallée, Canyon | Vale, Canhão |
| ⩧ Plain | Ebene | Llano | Plaine | Planície |
| ≻ Cape | Kap | Cabo | Cap | Cabo |
| I Island | Insel | Isla | Île | Ilha |
| II Islands | Inseln | Islas | Îles | Ilhas |
| ⊥ Other Topographic Features | Andere Topographische Objekte | Otros Elementos Topográficos | Autres données topographiques | Outros acidentes topográficos |

ESPAÑOL / FRANÇAIS / PORTUGUÊS


| Nombre / Nom / Nome | Página / Page | Lat.°′ | Long.°′ W = Oeste / Ouest |
|---|---|---|---|
| Kwanto Plain → Kantō-heiya ≚ | 94 | 36.00 N | 139.30 E |
| Kware | 150 | 13.12 N | 5.14 E |
| Kwa-Thema | 273d | 26.18 S | 28.23 E |
| Kwatisore | 164 | 3.15 S | 134.57 E |
| Kwazulu → KwaZulu-Natal □[4] | 158 | 28.40 S | 30.40 E |
| KwaZulu-Natal □[4] | 158 | 28.40 S | 30.40 E |
| Kweichow → Guizhou □[4] | 102 | 27.00 N | 107.00 E |
| Kweihwa → Hohhot | 102 | 40.51 N | 111.40 E |
| Kweijang → Guiyang | 102 | 26.35 N | 106.43 E |
| Kweilin → Guilin | 102 | 25.17 N | 110.17 E |
| Kweisui → Hohhot | 102 | 40.51 N | 111.40 E |
| Kweiyang → Guiyang | 102 | 26.35 N | 106.43 E |
| Kwekwe | 154 | 18.55 S | 29.49 E |
| Kweneng □[5] | 156 | 24.00 S | 24.00 E |
| Kwenge (Caengo) ≃ | 152 | 4.50 S | 18.42 E |
| Kwesimintim | 150 | 4.54 N | 1.47 W |
| Kwethluk | 180 | 60.49 N | 161.27 W |
| Kwethluk ≃ | 180 | 60.46 N | 161.26 W |
| Kwidzyn | 30 | 53.45 N | 18.56 E |
| Kwigillingok | 180 | 59.51 N | 163.08 W |
| Kwiguk | 180 | 62.45 N | 164.28 W |
| Kwiha | 144 | 13.31 N | 39.32 E |
| Kwikila | 164 | 9.48 S | 147.41 E |
| Kwilu (Cuilo) ≃ | 152 | 3.22 S | 17.22 E |
| Kwinana | 168a | 32.15 S | 115.48 E |
| Kwitaro ≃ | 246 | 3.19 N | 58.47 W |
| Kwobrup | 162 | 33.37 S | 117.46 E |
| Kwoka, Gunung ∧ | 164 | 0.31 S | 132.27 E |
| Kwolla | 150 | 9.00 N | 9.15 E |
| Kwun Tong | 271d | 22.19 N | 114.12 E |
| Kyabé | 146 | 9.27 N | 18.57 E |
| Kyabra | 166 | 26.18 S | 143.10 E |
| Kyabra Creek ≃ | 166 | 25.36 S | 142.55 E |
| Kyabram | 166 | 36.19 S | 145.03 E |
| Kyaikkami | 110 | 16.04 N | 97.34 E |
| Kyaiklat | 110 | 16.26 N | 95.44 E |
| Kyaikto | 110 | 17.18 N | 97.01 E |
| Kya-in | 110 | 16.02 N | 98.08 E |
| Kyaka | 154 | 1.16 S | 31.25 E |
| Kyalite | 166 | 34.57 S | 143.29 E |
| Kyancutta | 166 | 33.08 S | 135.34 E |
| Ky Anh | 110 | 18.05 N | 106.18 E |
| Kyat-aw | 110 | 12.29 N | 98.19 E |
| Kyaukhnyat | 110 | 18.15 N | 97.31 E |
| Kyaukkyi | 110 | 18.19 N | 96.46 E |
| Kyaukme | 110 | 22.32 N | 97.02 E |
| Kyaukpa | 110 | 13.05 N | 98.59 E |
| Kyaukpyu, Mya. | 110 | 19.05 N | 93.52 E |
| Kyaukpyu, Mya. | 110 | 19.26 N | 93.33 E |
| Kyaukse | 110 | 21.36 N | 96.08 E |
| Kyauktaw | 110 | 20.51 N | 92.59 E |
| Kyaunggon | 110 | 17.06 N | 95.11 E |
| Kybartai | 76 | 54.39 N | 22.45 E |
| Kybean | 171b | 36.22 S | 149.25 E |
| Kybeyan Range ⋏ | 171b | 36.10 S | 149.30 E |
| Kyburz | 226 | 38.47 N | 120.18 W |
| Kydra | 171b | 36.27 S | 149.23 E |
| Kyeamba | 171b | 35.26 S | 147.37 E |
| Kyeamba Creek ≃ | 171b | 35.06 S | 147.29 E |
| Kyebang-san ∧ | 98 | 37.43 N | 128.29 E |
| Kyegegwa | 154 | 0.29 N | 31.03 E |
| Kyeikdon | 110 | 16.00 N | 98.24 E |
| Kyeintali | 110 | 18.00 N | 94.29 E |
| Kyenjojo | 154 | 0.37 N | 30.38 E |
| Kyeryong-san Kukrip Kongwŏn ♠ | 98 | 36.21 N | 127.13 E |
| Kyes Peak ∧ | 224 | 47.57 N | 121.19 W |
| Kyffhäuser ⋏ | 54 | 51.23 N | 11.05 E |
| Kyffhäuser-Denkmal ⊥ | 54 | 51.23 N | 11.06 E |
| Kyidaunggan | 110 | 19.53 N | 96.12 E |
| Kyindwe | 110 | 20.58 N | 93.51 E |
| Kyje ◆[8] | 54 | 50.04 N | 14.32 E |
| Kyjov | 30 | 49.01 N | 17.08 E |
| Kykladen → Kikládhes II | 38 | 37.30 N | 25.00 E |
| Kykotsmovi Village | 200 | 35.52 N | 110.37 W |
| Kykva | 80 | 57.22 N | 53.50 E |
| Kylās ∧ | 124 | 25.18 N | 90.45 E |
| Kyle, Sk., Can. | 184 | 50.50 N | 108.02 W |
| Kyle, S.D., U.S. | 198 | 43.25 N | 102.10 W |
| Kyle, Tx., U.S. | 196 | 29.59 N | 97.52 W |
| Kyle □[9] | 46 | 55.29 N | 4.24 W |
| Kyle, Lake ⊜[1] | 154 | 20.14 S | 31.00 E |
| Kyleakin | 46 | 57.16 N | 5.44 W |
| Kyle of Lochalsh | 46 | 57.17 N | 5.43 W |
| Kylerhea | 46 | 57.14 N | 5.41 W |
| Kylertown | 214 | 41.00 N | 78.10 W |
| Kylestrome | 46 | 58.16 N | 5.02 W |
| Kyll ≃ | 56 | 49.48 N | 6.42 E |
| Kyllburg | 56 | 50.02 N | 6.35 E |
| Kym ≃ | 42 | 52.14 N | 0.17 W |
| Kymen lääni □[4] | 26 | 61.00 N | 28.00 E |
| Kymijoki ≃ | 26 | 60.30 N | 26.52 E |
| Kyn | 86 | 57.52 N | 58.38 E |
| Kyndby | 41 | 55.48 N | 11.56 E |
| Kyneton | 169 | 37.15 S | 144.27 E |
| Kynnefjäll ∧[2] | 26 | 58.42 N | 11.41 E |
| Kynšperk nad Ohří | 54 | 50.04 N | 12.32 E |
| Kynuna | 166 | 21.35 S | 141.55 E |
| Kyodong-do I | 98 | 37.45 N | 126.16 E |
| Kyoga, Lake ⊜ | 154 | 1.30 N | 33.00 E |
| Kyōga-misaki ≻ | 96 | 35.46 N | 135.13 E |
| Kyogle | 166 | 28.37 S | 153.00 E |
| Kyoha-ri | 271b | 37.46 N | 126.46 E |
| Kyohyŏn-ni | 271b | 37.43 N | 126.58 E |
| Kyom ≃ | 140 | 8.58 N | 28.13 E |
| Kyŏmip'o → Songnim | 98 | 38.44 N | 125.38 E |
| Kyonan | 94 | 35.07 N | 139.50 E |
| Kyondo | 110 | 16.35 N | 98.03 E |
| Kyŏnggi Do □[4] | 98 | 37.30 N | 127.15 E |
| Kyŏnggi-man ⊂ | 98 | 37.25 N | 126.00 E |
| Kyŏngju | 98 | 35.51 N | 129.14 E |
| Kyŏngju Kukrip Kongwŏn ♠ | 98 | 35.47 N | 129.15 E |
| Kyŏngsan | 98 | 35.48 N | 128.43 E |
| Kyŏngsang Namdo □[4] | 98 | 35.15 N | 128.30 E |
| Kyŏngsang Pukdo □[4] | 98 | 36.15 N | 128.45 E |
| Kyŏngsŏng, C.M.I.K. | 98 | 41.35 N | 129.36 E |
| Kyŏngsŏng → Sŏul, Taehan | 98 | 37.33 N | 126.58 E |
| Kyŏngwŏn | 98 | 42.48 N | 130.09 E |
| Kyônkadun | 110 | 16.04 N | 95.38 E |
| Kyonmange | 110 | 16.30 N | 95.50 E |
| Kyonpyaw | 110 | 17.18 N | 95.12 E |
| Kyotera | 154 | 0.33 S | 31.19 E |
| Kyōto, Nihon | 94 | 35.00 N | 135.45 E |
| Kyōto, Nihon | 270 | 35.00 N | 135.45 E |
| Kyōto □[5] | 94 | 35.05 N | 135.45 E |
| Kyōto-bonchi ⋏ | 270 | 35.03 N | 135.45 E |
| Kyōto Race Track ♠ | 270 | 34.54 N | 135.44 E |
| Kyōto University ʊ[2] | 270 | 35.02 N | 135.46 E |
| Kyōwa | 94 | 36.19 N | 140.03 E |
| Kyōyomi-dake ∧ | 96 | 33.31 N | 131.02 E |
| Kypšak, ozero ⊜ | 86 | 50.09 N | 68.28 E |
| Kyra | 88 | 49.36 N | 111.58 E |
| Kyra ≃ | 88 | 49.24 N | 112.19 E |
| Kyrčany | 80 | 57.37 N | 50.10 E |
| Kyren | 88 | 51.41 N | 102.08 E |
| Kyrenia → Girne | 130 | 35.20 N | 33.19 E |
| Kyrgyzstan □[1], Asia | 72 | 41.30 N | 75.00 E |
| Kyrgyzstan □[1], Asia | 85 | 41.30 N | 75.00 E |
| Kyritz | 54 | 52.56 N | 12.23 E |
| Kyrkheden | 40 | 60.10 N | 13.29 E |
| Kyrkkazyk | 85 | 42.30 N | 72.20 E |
| Kyrksæterøra | 26 | 63.17 N | 9.06 E |
| Kyrkslätt (Kirkkonummi) | 26 | 60.07 N | 24.26 E |
| Kyrö | 26 | 60.42 N | 22.45 E |
| Kyrönjoki ≃ | 26 | 63.14 N | 21.45 E |
| Kyrösjärvi ⊜ | 26 | 61.45 N | 23.10 E |
| Kyröskoski | 26 | 61.40 N | 23.11 E |
| Kyrta | 24 | 64.04 N | 57.42 E |
| Kyrykivka | 78 | 50.22 N | 35.07 E |
| Kyrykkuduk | 80 | 49.51 N | 51.54 E |
| Kyshen'ky | 78 | 48.53 N | 34.08 E |
| Kyshyn | 78 | 51.08 N | 27.41 E |
| Kyslivka | 83 | 49.38 N | 37.53 E |
| Kyslyakivka | 78 | 46.44 N | 31.59 E |
| Ky Son | 110 | 19.24 N | 104.08 E |
| Kyštovka | 86 | 56.33 N | 76.38 E |
| Kyštym | 86 | 55.42 N | 60.34 E |
| Kysykkamys | 80 | 49.14 N | 50.19 E |
| Kyte ≃ | 190 | 42.00 N | 89.19 W |
| Kytlym | 86 | 59.30 N | 59.12 E |
| Kytmanovo | 86 | 53.28 N | 85.28 E |
| Kyūhōji | 270 | 34.38 N | 135.35 E |
| Kyunchaung | 110 | 15.33 N | 98.15 E |
| Kyundon | 110 | 20.31 N | 95.44 E |
| Kyungyi I | 110 | 15.04 N | 97.44 E |
| Kyunhla | 110 | 23.21 N | 95.18 E |
| Kyuquot | 182 | 50.02 N | 127.23 W |
| Kyuquot Sound Џ | 182 | 50.05 N | 127.15 W |
| Kyūroku-jima I | 92 | 40.32 N | 139.29 E |
| Kyū-shizudani-gakkō ⊥ | 96 | 34.45 N | 134.13 E |
| Kyūshū I | 92 | 33.00 N | 131.00 E |
| Kyushu-Palau Ridge ✢[3] | 14 | 20.00 N | 136.00 E |
| Kyūshū-sanchi ⋏ | 92 | 32.35 N | 131.17 E |
| Kywebwe | 110 | 18.42 N | 96.25 E |
| Kywong | 166 | 34.59 S | 146.44 E |
| Kyyiv (Kiev) | 78 | 50.26 N | 30.31 E |
| Kyyiv □[4] | 78 | 50.15 N | 30.30 E |
| Kyyivs'ke vodoskhovyshche ⊜[1] | 78 | 51.00 N | 30.25 E |
| Kyyjärvi | 26 | 63.02 N | 24.34 E |
| Kyyvesi ⊜ | 26 | 61.58 N | 27.07 E |
| Kyzas | 86 | 52.20 N | 89.20 E |
| Kyzyl | 88 | 51.42 N | 94.27 E |
| Kyzylagaš | 86 | 45.54 N | 81.37 E |
| Kyzylaryk | 85 | 43.57 N | 70.42 E |
| Kyzylbejit | 85 | 41.30 N | 72.24 E |
| Kyzyl-Chaja | 86 | 50.03 N | 89.54 E |
| Kyzyl-Chem (Šišchid) ≃ | 88 | 51.21 N | 96.58 E |
| Kyzyl-Džar | 85 | 41.17 N | 72.02 E |
| Kyzylemgek | 85 | 41.57 N | 74.56 F |
| Kyzylespe | 86 | 47.27 N | 73.53 E |
| Kyzylkak, ozero ⊜ | 86 | 53.25 N | 73.48 E |
| Kyzyl-Kija | 85 | 40.16 N | 72.08 E |
| Kyzyl-Kommuna | 86 | 48.44 N | 67.32 E |
| Kyzylkum ◆[2] | 72 | 42.00 N | 64.00 E |
| Kyzylkup | 128 | 40.38 N | 53.58 E |
| Kyzyl-Mažalyk | 86 | 51.10 N | 90.32 E |
| Kyzylmazar | 85 | 39.39 N | 68.25 E |
| Kyzyloba | 80 | 49.37 N | 50.38 E |
| Kyzylsu ≃ | 85 | 39.17 N | 71.23 E |
| Kyzyltas, gory ⋏ | 86 | 48.30 N | 74.50 E |
| Kyzyltau | 86 | 47.53 N | 72.05 E |
| Kyzylt'ob'o | 85 | 42.13 N | 75.16 E |
| Kyzyltu, Kaz. | 86 | 47.46 N | 59.08 E |
| Kyzyltu, Kaz. | 86 | 47.43 N | 75.42 E |
| Kyzyltu, Kyrg. | 85 | 42.11 N | 76.40 E |
| Kyzyluj | 86 | 48.07 N | 65.28 E |
| Kyzylžar | 86 | 48.17 N | 69.39 E |
| Kzyl-Kuga | 80 | 48.28 N | 53.01 E |
| Kzyl-Orda | 86 | 44.48 N | 65.28 E |
| Kzyl-Orda □[8] | 86 | 45.00 N | 64.00 E |
| Kzyltu | 86 | 53.38 N | 72.20 E |
| **L** | | | |
| La'a | 102 | 29.44 N | 101.26 E |
| Laa an der Thaya | 61 | 48.43 N | 16.23 E |
| Laaben | 61 | 48.06 N | 15.52 E |
| Laaber | 60 | 49.04 N | 11.53 E |
| Laab im Walde | 264b | 48.09 N | 16.11 E |
| Laacher See ⊜ | 56 | 50.25 N | 7.16 E |
| Laaerberg ∧[2] | 264b | 48.09 N | 16.24 E |
| Laage | 54 | 53.56 N | 12.20 E |
| La Aguja, Cabo de ≻ | 246 | 11.18 N | 74.12 W |
| Laakajärvi ⊜ | 26 | 63.50 N | 27.55 E |
| Laakirchen | 64 | 47.58 N | 13.49 E |
| La Albuera | 34 | 38.43 N | 6.49 W |
| La Alcarria ◆[1] | 34 | 40.45 N | 2.45 W |
| La Aldea | 234 | 20.54 N | 101.29 W |
| La Aldehuela | 266a | 40.18 N | 3.36 W |
| La Algaba | 34 | 37.28 N | 6.01 W |
| La Almarcha | 34 | 39.41 N | 2.22 W |
| La Almunia de Doña Godina | 34 | 41.29 N | 1.22 W |
| Laanecoorie Reservoir ⊜[1] | 169 | 36.52 S | 143.53 E |
| La Antigua, Salina ≚ | 252 | 30.00 S | 66.06 W |
| La Antorcha, Cerro ∧ | 234 | 21.43 N | 102.45 W |
| Laar | 52 | 52.37 N | 6.44 E |
| Laar ◆[8] | 263 | 51.28 N | 6.43 E |
| La Araucanía □[4] | 252 | 38.45 S | 72.30 W |
| La Arena, Pan. | 236 | 7.58 N | 80.28 W |
| La Arena, Perú | 248 | 5.20 S | 80.44 W |
| Laas → Lasa | 64 | 46.37 N | 10.42 E |
| Laas Caanood | 144 | 8.28 N | 47.21 E |
| La Ascención | 232 | 24.20 N | 99.55 W |
| Laas Dawaco | 144 | 10.28 N | 49.05 E |
| Laas Dhaareed | 144 | 10.10 N | 45.59 E |
| Laase | 54 | 53.04 N | 11.18 E |
| Laas Qoray | 144 | 11.10 N | 48.13 E |
| La Asunción | 246 | 11.02 N | 63.53 W |
| La Atravesada, Loma ∧[2] | 232 | 29.57 N | 112.12 W |
| Laatzen | 52 | 52.19 N | 9.47 E |
| Laau Point ≻ | 229a | 21.06 N | 157.19 W |
| La Aurora | 286e | 33.36 S | 70.38 W |
| La Azufrosa | 196 | 28.14 N | 100.50 W |
| Laba ≃ | 78 | 45.11 N | 39.42 E |
| La Babia | 232 | 28.34 N | 102.04 W |
| Labadie | 219 | 38.31 N | 90.51 W |
| Labadieville | 194 | 29.50 N | 90.57 W |
| La Baie | 186 | 48.19 N | 70.53 W |
| La Balme-de-Sillingy | 58 | 45.58 N | 6.02 E |
| La Balme-les-Grottes | 62 | 45.51 N | 5.20 E |
| Laban | 208 | 37.24 N | 76.17 W |
| La Banda | 252 | 27.44 S | 64.15 W |
| La Bandera, Cerro ∧ | 232 | 24.35 N | 105.07 W |
| La Bañeza | 34 | 42.18 N | 5.54 W |
| La Barca | 234 | 20.17 N | 102.34 W |
| La Barceloneta ◆[8] | 266d | 41.22 N | 2.11 E |
| La Barge | 200 | 42.15 N | 110.11 W |
| La Barge Creek ≃ | 200 | 42.14 N | 110.10 W |
| La Barra | 236 | 12.54 N | 83.32 W |
| La Barre-en-Ouche | 50 | 48.57 N | 0.40 E |
| La Barrita | 236 | 14.05 N | 91.03 W |
| La Barr Meadows | 226 | 39.11 N | 121.02 W |
| Labason | 116 | 8.04 N | 122.31 E |
| La Bassée | 50 | 50.32 N | 2.48 E |
| Labastide-Murat | 32 | 44.39 N | 1.34 E |
| La Bastide-Puylaurent | 62 | 44.36 N | 3.54 E |
| La Bâte | 261 | 48.35 N | 2.01 E |
| La Baule-Escoublac | 32 | 47.17 N | 2.24 W |
| La Bazoche-Gouet | 50 | 48.08 N | 0.59 E |
| L'Abbé | 261 | 48.34 N | 1.50 E |
| Labdah (Leptis Magna) ⊥ | 146 | 32.38 N | 14.18 E |
| Labé | 150 | 11.19 N | 12.17 W |
| Labe (Elbe) ≃ | 30 | 53.50 N | 9.00 E |
| Labégude | 62 | 44.39 N | 4.22 E |
| La Bégude-Blanche | 62 | 43.55 N | 6.08 E |
| La Bégude-de-Mazenc | 62 | 44.32 N | 4.56 E |
| Labelle, P.Q., Can. | 206 | 46.16 N | 74.44 W |
| La Belle, Fl., U.S. | 220 | 26.45 N | 81.26 W |
| La Belle, Mo., U.S. | 219 | 40.07 N | 91.54 W |
| Labelle □[6] | 206 | 46.20 N | 75.00 W |
| Labelle, Lac ⊜, P.Q., Can. | 206 | 46.13 N | 74.52 W |
| La Belle, Lac ⊜, Wi., U.S. | 216 | 43.08 N | 88.31 W |
| Labengke, Pulau I | 112 | 3.27 S | 122.25 E |
| La Bérarde | 62 | 44.56 N | 6.18 E |
| Laberge, Lake ⊜ | 180 | 61.11 N | 135.12 W |
| La Berra ∧ | 58 | 46.41 N | 7.11 E |
| Laberweinting | 60 | 48.48 N | 12.19 E |
| La Besace | 56 | 49.34 N | 4.58 E |
| Labette Creek ≃ | 198 | 37.03 N | 95.05 W |
| Labi | 112 | 4.25 N | 114.22 E |
| La Biche ≃ | 182 | 55.01 N | 112.44 W |
| Labico | 66 | 41.47 N | 12.53 E |
| Labin | 36 | 45.05 N | 14.07 E |
| Labinsk | 84 | 44.38 N | 40.44 E |
| Labis | 114 | 2.23 N | 103.02 E |
| La Bisbal | 34 | 41.57 N | 3.03 E |
| Łabiszyn | 30 | 52.57 N | 17.55 E |
| Labkovičy | 76 | 53.50 N | 31.45 E |
| Lablābah, Wādī al- V | 273c | 30.02 N | 31.19 E |
| La Blanca | 286e | 33.31 S | 70.41 W |
| La Blanca Grande, Laguna ⊜ | 252 | 38.26 S | 63.55 W |
| Labná ⊥ | 232 | 20.11 N | 89.34 W |
| Labo | 116 | 14.09 N | 122.51 E |
| Labo ≃ | 116 | 14.11 N | 122.56 E |
| Labo, Mount ∧ | 116 | 14.01 N | 122.48 E |
| Laboe | 54 | 54.24 N | 10.15 E |
| La Boissière | 261 | 48.46 N | 1.59 E |
| La Boissière-Ecole | 261 | 48.41 N | 1.39 E |
| La Bollène-Vésubie | 62 | 43.59 N | 7.20 E |
| La Bonneville-sur-Iton | 50 | 49.00 N | 1.02 E |
| Laboratory | 214 | 40.09 N | 80.13 W |
| Laborde, Arg. | 252 | 33.09 S | 62.51 W |
| La Borde, Fr. | 261 | 48.32 N | 2.50 E |
| Laborec ≃ | 30 | 48.36 N | 22.00 E |
| Laborie | 241f | 13.45 N | 61.00 W |
| Labouchere, Mount ∧ | 162 | 25.12 S | 118.18 E |
| Labouheyre | 32 | 44.13 N | 0.55 W |
| Laboulaye | 252 | 34.07 S | 63.24 W |
| La Bouverie | 50 | 50.24 N | 3.52 E |
| La Boyera, Ven. | 286c | 10.23 N | 66.57 W |
| La Boyera, Ven. | 286c | 10.25 N | 66.50 W |
| Lābpur | 126 | 23.50 N | 87.49 E |
| Labrador ◆[1] | 176 | 54.00 N | 62.00 W |
| Labrador Basin ✢[1] | 16 | 53.00 N | 48.00 W |
| Labrador City | 176 | 52.57 N | 66.55 W |
| Labrador Sea ⊤[2] | 176 | 57.00 N | 53.00 W |
| Lábrea, Bra. | 248 | 7.16 S | 64.47 W |
| La Brea, Trin. | 241r | 10.15 N | 61.37 W |
| Labrède | 32 | 44.41 N | 0.31 W |
| La Bresse | 58 | 48.00 N | 6.53 E |
| La Brévine | 58 | 46.59 N | 6.36 E |
| Labrieville, Réserve ♠ | 186 | 49.20 N | 69.40 W |
| La Brigue | 62 | 44.04 N | 7.37 E |
| La Brillanne | 62 | 43.55 N | 5.53 E |
| Labrit | 32 | 44.07 N | 0.33 W |
| La Broquerie | 184 | 49.28 N | 96.27 W |
| Labroye | 50 | 50.17 N | 1.59 E |
| Labry | 56 | 49.10 N | 5.52 E |
| Labuan, Pulau I | 112 | 5.21 N | 115.13 E |
| Labuha | 164 | 0.37 S | 127.29 E |
| Labuhan | 115a | 6.22 S | 105.50 E |
| Labuhanbajo | 115b | 8.29 S | 119.54 E |
| Labuhanbatu | 114 | 2.12 N | 100.12 E |
| Labuhanbilik | 114 | 2.31 N | 100.10 E |
| Labuhandeli | 114 | 3.45 N | 98.41 E |
| Labuhanhaji, Indon. | 114 | 3.33 N | 97.00 E |
| Labuhanhaji, Indon. | 115b | 8.42 S | 116.34 E |
| Labuhanmarege | 112 | 7.06 S | 120.40 E |
| Labuhanmaringgai | 115a | 5.21 S | 105.48 E |
| Labuhanruku | 114 | 3.13 N | 99.35 E |
| Labuk ≃ | 112 | 5.54 N | 117.30 E |
| Labuk, Telukan ⊂ | 116 | 6.07 N | 117.46 E |
| Labu Kananga | 115b | 8.08 S | 117.47 E |
| Labutta | 110 | 16.09 N | 94.46 E |
| Labytnangi | 72 | 66.39 N | 66.21 E |
| Lač, Ross. | 24 | 63.18 N | 54.28 E |
| Laç, Shq. | 38 | 41.38 N | 19.43 E |
| Lac □[5] | 146 | 13.30 N | 14.15 E |
| Lača, ozero ⊜ | 24 | 61.20 N | 38.48 E |
| La Cadena | 196 | 25.53 N | 104.12 W |
| L'Acadie | 275a | 45.19 N | 73.21 W |
| L'Acadie ≃ | 206 | 45.29 N | 73.16 W |
| La Cadière-d'Azur | 62 | 43.12 N | 5.46 E |
| Lacadivas, Islas → Lakshadweep II | 122 | 10.00 N | 73.00 E |
| Laca Jahuira ≃ | 248 | 19.21 S | 67.54 W |
| La Cal ≃ | 248 | 17.27 S | 58.15 W |
| Lac-à-la-Tortue | 206 | 46.37 N | 72.38 W |
| La Calera, Chile | 252 | 32.47 S | 71.12 W |
| La Calera, Perú | 286d | 12.12 S | 76.54 W |
| Lac-Allard | 186 | 50.33 N | 63.25 W |
| Lacamas Creek ≃ | 224 | 46.20 N | 122.55 W |
| Lacamas Lake ⊜ | 224 | 45.37 N | 122.26 W |
| La Campana, Esp. | 34 | 37.34 N | 5.26 W |
| La Campana, Méx. | 234 | 22.45 N | 105.35 W |
| La Cañada | 234 | 20.37 N | 100.19 W |
| La Cañada, Cerro ∧ | 234 | 21.24 N | 99.13 W |
| La Canada Flintridge | 228 | 34.12 N | 118.12 W |
| La Canada Verde Creek ≃ | 280 | 33.52 N | 118.02 W |
| Lacanau | 32 | 44.59 N | 1.05 W |
| Lacanau, Lac de ⊂ | 32 | 44.58 N | 1.07 W |
| La Candelaria, Arg. | 252 | 26.06 S | 65.06 W |
| La Candelaria, Méx. | 200 | 31.07 N | 106.29 W |
| La Canourgue | 32 | 44.26 N | 3.13 E |
| Lacantún ≃ | 232 | 16.36 N | 90.39 W |
| La Capelle-en-Thiérache | 50 | 49.58 N | 3.55 E |
| La Capelle-lès-Boulogne | 50 | 50.44 N | 1.42 E |
| Lacapelle-Marival | 32 | 44.44 N | 1.54 E |
| La Carlota, Arg. | 252 | 33.26 S | 63.18 W |
| La Carlota, Pil. | 116 | 10.25 N | 122.55 E |
| Lacarne | 214 | 41.31 N | 83.03 W |
| La Carolina | 34 | 38.15 N | 3.37 W |
| La Casita | 234 | 23.43 N | 104.46 W |
| La Castellana | 116 | 10.20 N | 123.03 E |
| Lacaune | 32 | 43.43 N | 2.42 E |
| Lac-Bellemare | 206 | 46.34 N | 72.55 W |
| Lac-Brome | 206 | 45.13 N | 72.31 W |
| Laccadive, Minicoy, and Amīndīvi → Lakshadweep □[3] | 122 | 10.00 N | 73.00 E |
| Laccadive Islands → Lakshadweep II | 122 | 10.00 N | 73.00 E |
| Lacchiarella | 62 | 45.19 N | 9.08 E |
| Lacco Ameno | 68 | 40.45 N | 13.54 E |
| Lac Courte Oreilles Indian Reservation ◆[4] | 190 | 45.55 N | 91.19 W |
| Lac du Flambeau | 190 | 45.59 N | 89.51 W |
| Lac du Flambeau Indian Reservation ◆[4] | 190 | 45.59 N | 89.53 W |
| Laceby | 44 | 53.32 N | 0.10 W |
| Lacedonia | 68 | 41.03 N | 15.25 E |
| La Ceiba, Hond. | 236 | 15.47 N | 86.50 W |
| La Ceiba, Ven. | 246 | 9.28 N | 71.04 W |
| La Celle-les-Bordes | 261 | 48.38 N | 1.57 E |
| La Celle-Saint-Cloud | 261 | 48.51 N | 2.08 E |
| La Celle-Saint-Cyr | 50 | 47.58 N | 3.18 E |
| La Center, Ky., U.S. | 194 | 37.04 N | 88.58 W |
| La Center, Wa., U.S. | 224 | 45.52 N | 122.40 W |
| Lacepede Bay ⊂ | 166 | 36.47 S | 139.45 E |
| Lacerdónia | 156 | 18.01 S | 35.30 E |
| Laces (Latsch) | 64 | 46.37 N | 10.52 E |
| Lac-Etchemin | 186 | 46.24 N | 70.30 W |
| Lacey | 224 | 47.02 N | 122.49 W |
| Lacey Creek ≃ | 278 | 41.50 N | 88.03 W |
| Laceyville | 210 | 41.39 N | 76.10 W |
| Lac-Frontière | 186 | 46.42 N | 70.00 W |
| La Chaise-Dieu | 62 | 45.19 N | 3.42 E |
| La Chambre | 62 | 45.22 N | 6.18 E |
| La Chapelle-d'Angillon | 50 | 47.22 N | 2.26 E |
| La Chapelle-en-Vercors | 62 | 44.58 N | 5.25 E |
| La Chapelle-Gauthier | 261 | 48.33 N | 2.54 E |
| La Chapelle-la-Reine | 50 | 48.19 N | 2.35 E |
| La Chapelle-Saint-Luc | 50 | 48.20 N | 4.03 E |
| La Chapelle-Vendômoise | 50 | 47.40 N | 1.15 E |
| La Charité-sur-Loire | 50 | 47.11 N | 3.01 E |
| La Chartre-sur-le-Loir | 50 | 47.44 N | 0.35 E |
| La Châtaigneraie | 32 | 46.39 N | 0.44 W |
| La Châtre | 32 | 46.35 N | 1.59 E |
| Lachaussée, Étang de ⊜ | 56 | 49.02 N | 5.48 E |
| La Chaux-de-Fonds | 58 | 47.06 N | 6.50 E |
| Lachay, Punta ≻ | 248 | 11.18 S | 77.39 W |
| Lach Dennis | 262 | 53.15 N | 2.26 W |
| Lachdenpochja | 24 | 61.31 N | 30.08 E |
| Lachen | 58 | 47.12 N | 8.51 E |
| Lachenaie | 275a | 45.42 N | 73.34 W |
| Lachendorf | 52 | 52.37 N | 10.14 E |
| Lachhmangarh Sīkar | 120 | 27.49 N | 75.02 E |
| L'achi | 80 | 55.20 N | 41.56 E |
| Lachine | 206 | 45.26 N | 73.40 W |
| Lachine, Canal de ≊ | 275a | 45.26 N | 73.40 W |
| Lachine, Rapides de ᒪ | 275a | 45.25 N | 73.36 W |
| La Chira, Punta ≻ | 286d | 12.13 S | 77.03 W |
| La Chivera | 286c | 10.37 N | 66.54 W |
| Lachkaltsap Indian Reserve ◆[4] | 182 | 55.03 N | 129.34 W |
| Lachlan ≃ | 166 | 34.21 S | 143.57 E |
| La Chorrera, Col. | 246 | 0.44 S | 73.01 W |
| La Chorrera, Pan. | 236 | 8.53 N | 79.47 W |
| L'achovskije ostrova II | 74 | 73.30 N | 141.00 E |
| La Choza | 258 | 34.47 S | 59.07 W |
| La Choza, Arroyo ≃ | 258 | 34.40 S | 58.58 W |
| Lachta ◆[8] | 265a | 60.00 N | 30.09 E |
| Lachtinskij Razliv, ozero ⊜ | 265a | 60.00 N | 30.11 E |
| Lachute | 206 | 45.38 N | 74.20 W |
| La Ciénaga | 252 | 27.30 S | 66.57 W |
| La Ciénega | 234 | 16.54 N | 96.46 W |
| Lâçin | 130 | 40.47 N | 34.54 E |
| La Cinta Creek ≃ | 196 | 35.24 N | 104.06 W |
| La Ciotat | 62 | 43.10 N | 5.36 E |
| La Cisterna | 286e | 33.33 S | 70.41 W |
| La Citadelle ⊥ | 238 | 19.35 N | 72.14 W |
| La Ciudad | 234 | 23.44 N | 105.42 W |
| Lack | 48 | 54.33 N | 7.35 W |
| Lackawanna | 210 | 42.49 N | 78.49 W |
| Lackawanna □[6] | 210 | 41.24 N | 75.40 W |
| Lackawanna ≃ | 210 | 41.21 N | 75.47 W |
| Lackawanna, Lake ⊜ | 276 | 40.57 N | 74.42 W |
| Lackawanna State Park ♠ | 210 | 41.33 N | 75.44 W |
| Lackawaxen | 210 | 41.29 N | 74.59 W |
| Lackawaxen ≃ | 210 | 41.29 N | 74.59 W |
| Lackey | 208 | 37.14 N | 76.33 W |
| Lackland Air Force Base ■ | 196 | 29.27 N | 98.37 W |
| Läckö | 26 | 58.41 N | 13.13 E |
| Lackoje | 76 | 58.05 N | 38.08 E |
| Lac La Belle | 216 | 43.09 N | 88.32 W |
| Lac la Biche | 182 | 54.46 N | 111.58 W |
| Lac la Hache | 182 | 51.49 N | 121.28 W |
| Lac la Ronge Provincial Park ♠ | 184 | 55.15 N | 104.55 W |
| La Clayette | 32 | 46.18 N | 4.19 E |
| Laclede, Id., U.S. | 182 | 48.10 N | 116.45 W |
| La Clede, Il., U.S. | 219 | 38.53 N | 88.43 W |
| Laclede, Mo., U.S. | 194 | 39.47 N | 93.09 W |
| La Clotilde | 252 | 27.08 S | 60.40 W |
| La Clusaz | 58 | 45.54 N | 6.25 E |
| La Cluse | 58 | 46.10 N | 5.34 E |
| La Cluse-et-Mijoux | 58 | 46.53 N | 6.23 E |
| Lacmalac | 171b | 35.19 S | 148.19 E |
| Lac-Masson | 206 | 46.02 N | 74.04 W |
| Lac-Mégantic | 188 | 45.36 N | 70.53 W |
| Lacob ti-duyong, Mount ∧ | 116 | 17.35 N | 121.09 E |
| La Cocha | 252 | 27.47 S | 65.34 W |
| Lacolle | 206 | 45.05 N | 73.22 W |
| Lacolle ≃ | 206 | 45.04 N | 73.20 W |
| La Colle-sur-Loup | 62 | 43.41 N | 7.06 E |
| La Colmena | 286a | 19.36 N | 99.18 W |
| La Colorada | 232 | 28.41 N | 110.25 W |
| La Columna → Bolívar, Pico ∧ | 246 | 8.30 N | 71.02 W |
| La Coma | 232 | 24.28 N | 98.19 W |
| Lacombe, Ab., Can. | 182 | 52.28 N | 113.44 W |
| Lacombe, La., U.S. | 194 | 30.18 N | 89.56 W |
| Lacon | 190 | 41.01 N | 89.24 W |
| Lacona, Ia., U.S. | 190 | 41.11 N | 93.22 W |
| Lacona, N.Y., U.S. | 212 | 43.38 N | 76.04 W |
| La Concepción, Pan. | 236 | 8.31 N | 82.37 W |
| La Concepción, Ven. | 246 | 10.38 N | 71.50 W |
| La Condamine-Châtelard | 62 | 44.27 N | 6.45 E |
| Laconi | 71 | 39.51 N | 9.03 E |
| Laconia | 188 | 43.31 N | 71.28 W |
| La Conner | 224 | 48.23 N | 122.29 W |
| La Consulta | 252 | 33.44 S | 69.07 W |
| Lacoochee | 220 | 28.27 N | 82.10 W |
| La Coruña □[4] | 34 | 43.00 N | 8.35 W |
| Lacoste, Fr. | 62 | 43.50 N | 5.18 E |
| La Coste, Tx., U.S. | 196 | 29.19 N | 98.49 W |
| La Côte-Saint-André | 62 | 45.23 N | 5.15 E |
| La Courneuve | 261 | 48.56 N | 2.23 E |
| La Couronne | 62 | 43.20 N | 5.03 E |
| La Courtine | 32 | 45.42 N | 2.16 E |
| Lac qui Parle ≃ | 198 | 45.01 N | 95.53 W |
| Lac qui Parle, West Branch ≃ | 198 | 44.55 N | 96.02 W |
| La Crau | 62 | 43.09 N | 6.04 E |
| Lacre Punt ≻ | 241s | 12.02 N | 68.15 W |
| La Crescent | 190 | 43.49 N | 91.18 W |
| La Crescenta | 228 | 34.13 N | 118.14 W |
| La Croft | 214 | 40.39 N | 80.35 W |
| Lacroix-Saint-Ouen | 50 | 49.21 N | 2.47 E |
| La Crosse, In., U.S. | 216 | 41.19 N | 86.53 W |
| La Crosse, Ks., U.S. | 198 | 38.31 N | 99.18 W |
| La Crosse, Va., U.S. | 192 | 36.41 N | 78.05 W |
| Lacrosse, Wa., U.S. | 202 | 46.49 N | 117.53 W |
| La Crosse, Wi., U.S. | 190 | 43.48 N | 91.14 W |
| La Crosse ≃ | 190 | 43.49 N | 91.16 W |
| La Cruz, Arg. | 252 | 29.10 S | 56.38 W |
| La Cruz, Col. | 246 | 1.35 N | 76.58 W |
| La Cruz, C.R. | 236 | 11.04 N | 85.39 W |
| La Cruz, Méx. | 196 | 28.33 N | 100.48 W |
| La Cruz, Ur. | 258 | 33.56 S | 56.15 W |
| La Cruz, Cerro ∧ | 234 | 17.55 N | 101.31 W |
| La Cruz de Río Grande | 236 | 13.06 N | 84.10 W |
| Lac-Saguay | 206 | 46.30 N | 75.09 W |
| Lac Seul | 184 | 50.20 N | 92.16 W |
| Lac Seul Indian Reserve ◆[4] | 184 | 50.15 N | 92.10 W |
| La Cuchilla | 234 | 18.54 N | 103.19 W |
| La Cuesta, C.R. | 236 | 8.30 N | 82.50 W |
| La Cuesta, Méx. | 234 | 20.10 N | 104.51 W |
| La Cuesta, P.R. | 240m | 18.25 N | 66.49 W |
| La Cumbre, Arg. | 252 | 30.58 S | 64.30 W |
| La Cumbre, Ven. | 286c | 10.32 N | 66.57 W |
| La Cumbre, Volcán ∧[1] | 246a | 0.20 S | 91.30 W |
| La Cure | 58 | 46.28 N | 6.05 E |
| Lacy Fork ≃ | 222 | 32.24 N | 96.08 W |
| La Cygne | 198 | 38.21 N | 94.45 W |
| Lacy-Lakeview | 222 | 31.37 N | 97.06 W |
| Lada, Teluk ⊂ | 115a | 6.29 S | 105.44 E |
| Ladainha | 255 | 17.39 S | 41.44 W |
| Ladākh □[9] | 120 | 35.10 N | 76.10 E |
| Ladākh Range ⋏ | 120 | 34.00 N | 78.00 E |
| Ladan | 78 | 50.31 N | 32.35 E |
| La Dang, Ko I | 114 | 6.33 N | 99.18 E |
| Ladang Jagor | 114 | 4.42 N | 101.35 E |
| Ladara | 114 | 1.28 N | 97.28 E |
| Ladário | 248 | 19.01 S | 57.35 W |
| Ladbergen | 52 | 52.08 N | 7.44 E |
| Ladby | 41 | 55.26 N | 10.38 E |
| Ladd | 190 | 41.22 N | 89.13 W |
| Låddenhøj ∧[2] | 41 | 56.13 N | 9.48 E |
| Ladder Creek ≃ | 198 | 38.48 N | 100.52 W |
| Laddingford | 260 | 51.12 N | 0.25 E |
| Laddonia | 219 | 39.14 N | 91.38 W |
| Ladeburg | 264a | 52.42 N | 13.35 E |
| La Défense ʊ | 261 | 48.53 N | 2.15 E |
| La Dehesa | 286e | 33.22 S | 70.33 W |
| Ladenburg | 56 | 49.28 N | 8.37 E |
| La Dent d'Oche ∧ | 58 | 46.21 N | 6.44 E |
| Ladera Heights | 280 | 33.59 N | 118.22 W |
| La Désirade I | 241o | 16.19 N | 61.03 W |
| Ládhi | 38 | 41.27 N | 26.17 E |
| Ladhurka | 126 | 23.22 N | 86.32 E |
| La Digue I | 138 | 4.21 S | 55.50 E |
| Lâdik | 130 | 40.55 N | 35.55 E |
| Ladinger Spitze ∧ | 61 | 46.51 N | 14.39 E |
| L'adiny | 24 | 61.33 N | 38.20 E |
| Ladismith | 158 | 33.30 S | 21.16 E |
| Ladispoli | 66 | 41.56 N | 12.05 E |
| Lādīz | 128 | 28.56 N | 61.19 E |
| Ladner | 224 | 49.05 N | 123.05 W |
| Lādnūn | 120 | 27.39 N | 74.23 E |
| Ladoga | 194 | 39.54 N | 86.48 W |
| Ladoga, Lake → Ladožskoje ozero ⊜ | 24 | 61.00 N | 31.30 E |
| La Dolorita | 286c | 10.29 N | 66.47 W |
| Ladon | 50 | 48.00 N | 2.32 E |
| Ladonia | 196 | 33.25 N | 95.56 W |
| La Dorada | 246 | 5.27 N | 74.40 W |
| La Dormida | 252 | 33.21 S | 67.55 W |
| Lado Sarāi ◆[8] | 272a | 28.32 N | 77.12 E |
| Ladovskaja Balka | 80 | 45.38 N | 41.25 E |
| Ladožskaja | 78 | 45.19 N | 39.54 E |
| Ladožskoje Ozero | 76 | 60.08 N | 31.04 E |
| Ladožskoje ozero (Lake Ladoga) ⊜ | 24 | 61.00 N | 31.30 E |
| Lādpur ◆[8] | 272a | 28.44 N | 76.59 E |
| Ladrillero, Golfo ⊂ | 254 | 49.20 S | 75.37 W |
| Ladson | 192 | 32.59 N | 80.06 W |
| Ladue | 219 | 38.38 N | 90.23 W |
| Ladue ≃ | 180 | 63.09 N | 140.25 W |
| Laduozong | 102 | 31.27 N | 97.19 E |
| Laduškin | 76 | 54.36 N | 20.11 E |
| Ladva | 24 | 61.21 N | 34.34 E |
| Ladva-Vetka | 24 | 61.21 N | 34.27 E |
| Lādwa | 124 | 29.59 N | 77.03 E |
| Lady, Fr. | 261 | 48.35 N | 2.54 E |
| L'ady, Ross. | 76 | 58.38 N | 28.47 E |
| Lady Ann Strait Џ | 176 | 75.40 N | 79.50 W |
| Ladybank | 46 | 56.16 N | 3.08 W |
| Lady Barron | 166 | 40.12 S | 148.14 E |
| Ladybower Reservoir ⊜[1] | 44 | 53.20 N | 1.45 W |
| Ladybrand | 158 | 29.19 S | 27.25 E |
| Lady Elliot Island I | 166 | 24.07 S | 152.42 E |
| Lady Evelyn Lake ⊜ | 190 | 47.20 N | 80.10 W |
| Lady Frere | 158 | 31.44 S | 27.16 E |
| Lady Grey | 158 | 30.45 S | 27.13 E |
| Lady Lake | 220 | 28.55 N | 81.55 W |
| Ladysmith, Austl. | 171b | 35.12 S | 147.31 E |
| Ladysmith, B.C., Can. | 182 | 48.58 N | 123.49 W |
| Ladysmith, S. Afr. | 158 | 28.34 S | 29.45 E |
| Ladysmith, Wi., U.S. | 190 | 45.27 N | 91.06 W |
| Ladyženka | 86 | 51.00 N | 68.42 E |
| Ladyzhyn | 78 | 48.41 N | 29.15 E |
| Ladžanurges | 84 | 42.37 N | 42.50 E |
| Lae | 164 | 6.45 S | 147.00 E |
| Lae I[1] | 14 | 8.56 N | 166.14 E |
| Laem, Khao ∧ | 110 | 14.27 N | 101.30 E |
| Laem Ngop | 110 | 12.10 N | 102.26 E |
| La Encantada | 232 | 25.17 N | 101.04 W |
| La Encarnacion | 234 | 23.23 N | 98.01 W |
| Laer | 52 | 52.03 N | 7.21 E |
| Laer ◆[8] | 263 | 51.28 N | 7.16 E |
| Lærdalsøyri | 26 | 61.06 N | 7.29 E |
| La Escondida | 196 | 26.17 N | 99.46 W |
| La Esmeralda, Méx. | 232 | 27.17 N | 103.39 W |
| La Esmeralda, Para. | 252 | 22.13 S | 62.38 W |
| La Esmeralda, Ven. | 246 | 3.10 N | 65.33 W |
| Læsø I | 26 | 57.16 N | 11.01 E |
| La Esperanza, Cuba | 240p | 22.46 N | 83.44 W |
| La Esperanza, Hond. | 236 | 14.20 N | 88.10 W |
| La Esperanza, Méx. | 196 | 26.46 N | 104.00 W |
| La Esperanza, Méx. | 200 | 32.06 N | 114.47 W |
| La Esperanza, Perú | 248 | 8.05 S | 79.04 W |
| La Esperanza, P.R. | 240m | 18.22 N | 66.07 W |
| La Estación ◆[8] | 266a | 40.27 N | 3.48 W |
| La Estrella, Bol. | 248 | 16.30 S | 63.45 W |
| La Estrella, Ven. | 286c | 10.25 N | 66.48 W |
| La Estrella, Cerro ∧ | 286a | 19.20 N | 99.05 W |
| Lafa | 89 | 43.50 N | 127.19 E |
| La Falda | 252 | 31.05 S | 64.30 W |
| La Farge | 190 | 43.34 N | 90.38 W |
| LaFargeville | 212 | 44.11 N | 75.57 W |
| Lafayette, Fr. | 62 | 45.35 N | 5.04 E |
| Lafayette, Al., U.S. | 194 | 32.53 N | 85.24 W |
| Lafayette, Ca., U.S. | 226 | 37.53 N | 122.07 W |
| Lafayette, Co., U.S. | 198 | 39.59 N | 105.05 W |
| Lafayette, Ga., U.S. | 192 | 34.42 N | 85.16 W |
| Lafayette, In., U.S. | 216 | 40.25 N | 86.52 W |
| Lafayette, La., U.S. | 194 | 30.13 N | 92.01 W |
| Lafayette, Mn., U.S. | 190 | 44.26 N | 94.23 W |
| Lafayette, N.J., U.S. | 210 | 41.05 N | 74.41 W |
| La Fayette, N.Y., U.S. | 210 | 42.54 N | 76.06 W |
| Lafayette, Oh., U.S. | 216 | 40.46 N | 83.57 W |
| Lafayette, Or., U.S. | 224 | 45.14 N | 123.06 W |
| La Fayette, R.I., U.S. | 207 | 41.34 N | 71.28 W |
| Lafayette, Tn., U.S. | 194 | 36.31 N | 86.01 W |
| La Fayette, Tx., U.S. | 222 | 32.54 N | 94.51 W |
| Lafayette, Mount ∧ | 188 | 44.10 N | 71.38 W |
| Lafayette Hill | 285 | 40.05 N | 75.15 W |
| Lafayette Reservoir ⊜[1] | 282 | 37.53 N | 122.08 W |
| Lafayette Water Tunnel ◆[5] | 282 | 37.54 N | 122.12 W |
| La Fé | 240p | 21.45 N | 82.45 W |
| La Fère | 50 | 49.40 N | 3.22 E |
| La Feria | 196 | 26.09 N | 97.49 W |
| Laferrere | 288 | 34.45 S | 58.35 W |
| La Ferrière-sur-Risle | 50 | 48.59 N | 0.48 E |
| La Ferté-Alais | 50 | 48.29 N | 2.21 E |
| La Ferté-Bernard | 50 | 48.11 N | 0.40 E |
| La Ferté-Frênel | 50 | 48.50 N | 0.30 E |
| La Ferté-Gaucher | 50 | 48.47 N | 3.18 E |
| La Ferté-Imbault | 50 | 47.23 N | 1.58 E |
| La Ferté-Macé | 32 | 48.36 N | 0.22 W |
| La Ferté-Milon | 50 | 49.10 N | 3.07 E |
| La Ferté-Saint-Aubin | 50 | 47.43 N | 1.56 E |
| La Ferté-sous-Jouarre | 50 | 48.57 N | 3.08 E |
| Laferté-sur-Amance | 58 | 47.50 N | 5.42 E |
| La Ferté-Vidame | 50 | 48.37 N | 0.55 E |
| La Ferté-Villeneuil | 50 | 47.59 N | 1.21 E |
| Lafferty | 214 | 40.06 N | 81.01 W |
| Laffrey | 62 | 45.02 N | 5.46 E |
| Lafia | 150 | 8.30 N | 8.30 E |
| Lafiagi | 150 | 8.52 N | 5.25 E |
| Laflamme ≃ | 190 | 48.56 N | 77.18 W |
| Laflèche, P.Q., Can. | 275a | 45.30 N | 73.28 W |
| Lafleche, Sk., Can. | 184 | 49.43 N | 106.35 W |
| La Flèche, Fr. | 32 | 47.42 N | 0.05 W |
| La Floresta | 266d | 41.27 N | 2.04 E |
| La Florida, Chile | 286e | 33.33 S | 70.34 W |
| La Florida, Esp. | 266d | 41.31 N | 2.12 E |
| La Florida, Guat. | 232 | 16.33 N | 90.27 W |
| Lafnitz ≃ | 61 | 46.57 N | 16.16 E |
| La Foa | 175f | 21.43 S | 165.50 E |
| La Foce | 62 | 44.08 N | 9.47 E |
| La Follette | 192 | 36.22 N | 84.07 W |
| Lafon | 154 | 5.02 N | 32.27 E |
| Lafontaine, P.Q., Can. | 206 | 45.48 N | 74.01 W |
| La Fontaine, In., U.S. | 216 | 40.40 N | 85.43 W |
| Lafontaine, Parc ♠ | 275a | 45.32 N | 73.34 W |
| Lafourche, Bayou ≃ | 194 | 29.05 N | 90.1- W |
| La Foux, Fr. | 62 | 43.16 N | 6.3- E |
| La Foux, Fr. | 62 | 44.17 N | 6.3- E |
| La Fragua | 252 | 26.05 S | 64.2- W |
| La Francia | 252 | 31.24 S | 62.3- W |
| La Fregeneda | 34 | 40.59 N | 6.5- W |
| La Frette-sur-Seine | 261 | 48.58 N | 2.1- E |
| La Fría | 246 | 8.13 N | 72.1- W |
| Lafrimbolle | 58 | 48.36 N | 7.01 E |
| La Fuente de San Esteban | 34 | 40.48 N | 6.15 W |
| Laga, Monti della ⋏ | 66 | 42.37 N | 13.24 E |
| La Gacilly | 28 | 47.46 N | 2.09 W |
| Lagaip ≃ | 164 | 5.05 S | 142.40 E |
| La Galite I | 36 | 37.32 N | 8.56 E |
| La Gallareta | 252 | 29.34 S | 60.23 W |
| La Gallega | 34 | 41.54 N | 3.16 W |
| Lagan | 26 | 56.55 N | 13.59 E |
| Lagan ≃, Sve. | 26 | 56.33 N | 12.56 E |
| Lagan ≃, N. Ire., U.K. | 48 | 54.37 N | 5.53 W |
| Lagangzong | 120 | 28.05 N | 91.04 |
| Lagantu | 102 | 42.20 N | 108.22 |
| La Garde | 62 | 43.07 N | 6.01 |
| La Garde-Freinet | 62 | 43.19 N | 6.28 |
| La Garenne-Colombes | 261 | 48.55 N | 2.15 E |
| Lagarina, Val V | 64 | 45.45 N | 11.00 E |
| Lagarto, Bra. | 250 | 10.54 S | 37.41 W |
| Lagarto, C.R. | 236 | 10.07 N | 84.56 W |
| Lagarto Creek ≃ | 196 | 28.08 N | 97.56 W |
| Lagawe | 116 | 16.49 N | 121.06 E |
| Lagay | 116 | 14.06 N | 122.12 E |
| Lagayan | 116 | 17.43 N | 120.42 E |
| Lage, Dtsch. | 52 | 51.59 N | 8.48 E |
| Lage, Zhg. | 120 | 29.26 N | 85.51 E |
| Lagedu | 102 | 26.24 N | 101.11 E |
| Lågen ≃, Nor. | 26 | 59.03 N | 10.05 E |
| Lågen ≃, Nor. | 26 | 61.08 N | 10.25 E |
| Lägerdorf | 52 | 53.53 N | 9.34 E |
| Lages | 252 | 27.48 S | 50.19 W |
| Lageuen | 114 | 4.44 N | 95.31 E |
| Lage Zwaluwe | 52 | 51.43 N | 4.41 E |
| Laggan | 46 | 57.02 N | 4.16 W |
| Laggan, Loch ⊜[1] | 46 | 56.57 N | 4.28 W |
| Laggan Bay ⊂ | 46 | 55.41 N | 6.19 W |
| Lagginhorn ∧ | 58 | 46.11 N | 8.01 E |
| Laghmān □[4] | 120 | 35.00 N | 70.15 E |
| Laghouat | 148 | 33.50 N | 2.59 E |
| Laghy | 48 | 54.37 N | 8.05 W |
| La Giettaz | 62 | 45.52 N | 6.30 E |
| La Giganta, Cerro ∧ | 234 | 21.08 N | 101.19 W |
| La Giustiniana ◆[8] | 267a | 41.59 N | 12.24 E |
| La Gleize | 56 | 50.25 N | 5.51 E |
| La Gloria | 246 | 8.37 N | 73.48 W |
| Lagnieu | 58 | 45.54 N | 5.21 E |
| Lagny | 50 | 48.52 N | 2.43 E |
| Lagny-le-Sac | 261 | 49.05 N | 2.45 E |
| Lago | 68 | 39.10 N | 16.09 E |
| Lago, Mount ∧ | 224 | 48.51 N | 120.32 W |
| Lagoa Branca | 256 | 21.54 S | 47.02 W |
| Lagoa da Prata | 255 | 20.01 S | 45.33 W |
| Lagoa Formosa | 255 | 18.47 S | 46.24 W |
| Lago Argentino → Calafate | 254 | 50.20 S | 72.18 W |
| Lagoa Santa | 255 | 19.38 S | 43.53 W |
| Lagoa Vermelha | 252 | 28.13 S | 51.32 W |
| Lago Blanco | 254 | 45.55 S | 71.15 W |
| Lago da Pedra | 250 | 4.20 S | 45.10 W |
| Lagodechi | 84 | 41.49 N | 46.18 E |
| Lagodechskij zapovednik ♠ | 84 | 41.53 N | 46.22 E |
| Lagoinha | 256 | 23.06 S | 45.11 W |
| Lagolândia | 255 | 15.37 S | 49.02 W |
| Lagolovo | 265a | 59.42 N | 30.00 E |
| Lagonegro | 68 | 40.07 N | 15.46 E |
| Lagonglong | 116 | 8.48 N | 124.47 E |
| Lagonoy | 116 | 13.44 N | 123.31 E |
| Lagonoy Gulf ⊂ | 116 | 13.35 N | 123.45 E |
| Lagopesole, Castel di ⊥ | 68 | 40.48 N | 15.45 E |
| Lago Posadas | 254 | 47.32 S | 71.45 W |
| Lagorai, Catena del ⋏ | 64 | 46.18 N | 11.35 E |
| Lago Ranco | 254 | 40.20 S | 72.38 W |
| La Gorgue | 50 | 50.38 N | 2.42 E |
| Lagos, Ang. | 152 | 16.04 S | 17.03 E |
| Lagos, Nig. | 150 | 6.27 N | 3.24 E |
| Lagos, Nig. | 273a | 6.27 N | 3.24 E |
| Lagos, Port. | 34 | 37.06 N | 8.40 W |
| Lagos (Ikeja) Airport ⊠ | 273a | 6.35 N | 3.20 E |
| Lagos, University of ʊ[2] | 273a | 6.32 N | 3.24 E |
| Lagosanto | 66 | 44.46 N | 12.08 E |
| Lagos de Moreno | 234 | 21.21 N | 101.55 W |
| Lagos Harbour ⊂ | 273a | 6.26 N | 3.24 E |
| Lagos Island I | 273a | 6.27 N | 3.26 E |
| Lagos Lagoon ⊂ | 273a | 6.30 N | 3.26 E |
| Lagos Terminus ◆[5] | 273a | 6.28 N | 3.23 E |
| La Gouèra | 148 | 20.48 N | 17.08 W |
| La Goulette | 148 | 36.49 N | 10.18 E |
| Lago Viedma | 254 | 49.48 S | 72.07 W |
| La Granadella | 34 | 41.21 N | 0.40 E |
| La Grand'Combe | 62 | 44.13 N | 4.02 E |
| La Grande | 202 | 45.19 N | 118.05 W |
| La Grande Deux, Réservoir ⊜[1] | 176 | 53.40 N | 76.55 W |
| La Grande Moucherolle ∧ | 62 | 45.00 N | 5.34 E |
| La Grande Quatre, Réservoir ⊜[1] | 176 | 54.00 N | 73.15 W |
| La Grange, Austl. | 162 | 18.41 S | 121.45 E |
| LaGrange, Ca., U.S. | 226 | 37.40 N | 120.28 W |
| La Grange, Ga., U.S. | 192 | 33.02 N | 85.01 W |
| La Grange, Il., U.S. | 216 | 41.48 N | 87.52 W |
| Lagrange, In., U.S. | 216 | 41.39 N | 85.25 W |
| La Grange, Ky., U.S. | 218 | 38.24 N | 85.22 W |
| La Grange, Mo., U.S. | 219 | 40.02 N | 91.29 W |
| La Grange, N.C., U.S. | 192 | 35.18 N | 77.47 W |
| Lagrange, Oh., U.S. | 214 | 41.14 N | 82.07 W |
| La Grange, Tx., U.S. | 222 | 29.54 N | 96.52 W |
| Lagrange, Wy., U.S. | 198 | 41.38 N | 104.10 W |
| Lagrange □[6] | 216 | 41.39 N | 85.25 W |
| Lagrange Bay ⊂ | 162 | 18.38 S | 121.42 E |
| La Grange Highlands | 278 | 41.50 N | 87.51 W |
| La Grange Lock and Dam ◆[5] | 219 | 39.57 N | 90.32 W |
| La Grange Park | 278 | 41.50 N | 87.51 W |
| Lagrangeville | 210 | 41.39 N | 73.46 W |
| La Granja | 286e | 33.32 S | 70.39 W |
| La Gran Piedra ∧ | 240p | 20.01 N | 75.38 W |
| La Gran Sabana ≚ | 246 | 5.30 N | 61.30 W |
| La Grave | 62 | 45.03 N | 6.18 E |
| La Grita | 246 | 8.08 N | 71.59 W |
| Lagro | 216 | 40.50 N | 85.43 W |
| La Groise | 50 | 50.05 N | 3.41 E |
| La Grue Bayou ≃ | 194 | 34.05 N | 91.10 W |
| Lagu | 102 | 26.26 N | 101.30 E |
| La Guadeloupe (Saint-Évariste) | 188 | 45.57 N | 70.56 W |
| La Guajira □[5] | 246 | 11.30 N | 72.30 W |
| La Guajira, Península de ≻[1] | 246 | 12.00 N | 71.40 W |
| La Guardia, Arg. | 252 | 29.33 S | 65.27 W |
| La Guardia, Bol. | 248 | 17.54 S | 63.20 W |
| Laguardia, Esp. | 34 | 42.33 N | 2.35 W |
| La Guardia Airport ⊠ | 210 | 40.46 N | 73.53 W |
| La Guêpière | 261 | 48.35 N | 1.50 E |
| La Guerche-de-Bretagne | 32 | 47.56 N | 1.14 W |
| La Guerche-sur-l'Aubois | 32 | 46.57 N | 2.57 E |
| Laguiole | 32 | 44.41 N | 2.51 E |
| Laguna, Bra. | 252 | 28.29 S | 48.47 W |
| Laguna, N.M., U.S. | 200 | 35.02 N | 107.22 W |
| Laguna □[4] | 116 | 14.10 N | 121.20 E |
| Laguna ≃ | 226 | 38.16 N | 121.23 W |
| Laguna, Arroyo de la ≃ | 282 | 37.35 N | 121.53 W |


| Symbol | English | Deutsch | Español | Français | Português |
|---|---|---|---|---|---|
| ≃ | River | Fluß | Río | Rivière | Rio |
| ≊ | Canal | Kanal | Canal | Canal | Canal |
| ᒪ | Waterfall, Rapids | Wasserfall, Stromschnellen | Cascada, Rápidos | Chute d'eau, Rapides | Cascata, Rápidos |
| Џ | Strait | Meeresstraße | Estrecho | Détroit | Estreito |
| ⊂ | Bay, Gulf | Bucht, Golf | Bahía, Golfo | Baie, Golfe | Baía, Golfo |
| ⊜ | Lake, Lakes | See, Seen | Lago, Lagos | Lac, Lacs | Lago, Lagos |
| ≚ | Swamp | Sumpf | Pantano | Marais | Pântano |
| ⊓ | Ice Features, Glacier | Eis- und Gletscherformen | Accidentes Glaciales | Formes glaciaires | Acidentes glaciares |
| ⊤ | Other Hydrographic Features | Andere Hydrographische Objekte | Otros Elementos Hidrográficos | Autres données hydrographiques | Outros acidentes hidrográficos |
| ✢ | Submarine Features | Untermeerische Objekte | Accidentes Submarinos | Formes de relief sous-marin | Acidentes submarinos |
| □ | Political Unit | Politische Einheit | Unidad Politica | Entité politique | Unidade política |
| ʊ | Cultural Institution | Kulturelle Institution | Institución Cultural | Institution culturelle | Instituição cultural |
| ⊥ | Historical Site | Historische Stätte | Sitio Histórico | Site historique | Sitio histórico |
| ♠ | Recreational Site | Erholungs- und Ferienort | Sitio de Recreo | Centre de loisirs | Area de Lazer |
| ⊠ | Airport | Flughafen | Aeropuerto | Aéroport | Aeroporto |
| ■ | Military Installation | Militäranlage | Instalación Militar | Installation militaire | Instalação militar |
| ◆ | Miscellaneous | Verschiedenes | Misceláneo | Divers | Diversos |

Laguna, Ilha da I 250 1.40 S 51.00 W
Laguna Beach 228 33.32 N 117.46 W
Laguna Blanca 240p 20.27 N 76.07 W
Laguna Blanca, Parque Nacional ♦ 254 39.00 S 70.18 W
Laguna Creek ≃ 200 36.54 N 109.45 W
Laguna Dam •[6] 200 32.50 N 114.31 W
Laguna de Pozuelos, Monumento Natural ♦, Arg. 248 22.20 S 66.00 W
Laguna de Pozuelos, Monumento Natural ♦, Arg. 252 22.20 S 66.00 W
Laguna Hills 228 33.36 N 117.42 W
Laguna Indian Reservation •[4] 200 35.00 N 107.20 W
Laguna Lake ⊜ 226 35.16 S 120.42 W
Laguna Larga 252 31.46 S 63.48 W
Laguna Limpia 252 26.29 S 59.41 W
Laguna Niguel 228 33.31 N 117.43 W
Laguna Paiva 252 31.19 S 60.39 W
Laguna Park 222 31.52 N 97.23 W
Lagunas 248 5.14 S 75.38 W
Laguna San Rafael, Parque Nacional ♦ 254 47.00 S 73.30 W
Lagunas de Chacagua, Parque Nacional ♦ 234 16.00 N 97.00 W
Lagunas de Montebello, Parque Nacional ♦ 236 16.05 N 91.45 W
Lagunas de Zempoala, Parque Nacional ♦ 234 19.08 N 99.20 W
Lagundo 64 46.41 N 11.08 E
Lagunillas, Bol. 248 19.38 S 63.43 W
Lagunillas, Méx. 234 21.34 N 99.35 W
Lagunillas, Ven. 246 8.31 N 71.24 W
Lagunillas → Ciudad Ojeda, Ven. 246 10.12 N 71.19 W
Lagunillás, Laguna ⊜ 248 15.44 S 70.43 W
Laguntara c 236 15.35 N 84.05 W
L'agušje 86 54.24 N 77.59 E
Laguyu 104 41.43 N 123.49 E
Laha 89 48.10 N 124.39 E
La Habana (Havana), Cuba 240p 23.08 N 82.22 W
La Habana (Havana), Cuba 286b 23.08 N 82.22 W
La Habana □[4] 240p 22.45 N 82.10 W
La Habana, Universidad de ᵿ[2] 286b 23.08 N 82.22 W
La Habra 228 33.55 N 117.56 W
La Habra Heights 280 33.57 N 117.57 W
Lahad Datu 112 5.02 N 118.19 E
Lahad Datu, Telukan c 112 4.50 N 118.30 E
Lahaina 229a 20.52 N 156.40 W
Laham 112 0.22 N 115.24 E
Lahār 124 26.12 N 78.57 E
La Harpe, Il., U.S. 190 40.35 N 90.58 W
La Harpe, Ks., U.S. 198 37.55 N 95.17 W
Lāharpur 124 27.43 N 80.54 E
Lahaska 208 40.21 N 75.02 W
Lahat, Indon. 112 3.48 S 103.32 E
Lahat, Malay. 114 4.33 N 101.02 E
La Hauteville 261 48.42 N 1.37 E
La Havane → La Habana 240p 23.08 N 82.22 W
LaHave ≃ 186 44.14 N 64.20 W
La Haye → 's-Gravenhage 52 52.06 N 4.18 E
La Haye-du-Puits 32 49.18 N 1.33 W
La Häy-les-Rosas 261 48.47 N 2.21 E
Lähden 52 52.45 N 7.34 E
Lāhe 110 26.20 N 95.26 E
Laheria Sarai 124 26.07 N 85.54 E
Lahewa 114 1.24 N 97.11 E
Lahfān, Bi'r ⊤[4] 132 31.01 N 33.52 E
Lahi, Ava ⊔ 174w 21.02 S 175.11 W
Lahıç 84 40.51 N 48.24 E
La Higuera 252 29.30 S 71.17 W
Lahij 144 13.02 N 44.54 E
Lāhījān 128 37.12 N 50.01 E
Lahišyn 76 52.20 N 25.59 E
Lāhithah 132 32.59 N 36.35 E
Lahn ≃ 56 50.18 N 7.37 E
Lahnstein 56 50.19 N 7.36 E
Lahojsk 76 54.12 N 27.49 E
Laholm 26 56.31 N 13.02 E
Laholmsbukten c 26 56.35 N 12.50 E
La Honda 226 37.19 N 122.16 W
La Honda Creek ≃ 282 37.18 N 122.16 W
Lahontan Reservoir ⊜[1] 226 39.23 N 119.09 W
Lahontan State Recreation Area ♦ 226 39.28 N 119.03 W
Lahor → Lahore, Pāk. 123 31.35 N 74.18 E
Lāhor, Pāk. 123 34.03 N 72.22 E
Lahore 123 31.35 N 74.18 E
La Horqueta 246 3.06 N 72.50 W
La Horqueta, Arroyo ≃ 288 34.41 S 58.51 W
La Houssaye-en-Brie 261 48.45 N 2.53 E
Lahr 58 48.20 N 7.52 E
Lahri 120 29.11 N 68.13 E
Lāhrūd 128 38.30 N 47.49 E
Lahstedt 52 52.14 N 10.12 E
Laḥṭah, Wādī V 142 29.44 N 32.45 E
Lahti 26 60.58 N 25.40 E
La Huaca 248 4.54 S 80.57 W
La Huacana 234 18.58 N 101.49 W
La Huerta, Méx. 234 19.28 N 104.39 W
La Huerta, N.M., U.S. 196 32.27 N 104.13 W
La Hunière 261 48.36 N 1.52 E
Lahuy Island I 116 13.56 N 123.50 E
Laḥva 76 52.13 N 27.04 E
Laï 146 9.24 N 16.18 E
Laiagam 164 5.30 S 143.20 E
Lai'an 100 32.27 N 118.25 E
Laibach → Ljubljana 36 46.03 N 14.31 E
Laibin 102 23.42 N 109.22 E
Lai Chau 110 22.02 N 103.10 E
Laichingen 58 48.29 N 9.41 E
Laichow Bay → Laizhou Wan c 98 37.36 N 119.30 E
Laide 46 57.52 N 5.32 W
Laidley 171a 27.38 S 152.24 E
Laidley Creek ≃ 171a 27.31 S 152.24 E
Laidon, Loch ⊜ 46 56.39 N 4.40 W
Laie 229c 21.39 N 157.55 W
Laifang 100 25.56 N 116.54 E
Laifeng, Zhg. 102 29.31 N 109.15 E
Laifeng, Zhg. 107 30.14 N 105.17 E
Laifengzhen 107 29.26 N 106.13 E
L'Aigle 50 48.45 N 0.38 E
L'Aigle Creek ≃ 194 33.12 N 92.08 W
Laignes 50 47.50 N 4.22 E
Laigou 100 33.56 N 117.06 E
Laigueglia 62 43.58 N 8.09 E
Laihia 26 62.58 N 22.01 E
Lai-hka 110 21.16 N 97.40 E
Lailly-en-Val 50 47.46 N 1.41 E
Laïmbélé, Mont ∧ 175f 16.20 S 167.31 E
Lainate 266b 45.34 N 9.02 E
Lainbach 61 47.38 N 14.46 E
La Independencia, Bahía de c 248 14.15 S 76.10 W
Laingsburg, S. Afr. 158 33.11 S 20.51 E
Laingsburg, Mi., U.S. 216 42.53 N 84.21 W
Lainioälven ≃ 24 67.22 N 23.39 E
La Inmaculada 232 29.55 N 111.48 W
Laino Borgo 68 39.57 N 15.59 E
Lainsitz (Lužnice) ≃ 61 49.13 N 14.42 E
Lainville 261 49.04 N 1.49 E
Lainz •[8] 264b 48.11 N 16.17 E
Lainzer Tiergarten ♦ 264b 48.10 N 16.14 E
Lair, Scot., U.K. 46 57.29 N 5.20 W
Lair, Ky., U.S. 218 38.20 N 84.18 W
Laird Hill 222 32.21 N 94.54 W
Lairdsville 210 41.14 N 76.37 W
Lairg 46 58.01 N 4.25 W
Laïri 146 10.49 N 17.06 E
Laïri, Batha de ≃ 146 12.28 N 16.45 E
Laïriri, Pic ∧ 175f 15.27 S 166.48 E
Lais, Indon. 112 0.47 N 120.27 E
Lais, Indon. 112 3.32 S 102.03 E
Lais, Pil. 116 6.20 N 125.39 E
Laisamis 154 1.36 N 37.48 E
Laiševo 80 55.24 N 49.32 E
Laishan 98 37.24 N 121.23 E
Laishui 105 39.23 N 115.42 E
Laissac 32 44.23 N 2.49 E
Laissey 58 47.18 N 6.14 E
Laisu 107 29.16 N 105.47 E
Laisvall 24 66.05 N 17.10 E
Laitan 107 29.06 N 106.10 E
Laitila 26 60.53 N 21.41 E
Laives (Leifers) 64 46.26 N 11.20 E
Laiwu 98 36.12 N 117.38 E
Laiwui 164 1.22 S 127.40 E
Laixi (Shuiji) 98 36.51 N 120.29 E
Laiya 116 13.40 N 121.24 E
Laiyang 98 36.58 N 120.44 E
Laiyuan, Zhg. 98 39.18 N 114.44 E
Laiyuan, Zhg. 100 25.36 N 117.01 E
Laizhou Wan (Laichow Bay) c 98 37.36 N 119.30 E
Laja ≃, Chile 252 37.16 S 72.43 W
Laja ≃, Méx. 234 20.30 N 100.46 W
Laja ≃, Ross. 24 66.20 N 56.16 E
Laja, Laguna de la ⊜ 252 37.21 S 71.19 W
Laja, Salto del ⌊ 252 37.22 S 71.25 W
Lajajalpan ≃ 234 20.17 N 97.32 W
La Jalca 248 6.29 S 77.43 W
La Jara 200 37.16 N 105.57 W
La Jara •[1] 34 39.42 N 4.54 W
La Jara Canyon V 200 36.50 N 107.30 W
La Jara Creek ≃ 200 37.22 N 105.46 W
La Jarrie 32 46.08 N 1.00 W
Lajas, Cuba 240p 22.25 N 80.18 W
Lajas, P.R. 240m 18.03 N 67.04 W
La Javie 62 44.10 N 6.21 E
Laje 255 13.10 S 39.25 W
Laje, Ilha da I 287a 22.57 S 43.09 W
Laje, Ponta da › 266c 38.40 N 9.19 W
Laje, Ribeira de ≃ 266c 38.41 N 9.19 W
Lajeado 252 29.27 S 51.58 W
Lajeado Velho •[8] 287b 23.32 S 46.23 W
Lajedo 250 8.40 S 36.19 W
Lajes 250 5.41 S 36.14 W
Lajes, Ribeirão das ≃ 256 22.38 S 43.42 W
Lajinha 255 20.09 S 41.37 W
Laji Shan ⋏ 102 36.13 N 102.15 E
Lajkovo 265b 55.42 N 37.13 E
La Jolla 204 32.51 N 117.16 W
La Jolla, Point › 228 32.51 N 117.17 W
Lajord 184 50.14 N 104.09 W
La Jose 214 40.50 N 78.41 W
Lajosmizse 30 47.02 N 19.34 E
La Joya, Méx. 196 26.26 N 101.08 W
La Joya, Perú 248 16.44 S 71.51 W
La Joya, Cerro ∧ 234 20.06 N 101.38 W
La Joya, Laguna c 234 15.55 N 93.40 W
La Joya de Atotonilco 234 23.35 N 104.20 W
Lajta (Leitha) ≃ 61 47.54 N 17.17 E
Lajtamak 86 58.25 N 67.25 E
Lajturi 84 41.55 N 41.55 E
La Junta 198 37.59 N 103.32 W
Lakaband 120 31.00 N 69.30 E
Lakahia, Teluk c 164 4.00 S 134.38 E
Lakamané 150 14.31 N 9.55 W
Lakar Kūh ∧ 128 31.02 N 57.06 E
Lakatoro 175f 16.07 S 167.25 E
Lake 194 32.20 N 89.19 W
Lake □[6], Ca., U.S. 226 39.01 N 122.33 W
Lake □[6], Fl., U.S. 220 28.42 N 81.39 W
Lake □[6], Il., U.S. 216 42.22 N 87.50 W
Lake □[6], In., U.S. 216 41.25 N 87.22 W
Lake □[6], Oh., U.S. 214 41.43 N 81.15 W
Lake Accotink Park ♦ 284c 38.48 N 77.14 W
Lake Albert 171b 35.10 S 147.23 E
Lake Alfred 220 28.05 N 81.43 W
Lake Alpine 226 38.28 N 120.00 W
Lake Andes 198 43.09 N 98.32 W
Lake Angelus 281 42.42 N 83.19 W
Lake Ariel 210 41.27 N 75.23 W
Lake Arrowhead 228 34.14 N 117.11 W
Lake Arthur, La., U.S. 194 30.04 N 92.40 W
Lake Arthur, N.M., U.S. 196 32.59 N 104.21 W
Lake Barcroft 284c 38.51 N 77.09 W
Lake Bathurst 170 35.01 S 149.36 E
Lake Benton 198 44.15 N 96.17 W
Lake Beseck 207 41.31 N 72.44 W
Lake Bluff 216 42.16 N 87.50 W
Lake Brownwood 196 31.49 N 99.02 W
Lake Buena Vista 220 28.23 N 81.31 W
Lake Butler 192 30.01 N 82.20 W
Lake Cable 214 40.52 N 81.27 W
Lake Camm 162 32.59 S 119.35 E
Lake Cargelligo 166 33.18 S 146.23 E
Lake Carmel 210 41.27 N 73.40 W
Lake Charles 194 30.13 N 93.13 W
Lake Chelan National Recreation Area ♦ 224 48.20 N 120.40 W
Lake City, Ar., U.S. 194 35.48 N 90.26 W
Lake City, Co., U.S. 200 38.01 N 107.18 W
Lake City, Fl., U.S. 192 30.11 N 82.38 W
Lake City, Il., U.S. 219 39.45 N 88.43 W
Lake City, Ia., U.S. 198 42.16 N 94.44 W
Lake City, Mi., U.S. 190 44.20 N 85.12 W
Lake City, Mn., U.S. 190 44.26 N 92.16 W
Lake City, Pa., U.S. 214 42.00 N 80.20 W
Lake City, S.C., U.S. 192 33.52 N 79.45 W
Lake City, Tn., U.S. 192 36.13 N 84.09 W
Lake Clarke Shores 220 26.39 N 80.04 W
Lake Clark National Park ♦ 180 60.30 N 153.15 W
Lake Coleridge 172 43.22 S 171.32 E
Lake Como, N.Y., U.S. 210 42.41 N 76.18 W
Lake Como, Pa., U.S. 210 41.51 N 75.20 W
Lake Corpus Christi State Park ♦ 196 28.05 N 97.52 W
Lake Cowichan 224 48.50 N 124.03 W
Lake Creek ≃ 222 30.16 N 95.29 W
Lake Crescent 224 48.06 N 123.50 W
Lake Crystal 190 44.06 N 94.13 W
Lake Dalecarlia 216 41.20 N 87.24 W
Lake Dallas 222 33.07 N 97.02 W
Lake Delta 210 43.17 N 75.28 W
Lake Delton 190 43.36 N 89.47 W
Lakedemonovka 83 47.12 N 38.33 E
Lake Dennison State Park ♦ 207 42.38 N 72.05 W
Lake District •[1] 44 54.30 N 3.10 W
Lake District National Park ♦ 44 54.30 N 3.05 W
Lake Eliza 216 41.26 N 87.10 W
Lake Elsinore 228 33.38 N 117.20 W
Lake Elsinore State Recreation Area ♦ 228 33.41 N 117.22 W
Lake Entrance ⊔ 170 33.05 S 151.39 E
Lake Errock 224 49.13 N 122.02 W
Lake Eyre National Park ♦ 166 28.30 S 137.30 E
Lake Fairfax County Park ♦ 284c 38.58 N 77.19 W
Lake Fenton 216 42.52 N 83.43 W
Lakefield, On., Can. 212 44.26 N 78.16 W
Lakefield, S. Afr. 273d 26.11 S 28.18 E
Lakefield, Mn., U.S. 198 43.40 N 95.10 W
Lakefield National Park ♦ 164 15.00 S 144.05 E
Lake Forest, Fl., U.S. 192 25.58 N 80.11 W
Lake Forest, Il., U.S. 216 42.12 N 87.53 W
Lake Forest, N.J., U.S. 276 40.58 N 74.36 W
Lake Forest Park 224 47.45 N 122.17 W
Lake Fork 219 39.58 N 89.21 W
Lake Fork ≃, Il., U.S. 219 40.05 N 89.25 W
Lake Fork ≃, Ut,. U.S. 200 40.13 N 110.07 W
Lake Fork, North Fork ≃ 219 39.56 N 89.14 W
Lake Fork Creek ≃ 222 32.36 N 95.21 W
Lake Fork Reservoir ⊜[1] 222 32.50 N 95.35 W
Lake Geneva 216 42.36 N 88.26 W
Lake George 188 43.25 N 73.42 W
Lake Grace 162 33.06 S 118.28 E
Lake Grinnell 276 41.06 N 74.38 W
Lake Grove 276 40.51 N 73.06 W
Lake Hamilton 220 28.07 N 81.42 W
Lake Harbor 220 26.42 N 80.48 W
Lake Harbour 176 62.51 N 69.53 W
Lake Harmony 210 41.04 N 75.36 W
Lake Havasu City 200 34.29 N 114.19 W
Lake Havasu State Park ♦ 200 34.29 N 114.21 W
Lake Helen 220 28.58 N 81.14 W
Lake Hiawatha 210 40.52 N 74.22 W
Lake Hill 210 42.04 N 74.11 W
Lake Hills 216 41.28 N 87.27 W
Lake Hopatcong 210 40.55 N 74.39 W
Lake Hughes 228 34.40 N 118.26 W
Lake Huntington 210 41.41 N 75.00 W
Lakehurst 208 40.00 N 74.18 W
Lakehurst Naval Air Station ■ 208 40.01 N 74.18 W
Lake Illawarra 170 34.33 S 150.52 E
Lake Intervale 276 40.53 N 74.25 W
Lake in the Hills 216 42.10 N 88.19 W
Lake Isabella 204 35.39 N 118.28 W
Lake Jackson 222 29.02 N 95.26 W
Lake Jem 220 28.45 N 81.40 W
Lakekamu ≃ 164 8.10 S 146.15 E
Lake Katrine 210 41.59 N 73.59 W
Lake King 162 33.05 S 119.40 E
Lake Lackawanna 210 40.57 N 74.42 W
Lakeland, Fl., U.S. 220 28.03 N 81.57 W
Lakeland, Ga., U.S. 192 31.02 N 83.04 W
Lakeland, Mi., U.S. 216 42.28 N 83.51 W
Lakeland, N.Y., U.S. 210 43.06 N 76.15 W
Lakeland Park 216 42.21 N 88.17 W
Lakeland Village 228 33.39 N 117.22 W
Lake Lenape 210 41.01 N 74.44 W
Lake Linden 190 47.11 N 88.26 W
Lake Lookover 276 41.09 N 74.24 W
Lake Loramie State Park ♦ 216 40.23 N 84.20 W
Lake Louise 182 51.26 N 116.11 W
Lake Lucerne 214 41.24 N 81.21 W
Lake Luzerne 210 43.18 N 73.50 W
Lake Mackay Reserve •[4] 162 22.00 S 129.45 E
Lake Magdalene 220 28.05 N 82.28 W
Lake Malawi National Park ♦ 154 14.00 S 34.55 E
Lake Manyara National Park ♦ 154 3.30 S 36.25 E
Lake Mary 220 28.45 N 81.19 W
Lakemba 274a 33.55 S 151.05 E
Lakemba Island I 175g 18.13 S 178.47 W
Lakemba Passage ⊔ 175g 17.53 S 178.32 W
Lake Mead National Recreation Area ♦ 200 36.00 N 114.30 W
Lake Meredith National Recreation Area ♦ 196 35.40 N 101.40 W
Lake Mills, Ia., U.S. 190 43.25 N 93.31 W
Lake Mills, Wi., U.S. 216 43.04 N 88.54 W
Lake Milton 214 41.06 N 80.58 W
Lake Minchumina 180 63.53 N 152.19 W
Lake Monroe 220 28.50 N 81.19 W
Lakemont, N.Y., U.S. 210 42.31 N 76.56 W
Lakemont, Pa., U.S. 214 40.28 N 78.23 W
Lakemoor 216 42.20 N 88.12 W
Lakemore 214 41.01 N 81.25 W
Lake Mountain ∧ 169 37.31 S 145.54 E
Lake Murray 164 7.00 S 141.29 E
Lake Murray State Park ♦ 196 34.01 N 97.00 W
Laken •[8] 50 50.52 N 4.25 E
Lake Nakuru National Park ♦ 154 0.20 S 36.05 E
Lake Nash 166 21.00 S 137.55 E
Lake Nepessing 216 43.02 N 83.22 W
Lakenheath 42 52.25 N 0.31 E
Lake Norden 198 44.34 N 97.12 W
Lake Normandy Estates 284c 39.03 N 77.11 W
Lake Odessa 216 42.47 N 85.08 W
Lake of the Ozarks State Park ♦ 194 38.08 N 92.40 W
Lake of the Woods 216 41.26 N 86.14 W
Lake on the Mountain Provincial Park ♦ 212 44.02 N 77.05 W
Lake Orion 216 42.47 N 83.14 W
Lake Orion Heights 216 42.46 N 83.18 W
Lake Oroville State Recreational Area ♦ 226 39.32 N 121.27 W
Lake Oswego 224 45.25 N 122.39 W
Lake Ozark 194 38.11 N 92.38 W
Lakepa 174v 18.59 S 169.48 W
Lake Panasoffkee 220 28.46 N 82.07 W
Lake Paringa 172 43.43 S 169.29 E
Lake Park, Fl., U.S. 220 26.48 N 80.04 W
Lake Park, Ia., U.S. 198 43.27 N 95.19 W
Lake Park, Mn., U.S. 198 46.53 N 96.05 W
Lake Pine 208 39.52 N 74.51 W
Lake Placid, Fl., U.S. 220 27.17 N 81.21 W
Lake Placid, N.Y., U.S. 188 44.16 N 73.58 W
Lake Pleasant 188 43.28 N 74.25 W
Lakeport, Ca., U.S. 204 39.02 N 122.54 W
Lakeport, Mi., U.S. 190 43.07 N 82.30 W
Lakeport, N.Y., U.S. 210 43.09 N 75.52 W
Lake Preston 198 44.21 N 97.22 W
Lake Providence 194 32.48 N 91.10 W
Lake Pukaki 172 44.11 S 170.09 E
Lakeridge, Nv., U.S. 226 39.02 N 119.56 W
Lake Ridge, N.J., U.S. 276 40.24 N 74.15 W
Lake Riviera 208 40.03 N 74.10 W
Lake Ronkonkoma 276 40.50 N 73.07 W
Lake Saint Louis 219 38.48 N 90.45 W
Lake Sammamish State Park ♦ 224 47.33 N 122.03 W
Lake San Marcos 228 33.09 N 117.12 W
Lake Sawyer 224 47.20 N 122.03 W
Lakes Bay c 208 39.22 N 74.30 W
Lakes District 224 47.10 N 122.31 W
Lakes Entrance 166 37.53 S 147.59 E
Lake Shawnee 276 40.59 N 74.36 W
Lakeshore, Ca., U.S. 226 37.15 N 119.12 W
Lake Shore, Md., U.S. 208 39.06 N 76.29 W
Lake Shore, Mi., U.S. 216 42.38 N 86.14 W
Lakeshore, Ms., U.S. 194 30.14 N 89.26 W
Lake Shore, Wa., U.S. 224 45.42 N 122.42 W
Lakeside, N.S., Can. 186 44.38 N 63.41 W
Lakeside, S. Afr. 273d 26.06 S 28.09 E
Lakeside, Az., U.S. 200 34.09 N 109.58 W
Lakeside, Ca., U.S. 228 32.51 N 116.55 W
Lakeside, Ct., U.S. 207 41.25 N 73.13 W
Lakeside, Ct., U.S. 207 41.40 N 73.14 W
Lakeside, Mi., U.S. 216 41.51 N 86.40 W
Lakeside, Mt., U.S. 202 48.01 N 114.13 W
Lakeside, Oh., U.S. 214 41.32 N 82.44 W
Lakeside, Or., U.S. 202 43.34 N 124.10 W
Lakeside, Va., U.S. 208 37.36 N 77.28 W
Lakeside •[9] 281 42.37 N 83.00 W
Lakeside Village 222 32.02 N 97.30 W
Lake Station 216 41.34 N 87.14 W
Lake Stevens 224 48.01 N 122.04 W
Lake Stockholm 276 41.04 N 74.31 W
Lake Success 276 40.46 N 73.43 W
Lake Superior Provincial Park ♦ 190 47.32 N 84.50 W
Lake Swannanoa 276 41.01 N 74.31 W
Lake Taghkanic State Park ♦ 210 42.06 N 73.43 W
Lake Tahoe Airport ⊠ 226 38.54 N 120.00 W
Lake Tahoe-Nevada State Park ♦ 226 39.13 N 119.55 W
Lake Tamarack 210 41.06 N 74.32 W
Lake Tekapo 172 44.01 S 170.30 E
Lake Telemark 276 40.57 N 74.30 W
Lake Temescal Regional Park ♦ 282 37.51 N 122.14 W
Laketon 216 40.58 N 85.50 W
Laketown 200 41.49 N 111.19 W
Lake Varley 162 32.46 S 119.27 E
Lake View, Ar., U.S. 194 34.24 N 90.50 W
Lakeview, Ca., U.S. 228 33.50 N 117.07 W
Lakeview, Ga., U.S. 192 34.58 N 85.15 W
Lake View, Ia., U.S. 198 42.18 N 95.03 W
Lakeview, Mi., U.S. 190 43.26 N 85.16 W
Lake View, N.Y., U.S. 210 42.42 N 78.56 W
Lakeview, Oh., U.S. 216 40.29 N 83.56 W
Lakeview, Or., U.S. 202 42.11 N 120.20 W
Lake View, S.C., U.S. 192 34.20 N 79.09 W
Lakeview, Tx., U.S. 194 29.55 N 93.54 W
Lakeview, Tx., U.S. 196 34.40 N 100.42 W
Lakeview, Wa., U.S. 224 47.10 N 122.30 W
Lakeview •[8] 278 41.57 N 87.39 W
Lakeview Mountain ∧, B.C., Can. 182 49.03 N 120.09 W
Lakeview Mountain ∧, Wa., U.S. 224 46.22 N 121.24 W
Lakeview Park ♦ 285 40.12 N 75.32 W
Lake Village, Ar., U.S. 194 33.19 N 91.16 W
Lake Village, In., U.S. 216 41.08 N 87.27 W
Lakeville, Ct., U.S. 207 41.57 N 73.26 W
Lakeville, In., U.S. 216 41.31 N 86.16 W
Lakeville, Mi., U.S. 214 42.49 N 83.09 W
Lakeville, Mn., U.S. 190 44.38 N 93.14 W
Lakeville, N.Y., U.S. 210 42.50 N 77.42 W
Lakeville, Oh., U.S. 214 40.40 N 82.07 W
Lakeville Lake ⊜ 214 42.50 N 83.09 W
Lake Wales 220 27.54 N 81.35 W
Lake Whitney State Park ♦ 222 31.55 N 97.22 W
Lake Wilson 198 43.59 N 95.57 W
Lake Winola 210 41.30 N 75.50 W
Lakewood, Ca., U.S. 228 33.51 N 118.07 W
Lakewood, Co., U.S. 200 39.42 N 105.04 W
Lakewood, Il., U.S. 216 39.19 N 88.54 W
Lakewood, Mi., U.S. 216 42.18 N 85.31 W
Lakewood, N.J., U.S. 208 40.05 N 74.13 W
Lakewood, N.Y., U.S. 214 42.06 N 79.20 W
Lakewood, Oh., U.S. 214 41.28 N 81.47 W
Lakewood, Pa., U.S. 210 41.51 N 75.22 W
Lakewood, Wa., U.S. 224 48.09 N 122.12 W
Lakewood, Wi., U.S. 190 45.18 N 88.31 W
Lakewood Center •[9] 280 33.51 N 118.09 W
Lakewood Park 198 48.04 N 98.56 W
Lakewood Park ♦ 279a 41.29 N 81.47 W
Lakewood Shores 216 41.17 N 88.10 W
Lake Worth, Fl., U.S. 220 26.36 N 80.03 W
Lake Worth, Tx., U.S. 222 32.49 N 97.27 W
Lake Zurich 216 42.11 N 88.05 W
Lakhdaria 34 36.34 N 3.35 E
Lākheri 124 25.40 N 76.10 E
Lakhīmpur 124 27.57 N 80.46 E
Lakhipur, India 120 24.48 N 93.01 E
Lakhipur, India 124 26.02 N 90.18 E
Lakhish 132 31.34 N 34.51 E
Lakhish V 132 31.49 N 34.38 E
Lakhnādon 124 22.36 N 79.36 E
Lakhya ≃ 126 23.35 N 90.31 E
Läki 84 40.34 N 47.26 E
Laki ≃ 115a 7.30 S 107.25 E
Lakin 198 37.56 N 101.15 W
Lakinsk 80 56.01 N 39.57 E
Lakkadiven → Lakshadweep II 122 10.00 N 73.00 E
Lakki 123 32.36 N 70.55 E
Laknau → Lucknow 124 26.51 N 80.55 E
Lakonikós Kólpos c 38 36.25 N 22.37 E
Lakor, Pulau I 164 8.14 S 128.10 E
Lakota, C. Iv. 150 5.51 N 5.41 W
Lakota, Ia., U.S. 190 43.22 N 94.05 W
Lakota, N.D., U.S. 198 48.02 N 98.20 W
Laksefjorden c[2] 24 70.58 N 27.00 E
Lakselv 24 70.04 N 24.56 E
Lakshadweep □[8] 122 10.00 N 73.00 E
Lakshadweep II 122 10.00 N 73.00 E
Lakshadweep Sea ⊤[2] 12 7.00 N 76.00 E
Lākshām 124 23.14 N 91.08 E
Lakshamannāth 126 21.51 N 87.13 E
Lakshmanpur 272b 22.38 N 88.16 E
Lakshmeshwar 122 15.08 N 75.28 E
Lakshmi, Char I 126 21.57 N 90.33 E
Lakshmikantapur 126 22.07 N 88.20 E
Lakshmi Narayan Temple ᵿ[1] 272a 28.38 N 77.12 E
Lakshmīpur 126 22.57 N 90.50 E
Lakshmisāgar 126 22.55 N 87.01 E
Lala 116 7.59 N 123.46 E
Lalafuta ≃ 154 13.57 S 24.41 E
La Laguna → San Cristóbal de la Laguna 148 28.29 N 16.19 W
La Lagunita 234 23.41 N 105.44 W
La Laja 252 37.16 S 72.42 W
La Lajilla 232 26.47 N 99.37 W
Lāla Mūsa 123 32.42 N 73.58 E
Lalana ≃ 234 17.49 N 95.09 W
Lalapansi 154 19.16 S 30.15 E
Lâlapaşa 130 41.50 N 26.44 E
Lalatuncun 104 41.44 N 122.00 E
La Lava 248 19.55 S 65.38 W
Lalbenque 32 44.20 N 1.33 E
L'Albufera ⊜ 34 39.20 N 0.22 W
Laleham, Austl. 166 23.58 S 148.46 E
Laleham, Eng., U.K. 260 51.25 N 0.30 W
Lāleh Zār, Kūh-e ∧ 128 29.24 N 56.45 E
Lalendorf 54 53.45 N 12.23 E
La Leona 196 25.52 N 101.05 W
La Leonesa 252 27.03 S 58.43 W
Lalera 152 0.22 N 11.28 E
Lalevade-d'Ardèche 62 44.39 N 4.19 E
Lālganj 124 25.52 N 85.11 E
Lālgarh 126 22.35 N 87.03 E
Lāliān 123 31.49 N 72.48 E
Lalibela 144 12.02 N 39.02 E
La Libertad, El Sal. 236 13.29 N 89.19 W
La Libertad, Guat. 232 16.47 N 90.07 W
La Libertad, Hond. 236 14.43 N 87.36 W
La Libertad, Nic. 236 12.13 N 85.10 W
La Libertad □[5] 248 8.00 S 78.30 W
La Ligua 252 32.27 S 71.14 W
La Lima, Hond. 236 15.24 N 87.56 W
La Lima, It. 66 44.04 N 10.46 E
La Limpia, Laguna ⊜ 258 35.37 S 57.49 W
Lalín 34 42.39 N 8.07 W
Lalin ≃ 89 45.29 N 125.26 E
Lalinde 32 44.51 N 0.44 E
Lalindi 115b 10.12 S 120.10 E
Lalindu ≃ 112 3.28 S 122.05 E
La Línea 34 36.10 N 5.19 W
L'alino 82 54.29 N 39.06 E
Lalitpur 124 24.41 N 78.25 E
La Llagosta 266d 41.31 N 2.12 E
Lalla Khedidja, Tamgout de ∧ 34 36.27 N 4.15 E
Lal Lal Reservoir ⊜[1] 169 37.40 S 144.04 E
Lalling 60 48.51 N 13.09 E
Lālmanir Hāt 124 25.54 N 89.27 E
Lālmohan 126 22.13 N 90.42 E
Laloa 112 4.50 S 121.54 E
La Loche 184 56.29 N 109.27 W
La Loche ≃ 184 56.09 N 109.08 W
La Loche, Lac ⊜ 184 56.25 N 109.30 W
Laloki 164 9.25 S 147.15 E
La Londe 62 43.08 N 6.14 E
La Lora ⋏[1] 34 42.45 N 4.00 W
Lalor Park 274a 33.45 S 150.56 E
La Loupe 50 48.28 N 1.01 E
Lalouvesc 62 45.07 N 4.32 E
La Louvière 50 50.28 N 4.11 E
L'Alpe-d'Huez 62 45.06 N 6.04 E
Lālpur, Bngl. 126 24.11 N 88.58 E
Lālpur, India 120 22.12 N 69.58 E
Lal'sk 24 60.44 N 47.34 E
Lālsot 124 26.34 N 76.20 E
Lālua 126 21.57 N 90.18 E
La Luz, Méx. 196 25.52 N 97.37 W
La Luz, Méx. 232 24.12 N 97.52 W
La Luz, Nic. 236 13.44 N 84.47 W
La Luz, N.M., U.S. 200 32.58 N 105.56 W
Lam 60 49.12 N 13.03 E
Lama ≃, Ross. 82 56.29 N 36.10 E
Lama ≃, Zhg. 104 42.11 N 123.29 E
Lama, ozero ⊜ 74 69.30 N 90.30 E
L'Amable Lake ⊜ 212 45.01 N 77.49 W
La Macarena, Parque Nacional ♦ 246 2.40 N 73.45 W
La Macarena, Serranía de ⋏ 246 2.45 N 73.55 W
La Maddalena 71 41.13 N 9.24 E
Lama dei Peligni 66 42.02 N 14.11 E
La Madeleine 50 50.39 N 3.04 E
Lamadong 98 40.39 N 119.39 E
La Madrague 62 43.14 N 5.22 E
La Madrid, Arg. 252 27.38 S 65.15 W
Lamadrid, Méx. 196 27.05 N 101.50 W
Lamag 112 5.29 N 117.49 E
La Magdalena, Río de ≃ 286a 19.21 N 99.11 W
Lamagoumen 105 40.52 N 116.39 E
Lamahuang 104 42.27 N 121.33 E
La Mailleraye-sur-Seine 50 49.29 N 0.46 E
Lamainong 114 3.49 N 96.46 E
La Majada 286c 10.27 N 67.01 W
Lama-Kara 150 9.33 N 1.12 E
La Malbaie 186 47.39 N 70.10 W
La Malinche, Parque Nacional ♦ 234 19.15 N 98.05 W
Lamaline 186 46.52 N 55.49 W
La Malmaison ⊥ 261 48.52 N 2.10 E
Lamaload Reservoir ⊜[1] 262 53.16 N 2.02 W
Lama Mocogno 64 44.18 N 10.45 E
La Mancha •[1] 34 39.15 N 1.45 W
La Mancha, Canal de → English Channel ⊔ 28 50.20 N 1.00 W
Lamandau ≃ 112 2.42 S 111.34 E
Lamap 175f 16.26 S 167.43 E
Lamar, Co., U.S. 198 38.05 N 102.37 W
Lamar, Mo., U.S. 194 37.29 N 94.16 W
Lamar, Pa., U.S. 210 41.01 N 77.32 W
Lamar, S.C., U.S. 192 34.10 N 80.03 W
Lamar ≃ 202 44.56 N 110.24 W
La Marañosa 266a 40.17 N 3.35 W
Lamarche 58 48.04 N 5.47 E
Lamarche-sur-Saône 58 47.16 N 5.23 E
Lamari ≃ 164 6.54 S 145.25 E
La Mariposa, Embalse ⊜[1] 286c 10.24 N 66.56 W
La Mariscala 252 34.03 S 54.47 W
La Marmora, Punta ∧ 71 39.59 N 9.20 E
La Marolle-en-Sologne 50 47.35 N 1.47 E
La Maroma 196 28.34 N 100.45 W
Lamarque, Arg. 252 39.24 S 65.42 W
La Marque, Tx., U.S. 222 29.22 N 94.58 W
La Marsa 36 36.53 N 10.20 E
La Martre 62 43.46 N 6.36 E
Lamas 248 6.25 S 76.35 W
La Masica 236 15.37 N 87.07 W
Lamastre 62 44.59 N 4.35 E
La Matanza → San Justo 258 34.40 S 58.33 W
La Matanza □[5] 288 34.46 S 58.37 W
Lama Temple ᵿ[1] 271a 39.56 N 116.25 E
La Mauricie, Parc National de (La Mauricie National Park) ♦ 206 46.50 N 73.00 W
La Maya, Cuba 240p 20.10 N 75.39 W
Lamaya, Zhg. 102 29.50 N 99.53 E
Lamayingzi 104 42.09 N 121.50 E
Lambach 60 48.05 N 13.53 E
Lamballe 32 48.28 N 2.31 W
Lambaréné 152 0.42 S 10.13 E
Lambari 256 21.58 S 45.21 W
Lambari ≃, Bra. 255 19.30 S 45.00 W
Lambari ≃, Bra. 256 21.47 S 45.13 W
Lambasa 175g 16.26 S 179.24 E
Lambayeque 248 6.42 S 79.55 W
Lambayeque □[5] 248 6.20 S 80.00 W
Lambayeque ≃ 248 6.43 S 79.54 W
Lambay Island I 48 53.29 N 6.01 W
Lambe 273a 6.42 N 3.21 E
Lambersart 50 50.39 N 3.02 E
Lambert, Ms., U.S. 194 34.12 N 90.17 W
Lambert, Mt., U.S. 198 47.41 N 104.37 W
Lambert, Cape ›, Austl. 162 20.35 S 117.10 E
Lambert, Cape ›, Pap. N. Gui. 164 4.12 S 151.32 E
Lambert Glacier ⩍ 9 71.00 S 70.00 E
Lamberton 198 44.13 N 95.15 W
Lambert-Saint Louis International Airport ⊠ 219 38.45 N 90.22 W
Lambertsbaai → Lambert's Bay 158 32.05 S 18.17 E
Lambert's Bay 158 32.05 S 18.17 E
Lambertville, Mi., U.S. 216 41.45 N 83.37 W
Lambertville, N.J., U.S. 208 40.21 N 74.56 W
Lambesc 62 43.39 N 5.16 E
Lambeth 214 42.54 N 81.18 W
Lambeth •[8] 42 51.30 N 0.07 W
L'ambir' 80 54.17 N 45.07 E
Lambo Katenga 154 5.02 S 28.48 E
Lambomakondro 157b 22.41 S 44.44 E
Lambourn 42 51.31 N 1.31 W
Lambourne ≃ 42 51.24 N 1.18 W
Lambourne End 260 51.38 N 0.08 E
Lambrama 248 13.52 S 72.46 W
Lambrate •[8] 266b 45.29 N 9.15 E
Lambrecht 56 49.22 N 8.04 E
Lambrechten 60 48.19 N 13.31 E
Lambrechts Drift 158 28.31 S 21.43 E
Lambro ≃ 62 45.08 N 9.32 E
Lambro, Parco ♦ 266b 45.30 N 9.15 E
Lambs Creek 210 41.51 N 77.06 W
Lambs Terrace 285 39.46 N 75.02 W
Lambton 273d 26.15 S 28.10 E
Lambton □[6] 214 42.45 N 82.15 W
Lambton, Cape › 176 71.05 N 123.10 W
Lambu 164 3.09 S 151.41 E
Lambunao 116 11.03 N 122.29 E
L'amca 24 64.27 N 37.04 E
Lamdessar 164 7.12 S 131.58 E
Lame, Nig. 150 10.23 N 9.13 E
Lamé, Tchad 146 9.15 N 14.32 E
La Meca → Makkah 144 21.27 N 39.49 E
La Mecque → Makkah 144 21.27 N 39.49 E
Lame Deer 202 45.37 N 106.39 W
La Media Luna, Arrecifes de ⊹[2] 236 15.13 N 82.36 W
La Méditerranée → Mediterranean Sea ⊤[2] 10 35.00 N 20.00 E
Lamego 34 41.06 N 7.49 W
La Meije ∧ 62 45.00 N 6.18 E
Lameirão, Morro do ∧[2] 287a 22.54 S 43.31 W
La Membrolle-sur-Choisille 50 47.26 N 0.38 E
La Mendieta 252 24.19 S 64.58 W
L'amen'ga 76 59.51 N 44.31 E
Lamentin 241o 16.16 N 61.38 W
Lamèque 186 47.47 N 64.38 W
Lamèque, Île I 186 47.48 N 64.36 W
La Merced, Arg. 252 28.10 S 65.41 W
La Merced, Arg. 252 24.58 S 65.29 W
La Merced, Perú 248 11.03 S 75.19 W
Lameroo 166 35.20 S 140.31 E
La Mesa, Pan. 236 8.09 N 81.11 W
La Mesa, Ca., U.S. 228 32.46 N 117.01 W
La Mesa, N.M., U.S. 200 32.07 N 106.42 W
Lamesa, Tx., U.S. 196 32.44 N 101.57 W
La Mesa Dam •[6] 269f 14.43 N 121.04 E
La Meta ∧ 66 41.41 N 13.56 E
Lamía 38 38.54 N 22.26 E
L'amin ≃ 74 61.18 N 71.48 E
Lamine ≃ 194 38.59 N 92.51 W
La Minerve 206 46.15 N 74.56 W
Laming ≃ 61 47.25 N 15.16 E
Lamington ≃ 210 40.38 N 74.41 W
Lamington, Mount ∧[1] 164 8.56 S 148.10 E
Lamington National Park ♦ 166 28.15 S 153.12 E
La Mira 234 18.02 N 102.19 W
La Mirada 228 33.55 N 118.00 W
La Mirada Creek ≃ 280 33.53 N 118.01 W
La Misión 204 32.05 N 116.50 W
Lamitan 116 6.39 N 122.08 E
Lamlam, Mount ∧[2] 174p 13.20 N 144.40 E
Lamlash 46 55.32 N 5.08 W
Lamma Island I 271d 22.12 N 114.07 E
Lammefjord c 41 55.48 N 11.43 E
Lammerlaw Top ∧ 172 45.40 S 169.38 E
Lammermuir •[1] 46 55.50 N 2.25 W
Lammermuir Hills ⋏[2] 46 55.50 N 2.44 W
Lammeulo 114 5.15 N 95.56 E
Lammhulf 26 57.10 N 14.35 E
Lammi 26 61.05 N 25.01 E
Lamming Mills 182 53.22 N 120.18 W
Lamogai 164 5.50 S 149.20 E
La Moille, Il., U.S. 190 41.31 N 89.16 W
Lamoille, Nv., U.S. 204 40.43 N 115.28 W
Lamoille ≃ 188 44.35 N 73.10 W
La Moine ≃ 194 39.59 N 90.31 W
La Moine, East Fork ≃ 194 40.24 N 90.56 W
Lamoka Lake ⊜ 210 42.24 N 77.05 W
La Molina 286d 12.05 S 76.57 W
Lamon Bay c 116 14.25 N 122.00 E
Lamone ≃ 66 44.31 N 12.15 E
Lamongan 115a 7.07 S 112.25 E
Lamongan, Gunung ∧ 115a 7.58 S 113.20 E
Lamoni 190 40.37 N 93.56 W
Lamont, Ab., Can. 182 53.46 N 112.48 W
Lamont, Ca., U.S. 228 35.15 N 118.54 W
Lamont, Ia., U.S. 190 42.35 N 91.38 W
Lamont, Mi., U.S. 216 43.01 N 86.09 W
Lamont, Ok., U.S. 196 36.41 N 97.33 W
La Monte 194 38.46 N 93.25 W
La Mosquitia □[9] 236 15.00 N 83.45 W
La Mothe, Lac ⊜[1] 186 48.46 N 71.09 W
La Mothe-Achard 32 46.37 N 1.40 W
Lamotrek I[1] 14 7.30 N 146.20 E
La Mott 285 40.04 N 75.08 W
La Motte, Lac ⊜ 190 48.24 N 78.03 W
Lamotte-Beuvron 50 47.36 N 2.01 E
La Motte-Chalançon 62 44.29 N 5.23 E
La Motte-du-Caire 62 44.21 N 6.02 E
Lamoura 58 46.24 N 5.58 E
La Moure 198 46.21 N 98.17 W
La Moustique ≃ 241o 16.11 N 61.35 W
Lampa 248 15.21 S 70.22 W
Lampang 110 18.18 N 99.31 E
Lampasas 196 31.03 N 98.10 W
Lampasas ≃ 196 30.59 N 97.24 W
Lampazos de Naranjo 232 27.01 N 100.31 W
Lampedusa 70a 35.30 N 12.36 E
Lampedusa, Isola di I 70a 35.31 N 12.35 E
Lampertheim 56 49.35 N 8.28 E
Lampeter, Wales, U.K. 42 52.07 N 4.05 W
Lampeter, Pa., U.S. 208 39.58 N 76.14 W
Lamphun 110 18.35 N 99.01 E
Lampinsaari 26 64.25 N 25.09 E
Lampione, Isolotto di I 70a 35.34 N 12.19 E
Lampman 184 49.23 N 102.45 W
Lamprechtshausen 64 47.59 N 12.57 E
Lampung □[4] 112 5.00 S 105.00 E
Lampung, Teluk c 115a 5.40 S 105.20 E
Lamskoje 76 52.57 N 38.02 E
Lamspringe 52 51.58 N 10.00 E
Lamstedt 52 53.38 N 9.05 E
Lāmta 124 22.08 N 80.07 E
Lam Tong Hoi Hap ⊔ 271d 22.15 N 114.15 E
Lamu, Kenya 154 2.16 S 40.54 E
Lāmu, Mya. 110 19.14 N 94.10 E
Lamud 248 6.09 S 77.55 W
La Muerte, Cerro ∧ 236 9.33 N 83.44 W
Lam Uk Wei 271d 22.26 N 114.22 E
La Mure 62 44.54 N 5.47 E
Lamure-sur-Azergues 58 46.04 N 4.30 E
La Mutua 234 22.23 N 99.18 W
Lan' ≃, Bela. 76 52.09 N 27.18 E
Lan ≃, Zhg. 104 41.14 N 123.32 E
Lan, Loi ∧ 110 19.40 N 97.55 E
Lana 64 46.37 N 11.09 E
Lanai I 229a 20.50 N 156.55 W
Lanai City 229a 20.49 N 156.55 W
Lanaihale ∧ 229a 20.49 N 156.52 W
Lanaken 56 50.53 N 5.39 E
Lanalhue, Lago ⊜ 252 37.55 S 73.18 W
La Nana, Bayou ≃ 222 31.27 N 94.43 W
Lanao del Norte □[4] 116 8.10 N 124.00 E
Lanao del Sur □[4] 116 7.50 N 124.25 E
La Napoule 62 43.31 N 6.56 E
Lanarce 62 44.44 N 4.00 E
Lanark, On., Can. 212 45.01 N 76.22 W
Lanark, Scot., U.K. 46 55.41 N 3.46 W
Lanark, Il., U.S. 190 42.06 N 89.50 W
Lanark, Pa., U.S. 208 40.33 N 75.26 W
Lanark □[6] 212 45.05 N 76.20 W
La Nartelle 62 43.19 N 6.39 E
Lanas 112 5.20 N 116.30 E
La Nava de Ricomalillo 34 39.39 N 4.59 W
Lanbi Kyun I 110 10.50 N 98.15 E
Lanboyan Point › 116 8.18 N 122.56 E
Lancang 102 23.00 N 100.02 E
Lancang → Mekong ≃ 12 10.33 N 105.24 E
Lancashire 285 39.49 N 75.29 W
Lancashire □[6] 44 53.45 N 2.40 W
Lancashire Plain ≚ 44 53.40 N 2.45 W
Lancaster, On., Can. 206 45.08 N 74.30 W
Lancaster, Eng., U.K. 44 54.03 N 2.48 W
Lancaster, Ca., U.S. 228 34.41 N 118.08 W
Lancaster, Ky., U.S. 192 37.37 N 84.34 W
Lancaster, Ma., U.S. 207 42.27 N 71.40 W
Lancaster, Mn., U.S. 198 48.51 N 96.48 W
Lancaster, Mo., U.S. 194 40.31 N 92.31 W
Lancaster, N.H., U.S. 188 44.29 N 71.34 W
Lancaster, N.Y., U.S. 210 42.54 N 78.40 W
Lancaster, Oh., U.S. 188 39.43 N 82.36 W


**Symbols** in the index entries represent the broad categories identified in the key at the right. Symbols with superior numbers (⋏[1]) identify subcategories (see complete key on page *I · 1).*

**Symbole** im Register stellen die rechts im Schlüssel erklärten Kategorien dar. Symbole mit hochgestellten Ziffern (⋏[1]) bezeichnen Unterabteilungen einer Kategorie (vgl. vollständiger Schlüssel auf Seite *I · 1).*

**Los símbolos** incluídos en el texto del índice representan las grandes categorías identificadas con la clave a la derecha. Los símbolos con numeros en su parte superior (⋏[1]) identifican las subcategorías (véase la clave completa en la página *I · 1).*

**Les symboles** de l'index représentent les catégories indiquées dans la légende à droite. Les symboles suivis d'un indice (⋏[1]) représentent des sous-catégories (voir légende complète à la page *I · 1).*

**Os símbolos** incluídos no texto do índice representam as grandes categorias identificadas com a chave à direita. Os símbolos com números em sua parte superior (⋏[1]) identificam as subcategorias (veja-se a chave completa à página *I · 1).*

| | English | Deutsch | Español | Français | Português |
|---|---|---|---|---|---|
| ∧ | Mountain | Berg | Montaña | Montagne | Montanha |
| ⋏ | Mountains | Gebirge | Montañas | Montagnes | Montanhas |
| )( | Pass | Paß | Paso | Col | Passo |
| V | Valley, Canyon | Tal, Cañon | Valle, Cañón | Vallée, Canyon | Vale, Canhão |
| ≚ | Plain | Ebene | Llano | Plaine | Planície |
| › | Cape | Kap | Cabo | Cap | Cabo |
| I | Island | Insel | Isla | Île | Ilha |
| II | Islands | Inseln | Islas | Îles | Ilhas |
| ⊥ | Other Topographic Features | Andere Topographische Objekte | Otros Elementos Topográficos | Autres données topographiques | Outros acidentes topográficos |

ESPAÑOL — Nombre / Página / Lat.°′ / Long.°′ W = Oeste
FRANÇAIS — Nom / Page / Lat.°′ / Long.°′ W = Ouest
PORTUGUÊS — Nome / Página / Lat.°′ / Long.°′ W = Oeste


| Nombre | Página | Lat.°′ | Long.°′ W = Oeste |
|---|---|---|---|
| Lancaster, Pa., U.S. | 208 | 40.02 N | 76.18 W |
| Lancaster, S.C., U.S. | 192 | 34.43 N | 80.46 W |
| Lancaster, Tx., U.S. | 222 | 32.38 N | 96.47 W |
| Lancaster, Va., U.S. | 208 | 37.46 N | 76.28 W |
| Lancaster, Wi., U.S. | 190 | 42.50 N | 90.42 W |
| Lancaster □[6], Pa., U.S. | 208 | 40.02 N | 76.19 W |
| Lancaster □[6], Va., U.S. | 208 | 37.45 N | 76.30 W |
| Lancaster Canal ≊ | 262 | 53.46 N | 2.43 W |
| Lancaster Sound ⊔ | 176 | 74.13 N | 84.00 W |
| Lancaster Village | 285 | 39.45 N | 75.35 W |
| Lančchuti | 84 | 42.06 N | 42.01 E |
| Lance Creek | 200 | 43.01 N | 104.38 W |
| Lance Creek ≃ | 198 | 43.22 N | 104.16 W |
| Lancefield | 169 | 37.17 S | 144.44 E |
| Lancelin | 162 | 31.02 S | 115.20 E |
| Lancelot, Mount ∧ | 162 | 26.13 S | 123.12 E |
| Lancey | 62 | 45.14 N | 5.53 E |
| Lanchang | 114 | 3.30 N | 102.11 E |
| Lanchester | 44 | 54.49 N | 1.44 W |
| Lanchow → Lanzhou | 102 | 36.03 N | 103.41 E |
| Lanchyn | 78 | 48.34 N | 24.45 E |
| Lanciano | 66 | 42.14 N | 14.23 E |
| Lancin | 62 | 45.43 N | 5.24 E |
| Lancing | 42 | 50.50 N | 0.19 W |
| Lanco | 254 | 39.24 S | 72.46 W |
| Lancones | 246 | 4.35 S | 80.30 W |
| Lancun | 98 | 36.24 N | 120.10 E |
| Łańcut | 30 | 50.05 N | 22.13 E |
| Lancy | 58 | 46.11 N | 6.07 E |
| Lândana | 152 | 5.13 S | 12.08 E |
| Landang Gua | 116 | 6.58 N | 122.15 E |
| Landau | 56 | 49.12 N | 8.07 E |
| Landau an der Isar | 60 | 48.40 N | 12.43 E |
| Landay | 128 | 30.31 N | 63.47 E |
| Land Between the Lakes ♠ | 194 | 36.55 N | 88.05 W |
| Landeck | 58 | 47.08 N | 10.34 E |
| Landen | 56 | 50.45 N | 5.05 E |
| Landenberg | 208 | 39.47 N | 75.46 W |
| Landenhausen | 56 | 50.36 N | 9.28 E |
| Lander | 200 | 42.49 N | 108.43 W |
| Lander ≃ | 162 | 20.25 S | 132.00 E |
| Landerneau | 32 | 48.27 N | 4.15 W |
| Landes □[5] | 32 | 44.20 N | 1.00 W |
| Landes ◆[1] | 32 | 44.15 N | 1.00 W |
| Landesbergen | 52 | 52.33 N | 9.07 E |
| Landeskrone ∧[2] | 54 | 51.08 N | 14.56 E |
| Landess | 216 | 40.37 N | 85.34 W |
| Landete | 34 | 39.54 N | 1.22 W |
| Landham Brook ≃ | 283 | 42.22 N | 71.25 W |
| Landhausen | 263 | 51.24 N | 7.45 E |
| Landi | 98 | 36.35 N | 119.59 E |
| Landi Kotal | 123 | 34.06 N | 71.09 E |
| Landina | 86 | 59.12 N | 67.02 E |
| Landing | 210 | 40.54 N | 74.40 W |
| Landing Lake ⊜ | 184 | 55.17 N | 97.26 W |
| Landis, Sk., Can. | 184 | 52.12 N | 108.28 W |
| Landis, N.C., U.S. | 192 | 35.32 N | 80.36 W |
| Landisburg | 208 | 40.20 N | 77.18 W |
| Landisville | 208 | 40.06 N | 76.25 W |
| Landivisiau | 32 | 48.31 N | 4.04 W |
| Landkey | 42 | 51.04 N | 4.00 W |
| Landkirchen | 54 | 54.27 N | 11.08 E |
| Lando | 192 | 34.46 N | 81.00 W |
| Land O'Lakes, Fl., U.S. | 220 | 28.11 N | 82.34 W |
| Land O'Lakes, Wi., U.S. | 190 | 46.10 N | 89.13 W |
| Landor | 162 | 25.09 S | 116.54 E |
| Landos | 62 | 44.51 N | 3.50 E |
| Landösjön ⊜ | 26 | 63.35 N | 14.04 E |
| Landover Estates | 284c | 38.56 N | 76.54 W |
| Landover Hills | 284c | 38.57 N | 76.53 W |
| Landover Mall ◆[9] | 284c | 38.55 N | 76.51 W |
| Landquart | 58 | 46.58 N | 9.33 E |
| Landquart ≃ | 58 | 46.58 N | 9.32 E |
| Landrecies | 50 | 50.08 N | 3.42 E |
| Landres | 56 | 49.19 N | 5.48 E |
| Landreth Draw V | 196 | 31.14 N | 102.29 W |
| Landriano | 62 | 45.19 N | 9.15 E |
| Landri Sales | 250 | 7.16 S | 43.55 W |
| Landro (Höhlenstein) | 64 | 46.39 N | 12.14 E |
| Landrum | 192 | 35.10 N | 82.11 W |
| Landry | 62 | 45.34 N | 6.45 E |
| Landsberg | 54 | 51.31 N | 12.10 E |
| Landsberg am Lech | 58 | 48.05 N | 10.55 E |
| Landsberg an der Warthe → Gorzów Wielkopolski | 30 | 52.44 N | 15.15 E |
| Landsborough | 166 | 26.49 S | 152.58 E |
| Landsborough Creek ≃ | 166 | 22.30 S | 144.33 E |
| Landsbro | 26 | 57.22 N | 14.54 E |
| Land's End ⟩, Eng., U.K. | 42 | 50.03 N | 5.44 W |
| Lands End ⟩, Ca., U.S. | 228 | 33.28 N | 118.36 W |
| Lands End ⟩, R.I., U.S. | 207 | 41.27 N | 71.19 W |
| Landshut | 60 | 48.33 N | 12.09 E |
| Landskrona | 41 | 55.52 N | 12.50 E |
| Landsman Creek ≃ | 198 | 39.35 N | 102.19 W |
| Landsmeer | 52 | 52.26 N | 4.52 E |
| Landštejn | 61 | 49.00 N | 15.13 E |
| Landstuhl | 56 | 49.25 N | 7.34 E |
| Landweg | 263 | 51.29 N | 7.37 E |
| Landwehrbach ≃ | 263 | 51.26 N | 6.26 E |
| Lane | 219 | 40.07 N | 88.51 W |
| Lane ≃ | 50 | 47.17 N | 0.05 E |
| Lane City | 222 | 29.13 N | 96.02 W |
| Lane Cove | 274a | 33.49 S | 151.10 E |
| Lane Cove ≃ | 274a | 33.48 S | 151.09 E |
| Lane Cove River Park ♠ | 274a | 33.47 S | 151.09 E |
| La Negra | 252 | 23.45 S | 70.19 W |
| Lane Mountain ∧ | 228 | 35.05 N | 116.56 W |
| Lanersbach | 64 | 47.09 N | 11.44 E |
| Lanesboro, Ma., U.S. | 207 | 42.31 N | 73.14 W |
| Lanesboro, Mn., U.S. | 190 | 43.43 N | 91.58 W |
| Lanesboro, Pa., U.S. | 210 | 41.57 N | 75.35 W |
| Lanester | 32 | 47.46 N | 3.21 W |
| Lanesville, In., U.S. | 218 | 38.14 N | 85.59 W |
| Lanesville, N.Y., U.S. | 210 | 42.08 N | 74.16 W |
| Lanesville, Va., U.S. | 208 | 37.37 N | 76.59 W |
| Lanett | 194 | 32.52 N | 85.11 W |
| La Neuveville | 58 | 47.04 N | 7.06 E |
| Laneville | 222 | 31.58 N | 94.49 W |
| Lanexa | 208 | 37.24 N | 76.55 W |
| Lanezi Lake ⊜ | 182 | 53.03 N | 120.56 W |
| Lang | 184 | 49.56 N | 104.23 W |
| La'nga Co ⊜ | 124 | 30.42 N | 81.16 E |
| Langadhás | 38 | 40.45 N | 23.04 E |
| Langádhia | 38 | 37.41 N | 22.02 E |
| Langa-Langa | 152 | 3.54 S | 15.56 E |
| Langan Creek ≃ | 216 | 40.57 N | 87.49 W |
| Langano, Lake ⊜ | 144 | 7.35 N | 38.48 E |
| Langao | 102 | 32.13 N | 109.02 E |
| Langar, Afg. | 120 | 37.02 N | 73.47 E |
| L'angar, Kyrg. | 85 | 40.25 N | 73.07 E |
| L'angar, Taj. | 123 | 37.02 N | 72.42 E |
| Langara | 112 | 4.02 S | 123.00 E |
| Langara Island I | 182 | 54.14 N | 133.00 W |
| Langarūd | 128 | 37.11 N | 50.10 E |
| L'angasovo | 80 | 58.32 N | 49.30 E |
| Langat ≃ | 114 | 2.54 N | 101.22 E |
| Langau | 61 | 48.49 N | 15.42 E |
| Langavat, Loch ⊜ | 46 | 58.04 N | 6.48 W |
| Långban | 40 | 59.51 N | 14.15 E |
| Langbank | 184 | 50.05 N | 102.20 W |
| Lang Bay | 182 | 49.47 N | 124.21 W |
| Langberg ⋏ | 158 | 28.20 S | 22.35 E |
| Langburkersdorf | 54 | 51.02 N | 14.14 E |
| Langda | 102 | 31.12 N | 96.59 E |
| Langdai | 102 | 26.06 N | 105.20 E |
| Langdon | 198 | 48.45 N | 98.22 W |
| Langdondale | 214 | 40.08 N | 78.15 W |
| Langdon Hills | 260 | 51.34 N | 0.25 E |
| Langeac | 32 | 45.06 N | 3.30 E |
| Langeais | 50 | 47.20 N | 0.24 E |
| Langebaan | 158 | 33.06 S | 18.02 E |
| Langeberg ⋏ | 158 | 33.55 S | 20.30 E |
| Lange Berge ⋏[2] | 56 | 50.20 N | 10.55 E |
| Langebrück | 54 | 51.07 N | 13.50 E |
| Langeland I | 41 | 55.00 N | 10.50 E |
| Langelandsbælt ⊔ | 41 | 54.50 N | 10.55 E |
| Längelmävesi ⊜ | 26 | 61.32 N | 24.22 E |
| Langeloth | 214 | 40.21 N | 80.24 W |
| Langelsheim | 52 | 51.56 N | 10.19 E |
| Langemark | 50 | 50.55 N | 2.55 E |
| Langen, Dtsch. | 52 | 53.36 N | 8.35 E |
| Langen, Dtsch. | 56 | 49.59 N | 8.41 E |
| Langenargen | 58 | 47.35 N | 9.32 E |
| Langenau, Dtsch. | 54 | 50.50 N | 13.18 E |
| Langenau, Dtsch. | 58 | 48.30 N | 10.07 E |
| Langenberg, Dtsch. | 52 | 51.46 N | 8.19 E |
| Langenberg, Dtsch. | 56 | 51.21 N | 7.09 E |
| Langenbernsdorf | 54 | 50.45 N | 12.19 E |
| Langenbielau → Bielawa | 30 | 50.41 N | 16.38 E |
| Langenbochum | 263 | 51.37 N | 7.07 E |
| Langenbruck | 58 | 47.21 N | 7.46 E |
| Langenburg, Sk., Can. | 184 | 50.50 N | 101.43 W |
| Langenburg, Dtsch. | 56 | 49.15 N | 9.50 E |
| Langendorf | 54 | 51.11 N | 11.58 E |
| Langendreer ◆[8] | 263 | 51.28 N | 7.19 E |
| Langeneichstädt | 54 | 51.20 N | 11.41 E |
| Langenfeld, Dtsch. | 56 | 51.07 N | 6.56 E |
| Längenfeld, Öst. | 64 | 47.04 N | 10.58 E |
| Langenhagen | 52 | 52.27 N | 9.44 E |
| Langenhessen | 54 | 50.45 N | 12.22 E |
| Langenhorn | 41 | 54.41 N | 8.53 E |
| Langenhorst | 263 | 51.22 N | 7.02 E |
| Langenlois | 61 | 48.28 N | 15.40 E |
| Langennaundorf | 54 | 51.36 N | 13.20 E |
| Langenneufnach | 58 | 48.16 N | 10.36 E |
| Langenselbold | 56 | 50.10 N | 9.02 E |
| Langensteinach | 56 | 49.30 N | 10.10 E |
| Langenthal | 58 | 47.13 N | 7.47 E |
| Langenwang | 61 | 47.34 N | 15.37 E |
| Langenweddingen | 54 | 52.02 N | 11.31 E |
| Langenwetzendorf | 54 | 50.41 N | 12.05 E |
| Langenzenn | 56 | 49.30 N | 10.48 E |
| Langenzersdorf | 61 | 48.18 N | 16.22 E |
| Langeoog | 52 | 53.45 N | 7.29 E |
| Langeoog I | 52 | 53.46 N | 7.32 E |
| Langerfeld ◆[8] | 263 | 51.16 N | 7.15 E |
| Langer See ⊜ | 264a | 52.25 N | 13.38 E |
| Langerwehe | 56 | 50.49 N | 6.22 E |
| Langeskov | 41 | 55.22 N | 10.36 E |
| Langesund | 26 | 59.00 N | 9.45 E |
| Langevåg | 26 | 62.27 N | 6.12 E |
| Langewiesen | 54 | 50.40 N | 10.58 E |
| Langfang → Anci | 105 | 39.31 N | 116.41 E |
| Langfjorden ⊂[2] | 26 | 62.43 N | 7.30 E |
| Langford, Eng., U.K. | 260 | 51.45 N | 0.40 E |
| Langford, N.Y., U.S. | 210 | 42.35 N | 78.51 W |
| Langford, S.D., U.S. | 198 | 45.36 N | 97.49 W |
| Langförden | 52 | 52.47 N | 8.14 E |
| Langgam | 112 | 0.15 N | 101.43 E |
| Langgapayung | 114 | 1.43 N | 99.59 E |
| Langgöns | 56 | 50.30 N | 8.40 E |
| Långhalsen ⊜ | 40 | 58.56 N | 16.41 E |
| Langham | 184 | 52.22 N | 106.57 W |
| Langhe □[9] | 62 | 44.30 N | 8.00 E |
| Langhirano | 64 | 44.37 N | 10.16 E |
| Langho | 262 | 53.48 N | 2.27 W |
| Langholm | 44 | 55.09 N | 3.00 W |
| Langhorne | 208 | 40.10 N | 74.55 W |
| Langhorne Acres | 284c | 38.51 N | 77.16 W |
| Langhorne Creek | 168b | 35.18 S | 139.02 E |
| Langhorne Gardens | 285 | 40.11 N | 74.53 W |
| Langhorne Manor | 285 | 40.10 N | 74.55 W |
| Langhorne Terrace | 285 | 40.10 N | 74.57 W |
| Langji Shan I | 100 | 28.32 N | 121.36 E |
| Langjökull ⊓ | 24a | 64.42 N | 20.12 W |
| Langju | 100 | 27.52 N | 116.36 E |
| Lang Ka, Doi ∧ | 110 | 19.00 N | 99.24 E |
| Langkawi, Pulau I | 114 | 6.22 N | 99.50 E |
| Langkesi, Kepulauan II | 112 | 5.18 S | 124.20 E |
| Langklip | 158 | 28.12 S | 20.20 E |
| Langkrans | 158 | 27.47 S | 31.03 E |
| Langlade I | 186 | 46.50 N | 56.20 W |
| Lang Lang ≃ | 169 | 38.17 S | 145.31 E |
| Langley, B.C., Can. | 224 | 49.06 N | 122.39 W |
| Langley, Eng., U.K. | 260 | 51.30 N | 0.33 W |
| Langley, Eng., U.K. | 260 | 51.14 N | 0.35 E |
| Langley, Eng., U.K. | 262 | 53.15 N | 2.05 W |
| Langley, Ok., U.S. | 196 | 36.27 N | 95.02 W |
| Langley, S.C., U.S. | 192 | 33.31 N | 81.50 W |
| Langley, Wa., U.S. | 224 | 48.02 N | 122.24 W |
| Langley Air Force Base ■ | 208 | 37.05 N | 76.21 W |
| Langley Forest | 284c | 38.57 N | 77.10 W |
| Langley Hill ∧[2] | 282 | 37.20 N | 122.14 W |
| Langley Park | 284c | 38.59 N | 76.58 W |
| Langleyville | 219 | 39.34 N | 89.21 W |
| Langlo ≃ | 166 | 26.26 S | 146.05 E |
| Langlois | 202 | 42.55 N | 124.26 W |
| Langmazong | 120 | 30.52 N | 89.58 E |
| Lang Mo | 110 | 17.14 N | 106.27 E |
| Långnäs | 26 | 60.06 N | 20.17 E |
| Langnau | 58 | 46.57 N | 7.47 E |
| Langogne | 62 | 44.43 N | 3.51 E |
| Langon | 32 | 44.33 N | 0.15 W |
| Langøya I | 24 | 68.44 N | 14.50 E |
| Langping | 102 | 30.38 N | 110.21 E |
| Langport | 42 | 51.02 N | 2.50 W |
| Langqiao | 100 | 30.30 N | 118.24 E |
| Langquaid | 60 | 48.49 N | 12.03 E |
| Langreo → Sama [de Langreo], Esp. | 34 | 43.18 N | 5.41 W |
| Langreo, Esp. | 34 | 43.18 N | 5.41 W |
| Langres | 58 | 47.52 N | 5.20 E |
| Langres, Plateau de ⋏[1] | 58 | 47.41 N | 5.03 E |
| Langruth | 184 | 50.24 N | 98.38 W |
| Langruzong | 120 | 31.50 N | 91.25 E |
| Langsa | 114 | 4.28 N | 97.58 E |
| Langsa, Teluk ⊂ | 114 | 4.35 N | 98.00 E |
| Langschede | 263 | 51.29 N | 7.43 E |
| Långsele | 26 | 63.11 N | 17.04 E |
| Langshan, Zhg. | 102 | 41.12 N | 107.22 E |
| Langshan, Zhg. | 105 | 40.22 N | 115.41 E |
| Långshyttan | 40 | 60.27 N | 16.01 E |
| Långsjön ⊜ | 40 | 59.00 N | 17.27 E |
| Langsnek ⊥ | 158 | 27.28 S | 29.55 E |
| Lang Son | 110 | 21.50 N | 106.44 E |
| Langstaff | 275b | 43.50 N | 79.25 W |
| Langst-Kierst | 263 | 51.18 N | 6.43 E |
| Lang Suan | 110 | 9.57 N | 99.04 E |
| Långsvan ⊜ | 40 | 59.43 N | 15.49 E |
| Langtang National Park ♠ | 124 | 28.10 N | 85.30 E |
| Langtian | 100 | 25.11 N | 113.28 E |
| Langting | 120 | 25.30 N | 93.07 E |
| Langton | 212 | 42.45 N | 80.35 W |
| Langtoutun | 89 | 46.51 N | 121.54 E |
| Langtuozi | 104 | 41.01 N | 121.43 E |
| Langu | 100 | 27.56 N | 118.11 E |
| Langue | 236 | 13.37 N | 87.39 W |
| Languedoc □[9] | 32 | 44.00 N | 4.00 E |
| Langui Layo, Laguna de ⊜ | 248 | 14.29 S | 71.13 W |
| L'Anguille ≃ | 194 | 34.44 N | 90.40 W |
| Langula | 54 | 51.09 N | 10.25 E |
| Langundu, Tanjung ⟩ | 115b | 8.49 S | 118.58 E |
| Langwarden | 52 | 53.36 N | 8.19 E |
| Langwedel | 52 | 52.59 N | 9.12 E |
| Langweer | 52 | 52.57 N | 5.43 E |
| Langweid | 58 | 48.29 N | 10.51 E |
| Langweiler | 56 | 49.40 N | 7.31 E |
| Langwies | 58 | 46.49 N | 9.43 E |
| Langwo | 104 | 41.13 N | 121.44 E |
| Langwozhuang | 105 | 39.05 N | 115.37 E |
| Langxi | 106 | 31.08 N | 119.10 E |
| Langxi ≃ | 106 | 31.10 N | 118.59 E |
| Langzhong | 102 | 31.35 N | 105.59 E |
| Langzishan | 104 | 41.02 N | 123.23 E |
| Lanham | 284c | 38.58 N | 76.51 W |
| Lanhil Island I | 116 | 6.46 N | 122.22 E |
| Lanibga, Mount ∧ | 116 | 10.27 N | 123.56 E |
| Lanigan | 184 | 51.52 N | 105.02 W |
| Lanigan Creek ≃ | 184 | 51.23 N | 105.13 W |
| Lanín, Parque Nacional ♠ | 254 | 39.36 S | 71.24 W |
| Lanín, Volcán ∧[1] | 254 | 39.38 S | 71.30 W |
| Lanivtsi | 78 | 49.52 N | 26.05 E |
| Lanjiang | 107 | 30.24 N | 105.11 E |
| Lankao (Lanfeng) | 98 | 34.50 N | 114.49 E |
| Länkäran | 84 | 38.45 N | 48.50 E |
| Lanker See ⊜ | 54 | 54.12 N | 10.17 E |
| Lankeys Creek | 171b | 35.49 S | 147.39 E |
| Länkipohja | 26 | 61.44 N | 24.48 E |
| Lanklaar | 56 | 51.01 N | 5.44 E |
| Lank-Latum | 263 | 51.18 N | 6.41 E |
| Lankou | 100 | 23.59 N | 115.05 E |
| Lankoviri | 146 | 9.00 N | 11.25 E |
| Lankwitz ◆[8] | 264a | 52.26 N | 13.21 E |
| Lanling | 89 | 45.15 N | 126.12 E |
| Lanna | 78 | 49.21 N | 35.16 E |
| Lannabruk | 40 | 59.14 N | 14.56 E |
| Lannach | 61 | 46.56 N | 15.19 E |
| Lännaholm | 40 | 59.53 N | 17.57 E |
| Lannemezan | 32 | 43.08 N | 0.23 E |
| Lannilis | 32 | 48.34 N | 4.31 W |
| Lannion | 32 | 48.44 N | 3.28 W |
| Lannon | 216 | 43.08 N | 88.09 W |
| L'Annonciation | 206 | 46.25 N | 74.52 W |
| Lanoka Harbor | 208 | 39.52 N | 74.10 W |
| Lanoraie | 206 | 45.58 N | 73.13 W |
| La Noria | 258 | 35.10 S | 58.48 W |
| Lanping | 102 | 26.29 N | 99.23 E |
| Lanqibao | 104 | 40.56 N | 122.25 E |
| Lanqikoucun | 104 | 40.52 N | 122.26 E |
| Lanqipuzi | 104 | 42.12 N | 123.15 E |
| Lanquín | 236 | 15.34 N | 89.58 W |
| Lans, Montagnes de ⋏ | 62 | 44.52 N | 5.29 E |
| Lansdale | 208 | 40.14 N | 75.17 W |
| Lansdowne, Austl. | 162 | 17.53 S | 126.39 E |
| Lansdowne, Austl. | 274a | 33.54 S | 150.59 E |
| Lansdowne, On., Can. | 212 | 44.24 N | 76.01 W |
| Lansdowne, India | 124 | 29.50 N | 78.41 E |
| Lansdowne, Md., U.S. | 284b | 39.14 N | 76.39 W |
| Lansdowne, Pa., U.S. | 285 | 39.56 N | 75.16 W |
| L'Anse, Mi., U.S. | 190 | 46.45 N | 88.27 W |
| Lanse, Pa., U.S. | 214 | 40.59 N | 78.08 W |
| L'Anse-aux-Meadows National Historic Park ♠ | 186 | 51.36 N | 55.32 W |
| L'anse Creuse Bay ⊂ | 214 | 42.34 N | 82.49 W |
| L'Anse Indian Reservation ◆[4] | 190 | 46.48 N | 88.22 W |
| Lans-en-Vercors | 62 | 45.07 N | 5.35 E |
| Lansford, N.D., U.S. | 198 | 48.37 N | 101.22 W |
| Lansford, Pa., U.S. | 210 | 40.49 N | 75.52 W |
| Lanshan | 102 | 25.18 N | 111.52 E |
| Lanshantou | 98 | 35.07 N | 119.21 E |
| Lansing, Il., U.S. | 216 | 41.33 N | 87.32 W |
| Lansing, Ia., U.S. | 190 | 43.21 N | 91.12 W |
| Lansing, Ks., U.S. | 198 | 39.14 N | 94.54 W |
| Lansing, Mi., U.S. | 216 | 42.43 N | 84.33 W |
| Lansing, N.Y., U.S. | 210 | 42.32 N | 76.30 W |
| Lansing, Oh., U.S. | 214 | 40.04 N | 80.47 W |
| Lansing ◆[8] | 275b | 43.45 N | 79.25 W |
| Lansing, Lake ⊜ | 216 | 42.46 N | 84.25 W |
| Lansing Municipal Airport ⊠ | 278 | 41.32 N | 87.32 W |
| Lanškroun | 30 | 49.55 N | 16.37 E |
| Lanslebourg | 62 | 45.17 N | 6.52 E |
| Lanslevillard | 62 | 45.17 N | 6.55 E |
| Lanstrop ◆[8] | 263 | 51.34 N | 7.34 E |
| Lantana | 220 | 26.35 N | 80.03 W |
| Lantang | 100 | 23.25 N | 114.56 E |
| Lantau Island I | 100 | 22.17 N | 113.59 E |
| Lanta Yai, Ko I | 110 | 7.35 N | 99.05 E |
| Lanterne ≃ | 58 | 47.44 N | 6.03 E |
| Lantewa | 146 | 12.16 N | 11.44 E |
| Lantian | 102 | 34.03 N | 109.12 E |
| Lantianba | 107 | 28.52 N | 105.26 E |
| Lantianchang | 271a | 39.58 N | 116.17 E |
| Lantsch | 58 | 46.41 N | 9.34 E |
| Lantschou → Lanzhou | 102 | 36.03 N | 103.41 E |
| Lantzville | 224 | 49.15 N | 124.05 W |
| La Nurra ◆[1] | 71 | 40.45 N | 8.15 E |
| Lanús | 258 | 34.43 S | 58.24 W |
| Lanús □[5] | 288 | 34.42 S | 58.28 W |
| Lanusei | 71 | 39.53 N | 9.32 E |
| Lanuvio | 66 | 41.40 N | 12.42 E |
| Lanuza | 116 | 9.14 N | 126.04 E |
| Lanuza Bay ⊂ | 116 | 9.17 N | 126.04 E |
| Lanxi, Zhg. | 89 | 46.15 N | 126.14 E |
| Lanxi, Zhg. | 100 | 29.12 N | 119.28 E |
| Lanxian | 102 | 38.22 N | 111.46 E |
| Lány | 54 | 50.06 N | 13.58 E |
| Lan Yü I | 100 | 22.03 N | 121.32 E |
| Lanzada | 64 | 46.15 N | 9.51 E |
| Lanzarote I | 148 | 29.00 N | 13.40 W |
| Lanzendorf | 264b | 48.06 N | 16.26 E |
| Lanzhou (Lanchow) | 102 | 36.03 N | 103.41 E |
| Lanzo Torinese | 62 | 45.16 N | 7.28 E |
| Lao → Laos □[1] | 110 | 18.00 N | 105.00 E |
| Lao ≃, It. | 68 | 39.47 N | 15.48 E |
| Lao ≃, Thai | 110 | 19.55 N | 99.54 E |
| Lao ≃, Zhg. | 100 | 29.11 N | 116.00 E |
| Laoag | 116 | 18.12 N | 120.36 E |
| Laoag ≃ | 116 | 18.12 N | 120.31 E |
| Laoang | 116 | 12.34 N | 125.00 E |
| Laoang Island I | 116 | 12.35 N | 125.01 E |
| Lao Bao | 110 | 16.37 N | 106.36 E |
| Laobian, Zhg. | 104 | 40.42 N | 122.21 E |
| Laobian, Zhg. | 104 | 41.58 N | 123.10 E |
| Lao Cai | 110 | 22.30 N | 103.57 E |
| Laochang, Zhg. | 102 | 24.34 N | 104.11 E |
| Laochang, Zhg. | 107 | 29.30 N | 106.36 E |
| Laocheng | 104 | 42.37 N | 124.04 E |
| Laodafang | 104 | 41.40 N | 122.40 E |
| Laodao ≃ | 100 | 23.16 N | 112.58 E |
| Laodaodian | 89 | 51.16 N | 126.40 E |
| Laofengkou | 86 | 46.11 N | 83.38 E |
| Laofu | 98 | 42.13 N | 118.17 E |
| Laogang | 106 | 31.01 N | 121.49 E |
| Laoge | 100 | 32.49 N | 119.52 E |
| Laoguan | 100 | 27.38 N | 113.36 E |
| Laoguanpu | 104 | 40.53 N | 120.51 E |
| Laoha ≃ | 90 | 43.24 N | 120.39 E |
| Laohaotuo | 104 | 41.25 N | 122.46 E |
| Laoheba | 107 | 28.51 N | 103.49 E |
| Laoheishan | 89 | 43.45 N | 130.52 E |
| Laoheshangtai | 104 | 40.43 N | 120.49 E |
| Laohokow → Guanghua | 102 | 32.25 N | 111.36 E |
| Laohuk'ou | 100 | 24.53 N | 121.03 E |
| Laohumiao | 271a | 39.58 N | 116.20 E |
| Laohutuozi | 104 | 42.25 N | 122.34 E |
| Laois □[6] | 48 | 53.00 N | 7.24 W |
| Laojunguan | 105 | 40.22 N | 114.47 E |
| Laojunmiao → Yumen | 102 | 39.56 N | 97.51 E |
| Laoka | 89 | 52.47 N | 125.52 E |
| Laolao, Bahia ⊂ | 174n | 15.08 N | 145.46 E |
| Lao Ling ∧ | 89 | 43.27 N | 130.11 E |
| Laolong ≃ | 106 | 32.11 N | 120.00 E |
| Laolongtan | 107 | 30.01 N | 104.48 E |
| Laomocun | 106 | 30.51 N | 119.11 E |
| Laon | 50 | 49.34 N | 3.40 E |
| Laona, N.Y., U.S. | 214 | 42.25 N | 79.19 W |
| Laona, Wi., U.S. | 190 | 45.33 N | 88.40 W |
| La Orchila, Isla I | 246 | 11.48 N | 66.09 W |
| La Orotava | 148 | 28.23 N | 16.31 W |
| La Oroya | 248 | 11.32 S | 75.54 W |
| Laos (Lao) □[1], Asia | 108 | 18.00 N | 105.00 E |
| Laos (Lao) □[1], Asia | 110 | 18.00 N | 105.00 E |
| Laoshan (Licun) | 98 | 36.10 N | 120.25 E |
| Laoshan Wan ⊂ | 98 | 36.24 N | 120.45 E |
| Laosolu | 114 | 3.11 N | 98.02 E |
| Laotto | 216 | 41.17 N | 85.12 W |
| Laou, Oued ≃ | 34 | 35.29 N | 5.04 W |
| Laowushi | 106 | 31.43 N | 121.00 E |
| Laoxinkou | 100 | 30.12 N | 112.50 E |
| Laoyemiao | 98 | 41.03 N | 119.53 E |
| Laoyezhuang | 106 | 32.16 N | 120.04 E |
| Laoyingpan | 100 | 26.34 N | 115.10 E |
| Laozha | 106 | 31.35 N | 121.07 E |
| Laozhen | 100 | 31.34 N | 118.19 E |
| Laozhong | 98 | 33.56 N | 114.51 E |
| Laozhuangzi | 105 | 39.44 N | 118.05 E |
| Laozishan | 100 | 33.11 N | 118.36 E |
| Lapa | 252 | 25.45 S | 49.42 W |
| Lapa ◆[8], Bra. | 287a | 22.55 S | 43.11 W |
| Lapa ◆[8], Bra. | 287b | 23.32 S | 46.42 W |
| Lapacičy | 76 | 53.34 N | 30.53 E |
| Lapac Island I | 116 | 5.32 N | 120.47 E |
| Lapai | 150 | 9.06 N | 6.45 E |
| Lapaich, Sgurr na ∧ | 46 | 57.21 N | 5.04 W |
| Lapalisse | 32 | 46.15 N | 3.38 E |
| La Palma, Col. | 246 | 5.22 N | 74.24 W |
| La Palma, Cuba | 240p | 22.45 N | 83.33 W |
| La Palma, El Sal. | 236 | 14.19 N | 89.11 W |
| La Palma, Méx. | 234 | 17.05 N | 99.29 W |
| La Palma, Méx. | 234 | 20.09 N | 102.46 W |
| La Palma, Pan. | 246 | 8.25 N | 78.09 W |
| La Palma, Pan. | 246 | 7.42 N | 80.12 W |
| La Palma, Ca., U.S. | 280 | 33.50 N | 118.02 W |
| La Palma I | 148 | 28.40 N | 17.52 W |
| La Palma ≃ | 240p | 23.03 N | 80.54 W |
| La Palma de Cervelló | 266d | 41.25 N | 1.58 E |
| La Palma del Condado | 34 | 37.23 N | 6.33 W |
| La Palmita | 196 | 25.57 N | 99.18 W |
| La Paloma | 252 | 34.40 S | 54.10 W |
| La Palud | 62 | 43.47 N | 6.20 E |
| La Pampa □[4] | 252 | 37.00 S | 66.00 W |
| La Panza Range ⋏ | 226 | 35.18 N | 120.18 W |
| Lapão | 250 | 11.24 S | 41.50 W |
| La Paragua | 246 | 6.50 N | 63.20 W |
| Laparan Island I | 116 | 5.54 N | 119.59 E |
| La Parota | 234 | 18.20 N | 101.08 W |
| La Pasión, Laguna ⊂ | 234 | 15.59 N | 97.40 W |
| La Pasión, Río de ≃ | 232 | 16.28 N | 90.33 W |
| La Patrie | 206 | 45.24 N | 71.15 W |
| La Paz, Arg. | 252 | 30.45 S | 59.39 W |
| La Paz, Arg. | 252 | 33.28 S | 67.33 W |
| La Paz, Bol. | 248 | 16.30 S | 68.09 W |
| La Paz, Col. | 246 | 10.23 N | 73.10 W |
| La Paz, Hond. | 236 | 14.16 N | 87.40 W |
| La Paz, Méx. | 232 | 24.10 N | 110.18 W |
| La Paz, Méx. | 234 | 23.41 N | 100.43 W |
| La Paz, Pil. | 116 | 8.19 N | 125.43 E |
| Lapaz, In., U.S. | 216 | 41.28 N | 86.18 W |
| La Paz, Ur. | 258 | 34.21 S | 57.18 W |
| La Paz, Ur. | 258 | 34.46 S | 56.15 W |
| La Paz □[5], Bol. | 248 | 15.30 S | 68.00 W |
| La Paz □[5], Hond. | 236 | 14.15 N | 87.50 W |
| La Paz, Bahía ⊂ | 232 | 24.09 N | 110.25 W |
| La Paz, Río de ≃ | 248 | 16.27 S | 67.19 W |
| La Paz Centro | 236 | 12.20 N | 86.41 W |
| Lape | 115b | 8.39 S | 117.37 E |
| La Pedrera | 246 | 1.18 S | 69.43 W |
| Lapeer | 216 | 43.03 N | 83.19 W |
| Lapeer □[6] | 216 | 43.00 N | 83.20 W |
| Lapel | 218 | 40.04 N | 85.50 W |
| La Penne-sur-Huveaune | 62 | 43.17 N | 5.31 E |
| La Perla, Méx. | 196 | 28.18 N | 104.33 W |
| La Perla, Méx. | 232 | 28.18 N | 104.38 W |
| La Perla, Perú | 286d | 12.05 S | 77.08 W |
| La Perouse | 170 | 33.59 S | 151.14 E |
| La Perouse, Bahía ⊂ | 174z | 27.04 S | 109.18 W |
| La Perouse Bay ⊂ | 229a | 20.35 N | 156.25 W |
| La Perouse Strait ⊔ | 89 | 45.45 N | 142.00 E |
| La Pesca | 234 | 23.46 N | 97.47 W |
| La Pesse | 58 | 46.18 N | 5.51 E |
| La Petite-Pierre | 56 | 48.52 N | 7.19 E |
| Lapford | 42 | 50.55 N | 3.47 W |
| Lapham Hill ∧[2] | 216 | 43.02 N | 88.24 W |
| L'apičev | 80 | 48.30 N | 43.32 E |
| La Piedad de Cabadas | 234 | 20.21 N | 102.00 W |
| La Pimienta | 234 | 21.28 N | 99.01 W |
| La Pine | 202 | 43.40 N | 121.30 W |
| Lapinin Island I | 116 | 10.06 N | 124.34 E |
| Lapinjärvi (Lappträsk) | 26 | 60.38 N | 26.13 E |
| Lapin lääni □[4] | 24 | 68.00 N | 27.00 E |
| Lapinlahti | 26 | 63.22 N | 27.24 E |
| Lapino | 82 | 54.57 N | 37.49 E |
| La Pintada | 236 | 8.36 N | 80.27 W |
| La Pintana | 286e | 33.37 S | 70.38 W |
| La Pizzuta ∧ | 70 | 38.00 N | 13.16 E |
| La Place, Il., U.S. | 219 | 39.48 N | 88.43 W |
| La Place, La., U.S. | 194 | 30.03 N | 90.28 W |
| Lap Lae | 110 | 17.39 N | 100.02 E |
| La Plaine | 240d | 15.20 N | 61.15 W |
| Lapland □[9] | 24 | 68.00 N | 25.00 E |
| Laplandija | 24 | 68.16 N | 33.19 E |
| Laplandskij zapovednik ◆[4] | 24 | 67.50 N | 32.10 E |
| La Plata, Arg. | 258 | 34.55 S | 57.57 W |
| La Plata, Col. | 246 | 2.23 N | 75.53 W |
| La Plata, Md., U.S. | 208 | 38.31 N | 76.58 W |
| La Plata, Mo., U.S. | 194 | 40.01 N | 92.29 W |
| La Plata □[5] | 288 | 34.55 S | 58.04 W |
| La Plata ≃ | 200 | 36.54 N | 108.15 W |
| La Plata, Lago ⊜ | 254 | 44.53 S | 71.50 W |
| La Plata, Lago ⊜[1] | 240m | 18.20 N | 66.14 W |
| La Plata, Universidad Nacional de ⊍[2] | 288 | 35.55 S | 57.57 W |
| La Plata Peak ∧ | 200 | 39.02 N | 106.28 W |
| La Playa ◆[8] | 286b | 23.06 N | 82.27 W |
| La Playa Corrida de San Juan, Punta ⟩ | 234 | 18.36 N | 103.42 W |
| La Plonge Indian Reserve ◆[4] | 184 | 55.15 N | 107.36 W |
| La Plume | 210 | 41.34 N | 75.45 W |
| La Pobla de Segur | 34 | 42.14 N | 0.59 E |
| La Pocatière | 186 | 47.22 N | 70.02 W |
| La Poile | 186 | 47.41 N | 58.24 W |
| La Poile Bay ⊂ | 186 | 47.38 N | 58.20 W |
| Lapominka | 24 | 64.48 N | 40.28 E |
| La Pomme | 62 | 43.25 N | 5.35 E |
| Laponie → Lapland □[9] | 24 | 68.00 N | 25.00 E |
| Laporte, Co., U.S. | 200 | 40.38 N | 105.08 W |
| La Porte, In., U.S. | 216 | 41.36 N | 86.43 W |
| La Porte, Oh., U.S. | 279a | 41.19 N | 82.05 W |
| Laporte, Pa., U.S. | 210 | 41.25 N | 76.30 W |
| La Porte, Tx., U.S. | 222 | 29.39 N | 95.01 W |
| La Porte □[6] | 216 | 41.36 N | 86.43 W |
| La Porte City | 190 | 42.18 N | 92.11 W |
| Laposo, Bulu ∧ | 112 | 4.29 S | 119.47 E |
| La Potherie, Lac ⊜ | 176 | 58.50 N | 72.24 W |
| Lapoutroie | 58 | 48.09 N | 7.10 E |
| La Poveda | 266a | 40.19 N | 3.29 W |
| La Poza Grande | 232 | 25.50 N | 112.05 W |
| Lappago (Lappach) | 64 | 46.55 N | 11.48 E |
| Lappajärvi | 26 | 63.12 N | 23.38 E |
| Lappajärvi ⊜ | 26 | 63.08 N | 23.40 E |
| Lappeenranta | 26 | 61.04 N | 28.11 E |
| Lappersdorf | 60 | 49.03 N | 12.05 E |
| Lappfjärd (Lapväärtti) | 26 | 62.15 N | 21.32 E |
| Lappi | 26 | 61.06 N | 21.50 E |
| Lappland → Lapland □[9] | 24 | 68.00 N | 25.00 E |
| Lappträsk → Lapinjärvi | 26 | 60.38 N | 26.13 E |
| La Prairie | 206 | 45.25 N | 73.30 W |
| Laprairie □[6] | 206 | 45.20 N | 73.35 W |
| La Prele Creek ≃ | 198 | 42.50 N | 105.30 W |
| La Presa ≃ | 232 | 24.25 N | 111.34 W |
| Laprida, Arg. | 252 | 37.33 S | 60.49 W |
| Laprida, Arg. | 252 | 28.23 S | 64.33 W |
| La Pryor | 196 | 28.57 N | 99.51 W |
| Lapšanga | 80 | 57.27 N | 45.03 E |
| Lâpseki | 130 | 40.20 N | 26.41 E |
| Lapta | 130 | 35.20 N | 33.10 E |
| Laptev Sea → Laptevych, more ⊤[2] | 74 | 76.00 N | 126.00 E |
| Laptevych, more (Laptev Sea) ⊤[2] | 74 | 76.00 N | 126.00 E |
| Lapua | 26 | 62.57 N | 23.00 E |
| Lapuanjoki ≃ | 26 | 63.34 N | 22.30 E |
| La Puebla de Cazalla | 34 | 37.14 N | 5.19 W |
| La Puebla de Montalbán | 34 | 39.52 N | 4.21 W |
| La Puente | 228 | 34.01 N | 117.56 W |
| La Puerta | 252 | 28.10 S | 65.48 W |
| Lapu-Lapu (Opon) | 116 | 10.19 N | 123.57 E |
| La Punt | 58 | 46.35 N | 9.55 E |
| La Punta | 286d | 12.05 S | 77.11 W |
| La Purísima, Chile | 286e | 33.34 S | 70.39 W |
| La Purísima, Méx. | 232 | 26.10 N | 112.04 W |
| Lăpuș | 38 | 47.30 N | 24.01 E |
| La Push | 224 | 47.54 N | 124.38 W |
| Lapuyan | 116 | 7.36 N | 123.12 E |
| Lapväärtti → Lappfjärd | 26 | 62.15 N | 21.32 E |
| Lapwai | 202 | 46.24 N | 116.48 W |
| Łapy | 30 | 53.00 N | 22.53 E |
| La Queue-en-Brie | 261 | 48.47 N | 2.35 E |
| La Queue-lès-Yvelines | 261 | 48.48 N | 1.46 E |
| La Quiaca | 252 | 22.06 S | 65.37 W |
| L'Aquila | 66 | 42.22 N | 13.22 E |
| L'Aquila □[4] | 66 | 42.05 N | 13.40 E |
| Lār | 128 | 27.41 N | 54.17 E |
| Lara | 169 | 38.01 S | 144.24 E |
| Lara □[3] | 246 | 10.10 N | 69.50 W |
| Larabanga | 150 | 9.13 N | 1.51 W |
| Laracha | 34 | 43.15 N | 8.35 W |
| Larache | 148 | 35.12 N | 6.10 W |
| Laragne-Montéglin | 62 | 44.19 N | 5.49 E |
| Lārak, Jazīreh-ye I | 128 | 26.52 N | 56.22 E |
| Laramate | 248 | 14.15 S | 74.52 W |
| La Rambla | 34 | 37.36 N | 4.44 W |
| Laramie | 200 | 41.18 N | 105.35 W |
| Laramie ≃ | 200 | 42.12 N | 104.32 W |
| Laramie Mountains ⋏ | 200 | 42.00 N | 105.40 W |
| Laramie Peak ∧ | 200 | 42.17 N | 105.27 W |
| Laranjaí ≃ | 255 | 23.12 S | 53.45 W |
| Laranjal | 255 | 21.22 S | 42.28 W |
| Laranjeiras | 250 | 10.48 S | 37.10 W |
| Laranjeiras ◆[8] | 287a | 22.56 S | 43.11 W |
| Laranjeiras do Sul | 252 | 25.25 S | 52.25 W |
| Larantuka | 115b | 8.21 S | 122.59 E |
| Laraos | 248 | 12.17 S | 75.50 W |
| Larap | 116 | 14.18 N | 122.39 E |
| Larat | 164 | 7.09 S | 131.45 E |
| Larat, Pulau I | 164 | 7.10 S | 131.50 E |
| Laravale | 171a | 28.05 S | 152.56 E |
| La Raya, Abra )( | 248 | 14.35 S | 70.59 W |
| L'Arbaa Naït Irathen | 34 | 36.38 N | 4.12 E |
| Larb Creek ≃ | 202 | 48.25 N | 107.16 W |
| L'Arbresle | 62 | 45.50 N | 4.37 E |
| Lärbro | 26 | 57.47 N | 18.47 E |
| Larbut, Jazīrat I | 140 | 18.47 N | 37.33 E |
| Larche, Col de (Colle della Maddalena) )( | 62 | 44.25 N | 6.53 E |
| Larchmont | 210 | 40.55 N | 73.45 W |
| Larchmont Harbor ⊂ | 276 | 40.55 N | 73.45 W |
| Larchwood | 198 | 43.27 N | 96.26 W |
| Lardaro | 64 | 45.58 N | 10.39 E |
| Larde | 154 | 16.28 S | 39.43 E |
| Lardeau | 182 | 50.09 N | 116.57 W |
| Larderello | 66 | 43.14 N | 10.53 E |
| Larder Lake ⊜ | 190 | 48.05 N | 79.36 W |
| Lardier, Cap ⟩ | 62 | 43.09 N | 6.37 E |
| L'Ardoise | 186 | 45.37 N | 60.45 W |
| Lardy | 261 | 48.31 N | 2.16 E |
| Lare | 154 | 0.20 N | 37.56 E |
| Laredo, Esp. | 34 | 43.24 N | 3.25 W |
| Laredo, Tx., U.S. | 196 | 27.30 N | 99.30 W |
| Laredo Sound ⊔ | 182 | 52.32 N | 128.53 W |
| La Reforma, Méx. | 232 | 25.06 N | 108.05 W |
| La Reforma, Méx. | 234 | 16.34 N | 97.51 W |
| La Reina | 286e | 33.27 S | 70.33 W |
| Laren | 52 | 52.15 N | 5.14 E |
| Larena | 116 | 9.15 N | 123.35 E |
| La Réole | 32 | 44.35 N | 0.02 W |
| Lares, Perú | 248 | 13.04 S | 72.05 W |
| Lares, P.R. | 240m | 18.18 N | 66.53 W |
| Larga | 38 | 48.23 N | 26.50 E |
| Larga, Laguna ⊜ | 196 | 27.30 N | 97.25 W |
| Large, Île du I | 275a | 45.19 N | 73.52 W |
| Largentière | 62 | 44.32 N | 4.18 E |
| L'Argentière-la-Bessée | 62 | 44.47 N | 6.33 E |
| Lar Gerd | 120 | 35.29 N | 66.40 E |
| Largo | 220 | 27.54 N | 82.47 W |
| Largo, Cañon V | 200 | 36.40 N | 107.43 W |
| Largo, Cayo I | 240p | 21.38 N | 81.28 W |
| Largo Creek ≃ | 200 | 34.29 N | 108.51 W |
| Largoward | 46 | 56.15 N | 2.51 W |
| Largs | 46 | 55.48 N | 4.52 W |
| Largue ≃ | 62 | 43.51 N | 5.52 E |
| Lari, It. | 66 | 43.34 N | 10.35 E |
| Lari, Perú | 248 | 15.37 S | 71.46 W |
| Lariang | 112 | 1.26 S | 119.17 E |
| Lariang ≃ | 112 | 1.25 S | 119.17 E |
| La Ricamarie | 62 | 45.24 N | 4.22 E |
| Larimer | 214 | 40.21 N | 79.44 W |
| Larimore | 198 | 47.54 N | 97.37 W |
| Larino | 66 | 41.48 N | 14.54 E |
| La Rioja | 252 | 29.26 S | 66.51 W |
| La Rioja □[3] | 34 | 42.15 N | 2.30 W |
| La Rioja □[4] | 252 | 30.00 S | 67.30 W |
| Lárisa | 38 | 39.38 N | 22.25 E |
| Larisa Station ◆[5] | 267c | 37.59 N | 23.43 E |
| Larjak | 74 | 61.16 N | 80.15 E |
| Larjan | 76 | 59.30 N | 33.47 E |
| Larjegan ≃ | 86 | 60.30 N | 77.44 E |
| Lārkāna | 120 | 27.33 N | 68.13 E |
| Larkhall | 46 | 55.45 N | 3.59 W |
| Lark Harbour | 186 | 49.06 N | 58.23 W |
| Larkhill | 42 | 51.12 N | 1.50 W |
| Larkspur | 226 | 37.56 N | 122.30 W |
| Larksville | 210 | 41.14 N | 75.55 W |
| Larnaca → Lárnax | 130 | 34.55 N | 33.38 E |
| Lárnakos, Kólpos ⊂ | 130 | 34.55 N | 33.45 E |
| Lárnax (Larnaca) | 130 | 34.55 N | 33.38 E |
| Larne | 48 | 54.51 N | 5.49 W |
| Larned | 198 | 38.10 N | 99.05 W |
| Larne Lough ⊜ | 48 | 54.47 N | 5.45 W |
| Laro | 146 | 8.17 N | 12.18 E |
| La Robla | 34 | 42.48 N | 5.37 W |
| La Roca de la Sierra | 34 | 39.07 N | 6.41 W |
| La Roche | 58 | 46.42 N | 7.08 E |
| La Roche-Bernard | 32 | 47.31 N | 2.18 W |
| La Roche-de-Rame | 62 | 44.45 N | 6.35 E |
| La Roche-Derrien | 28 | 48.45 N | 3.16 W |
| La Roche-des-Arnauds | 62 | 44.34 N | 5.57 E |
| La Roche-en-Ardenne | 56 | 50.11 N | 5.35 E |
| La Roche-en-Brenil | 50 | 47.22 N | 4.10 E |
| La Rochefoucauld | 32 | 45.45 N | 0.23 E |
| La Roche-Guyon | 50 | 49.05 N | 1.38 E |
| La Rochelle | 32 | 46.10 N | 1.10 W |
| Laroche-Saint-Cydroine | 50 | 47.58 N | 3.31 E |
| La Roche-sur-Foron | 58 | 46.04 N | 6.19 E |
| La Roche-sur-Yon | 32 | 46.40 N | 1.26 W |
| La Rochette, Fr. | 62 | 45.28 N | 6.07 E |
| La Rochette, Fr. | 261 | 48.30 N | 2.40 E |
| Larochette, Lux. | 56 | 49.47 N | 6.15 E |
| La Roda | 34 | 39.13 N | 2.09 W |
| La Romaine | 186 | 50.13 N | 60.40 W |
| La Romana | 238 | 18.25 N | 68.58 W |
| Larona | 112 | 2.45 S | 121.20 E |
| La Ronge | 184 | 55.06 N | 105.17 W |
| Laroquebrou | 32 | 44.58 N | 2.11 E |
| La Roquebrussanne | 62 | 43.20 N | 5.59 E |
| Larose | 194 | 29.34 N | 90.22 W |
| La Rosita | 236 | 13.53 N | 84.24 W |
| La Route | 261 | 48.48 N | 2.47 E |
| Larrabee State Park ♠ | 224 | 48.41 N | 122.29 W |
| Larreynaga | 236 | 12.40 N | 86.34 W |
| Larrey Point ⟩ | 162 | 19.58 S | 119.07 E |
| Larrimah | 164 | 15.35 S | 133.12 E |
| Larringes | 58 | 46.22 N | 6.35 E |
| Larrison Creek ≃ | 222 | 31.27 N | 95.03 W |
| Larroque | 252 | 33.02 S | 59.01 W |
| Larrys Creek ≃ | 210 | 41.13 N | 77.13 W |
| Larrys River | 186 | 45.13 N | 61.23 W |
| Larsen Air Park ⊠ | 281 | 42.11 N | 83.33 W |
| Larsen Bay | 180 | 57.33 N | 154.00 W |
| Larsen Ice Shelf ⊓ | 9 | 68.30 S | 62.30 W |
| Larteh Aheneasi | 150 | 5.56 N | 0.04 E |
| La Rubia | 252 | 30.06 S | 61.48 W |
| La Rue, Oh., U.S. | 214 | 40.35 N | 83.23 W |
| Larue, Tx., U.S. | 222 | 32.07 N | 95.41 W |
| La Rumorosa | 204 | 32.34 N | 116.06 W |
| Laruns | 32 | 42.59 N | 0.25 W |
| Larus Lake ⊜ | 184 | 51.17 N | 94.40 W |
| Larvik | 26 | 59.04 N | 10.00 E |
| Larwill | 216 | 41.10 N | 85.37 W |
| Laryne | 83 | 47.53 N | 37.56 E |
| Larzac, Causse du ⋏[1] | 32 | 43.50 N | 3.25 E |
| Lasa (Laas) | 64 | 46.37 N | 10.42 E |
| La Sabana | 252 | 27.52 S | 59.57 W |
| Las Adjuntas | 286c | 10.26 N | 67.01 W |
| La Sagne | 58 | 47.03 N | 6.48 E |
| La Sal | 200 | 38.18 N | 109.14 W |
| La Salada, Laguna ⊜ | 234 | 22.28 N | 98.20 W |
| La Salette-Fallavaux | 62 | 44.51 N | 5.59 E |
| La Salle, On., Can. | 214 | 42.14 N | 83.06 W |
| La Salle, P.Q., Can. | 206 | 45.26 N | 73.38 W |
| Lasalle, Fr. | 62 | 44.03 N | 3.51 E |
| La Salle, It. | 62 | 45.45 N | 7.04 E |
| La Salle, Co., U.S. | 200 | 40.20 N | 104.42 W |
| La Salle, Il., U.S. | 216 | 41.20 N | 89.06 W |
| La Salle □[6] | 216 | 41.21 N | 88.51 W |
| La Salle ≃ | 184 | 49.45 N | 97.08 W |
| Lasalle, Parc ♠ | 275a | 45.26 N | 73.40 W |
| La Salle College ⊍[2] | 285 | 40.02 N | 75.09 W |
| La Salle Gardens | 216 | 42.39 N | 83.21 W |
| Las Almejas, Bahía ⊂ | 232 | 24.29 N | 111.44 W |
| La Sal Mountains ⋏ | 200 | 38.30 N | 109.10 W |
| Lasan | 112 | 1.14 N | 115.13 E |
| Lasanga Island I | 164 | 7.25 S | 147.16 E |
| Las Animas | 198 | 38.04 N | 103.13 W |
| La Santa, Cerro ∧ | 240m | 18.07 N | 66.03 W |
| Las Arenas | 240m | 18.02 N | 67.09 W |
| La Sarraz | 58 | 46.40 N | 6.31 E |
| La Sarre | 190 | 48.48 N | 79.12 W |
| La Sarre ≃ | 190 | 48.43 N | 79.16 W |
| Las Arrias | 252 | 30.21 S | 63.35 W |
| La Sauceda | 196 | 28.26 N | 100.38 W |
| La Saulce | 62 | 44.25 N | 6.01 E |
| Las Auras | 196 | 26.25 N | 99.20 W |
| Las Aves, Isla I | 238 | 15.42 N | 63.38 W |
| Las Aves, Islas II | 246 | 12.00 N | 67.30 W |
| Las Ballenas, Canal de ⊔ | 232 | 29.10 N | 113.29 W |
| Lasberg | 61 | 48.28 N | 14.32 E |
| Las Blancas | 196 | 25.42 N | 97.35 W |
| Las Bonitas | 246 | 7.52 N | 65.40 W |
| Las Breñas | 252 | 27.05 S | 61.05 W |
| Låsby | 41 | 56.09 N | 9.49 E |
| Las Cabezas de San Juan | 34 | 36.59 N | 5.56 W |
| Las Cabras | 252 | 34.18 S | 71.19 W |
| Las Cañas ≃ | 234 | 22.29 N | 105.36 W |
| Lascano | 252 | 33.40 S | 54.12 W |
| Lascar, Volcán ∧[1] | 252 | 23.23 S | 67.45 W |
| Lascari | 70 | 38.00 N | 13.56 E |
| Las Casas → San Cristóbal de las Casas | 234 | 16.45 N | 92.38 W |
| Las Catitas | 252 | 33.18 S | 68.02 W |
| Las Catonas, Arroyo ≃ | 288 | 34.37 S | 58.43 W |
| Lascaux, Grotte de ⊥[5] | 32 | 45.01 N | 1.08 E |
| Las Cejas | 252 | 26.53 S | 64.44 W |
| L'Ascension | 206 | 46.33 N | 74.50 W |
| Las Chacras | 258 | 35.05 S | 59.10 W |
| Las Choapas | 234 | 17.55 N | 94.05 W |
| La Scie | 186 | 49.57 N | 55.36 W |
| Las Coloradas | 254 | 39.33 S | 70.35 W |
| Las Condes | 286e | 33.22 S | 70.31 W |
| Lascone, Monte ∧[2] | 267a | 41.59 N | 12.23 E |
| Las Cruces | 200 | 32.18 N | 106.46 W |
| Las Cuevas | 232 | 29.38 N | 101.19 W |
| Las Delicias | 232 | 15.58 N | 91.50 W |
| La Selle, Morne ∧ | 238 | 18.22 N | 71.59 W |
| La Selva Beach | 226 | 36.55 N | 121.51 W |
| Lasem | 115a | 6.42 S | 111.26 E |
| La Serena | 252 | 29.54 S | 71.16 W |
| La Serena ◆[1] | 34 | 38.45 N | 5.30 W |
| La Seyne-sur-Mer | 62 | 43.06 N | 5.53 E |
| Las Flores, Arg. | 252 | 36.03 S | 59.07 W |
| Las Flores, Arg. | 252 | 30.19 S | 69.12 W |
| Las Flores, Méx. | 234 | 18.22 N | 93.10 W |
| Las Flores, P.R. | 240m | 18.03 N | 66.22 W |
| Las Flores, Ven. | 286c | 10.34 N | 66.56 W |
| Las Flores, Arroyo ≃ | 252 | 35.36 S | 59.01 W |
| Las Flores, Cerro ∧ | 234 | 16.43 N | 95.30 W |
| Las Flores Canyon V | 280 | 34.03 N | 118.38 W |
| Las Flores Chica, Laguna ⊜ | 258 | 35.30 S | 59.01 W |
| Las Flores Grande, Laguna ⊜ | 258 | 35.34 S | 59.02 W |
| Las Garcitas | 252 | 26.35 S | 59.48 W |
| Las Guacamayas | 234 | 18.02 N | 102.12 W |
| Las Guayabas | 232 | 24.00 N | 97.45 W |
| Lasham | 42 | 51.11 N | 1.03 W |
| Las Harquetas, Arroyo ≃ | 288 | 34.29 S | 58.38 W |
| Lashburn | 184 | 53.08 N | 109.36 W |
| Lāsh-e Joveyn | 128 | 31.43 N | 61.37 E |
| Las Heras, Arg. | 252 | 32.51 S | 68.49 W |
| Las Heras, Arg. | 254 | 46.33 S | 68.57 W |
| Lashio | 110 | 22.56 N | 97.45 E |
| Lashkar → Gwalior | 124 | 26.13 N | 78.10 E |
| Lashkar Gāh | 128 | 31.35 N | 64.21 E |
| Las Hormigas | 232 | 25.30 N | 98.44 W |
| Lasht | 123 | 36.48 N | 73.01 E |
| Lasia, Pulau I | 114 | 2.10 N | 96.39 E |
| La Sierra, Montaña ⋏ | 236 | 14.04 N | 87.54 W |
| Las Iglesias | 196 | 27.35 N | 101.21 W |
| Las Iglesias, Cerro ∧ | 232 | 26.16 N | 106.38 W |
| La Sila ⋏ | 68 | 39.15 N | 16.30 E |
| La Siligata | 66 | 43.56 N | 12.45 E |
| La Silla de Caracas ∧ | 286c | 10.33 N | 66.51 W |
| Łasin | 30 | 53.32 N | 19.05 E |
| Lašino | 80 | 58.16 N | 49.59 E |
| Lāsjerd | 128 | 35.24 N | 53.04 E |
| Łask | 30 | 51.36 N | 19.07 E |
| Łaskarzew | 30 | 51.48 N | 21.35 E |
| L'askel'a | 24 | 61.45 N | 30.59 E |
| Laško | 36 | 46.09 N | 15.14 E |
| Las Lajas, Arg. | 252 | 38.31 S | 70.22 W |
| Las Lajas, Pan. | 236 | 8.15 N | 81.52 W |
| Las Lajitas | 252 | 24.41 S | 64.15 W |
| Las Lomas | 246 | 4.40 S | 80.15 W |
| Las Lomitas | 252 | 24.42 S | 60.36 W |
| Lašma | 80 | 54.56 N | 41.09 E |
| Las Malvinas | 252 | 34.50 S | 68.15 W |
| Lašmanka | 80 | 54.44 N | 51.28 E |
| Las Mareas | 240m | 17.56 N | 66.09 W |
| Las Margaritas | 232 | 16.19 N | 91.59 W |
| Las Margaritas, Laguna ⊜ | 258 | 35.28 S | 57.56 W |
| Las Marianas | 258 | 35.04 S | 59.31 W |


| Symbol | English | Deutsch | Español | Français | Português |
|---|---|---|---|---|---|
| ≃ | River | Fluß | Río | Rivière | Rio |
| ≊ | Canal | Kanal | Canal | Canal | Canal |
| ⌊ | Waterfall, Rapids | Wasserfall, Stromschnellen | Cascada, Rápidos | Chute d'eau, Rapides | Cascata, Rápidos |
| ⊔ | Strait | Meeresstraße | Estrecho | Détroit | Estreito |
| ⊂ | Bay, Gulf | Bucht, Golf | Bahía, Golfo | Baie, Golfe | Baía, Golfo |
| ⊜ | Lake, Lakes | See, Seen | Lago, Lagos | Lac, Lacs | Lago, Lagos |
| ≡ | Swamp | Sumpf | Pantano | Marais | Pântano |
| ⊓ | Ice Features, Glacier | Eis- und Gletscherformen | Accidentes Glaciales | Formes glaciaires | Acidentes glaciares |
| ⊤ | Other Hydrographic Features | Andere Hydrographische Objekte | Otros Elementos Hidrográficos | Autres données hydrographiques | Outros acidentes hidrográficos |
| ◆ | Submarine Features | Untermeerische Objekte | Accidentes Submarinos | Formes de relief sous-marin | Acidentes submarinos |
| □ | Political Unit | Politische Einheit | Unidad Política | Entité politique | Unidade política |
| ⊍ | Cultural Institution | Kulturelle Institution | Institución Cultural | Institution culturelle | Instituição cultural |
| ⊥ | Historical Site | Historische Stätte | Sitio Histórico | Site historique | Sitio histórico |
| ♠ | Recreational Site | Erholungs- und Ferienort | Sitio de Recreo | Centre de loisirs | Area de Lazer |
| ⊠ | Airport | Flughafen | Aeropuerto | Aéroport | Aeroporto |
| ■ | Military Installation | Militäranlage | Instalación Militar | Installation militaire | Instalação militar |
| ◆ | Miscellaneous | Verschiedenes | Misceláneo | Divers | Diversos |

**ENGLISH** — Name, Page, Lat.°′, Long.°′
**DEUTSCH** — Name, Seite, Breite°′, Länge°′ E = Ost


| Name | Page | Lat.°′ | Long.°′ |
|---|---|---|---|
| Las Marías | 240m | 18.15 N | 67.00 W |
| Las Mayas | 286c | 10.26 N | 66.56 W |
| Las Mercedes | 246 | 9.07 N | 66.24 W |
| Las Mesas de San Isidro | 234 | 21.55 N | 100.15 W |
| Las Minas | 286c | 10.27 N | 66.52 W |
| Las Minas, Cerro ∧ | 236 | 14.33 N | 88.39 W |
| Las Minillas, Cerro ∧ | 286e | 33.31 S | 70.29 W |
| Las Moras Creek ≃ | 196 | 29.00 N | 100.39 W |
| Las Mulas, Laguna ⊜ | 258 | 35.32 S | 57.54 W |
| Las Navas | 116 | 12.21 N | 125.02 E |
| Las Nieves | 232 | 26.24 N | 105.22 W |
| Las Nopaleras, Cerro ∧ | 232 | 25.08 N | 103.14 W |
| La Solana | 34 | 38.56 N | 3.14 W |
| La Soledad, Cerro ∧ | 232 | 26.32 N | 107.17 W |
| Lasolo | 112 | 3.29 S | 122.04 E |
| Lasolo ≃ | 112 | 3.28 S | 122.06 E |
| Las Ortegas, Arroyo ≃ | 288 | 34.45 S | 58.32 W |
| Las Ovejas | 252 | 37.01 S | 70.45 W |
| Las Palmas, Arg. | 252 | 27.04 S | 58.42 W |
| Las Palmas, Arg. | 258 | 34.05 S | 59.10 W |
| Las Palmas, Pan. | 236 | 8.08 N | 81.27 W |
| Las Palmas, P.R. | 240m | 17.59 N | 66.02 W |
| Las Palmas □[4] | 148 | 28.25 N | 14.15 W |
| Las Palmas de Gran Canaria | 148 | 28.06 N | 15.24 W |
| Las Palomas | 200 | 31.44 N | 107.37 W |
| Las Perdices, Canal ≡ | 286e | 33.31 S | 70.33 W |
| La Spezia | 62 | 44.07 N | 9.50 E |
| La Spezia □[4] | 62 | 44.15 N | 9.42 E |
| Las Piedras, P.R. | 240m | 18.11 N | 65.52 W |
| Las Piedras, Ur. | 258 | 34.44 S | 56.13 W |
| Las Piedras, Río de ≃ | 248 | 12.30 S | 69.14 W |
| Las Piñas, Pil. | 269f | 14.29 N | 120.59 E |
| Las Piñas, P.R. | 240m | 18.15 N | 65.55 W |
| Las Plumas | 254 | 43.43 S | 67.15 W |
| Lasqueti Island I | 182 | 49.29 N | 124.17 W |
| Las Raices Creek ≃ | 196 | 28.09 N | 99.02 W |
| Las Ratas, Cerro ∧ | 234 | 18.37 N | 103.37 W |
| Las Rejas | 286e | 33.28 S | 70.44 W |
| Las Rosas, Arg. | 252 | 32.28 S | 61.34 W |
| Las Rosas, Chile | 286e | 33.35 S | 70.37 W |
| Las Rosas, Méx. | 232 | 16.24 N | 92.23 W |
| Las Rozas de Madrid | 266a | 40.29 N | 3.52 W |
| Las Sales, Canal ≡ | 286a | 19.26 N | 99.03 W |
| Lassan | 54 | 53.57 N | 13.50 E |
| Lassance | 255 | 17.54 S | 44.34 W |
| Lassater | 222 | 32.49 N | 94.30 W |
| Lassay | 32 | 48.26 N | 0.30 W |
| Lassee | 61 | 48.13 N | 16.49 E |
| Lassellsville | 210 | 43.03 N | 74.36 W |
| Lassen Peak ∧[1] | 204 | 40.29 N | 121.31 W |
| Lassen Volcanic National Park ♦ | 204 | 40.30 N | 121.19 W |
| Lassigny | 50 | 49.35 N | 2.51 E |
| Lassnitz ≃ | 61 | 46.46 N | 15.32 E |
| Lassnitzhöhe | 61 | 47.05 N | 15.35 E |
| Lasso ∧[2] | 174n | 15.02 N | 145.38 E |
| L'Assomption | 206 | 45.50 N | 73.25 W |
| L'Assomption □[6] | 206 | 45.48 N | 73.35 W |
| L'Assomption ≃ | 206 | 45.43 N | 73.29 W |
| Lasswade | 46 | 55.53 N | 3.08 W |
| Lassy | 261 | 49.06 N | 2.27 E |
| Las Tablas | 246 | 7.46 N | 80.17 W |
| Lastarrio, Parque Nacional ♦ | 254 | 44.50 S | 72.05 W |
| Las Tinajas | 252 | 27.27 S | 62.55 W |
| Last Mountain ∧ | 184 | 51.07 N | 104.54 W |
| Last Mountain Lake ⊜ | 184 | 51.05 N | 105.10 W |
| Las Toscas | 252 | 28.21 S | 59.17 W |
| Lastoursville | 152 | 0.49 S | 12.42 E |
| Lastovo, Otok I | 36 | 42.45 N | 16.53 E |
| Lastovski Kanal ʊ | 36 | 42.50 N | 16.59 E |
| Lastra a Signa | 66 | 43.46 N | 11.06 E |
| Las Trampas Creek ≃ | 282 | 37.53 N | 122.03 W |
| Las Trampas Peak ∧ | 282 | 37.50 N | 122.03 W |
| Las Trampas Regional Park ♦ | 282 | 37.50 N | 122.03 W |
| Las Trampas Ridge ∧ | 282 | 37.49 N | 122.02 W |
| Lästringe | 40 | 58.54 N | 17.18 E |
| Las Truchas | 234 | 17.55 N | 102.12 W |
| Lastrup | 52 | 52.48 N | 7.52 E |
| Las Tunas | 240p | 20.58 N | 76.57 W |
| Las Tunas □[4] | 240p | 21.00 N | 77.00 W |
| Las Tunas, Arroyo ≃ | 288 | 34.27 S | 58.41 W |
| Las Tunas, Punta ≻ | 240m | 18.30 N | 66.38 W |
| Las Tunas Beach ♦ | 280 | 34.02 N | 118.36 W |
| Las Tunas Grandes, Laguna ⊜ | 252 | 35.58 S | 62.25 W |
| La Suze | 32 | 47.54 N | 0.02 E |
| Las Varas, Méx. | 232 | 29.29 N | 108.01 W |
| Las Varas, Méx. | 234 | 21.10 N | 105.10 W |
| Las Varillas | 252 | 31.52 S | 62.43 W |
| Las Vegas, P.R. | 240m | 18.11 N | 67.02 W |
| Las Vegas, Nv., U.S. | 204 | 36.10 N | 115.08 W |
| Las Vegas, N.M., U.S. | 200 | 35.36 N | 105.13 W |
| Las Vegas, Ven. | 246 | 9.35 N | 68.37 W |
| Las Vigas de Ramirez | 234 | 19.38 N | 97.05 W |
| La Tabatière | 186 | 50.50 N | 58.58 W |
| Latacunga | 246 | 0.56 S | 78.37 W |
| Latady Island I | 9 | 70.45 S | 74.35 W |
| La Tagua | 246 | 0.03 S | 74.40 W |
| Latakia → Al-Lādhiqīyah | 130 | 35.31 N | 35.47 E |
| Latakia □[9] | 130 | 35.20 N | 36.00 E |
| Latambar | 123 | 33.07 N | 70.52 E |
| Lata Mountain ∧ | 174y | 14.14 S | 169.29 W |
| La Tapona | 234 | 22.48 N | 100.38 W |
| Låtefossen ⌊ | 26 | 59.57 N | 6.37 E |
| Latehar | 124 | 23.45 N | 84.30 E |
| Lately Common | 262 | 53.29 N | 2.30 W |
| Latera | 66 | 42.38 N | 11.50 E |
| Laterina | 66 | 43.31 N | 11.43 E |
| Laterns | 58 | 47.16 N | 9.43 E |
| Laterrière | 186 | 48.18 N | 71.06 W |
| Laterza | 68 | 40.37 N | 16.48 E |
| La Teste-de-Buch | 32 | 44.38 N | 1.09 W |
| La Tetilla, Cerro ∧ | 234 | 20.21 N | 104.59 W |
| Latexo | 222 | 31.24 N | 95.29 W |
| Latgale □[9] | 76 | 56.20 N | 27.10 E |
| Latham, Austl. | 162 | 29.45 S | 116.26 E |
| Latham, Il., U.S. | 219 | 39.58 N | 89.10 W |
| Latham, N.Y., U.S. | 210 | 42.44 N | 73.45 W |
| Latham, Oh., U.S. | 218 | 39.06 N | 83.15 W |
| Lathan ≃ | 50 | 47.27 N | 0.08 E |
| Lathen | 52 | 52.52 N | 7.19 E |
| Latheron | 46 | 58.17 N | 3.23 W |
| Lāthi | 120 | 21.43 N | 71.23 E |
| Lathrop, Ca., U.S. | 226 | 37.49 N | 121.16 W |
| Lathrop, Mo., U.S. | 194 | 39.32 N | 94.19 W |
| Lathrup Village | 281 | 42.29 N | 83.14 W |
| La Thuile | 62 | 45.43 N | 6.57 E |
| La Tiama | 286c | 10.26 N | 66.46 W |
| Latian, Mount ∧ | 116 | 6.13 N | 125.30 E |
| Latiano | 68 | 40.33 N | 17.43 E |
| Latimer, Eng., U.K. | 260 | 51.41 N | 0.33 W |
| Latimer, Ia., U.S. | 190 | 42.45 N | 93.22 W |
| Latina | 66 | 41.28 N | 12.52 E |
| Latina □[4] | 66 | 41.27 N | 13.06 E |
| Latiri | 140 | 9.10 N | 25.43 E |
| Latisana | 64 | 45.47 N | 13.00 E |
| Latjuga | 24 | 64.16 N | 48.46 E |
| Latnaja | 78 | 51.43 N | 38.55 E |
| La Toma | 252 | 33.03 S | 65.37 W |
| Laton | 226 | 36.26 N | 119.41 W |
| Latonovo | 83 | 47.29 N | 38.38 E |
| Latornell ≃ | 182 | 54.58 N | 118.00 W |
| La Torrecilla ∧ | 240m | 18.12 N | 66.20 W |
| La Tortuga, Isla I | 246 | 10.56 N | 65.20 W |
| Latorytsya ≃ | 30 | 48.28 N | 21.50 E |
| Latouche Island I | 180 | 60.00 N | 147.55 W |
| Latouche Treville, Cape ≻ | 162 | 18.27 S | 121.49 E |
| La Tour | 62 | 43.57 N | 7.11 E |
| La Tour-d'Aigues | 62 | 43.44 N | 5.33 E |
| La Tour-d'Auvergne | 32 | 45.32 N | 2.41 E |
| La Tour-de-Peilz | 58 | 46.27 N | 6.49 E |
| La Tour-du-Pin | 62 | 45.34 N | 5.27 E |
| La Tourette Park ♦ | 276 | 40.35 N | 74.08 W |
| Latowicz | 30 | 52.02 N | 21.48 E |
| Lat Phrao, Khlong ≡ | 269a | 13.48 N | 100.35 E |
| La Tremblade | 32 | 45.46 N | 1.08 W |
| La Trimouille | 32 | 46.28 N | 1.02 E |
| La Trinidad, Arg. | 252 | 27.24 S | 65.31 W |
| La Trinidad, Nic. | 236 | 12.58 N | 86.14 W |
| La Trinidad, Pil. | 116 | 16.28 N | 120.35 E |
| La Trinidad, Ven. | 286c | 10.27 N | 66.52 W |
| La Trinidad de Orichuna | 246 | 7.07 N | 69.45 W |
| La Trinitaria | 232 | 16.07 N | 92.03 W |
| La Trinité | 240e | 14.44 N | 60.58 W |
| Latrobe, Austl. | 166 | 41.14 S | 146.24 E |
| Latrobe, Pa., U.S. | 214 | 40.19 N | 79.22 W |
| La Trobe ≃ | 169 | 38.10 S | 146.32 E |
| Latrobe University ʋ[2] | 274b | 37.43 S | 145.03 E |
| La Tronche | 62 | 45.12 N | 5.44 E |
| Latronico | 68 | 40.05 N | 16.01 E |
| Latsch → Laces | 64 | 46.37 N | 10.52 E |
| Latta | 192 | 34.20 N | 79.25 W |
| Lattarico | 68 | 39.28 N | 16.08 E |
| Lattasburg | 214 | 40.53 N | 82.06 W |
| Latterbach | 58 | 46.40 N | 7.35 E |
| Lattingtown | 276 | 40.54 N | 73.36 W |
| Latty | 216 | 41.05 N | 84.35 W |
| La Tuilerie | 261 | 48.34 N | 2.08 E |
| La Tuilière | 62 | 44.11 N | 5.32 E |
| Latuna | 112 | 8.23 S | 124.06 E |
| La Tuque | 176 | 47.26 N | 72.47 W |
| Lātūr | 122 | 18.24 N | 76.35 E |
| La Turbie | 62 | 43.45 N | 7.24 E |
| Latvia (Latvija) □[1], Europe | 22 | 57.00 N | 25.00 E |
| Latvia (Latvija) □[1], Europe | 76 | 57.00 N | 25.00 E |
| Lau, Nig. | 146 | 9.13 N | 11.17 E |
| Lau, Pap. N. Gui. | 164 | 5.50 S | 151.20 E |
| Laubach | 56 | 50.33 N | 8.59 E |
| Lau Basin ⊹[1] | 14 | 20.00 S | 177.00 W |
| Laubusch | 54 | 51.28 N | 14.10 E |
| Laubuseschbach | 56 | 50.24 N | 8.20 E |
| Lauca ≃ | 248 | 19.10 S | 68.10 W |
| Lauca, Parque Nacional ♦ | 248 | 18.20 S | 69.15 W |
| Laucha | 54 | 51.13 N | 11.41 E |
| Lauchhammer | 54 | 51.30 N | 13.47 E |
| Lauchheim | 56 | 48.52 N | 10.14 E |
| Lauchringen | 58 | 47.38 N | 8.19 E |
| Lauda-Königshofen | 56 | 49.34 N | 9.41 E |
| Lauder | 46 | 55.43 N | 2.45 W |
| Lauderdale | 194 | 32.31 N | 88.30 W |
| Lauderdale V | 46 | 55.43 N | 2.42 W |
| Lauderdale-by-the-Sea | 220 | 26.12 N | 80.07 W |
| Lauderdale Lakes | 220 | 26.09 N | 80.12 W |
| Lauderhill | 220 | 26.08 N | 80.12 W |
| Laudun | 62 | 44.06 N | 4.40 E |
| Lauenbrück | 52 | 53.12 N | 9.33 E |
| Lauenburg, Dtsch. | 52 | 53.22 N | 10.33 E |
| Lauenburg → Lębork, Pol. | 30 | 54.33 N | 17.44 E |
| Lauenförde | 52 | 51.39 N | 9.23 E |
| Lauenstein, Dtsch. | 52 | 52.04 N | 9.33 E |
| Lauenstein, Dtsch. | 54 | 50.47 N | 13.49 E |
| Lauenstein, Dtsch. | 54 | 50.31 N | 11.20 E |
| Lauer ≃ | 56 | 50.18 N | 10.10 E |
| Lauerzer See ⊜ | 58 | 47.02 N | 8.36 E |
| Lauf an der Pegnitz | 60 | 49.30 N | 11.17 E |
| Läufelfingen | 58 | 47.24 N | 7.51 E |
| Laufen, Dtsch. | 64 | 47.57 N | 12.56 E |
| Laufen, Schw. | 58 | 47.25 N | 7.30 E |
| Laufenburg (Baden), Dtsch. | 58 | 47.35 N | 8.04 E |
| Laufenburg (Baden), Schw. | 58 | 47.33 N | 8.04 E |
| Laufersfort, Schloss ⊥ | 263 | 51.25 N | 6.37 E |
| Lauffen am Neckar | 56 | 49.05 N | 9.10 E |
| Laugharne | 42 | 51.47 N | 4.28 W |
| Laughery Creek ≃ | 218 | 39.02 N | 84.53 W |
| Laughlen, Mount ∧ | 162 | 23.23 S | 134.23 E |
| Laughlin Air Force Base ■ | 196 | 29.22 N | 100.47 W |
| Laughlin Peak ∧ | 196 | 36.38 N | 104.12 W |
| Laughlintown | 214 | 40.13 N | 79.12 W |
| Lau Group II | 175g | 18.20 S | 178.30 W |
| Lauingen | 56 | 48.34 N | 10.25 E |
| Lauis → Lugano | 58 | 46.01 N | 8.58 E |
| Laukaa | 26 | 62.25 N | 25.57 E |
| Laukuva | 76 | 55.37 N | 22.14 E |
| Laul'u | 89 | 45.46 N | 135.16 E |
| Laun | 110 | 10.07 N | 98.46 E |
| Launceston, Austl. | 166 | 41.26 S | 147.08 E |
| Launceston, Eng., U.K. | 42 | 50.38 N | 4.21 W |
| Laundi, Tanjung ≻ | 115b | 9.28 S | 120.12 E |
| Laune ≃ | 48 | 52.07 N | 9.48 W |
| Launglon | 110 | 13.58 N | 98.07 E |
| Laungowāl | 123 | 30.13 N | 75.41 E |
| La Unión, Chile | 254 | 40.17 S | 73.05 W |
| La Unión, Col. | 246 | 1.36 N | 77.09 W |
| La Unión, El Sal. | 236 | 13.20 N | 87.51 W |
| La Unión, Esp. | 34 | 37.37 N | 0.52 W |
| La Unión, Méx. | 234 | 17.58 N | 101.49 W |
| La Unión, Perú | 248 | 9.46 S | 76.48 W |
| La Unión, Perú | 248 | 5.24 S | 80.45 W |
| La Union, Pil. | 116 | 6.42 N | 126.05 E |
| La Union, N.M., U.S. | 200 | 31.57 N | 106.39 W |
| La Unión, Ven. | 246 | 8.13 N | 67.46 W |
| La Unión, Ven. | 286c | 10.25 N | 66.48 W |
| La Union □[4] | 116 | 16.35 N | 120.25 E |
| Launois-sur-Vence | 56 | 49.39 N | 4.32 E |
| Launsdorf | 61 | 46.46 N | 14.27 E |
| Laupen | 58 | 46.54 N | 7.14 E |
| Laupendahl ⊕[8] | 263 | 51.21 N | 6.56 E |
| Laupheim | 58 | 48.14 N | 9.52 E |
| Laur | 116 | 15.35 N | 121.11 E |
| Laura, Austl. | 164 | 15.34 S | 144.28 E |
| Laura, Oh., U.S. | 218 | 39.59 N | 84.24 W |
| La Urbana | 246 | 7.08 N | 66.56 W |
| Laureana di Borrello | 68 | 38.30 N | 16.05 E |
| Laurel, De., U.S. | 208 | 38.33 N | 75.34 W |
| Laurel, Fl., U.S. | 220 | 27.07 N | 82.27 W |
| Laurel, In., U.S. | 218 | 39.30 N | 85.11 W |
| Laurel, Md., U.S. | 208 | 39.05 N | 76.50 W |
| Laurel, Ms., U.S. | 194 | 31.41 N | 89.07 W |
| Laurel, Mt., U.S. | 202 | 45.40 N | 108.46 W |
| Laurel, Ne., U.S. | 198 | 42.25 N | 97.05 W |
| Laurel, Va., U.S. | 208 | 37.38 N | 77.30 W |
| Laurel, Wa., U.S. | 224 | 45.57 N | 121.23 W |
| Laurel ≃ | 192 | 36.57 N | 84.18 W |
| Laurel, Mount ∧[2] | 285 | 39.56 N | 74.53 W |
| Laurel Bay | 192 | 32.33 N | 80.44 W |
| Laureldale, N.J., U.S. | 208 | 39.29 N | 74.41 W |
| Laureldale, Pa., U.S. | 208 | 40.23 N | 75.55 W |
| Laureles | 252 | 31.22 S | 55.51 W |
| Laureles, Isla de los I | 258 | 33.45 S | 59.23 W |
| Laurel Gardens | 279b | 40.31 N | 80.01 W |
| Laurel Hill, Austl. | 171b | 35.37 S | 148.05 E |
| Laurel Hill, N.C., U.S. | 192 | 34.48 N | 79.32 W |
| Laurel Hill ∧ | 214 | 40.15 N | 79.05 W |
| Laurel Hollow | 276 | 40.52 N | 73.28 W |
| Laurel Reservoir ⊜[1] | 276 | 41.10 N | 73.33 W |
| Laurel Ridge State Park ♦ | 188 | 39.58 N | 79.23 W |
| Laurel River Lake ⊜[1] | 192 | 36.55 N | 84.15 W |
| Laurel Run | 210 | 41.13 N | 75.51 W |
| Laurel Run ≃ | 208 | 40.20 N | 77.20 W |
| Laurel Springs | 285 | 39.49 N | 75.00 W |
| Laurelton | 210 | 40.52 N | 77.11 W |
| Laurelville, Oh., U.S. | 188 | 39.28 N | 82.44 W |
| Laurelville, Pa., U.S. | 214 | 40.09 N | 79.29 W |
| Laurenburg | 56 | 50.20 N | 7.54 E |
| Laurence Harbor | 276 | 40.27 N | 74.14 W |
| Laurencekirk | 46 | 56.50 N | 2.29 W |
| Laurens, Ia., U.S. | 198 | 42.50 N | 94.51 W |
| Laurens, N.Y., U.S. | 210 | 42.32 N | 75.06 W |
| Laurens, S.C., U.S. | 192 | 34.29 N | 82.00 W |
| Laurentides | 206 | 45.51 N | 73.46 W |
| Laurentides, Les ⋀[1] | 176 | 48.00 N | 71.00 W |
| Laurentides, Parc Provincial des ♦ | 186 | 47.40 N | 71.30 W |
| Laurenzana | 68 | 40.28 N | 15.58 E |
| Lauria | 68 | 40.02 N | 15.50 E |
| Lau Ridge ⊹[3] | 14 | 21.00 S | 178.30 W |
| Laurie Island I | 9 | 60.45 S | 44.35 W |
| Laurie Lake ⊜ | 184 | 56.34 N | 101.54 W |
| Laurier, Mb., Can. | 184 | 50.54 N | 99.33 W |
| Laurier, P.Q., Can. | 206 | 46.32 N | 71.38 W |
| Laurière | 32 | 46.05 N | 1.28 E |
| Laurierville | 206 | 46.18 N | 71.39 W |
| Laurinburg | 192 | 34.46 N | 79.27 W |
| Laurino | 68 | 40.20 N | 15.20 E |
| Laurito | 68 | 40.10 N | 15.24 E |
| Lauritsala | 26 | 61.04 N | 28.16 E |
| Lauritzen Bay C | 9 | 69.05 S | 156.50 E |
| Laurium | 190 | 47.14 N | 88.26 W |
| Lauriya Nandangarh | 124 | 26.59 N | 84.24 E |
| Lauro, Monte ∧ | 70 | 37.07 N | 14.49 E |
| Laurys Station | 208 | 40.43 N | 75.32 W |
| Lausanne | 58 | 46.31 N | 6.38 E |
| Lauscha | 54 | 50.28 N | 11.10 E |
| Laussig, Dtsch. | 54 | 51.33 N | 12.38 E |
| Laussig, Dtsch. | 54 | 51.33 N | 12.38 E |
| Laut | 86 | 59.18 N | 66.02 E |
| Laut, Pulau I, Indon. | 112 | 3.40 S | 116.10 E |
| Laut, Pulau I, Indon. | 112 | 4.43 N | 107.59 E |
| Laut, Selat ʊ | 112 | 3.25 S | 116.03 E |
| Lauta | 54 | 51.27 N | 14.04 E |
| Lautaro | 252 | 38.31 S | 72.27 W |
| Lautaro, Volcán ∧[1] | 254 | 49.00 S | 73.32 W |
| Lautem | 112 | 8.22 S | 126.54 E |
| Lautenbach | 58 | 47.57 N | 7.09 E |
| Lautenthal | 52 | 51.52 N | 10.17 E |
| Lauter ≃, Dtsch. | 56 | 49.39 N | 7.35 E |
| Lauter ≃, Europe | 56 | 48.58 N | 8.11 E |
| Lauterach | 58 | 47.29 N | 9.44 E |
| Lauterbach, Dtsch. | 56 | 50.38 N | 9.24 E |
| Lauterbach, Dtsch. | 58 | 48.14 N | 8.20 E |
| Lauterbourg | 56 | 48.59 N | 8.11 E |
| Lauterbrunnen | 58 | 46.36 N | 7.55 E |
| Lauterecken | 56 | 49.39 N | 7.35 E |
| Lauterhofen | 60 | 49.22 N | 11.37 E |
| Lauter [Sachsen] | 54 | 50.33 N | 12.44 E |
| Lauterstein | 56 | 48.42 N | 9.53 E |
| Laut Kecil, Kepulauan II | 112 | 4.50 S | 115.45 E |
| Lautoka | 175g | 17.37 S | 177.27 E |
| Lauttakylä → Huittinen | 26 | 61.11 N | 22.42 E |
| Laut Tawar, Danau ⊜ | 114 | 4.38 N | 96.54 E |
| Lauwe | 50 | 50.48 N | 3.11 E |
| Lauwerszee C | 52 | 53.20 N | 6.12 E |
| Lauzerte | 32 | 44.15 N | 1.08 E |
| Lauzon | 206 | 46.50 N | 71.10 W |
| Lauzun | 32 | 44.38 N | 0.28 E |
| Lava (Łyna) ≃ | 76 | 54.37 N | 21.14 E |
| Lava, Nosy I | 157b | 14.33 S | 47.36 E |
| Lava Beds National Monument ♦ | 204 | 41.42 N | 121.30 W |
| Lavaca □[6] | 222 | 29.22 N | 96.55 W |
| Lavaca ≃ | 196 | 28.50 N | 96.36 W |
| Lavaca Bay C | 196 | 28.35 N | 96.35 W |
| La Vacherie | 62 | 44.53 N | 5.11 E |
| Lavagh More ∧ | 48 | 54.45 N | 8.05 W |
| Lavagna | 62 | 44.18 N | 9.20 E |
| Lavagna ≃ | 62 | 44.21 N | 9.20 E |
| Lava Hot Springs | 202 | 42.37 N | 112.00 W |
| Lavaisse | 252 | 33.49 S | 65.25 W |
| Laval, P.Q., Can. | 206 | 45.35 N | 73.45 W |
| Laval, Fr. | 32 | 48.04 N | 0.46 W |
| Laval-des-Rapides ⊕[8] | 275a | 45.33 N | 73.42 W |
| La Valette → Valletta | 36 | 35.54 N | 14.31 E |
| La Valette-du-Var | 62 | 43.08 N | 5.59 E |
| La Vall d'Uixo | 34 | 39.49 N | 0.14 W |
| Lavalle, Arg. | 252 | 29.01 S | 59.11 W |
| Lavalle, Arg. | 252 | 28.12 S | 65.08 W |
| Lavalleja → Minas | 252 | 34.23 S | 55.14 W |
| Lavallette | 208 | 39.58 N | 74.04 W |
| La Valley | 200 | 37.06 N | 105.20 W |
| Laval-Ouest ⊕[8] | 275a | 45.33 N | 73.52 W |
| Lavaltrie | 206 | 45.53 N | 73.17 W |
| Lavamünd | 61 | 46.39 N | 14.56 E |
| Lāvān, Jazīreh-ye I | 128 | 26.48 N | 53.15 E |
| Lavan, Naḥal V | 132 | 30.57 N | 34.21 E |
| Lavanono | 157b | 25.24 S | 44.55 E |
| Lavant ≃ | 61 | 46.38 N | 14.57 E |
| Lavapié, Punta ≻ | 252 | 37.09 S | 73.35 W |
| Lávara | 38 | 41.16 N | 26.22 E |
| Lavaraty | 157b | 23.16 S | 46.59 E |
| Lavardac | 32 | 44.11 N | 0.18 E |
| Lavarone | 64 | 45.56 N | 11.15 E |
| Lavassaare | 76 | 58.31 N | 24.22 E |
| Lava-Tudo ≃ | 252 | 28.26 S | 50.25 W |
| Laveaga Peak ∧ | 226 | 36.53 N | 121.11 W |
| La Vecilla de Curueño | 34 | 42.51 N | 5.24 W |
| La Vega | 238 | 19.13 N | 70.31 W |
| La Vega ⊕[8] | 286c | 10.28 N | 66.57 W |
| Lavela | 24 | 63.38 N | 45.31 E |
| La Vela, Cabo de ≻ | 246 | 12.15 N | 72.11 W |
| La Vela de Coro | 246 | 11.27 N | 69.34 W |
| Lavelanet | 32 | 42.56 N | 1.51 E |
| Lavelle | 208 | 40.46 N | 76.22 W |
| Lavello | 68 | 41.03 N | 15.48 E |
| Laven | 41 | 56.07 N | 9.43 E |
| La Venada | 196 | 25.50 N | 97.30 W |
| Lavendon | 42 | 52.11 N | 0.40 W |
| Lavenham | 42 | 52.06 N | 0.47 E |
| Laveno | 58 | 45.55 N | 8.37 E |
| Lavenone | 64 | 45.44 N | 10.26 E |
| La Venta ≃ | 234 | 16.59 N | 93.46 W |
| La Venta ⊥ | 234 | 18.08 N | 94.03 W |
| Laventie | 50 | 50.38 N | 2.46 E |
| La Ventura | 232 | 24.38 N | 100.54 W |
| Laver ≃ | 44 | 54.08 N | 1.30 W |
| Lavéra | 62 | 43.23 N | 5.02 E |
| La Vera ⊕[1] | 34 | 40.20 N | 5.30 W |
| La Verde, Arg. | 252 | 27.08 S | 59.23 W |
| La Verde, Arg. | 258 | 34.44 S | 59.16 W |
| Laverdière, Lac ⊜ | 206 | 46.50 N | 74.28 W |
| L'averdy, Cape ≻ | 175e | 5.33 S | 155.04 E |
| La Vérendrye, Réserve ♦ | 190 | 47.30 N | 77.30 W |
| La Vergne | 194 | 36.00 N | 86.34 W |
| La Verna ʋ[1] | 66 | 43.42 N | 11.54 E |
| La Verne, Ca., U.S. | 280 | 34.06 N | 117.46 W |
| Laverne, Ok., U.S. | 196 | 36.42 N | 99.53 W |
| La Vernia | 196 | 29.21 N | 98.07 W |
| Laverock | 285 | 40.05 N | 75.11 W |
| La Verpillière | 62 | 45.38 N | 5.09 E |
| La Verrière | 261 | 48.45 N | 1.57 E |
| Lavers Hill | 169 | 38.40 S | 143.24 E |
| Laverton, Austl. | 162 | 28.38 S | 122.25 E |
| Laverton, Austl. | 169 | 37.52 S | 144.45 E |
| Laverton Royal Australian Air Force Base ■ | 169 | 37.52 S | 144.43 E |
| La Veta | 200 | 37.30 N | 105.00 W |
| Lavezares | 116 | 12.32 N | 124.20 E |
| Lavezzi, Îles II | 71 | 41.20 N | 9.15 E |
| Lavezzola | 66 | 44.34 N | 11.52 E |
| Lavia | 26 | 61.36 N | 22.36 E |
| Laviano | 68 | 40.47 N | 15.18 E |
| Lavic Lake ⊜ | 204 | 34.40 N | 116.21 W |
| La Victoria, Perú | 286d | 12.04 S | 77.02 W |
| La Victoria, Ven. | 246 | 10.14 N | 67.20 W |
| Lavieille, Lake ⊜ | 190 | 45.51 N | 78.14 W |
| Lavik | 26 | 61.06 N | 5.30 E |
| La Vila Joiosa | 34 | 38.30 N | 0.14 W |
| La Villa | 64 | 46.36 N | 11.54 E |
| La Villa ≃ | 236 | 7.59 N | 80.23 W |
| La Ville-du-Bois | 261 | 48.40 N | 2.16 E |
| La Villeneuve-Saint-Martin | 261 | 49.04 N | 1.58 E |
| Lavillette | 186 | 47.16 N | 65.18 W |
| Lavin | 58 | 46.46 N | 10.06 E |
| La Viña, Arg. | 252 | 25.27 S | 65.35 W |
| Lavina, Mt., U.S. | 202 | 46.17 N | 108.56 W |
| Lavinio Lido di Enea | 66 | 41.30 N | 12.05 E |
| Laviolette, Lac ⊜ | 206 | 46.51 N | 73.58 W |
| La Virginia | 246 | 4.54 N | 75.53 W |
| Lavis | 64 | 46.08 N | 11.07 E |
| La Vista | 198 | 41.11 N | 96.01 W |
| Lavon | 222 | 33.02 N | 96.26 W |
| Lavonia | 192 | 34.26 N | 83.06 W |
| Lavon Lake ⊜[1] | 222 | 33.05 N | 96.28 W |
| Lavougba | 152 | 5.46 N | 23.21 E |
| La Voulte-sur-Rhône | 62 | 44.48 N | 4.47 E |
| Lavoûte-sur-Loire | 62 | 45.07 N | 3.54 E |
| Lavoutte, Anse C | 241f | 14.06 N | 60.56 W |
| Lavradia | 266c | 38.40 N | 9.03 W |
| Lavras | 256 | 21.14 S | 45.00 W |
| Lavras ≃ | 287a | 23.00 S | 43.33 W |
| Lavras da Mangabeira | 250 | 6.45 S | 38.57 W |
| Lavras do Sul | 252 | 30.49 S | 53.55 W |
| Lavrentija | 180 | 65.35 N | 171.00 W |
| Lavrentija, zaliv C | 180 | 65.40 N | 171.15 W |
| Lavrinhas | 256 | 22.35 S | 44.54 W |
| Lávrion | 38 | 37.44 N | 24.04 E |
| Lavumisa | 158 | 27.19 S | 31.54 E |
| Lavushi Manda National Park ♦ | 154 | 12.20 S | 30.50 E |
| Lawa | 116 | 6.12 N | 125.41 E |
| Lawai | 229b | 21.55 N | 159.30 W |
| Lawang | 115a | 7.49 S | 112.42 E |
| La Wantzenau | 58 | 48.40 N | 7.50 E |
| La Ward | 222 | 28.51 N | 96.28 W |
| Lawas | 112 | 4.51 N | 115.24 E |
| Lawatu | 112 | 2.53 S | 120.18 E |
| Lawdar | 144 | 13.53 N | 45.52 E |
| Lawele | 112 | 5.13 S | 122.57 E |
| Lawers, Ben ∧ | 46 | 56.34 N | 4.13 W |
| Laweueng | 114 | 5.31 N | 95.52 E |
| Lawford Lake ⊜ | 184 | 54.30 N | 96.43 W |
| Lawgi | 166 | 24.34 S | 150.39 E |
| Lawin | 114 | 5.18 N | 101.04 E |
| Lawin, Pulau I | 164 | 1.31 S | 128.44 E |
| Lawit, Gunong ∧ | 114 | 5.25 N | 102.35 E |
| Lawksawk | 110 | 21.15 N | 96.52 E |
| Lawler | 190 | 43.04 N | 92.09 W |
| Lawlor, Mount ∧ | 280 | 34.16 N | 118.06 W |
| Lawn, Nf., Can. | 186 | 46.57 N | 55.32 W |
| Lawn, Pa., U.S. | 208 | 40.13 N | 76.32 W |
| Lawn, Tx., U.S. | 196 | 32.08 N | 99.49 W |
| Lawn Bay C | 186 | 46.53 N | 55.35 W |
| Lawndale, Ca., U.S. | 228 | 33.53 N | 118.21 W |
| Lawndale, Il., U.S. | 219 | 40.13 N | 89.17 W |
| Lawndale, N.C., U.S. | 192 | 35.24 N | 81.33 W |
| Lawndale ⊕[8], Il., U.S. | 278 | 41.51 N | 87.43 W |
| Lawndale ⊕[8], Pa., U.S. | 285 | 40.03 N | 75.05 W |
| Lawnes Creek ≃ | 208 | 37.08 N | 76.40 W |
| Lawn Hill | 166 | 18.35 S | 138.35 E |
| Lawn Hill Creek ≃ | 166 | 18.03 S | 139.09 E |
| Lawn Hill National Park ♦ | 166 | 18.45 S | 138.27 E |
| Lawnside | 285 | 39.51 N | 75.01 W |
| Lawowa | 112 | 4.26 S | 122.56 E |
| Lawqah | 128 | 29.49 N | 42.45 E |
| Lawra | 150 | 10.39 N | 2.52 W |
| Lawrence, N.Z. | 172 | 45.55 S | 169.41 E |
| Lawrence, In., U.S. | 218 | 39.50 N | 86.01 W |
| Lawrence, Ks., U.S. | 198 | 38.58 N | 95.14 W |
| Lawrence, Ma., U.S. | 207 | 42.42 N | 71.09 W |
| Lawrence, Mi., U.S. | 216 | 42.13 N | 86.03 W |
| Lawrence, Ne., U.S. | 198 | 40.17 N | 98.15 W |
| Lawrence, N.Y., U.S. | 276 | 40.36 N | 73.43 W |
| Lawrence, Pa., U.S. | 279b | 40.18 N | 80.09 W |
| Lawrence, Tx., U.S. | 222 | 32.45 N | 96.21 W |
| Lawrence □[6], In., U.S. | 218 | 38.52 N | 86.29 W |
| Lawrence □[6], Pa., U.S. | 214 | 41.00 N | 80.20 W |
| Lawrence, Lake ⊜ | 224 | 46.51 N | 122.34 W |
| Lawrence Brook ≃ | 276 | 40.29 N | 74.24 W |
| Lawrenceburg, In., U.S. | 218 | 39.05 N | 84.51 W |
| Lawrenceburg, Ky., U.S. | 218 | 38.02 N | 84.54 W |
| Lawrenceburg, Tn., U.S. | 194 | 35.14 N | 87.20 W |
| Lawrence Fork ≃ | 198 | 41.36 N | 103.14 W |
| Lawrence Institute of Technology ʋ[2] | 281 | 42.28 N | 83.15 W |
| Lawrence Marsh ≋ | 276 | 40.36 N | 73.42 W |
| Lawrence Municipal Airport ⊠ | 283 | 42.43 N | 71.07 W |
| Lawrence Park | 214 | 42.09 N | 80.01 W |
| Lawrencepur | 123 | 33.50 N | 72.30 E |
| Lawrenceville, Il., U.S. | 194 | 38.43 N | 87.40 W |
| Lawrenceville, N.J., U.S. | 208 | 40.17 N | 74.43 W |
| Lawrenceville, Pa., U.S. | 210 | 42.00 N | 77.08 W |
| Lawrenceville, Va., U.S. | 192 | 36.45 N | 77.50 W |
| Lawrenceville ⊕[8] | 279b | 40.28 N | 79.57 W |
| Lawson, Austl. | 170 | 33.43 S | 150.26 E |
| Lawson, Mo., U.S. | 194 | 39.26 N | 94.12 W |
| Lawson Heights | 214 | 40.18 N | 79.23 W |
| Lawsonia | 208 | 37.58 N | 75.50 W |
| Lawsons Creek ≃ | 170 | 32.35 S | 149.43 E |
| Lawtey | 192 | 30.02 N | 82.04 W |
| Lawton, Ky., U.S. | 218 | 38.16 N | 83.13 W |
| Lawton, Mi., U.S. | 216 | 42.10 N | 85.50 W |
| Lawton, N.D., U.S. | 198 | 48.18 N | 98.22 W |
| Lawton, Ok., U.S. | 196 | 34.36 N | 98.23 W |
| Lawton ⊕[8] | 286b | 23.06 N | 82.21 W |
| Lawu, Gunung ∧ | 115a | 7.38 S | 111.11 E |
| Lawyer Creek ≃ | 202 | 46.14 N | 116.01 W |
| Lawyersville | 210 | 42.42 N | 74.30 W |
| Lawz, Jabal al- ∧ | 128 | 28.40 N | 35.18 E |
| Laxå | 40 | 58.59 N | 14.37 E |
| Laxay | 46 | 58.09 N | 6.35 W |
| Laxe | 34 | 43.13 N | 9.00 W |
| Laxenburg | 264b | 48.04 N | 16.21 E |
| Laxenburger Park ♦ | 264b | 48.04 N | 16.22 E |
| Laxey | 44 | 54.14 N | 4.23 W |
| Laxford, Loch C | 46 | 58.23 N | 5.06 W |
| Lax Kw'alaams | 182 | 54.33 N | 130.25 W |
| Laxou | 58 | 48.41 N | 6.09 E |
| Layang Layang | 114 | 1.49 N | 103.29 E |
| Laye ≃ | 62 | 43.54 N | 5.48 E |
| La Yesca | 234 | 21.19 N | 104.02 W |
| Layhill | 208 | 39.05 N | 77.03 W |
| Laylā | 144 | 22.17 N | 46.45 E |
| Lay Lake ⊜[1] | 194 | 33.10 N | 86.35 W |
| Layou | 241h | 13.12 N | 61.17 W |
| Layou ≃ | 240d | 15.23 N | 61.26 W |
| La'youn □[4] | 148 | 27.55 N | 12.15 W |
| Lay-Saint-Christophe | 56 | 48.45 N | 6.12 E |
| Laysan Island I | 14 | 25.50 N | 171.50 W |
| Layton, N.J., U.S. | 210 | 41.13 N | 74.50 W |
| Layton, Ut,. U.S. | 200 | 41.03 N | 111.58 W |
| Laytons Lake ⊜ | 285 | 39.42 N | 75.26 W |
| Laytonville | 204 | 39.41 N | 123.28 W |
| Laytown | 48 | 53.40 N | 6.14 W |
| Laž | 80 | 57.11 N | 49.14 E |
| La Zarca | 232 | 25.50 N | 104.44 W |
| Lazarev | 89 | 52.13 N | 141.32 E |
| Lazarevo | 80 | 56.49 N | 50.15 E |
| Lazarevskoje | 84 | 43.55 N | 39.20 E |
| Lazarivo | 157b | 23.54 S | 44.59 E |
| Lazaro Cárdenas, Méx. | 196 | 25.23 N | 103.10 W |
| Lázaro Cárdenas, Méx. | 232 | 30.33 N | 115.56 W |
| Lázaro Cárdenas, Méx. | 234 | 17.57 N | 102.12 W |
| Lázaro Cárdenas, Presa ⊜[1] | 232 | 25.35 N | 105.02 W |
| Lazdijai | 76 | 54.14 N | 23.31 E |
| Lazha | 102 | 26.26 N | 101.50 E |
| Lazhulong | 120 | 35.08 N | 81.33 E |
| Lazi | 116 | 9.08 N | 123.38 E |
| Lazio □[4] | 66 | 42.00 N | 12.30 E |
| Lazirky | 78 | 50.06 N | 32.39 E |
| Lazise | 64 | 45.30 N | 10.44 E |
| Lazo | 89 | 43.25 N | 133.55 E |
| La Zorra, Quebrada ≃ | 286c | 10.36 N | 67.03 W |
| Lazovskij zapovednik ♦ | 89 | 43.00 N | 133.55 E |
| Lazzaro | 68 | 37.58 N | 15.40 E |
| Lazzate | 266b | 45.40 N | 9.05 E |
| Lea ≃ | 42 | 51.30 N | 0.01 E |
| Léach | 110 | 12.21 N | 103.46 E |
| Leach ≃ | 42 | 51.41 N | 1.39 W |
| Leach Pond ⊜ | 283 | 42.04 N | 71.09 W |
| Leachville | 194 | 35.56 N | 90.15 W |
| Leacock | 208 | 40.05 N | 76.12 W |
| Lead | 198 | 44.21 N | 103.45 W |
| Leadbetter Point ≻ | 224 | 46.38 N | 124.03 W |
| Leadburn | 46 | 55.47 N | 3.14 W |
| Leadenham | 44 | 53.05 N | 0.34 W |
| Leaden Roding | 260 | 51.48 N | 0.19 E |
| Leader | 184 | 50.53 N | 109.31 W |
| Leader Water ≃ | 46 | 55.36 N | 2.41 W |
| Leadgate | 44 | 54.52 N | 1.48 W |
| Lead Hill ∧[2] | 194 | 37.06 N | 92.38 W |
| Leadhills | 44 | 55.25 N | 3.47 W |
| Leadon ≃ | 42 | 51.53 N | 2.16 W |
| Leadore | 202 | 44.40 N | 113.21 W |
| Leadville | 200 | 39.15 N | 106.17 W |
| Leaf ≃, Mn., U.S. | 198 | 46.29 N | 94.53 W |
| Leaf ≃, Ms., U.S. | 194 | 31.00 N | 88.45 W |
| Leaf Lake ⊜ | 184 | 53.02 N | 102.07 W |
| Leaghur, Lake ⊜ | 166 | 33.35 S | 143.04 E |
| League, Slieve ∧ | 48 | 54.39 N | 8.44 W |
| League City | 222 | 29.30 N | 95.05 W |
| Leakesville | 194 | 31.09 N | 88.33 W |
| Leakey | 196 | 29.43 N | 99.45 W |
| Leakin Park ♦ | 284b | 39.18 N | 76.42 W |
| Leak Run ≃ | 279b | 40.27 N | 79.47 W |
| Leaksville | 192 | 36.29 N | 79.53 W |
| Lealman | 220 | 27.49 N | 82.40 W |
| Lealui | 152 | 15.10 S | 23.02 E |
| Leam ≃ | 42 | 52.17 N | 1.14 W |
| Leamington | 214 | 42.03 N | 82.36 W |
| Leamington Spa → Royal Leamington Spa | 42 | 52.18 N | 1.31 W |
| Le'an | 100 | 27.24 N | 115.48 E |
| Leán ≃ | 236 | 15.47 N | 87.20 W |
| Leander Point ≻ | 162 | 29.16 S | 114.56 E |
| Leandro | 250 | 5.59 S | 44.55 W |
| Leandro N. Alem | 252 | 27.36 S | 55.19 W |
| Leane, Lough ⊜ | 48 | 52.05 N | 9.35 W |
| Leannan ≃ | 48 | 55.02 N | 7.38 W |
| Leano, Monte ∧ | 66 | 41.20 N | 13.13 E |
| Learmonth | 162 | 22.15 S | 114.05 E |
| Leary | 192 | 31.29 N | 84.30 W |
| Leaside □[8] | 275b | 43.42 N | 79.22 W |
| Leask | 184 | 53.00 N | 106.45 W |
| Leatherhead | 42 | 51.18 N | 0.20 W |
| Leatherman Peak ∧ | 202 | 44.05 N | 113.44 W |
| Leatherwood Creek ≃ | 218 | 38.49 N | 86.30 W |
| Lea Town | 262 | 53.46 N | 2.48 W |
| Leavenworth, Ks., U.S. | 198 | 39.18 N | 94.55 W |
| Leavenworth, Wa., U.S. | 224 | 47.35 N | 120.39 W |
| Leavesden Aerodrome ⊠ | 260 | 51.42 N | 0.27 W |
| Leavittsburg | 214 | 41.14 N | 80.52 W |
| Leawood | 194 | 37.03 N | 94.31 W |
| Łeba | 30 | 54.47 N | 17.33 E |
| Łeba ≃ | 30 | 54.47 N | 17.33 E |
| Lebach | 56 | 49.24 N | 6.54 E |
| Lebak | 116 | 6.32 N | 124.03 E |
| Lebam | 224 | 46.33 N | 123.32 W |
| Lébamba | 152 | 2.12 S | 11.30 E |
| Leban □[8] | 128 | 38.51 N | 63.34 E |
| Lebango | 152 | 0.22 N | 14.49 E |
| Lebanon, Ct., U.S. | 207 | 41.38 N | 72.13 W |
| Lebanon, Il., U.S. | 219 | 38.36 N | 89.48 W |
| Lebanon, In., U.S. | 218 | 40.02 N | 86.28 W |
| Lebanon, Ks., U.S. | 198 | 39.48 N | 98.33 W |
| Lebanon, Ky., U.S. | 194 | 37.34 N | 85.15 W |
| Lebanon, Mo., U.S. | 194 | 37.40 N | 92.39 W |
| Lebanon, N.H., U.S. | 188 | 43.38 N | 72.15 W |
| Lebanon, N.J., U.S. | 210 | 40.38 N | 74.50 W |
| Lebanon, N.Y., U.S. | 210 | 42.47 N | 75.39 W |
| Lebanon, Oh., U.S. | 218 | 39.26 N | 84.12 W |
| Lebanon, Or., U.S. | 202 | 44.32 N | 122.54 W |
| Lebanon, Pa., U.S. | 208 | 40.20 N | 76.24 W |
| Lebanon, S.D., U.S. | 198 | 45.04 N | 99.46 W |
| Lebanon, Tn., U.S. | 194 | 36.12 N | 86.17 W |
| Lebanon, Va., U.S. | 192 | 36.54 N | 82.04 W |
| Lebanon □[6] | 208 | 40.20 N | 76.25 W |
| Lebanon (Lubnān) □[1], Asia | 118 | 34.00 N | 36.00 E |
| Lebanon (Lubnān) □[1], Asia | 128 | 34.00 N | 36.00 E |
| Lebanon Junction | 194 | 37.50 N | 85.43 W |
| Lebanon Mountains → Lubnān, Jabal ⋀ | 132 | 34.00 N | 36.00 E |
| Lebanon Springs | 210 | 42.29 N | 73.23 W |
| Le Bar-sur-le-Loup | 62 | 43.42 N | 6.59 E |
| Leb'ažje, Kaz. | 86 | 51.28 N | 77.46 E |
| Leb'ažje, Ross. | 80 | 57.25 N | 49.32 E |
| Leb'ažje, Ross. | 86 | 55.16 N | 66.29 E |
| Lebbeke | 50 | 51.00 N | 4.08 E |
| Le Béage | 62 | 44.51 N | 4.07 E |
| Le Beausset | 62 | 43.12 N | 5.48 E |
| Lebec | 228 | 34.50 N | 118.51 W |
| Lebed'an' | 76 | 53.01 N | 39.09 E |
| Lebedevka, Kaz. | 86 | 50.09 N | 54.07 E |
| Lebedevka, Ross. | 80 | 51.06 N | 47.09 E |
| Lebedevka, Ross. | 86 | 56.48 N | 66.57 E |
| Lebedi | 78 | 51.17 N | 37.38 E |
| Lebedino | 80 | 55.14 N | 49.50 E |
| Lebedyn, Ukr. | 78 | 48.59 N | 31.31 E |
| Lebedyn, Ukr. | 78 | 50.36 N | 34.30 E |
| Leben, Oued el V | 148 | 34.37 N | 10.01 E |
| Lebesby | 24 | 70.34 N | 26.59 E |
| Le Bessat | 62 | 45.22 N | 4.31 E |
| Le Bihan Falls ⌊ | 158 | 29.51 S | 28.03 E |
| Le Biot | 58 | 46.16 N | 6.38 E |
| Lebir ≃ | 114 | 5.33 N | 102.12 E |
| Le Blanc | 32 | 46.38 N | 1.04 E |
| Le Blanc-Mesnil | 261 | 48.56 N | 2.28 E |
| Le Bleymard | 62 | 44.29 N | 3.44 E |
| Leblon ⊕[8] | 287a | 22.59 S | 43.13 W |
| Lebo, Ks., U.S. | 198 | 38.25 N | 95.51 W |
| Lebo, Zaïre | 152 | 4.29 N | 23.57 E |
| Le Bois-de-Cise | 50 | 50.05 N | 1.26 E |
| Le Bois-Dieu | 261 | 48.39 N | 1.43 E |
| Le Bois-d'Oingt | 58 | 45.55 N | 4.35 E |
| Lebombo Mountains ⋀[2] | 156 | 25.15 S | 32.00 E |
| Lebongtandai | 112 | 3.01 S | 101.54 E |
| Le Boréon | 62 | 44.07 N | 7.17 E |
| Lębork | 30 | 54.33 N | 17.44 E |
| Le Boulay | 261 | 48.47 N | 1.40 E |
| Le Bourg-d'Oisans | 62 | 45.03 N | 6.02 E |
| Le Bourget | 261 | 48.56 N | 2.26 E |
| Le Bourget-du-Lac | 62 | 45.39 N | 5.52 E |
| Le Brassus | 58 | 46.35 N | 6.13 E |
| Lebrija | 34 | 36.55 N | 6.04 W |
| Lebrija ≃ | 246 | 8.08 N | 73.47 W |
| Le Broc | 62 | 43.49 N | 7.10 E |
| Le Brugeron | 62 | 45.43 N | 3.43 E |
| Łebsko, Jezioro C | 30 | 54.44 N | 17.24 E |
| Lebu | 252 | 37.37 S | 73.39 W |
| Le Bugue | 32 | 44.55 N | 0.56 E |
| Le Buisson de Massoury ≋ | 261 | 48.30 N | 2.43 E |
| Lebus | 54 | 52.25 N | 14.32 E |
| Le Caire → Al-Qāhirah | 142 | 30.03 N | 31.15 E |
| Le Camp-du-Castellet | 62 | 43.15 N | 5.45 E |
| Le Cannet | 62 | 43.34 N | 7.01 E |
| Lecanto | 220 | 28.51 N | 82.29 W |
| Le Cap → Cap-Haïtien, Haï. | 238 | 19.45 N | 72.12 W |
| Le Cap → Cape Town, S. Afr. | 158 | 33.55 S | 18.22 E |
| Le Carbet | 240e | 14.43 N | 61.11 W |
| Le Cateau | 50 | 50.06 N | 3.33 E |
| Le Catelet | 50 | 50.00 N | 3.15 E |
| Lecce | 68 | 40.23 N | 18.11 E |
| Lecce □[4] | 68 | 40.13 N | 18.10 E |
| Lecce, Tavoliere di ≚ | 68 | 40.30 N | 17.35 E |
| Lecce nei Marsi | 66 | 41.56 N | 13.41 E |
| Lečchumskij chrebet ⋀ | 84 | 42.45 N | 43.05 E |
| Lecco | 62 | 45.51 N | 9.23 E |
| Lecco □[4] | 58 | 45.55 N | 9.25 E |
| Lecco, Lago di ⊜ | 58 | 45.55 N | 9.19 E |
| Le Center | 190 | 44.23 N | 93.43 W |
| Lech | 58 | 47.12 N | 10.09 E |
| Lech ≃ | 30 | 48.44 N | 10.56 E |
| Le Châble, Fr. | 58 | 46.06 N | 6.06 E |
| Le Châble, Schw. | 58 | 46.05 N | 7.12 E |
| L'Échalp | 62 | 44.45 N | 7.00 E |
| Le Chambon-Feugerolles | 62 | 45.24 N | 4.19 E |
| Le Chambon-sur-Lignon | 62 | 45.03 N | 4.18 E |
| Le Champ-Renault | 261 | 49.06 N | 2.31 E |
| Lechang | 100 | 25.09 N | 113.21 E |
| Le Chasseral ∧ | 58 | 47.08 N | 7.03 E |
| Le-Château-d'Oléron | 32 | 45.53 N | 1.11 W |
| Le Châtelard, Fr. | 62 | 45.41 N | 6.08 E |
| Le Châtelard, Schw. | 58 | 46.04 N | 6.58 E |
| Le Châtelet | 32 | 46.39 N | 2.17 E |
| Le Châtelet-en-Brie | 50 | 48.30 N | 2.48 E |
| Lechbruck | 58 | 47.42 N | 10.47 E |
| Leche, Laguna de la C | 240p | 22.13 N | 78.38 W |
| Le Chêne-Rogneux | 261 | 48.46 N | 1.46 E |
| Le Chesnay | 261 | 48.50 N | 2.07 E |
| Le Chesne | 56 | 49.31 N | 4.46 E |
| Le Cheylard | 62 | 44.54 N | 4.25 E |
| Lechfeld ≚ | 58 | 48.10 N | 10.50 E |
| Lechiguanas, Islas de las II | 252 | 33.26 S | 59.42 W |
| Lechlade | 42 | 51.43 N | 1.41 W |
| Lechleiten | 58 | 47.16 N | 10.12 E |
| Lechta | 24 | 60.49 N | 48.28 E |
| Lechtaler Alpen ⋀ | 64 | 47.15 N | 10.30 E |
| Lechuga, Arroyo ≃ | 286b | 23.01 N | 82.16 W |
| Lechuguilla, Cerro ∧ | 234 | 22.19 N | 104.15 W |
| Lecinone, Monte ∧ | 267a | 41.59 N | 12.48 E |
| Leck | 41 | 54.46 N | 8.58 E |
| Le Claire | 190 | 41.36 N | 90.21 W |
| Lecompte | 194 | 31.05 N | 92.24 W |
| Leconfield | 44 | 53.52 N | 0.27 W |
| Léconi | 152 | 1.35 S | 14.14 E |
| Lecontes Mills | 214 | 41.05 N | 78.17 W |
| Le Cornate ∧ | 66 | 43.10 N | 10.57 E |
| Le Coudray-Montceaux | 261 | 48.34 N | 2.31 E |
| Le Coudray-Saint-Germer | 50 | 49.25 N | 1.50 E |
| Le Creusot | 58 | 46.48 N | 4.26 E |
| Le Croci di Acerno )( | 68 | 40.47 N | 15.02 E |
| Le Croisic | 32 | 47.18 N | 2.31 W |
| Le Crotoy | 50 | 50.13 N | 1.37 E |
| Łęczna | 30 | 51.19 N | 22.52 E |
| Łęczyca | 30 | 52.04 N | 19.13 E |
| Leda ≃ | 52 | 53.12 N | 7.26 E |
| Ledaig | 46 | 56.30 N | 5.23 W |
| Led'anaja, gora ∧ | 74 | 61.53 N | 171.09 E |
| Ledang, Gunong ∧ | 114 | 2.22 N | 102.37 E |
| Ledava ≃ | 61 | 46.29 N | 16.35 E |
| Ledbetter | 222 | 30.09 N | 96.48 W |
| Ledbury | 42 | 52.02 N | 2.25 W |
| Lede | 50 | 50.58 N | 3.58 E |
| Ledenice | 61 | 48.57 N | 14.37 E |
| Lederach | 285 | 40.16 N | 75.24 W |
| Le Deschaux | 58 | 46.57 N | 5.30 E |
| Ledesma | 34 | 41.05 N | 6.00 W |
| Ledgewood | 276 | 40.52 N | 74.39 W |
| Ledi, Ben ∧ | 46 | 56.15 N | 4.19 W |
| Le Diamant | 240e | 14.29 N | 61.02 W |
| Lediba | 152 | 3.03 S | 16.32 E |
| Lédignan | 62 | 43.59 N | 4.06 E |
| Ledkovo | 24 | 67.14 N | 50.30 E |
| Lednice | 61 | 48.48 N | 16.48 E |
| Ledo, India | 120 | 27.18 N | 95.44 E |
| Ledo, Indon. | 112 | 1.02 N | 109.36 E |
| Lêdo, Cabo ≻ | 152 | 9.41 S | 13.12 E |
| Ledong | 110 | 18.45 N | 109.12 E |
| Le Donjon | 32 | 46.21 N | 3.48 E |
| Le Dorat | 32 | 46.13 N | 1.05 E |
| Le Doré, Lac ⊜ | 186 | 51.17 N | 61.23 W |
| Ledra ≃ | 64 | 46.13 N | 13.02 E |
| Ledsham | 262 | 53.16 N | 2.58 W |
| Ledu | 102 | 36.32 N | 102.25 E |
| Leduc | 182 | 53.16 N | 113.33 W |
| Ledung | 114 | 2.45 N | 99.59 E |
| Ledyard Bay C | 180 | 69.30 N | 164.30 W |
| Lędyczek | 30 | 53.33 N | 16.58 E |
| Lee, Il., U.S. | 216 | 41.48 N | 88.56 W |
| Lee, Ma., U.S. | 207 | 42.18 N | 73.14 W |
| Lee □[6], Fl., U.S. | 220 | 26.34 N | 81.55 W |
| Lee □[6], Il., U.S. | 216 | 41.50 N | 89.29 W |
| Lee □[6], Tx., U.S. | 222 | 30.20 N | 96.55 W |
| Lee ≃ | 48 | 51.54 N | 8.22 W |
| Lee Boulevard Heights | 284c | 38.52 N | 77.09 W |
| Lee Center | 210 | 43.18 N | 75.31 W |
| Leechburg | 214 | 40.37 N | 79.36 W |
| Leechburg Airport ⊠ | 279b | 40.37 N | 79.34 W |
| Leech Lake ⊜, Sk., Can. | 184 | 51.04 N | 102.30 W |
| Leech Lake ⊜, Mn., U.S. | 190 | 47.09 N | 94.23 W |
| Leech Lake Indian Reservation ⊕[4] | 190 | 47.30 N | 94.27 W |
| Leechtown | 224 | 48.30 N | 123.42 W |
| Leedey | 196 | 35.52 N | 99.20 W |
| Leedom Estates | 285 | 39.41 N | 75.35 W |
| Leeds, Eng., U.K. | 44 | 53.50 N | 1.35 W |
| Leeds, Al., U.S. | 194 | 33.32 N | 86.32 W |
| Leeds, N.Y., U.S. | 210 | 42.15 N | 73.54 W |
| Leeds, N.D., U.S. | 198 | 48.17 N | 99.26 W |
| Leeds and Bradford (Yeadon) Airport ⊠ | 44 | 53.52 N | 1.38 W |
| Leeds and Grenville □[6] | 212 | 44.45 N | 75.50 W |
| Leeds and Liverpool Canal ≡ | 262 | 53.25 N | 2.59 W |
| Leeds Point | 208 | 39.29 N | 74.25 W |
| Leedstown | 42 | 50.10 N | 5.22 W |
| Leegebruch | 54 | 52.43 N | 13.11 E |
| Leek, Ned. | 52 | 53.09 N | 6.24 E |
| Leek, Eng., U.K. | 44 | 53.06 N | 2.01 W |
| Leelanau, Lake ⊜ | 190 | 44.55 N | 85.43 W |
| Leelanau Peninsula ≻[1] | 190 | 45.10 N | 85.35 W |
| Leeming | 44 | 54.17 N | 1.32 W |
| Leenaun | 48 | 53.36 N | 9.45 W |
| Leende | 52 | 51.21 N | 5.33 E |
| Lee-on-the-Solent | 42 | 50.47 N | 1.12 W |
| Lee Park | 210 | 41.14 N | 75.55 W |
| Leeper | 214 | 41.22 N | 79.18 W |
| Leer | 52 | 53.14 N | 7.26 E |
| Leerdam | 52 | 51.54 N | 5.05 E |
| Leerhafe | 52 | 53.32 N | 7.47 E |
| Leersum | 52 | 52.01 N | 5.26 E |
| Lees | 262 | 53.32 N | 2.04 W |
| Leesburg, Fl., U.S. | 220 | 28.48 N | 81.52 W |


**Symbols** in the index entries represent the broad categories identified in the key at the right. Symbols with superior numbers (⋀[1]) identify subcategories (see complete key on page *I · 1*).

**Symbole** im Register stellen die rechts im Schlüssel erklärten Kategorien dar. Symbole mit hochgestellten Ziffern (⋀[1]) bezeichnen Unterabteilungen einer Kategorie (vgl. vollständiger Schlüssel auf Seite *I · 1*).

**Los símbolos** incluídos en el texto del índice representan las grandes categorías identificadas con la clave a la derecha. Los símbolos con numeros en su parte superior (⋀[1]) identifican las subcategorías (véase la clave completa en la página *I · 1*).

**Les symboles** de l'index représentent les catégories indiquées dans la légende à droite. Les symboles suivis d'un indice (⋀[1]) représentent des sous-catégories (voir légende complète à la page *I · 1*).

**Os símbolos** incluídos no texto do índice representam as grandes categorias identificadas com a chave à direita. Os símbolos com números em sua parte superior (⋀[1]) identificam as subcategorias (veja-se a chave completa à página *I · 1*).

| | | | | |
|---|---|---|---|---|
| ∧ Mountain | Berg | Montaña | Montagne | Montanha |
| ⋀ Mountains | Gebirge | Montañas | Montagnes | Montanhas |
| )( Pass | Paß | Paso | Col | Passo |
| V Valley, Canyon | Tal, Cañon | Valle, Cañón | Vallée, Canyon | Vale, Canhão |
| ≚ Plain | Ebene | Llano | Plaine | Planície |
| ≻ Cape | Kap | Cabo | Cap | Cabo |
| I Island | Insel | Isla | Île | Ilha |
| II Islands | Inseln | Islas | Îles | Ilhas |
| ⊥ Other Topographic Features | Andere Topographische Objekte | Otros Elementos Topográficos | Autres données topographiques | Outros acidentes topográficos |

ESPAÑOL — Nombre, Página, Lat.°', Long.°' W = Oeste
FRANÇAIS — Nom, Page, Lat.°', Long.°' W = Ouest
PORTUGUÊS — Nome, Página, Lat.°', Long.°' W = Oeste


| Nombre | Página | Lat.°' | Long.°' W = Oeste |
|---|---|---|---|
| Leesburg, Ga., U.S. | 192 | 31.43 N | 84.10 W |
| Leesburg, In., U.S. | 216 | 41.19 N | 85.51 W |
| Leesburg, N.J., U.S. | 208 | 39.15 N | 74.59 W |
| Leesburg, Oh., U.S. | 218 | 39.20 N | 83.33 W |
| Leesburg, Tx., U.S. | 222 | 32.59 N | 95.05 W |
| Leesburg, Va., U.S. | 208 | 39.06 N | 77.33 W |
| Lees Creek ≃ | 218 | 39.21 N | 83.29 W |
| Leese | 52 | 52.30 N | 9.06 E |
| Leesport | 208 | 40.27 N | 75.58 W |
| Lees Summit | 194 | 38.55 N | 94.23 W |
| Leeste | 52 | 52.59 N | 8.49 E |
| Leeston | 172 | 43.46 S | 172.18 E |
| Leesville, Il., U.S. | 216 | 41.01 N | 87.33 W |
| Leesville, In., U.S. | 218 | 38.51 N | 86.18 W |
| Leesville, La., U.S. | 194 | 31.08 N | 93.15 W |
| Leesville, Oh., U.S. | 214 | 40.27 N | 81.13 W |
| Leesville, S.C., U.S. | 192 | 33.54 N | 81.30 W |
| Leesville, Tx., U.S. | 222 | 29.24 N | 97.45 W |
| Leesville Lake ⊜[1], Oh., U.S. | 214 | 40.30 N | 81.10 W |
| Leesville Lake ⊜[1], Va., U.S. | 192 | 37.05 N | 79.25 W |
| Leeton | 166 | 34.33 S | 146.24 E |
| Leetonia | 214 | 40.52 N | 80.45 W |
| Leetsdale | 214 | 40.33 N | 80.12 W |
| Leeudoringstad | 158 | 27.15 S | 26.10 E |
| Leeu-Gamka | 158 | 32.47 S | 21.59 E |
| Leeupan ≃ | 273d | 26.14 S | 28.19 E |
| Leeuwarden | 52 | 53.12 N | 5.46 E |
| Leeuwin, Cape ≻ | 162 | 34.22 S | 115.08 E |
| Lee Vining | 226 | 37.57 N | 119.07 W |
| Leeward Islands II | 238 | 17.00 N | 63.00 W |
| Le Faouët | 28 | 48.02 N | 3.29 W |
| Le Fayet | 58 | 45.55 N | 6.42 E |
| Lefèvre, Pointe ≻ | 175f | 20.54 S | 167.01 E |
| Leffe | 62 | 45.48 N | 9.53 E |
| Lefferts, Lake ⊜ | 276 | 40.25 N | 74.14 W |
| Léfini ≃ | 152 | 2.57 S | 16.10 E |
| Léfini, Réserve de Chasse de la -◆-[4] | 152 | 2.58 S | 15.25 E |
| Lefke | 130 | 35.07 N | 32.51 E |
| Le Focette | 64 | 43.55 N | 10.13 E |
| Leforest | 50 | 50.26 N | 3.04 E |
| Lefors | 196 | 35.26 N | 100.48 W |
| Le François | 240e | 14.37 N | 60.54 W |
| Le Freney-d'Oisans | 62 | 45.02 N | 6.07 E |
| Lefroy | 212 | 44.16 N | 79.34 W |
| Lefroy, Lake ⊜ | 162 | 31.15 S | 121.40 E |
| Leftrook Lake ⊜ | 184 | 56.05 N | 98.36 W |
| Lega Hida | 144 | 7.56 N | 41.04 E |
| Legal | 182 | 53.57 N | 113.35 W |
| Leganés | 34 | 40.19 N | 3.45 W |
| Le Gardeur | 206 | 45.45 N | 73.28 W |
| Legaspi | 116 | 13.08 N | 123.44 E |
| Legau | 58 | 47.51 N | 10.07 E |
| Legden | 52 | 52.02 N | 7.07 E |
| Legendre ≃ | 206 | 45.44 N | 71.08 W |
| Legendre Island I | 162 | 20.23 S | 116.54 E |
| Leggett, Ca., U.S. | 204 | 39.51 N | 123.42 W |
| Leggett, Tx., U.S. | 222 | 30.49 N | 94.52 W |
| Leghorn → Livorno | 66 | 43.33 N | 10.19 E |
| Legion Mine | 154 | 21.23 S | 28.33 E |
| Legion of Honor, Palace of the υ | 282 | 37.47 N | 122.30 W |
| Legionowo | 30 | 52.25 N | 20.56 E |
| Legnago | 64 | 45.11 N | 11.18 E |
| Legnano | 62 | 45.36 N | 8.54 E |
| Legnica (Liegnitz) | 30 | 51.13 N | 16.09 E |
| Legnica □[4] | 30 | 51.25 N | 16.10 E |
| Le Gosier | 241o | 16.12 N | 61.30 W |
| Le Grand | 226 | 37.13 N | 120.14 W |
| LeGrand, Cape ≻ | 162 | 34.01 S | 122.06 E |
| Le Grand-Lucé | 50 | 47.52 N | 0.28 E |
| Le Grand-Quevilly | 50 | 49.25 N | 1.02 E |
| Le Grand-Serre | 62 | 45.16 N | 5.06 E |
| Le Grand Wintersberg ∧[2] | 56 | 48.59 N | 7.37 E |
| Le Grau-du-Roi | 62 | 43.32 N | 4.08 E |
| Le Gua | 62 | 45.01 N | 5.37 E |
| Le Guelta | 34 | 36.22 N | 0.50 E |
| Leguga | 154 | 3.23 N | 25.02 E |
| Legume | 166 | 28.25 S | 152.19 E |
| Legundi, Pulau I | 115a | 5.50 S | 105.16 E |
| Leh | 123 | 34.10 N | 77.35 E |
| Le Havre | 50 | 49.30 N | 0.08 E |
| Lehčevo | 38 | 43.32 N | 23.32 E |
| Le Hérie-la-Viéville | 50 | 49.49 N | 3.38 E |
| Lehesten | 54 | 50.29 N | 11.28 E |
| Lehi | 200 | 40.23 N | 111.50 W |
| Lehigh, Ia., U.S. | 190 | 42.21 N | 94.03 W |
| Lehigh, Ok., U.S. | 196 | 34.28 N | 96.12 W |
| Lehigh □[6] | 208 | 40.36 N | 75.29 W |
| Lehigh ≃ | 210 | 40.41 N | 75.12 W |
| Lehigh Acres | 220 | 26.37 N | 81.37 W |
| Lehighton | 210 | 40.50 N | 75.42 W |
| Lehinch | 48 | 52.56 N | 9.21 W |
| Lehnin | 54 | 52.19 N | 12.44 E |
| Lehnitz | 54 | 52.44 N | 13.15 E |
| Lehnitz See ⊜ | 264a | 52.45 N | 13.16 E |
| Leho | 140 | 7.07 N | 33.52 E |
| Le Hohwald | 58 | 48.24 N | 7.20 E |
| Le Houlme | 50 | 49.31 N | 1.02 E |
| Lehr | 198 | 45.59 N | 99.32 W |
| Lehra Gāga | 123 | 29.55 N | 75.49 E |
| Lehrbach | 56 | 50.47 N | 9.04 E |
| Lehrberg | 56 | 49.21 N | 10.30 E |
| Lehre | 54 | 52.19 N | 10.40 E |
| Lehrte | 52 | 52.22 N | 9.59 E |
| Lehtimäki | 26 | 62.47 N | 23.55 E |
| Lehtrār Bāla | 123 | 33.42 N | 73.26 E |
| Lehtse | 76 | 59.15 N | 25.50 E |
| Lehua I | 229b | 22.01 N | 160.06 W |
| Lehututu | 156 | 23.58 S | 21.51 E |
| Lei ≃ | 100 | 26.54 N | 112.39 E |
| Leiah | 123 | 30.58 N | 70.56 E |
| Leião | 266c | 38.44 N | 9.18 W |
| Leibnitz | 61 | 46.47 N | 15.32 E |
| Leibo | 102 | 28.19 N | 103.21 E |
| Leicester, Eng., U.K. | 42 | 52.38 N | 1.05 W |
| Leicester, Ma., U.S. | 207 | 42.14 N | 71.54 W |
| Leicester, N.Y., U.S. | 210 | 42.46 N | 77.53 W |
| Leicestershire □[6] | 42 | 52.40 N | 1.10 W |
| Leichhardt | 274a | 33.53 S | 151.07 E |
| Leichhardt ≃ | 166 | 17.35 S | 139.48 E |
| Leichhardt Falls ∟ | 166 | 18.14 S | 139.53 E |
| Leichhardt Range ⋏ | 166 | 20.40 S | 147.25 E |
| Leichlingen | 56 | 51.06 N | 7.01 E |
| Leiden | 52 | 52.09 N | 4.30 E |
| Leiderdorp | 52 | 52.09 N | 4.32 E |
| Leidschendam | 52 | 52.05 N | 4.24 E |
| Leie (Lys) ≃ | 50 | 51.03 N | 3.43 E |
| Leiferde | 52 | 52.26 N | 10.26 E |
| Leigh, N.Z. | 172 | 36.17 S | 174.49 E |
| Leigh, Eng., U.K. | 44 | 53.30 N | 2.33 W |
| Leigh, Eng., U.K. | 260 | 51.12 N | 0.13 E |
| Leigh ≃ | 169 | 38.06 S | 144.03 E |
| Leigh Canal ≍ | 262 | 53.28 N | 2.21 W |
| Leigh Creek | 166 | 30.28 S | 138.25 E |
| Leighlinbridge | 48 | 52.44 N | 6.59 W |
| Leigh-on-Sea | 42 | 51.33 N | 0.38 E |
| Leighton | 194 | 34.42 N | 87.31 W |
| Leighton Buzzard | 42 | 51.55 N | 0.40 W |
| Leikanger | 26 | 61.10 N | 6.52 E |
| Leiktho | 110 | 19.13 N | 96.35 E |
| Leimen | 56 | 49.21 N | 8.41 E |
| Leimstruth | 56 | 50.59 N | 8.19 E |
| Lein ≃ | 56 | 48.54 N | 10.01 E |
| Leinan | 184 | 50.30 N | 107.46 W |
| Leinburg | 60 | 49.27 N | 11.19 E |
| Leine ≃ | 52 | 52.43 N | 9.36 E |
| Leinefelde, Dtsch. | 52 | 51.23 N | 10.20 E |
| Leinefelde, Dtsch. | 54 | 51.23 N | 10.20 E |
| Leinfelden-Echterdingen | 56 | 48.41 N | 9.08 E |
| Leingarten | 56 | 49.09 N | 9.07 E |
| Leinster | 162 | 27.51 S | 120.36 E |
| Leinster □[9] | 48 | 53.05 N | 7.00 W |
| Leinster, Mount ∧ | 48 | 52.37 N | 6.44 W |
| Leintwardine | 42 | 52.23 N | 2.51 W |
| Leipalingis | 76 | 54.05 N | 23.51 E |
| Leipheim | 58 | 48.27 N | 10.13 E |
| Leipoldtville | 158 | 32.14 S | 18.30 E |
| Leipsic, De., U.S. | 208 | 39.14 N | 75.31 W |
| Leipsic, In., U.S. | 218 | 38.40 N | 86.22 W |
| Leipsic, Oh., U.S. | 216 | 41.05 N | 83.59 W |
| Leipsic ≃ | 208 | 39.15 N | 75.24 W |
| Leipzig | 54 | 51.19 N | 12.20 E |
| Leiria | 34 | 39.45 N | 8.48 W |
| Leirvik | 26 | 59.45 N | 5.30 E |
| Leisach | 64 | 46.48 N | 12.45 E |
| Leishendian | 107 | 28.58 N | 106.40 E |
| Leisi | 76 | 58.34 N | 22.39 E |
| Leisler, Mount ∧ | 162 | 23.28 S | 129.17 E |
| Leisnig | 54 | 51.09 N | 12.56 E |
| Leiston | 42 | 52.12 N | 1.34 E |
| Leisure City | 220 | 25.29 N | 80.25 W |
| Leitariegos, Puerto de )( | 34 | 43.00 N | 6.25 W |
| Leitchfield | 194 | 37.28 N | 86.17 W |
| Leiters Ford | 216 | 41.07 N | 86.23 W |
| Leith | 46 | 55.59 N | 3.10 W |
| Leith, Water of ≃ | 46 | 55.59 N | 3.11 W |
| Leitha (Lajta) ≃ | 61 | 47.54 N | 17.17 E |
| Leithagebirge ⋏ | 61 | 47.52 N | 16.35 E |
| Leithe -◆-[8] | 263 | 51.29 N | 7.06 E |
| Leith Hill ∧[2] | 42 | 51.11 N | 0.23 W |
| Leitre | 164 | 2.50 S | 141.40 E |
| Leitrim | 48 | 54.00 N | 8.04 W |
| Leitrim □[6] | 48 | 54.20 N | 8.20 W |
| Leitzkau | 54 | 52.03 N | 11.57 E |
| Leixi | 100 | 27.10 N | 112.52 E |
| Leixlip | 48 | 53.22 N | 6.29 W |
| Leiyang | 100 | 26.24 N | 112.51 E |
| Lei Yue Mun ʮ | 271d | 22.16 N | 114.14 E |
| Leizhou Bandao ≻[1] | 102 | 21.15 N | 110.09 E |
| Leizhuang | 98 | 39.47 N | 118.34 E |
| Lejasciems | 76 | 57.17 N | 26.35 E |
| Lek ≃ | 52 | 51.55 N | 4.34 E |
| Lékana | 152 | 2.19 S | 14.36 E |
| Le Kef → El Kef | 148 | 36.11 N | 8.43 E |
| Lékéti ≃ | 152 | 1.36 S | 14.57 E |
| Lekhainá | 38 | 37.56 N | 21.17 E |
| Lekir | 114 | 4.07 N | 100.44 E |
| Lekitobi | 112 | 1.58 S | 124.33 E |
| Lekkeroog | 158 | 30.43 S | 20.00 E |
| Lekkerwater | 156 | 23.38 S | 17.14 E |
| Lekma ≃ | 80 | 58.18 N | 52.04 E |
| Łeknice | 54 | 51.35 N | 14.45 E |
| Lékoni ≃ | 152 | 1.11 S | 13.16 E |
| Lekotero | 152 | 0.46 S | 23.51 E |
| Lékoumou □[5] | 152 | 3.00 S | 13.30 E |
| Le Kreïder | 148 | 34.06 N | 0.02 E |
| Le Kremlin-Bicêtre | 261 | 48.49 N | 2.21 E |
| Leksand | 26 | 60.44 N | 14.59 E |
| Leksberg | 40 | 58.41 N | 13.49 E |
| Leksozero, ozero ⊜ | 24 | 63.46 N | 30.58 E |
| Leksvik | 26 | 63.40 N | 10.37 E |
| Lela | 152 | 5.03 S | 12.29 E |
| Le Lac-d'Issarlès | 62 | 44.49 N | 4.04 E |
| Le Lamentin | 240e | 14.37 N | 61.01 W |
| Leland, Il., U.S. | 216 | 41.37 N | 88.48 W |
| Leland, Mi., U.S. | 190 | 45.01 N | 85.45 W |
| Leland, Ms., U.S. | 194 | 33.24 N | 90.53 W |
| Leland Grove | 219 | 39.47 N | 89.41 W |
| Leland Lake ⊜ | 224 | 47.53 N | 122.53 W |
| Lelång ⊜ | 26 | 59.08 N | 12.10 E |
| Lelant | 42 | 50.11 N | 5.26 W |
| Le Laus | 62 | 44.31 N | 6.09 E |
| Le Lauzet-Ubaye | 62 | 44.26 N | 6.26 E |
| Le Lavandou | 62 | 43.08 N | 6.22 E |
| Lel'čycy | 78 | 51.47 N | 28.19 E |
| Leleiwi Point ≻ | 229d | 19.44 N | 155.00 W |
| Leleque | 254 | 42.23 S | 71.03 W |
| Leles | 115a | 7.07 S | 107.53 E |
| Lelewau | 112 | 3.02 S | 121.05 E |
| Lélex | 58 | 46.18 N | 5.57 E |
| Le Liège | 50 | 47.13 N | 1.06 E |
| Le Limbé | 238 | 19.42 N | 72.24 W |
| Leling | 98 | 37.45 N | 117.12 E |
| Lelingluang | 164 | 7.09 S | 131.43 E |
| Lelintah | 164 | 2.03 S | 130.16 E |
| Le Lion-d'Angers | 32 | 47.38 N | 0.43 W |
| Leli Shan ∧ | 120 | 33.26 N | 81.42 E |
| Le Locle | 58 | 47.03 N | 6.45 E |
| Lelogama | 112 | 9.44 S | 123.57 E |
| Le Lorrain | 240e | 14.50 N | 61.04 W |
| Le Luc | 62 | 43.23 N | 6.19 E |
| Le Lude | 50 | 47.39 N | 0.09 E |
| Lelydorp | 250 | 5.42 N | 55.16 W |
| Lelystad | 52 | 52.31 N | 5.27 E |
| Lema | 150 | 12.57 N | 4.14 E |
| Lemahabang | 115a | 6.17 S | 107.27 E |
| Le Maire, Estrecho de ʮ | 254 | 54.50 S | 65.00 W |
| Léman, Lac → Geneva, Lake ⊜ | 58 | 46.25 N | 6.30 E |
| Lemankoa | 175e | 5.02 S | 154.35 E |
| Le Mans | 50 | 48.00 N | 0.12 E |
| Le Marin | 240e | 14.28 N | 60.53 W |
| Le Markstein | 58 | 47.56 N | 7.02 E |
| Le Mars | 198 | 42.47 N | 96.09 W |
| Lema Shilindi | 144 | 4.55 N | 42.02 E |
| Lemay | 219 | 38.32 N | 90.17 W |
| Lemay, Lac ⊜ | 186 | 50.35 N | 68.25 W |
| Lembach | 56 | 49.00 N | 7.48 E |
| Lembach im Mühlkreis | 60 | 48.29 N | 13.53 E |
| Lemba-Gaba | 273b | 4.27 S | 15.18 E |
| Lembak | 112 | 0.52 N | 117.32 E |
| Lembang | 115a | 6.49 S | 107.36 E |
| Lembeck | 52 | 51.45 N | 7.00 E |
| Lembeek | 50 | 50.43 N | 4.13 E |
| Lembeh, Pulau I | 112 | 1.26 N | 125.13 E |
| Lembeni | 154 | 3.47 S | 37.37 E |
| Lemberg, Sk., Can. | 184 | 50.44 N | 103.13 W |
| Lemberg, Dtsch. | 56 | 49.10 N | 7.39 E |
| Lemberg, Fr. | 56 | 49.00 N | 7.23 E |
| Lemberg → L'viv, Ukr. | 78 | 49.50 N | 24.00 E |
| Lemberg ∧ | 58 | 48.09 N | 8.45 E |
| Lembruch | 52 | 52.31 N | 8.22 E |
| Lembu, Gunung ∧ | 114 | 4.12 N | 97.24 E |
| Lemdiyya | 148 | 36.12 N | 2.50 E |
| Leme | 255 | 22.12 S | 47.24 W |
| Leme, Morro do ∧[2] | 287a | 22.58 S | 43.10 W |
| Le Mée-sur-Seine | 261 | 48.32 N | 2.38 E |
| Lemei Rock ∧ | 224 | 46.01 N | 121.46 W |
| Lemele | 52 | 52.27 N | 6.25 E |
| Le Mêle-sur-Sarthe | 50 | 48.31 N | 0.21 E |
| Lemene ≃ | 64 | 45.37 N | 12.53 E |
| Lemeris, Cape ≻ | 164 | 3.15 S | 152.03 E |
| Le Merlerault | 50 | 48.42 N | 0.18 E |
| Lemery | 116 | 13.53 N | 120.55 E |
| Lemeškino | 80 | 51.01 N | 44.27 E |
| Le Mesle | 261 | 48.43 N | 1.41 E |
| Le Mesnil-Amelot | 261 | 49.01 N | 2.36 E |
| Le Mesnil-Aubry | 261 | 49.03 N | 2.24 E |
| Le Mesnil-le-Roi | 261 | 48.56 N | 2.08 E |
| Le Mesnil-Saint-Denis | 261 | 48.45 N | 1.58 E |
| Le Mesnil-sur-Oger | 50 | 48.57 N | 4.01 E |
| Lemesós (Limassol) | 130 | 34.40 N | 33.02 E |
| Lemeta | 180 | 64.52 N | 147.44 W |
| Lemförde | 52 | 52.28 N | 8.22 E |
| Lemfu | 152 | 5.18 S | 15.13 E |
| Lemgo | 52 | 52.02 N | 8.54 E |
| Lemhi ≃ | 202 | 45.12 N | 113.53 W |
| Lemhi Pass )( | 202 | 44.58 N | 113.27 W |
| Lemhi Range ⋏ | 202 | 44.30 N | 113.25 W |
| Lemie | 62 | 45.14 N | 7.17 E |
| Lemierzyce | 54 | 52.35 N | 14.56 E |
| Lemieux Islands II | 176 | 64.30 N | 64.40 W |
| Lemin | 102 | 21.11 N | 109.42 E |
| Leming | 196 | 29.04 N | 98.29 W |
| Lemitar | 200 | 34.09 N | 106.54 W |
| Lemland I | 26 | 60.03 N | 20.09 E |
| Lemmatsi | 76 | 58.20 N | 26.37 E |
| Lemmenjoen kansallispuisto ♦ | 24 | 68.40 N | 26.00 E |
| Lemmer | 52 | 52.50 N | 5.42 E |
| Lemmon | 198 | 45.56 N | 102.09 W |
| Lemmon, Mount ∧ | 200 | 32.26 N | 110.47 W |
| Lemnos → Límnos I | 38 | 39.54 N | 25.21 E |
| Lemoenshoek | 158 | 33.51 S | 20.51 E |
| Lemoine, Lac ⊜ | 190 | 48.00 N | 78.00 W |
| Lemon, Lake ⊜ | 218 | 39.16 N | 86.25 W |
| Le Monastier | 62 | 44.56 N | 4.00 E |
| Lemoncove | 204 | 36.23 N | 119.01 W |
| Lemon Creek ≃ | 276 | 40.31 N | 74.12 W |
| Le Monêtier-les-Bains | 62 | 44.59 N | 6.31 E |
| Lemon Grove | 228 | 32.44 N | 117.01 W |
| Lemon Heights | 280 | 33.46 N | 117.48 W |
| Lemont, Il., U.S. | 216 | 41.40 N | 88.00 W |
| Lemont, Pa., U.S. | 214 | 40.49 N | 77.49 W |
| Le Montet | 32 | 46.25 N | 3.03 E |
| Le Mont-Saint-Michel υ[1] | 32 | 48.38 N | 1.32 W |
| Lemoore | 226 | 36.18 N | 119.46 W |
| Lemoore Naval Air Station ■ | 226 | 36.15 N | 119.57 W |
| Lemoro | 112 | 1.25 S | 121.05 E |
| Le Moule | 241o | 16.20 N | 61.21 W |
| Le Moutier | 261 | 48.50 N | 1.42 E |
| LeMoyne, P.Q., Can. | 275a | 45.31 N | 73.29 W |
| Lemoyne, Oh., U.S. | 214 | 41.30 N | 83.28 W |
| Lemoyne, Pa., U.S. | 208 | 40.15 N | 76.54 W |
| Lempa ≃ | 236 | 13.14 N | 88.49 W |
| Lempäälä | 26 | 61.19 N | 23.45 E |
| Lempe | 112 | 1.40 S | 120.14 E |
| Lempira □[5] | 236 | 14.20 N | 88.40 W |
| Lemro ≃ | 110 | 20.25 N | 93.20 E |
| Lemsid | 148 | 26.32 N | 13.49 W |
| Lemukutan, Pulau I | 112 | 0.45 N | 108.43 E |
| Le Murge ⋏[1] | 68 | 40.52 N | 16.42 E |
| Lemutan | 112 | 3.03 N | 115.49 E |
| Le Muy | 62 | 43.28 N | 6.33 E |
| Lemva ≃ | 24 | 66.30 N | 61.48 E |
| Lemvig | 26 | 56.32 N | 8.18 E |
| Lemwerder | 52 | 53.10 N | 8.37 E |
| Lemyethna | 110 | 17.36 N | 95.09 E |
| Len ≃ | 260 | 51.16 N | 0.31 E |
| Lena, Il., U.S. | 190 | 42.22 N | 89.49 W |
| Lena, Wi., U.S. | 190 | 44.57 N | 88.02 W |
| Lena ≃ | 74 | 72.25 N | 126.40 E |
| Lenangguar | 115b | 8.44 S | 117.24 E |
| Lenape | 285 | 39.55 N | 75.38 W |
| Lenart | 36 | 46.35 N | 15.50 E |
| Lenasia | 273d | 26.17 S | 27.50 E |
| Lenawee □[6] | 216 | 41.53 N | 84.04 W |
| Lencloître | 32 | 46.49 N | 0.20 E |
| Lençóis | 255 | 12.34 S | 41.23 W |
| Lençois Maranhenses, Parque Nacional dos ♦ | 250 | 2.25 S | 43.15 W |
| Lend | 64 | 47.18 N | 13.04 E |
| Lenda ≃ | 154 | 1.20 N | 28.01 E |
| Lendava | 61 | 46.34 N | 16.27 E |
| Lendelede | 50 | 50.53 N | 3.14 E |
| Lendery | 24 | 63.26 N | 31.03 E |
| Lendinara | 64 | 45.05 N | 11.36 E |
| Lendorf | 64 | 46.50 N | 13.26 E |
| Lendringsen | 56 | 51.24 N | 7.49 E |
| Le Neubourg | 50 | 49.09 N | 0.55 E |
| Lenga | 114 | 2.17 N | 102.49 E |
| Lengduqiao | 106 | 30.27 N | 119.15 E |
| Lengede | 52 | 52.12 N | 10.18 E |
| Lengefeld, Dtsch. | 54 | 50.43 N | 13.11 E |
| Lengefeld, Dtsch. | 54 | 50.50 N | 11.20 E |
| Lengelscheid | 263 | 51.08 N | 7.40 E |
| Lengenfeld, Dtsch. | 54 | 50.34 N | 12.22 E |
| Lengenfeld, Dtsch. | 56 | 51.13 N | 10.13 E |
| Lenger | 85 | 42.12 N | 69.54 E |
| Lengerich, Dtsch. | 52 | 52.11 N | 7.50 E |
| Lengerich, Dtsch. | 52 | 52.33 N | 7.32 E |
| Lenggor ≃ | 114 | 2.25 N | 103.37 E |
| Lenggries | 64 | 47.41 N | 11.34 E |
| Lenghu | 90 | 38.30 N | 93.15 E |
| Lengjiagou | 104 | 41.40 N | 121.37 E |
| Lengkong | 115a | 7.32 S | 112.04 E |
| Lenglingen ⊜ | 26 | 64.14 N | 13.45 E |
| Lengnau | 58 | 47.11 N | 7.22 E |
| Lengoué | 152 | 1.13 N | 15.43 E |
| Lengoué ≃ | 152 | 0.49 N | 15.47 E |
| Lengshuichang | 107 | 29.27 N | 106.26 E |
| Lengshuikeng | 100 | 27.55 N | 117.08 E |
| Lengshuitan | 102 | 26.27 N | 111.35 E |
| Lengua de Vaca, Punta ≻ | 252 | 30.14 S | 71.38 W |
| Lengulu | 154 | 3.15 N | 26.30 E |
| Lengwe National Park ♦ | 154 | 16.15 S | 34.45 E |
| Lengzipu | 104 | 41.42 N | 122.47 E |
| Lenham | 42 | 51.14 N | 0.43 E |
| Lenhartsville | 208 | 40.34 N | 75.53 W |
| Lenhovda | 26 | 57.00 N | 15.17 E |
| Lenina, gora ∧[2] | 265b | 55.42 N | 37.31 E |
| Lenina, ozero ⊜ | 78 | 48.33 N | 35.12 E |
| Lenina, pik ∧ | 85 | 39.20 N | 72.55 E |
| Leninabad → Chudžand | 85 | 40.17 N | 69.37 E |
| Leninakan → Kumajri | 84 | 40.48 N | 43.50 E |
| Lenin Central Stadium ♦ | 265b | 55.43 N | 37.33 E |
| Lenin-Džol | 85 | 41.03 N | 72.38 E |
| Lenine | 78 | 45.18 N | 35.47 E |
| Leningori | 84 | 42.07 N | 44.29 E |
| Leningrad → Sankt-Peterburg | 76 | 59.55 N | 30.15 E |
| Leningrado → Sankt-Peterburg | 76 | 59.55 N | 30.15 E |
| Leningrad Oblast' □[4] | 24 | 60.00 N | 32.00 E |
| Leningradskaja | 78 | 46.19 N | 39.24 E |
| Leningradskij | 85 | 38.06 N | 70.01 E |
| Leningradskoje | 86 | 53.33 N | 71.35 E |
| Lenino -◆-[8] | 265b | 55.37 N | 37.41 E |
| Leninogorsk, Kaz. | 86 | 50.27 N | 83.32 E |
| Leninogorsk, Ross. | 80 | 54.36 N | 52.30 E |
| Leninpol' | 85 | 42.29 N | 71.55 E |
| Leninsk, Kaz. | 86 | 45.40 N | 63.20 E |
| Leninsk, Ross. | 80 | 48.08 N | 43.46 E |
| Leninsk, Ross. | 80 | 48.42 N | 45.11 E |
| Leninsk, Ross. | 86 | 54.55 N | 59.54 E |
| Leninsk, Uzb. | 85 | 40.38 N | 72.15 E |
| Leninskaja Sloboda | 80 | 56.05 N | 44.28 E |
| Lenins'ke, Ukr. | 78 | 45.16 N | 35.54 E |
| Lenins'ke, Ukr. | 78 | 51.27 N | 33.18 E |
| Lenins'ke, Ukr. | 83 | 48.05 N | 39.31 E |
| Leninskij, Kaz. | 86 | 52.13 N | 76.47 E |
| Leninskij, Ross. | 80 | 46.31 N | 44.28 E |
| Leninskij, Ross. | 80 | 56.34 N | 45.56 E |
| Leninskij, Ross. | 82 | 54.18 N | 37.28 E |
| Leninsk-Kuzneckij | 86 | 54.38 N | 86.10 E |
| Leninskoje, Kaz. | 80 | 49.03 N | 49.56 E |
| Leninskoje, Kaz. | 85 | 41.45 N | 69.23 E |
| Leninskoje, Kaz. | 86 | 54.04 N | 65.22 E |
| Leninskoje, Kaz. | 86 | 50.44 N | 57.53 E |
| Leninskoje, Kyrg. | 85 | 40.42 N | 73.11 E |
| Leninskoje, Ross. | 80 | 58.19 N | 47.06 E |
| Leninskoje, Ross. | 89 | 47.56 N | 132.38 E |
| Lenin-Stausee → Kujbyševskoje vodochranilišče ⊜[1] | 80 | 54.30 N | 48.30 E |
| Leninžol | 80 | 49.20 N | 47.05 E |
| Lenk | 58 | 46.28 N | 7.27 E |
| Lenkerville | 208 | 40.32 N | 76.58 W |
| Len'ki | 86 | 52.57 N | 80.26 E |
| Lenmalu | 164 | 1.44 S | 130.13 E |
| Lennard, Mount ∧[2] | 168a | 33.21 S | 115.53 E |
| Lenne ≃ | 56 | 51.25 N | 7.30 E |
| Lennegebirge ⋏ | 52 | 51.15 N | 8.00 E |
| Lennep | 56 | 51.12 N | 7.16 E |
| Lennep -◆-[8] | 52 | 51.12 N | 7.16 E |
| Lennestadt | 56 | 51.08 N | 8.01 E |
| Lenni | 285 | 39.54 N | 75.27 W |
| Lenningen | 58 | 48.33 N | 9.28 E |
| Lennon | 216 | 42.59 N | 83.56 W |
| Lennonville | 162 | 27.58 S | 117.50 E |
| Lennox, Ca., U.S. | 228 | 33.56 N | 118.21 W |
| Lennox, S.D., U.S. | 198 | 43.21 N | 96.53 W |
| Lennox □[9] | 46 | 56.02 N | 4.15 W |
| Lennox, Isla I | 254 | 55.18 S | 66.50 W |
| Lennox and Addington □[6] | 212 | 44.30 N | 77.00 W |
| Lennoxtown | 46 | 55.59 N | 4.12 W |
| Lennoxville | 206 | 45.22 N | 71.51 W |
| Leno | 64 | 45.22 N | 10.13 E |
| Lenoir | 192 | 35.54 N | 81.32 W |
| Lenoir City | 192 | 35.47 N | 84.15 W |
| Le Noirmont | 58 | 47.13 N | 6.58 E |
| Lenola | 66 | 41.24 N | 13.28 E |
| Lenora | 60 | 48.56 N | 13.48 E |
| Lenore Lake ⊜ | 184 | 52.30 N | 105.00 W |
| Le Nouvion-en-Thiérache | 50 | 50.01 N | 3.47 E |
| Lenox, Ga., U.S. | 192 | 31.16 N | 83.27 W |
| Lenox, Ia., U.S. | 198 | 40.52 N | 94.33 W |
| Lenox, Ma., U.S. | 207 | 42.22 N | 73.17 W |
| Lenox, Tn., U.S. | 194 | 36.05 N | 89.29 W |
| Lenox Dale | 207 | 42.20 N | 73.14 W |
| Lens | 50 | 50.26 N | 2.50 E |
| Lensahn | 54 | 54.13 N | 10.52 E |
| Lensk | 74 | 61.00 N | 114.50 E |
| Lenskoje | 86 | 58.09 N | 63.11 E |
| Lenswood | 168b | 34.55 S | 138.49 E |
| Lentate sul Seveso | 266b | 45.41 N | 9.07 E |
| Lentechi | 84 | 42.48 N | 42.44 E |
| Lenti | 30 | 46.37 N | 16.33 E |
| Lenting | 60 | 48.48 N | 11.28 E |
| Lentini | 70 | 37.17 N | 15.00 E |
| Lentner | 219 | 39.43 N | 92.09 W |
| Lentua ⊜ | 26 | 64.14 N | 29.36 E |
| Lentvaris | 76 | 54.39 N | 25.03 E |
| Lenwood | 228 | 34.53 N | 117.07 W |
| Lenya | 110 | 11.28 N | 99.00 E |
| Lenya ≃ | 110 | 11.40 N | 98.43 E |
| Lenz | 273d | 26.19 S | 27.49 E |
| Lenzburg | 58 | 47.23 N | 8.11 E |
| Lenzen | 54 | 53.05 N | 11.28 E |
| Lenzerheide (Lai) | 58 | 46.44 N | 9.33 E |
| Lenzkirch | 58 | 47.52 N | 8.12 E |
| Léo, Burkina | 150 | 11.06 N | 2.06 W |
| Leo, In., U.S. | 216 | 41.13 N | 85.00 W |
| Leoben | 61 | 47.23 N | 15.06 E |
| Leo Carrillo State Beach ♦ | 228 | 34.03 N | 118.56 W |
| Léogâne | 238 | 18.31 N | 72.38 W |
| Leogang | 64 | 47.26 N | 12.45 E |
| Leola, Ar., U.S. | 194 | 34.10 N | 92.35 W |
| Leola, Pa., U.S. | 208 | 40.05 N | 76.11 W |
| Leola, S.D., U.S. | 198 | 45.43 N | 98.56 W |
| Leominster, Eng., U.K. | 42 | 52.14 N | 2.45 W |
| Leominster, Ma., U.S | 207 | 42.31 N | 71.45 W |
| León, Esp. | 34 | 42.36 N | 5.34 W |
| Léon, Fr. | 32 | 43.53 N | 1.18 W |
| León, Nic. | 236 | 12.26 N | 86.53 W |
| Leon, Pil. | 116 | 10.47 N | 122.23 E |
| Leon, Ia., U.S. | 190 | 40.44 N | 93.44 W |
| Leon, Ks., U.S. | 198 | 37.41 N | 96.46 W |
| Leon, N.Y., U.S. | 210 | 42.18 N | 79.01 W |
| León □[4] | 34 | 42.35 N | 6.00 W |
| León □[5] | 236 | 12.35 N | 86.35 W |
| Leon □[6] | 222 | 31.18 N | 95.55 W |
| León □[9] | 34 | 42.00 N | 6.00 W |
| Leon ≃ | 196 | 30.59 N | 97.24 W |
| Leon, Arroyo ≃ | 282 | 37.28 N | 122.25 W |
| León, Montes de ⋏ | 34 | 42.30 N | 6.18 W |
| Leona | 222 | 31.09 N | 95.58 W |
| Leona ≃ | 196 | 28.45 N | 99.11 W |
| Leona, Punta ≻ | 236 | 9.41 N | 84.41 W |
| Leonard, Mi., U.S. | 214 | 42.51 N | 83.08 W |
| Leonard, Mo., U.S. | 219 | 39.53 N | 92.10 W |
| Leonard, N.D., U.S. | 198 | 46.39 N | 97.14 W |
| Leonard, Tx., U.S. | 196 | 33.22 N | 96.14 W |
| Leonardo | 276 | 40.25 N | 74.03 W |
| Leonardo da Vinci, Aeroporto Intercontinentale ⊠ | 66 | 41.48 N | 12.13 E |
| Leonardsburg | 214 | 40.21 N | 82.59 W |
| Leonardsville | 210 | 42.48 N | 75.15 W |
| Leonardtown | 208 | 38.17 N | 76.38 W |
| Leonardville, Namibia | 156 | 23.29 S | 18.49 E |
| Leonardville, Ks., U.S. | 198 | 39.21 N | 96.51 W |
| Leona Vicario | 200 | 32.10 N | 115.10 W |
| Leonberg | 56 | 48.48 N | 9.01 E |
| Leondale | 273d | 26.18 S | 28.12 E |
| Leondárion | 267c | 37.59 N | 23.51 E |
| León [de los Aldamas] | 234 | 21.07 N | 101.40 W |
| Leonding | 61 | 48.16 N | 14.15 E |
| Leone | 174u | 14.20 S | 170.47 W |
| Leone, Golfo del → Lion, Golfe du ⊂ | 32 | 43.00 N | 4.00 E |
| Leone, Monte ∧ | 58 | 46.15 N | 8.06 E |
| Leones | 252 | 32.39 S | 62.18 W |
| Leonessa | 66 | 42.34 N | 12.58 E |
| Leonforte | 70 | 37.38 N | 14.23 E |
| Leongatha | 169 | 38.29 S | 145.57 E |
| León Guzmán | 195 | 25.31 N | 103.34 W |
| Leonia | 276 | 40.51 N | 73.59 W |
| Leonicha | 76 | 59.37 N | 38.51 E |
| Leonidas | 216 | 42.01 N | 85.21 W |
| Leonídhion | 38 | 37.10 N | 22.52 E |
| Leonidovo | 89 | 49.17 N | 142.50 E |
| Leon Junction | 222 | 31.20 N | 97.36 W |
| Leonora | 162 | 28.53 S | 121.20 E |
| Leonovo | 82 | 55.26 N | 38.42 E |
| Leontjevka | 85 | 43.03 N | 69.50 E |
| Leontjevo | 76 | 58.58 N | 36.37 E |
| Leonville | 194 | 30.28 N | 91.58 W |
| Leopard | 285 | 40.01 N | 75.27 W |
| Leopold | 169 | 38.11 S | 144.28 E |
| Leopold and Astrid Coast ⊥[2] | 9 | 67.10 S | 84.10 E |
| Leopoldau -◆-[8] | 264b | 48.16 N | 16.27 E |
| Leopold Downs | 162 | 17.52 S | 125.25 E |
| Léopold II, Lac → Mai-Ndombe, Lac ⊜ | 152 | 2.00 S | 18.20 E |
| Leopoldina | 256 | 21.32 S | 42.38 W |
| Leopoldkanaal ≍ | 50 | 51.14 N | 3.46 E |
| Leopoldo de Bulhões | 255 | 16.37 S | 48.46 W |
| Leopoldo y Astrid, Costa → Leopold and Astrid Coast ⊥[2] | 9 | 67.10 S | 84.10 E |
| Leopoldsburg | 56 | 51.07 N | 5.15 E |
| Leopoldsdorf | 264b | 48.06 N | 16.24 E |
| Leopoldshagen | 54 | 53.46 N | 13.53 E |
| Leopoldstadt -◆-[8] | 264b | 48.13 N | 16.23 E |
| Léopoldville → Kinshasa | 152 | 4.18 S | 15.18 E |
| Leoti | 198 | 38.28 N | 101.21 W |
| Leova | 38 | 46.29 N | 28.15 E |
| Leoville | 184 | 53.37 N | 107.35 W |
| Le Pailly | 58 | 47.48 N | 5.25 E |
| Le Palais | 32 | 47.21 N | 3.09 W |
| Lepanto, C.R. | 236 | 9.57 N | 85.02 W |
| Lepanto → Návpaktos, Ellás | 38 | 38.23 N | 21.50 E |
| Lepanto, Ar., U.S. | 194 | 35.36 N | 90.19 W |
| Lepar, Pulau I | 112 | 2.57 S | 106.50 E |
| Le Parcq | 50 | 50.23 N | 2.06 E |
| Le Pâté | 261 | 48.32 N | 2.18 E |
| Lepe | 34 | 37.15 N | 7.12 W |
| Le Péage-de-Roussillon | 62 | 45.22 N | 4.48 E |
| Le Pecq | 261 | 48.54 N | 2.07 E |
| Lepel' | 76 | 54.53 N | 28.42 E |
| Le Pellerin | 32 | 47.12 N | 1.45 W |
| Lepembusu, Keli ∧ | 115b | 8.40 S | 121.49 E |
| Le Perray-en-Yuelines | 261 | 48.42 N | 1.51 E |
| Le Perreux-sur-Marne | 261 | 48.51 N | 2.30 E |
| Lepeški | 82 | 56.05 N | 38.07 E |
| Le Petit-Clamart υ | 261 | 48.47 N | 2.14 E |
| Le Petit-Couronne | 50 | 49.23 N | 1.01 E |
| Le Petit-Quevilly | 50 | 49.26 N | 1.02 E |
| Lephepe | 156 | 23.20 S | 25.50 E |
| Lépi | 152 | 12.52 S | 15.26 E |
| Le Piastre | 66 | 44.00 N | 10.50 E |
| Lepihué | 254 | 41.37 S | 73.36 W |
| Le Pin | 261 | 48.55 N | 2.38 E |
| Le Pin-au-Haras | 50 | 48.44 N | 0.09 E |
| L'Épine, Fr. | 56 | 48.58 N | 4.28 E |
| L'Épine, Fr. | 261 | 48.32 N | 2.21 E |
| Leping | 100 | 28.57 N | 117.05 E |
| Lepini, Monti ⋏ | 66 | 41.35 N | 13.00 E |
| Lépin-le-Lac | 62 | 45.32 N | 5.47 E |
| L'Épiphanie | 206 | 45.51 N | 73.30 W |
| Le Plessis-aux-Bois | 261 | 49.00 N | 2.46 E |
| Le Plessis-Belleville | 50 | 49.06 N | 2.46 E |
| Le Plessis-Bouchard | 261 | 49.00 N | 2.14 E |
| Le Plessis-Pâté | 261 | 48.37 N | 2.20 E |
| Le Plessis-Trévise | 261 | 48.49 N | 2.34 E |
| Leplyavo | 78 | 49.48 N | 31.32 E |
| Lépo, Lagoa de ⊜ | 152 | 17.08 S | 19.00 E |
| Le Poët | 62 | 44.17 N | 5.53 E |
| Le Pont | 58 | 46.40 N | 6.20 E |
| Le Pont-de-Beauvoisin | 62 | 45.32 N | 5.40 E |
| Le Pont-de-Montvert | 62 | 44.22 N | 3.45 E |
| Le Pontel | 261 | 48.49 N | 1.53 E |
| Lepontine, Alpi ⋏ | 58 | 46.25 N | 8.40 E |
| Leporano | 68 | 40.23 N | 17.20 E |
| Le Port | 157c | 20.55 S | 55.18 E |
| Le Portel | 50 | 50.42 N | 1.34 E |
| Le Port-Marly | 261 | 48.53 N | 2.06 E |
| Le Pouzin | 62 | 44.45 N | 4.45 E |
| Leppävirta | 26 | 62.29 N | 27.47 E |
| Lepperton | 172 | 39.04 S | 174.13 E |
| Leppin | 54 | 52.53 N | 11.34 E |
| Leppington | 274a | 33.58 S | 150.49 E |
| Le Pradet | 62 | 43.06 N | 6.01 E |
| Lepreau, Point ≻ | 186 | 45.04 N | 66.27 W |
| Le Prêcheur | 240e | 14.48 N | 61.14 W |
| Le Pré-Saint-Gervais | 261 | 48.53 N | 2.25 E |
| Le Prese | 58 | 46.18 N | 10.04 E |
| Lepsinsk | 86 | 45.32 N | 80.37 E |
| Lepsy, Kaz. | 86 | 46.18 N | 78.20 E |
| Lepsy, Kaz. | 86 | 46.15 N | 78.55 E |
| Le Puy | 62 | 45.02 N | 3.53 E |
| Le Quesnoy | 50 | 50.15 N | 3.38 E |
| Léraba ≃ | 150 | 9.42 N | 4.35 W |
| Le Raincy | 261 | 48.54 N | 2.31 E |
| Le Rayol-Canadel-sur-Mer | 62 | 43.10 N | 6.28 E |
| Le Raysville | 210 | 41.51 N | 76.11 W |
| Lerberget | 41 | 56.11 N | 12.33 E |
| Lercara Friddi | 70 | 37.45 N | 13.36 E |
| Lerche -◆-[8] | 263 | 51.37 N | 7.43 E |
| Lerderderg ≃ | 169 | 37.42 S | 144.30 E |
| Lerdo → Ciudad Lerdo | 196 | 25.32 N | 103.32 W |
| Léré, Fr. | 50 | 47.28 N | 2.52 E |
| Léré, Mali | 150 | 15.43 N | 4.55 W |
| Lere, Nig. | 150 | 9.43 N | 9.21 E |
| Léré, Tchad | 146 | 9.39 N | 14.13 E |
| Lereh | 164 | 3.08 S | 139.54 E |
| Lerek ∧ | 114 | 3.47 N | 102.47 E |
| Le Reposoir | 58 | 46.00 N | 6.33 E |
| Leri ≃ | 42 | 52.32 N | 4.02 W |
| Leribe | 158 | 28.58 S | 28.00 E |
| Lerici | 64 | 44.04 N | 9.55 E |
| Lérida, Col. | 246 | 0.10 N | 70.42 W |
| Lérida → Lleida, Esp. | 34 | 41.37 N | 0.37 E |
| Lerik | 84 | 38.46 N | 48.25 E |
| Lérins, Îles de II | 62 | 43.31 N | 7.03 E |
| Lerma | 34 | 42.02 N | 3.45 W |
| Lerma ≃ | 234 | 20.13 N | 102.46 W |
| Lermontovka | 89 | 47.10 N | 134.20 E |
| Lermoos | 64 | 47.24 N | 10.53 E |
| Lerno, Monte ∧ | 71 | 40.37 N | 9.10 E |
| Le Robert | 240e | 14.41 N | 60.57 W |
| Léros I, Ellás | 38 | 37.08 N | 26.52 E |
| Léros I, Ellás | 267c | 37.59 N | 23.32 E |
| Lérouville | 56 | 48.47 N | 5.33 E |
| Leroux Wash ∨ | 200 | 34.54 N | 110.12 W |
| Le Roy, Il., U.S. | 216 | 40.21 N | 88.45 W |
| Leroy, In., U.S. | 216 | 41.22 N | 87.16 W |
| Le Roy, Ks., U.S. | 198 | 38.05 N | 95.38 W |
| Le Roy, Mn., U.S. | 190 | 43.30 N | 92.30 W |
| Le Roy, N.Y., U.S. | 210 | 42.58 N | 77.59 W |
| Le Roy, Pa., U.S. | 210 | 41.41 N | 76.43 W |
| Leroy, Tx., U.S. | 222 | 31.44 N | 97.01 W |
| Lerum | 26 | 57.46 N | 12.16 E |
| Le Russey | 58 | 47.10 N | 6.44 E |
| Lerwick | 46a | 60.09 N | 1.09 W |
| Léry | 206 | 45.21 N | 73.48 W |
| Lesa | 62 | 45.50 N | 8.34 E |
| Les Abrets | 62 | 45.32 N | 5.35 E |
| Les Abymes | 241o | 16.16 N | 61.31 W |
| Lesage, Lac ⊜ | 206 | 46.19 N | 75.03 W |
| Le Saint-Esprit | 240e | 14.34 N | 60.57 W |
| Les Aix-d'Angillon | 50 | 47.12 N | 2.34 E |
| Les Allues | 62 | 45.26 N | 6.33 E |
| Les Alluets-le-Roi | 261 | 48.55 N | 1.55 E |
| Les Andelys | 50 | 49.15 N | 1.25 E |
| Les Anses-d'Arlets | 240e | 14.29 N | 61.05 W |
| Le Sappy-en-Chartreuse | 62 | 45.16 N | 5.47 E |
| Les Arcs | 62 | 43.27 N | 6.29 E |
| Lesatima, Oldoinyo ∧ | 154 | 0.19 S | 36.37 E |
| Le Sauze | 62 | 44.22 N | 6.41 E |
| Les Baux-en-Provence | 62 | 43.45 N | 4.48 E |
| Les Bézards | 50 | 47.48 N | 2.44 E |
| Les Bordes | 261 | 48.39 N | 1.58 E |
| Les Borges Blanques | 34 | 41.31 N | 0.52 E |
| Lesbos → Lésvos I | 38 | 39.10 N | 26.20 E |
| Les Bouchoux | 58 | 46.18 N | 5.49 E |
| Les Bréviaires | 261 | 48.42 N | 1.49 E |
| Lesbury | 44 | 55.24 N | 1.36 W |
| L'Escarène | 62 | 43.50 N | 7.21 E |
| Les Cayes | 238 | 18.12 N | 73.45 W |
| Les Chaises | 261 | 48.39 N | 1.42 E |
| Les Chapieux | 62 | 45.42 N | 6.44 E |
| Leschenault, Cape ≻ | 162 | 31.18 S | 115.27 E |
| Leschenault Estuary ⊂[1] | 168a | 33.15 S | 115.42 E |
| Lesches | 261 | 48.54 N | 2.47 E |
| Les Clayes-sous-Bois | 261 | 48.49 N | 1.59 E |
| Les Contamines-Montjoie | 62 | 45.50 N | 6.44 E |
| Les Diablerets | 58 | 46.21 N | 7.10 E |
| Les Diablerets ∧ | 58 | 46.19 N | 7.12 E |
| Lesdiboderi | 146 | 8.28 N | 12.35 E |
| Les Echarmeaux | 58 | 46.10 N | 4.27 E |
| Les Échelles | 62 | 45.26 N | 5.45 E |
| Les Écureuils | 206 | 46.39 N | 71.43 W |
| Le Semnoz ∧ | 62 | 45.48 N | 6.07 E |
| Leseru | 154 | 0.35 N | 35.10 E |
| Les Essarts | 32 | 46.46 N | 1.14 W |
| Les Essarts-le-Roi | 261 | 48.43 N | 1.54 E |
| Les Estables | 62 | 44.54 N | 4.10 E |
| Les Étangs | 56 | 49.09 N | 6.23 E |
| Les Fonts | 266d | 41.32 N | 2.02 E |
| Les Fourgs | 58 | 46.50 N | 6.25 E |
| Les Galleries d'Anjou -◆-[9] | 275a | 45.35 N | 73.34 W |
| Les Gâtines | 261 | 48.48 N | 1.58 E |
| Les Gets | 58 | 46.09 N | 6.40 E |
| Les Granges-le-Roi | 261 | 48.30 N | 2.01 E |
| Les Grésillons | 261 | 48.56 N | 2.01 E |
| Les Halles | 62 | 45.43 N | 4.26 E |
| Leshan | 107 | 29.34 N | 103.45 E |
| Les Haudères | 58 | 46.05 N | 7.31 E |
| Les Hautes-Rivières | 56 | 49.53 N | 4.50 E |
| Les Herbiers | 32 | 46.52 N | 1.01 W |
| Les Houches | 62 | 45.53 N | 6.48 E |
| Lesignano de'Bagni | 64 | 44.39 N | 10.18 E |
| Lésigny | 261 | 48.45 N | 2.37 E |
| Lesima, Monte ∧ | 62 | 44.41 N | 9.15 E |
| Lesina | 68 | 41.52 N | 15.21 E |
| Lesina, Lago di ⊂ | 68 | 41.53 N | 15.26 E |
| Les Islettes | 56 | 49.06 N | 5.00 E |
| Lesjaskog | 26 | 62.15 N | 8.22 E |
| Lesjöfors | 40 | 59.59 N | 14.11 E |
| Lesken | 84 | 43.16 N | 43.48 E |
| Lesko | 30 | 49.29 N | 22.21 E |
| Leskovac | 38 | 42.59 N | 21.57 E |
| Leskov Island I | 18 | 56.40 S | 28.10 W |
| Les'ky | 78 | 49.19 N | 32.13 E |
| Les Laumes | 58 | 47.32 N | 4.27 E |
| Les Lecques | 62 | 43.11 N | 5.40 E |
| Leslie, S. Afr. | 158 | 26.27 S | 28.55 E |
| Leslie, Scot., U.K. | 46 | 56.12 N | 3.13 W |
| Leslie, Ar., U.S. | 194 | 35.49 N | 92.33 W |
| Leslie, Ga., U.S. | 192 | 31.57 N | 84.05 W |
| Leslie, Mi., U.S. | 216 | 42.27 N | 84.25 W |
| Leslie, W.V., U.S. | 188 | 38.02 N | 80.43 W |
| Les Lilas | 261 | 48.53 N | 2.25 E |
| Les Loges | 261 | 48.34 N | 2.03 E |
| Les Loges-en-Josas | 261 | 48.46 N | 2.09 E |
| Lesmahagow | 46 | 55.39 N | 3.55 W |
| Les Marécottes | 58 | 46.07 N | 7.00 E |
| Les Mées | 62 | 44.02 N | 5.59 E |
| Les Mesnuls | 50 | 48.45 N | 1.50 E |
| Lesmo | 266b | 45.39 N | 9.18 E |
| Les Molières | 261 | 48.40 N | 2.04 E |
| Les Monges ∧ | 62 | 44.16 N | 6.12 E |
| Lesmont | 50 | 48.26 N | 4.25 E |
| Les Mosses | 58 | 46.24 N | 7.07 E |
| Lesmurdie Falls National Park ♦ | 168a | 32.01 S | 116.04 E |
| Les Mureaux | 261 | 49.00 N | 1.55 E |
| Leśna | 30 | 51.02 N | 15.16 E |
| Lesneven | 32 | 48.34 N | 4.19 W |
| Les Neyrolles | 58 | 46.08 N | 5.38 E |
| Lešnica | 38 | 44.39 N | 19.19 E |
| Lesnoj, Ross. | 24 | 59.48 N | 52.08 E |
| Lesnoj, Ross. | 80 | 54.11 N | 40.27 E |
| Lesnoj, Ross. | 86 | 56.57 N | 67.15 E |
| Lesnoj -◆-[8] | 265a | 60.00 N | 30.19 E |
| Lesnoje | 76 | 58.17 N | 35.32 E |
| Lesnoje Konobejevo | 80 | 54.02 N | 41.55 E |
| Lesnoje Mat'unino | 80 | 53.27 N | 47.26 E |
| Lesnoj Gorodok | 265b | 55.39 N | 37.13 E |
| Lesnoj park ♦ | 265a | 59.59 N | 30.21 E |
| Lesnyje Pol'any, Ross. | 24 | 58.58 N | 52.26 E |
| Lesnyje Pol'any, Ross. | 265b | 55.57 N | 37.53 E |
| Lesogorsk, Ross. | 80 | 55.06 N | 43.56 E |
| Lesogorsk, Ross. | 88 | 56.03 N | 99.33 E |
| Lesogorsk, Ross. | 89 | 49.27 N | 142.08 E |
| Lesogorskij | 24 | 61.02 N | 28.53 E |
| Lesong, Gunong ∧ | 114 | 2.44 N | 103.17 E |
| Lesopil'noje | 89 | 46.44 N | 134.20 E |
| Lesosibirsk | 86 | 58.16 N | 92.29 E |
| Lesotho □[1], Afr. | 138 | 29.30 S | 28.30 E |
| Lesotho □[1], Afr. | 158 | 29.30 S | 28.30 E |
| Lesozavodsk | 89 | 45.28 N | 133.27 E |
| Lesozavodskij | 24 | 66.44 N | 32.49 E |
| Les Pavillons-sous-Bois | 261 | 48.55 N | 2.30 E |
| Les Pieux | 32 | 49.31 N | 1.48 W |
| Les Planches-en-Montagne | 58 | 46.40 N | 6.01 E |
| Les Ponts-de-Martel | 58 | 46.54 N | 6.41 E |
| Les Posets ∧ | 34 | 42.39 N | 0.25 E |
| Les Praz-de-Chamonix | 58 | 45.56 N | 6.52 E |
| Lesquin | 50 | 50.35 N | 3.07 E |
| Les Riceys | 50 | 47.59 N | 4.22 E |
| Les Roches-l'Evêque | 50 | 47.47 N | 0.53 E |
| Les Rousses | 58 | 46.29 N | 6.04 E |
| Les Ruelles | 261 | 48.40 N | 1.37 E |
| Les Sables-d'Olonne | 32 | 46.30 N | 1.47 W |
| Lessach | 64 | 47.11 N | 13.49 E |
| Les Saintes II | 241o | 15.52 N | 61.37 W |
| Les Salles-sur-Verdon | 62 | 43.46 N | 6.12 E |
| Lessay | 32 | 49.13 N | 1.32 W |
| Les Scaffarels | 62 | 43.57 N | 6.41 E |
| Lesse ≃ | 56 | 50.14 N | 4.54 E |
| Lessebo | 26 | 56.45 N | 15.16 E |
| Lessen → Lessines | 50 | 50.43 N | 3.50 E |
| Lesser Antilles II | 238 | 15.00 N | 61.00 W |
| Lesser Caucasus ⋏ | 84 | 41.00 N | 44.35 E |
| Lesser Khingan Range → Xiao Hinggan Ling ⋏ | 89 | 48.45 N | 127.00 E |
| Lesser Slave ≃ | 182 | 55.10 N | 114.03 W |
| Lesser Slave Lake ⊜ | 182 | 55.25 N | 115.30 W |
| Lesser Sunda Islands → Tenggara, Nusa II | 108 | 9.00 S | 120.00 E |
| Lessines (Lessen) | 50 | 50.43 N | 3.50 E |
| Lessini, Monti ⋏ | 64 | 45.41 N | 11.13 E |
| L'Estaque | 62 | 43.22 N | 5.20 E |
| Leste ≃ | 250 | 6.20 S | 57.46 W |
| Lester, Pa., U.S. | 285 | 39.52 N | 75.17 W |
| Lester, Wa., U.S. | 224 | 47.12 N | 121.29 W |
| Lester B. Pearson International Airport ⊠ | 212 | 43.41 N | 79.38 W |
| Les Tessiers | 62 | 44.24 N | 4.16 E |
| Les Thilliers-en-Vexin | 50 | 49.14 N | 1.36 E |
| Lestijärvi | 26 | 63.32 N | 24.39 E |
| Lestijoki ≃ | 26 | 64.04 N | 23.38 E |
| Lestkov | 60 | 49.54 N | 12.52 E |
| Lestock | 184 | 51.18 N | 104.00 W |
| L'Estréchure | 62 | 44.06 N | 3.47 E |
| Les Trois-Îlets | 240e | 14.32 N | 61.02 W |
| Les Trois Lacs ⊜ | 206 | 45.48 N | 71.54 W |
| Le Sueur | 190 | 44.30 N | 93.52 W |
| Le Sueur ≃ | 190 | 44.07 N | 94.03 W |
| Lesueur, Mount ∧[2] | 162 | 30.10 S | 115.11 E |
| Lešukonskoje | 24 | 64.54 N | 45.40 E |
| Les Ulis | 261 | 48.41 N | 2.11 E |
| Lesung, Tanjung ≻ | 115a | 6.28 S | 105.40 E |
| Lesunovo | 80 | 55.40 N | 43.07 E |
| Les Vans | 62 | 44.24 N | 4.08 E |
| Les Verrières | 58 | 46.54 N | 6.30 E |
| Lésvos (Lesbos) I | 38 | 39.10 N | 26.20 E |
| Leszno | 30 | 51.51 N | 16.35 E |
| Leszno □[4] | 30 | 51.45 N | 16.45 E |
| Letälven ≃ | 40 | 59.05 N | 14.20 E |
| L'Étang-la-Ville | 261 | 48.52 N | 2.05 E |
| Letcher | 198 | 43.53 N | 98.08 W |
| Letchmore Heath | 260 | 51.40 N | 0.20 W |
| Letchworth | 42 | 51.58 N | 0.14 W |
| Letchworth State Park ♦ | 210 | 42.42 N | 77.56 W |
| Letea, Ostrovul I | 38 | 45.20 N | 29.20 E |
| Le Teil | 62 | 44.33 N | 4.41 E |
| Le Temple | 261 | 49.00 N | 1.58 E |
| Letenye | 30 | 46.26 N | 16.43 E |
| Le Tertre-Saint-Denis | 261 | 48.56 N | 1.36 E |
| Lethbridge, Austl. | 274a | 33.44 S | 150.48 E |
| Lethbridge, Ab., Can. | 182 | 49.42 N | 112.50 W |
| Lethbridge, Nf., Can. | 186 | 48.21 N | 53.52 W |
| Le Theil-sur-Huisne | 50 | 48.16 N | 0.42 E |
| Lethem | 246 | 3.23 N | 59.48 W |
| Le Thillay | 261 | 49.00 N | 2.28 E |
| Le Thillot | 58 | 47.53 N | 6.46 E |
| Le Tholy | 58 | 48.05 N | 6.45 E |
| Le Thor | 62 | 43.56 N | 5.00 E |
| Le Thoronet | 62 | 43.27 N | 6.18 E |
| Leti, Kepulauan II | 164 | 8.13 S | 127.50 E |
| Leti, Pulau I | 112 | 8.12 S | 127.41 E |
| Leticia | 246 | 4.09 S | 69.57 W |
| Leting | 98 | 39.27 N | 118.53 E |
| Letino | 68 | 41.26 N | 14.17 E |
| Letjiesbos | 158 | 32.34 S | 22.16 E |
| Letka | 24 | 59.36 N | 49.22 E |
| Letlhakane | 156 | 21.27 S | 25.30 E |
| Letlhakeng | 156 | 24.08 S | 25.02 E |
| Letmathe | 56 | 51.22 N | 7.37 E |


| Symbol | English | Deutsch | Español | Français | Português |
|---|---|---|---|---|---|
| ≃ | River | Fluß | Río | Rivière | Rio |
| ≍ | Canal | Kanal | Canal | Canal | Canal |
| ∟ | Waterfall, Rapids | Wasserfall, Stromschnellen | Cascada, Rápidos | Chute d'eau, Rapides | Cascata, Rápidos |
| ʮ | Strait | Meeresstraße | Estrecho | Détroit | Estreito |
| ⊂ | Bay, Gulf | Bucht, Golf | Bahía, Golfo | Baie, Golfe | Baía, Golfo |
| ⊜ | Lake, Lakes | See, Seen | Lago, Lagos | Lac, Lacs | Lago, Lagos |
| ≡ | Swamp | Sumpf | Pantano | Marais | Pântano |
| ⍓ | Ice Features, Glacier | Eis- und Gletscherformen | Accidentes Glaciales | Formes glaciaires | Acidentes glaciares |
| ⍑ | Other Hydrographic Features | Andere Hydrographische Objekte | Otros Elementos Hidrográficos | Autres données hydrographiques | Outros acidentes hidrográficos |

| Symbol | English | Deutsch | Español | Français | Português |
|---|---|---|---|---|---|
| ✢ | Submarine Features | Untermeerische Objekte | Accidentes Submarinos | Formes de relief sous-marin | Acidentes submarinos |
| □ | Political Unit | Politische Einheit | Unidad Politica | Entité politique | Unidade política |
| υ | Cultural Institution | Kulturelle Institution | Institución Cultural | Institution culturelle | Instituição cultural |
| ⊥ | Historical Site | Historische Stätte | Sitio Histórico | Site historique | Sitio histórico |
| ♦ | Recreational Site | Erholungs- und Ferienort | Sitio de Recreo | Centre de loisirs | Area de Lazer |
| ⊠ | Airport | Flughafen | Aeropuerto | Aéroport | Aeroporto |
| ■ | Military Installation | Militäranlage | Instalación Militar | Installation militaire | Instalação militar |
| -◆- | Miscellaneous | Verschiedenes | Misceláneo | Divers | Diversos |

| Name | Page | Lat.°′ | Long.°′ |
|---|---|---|---|
| Letn'aja Zolotica | **24** | 64.57 N | 36.50 E |
| Letnerečenskij | **24** | 64.17 N | 34.23 E |
| Le Touquet-Paris-Plage | **50** | 50.31 N | 1.35 E |
| Le Touvet | **62** | 45.21 N | 5.57 E |
| Letovo | **265b** | 55.34 N | 37.24 E |
| Letpadan | **110** | 17.47 N | 95.45 E |
| Le Trait | **50** | 49.28 N | 0.49 E |
| Le Trayas | **62** | 43.28 N | 6.55 E |
| Le Tremblay-sur-Mauldre | **261** | 48.47 N | 1.53 E |
| Le Tréport | **50** | 50.04 N | 1.22 E |
| Letschin | **54** | 52.39 N | 14.21 E |
| Letsôk-aw Kyun I | **110** | 11.37 N | 98.15 E |
| Letter | **52** | 52.24 N | 9.38 E |
| Letterfrack | **48** | 53.33 N | 10.00 W |
| Letterkenny | **48** | 54.57 N | 7.44 W |
| Lettermullan | **48** | 53.13 N | 9.42 W |
| Letterston | **42** | 51.56 N | 5.00 W |
| Lettonie → Latvia □[1] | **72** | 57.00 N | 25.00 E |
| Letts | **218** | 39.14 N | 85.35 W |
| Letung | **112** | 2.58 N | 105.42 E |
| Letychiv | **78** | 49.23 N | 27.37 E |
| Letzlingen | **54** | 52.26 N | 11.29 E |
| Leu | **38** | 44.11 N | 24.00 E |
| Léua | **152** | 11.34 S | 20.32 E |
| Leuben | **54** | 51.10 N | 13.18 E |
| Leubnitz | **54** | 50.43 N | 12.21 E |
| Leubsdorf | **54** | 50.48 N | 13.08 E |
| Leuca | **68** | 39.48 N | 18.21 E |
| Leucate, Étang de ⊂ | **32** | 42.51 N | 3.00 E |
| Leuchars | **46** | 56.23 N | 2.53 W |
| Leuchtenberg | **60** | 49.36 N | 12.15 E |
| Leudeville | **261** | 48.34 N | 2.20 E |
| Leuenberger Forst ◆[3] | **264a** | 52.40 N | 13.53 E |
| Leuglay | **58** | 47.49 N | 4.48 E |
| Leuk | **58** | 46.19 N | 7.38 E |
| Leukerbad | **58** | 46.23 N | 7.38 E |
| Leulumoega | **175a** | 13.49 S | 171.55 W |
| Leumeah | **274a** | 34.03 S | 150.50 E |
| Leun | **56** | 50.33 N | 8.21 E |
| Leuna | **54** | 51.19 N | 12.01 E |
| Leupoldsgrün | **54** | 50.17 N | 11.47 E |
| Leura | **170** | 33.43 S | 150.20 E |
| Leura, Mount ∧[2] | **169** | 38.15 S | 143.09 E |
| Leuser, Gunung ∧ | **114** | 3.45 N | 97.11 E |
| Leušinskij Tuman, ozero ⊜ | **86** | 59.42 N | 65.35 E |
| Leutenberg | **54** | 50.34 N | 11.28 E |
| Leutersdorf | **54** | 50.57 N | 14.40 E |
| Leutershausen | **56** | 49.18 N | 10.24 E |
| Leutesdorf | **56** | 50.27 N | 7.23 E |
| Leutkirch | **58** | 47.49 N | 10.01 E |
| Leuven (Louvain) | **56** | 50.53 N | 4.42 E |
| Leuville-sur-Orge | **261** | 48.37 N | 2.16 E |
| Leuwiliang | **115a** | 6.34 S | 106.37 E |
| Leuze, Bel. | **50** | 50.36 N | 3.36 E |
| Leuze, Bel. | **56** | 50.34 N | 4.54 E |
| Levack | **190** | 46.38 N | 81.23 W |
| Levádhia | **38** | 38.25 N | 22.54 E |
| Levaja Mama ≃ | **88** | 57.10 N | 111.54 E |
| Le Val-d'Ajol | **58** | 47.55 N | 6.29 E |
| Le Val-d'Albian | **261** | 48.45 N | 2.11 E |
| Levallois-Perret | **261** | 48.54 N | 2.18 E |
| Le Val-Saint-Germain | **261** | 48.34 N | 2.04 E |
| Levan | **200** | 39.33 N | 111.51 W |
| Levanger | **26** | 63.45 N | 11.18 E |
| Levanna, Monte ∧ | **62** | 45.24 N | 7.12 E |
| Levant, Île du I | **62** | 43.03 N | 6.28 E |
| Levante, Riviera di ⊥[2] | **62** | 44.15 N | 9.30 E |
| Levanto | **62** | 44.10 N | 9.38 E |
| Levanzo | **70** | 37.59 N | 12.20 E |
| Levanzo, Isola di I | **70** | 38.00 N | 12.20 E |
| Levaši | **84** | 42.27 N | 47.20 E |
| Le Vauclin | **240e** | 14.33 N | 60.51 W |
| Levdym | **86** | 60.29 N | 66.19 E |
| Leveaux Mountain ∧[2] | **190** | 47.37 N | 90.47 W |
| Levél | **61** | 47.54 N | 17.12 E |
| Level, Isla I | **254** | 44.29 S | 74.23 W |
| Level Green | **279b** | 40.24 N | 79.43 W |
| Levelland | **196** | 33.35 N | 102.22 W |
| Levelock | **180** | 59.07 N | 156.52 W |
| Level Park | **216** | 42.22 N | 85.18 W |
| Leven, Eng., U.K. | **44** | 53.53 N | 0.19 W |
| Leven, Scot., U.K. | **46** | 56.12 N | 3.00 W |
| Leven ≃, Eng., U.K. | **44** | 54.14 N | 3.01 W |
| Leven ≃, Eng., U.K. | **44** | 54.31 N | 1.21 W |
| Leven, Loch ⊜, Scot., U.K. | **46** | 56.41 N | 5.07 W |
| Leven, Loch ⊜, Scot., U.K. | **46** | 56.12 N | 3.22 W |
| Leven Point ≻ | **158** | 27.55 S | 32.35 E |
| Levens | **62** | 43.52 N | 7.13 E |
| Levenshulme ◆[8] | **262** | 53.27 N | 2.10 W |
| Levent | **130** | 38.27 N | 37.52 E |
| Leventina, Valle V | **58** | 46.25 N | 8.52 E |
| Leveque, Cape ≻ | **162** | 16.24 S | 122.56 E |
| Leverano | **68** | 40.17 N | 18.00 E |
| Leverburgh | **46** | 57.45 N | 7.00 W |
| Leveretts Chapel | **222** | 32.19 N | 94.55 W |
| Levering | **190** | 45.38 N | 84.47 W |
| Leverkusen | **56** | 51.03 N | 6.59 E |
| Levern | **52** | 52.22 N | 8.26 E |
| Lever Park ♦ | **262** | 53.37 N | 2.34 W |
| Le Vésinet | **261** | 48.54 N | 2.08 E |
| Le Vésuve → Vesuvio ∧[1] | **68** | 40.49 N | 14.26 E |
| Leviathan Peak ∧ | **226** | 38.41 N | 119.37 W |
| Levice | **30** | 48.13 N | 18.37 E |
| Levicha | **86** | 57.36 N | 59.55 E |
| Levick, Mount ∧ | **9** | 74.08 S | 163.12 E |
| Levico | **64** | 46.01 N | 11.18 E |
| Levie | **36** | 41.42 N | 9.07 E |
| Levier | **58** | 46.57 N | 6.08 E |
| Le Vigan | **32** | 43.59 N | 3.35 E |
| Levin | **172** | 40.37 S | 175.17 E |
| Levino | **76** | 60.29 N | 37.30 E |
| Lévis | **206** | 46.48 N | 71.11 W |
| Lévis □[6] | **206** | 46.40 N | 71.15 W |
| Levisa Fork ≃ | **192** | 38.06 N | 82.36 W |
| Lévis-Saint Nom | **261** | 48.43 N | 1.58 E |
| Levítha I | **38** | 37.00 N | 26.28 E |
| Levittown, P.R. | **240m** | 18.27 N | 66.14 W |
| Levittown → Willingboro, N.J., U.S. | **208** | 40.03 N | 74.53 W |
| Levittown, N.Y., U.S. | **210** | 40.43 N | 73.30 W |
| Levittown, Pa., U.S. | **208** | 40.09 N | 74.49 W |
| Levittown Discount World ◆[9] | **285** | 40.09 N | 74.49 W |
| Lévka Óri ∧ | **38** | 35.18 N | 24.01 E |
| Levkás | **38** | 38.50 N | 20.41 E |
| Levkás I | **38** | 38.39 N | 20.27 E |
| Levkímmi | **38** | 39.25 N | 20.04 E |
| Levoča | **30** | 49.02 N | 20.36 E |
| Levokumskoje | **84** | 44.48 N | 44.39 E |
| Levroux | **32** | 46.59 N | 1.37 E |
| Levski | **38** | 43.22 N | 25.08 E |
| Lev Tolstoj | **76** | 53.13 N | 39.27 E |
| Levuka | **175g** | 17.41 S | 178.50 E |
| Lėvuo ≃ | **76** | 56.04 N | 24.23 E |
| Levyj Tuzlov ≃ | **83** | 47.35 N | 39.23 E |
| Lewapaku | **115b** | 9.43 S | 119.55 E |
| Lewbeach | **210** | 42.00 N | 74.47 W |
| Lewe | **110** | 19.38 N | 96.07 E |
| Lewedorp | **52** | 51.30 N | 3.45 E |
| Lewellen | **198** | 41.19 N | 102.08 W |
| Lewer ≃ | **156** | 25.30 S | 17.45 E |
| Lewes, Eng., U.K. | **42** | 50.52 N | 0.01 E |
| Lewes, De., U.S. | **208** | 38.46 N | 75.08 W |
| Lewin Brzeski | **30** | 50.46 N | 17.37 E |
| Lewis, Ia., U.S. | **198** | 41.18 N | 95.04 W |
| Lewis, Ks., U.S. | **198** | 37.56 N | 99.15 W |
| Lewis □[6], Ky., U.S. | **218** | 38.32 N | 83.21 W |
| Lewis □[6], Mo., U.S. | **219** | 40.08 N | 91.45 W |
| Lewis □[6], N.Y., U.S. | **212** | 43.47 N | 75.29 W |
| Lewis □[6], Wa., U.S. | **224** | 46.35 N | 122.22 W |
| Lewis ≃ | **224** | 45.51 N | 122.48 W |
| Lewis, Butt of ≻ | **46** | 58.31 N | 6.16 W |
| Lewis, East Fork ≃ | **224** | 45.52 N | 122.43 W |
| Lewis, Isle of I | **46** | 58.10 N | 6.40 W |
| Lewis, Mount ∧ | **204** | 40.24 N | 116.51 W |
| Lewis and Clark ≃ | **224** | 46.10 N | 123.52 W |
| Lewis and Clark Cavern State Park ♦ | **202** | 45.49 N | 111.13 W |
| Lewis and Clark Lake ⊜[1] | **198** | 42.50 N | 97.45 W |
| Lewis and Clark Range ⋏ | **202** | 47.30 N | 113.00 W |
| Lewisberry | **208** | 40.08 N | 76.52 W |
| Lewisburg, Ky., U.S. | **194** | 36.59 N | 86.56 W |
| Lewisburg, Oh., U.S. | **218** | 39.50 N | 84.32 W |
| Lewisburg, Pa., U.S. | **210** | 40.57 N | 76.53 W |
| Lewisburg, Tn., U.S. | **194** | 35.26 N | 86.47 W |
| Lewisburg, W.V., U.S. | **188** | 37.48 N | 80.26 W |
| Lewis Center | **214** | 40.12 N | 83.01 W |
| Lewis Creek ≃, Ca., U.S. | **226** | 35.17 N | 120.58 W |
| Lewis Creek ≃, In., U.S. | **218** | 39.22 N | 85.51 W |
| Lewis Creek Reservoir ⊜[1] | **222** | 30.26 N | 95.32 W |
| Lewisdale | **284c** | 38.58 N | 76.58 W |
| Lewisetta | **208** | 38.01 N | 76.28 W |
| Lewis Gut ⊂ | **276** | 41.09 N | 73.09 W |
| Lewisham | **273d** | 26.07 S | 27.49 E |
| Lewisham ◆[8] | **42** | 51.27 N | 0.01 E |
| Lewisham Location | **273d** | 26.10 S | 27.47 E |
| Lewis-Lockport Airport ⊠ | **278** | 41.36 N | 88.05 W |
| Lewis Pass )( | **172** | 42.23 S | 172.24 E |
| Lewisport | **194** | 37.56 N | 86.54 W |
| Lewisporte | **186** | 49.15 N | 55.03 W |
| Lewis Range ⋏, Austl. | **162** | 20.20 S | 128.40 E |
| Lewis Range ⋏, Mt., U.S. | **202** | 48.35 N | 113.40 W |
| Lewis Run | **214** | 41.52 N | 78.39 W |
| Lewis Run ≃ | **279b** | 40.17 N | 79.55 W |
| Lewis Smith Lake ⊜[1] | **194** | 34.05 N | 87.07 W |
| Lewiston, Ca., U.S. | **204** | 40.43 N | 122.48 W |
| Lewiston, Id., U.S. | **202** | 46.25 N | 117.01 W |
| Lewiston, Me., U.S. | **188** | 44.06 N | 70.12 W |
| Lewiston, Mi., U.S. | **190** | 44.53 N | 84.18 W |
| Lewiston, Mn., U.S. | **190** | 43.59 N | 91.52 W |
| Lewiston, N.Y., U.S. | **210** | 43.10 N | 79.02 W |
| Lewiston, Ut,. U.S. | **200** | 41.58 N | 111.51 W |
| Lewiston Orchards | **202** | 46.23 N | 116.59 W |
| Lewistown, Il., U.S. | **194** | 40.23 N | 90.09 W |
| Lewistown, Md., U.S. | **208** | 39.32 N | 77.24 W |
| Lewistown, Mo., U.S. | **219** | 40.05 N | 91.48 W |
| Lewistown, Mt., U.S. | **202** | 47.03 N | 109.25 W |
| Lewistown, Oh., U.S. | **216** | 40.25 N | 83.53 W |
| Lewistown, Pa., U.S. | **208** | 40.35 N | 77.34 W |
| Lewisville, N.B., Can. | **186** | 46.06 N | 64.46 W |
| Lewisville, Ar., U.S. | **194** | 33.21 N | 93.34 W |
| Lewisville, In., U.S. | **218** | 39.48 N | 85.21 W |
| Lewisville, Pa., U.S. | **208** | 39.43 N | 75.53 W |
| Lewisville, Tx., U.S. | **222** | 33.02 N | 96.59 W |
| Lewisville Dam ◆[6] | **222** | 33.05 N | 96.55 W |
| Lewisville Lake ⊜[1] | **196** | 33.08 N | 97.00 W |
| Lewoleba | **112** | 8.23 S | 123.24 E |
| Lewotobi-lakilaki, Ili ∧ | **115b** | 8.32 S | 122.46 E |
| Lewvan | **184** | 50.00 N | 104.06 W |
| Lexa | **194** | 34.35 N | 90.44 W |
| Lexington, Ga., U.S. | **192** | 33.52 N | 83.06 W |
| Lexington, Il., U.S. | **216** | 40.38 N | 88.47 W |
| Lexington, In., U.S. | **218** | 38.39 N | 85.37 W |
| Lexington, Ky., U.S. | **218** | 38.02 N | 84.30 W |
| Lexington, Ma., U.S. | **207** | 42.26 N | 71.13 W |
| Lexington, Mi., U.S. | **190** | 43.16 N | 82.31 W |
| Lexington, Ms., U.S. | **194** | 33.06 N | 90.03 W |
| Lexington, Mo., U.S. | **194** | 39.11 N | 93.52 W |
| Lexington, Ne., U.S. | **198** | 40.46 N | 99.44 W |
| Lexington, N.Y., U.S. | **210** | 42.15 N | 74.22 W |
| Lexington, N.C., U.S. | **192** | 35.49 N | 80.15 W |
| Lexington, Oh., U.S. | **214** | 40.40 N | 82.34 W |
| Lexington, Ok., U.S. | **196** | 35.00 N | 97.20 W |
| Lexington, Or., U.S. | **202** | 45.26 N | 119.41 W |
| Lexington, S.C., U.S. | **192** | 33.58 N | 81.14 W |
| Lexington, Tn., U.S. | **194** | 35.39 N | 88.23 W |
| Lexington, Tx., U.S. | **222** | 30.25 N | 97.01 W |
| Lexington, Va., U.S. | **192** | 37.47 N | 79.26 W |
| Lexington Park | **208** | 38.16 N | 76.27 W |
| Lexington Reservoir ⊜[1] | **226** | 37.12 N | 121.59 W |
| Lexton | **169** | 37.17 S | 143.31 E |
| Leybourne | **260** | 51.18 N | 0.25 E |
| Leyburn | **44** | 54.19 N | 1.49 W |
| Leyden → Leiden | **52** | 52.09 N | 4.30 E |
| Leye | **102** | 24.48 N | 106.34 E |
| Leyland | **44** | 53.42 N | 2.42 W |
| Leyond ≃ | **184** | 51.40 N | 96.32 W |
| Léyou ≃ | **152** | 1.07 S | 13.08 E |
| Leyre ≃ | **32** | 44.39 N | 1.01 W |
| Leysdown-on-Sea | **42** | 51.24 N | 0.55 E |
| Leysin | **58** | 46.21 N | 7.01 E |
| Leyte | **116** | 11.23 N | 124.29 E |
| Leyte □[4] | **116** | 10.50 N | 124.55 E |
| Leyte I | **116** | 10.50 N | 124.50 E |
| Leyte Gulf ⊂ | **116** | 10.50 N | 125.25 E |
| Leyton ◆[8] | **260** | 51.33 N | 0.01 W |
| Leyu | **106** | 31.55 N | 120.43 E |
| Lèz ≊ | **62** | 43.31 N | 3.55 E |
| Leža | **76** | 58.56 N | 40.45 E |
| Leža ≃ | **76** | 59.15 N | 40.10 E |
| Leżajsk | **30** | 50.16 N | 22.24 E |
| Lezama | **246** | 9.43 N | 66.24 W |
| Lézarde ≃ | **240e** | 14.36 N | 61.01 W |
| Lézat | **58** | 46.30 N | 5.56 E |
| Lèze ≃ | **62** | 43.40 N | 5.28 E |
| Lezhë | **38** | 41.47 N | 19.39 E |
| Lezhi | **107** | 30.17 N | 105.02 E |
| Lëzna | **76** | 55.02 N | 30.48 E |
| Ležn'ovo | **80** | 56.46 N | 40.53 E |
| Lezzeno | **58** | 45.56 N | 9.11 E |
| L'gov | **78** | 51.43 N | 35.17 E |
| Lhasa | **120** | 29.40 N | 91.09 E |
| Lhasa ≃ | **120** | 29.21 N | 90.45 E |
| L'Hautil | **261** | 49.00 N | 2.01 E |
| Lhazê | **120** | 29.10 N | 87.42 E |
| L'Hillil | **34** | 35.41 N | 0.19 E |
| Lhokkruet | **114** | 4.52 N | 95.24 E |
| Lhoknga | **114** | 5.29 N | 95.15 E |
| Lhokseumawe | **114** | 5.10 N | 97.08 E |
| Lhoksukon | **114** | 5.03 N | 97.19 E |
| L'Hôpital-sous-Rochefort | **62** | 45.46 N | 3.56 E |
| Lhorong | **102** | 30.45 N | 96.09 E |
| L'Hospitalet de Llobregat | **34** | 41.22 N | 2.08 E |
| Lhotse ∧ | **124** | 27.57 N | 86.56 E |
| Lhozhag | **120** | 28.24 N | 90.49 E |
| Lhuis | **62** | 45.45 N | 5.32 E |
| Lhuntsi Dzong | **120** | 27.39 N | 91.09 E |
| Lhünzê | **120** | 28.25 N | 92.31 E |
| Li | **110** | 17.48 N | 98.57 E |
| Li ≃, Thai | **110** | 18.26 N | 98.42 E |
| Li ≃, Zhg. | **100** | 33.11 N | 115.07 E |
| Li ≃, Zhg. | **102** | 29.24 N | 112.01 E |
| Lian ≃, Zhg. | **100** | 25.46 N | 115.38 E |
| Lian ≃, Zhg. | **100** | 24.02 N | 113.18 E |
| Lian ≃, Zhg. | **102** | 24.02 N | 113.18 E |
| Lian ≃, Zhg. | **102** | 27.48 N | 112.52 E |
| Liancheng | **100** | 25.44 N | 116.46 E |
| Liancourt | **50** | 49.20 N | 2.28 E |
| Liane ≃ | **50** | 50.43 N | 1.36 E |
| Liang | **164** | 3.30 S | 128.19 E |
| Lianga | **116** | 8.38 N | 126.06 E |
| Lianga Bay ⊂ | **116** | 8.37 N | 126.12 E |
| Liang'anchang | **107** | 30.30 N | 104.56 E |
| Liangbao | **102** | 34.37 N | 110.45 E |
| Liangbingbao | **89** | 45.48 N | 128.19 E |
| Liangbingtai | **89** | 43.12 N | 128.47 E |
| Liangbuaya | **112** | 0.05 N | 116.46 E |
| Liangchahe | **107** | 29.03 N | 106.18 E |
| Liangcheng | **98** | 35.35 N | 119.35 E |
| Liangcun | **100** | 26.36 N | 115.34 E |
| Liangdang | **102** | 33.56 N | 106.12 E |
| Liangdawa | **105** | 40.39 N | 117.37 E |
| Liangfengwu | **107** | 30.11 N | 105.22 E |
| Lianggezhuang | **105** | 39.21 N | 115.22 E |
| Lianghe, Zhg. | **89** | 45.09 N | 128.45 E |
| Lianghe, Zhg. | **102** | 24.51 N | 98.25 E |
| Liangheguan | **102** | 32.52 N | 109.19 E |
| Lianghekou, Zhg. | **102** | 33.42 N | 104.25 E |
| Lianghekou, Zhg. | **102** | 29.14 N | 108.40 E |
| Lianghekou, Zhg. | **102** | 31.27 N | 102.13 E |
| Lianghekou, Zhg. | **107** | 28.55 N | 106.03 E |
| Liangiu | **98** | 35.12 N | 117.47 E |
| Liangjia | **107** | 29.29 N | 105.33 E |
| Liangjiadian | **98** | 39.10 N | 121.54 E |
| Liangjiafang | **98** | 41.04 N | 117.18 E |
| Liangjianfang | **105** | 40.45 N | 117.20 E |
| Liangjiang | **102** | 23.23 N | 108.22 E |
| Liangjiangkou | **98** | 42.38 N | 128.05 E |
| Liangjiawazi | **104** | 40.40 N | 120.42 E |
| Liangjiazi | **104** | 42.13 N | 122.31 E |
| Liangkou | **100** | 23.43 N | 113.43 E |
| Lianglukou | **107** | 29.18 N | 106.15 E |
| Liangmen | **98** | 35.34 N | 114.54 E |
| Liangmentou | **100** | 28.58 N | 121.12 E |
| Liangmushi | **106** | 30.46 N | 119.35 E |
| Liangpa | **102** | 24.10 N | 106.13 E |
| Liangpeng | **106** | 30.47 N | 119.38 E |
| Liangping | **102** | 30.41 N | 107.49 E |
| Liang Shan ∧ | **102** | 23.45 N | 99.45 E |
| Liangshui ≃ | **271a** | 39.49 N | 116.40 E |
| Liangtian | **100** | 25.37 N | 113.00 E |
| Liangtinghe | **100** | 30.20 N | 116.12 E |
| Liangtoumen | **100** | 29.31 N | 120.45 E |
| Liangtun | **98** | 40.14 N | 122.34 E |
| Liangwangzhuang | **105** | 39.01 N | 116.58 E |
| Liangxiangzhen | **105** | 39.44 N | 116.08 E |
| Liangying | **100** | 23.14 N | 116.21 E |
| Liangyuan | **100** | 32.00 N | 117.34 E |
| Liangzhu | **106** | 30.23 N | 120.03 E |
| Liangzi Hu ⊜ | **100** | 30.16 N | 114.34 E |
| Lianhe | **98** | 42.36 N | 125.37 E |
| Lian Hu ⊜ | **106** | 32.02 N | 119.32 E |
| Lianhua | **100** | 27.07 N | 113.57 E |
| Lianhuachi | **105** | 40.28 N | 116.33 E |
| Lianhuapao | **89** | 45.32 N | 129.50 E |
| Lianhua Shan ⋏ | **100** | 23.40 N | 116.00 E |
| Lianjiang, Zhg. | **100** | 26.12 N | 119.31 E |
| Lianjiang, Zhg. | **102** | 21.38 N | 110.15 E |
| Lianjiechang | **107** | 29.41 N | 104.30 E |
| Liannan (Sanjiang) | **102** | 24.38 N | 112.10 E |
| Lianozovo ◆[8] | **265b** | 55.54 N | 37.35 E |
| Lianping | **100** | 24.22 N | 114.31 E |
| Lianpu | **100** | 26.02 N | 118.38 E |
| Lianshanguan | **104** | 40.58 N | 123.46 E |
| Lianshi | **106** | 30.42 N | 120.26 E |
| Lianshui | **100** | 33.47 N | 119.16 E |
| Liansiji | **98** | 33.58 N | 114.24 E |
| Liantang | **106** | 31.37 N | 120.38 E |
| Lianxian | **102** | 24.48 N | 112.25 E |
| Lianyin | **89** | 53.28 N | 123.51 E |
| Lianyuan (Lantian) | **102** | 27.42 N | 111.19 E |
| Lianyungang, Zhg. | **98** | 34.44 N | 119.30 E |
| Lianyungang (Xinpu), Zhg. | **98** | 34.39 N | 119.16 E |
| Lianyun Shan ∧ | **100** | 28.32 N | 113.50 E |
| Lianzhou → Hepu | **102** | 21.39 N | 109.11 E |
| Liao ≃ | **90** | 40.50 N | 121.48 E |
| Liaobinta | **104** | 42.08 N | 123.04 E |
| Liaocheng | **98** | 36.30 N | 115.59 E |
| Liaodong Bandao (Liaotung Peninsula) ≻[1] | **98** | 40.00 N | 122.20 E |
| Liaodong Wan (Gulf of Liaotung) ⊂ | **98** | 40.30 N | 121.30 E |
| Liaohe Kou ⊂[1] | **104** | 40.42 N | 122.05 E |
| Liaojiangshi | **100** | 26.05 N | 113.17 E |
| Liaoning □[4] | **90** | 41.00 N | 123.00 E |
| Liaotung, Gulf of → Liaodong Wan ⊂ | **98** | 40.30 N | 121.30 E |
| Liaotung Peninsula → Liaodong Bandao ≻[1] | **98** | 40.00 N | 122.20 E |
| Liaoyang | **104** | 41.17 N | 123.11 E |
| Liaoyangwopu | **89** | 43.00 N | 123.28 E |
| Liaoyuan | **89** | 42.54 N | 125.07 E |
| Liaozhong | **104** | 41.31 N | 122.44 E |
| Liapádhes | **38** | 39.40 N | 19.44 E |
| Liāquatpur | **123** | 28.56 N | 70.57 E |
| Liard ≃ | **176** | 61.52 N | 121.18 W |
| Liāri | **120** | 25.41 N | 66.29 E |
| Liart | **50** | 49.46 N | 4.20 E |
| Liat, Pulau I | **112** | 2.53 S | 107.05 E |
| Liathach ∧ | **46** | 57.35 N | 5.29 W |
| Lib I | **14** | 8.19 N | 167.25 E |
| Libagon | **116** | 10.18 N | 125.03 E |
| Liban → Lebanon □[1] | **128** | 34.00 N | 36.00 E |
| Libanga | **152** | 0.19 N | 18.41 E |
| Líbano | **246** | 4.55 N | 75.04 W |
| Libano → Lebanon □[1] | **128** | 34.00 N | 36.00 E |
| Libanon → Lebanon □[1] | **128** | 34.00 N | 36.00 E |
| Libau → Liepāja | **76** | 56.31 N | 21.01 E |
| Libby | **202** | 48.23 N | 115.33 W |
| Libby Dam ◆[6] | **202** | 48.24 N | 115.20 W |
| Libčeves | **54** | 50.26 N | 13.50 E |
| Libčice nad Vltavou | **54** | 50.10 N | 14.20 E |
| Liběchov | **54** | 50.20 N | 14.28 E |
| Libenge | **152** | 3.39 N | 18.38 E |
| Liberal, Ks., U.S. | **198** | 37.02 N | 100.55 W |
| Liberal, Mo., U.S. | **194** | 37.33 N | 94.31 W |
| Liberdade | **256** | 22.01 S | 44.19 W |
| Liberdade ◆[8] | **287b** | 23.35 S | 46.37 W |
| Liberdade ≃, Bra. | **248** | 7.10 S | 71.51 W |
| Liberdade ≃, Bra. | **250** | 9.40 S | 52.17 W |
| Liberec | **30** | 50.46 N | 15.03 E |
| Liberia | **236** | 10.38 N | 85.27 W |
| Liberia □[1], Afr. | **134** | 6.30 N | 9.30 W |
| Liberia □[1], Afr. | **150** | 6.30 N | 9.30 W |
| Liberta | **240c** | 17.02 N | 61.47 W |
| Libertad, Arg. | **258** | 34.42 S | 58.41 W |
| Libertad, Ur. | **258** | 34.38 S | 56.39 W |
| Libertad, Ven. | **246** | 8.20 N | 69.37 W |
| Libertad, Ven. | **246** | 9.23 N | 68.44 W |
| Libertador □[5] | **286c** | 10.27 N | 66.57 W |
| Libertador General Bernardo O'Higgins □[4] | **252** | 34.30 S | 71.00 W |
| Libertador General San Martín | **252** | 23.48 S | 64.48 W |
| Liberty, Il., U.S. | **219** | 39.53 N | 91.06 W |
| Liberty, In., U.S. | **218** | 39.38 N | 84.55 W |
| Liberty, Ky., U.S. | **194** | 37.19 N | 84.56 W |
| Liberty, Ms., U.S. | **194** | 31.09 N | 90.48 W |
| Liberty, Mo., U.S. | **194** | 39.14 N | 94.25 W |
| Liberty, Ne., U.S. | **198** | 40.05 N | 96.28 W |
| Liberty, N.Y., U.S. | **210** | 41.48 N | 74.44 W |
| Liberty, N.C., U.S. | **192** | 35.51 N | 79.34 W |
| Liberty, Pa., U.S. | **210** | 41.34 N | 77.06 W |
| Liberty, Pa., U.S. | **279b** | 40.20 N | 79.51 W |
| Liberty, S.C., U.S. | **192** | 34.47 N | 82.41 W |
| Liberty, Tx., U.S. | **222** | 30.03 N | 94.47 W |
| Liberty □[6] | **222** | 30.12 N | 94.50 W |
| Liberty Acres | **280** | 34.04 N | 118.12 W |
| Liberty Center, In., U.S. | **216** | 40.41 N | 85.16 W |
| Liberty Center, Oh., U.S. | **216** | 41.26 N | 84.00 W |
| Liberty City | **222** | 32.27 N | 94.57 W |
| Liberty Corner | **276** | 40.39 N | 74.34 W |
| Liberty Ditch ≊ | **226** | 36.31 N | 120.02 W |
| Liberty Farms | **226** | 38.19 N | 121.42 W |
| Liberty Hill | **196** | 30.40 N | 97.55 W |
| Liberty Island I | **276** | 40.41 N | 74.03 W |
| Liberty Lake ⊜[1] | **208** | 39.25 N | 76.53 W |
| Liberty Manor | **284b** | 39.21 N | 76.47 W |
| Liberty Mills | **216** | 41.02 N | 85.44 W |
| Liberty Park | **216** | 41.26 N | 87.22 W |
| Libertytown | **208** | 39.29 N | 77.14 W |
| Liberty Tree Mall ◆[9] | **283** | 42.33 N | 70.57 W |
| Liberty Tunnel ◆[5] | **279b** | 40.26 N | 80.01 W |
| Libertyville | **216** | 42.16 N | 87.57 W |
| Líbeznice | **54** | 50.10 N | 14.30 E |
| Libia → Libya □[1] | **146** | 27.00 N | 17.00 E |
| Libibi | **152** | 14.42 S | 17.44 E |
| Libishan | **106** | 30.45 N | 119.20 E |
| Lībiyā → Libya □[1] | **146** | 27.00 N | 17.00 E |
| Lībīyah, Aṣ-Ṣaḥrā' al- (Libyan Desert) ◆[2] | **136** | 24.00 N | 25.00 E |
| Liblín | **60** | 49.55 N | 13.32 E |
| Libni, Jabal ∧[2] | **132** | 30.44 N | 33.50 E |
| Libo | **102** | 25.28 N | 107.53 E |
| Libobo, Tanjung ≻ | **164** | 0.54 S | 128.28 E |
| Liboc ≃ | **54** | 50.10 N | 13.31 E |
| Libochovice | **54** | 50.22 N | 14.03 E |
| Libode | **158** | 31.33 S | 29.02 E |
| Liboi | **154** | 0.24 N | 40.57 E |
| Liboko | **152** | 2.43 N | 21.28 E |
| Libomyšl | **60** | 49.52 N | 14.00 E |
| Libona | **116** | 8.20 N | 124.44 E |
| Liboumba ≃ | **152** | 0.38 N | 12.54 E |
| Libourne | **32** | 44.55 N | 0.14 W |
| Libramont | **56** | 49.55 N | 5.23 E |
| Library | **214** | 40.18 N | 80.02 W |
| Librazhd | **38** | 41.11 N | 20.19 E |
| Libres | **234** | 19.28 N | 97.41 W |
| Libreville | **152** | 0.23 N | 9.27 E |
| Librizzi | **70** | 38.06 N | 14.57 E |
| Libro Point ≻ | **116** | 11.26 N | 119.29 E |
| Libu | **102** | 23.41 N | 111.30 E |
| Libucan Island I | **116** | 11.54 N | 124.39 E |
| Libuganon ≃ | **116** | 7.27 N | 125.47 E |
| Libunga | **154** | 1.49 N | 26.35 E |
| Liburung | **112** | 3.55 S | 120.09 E |
| Libušín | **54** | 50.09 N | 14.04 E |
| Libya (Lībiyā) □[1], Afr. | **136** | 27.00 N | 17.00 E |
| Libya (Lībiyā) □[1], Afr. | **146** | 27.00 N | 17.00 E |
| Libyan Desert → Lībīyah, Aṣ-Ṣaḥrā' al- ◆[2] | **136** | 24.00 N | 25.00 E |
| Libyan Plateau → Aḍ-Diffah ⋏[1] | **140** | 30.30 N | 25.30 E |
| Libye → Libya □[1] | **146** | 27.00 N | 17.00 E |
| Libyen → Libya □[1] | **146** | 27.00 N | 17.00 E |
| Libysche Wüste → Lībīyah, Aṣ-Ṣaḥrā' al- ◆[2] | **136** | 24.00 N | 25.00 E |
| Licancábur, Volcán ∧[1] | **248** | 22.50 S | 67.50 W |
| Licantén | **252** | 34.59 S | 72.00 W |
| Licata | **70** | 37.06 N | 13.56 E |
| Licciana Nardi | **64** | 44.16 N | 10.02 E |
| Lice | **130** | 38.28 N | 40.39 E |
| Lich | **56** | 50.33 N | 8.50 E |
| Lichačova, mys ≻ | **89** | 42.44 N | 132.51 E |
| Lichaja ≃ | **83** | 48.08 N | 40.15 E |
| Lichang | **107** | 28.53 N | 104.26 E |
| Licheng | **102** | 36.30 N | 113.21 E |
| Lichères-Près-Aigremont | **50** | 47.43 N | 3.51 E |
| Lichfield | **42** | 52.42 N | 1.48 W |
| Lichinga | **154** | 13.18 S | 35.14 E |
| Lichitişeni | **38** | 46.23 N | 27.17 E |
| Lichoborka ≃ | **265b** | 55.50 N | 37.38 E |
| Lichoslavl' | **76** | 57.07 N | 35.28 E |
| Lichovskoj | **83** | 48.07 N | 40.12 E |
| Lichtaart | **56** | 51.14 N | 4.54 E |
| Lichte | **54** | 50.31 N | 11.10 E |
| Lichtenau, Dtsch. | **56** | 49.17 N | 10.41 E |
| Lichtenau, Dtsch. | **56** | 48.43 N | 8.01 E |
| Lichtenberg, Dtsch. | **54** | 50.23 N | 11.40 E |
| Lichtenberg, Fr. | **56** | 48.55 N | 7.29 E |
| Lichtenberg ◆[8] | **264a** | 52.31 N | 13.29 E |
| Lichtenburg | **158** | 26.08 S | 26.08 E |
| Lichtendorf | **263** | 51.28 N | 7.37 E |
| Lichtenfels, Dtsch. | **56** | 50.09 N | 11.04 E |
| Lichtenfels, Dtsch. | **56** | 51.14 N | 8.49 E |
| Lichtenplatz ◆[8] | **263** | 51.15 N | 7.12 E |
| Lichtenrade ◆[8] | **264a** | 52.23 N | 13.25 E |
| Lichtensee | **54** | 51.23 N | 13.22 E |
| Lichtensteig | **58** | 47.19 N | 9.05 E |
| Lichtenstein | **54** | 50.45 N | 12.37 E |
| Lichtenstein, Schloss ʊ | **58** | 48.24 N | 9.15 E |
| Lichtentanne | **54** | 50.42 N | 12.25 E |
| Lichtenvoorde | **52** | 51.59 N | 6.34 E |
| Lichterfelde ◆[8] | **264a** | 52.26 N | 13.19 E |
| Lichtervelde | **50** | 51.02 N | 3.09 E |
| Lichuan, Zhg. | **100** | 27.18 N | 116.53 E |
| Lichuan, Zhg. | **102** | 30.18 N | 108.51 E |
| Lick Creek ≃, Il., U.S. | **219** | 39.42 N | 89.41 W |
| Lick Creek ≃, In., U.S. | **218** | 38.33 N | 86.31 W |
| Lick Creek ≃, Mo., U.S. | **219** | 39.31 N | 91.39 W |
| Lick Creek ≃, Oh., U.S. | **216** | 41.21 N | 84.25 W |
| Lick Creek ≃, Tn., U.S. | **192** | 36.11 N | 83.10 W |
| Lickershamn | **26** | 57.50 N | 18.31 E |
| Licking | **194** | 37.29 N | 91.51 W |
| Licking □[6] | **214** | 40.10 N | 82.30 W |
| Licking ≃, Ky., U.S. | **188** | 39.06 N | 84.30 W |
| Licking ≃, Oh., U.S. | **214** | 40.03 N | 82.20 W |
| Licking, North Fork ≃, Ky., U.S. | **218** | 38.35 N | 84.13 W |
| Licking, North Fork ≃, Oh., U.S. | **214** | 40.03 N | 82.23 W |
| Licking, South Fork ≃ | **218** | 38.41 N | 84.20 W |
| Lickingville | **214** | 41.23 N | 79.22 W |
| Lick Observatory ʊ[3] | **226** | 37.22 N | 121.37 W |
| Ličko Polje ≚ | **36** | 44.35 N | 15.25 E |
| Lick Run ≃, Pa., U.S. | **210** | 41.12 N | 77.32 W |
| Lick Run ≃, Pa., U.S. | **279b** | 40.17 N | 79.57 W |
| Licodia Eubea | **70** | 37.09 N | 14.42 E |
| Licosa, Punta ≻ | **68** | 40.15 N | 14.54 E |
| Licun | **98** | 38.32 N | 117.08 E |
| Licungo ≃ | **154** | 17.40 S | 37.15 E |
| Lid' | **76** | 59.39 N | 35.05 E |
| Lida | **76** | 53.53 N | 25.18 E |
| Lidan ≃ | **26** | 58.31 N | 13.09 E |
| Lidao | **98** | 37.15 N | 122.32 E |
| Lidarentuncun | **104** | 41.32 N | 123.12 E |
| Lidcombe | **274a** | 33.52 S | 151.03 E |
| Liddel Water ≃ | **44** | 55.04 N | 2.57 W |
| Liddesdale V | **44** | 55.12 N | 2.46 W |
| Liddon Gulf ⊂ | **176** | 75.03 N | 113.00 W |
| Liden | **26** | 62.42 N | 16.48 E |
| Lidesi | **100** | 33.33 N | 115.53 E |
| Lidgerwood | **198** | 46.04 N | 97.09 W |
| Lidgetton | **158** | 29.25 S | 30.05 E |
| Lidian | **107** | 28.57 N | 103.44 E |
| Lídice, Bra. | **256** | 22.51 S | 44.12 W |
| Lídice, Pan. | **236** | 8.45 N | 79.54 W |
| Lidice ⊥ | **54** | 50.03 N | 14.08 E |
| Lidingö | **40** | 59.22 N | 18.08 E |
| Lidköping | **26** | 58.30 N | 13.10 E |
| Lido | **64** | 45.25 N | 12.22 E |
| Lido, Litorale di ⊥[2] | **64** | 45.23 N | 12.21 E |
| Lido, Porto di ⊂ | **64** | 45.26 N | 12.25 E |
| Lido Beach | **276** | 40.35 N | 73.38 W |
| Lido di Camaiore | **64** | 43.54 N | 10.13 E |
| Lido di Castel Fusano ◆[8] | **66** | 41.43 N | 12.20 E |
| Lido di Iesolo | **64** | 45.30 N | 12.39 E |
| Lido di Metaponto | **68** | 40.22 N | 16.50 E |
| Lido di Ostia ◆[8] | **66** | 41.44 N | 12.14 E |
| Lido di Pomposa | **66** | 44.45 N | 12.14 E |
| Lido di Siponto | **68** | 41.37 N | 15.55 E |
| Lido Key I | **220** | 27.19 N | 82.35 W |
| Lidsjön ⊜ | **40** | 58.55 N | 16.51 E |
| Lidu | **107** | 30.35 N | 106.04 E |
| Lidzbark | **30** | 53.17 N | 19.49 E |
| Lidzbark Warmiński | **30** | 54.09 N | 20.35 E |
| Liebenau, Dtsch. | **52** | 52.36 N | 9.05 E |
| Liebenau, Dtsch. | **52** | 51.30 N | 9.17 E |
| Liebenau, Öst. | **61** | 48.32 N | 14.49 E |
| Liebenbergsvlei ≃ | **158** | 27.20 S | 28.31 E |
| Liebenburg | **52** | 52.01 N | 10.26 E |
| Liebenwalde | **54** | 52.52 N | 13.23 E |
| Lieberhausen | **56** | 51.03 N | 7.40 E |
| Lieberose | **54** | 51.59 N | 14.17 E |
| Liebertwolkwitz | **54** | 51.17 N | 12.28 E |
| Liebig, Mount ∧ | **162** | 23.18 S | 131.22 E |
| Liebstadt | **54** | 50.52 N | 13.51 E |
| Liechtenstein □[1], Europe | **22** | 47.09 N | 9.35 E |
| Liechtenstein □[1], Europe | **58** | 47.09 N | 9.35 E |
| Liechtensteinklamm V | **64** | 47.18 N | 13.12 E |
| Liedberg | **263** | 51.10 N | 6.32 E |
| Liedekerke | **50** | 50.52 N | 4.05 E |
| Liège (Luik) | **56** | 50.38 N | 5.34 E |
| Liège □[4] | **56** | 50.30 N | 5.30 E |
| Liège, Aéroport ⊠ | **56** | 50.39 N | 5.30 E |
| Liegnitz → Legnica | **30** | 51.13 N | 16.09 E |
| Lieja → Liège | **56** | 50.38 N | 5.34 E |
| Lieksa | **26** | 63.19 N | 30.01 E |
| Lielais Liepu kalns ∧[2] | **76** | 56.25 N | 27.50 E |
| Lielupe ≃ | **76** | 57.01 N | 23.56 E |
| Lielvārde | **76** | 56.43 N | 24.51 E |
| Liemienzhen | **107** | 30.29 N | 106.05 E |
| Lienart | **154** | 3.04 N | 25.31 E |
| Lienchou → Hepu | **102** | 21.39 N | 109.11 E |
| Lienen | **52** | 52.09 N | 7.58 E |
| Lienz | **64** | 46.50 N | 12.47 E |
| Liepāja | **76** | 56.31 N | 21.01 E |
| Liepājas ezers ⊜ | **76** | 56.27 N | 21.03 E |
| Liepe | **54** | 53.58 N | 13.56 E |
| Liepna | **76** | 57.25 N | 27.25 E |
| Liepnitzsee ⊜ | **264a** | 52.45 N | 13.30 E |
| Lièpvre | **58** | 48.16 N | 7.17 E |
| Lier (Lierre) | **50** | 51.08 N | 4.34 E |
| Lierenfeld ◆[8] | **263** | 51.13 N | 6.51 E |
| Lierna | **58** | 45.57 N | 9.18 E |
| Liernais | **50** | 47.12 N | 4.17 E |
| Lierneux | **56** | 50.18 N | 5.48 E |
| Liershizhai | **104** | 41.49 N | 123.43 E |
| Liesborn | **52** | 51.43 N | 8.15 E |
| Lieser ≃, Dtsch. | **56** | 49.55 N | 7.01 E |
| Lieser ≃, Öst. | **64** | 46.47 N | 13.39 E |
| Lieshout | **52** | 51.32 N | 5.35 E |
| Liesing ◆[8] | **264b** | 48.08 N | 16.17 E |
| Liesing ≃, Öst. | **61** | 47.20 N | 15.02 E |
| Liesing ≃, Öst. | **264b** | 48.08 N | 16.28 E |
| Liesjärven kansallispuisto ♦ | **26** | 60.40 N | 23.54 E |
| Lieskau | **54** | 51.37 N | 13.48 E |
| Liesse | **50** | 49.37 N | 3.48 E |
| Liessies | **50** | 50.07 N | 4.05 E |
| Liestal | **58** | 47.29 N | 7.44 E |
| Lieşti | **38** | 45.38 N | 27.32 E |
| Lietuva → Lithuania □[1] | **72** | 56.00 N | 24.00 E |
| Lietzow | **54** | 54.29 N | 13.30 E |
| Lieurey | **50** | 49.14 N | 0.29 E |
| Lieusaint | **261** | 48.38 N | 2.33 E |
| Lieutel ≃ | **261** | 48.49 N | 1.52 E |
| Lieutenant Robert J. Palenscar Memorial Airport ⊠ | **285** | 39.51 N | 75.03 W |
| Liévin | **50** | 50.25 N | 2.46 E |
| Lièvre, Rivière du ≃ | **176** | 45.31 N | 75.26 W |
| Lièvres, Île aux I | **186** | 47.51 N | 69.44 W |
| Liezen | **61** | 47.35 N | 14.15 E |
| Lifanga | **152** | 0.19 N | 21.57 E |
| Liffey ≃ | **48** | 53.21 N | 6.16 W |
| Liffol-le-Grand | **58** | 48.19 N | 5.35 E |
| Lifford | **48** | 54.50 N | 7.29 W |
| Liffré | **32** | 48.13 N | 1.30 W |
| Lifjell ∧ | **26** | 59.30 N | 8.52 E |
| Lifoku | **152** | 0.04 S | 21.18 E |
| Lifou I | **175f** | 20.53 S | 167.13 E |
| Lifoula | **273b** | 4.06 S | 15.25 E |
| Lifton | **42** | 50.39 N | 4.17 W |
| Liftwood | **285** | 39.47 N | 75.31 W |
| Lifune ≃ | **152** | 8.21 S | 13.22 E |
| Ligačovo | **265b** | 55.56 N | 37.15 E |
| Ligang | **100** | 30.04 N | 121.52 E |
| Ligao, Pil. | **116** | 13.14 N | 123.32 E |
| Ligao, Pil. | **116** | 6.17 N | 124.09 E |
| Ligasa | **152** | 0.42 N | 23.45 E |
| Ligezhuang, Zhg. | **105** | 39.49 N | 115.56 E |
| Ligezhuang, Zhg. | **105** | 39.42 N | 118.12 E |
| Light ≃ | **168b** | 34.35 S | 138.22 E |
| Lightfoot | **208** | 37.20 N | 76.45 W |
| Lighthouse Beach ⊥[2] | **273a** | 6.24 N | 3.22 E |
| Lighthouse Point | **220** | 26.16 N | 80.05 W |
| Lighthouse Point ≻, On., Can. | **214** | 41.50 N | 82.38 W |
| Lighthouse Point ≻, Fl., U.S. | **192** | 29.54 N | 84.21 W |
| Lighthouse Point ≻, Mi., U.S. | **190** | 45.13 N | 85.32 W |
| Lighthouse Reef ✢[2] | **232** | 17.20 N | 87.32 W |
| Lightning Creek ≃, Sk., Can. | **184** | 49.12 N | 101.43 W |
| Lightning Creek ≃, N.A. | **224** | 48.50 N | 121.03 W |
| Lightning Creek ≃, Wy., U.S. | **198** | 43.11 N | 104.44 W |
| Lightning Ridge | **166** | 29.26 S | 147.59 E |
| Lightstreet | **210** | 41.02 N | 76.25 W |
| Lightsville | **216** | 40.18 N | 84.42 W |
| Ligist | **61** | 46.59 N | 15.12 E |
| Lignano Pineta | **64** | 45.40 N | 13.07 E |
| Lignano Sabbiadoro | **64** | 45.42 N | 13.09 E |
| Lignières | **32** | 46.45 N | 2.11 E |
| Lignite | **198** | 48.52 N | 102.33 W |
| Lignon ≃ | **62** | 45.44 N | 4.08 E |
| Lignumvitae Key I | **220** | 24.55 N | 80.42 W |
| Ligny-en-Barrois | **58** | 48.41 N | 5.20 E |
| Ligny-en-Cambrésis | **50** | 50.06 N | 3.22 E |
| Ligny-le-Châtel | **50** | 47.54 N | 3.45 E |
| Ligny-le-Ribault | **50** | 47.41 N | 1.47 E |
| Ligonha ≃ | **154** | 16.54 S | 39.09 E |
| Ligonier, In., U.S. | **216** | 41.27 N | 85.35 W |
| Ligonier, Pa., U.S. | **214** | 40.14 N | 79.14 W |
| Ligovo | **76** | 60.13 N | 31.48 E |
| Ligovo ◆[8] | **265a** | 59.50 N | 30.12 E |
| Ligovskij kanal ≊ | **265a** | 59.47 N | 30.10 E |
| Liguantu | **105** | 40.24 N | 115.45 E |
| Ligueil | **32** | 47.03 N | 0.49 E |
| Ligui | **232** | 25.43 N | 111.16 W |
| Ligure, Mar → Ligurian Sea ⊤[2] | **36** | 43.30 N | 9.00 E |
| Liguria □[4] | **36** | 44.30 N | 8.50 E |
| Liguria, Mar de → Ligurian Sea ⊤[2] | **36** | 43.30 N | 9.00 E |
| Ligurian Sea ⊤[2] | **36** | 43.30 N | 9.00 E |
| Ligurisches Meer → Ligurian Sea ⊤[2] | **36** | 43.30 N | 9.00 E |
| Lihir Group II | **164** | 3.05 S | 152.40 E |
| Lihir Island I | **164** | 3.05 S | 152.35 E |
| Lihoi Seamount ✢[3] | **14** | 18.56 N | 155.16 W |
| Lihou Reef and Cays ✢[2] | **166** | 17.25 S | 151.40 E |
| Lihu | **100** | 23.23 N | 116.03 E |
| Lihue | **229b** | 21.58 N | 159.22 W |
| Lihue Airport ⊠ | **229b** | 21.59 N | 159.21 W |
| Lihuel Calel, Parque Nacional ♦, Arg. | **252** | 37.58 S | 65.32 W |
| Lihuel Calel, Parque Nacional ♦, Arg. | **254** | 37.58 S | 65.32 W |
| Lihula | **76** | 58.41 N | 23.50 E |
| Liji, Zhg. | **100** | 31.59 N | 115.51 E |
| Liji, Zhg. | **100** | 33.48 N | 117.48 E |
| Lijia, Zhg. | **98** | 37.49 N | 118.01 E |
| Lijia, Zhg. | **104** | 41.43 N | 122.20 E |
| Lijiaba | **107** | 29.37 N | 105.33 E |
| Lijiadian | **104** | 42.07 N | 121.14 E |
| Lijiajie | **107** | 29.49 N | 105.30 E |
| Lijiakou | **105** | 39.12 N | 116.29 E |
| Lijiang | **102** | 26.57 N | 100.15 E |
| Lijiapuzi | **104** | 40.59 N | 123.38 E |
| Lijiaqiao, Zhg. | **105** | 40.03 N | 116.40 E |
| Lijiaqiao, Zhg. | **105** | 39.47 N | 117.47 E |
| Lijiaqiao, Zhg. | **106** | 31.38 N | 120.00 E |
| Lijiatun | **104** | 41.19 N | 121.23 E |
| Lijiatuo | **107** | 29.28 N | 106.33 E |
| Lijiawobao | **104** | 41.00 N | 122.26 E |
| Lijiaxiang | **106** | 30.57 N | 119.59 E |
| Lijiazao | **105** | 39.17 N | 118.19 E |
| Lijin, Zhg. | **98** | 37.29 N | 118.16 E |
| Lijin, Zhg. | **104** | 41.40 N | 121.20 E |
| Lik ≃ | **110** | 18.31 N | 102.31 E |
| Likako | **152** | 0.15 N | 21.00 E |
| Likang | **100** | 22.47 N | 120.29 E |
| Likasi (Jadotville) | **154** | 10.59 S | 26.44 E |
| Likati | **152** | 3.21 N | 23.53 E |
| Likati ≃ | **152** | 2.53 N | 24.03 E |
| Likely | **182** | 52.37 N | 121.34 W |
| Likėnai | **76** | 56.12 N | 24.37 E |
| Likete | **152** | 0.43 S | 21.25 E |
| Likhu ≃ | **124** | 27.15 N | 86.12 E |
| Liki | **112** | 1.36 S | 101.11 E |
| Likimi | **152** | 2.50 N | 20.45 E |
| Likino | **82** | 55.38 N | 37.08 E |
| Likino-Dulevo | **82** | 55.43 N | 38.58 E |
| Liknes | **26** | 58.19 N | 6.59 E |
| Likoma Island I | **154** | 12.05 S | 34.45 E |
| Likou, Zhg. | **100** | 29.53 N | 117.28 E |
| Likou, Zhg. | **100** | 33.51 N | 113.20 E |
| Likou, Zhg. | **106** | 31.24 N | 120.37 E |
| Likouala □[5] | **152** | 2.00 N | 17.30 E |
| Likouala ≃ | **152** | 1.13 S | 16.48 E |
| Likouala aux Herbes ≃ | **152** | 0.50 S | 17.11 E |
| Likova ≃ | **265b** | 55.34 N | 37.21 E |
| Likstammen ⊜ | **40** | 58.58 N | 17.12 E |
| Liku | **174v** | 19.02 S | 169.47 W |
| Likupang | **112** | 1.41 N | 125.04 E |
| Likus ≃ | **236** | 14.14 N | 83.35 W |
| Likuyu | **154** | 10.20 S | 36.14 E |
| Lilanchengzhen | **105** | 39.12 N | 116.43 E |
| Lilanga | **152** | 0.34 S | 23.55 E |
| Lilasi | **124** | 29.22 N | 84.30 E |
| Lilbert | **222** | 31.44 N | 94.54 W |
| Lilbourn | **194** | 36.35 N | 89.36 W |
| L'Île-Bouchard | **32** | 47.07 N | 0.25 E |
| Lilenga | **152** | 0.54 N | 22.06 E |
| L'Île-Rousse | **36** | 42.38 N | 8.56 E |
| Lili | **106** | 31.00 N | 120.42 E |
| Lilian Point ≻ | **174d** | 0.53 S | 169.35 E |
| Lilienfeld | **61** | 48.03 N | 15.36 E |
| Lilienthal | **52** | 53.08 N | 8.55 E |
| Liling | **100** | 27.40 N | 113.30 E |
| Lilio | **116** | 14.08 N | 121.26 E |
| Liljendal | **40** | 60.08 N | 14.04 E |
| Lilla Bharwana | **123** | 32.34 N | 72.45 E |
| Lilla Edet | **26** | 58.08 N | 12.08 E |
| Lillån | **40** | 59.19 N | 15.13 E |
| Lillby | **26** | 63.28 N | 23.00 E |
| Lille | **50** | 50.38 N | 3.04 E |
| Lillebælt ≍ | **41** | 55.20 N | 9.45 E |
| Lillebonne | **50** | 49.31 N | 0.33 E |
| Lillehammer | **26** | 61.08 N | 10.30 E |
| Lille-Lesquin, Aéroport ⊠ | **50** | 50.35 N | 3.07 E |
| Lillerød | **41** | 55.52 N | 12.22 E |
| Lillers | **50** | 50.34 N | 2.29 E |
| Lillesand | **26** | 58.15 N | 8.24 E |
| Lilleshall | **42** | 52.44 N | 2.21 W |
| Lillestrøm | **26** | 59.57 N | 11.05 E |
| Lille Værløse | **41** | 55.47 N | 12.23 E |
| Lillhärdal | **26** | 61.51 N | 14.04 E |
| Lillian | **222** | 32.30 N | 97.11 W |
| Lillington | **192** | 35.23 N | 78.48 W |
| Lillinonah Lake ⊜[1] | **207** | 41.28 N | 73.21 W |
| Lilli Pilli | **274a** | 34.04 S | 151.07 E |
| Lillo | **34** | 39.43 N | 3.18 W |
| Lillooet | **182** | 50.42 N | 121.56 W |
| Lillooet ≃ | **182** | 49.45 N | 122.08 W |
| Lillooet Lake ⊜ | **182** | 50.13 N | 122.29 W |
| Lilly | **214** | 40.25 N | 78.37 W |
| Lilly Creek ≃ | **222** | 32.47 N | 94.56 W |
| Liloan | **116** | 10.09 N | 125.07 E |
| Lilongwe | **154** | 13.59 S | 33.44 E |
| Lilo Viejo | **252** | 26.56 S | 62.58 W |
| Liloy | **116** | 8.08 N | 122.40 E |
| Liluāh | **272b** | 22.35 N | 88.23 E |
| Lily | **192** | 37.01 N | 84.04 W |
| Lily Cache Creek ≃ | **278** | 41.41 N | 88.07 W |
| Lilydale, Austl. | **166** | 41.15 S | 147.13 E |
| Lilydale, Austl. | **169** | 37.45 S | 145.21 E |
| Lily Dale, N.Y., U.S. | **214** | 42.21 N | 79.19 W |
| Lilyfield | **274a** | 33.52 S | 151.10 E |
| Lilyvale | **273d** | 26.06 S | 28.25 E |
| Lim ≃, Afr. | **152** | 7.54 N | 15.46 E |
| Lim ≃, Europe | **38** | 43.45 N | 19.13 E |
| Lima, Arg. | **258** | 34.03 S | 59.12 W |
| Lima, Para. | **252** | 23.54 S | 56.20 W |
| Lima, Perú | **248** | 12.03 S | 77.03 W |
| Lima, Perú | **286d** | 12.03 S | 77.03 W |
| Lima, Sve. | **26** | 60.56 N | 13.26 E |
| Lima, Il., U.S. | **219** | 40.11 N | 91.23 W |
| Lima, Mt., U.S. | **202** | 44.38 N | 112.35 W |
| Lima, N.Y., U.S. | **210** | 42.54 N | 77.36 W |
| Lima, Oh., U.S. | **216** | 40.44 N | 84.06 W |
| Lima, Pa., U.S. | **285** | 39.55 N | 75.26 W |
| Lima □[5] | **248** | 12.00 S | 76.35 W |
| Lima (Limia) ≃, Europe | **34** | 41.41 N | 8.50 W |
| Lima ≃, It. | **64** | 44.00 N | 10.35 E |
| Lima, Punta ≻ | **240m** | 18.11 N | 65.41 W |
| Lima Center | **216** | 42.47 N | 88.49 W |
| Limache | **252** | 33.01 S | 71.16 W |
| Lima Duarte | **256** | 21.51 S | 43.48 W |
| Liman, Ross. | **80** | 45.47 N | 47.14 E |
| Liman, Yis. | **132** | 33.03 N | 35.06 E |
| Liman ≃ | **115a** | 6.29 S | 105.48 E |
| Limanowa | **30** | 49.43 N | 20.26 E |
| Limão ◆[8] | **287b** | 23.30 S | 46.40 W |
| Limapuluh | **114** | 3.10 N | 99.26 E |
| Lima Reservoir ⊜[1] | **202** | 44.38 N | 112.17 W |
| Limarí ≃ | **252** | 30.44 S | 71.43 W |
| Limas | **112** | 0.14 N | 104.31 E |
| Limasawa Island I | **116** | 9.56 N | 125.05 E |
| Limassa | **152** | 4.14 N | 22.02 E |
| Limassol → Lemesós | **130** | 34.40 N | 33.02 E |
| Limavady | **48** | 55.03 N | 6.57 W |
| Limaville | **214** | 40.59 N | 81.09 W |
| Limay, Fr. | **50** | 49.00 N | 1.44 E |
| Limay, Pil. | **116** | 14.34 N | 120.36 E |
| Limay ≃ | **254** | 38.59 S | 68.00 W |
| Limay Mahuida | **252** | 37.12 S | 66.42 W |
| Limbach-Oberfrohna | **54** | 50.51 N | 12.45 E |
| Limbadi | **68** | 38.33 N | 15.58 E |
| Limbang | **112** | 4.45 N | 115.00 E |
| Limbang ≃ | **112** | 4.50 N | 115.01 E |
| Limbani | **248** | 14.08 S | 69.42 W |
| Limbara, Monte ∧ | **71** | 40.51 N | 9.10 E |
| Limbaži | **76** | 57.31 N | 24.42 E |
| Līmbdi | **120** | 22.34 N | 71.48 E |
| Limbe, Cam. | **152** | 4.01 N | 9.12 E |
| Limbe, Malaŵi | **154** | 15.49 S | 35.03 E |
| Limbiate | **62** | 45.36 N | 9.07 E |
| Limboto | **112** | 0.37 N | 122.57 E |
| Limbourg | **56** | 50.37 N | 5.56 E |
| Limbrick | **262** | 53.38 N | 2.36 W |
| Limbueta | **152** | 12.30 S | 18.42 E |
| Limbunya | **164** | 17.14 S | 129.50 E |
| Limburg □[4], Bel. | **56** | 51.00 N | 5.30 E |
| Limburg □[4], Ned. | **52** | 51.14 N | 5.50 E |
| Limburg an der Lahn | **56** | 50.23 N | 8.04 E |
| Limburgerhof | **56** | 49.25 N | 8.24 E |


**Symbols** in the index entries represent the broad categories identified in the key at the right. Symbols with superior numbers (⋏[1]) identify subcategories (see complete key on page *I · 1).*

**Symbole** im Register stellen die rechts im Schlüssel erklärten Kategorien dar. Symbole mit hochgestellten Ziffern (⋏[1]) bezeichnen Unterabteilungen einer Kategorie (vgl. vollständiger Schlüssel auf Seite *I · 1).*

**Los símbolos** incluídos en el texto del índice representan las grandes categorías identificadas con la clave a la derecha. Los símbolos con numeros en su parte superior (⋏[1]) identifican las subcategorías (véase la clave completa en la página *I · 1).*

**Les symboles** de l'index représentent les catégories indiquées dans la légende à droite. Les symboles suivis d'un indice (⋏[1]) représentent des sous-catégories (voir légende complète à la page *I · 1).*

**Os símbolos** incluídos no texto do índice representam as grandes categorias identificadas com a chave à direita. Os símbolos com números em sua parte superior (⋏[1]) identificam as subcategorias (veja-se a chave completa à página *I · 1).*

| | | | | |
|---|---|---|---|---|
| ∧ Mountain | Berg | Montaña | Montagne | Montanha |
| ⋏ Mountains | Gebirge | Montañas | Montagnes | Montanhas |
| )( Pass | Paß | Paso | Col | Passo |
| V Valley, Canyon | Tal, Cañon | Valle, Cañón | Vallée, Canyon | Vale, Canhão |
| ≚ Plain | Ebene | Llano | Plaine | Planície |
| ≻ Cape | Kap | Cabo | Cap | Cabo |
| I Island | Insel | Isla | Île | Ilha |
| II Islands | Inseln | Islas | Îles | Ilhas |
| ⊥ Other Topographic Features | Andere Topographische Objekte | Otros Elementos Topográficos | Autres données topographiques | Outros acidentes topográficos |

## ESPAÑOL

| Nombre | Página | Lat.°′ | Long.°′ W = Oeste |
|---|---|---|---|
| Lim Chu Kang | 271c | 1.26 N | 103.43 E |
| Limecrest | 218 | 39.54 N | 83.48 W |
| Limefield | 262 | 53.37 N | 2.18 W |
| Limeira | 255 | 22.34 S | 47.24 W |
| Limekiln Canyon V | 280 | 34.18 N | 118.33 W |
| Lime Lake | 210 | 42.26 N | 78.29 W |
| Limen | 100 | 27.07 N | 119.19 E |
| Limena | 64 | 45.29 N | 11.50 E |
| Limentra ≃ | 64 | 44.14 N | 11.03 E |
| Limerick, Sk., Can. | 184 | 49.40 N | 106.15 W |
| Limerick (Luimneach), Ire. | 48 | 52.40 N | 8.38 W |
| Limerick, Pa., U.S. | 285 | 40.14 N | 75.32 W |
| Limerick □[6] | 48 | 52.30 N | 8.45 W |
| Limerick Lake ⊜ | 212 | 44.54 N | 77.37 W |
| Limerock | 207 | 41.55 N | 71.28 W |
| Lime Springs | 190 | 43.27 N | 92.17 W |
| Limestone, Austl. | 162 | 21.11 S | 119.50 E |
| Limestone, Fl., U.S. | 220 | 27.21 N | 81.53 W |
| Limestone, Me., U.S. | 186 | 46.54 N | 67.49 W |
| Limestone, N.Y., U.S. | 210 | 42.01 N | 78.37 W |
| Limestone, Pa., U.S. | 214 | 41.08 N | 79.20 W |
| Limestone □[6] | 222 | 31.35 N | 96.35 W |
| Limestone ≃ | 184 | 56.31 N | 94.07 W |
| Limestone, Lake ⊜[1] | 222 | 31.25 N | 96.20 W |
| Limestone Bay c | 184 | 53.50 N | 98.50 W |
| Limestone Canyon V | 280 | 33.45 N | 117.41 W |
| Limestone Creek ≃ | 210 | 43.06 N | 75.58 W |
| Limestone Lake ⊜, Mb., Can. | 184 | 56.35 N | 96.00 W |
| Limestone Lake ⊜, Sk., Can. | 184 | 54.36 N | 103.18 W |
| Limestone Point ›[1] | 184 | 53.50 N | 98.50 W |
| Limestone Point Lake ⊜ | 184 | 55.07 N | 100.32 W |
| Lime Street Station ◈[5] | 262 | 53.25 N | 2.59 W |
| Lime Village | 180 | 61.21 N | 155.28 W |
| Limfjorden ⋓ | 26 | 56.55 N | 9.10 E |
| Limhamn ◈[8] | 41 | 55.35 N | 12.54 E |
| Limia (Lima) ≃ | 34 | 41.41 N | 8.50 W |
| Limina | 70 | 37.56 N | 15.17 E |
| Liminka | 26 | 64.49 N | 25.24 E |
| Liminzhen | 98 | 34.31 N | 115.56 E |
| Limit Brook ≃ | 283 | 42.42 N | 71.25 W |
| Limmared | 26 | 57.32 N | 13.21 E |
| Limmaren ⊜ | 40 | 59.44 N | 18.43 E |
| Limmen | 52 | 52.34 N | 4.41 E |
| Limmen Bight c[3] | 164 | 14.45 S | 135.40 E |
| Limmen Bight ≃ | 164 | 15.07 S | 135.44 E |
| Límnos I | 38 | 39.54 N | 25.21 E |
| Limoeiro | 250 | 7.52 S | 35.27 W |
| Limoeiro do Norte | 250 | 5.08 S | 38.05 W |
| Limoges, On., Can. | 212 | 45.20 N | 75.15 W |
| Limoges, Fr. | 32 | 45.50 N | 1.16 E |
| Limoges-Fourches | 261 | 48.38 N | 2.40 E |
| Limogne | 32 | 44.24 N | 1.46 E |
| Limón, Hond. | 236 | 15.52 N | 85.33 W |
| Limon, Co., U.S. | 198 | 39.15 N | 103.41 W |
| Limón □[4] | 236 | 10.00 N | 83.15 W |
| Limonar | 240p | 22.57 N | 81.24 W |
| Limone Piemonte | 62 | 44.12 N | 7.34 E |
| Limone sul Garda | 64 | 45.49 N | 10.47 E |
| Limours | 50 | 48.39 N | 2.05 E |
| Limousin, Plateaux du ⋏[1] | 32 | 45.50 N | 1.15 E |
| Limoux | 32 | 43.04 N | 2.14 E |
| Limpopo ≃ | 156 | 25.15 S | 33.30 E |
| Limpsfield | 42 | 51.16 N | 0.01 E |
| Limski kanal c | 64 | 45.07 N | 13.38 E |
| Limu | 102 | 25.02 N | 110.51 E |
| Limuru | 154 | 1.06 S | 36.39 E |
| Linachamari | 24 | 69.40 N | 31.20 E |
| Līnah | 128 | 28.42 N | 43.48 E |
| Lin'an | 106 | 30.14 N | 119.43 E |
| Linanäs | 40 | 59.28 N | 18.31 E |
| Linao Bay c | 116 | 6.45 N | 124.00 E |
| Linapacan Island I | 116 | 11.27 N | 119.49 E |
| Linapacan Strait ⋓ | 116 | 11.37 N | 119.56 E |
| Linares, Chile | 252 | 35.51 S | 71.36 W |
| Linares, Col. | 246 | 1.23 N | 77.31 W |
| Linares, Esp. | 34 | 38.05 N | 3.38 W |
| Linares, Méx. | 232 | 24.52 N | 99.34 W |
| Linariá | 38 | 38.50 N | 24.32 E |
| Linaro, Capo › | 66 | 42.02 N | 11.50 E |
| Linas | 261 | 48.38 N | 2.16 E |
| Linas, Monte ∧ | 71 | 39.27 N | 8.37 E |
| Linas-Montlhéry, Domaine Militaire de ■ | 261 | 48.37 N | 2.13 E |
| Linate, Aeroporto di ⊠ | 62 | 45.27 N | 9.16 E |
| Lincai | 100 | 33.50 N | 114.56 E |
| Lincang | 102 | 23.45 N | 102.20 E |
| Lince | 286d | 12.06 S | 77.03 W |
| Linch | 200 | 43.36 N | 106.11 W |
| Lincheng, Zhg. | 98 | 37.27 N | 114.29 E |
| Lincheng, Zhg. | 106 | 30.55 N | 119.47 E |
| Linch'ing → Linqing | 98 | 36.53 N | 115.41 E |
| Lincoln, Arg. | 252 | 34.52 S | 61.32 W |
| Lincoln, On., Can. | 212 | 43.10 N | 79.29 W |
| Lincoln, N.Z. | 172 | 43.39 S | 172.29 E |
| Lincoln, Eng., U.K. | 44 | 53.14 N | 0.33 W |
| Lincoln, Ar., U.S. | 194 | 35.56 N | 94.25 W |
| Lincoln, Ca., U.S. | 226 | 38.53 N | 121.17 W |
| Lincoln, De., U.S. | 208 | 38.52 N | 75.25 W |
| Lincoln, Il., U.S. | 219 | 40.08 N | 89.21 W |
| Lincoln, In., U.S. | 216 | 40.37 N | 86.12 W |
| Lincoln, Ks., U.S. | 198 | 39.02 N | 98.08 W |
| Lincoln, Me., U.S. | 188 | 45.21 N | 68.30 W |
| Lincoln, Ma., U.S. | 207 | 42.25 N | 71.18 W |
| Lincoln, Mi., U.S. | 190 | 44.41 N | 83.24 W |
| Lincoln, Mo., U.S. | 194 | 38.23 N | 93.20 W |
| Lincoln, Mt., U.S. | 202 | 46.57 N | 112.40 W |
| Lincoln, Ne., U.S. | 198 | 40.48 N | 96.40 W |
| Lincoln, N.H., U.S. | 188 | 44.02 N | 71.40 W |
| Lincoln, Pa., U.S. | 208 | 40.12 N | 76.12 W |
| Lincoln, Pa., U.S. | 279b | 40.18 N | 79.51 W |
| Lincoln, R.I., U.S. | 207 | 41.54 N | 71.25 W |
| Lincoln, Tx., U.S. | 222 | 30.17 N | 96.52 W |
| Lincoln □[6], Mo., U.S. | 219 | 39.05 N | 90.57 W |
| Lincoln □[6], Or., U.S. | 224 | 44.59 N | 123.52 W |
| Lincoln, Mount ∧ | 200 | 39.21 N | 106.07 W |
| Lincoln Acres | 228 | 32.40 N | 117.04 W |
| Lincoln Boyhood National Memorial ⊥ | 194 | 38.10 N | 86.58 W |
| Lincoln Cathedral ◡[1] | 44 | 53.14 N | 0.33 W |
| Lincoln Center ◡ | 276 | 40.46 N | 73.59 W |
| Lincoln City | 224 | 44.57 N | 124.00 W |
| Lincoln Creek ≃, Ne., U.S. | 198 | 40.54 N | 97.06 W |
| Lincoln Creek ≃, Wa., U.S. | 224 | 46.45 N | 123.02 W |
| Lincolndale | 210 | 41.19 N | 73.43 W |
| Lincoln Estates | 278 | 41.31 N | 87.49 W |
| Lincoln Heights, Oh., U.S. | 214 | 40.47 N | 82.30 W |
| Lincoln Heights, Oh., U.S. | 218 | 39.15 N | 84.28 W |
| Lincoln Heights, Pa., U.S. | 279b | 40.19 N | 79.37 W |
| Lincoln Home National Historic Site ⊥ | 219 | 39.47 N | 89.38 W |
| Lincolnia Heights | 284c | 38.50 N | 77.09 W |
| Lincoln Memorial ⊥ | 284c | 38.53 N | 77.03 W |
| Lincoln Park, Co., U.S. | 200 | 38.25 N | 105.13 W |
| Lincoln Park, Ga., U.S. | 192 | 32.52 N | 84.19 W |
| Lincoln Park, Mi., U.S. | 216 | 42.15 N | 83.10 W |
| Lincoln Park, N.J., U.S. | 276 | 40.55 N | 74.18 W |
| Lincoln Park, N.Y., U.S. | 210 | 41.57 N | 74.00 W |
| Lincoln Park ♠, Ca., U.S. | 282 | 37.46 N | 122.30 W |

## FRANÇAIS

| Nom | Page | Lat.°′ | Long.°′ W = Ouest |
|---|---|---|---|
| Lincoln Park ♠, Il., U.S. | 278 | 41.56 N | 87.38 W |
| Lincoln Park Airport ⊠ | 276 | 40.57 N | 74.19 W |
| Lincoln Place ◈[8] | 279b | 40.22 N | 79.55 W |
| Lincoln Sea ⊤[2] | 16 | 83.00 N | 56.00 W |
| Lincolnshire | 216 | 42.11 N | 87.54 W |
| Lincolnshire □[6] | 28 | 52.55 N | 0.22 W |
| Lincoln's New Salem State Park ♠ | 219 | 39.58 N | 89.52 W |
| Lincoln Tomb State Memorial ⊥ | 219 | 39.50 N | 89.39 W |
| Lincolnton, Ga., U.S. | 192 | 33.47 N | 82.28 W |
| Lincolnton, N.C., U.S. | 192 | 35.28 N | 81.15 W |
| Lincoln Tunnel ◈[5] | 276 | 40.46 N | 74.01 W |
| Lincoln University | 208 | 39.48 N | 75.55 W |
| Lincoln Village, Ca., U.S. | 226 | 38.00 N | 121.19 W |
| Lincoln Village, Oh., U.S. | 218 | 39.57 N | 83.08 W |
| Lincolnville | 214 | 41.47 N | 79.51 W |
| Lincolnwood | 278 | 42.00 N | 87.43 W |
| Lincolnwood Hills | 278 | 41.31 N | 87.54 W |
| Linconia | 285 | 40.08 N | 74.59 W |
| Lincroft | 208 | 40.19 N | 74.07 W |
| Lind | 202 | 46.58 N | 118.36 W |
| Linda, Ross. | 80 | 56.37 N | 44 07 E |
| Linda, Ca., U.S. | 226 | 39.07 N | 121 32 W |
| Linda-a-Velha | 266c | 38.43 N | 9.14 W |
| Lindale, Ga., U.S. | 192 | 34.11 N | 85.10 W |
| Lindale, Tx., U.S. | 222 | 32.30 N | 95.24 W |
| Lindau, Dtsch. | 41 | 54.36 N | 9.47 E |
| Lindau, Dtsch. | 52 | 51.39 N | 10.07 E |
| Lindau, Dtsch. | 54 | 52.02 N | 12.06 E |
| Lindau, Dtsch. | 58 | 47.33 N | 9.41 E |
| Lindbergh | 219 | 39.02 N | 92.08 W |
| Lindbergh Field ⊠ | 228 | 32.44 N | 117.11 W |
| Lind Coulee V | 202 | 47.00 N | 119.10 W |
| Linde ≃ | 74 | 64.57 N | 124.36 E |
| Lindelse | 41 | 54.52 N | 10.44 E |
| Linden, Dtsch. | 56 | 50.31 N | 8.39 E |
| Linden, Guy. | 246 | 6.00 N | 58.18 W |
| Linden, Al., U.S. | 194 | 32.18 N | 87.47 W |
| Linden, Ca., U.S. | 226 | 38.01 N | 121.05 W |
| Linden, In., U.S. | 194 | 40.11 N | 86.54 W |
| Linden, Mi., U.S. | 216 | 42.48 N | 83.46 W |
| Linden, N.J., U.S. | 210 | 40.37 N | 74.14 W |
| Linden, Pa., U.S. | 210 | 41.14 N | 77.08 W |
| Linden, Pa., U.S. | 279b | 40.14 N | 80.08 W |
| Linden, Tn., U.S. | 194 | 35.37 N | 87.50 W |
| Linden, Tx., U.S. | 194 | 33.00 N | 94.21 W |
| Linden ◈[8] | 273d | 26.08 S | 28.00 E |
| Linden Airport ⊠ | 276 | 40.37 N | 74.15 W |
| Lindenberg, Dtsch. | 54 | 53.02 N | 12.07 E |
| Lindenberg, Dtsch. | 54 | 52.36 N | 13.31 E |
| Lindenberg, Dtsch. | 54 | 52.12 N | 14.07 E |
| Lindenberg im Allgäu | 58 | 47.36 N | 9.53 E |
| Linden-Dahlhausen ◈[8] | 263 | 51.26 N | 7.09 E |
| Lindenfels | 56 | 49.41 N | 8.47 E |
| Lindenhorst ◈[8] | 263 | 51.33 N | 7.27 E |
| Lindenhurst, Il., U.S. | 216 | 42.24 N | 88.01 W |
| Lindenhurst, N.Y., U.S. | 210 | 40.41 N | 73.22 W |
| Lindenhurst, Pa., U.S. | 285 | 40.14 N | 74.54 W |
| Linden Park | 216 | 40.13 N | 85.23 W |
| Lindenthal | 54 | 51.24 N | 12.20 E |
| Lindenwold | 208 | 39.49 N | 74.59 W |
| Lindenwood, Il., U.S. | 216 | 42.03 N | 89.02 W |
| Lindenwood, In., U.S. | 218 | 39.41 N | 86.09 W |
| Linderhausen | 263 | 51.18 N | 7.17 E |
| Linderhof, Schloss ⊥ | 64 | 47.34 N | 10.57 E |
| Lindern | 52 | 52.50 N | 7.46 E |
| Linderöd | 41 | 55.56 N | 13.49 E |
| Linderödsåsen ⋏[2] | 26 | 55.53 N | 13.56 E |
| Lindesay, Mount ∧[2] | 162 | 34.49 S | 117.18 E |
| Lindesberg | 40 | 59.35 N | 15.15 E |
| Lindesnäs | 40 | 60.20 N | 14.32 E |
| Lindesnes › | 26 | 58.00 N | 7.02 E |
| Lindfield, Austl. | 274a | 33.47 S | 151.10 E |
| Lindfield, Eng., U.K. | 42 | 51.01 N | 0.05 W |
| Lindfors | 40 | 59.36 N | 13.49 E |
| Lindholmen | 40 | 59.35 N | 18.06 E |
| Lindhorst | 52 | 52.21 N | 9.17 E |
| Líndhos | 38 | 36.06 N | 28.04 E |
| Líndhos ⊥ | 38 | 36.06 N | 28.05 E |
| Lindi | 154 | 10.00 S | 39.43 E |
| Lindi □[4] | 154 | 9.15 S | 38.45 E |
| Lindi ≃ | 154 | 0.33 N | 25.05 E |
| Lindian | 89 | 47.11 N | 124.52 E |
| Lindis Pass )( | 172 | 44.36 S | 169.40 E |
| Lindkirchen | 60 | 48.40 N | 11.47 E |
| Lindlar | 56 | 51.01 N | 7.23 E |
| Lindley, S. Afr. | 158 | 28.00 S | 27.57 E |
| Lindley, N.Y., U.S. | 210 | 42.02 N | 77.08 W |
| Lind National Park ♠ | 166 | 37.35 S | 149.05 E |
| Lindö | 40 | 58.37 N | 16.15 E |
| Lindóia | 256 | 22.31 S | 46.39 W |
| Lindome | 26 | 57.34 N | 12.05 E |
| Lindon | 198 | 39.44 N | 103.24 W |
| Lindong, Zhg. | 100 | 26.03 N | 118.49 E |
| Lindong, Zhg. | 105 | 39.51 N | 117.41 E |
| Lindow | 54 | 52.58 N | 13.00 E |
| Lind Point › | 240m | 18.20 N | 64.48 W |
| Lindre, Étang de ⊜[1] | 56 | 48.47 N | 6.45 E |
| Lindsay, On., Can. | 212 | 44.21 N | 78.44 W |
| Lindsay, Ca., U.S. | 204 | 36.12 N | 119.05 W |
| Lindsay, Ne., U.S. | 198 | 41.42 N | 97.41 W |
| Lindsay, Ok., U.S. | 196 | 34.50 N | 97.36 W |
| Lindsborg | 198 | 38.34 N | 97.40 W |
| Lindsey | 214 | 41.25 N | 83.13 W |
| Lindved | 41 | 55.47 N | 9.35 E |
| Lindy Lake | 276 | 41.05 N | 74.22 W |
| Lineboro | 208 | 39.43 N | 76.50 W |
| Line Creek ≃ | 194 | 33.34 N | 88.42 W |
| Line Islands II | 14 | 0.05 N | 157.00 W |
| Line Lexington | 208 | 40.17 N | 75.16 W |
| Line Mountain ∧ | 210 | 40.45 N | 76.37 W |
| Linesville | 214 | 41.39 N | 80.25 W |
| Lineville, Al., U.S. | 194 | 33.18 N | 85.45 W |
| Lineville, Ia., U.S. | 190 | 40.34 N | 93.31 W |
| Línevo | 86 | 54.05 N | 83.24 E |
| Linfen | 102 | 36.05 N | 111.32 E |
| Linfield | 208 | 40.13 N | 75.34 W |
| Linford | 260 | 51.29 N | 0.25 W |
| Ling ≃ | 46 | 57.19 N | 5.27 W |
| Ling'an | 106 | 30.36 N | 120.30 E |
| Linganamakki Reservoir ⊜[1] | 122 | 14.04 N | 74.54 E |
| Lingao | 102 | 19.54 N | 109.40 E |
| Lingayen | 116 | 16.01 N | 120.14 E |
| Lingayen Gulf c | 116 | 16.15 N | 120.14 E |
| Lingbi | 100 | 33.33 N | 117.33 E |
| Lingbo | 26 | 61.03 N | 16.41 E |
| Lingchuan, Zhg. | 102 | 25.26 N | 110.15 E |
| Lingchuan, Zhg. | 102 | 35.46 N | 113.26 E |
| Lingda | 106 | 31.12 N | 119.18 E |
| Lingdale | 44 | 54.32 N | 0.57 W |
| Lingdianzhen | 106 | 31.51 N | 121.25 E |
| Lingdou | 100 | 26.22 N | 118.56 E |
| Lingen | 52 | 52.31 N | 7.19 E |
| Lingesestausee ⊜[1] | 263 | 51.06 N | 7.32 E |
| Lingfengwei | 100 | 24.44 N | 115.35 E |
| Lingfield | 42 | 51.11 N | 0.01 W |
| Lingga, Kepulauan II | 112 | 0.05 S | 104.35 E |
| Lingga, Pulau I | 112 | 0.12 S | 104.35 E |
| Lingham Lake ⊜ | 212 | 44.46 N | 77.25 W |
| Linghe | 98 | 36.23 N | 119.03 E |
| Linghu | 106 | 30.44 N | 120.10 E |
| Lingig | 116 | 8.02 N | 126.24 E |
| Lingjiachang | 107 | 29.28 N | 104.54 E |
| Lingjiaqiao | 106 | 30.09 N | 120.04 E |
| Lingkar Dzong | 124 | 28.45 N | 90.36 E |
| Lingkou, Zhg. | 100 | 29.16 N | 120.38 E |
| Lingkou, Zhg. | 106 | 31.57 N | 119.38 E |
| Lingle | 200 | 42.08 N | 104.20 W |
| Linglestown | 208 | 40.21 N | 76.48 W |
| Lingling | 102 | 26.13 N | 111.37 E |
| Linglongta | 98 | 40.54 N | 119.59 E |
| Lingma | 102 | 23.22 N | 107.53 E |

## PORTUGUÊS

| Nome | Página | Lat.°′ | Long.°′ W = Oeste |
|---|---|---|---|
| Lingolsheim | 58 | 48.34 N | 7.41 E |
| Lingomo | 152 | 0.38 N | 21.59 E |
| Lingqiu | 98 | 39.24 N | 114.13 E |
| Lingshan, Zhg. | 98 | 36.33 N | 120.27 E |
| Lingshan, Zhg. | 102 | 22.28 N | 109.17 E |
| Lingshanwei | 98 | 35.58 N | 120.13 E |
| Lingshi | 102 | 36.54 N | 111.43 E |
| Lingshou | 98 | 38.18 N | 114.24 E |
| Lingshui | 110 | 18.31 N | 110.01 E |
| Lingtangqiao | 100 | 32.43 N | 119.14 E |
| Linguaglossa | 70 | 37.50 N | 15.08 E |
| Linguère | 150 | 15.24 N | 15.07 W |
| Lingwala | 273b | 4.22 S | 15.17 E |
| Lingwood | 42 | 52.37 N | 1.29 E |
| Lingwu | 102 | 38.06 N | 106.21 E |
| Lingxian, Zhg. | 98 | 37.21 N | 116.34 E |
| Lingxian, Zhg. | 100 | 26.30 N | 113.46 E |
| Lingxiazhu | 100 | 29.03 N | 119.46 E |
| Lingyuan | 98 | 41.15 N | 119.16 E |
| Lingzhuangzi | 105 | 39.04 N | 117.09 E |
| Lingzinan | 105 | 39.29 N | 115.15 E |
| Linh, Ngoc ∧ | 110 | 15.04 N | 107.59 E |
| Linhai | 100 | 28.51 N | 121.07 E |
| Linhares | 255 | 19.25 S | 40.04 W |
| Linh Cam | 110 | 18.31 N | 105.34 E |
| Linhe | 102 | 40.51 N | 107.30 E |
| Linhezhuang | 105 | 40.04 N | 117.39 E |
| Linhigh | 284b | 39.21 N | 76.31 W |
| Linhó | 266c | 38.46 N | 9.23 W |
| Linhsia → Linxia | 102 | 35.35 N | 103.13 E |
| Linhuaiguan | 100 | 32.55 N | 117.40 E |
| Linhuanji | 100 | 33.42 N | 116.33 E |
| Lini → Linyi | 98 | 35.04 N | 118.22 E |
| Linjiang, Zhg. | 98 | 41.44 N | 126.55 E |
| Linjiang, Zhg. | 100 | 27.50 N | 118.26 E |
| Linjiang, Zhg. | 100 | 28.04 N | 115.21 E |
| Linjiang, Zhg. | 102 | 33.01 N | 105.01 E |
| Linjiangchang | 107 | 29.14 N | 105.58 E |
| Linjianghu | 100 | 28.41 N | 117.54 E |
| Linjiangsi | 107 | 30.15 N | 104.37 E |
| Linjiatai | 104 | 40.43 N | 123.57 E |
| Linkenheim-Hochstetten | 56 | 49.07 N | 8.24 E |
| Linköping | 26 | 58.25 N | 15.37 E |
| Linkou | 89 | 45.15 N | 130.16 E |
| Linksfield ◈[8] | 273d | 26.10 S | 28.06 E |
| Linksmakalnis | 76 | 54.45 N | 23.55 E |
| Linksness | 46 | 58.56 N | 3.19 W |
| Linkuva | 76 | 56.05 N | 23.59 E |
| Linkwood | 208 | 38.32 N | 75.57 W |
| Linli | 102 | 29.18 N | 111.30 E |
| Linlithgow | 46 | 55.59 N | 3.37 W |
| Linmeyer | 273d | 26.16 S | 28.04 E |
| Linn, Ks., U.S. | 198 | 39.40 N | 97.05 W |
| Linn, Mo., U.S. | 219 | 38.29 N | 91.51 W |
| Linn ◈[8] | 263 | 51.20 N | 6.38 E |
| Linnancang | 105 | 39.50 N | 117.37 E |
| Linnansaaren kansallispuisto ♠ | 26 | 62.07 N | 28.31 E |
| Linndale | 279a | 41.27 N | 81.46 W |
| Linne | 52 | 51.10 N | 5.57 E |
| Linnell | 226 | 36.21 N | 119.11 W |
| Linnés Hammarby ⊥ | 40 | 59.49 N | 17.46 E |
| Linn Grove | 216 | 40.38 N | 85.01 W |
| Linnhe, Loch c | 46 | 56.39 N | 5.21 W |
| Linnich | 56 | 50.59 N | 6.16 E |
| Linntown | 210 | 40.58 N | 76.54 W |
| Linnville Bayou ≃ | 222 | 28.57 N | 95.42 W |
| Linosa | 70a | 35.51 N | 12.52 E |
| Linosa, Isola di I | 70a | 35.51 N | 12.52 E |
| Lin'ovo | 80 | 50.53 N | 44.51 E |
| Linow | 54 | 53.06 N | 12.49 E |
| Linping → Yuhang | 106 | 30.25 N | 120.18 E |
| Linpu | 100 | 30.03 N | 120.15 E |
| Linqi, Zhg. | 98 | 35.48 N | 113.53 E |
| Linqi, Zhg. | 100 | 29.51 N | 119.06 E |
| Linqing | 98 | 36.53 N | 115.41 E |
| Linqu | 98 | 36.32 N | 118.31 E |
| Linquan | 100 | 33.06 N | 115.13 E |
| Linru | 100 | 34.11 N | 112.49 E |
| Linruzhen | 100 | 34.17 N | 112.35 E |
| Lins | 255 | 21.40 S | 49.45 W |
| Linshan | 100 | 30.09 N | 120.59 E |
| Linshanhe | 100 | 30.44 N | 114.52 E |
| Linshengpu | 104 | 41.34 N | 123.20 E |
| Linshui | 102 | 30.21 N | 106.59 E |
| Linslade | 42 | 51.55 N | 0.41 W |
| Linstead | 241q | 18.08 N | 77.02 W |
| Linta ≃ | 157b | 25.02 S | 44.05 E |
| Lintan | 102 | 34.37 N | 103.40 E |
| Lintao | 102 | 35.27 N | 103.46 E |
| Linté | 152 | 5.24 N | 11.42 E |
| Linth ≃ | 58 | 47.07 N | 9.07 E |
| Linthal, Fr. | 58 | 47.56 N | 7.08 E |
| Linthal, Schw. | 58 | 46.55 N | 9.00 E |
| Linthicum Heights | 284b | 39.12 N | 76.39 W |
| Linthkanal ≅ | 58 | 47.13 N | 8.57 E |
| Linthwaite | 262 | 53 37 N | 1.51 W |
| Lintingkou | 105 | 39.39 N | 117.30 E |
| Linton, Austl. | 169 | 37.41 S | 143.34 E |
| Linton, N.Z. | 172 | 40.26 S | 175.33 E |
| Linton, Eng., U.K. | 42 | 52.06 N | 0.17 E |
| Linton, Eng., U.K. | 260 | 51.13 N | 0.31 E |
| Linton, In., U.S. | 194 | 39.02 N | 87.09 W |
| Linton, N.D., U.S. | 198 | 46.16 N | 100.13 W |
| Lintong | 102 | 34.21 N | 109.11 E |
| Linton Park ♠ | 260 | 51.13 N | 0.31 E |
| Lintorf | 52 | 51.20 N | 6.49 E |
| Linum | 264a | 52.46 N | 12.53 E |
| Linville, Austl. | 171a | 26.51 S | 152.16 E |
| Linville, N.C., U.S. | 192 | 36.03 N | 81.52 W |
| Linwood, Austl. | 168b | 34.21 S | 138.46 E |
| Linwood, In., U.S. | 218 | 40.12 N | 85.41 W |
| Linwood, Ma., U.S. | 207 | 42.05 N | 71.38 W |
| Linwood, N.J., U.S. | 208 | 39.20 N | 74.34 W |
| Linwood, Pa., U.S. | 285 | 39.49 N | 75.24 W |
| Linworth | 214 | 40.06 N | 83.04 W |
| Linwu, Zhg. | 98 | 36.14 N | 119.17 E |
| Linwu, Zhg. | 102 | 25.16 N | 112.20 E |
| Linxi, Zhg. | 90 | 43.30 N | 118.00 E |
| Linxi, Zhg. | 98 | 36.52 N | 115.32 E |
| Linxia | 102 | 35.35 N | 103.13 E |
| Linxian, Zhg. | 98 | 36.04 N | 113.50 E |
| Linxian, Zhg. | 102 | 37.58 N | 110.59 E |
| Linxiang | 100 | 29.28 N | 113.30 E |
| Linyanti | 156 | 18.04 S | 24.01 E |
| Linyanti ≃ | 156 | 17.58 S | 24.16 E |
| Linyi, Zhg. | 98 | 35.04 N | 118.22 E |
| Linyi, Zhg. | 98 | 37.13 N | 116.51 E |
| Linyi, Zhg. | 102 | 35.15 N | 110.59 E |
| Linying | 100 | 33.50 N | 113.57 E |
| Linyü → Shanhaiguan | 98 | 40.01 N | 119.44 E |
| Linyüan | 100 | 22.30 N | 120.23 E |
| Linz, Dtsch. | 56 | 50.34 N | 7.17 E |
| Linz, Öst. | 61 | 48.18 N | 14.18 E |
| Linze, Zhg. | 100 | 33.03 N | 119.38 E |
| Linze, Zhg. | 102 | 39.19 N | 100.17 E |
| Linzgau ◈[1] | 58 | 47.45 N | 9.16 E |
| Linzhai | 100 | 24.18 N | 115.03 E |
| Linzhang | 98 | 36.21 N | 114.36 E |
| Linzhi | 120 | 29.25 N | 94.22 E |
| Linzikou | 100 | 28.42 N | 112.46 E |
| Linzolo | 152 | 4.25 S | 15.07 E |
| Lioko, Zaïre | 152 | 0.02 N | 22.04 E |
| Lioko, Zaïre | 152 | 1.25 N | 23.07 E |
| Lio Matoh | 112 | 3.10 N | 115.14 E |
| Liomer | 50 | 49.51 N | 1.49 E |
| Lion, Golfe du c | 32 | 43.00 N | 4.00 E |
| Lionel Town | 241q | 17.48 N | 77.14 W |
| Lioni | 68 | 40.52 N | 15.11 E |
| Lion Rock ∧[2] | 271d | 22.22 N | 114.11 E |
| Lion Rock Tunnel ◈[5] | 271d | 22.21 N | 114.09 E |
| Lions Den | 154 | 17.16 S | 30.02 E |
| Lion's Head | 212 | 44.59 N | 81.15 W |
| Lionville | 208 | 40.03 N | 75.39 W |
| Lioppa | 112 | 7.40 S | 126.00 E |
| Liouesso | 152 | 1.02 N | 15.43 E |
| Lipa | 116 | 13.57 N | 121.10 E |
| Lipan | 196 | 32.31 N | 98.03 W |
| Lipany | 30 | 49.10 N | 20.58 E |
| Lipari | 70 | 38.28 N | 14.57 E |
| Lipari, Isola I | 70 | 38.29 N | 14.56 E |
| Lipatkain | 112 | 0.01 S | 101.13 E |
| Lipayan | 104 | 42.13 N | 123.23 E |
| Lipeck | 76 | 52.37 N | 39.35 E |
| Lipeck Oblast □[4] | 76 | 52.30 N | 39.00 E |
| Liperi | 26 | 62.32 N | 29.22 E |
| Lipetsk → Lipeck | 76 | 52.37 N | 39.35 E |
| Lipez, Cerro ∧ | 248 | 21.53 S | 66.52 W |
| Liphook | 42 | 51.05 N | 0.49 W |
| Lipiany | 30 | 53.00 N | 14.59 E |
| Lipicy | 76 | 53.22 N | 37.17 E |
| Lipin Bor | 76 | 60.16 N | 37.57 E |
| Liping | 102 | 26.17 N | 109.00 E |
| Lipis ≃ | 114 | 4.10 N | 102.04 E |
| Lipiyu | 104 | 41.09 N | 123.36 E |
| Lipka ≃ | 265b | 55.45 N | 37.11 E |
| Lipki | 76 | 53.58 N | 37.42 E |
| Lipník nad Bečvou | 30 | 49.31 N | 17.35 E |
| Lipniški | 76 | 54.00 N | 25.37 E |
| Lipno | 30 | 52.51 N | 19.10 E |
| Lipno, údolní Nádrž ⊜[1] | 61 | 48.43 N | 14.04 E |
| Lipno nad Vltavou | 61 | 48.38 N | 14.14 E |
| Lipoa Point › | 229a | 21.02 N | 156.38 W |
| Lipova | 38 | 46.05 N | 21.40 E |
| Lipovcy | 89 | 44.11 N | 131.44 E |
| Lipovka, Ross. | 78 | 50.52 N | 40.02 E |
| Lipovka, Ross. | 80 | 52.26 N | 46.11 E |
| Lipovka, Ross. | 80 | 49.46 N | 44.56 E |
| Lippborg | 52 | 51.40 N | 8.02 E |
| Lippe ≃ | 52 | 51.39 N | 6.38 E |
| Lipperode | 52 | 51.41 N | 8.22 E |
| Lippetal | 52 | 51.40 N | 8.06 E |
| Lippoldsberg | 52 | 51.37 N | 9.33 E |
| Lippstadt | 52 | 51.40 N | 8.19 E |
| Lipscomb | 196 | 36.14 N | 100.16 W |
| Lipsko | 30 | 51.09 N | 21.39 E |
| Lipsoí I, Ellás | 38 | 37.20 N | 26.45 E |
| Lipsoí I, Ellás | 130 | 37.20 N | 26.45 E |
| Lipton | 184 | 50.54 N | 103.50 W |
| Liptovská Teplička | 30 | 48.59 N | 20.06 E |
| Liptovský Mikuláš | 30 | 49.06 N | 19.37 E |
| Liptrap, Cape › | 166 | 38.54 S | 145.55 E |
| Lipu | 102 | 24.25 N | 110.29 E |
| Lipu La )( | 124 | 30.21 N | 81.05 E |
| Liqiao | 107 | 29.03 N | 104.48 E |
| Lira, Ug. | 154 | 2.15 N | 32.54 E |
| Lira, Ven. | 286c | 10.26 N | 66.46 W |
| Liranga | 152 | 0.40 S | 17.36 E |
| Lirangdian | 105 | 39.14 N | 116.14 E |
| Lircay | 248 | 12.56 S | 74.43 W |
| Liren | 100 | 33.55 N | 118.47 E |
| Lirentuncun | 104 | 41.24 N | 122.59 E |
| Liri ≃ | 66 | 41.25 N | 13.52 E |
| Liro | 175f | 16.27 S | 168.13 E |
| Liro ≃ | 58 | 46.18 N | 9.23 E |
| Lisakovsk | 86 | 52.36 N | 62.37 E |
| Lisala | 152 | 2.09 N | 21.31 E |
| Lisavy | 82 | 56.33 N | 38.32 E |
| Lisboa (Lisbon), Port. | 34 | 38.43 N | 9.08 W |
| Lisboa (Lisbon), Port. | 266c | 38.43 N | 9.08 W |
| Lisboa □[5] | 266c | 38.48 N | 9.16 W |
| Lisbon → Lisboa, Port. | 34 | 38.43 N | 9.08 W |
| Lisbon, Il., U.S. | 216 | 41.29 N | 88.29 W |
| Lisbon, Md., U.S. | 208 | 39.20 N | 77.04 W |
| Lisbon, N.H., U.S. | 188 | 44.12 N | 71.54 W |
| Lisbon, N.D., U.S. | 198 | 46.26 N | 97.40 W |
| Lisbon, Oh., U.S. | 214 | 40.46 N | 80.46 W |
| Lisbon Falls | 188 | 43.59 N | 70.03 W |
| Lisbonne → Lisboa | 34 | 38.43 N | 9.08 W |
| Lisburn | 48 | 54.31 N | 6.03 W |
| Lisburne, Cape › | 180 | 68.52 N | 166.14 W |
| Lisburne Peninsula ›[1] | 180 | 68.30 N | 165.15 W |
| Liscannor Bay c | 48 | 52.55 N | 9.25 W |
| Liscarney | 48 | 53.43 N | 9.35 W |
| Liscia ≃ | 71 | 41.11 N | 9.19 E |
| Liscia, Lago di ⊜ | 71 | 41.00 N | 9.16 E |
| Lisdoonvarna | 48 | 53.01 N | 9.15 W |
| Liseleje | 41 | 56.01 N | 11.59 E |
| Lishan, Zhg. | 100 | 31.50 N | 113.16 E |
| Lishan, Zhg. | 104 | 41.10 N | 123.00 E |
| Lishangzhuang | 105 | 39.35 N | 118.11 E |
| Lishanke | 98 | 40.41 N | 119.53 E |
| Lishchynivka | 78 | 49.16 N | 34.14 E |
| Lishe | 100 | 29.48 N | 121.28 E |
| Lishe ≃ | 102 | 24.18 N | 101.32 E |
| Lishi, Zhg. | 102 | 37.32 N | 111.09 E |
| Lishi, Zhg. | 106 | 31.14 N | 120.37 E |
| Lishi, Zhg. | 107 | 29.10 N | 105.42 E |
| Lishizhen, Zhg. | 107 | 29.20 N | 105.24 E |
| Lishizhen, Zhg. | 107 | 29.04 N | 106.15 E |
| Lishu | 89 | 43.21 N | 124.37 E |
| Lishui, Zhg. | 100 | 28.27 N | 119.54 E |
| Lishui, Zhg. | 106 | 31.39 N | 119.01 E |
| Lishuzhen | 89 | 45.05 N | 130.41 E |
| Lisianski Island I | 14 | 26.02 N | 174.00 W |
| Lisica ≃ | 86 | 58.34 N | 85.11 E |
| Lisichansk → Lysychans'k | 83 | 48.55 N | 38.26 E |
| Lisicy | 82 | 56.47 N | 36.21 E |
| Lisieux, Sk., Can. | 184 | 49.17 N | 105.59 W |
| Lisieux, Fr. | 50 | 49.09 N | 0.14 E |
| Lisij Nos | 265a | 60.01 N | 30.00 E |
| Líšina | 60 | 49.37 N | 13.10 E |
| Lisitu | 154 | 9.39 S | 34.39 E |
| Lisivshchyna | 78 | 50.47 N | 28.35 E |
| Lisizhuang | 105 | 38.55 N | 115.07 E |
| Lisja | 80 | 57.15 N | 54.22 E |
| Liska ≃ | 80 | 48.32 N | 43.08 E |
| Liskeard | 42 | 50.28 N | 4.28 W |
| Liski, Ross. | 78 | 50.59 N | 39.30 E |
| Liski, Ross. | 78 | 50.56 N | 39.29 E |
| Lískova | 60 | 49.25 N | 12.43 E |
| L'Isle, Schw. | 58 | 46.37 N | 6.25 E |
| Lisle, Il., U.S. | 216 | 41.48 N | 88.04 W |
| Lisle, N.Y., U.S. | 210 | 42.21 N | 76.00 W |
| L'Isle-Adam | 50 | 49.07 N | 2.14 E |
| L'Isle Jourdain | 32 | 46.14 N | 0.41 E |
| L'Isle-sur-la-Sorgue | 62 | 43.55 N | 5.03 E |
| L'Isle-sur-le-Doubs | 58 | 47.27 N | 6.35 E |
| L'Isle-sur-Serein | 50 | 47.35 N | 4.00 E |
| Lisman | 194 | 32.10 N | 88.16 W |
| Lismore, Austl. | 166 | 28.48 S | 153.17 E |
| Lismore, Austl. | 169 | 37.58 S | 143.20 E |
| Lismore, N.S., Can. | 186 | 45.42 N | 62.16 W |
| Lismore, Ire. | 48 | 52.08 N | 7.55 W |
| Lismore Castle ⊥ | 48 | 52.08 N | 7.52 W |
| Lismore Island I | 46 | 56.29 N | 5.33 W |
| Lisnaskea | 48 | 54.15 N | 7.27 W |
| Lisö ›[1] | 40 | 58.55 N | 17.45 E |
| Lišov | 61 | 49.01 N | 14.37 E |
| Liss | 42 | 51.03 N | 0.55 W |
| Lissabon → Lisboa | 34 | 38.43 N | 9.08 W |
| Lissberg | 56 | 50.22 N | 9.05 E |
| Lisse | 52 | 52.15 N | 4.33 E |
| Lisses | 261 | 48.36 N | 2.26 E |
| Lissewege | 50 | 51.18 N | 3.11 E |
| Lissie | 222 | 29.33 N | 96.13 W |
| Lissingen | 56 | 50.14 N | 6.38 E |
| Lissone | 62 | 45.37 N | 9.14 E |
| Lissy | 261 | 48.38 N | 2.42 E |
| Lista | 80 | 47.44 N | 45.54 E |
| Lista ›[1] | 26 | 58.07 N | 6.40 E |
| Lister ≃ | 263 | 51.05 N | 7.45 E |
| Lištica | 36 | 43.23 N | 17.36 E |
| Listowel, On., Can. | 212 | 43.44 N | 80.57 W |
| Listowel, Ire. | 48 | 52.27 N | 9.29 W |
| Listv'anka | 88 | 51.52 N | 104.51 E |
| Listv'anskij | 86 | 54.27 N | 83.29 E |
| Lisui | 105 | 40.05 N | 116.44 E |
| Lit | 26 | 63.19 N | 14.49 E |
| Lita | 100 | 27.22 N | 116.34 E |
| Litang, Malay. | 112 | 5.20 N | 118.31 E |
| Litang, Zhg. | 102 | 23.11 N | 109.05 E |
| Litang, Zhg. | 102 | 30.00 N | 100.16 E |
| Litang ≃ | 102 | 28.04 N | 101.30 E |
| Litani ≃ | 250 | 3.40 N | 54.00 W |
| Līṭānī, Nahr al- ≃ | 132 | 33.20 N | 35.14 E |
| Litava ≃ | 61 | 49.02 N | 16.36 E |
| Litcham | 42 | 52.44 N | 0.47 E |
| Litchfield, Ct., U.S. | 207 | 41.44 N | 73.11 W |
| Litchfield, Il., U.S. | 219 | 39.10 N | 89.39 W |
| Litchfield, Mi., U.S. | 216 | 42.02 N | 84.45 W |
| Litchfield, Mn., U.S. | 190 | 45.07 N | 94.31 W |
| Litchfield, Ne., U.S. | 198 | 41.09 N | 99.09 W |
| Litchfield, Oh., U.S. | 214 | 41.10 N | 82.02 W |
| Litchfield □[6] | 207 | 41.45 N | 73.11 W |
| Litchfield Park | 200 | 33.29 N | 112.21 W |
| Litchville | 198 | 46.39 N | 98.11 W |
| Literberry | 219 | 39.51 N | 90.12 W |
| Līth, Wādī al- V | 144 | 20.40 N | 40.35 E |
| Litherland | 44 | 53.28 N | 2.59 W |
| Lithgow | 170 | 33.29 S | 150.09 E |
| Lithia | 220 | 27.51 N | 82.10 W |
| Líthinon, Ákra › | 38 | 34.55 N | 24.44 E |
| Lithonia | 192 | 33.42 N | 84.06 W |
| Lithuania (Lietuva) □[1], Europe | 22 | 56.00 N | 24.00 E |
| Lithuania (Lietuva) □[1], Europe | 76 | 56.00 N | 24.00 E |
| Litian | 100 | 26.58 N | 114.10 E |
| Litija | 36 | 46.03 N | 14.50 E |
| Litipāra | 124 | 24.42 N | 87.37 E |
| Lititz | 208 | 40.09 N | 76.18 W |
| Litke | 89 | 53.57 N | 140.15 E |
| Litókhoron | 38 | 40.06 N | 22.30 E |
| Litoko | 154 | 1.13 S | 24.47 E |
| Litoměřice | 54 | 50.35 N | 14.09 E |
| Litomyšl | 30 | 49.52 N | 16.19 E |
| Litoo | 154 | 9.54 S | 38.24 E |
| Litouqiao | 106 | 31.15 N | 118.54 E |
| Litovel | 30 | 49.42 N | 17.05 E |
| Litovko | 89 | 49.15 N | 135.11 E |
| Litschau | 61 | 48.57 N | 15.03 E |
| Littau | 58 | 47.03 N | 8.16 E |
| Little ≃, Austl. | 169 | 38.01 S | 144.35 E |
| Little ≃, On., Can. | 281 | 42.20 N | 82.56 W |
| Little ≃, U.S. | 194 | 33.37 N | 93.52 W |
| Little ≃, U.S. | 194 | 35.32 N | 90.25 W |
| Little ≃, Al., U.S. | 194 | 31.18 N | 87.46 W |
| Little ≃, Al., U.S. | 194 | 34.16 N | 85.40 W |
| Little ≃, Ct., U.S. | 207 | 41.36 N | 72.03 W |
| Little ≃, Ga., U.S. | 192 | 30.51 N | 83.21 W |
| Little ≃, Ga., U.S. | 192 | 33.39 N | 82.32 W |
| Little ≃, Ga., U.S. | 192 | 33.14 N | 83.24 W |
| Little ≃, In., U.S. | 216 | 40.53 N | 85.32 W |
| Little ≃, Ky., U.S. | 194 | 36.51 N | 87.58 W |
| Little ≃, La., U.S. | 194 | 31.38 N | 91.49 W |
| Little ≃, Ma., U.S. | 283 | 42.37 N | 70.42 W |
| Little ≃, Ma., U.S. | 283 | 42.46 N | 70.51 W |
| Little ≃, N.Y., U.S. | 210 | 43.18 N | 75.43 W |
| Little ≃, N.C., U.S. | 192 | 35.21 N | 78.02 W |
| Little ≃, N.C., U.S. | 192 | 35.15 N | 78.42 W |
| Little ≃, Ok., U.S. | 196 | 35.00 N | 96.25 W |
| Little ≃, S.C., U.S. | 192 | 34.10 N | 81.11 W |
| Little ≃, S.C., U.S. | 192 | 33.56 N | 82.25 W |
| Little ≃, S.C., U.S. | 192 | 34.11 N | 81.45 W |
| Little ≃, Tn., U.S. | 192 | 35.51 N | 83.57 W |
| Little ≃, Tx., U.S. | 222 | 30.51 N | 96.41 W |
| Little ≃, Va., U.S. | 192 | 37.05 N | 80.32 W |
| Little ≃, Va., U.S. | 208 | 37.49 N | 77.26 W |
| Little, Mountain Fork ≃ | 194 | 33.57 N | 94.34 W |
| Little Abaco I | 238 | 26.53 N | 77.43 W |
| Little Alfoid → Kis Alföld ≚ | 61 | 47.30 N | 17.00 E |
| Little Amwell | 260 | 51.47 N | 0.02 W |
| Little Andaman I | 110 | 10.45 N | 92.30 E |
| Little Arkansas ≃ | 198 | 37.43 N | 97.22 W |
| Little Auglaize ≃ | 216 | 41.07 N | 84.25 W |
| Little Averill Lake ⊜ | 206 | 44.57 N | 71.44 W |
| Little Baddow | 260 | 51.44 N | 0.35 E |
| Little Barrier Island I | 172 | 36.12 S | 175.05 E |
| Little Bay | 186 | 47.41 N | 58.24 W |
| Little Bay c | 276 | 40.48 N | 73.47 W |
| Little Bay Islands | 186 | 49.39 N | 55.47 W |
| Little Bear ≃ | 200 | 41.42 N | 111.57 W |
| Little Bear Creek ≃ | 196 | 37.43 N | 101.43 W |
| Little Bear Creek Reservoir ⊜[1] | 194 | 34.25 N | 87.57 W |
| Little Beaver Creek ≃, U.S. | 198 | 46.17 N | 103.56 W |
| Little Beaver Creek ≃, U.S. | 198 | 39.49 N | 101.03 W |
| Little Beaver Creek ≃, U.S. | 214 | 40.38 N | 80.31 W |
| Little Beaver Creek ≃, Wa., U.S. | 224 | 48.54 N | 121.06 W |
| Little Beaver Creek, Middle Fork ≃ | 214 | 40.43 N | 80.37 W |
| Little Beaver Creek, North Fork ≃ | 214 | 40.43 N | 80.33 W |
| Little Beaver Creek, West Fork ≃ | 214 | 40.43 N | 80.37 W |
| Little Belt → Lillebælt ⋓ | 41 | 55.20 N | 9.45 E |
| Little Belt Mountains ⋏ | 202 | 46.45 N | 110.35 W |
| Little Berkhamsted | 260 | 51.45 N | 0.08 W |
| Little Bighorn ≃ | 202 | 45.44 N | 107.34 W |
| Little Bighorn Battlefield National Monunent ♠ | 202 | 45.32 N | 107.20 W |
| Little Billabong | 171b | 35.35 S | 147.32 E |
| Little Bitter Lake → Murrah aṣ-Ṣughrā, Al-Buḥayrah al- ⊜ | 142 | 30.13 N | 32.33 E |
| Little Bitterroot ≃ | 202 | 47.30 N | 114.19 W |
| Little Black ≃, U.S. | 194 | 36.25 N | 90.45 W |
| Little Black ≃, Ak., U.S. | 180 | 66.26 N | 143.49 W |
| Little Black Bear Indian Reserve ◈[4] | 184 | 51.00 N | 103.23 W |
| Little Blackfoot ≃ | 202 | 46.31 N | 112.48 W |
| Little Blue ≃, U.S. | 198 | 39.41 N | 96.40 W |
| Little Blue ≃, In., U.S. | 218 | 39.32 N | 85.46 W |
| Littleborough | 44 | 53.39 N | 2.05 W |
| Little Bow ≃ | 182 | 49.53 N | 112.29 W |
| Little Brazos ≃ | 222 | 30.38 N | 96.31 W |
| Little Brokenstraw Creek ≃ | 214 | 41.50 N | 79.23 W |
| Little Brosna ≃ | 48 | 53.10 N | 8.05 W |
| Little Buffalo ≃ | 176 | 61.00 N | 113.46 W |
| Little Bullhead | 184 | 51.40 N | 96.51 W |
| Little Burstead | 260 | 51.36 N | 0.24 E |
| Little Calumet ≃ | 278 | 41.39 N | 87.34 W |
| Little Catalina | 186 | 48.33 N | 53.02 W |
| Little Cayman I | 238 | 19.41 N | 80.03 W |
| Little Cedar ≃ | 190 | 42.57 N | 92.31 W |
| Little Chalfont | 260 | 51.40 N | 0.34 W |
| Little Chartiers Creek ≃ | 279b | 40.17 N | 80.08 W |
| Little Choptank River c | 208 | 38.32 N | 76.13 W |
| Little Churchill ≃ | 184 | 57.15 N | 95.21 W |
| Little Chute | 190 | 44.16 N | 88.19 W |
| Little Coco Island I | 110 | 14.00 N | 93.13 E |
| Little Colorado ≃ | 200 | 36.11 N | 111.48 W |
| Little Compton | 207 | 41.30 N | 71.10 W |
| Little Cooley | 214 | 41.44 N | 79.53 W |
| Little Cottonwood ≃ | 198 | 44.15 N | 94.20 W |
| Little Creek | 208 | 39.10 N | 75.26 W |
| Little Creek ≃ | 285 | 39.56 N | 74.48 W |
| Little Creek Naval Amphibious Base ■ | 208 | 36.55 N | 76.10 W |
| Little Creek Reservoir ⊜[1] | 208 | 37.20 N | 76.50 W |
| Little Cumbrae Island I | 46 | 55.43 N | 4.57 W |
| Little Current | 190 | 45.58 N | 81.56 W |
| Little Current ≃ | 176 | 50.57 N | 84.36 W |
| Little Cypress Bayou ≃ | 194 | 32.41 N | 94.15 W |
| Little Cypress Creek ≃ | 222 | 32.39 N | 94.42 W |
| Little Darby Creek ≃ | 218 | 39.53 N | 83.13 W |
| Little Dart ≃ | 42 | 50.54 N | 3.51 W |
| Little Deep Creek ≃ | 198 | 48.35 N | 100.52 W |
| Little Deer Creek ≃, In., U.S. | 216 | 40.36 N | 86.28 W |
| Little Deer Creek ≃, Pa., U.S. | 279b | 40.33 N | 79.50 W |
| Little Deschutes ≃ | 202 | 43.51 N | 121.27 W |
| Little Desert ◈[2] | 166 | 36.35 S | 141.20 E |
| Little Desert National Park ♠ | 166 | 36.25 S | 141.25 E |
| Little Diomede Island I | 180 | 65.45 N | 168.57 W |
| Little Don ≃ | 275b | 43.42 N | 79.20 W |
| Little Dry Creek ≃, Ca., U.S. | 226 | 39.22 N | 121.52 W |
| Little Dry Creek ≃, Mt., U.S. | 202 | 47.21 N | 106.22 W |
| Little Ease Run ≃ | 285 | 39.39 N | 75.04 W |
| Little Eau Pleine ≃ | 190 | 44.40 N | 89.41 W |
| Little Egg Harbor c | 208 | 39.35 N | 74.18 W |
| Little Elkhart ≃ | 216 | 41.43 N | 85.49 W |
| Little End | 260 | 51.41 N | 0.14 E |
| Little Etobicoke Creek ≃ | 275b | 43.37 N | 79.34 W |
| Little Exuma I | 238 | 23.27 N | 75.37 W |
| Little Fabius ≃ | 219 | 39.59 N | 91.59 W |
| Little Falls, Mn., U.S. | 190 | 45.58 N | 94.21 W |
| Little Falls, N.J., U.S. | 276 | 40.52 N | 74.12 W |
| Little Falls, N.Y., U.S. | 210 | 43.02 N | 74.51 W |
| Little Falls ≃ | 208 | 39.36 N | 76.38 W |
| Little Falls Dam ◈[6] | 284c | 38.57 N | 77.08 W |
| Little Farms | 218 | 39.57 N | 83.10 W |
| Little Ferry | 276 | 40.51 N | 74.02 W |
| Littlefield | 196 | 33.55 N | 102.19 W |
| Little Flatrock ≃ | 218 | 39.26 N | 85.33 W |
| Littlefork | 190 | 48.23 N | 93.33 W |
| Little Fork ≃ | 190 | 48.31 N | 93.35 W |
| Little Fort | 182 | 51.25 N | 120.12 W |
| Little Genesee | 210 | 42.02 N | 78.13 W |
| Little Gold ≃ | 162 | 18.01 S | 126.29 E |
| Little Gunpowder Falls ≃ | 208 | 39.23 N | 76.22 W |
| Littlehampton | 42 | 50.48 N | 0.33 W |
| Little Harbour Deep | 186 | 50.15 N | 56.33 W |
| Little Haw Creek ≃ | 192 | 29.23 N | 81.24 W |
| Little Hawk Lake ⊜ | 212 | 45.10 N | 78.42 W |
| Little Hoosic ≃ | 210 | 42.49 N | 73.20 W |
| Little Hope | 214 | 42.06 N | 79.49 W |
| Little Hulton | 262 | 53.32 N | 2.25 W |
| Little Humboldt ≃ | 204 | 41.00 N | 117.43 W |
| Little Humboldt, North Fork ≃ | 204 | 41.27 N | 117.09 W |
| Little Humboldt, South Fork ≃ | 204 | 41.26 N | 117.07 W |
| Little Hurricane Creek ≃ | 192 | 31.23 N | 82.19 W |
| Little Inagua I | 238 | 21.30 N | 73.00 W |
| Little Indian Creek ≃, Il., U.S. | 216 | 41.31 N | 88.46 W |
| Little Indian Creek ≃, In., U.S. | 218 | 38.12 N | 86.08 W |
| Little Island Pond ⊜ | 283 | 42.43 N | 71.17 W |
| Littlejohns Creek ≃ | 226 | 37.52 N | 121.14 W |
| Little Juniata ≃ | 214 | 40.34 N | 78.03 W |
| Little Juniata Creek ≃ | 208 | 40.23 N | 77.02 W |
| Little Kanawha ≃ | 188 | 39.16 N | 81.34 W |
| Little Kanawha, West Fork ≃ | 188 | 38.57 N | 81.16 W |
| Little Karroo (Klein Karroo) ⋏[1] | 158 | 33.45 S | 21.30 E |
| Little Kentucky ≃ | 218 | 38.41 N | 85.12 W |
| Little Klickitat ≃ | 224 | 45.51 N | 121.04 W |
| Little Koniuji Island I | 180 | 55.01 N | 159.26 W |
| Little Lake ⊜, On., Can. | 212 | 44.26 N | 79.40 W |
| Little Lake ⊜, La., U.S. | 194 | 29.30 N | 90.10 W |
| Little Laramie ≃ | 200 | 41.28 N | 105.44 W |
| Little Laver | 260 | 51.46 N | 0.14 E |
| Little Leigh | 262 | 53.17 N | 2.35 W |
| Little Lever | 262 | 53.34 N | 2.22 W |
| Little Limestone Lake ⊜ | 184 | 53.46 N | 99.18 W |
| Little London | 241q | 18.15 N | 78.13 W |
| Little Lost ≃ | 202 | 43.46 N | 112.58 W |
| Little Lun ≃ | 116 | 6.02 N | 125.17 E |
| Little Mahoning Creek ≃ | 214 | 40.49 N | 79.00 W |
| Little Maitland ≃ | 212 | 43.52 N | 81.18 W |
| Little Manatee ≃ | 220 | 27.42 N | 82.28 W |
| Little Manatee, South Fork ≃ | 220 | 27.39 N | 82.18 W |
| Little Manistee ≃ | 190 | 44.15 N | 86.19 W |
| Little Manitou Lake ⊜ | 184 | 51.45 N | 105.30 W |
| Little Marco Pass c | 220 | 26.01 N | 81.46 W |
| Little Marsh | 210 | 41.53 N | 77.24 W |
| Little Meadows | 210 | 41.59 N | 76.08 W |
| Little Mecatina ≃ | 176 | 50.28 N | 59.35 W |
| Little Medicine Bow ≃ | 200 | 41.58 N | 106.18 W |
| Little Mexico | 196 | 30.57 N | 102.52 W |
| Little Miami ≃ | 218 | 39.05 N | 84.26 W |
| Little Miami, East Fork ≃ | 218 | 39.09 N | 84.18 W |
| Little Miami, North Fork ≃ | 218 | 39.48 N | 83.47 W |
| Littlemill | 46 | 57.32 N | 3.49 W |
| Little Mississippi ≃ | 212 | 45.17 N | 77.35 W |
| Little Missouri ≃, U.S. | 198 | 47.30 N | 102.25 W |
| Little Missouri ≃, Ar., U.S. | 194 | 33.49 N | 92.54 W |
| Little Mountain ∧ | 208 | 40.47 N | 76.40 W |
| Little Muddy ≃, Il., U.S. | 194 | 37.50 N | 89.11 W |
| Little Muddy ≃, N.D., U.S. | 198 | 48.12 N | 103.36 W |
| Little Mulberry Creek ≃ | 194 | 32.26 N | 86.51 W |
| Little Naches ≃ | 224 | 46.58 N | 121.08 W |
| Little Nahant | 283 | 42.25 N | 70.56 W |
| Little Namaqualand □[9] | 156 | 29.00 S | 17.00 E |
| Little Neck | 283 | 42.42 N | 70.48 W |
| Little Neck ◈[8] | 276 | 40.46 N | 73.44 W |
| Little Neck Bay c | 276 | 40.47 N | 73.46 W |
| Little Nemaha ≃ | 198 | 40.19 N | 95.40 W |
| Little Neshaminy Creek ≃ | 285 | 40.15 N | 75.02 W |
| Little Niangua ≃ | 194 | 38.04 N | 92.54 W |
| Little Nicobar I | 110 | 7.20 N | 93.40 E |
| Little Ohoopee ≃ | 192 | 32.27 N | 82.24 W |
| Little Osage ≃ | 194 | 38.02 N | 94.14 W |
| Little Otter Creek ≃ | 212 | 42.44 N | 80.51 W |
| Little Ouse ≃ | 42 | 52.30 N | 0.22 E |
| Little Panoche Creek ≃ | 226 | 36.50 N | 120.42 W |
| Little Patuxent ≃ | 284b | 39.11 N | 76.52 W |
| Little Paxton | 42 | 52.15 N | 0.15 W |
| Little Peconic Bay c | 207 | 40.59 N | 72.24 W |
| Little Pee Dee ≃ | 192 | 33.42 N | 79.11 W |
| Little Pic ≃ | 190 | 48.48 N | 86.37 W |
| Little Pine and Lucky Man Indian Reserve ◈[4] | 184 | 52.56 N | 109.05 W |
| Little Pine Creek ≃, Pa., U.S. | 210 | 41.18 N | 77.22 W |
| Little Pine Creek ≃, Pa., U.S. | 279b | 40.31 N | 79.57 W |
| Little Pine Island I | 220 | 26.36 N | 82.05 W |


| Symbol | English | Deutsch | Español | Français | Português |
|---|---|---|---|---|---|
| ≃ | River | Fluß | Río | Rivière | Rio |
| ≅ | Canal | Kanal | Canal | Canal | Canal |
| ∟ | Waterfall, Rapids | Wasserfall, Stromschnellen | Cascada, Rápidos | Chute d'eau, Rapides | Cascata, Rápidos |
| ⋓ | Strait | Meeresstraße | Estrecho | Détroit | Estreito |
| c | Bay, Gulf | Bucht, Golf | Bahía, Golfo | Baie, Golfe | Baía, Golfo |
| ⊜ | Lake, Lakes | See, Seen | Lago, Lagos | Lac, Lacs | Lago, Lagos |
| ≡ | Swamp | Sumpf | Pantano | Marais | Pântano |
| ⊓ | Ice Features, Glacier | Eis- und Gletscherformen | Accidentes Glaciales | Formes glaciaires | Acidentes glaciares |
| ⊤ | Other Hydrographic Features | Andere Hydrographische Objekte | Otros Elementos Hidrográficos | Autres données hydrographiques | Outros acidentes hidrográficos |

| Symbol | English | Deutsch | Español | Français | Português |
|---|---|---|---|---|---|
| ↞ | Submarine Features | Untermeerische Objekte | Accidentes Submarinos | Formes de relief sous-marin | Acidentes submarinos |
| □ | Political Unit | Politische Einheit | Unidad Politica | Entité politique | Unidade política |
| ◡ | Cultural Institution | Kulturelle Institution | Institución Cultural | Institution culturelle | Institução cultural |
| ⊥ | Historical Site | Historische Stätte | Sitio Histórico | Site historique | Sitio histórico |
| ♠ | Recreational Site | Erholungs- und Ferienort | Sitio de Recreo | Centre de loisirs | Area de Lazer |
| ⊠ | Airport | Flughafen | Aeropuerto | Aéroport | Aeroporto |
| ■ | Military Installation | Militäranlage | Instalación Militar | Installation militaire | Instalação militar |
| ◈ | Miscellaneous | Verschiedenes | Misceláneo | Divers | Diversos |

| Name | Page | Lat.°′ | Long.°′ |
|---|---|---|---|
| Little Pine Key I | 220 | 24.44 N | 81.19 W |
| Little Pine State Park ♦ | 210 | 41.22 N | 77.20 W |
| Little Pipe Creek ≃ | 208 | 39.36 N | 77.16 W |
| Little Platte ≃ | 194 | 39.24 N | 94.41 W |
| Little Plum Creek ≃ | 279b | 40.30 N | 79.51 W |
| Little Popo Aggie ≃ | 202 | 42.54 N | 108.35 W |
| Little Porcupine Creek ≃, Mt., U.S. | 202 | 46.18 N | 106.34 W |
| Little Porcupine Creek ≃, Mt., U.S. | 202 | 48.02 N | 106.04 W |
| Littleport | 42 | 52.28 N | 0.19 E |
| Little Portage Creek ≃ | 216 | 42.00 N | 85.27 W |
| Little Powder ≃ | 198 | 45.28 N | 105.20 W |
| Little Pucketa Creek ≃ | 279b | 40.33 N | 79.45 W |
| Little Quill Lake ⊜ | 184 | 51.55 N | 104.05 W |
| Little Rann of Kachchh ≚ | 120 | 23.25 N | 71.15 E |
| Little Red ≃ | 194 | 35.11 N | 91.27 W |
| Little Red, Middle Fork ≃ | 194 | 35.37 N | 92.11 W |
| Little Red Deer ≃ | 182 | 52.04 N | 114.09 W |
| Little Red River Indian Reserve ◆[4] | 184 | 53.30 N | 105.58 W |
| Little Redstone Lake ⊜ | 212 | 45.13 N | 78.34 W |
| Little River, Austl. | 169 | 37.58 S | 144.30 E |
| Little River, N.Z. | 172 | 43.46 S | 172.47 E |
| Little River, Ks., U.S. | 198 | 38.23 N | 98.00 W |
| Little River, Tx., U.S. | 222 | 30.59 N | 97.22 W |
| Little Rock, Ar., U.S. | 194 | 34.44 N | 92.17 W |
| Littlerock, Ca., U.S. | 228 | 34.31 N | 117.59 W |
| Little Rock, Il., U.S. | 216 | 41.43 N | 88.34 W |
| Little Rock, Ia., U.S. | 198 | 43.26 N | 95.52 W |
| Littlerock, Wa., U.S. | 224 | 46.54 N | 123.01 W |
| Little Rock ≃ | 198 | 43.16 N | 96.15 W |
| Little Rock Air Force Base ■ | 194 | 34.55 N | 92.10 W |
| Little Rock Creek ≃ | 228 | 34.28 N | 118.01 W |
| Little Rock Wash V | 228 | 34.42 N | 118.02 W |
| Little Rocky Mountains ⋏ | 202 | 47.50 N | 108.10 W |
| Little Rouge Creek ≃ | 212 | 43.48 N | 79.08 W |
| Little Ruaha ≃ | 154 | 7.17 S | 35.28 E |
| Little Sable Point > | 190 | 43.38 N | 86.32 W |
| Little Sac ≃ | 194 | 37.39 N | 93.46 W |
| Little Sachigo Lake ⊜ | 184 | 54.09 N | 92.11 W |
| Little Saint Bernard Pass → Petit-Saint-Bernard, Col du )( | 62 | 45.41 N | 6.53 E |
| Little Salkehatchie ≃ | 192 | 32.37 N | 80.53 W |
| Little Salmon ≃, Id., U.S. | 202 | 45.25 N | 116.19 W |
| Little Salmon ≃, N.Y., U.S. | 212 | 43.32 N | 76.16 W |
| Little Salmon, North Branch ≃ | 212 | 43.24 N | 76.09 W |
| Little Salmon, South Branch ≃ | 212 | 43.24 N | 76.09 W |
| Little Salmon Lake ⊜ | 180 | 62.12 N | 134.45 W |
| Little Salt Lake ⊜ | 200 | 37.55 N | 112.53 W |
| Little Sandy ≃ | 188 | 38.35 N | 82.51 W |
| Little Sandy, East Fork ≃ | 188 | 38.30 N | 82.50 W |
| Little Sandy Creek ≃ | 200 | 42.06 N | 109.27 W |
| Little Sandy Desert ◆[2] | 162 | 24.20 S | 120.50 E |
| Little Saskatchewan ≃ | 184 | 49.52 N | 100.07 W |
| Little Scarcies ≃ | 150 | 8.51 N | 13.09 W |
| Little Scioto ≃, Oh., U.S. | 214 | 40.31 N | 83.12 W |
| Little Scioto ≃, Oh., U.S. | 218 | 38.46 N | 82.53 W |
| Little Sewickley Creek ≃, Pa., U.S. | 279b | 40.15 N | 79.45 W |
| Little Sewickley Creek ≃, Pa., U.S. | 279b | 40.33 N | 80.12 W |
| Little Silver | 276 | 40.20 N | 74.02 W |
| Little Sioux ≃ | 198 | 41.49 N | 96.04 W |
| Little Sioux, West Fork ≃ | 198 | 42.04 N | 96.00 W |
| Little Sitkin Island I | 181a | 51.55 N | 178.30 E |
| Little Smoky ≃ | 182 | 55.42 N | 117.38 W |
| Little Snake ≃ | 200 | 40.27 N | 108.26 W |
| Little Sodus Bay ⊂ | 210 | 43.20 N | 76.43 W |
| Little Southwest Miramichi ≃ | 186 | 46.57 N | 65.50 W |
| Little Stanney | 262 | 53.15 N | 2.53 W |
| Little Stony Creek ≃ | 226 | 39.20 N | 122.31 W |
| Little Stour ≃ | 42 | 51.19 N | 1.15 E |
| Littlestown | 208 | 39.44 N | 77.05 W |
| Little Stukeley | 42 | 52.21 N | 0.13 W |
| Little Sugarloaf ∧[2] | 274b | 37.41 S | 145.19 E |
| Little Sur ≃ | 226 | 36.20 N | 121.54 W |
| Little Sutton | 262 | 53.17 N | 2.57 W |
| Little Swatara Creek ≃ | 208 | 40.24 N | 76.29 W |
| Little Tallapoosa ≃ | 192 | 33.18 N | 85.34 W |
| Little Tanaga Island I | 180 | 51.48 N | 176.10 W |
| Little Tennessee ≃ | 192 | 35.47 N | 84.15 W |
| Little Thurrock | 260 | 51.28 N | 0.21 E |
| Little Timber Creek ≃ | 285 | 39.53 N | 75.08 W |
| Little Tinicum Island I | 285 | 39.51 N | 75.17 W |
| Little Tobago I, Br. Vir. Is. | 240m | 18.26 N | 64.51 W |
| Little Tobago I, Trin. | 241r | 11.18 N | 60.30 W |
| Little Toby Creek ≃ | 214 | 41.22 N | 78.49 W |
| Littleton, Eng., U.K. | 260 | 51.24 N | 0.28 W |
| Littleton, Co., U.S. | 200 | 39.36 N | 105.00 W |
| Littleton, Ma., U.S. | 207 | 42.32 N | 71.30 W |
| Littleton, N.H., U.S. | 188 | 44.18 N | 71.46 W |
| Littleton, N.C., U.S. | 192 | 36.26 N | 77.54 W |
| Littleton, W.V., U.S. | 188 | 39.41 N | 80.31 W |
| Little Traverse Bay ⊂ | 190 | 45.24 N | 85.03 W |
| Little Truckee ≃ | 226 | 39.25 N | 120.05 W |
| Little Turtle ≃ | 184 | 48.46 N | 92.36 W |
| Little Turtle State Recreation Area ♦ | 216 | 40.50 N | 85.26 W |
| Little Valley | 210 | 42.15 N | 78.48 W |
| Little Vermilion ≃ | 216 | 41.20 N | 89.05 W |
| Little Vermilion Lake ⊜ | 184 | 51.16 N | 93.50 W |
| Little Vienna Estates | 284c | 38.54 N | 77.18 W |
| Little Wabash ≃ | 194 | 37.54 N | 88.05 W |
| Little Walsingham | 42 | 52.54 N | 0.51 E |
| Little Waltham | 260 | 51.47 N | 0.29 E |
| Little Warley | 260 | 51.35 N | 0.19 E |
| Little Washita ≃ | 196 | 34.58 N | 97.51 W |
| Little Wellington, Isla I | 254 | 48.30 S | 74.45 W |
| Little White ≃ | 198 | 43.44 N | 100.40 W |
| Little White Mountain ∧ | 182 | 49.42 N | 119.20 W |
| Little White Salmon ≃ | 224 | 45.43 N | 121.38 W |
| Little Wichita ≃ | 196 | 33.54 N | 97.59 W |
| Little Wichita, East Fork ≃ | 196 | 33.52 N | 98.07 W |
| Little Wind ≃ | 202 | 42.57 N | 108.29 W |
| Little Wind, North Fork ≃ | 202 | 43.01 N | 108.53 W |
| Little Wind, South Fork ≃ | 202 | 43.01 N | 108.53 W |
| Little Wolf ≃ | 190 | 44.23 N | 88.48 W |
| Little Wood ≃ | 202 | 42.57 N | 114.21 W |
| Little York, In., U.S. | 218 | 38.42 N | 85.54 W |
| Little York, N.Y., U.S. | 210 | 42.42 N | 76.10 W |
| Little Zab (Zāb-e Kūchek) (Az-Zāb aṣ-Ṣaghīr) ≃ | 128 | 35.12 N | 43.25 E |
| Littoral □[4] | 152 | 4.13 N | 10.25 E |
| Litunga | 152 | 13.17 S | 16.43 E |
| Litvínov | 54 | 50.37 N | 13.36 E |
| Litvinovo | 76 | 59.34 N | 38.01 E |
| Litvinskoje | 86 | 50.42 N | 72.42 E |
| Lityn | 78 | 49.20 N | 28.05 E |
| Litzmannstadt → Łódź | 30 | 51.46 N | 19.30 E |
| Liu ≃, Zhg. | 98 | 41.48 N | 122.43 E |
| Liu ≃, Zhg. | 98 | 42.45 N | 126.04 E |
| Liu ≃, Zhg. | 98 | 40.38 N | 118.09 E |
| Liu ≃, Zhg. | 102 | 23.52 N | 109.45 E |
| Liu ≃, Zhg. | 105 | 40.38 N | 118.09 E |
| Liu ≃, Zhg. | 106 | 31.31 N | 121.18 E |
| Liuanzhuang | 105 | 39.14 N | 117.11 E |
| Liuba | 102 | 33.32 N | 107.07 E |
| Liubotong | 100 | 31.26 N | 116.00 E |
| Liucao | 106 | 31.07 N | 121.41 E |
| Liuchen | 102 | 23.09 N | 110.29 E |
| Liucheng, Zhg. | 100 | 24.03 N | 115.08 E |
| Liucheng, Zhg. | 100 | 28.36 N | 119.34 E |
| Liucheng, Zhg. | 102 | 24.32 N | 109.21 E |
| Liuchengba | 102 | 27.27 N | 102.53 E |
| Liuch'iu Hsü I | 100 | 22.21 N | 120.22 E |
| Liuchow → Liuzhou | 102 | 24.19 N | 109.24 E |
| Liucun | 106 | 30.44 N | 119.23 E |
| Liucura | 252 | 38.39 S | 71.05 W |
| Liudaogou | 98 | 41.34 N | 127.12 E |
| Liudaohe | 105 | 40.39 N | 116.12 E |
| Liudongqiao | 106 | 31.03 N | 119.32 E |
| Liudu | 100 | 26.44 N | 119.33 E |
| Liuduo | 100 | 34.01 N | 120.17 E |
| Liuduzhuang | 105 | 39.27 N | 117.50 E |
| Liuerbao | 104 | 41.13 N | 122.55 E |
| Liufang | 100 | 27.56 N | 116.22 E |
| Liufangling | 100 | 30.27 N | 114.27 E |
| Liufentzu | 269d | 24.57 N | 121.35 E |
| Liugezhuang, Zhg. | 98 | 38.33 N | 116.30 E |
| Liugezhuang, Zhg. | 105 | 40.03 N | 118.16 E |
| Liugou | 105 | 40.57 N | 118.18 E |
| Liugu ≃ | 98 | 40.22 N | 120.26 E |
| Liuguan | 100 | 29.56 N | 113.08 E |
| Liuguantun | 104 | 41.20 N | 121.21 E |
| Liuhang | 106 | 31.21 N | 121.22 E |
| Liuhe, Zhg. | 98 | 42.15 N | 125.43 E |
| Liuhe, Zhg. | 100 | 33.20 N | 112.48 E |
| Liuhe, Zhg. | 100 | 30.46 N | 113.12 E |
| Liuhe, Zhg. | 100 | 32.22 N | 118.49 E |
| Liuhe, Zhg. | 100 | 30.20 N | 115.36 E |
| Liuhe, Zhg. | 105 | 39.31 N | 118.17 E |
| Liuhe, Zhg. | 106 | 31.30 N | 121.15 E |
| Liuhegou | 104 | 41.56 N | 122.44 E |
| Liuheita | 104 | 42.09 N | 123.56 E |
| Liuhejie | 102 | 24.26 N | 101.35 E |
| Liuhekou | 105 | 40.39 N | 118.09 E |
| Liuheng Dao I | 100 | 29.43 N | 122.08 E |
| Liuhuang | 100 | 23.58 N | 116.28 E |
| Liuhudang | 104 | 42.31 N | 122.22 E |
| Liujia | 102 | 24.54 N | 107.49 E |
| Liujiachang | 107 | 29.46 N | 103.49 E |
| Liujiachuan | 105 | 40.07 N | 114.47 E |
| Liujiadai | 106 | 31.57 N | 120.23 E |
| Liujiadian | 89 | 50.07 N | 124.17 E |
| Liujiadu | 106 | 32.15 N | 120.33 E |
| Liujiafen | 105 | 39.58 N | 115.47 E |
| Liujiagangzi | 104 | 41.28 N | 122.33 E |
| Liujiagou | 98 | 37.47 N | 120.53 E |
| Liujiahe, Zhg. | 100 | 32.06 N | 113.21 E |
| Liujiahe, Zhg. | 104 | 40.40 N | 123.58 E |
| Liujiang | 98 | 40.04 N | 119.34 E |
| Liujiashan | 105 | 40.14 N | 114.49 E |
| Liujiatun, Zhg. | 104 | 41.52 N | 122.44 E |
| Liujiatun, Zhg. | 104 | 41.51 N | 122.05 E |
| Liujiatun, Zhg. | 104 | 42.08 N | 122.44 E |
| Liujiawopeng | 104 | 42.16 N | 123.01 E |
| Liujiazhai | 269b | 31.21 N | 121.27 E |
| Liujiazhen | 106 | 32.04 N | 121.30 E |
| Liujiazi, Zhg. | 98 | 41.00 N | 120.13 E |
| Liujiazi, Zhg. | 104 | 42.36 N | 122.15 E |
| Liujiazi, Zhg. | 104 | 41.48 N | 123.47 E |
| Liujingcun | 105 | 39.27 N | 115.26 E |
| Liujisu | 105 | 40.01 N | 117.13 E |
| Liukeshu | 86 | 44.59 N | 90.12 E |
| Liuku | 102 | 25.48 N | 98.52 E |
| Liuli | 154 | 11.05 S | 34.38 E |
| Liulicun | 271a | 39.56 N | 116.28 E |
| Liulidian | 106 | 31.31 N | 119.17 E |
| Liuligou | 104 | 41.24 N | 121.29 E |
| Liulihezhen | 105 | 39.36 N | 116.01 E |
| Liulin | 100 | 31.34 N | 113.14 E |
| Liuliwei | 100 | 24.20 N | 114.03 E |
| Liulongtai | 104 | 41.32 N | 120.56 E |
| Liumachang | 107 | 29.51 N | 104.54 E |
| Liumaogou | 89 | 48.12 N | 127.13 E |
| Liupangtun | 104 | 41.36 N | 123.28 E |
| Liupan Shan ⋏ | 102 | 35.40 N | 106.40 E |
| Liuqianhutun | 104 | 42.01 N | 123.41 E |
| Liuqiao | 106 | 32.11 N | 120.51 E |
| Liuquan, Zhg. | 98 | 34.27 N | 117.20 E |
| Liuquan, Zhg. | 105 | 39.22 N | 116.18 E |
| Liurenba | 100 | 29.57 N | 114.49 E |
| Liushi, Zhg. | 98 | 38.33 N | 115.44 E |
| Liushi, Zhg. | 100 | 28.03 N | 120.51 E |
| Liushilipu | 100 | 32.45 N | 115.58 E |
| Liushi Shan ∧ | 120 | 36.15 N | 82.05 E |
| Liushouying | 98 | 39.48 N | 119.19 E |
| Liushudian | 98 | 35.54 N | 119.30 E |
| Liushudixia | 104 | 42.26 N | 121.14 E |
| Liushui | 89 | 44.17 N | 124.15 E |
| Liushuigou | 100 | 31.34 N | 112.27 E |
| Liushuquan | 105 | 39.21 N | 118.06 E |
| Liusiqiao | 100 | 29.47 N | 116.21 E |
| Liusong | 105 | 39.40 N | 117.08 E |
| Liuta | 98 | 35.52 N | 115.18 E |
| Liutai | 98 | 41.20 N | 113.43 E |
| Liutaizi | 104 | 41.46 N | 122.39 E |
| Liutang | 102 | 24.58 N | 110.21 E |
| Liutiaozhaicun | 104 | 41.29 N | 123.12 E |
| Liutuan | 98 | 36.56 N | 119.22 E |
| Liutuhutun | 104 | 40.44 N | 120.32 E |
| Liuwanglou | 98 | 34.48 N | 116.28 E |
| Liuwa Plain ≚ | 152 | 14.30 S | 22.40 E |
| Liuwa Plain National Park ♦ | 152 | 14.30 S | 22.40 E |
| Liuwei | 106 | 32.16 N | 119.28 E |
| Liuwudian | 100 | 24.36 N | 118.13 E |
| Liuxi ≃ | 100 | 23.22 N | 112.54 E |
| Liuxia | 106 | 30.15 N | 120.03 E |
| Liuyang | 100 | 28.09 N | 113.38 E |
| Liuyang ≃ | 100 | 28.13 N | 112.58 E |
| Liuyuan | 98 | 36.10 N | 114.34 E |
| Liuyuankou | 98 | 34.54 N | 114.20 E |
| Liuzhai | 102 | 25.15 N | 107.20 E |
| Liuzhou | 102 | 24.19 N | 109.24 E |
| Liuzhuang | 100 | 33.10 N | 120.19 E |
| Livada | 38 | 47.52 N | 23.07 E |
| Livadija | 89 | 42.50 N | 132.39 E |
| Livanátai | 38 | 38.42 N | 23.03 E |
| Līvāni | 76 | 56.22 N | 26.11 E |
| Livanjsko Polje ≚ | 36 | 43.55 N | 16.45 E |
| Livanovka | 86 | 52.06 N | 61.59 E |
| Livarot | 50 | 49.01 N | 0.09 E |
| Lively, On., Can. | 190 | 46.26 N | 81.09 W |
| Lively, Va., U.S. | 208 | 37.47 N | 76.31 W |
| Lively Island I | 254 | 52.02 S | 58.30 W |
| Livengood | 180 | 65.32 N | 148.33 W |
| Livenka, Ross. | 78 | 50.26 N | 38.18 E |
| Livenka, Ross. | 78 | 50.44 N | 40.14 E |
| Livenza ≃ | 64 | 45.35 N | 12.51 E |
| Live Oak, Ca., U.S. | 226 | 39.16 N | 121.39 W |
| Live Oak, Fl., U.S. | 192 | 30.17 N | 82.59 W |
| Live Oak Creek ≃ | 196 | 30.39 N | 101.42 W |
| Liverdun | 56 | 48.45 N | 6.03 E |
| Liverdy-en-Brie | 261 | 48.42 N | 2.47 E |
| Livergnano | 66 | 44.19 N | 11.21 E |
| Liveringa | 162 | 18.03 S | 124.10 E |
| Livermore, Ca., U.S. | 226 | 37.40 N | 121.46 W |
| Livermore, Ia., U.S. | 190 | 42.52 N | 94.11 W |
| Livermore, Ky., U.S. | 194 | 37.29 N | 87.07 W |
| Livermore, Mount ∧ | 196 | 30.38 N | 104.10 W |
| Livermore Falls | 188 | 44.28 N | 70.11 W |
| Liverpool, Austl. | 170 | 33.54 S | 150.56 E |
| Liverpool, N.S., Can. | 186 | 44.02 N | 64.43 W |
| Liverpool, Eng., U.K. | 44 | 53.25 N | 2.55 W |
| Liverpool, Eng., U.K. | 262 | 53.25 N | 2.55 W |
| Liverpool, In., U.S. | 216 | 41.34 N | 87.18 W |
| Liverpool, N.Y., U.S. | 210 | 43.06 N | 76.13 W |
| Liverpool, Pa., U.S. | 208 | 40.34 N | 76.59 W |
| Liverpool, Tx., U.S. | 222 | 29.18 N | 95.17 W |
| Liverpool □[8] | 262 | 53.25 N | 2.55 W |
| Liverpool ≃ | 164 | 12.02 S | 134.13 E |
| Liverpool (Speke) Airport ⊠ | 44 | 53.21 N | 2.52 W |
| Liverpool, Cape > | 176 | 73.38 N | 78.06 W |
| Liverpool, University of ʊ[2] | 262 | 53.24 N | 2.58 W |
| Liverpool Bay ⊂, N.T., Can. | 180 | 69.45 N | 130.00 W |
| Liverpool Bay ⊂, N.S., Can. | 186 | 44.02 N | 64.41 W |
| Liverpool Bay ⊂, Eng., U.K. | 44 | 53.30 N | 3.16 W |
| Liverpool Football Ground ♦ | 262 | 53.26 N | 2.57 W |
| Liverpool Heights | 210 | 43.07 N | 76.13 W |
| Liverpool Range ⋏ | 166 | 31.40 S | 150.30 E |
| Livet-et-Gavet | 62 | 45.06 N | 5.56 E |
| Livigno | 64 | 46.32 N | 10.04 E |
| Livigno, Lago di ⊜[1], It. | 58 | 46.37 N | 10.10 E |
| Livigno, Lago di ⊜[1], It. | 64 | 46.37 N | 10.10 E |
| Livilliers | 261 | 49.06 N | 2.06 E |
| Lívingston, Guat. | 236 | 15.50 N | 88.45 W |
| Livingston, Scot., U.K. | 46 | 55.53 N | 3.32 W |
| Livingston, Al., U.S. | 194 | 32.35 N | 88.11 W |
| Livingston, Ca., U.S. | 226 | 37.23 N | 120.43 W |
| Livingston, Il., U.S. | 194 | 38.58 N | 89.45 W |
| Livingston, Ky., U.S. | 192 | 37.17 N | 84.12 W |
| Livingston, La., U.S. | 194 | 30.30 N | 90.44 W |
| Livingston, Mt., U.S. | 202 | 45.39 N | 110.33 W |
| Livingston, N.J., U.S. | 210 | 40.47 N | 74.18 W |
| Livingston, N.Y., U.S. | 210 | 42.09 N | 73.47 W |
| Livingston, Tn., U.S. | 194 | 36.23 N | 85.19 W |
| Livingston, Tx., U.S. | 222 | 30.42 N | 94.55 W |
| Livingston, Wi., U.S. | 190 | 42.54 N | 90.25 W |
| Livingston □[6], Il., U.S. | 216 | 40.53 N | 88.38 W |
| Livingston □[6], Mi., U.S. | 216 | 42.38 N | 83.50 W |
| Livingston □[6], N.Y., U.S. | 210 | 42.48 N | 77.49 W |
| Livingstone | 154 | 17.50 S | 25.53 E |
| Livingstone, Chutes de (Livingstone Falls) ㇄ | 152 | 4.50 S | 14.30 E |
| Livingstone, Lake ⊜[1] | 222 | 30.50 N | 95.30 W |
| Livingstone Falls → Livingstone, Chutes de ㇄ | 152 | 4.50 S | 14.30 E |
| Livingstone Lake ⊜ | 212 | 45.22 N | 78.43 W |
| Livingstonia | 154 | 10.36 S | 34.07 E |
| Livingston Island I | 9 | 62.35 S | 60.30 W |
| Livingston Mall ◆[9] | 276 | 40.47 N | 74.21 W |
| Livingston Manor | 210 | 41.54 N | 74.49 W |
| Livno | 36 | 43.50 N | 17.01 E |
| Livny | 76 | 52.25 N | 37.37 E |
| Livojoki ≃ | 26 | 65.24 N | 26.48 E |
| Livonia, In., U.S. | 218 | 38.34 N | 86.17 W |
| Livonia, La., U.S. | 194 | 30.33 N | 91.33 W |
| Livonia, Mi., U.S. | 216 | 42.22 N | 83.21 W |
| Livonia, N.Y., U.S. | 210 | 42.49 N | 77.40 W |
| Livonia Center | 210 | 42.49 N | 77.38 W |
| Livonia Mall ◆[9] | 281 | 42.26 N | 83.20 W |
| Livorno (Leghorn) | 66 | 43.33 N | 10.19 E |
| Livorno □[4] | 66 | 43.14 N | 10.35 E |
| Livorno Ferraris | 62 | 45.17 N | 8.05 E |
| Livourne → Livorno | 66 | 43.33 N | 10.19 E |
| Livramento → Santana do Livramento | 252 | 30.53 S | 55.31 W |
| Livramento do Brumado | 255 | 13.39 S | 41.50 W |
| Livron-sur-Drôme | 62 | 44.46 N | 4.51 E |
| Livry-Gargan | 261 | 48.56 N | 2.33 E |
| Livry-sur-Seine | 261 | 48.31 N | 2.41 E |
| Liwa | 112 | 5.04 S | 104.06 E |
| Liwale | 154 | 9.46 S | 37.56 E |
| Liwale Chini | 154 | 9.41 S | 38.01 E |
| Liwan | 154 | 4.54 N | 35.40 E |
| Liwonde | 154 | 14.52 S | 35.28 E |
| Liwonde National Park ♦ | 154 | 14.50 S | 35.20 E |
| Liwung ≃ | 115a | 6.08 S | 106.49 E |
| Lixi, Zhg. | 100 | 29.15 N | 114.46 E |
| Lixi, Zhg. | 100 | 27.39 N | 116.19 E |
| Lixian, Zhg. | 98 | 38.29 N | 115.34 E |
| Lixian, Zhg. | 102 | 34.11 N | 105.02 E |
| Lixian, Zhg. | 102 | 29.30 N | 111.37 E |
| Lixian, Zhg. | 105 | 39.33 N | 116.26 E |
| Lixian → Black ≃ | 110 | 21.15 N | 105.20 E |
| Lixin, Zhg. | 100 | 26.52 N | 116.42 E |
| Lixin, Zhg. | 100 | 33.06 N | 116.08 E |
| Lixing | 100 | 33.28 N | 115.28 E |
| Lixingzhuang | 105 | 39.25 N | 117.56 E |
| Lixoúrion | 38 | 38.12 N | 20.26 E |
| Lixus ⊥ | 34 | 35.16 N | 6.13 W |
| Liyang, Zhg. | 98 | 37.28 N | 113.37 E |
| Liyang, Zhg. | 106 | 31.26 N | 119.29 E |
| Liyuanbao | 100 | 25.16 N | 112.55 E |
| Liyujiang | 100 | 25.57 N | 113.15 E |
| Lizard | 42 | 49.58 N | 5.12 W |
| Lizarda | 250 | 9.36 S | 46.41 W |
| Lizard Head Peak ∧ | 200 | 42.47 N | 109.11 W |
| Lizard Island I | 164 | 14.40 S | 145.28 E |
| Lizard Point > | 42 | 49.56 N | 5.13 W |
| Lizard Point Indian Reserve ◆[4] | 184 | 50.40 N | 100.57 W |
| Lize | 107 | 30.08 N | 106.11 E |
| Lizhai | 106 | 31.34 N | 121.45 E |
| Lizhou | 102 | 28.08 N | 102.10 E |
| Lizhu | 100 | 29.56 N | 120.30 E |
| Lizhuang, Zhg. | 100 | 34.24 N | 116.30 E |
| Lizhuang, Zhg. | 107 | 28.47 N | 104.46 E |
| Lizhuangqiao | 106 | 31.48 N | 119.37 E |
| Lizinovka | 78 | 50.08 N | 39.28 E |
| Liziwei | 107 | 30.19 N | 106.39 E |
| Lizy-sur-Ourcq | 50 | 49.01 N | 3.02 E |
| Lizzana | 64 | 45.51 N | 11.03 E |
| Lizzanello | 68 | 40.18 N | 18.13 E |
| Lizzano | 68 | 40.23 N | 17.27 E |
| Lizzano in Belvedere | 64 | 44.10 N | 10.53 E |
| Ljady | 76 | 54.36 N | 31.10 E |
| Ljahavičy | 76 | 53.02 N | 26.16 E |
| Ljalovo | 82 | 56.03 N | 37.14 E |
| Ljan | 26 | 59.51 N | 10.48 E |
| Ljaskavičy | 78 | 52.07 N | 28.09 E |
| Ljasnaja | 76 | 52.59 N | 25.46 E |
| Ljasnaja ≃ | 76 | 52.10 N | 23.33 E |
| Ljuban', Bela. | 76 | 52.37 N | 29.08 E |
| Ljuban', Bela. | 76 | 52.48 N | 27.59 E |
| Ljubča | 76 | 53.45 N | 26.03 E |
| Ljubelj (Loiblpass) )( | 61 | 46.26 N | 14.16 E |
| Ljubija | 36 | 44.56 N | 16.37 E |
| Ljubimec | 38 | 41.50 N | 26.05 E |
| Ljubinje | 38 | 42.57 N | 18.05 E |
| Ljubljana | 36 | 46.03 N | 14.31 E |
| Ljubovija | 38 | 44.11 N | 19.22 E |
| Ljubuški | 36 | 43.12 N | 17.33 E |
| Ljugarn | 26 | 57.19 N | 18.42 E |
| Ljunga | 40 | 58.31 N | 16.21 E |
| Ljungan ≃ | 26 | 62.19 N | 17.23 E |
| Ljungaverk | 26 | 62.29 N | 16.03 E |
| Ljungby | 26 | 56.50 N | 13.56 E |
| Ljungbyhed | 41 | 56.04 N | 13.12 E |
| Ljungbyholm | 26 | 56.38 N | 16.10 E |
| Ljungdalen | 26 | 62.51 N | 12.47 E |
| Ljungsbro | 26 | 58.31 N | 15.30 E |
| Ljungskile | 26 | 58.14 N | 11.55 E |
| Ljusdal | 26 | 61.50 N | 16.05 E |
| Ljusfallshammar | 40 | 58.47 N | 15.29 E |
| Ljusina | 76 | 52.38 N | 26.31 E |
| Ljusnan ≃ | 26 | 61.12 N | 17.08 E |
| Ljusnaren ⊜ | 40 | 59.51 N | 14.56 E |
| Ljusne | 26 | 61.13 N | 17.08 E |
| Ljusterö I | 40 | 59.31 N | 18.37 E |
| Ljutomer | 36 | 46.31 N | 16.12 E |
| Llagas Creek ≃ | 226 | 36.58 N | 121.31 W |
| Llaima, Volcán ∧[1] | 252 | 38.43 S | 71.43 W |
| Llamara, Salar de ≚ | 248 | 21.13 S | 69.40 W |
| Llanaber | 42 | 52.45 N | 4.05 W |
| Llanaelhaearn | 42 | 52.59 N | 4.24 W |
| Llanarth | 42 | 52.12 N | 4.18 W |
| Llanarthney | 42 | 51.52 N | 4.09 W |
| Llanbedrog | 42 | 52.52 N | 4.29 W |
| Llanberis, Pass of V | 44 | 53.06 N | 4.04 W |
| Llanbister | 42 | 52.21 N | 3.18 W |
| Llanboidy | 42 | 51.54 N | 4.36 W |
| Llanbryde | 46 | 57.37 N | 3.13 W |
| Llanbrynmair | 42 | 52.37 N | 3.57 W |
| Llançà | 34 | 42.22 N | 3.09 E |
| Llancanelo, Laguna ⊜ | 252 | 35.35 S | 69.09 W |
| Llandaff | 42 | 51.30 N | 3.14 W |
| Llandaff Cathedral ʊ[1] | 42 | 51.29 N | 3.15 W |
| Llanddewi Brefi | 42 | 52.10 N | 3.57 W |
| Llandeilo | 42 | 51.52 N | 3.59 W |
| Llandilo | 274a | 33.43 S | 150.45 E |
| Llandinam | 42 | 52.29 N | 3.26 W |
| Llandissilio | 42 | 51.53 N | 4.44 W |
| Llandovery | 42 | 51.59 N | 3.48 W |
| Llandrindod Wells | 42 | 52.15 N | 3.23 W |
| Llandudno | 44 | 53.19 N | 3.49 W |
| Llandybie | 42 | 51.50 N | 4.00 W |
| Llandysul | 42 | 52.02 N | 4.19 W |
| Llanelli | 42 | 51.42 N | 4.10 W |
| Llanelltyd | 42 | 52.45 N | 3.54 W |
| Llanelly | 169 | 36.44 S | 143.51 E |
| Llanenddwyn | 42 | 52.49 N | 4.06 W |
| Llanerchymedd | 44 | 53.20 N | 4.22 W |
| Llanes | 34 | 43.25 N | 4.45 W |
| Llanfaethlu | 44 | 53.21 N | 4.32 W |
| Llanfair-Caereinion | 42 | 52.39 N | 3.20 W |
| Llanfairfechan | 44 | 53.15 N | 3.58 W |
| Llanfairpwllgwyngyll | 44 | 53.13 N | 4.12 W |
| Llanfrynach | 42 | 51.56 N | 3.21 W |
| Llanfyllin | 42 | 52.46 N | 3.17 W |
| Llanfynydd | 42 | 51.56 N | 4.06 W |
| Llanfyrnach | 42 | 51.57 N | 4.35 W |
| Llangadog | 42 | 51.56 N | 3.53 W |
| Llangefni | 44 | 53.16 N | 4.18 W |
| Llangennech | 42 | 51.41 N | 4.04 W |
| Llangollen | 42 | 52.58 N | 3.10 W |
| Llangollen Estates | 208 | 39.39 N | 75.37 W |
| Llangranog | 42 | 52.09 N | 4.29 W |
| Llangurig | 42 | 52.25 N | 3.36 W |
| Llangwyryfon | 42 | 52.19 N | 4.03 W |
| Llangynog | 42 | 52.50 N | 3.25 W |
| Llanharan | 42 | 51.33 N | 3.25 W |
| Llanidloes | 42 | 52.27 N | 3.32 W |
| Llanilar | 42 | 52.21 N | 4.01 W |
| Llanllyfni | 44 | 53.03 N | 4.17 W |
| Llano | 196 | 30.45 N | 98.40 W |
| Llano ≃ | 196 | 30.35 N | 98.25 W |
| Llano Colorado | 204 | 31.38 N | 115.55 W |
| Llanon | 42 | 52.17 N | 4.10 W |
| Llanos ≚ | 246 | 5.00 N | 70.00 W |
| Llanpumsaint | 42 | 51.56 N | 4.18 W |
| Llanquihue | 254 | 41.15 S | 73.01 W |
| Llanquihue, Lago ⊜ | 254 | 41.08 S | 72.48 W |
| Llanrhaeadr-ym-Mochnant | 42 | 52.51 N | 3.17 W |
| Llanrhidian | 42 | 51.37 N | 4.11 W |
| Llanrhystud | 42 | 52.18 N | 4.09 W |
| Llanrwst | 44 | 53.08 N | 3.48 W |
| Llansantffraid-ym-Mechain | 42 | 52.47 N | 3.08 W |
| Llansawel | 42 | 52.01 N | 4.00 W |
| Llantrisant | 42 | 51.33 N | 3.23 W |
| Llantwit Major | 42 | 51.25 N | 3.30 W |
| Llanuwchllyn | 42 | 52.52 N | 3.41 W |
| Llanwenog | 42 | 52.06 N | 4.12 W |
| Llanwrda | 42 | 51.58 N | 3.53 W |
| Llanwrtyd Wells | 42 | 52.07 N | 3.38 W |
| Llanybydder | 42 | 52.04 N | 4.09 W |
| Llata | 248 | 9.25 S | 76.47 W |
| Llavallol ◆[8] | 288 | 34.48 S | 58.28 W |
| Llay | 44 | 53.06 N | 2.59 W |
| Lleida | 34 | 41.37 N | 0.37 E |
| Lleida □[4] | 34 | 42.00 N | 1.10 E |
| Llentrisca, Cap > | 34 | 38.51 N | 1.14 E |
| Llera de Canales | 234 | 23.19 N | 99.01 W |
| Llerena | 34 | 38.14 N | 6.01 W |
| Lleulleu, Lago ⊜ | 252 | 38.09 S | 73.20 W |
| Lleyn Peninsula >[1] | 42 | 52.54 N | 4.30 W |
| Llica | 248 | 19.52 S | 68.16 W |
| Llico | 252 | 34.46 S | 72.05 W |
| Lliria | 34 | 39.38 N | 0.36 W |
| Llivia | 32 | 42.28 N | 1.59 E |
| Llobregat ≃ | 34 | 41.19 N | 2.09 E |
| Llobregat, Delta del ≚[2] | 266d | 41.17 N | 2.08 E |
| Llorente | 116 | 11.25 N | 125.33 E |
| Llorente ≃ | 116 | 11.25 N | 125.33 E |
| Llorona, Punta > | 236 | 8.39 N | 83.45 W |
| Lloyd | 218 | 38.37 N | 82.51 W |
| Lloyd Harbor | 210 | 40.54 N | 73.27 W |
| Lloyd Harbor ⊂ | 276 | 40.55 N | 73.27 W |
| Lloydminster | 184 | 53.17 N | 110.00 W |
| Lloyd Neck >[1] | 276 | 40.56 N | 73.28 W |
| Lloyd Point > | 210 | 40.57 N | 73.29 W |
| Lloyds ≃ | 186 | 48.33 N | 57.13 W |
| Llucena | 34 | 40.08 N | 0.17 W |
| Llucmajor | 34 | 39.29 N | 2.54 E |
| Llullaillaco, Volcán ∧[1] | 252 | 24.43 S | 68.33 W |
| Llusco | 248 | 14.21 S | 72.07 W |
| Lluta ≃ | 248 | 18.24 S | 70.19 W |
| Llyn Brianne Reservoir ⊜[1] | 42 | 52.08 N | 3.45 W |
| Llyswen | 42 | 52.02 N | 3.17 W |
| Llys-y-frân Reservoir ⊜[1] | 42 | 51.53 N | 4.51 W |
| Lnáře | 60 | 49.28 N | 13.47 E |
| Lo (Panlong) ≃ | 110 | 21.18 N | 105.25 E |
| Loa | 200 | 38.24 N | 111.38 W |
| Loa ≃, Chile | 244 | 21.26 S | 70.04 W |
| Loa ≃, Congo | 273b | 4.20 S | 15.11 E |
| Loami | 194 | 39.40 N | 89.51 W |
| Loanda → Luanda, Ang. | 152 | 8.48 S | 13.14 E |
| Loanda, Bra. | 255 | 22.54 S | 53.10 W |
| Loanda, Gabon | 152 | 0.55 S | 9.00 E |
| Loande ≃ | 152 | 8.41 S | 17.56 E |
| Loange (Luangue) ≃ | 152 | 4.17 S | 20.02 E |
| Loango Buele | 152 | 5.10 S | 12.59 E |
| Loanhead | 46 | 55.53 N | 3.09 W |
| Loanja ≃ | 154 | 17.22 S | 24.48 E |
| Loano | 62 | 44.08 N | 8.15 E |
| Loantaka Brook ≃ | 276 | 40.43 N | 74.28 W |
| Lo Aranguiz | 286e | 33.23 S | 70.40 W |
| Loay | 116 | 9.36 N | 124.01 E |
| Lob' ≃ | 82 | 56.29 N | 35.51 E |
| Lobamba | 158 | 26.27 S | 31.12 E |
| Loban | 24 | 65.44 N | 45.25 E |
| Loban' ≃ | 80 | 56.58 N | 51.12 E |
| Lobanovo | 76 | 53.04 N | 38.14 E |
| Lobanovskije Vyselki | 82 | 54.18 N | 38.58 E |
| Lo Barnechea | 286e | 33.21 S | 70.31 W |
| Lobaski | 80 | 54.38 N | 45.09 E |
| Lobatos | 234 | 22.49 N | 103.24 W |
| Lobatse | 156 | 25.11 S | 25.40 E |
| Löbau | 54 | 51.05 N | 14.40 E |
| Lobau ≚ | 264b | 48.10 N | 16.32 E |
| Lobaye □[5] | 152 | 4.00 N | 18.30 E |
| Lobaye ≃ | 152 | 3.41 N | 18.35 E |
| Lobbes | 50 | 50.21 N | 4.15 E |
| Lobbs Run ≃ | 279b | 40.15 N | 79.55 W |
| Lobdell Lake ⊜ | 216 | 42.48 N | 83.48 W |
| Löbejün | 54 | 51.38 N | 11.53 E |
| Lobelville | 194 | 35.46 N | 87.47 W |
| Lo Benitez | 286e | 33.34 S | 70.42 W |
| Lobería | 252 | 38.09 S | 58.47 W |
| Lo Bernales | 286e | 33.34 S | 70.34 W |
| Löberöd | 41 | 55.47 N | 13.30 E |
| Lobethal | 168b | 34.54 S | 138.52 E |
| Łobez | 30 | 53.39 N | 15.36 E |
| Lobito | 152 | 12.20 S | 13.34 E |
| Lobitos | 246 | 4.26 S | 81.17 W |
| Lobitos Creek ≃ | 282 | 37.22 N | 122.24 W |
| Lobn'a | 82 | 56.01 N | 37.30 E |
| Löbnitz, Dtsch. | 54 | 51.35 N | 12.28 E |
| Löbnitz, Dtsch. | 54 | 54.17 N | 12.43 E |
| Lobo, Indon. | 164 | 3.45 S | 134.05 E |
| Lobo, Pil. | 116 | 13.39 N | 121.13 E |
| Lobo ≃ | 150 | 6.02 N | 6.47 W |
| Loboko | 152 | 0.45 S | 16.38 E |
| Lobos | 258 | 35.11 S | 59.06 W |
| Lobos, Cay I | 238 | 22.24 N | 77.32 W |
| Lobos, Isla I | 232 | 27.20 N | 110.36 W |
| Lobos, Isla de I, Esp. | 148 | 28.45 N | 13.49 W |
| Lobos, Isla de I, Méx. | 234 | 21.27 N | 97.13 W |
| Lobos, Laguna de ⊜ | 258 | 35.17 S | 59.07 W |
| Lobos, Point > | 226 | 37.47 N | 122.31 W |
| Lobos, Punta > | 248 | 21.01 S | 70.11 W |
| Lobos de Afuera, Islas II | 248 | 6.57 S | 80.42 W |
| Lobos de Tierra, Isla I | 248 | 6.27 S | 80.52 W |
| Lo Boza | 286e | 33.23 S | 70.46 W |
| Lobskoje | 24 | 62.45 N | 35.16 E |
| Lobstädt | 54 | 51.08 N | 12.29 E |
| Loburg | 54 | 52.07 N | 12.05 E |
| Lobva | 86 | 59.12 N | 60.30 E |
| Łobżenica | 30 | 53.16 N | 17.15 E |
| Locana | 62 | 45.25 N | 7.27 E |
| Locana, Val di V | 62 | 45.25 N | 7.27 E |
| Locarno | 58 | 46.10 N | 8.48 E |
| Lo Castillo, Aeropuerto ⊠ | 286e | 33.23 S | 70.36 W |
| Locate Triulzi | 62 | 45.21 N | 9.13 E |
| Loccum | 52 | 52.27 N | 9.08 E |
| Loceri | 71 | 39.51 N | 9.35 E |
| Loch | 169 | 38.22 S | 145.43 E |
| Lochaber ◆[1] | 46 | 56.57 N | 5.06 W |
| Lochailort | 46 | 56.53 N | 5.40 W |
| Lochaline | 46 | 56.32 N | 5.47 W |
| Locharbriggs | 44 | 55.06 N | 3.35 W |
| Lochar Water ≃ | 44 | 54.59 N | 3.27 W |
| Lochboisdale | 46 | 57.09 N | 7.19 W |
| Lochcarron | 46 | 57.24 N | 5.30 W |
| Lochdon | 46 | 56.26 N | 5.41 W |
| Lochearn | 284b | 39.21 N | 76.43 W |
| Lochearnhead | 46 | 56.23 N | 4.17 W |
| Lochem | 52 | 52.09 N | 6.25 E |
| Loches | 50 | 47.08 N | 1.00 E |
| Lochgair | 46 | 56.03 N | 5.20 W |
| Loch Garman → Wexford | 48 | 52.20 N | 6.27 W |
| Lochgelly | 46 | 56.08 N | 3.19 W |
| Lochgilphead | 46 | 56.03 N | 5.26 W |
| Lochgoilhead | 46 | 56.10 N | 4.54 W |
| Lochiel | 168b | 33.56 S | 138.10 E |
| Lochindorb ⊜ | 46 | 57.24 N | 3.43 W |
| Lochino | 265b | 55.42 N | 37.19 E |
| Lochinvar National Park ♦ | 154 | 15.55 S | 27.15 E |
| Lochinver | 46 | 58.09 N | 5.15 W |
| Lochmaben | 44 | 55.08 N | 3.27 W |
| Lochmaddy | 46 | 57.36 N | 7.11 W |
| Lochnagar ∧ | 46 | 56.57 N | 3.16 W |
| Lochovice | 60 | 49.51 N | 13.59 E |
| Lochranza | 46 | 55.42 N | 5.18 W |
| Loch Raven Dam ◆[6] | 284b | 39.26 N | 76.33 W |
| Loch Raven Reservoir ⊜[1] | 208 | 39.27 N | 76.34 W |
| Lochristi | 50 | 51.06 N | 3.50 E |
| Lochsa ≃ | 202 | 46.08 N | 115.36 W |
| Loch Sheldrake | 210 | 41.46 N | 74.39 W |
| Loch Sport | 166 | 38.03 S | 147.36 E |
| Lochwinnoch | 46 | 55.48 N | 4.39 W |
| Lochy, Loch ⊜ | 46 | 56.57 N | 4.53 W |
| Lock | 166 | 33.34 S | 135.46 E |
| Lock and Dam No. 20 ◆[6], U.S. | 219 | 40.09 N | 91.30 W |
| Lock and Dam No. 21 ◆[6], U.S. | 219 | 39.54 N | 91.26 W |
| Lock and Dam No. 24 ◆[6], U.S. | 219 | 39.22 N | 90.55 W |
| Lock and Dam No. 25 ◆[6], U.S. | 219 | 39.01 N | 90.41 W |
| Lock and Dam No. 22 ◆[6], U.S. | 219 | 39.39 N | 91.16 W |
| Locke, Ca., U.S. | 226 | 38.15 N | 121.31 W |
| Locke, In., U.S. | 216 | 41.28 N | 86.00 W |
| Locke, N.Y., U.S. | 210 | 42.39 N | 76.25 W |
| Lockeford | 226 | 38.10 N | 121.09 W |
| Lockenhaus | 61 | 47.24 N | 16.25 E |
| Lockeport | 186 | 43.42 N | 65.07 W |
| Lockerbie | 44 | 55.07 N | 3.22 W |
| Lockesburg | 194 | 33.58 N | 94.10 W |
| Lockhart, Austl. | 166 | 35.14 S | 146.43 E |
| Lockhart, Fl., U.S. | 220 | 28.37 N | 81.26 W |
| Lockhart, Tx., U.S. | 222 | 29.53 N | 97.40 W |
| Lockhart River Aboriginal Reserve ◆[4] | 164 | 13.00 S | 143.15 E |
| Lock Haven | 210 | 41.08 N | 77.26 W |
| Lockheed Aircraft Corporation ʊ[3], Ca., U.S. | 280 | 34.12 N | 118.22 W |
| Lockheed Aircraft Corporation ʊ[3], Ca., U.S. | 282 | 37.25 N | 122.02 W |
| Lockington | 216 | 40.12 N | 84.13 W |
| Lockington Dam ◆[6] | 216 | 40.17 N | 84.15 W |
| Lock Mountain ∧ | 214 | 40.25 N | 78.18 W |
| Lockney | 196 | 34.07 N | 101.26 W |
| Löcknitz | 54 | 53.27 N | 14.12 E |
| Löcknitz ≃, Dtsch. | 54 | 53.07 N | 11.16 E |
| Löcknitz ≃, Dtsch. | 264a | 52.25 N | 13.49 E |
| Lockport, Mb., Can. | 184 | 50.05 N | 96.56 W |
| Lockport, Il., U.S. | 216 | 41.35 N | 88.03 W |
| Lockport, La., U.S. | 194 | 29.39 N | 90.32 W |
| Lockport, N.Y., U.S. | 210 | 43.10 N | 78.41 W |
| Lockport Lock ◆[5] | 278 | 41.35 N | 88.04 W |
| Locks Heath | 42 | 50.52 N | 1.15 W |
| Locksley Park | 210 | 42.45 N | 78.52 W |
| Lockvattnet ⊜ | 40 | 59.03 N | 17.05 E |
| Lockview | 279b | 40.10 N | 79.55 W |
| Lockwood, Ca., U.S. | 226 | 35.56 N | 121.05 W |
| Lockwood, Mo., U.S. | 194 | 37.23 N | 93.57 W |
| Lockwood Corners | 214 | 41.00 N | 81.34 W |
| Lockyer Creek ≃ | 171a | 27.25 S | 152.36 E |
| Locminé | 28 | 47.53 N | 2.50 W |
| Loc Ninh | 110 | 11.51 N | 106.36 E |
| Loco, Bayou ≃ | 222 | 31.28 N | 94.44 W |
| Locon | 50 | 50.34 N | 2.40 E |
| Locorotondo | 68 | 40.45 N | 17.20 E |
| Locri | 68 | 38.14 N | 16.16 E |
| Locri Epizefiri ⊥ | 68 | 38.12 N | 16.13 E |
| Locroja | 248 | 12.41 S | 74.26 W |
| Locsin | 116 | 13.09 N | 123.43 E |
| Locumba | 248 | 17.36 S | 70.46 W |
| Locumba ≃ | 248 | 17.54 S | 70.57 W |
| Locust | 208 | 40.18 N | 73.59 W |
| Locust Creek ≃ | 194 | 39.40 N | 93.17 W |
| Locust Fork ≃ | 194 | 33.33 N | 87.11 W |
| Locust Grove, N.Y., U.S. | 276 | 40.48 N | 73.30 W |
| Locust Grove, Ok., U.S. | 196 | 36.12 N | 95.10 W |
| Locust Lake State Park ♦ | 208 | 40.46 N | 76.08 W |
| Locust Point > | 276 | 40.49 N | 73.48 W |
| Locust Valley | 210 | 40.53 N | 73.36 W |
| Lod (Lydda) | 132 | 31.58 N | 34.54 E |
| Lod, Nemel-Te'ufa (Ben Gurion Airport) ⊠ | 132 | 31.59 N | 34.53 E |
| Loda | 216 | 40.31 N | 88.04 W |
| Lodal Creek ≃ | 285 | 40.14 N | 75.27 W |
| Löddeköpinge | 41 | 55.46 N | 13.01 E |
| Loddon | 42 | 52.32 N | 1.29 E |
| Loddon ≃, Austl. | 166 | 35.32 S | 143.52 E |
| Loddon ≃, Eng., U.K. | 42 | 51.30 N | 0.53 W |
| Lodè | 71 | 40.35 N | 9.32 E |
| Lodejnoje Pole | 76 | 60.44 N | 33.30 E |
| Lodenau | 54 | 51.24 N | 14.57 E |
| Löderburg | 54 | 51.52 N | 11.32 E |
| Lodève | 32 | 43.43 N | 3.19 E |
| Lodge Creek ≃ | 202 | 48.35 N | 109.10 W |
| Lodge Grass | 202 | 45.18 N | 107.21 W |
| Lodgepole, Ab., Can. | 182 | 53.06 N | 115.19 W |
| Lodgepole, Ne., U.S. | 198 | 41.08 N | 102.38 W |
| Lodgepole Creek ≃ | 198 | 40.57 N | 102.22 W |
| Lodhāsuli | 126 | 22.19 N | 87.03 E |
| Lodhrān | 123 | 29.32 N | 71.38 E |
| Lodi, It. | 62 | 45.19 N | 9.30 E |
| Lodi, Ca., U.S. | 226 | 38.07 N | 121.16 W |
| Lodi, N.J., U.S. | 210 | 40.52 N | 74.05 W |
| Lodi, N.Y., U.S. | 210 | 42.36 N | 76.49 W |
| Lodi, Oh., U.S. | 214 | 41.02 N | 82.00 W |
| Lodi, Wi., U.S. | 190 | 43.18 N | 89.31 W |
| Lodi □[4] | 62 | 45.15 N | 9.35 E |
| Lodi Park ♦ | 272a | 28.36 N | 77.13 E |
| Lodi Vecchio | 62 | 45.18 N | 9.24 E |
| Lodja | 152 | 3.29 S | 23.26 E |
| Lodosa | 34 | 42.25 N | 2.05 W |
| Lodoyo | 115a | 8.10 S | 112.13 E |
| Lodrone | 64 | 45.50 N | 10.32 E |
| Lods | 58 | 47.03 N | 6.15 E |
| Lodsch → Łódź | 30 | 51.46 N | 19.30 E |
| Lodwar | 154 | 3.07 N | 35.36 E |
| Łódź | 30 | 51.46 N | 19.30 E |
| Łódź □[4] | 30 | 51.50 N | 19.25 E |
| Loe Āgra | 123 | 34.35 N | 71.43 E |
| Loei | 110 | 17.29 N | 101.35 E |
| Loei ≃ | 110 | 17.51 N | 101.37 E |
| Loen | 26 | 61.52 N | 6.52 E |
| Loenen | 52 | 52.07 N | 6.01 E |
| Loengo | 154 | 4.45 S | 26.27 E |
| Loeriesfontein | 158 | 30.56 S | 19.26 E |
| Lo Espejo | 286e | 33.32 S | 70.43 W |
| Lo Espejo, Canal ≍ | 286e | 33.32 S | 70.43 W |
| Loeų | 78 | 51.56 N | 30.46 E |
| Lofa ≃ | 150 | 6.36 N | 11.08 W |
| Lofer | 64 | 47.35 N | 12.41 E |
| Löffingen | 58 | 47.53 N | 8.20 E |
| Lofoten II | 24 | 68.30 N | 15.00 E |
| Lofoten Basin ✦[1] | 10 | 70.00 N | 4.00 E |
| Lofthouse | 44 | 53.44 N | 1.29 W |
| Lofthus | 26 | 60.20 N | 6.40 E |
| Loftus, Austl. | 274a | 34.03 S | 151.03 E |
| Loftus, Eng., U.K. | 44 | 54.33 N | 0.53 W |
| Lofty, Mount ∧, Austl. | 168b | 34.59 S | 138.42 E |
| Lofty, Mount ∧, Austl. | 274b | 37.43 S | 145.17 E |
| Log | 80 | 49.29 N | 43.52 E |
| Loga, Dtsch. | 52 | 53.14 N | 7.29 E |
| Loga, Niger | 150 | 13.37 N | 3.14 E |
| Logačovka | 80 | 52.23 N | 52.21 E |
| Logan, Ia., U.S. | 198 | 41.38 N | 95.47 W |
| Logan, Ks., U.S. | 198 | 39.39 N | 99.34 W |
| Logan, N.M., U.S. | 196 | 35.22 N | 103.25 W |
| Logan, Oh., U.S. | 188 | 39.32 N | 82.24 W |
| Logan, Ut,. U.S. | 200 | 41.44 N | 111.50 W |
| Logan, W.V., U.S. | 188 | 37.50 N | 81.59 W |
| Logan □[6], Il., U.S. | 219 | 40.09 N | 89.22 W |
| Logan □[6], Oh., U.S. | 216 | 40.22 N | 83.46 W |
| Logan ◆[8] | 285 | 40.02 N | 75.09 W |
| Logan ≃, Austl. | 171a | 27.43 S | 153.18 E |
| Logan ≃, Ab., Can. | 182 | 55.09 N | 111.42 W |
| Logan ≃, Ut,. U.S. | 200 | 41.44 N | 111.57 W |
| Logan, Mount ∧, Yk., Can. | 180 | 60.34 N | 140.24 W |
| Logan, Mount ∧, Wa., U.S. | 224 | 48.32 N | 120.57 W |
| Logan Creek ≃, Ca., U.S. | 226 | 39.22 N | 122.06 W |
| Logan Creek ≃, Mo., U.S. | 194 | 37.11 N | 90.49 W |
| Logan Creek ≃, Ne., U.S. | 198 | 41.37 N | 96.29 W |
| Logandale | 204 | 36.35 N | 114.29 W |
| Logan International Airport ⊠ | 283 | 42.22 N | 71.00 W |
| Logan Lake ⊜ | 212 | 44.52 N | 78.59 W |
| Logan Martin Lake ⊜[1] | 194 | 33.40 N | 86.15 W |
| Logan Mountains ⋏ | 180 | 61.45 N | 128.38 W |
| Logan Pass )( | 202 | 48.42 N | 113.43 W |
| Logansport, In., U.S. | 216 | 40.45 N | 86.21 W |
| Logansport, La., U.S. | 194 | 31.58 N | 93.59 W |
| Logan Square ◆[8] | 278 | 41.56 N | 87.42 W |
| Loganton | 210 | 41.02 N | 77.18 W |
| Loganville, Ga., U.S. | 192 | 33.50 N | 83.54 W |
| Loganville, Pa., U.S. | 208 | 39.52 N | 76.42 W |
| Logärden ⊜ | 40 | 60.37 N | 16.00 E |
| Lögdeälven ≃ | 26 | 63.33 N | 19.25 E |
| Logduz | 76 | 60.00 N | 44.41 E |
| Loge ≃, Ang. | 152 | 10.12 S | 17.00 E |
| Loge ≃, Ang. | 152 | 7.49 S | 13.06 E |
| Logia | 164 | 2.55 S | 151.27 E |
| Loginovo | 82 | 55.42 N | 38.44 E |
| Logirim | 154 | 4.43 N | 33.14 E |
| Lognes | 261 | 48.50 N | 2.38 E |
| Lognes-Émerainville, Aérodrome de ⊠ | 261 | 48.49 N | 2.37 E |
| Logo | 154 | 5.20 N | 30.18 E |
| Logone ≃ | 146 | 12.06 N | 15.02 E |
| Logone Birni | 146 | 11.47 N | 15.06 E |
| Logone Gana | 146 | 11.33 N | 15.09 E |
| Logone-Occidental □[5] | 146 | 8.50 N | 16.00 E |
| Logone Occidental ≃ | 146 | 9.07 N | 16.26 E |
| Logone-Oriental □[5] | 146 | 8.15 N | 16.20 E |
| Logone Oriental ≃ | 146 | 9.07 N | 16.26 E |
| Logoualé | 150 | 7.07 N | 7.33 W |
| Logovskij | 80 | 48.26 N | 43.23 E |
| Log pod Mangartom | 64 | 46.24 N | 13.36 E |
| Logroño | 34 | 42.28 N | 2.27 W |
| Logrosán | 34 | 39.20 N | 5.29 W |
| Løgstør | 26 | 56.58 N | 9.15 E |
| Logtāk Lake ⊜ | 120 | 24.33 N | 93.50 E |
| Løgten | 41 | 56.17 N | 10.19 E |
| Logudoro ◆[1] | 71 | 40.35 N | 8.40 E |
| Logue Brook Dam ◆[6] | 168a | 33.00 S | 115.57 E |
| Løgumgårde | 41 | 55.05 N | 8.57 E |
| Løgumkloster | 41 | 55.03 N | 8.57 E |
| Logumukum | 154 | 0.27 N | 36.05 E |
| Logy Creek ≃ | 224 | 46.11 N | 120.35 W |
| Loh I | 175f | 13.21 S | 166.38 E |
| Lohāgara | 126 | 23.11 N | 89.39 E |
| Lohals | 41 | 55.08 N | 10.55 E |
| Lohārdaga | 124 | 23.26 N | 84.41 E |
| Lohāru | 120 | 28.27 N | 75.49 E |
| Lohatlha | 158 | 28.02 S | 23.04 E |
| Lohausen ◆[8] | 263 | 51.16 N | 6.44 E |
| Lohauserholz ◆[8] | 263 | 51.39 N | 7.48 E |
| Lohberg | 263 | 51.35 N | 6.46 E |
| Löhdorf ◆[8] | 263 | 51.09 N | 7.01 E |
| Lo Hermida | 286e | 33.29 S | 70.33 W |
| Lohfelden | 56 | 51.16 N | 9.32 E |
| Lohheide ◆[8] | 263 | 51.30 N | 6.40 E |
| Lohiān | 123 | 31.10 N | 75.11 E |
| Lohiniva | 24 | 67.10 N | 24.58 E |
| Lohit ≃ | 120 | 27.48 N | 95.28 E |
| Lohja | 26 | 60.15 N | 24.05 E |
| Lohjanharju ∧ | 26 | 60.15 N | 24.30 E |
| Lohjanjärvi ⊜ | 26 | 60.15 N | 23.55 E |
| Löhlbach | 56 | 51.04 N | 8.58 E |
| Lohmar | 56 | 50.50 N | 7.13 E |
| Lohme, Dtsch. | 54 | 54.35 N | 13.37 E |
| Löhme, Dtsch. | 264a | 52.37 N | 13.40 E |
| Lohmen, Dtsch. | 54 | 50.59 N | 13.59 E |
| Lohmen, Dtsch. | 54 | 53.41 N | 12.05 E |
| Lohmühle | 263 | 51.31 N | 6.40 E |
| Löhnberg | 56 | 50.31 N | 8.17 E |
| Lohne, Dtsch. | 52 | 52.42 N | 8.12 E |
| Löhne, Dtsch. | 52 | 52.11 N | 8.41 E |
| Löhnen | 263 | 51.36 N | 6.39 E |
| Lohnsburg | 60 | 48.09 N | 13.24 E |
| Loho → Luohe | 100 | 33.35 N | 114.01 E |
| Lohr am Main | 56 | 50.00 N | 9.34 E |
| Lohrville | 198 | 42.16 N | 94.32 W |


**Symbols** in the index entries represent the broad categories identified in the key at the right. Symbols with superior numbers (⋏[1]) identify subcategories (see complete key on page *I · 1).*

**Symbole** im Register stellen die rechts im Schlüssel erklärten Kategorien dar. Symbole mit hochgestellten Ziffern (⋏[1]) bezeichnen Unterabteilungen einer Kategorie (vgl. vollständiger Schlüssel auf Seite *I · 1).*

**Los símbolos** incluídos en el texto del índice representan las grandes categorías identificadas con la clave a la derecha. Los símbolos con numeros en su parte superior (⋏[1]) identifican las subcategorías (véase la clave completa en la página *I · 1).*

**Les symboles** de l'index représentent les catégories indiquées dans la légende à droite. Les symboles suivis d'un indice (⋏[1]) représentent des sous-catégories (voir légende complète à la page *I · 1).*

**Os símbolos** incluídos no texto do índice representam as grandes categorias identificadas com a chave à direita. Os símbolos com números em sua parte superior (⋏[1]) identificam as subcategorias (veja-se a chave completa à página *I · 1).*

| | English | Deutsch | Español | Français | Português |
|---|---|---|---|---|---|
| ∧ | Mountain | Berg | Montaña | Montagne | Montanha |
| ⋏ | Mountains | Gebirge | Montañas | Montagnes | Montanhas |
| )( | Pass | Paß | Paso | Col | Passo |
| V | Valley, Canyon | Tal, Cañon | Valle, Cañón | Vallée, Canyon | Vale, Canhão |
| ≚ | Plain | Ebene | Llano | Plaine | Planície |
| > | Cape | Kap | Cabo | Cap | Cabo |
| I | Island | Insel | Isla | Île | Ilha |
| II | Islands | Inseln | Islas | Îles | Ilhas |
| ± | Other Topographic Features | Andere Topographische Objekte | Otros Elementos Topográficos | Autres données topographiques | Outros acidentes topográficos |

ESPAÑOL — Nombre | Página | Lat.°′ | Long.°′ W = Oeste
FRANÇAIS — Nom | Page | Lat.°′ | Long.°′ W = Ouest
PORTUGUÊS — Nome | Página | Lat.°′ | Long.°′ W = Oeste


| Nombre | Página | Lat.°′ | Long.°′ W = Oeste |
|---|---|---|---|
| Lohsa | 54 | 51.23 N | 14.24 E |
| Loi ≃ | 110 | 21.19 N | 100.44 E |
| Loi, Phou ∧ | 110 | 20.16 N | 103.12 E |
| Loiano | 66 | 44.16 N | 11.19 E |
| Loiblpass (Ljubelj) )( | 61 | 46.26 N | 14.16 E |
| Loiborsoit | 154 | 3.52 S | 36.26 E |
| Loi-kaw | 110 | 19.41 N | 97.13 E |
| Loile ≃ | 152 | 0.52 S | 20.12 E |
| Loimaa | 26 | 60.51 N | 23.03 E |
| Loimijoki ≃ | 26 | 61.13 N | 22.38 E |
| Loi Mwe | 110 | 21.11 N | 99.46 E |
| Loing ≃ | 50 | 48.23 N | 2.48 E |
| Loing, Canal du ≅ | 50 | 48.22 N | 2.50 E |
| Loir ≃ | 32 | 47.33 N | 0.32 W |
| Loira → Loire ≃ | 32 | 47.16 N | 2.11 W |
| Loire | 62 | 45.33 N | 4.48 E |
| Loire □[5] | 32 | 45.30 N | 4.00 E |
| Loire ≃ | 32 | 47.16 N | 2.11 W |
| Loire, Canal latéral à la ≅ | 50 | 47.37 N | 2.44 E |
| Loire-Atlantique □[5] | 32 | 47.20 N | 1.35 W |
| Loiret □[5] | 50 | 47.55 N | 2.20 E |
| Loiret ≃ | 50 | 47.52 N | 1.48 E |
| Loir-et-Cher □[5] | 50 | 47.30 N | 1.30 E |
| Loïs, Lac ⊜ | 190 | 48.34 N | 78.44 W |
| Loisach ≃ | 64 | 47.56 N | 11.27 E |
| Loisdale | 284c | 38.46 N | 77.11 W |
| Loisia | 58 | 46.29 N | 5.27 E |
| Loison ≃ | 56 | 49.30 N | 5.17 E |
| Loitz | 54 | 53.58 N | 13.07 E |
| Loíza, Lago ⊜[1] | 240m | 18.17 N | 66.00 W |
| Loíza Aldea | 240m | 18.26 N | 65.53 W |
| Loja, Ec. | 246 | 4.00 S | 79.13 W |
| Loja, Esp. | 34 | 37.10 N | 4.09 W |
| Loja □[4] | 246 | 4.10 S | 79.30 W |
| Lojang → Luoyang | 102 | 34.41 N | 112.28 E |
| Lojga | 24 | 61.05 N | 44.37 E |
| Lojno | 24 | 59.44 N | 52.39 E |
| Løjt Kirkeby | 41 | 55.05 N | 9.28 E |
| Loka, Sūd. | 154 | 4.16 N | 31.01 E |
| Loka, Zaïre | 152 | 0.20 N | 17.57 E |
| Loka brunn | 40 | 59.36 N | 14.28 E |
| Lokachi | 78 | 50.44 N | 24.39 E |
| Lokako | 152 | 2.14 S | 21.45 E |
| Lokalema | 152 | 1.59 N | 22.17 E |
| Lokan ≃ | 116 | 5.25 N | 117.44 E |
| Lokandu | 154 | 2.31 S | 25.47 E |
| Lokan tekojärvi ⊜[1] | 24 | 67.55 N | 27.40 E |
| Lökbatan | 84 | 40.20 N | 49.43 E |
| Løken | 26 | 59.48 N | 11.29 E |
| Lokeren | 50 | 51.06 N | 4.00 E |
| Loket | 54 | 50.09 N | 12.43 E |
| Lokhvytsya | 78 | 50.22 N | 33.16 E |
| Lokichar | 154 | 2.23 N | 35.39 E |
| Lokichokio | 154 | 4.12 N | 34.21 E |
| Lokitaung | 154 | 4.16 N | 35.45 E |
| Lokka | 24 | 67.49 N | 27.44 E |
| Løkken | 26 | 57.22 N | 9.43 E |
| Løkken verk | 26 | 63.08 N | 9.42 E |
| Lokn'a | 76 | 56.50 N | 30.09 E |
| Loknaš ≃ | 82 | 56.11 N | 36.04 E |
| Loko | 150 | 8.02 N | 7.49 E |
| Lokofa-Bokolongo | 152 | 0.12 N | 19.22 E |
| Lokoja | 150 | 7.47 N | 6.45 E |
| Lokolama | 152 | 2.34 S | 19.53 E |
| Lokolenge | 152 | 1.11 N | 22.40 E |
| Lokolo ≃ | 152 | 0.43 S | 19.40 E |
| Lokomo | 152 | 2.41 N | 15.19 E |
| Lokoro ≃ | 152 | 1.43 S | 18.23 E |
| Lokossa | 150 | 6.38 N | 1.43 E |
| Lokosso | 150 | 10.19 N | 3.40 W |
| Lokot', Ross. | 76 | 52.34 N | 34.34 E |
| Lokot', Ross. | 86 | 51.11 N | 81.11 E |
| Lokoua ≃ | 273b | 4.06 S | 15.16 E |
| Loksa | 76 | 59.35 N | 25.45 E |
| Loks Land I | 176 | 62.26 N | 64.38 W |
| Lokve | 64 | 46.01 N | 13.49 E |
| Loky | 157b | 12.47 S | 49.39 E |
| Lol | 140 | 6.26 N | 29.37 E |
| Lol ≃ | 140 | 9.13 N | 28.59 E |
| Lóla, Ang. | 152 | 14.22 S | 13.42 E |
| Lola, Guinée | 150 | 7.48 N | 8.32 W |
| Lola, Mount ∧ | 226 | 39.26 N | 120.22 W |
| Lolengi | 152 | 0.07 N | 20.59 E |
| Loleta | 204 | 40.38 N | 124.13 W |
| Lolingo | 152 | 0.55 N | 22.38 E |
| Loliondo | 154 | 2.03 S | 35.37 E |
| Lolita | 222 | 28.50 N | 96.32 W |
| Lolland I | 41 | 54.46 N | 11.30 E |
| Lollar | 56 | 50.39 N | 8.42 E |
| Lolo, Mt., U.S. | 202 | 46.45 N | 114.04 W |
| Lolo, Zaïre | 152 | 2.13 N | 23.00 E |
| Lolo ≃ | 152 | 1.07 S | 12.28 E |
| Lolobau Island I | 164 | 4.55 S | 151.10 E |
| Lolo Creek ≃, Id., U.S. | 202 | 46.26 N | 116.10 W |
| Lolo Creek ≃, Mt., U.S. | 202 | 46.45 N | 114.03 W |
| Lolodorf | 152 | 3.14 N | 10.44 E |
| Lolo Pass )( | 202 | 46.38 N | 114.35 W |
| Lolotique | 236 | 13.33 N | 88.21 W |
| Lolowai | 175f | 15.18 S | 168.00 E |
| Loltong | 175f | 15.33 S | 168.08 E |
| Lolvavana, Passage ʮ | 175f | 15.26 S | 168.12 E |
| Lolwa | 154 | 1.22 N | 29.31 E |
| Lolworth Range ⩘ | 166 | 20.20 S | 145.15 E |
| Lom, Blg. | 38 | 43.49 N | 23.14 E |
| Lom, Česká Rep. | 54 | 50.37 N | 13.40 E |
| Lom, Nor. | 26 | 61.50 N | 8.33 E |
| Lom, Ross. | 80 | 57.54 N | 39.12 E |
| Lom ∧ | 60 | 49.54 N | 13.12 E |
| Lom ≃, Afr. | 152 | 5.20 N | 13.24 E |
| Lom ≃, Blg. | 38 | 43.50 N | 23.15 E |
| Loma | 144 | 6.55 N | 37.34 E |
| Loma, Point › | 228 | 32.41 N | 117.14 W |
| Loma Blanca, Chile | 286e | 33.30 S | 70.47 W |
| Loma Blanca, Méx. | 200 | 31.35 N | 106.17 W |
| Loma Bonita | 234 | 18.07 N | 95.53 W |
| Loma Echegareña | 234 | 22.53 N | 105.51 W |
| Lomakino | 85 | 40.05 N | 68.10 E |
| Lomako ≃ | 152 | 0.50 N | 20.50 E |
| Loma Linda | 228 | 34.02 N | 117.15 W |
| Lomaloma | 175g | 17.17 S | 178.59 W |
| Lomami ≃ | 138 | 0.46 N | 24.16 E |
| Loma Mountains ⩘ | 150 | 9.10 N | 11.07 W |
| Loma Ridge ∧ | 280 | 33.45 N | 117.43 W |
| Lomas, Bahía ⊂ | 254 | 52.35 S | 69.05 W |
| Lomas Alegres | 234 | 17.38 N | 92.36 W |
| Lomas Chapultepec ➛[8] | 286a | 19.26 N | 99.13 W |
| Lomas del Real | 234 | 22.30 N | 97.54 W |
| Lomas de Monreal | 200 | 31.17 N | 110.56 W |
| Lomas de Zamora | 258 | 34.46 S | 58.24 W |
| Lomas de Zamora □[5] | 288 | 34.45 S | 58.24 W |
| Loma Verde | 258 | 35.16 S | 58.24 W |
| Lomax, Il., U.S. | 190 | 40.41 N | 91.04 W |
| Lomax, Tx., U.S. | 222 | 29.41 N | 95.04 W |
| Łomazy | 30 | 51.55 N | 23.10 E |
| Lomazzo | 62 | 45.42 N | 9.02 E |
| Lomba ≃ | 152 | 15.36 S | 21.32 E |
| Lombagin | 112 | 0.55 N | 124.04 E |
| Lombard | 216 | 41.52 N | 88.00 W |
| Lombardia □[4] | 36 | 45.40 N | 9.30 E |
| Lombardy East | 273d | 26.07 S | 28.08 E |
| Lombe | 152 | 9.27 S | 16.13 E |
| Lomblen, Pulau I | 112 | 8.25 S | 123.30 E |
| Lombo do Tejo, Mouchão do I | 266c | 38.52 N | 9.00 W |
| Lombok | 115b | 8.30 S | 116.40 E |
| Lombok I | 115b | 8.45 S | 116.30 E |
| Lombok, Selat ʮ | 115b | 8.30 S | 115.50 E |
| Lombong | 114 | 1.48 N | 103.51 E |
| Lomé | 150 | 6.08 N | 1.13 E |
| Lomela | 152 | 2.18 S | 23.17 E |
| Lomela ≃ | 152 | 0.14 S | 20.42 E |
| Lomellina □[9] | 62 | 45.15 N | 8.45 E |
| Lometa | 196 | 31.13 N | 98.23 W |
| Lomi | 24 | 67.05 N | 16.09 E |
| Lomié | 152 | 3.10 N | 13.37 E |
| Lomira | 190 | 43.35 N | 88.26 W |
| Lo Miranda | 252 | 34.11 S | 70.54 W |
| Lomita | 228 | 33.47 N | 118.18 W |
| Lom Kao | 110 | 16.53 N | 101.14 E |
| Lomma | 41 | 55.41 N | 13.05 E |
| Lommabukten ⊂ | 41 | 55.40 N | 12.58 E |
| Lommatzsch | 54 | 51.12 N | 13.18 E |
| Lomme | 50 | 50.39 N | 2.59 E |
| Lomme ≃ | 56 | 50.08 N | 5.10 E |
| Lommel | 56 | 51.14 N | 5.18 E |
| Lomnice ≃ | 60 | 49.26 N | 14.04 E |
| Lomnice nad Popelkou | 30 | 50.32 N | 15.22 E |
| Lomond | 182 | 50.21 N | 112.39 W |
| Lomond, Loch ⊜, N.S., Can. | 186 | 45.46 N | 60.35 W |
| Lomond, Loch ⊜, On., Can. | 190 | 48.15 N | 89.20 W |
| Lomond, Loch ⊜, Scot., U.K. | 46 | 56.08 N | 4.38 W |
| Lomond, Loch ⊜, Il., U.S. | 278 | 42.17 N | 88.01 W |
| Lomonosov | 265a | 59.55 N | 29.46 E |
| Lomonosovka | 86 | 52.50 N | 66.28 E |
| Lomonosov Moscow State University Ʊ[2] | 265b | 55.43 N | 37.32 E |
| Lomovoje | 24 | 64.01 N | 40.40 E |
| Lompobatang, Gunung ∧ | 112 | 5.20 S | 119.55 E |
| Lompoc | 204 | 34.38 N | 120.27 W |
| Lom Sak | 110 | 16.47 N | 101.15 E |
| Lomuvatka | 83 | 48.27 N | 38.34 E |
| Lomy | 88 | 52.17 N | 117.59 E |
| Łomża | 30 | 53.11 N | 22.05 E |
| Łomża □[4] | 30 | 53.00 N | 22.15 E |
| Lonaconing | 188 | 39.33 N | 78.58 W |
| Lonate Pozzolo | 62 | 45.36 N | 8.45 E |
| Lonato | 64 | 45.27 N | 10.29 E |
| Lonāvale | 122 | 18.45 N | 73.25 E |
| Lončakovo | 89 | 47.05 N | 134.10 E |
| Loncoche | 254 | 39.22 S | 72.38 W |
| Loncon ≃ | 64 | 45.42 N | 12.47 E |
| Loncopué | 252 | 38.04 S | 70.37 W |
| Londela-Kaye | 152 | 4.51 S | 13.24 E |
| Londerzeel | 50 | 51.00 N | 4.18 E |
| Londinières | 50 | 49.50 N | 1.24 E |
| Londo | 154 | 2.03 N | 25.43 E |
| Londoko | 89 | 49.02 N | 131.59 E |
| London, On., Can. | 212 | 42.59 N | 81.14 W |
| London, Kiribati | 174o | 1.58 N | 157.28 W |
| London, Eng., U.K. | 42 | 51.30 N | 0.10 W |
| London, Eng., U.K. | 260 | 51.30 N | 0.10 W |
| London, Ar., U.S. | 194 | 35.19 N | 93.15 W |
| London, Ca., U.S. | 226 | 36.30 N | 119.25 W |
| London, Ky., U.S. | 192 | 37.07 N | 84.05 W |
| London, Oh., U.S. | 218 | 39.53 N | 83.26 W |
| London, Tx., U.S. | 196 | 30.41 N | 99.35 W |
| London, Wi., U.S. | 216 | 43.03 N | 89.01 W |
| London (Gatwick) Airport ⊠, Eng., U.K. | 42 | 51.09 N | 0.21 W |
| London (Heathrow) Airport ⊠, Eng., U.K. | 42 | 51.27 N | 0.28 W |
| London Colney | 260 | 51.43 N | 0.18 W |
| Londonderry, N.S., Can. | 186 | 45.29 N | 63.36 W |
| Londonderry (Derry), N. Ire., U.K. | 48 | 54.59 N | 7.20 W |
| Londonderry, N.H., U.S. | 207 | 42.51 N | 71.22 W |
| Londonderry, Oh., U.S. | 214 | 39.16 N | 82.47 W |
| Londonderry, Cape › | 164 | 13.45 S | 126.55 E |
| Londonderry, Isla I | 254 | 55.03 S | 70.35 W |
| Londontowne | 208 | 38.59 N | 76.32 W |
| London Zoo ♦ | 260 | 51.32 N | 0.09 W |
| Londres, Arg. | 252 | 27.43 S | 67.07 W |
| Londres → London, Eng., U.K. | 42 | 51.30 N | 0.10 W |
| Londrina | 255 | 23.18 S | 51.09 W |
| Lonedell | 219 | 38.18 N | 90.50 W |
| Lone Grove | 196 | 34.10 N | 97.15 W |
| Lonely Lake ⊜ | 184 | 51.09 N | 99.05 W |
| Lonelyville | 276 | 40.39 N | 73.11 W |
| Lone Mountain ∧ | 204 | 38.02 N | 117.29 W |
| Lone Oak, Ky., U.S. | 194 | 37.02 N | 88.39 W |
| Lone Oak, Tx., U.S. | 222 | 33.01 N | 95.57 W |
| Lone Pine | 204 | 36.36 N | 118.03 W |
| Lone Pine Koala Sanctuary ♦ | 171a | 27.32 S | 152.57 E |
| Lone Rock | 190 | 43.11 N | 90.11 W |
| Lone Star | 222 | 32.56 N | 94.43 W |
| Lone Tree | 190 | 41.29 N | 91.25 W |
| Lone Tree Creek ≃, U.S. | 200 | 40.25 N | 104.35 W |
| Lone Tree Creek ≃, Ca., U.S. | 226 | 37.53 N | 121.14 W |
| Lone Wolf | 196 | 34.59 N | 99.14 W |
| Long | 110 | 18.05 N | 99.50 E |
| Long ≃, Fr. | 50 | 47.41 N | 0.28 E |
| Long ≃, Zhg. | 100 | 23.26 N | 114.38 E |
| Long ≃, Zhg. | 102 | 24.32 N | 109.15 E |
| Long ≃, Zhg. | 105 | 39.23 N | 116.49 E |
| Longa | 152 | 14.42 S | 18.32 E |
| Longa ≃, Ang. | 152 | 16.25 N | 19.04 E |
| Longa ≃, Ang. | 152 | 10.15 S | 13.30 E |
| Longá ≃, Bra. | 250 | 3.09 S | 41.56 W |
| Longa, proliv ʮ | 74 | 70.20 N | 178.00 E |
| Longairo | 154 | 4.30 N | 32.17 E |
| Long Akah | 112 | 3.19 N | 114.47 E |
| Long'an | 102 | 25.03 N | 109.00 E |
| Longana | 175f | 15.20 S | 167.55 E |
| Long'anqiao | 89 | 47.31 N | 124.27 E |
| Longare | 64 | 45.29 N | 11.36 E |
| Longarone | 64 | 46.16 N | 12.18 E |
| Long Arroyo V | 196 | 33.04 N | 104.17 W |
| Longasy | 24 | 61.58 N | 35.09 E |
| Longaví | 252 | 35.58 S | 71.41 W |
| Longbangun | 112 | 0.36 N | 115.11 E |
| Long Bar Harbor | 208 | 39.27 N | 76.15 W |
| Long Barn | 226 | 38.05 N | 120.08 W |
| Long Bay ⊂, Austl. | 274a | 33.58 S | 151.16 E |
| Long Bay ⊂, U.S. | 192 | 33.35 N | 78.45 W |
| Long Beach, Ca., U.S. | 228 | 33.46 N | 118.11 W |
| Long Beach, In., U.S. | 216 | 41.44 N | 86.51 W |
| Long Beach, Ms., U.S. | 194 | 30.21 N | 89.09 W |
| Long Beach, N.Y., U.S. | 210 | 40.35 N | 73.39 W |
| Long Beach, Wa., U.S. | 224 | 46.21 N | 124.03 W |
| Long Beach ⩸[2] | 208 | 39.39 N | 74.11 W |
| Long Beach Breakwater ➛[5] | 280 | 33.43 N | 118.09 W |
| Long Beach Middle Harbor ⊂ | 280 | 33.45 N | 118.13 W |
| Long Beach Municipal Airport ⊠ | 280 | 33.49 N | 118.09 W |
| Long Beach Naval Station ■ | 280 | 33.45 N | 118.14 W |
| Longbeleh | 112 | 0.16 N | 116.11 E |
| Long Belepai | 112 | 2.45 N | 114.04 E |
| Longbenton | 44 | 55.02 N | 1.35 W |
| Longboat Key | 220 | 27.24 N | 82.39 W |
| Longboat Key I | 220 | 27.23 N | 82.39 W |
| Long Branch, N.J., U.S. | 208 | 40.18 N | 73.59 W |
| Longbranch, Wa., U.S. | 224 | 47.12 N | 122.45 W |
| Long Branch □[8] | 275b | 43.35 N | 79.32 W |
| Long Branch ≃ | 219 | 39.23 N | 91.49 W |
| Long Branch Lake ⊜[1] | 194 | 39.49 N | 92.31 W |
| Longbu | 100 | 25.32 N | 115.24 E |
| Long Buckby | 42 | 52.19 N | 1.04 W |
| Long Cane Creek ≃ | 192 | 33.57 N | 82.24 W |
| Long Canyon V | 226 | 38.59 N | 120.41 W |
| Long Cay I | 238 | 22.37 N | 74.20 W |
| Longchamp, Hippodrome de ♦ | 261 | 48.51 N | 2.14 E |
| Longchamps, Arg. | 258 | 34.52 S | 58.23 W |
| Longchamps, Bel. | 56 | 50.03 N | 5.42 E |
| Longchang, Zhg. | 104 | 40.53 N | 123.08 E |
| Longchang, Zhg. | 107 | 29.21 N | 105.17 E |
| Longchaumois | 58 | 46.27 N | 5.56 E |
| Longchêne | 261 | 48.38 N | 2.00 E |
| Longchuan, Zhg. | 100 | 24.07 N | 115.17 E |
| Longchuan, Zhg. | 102 | 24.14 N | 97.45 E |
| Longchuan (Shweli) ≃ | 102 | 23.56 N | 96.17 E |
| Long Creek, Il., U.S. | 219 | 39.48 N | 88.50 W |
| Long Creek, Or., U.S. | 202 | 44.42 N | 119.06 W |
| Long Creek ≃ | 184 | 49.07 N | 103.00 W |
| Long Crendon | 42 | 51.47 N | 1.01 W |
| Longcun | 100 | 23.34 N | 115.33 E |
| Longde | 102 | 35.28 N | 106.22 E |
| Longdendale V | 262 | 53.29 N | 1.56 W |
| Long Ditton | 260 | 51.23 N | 0.20 W |
| Longdongtuo | 107 | 29.59 N | 106.21 E |
| Longdor, gora ∧ | 88 | 58.24 N | 116.47 E |
| Longdou | 100 | 27.25 N | 117.24 E |
| Longdu | 106 | 31.51 N | 118.56 E |
| Long Eaton | 42 | 52.54 N | 1.15 W |
| Longeau | 58 | 47.46 N | 5.18 E |
| Long Eddy | 210 | 41.51 N | 75.08 W |
| Longfellow National Historic Site ⊥ | 283 | 42.23 N | 71.08 W |
| Longfengchang | 107 | 30.26 N | 105.38 E |
| Longfengkan | 104 | 41.51 N | 124.01 E |
| Longfengyutun | 104 | 40.39 N | 122.57 E |
| Longfield | 260 | 51.24 N | 0.18 E |
| Longford, Austl. | 166 | 38.10 S | 147.05 E |
| Longford, Ire. | 48 | 53.44 N | 7.47 W |
| Longford, Md., U.S. | 284b | 39.25 N | 76.39 W |
| Longford □[6] | 48 | 53.40 N | 7.40 W |
| Longford Park ♦ | 262 | 53.27 N | 2.17 W |
| Longframlington | 44 | 55.18 N | 1.47 W |
| Longgang, Zhg. | 100 | 29.38 N | 114.57 E |
| Longgang, Zhg. | 100 | 33.22 N | 120.04 E |
| Longgang, Zhg. | 102 | 24.41 N | 101.09 E |
| Longgangzi | 104 | 42.09 N | 123.26 E |
| Long Green | 208 | 39.23 N | 76.31 W |
| Long Grove | 216 | 42.11 N | 88.00 W |
| Longguan | 105 | 40.47 N | 115.34 E |
| Longgudu | 100 | 27.45 N | 116.14 E |
| Longguntur | 112 | 0.13 N | 112.12 E |
| Long Harbour | 186 | 47.26 N | 53.48 W |
| Long Harbour ⊂, Nf., Can. | 186 | 47.44 N | 55.01 W |
| Long Harbour ⊂, H.K. | 271d | 22.27 N | 114.20 E |
| Longhorn Cavern State Park ♦ | 196 | 30.20 N | 98.30 W |
| Longhorsley | 44 | 55.15 N | 1.46 W |
| Longhoughton | 44 | 55.26 N | 1.36 W |
| Long Hu ⊜ | 100 | 29.58 N | 116.10 E |
| Longhua, Zhg. | 98 | 41.17 N | 117.37 E |
| Longhua, Zhg. | 100 | 22.42 N | 113.59 E |
| Longhua, Zhg. | 100 | 23.37 N | 114.14 E |
| Longhua, Zhg. | 106 | 31.09 N | 121.26 E |
| Longhua Airport ⊠ | 269b | 31.10 N | 121.26 E |
| Longhua Pagoda Ʊ[1] | 269b | 31.11 N | 121.26 E |
| Longhui, Zhg. | 100 | 25.32 N | 114.47 E |
| Longhui (Taohuaping), Zhg. | 102 | 27.00 N | 110.59 E |
| Longhui, Zhg. | 107 | 29.32 N | 104.48 E |
| Longhutang | 106 | 31.52 N | 119.59 E |
| Longi | 70 | 38.01 N | 14.45 E |
| Longido | 154 | 2.44 S | 36.41 E |
| Longiram | 112 | 0.02 S | 115.38 E |
| Long Island I, Antig. | 240c | 17.08 N | 61.45 W |
| Long Island I, Austl. | 166 | 22.09 S | 149.54 E |
| Long Island I, Ba. | 238 | 23.15 N | 75.07 W |
| Long Island I, Nf., Can. | 186 | 47.35 N | 54.05 W |
| Long Island I, N.T., Can. | 176 | 54.50 N | 79.20 W |
| Long Island I, N.S., Can. | 186 | 44.20 N | 66.15 W |
| Long Island I, Ak., U.S. | 182 | 54.54 N | 132.45 W |
| Long Island I, Ma., U.S. | 283 | 42.19 N | 70.58 W |
| Long Island I, N.Y., U.S. | 188 | 40.50 N | 73.00 W |
| Long Island I, Wa., U.S. | 224 | 46.27 N | 123.58 W |
| Long Island City ➛[8] | 276 | 40.45 N | 73.56 W |
| Long Island MacArthur Airport ⊠ | 210 | 40.48 N | 73.06 W |
| Long Island Sound ʮ | 188 | 41.05 N | 72.58 W |
| Long Island University Ʊ[2], N.Y., U.S. | 276 | 40.41 N | 73.59 W |
| Long Island University (C.W. Post Center) Ʊ[2], N.Y., U.S. | 276 | 40.49 N | 73.36 W |
| Longitudinal, Valle V | 252 | 36.00 S | 72.00 W |
| Long Jetty | 170 | 33.22 S | 151.29 E |
| Longji | 107 | 29.23 N | 106.04 E |
| Longjiadian | 104 | 42.10 N | 120.47 E |
| Longjiang, Zhg. | 89 | 47.19 N | 123.12 E |
| Longjiang, Zhg. | 100 | 22.53 N | 113.04 E |
| Longjiang, Zhg. | 100 | 22.59 N | 116.13 E |
| Longjiang, Zhg. | 107 | 29.48 N | 105.03 E |
| Longjie | 107 | 29.53 N | 104.32 E |
| Longjin | 100 | 28.37 N | 116.37 E |
| Longjing | 100 | 23.53 N | 112.52 E |
| Longjohn Slough ≃ | 278 | 41.43 N | 87.53 W |
| Longjumeau | 50 | 48.42 N | 2.18 E |
| Longka | 120 | 33.12 N | 79.47 E |
| Longkamp | 56 | 49.53 N | 7.07 E |
| Longkangji | 100 | 33.09 N | 116.54 E |
| Long Ke | 271d | 22.23 N | 114.22 E |
| Long Key I, Fl., U.S. | 220 | 24.49 N | 80.49 W |
| Long Key I, Fl., U.S. | 220 | 27.44 N | 82.45 W |
| Long King Creek ≃ | 222 | 30.34 N | 94.58 W |
| Longkou, Zhg. | 98 | 37.38 N | 120.18 E |
| Longkou, Zhg. | 100 | 32.56 N | 114.57 E |
| Longkou, Zhg. | 100 | 29.57 N | 113.47 E |
| Longkou, Zhg. | 100 | 26.11 N | 115.15 E |
| Longkouqiao | 85 | 39.40 N | 77.09 E |
| Long Lake, Il., U.S. | 216 | 42.22 N | 88.08 W |
| Long Lake, N.Y., U.S. | 188 | 43.58 N | 74.25 W |
| Long Lake, Tx., U.S. | 222 | 31.39 N | 95.47 W |
| Long Lake ⊜, On., Can. | 212 | 44.41 N | 76.45 W |
| Long Lake ⊜, Mi., U.S. | 190 | 45.12 N | 83.30 W |
| Long Lake ⊜, Mi., U.S. | 281 | 42.37 N | 83.44 W |
| Long Lake ⊜, Mi., U.S. | 281 | 42.36 N | 83.28 W |
| Long Lake ⊜, N.Y., U.S. | 188 | 44.04 N | 74.20 W |
| Long Lake ⊜, N.D., U.S. | 198 | 46.43 N | 100.07 W |
| Long Lake ⊜, Wa., U.S. | 224 | 47.03 N | 122.47 W |
| Long Lake ⊜[1] | 202 | 47.50 N | 117.40 W |
| Long Lake Creek ≃ | 198 | 46.40 N | 100.13 W |
| Long Lake Shores | 281 | 42.35 N | 83.19 W |
| Long Lama | 112 | 3.46 N | 114.24 E |
| Longlaville | 56 | 49.32 N | 5.47 E |
| Longleaf | 194 | 31.00 N | 92.34 W |
| Long Leaf Park | 192 | 34.12 N | 77.56 W |
| Longleat Ʊ | 42 | 51.12 N | 2.17 W |
| Longlegged Lake ⊜ | 184 | 50.46 N | 94.08 W |
| Longli | 102 | 26.26 N | 106.58 E |
| Longlin | 102 | 24.49 N | 105.31 E |
| Longling | 102 | 24.39 N | 98.40 E |
| Longmeadow | 207 | 42.03 N | 72.35 W |
| Long Melford | 42 | 52.05 N | 0.43 E |
| Longmen, Zhg. | 89 | 48.55 N | 126.54 E |
| Longmen, Zhg. | 100 | 29.53 N | 119.57 E |
| Longmen, Zhg. | 100 | 24.56 N | 118.04 E |
| Longmen, Zhg. | 100 | 25.06 N | 116.58 E |
| Longmen, Zhg. | 100 | 23.44 N | 114.15 E |
| Longmen, Zhg. | 107 | 29.27 N | 104.59 E |
| Longmen, Zhg. | 107 | 29.12 N | 106.13 E |
| Longmenchang | 107 | 30.53 N | 106.10 E |
| Longmensuo | 98 | 40.56 N | 115.54 E |
| Longmenzhang | 107 | 28.59 N | 106.13 E |
| Longming | 102 | 22.59 N | 107.11 E |
| Longmire | 224 | 46.45 N | 121.49 W |
| Long Moc | 110 | 18.51 N | 105.01 E |
| Longmont | 200 | 40.10 N | 105.06 W |
| Longmorn | 46 | 57.36 N | 3.17 W |
| Long Mountain ∧ | 194 | 36.41 N | 92.26 W |
| Long Mountain ∧[2] | 42 | 52.39 N | 3.09 W |
| Longmu | 100 | 24.16 N | 115.28 E |
| Longnan | 100 | 24.54 N | 114.48 E |
| Longnawan | 112 | 1.54 N | 114.53 E |
| Long Neck ›[1] | 276 | 41.03 N | 73.29 W |
| Long Neck Point › | 276 | 41.02 N | 73.29 W |
| Longniddry | 46 | 55.58 N | 2.53 W |
| Longnüsi | 107 | 30.23 N | 106.11 E |
| Longny-au-Perche | 50 | 48.32 N | 0.45 E |
| Longobucco | 68 | 39.27 N | 16.37 E |
| Longperrier | 261 | 49.03 N | 2.40 E |
| Long Pine | 198 | 42.32 N | 99.42 W |
| Longping | 100 | 29.53 N | 115.41 E |
| Long Plains | 168b | 34.21 S | 138.22 E |
| Long Point, Austl. | 274a | 34.01 S | 150.54 E |
| Long Point, Il., U.S. | 216 | 41.00 N | 88.54 W |
| Long Point ›, Ba. | 240b | 25.01 N | 77.20 W |
| Long Point ›, Nf., Can. | 186 | 48.48 N | 58.46 W |
| Long Point ›, N.S., Can. | 186 | 46.51 N | 60.18 W |
| Long Point ›, On., Can. | 212 | 44.06 N | 76.29 W |
| Long Point ›, On., Can. | 212 | 44.32 N | 80.18 W |
| Long Point ›, Pil. | 116 | 9.39 N | 118.20 E |
| Long Point ›, Ca., U.S. | 280 | 33.44 N | 118.23 W |
| Long Point ›, Vir. Is., U.S. | 240m | 18.18 N | 64.53 W |
| Long Point ›[1], Mb., Can. | 184 | 53.02 N | 98.40 W |
| Long Point ›[1], On., Can. | 214 | 42.34 N | 80.15 W |
| Long Point Bay ⊂ | 212 | 42.40 N | 80.14 W |
| Long Point Creek ≃ | 216 | 41.02 N | 88.48 W |
| Long Point Provincial Park ♦ | 214 | 42.35 N | 80.35 W |
| Long Pond ⊜, U.S. | 283 | 42.41 N | 71.21 W |
| Long Pond ⊜, Ma., U.S. | 207 | 41.48 N | 70.57 W |
| Long Pond ⊜, Ma., U.S. | 207 | 41.43 N | 70.04 W |
| Longpont, Fr. | 50 | 49.16 N | 3.13 E |
| Longpont, Fr. | 261 | 48.38 N | 2.17 E |
| Longport | 208 | 39.18 N | 74.31 W |
| Long Prairie | 198 | 45.58 N | 94.51 W |
| Long Prairie ≃ | 198 | 46.20 N | 94.36 W |
| Longpré-les-Corps-Sants | 50 | 50.01 N | 1.59 E |
| Long Preston | 44 | 54.02 N | 2.15 W |
| Longqiantai | 104 | 41.23 N | 120.52 E |
| Longqu, Zhg. | 98 | 34.16 N | 114.49 E |
| Longqu, Zhg. | 98 | 34.54 N | 116.47 E |
| Longquan | 100 | 28.04 N | 119.07 E |
| Longquan ≃ | 100 | 28.17 N | 119.44 E |
| Longquanguan | 98 | 38.55 N | 113.51 E |
| Longquan Shan ⩘ | 107 | 30.25 N | 104.15 E |
| Longquanyi | 107 | 30.34 N | 104.16 E |
| Longquanzhen | 107 | 30.21 N | 104.39 E |
| Long Range Mountains ⩘ | 186 | 49.20 N | 57.30 W |
| Longreach | 166 | 23.26 S | 144.15 E |
| Long Reach ⊂ | 186 | 45.26 N | 66.09 W |
| Long Reach ʮ | 212 | 44.07 N | 77.04 W |
| Long Reef ✢[2] | 164 | 11.11 S | 151.40 E |
| Long Reef Point › | 274a | 33.45 S | 151.19 E |
| Longridge | 44 | 53.51 N | 2.36 W |
| Long Run ≃, Il., U.S. | 278 | 41.37 N | 88.03 W |
| Long Run ≃, Pa., U.S. | 279b | 40.20 N | 79.48 W |
| Long-Sault | 206 | 45.02 N | 74.53 W |
| Long Sault Dam ➛[6] | 206 | 45.00 N | 74.45 W |
| Long Sault Islands II | 206 | 45.00 N | 74.55 W |
| Longsegah | 112 | 2.15 N | 116.42 E |
| Longshan, Zhg. | 100 | 33.36 N | 116.18 E |
| Longshan, Zhg. | 102 | 29.28 N | 109.20 E |
| Longshansuo | 100 | 30.05 N | 121.33 E |
| Longsheng, Zhg. | 102 | 25.48 N | 110.00 E |
| Longsheng, Zhg. | 107 | 30.36 N | 105.21 E |
| Longshizhen, Zhg. | 107 | 30.12 N | 106.26 E |
| Longshizhen, Zhg. | 107 | 29.23 N | 105.10 E |
| Longshu | 107 | 29.33 N | 105.45 E |
| Longs Peak ∧ | 200 | 40.15 N | 105.37 W |
| Long Stratton | 42 | 52.29 N | 1.14 E |
| Long Sutton | 42 | 52.47 N | 0.08 E |
| Longtaichang | 107 | 30.04 N | 105.34 E |
| Longtan, Zhg. | 100 | 23.40 N | 113.24 E |
| Longtan, Zhg. | 102 | 28.20 N | 108.52 E |
| Longtan, Zhg. | 106 | 32.11 N | 119.04 E |
| Longtan, Zhg. | 106 | 31.20 N | 118.45 E |
| Longtansi | 107 | 30.42 N | 104.10 E |
| Longtanzhen | 107 | 29.19 N | 104.35 E |
| Long Teru | 112 | 3.52 N | 114.15 E |
| Long Thanh | 110 | 10.47 N | 106.57 E |
| Longtian | 100 | 25.38 N | 119.28 E |
| Longtian'an | 106 | 31.10 N | 120.49 E |
| Long Tom ≃ | 202 | 44.23 N | 123.15 W |
| Longton, Eng., U.K. | 44 | 53.43 N | 2.48 W |
| Longton, Eng., U.K. | 262 | 53.43 N | 2.48 W |
| Longton, Ks., U.S. | 198 | 37.22 N | 96.04 W |
| Longtou | 98 | 38.51 N | 121.18 E |
| Longtoupu | 100 | 27.54 N | 113.12 E |
| Longtouwei | 100 | 25.14 N | 115.24 E |
| Longtown | 44 | 55.01 N | 2.58 W |
| Long Truong | 269c | 10.49 N | 106.49 E |
| Longué | 32 | 47.23 N | 0.06 W |
| Longueau | 50 | 49.52 N | 2.21 E |
| Longuenesse | 50 | 50.44 N | 1.24 E |
| Longuesse | 261 | 49.04 N | 1.56 E |
| Longueuil | 206 | 45.32 N | 73.30 W |
| Longueville, Austl. | 274a | 33.50 S | 151.10 E |
| Longueville, Fr. | 50 | 48.31 N | 3.15 E |
| Longueville-sur-Scie | 50 | 49.43 N | 1.06 E |
| Longuyon | 56 | 49.26 N | 5.36 E |
| Long Valley | 210 | 40.47 N | 74.46 W |
| Long Valley Creek ≃, Ca., U.S. | 226 | 39.03 N | 122.34 W |
| Long Valley Creek ≃, Nv., U.S. | 226 | 39.31 N | 119.39 W |
| Longvic | 58 | 47.17 N | 5.04 E |
| Longview, Ab., Can. | 182 | 50.32 N | 114.14 W |
| Longview, N.C., U.S. | 192 | 35.43 N | 81.23 W |
| Longview, Tx., U.S. | 222 | 32.30 N | 94.44 W |
| Longview, Wa., U.S. | 224 | 46.08 N | 122.56 W |
| Longview Heights | 222 | 32.30 N | 94.41 W |
| Longvilliers | 261 | 48.35 N | 2.00 E |
| Longvilly | 56 | 50.01 N | 5.50 E |
| Longwai | 112 | 0.42 N | 116.39 E |
| Longwan | 105 | 38.57 N | 116.10 E |
| Longwangmiao, Zhg. | 98 | 36.12 N | 115.13 E |
| Longwangmiao, Zhg. | 102 | 40.36 N | 95.52 E |
| Longwangmiao, Zhg. | 104 | 41.38 N | 121.04 E |
| Longwangmiao, Zhg. | 104 | 42.35 N | 123.42 E |
| Longwarry | 169 | 38.07 S | 145.46 E |
| Longwen | 100 | 24.36 N | 116.21 E |
| Longwo | 100 | 23.28 N | 115.17 E |
| Longwokou | 106 | 32.18 N | 119.52 E |
| Longwood | 220 | 28.42 N | 81.20 W |
| Longwood Gardens ♦ | 285 | 39.52 N | 75.40 W |
| Longwood Lake | 276 | 40.59 N | 74.52 W |
| Longwood Park | 192 | 34.55 N | 79.42 W |
| Longworth | 182 | 53.55 N | 121.28 W |
| Longwy | 56 | 49.31 N | 5.46 E |
| Longxi → Zhangzhou, Zhg. | 100 | 24.33 N | 117.39 E |
| Longxi, Zhg. | 102 | 34.56 N | 104.47 E |
| Longxi, Zhg. | 107 | 29.59 N | 106.09 E |
| Longxian, Zhg. | 102 | 34.51 N | 106.59 E |
| Longxian, Zhg. | 107 | 29.09 N | 105.50 E |
| Long Xuyen | 110 | 10.23 N | 105.25 E |
| Longyan | 100 | 25.08 N | 117.02 E |
| Longyao | 98 | 37.23 N | 114.41 E |
| Longyou | 100 | 29.02 N | 119.10 E |
| Longyou ≃ | 106 | 32.08 N | 120.38 E |
| Longyuanba | 100 | 24.56 N | 114.27 E |
| Longzhaogou | 98 | 40.49 N | 124.36 E |
| Longzhen | 89 | 48.41 N | 126.42 E |
| Longzhou | 102 | 22.22 N | 106.52 E |
| Loni | 272a | 28.45 N | 77.17 E |
| Lonigo | 64 | 45.23 N | 11.23 E |
| Löningen | 52 | 52.44 N | 7.46 E |
| Lonja ≃ | 36 | 45.27 N | 16.41 E |
| Lonkala | 152 | 4.37 S | 23.14 E |
| Lönnewitz | 54 | 51.34 N | 13.11 E |
| Lonny | 56 | 49.49 N | 4.35 E |
| Lonoke | 194 | 34.47 N | 91.53 W |
| Lonquimay, Volcán ∧[1] | 252 | 38.22 S | 71.34 W |
| Lönsboda | 26 | 56.24 N | 14.19 E |
| Lønsdal | 24 | 66.44 N | 15.28 E |
| Lonsdale | 190 | 44.28 N | 93.25 W |
| Lonsdale, Point › | 169 | 38.17 S | 144.37 E |
| Lonsee | 58 | 48.33 N | 9.55 E |
| Lons-le-Saunier | 58 | 46.40 N | 5.33 E |
| Lonton | 110 | 25.06 N | 96.17 E |
| Lontra ≃ | 250 | 6.37 S | 48.39 W |
| Lontra, Ribeirão da ≃ | 255 | 21.28 S | 53.37 W |
| Lonua ≃ | 152 | 1.16 N | 22.38 E |
| Lonzhen | 107 | 30.00 N | 103.59 E |
| Loo | 84 | 43.43 N | 39.36 E |
| Looc | 116 | 12.16 N | 121.59 E |
| Looe | 42 | 50.21 N | 4.28 W |
| Loogootee | 194 | 38.40 N | 86.54 W |
| Looking Glass ≃ | 216 | 42.52 N | 84.54 W |
| Lookout | 210 | 41.47 N | 75.11 W |
| Lookout, Cape ›, N.C., U.S. | 192 | 34.35 N | 76.32 W |
| Lookout, Cape ›, Or., U.S. | 224 | 45.20 N | 124.00 W |
| Lookout, Point ›, Austl. | 171a | 27.26 S | 153.33 E |
| Lookout, Point ›, Md., U.S. | 208 | 38.02 N | 76.19 W |
| Lookout Mountain ∧, U.S. | 194 | 34.25 N | 85.40 W |
| Lookout Mountain ∧, Or., U.S. | 202 | 44.20 N | 120.22 W |
| Lookout Mountain ∧, Or., U.S. | 224 | 45.21 N | 121.31 W |
| Lookout Mountain ∧, Wa., U.S. | 224 | 48.40 N | 122.22 W |
| Lookout Pass )( | 202 | 47.27 N | 115.42 W |
| Lookout Point Lake ⊜[1] | 202 | 43.52 N | 122.40 W |
| Lookout Ridge ⩘ | 180 | 69.07 N | 158.36 W |
| Loolmalassin ∧[1] | 154 | 3.03 S | 35.49 E |
| Loomis, Ca., U.S. | 226 | 38.49 N | 121.12 W |
| Loomis, Ne., U.S. | 198 | 40.28 N | 99.30 W |
| Loomis, Wa., U.S. | 182 | 48.49 N | 119.37 W |
| Loon | 116 | 9.48 N | 123.47 E |
| Loon ≃ | 184 | 55.50 N | 101.59 W |
| Loon Creek ≃ | 202 | 44.49 N | 114.49 W |
| Loongana | 162 | 30.57 S | 127.02 E |
| Loon Lake ⊜, Can. | 184 | 55.51 N | 102.00 W |
| Loon Lake ⊜, Mi., U.S. | 281 | 42.41 N | 83.22 W |
| Loon Lake ⊜[1] | 226 | 39.00 N | 120.18 W |
| Loon op Zand | 52 | 51.38 N | 5.04 E |
| Loop | 196 | 32.55 N | 102.25 W |
| Loop ➛[8] | 278 | 41.53 N | 87.38 W |
| Loop Head › | 48 | 52.34 N | 9.56 W |
| Loosdorf | 61 | 48.12 N | 15.24 E |
| Loosduinen ➛[8] | 52 | 52.04 N | 4.13 E |
| Loose, Dtsch. | 41 | 54.31 N | 9.53 E |
| Loose, Eng., U.K. | 260 | 51.14 N | 0.31 E |
| Loose Creek | 219 | 38.30 N | 91.57 W |
| Lop | 120 | 37.02 N | 80.15 E |
| Lop ≃ | 110 | 13.18 N | 107.37 E |
| Lopandino | 76 | 52.28 N | 34.49 E |
| Lopanka | 80 | 46.24 N | 40.59 E |
| Lopar'ovo | 80 | 58.20 N | 42.41 E |
| Lopasn'a ≃ | 82 | 54.51 N | 37.52 E |
| Lopatin | 84 | 43.53 N | 47.41 E |
| Lopatina, gora ∧ | 89 | 50.52 N | 143.10 E |
| Lopatino, Ross. | 80 | 52.37 N | 45.47 E |
| Lopatino, Ross. | 82 | 54.45 N | 37.00 E |
| Lopatino, Ross. | 89 | 48.24 N | 142.15 E |
| Lopatinskij | 82 | 55.21 N | 38.34 E |
| Lopatka, mys › | 74 | 50.52 N | 156.40 E |
| Lopatovo | 76 | 56.08 N | 29.12 E |
| Lopatyn | 78 | 50.13 N | 24.50 E |
| Lop Buri | 110 | 14.48 N | 100.37 E |
| Lopé-Okanda, Réserve de Chasse de ➛[4] | 152 | 0.30 S | 11.40 E |
| Lopévi I | 175f | 16.30 S | 168.21 E |
| López, Méx. | 232 | 27.00 N | 105.02 W |
| Lopez, Pa., U.S. | 210 | 41.27 N | 76.20 W |
| Lopez, Wa., U.S. | 224 | 48.31 N | 122.54 W |
| López, Arroyo de ≃ | 258 | 35.26 S | 57.35 W |
| Lopez, Cap › | 152 | 0.37 S | 8.43 E |
| Lopez Bay ⊂ | 116 | 13.56 N | 122.12 E |
| Lopez Island I | 224 | 48.30 N | 122.54 W |
| Lopez Lake ⊜[1] | 226 | 35.12 N | 120.28 W |
| Lopez Point › | 226 | 36.01 N | 121.34 W |
| Lopik | 52 | 51.58 N | 4.56 E |
| Lop Nor → Lop Nur ⊜ | 90 | 40.20 N | 90.15 E |
| Lop Nur (Lop Nor) ⊜ | 90 | 40.20 N | 90.15 E |
| Lopori ≃ | 152 | 1.14 N | 19.49 E |
| Lopotovo | 82 | 56.04 N | 36.49 E |
| Loppersum | 52 | 53.19 N | 6.45 E |
| Loppi | 26 | 60.43 N | 24.27 E |
| Lo Prado | 286e | 33.26 S | 70.45 W |
| Lopšen'ga | 24 | 64.58 N | 37.41 E |
| Lopt'uga | 24 | 63.16 N | 47.56 E |
| Lopuchovka, Ross. | 80 | 51.59 N | 44.42 E |
| Lopuchovka, Ross. | 80 | 50.37 N | 44.29 E |
| Łopuszno | 30 | 50.57 N | 20.15 E |
| Lora | 123 | 33.53 N | 73.17 E |
| Lora ≃ | 246 | 9.25 N | 72.25 W |
| Lora, Hāmūn-i- ⊜ | 128 | 29.20 N | 64.50 E |
| Lora Creek ≃ | 162 | 28.10 S | 135.22 E |
| Lora del Río | 34 | 37.39 N | 5.32 W |
| Lorain | 214 | 41.27 N | 82.10 W |
| Lorain □[6] | 214 | 41.22 N | 82.06 W |
| Lorain County Regional Airport ⊠ | 279a | 41.20 N | 82.11 W |
| Loraine, Ca., U.S. | 228 | 35.19 N | 118.25 W |
| Loraine, Il., U.S. | 219 | 40.09 N | 91.13 W |
| Loraine, Tx., U.S. | 196 | 32.24 N | 100.42 W |
| Loralai | 120 | 30.22 N | 68.36 E |
| Loramie, Lake ⊜[1] | 216 | 40.23 N | 84.18 W |
| Loramie Creek ≃ | 216 | 40.11 N | 84.14 W |
| Lorca | 34 | 37.40 N | 1.42 W |
| Lorch, Dtsch. | 56 | 48.49 N | 9.40 E |
| Lorch, Dtsch. | 56 | 50.02 N | 7.48 E |
| Lorchhausen | 56 | 50.03 N | 7.47 E |
| Lord Howe Island I | 160 | 31.33 S | 159.05 E |
| Lord Howe Rise ✢[3] | 14 | 32.00 S | 162.00 E |
| Lord Howe Seamounts ✢[3] | 14 | 28.00 S | 159.00 E |
| Lord Mayor Bay ⊂ | 176 | 69.44 N | 92.00 W |
| Lordsburg | 200 | 32.21 N | 108.42 W |
| Lord's Cricket Ground ♦ | 260 | 51.32 N | 0.10 W |
| Lordstown | 214 | 41.09 N | 80.53 W |
| Lords Valley | 210 | 41.23 N | 75.04 W |
| Loreauville | 194 | 30.03 N | 91.44 W |
| Loreley ♦ | 56 | 50.08 N | 7.44 E |
| Lorena, Bra. | 256 | 22.44 S | 45.08 W |
| Lorena, Tx., U.S. | 222 | 31.23 N | 97.13 W |
| Lorengau | 164 | 2.00 S | 147.15 E |
| Lorentz ≃ | 164 | 5.23 S | 138.04 E |
| Lorentzen | 56 | 48.57 N | 7.10 E |
| Lorenzago di Cadore | 64 | 46.29 N | 12.28 E |
| Lorenzo | 196 | 33.40 N | 101.32 W |
| Lorenzo Geyres (Queguay) | 252 | 32.05 S | 57.55 W |
| Loreo | 64 | 45.04 N | 12.11 E |
| Lorestān □[4] | 128 | 33.30 N | 48.30 E |
| Loreto, Arg. | 252 | 27.46 S | 57.17 W |
| Loreto, Bol. | 248 | 15.13 S | 64.40 W |
| Loreto, Bra. | 250 | 7.05 S | 45.09 W |
| Loreto, It. | 66 | 43.26 N | 13.36 E |
| Loreto, Méx. | 232 | 26.01 N | 111.21 W |
| Loreto, Méx. | 234 | 22.16 N | 101.58 W |
| Loreto, Para. | 252 | 23.16 S | 57.11 W |
| Loreto, Pil. | 116 | 8.12 N | 125.45 E |
| Loreto, Pil. | 116 | 10.21 N | 125.34 E |
| Loreto □[5] | 246 | 3.00 S | 75.00 W |
| Loreto Aprutino | 66 | 42.26 N | 13.59 E |
| Loreto Mocagua | 246 | 3.48 S | 70.15 W |
| Lorette, Mb., Can. | 184 | 49.44 N | 96.52 W |
| Lorette, Fr. | 62 | 45.31 N | 4.35 E |
| Loretteville | 206 | 46.51 N | 71.21 W |
| Loretto → Loreto, It. | 66 | 43.26 N | 13.36 E |
| Loretto, Ky., U.S. | 194 | 37.38 N | 85.24 W |
| Loretto, Pa., U.S. | 214 | 40.30 N | 78.37 W |
| Loretto, Tn., U.S. | 194 | 35.04 N | 87.26 W |
| Lorgues | 62 | 43.29 N | 6.22 E |
| Lorian Swamp ⩩ | 154 | 0.40 N | 39.35 E |
| Lorica | 246 | 9.14 N | 75.49 W |
| Lorida | 220 | 27.26 N | 81.15 W |
| Lorient | 32 | 47.45 N | 3.22 W |
| L'Orignal | 206 | 45.37 N | 74.42 W |
| Lorimer Park ♦ | 285 | 40.06 N | 75.05 W |
| Lorimor | 194 | 41.07 N | 94.03 W |
| Loring, Aeródromo de ⊠ | 266a | 40.22 N | 3.47 W |
| Loring Air Force Base ■ | 186 | 46.57 N | 67.54 W |
| Lorino | 180 | 65.30 N | 171.43 W |
| Loriol-sur-Drôme | 62 | 44.45 N | 4.49 E |
| Loris | 192 | 34.03 N | 78.53 W |
| Lorman | 194 | 31.49 N | 91.03 W |
| L'Orme | 261 | 48.39 N | 1.41 E |
| Lormes | 50 | 47.17 N | 3.49 E |
| Lorn, Firth of ⊂[1] | 46 | 56.20 N | 5.45 W |
| Lorna Glen | 162 | 26.14 S | 121.33 E |
| Lorne, Austl. | 169 | 38.33 S | 143.59 E |
| Lorne, N.B., Can. | 186 | 47.53 N | 66.08 W |
| Loro Ciuffenna | 66 | 43.35 N | 11.38 E |
| Loronyo | 154 | 4.39 N | 32.38 E |
| Lorquin | 58 | 48.40 N | 7.00 E |
| Lörrach | 58 | 47.37 N | 7.40 E |
| Lorraine □[9] | 32 | 49.00 N | 6.00 E |
| Lorrez-le-Bocage | 50 | 48.14 N | 2.54 E |
| Lorris | 50 | 47.53 N | 2.31 E |
| Lorsch | 56 | 49.39 N | 8.34 E |
| Lorsica | 62 | 44.26 N | 9.16 E |
| Lorup | 52 | 52.55 N | 7.38 E |
| Lorze ≃ | 58 | 47.15 N | 8.25 E |
| Los | 26 | 61.44 N | 15.10 E |
| Los, Îles de II | 150 | 9.30 N | 13.48 W |
| Losa, Nuraghe ⊥ | 71 | 40.07 N | 8.46 E |
| Losada ≃ | 246 | 2.12 N | 73.55 W |
| Los Aguacates | 286c | 10.35 N | 66.48 W |
| Los Alamitos | 280 | 33.48 N | 118.04 W |
| Los Alamitos Armed Forces Reserve Center ■ | 280 | 33.47 N | 118.03 W |
| Los Alamitos Race Course ♦ | 280 | 33.48 N | 118.03 W |
| Los Alamos, Ca., U.S. | 204 | 34.44 N | 120.16 W |
| Los Alamos, N.M., U.S. | 200 | 35.53 N | 106.19 W |
| Los Aldamas | 232 | 26.03 N | 99.11 W |
| Los Alerces, Parque Nacional ♦ | 254 | 42.50 S | 71.52 W |
| Los Altos, Méx. | 196 | 26.14 N | 98.28 W |
| Los Altos, Ca., U.S. | 226 | 37.23 N | 122.06 W |
| Los Altos Hills | 226 | 37.22 N | 122.08 W |
| Los Amates, Guat. | 236 | 15.16 N | 89.06 W |
| Los Amates, Méx. | 234 | 18.08 N | 102.15 W |
| Los Americanos, Barra I | 232 | 24.50 N | 97.35 W |
| Los Andes | 252 | 32.50 S | 70.37 W |
| Los Ángeles, Chile | 252 | 37.28 S | 72.21 W |
| Los Angeles, Ca., U.S. | 228 | 34.03 N | 118.14 W |
| Los Angeles, Ca., U.S. | 280 | 34.03 N | 118.14 W |
| Los Angeles □[6] | 228 | 34.20 N | 118.10 W |
| Los Angeles ≃ | 228 | 33.46 N | 118.12 W |
| Los Angeles Aqueduct ≅[1] | 204 | 35.22 N | 118.05 W |
| Los Angeles Coliseum and Sports Arena ♦ | 280 | 34.01 N | 118.17 W |
| Los Angeles Convention Center Ʊ | 280 | 34.03 N | 118.17 W |
| Los Angeles County Fairgrounds ♦ | 280 | 34.05 N | 117.46 W |
| Los Angeles County Museum of Art Ʊ | 280 | 34.05 N | 118.22 W |
| Los Angeles Harbor ⊂ | 280 | 33.42 N | 118.16 W |
| Los Angeles International Airport ⊠ | 228 | 33.56 N | 118.24 W |
| Los Antiguos | 254 | 46.33 S | 71.37 W |
| Losantville | 218 | 40.01 N | 85.10 W |
| Losap I[1] | 14 | 6.54 N | 152.44 E |
| Los Arabos | 240p | 22.44 N | 80.43 W |
| Losarang | 115a | 6.24 S | 108.10 E |
| Los Aros | 234 | 22.46 N | 102.57 W |
| Los Banos | 226 | 37.03 N | 120.50 W |
| Los Banos Creek ≃ | 226 | 37.20 N | 120.57 W |
| Los Banos Creek, North Fork ≃ | 226 | 36.57 N | 121.07 W |
| Los Banos Creek, South Fork ≃ | 226 | 36.57 N | 121.07 W |
| Los Banos Reservoir ⊜[1] | 226 | 36.59 N | 120.57 W |
| Los Berros | 252 | 31.57 S | 68.39 W |
| Los Blancos | 252 | 23.36 S | 62.36 W |
| Los Bolones, Cerro ∧, Méx. | 232 | 16.50 N | 92.38 W |
| Los Bolones, Cerro ∧, Méx. | 234 | 16.39 N | 92.34 W |
| Los Cardales | 258 | 34.20 S | 58.59 W |
| Los Cerrillos, Arg. | 252 | 31.57 S | 65.28 W |
| Los Cerrillos, Ur. | 258 | 34.37 S | 56.22 W |
| Los Cerrillos, Aeropuerto ⊠ | 286e | 33.30 S | 70.43 W |
| Los Cerritos Center ➛[9] | 280 | 33.52 N | 118.05 W |
| Los Chacos | 248 | 14.33 S | 62.11 W |
| Los Chiles | 236 | 11.02 N | 84.43 W |
| Los Conquistadores | 252 | 30.36 S | 58.28 W |
| Los Coronados, Islas II | 204 | 32.25 N | 117.15 W |
| Los Coyotes Indian Reservation ➛[4] | 204 | 33.20 N | 116.35 W |
| Los Cuatro Álamos | 286e | 33.32 S | 70.44 W |
| Los Dos Caminos | 286c | 10.31 N | 66.50 W |
| Los Ebanos | 196 | 26.14 N | 98.34 W |
| Loseley House ⊥ | 260 | 51.13 N | 0.36 W |
| Los Esclavos ≃ | 236 | 13.50 N | 90.20 W |
| Losevo | 78 | 50.40 N | 40.02 E |
| Los Flamencos, Laguna ⊜ | 258 | 35.36 S | 58.42 W |
| Los Frailes, Picacho ∧ | 234 | 23.53 N | 106.03 W |
| Los Frentones | 252 | 26.25 S | 61.25 W |
| Los Fresnos | 196 | 26.04 N | 97.29 W |


| Symbol | English | Deutsch | Español | Français | Português |
|---|---|---|---|---|---|
| ≃ | River | Fluß | Río | Rivière | Rio |
| ≅ | Canal | Kanal | Canal | Canal | Canal |
| ᒪ | Waterfall, Rapids | Wasserfall, Stromschnellen | Cascada, Rápidos | Chute d'eau, Rapides | Cascata, Rápidos |
| ʮ | Strait | Meeresstraße | Estrecho | Détroit | Estreito |
| ⊂ | Bay, Gulf | Bucht, Golf | Bahía, Golfo | Baie, Golfe | Baía, Golfo |
| ⊜ | Lake, Lakes | See, Seen | Lago, Lagos | Lac, Lacs | Lago, Lagos |
| ⩩ | Swamp | Sumpf | Pantano | Marais | Pântano |
| ⍓ | Ice Features, Glacier | Eis- und Gletscherformen | Accidentes Glaciales | Formes glaciaires | Acidentes glaciares |
| ⍑ | Other Hydrographic Features | Andere Hydrographische Objekte | Otros Elementos Hidrográficos | Autres données hydrographiques | Outros acidentes hidrográficos |
| ✢ | Submarine Features | Untermeerische Objekte | Accidentes Submarinos | Formes de relief sous-marin | Acidentes submarinos |
| □ | Political Unit | Politische Einheit | Unidad Politica | Entité politique | Unidade política |
| Ʊ | Cultural Institution | Kulturelle Institution | Institución Cultural | Institution culturelle | Instituição cultural |
| ⊥ | Historical Site | Historische Stätte | Sitio Histórico | Site historique | Sitio histórico |
| ♦ | Recreational Site | Erholungs- und Ferienort | Sitio de Recreo | Centre de loisirs | Area de Lazer |
| ⊠ | Airport | Flughafen | Aeropuerto | Aéroport | Aeroporto |
| ■ | Military Installation | Militäranlage | Instalación Militar | Installation militaire | Instalação militar |
| ➛ | Miscellaneous | Verschiedenes | Misceláneo | Divers | Diversos |

ENGLISH — Name, Page, Lat.°′, Long.°′
DEUTSCH — Name, Seite, Breite°′, Länge°′ E = Ost


| Name | Page | Lat.°′ | Long.°′ |
|---|---|---|---|
| Los Garzas | 196 | 26.23 N | 99.46 W |
| Los Gatos | 226 | 37.13 N | 121.58 W |
| Los Gatos Creek ≃, Ca., U.S. | 226 | 36.13 N | 120.08 W |
| Los Gatos Creek ≃, Ca., U.S. | 226 | 37.20 N | 121.54 W |
| Los Glaciares, Parque Nacional ♦ | 254 | 49.52 S | 73.05 W |
| Los Guerras | 196 | 26.25 N | 99.05 W |
| Loshan → Leshan | 107 | 29.34 N | 103.45 E |
| Losheim | 56 | 49.30 N | 6.44 E |
| Los Hermanos, Islas II | 246 | 11.45 N | 64.25 W |
| Los Herreras | 196 | 25.55 N | 99.24 W |
| Loshkarivka | 78 | 47.57 N | 34.12 E |
| Los Huacales, Cerro ∧ | 234 | 22.19 N | 101.34 W |
| Losi | 273a | 6.40 N | 3.31 E |
| Łosice | 30 | 52.14 N | 22.43 E |
| Los Idolos, Parque Arquelógico de ⊥ | 246 | 1.55 N | 76.10 W |
| Lošinj, Otok I | 36 | 44.36 N | 14.24 E |
| Losinoborskaja | 86 | 58.27 N | 89.28 E |
| Losino-Petrovskij | 82 | 55.52 N | 38.12 E |
| Los Jazmines, Presa ⊜[1] | 286a | 19.25 N | 99.16 W |
| Los Juríes | 252 | 28.28 S | 62.06 W |
| Loskopdam ⊜[1] | 156 | 25.23 S | 29.20 E |
| Loskop Dam Game Reserve ◆[4] | 156 | 25.23 S | 29.20 E |
| Los Lagos | 254 | 39.51 S | 72.50 W |
| Los Lagos □[4] | 254 | 41.45 S | 73.00 W |
| Los Llanos | 240m | 18.03 N | 66.24 W |
| Los Llanos [de Aridane] | 148 | 28.39 N | 17.54 W |
| Los López | 196 | 26.15 N | 99.05 W |
| Los Lunas | 200 | 34.48 N | 106.43 W |
| Los Manglares de Tumbes, Santuario Nacional ♦ | 246 | 2.25 S | 80.20 W |
| Los Maribios, Cordillera ⋏ | 236 | 12.35 N | 86.50 W |
| Los Médanos, Istmo de ⊥[3] | 241s | 11.35 N | 69.45 W |
| Los Menucos | 254 | 40.50 S | 68.08 W |
| Los Micos, Laguna de ⊂ | 236 | 15.45 N | 87.36 W |
| Los'mino | 76 | 55.04 N | 34.24 E |
| Los Mochis | 232 | 25.45 N | 108.57 W |
| Los Molinos | 204 | 40.01 N | 122.05 W |
| Los Muermos | 254 | 41.24 S | 73.29 W |
| Los Naranjos | 286c | 10.27 N | 66.48 W |
| Los Navalmorales | 34 | 39.43 N | 4.38 W |
| Lošnica | 76 | 54.17 N | 28.46 E |
| Los Nietos | 280 | 33.58 N | 118.04 W |
| Løsning | 41 | 55.48 N | 9.42 E |
| Los Nogales | 196 | 26.16 N | 99.43 W |
| Losolava | 175f | 14.11 S | 167.34 E |
| Los Olmos Creek ≃, Tx., U.S. | 196 | 27.20 N | 97.40 W |
| Los Olmos Creek ≃, Tx., U.S. | 196 | 26.21 N | 98.48 W |
| Los Osos | 226 | 35.19 N | 120.50 W |
| Los Oyameles | 234 | 19.43 N | 97.32 W |
| Los Padillas | 200 | 34.58 N | 106.41 W |
| Los Palacios, Arg. | 252 | 29.22 S | 68.11 W |
| Los Palacios, Cuba | 240p | 22.35 N | 83.15 W |
| Los Palacios y Villafranca | 34 | 37.10 N | 5.56 W |
| Los Perros, Arroyo ≃ | 288 | 34.37 S | 58.46 W |
| Los Pinos ◆[8] | 286b | 23.04 N | 82.23 W |
| Los Pinos ≃ | 200 | 36.56 N | 107.36 W |
| Los Placeres del Oro | 234 | 18.13 N | 100.54 W |
| Los Polvorines | 288 | 34.30 S | 58.41 W |
| Los Quillayes | 286e | 33.34 S | 70.37 W |
| Los Quirquinchos | 252 | 33.22 S | 61.43 W |
| Los Rábanos | 240m | 18.11 N | 66.50 W |
| Los Ramones | 196 | 25.42 N | 99.37 W |
| Los Remedios ≃ | 286a | 19.31 N | 99.05 W |
| Los Reyes de Salgado | 234 | 19.35 N | 102.29 W |
| Los Reyes la Paz | 286a | 19.21 N | 98.58 W |
| Los Ríos □[4] | 246 | 1.30 S | 79.25 W |
| Los Rodríguez | 232 | 27.11 N | 101.21 W |
| Los Roques, Islas II | 246 | 11.50 N | 66.45 W |
| Lossa ≃ | 54 | 51.18 N | 11.10 E |
| Los Santos □[4] | 236 | 7.55 N | 80.25 W |
| Los Santos de Maimona | 34 | 38.27 N | 6.23 W |
| Los Sauces | 252 | 37.58 S | 72.50 W |
| Lossburg | 58 | 48.25 N | 8.27 E |
| Lössel | 263 | 51.21 N | 7.39 E |
| Losser | 52 | 52.15 N | 7.00 E |
| Los Serranos | 228 | 33.59 N | 117.42 W |
| Lossie ≃ | 46 | 57.43 N | 3.16 W |
| Lossiemouth | 46 | 57.43 N | 3.18 W |
| Lössnitz | 54 | 50.37 N | 12.43 E |
| Lost ≃, U.S. | 202 | 41.56 N | 121.30 W |
| Lost ≃, In., U.S. | 194 | 38.33 N | 86.49 W |
| Lost ≃, Mn., U.S. | 198 | 47.51 N | 96.02 W |
| Lost ≃, W.V., U.S. | 188 | 39.05 N | 78.36 W |
| Lostant | 216 | 41.09 N | 89.04 W |
| Los Taques | 246 | 11.50 N | 70.16 W |
| Lost Bridge State Recreation Area ♦ | 216 | 40.45 N | 85.37 W |
| Lost Creek ≃, Al., U.S. | 194 | 33.38 N | 87.14 W |
| Lost Creek ≃, Ar., U.S. | 194 | 34.10 N | 92.31 W |
| Lost Creek ≃, Oh., U.S. | 218 | 39.58 N | 84.09 W |
| Lost Creek ≃, Ut,. U.S. | 200 | 41.04 N | 111.32 W |
| Lost Creek ≃, Wy., U.S. | 200 | 42.01 N | 108.11 W |
| Lost Draw V | 196 | 32.58 N | 102.02 W |
| Los Telares | 252 | 28.59 S | 63.26 W |
| Los Teques | 246 | 10.21 N | 67.02 W |
| Los Testigos, Islas II | 246 | 11.22 N | 63.06 W |
| Lost Hills | 226 | 35.36 N | 119.41 W |
| Lostine ≃ | 202 | 45.33 N | 117.29 W |
| Lost Lake ⊜, Or., U.S. | 224 | 45.29 N | 121.49 W |
| Lost Lake ⊜, Wa., U.S. | 224 | 47.20 N | 121.24 W |
| Lost Nation | 190 | 41.57 N | 90.49 W |
| Lostock ≃ | 262 | 53.40 N | 2.48 W |
| Lostock Gralam | 262 | 53.16 N | 2.28 W |
| Los Trancos Creek ≃ | 282 | 37.25 N | 122.12 W |
| Los Trancos Woods | 282 | 37.21 N | 122.12 W |
| Lost River Range ⋏ | 202 | 44.10 N | 113.35 W |
| Lost Trail Pass )( | 202 | 45.41 N | 113.57 W |
| Lostwithiel | 42 | 50.25 N | 4.40 W |
| Losuia | 164 | 8.32 S | 151.04 E |
| Los Vidrios | 232 | 31.59 N | 113.28 W |
| Los Vilos | 252 | 31.55 S | 71.31 W |
| Los Yébenes | 34 | 39.34 N | 3.53 W |
| Losynivka | 78 | 50.51 N | 31.54 E |
| Lot □[5] | 32 | 44.35 N | 1.40 E |
| Lot ≃ | 32 | 44.18 N | 0.20 E |
| Lota | 252 | 37.05 S | 73.10 W |
| Lotagipi Swamp (Lotikipi Plain) ≚ | 144 | 4.36 N | 34.55 E |
| Lotak | 112 | 0.11 S | 115.54 E |
| Lotbinière □[6] | 206 | 46.30 N | 71.40 W |
| Lotela, Lake ⊜ | 220 | 27.34 N | 81.29 W |
| Løten | 26 | 60.49 N | 11.19 E |
| Lot-et-Garonne □[5] | 32 | 44.20 N | 0.20 E |
| Lotfābād | 128 | 37.32 N | 59.20 E |
| Lothair, S. Afr. | 158 | 26.26 S | 30.27 E |
| Lothair, Ky., U.S. | 192 | 37.14 N | 83.10 W |
| Lothian □[4] | 46 | 55.55 N | 3.05 W |
| Lothringen → Lorraine □[9] | 32 | 49.00 N | 6.00 E |
| Lotikipi Plain (Lotagipi Swamp) ≚ | 144 | 4.36 N | 34.55 E |
| Loto | 152 | 2.49 S | 22.29 E |
| Loto ≃ | 152 | 1.55 S | 22.09 E |
| Lotofaga | 175a | 13.59 S | 171.50 W |
| Lotoi ≃ | 152 | 1.35 S | 18.30 E |
| Lotorp | 40 | 58.44 N | 15.50 E |
| Lotošino | 76 | 56.14 N | 35.38 E |
| Lotrului, Munţii ⋏ | 38 | 45.30 N | 23.52 E |
| Lotsane ≃ | 156 | 22.41 S | 28.11 E |
| Lötschberg Tunnel ◆[5] | 58 | 46.25 N | 7.45 E |
| Lötschental V | 58 | 46.25 N | 7.50 E |
| Lotseninsel I | 41 | 54.40 N | 10.01 E |
| Lott | 222 | 31.12 N | 97.02 W |
| Lotta ≃ | 24 | 68.36 N | 31.06 E |
| Lotte | 52 | 52.17 N | 7.55 E |
| Lottivue | 214 | 42.40 N | 82.46 W |
| Löttringhausen ◆[8] | 263 | 51.27 N | 7.27 E |
| Lottsburg | 208 | 37.57 N | 76.31 W |
| Lotts Creek ≃ | 192 | 32.09 N | 81.47 W |
| Lottsford Branch ≃ | 284c | 38.55 N | 76.49 W |
| Lottstetten | 58 | 47.38 N | 8.34 E |
| Lotuke, Jabal ∧ | 154 | 4.07 N | 33.48 E |
| Lotung | 100 | 24.41 N | 121.46 E |
| Lotzorai | 71 | 39.58 N | 9.39 E |
| Louang Namtha | 110 | 20.57 N | 101.25 E |
| Louangphrabang | 110 | 19.52 N | 102.08 E |
| L'Ouarsenis, Massif de ⋏ | 34 | 35.40 N | 1.50 E |
| Loubaresse | 62 | 44.36 N | 4.03 E |
| Loube, Montagne de la ∧ | 62 | 43.22 N | 5.59 E |
| Loubetsi | 152 | 3.12 S | 12.10 E |
| Louchi | 24 | 66.04 N | 33.00 E |
| Loučim | 60 | 49.22 N | 13.07 E |
| Loučná ∧ | 54 | 50.39 N | 13.37 E |
| Loude | 98 | 35.54 N | 117.18 E |
| Loudéac | 32 | 48.10 N | 2.45 W |
| Louden Cove ⊂ | 276 | 41.05 N | 73.43 W |
| Loudes | 62 | 45.05 N | 3.45 E |
| Loudima Poste | 152 | 4.07 S | 13.04 E |
| Loudon | 192 | 35.43 N | 84.20 W |
| Loudonville, N.Y., U.S. | 210 | 42.42 N | 73.45 W |
| Loudonville, Oh., U.S. | 214 | 40.38 N | 82.14 W |
| Loudoun □[6] | 208 | 39.05 N | 77.30 W |
| Loudun | 32 | 47.01 N | 0.05 E |
| Loué | 32 | 48.00 N | 0.09 W |
| Loue ≃ | 58 | 47.01 N | 5.27 E |
| Louga | 150 | 15.37 N | 16.13 W |
| Louga □[4] | 150 | 15.25 N | 15.30 W |
| Louge | 252 | 36.57 S | 61.40 W |
| Louge ≃ | 32 | 43.27 N | 1.20 E |
| Lougguéré ≃ | 150 | 15.35 N | 14.47 W |
| Loughborough | 42 | 52.47 N | 1.11 W |
| Loughborough Lake ⊜ | 212 | 44.23 N | 76.30 W |
| Loughermore ∧[2] | 48 | 54.59 N | 7.05 W |
| Loughman | 220 | 28.14 N | 81.34 W |
| Loughor | 42 | 51.40 N | 4.04 W |
| Loughor ≃ | 42 | 51.40 N | 4.04 W |
| Loughrea | 48 | 53.12 N | 8.34 W |
| Loughros More Bay ⊂ | 48 | 54.47 N | 8.35 W |
| Loughton | 260 | 51.39 N | 0.03 E |
| Louhans | 58 | 46.38 N | 5.13 E |
| Louin | 194 | 32.04 N | 89.15 W |
| Louisa, Ky., U.S. | 192 | 38.06 N | 82.36 W |
| Louisa, Va., U.S. | 192 | 38.01 N | 78.00 W |
| Louisa, Lake ⊜, On., Can. | 212 | 45.28 N | 78.30 W |
| Louisa, Lake ⊜, Fl., U.S. | 220 | 28.29 N | 81.44 W |
| Louisbourg | 186 | 45.55 N | 59.58 W |
| Louis Bull Indian Reserve ◆[4] | 182 | 52.53 N | 113.31 W |
| Louisburg, Ks., U.S. | 198 | 38.37 N | 94.40 W |
| Louisburg, N.C., U.S. | 192 | 36.05 N | 78.18 W |
| Louisburgh | 48 | 53.46 N | 9.51 W |
| Louisdale | 186 | 45.36 N | 61.04 W |
| Louise, Ms., U.S. | 194 | 32.58 N | 90.35 W |
| Louise, Tx., U.S. | 222 | 29.06 N | 96.25 W |
| Louise, Lac ⊜, P.Q., Can. | 206 | 45.46 N | 74.25 W |
| Louise, Lac ⊜, P.Q., Can. | 206 | 45.43 N | 71.25 W |
| Louise, Lake ⊜ | 180 | 62.20 N | 146.30 W |
| Louise Island I | 182 | 52.58 N | 131.50 W |
| Louiseville | 206 | 46.15 N | 72.57 W |
| Louis Gentil → Youssoufia | 148 | 32.16 N | 8.33 W |
| Louisiade Archipelago II | 160 | 11.00 S | 153.00 E |
| Louisiana | 219 | 39.26 N | 91.03 W |
| Louisiana □[3], U.S. | 178 | 31.15 N | 92.15 W |
| Louisiana □[3], U.S. | 194 | 31.15 N | 92.15 W |
| Louisiana ⚘ | 41 | 55.58 N | 12.33 E |
| Lou Island I | 164 | 2.25 S | 147.20 E |
| Louis Trichardt | 156 | 23.01 S | 29.43 E |
| Louisvale | 158 | 28.33 S | 21.12 E |
| Louisville, On., Can. | 214 | 42.28 N | 82.07 W |
| Louisville, Al., U.S. | 194 | 31.47 N | 85.33 W |
| Louisville, Ga., U.S. | 192 | 33.00 N | 82.24 W |
| Louisville, Il., U.S. | 194 | 38.46 N | 88.30 W |
| Louisville, Ky., U.S. | 218 | 38.15 N | 85.45 W |
| Louisville, Ms., U.S. | 194 | 33.07 N | 89.03 W |
| Louisville, Ne., U.S. | 198 | 40.59 N | 96.09 W |
| Louisville, Oh., U.S. | 214 | 40.50 N | 81.15 W |
| Louisville Ridge ✦[3] | 14 | 31.00 S | 172.30 W |
| Louisville Seamount ✦[3] | 14 | 31.15 S | 172.15 W |
| Louis-XIV, Pointe › | 176 | 54.37 N | 79.45 W |
| Loujiaying | 98 | 42.04 N | 116.04 E |
| Loukanga | 273b | 4.20 S | 15.09 E |
| Loukkos, Oued ≃ | 34 | 35.12 N | 6.09 W |
| Loukoua ≃ | 273b | 4.09 S | 15.08 E |
| Loulé | 34 | 37.08 N | 8.02 W |
| Loum | 152 | 4.43 N | 9.44 E |
| Loumou | 273b | 4.08 S | 15.09 E |
| Lount Lake ⊜ | 184 | 50.10 N | 94.20 W |
| Louny | 54 | 50.19 N | 13.46 E |
| Loup ≃, Fr. | 62 | 43.38 N | 7.09 E |
| Loup ≃, Ne., U.S. | 198 | 41.24 N | 97.19 W |
| Loup, Gorge du V | 56 | 49.47 N | 6.23 E |
| Loup, Rivière du ≃ | 206 | 46.13 N | 72.55 W |
| Loup City | 198 | 41.16 N | 98.57 W |
| Loups Marins, Lacs des ⊜ | 176 | 56.30 N | 73.45 W |
| Lourches | 50 | 50.19 N | 3.21 E |
| Lourdes, Nf., Can. | 186 | 48.39 N | 59.00 W |
| Lourdes, Fr. | 32 | 43.06 N | 0.03 W |
| Lourel de Baixo | 266c | 38.49 N | 9.22 W |
| Lourenço | 250 | 2.30 N | 51.40 W |
| Lourenço Marques → Maputo | 156 | 25.58 S | 32.35 E |
| Lourenço Velho | 256 | 22.22 S | 45.19 W |
| Lourenço Velho ≃, Bra. | 256 | 23.26 S | 45.35 W |
| Lourenço Velho ≃, Bra. | 256 | 22.22 S | 45.31 W |
| Loures | 34 | 38.50 N | 9.10 W |
| Loures ≃ | 266c | 38.50 N | 9.08 W |
| Lourinhã | 34 | 39.14 N | 9.19 W |
| Lourmarin | 62 | 43.46 N | 5.22 E |
| Lourosa | 34 | 40.19 N | 7.56 W |
| Loury | 50 | 48.00 N | 2.05 E |
| Lousã, Port. | 34 | 40.07 N | 8.15 W |
| Lousa, Port. | 266c | 38.53 N | 9.12 W |
| Louse Creek ≃ | 198 | 46.22 N | 100.57 W |
| Lou Shan ∧ | 89 | 45.15 N | 128.58 E |
| Louta | 150 | 13.30 N | 3.10 W |
| Loutang | 106 | 31.26 N | 121.12 E |
| Loutézou, Île de I | 273b | 4.22 S | 15.10 E |
| Louth, Austl. | 166 | 30.32 S | 145.07 E |
| Louth, Ire. | 44 | 53.57 N | 6.33 W |
| Louth, Ire. | 48 | 53.57 N | 6.33 W |
| Louth, Eng., U.K. | 44 | 53.22 N | 0.01 W |
| Louth □[6] | 48 | 53.55 N | 6.30 W |
| Louth Bay ⊂ | 166 | 34.34 S | 136.02 E |
| Louti, Mayo ≃ | 146 | 9.38 N | 13.56 E |
| Loutit Bay ⊂ | 169 | 38.33 S | 144.00 E |
| Loutrá Aidhipsoú | 38 | 38.51 N | 23.02 E |
| Loutre ≃ | 219 | 38.42 N | 91.25 W |
| Loutre, Bayou de ≃ | 194 | 32.41 N | 92.08 W |
| Loutrópirgos | 267c | 38.02 N | 23.28 E |
| Louvain → Leuven | 56 | 50.53 N | 4.42 E |
| Louveciennes | 261 | 48.52 N | 2.07 E |
| Louveigné | 56 | 50.32 N | 5.42 E |
| Louveira | 256 | 23.04 S | 46.58 W |
| Louviers, Fr. | 50 | 49.13 N | 1.10 E |
| Louviers, Co., U.S. | 200 | 39.28 N | 105.00 W |
| Louvre ⚘ | 261 | 48.52 N | 2.20 E |
| Louvres | 50 | 49.02 N | 2.30 E |
| Louvroil | 50 | 50.16 N | 3.58 E |
| Louwsburg | 158 | 27.37 S | 31.07 E |
| Lou Yaeger, Lake ⊜[1] | 219 | 39.10 N | 89.37 W |
| Lövånger | 26 | 64.22 N | 21.18 E |
| Lovászi | 61 | 46.33 N | 16.34 E |
| Lovat' ≃ | 76 | 58.14 N | 31.28 E |
| Lovcy | 82 | 55.00 N | 39.15 E |
| Love | 184 | 53.29 N | 104.09 W |
| Loveč | 38 | 43.08 N | 24.43 E |
| Loveč □[4] | 38 | 43.11 N | 25.10 E |
| Love Clough | 262 | 53.44 N | 2.17 W |
| Lovedale | 279b | 40.17 N | 79.52 W |
| Lovejoy | 219 | 38.39 N | 90.10 W |
| Lovelady | 222 | 31.08 N | 95.27 W |
| Loveland, Co., U.S. | 200 | 40.23 N | 105.04 W |
| Loveland, Oh., U.S. | 218 | 39.16 N | 84.16 W |
| Lovell | 202 | 44.50 N | 108.23 W |
| Lovell Island I | 283 | 42.20 N | 70.56 W |
| Lovelock | 204 | 40.10 N | 118.28 W |
| Lovely | 192 | 37.49 N | 82.24 W |
| Love Point › | 208 | 39.02 N | 76.18 W |
| Lovere | 64 | 45.49 N | 10.04 E |
| Lovering, Lac ⊜ | 206 | 45.10 N | 72.09 W |
| Lovero | 64 | 46.14 N | 10.14 E |
| Loves Green | 260 | 51.43 N | 0.24 E |
| Loves Park | 216 | 42.19 N | 89.03 W |
| Loviisa → Lovisa | 26 | 60.27 N | 26.14 E |
| Lovilia | 190 | 41.08 N | 92.54 W |
| Loving, N.M., U.S. | 196 | 32.17 N | 104.05 W |
| Loving, Tx., U.S. | 196 | 33.16 N | 98.31 W |
| Lovingston | 192 | 37.45 N | 78.52 W |
| Lovington, Il., U.S. | 219 | 39.42 N | 88.37 W |
| Lovington, N.M., U.S. | 196 | 32.56 N | 103.20 W |
| Lovisa (Loviisa) | 26 | 60.27 N | 26.14 E |
| Lövő | 61 | 47.30 N | 16.47 E |
| Lovö I | 40 | 59.20 N | 17.50 E |
| Lovoi ≃ | 154 | 8.14 S | 26.39 E |
| Lovosice | 54 | 50.31 N | 14.03 E |
| Lovozero, Ross. | 24 | 68.00 N | 35.00 E |
| Lovozero, Ross. | 24 | 65.00 N | 29.50 E |
| Lovozero, ozero ⊜ | 24 | 67.54 N | 35.12 E |
| Lovrenc | 61 | 46.32 N | 15.23 E |
| Lövstabruk | 40 | 60.24 N | 17.53 E |
| Lövstabukten ⊂ | 40 | 60.35 N | 17.45 E |
| Lövstad slott ⊥ | 40 | 58.33 N | 16.02 E |
| Lóvua, Ang. | 152 | 11.36 S | 23.53 E |
| Lóvua, Ang. | 152 | 7.20 S | 20.16 E |
| Lovua (Lóvua) ≃ | 152 | 6.07 S | 20.35 E |
| Low | 188 | 45.48 N | 75.57 W |
| Low, Cape › | 176 | 63.07 N | 85.18 W |
| Lowa | 154 | 1.24 S | 25.51 E |
| Lowa ≃ | 154 | 1.24 S | 25.51 E |
| Lowāda | 126 | 22.27 N | 87.37 E |
| Lowat → Lovat' ≃ | 76 | 58.14 N | 31.28 E |
| Lowber | 279b | 40.15 N | 79.46 W |
| Lowden | 190 | 41.51 N | 90.55 W |
| Lowder Brook ≃ | 283 | 43.14 N | 71.11 W |
| Lowell, Ar., U.S. | 194 | 36.15 N | 94.07 W |
| Lowell, In., U.S. | 216 | 41.17 N | 87.25 W |
| Lowell, Ma., U.S. | 207 | 42.38 N | 71.19 W |
| Lowell, Mi., U.S. | 216 | 42.56 N | 85.20 W |
| Lowell, Or., U.S. | 202 | 43.55 N | 122.46 W |
| Lowell, Lake ⊜[1] | 202 | 43.33 N | 116.40 W |
| Lowell, University of ⚘[2] | 283 | 42.39 N | 71.20 W |
| Lowell-Dracut State Forest ♦ | 283 | 42.40 N | 71.22 W |
| Lowelli | 140 | 5.59 N | 33.45 E |
| Lowellville | 214 | 41.02 N | 80.32 W |
| Löwen → Leuven | 56 | 50.53 N | 4.42 E |
| Löwen ≃ | 158 | 26.51 S | 18.17 E |
| Löwenberg | 54 | 52.54 N | 13.08 E |
| Löwenbruch | 264a | 52.18 N | 13.19 E |
| Löwenstein | 56 | 49.06 N | 9.22 E |
| Lowe Pond ⊜ | 283 | 42.41 N | 70.59 W |
| Lower Aetna Lake ⊜ | 285 | 39.51 N | 74.48 W |
| Lower Arrow Lake ⊜ | 182 | 49.40 N | 118.08 W |
| Lower Bay ⊂ | 208 | 40.33 N | 74.02 W |
| Lower Bear River Reservoir ⊜[1] | 226 | 38.33 N | 120.14 W |
| Lower Bershire Valley | 276 | 40.54 N | 74.37 W |
| Lower Beverley Lake ⊜ | 212 | 44.36 N | 76.09 W |
| Lower Broughton ◆[8] | 262 | 53.29 N | 2.15 W |
| Lower Brule Indian Reservation ◆[4] | 198 | 44.05 N | 99.44 W |
| Lower Buckhorn Lake ⊜ | 212 | 44.33 N | 78.17 W |
| Lower Burrell | 214 | 40.33 N | 79.45 W |
| Lower California → Baja California ›[1] | 232 | 28.00 N | 113.30 W |
| Lower Chittering | 168a | 31.34 S | 116.06 E |
| Lower Crystal Springs Reservoir ⊜[1] | 226 | 37.32 N | 122.22 W |
| Lower Darwen | 262 | 53.43 N | 2.28 W |
| Lower Egypt → Mişr Baḩrī □[9] | 140 | 31.00 N | 31.00 E |
| Lower Eltham Park ♦ | 274b | 37.45 S | 145.09 E |
| Lower Elwha Indian Reservation ◆[4] | 224 | 48.09 N | 123.33 W |
| Lower Fort Garry National Historic Park ♦ | 184 | 50.07 N | 96.55 W |
| Lower Ganga Canal ≊ | 124 | 26.27 N | 80.17 E |
| Lower Gap ⊂ | 212 | 44.10 N | 76.35 W |
| Lower Halstow | 260 | 51.22 N | 0.40 E |
| Lower Hay Lake ⊜ | 212 | 45.25 N | 78.13 W |
| Lower Higham | 260 | 51.26 N | 0.28 E |
| Lower Huron Metropolitan Park ♦ | 281 | 42.12 N | 83.25 W |
| Lower Hutt | 172 | 41.13 S | 174.55 E |
| Lower Kalskag | 180 | 61.31 N | 160.22 W |
| Lower Keechi Creek ≃ | 222 | 31.08 N | 95.46 W |
| Lower Klamath Lake ⊜ | 204 | 41.55 N | 121.42 W |
| Lower Lake | 226 | 38.55 N | 122.36 W |
| Lower Lake ⊜ | 204 | 41.15 N | 120.02 W |
| Lower Loteni | 158 | 29.32 S | 29.36 E |
| Lower Manitou Lake ⊜ | 184 | 49.15 N | 93.00 W |
| Lower Matecumbe Key I | 220 | 24.51 N | 80.43 W |
| Lower Montville | 276 | 40.54 N | 74.22 W |
| Lower Mystic Lake ⊜ | 283 | 42.26 N | 71.09 W |
| Lower Nazeing | 260 | 51.44 N | 0.01 E |
| Lower Otay Lake ⊜[1] | 228 | 32.37 N | 116.55 W |
| Lower Paia | 229a | 20.55 N | 156.23 W |
| Lower Paudash Lake ⊜ | 212 | 44.58 N | 78.01 W |
| Lower Peirce Reservoir ⊜[1] | 271c | 1.22 N | 103.49 E |
| Lower Peover | 262 | 53.16 N | 2.23 W |
| Lower Place | 262 | 53.36 N | 2.09 W |
| Lower Plenty | 274b | 37.44 S | 145.06 E |
| Lower Portland | 170 | 33.27 S | 150.53 E |
| Lower Post | 176 | 59.55 N | 128.30 W |
| Lower Red Lake ⊜ | 198 | 48.00 N | 94.50 W |
| Lower River Rouge ≃ | 281 | 42.18 N | 83.14 W |
| Lower Rouge Parkway ♦ | 281 | 42.18 N | 83.20 W |
| Lower Saxony → Niedersachsen □[3] | 30 | 52.40 N | 9.00 E |
| Lower Stoke | 260 | 51.27 N | 0.38 E |
| Lower Trajan's Wall ⊥ | 38 | 45.40 N | 28.30 E |
| Lower Ugashik Lake ⊜ | 180 | 57.30 N | 156.56 W |
| Lower Van Norman Lake ⊜[1] | 280 | 34.17 N | 118.29 W |
| Lower West Pubnico | 186 | 43.38 N | 65.48 W |
| Lower Whitley | 262 | 53.18 N | 2.35 W |
| Lower Wood's Harbour | 186 | 43.31 N | 65.44 W |
| Lowery, Lake ⊜ | 220 | 28.07 N | 81.41 W |
| Lower Zambezi International Game Park ◆[4] | 154 | 15.30 S | 29.35 E |
| Lowestoft | 42 | 52.29 N | 1.45 E |
| Lowgar □[4] | 120 | 33.50 N | 69.00 E |
| Lowick | 44 | 55.38 N | 2.00 W |
| Łowicz | 30 | 52.07 N | 19.56 E |
| Lowman | 210 | 42.02 N | 76.44 W |
| Lowmoor | 192 | 37.47 N | 79.53 W |
| Lowood | 171a | 27.28 S | 152.35 E |
| Lowrah (Pishīn Lora) ≃ | 120 | 29.09 N | 64.55 E |
| Lowries Run ≃ | 279b | 40.30 N | 80.05 W |
| Low Rocky Point › | 166 | 43.00 S | 145.30 E |
| Lowry Air Force Base ■ | 198 | 39.43 N | 104.53 W |
| Lowry City | 194 | 38.08 N | 93.43 W |
| Lowther ≃ | 44 | 54.39 N | 2.44 W |
| Lowther Hills ⋏[2] | 44 | 55.19 N | 3.38 W |
| Lowton | 262 | 53.28 N | 2.35 W |
| Lowton Common | 262 | 53.29 N | 2.33 W |
| Lowville, N.Y., U.S. | 212 | 43.47 N | 75.29 W |
| Lowville, Pa., U.S. | 214 | 42.01 N | 79.49 W |
| Loxahatchee | 220 | 26.49 N | 80.13 W |
| Loxley | 194 | 30.37 N | 87.45 W |
| Loxstedt | 52 | 53.28 N | 8.38 E |
| Loxten | 52 | 52.03 N | 8.08 E |
| Loxton, Austl. | 166 | 34.27 S | 140.35 E |
| Loxton, S. Afr. | 158 | 31.30 S | 22.22 E |
| Loyal | 190 | 44.44 N | 90.29 W |
| Loyal, Loch ⊜ | 46 | 58.23 N | 4.22 W |
| Loyalhanna | 214 | 40.19 N | 79.21 W |
| Loyalhanna Creek ≃ | 214 | 40.28 N | 79.27 W |
| Loyalhanna Lake ⊜[1] | 214 | 40.25 N | 79.28 W |
| Loyalsock Creek ≃ | 210 | 41.14 N | 76.56 W |
| Loyalton | 204 | 39.40 N | 120.14 W |
| Loyalty Islands → Loyauté, Îles II | 175f | 21.00 S | 167.00 E |
| Loyang, Sing. | 271c | 1.22 N | 103.58 E |
| Loyang → Luoyang, Zhg. | 102 | 34.41 N | 112.28 E |
| Loyauté, Îles (Loyalty Islands) II | 175f | 21.00 S | 167.00 E |
| Loyne, Loch ⊜ | 46 | 57.06 N | 5.00 W |
| Loyola College ⚘[2] | 284b | 39.21 N | 76.37 W |
| Loyola Marymount University ⚘[2] | 280 | 33.58 N | 118.25 W |
| Loyola University ⚘[2] | 278 | 42.00 N | 87.39 W |
| Loyoro | 154 | 3.21 N | 34.16 E |
| Loysburg | 214 | 40.10 N | 78.23 W |
| Loysville | 208 | 40.22 N | 77.21 W |
| Lozano | 258 | 34.51 S | 59.03 W |
| Lozère □[5] | 32 | 44.30 N | 3.30 E |
| Lozère, Mont ⋏ | 62 | 44.25 N | 3.46 E |
| Loznica | 38 | 44.32 N | 19.13 E |
| Ložnikovo, Ross. | 86 | 56.54 N | 73.56 E |
| Ložnikovo, Ross. | 88 | 51.22 N | 117.03 E |
| Loznoje | 80 | 49.17 N | 44.26 E |
| Lozno-Oleksandrivka | 78 | 49.50 N | 38.44 E |
| L'Ozone ◆[8] | 273b | 4.21 S | 15.14 E |
| Lozova | 78 | 48.54 N | 36.20 E |
| Lozove, Ukr. | 78 | 49.18 N | 27.18 E |
| Lozove, Ukr. | 83 | 49.28 N | 37.54 E |
| Lozove, Ukr. | 83 | 49.13 N | 37.36 E |
| Lozovoje | 86 | 53.17 N | 77.45 E |
| Lozoyuela | 34 | 40.55 N | 3.37 W |
| Loz'va ≃ | 86 | 59.36 N | 62.20 E |
| Lozzo di Cadore | 64 | 46.29 N | 12.27 E |
| Lu | 62 | 45.00 N | 8.29 E |
| Lu ≃ | 100 | 27.04 N | 115.00 E |
| Lua ≃ | 152 | 2.46 N | 18.26 E |
| Luabo | 156 | 18.30 S | 36.10 E |
| Luabu ≃ | 152 | 2.46 S | 18.19 E |
| Luachimo ≃ | 152 | 6.33 S | 20.59 E |
| Luaha-sibuha | 110 | 0.31 S | 98.28 E |
| Luala ≃ | 154 | 17.57 S | 36.30 E |
| Lualaba ≃ | 154 | 0.26 N | 25.20 E |
| Luali | 152 | 5.06 S | 12.29 E |
| Lualoje ≃ | 152 | 12.18 S | 21.38 E |
| Luama ≃ | 154 | 4.46 S | 26.53 E |
| Luambe National Park ♦ | 154 | 12.25 S | 32.15 E |
| Luambimba ≃ | 152 | 15.00 S | 22.48 E |
| Luampa | 154 | 15.03 S | 24.28 E |
| Luampa ≃ | 154 | 14.33 S | 24.10 E |
| Lu'an | 100 | 31.44 N | 116.31 E |
| Luan ≃ | 98 | 39.20 N | 119.10 E |
| Luana ≃ | 152 | 7.56 S | 21.06 E |
| Luan Balu | 114 | 2.38 N | 96.13 E |
| Luancheng, Zhg. | 98 | 37.53 N | 114.39 E |
| Luancheng, Zhg. | 102 | 22.45 N | 108.51 E |
| Luanchuan | 102 | 33.51 N | 111.36 E |
| Luancundo ≃ | 152 | 16.25 S | 21.27 E |
| Luanda | 152 | 8.48 S | 13.14 E |
| Luanda □[5] | 152 | 9.00 S | 13.15 E |
| Luando ≃ | 152 | 10.19 S | 16.40 E |
| Luando, Réserva do ◆[4] | 152 | 11.10 S | 17.30 E |
| Luang, Khao ∧ | 110 | 8.31 N | 99.47 E |
| Luang, Thale ⊂ | 110 | 7.30 N | 100.15 E |
| Luang Chiang Dao, Doi ∧ | 110 | 19.23 N | 98.54 E |
| Luanginga (Luanguinga) ≃ | 152 | 15.11 S | 22.56 E |
| Luang Prabang → Louangphrabang | 110 | 19.52 N | 102.08 E |
| Luang Prabang Range ⋏ | 110 | 18.30 N | 101.15 E |
| Luangue | 152 | 7.19 S | 19.38 E |
| Luangue (Loange) ≃ | 152 | 4.17 S | 20.02 E |
| Luanguinga (Luanginga) ≃ | 152 | 15.11 S | 22.56 E |
| Luangwa (Aruângua) ≃ | 154 | 15.36 S | 30.25 E |
| Luanhaizi | 120 | 34.27 N | 93.12 E |
| Luanhe | 105 | 40.57 N | 117.44 E |
| Luannan (Bencheng) | 98 | 39.32 N | 118.39 E |
| Luanping (Anjiangying) | 98 | 40.57 N | 117.20 E |
| Luanshishan | 104 | 42.10 N | 123.41 E |
| Luanshya | 154 | 13.08 S | 28.24 E |
| Luán Toro | 252 | 36.12 S | 65.06 W |
| Luanxian | 98 | 39.45 N | 118.44 E |
| Luanza | 154 | 8.42 S | 28.42 E |
| Luapula □[4] | 154 | 10.55 S | 29.00 E |
| Luapula ≃ | 154 | 9.26 S | 28.33 E |
| Luar, Danau ⊜ | 112 | 0.55 N | 112.15 E |
| Luarca | 34 | 43.32 N | 6.32 W |
| Luashi | 152 | 10.56 S | 23.37 E |
| Luashi ≃ | 152 | 10.41 S | 22.55 E |
| Luassinga ≃ | 152 | 15.47 S | 18.50 E |
| Luati | 152 | 14.35 S | 21.13 E |
| Luatira | 152 | 12.52 S | 17.14 E |
| Luau | 152 | 10.42 S | 22.12 E |
| Lua-Vindu ≃ | 152 | 3.38 N | 19.16 E |
| Luba | 152 | 3.27 N | 8.33 E |
| Lubaantun ⊥ | 232 | 16.17 N | 88.58 W |
| Lubaczów | 30 | 50.10 N | 23.07 E |
| Lubalo | 152 | 9.12 S | 19.16 E |
| Lubalo ≃ | 152 | 7.22 S | 19.20 E |
| Lubamiti | 152 | 2.29 S | 17.47 E |
| Lubań, Pol. | 30 | 51.08 N | 15.18 E |
| L'uban', Ross. | 76 | 59.21 N | 31.13 E |
| Lubāna | 76 | 56.54 N | 26.43 E |
| Lubang | 116 | 13.52 N | 120.07 E |
| Lubang Island I | 116 | 13.46 N | 120.11 E |
| Lubang Islands II | 116 | 13.46 N | 120.15 E |
| Lubango | 152 | 14.55 S | 13.30 E |
| Lubanowo | 54 | 53.09 N | 14.36 E |
| Lubāns ⊜ | 76 | 56.46 N | 26.53 E |
| Lubansenshi ≃ | 154 | 11.21 S | 30.35 E |
| Lub'any | 80 | 56.02 N | 51.24 E |
| Lubao | 100 | 23.22 N | 112.55 E |
| Lübars | 54 | 52.39 N | 12.02 E |
| Lübars ◆[8] | 264a | 52.37 N | 13.22 E |
| Lubartów | 30 | 51.28 N | 22.38 E |
| Lubawa | 30 | 53.30 N | 19.45 E |
| Lubaynī, Baḩr al- ≊ | 273c | 29.56 N | 31.11 E |
| Lübbecke | 52 | 52.18 N | 8.36 E |
| Lübben | 54 | 51.56 N | 13.53 E |
| Lübbenau | 54 | 51.52 N | 13.57 E |
| Lubber Brook ≃ | 283 | 42.33 N | 71.09 W |
| Lubbers Run ≃ | 276 | 40.56 N | 74.43 W |
| Lübbesee ⊜ | 54 | 53.05 N | 13.34 E |
| Lubbock | 196 | 33.34 N | 101.51 W |
| Lübbow | 54 | 52.54 N | 11.10 E |
| Lubbub Creek ≃ | 194 | 33.04 N | 88.10 W |
| Lubec | 188 | 44.51 N | 66.59 W |
| Lübeck | 54 | 53.52 N | 10.40 E |
| Lübecker Bucht ⊂ | 54 | 54.00 N | 10.55 E |
| Lubefu | 152 | 4.43 S | 24.25 E |
| Lubefu ≃ | 152 | 4.10 S | 23.00 E |
| Lubelska, Wyżyna ⋏[2] | 30 | 51.00 N | 23.00 E |
| Lubembe (Luembe) ≃ | 152 | 6.37 S | 21.05 E |
| Lüben → Lubin | 30 | 51.24 N | 16.13 E |
| Lubenec | 54 | 50.06 N | 13.20 E |
| L'ubercy | 82 | 55.41 N | 37.53 E |
| Lubéron, Montagne du ⋏ | 62 | 43.48 N | 5.22 E |
| Lubersac | 32 | 45.27 N | 1.24 E |
| Lübesse | 54 | 53.29 N | 11.28 E |
| Lubi ≃ | 152 | 4.58 S | 23.26 E |
| Lubiana → Ljubljana | 36 | 46.03 N | 14.31 E |
| Lubic Island I | 116 | 10.58 N | 120.44 E |
| L'ubickoje | 80 | 51.46 N | 49.19 E |
| Lubień Kujawski | 30 | 52.25 N | 19.10 E |
| Lubilash ≃ | 152 | 6.02 S | 23.45 E |
| Lubile | 154 | 2.55 S | 26.45 E |
| L'ubim | 80 | 58.22 N | 40.41 E |
| L'ubimovka, Kaz. | 86 | 52.15 N | 66.45 E |
| L'ubimovka, Ross. | 78 | 51.31 N | 35.37 E |
| Lubin, Pol. | 30 | 51.24 N | 16.13 E |
| Lubin, Pol. | 54 | 53.50 N | 14.25 E |
| L'ubino | 86 | 57.30 N | 88.47 E |
| L'ubinskij | 86 | 55.09 N | 72.42 E |
| Lubishi ≃ | 152 | 6.54 S | 24.09 E |
| Lubja ≃ | 265a | 59.58 N | 30.30 E |
| Lublin | 30 | 51.15 N | 22.35 E |
| Lublin □[4] | 30 | 51.30 N | 22.30 E |
| Lubliniec | 30 | 50.40 N | 18.41 E |
| L'ublino ◆[8] | 265b | 55.41 N | 37.44 E |
| Lubmin | 54 | 54.08 N | 13.37 E |
| Lubnān → Lebanon □[1] | 128 | 34.00 N | 36.00 E |
| Lubnān, Jabal (Lebanon Mountains) ⋏ | 132 | 34.00 N | 36.00 E |
| L'ubnica | 76 | 57.58 N | 32.42 E |
| Lubny | 78 | 50.01 N | 33.00 E |
| L'ubochna | 76 | 53.31 N | 34.23 E |
| Lubok China | 114 | 2.27 N | 102.04 E |
| Lubomierz | 30 | 51.01 N | 15.30 E |
| Luboń | 30 | 52.23 N | 16.54 E |
| Lubondai | 152 | 6.34 S | 22.39 E |
| Lubondoi | 154 | 8.02 S | 26.31 E |
| L'ubostan' | 78 | 51.19 N | 35.44 E |
| Lubraniec | 30 | 52.33 N | 18.50 E |
| Lubsko | 30 | 51.46 N | 14.59 E |
| Lubsza ≃ | 54 | 51.56 N | 14.43 E |
| Lübtheen | 54 | 53.18 N | 11.04 E |
| Lubu, Indon. | 112 | 0.46 S | 122.30 E |
| Lubu, Zhg. | 102 | 23.09 N | 112.13 E |
| Lubuagan | 116 | 17.21 N | 121.10 E |
| L'ubučany | 82 | 55.15 N | 37.33 E |
| Lubudi, Zaïre | 152 | 6.51 S | 21.18 E |
| Lubudi, Zaïre | 154 | 9.57 S | 25.58 E |
| Lubudi ≃, Zaïre | 152 | 4.03 S | 21.23 E |
| Lubudi ≃, Zaïre | 154 | 9.13 S | 25.38 E |
| Lubue | 152 | 4.09 S | 19.52 E |
| Lubue ≃ | 152 | 4.10 S | 19.53 E |
| Lubukambacang | 112 | 0.37 S | 101.25 E |
| Lubukbatang | 112 | 4.03 S | 104.12 E |
| Lubukbertubung | 112 | 0.02 N | 102.08 E |
| Lubuklinggau | 112 | 3.18 S | 102.52 E |
| Lubukpakam | 114 | 3.33 N | 98.52 E |
| Lubukraya, Dolok ∧ | 114 | 1.29 N | 99.13 E |
| Lubuksikaping | 112 | 0.08 N | 100.10 E |
| Lubumbaschi → Lubumbashi | 154 | 11.40 S | 27.28 E |
| Lubumbashi (Élisabethville) | 154 | 11.40 S | 27.28 E |
| Lubunda | 154 | 5.10 S | 26.40 E |
| Lubutu | 154 | 0.44 S | 26.35 E |
| Luby | 54 | 50.12 N | 12.25 E |
| L'ubytino | 76 | 58.49 N | 33.23 E |
| Lübz | 54 | 53.27 N | 12.01 E |
| Lučak | 85 | 38.23 N | 67.25 E |
| Lucala | 152 | 9.16 S | 15.15 E |
| Lucala ≃, Ang. | 152 | 6.38 S | 12.34 E |
| Lucala ≃, Ang. | 152 | 9.37 S | 14.14 E |
| Lucan, On., Can. | 190 | 43.11 N | 81.24 W |
| Lucan, Ire. | 48 | 53.22 N | 6.27 W |
| Lucanas | 248 | 14.36 S | 74.15 W |
| Lucania □[9] | 68 | 40.30 N | 16.00 E |
| Lucania, Mount ∧ | 180 | 61.01 N | 140.28 W |
| Lucano | 152 | 11.16 S | 21.38 E |
| Lucaogou | 102 | 42.26 N | 96.55 E |
| Lucapa | 152 | 8.36 S | 20.54 E |
| Lucas, Ia., U.S. | 190 | 41.01 N | 93.27 W |
| Lucas, Ks., U.S. | 198 | 39.03 N | 98.32 W |
| Lucas, Oh., U.S. | 214 | 40.45 N | 82.30 W |
| Lucas, Tx., U.S. | 222 | 33.05 N | 96.35 W |
| Lucas □[6] | 214 | 41.39 N | 83.32 W |
| Lucas González | 252 | 32.24 S | 59.33 W |
| Lucas Heights | 274a | 34.02 S | 150.58 E |
| Lucas Valley | 282 | 38.03 N | 122.35 W |
| Lucasville | 218 | 38.52 N | 82.59 W |
| Lucban | 116 | 14.06 N | 121.33 E |
| Lucca | 66 | 43.50 N | 10.29 E |
| Lucca □[4] | 64 | 44.02 N | 10.27 E |
| Lucca Sicula | 70 | 37.35 N | 13.18 E |
| Lucé | 50 | 48.26 N | 1.28 E |
| Luce, Water of ≃ | 44 | 54.52 N | 4.48 W |
| Lucea | 241q | 18.27 N | 78.10 W |
| Luce Bay ⊂ | 44 | 54.47 N | 4.50 W |
| Luce Bayou ≃ | 222 | 30.03 N | 95.07 W |
| Lucedale | 194 | 30.55 N | 88.35 W |
| Lucena, Esp. | 34 | 37.24 N | 4.29 W |
| Lucena, Pil. | 116 | 13.56 N | 121.37 E |
| Lucenay-l'Évêque | 32 | 47.05 N | 4.15 E |
| Luc-en-Diois | 62 | 44.37 N | 5.27 E |
| Lučenec | 30 | 48.20 N | 19.40 E |
| Lucens | 58 | 46.42 N | 6.50 E |
| Luceque | 152 | 14.41 S | 15.04 E |
| Lucera | 68 | 41.30 N | 15.20 E |
| Lucéram | 62 | 43.53 N | 7.22 E |
| Lucerne → Luzern, Schw. | 58 | 47.03 N | 8.18 E |
| Lucerne, Ca., U.S. | 204 | 39.05 N | 122.47 W |
| Lucerne, In., U.S. | 216 | 40.52 N | 86.24 W |
| Lucerne, Lake → Vierwaldstätter See ⊜ | 58 | 47.00 N | 8.28 E |
| Lucerne Lake ⊜ | 228 | 34.31 N | 116.57 W |
| Lucernemines | 214 | 40.33 N | 79.09 W |
| Lucerne Valley | 228 | 34.26 N | 116.58 W |
| Lucero | 200 | 30.49 N | 106.30 W |
| Lucero, Lake ⊜ | 200 | 32.42 N | 106.25 W |
| Luch | 80 | 57.01 N | 42.15 E |
| Luch ≃ | 80 | 56.14 N | 42.25 E |
| Luchang | 102 | 26.23 N | 102.18 E |
| Lucheng, Zhg. | 102 | 24.21 N | 106.00 E |
| Lücheng, Zhg. | 106 | 31.55 N | 119.44 E |
| Lucheng, Zhg. | 106 | 31.47 N | 120.02 E |
| Luché-Pringé | 50 | 47.42 N | 0.05 E |
| Lucheringo ≃ | 154 | 11.43 S | 36.17 E |
| Luchibe ≃ | 152 | 12.07 S | 21.13 E |
| Luchico (Lushiko) ≃ | 152 | 6.13 S | 19.40 E |
| Luchou | 269d | 25.05 N | 121.28 E |
| Luchovicy | 82 | 54.59 N | 39.03 E |
| Lüchow, Dtsch. | 54 | 52.58 N | 11.10 E |
| Luchow → Luzhou, Zhg. | 107 | 28.54 N | 105.27 E |
| Lüchtringen | 52 | 51.47 N | 9.25 E |
| Luchuan | 102 | 22.19 N | 110.11 E |
| Luci | 100 | 29.52 N | 119.47 E |
| Luciara | 250 | 10.27 S | 50.32 W |
| Lucie ≃ | 250 | 3.35 N | 57.38 W |
| Lucikou | 100 | 28.56 N | 116.04 E |
| Lucinda, Austl. | 166 | 18.32 S | 146.20 E |
| Lucinda, Pa., U.S. | 214 | 41.19 N | 79.22 W |
| Lucindale | 166 | 36.59 S | 140.22 E |
| Lucio Vázquez | 234 | 22.47 N | 99.46 W |
| Lucipara, Kepulauan II | 164 | 5.30 S | 127.33 E |
| Lucira | 152 | 13.51 S | 12.31 E |
| Lucito | 66 | 41.44 N | 14.41 E |
| Luci Yu I | 100 | 25.07 N | 119.22 E |
| Luck | 190 | 45.34 N | 92.28 W |
| Luck, Mount ∧[2] | 162 | 28.47 S | 123.33 E |
| Lucka | 54 | 51.06 N | 12.20 E |
| Luckau | 54 | 51.51 N | 13.43 E |
| Luckeesarai | 124 | 25.11 N | 86.05 E |
| Luckenwalde | 54 | 52.05 N | 13.10 E |
| Luckey | 214 | 41.27 N | 83.29 W |
| Luckhoff | 158 | 29.44 S | 24.43 E |
| Luckiamute ≃ | 202 | 44.45 N | 123.09 W |
| Luck Lake ⊜ | 184 | 51.05 N | 107.07 W |
| Lucknow, On., Can. | 190 | 43.57 N | 81.31 W |
| Lucknow, India | 124 | 26.51 N | 80.55 E |
| Lucknow, Pa., U.S. | 208 | 40.20 N | 76.54 W |
| Lucknow Branch ≊ | 124 | 27.57 N | 80.03 E |
| Lückstedt | 54 | 52.49 N | 11.35 E |
| Lucky Lake | 184 | 51.00 N | 107.10 W |
| Lucky Peak Lake ⊜[1] | 202 | 43.33 N | 116.00 W |
| Luco dei Marsi | 66 | 41.58 N | 13.28 E |
| Lucomagno, Passo del )( | 58 | 46.33 N | 8.49 E |
| Luçon, Fr. | 32 | 46.27 N | 1.10 W |
| Lucon, Pa., U.S. | 285 | 40.14 N | 75.25 W |
| Luconha ≃ | 152 | 12.54 S | 21.15 E |
| Lučosa ≃ | 76 | 55.10 N | 30.11 E |
| Lucun, Zhg. | 98 | 36.12 N | 118.01 E |
| Lucun, Zhg. | 106 | 30.49 N | 119.26 E |
| Lucunga ≃ | 152 | 6.57 S | 12.48 E |
| Lucungu ≃ | 152 | 6.41 S | 14.26 E |
| Lucusse | 152 | 12.32 S | 20.48 E |
| Lucy Creek | 166 | 22.25 S | 136.20 E |
| Lučyn | 76 | 53.01 N | 30.01 E |
| Lüda → Dalian | 98 | 38.53 N | 121.35 E |
| Luda Kamčija ≃ | 38 | 43.03 N | 27.29 E |
| Ludao | 89 | 43.51 N | 129.19 E |
| Ludbreg | 36 | 46.15 N | 16.37 E |
| Luddan | 123 | 29.54 N | 72.34 E |
| Luddenden | 262 | 53.44 N | 1.56 W |
| Luddenham | 274a | 33.53 S | 150.41 E |
| Luddesdown | 260 | 51.22 N | 0.24 E |
| Lüdenscheid | 56 | 51.13 N | 7.38 E |
| Lüder ≃ | 56 | 50.31 N | 9.27 E |
| Lüderitz, Dtsch. | 54 | 52.30 N | 11.44 E |
| Lüderitz, Namibia | 156 | 26.38 S | 15.10 E |
| Lüdersdorf | 54 | 53.47 N | 10.46 E |
| Ludgershall | 42 | 51.16 N | 1.37 W |
| Ludgo | 40 | 58.55 N | 17.08 E |
| Ludhiāna | 123 | 30.54 N | 75.51 E |
| Ludian | 102 | 27.11 N | 103.33 E |
| Luding | 102 | 29.55 N | 102.15 E |
| Lüdinghausen | 52 | 51.46 N | 7.26 E |
| Ludington | 190 | 43.57 N | 86.27 W |
| Ludingtonville | 210 | 41.29 N | 73.39 W |
| L'udinovo | 76 | 53.52 N | 34.27 E |
| L'udkovo | 76 | 54.36 N | 34.43 E |
| Ludlam Bay ⊂ | 208 | 39.10 N | 74.42 W |
| Ludlow, Eng., U.K. | 42 | 52.22 N | 2.43 W |
| Ludlow, Il., U.S. | 216 | 40.23 N | 88.08 W |
| Ludlow, Ky., U.S. | 218 | 39.05 N | 84.32 W |
| Ludlow, Ma., U.S. | 207 | 42.09 N | 72.28 W |
| Ludlow, Pa., U.S. | 214 | 41.43 N | 78.56 W |
| Ludlow, Vt., U.S. | 188 | 43.23 N | 72.42 W |
| Ludlow Falls | 218 | 40.00 N | 84.20 W |
| Ludlowville | 210 | 42.33 N | 76.32 W |
| Ludogorie ◆[1] | 38 | 43.46 N | 26.56 E |
| Ludonghe | 102 | 25.53 N | 103.33 E |
| Ludoni | 76 | 58.12 N | 29.21 E |
| Ludowici | 192 | 31.42 N | 81.44 W |
| Luduș | 38 | 46.29 N | 24.05 E |
| Ludvika | 40 | 60.09 N | 15.11 E |
| Ludwigkanal ≊ | 60 | 49.05 N | 11.27 E |
| Ludwigsburg | 56 | 48.53 N | 9.11 E |
| Ludwigsfelde | 54 | 52.17 N | 13.16 E |
| Ludwigsfelder-Heide ◆[3] | 264a | 52.18 N | 13.14 E |
| Ludwigshafen, Dtsch. | 56 | 49.29 N | 8.26 E |
| Ludwigshafen, Dtsch. | 58 | 47.49 N | 9.03 E |
| Ludwigslust | 54 | 53.19 N | 11.30 E |
| Ludwigsort → Laduškin | 76 | 54.36 N | 20.11 E |
| Ludwigsstadt | 54 | 50.30 N | 11.23 E |
| Ludwigstein, Burg ⊥ | 56 | 51.20 N | 9.55 E |
| Ludza | 76 | 56.33 N | 27.43 E |
| Lue | 170 | 32.39 S | 149.51 E |
| Luebo | 152 | 5.21 S | 21.25 E |
| Lueders | 196 | 32.48 N | 99.37 W |
| Lueg, Pass )( | 64 | 47.34 N | 13.12 E |
| Lueki | 154 | 3.22 S | 25.51 E |
| Luele ≃ | 152 | 7.55 S | 20.09 E |
| Luemba | 154 | 3.42 S | 28.40 E |
| Luembe (Lubembe) ≃, Afr. | 152 | 6.37 S | 21.05 E |
| Luembé ≃, Zaïre | 154 | 6.43 S | 24.11 E |
| Luena, Ang. | 152 | 11.47 S | 19.52 E |
| Luena, Zaïre | 154 | 9.27 S | 25.47 E |
| Luena ≃, Ang. | 152 | 12.31 S | 22.34 E |
| Luena ≃, Zam. | 152 | 14.45 S | 23.25 E |
| Luena Flats ≚ | 152 | 14.50 S | 23.20 E |
| Luengué ≃ | 152 | 16.54 S | 21.52 E |
| Luenha (Ruenya) ≃ | 154 | 16.24 S | 33.48 E |
| Lueo ≃ | 152 | 9.06 S | 23.51 E |
| Luepa | 246 | 5.43 N | 61.31 W |
| Lueta | 152 | 7.19 S | 22.06 E |
| Lueta ≃ | 152 | 7.04 S | 21.40 E |
| Lueyang | 102 | 33.20 N | 106.10 E |
| Lüfangsicun | 104 | 41.25 N | 123.22 E |
| Lufeng, Zhg. | 100 | 22.57 N | 115.38 E |
| Lufeng, Zhg. | 102 | 25.07 N | 102.07 E |
| Lufico | 152 | 6.24 S | 13.23 E |
| Lufira ≃ | 154 | 8.16 S | 26.27 E |
| Lufkin | 222 | 31.20 N | 94.43 W |
| Luftekopf ∧[2] | 56 | 50.05 N | 7.37 E |
| Lufubu ≃ | 154 | 8.36 S | 30.47 E |
| Lufuidje ≃ | 152 | 12.52 S | 22.47 E |
| Lufupa | 154 | 10.37 S | 24.56 E |
| Lufupa ≃ | 154 | 14.37 S | 26.12 E |
| Luga | 76 | 58.44 N | 29.52 E |
| Luga ≃ | 76 | 59.40 N | 28.18 E |
| Lugagnano Val d'Arda | 62 | 44.49 N | 9.50 E |
| Lugang, Zhg. | 100 | 31.17 N | 118.22 E |
| Lugang, Zhg. | 100 | 27.23 N | 115.36 E |
| Luganga | 154 | 7.31 S | 35.32 E |
| Lugano | 58 | 46.01 N | 8.58 E |
| Lugano, Lago di ⊜ | 58 | 46.00 N | 9.00 E |
| Lugansk → Luhans'k | 83 | 48.34 N | 39.20 E |
| Luganville | 175f | 15.32 S | 167.10 E |
| Lugards Falls ⌞ | 154 | 3.03 S | 38.42 E |
| Lugareño | 240p | 21.33 N | 77.28 W |
| Lugarno | 274a | 33.59 S | 151.03 E |
| Lugau | 54 | 50.44 N | 12.44 E |
| Lügde | 52 | 51.57 N | 9.15 E |
| Lugela | 154 | 16.25 S | 36.43 E |
| Lugenda | 154 | 12.30 S | 37.43 E |
| Lugenda ≃ | 154 | 11.25 S | 38.33 E |


**Symbols** in the index entries represent the broad categories identified in the key at the right. Symbols with superior numbers (⋏[1]) identify subcategories (see complete key on page *I · 1)*.

**Symbole** im Register stellen die rechts im Schlüssel erklärten Kategorien dar. Symbole mit hochgestellten Ziffern (⋏[1]) bezeichnen Unterabteilungen einer Kategorie (vgl. vollständiger Schlüssel auf Seite *I · 1)*.

**Los símbolos** incluídos en el texto del índice representan las grandes categorías identificadas con la clave a la derecha. Los símbolos con numeros en su parte superior (⋏[1]) identifican las subcategorías (véase la clave completa en la página *I · 1)*.

**Les symboles** de l'index représentent les catégories indiquées dans la légende à droite. Les symboles suivis d'un indice (⋏[1]) représentent des sous-catégories (voir légende complète à la page *I · 1)*.

**Os símbolos** incluídos no texto do índice representam as grandes categorias identificadas com a chave à direita. Os símbolos com números em sua parte superior (⋏[1]) identificam as subcategorias (veja-se a chave completa à página *I · 1)*.

| | English | Deutsch | Español | Français | Português |
|---|---|---|---|---|---|
| ∧ | Mountain | Berg | Montaña | Montagne | Montanha |
| ⋏ | Mountains | Gebirge | Montañas | Montagnes | Montanhas |
| )( | Pass | Paß | Paso | Col | Passo |
| V | Valley, Canyon | Tal, Cañon | Valle, Cañón | Vallée, Canyon | Vale, Canhão |
| ≚ | Plain | Ebene | Llano | Plaine | Planície |
| › | Cape | Kap | Cabo | Cap | Cabo |
| I | Island | Insel | Isla | Île | Ilha |
| II | Islands | Inseln | Islas | Îles | Ilhas |
| ⊥ | Other Topographic Features | Andere Topographische Objekte | Otros Elementos Topográficos | Autres données topographiques | Outros acidentes topográficos |

ESPAÑOL | FRANÇAIS | PORTUGUÊS

| Nombre | Página | Lat.°′ | Long.°′ W = Oeste |
|---|---|---|---|
| Lugg ≃ | 42 | 52.02 N | 2.38 W |
| Luggarus → Locarno | 58 | 46.10 N | 8.48 E |
| Luginino | 76 | 57.43 N | 35.17 E |
| Lugnano in Teverina | 66 | 42.34 N | 12.20 E |
| Lugnaquillia Mountain ∧ | 48 | 52.58 N | 6.27 W |
| Lugnås | 40 | 58.39 N | 13.42 E |
| Lugny | 58 | 46.28 N | 4.49 E |
| Lugo, Esp. | 34 | 43.00 N | 7.34 W |
| Lugo, It. | 66 | 44.25 N | 11.54 E |
| Lugo □[4] | 34 | 43.00 N | 7.25 W |
| Lugoj | 38 | 45.41 N | 21.54 E |
| Lugongshi | 106 | 31.38 N | 121.12 E |
| Lugos → Lugoj | 38 | 45.41 N | 21.54 E |
| Lugouqiao | 105 | 39.51 N | 116.13 E |
| Lugovaja Subbota | 86 | 59.52 N | 69.45 E |
| Lugovoj, Kaz. | 85 | 42.56 N | 72.45 E |
| Lugovoj, Ross. | 86 | 59.44 N | 65.55 E |
| Lugovoje | 85 | 42.55 N | 72.43 E |
| Lugovskij | 88 | 58.02 N | 112.54 E |
| Lugovskoje | 80 | 50.38 N | 46.28 E |
| Lugu | 102 | 28.21 N | 102.09 E |
| Lugulu ≃ | 154 | 2.17 S | 26.32 E |
| Lugunga ∧ | 154 | 6.47 S | 36.19 E |
| Luguru | 154 | 2.55 S | 33.58 E |
| Lugus Island I | 116 | 5.41 N | 120.50 E |
| Luhan' ≃ | 83 | 48.37 N | 39.27 E |
| Luhanchyk ≃ | 83 | 48.35 N | 39.32 E |
| Luhanka | 26 | 61.47 N | 25.42 E |
| Luhans'k | 83 | 48.34 N | 39.20 E |
| Luhans'k □[4] | 78 | 49.00 N | 39.00 E |
| Luhans'ke | 83 | 48.26 N | 38.15 E |
| Luhe ≃ | 52 | 53.18 N | 10.11 E |
| Lühedian | 100 | 32.33 N | 114.28 E |
| Luhe-Wildenau | 60 | 49.35 N | 12.09 E |
| Lühmannsdorf | 54 | 54.00 N | 13.38 E |
| Luhombero ≃ | 154 | 8.24 S | 37.12 E |
| Luhsien → Luzhou | 107 | 28.54 N | 105.27 E |
| Luhuo | 102 | 31.26 N | 100.48 E |
| Luhyny | 78 | 51.04 N | 28.24 E |
| Lui ≃, Ang. | 152 | 8.41 S | 17.56 E |
| Lui ≃, Zam. | 152 | 16.21 S | 23.18 E |
| Lui, Beinn ∧ | 46 | 56.24 N | 4.49 W |
| Luia | 152 | 8.26 S | 21.45 E |
| Luia (Ruya) ≃, Afr. | 154 | 16.34 S | 33.12 E |
| Luia ≃, Ang. | 152 | 8.24 S | 21.42 E |
| Lúia ≃, Moç. | 154 | 15.34 S | 32.58 E |
| Luiana | 152 | 17.23 S | 23.03 E |
| Luiana ≃ | 152 | 17.27 S | 23.14 E |
| Luichart, Loch ⊜ | 46 | 57.37 N | 4.46 W |
| Luido | 156 | 21.31 S | 34.41 E |
| Luie ≃ | 152 | 4.33 S | 17.41 E |
| Luik → Liège | 56 | 50.38 N | 5.34 E |
| Luilaka ≃ | 152 | 0.52 S | 20.12 E |
| Luilu ≃ | 152 | 6.22 S | 23.50 E |
| Luimbale | 152 | 12.15 S | 15.19 E |
| Luimneach → Limerick | 48 | 52.40 N | 8.38 W |
| Luing I | 46 | 56.13 N | 5.40 W |
| Luino | 58 | 46.00 N | 8.44 E |
| Luio ≃ | 152 | 13.15 S | 21.39 E |
| Luipaardsvlei | 273d | 26.16 S | 27.42 E |
| Luiro ≃ | 24 | 67.08 N | 27.29 E |
| Luisant | 50 | 48.25 N | 1.29 E |
| Luís Correia | 250 | 2.53 S | 41.40 W |
| Luisen-Berg ∧[2] | 264a | 52.27 N | 13.07 E |
| Luisenthal | 54 | 50.47 N | 10.43 E |
| Luís Gomes | 250 | 6.25 S | 38.23 W |
| Luis Guillón | 288 | 34.48 S | 58.27 W |
| Luishia | 154 | 11.10 S | 27.02 E |
| Luis Moya, Méx. | 234 | 22.25 N | 102.15 W |
| Luis Moya, Méx. | 234 | 23.05 N | 103.56 W |
| Luis Muñoz Marin, Aeropuerto Internacional ⊠ | 240m | 18.27 N | 66.00 W |
| Luis Peña, Cayo de I | 240m | 18.18 N | 65.20 W |
| Luis Pereira, Arroyo ≃ | 258 | 34.33 S | 57.02 W |
| Luita | 152 | 8.04 S | 19.25 E |
| Luitpold Coast ±[2] | 9 | 78.30 S | 32.00 W |
| Luiza | 152 | 7.12 S | 22.25 E |
| Luiza ≃ | 152 | 7.35 S | 22.40 E |
| Luizavo ≃ | 152 | 11.42 S | 23.12 E |
| Luizi | 154 | 6.03 S | 27.28 E |
| Luiziânia | 255 | 21.41 S | 50.17 W |
| Luján, Arg. | 252 | 33.03 S | 68.52 W |
| Luján, Arg. | 252 | 32.22 S | 65.57 W |
| Luján, Arg. | 258 | 34.34 S | 59.07 W |
| Luján ≃ | 288 | 34.26 S | 58.32 W |
| Lujia, Zhg. | 106 | 31.15 N | 121.37 E |
| Lujia, Zhg. | 106 | 31.19 N | 121.03 E |
| Lujia, Zhg. | 269b | 31.22 N | 121.18 E |
| Lujiabang | 106 | 31.20 N | 121.01 E |
| Lujiachang | 107 | 30.14 N | 105.34 E |
| Lujiagangzi | 104 | 42.05 N | 122.59 E |
| Lujiang | 100 | 31.14 N | 117.17 E |
| Lujiao | 100 | 29.10 N | 112.52 E |
| Lujiaoxi | 107 | 28.55 N | 105.48 E |
| Lujiaqiao, Zhg. | 106 | 31.47 N | 120.27 E |
| Lujiaqiao, Zhg. | 107 | 28.50 N | 106.21 E |
| Lujiatun, Zhg. | 98 | 40.14 N | 122.11 E |
| Lujiatun, Zhg. | 104 | 41.58 N | 122.38 E |
| Lujiatun, Zhg. | 104 | 42.18 N | 124.15 E |
| Lujiatun, Zhg. | 104 | 41.10 N | 121.56 E |
| Lujiazhou | 100 | 28.16 N | 114.35 E |
| L'uk | 80 | 56.55 N | 52.48 E |
| Lukachukai Wash V | 200 | 36.39 N | 109.36 W |
| Lukačok | 89 | 53.03 N | 132.16 E |
| Lukala | 152 | 5.31 S | 14.32 E |
| Lukang | 100 | 24.03 N | 120.25 E |
| Lukanga, Zaïre | 152 | 1.00 S | 18.08 E |
| Lukanga, Zaïre | 152 | 1.41 S | 18.09 E |
| Lukanga Swamp ≋ | 154 | 14.25 S | 27.45 E |
| Luk'anovo | 82 | 54.52 N | 37.25 E |
| Lukašin | 84 | 40.12 N | 44.01 E |
| Lukaškin Jar | 86 | 60.20 N | 78.24 E |
| Luke, Mount ∧ | 162 | 27.13 S | 116.48 E |
| Luke Air Force Base ■ | 200 | 33.32 N | 112.22 W |
| Lukenie ≃ | 152 | 2.44 S | 18.09 E |
| Lukens, Mount ∧ | 280 | 34.16 N | 118.14 W |
| Lukeville | 200 | 31.52 N | 112.48 W |
| Luki | 76 | 53.29 N | 26.15 E |
| Lukino, Ross. | 82 | 55.26 N | 37.04 E |
| Lukino, Ross. | 82 | 55.50 N | 36.49 E |
| Lukiv | 78 | 51.13 N | 24.19 E |
| Lukka | 140 | 14.33 N | 23.42 E |
| Luknovo | 80 | 56.12 N | 42.03 E |
| Lukojanov | 80 | 55.02 N | 44.30 E |
| Lukolela, Zaïre | 152 | 5.23 S | 24.32 E |
| Lukolela, Zaïre | 152 | 1.03 S | 17.12 E |
| Lukong | 107 | 29.31 N | 105.39 E |
| Lukoshi ≃ | 152 | 10.05 S | 22.59 E |
| Lukosi | 154 | 18.30 S | 26.30 E |
| Lukoškino | 82 | 55.19 N | 37.16 E |
| Lukou, Zhg. | 100 | 27.14 N | 114.04 E |
| Lukou, Zhg. | 106 | 31.48 N | 118.52 E |
| Lukoupu | 100 | 29.30 N | 113.26 E |
| Lukouyu | 100 | 28.24 N | 113.18 E |
| Lukovit | 38 | 43.12 N | 24.10 E |
| Lukovskaja | 80 | 50.35 N | 41.52 E |
| Łuków | 30 | 51.56 N | 22.23 E |
| Lükqün | 86 | 42.44 N | 89.42 E |
| Lukuga ≃ | 154 | 5.40 S | 26.55 E |
| Lukula | 152 | 5.23 S | 12.57 E |
| Lukula ≃, Afr. | 152 | 5.08 S | 12.28 E |
| Lukula ≃, Zaïre | 152 | 4.13 S | 17.58 E |
| Lukuledi ≃ | 154 | 10.05 S | 39.42 E |
| Lukulu | 152 | 14.25 S | 23.12 E |
| Lukulu ≃ | 154 | 10.56 S | 31.05 E |
| Lukumburu | 154 | 9.45 S | 35.09 E |
| Lukunga ≃ | 273b | 4.25 S | 15.14 E |
| Lukuni | 152 | 5.52 S | 17.11 E |
| Lukusashi ≃ | 154 | 14.38 S | 30.00 E |
| Lukusuzi National Park ♠ | 154 | 12.50 S | 32.35 E |

| Nom | Page | Lat.°′ | Long.°′ W = Ouest |
|---|---|---|---|
| Lula, It. | 71 | 40.28 N | 9.29 E |
| Lula, Ms., U.S. | 194 | 34.27 N | 90.28 W |
| Lula, Zaïre | 152 | 5.22 S | 16.02 E |
| Luleå | 26 | 65.34 N | 22.10 E |
| Luleälven ≃ | 24 | 65.35 N | 22.03 E |
| Lüleburgaz | 130 | 41.24 N | 27.21 E |
| Lules | 252 | 26.56 S | 65.21 W |
| Luliang | 102 | 25.05 N | 103.36 E |
| Lüliang Shan ∧∧ | 102 | 37.25 N | 111.20 E |
| Luliāni | 123 | 31.15 N | 74.25 E |
| Luliao | 269d | 25.07 N | 121.39 E |
| Luling | 222 | 29.40 N | 97.38 W |
| Lullingstone Castle ⊥ | 260 | 51.21 N | 0.12 E |
| Lulo ≃ | 152 | 9.25 S | 18.14 E |
| Lulong | 98 | 39.54 N | 118.50 E |
| Lulonga | 152 | 0.37 N | 18.23 E |
| Lulonga ≃ | 152 | 0.43 N | 18.23 E |
| Lulu ≃ | 152 | 1.18 N | 23.42 E |
| Lulua ≃ | 152 | 5.02 S | 21.07 E |
| Luluabourg → Kananga | 152 | 5.54 S | 22.25 E |
| Lulu Island I, B.C., Can. | 224 | 49.09 N | 123.05 W |
| Lulu Island I, Ak., U.S. | 182 | 55.28 N | 133.30 W |
| Luluo | 98 | 37.06 N | 113.58 E |
| Lulworth, Mount ∧ | 162 | 26.53 S | 117.42 E |
| Lumai | 152 | 13.31 S | 21.21 E |
| Lumajang | 115a | 8.08 S | 113.13 E |
| Lumajangdong Co ⊜ | 120 | 34.00 N | 81.45 E |
| Lumaku, Gunong ∧ | 112 | 4.52 N | 115.38 E |
| Lumaling | 120 | 29.53 N | 92.37 E |
| Lumb | 262 | 53.42 N | 1.58 W |
| Lumbala ≃ | 152 | 12.38 S | 22.34 E |
| Lumbala Kaquengue | 152 | 12.39 S | 22.34 E |
| Lumbala N'guimbo | 152 | 14.08 S | 21.25 E |
| Lumbangaraga | 114 | 1.53 N | 99.04 E |
| Lumbanlobu | 114 | 2.31 N | 99.08 E |
| Lumbe ≃ | 152 | 16.42 S | 23.42 E |
| Lumber ≃ | 192 | 34.12 N | 79.10 W |
| Lumber City | 192 | 31.55 N | 82.40 W |
| Lumberport | 188 | 39.22 N | 80.20 W |
| Lumberton, Ms., U.S. | 194 | 31.00 N | 89.27 W |
| Lumberton, N.J., U.S. | 285 | 39.57 N | 74.48 W |
| Lumberton, N.C., U.S. | 192 | 34.37 N | 79.00 W |
| Lumberton, Tx., U.S. | 194 | 30.16 N | 94.10 W |
| Lumbinī □[8] | 124 | 27.45 N | 83.30 E |
| Lumbis | 112 | 4.18 N | 116.15 E |
| Lumbo | 154 | 15.00 S | 40.44 E |
| Lumbovka | 24 | 67.44 N | 40.30 E |
| Lumbrales | 34 | 40.56 N | 6.43 W |
| Lumbrein | 58 | 46.41 N | 9.08 E |
| Lumbres | 50 | 50.42 N | 2.08 E |
| Lumbwa | 154 | 0.12 S | 35.28 E |
| Lumby | 182 | 50.15 N | 118.58 W |
| Lumding | 120 | 25.45 N | 93.10 E |
| Lumege ≃ | 152 | 11.55 S | 20.58 E |
| Lumerau ≃ | 116 | 5.21 N | 118.53 E |
| Lumi | 164 | 3.29 S | 142.02 E |
| Lumiei ≃ | 64 | 46.24 N | 12.51 E |
| Luminárias | 256 | 21.30 S | 44.54 W |
| Luminosa | 256 | 22.35 S | 45.38 W |
| Lumintao ≃ | 116 | 12.43 N | 120.55 E |
| Lummen | 56 | 50.59 N | 5.12 E |
| Lummi Bay c | 224 | 48.46 N | 122.41 W |
| Lummi Indian Reservation ✦[4] | 224 | 48.48 N | 122.38 W |
| Lummi Island | 224 | 48.42 N | 122.40 W |
| Lummi Island I | 224 | 48.42 N | 122.40 W |
| Lumphanan | 46 | 57.07 N | 2.41 W |
| Lumphăt | 110 | 13.30 N | 106.59 E |
| Lumphini Park ♠ | 269a | 13.44 N | 100.33 E |
| Lumpkin | 192 | 32.03 N | 84.47 W |
| Lumpun ≃ | 80 | 57.01 N | 51.22 E |
| Lumsån ≃ | 40 | 59.59 N | 15.26 E |
| Lumsås | 41 | 55.57 N | 11.31 E |
| Lumsden, Nf., Can. | 186 | 49.19 N | 53.37 W |
| Lumsden, Sk., Can. | 184 | 50.34 N | 104.53 W |
| Lumsden, N.Z. | 172 | 45.44 S | 168.27 E |
| Lumsden, Scot., U.K. | 46 | 57.15 N | 2.52 W |
| Lumsheden | 40 | 60.43 N | 16.15 E |
| Lums Pond State Park ♠ | 208 | 39.34 N | 75.43 W |
| Lumu, Indon. | 112 | 2.11 S | 119.09 E |
| Lumu, Zhg. | 106 | 31.22 N | 120.37 E |
| Lumuna | 154 | 3.46 S | 26.24 E |
| Lumuna ≃ | 152 | 16.59 S | 21.25 E |
| Lumut, Indon. | 114 | 1.33 N | 98.56 E |
| Lumut, Malay. | 114 | 4.14 N | 100.38 E |
| Lumut, Tanjung > | 112 | 3.50 S | 105.57 E |
| Lumwana | 154 | 11.50 S | 25.10 E |
| Lün, Mong. | 88 | 47.24 N | 102.52 E |
| Lün, Mong. | 88 | 47.52 N | 105.15 E |
| Luna, Pil. | 116 | 16.51 N | 120.23 E |
| Luna, Pil. | 116 | 18.18 N | 121.21 E |
| Luna ≃ | 246 | 4.32 S | 60.41 W |
| Lunada Bay c | 280 | 33.46 N | 118.25 W |
| Lunain ≃ | 50 | 48.20 N | 2.47 E |
| Lunamatrona | 71 | 39.39 N | 8.54 E |
| Lunan | 102 | 24.49 N | 103.16 E |
| Lunan Bay c | 46 | 56.39 N | 2.28 W |
| Lunano | 66 | 43.44 N | 12.26 E |
| Luna Pier | 216 | 41.48 N | 83.26 W |
| Lūnāvāda | 120 | 23.08 N | 73.37 E |
| Luncarty | 46 | 56.27 N | 3.28 W |
| Lund, B.C., Can. | 182 | 49.58 N | 124.44 W |
| Lund, Sve. | 41 | 55.42 N | 13.11 E |
| Lund, Nv., U.S. | 204 | 38.51 N | 115.00 W |
| Lunda ≃, Ang. | 152 | 6.07 S | 13.52 E |
| L'unda ≃, Ross. | 80 | 56.32 N | 46.03 E |
| Lundåkrabukten c | 41 | 55.48 N | 12.53 E |
| Lundale | 188 | 37.48 N | 81.44 W |
| Lunda Norte □[5] | 152 | 8.45 S | 19.45 E |
| Lundar | 184 | 50.42 N | 98.02 W |
| Lunda Sul □[5] | 152 | 10.00 S | 20.30 E |
| Lundazi | 154 | 12.19 S | 33.13 E |
| Lundby | 41 | 55.07 N | 11.53 E |
| Lunde | 41 | 55.29 N | 10.21 E |
| Lundeborg | 41 | 55.08 N | 10.47 E |
| Lunden | 41 | 54.20 N | 9.01 E |
| Lunderskov | 41 | 55.29 N | 9.18 E |
| Lundevatn ⊜ | 26 | 58.22 N | 6.36 E |
| Lundi ≃ | 154 | 21.43 S | 32.34 E |
| Lundsberg | 40 | 59.30 N | 14.10 E |
| Lundsfjärden ⊜ | 40 | 59.38 N | 14.41 E |
| Lundy I | 42 | 51.10 N | 4.40 W |
| Lundys Lane | 214 | 41.53 N | 80.21 W |
| Lune ≃ | 44 | 54.02 N | 2.50 W |
| Lüneburg | 52 | 53.15 N | 10.23 E |
| Lüneburg □[5] | 52 | 53.15 N | 10.00 E |
| Lüneburger Heide ✦[1] | 52 | 53.10 N | 10.20 E |
| Lunel | 62 | 43.41 N | 4.08 E |
| Lünen | 52 | 51.36 N | 7.32 E |
| Lunenburg, N.S., Can. | 186 | 44.23 N | 64.19 W |
| Lunenburg, Ma., U.S. | 207 | 42.35 N | 71.43 W |
| Lunenburg, Va., U.S. | 192 | 36.57 N | 78.15 W |
| Luneray | 50 | 49.50 N | 0.55 E |
| Lünern | 263 | 51.33 N | 7.46 E |
| Lunéville | 56 | 48.36 N | 6.30 E |
| Lunga I | 46 | 56.13 N | 5.42 W |
| Lunga ≃, Ang. | 152 | 5.59 S | 16.20 E |
| Lunga ≃, Zam. | 154 | 14.34 S | 26.25 E |
| Lungälven ≃ | 40 | 59.34 N | 14.10 E |
| Lunga Reservoir ⊜[1] | 208 | 38.32 N | 77.28 W |
| Lungau ✦[1] | 64 | 47.07 N | 13.39 E |
| Lungavilla | 62 | 45.02 N | 9.04 E |
| Lungch'i → Zhangzhou | 100 | 24.33 N | 117.39 E |
| Lunge | 152 | 12.12 S | 16.05 E |
| Lunge'nake | 120 | 31.45 N | 85.55 E |
| Lungern | 58 | 46.47 N | 8.10 E |
| Lunggar | 120 | 31.10 N | 84.00 E |
| Lunghezza ✦[8] | 267a | 41.55 N | 12.40 E |
| Lungi | 150 | 8.38 N | 13.13 W |
| Lunglei | 120 | 22.53 N | 92.44 E |
| Lungro | 68 | 39.44 N | 16.07 E |
| Lungsang | 124 | 29.51 N | 88.41 E |

| Nome | Página | Lat.°′ | Long.°′ W = Oeste |
|---|---|---|---|
| Lungt'an | 100 | 24.52 N | 121.12 E |
| Lungué-Bungo (Lungwebungu) ≃ | 152 | 14.19 S | 23.14 E |
| Lunguya | 154 | 3.23 S | 32.24 E |
| Lungwebungu (Lungué-Bungo) ≃ | 152 | 14.19 S | 23.14 E |
| Lūni | 120 | 26.00 N | 73.00 E |
| Lūni ≃ | 120 | 24.41 N | 71.15 E |
| Luni ⊥ | 64 | 44.04 N | 10.01 E |
| Lunia-Bubi | 154 | 7.30 S | 24.49 E |
| Lunigiana ✦[1] | 64 | 44.15 N | 9.50 E |
| Lunin | 76 | 52.18 N | 26.38 E |
| Luninec | 76 | 52.15 N | 26.48 E |
| Lunino, Ross. | 80 | 53.35 N | 45.14 E |
| Lunino, Ross. | 82 | 54.09 N | 38.29 E |
| Lunjiao | 100 | 22.53 N | 113.13 E |
| Lūnkaransar | 120 | 28.29 N | 73.44 E |
| Lunna | 76 | 53.27 N | 24.16 E |
| Lunnaja, gora ∧ | 180 | 68.14 N | 174.20 E |
| Lunndörrsfjällen ∧ | 26 | 63.00 N | 13.00 E |
| Lunongzha | 106 | 31.59 N | 120.55 E |
| Lunsar | 150 | 8.41 N | 12.32 W |
| Lunsemfwa ≃ | 154 | 14.54 S | 30.12 E |
| Lunt | 262 | 53.31 N | 2.59 W |
| Lunteren | 52 | 52.05 N | 5.37 E |
| Lunyuk | 115b | 8.57 S | 117.14 E |
| Lunz am See | 61 | 47.51 N | 15.03 E |
| Lunzenau | 54 | 50.58 N | 12.45 E |
| Lunzhen | 98 | 36.47 N | 116.34 E |
| Luo ≃, Zhg. | 102 | 34.42 N | 110.15 E |
| Luo ≃, Zhg. | 102 | 34.48 N | 113.04 E |
| Luoba, Zhg. | 100 | 24.51 N | 114.13 E |
| Luoba, Zhg. | 107 | 29.08 N | 106.11 E |
| Luobei (Fengxiang) | 89 | 47.34 N | 130.50 E |
| Luobo | 102 | 28.22 N | 101.38 E |
| Luobu | 102 | 24.30 N | 109.40 E |
| Luobumiao | 102 | 40.19 N | 107.30 E |
| Luochanghe | 100 | 31.01 N | 117.18 E |
| Luocheng, Zhg. | 102 | 24.51 N | 108.59 E |
| Luocheng, Zhg. | 107 | 29.23 N | 104.01 E |
| Luochuan | 102 | 35.55 N | 109.26 E |
| Luoci | 102 | 25.19 N | 102.18 E |
| Luodian | 106 | 31.25 N | 121.20 E |
| Luoding | 102 | 22.47 N | 111.31 E |
| Luoduzhen | 107 | 30.22 N | 106.35 E |
| Luofa | 105 | 39.25 N | 116.50 E |
| Luofang, Zhg. | 100 | 28.40 N | 115.04 E |
| Luofang, Zhg. | 100 | 27.52 N | 115.06 E |
| Luofu, Zaïre | 154 | 0.10 S | 29.14 E |
| Luofu, Zhg. | 100 | 24.32 N | 115.35 E |
| Luogang, Zhg. | 100 | 23.11 N | 113.30 E |
| Luogang, Zhg. | 100 | 24.25 N | 115.38 E |
| Luogosanto | 71 | 41.03 N | 9.13 E |
| Luoguhe | 89 | 53.18 N | 121.30 E |
| Luohan Shan ∧ | 100 | 25.51 N | 119.13 E |
| Luohe | 100 | 33.35 N | 114.01 E |
| Luoheya | 98 | 35.46 N | 118.54 E |
| Luohua | 100 | 26.35 N | 118.43 E |
| Luoji | 100 | 32.06 N | 117.16 E |
| Luojiachang | 107 | 30.49 N | 106.32 E |
| Luojiang | 102 | 31.21 N | 104.28 E |
| Luojiatang | 106 | 30.18 N | 120.13 E |
| Luojiatun, Zhg. | 98 | 40.11 N | 118.34 E |
| Luojiatun, Zhg. | 104 | 42.06 N | 122.44 E |
| Luojiatun, Zhg. | 104 | 40.55 N | 122.04 E |
| Luojiawei | 100 | 26.55 N | 115.02 E |
| Luoke | 100 | 24.07 N | 114.28 E |
| Luokeng | 100 | 24.32 N | 113.23 E |
| Luokou, Zhg. | 100 | 28.54 N | 117.24 E |
| Luokou, Zhg. | 100 | 25.46 N | 115.39 E |
| Luolong | 107 | 28.49 N | 104.46 E |
| L'Uomo di Cagna ∧ | 71 | 41.33 N | 9.04 E |
| Luonan | 102 | 34.05 N | 110.04 E |
| Luoning | 102 | 34.25 N | 111.42 E |
| Luoping | 102 | 24.59 N | 104.21 E |
| Luoqi | 102 | 29.48 N | 106.56 E |
| Luoqiao | 100 | 26.28 N | 119.01 E |
| Luoquanzhen | 107 | 29.50 N | 104.31 E |
| Luoshan, Zhg. | 100 | 32.13 N | 114.32 E |
| Luoshan, Zhg. | 100 | 29.41 N | 113.18 E |
| Luoshan, Zhg. | 105 | 39.55 N | 117.33 E |
| Luoshe, Zhg. | 106 | 31.39 N | 120.11 E |
| Luoshe, Zhg. | 106 | 30.41 N | 120.04 E |
| Luoshuihe | 98 | 39.27 N | 114.19 E |
| Luossa ≃ | 152 | 8.24 S | 17.03 E |
| Luotian | 100 | 30.48 N | 115.22 E |
| Luotuodian | 100 | 32.13 N | 113.49 E |
| Luotuoqiao | 100 | 29.56 N | 121.32 E |
| Luotuo Shan ∧ | 104 | 42.14 N | 121.42 E |
| Luowenba | 102 | 31.48 N | 107.48 E |
| Luowenyu | 105 | 40.16 N | 117.57 E |
| Luoxi | 100 | 29.05 N | 114.58 E |
| Luoxiao Shan ∧∧ | 100 | 26.00 N | 114.00 E |
| Luoyang (Loyang), Zhg. | 102 | 34.41 N | 112.28 E |
| Luoyang, Zhg. | 106 | 31.39 N | 120.05 E |
| Luoyuan | 100 | 26.31 N | 119.32 E |
| Luoyuan Wan c | 100 | 26.25 N | 119.43 E |
| Luoyukou | 102 | 38.23 N | 110.43 E |
| Luozhexi | 107 | 29.02 N | 103.54 E |
| Luozi | 152 | 4.57 S | 14.08 E |
| Lupala | 156 | 17.50 S | 19.06 E |
| Lupani | 154 | 18.54 S | 27.44 E |
| Lupao | 116 | 15.53 N | 120.54 E |
| Lupar ≃ | 112 | 1.30 N | 111.00 E |
| Łupawa | 30 | 54.26 N | 17.24 E |
| Lupberg | 60 | 49.09 N | 11.45 E |
| Lupembe | 154 | 9.15 S | 35.15 E |
| Lupeni | 38 | 45.22 N | 23.13 E |
| Lupire | 152 | 14.36 S | 19.29 E |
| Lupiro | 154 | 8.23 S | 36.40 E |
| Lupon | 116 | 6.54 N | 126.00 E |
| Luppa | 54 | 51.20 N | 12.57 E |
| Luputa | 152 | 7.10 S | 23.42 E |
| Luqiao, Zhg. | 100 | 32.34 N | 117.14 E |
| Luqiao, Zhg. | 100 | 28.35 N | 121.22 E |
| Luqu | 102 | 34.41 N | 102.22 E |
| Luque | 34 | 37.33 N | 4.16 W |
| Luquillo | 240m | 18.22 N | 65.43 W |
| Luquillo, Sierra de ∧∧ | 240m | 18.17 N | 65.47 W |
| Lūrah ≃ | 120 | 31.33 N | 66.33 E |
| Luray | 188 | 38.39 N | 78.27 W |
| Lure | 58 | 47.41 N | 6.30 E |
| Lure, Montagne de ∧∧ | 62 | 44.07 N | 5.47 E |
| Lureco ≃ | 154 | 12.28 S | 37.40 E |
| Luremo | 152 | 8.31 S | 17.50 E |
| Lurgan | 48 | 54.28 N | 6.20 W |
| Luribay | 248 | 17.06 S | 67.39 W |
| Lurigancho | 286d | 12.02 S | 77.01 W |
| Lurín | 248 | 12.17 S | 76.52 W |
| Lúrio | 154 | 13.35 S | 40.30 E |
| Lúrio ≃ | 154 | 13.35 S | 40.32 E |
| Lurisia | 62 | 44.18 N | 7.42 E |
| Lurnea | 274a | 33.56 S | 150.54 E |
| Lurö I | 26 | 58.48 N | 13.14 E |
| Lürrip ✦[8] | 263 | 51.12 N | 6.28 E |
| Lusahunga | 154 | 2.52 S | 31.15 E |
| Lusaka, Zaïre | 154 | 7.10 S | 29.27 E |
| Lusaka, Zam. | 154 | 15.25 S | 28.17 E |
| Lusaka □[4] | 154 | 15.25 S | 29.00 E |
| Lusakert | 84 | 40.23 N | 44.36 E |
| Lusambo | 152 | 4.58 S | 23.27 E |
| Lusancay Islands and Reefs II | 164 | 8.25 S | 150.20 E |
| Lusanga | 152 | 4.50 S | 18.44 E |
| Lusangaye | 154 | 4.54 S | 26.00 E |
| Lusangi | 154 | 4.37 S | 27.08 E |
| Luscar | 182 | 53.04 N | 117.24 W |
| Luseke | 152 | 2.51 S | 23.08 E |
| Luseland | 184 | 52.05 N | 109.24 W |
| Lusen ∧ | 60 | 48.56 N | 13.31 E |
| Lusenga Plain National Park ♠ | 154 | 9.30 S | 29.10 E |
| Lusengo | 152 | 1.46 N | 19.29 E |
| Luserna San Giovanni | 62 | 44.48 N | 7.15 E |
| Lush, Mount ∧ | 164 | 17.02 S | 127.30 E |
| Lushan, Zhg. | 100 | 33.45 N | 112.53 E |
| Lushan, Zhg. | 102 | 30.15 N | 102.58 E |
| Lu Shan ∧ | 100 | 29.31 N | 115.58 E |

| | | | |
|---|---|---|---|
| Lu Shan ∧∧ | 98 | 36.05 N | 118.05 E |
| Lushanguanliju | 100 | 29.33 N | 115.58 E |
| Lushi | 102 | 34.05 N | 111.01 E |
| Lushiko (Luchico) ≃ | 152 | 6.13 S | 19.40 E |
| Lüshikou | 100 | 29.16 N | 120.17 E |
| Lushnje | 38 | 40.56 N | 19.42 E |
| Lushoto | 154 | 4.47 S | 38.17 E |
| Lushui | 102 | 26.00 N | 98.51 E |
| Lüshun (Port Arthur) | 98 | 38.48 N | 121.16 E |
| Lüsi | 106 | 32.03 N | 121.36 E |
| Lusi ≃ | 115a | 7.05 S | 110.55 E |
| Lusiana | 64 | 45.47 N | 11.34 E |
| Lusignan | 32 | 46.26 N | 0.07 E |
| Lusignan, Lac ⊜ | 206 | 46.40 N | 74.09 W |
| Lusigny-sur-Barse | 50 | 48.15 N | 4.16 E |
| Lusikisiki | 158 | 31.25 S | 29.30 E |
| Lusk, Ire. | 48 | 53.32 N | 6.10 W |
| Lusk, Wy., U.S. | 200 | 42.45 N | 104.27 W |
| Lus-la-Croix-Haute | 62 | 44.40 N | 5.42 E |
| Lusongwa | 152 | 12.58 S | 24.16 E |
| Luspebryggan | 24 | 67.01 N | 19.51 E |
| Lussac-les-Châteaux | 32 | 46.24 N | 0.44 E |
| Lussan | 62 | 44.09 N | 4.22 E |
| Luṣṣān, Wādī V | 132 | 30.30 N | 34.18 E |
| Lüssow | 54 | 53.50 N | 12.09 E |
| Lustenau | 58 | 47.26 N | 9.39 E |
| Luster | 26 | 61.26 N | 7.24 E |
| Lustin | 56 | 50.23 N | 4.53 E |
| Lustrafjorden c[2] | 26 | 61.20 N | 7.22 E |
| Lüstringen | 52 | 52.16 N | 8.08 E |
| Lusutfu (Maputo) (Great Usutu) ≃ | 158 | 26.11 S | 32.42 E |
| Luswishi ≃ | 154 | 13.55 S | 27.24 E |
| Lūt, Dasht-e ✦[2] | 128 | 32.00 N | 58.00 E |
| Lü-ta → Dalian | 98 | 38.53 N | 121.35 E |
| L'uta ≃ | 76 | 58.37 N | 28.40 E |
| Lutago (Luttach) | 64 | 46.57 N | 11.55 E |
| Lutai | 100 | 33.32 N | 115.03 E |
| Lütan, Zhg. | 98 | 34.07 N | 114.27 E |
| Lütan, Zhg. | 100 | 28.57 N | 119.46 E |
| Lutang | 100 | 25.39 N | 112.46 E |
| Lutao | 116 | 10.00 N | 124.04 E |
| Lü Tao I | 100 | 22.40 N | 121.29 E |
| Lutcher | 194 | 30.02 N | 90.41 W |
| Lute | 284c | 39.04 N | 77.03 W |
| Lutembo | 152 | 13.26 S | 21.16 E |
| Lutembo ≃ | 152 | 12.03 S | 22.15 E |
| Lutesville | 194 | 37.18 N | 89.58 W |
| Lutéte ≃ | 152 | 9.21 S | 15.14 E |
| Lutexu ≃ | 273b | 4.24 S | 15.12 E |
| Lütgendortmund ✦[8] | 263 | 51.30 N | 7.21 E |
| Luthe | 52 | 52.26 N | 9.28 E |
| Luther, Mi., U.S. | 190 | 44.02 N | 85.40 W |
| Luther, Ok., U.S. | 196 | 35.39 N | 97.11 W |
| Luther Lake ⊜ | 212 | 43.55 N | 80.26 W |
| Luthersburg | 214 | 41.03 N | 78.43 W |
| Lutherstadt Eisleben | 54 | 51.31 N | 11.32 E |
| Lutherstadt Wittenberg | 54 | 51.52 N | 12.39 E |
| Lutherville-Timonium | 284b | 39.25 N | 76.37 W |
| Luthrie | 46 | 56.21 N | 3.05 W |
| Luti | 175e | 7.14 S | 156.59 E |
| Lutian, Zhg. | 100 | 26.33 N | 114.38 E |
| Lütian, Zhg. | 100 | 23.48 N | 113.56 E |
| Lütjenburg | 54 | 54.17 N | 10.35 E |
| Lütjensee | 52 | 53.39 N | 10.22 E |
| Luton, Eng., U.K. | 42 | 51.53 N | 0.25 W |
| Luton, Eng., U.K. | 260 | 51.22 N | 0.32 E |
| Lutong | 112 | 4.28 N | 114.00 E |
| Lutosn'a ≃ | 82 | 56.26 N | 36.52 E |
| Lutou | 100 | 32.16 N | 112.53 E |
| Lutry | 58 | 46.30 N | 6.41 E |
| Lutshi | 154 | 4.09 S | 26.30 E |
| Lutshima ≃ | 152 | 5.22 S | 18.59 E |
| Luts'k | 78 | 50.44 N | 25.20 E |
| Luttach → Lutago | 64 | 46.57 N | 11.55 E |
| Lutter | 52 | 51.59 N | 10.16 E |
| Lutterbach | 58 | 47.46 N | 7.17 E |
| Lutterworth | 42 | 52.28 N | 1.10 W |
| Lüttich → Liège | 56 | 50.38 N | 5.34 E |
| Luttrell | 192 | 36.11 N | 83.44 W |
| Lüttringhausen ✦[8] | 263 | 51.13 N | 7.14 E |
| Lutuai ≃ | 152 | 12.33 S | 20.16 E |
| Lutuhyne | 83 | 48.24 N | 39.13 E |
| Lutz | 220 | 28.09 N | 82.27 W |
| Lützel | 56 | 50.58 N | 8.10 E |
| Lutzelbourg | 56 | 48.44 N | 7.15 E |
| Lützelflüh | 58 | 47.00 N | 7.41 E |
| Lützen | 54 | 51.15 N | 12.08 E |
| Lutzerath | 56 | 50.07 N | 7.00 E |
| Lutz Hill | 284b | 39.20 N | 76.32 W |
| Lützow | 54 | 53.40 N | 11.11 E |
| Lützow-Holm Bay c | 9 | 69.10 S | 37.30 E |
| Lutzputs | 158 | 28.03 S | 20.40 E |
| Lützschena | 54 | 51.23 N | 12.16 E |
| Lutzville | 158 | 31.33 S | 18.22 E |
| Luud, Waadi V | 144 | 10.17 N | 50.14 E |
| Luuq | 144 | 3.48 N | 42.33 E |
| Luus | 102 | 45.30 N | 105.45 E |
| Luverne, Al., U.S. | 194 | 31.42 N | 86.15 W |
| Lu Verne, Ia., U.S. | 190 | 42.54 N | 94.04 W |
| Luverne, Mn., U.S. | 198 | 43.39 N | 96.12 W |
| Luvo | 152 | 5.51 S | 14.05 E |
| Luvo ≃ | 152 | 10.18 S | 17.08 E |
| Luvua | 154 | 8.48 S | 25.19 E |
| Lúvua ≃, Ang. | 152 | 11.57 S | 22.30 E |
| Luvua ≃, Zaïre | 154 | 6.46 S | 26.58 E |
| Luvuvhu ≃ | 156 | 22.40 S | 30.55 E |
| Luwegu ≃ | 154 | 8.31 S | 37.23 E |
| Luwingu | 154 | 10.15 S | 29.55 E |
| Luwuk, Indon. | 112 | 0.56 S | 122.47 E |
| Luwuk → Banggai, Indon. | 112 | 1.34 S | 123.30 E |
| Luxana Bay c | 182 | 52.03 N | 131.00 W |
| Luxapallila Creek ≃ | 194 | 33.28 N | 88.26 W |
| Luxembourg | 56 | 49.36 N | 6.09 E |
| Luxembourg □[4] | 56 | 50.00 N | 5.30 E |
| Luxembourg □[1], Europe | 22 | 49.45 N | 6.05 E |
| Luxembourg □[1], Europe | 56 | 49.45 N | 6.05 E |
| Luxembourg, Aéroport de ⊠ | 56 | 49.37 N | 6.10 E |
| Luxembourg, Jardin du ♠ | 261 | 48.51 N | 2.19 E |
| Luxemburg | 190 | 44.32 N | 87.42 W |
| Luxemburg → Luxembourg □[1] | 56 | 49.45 N | 6.05 E |
| Luxemburgo → Luxembourg □[1] | 56 | 49.45 N | 6.05 E |
| Luxeuil-les-Bains | 58 | 47.49 N | 6.23 E |
| Luxi, Zhg. | 102 | 24.32 N | 103.41 E |
| Luxi (Mangshi), Zhg. | 102 | 24.20 N | 98.25 E |
| Lüxia | 100 | 26.41 N | 120.06 E |
| Luxian | 107 | 28.55 N | 105.29 E |
| Luxiang, Zhg. | 106 | 31.32 N | 120.45 E |
| Lüxiang, Zhg. | 106 | 30.50 N | 121.10 E |
| Luxi Dao I | 100 | 27.59 N | 121.11 E |
| Luxikou | 100 | 29.54 N | 113.42 E |
| Luxmanor | 284c | 39.02 N | 77.07 W |
| Luxor → Al-Uqṣur | 140 | 25.41 N | 32.39 E |
| Luxora | 194 | 35.45 N | 89.55 W |
| Luxu | 106 | 31.01 N | 120.50 E |
| Lu Xun Museum ❦ | 269b | 31.16 N | 121.28 E |
| Lüxuqiao | 106 | 31.50 N | 119.31 E |
| Luy ≃ | 32 | 43.39 N | 1.08 W |
| Luyan | 106 | 30.25 N | 120.53 E |
| Lüyang | 104 | 41.23 N | 121.40 E |
| Luyanó ≃ | 286b | 23.07 N | 82.21 W |
| Luyeh | 100 | 22.55 N | 121.08 E |
| Luyi | 100 | 33.53 N | 115.28 E |
| Luynes | 50 | 47.23 N | 0.33 E |
| Luyu | 106 | 31.34 N | 121.41 E |
| Luyuan, Zhg. | 106 | 31.51 N | 120.38 E |
| Luyuan, Zhg. | 271a | 39.54 N | 116.27 E |
| Luz, Bra. | 255 | 19.48 S | 45.40 W |

| | | | |
|---|---|---|---|
| Luz, Bra. | 287a | 22.48 S | 43.05 W |
| Luz ✦[8] | 266c | 38.46 N | 9.10 W |
| Luz, Estação da ✦[5] | 287b | 23.32 S | 46.38 W |
| Luz, Isla I | 254 | 45.30 S | 73.59 W |
| Luz, Ponta da > | 287a | 22.47 S | 43.05 W |
| Luza, Ross. | 24 | 62.42 N | 37.06 E |
| Luza, Ross. | 24 | 60.39 N | 47.10 E |
| Luža, Ross. | 76 | 59.58 N | 31.56 E |
| Luža ≃ | 82 | 55.03 N | 36.35 E |
| Luzarches | 50 | 49.07 N | 2.25 E |
| Luzern | 58 | 47.03 N | 8.18 E |
| Luzern □[3] | 58 | 47.05 N | 8.05 E |
| Luzerne | 210 | 41.17 N | 75.54 W |
| Luzerne □[6] | 210 | 41.14 N | 75.53 W |
| Luzhai, Zhg. | 102 | 24.31 N | 109.50 E |
| Luzhai, Zhg. | 269b | 31.20 N | 121.22 E |
| Luzhi | 106 | 31.16 N | 120.52 E |
| Luzhou | 107 | 28.54 N | 105.27 E |
| Luziânia | 255 | 16.15 S | 47.56 W |
| Lužické hory ∧∧ | 54 | 50.48 N | 14.40 E |
| Luzilândia | 250 | 3.28 S | 42.22 W |
| Lužki, Bela. | 76 | 55.21 N | 27.52 E |
| Lužki, Ross. | 82 | 54.51 N | 37.36 E |
| Lužná | 54 | 50.06 N | 13.45 E |
| Lužnice ≃ | 30 | 49.14 N | 14.23 E |
| Lužniki ✦[8] | 265b | 55.43 N | 37.33 E |
| Luzon I | 116 | 16.00 N | 121.00 E |
| Luzon Strait ɰ | 108 | 20.30 N | 121.00 E |
| Lužskaja guba c | 76 | 59.45 N | 28.20 E |
| Luzy | 32 | 46.48 N | 3.58 E |
| Luzzara | 64 | 44.58 N | 10.41 E |
| Luzzi | 68 | 39.27 N | 16.17 E |
| L'va ≃ | 78 | 52.00 N | 27.36 E |
| L'va Tolstogo | 82 | 54.37 N | 36.03 E |
| L'viv | 78 | 49.50 N | 24.00 E |
| L'viv □[4] | 78 | 49.30 N | 24.00 E |
| Lvov → L'viv | 78 | 49.50 N | 24.00 E |
| L'vovskij | 82 | 55.19 N | 37.31 E |
| Lwów → L'viv | 78 | 49.50 N | 24.00 E |
| Lwówek | 30 | 52.28 N | 16.10 E |
| Lwówek Śląski | 30 | 51.07 N | 15.35 E |
| Lyadova ≃ | 78 | 48.28 N | 27.37 E |
| Lyall, Mount ∧ | 172 | 45.17 S | 167.34 E |
| Lyallpur → Faisalabad | 123 | 31.25 N | 73.05 E |
| Lyantonde | 154 | 0.24 S | 31.09 E |
| Lyashchivka | 78 | 49.33 N | 32.41 E |
| Lybster | 46 | 58.18 N | 3.18 W |
| Lycaonia □[9] | 130 | 37.50 N | 33.15 E |
| Lychen | 54 | 53.12 N | 13.19 E |
| Lychkove | 78 | 49.06 N | 35.12 E |
| Lycia □[9] | 130 | 36.20 N | 30.00 E |
| Lyck → Ełk | 30 | 53.50 N | 22.22 E |
| Lyckeby | 26 | 56.12 N | 15.39 E |
| Lyčkovo | 76 | 57.55 N | 32.24 E |
| Lycksele | 26 | 64.36 N | 18.40 E |
| Lycoming □[6] | 210 | 41.14 N | 77.00 W |
| Lycoming Creek ≃ | 210 | 41.13 N | 77.02 W |
| Lydd | 42 | 50.57 N | 0.55 E |
| Lydda → Lod | 132 | 31.58 N | 34.54 E |
| Lydden ≃ | 42 | 50.56 N | 2.22 W |
| Lydenburg | 156 | 25.10 S | 30.29 E |
| Lydenburgh County Park ♠ | 276 | 40.50 N | 73.14 W |
| Lydford | 42 | 50.39 N | 4.06 W |
| Lydgate | 262 | 53.44 N | 2.07 W |
| Lydham | 42 | 52.31 N | 2.58 W |
| Lydia □[9] | 130 | 38.40 N | 27.30 E |
| Lydia Mills | 192 | 34.28 N | 81.55 W |
| Lydiate | 262 | 53.32 N | 2.57 W |
| Lydick | 216 | 41.42 N | 86.22 W |
| Lydney | 42 | 51.44 N | 2.32 W |
| Lye Green | 260 | 51.43 N | 0.35 W |
| Lyell, Mount ∧, Can. | 182 | 51.57 N | 117.06 W |
| Lyell, Mount ∧, Ca., U.S. | 226 | 37.44 N | 119.16 W |
| Lyell Brown, Mount ∧ | 162 | 23.21 S | 130.24 E |
| Lyell Island I | 182 | 52.40 N | 131.30 W |
| Lyerly | 192 | 34.24 N | 85.24 W |
| Lyford | 196 | 26.24 N | 97.47 W |
| Lygnern ⊜ | 26 | 57.29 N | 12.20 E |
| Lyhivka | 78 | 49.08 N | 36.03 E |
| Lykens | 208 | 40.34 N | 76.42 W |
| Lykhivka | 78 | 48.41 N | 33.55 E |
| Lykošino | 76 | 58.07 N | 33.43 E |
| Lyle, Mn., U.S. | 190 | 43.30 N | 92.56 W |
| Lyle, Wa., U.S. | 224 | 45.41 N | 121.17 W |
| Lyles | 194 | 35.55 N | 87.20 W |
| Lyman, Ukr. | 78 | 49.36 N | 36.27 E |
| Lyman, Ukr. | 78 | 45.41 N | 29.45 E |
| Lyman, Ukr. | 83 | 49.21 N | 38.57 E |
| Lyman, Ne., U.S. | 198 | 41.55 N | 104.02 W |
| Lyman, S.C., U.S. | 192 | 34.56 N | 82.07 W |
| Lyman, Wa., U.S. | 224 | 48.31 N | 122.03 W |
| Lyman, Wy., U.S. | 200 | 41.19 N | 110.17 W |
| Lymans'ke | 78 | 46.38 N | 30.00 E |
| Lymbel'karamo | 86 | 60.15 N | 83.32 E |
| Lyme | 207 | 41.18 N | 72.19 W |
| Lyme Bay c | 42 | 50.38 N | 3.00 W |
| Lyme Hall ⊥ | 262 | 53.20 N | 2.03 W |
| Lyme Park ♠ | 262 | 53.21 N | 2.04 W |
| Lyme Regis | 42 | 50.44 N | 2.57 W |
| Lyminge | 42 | 51.08 N | 1.05 E |
| Lymington | 42 | 50.46 N | 1.33 W |
| Lymkoj | 86 | 59.31 N | 70.22 E |
| Lymm | 262 | 53.23 N | 2.29 W |
| Lympne | 42 | 51.05 N | 1.02 E |
| Lympstone | 42 | 50.39 N | 3.25 W |
| Lymyshivka | 78 | 52.04 N | 31.38 E |
| Lyn | 212 | 44.35 N | 75.47 W |
| Łyna (Lava) ≃ | 76 | 54.37 N | 21.14 E |
| Lynæs | 41 | 55.57 N | 11.52 E |
| Lynbrook | 276 | 40.39 N | 73.41 W |
| Lynch, Ky., U.S. | 192 | 36.57 N | 82.55 W |
| Lynch, Ne., U.S. | 198 | 42.49 N | 98.27 W |
| Lynch, Lac ⊜ | 190 | 46.25 N | 77.05 W |
| Lynchburg, Oh., U.S. | 218 | 39.14 N | 83.47 W |
| Lynchburg, S.C., U.S. | 192 | 34.03 N | 80.04 W |
| Lynchburg, Tn., U.S. | 194 | 35.16 N | 86.22 W |
| Lynchburg, Va., U.S. | 192 | 37.24 N | 79.08 W |
| Lynches ≃ | 192 | 33.50 N | 79.22 W |
| Lynchville | 214 | 41.26 N | 78.34 W |
| Lynd ≃ | 164 | 16.28 S | 143.18 E |
| Lynde Creek ≃ | 212 | 43.51 N | 78.57 W |
| Lynden, On., Can. | 212 | 43.14 N | 80.09 W |
| Lynden, Wa., U.S. | 224 | 48.56 N | 122.27 W |
| Lyndhurst, Austl. | 166 | 19.12 S | 144.23 E |
| Lyndhurst, Austl. | 166 | 30.17 S | 138.21 E |
| Lyndhurst, Austl. | 274b | 38.03 S | 145.15 E |
| Lyndhurst, Eng., U.K. | 42 | 50.52 N | 1.34 W |
| Lyndhurst, N.J., U.S. | 276 | 40.48 N | 74.07 W |
| Lyndhurst, Oh., U.S. | 214 | 41.31 N | 81.29 W |
| Lyndoch | 168b | 34.37 S | 138.53 E |
| Lyndon, Austl. | 162 | 23.37 S | 115.15 E |
| Lyndon, Ks., U.S. | 198 | 38.38 N | 95.41 W |
| Lyndon, Ky., U.S. | 218 | 38.15 N | 85.36 W |
| Lyndon ≃ | 162 | 23.29 S | 114.06 E |
| Lyndon B. Johnson, Lake ⊜[1] | 196 | 30.35 N | 98.25 W |
| Lyndon B. Johnson Historical Park ♠ | 196 | 30.15 N | 98.38 W |
| Lyndon B. Johnson Space Center ❦[3] | 222 | 29.34 N | 95.05 W |
| Lyndonville, N.Y., U.S. | 210 | 43.19 N | 78.23 W |
| Lyndonville, Vt., U.S. | 188 | 44.32 N | 72.00 W |
| Lyndora | 214 | 40.51 N | 79.55 W |
| Lyne | 260 | 51.23 N | 0.33 W |
| Lyne ≃, Eng., U.K. | 44 | 54.58 N | 3.01 W |
| Lyne ≃, Eng., U.K. | 44 | 55.12 N | 1.31 W |
| Lyneham | 42 | 51.31 N | 1.58 W |
| Lynemouth | 44 | 55.12 N | 1.31 W |
| Lyne Water ≃ | 46 | 55.39 N | 3.16 W |
| Lynga | 80 | 57.17 N | 53.04 E |
| Lyngdal | 26 | 58.08 N | 7.05 E |

| | | | |
|---|---|---|---|
| Lynge | 41 | 55.51 N | 12.17 E |
| Lyngen | 24 | 69.34 N | 20.10 E |
| Lyngen c[2] | 24 | 69.58 N | 20.30 E |
| Lyngør | 26 | 58.38 N | 9.10 E |
| Lynher ≃ | 42 | 50.28 N | 4.12 W |
| Lynmouth | 42 | 51.15 N | 3.50 W |
| Lynn, Al., U.S. | 194 | 34.02 N | 87.32 W |
| Lynn, In., U.S. | 218 | 40.02 N | 84.56 W |
| Lynn, Ma., U.S. | 207 | 42.28 N | 70.57 W |
| Lynn ≃ | 212 | 42.47 N | 80.12 W |
| Lynn Canal c | 180 | 58.50 N | 135.15 W |
| Lynndyl | 200 | 39.31 N | 112.22 W |
| Lynne Acres | 284b | 39.21 N | 76.45 W |
| Lynnfield | 207 | 42.32 N | 71.02 W |
| Lynn Garden | 192 | 36.34 N | 82.34 W |
| Lynn Harbor c | 283 | 42.27 N | 70.57 W |
| Lynn Haven | 194 | 30.14 N | 85.38 W |
| Lynn Lake | 184 | 56.51 N | 101.03 W |
| Lynnville | 190 | 41.34 N | 92.47 W |
| Lynnwood, Pa., U.S. | 210 | 41.14 N | 75.56 W |
| Lynnwood, Pa., U.S. | 214 | 40.07 N | 79.51 W |
| Lynnwood, Wa., U.S. | 224 | 47.49 N | 122.18 W |
| Lynn Woods ♠ | 283 | 42.29 N | 70.59 W |
| Lynovytsya | 78 | 50.28 N | 32.22 E |
| Lynton | 42 | 51.15 N | 3.50 W |
| Lyntupy | 76 | 55.03 N | 26.19 E |
| Lynwood, Ca., U.S. | 228 | 33.55 N | 118.12 W |
| Lynwood, Il., U.S. | 278 | 41.32 N | 87.32 W |
| Lynx Lake ⊜ | 176 | 62.25 N | 106.15 W |
| Lyø I | 41 | 55.02 N | 10.10 E |
| Lyon | 62 | 45.45 N | 4.51 E |
| Lyon □[6] | 226 | 39.00 N | 119.15 W |
| Lyon ≃ | 46 | 56.37 N | 4.01 W |
| Lyon, Gare ✦[5] | 261 | 48.51 N | 2.23 E |
| Lyon, Glen V | 46 | 56.35 N | 4.20 W |
| Lyon, Loch ⊜ | 46 | 56.32 N | 4.36 W |
| Lyon Inlet c | 176 | 66.32 N | 83.53 W |
| Lyon Mountain | 188 | 44.43 N | 73.54 W |
| Lyon Mountain ∧ | 188 | 44.41 N | 73.53 W |
| Lyonnais □[9] | 62 | 45.45 N | 4.30 E |
| Lyonnais, Monts du ∧∧ | 62 | 45.40 N | 4.30 E |
| Lyons, Co., U.S. | 200 | 40.13 N | 105.16 W |
| Lyons, Ga., U.S. | 192 | 32.12 N | 82.19 W |
| Lyons, Il., U.S. | 216 | 41.48 N | 87.49 W |
| Lyons, In., U.S. | 194 | 38.59 N | 87.04 W |
| Lyons, Ks., U.S. | 198 | 38.20 N | 98.12 W |
| Lyons, Mi., U.S. | 216 | 42.58 N | 84.56 W |
| Lyons, Ne., U.S. | 198 | 41.56 N | 96.28 W |
| Lyons, N.Y., U.S. | 210 | 43.03 N | 76.59 W |
| Lyons, Oh., U.S. | 216 | 41.41 N | 84.04 W |
| Lyons, Tx., U.S. | 222 | 30.23 N | 96.34 W |
| Lyons, Wi., U.S. | 216 | 42.39 N | 88.21 W |
| Lyons ≃ | 162 | 25.02 S | 115.09 E |
| Lyon-Satolas, Aéroport de ⊠ | 62 | 45.43 N | 5.04 E |
| Lyons Creek ≃ | 284a | 43.03 N | 79.04 W |
| Lyons Falls | 212 | 43.37 N | 75.22 W |
| Lyons-la-Forêt | 50 | 49.24 N | 1.28 E |
| Lyons Plains | 207 | 41.13 N | 73.21 W |
| Lyons Run ≃ | 279b | 40.25 N | 79.43 W |
| Lyon Station | 208 | 40.28 N | 75.45 W |
| Lyonsville | 276 | 40.57 N | 74.25 W |
| Lypets'ke Druhe | 78 | 47.46 N | 29.41 E |
| Lypova Dolyna | 78 | 50.35 N | 33.48 E |
| Lypovets' | 78 | 49.14 N | 29.03 E |
| Lyptsi | 78 | 50.13 N | 36.25 E |
| Lyracrumpane | 48 | 52.20 N | 9.30 W |
| Lyrestad | 40 | 58.48 N | 14.04 E |
| Lys (Leie) ≃, Europe | 50 | 51.03 N | 3.43 E |
| Lys ≃, It. | 62 | 45.36 N | 7.47 E |
| Lysá ∧ | 60 | 49.29 N | 12.42 E |
| Lysa Hora | 78 | 48.11 N | 31.06 E |
| Lysaker | 26 | 59.54 N | 10.36 E |
| Lysá pod Makytou | 30 | 49.12 N | 18.13 E |
| Lysefjorden c[2] | 26 | 59.00 N | 6.14 E |
| Lysekil | 26 | 58.16 N | 11.26 E |
| Lysets' | 78 | 48.52 N | 24.36 E |
| Lyshnivka | 78 | 51.28 N | 25.25 E |
| Łysica ∧ | 30 | 50.54 N | 20.55 E |
| Lysina ∧ | 60 | 50.02 N | 12.37 E |
| Lysjön ⊜ | 40 | 60.07 N | 14.18 E |
| Lyskovo | 80 | 56.04 N | 45.02 E |
| Lysogorka | 83 | 47.42 N | 39.12 E |
| Lyss | 58 | 47.04 N | 7.18 E |
| Lysterfield | 274b | 37.56 S | 145.18 E |
| Lysterfield ∧[2] | 274b | 37.56 S | 145.16 E |
| Lysterfield Reservoir ⊜[1] | 274b | 37.58 S | 145.18 E |
| Lyster Station | 206 | 46.22 N | 71.37 W |
| Lys'va | 86 | 58.07 N | 57.47 E |
| Lys'va ≃ | 80 | 58.15 N | 54.47 E |
| Lysyanka | 78 | 49.16 N | 30.50 E |
| Lysychans'k | 83 | 48.55 N | 38.26 E |
| Lysyje Gory | 80 | 51.32 N | 44.46 E |
| Lytham Saint Anne's | 44 | 53.45 N | 2.57 W |
| Lytkarino | 82 | 55.35 N | 37.54 E |
| Lytle | 196 | 29.13 N | 98.47 W |
| Lytle Creek ≃ | 228 | 34.09 N | 117.23 W |
| Lyttelton, N.Z. | 172 | 43.35 S | 172.42 E |
| Lyttelton, S. Afr. | 158 | 25.50 S | 28.11 E |
| Lytton | 182 | 50.14 N | 121.34 W |
| Lytton Springs | 222 | 30.00 N | 97.37 W |
| Lytvynivka | 83 | 49.18 N | 39.27 E |
| Lyubar | 78 | 49.55 N | 27.44 E |
| Lyubashivka | 78 | 47.51 N | 30.15 E |
| Lyubech | 78 | 51.42 N | 30.39 E |
| Lyubertsy → L'ubercy | 82 | 55.41 N | 37.53 E |
| Lyubeshiv | 78 | 51.46 N | 25.31 E |
| Lyuboml' | 78 | 51.14 N | 24.01 E |
| Lyubotyn | 78 | 49.57 N | 35.57 E |
| Lyubymivka | 78 | 46.47 N | 33.34 E |
| Lyuten'ka | 78 | 50.13 N | 34.02 E |
| Lyzyne | 83 | 49.33 N | 38.51 E |

## M

| | | | |
|---|---|---|---|
| Ma ≃ | 110 | 19.47 N | 105.56 E |
| Ma, Oued el V, Alg. | 148 | 27.45 N | 7.45 W |
| Ma, Oued el V, Maur. | 148 | 24.03 N | 9.10 W |
| Maadid, Djebel ∧ | 34 | 35.52 N | 4.46 E |
| Maalaea Bay c | 229a | 20.47 N | 156.29 W |
| Ma'alot-Tarshiḥa | 132 | 33.01 N | 35.17 E |
| Maam Cross | 48 | 53.27 N | 9.31 W |
| Ma'ān | 132 | 30.12 N | 35.44 E |
| Ma'ān □[8] | 132 | 30.20 N | 36.30 E |
| Maaninka | 26 | 63.09 N | 27.18 E |
| Ma'anshan, Zhg. | 100 | 31.42 N | 118.30 E |
| Maanshan, Zhg. | 107 | 29.52 N | 104.59 E |
| Ma-ao | 116 | 10.29 N | 122.59 E |
| Maap I | 174q | 9.35 N | 138.11 E |
| Maar | 140 | 6.54 N | 31.33 E |
| Maardu | 76 | 59.28 N | 25.02 E |
| Maarianhamina → Mariehamn | 26 | 60.06 N | 19.57 E |
| Ma'āriк, Qārat al- ∧[2] | 142 | 29.59 N | 30.52 E |
| Ma'arrat an-Nu'mān | 130 | 35.38 N | 36.40 E |
| Ma'arrat Miṣrīn | 130 | 36.01 N | 36.40 E |
| Ma'arrat Ṣaydnāyā | 132 | 33.41 N | 36.23 E |
| Maarssen | 52 | 52.08 N | 5.08 E |
| Maas | 48 | 54.50 N | 8.22 W |
| Maas (Meuse) ≃ | 30 | 51.49 N | 5.01 E |
| Maasbracht | 52 | 51.08 N | 5.53 E |
| Maasdam | 52 | 51.47 N | 4.32 E |
| Maaseik | 56 | 51.06 N | 5.48 E |
| Maasholm | 41 | 54.41 N | 9.59 E |
| Maasin | 116 | 10.08 N | 124.50 E |
| Maasmechelen | 56 | 50.58 N | 5.42 E |
| Maasniel | 52 | 51.13 N | 6.01 E |
| Maassluis | 52 | 51.55 N | 4.15 E |
| Maastricht | 56 | 50.52 N | 5.43 E |
| Maave | 156 | 21.03 S | 34.47 E |
| Ma-ayon ≃ | 116 | 11.25 N | 122.46 E |
| Maba | 100 | 32.59 N | 118.48 E |
| Maba, Ouadi V | 146 | 15.10 N | 21.00 E |
| Mababe Depression ±[7] | 156 | 18.50 S | 24.15 E |

| | | | | | |
|---|---|---|---|---|---|
| ≃ | River | Fluß | Río | Rivière | Rio |
| ≅ | Canal | Kanal | Canal | Canal | Canal |
| ʟ | Waterfall, Rapids | Wasserfall, Stromschnellen | Cascada, Rápidos | Chute d'eau, Rapides | Cascata, Rápidos |
| ɰ | Strait | Meeresstraße | Estrecho | Détroit | Estreito |
| c | Bay, Gulf | Bucht, Golf | Bahía, Golfo | Baie, Golfe | Baía, Golfo |
| ⊜ | Lake, Lakes | See, Seen | Lago, Lagos | Lac, Lacs | Lago, Lagos |
| ≋ | Swamp | Sumpf | Pantano | Marais | Pântano |
| ⩍ | Ice Features, Glacier | Eis- und Gletscherformen | Accidentes Glaciales | Formes glaciaires | Acidentes glaciares |
| ᵳ | Other Hydrographic Features | Andere Hydrographische Objekte | Otros Elementos Hidrográficos | Autres données hydrographiques | Outros acidentes hidrográficos |

| | | | | | |
|---|---|---|---|---|---|
| ✢ | Submarine Features | Untermeerische Objekte | Accidentes Submarinos | Formes de relief sous-marin | Acidentes submarinos |
| □ | Political Unit | Politische Einheit | Unidad Politica | Entité politique | Unidade política |
| ❦ | Cultural Institution | Kulturelle Institution | Institución Cultural | Institution culturelle | Instituição cultural |
| ⊥ | Historical Site | Historische Stätte | Sitio Histórico | Site historique | Sitio histórico |
| ♠ | Recreational Site | Erholungs- und Ferienort | Sitio de Recreo | Centre de loisirs | Area de Lazer |
| ⊠ | Airport | Flughafen | Aeropuerto | Aéroport | Aeroporto |
| ■ | Military Installation | Militäranlage | Instalación Militar | Installation militaire | Instalação militar |
| ✦ | Miscellaneous | Verschiedenes | Misceláneo | Divers | Diversos |

ENGLISH: Name · Page · Lat.°′ · Long.°′ — DEUTSCH: Name · Seite · Breite°′ · Länge°′ E = Ost


Mabaduan 164 9.16 S 142.44 E
Mabaho, Mount ∧ 116 9.15 N 125.42 E
Mabaia 152 7.13 S 14.03 E
Mabalacat 116 15.14 N 120.34 E
Mabalane 156 23.37 S 32.31 E
Mabana 224 48.05 N 122.24 W
Mabanga 152 1.30 N 19.06 E
Mabank 222 32.21 N 96.06 W
Mabaoquan 105 40.09 N 115.53 E
Ma'barot 132 32.22 N 34.54 E
Mabaruma 246 8.12 N 59.47 W
Mabashi 268 35.49 N 139.55 E
Mabau 112 2.14 S 111.54 E
Mabay 240p 20.16 N 76.40 W
Mabber, Ras › 144 9.28 N 50.50 E
Mabel Creek 162 29.01 S 134.17 E
Mabeleapodi 156 20.58 S 22.36 E
Mabel Lake ⊜ 182 50.35 N 118.44 W
Maben 194 33.33 N 89.05 W
Mabenga-Cité 152 3.39 S 18.40 E
Mabenge 152 4.14 N 24.09 E
Maberry, Loch ⊜ 44 55.02 N 4.41 W
Mabeti ≃ 92 40.31 N 141.31 E
Mabeul 36 36.27 N 10.46 E
Mabi, Nihon 96 34.38 N 133.41 E
Mabi, Zhg. 100 26.21 N 119.36 E
Mabi, Zhg. 102 35.59 N 112.15 E
Mabian 107 28.48 N 103.41 E
Mabian ≃ 107 29.08 N 103.58 E
Mablethorpe 44 53.21 N 0.15 E
Mableton 192 33.49 N 84.34 W
Mabole ≃ 150 9.01 N 12.44 W
Maboma 154 2.32 N 28.13 E
Mabonto 150 8.52 N 11.49 W
Mabote 156 22.03 S 34.09 E
Mabou 186 46.05 N 61.22 W
Mabrak, Jabal ∧ 132 30.13 N 35.29 E
Mabrous ⊤[4] 146 21.13 N 13.38 E
Mabrūk, Lībiyā 146 29.50 N 17.10 E
Mabrūk, Sūd. 140 8.07 N 29.25 E
Mabton 202 46.12 N 119.59 W
Mabuasehube Game Reserve ⬥[4] 156 25.10 S 22.10 E
Mabuguai 100 29.49 N 112.42 E
Mabuki 154 2.59 S 33.11 E
Mabuni 174m 26.05 N 127.43 E
Mabwe 154 8.39 S 26.31 E
Mača, Ross. 74 59.54 N 117.35 E
Maca, Ven. 286c 10.28 N 66.48 W
Maca, Cerro ∧ 254 45.06 S 73.12 W
Macachín 252 37.09 S 63.39 W
Macaco, Morro do ∧[2] 287a 22.56 S 43.07 W
Macacos, Ilha dos I 250 1.20 S 50.35 W
Macacu ≃ 256 22.42 S 43.02 W
Macaé 255 22.23 S 41.47 W
Macaíba 250 5.51 S 35.21 W
Macajalar Bay ⊂ 116 8.37 N 124.38 E
Macajuba 255 12.09 S 40.22 W
Macalaya 116 12.53 N 123.46 E
Macalelon 116 13.45 N 122.08 E
Macalister 182 52.27 N 122.24 W
Macalister ≃ 166 38.02 S 146.59 E
Macalister, Mount ∧ 170 34.27 S 149.45 E
Macallum Lake ⊜ 184 55.02 N 108.25 W
Macaloge 154 12.25 S 35.25 E
MacAlpine Lake ⊜ 176 66.40 N 103.15 W
Macamic, Lac ⊜ 190 48.48 N 78.59 W
Macan, Kepulauan II 112 7.00 S 121.00 E
Macao → Macau, Macau 100 22.14 N 113.35 E
Macão, Port. 34 39.33 N 8.00 W
Macao → Macau □[2] 100 22.10 N 113.33 E
Macapá 250 0.02 N 51.03 W
Macará 246 4.23 S 79.57 W
Macarani 255 15.33 S 40.24 W
Macarao 286c 10.26 N 67.02 W
Macarao ≃ 286c 10.26 N 67.01 W
Macareo, Caño ≃[1] 246 9.47 N 61.37 W
Macari ≃ 250 1.52 N 50.31 W
MacArthur, Pil. 116 10.50 N 125.00 E
MacArthur, Il., U.S. 278 41.39 N 87.44 W
Macas 246 2.19 S 78.07 W
Macatawa ≃ 216 42.48 N 86.05 W
Macatawa, Lake ⊂ 216 42.47 N 86.10 W
Macaterick, Loch ⊜ 44 55.12 N 4.26 W
Macau, Bra. 250 5.07 S 36.38 W
Macau (Aomen), Macau 100 22.14 N 113.35 E
Macau □[2], Asia 90 22.10 N 113.33 E
Macau □[2], Asia 100 22.10 N 113.33 E
Macau, Ilha I 156 20.55 S 35.05 E
Macauã ≃ 248 9.13 S 68.44 W
Macaúbas 255 13.02 S 42.42 W
Macaya, Pic ∧ 238 18.25 N 74.00 W
Macaza ≃ 206 46.21 N 74.47 W
Maccarese ⬥[8] 267a 41.53 N 12.13 E
Maccarese, Bonifica di ⬥[1] 267a 41.51 N 12.13 E
Macchiagodena 66 41.33 N 14.24 E
MacClenny 192 30.16 N 82.07 W
Macclesfield, Austl. 168b 35.10 S 138.50 E
Macclesfield, Eng., U.K. 44 53.16 N 2.07 W
Macclesfield □[8] 262 53.17 N 2.15 W
Macclesfield Canal ≊ 262 53.24 N 2.03 W
Macclesfield Forest ⬥[3] 262 53.15 N 2.03 W
Macdhui, Ben ∧ 158 30.39 S 27.58 E
MacDill Air Force Base ■ 220 27.51 N 82.29 W
Macdonald ≃ 170 33.23 S 150.59 E
Macdonald, Lake ⊜ 162 23.30 S 129.00 E
MacDonald Downs 162 22.27 S 135.13 E
Macdonald Lake ⊜ 212 45.14 N 78.34 W
MacDonald Pass )( 202 46.34 N 112.18 W
Macdonald Range ⋏ 182 49.12 N 114.46 W
MacDonnell Ranges ⋏ 162 23.45 S 133.20 E
Macdonnel Peninsula ›[1] 168b 35.47 S 138.00 E
MacDowell Lake ⊜ 184 52.15 N 92.45 W
Macduff 46 57.40 N 2.29 W
Macdui, Ben ∧ 46 57.05 N 3.38 W
Mačecha 80 50.48 N 43.17 E
Maceday Lake ⊜ 281 42.42 N 83.26 W
Macedo de Cavaleiros 34 41.32 N 6.58 W
Macedon, Austl. 169 37.25 S 144.34 E
Macedon, N.Y., U.S. 210 43.04 N 77.17 W
Macedonia, Ct., U.S. 207 41.47 N 73.30 W
Macedonia, Oh., U.S. 214 41.18 N 81.30 W
Macedonia □[9] 38 41.00 N 23.00 E
Macedonia □[1], Europe 22 41.50 N 22.00 E
Macedonia (Makedonija) □[1], Europe 38 41.50 N 22.00 E
Macedonia Brook State Park ♠ 207 41.47 N 73.29 W
Maceió 250 9.40 S 35.43 W
Maceira 266c 38.52 N 9.19 W
Macenta 150 8.33 N 9.28 W
Maceo 246 6.33 N 74.47 W
Macerata 66 43.18 N 13.27 E
Macerata □[4] 66 43.12 N 13.10 E
Macerata Feltria 66 43.48 N 12.26 E
MacFarlane ≃ 176 59.12 N 107.58 W
Macfarlane, Lake ⊜ 166 31.55 S 136.42 E
Macfarlane, Mount ∧ 172 43.56 S 169.23 E
Macgillycuddy's Reeks ⋏ 48 51.55 N 9.45 W
MacGregor 184 49.57 N 98.49 W
Machacamarca 248 18.10 S 67.02 W
Machache ∧ 158 29.21 S 27.55 E
Machachi 246 0.30 S 78.34 W
Machačkala 84 42.58 N 47.30 E
Machada, Mata Nacional da ♠ 266c 38.36 N 9.02 W
Machadinho ≃ 248 9.00 S 61.52 W
Machado 256 21.41 S 45.56 W
Machado ≃, Bra. 248 8.03 S 62.52 W
Machado ≃, Bra. 256 21.38 S 45.52 W
Machadodorp 156 25.40 S 30.14 E
Machagai 252 26.56 S 60.03 W
Machaíla 156 22.15 S 32.55 E
Machakos 154 1.31 S 37.16 E
Machala 246 3.16 S 79.58 W
Machalí 252 34.11 S 70.40 W
Machalilla, Parque Nacional ♠ 246 1.30 S 80.45 W
Machalino 80 53.05 N 46.14 E
Māchalpur 124 24.08 N 76.18 E
Machaneng 156 23.10 S 27.26 E
Machang, Malay. 114 5.46 N 102.13 E
Machang, Zhg. 98 34.06 N 119.02 E
Machang, Zhg. 98 42.05 N 119.42 E
Machanga 156 20.58 S 34.59 E
Machangcun 105 38.54 N 115.26 E
Machangfu 102 25.14 N 103.45 E
Machang Jianhe ≃ 105 39.00 N 117.40 E
Machaquilá ≃ 236 16.13 N 90.01 W
Machattie, Lake ⊜ 166 24.50 S 139.48 E
Machault 50 49.21 N 4.30 E
Machava 156 25.54 S 32.29 E
Machaze 156 20.51 S 33.26 E
Machecoul 32 47.00 N 1.50 W
Macheke 154 18.05 S 31.51 E
Machekhy 78 49.31 N 34.26 E
Machelen 50 50.55 N 4.26 E
Macheng 100 31.13 N 115.00 E
Macherio 266b 45.38 N 9.16 E
Māčherla 122 16.29 N 79.26 E
Machern 54 51.21 N 12.37 E
Machery 261 48.36 N 2.05 E
Machesna Mountain ∧ 226 35.17 N 120.14 W
Machesney Park 216 42.20 N 89.03 W
Māchhīwāra 123 30.55 N 76.12 E
Machhlīshahr 124 25.41 N 82.25 E
Machias, Me., U.S. 188 44.42 N 67.27 W
Machias, N.Y., U.S. 210 42.25 N 78.30 W
Machias ≃ 188 44.43 N 67.22 W
Machias Bay ⊂ 188 44.40 N 67.20 W
Machichi ≃ 184 57.03 N 92.06 W
Machico 148 32.42 N 16.46 W
Machida 94 35.32 N 139.27 E
Machile ≃ 154 17.26 S 25.02 E
Machilīpatnam (Bandar) 122 16.10 N 81.08 E
Machindžauri 84 41.40 N 41.43 E
Machiques 246 10.04 N 72.34 W
Machiya ≃ 94 35.01 N 136.42 E
Machkund ⊜[1] 122 18.26 N 82.35 E
Machmud-Mekteb 84 44.26 N 45.13 E
Machn'ovo 86 58.27 N 61.42 E
Macho, Arroyo del V 196 33.36 N 104.28 W
Machočen, porog ⌊ 88 57.23 N 121.29 E
Machona, Laguna ⊂ 234 18.20 N 93.40 W
Machrihanish 46 55.26 N 5.45 W
Machtaly 85 41.22 N 68.02 E
Machupicchu 248 13.07 S 72.34 W
Machupicchu ⊥ 248 13.07 S 72.34 W
Machupo ≃ 248 12.34 S 64.25 W
Machynlleth 42 52.35 N 3.51 W
Maciá, Arg. 252 32.10 S 59.23 W
Macia, Moç. 156 25.03 S 33.10 E
Maciel, Arroyo ≃, Ur. 258 33.42 S 57.59 W
Maciel, Arroyo ≃, Ur. 258 33.36 S 56.31 W
Măcin 38 45.15 N 28.08 E
Macina → Massina ⬥[1] 150 14.30 N 5.00 W
Macintyre ≃ 166 28.38 N 149.41 E
Maçka 130 40.48 N 39.38 E
Mačkassy 80 52.46 N 45.34 E
Mackay, Austl. 166 21.09 S 149.11 E
Mackay, Id., U.S. 202 43.54 N 113.36 W
MacKay ≃ 184 57.03 N 111.55 W
Mackay, Lake ⊜ 162 22.30 S 129.00 E
MacKay Lake ⊜ 176 63.55 N 110.25 W
Mackenrode 54 51.33 N 10.33 E
Mackenzie 246 6.00 N 58.17 W
Mackenzie ≃, Austl. 166 23.38 S 149.46 E
Mackenzie ≃, N.T., Can. 176 69.15 N 134.08 W
MacKenzie Bay ⊂, Ant. 9 68.20 S 71.15 E
Mackenzie Bay ⊂, Can. 180 69.00 N 136.30 W
Mackenzie Delta ≚[2] 180 68.50 N 135.25 W
Mackenzie Mountains ⋏ 180 64.00 N 130.00 W
Mackeyville 210 41.03 N 77.28 W
Mackinac, Straits of ʉ 190 45.49 N 84.42 W
Mackinac Bridge ⬥[5] 190 45.50 N 84.45 W
Mackinac Island 190 45.50 N 84.37 W
Mackinac Island I 190 45.51 N 84.38 W
Mackinac Island State Park ♠ 190 45.52 N 84.40 W
Mackinaw 190 40.32 N 89.21 W
Mackinaw ≃ 194 40.33 N 89.44 W
Mackinaw City 190 45.47 N 84.43 W
Mackinnon Road 154 3.44 S 39.03 E
Macklin 184 52.20 N 109.56 W
Mačkovci 61 46.47 N 16.09 E
M'ačkovo, Ross. 82 55.13 N 38.40 E
M'ačkovo, Ross. 82 56.21 N 39.03 E
Macksville, Austl. 166 30.43 S 152.55 E
Macksville, Ks., U.S. 198 38.57 N 98.58 W
Maclean 166 29.28 S 153.13 E
Macleantown 158 32.47 S 27.45 E
Maclear 158 31.02 S 28.23 E
Macleay ≃ 166 30.52 S 153.01 E
Macleod 274b 37.43 S 145.04 E
Macleod, Lake ⊜ 162 24.00 S 113.35 E
Maclovia Herrera 232 29.05 N 105.08 W
Macmillan ≃ 180 62.52 N 135.55 W
Macocolo 152 6.47 S 16.08 E
Macolin 58 47.09 N 7.14 E
Macolla, Punta › 241s 12.06 N 70.13 W
Macolo 152 7.05 S 16.48 E
Macomb 190 40.27 N 90.40 W
Macomb □[6] 214 42.40 N 82.54 W
Macomb Mall ⬥[9] 281 42.32 N 82.55 W
Macomer 71 40.16 N 8.47 E
Macomia 154 12.15 S 40.08 E
Macon, Bel. 50 50.03 N 4.13 E
Mâcon, Fr. 58 46.18 N 4.50 E
Macon, Ga., U.S. 192 32.50 N 83.37 W
Macon, Il., U.S. 219 39.42 N 88.59 W
Macon, Ms., U.S. 194 33.06 N 88.33 W
Macon, Mo., U.S. 194 39.44 N 92.28 W
Macon □[6], Il., U.S. 219 39.51 N 89.32 W
Macon □[6], Mo., U.S. 219 39.50 N 92.20 W
Macon, Bayou ≃ 194 31.55 N 91.33 W
Macon Creek ≃ 216 41.58 N 83.38 W
Macondo 152 12.35 S 23.44 E
Macondo ≃ 152 13.23 S 23.03 E
Mâconnais, Monts du ⋏ 58 46.18 N 4.45 E
Macorís, Cabo › 238 19.47 N 70.28 W
Macosquin 48 55.06 N 6.43 W
Macossa 156 17.52 S 33.56 E
Macouba, Pointe de › 240e 14.53 N 61.09 W
Macoun Lake ⊜ 184 56.32 N 103.50 W
Macoupin □[6] 219 39.17 N 89.53 W
Macoupin Creek ≃ 219 39.11 N 90.36 W
Macovane 156 21.28 S 35.04 E
Macpherson, Mount ∧[2] 162 21.49 S 121.35 E
Macquarie ≃, Austl. 166 41.44 S 147.08 E
Macquarie ≃, Austl. 166 30.07 S 147.24 E
Macquarie, Lake ⊜ 170 33.05 S 151.35 E
Macquarie Fields 274a 33.59 S 150.53 E
Macquarie Harbour ⊂ 166 42.19 S 145.23 E
Macquarie Island I 9 54.30 S 158.56 E
Macquarie Marshes ≋ 166 30.50 S 147.32 E
Macquarie Pass National Park ♠ 170 34.34 S 150.39 E
Macquarie Ridge ✦[3] 9 57.00 S 159.00 E
Macquarie University ✝[2] 274a 33.46 S 151.06 E
MacRitchie Reservoir ⊜[1] 271c 1.21 N 103.50 E
Mac. Robertson Land ⬥[1] 9 68.10 S 65.00 E
Macrohon 116 10.05 N 124.56 E
Macroom 48 51.54 N 8.57 W
Mactan Island I 116 10.18 N 123.58 E
MacTier 212 45.08 N 79.47 W
Macuco de Minas 256 21.46 S 44.47 W
Macucuau ≃ 246 0.37 S 61.24 W
Macuelizo 236 15.18 N 88.31 W
Macugnaga 58 45.58 N 7.58 E
Macujer 246 0.23 N 72.55 W
Macul 286e 33.30 S 70.34 W
Maculabo Island I 116 14.24 N 122.49 E
Macumba ≃ 162 27.52 S 137.12 E
Macungie 208 40.30 N 75.33 W
Macunqiao 100 33.50 N 116.13 E
Macuro 246 10.39 N 61.56 W
Macusani 248 14.05 S 70.26 W
Macuspana 234 17.46 N 92.36 W
Macusse 152 17.51 S 20.21 E
Macuto 286c 10.37 N 66.53 W
Macuze 156 17.42 S 37.11 E
Macy 216 40.57 N 86.07 W
Mad ≃, On., Can. 212 44.25 N 79.54 W
Mad ≃, Ca., U.S. 204 40.57 N 124.07 W
Mad ≃, N.Y., U.S. 212 43.20 N 75.44 W
Mad ≃, Oh., U.S. 188 39.46 N 84.11 W
Mad ≃, Vt., U.S. 188 44.18 N 72.41 W
Mada ≃ 150 7.59 N 7.55 E
Ma'dabā 132 31.43 N 35.48 E
Madagascar (Madagasikara) □[1], Afr. 138 19.00 S 46.00 E
Madagascar (Madagasikara) □[1], Afr. 157b 19.00 S 46.00 E
Madagascar Basin ✦[1] 12 27.00 S 53.00 E
Madagascar Plateau ✦[3] 10 30.00 S 45.00 E
Madagasikara → Madagascar □[1] 157b 19.00 S 46.00 E
Madagaskar → Madagascar □[1] 157b 19.00 S 46.00 E
Madagiz 84 40.19 N 46.44 E
Madagoi, Bohol V 144 0.44 N 42.56 E
Madā'in Şāliḥ 128 26.48 N 37.53 E
Madajevo 80 54.48 N 44.31 E
Madama 146 21.58 N 13.39 E
Madame, Isle I 186 45.33 N 61.02 W
Madan 38 41.30 N 24.57 E
Madanapalle 122 13.33 N 78.30 E
Madang, Pap. N. Gui. 164 5.15 S 145.50 E
Madang, Zhg. 100 29.58 N 116.40 E
Madang □[5] 164 5.00 S 145.30 E
Madanpur 272b 22.40 N 88.32 E
Madanpur Dabās ⬥[8] 272a 28.43 N 77.02 E
Madaoua 150 14.05 N 5.58 E
Mādār Gāng ≃[1] 126 22.12 N 89.04 E
Mādāri Hāt 124 26.42 N 89.17 E
Mādārīpur 124 23.10 N 90.12 E
Madarounfa 150 13.18 N 7.09 E
Mādārpur 272b 22.54 N 88.27 E
Madau Island I 164 8.58 S 152.28 E
Madawaska, On., Can. 212 45.30 N 77.59 W
Madawaska, Me., U.S. 186 47.21 N 68.19 W
Madawaska ≃ 212 45.27 N 76.21 W
Madawaska Highlands ⋏[1] 212 45.15 N 77.35 W
Madawaska Lake ⊜ 212 45.20 N 78.23 W
Madaxmaroodi 144 2.39 N 44.36 E
Madaya, Mya. 110 22.13 N 96.07 E
Maḍāyā, Sūrīy. 132 33.41 N 36.06 E
Madbar 140 6.19 N 30.40 E
Mad Creek ≃ 210 42.55 N 77.59 W
Maddalena, Colle della (Col de Larche) )( 62 44.25 N 6.53 E
Maddalena, Isola I 71 41.14 N 9.25 E
Maddaloni 68 41.02 N 14.23 E
Maddela 116 16.21 N 121.41 E
Madden, Mount ∧ 162 33.12 S 119.51 E
Maddington 168a 32.03 S 115.59 E
Maddock 198 47.57 N 99.31 W
Maddy, Loch ⊂ 46 57.36 N 7.08 W
Made 52 51.41 N 4.46 E
Madeir 140 7.50 N 29.12 E
Madeira 218 39.11 N 84.21 W
Madeira I 148 32.44 N 17.00 W
Madeira ≃ 242 3.22 S 58.45 W
Madeira, Arquipélago da II 148 32.40 N 16.45 W
Madeira Beach 220 27.48 N 82.48 W
Madeirinha ≃ 248 8.31 S 60.46 W
Madeirinha, Paraná ≃[1] 246 3.25 S 58.51 W
Mädelegabel ∧ 58 47.18 N 10.18 E
Madeleine, Îles de la II 186 47.30 N 61.45 W
Madeleine, Pointe › 275a 45.27 N 73.57 W
Madeleine-Centre 186 49.15 N 65.21 W
Madeley, Eng., U.K. 42 52.59 N 2.20 W
Madeley, Eng., U.K. 42 52.39 N 2.28 W
Madelia 190 44.03 N 94.25 W
Madeline Island I 190 46.50 N 90.40 W
Maden, Tür. 130 38.23 N 39.40 E
Maden, Tür. 130 40.11 N 40.25 E
Madenijet 86 47.53 N 78.37 E
Madera, Méx. 232 29.12 N 108.07 W
Madera, Ca., U.S. 226 36.57 N 120.03 W
Madera, Pa., U.S. 214 40.49 N 78.26 W
Madera □[6] 226 37.15 N 119.45 W
Madera Canal ≊ 226 37.05 N 119.59 W
Madera Lake ⊜[1] 226 37.02 N 119.59 W
Madera Peak ∧ 226 37.32 N 119.23 W
Maderas, Islas → Madeira, Arquipélago da II 148 32.40 N 16.45 W
Maderas, Volcán ∧[1] 236 11.27 N 85.31 W
Maderno 64 45.38 N 10.35 E
Madgaon (Margao) 122 15.18 N 73.57 E
Madh ⬥[8] 272c 19.08 N 72.47 E
Madhepura 124 25.55 N 86.47 E
Madhkūr, Bi'r ⊤[4] 142 30.42 N 32.32 E
Mādhopur 123 32.22 N 75.36 E
Madhubani 124 26.22 N 86.05 E
Madhudaha 272b 22.31 N 88.25 E
Madhugiri 122 13.40 N 77.12 E
Madhumati ≃[1] 126 22.53 N 89.52 E
Madhupar 126 22.54 N 86.28 E
Madhupur 126 24.16 N 86.39 E
Madhya Bhārat Pathār ⬥[1] 124 25.00 N 77.00 E
Madhyamgrām 272b 22.42 N 88.27 E
Madhya Pradesh □[3] 118 23.00 N 79.00 E
Madia 154 7.08 S 26.00 E
Madian 106 32.15 N 119.58 E
Madibi 152 4.18 S 18.24 E
Madibira 154 8.12 S 34.49 E
Madibogo 158 26.25 S 25.10 E
Madida 98 42.57 N 130.48 E
Madidi ≃ 248 12.32 S 66.52 W
Madill 196 34.05 N 96.46 W
Madimba, Ang. 152 6.31 S 14.21 E
Madimba, Zaïre 152 4.58 S 15.08 E
Madina 150 13.24 N 8.51 W
Madina do Boé 150 11.45 N 14.13 W
Madinani 150 9.37 N 6.57 W
Madinat al-Abyār 146 32.11 N 20.36 E
Madīnat ash-Sha'b (Al-Ittihad) 144 12.50 N 44.56 E
Madīnat ath Thawrah 130 35.52 N 38.34 E
Madine, Lac de ⊜ 56 48.54 N 5.42 E
Madingo 152 4.07 S 11.22 E
Madingou 152 4.09 S 13.34 E
Madingzi 104 42.08 N 120.52 E
Madi Opei 154 3.37 N 33.05 E
Madirobe 157b 16.04 S 46.15 E
Madirovalo 157b 16.26 S 46.30 E
Madison, Al., U.S. 194 34.41 N 86.44 W
Madison, Ca., U.S. 226 38.41 N 121.58 W
Madison, Ct., U.S. 207 41.16 N 72.35 W
Madison, Fl., U.S. 192 30.28 N 83.24 W
Madison, Ga., U.S. 192 33.35 N 83.28 W
Madison, Il., U.S. 219 38.40 N 90.09 W
Madison, In., U.S. 218 38.44 N 85.22 W
Madison, Ks., U.S. 198 38.08 N 96.08 W
Madison, Me., U.S. 188 44.47 N 69.52 W
Madison, Md., U.S. 208 38.30 N 76.13 W
Madison, Mn., U.S. 198 45.00 N 96.11 W
Madison, Mo., U.S. 219 39.28 N 92.12 W
Madison, Ne., U.S. 198 41.49 N 97.27 W
Madison, N.J., U.S. 210 40.45 N 74.25 W
Madison, N.Y., U.S. 210 42.53 N 75.30 W
Madison, N.C., U.S. 192 36.23 N 79.57 W
Madison, Oh., U.S. 214 41.46 N 81.03 W
Madison, Pa., U.S. 279b 40.15 N 79.41 W
Madison, S.D., U.S. 198 44.00 N 97.06 W
Madison, Va., U.S. 188 38.22 N 78.15 W
Madison, W.V., U.S. 188 38.04 N 81.49 W
Madison, Wi., U.S. 216 43.04 N 89.24 W
Madison □[6], Il., U.S. 219 38.49 N 89.58 W
Madison □[6], In., U.S. 218 40.10 N 85.41 W
Madison □[6], N.Y., U.S. 210 43.05 N 75.42 W
Madison □[6], Oh., U.S. 218 39.53 N 83.27 W
Madison □[6], Tx., U.S. 222 30.58 N 95.55 W
Madison ≃ 202 45.56 N 111.30 W
Madison, West Fork ≃ 202 44.55 N 111.35 W
Madisonburg, Oh., U.S. 214 40.51 N 81.55 W
Madisonburg, Pa., U.S. 210 40.55 N 77.31 W
Madison Heights, Mi., U.S. 216 42.29 N 83.06 W
Madison Heights, Va., U.S. 192 37.25 N 79.07 W
Madison Mills 218 39.40 N 83.20 W
Madison-on-the-Lake 214 41.42 N 81.24 W
Madison Park 276 40.26 N 74.19 W
Madison Range ⋏ 202 45.15 N 111.20 W
Madison Square Garden ♠ 276 40.45 N 74.00 W
Madisonville, Ky., U.S. 194 37.19 N 87.29 W
Madisonville, La., U.S. 194 30.24 N 90.09 W
Madisonville, Tn., U.S. 192 35.31 N 84.21 W
Madisonville, Tx., U.S. 222 30.56 N 95.54 W
Madiun 115a 7.37 S 111.31 E
Madiun ≃ 115a 7.23 S 111.27 E
Madiyi 102 28.14 N 110.30 E
Madjingo 152 1.23 N 14.06 E
Madjoari 150 11.26 N 1.15 E
Madley, Mount ∧ 162 24.31 S 123.58 E
Madoc 212 44.30 N 77.28 W
Mado Gashi 154 0.44 N 39.10 E
Madoi 102 34.53 N 98.24 E
Madol 140 9.02 N 27.46 E
Madon ≃ 58 48.36 N 6.06 E
Madona 76 56.51 N 26.13 E
Madonie ⋏ 70 37.52 N 13.58 E
Madonna (Unserfrau) 64 46.43 N 10.52 E
Madonna della Guardia ✝[1] 62 44.29 N 8.51 E
Madonna della Quercia ✝[1] 66 42.25 N 12.06 E
Madonna dell'Olmo 62 44.25 N 7.32 E
Madonna del Sasso ✝[1] 58 46.11 N 8.33 E
Madonna di Campiglio 64 46.14 N 10.49 E
Madonna di Tirano 64 46.13 N 10.09 E
Madora 76 53.09 N 30.11 E
Madougou 150 14.24 N 3.05 W
Madrakah 144 21.59 N 39.59 E
Madrakah, Ra's al- › 118 19.00 N 57.50 E
Madras, India 118 13.05 N 80.17 E
Madras, India 122 13.05 N 80.17 E
Madras, Or., U.S. 202 44.38 N 121.07 W
Madras → Tamil Nādu □[3] 122 11.00 N 78.15 E
Madre, Laguna ⊂, Méx. 232 25.00 N 97.40 W
Madre, Laguna ⊂, Tx., U.S. 196 27.00 N 97.35 W
Madre, Sierra ⋏ 116 16.20 N 122.00 E
Madre de Chiapas, Sierra ⋏ 232 15.30 N 92.35 W
Madre de Deus de Minas 256 21.29 S 44.20 W
Madre de Dios □[5] 248 12.00 S 70.15 W
Madre de Dios ≃ 248 10.23 S 65.24 W
Madre de Dios, Isla I 254 50.15 S 75.05 W
Madre del Sur, Sierra ⋏ 234 17.00 N 100.00 W
Madre Occidental, Sierra ⋏ 232 25.00 N 105.00 W
Madre Oriental, Sierra ⋏ 232 22.00 N 99.30 W
Madre Vieja ≃ 236 14.01 N 91.26 W
Madrid, Col. 246 4.44 N 74.16 W
Madrid, Esp. 34 40.24 N 3.41 W
Madrid, Esp. 266a 40.24 N 3.41 W
Madrid, Pil. 116 9.15 N 126.00 E
Madrid, Al., U.S. 194 31.02 N 85.23 W
Madrid, Ia., U.S. 190 41.52 N 93.49 W
Madrid, Ne., U.S. 198 40.51 N 101.32 W
Madrid □[3] 34 40.30 N 3.40 W
Madridejos, Esp. 34 39.28 N 3.32 W
Madridejos, Pil. 116 11.18 N 123.44 E
Madrigalejo 34 39.09 N 5.37 W
Madrillon 284c 38.55 N 77.14 W
Madriz □[5] 236 13.30 N 86.30 W
Madroñera 34 39.26 N 5.46 W
Madruga 240p 22.55 N 81.51 W
Madrūsah 146 24.48 N 14.32 E
Madsen 184 50.58 N 93.55 W
Madsūs, Bi'r ⊤[4] 142 29.15 N 32.19 E
Maducang Island I 116 10.42 N 120.15 E
Maduda 152 4.55 S 13.06 E
Maduo 152 1.24 S 20.44 E
Madura, Austl. 162 31.55 S 127.00 E
Madura → Madurai, India 122 9.56 N 78.07 E
Madura I 115a 7.00 S 113.20 E
Madura, Selat ʉ 115a 7.25 S 113.25 E
Madurai 122 9.56 N 78.07 E
Madurāntakam 122 12.31 N 79.54 E
Madureira, Serra de ⋏ 287a 22.49 S 43.31 W
Maduru ≃ 122 7.52 N 81.31 E
Madwar al-Bighāl ∧[2] 142 29.09 N 29.54 E
Madžalis 84 42.08 N 47.50 E
Mãe, Ilha da I 287a 22.59 S 43.04 W
Maeander Reef ✦[2] 116 8.05 N 119.18 E
Maebaru 92 33.33 N 130.12 E
Maebashi 94 36.23 N 139.04 E
Maeda 270 34.55 N 135.08 E
Mãe dos Homens 256 22.52 S 46.37 W
Maegye-ri 98 34.45 N 126.18 E
Mae Hong Son 110 19.16 N 97.56 E
Mae Klong ≃ 110 13.21 N 100.00 E
Maenclochog 42 51.54 N 4.48 W
Maengsan 98 39.40 N 126.30 E
Maeno ⬥[8] 268 35.46 N 139.42 E
Maenza 66 41.31 N 13.11 E
Mae Ramat 110 16.58 N 98.31 E
Mae Rim 110 18.54 N 98.57 E
Maerkansu 85 39.19 N 73.53 E
Ma'erna 102 31.13 N 102.02 E
Maer Shan ∧ 102 26.18 N 100.20 E
Mae Sariang 110 18.10 N 97.56 E
Maeser 200 40.28 N 109.35 W
Mae Sot 110 16.43 N 98.34 E
Maesteg 42 51.37 N 3.40 W
Maestra, Sierra ⋏ 240p 20.00 N 76.45 W
Maestre de Campo Island I 116 12.56 N 121.42 E
Maestu 34 42.44 N 2.27 W
Mae Tha 110 18.28 N 99.08 E
Maevarano ≃ 157b 14.35 S 47.58 E
Maevatanana 157b 16.56 S 46.49 E
Maéwo I 175f 15.10 S 168.10 E
Ma'fan 146 25.55 N 14.29 E
Mafang 105 40.02 N 117.01 E
Mafangchang 107 29.24 N 106.06 E
Mafangcun 105 40.09 N 116.24 E
Ma Faro ✦[2] 122 5.50 N 73.26 E
Mafeking 184 52.41 N 101.06 W
Mafembage 152 14.32 S 21.42 E
Mafengtun 104 40.49 N 122.54 E
Mafeteng 158 29.51 S 27.15 E
Maffliers 261 49.05 N 2.19 E
Maffra 166 37.58 S 146.59 E
Mafia Channel ʉ 154 8.10 S 39.40 E
Mafia Island I 154 7.50 S 39.50 E
Mafikeng 156 25.53 S 25.39 E
Mafou ≃ 150 10.32 N 10.08 W
Mafra, Bra. 252 26.07 S 49.49 W
Mafra, Port. 34 38.56 N 9.20 W
Magadan 74 59.34 N 150.48 E
Magadi 154 1.54 S 36.17 E
Magadi, Lake ⊜ 154 1.52 S 36.17 E
Magaguadavic Lake ⊜ 186 45.43 N 67.12 W
Magai-butsu ✝[1] 96 33.05 N 131.45 E
Magalhães Bastos ⬥[8] 287a 22.53 S 43.23 W
Magalhães de Almeida 250 3.24 S 42.12 W
Magaliesberg ⋏ 158 25.50 S 27.30 E
Magallanes → Punta Arenas, Chile 254 53.09 S 70.55 W
Magallanes, Pil. 116 12.50 N 123.50 E
Magallanes, Estrecho de (Strait of Magellan) ʉ 254 54.00 S 71.00 W
Magallanes y de la Antártica Chilena □[4] 254 53.00 S 72.00 W
Maganga 154 0.51 N 26.22 E
Magangué 246 9.14 N 74.45 W
Magansk 88 55.52 N 93.15 E
Maganuy ≃ 116 6.55 N 124.30 E
Magara, India 126 22.34 N 87.34 E
Mağara, Tür. 130 36.43 N 33.52 E
Magaramkent 84 41.37 N 48.21 E
Magaria 150 13.00 N 8.54 E
Magat ≃ 116 17.02 N 121.49 E
Magazine Mountain ∧ 194 35.10 N 93.38 W
Magazzolo ≃ 70 37.25 N 13.15 E
Magboro 273a 6.43 N 3.24 E
Magburaka 150 8.43 N 11.57 W
Magdagači 89 53.27 N 125.48 E
Magdalena, Arg. 258 35.04 S 57.32 W
Magdalena, Bol. 248 13.20 S 64.08 W
Magdalena, Méx. 234 20.55 N 103.57 W
Magdalena, Perú 248 6.21 S 77.49 W
Magdalena, Perú 286d 12.06 S 77.05 W
Magdalena, N.M., U.S. 200 34.07 N 107.14 W
Magdalena □[5] 246 10.00 N 74.00 W
Magdalena ≃, Col. 246 11.06 N 74.51 W
Magdalena ≃, Méx. 232 30.48 N 112.32 W
Magdalena, Bahía ⊂ 232 24.35 N 112.00 W
Magdalena, Isla I, Chile 254 44.40 S 73.10 W
Magdalena, Isla I, Méx. 232 24.55 N 112.15 W
Magdalena, Punta › 246 3.56 N 77.21 W
Magdalena Contreras ⬥[8] 286a 19.18 N 99.17 W
Magdalena de Kino 232 30.38 N 110.57 W
Magdalena Peñasco 234 17.14 N 97.34 W
Magdalena Teitipac 234 16.54 N 96.34 W
Magdalena Tequisistlán 234 16.22 N 95.15 W
Magdalen Laver 260 51.45 N 0.11 E
Magdeburg 54 52.07 N 11.38 E
Magdeburger Börde ≚ 54 52.00 N 11.30 E
Magdeburgo → Magdeburg 54 52.07 N 11.38 E
Magdiwang 116 12.30 N 122.31 E
Magdonskij, porog ⌊ 88 57.45 N 100.55 E
Māge 110 26.33 N 98.33 E
Magé □[7] 287a 22.41 S 43.07 W
Magee 194 31.52 N 89.44 W
Magee, Island ›[1] 48 54.49 N 5.42 W
Magelang 115a 7.28 S 110.13 E
Magellan, Strait of → Magallanes, Estrecho de ʉ 254 54.00 S 71.00 W
Magellan-Strasse → Magallanes, Estrecho de ʉ 254 54.00 S 71.00 W
Magén 132 31.18 N 34.26 E
Magenta 62 45.28 N 8.53 E
Magenta, Lake ⊜ 162 33.26 S 119.10 E
Magerøy I 24 71.03 N 25.45 E
Magetan 115a 7.39 S 111.20 E
Magezhuang 105 40.08 N 117.59 E
Maggia 58 46.15 N 8.42 E
Maggia ≃ 58 46.09 N 8.48 E
Maggia, Valle V 58 46.17 N 8.40 E
Maggie Creek ≃ 204 40.43 N 116.05 W
Maggiorasca, Monte ∧ 62 44.33 N 9.29 E
Maggiore ≃ 267a 41.54 N 12.16 E
Maggiore, Lago ⊜ 36 46.00 N 8.40 E
Maggiore, Monte ∧ 68 41.14 N 14.12 E
Maghāghah 142 28.39 N 30.50 E
Maghama 150 15.31 N 12.51 W
Maghar 132 32.53 N 35.24 E
Maghdūshah 132 33.31 N 35.23 E
Maghera 48 54.51 N 6.40 W
Magherafelt 48 54.45 N 6.36 W
Maghniyya 148 34.50 N 1.50 W
Magholpur ⬥[8] 272a 28.42 N 77.06 E
Maghull 44 53.32 N 2.57 W
Magician Lake ⊜ 216 42.04 N 86.10 W
Magic Mountain ♠ 228 34.26 N 118.36 W
Magic Reservoir ⊜[1] 202 43.17 N 114.23 W
Magill, Lac ⊜ 206 45.35 N 71.17 W
Magill Heights 279b 40.37 N 79.52 W
Magill Lake ⊜ 184 54.45 N 94.58 W
Maginu 268 35.35 N 139.36 E
Magione 66 43.08 N 12.12 E
Magisano 68 39.01 N 16.37 E
Magiscatzín 234 22.48 N 98.42 W
Magiss Lake ⊜ 184 52.59 N 91.40 W
Maglaj 38 44.33 N 18.06 E
Magliana ⬥[8] 267a 41.50 N 12.25 E
Magliana, Fosso ≃ 267a 41.49 N 12.25 E
Magliano dei Marsi 66 42.05 N 13.22 E
Magliano in Toscana 66 42.36 N 11.17 E
Magliano Sabina 66 42.22 N 12.29 E
Maglie 68 40.07 N 18.19 E
Maglód 264c 47.27 N 19.21 E
M'aglovo 265a 59.53 N 30.41 E
Magnago 266b 45.35 N 8.48 E
Magnanville 261 48.58 N 1.41 E
Magnet 184 51.19 N 99.30 W
Magnetawan ≃ 190 45.46 N 80.37 W
Magnetic Island I 166 19.08 S 146.50 E
Magnetic Springs 214 40.21 N 83.16 W
Magnetischer Nordpol → North Magnetic Pole ⬥ 16 77.19 N 101.49 W
Magnetischer Südpol → South Magnetic Pole ⬥ 9 65.18 S 139.30 E
Magnières 58 48.27 N 6.34 E
Magnitka 86 55.21 N 59.43 E
Magnitogorsk 86 53.27 N 59.04 E
Magnitostroj 80 51.43 N 53.05 E
Magnolia, Ar., U.S. 194 33.16 N 93.14 W
Magnolia, De., U.S. 208 39.04 N 75.28 W
Magnolia, Ma., U.S. 283 42.35 N 70.43 W
Magnolia, Mn., U.S. 198 43.38 N 96.04 W
Magnolia, Ms., U.S. 194 31.08 N 90.27 W
Magnolia, N.J., U.S. 285 39.51 N 75.02 W
Magnolia, Oh., U.S. 214 40.39 N 81.17 W
Magnolia, Tx., U.S. 222 30.13 N 95.45 W
Magnor 26 59.57 N 12.12 E
Magny-en-Vexin 50 49.09 N 1.47 E
Magny-le-Hongre 261 48.52 N 2.49 E
Magny-les-Hameaux 261 48.44 N 2.04 E
Mago 89 53.15 N 140.13 E
Magog 206 45.16 N 72.09 W
Magog ≃ 206 45.24 N 71.54 W
Magog, Lake ⊜ 206 45.18 N 72.03 W
Magoito 266c 38.52 N 9.26 W
Magome ⬥[8] 268 35.35 N 139.43 E
Mago National Park ♠ 144 5.30 N 36.15 E
Magonoy 116 6.54 N 124.33 E
Magoro 154 1.44 N 34.06 E
Magothy Bay ⊂ 208 37.10 N 75.55 W
Magothy River ⊂ 208 39.04 N 76.28 W
Magoúla 267c 38.04 N 23.32 E
Magoye 154 16.00 S 27.37 E
Magozal, Méx. 232 21.34 N 97.59 W
Magozal, Méx. 234 21.34 N 97.59 W
M'agozero 76 60.21 N 34.50 E
Magpie 186 50.19 N 64.30 W
Magpie ≃, On., Can. 190 47.56 N 84.50 W
Magpie ≃, P.Q., Can. 186 50.19 N 64.27 W
Magpie, Lac ⊜ 186 51.00 N 64.41 W
Magpie Ouest ≃ 186 51.02 N 64.42 W
Magra 126 22.59 N 88.22 E
Magra ≃ 64 44.03 N 9.58 E
Magra Hāt 126 22.14 N 88.23 E
Magrath 182 49.25 N 112.52 W
Magrè (Margreid) 64 46.17 N 11.12 E
Magro ≃ 34 39.11 N 0.25 W
Magruder Mountain ∧ 204 37.25 N 117.33 W
Magsaysay (Linugos) 116 9.01 N 125.11 E
Magsingal 116 17.41 N 120.25 E
Magstadt 56 48.45 N 8.58 E
Magu ≃ 250 2.56 S 41.55 W
Maguan 102 22.59 N 104.19 E
Maguanying 271a 39.52 N 116.17 E
Maguari, Cabo › 250 0.18 S 48.22 W
Magude 156 25.02 S 32.40 E
Magudu 158 27.31 S 31.40 E
Magueyes 196 25.44 N 97.47 W
Maguindanao □[4] 116 6.55 N 124.20 E
Magumeri 146 12.08 N 12.50 E
Māgura 124 23.29 N 89.25 E
Maguru 150 12.28 N 6.35 E
Maguse Lake ⊜ 176 61.40 N 95.10 W
Maguzhan 120 31.15 N 88.00 E
Magway, Mya. 110 20.09 N 94.55 E
Magway, Mya. 110 20.30 N 94.30 E
Magwe 154 4.08 N 32.17 E
Magwood Park ♠ 275b 43.39 N 79.30 W
Magyarország → Hungary □[1] 30 47.00 N 20.00 E
Mahābād 128 36.45 N 45.43 E
Mahābaleshwar 122 17.55 N 73.40 E
Mahabe 157b 17.05 S 45.20 E
Mahābhārat Lek ⋏ 124 27.40 N 84.30 E
Mahabo, Madag. 157b 23.40 S 46.08 E
Mahabo, Madag. 157b 20.23 S 44.40 E
Mahād 122 18.05 N 73.25 E
Mahadday Weyn 144 2.58 N 45.32 E
Mahādebpur 126 23.51 N 89.53 E
Mahādeo Hills ⋏[2] 122 22.22 N 78.34 E
Mahādeo Range ⋏ 122 17.50 N 74.15 E
Mahaffey 214 40.52 N 78.43 W
Mahagi 154 2.18 N 30.59 E
Mahagi Port 154 2.09 N 31.14 E
Mahai 102 38.17 N 94.13 E
Mahaica-Berbice □[4] 246 6.20 N 57.50 W
Mahaicony Village 246 6.36 N 57.48 W
Mahajamba ≃ 157b 15.33 S 47.08 E
Mahajamba, Helodranon' i ⊂ 157b 15.24 S 47.05 E
Mahājan 123 28.47 N 73.50 E
Mahajanga 157b 15.43 S 46.19 E
Mahajanga □[4] 157b 17.00 S 46.00 E
Mahajilo ≃ 157b 19.42 S 45.22 E
Maḥajjah 132 32.57 N 36.14 E
Mahākālī □[8] 124 29.30 N 80.30 E
Mahākālī (Sārda) ≃ 124 27.21 N 81.23 E
Mahakam ≃ 112 0.35 S 117.17 E
Mahālandi 126 24.04 N 88.07 E
Mahalatswe 156 23.05 S 26.51 E
Mahalla el-Kubra → Al-Maḥallah al-Kubrā 142 30.58 N 31.10 E
Maḥallāt 128 33.55 N 50.27 E
Maḥallat Kayl 142 31.01 N 30.17 E
Maḥallat Marḥūm 142 30.48 N 30.57 E
Maḥallat Minūf 142 30.53 N 30.58 E
Maḥallat Zayyād 142 31.02 N 31.14 E
Maham 124 28.59 N 76.18 E
Mahamba 158 27.07 S 31.10 E
Mahānadi ≃ 118 20.19 N 86.45 E
Mahānadpati 126 23.00 N 88.16 E
Mahānanda ≃ 124 24.29 N 88.18 E
Mahanay Island I 116 10.12 N 124.14 E
Mahanoro 157b 19.54 S 48.48 E
Mahanoy City 208 40.48 N 76.08 W
Mahanoy Creek ≃ 208 40.42 N 76.51 W
Mahantango Creek ≃ 208 40.47 N 76.56 W
Mahantango Mountain ∧ 208 40.40 N 76.45 W
Mahao 89 43.10 N 127.59 E
Mahape 272c 19.07 N 73.01 E
Mahārājganj, India 124 26.07 N 84.29 E
Mahārājganj, India 124 27.09 N 83.34 E
Mahārājpur, India 124 25.01 N 79.44 E
Mahārājpur, India 272a 28.39 N 77.20 E
Mahārāshtra □[3] 122 19.00 N 76.00 E
Maḥārīq, Wādī V 142 27.48 N 31.47 E
Mahārlū, Daryācheh-ye ⊜ 128 29.25 N 52.50 E
Mahāsamund 120 21.06 N 82.06 E
Maha Sarakham 110 16.11 N 103.18 E
Maha Sawat, Khlong ≊ 269a 13.47 N 100.28 E
Mahasoa 157b 22.12 S 46.06 E
Mahasolo 157b 19.07 S 46.22 E
Mahates 246 10.14 N 75.12 W
Mahatsinjo 157b 21.26 S 45.51 E
Maḥaṭṭat al-Ḥafīf 132 32.12 N 37.08 E
Mahaut 240d 15.21 N 61.25 W
Mahavavy ≃, Madag. 157b 15.57 S 45.54 E
Mahavavy ≃, Madag. 157b 13.00 S 48.55 E
Mahaweli ≃ 122 8.27 N 81.13 E
Mahaxai 110 17.25 N 105.12 E
Maḥbas, Wādī al- V 140 15.50 N 29.45 E
Mahbūbābād 122 17.37 N 80.01 E
Mahbūbnagar 122 16.44 N 77.59 E
Mahd adh-Dhahab 128 23.30 N 40.52 E
Mahdalynivka 78 48.55 N 34.54 E
Mahdāt, Bi'r al- ⊤[4] 142 30.44 N 32.32 E
Mahdia, Guy. 246 5.16 N 59.09 W
Mahdia, Tun. 148 35.30 N 11.04 E
Mahe 122 11.42 N 75.32 E
Mahébourg 157c 20.24 S 57.42 E
Mahé Island I 138 4.40 S 55.28 E
Mahendraganj 124 25.20 N 89.45 E
Mahendragarh 124 28.17 N 76.09 E
Mahendra Giri ∧ 122 18.58 N 84.21 E


**Symbols** in the index entries represent the broad categories identified in the key at the right. Symbols with superior numbers (⋏[1]) identify subcategories (see complete key on page *I · 1).*

**Symbole** im Register stellen die rechts im Schlüssel erklärten Kategorien dar. Symbole mit hochgestellten Ziffern (⋏[1]) bezeichnen Unterabteilungen einer Kategorie (vgl. vollständiger Schlüssel auf Seite *I · 1).*

**Los símbolos** incluídos en el texto del índice representan las grandes categorías identificadas con la clave a la derecha. Los símbolos con numeros en su parte superior (⋏[1]) identifican las subcategorías (véase la clave completa en la página *I · 1).*

**Les symboles** de l'index représentent les catégories indiquées dans la légende à droite. Les symboles suivis d'un indice (⋏[1]) représentent des sous-catégories (voir légende complète à la page *I · 1).*

**Os símbolos** incluídos no texto do índice representam as grandes categorias identificadas com a chave à direita. Os símbolos com números em sua parte superior (⋏[1]) identificam as subcategorias (veja-se a chave completa à página *I · 1).*

| | | | | |
|---|---|---|---|---|
| ∧ Mountain | Berg | Montaña | Montagne | Montanha |
| ⋏ Mountains | Gebirge | Montañas | Montagnes | Montanhas |
| )( Pass | Paß | Paso | Col | Passo |
| V Valley, Canyon | Tal, Cañon | Valle, Cañón | Vallée, Canyon | Vale, Canhão |
| ≚ Plain | Ebene | Llano | Plaine | Planície |
| › Cape | Kap | Cabo | Cap | Cabo |
| I Island | Insel | Isla | Île | Ilha |
| II Islands | Inseln | Islas | Îles | Ilhas |
| ⊥ Other Topographic Features | Andere Topographische Objekte | Otros Elementos Topográficos | Autres données topographiques | Outros acidentes topográficos |

ESPAÑOL / FRANÇAIS / PORTUGUÊS


| Nombre / Nom / Nome | Página / Page | Lat.°′ | Long.°′ W = Oeste / W = Ouest |
|---|---|---|---|
| Mahendranagar | 124 | 28.52 N | 80.17 E |
| Mahenge, Tan. | 154 | 7.38 S | 36.16 E |
| Mahenge, Tan. | 154 | 8.41 S | 36.43 E |
| Maheno | 172 | 45.10 S | 170.50 E |
| Maheriv | 78 | 50.08 N | 23.43 E |
| Mahesāna | 120 | 23.36 N | 72.24 E |
| Mahesgādi | 272b | 22.39 N | 88.33 E |
| Maheshmunda | 126 | 24.13 N | 86.24 E |
| Maheshtala | 272b | 22.30 N | 88.15 E |
| Maheshwar | 120 | 22.11 N | 75.35 E |
| Mahespur | 124 | 23.21 N | 88.55 E |
| Mahgawān | 124 | 26.29 N | 78.37 E |
| Mahi ≃ | 120 | 22.16 N | 72.58 E |
| Mahia Peninsula ›[1] | 172 | 39.10 S | 177.53 E |
| Mahiāri | 272b | 22.35 N | 88.14 E |
| Māhikpur | 272b | 22.32 N | 88.14 E |
| Mahilāra | 126 | 22.56 N | 90.16 E |
| Mahilëu | 76 | 53.54 N | 30.21 E |
| Mahilëu □[8] | 76 | 53.45 N | 30.30 E |
| Māhīm ◆[8] | 272c | 19.03 N | 72.49 E |
| Māhīm ≃ | 272c | 19.03 N | 72.51 E |
| Māhīm Bay ⊂ | 272c | 19.02 N | 72.50 E |
| Mahina, Mali | 150 | 13.46 N | 10.51 W |
| Mahina, Poly. fr. | 174s | 17.31 S | 149.30 W |
| Mahinerangi, Lake ⊜ | 172 | 45.51 S | 169.57 E |
| Mahinog | 116 | 9.09 N | 124.47 E |
| Mahīshādal | 126 | 22.11 N | 87.59 E |
| Mahishdānga | 272b | 22.54 N | 88.11 E |
| Mahlabatini | 158 | 28.14 S | 31.30 E |
| Mahlangasi | 158 | 27.37 S | 31.42 E |
| Mahlberg | 58 | 48.17 N | 7.48 E |
| Mahlow | 54 | 52.22 N | 13.24 E |
| Mahlsdorf | 54 | 52.47 N | 11.13 E |
| Mahlsdorf ◆[8] | 264a | 52.31 N | 13.37 E |
| Mahlsdorf-Süd ◆[8] | 264a | 52.29 N | 13.36 E |
| Mahmūdābād, India | 124 | 27.18 N | 81.07 E |
| Maḥmūdābād, Īrān | 128 | 36.38 N | 52.15 E |
| Maḥmūd-e Rāqī | 120 | 35.01 N | 69.20 E |
| Maḥmūdīyah, Tur'at al- ≍ | 142 | 31.11 N | 29.53 E |
| Mahmudiye | 130 | 39.30 N | 31.00 E |
| Mahmūdpur, India | 272a | 28.46 N | 77.22 E |
| Mahmudpur, India | 272b | 22.41 N | 88.09 E |
| Mahmutbey ◆[8] | 267b | 41.03 N | 28.49 E |
| Mahmutşevketpaşa | 130 | 41.05 N | 29.19 E |
| Mahmutşevketpaşa ◆[8] | 267b | 41.09 N | 29.11 E |
| Mahnomen | 198 | 47.18 N | 95.58 W |
| Mahoba | 124 | 25.17 N | 79.52 E |
| Mahogany Mountain ∧ | 202 | 43.14 N | 117.16 W |
| Mahomet | 216 | 40.11 N | 88.24 W |
| Mahone Bay | 186 | 44.27 N | 64.23 W |
| Mahone Bay ⊂ | 186 | 44.30 N | 64.15 W |
| Mahoning □[6] | 214 | 41.06 N | 80.39 W |
| Mahoning ≃ | 214 | 40.58 N | 80.23 W |
| Mahoning, West Branch ≃ | 214 | 41.12 N | 80.57 W |
| Mahoning Creek ≃ | 214 | 40.55 N | 79.27 W |
| Mahoning Creek Lake ⊜[1] | 214 | 40.50 N | 79.10 W |
| Mahony Lake ⊜ | 180 | 65.30 N | 125.20 W |
| Mahood Falls | 182 | 51.50 N | 120.39 W |
| Mahood Lake ⊜ | 182 | 51.55 N | 120.24 W |
| Mahopac | 210 | 41.22 N | 73.44 W |
| Mahopac Falls | 210 | 41.22 N | 73.46 W |
| Mahora | 34 | 39.13 N | 1.44 W |
| Mahoras Brook ≃ | 276 | 40.25 N | 74.08 W |
| Mahrāt, Jabal ⋏[1] | 144 | 17.05 N | 51.30 E |
| Mahrauli ◆[8] | 272a | 28.31 N | 77.11 E |
| Mahrauni | 124 | 24.35 N | 78.43 E |
| Mähren → Morava □[9] | 30 | 49.20 N | 17.00 E |
| Mahres | 148 | 34.32 N | 10.30 E |
| Mähring | 60 | 49.55 N | 12.32 E |
| Mahuiling | 100 | 29.24 N | 115.48 E |
| Māhul ◆[8] | 272c | 19.01 N | 72.53 E |
| Mahulia | 126 | 22.39 N | 86.24 E |
| Mahur Island I | 164 | 2.50 S | 152.40 E |
| Mahuta | 154 | 10.52 S | 39.27 E |
| Mahuva | 120 | 21.05 N | 71.48 E |
| Mahwa | 124 | 27.03 N | 76.56 E |
| Mahwah | 276 | 41.06 N | 74.09 W |
| Mahwah ≃ | 276 | 41.06 N | 74.10 W |
| Mai, Île de I | 275a | 45.36 N | 73.50 W |
| Maia, Am. Sam. | 174y | 14.13 S | 169.28 W |
| Maia, Port. | 34 | 41.14 N | 8.37 W |
| Mai Aini | 144 | 14.47 N | 39.06 E |
| Maiala National Park ♠ | 171a | 27.19 S | 152.46 E |
| Maianga | 152 | 14.12 S | 21.45 E |
| Maiano | 64 | 46.11 N | 13.04 E |
| Maiauatá | 250 | 1.51 S | 49.02 W |
| Maicao | 246 | 11.23 N | 72.13 W |
| Maîche | 58 | 47.15 N | 6.48 E |
| Maichen | 102 | 20.29 N | 109.59 E |
| Maici ≃ | 248 | 6.30 S | 61.43 W |
| Maicuru ≃ | 250 | 2.14 S | 54.17 W |
| Maida | 68 | 38.51 N | 16.22 E |
| Maidan ♠ | 272b | 22.33 N | 88.21 E |
| Maiden | 192 | 35.34 N | 81.12 W |
| Maidenhead | 42 | 51.32 N | 0.44 W |
| Maiden Newton | 42 | 50.46 N | 2.35 W |
| Maidstone, Austl. | 274b | 37.47 S | 144.52 E |
| Maidstone, On., Can. | 214 | 42.13 N | 82.53 W |
| Maidstone, Sk., Can. | 184 | 53.06 N | 109.18 W |
| Maidstone, Eng., U.K. | 42 | 51.17 N | 0.32 E |
| Maidstone □[8] | 260 | 51.17 N | 0.35 E |
| Maiduguri | 146 | 11.51 N | 13.10 E |
| Maie | 154 | 2.46 N | 30.34 E |
| Maiella, Montagna della ⋏ | 66 | 42.05 N | 14.07 E |
| Maienfeld | 58 | 47.00 N | 9.32 E |
| Maierato | 68 | 38.42 N | 16.11 E |
| Maifeld ◆[1] | 56 | 50.20 N | 7.20 E |
| Maigatari | 150 | 12.46 N | 9.27 E |
| Maignelay | 50 | 49.33 N | 2.31 E |
| Maigo | 116 | 8.10 N | 123.57 E |
| Mai Gudo ∧ | 144 | 7.29 N | 37.12 E |
| Maigue ≃ | 48 | 52.39 N | 8.48 W |
| Maihar | 124 | 24.16 N | 80.45 E |
| Maihara | 94 | 35.19 N | 136.17 E |
| Maijoma | 196 | 28.55 N | 104.21 W |
| Maikala Plateau ⋏[1] | 124 | 22.30 N | 81.00 E |
| Maikala Range ⋏ | 122 | 22.30 N | 81.30 E |
| Maikammer | 56 | 49.18 N | 8.08 E |
| Maiko ≃ | 154 | 0.14 N | 25.33 E |
| Maiko, Parc National de la ♠ | 154 | 0.30 S | 27.45 E |
| Maikoor, Pulau I | 164 | 6.15 S | 134.15 E |
| Mailand → Milano | 62 | 45.28 N | 9.12 E |
| Mailāni | 124 | 28.17 N | 80.21 E |
| Mailasqui | 256 | 23.33 S | 47.04 W |
| Maili | 229c | 21.25 N | 158.10 W |
| Maillane | 62 | 43.50 N | 4.47 E |
| Mailley-et-Chazelot | 58 | 47.32 N | 6.03 E |
| Maillezais | 32 | 46.22 N | 0.44 W |
| Mailly-le-Camp | 50 | 48.40 N | 4.13 E |
| Mailly-le-Château | 50 | 47.36 N | 3.38 E |
| Mailly-Maillet | 50 | 50.04 N | 2.36 E |
| Mailsi | 123 | 29.48 N | 72.11 E |
| Maimbung | 116 | 5.56 N | 121.02 E |
| Mai Mefales | 144 | 14.59 N | 38.16 E |
| Mā'īn | 132 | 31.41 N | 35.44 E |
| Main ≃, Dtsch. | 30 | 50.00 N | 8.18 E |
| Main ≃, N. Ire., U.K. | 48 | 54.43 N | 6.18 W |
| Maināguri | 124 | 26.34 N | 88.49 E |
| Mainau | 58 | 47.42 N | 9.11 E |
| Mainbernheim | 56 | 49.43 N | 10.13 E |
| Mainburg | 60 | 48.38 N | 11.47 E |
| Main Camp | 174o | 2.01 N | 157.25 W |
| Main Canal ≍, Ca., U.S. | 226 | 37.25 N | 121.05 W |
| Main Canal ≍, Ca., U.S. | 226 | 37.23 N | 120.26 W |
| Main Canal ≍, Wa., U.S. | 224 | 47.07 N | 120.44 W |
| Main Channel ʉ | 190 | 45.22 N | 81.50 W |
| Maincourt-sur-Yvette | 261 | 48.43 N | 1.58 E |
| Main Creek ≃ | 276 | 40.34 N | 74.11 W |
| Maincy | 261 | 48.33 N | 2.42 E |
| Mai-Ndombe, Lac ⊜ | 152 | 2.00 S | 18.20 E |
| Main-Donau-Kanal ≍ | 60 | 49.02 N | 11.36 E |
| Main Duck Island I | 212 | 43.56 N | 76.37 W |
| Maine | 210 | 42.11 N | 76.03 W |
| Maine □[9] | 32 | 48.15 N | 0.05 W |
| Maine □[3], U.S. | 178 | 45.15 N | 69.15 W |
| Maine □[3], U.S. | 188 | 45.15 N | 69.15 W |
| Maine ≃ | 48 | 52.09 N | 9.45 W |
| Maine, Gulf of ⊂ | 178 | 43.00 N | 68.00 W |
| Maine-et-Loire □[5] | 32 | 47.25 N | 0.30 W |
| Mainesburg | 210 | 41.47 N | 77.07 W |
| Maïné-Soroa | 146 | 13.12 N | 12.02 E |
| Maineville | 218 | 39.18 N | 84.13 W |
| Mainguerin | 261 | 48.32 N | 1.51 E |
| Mainhardt | 56 | 49.04 N | 9.33 E |
| Mainit | 116 | 9.32 N | 125.32 E |
| Mainit, Lake ⊜ | 116 | 9.26 N | 125.32 E |
| Mainland | 285 | 40.15 N | 75.22 W |
| Mainland I, Scot., U.K. | 46 | 59.00 N | 3.15 W |
| Mainland I, Scot., U.K. | 46a | 60.16 N | 1.16 W |
| Mainleus | 54 | 50.06 N | 11.22 E |
| Mainoru | 164 | 14.02 S | 134.05 E |
| Mainpuri | 124 | 27.14 N | 79.01 E |
| Main Range National Park ♠ | 171a | 28.01 S | 152.22 E |
| Maintal | 56 | 50.09 N | 8.54 E |
| Maintenon | 50 | 48.35 N | 1.35 E |
| Maintirano | 157b | 18.03 S | 44.01 E |
| Main Topsail ∧ | 186 | 49.08 N | 56.33 W |
| Mainvilliers | 50 | 48.27 N | 1.28 E |
| Mainz | 56 | 50.01 N | 8.16 E |
| Maio I | 150a | 15.15 N | 23.10 W |
| Maiolati Spontini | 66 | 43.28 N | 13.06 E |
| Maiori | 68 | 40.39 N | 14.38 E |
| Maiori, Nuraghe ⊥ | 71 | 40.56 N | 9.06 E |
| Maipa | 164 | 8.21 S | 146.33 E |
| Maipo ≃ | 252 | 33.37 S | 71.39 W |
| Maipo, Volcán ∧[1] | 252 | 34.10 S | 69.50 W |
| Maipú, Arg. | 252 | 36.52 S | 57.52 W |
| Maipú, Arg. | 252 | 32.58 S | 68.47 W |
| Maipú, Chile | 252 | 33.31 S | 70.46 W |
| Maiqihamiao | 89 | 43.22 N | 120.46 E |
| Maiquetía | 246 | 10.36 N | 66.57 W |
| Maira ≃ | 62 | 44.49 N | 7.38 E |
| Maira, Valle ∨ | 62 | 44.30 N | 7.08 E |
| Mairābāri | 120 | 26.28 N | 92.26 E |
| Mairi | 250 | 11.43 S | 40.08 W |
| Mairinque | 256 | 23.33 S | 47.10 W |
| Mairiporã | 256 | 23.19 S | 46.35 W |
| Mairiporã □[7] | 287b | 23.24 S | 46.37 W |
| Mairipotaba | 255 | 17.18 S | 49.28 W |
| Maisach | 60 | 48.13 N | 11.16 E |
| Maisaka | 94 | 34.41 N | 137.37 E |
| Maishi | 100 | 29.11 N | 113.58 E |
| Maišiagala | 76 | 54.52 N | 25.04 E |
| Maiskhāl Island I | 120 | 21.36 N | 91.56 E |
| Maison de Pierre, Lac de la ⊜ | 206 | 46.53 N | 74.42 W |
| Maisonneuve, Parc ♠ | 275a | 45.33 N | 73.34 W |
| Maisons-Alfort | 261 | 48.48 N | 2.26 E |
| Maisons-Laffitte | 50 | 48.57 N | 2.09 E |
| Maisons-Laffitte, Château de ⊥ | 261 | 48.57 N | 2.09 E |
| Maisse | 50 | 48.24 N | 2.23 E |
| Maissin | 56 | 49.58 N | 5.11 E |
| Maitani | 270 | 34.49 N | 135.22 E |
| Maitengwe | 156 | 20.06 S | 27.13 E |
| Maitengwe ≃ | 156 | 19.59 S | 26.26 E |
| Maithon Reservoir ⊜[1] | 126 | 23.50 N | 86.43 E |
| Maitland, Austl. | 168b | 34.22 S | 137.40 E |
| Maitland, Austl. | 170 | 32.44 S | 151.33 E |
| Maitland, N.S., Can. | 186 | 45.19 N | 63.30 W |
| Maitland, On., Can. | 212 | 44.38 N | 75.37 W |
| Maitland, Fl., U.S. | 220 | 28.37 N | 81.21 W |
| Maitland ≃ | 190 | 43.45 N | 81.43 W |
| Maitland, Lake ⊜ | 162 | 27.11 S | 121.03 E |
| Maitri ⊍[3] | 9 | 70.46 S | 11.44 E |
| Maixie | 100 | 27.38 N | 115.29 E |
| Maíz ≃ | 236 | 11.17 N | 83.52 W |
| Maíz, Islas del II | 236 | 12.15 N | 83.00 W |
| Maizefield | 158 | 26.28 S | 29.31 E |
| Maizhokunggar | 120 | 29.50 N | 91.45 E |
| Maizières-lès-Metz | 56 | 49.13 N | 6.09 E |
| Maizières-lès-Vic | 58 | 48.43 N | 6.46 E |
| Maizuru | 96 | 35.28 N | 135.24 E |
| Maja ≃, Ross. | 74 | 60.24 N | 134.30 E |
| Maja ≃, Ross. | 89 | 54.31 N | 134.41 E |
| Majābirah, Minqār al- ⊥[4] | 142 | 30.16 N | 29.49 E |
| Majačnyj | 86 | 52.41 N | 55.44 E |
| Majadahonda | 266a | 40.29 N | 3.52 W |
| Majagua | 240p | 21.55 N | 79.00 W |
| Majagual | 246 | 8.33 N | 74.38 W |
| Majalaya | 115a | 7.03 S | 107.45 E |
| Majalengka | 115a | 6.50 S | 108.13 E |
| Majana, Ensenada de ⊂ | 240p | 22.41 N | 82.45 W |
| Majanji | 154 | 0.15 N | 33.59 E |
| Majari ≃ | 246 | 3.29 N | 60.58 W |
| Majayjay | 116 | 14.09 N | 121.28 E |
| Majchura | 85 | 39.02 N | 68.35 E |
| Majdantal | 85 | 43.41 N | 68.02 E |
| Majd el Kurūm | 132 | 32.55 N | 35.15 E |
| Majé | 256 | 22.39 S | 43.02 W |
| Majeigha | 140 | 11.33 N | 24.40 E |
| Majenang | 115a | 7.18 S | 108.45 E |
| Majene | 112 | 3.33 S | 118.57 E |
| Majenica | 216 | 40.46 N | 85.27 W |
| Majevica ⋏ | 38 | 44.30 N | 18.55 E |
| Maji | 144 | 6.11 N | 35.38 E |
| Majia | 100 | 32.32 N | 118.50 E |
| Majia ≃ | 98 | 38.09 N | 117.53 E |
| Majiacun | 106 | 30.08 N | 119.58 E |
| Majiahe | 102 | 35.20 N | 104.46 E |
| Majian, Zhg. | 100 | 29.19 N | 119.36 E |
| Majian, Zhg. | 100 | 29.43 N | 120.00 E |
| Majiang, Zhg. | 102 | 23.48 N | 111.09 E |
| Majiang, Zhg. | 110 | 26.28 N | 107.28 E |
| Majiangzong | 120 | 30.27 N | 90.03 E |
| Majiaoba | 102 | 32.14 N | 104.35 E |
| Majiaping | 102 | 36.31 N | 103.20 E |
| Majiasi | 105 | 39.03 N | 117.05 E |
| Majiawopu | 104 | 41.46 N | 121.06 E |
| Majiayan | 100 | 27.26 N | 112.56 E |
| Majiazhai | 104 | 42.22 N | 124.04 E |
| Majiazhou | 100 | 26.46 N | 114.47 E |
| Majidun Creek ≃ | 273a | 6.38 N | 3.28 E |
| Majie, Zhg. | 102 | 23.50 N | 105.07 E |
| Majie, Zhg. | 102 | 25.03 N | 103.45 E |
| Majin | 100 | 29.18 N | 118.24 E |
| Majin ≃ | 100 | 29.00 N | 118.21 E |
| Majinzhuangzi | 104 | 41.55 N | 123.53 E |
| Maji Shan I | 106 | 31.26 N | 120.06 E |
| Majītha | 123 | 31.46 N | 74.57 E |
| Majja | 74 | 61.44 N | 130.18 E |
| Majkain | 86 | 51.27 N | 75.52 E |
| Majkop | 84 | 44.35 N | 40.07 E |
| Majkor | 86 | 59.01 N | 55.54 E |
| Majli-Saj | 85 | 41.17 N | 72.29 E |
| Majlispur | 126 | 24.13 N | 90.53 E |
| Majlybas | 86 | 45.49 N | 62.39 E |
| Majmak | 85 | 42.40 N | 71.15 E |
| Majna, Ross. | 80 | 54.07 N | 47.37 E |
| Majna, Ross. | 86 | 53.00 N | 91.28 E |
| Majnan | 272b | 22.59 N | 88.09 E |
| Majnic, ozero ⊜ | 180 | 63.15 N | 176.40 E |
| Majno-Gytkino | 180 | 63.36 N | 176.30 E |
| Majŏn-ni, C.M.I.K. | 98 | 39.06 N | 127.07 E |
| Majŏn-ni, Taehan | 271b | 37.36 N | 126.41 E |
| Major, Puig ∧ | 34 | 39.48 N | 2.48 E |
| Majorca → Mallorca I | 34 | 39.30 N | 3.00 E |
| Major Creek ≃ | 169 | 36.51 S | 145.05 E |
| Major Isidoro | 250 | 9.32 S | 37.00 W |
| Majorque, Île → Mallorca I | 34 | 39.30 N | 3.00 E |
| Majrūr | 140 | 14.01 N | 30.27 E |
| Majrūr, Wādī ∨ | 140 | 15.44 N | 26.26 E |
| Majseevičy | 76 | 53.13 N | 28.17 E |
| Majsk | 86 | 57.49 N | 77.16 E |
| Majskij, Ross. | 83 | 47.43 N | 40.03 E |
| Majskij, Ross. | 84 | 43.38 N | 44.04 E |
| Majskij, Ross. | 89 | 52.18 N | 129.38 E |
| Majskij, Ross. | 89 | 49.00 N | 140.10 E |
| Majskoje, Kaz. | 86 | 50.55 N | 78.15 E |
| Majskoje, Ross. | 82 | 56.08 N | 37.55 E |
| Majtan | 86 | 45.46 N | 74.20 E |
| Majtobe | 85 | 43.01 N | 70.35 E |
| Māju | 126 | 22.37 N | 88.05 E |
| Majuba Hill ⊥ | 158 | 27.28 S | 29.51 E |
| Majuqiao | 105 | 39.46 N | 116.32 E |
| Majuro I[1] | 14 | 7.09 N | 171.12 E |
| Majuzigou | 104 | 41.49 N | 121.38 E |
| Maka | 150 | 13.40 N | 14.17 W |
| Makabana | 152 | 2.48 S | 12.29 E |
| Makabe | 94 | 36.16 N | 140.06 E |
| Makadasa ≃ | 116 | 7.22 N | 124.36 E |
| Makaha, Hi., U.S. | 229c | 21.28 N | 158.13 W |
| Makaha, Zimb. | 154 | 17.17 S | 32.37 E |
| Makaha Point › | 229b | 22.08 N | 159.44 W |
| Makah Bay ⊂ | 224 | 48.19 N | 124.40 W |
| Makah Indian Reservation ◆[4] | 224 | 48.20 N | 124.41 W |
| Makahuena Point › | 229b | 21.52 N | 159.27 W |
| Makak | 152 | 3.33 N | 11.02 E |
| Makala | 273b | 4.25 S | 15.17 E |
| Makalamabedi | 156 | 20.19 S | 23.51 E |
| Makale | 112 | 3.06 S | 119.51 E |
| Makallé | 252 | 27.13 S | 59.17 W |
| Makālu ∧ | 124 | 27.54 N | 87.06 E |
| Makamba | 154 | 4.08 S | 29.49 E |
| Makanapur | 272a | 28.38 N | 77.21 E |
| Makanči | 86 | 46.48 N | 82.00 E |
| Makanya | 154 | 4.20 S | 37.51 E |
| Makanza | 152 | 1.36 N | 19.07 E |
| Makaoo Indian Reserve ◆[4] | 184 | 53.40 N | 110.02 W |
| Makapu Point › | 174v | 18.59 S | 169.56 W |
| Makapuu Head › | 229c | 21.19 N | 157.39 W |
| Makarakomburu, Mount ∧ | 175e | 9.43 S | 160.02 E |
| Makarakskij | 86 | 55.36 N | 88.03 E |
| Makarapan Mountain ∧ | 246 | 4.00 N | 58.51 W |
| Makarewa | 172 | 46.20 S | 168.21 E |
| Makari | 146 | 12.35 N | 14.28 E |
| Makar-Ib | 24 | 63.39 N | 49.24 E |
| Makaricha | 24 | 66.15 N | 58.20 E |
| Makariv | 78 | 50.28 N | 29.49 E |
| Makarje | 80 | 58.35 N | 48.11 E |
| Makarjev | 80 | 57.52 N | 43.48 E |
| Makarjevo | 80 | 56.06 N | 45.06 E |
| Makarov | 89 | 48.38 N | 142.48 E |
| Makarovo, Ross. | 80 | 52.18 N | 43.20 E |
| Makarovo, Ross. | 82 | 54.22 N | 36.40 E |
| Makarovo, Ross. | 88 | 57.29 N | 107.52 E |
| Makarska | 36 | 43.18 N | 17.02 E |
| Makasar → Ujungpandang | 112 | 5.07 S | 119.24 E |
| Makasar, Selat (Makassar Strait) ʉ | 112 | 2.00 S | 117.30 E |
| Makaševka | 80 | 51.30 N | 42.36 E |
| Makassar Strait → Makasar, Selat ʉ | 112 | 2.00 S | 117.30 E |
| Makasuko | 154 | 6.00 S | 34.56 E |
| Makat | 80 | 47.39 N | 53.19 E |
| Makatea I | 14 | 15.50 S | 148.15 W |
| Makati | 269f | 14.34 N | 121.02 E |
| Makaw, Mya. | 110 | 26.27 N | 96.42 E |
| Makaw, Zaïre | 152 | 3.29 S | 18.19 E |
| Makawao | 229a | 20.51 N | 156.18 W |
| Makaweli | 229b | 21.55 N | 159.38 W |
| Makay, Massif du ⋏ | 157b | 21.15 S | 45.15 E |
| Makaya | 152 | 3.22 S | 18.02 E |
| Makedonija → Macedonia □[1] | 38 | 41.50 N | 22.00 E |
| Makefu | 174v | 18.59 S | 169.55 W |
| Makemie Park | 208 | 37.55 N | 75.34 W |
| Makemo I[1] | 14 | 16.35 S | 143.40 W |
| Makena | 229a | 20.39 N | 156.27 W |
| Makeni | 150 | 8.53 N | 12.03 W |
| Makere | 154 | 4.17 S | 30.25 E |
| Maketu | 172 | 37.46 S | 176.27 E |
| Makeyevka → Makiyivka, Ukr. | 83 | 48.02 N | 37.58 E |
| Makeyevka → Makiyivka, Ukr. | 83 | 48.02 N | 37.58 E |
| Makgadikgadi ≡ | 156 | 20.45 S | 25.30 E |
| Makgadikgadi Pans Game Reserve ◆[4] | 156 | 20.30 S | 24.45 E |
| Makhachkala → Machačkala | 84 | 42.58 N | 47.30 E |
| Makhad | 123 | 33.08 N | 71.44 E |
| Makhaleng ≃ | 158 | 30.20 S | 27.23 E |
| Mākhālpur | 272b | 22.56 N | 88.10 E |
| Makham | 110 | 12.40 N | 102.12 E |
| Makhdūmnagar | 124 | 26.28 N | 82.46 E |
| Makhfar al-Quwayrah | 132 | 29.48 N | 35.19 E |
| Makhfar Ramn | 132 | 29.42 N | 35.25 E |
| Makhrūq, Wādī al- ∨ | 132 | 31.30 N | 37.10 E |
| Makhyah, Wādī ∨ | 144 | 17.40 N | 49.01 E |
| Maki, Indon. | 164 | 3.11 S | 134.14 E |
| Maki, Nihon | 92 | 37.45 N | 138.53 E |
| Maki, Nihon | 94 | 37.05 N | 138.23 E |
| Maki, Nihon | 270 | 34.52 N | 135.04 E |
| Makika, Lua ⊥[6] | 229a | 20.34 N | 156.34 W |
| Makikihi | 172 | 44.38 S | 171.09 E |
| Makilala | 116 | 6.55 N | 125.05 E |
| Makindu | 154 | 2.17 S | 37.49 E |
| Makino, Nihon | 94 | 35.28 N | 136.05 E |
| M'akino, Ross. | 265b | 55.48 N | 37.22 E |
| Makinsk | 86 | 52.37 N | 70.26 E |
| Makio-dam ◆[6] | 94 | 35.50 N | 137.36 E |
| Makioka | 94 | 35.45 N | 138.43 E |
| Makira □[4] | 175e | 11.00 S | 162.30 E |
| Makira Harbour ⊂ | 175e | 10.25 S | 161.29 E |
| M'akiševo | 76 | 56.34 N | 28.53 E |
| M'akit | 74 | 61.24 N | 152.09 E |
| Makiyivka, Ukr. | 78 | 50.40 N | 31.50 E |
| Makiyivka, Ukr. | 83 | 49.14 N | 37.59 E |
| Makiyivka, Ukr. | 83 | 48.02 N | 37.58 E |
| Makkah (Mecca) | 144 | 21.27 N | 39.49 E |
| Makkavejevo | 88 | 51.44 N | 113.58 E |
| Makkum | 52 | 53.04 N | 5.24 E |
| Makó, Magy. | 30 | 46.13 N | 20.29 E |
| Mako, Sén. | 150 | 12.52 N | 12.21 W |
| Makoaneng ∧ | 158 | 29.47 S | 28.57 E |
| Makobe Lake ⊜ | 190 | 47.27 N | 80.25 W |
| Makoka | 154 | 2.34 S | 25.29 E |
| Makok-ni | 271b | 37.43 N | 126.38 E |
| Makokou | 152 | 0.34 N | 12.52 E |
| Makoli | 154 | 17.27 S | 26.05 E |
| Makongai Island I | 175g | 17.27 S | 178.58 E |
| Makongo | 154 | 3.25 N | 26.22 E |
| Makongolosi | 154 | 8.24 S | 33.09 E |
| Makopse | 84 | 43.59 N | 39.13 E |
| Makorako ∧ | 172 | 39.09 S | 176.02 E |
| Makoro | 154 | 3.08 N | 29.44 E |
| Makoshika State Park ♠ | 198 | 47.03 N | 104.41 W |
| Makoshyne | 78 | 51.27 N | 32.18 E |
| Makotuku | 172 | 40.07 S | 176.14 E |
| Makoua | 152 | 0.01 N | 15.39 E |
| Makov | 30 | 49.23 N | 18.30 E |
| Makovskoje | 86 | 58.12 N | 90.52 E |
| Maków Mazowiecki | 30 | 52.52 N | 21.06 E |
| Maków Podhalański | 30 | 49.44 N | 19.41 E |
| Makrai | 124 | 22.04 N | 77.06 E |
| Makrampur | 126 | 22.44 N | 90.14 E |
| Makrāna | 120 | 27.03 N | 74.43 E |
| Makran Coast ⊥[2] | 128 | 25.15 N | 61.00 E |
| Makrany | 78 | 51.50 N | 24.14 E |
| M'aksa | 76 | 58.54 N | 38.12 E |
| Maksaticha | 76 | 57.48 N | 35.53 E |
| Maksimicha | 88 | 53.15 N | 108.43 E |
| Maksimkin Jar | 86 | 58.42 N | 86.48 E |
| Maksimovka, Ross. | 80 | 52.59 N | 51.10 E |
| Maksimovka, Ross. | 89 | 46.04 N | 137.51 E |
| Maksimovo | 82 | 56.20 N | 35.58 E |
| Maksudangarh | 124 | 24.03 N | 77.15 E |
| Maksymovychi | 78 | 51.13 N | 29.37 E |
| Maktar | 148 | 35.51 N | 9.12 E |
| Maktau | 154 | 3.24 S | 38.08 E |
| Mākū, Īrān | 128 | 39.17 N | 44.31 E |
| Maku, Zhg. | 105 | 39.33 N | 114.46 E |
| Makuhari | 268 | 35.39 N | 140.03 E |
| Makuliro | 154 | 9.35 S | 37.26 E |
| Makumbako | 154 | 8.51 S | 34.50 E |
| Makumbi | 152 | 5.51 S | 20.41 E |
| Makung (P'enghu) | 100 | 23.34 N | 119.34 E |
| Makunudu I | 122 | 6.25 N | 72.41 E |
| Makunudu Atoll I[1] | 122 | 6.20 N | 72.36 E |
| Makuragi-san ∧ | 96 | 35.32 N | 133.08 E |
| Makurazaki | 92 | 31.16 N | 130.19 E |
| Makurdi | 150 | 7.45 N | 8.32 E |
| Makushin Volcano ∧[1] | 180 | 53.53 N | 166.50 W |
| Makušino | 86 | 55.13 N | 67.13 E |
| Makuyuni | 154 | 3.33 S | 36.06 E |
| Makwa Lake ⊜ | 184 | 54.04 N | 109.15 W |
| Makwassie | 158 | 27.26 S | 26.00 E |
| Makwende-Bayo | 154 | 7.08 S | 28.06 E |
| Makwiro | 154 | 17.58 S | 30.28 E |
| Māl, India | 124 | 26.52 N | 88.44 E |
| Mal, Maur. | 150 | 16.58 N | 13.23 W |
| Mala, Perú | 248 | 12.39 S | 76.38 W |
| Malå, Sve. | 26 | 65.11 N | 18.44 E |
| Mala ≃ | 248 | 12.40 S | 76.41 W |
| Mala, Punta › | 246 | 7.28 N | 80.00 W |
| Malabang | 116 | 7.38 N | 124.03 E |
| Malabar, Austl. | 274a | 33.58 S | 151.15 E |
| Malabar, Fl., U.S. | 220 | 28.00 N | 80.33 W |
| Malabar Coast ⊥[2] | 122 | 11.00 N | 75.00 E |
| Malabar Farm State Park ♠ | 214 | 40.38 N | 82.25 W |
| Malabar Hill ∧[2] | 272c | 18.57 N | 72.48 E |
| Malabar Point › | 272c | 18.57 N | 72.47 E |
| Mala Bilozirka | 78 | 47.14 N | 34.56 E |
| Malabo | 152 | 3.45 N | 8.47 E |
| Mal Abrigo | 258 | 34.09 S | 56.57 W |
| Malabrigo Point › | 116 | 13.36 N | 121.15 E |
| Malabuyoc | 116 | 9.39 N | 123.19 E |
| Malaca, Estrecho de → Malacca, Strait of ʉ | 110 | 2.30 N | 101.20 E |
| Malacacheta | 255 | 17.50 S | 42.05 W |
| Malacañang Palace ⊍ | 269f | 14.36 N | 120.59 E |
| Malacatepec, Volcán ∧[1] | 286a | 19.10 N | 99.16 W |
| Malacca, Strait of ʉ | 110 | 2.30 N | 101.20 E |
| Malachovka | 82 | 55.39 N | 38.00 E |
| Malachovo, Ross. | 82 | 54.45 N | 37.27 E |
| Malachovo, Ross. | 82 | 54.22 N | 37.31 E |
| Malachovskij | 80 | 49.08 N | 41.43 E |
| Malacky | 30 | 48.27 N | 17.00 E |
| Mālād ◆[8] | 272c | 19.11 N | 72.51 E |
| Malad ≃ | 200 | 41.35 N | 112.07 W |
| Malad City | 202 | 42.11 N | 112.15 W |
| Malad Creek ≃ | 272c | 19.08 N | 72.48 E |
| Mala Divytsya | 78 | 50.41 N | 32.10 E |
| Maladzečna | 76 | 54.19 N | 26.49 E |
| Malafede ≃ | 267a | 41.47 N | 12.24 E |
| Málaga, Col. | 246 | 6.42 N | 72.44 W |
| Málaga, Esp. | 34 | 36.43 N | 4.25 W |
| Malaga, Ca., U.S. | 226 | 36.42 N | 119.46 W |
| Malaga, N.J., U.S. | 208 | 39.34 N | 75.02 W |
| Malaga, N.M., U.S. | 196 | 32.13 N | 104.04 W |
| Málaga □[4] | 34 | 36.50 N | 4.40 W |
| Malagarasi | 154 | 5.06 S | 30.50 E |
| Malagarasi ≃ | 154 | 5.12 S | 29.47 E |
| Malagash | 186 | 45.46 N | 63.23 W |
| Malagasy Republic → Madagascar □[1] | 157b | 19.00 S | 46.00 E |
| Malago ≃ | 116 | 10.55 N | 123.02 E |
| Malagón | 34 | 39.10 N | 3.51 W |
| Malagrotta ◆[8] | 66 | 41.53 N | 12.20 E |
| Mal'agurt | 80 | 57.39 N | 52.32 E |
| Malahat | 224 | 48.32 N | 123.34 W |
| Malahide | 48 | 53.27 N | 6.09 W |
| Mălăiești | 38 | 46.59 N | 29.33 E |
| Malaimbandy | 157b | 20.20 S | 45.36 E |
| Malaisie → Malaysia □[1] | 112 | 2.30 N | 112.30 E |
| Malaita □[4] | 175e | 9.00 S | 161.00 E |
| Malaita I | 175e | 9.00 S | 161.00 E |
| Malaja Bessergenovka | 83 | 47.09 N | 38.36 E |
| Malaja Borščovka | 82 | 56.33 N | 36.53 E |
| Malaja Bykovka | 80 | 51.54 N | 47.45 E |
| Malaja Čuja ≃ | 88 | 58.56 N | 112.13 E |
| Malaja Doroginka | 82 | 54.06 N | 38.56 E |
| Malaja Dubna | 82 | 55.52 N | 38.58 E |
| Malaja Istra ≃ | 82 | 55.54 N | 36.50 E |
| Malaja Ižmora | 80 | 53.32 N | 42.48 E |
| Malaja Jekaterinovka | 80 | 51.26 N | 44.17 E |
| Malaja Kinel' ≃ | 80 | 53.29 N | 51.30 E |
| Malaja Kokšaga ≃ | 80 | 56.09 N | 47.53 E |
| Malaja Konkudera ≃ | 88 | 57.26 N | 112.37 E |
| Malaja Kuril'skaja Gr'ada (Habomai-Shotō) II | 92a | 43.30 N | 146.10 E |
| Malaja Laba ≃ | 84 | 44.16 N | 40.53 E |
| Malaja Neva ≃[1] | 265a | 59.57 N | 30.15 E |
| Malaja Ochta ◆[8] | 265a | 59.56 N | 30.24 E |
| Malaja Orlovka | 80 | 47.18 N | 41.24 E |
| Malaja Pera | 24 | 64.11 N | 54.47 E |
| Malaja Serdoba | 80 | 52.28 N | 44.56 E |
| Malaja Sestra ≃ | 82 | 56.17 N | 35.57 E |
| Malaja Višera | 76 | 58.51 N | 32.14 E |
| Malaka → Melaka | 114 | 2.12 N | 102.15 E |
| Malaka, Sempitan ʉ | 114 | 5.44 N | 95.30 E |
| Malakāl | 140 | 9.31 N | 31.39 E |
| Malākand | 123 | 34.34 N | 71.56 E |
| Mala Kapela ⋏ | 36 | 44.50 N | 15.30 E |
| Malakka, Strasse von → Malacca, Strait of ʉ | 110 | 2.30 N | 101.20 E |
| Malakoff, Fr. | 261 | 48.49 N | 2.19 E |
| Malakoff, Tx., U.S. | 222 | 32.10 N | 96.00 W |
| Malakpur ◆[8] | 272a | 28.42 N | 77.12 E |
| Malakula □[8] | 175f | 16.20 S | 167.20 E |
| Malakula I | 175f | 16.15 S | 167.30 E |
| Malakwāl | 123 | 32.34 N | 73.13 E |
| Malala | 164 | 5.15 S | 147.10 E |
| Malalag | 116 | 6.36 N | 125.24 E |
| Malalbergo | 64 | 44.43 N | 11.32 E |
| Malamala | 112 | 3.21 S | 120.55 E |
| Mala Mala Game Reserve ◆[4] | 156 | 24.52 S | 31.30 E |
| Malamaui Island I | 116 | 6.44 N | 121.58 E |
| Malambo | 246 | 10.52 N | 74.47 W |
| Malambo, Arroyo ≃ | 258 | 33.43 S | 58.46 W |
| Malambunga | 116 | 9.02 N | 117.38 E |
| Malamocco | 64 | 45.22 N | 12.20 E |
| Malampaya Sound ʉ | 116 | 10.51 N | 119.20 E |
| Malān | 110 | 25.37 N | 96.21 E |
| Malān, Rās › | 128 | 25.18 N | 65.11 E |
| Malanao Island I | 116 | 9.27 N | 118.37 E |
| Malanas ≃ | 116 | 17.41 N | 120.43 E |
| Mālancha | 272b | 22.55 N | 88.26 E |
| Mālancha ≃[1] | 126 | 21.40 N | 89.20 E |
| Mālandighi | 126 | 23.33 N | 87.24 E |
| Malandji | 152 | 5.56 S | 22.18 E |
| Malang | 115a | 7.59 S | 112.37 E |
| Malang, Gunung ∧ | 115a | 7.02 S | 107.01 E |
| Malangali | 154 | 8.34 S | 34.51 E |
| Malangas | 116 | 7.37 N | 123.01 E |
| Malanggwā | 124 | 26.52 N | 85.34 E |
| Malangka, Tanjung › | 112 | 1.20 N | 120.48 E |
| Malan Guan )( | 105 | 40.16 N | 117.39 E |
| Malanipa Island I | 116 | 6.53 N | 122.16 E |
| Malanje | 152 | 9.32 S | 16.20 E |
| Malanje □[5] | 152 | 9.30 S | 16.30 E |
| Malanut Bay ⊂ | 116 | 9.16 N | 117.59 E |
| Malanville | 150 | 11.52 N | 3.23 E |
| Malanyu | 105 | 40.11 N | 117.42 E |
| Malanzán | 252 | 30.48 S | 66.37 W |
| Mała Panew ≃ | 30 | 50.44 N | 17.52 E |
| Malapantao, Mount ∧ | 116 | 9.54 N | 122.37 E |
| Malapardis Brook ≃ | 276 | 40.49 N | 74.25 W |
| Mälaren ⊜ | 40 | 59.30 N | 17.12 E |
| Malargüe | 252 | 35.28 S | 69.35 W |
| Mälar-See → Mälaren ⊜ | 40 | 59.30 N | 17.12 E |
| Malartic | 190 | 48.08 N | 78.08 W |
| Malartic, Lac ⊜ | 190 | 48.15 N | 78.07 W |
| Malaryta | 78 | 51.47 N | 24.05 E |
| Malasia → Malaysia □[1] | 112 | 2.30 N | 112.30 E |
| Malasiqui | 116 | 15.55 N | 120.25 E |
| Malaspina | 254 | 44.56 S | 66.54 W |
| Malaspina Glacier ⊓ | 180 | 59.50 N | 140.30 W |
| Malaspina Strait ʉ | 182 | 49.44 N | 124.20 W |
| Malassis | 261 | 48.38 N | 2.03 E |
| Malāṭīyah | 142 | 28.42 N | 30.51 E |
| Mala Tokmachivka | 78 | 47.32 N | 35.54 E |
| Malatya | 130 | 38.21 N | 38.19 E |
| Malatya □[4] | 130 | 38.30 N | 38.10 E |
| Malau | 175f | 15.10 S | 166.48 E |
| Malaucène | 62 | 44.10 N | 5.08 E |
| Malaunay | 50 | 49.32 N | 1.02 E |
| Malaut | 123 | 30.13 N | 74.29 E |
| Malavalli | 122 | 12.23 N | 77.05 E |
| Mala Vyska | 78 | 48.39 N | 31.38 E |
| Malawali, Pulau I | 116 | 7.03 N | 117.18 E |
| Malawi □[1], Afr. | 138 | 13.30 S | 34.00 E |
| Malawi □[1], Afr. | 154 | 13.30 S | 34.00 E |
| Malawi, Lake → Nyasa, Lake ⊜ | 154 | 12.00 S | 34.30 E |
| Malawiya | 140 | 15.16 N | 36.12 E |
| Malaya → Semenanjung Malaysia □[9] | 114 | 4.00 N | 102.00 E |
| Malayagiri ∧ | 120 | 21.23 N | 85.16 E |
| Malayal | 116 | 7.12 N | 121.57 E |
| Malaybalay | 116 | 8.09 N | 125.05 E |
| Malāyer | 128 | 34.17 N | 48.50 E |
| Malay Peninsula ›[1] | 110 | 6.00 N | 101.00 E |
| Malay Reef ⊹[2] | 166 | 17.59 S | 149.18 E |
| Malaysia □[1], Asia | 108 | 2.30 N | 112.30 E |
| Malaysia □[1], Asia | 112 | 2.30 N | 112.30 E |
| Malazgirt | 130 | 39.09 N | 42.31 E |
| Malbaie ≃ | 186 | 47.39 N | 70.09 W |
| Malbaie, La ⊂ | 186 | 48.35 N | 64.14 W |
| Malbon | 166 | 21.04 S | 140.18 E |
| Malbooma | 162 | 30.41 S | 134.11 E |
| Malborghetto Valbruna | 64 | 46.30 N | 13.26 E |
| Malbork | 30 | 54.02 N | 19.01 E |
| Malbrán | 252 | 29.21 S | 62.27 W |
| Malbuisson | 58 | 46.48 N | 6.18 E |
| Malbun | 58 | 47.35 N | 9.33 E |
| Malcesine | 64 | 45.46 N | 10.48 E |
| Mal'cevo | 265b | 55.56 N | 37.57 E |
| Mal'čevskaja | 78 | 49.04 N | 40.21 E |
| Mal'čevsko-Polnenskaja | 83 | 48.58 N | 40.12 E |
| Malchanskij chrebet ⋏ | 88 | 50.45 N | 109.30 E |
| Malchin | 54 | 53.44 N | 12.46 E |
| Malchiner See ⊜ | 54 | 53.43 N | 12.38 E |
| Malching | 60 | 48.19 N | 13.12 E |
| Malchow | 54 | 53.28 N | 12.25 E |
| Malchow ◆[8] | 264a | 52.35 N | 13.29 E |
| Malčin | 88 | 49.44 N | 93.18 E |
| Malcolm | 162 | 28.56 S | 121.30 E |
| Malcolm, Point › | 162 | 33.48 S | 123.45 E |
| Malcolm Island I | 182 | 50.40 N | 127.00 W |
| Malcom | 190 | 41.42 N | 92.33 W |
| Malcompeth → Mahābaleshwar | 122 | 17.55 N | 73.40 E |
| Malcontenta | 64 | 45.25 N | 12.13 E |
| Malczyce | 30 | 51.14 N | 16.29 E |
| Māldah | 124 | 25.02 N | 88.09 E |
| Maldegem | 50 | 51.13 N | 3.27 E |
| Malden, Ma., U.S. | 207 | 42.25 N | 71.04 W |
| Malden, Mo., U.S. | 194 | 36.33 N | 89.57 W |
| Malden I | 14 | 4.03 S | 154.59 W |
| Malden ≃ | 283 | 42.24 N | 71.05 W |
| Malden Bridge | 210 | 42.28 N | 73.35 W |
| Malden on Hudson | 210 | 42.06 N | 73.56 W |
| Maldivas → Maldives □[1] | 12 | 3.15 N | 73.00 E |
| Maldive Islands → Maldives □[1] | 12 | 3.15 N | 73.00 E |
| Mal di Ventre, Isola di I | 71 | 39.59 N | 8.18 E |
| Maldives □[1] | 12 | 3.15 N | 73.00 E |
| Maldon, Austl. | 169 | 37.00 S | 144.04 E |
| Maldon, Eng., U.K. | 42 | 51.45 N | 0.40 E |
| Maldon □[8] | 260 | 51.43 N | 0.40 E |
| Maldonado | 252 | 34.54 S | 54.57 W |
| Maldonado, Punta › | 234 | 16.20 N | 98.35 W |
| Male, It. | 64 | 46.21 N | 10.55 E |
| Male', Mald. | 12 | 4.10 N | 73.30 E |
| Male, Mya. | 110 | 23.02 N | 95.58 E |
| Maléa, Ákra › | 38 | 36.26 N | 23.12 E |
| Malea, Dolok ∧ | 114 | 0.56 N | 99.38 E |
| Malebo, Pool ⊜ | 152 | 4.17 S | 15.20 E |
| Malediven → Maldives □[1] | 12 | 3.15 N | 73.00 E |
| Mālegaon | 122 | 20.33 N | 74.32 E |
| Malegno, It. | 64 | 45.56 N | 10.14 E |
| Malegno, It. | 64 | 46.40 N | 11.08 E |
| Malehra | 124 | 24.34 N | 79.19 E |
| Maleit, Lake ⊜ | 140 | 7.55 N | 28.35 E |
| Malek, Kaz. | 85 | 40.47 N | 68.37 E |
| Malek, Sūd. | 140 | 6.04 N | 31.36 E |
| Malé Karpaty ⋏ | 30 | 48.30 N | 17.20 E |
| Malek Dīn | 120 | 32.25 N | 68.04 E |
| Malek Kandī | 128 | 37.09 N | 46.06 E |
| Malek Sīāh, Kūh-e ∧ | 128 | 29.51 N | 60.52 E |
| Malela, Zaïre | 154 | 2.28 S | 26.09 E |
| Malela, Zaïre | 154 | 4.22 S | 26.08 E |
| Malema | 154 | 14.57 S | 37.20 E |
| Malen'ga | 24 | 63.50 N | 36.25 E |
| Malengoya | 154 | 3.32 N | 25.25 E |
| Malente | 54 | 54.10 N | 10.33 E |
| Maleo | 62 | 45.10 N | 9.46 E |
| Male Polissya ◆[1] | 78 | 50.10 N | 25.00 E |
| Māler Kotla | 124 | 30.31 N | 75.53 E |
| Malesco | 58 | 46.08 N | 8.30 E |
| Malesherbes | 50 | 48.18 N | 2.25 E |
| Malestroit | 32 | 47.49 N | 2.23 W |
| Maleta | 88 | 50.50 N | 108.25 E |
| Maletto | 70 | 37.49 N | 14.52 E |
| Malfa | 70 | 38.35 N | 14.50 E |
| Malgas | 158 | 34.18 S | 20.35 E |
| Malgersdorf | 60 | 48.32 N | 12.45 E |
| Malgobek | 84 | 43.32 N | 44.34 E |
| Malgomaj ⊜ | 26 | 64.47 N | 16.12 E |
| Malha Wells | 140 | 15.08 N | 26.12 E |
| Malheur ≃ | 202 | 44.03 N | 116.59 W |
| Malheur, North Fork ≃ | 202 | 43.45 N | 118.04 W |
| Malheur, South Fork ≃ | 202 | 43.33 N | 118.10 W |
| Malheureux, Cap › | 157c | 19.59 S | 57.36 E |
| Malheur Lake ⊜ | 202 | 43.20 N | 118.45 W |
| Mali, Guinée | 150 | 12.05 N | 12.18 W |
| Mali, Zaïre | 154 | 2.48 S | 26.08 E |
| Mali □[1], Afr. | 134 | 17.00 N | 4.00 W |
| Mali □[1], Afr. | 150 | 17.00 N | 4.00 W |
| Mali ≃ | 102 | 25.43 N | 97.29 E |
| Maliangping | 102 | 31.29 N | 111.20 E |
| Malianjingzi | 102 | 41.32 N | 95.23 E |
| Malibamatšo ≃ | 158 | 29.20 S | 29.28 E |
| Malibu | 228 | 34.02 N | 118.42 W |
| Malibu Lake ⊜[1] | 228 | 34.07 N | 118.45 W |
| Malien ≃ | 269d | 25.11 N | 121.41 E |
| Malienkang | 269d | 25.10 N | 121.39 E |
| Maligay Bay ⊂ | 116 | 7.30 N | 123.14 E |
| Malighati | 126 | 22.33 N | 87.40 E |
| Maligne ≃ | 182 | 52.56 N | 118.02 W |
| Maligne Lake ⊜ | 182 | 52.40 N | 117.[illegible] W |
| Malīhābād | 124 | 26.55 N | 80.[illegible] E |
| Māliḥah, Wādī ∨ | 142 | 29.21 N | 32.[illegible] E |
| Malik | 112 | 0.34 S | 123.1[illegible] E |
| Malik, Wādī al- ∨ | 140 | 18.02 N | 30.5[illegible] E |
| Mali Kyun I | 110 | 13.06 N | 98.1[illegible] E |
| Malili | 112 | 2.38 S | 121.0[illegible] E |
| Målilla | 26 | 57.23 N | 15.4[illegible] E |
| Malimba, Monts ⋏ | 154 | 7.32 S | 29.3[illegible] E |
| Malim Nawar | 114 | 4.21 N | 101.0[illegible] E |
| Malimono | 116 | 9.34 N | 125.2[illegible] E |
| Malin, Ire. | 48 | 55.18 N | 7.15 W |
| Malin, Or., U.S. | 202 | 42.00 N | 121.24 W |
| Malinalco ⊥ | 234 | 18.57 N | 99.30 W |
| Malinaltepec | 234 | 17.03 N | 98.40 W |
| Malinau | 112 | 3.35 N | 116.38 E |
| Malin Beg | 48 | 54.40 N | 8.48 W |
| Malindang, Mount ∧ | 116 | 8.13 N | 123.38 E |
| Malindi | 154 | 3.13 S | 40.07 E |
| Malindi Marine National Park ♠ | 154 | 3.15 S | 40.10 [illegible] |
| Malines → Mechelen | 50 | 51.02 N | 4.28 [illegible] |
| Malinga | 152 | 2.25 S | 12.14 E |
| Malingping | 115a | 6.46 S | 106.01 E |
| Malingsbosjön ⊜ | 40 | 59.55 N | 15.27 E |
| Malin Head › | 48 | 55.23 N | 7.24 W |
| Malinki | 82 | 54.05 N | 38.59 E |
| Malinniki | 82 | 56.17 N | 38.24 E |
| Malino, Indon. | 112 | 5.15 S | 119.51 E |
| Malino, Ross. | 82 | 55.06 N | 38.11 E |
| Malino, Ross. | 265b | 55.58 N | 37.13 E |
| Malino, Bukit ∧ | 112 | 0.45 N | 120.47 E |
| Malinoa I | 174w | 21.02 S | 175.08 W |
| Malinovka, Ross. | 80 | 51.47 N | 43.26 E |
| Malinovka, Ross. | 86 | 53.24 N | 87.17 E |
| Malinta | 216 | 41.19 N | 84.02 W |
| Malinyi | 154 | 8.56 S | 36.08 E |
| Malipara | 272b | 22.57 N | 88.14 E |
| Mali Rajinac ∧ | 36 | 44.48 N | 15.02 E |
| Malita | 116 | 6.25 N | 125.36 E |
| Malitbog | 116 | 10.10 N | 125.00 E |
| Maliuchang | 107 | 29.05 N | 104.07 E |
| Maliuping | 107 | 29.55 N | 106.23 E |
| Ma Liu Shui | 271d | 22.25 N | 114.12 E |
| Malivo | 82 | 55.07 N | 39.02 E |
| Maliwun | 110 | 10.14 N | 98.37 E |
| Maliyivka | 78 | 47.29 N | 32.43 E |
| Malizhen | 102 | 23.10 N | 104.35 E |
| Maljamar | 196 | 32.51 N | 103.46 W |
| Malka, Ross. | 74 | 53.20 N | 157.30 E |
| Malka, Ross. | 84 | 43.47 N | 43.21 E |
| Malka ≃ | 84 | 43.44 N | 44.15 E |
| Malkāpur | 120 | 20.53 N | 76.12 E |
| Malkara | 130 | 40.53 N | 26.54 E |
| Malkerns | 158 | 26.32 S | 31.11 E |
| Malko Tărnovo | 38 | 41.59 N | 27.32 E |
| Mallāḥ | 132 | 32.30 N | 36.51 E |
| Mallaig, Ab., Can. | 182 | 54.13 N | 111.22 W |
| Mallaig, Scot., U.K. | 46 | 57.00 N | 5.50 W |
| Mallala | 168b | 34.26 S | 138.30 E |
| Mallaoua | 150 | 13.02 N | 9.36 E |
| Mallapunyah | 164 | 16.59 S | 135.49 E |
| Mallaranny | 48 | 53.54 N | 9.49 W |
| Mallard Reservoir ⊜[1] | 282 | 38.01 N | 122.03 W |
| Mallawī | 142 | 27.44 N | 30.50 E |
| Mallee Cliffs National Park ♠ | 166 | 34.15 S | 142.40 E |
| Mallemort | 62 | 43.44 N | 5.11 E |
| Mallersdorf-Pfaffenberg | 60 | 48.47 N | 12.16 E |
| Mallery Lake ⊜ | 176 | 63.55 N | 98.25 W |
| Malles Venosta (Mals) | 64 | 46.41 N | 10.32 E |
| Mallet | 252 | 25.55 S | 50.50 W |
| Mallig | 116 | 17.08 N | 121.41 E |
| Malligasta | 252 | 29.11 S | 67.26 W |
| Mallina | 162 | 20.53 S | 118.02 E |
| Malling | 41 | 56.02 N | 10.10 E |
| Malliss, Dtsch. | 54 | 53.13 N | 11.19 E |
| Malliss, Dtsch. | 54 | 53.13 N | 11.19 E |
| Mallnitz | 64 | 46.59 N | 13.10 E |
| Mallorca I | 34 | 39.30 N | 3.00 E |
| Mallorytown | 212 | 44.29 N | 75.53 W |
| Mallow | 48 | 52.08 N | 8.39 W |
| Mallwood | 216 | 42.51 N | 89.02 W |
| Malm | 26 | 64.04 N | 11.13 E |
| Malmbäck | 26 | 57.35 N | 14.28 E |
| Malmberget | 24 | 67.10 N | 20.40 E |
| Malmédy | 56 | 50.25 N | 6.02 E |
| Malmesbury, S. Afr. | 158 | 33.28 S | 18.44 E |
| Malmesbury, Eng., U.K. | 42 | 51.36 N | 2.06 W |
| Malmesbury, Vale of ∨ | 42 | 51.22 N | 2.10 W |
| Malmköping | 40 | 59.08 N | 16.44 E |
| Malmlången ⊜ | 40 | 59.27 N | 14.42 E |
| Malmö | 41 | 55.36 N | 13.00 E |
| Malmöhus Län □[6] | 26 | 55.45 N | 13.30 E |
| Malmsbury | 169 | 37.12 S | 144.23 E |
| Malmsbury Reservoir ⊜[1] | 169 | 37.13 S | 144.22 E |
| Malmslätt | 26 | 58.25 N | 15.30 E |
| Malmstrom Air Force Base ■ | 202 | 47.30 N | 111.10 W |
| Malmyž | 80 | 56.31 N | 50.41 E |
| Malna | 116 | 8.08 N | 124.27 E |
| Malnate | 62 | 45.48 N | 8.53 E |
| Malnoue | 261 | 48.50 N | 2.36 E |
| Malo | 64 | 45.39 N | 11.24 E |
| Malo I | 175f | 15.40 S | 167.11 E |
| Malo, Arroyo ≃ | 258 | 33.43 S | 58.52 W |
| Maloarchangel'sk | 76 | 52.24 N | 36.30 E |
| Maloarchangel'skoje | 88 | 50.24 N | 108.50 E |
| Maloba | 154 | 6.18 S | 27.39 E |
| Malodel'skaja | 80 | 50.11 N | 43.53 E |
| Maloduša | 76 | 52.09 N | 30.14 E |
| Maloelap I[1] | 14 | 8.45 N | 171.03 E |
| Maloja | 58 | 46.24 N | 9.41 E |
| Malojapass )( | 58 | 46.24 N | 9.41 E |
| Malojaroslavec | 82 | 55.01 N | 36.28 E |
| Malojaz | 86 | 55.13 N | 58.09 E |
| Maloje Goloustnoje | 88 | 52.18 N | 105.18 E |
| Maloje Kozino | 80 | 56.26 N | 43.41 E |
| Maloje-Ščerbedino | 80 | 51.59 N | 42.50 E |
| Maloje Skuratovo | 76 | 53.33 N | 37.00 E |
| Malokaterynivka | 78 | 47.39 N | 35.16 E |
| Malokirsanovka | 83 | 47.28 N | 38.31 E |
| Malokrasnojarka | 86 | 56.28 N | 76.01 E |
| Malo-les-Bains | 50 | 51.03 N | 2.24 E |
| Malolo | 154 | 7.18 S | 36.35 E |
| Malolos, Guam | 174p | 13.18 N | 144.46 E |
| Malolos, Pil. | 116 | 14.51 N | 120.49 E |
| Malom | 164 | 3.10 S | 151.50 E |
| Maloma | 158 | 27.00 S | 31.40 E |
| Malombe, Lake ⊜ | 154 | 14.38 S | 35.12 E |
| Malomykhaylivka | 78 | 48.06 N | 36.23 E |
| Malomykolaivka | 83 | 48.18 N | 39.01 E |
| Malonabatovskij | 80 | 48.57 N | 43.40 E |
| Malone, Fl., U.S. | 192 | 30.57 N | 85.09 W |
| Malone, N.Y., U.S. | 188 | 44.50 N | 74.17 W |
| Malone, Tx., U.S. | 222 | 31.55 N | 96.54 W |
| Malone, Wa., U.S. | 224 | 46.58 N | 123.20 W |
| Malonga | 152 | 10.24 S | 23.10 E |
| Malonno | 64 | 46.07 N | 10.18 E |
| Malonty | 61 | 48.41 N | 14.35 E |
| Małopolska ◆[1] | 30 | 50.10 N | 21.30 E |
| Malorossijka | 86 | 53.12 N | 62.30 E |
| Malošujka | 24 | 63.45 N | 37.22 E |
| Malotkavičy | 76 | 52.07 N | 25.56 E |
| Malott | 182 | 48.16 N | 119.42 W |
| Måløv | 41 | 55.45 N | 12.20 E |
| Małowice | 30 | 51.34 N | 15.27 E |
| Måløy | 26 | 61.56 N | 5.07 E |
| Malozemel'skaja Tundra ◆[1] | 24 | 67.50 N | 51.00 E |
| Malpaisillo | 236 | 12.35 N | 86.41 W |
| Malpartida de Plasencia | 34 | 39.59 N | 6.02 W |
| Malpas, Austl. | 166 | 34.43 S | 140.37 E |


| | | | | | |
|---|---|---|---|---|---|
| ≃ | River | Fluß | Río | Rivière | Rio |
| ≍ | Canal | Kanal | Canal | Canal | Canal |
| ʟ | Waterfall, Rapids | Wasserfall, Stromschnellen | Cascada, Rápidos | Chute d'eau, Rapides | Cascata, Rápidos |
| ʉ | Strait | Meeresstraße | Estrecho | Détroit | Estreito |
| ⊂ | Bay, Gulf | Bucht, Golf | Bahía, Golfo | Baie, Golfe | Baía, Golfo |
| ⊜ | Lake, Lakes | See, Seen | Lago, Lagos | Lac, Lacs | Lago, Lagos |
| ≡ | Swamp | Sumpf | Pantano | Marais | Pântano |
| ⊓ | Ice Features, Glacier | Eis- und Gletscherformen | Accidentes Glaciales | Formes glaciaires | Acidentes glaciares |
| ⊤ | Other Hydrographic Features | Andere Hydrographische Objekte | Otros Elementos Hidrográficos | Autres données hydrographiques | Outros acidentes hidrográficos |

| | | | | | |
|---|---|---|---|---|---|
| ⊹ | Submarine Features | Untermeerische Objekte | Accidentes Submarinos | Formes de relief sous-marin | Acidentes submarinos |
| □ | Political Unit | Politische Einheit | Unidad Politica | Entité politique | Unidade política |
| ⊍ | Cultural Institution | Kulturelle Institution | Institución Cultural | Institution culturelle | Instituição cultural |
| ⊥ | Historical Site | Historische Stätte | Sitio Histórico | Site historique | Sitio histórico |
| ♠ | Recreational Site | Erholungs- und Ferienort | Sitio de Recreo | Centre de loisirs | Area de Lazer |
| ⊠ | Airport | Flughafen | Aeropuerto | Aéroport | Aeroporto |
| ■ | Military Installation | Militäranlage | Instalación Militar | Installation militaire | Instalação militar |
| ◆ | Miscellaneous | Verschiedenes | Misceláneo | Divers | Diversos |

ENGLISH / DEUTSCH


| Name / Name | Page / Seite | Lat.°′ / Breite°′ | Long.°′ / Länge°′ E = Ost |
|---|---|---|---|
| Malpas, Eng., U.K. | 44 | 53.01 N | 2.46 W |
| Malpaso | 234 | 22.37 N | 102.46 W |
| Malpe | 122 | 13.21 N | 74.43 E |
| Malpelo, Isla de I | 242 | 3.59 N | 81.35 W |
| Malpensa, Aeroporto della ⊠ | 62 | 45.38 N | 8.44 E |
| Malpeque Bay c | 186 | 46.30 N | 63.47 W |
| Malprabha ≃ | 122 | 16.12 N | 76.03 E |
| Mālpura | 120 | 26.17 N | 75.23 E |
| Mals → Malles Venosta | 64 | 46.41 N | 10.32 E |
| Mälsåker slott ⊥ | 40 | 59.23 N | 17.18 E |
| Malsch | 56 | 48.53 N | 8.19 E |
| Malše (Maltsch) ≃ | 61 | 48.58 N | 14.28 E |
| Målselva ≃ | 24 | 69.14 N | 18.30 E |
| Malsfeld | 56 | 51.06 N | 9.32 E |
| Malta, Bra. | 250 | 6.54 S | 37.31 W |
| Malta, Lat. | 76 | 56.21 N | 27.10 E |
| Malta, Öst. | 64 | 46.57 N | 13.30 E |
| Malta, Il., U.S. | 216 | 41.56 N | 88.52 W |
| Malta, Mt., U.S. | 202 | 48.21 N | 107.52 W |
| Malta, Oh., U.S. | 188 | 39.38 N | 81.51 W |
| Malta □[1], Europe | 22 | 35.50 N | 14.35 E |
| Malta □[1], Europe | 36 | 35.50 N | 14.35 E |
| Malta I | 36 | 35.53 N | 14.27 E |
| Malta ≃ | 76 | 56.44 N | 26.53 E |
| Malta Channel ʯ | 36 | 36.20 N | 15.00 E |
| Maltahöhe | 156 | 24.50 S | 17.00 E |
| Maltatal V | 64 | 47.03 N | 13.24 E |
| Maltby | 44 | 53.26 N | 1.11 W |
| Malte → Malta □[1] | 36 | 35.50 N | 14.35 E |
| Malte Brun ∧ | 172 | 43.34 S | 170.18 E |
| Maltepe ◆[8] | 267b | 40.55 N | 29.08 E |
| Malton | 44 | 54.08 N | 0.48 W |
| Malton ◆[8] | 275b | 43.42 N | 79.38 W |
| Maltrata | 234 | 18.48 N | 97.16 W |
| Maltsch (Malše) ≃ | 61 | 48.58 N | 14.28 E |
| Malugou | 89 | 43.39 N | 128.27 E |
| Maluku □[4] | 164 | 5.00 S | 130.00 E |
| Maluku (Moluccas) II | 108 | 2.00 S | 128.00 E |
| Maluku, Laut (Molucca Sea) ▼[2] | 108 | 0.00 | 125.00 E |
| Maluku-Maes | 152 | 4.06 S | 15.31 E |
| Ma'lūlā | 130 | 33.50 N | 36.33 E |
| Ma'lūlā, Jabal ∧ | 132 | 33.54 N | 36.36 E |
| Malu Mare | 38 | 44.15 N | 23.51 E |
| Malumfashi | 150 | 11.47 N | 7.37 E |
| Malunda | 112 | 3.00 S | 118.50 E |
| Malung | 26 | 60.40 N | 13.44 E |
| Maluso | 116 | 6.33 N | 121.53 E |
| Malūṭ | 140 | 10.26 N | 32.12 E |
| Maluti | 126 | 24.09 N | 87.41 E |
| Maluwe | 150 | 8.40 N | 2.17 W |
| Maluzhen | 106 | 31.20 N | 121.16 E |
| Malvaglia | 58 | 46.25 N | 8.59 E |
| Malvaglio | 266b | 45.31 N | 8.47 E |
| Malvagna | 70 | 37.55 N | 15.04 E |
| Mālvan | 122 | 16.04 N | 73.28 E |
| Malveira | 266c | 38.45 N | 9.27 W |
| Malvern, Austl. | 274b | 37.52 S | 145.02 E |
| Malvern, Ar., U.S. | 194 | 34.21 N | 92.48 W |
| Malvern, Ia., U.S. | 198 | 41.00 N | 95.35 W |
| Malvern, Oh., U.S. | 214 | 40.41 N | 81.10 W |
| Malvern, Pa., U.S. | 285 | 40.02 N | 75.31 W |
| Malvern ◆[8] | 273d | 26.12 S | 28.06 E |
| Malverne | 276 | 40.40 N | 73.40 W |
| Malvern Hills ∧∧[2] | 42 | 52.05 N | 2.21 W |
| Malvérnia | 156 | 22.06 S | 31.42 E |
| Malvern Link | 42 | 52.08 N | 2.18 W |
| Malvinas | 252 | 29.37 S | 58.59 W |
| Malvinas, Islas → Falkland Islands □[2] | 254 | 51.45 S | 59.00 W |
| Malvito | 68 | 39.36 N | 16.03 E |
| Malwal | 140 | 9.19 N | 31.35 E |
| Mālwa Plateau ∧∧[1] | 124 | 23.50 N | 77.30 E |
| Malybaj | 85 | 43.30 N | 78.25 E |
| Malý Dunaj ≃ | 30 | 47.45 N | 18.09 E |
| Malyj Nesvetaj ≃ | 83 | 47.32 N | 39.49 E |
| Malyj, ostrov I | 76 | 60.02 N | 28.02 E |
| Malyja Haradzjacičy | 76 | 52.33 N | 28.20 E |
| Malyj An'uj ≃ | 74 | 68.30 N | 160.49 E |
| Malyj Čeremšan ≃ | 80 | 54.18 N | 50.01 E |
| Malyj Chamar-Daban, chrebet ∧∧ | 88 | 51.00 N | 105.00 E |
| Malyj Civil' ≃ | 80 | 55.54 N | 47.28 E |
| Malyje Alabuchi | 80 | 51.33 N | 42.10 E |
| Malyje Čany, ozero ⊜ | 86 | 54.33 N | 78.02 E |
| Malyje Jagury | 80 | 45.26 N | 43.01 E |
| Malyje Kamkaly | 86 | 44.44 N | 71.31 E |
| Malyje Karmakuly | 72 | 72.23 N | 52.44 E |
| Malyje Porogi | 265a | 59.47 N | 30.42 E |
| Malyj Irgiz ≃ | 80 | 52.12 N | 47.58 E |
| Malyj Jenisej (Ka-Chem) ≃ | 88 | 51.43 N | 94.26 E |
| Malyj Jugan ≃ | 86 | 60.40 N | 73.54 E |
| Malyj Kundyš ≃ | 80 | 56.22 N | 47.53 E |
| Malyj Šantar, ostrov I | 89 | 54.30 N | 137.36 E |
| Malyj Sarybulak | 86 | 52.10 N | 72.35 E |
| Malyj Tajmyr, ostrov I | 74 | 78.08 N | 107.12 E |
| Malyj T'uters, ostrov I | 76 | 59.49 N | 26.56 E |
| Malyj Uran ≃ | 80 | 52.30 N | 53.01 E |
| Malyj Uzen' ≃ | 80 | 48.50 N | 49.39 E |
| Malyj Zelenčuk ≃ | 84 | 44.24 N | 41.56 E |
| Malyn', Ross. | 82 | 54.36 N | 38.40 E |
| Malyn, Ukr. | 78 | 50.46 N | 29.15 E |
| Malynivka | 78 | 49.47 N | 36.43 E |
| Malyševo | 76 | 57.50 N | 35.36 E |
| Malzéville | 58 | 48.43 N | 6.12 E |
| Mama | 88 | 58.18 N | 112.54 E |
| Mama ≃ | 88 | 58.18 N | 112.55 E |
| Ma Ma Creek ≃ | 171a | 27.35 S | 152.13 E |
| Mamadyš | 80 | 55.44 N | 51.25 E |
| Mamagota | 175e | 6.46 S | 155.24 E |
| Mamahuolang | 104 | 42.24 N | 124.12 E |
| Mamajiecun | 104 | 41.26 N | 122.51 E |
| Mamakan | 88 | 57.48 N | 114.01 E |
| Mamaku | 172 | 38.06 S | 176.05 E |
| Mamakwash Lake ⊜ | 184 | 51.38 N | 92.56 W |
| Mamala Bay c | 229a | 21.18 N | 157.57 W |
| Mamalu Bay c | 229a | 20.37 N | 156.09 W |
| Mamanguape | 250 | 6.50 S | 35.07 W |
| Mama'o, Hakau ✢[2] | 174w | 21.00 S | 175.12 W |
| Mamara | 248 | 14.14 S | 72.35 W |
| Mamaroneck | 210 | 40.56 N | 73.43 W |
| Mamaroneck ≃ | 276 | 40.57 N | 73.44 W |
| Mamaroneck Harbor c | 276 | 40.56 N | 73.43 W |
| Mamasa | 112 | 2.56 S | 119.22 E |
| Mamasa ≃ | 112 | 3.30 S | 119.42 E |
| Mamba | 94 | 36.07 N | 138.55 E |
| Mambaí | 255 | 14.28 S | 46.07 W |
| Mambajao | 116 | 9.15 N | 124.43 E |
| Mambajao, Mount ∧ | 116 | 9.10 N | 124.44 E |
| Mambali | 154 | 4.33 S | 32.41 E |
| Mambalot | 116 | 8.51 N | 117.55 E |
| Mambare ≃ | 164 | 8.20 S | 147.55 E |
| Mambasa | 154 | 1.21 N | 29.03 E |
| Mamberamo ≃ | 164 | 1.26 S | 137.53 E |
| Mambéré ≃ | 152 | 3.31 N | 16.03 E |
| Mambili ≃ | 152 | 0.07 N | 16.08 E |
| Mambrui | 154 | 3.07 S | 40.09 E |
| Mambucaba | 256 | 23.01 S | 44.31 W |
| Mambucaba ≃ | 256 | 23.02 S | 44.32 W |
| Mamburao | 116 | 13.14 N | 120.35 E |
| Mambusao ≃ | 116 | 11.24 N | 122.41 E |
| Mamdūḥ, Rujm ∧ | 132 | 32.14 N | 36.15 E |
| Mamedkala | 84 | 42.10 N | 48.06 E |
| Mamehaktebo | 112 | 0.08 N | 115.32 E |
| Mamelodi | 158 | 25.42 S | 28.21 E |
| Ma-Me-O Beach | 182 | 52.58 N | 113.59 W |
| Mamera | 286c | 10.27 N | 66.59 W |
| Mamera, Quebrada ≃ | 286c | 10.27 N | 66.59 W |
| Mamers | 50 | 48.21 N | 0.23 E |
| Mamfe | 152 | 5.46 N | 9.17 E |
| Mamiá ≃ | 250 | 1.55 S | 55.07 W |
| Mamiá, Lago ⊜ | 246 | 4.15 S | 63.03 W |
| Mamiao | 98 | 35.04 N | 116.10 E |
| Mamie | 192 | 36.07 N | 75.50 W |
| Mamiña | 248 | 20.05 S | 69.14 W |
| Maminigui | 150 | 7.24 N | 5.50 W |
| Mamirolle | 58 | 47.12 N | 6.10 E |
| Mamisonskij, pereval )( | 84 | 42.43 N | 43.48 E |
| Maml'utka | 86 | 54.57 N | 68.35 E |
| Mammendorf | 60 | 48.12 N | 11.09 E |
| Mammola | 68 | 38.22 N | 16.15 E |
| Mammoth, Az., U.S. | 200 | 32.43 N | 110.38 W |
| Mammoth, W.V., U.S. | 188 | 38.15 N | 81.22 W |
| Mammoth Cave National Park ♦ | 194 | 37.08 N | 86.13 W |
| Mammoth Lakes | 204 | 37.38 N | 118.58 W |
| Mammoth Pool Reservoir ⊜[1] | 226 | 37.20 N | 119.20 W |
| Mammoth Spring | 194 | 36.29 N | 91.32 W |
| Mamoiada | 71 | 40.13 N | 9.17 E |
| Mamonovo, Ross. | 76 | 54.28 N | 19.57 E |
| Mamonovo, Ross. | 265b | 55.36 N | 37.49 E |
| Mamonovo, Ross. | 265b | 55.41 N | 37.19 E |
| Mamont | 279b | 40.29 N | 79.36 W |
| Mamontovo, Ross. | 86 | 52.43 N | 81.37 E |
| Mamontovo, Ross. | 86 | 51.45 N | 81.25 E |
| Mamoré ≃ | 248 | 10.23 S | 65.23 W |
| Mamori, Lago ⊜ | 246 | 3.38 S | 60.07 W |
| Mamoriá ≃ | 248 | 7.30 S | 66.21 W |
| Mamou, Guinée | 150 | 10.23 N | 12.05 W |
| Mamou, La., U.S. | 194 | 30.38 N | 92.25 W |
| Mamoutzou | 157a | 12.47 S | 45.14 E |
| Mampikony | 157b | 16.06 S | 47.38 E |
| Mampong | 150 | 7.04 N | 1.24 W |
| Mamraš | 84 | 41.44 N | 48.19 E |
| Mamre | 158 | 33.30 S | 18.29 E |
| Mamry, Jezioro ⊜ | 30 | 54.08 N | 21.42 E |
| Mamuchi | 98 | 35.41 N | 118.17 E |
| Mamué | 152 | 13.35 S | 13.13 E |
| Mamuil, Paso de )( | 254 | 39.35 S | 71.28 W |
| Mamuju | 112 | 2.41 S | 118.54 E |
| Mamulique | 196 | 26.08 N | 100.20 W |
| Ma'mūn | 140 | 12.15 N | 22.41 E |
| Mamuno | 156 | 22.16 S | 20.01 E |
| Mamuripi (Manuripe) ≃ | 248 | 11.06 S | 67.36 W |
| Mamuru ≃ | 250 | 2.42 S | 56.44 W |
| Mamykovo | 80 | 54.38 N | 50.37 E |
| Mamyl' | 24 | 61.57 N | 56.41 E |
| Man, C. Iv. | 150 | 7.24 N | 7.33 W |
| Man, India | 120 | 33.51 N | 78.32 E |
| Man, W.V., U.S. | 192 | 37.44 N | 81.52 W |
| Man (Île de) → Isle of Man □[2] | 44 | 54.15 N | 4.30 W |
| Man, Isle of → Isle of Man □[2] | 44 | 54.15 N | 4.30 W |
| Mana, Guy. fr. | 250 | 5.40 N | 53.47 W |
| Mana, Hi., U.S. | 229b | 22.02 N | 159.46 W |
| Mana ≃, Guy. fr. | 250 | 5.44 N | 53.54 W |
| Mana ≃, Ross. | 86 | 55.57 N | 92.28 E |
| Manabí □[4] | 246 | 0.40 S | 80.05 W |
| Manacacías ≃ | 246 | 4.23 N | 72.04 W |
| Manacapuru | 246 | 3.18 S | 60.37 W |
| Manacapuru ≃ | 246 | 3.18 S | 60.38 W |
| Manacle Point > | 42 | 50.03 N | 5.03 W |
| Manacor | 34 | 39.34 N | 3.12 E |
| Manado | 112 | 1.29 N | 124.51 E |
| Managua | 236 | 12.09 N | 86.17 W |
| Managua □[5] | 236 | 12.00 N | 86.25 W |
| Managua, Aeropuerto ⊠ | 286b | 23.00 N | 82.17 W |
| Managua, Lago de ⊜ | 236 | 12.20 N | 86.20 W |
| Manahawkin | 208 | 39.41 N | 74.15 W |
| Manahawkin Bay c | 208 | 39.40 N | 74.12 W |
| Manaia | 172 | 39.33 S | 174.08 E |
| Manā'if, Bi'r al- ▼[4] | 142 | 30.31 N | 32.12 E |
| Manajenki | 76 | 53.42 N | 36.27 E |
| Manakalampona ∧ | 157b | 15.23 S | 48.50 E |
| Manakara | 157b | 22.08 S | 48.01 E |
| Manakau | 172 | 40.43 S | 175.13 E |
| Manakau ∧ | 172 | 42.14 S | 173.37 E |
| Manākhah | 144 | 15.07 N | 43.44 E |
| Manalapan Brook ≃ | 276 | 40.24 N | 74.23 W |
| Manāli | 123 | 32.15 N | 77.10 E |
| Manama → Al-Manāmah | 128 | 26.13 N | 50.35 E |
| Manamansalo I | 26 | 64.21 N | 27.04 E |
| Manambaho ≃ | 157b | 17.41 S | 44.04 E |
| Manambato, Madag. | 157b | 13.14 S | 49.54 E |
| Manambato, Madag. | 157b | 13.43 S | 49.07 E |
| Manambolo ≃ | 157b | 19.18 S | 44.24 E |
| Manambolosy | 157b | 16.02 S | 49.40 E |
| Manam Island I | 164 | 4.05 S | 145.05 E |
| Mánamo, Caño ≃[1] | 246 | 9.55 N | 62.16 W |
| Manamoc Island I | 116 | 11.19 N | 120.41 E |
| Manana Island I | 229c | 21.20 N | 157.40 W |
| Mananantanana ≃ | 157b | 21.25 S | 45.33 E |
| Mananao | 116 | 13.30 N | 120.34 E |
| Mananara | 157b | 16.10 S | 49.46 E |
| Mananara ≃ | 157b | 23.21 S | 47.42 E |
| Manandaza | 157b | 19.19 S | 45.23 E |
| Mananjary | 157b | 21.13 S | 48.20 E |
| Manankoro | 150 | 10.28 N | 7.27 W |
| Manantenina | 157b | 24.17 S | 47.19 E |
| Manantiales Behr | 254 | 45.41 S | 67.31 W |
| Manaoag | 116 | 16.03 N | 120.29 E |
| Manáos → Manaus | 246 | 3.08 S | 60.01 W |
| Manapatrana | 157b | 21.40 S | 47.35 E |
| Manapiare ≃ | 246 | 5.04 N | 66.30 W |
| Manapire ≃ | 246 | 7.42 N | 66.07 W |
| Manapla | 116 | 10.58 N | 123.07 E |
| Mana Point > | 229b | 22.03 N | 159.47 W |
| Mana Pools National Park ♦ | 154 | 16.00 S | 28.35 E |
| Manapouri | 172 | 45.34 S | 167.36 E |
| Manapouri, Lake ⊜ | 172 | 45.30 S | 167.30 E |
| Manappārai | 122 | 10.36 N | 78.25 E |
| Manaquiri, Lago ⊜ | 246 | 3.29 S | 60.31 W |
| Manār ≃ | 122 | 18.39 N | 77.44 E |
| Manaravolo | 157b | 23.59 S | 45.39 E |
| Manas, Som. | 144 | 2.57 N | 43.28 E |
| Manas, Zhg. | 86 | 44.18 N | 86.13 E |
| Manās ≃, Asia | 120 | 26.13 N | 90.38 E |
| Manas ≃, Zhg. | 86 | 45.38 N | 85.12 E |
| Manas, gora ∧ | 85 | 42.18 N | 71.01 E |
| Manasarowar Lake → Mapam Yumco ⊜ | 120 | 30.42 N | 81.27 E |
| Manas Hu ⊜ | 86 | 45.45 N | 85.55 E |
| Manāslu ∧ | 124 | 28.33 N | 84.33 E |
| Manasota Key I | 220 | 26.58 N | 82.23 W |
| Manasquan | 208 | 40.07 N | 74.02 W |
| Manasquan ≃ | 208 | 40.06 N | 74.02 W |
| Manassa | 200 | 37.10 N | 105.56 W |
| Manassas | 208 | 38.45 N | 77.28 W |
| Manassas National Battlefield Park ♦ | 208 | 38.50 N | 77.32 W |
| Manassas Park | 208 | 38.46 N | 77.27 W |
| Manastash Creek ≃ | 224 | 46.59 N | 120.35 W |
| Manastash Creek, North Fork ≃ | 224 | 46.57 N | 120.44 W |
| Manastash Creek, South Fork ≃ | 224 | 46.57 N | 120.44 W |
| Manastash Ridge ∧ | 224 | 46.55 N | 120.30 W |
| Mânăstirea | 38 | 44.13 N | 26.54 E |
| Manatang | 112 | 8.26 S | 124.28 E |
| Manatawny | 208 | 40.17 N | 75.41 W |
| Manatawny Creek ≃ | 208 | 40.14 N | 75.39 W |
| Manatee □[6] | 220 | 27.26 N | 82.25 W |
| Manatee ≃ | 220 | 27.32 N | 82.38 W |
| Manatee, Lake ⊜[1] | 220 | 27.29 N | 82.20 W |
| Manatí, Col. | 246 | 10.27 N | 74.58 W |
| Manatí, Cuba | 240p | 21.19 N | 76.56 W |
| Manatí, P.R. | 240m | 18.26 N | 66.29 W |
| Manatí ≃ | 240p | 21.40 N | 79.50 W |
| Manatí, Bahía de c | 240p | 21.24 N | 76.48 W |
| Manatuto | 112 | 8.30 S | 126.01 E |
| Manaul | 116 | 12.27 N | 121.25 E |
| Manaung | 110 | 18.51 N | 93.44 E |
| Manaus | 246 | 3.08 S | 60.01 W |
| Manavgat | 130 | 36.47 N | 31.26 E |
| Manawa | 190 | 44.27 N | 88.55 W |
| Mānāwāla | 123 | 31.35 N | 73.41 E |
| Manawan Lake ⊜ | 184 | 55.24 N | 103.14 W |
| Manāwar | 120 | 22.14 N | 75.05 E |
| Manawatu ≃ | 172 | 40.28 S | 175.13 E |
| Manawoka, Pulau I | 164 | 4.05 S | 131.20 E |
| Manay | 116 | 7.13 N | 126.32 E |
| Manayunk ◆[8] | 285 | 40.01 N | 75.13 W |
| Manazuru | 94 | 35.09 N | 139.08 E |
| Manazuru-misaki > | 94 | 35.08 N | 139.10 E |
| Manban | 102 | 23.04 N | 103.11 E |
| Mānbāzār | 126 | 23.04 N | 86.39 E |
| Manbian | 102 | 24.19 N | 100.32 E |
| Manbij | 130 | 36.31 N | 37.57 E |
| Manby | 44 | 53.22 N | 0.06 E |
| Mancelona | 190 | 44.54 N | 85.03 W |
| Mancha Blanca | 254 | 40.47 S | 65.27 W |
| Mancha Real | 34 | 37.47 N | 3.37 W |
| Manchaug | 207 | 42.05 N | 71.44 W |
| Manche □[5] | 32 | 49.00 N | 1.10 W |
| Mancheng | 105 | 38.56 N | 115.20 E |
| Mancherāl | 122 | 18.52 N | 79.26 E |
| Manchester, Eng., U.K. | 44 | 53.28 N | 2.15 W |
| Manchester, Eng., U.K. | 262 | 53.28 N | 2.15 W |
| Manchester, Ct., U.S. | 207 | 41.46 N | 72.31 W |
| Manchester, Ga., U.S. | 192 | 32.51 N | 84.37 W |
| Manchester, Il., U.S. | 219 | 39.33 N | 90.20 W |
| Manchester, Ia., U.S. | 190 | 42.29 N | 91.27 W |
| Manchester, Ky., U.S. | 192 | 37.09 N | 83.45 W |
| Manchester, Md., U.S. | 208 | 39.39 N | 76.53 W |
| Manchester, Ma., U.S. | 207 | 42.34 N | 70.46 W |
| Manchester, Mi., U.S. | 216 | 42.09 N | 84.02 W |
| Manchester, N.H., U.S. | 188 | 42.59 N | 71.27 W |
| Manchester, N.Y., U.S. | 210 | 42.58 N | 77.13 W |
| Manchester, Oh., U.S. | 218 | 38.41 N | 83.36 W |
| Manchester, Pa., U.S. | 208 | 40.03 N | 76.43 W |
| Manchester, Tn., U.S. | 194 | 35.28 N | 86.05 W |
| Manchester, Vt., U.S. | 210 | 43.09 N | 73.04 W |
| Manchester, Wa., U.S. | 224 | 47.33 N | 122.33 W |
| Manchester □[8] | 262 | 53.27 N | 2.13 W |
| Manchester Bridge | 210 | 41.41 N | 73.52 W |
| Manchester City Football Ground ♦ | 262 | 53.27 N | 2.14 W |
| Manchester Docks ◆[5] | 262 | 53.28 N | 2.17 W |
| Manchester International Airport ⊠ | 44 | 53.21 N | 2.15 W |
| Manchester Race Course ♦ | 262 | 53.30 N | 2.16 W |
| Manchester Ship Canal ≅ | 262 | 53.19 N | 2.57 W |
| Manchester United Football Ground ♦ | 262 | 53.28 N | 2.18 W |
| Manching | 60 | 48.43 N | 11.30 E |
| Manchioneal | 241q | 18.02 N | 76.17 W |
| Manchón | 236 | 14.23 N | 92.02 W |
| Manchouli → Manzhouli | 88 | 49.35 N | 117.22 E |
| Manchuria □[9] | 90 | 47.00 N | 125.00 E |
| Manciano | 66 | 42.35 N | 11.31 E |
| Mancieulles | 56 | 49.17 N | 5.53 E |
| Máncora | 246 | 4.06 S | 81.05 W |
| Mancos | 200 | 37.20 N | 108.17 W |
| Mancos ≃ | 200 | 36.59 N | 108.59 W |
| Mand | 128 | 26.07 N | 62.03 E |
| Mānd ≃, India | 120 | 21.42 N | 83.15 E |
| Mand ≃, Īrān | 128 | 28.11 N | 51.17 E |
| Manda, India | 126 | 22.06 N | 86.14 E |
| Manda, Tan. | 154 | 7.58 S | 32.26 E |
| Manda, Tan. | 154 | 8.30 S | 32.44 E |
| Manda, Tan. | 154 | 10.28 S | 34.35 E |
| Manda, Tchad | 146 | 9.12 N | 18.10 E |
| Manda, Jabal ∧ | 140 | 8.39 N | 24.27 E |
| Mandabe, Madag. | 157b | 21.03 S | 44.55 E |
| Mandabe, Madag. | 157b | 20.55 S | 45.49 E |
| Mandach | 102 | 44.28 N | 108.11 E |
| Mandaguari | 255 | 23.32 S | 51.42 W |
| Mandai Orchard Gardens ♦ | 271c | 1.24 N | 103.47 E |
| Manda Island I | 154 | 2.15 S | 40.57 E |
| Mandal | 26 | 58.02 N | 7.27 E |
| Mandal, Jibāl ∧[2] | 140 | 12.09 N | 29.31 E |
| Mandala, Puncak ∧ | 164 | 4.44 S | 140.20 E |
| Mandalay | 110 | 22.00 N | 96.05 E |
| Mandalay □[5] | 110 | 21.00 N | 96.00 E |
| Mandale | 216 | 41.01 N | 84.20 W |
| Mandale Station ◆[5] | 272c | 19.03 N | 72.56 E |
| Mandalgov' | 102 | 45.45 N | 106.12 E |
| Mandalī | 128 | 33.45 N | 45.32 E |
| Mandalkia | 272b | 22.43 N | 88.08 E |
| Mandal-Ovoo | 102 | 44.35 N | 104.05 E |
| Mandalselva ≃ | 26 | 58.02 N | 7.28 E |
| Mandaluyong | 269f | 14.35 N | 121.02 E |
| Mandan | 198 | 46.49 N | 100.53 W |
| Mandanici | 70 | 38.00 N | 15.19 E |
| Mandāoli ◆[8] | 272a | 28.38 N | 77.18 E |
| Mandaon | 116 | 12.14 N | 123.17 E |
| Mandapur | 126 | 23.00 N | 88.29 E |
| Mandar, Teluk c | 112 | 3.40 S | 119.15 E |
| Mandara Mountains (Monts Mandara) ∧∧ | 146 | 10.45 N | 13.40 E |
| Mandas | 71 | 39.38 N | 9.07 E |
| Mandatoriccio | 68 | 39.28 N | 16.50 E |
| Mandau ≃ | 114 | 0.48 N | 101.47 E |
| Mandaue | 116 | 10.20 N | 123.56 E |
| Mandāwar | 124 | 29.30 N | 78.08 E |
| Mandeb, Bab el ʯ | 144 | 12.40 N | 43.20 E |
| Mandehu | 104 | 42.07 N | 121.33 E |
| Mandel | 128 | 33.17 N | 61.52 E |
| Mandélia | 146 | 11.43 N | 15.15 E |
| Mandelieu | 62 | 43.33 N | 6.56 E |
| Mandello del Lario | 58 | 45.54 N | 9.19 E |
| Mandera | 154 | 3.56 N | 41.52 E |
| Manderfeld | 56 | 50.20 N | 6.20 E |
| Manderscheid | 56 | 50.05 N | 6.49 E |
| Manderson | 202 | 44.16 N | 107.57 W |
| Mandeure | 58 | 47.27 N | 6.48 E |
| Mandeville, P.Q., Can. | 206 | 46.22 N | 73.22 W |
| Mandeville, Jam. | 241q | 18.02 N | 77.30 W |
| Mandeville, N.Z. | 172 | 46.00 S | 168.49 E |
| Mandeville, La., U.S. | 194 | 30.21 N | 90.03 W |
| Mandi | 123 | 31.43 N | 76.55 E |
| Mandiana | 150 | 10.38 N | 8.41 W |
| Mandiangin | 112 | 2.01 S | 102.58 E |
| Mandi Angin, Gunong ∧ | 114 | 4.42 N | 102.52 E |
| Mandi Bahāuddīn | 123 | 32.35 N | 73.30 E |
| Mandi Būrewāla | 123 | 30.09 N | 72.41 E |
| Mandi Dabwāli | 123 | 29.58 N | 74.42 E |
| Mandié | 154 | 16.30 S | 33.30 E |
| Mandimba | 154 | 14.21 S | 35.39 E |
| Mandini | 158 | 29.09 S | 31.25 E |
| Mandioli, Pulau I | 108 | 0.44 S | 127.14 E |
| Mandioré, Lagoa ⊜ | 248 | 18.08 S | 57.33 W |
| Mandira ⊜[1] | 124 | 22.20 N | 84.35 E |
| Mandiri ≃ | 115a | 7.02 S | 106.32 E |
| Mandi Sādiqganj | 123 | 30.10 N | 73.44 E |
| Mandjafa | 146 | 11.11 N | 15.25 E |
| Mandjé, Lac ⊜ | 152 | 2.50 S | 10.22 E |
| Mandji | 152 | 1.36 S | 10.26 E |
| Mandla | 124 | 22.36 N | 80.23 E |
| Mandora | 162 | 19.44 S | 120.51 E |
| Mandoto | 157b | 19.34 S | 46.17 E |
| Mandoul ≃ | 146 | 8.56 N | 17.58 E |
| Mandouri | 150 | 10.51 N | 0.49 E |
| Mándra, Ellás | 267c | 38.04 N | 23.30 E |
| Māndrā, India | 272b | 22.55 N | 88.07 E |
| Mandra, Pāk. | 123 | 33.22 N | 73.14 E |
| Mandrare ≃ | 157b | 25.10 S | 46.27 E |
| Mandres-les-Roses | 261 | 48.42 N | 2.33 E |
| Mandriola ◆[8] | 267a | 41.45 N | 12.30 E |
| Mandriole | 64 | 44.33 N | 12.14 E |
| Mandrioli, Passo dei )( | 66 | 43.48 N | 11.55 E |
| Mandritsara | 157b | 15.50 S | 48.49 E |
| Mandronarivo | 157b | 21.07 S | 45.38 E |
| Mandsaur | 120 | 24.04 N | 75.04 E |
| Māndu | 122 | 22.22 N | 75.23 E |
| Mandu, Ribeirão do ≃ | 256 | 22.14 S | 45.55 W |
| Manduba, Ponta > | 256 | 24.05 S | 46.18 W |
| Manduhu | 104 | 41.36 N | 122.38 E |
| Mandun | 102 | 22.17 N | 100.05 E |
| Mandurah | 168a | 32.32 S | 115.43 E |
| Manduria | 68 | 40.24 N | 17.38 E |
| Māndvi, India | 120 | 21.15 N | 73.18 E |
| Māndvi, India | 120 | 22.50 N | 69.22 E |
| Mandvi ◆[8] | 272c | 18.57 N | 72.50 E |
| Mandya | 122 | 12.33 N | 76.54 E |
| Mané | 150 | 12.59 N | 1.21 W |
| Måne ≃ | 26 | 59.00 N | 9.40 E |
| Manea | 42 | 52.30 N | 0.11 E |
| Manebach | 54 | 50.41 N | 10.51 E |
| Manek Urai | 114 | 5.23 N | 102.14 E |
| Manendragarh | 124 | 23.13 N | 82.13 E |
| Manera | 157b | 22.55 S | 44.20 E |
| Manerbio | 64 | 45.21 N | 10.08 E |
| Manětím | 60 | 49.59 N | 13.14 E |
| Manevychi | 78 | 51.17 N | 25.33 E |
| Manfalūṭ | 142 | 27.19 N | 30.58 E |
| Manfredonia | 68 | 41.38 N | 15.55 E |
| Manfredonia, Golfo di c | 68 | 41.35 N | 16.05 E |
| Manga, Bra. | 255 | 14.46 S | 43.56 W |
| Manga, Burkina | 150 | 11.40 N | 1.04 W |
| Manga, Ur. | 258 | 34.49 S | 56.06 W |
| Manga ◆[1] | 146 | 15.00 N | 14.00 E |
| Mangabeiras, Chapada das ∧∧[2] | 250 | 10.00 S | 46.30 W |
| Mangagoy | 116 | 8.11 N | 126.21 E |
| Mangahao ≃ | 172 | 40.23 S | 175.50 E |
| Mangai | 164 | 2.45 S | 151.05 E |
| Mangaia I | 14 | 21.55 S | 157.55 W |
| Mangakino | 172 | 38.22 S | 175.47 E |
| Mangala | 152 | 1.02 N | 23.50 E |
| Mangalagiri | 122 | 16.26 N | 80.33 E |
| Mangaldai | 120 | 26.26 N | 92.02 E |
| Mangaldan | 116 | 16.04 N | 120.24 E |
| Mangalia | 38 | 43.50 N | 28.35 E |
| Mangalkot | 126 | 23.33 N | 87.54 E |
| Mangalmé | 146 | 12.21 N | 19.37 E |
| Mangalore | 122 | 12.52 N | 74.53 E |
| Mangalpaita | 126 | 23.19 N | 89.11 E |
| Mangalvedha | 122 | 17.31 N | 75.28 E |
| Mangamahu | 172 | 39.49 S | 175.22 E |
| Manganês ≃ | 250 | 10.21 S | 48.27 W |
| Manganji | 268 | 35.40 N | 139.26 E |
| Mangaoka | 157b | 12.19 S | 49.07 E |
| Mangapehi | 172 | 38.31 S | 175.18 E |
| Mangaratiba | 256 | 22.57 S | 44.02 W |
| Mangart, Monte (Mangrt) ∧ | 64 | 46.25 N | 13.40 E |
| Mangatarem | 116 | 15.47 N | 120.17 E |
| Mangawān | 124 | 24.41 N | 81.33 E |
| Mangaweka | 172 | 39.48 S | 175.47 E |
| Mangaweka ∧ | 172 | 39.49 S | 176.05 E |
| Mangcao Point > | 116 | 11.02 N | 123.54 E |
| Mangchang | 102 | 25.08 N | 107.31 E |
| Mangde ≃ | 124 | 27.35 N | 90.28 E |
| Mange, S.L. | 150 | 8.55 N | 12.51 W |
| Mange, Zaïre | 152 | 0.54 N | 20.30 E |
| Mange, Zhg. | 120 | 32.25 N | 83.35 E |
| Mangeigne | 146 | 10.31 N | 21.19 E |
| Mangerton Mountain ∧ | 48 | 51.57 N | 9.29 W |
| Mangfall ≃ | 64 | 47.51 N | 12.08 E |
| Manggar | 112 | 2.53 S | 108.16 E |
| Manggeng | 114 | 3.36 N | 96.55 E |
| Manggonggri | 164 | 3.30 S | 133.19 E |
| Mangguar, Tanjung > | 164 | 2.53 S | 134.51 E |
| Mangham | 194 | 32.18 N | 91.46 W |
| Mangichu ≃ | 126 | 23.24 N | 90.48 E |
| Mangindrano | 157b | 14.17 S | 48.58 E |
| Mangin Range ∧∧ | 110 | 24.20 N | 95.42 E |
| Mangistau □[8] | 86 | 44.00 N | 54.30 E |
| Mangkalihat, Tanjung > | 112 | 1.02 N | 118.59 E |
| Mangkutana | 112 | 2.24 S | 120.48 E |
| Manglares, Cabo > | 246 | 1.36 N | 79.02 W |
| Mangla Reservoir ⊜[1] | 123 | 33.10 N | 73.40 E |
| Manglaur | 124 | 29.48 N | 77.52 E |
| Manglisi | 84 | 41.43 N | 44.24 E |
| Mangnai | 120 | 37.40 N | 91.50 E |
| Mangniu ≃, Zhg. | 104 | 41.45 N | 120.53 E |
| Mangniu ≃, Zhg. | 105 | 39.04 N | 116.26 E |
| Mangnuiyingzi | 104 | 41.37 N | 120.43 E |
| Mango | 220 | 28.00 N | 82.19 W |
| Mangochi | 154 | 14.28 S | 35.16 E |
| Mango Island I | 175g | 17.27 S | 179.09 W |
| Mangoky ≃, Madag. | 157b | 21.29 S | 43.41 E |
| Mangoky ≃, Madag. | 157b | 23.27 S | 45.13 E |
| Mangole, Pulau I | 112 | 1.53 S | 125.50 E |
| Mangombe | 154 | 1.25 S | 26.54 E |
| Mangone | 68 | 39.12 N | 16.20 E |
| Mangonia Park | 220 | 26.46 N | 80.05 W |
| Mangonui | 172 | 34.59 S | 173.32 E |
| Mangoplah | 171b | 35.23 S | 147.15 E |
| Mangoro ≃ | 157b | 20.00 S | 48.45 E |
| Mangotsfield | 42 | 51.28 N | 2.28 W |
| Mangoupa | 140 | 5.53 N | 24.40 E |
| Mangrol | 120 | 21.07 N | 70.07 E |
| Mangrove Cay I | 238 | 24.10 N | 77.45 W |
| Mangrove Creek ≃ | 170 | 33.28 S | 151.10 E |
| Mangrove Creek Dam ◆[6] | 170 | 33.13 S | 151.07 E |
| Mangrove Mountain | 170 | 33.19 S | 151.14 E |
| Mangrove Point > | 220 | 26.56 N | 82.08 W |
| Mangrt (Monte Mangart) ∧ | 64 | 46.25 N | 13.40 E |
| Mangrullo, Cuchilla ∧∧[2] | 258 | 34.34 S | 56.42 W |
| Mangrūl Pīr | 122 | 20.19 N | 77.21 E |
| Mångsälven ≃ | 40 | 59.59 N | 14.36 E |
| Mangsang | 112 | 2.10 S | 104.00 E |
| Mangu ≃ | 273b | 4.24 S | 15.24 E |
| Mangualde | 34 | 40.36 N | 7.46 W |
| Mangueira, Lagoa c | 252 | 33.06 S | 52.48 W |
| Mangueirinha | 252 | 25.57 S | 52.09 W |
| Manguéni, Plateau du ∧∧[1] | 146 | 22.35 N | 12.40 E |
| Mangui | 89 | 52.03 N | 122.13 E |
| Manguito | 240p | 22.35 N | 80.55 W |
| Mangulile | 236 | 15.03 N | 86.49 W |
| Mangum | 196 | 34.52 N | 99.30 W |
| Mangungu | 152 | 5.13 S | 19.35 E |
| Mangut, Ross. | 86 | 55.47 N | 70.46 E |
| Mangut, Ross. | 88 | 49.46 N | 112.38 E |
| Mangya | 90 | 37.40 N | 90.50 E |
| Man'gyŏng | 98 | 35.52 N | 126.48 E |
| Manhan ≃ | 207 | 42.17 N | 72.38 W |
| Manhartsberg ∧ | 61 | 48.32 N | 15.44 E |
| Manhasset | 276 | 40.47 N | 73.42 W |
| Manhasset Bay c | 276 | 40.50 N | 73.43 W |
| Manhasset Hills | 276 | 40.46 N | 73.41 W |
| Manhasset Neck >[1] | 276 | 40.50 N | 73.42 W |
| Manhattan, Il., U.S. | 216 | 41.25 N | 87.59 W |
| Manhattan, Ks., U.S. | 198 | 39.11 N | 96.34 W |
| Manhattan, Mt., U.S. | 202 | 45.51 N | 111.19 W |
| Manhattan □[8] | 276 | 40.46 N | 73.55 W |
| Manhattan Beach | 228 | 33.53 N | 118.24 W |
| Manhattan Beach State Park ♦ | 280 | 33.54 N | 118.25 W |
| Manhattan Bridge ◆[5] | 276 | 40.42 N | 73.59 W |
| Manhattan College ♁[2] | 276 | 40.53 N | 73.54 W |
| Manheim | 208 | 40.09 N | 76.23 W |
| Manhiça | 156 | 25.24 S | 32.48 E |
| Mān Hpāng | 110 | 22.41 N | 98.36 E |
| Manhuaçu | 255 | 20.15 S | 42.02 W |
| Manhuaçu ≃ | 255 | 19.30 S | 41.06 W |
| Manhumirim | 255 | 20.22 S | 41.57 W |
| Maní, P.R. | 240m | 18.15 N | 67.10 W |
| Mani, Zaïre | 154 | 6.27 S | 25.20 E |
| Māni', Jabal al- ∧ | 132 | 33.19 N | 36.17 E |
| Mania ≃ | 157b | 19.42 S | 45.22 E |
| Maniago | 64 | 46.10 N | 12.43 E |
| Maniamba | 154 | 12.43 S | 35.00 E |
| Manianga | 273b | 4.10 S | 15.19 E |
| Manica □[5] | 156 | 19.00 S | 33.15 E |
| Manicahan | 116 | 7.01 N | 122.12 E |
| Manicaland □[4] | 154 | 19.30 S | 32.15 E |
| Manicani Island I | 116 | 10.59 N | 125.38 E |
| Manicaragua | 240p | 22.09 N | 79.58 W |
| Manic Deux, Réservoir ⊜[1] | 186 | 49.25 N | 68.25 W |
| Manicoré | 248 | 5.49 S | 61.17 W |
| Manicoré ≃ | 248 | 5.51 S | 61.19 W |
| Manicouagan ≃ | 186 | 49.11 N | 68.13 W |
| Manicouagan, Réservoir ⊜[1] | 186 | 51.30 N | 68.19 W |
| Manic Trois, Réservoir ⊜[1] | 186 | 50.00 N | 68.40 W |
| Maniema □[4] | 154 | 3.00 S | 26.30 E |
| Manifold ≃ | 44 | 53.03 N | 1.47 W |
| Maniganggo | 102 | 32.01 N | 99.11 E |
| Manignan | 150 | 10.00 N | 7.50 W |
| Manigotagan | 184 | 51.06 N | 96.18 W |
| Manigotagan ≃ | 184 | 51.07 N | 96.20 W |
| Manihāri | 124 | 25.21 N | 87.38 E |
| Manihiki I[1] | 14 | 10.24 S | 161.01 W |
| Manika, Plateau de la ∧∧[1] | 154 | 10.00 S | 26.00 E |
| Manikanāli | 126 | 23.19 N | 87.03 E |
| Mānikganj | 124 | 23.52 N | 90.00 E |
| Mānikpur | 124 | 25.04 N | 81.07 E |
| Manila, Pil. | 116 | 14.35 N | 121.00 E |
| Manila, Pil. | 269f | 14.35 N | 121.00 E |
| Manila, Ar., U.S. | 194 | 35.52 N | 90.10 W |
| Manila, Ut., U.S. | 200 | 40.59 N | 109.43 W |
| Manila Bay c | 116 | 14.30 N | 120.45 E |
| Manila Cathedral ♁[1] | 269f | 14.35 N | 120.59 E |
| Manila International Airport ⊠ | 269f | 14.31 N | 121.01 E |
| Manilla, Austl. | 166 | 30.45 S | 150.43 E |
| Manilla, In., U.S. | 218 | 39.34 N | 85.37 W |
| Manilla, Ia., U.S. | 198 | 41.53 N | 95.13 W |
| Manille → Manila | 116 | 14.35 N | 121.00 E |
| Manily | 74 | 62.29 N | 165.36 E |
| Mani Majra | 123 | 30.43 N | 76.50 E |
| Manimbaya, Tanjung > | 112 | 0.01 N | 119.36 E |
| Manimpé | 150 | 14.09 N | 5.31 W |
| Maningory ≃ | 157b | 17.13 S | 49.28 E |
| Maningrida | 164 | 12.03 S | 134.13 E |
| Maninjau, Danau ⊜ | 112 | 0.20 S | 100.11 E |
| Manino | 76 | 53.58 N | 34.20 E |
| Manipa, Pulau I | 164 | 3.17 S | 127.35 E |
| Manipa, Selat ʯ | 164 | 3.20 S | 127.23 E |
| Manipur □[3] | 120 | 25.00 N | 94.00 E |
| Manipur ≃ | 110 | 22.52 N | 94.05 E |
| Manique de Baixo | 266c | 38.44 N | 9.22 W |
| Maniquin Island I | 116 | 11.36 N | 121.45 E |
| Manirāmpur | 126 | 23.01 N | 89.14 E |
| Manisa | 130 | 38.36 N | 27.26 E |
| Manisa □[4] | 130 | 38.50 N | 28.10 E |
| Manissauá-Miçu ≃ | 250 | 10.58 S | 53.20 W |
| Manistee | 190 | 44.14 N | 86.19 W |
| Manistee ≃ | 190 | 44.15 N | 86.21 W |
| Manistique | 190 | 45.57 N | 86.14 W |
| Manistique ≃ | 190 | 45.57 N | 86.15 W |
| Manistique, West Branch ≃ | 190 | 46.02 N | 86.09 W |
| Manistique Lake ⊜ | 190 | 46.15 N | 85.45 W |
| Manito | 194 | 40.25 N | 89.46 W |
| Manitoba □[4], Can. | 176 | 54.00 N | 97.00 W |
| Manitoba □[4], Can. | 184 | 54.00 N | 97.00 W |
| Manitoba, Lake ⊜ | 184 | 51.00 N | 98.45 W |
| Manitou | 184 | 49.15 N | 98.31 W |
| Manitou ≃, On., Can. | 184 | 48.58 N | 93.20 W |
| Manitou ≃, P.Q., Can. | 186 | 50.18 N | 65.15 W |
| Manitou, Lac ⊜, P.Q., Can. | 186 | 50.29 N | 63.54 W |
| Manitou, Lac ⊜, P.Q., Can. | 186 | 50.54 N | 65.18 W |
| Manitou, Lac ⊜, P.Q., Can. | 206 | 46.03 N | 74.23 W |
| Manitou, Lake ⊜, On., Can. | 190 | 45.48 N | 82.00 W |
| Manitou, Lake ⊜, In., U.S. | 216 | 41.03 N | 86.11 W |
| Manitou Beach, Sk., Can. | 184 | 51.43 N | 105.26 W |
| Manitou Beach, Mi., U.S. | 216 | 41.58 N | 84.19 W |
| Manitou Lake ⊜, On., Can. | 190 | 46.01 N | 79.00 W |
| Manitou Lake ⊜, Sk., Can. | 184 | 52.45 N | 109.45 W |
| Manitoulin Island I | 190 | 45.50 N | 82.20 W |
| Manitou Springs | 200 | 38.51 N | 104.55 W |
| Manitouwabing Lake ⊜ | 212 | 45.29 N | 79.54 W |
| Manitowaning | 190 | 45.45 N | 81.49 W |
| Manitowik Lake ⊜ | 190 | 48.10 N | 84.24 W |
| Manitowish Waters | 190 | 46.09 N | 89.53 W |
| Manitowoc | 190 | 44.05 N | 87.39 W |
| Manitowoc ≃ | 190 | 44.05 N | 87.39 W |
| Maniwaki | 188 | 46.23 N | 75.58 W |
| Ma'nīyā | 142 | 30.50 N | 30.39 E |
| Manizales | 246 | 5.05 N | 75.32 W |
| Manja, Madag. | 157b | 21.26 S | 44.20 E |
| Manjā, Urd. | 132 | 31.45 N | 35.51 E |
| Manjacaze | 156 | 24.44 S | 33.53 E |
| Manjakandriana | 157b | 18.55 S | 47.47 E |
| Manjeri | 122 | 11.07 N | 76.07 E |
| Manjiang | 98 | 41.57 N | 127.36 E |
| Manjimup | 162 | 34.14 S | 116.09 E |
| Manjing | 107 | 29.55 N | 104.07 E |
| Mānjra ≃ | 122 | 18.49 N | 77.52 E |
| Manjuyod | 116 | 9.41 N | 123.09 E |
| Mank | 61 | 48.06 N | 15.20 E |
| Mankanaj | 86 | 48.58 N | 60.58 E |
| Månkarbo | 40 | 60.14 N | 17.28 E |
| Mān Kāt | 110 | 22.05 N | 98.01 E |
| Mankato, Ks., U.S. | 198 | 39.47 N | 98.12 W |
| Mankato, Mn., U.S. | 190 | 44.09 N | 93.59 W |
| Mankayane | 158 | 26.42 S | 31.00 E |
| Mankent | 85 | 42.25 N | 69.50 E |
| Mankera | 123 | 31.23 N | 71.26 E |
| Mankim | 152 | 5.01 N | 12.00 E |
| Mankinholes | 262 | 53.42 N | 2.03 W |
| Man'kivka, Ukr. | 78 | 48.58 N | 30.20 E |
| Man'kivka, Ukr. | 83 | 49.34 N | 38.27 E |
| Mankono | 150 | 8.04 N | 6.12 W |
| Mankota | 184 | 49.25 N | 107.04 W |
| Man'kovo | 83 | 49.24 N | 40.17 E |
| Man'kovo-Ber'ozovskaja | 80 | 48.47 N | 41.33 E |
| Mankoya | 154 | 14.47 S | 24.48 E |
| Mānkundu | 272b | 22.50 N | 88.22 E |
| Mānkur, India | 126 | 22.30 N | 87.54 E |
| Mānkur, India | 126 | 23.20 N | 87.33 E |
| Manlaj | 102 | 44.07 N | 106.50 E |
| Manley | 262 | 53.14 N | 2.45 W |
| Manley Hot Springs | 180 | 65.00 N | 150.37 W |
| Manleys Corner | 283 | 42.03 N | 71.04 W |
| Manlius | 210 | 43.00 N | 75.58 W |
| Manlleu | 34 | 42.00 N | 2.17 E |
| Manly, Austl. | 170 | 33.48 S | 151.17 E |
| Manly, Austl. | 171a | 27.28 S | 153.15 E |
| Manly, Ia., U.S. | 190 | 43.17 N | 93.12 W |
| Manly Warringah War Memorial Park ♦ | 274a | 33.46 S | 151.15 E |
| Manmād | 122 | 20.15 N | 74.27 E |
| Mann ≃ | 164 | 12.20 S | 134.07 E |
| Mann, Mount ∧ | 162 | 25.59 S | 129.42 E |
| Manna, Indon. | 112 | 4.27 S | 102.55 E |
| Mān Na, Mya. | 110 | 23.27 N | 97.14 E |
| Mannahill | 166 | 32.26 S | 139.59 E |
| Mannar | 122 | 8.59 N | 79.54 E |
| Mannar, Gulf of c | 122 | 8.30 N | 79.00 E |
| Mannārgudi | 122 | 10.40 N | 79.26 E |
| Mannar Island I | 122 | 9.03 N | 79.50 E |
| Mann Creek ≃ | 281 | 42.32 N | 83.44 W |
| Männedorf | 58 | 47.15 N | 8.42 E |
| Mannersdorf am Leithagebirge | 61 | 47.58 N | 16.36 E |
| Mannersdorf an der Rabnitz | 61 | 47.25 N | 16.31 E |
| Mannford | 196 | 36.09 N | 96.23 W |
| Mannheim | 56 | 49.29 N | 8.29 E |
| Manni | 120 | 34.48 N | 87.15 E |
| Manning, Ia., U.S. | 198 | 41.54 N | 95.03 W |
| Manning, N.D., U.S. | 198 | 47.13 N | 102.46 W |
| Manning, S.C., U.S. | 192 | 33.41 N | 80.12 W |
| Manning, Cape > | 174o | 2.02 N | 157.26 W |
| Manning Provincial Park ♦ | 224 | 49.07 N | 120.54 W |
| Manning Strait ʯ | 175e | 7.24 S | 158.00 E |
| Mannington | 188 | 39.31 N | 80.20 W |
| Manningtree | 42 | 51.57 N | 1.04 E |
| Mannō | 96 | 34.11 N | 133.51 E |
| Mann Ranges ∧∧ | 162 | 26.00 S | 129.30 E |
| Mannsville | 212 | 43.42 N | 76.03 W |
| Mannswörth ◆[8] | 264b | 48.09 N | 16.31 E |
| Mannu ≃, It. | 71 | 39.16 N | 9.00 E |
| Mannu ≃, It. | 71 | 40.50 N | 8.23 E |
| Mannu, Capo > | 71 | 40.02 N | 8.22 E |
| Mannu, Monte ∧ | 71 | 40.23 N | 8.25 E |
| Mannum | 166 | 34.55 S | 139.18 E |
| Mannus | 171b | 35.48 S | 147.57 E |
| Mannus Creek ≃ | 171b | 35.58 S | 148.03 E |
| Mannville | 182 | 53.20 N | 111.10 W |
| Mano | 150 | 8.02 N | 12.06 W |
| Mano ≃ | 150 | 6.56 N | 11.31 W |
| Manoa | 248 | 9.40 S | 65.27 W |
| Manoel Ribas | 252 | 24.31 S | 51.39 W |
| Manohardi | 126 | 24.08 N | 90.43 E |
| Manoharpur, India | 124 | 22.23 N | 85.12 E |
| Manoharpur, India | 126 | 21.59 N | 87.18 E |
| Manokin ≃ | 208 | 38.05 N | 75.55 W |
| Manokotak | 180 | 58.40 N | 159.09 W |
| Manokwari | 164 | 0.52 S | 134.05 E |
| Manolo Fortich (Maluko) | 116 | 8.25 N | 124.58 E |
| Manoma ≃ | 89 | 49.18 N | 136.37 E |
| Manombo | 157b | 22.57 S | 43.28 E |
| Manomet | 207 | 41.55 N | 70.34 W |
| Manomet Hill ∧[2] | 207 | 41.55 N | 70.36 W |
| Manong | 114 | 4.36 N | 100.53 E |
| Manonga ≃ | 154 | 4.08 S | 34.12 E |
| Manono | 154 | 7.18 S | 27.25 E |
| Manono I | 175a | 13.50 S | 172.05 W |
| Manoora | 168b | 34.00 S | 138.49 E |
| Manoppello | 66 | 42.15 N | 14.03 E |
| Manor, Sk., Can. | 184 | 49.36 N | 102.05 W |
| Manor, Pa., U.S. | 214 | 40.20 N | 79.40 W |
| Manor, Tx., U.S. | 222 | 30.20 N | 97.33 W |
| Manorbier | 42 | 51.39 N | 4.48 W |
| Manorhamilton | 48 | 54.18 N | 8.10 W |
| Manorhaven | 276 | 40.50 N | 73.42 W |
| Manor Hill | 214 | 40.38 N | 77.55 W |
| Manori ◆[8] | 272c | 19.12 N | 72.47 E |
| Manori Creek c | 272c | 19.12 N | 72.48 E |
| Manorina National Park ♦ | 171a | 27.23 S | 152.47 E |
| Manori Point > | 272c | 19.11 N | 72.47 E |
| Manoron | 110 | 11.38 N | 99.04 E |
| Manorville | 214 | 40.47 N | 79.31 W |
| Manosque | 62 | 43.50 N | 5.47 E |
| Manotick | 212 | 45.13 N | 75.41 W |
| Manouane ≃ | 186 | 49.30 N | 71.11 W |
| Manouane, Lac ⊜ | 186 | 50.41 N | 70.45 W |
| Manouanis ≃ | 186 | 50.28 N | 70.08 W |
| Manouanis, Lac ⊜ | 186 | 50.51 N | 70.20 W |
| Manown | 279b | 40.13 N | 79.54 W |
| Manpaka | 273b | 4.18 S | 15.12 E |
| Manpitou | 100 | 22.17 N | 112.52 E |
| Manp'o | 98 | 41.10 N | 126.17 E |
| Mānpur, India | 122 | 20.22 N | 80.43 E |
| Mānpur, India | 124 | 23.46 N | 81.08 E |
| Manqabād | 142 | 27.12 N | 31.07 E |
| Manqaṭīn | 142 | 28.20 N | 30.40 E |
| Manquehue, Cerro ∧ | 286e | 33.21 S | 70.36 W |
| Manra I[1] | 14 | 4.27 S | 171.15 W |
| Manresa | 34 | 41.44 N | 1.50 E |
| Manresa Island I | 276 | 41.04 N | 73.25 W |
| Mānsa, India | 120 | 23.26 N | 72.40 E |
| Mānsa, India | 123 | 29.59 N | 75.23 E |
| Mansa (Fort Rosebery), Zam. | 154 | 11.12 S | 28.53 E |
| Mansabá | 150 | 12.18 N | 15.15 W |
| Mansafīs | 142 | 28.00 N | 30.49 E |
| Mansalay | 116 | 12.31 N | 121.26 E |
| Mansara | 150 | 13.20 N | 4.39 W |
| Manse ≃ | 50 | 47.08 N | 0.25 E |
| Manseau | 206 | 46.22 N | 72.00 W |
| Mānsehra | 123 | 34.20 N | 73.12 E |
| Mansein | 110 | 25.12 N | 95.58 E |
| Mansel Island I | 176 | 62.00 N | 79.50 W |
| Mansfeld | 54 | 51.35 N | 11.27 E |
| Mansfield, Austl. | 169 | 37.03 S | 146.05 E |
| Mansfield, Eng., U.K. | 44 | 53.09 N | 1.11 W |
| Mansfield, Ar., U.S. | 194 | 35.04 N | 94.13 W |
| Mansfield, Ga., U.S. | 192 | 33.31 N | 83.44 W |
| Mansfield, Il., U.S. | 216 | 40.12 N | 88.30 W |
| Mansfield, La., U.S. | 194 | 32.02 N | 93.42 W |
| Mansfield, Ma., U.S. | 207 | 42.02 N | 71.13 W |
| Mansfield, Mo., U.S. | 194 | 37.06 N | 92.34 W |
| Mansfield, N.J., U.S. | 285 | 40.05 N | 74.43 W |
| Mansfield, Oh., U.S. | 214 | 40.45 N | 82.30 W |
| Mansfield, Pa., U.S. | 210 | 41.48 N | 77.04 W |
| Mansfield, Tx., U.S. | 222 | 32.33 N | 97.08 W |
| Mansfield, Mount ∧ | 188 | 44.33 N | 72.49 W |
| Mansfield Center | 207 | 41.45 N | 72.11 W |
| Mansfield Hollow Lake ⊜[1] | 207 | 41.45 N | 72.11 W |
| Mansfield Hollow State Park ♦ | 207 | 41.46 N | 72.10 W |
| Mansfield Municipal Airport ⊠ | 283 | 42.00 N | 71.12 W |
| Mansfield Woodhouse | 44 | 53.11 N | 1.12 W |
| Man Shan I | 106 | 31.14 N | 120.17 E |
| Mansieville Location | 273d | 26.05 S | 27.45 E |
| Mānsinhapur | 272b | 22.39 N | 88.09 E |
| Mansión | 236 | 10.06 N | 85.22 W |
| Manskoje belogorje ∧∧ | 88 | 54.35 N | 94.00 E |
| Mansle | 32 | 45.53 N | 0.11 E |
| Manso ≃ | 248 | 14.42 S | 56.16 W |
| Mansôa | 150 | 12.10 N | 14.36 W |
| Manson, Ia., U.S. | 198 | 42.32 N | 94.32 W |
| Manson, Wa., U.S. | 182 | 47.53 N | 120.09 W |
| Manson ≃ | 182 | 55.42 N | 123.47 W |
| Manson Creek | 182 | 55.41 N | 124.29 W |
| Mansonville | 206 | 45.03 N | 72.23 W |
| Mansourah | 34 | 36.04 N | 4.28 E |
| Mansucum | 246 | 9.02 N | 77.49 W |
| Mansura → Al-Manṣūrah, Miṣr | 142 | 31.03 N | 31.23 E |
| Mansura, La., U.S. | 194 | 31.03 N | 92.02 W |
| Manṣūrīyah, Tur'at al- ≅ | 142 | 31.03 N | 31.24 E |
| Mansurovo | 82 | 55.52 N | 36.36 E |
| Manta, Ec. | 246 | 0.57 S | 80.44 W |
| Manta, It. | 62 | 44.37 N | 7.29 E |
| Manta, Bahía de c | 246 | 0.54 S | 80.42 W |
| Mantabuan Island I | 116 | 5.02 N | 120.13 E |
| Mantagao ≃ | 184 | 51.50 N | 97.48 W |
| Mantalingajan, Mount ∧ | 116 | 8.48 N | 117.40 E |
| Mantalingajan Range ∧∧ | 116 | 8.46 N | 117.40 E |
| Mantanani Besar, Pulau I | 112 | 6.45 N | 116.17 E |
| Mantangule Island I | 116 | 8.10 N | 117.10 E |


**Symbols** in the index entries represent the broad categories identified in the key at the right. Symbols with superior numbers (∧∧[1]) identify subcategories (see complete key on page *I · 1).*

**Symbole** im Register stellen die rechts im Schlüssel erklärten Kategorien dar. Symbole mit hochgestellten Ziffern (∧∧[1]) bezeichnen Unterabteilungen einer Kategorie (vgl. vollständiger Schlüssel auf Seite *I · 1).*

**Los símbolos** incluídos en el texto del índice representan las grandes categorías identificadas con la clave a la derecha. Los símbolos con numeros en su parte superior (∧∧[1]) identifican las subcategorías (véase la clave completa en la página *I · 1).*

**Les symboles** de l'index représentent les catégories indiquées dans la légende à droite. Les symboles suivis d'un indice (∧∧[1]) représentent des sous-catégories (voir légende complète à la page *I · 1).*

**Os símbolos** incluídos no texto do índice representam as grandes categorias identificadas com a chave à direita. Os símbolos com números em sua parte superior (∧∧[1]) identificam as subcategorias (veja-se a chave completa à página *I · 1).*

| Symbol | English | Deutsch | Español | Français | Português |
|---|---|---|---|---|---|
| ∧ | Mountain | Berg | Montaña | Montagne | Montanha |
| ∧∧ | Mountains | Gebirge | Montañas | Montagnes | Montanhas |
| )( | Pass | Paß | Paso | Col | Passo |
| V | Valley, Canyon | Tal, Cañon | Valle, Cañón | Vallée, Canyon | Vale, Canhão |
| ≚ | Plain | Ebene | Llano | Plaine | Planície |
| > | Cape | Kap | Cabo | Cap | Cabo |
| I | Island | Insel | Isla | Île | Ilha |
| II | Islands | Inseln | Islas | Îles | Ilhas |
| ⊥ | Other Topographic Features | Andere Topographische Objekte | Otros Elementos Topográficos | Autres données topographiques | Outros acidentes topográficos |

ESPAÑOL — Nombre · Página · Lat.°′ · Long.°′ W = Oeste
FRANÇAIS — Nom · Page · Lat.°′ · Long.°′ W = Ouest
PORTUGUÊS — Nome · Página · Lat.°′ · Long.°′ W = Oeste


| Nombre | Página | Lat.°′ | Long.°′ W = Oeste |
|---|---|---|---|
| Mantantale | 152 | 2.10 S | 20.06 E |
| Mantare | 154 | 2.43 S | 33.13 E |
| Mantaro ≃ | 248 | 12.15 S | 73.58 W |
| Manteca | 226 | 37.47 N | 121.12 W |
| Mantecal | 246 | 7.33 N | 69.09 W |
| Mantel | 60 | 49.39 N | 12.03 E |
| Mantena | 255 | 18.47 S | 40.59 W |
| Manteno | 216 | 41.15 N | 87.49 W |
| Manteo | 192 | 35.54 N | 75.40 W |
| Mantes-Chérence, Aérodrome de ⊠ | 261 | 49.05 N | 1.41 E |
| Mantes-la-Jolie | 50 | 48.59 N | 1.43 E |
| Mantes-la-Ville | 261 | 48.58 N | 1.42 E |
| Manteswar | 126 | 23.26 N | 88.06 E |
| Manteuil-le-Haudouin | 50 | 49.08 N | 2.48 E |
| Manthelan | 50 | 47.08 N | 0.47 E |
| Manti | 200 | 39.16 N | 111.38 W |
| Manticao | 116 | 8.24 N | 124.17 E |
| Mantilla ◆[8] | 286b | 23.04 N | 82.20 W |
| Mantin | 114 | 2.49 N | 101.54 E |
| Mantiqueira, Serra da ⋏ | 256 | 22.00 S | 44.45 W |
| Mantok | 112 | 1.09 S | 123.14 E |
| Manton | 190 | 44.24 N | 85.23 W |
| Mantorville | 190 | 44.04 N | 92.45 W |
| Mantos Blancos | 252 | 23.25 S | 70.05 W |
| Mantou | 104 | 42.27 N | 122.26 E |
| Mantova | 64 | 45.09 N | 10.48 E |
| Mantova □[4] | 64 | 45.10 N | 10.47 E |
| Māntri | 126 | 21.39 N | 86.49 E |
| Mänttä | 26 | 62.02 N | 24.38 E |
| Mantua, Cuba | 240p | 22.17 N | 84.17 W |
| Mantua → Mantova, It. | 64 | 45.09 N | 10.48 E |
| Mantua, N.J., U.S. | 208 | 39.47 N | 75.10 W |
| Mantua, Oh., U.S. | 214 | 41.17 N | 81.13 W |
| Mantua, Va., U.S. | 284c | 38.51 N | 77.15 W |
| Mantua ≃ | 240p | 22.12 N | 84.25 W |
| Mantua Creek ≃ | 285 | 39.51 N | 75.14 W |
| Mantua Creek, Chestnut Branch ≃ | 285 | 39.47 N | 75.10 W |
| Mantua Creek, Porch Branch ≃ | 285 | 39.46 N | 75.07 W |
| Mantua Hills | 284c | 38.51 N | 77.16 W |
| Mantua Terrace | 285 | 39.48 N | 75.10 W |
| Manturovo, Ross. | 78 | 51.28 N | 37.07 E |
| Manturovo, Ross. | 80 | 58.20 N | 44.46 E |
| Mäntyharju | 26 | 61.25 N | 26.53 E |
| Mäntyluoto | 26 | 61.35 N | 21.29 E |
| Manu | 248 | 12.15 S | 70.50 W |
| Manú ≃ | 248 | 12.16 S | 70.51 W |
| Manu, Parque Nacional del ♦ | 248 | 12.15 S | 71.40 W |
| Manuae I[1], Cook Is. | 14 | 19.21 S | 158.56 W |
| Manuae I[1], Poly. fr. | 14 | 16.30 S | 154.40 W |
| Manua Islands II | 174y | 14.13 S | 169.35 W |
| Manuel | 234 | 22.44 N | 98.19 W |
| Manuel Alves ≃ | 250 | 11.19 S | 48.28 W |
| Manuel Alves Grande ≃ | 250 | 7.27 S | 47.35 W |
| Manuel Antonio, Parque Nacional ♦ | 236 | 9.25 N | 84.10 W |
| Manuel Avila Camacho, Presa ⊜[1] | 234 | 18.55 N | 98.10 W |
| Manuel Benavides | 232 | 29.05 N | 103.55 W |
| Manuel Derqui | 252 | 27.50 S | 58.48 W |
| Manuel Duarte | 256 | 22.06 S | 43.34 W |
| Manuel Ribeiro | 256 | 22.54 S | 42.47 W |
| Manuel Rodríguez, Isla I | 254 | 52.35 S | 73.50 W |
| Manuel Urbano | 248 | 8.53 S | 69.18 W |
| Manués-Açu ≃ | 250 | 3.22 S | 57.44 W |
| Manuguru | 122 | 17.59 N | 80.43 E |
| Manuhangi I[1] | 14 | 19.12 S | 141.16 W |
| Manuherikia ≃ | 172 | 45.16 S | 169.24 E |
| Manui, Pulau I | 112 | 3.35 S | 123.08 E |
| Manuilovskaja | 76 | 60.29 N | 40.40 E |
| Manu Island I | 164 | 1.17 S | 143.35 E |
| Manūjān | 128 | 27.24 N | 57.32 E |
| Manuk ≃ | 115a | 6.14 S | 108.13 E |
| Manuk, Pulau I | 164 | 5.33 S | 130.18 E |
| Manukan | 116 | 8.31 N | 123.06 E |
| Manukau | 172 | 37.02 S | 174.54 E |
| Manukau Harbour c | 172 | 37.01 S | 174.44 E |
| Manulla ≃ | 48 | 53.57 N | 9.12 W |
| Manulu Lagoon c | 174o | 1.56 N | 157.20 W |
| Manumuskin ≃ | 208 | 39.18 N | 75.00 W |
| Manundi, Tanjung › | 164 | 0.38 S | 135.22 E |
| Manunui | 172 | 38.53 S | 175.20 E |
| Manuoha ∧ | 172 | 38.39 S | 177.07 E |
| Manuripe (Mamuripi) ≃ | 248 | 11.06 S | 67.36 W |
| Manuripi ≃ | 248 | 11.42 S | 67.16 W |
| Manursing Island I | 276 | 40.58 N | 73.40 W |
| Manursing Island Park ♦ | 276 | 40.58 N | 73.40 W |
| Manus □[5] | 164 | 2.00 S | 147.00 E |
| Mānushmuria | 126 | 22.22 N | 86.47 E |
| Manus Island I | 164 | 2.05 S | 147.00 E |
| Manutahi | 172 | 39.40 S | 174.24 E |
| Manutuke | 172 | 38.41 S | 177.55 E |
| Manvel, N.D., U.S. | 198 | 48.04 N | 97.10 W |
| Manvel, Tx., U.S. | 222 | 29.28 N | 95.22 W |
| Manville, N.J., U.S. | 210 | 40.32 N | 74.35 W |
| Manville, R.I., U.S. | 207 | 41.58 N | 71.28 W |
| Mānwat | 122 | 19.18 N | 76.30 E |
| Many | 194 | 31.34 N | 93.29 W |
| Manyal Shīḩah | 273c | 29.57 N | 31.14 E |
| Manyana | 156 | 23.23 S | 21.44 E |
| Manyani | 154 | 3.05 S | 38.30 E |
| Manyara, Lake ⊜ | 154 | 3.35 S | 35.50 E |
| Manyberries | 184 | 49.24 N | 110.42 W |
| Manyč ≃ | 72 | 47.15 N | 40.00 E |
| Manyč-Gudilo, ozero ⊜ | 80 | 46.24 N | 42.38 E |
| Manyeleti Game Reserve ◆[4] | 156 | 25.42 S | 31.30 E |
| Many Island Lake ⊜ | 184 | 50.08 N | 110.03 W |
| Manyoni | 154 | 5.45 S | 34.50 E |
| Many Peaks | 166 | 24.33 S | 151.23 E |
| Manytsch → Manyč ≃ | 72 | 47.15 N | 40.00 E |
| Manz'a | 86 | 58.29 N | 96.15 E |
| Mānzai | 120 | 30.07 N | 68.52 E |
| Manzanares | 34 | 39.00 N | 3.22 W |
| Manzanares ≃ | 34 | 40.19 N | 3.32 W |
| Manzanares, Canal del ≍ | 266a | 40.23 N | 3.41 W |
| Manzanillo, Cuba | 240p | 20.21 N | 77.07 W |
| Manzanillo, Méx. | 234 | 19.03 N | 104.20 W |
| Manzanillo, Bahía c | 234 | 19.04 N | 104.22 W |
| Manzanillo, Bahía de c | 234 | 19.12 N | 104.43 W |
| Manzanillo, Punta ›, Pan. | 236 | 9.38 N | 79.32 W |
| Manzanillo, Punta ›, Ven. | 241s | 11.32 N | 69.17 W |
| Manzanillo Bay c | 238 | 19.45 N | 71.46 W |
| Manzanita, Or., U.S. | 224 | 45.43 N | 123.56 W |
| Manzanita, Wa., U.S. | 224 | 47.42 N | 122.33 W |
| Manzano, It. | 64 | 45.59 N | 13.23 E |
| Manzano, N.M., U.S. | 200 | 34.38 N | 106.20 W |
| Manzanola | 198 | 38.06 N | 103.51 W |
| Manzano Peak ∧ | 200 | 34.35 N | 106.26 W |
| Manzheliya | 78 | 49.19 N | 33.38 E |
| Manzhouli | 88 | 49.35 N | 117.22 E |
| Manziana | 66 | 42.08 N | 12.08 E |
| Manzil | 128 | 29.15 N | 63.05 E |
| Manzilah, Birkat al- ⊜ | 142 | 31.08 N | 31.56 E |
| Manzilah, Buḩayrat al- ⊜ | 142 | 31.15 N | 32.00 E |
| Manzini | 158 | 26.30 S | 31.25 E |
| Manzone | 258 | 34.29 S | 58.52 W |
| Manzurka | 88 | 53.30 N | 106.04 E |
| Maó, Esp. | 34 | 39.53 N | 4.15 E |
| Mao, Rep. Dom. | 238 | 19.34 N | 71.05 W |
| Mao, Tchad | 136 | 14.07 N | 15.19 E |
| Maoba | 102 | 30.02 N | 108.59 E |
| Maocifan | 100 | 31.40 N | 112.53 E |
| Maocun | 98 | 34.25 N | 117.16 E |
| Maodianzi, Zhg. | 107 | 30.42 N | 104.25 E |
| Maodianzi, Zhg. | 107 | 29.45 N | 104.55 E |
| Mao'ertuo | 107 | 29.19 N | 106.24 E |
| Maojiagou | 104 | 40.58 N | 120.51 E |
| Maojiaji | 100 | 31.32 N | 114.16 E |
| Maojiakou | 100 | 29.53 N | 112.58 E |
| Maojiaping | 105 | 40.34 N | 114.43 E |
| Maojiapuzi | 104 | 41.10 N | 123.32 E |
| Maojiatun | 104 | 41.05 N | 121.58 E |
| Maojiazao | 98 | 39.53 N | 113.26 E |
| Maoke, Pegunungan ⋏ | 164 | 4.00 S | 138.00 E |
| Maolin, Zhg. | 89 | 43.58 N | 123.24 E |
| Maolin, Zhg. | 100 | 30.32 N | 118.14 E |
| Maomao Shan ∧ | 102 | 37.12 N | 103.10 E |
| Maoming | 102 | 21.39 N | 110.54 E |
| Maomu | 102 | 40.18 N | 99.28 E |
| Ma On Shan ∧ | 271d | 22.25 N | 114.15 E |
| Ma On Shan Tsuen | 271d | 22.24 N | 114.14 E |
| Maoping | 102 | 30.23 N | 110.33 E |
| Maopora, Pulau I | 112 | 7.35 S | 127.35 E |
| Maoshan | 105 | 40.17 N | 117.26 E |
| Mao Shan ⋏ | 106 | 31.43 N | 119.17 E |
| Maoshi | 100 | 26.57 N | 113.05 E |
| Maospati | 115a | 7.36 S | 111.26 E |
| Maouri, Dallol V | 150 | 12.05 N | 3.32 E |
| Maowen | 102 | 31.30 N | 103.39 E |
| Maoxing | 89 | 45.32 N | 124.33 E |
| Mao Yü I | 100 | 23.19 N | 119.19 E |
| Maozhou | 105 | 38.51 N | 116.06 E |
| Mapaga | 112 | 0.06 S | 119.48 E |
| Mapam Yumco ⊜ | 120 | 30.42 N | 81.27 E |
| Mapan | 112 | 2.21 S | 111.10 E |
| Mapanda | 152 | 9.32 S | 24.16 E |
| Mapane | 112 | 1.24 S | 120.40 E |
| Mapanza | 154 | 16.15 S | 26.55 E |
| Mapaoni ≃ | 250 | 1.55 N | 54.13 W |
| Mapari ≃, Bra. | 246 | 1.49 S | 66.48 W |
| Mapari ≃, Bra. | 250 | 0.45 N | 53.07 W |
| Mapastepec | 234 | 15.26 N | 92.54 W |
| Mapaville | 219 | 38.14 N | 90.29 W |
| Mapi | 164 | 7.07 S | 139.23 E |
| Mapi ≃ | 164 | 7.00 S | 139.16 E |
| Mapia, Kepulauan II | 108 | 0.50 N | 134.20 E |
| Mapida | 112 | 0.33 S | 119.46 E |
| Mapimí | 232 | 25.49 N | 103.51 W |
| Mapimí, Bolsón de ◆[2] | 232 | 26.30 N | 104.00 W |
| Mapimí, Bufa de ∧ | 196 | 25.47 N | 103.48 W |
| Maping, Zhg. | 100 | 24.16 N | 117.54 E |
| Maping, Zhg. | 100 | 31.36 N | 113.32 E |
| Mapinga | 154 | 6.36 S | 39.04 E |
| Mapinhane | 156 | 22.19 S | 35.03 E |
| Mapire | 246 | 7.45 N | 64.42 W |
| Mapiri | 248 | 15.15 S | 68.10 W |
| Mapiri ≃ | 248 | 9.52 S | 66.21 W |
| Mapixari, Ilha I | 246 | 2.10 S | 65.08 W |
| Maple ◆[8] | 275b | 43.51 N | 79.31 W |
| Maple ≃, U.S. | 198 | 45.47 N | 98.33 W |
| Maple ≃, Ia., U.S. | 198 | 42.00 N | 95.59 W |
| Maple ≃, Mi., U.S. | 190 | 42.59 N | 84.57 W |
| Maple ≃, Mn., U.S. | 190 | 44.05 N | 94.00 W |
| Maple ≃, N.D., U.S. | 198 | 46.56 N | 96.55 W |
| Maple Airfield ⊠ | 275b | 43.51 N | 79.32 W |
| Maple Bay | 224 | 48.49 N | 123.36 W |
| Maple Bluff | 216 | 43.07 N | 89.22 W |
| Maple Creek | 184 | 49.55 N | 109.27 W |
| Maple Creek ≃ | 198 | 41.33 N | 96.27 W |
| Maplecrest | 210 | 42.17 N | 74.11 W |
| Maple Cross | 260 | 51.37 N | 0.30 W |
| Mapledale | 214 | 41.23 N | 79.51 W |
| Maple Falls | 224 | 48.55 N | 122.04 W |
| Maple Glen | 285 | 40.11 N | 75.11 W |
| Maple Grove, On., Can. | 212 | 43.55 N | 78.44 W |
| Maple Grove, P.Q., Can. | 206 | 45.19 N | 73.50 W |
| Maple Heights | 214 | 41.24 N | 81.33 W |
| Maple Lake | 190 | 45.13 N | 94.00 W |
| Maple Lake ⊜ | 212 | 45.06 N | 78.40 W |
| Maple Lane | 216 | 41.45 N | 86.14 W |
| Maple Leaf Gardens ♦ | 275b | 43.40 N | 79.23 W |
| Maple Meadow Brook ≃ | 283 | 42.33 N | 71.09 W |
| Maple Mount | 194 | 37.42 N | 87.26 W |
| Maple Park | 216 | 41.55 N | 88.36 W |
| Maple Ridge | 224 | 49.13 N | 122.36 W |
| Maples | 216 | 41.01 N | 84.58 W |
| Maple Shade | 285 | 39.57 N | 74.59 W |
| Maple Springs | 214 | 42.12 N | 79.25 W |
| Maplesville | 194 | 32.47 N | 86.52 W |
| Mapleton, S. Afr. | 158 | 26.20 S | 28.14 E |
| Mapleton, Ia., U.S. | 198 | 42.09 N | 95.47 W |
| Mapleton, Mn., U.S. | 190 | 43.55 N | 93.57 W |
| Mapleton, Or., U.S. | 202 | 44.01 N | 123.51 W |
| Mapleton, Ut,. U.S. | 200 | 40.07 N | 111.34 W |
| Mapleton Depot | 214 | 40.24 N | 77.57 W |
| Maple Valley | 224 | 47.25 N | 122.03 W |
| Mapleville | 207 | 41.56 N | 71.38 W |
| Maplewood, Mo., U.S. | 219 | 38.36 N | 90.19 W |
| Maplewood, N.J., U.S. | 276 | 40.43 N | 74.14 W |
| Maplewood, Oh., U.S. | 216 | 40.23 N | 84.02 W |
| Maplewood, Wa., U.S. | 224 | 47.30 N | 122.07 W |
| Maplewood Terrace | 279b | 40.17 N | 79.32 W |
| Mapocho ≃ | 286e | 33.25 S | 70.47 W |
| Mapocho, Estación ◆[5] | 286e | 33.26 S | 70.40 W |
| Mapoi | 154 | 5.28 N | 27.40 E |
| Mapoon Aboriginal Reserve ◆[4] | 164 | 11.40 S | 142.25 E |
| Mappsville | 208 | 37.51 N | 75.34 W |
| Maprik | 164 | 3.40 S | 143.05 E |
| Mapuera ≃ | 250 | 1.05 S | 57.02 W |
| Mapujiang | 105 | 40.24 N | 114.56 E |
| Mapulanguene | 156 | 24.29 S | 32.06 E |
| Mapumulo | 158 | 29.11 S | 31.02 E |
| Maputa | 158 | 26.59 S | 32.46 E |
| Maputo | 156 | 25.58 S | 32.35 E |
| Maputo □[5] | 156 | 26.00 S | 32.25 E |
| Maputo (Great Usutu) (Lusutfu) ≃ | 158 | 26.11 S | 32.42 E |
| Maputo, Baia de c | 158 | 25.48 S | 32.51 E |
| Maqên Gangri ∧ | 102 | 34.55 N | 99.18 E |
| Maqiangou | 105 | 39.30 N | 115.02 E |
| Maqiao, Zhg. | 100 | 29.48 N | 114.22 E |
| Maqiao, Zhg. | 106 | 30.28 N | 120.42 E |
| Maqna | 128 | 28.24 N | 34.45 E |
| Maqṭeïr ⊤[4] | 148 | 22.10 N | 10.50 W |
| Maquan ≃ | 124 | 29.35 N | 84.10 E |
| Maqueda | 34 | 40.04 N | 4.22 W |
| Maqueda Bay c | 116 | 11.44 N | 124.58 E |
| Maqueda Channel ⊔ | 116 | 13.42 N | 124.01 E |
| Maquela do Zombo | 152 | 6.03 S | 15.07 E |
| Maquereau, Pointe au › | 186 | 48.12 N | 64.47 W |
| Maquilaú ≃ | 246 | 1.23 N | 63.24 W |
| Maquiling, Mount ∧ | 116 | 14.08 N | 121.12 E |
| Maquinchao | 254 | 41.15 S | 68.44 W |
| Maquinchao ≃ | 254 | 41.13 S | 69.25 W |
| Maquoketa | 190 | 42.04 N | 90.39 W |
| Maquoketa ≃ | 190 | 42.11 N | 90.19 W |
| Maquoketa, North Fork ≃ | 190 | 42.05 N | 90.40 W |
| Mar, Laguna c | 286b | 23.05 N | 82.30 W |
| Mar, Serra do ±[4] | 252 | 26.00 S | 48.00 W |
| Mara, India | 120 | 28.11 N | 94.06 E |
| Mara, Perú | 248 | 14.06 S | 72.07 W |
| Mara, Zhg. | 120 | 28.11 N | 94.08 E |
| Mara □[4] | 154 | 1.45 S | 34.30 E |
| Mara ≃, Afr. | 154 | 1.31 S | 33.56 E |
| Mara ≃, Ross. | 88 | 58.06 N | 104.06 E |
| Maraã, Bra. | 246 | 1.50 S | 65.22 W |
| Maraa, Poly. fr. | 174s | 17.46 S | 149.34 W |
| Marabá | 250 | 5.21 S | 49.07 W |
| Marabahan | 112 | 3.00 S | 114.45 E |
| Marabut | 116 | 11.07 N | 125.13 E |
| Maracá, Ilha de I, Bra. | 246 | 3.25 N | 61.40 W |
| Maracá, Ilha de I, Bra. | 250 | 2.05 N | 50.25 W |
| Maracaçumé ≃ | 250 | 1.23 S | 45.42 W |
| Maracaí | 255 | 22.36 S | 50.39 W |
| Maracaibo | 246 | 10.40 N | 71.37 W |
| Maracaibo, Lago de ⊜ | 246 | 9.50 N | 71.30 W |
| Maracaju | 255 | 21.38 S | 55.09 W |
| Maracaju, Serra de ⋏[2] | 255 | 20.45 S | 55.00 W |
| Maracalagonis | 71 | 39.17 N | 9.13 E |
| Maracanã | 250 | 0.46 S | 47.27 W |
| Maracanã ◆[8] | 287a | 22.54 S | 43.14 W |
| Maracanã ≃ | 248 | 8.22 S | 59.41 W |
| Maracanã, Estádio do ♦ | 287a | 22.55 S | 43.14 W |
| Maracanaú | 250 | 3.52 S | 38.38 W |
| Maracás | 255 | 13.26 S | 40.27 W |
| Maracay | 246 | 10.15 N | 67.36 W |
| Maracossic Creek ≃ | 208 | 37.53 N | 77.11 W |
| Marādah | 146 | 29.14 N | 19.13 E |
| Maradi | 150 | 13.29 N | 7.06 E |
| Maradi □[5] | 150 | 14.00 N | 7.00 E |
| Maradi, Goulbin ≃ | 150 | 13.38 N | 6.20 E |
| Marāghah, Sabkhat al- ⊜ | 130 | 35.39 N | 37.39 E |
| Marāgheh | 128 | 37.23 N | 46.13 E |
| Maragiu, Capo › | 71 | 40.20 N | 8.23 E |
| Maragogi | 250 | 9.01 S | 35.13 W |
| Maragogipe | 255 | 12.46 S | 38.55 W |
| Marahoué, Parc National de la ♦ | 150 | 7.00 N | 6.00 W |
| Mārahra | 124 | 27.44 N | 78.35 E |
| Marahuaca, Cerro ∧ | 246 | 3.34 N | 65.27 W |
| Maraial | 250 | 8.47 S | 35.50 W |
| Maraiche Lake ⊜ | 184 | 54.28 N | 102.01 W |
| Marainviller | 58 | 48.35 N | 6.36 E |
| Maraisburg → Roodepoort-Maraisburg | 273d | 26.11 S | 27.56 E |
| Marais des Cygnes ≃ | 194 | 38.02 N | 94.14 W |
| Marais Temps Clair ⊜ | 219 | 38.54 N | 90.24 W |
| Marajó, Baía de c | 250 | 1.00 S | 48.30 W |
| Marajó, Ilha de I | 250 | 1.00 S | 49.30 W |
| Marakabei | 158 | 29.32 S | 28.09 E |
| Ma'rakah | 132 | 33.16 N | 35.18 E |
| Mārākand | 84 | 38.52 N | 45.14 E |
| Marakwini | 164 | 3.42 S | 141.31 E |
| Maralal | 154 | 1.06 N | 36.42 E |
| Maralaleng | 156 | 25.47 S | 22.45 E |
| Maralal Game Sanctuary ◆[4] | 154 | 1.09 N | 36.38 E |
| Maraldy | 86 | 52.26 N | 77.45 E |
| Marali | 152 | 6.01 N | 18.24 E |
| Maralik | 84 | 40.35 N | 43.52 E |
| Maralinga | 162 | 30.10 S | 131.35 E |
| Maralinga Lands ◆[4] | 162 | 29.15 S | 130.50 E |
| Maram | 120 | 25.25 N | 94.06 E |
| Maramag | 116 | 7.46 N | 125.00 E |
| Maramasike I | 175e | 9.32 S | 161.27 E |
| Marambaia ≃ | 256 | 21.44 S | 46.25 W |
| Marambaia, Ilha da I | 256 | 23.04 S | 43.58 W |
| Marambaia, Pico da ∧ | 256 | 23.04 S | 43.59 W |
| Marambaia, Restinga de ±[2] | 256 | 23.04 S | 43.45 W |
| Marambio ☋[3] | 9 | 64.14 S | 56.43 W |
| Marampa | 150 | 8.41 N | 12.28 W |
| Maramsilli Reservoir ⊜[1] | 122 | 20.32 N | 81.41 E |
| Maramureș □[6] | 38 | 47.40 N | 24.00 E |
| Maran | 114 | 3.35 N | 102.46 E |
| Mārān, Koh-i- ∧ | 120 | 29.26 N | 66.48 E |
| Marana, Mali | 150 | 14.38 N | 11.55 W |
| Marana, Az., U.S. | 200 | 32.26 N | 111.13 W |
| Maranalgo | 162 | 29.23 S | 117.48 E |
| Maranboy | 164 | 14.30 S | 132.45 E |
| Maranchón | 34 | 41.03 N | 2.12 W |
| Marand | 128 | 38.26 N | 45.46 E |
| Maranello | 64 | 44.32 N | 10.52 E |
| Marang, Malay. | 114 | 5.12 N | 103.13 E |
| Marang, Mya. | 110 | 10.27 N | 98.47 E |
| Marangá ≃ | 287a | 22.51 S | 43.23 W |
| Marangani | 248 | 14.22 S | 71.10 W |
| Marangas | 116 | 8.40 N | 117.38 E |
| Marange-Zondrange | 56 | 49.07 N | 6.32 E |
| Maranguape | 250 | 3.53 S | 38.40 W |
| Maranhão □[3] | 250 | 5.00 S | 45.00 W |
| Maranhão ≃ | 255 | 13.51 S | 48.20 W |
| Marano | 266b | 45.38 N | 8.38 E |
| Marano, Laguna di c | 64 | 45.44 N | 13.10 E |
| Maranoa ≃ | 166 | 27.50 S | 148.37 E |
| Marano di Napoli | 68 | 40.54 N | 14.11 E |
| Marano Lagunare | 64 | 45.46 N | 13.10 E |
| Marañón ≃ | 242 | 4.30 S | 73.27 W |
| Marano sul Panaro | 64 | 44.27 N | 10.58 E |
| Marano Vicentino | 64 | 45.41 N | 11.25 E |
| Marans | 32 | 46.19 N | 1.00 W |
| Maraoli ◆[8] | 272c | 19.03 N | 72.54 E |
| Marapanim | 250 | 0.42 S | 47.42 W |
| Marapendi, Lagoa de c | 287a | 23.01 S | 43.24 W |
| Marapi ≃ | 250 | 0.37 N | 55.58 W |
| Marapicu, Morro do ∧ | 287a | 22.50 S | 43.36 W |
| Mararoa ≃ | 172 | 45.34 S | 167.36 E |
| Mararui | 154 | 1.56 S | 41.18 E |
| Maras, Perú | 248 | 13.20 S | 72.09 W |
| Maraş → Kahramanmaraş, Tür. | 130 | 37.36 N | 36.55 E |
| Marasany | 80 | 57.27 N | 54.25 E |
| Marasende, Pulau I | 112 | 5.08 S | 118.09 E |
| Mărășești | 38 | 45.52 N | 27.14 E |
| Maratasã ≃ | 250 | 4.14 S | 42.15 W |
| Maratea | 68 | 39.59 N | 15.45 E |
| Marathon, Austl. | 166 | 20.49 S | 143.34 E |
| Marathon, On., Can. | 190 | 48.43 N | 86.23 W |
| Marathón, Ellás | 38 | 38.10 N | 23.58 E |
| Marathon, Fl., U.S. | 220 | 24.42 N | 81.05 W |
| Marathon, N.Y., U.S. | 210 | 42.26 N | 76.01 W |
| Marathon, Tx., U.S. | 196 | 30.12 N | 103.15 W |
| Marathon, Wi., U.S. | 190 | 44.55 N | 89.50 W |
| Maratua, Pulau I | 112 | 2.15 N | 118.36 E |
| Marau, Bra. | 252 | 28.27 S | 52.12 W |
| Maraú, Bra. | 255 | 14.06 S | 39.00 W |
| Marauiá ≃ | 246 | 0.23 S | 65.13 W |
| Marausa | 70 | 37.56 N | 12.30 E |
| Maravari | 175e | 7.51 S | 156.42 E |
| Maravatío de Ocampo | 234 | 19.54 N | 100.27 W |
| Maravilha | 252 | 26.47 S | 53.09 W |
| Maravillas | 232 | 27.22 N | 104.29 W |
| Maravillas Creek ≃ | 196 | 29.34 N | 102.47 W |
| Mara Vista | 207 | 41.33 N | 70.34 W |
| Marav Lake ⊜ | 120 | 29.04 N | 69.18 E |
| Maravovo | 175e | 9.17 S | 159.38 E |
| Marāwah | 146 | 32.29 N | 21.25 E |
| Marawi, Pil. | 116 | 8.01 N | 124.18 E |
| Marawī, Sūd. | 140 | 18.29 N | 31.49 E |
| Marawwah I | 128 | 24.18 N | 53.18 E |
| Maraye-en-Othe | 50 | 48.10 N | 3.51 E |
| Marayes | 252 | 31.29 S | 67.20 W |
| Marayong | 274a | 33.45 S | 150.54 E |
| Märäzä | 84 | 40.33 N | 48.56 E |
| Marazion | 42 | 50.08 N | 5.28 W |
| Marbach, Dtsch. | 54 | 51.02 N | 13.13 E |
| Marbach, Dtsch. | 56 | 50.37 N | 9.43 E |
| Marbach, Dtsch. | 56 | 51.28 N | 8.50 E |
| Marbach, Schw. | 58 | 46.52 N | 7.55 E |
| Marbach am Neckar | 56 | 48.56 N | 9.14 E |
| Marbache | 56 | 48.48 N | 6.05 E |
| Marbais | 50 | 50.33 N | 4.31 E |
| Marbeck | 52 | 51.49 N | 6.52 E |
| Marbella | 34 | 36.31 N | 4.53 W |
| Marble, Mn., U.S. | 190 | 47.19 N | 93.17 W |
| Marble, N.C., U.S. | 192 | 35.10 N | 83.55 W |
| Marble, Pa., U.S. | 214 | 41.20 N | 79.26 W |
| Marble Arch ⊥ | 146 | 30.29 N | 18.35 E |
| Marble Bar | 162 | 21.11 S | 119.44 E |
| Marble Canyon V | 200 | 36.30 N | 111.50 W |
| Marble Falls | 196 | 30.34 N | 98.16 W |
| Marble Hall | 156 | 24.57 S | 29.13 E |
| Marblehead, Il., U.S. | 219 | 39.50 N | 91.22 W |
| Marblehead, Ma., U.S. | 207 | 42.30 N | 70.51 W |
| Marblehead, Oh., U.S. | 214 | 41.32 N | 82.44 W |
| Marblehead Neck ›[1] | 283 | 42.29 N | 70.51 W |
| Marble Hill | 194 | 37.18 N | 89.58 W |
| Marble Lake ⊜ | 216 | 41.54 N | 84.54 W |
| Marblemount | 224 | 48.31 N | 121.26 W |
| Marble Rock | 190 | 42.57 N | 92.52 W |
| Marbleton | 206 | 45.37 N | 71.35 W |
| Marburg, Austl. | 171a | 27.34 S | 152.35 E |
| Marburg, Dtsch. | 56 | 50.49 N | 8.46 E |
| Marburg, S. Afr. | 158 | 30.44 S | 30.26 E |
| Marburg, Lake ⊜[1] | 208 | 39.48 N | 76.53 W |
| Marburg an der Drau → Maribor | 36 | 46.33 N | 15.39 E |
| Marbury | 208 | 38.34 N | 77.09 W |
| Marc ≃ | 50 | 50.43 N | 3.50 E |
| Marca, Ponta da › | 152 | 16.31 S | 11.42 E |
| Marcal ≃ | 30 | 47.41 N | 17.32 E |
| Marcala | 236 | 14.07 N | 88.00 W |
| Marcali | 30 | 46.35 N | 17.25 E |
| Marcallo con Casone | 266b | 45.29 N | 8.52 E |
| Marcaria | 64 | 45.07 N | 10.32 E |
| Marceau, Lac ⊜ | 186 | 51.25 N | 66.41 W |
| Marcedusa | 68 | 39.02 N | 16.50 E |
| Marcelin | 184 | 52.55 N | 106.47 W |
| Marceline | 194 | 39.42 N | 92.56 W |
| Marcelino Ramos | 252 | 27.28 S | 51.54 W |
| Marcella | 276 | 40.59 N | 74.28 W |
| Marcellina | 66 | 42.01 N | 12.48 E |
| Marcellus, Mi., U.S. | 216 | 42.01 N | 85.48 W |
| Marcellus, N.Y., U.S. | 210 | 42.59 N | 76.20 W |
| Marcellus Falls | 210 | 43.00 N | 76.20 W |
| Marcevo | 83 | 47.15 N | 38.53 E |
| March, Dtsch. | 58 | 48.03 N | 7.47 E |
| March, Eng., U.K. | 42 | 52.33 N | 0.06 E |
| March (Morava) ≃ | 30 | 48.10 N | 16.59 E |
| Marcha | 74 | 60.37 N | 123.18 E |
| Marcha ≃ | 74 | 63.28 N | 118.50 E |
| March Air Force Base ■ | 228 | 33.54 N | 117.15 W |
| Marchais | 261 | 48.31 N | 2.03 E |
| Marchal | 152 | 5.16 S | 14.58 E |
| Marchamat | 85 | 40.30 N | 72.19 E |
| Marchand | 214 | 40.51 N | 79.02 W |
| Marchaux | 58 | 47.19 N | 6.08 E |
| Marche □[4] | 66 | 43.30 N | 13.15 E |
| Marche □[9] | 32 | 46.05 N | 2.10 E |
| Marche-en-Famenne | 56 | 50.12 N | 5.20 E |
| Marchegg | 61 | 48.17 N | 16.55 E |
| Marche-les-Dames | 56 | 50.29 N | 4.58 E |
| Marchémoret | 261 | 49.03 N | 2.46 E |
| Marchena | 34 | 37.20 N | 5.24 W |
| Marchena, Isla I | 246a | 0.21 N | 90.29 W |
| Marchenoir | 50 | 47.49 N | 1.24 E |
| Marchesato ◆[1] | 68 | 39.07 N | 16.58 E |
| Marchfeld ◆[1] | 264b | 48.17 N | 16.31 E |
| Marchienne-au-Pont | 50 | 50.24 N | 4.23 E |
| Marchinbar Island I | 164 | 11.15 S | 136.45 E |
| Mar Chiquita, Laguna c | 252 | 37.37 S | 57.24 W |
| Mar Chiquita, Laguna ⊜ | 252 | 30.42 S | 62.36 W |
| Marchtrenk | 61 | 48.11 N | 14.07 E |
| Marchykhyna Buda | 78 | 51.58 N | 34.03 E |
| Marciana | 66 | 42.47 N | 10.10 E |
| Marciana Marina | 66 | 42.48 N | 10.12 E |
| Marcianise | 68 | 41.02 N | 14.17 E |
| Marciano della Chiana | 66 | 43.18 N | 11.47 E |
| Marcigny | 32 | 46.17 N | 4.02 E |
| Marcillac-Vallon | 32 | 44.29 N | 2.28 E |
| Marcilloles | 62 | 45.20 N | 5.11 E |
| Marcilly | 261 | 49.02 N | 2.53 E |
| Marcilly-la-Campagne | 50 | 48.50 N | 1.13 E |
| Marcilly-le-Hayer | 50 | 48.21 N | 3.38 E |
| Marcilly-sur-Eure | 50 | 48.49 N | 1.21 E |
| Marck | 50 | 50.57 N | 1.57 E |
| Marckolsheim | 58 | 48.10 N | 7.33 E |
| Marco, Bra. | 250 | 3.08 S | 40.09 W |
| Marco, It. | 64 | 45.51 N | 11.01 E |
| Marco, Fl., U.S. | 220 | 25.58 N | 81.43 W |
| Marcoing | 50 | 50.07 N | 3.11 E |
| Marco Island I | 220 | 25.55 N | 81.45 W |
| Marcola | 202 | 44.10 N | 122.51 W |
| Marcona | 248 | 15.03 S | 75.01 W |
| Marco Polo, Aeroporto ⊠ | 64 | 45.30 N | 12.21 E |
| Marco Polo Bridge ◆[5] | 271a | 39.52 N | 116.12 E |
| Marcos Juárez | 252 | 32.42 S | 62.06 W |
| Marcos Paz | 258 | 34.46 S | 58.50 W |
| Marcos Paz □[5] | 288 | 34.49 S | 58.49 W |
| Marcotte, Lac ⊜ | 206 | 46.47 N | 73.12 W |
| Marcoussis | 261 | 48.39 N | 2.14 E |
| Marcq | 261 | 48.52 N | 1.49 E |
| Marcq-en-Barœul | 50 | 50.40 N | 3.05 E |
| Marčugi | 82 | 55.21 N | 38.33 E |
| Mârculești | 38 | 47.52 N | 28.14 E |
| Marcus | 198 | 42.49 N | 95.48 W |
| Marcus Baker, Mount ∧ | 180 | 61.26 N | 147.45 W |
| Marcus Hook | 208 | 39.49 N | 75.25 W |
| Marcus Hook Creek ≃ | 285 | 39.49 N | 75.25 W |
| Marcus Island → Minami-Tori-shima I | 14 | 24.18 N | 153.58 E |
| Marcy, Mount ∧ | 188 | 44.07 N | 73.56 W |
| Marda | 162 | 30.13 S | 119.17 E |
| Mardalsfossen ∟ | 26 | 62.30 N | 8.07 E |
| Mardān | 123 | 34.12 N | 72.02 E |
| Mardarivka | 78 | 47.32 N | 29.44 E |
| Mar de Cães, Vala de ≍ | 266c | 38.51 N | 8.59 W |
| Mar de Espanha | 256 | 21.52 S | 43.00 W |
| Mardela Springs | 208 | 38.27 N | 75.45 W |
| Mar del Plata | 252 | 38.00 S | 57.33 W |
| Marden | 42 | 51.10 N | 0.29 E |
| Mardie | 162 | 21.11 S | 115.57 E |
| Mardin | 130 | 37.18 N | 40.44 E |
| Mardin □[4] | 128 | 37.25 N | 41.00 E |
| Mar Dyke ≃ | 260 | 51.29 N | 0.14 E |
| Maré I | 175f | 21.30 S | 168.00 E |
| Mare a Brăilei, Insula I | 38 | 45.00 N | 28.00 E |
| Marea de Portillo | 240p | 19.55 N | 77.11 W |
| Marecchia ≃ | 66 | 44.04 N | 12.34 E |
| Marechal Cândido Rondon | 252 | 24.34 S | 54.04 W |
| Marechal Deodoro | 250 | 9.43 S | 35.54 W |
| Marechal Taumaturgo | 248 | 8.57 S | 72.48 W |
| Maree, Loch ⊜ | 46 | 57.42 N | 5.30 W |
| Mareeba | 166 | 17.00 S | 145.26 E |
| Mareetsane | 158 | 26.09 S | 25.25 E |
| Mareil-en-France | 261 | 49.04 N | 2.26 E |
| Mareil-le-Guyon | 261 | 48.47 N | 1.51 E |
| Mareil-Marly | 261 | 48.53 N | 2.05 E |
| Mare Island I | 226 | 38.06 N | 122.16 W |
| Mare Island Naval Shipyard ■ | 226 | 38.06 N | 122.17 W |
| Mare Island Strait ⊔ | 282 | 38.06 N | 122.17 W |
| Mareje, Gunung ∧ | 115b | 8.46 S | 116.08 E |
| Marek | 112 | 4.48 S | 120.21 E |
| Maremma ◆[1] | 66 | 42.30 N | 11.30 E |
| Marene | 62 | 44.39 N | 7.44 E |
| Marengo, Il., U.S. | 216 | 42.14 N | 88.36 W |
| Marengo, In., U.S. | 218 | 38.22 N | 86.20 W |
| Marengo, Ia., U.S. | 190 | 41.47 N | 92.04 W |
| Marengo, Mi., U.S. | 216 | 42.17 N | 84.51 W |
| Marengo, Oh., U.S. | 214 | 40.24 N | 82.49 W |
| Marengo ⊥ | 62 | 44.49 N | 8.40 E |
| Marengo Cave ±[5] | 218 | 38.23 N | 86.21 W |
| Marenisco | 190 | 46.22 N | 89.41 W |
| Marennes | 32 | 45.50 N | 1.06 W |
| Marerano | 157b | 21.23 S | 44.52 E |
| Maresias | 256 | 23.48 S | 45.33 W |
| Marettimo | 70 | 37.58 N | 12.04 E |
| Marettimo, Isola I | 70 | 37.58 N | 12.03 E |
| Mareuil-en-Brie | 50 | 48.57 N | 3.45 E |
| Mareuil-lès-Meaux | 261 | 48.56 N | 2.52 E |
| Mareuil-sur-Aÿ | 50 | 49.03 N | 4.02 E |
| Mareuil-sur-Belle | 32 | 45.28 N | 0.28 E |
| Marevo | 76 | 57.19 N | 32.05 E |
| Marey-sur-Tille | 58 | 47.35 N | 5.03 E |
| Marfa | 196 | 30.18 N | 104.01 W |
| Marfinka | 83 | 47.36 N | 38.32 E |
| Marfino | 80 | 46.25 N | 48.44 E |
| Mar Forest ◆[3] | 46 | 57.00 N | 3.35 W |
| Margai Caka ⊜ | 120 | 35.00 N | 87.00 E |
| Margam, Īrān | 84 | 39.09 N | 44.57 E |
| Margam, Wales, U.K. | 42 | 51.34 N | 3.44 W |
| Margao → Madgaon | 122 | 15.18 N | 73.57 E |
| Margaree | 186 | 46.24 N | 61.05 W |
| Margaree Harbour | 186 | 46.26 N | 61.07 W |
| Margaret ≃ | 162 | 18.10 S | 125.37 E |
| Margaret, Mount ∧ | 224 | 46.18 N | 122.08 W |
| Margaret Bay | 182 | 51.20 N | 127.29 W |
| Margaret Creek ≃ | 166 | 29.26 S | 137.07 E |
| Margarethenhöhe ◆[8] | 263 | 51.26 N | 6.58 E |
| Margaret River, Austl. | 162 | 33.57 S | 115.04 E |
| Margaret River, Austl. | 162 | 18.38 S | 126.52 E |
| Margaret Roding | 260 | 51.47 N | 0.19 E |
| Margaretting | 260 | 51.41 N | 0.25 E |
| Margarettsville | 208 | 36.32 N | 77.21 W |
| Margaretville | 210 | 42.08 N | 74.38 W |
| Margarita, Bahía → Marguerite Bay c | 9 | 68.30 S | 68.30 W |
| Margarita, Isla de I | 246 | 11.00 N | 64.00 W |
| Margarita Belén | 252 | 27.16 S | 58.58 W |
| Margarita Peak ∧ | 228 | 33.26 N | 117.23 W |
| Margaritovka | 83 | 46.55 N | 38.52 E |
| Margate, S. Afr. | 158 | 30.55 S | 30.15 E |
| Margate, Eng., U.K. | 42 | 51.24 N | 1.24 E |
| Margate, Fl., U.S. | 220 | 26.14 N | 80.12 W |
| Margate City | 208 | 39.19 N | 74.30 W |
| Margecany | 30 | 48.54 N | 21.01 E |
| Margelan → Margilan | 85 | 40.28 N | 71.44 E |
| Margeride, Monts de la ⋏ | 32 | 44.50 N | 3.30 E |
| Margès | 62 | 45.09 N | 5.03 E |
| Mārgherita, India | 120 | 27.17 N | 95.41 E |
| Margherita → Jamaame, Som. | 144 | 0.04 N | 42.45 E |
| Margherita di Savoia | 68 | 41.23 N | 16.09 E |
| Margherita Peak ∧ | 154 | 0.22 N | 29.51 E |
| Marghī | 120 | 34.58 N | 66.31 E |
| Marghita | 38 | 47.21 N | 22.21 E |
| Margi ≃ | 70 | 37.16 N | 14.58 E |
| Margilan | 85 | 40.28 N | 71.44 E |
| Margit Híd ◆[5] | 264c | 47.31 N | 19.02 E |
| Margit-sziget I | 264c | 47.32 N | 19.03 E |
| Margny-lès-Compiègne | 50 | 49.26 N | 2.49 E |
| Margone | 62 | 45.13 N | 7.11 E |
| Margonin | 30 | 52.59 N | 17.05 E |
| Margos | 248 | 10.04 S | 76.26 W |
| Margosatubig | 116 | 7.34 N | 123.10 E |
| Margot Lake ⊜ | 184 | 52.28 N | 93.10 W |
| Māṛgow, Dasht-e ◆[2] | 128 | 30.45 N | 63.10 E |
| Margreid → Magrè | 64 | 46.17 N | 11.12 E |
| Marguerite, Pic → Margherita Peak ∧ | 154 | 0.22 N | 29.51 E |
| Marguerite Bay c | 9 | 68.30 S | 68.30 W |
| Marguerittes | 62 | 43.51 N | 4.27 E |
| Margut | 56 | 49.35 N | 5.16 E |
| Margyang | 124 | 29.57 N | 90.09 E |
| Marhanets' | 78 | 47.38 N | 34.40 E |
| Mari | 164 | 9.10 S | 141.40 E |
| Maria | 116 | 9.12 N | 123.39 E |
| Maria, Îles II | 14 | 21.48 S | 154.41 W |
| Mariabrunn ◆[8] | 264b | 48.12 N | 16.14 E |
| María Cleofas, Isla I | 234 | 21.16 N | 106.14 W |
| Maria da Fé | 256 | 22.18 S | 45.23 W |
| María Elena | 252 | 22.21 S | 69.40 W |
| Maria Enzersdorf | 61 | 48.06 N | 16.17 E |
| Maria Gail | 64 | 46.36 N | 13.52 E |
| Mariager | 26 | 56.39 N | 10.00 E |
| Mariāhu | 124 | 25.37 N | 82.37 E |
| María Ignacia (Vela) | 252 | 37.24 S | 59.30 W |
| Maria Island I, Austl. | 164 | 14.52 S | 135.40 E |
| Maria Island I, Austl. | 166 | 42.39 S | 148.04 E |
| Maria Island National Park ♦ | 166 | 42.39 S | 148.06 E |
| Mariakani | 154 | 3.52 S | 39.28 E |
| Maria Laach ☋[1] | 56 | 50.24 N | 7.14 E |
| María la Baja | 246 | 9.59 N | 75.17 W |
| Maria Lanzendorf | 264b | 48.06 N | 16.25 E |
| Maria Luggau | 64 | 46.42 N | 12.45 E |
| María Madre, Isla I | 234 | 21.35 N | 106.33 W |
| María Magdalena, Isla I | 234 | 21.25 N | 106.24 W |
| Marian, Lake ⊜ | 220 | 27.52 N | 81.06 W |
| Mariana | 255 | 20.23 S | 43.25 W |
| Mariana Basin ✣[1] | 14 | 17.30 N | 145.00 E |
| Mariana Islands II | 108 | 16.00 N | 145.30 E |
| Mariana Ridge ✣[3] | 14 | 17.00 N | 146.00 E |
| Mariana Trench ✣[1] | 14 | 15.00 N | 147.30 E |
| Mariāni | 120 | 26.40 N | 94.20 E |
| Marian Lake ⊜ | 176 | 63.00 N | 116.10 W |
| Marianna, Ar., U.S. | 194 | 34.46 N | 90.45 W |
| Marianna, Fl., U.S. | 192 | 30.46 N | 85.13 W |
| Mariannelund | 26 | 57.37 N | 15.34 E |
| Mariannhill | 158 | 29.52 S | 30.50 E |
| Mariano Acosta | 258 | 34.43 S | 58.48 W |
| Mariano Comense | 62 | 45.42 N | 9.11 E |
| Mariano del Friuli | 64 | 45.55 N | 13.27 E |
| Mariano I. Loza | 252 | 29.22 S | 58.12 W |
| Mariano J. Haedo | 288 | 34.38 S | 58.36 W |
| Mariano Moreno, Arg. | 252 | 38.44 S | 70.01 W |
| Mariano Moreno → Moreno, Arg. | 258 | 34.39 S | 58.48 W |
| Marianopoli | 70 | 37.36 N | 13.55 E |
| Mariánské Lázně | 60 | 49.59 N | 12.43 E |
| Mariar | 164 | 2.48 S | 132.50 E |
| Mariarano | 157b | 15.29 S | 46.42 E |
| Marias ≃ | 202 | 47.56 N | 110.30 W |
| Marias, Dry Fork ≃ | 202 | 48.22 N | 111.45 W |
| Marías, Islas II | 234 | 21.25 N | 106.28 W |
| Maria Saal | 61 | 46.41 N | 14.21 E |
| Marias Pass )( | 202 | 48.19 N | 113.21 W |
| Maria Stein | 216 | 40.24 N | 84.28 W |
| María Teresa | 252 | 34.01 S | 61.54 W |
| Maria-Theresiopel → Subotica | 38 | 46.06 N | 19.39 E |
| Mariato, Punta › | 246 | 7.13 N | 80.53 W |
| Maria van Diemen, Cape › | 172 | 34.28 S | 172.39 E |
| Mariaville | 210 | 42.49 N | 74.08 W |
| Mariazell | 61 | 47.47 N | 15.19 E |
| Ma'rib | 144 | 15.30 N | 45.20 E |
| Maribo | 41 | 54.46 N | 11.31 E |
| Maribojoc Bay c | 116 | 9.42 N | 123.50 E |
| Maribor | 36 | 46.33 N | 15.39 E |
| Maribyrnong | 274b | 37.46 S | 144.54 E |
| Maricá, Bra. | 256 | 22.55 S | 42.49 W |
| Marica, Ross. | 78 | 51.45 N | 35.16 E |
| Maricá □[7] | 287a | 22.57 S | 42.59 W |
| Marica (Évros) (Meriç) ≃ | 38 | 40.52 N | 26.12 E |
| Maricá, Lagoa de c | 256 | 22.56 S | 42.5 W |
| Maricaban Island I | 116 | 13.39 N | 120.5 E |
| Maricao | 240m | 18.11 N | 66.5 W |
| Maricás, Ilhas II | 256 | 23.01 S | 42.5 W |
| Maricha Bil ⊜ | 272b | 22.55 N | 88.3 E |
| Marico ≃ | 156 | 24.12 S | 26.5 E |
| Maricopa, Az., U.S. | 200 | 33.03 N | 112.0 W |
| Maricopa, Ca., U.S. | 204 | 35.03 N | 119.2 W |
| Maricopa Indian Reservation ◆[4] | 200 | 33.02 N | 112.05 W |
| Maricunga, Salar de ≡ | 252 | 26.55 S | 69.05 W |
| Maridagao ≃ | 116 | 7.13 N | 124.41 E |
| Marīdī | 154 | 4.55 N | 29.28 E |
| Maridi ≃ | 140 | 6.05 N | 29.24 E |
| Marié ≃ | 246 | 0.27 S | 66.26 W |
| Marie Byrd Land ◆[1] | 9 | 80.00 S | 120.00 W |
| Marie Curtis Park ♦ | 275b | 43.35 N | 79.33 W |
| Mariedamm | 40 | 58.51 N | 15.09 E |
| Mariefred | 40 | 59.16 N | 17.13 E |
| Marie-Galante I | 241o | 15.56 N | 61.16 W |
| Mariehamn | 26 | 60.06 N | 19.57 E |
| Marieholm | 41 | 55.52 N | 13.09 E |
| Mariel | 240p | 22.59 N | 82.45 W |
| Mari El → Marij El □[3] | 80 | 56.30 N | 48.00 |
| Marie Lake ⊜ | 184 | 54.37 N | 110.18 W |
| Marie-Lefranc, Lac ⊜ | 206 | 46.08 N | 75.00 W |
| Mariembourg | 50 | 50.06 N | 4.31 E |
| Marienbad → Mariánské Lázně | 60 | 49.59 N | 12.43 E |
| Marienbaum | 52 | 51.41 N | 6.22 E |
| Marienberg, Dtsch. | 54 | 50.39 N | 13.10 E |
| Marienberg, Pap. N. Gui. | 164 | 3.55 S | 144.15 E |
| Marien-Berg ∧[2] | 264a | 52.22 N | 13.32 E |
| Marienborn | 54 | 52.12 N | 11.08 E |
| Marienburg → Malbork | 30 | 54.02 N | 19.01 E |
| Mariendorf ◆[8] | 264a | 52.26 N | 13.23 E |
| Marienfelde ◆[8] | 54 | 52.25 N | 13.22 E |
| Marienhafe | 52 | 53.31 N | 7.16 E |
| Marienheide | 56 | 51.05 N | 7.32 E |
| Marienmünster | 52 | 51.50 N | 9.13 E |
| Mariental, Dtsch. | 54 | 52.16 N | 10.59 E |
| Mariental, Namibia | 156 | 24.36 S | 17.59 E |
| Marienville | 214 | 41.28 N | 79.07 W |
| Maries □[6] | 219 | 38.15 N | 91.55 W |
| Maries ≃ | 194 | 38.30 N | 92.01 W |
| Mariestad | 40 | 58.43 N | 13.51 E |
| Marieta ≃ | 246 | 5.02 N | 66.38 W |
| Marietta, Ga., U.S. | 192 | 33.57 N | 84.33 W |
| Marietta, In., U.S. | 218 | 39.26 N | 85.53 W |
| Marietta, Mn., U.S. | 198 | 45.00 N | 96.25 W |
| Marietta, Oh., U.S. | 188 | 39.24 N | 81.27 W |
| Marietta, Ok., U.S. | 196 | 33.56 N | 97.06 W |
| Marietta, Pa., U.S. | 208 | 40.03 N | 76.33 W |
| Marietta, Tx., U.S. | 222 | 33.10 N | 94.33 W |
| Marietta, Wa., U.S. | 224 | 48.47 N | 122.34 W |
| Marieville | 206 | 45.26 N | 73.10 W |
| Mariga ≃ | 150 | 9.40 N | 5.55 E |
| Marignane | 62 | 43.25 N | 5.13 E |
| Marignier | 58 | 46.06 N | 6.31 E |
| Marigny-le-Châtel | 50 | 48.24 N | 3.44 E |
| Marigny-L'Église | 50 | 47.22 N | 3.56 E |
| Marigot, Dom. | 240d | 15.32 N | 61.18 W |
| Marigot, Guad. | 238 | 18.04 N | 63.06 W |
| Marihatag | 116 | 8.48 N | 126.18 E |
| Mariinsk | 86 | 56.13 N | 87.45 E |
| Mariinskoje | 89 | 51.43 N | 140.13 E |
| Marijampole | 76 | 54.33 N | 23.21 E |
| Marijec | 80 | 56.32 N | 49.50 E |
| Marij El □[3], Ross. | 72 | 56.30 N | 48.00 E |
| Marij El □[3], Ross. | 80 | 56.30 N | 48.00 E |
| Marikana | 158 | 25.42 S | 27.30 E |
| Marikina | 269f | 14.38 N | 121.06 E |
| Marikina ≃ | 269f | 14.33 N | 121.04 E |
| Marília | 255 | 22.13 S | 49.56 W |
| Marilla | 210 | 42.50 N | 78.33 W |
| Mari-Malmyž | 80 | 56.30 N | 50.52 E |
| Marimari ≃ | 246 | 3.58 S | 58.49 W |
| Marimba | 152 | 8.28 S | 17.08 E |
| Marín | 34 | 42.23 N | 8.42 W |
| Marin □[6] | 226 | 38.03 N | 122.33 W |
| Marina | 226 | 36.41 N | 121.48 W |
| Marina ◆[8] | 282 | 37.47 N | 122.27 W |
| Marina del Rey | 280 | 33.50 N | 118.25 W |
| Marina del Rey c | 280 | 33.58 N | 118.27 W |
| Marina di Andora | 62 | 43.57 N | 8.08 E |
| Marina di Campo | 66 | 42.44 N | 10.14 E |
| Marina di Caronia | 70 | 38.02 N | 14.28 E |
| Marina di Carrara | 64 | 44.02 N | 10.02 E |
| Marina di Cecina | 66 | 43.18 N | 10.29 E |
| Marina di Gioiosa Ionica | 68 | 38.18 N | 16.20 E |
| Marina di Grosseto | 66 | 42.43 N | 10.59 E |
| Marina di Massa | 64 | 44.00 N | 10.06 E |
| Marina di Minturno | 66 | 41.16 N | 13.45 E |
| Marina di Orosei | 71 | 40.22 N | 9.43 E |
| Marina di Palma ◆[8] | 70 | 37.10 N | 13.43 E |
| Marina di Pietrasanta | 64 | 43.56 N | 10.12 E |
| Marina di Pisa | 66 | 43.40 N | 10.16 E |
| Marina di Ragusa | 70 | 36.47 N | 14.33 E |
| Marina di Ravenna | 66 | 44.29 N | 12.17 E |
| Marina Fall ∟ | 246 | 5.22 N | 59.29 W |
| Mar'ina Horka | 76 | 53.31 N | 28.09 E |
| Marin City | 282 | 37.52 N | 122.21 W |
| Marinduque □[4] | 116 | 13.25 N | 121.55 E |
| Marinduque Island I | 116 | 13.24 N | 121.58 E |
| Marine | 219 | 38.47 N | 89.46 W |
| Marine City | 214 | 42.43 N | 82.29 W |
| Marine-Ehrenmal ⊥ | 54 | 54.23 N | 10.15 E |
| Marineland of the Pacific ☋[3] | 228 | 33.44 N | 118.24 W |
| Marinella | 70 | 37.35 N | 12.50 E |
| Marine Museum ☋ | 280 | 33.43 N | 118.17 W |
| Marineo | 70 | 37.57 N | 13.25 E |
| Marine Park ♦ | 283 | 42.20 N | 71.01 W |
| Marine Parkway Bridge ◆[5] | 276 | 40.34 N | 73.53 W |
| Mariners Museum ☋ | 208 | 37.03 N | 76.30 W |
| Marines | 50 | 49.09 N | 1.59 E |
| Marinette | 190 | 45.06 N | 87.37 W |
| Maringá | 255 | 23.25 S | 51.55 W |
| Maringa ≃ | 152 | 1.14 N | 19.48 E |
| Maringouin | 194 | 30.29 N | 91.31 W |
| Maríngué | 154 | 17.55 S | 34.24 E |
| Marinha Grande | 34 | 39.45 N | 8.56 W |
| Marinho ≃ | 287a | 23.00 S | 43.27 W |
| Marin Mall ◆[9] | 282 | 37.56 N | 122.31 W |
| Marino, It. | 66 | 41.46 N | 12.39 E |
| Marino, Vanuatu | 175f | 15.00 S | 168.09 E |
| Marinovka | 80 | 48.41 N | 43.49 E |
| Marin Peninsula ›[1] | 282 | 37.51 N | 122.31 W |
| Marinskij Posad | 80 | 56.07 N | 47.43 E |
| Marintu | 112 | 0.34 N | 110.00 E |
| Marinwood | 226 | 38.02 N | 122.32 W |
| Mario, Monte ∧[2] | 267a | 41.55 N | 12.27 E |
| Marion, Austl. | 168b | 35.01 S | 138.34 E |
| Marion, Al., U.S. | 194 | 32.37 N | 87.19 W |
| Marion, Ar., U.S. | 194 | 35.12 N | 90.11 W |
| Marion, Ct., U.S. | 207 | 41.33 N | 72.55 W |
| Marion, Il., U.S. | 194 | 37.43 N | 88.55 W |
| Marion, In., U.S. | 216 | 40.33 N | 85.39 W |
| Marion, Ia., U.S. | 190 | 42.02 N | 91.35 W |
| Marion, Ks., U.S. | 198 | 38.20 N | 97.01 W |
| Marion, Ky., U.S. | 194 | 37.19 N | 88.04 W |
| Marion, La., U.S. | 194 | 32.54 N | 92.14 W |
| Marion, Ma., U.S. | 207 | 41.42 N | 70.45 W |
| Marion, Mi., U.S. | 190 | 44.06 N | 85.08 W |
| Marion, Ms., U.S. | 194 | 32.25 N | 88.38 W |
| Marion, N.Y., U.S. | 210 | 43.08 N | 77.11 W |
| Marion, N.C., U.S. | 192 | 35.41 N | 82.00 W |
| Marion, N.D., U.S. | 198 | 46.36 N | 98.19 W |
| Marion, Oh., U.S. | 214 | 40.35 N | 83.07 W |
| Marion, S.C., U.S. | 192 | 34.10 N | 79.24 W |
| Marion, S.D., U.S. | 198 | 43.25 N | 97.15 W |
| Marion, Va., U.S. | 192 | 36.50 N | 81.30 W |
| Marion, Wi., U.S. | 190 | 44.40 N | 88.53 W |


| | | | | |
|---|---|---|---|---|
| ≃ River | Fluß | Río | Rivière | Rio |
| ≍ Canal | Kanal | Canal | Canal | Canal |
| ∟ Waterfall, Rapids | Wasserfall, Stromschnellen | Cascada, Rápidos | Chute d'eau, Rapides | Cascata, Rápidos |
| ⊔ Strait | Meeresstraße | Estrecho | Détroit | Estreito |
| c Bay, Gulf | Bucht, Golf | Bahía, Golfo | Baie, Golfe | Baía, Golfo |
| ⊜ Lake, Lakes | See, Seen | Lago, Lagos | Lac, Lacs | Lago, Lagos |
| ≡ Swamp | Sumpf | Pantano | Marais | Pântano |
| ⊞ Ice Features, Glacier | Eis- und Gletscherformen | Accidentes Glaciales | Formes glaciaires | Acidentes glaciares |
| ⊤ Other Hydrographic Features | Andere Hydrographische Objekte | Otros Elementos Hidrográficos | Autres données hydrographiques | Outros acidentes hidrográficos |

| | | | | |
|---|---|---|---|---|
| ✣ Submarine Features | Untermeerische Objekte | Accidentes Submarinos | Formes de relief sous-marin | Acidentes submarinos |
| □ Political Unit | Politische Einheit | Unidad Politica | Entité politique | Unidade política |
| ☋ Cultural Institution | Kulturelle Institution | Institución Cultural | Institution culturelle | Institução cultural |
| ⊥ Historical Site | Historische Stätte | Sitio Histórico | Site historique | Sitio histórico |
| ♦ Recreational Site | Erholungs- und Ferienort | Sitio de Recreo | Centre de loisirs | Area de Lazer |
| ⊠ Airport | Flughafen | Aeropuerto | Aéroport | Aeroporto |
| ■ Military Installation | Militäranlage | Instalación Militar | Installation militaire | Instalação militar |
| ◆ Miscellaneous | Verschiedenes | Misceláneo | Divers | Diversos |

| Name (ENGLISH) / Name (DEUTSCH) | Page / Seite | Lat.°′ / Breite°′ | Long.°′ / Länge°′ E = Ost |
|---|---|---|---|
| Marion □[6], Fl., U.S. | 220 | 29.00 N | 82.03 W |
| Marion □[6], Il., U.S. | 219 | 38.38 N | 88.57 W |
| Marion □[6], In., U.S. | 218 | 39.46 N | 86.09 W |
| Marion □[6], Mo., U.S. | 219 | 39.50 N | 91.37 W |
| Marion □[6], Oh., U.S. | 214 | 40.35 N | 83.08 W |
| Marion □[6], Or., U.S. | 224 | 45.06 N | 122.47 W |
| Marion □[6], Tx., U.S. | 222 | 32.48 N | 94.33 W |
| Marion, Lake ⊜ | 220 | 28.05 N | 81.32 W |
| Marion, Lake ⊜[1] | 192 | 33.30 N | 80.25 W |
| Marion Bay C | 166 | 42.48 S | 147.55 E |
| Marion Center | 214 | 40.46 N | 79.03 W |
| Marion Downs | 166 | 23.22 S | 139.39 E |
| Marion Heights | 210 | 40.48 N | 76.28 W |
| Marion Hill | 214 | 40.44 N | 80.18 W |
| Marion Junction | 194 | 32.26 N | 87.14 W |
| Marion Lake ⊜[1] | 198 | 38.24 N | 97.08 W |
| Marion Reef ✢[2] | 166 | 19.10 S | 152.17 E |
| Marion Station | 208 | 38.02 N | 75.46 W |
| Marionville | 194 | 37.00 N | 93.38 W |
| Mariópolis | 252 | 26.20 S | 52.33 W |
| Maripa | 246 | 7.26 N | 65.09 W |
| Maripá de Minas | 256 | 21.48 S | 42.58 W |
| Maripasoula | 250 | 3.38 N | 54.02 W |
| Maripipi Island I | 116 | 11.47 N | 124.19 E |
| Mariposa | 226 | 37.29 N | 119.57 W |
| Mariposa □[6] | 226 | 37.29 N | 119.58 W |
| Mariposa Creek ≐ | 226 | 37.14 N | 120.26 W |
| Mariposa Slough ≐ | 226 | 37.12 N | 120.46 W |
| Mariquita | 246 | 5.12 N | 74.54 W |
| Marisa | 112 | 0.28 N | 121.56 E |
| Marisa ≐ | 112 | 0.28 N | 121.56 E |
| Mariscal Estigarribia | 252 | 22.02 S | 60.38 W |
| Marisco, Ponta do › | 287a | 23.01 S | 43.17 W |
| Mariškino | 82 | 55.21 N | 38.37 E |
| Marismas del Guadalquivir ≡ | 34 | 37.00 N | 6.15 W |
| Marissa | 219 | 38.15 N | 89.45 W |
| Maritime Alps (Alpes Maritimes) (Alpi Marittime) ⋏ | 62 | 44.15 N | 7.10 E |
| Maritime Atlas → Atlas Tellien ⋏ | 148 | 36.00 N | 3.00 E |
| Maritimes, Alpes → Maritime Alps ⋏ | 62 | 44.15 N | 7.10 E |
| Marittime, Alpi → Maritime Alps ⋏ | 62 | 44.15 N | 7.10 E |
| Mari-Turek | 80 | 56.47 N | 49.36 E |
| Maritzburg → Pietermaritzburg | 158 | 29.37 S | 30.16 E |
| Mariupol' | 83 | 47.06 N | 37.33 E |
| Mariusa, Caño ≐[1] | 246 | 9.43 N | 61.26 W |
| Mariusa, Isla I | 241r | 9.39 N | 61.19 W |
| Marīvān | 128 | 35.31 N | 46.10 E |
| Mariveles | 116 | 14.26 N | 120.29 E |
| Märjamaa | 76 | 58.54 N | 24.26 E |
| Marjanovka | 86 | 54.58 N | 72.38 E |
| Marjanskaja | 78 | 45.06 N | 38.38 E |
| Marjevka | 86 | 53.46 N | 67.24 E |
| Marjino, Ross. | 82 | 54.28 N | 37.12 E |
| Marjino, Ross. | 89 | 48.31 N | 130.38 E |
| Marjino, Ross. | 265a | 59.50 N | 29.56 E |
| Marjino, Ross. | 265a | 59.54 N | 31.00 E |
| Marjino, Ross. | 265b | 55.52 N | 37.18 E |
| Marjinskaja | 84 | 43.53 N | 43.29 E |
| Marjinsko | 76 | 58.49 N | 28.32 E |
| Mār Jirjis, Jūn C | 132 | 33.54 N | 35.33 E |
| Marj 'Uyūn | 132 | 33.22 N | 35.35 E |
| Marka, Som. | 144 | 1.43 N | 44.53 E |
| Mārkā, Urd. | 132 | 31.59 N | 35.59 E |
| Markā I | 144 | 18.13 N | 41.19 E |
| Mark Acres | 279b | 40.21 N | 79.42 W |
| Markakol', ozero ⊜ | 86 | 48.45 N | 85.48 E |
| Markala | 150 | 13.41 N | 6.05 W |
| Markam | 102 | 29.40 N | 98.30 E |
| Markansu | 85 | 39.18 N | 73.20 E |
| Mārkāpur | 122 | 15.44 N | 79.17 E |
| Markaryd | 26 | 56.26 N | 13.36 E |
| Markazī □[4] | 128 | 34.30 N | 50.30 E |
| Markdale | 212 | 44.19 N | 80.39 W |
| Markdorf | 58 | 47.43 N | 9.23 E |
| Marked Tree | 194 | 35.31 N | 90.25 W |
| Markelo | 52 | 52.14 N | 6.30 E |
| Markelovo | 86 | 56.42 N | 83.33 E |
| Marken I | 52 | 52.28 N | 5.03 E |
| Markendorf | 54 | 51.59 N | 13.10 E |
| Markermeer ⊜ | 52 | 52.33 N | 5.15 E |
| Markesan | 190 | 43.42 N | 88.59 W |
| Märket I | 40 | 60.18 N | 19.08 E |
| Market Bosworth | 42 | 52.37 N | 1.24 W |
| Market Deeping | 42 | 52.41 N | 0.19 W |
| Market Drayton | 42 | 52.54 N | 2.29 W |
| Market Harborough | 42 | 52.29 N | 0.55 W |
| Markethill | 48 | 54.18 N | 6.31 W |
| Market Lavington | 42 | 51.18 N | 1.59 W |
| Market Rasen | 44 | 53.24 N | 0.21 W |
| Market Weighton | 44 | 53.52 N | 0.40 W |
| Markfield | 42 | 52.40 N | 1.17 W |
| Markgröningen | 56 | 48.54 N | 9.05 E |
| Markham, On., Can. | 212 | 43.52 N | 79.16 W |
| Markham, Il., U.S. | 278 | 41.35 N | 87.41 W |
| Markham, Tx., U.S. | 222 | 28.57 N | 96.04 W |
| Markham ≐ | 164 | 6.35 S | 146.25 E |
| Markham, Mount ∧ | 9 | 82.51 S | 161.21 E |
| Markham Bay C | 176 | 63.30 N | 71.48 W |
| Markinch | 46 | 56.12 N | 3.08 W |
| Märkisch Buchholz | 54 | 52.07 N | 13.46 E |
| Markit | 85 | 38.55 N | 77.38 E |
| Markivka | 83 | 49.31 N | 39.34 E |
| Markkleeberg | 54 | 51.17 N | 12.23 E |
| Markland Dam ◆[6] | 218 | 38.47 N | 84.58 W |
| Markle, In., U.S. | 216 | 40.50 N | 85.20 W |
| Markle, Pa., U.S. | 279b | 40.34 N | 79.39 W |
| Markleeville | 226 | 38.41 N | 119.46 W |
| Markleville | 218 | 39.58 N | 85.36 W |
| Markley Canyon V | 282 | 38.00 N | 121.50 W |
| Marklohe | 52 | 52.40 N | 9.09 E |
| Marknesse | 52 | 52.43 N | 5.52 E |
| Markneukirchen | 54 | 50.18 N | 12.19 E |
| Markoldendorf | 52 | 51.48 N | 9.46 E |
| Markópoulon | 267c | 37.54 N | 23.54 E |
| Markounda | 152 | 7.37 N | 16.59 E |
| Markovo, Ross. | 74 | 64.40 N | 170.25 E |
| Markovo, Ross. | 80 | 57.01 N | 40.30 E |
| Markovo, Ross. | 82 | 55.52 N | 39.17 E |
| Markovo, Ross. | 88 | 57.20 N | 107.04 E |
| Markoy | 150 | 14.39 N | 0.02 E |
| Markranstädt | 54 | 51.18 N | 12.13 E |
| Marks, Ross. | 80 | 51.42 N | 46.46 E |
| Marks, Ms., U.S. | 194 | 34.15 N | 90.16 W |
| Marks Tey | 42 | 51.52 N | 0.47 E |
| Marksuhl | 56 | 50.55 N | 10.11 E |
| Marksville | 194 | 31.07 N | 92.03 W |
| Markt Bibart | 56 | 49.39 N | 10.26 E |
| Marktbreit | 56 | 49.40 N | 10.08 E |
| Markt Erlbach | 56 | 49.29 N | 10.38 E |
| Marktheidenfeld | 56 | 49.50 N | 9.36 E |
| Markt Indersdorf | 60 | 48.22 N | 11.23 E |
| Marktl | 60 | 48.15 N | 12.51 E |
| Marktleugast | 54 | 50.10 N | 11.38 E |
| Marktleuthen | 54 | 50.08 N | 12.00 E |
| Marktoberdorf | 58 | 47.47 N | 10.37 E |
| Marktredwitz | 60 | 50.00 N | 12.06 E |
| Markt Rettenbach | 58 | 47.57 N | 10.23 E |
| Marktschellenberg | 64 | 47.42 N | 13.02 E |
| Markt Schwaben | 60 | 48.11 N | 11.51 E |
| Mark Twain Cave ±[5] | 219 | 39.42 N | 91.21 W |
| Mark Twain Lake ⊜[1] | 219 | 39.30 N | 91.45 W |
| Mark Twain State Park ♦ | 219 | 39.29 N | 91.48 W |
| Markundi | 140 | 11.33 N | 23.49 E |
| Markvue Manor | 279b | 40.20 N | 79.46 W |
| Mark West Creek ≐ | 226 | 38.30 N | 122.42 W |
| Marl | 52 | 51.38 N | 7.05 E |
| Marlasi | 164 | 5.30 S | 134.38 E |
| Marlboro, Ab., Can. | 182 | 53.33 N | 116.45 W |
| Marlboro, N.J., U.S. | 208 | 40.18 N | 74.14 W |
| Marlboro, N.Y., U.S. | 210 | 41.36 N | 73.56 W |
| Marlboro, Oh., U.S. | 214 | 40.53 N | 81.12 W |
| Marlboro, Pa., U.S. | 285 | 39.54 N | 75.42 W |
| Marlborough, Austl. | 166 | 22.49 S | 149.53 E |
| Marlborough, Guy. | 246 | 7.29 N | 58.38 W |
| Marlborough, Eng., U.K. | 42 | 51.26 N | 1.43 W |
| Marlborough, Ct., U.S. | 207 | 41.37 N | 72.27 W |
| Marlborough, Ma., U.S. | 207 | 42.20 N | 71.33 W |
| Marlborough Downs ⋏[1] | 42 | 51.30 N | 1.45 W |
| Marldon | 42 | 50.28 N | 3.36 W |
| Marle | 50 | 49.44 N | 3.46 E |
| Marlenheim | 58 | 48.37 N | 7.30 E |
| Marles-en-Brie | 261 | 48.44 N | 2.53 E |
| Marles-les-Mines | 50 | 50.30 N | 2.31 E |
| Marlette | 190 | 43.19 N | 83.04 W |
| Marlette Lake ⊜ | 226 | 39.10 N | 119.54 W |
| Marley, Il., U.S. | 278 | 41.33 N | 87.55 W |
| Marley, Md., U.S. | 208 | 39.09 N | 76.35 W |
| Marley Creek ≐ | 278 | 41.31 N | 87.57 W |
| Marley Neck ›[1] | 284b | 39.12 N | 76.33 W |
| Marlieux | 58 | 46.04 N | 5.04 E |
| Marlin | 222 | 31.18 N | 96.53 W |
| Marlinton | 188 | 38.13 N | 80.05 W |
| Marl-Loemühle, Flughafen ⊠ | 263 | 51.39 N | 7.10 E |
| Marlow, Dtsch. | 54 | 54.09 N | 12.34 E |
| Marlow, Eng., U.K. | 42 | 51.35 N | 0.48 W |
| Marlow, Ok., U.S. | 196 | 34.38 N | 97.57 W |
| Marlpit Hill | 260 | 51.13 N | 0.04 E |
| Marlton | 208 | 39.53 N | 74.55 W |
| Marlton Heights | 285 | 39.40 N | 75.21 W |
| Marly | 50 | 50.20 N | 3.32 E |
| Marly, Forêt de ♦ | 261 | 48.52 N | 2.03 E |
| Marly-la-Ville | 261 | 49.05 N | 2.30 E |
| Marly-le-Roi | 50 | 48.52 N | 2.05 E |
| Marma, Sve. | 26 | 61.16 N | 16.52 E |
| Marma, Sve. | 40 | 60.30 N | 17.25 E |
| Marmaduke | 194 | 36.11 N | 90.22 W |
| Marmagne | 58 | 46.50 N | 4.21 E |
| Marmande | 32 | 44.30 N | 0.10 E |
| Marmara, Sea of → Marmara Denizi ▾[2] | 130 | 40.40 N | 28.15 E |
| Marmara Adası I | 130 | 40.38 N | 27.37 E |
| Marmara Denizi (Sea of Marmara) ▾[2] | 130 | 40.40 N | 28.15 E |
| Marmara Ereğlisi | 130 | 40.58 N | 27.57 E |
| Marmara Gölü ⊜ | 130 | 38.37 N | 28.02 E |
| Marmaris | 130 | 36.51 N | 28.16 E |
| Marmarītā | 130 | 34.47 N | 36.15 E |
| Marmarth | 198 | 46.17 N | 103.55 W |
| Marmaton ≐ | 194 | 38.00 N | 94.19 W |
| Marmelópolis | 256 | 22.27 S | 45.10 W |
| Marmelos | 248 | 6.08 S | 61.50 W |
| Marmelos, Rio dos ≐ | 248 | 6.06 S | 61.46 W |
| Marmet | 188 | 38.14 N | 81.34 W |
| Marmion Lake ⊜[1] | 190 | 48.54 N | 91.30 W |
| Marmirolo | 64 | 45.13 N | 10.45 E |
| Marmolada ∧ | 64 | 46.26 N | 11.51 E |
| Marmora, On., Can. | 212 | 44.29 N | 77.41 W |
| Marmora, N.J., U.S. | 208 | 39.16 N | 74.38 W |
| Marmore | 66 | 42.33 N | 12.43 E |
| Marmore ≐ | 62 | 45.44 N | 7.37 E |
| Marmore, Cascàta delle ∟ | 66 | 42.33 N | 12.43 E |
| Marmot Bay C | 180 | 58.00 N | 152.20 W |
| Marmot Island I | 180 | 58.13 N | 151.51 W |
| Marmoutier | 58 | 48.41 N | 7.23 E |
| Mar Muerto, Laguna C | 234 | 16.10 N | 94.10 W |
| Marnate | 266b | 45.38 N | 8.54 E |
| Marnay | 58 | 47.17 N | 5.46 E |
| Marnaz | 58 | 46.04 N | 6.32 E |
| Marne, Dtsch. | 52 | 53.57 N | 9.00 E |
| Marne, Mi., U.S. | 216 | 43.02 N | 85.49 W |
| Marne □[5] | 32 | 48.55 N | 4.10 E |
| Marne ≐, Austl. | 168b | 34.40 S | 139.18 E |
| Marne ≐, Fr. | 32 | 48.49 N | 2.24 E |
| Marne à la Saône, Canal de la ≊ | 58 | 48.44 N | 4.36 E |
| Marne au Rhin, Canal de la ≊ | 56 | 48.35 N | 7.47 E |
| Marneuli | 84 | 41.28 N | 44.50 E |
| Marnhull | 42 | 50.58 N | 2.18 W |
| Marnitz | 54 | 53.19 N | 11.56 E |
| Maroa, Il., U.S. | 219 | 40.02 N | 88.57 W |
| Maroa, Ven. | 246 | 2.43 N | 67.33 W |
| Maroala | 157b | 15.23 S | 47.59 E |
| Maroantsetra | 157b | 15.26 S | 49.44 E |
| Marobi Raghza | 120 | 32.36 N | 69.52 E |
| Maroc → Morocco □[1] | 148 | 32.00 N | 5.00 W |
| Maroelaboom | 156 | 19.15 S | 18.53 E |
| Marofandilia | 157b | 20.07 S | 44.34 E |
| Marogio ≐ | 70 | 37.03 N | 14.15 E |
| Marokko → Morocco □[1] | 148 | 32.00 N | 5.00 W |
| Marol ◆[8] | 272c | 19.07 N | 72.53 E |
| Marolambo | 157b | 20.02 S | 48.07 E |
| Maroldsweisach | 56 | 50.12 N | 10.39 E |
| Marolles-en-Brie | 261 | 48.44 N | 2.33 E |
| Marolles-en-Hurepoix | 261 | 48.34 N | 2.18 E |
| Marolles-les-Braults | 50 | 48.15 N | 0.19 E |
| Maromandia | 157b | 14.13 S | 48.08 E |
| Maromme | 50 | 49.28 N | 1.02 E |
| Maromokotro ∧ | 157b | 14.01 S | 48.59 E |
| Marondera | 154 | 18.10 S | 31.36 E |
| Marone | 64 | 45.44 N | 10.05 E |
| Marong | 102 | 31.07 N | 99.20 E |
| Maronghi Creek ≐ | 171a | 26.58 S | 152.22 E |
| Maroni (Marowijne) ≐ | 250 | 5.45 N | 53.58 W |
| Maroon | 171a | 28.10 S | 152.44 E |
| Maroon, Mount ∧ | 171a | 28.13 S | 152.44 E |
| Maroondah Aqueduct ≊[1] | 274b | 37.42 S | 145.01 E |
| Maros | 112 | 5.00 S | 119.34 E |
| Maros (Mureș) ≐ | 38 | 46.15 N | 20.13 E |
| Maroseranana | 157b | 18.32 S | 48.51 E |
| Marostica | 64 | 45.45 N | 11.39 E |
| Marosvásárhely → Târgu Mureș | 38 | 46.33 N | 24.33 E |
| Marotandrano | 157b | 16.10 S | 48.50 E |
| Marotiri, Îles II | 14 | 27.55 S | 143.26 W |
| Marotta | 66 | 43.46 N | 13.08 E |
| Maroua | 146 | 10.36 N | 14.20 E |
| Maroubra | 274a | 33.57 S | 151.16 E |
| Marouini ≐ | 250 | 3.18 N | 54.04 W |
| Marovato, Madag. | 157b | 13.59 S | 48.36 E |
| Marovato, Madag. | 157b | 15.48 S | 48.05 E |
| Marovato, Madag. | 157b | 16.28 S | 48.25 E |
| Marovoay | 157b | 16.06 S | 46.39 E |
| Marovoay Nord | 157b | 16.57 S | 44.34 E |
| Marowijne □[5] | 250 | 5.40 N | 54.20 W |
| Marowijne (Maroni) ≐ | 250 | 5.45 N | 53.58 W |
| Marpent | 50 | 50.18 N | 4.05 E |
| Marpingen | 56 | 49.27 N | 7.03 E |
| Marple | 44 | 53.24 N | 2.03 W |
| Marquam | 224 | 45.04 N | 122.41 W |
| Marquand | 194 | 37.25 N | 90.10 W |
| Marquard | 158 | 28.54 S | 27.28 E |
| Marquardt | 54 | 52.27 N | 12.57 E |
| Marquartstein | 64 | 47.45 N | 12.28 E |
| Marquesas Islands → Marquises, Îles II | 6 | 9.00 S | 139.30 W |
| Marquesas Keys II | 220 | 24.34 N | 82.08 W |
| Marquette, Ks., U.S. | 198 | 38.33 N | 97.50 W |
| Marquette, Mi., U.S. | 190 | 46.32 N | 87.23 W |
| Marquette Park ♦ | 278 | 41.46 N | 87.42 W |
| Márquez, Perú | 286d | 11.57 S | 77.08 W |
| Marquez, Tx., U.S. | 222 | 31.14 N | 96.15 W |
| Marquion | 50 | 50.13 N | 3.05 E |
| Marquis | 241k | 12.06 N | 61.37 W |
| Marquis, Cape › | 241f | 14.03 N | 60.54 W |
| Marquise | 50 | 50.49 N | 1.42 E |
| Marquises, Îles (Marquesas Islands) II | 6 | 9.00 S | 139.30 W |
| Marrabel | 168b | 34.08 S | 138.53 E |
| Marra Creek ≐ | 166 | 30.05 S | 147.05 E |
| Marradi | 66 | 44.04 N | 11.37 E |
| Marradong | 168a | 32.52 S | 116.27 E |
| Marrah, Jabal ∧ | 140 | 13.04 N | 24.21 E |
| Marra Hills ⋏[2] | 140 | 6.05 N | 27.33 E |
| Marrakech | 148 | 31.38 N | 8.00 W |
| Marrakech □[4] | 148 | 31.30 N | 8.05 W |
| Marramarra National Park ♦ | 170 | 33.32 S | 151.04 E |
| Marrawah | 166 | 40.56 S | 144.41 E |
| Marree | 166 | 29.39 S | 138.04 E |
| Marrero | 194 | 29.53 N | 90.06 W |
| Marrickville | 274a | 33.55 S | 151.09 E |
| Marromeu | 156 | 18.20 S | 35.56 E |
| Marrowstone Island I | 224 | 48.04 N | 122.41 W |
| Marrubiu | 71 | 39.45 N | 8.38 E |
| Marruecos → Morocco □[1] | 148 | 32.00 N | 5.00 W |
| Marrupa | 154 | 13.08 S | 37.30 E |
| Mars | 214 | 40.41 N | 80.00 W |
| Marsā al-Burayqah | 146 | 30.25 N | 19.34 E |
| Marsabit | 154 | 2.20 N | 37.59 E |
| Marsabit National Park ♦ | 154 | 2.20 N | 38.00 E |
| Marsac-en-Livradois | 62 | 45.29 N | 3.44 E |
| Marṣafā wa Kafr Aḥmad Ḥashīsh | 142 | 30.25 N | 31.15 E |
| Marsal | 56 | 48.48 N | 6.36 E |
| Marsala | 70 | 37.48 N | 12.26 E |
| Marsā Maṭrūḥ | 140 | 31.21 N | 27.14 E |
| Marsā Maṭrūḥ □[4] | 142 | 29.00 N | 30.00 E |
| Marsange ≐ | 261 | 48.43 N | 2.45 E |
| Marsangue ≐ | 261 | 48.40 N | 2.47 E |
| Marsannay-la-Côte | 58 | 47.16 N | 4.59 E |
| Marsanne | 62 | 44.39 N | 4.52 E |
| Marsassoum | 150 | 12.50 N | 16.00 W |
| Mars'aty | 86 | 60.05 N | 60.29 E |
| Marsberg, Dtsch. | 52 | 51.28 N | 8.50 E |
| Marsberg, Dtsch. | 56 | 51.28 N | 8.51 E |
| Marscheid ◆[8] | 263 | 51.14 N | 7.14 E |
| Marsciano | 66 | 42.54 N | 12.20 E |
| Marsden, Austl. | 166 | 33.45 S | 147.32 E |
| Marsden, Eng., U.K. | 262 | 53.36 N | 1.56 W |
| Marsden, Point › | 168b | 35.35 S | 137.38 E |
| Marsden Park | 274a | 33.42 S | 150.50 E |
| Marsdiep U | 52 | 52.59 N | 4.45 E |
| Marseille | 62 | 43.18 N | 5.24 E |
| Marseille-en-Beauvaisis | 50 | 49.35 N | 1.57 E |
| Marseille-Marignane, Aéroport de ⊠ | 62 | 43.27 N | 5.13 E |
| Marseilles, Il., U.S. | 216 | 41.19 N | 88.42 W |
| Marseilles, Oh., U.S. | 214 | 40.42 N | 83.23 W |
| Marsella → Marseille | 62 | 43.18 N | 5.24 E |
| Marsfield | 274a | 33.47 S | 151.07 E |
| Marsfjället ∧ | 24 | 65.05 N | 15.28 E |
| Marshall, Liber. | 150 | 6.10 N | 10.23 W |
| Marshall, Ar., U.S. | 194 | 35.54 N | 92.37 W |
| Marshall, Il., U.S. | 194 | 39.23 N | 87.41 W |
| Marshall, Mi., U.S. | 216 | 42.16 N | 84.57 W |
| Marshall, Mn., U.S. | 198 | 44.26 N | 95.47 W |
| Marshall, Mo., U.S. | 194 | 39.07 N | 93.11 W |
| Marshall, N.C., U.S. | 192 | 35.47 N | 82.41 W |
| Marshall, Tx., U.S. | 194 | 32.32 N | 94.22 W |
| Marshall, Va., U.S. | 188 | 38.51 N | 77.51 W |
| Marshall, Wi., U.S. | 216 | 43.10 N | 89.04 W |
| Marshall □[6], Il., U.S. | 216 | 41.02 N | 89.24 W |
| Marshall □[6], In., U.S. | 216 | 41.21 N | 86.19 W |
| Marshall ≐ | 162 | 22.59 S | 136.59 E |
| Marshall Bennett Islands II | 164 | 8.50 S | 151.50 E |
| Marshallberg | 192 | 34.43 N | 76.30 W |
| Marshall Canyon Regional Park ♦ | 280 | 34.09 N | 117.43 W |
| Marshall Gold Discovery State Historical Park ♦ | 226 | 38.48 N | 120.53 W |
| Marshall Hall | 208 | 38.41 N | 77.06 W |
| Marshall Islands □[1] | 14 | 11.00 N | 168.00 E |
| Marshall Islands II | 14 | 9.00 N | 168.00 E |
| Marshalls Creek | 210 | 41.03 N | 75.08 W |
| Marshallton, De., U.S. | 208 | 39.43 N | 75.39 W |
| Marshallton, Pa., U.S. | 210 | 40.47 N | 76.33 W |
| Marshallton, Pa., U.S. | 285 | 39.57 N | 75.41 W |
| Marshalltown | 190 | 42.02 N | 92.54 W |
| Marshallville, Ga., U.S. | 192 | 32.27 N | 83.56 W |
| Marshallville, Oh., U.S. | 214 | 40.54 N | 81.44 W |
| Marshbank Metropolitan Park ♦ | 281 | 42.36 N | 83.23 W |
| Marsh Creek ≐, Ca., U.S. | 282 | 37.53 N | 121.49 W |
| Marsh Creek ≐, Mi., U.S. | 281 | 42.06 N | 83.13 W |
| Marsh Creek ≐, Pa., U.S. | 214 | 41.03 N | 77.36 W |
| Marsh Creek ≐, Pa., U.S. | 285 | 40.03 N | 75.43 W |
| Marsh Creek ≐, Wi., U.S. | 216 | 42.13 N | 89.04 W |
| Marsh Creek Lake ⊜[1] | 208 | 40.04 N | 75.44 W |
| Marshes Creek ≐ | 276 | 40.36 N | 74.13 W |
| Marshfield, Eng., U.K. | 42 | 51.28 N | 2.19 W |
| Marshfield, Ma., U.S. | 207 | 42.05 N | 70.42 W |
| Marshfield, Mo., U.S. | 194 | 37.20 N | 92.54 W |
| Marshfield, Wi., U.S. | 190 | 44.40 N | 90.10 W |
| Marshfield Airport ⊠ | 283 | 42.06 N | 70.40 W |
| Marshfield Center | 283 | 42.07 N | 70.43 W |
| Marshfield Hills | 207 | 42.08 N | 70.44 W |
| Marsh Harbour | 238 | 26.33 N | 77.03 W |
| Marsh Hill | 210 | 41.29 N | 76.58 W |
| Mars Hill, In., U.S. | 218 | 39.43 N | 86.09 W |
| Mars Hill, Me., U.S. | 186 | 46.30 N | 67.52 W |
| Mars Hill, N.C., U.S. | 192 | 35.49 N | 82.32 W |
| Marsh Island I | 194 | 29.35 N | 91.53 W |
| Marsh Lake ⊜ | 180 | 60.25 N | 134.18 W |
| Marsh Peak ∧ | 200 | 40.43 N | 109.50 W |
| Marshside | 262 | 53.40 N | 2.58 W |
| Marshville | 192 | 34.59 N | 80.22 W |
| Marshyhope Creek ≐ | 208 | 38.32 N | 75.45 W |
| Marsica ◆[1] | 66 | 41.50 N | 13.45 E |
| Marsico Nuovo | 68 | 40.25 N | 15.44 E |
| Marsico Vetere | 68 | 40.23 N | 15.49 E |
| Marsillargues | 62 | 43.40 N | 4.11 E |
| Marsimang, Tanjung › | 164 | 3.27 S | 130.49 E |
| Marsing | 202 | 43.32 N | 116.48 W |
| Marske-by-the-Sea | 44 | 54.36 N | 1.01 W |
| Mars-la-Tour | 56 | 49.06 N | 5.54 E |
| Marson | 56 | 48.55 N | 4.32 E |
| Marssum | 52 | 53.12 N | 5.42 E |
| Märsta | 40 | 59.37 N | 17.51 E |
| Marstal | 41 | 54.51 N | 10.31 E |
| Marsteller | 214 | 40.39 N | 78.48 W |
| Märstetten | 58 | 47.36 N | 9.04 E |
| Marston | 262 | 53.16 N | 2.30 W |
| Marston Moor ≚ | 44 | 53.57 N | 1.17 W |
| Marston Moor Battlesite ⊥ | 44 | 53.57 N | 1.17 W |
| Marstons Mills | 207 | 41.39 N | 70.25 W |
| Marstrand | 26 | 57.53 N | 11.35 E |
| Marsyāngdī ≐ | 124 | 28.05 N | 84.28 E |
| Mart | 222 | 31.32 N | 96.50 W |
| Marta | 66 | 42.32 N | 11.55 E |
| Marta ≐ | 66 | 42.14 N | 11.42 E |
| Martaban | 110 | 16.32 N | 97.37 E |
| Martaban, Gulf of C | 110 | 16.30 N | 97.00 E |
| Martano | 68 | 40.12 N | 18.18 E |
| Martap | 152 | 6.54 N | 13.03 E |
| Martapura, Indon. | 112 | 3.25 S | 114.51 E |
| Martapura, Indon. | 112 | 4.19 S | 104.22 E |
| Marte | 146 | 12.22 N | 13.51 E |
| Marteg ≐ | 42 | 52.20 N | 3.33 W |
| Martel, Fr. | 32 | 44.56 N | 1.37 E |
| Martel, Oh., U.S. | 214 | 40.40 N | 82.55 W |
| Martelange | 56 | 49.50 N | 5.44 E |
| Martell | 226 | 38.22 N | 120.48 W |
| Martello | 64 | 46.34 N | 10.47 E |
| Martello, Val V | 64 | 46.31 N | 10.45 E |
| Martemjanovskij | 86 | 55.54 N | 80.22 E |
| Marten ◆[8] | 263 | 51.31 N | 7.23 E |
| Marten Lake ⊜ | 190 | 46.42 N | 79.41 W |
| Marten Mountain ∧ | 182 | 55.28 N | 114.43 W |
| Marte R. Gomez, Presa ⊜[1] | 196 | 26.10 N | 99.00 W |
| Martfeld | 52 | 52.52 N | 9.04 E |
| Marthaguy Creek ≐ | 166 | 30.16 S | 147.35 E |
| Martha Lake | 224 | 47.51 N | 122.20 W |
| Marthall | 262 | 53.17 N | 2.18 W |
| Martham | 42 | 52.42 N | 1.38 E |
| Marthasville | 219 | 38.37 N | 91.03 W |
| Martha's Vineyard I | 207 | 41.25 N | 70.40 W |
| Martí, Cuba | 240p | 21.09 N | 77.27 W |
| Martí, Cuba | 240p | 22.57 N | 80.55 W |
| Martí, Pico ∧ | 240p | 20.01 N | 76.35 W |
| Martignacco | 64 | 46.05 N | 13.08 E |
| Martignat | 58 | 46.13 N | 5.36 E |
| Martigny | 58 | 46.06 N | 7.04 E |
| Martigny-les-Bains | 58 | 48.06 N | 5.49 E |
| Martigues | 62 | 43.24 N | 5.03 E |
| Martil | 34 | 35.37 N | 5.17 W |
| Martim Francisco | 256 | 22.31 S | 46.57 W |
| Martin, Slvk. | 30 | 49.05 N | 18.55 E |
| Martin, Ky., U.S. | 192 | 37.34 N | 82.45 W |
| Martin, Mi., U.S. | 216 | 42.32 N | 85.38 W |
| Martin, N.D., U.S. | 198 | 47.49 N | 100.06 W |
| Martin, Oh., U.S. | 214 | 41.33 N | 83.20 W |
| Martin, S.D., U.S. | 198 | 43.10 N | 101.43 W |
| Martin, Tn., U.S. | 194 | 36.20 N | 88.51 W |
| Martin □[6] | 220 | 27.07 N | 80.31 W |
| Martín ≐ | 34 | 41.18 N | 0.19 W |
| Martín, Arroyo ≐ | 288 | 34.51 S | 58.04 W |
| Martin, Isle I | 46 | 57.55 N | 5.14 W |
| Martina | 58 | 46.53 N | 10.30 E |
| Martina Franca | 68 | 40.42 N | 17.21 E |
| Martinborough | 172 | 41.13 S | 175.28 E |
| Martín Chico, Punta › | 258 | 34.10 S | 58.13 W |
| Martindale | 196 | 29.50 N | 97.51 W |
| Martindale Creek ≐, Austl. | 170 | 32.32 S | 150.42 E |
| Martindale Creek ≐, In., U.S. | 218 | 39.48 N | 85.09 W |
| Martindale Pond ⊜ | 284a | 43.11 N | 79.16 W |
| Martin-Église | 50 | 49.54 N | 1.09 E |
| Martinengo | 62 | 45.34 N | 9.46 E |
| Mărtinești | 38 | 45.30 N | 27.18 E |
| Martinez, Ca., U.S. | 226 | 38.01 N | 122.07 W |
| Martinez, Ga., U.S. | 192 | 33.31 N | 82.04 W |
| Martínez ◆[8] | 258 | 34.29 S | 58.30 W |
| Martínez de la Torre | 234 | 20.04 N | 97.03 W |
| Martín García, Isla I | 258 | 34.13 S | 58.15 W |
| Martinho Campos | 255 | 19.20 S | 45.13 W |
| Martinica → Martinique □[2] | 240e | 14.40 N | 61.00 W |
| Martini Creek ≐ | 282 | 37.33 N | 122.31 W |
| Martinique □[2], N.A. | 230 | 14.40 N | 61.00 W |
| Martinique □[2], N.A. | 240e | 14.40 N | 61.00 W |
| Martinique Passage U | 238 | 15.10 N | 61.15 W |
| Martin Lake ⊜[1], Al., U.S. | 194 | 32.50 N | 85.55 W |
| Martin Lake ⊜[1], Tx., U.S. | 222 | 32.15 N | 94.35 W |
| Martin Marietta Corporation ᵾ[3] | 284b | 39.20 N | 76.26 W |
| Martinniemi | 26 | 65.13 N | 25.18 E |
| Martinópole | 250 | 3.15 S | 40.41 W |
| Martin Peninsula ›[1] | 9 | 74.25 S | 114.10 W |
| Martín Pérez ≐ | 286b | 23.07 N | 82.20 W |
| Martin Point › | 180 | 70.08 N | 143.16 W |
| Martin Run ≐ | 279a | 41.27 N | 82.12 W |
| Martins | 250 | 6.05 S | 37.55 W |
| Martinsberg | 61 | 48.22 N | 15.09 E |
| Martins Brook ≐ | 283 | 42.34 N | 71.06 W |
| Martinsburg, Mo., U.S. | 219 | 39.06 N | 91.38 W |
| Martinsburg, N.Y., U.S | 212 | 43.44 N | 75.28 W |
| Martinsburg, Oh., U.S. | 214 | 40.16 N | 82.21 W |
| Martinsburg, Pa., U.S. | 214 | 40.18 N | 78.19 W |
| Martinsburg, W.V., U.S. | 188 | 39.27 N | 77.57 W |
| Martins Creek | 208 | 40.47 N | 75.11 W |
| Martins Creek ≐ | 210 | 41.37 N | 75.46 W |
| Martinscroft | 262 | 53.24 N | 2.31 W |
| Martins Ferry | 214 | 40.05 N | 80.43 W |
| Martins Mills | 222 | 32.25 N | 95.47 W |
| Martins Pond ⊜ | 283 | 42.36 N | 71.08 W |
| Martinstein | 56 | 49.48 N | 7.32 E |
| Martinsthal | 56 | 50.03 N | 8.07 E |
| Martinsville, Austl. | 170 | 33.03 S | 151.25 E |
| Martinsville, Il., U.S. | 194 | 39.20 N | 87.52 W |
| Martinsville, In., U.S. | 218 | 39.25 N | 86.25 W |
| Martinsville, N.J., U.S. | 276 | 40.36 N | 74.34 W |
| Martinsville, Oh., U.S. | 218 | 39.19 N | 83.48 W |
| Martinsville, Va., U.S. | 192 | 36.41 N | 79.52 W |
| Martinton | 216 | 40.55 N | 87.44 W |
| Martintown | 206 | 45.09 N | 74.42 W |
| Martin Van Buren National Historic Site ⊥ | 210 | 42.22 N | 73.43 W |
| Martin Vaz, Ilhas II | 244 | 20.30 S | 28.51 W |
| Martis | 71 | 40.47 N | 8.49 E |
| Martisovo | 76 | 56.34 N | 31.55 E |
| Martock | 42 | 50.59 N | 2.46 W |
| Martofte | 41 | 55.33 N | 10.40 E |
| Marton, N.Z. | 172 | 40.05 S | 175.23 E |
| Marton, Eng., U.K. | 262 | 53.12 N | 2.13 W |
| Martorell | 266d | 41.28 N | 1.56 E |
| Martorelles de Baix | 266d | 41.32 N | 2.14 E |
| Martos | 34 | 37.43 N | 3.58 W |
| Martova | 78 | 49.57 N | 36.57 E |
| Martre, Lac la ⊜ | 176 | 63.15 N | 117.55 W |
| Martti | 24 | 67.28 N | 28.28 E |
| Martūbah | 146 | 32.35 N | 22.46 E |
| Martuk | 86 | 50.46 N | 56.31 E |
| Martuni | 84 | 40.08 N | 45.19 E |
| Martvili | 84 | 42.25 N | 42.22 E |
| Martville | 210 | 43.17 N | 76.38 W |
| Martynivka | 78 | 49.38 N | 31.18 E |
| Martynovo | 80 | 50.43 N | 50.23 E |
| Martynovskij | 80 | 50.29 N | 42.18 E |
| Martynovychi | 78 | 51.17 N | 29.37 E |
| Maru | 150 | 12.22 N | 6.22 E |
| Marua | 164 | 9.30 S | 149.20 E |
| Marudi | 112 | 4.11 N | 114.19 E |
| Marudu, Telukan C | 112 | 6.45 N | 116.55 E |
| Marugame | 96 | 34.17 N | 133.47 E |
| Maruggio | 68 | 40.19 N | 17.34 E |
| Maruia | 172 | 42.11 S | 172.13 E |
| Maruia ≐ | 172 | 41.47 S | 172.12 E |
| Maruim | 250 | 10.45 S | 37.05 W |
| Maruko | 94 | 36.19 N | 138.16 E |
| Marula | 154 | 20.26 S | 28.06 E |
| Marulan | 170 | 34.43 S | 150.00 E |
| Marulan South | 170 | 34.46 S | 150.02 E |
| Marum | 52 | 53.08 N | 6.16 E |
| Marum, Mont ∧ | 175f | 16.15 S | 168.07 E |
| Marunga | 152 | 17.27 S | 20.02 E |
| Marungu | 154 | 3.44 S | 30.48 E |
| Marungu ⋏ | 154 | 7.42 S | 30.00 E |
| Maruoka | 94 | 36.09 N | 136.16 E |
| Mårup | 41 | 55.57 N | 10.35 E |
| Marusino | 265b | 55.42 N | 37.59 E |
| Maruškino | 82 | 55.36 N | 37.12 E |
| Ma'rūt | 120 | 31.34 N | 67.03 E |
| Marutea I[1] | 14 | 17.00 S | 143.10 W |
| Maruyama | 94 | 35.01 N | 139.58 E |
| Maruyama ≐ | 96 | 35.39 N | 134.50 E |
| Marv Dasht | 128 | 29.50 N | 52.40 E |
| Marve ◆[8] | 272c | 19.12 N | 72.49 E |
| Marvejols | 32 | 44.33 N | 3.18 E |
| Marvell | 194 | 34.33 N | 90.54 W |
| Marvel Loch | 162 | 31.28 S | 119.28 E |
| Marviken | 40 | 58.34 N | 16.51 E |
| Marvila ◆[8] | 266c | 38.44 N | 9.06 W |
| Marville | 56 | 49.27 N | 5.27 E |
| Marvin Creek ≐ | 214 | 41.48 N | 78.26 W |
| Marvine, Mount ∧ | 200 | 38.40 N | 111.39 W |
| Mar Vista ◆[8] | 280 | 34.00 N | 118.27 W |
| Mārwār | 120 | 25.44 N | 73.36 E |
| Marwayne | 184 | 53.32 N | 110.20 W |
| Marwitz | 264a | 52.41 N | 13.09 E |
| Marwitzer Heide ◆[3] | 264a | 52.40 N | 13.06 E |
| Marwood | 214 | 40.48 N | 79.47 W |
| Marxhagen | 54 | 53.37 N | 12.36 E |
| Marxloh ◆[8] | 263 | 51.31 N | 6.46 E |
| Mary | 128 | 37.36 N | 61.50 E |
| Mary ≐, Austl. | 164 | 12.53 S | 131.38 E |
| Mary ≐, Austl. | 166 | 25.26 S | 152.55 E |
| Mar'yanivka | 78 | 50.28 N | 24.48 E |
| Mary Anne Group II | 162 | 21.13 S | 115.32 E |
| Maryborough, Austl. | 166 | 25.32 S | 152.42 E |
| Maryborough, Austl. | 169 | 37.03 S | 143.45 E |
| Maryborough → Port Laoise, Ire. | 48 | 53.02 N | 7.17 W |
| Mary D | 208 | 40.45 N | 76.04 W |
| Marydale | 158 | 29.23 S | 22.05 E |
| Marydel | 208 | 39.06 N | 75.44 W |
| Maryfield | 184 | 49.48 N | 101.32 W |
| Maryhill | 224 | 45.41 N | 120.49 W |
| Mar'yinka | 83 | 47.56 N | 37.31 E |
| Maryj □[8] | 128 | 37.30 N | 62.30 E |
| Mary Jane, Lake ⊜ | 220 | 28.22 N | 81.11 W |
| Mary Kathleen | 166 | 20.49 S | 139.58 E |
| Maryknoll | 210 | 41.11 N | 73.50 W |
| Mary Lake ⊜ | 212 | 45.15 N | 79.15 W |
| Maryland | 210 | 42.32 N | 74.53 W |
| Maryland □[3], U.S. | 178 | 39.00 N | 76.45 W |
| Maryland □[3], U.S. | 188 | 39.00 N | 76.45 W |
| Maryland, University of (Baltimore County Campus) ᵾ[2], Md., U.S. | 284b | 39.15 N | 76.43 W |
| Maryland, University of ᵾ[2], Md., U.S. | 284c | 38.59 N | 76.57 W |
| Maryland City | 208 | 39.05 N | 76.49 W |
| Maryland Gardens Park ♦ | 275b | 43.47 N | 79.32 W |
| Maryland Heights | 219 | 38.42 N | 90.25 W |
| Maryland Historical Society ᵾ | 284b | 39.18 N | 76.37 W |
| Maryland Line | 208 | 39.42 N | 76.39 W |
| Maryland Park | 284c | 38.53 N | 76.54 W |
| Marylebone | 262 | 53.34 N | 2.38 W |
| Maryneal | 196 | 32.14 N | 100.27 W |
| Marynivka | 78 | 47.46 N | 30.53 E |
| Marypark | 46 | 57.26 N | 3.21 W |
| Maryport | 44 | 54.43 N | 3.30 W |
| Marys ≐, Il., U.S. | 194 | 37.53 N | 89.47 W |
| Marys ≐, Nv., U.S. | 204 | 41.04 N | 115.16 W |
| Marys Creek ≐ | 202 | 42.18 N | 115.48 W |
| Mary's Igloo | 180 | 65.09 N | 165.04 W |
| Marys Peak ∧ | 202 | 44.30 N | 123.33 W |
| Marystown | 186 | 47.10 N | 55.09 W |
| Marysvale | 200 | 38.26 N | 112.13 W |
| Marysville, Austl. | 169 | 37.31 S | 145.45 E |
| Marysville, B.C., Can. | 182 | 49.38 N | 115.57 W |
| Marysville, N.B., Can. | 186 | 45.59 N | 66.35 W |
| Marysville, Ca., U.S. | 226 | 39.08 N | 121.35 W |
| Marysville, Ks., U.S. | 198 | 39.50 N | 96.38 W |
| Marysville, Mi., U.S. | 214 | 42.54 N | 82.29 W |
| Marysville, Oh., U.S. | 214 | 40.14 N | 83.22 W |
| Marysville, Pa., U.S. | 208 | 40.20 N | 76.55 W |
| Marysville, Wa., U.S. | 224 | 48.03 N | 122.10 W |
| Maryūṭ, Buḥayrat ⊜ | 142 | 31.08 N | 29.56 E |
| Maryvale | 171a | 28.05 S | 152.15 E |
| Maryvale ◆[8] | 275b | 43.46 N | 79.18 W |
| Maryville, Mo., U.S. | 194 | 40.20 N | 94.52 W |
| Maryville, Tn., U.S. | 192 | 35.45 N | 83.58 W |
| Marywell | 46 | 57.02 N | 2.42 W |
| Marywood | 216 | 41.48 N | 88.18 W |
| Marzabotto | 64 | 44.20 N | 11.12 E |
| Marzagão | 255 | 17.59 S | 48.39 W |
| Marzahn ◆[8] | 264a | 52.33 N | 13.33 E |
| Marzahna | 54 | 52.00 N | 12.46 E |
| Marzahne | 54 | 52.31 N | 12.31 E |
| Marzal, Aven de ±[5] | 62 | 44.22 N | 4.31 E |
| Marzo, Punta › | 246 | 6.50 N | 77.42 W |
| Marzolara | 64 | 44.38 N | 10.10 E |
| Marzūq | 146 | 25.55 N | 13.55 E |
| Marzūq, Ḥamādat ◆[2] | 146 | 26.10 N | 12.45 E |
| Marzūq, Ṣaḥrā' ◆[2] | 146 | 24.30 N | 13.00 E |
| Masa | 152 | 3.45 S | 15.29 E |
| Masachapa | 236 | 11.47 N | 86.31 W |
| Masada → Meẓada, Ḥorvot ⊥ | 132 | 31.19 N | 35.21 E |
| Mas'adah (Cæsarea Philippi) | 132 | 33.14 N | 35.45 E |
| Más Afuera, Isla → Alejandro Selkirk, Isla I | 244 | 33.45 S | 80.46 W |
| Masagua | 236 | 14.12 N | 90.51 W |
| Masaguisi | 116 | 12.41 N | 121.32 E |
| Masai | 114 | 1.29 N | 103.53 E |
| Masai Mara Game Reserve ◆[4] | 154 | 1.15 S | 35.15 E |
| Masai Steppe ⋏[1] | 154 | 4.45 S | 37.00 E |
| Masak | 85 | 43.37 N | 78.18 E |
| Masaka | 154 | 0.20 S | 31.44 E |
| Masaki, Nihon | 96 | 33.47 N | 132.42 E |
| Masaki, Nihon | 268 | 35.13 N | 140.02 E |
| Masalembu Besar, Pulau I | 112 | 5.34 S | 114.26 E |
| Masallı | 84 | 39.03 N | 48.40 E |
| Masalok, Puntan › | 174n | 15.01 N | 145.41 E |
| Masamba | 112 | 2.32 S | 120.20 E |
| Masan | 98 | 35.11 N | 128.32 E |
| Masandra | 78 | 44.32 N | 34.12 E |
| Masangwe ∧ | 154 | 5.28 S | 30.05 E |
| Masānjor | 126 | 24.07 N | 87.19 E |
| Masapelid Island I | 116 | 9.42 N | 125.39 E |
| Masapun | 112 | 7.47 S | 126.38 E |
| Masārah | 142 | 27.29 N | 30.50 E |
| Masaran | 115a | 7.28 S | 110.55 E |
| Ma'ṣarat Samālūṭ | 142 | 28.19 N | 30.43 E |
| Masaryktown | 220 | 28.26 N | 82.27 W |
| Masasi | 154 | 10.43 S | 38.48 E |
| Masatepe | 236 | 11.55 N | 86.09 W |
| Más a Tierra, Isla → Róbinson Crusoe, Isla I | 244 | 33.38 S | 78.52 W |
| Masaya | 236 | 11.58 N | 86.06 W |
| Masaya □[5] | 236 | 12.00 N | 86.10 W |
| Masba | 146 | 11.30 N | 13.00 E |
| Masbate | 116 | 12.22 N | 123.36 E |
| Masbate □[4] | 116 | 12.20 N | 123.30 E |
| Masbate Island I | 116 | 12.15 N | 123.30 E |
| Masbate Pass U | 116 | 12.30 N | 123.35 E |
| Mascali | 70 | 37.45 N | 15.12 E |
| Mascarene Basin ✢[1] | 12 | 15.00 S | 56.00 E |
| Mascarene Islands II | 157c | 21.00 S | 57.00 E |
| Mascarene Plateau ✢[3] | 12 | 10.00 S | 60.00 E |
| Mascasín | 252 | 31.22 S | 66.59 W |
| Maschen | 52 | 53.24 N | 10.02 E |
| Maschito | 68 | 40.54 N | 15.50 E |
| Mascot, Austl. | 274a | 33.56 S | 151.12 E |
| Mascot, Tn., U.S. | 192 | 36.03 N | 83.44 W |
| Mascota | 234 | 20.32 N | 104.49 W |
| Mascota ≐ | 234 | 20.38 N | 104.59 W |
| Mascotte | 220 | 28.35 N | 81.53 W |
| Mascouche | 206 | 45.45 N | 73.36 W |
| Mascouche ≐ | 206 | 45.41 N | 73.40 W |
| Mascoutah | 219 | 38.29 N | 89.47 W |
| Mascuppic Lake ⊜ | 283 | 42.41 N | 71.23 W |
| Mase | 102 | 27.16 N | 104.08 E |
| Masefield | 184 | 49.09 N | 107.48 W |
| Masela, Pulau I | 164 | 8.09 S | 129.50 E |
| Maselheim, Dtsch. | 58 | 48.08 N | 9.53 E |
| Maselheim, Dtsch. | 64 | 48.08 N | 9.53 E |
| Masenberg ∧ | 61 | 47.21 N | 15.53 E |
| Maser | 64 | 45.48 N | 11.59 E |
| Maserada sul Piave | 64 | 45.45 N | 12.17 E |
| Maseru | 158 | 29.28 S | 27.30 E |
| Masevaux | 58 | 47.47 N | 7.00 E |
| Masha | 100 | 27.26 N | 117.50 E |
| Mashaba | 154 | 20.02 S | 30.29 E |
| Mashaba Mountains ⋏ | 154 | 18.45 S | 30.32 E |
| Mash'abbe' Sade | 132 | 31.00 N | 34.47 E |
| Mashābih I | 128 | 25.37 N | 36.29 E |
| Mashalah | 142 | 30.44 N | 31.08 E |
| Masham | 44 | 54.13 N | 1.40 W |
| Mashan, Zhg. | 89 | 45.13 N | 130.35 E |
| Mashan, Zhg. | 100 | 27.33 N | 113.46 E |
| Mashan, Zhg. | 102 | 23.50 N | 108.16 E |
| Mashar | 140 | 9.14 N | 26.52 E |
| Mashbury | 260 | 51.47 N | 0.24 E |
| Mashel ≐ | 224 | 46.51 N | 122.20 W |
| Mashenqiao | 105 | 40.04 N | 117.36 E |
| Masherbrum ∧ | 123 | 35.43 N | 76.18 E |
| Masheve | 78 | 52.06 N | 32.48 E |
| Mashgharah | 132 | 33.32 N | 35.39 E |
| Mashhad, Īrān | 128 | 36.18 N | 59.36 E |
| Mash-had, Yis. | 132 | 32.44 N | 35.19 E |
| Mashi, Nig. | 150 | 13.00 N | 7.54 E |
| Mashi, Zhg. | 100 | 29.05 N | 114.22 E |
| Mashi, Zhg. | 100 | 25.01 N | 114.09 E |
| Mashike | 92a | 43.51 N | 141.31 E |
| Mashiko | 94 | 36.28 N | 140.06 E |
| Mashita ≐ | 94 | 35.40 N | 137.10 E |
| Mashivka | 78 | 49.26 N | 34.52 E |
| Mashīz | 128 | 29.56 N | 56.37 E |
| Mashkai ≐ | 128 | 26.02 N | 65.19 E |
| Māshkel, Hāmūn-i- ⊜ | 128 | 28.15 N | 63.00 E |
| Māshkel, Rūd-i- (Māshkīd) ≐ | 128 | 28.02 N | 63.25 E |
| Mashki Chāh | 128 | 29.01 N | 62.27 E |
| Māshkīd (Rūd-i-Māshkel) ≐ | 128 | 28.02 N | 63.25 E |
| Mashonaland North □[4] | 154 | 16.30 S | 30.00 E |
| Mashonaland South □[4] | 154 | 18.15 S | 30.45 E |
| Mashpee | 207 | 41.38 N | 70.28 W |
| Mashra'ur-Raqq | 140 | 8.25 N | 29.16 E |
| Mashtūl as-Sūq | 142 | 30.22 N | 31.22 E |
| Mashū-ko ⊜ | 92a | 43.35 N | 144.32 E |
| Masibi | 152 | 11.08 S | 22.42 E |
| Masihi | 114 | 2.47 N | 99.40 E |
| Masīlah, Wādī al- V | 144 | 15.10 N | 51.08 E |
| Masi-Manimba | 152 | 4.46 S | 17.55 E |
| Masin | 164 | 6.15 S | 139.19 E |
| Masina | 272b | 22.55 N | 88.32 E |
| Masindi | 154 | 1.41 N | 31.43 E |
| Masini Port | 154 | 1.42 N | 32.05 E |
| Masinloc | 116 | 15.32 N | 119.57 E |
| Masīr | 142 | 31.03 N | 31.00 E |
| Maṣīrah I | 118 | 20.25 N | 58.50 E |
| Maṣīrah, Khalīj C | 118 | 20.10 N | 58.15 E |
| Masis | 84 | 40.00 N | 44.29 E |
| Masisea | 248 | 8.36 S | 74.19 W |
| Masisi | 154 | 1.24 S | 28.49 E |
| Masjed-e Soleymān | 128 | 31.58 N | 49.18 E |
| Masjid Tanah | 114 | 2.21 N | 102.07 E |
| Mask, Lough ⊜ | 48 | 53.35 N | 9.20 W |
| Maska | 150 | 11.20 N | 7.20 E |
| Maskan, Ras › | 144 | 11.10 N | 43.33 E |
| Maskanah | 130 | 36.01 N | 38.05 E |
| Maskin | 128 | 23.35 N | 56.39 E |
| Maškino | 82 | 54.53 N | 36.08 E |
| Maskinongé □[6] | 206 | 46.35 N | 73.30 W |
| Maskinongé ≐, P.Q., Can. | 206 | 46.10 N | 73.01 W |
| Maskinongé ≐, P.Q., Can. | 206 | 45.49 N | 74.40 W |
| Maskinongé, Lac ⊜ | 206 | 46.19 N | 73.23 W |
| Maškoviči | 82 | 54.11 N | 36.17 E |
| Masku | 26 | 60.34 N | 22.06 E |
| Maskūtān | 128 | 26.51 N | 59.49 E |
| Maskwa ≐ | 184 | 50.33 N | 96.08 W |
| Masl'anino | 86 | 54.20 N | 84.13 E |
| Masl'anskaja | 86 | 55.56 N | 70.08 E |
| Maslova | 265a | 59.47 N | 30.48 E |
| Maslovka | 78 | 51.33 N | 39.14 E |
| Maslovo | 86 | 60.07 N | 60.30 E |
| Masnières | 50 | 50.07 N | 3.13 E |
| Maso | 150 | 7.14 N | 2.53 W |
| Masoala | 157b | 15.59 S | 50.10 E |
| Masoala, Cap › | 157b | 15.59 S | 50.13 E |
| Masoala, Presqu'île de ›[1] | 157b | 15.40 S | 50.12 E |
| Masoarivo | 157b | 19.03 S | 44.19 E |
| Masomeloka | 157b | 20.17 S | 48.37 E |
| Mason, Mi., U.S. | 216 | 42.34 N | 84.26 W |
| Mason, Oh., U.S. | 218 | 39.21 N | 84.18 W |
| Mason, Tn., U.S. | 194 | 35.24 N | 89.31 W |
| Mason, Tx., U.S. | 196 | 30.44 N | 99.13 W |
| Mason, W.V., U.S. | 188 | 39.01 N | 82.01 W |
| Mason □[6], Il., U.S. | 219 | 40.18 N | 90.04 W |
| Mason □[6], Ky., U.S. | 218 | 38.35 N | 83.48 W |
| Mason □[6], Wa., U.S. | 224 | 47.20 N | 123.09 W |
| Mason, Lake ⊜ | 162 | 27.39 S | 119.34 E |
| Mason Bay C | 172 | 46.56 S | 167.44 E |
| Mason City, Il., U.S. | 219 | 40.12 N | 89.41 W |
| Mason City, Ia., U.S. | 190 | 43.09 N | 93.12 W |
| Mason City, Ne., U.S. | 198 | 41.13 N | 99.18 W |
| Masone | 62 | 44.30 N | 8.42 E |
| Masonicus Brook ≐ | 276 | 41.06 N | 74.09 W |
| Mason Lake ⊜ | 224 | 47.20 N | 122.57 W |
| Masons Creek ≐ | 285 | 39.59 N | 74.51 W |
| Mason Valley V | 226 | 39.07 N | 119.10 W |
| Masonville, N.J., U.S. | 285 | 39.59 N | 74.52 W |
| Masonville, N.Y., U.S. | 210 | 42.15 N | 75.23 W |
| Maspeth ◆[8] | 276 | 40.43 N | 73.55 W |
| Masqaṭ (Muscat) | 128 | 23.37 N | 58.35 E |
| Maṣra' | 142 | 27.14 N | 31.02 E |
| Massa | 64 | 44.01 N | 10.09 E |
| Massa-Carrara □[4] | 64 | 44.15 N | 10.03 E |
| Massachusetts □[3], U.S. | 178 | 42.15 N | 71.50 W |
| Massachusetts □[3], U.S. | 207 | 42.15 N | 71.50 W |
| Massachusetts (Boston), University of ᵾ[2] | 283 | 42.19 N | 71.03 W |
| Massachusetts Bay C | 207 | 42.20 N | 70.50 W |
| Massachusetts Correctional Institution ᵾ | 283 | 42.07 N | 71.18 W |
| Massachusetts Institute of Technology ᵾ[2] | 283 | 42.21 N | 71.06 W |
| Massaciuccoli, Lago di ⊜ | 66 | 43.50 N | 10.20 E |
| Massacre Lake ⊜ | 204 | 41.39 N | 119.35 W |
| Massa Fermana | 66 | 43.09 N | 13.28 E |
| Massa Fiscaglia | 66 | 44.48 N | 12.01 E |
| Massafra | 68 | 40.35 N | 17.07 E |
| Massaguet | 146 | 12.28 N | 15.26 E |
| Massakory | 146 | 13.00 N | 15.44 E |
| Massalassef | 146 | 11.43 N | 17.08 E |
| Massa Lombarda | 66 | 44.27 N | 11.49 E |
| Massa Lubrense | 68 | 40.36 N | 14.20 E |
| Massa Marittima | 66 | 43.03 N | 10.53 E |
| Massa Martana | 66 | 42.46 N | 12.31 E |
| Massangano | 152 | 9.37 S | 14.15 E |
| Massangena | 156 | 21.32 S | 32.57 E |
| Massapê | 250 | 3.31 S | 40.19 W |
| Massapequa | 210 | 40.40 N | 73.28 W |
| Massapequa Park | 276 | 40.40 N | 73.27 W |
| Massapequa Reserve County Park ♦ | 276 | 40.42 N | 73.27 W |
| Massapoag Brook ≐ | 283 | 42.09 N | 71.09 W |
| Massapoag Lake ⊜ | 283 | 42.06 N | 71.11 W |
| Massara | 156 | 18.20 S | 34.09 E |
| Massarosa | 66 | 43.52 N | 10.20 E |
| Massasoit State Park ♦ | 207 | 41.53 N | 71.01 W |
| Massaua → Mitsiwa | 144 | 15.38 N | 39.28 E |
| Massawa → Mitsiwa | 144 | 15.38 N | 39.28 E |
| Massawippi ≐ | 206 | 45.22 N | 71.51 W |
| Massawippi, Lake ⊜ | 206 | 45.14 N | 72.00 W |
| Massay | 50 | 47.09 N | 2.00 E |


**Symbols** in the index entries represent the broad categories identified in the key at the right. Symbols with superior numbers (⋏[1]) identify subcategories (see complete key on page *I · 1).*

**Symbole** im Register stellen die rechts im Schlüssel erklärten Kategorien dar. Symbole mit hochgestellten Ziffern (⋏[1]) bezeichnen Unterabteilungen einer Kategorie (vgl. vollständiger Schlüssel auf Seite *I · 1).*

**Los símbolos** incluídos en el texto del índice representan las grandes categorías identificadas con la clave a la derecha. Los símbolos con numeros en su parte superior (⋏[1]) identifican las subcategorías (véase la clave completa en la página *I · 1).*

**Les symboles** de l'index représentent les catégories indiquées dans la légende à droite. Les symboles suivis d'un indice (⋏[1]) représentent des sous-catégories (voir légende complète à la page *I · 1).*

**Os símbolos** incluídos no texto do índice representam as grandes categorias identificadas com a chave à direita. Os símbolos com números em sua parte superior (⋏[1]) identificam as subcategorias (veja-se a chave completa à página *I · 1).*

| | | | | |
|---|---|---|---|---|
| ∧ Mountain | Berg | Montaña | Montagne | Montanha |
| ⋏ Mountains | Gebirge | Montañas | Montagnes | Montanhas |
| )( Pass | Paß | Paso | Col | Passo |
| V Valley, Canyon | Tal, Cañon | Valle, Cañón | Vallée, Canyon | Vale, Canhão |
| ≚ Plain | Ebene | Llano | Plaine | Planície |
| › Cape | Kap | Cabo | Cap | Cabo |
| I Island | Insel | Isla | Île | Ilha |
| II Islands | Inseln | Islas | Îles | Ilhas |
| ± Other Topographic Features | Andere Topographische Objekte | Otros Elementos Topográficos | Autres données topographiques | Outros acidentes topográficos |

ESPAÑOL — Nombre · Página · Lat.°′ · Long.°′ W = Oeste
FRANÇAIS — Nom · Page · Lat.°′ · Long.°′ W = Ouest
PORTUGUÊS — Nome · Página · Lat.°′ · Long.°′ W = Oeste


| Nombre | Página | Lat.°′ | Long.°′ W = Oeste |
|---|---|---|---|
| Massé, Ruisseau ≃ | 275a | 45.28 N | 73.17 W |
| Massello | 62 | 44.57 N | 7.04 E |
| Massen | 52 | 51.32 N | 7.38 E |
| Massena, Ia., U.S. | 198 | 41.15 N | 94.46 W |
| Massena, N.Y., U.S. | 206 | 44.55 N | 74.53 W |
| Massenya | 146 | 11.24 N | 16.10 E |
| Masset | 182 | 54.02 N | 132.09 W |
| Masset Inlet c | 182 | 53.42 N | 132.20 W |
| Masseube | 32 | 43.26 N | 0.35 E |
| Massey | 190 | 46.12 N | 82.05 W |
| Massiac | 32 | 45.15 N | 3.12 E |
| Massiaru | 76 | 58.00 N | 24.35 E |
| Massico, Monte ∧ | 68 | 41.10 N | 13.55 E |
| Massieville | 218 | 39.16 N | 82.58 W |
| Massif Central → Central, Massif ⋏ | 32 | 45.00 N | 3.10 E |
| Massillon | 214 | 40.48 N | 81.32 W |
| Massima Camp | 152 | 1.27 S | 11.42 E |
| Massina | 273b | 4.22 S | 15.22 E |
| Massina ◆1 | 150 | 14.30 N | 5.00 W |
| Massing | 60 | 48.24 N | 12.36 E |
| Massinga | 156 | 23.20 S | 35.25 E |
| Massingir | 156 | 23.51 S | 32.04 E |
| Massive, Mount ∧ | 200 | 39.12 N | 106.28 W |
| Masson, Lac ⊜ | 206 | 46.03 N | 74.02 W |
| Masson Island I | 9 | 66.08 S | 96.34 E |
| Massy | 261 | 48.44 N | 2.17 E |
| Mastābah | 144 | 20.49 N | 39.20 E |
| Maştağa | 84 | 40.32 N | 50.00 E |
| Masterson | 196 | 35.38 N | 101.58 W |
| Masterton | 172 | 40.57 S | 175.40 E |
| Mas-Thibert | 62 | 43.34 N | 4.44 E |
| Mastic Point | 192 | 25.03 N | 77.57 W |
| Mastigouche ≃ | 206 | 46.20 N | 73.24 W |
| Mastigouche Nord ≃ | 206 | 46.24 N | 73.25 W |
| Mastok | 76 | 53.59 N | 30.28 E |
| Mastūj | 123 | 36.17 N | 72.31 E |
| Mastūj ≃ | 123 | 35.54 N | 71.49 E |
| Mastung | 120 | 29.48 N | 66.51 E |
| Mastūrah | 128 | 23.06 N | 38.50 E |
| Masty | 76 | 53.25 N | 24.32 E |
| Masu | 146 | 12.10 N | 13.19 E |
| Masua | 126 | 24.16 N | 90.46 E |
| Masuda | 96 | 34.40 N | 131.51 E |
| Masuho | 94 | 35.34 N | 138.28 E |
| Masuika | 152 | 7.37 S | 22.32 E |
| Masuku | 154 | 17.12 S | 27.07 E |
| Māsūleh | 128 | 37.10 N | 48.59 E |
| Masulipatam → Machilīpatnam | 122 | 16.10 N | 81.08 E |
| Masura | 126 | 23.16 N | 90.24 E |
| Masurai, Gunung ∧ | 112 | 2.30 S | 101.51 E |
| Masury | 214 | 41.12 N | 80.32 W |
| Masvingo | 154 | 20.05 S | 30.50 E |
| Maşyāf | 130 | 35.03 N | 36.21 E |
| Maszewo, Pol. | 30 | 53.29 N | 15.02 E |
| Maszewo, Pol. | 54 | 52.06 N | 14.55 E |
| Mat ≃ | 38 | 41.39 N | 19.34 E |
| Mata, Indon. | 115b | 8.12 S | 122.56 E |
| Mata, Zaïre | 152 | 7.53 S | 21.58 E |
| Mata Amarilla | 254 | 49.36 S | 71.13 W |
| Mataba, Mount ∧ | 269f | 14.42 N | 121.10 E |
| Matabeleland North □4 | 154 | 19.00 S | 27.15 E |
| Matabeleland South □4 | 154 | 21.00 S | 29.15 E |
| Mātābhānga | 124 | 26.20 N | 89.13 E |
| Matabuena | 34 | 41.10 N | 3.40 W |
| Matachel ≃ | 34 | 38.50 N | 6.17 W |
| Matachewan | 190 | 47.56 N | 80.39 W |
| Matacuni ≃ | 246 | 3.02 N | 65.16 W |
| Matad | 88 | 46.58 N | 115.18 E |
| Mata de Plátano, Quebrada ≃ | 286c | 10.35 N | 66.46 W |
| Matadero Creek ≃ | 282 | 37.26 N | 122.08 W |
| Mata de São João | 255 | 12.31 S | 38.17 W |
| Matadi | 152 | 5.49 S | 13.27 E |
| Matador | 196 | 34.00 N | 100.49 W |
| Matagalpa | 236 | 12.55 N | 85.55 W |
| Matagalpa □5 | 236 | 13.00 N | 85.30 W |
| Matagami | 176 | 49.45 N | 77.38 W |
| Matag-ob | 116 | 11.07 N | 124.29 E |
| Matagorda | 196 | 28.41 N | 95.58 W |
| Matagorda □6 | 222 | 28.57 N | 96.00 W |
| Matagorda Bay c | 196 | 28.35 N | 96.20 W |
| Matagorda Island I | 196 | 28.15 N | 96.30 W |
| Matagorda Peninsula ≻1 | 196 | 28.32 N | 96.07 W |
| Mata Grande | 250 | 9.07 S | 37.44 W |
| Matahiae, Pointe ≻ | 174s | 17.49 S | 149.17 W |
| Mataiea | 174s | 17.45 S | 149.23 W |
| Mataiva I1 | 14 | 14.53 S | 148.40 W |
| Mataj | 86 | 45.53 N | 78.43 E |
| Matajing | 107 | 29.32 N | 104.00 E |
| Matak, Pulau I | 112 | 3.18 N | 106.16 E |
| Matakana, Austl. | 166 | 33.00 S | 145.54 E |
| Matakana, N.Z. | 172 | 36.21 S | 174.43 E |
| Matakana Island I | 172 | 37.35 S | 176.05 E |
| Matakitaki ≃ | 172 | 41.48 S | 172.19 E |
| Matala | 152 | 14.46 S | 15.04 E |
| Matale | 122 | 7.28 N | 80.37 E |
| Matam | 150 | 15.40 N | 13.15 W |
| Matama | 96 | 33.36 N | 131.28 E |
| Matama, Cerro ∧ | 236 | 9.47 N | 83.15 W |
| Matamata | 172 | 37.49 S | 175.47 E |
| Matameye | 150 | 13.26 N | 8.28 E |
| Matamoras | 210 | 41.22 N | 74.42 W |
| Matamoros, Méx. | 232 | 25.53 N | 97.30 W |
| Matamoros, Méx. | 232 | 25.32 N | 103.15 W |
| Matan | 112 | 1.52 S | 110.00 E |
| Matana | 154 | 3.46 S | 29.41 E |
| Matana, Danau ⊜ | 112 | 2.28 S | 121.20 E |
| Matanalem, Cape ≻ | 164 | 2.28 S | 149.57 E |
| Matandu ≃ | 154 | 8.45 S | 39.19 E |
| Matane | 186 | 48.51 N | 67.32 W |
| Matang, Malay. | 114 | 4.49 N | 100.41 E |
| Matang, Zhg. | 100 | 29.17 N | 113.05 E |
| Matang, Zhg. | 100 | 32.20 N | 121.04 E |
| Matangi | 172 | 37.49 S | 175.25 E |
| Matani | 84 | 42.06 N | 45.13 E |
| Matanni | 123 | 33.48 N | 71.34 E |
| Matanuska ≃ | 180 | 61.30 N | 149.15 W |
| Matanza → San Justo | 258 | 34.40 S | 58.33 W |
| Matanza, Aeródromo ⊠ | 288 | 34.44 S | 58.30 W |
| Matanza, Río de la ≃ | 258 | 34.42 S | 58.28 W |
| Matanzas, Cuba | 240p | 23.03 N | 81.35 W |
| Matanzas, Méx. | 234 | 21.37 N | 101.38 W |
| Matanzas □4 | 240p | 22.40 N | 81.20 W |
| Matanzas, Bahía de c | 240p | 23.04 N | 81.30 W |
| Matapa | 156 | 23.11 S | 24.39 E |
| Matapalo, Cabo ≻ | 236 | 8.23 N | 83.19 W |
| Matape ≃ | 232 | 28.25 N | 110.26 W |
| Matapédia | 186 | 47.58 N | 66.57 W |
| Matapédia, Lac ⊜ | 186 | 48.33 N | 67.33 W |
| Matapi ≃ | 250 | 0.03 S | 51.12 W |
| Mata Point ≻ | 174v | 19.07 S | 169.51 W |
| Matapu | 172 | 39.29 S | 174.14 E |
| Mataquito ≃ | 252 | 34.59 S | 72.12 W |
| Matará, Perú | 248 | 7.16 S | 78.16 W |
| Matara, S. Lan. | 122 | 5.56 N | 80.33 E |
| Mataram | 115b | 8.35 S | 116.07 E |
| Matarani | 248 | 17.00 S | 72.06 W |
| Mataranka | 164 | 14.56 S | 133.07 E |
| Matārimah, Ra's ≻ | 142 | 29.27 N | 32.42 E |
| Matarinao Bay c | 116 | 11.14 N | 125.34 E |
| Mataró | 34 | 41.32 N | 2.27 E |
| Matarraña ≃ | 34 | 41.14 N | 0.22 E |
| Matas ∧ | 266d | 41.30 N | 2.16 E |
| Matasiri, Pulau I | 112 | 4.48 S | 115.48 E |
| Mätäsvaara | 26 | 63.26 N | 29.36 E |
| Matata | 172 | 37.53 S | 176.45 E |
| Matatepai, Pointe ≻ | 174v | 9.43 S | 139.02 W |
| Matatiele | 158 | 30.24 S | 28.43 E |
| Mātātīla Dam ◆6 | 124 | 25.06 N | 78.22 E |
| Matatindoc Point ≻ | 116 | 9.43 N | 122.23 E |
| Matatula, Cape ≻ | 174u | 14.15 S | 170.34 W |
| Mataura | 172 | 46.11 S | 168.52 E |
| Matauá ≃, Bra. | 248 | 5.30 S | 60.45 W |
| Mataura ≃, N.Z. | 172 | 46.34 S | 168.43 E |
| Matāutu | 175a | 13.57 S | 171.56 W |
| Mataval, Baie de c | 174s | 17.30 S | 149.30 W |
| Matavera | 174k | 21.13 S | 159.44 W |
| Mataveri | 174z | 27.10 S | 109.27 E |
| Mataveri Airstrip ⊠ | 174z | 27.10 S | 109.25 W |
| Matawai | 172 | 38.21 S | 177.32 E |
| Matawan | 208 | 40.24 N | 74.13 W |
| Matawin ≃ | 206 | 46.54 N | 72.56 W |
| Matāy | 142 | 28.25 N | 30.46 E |
| Matbūl | 142 | 31.05 N | 31.02 E |
| Matča | 85 | 39.27 N | 69.39 E |
| Matchaponix Brook ≃ | 276 | 40.23 N | 74.23 W |
| Matchi-Manitou, Lac ⊜ | 190 | 48.00 N | 77.04 W |
| Matching | 260 | 51.47 N | 0.13 E |
| Matching Green | 260 | 51.47 N | 0.14 E |
| Matching Tye | 260 | 51.47 N | 0.12 E |
| Mateare | 236 | 12.14 N | 86.26 W |
| Mateba, Île de I | 152 | 5.54 S | 12.50 E |
| Matehuala | 234 | 23.39 N | 100.39 W |
| Mateke Hills ⋏2 | 154 | 21.48 S | 31.00 E |
| Mateko | 152 | 4.03 S | 18.55 E |
| Matelica | 66 | 43.15 N | 13.00 E |
| Matemo, Ilha I | 154 | 12.13 S | 40.36 E |
| Matera | 68 | 40.40 N | 16.37 E |
| Matera □4 | 68 | 40.30 N | 16.25 E |
| Materborn | 52 | 51.46 N | 6.06 E |
| Matese, Lago del ⊜ | 68 | 41.25 N | 14.25 E |
| Matese, Monti del ⋏ | 66 | 41.27 N | 14.22 E |
| Mátészalka | 30 | 47.57 N | 22.19 E |
| Matete ≃ | 273b | 4.24 S | 15.20 E |
| Matetsi | 154 | 18.16 S | 25.56 E |
| Mateur | 148 | 37.03 N | 9.40 E |
| Matewan | 192 | 37.37 N | 82.09 W |
| Matfield | 207 | 42.02 N | 70.59 W |
| Matfors | 26 | 62.21 N | 17.02 E |
| Matha | 32 | 45.52 N | 0.19 W |
| Mathbaria | 126 | 22.18 N | 89.57 E |
| Mathematicians Seamounts ✢3 | 16 | 15.00 N | 111.00 W |
| Mather, Mb., Can. | 184 | 49.06 N | 99.07 W |
| Mather, Pa., U.S. | 188 | 39.56 N | 80.04 W |
| Mather Air Force Base ■ | 226 | 38.34 N | 121.18 W |
| Mather Gorge V | 284c | 38.59 N | 77.15 W |
| Matheson | 190 | 48.32 N | 80.28 W |
| Matheson Island | 184 | 51.44 N | 96.56 W |
| Matheu | 258 | 34.22 S | 58.50 W |
| Mathews | 208 | 37.26 N | 76.19 W |
| Mathews □6 | 208 | 37.25 N | 76.20 W |
| Mathews, Lake ⊜ | 228 | 33.51 N | 117.26 W |
| Mathi | 62 | 45.15 N | 7.32 E |
| Mathis | 196 | 28.05 N | 97.49 W |
| Māthle | 272b | 22.35 N | 88.14 E |
| Mathry | 42 | 51.57 N | 5.05 W |
| Mathura, India | 122 | 10.57 N | 78.27 E |
| Mathura, India | 124 | 27.30 N | 77.41 E |
| Mathura Bil ⊜ | 272b | 22.56 N | 88.29 E |
| Mathurai → Madurai | 122 | 9.56 N | 78.07 E |
| Mathurāpur, Bngl. | 126 | 24.02 N | 88.47 E |
| Mathurāpur, Bngl. | 126 | 23.17 N | 89.15 E |
| Mati | 116 | 6.57 N | 126.13 E |
| Matiacoali | 150 | 12.22 N | 1.02 E |
| Matiakhola | 126 | 23.16 N | 86.56 E |
| Mātiāli | 124 | 26.56 N | 88.49 E |
| Matiāri | 120 | 25.36 N | 68.27 E |
| Matias Barbosa | 256 | 21.53 S | 43.20 W |
| Matías Romero | 234 | 16.53 N | 95.02 W |
| Mātibhānga | 126 | 22.49 N | 89.56 E |
| Matícora ≃ | 246 | 11.03 N | 71.09 W |
| Matiere | 172 | 38.45 S | 175.06 E |
| Matignon | 32 | 48.36 N | 2.18 W |
| Matiguás | 236 | 12.50 N | 85.28 W |
| Matinecock | 276 | 40.53 N | 73.38 W |
| Matinenda Lake ⊜ | 190 | 46.22 N | 82.57 W |
| Matinha | 250 | 3.06 S | 45.02 W |
| Matinicock Point ≻ | 276 | 40.54 N | 73.38 W |
| Matinicus Island I | 188 | 43.54 N | 68.55 W |
| Matino | 68 | 40.02 N | 18.08 E |
| Matipó | 255 | 20.17 S | 42.21 W |
| Maţir Ţāris | 142 | 29.22 N | 30.54 E |
| Matiyure ≃ | 246 | 7.36 N | 67.39 W |
| Matjiesfontein | 158 | 33.14 S | 20.35 E |
| Matkasel'kja | 26 | 61.58 N | 30.33 E |
| Mātla ≃1 | 126 | 22.04 N | 88.38 E |
| Matlab Bāzār | 126 | 23.20 N | 90.43 E |
| Matlacha | 220 | 26.37 N | 82.05 W |
| Matlacha Pass ɥ | 220 | 26.37 N | 82.04 W |
| Matlamanyane | 156 | 19.33 S | 25.57 E |
| Matlapa | 234 | 21.15 N | 98.50 W |
| M'atlevo | 76 | 54.54 N | 35.39 E |
| Mātli | 120 | 25.02 N | 68.39 E |
| Matlock, Eng., U.K. | 44 | 53.08 N | 1.32 W |
| Matlock, Wa., U.S. | 224 | 47.14 N | 123.25 W |
| Matlock, Mount ∧ | 169 | 37.35 S | 146.11 E |
| Matmata | 148 | 33.33 N | 9.58 E |
| Matnog | 116 | 12.35 N | 124.05 E |
| Mato | 154 | 8.01 S | 24.55 E |
| Mato ≃ | 246 | 7.09 N | 65.07 W |
| Mato, Cerro ∧ | 246 | 7.15 N | 65.14 W |
| Matoaca | 208 | 37.13 N | 77.28 W |
| Matobe | 112 | 2.42 S | 100.11 E |
| Matočkin Šar | 72 | 73.16 N | 56.27 E |
| Matočkin Šar, proliv ɥ | 72 | 73.20 N | 55.21 E |
| Mato Grosso □3 | 242 | 12.00 S | 57.00 W |
| Mato Grosso, Planalto do ⋏1 | 242 | 15.30 S | 56.00 W |
| Mato Grosso do Sul □3 | 242 | 20.00 S | 55.00 W |
| Matola-Rio | 156 | 25.58 S | 32.26 E |
| Matombo | 154 | 7.03 S | 37.46 E |
| Mato Mole, Serra do ⋏2 | 256 | 23.00 S | 46.12 W |
| Matong | 164 | 5.35 S | 151.45 E |
| Matonipi ≃ | 186 | 51.21 N | 69.45 W |
| Matope | 154 | 15.20 S | 34.59 E |
| Matopos | 154 | 20.24 S | 28.28 E |
| Matos ≃ | 248 | 14.07 S | 65.25 W |
| Matosinhos | 34 | 41.11 N | 8.42 W |
| Matoso, Ponta do ≻ | 287a | 22.50 S | 43.11 W |
| Matou, T'aiwan | 100 | 23.11 N | 120.14 E |
| Matou, Zhg. | 98 | 36.29 N | 114.26 E |
| Matou, Zhg. | 100 | 25.14 N | 118.22 E |
| Matou, Zhg. | 100 | 29.49 N | 115.35 E |
| Matou, Zhg. | 100 | 30.48 N | 118.29 E |
| Matou, Zhg. | 105 | 39.46 N | 116.49 E |
| Matou, Zhg. | 105 | 39.18 N | 116.45 E |
| Matou, Zhg. | 105 | 39.33 N | 116.07 E |
| Matouji | 98 | 35.02 N | 115.07 E |
| Matour | 58 | 46.18 N | 4.29 E |
| Matoury | 250 | 4.51 N | 52.20 W |
| Matouxi | 107 | 30.15 N | 106.31 E |
| Matouying | 98 | 39.18 N | 118.47 E |
| Matouzhen, Zhg. | 98 | 34.39 N | 118.18 E |
| Matouzhen, Zhg. | 100 | 33.32 N | 118.56 E |
| Mato Verde | 255 | 15.23 S | 42.52 W |
| Matozinhos | 255 | 19.35 S | 44.07 W |
| Mátra ⋏ | 30 | 47.55 N | 20.00 E |
| Maţraḩ | 128 | 23.38 N | 58.34 E |
| Matraville | 274a | 33.54 S | 151.18 E |
| Matrei am Brenner | 64 | 47.08 N | 11.27 E |
| Matrei in Osttirol | 64 | 47.00 N | 12.32 E |
| Matru | 150 | 7.36 N | 12.11 W |
| Matsap | 158 | 28.38 S | 22.47 E |
| Matsapha | 158 | 26.29 S | 31.23 E |
| Matsari | 152 | 5.21 N | 12.14 E |
| Matsena | 150 | 13.05 N | 10.05 E |
| Matsiatra ≃ | 157b | 21.25 S | 45.33 E |
| Matsieng | 158 | 29.36 S | 27.32 E |
| Matsiketsgårdarna | 40 | 60.28 N | 15.22 E |
| Matsqui | 224 | 49.12 N | 122.25 W |
| Matsu → Matsu Tao I | 100 | 26.09 N | 119.56 E |
| Matsubara | 96 | 34.33 N | 135.33 E |
| Matsubushi | 268 | 35.55 N | 139.49 E |
| Matsuda | 94 | 35.21 N | 139.09 E |
| Matsudai | 94 | 37.08 N | 138.37 E |
| Matsudo | 94 | 35.47 N | 139.54 E |
| Matsudo Race Track ♦ | 268 | 35.48 N | 139.55 E |
| Matsue | 96 | 35.28 N | 133.04 E |
| Matsugasaki | 268 | 35.53 N | 139.58 E |
| Matsuida | 94 | 36.19 N | 138.48 E |
| Matsukawa, Nihon | 94 | 36.25 N | 137.51 E |
| Matsukawa, Nihon | 94 | 35.36 N | 137.55 E |
| Matsumae | 92 | 41.26 N | 140.07 E |
| Matsumoto | 94 | 36.14 N | 137.58 E |
| Matsuno | 96 | 33.13 N | 132.42 E |
| Matsunoyama | 94 | 37.05 N | 138.37 E |
| Matsuo | 94 | 35.38 N | 140.28 E |
| Matsuōji | 268 | 35.08 N | 140.01 E |
| Matsuoka | 94 | 36.05 N | 136.18 E |
| Matsuo-san ∧ | 270 | 34.38 N | 135.44 E |
| Matsusaka | 94 | 34.34 N | 136.32 E |
| Matsushima | 92 | 38.22 N | 141.04 E |
| Matsu Tao I | 100 | 26.09 N | 119.56 E |
| Matsutō | 94 | 36.31 N | 136.34 E |
| Matsuura | 92 | 33.22 N | 129.42 E |
| Matsuyama | 96 | 33.50 N | 132.45 E |
| Matsuzaki | 94 | 34.45 N | 138.47 E |
| Matta ≃ | 208 | 38.07 N | 77.26 W |
| Mattagami ≃ | 176 | 50.43 N | 81.29 W |
| Mattagami Heights | 190 | 48.29 N | 81.22 W |
| Mattagami Lake ⊜ | 190 | 47.54 N | 81.35 W |
| Mattamuskeet, Lake ⊜ | 192 | 35.30 N | 76.11 W |
| Mattapan ◆8 | 283 | 42.16 N | 71.06 W |
| Mattapoisett | 207 | 41.39 N | 70.49 W |
| Mattaponi | 208 | 37.32 N | 76.46 W |
| Mattaponi ≃ | 208 | 37.31 N | 76.47 W |
| Mattarana | 62 | 44.15 N | 9.37 E |
| Mattarello | 64 | 46.00 N | 11.07 E |
| Mattawa, On., Can. | 190 | 46.19 N | 78.42 W |
| Mattawa, Wa., U.S. | 202 | 46.44 N | 119.54 W |
| Mattawa ≃ | 190 | 46.19 N | 78.43 W |
| Mattawamkeag | 188 | 45.30 N | 68.21 W |
| Mattawamkeag ≃ | 188 | 45.30 N | 68.24 W |
| Mattawan | 216 | 42.12 N | 85.47 W |
| Mattawana | 214 | 40.30 N | 77.44 W |
| Mattawoman Creek ≃ | 208 | 38.34 N | 77.12 W |
| Matterhorn (Cervino) ∧, Europe | 58 | 45.59 N | 7.43 E |
| Matterhorn ∧, Nv., U.S. | 204 | 41.49 N | 115.23 W |
| Mattersburg | 61 | 47.44 N | 16.25 E |
| Mattertal V | 58 | 46.10 N | 7.49 E |
| Matteson | 216 | 41.30 N | 87.42 W |
| Matteson Lake ⊜ | 216 | 41.56 N | 85.12 W |
| Matthew Flinders Memorial ⊥ | 169 | 38.19 S | 145.04 E |
| Matthews | 216 | 40.23 N | 85.29 W |
| Matthews Mountain ∧2 | 194 | 37.29 N | 90.21 W |
| Matthews Ridge | 246 | 7.30 N | 60.10 W |
| Matthew Town | 238 | 20.57 N | 73.40 W |
| Matthias Church ɵ1 | 264c | 47.30 N | 19.02 E |
| Matthiessen State Park ♦ | 216 | 41.17 N | 89.01 W |
| Maţţī, Sabkhat ⊜ | 128 | 23.30 N | 52.00 E |
| Mattie, Lake ⊜ | 220 | 28.08 N | 81.46 W |
| Mattig ≃ | 60 | 48.16 N | 13.04 E |
| Mattighofen | 60 | 48.06 N | 13.09 E |
| Mattinata | 68 | 41.42 N | 16.03 E |
| Mattishall | 42 | 52.39 N | 1.02 E |
| Mattituck | 207 | 40.59 N | 72.32 W |
| Mattole ≃ | 204 | 40.18 N | 124.21 W |
| Mattoon, Il., U.S. | 194 | 39.28 N | 88.22 W |
| Mattoon, Wi., U.S. | 190 | 45.00 N | 89.02 W |
| Mattox Creek ≃ | 208 | 38.12 N | 76.58 W |
| Mattox Draw V | 198 | 38.03 N | 101.11 W |
| Mattsee | 64 | 47.58 N | 13.06 E |
| Mattsee ⊜ | 60 | 47.59 N | 13.07 E |
| Mattydale | 210 | 43.05 N | 76.08 W |
| Matu | 112 | 2.41 N | 111.32 E |
| Matua | 112 | 2.59 S | 110.45 E |
| Matuba | 156 | 24.27 S | 32.55 E |
| Matucana | 248 | 11.51 S | 76.24 W |
| Matudo → Matsudo | 94 | 35.47 N | 139.54 E |
| Matue → Matsue | 96 | 35.28 N | 133.04 E |
| Matuku Island I | 175g | 19.10 S | 179.46 E |
| Matumoto → Matsumoto | 94 | 36.14 N | 137.58 E |
| Matungo ≃ | 152 | 16.25 S | 21.27 E |
| Matunuck | 207 | 41.23 N | 71.32 W |
| Matuog | 116 | 9.55 N | 123.09 E |
| Matura Bay c | 241r | 10.38 N | 61.01 W |
| Maturín | 246 | 9.45 N | 63.11 W |
| Maturino | 76 | 59.06 N | 37.55 E |
| Matusadona National Park ♦ | 154 | 16.25 S | 28.35 E |
| Matutina | 255 | 19.13 S | 45.58 W |
| Matuto | 154 | 14.46 S | 35.59 E |
| Matutum, Mount ∧ | 116 | 6.22 N | 125.05 E |
| Matuzaka → Matsusaka | 94 | 34.34 N | 136.32 E |
| Matvejevka | 80 | 53.32 N | 53.29 E |
| Matvejev Kurgan | 83 | 47.35 N | 38.52 E |
| Matvejevo, Ross. | 76 | 58.38 N | 43.30 E |
| Matvejevo, Ross. | 86 | 57.47 N | 57.51 E |
| Matxixako, Cabo ≻ | 34 | 43.27 N | 2.45 W |
| Mátyásföld ◆8 | 264c | 47.31 N | 19.13 E |
| Matyra ≃ | 76 | 52.38 N | 39.38 E |
| Matyševo | 80 | 50.49 N | 44.12 E |
| Matysiv | 78 | 49.03 N | 31.34 E |
| Mau | 124 | 25.17 N | 81.23 E |
| Maú (Ireng) ≃ | 246 | 3.33 N | 59.51 W |
| Mauá, Bra. | 256 | 23.40 S | 46.27 W |
| Maúa, Moç. | 154 | 13.51 S | 37.10 E |
| Mauá □7 | 287b | 23.40 S | 46.27 W |
| Mau Aimma | 124 | 25.42 N | 81.55 E |
| Mauban | 116 | 14.12 N | 121.44 E |
| Maubara | 112 | 8.37 S | 125.12 E |
| Maubeuge | 50 | 50.17 N | 3.58 E |
| Mauchamps | 261 | 48.32 N | 2.12 E |
| Mauchline | 46 | 55.31 N | 4.24 W |
| Maud, Scot., U.K. | 46 | 57.31 N | 2.06 W |
| Maud, Mo., U.S. | 219 | 39.37 N | 92.15 W |
| Maud, Oh., U.S. | 218 | 39.21 N | 84.23 W |
| Maud, Ok., U.S. | 196 | 35.08 N | 96.46 W |
| Maud, Tx., U.S. | 194 | 33.20 N | 94.21 W |
| Maud, Point ≻ | 162 | 23.06 S | 113.45 E |
| Maudaha | 124 | 25.41 N | 80.07 E |
| Maude | 166 | 34.28 S | 144.18 E |
| Maudétour-en-Vexin | 261 | 49.06 N | 1.47 E |
| Mau-é-ele | 156 | 24.21 S | 34.07 E |
| Mauensee | 58 | 47.10 N | 8.04 E |
| Mauer ◆8 | 264b | 48.09 N | 16.16 E |
| Mauerbach | 264b | 48.15 N | 16.10 E |
| Mauerbach ≃ | 264b | 48.12 N | 16.14 E |
| Mauerkirchen | 60 | 48.11 N | 13.08 E |
| Maués | 250 | 3.24 S | 57.42 W |
| Maués ≃ | 246 | 3.22 S | 57.44 W |
| Maug ≃ | 116 | 8.20 N | 125.53 E |
| Mauganj | 124 | 24.41 N | 81.53 E |
| Mauga Silisili ∧ | 175a | 13.35 S | 172.27 W |
| Maughold | 44 | 54.18 N | 4.17 W |
| Maug Islands II | 108 | 20.01 N | 145.13 E |
| Mauguio | 62 | 43.37 N | 4.01 E |
| Mauguio, Étang de c | 62 | 43.35 N | 4.02 E |
| Maui □6 | 229a | 20.53 N | 156.30 W |
| Maui I | 229a | 20.45 N | 156.15 W |
| Mauk | 115a | 6.04 S | 106.30 E |
| Mauke I | 14 | 20.09 S | 157.23 W |
| Maulbach | 56 | 50.43 N | 9.04 E |
| Maulbronn | 56 | 49.00 N | 8.49 E |
| Maulde | 50 | 50.30 N | 3.26 E |
| Mauldin | 192 | 34.46 N | 82.18 W |
| Mauldre ≃ | 261 | 48.59 N | 1.48 E |
| Maule | 50 | 48.55 N | 1.51 E |
| Maule □4 | 252 | 35.30 S | 71.30 W |
| Maule ≃ | 252 | 35.19 S | 72.25 W |
| Maule, Laguna del ⊜ | 252 | 36.04 S | 70.30 W |
| Mauléon | 32 | 46.56 N | 0.45 W |
| Mauléon-Licharre | 32 | 43.14 N | 0.53 W |
| Maulette | 261 | 48.48 N | 1.37 E |
| Maullín | 254 | 41.38 S | 73.37 W |
| Maulvi Bāzār | 120 | 24.29 N | 91.47 E |
| Maumaupaki ∧ | 172 | 36.58 S | 175.35 E |
| Maumee | 214 | 41.33 N | 83.39 W |
| Maumee ≃ | 216 | 41.42 N | 83.28 W |
| Maumee Bay c | 214 | 41.43 N | 83.26 W |
| Maumelle, Lake ⊜1 | 194 | 34.55 N | 92.40 W |
| Maumere | 115b | 8.37 S | 122.14 E |
| Maun | 156 | 20.00 S | 23.25 E |
| Maunabo | 240m | 18.01 N | 65.54 W |
| Mauna Kea ∧1 | 229d | 19.50 N | 155.28 W |
| Maunaloa | 229a | 21.08 N | 157.13 W |
| Mauna Loa ∧1 | 229d | 19.29 N | 155.36 W |
| Maunalua Bay c | 229c | 21.17 N | 157.44 W |
| Maunath Bhanjan | 124 | 25.57 N | 83.33 E |
| Maunatlala | 156 | 22.32 S | 27.28 E |
| Maunesha ≃ | 216 | 43.13 N | 88.57 W |
| Maungahaumi ∧ | 172 | 38.18 S | 177.40 E |
| Maunga Roa ∧ | 174k | 21.13 S | 159.48 W |
| Maungatapere | 172 | 35.45 S | 174.12 E |
| Maungaturoto | 172 | 36.06 S | 174.22 E |
| Maungdaw | 110 | 20.50 N | 92.21 E |
| Maungmagan | 110 | 14.09 N | 98.06 E |
| Maungu | 154 | 3.33 S | 38.45 E |
| Maunoir, Lac ⊜ | 180 | 67.30 N | 125.00 W |
| Maupihaa I1 | 14 | 16.50 S | 153.55 W |
| Maupin | 224 | 45.10 N | 121.04 W |
| Maur | 123 | 30.05 N | 75.15 E |
| Mau Rānīpur | 124 | 25.15 N | 79.08 E |
| Maurecourt | 261 | 49.00 N | 2.04 E |
| Maure-de-Bretagne | 32 | 47.54 N | 1.59 W |
| Mauregard | 261 | 49.02 N | 2.35 E |
| Maurepas | 261 | 48.45 N | 1.55 E |
| Maurepas, Lake ⊜ | 194 | 30.15 N | 90.30 W |
| Maures ⋏ | 62 | 43.16 N | 6.23 E |
| Mauretanien → Mauritania □1 | 134 | 20.00 N | 12.00 W |
| Mauri ≃ | 248 | 17.18 S | 68.41 W |
| Mauria, Passo della )( | 64 | 46.27 N | 12.31 E |
| Mauriac | 32 | 45.13 N | 2.20 E |
| Maurice (Île) → Mauritius □1 | 157c | 20.17 S | 57.33 E |
| Maurice ≃ | 208 | 39.13 N | 75.02 W |
| Maurice, Lake ⊜ | 162 | 29.28 S | 130.58 E |
| Maurice K. Goddard State Park ♦ | 214 | 41.23 N | 81.10 W |
| Mauricetown | 208 | 39.17 N | 74.58 W |
| Mauriceville | 172 | 40.47 S | 175.42 E |
| Mauricio → Mauritius □1 | 157c | 20.17 S | 57.33 E |
| Maurienne V | 62 | 45.13 N | 6.30 E |
| Maurino, Canal ≊ | 286e | 33.34 S | 70.32 W |
| Mauritania (Mauritanie) □1 | 134 | 20.00 N | 12.00 W |
| Mauritanie → Mauritania □1 | 134 | 20.00 N | 12.00 W |
| Mauriti | 250 | 7.23 S | 38.46 W |
| Mauritius □1, Afr. | 138 | 20.17 S | 57.33 E |
| Mauritius □1, Afr. | 157c | 20.17 S | 57.33 E |
| Mauritius I | 157c | 20.17 S | 57.33 E |
| Mauron | 32 | 48.05 N | 2.18 W |
| Maurs | 32 | 44.43 N | 2.11 E |
| Maurui | 154 | 5.07 S | 38.23 E |
| Maury ≃ | 192 | 37.37 N | 79.27 W |
| Maury Channel ɥ | 176 | 75.44 N | 94.40 W |
| Maury Island ≻1 | 224 | 47.20 N | 122.24 W |
| Maussane | 62 | 43.43 N | 4.48 E |
| Mauston | 190 | 43.47 N | 90.04 W |
| Mautala | 126 | 22.25 N | 89.05 E |
| Mautau, Pointe ≻ | 174x | 9.42 S | 138.58 W |
| Mautern an der Donau | 61 | 48.24 N | 15.35 E |
| Mauterndorf | 64 | 47.08 N | 13.40 E |
| Mautern in Steiermark | 61 | 47.24 N | 14.50 E |
| Mauth | 60 | 48.53 N | 13.35 E |
| Mauthausen | 61 | 48.14 N | 14.32 E |
| Mauthen | 64 | 46.40 N | 13.00 E |
| Mauvais Coulee V | 198 | 48.21 N | 99.06 W |
| Mauvaise Terre Creek ≃ | 219 | 39.43 N | 90.38 W |
| Mauvaise Terre Lake ⊜1 | 219 | 39.42 N | 90.12 W |
| Mauvezin | 32 | 43.44 N | 0.55 E |
| Mava | 164 | 6.50 S | 141.25 E |
| Mavaca ≃ | 246 | 2.31 N | 65.11 W |
| Mavanza | 156 | 22.43 S | 35.08 E |
| Māvelikara | 122 | 9.16 N | 76.33 E |
| Maverick | 200 | 33.43 N | 109.32 W |
| Mavinga | 152 | 15.50 S | 20.21 E |
| Mavita | 156 | 19.33 S | 33.10 E |
| Mavonde | 156 | 18.32 S | 33.02 E |
| Mavuradona Mountains ⋏ | 154 | 16.30 S | 31.20 E |
| Mawa | 154 | 2.43 N | 26.42 E |
| Mawai | 114 | 1.52 N | 103.57 E |
| Ma Wan I | 271d | 22.21 N | 114.03 E |
| Mawāna | 124 | 29.06 N | 77.55 E |
| Mawangkanli Shan ∧ | 120 | 34.19 N | 80.03 E |
| Mawangtang | 106 | 30.42 N | 120.42 E |
| Mawasangka | 112 | 5.17 S | 122.18 E |
| Mawchi | 110 | 18.49 N | 97.09 E |
| Maw-daung Pass )( | 110 | 11.47 N | 99.39 E |
| Mawdesley | 262 | 53.38 N | 2.46 W |
| Mawdesley Lake ⊜ | 184 | 54.01 N | 100.39 W |
| Mawgan | 42 | 50.06 N | 5.12 W |
| Mawi | 272a | 28.39 N | 77.25 E |
| Mawiwi | 154 | 3.06 N | 27.40 E |
| Māwiyah | 144 | 13.35 N | 44.21 E |
| Mawjib, Wādī al- V | 132 | 31.28 N | 35.34 E |
| Mawkhi | 110 | 16.17 N | 98.53 E |
| Mawlaik | 110 | 23.38 N | 94.24 E |
| Mawlamyaing → Mawlamyine | 110 | 16.30 N | 97.38 E |
| Mawlamyine (Moulmein) | 110 | 16.30 N | 97.38 E |
| Mawr, Wādī V | 144 | 15.41 N | 42.42 E |
| Mawshij | 144 | 13.43 N | 43.17 E |
| Mawson ɵ3 | 9 | 67.40 S | 63.43 E |
| Mawson Escarpment ⏊4 | 9 | 73.05 S | 68.10 E |
| Mawson Peninsula ≻1 | 9 | 68.35 S | 154.11 E |
| Maw Taung ∧ | 110 | 11.39 N | 99.35 E |
| Mawuba | 102 | 29.50 N | 108.11 E |
| Max | 198 | 47.49 N | 101.17 W |
| Maxaranguape | 250 | 5.31 S | 35.16 W |
| Maxatawny | 208 | 40.33 N | 75.41 W |
| Maxcanú | 232 | 20.35 N | 89.59 W |
| Maxéville | 58 | 48.43 N | 6.10 E |
| Maxglan, Flughafen ⊠ | 64 | 47.48 N | 13.02 E |
| Maxhütte-Haidhof | 60 | 49.12 N | 12.05 E |
| Maxiang | 100 | 24.41 N | 118.15 E |
| Maximo | 214 | 40.53 N | 81.11 W |
| Maximo Paz | 258 | 34.56 S | 58.37 W |
| Maxinkuckee, Lake ⊜ | 216 | 41.12 N | 86.24 W |
| Maxixe | 156 | 23.51 S | 35.21 E |
| Maxon Creek ≃ | 196 | 29.53 N | 102.24 W |
| Maxton | 192 | 34.44 N | 79.20 W |
| Maxville | 206 | 45.17 N | 74.51 W |
| Maxwell, Ca., U.S. | 226 | 39.16 N | 122.11 W |
| Maxwell, In., U.S. | 218 | 39.51 N | 85.46 W |
| Maxwell, Ia., U.S. | 190 | 41.53 N | 93.23 W |
| Maxwell, Ne., U.S. | 198 | 41.04 N | 100.31 W |
| Maxwell, N.M., U.S. | 196 | 36.32 N | 104.32 W |
| Maxwell, Tx., U.S. | 222 | 29.53 N | 97.48 W |
| Maxwell Air Force Base ■ | 194 | 32.23 N | 86.21 W |
| Maxwell Bay c | 176 | 74.35 N | 89.00 W |
| May | 196 | 31.59 N | 98.55 W |
| May ≃, Austl. | 162 | 17.07 S | 123.50 E |
| May ≃, Ab., Can. | 182 | 55.43 N | 111.22 W |
| May ≃, Pap. N. Gui. | 164 | 4.35 S | 141.35 E |
| May, Cape ≻1 | 208 | 38.58 N | 74.55 W |
| May, Isle of I | 46 | 56.11 N | 2.34 W |
| May, Mount ∧ | 182 | 54.02 N | 119.58 W |
| Maya, Pulau I | 112 | 1.10 S | 109.35 E |
| May Aché | 146 | 12.00 N | 15.44 E |
| Mayachka ≃ | 83 | 48.44 N | 37.33 E |
| Mayaguana I | 238 | 22.23 N | 72.57 W |
| Mayaguana Passage ɥ | 238 | 22.32 N | 73.15 W |
| Mayagüez | 240m | 18.12 N | 67.09 W |
| Mayagüez, Aeropuerto ⊠ | 240m | 18.15 N | 67.09 W |
| Mayagüez, Bahía de c | 240m | 18.12 N | 67.10 W |
| Mayahi | 150 | 13.58 N | 7.40 E |
| Mayajigua | 240p | 22.14 N | 79.04 W |
| Mayaka | 152 | 5.17 N | 16.52 E |
| Mayaky, Ukr. | 78 | 46.25 N | 30.16 E |
| Mayaky, Ukr. | 83 | 48.57 N | 37.37 E |
| Mayala | 273b | 4.21 S | 15.09 E |
| Mayales, Punta ≻ | 236 | 11.52 N | 85.26 W |
| Mayama | 152 | 3.51 S | 14.54 E |
| Mayamba | 152 | 4.46 S | 16.52 E |
| Mayāmey | 128 | 36.24 N | 55.42 E |
| Maya Mountains ⋏ | 232 | 16.40 N | 88.50 W |
| Mayang | 102 | 27.41 N | 109.35 E |
| Mayang-do I | 98 | 40.00 N | 128.12 E |
| Mayantoc | 116 | 15.37 N | 120.23 E |
| Mayao | 106 | 30.50 N | 120.23 E |
| Mayapan ⊥ | 232 | 20.38 N | 89.27 W |
| Māyāpur | 272b | 22.27 N | 88.08 E |
| Mayarí | 240p | 20.40 N | 75.41 W |
| Mayarí Arriba | 240p | 20.25 N | 75.32 W |
| Mayaro Bay c | 241r | 10.15 N | 60.58 W |
| Maya-san ∧ | 96 | 34.44 N | 135.12 E |
| Maybee | 216 | 42.00 N | 83.30 W |
| Maybeury | 192 | 37.22 N | 81.22 W |
| Maybole | 44 | 55.21 N | 4.41 W |
| Maybrook | 210 | 41.29 N | 74.13 W |
| Maychew | 144 | 13.02 N | 39.34 E |
| Maydelle | 222 | 31.48 N | 95.18 W |
| Maydena | 166 | 42.55 S | 146.30 E |
| Maydh | 144 | 11.00 N | 47.07 E |
| Maydī | 144 | 16.20 N | 42.46 E |
| Maydolong | 116 | 11.30 N | 125.30 E |
| Maydūm | 142 | 29.22 N | 31.10 E |
| Mayen | 56 | 50.19 N | 7.13 E |
| Mayence → Mainz | 56 | 50.01 N | 8.16 E |
| Mayenne | 32 | 48.18 N | 0.37 W |
| Mayenne □5 | 32 | 48.05 N | 0.40 W |
| Mayenne ≃ | 32 | 47.30 N | 0.33 W |
| Mayer | 200 | 34.23 N | 112.14 W |
| Mayerling | 61 | 48.03 N | 16.06 E |
| Mayersville | 194 | 32.54 N | 91.03 W |
| Mayerthorpe | 182 | 53.57 N | 115.08 W |
| Mayet | 50 | 47.46 N | 0.17 E |
| Mayfair ◆8, S. Afr. | 273d | 26.12 S | 28.01 E |
| Mayfair ◆8, Pa., U.S. | 285 | 40.02 N | 75.03 W |
| Mayfield, N.Z. | 172 | 43.49 S | 171.25 E |
| Mayfield, Eng., U.K. | 42 | 51.01 N | 0.15 E |
| Mayfield, Eng., U.K. | 44 | 53.01 N | 1.45 W |
| Mayfield, Scot., U.K. | 46 | 55.52 N | 3.02 W |
| Mayfield, In., U.S. | 218 | 40.11 N | 85.21 W |
| Mayfield, Ky., U.S. | 194 | 36.44 N | 88.38 W |
| Mayfield, N.Y., U.S. | 210 | 43.06 N | 74.15 W |
| Mayfield, Oh., U.S. | 279a | 41.33 N | 81.26 W |
| Mayfield, Pa., U.S. | 210 | 41.32 N | 75.32 W |
| Mayfield, Ut,. U.S. | 200 | 39.06 N | 111.42 W |
| Mayfield Creek ≃ | 194 | 36.57 N | 89.05 W |
| Mayfield Dam ◆6 | 224 | 46.30 N | 122.35 W |
| Mayfield Heights | 214 | 41.31 N | 81.27 W |
| Mayfield Lake ⊜1 | 224 | 46.31 N | 122.32 W |
| Mayflower | 194 | 34.57 N | 92.25 W |
| Mayford | 260 | 51.18 N | 0.34 W |
| May Inlet c | 176 | 76.15 N | 100.45 W |
| Māyir, Sūrīy. | 130 | 36.23 N | 37.02 E |
| Māyir, Sūrīy. | 130 | 36.28 N | 37.11 E |
| May Jirgui | 150 | 13.44 N | 8.08 E |
| Maykop → Majkop | 84 | 44.35 N | 40.07 E |
| Mayland | 42 | 51.39 N | 0.47 E |
| Maymont | 184 | 52.33 N | 107.40 W |
| Maymūn, Wādī V | 146 | 30.10 N | 10.27 E |
| Maymyo | 110 | 22.02 N | 96.28 E |
| Mayna | 126 | 22.14 N | 87.47 E |
| Maynāmati | 124 | 23.29 N | 91.07 E |
| Maynard, Ia., U.S. | 190 | 42.46 N | 91.52 W |
| Maynard, Ma., U.S. | 207 | 42.26 N | 71.27 W |
| Maynard, Oh., U.S. | 214 | 40.07 N | 80.53 W |
| Maynardville | 192 | 36.15 N | 83.47 W |
| Mayne | 224 | 48.51 N | 123.18 W |
| Mayne ≃ | 166 | 23.34 S | 141.18 E |
| Mayne Island I | 224 | 48.51 N | 123.17 W |
| Maynooth | 48 | 53.23 N | 6.35 W |
| Mayo, Yk., Can. | 180 | 63.35 N | 135.54 W |
| Mayo, Fl., U.S. | 192 | 30.03 N | 83.10 W |
| Mayo, Md., U.S. | 208 | 38.53 N | 76.30 W |
| Mayo □6 | 48 | 53.54 N | 9.15 W |
| Mayo ≃, Arg. | 254 | 45.46 S | 69.43 W |
| Mayo ≃, Col. | 246 | 1.40 N | 77.21 W |
| Mayo ≃, Méx. | 232 | 26.45 N | 109.47 W |
| Mayo ≃, Perú | 248 | 6.37 S | 76.16 W |
| Mayoba | 154 | 17.13 S | 26.16 E |
| Mayo Bay c | 116 | 6.56 N | 126.22 E |
| Mayodan | 192 | 36.24 N | 79.58 W |
| Mayo Faran | 146 | 8.57 N | 12.04 E |
| Mayo-Kébbi □5 | 146 | 10.00 N | 15.30 E |
| Mayoko, Congo | 152 | 2.18 S | 12.49 E |
| Mayoko, Zaïre | 152 | 1.05 S | 23.49 E |
| Mayo Lake ⊜ | 180 | 63.46 N | 135.10 W |
| Mayo Ndaga | 146 | 6.54 N | 11.25 E |
| Mayon Volcano ∧1 | 116 | 13.15 N | 123.41 E |
| Mayor Buratovich | 252 | 39.15 S | 62.37 W |
| Mayo Reservoir ⊜1 | 192 | 36.00 N | 78.53 W |
| Mayor Island I | 172 | 37.18 S | 176.16 E |
| Mayor Pablo Lagerenza | 248 | 19.58 S | 60.45 W |
| Mayotte □2, Afr. | 138 | 12.50 S | 45.10 E |
| Mayotte □2, Afr. | 157a | 12.50 S | 45.10 E |
| Mayoyao | 116 | 16.59 N | 121.14 E |
| Mayoyoque | 246 | 0.41 N | 75.18 W |
| Maypearl | 222 | 32.19 N | 97.01 W |
| May Pen | 241q | 17.58 N | 77.14 W |
| Mayport Naval Station ■ | 192 | 30.22 N | 81.24 W |
| Mayraira Point ≻ | 116 | 18.39 N | 120.51 E |
| Mayrán, Desierto de ◆2 | 196 | 25.45 N | 102.45 W |
| Mayres | 62 | 44.40 N | 4.07 E |
| Mayrhofen | 64 | 47.10 N | 11.52 E |
| Mays | 218 | 39.45 N | 85.26 W |
| Maysah, Tall al- ∧ | 132 | 31.08 N | 35.40 E |
| Maysān □4 | 128 | 32.00 N | 47.00 E |
| Maysfield | 222 | 30.54 N | 96.51 W |
| Mays Landing | 208 | 39.27 N | 74.43 W |
| Mays Lick | 218 | 38.31 N | 83.50 W |
| Maysville, Ky., U.S. | 218 | 38.38 N | 83.44 W |
| Maysville, Mo., U.S. | 194 | 39.53 N | 94.21 W |
| Maysville, N.C., U.S. | 192 | 34.54 N | 77.13 W |
| Maysville, Ok., U.S. | 196 | 34.49 N | 97.24 W |
| Maythalūn | 132 | 32.21 N | 35.16 E |
| Maytiguid Island I | 116 | 11.03 N | 119.36 E |
| Maytown | 208 | 40.04 N | 76.35 W |
| Mayu | 100 | 27.48 N | 120.26 E |
| Mayumba | 152 | 3.25 S | 10.39 E |
| Mayung | 114 | 0.49 N | 103.03 E |
| Māyūram | 122 | 11.06 N | 79.40 E |
| Mayville, Mi., U.S. | 190 | 43.20 N | 83.21 W |
| Mayville, N.Y., U.S. | 214 | 42.15 N | 79.30 W |
| Mayville, N.D., U.S. | 198 | 47.29 N | 97.19 W |
| Mayville, Wi., U.S. | 190 | 43.29 N | 88.32 W |
| Maywood, Ca., U.S. | 280 | 33.59 N | 118.11 W |
| Maywood, Il., U.S. | 216 | 41.52 N | 87.50 W |
| Maywood, Mo., U.S. | 219 | 39.57 N | 91.36 W |
| Maywood, Ne., U.S. | 198 | 40.39 N | 100.37 W |
| Maywood, N.J., U.S. | 276 | 40.54 N | 74.03 W |
| Maywood, N.Y., U.S. | 210 | 42.42 N | 73.52 W |
| Maywood Race Track ♦ | 278 | 41.44 N | 87.51 W |
| Mayyit, Al-Bahr al- → Dead Sea ⊜ | 132 | 31.30 N | 35.30 E |
| Maza, Arg. | 252 | 36.50 S | 63.19 W |
| Maza, Ross. | 80 | 57.14 N | 44.1[illegible] E |
| Mazabuka | 154 | 15.51 S | 27.4[illegible] E |
| Mazagan → El-Jadida | 148 | 33.16 N | 8.30 W |
| Mazagão | 250 | 0.07 S | 51.17 W |
| Mazagaon ◆8 | 272c | 18.57 N | 72.50 E |
| Mazagão Velho | 250 | 0.13 S | 51.25 W |
| Ma'zah, Jabal ∧ | 130 | 35.51 N | 40.38 E |
| Mazamet | 32 | 43.30 N | 2.24 E |
| Mazamitla | 234 | 19.55 N | 103.02 W |
| Mazán ≃ | 246 | 3.28 S | 73.11 W |
| Māzandarān □4 | 128 | 36.30 N | 53.30 E |
| Mazanovo | 89 | 51.40 N | 128.52 E |
| Mazār, Jabal ∧ | 132 | 33.34 N | 36.03 E |
| Mazar, Oued V | 148 | 31.50 N | 1.36 E |
| Mazara, Val di ◆1 | 70 | 37.50 N | 13.00 E |
| Mazara del Vallo | 70 | 37.39 N | 12.35 E |
| Mazār-e Sharīf | 120 | 36.42 N | 67.06 E |
| Mazargues | 62 | 43.15 N | 5.24 E |
| Mazaro ≃ | 70 | 37.39 N | 12.35 E |
| Mazarredo | 254 | 47.05 S | 66.42 W |
| Mazarrón | 34 | 37.36 N | 1.19 W |
| Mazarrón, Golfo de c | 34 | 37.30 N | 1.18 W |
| Mazarsu | 85 | 41.56 N | 72.40 E |
| Mazaruni ≃ | 246 | 6.25 N | 58.38 W |
| Mazatenango | 236 | 14.32 N | 91.30 W |
| Mazatlán | 234 | 23.13 N | 106.25 W |
| Mazatlán Villa de Flores | 234 | 18.02 N | 96.54 W |
| Mazatzal Mountains ⋏ | 200 | 34.00 N | 111.55 W |
| Mazatzal Peak ∧ | 200 | 34.03 N | 111.28 W |
| Maze | 94 | 35.52 N | 137.10 E |
| Maze ≃ | 94 | 35.40 N | 137.10 E |
| Mažeikiai | 76 | 56.19 N | 22.20 E |
| Mazenod | 184 | 49.53 N | 106.14 W |
| Mazeppa, Mn., U.S. | 190 | 44.16 N | 92.32 W |
| Mazeppa, Pa., U.S. | 210 | 40.59 N | 76.59 W |
| Mazha | 100 | 23.27 N | 114.00 E |
| Māzhān, Īrān | 128 | 32.35 N | 59.01 E |
| Mazhan, Zhg. | 98 | 36.04 N | 118.45 E |
| Mazhangfang, Zhg. | 104 | 42.23 N | 122.26 E |
| Mazhangfang, Zhg. | 104 | 40.44 N | 120.53 E |
| Mazhuang, Zhg. | 98 | 37.47 N | 115.17 E |
| Mazhuang, Zhg. | 100 | 32.54 N | 114.03 E |
| Mazhuang, Zhg. | 105 | 39.11 N | 116.15 E |
| Mazhūr, Khubb al- ⏊8 | 128 | 27.45 N | 43.55 E |
| Mazıdağı | 130 | 37.30 N | 40.30 E |
| Mazigou | 105 | 40.28 N | 114.48 E |
| Mazilovo ◆8 | 265b | 55.44 N | 37.26 E |
| Mazīnān | 128 | 36.18 N | 56.46 E |
| Mazinaw Lake ⊜ | 212 | 44.55 N | 77.12 W |
| Mazirbe | 76 | 57.41 N | 22.21 E |
| Mazoco | 154 | 11.40 S | 35.48 E |
| Mazoe ≃ | 154 | 16.32 S | 33.25 E |
| Mazomanie | 190 | 43.10 N | 89.47 W |
| Mazomba ≃ | 256 | 22.53 S | 43.45 W |
| Mazon | 216 | 41.14 N | 88.25 W |
| Mazon ≃ | 216 | 41.21 N | 88.25 W |
| Mazon, East Fork ≃ | 216 | 41.11 N | 88.18 W |
| Mazon, West Fork ≃ | 216 | 41.15 N | 88.21 W |
| Mazong Shan ∧ | 102 | 41.28 N | 97.10 E |
| Mazong Shan ⋏ | 102 | 41.30 N | 97.30 E |
| Mazou ≃ | 50 | 47.15 N | 2.59 E |
| Mazra'at-Bayt Jinn | 132 | 33.19 N | 35.55 E |
| Mazsalaca | 76 | 57.52 N | 25.03 E |
| Mazul'skij | 86 | 56.16 N | 90.28 E |
| Mazunga | 154 | 21.45 S | 29.52 E |
| Mazury ◆1 | 30 | 53.45 N | 21.00 E |
| Mazyr | 78 | 52.03 N | 29.14 E |
| Mazzarino | 70 | 37.18 N | 14.13 E |
| Mazzarrà Sant'andrea | 70 | 38.05 N | 15.08 E |
| Mazzin | 64 | 46.27 N | 11.42 E |
| Mba | 175g | 17.33 S | 177.41 E |
| Mbabala Island I | 154 | 11.18 S | 29.44 E |
| Mbabane | 158 | 26.18 S | 31.06 E |
| Mbabo, Tchabal ∧ | 152 | 7.16 N | 12.09 E |
| Mbacké | 150 | 14.48 N | 15.55 W |
| Mbaéré ≃ | 152 | 3.47 N | 17.31 E |
| Mbage | 140 | 5.30 N | 25.13 E |
| M'bahiakro | 150 | 7.27 N | 4.20 W |
| Mbaïki | 152 | 3.53 N | 18.00 E |
| Mbakaou, Barrage de ◆5 | 152 | 6.15 N | 12.46 E |
| Mbala, Centraf. | 152 | 7.48 N | 20.51 E |
| Mbala (Abercorn), Zam. | 154 | 8.50 S | 31.22 E |
| Mbalam | 152 | 2.13 N | 13.49 E |
| Mbale | 154 | 1.05 N | 34.10 E |
| Mbali | 152 | 2.50 S | 16.12 E |
| Mbali ≃ | 152 | 4.26 N | 18.20 E |
| Mbalizi | 154 | 8.56 S | 33.22 E |
| Mbalmayo | 152 | 3.31 N | 11.30 E |
| Mbalouro ≃ | 273b | 4.09 S | 15.21 E |
| Mbalourou | 273b | 4.09 S | 15.21 E |
| Mbam ≃ | 152 | 4.24 N | 11.17 E |
| Mbamba Bay | 154 | 11.17 S | 34.46 E |
| Mbamou, Île I | 152 | 4.13 S | 15.25 E |
| Mbamou, Pointe ≻ | 273b | 4.16 S | 15.19 E |
| Mbandaka (Coquilhatville) | 152 | 0.04 N | 18.16 E |
| Mbanga | 152 | 4.30 N | 9.34 E |
| Mbanika Island I | 175e | 9.05 S | 159.12 E |
| M'banza Congo | 152 | 6.16 S | 14.15 E |
| Mbanza-Ngungu | 152 | 5.15 S | 14.52 E |
| Mbarangandu ≃ | 154 | 8.57 S | 37.24 E |
| Mbarara | 154 | 0.37 S | 30.39 E |
| Mbari ≃ | 152 | 4.34 N | 22.43 E |
| Mbarizunga Game Reserve ◆4 | 154 | 4.45 N | 28.06 E |
| Mbashe ≃ | 158 | 32.15 S | 28.53 E |
| Mbassay | 146 | 7.39 N | 15.40 E |
| Mbate | 154 | 8.52 S | 39.10 E |
| M'batto | 150 | 6.28 N | 4.22 W |
| Mbava Island I | 175e | 7.49 S | 156.33 E |
| Mbé, Cam. | 152 | 7.43 N | 13.30 E |
| Mbé, Congo | 152 | 3.18 S | 15.54 E |
| Mbé ≃ | 152 | 0.27 N | 9.41 E |
| Mbemba | 154 | 10.03 S | 38.36 E |
| Mbengga I | 175g | 18.23 S | 178.08 E |
| M'bengué | 150 | 10.00 N | 5.54 W |
| Mbéré | 146 | 10.49 N | 15.44 E |
| Mbéré ≃ | 152 | 7.45 N | 15.36 E |
| Mberengwa | 154 | 20.30 S | 29.53 E |
| Mbereshi Mission | 154 | 9.45 S | 28.46 E |
| Mberubu | 150 | 6.10 N | 7.38 E |
| Mbeya | 154 | 8.54 S | 33.27 E |
| Mbeya □4 | 154 | 8.00 S | 33.30 E |
| Mbi ≃ | 152 | 4.26 N | 18.16 E |
| Mbia | 140 | 6.15 N | 29.19 E |
| M'bigou | 152 | 1.53 S | 11.56 E |
| Mbinda | 152 | 2.00 S | 12.55 E |
| Mbindawina | 152 | 15.57 S | 23.18 E |
| Mbinga | 154 | 10.56 S | 35.01 E |
| Mbini | 152 | 1.35 N | 9.37 E |
| Mbini ≃ | 152 | 1.35 N | 9.37 E |
| Mbirira | 154 | 4.21 S | 30.10 E |
| Mbirizi | 154 | 0.23 S | 31.27 E |
| Mbogo | 154 | 7.26 S | 33.26 E |
| Mboie | 152 | 6.56 S | 21.54 E |
| Mbola | 175e | 9.37 S | 160.39 E |
| Mboli | 152 | 4.08 N | 23.09 E |
| Mbomou □5 | 152 | 5.00 N | 23.30 E |
| Mbomou (Bomu) ≃ | 136 | 4.08 N | 22.26 E |
| Mbonge | 152 | 4.33 N | 9.05 E |
| Mboro, Sén. | 150 | 15.09 N | 16.54 W |
| Mboro, Sūd. | 140 | 6.18 N | 28.45 E |
| Mborokua I | 175e | 9.00 S | 158.40 E |
| Mborong | 115b | 8.49 S | 120.37 E |
| Mboté | 152 | 3.56 S | 12.43 E |
| Mbotou ≃ | 152 | 6.49 N | 24.14 E |
| Mbouda | 152 | 5.38 N | 10.15 E |
| Mboula | 152 | 4.27 N | 16.29 E |
| Mbour | 150 | 14.24 N | 16.58 W |
| Mbout | 150 | 16.02 N | 12.35 W |
| Mbrès | 152 | 6.40 N | 19.48 E |
| M'Bridge ≃ | 152 | 7.15 S | 12.50 E |
| Mbua | 175g | 16.48 S | 178.37 E |


| Symbol | English | Deutsch | Español | Français | Português |
|---|---|---|---|---|---|
| ≃ | River | Fluß | Río | Rivière | Rio |
| ≊ | Canal | Kanal | Canal | Canal | Canal |
| ʟ | Waterfall, Rapids | Wasserfall, Stromschnellen | Cascada, Rápidos | Chute d'eau, Rapides | Cascata, Rápidos |
| ɥ | Strait | Meeresstraße | Estrecho | Détroit | Estreito |
| c | Bay, Gulf | Bucht, Golf | Bahía, Golfo | Baie, Golfe | Baía, Golfo |
| ⊜ | Lake, Lakes | See, Seen | Lago, Lagos | Lac, Lacs | Lago, Lagos |
| ≋ | Swamp | Sumpf | Pantano | Marais | Pântano |
| ⊻ | Ice Features, Glacier | Eis- und Gletscherformen | Accidentes Glaciales | Formes glaciaires | Acidentes glaciares |
| ⊜ | Other Hydrographic Features | Andere Hydrographische Objekte | Otros Elementos Hidrográficos | Autres données hydrographiques | Outros acidentes hidrográficos |

| Symbol | English | Deutsch | Español | Français | Português |
|---|---|---|---|---|---|
| ✢ | Submarine Features | Untermeerische Objekte | Accidentes Submarinos | Formes de relief sous-marin | Acidentes submarinos |
| □ | Political Unit | Politische Einheit | Unidad Política | Entité politique | Unidade política |
| ɵ | Cultural Institution | Kulturelle Institution | Institución Cultural | Institution culturelle | Instituição cultural |
| ⊥ | Historical Site | Historische Stätte | Sitio Histórico | Site historique | Sítio histórico |
| ♦ | Recreational Site | Erholungs- und Ferienort | Sitio de Recreo | Centre de loisirs | Área de Lazer |
| ⊠ | Airport | Flughafen | Aeropuerto | Aéroport | Aeroporto |
| ■ | Military Installation | Militäranlage | Instalación Militar | Installation militaire | Instalação militar |
| ◆ | Miscellaneous | Verschiedenes | Misceláneo | Divers | Diversos |

Mbua Bay ⊂ 175g 16.49 S 178.35 E
Mbuji-Mayi (Bakwanga) 152 6.09 S 23.38 E
Mbulu 154 3.51 S 35.32 E
Mbulula 154 5.26 S 27.26 E
Mbuluzane ≃ 158 26.08 S 31.52 E
Mbuluzi ≃ 158 26.08 S 31.52 E
Mbuma 154 3.32 N 24.50 E
Mburucuyá 252 28.03 S 58.14 W
Mbutha 175g 16.39 S 179.50 E
Mbwemkuru ≃ 154 9.29 S 39.39 E
McAdam 186 45.36 N 67.20 W
McAdam National Park ♠ 164 7.15 S 145.40 E
McAdams Peak ∧[2] 219 38.58 N 90.32 W
McAdoo 210 40.54 N 75.59 W
McAdoo Heights 210 40.54 N 76.01 W
McAfee 210 41.10 N 74.32 W
McAlester 196 34.56 N 95.46 W
McAlisterville 208 40.38 N 77.16 W
McAllen 196 26.12 N 98.13 W
McAlpine 208 39.16 N 76.50 W
McAlpine Dam ✦[6] 218 38.16 N 85.47 W
McAlveys Fort 214 40.39 N 77.50 W
McArthur 188 39.14 N 82.28 W
McArthur ≃ 164 15.54 S 136.40 E
McArthur River 164 16.27 S 136.07 E
McAuley 184 50.16 N 101.23 W
McBain 190 44.11 N 85.12 W
McBee 192 34.28 N 80.15 W
McBeth 222 29.11 N 95.30 W
McBeth Fjord ⊂[2] 176 69.38 N 68.30 W
McBride 182 53.18 N 120.10 W
McCall 202 44.54 N 116.05 W
McCall Creek 194 31.30 N 90.41 W
McCallum 186 47.38 N 56.15 W
McCallum Creek ≃ 169 37.03 S 143.49 E
McCamey 196 31.08 N 102.13 W
McCammon 202 42.39 N 112.11 W
McCandless, Pa., U.S. 214 40.35 N 80.01 W
McCandless, Pa., U.S. 279b 40.34 N 80.02 W
McCarteney Creek ≃ 202 47.13 N 120.05 W
McCarthy 180 61.26 N 142.55 W
McCauley Island I 182 53.40 N 130.15 W
McCaysville 192 34.59 N 84.22 W
McChord Air Force Base ■ 224 47.08 N 122.29 W
McClarens Run ≃ 279b 40.27 N 80.12 W
McClarty Lake ⊜ 184 54.28 N 100.20 W
McCleary 224 47.03 N 123.15 W
McClees Creek ≃ 276 40.22 N 74.03 W
McClellan Air Force Base ■ 226 38.39 N 121.23 W
McClellan Creek ≃ 196 35.22 N 100.34 W
McClellanville 192 33.05 N 79.27 W
McClintock, Mount ∧ 9 80.13 S 157.26 E
McCloud 204 41.15 N 122.08 W
McCloud ≃ 204 40.46 N 122.18 W
McClure, Il., U.S. 194 37.19 N 89.26 W
McClure, Oh., U.S. 216 41.22 N 83.56 W
McClure, Pa., U.S. 210 40.42 N 77.18 W
McClure, Lake ⊜[1] 226 37.37 N 120.16 W
McClusky 198 47.29 N 100.26 W
McColl 192 34.40 N 79.32 W
McComas 192 37.23 N 81.17 W
McComb, Ms., U.S. 194 31.14 N 90.27 W
McComb, Oh., U.S. 216 41.06 N 83.47 W
McConaughy, Lake ⊜[1] 198 41.15 N 101.50 W
McConnell Air Force Base ■ 198 37.38 N 97.15 W
McConnell Range ⩕ 180 64.00 N 123.50 W
McConnellsburg 188 39.55 N 77.59 W
McConnells Mill 279b 40.15 N 80.15 W
McConnells Mill State Park ♠ 214 40.57 N 80.11 W
McConnellstown 214 40.27 N 78.05 W
McConnellsville 210 43.16 N 75.42 W
McConnelsville 188 39.38 N 81.51 W
McCook, Il., U.S. 278 41.48 N 87.50 W
McCook, Ne., U.S. 198 40.12 N 100.37 W
McCordsville 218 39.53 N 85.55 W
McCormick 192 33.54 N 82.17 W
McCormick Place ⊍ 278 41.51 N 87.37 W
McCoy 224 45.03 N 123.13 W
McCoy Creek ≃ 202 43.02 N 118.50 W
McCoy Lake ⊜ 184 52.35 N 92.19 W
McCraney Creek ≃ 219 39.39 N 91.12 W
McCreary 184 50.46 N 99.30 W
McCrory 194 35.15 N 91.12 W
McCulloch, Mount ∧ 162 25.10 S 129.52 E
McCullom Lake 216 42.22 N 88.18 W
McCullough 279b 40.22 N 79.38 W
McCullough Mountain ∧ 204 35.36 N 115.11 W
McCune 198 37.21 N 95.00 W
McCurtain 196 35.08 N 94.58 W
McCusker ≃ 184 55.32 N 108.40 W
McCutchenville 214 40.59 N 83.15 W
McDade 222 30.17 N 97.15 W
McDavid 194 30.51 N 87.19 W
McDermitt 204 41.59 N 117.43 W
McDermott 218 38.50 N 83.03 W
McDonald, Ks., U.S. 198 39.47 N 101.22 W
McDonald, Pa., U.S. 214 40.22 N 80.14 W
McDonald, Lac ⊜ 206 45.52 N 74.35 W
McDonald, Lake ⊜ 202 48.35 N 113.55 W
McDonald Park ♠ 282 37.18 N 122.17 W
McDonogh 284b 39.24 N 76.46 W
McDonough, Ga., U.S. 192 33.26 N 84.08 W
McDonough, N.Y., U.S. 210 42.30 N 75.46 W
McDouall Peak 162 29.51 S 134.55 E
McDougal, Mount ∧ 200 42.54 N 110.36 W
McDowell Peak ∧ 200 33.40 N 111.50 W
McElhattan 210 41.09 N 77.22 W
McElmo Creek ≃ 200 37.13 N 109.12 W
Mc Ennen Airport ⊠ 281 42.12 N 83.37 W
Mcensk 76 53.17 N 36.35 E
McEwen 194 36.06 N 87.37 W
McEwensville 210 41.05 N 76.49 W
McFadden 200 41.39 N 106.07 W
McFarland, Ca., U.S. 226 35.40 N 119.13 W
McFarland, Wi., U.S. 216 43.00 N 89.17 W
McGavock Lake ⊜ 184 56.32 N 101.25 W
McGehee 194 33.37 N 91.23 W
McGill 204 39.24 N 114.46 W
McGill, Université ⊍[2] 275a 45.30 N 73.35 W
McGillivray, Lac ⊜ 190 46.04 N 77.06 W
McGinnis Slough Wildlife Refuge ✦[4] 278 41.39 N 87.52 W
McGovern 214 40.14 N 80.13 W
McGrann 214 40.47 N 79.31 W
McGrath 180 62.58 N 155.38 W
McGraw 210 42.35 N 76.05 W
McGregor, On., Can. 214 42.09 N 82.58 W
McGregor, S. Afr. 158 33.57 S 19.50 E
McGregor, Ia., U.S. 190 43.01 N 91.10 W
McGregor, Tx., U.S. 222 31.26 N 97.24 W
McGregor ≃ 182 54.11 N 122.00 W
McGregor Creek ≃ 214 42.24 N 82.11 W
McGregor Lake ⊜ 182 50.31 N 112.53 W
McGregor Range ⩕ 166 26.40 S 142.45 E
McGuffey 216 40.41 N 83.47 W
McGuire, Mount ∧ 202 45.10 N 114.36 W
McGuire Air Force Base ■ 208 40.02 N 74.35 W
McGuire Reservoir ⊜ 224 45.19 N 123.26 W
M'Chedallah 34 36.21 N 4.16 E
McHenry, Il., U.S. 216 42.20 N 88.16 W
McHenry, Ms., U.S. 194 30.42 N 89.08 W
McHenry □[6] 216 42.19 N 88.27 W
Mcherrah ✦[1] 148 27.00 N 4.40 W
Mchinga 154 9.44 S 39.42 E
Mchinji 154 13.41 S 32.55 E
Mchungo 154 7.42 S 39.17 E
McInnes Lake ⊜ 184 52.12 N 93.45 W
McIntosh, Al., U.S. 194 31.15 N 88.01 W
McIntosh, Il., U.S. 216 42.03 N 88.23 W
McIntosh, Mn., U.S. 198 47.38 N 95.53 W
McIntosh, S.D., U.S. 198 45.55 N 101.20 W
McIntosh Lake ⊜ 184 55.45 N 105.08 W
McIntyre 214 40.34 N 79.17 W
McIntyre Bay ⊂ 182 54.05 N 131.55 W
McKay, Mount ∧ 162 22.26 S 120.01 E
McKay Creek ≃ 202 45.40 N 118.50 W
McKean 214 41.59 N 80.09 W
McKean □[6] 214 41.49 N 78.27 W
McKeand ≃ 176 65.26 N 68.10 W
McKee 192 37.25 N 83.59 W
McKee City 208 39.27 N 74.38 W
McKee Creek ≃ 219 39.46 N 90.36 W
McKeesport 214 40.20 N 79.51 W
McKees Rocks 214 40.27 N 80.03 W
McKenna 224 46.56 N 122.33 W
McKenzie, Al., U.S. 194 31.32 N 86.42 W
McKenzie, Tn., U.S. 194 36.07 N 88.31 W
McKenzie ≃ 202 44.07 N 123.06 W
McKenzie Bridge 202 44.10 N 122.09 W
McKenzie Creek ≃ 212 43.02 N 79.53 W
McKenzie Island 184 51.05 N 93.48 W
McKenzie Lake ⊜, On., Can. 212 45.22 N 78.02 W
McKenzie Lake ⊜, Sk., Can. 184 54.12 N 102.30 W
McKerrow, Lake ⊜ 172 44.26 S 168.03 E
McKillip Ditch ≡ 216 40.50 N 86.51 W
McKinlay 166 21.16 S 141.17 E
McKinlay ≃ 166 20.50 S 141.28 E
McKinley, Mount ∧ 180 63.04 N 151.00 W
McKinley Airport ⊠ 281 42.33 N 82.58 W
McKinley Park ♠ 279b 40.25 N 80.00 W
McKinleyville, Ca., U.S. 204 40.56 N 124.05 W
McKinleyville, W.V., U.S. 214 40.15 N 80.36 W
McKinney 222 33.11 N 96.36 W
McKittrick, Ca., U.S. 226 35.18 N 119.37 W
McKittrick, Mo., U.S. 219 38.44 N 91.27 W
McKittrick Summit ∧ 226 35.18 N 119.46 W
McKnight Lake ⊜ 184 56.03 N 101.08 W
McKnightstown 208 39.52 N 77.20 W
McKnight Village 279b 40.31 N 80.00 W
McKownville 210 42.41 N 73.50 W
McLain 194 31.06 N 88.49 W
McLaren Vale 168b 35.14 S 138.32 E
McLarty Hills ⩕[2] 162 19.29 S 123.33 E
McLaughlin 198 45.48 N 100.48 W
McLaughlin ≃ 184 53.46 N 97.38 W
McLaughlin Run ≃ 279b 40.22 N 80.07 W
McLaurin 194 31.10 N 89.13 W
McLean, Sk., Can. 184 50.30 N 104.04 W
McLean, Il., U.S. 194 40.18 N 89.10 W
McLean, N.Y., U.S. 210 42.33 N 76.17 W
McLean, Tx., U.S. 196 35.13 N 100.35 W
McLean, Va., U.S. 208 38.56 N 77.10 W
McLean □[6] 216 40.29 N 88.45 W
McLean Hamlet 284c 38.56 N 77.13 W
McLean Lake ⊜ 184 56.27 N 109.15 W
McLean Mountain ∧ 186 47.07 N 68.50 W
McLeansboro 194 38.05 N 88.32 W
McLennan 182 55.42 N 116.54 W
McLennan □[6] 222 31.35 N 97.13 W
McLeod ≃ 182 54.08 N 115.42 W
McLeod Bay ⊂ 176 62.53 N 110.00 W
McLeodganj 123 30.15 N 73.42 E
McLeod Lake 182 54.59 N 123.02 W
M'Clintock Channel ⊔ 176 72.00 N 102.00 W
McLoughlin, Mount ∧ 202 42.27 N 122.19 W
McLoughlin Bay ⊂ 176 67.50 N 99.00 W
McLoughlin House National Historic Site ⊥ 224 45.20 N 122.33 W
McLouth 198 39.11 N 95.12 W
McLure 182 51.03 N 120.14 W
M'Clure Strait ⊔ 176 74.30 N 116.00 W
McMahan 222 29.51 N 97.31 W
McMahon 184 50.05 N 107.32 W
McMasterville 206 45.33 N 73.15 W
McMichael Art Collection ⊍ 275b 43.50 N 79.37 W
McMillan, Lake ⊜[1] 196 32.40 N 104.20 W
McMinnville, Or., U.S. 224 45.12 N 123.11 W
McMinnville, Tn., U.S. 194 35.41 N 85.46 W
McMurdo ⊍[3] 9 77.50 S 166.25 E
McMurdo Sound ⊔ 9 77.30 S 165.00 E
McMurray 214 40.17 N 80.05 W
McNair 222 29.48 N 95.02 W
McNary 200 34.04 N 109.51 W
McNeil, Ar., U.S. 194 33.20 N 93.12 W
McNeil, Tx., U.S. 222 30.27 N 97.43 W
McNeil, Mount ∧ 182 54.35 N 130.14 W
McNeil Island I 224 47.13 N 122.41 W
McNeill 194 30.40 N 89.38 W
McNulty 224 45.50 N 122.50 W
McPhail ≃ 184 52.44 N 96.31 W
McPhee Bay ⊂ 212 44.35 N 79.19 W
McPhee Reservoir ⊜[1] 200 37.32 N 108.35 W
McPherson 198 38.22 N 97.39 W
McPherson Range ⩕ 166 28.20 S 153.00 E
McQueeney 196 29.35 N 98.02 W
McRae, Ar., U.S. 194 35.06 N 91.49 W
McRae, Ga., U.S. 192 32.04 N 82.54 W
McRae, Mount ∧ 162 22.17 S 117.35 E
McRae Point Provincial Park ♠ 212 44.34 N 79.19 W
McRoberts 192 37.12 N 82.40 W
McSherrystown 208 39.48 N 77.00 W
McVeigh 192 37.32 N 82.15 W
McVeytown 214 40.30 N 77.44 W
McVickers Brook ≃ 276 40.45 N 74.38 W
McVille 198 47.45 N 98.10 W
McWilliams 194 31.49 N 87.05 W
Mdandu 154 9.09 S 34.42 E
Mdantsana 158 32.56 S 27.42 E
M'Daourouch 36 36.05 N 7.49 E
Meacham 184 52.08 N 105.45 W
Mead 198 41.14 N 96.30 W
Mead, Lake ⊜[1] 200 36.05 N 114.25 W
Meade, Ks., U.S. 198 37.17 N 100.20 W
Meade, Mi., U.S. 214 42.43 N 82.52 W
Meade ≃ 180 70.50 N 156.25 W
Meaden Peak ∧ 200 40.46 N 107.03 W
Meade Peak ∧ 202 42.30 N 111.15 W
Meadie, Loch ⊜ 46 58.20 N 4.33 W
Meadow, Tx., U.S. 196 33.20 N 102.12 W
Meadow, Ut., U.S. 200 38.53 N 112.24 W
Meadowbank Park ♠ 274a 33.49 S 151.06 E
Meadowbrook, Il., U.S. 219 38.54 N 90.01 W
Meadowbrook, In., U.S. 216 41.03 N 85.03 W
Meadow Brook ≃, Ma., U.S. 283 42.03 N 70.58 W
Meadow Brook ≃, Pa., U.S. 285 40.07 N 75.04 W
Meadow Creek ≃ 202 46.03 N 115.18 W
Meadow Flat 170 33.26 S 149.56 E
Meadow Island I 276 40.36 N 73.33 W
Meadow Lake 184 54.08 N 108.26 W
Meadow Lake ⊜, Sk., Can. 184 54.07 N 108.20 W
Meadow Lake ⊜, N.Y., U.S. 276 40.44 N 73.50 W
Meadow Lake Provincial Park ♠ 184 54.28 N 109.10 W
Meadow Lands 214 40.13 N 80.13 W
Meadowlands Race Track ♠ 276 40.49 N 74.05 W
Meadowlark Airport ⊠ 280 33.43 N 118.02 W
Meadowood, De., U.S. 285 39.43 N 75.47 W
Meadowood, Md., U.S. 284c 39.04 N 77.00 W
Meadows 168b 35.11 S 138.46 E
Meadows, Island of I 276 40.34 N 74.12 W
Meadows Field ⊠ 226 35.26 N 119.03 W
Meadowvale ✦[8] 275b 43.37 N 79.43 W
Meadow Valley Wash V 204 36.39 N 114.35 W
Meadowview 192 36.46 N 81.52 W
Meadow Vista 226 39.06 N 121.01 W
Meads Creek ≃ 210 42.10 N 77.07 W
Meadville, Ms., U.S. 194 31.28 N 90.53 W
Meadville, Mo., U.S. 194 39.47 N 93.18 W
Meadville, Pa., U.S. 214 41.38 N 80.09 W
Meaford 212 44.36 N 80.35 W
Meaghers Grant 186 44.55 N 63.15 W
Me-akan-dake ∧ 92a 43.23 N 144.01 E
Mealasta Isle I 46 58.05 N 7.08 W
Mealhada 34 40.22 N 8.27 W
Méan 56 50.22 N 5.20 E
Meana 128 36.55 N 60.30 E
Meana Sardo 71 39.57 N 9.04 E
Meandarra 166 27.20 S 149.53 E
Meander Creek Reservoir ⊜[1] 214 41.09 N 80.47 W
Meander River 176 59.02 N 117.42 W
Mearim ≃ 250 3.04 S 44.35 W
Measham 42 52.43 N 1.29 W
Meath □[6] 48 53.35 N 6.40 W
Meath □[9] 48 53.40 N 7.00 W
Meaux 50 48.57 N 2.52 E
Meaux-Esbly, Aérodrome de ⊠ 261 48.55 N 2.50 E
Mebane 192 36.05 N 79.16 W
Mebisere 273a 6.42 N 3.31 E
Mebtoûh, Oued el ≃ 34 35.16 N 0.32 W
Meča ≃ 82 54.50 N 39.10 E
Meca, La → Makkah 144 21.27 N 39.49 E
Mecanhelas 154 15.12 S 35.54 E
Mecatán 234 21.32 N 105.08 W
Mecatlán 234 20.13 N 97.41 W
Mecaya ≃ 246 0.29 N 75.11 W
Mecca → Makkah 144 21.27 N 39.49 E
Mečetinskaja 78 46.46 N 40.27 E
Mečetka 78 50.54 N 40.05 E
Mechanic Falls 188 44.06 N 70.23 W
Mechanicsburg, Il., U.S. 219 39.48 N 89.24 W
Mechanicsburg, In., U.S. 218 40.09 N 86.28 W
Mechanicsburg, Oh., U.S. 218 40.04 N 83.33 W
Mechanicsburg, Pa., U.S. 208 40.12 N 77.00 W
Mechanicstown, N.Y., U.S. 210 41.27 N 74.24 W
Mechanicstown, Oh., U.S. 214 40.37 N 80.57 W
Mechanicsville, Ia., U.S. 190 41.54 N 91.15 W
Mechanicsville, Md., U.S. 208 38.26 N 76.44 W
Mechanicsville, Va., U.S. 192 37.36 N 77.22 W
Mechanicville 210 42.54 N 73.41 W
Mechara 144 8.32 N 40.22 E
Mecharchar I 175b 7.09 N 134.22 E
Mechebylove 78 49.04 N 36.41 E
Mechelen (Malines) 50 51.02 N 4.28 E
Mechel'ta 84 42.48 N 46.30 E
Mechernich 56 50.35 N 6.38 E
Mechī □[8] 124 27.15 N 87.45 E
Mechī ≃ 124 26.14 N 87.58 E
Mechita 252 35.04 S 60.24 W
Mechlin → Mechelen 50 51.02 N 4.28 E
Mechonskoje 86 56.09 N 64.34 E
Mechra Safsaf 34 34.52 N 2.36 W
Mechren'ga 24 61.46 N 40.57 E
Mechrenga ≃ 24 63.15 N 41.20 E
Mechriyya 148 33.35 N 0.18 W
Mechroha 36 36.21 N 7.51 E
Mecidiye, Tür. 130 40.38 N 26.32 E
Mecidiye, Tür. 130 38.53 N 27.42 E
Mečigmen 180 65.28 N 172.05 W
Mečigmeskij zaliv ⊂ 180 65.25 N 172.00 W
Meçitözü 130 40.31 N 35.19 E
Meckelfeld 52 53.25 N 10.01 E
Meckenbeuren 58 47.42 N 9.34 E
Meckenheim 56 50.37 N 7.07 E
Meckering 162 31.38 S 117.01 E
Meckesheim 56 49.19 N 8.49 E
Meckinghoven 263 51.37 N 7.19 E
Mecklenburg, Dtsch. 54 53.47 N 11.28 E
Mecklenburg, N.Y., U.S. 210 42.27 N 76.43 W
Mecklenburg □[9] 54 53.30 N 13.00 E
Mecklenburger Bucht ⊂ 54 54.20 N 11.40 E
Mecklenburgische Seenplatte ✦[1] 54 53.30 N 12.00 E
Mecklenburg-Vorpommern □[3] 54 53.45 N 12.30 E
Meclov 60 49.31 N 12.52 E
Meco 210 43.03 N 74.23 W
Mecoacán 234 18.23 N 93.07 W
Mecoacán, Laguna ⊂ 234 18.22 N 93.09 W
Meconta 154 14.49 S 39.50 E
Mecox Bay ⊂ 207 40.54 N 72.20 W
Mecque, La → Makkah 144 21.27 N 39.49 E
Mecsek ⩕ 30 46.15 N 18.05 E
Mecubúri 154 14.39 S 38.54 E
Mecubúri ≃ 154 14.10 S 40.31 E
Mecúfi 154 13.17 S 40.30 E
Mecula 154 12.04 S 37.40 E
Meda, It. 62 45.40 N 9.09 E
Meda, Port. 34 40.58 N 7.16 W
Medak 122 18.02 N 78.16 E
Medākul 126 23.03 N 90.11 E
Médan, Fr. 261 48.57 N 2.00 E
Medan, Indon. 114 3.35 N 98.40 E
Medang 114 2.06 N 101.38 E
Medang, Pulau I 115b 8.09 S 117.23 E
Medang, Tanjung › 114 2.08 N 101.39 E
Médanos 252 38.50 S 62.41 W
Medanosa, Punta › 254 48.06 S 65.55 W
Medaryville 216 41.04 N 86.53 W
Mede 62 45.06 N 8.44 E
Medebach 56 51.12 N 8.42 E
Medeiros Neto 255 17.20 S 40.14 W
Medel, Val V 58 46.37 N 8.50 E
Medellín, Col. 246 6.15 N 75.35 W
Medellin, Pil. 116 11.08 N 123.58 E
Medelpad □[9] 26 62.40 N 16.15 E
Medemblik 52 52.46 N 5.06 E
Měděnec 54 50.25 N 13.05 E
Médenine 148 33.21 N 10.30 E
Medenytsya 78 49.26 N 23.45 E
Mederdra 150 16.55 N 15.39 W
Medesano 64 44.45 N 10.08 E
Medevi 40 58.40 N 14.57 E
Medfield 207 42.11 N 71.18 W
Medford, Ma., U.S. 207 42.25 N 71.06 W
Medford, N.J., U.S. 208 39.54 N 74.49 W
Medford, N.Y., U.S. 210 40.49 N 73.00 W
Medford, Ok., U.S. 196 36.48 N 97.44 W
Medford, Or., U.S. 202 42.19 N 122.52 W
Medford, Wi., U.S. 190 45.08 N 90.20 W
Medford Farms 285 39.52 N 74.45 W
Medford Lakes 285 39.51 N 74.48 W
Medfra 180 63.06 N 154.44 W
Medgidia 38 44.15 N 28.16 E
Medgyes → Mediaș 38 46.10 N 24.21 E
Medi 154 5.04 N 30.44 E
Media 208 39.55 N 75.23 W
Mediapolis 190 41.00 N 91.09 W
Mediaș 38 46.10 N 24.21 E
Medical Lake 202 47.34 N 117.40 W
Medicina 66 44.28 N 11.38 E
Medicine Bow 200 41.53 N 106.12 W
Medicine Bow ≃ 200 42.00 N 106.40 W
Medicine Bow Mountains ⩕ 200 41.10 N 106.10 W
Medicine Bow Peak ∧ 200 41.21 N 106.19 W
Medicine Creek ≃, Mo., U.S. 194 39.43 N 93.24 W
Medicine Creek ≃, Ne., U.S. 198 40.17 N 100.10 W
Medicine Creek ≃, S.D., U.S. 198 44.06 N 99.42 W
Medicine Hat 184 50.03 N 110.40 W
Medicine Knoll Creek ≃ 198 44.19 N 100.05 W
Medicine Lake 198 48.30 N 104.30 W
Medicine Lake ⊜ 198 48.28 N 104.24 W
Medicine Lodge 198 37.16 N 98.34 W
Medicine Lodge ≃ 196 36.49 N 98.20 W
Medicine Rocks State Park ♠ 198 46.01 N 104.35 W
Medina → Al-Madīnah, Ar. Su. 128 24.28 N 39.36 E
Medina, Bra. 255 16.15 S 41.29 W
Medina, Pil. 116 8.55 N 125.01 E
Medina, N.Y., U.S. 210 43.13 N 78.23 W
Medina, N.D., U.S. 198 46.53 N 99.17 W
Medina, Oh., U.S. 214 41.08 N 81.51 W
Medina, Tx., U.S. 196 29.48 N 99.15 W
Medina, Wa., U.S. 224 47.37 N 122.13 W
Medina □[6] 214 41.08 N 81.52 W
Medina ≃ 196 29.12 N 98.20 W
Medinaceli 34 41.10 N 2.26 W
Medina del Campo 34 41.18 N 4.55 W
Medina de Ríoseco 34 41.53 N 5.02 W
Médina Gonasse 150 13.08 N 13.45 W
Medinah 278 41.59 N 88.01 W
Medina Lake ⊜[1] 196 29.35 N 98.58 W
Médina Sabak 150 13.36 N 15.35 W
Medina-Sidonia 34 36.27 N 5.55 W
Medinat al-Faiyum → Al-Fayyūm 142 29.19 N 30.50 E
Medininkai 76 54.32 N 25.40 E
Medinīpur 126 22.26 N 87.20 E
Medino 164 9.40 S 149.40 E
Medio, Arroyo del ≃ 258 33.49 S 57.43 W
Medio, Punta › 252 27.07 S 70.57 W
Medio Creek ≃ 196 28.19 N 97.19 W
Mediterranean Sea ⚲[2] 10 35.00 N 20.00 E
Mediterraneo, Mare → Mediterranean Sea ⚲[2] 10 35.00 N 20.00 E
Medjana 34 36.08 N 4.41 E
Medje 154 2.25 N 27.18 E
Medjerda, Monts de la ⩕ 36 36.35 N 8.15 E
Medkovec 38 43.37 N 23.10 E
Mednogorsk 86 51.24 N 57.37 E
Mednoje 76 56.56 N 35.29 E
Mednyj, ostrov I 74 54.45 N 167.35 E
Médoc ✦[1] 32 45.20 N 1.00 W
Mêdog 120 29.20 N 95.15 E
Medolla 64 44.51 N 11.04 E
Medora, Il., U.S. 219 39.11 N 90.09 W
Medora, In., U.S. 218 38.49 N 86.10 W
Medora, N.D., U.S. 198 46.54 N 103.31 W
Médouneu 152 0.57 N 10.47 E
Medow 54 53.50 N 13.32 E
Medstead, Sk., Can. 184 53.19 N 108.02 W
Medstead, Eng., U.K. 42 51.08 N 1.04 W
Medua 126 22.38 N 90.44 E
Meductic 186 46.00 N 67.29 W
Medulla 220 27.58 N 81.58 W
Međumurje ✦[1] 61 46.25 N 16.30 E
Meduna ≃ 64 45.49 N 12.34 E
Medveđa 38 42.50 N 21.35 E
Medvedevo, Ross. 76 60.02 N 43.01 E
Medvedevo, Ross. 80 56.37 N 47.47 E
Medvedevo, Ross. 86 60.37 N 77.21 E
Medvedevskoje 76 58.58 N 35.58 E
Medvedica ≃, Ross. 76 57.05 N 37.32 E
Medvedica ≃, Ross. 80 49.35 N 42.41 E
Medvedickij 80 50.47 N 44.43 E
Medvědí hora ∧ 60 48.59 N 13.25 E
Medvedkovo ✦[8] 265b 55.53 N 37.38 E
Medvedok 80 57.23 N 50.05 E
Medvedovskaja 78 45.27 N 39.01 E
Medvėgalis ∧[2] 76 55.38 N 22.45 E
Medvenka, Ross. 78 51.26 N 36.07 E
Medvenka, Ross. 82 54.15 N 37.42 E
Medvežij, ostrov I 89 54.41 N 136.18 E
Medvežje, ozero ⊜ 86 55.07 N 68.00 E
Medvežjegorsk 24 62.55 N 34.23 E
Medvežji ostrova II 74 70.52 N 161.26 E
Medvežji ozera ⊜ 265b 55.52 N 38.00 E
Medvežji Oz'ora 265b 55.52 N 37.59 E
Medvežskaja 24 64.57 N 57.34 E
Medv'onka ≃ 265b 55.44 N 37.12 E
Medvyn 78 49.23 N 30.47 E
Medway, Ma., U.S. 207 42.08 N 71.23 W
Medway, Oh., U.S. 218 39.53 N 83.59 W
Medway □[8] 260 51.24 N 0.31 E
Medway ≃, N.S., Can. 186 44.08 N 64.36 W
Medway ≃, Eng., U.K. 42 51.27 N 0.44 E
Medyn' 82 54.58 N 35.52 E
Medynka ≃ 82 54.44 N 36.02 E
Medynskij Zavorot, mys › 24 68.58 N 59.17 E
Medzhybizh 78 49.26 N 27.25 E
Medzilaborce 30 49.16 N 21.55 E
Meeberrie 162 26.58 S 115.58 E
Meekatharra 162 26.36 S 118.29 E
Meeker, Co., U.S. 200 40.02 N 107.54 W
Meeker, Oh., U.S. 214 40.39 N 83.18 W
Meeks Bay 226 39.02 N 120.08 W
Meelpaeg Lake ⊜[1] 186 48.16 N 56.35 W
Meenaar 168a 31.38 S 116.53 E
Meentheena 162 21.17 S 120.28 E
Meer 56 51.27 N 4.44 E
Meeralpen → Maritime Alps ⩕ 62 44.15 N 7.10 E
Meerane 54 50.51 N 12.28 E
Meerbeck 263 51.28 N 6.39 E
Meerbeke 50 50.50 N 4.02 E
Meerbusch 56 51.15 N 6.41 E
Meerhout 56 51.08 N 5.05 E
Meerhusener Moor ✦[3] 52 53.35 N 7.30 E
Meerkerk 52 51.55 N 5.00 E
Meerle 52 51.28 N 4.48 E
Meersburg 58 47.41 N 9.16 E
Meerssen 56 50.53 N 5.45 E
Meerut 124 28.59 N 77.42 E
Meese ≃ 42 52.40 N 2.39 W
Meeteetse 202 44.09 N 108.52 W
Mega, Indon. 164 0.41 S 131.53 E
Mega, Ityo. 144 4.07 N 38.16 E
Mega, Pulau I 112 4.00 S 101.02 E
Megalo 144 6.55 N 41.48 E
Megálon Khoríon 38 36.27 N 27.21 E
Megalópolis 38 37.24 N 22.08 E
Mégantic □[6] 206 46.10 N 71.30 W
Mégantic, Lac ⊜ 188 45.32 N 70.53 W
Mégantic, Mont ∧ 206 45.28 N 71.09 W
Mégara 38 38.01 N 23.21 E
Megargel 196 33.27 N 98.56 W
Mégaron, Kólpos ⊂ 267c 37.56 N 23.20 E
Megaruma ≃ 154 13.28 S 40.32 E
Megasini ∧ 126 21.38 N 86.21 E
Meget 88 52.24 N 104.03 E
Megève 62 45.52 N 6.37 E
Mégevette 58 46.12 N 6.30 E
Megezez ∧ 144 9.17 N 39.32 E
Megget Reservoir ⊜[1] 46 55.29 N 3.17 W
Meghālaya □[3] 120 25.30 N 91.15 E
Meghna ≃ 120 22.50 N 90.50 E
Megi-jima I 96 34.24 N 134.03 E
Mégiscane ≃ 190 48.29 N 77.08 W
Mégiscane, Lac ⊜ 190 48.35 N 75.55 W
Meglino, ozero ⊜ 76 58.25 N 35.07 E
Megra, Ross. 24 66.09 N 41.37 E
Megra, Ross. 76 60.10 N 37.13 E
Megri 84 38.56 N 46.16 E
Meguro ✦[8] 268 35.38 N 139.42 E
Meguro ≃ 268 35.37 N 139.45 E
Mehadia 38 44.55 N 22.22 E
Méhaigne ≃ 56 50.32 N 5.13 E
Mehaïguene, Oued V 148 32.15 N 2.59 E
Mehakit 112 2.51 S 115.57 E
Mehanom, mys › 78 44.48 N 35.05 E
Mehar 120 27.11 N 67.49 E
Meharry, Mount ∧ 162 22.59 S 118.35 E
Mehdia 148 35.26 N 1.40 E
Mehede 40 60.27 N 17.24 E
Mehedinți □[6] 38 44.30 N 22.50 E
Meheisa 140 19.37 N 32.57 E
Mehekar 122 20.09 N 76.34 E
Mehendiganj 126 22.49 N 90.32 E
Meherpur 124 23.46 N 88.38 E
Meherrin ≃ 192 36.26 N 76.57 W
Mehetia I 14 17.52 S 148.03 W
Mehidpur 120 23.49 N 75.40 E
Mehikoorma 76 58.14 N 27.28 E
Mehlville 219 38.30 N 90.19 W
Mehnagar 124 25.53 N 83.07 E
Mehndāwal 124 26.59 N 83.07 E
Mehoopany 210 41.34 N 76.04 W
Mehoopany Creek ≃ 210 41.34 N 76.03 W
Mehpālpur ✦[8] 272a 28.33 N 77.08 E
Mehrābād 128 36.53 N 47.55 E
Mehrābād ✦[8] 267d 35.40 N 51.20 E
Mehram Nagar ✦[8] 272a 28.34 N 77.07 E
Mehrān 128 33.07 N 46.10 E
Mehrān ≃ 128 26.52 N 55.24 E
Mehring 56 49.48 N 6.49 E
Mehrīz 128 31.35 N 54.28 E
Mehrow 264a 52.34 N 13.37 E
Mehrum 263 51.35 N 6.37 E
Mè-hsa-tè 110 19.33 N 97.38 E
Mehtarlām 120 34.39 N 70.10 E
Mehun-sur-Yèvre 50 47.09 N 2.13 E
Mei ≃, Zhg. 100 24.24 N 116.34 E
Mei ≃, Zhg. 100 26.00 N 115.23 E
Mei ≃, Zhg. 105 39.21 N 117.50 E
Meia Meia 154 5.49 S 35.48 E
Meia Ponte, Rio da ≃ 255 18.32 S 49.36 W
Meichang 105 39.22 N 117.10 E
Meichuan 100 30.10 N 115.36 E
Meicun, Zhg. 100 25.30 N 116.56 E
Meicun, Zhg. 106 30.22 N 119.01 E
Meicun, Zhg. 106 30.40 N 119.04 E
Meicun, Zhg. 106 31.33 N 120.24 E
Meide 263 51.11 N 6.55 E
Meiderich ✦[8] 263 51.28 N 6.46 E
Meidling ✦[8] 264b 48.11 N 16.20 E
Meierij ✦[1] 52 51.35 N 5.40 E
Meierkaisong 120 30.54 N 84.31 E
Meiersberg 263 51.17 N 6.57 E
Meig ≃ 46 57.34 N 4.41 W
Meiganga 152 6.31 N 14.11 E
Meigle 46 56.35 N 3.09 W
Meigs 192 31.04 N 84.05 W
Meigs Field ⊠ 278 41.51 N 87.36 W
Meihsien → Meixian 100 24.21 N 116.08 E
Meihua 100 26.02 N 119.40 E
Meihuajie 100 25.14 N 113.05 E
Meijel 52 51.21 N 5.53 E
Meijino-Mori-Minō-kokutei-kōen ♠ 94 34.51 N 135.29 E
Meiji Shrine ⊍[1] 268 35.41 N 139.42 E
Meikeng 100 23.59 N 114.05 E
Meikle Millyea ∧ 44 55.07 N 4.19 W
Meikle Says Law ∧ 46 55.55 N 2.40 W
Meiktila 110 20.52 N 95.52 E
Meilen 58 47.16 N 8.38 E
Meili 106 31.42 N 120.53 E
Meilie 100 26.18 N 117.38 E
Meilin, Zhg. 100 23.18 N 115.58 E
Meilin, Zhg. 106 30.35 N 119.04 E
Meillerie 58 46.24 N 6.43 E
Meilong 100 22.56 N 115.17 E
Meilunyingzi 104 42.18 N 122.10 E
Meina 62 45.47 N 8.32 E
Meine 52 52.23 N 10.32 E
Meinersen 52 52.29 N 10.22 E
Meiners Oaks 228 34.26 N 119.17 W
Meinerzhagen 56 51.06 N 7.38 E
Meiningen 54 50.34 N 10.25 E
Meinung 100 22.54 N 120.32 E
Meio, Ilha do I 287a 23.02 S 43.17 W
Meiringen 58 46.43 N 8.12 E
Meisburg 56 50.06 N 6.41 E
Meisenheim 56 49.42 N 7.40 E
Meishan, Zhg. 106 31.06 N 119.43 E
Meishan, Zhg. 107 30.02 N 103.49 E
Meissen 54 51.10 N 13.28 E
Meissendorf 52 52.43 N 9.50 E
Meiss Lake ⊜ 204 41.52 N 122.04 W
Meissner ∧ 56 51.12 N 9.50 E
Meitan 102 27.46 N 107.35 E
Meitian 100 25.21 N 112.47 E
Meitingen 56 48.32 N 10.50 E
Meiwa 94 34.33 N 136.39 E
Meixi 106 30.48 N 119.45 E
Meixian, Zhg. 100 24.21 N 116.08 E
Meixian, Zhg. 100 28.52 N 113.38 E
Meiyao 89 49.37 N 124.30 E
Meiyino 140 6.12 N 34.40 E
Meizhai 102 25.30 N 108.50 E
Meizhou 100 23.50 N 117.20 E
Meizhou Dao I 100 25.06 N 119.07 E
Meizhou Wan ⊂ 100 25.06 N 119.00 E
Meizhu 106 31.16 N 119.13 E
Meječkyn, ostrov I 180 65.26 N 178.00 W
Mejerda, Oued (Oued Medjerda) ≃ 36 37.07 N 10.13 E
Mejez el Bab 148 36.39 N 9.37 E
Mejia 126 23.34 N 87.06 E
Mejicanos 236 13.43 N 89.12 W
Mejillones 252 23.06 S 70.27 W
Mejillones, Península ›[1] 252 23.17 S 70.34 W
Mejillones del Sur, Bahía de ⊂ 252 23.03 S 70.27 W
Mejnypil'gyno 74 62.32 N 177.02 E
Mejorada del Campo 266a 40.24 N 3.29 W
Meka 162 27.26 S 116.48 E
Mekada, Garaet el ≡ 36 36.48 N 8.00 E
Mékambo 152 1.01 N 13.56 E
Mekele 144 13.33 N 39.30 E
Mekerra, Oued ≃ 34 35.00 N 0.45 W
Mekhé 150 15.07 N 16.38 W
Mekhliganj 124 26.21 N 88.55 E
Mekhtar 120 30.28 N 69.22 E
Mékinac ≃ 206 46.51 N 72.46 W
Mekka → Makkah 144 21.27 N 39.49 E
Meknès 148 33.53 N 5.37 W
Meknès □[4] 148 33.50 N 5.30 W
Mekong ≃ 12 10.33 N 105.24 E
Mekongga, Gunung ∧ 112 3.38 S 121.15 E
Mekongga, Pegunungan ⩕ 112 3.35 S 121.15 E
Mékôngk → Mekong ≃ 12 10.33 N 105.24 E
Mekoryuk 180 60.23 N 166.12 W
Mékrou ≃ 150 12.24 N 2.49 E
Mel 64 46.04 N 12.05 E
Melado ≃ 252 35.43 S 71.05 W
Melah, Oued el V, Alg. 148 28.21 N 6.00 E
Melah, Oued el V, Tun. 148 34.03 N 8.06 E
Melah, Sebkhet el ⊜ 148 29.05 N 1.10 W
Melaka 114 2.12 N 102.15 E
Melaka □[3] 114 2.15 N 102.15 E
Melalap 112 5.14 N 116.00 E
Melandro ≃ 68 40.37 N 15.27 E
Melanesia II 14 13.00 S 164.00 E
Melanesian Basin ✢[1] 14 0.05 N 160.35 E
Melappālaiyam 122 8.42 N 77.43 E
Melara 64 45.03 N 11.11 E
Melaune 54 51.11 N 14.44 E
Melawi ≃ 112 0.05 N 111.29 E
Melayu ≃ 271c 1.27 N 103.42 E
Melbeck 52 53.11 N 10.24 E
Melbern 216 41.28 N 84.39 W
Melbost 46 58.15 N 6.22 W
Melbourn 42 52.05 N 0.01 E
Melbourne, Austl. 169 37.49 S 144.58 E
Melbourne, Austl. 274b 37.49 S 144.58 E
Melbourne, On., Can. 214 42.49 N 81.33 W
Melbourne, Eng., U.K. 42 52.49 N 1.25 W
Melbourne, Ar., U.S. 194 36.03 N 91.54 W
Melbourne, Fl., U.S. 220 28.04 N 80.36 W
Melbourne, Ia., U.S. 190 41.56 N 93.06 W
Melbourne, University of ⊍[2] 274b 37.48 S 144.58 E
Melbourne Beach 220 28.04 N 80.33 W
Melbourne Island I 176 68.30 N 104.45 W
Melbourne Regional Airport ⊠ 220 28.06 N 80.38 W
Mel'cany 80 54.28 N 44.43 E
Melcher 190 41.13 N 93.14 W
Melchor, Isla I 254 45.08 S 73.57 W
Melchor Múzquiz 232 27.53 N 101.31 W
Melchor Ocampo 196 26.03 N 99.33 W
Melchor Romero ✦[8] 258 34.56 S 58.03 W
Melchtal 58 46.50 N 8.17 E
Melcroft 214 40.03 N 79.24 W
Melderskin ∧ 26 60.01 N 6.05 E
Meldola 66 44.07 N 12.05 E
Meldorf 30 54.05 N 9.05 E
Meldrum Bay 190 45.56 N 83.07 W
Meldrum Creek 182 52.07 N 122.20 W
Mélé, Centraf. 146 9.46 N 21.33 E
Mele, India 272b 22.49 N 88.09 E
Mele, It. 62 44.27 N 8.45 E
Mélé, Baie ⊂ 175f 17.43 S 168.15 E
Mele, Capo › 62 43.57 N 8.10 E
Melechovo 80 56.17 N 41.17 E
Meleck 86 57.25 N 90.12 E
Meleden 144 10.25 N 49.51 E
Melegnano 62 45.21 N 9.19 E
Melekeok 175b 7.29 N 134.38 E
Melekess → Dimitrovgrad 80 54.14 N 49.39 E
Melela ≃ 154 17.04 S 38.36 E
Melena del Sur 240p 22.47 N 82.09 W
Melendiz Dağı ∧ 130 38.07 N 34.25 E
Melendugno 68 40.16 N 18.20 E
Melenki 80 55.20 N 41.38 E
Meleuz 86 52.58 N 55.55 E
Mélèzes, Rivière aux ≃ 176 57.40 N 69.29 W
Melfa 208 37.39 N 75.45 W
Melfa ≃ 66 41.30 N 13.35 E
Melfi, It. 68 41.00 N 15.39 E
Melfi, Tchad 146 11.04 N 17.56 E
Melfort, Sk., Can. 184 52.52 N 104.36 W
Melfort, Zimb. 154 17.59 S 31.19 E
Melfort, Loch ⊂ 46 56.15 N 5.31 W
Melgaço, Bra. 250 1.47 S 50.44 W
Melgaço, Port. 34 42.07 N 8.16 W
Melgar 246 4.12 N 74.39 W
Melghir, Chott ⊜ 148 34.20 N 6.20 E
Mel'guny 80 52.09 N 40.52 E
Melhus 26 63.17 N 10.16 E
Meli ≃ 150 8.16 N 10.42 W
Meliane, Oued ≃ 36 36.46 N 10.18 E
Meliau 112 0.08 S 110.18 E
Meliau, Gunong ∧ 116 5.50 N 117.14 E
Melibocus ∧ 56 49.42 N 8.40 E
Melichovo, Ross. 78 50.42 N 36.48 E
Melichovo, Ross. 82 55.07 N 37.39 E
Melicuccà 68 38.18 N 15.53 E
Melide, Esp. 34 42.55 N 8.00 W
Melide, Schw. 58 45.57 N 8.57 E
Meligalás 38 37.13 N 21.59 E
Melilla 34 35.19 N 2.58 W
Melilli 70 37.11 N 15.07 E
Melimoyu, Cerro ∧ 254 44.05 S 72.52 W
Melincué 252 33.39 S 61.27 W
Melipilla 252 33.42 S 71.13 W
Mélisey 58 47.45 N 6.35 E
Melissa 68 39.18 N 17.01 E
Melissano 68 39.58 N 18.07 E
Melíssia 267c 38.03 N 23.50 E
Melita 184 49.16 N 101.00 W
Melito di Porto Salvo 68 37.55 N 15.47 E
Melitopol' 78 46.50 N 35.22 E
Melívoia 38 39.45 N 22.48 E
Melk 61 48.14 N 15.20 E
Melk ≃ 61 48.14 N 15.19 E
Melk ⊍[1] 61 48.14 N 15.20 E
Melka Teka 144 6.05 N 43.08 E
Melkbosstrand 158 33.43 S 18.27 E
Melksham 42 51.23 N 2.09 W
Mella ≃ 64 45.13 N 10.13 E
Mellansel 26 63.26 N 18.19 E
Mellau 58 47.21 N 9.53 E
Melle, Dtsch. 52 52.12 N 8.20 E
Melle, Fr. 32 46.13 N 0.09 W
Mellègue, Oued ≃ 36 36.32 N 8.51 E
Mellen 190 46.19 N 90.39 W
Mellendorf 52 52.33 N 9.43 E
Mellenville 210 42.15 N 73.40 W
Mellerud 26 58.42 N 12.28 E
Mellette 198 45.09 N 98.29 W
Mellier ≃ 56 49.43 N 5.32 E
Melling 262 53.30 N 2.56 W
Mellingen 54 50.56 N 11.23 E
Mellish Reef I[1] 160 17.25 S 155.50 E
Mellish Rise ✢[3] 14 17.00 S 156.00 E
Mellit 140 14.08 N 25.33 E
Mellone, Monte ∧[2] 267a 41.50 N 12.43 E
Mellong Range ⩕ 170 33.06 S 150.43 E
Mellon Udrigle 46 57.55 N 5.39 W
Mellor 262 53.46 N 2.32 W
Mellor Brook 262 53.47 N 2.33 W
Mellösa 40 59.06 N 16.33 E
Mellrichstadt 56 50.26 N 10.18 E
Mellum I 52 53.40 N 8.10 E
Melmerby 44 54.44 N 2.35 W
Melmore 214 41.02 N 83.07 W
Melmoth 158 28.38 S 31.24 E
Mělník 54 50.20 N 14.29 E
Mel'nikovo, Ross. 26 61.05 N 29.22 E
Mel'nikovo, Ross. 86 56.34 N 84.05 E
Mel'nikovo, Taj. 85 40.19 N 70.19 E
Mel'nytsya-Podil's'ka 78 48.37 N 26.10 E
Melo 252 32.22 S 54.11 W
Melo ≃ 248 21.27 S 57.52 W
Melo, Ilha de I 150 11.02 N 15.13 W
Melocheville 206 45.19 N 73.56 W
Meloco 154 13.25 S 39.08 E
Melolo 115b 9.53 S 120.40 E
Melolo ≃ 115b 9.52 S 120.41 E
Melong 152 5.07 N 9.57 E
Melos → Mílos I 38 36.41 N 24.15 E
Melovaja ≃ 83 49.23 N 40.16 E
Melovoj Syrt ∧ 80 52.15 N 52.35 E
Melozitna ≃ 180 64.46 N 155.29 W
Melrose, Austl. 162 27.56 S 121.19 E
Melrose, Austl. 166 32.42 S 146.58 E
Melrose, Scot., U.K. 46 55.36 N 2.44 W
Melrose, Ma., U.S. 207 42.27 N 71.04 W
Melrose, Mn., U.S. 198 45.40 N 94.48 W
Melrose, N.M., U.S. 196 34.25 N 103.37 W
Melrose, N.Y., U.S. 210 42.50 N 73.37 W
Melrose, Oh., U.S. 216 41.05 N 84.25 W
Melrose, Wi., U.S. 190 44.07 N 90.59 W
Melrose ✦[8] 276 40.49 N 73.55 W
Melrose Abbey ⊍[1] 46 55.37 N 2.45 W
Melrose Park, Fl., U.S. 220 26.06 N 80.12 W
Melrose Park, Il., U.S. 216 41.54 N 87.51 W


**Symbols** in the index entries represent the broad categories identified in the key at the right. Symbols with superior numbers (⩕[1]) identify subcategories (see complete key on page *I · 1*).

**Symbole** im Register stellen die rechts im Schlüssel erklärten Kategorien dar. Symbole mit hochgestellten Ziffern (⩕[1]) bezeichnen Unterabteilungen einer Kategorie (vgl. vollständiger Schlüssel auf Seite *I · 1*).

**Los símbolos** incluídos en el texto del índice representan las grandes categorías identificadas con la clave a la derecha. Los símbolos con numeros en su parte superior (⩕[1]) identifican las subcategorías (véase la clave completa en la página *I · 1*).

**Les symboles** de l'index représentent les catégories indiquées dans la légende à droite. Les symboles suivis d'un indice (⩕[1]) représentent des sous-catégories (voir légende complète à la page *I · 1*).

**Os símbolos** incluídos no texto do índice representam as grandes categorias identificadas com a chave à direita. Os símbolos com números em sua parte superior (⩕[1]) identificam as subcategorias (veja-se a chave completa à página *I · 1*).

| | | | | | |
|---|---|---|---|---|---|
| ∧ | Mountain | Berg | Montaña | Montagne | Montanha |
| ⩕ | Mountains | Gebirge | Montañas | Montagnes | Montanhas |
| ✕ | Pass | Paß | Paso | Col | Passo |
| V | Valley, Canyon | Tal, Cañon | Valle, Cañón | Vallée, Canyon | Vale, Canhão |
| ≚ | Plain | Ebene | Llano | Plaine | Planície |
| › | Cape | Kap | Cabo | Cap | Cabo |
| I | Island | Insel | Isla | Île | Ilha |
| II | Islands | Inseln | Islas | Îles | Ilhas |
| ✦ | Other Topographic Features | Andere Topographische Objekte | Otros Elementos Topográficos | Autres données topographiques | Outros acidentes topográficos |

ESPAÑOL · FRANÇAIS · PORTUGUÊS


| Nombre / Nom / Nome | Página / Page / Página | Lat.°′ | Long.°′ W = Oeste / W = Ouest / W = Oeste |
|---|---|---|---|
| Melrose Park, N.Y., U.S. | 212 | 42.54 N | 76.32 W |
| Melrose Park, Pa., U.S. | 285 | 40.04 N | 75.08 W |
| Mels | 58 | 47.03 N | 9.25 E |
| Melstone | 202 | 46.35 N | 107.52 W |
| Melsungen | 56 | 51.08 N | 9.32 E |
| Meltaus | 24 | 66.54 N | 25.22 E |
| Meltham, Eng., U.K. | 44 | 53.35 N | 1.51 W |
| Meltham, Eng., U.K. | 262 | 53.36 N | 1.51 W |
| Melton, Austl. | 168b | 34.05 S | 137.59 E |
| Melton, Austl. | 169 | 37.41 S | 144.35 E |
| Melton Constable | 42 | 52.53 N | 1.01 E |
| Melton Hill Lake ⊜[1] | 192 | 36.00 N | 84.15 W |
| Melton Mowbray | 42 | 52.46 N | 0.53 W |
| Melton Reservoir ⊜[1] | 169 | 37.43 S | 144.32 E |
| Melúa | 246 | 3.55 N | 72.50 W |
| Meluan | 112 | 1.52 N | 111.56 E |
| Meluco | 154 | 12.36 S | 39.38 E |
| Melúli ≃ | 154 | 16.28 S | 39.44 E |
| Melun, Fr. | 50 | 48.32 N | 2.40 E |
| Melun, Mya. | 110 | 20.14 N | 93.24 E |
| Melunga | 152 | 17.16 S | 16.24 E |
| Melūr | 122 | 10.03 N | 78.20 E |
| Melvaig | 46 | 57.48 N | 5.49 W |
| Melvern | 198 | 38.30 N | 95.38 W |
| Melvern Lake ⊜[1] | 198 | 38.30 N | 95.50 W |
| Melvich | 46 | 58.33 N | 3.55 W |
| Melville, Austl. | 168a | 32.03 S | 115.49 E |
| Melville, Sk., Can. | 184 | 50.55 N | 102.48 W |
| Melville, La., U.S. | 194 | 30.41 N | 91.44 W |
| Melville, N.Y., U.S. | 276 | 40.47 N | 73.24 W |
| Melville ◆[8] | 273d | 26.11 S | 28.00 E |
| Melville, Cape ≻, Austl. | 164 | 14.11 S | 144.30 E |
| Melville, Cape ≻, Pil. | 116 | 7.49 N | 117.01 E |
| Melville, Détroit de → Viscount Melville Sound u | 176 | 74.10 N | 108.00 W |
| Melville, Lake ⊜ | 176 | 53.45 N | 59.30 W |
| Melville Bugt c | 16 | 75.30 N | 63.00 W |
| Melville Hall Airport ⊠ | 240d | 15.33 N | 61.18 W |
| Melville Hills ⋏[2] | 180 | 69.15 N | 124.00 W |
| Melville Island I, Austl. | 164 | 11.40 S | 131.00 E |
| Melville Island I, N.T., Can. | 16 | 75.15 N | 110.00 W |
| Melville Island Aboriginal Reserve ◆[4] | 164 | 11.40 S | 131.00 E |
| Melville Peninsula ≻[1] | 176 | 68.00 N | 84.00 W |
| Melville Sound u, N.T., Can. | 176 | 68.05 N | 107.30 W |
| Melville Sound u, On., Can. | 212 | 44.57 N | 81.05 W |
| Melvin, Il., U.S. | 216 | 40.34 N | 88.15 W |
| Melvin, Ky., U.S. | 192 | 37.21 N | 82.41 W |
| Melvin, Tx., U.S. | 196 | 31.13 N | 99.35 W |
| Melvin, Lough ⊜ | 48 | 54.26 N | 8.10 W |
| Melvindale | 281 | 42.16 N | 83.10 W |
| Melvin Lake ⊜ | 184 | 57.08 N | 100.15 W |
| Melyana | 148 | 36.15 N | 2.15 E |
| Mélykút | 30 | 46.13 N | 19.24 E |
| Melzo | 62 | 45.30 N | 9.25 E |
| Memala | 112 | 1.44 S | 112.36 E |
| Mêmar Co ⊜ | 120 | 34.15 N | 82.20 E |
| Memāri | 126 | 23.12 N | 88.07 E |
| Memba | 154 | 14.11 S | 40.30 E |
| Membalong | 112 | 3.09 S | 107.38 E |
| Memboro | 115b | 9.22 S | 119.32 E |
| Membre | 56 | 49.52 N | 4.54 E |
| Même ≃ | 50 | 48.11 N | 0.39 E |
| Memel → Klaipėda, Liet. | 76 | 55.43 N | 21.07 E |
| Memel, S. Afr. | 158 | 27.43 S | 29.30 E |
| Memel → Nemunas ≃ | 76 | 55.18 N | 21.23 E |
| Mēmele ≃ | 76 | 56.24 N | 24.10 E |
| Memewin, Lac ⊜ | 190 | 46.29 N | 78.42 W |
| Memmert I | 52 | 53.39 N | 6.53 E |
| Memmingen | 58 | 47.59 N | 10.11 E |
| Memo ≃ | 246 | 9.16 N | 66.40 W |
| Memori, Tanjung ≻ | 164 | 0.52 S | 134.08 E |
| Memorial Bridge ◆[5] | 269a | 13.44 N | 100.30 E |
| Memorial Stadium ♠ | 284b | 39.20 N | 76.36 W |
| Mémót | 110 | 11.49 N | 106.11 E |
| Mempawah | 112 | 0.22 N | 108.58 E |
| Memphis, Fl., U.S. | 220 | 27.32 N | 82.33 W |
| Memphis, In., U.S. | 218 | 38.29 N | 85.45 W |
| Memphis, Mi., U.S. | 214 | 42.54 N | 82.46 W |
| Memphis, Mo., U.S. | 194 | 40.27 N | 92.10 W |
| Memphis, Tn., U.S. | 194 | 35.08 N | 90.02 W |
| Memphis, Tx., U.S. | 196 | 34.43 N | 100.32 W |
| Memphis → Mīt Ruhaynah ⊥ | 142 | 29.51 N | 31.15 E |
| Memphis Naval Air Station ■ | 194 | 35.21 N | 89.52 W |
| Memphremagog, Lake ⊜ | 206 | 45.05 N | 72.15 W |
| Memsie | 46 | 57.39 N | 2.02 W |
| Mena, Ityo. | 144 | 6.25 N | 39.51 E |
| Mena, Ukr. | 78 | 51.31 N | 32.13 E |
| Mena, Ar., U.S. | 194 | 34.35 N | 94.14 W |
| Menado → Manado | 112 | 1.29 N | 124.51 E |
| Menaggio | 58 | 46.01 N | 9.14 E |
| Menahga | 198 | 46.45 N | 95.06 W |
| Menai | 274a | 34.01 S | 151.01 E |
| Menai Bridge | 44 | 53.14 N | 4.10 W |
| Menai Strait u | 44 | 53.12 N | 4.12 W |
| Ménaka | 150 | 15.55 N | 2.24 E |
| Menaldum | 52 | 53.12 N | 5.39 E |
| Menan | 202 | 43.43 N | 111.59 W |
| Menands | 210 | 42.41 N | 73.43 W |
| Menangina | 162 | 29.50 S | 121.54 E |
| Menantico Creek ≃ | 208 | 39.20 N | 75.00 W |
| Menarandra ≃ | 157b | 25.17 S | 44.30 E |
| Menard | 196 | 30.55 N | 99.47 W |
| Menard □[6] | 219 | 40.01 N | 89.51 W |
| Menard Creek ≃ | 222 | 30.29 N | 94.50 W |
| Menars | 50 | 47.38 N | 1.24 E |
| Menasha | 190 | 44.12 N | 88.26 W |
| Menate | 112 | 0.14 S | 113.02 E |
| Menawashei | 140 | 12.40 N | 24.59 E |
| Menchang | 105 | 38.54 N | 117.01 E |
| Menchykury | 78 | 47.04 N | 34.48 E |
| Mencué | 254 | 40.25 S | 69.38 W |
| Mend | 89 | 43.40 N | 123.08 E |
| Mendanau, Pulau I | 112 | 2.51 S | 107.26 E |
| Mendarik, Pulau I | 112 | 1.18 N | 107.02 E |
| Mendatai | 102 | 38.51 N | 94.39 E |
| Mendatica | 62 | 44.05 N | 7.49 E |
| Mendawai | 112 | 2.59 S | 113.16 E |
| Mendawai ≃ | 112 | 3.17 S | 113.21 E |
| Mendaya | 115a | 8.23 S | 114.42 E |
| Mende | 32 | 44.30 N | 3.30 E |
| Mendebo ⋏ | 144 | 6.50 N | 39.40 E |
| Mendel' ≃ | 86 | 58.13 N | 90.08 E |
| Mendelejevsk | 80 | 55.54 N | 52.20 E |
| Menden | 56 | 51.26 N | 7.47 E |
| Menden ◆[8] | 263 | 51.24 N | 6.54 E |
| Mendenhall, Ms., U.S. | 194 | 31.57 N | 89.52 W |
| Mendenhall, Pa., U.S. | 285 | 39.51 N | 75.38 W |
| Mendenhall, Cape ≻ | 180 | 59.51 N | 166.15 W |
| Mendes | 256 | 22.32 S | 43.44 W |
| Méndez | 232 | 25.07 N | 98.34 W |
| Mendez-Nuñez | 116 | 14.08 N | 120.54 E |
| Mendham | 210 | 40.46 N | 74.36 W |
| Mendi, Ityo. | 144 | 9.50 N | 35.06 E |
| Mendi, Pap. N. Gui. | 164 | 6.10 S | 143.40 E |
| Mendig | 56 | 50.21 N | 7.15 E |
| Mendip Hills ⋏[2] | 42 | 51.15 N | 2.40 W |
| Mendlesham | 42 | 52.16 N | 1.05 E |
| Mendocino | 204 | 39.18 N | 123.47 W |
| Mendocino, Cape ≻ | 204 | 40.25 N | 124.25 W |
| Mendocino Fracture Zone ✦ | 16 | 40.00 N | 145.00 W |
| Mendola ≃ | 70 | 37.44 N | 13.32 E |
| Mendon, Il., U.S. | 219 | 40.05 N | 91.17 W |
| Mendon, Ma., U.S. | 207 | 42.06 N | 71.33 W |
| Mendon, Mi., U.S. | 216 | 42.00 N | 85.27 W |
| Mendon, N.Y., U.S. | 210 | 43.00 N | 77.34 W |
| Mendon, Oh., U.S. | 216 | 40.40 N | 84.31 W |
| Mendon, Pa., U.S. | 279b | 40.11 N | 79.41 W |
| Mendota, Ca., U.S. | 226 | 36.45 N | 120.22 W |
| Mendota, Il., U.S. | 216 | 41.32 N | 89.07 W |
| Mendota, Lake ⊜ | 216 | 43.05 N | 89.25 W |
| Mendota Dam ◆[6] | 226 | 36.48 N | 120.22 W |
| Mendoza, Arg. | 252 | 32.53 S | 68.49 W |
| Mendoza, Perú | 248 | 6.20 S | 77.24 W |
| Mendoza, Ur. | 258 | 34.17 S | 56.13 W |
| Mendoza □[4] | 252 | 34.30 S | 68.30 W |
| Mendoza ≃ | 252 | 32.21 S | 68.18 W |
| Mendoza, Arroyo de ≃ | 258 | 34.21 S | 56.18 W |
| Mendrisio | 58 | 45.52 N | 8.59 E |
| Mend'ukino | 82 | 54.47 N | 38.51 E |
| Mendung | 112 | 0.31 N | 103.13 E |
| Ménéac | 32 | 48.09 N | 2.28 W |
| Mene de Mauroa | 246 | 10.43 N | 71.01 W |
| Mene Grande | 246 | 9.49 N | 70.56 W |
| Menemen | 130 | 38.36 N | 27.04 E |
| Menen | 50 | 50.48 N | 3.07 E |
| Meneng Point ≻ | 174b | 0.32 S | 166.57 E |
| Menes | 115a | 6.23 S | 105.55 E |
| Menfi | 70 | 37.36 N | 12.58 E |
| Mengalum, Pulau I | 112 | 6.16 N | 115.12 E |
| Mengban | 102 | 23.08 N | 100.19 E |
| Mengbang | 102 | 21.28 N | 101.19 E |
| Mengcheng | 100 | 33.17 N | 116.33 E |
| Mengchi ≃ | 107 | 29.47 N | 104.56 E |
| Mengcun | 98 | 38.06 N | 117.05 E |
| Mengdapu | 104 | 41.35 N | 123.12 E |
| Mengede ◆[8] | 263 | 51.34 N | 7.23 E |
| Mengeh Jek | 120 | 37.02 N | 66.07 E |
| Mengen, Dtsch. | 58 | 48.03 N | 9.20 E |
| Mengen, Tür. | 130 | 40.56 N | 32.04 E |
| Mengeringhausen | 56 | 51.22 N | 8.59 E |
| Mengersgereuth-Hämmern | 54 | 50.24 N | 11.07 E |
| Menges Mills | 208 | 39.52 N | 76.54 W |
| Menggala | 112 | 4.28 S | 105.17 E |
| Menggu | 102 | 26.34 N | 102.57 E |
| Menggubao | 104 | 42.27 N | 122.23 E |
| Menggudai | 102 | 38.10 N | 108.15 E |
| Menghai | 102 | 22.00 N | 100.26 E |
| Menghe | 106 | 32.03 N | 119.47 E |
| Menghun | 102 | 21.44 N | 100.23 E |
| Mengjiacun | 106 | 31.33 N | 118.46 E |
| Mengjiagang | 89 | 46.22 N | 130.40 E |
| Mengjiatai | 104 | 42.06 N | 123.21 E |
| Mengjiawan | 102 | 38.35 N | 109.25 E |
| Mengjiawopeng | 104 | 41.22 N | 121.51 E |
| Mengjiayuanjia | 105 | 40.52 N | 118.08 E |
| Mengjiazhai | 269b | 31.18 N | 121.19 E |
| Mengka | 102 | 25.10 N | 98.01 E |
| Mengkibol | 114 | 1.58 N | 103.20 E |
| Mengkofen | 60 | 48.43 N | 12.27 E |
| Mengkuang | 114 | 3.11 N | 102.24 E |
| Menglian | 102 | 22.20 N | 99.38 E |
| Menglinghausen ◆[8] | 263 | 51.28 N | 7.25 E |
| Mengluchang | 107 | 29.19 N | 103.35 E |
| Mengmucun | 106 | 31.59 N | 119.01 E |
| Mengong | 152 | 2.56 N | 11.25 E |
| Mengqigou | 104 | 42.00 N | 121.08 E |
| Mengshan | 102 | 24.07 N | 110.33 E |
| Meng Shan ⋏, Zhg. | 98 | 35.44 N | 117.45 E |
| Meng Shan ⋏, Zhg. | 104 | 41.50 N | 121.10 E |
| Mengtong | 107 | 30.44 N | 105.53 E |
| Mengulek, gora ∧ | 86 | 50.58 N | 89.30 E |
| Mengwang | 102 | 22.26 N | 100.34 E |
| Mengyin | 98 | 35.45 N | 117.57 E |
| Mengzhe | 102 | 22.02 N | 100.16 E |
| Mengzhi | 102 | 24.10 N | 99.46 E |
| Mengzi | 102 | 23.22 N | 103.20 E |
| Menihek Lakes ⊜ | 176 | 54.00 N | 66.35 W |
| Ménil-la-Tour | 56 | 48.46 N | 5.52 E |
| Menindee | 166 | 32.24 S | 142.26 E |
| Menindee Lake ⊜ | 166 | 32.21 S | 142.20 E |
| Meningie | 166 | 35.42 S | 139.20 E |
| Menjiaqiangzi | 104 | 42.29 N | 121.19 E |
| Menkoutang | 106 | 31.01 N | 119.27 E |
| Menlo | 224 | 46.37 N | 123.38 W |
| Menlo Park | 226 | 37.27 N | 122.10 W |
| Menlo Park Mall ◆[9] | 276 | 40.32 N | 74.20 W |
| Menlo Park Terrace | 276 | 40.32 N | 74.20 W |
| Mennecy | 261 | 48.34 N | 2.26 E |
| Mennetou-sur-Cher | 50 | 47.16 N | 1.53 E |
| Mennighüffen | 52 | 52.13 N | 8.43 E |
| Menno | 198 | 43.14 N | 97.34 W |
| Meno, Indon. | 164 | 3.52 S | 135.31 E |
| Meno, Ok., U.S. | 196 | 36.23 N | 98.10 W |
| Menominee | 190 | 45.06 N | 87.36 W |
| Menominee ≃ | 190 | 45.05 N | 87.36 W |
| Menominee Indian Reservation ◆[4] | 190 | 45.00 N | 88.45 W |
| Menomonee ≃ | 216 | 43.02 N | 87.54 W |
| Menomonee Falls | 216 | 43.10 N | 88.07 W |
| Menomonie | 190 | 44.52 N | 91.55 W |
| Menongue | 152 | 14.36 S | 17.48 E |
| Menor, Mar c | 34 | 37.43 N | 0.48 W |
| Menorca I | 34 | 40.00 N | 4.00 E |
| Mens | 62 | 44.49 N | 5.45 E |
| Menslage | 52 | 52.41 N | 7.49 E |
| Menston | 44 | 53.53 N | 1.44 W |
| Menstrup | 41 | 55.13 N | 11.36 E |
| Mentana | 66 | 42.02 N | 12.38 E |
| Mentasta Lake | 180 | 62.55 N | 143.45 W |
| Mentasta Mountains ⋏ | 180 | 62.40 N | 143.07 W |
| Mentawai, Kepulauan II | 108 | 2.00 S | 99.30 E |
| Mentawai, Selat u | 108 | 1.45 S | 100.00 E |
| Mentekab | 114 | 3.29 N | 102.21 E |
| Menteke, peski ◆[2] | 80 | 47.20 N | 50.40 E |
| Menteng ◆[8] | 269e | 6.12 S | 106.50 E |
| Menteroda | 54 | 51.18 N | 10.33 E |
| Menthon-Saint-Bernard | 62 | 45.51 N | 6.12 E |
| Menton | 62 | 43.47 N | 7.30 E |
| Mentone, Austl. | 274b | 37.59 S | 145.05 E |
| Mentone → Menton, Fr. | 62 | 43.47 N | 7.30 E |
| Mentone, Ca., U.S. | 228 | 34.05 N | 117.08 W |
| Mentone, In., U.S. | 216 | 41.10 N | 86.02 W |
| Mentone, Tx., U.S. | 196 | 31.42 N | 103.36 W |
| Mentor, Ky., U.S. | 218 | 38.53 N | 84.14 W |
| Mentor, Oh., U.S. | 214 | 41.39 N | 81.20 W |
| Mentor-on-the-Lake | 214 | 41.42 N | 81.21 W |
| Mentougou | 105 | 39.56 N | 116.03 E |
| Mentzdam ⊜[1] | 158 | 33.10 S | 25.09 E |
| Menucourt | 261 | 49.02 N | 1.59 E |
| Menuma | 94 | 36.13 N | 139.23 E |
| Men'uša | 76 | 58.23 N | 30.42 E |
| Menyamya | 164 | 7.10 S | 146.00 E |
| Menyapa, Gunung ∧ | 112 | 1.05 N | 116.05 E |
| Menyuan | 102 | 37.27 N | 101.48 E |
| Menza ≃ | 88 | 50.14 N | 108.38 E |
| Menzel Bourguiba | 148 | 37.10 N | 9.48 E |
| Menzel Bou Zelfa | 36 | 36.41 N | 10.36 E |
| Menzel Djemil | 36 | 37.14 N | 9.55 E |
| Menzelen | 52 | 51.37 N | 6.32 E |
| Menzelerheide | 263 | 51.37 N | 6.31 E |
| Menzelinsk | 80 | 55.43 N | 53.08 E |
| Menzel Temime | 148 | 36.47 N | 10.59 E |
| Menzenschwand | 58 | 47.49 N | 8.04 E |
| Menzies | 162 | 29.41 S | 121.02 E |
| Menzies, Mount ∧ | 9 | 73.30 S | 61.50 E |
| Menziken | 58 | 47.14 N | 8.12 E |
| Meobbaai c | 156 | 24.25 S | 14.34 E |
| Meola Āgri | 272a | 28.42 N | 77.23 E |
| Meolo | 64 | 45.37 N | 12.27 E |
| Meon ≃ | 42 | 50.48 N | 1.15 W |
| Meopham | 260 | 51.22 N | 0.22 E |
| Meopham Station | 260 | 51.23 N | 0.21 E |
| Meoqui | 232 | 28.17 N | 105.29 W |
| Meota | 184 | 53.02 N | 108.27 W |
| Méouge ≃ | 62 | 44.16 N | 5.50 E |
| Méounes-lès-Montrieux | 62 | 43.17 N | 5.58 E |
| Mepal | 42 | 52.24 N | 0.07 E |
| Mepisckaro, gora ∧ | 84 | 41.50 N | 42.40 E |
| Meppel | 52 | 52.42 N | 6.11 E |
| Meppen | 52 | 52.41 N | 7.17 E |
| Meqerghane, Sebkha ≚ | 148 | 26.19 N | 1.20 E |
| Meqruur | 174q | 9.31 N | 138.09 E |
| Mequinenza, Embalse de ⊜[1] | 34 | 41.20 N | 0.05 E |
| Mequon | 216 | 43.13 N | 87.59 W |
| Mer | 50 | 47.42 N | 1.30 E |
| Mera ≃ | 58 | 46.11 N | 9.25 E |
| Merah | 112 | 0.50 N | 116.48 E |
| Merai | 164 | 4.50 S | 152.20 E |
| Meråker | 26 | 63.26 N | 11.45 E |
| Merakurak | 115a | 6.53 S | 111.59 E |
| Meramangye, Lake ⊜ | 162 | 28.25 S | 132.13 E |
| Merambéllou, Kólpos c | 38 | 35.14 N | 25.47 E |
| Meramec ≃ | 194 | 38.23 N | 90.21 W |
| Meramec Caverns ⊥[5] | 219 | 38.15 N | 91.06 W |
| Meramec State Park ♠ | 219 | 38.14 N | 91.05 W |
| Meran → Merano, It. | 64 | 46.40 N | 11.09 E |
| Meran, Nig. | 273a | 6.38 N | 3.16 E |
| Meranggau | 112 | 0.12 S | 110.17 E |
| Merangin ≃ | 112 | 2.09 S | 102.47 E |
| Merano (Meran) | 64 | 46.40 N | 11.09 E |
| Merapi, Gunung ∧ | 115a | 8.03 S | 114.15 E |
| Merapoh | 114 | 4.41 N | 101.59 E |
| Merasheen | 186 | 47.25 N | 54.21 W |
| Merasheen Island I | 186 | 47.30 N | 54.15 W |
| Merate | 62 | 45.42 N | 9.25 E |
| Meratus, Pegunungan ⋏ | 112 | 2.45 S | 115.40 E |
| Merauke | 164 | 8.28 S | 140.20 E |
| Merauke ≃ | 164 | 8.30 S | 140.24 E |
| Merbabu, Gunung ∧ | 115a | 7.27 S | 110.26 E |
| Merbau, Indon. | 114 | 1.07 N | 102.33 E |
| Merbau, Indon. | 114 | 2.16 N | 99.50 E |
| Merbein | 166 | 34.11 S | 142.04 E |
| Merca → Marka | 144 | 1.43 N | 44.53 E |
| Mercaderes | 246 | 1.47 N | 77.10 W |
| Mercantour, Parc National du ♠ | 62 | 44.10 N | 7.00 E |
| Mercāra | 122 | 12.25 N | 75.44 E |
| Mercatale | 66 | 43.15 N | 12.08 E |
| Mercato San Severino | 68 | 40.47 N | 14.46 E |
| Mercato Saraceno | 66 | 43.57 N | 12.12 E |
| Merced | 226 | 37.18 N | 120.28 W |
| Merced □[6] | 226 | 37.15 N | 120.40 W |
| Merced ≃ | 226 | 37.21 N | 120.58 W |
| Merced, Lake ⊜ | 282 | 37.43 N | 122.29 W |
| Merced, North Fork ≃ | 226 | 37.37 N | 120.03 W |
| Merced, South Fork ≃ | 226 | 37.39 N | 119.53 W |
| Merced Airport ⊠ | 226 | 37.17 N | 120.31 W |
| Mercedario, Cerro ∧ | 252 | 31.59 S | 70.07 W |
| Mercedes, Arg. | 252 | 29.12 S | 58.05 W |
| Mercedes, Arg. | 252 | 33.40 S | 65.28 W |
| Mercedes, Arg. | 258 | 34.39 S | 59.27 W |
| Mercedes, Pil. | 116 | 14.07 N | 123.01 E |
| Mercedes, Tx., U.S. | 196 | 26.08 N | 97.54 W |
| Mercedes, Ur. | 252 | 33.16 S | 58.01 W |
| Mercer, N.Z. | 172 | 37.16 S | 175.03 E |
| Mercer, Mo., U.S. | 194 | 40.30 N | 93.31 W |
| Mercer, Oh., U.S. | 216 | 40.40 N | 84.35 W |
| Mercer, Pa., U.S. | 214 | 41.13 N | 80.14 W |
| Mercer, Wi., U.S. | 190 | 46.09 N | 90.03 W |
| Mercer □[6], N.J., U.S. | 208 | 40.13 N | 74.45 W |
| Mercer □[6], Oh., U.S. | 216 | 40.33 N | 84.34 W |
| Mercer □[6], Pa., U.S. | 214 | 41.14 N | 80.15 W |
| Mercer Island | 224 | 47.35 N | 122.15 W |
| Mercersburg | 188 | 39.49 N | 77.54 W |
| Mercerville | 208 | 40.14 N | 74.41 W |
| Mercês, Bra. | 256 | 21.12 S | 43.21 W |
| Mercês, Port. | 266c | 38.47 N | 9.19 W |
| Merchants Bay c | 176 | 67.10 N | 62.50 W |
| Merchants Millpond ⊜ | 208 | 36.26 N | 76.41 W |
| Merchantville | 285 | 39.56 N | 75.04 W |
| Merchong ≃ | 114 | 3.03 N | 103.27 E |
| Merchtem | 50 | 50.58 N | 4.14 E |
| Mercier (Saint-Philomène) | 275a | 45.19 N | 73.45 W |
| Mercier, Pont ◆[5] | 275a | 45.25 N | 73.39 W |
| Mercoal | 182 | 53.10 N | 117.05 W |
| Mercogliano | 68 | 40.55 N | 14.44 E |
| Mercury | 204 | 36.40 N | 115.59 W |
| Mercury Islands II | 172 | 36.35 S | 175.55 E |
| Mercy, Cape ≻ | 176 | 64.53 N | 63.32 W |
| Mercy Bay c | 176 | 74.05 N | 119.00 W |
| Mercy-le-Bas | 56 | 49.23 N | 5.45 E |
| Merdeka Bridge ◆[5] | 271c | 1.18 N | 103.53 E |
| Méré, Fr. | 261 | 48.47 N | 1.49 E |
| Mere, Eng., U.K. | 42 | 51.06 N | 2.16 W |
| Mere, Eng., U.K. | 262 | 53.20 N | 2.25 W |
| Mere Brow | 262 | 53.40 N | 2.53 W |
| Mereckij | 85 | 43.48 N | 74.42 E |
| Mereclough | 262 | 53.46 N | 2.11 W |
| Meredale | 273d | 26.17 S | 27.59 E |
| Meredith, Austl. | 169 | 37.51 S | 144.04 E |
| Meredith, N.H., U.S. | 188 | 43.39 N | 71.30 W |
| Meredith, Cape ≻ | 254 | 52.15 S | 60.39 W |
| Meredith, Lake ⊜[1] | 196 | 35.36 N | 101.42 W |
| Meredosia | 219 | 39.50 N | 90.34 W |
| Meredosia Lake ⊜ | 219 | 39.52 N | 90.33 W |
| Mereeg | 144 | 3.46 N | 47.18 E |
| Merefa | 78 | 49.49 N | 36.03 E |
| Méré Lava I | 175f | 14.25 S | 168.03 E |
| Merelbeke | 50 | 51.00 N | 3.45 E |
| Mereni | 38 | 46.58 N | 29.04 E |
| Merenkurkku (Norra Kvarken) u | 26 | 63.36 N | 20.43 E |
| Merevari ≃ | 246 | 4.28 N | 63.57 W |
| Méréville | 50 | 48.19 N | 2.05 E |
| Merewa | 144 | 7.40 N | 37.00 E |
| Merewether | 170 | 32.57 S | 151.46 E |
| Mereworth | 260 | 51.15 N | 0.23 E |
| Mergenevo | 80 | 49.56 N | 51.17 E |
| Mergozzo | 58 | 45.58 N | 8.26 E |
| Mergui (Myeik) | 110 | 12.26 N | 98.36 E |
| Mergui Archipelago II | 110 | 12.00 N | 98.00 E |
| Merḥavya | 132 | 32.36 N | 35.19 E |
| Meria | 272b | 22.59 N | 88.20 E |
| Meribah | 166 | 34.42 S | 140.51 E |
| Méribel | 62 | 45.25 N | 6.34 E |
| Meriç | 130 | 41.11 N | 26.25 E |
| Meriç (Marica) (Évros) ≃ | 38 | 40.52 N | 26.12 E |
| Méricourt | 50 | 50.24 N | 2.52 E |
| Mérida, Esp. | 34 | 38.55 N | 6.20 W |
| Mérida, Méx. | 200 | 32.39 N | 114.58 W |
| Mérida, Méx. | 232 | 20.58 N | 89.37 W |
| Merida, Pil. | 116 | 10.55 N | 124.32 E |
| Mérida, Ven. | 246 | 8.36 N | 71.08 W |
| Mérida □[3] | 246 | 8.30 N | 71.10 W |
| Mérida, Cordillera de ⋏ | 246 | 8.40 N | 71.00 W |
| Meridale | 210 | 42.22 N | 74.57 W |
| Meriden, Eng., U.K. | 42 | 52.26 N | 1.37 W |
| Meriden, Ct., U.S. | 207 | 41.32 N | 72.48 W |
| Meriden, N.J., U.S. | 276 | 40.57 N | 74.28 W |
| Meridian, Ca., U.S. | 226 | 39.09 N | 121.55 W |
| Meridian, Ga., U.S. | 192 | 31.27 N | 81.22 W |
| Meridian, Id., U.S. | 202 | 43.36 N | 116.23 W |
| Meridian, Ms., U.S. | 194 | 32.21 N | 88.42 W |
| Meridian, N.Y., U.S. | 210 | 43.09 N | 76.32 W |
| Meridian, Pa., U.S. | 214 | 40.51 N | 79.58 W |
| Meridian, Tx., U.S. | 222 | 31.55 N | 97.39 W |
| Meridian Hills | 218 | 39.53 N | 86.09 W |
| Meridian Naval Air Station ■ | 194 | 32.33 N | 88.34 W |
| Meridianville | 194 | 34.51 N | 86.34 W |
| Mériel | 261 | 49.05 N | 2.12 E |
| Mérignac | 32 | 44.50 N | 0.42 W |
| Merigold | 194 | 33.50 N | 90.43 W |
| Merikarvia | 26 | 61.51 N | 21.30 E |
| Merille, Laga ≃ | 154 | 1.25 N | 38.26 E |
| Merimbula | 166 | 36.53 S | 149.54 E |
| Merín, Laguna (Lagoa Mirim) c | 252 | 32.45 S | 52.50 W |
| Merinda | 166 | 20.01 S | 148.10 E |
| Mering | 60 | 48.16 N | 10.59 E |
| Meringa | 146 | 10.44 N | 12.09 E |
| Merin Gubai | 144 | 1.26 N | 44.20 E |
| Meringur | 166 | 34.24 S | 141.16 E |
| Merino | 198 | 40.28 N | 103.21 W |
| Merinos | 252 | 32.24 S | 56.54 W |
| Merion Station | 285 | 39.59 N | 75.15 W |
| Merir I | 108 | 4.19 N | 132.19 E |
| Merishausen | 58 | 47.45 N | 8.37 E |
| Merit | 222 | 33.13 N | 96.17 W |
| Merivale Gardens | 212 | 45.19 N | 75.44 W |
| Meriwether Farms | 285 | 39.58 N | 75.34 W |
| Merizo | 174p | 13.16 N | 144.40 E |
| Merke | 85 | 42.52 N | 73.11 E |
| Merkel | 196 | 32.28 N | 100.00 W |
| Merkem | 50 | 50.57 N | 2.51 E |
| Merkendorf | 56 | 49.12 N | 10.42 E |
| Merkinė | 76 | 54.10 N | 24.10 E |
| Merklín | 60 | 49.34 N | 13.07 E |
| Merklingen | 58 | 48.30 N | 9.44 E |
| Merkourovoúni ∧ | 267c | 37.54 N | 23.48 E |
| Merksem | 50 | 51.15 N | 4.27 E |
| Merksplas | 56 | 51.22 N | 4.52 E |
| Merkulavičy | 76 | 52.58 N | 30.36 E |
| Merkys ≃ | 76 | 54.10 N | 24.11 E |
| Merlara | 64 | 45.10 N | 11.26 E |
| Merlejevo | 82 | 55.05 N | 37.13 E |
| Merlimau, Pulau I | 271c | 1.17 N | 103.42 E |
| Merlimont-Plage | 50 | 50.28 N | 1.35 E |
| Merlin, On., Can. | 214 | 42.14 N | 82.14 W |
| Merlin, Or., U.S. | 202 | 42.31 N | 123.25 W |
| Merlin Seamount ✦[3] | 14 | 9.05 S | 150.44 W |
| Merlo, Arg. | 252 | 32.21 S | 65.02 W |
| Merlo, Arg. | 258 | 34.40 S | 58.45 W |
| Merlo □[5] | 288 | 34.40 S | 58.45 W |
| Merlo, Aeródromo ⊠ | 288 | 34.41 S | 58.45 W |
| Merlynston | 274b | 37.43 S | 144.58 E |
| Mermaid Beach | 171a | 28.03 S | 153.27 E |
| Mern | 41 | 55.03 N | 12.04 E |
| Merna | 198 | 41.29 N | 99.45 W |
| Mernye | 30 | 46.30 N | 17.50 E |
| Meroe ⊥ | 140 | 16.56 N | 33.43 E |
| Meron | 132 | 32.59 N | 35.26 E |
| Meron, Hare ∧ | 132 | 32.58 N | 35.25 E |
| Meros, Ponta dos ≻ | 256 | 23.13 S | 44.21 W |
| Merotai Besar | 112 | 4.26 N | 117.46 E |
| Merouana | 34 | 35.38 N | 5.55 E |
| Merouane, Chott ⊜ | 148 | 34.00 N | 6.02 E |
| Mer'oža | 76 | 59.02 N | 36.23 E |
| Merredin | 162 | 31.29 S | 118.16 E |
| Merrick | 276 | 40.39 N | 73.33 W |
| Merrick ∧ | 44 | 55.08 N | 4.29 W |
| Merrick Bay c | 276 | 40.38 N | 73.33 W |
| Merrickville | 212 | 44.55 N | 75.50 W |
| Merri Creek ≃ | 169 | 37.48 S | 145.01 E |
| Merriewold Lake | 210 | 41.22 N | 74.12 W |
| Merrifield | 284c | 38.52 N | 77.13 W |
| Merrill, Ia., U.S. | 198 | 42.43 N | 96.14 W |
| Merrill, Mi., U.S. | 190 | 43.24 N | 84.19 W |
| Merrill, Or., U.S. | 202 | 42.01 N | 121.35 W |
| Merrill, Wi., U.S. | 190 | 45.10 N | 89.41 W |
| Merrillan | 190 | 44.27 N | 90.50 W |
| Merrill C. Meigs Field ⊠ | 278 | 41.52 N | 87.37 W |
| Merrill Lake ⊜ | 212 | 44.55 N | 77.24 W |
| Merrill Lake ⊜[1] | 224 | 46.05 N | 122.19 W |
| Merrillville | 216 | 41.28 N | 87.19 W |
| Merrimac | 207 | 42.49 N | 71.00 W |
| Merrimack ≃ | 188 | 42.49 N | 70.49 W |
| Merrimack College ʋ[2] | 283 | 42.40 N | 71.08 W |
| Merrimac Terrace | 283 | 42.49 N | 71.00 W |
| Merriman, S. Afr. | 158 | 31.13 S | 23.38 E |
| Merriman, Ne., U.S. | 198 | 42.55 N | 101.42 W |
| Merrionette Park | 278 | 41.41 N | 87.42 W |
| Merriott | 42 | 50.54 N | 2.48 W |
| Merritt, B.C., Can. | 182 | 50.07 N | 120.47 W |
| Merritt, Wa., U.S. | 224 | 47.47 N | 120.51 W |
| Merritt, Lake ⊜[1] | 282 | 37.48 N | 122.16 W |
| Merritt Island | 220 | 28.21 N | 80.42 W |
| Merritt Island I | 220 | 28.33 N | 80.40 W |
| Merritt Reservoir ⊜[1] | 198 | 42.35 N | 100.55 W |
| Merriwa | 166 | 32.08 S | 150.21 E |
| Mer Rouge | 194 | 32.46 N | 91.47 W |
| Merrow | 207 | 41.49 N | 72.18 W |
| Merrygoen | 166 | 31.50 S | 149.14 E |
| Merrylands | 274a | 33.50 S | 150.59 E |
| Merrymount Park ♠ | 283 | 42.16 N | 71.01 W |
| Merryville | 194 | 30.45 N | 93.32 W |
| Mersa Fatma | 144 | 14.55 N | 40.20 E |
| Mersa Matruh → Marsā Maṭrūḥ | 140 | 31.21 N | 27.14 E |
| Mersch | 56 | 49.46 N | 6.06 E |
| Merscheid ◆[8] | 263 | 51.10 N | 7.01 E |
| Merse V | 46 | 55.39 N | 2.15 W |
| Merse ≃ | 66 | 43.05 N | 11.22 E |
| Mersea Island I | 42 | 51.47 N | 0.55 E |
| Merseburg | 54 | 51.21 N | 11.59 E |
| Mersey ≃, Austl. | 166 | 41.10 S | 146.22 E |
| Mersey ≃, N.S., Can. | 186 | 44.02 N | 64.43 W |
| Mersey ≃, Eng., U.K. | 44 | 53.25 N | 3.00 W |
| Merseyside □[6] | 44 | 53.25 N | 2.50 W |
| Mersey Tunnel ◆[5] | 262 | 53.24 N | 3.00 W |
| Mersin → İçel | 130 | 36.48 N | 34.38 E |
| Mersing | 114 | 2.26 N | 103.50 E |
| Mers-les-Bains | 50 | 50.04 N | 1.23 E |
| Mērsrags | 76 | 57.21 N | 23.07 E |
| Merstham | 260 | 51.16 N | 0.09 W |
| Merta | 120 | 26.39 N | 74.02 E |
| Merta Road | 120 | 26.43 N | 73.55 E |
| Merthyr Tydfil | 42 | 51.46 N | 3.23 W |
| Merti | 154 | 1.04 N | 38.40 E |
| Mertingen | 56 | 48.39 N | 10.47 E |
| Mértola | 34 | 37.38 N | 7.40 W |
| Merton, Austl. | 169 | 36.59 S | 145.42 E |
| Merton, Wi., U.S. | 216 | 43.08 N | 88.18 W |
| Merton ◆[8] | 42 | 51.25 N | 0.12 W |
| Mertz Glacier Tongue Π | 9 | 67.40 S | 144.45 E |
| Mertzon | 196 | 31.16 N | 100.49 W |
| Mertztown | 208 | 40.30 N | 75.40 W |
| Méru, Fr. | 50 | 49.14 N | 2.08 E |
| Meru, Kenya | 154 | 0.03 N | 37.39 E |
| Meru, Mount ∧ | 154 | 3.14 S | 36.45 E |
| Meru National Park ♠ | 154 | 0.10 N | 38.15 E |
| Meruoca | 250 | 3.28 S | 40.28 W |
| Merv → Mary | 128 | 37.36 N | 61.50 E |
| Mervans | 58 | 46.48 N | 5.11 E |
| Merville | 50 | 50.38 N | 2.38 E |
| Mervin | 184 | 53.20 N | 108.53 W |
| Merwede | 158 | 31.38 S | 23.48 E |
| Merweville | 158 | 32.40 S | 21.31 E |
| Merwin, Lake ⊜[1] | 224 | 45.59 N | 122.26 W |
| Merxleben | 54 | 51.07 N | 10.40 E |
| Mëry, Bela. | 76 | 55.37 N | 27.38 E |
| Mery, Ross. | 82 | 55.49 N | 36.36 E |
| Méry-la-Bataille | 50 | 49.33 N | 2.38 E |
| Méry-sur-Oise | 261 | 49.04 N | 2.11 E |
| Méry-sur-Seine | 50 | 48.30 N | 3.53 E |
| Merzen | 52 | 52.29 N | 7.50 E |
| Merzenich | 56 | 50.50 N | 6.32 E |
| Merzhausen | 58 | 47.58 N | 7.49 E |
| Merzifon | 130 | 40.53 N | 35.29 E |
| Merzig | 56 | 49.27 N | 6.36 E |
| Mesa, Micron. | 175c | 7.21 N | 151.51 E |
| Mesa, Moç. | 154 | 13.00 S | 39.33 E |
| Mesa, S. Afr. | 158 | 26.29 S | 26.59 E |
| Mesa, Az., U.S. | 200 | 33.25 N | 111.49 W |
| Mesa ≃ | 34 | 41.15 N | 1.48 W |
| Mesa, Cerro ∧ | 254 | 48.46 S | 71.29 W |
| Mesabi Range ⋏[2] | 190 | 47.30 N | 92.50 W |
| Mesachie Lake | 224 | 48.49 N | 124.07 W |
| Mesa del Nayar | 234 | 22.16 N | 104.35 W |
| Mesa de Santa Rita | 234 | 23.04 N | 105.31 W |
| Mesagne | 68 | 40.33 N | 17.49 E |
| Mes'agutovo | 86 | 55.35 N | 58.20 E |
| Mesaména | 152 | 3.44 N | 12.50 E |
| Mesa Mountain ∧ | 200 | 37.55 N | 106.38 W |
| Mesarás, Kólpos c | 38 | 34.58 N | 24.36 E |
| Mesa Verde National Park ♠ | 200 | 37.13 N | 108.30 W |
| Mescalero | 200 | 33.09 N | 105.46 W |
| Mescalero Apache Indian Reservation ◆[4] | 200 | 33.12 N | 105.40 W |
| Meščerino, Ross. | 76 | 53.37 N | 37.23 E |
| Meščerino, Ross. | 82 | 55.11 N | 38.21 E |
| Meščerskij | 265b | 55.40 N | 37.25 E |
| Meščerskoje | 82 | 55.17 N | 37.38 E |
| Meschede | 56 | 51.20 N | 8.17 E |
| Meschetskij chrebet ⋏ | 84 | 41.48 N | 42.30 E |
| Mescit Tepe ∧ | 130 | 40.22 N | 41.11 E |
| Meščovsk | 76 | 54.19 N | 35.17 E |
| Meščura | 24 | 63.20 N | 50.52 E |
| Mese | 58 | 46.17 N | 9.21 E |
| Mèsè Atet | 110 | 18.38 N | 97.39 E |
| Mesen-Bucht → Mezenskaja guba c | 24 | 66.40 N | 43.45 E |
| Mesero | 266b | 45.30 N | 8.51 E |
| Mesewa → Mitsiwa | 144 | 15.38 N | 39.28 E |
| Mesfinto | 144 | 13.20 N | 37.19 E |
| Mesgarābād | 267d | 35.37 N | 51.31 E |
| Mesgouez, Lac ⊜ | 176 | 51.24 N | 75.05 W |
| Meshed → Mashhad | 128 | 36.18 N | 59.36 E |
| Meshgīn Shahr | 128 | 38.24 N | 47.40 E |
| Meshomasic Mountain ∧ | 207 | 41.38 N | 72.32 W |
| Meshoppen | 210 | 41.34 N | 76.03 W |
| Meshoppen Creek ≃ | 210 | 41.37 N | 76.03 W |
| Mesick | 190 | 44.24 N | 85.42 W |
| Mesier, Canal u | 254 | 48.20 S | 74.33 W |
| Mesilinka ≃ | 182 | 56.09 N | 124.28 W |
| Mesilla | 200 | 32.16 N | 106.48 W |
| Mesillas, Méx. | 234 | 23.14 N | 106.03 W |
| Mesillas, Méx. | 234 | 23.33 N | 103.35 W |
| Mesima ≃ | 68 | 38.30 N | 15.55 E |
| Meskiana | 148 | 35.39 N | 7.41 E |
| Meskiana, Oued ≃ | 36 | 35.49 N | 7.53 E |
| Meskine | 146 | 11.25 N | 15.21 E |
| Meškuičiai | 76 | 56.05 N | 23.28 E |
| Meskum | 114 | 1.34 N | 102.01 E |
| Meslay-du-Maine | 32 | 47.57 N | 0.33 W |
| Meslay-le-Grenet | 50 | 48.22 N | 1.23 E |
| Mesnil-Val-Plage | 50 | 50.03 N | 1.20 E |
| Mesocco | 58 | 46.23 N | 9.14 E |
| Mesola | 66 | 44.55 N | 12.14 E |
| Mesolcina, Valle V | 58 | 46.20 N | 9.10 E |
| Mesolóngion | 38 | 38.21 N | 21.17 E |
| Mesomikenda Lake ⊜ | 190 | 47.40 N | 81.53 W |
| Mesopotamia | 214 | 41.27 N | 80.57 W |
| Mesopotamia □[9] | 128 | 34.00 N | 44.00 E |
| Mesoraca | 68 | 39.05 N | 16.48 E |
| Mesóyia □[9] | 267c | 37.56 N | 23.53 E |
| Mespelbrunn ⊥ | 56 | 49.54 N | 9.19 E |
| Mesquita, Bra. | 255 | 19.13 S | 42.35 W |
| Mesquita, Bra. | 256 | 22.48 S | 43.26 W |
| Mesquite, Nv., U.S. | 204 | 36.48 N | 114.03 W |
| Mesquite, Tx., U.S. | 222 | 32.46 N | 96.35 W |
| Messach Mellet ⋏[2] | 146 | 24.30 N | 11.35 E |
| Messalo ≃ | 154 | 11.40 S | 40.26 E |
| Messaoud, Oued V | 148 | 27.28 N | 0.21 W |
| Messdorf | 54 | 52.43 N | 11.33 E |
| Messina, It. | 70 | 38.11 N | 15.33 E |
| Messina, S. Afr. | 156 | 22.23 S | 30.00 E |
| Messina □[4] | 70 | 38.03 N | 14.52 E |
| Messina, Stretto di u | 70 | 38.15 N | 15.35 E |
| Messinge ≃ | 154 | 11.34 S | 35.25 E |
| Messingham | 44 | 53.32 N | 0.39 W |
| Messíni | 38 | 37.04 N | 22.00 E |
| Messíni ⊥ | 38 | 37.11 N | 21.57 E |
| Messiniakós Kólpos c | 38 | 36.58 N | 22.00 E |
| Messix Peak ∧ | 202 | 41.29 N | 112.31 W |
| Messkirch | 58 | 47.59 N | 9.07 E |
| Messojacha ≃ | 74 | 67.52 N | 77.27 E |
| Messondo | 152 | 3.43 N | 10.28 E |
| Messtetten | 58 | 48.11 N | 8.58 E |
| Messy | 261 | 48.58 N | 2.42 E |
| Mestá | 38 | 38.15 N | 25.55 E |
| Mesta (Néstos) ≃ | 38 | 40.41 N | 24.44 E |
| Mestasa | 148 | 35.07 N | 4.25 W |
| Městečko | 60 | 50.03 N | 13.52 E |
| Mestghanem | 148 | 35.51 N | 0.07 E |
| Mestia | 84 | 43.03 N | 42.43 E |
| Mestlin | 54 | 53.35 N | 11.56 E |
| Město Touškov | 60 | 49.46 N | 13.15 E |
| Mestre | 64 | 45.29 N | 12.15 E |
| Mestrino | 64 | 45.26 N | 11.45 E |
| Mesudiye | 130 | 40.28 N | 37.46 E |
| Mesuji ≃ | 112 | 4.08 S | 105.52 E |
| Mesum | 52 | 52.13 N | 7.29 E |
| Meszah Peak ∧ | 180 | 58.28 N | 131.26 W |
| Meta, It. | 68 | 40.39 N | 14.24 E |
| Meta, Mo., U.S. | 219 | 38.18 N | 92.09 W |
| Meta □[5] | 246 | 3.30 N | 73.00 W |
| Meta ≃ | 246 | 6.12 N | 67.28 W |
| Métabief | 58 | 46.47 N | 6.21 E |
| Metagācha | 272b | 22.38 N | 88.31 E |
| Metahara | 144 | 8.54 N | 39.55 E |
| Meta Incognita Peninsula ≻[1] | 176 | 62.45 N | 68.30 W |
| Metairie | 194 | 29.59 N | 90.09 W |
| Metaline Falls | 202 | 48.51 N | 117.22 W |
| Metallifere, Colline ⋏ | 66 | 43.15 N | 11.00 E |
| Metallostroj | 265a | 59.47 N | 30.33 E |
| Metamora, Il., U.S. | 190 | 40.47 N | 89.21 W |
| Metamora, In., U.S. | 218 | 39.26 N | 85.08 W |
| Metamora, Mi., U.S. | 216 | 42.56 N | 83.17 W |
| Metamora, Oh., U.S. | 216 | 41.42 N | 83.54 W |
| Metán | 252 | 25.29 S | 64.57 W |
| Metangula | 154 | 12.43 S | 34.49 E |
| Metapán | 236 | 14.20 N | 89.27 W |
| Metapontum ⊥ | 68 | 40.23 N | 16.50 E |
| Metarica | 154 | 14.20 S | 36.48 E |
| Metates | 234 | 23.46 N | 106.02 W |
| Metaurilia | 66 | 43.49 N | 13.03 E |
| Metauro ≃ | 66 | 43.50 N | 13.03 E |
| Metcalfe | 212 | 45.14 N | 75.28 W |
| Metchosin | 224 | 48.22 N | 123.33 W |
| Metechi | 84 | 41.55 N | 44.21 E |
| Metedeconk, South Branch ≃ | 208 | 40.04 N | 74.09 W |
| Meteghan | 186 | 44.11 N | 66.10 W |
| Metelen | 52 | 52.08 N | 7.12 E |
| Metema | 144 | 12.57 N | 36.12 E |
| Metéora ʋ[1] | 38 | 39.46 N | 21.36 E |
| Meteor Crater ⊥[6] | 200 | 35.02 N | 111.02 W |
| Meteor Seamount ✦[3] | 8 | 48.00 S | 8.30 E |
| Metepec, Méx. | 234 | 19.15 N | 99.36 W |
| Metepec, Méx. | 234 | 18.56 N | 98.28 W |
| Metharaw | 110 | 16.12 N | 98.08 E |
| Metheringham | 44 | 53.08 N | 0.24 W |
| Methil | 46 | 56.10 N | 3.01 W |
| Methler | 263 | 51.35 N | 7.37 E |
| Methlick | 46 | 57.25 N | 2.14 W |
| Methóni | 38 | 36.50 N | 21.43 E |
| Methow | 182 | 48.07 N | 120.00 W |
| Methow ≃ | 202 | 48.03 N | 119.53 W |
| Methuen | 207 | 42.43 N | 71.11 W |
| Methven, N.Z. | 172 | 43.38 S | 171.39 E |
| Methven, Scot., U.K. | 46 | 56.25 N | 3.34 W |
| Methwold | 42 | 52.31 N | 0.33 E |
| Metica ≃ | 246 | 4.09 N | 72.55 W |
| Metiskow | 184 | 52.24 N | 110.38 W |
| Metković | 36 | 43.03 N | 17.39 E |
| Metlakatla, B.C., Can. | 182 | 54.20 N | 130.27 W |
| Metlakatla, Ak., U.S. | 182 | 55.08 N | 131.35 W |
| Metlaoui | 148 | 34.20 N | 8.24 E |
| Metlatonoc | 234 | 17.11 N | 98.20 W |
| Metlika | 36 | 45.39 N | 15.19 E |
| Metlili, Oued V | 148 | 31.54 N | 4.53 E |
| Metlili ech Chaâmba | 148 | 32.18 N | 3.40 E |
| Metnitz | 61 | 46.59 N | 14.13 E |
| Meto, Bayou ≃ | 194 | 34.05 N | 91.26 W |
| Metolius ≃ | 202 | 44.36 N | 121.17 W |
| Metompkin Bay c | 208 | 37.43 N | 75.35 W |
| Metompkin Inlet c | 208 | 37.41 N | 75.35 W |
| Metro | 115a | 5.05 S | 105.20 E |
| Metropolis | 194 | 37.09 N | 88.43 W |
| Metropolitan | 190 | 46.00 N | 87.53 W |
| Metropolitan Beach ♠ | 281 | 42.35 N | 82.48 W |
| Metropolitan Museum of Art ʋ | 276 | 40.47 N | 73.58 W |
| Metropolitan Oakland International Airport ⊠ | 226 | 37.43 N | 122.13 W |
| Metschow | 54 | 53.49 N | 12.58 E |
| Metsematluku | 156 | 24.01 S | 24.40 E |
| Metsera | 154 | 2.35 S | 26.07 E |
| Métsovon | 38 | 39.46 N | 21.11 E |
| Mettawa | 278 | 42.14 N | 87.56 W |
| Metten | 60 | 48.52 N | 12.55 E |
| Mettendorf | 56 | 49.57 N | 6.19 E |
| Metter | 192 | 32.23 N | 82.03 W |
| Mettet | 56 | 50.19 N | 4.40 E |
| Mettetal Airport ⊠ | 281 | 42.21 N | 83.27 W |
| Mettingen | 52 | 52.18 N | 7.46 E |
| Mettlach | 56 | 49.30 N | 6.36 E |
| Mettmach | 60 | 48.10 N | 13.21 E |
| Mettmann | 56 | 51.15 N | 6.58 E |
| Mettray | 50 | 47.27 N | 0.39 E |
| Mettuppālaiyam | 122 | 11.18 N | 76.57 E |
| Mettūr | 122 | 11.48 N | 77.48 E |
| Metu | 144 | 8.20 N | 35.36 E |
| Metuchen | 210 | 40.32 N | 74.21 W |
| Metuge | 154 | 12.58 S | 40.20 E |
| Metulla | 132 | 33.16 N | 35.35 E |
| Metundo, Ilha I | 154 | 11.10 S | 40.41 E |
| Metz | 56 | 49.08 N | 6.10 E |
| Metzervisse | 56 | 49.19 N | 6.17 E |
| Metzger | 224 | 45.26 N | 122.45 W |
| Metzingen | 56 | 48.32 N | 9.17 E |
| Metzkausen | 263 | 51.16 N | 6.57 E |
| Metztitlán | 234 | 20.36 N | 98.45 W |
| Metztitlán, Laguna ⊜ | 234 | 20.40 N | 98.50 W |
| Meu ≃ | 32 | 48.02 N | 1.47 W |
| Meudon | 261 | 48.48 N | 2.14 E |
| Meudon, Bois de ♠ | 261 | 48.47 N | 2.12 E |
| Meul ≃ | 158 | 27.56 S | 28.50 E |
| Meulaboh | 114 | 4.09 N | 96.08 E |
| Meulan | 50 | 49.01 N | 1.54 E |
| Meulebeke | 50 | 50.57 N | 3.17 E |
| Meung-sur-Loire | 50 | 47.50 N | 1.42 E |
| Meureubo ≃ | 114 | 4.09 N | 96.09 E |
| Meureudu | 114 | 5.16 N | 96.16 E |
| Meursault | 58 | 46.59 N | 4.46 E |
| Meurthe ≃ | 32 | 48.47 N | 6.09 E |
| Meurthe-et-Moselle □[5] | 32 | 48.35 N | 6.10 E |
| Meuse | 58 | 47.59 N | 5.33 E |
| Meuse □[5] | 32 | 49.00 N | 5.30 E |
| Meuse (Maas) ≃ | 30 | 51.49 N | 5.01 E |
| Meuselwitz | 54 | 51.02 N | 12.17 E |
| Meuvette ≃ | 50 | 48.45 N | 1.08 E |
| Meux Creek ≃ | 212 | 44.07 N | 81.02 W |
| Mevagissey | 42 | 50.16 N | 4.48 W |
| Mevang | 152 | 0.07 N | 11.05 E |
| Mewāt Plain ≚ | 124 | 27.40 N | 77.15 E |
| Mexborough | 44 | 53.30 N | 1.17 W |
| Mexia | 222 | 31.40 N | 96.28 W |
| Mexia Lake ⊜[1] | 222 | 31.39 N | 96.36 W |
| Mexiana, Ilha I | 250 | 0.02 S | 49.35 W |
| Mexicali | 232 | 32.40 N | 115.29 W |
| Mexican Hat | 200 | 37.09 N | 109.52 W |
| Mexico, In., U.S. | 216 | 40.49 N | 86.06 W |
| Mexico, Me., U.S. | 188 | 44.33 N | 70.32 W |
| Mexico, Mo., U.S. | 219 | 39.10 N | 91.52 W |
| Mexico, N.Y., U.S. | 212 | 43.27 N | 76.13 W |
| Mexico, Pa., U.S. | 208 | 40.32 N | 77.21 W |
| México □[3] | 234 | 19.20 N | 99.45 W |
| Mexico (México) □[1], N.A. | 230 | 23.00 N | 102.00 W |
| Mexico (México) □[1], N.A. | 232 | 23.00 N | 102.00 W |
| México, Golfo de → Mexico, Gulf of c | 230 | 25.00 N | 90.00 W |
| Mexico, Gulf of c | 230 | 25.00 N | 90.00 W |
| Mexico Basin ✦[1] | 16 | 25.00 N | 92.00 W |
| Mexico Bay c | 212 | 43.31 N | 76.17 W |
| Mexico Beach | 192 | 29.58 N | 85.24 W |
| Mexico City → Ciudad de México | 234 | 19.24 N | 99.09 W |
| Mexiko → Ciudad de México | 234 | 19.24 N | 99.09 W |
| Mexiko → Mexico □[1] | 232 | 23.00 N | 102.00 W |
| Mexiko, Golf von → Mexico, Gulf of c | 230 | 25.00 N | 90.00 W |
| Meximieux | 58 | 45.54 N | 5.12 E |
| Mexique → Mexico □[1] | 230 | 23.00 N | 102.00 W |
| Mexique, Golfe du → Mexico, Gulf of c | 230 | 25.00 N | 90.00 W |
| Mexticacán | 234 | 21.13 N | 102.43 W |
| Mey, Castle of ⊥ | 46 | 58.38 N | 3.14 W |
| Meyanodas | 164 | 7.38 S | 131.38 E |
| Meycauayan | 116 | 14.44 N | 120.58 E |
| Meydan | 130 | 38.21 N | 41.47 E |
| Meydancık | 130 | 41.25 N | 42.14 E |
| Meydān-e Gel ≚ | 128 | 29.04 N | 54.50 E |
| Meydān Khvolah | 120 | 33.36 N | 69.51 E |
| Meyenburg | 54 | 53.18 N | 12.14 E |
| Meyers Chuck | 182 | 55.44 N | 132.15 W |
| Meyersdale | 188 | 39.48 N | 79.01 W |
| Meyers Lake | 214 | 40.52 N | 81.24 W |
| Meyersville | 222 | 28.55 N | 97.21 W |
| Meyerton | 158 | 26.33 S | 28.01 E |
| Meyísti I | 130 | 36.08 N | 29.34 E |
| Meymac | 32 | 45.32 N | 2.09 E |
| Meymaneh | 120 | 35.55 N | 64.47 E |
| Meymeh | 128 | 33.27 N | 51.10 E |
| Meymeh ≃ | 128 | 32.05 N | 47.16 E |
| Meynypilgino | 180 | 62.32 N | 177.02 E |
| Meyo Centre | 152 | 2.33 N | 11.02 E |
| Meyrargues | 62 | 43.38 N | 5.32 E |
| Meyrin | 58 | 46.14 N | 6.05 E |
| Meyronne | 184 | 49.39 N | 106.50 W |
| Meyrueis | 32 | 44.10 N | 3.26 E |
| Meyungs | 175b | 7.20 N | 134.27 E |
| Meža ≃ | 61 | 46.35 N | 15.02 E |
| Meẕada, Ḥorvot (Masada) ⊥ | 132 | 31.19 N | 35.21 E |
| Mezapa | 236 | 15.33 N | 87.23 W |
| Mezcala | 234 | 17.56 N | 99.37 W |
| Mezcala ≃ | 234 | 18.00 N | 99.47 W |
| Mezcalapa | 234 | 17.37 N | 93.22 W |
| Mezcalapa ≃ | 234 | 18.00 N | 92.54 W |
| Mezdra | 38 | 43.09 N | 23.42 E |
| Meždurečensk | 86 | 53.42 N | 88.03 E |
| Meždurečenskij | 86 | 59.36 N | 65.53 E |
| Mèze | 32 | 43.25 N | 3.36 E |
| Mézel | 62 | 43.59 N | 6.12 E |
| Mezen' | 24 | 65.50 N | 44.13 E |
| Mezen' ≃ | 24 | 66.11 N | 43.59 E |
| Mézenc, Mont ∧ | 62 | 44.55 N | 4.11 E |
| Mezenskaja guba c | 24 | 66.40 N | 43.45 E |
| Mezhova | 78 | 48.16 N | 36.44 E |
| Mezhyrich | 78 | 50.43 N | 34.29 E |
| Meziadin Lake ⊜ | 182 | 56.04 N | 129.18 W |


| | English | Deutsch | Español | Français | Português |
|---|---|---|---|---|---|
| ≃ | River | Fluß | Río | Rivière | Rio |
| ≡ | Canal | Kanal | Canal | Canal | Canal |
| ⊥ | Waterfall, Rapids | Wasserfall, Stromschnellen | Cascada, Rápidos | Chute d'eau, Rapides | Cascata, Rápidos |
| u | Strait | Meeresstraße | Estrecho | Détroit | Estreito |
| c | Bay, Gulf | Bucht, Golf | Bahía, Golfo | Baie, Golfe | Baía, Golfo |
| ⊜ | Lake, Lakes | See, Seen | Lago, Lagos | Lac, Lacs | Lago, Lagos |
| ≚ | Swamp | Sumpf | Pantano | Marais | Pântano |
| Π | Ice Features, Glacier | Eis- und Gletscherformen | Accidentes Glaciales | Formes glaciaires | Acidentes glaciares |
| ≈ | Other Hydrographic Features | Andere Hydrographische Objekte | Otros Elementos Hidrográficos | Autres données hydrographiques | Outros acidentes hidrográficos |
| ✦ | Submarine Features | Untermeerische Objekte | Accidentes Submarinos | Formes de relief sous-marin | Acidentes submarinos |
| □ | Political Unit | Politische Einheit | Unidad Política | Entité politique | Unidade política |
| ʋ | Cultural Institution | Kulturelle Institution | Institución Cultural | Institution culturelle | Instituição cultural |
| ⊥ | Historical Site | Historische Stätte | Sitio Histórico | Site historique | Sitio histórico |
| ♠ | Recreational Site | Erholungs- und Ferienort | Sitio de Recreo | Centre de loisirs | Area de Lazer |
| ⊠ | Airport | Flughafen | Aeropuerto | Aéroport | Aeroporto |
| ■ | Military Installation | Militäranlage | Instalación Militar | Installation militaire | Instalação militar |
| ◆ | Miscellaneous | Verschiedenes | Misceláneo | Divers | Diversos |

Mežica 61 46.31 N 14.52 E
Mézières-en-Brenne 32 46.49 N 1.13 E
Mézières-sur-Seine 261 48.58 N 1.48 E
Mézilhac 62 44.48 N 4.21 E
Mézin 32 44.03 N 0.16 E
Mezinovskij 76 55.30 N 40.21 E
Mezőberény 30 46.50 N 21.02 E
Mezőcsát 30 47.49 N 20.55 E
Mezőkovácsháza 30 46.25 N 20.55 E
Mezőkövesd 30 47.50 N 20.34 E
Mezőtúr 30 47.00 N 20.38 E
Mežoz'ornyj 86 54.09 N 59.23 E
Mezquital 234 23.29 N 104.23 W
Mezquital ≃ 232 22.35 N 104.54 W
Mezquital del Oro 234 21.10 N 103.23 W
Mezquitic 234 22.23 N 103.41 W
Mezraa 130 41.12 N 35.08 E
Mézy 261 49.00 N 1.53 E
Mezzana 64 46.19 N 10.48 E
Mezzano 64 46.09 N 11.48 E
Mezzenile 62 45.17 N 7.23 E
Mezzocorona 64 46.13 N 11.07 E
Mezzoiuso 70 37.52 N 13.28 E
Mezzola, Lago di ⊜ 58 46.12 N 9.26 E
Mezzoldo 58 46.01 N 9.40 E
Mezzolombardo 64 46.13 N 11.05 E
Mezzomerico 266b 45.37 N 8.36 E
Mfangano Island I 154 0.28 S 34.01 E
Mfolozi ≃ 158 28.25 S 32.26 E
Mfou 152 3.43 N 11.38 E
Mfuwe 154 13.04 S 31.46 E
Mgači 89 51.05 N 142.17 E
Mgeni ≃ 158 29.48 S 31.02 E
Mgeta 154 8.19 S 36.08 E
Mglin 76 53.04 N 32.51 E
M'Goun, Irhil ʌ 148 31.31 N 6.25 W
M'hai, B'nom ʌ 110 11.21 N 107.50 E
Mhasvād 122 17.38 N 74.47 E
Mhlatuze ≃ 158 28.47 S 32.06 E
Mhlume 158 26.02 S 31.50 E
Mholach, Beinn ʌ 2 46 58.14 N 6.31 W
Mhòr, Beinn ʌ 46 57.17 N 7.19 W
Mhòr, Loch ⊜ 46 57.14 N 4.26 W
Mhow 120 22.33 N 75.46 E
Mi ≃, Zhg. 98 37.12 N 119.10 E
Mi ≃, Zhg. 100 27.09 N 112.51 E
Mia, Oued V 148 30.47 N 4.54 E
Miacatlán 234 18.46 N 99.22 W
Mia-dong ◆ 8 271b 37.37 N 127.01 E
Miagao 116 10.39 N 122.14 E
Miahuatlán de Porfirio Díaz 234 16.20 N 96.36 W
Miajadas 34 39.09 N 5.54 W
Miaméré 146 8.52 N 19.50 E
Miami, Mb., Can. 184 49.21 N 98.11 W
Miami, Az., U.S. 200 33.23 N 110.52 W
Miami, Fl., U.S. 220 25.46 N 80.11 W
Miami, In., U.S. 216 40.36 N 86.06 W
Miami, Ok., U.S. 196 36.52 N 94.52 W
Miami, Tx., U.S. 196 35.42 N 100.38 W
Miami □ 6, In., U.S. 216 40.45 N 86.04 W
Miami □ 6, Oh., U.S. 218 40.02 N 84.13 W
Miami ≃ 224 45.33 N 123.53 W
Miami Beach, On., Can. 212 44.13 N 79.29 W
Miami Beach, Fl., U.S. 220 25.47 N 80.07 W
Miami Canal ≋ 220 25.47 N 80.15 W
Miami Creek ≃ 226 37.21 N 119.44 W
Miami International Airport ⊠ 220 25.48 N 80.17 W
Miami Lakes 220 25.53 N 80.18 W
Miamisburg 218 39.38 N 84.17 W
Miamisburg Mound State Memorial ⊥ 218 39.38 N 84.17 W
Miami Shores 220 25.51 N 80.11 W
Miami Springs 220 25.49 N 80.17 W
Miami State Recreation Area ♠ 216 40.40 N 85.55 W
Miamiville 218 39.13 N 84.18 W
Miān Channūn 123 30.27 N 72.22 E
Mianchi 102 34.48 N 111.49 E
Miāndoāb 128 36.58 N 46.06 E
Miandrivazo 157b 19.31 S 45.28 E
Mianduhe 89 49.05 N 121.06 E
Miane 64 45.57 N 12.06 E
Miāneh 128 37.26 N 47.42 E
Miang, Phu ʌ 110 17.42 N 101.01 E
Miangas, Pulau I 108 5.35 N 126.35 E
Mianhu 100 23.28 N 116.09 E
Mianhuadi 104 41.15 N 120.49 E
Miāni 123 32.32 N 73.04 E
Miāni Hōr c 120 25.34 N 66.19 E
Mianning 102 28.39 N 102.09 E
Mianus ≃ 207 41.03 N 73.35 W
Mianus, East Branch ≃ 276 41.06 N 73.35 W
Mianus Reservoir ⊜ 1 276 41.08 N 73.37 W
Miānwāli 123 32.35 N 71.33 E
Mianxian 102 33.09 N 106.48 E
Mianyang, Zhg. 100 30.23 N 113.25 E
Mianyang, Zhg. 102 31.30 N 104.49 E
Mianzhu 102 31.20 N 104.09 E
Miao Dao I 98 37.56 N 120.45 E
Miaodao Qundao II 98 38.10 N 120.40 E
Miao'ergou 86 45.32 N 83.52 E
Miaofengshan 105 40.04 N 116.13 E
Miaogou 104 41.12 N 120.40 E
Miaojiagou 104 42.16 N 123.22 E
Miaojiatun 104 40.54 N 120.55 E
Miaokou 98 35.48 N 114.09 E
Miaoli 100 24.34 N 120.49 E
Miao Ling ʌʌ 102 26.15 N 107.26 E
Miaopu 106 31.00 N 118.44 E
Miaoqian 100 30.33 N 117.44 E
Miaotou 106 30.58 N 120.33 E
Miaowan 100 33.07 N 114.41 E
Miaoyang 98 40.49 N 124.24 E
Miaozhen 106 31.43 N 121.21 E
Miaozigou 107 30.17 N 104.35 E
Miarayon 116 8.04 N 124.50 E
Miarinarivo, Madag. 157b 16.38 S 48.15 E
Miarinarivo, Madag. 157b 18.57 S 46.55 E
Miarinavaratra 157b 20.13 S 47.31 E
Miasa 94 36.34 N 137.53 E
Miass 86 54.59 N 60.06 E
Miass ≃ 86 56.06 N 64.30 E
Miasteczko Krajeńskie 30 53.06 N 17.01 E
Miastko 30 54.01 N 17.00 E
Miboro-dam ◆ 6 94 36.08 N 136.55 E
Mibu 94 36.25 N 139.48 E
Mibu ≃ 94 35.49 N 137.57 E
Mica 156 24.10 S 30.48 E
Mica Mountain ʌ 200 32.13 N 110.33 W
Micang Shan ʌʌ 102 32.45 N 107.20 E
Micanopy 192 29.30 N 82.16 W
Micaúne 156 18.18 S 36.35 E
Mičavičevnik 24 64.14 N 57.58 E
Miccosukee, Lake ⊜ 1 192 30.34 N 83.58 W
Miccosukee Indian Reservation ◆ 4 220 26.10 N 80.50 W
Michael, Mount ʌ 164 6.25 S 145.20 E
Michael J. Kirwan Reservoir ⊜ 1 214 41.10 N 81.10 W
Michajlov 82 54.14 N 39.02 E
Michajlovka, Kaz. 85 43.06 N 71.36 E
Michajlovka, Kaz. 85 42.50 N 75.42 E
Michajlovka, Kaz. 86 53.51 N 76.32 E
Michajlovka, Kyrg. 85 42.37 N 78.20 E
Michajlovka, Ross. 78 49.53 N 39.38 E
Michajlovka, Ross. 80 47.38 N 46.54 E
Michajlovka, Ross. 80 50.05 N 43.15 E
Michajlovka, Ross. 86 51.49 N 79.45 E
Michajlovka, Ross. 86 56.26 N 78.53 E
Michajlovka, Ross. 88 50.26 N 104.10 E
Michajlovka, Ross. 88 55.30 N 114.09 E
Michajlovka, Ross. 88 51.07 N 119.20 E
Michajlovka, Ross. 88 52.57 N 103.18 E
Michajlovka, Ross. 89 49.13 N 129.56 E
Michajlovka, Ross. 89 43.56 N 132.00 E
Michajlovka, Ross. 265a 60.04 N 30.14 E
Michajlovka, Ross. 265a 59.43 N 30.01 E
Michajlovo 80 56.56 N 45.04 E
Michajlovo-Aleksandrovskij 83 49.13 N 40.15 E
Michajlovska 86 50.17 N 55.23 E
Michajlovskaja 80 50.58 N 41.52 E
Michajlovskij, Ross. 76 60.05 N 43.29 E
Michajlovskij, Ross. 86 51.41 N 79.47 E
Michajlovskoje, Ross. 76 58.23 N 37.40 E
Michajlovskoje, Ross. 80 56.11 N 45.47 E
Michajlovskoje, Ross. 82 55.50 N 36.20 E
Michajlovskoje, Ross. 265b 55.35 N 37.35 E
Michalevo 82 55.27 N 38.26 E
Michali 82 55.17 N 39.05 E
Michalkovo 82 54.11 N 37.33 E
Michalovce 30 48.45 N 21.55 E
Michalovy Hory 60 49.55 N 12.47 E
Michaud, Point ≻ 186 45.34 N 60.40 W
Micheal Peak ʌ 182 53.35 N 126.26 W
Michejevo 88 57.10 N 104.53 E
Michel 182 49.43 N 114.49 W
Michelago 171b 35.43 S 149.10 E
Michelau 56 50.10 N 11.06 E
Micheldever 42 51.09 N 1.15 W
Micheldorf in Oberösterreich 61 47.52 N 14.08 E
Michelsneukirchen 60 49.08 N 12.33 E
Michelson, Mount ʌ 180 69.19 N 144.17 W
Michel'sonovskij 265b 55.42 N 37.54 E
Michelstadt 56 49.41 N 9.00 E
Michendorf 54 52.18 N 13.01 E
Miches 238 18.59 N 69.03 W
Micheta 84 41.52 N 44.44 E
Michiana 216 41.46 N 86.48 W
Michiana Regional Airport ⊠ 216 41.42 N 86.19 W
Michigamme ≃ 190 46.04 N 88.13 W
Michigan 198 48.01 N 98.07 W
Michigan □ 3, U.S. 178 44.00 N 85.00 W
Michigan □ 3, U.S. 190 44.00 N 85.00 W
Michigan ≃ 200 40.52 N 106.20 W
Michigan, Lake ⊜ 190 44.00 N 87.00 W
Michigan, University of ⊕ 2 281 42.17 N 83.44 W
Michigan Center 216 42.13 N 84.19 W
Michigan City 216 41.42 N 86.53 W
Michigan International Speedway ♠ 216 42.03 N 84.15 W
Michigan Stadium ♠ 281 42.16 N 83.45 W
Michigan State Fair Grounds ♠ 281 42.27 N 83.07 W
Michigantown 216 40.19 N 86.23 W
Michika 146 10.38 N 13.24 E
Michillinda 280 34.07 N 118.05 W
Michinmahuida, Volcán ʌ 1 254 42.49 S 72.28 W
Michipicoten Bay c 190 47.55 N 84.56 W
Michipicoten Island I 190 47.45 N 85.45 W
Michnevo 82 55.07 N 37.58 E
Michninskaja 24 60.26 N 46.14 E
Michoacán 204 32.28 N 115.20 W
Michoacán □ 3 234 19.10 N 101.50 W
Michoacanejo 234 21.33 N 102.36 W
Michów 30 51.32 N 22.19 E
Michurinsk → Mičurinsk 80 52.54 N 40.30 E
Mickle Fell ʌ 44 54.37 N 2.18 W
Mickleham 260 51.16 N 0.19 W
Mickleover 42 52.54 N 1.32 W
Mickleton, Eng., U.K. 42 52.05 N 1.46 W
Mickleton, N.J., U.S. 285 39.47 N 75.14 W
Mickle Trafford 262 53.13 N 2.50 W
Mickleyville 218 39.45 N 86.16 W
Mico ≃ 236 12.11 N 84.16 W
Mico, Montañas del ʌʌ 236 15.30 N 88.55 W
Miconge 152 4.26 S 12.51 E
Micoud 241f 13.50 N 60.54 W
Micronesia II 14 11.00 N 159.00 E
Micronesia, Federated States of □ 1 14 5.00 N 152.00 E
Mičurinsk 80 52.54 N 40.30 E
Midai, Pulau I 112 3.00 N 107.47 E
Midale 184 49.22 N 103.27 W
Midar 148 34.58 N 3.30 W
Mid-Atlantic Ridge ✦ 3 8 0.00 20.00 W
Midbar Yehuda → Wilderness of Judæa ◆ 2 132 31.30 N 35.18 E
Middalya 162 23.55 S 114.45 E
Middelburg, Ned. 52 51.30 N 3.37 E
Middelburg, S. Afr. 158 25.47 S 29.28 E
Middelburg, S. Afr. 158 31.30 S 25.00 E
Middelfart 41 55.30 N 9.45 E
Middelharnis 52 51.45 N 4.11 E
Middelkerke 50 51.11 N 2.49 E
Middelkerke, Vliegveld ⊠ 50 51.12 N 2.52 E
Middelpos 158 31.55 S 20.13 E
Middelstum 52 53.20 N 6.38 E
Middelwater 156 23.17 S 30.16 E
Middelwit 156 24.58 S 27.00 E
Middenbeemster 52 52.33 N 4.55 E
Middenin 158 27.43 S 28.02 E
Middenmeer 52 52.47 N 5.00 E
Middle ≃, B.C., Can. 182 54.50 N 125.08 W
Middle ≃, Ca., U.S. 226 38.03 N 121.31 W
Middle ≃, Ia., U.S. 194 41.29 N 93.24 W
Middle ≃, Mn., U.S. 198 48.22 N 97.04 W
Middle ≃, Mo., U.S. 219 38.39 N 91.53 W
Middle Alkali Lake ⊜ 204 41.28 N 120.04 W
Middle America Trench ✦ 1 16 15.00 N 95.00 W
Middle Andaman I 110 12.30 N 92.50 E
Middle Barton 42 51.56 N 1.22 W
Middle Bass 214 41.41 N 82.50 W
Middle Bass Island I 214 41.41 N 82.49 W
Middle-Bay 186 51.28 N 57.30 W
Middle Bay c 276 40.37 N 73.36 W
Middleboro 207 41.53 N 70.54 W
Middle Bosque ≃ 222 31.31 N 97.16 W
Middlebourne 188 39.29 N 80.54 W
Middlebranch 214 40.54 N 81.20 W
Middle Breakwater ◆ 5 280 33.43 N 118.13 W
Middlebro 184 49.01 N 95.21 W
Middle Brook 186 48.45 N 54.13 W
Middle Brook ≃, N.J., U.S. 276 40.39 N 74.41 W
Middle Brook ≃, N.J., U.S. 276 40.33 N 74.33 W
Middle Brook, East Branch ≃ 276 40.35 N 74.33 W
Middle Brook, West Branch ≃ 276 40.35 N 74.33 W
Middleburg, Md., U.S. 208 39.35 N 77.12 W
Middleburg, N.Y., U.S. 210 42.36 N 74.20 W
Middleburg, Oh., U.S. 216 40.17 N 83.34 W
Middleburg, Pa., U.S. 208 40.47 N 77.02 W
Middleburg Heights 214 41.22 N 81.48 W
Middlebury, Ct., U.S. 207 41.31 N 73.07 W
Middlebury, In., U.S. 216 41.40 N 85.42 W
Middlebury, Vt., U.S. 188 44.00 N 73.10 W
Middlebush 276 40.29 N 74.32 W
Middle Caicos I 238 21.47 N 71.43 W
Middle Cape ≻ 220 25.09 N 81.09 W
Middle Castor ≃ 212 45.16 N 75.24 W
Middle Channel ≃ 1, N.T., Can. 180 69.21 N 135.33 W
Middle Channel ≃ 1, Mi., U.S. 281 42.33 N 82.42 W
Middle Concho ≃ 196 31.27 N 100.25 W
Middle Creek ≃, U.S. 208 39.41 N 76.18 W
Middle Creek ≃, Pa., U.S. 210 40.46 N 76.52 W
Middle Creek ≃, Pa., U.S. 210 41.28 N 75.11 W
Middle Fabius ≃ 194 39.58 N 91.35 W
Middle Falls 210 43.07 N 73.32 W
Middlefield, Ct., U.S. 207 41.31 N 72.42 W
Middlefield, N.Y., U.S. 210 42.41 N 74.50 W
Middlefield, Oh., U.S. 214 41.27 N 81.04 W
Middle Fork Reservoir ⊜ 1 218 39.51 N 84.51 W
Middle Ground I 272c 18.55 N 72.51 E
Middle Ground ✦ 2 174g 28.15 N 177.25 W
Middle Grove, Mo., U.S. 219 39.24 N 92.16 W
Middle Grove, N.Y., U.S. 210 43.05 N 73.55 W
Middle Haddam 207 41.33 N 72.33 W
Middleham 44 54.17 N 1.49 W
Middle Harbour c 274a 33.48 S 151.14 E
Middle Head ≻ 274a 33.50 S 151.16 E
Middle Hope 210 41.34 N 74.01 W
Middle Island 210 40.53 N 72.56 W
Middle Island I, Austl. 162 34.07 S 123.12 E
Middle Island I, On., Can. 214 41.41 N 82.41 W
Middle Level Main Drain ≋ 42 52.43 N 0.22 E
Middle Loup ≃ 198 41.17 N 98.23 W
Middle Maitland ≃ 212 43.53 N 81.19 W
Middlemarch 172 45.31 S 170.07 E
Middlemount 166 22.49 S 148.40 E
Middle Musquodoboit 186 45.03 N 63.09 W
Middle Nodaway ≃ 194 40.54 N 95.00 W
Middle Pease ≃ 196 34.15 N 100.07 W
Middle Point 216 40.51 N 84.27 W
Middleport, N.Y., U.S. 210 43.12 N 78.28 W
Middleport, Oh., U.S. 188 39.00 N 82.02 W
Middleport, Pa., U.S. 208 40.44 N 76.05 W
Middle Raccoon ≃ 198 41.34 N 94.12 W
Middle Reservoir ⊜ 1 283 42.27 N 71.07 W
Middle River 208 39.20 N 76.26 W
Middle River c 208 39.19 N 76.25 W
Middle River Neck ≻ 1 284b 39.22 N 76.23 W
Middle River Rouge ≃ 281 42.20 N 83.15 W
Middle Rouge Parkway ♠ 281 42.21 N 83.21 W
Middle Run ≃ 285 39.41 N 75.43 W
Middlesboro 192 36.36 N 83.43 W
Middlesbrough 44 54.35 N 1.14 W
Middlesex, Belize 232 17.02 N 88.31 W
Middlesex, N.J., U.S. 276 40.34 N 74.29 W
Middlesex, N.Y., U.S. 210 42.42 N 77.16 W
Middlesex, N.C., U.S. 192 35.47 N 78.12 W
Middlesex □ 6, On., Can. 212 43.00 N 81.08 W
Middlesex □ 6, Ct., U.S. 207 41.33 N 72.39 W
Middlesex □ 6, Ma., U.S. 207 42.30 N 71.25 W
Middlesex □ 6, N.J., U.S. 208 40.29 N 74.27 W
Middlesex □ 6, Va., U.S. 208 37.40 N 76.35 W
Middlesex Fells Reservation ♠ 283 42.27 N 71.07 W
Middlesex Reservoir ⊜ 1 276 40.37 N 74.19 W
Middle Stewiacke 186 45.13 N 63.08 W
Middle Swan 168a 31.52 S 116.00 E
Middle Thames ≃ 212 42.59 N 80.58 W
Middleton, Austl. 166 22.22 S 141.32 E
Middleton, N.S., Can. 186 44.57 N 65.04 W
Middleton, Eng., U.K. 42 52.43 N 0.28 E
Middleton, Eng., U.K. 44 53.33 N 2.13 W
Middleton, Ma., U.S. 207 42.35 N 71.01 W
Middleton, Mi., U.S. 190 43.11 N 84.42 W
Middleton, Tn., U.S. 194 35.03 N 88.53 W
Middleton, Wi., U.S. 216 43.05 N 89.30 W
Middleton-in-Teesdale 44 54.38 N 2.04 W
Middleton Island I 180 59.25 N 146.25 W
Middleton-on-the-Wolds 44 53.56 N 0.33 W
Middleton Pond ⊜ 283 42.36 N 71.02 W
Middleton Reef I 1 160 29.28 S 159.06 E
Middleton Saint George 44 54.30 N 1.28 W
Middletown, N. Ire., U.K. 48 54.18 N 6.50 W
Middletown, Ca., U.S. 226 38.45 N 122.36 W
Middletown, Ct., U.S. 207 41.33 N 72.39 W
Middletown, De., U.S. 208 39.26 N 75.43 W
Middletown, Il., U.S. 219 40.11 N 89.35 W
Middletown, In., U.S. 218 40.03 N 85.32 W
Middletown, Ky., U.S. 218 38.14 N 85.32 W
Middletown, Md., U.S. 208 39.26 N 77.32 W
Middletown, Mo., U.S. 219 39.07 N 91.24 W
Middletown, N.J., U.S. 208 40.23 N 74.07 W
Middletown, N.Y., U.S. 210 41.26 N 74.25 W
Middletown, Oh., U.S. 218 39.30 N 84.23 W
Middletown, Pa., U.S. 208 40.11 N 76.43 W
Middletown, R.I., U.S. 207 41.32 N 71.17 W
Middletown, Va., U.S. 188 39.01 N 78.16 W
Middletown Park 218 40.09 N 85.26 W
Middle Tuolumne ≃ 226 37.50 N 120.01 W
Middleville, Mi., U.S. 216 42.42 N 85.27 W
Middleville, N.Y., U.S. 210 43.08 N 74.58 W
Middleville, N.Y., U.S. 276 43.08 N 74.58 W
Middlewich 44 53.11 N 2.27 W
Middle Yegua Creek ≃ 222 30.19 N 96.47 W
Middle Yuba ≃ 226 39.22 N 121.12 W
Midelt 148 32.41 N 4.43 W
Midfield 222 28.56 N 96.13 W
Midge Hall 262 53.42 N 2.45 W
Midgic 186 45.59 N 64.18 W
Mid Glamorgan □ 6 42 51.40 N 3.30 W
Midgley 262 53.44 N 1.58 W
Midhurst, On., Can. 212 44.27 N 79.44 W
Midhurst, Eng., U.K. 42 50.59 N 0.45 W
Midi, Aiguille du ʌ 62 45.52 N 6.53 E
Midi, Canal du ≋ 32 43.26 N 1.58 E
Midi de Bigorre, Pic du ʌ 32 42.56 N 0.08 E
Mid Illovo 158 29.59 S 30.25 E
Mid-Indian Basin ✦ 1 12 10.00 S 80.00 E
Mid-Indian Ridge ✦ 3 6 12.00 S 66.00 E
Midland, Austl. 168a 31.53 S 116.00 E
Midland, On., Can. 212 44.45 N 79.53 W
Midland, Ca., U.S. 204 33.52 N 114.48 W
Midland, Mi., U.S. 190 43.36 N 84.14 W
Midland, N.C., U.S. 192 35.13 N 80.30 W
Midland, Oh., U.S. 218 39.18 N 83.54 W
Midland, Pa., U.S. 214 40.37 N 80.26 W
Midland, Pa., U.S. 214 40.37 N 80.26 W
Midland, S.D., U.S. 198 44.04 N 101.09 W
Midland, Tx., U.S. 196 31.59 N 102.04 W
Midland, Wa., U.S. 224 47.10 N 122.24 W
Midland Bay c 212 44.47 N 79.52 W
Midland Beach ◆ 8 276 40.34 N 74.05 W
Midland City 219 40.09 N 89.08 W
Midland Park, Mi., U.S. 216 42.23 N 85.22 W
Midland Park, N.J., U.S. 276 40.59 N 74.08 W
Midland Park Lake ⊜ 212 44.44 N 79.53 W
Midlands □ 4 154 19.00 S 29.45 E
Midleton 48 51.55 N 8.10 W
Midlothian, Il., U.S. 216 41.37 N 87.43 W
Midlothian, Tx., U.S. 222 32.28 N 96.59 W
Midlothian Creek ≃ 278 41.39 N 87.40 W
Midlum 52 53.43 N 8.37 E
Midnapore 182 50.55 N 114.05 W
Midnapore Canal ≋ 126 22.25 N 87.53 E
Midnapore Plain ≚ 126 22.00 N 87.45 E
Mid-Ohio Sports Car Course ♠ 214 40.40 N 82.38 W
Midongy Nord 157b 20.45 S 46.13 E
Midongy Sud 157b 23.35 S 47.01 E
Midori 96 34.43 N 132.37 E
Midori ◆ 8 268 35.32 N 139.34 E
Midori ≃ 92 32.42 N 130.37 E
Midou ≃ 32 43.54 N 0.30 W
Mid-Pacific Mountains ✦ 3 14 20.00 N 170.00 E
Midpines 226 37.32 N 119.55 W
Midreshet Ben Gurion 132 30.51 N 34.46 E
Midsayap 116 7.12 N 124.32 E
Midshipman Point ≻ 282 38.07 N 122.27 W
Midsland 52 53.22 N 5.16 E
Midsomer Norton 42 51.18 N 2.28 W
Midu 102 25.22 N 100.31 E
Midvale, De., U.S. 285 39.39 N 75.37 W
Midvale, Id., U.S. 202 44.28 N 116.44 W
Midvale, Oh., U.S. 214 40.26 N 81.22 W
Midville 192 32.49 N 82.14 W
Midway, B.C., Can. 182 49.01 N 118.47 W
Midway, B.C., Can. 202 49.01 N 118.46 W
Midway, Al., U.S. 194 32.04 N 85.31 W
Midway, In., U.S. 216 41.37 N 85.55 W
Midway, Ky., U.S. 218 38.09 N 84.41 W
Midway, Pa., U.S. 279b 40.22 N 80.17 W
Midway, Tx., U.S. 222 31.02 N 95.45 W
Midway, Ut,. U.S. 200 40.30 N 111.28 W
Midway City 280 33.45 N 118.00 W
Midway Islands □ 2, Oc. 6 28.13 N 177.22 W
Midway Islands □ 2, Oc. 174g 28.13 N 177.22 W
Midway Mall ◆ 9 279a 41.24 N 82.07 W
Midway Naval Station ■ 174g 28.13 N 177.26 W
Midway Park 192 34.43 N 77.21 W
Midwest 200 43.24 N 106.16 W
Midwest City 196 35.26 N 97.23 W
Midwolda 52 53.12 N 7.00 E
Midyan ◆ 1 128 27.40 N 35.35 E
Midyat 130 37.25 N 41.23 E
Midyobe 152 1.21 N 10.18 E
Midžor (Midžur) ʌ 38 43.23 N 22.42 E
Mie 96 32.58 N 131.35 E
Mie □ 5 92 34.30 N 136.30 E
Miechów 30 50.23 N 20.01 E
Miedwie, Jezioro ⊜ 54 53.17 N 14.52 E
Międzybórz 30 51.24 N 17.40 E
Międzychód 30 52.36 N 15.55 E
Międzylesie 30 50.10 N 16.40 E
Międzyrzec Podlaski 30 52.00 N 22.47 E
Międzyrzecz 30 52.28 N 15.35 E
Międzyzdroje 30 53.55 N 14.28 E
Miehuapu 105 39.11 N 117.44 E
Miejska Górka 30 51.40 N 16.58 E
Miélan 32 43.26 N 0.19 E
Mielec 30 50.18 N 21.25 E
Mielno 30 54.16 N 16.01 E
Mien ⊜ 26 56.25 N 14.51 E
Mienga 152 17.17 S 19.48 E
Mienhua Yü I 100 25.29 N 122.06 E
Mient'ienhuo Shan ʌ 269d 25.11 N 121.30 E
Mier 232 26.26 N 99.09 W
Miercurea-Ciuc 38 46.22 N 25.48 E
Mieres 34 43.15 N 5.46 W
Mierlo 52 51.27 N 5.37 E
Mieroszów 30 50.41 N 16.10 E
Miersdorf 264a 52.20 N 13.37 E
Miersig 38 46.53 N 21.51 E
Mier y Noriega 234 23.25 N 100.07 W
Miesaituo 120 35.52 N 93.40 E
Miesbach 64 47.47 N 11.50 E
Miesenbach 61 47.22 N 15.46 E
Mieso 144 9.15 N 40.48 E
Mieste 54 52.28 N 11.11 E
Miesterhorst 54 52.27 N 11.09 E
Mieszkowice 30 52.46 N 14.30 E
Mifflin, Oh., U.S. 214 40.47 N 82.22 W
Mifflin, Pa., U.S. 208 40.34 N 77.24 W
Mifflin □ 6 210 40.40 N 77.33 W
Mifflinburg 210 40.55 N 77.02 W
Mifflintown 208 40.34 N 77.23 W
Mifflinville 210 41.01 N 76.18 W
Miftāḥ, Wādī V 142 30.15 N 31.46 E
Migdal 132 32.50 N 35.30 E
Migdal Ha'Emeq 132 32.41 N 35.15 E
Migdol 158 26.54 S 25.27 E
Migennes 50 47.58 N 3.31 E
Migliarino 66 44.46 N 11.56 E
Migliaro 64 44.48 N 11.58 E
Miglionico 68 40.34 N 16.30 E
Mignano Monte Lungo 68 41.23 N 13.58 E
Mignone ≃ 66 42.11 N 11.44 E
Mignovillard 58 46.48 N 6.08 E
Migori ≃ 154 0.59 S 34.15 E
Miguel Alemán, Presa ⊜ 1 234 18.13 N 96.32 W
Miguel Alves 250 4.10 S 42.54 W
Miguel Auza 232 24.18 N 103.25 W
Miguel Calmon 250 11.26 S 40.36 W
Miguel Couto 287a 22.43 S 43.27 W
Miguel de la Borda 236 9.09 N 80.19 W
Migueles, Arroyo de los ≃ 266a 40.20 N 3.32 W
Miguelete 258 34.01 S 57.39 W
Miguelete, Arroyo ≃ 258 34.14 S 57.54 W
Miguel Hidalgo, Presa ⊜ 1 232 26.30 N 108.35 W
Miguelópolis 255 20.12 S 48.03 W
Miguel Pereira 256 22.27 S 43.22 W
Miguel Riglos 252 36.51 S 63.42 W
Migulinskaja 80 49.42 N 41.16 E
Migvie 46 57.08 N 2.56 W
Migyaunglaung 110 14.40 N 98.09 E
Mihăești 38 45.07 N 25.00 E
Mihai Viteazu 38 44.39 N 28.41 E
Mihajlovgrad □ 4 38 43.32 N 23.32 E
Mihalgazi 130 40.02 N 30.34 E
Mihalıççık 130 39.52 N 31.30 E
Mihama, Nihon 94 34.46 N 136.54 E
Mihama, Nihon 94 35.36 N 135.56 E
Mihama, Nihon 96 33.54 N 135.08 E
Mihanavičy 76 53.45 N 27.40 E
Mihara, Nihon 96 34.32 N 135.34 E
Mihara, Nihon 96 34.24 N 133.05 E
Mihara, Nihon 96 34.17 N 134.46 E
Mihara-yama ʌ 94 34.43 N 139.23 E
Mihla 54 51.04 N 10.20 E
Miho 94 36.00 N 140.18 E
Mihonoseki 96 35.34 N 133.19 E
Miho-wan c 96 35.30 N 133.23 E
Mihuangzhuang 105 39.07 N 116.12 E
Mijaly 86 48.57 N 53.42 E
Mijares ≃ 34 39.55 N 0.01 W
Mijdaḥah 144 14.00 N 48.26 E
Mijdrecht 52 52.13 N 4.52 E
Mijiang 98 43.01 N 130.08 E
Mijoux 58 46.22 N 6.00 E
Mikabo-yama ʌ 94 36.09 N 138.55 E
Mikame 96 33.25 N 132.27 E
Mikamo, Nihon 96 35.09 N 133.37 E
Mikamo, Nihon 96 34.05 N 133.57 E
Mikasa 92a 43.14 N 141.53 E
Mikaševičy 76 52.13 N 27.28 E
Mikata 94 35.33 N 135.55 E
Mikata-ko ⊜ 94 35.34 N 135.53 E
Mikatou 273b 4.16 S 15.08 E
Mikawa, Nihon 94 36.29 N 136.29 E
Mikawa, Nihon 96 33.37 N 132.58 E
Mikawa-wan c 94 34.43 N 137.10 E
Mikawa-wan-kokutei-kōen ♠ 94 34.42 N 137.10 E
Mikazuki 96 34.58 N 134.27 E
Mikese 154 6.46 S 37.54 E
Mikhaylo-Kotsyubyns'ke 78 51.27 N 31.04 E
Mikhaylov, Cape ≻ 9 66.51 S 118.33 E
Mikhrot Shelomo Hamelekh (Timna') (King Solomon's Mines) ⊥ 132 29.45 N 34.56 E
Miki, Nihon 96 34.48 N 134.59 E
Miki, Nihon 96 34.17 N 134.05 E
Mikínai ⊥ 38 37.44 N 22.45 E
Mikindani 154 10.17 S 40.07 E
Mikinduri 154 0.07 N 37.50 E
Mikkabi 94 34.48 N 137.33 E
Mikkaichi 270 34.26 N 135.35 E
Mikkeli 26 61.41 N 27.15 E
Mikkelin lääni □ 4 26 62.00 N 27.30 E
Mikkwa ≃ 176 58.25 N 114.45 W
Mikołajki 30 53.49 N 21.36 E
Mikołów 30 50.11 N 18.55 E
Mikomeseng 152 2.08 N 10.37 E
Mikomoto-jima I 94 34.34 N 138.56 E
Míkonos 38 37.26 N 25.20 E
Míkonos I 38 37.29 N 25.25 E
Mikope 152 5.03 S 20.48 E
Mikrá Préspa, Límni ⊜ 38 40.46 N 21.04 E
Mikre 38 43.02 N 24.31 E
Miksimil 126 22.52 N 89.23 E
Mikšino 76 57.15 N 35.43 E
Mikstat 30 51.32 N 17.59 E
Mikulášovice 54 50.58 N 14.20 E
Mikulino 76 55.02 N 31.07 E
Mikulkin, mys ≻ 24 67.48 N 46.40 E
Mikulov 61 48.49 N 16.39 E
Mikumi 154 7.24 S 36.59 E
Mikumi National Park ♠ 154 7.12 S 37.05 E
Mikun' 24 62.21 N 50.06 E
Mikuni 94 36.13 N 136.09 E
Mikuni-sammyaku ʌʌ 94 36.50 N 138.40 E
Mikuni-tōge )( 94 36.46 N 138.50 E
Mikuni-yama ʌ 94 35.59 N 138.43 E
Mikura-jima I 92 33.52 N 139.36 E
Mila 34 36.27 N 6.16 E
Milaca 190 45.45 N 93.39 W
Miladummadulu Atoll I 1 122 6.15 N 73.15 E
Milagre 256 21.18 S 47.00 W
Milagres 250 7.17 S 38.57 W
Milagro 246 2.07 S 79.36 W
Milagros 116 12.13 N 123.30 E
Milam □ 6 222 30.47 N 96.57 W
Milan → Milano, It. 62 45.28 N 9.12 E
Milan, Ga., U.S. 192 32.01 N 83.03 W
Milan, In., U.S. 218 39.07 N 85.07 W
Milan, Mi., U.S. 216 42.05 N 83.40 W
Milan, Mn., U.S. 198 45.06 N 95.54 W
Milan, Mo., U.S. 194 40.12 N 93.07 W
Milan, N.M., U.S. 200 35.10 N 107.53 W
Milan, Oh., U.S. 214 41.17 N 82.36 W
Milan, Pa., U.S. 210 41.54 N 76.32 W
Milan, Tn., U.S. 194 35.55 N 88.45 W
Milando 152 8.45 S 17.36 E
Milan Federal Correctional Institution ⊕ 281 42.06 N 83.40 W
Milang 168b 35.25 S 138.58 E
Milano (Milan), It. 62 45.28 N 9.12 E
Milano (Milan), It. 266b 45.28 N 9.12 E
Milano, Tx., U.S. 222 30.43 N 96.52 W
Milano □ 4 62 45.30 N 9.10 E
Milanoa 157b 13.35 S 49.47 E
Milano Marittima 66 44.16 N 12.21 E
Milanville 210 41.40 N 75.04 W
Milâs 130 37.19 N 27.47 E
Milašavičy 78 51.39 N 27.56 E
Milaslavičy 76 53.41 N 32.15 E
Mil'atino, Ross. 76 54.29 N 34.18 E
Mil'atino, Ross. 82 55.41 N 35.48 E
Milavidy 76 52.55 N 25.44 E
Milazzo 70 38.13 N 15.14 E
Milazzo, Capo di ≻ 70 38.16 N 15.14 E
Milazzo, Golfo di c 70 38.15 N 15.20 E
Milbank 198 45.13 N 96.38 W
Milbanke Sound ʁ 182 52.18 N 128.33 W
Milborne Port 42 50.58 N 2.27 W
Milbuk 116 6.10 N 124.16 E
Milburn 196 34.14 N 96.32 W
Milburn Creek ≃ 276 40.38 N 73.36 W
Milden 184 51.30 N 107.31 W
Mildenau 54 50.35 N 13.04 E
Mildenberg 54 53.01 N 13.17 E
Mildenhall 42 52.21 N 0.30 E
Milders 64 47.06 N 11.16 E
Mildmay 212 44.03 N 81.07 W
Mildred, Il., U.S. 219 39.46 N 89.38 W
Mildred, Pa., U.S. 210 41.28 N 76.22 W
Mildura 166 34.12 S 142.09 E
Mil düzü ≚ 84 40.00 N 48.00 E
Mile 102 24.26 N 103.26 E
Miléai 38 39.20 N 23.09 E
Milena 70 37.28 N 13.44 E
Milendella 168b 34.49 S 139.12 E
Milepa 154 11.43 S 36.20 E
Miles, Austl. 166 26.40 S 150.11 E
Miles, Tx., U.S. 196 31.35 N 100.10 W
Miles ≃ 283 42.40 N 70.51 W
Milesburg 214 40.56 N 77.47 W
Miles City 202 46.24 N 105.50 W
Miles Creek c 208 38.46 N 76.12 W
Miles Creek ≃ 226 37.12 N 120.21 W
Mile Seven Hundred Thirty Three 180 60.03 N 131.07 W
Milešovka ʌ 54 50.33 N 13.56 E
Milestone 184 50.00 N 104.30 W
Milesville 279b 40.12 N 79.52 W
Milet (Miletus) ⊥ 130 37.28 N 27.15 E
Mileto 68 38.36 N 16.04 E
Miletto, Monte ʌ 68 41.27 N 14.22 E
Miletus → Milet ⊥ 130 37.28 N 27.15 E
Mileura 162 26.23 S 117.20 E
Milevsko 30 49.27 N 14.22 E
Milford, Eng., U.K. 42 51.11 N 0.38 W
Milford, Ct., U.S. 207 41.13 N 73.04 W
Milford, De., U.S. 208 38.54 N 75.25 W
Milford, Il., U.S. 216 40.37 N 87.41 W
Milford, In., U.S. 216 41.24 N 85.50 W
Milford, Ia., U.S. 198 43.19 N 95.08 W
Milford, Ky., U.S. 218 38.34 N 84.09 W
Milford, Me., U.S. 188 44.56 N 68.38 W
Milford, Md., U.S. 284b 39.21 N 76.44 W
Milford, Ma., U.S. 207 42.08 N 71.31 W
Milford, Mi., U.S. 216 42.35 N 83.35 W
Milford, N.H., U.S. 207 42.50 N 71.38 W
Milford, N.J., U.S. 210 40.34 N 75.05 W
Milford, N.Y., U.S. 210 42.35 N 74.56 W
Milford, Oh., U.S. 218 39.10 N 84.17 W
Milford, Pa., U.S. 210 41.19 N 74.48 W
Milford, Tx., U.S. 222 32.07 N 96.57 W
Milford, Ut,. U.S. 200 38.23 N 113.00 W
Milford, Va., U.S. 208 38.01 N 77.22 W
Milford Brook ≃ 276 40.19 N 74.17 W
Milford Center 218 40.10 N 83.26 W
Milford Cross Roads 285 39.43 N 75.44 W
Milford Haven 42 51.40 N 5.02 W
Milford Haven c 42 51.42 N 5.03 W
Milford Lake ⊜ 1 198 39.15 N 97.00 W
Milford on Sea 42 50.44 N 1.36 W
Milford Ridge 284b 39.21 N 76.45 W
Milford Sound 172 44.40 S 167.54 E
Milford Sound ʁ 172 44.35 S 167.47 E
Milford Station 186 45.03 N 63.26 W
Milgis ≃ 154 1.48 N 38.06 E
Milgoo ʌ 162 28.51 S 118.07 E
Mil'guvejem ≃ 180 68.22 N 171.30 E
Milḥ, Baḥr al- ⊜ 128 32.40 N 43.35 E
Milḥat Ashqar ≡, 'Īrāq 128 35.18 N 41.55 E
Milḥat Ashqar ≡, 'Īrāq 130 35.18 N 41.55 E
Milhaud 62 43.47 N 4.18 E
Mili I 1 14 6.08 N 171.55 E
Milian ≃ 112 5.13 N 117.25 E
Milicia ≃ 70 38.04 N 13.33 E
Milicz 30 51.32 N 17.17 E
Milieu, Rivière du ≃ 206 46.47 N 73.56 W
Milīj 142 30.36 N 31.03 E
Milim 164 5.10 S 152.00 E
Milín 60 49.39 N 14.02 E
Miling 162 30.30 S 116.21 E
Milis 71 40.03 N 8.38 E
Militello in Val di Catania 70 37.16 N 14.48 E
Militello Rosmarino 70 38.03 N 14.41 E
Milk ≃ 202 48.05 N 106.15 W
Milk Creek ≃, Co., U.S. 200 40.24 N 107.45 W
Milk Creek ≃, Or., U.S. 224 45.15 N 122.41 W
Milk Hill ʌ 2 42 51.23 N 1.51 W
Mil'kovo 74 54.43 N 158.37 E
Milk River 182 49.09 N 112.05 W
Milk River Ridge Reservoir ⊜ 1 182 49.22 N 112.35 W
Mill 52 51.41 N 5.47 E
Mill ≃, Ct., U.S. 276 41.08 N 73.16 W
Mill ≃, Ma., U.S. 207 42.18 N 72.37 W
Mill ≃, Ma., U.S. 283 42.38 N 70.41 W
Mill ≃, Ma., U.S. 283 42.12 N 70.57 W
Mill ≃, Ma., U.S. 283 42.08 N 71.21 W
Mill ≃, Ma., U.S. 283 42.44 N 70.52 W
Mill ≃, N.Y., U.S. 276 40.38 N 73.39 W
Millard 198 41.13 N 96.07 W
Millau 32 44.06 N 3.05 E
Mill Bay 224 48.39 N 123.34 W
Millboro 192 37.59 N 79.36 W
Millbourne 285 39.58 N 75.15 W
Millbrae 226 37.35 N 122.23 W
Millbrook, On., Can. 212 44.09 N 78.27 W
Millbrook, Eng., U.K. 42 50.20 N 4.13 W
Millbrook, Ma., U.S. 283 42.03 N 70.41 W
Millbrook, N.J., U.S. 276 40.52 N 74.33 W
Millbrook, N.Y., U.S. 210 41.47 N 73.41 W
Mill Brook ≃, Ma., U.S. 283 42.31 N 71.18 W
Mill Brook ≃, N.J., U.S. 276 40.53 N 74.32 W
Mill Brook ≃, N.J., U.S. 276 40.25 N 74.06 W
Mill Brook ≃, N.J., U.S. 276 40.29 N 74.23 W
Millburn 276 40.44 N 74.18 W
Millbury, Ma., U.S. 207 42.11 N 71.45 W
Millbury, Oh., U.S. 214 41.33 N 83.25 W
Mill City 202 44.45 N 122.29 W
Mill Creek, Pa., U.S. 214 40.26 N 77.56 W
Millcreek, Ut,. U.S. 200 40.27 N 111.54 W
Mill Creek, W.V., U.S. 188 38.43 N 79.58 W
Mill Creek ≃, Austl. 274a 33.59 S 151.01 E
Mill Creek ≃, Ca., U.S. 226 36.49 N 119.21 W
Mill Creek ≃, Ca., U.S. 228 34.05 N 117.06 W
Mill Creek ≃, De., U.S. 285 39.42 N 75.39 W
Mill Creek ≃, Il., U.S. 219 39.50 N 91.24 W
Mill Creek ≃, In., U.S. 194 39.30 N 86.57 W
Mill Creek ≃, In., U.S. 216 41.01 N 86.36 W
Mill Creek ≃, Ia., U.S. 198 42.47 N 95.31 W
Mill Creek ≃, Ks., U.S. 198 39.55 N 96.56 W
Mill Creek ≃, Ky., U.S. 218 38.28 N 84.20 W
Mill Creek ≃, N.J., U.S. 276 40.48 N 74.03 W
Mill Creek ≃, N.J., U.S. 285 40.02 N 74.55 W
Mill Creek ≃, N.Y., U.S. 212 43.57 N 76.08 W
Mill Creek ≃, Oh., U.S. 214 41.06 N 80.40 W
Mill Creek ≃, Oh., U.S. 214 40.14 N 83.09 W
Mill Creek ≃, Oh., U.S. 218 39.06 N 84.32 W
Mill Creek ≃, Oh., U.S. 279a 41.25 N 81.38 W
Mill Creek ≃, Or., U.S. 224 45.36 N 121.11 W
Mill Creek ≃, Pa., U.S. 208 40.00 N 76.18 W
Mill Creek ≃, Pa., U.S. 210 41.53 N 77.08 W
Mill Creek ≃, Pa., U.S. 214 41.09 N 79.03 W
Mill Creek ≃, Pa., U.S. 285 40.03 N 75.16 W
Mill Creek ≃, Pa., U.S. 285 40.08 N 74.52 W
Mill Creek ≃, Tx., U.S. 222 32.10 N 96.42 W
Mill Creek ≃, Tx., U.S. 222 30.08 N 95.37 W
Mill Creek ≃, Tx., U.S. 222 32.46 N 95.46 W
Mill Creek ≃, Tx., U.S. 222 29.50 N 96.07 W
Mill Creek ≃, Va., U.S. 208 38.09 N 77.10 W
Mill Creek, North Fork ≃ 224 45.33 N 121.18 W
Mill Creek, South Fork ≃ 224 45.36 N 121.12 W
Millcreek Township 214 42.05 N 80.10 W
Milldale 207 41.33 N 72.53 W
Milledgeville, Ga., U.S. 192 33.04 N 83.13 W
Milledgeville, Il., U.S. 190 41.57 N 89.46 W
Milledgeville, Oh., U.S. 218 39.36 N 83.35 W
Mille Îles, Rivière des ≃ 206 45.42 N 73.32 W
Mille Lacs, Lac des ⊜ 190 48.50 N 90.30 W
Mille Lacs Kathio State Park ♠ 190 46.08 N 93.43 W
Mille Lacs Lake ⊜ 190 46.15 N 93.40 W
Millemont 261 48.49 N 1.45 E
Millen 192 32.48 N 81.56 W
Millendon 168a 31.48 S 116.02 E
Miller, Mo., U.S. 194 37.13 N 93.50 W
Miller, S.D., U.S. 198 44.31 N 98.59 W
Miller □ 6 219 38.15 N 92.15 W
Miller, Mount ʌ 180 60.25 N 142.23 W
Miller City 216 41.06 N 84.08 W
Miller Creek ≃ 282 38.02 N 122.30 W
Miller House 180 65.32 N 145.11 W
Miller Mountain ʌ 204 38.03 N 118.12 W
Millerovo, Ross. 78 48.55 N 40.25 E
Millerovo, Ross. 83 47.49 N 39.15 E
Miller Peak ʌ 200 31.23 N 110.17 W
Miller Place 210 40.58 N 73.00 W
Millers ≃ 207 42.35 N 72.30 W
Millersburg, In., U.S. 216 41.31 N 85.41 W
Millersburg, In., U.S. 218 41.31 N 85.41 W
Millersburg, Ky., U.S. 218 38.18 N 84.08 W
Millersburg, Mi., U.S. 190 45.20 N 84.03 W
Millersburg, Oh., U.S. 214 40.33 N 81.55 W
Millersburg, Pa., U.S. 208 40.32 N 76.57 W
Millers Creek ≃ 196 33.27 N 99.14 W
Miller Seamount ✦ 3 16 53.30 N 144.20 W
Millers Falls 207 42.34 N 72.29 W
Millers Ferry 194 32.05 N 87.22 W
Millers Flat 172 45.40 S 169.25 E
Millers Island 284b 39.14 N 76.24 W
Millers Pond ⊜ 276 40.51 N 73.12 W
Millersport 188 39.54 N 82.32 W
Millers Run ≃ 279b 40.22 N 80.07 W
Millerstown 210 40.32 N 77.09 W

**Symbols** in the index entries represent the broad categories identified in the key at the right. Symbols with superior numbers (ʌʌ 1) identify subcategories (see complete key on page *I · 1).*

**Symbole** im Register stellen die rechts im Schlüssel erklärten Kategorien dar. Symbole mit hochgestellten Ziffern (ʌʌ 1) bezeichnen Unterabteilungen einer Kategorie (vgl. vollständiger Schlüssel auf Seite *I · 1).*

**Los símbolos** incluídos en el texto del índice representan las grandes categorías identificadas con la clave a la derecha. Los símbolos con numeros en su parte superior (ʌʌ 1) identifican las subcategorías (véase la clave completa en la página *I · 1).*

**Les symboles** de l'index représentent les catégories indiquées dans la légende à droite. Les symboles suivis d'un indice (ʌʌ 1) représentent des sous-catégories (voir légende complète à la page *I · 1).*

**Os símbolos** incluídos no texto do índice representam as grandes categorias identificadas com a chave à direita. Os símbolos com números em sua parte superior (ʌʌ 1) identificam as subcategorias (veja-se a chave completa à página *I · 1).*

| | English | Deutsch | Español | Français | Português |
|---|---|---|---|---|---|
| ʌ | Mountain | Berg | Montaña | Montagne | Montanha |
| ʌʌ | Mountains | Gebirge | Montañas | Montagnes | Montanhas |
| )( | Pass | Paß | Paso | Col | Passo |
| V | Valley, Canyon | Tal, Cañon | Valle, Cañón | Vallée, Canyon | Vale, Canhão |
| ≚ | Plain | Ebene | Llano | Plaine | Planície |
| ≻ | Cape | Kap | Cabo | Cap | Cabo |
| I | Island | Insel | Isla | Île | Ilha |
| II | Islands | Inseln | Islas | Îles | Ilhas |
| ⊥ | Other Topographic Features | Andere Topographische Objekte | Otros Elementos Topográficos | Autres données topographiques | Outros acidentes topográficos |

| ESPAÑOL Nombre / FRANÇAIS Nom / PORTUGUÊS Nome | Página / Page | Lat.°′ | Long.°′ W = Oeste / W = Ouest |
|---|---|---|---|
| Millersville, Il., U.S. | 219 | 39.25 N | 89.07 W |
| Millersville, Oh., U.S. | 214 | 41.18 N | 83.16 W |
| Millersville, Pa., U.S. | 208 | 39.59 N | 76.21 W |
| Millerton, N.Y., U.S. | 210 | 41.57 N | 73.30 W |
| Millerton, Pa., U.S. | 210 | 41.59 N | 76.56 W |
| Millerton Lake ⊜[1] | 226 | 37.01 N | 119.41 W |
| Millerton Lake State Recreation Area ♠ | 226 | 37.02 N | 119.37 W |
| Millertown | 186 | 48.49 N | 56.33 W |
| Millertown Junction | 186 | 49.01 N | 56.21 W |
| Millesimo | 62 | 44.22 N | 8.12 E |
| Millet | 182 | 53.06 N | 113.28 W |
| Millett, Mi., U.S. | 216 | 42.42 N | 84.38 W |
| Millett, Tx., U.S. | 196 | 28.35 N | 99.12 W |
| Milleur Point › | 44 | 55.01 N | 5.06 W |
| Millevaches, Plateau de ⩘[1] | 32 | 45.30 N | 2.10 E |
| Millford | 48 | 55.07 N | 7.43 W |
| Mill Green | 260 | 51.41 N | 0.22 E |
| Mill Grove | 216 | 40.25 N | 85.17 W |
| Mill Hall | 210 | 41.06 N | 77.29 W |
| Millheim | 210 | 40.53 N | 77.28 W |
| Mill Hill ◆[8] | 260 | 51.37 N | 0.13 W |
| Mill Hill ∧[2] | 262 | 53.25 N | 1.54 W |
| Millhousen | 218 | 39.13 N | 85.26 W |
| Millican | 222 | 30.28 N | 96.12 W |
| Millicent | 166 | 37.36 S | 140.22 E |
| Milligan, Fl., U.S. | 194 | 30.45 N | 86.38 W |
| Milligan, Ne., U.S. | 198 | 40.30 N | 97.23 W |
| Milligan Gulch V | 200 | 33.37 N | 107.02 W |
| Milligantown | 279b | 40.33 N | 79.41 W |
| Milliken | 275b | 43.49 N | 79.18 W |
| Millingen aan de Rijn | 52 | 51.52 N | 6.02 E |
| Millington, Il., U.S. | 216 | 41.34 N | 88.36 W |
| Millington, Md., U.S. | 208 | 39.15 N | 75.50 W |
| Millington, Mi., U.S. | 190 | 43.16 N | 83.31 W |
| Millington, N.J., U.S. | 210 | 40.40 N | 74.31 W |
| Millington, Tn., U.S. | 194 | 35.20 N | 89.53 W |
| Millinocket | 188 | 45.39 N | 68.42 W |
| Millionnyj | 89 | 54.30 N | 126.19 E |
| Millis | 207 | 42.10 N | 71.21 W |
| Mill Island I, Ant. | 9 | 65.30 S | 100.40 E |
| Mill Island I, N.T., Can. | 176 | 64.00 N | 78.00 W |
| Millisle | 48 | 54.36 N | 5.32 W |
| Mill Lake ⊜ | 212 | 45.22 N | 80.00 W |
| Millmerran | 166 | 27.52 S | 151.16 E |
| Millmont | 210 | 40.53 N | 77.08 W |
| Mill Neck | 276 | 40.52 N | 73.34 W |
| Mill Neck ›[1] | 276 | 40.53 N | 73.33 W |
| Mill Neck Creek c | 276 | 40.54 N | 73.33 W |
| Millom | 44 | 54.13 N | 3.18 W |
| Mill Pond ⊜ | 276 | 40.53 N | 73.22 W |
| Millport, Scot., U.K. | 46 | 55.46 N | 4.55 W |
| Millport, Al., U.S. | 194 | 33.33 N | 88.04 W |
| Millport, N.Y., U.S. | 210 | 42.16 N | 76.50 W |
| Millport, Pa., U.S. | 214 | 41.55 N | 78.07 W |
| Millrift | 210 | 41.25 N | 74.45 W |
| Mill River | 207 | 42.06 N | 73.16 W |
| Mill Run Acres | 284c | 38.58 N | 77.17 W |
| Millry | 194 | 31.38 N | 88.18 W |
| Mills, Pa., U.S. | 214 | 41.57 N | 77.41 W |
| Mills, Wy., U.S. | 202 | 42.50 N | 106.21 W |
| Mills, Lake ⊜[1] | 224 | 47.59 N | 123.36 W |
| Millsboro | 208 | 38.35 N | 75.17 W |
| Mills Creek ≃, Austl. | 166 | 22.23 S | 143.05 E |
| Mills Creek ≃, Ca., U.S. | 282 | 37.27 N | 122.25 W |
| Mills Lake ⊜ | 176 | 61.30 N | 118.10 W |
| Mills Mansion State Historic Site ⊥ | 210 | 41.52 N | 73.57 W |
| Millstadt | 219 | 38.27 N | 90.05 W |
| Millstatt | 64 | 46.48 N | 13.35 E |
| Millstätter See ⊜ | 64 | 46.47 N | 13.35 E |
| Millstone | 276 | 40.29 N | 74.35 W |
| Millstone ≃ | 276 | 40.33 N | 74.34 W |
| Millstream, Austl. | 162 | 21.35 S | 117.04 E |
| Millstream, B.C., Can. | 224 | 48.30 N | 123.31 W |
| Millstream Chichester National Park ♠ | 162 | 21.25 S | 117.20 E |
| Millstreet | 48 | 52.03 N | 9.04 W |
| Milltown, Scot., U.K. | 46 | 57.14 N | 2.52 W |
| Milltown, In., U.S. | 218 | 38.20 N | 86.16 W |
| Milltown, Mt., U.S. | 202 | 46.52 N | 113.52 W |
| Milltown, N.J., U.S. | 208 | 40.27 N | 74.26 W |
| Milltown, Wi., U.S. | 190 | 45.31 N | 92.30 W |
| Milltown Malbay | 48 | 52.50 N | 9.23 W |
| Millvale | 279b | 40.28 N | 79.58 W |
| Mill Valley | 226 | 37.54 N | 122.32 W |
| Mill Village | 214 | 41.53 N | 79.58 W |
| Millville, Ma., U.S. | 207 | 42.01 N | 71.34 W |
| Millville, N.J., U.S. | 208 | 39.24 N | 75.02 W |
| Millville, Oh., U.S. | 218 | 39.24 N | 84.40 W |
| Millville, Pa., U.S. | 210 | 41.07 N | 76.31 W |
| Millville Lake | 283 | 42.48 N | 71.13 W |
| Millville Lake ⊜ | 283 | 42.48 N | 71.13 W |
| Millwood, Md., U.S. | 284c | 38.53 N | 76.53 W |
| Millwood, N.Y., U.S. | 210 | 41.11 N | 73.48 W |
| Millwood, Va., U.S. | 188 | 39.04 N | 78.02 W |
| Millwood Lake ⊜[1] | 194 | 33.45 N | 94.00 W |
| Milly-la-Forêt | 50 | 48.24 N | 2.28 E |
| Milly-Lamartine | 58 | 46.21 N | 4.42 E |
| Milmay | 208 | 39.26 N | 74.51 W |
| Milmersdorf | 54 | 53.06 N | 13.38 E |
| Milmine | 219 | 39.54 N | 88.39 W |
| Milmont Park | 285 | 39.53 N | 75.20 W |
| Milne Bay □[5] | 164 | 10.00 S | 152.30 E |
| Milne Bay c | 164 | 10.22 S | 150.30 E |
| Milner | 224 | 49.20 N | 122.42 W |
| Milnesville | 210 | 40.59 N | 75.59 W |
| Milngavie | 46 | 55.57 N | 4.20 W |
| Milnor | 198 | 46.15 N | 97.27 W |
| Milnrow | 44 | 53.37 N | 2.06 W |
| Milnthorpe | 44 | 54.14 N | 2.46 W |
| Milo, Ab., Can. | 182 | 50.34 N | 112.53 W |
| Milo, Ia., U.S. | 190 | 41.17 N | 93.26 W |
| Milo, Me., U.S. | 188 | 45.15 N | 68.59 W |
| Milo ≃ | 150 | 11.04 N | 9.14 W |
| Milon-la-Chapelle | 261 | 48.44 N | 2.03 E |
| Mílos | 38 | 36.45 N | 24.27 E |
| Mílos I | 38 | 36.41 N | 24.15 E |
| Miloslavskoje | 76 | 53.34 N | 39.24 E |
| Miłosław | 30 | 52.13 N | 17.29 E |
| Milove | 83 | 49.22 N | 40.06 E |
| Milow, Dtsch. | 54 | 53.11 N | 11.32 E |
| Milow, Dtsch. | 54 | 52.31 N | 12.18 E |
| Milpa Alta ◆[8] | 286a | 19.11 N | 99.01 W |
| Milparinka | 166 | 29.44 S | 141.53 E |
| Milpitas | 226 | 37.25 N | 121.54 W |
| Milpitas Wash V | 204 | 33.18 N | 114.44 W |
| Milroy, In., U.S. | 218 | 39.29 N | 85.28 W |
| Milroy, Pa., U.S. | 208 | 40.42 N | 77.35 W |
| Milseburg ∧ | 56 | 50.32 N | 9.53 E |
| Milspe | 263 | 51.18 N | 7.21 E |
| Miltach | 60 | 49.09 N | 12.46 E |
| Miltenberg | 56 | 49.42 N | 9.15 E |
| Miltitz | 54 | 51.19 N | 12.16 E |
| Milton, Austl. | 170 | 35.19 S | 150.26 E |
| Milton, On., Can. | 212 | 43.31 N | 79.53 W |
| Milton, N.Z. | 172 | 46.07 S | 169.58 E |
| Milton, Eng., U.K. | 42 | 52.14 N | 0.09 E |
| Milton, De., U.S. | 208 | 38.46 N | 75.18 W |
| Milton, Fl., U.S. | 194 | 30.37 N | 87.02 W |
| Milton, Il., U.S. | 219 | 39.34 N | 90.39 W |
| Milton, In., U.S. | 218 | 39.47 N | 85.09 W |
| Milton, In., U.S. | 218 | 38.58 N | 85.01 W |
| Milton, Ia., U.S. | 190 | 40.40 N | 92.09 W |
| Milton, Ky., U.S. | 218 | 38.43 N | 85.22 W |
| Milton, Ma., U.S. | 207 | 42.15 N | 71.05 W |
| Milton, N.J., U.S. | 276 | 41.02 N | 74.32 W |
| Milton, N.Y., U.S. | 210 | 41.39 N | 73.57 W |
| Milton, N.D., U.S. | 198 | 48.37 N | 98.02 W |
| Milton, Pa., U.S. | 210 | 41.00 N | 76.50 W |
| Milton, Vt., U.S. | 188 | 44.38 N | 73.06 W |
| Milton, Wa., U.S. | 224 | 47.14 N | 122.18 W |
| Milton, W.V., U.S. | 188 | 38.26 N | 82.07 W |
| Milton, Wi., U.S. | 216 | 42.46 N | 88.56 W |
| Milton, Lake ⊜ | 214 | 41.06 N | 80.58 W |
| Milton Abbot | 42 | 50.35 N | 4.15 W |
| Milton-Freewater | 202 | 45.55 N | 118.23 W |
| Milton Harbor c | 276 | 40.57 N | 73.42 W |
| Milton Keynes | 42 | 52.02 N | 0.42 W |
| Milton Point › | 276 | 40.57 N | 73.42 W |
| Miltonvale | 198 | 39.20 N | 97.26 W |
| Miltou | 146 | 10.14 N | 17.26 E |
| Miltzow | 54 | 54.12 N | 13.13 E |
| Milumba | 154 | 7.06 S | 31.04 E |
| Miluo | 100 | 28.50 N | 113.04 E |
| Miluo ≃ | 100 | 28.50 N | 113.06 E |
| Mil'utinskaja | 80 | 48.38 N | 41.40 E |
| Mil'utkej, gora ∧ | 180 | 65.42 N | 178.03 W |
| Miluvatka | 83 | 49.21 N | 38.11 E |
| Milverton, On., Can. | 212 | 43.34 N | 80.55 W |
| Milverton, Eng., U.K. | 42 | 51.02 N | 3.16 W |
| Milwaukee | 216 | 43.02 N | 87.54 W |
| Milwaukee □[6] | 216 | 43.02 N | 87.58 W |
| Milwaukee ≃ | 190 | 43.02 N | 87.54 W |
| Milwaukee Bay c | 216 | 43.02 N | 87.53 W |
| Milwaukie | 224 | 45.26 N | 122.38 W |
| Milybulak | 86 | 48.57 N | 75.13 E |
| Mim | 150 | 6.54 N | 2.34 W |
| Mima | 96 | 33.17 N | 132.36 E |
| Mimasaka | 96 | 35.00 N | 134.10 E |
| Mimbres ≃ | 200 | 32.13 N | 107.28 W |
| Mimbres Mountains ⩘ | 200 | 32.45 N | 107.45 W |
| Mimi ≃ | 92 | 32.20 N | 131.37 E |
| Mimico ◆[8] | 275b | 43.37 N | 79.30 W |
| Mimico Creek ≃ | 275b | 43.37 N | 79.29 W |
| Mimizan | 32 | 44.12 N | 1.14 W |
| Mimmaya | 92 | 41.12 N | 140.26 E |
| Mimoň | 54 | 50.40 N | 14.44 E |
| Mimongo | 152 | 1.11 S | 11.36 E |
| Mimoso, Bra. | 248 | 16.17 S | 55.48 W |
| Mimoso, Bra. | 255 | 15.10 S | 48.05 W |
| Mimoso do Sul | 255 | 21.04 S | 41.22 W |
| Mims | 220 | 28.39 N | 80.50 W |
| Mimuro-yama ∧ | 96 | 35.14 N | 134.28 E |
| Min ≃, Zhg. | 100 | 26.05 N | 119.32 E |
| Min ≃, Zhg. | 102 | 28.46 N | 104.38 E |
| Mina, Méx. | 196 | 26.01 N | 100.32 W |
| Mina, Nv., U.S. | 204 | 38.23 N | 118.06 W |
| Mina ≃ | 112 | 10.09 S | 124.12 E |
| Mîna, Oued ≃ | 34 | 35.47 N | 0.30 E |
| Mīnā' al-Aḥmadī | 128 | 29.04 N | 48.08 E |
| Mīnāb | 128 | 27.09 N | 57.05 E |
| Mīnāb ≃ | 128 | 27.01 N | 56.53 E |
| Minabe | 96 | 33.46 N | 135.19 E |
| Minabegawa | 96 | 33.47 N | 135.20 E |
| Mina El Limón | 236 | 12.45 N | 86.44 W |
| Minago ≃ | 184 | 54.34 N | 98.08 W |
| Minahasa ›[1] | 112 | 1.00 N | 124.35 E |
| Mināj ≃[1] | 126 | 22.31 N | 89.22 E |
| Minakami | 94 | 36.46 N | 138.58 E |
| Minakuchi | 94 | 34.58 N | 136.10 E |
| Minam ≃ | 202 | 45.37 N | 117.43 W |
| Minamata | 92 | 32.13 N | 130.24 E |
| Minami | 94 | 35.39 N | 136.57 E |
| Minami ◆[8], Nihon | 268 | 35.24 N | 139.36 E |
| Minami ◆[8], Nihon | 270 | 34.40 N | 135.31 E |
| Minami ◆[8], Nihon | 270 | 34.58 N | 135.45 E |
| Minami ≃ | 94 | 35.30 N | 135.49 E |
| Minamiaiki | 94 | 36.02 N | 138.33 E |
| Minami-Alps-kokuritsu-kōen ♠ | 94 | 35.40 N | 138.13 E |
| Minamiashigara | 94 | 35.19 N | 139.07 E |
| Minami-Bōsō-kokutei-kōen ♠ | 94 | 35.10 N | 140.05 E |
| Minamichita | 94 | 34.44 N | 136.52 E |
| Minami-Daitō-jima I | 90 | 25.50 N | 131.15 E |
| Minami-Iō-jima I | 14 | 24.14 N | 141.28 E |
| Minamiizu | 94 | 34.39 N | 138.50 E |
| Minamimaki | 94 | 36.00 N | 138.30 E |
| Minaminasu | 94 | 36.39 N | 140.06 E |
| Minamisenju ◆[8] | 268 | 35.44 N | 139.48 E |
| Minamishinano | 94 | 35.19 N | 137.56 E |
| Minami-Tori-shima (Marcus Island) I | 14 | 24.18 N | 153.58 E |
| Minano | 94 | 36.04 N | 139.06 E |
| Mina Pirquitas | 252 | 22.41 S | 66.31 W |
| Minard, S. Afr. | 158 | 31.17 S | 27.35 E |
| Minard, Scot., U.K. | 46 | 56.07 N | 5.15 W |
| Minas, Cuba | 240p | 21.29 N | 77.37 W |
| Minas, Indon. | 114 | 0.50 N | 101.29 E |
| Minas, Ur. | 252 | 34.23 S | 55.14 W |
| Minas, Sierra de las ⩘ | 236 | 15.10 N | 89.40 W |
| Minas Basin c | 186 | 45.20 N | 64.00 W |
| Minas Channel ʉ | 186 | 45.15 N | 64.45 W |
| Minas de Barroterán | 232 | 27.40 N | 101.20 W |
| Minas de Corrales | 252 | 31.35 S | 55.28 W |
| Minas de Matahambre | 240p | 22.35 N | 83.57 W |
| Minas de Oro | 236 | 14.46 N | 87.20 W |
| Minas de Ríotinto | 34 | 37.42 N | 6.35 W |
| Minas Gerais □[3] | 255 | 18.00 S | 44.00 W |
| Minas Novas | 255 | 17.15 S | 42.36 W |
| Minatare | 198 | 41.48 N | 103.30 W |
| Minatitlán | 234 | 17.59 N | 94.31 W |
| Minato | 268 | 35.13 N | 139.52 E |
| Minato ◆[8], Nihon | 268 | 35.39 N | 139.45 E |
| Minato ◆[8], Nihon | 270 | 34.39 N | 135.26 E |
| Minato ≃ | 268 | 35.13 N | 139.52 E |
| Minbāl | 142 | 28.24 N | 30.41 E |
| Minbu | 110 | 20.11 N | 94.52 E |
| Minbulak | 85 | 41.30 N | 75.53 E |
| Minbya | 110 | 20.22 N | 93.15 E |
| Minbyin | 110 | 19.17 N | 93.32 E |
| Minchinābād | 123 | 30.10 N | 73.34 E |
| Minchinhampton | 42 | 51.42 N | 2.10 W |
| Minchumina, Lake ⊜ | 180 | 63.52 N | 152.15 W |
| Mincio ≃ | 64 | 45.04 N | 10.59 E |
| Mincivan | 84 | 39.03 N | 46.42 E |
| Minco | 196 | 35.18 N | 97.56 W |
| Minčol ∧ | 30 | 49.15 N | 20.59 E |
| Mind'ak | 86 | 54.02 N | 58.48 E |
| Mindanao I | 116 | 8.00 N | 125.00 E |
| Mindanao ≃ | 116 | 7.07 N | 124.24 E |
| Mindego Creek ≃ | 282 | 37.18 N | 122.15 W |
| Mindego Hill ∧[2] | 282 | 37.18 N | 122.13 W |
| Mindel ≃ | 58 | 48.31 N | 10.23 E |
| Mindelheim | 58 | 48.03 N | 10.29 E |
| Mindelo | 150a | 16.53 N | 25.00 W |
| Mindemoya | 190 | 45.44 N | 82.10 W |
| Minden, On., Can. | 212 | 44.55 N | 78.43 W |
| Minden, Dtsch. | 52 | 52.17 N | 8.55 E |
| Minden, La., U.S. | 194 | 32.36 N | 93.17 W |
| Minden, Ne., U.S. | 198 | 40.29 N | 98.56 W |
| Minden, Nv., U.S. | 226 | 38.57 N | 119.45 W |
| Minden, W.V., U.S. | 188 | 37.58 N | 81.07 W |
| Minden City | 190 | 43.40 N | 82.46 W |
| Mindenmines | 194 | 37.28 N | 94.35 W |
| Minderoo | 162 | 22.00 S | 115.02 E |
| Mindif | 146 | 10.24 N | 14.26 E |
| Mindiptana | 164 | 5.45 S | 140.42 E |
| Mindon | 110 | 19.21 N | 94.44 E |
| Mindoro I | 116 | 12.50 N | 121.05 E |
| Mindoro Occidental □[4] | 116 | 13.00 N | 121.00 E |
| Mindoro Oriental □[4] | 116 | 13.00 N | 121.20 E |
| Mindoro Strait ʉ | 116 | 12.20 N | 120.40 E |
| Mindouli | 152 | 4.17 S | 14.21 E |
| Mindourou, Cam. | 152 | 3.25 N | 13.32 E |
| Mindourou, Cam. | 152 | 4.06 N | 14.34 E |
| Minduri | 256 | 21.41 S | 44.37 W |
| Mine, Ityo. | 144 | 8.20 N | 40.09 E |
| Mine, Nihon | 96 | 33.17 N | 130.26 E |
| Mine, Nihon | 96 | 34.10 N | 131.13 E |
| Minear Lake ⊜ | 278 | 42.17 N | 87.57 W |
| Minebank Run ≃ | 284b | 39.25 N | 76.32 W |
| Mine Brook ≃, Ma., U.S. | 283 | 42.08 N | 71.26 W |
| Mine Brook ≃, Ma., U.S. | 283 | 42.09 N | 71.15 W |
| Mine Brook ≃, N.J., U.S. | 276 | 40.41 N | 74.38 W |
| Mine Centre | 190 | 48.45 N | 92.37 W |
| Minehead | 42 | 51.13 N | 3.29 W |
| Mine Hill | 210 | 40.52 N | 74.35 W |
| Mineiros | 255 | 17.34 S | 52.34 W |
| Mineo | 70 | 37.16 N | 14.42 E |
| Mineola, N.Y., U.S. | 210 | 40.44 N | 73.38 W |
| Mineola, Tx., U.S. | 222 | 32.39 N | 95.29 W |
| Miner ≃ | 180 | 66.30 N | 138.25 W |
| Mineral | 224 | 46.43 N | 122.10 W |
| Mineral City | 214 | 40.36 N | 81.21 W |
| Mineral Creek ≃ | 224 | 46.45 N | 122.08 W |
| Mineral de Cucharas | 234 | 22.52 N | 105.19 W |
| Mineral del Monte | 234 | 20.08 N | 98.40 W |
| Mineral de Pozos | 234 | 21.14 N | 100.29 W |
| Mineral'nyje Vody | 84 | 44.12 N | 43.08 E |
| Mineral Point, Pa., U.S. | 214 | 40.23 N | 78.50 W |
| Mineral Point, Wi., U.S. | 190 | 42.51 N | 90.10 W |
| Mineral Ridge | 214 | 41.08 N | 80.46 W |
| Mineral Springs, Ar., U.S. | 194 | 33.52 N | 93.54 W |
| Mineral Springs, Pa., U.S. | 214 | 41.00 N | 78.22 W |
| Mineral Wells | 196 | 32.48 N | 98.06 W |
| Minerbe | 64 | 45.14 N | 11.20 E |
| Minerbio | 64 | 44.37 N | 11.29 E |
| Minersville, Pa., U.S. | 208 | 40.41 N | 76.16 W |
| Minersville, Ut., U.S. | 200 | 38.12 N | 112.55 W |
| Mine Run ≃ | 285 | 40.15 N | 75.28 W |
| Minerva, Ky., U.S. | 218 | 38.42 N | 83.55 W |
| Minerva, Oh., U.S. | 214 | 40.43 N | 81.06 W |
| Minerva, Tx., U.S. | 222 | 30.46 N | 96.59 W |
| Minerva, Embalse ⊜[1] | 240p | 22.25 N | 79.48 W |
| Minerva Park | 214 | 40.04 N | 83.00 W |
| Minervino Murge | 68 | 41.05 N | 16.05 E |
| Minesing Swamp ≣ | 212 | 44.23 N | 79.51 W |
| Minetto | 210 | 43.23 N | 76.28 W |
| Mineville | 188 | 44.05 N | 73.31 W |
| Mineyama | 96 | 35.37 N | 135.04 E |
| Minfeng | 120 | 37.05 N | 82.40 E |
| Minga | 154 | 11.08 S | 27.57 E |
| Mingäçevir | 84 | 40.45 N | 47.03 E |
| Mingäçevir su anbarı ⊜[1] | 84 | 40.50 N | 46.50 E |
| Mingala | 152 | 5.06 N | 21.49 E |
| Mingan | 186 | 50.18 N | 64.02 W |
| Mingan ≃ | 186 | 50.18 N | 63.59 W |
| Mingan, Îles de II | 186 | 50.12 N | 63.35 W |
| Mingan Archipelago National Park ♠ | 186 | 50.12 N | 63.35 W |
| Mingan Mountains ⩘ | 116 | 15.29 N | 121.24 E |
| Mingāora | 123 | 34.47 N | 72.22 E |
| Mingardo ≃ | 68 | 40.02 N | 15.18 E |
| Mingary | 166 | 32.08 S | 140.44 E |
| Mingcheng | 89 | 43.11 N | 125.59 E |
| Mingela | 166 | 19.53 S | 146.38 E |
| Mingenew | 162 | 29.11 S | 115.26 E |
| Mingera Creek ≃ | 166 | 20.38 S | 138.10 E |
| Minggang | 100 | 32.29 N | 114.03 E |
| Minggao | 100 | 34.20 N | 112.15 E |
| Minghuang | 106 | 31.41 N | 119.56 E |
| Mingin | 110 | 22.52 N | 94.39 E |
| Mingir | 38 | 46.40 N | 28.19 E |
| Mingjuesi | 106 | 31.34 N | 118.53 E |
| Minglanilla | 34 | 39.32 N | 1.36 W |
| Ming Ming | 164 | 5.30 S | 146.10 E |
| Mingo, Congo | 152 | 1.55 S | 14.59 E |
| Mingo, Oh., U.S. | 216 | 40.13 N | 83.38 W |
| Mingo Creek ≃, Pa., U.S. | 279b | 40.13 N | 79.57 W |
| Mingo Creek ≃, Pa., U.S. | 285 | 40.10 N | 75.32 W |
| Mingo Junction | 214 | 40.19 N | 80.36 W |
| Mingorría | 34 | 40.45 N | 4.40 W |
| Mingoville | 214 | 40.56 N | 77.39 W |
| Mingoyo | 154 | 10.06 S | 39.38 E |
| Mingrel'skaja | 78 | 45.01 N | 38.20 E |
| Mingshantou | 100 | 29.18 N | 112.33 E |
| Mingshui, Zhg. | 89 | 47.10 N | 125.55 E |
| Mingshui, Zhg. | 102 | 42.06 N | 96.04 E |
| Mingulay I | 46 | 56.49 N | 7.38 W |
| Mingwan | 106 | 31.04 N | 120.17 E |
| Mingxi | 100 | 26.24 N | 117.13 E |
| Mingyuegou | 89 | 43.07 N | 128.54 E |
| Mingyuelu | 85 | 39.34 N | 75.26 E |
| Minhang | 106 | 31.01 N | 121.24 E |
| Minhla, Mya. | 110 | 19.58 N | 95.03 E |
| Minhla, Mya. | 110 | 17.59 N | 95.43 E |
| Minho □[9] | 34 | 41.40 N | 8.30 W |
| Minho (Miño) ≃ | 34 | 41.52 N | 8.51 W |
| Minhou | 100 | 26.12 N | 119.06 E |
| Minianko | 150 | 9.58 N | 8.22 W |
| Minićevo | 38 | 43.41 N | 22.18 E |
| Minicoy Island I | 122 | 8.17 N | 73.02 E |
| Minier | 194 | 40.26 N | 89.18 W |
| Minigwal, Lake ⊜ | 162 | 29.35 S | 123.12 E |
| Minija ≃ | 76 | 55.21 N | 21.17 E |
| Minilya | 162 | 23.51 S | 113.58 E |
| Minilya ≃ | 162 | 23.56 S | 113.51 E |
| Minimarg | 123 | 34.47 N | 75.05 E |
| Minīn | 132 | 33.39 N | 36.18 E |
| Miniota | 184 | 50.08 N | 101.00 W |
| Minisinakwa Lake ⊜ | 190 | 47.40 N | 81.43 W |
| Ministikwan Lake ⊜ | 184 | 54.01 N | 109.39 W |
| Ministro Ramos Mexía | 254 | 40.30 S | 67.17 W |
| Ministro Rivadavia | 288 | 34.51 S | 58.22 W |
| Minitonas | 184 | 52.07 N | 101.00 W |
| Minj | 164 | 5.54 S | 144.39 E |
| Minjar | 86 | 55.04 N | 57.33 E |
| Minjary, Mount ∧ | 171b | 35.14 S | 148.08 E |
| Minjiadianzi | 104 | 41.35 N | 121.41 E |
| Minjiaji | 100 | 31.08 N | 115.01 E |
| Minkamman | 140 | 6.03 N | 31.32 E |
| Min'kovo | 76 | 59.42 N | 43.28 E |
| Min-Kuš | 85 | 41.41 N | 74.28 E |
| Minlaton | 168b | 34.46 S | 137.36 E |
| Minle, Zhg. | 100 | 22.59 N | 112.58 E |
| Minle, Zhg. | 102 | 38.27 N | 100.56 E |
| Minna | 150 | 9.37 N | 6.33 E |
| Minna Bluff ›[1] | 9 | 78.32 S | 166.30 E |
| Minna-shima I, Nihon | 174m | 26.39 N | 127.49 E |
| Minna-shima I, Nihon | 175d | 24.45 N | 124.42 E |
| Minneapolis, Ks., U.S. | 198 | 39.07 N | 97.42 W |
| Minneapolis, Mn., U.S. | 190 | 44.58 N | 93.15 W |
| Minnechaduza Creek ≃ | 198 | 42.54 N | 100.29 W |
| Minnedosa | 184 | 50.14 N | 99.51 W |
| Minnehaha | 224 | 45.39 N | 122.37 W |
| Minnehaha, Lake ⊜ | 220 | 28.31 N | 81.46 W |
| Minneola, Fl., U.S. | 220 | 28.35 N | 81.45 W |
| Minneola, Ks., U.S. | 198 | 37.26 N | 100.00 W |
| Minneola, Lake ⊜ | 220 | 28.34 N | 81.46 W |
| Minneosa Creek ≃ | 196 | 35.31 N | 102.48 W |
| Minneota | 198 | 44.34 N | 95.59 W |
| Minnertsga | 52 | 53.15 N | 5.35 E |
| Minnesota □[3] | 178 | 46.00 N | 94.15 W |
| Minnesota ≃ | 178 | 44.54 N | 93.10 W |
| Minnesota Lake | 190 | 43.50 N | 93.49 W |
| Minnewanka, Lake ⊜ | 182 | 51.15 N | 115.20 W |
| Minnewaukan | 198 | 48.04 N | 99.15 W |
| Minnie Creek | 162 | 24.02 S | 115.42 E |
| Minnigaff | 44 | 54.58 N | 4.30 W |
| Minnipa | 162 | 32.51 S | 135.09 E |
| Minnitaki Lake ⊜ | 184 | 49.58 N | 92.00 W |
| Minnoch, Water of ≃ | 44 | 55.02 N | 4.33 W |
| Mino, Nihon | 94 | 35.32 N | 136.55 E |
| Minō, Nihon | 96 | 34.50 N | 135.28 E |
| Miño (Minho) ≃, Europe | 34 | 41.52 N | 8.51 W |
| Minō ≃, Nihon | 270 | 34.47 N | 134.57 E |
| Minoa | 210 | 43.04 N | 76.00 W |
| Minobu | 94 | 35.22 N | 138.26 E |
| Minobu-san ∧ | 94 | 35.24 N | 138.25 E |
| Minobu-sanchi ⩘ | 94 | 35.14 N | 138.20 E |
| Minocqua | 190 | 45.52 N | 89.42 W |
| Minokamo | 94 | 35.26 N | 137.01 E |
| Mino-Mikawa-kōgen ⩘[1] | 94 | 35.11 N | 137.23 E |
| Minong | 190 | 46.05 N | 91.49 W |
| Minonk | 216 | 40.54 N | 89.02 W |
| Minooka | 216 | 41.27 N | 88.16 W |
| Minorca → Menorca I | 34 | 40.00 N | 4.00 E |
| Minori | 94 | 36.14 N | 140.21 E |
| Minorsville | 218 | 38.20 N | 84.42 W |
| Minoshō | 270 | 34.39 N | 135.49 E |
| Minot, Ma., U.S. | 283 | 42.14 N | 70.45 W |
| Minot, N.D., U.S. | 198 | 48.13 N | 101.17 W |
| Minot Air Force Base ■ | 198 | 48.26 N | 101.21 W |
| Minowa | 94 | 35.55 N | 137.59 E |
| Minqiao | 100 | 32.53 N | 119.13 E |
| Minqin | 102 | 38.42 N | 103.11 E |
| Minqing | 100 | 26.12 N | 118.51 E |
| Minquadale | 285 | 39.42 N | 75.34 W |
| Minquan | 98 | 34.41 N | 115.11 E |
| Minquiers, Plateau des II | 32 | 48.57 N | 2.09 W |
| Minsen | 52 | 53.42 N | 7.58 E |
| Min Shan ⩘ | 102 | 33.35 N | 103.00 E |
| Minshāt adh-Dhahab | 142 | 28.00 N | 30.42 E |
| Minshat al-Amir Muhammad ʿAli | 142 | 29.10 N | 30.38 E |
| Minshāt al-Bakkārī | 273c | 30.01 N | 31.08 E |
| Minshāt al-Ikhwah | 142 | 30.56 N | 31.21 E |
| Minshāt al-Mughālaqah | 142 | 27.44 N | 30.47 E |
| Minshāt Būlīn | 142 | 31.11 N | 30.10 E |
| Minshāt Sulṭān | 142 | 30.32 N | 30.55 E |
| Minsk | 76 | 53.54 N | 27.34 E |
| Minsk □[8] | 76 | 53.45 N | 27.45 E |
| Minskae ųzvyšša ⩘[1] | 76 | 54.00 N | 27.10 E |
| Mińsk Mazowiecki | 30 | 52.11 N | 21.34 E |
| Minster, Eng., U.K. | 42 | 51.20 N | 1.19 E |
| Minster, Eng., U.K. | 42 | 51.26 N | 0.49 E |
| Minster, Oh., U.S. | 216 | 40.24 N | 84.23 W |
| Minsterley | 42 | 52.39 N | 2.55 W |
| Minta | 152 | 4.35 N | 12.48 E |
| Mintaka Pass )( | 123 | 37.00 N | 74.50 E |
| Mintard | 263 | 51.22 N | 6.54 E |
| Mintaro | 168b | 33.55 S | 138.43 E |
| Mintlaw | 46 | 57.31 N | 2.00 W |
| Minto, Austl. | 274a | 34.01 S | 150.51 E |
| Minto, Mb., Can. | 184 | 49.25 N | 100.01 W |
| Minto, N.B., Can. | 186 | 46.05 N | 66.05 W |
| Minto, Yk., Can. | 180 | 62.34 N | 136.51 W |
| Minto, Ak., U.S. | 180 | 65.09 N | 149.21 W |
| Minto, N.D., U.S. | 198 | 48.17 N | 97.22 W |
| Minto, Lac ⊜ | 176 | 57.13 N | 75.00 W |
| Minto Inlet c | 176 | 71.20 N | 117.00 W |
| Mintom II | 152 | 2.42 N | 13.17 E |
| Minton | 184 | 49.10 N | 104.35 W |
| Mintoum | 152 | 0.27 N | 12.16 E |
| Minturn | 200 | 39.35 N | 106.25 W |
| Minturnae ⊥ | 68 | 41.14 N | 13.45 E |
| Minturno | 66 | 41.15 N | 13.45 E |
| Minūf | 142 | 30.28 N | 30.56 E |
| Minulovo | 265a | 60.03 N | 30.45 E |
| Minumadai-yōsui ≊ | 268 | 35.50 N | 139.42 E |
| Minur'uk | 85 | 40.56 N | 73.22 E |
| Minusinsk | 86 | 53.43 N | 91.42 E |
| Minutang | 120 | 28.13 N | 96.32 E |
| Minute Man National Historical Park ♠ | 207 | 42.27 N | 71.17 W |
| Minvoul | 152 | 2.09 N | 12.08 E |
| Minwakh | 144 | 16.50 N | 48.05 E |
| Minxian | 102 | 34.26 N | 104.02 E |
| Minya → Al-Minyā | 142 | 28.06 N | 30.45 E |
| Minyā al-Qamḥ | 142 | 30.31 N | 31.21 E |
| Minya Konka → Gongga Shan ∧ | 102 | 29.35 N | 101.51 E |
| Minyat an-Naṣr | 142 | 31.07 N | 31.39 E |
| Minyat as-Sīrij ◆[8] | 273c | 30.05 N | 31.15 E |
| Minyat Sandūb | 142 | 31.00 N | 31.23 E |
| Minzow | 54 | 53.23 N | 12.30 E |
| Mio | 190 | 44.39 N | 84.07 W |
| Mioglia | 62 | 44.29 N | 8.25 E |
| Mionica | 38 | 44.15 N | 20.05 E |
| Mipi | 120 | 28.57 N | 95.48 E |
| Miquan | 86 | 44.06 N | 87.35 E |
| Miquelon I | 186 | 47.03 N | 56.20 W |
| Miquihuana | 234 | 23.34 N | 99.47 W |
| Miquon | 285 | 40.04 N | 75.16 W |
| Mir, Bela. | 76 | 53.27 N | 26.28 E |
| Mir, Cuba | 240p | 20.46 N | 76.36 W |
| Mīr, Miṣr | 142 | 27.27 N | 30.44 E |
| Mir, Niger | 146 | 14.05 N | 11.59 E |
| Mira | 34 | 40.26 N | 8.44 W |
| Mira ≃, N.S., Can. | 186 | 46.03 N | 60.00 W |
| Mira ≃, Col. | 246 | 1.36 N | 79.01 W |
| Mira ≃, Port. | 34 | 37.43 N | 8.47 W |
| Mīrābād | 128 | 30.25 N | 61.50 E |
| Mira Bay c | 186 | 46.02 N | 59.56 W |
| Mirabeau | 62 | 43.42 N | 5.39 E |
| Mirabel | 206 | 45.39 N | 74.05 W |
| Mirabel, Aéroport International de ⊠ | 206 | 45.41 N | 74.02 W |
| Mirabella Eclano | 68 | 41.02 N | 14.59 E |
| Mirabella Imbaccari | 70 | 37.19 N | 14.27 E |
| Mirabello, Ippodromo ♠ | 266b | 45.36 N | 9.17 E |
| Mirabello Monferrato | 62 | 45.02 N | 8.31 E |
| Miracema do Tocantins | 250 | 9.33 S | 48.24 W |
| Mirada Hills → La Mirada | 228 | 33.54 N | 118.01 W |
| Mirador | 250 | 6.22 S | 44.22 W |
| Mirador, Cerro ∧ | 286d | 11.57 S | 77.02 W |
| Mirador, Paso de )( | 254 | 40.42 S | 71.56 W |
| Miradouro | 255 | 20.53 S | 42.21 W |
| Miraflores, Arg. | 252 | 28.36 S | 65.55 W |
| Miraflores, Col. | 246 | 5.12 N | 73.12 W |
| Miraflores, Col. | 246 | 1.25 N | 72.13 W |
| Miraflores, Perú | 286d | 12.07 S | 77.02 W |
| Miraflores, Esclusas de ◆[5] | 236 | 9.00 N | 79.36 W |
| Miraflores, Palacio ʊ | 286c | 10.31 N | 66.55 W |
| Mīrah, Wādī al- V | 128 | 32.26 N | 41.42 E |
| Miraí | 256 | 21.12 S | 42.37 W |
| Miraj | 122 | 16.50 N | 74.38 E |
| Miraki | 85 | 39.02 N | 67.10 E |
| Mira Loma | 228 | 34.01 N | 117.31 W |
| Miramar, Arg. | 252 | 38.16 S | 57.51 W |
| Miramar, Arg. | 252 | 30.54 S | 62.40 W |
| Miramar, C.R. | 236 | 10.06 N | 84.44 W |
| Miramar, Fr. | 62 | 43.30 N | 6.57 E |
| Miramar, Moç. | 156 | 23.50 S | 35.34 E |
| Miramar, Fl., U.S. | 220 | 25.59 N | 80.13 W |
| Miramar ◆[8] | 286b | 23.07 N | 82.25 W |
| Miramar, Laguna ⊜ | 236 | 16.23 N | 91.16 W |
| Miramare | 66 | 44.02 N | 12.38 E |
| Miramare, Aeroporto di ⊠ | 66 | 44.02 N | 12.35 E |
| Miramare, Castello di ⊥ | 64 | 45.42 N | 13.43 E |
| Miramar Naval Air Station ■ | 228 | 32.52 N | 117.07 W |
| Miramas | 62 | 43.35 N | 5.00 E |
| Mirambeau | 32 | 45.23 N | 0.34 W |
| Miramichi Bay c | 186 | 47.08 N | 65.08 W |
| Mira Monte | 228 | 36.42 N | 119.03 W |
| Mīram Shāh | 120 | 33.01 N | 70.04 E |
| Mīrān | 123 | 31.24 N | 70.43 E |
| Miranda, Austl. | 274a | 34.02 S | 151.06 E |
| Miranda, Bra. | 248 | 20.14 S | 56.22 W |
| Miranda, Col. | 246 | 3.15 N | 76.14 W |
| Miranda, Ca., U.S. | 204 | 40.14 N | 123.49 W |
| Miranda □[3] | 246 | 10.15 N | 66.25 W |
| Miranda ≃ | 248 | 19.25 S | 57.20 W |
| Miranda, Aerodromo ⊠ | 286c | 10.29 N | 66.50 W |
| Miranda de Ebro | 34 | 42.41 N | 2.57 W |
| Miranda do Douro | 34 | 41.30 N | 6.16 W |
| Mirande | 32 | 43.31 N | 0.25 E |
| Mirandela | 34 | 41.29 N | 7.11 W |
| Mirando City | 196 | 27.26 N | 99.00 W |
| Mirandola | 64 | 44.53 N | 11.04 E |
| Mirano | 64 | 45.30 N | 12.07 E |
| Mirantão | 256 | 22.15 S | 44.30 W |
| Mirante do Paranapanema | 255 | 22.17 S | 51.54 W |
| Mirapuxi ≃ | 255 | 13.06 S | 51.10 W |
| Mirasaka | 96 | 34.46 N | 132.58 E |
| Mira Taglio | 64 | 45.26 N | 12.08 E |
| Miravalles, Volcán ∧[1] | 236 | 10.45 N | 85.10 W |
| Mīr Bacheh Kowt | 120 | 34.45 N | 69.08 E |
| Mirbāṭ | 118 | 17.00 N | 54.45 E |
| Mirboo North | 169 | 38.24 S | 146.10 E |
| Mirebeau-sur-Bèze | 58 | 47.24 N | 5.19 E |
| Mirecourt | 58 | 48.18 N | 6.08 E |
| Miren | 64 | 45.54 N | 13.37 E |
| Mirfield | 44 | 53.40 N | 1.41 W |
| Mirgorodka | 80 | 50.58 N | 53.33 E |
| Miri | 112 | 4.23 N | 113.59 E |
| Miriam Vale | 166 | 24.20 S | 151.34 E |
| Mirim, Lagoa (Laguna Merín) c | 252 | 32.45 S | 52.50 W |
| Mirimichi, Lake ⊜ | 283 | 42.02 N | 71.18 W |
| Mírina | 38 | 39.52 N | 25.04 E |
| Miriñay ≃ | 252 | 30.10 S | 57.39 W |
| Mirinzal | 250 | 2.01 S | 44.43 W |
| Miritiparaná ≃ | 246 | 1.11 S | 70.02 W |
| Miriyama | 164 | 3.57 S | 141.45 E |
| Mīrjāveh | 128 | 29.01 N | 61.28 E |
| Mirke ◆[8] | 263 | 51.16 N | 7.09 E |
| Mirna ≃ | 64 | 45.19 N | 13.36 E |
| Mirnock ∧ | 64 | 46.46 N | 13.43 E |
| Mirnoje Ozero | 86 | 57.44 N | 78.45 E |
| Mirnyj, Ross. | 74 | 62.33 N | 113.53 E |
| Mirnyj, Ross. | 80 | 53.30 N | 50.18 E |
| Mirnyy ʊ[3] | 9 | 66.33 S | 93.00 E |
| Mirond Lake ⊜ | 184 | 55.06 N | 102.47 W |
| Mironeasa | 38 | 46.58 N | 27.25 E |
| Mironovo | 88 | 58.19 N | 109.38 E |
| Miroslav | 61 | 48.57 N | 16.18 E |
| Mirosławiec | 30 | 53.21 N | 16.05 E |
| Mirošov | 60 | 49.41 N | 13.40 E |
| Mirotice | 60 | 49.26 N | 14.02 E |
| Mirove | 78 | 47.45 N | 34.45 E |
| Mirovice | 60 | 49.31 N | 14.02 E |
| Mirow | 54 | 53.16 N | 12.49 E |
| Mīrpur, Bngl. | 126 | 23.47 N | 90.21 E |
| Mīrpur, Bngl. | 126 | 23.56 N | 88.59 E |
| Mīrpur, Pāk. | 123 | 33.11 N | 73.47 E |
| Mīrpur Batoro | 120 | 24.44 N | 68.16 E |
| Mīrpur Bībīwāri | 120 | 28.32 N | 67.44 E |
| Mīrpur Khās | 120 | 25.32 N | 69.00 E |
| Mīrpur Sakro | 120 | 24.33 N | 67.37 E |
| Mirria | 150 | 13.43 N | 9.07 E |
| Mirror | 182 | 52.28 N | 113.07 W |
| Mirror Lake ⊜, Ma., U.S. | 283 | 42.05 N | 71.20 W |
| Mirror Lake ⊜, N.J., U.S. | 276 | 40.29 N | 74.22 W |
| Mirtağ | 130 | 38.23 N | 41.56 E |
| Mirto | 70 | 38.05 N | 14.45 E |
| Mirtóön Pélagos ⫪[2] | 38 | 36.51 N | 23.18 E |
| Miryang | 98 | 35.31 N | 128.44 E |
| Miry Run ≃ | 285 | 40.15 N | 74.49 W |
| Mirza-Aki | 85 | 40.45 N | 73.25 E |
| Mirzaani | 84 | 41.23 N | 46.09 E |
| Mirzāganj | 126 | 22.21 N | 90.14 E |
| Mīrzākalu | 126 | 22.29 N | 90.48 E |
| Mirzāpur, Bngl. | 126 | 24.06 N | 90.06 E |
| Mirzāpur, India | 124 | 25.09 N | 82.35 E |
| Mirzāpur, India | 272b | 22.50 N | 88.24 E |
| Mis, It. | 64 | 46.09 N | 12.05 E |
| Mis, It. | 64 | 46.12 N | 11.57 E |
| Misa ≃ | 66 | 43.43 N | 13.14 E |
| Misāḥah, Bi'r ⫪[4] | 140 | 22.12 N | 27.57 E |
| Misailovo | 265b | 55.34 N | 37.49 E |
| Misaka | 94 | 35.38 N | 138.40 E |
| Misaka-tōge )( | 96 | 33.42 N | 132.52 E |
| Misaki, Nihon | 94 | 35.18 N | 140.22 E |
| Misaki → Miura, Nihon | 94 | 35.08 N | 139.37 E |
| Misaki, Nihon | 96 | 33.23 N | 132.07 E |
| Misaki, Nihon | 96 | 34.19 N | 135.09 E |
| Misakubo | 94 | 35.09 N | 137.52 E |
| Misallah, Ra's › | 142 | 29.50 N | 32.36 E |
| Misamis Occidental □[4] | 116 | 8.20 N | 123.42 E |
| Misamis Oriental □[4] | 116 | 8.45 N | 125.00 E |
| Misano Adriatico | 66 | 43.57 N | 12.39 E |
| Misantla | 234 | 19.56 N | 96.50 W |
| Misasa | 96 | 35.24 N | 133.54 E |
| Misasagi → Fujiidera | 96 | 34.34 N | 135.36 E |
| Misato, Nihon | 94 | 36.23 N | 138.57 E |
| Misato, Nihon | 94 | 34.43 N | 136.24 E |
| Misato, Nihon | 94 | 36.15 N | 137.54 E |
| Misato, Nihon | 96 | 34.09 N | 135.22 E |
| Misato, Nihon | 268 | 35.50 N | 139.53 E |
| Misawa | 92 | 40.41 N | 141.24 E |
| Misbourne ≃ | 260 | 51.34 N | 0.29 W |
| Misburg | 52 | 52.23 N | 9.51 E |
| Miscou Centre | 186 | 47.57 N | 64.34 W |
| Miscou Island I | 186 | 47.57 N | 64.33 W |
| Miscou Point › | 186 | 48.03 N | 64.32 W |
| Mišelevka | 88 | 52.51 N | 103.09 E |
| Misema ≃ | 190 | 47.54 N | 79.53 W |
| Mi-sen ∧ | 96 | 34.16 N | 132.19 E |
| Misenheimer | 192 | 35.29 N | 80.17 W |
| Miseno | 68 | 40.47 N | 14.05 E |
| Misericórdia, Serra da ∧ | 287a | 22.51 S | 43.17 W |
| Misery, Mount ∧ | 169 | 37.24 S | 143.36 E |
| Misgār | 123 | 36.47 N | 74.47 E |
| Mish'āb, Ra's al- › | 128 | 28.12 N | 48.39 E |
| Mishagua ≃ | 248 | 11.13 S | 72.59 W |
| Mishan | 89 | 45.33 N | 131.52 E |
| Mishawaka | 216 | 41.39 N | 86.09 W |
| Mishawum Lake ⊜ | 283 | 42.30 N | 71.08 W |
| Mishbiḥ, Jabal ∧ | 140 | 22.38 N | 34.44 E |
| Misheguk Mountain ∧ | 180 | 68.15 N | 161.03 W |
| Mishe-Mokwa, Lake ⊜ | 285 | 39.52 N | 74.48 W |
| Mishibishu Lake ⊜ | 190 | 48.05 N | 85.25 W |
| Mishicot | 190 | 44.14 N | 87.38 W |
| Mishima, Nihon | 94 | 35.07 N | 138.55 E |
| Mishima → Settsu, Nihon | 96 | 34.46 N | 135.33 E |
| Mi-shima I | 96 | 34.46 N | 131.09 E |
| Mishmar HaNegev | 132 | 31.21 N | 34.43 E |
| Mishmi Hills ⩘[2] | 120 | 29.00 N | 96.00 E |
| Mishō | 96 | 32.57 N | 132.34 E |
| Mishqal, Jabal al- ∧ | 132 | 31.53 N | 36.08 E |
| Mišicha | 88 | 51.38 N | 105.35 E |
| Misikan | 120 | 35.45 N | 89.25 E |
| Misilmeri | 70 | 38.02 N | 13.27 E |
| Misima Island I | 164 | 10.40 S | 152.45 E |
| Misinto | 266b | 45.40 N | 9.05 E |
| Misiones □[4] | 252 | 27.00 S | 55.00 W |
| Misiones □[5] | 252 | 27.00 S | 57.00 W |
| Misión San Francisco de Laishí | 252 | 26.14 S | 58.38 W |
| Misión San Vicente | 232 | 31.20 N | 116.15 W |
| Misirevo | 82 | 56.16 N | 36.45 E |
| Miskī | 140 | 14.51 N | 24.13 E |
| Miski, Enneri V | 146 | 20.00 N | 17.55 E |
| Miškino, Ross. | 86 | 55.20 N | 63.55 E |
| Miškino, Ross. | 265a | 59.42 N | 30.45 E |
| Miskito Channel ʉ | 236 | 14.20 N | 83.08 W |
| Miskitos, Cayos II | 236 | 14.23 N | 82.46 W |
| Miskitos Reef ✣[2] | 236 | 14.28 N | 82.42 W |
| Miskolc | 30 | 48.06 N | 20.47 E |
| Misli | 130 | 38.10 N | 34.52 E |
| Mislinja | 61 | 46.28 N | 15.14 E |
| Mislinja ≃ | 61 | 46.35 N | 15.02 E |
| Mislippi | 146 | 10.00 N | 15.37 E |
| Mislivna ∧ | 61 | 48.40 N | 14.44 E |
| Mismār | 140 | 18.13 N | 35.38 E |
| Mismār, Jabal ∧ | 140 | 18.06 N | 35.42 E |
| Mismi, Nevado ∧ | 248 | 15.30 S | 71.42 W |
| Mišn'ovo | 76 | 53.58 N | 36.21 E |
| Misoke | 154 | 1.06 S | 28.38 E |
| Misool, Pulau I | 164 | 1.52 S | 130.10 E |
| Mispillion ≃ | 208 | 38.57 N | 75.20 W |
| Misquamaebin Lake ⊜ | 184 | 53.30 N | 91.05 W |
| Misquamicut | 207 | 41.20 N | 71.49 W |
| Miṣr → Egypt □[1] | 140 | 27.00 N | 30.00 E |
| Miṣr al-Jadīdah (Heliopolis) ◆[8] | 273c | 30.06 N | 31.20 E |
| Miṣr al-Qadīmah (Old Cairo) ◆[8] | 273c | 30.00 N | 31.14 E |
| Misrātah | 146 | 32.23 N | 15.06 E |
| Miṣr Baḥrī □[9] | 140 | 31.00 N | 31.00 E |
| Misrikh | 124 | 27.27 N | 80.31 E |
| Missanello | 68 | 40.17 N | 16.10 E |
| Missão Santa Cruz | 152 | 16.14 S | 21.57 E |
| Missão Velha | 250 | 7.15 S | 39.08 W |
| Misserghin | 34 | 35.37 N | 0.45 W |
| Missinaibi ≃ | 176 | 50.44 N | 81.29 W |
| Missinaibi Lake ⊜ | 190 | 48.23 N | 83.40 W |
| Missinaibi Lake Provincial Park ♠ | 190 | 48.25 N | 83.35 W |
| Mission, B.C., Can. | 224 | 49.08 N | 122.18 W |
| Mission, S.D., U.S. | 198 | 43.18 N | 100.39 W |
| Mission, Tx., U.S. | 196 | 26.12 N | 98.19 W |
| Mission ◆[8] | 282 | 37.45 N | 122.25 W |
| Mission Bay c | 228 | 32.47 N | 117.15 W |
| Mission Beach | 166 | 17.52 S | 146.06 E |
| Mission Creek ≃ | 282 | 37.32 N | 121.55 W |
| Mission Hills ◆[8] | 280 | 34.16 N | 118.27 W |
| Mission Mountain ∧[2] | 194 | 36.02 N | 94.35 W |
| Mission Peak ∧ | 282 | 37.31 N | 121.53 W |
| Mission Range ⩘ | 202 | 47.30 N | 113.55 W |
| Mission Texas State Historic Park ♠ | 222 | 31.33 N | 95.15 W |
| Mission Valley | 222 | 28.54 N | 97.12 W |
| Mission Viejo | 228 | 33.36 N | 117.40 W |
| Missisquoi □[6] | 206 | 45.10 N | 72.55 W |
| Missisquoi ≃ | 206 | 45.00 N | 73.08 W |
| Missisquoi Bay c | 206 | 45.05 N | 73.10 W |
| Missisquoi-Nord ≃ | 206 | 45.02 N | 72.26 W |
| Mississagagon Lake ⊜ | 212 | 44.52 N | 77.05 W |
| Mississagi ≃ | 190 | 46.10 N | 83.01 W |
| Mississagi Provincial Park ♠ | 190 | 46.35 N | 82.45 W |
| Mississagua ≃ | 212 | 44.34 N | 78.20 W |
| Mississagua Lake ⊜ | 212 | 44.42 N | 78.19 W |
| Mississauga | 212 | 43.35 N | 79.39 W |
| Mississinewa ≃ | 216 | 40.46 N | 86.02 W |
| Mississinewa Lake ⊜[1] | 216 | 40.42 N | 85.52 W |
| Mississippi □[3], U.S. | 178 | 32.50 N | 89.30 W |
| Mississippi □[3], U.S. | 194 | 32.50 N | 89.30 W |
| Mississippi ≃, On., Can. | 212 | 45.26 N | 76.16 W |
| Mississippi ≃, U.S. | 178 | 29.00 N | 89.15 W |
| Mississippi Bay c | 162 | 34.00 S | 122.17 E |
| Mississippi Delta ≃[2] | 194 | 29.10 N | 89.15 W |
| Mississippi Lake ⊜ | 212 | 45.05 N | 76.12 W |
| Mississippi Sound ʉ | 194 | 30.15 N | 88.40 W |
| Mississippi State | 194 | 33.26 N | 88.47 W |
| Missolonghi → Mesolóngion | 38 | 38.21 N | 21.17 E |
| Missoula | 202 | 46.52 N | 113.59 W |
| Missouri □[3], U.S. | 178 | 38.30 N | 93.30 W |
| Missouri □[3], U.S. | 194 | 38.30 N | 93.30 W |
| Missouri ≃ | 178 | 38.50 N | 90.08 W |
| Missouri, Coteau du ⩘[2] | 198 | 46.00 N | 99.30 W |
| Missouri Buttes ∧ | 198 | 44.37 N | 104.47 W |
| Missouri City | 222 | 29.37 N | 95.32 W |
| Missouri Creek ≃ | 219 | 40.07 N | 90.43 W |
| Missouri Valley | 198 | 41.33 N | 95.53 W |
| Mistake, Mount ∧ | 171a | 27.52 S | 152.20 E |
| Mistake Creek | 164 | 17.06 S | 129.04 E |
| Mistake Creek ≃ | 166 | 21.38 S | 146.50 E |
| Mistake Mountains ⩘ | 171a | 27.52 S | 152.22 E |
| Mistaken Point › | 186 | 46.38 N | 53.10 W |
| Mistanipisipou ≃ | 186 | 51.32 N | 61.50 W |
| Mistassibi ≃ | 176 | 48.53 N | 72.13 W |
| Mistassibi Nord-Est ≃ | 186 | 49.50 N | 71.56 W |
| Mistassini | 176 | 50.25 N | 73.52 W |
| Mistassini, Lac ⊜ | 176 | 51.00 N | 73.37 W |
| Mistatim | 184 | 52.52 N | 103.22 W |
| Mistawasis Indian Reserve ◆[4] | 184 | 53.06 N | 106.48 W |
| Mistelbach, Dtsch. | 60 | 49.55 N | 11.31 E |
| Mistelbach, Öst. | 61 | 48.34 N | 16.35 E |
| Mistelgau | 60 | 49.55 N | 11.28 E |
| Misteln ⊜ | 40 | 59.07 N | 16.57 E |
| Misterbianco | 70 | 37.31 N | 15.00 E |
| Misterei | 140 | 13.07 N | 22.09 E |
| Misteriosa Bank ✣[2] | 238 | 18.50 N | 83.50 W |
| Misterton, Eng., U.K. | 42 | 50.52 N | 2.47 W |
| Misterton, Eng., U.K. | 44 | 53.27 N | 0.51 W |
| Misti, Volcán ∧[1] | 248 | 16.18 S | 71.24 W |
| Mistikokan ≃ | 184 | 57.01 N | 91.27 W |
| Mistky | 83 | 49.19 N | 38.30 E |
| Mistley | 42 | 51.56 N | 1.05 E |
| Mistrás ⊥ | 38 | 37.04 N | 22.21 E |
| Mistretta | 70 | 37.56 N | 14.22 E |
| Misugi | 94 | 34.33 N | 136.16 E |
| Misumi, Nihon | 92 | 32.37 N | 130.27 E |
| Misumi, Nihon | 96 | 34.46 N | 131.58 E |
| Misumi, Nihon | 96 | 34.22 N | 131.15 E |
| Misumi ≃ | 96 | 34.47 N | 131.56 E |
| Misurina | 64 | 46.35 N | 12.15 E |
| Mišutino, Ross. | 76 | 59.31 N | 36.01 E |
| Mišutino, Ross. | 82 | 56.23 N | 38.06 E |
| Mita, Punta › | 234 | 20.47 N | 105.33 W |
| Mīt Abū Ghālib | 142 | 31.17 N | 31.40 E |
| Mita Hills Dam ◆[6] | 154 | 14.15 S | 29.06 E |
| Mit'ajevo, Ross. | 82 | 55.16 N | 36.32 E |
| Mit'ajevo, Ross. | 86 | 60.17 N | 61.06 E |
| Mitaka | 94 | 35.40 N | 139.33 E |
| Mitake, Nihon | 94 | 35.25 N | 137.08 E |
| Mitake, Nihon | 94 | 35.51 N | 137.37 E |
| Mit'akinka ≃ | 83 | 48.35 N | 39.50 E |
| Mit'akino | 82 | 54.24 N | 38.50 E |
| Mit'akinskaja | 83 | 48.36 N | 39.47 E |
| Mīt al-ʿĀmil | 142 | 30.54 N | 31.21 E |
| Mitatib | 140 | 16.03 N | 36.11 E |
| Mitau → Jelgava | 76 | 56.39 N | 23.42 E |
| Mīt Badr Ḥalāwah | 142 | 30.51 N | 31.14 E |
| Mīt Bashshār | 142 | 30.31 N | 31.24 E |
| Mitcham, Austl. | 168b | 34.59 S | 138.36 E |
| Mitcham, Austl. | 274b | 37.49 S | 145.12 E |
| Mitcham ◆[8] | 260 | 51.24 N | 0.10 W |
| Mitcheldean | 42 | 51.53 N | 2.30 W |
| Mitchell, Austl. | 166 | 26.29 S | 147.58 E |
| Mitchell, On., Can. | 212 | 43.28 N | 81.12 W |
| Mitchell, Il., U.S. | 219 | 38.46 N | 90.06 W |
| Mitchell, In., U.S. | 218 | 38.43 N | 86.28 W |
| Mitchell, Ne., U.S. | 198 | 41.56 N | 103.48 W |
| Mitchell, Or., U.S. | 202 | 44.34 N | 120.09 W |
| Mitchell, S.D., U.S. | 198 | 43.42 N | 98.01 W |
| Mitchell ≃, Austl. | 164 | 15.12 S | 141.35 E |
| Mitchell ≃, Austl. | 164 | 14.28 S | 125.43 E |
| Mitchell ≃, Austl. | 166 | 37.53 S | 147.41 E |
| Mitchell, Lake ⊜[1] | 194 | 32.50 N | 86.30 W |
| Mitchell, Mount ∧ | 192 | 35.46 N | 82.16 W |
| Mitchell and Alice Rivers National Park ♠ | 164 | 15.30 S | 142.05 E |
| Mitchell Bay c | 214 | 42.28 N | 82.26 W |
| Mitchell Corners | 212 | 43.57 N | 78.48 W |
| Mitchell Field ⊠ | 278 | 41.55 N | 88.15 W |
| Mitchell Lake ⊜, B.C., Can. | 182 | 52.53 N | 120.36 W |
| Mitchell Lake ⊜, On., Can. | 212 | 44.34 N | 78.58 W |
| Mitchell Point › | 214 | 42.26 N | 82.26 W |
| Mitchellville | 190 | 41.40 N | 93.21 W |
| Mitchelstown | 48 | 52.16 N | 8.16 W |
| Mīt Fāris | 142 | 31.02 N | 31.36 E |
| Mīt Ghamr | 142 | 30.43 N | 31.16 E |
| Mīt Ḥalfah | 273c | 30.10 N | 31.14 E |
| Mīt Ḥamal | 142 | 30.26 N | 31.32 E |
| Mithapur | 120 | 22.25 N | 69.00 E |


| Symbol | English | Deutsch | Español | Français | Português |
|---|---|---|---|---|---|
| ≃ | River | Fluß | Río | Rivière | Rio |
| ≊ | Canal | Kanal | Canal | Canal | Canal |
| ᒪ | Waterfall, Rapids | Wasserfall, Stromschnellen | Cascada, Rápidos | Chute d'eau, Rapides | Cascata, Rápidos |
| ʉ | Strait | Meeresstraße | Estrecho | Détroit | Estreito |
| c | Bay, Gulf | Bucht, Golf | Bahía, Golfo | Baie, Golfe | Baía, Golfo |
| ⊜ | Lake, Lakes | See, Seen | Lago, Lagos | Lac, Lacs | Lago, Lagos |
| ≣ | Swamp | Sumpf | Pantano | Marais | Pântano |
| ⊓ | Ice Features, Glacier | Eis- und Gletscherformen | Accidentes Glaciales | Formes glaciaires | Acidentes glaciares |
| ⫪ | Other Hydrographic Features | Andere Hydrographische Objekte | Otros Elementos Hidrográficos | Autres données hydrographiques | Outros acidentes hidrográficos |
| ✣ | Submarine Features | Untermeerische Objekte | Accidentes Submarinos | Formes de relief sous-marin | Acidentes submarinos |
| □ | Political Unit | Politische Einheit | Unidad Politica | Entité politique | Unidade política |
| ʊ | Cultural Institution | Kulturelle Institution | Institución Cultural | Institution culturelle | Instituição cultural |
| ⊥ | Historical Site | Historische Stätte | Sitio Histórico | Site historique | Sitio histórico |
| ♠ | Recreational Site | Erholungs- und Ferienort | Sitio de Recreo | Centre de loisirs | Area de Lazer |
| ⊠ | Airport | Flughafen | Aeropuerto | Aéroport | Aeroporto |
| ■ | Military Installation | Militäranlage | Instalación Militar | Installation militaire | Instalação militar |
| ◆ | Miscellaneous | Verschiedenes | Misceláneo | Divers | Diversos |

| Name | Page | Lat. | Long. |
|---|---|---|---|
| Mitha Tiwāna | 123 | 32.15 N | 72.07 E |
| Mithi | 120 | 24.44 N | 69.48 E |
| Míthimna | 38 | 39.22 N | 26.10 E |
| Mitiaro I | 14 | 19.49 S | 157.43 W |
| Mitidja, Plaine de la ≃ | 34 | 36.45 N | 3.00 E |
| Mitilíni | 38 | 39.06 N | 26.32 E |
| Mitino | 265b | 55.51 N | 37.21 E |
| Mitis, Lac ⊜ | 186 | 48.17 N | 67.45 W |
| Mitishto ≃ | 184 | 54.50 N | 98.58 W |
| Mitiškovo | 76 | 54.40 N | 33.31 E |
| Mitiwanga | 214 | 41.22 N | 82.27 W |
| Mitkof Island I | 180 | 56.45 N | 132.50 W |
| Mitla ⊥ | 234 | 16.55 N | 96.17 W |
| Mitla, Laguna ⊂ | 234 | 17.03 N | 100.25 W |
| Mitla, Mamarr (Mitla Pass) )( | 142 | 30.00 N | 32.53 E |
| Mitla Pass → Mitla, Mamarr )( | 142 | 30.00 N | 32.53 E |
| Mito, Nihon | 94 | 34.49 N | 137.19 E |
| Mito, Nihon | 94 | 36.22 N | 140.28 E |
| Mito, Nihon | 96 | 34.40 N | 131.59 E |
| Mitō, Nihon | 96 | 34.13 N | 131.21 E |
| Mito, Nihon | 268 | 35.10 N | 139.37 E |
| Mitomi | 94 | 35.47 N | 138.44 E |
| Mitoya | 96 | 35.17 N | 132.52 E |
| Mitra, Monte ∧ | 152 | 1.23 N | 9.57 E |
| Mitra do Bispo ∧ | 256 | 22.10 S | 44.34 W |
| Mitre ∧ | 172 | 40.48 S | 175.27 E |
| Mitre, Península >[1] | 254 | 54.48 S | 65.40 W |
| Mitre Peak ∧ | 172 | 44.38 S | 167.50 E |
| Mitrofania Island I | 180 | 55.51 N | 158.49 W |
| Mitrofanovka | 78 | 49.58 N | 39.42 E |
| Mitrofanovo | 24 | 63.13 N | 56.00 E |
| Mīt Ruhaynah | 273c | 29.51 N | 31.15 E |
| Mīt Ruhaynah (Memphis) ⊥ | 142 | 29.51 N | 31.15 E |
| Mitry-le-Neuf | 261 | 48.57 N | 2.36 E |
| Mitry-Mory | 261 | 48.59 N | 2.37 E |
| Mitsamiouli | 157a | 11.23 S | 43.18 E |
| Mitsinjo | 157b | 16.01 S | 45.52 E |
| Mitsio, Nosy I | 157b | 12.54 S | 48.36 E |
| Mitsiwa (Massawa) | 144 | 15.38 N | 39.28 E |
| Mitsiwa Channel ⊔ | 144 | 15.30 N | 40.00 E |
| Mitsu, Nihon | 96 | 34.47 N | 134.33 E |
| Mitsu, Nihon | 96 | 34.48 N | 133.56 E |
| Mitsubori | 268 | 35.56 N | 139.56 E |
| Mitsue | 94 | 34.29 N | 136.10 E |
| Mitsugi | 96 | 34.30 N | 133.09 E |
| Mitsuike Park ♦ | 268 | 35.31 N | 139.39 E |
| Mitsukaidō | 94 | 36.01 N | 139.59 E |
| Mitsuke | 92 | 37.32 N | 138.56 E |
| Mitsumarenge-dake ∧ | 94 | 36.23 N | 137.35 E |
| Mitsushima | 92 | 34.16 N | 129.19 E |
| Mitsuzaku | 268 | 35.25 N | 140.00 E |
| Mitsuzawa Park Race Track ♦ | 268 | 35.27 N | 139.36 E |
| Mitta, Oued el V | 148 | 34.20 N | 6.44 E |
| Mittagong | 170 | 34.27 S | 150.27 E |
| Mittagskogel (Kepa) ∧ | 61 | 46.31 N | 13.57 E |
| Mittainville | 261 | 48.40 N | 1.39 E |
| Mitta Mitta ≃ | 171b | 36.12 S | 147.11 E |
| Mitte ◆[8] | 264a | 52.31 N | 13.24 E |
| Mittelberg | 58 | 47.20 N | 10.10 E |
| Mittelfischach | 56 | 49.02 N | 9.52 E |
| Mittelfranken □[5] | 56 | 49.20 N | 10.40 E |
| Mittellandkanal ≍ | 30 | 52.16 N | 11.41 E |
| Mittelmeer → Mediterranean Sea ▽[2] | 10 | 35.00 N | 20.00 E |
| Mittelsaida | 54 | 50.46 N | 13.18 E |
| Mittelstetten | 60 | 48.15 N | 11.06 E |
| Mittenwald | 64 | 47.27 N | 11.15 E |
| Mittenwalde, Dtsch. | 54 | 53.11 N | 13.39 E |
| Mittenwalde, Dtsch. | 54 | 52.16 N | 13.32 E |
| Mitterndorf | 64 | 47.33 N | 13.55 E |
| Mittersill | 64 | 47.16 N | 12.29 E |
| Mitterskirchen | 60 | 48.21 N | 12.44 E |
| Mitterteich | 60 | 49.57 N | 12.15 E |
| Mittewald an der Drau | 64 | 46.46 N | 12.36 E |
| Mittweida | 54 | 50.59 N | 12.59 E |
| Mitú | 246 | 1.08 N | 70.03 W |
| Mitumba, Monts ⩕ | 154 | 6.00 S | 29.00 E |
| Mituo | 107 | 28.53 N | 105.37 E |
| Mitwaba | 154 | 8.38 S | 27.20 E |
| Mitwitz | 56 | 50.15 N | 11.12 E |
| Mityana | 154 | 0.24 N | 32.03 E |
| Mīt Yazīd | 142 | 30.30 N | 31.20 E |
| Mitzic | 152 | 0.47 N | 11.34 E |
| Miura | 94 | 35.08 N | 139.37 E |
| Miura-chosuichi ⊜[1] | 94 | 35.49 N | 137.23 E |
| Miura-dam ◆[6] | 94 | 35.49 N | 137.24 E |
| Miura-hantō >[1] | 94 | 35.15 N | 139.39 E |
| Mius | 80 | 51.26 N | 47.56 E |
| Mius ≃ | 83 | 47.18 N | 38.49 E |
| Miusskij liman ⊂[1] | 83 | 47.15 N | 38.40 E |
| Miusyns'k | 83 | 48.05 N | 38.53 E |
| Miwa, Nihon | 94 | 35.11 N | 136.47 E |
| Miwa, Nihon | 94 | 36.39 N | 140.18 E |
| Miwa, Nihon | 96 | 35.12 N | 135.14 E |
| Miwa, Nihon | 96 | 34.13 N | 132.06 E |
| Miwa, Nihon | 96 | 34.39 N | 132.51 E |
| Miwa, Nihon | 270 | 34.31 N | 135.51 E |
| Mi-Wuk Village | 226 | 38.05 N | 120.13 W |
| Mixcoac ◆[8] | 286a | 19.23 N | 99.12 W |
| Mixcoac, Presa de ⊜[1] | 286a | 19.22 N | 99.14 W |
| Mixco Viejo ⊥ | 236 | 14.52 N | 90.40 W |
| Mixian | 100 | 34.31 N | 113.22 E |
| Mixin | 107 | 30.23 N | 105.46 E |
| Mixquiahuala | 234 | 20.14 N | 99.13 W |
| Mixtán | 234 | 17.55 N | 95.51 W |
| Mixteco ≃ | 234 | 18.11 N | 98.30 W |
| Mixtlán | 234 | 20.26 N | 104.25 W |
| Miya | 94 | 36.05 N | 137.15 E |
| Miya ≃, Nihon | 94 | 36.28 N | 137.15 E |
| Miya ≃, Nihon | 94 | 34.32 N | 136.44 E |
| Miyagawa, Nihon | 94 | 36.19 N | 137.09 E |
| Miyagawa, Nihon | 94 | 34.22 N | 136.21 E |
| Miyagi □[5] | 92 | 38.22 N | 140.52 E |
| Miyagi-jima I | 174m | 26.21 N | 127.57 E |
| Miyāh, Wādī al- V | 140 | 25.00 N | 33.23 E |
| Miyahara | 268 | 35.56 N | 139.37 E |
| Miyajima | 96 | 34.18 N | 132.19 E |
| Miyake | 270 | 34.35 N | 135.47 E |
| Miyake-jima I | 92 | 34.05 N | 139.32 E |
| Miyako | 92 | 39.38 N | 141.57 E |
| Miyakojima ◆[8] | 270 | 34.43 N | 135.33 E |
| Miyako-jima I | 175d | 24.47 N | 125.20 E |
| Miyakonojō | 92 | 31.44 N | 131.04 E |
| Miyako-rettō II | 175d | 24.24 N | 125.00 E |
| Miyama, Nihon | 92 | 34.06 N | 136.14 E |
| Miyama, Nihon | 94 | 36.00 N | 136.22 E |
| Miyama, Nihon | 94 | 35.33 N | 136.45 E |
| Miyama, Nihon | 96 | 35.16 N | 135.33 E |
| Miyama, Nihon | 96 | 33.59 N | 135.22 E |
| Miyāni | 120 | 21.51 N | 69.23 E |
| Miyanojō | 92 | 31.54 N | 130.27 E |
| Miyanoura-dake ∧ | 93b | 30.20 N | 130.31 E |
| Miyara | 175d | 24.20 N | 124.14 E |
| Miyata | 96 | 33.44 N | 130.40 E |
| Miyazaki, Nihon | 92 | 31.54 N | 131.26 E |
| Miyazaki, Nihon | 94 | 35.56 N | 136.05 E |
| Miyazakino-hana > | 96 | 34.04 N | 135.05 E |
| Miyazu | 96 | 35.32 N | 135.11 E |
| Miyi | 102 | 27.00 N | 102.08 E |
| Miyoshi, Nihon | 96 | 33.57 N | 133.03 E |
| Miyoshi, Nihon | 96 | 34.48 N | 132.51 E |
| Miyoshi, Nihon | 96 | 34.02 N | 133.52 E |
| Miyoshi, Nihon | 268 | 35.50 N | 139.31 E |
| Miyota | 94 | 36.18 N | 138.30 E |
| Miyun | 105 | 40.22 N | 116.50 E |
| Miyun Shuiku ⊜[1] | 105 | 40.30 N | 116.58 E |
| Mizan Teferi | 144 | 6.53 N | 35.28 E |
| Mizdah | 146 | 31.26 N | 12.59 E |
| Mize | 194 | 31.52 N | 89.33 W |
| Mizen Head >, Ire. | 48 | 52.51 N | 6.01 W |
| Mizen Head >, Ire. | 48 | 51.27 N | 9.49 W |
| Mižèvičy | 76 | 52.59 N | 25.05 E |
| Mizhhir'ya | 78 | 48.32 N | 23.30 E |
| Mizhi | 102 | 37.49 N | 110.02 E |
| Mizil | 38 | 45.00 N | 26.26 E |
| Mizoch | 78 | 50.24 N | 26.09 E |
| Mizoguchi | 96 | 35.21 N | 133.26 E |
| Mizonokuchi | 268 | 35.36 N | 139.37 E |
| Mizonuma | 268 | 35.48 N | 139.36 E |
| Mizoram □[3] | 120 | 23.30 N | 93.00 E |
| Mizpah | 208 | 39.29 N | 74.50 W |
| Mizpah Creek ≃ | 198 | 46.16 N | 105.17 W |
| Mizpé Ramon | 132 | 30.36 N | 34.48 E |
| Mizque | 248 | 17.56 S | 65.19 W |
| Mizque ≃ | 248 | 18.39 S | 64.20 W |
| Mizue ◆[8] | 268 | 35.41 N | 139.54 E |
| Mizuho, Nihon | 94 | 35.46 N | 139.21 E |
| Mizuho, Nihon | 96 | 35.10 N | 135.22 E |
| Mizuho, Nihon | 96 | 34.51 N | 132.31 E |
| Mizukaidō → Mitsukaidō | 94 | 36.01 N | 139.59 E |
| Mizuko | 268 | 35.50 N | 139.34 E |
| Mizumaki | 96 | 33.51 N | 130.42 E |
| Mizunami | 94 | 35.22 N | 137.15 E |
| Mizunoko-jima I | 96 | 33.02 N | 132.11 E |
| Mizusawa | 92 | 39.08 N | 141.08 E |
| Mizushima-nada ⊂ | 96 | 34.25 N | 133.40 E |
| Mizutori | 270 | 34.47 N | 135.45 E |
| Mizuwake-tōge )( | 96 | 33.15 N | 131.17 E |
| Mjadzel | 76 | 54.53 N | 26.57 E |
| Mjaleškavičy | 78 | 51.56 N | 28.59 E |
| Mjälgen | 40 | 60.33 N | 15.07 E |
| Mjällom | 26 | 62.59 N | 18.26 E |
| Mjangad | 86 | 48.15 N | 91.57 E |
| Mjanyana | 158 | 31.50 S | 28.10 E |
| Mjölby | 26 | 58.19 N | 15.08 E |
| Mjøndalen | 26 | 59.45 N | 10.01 E |
| Mjörn ⊜ | 26 | 57.54 N | 12.25 E |
| Mjøsa ⊜ | 26 | 60.40 N | 11.00 E |
| Mkalama | 154 | 4.07 S | 34.38 E |
| Mkata | 154 | 5.47 S | 38.17 E |
| Mkhondvo ≃ | 158 | 26.39 S | 31.25 E |
| Mkokotoni | 154 | 5.52 S | 39.15 E |
| Mkomazi ≃ | 158 | 30.12 S | 30.50 E |
| Mkomazi Game Reserve ◆[4] | 154 | 4.10 S | 38.10 E |
| Mkulwe | 154 | 8.35 S | 32.19 E |
| Mkumvura ≃ | 154 | 15.55 S | 31.07 E |
| Mkunumbi | 154 | 2.18 S | 40.42 E |
| Mkushi | 154 | 13.40 S | 29.20 E |
| Mkushi ≃ | 154 | 14.40 S | 29.07 E |
| Mkushi River | 154 | 13.32 S | 29.45 E |
| Mkuze | 158 | 27.37 S | 32.02 E |
| Mkuze ≃ | 158 | 27.53 S | 32.29 E |
| Mkuzi Game Reserve ◆[4] | 158 | 27.40 S | 32.15 E |
| Mkwaja | 154 | 5.47 S | 38.51 E |
| Mkwaya | 154 | 10.06 S | 39.40 E |
| Mladá Boleslav | 54 | 50.23 N | 14.59 E |
| Mladenovac | 38 | 44.26 N | 20.42 E |
| Mladotice | 60 | 49.58 N | 13.18 E |
| Mlala Hills ⩕[2] | 154 | 6.47 S | 31.45 E |
| M'Lang | 116 | 6.55 N | 124.53 E |
| M'Lang ≃ | 116 | 6.52 N | 124.45 E |
| Mlanje Peak → Sapitwa ∧ | 154 | 15.57 S | 35.36 E |
| Mlava ≃ | 38 | 44.45 N | 21.13 E |
| Mława | 30 | 53.06 N | 20.23 E |
| Mlawula | 158 | 26.11 S | 32.01 E |
| Mliba | 158 | 26.14 S | 31.36 E |
| Mljet, Otok I | 36 | 42.45 N | 17.30 E |
| Mljet Nacionalni Park ♦ | 36 | 42.47 N | 17.25 E |
| Mljetski Kanal ⊔ | 36 | 42.48 N | 17.35 E |
| Mlyniv | 78 | 50.31 N | 25.37 E |
| Mmabatho | 156 | 25.51 S | 25.38 E |
| Mmadinare | 156 | 21.57 S | 27.52 E |
| Mnazi | 154 | 8.54 S | 39.06 E |
| Mnevniki ◆[8] | 265b | 55.45 N | 37.28 E |
| Mnichov | 60 | 50.03 N | 12.49 E |
| Mníšek pod Brdy | 30 | 49.52 N | 14.16 E |
| Mo | 24 | 66.15 N | 14.08 E |
| Mo ≃ | 150 | 8.45 N | 0.11 E |
| Moa | 240p | 20.40 N | 74.56 W |
| Moa ≃, Afr. | 150 | 6.59 N | 11.36 W |
| Moa ≃, Bra. | 248 | 7.39 S | 72.41 W |
| Moa, Pulau I | 164 | 8.10 S | 127.56 E |
| Moab | 200 | 38.34 N | 109.32 W |
| Moabi | 152 | 2.15 S | 11.00 E |
| Moaco ≃ | 248 | 7.41 S | 68.18 W |
| Moa Island I | 164 | 10.12 S | 142.16 E |
| Moala Island I | 175g | 18.36 S | 179.53 E |
| Moalboal | 116 | 9.56 N | 123.23 E |
| Moama | 166 | 36.07 S | 144.47 E |
| Moamba | 156 | 25.35 S | 32.13 E |
| Moana | 168b | 35.13 S | 138.29 E |
| Moanda | 152 | 1.34 S | 13.11 E |
| Moanza | 152 | 5.25 S | 17.30 E |
| Moar Lake ⊜ | 184 | 52.00 N | 95.09 W |
| Moate | 48 | 53.23 N | 7.43 W |
| Moatize | 154 | 16.08 S | 33.45 E |
| Moawhango | 172 | 39.35 S | 175.52 E |
| Moba, Nig. | 273a | 6.27 N | 3.28 E |
| Moba, Zaïre | 154 | 7.03 S | 29.47 E |
| Mobara | 94 | 35.25 N | 140.18 E |
| Mobārakpur | 126 | 22.58 N | 89.10 E |
| Mobaye | 152 | 4.19 N | 21.11 E |
| Mobayi-Mbongo | 152 | 4.18 N | 21.11 E |
| Mobberley | 262 | 53.19 N | 2.20 W |
| Mobeetie | 196 | 35.31 N | 100.26 W |
| Mobeka | 152 | 1.53 N | 19.46 E |
| Mobenzélé | 152 | 0.54 N | 17.51 E |
| Moberly | 194 | 39.25 N | 92.26 W |
| Moberly ≃ | 182 | 56.12 N | 120.55 W |
| Moberly Lake | 182 | 55.48 N | 121.45 W |
| Moberly Lake ⊜ | 182 | 55.49 N | 121.45 W |
| Mobile, Al., U.S. | 194 | 30.41 N | 88.02 W |
| Mobile, Az., U.S. | 200 | 33.03 N | 112.16 W |
| Mobile ≃ | 194 | 30.29 N | 88.01 W |
| Mobile Bay ⊂ | 194 | 30.25 N | 88.00 W |
| Mobjack | 208 | 37.23 N | 76.21 W |
| Mobjack Bay ⊂ | 208 | 37.19 N | 76.21 W |
| Mobridge | 198 | 45.32 N | 100.25 W |
| Moca, P.R. | 240m | 18.24 N | 67.07 W |
| Moca, Rep. Dom. | 238 | 19.24 N | 70.31 W |
| Moča ≃ | 82 | 55.25 N | 37.28 E |
| Mocajuba | 250 | 2.35 S | 49.30 W |
| Mocal ≃ | 236 | 14.00 N | 88.33 W |
| Močalejevka | 80 | 53.38 N | 51.46 E |
| Močališče | 80 | 56.21 N | 48.23 E |
| Moçambique | 154 | 15.03 S | 40.45 E |
| Moçambique → Mozambique □[1] | 138 | 18.15 S | 35.00 E |
| Mocanaqua | 210 | 41.08 N | 76.08 W |
| Mocassins, Lac des ⊜ | 206 | 46.35 N | 74.25 W |
| Mo Cay | 110 | 10.08 N | 106.20 E |
| Moccasin, Ca., U.S. | 226 | 37.49 N | 120.18 W |
| Moccasin, Il., U.S. | 219 | 39.09 N | 88.45 W |
| Moc Chau | 110 | 20.51 N | 104.37 E |
| Moccoidumis | 144 | 1.36 N | 44.26 E |
| Mocha → Al-Makhā' | 144 | 13.19 N | 43.15 E |
| Mocha, Isla I | 252 | 38.22 S | 73.56 W |
| Moche ≃ | 248 | 8.10 S | 79.03 W |
| Moche ⊥ | 248 | 8.06 S | 79.05 W |
| Mocheng | 106 | 31.35 N | 120.43 E |
| Mochh | 123 | 32.45 N | 71.31 E |
| Mochigase | 96 | 35.20 N | 134.12 E |
| Mochitlan | 234 | 17.30 N | 99.18 W |
| Mochizuki | 94 | 36.16 N | 138.22 E |
| Mocho, Arroyo ≃ | 226 | 37.41 N | 121.55 W |
| Mochonap ⊔ | 175c | 7.41 N | 151.48 E |
| Mochov | 54 | 50.08 N | 14.50 E |
| Mochtín | 60 | 49.22 N | 13.21 E |
| Mochudi | 156 | 24.28 S | 26.05 E |
| Močily | 82 | 54.20 N | 38.41 E |
| Mocímboa da Praia | 154 | 11.20 S | 40.21 E |
| Mocímboa do Rovuma | 154 | 11.20 S | 39.18 E |
| Möckeln ⊜, Sve. | 26 | 56.40 N | 14.10 E |
| Möckeln ⊜, Sve. | 40 | 59.18 N | 14.30 E |
| Möckern | 54 | 52.08 N | 11.57 E |
| Mockfjärd | 40 | 60.30 N | 14.58 E |
| Mockhorn Island I | 208 | 37.13 N | 75.53 W |
| Möckmühl | 56 | 49.19 N | 9.22 E |
| Mockrehna | 54 | 51.30 N | 12.49 E |
| Mocksville | 192 | 35.53 N | 80.33 W |
| Moclips | 224 | 47.14 N | 124.12 W |
| Môco, Serra do ∧ | 152 | 12.28 S | 15.10 E |
| Mocoa | 246 | 1.09 N | 76.37 W |
| Mococa | 256 | 21.28 S | 47.01 W |
| Mocoduene | 156 | 23.40 S | 35.10 E |
| Mocoretá | 252 | 30.38 S | 57.58 W |
| Mocorito | 232 | 25.29 N | 107.55 W |
| Moctezuma, Méx. | 232 | 29.48 N | 109.42 W |
| Moctezuma, Méx. | 234 | 22.45 N | 101.05 W |
| Moctezuma ≃, Méx. | 232 | 29.09 N | 109.40 W |
| Moctezuma ≃, Méx. | 234 | 21.59 N | 98.34 W |
| Mocuba | 154 | 16.50 S | 36.59 E |
| Močurica ≃ | 38 | 42.31 N | 26.32 E |
| Modane | 62 | 45.12 N | 6.40 E |
| Modāsa | 120 | 23.28 N | 73.18 E |
| Modau ≃ | 56 | 49.49 N | 8.28 E |
| Modbury | 42 | 50.21 N | 3.53 W |
| Modder ≃ | 158 | 29.02 S | 24.37 E |
| Modderbee | 273d | 26.10 S | 28.24 E |
| Modder East | 273d | 26.11 S | 28.26 E |
| Modderfontein | 273d | 26.06 S | 28.09 E |
| Modderfontein ≃ | 273d | 26.13 S | 28.10 E |
| Modderrivier | 158 | 29.02 S | 24.38 E |
| Model City | 284a | 43.11 N | 78.59 W |
| Modena, It. | 64 | 44.40 N | 10.55 E |
| Modena, N.Y., U.S. | 210 | 41.40 N | 74.07 W |
| Modena □[4] | 64 | 44.30 N | 10.54 E |
| Moder ≃ | 56 | 48.49 N | 8.06 E |
| Möderbrugg | 61 | 47.17 N | 14.29 E |
| Modern Art, Museum of ʊ | 276 | 40.46 N | 73.58 W |
| Modeste, Mount ∧ | 224 | 48.37 N | 124.06 W |
| Modesto, Ca., U.S. | 226 | 37.38 N | 120.59 W |
| Modesto, Il., U.S. | 219 | 39.29 N | 89.59 W |
| Modesto City-County Airport ⊠ | 226 | 37.39 N | 120.57 W |
| Modesto Main Canal ≍ | 226 | 37.39 N | 120.27 W |
| Modesto Reservoir ⊜[1] | 226 | 37.26 N | 121.58 W |
| Modica | 70 | 36.52 N | 14.46 E |
| Modigliana | 66 | 44.09 N | 11.47 E |
| Modinagar | 124 | 28.51 N | 77.37 E |
| Modione ≃ | 70 | 37.34 N | 12.49 E |
| Modjamboli | 152 | 2.28 N | 22.06 E |
| Modjeska | 280 | 33.43 N | 117.37 W |
| Mödling | 61 | 48.05 N | 16.17 E |
| Mödling ≃ | 264b | 48.04 N | 16.22 E |
| Modoc | 218 | 40.02 N | 85.07 W |
| Modon ≃ | 50 | 47.16 N | 1.27 E |
| Modowi | 164 | 4.05 S | 134.39 E |
| Modra, Slvk. | 30 | 48.21 N | 17.17 E |
| Modra, Tchad | 146 | 20.43 N | 17.42 E |
| Modra špilja ⊥[5] | 36 | 43.00 N | 16.02 E |
| Mödrath | 56 | 50.53 N | 6.43 E |
| Modriča | 38 | 44.57 N | 18.18 E |
| Modřice | 61 | 49.07 N | 16.37 E |
| Mo Duc | 110 | 14.57 N | 108.53 E |
| Modugno | 68 | 41.05 N | 16.47 E |
| Moe | 169 | 38.10 S | 146.15 E |
| Moe ≃, Austl. | 169 | 38.08 S | 146.17 E |
| Moe ≃, P.Q., Can. | 206 | 45.19 N | 71.49 W |
| Moecherville | 216 | 41.44 N | 88.17 W |
| Moeda | 255 | 20.20 S | 44.03 W |
| Moehau ∧ | 172 | 36.35 S | 175.24 E |
| Moel Fferna ∧ | 42 | 52.57 N | 3.18 W |
| Moelv | 26 | 60.56 N | 10.42 E |
| Moema | 255 | 19.50 S | 45.24 W |
| Moen | 50 | 50.46 N | 3.24 E |
| Moena | 64 | 46.22 N | 11.39 E |
| Moengo | 250 | 5.37 N | 54.24 W |
| Moen-jo-Daro ⊥ | 120 | 27.18 N | 68.15 E |
| Moenkopi | 200 | 36.06 N | 111.13 W |
| Moenkopi Wash V | 200 | 35.54 N | 111.26 W |
| Moeraki Point > | 172 | 45.22 S | 170.52 E |
| Moerbeke, Bel. | 50 | 50.45 N | 3.55 E |
| Moerbeke, Bel. | 50 | 51.10 N | 3.56 E |
| Moerdijk | 52 | 51.43 N | 4.38 E |
| Moerewa | 172 | 35.23 S | 174.02 E |
| Moergestel | 52 | 51.33 N | 5.11 E |
| Moero, Lago → Mweru, Lake ⊜ | 154 | 9.00 S | 28.45 E |
| Moers | 56 | 51.27 N | 6.37 E |
| Moersbach ≃ | 263 | 51.33 N | 6.36 E |
| Moesa ≃ | 58 | 46.13 N | 9.03 E |
| Moffat | 44 | 55.20 N | 3.27 W |
| Moffat Peak ∧ | 172 | 45.02 S | 168.07 E |
| Moffatt | 222 | 31.12 N | 97.28 W |
| Moffatt, Lac ⊜ | 206 | 45.34 N | 71.19 W |
| Moffat Water ≃ | 44 | 55.18 N | 3.25 W |
| Moffet Point > | 180 | 55.26 N | 162.32 W |
| Moffett Field Naval Air Station ■ | 226 | 37.24 N | 122.03 W |
| Moffit | 198 | 46.40 N | 100.17 W |
| Mofoluku | 273a | 6.33 N | 3.20 E |
| Moga | 123 | 30.48 N | 75.10 E |
| Mogadiscio → Muqdisho | 144 | 2.04 N | 45.22 E |
| Mogadishu → Muqdisho | 144 | 2.04 N | 45.22 E |
| Mogador → Essaouira | 148 | 31.30 N | 9.47 W |
| Mogadore | 214 | 41.02 N | 81.23 W |
| Mogadore Reservoir ⊜[1] | 214 | 41.04 N | 81.21 W |
| Mogadouro | 34 | 41.20 N | 6.39 W |
| Mogalakwena ≃ | 156 | 23.00 S | 28.40 E |
| Mogalo | 152 | 3.10 N | 19.04 E |
| Mogami ≃ | 92 | 38.55 N | 139.48 E |
| Mogan Shan ∧ | 106 | 30.36 N | 119.52 E |
| Mogapinyana | 156 | 22.19 S | 27.27 E |
| Mogaung | 110 | 25.18 N | 96.56 E |
| Mogdy | 89 | 50.35 N | 133.51 E |
| Mogees | 285 | 40.06 N | 75.19 W |
| Møgeltønder | 41 | 54.56 N | 8.49 E |
| Mogenstrup | 41 | 55.11 N | 11.53 E |
| Mogent ≃ | 266d | 41.33 N | 2.15 E |
| Moggio Udinese | 64 | 46.25 N | 13.12 E |
| Mogi, Serra do ⩕ | 287b | 23.47 S | 46.20 W |
| Mogielnica | 30 | 51.42 N | 20.43 E |
| Mogilev → Mahilëu | 76 | 53.54 N | 30.21 E |
| Mogilno | 30 | 52.40 N | 17.58 E |
| Mogincual | 154 | 15.35 S | 40.25 E |
| Moglal, Wādī V | 140 | 19.18 N | 34.29 E |
| Moglia | 64 | 44.56 N | 10.55 E |
| Mogliano Veneto | 64 | 45.33 N | 12.14 E |
| Mogoča | 88 | 53.44 N | 119.44 E |
| Mogoča ≃ | 76 | 58.00 N | 36.26 E |
| Mogočin | 86 | 57.43 N | 83.34 E |
| Mogod | 88 | 48.24 N | 103.00 E |
| Mogogh | 140 | 8.26 N | 31.19 E |
| Mogojto | 88 | 54.25 N | 110.27 E |
| Mogojtuj | 88 | 51.17 N | 114.55 E |
| Mogok | 110 | 22.55 N | 96.30 E |
| Mogollon Mountains ⩕ | 200 | 33.25 N | 108.40 W |
| Mogollon Rim ⊥[4] | 200 | 34.25 N | 110.50 W |
| Mogor | 120 | 32.52 N | 67.47 E |
| Mogorella | 71 | 39.52 N | 8.51 E |
| Mogoro | 71 | 39.41 N | 8.47 E |
| Mogotes | 246 | 6.30 N | 72.58 W |
| Mogotón ∧ | 236 | 13.45 N | 86.23 W |
| Mograt Island I | 140 | 19.30 N | 33.15 E |
| Mogroum | 146 | 11.06 N | 15.25 E |
| Moguer | 34 | 37.16 N | 6.50 W |
| Mogyoród | 264c | 47.36 N | 19.15 E |
| Mogyoródi-patak ≃ | 264c | 47.36 N | 19.05 E |
| Mogzon | 88 | 51.45 N | 111.58 E |
| Mohács | 30 | 45.59 N | 18.42 E |
| Mohaka | 172 | 39.07 S | 177.11 E |
| Mohaka ≃ | 172 | 39.07 S | 177.12 E |
| Mohall | 198 | 48.45 N | 101.30 W |
| Moḥammadābād | 128 | 30.53 N | 61.28 E |
| Mohammedia (Fedala) | 148 | 33.44 N | 7.24 W |
| Mohana | 124 | 25.54 N | 77.45 E |
| Mohangi | 154 | 0.03 N | 29.05 E |
| Mohania | 124 | 25.11 N | 83.37 E |
| Mohanpur, Bngl. | 126 | 23.24 N | 90.36 E |
| Mohanpur, India | 126 | 21.51 N | 87.26 E |
| Mohanpur, India | 272a | 28.44 N | 77.10 E |
| Mohave, Lake ⊜[1] | 204 | 35.25 N | 114.38 W |
| Mohawk, Mi., U.S. | 190 | 47.18 N | 88.21 W |
| Mohawk, N.Y., U.S. | 210 | 43.00 N | 75.00 W |
| Mohawk ≃ | 210 | 42.47 N | 73.42 W |
| Mohawk, East Branch ≃ | 212 | 43.22 N | 75.28 W |
| Mohawk, Lake ⊜ | 276 | 41.02 N | 74.41 W |
| Mohawk Dam ◆[6] | 214 | 40.20 N | 82.05 W |
| Mohawk Mountain ∧ | 207 | 41.49 N | 73.17 W |
| Mohawk Point > | 212 | 42.51 N | 79.29 W |
| Mohe | 89 | 53.29 N | 122.19 E |
| Moheda | 26 | 57.00 N | 14.34 E |
| Mohegan | 207 | 41.28 N | 72.06 W |
| Mohegan Lake | 210 | 41.19 N | 73.51 W |
| Mohelnice | 30 | 49.46 N | 16.55 E |
| Moher, Cliffs of ⊥[4] | 48 | 52.57 N | 9.26 W |
| Mohican ≃ | 214 | 40.22 N | 82.09 W |
| Mohican, Black Fork ≃ | 214 | 40.35 N | 82.17 W |
| Mohican, Cape > | 180 | 60.12 N | 167.28 W |
| Mohican, Clear Fork ≃ | 214 | 40.35 N | 82.12 W |
| Mohican, Jerome Fork ≃ | 214 | 40.45 N | 82.23 W |
| Mohican, Lake Fork ≃ | 214 | 40.27 N | 82.12 W |
| Mohican, Muddy Fork ≃ | 214 | 40.45 N | 82.08 W |
| Mohican State Park ♦ | 214 | 40.37 N | 82.16 W |
| Mohicanville Dam ◆[6] | 214 | 40.44 N | 82.09 W |
| Mohili ◆[8] | 272c | 19.06 N | 72.53 E |
| Mohill | 48 | 53.54 N | 7.52 W |
| Mohlakeng | 273d | 26.13 S | 27.42 E |
| Möhlau | 54 | 51.44 N | 12.21 E |
| Möhlin | 58 | 47.34 N | 7.51 E |
| Möhne ≃ | 52 | 51.27 N | 7.57 E |
| Möhnestausee ⊜[1] | 52 | 51.29 N | 8.08 E |
| Mohns Ridge ✢[3] | 16 | 72.30 N | 5.00 E |
| Mohnton | 208 | 40.17 N | 75.59 W |
| Mohnyin | 110 | 24.47 N | 96.22 E |
| Moho ≃ | 236 | 16.04 N | 88.52 W |
| Mohokare (Caledon) ≃ | 158 | 30.31 S | 26.05 E |
| Moholm | 40 | 58.37 N | 14.02 E |
| Mohon | 56 | 49.45 N | 4.44 E |
| Mohorn | 54 | 51.00 N | 13.28 E |
| Mohoro | 154 | 8.08 S | 39.10 E |
| Möhringen | 58 | 47.57 N | 8.46 E |
| Mohrsville | 208 | 40.28 N | 75.59 W |
| Mohyla-Bel'mak, hora ∧[2] | 78 | 47.20 N | 36.35 E |
| Mohyla-Mechetna, hora ∧[2] | 83 | 48.16 N | 38.53 E |
| Mohyliv | 78 | 48.52 N | 34.29 E |
| Mohyliv-Podil's'kyy | 78 | 48.27 N | 27.48 E |
| Moi | 26 | 58.28 N | 6.32 E |
| Moiano, It. | 68 | 40.39 N | 14.28 E |
| Moiano, It. | 68 | 41.05 N | 14.32 E |
| Moindou | 175f | 21.42 S | 165.41 E |
| Moinești | 38 | 46.28 N | 26.29 E |
| Moingbi | 140 | 5.46 N | 28.49 E |
| Moio Alcantara | 70 | 37.54 N | 15.03 E |
| Moiporá | 255 | 16.34 S | 50.42 W |
| Moira | 48 | 54.30 N | 6.17 W |
| Moira ≃ | 212 | 44.09 N | 77.23 W |
| Moiraba | 250 | 2.27 S | 49.25 W |
| Moira Lake ⊜ | 212 | 44.29 N | 77.27 W |
| Moirans | 62 | 45.20 N | 5.34 E |
| Moirans-en-Montagne | 58 | 46.26 N | 5.44 E |
| Mõisaküla | 76 | 58.06 N | 25.11 E |
| Moisdon | 32 | 47.37 N | 1.22 W |
| Moisejevka | 86 | 58.05 N | 76.16 E |
| Moisejevo Alabuška | 76 | 51.54 N | 42.06 E |
| Moisenay | 261 | 48.34 N | 2.44 E |
| Moisés Ville | 252 | 30.43 S | 61.29 W |
| Moisie | 186 | 50.11 N | 66.05 W |
| Moisie ≃ | 176 | 50.11 N | 66.05 W |
| Moisie, Baie de ⊂ | 186 | 50.16 N | 65.56 W |
| Moisling ◆[8] | 54 | 53.50 N | 10.38 E |
| Moison Creek ≃ | 281 | 42.18 N | 82.40 W |
| Moissac | 32 | 44.06 N | 1.05 E |
| Moïssala | 146 | 8.21 N | 17.46 E |
| Moisselles | 261 | 49.03 N | 2.20 E |
| Moisson | 261 | 49.05 N | 1.40 E |
| Moisson, Forêt de ♦ | 261 | 49.03 N | 1.39 E |
| Moissy-Cramayel | 261 | 48.38 N | 2.36 E |
| Moita | 34 | 38.39 N | 8.59 W |
| Moitaco | 246 | 8.01 N | 64.21 W |
| Moivre ≃ | 56 | 48.52 N | 4.28 E |
| Mojácar | 34 | 37.08 N | 1.51 W |
| Mojana, Brazo ≃[1] | 246 | 9.02 N | 74.46 W |
| Mojave | 228 | 35.03 N | 118.10 W |
| Mojave ≃ | 204 | 35.06 N | 116.04 W |
| Mojave Desert ◆[2] | 204 | 35.00 N | 117.00 W |
| Mojave River Forks Reservoir ⊜[1] | 228 | 34.20 N | 117.15 W |
| Moji | 85 | 38.59 N | 74.24 E |
| Mojiang | 102 | 23.28 N | 101.39 E |
| Mojicuaçu ≃ | 255 | 20.53 S | 48.10 W |
| Moji das Cruzes | 256 | 23.31 S | 46.11 W |
| Mojiguaçu | 256 | 22.22 S | 46.57 W |
| Mojimirim | 256 | 22.26 S | 46.57 W |
| Mojjero ≃ | 74 | 68.44 N | 103.42 E |
| Mojnalyk | 88 | 51.18 N | 95.33 E |
| Mojo | 144 | 8.36 N | 39.07 E |
| Mojoagung | 115a | 7.34 S | 112.21 E |
| Mojokerto | 115a | 7.28 S | 112.26 E |
| Mojosari | 115a | 7.31 S | 112.33 E |
| Mojstrana | 64 | 46.27 N | 13.56 E |
| Moju | 250 | 1.53 S | 48.46 W |
| Moju ≃ | 250 | 1.40 S | 48.25 W |
| Mojynkum | 85 | 43.48 N | 73.41 E |
| Mojynkum, peski ◆[2] | 86 | 44.20 N | 71.00 E |
| Mojynty | 86 | 47.13 N | 73.21 E |
| Mōka | 94 | 36.26 N | 140.01 E |
| Mokai | 172 | 38.32 S | 175.54 E |
| Mokāma | 124 | 25.24 N | 85.55 E |
| Mokambo | 154 | 12.25 S | 28.21 E |
| Mokane | 219 | 38.40 N | 91.52 W |
| Mokapu Peninsula >[1] | 229c | 21.27 N | 157.45 W |
| Mokaria | 152 | 2.00 N | 23.20 E |
| Mokarta, Castello di ⊥ | 70 | 37.48 N | 12.45 E |
| Mokau | 172 | 38.41 S | 174.37 E |
| Mokau ≃ | 172 | 38.42 S | 174.37 E |
| Moke | 102 | 30.14 N | 100.01 E |
| Mokelumne ≃ | 226 | 38.13 N | 121.28 W |
| Mokelumne, Middle Fork ≃ | 226 | 38.22 N | 120.37 W |
| Mokelumne, North Fork ≃ | 226 | 38.22 N | 120.37 W |
| Mokelumne, South Fork ≃ | 226 | 38.23 N | 120.35 W |
| Mokelumne Aqueduct ≍[1] | 226 | 37.54 N | 122.07 W |
| Mokelumne Hill | 226 | 38.18 N | 120.42 W |
| Mokena | 216 | 41.31 N | 87.53 W |
| Mokhotlong | 158 | 29.22 S | 29.02 E |
| Mokil I[1] | 14 | 6.40 N | 159.47 E |
| Mokimbo | 154 | 6.20 S | 28.42 E |
| Mokino | 80 | 57.27 N | 49.11 E |
| Moklakan | 88 | 54.56 N | 118.56 E |
| Möklinta | 40 | 60.05 N | 16.32 E |
| Moknine | 148 | 35.38 N | 10.54 E |
| Mokochu, Khao ∧ | 110 | 15.56 N | 99.06 E |
| Mokohinau Islands II | 172 | 35.55 S | 175.07 E |
| Mokokchūng | 120 | 26.20 N | 94.32 E |
| Mokolo, Cam. | 146 | 10.45 N | 13.48 E |
| Mokolo, Zaïre | 152 | 1.57 N | 18.05 E |
| Mokolo ≃ | 156 | 23.14 S | 27.43 E |
| Mokombe | 152 | 0.14 S | 23.48 E |
| Mokoreta ≃ | 172 | 46.21 S | 168.51 E |
| Mokou | 273b | 4.13 S | 15.13 E |
| Mokpalin | 110 | 17.26 N | 96.53 E |
| Mokp'o | 98 | 34.48 N | 126.22 E |
| Mokraja Jel'muta | 80 | 46.51 N | 41.41 E |
| Mokraja Ol'chovka | 80 | 50.28 N | 44.59 E |
| Mokra Sura ≃ | 78 | 48.19 N | 35.09 E |
| Mokra Volnovakha ≃ | 83 | 47.30 N | 37.15 E |
| Mokrisset | 34 | 34.59 N | 5.20 W |
| Mokri Yaly ≃ | 78 | 48.05 N | 36.44 E |
| Mokrous | 80 | 51.14 N | 47.37 E |
| Mokrousovo | 86 | 55.48 N | 66.45 E |
| Mokroyelanchyk | 83 | 47.42 N | 38.31 E |
| Mokrušinskoje | 86 | 57.31 N | 93.11 E |
| Mokryj Gašun | 80 | 46.53 N | 42.45 E |
| Mokryj Jelančik ≃ | 83 | 47.08 N | 38.20 E |
| Mokryj Kor | 82 | 54.34 N | 37.58 E |
| Mokša ≃ | 80 | 54.44 N | 41.53 E |
| Mokšan | 80 | 53.26 N | 44.37 E |
| Moku | 154 | 2.57 N | 29.22 E |
| Mokuleia | 229c | 21.35 N | 158.09 W |
| Mokumbusu | 152 | 1.44 N | 21.04 E |
| Mokvyn | 78 | 50.57 N | 26.48 E |
| Mokwa | 150 | 9.20 N | 5.02 E |
| Mol | 56 | 51.11 N | 5.06 E |
| Mola di Bari | 68 | 41.04 N | 17.05 E |
| Molale | 144 | 10.08 N | 39.42 E |
| Molalla | 224 | 45.08 N | 122.34 W |
| Molalla ≃ | 224 | 45.18 N | 122.43 W |
| Molalla, North Fork ≃ | 224 | 45.05 N | 122.29 W |
| Molanda | 152 | 2.28 N | 20.48 E |
| Molango | 234 | 20.53 N | 98.46 W |
| Molanosa | 184 | 54.30 N | 105.33 W |
| Moláoi | 38 | 36.48 N | 22.52 E |
| Molara, Isola I | 71 | 40.52 N | 9.43 E |
| Molaretto | 62 | 45.10 N | 7.00 E |
| Molat, Otok I | 36 | 44.15 N | 14.49 E |
| Molbergen | 52 | 52.51 N | 7.55 E |
| Molčanovka | 83 | 46.52 N | 38.37 E |
| Molčanovo | 86 | 57.35 N | 83.48 E |
| Mold | 44 | 53.10 N | 3.08 W |
| Moldary | 86 | 50.47 N | 78.29 E |
| Moldau → Vltava ≃ | 30 | 50.21 N | 14.30 E |
| Moldavia □[9] | 38 | 47.00 N | 27.15 E |
| Moldavia → Moldova □[1] | 38 | 47.00 N | 29.00 E |
| Moldavija → Moldova □[1] | 38 | 47.00 N | 29.00 E |
| Molde | 26 | 62.44 N | 7.11 E |
| Moldotau, chrebet ⩕ | 85 | 41.35 N | 74.40 E |
| Moldova □[1], Europe | 22 | 47.00 N | 29.00 E |
| Moldova □[1], Europe | 38 | 47.00 N | 29.00 E |
| Moldova ≃ | 38 | 46.54 N | 26.58 E |
| Moldova Nouă | 38 | 44.44 N | 21.40 E |
| Moldoveanu, Vârful ∧ | 38 | 45.36 N | 24.44 E |
| Môle ≃, Fr. | 62 | 43.15 N | 6.32 E |
| Mole ≃, Eng., U.K. | 42 | 50.57 N | 3.54 W |
| Mole ≃, Eng., U.K. | 42 | 51.24 N | 0.21 W |
| Môle, Cap du > | 238 | 19.50 N | 73.25 W |
| Mole Creek | 166 | 41.33 S | 146.24 E |
| Moledet | 132 | 32.35 N | 35.26 E |
| Molega Lake ⊜ | 186 | 44.22 N | 64.53 W |
| Mole Game Reserve ◆[4] | 150 | 9.30 N | 2.00 W |
| Molegbe | 152 | 4.14 N | 20.53 E |
| Molenbeek-St.-Jean | 50 | 50.51 N | 4.19 E |
| Molepolole | 156 | 24.25 S | 25.30 E |
| Moléson ∧ | 58 | 46.33 N | 7.01 E |
| Molėtai | 76 | 55.14 N | 25.25 E |
| Mole Valley □[8] | 260 | 51.16 N | 0.18 W |
| Molfetta | 68 | 41.12 N | 16.36 E |
| Molibagu | 112 | 0.23 N | 123.59 E |
| Molières-sur-Cèze | 62 | 44.15 N | 4.09 E |
| Molimiao | 89 | 43.34 N | 121.54 E |
| Molina | 252 | 35.07 S | 71.17 W |
| Molina de Aragón | 34 | 40.51 N | 1.53 W |
| Molina de Segura | 34 | 38.03 N | 1.12 W |
| Molina di Ledro | 64 | 45.56 N | 10.46 E |
| Molinara | 68 | 41.18 N | 14.54 E |
| Moline, Il., U.S. | 190 | 41.30 N | 90.30 W |
| Moline, Ks., U.S. | 198 | 37.21 N | 96.18 W |
| Moline, Mi., U.S. | 216 | 42.44 N | 85.39 W |
| Molinella | 64 | 44.37 N | 11.40 E |
| Molinges | 58 | 46.21 N | 5.46 E |
| Molingguan | 106 | 31.50 N | 118.50 E |
| Molini di Tures (Mühlen) | 64 | 46.54 N | 11.56 E |
| Molinière Point > | 241k | 12.05 N | 61.45 W |
| Molino | 194 | 30.43 N | 87.18 W |
| Molino de Rosas ◆[8] | 286a | 19.22 N | 99.13 W |
| Molinos | 252 | 25.25 S | 66.19 W |
| Molins de Rei | 34 | 41.25 N | 2.01 E |
| Moliro | 154 | 8.13 S | 30.34 E |
| Molise □[4] | 66 | 41.35 N | 14.30 E |
| Moliterno | 68 | 40.14 N | 15.52 E |
| Mölkau | 54 | 51.20 N | 12.26 E |
| Molkom | 40 | 59.36 N | 13.43 E |
| Möll ≃ | 64 | 46.50 N | 13.26 E |
| Mollahasan | 130 | 39.22 N | 42.37 E |
| Mollāhāt | 126 | 22.56 N | 89.48 E |
| Mollakendi | 130 | 38.36 N | 39.20 E |
| Mollaro | 64 | 46.16 N | 11.05 E |
| Möllbrücke | 64 | 46.50 N | 13.22 E |
| Mölle | 41 | 56.17 N | 12.29 E |
| Möllen | 263 | 51.35 N | 6.42 E |
| Möllenbeck, Dtsch. | 54 | 53.17 N | 11.44 E |
| Möllenbeck, Dtsch. | 54 | 53.23 N | 13.20 E |
| Mollendo | 248 | 17.02 S | 72.01 W |
| Möllenhagen | 54 | 53.32 N | 12.56 E |
| Möllensee ⊜ | 264a | 52.26 N | 13.51 E |
| Mollepata | 248 | 13.31 S | 72.32 W |
| Moller, Port ⊂ | 180 | 55.51 N | 160.25 W |
| Möllersdorf | 264b | 48.02 N | 16.18 E |
| Mollet del Vallès | 266d | 41.33 N | 2.13 E |
| Mollia | 62 | 45.49 N | 8.02 E |
| Molliens-Vidame | 50 | 49.53 N | 2.01 E |
| Mollington | 262 | 53.13 N | 2.55 W |
| Mollis | 58 | 47.05 N | 9.04 E |
| Mölln, Dtsch. | 54 | 53.37 N | 10.41 E |
| Molln, Öst. | 61 | 47.53 N | 14.15 E |
| Mollösund | 26 | 58.04 N | 11.28 E |
| Mollusk | 208 | 37.43 N | 76.32 W |
| Molly Ann Brook ≃ | 276 | 40.55 N | 74.11 W |
| Mölnbo | 40 | 59.03 N | 17.25 E |
| Mölndal | 26 | 57.39 N | 12.01 E |
| Mölnlycke | 26 | 57.39 N | 12.09 E |
| Mölntorp | 40 | 59.33 N | 16.15 E |
| Molocaboc Island I | 116 | 10.58 N | 123.34 E |
| Molochans'k | 78 | 47.12 N | 35.36 E |
| Molochio | 68 | 38.18 N | 16.02 E |
| Molochna ≃ | 78 | 46.42 N | 35.20 E |
| Molochnyy lyman ⊜ | 78 | 46.30 N | 35.20 E |
| Moločnoje | 76 | 59.17 N | 39.41 E |
| Molócuè ≃ | 154 | 17.03 S | 38.52 E |
| Molodežnaja ʊ[3] | 9 | 67.35 S | 46.35 E |
| Molodi | 82 | 55.17 N | 37.31 E |
| Molodo | 150 | 14.14 N | 6.02 W |
| Molodogvardejskoje | 86 | 54.03 N | 70.44 E |
| Molodohvariys'k | 83 | 48.20 N | 39.40 E |
| Molodoj Tud | 76 | 56.26 N | 33.36 E |
| Molod'ožnyj | 89 | 50.23 N | 136.48 E |
| Mologa ≃ | 76 | 58.50 N | 37.11 E |
| Molokai I | 229a | 21.07 N | 157.00 W |
| Molokai Fracture Zone ✢ | 16 | 23.00 N | 130.00 W |
| Molokča ≃ | 82 | 56.15 N | 38.45 E |
| Molokini I | 229a | 20.38 N | 156.30 W |
| Molokovo, Ross. | 76 | 58.10 N | 36.45 E |
| Molokovo, Ross. | 82 | 55.34 N | 37.52 E |
| Moloma ≃ | 24 | 58.20 N | 48.28 E |
| Molong | 166 | 33.06 S | 148.52 E |
| Molonglo ≃ | 171b | 35.15 S | 148.58 E |
| Molopo ≃ | 156 | 28.30 S | 20.13 E |
| Molotov → Perm' | 86 | 58.00 N | 56.15 E |
| Molotovsk → Severodvinsk | 24 | 64.34 N | 39.50 E |
| Molou | 146 | 13.42 N | 21.44 E |
| Moloundou | 152 | 2.03 N | 15.10 E |
| Molowaie | 152 | 5.47 S | 23.20 E |
| Moloy | 58 | 47.32 N | 4.55 E |
| Molsheim | 58 | 48.32 N | 7.29 E |
| Molson Lake ⊜ | 184 | 54.12 N | 96.45 W |
| Molteno | 158 | 31.22 S | 26.22 E |
| Moltrasio | 58 | 45.52 N | 9.05 E |
| Molu, Pulau I | 164 | 6.45 S | 131.33 E |
| Molucas, Islas → Maluku II | 108 | 2.00 S | 128.00 E |
| Molucas, Mar de la → Maluku, Laut ▽[2] | 108 | 0.00 | 125.00 E |
| Moluccas → Maluku II | 108 | 2.00 S | 128.00 E |
| Molucca Sea → Maluku, Laut ▽[2] | 108 | 0.00 | 125.00 E |
| Molukken → Maluku II | 108 | 2.00 S | 128.00 E |
| Molumbo | 154 | 15.27 S | 30.15 E |
| Molundo | 116 | 7.56 N | 124.23 E |
| Moluques → Maluku II | 108 | 2.00 S | 128.00 E |
| Molveno, Lago di ⊜ | 64 | 46.08 N | 10.57 E |
| Molvoticy | 76 | 57.25 N | 32.20 E |
| Molžaninovo | 82 | 55.56 N | 37.22 E |
| Moma, Moç. | 154 | 16.44 S | 39.14 E |
| Moma, Zaïre | 152 | 1.36 S | 23.57 E |
| Moma ≃ | 74 | 66.26 N | 143.06 E |
| Momanga | 156 | 18.12 S | 21.42 E |
| Momats ≃ | 164 | 5.20 S | 137.47 E |
| Momax | 234 | 21.56 N | 103.19 W |
| Momba ≃ | 154 | 8.28 S | 32.40 E |
| Mombaça | 250 | 5.45 S | 39.38 W |
| Mombaça, Corrego ≃ | 287b | 23.46 S | 46.47 W |
| Mombachito, Cerro ∧ | 236 | 12.24 N | 85.34 W |
| Mombacho, Volcán ∧[1] | 236 | 11.50 N | 85.58 W |
| Mombango | 152 | 1.45 N | 24.26 E |
| Mombaruzzo | 62 | 44.46 N | 8.27 E |
| Mombasa | 154 | 4.03 S | 39.40 E |
| Mombetsu | 92a | 44.21 N | 143.22 E |
| Mombo | 154 | 4.53 S | 38.17 E |
| Mombongo | 152 | 1.39 N | 23.09 E |
| Momboyo ≃ | 152 | 0.16 S | 19.00 E |
| Mombuey | 34 | 42.02 N | 6.20 W |
| Mombum | 164 | 8.23 S | 138.51 E |
| Momčilgrad | 38 | 41.32 N | 25.25 E |
| Momence | 216 | 41.10 N | 87.39 W |
| Momfafa, Tanjung > | 164 | 0.18 S | 131.20 E |
| Momi | 175g | 17.55 S | 177.17 E |
| Momignies | 50 | 50.02 N | 4.10 E |
| Mömlingen | 56 | 49.52 N | 9.05 E |
| Mommark | 41 | 54.55 N | 10.03 E |
| Mommenheim | 56 | 48.45 N | 7.39 E |
| Momo | 152 | 1.52 N | 11.48 E |
| Momotombo, Volcán ∧[1] | 236 | 12.26 N | 86.33 W |
| Momozaka | 270 | 34.51 N | 135.02 E |
| Mompog Island I | 116 | 13.31 N | 122.11 E |
| Mompog Pass ⊔ | 116 | 13.34 N | 122.13 E |
| Mompono | 152 | 0.04 N | 21.48 E |
| Mompós | 246 | 9.14 N | 74.26 W |
| Momskij chrebet ⩕ | 74 | 66.00 N | 146.00 E |
| Mon | 110 | 18.31 N | 96.38 E |
| Mon □[8] | 110 | 17.30 N | 97.00 E |
| Møn I | 41 | 55.00 N | 12.20 E |
| Mon ≃ | 110 | 20.20 N | 94.54 E |
| Mona | 200 | 39.48 N | 111.51 W |
| Mona, Canal de la ⊔ | 238 | 18.30 N | 67.45 W |
| Mona, Isla de I | 238 | 18.05 N | 67.54 W |
| Mona, Punta > | 236 | 9.38 N | 82.37 W |
| Monaca | 214 | 40.41 N | 80.16 W |
| Monach, Sound of ⊔ | 46 | 57.34 N | 7.35 W |
| Monach Islands II | 46 | 57.31 N | 7.40 W |
| Monaci, Fiume dei ≃ | 70 | 37.24 N | 14.48 E |
| Monaco | 62 | 43.42 N | 7.23 E |
| Monaco □[1], Europe | 22 | 43.45 N | 7.25 E |
| Monaco □[1], Europe | 62 | 43.45 N | 7.25 E |
| Monadhliath Mountains ⩕ | 46 | 57.10 N | 4.00 W |
| Monadnock Mountain ∧ | 207 | 42.52 N | 72.07 W |
| Monagas □[3] | 246 | 9.20 N | 63.00 W |
| Monaghan | 48 | 54.15 N | 6.58 W |
| Monaghan □[6] | 48 | 54.10 N | 7.00 W |
| Monagrillo | 236 | 7.59 N | 80.26 W |
| Monahans | 196 | 31.35 N | 102.53 W |
| Monahans Draw V | 196 | 31.55 N | 101.46 W |
| Monahans Sandhills State Park ♦ | 196 | 31.38 N | 102.50 W |
| Monakino | 89 | 43.24 N | 133.29 E |
| Mona Lake ⊜ | 216 | 43.11 N | 86.17 W |
| Monamolin | 48 | 52.33 N | 6.20 W |
| Monango | 198 | 46.10 N | 98.35 W |
| Monapo | 154 | 14.57 S | 40.17 E |
| Monapo ≃ | 154 | 15.07 S | 40.33 E |
| Mona Quimbundo | 152 | 9.55 S | 19.58 E |
| Monar, Loch ⊜ | 46 | 57.25 N | 5.06 W |
| Monarch | 192 | 34.43 N | 81.35 W |
| Monarch Mountain ∧ | 182 | 51.54 N | 125.53 W |
| Monarch Pass )( | 200 | 38.30 N | 106.19 W |
| Monaro Range ⩕ | 171b | 36.22 S | 149.03 E |
| Monarto South | 168b | 35.08 S | 139.08 E |
| Monaš | 80 | 46.58 N | 50.36 E |
| Monashee Mountains ⩕ | 182 | 50.30 N | 118.30 W |
| Monashee Provincial Park ♦ | 182 | 50.28 N | 118.11 W |
| Monash University ʊ[2] | 274b | 37.55 S | 145.08 E |
| Monasterace | 68 | 38.27 N | 16.33 E |
| Monasterevin | 48 | 53.07 N | 7.02 W |
| Monasterolo di Savigliano | 62 | 44.40 N | 7.37 E |
| Monastir, It. | 71 | 39.23 N | 9.02 E |
| Monastir → Bitola, Mak. | 38 | 41.01 N | 21.20 E |
| Monastir, Tun. | 148 | 35.47 N | 10.50 E |
| Monastyrščina | 76 | 54.21 N | 31.50 E |
| Monastyryshche | 78 | 49.00 N | 29.49 E |
| Monastyrys'ka | 78 | 49.06 N | 25.11 E |
| Monatélé | 152 | 4.16 N | 11.12 E |
| Mona Vale | 170 | 33.41 S | 151.18 E |
| Monbulk | 274b | 37.52 S | 145.25 E |
| Monbulk Creek ≃ | 274b | 37.54 S | 145.15 E |
| Moncada | 116 | 15.44 N | 120.34 E |
| Moncalieri | 62 | 45.00 N | 7.41 E |
| Moncalvo | 62 | 45.03 N | 8.16 E |
| Monção, Bra. | 250 | 3.30 S | 45.15 W |
| Moncão, Port. | 34 | 42.05 N | 8.29 W |
| Monceau-sur-Sambre | 50 | 50.25 N | 4.22 E |
| Mončegorsk | 24 | 67.54 N | 32.58 E |
| Mönch ∧ | 58 | 46.34 N | 7.59 E |
| Mönchdorf | 61 | 48.21 N | 14.48 E |
| Mönchengladbach | 56 | 51.12 N | 6.28 E |
| Mönchengladbach, Flughafen ⊠ | 263 | 51.14 N | 6.29 E |
| Mönchhof | 61 | 47.52 N | 16.56 E |
| Monchique | 34 | 37.19 N | 8.33 W |
| Mönchweiler | 58 | 48.06 N | 8.25 E |
| Moncks Corner | 192 | 33.11 N | 80.00 W |
| Monclova | 232 | 26.54 N | 101.25 W |
| Moncontour | 32 | 48.21 N | 2.39 W |
| Moncoutant | 32 | 46.43 N | 0.35 W |
| Moncton | 186 | 46.06 N | 64.47 W |
| Mondaí | 252 | 27.05 S | 53.25 W |
| Mondaino | 66 | 43.51 N | 12.41 E |
| Mondavio | 66 | 43.40 N | 12.58 E |
| Monday ≃ | 252 | 25.33 S | 54.41 W |
| Mondego ≃ | 34 | 40.09 N | 8.52 W |
| Mondego, Cabo > | 34 | 40.11 N | 8.55 W |
| Mondello | 70 | 38.13 N | 13.20 E |
| Mondeodo | 112 | 3.33 S | 122.12 E |
| Mondeor | 273d | 26.17 S | 28.00 E |
| Mondimbi | 152 | 1.43 N | 22.58 E |
| Mondo, Tan. | 154 | 4.59 S | 35.54 E |
| Mondo, Tchad | 146 | 13.47 N | 15.32 E |
| Mondolè, Monte ∧ | 62 | 44.13 N | 7.46 E |
| Mondolfo | 66 | 43.45 N | 13.06 E |
| Mondombe | 152 | 0.53 S | 22.45 E |
| Mondoñedo | 34 | 43.26 N | 7.22 W |
| Mondorf-les-Bains | 56 | 49.31 N | 6.16 E |
| Mondoro | 150 | 14.40 N | 1.57 W |
| Mondoubleau | 50 | 47.59 N | 0.54 E |
| Mondovi | 190 | 44.34 N | 91.40 W |


**Symbols** in the index entries represent the broad categories identified in the key at the right. Symbols with superior numbers (⩕[1]) identify subcategories (see complete key on page *I · 1).*

**Symbole** im Register stellen die rechts im Schlüssel erklärten Kategorien dar. Symbole mit hochgestellten Ziffern (⩕[1]) bezeichnen Unterabteilungen einer Kategorie (vgl. vollständiger Schlüssel auf Seite *I · 1).*

**Los símbolos** incluídos en el texto del índice representan las grandes categorías identificadas con la clave a la derecha. Los símbolos con numeros en su parte superior (⩕[1]) identifican las subcategorías (véase la clave completa en la página *I · 1).*

**Les symboles** de l'index représentent les catégories indiquées dans la légende à droite. Les symboles suivis d'un indice (⩕[1]) représentent des sous-catégories (voir légende complète à la page *I · 1).*

**Os símbolos** incluídos no texto do índice representam as grandes categorias identificadas com a chave à direita. Os símbolos com números em sua parte superior (⩕[1]) identificam as subcategorias (veja-se a chave completa à página *I · 1).*

| | English | Deutsch | Español | Français | Português |
|---|---|---|---|---|---|
| ∧ | Mountain | Berg | Montaña | Montagne | Montanha |
| ⩕ | Mountains | Gebirge | Montañas | Montagnes | Montanhas |
| )( | Pass | Paß | Paso | Col | Passo |
| V | Valley, Canyon | Tal, Cañon | Valle, Cañón | Vallée, Canyon | Vale, Canhão |
| ≃ | Plain | Ebene | Llano | Plaine | Planície |
| > | Cape | Kap | Cabo | Cap | Cabo |
| I | Island | Insel | Isla | Île | Ilha |
| II | Islands | Inseln | Islas | Îles | Ilhas |
| ⊥ | Other Topographic Features | Andere Topographische Objekte | Otros Elementos Topográficos | Autres données topographiques | Outros acidentes topográficos |

| ESPAÑOL Nombre / FRANÇAIS Nom / PORTUGUÊS Nome | Página / Page / Página | Lat.°′ | Long.°′ W = Oeste / W = Ouest / W = Oeste |
|---|---|---|---|
| Mondragon, Fr. | 62 | 44.14 N | 4.43 E |
| Mondragon, Pil. | 116 | 12.31 N | 124.45 E |
| Mondragone | 68 | 41.07 N | 13.53 E |
| Mondrain Island I | 162 | 34.08 S | 122.15 E |
| Mondsee | 64 | 47.52 N | 13.21 E |
| Mondsee ⊜ | 64 | 47.49 N | 13.23 E |
| Monds Island I | 285 | 39.50 N | 75.19 W |
| Mondy | 88 | 51.40 N | 100.59 E |
| Monee | 216 | 41.25 N | 87.45 W |
| Moneglia | 62 | 44.14 N | 9.30 E |
| Monemvasía | 38 | 36.41 N | 23.03 E |
| Monero | 200 | 36.54 N | 106.52 W |
| Moneron, ostrov I | 89 | 46.17 N | 141.15 E |
| Monesiglio | 62 | 44.28 N | 8.07 E |
| Monessen | 214 | 40.08 N | 79.53 W |
| Monesterio | 34 | 38.05 N | 6.16 W |
| Monestier-de-Clermont | 62 | 44.54 N | 5.38 E |
| Monetnyj | 86 | 57.03 N | 60.53 E |
| Monett | 194 | 36.55 N | 93.55 W |
| Monette | 194 | 35.53 N | 90.20 W |
| Money Creek ≃ | 216 | 40.40 N | 88.58 W |
| Moneygall | 48 | 52.53 N | 7.57 W |
| Moneymore | 48 | 54.42 N | 6.40 W |
| Monfalcone | 64 | 45.49 N | 13.32 E |
| Monferrato □9 | 62 | 44.55 N | 8.05 E |
| Monflanquin | 32 | 44.32 N | 0.46 E |
| Monforte | 34 | 39.03 N | 7.26 W |
| Monforte de Lemos | 34 | 42.31 N | 7.30 W |
| Monforte San Giorgio | 70 | 38.09 N | 15.23 E |
| Monfort Heights | 218 | 39.12 N | 84.37 W |
| Monga | 152 | 4.12 N | 22.49 E |
| Mongaguá | 256 | 24.06 S | 46.37 W |
| Mongai-Musenge | 152 | 4.04 S | 19.34 E |
| Mongala ≃ | 152 | 1.53 N | 19.46 E |
| Mongalla | 154 | 5.12 N | 31.46 E |
| Mongalla Game Reserve ◆4 | 154 | 5.12 N | 31.33 E |
| Mongandjo | 152 | 1.21 N | 24.20 E |
| Mongarlowe ≃ | 170 | 35.15 S | 149.52 E |
| Mongat | 266d | 41.28 N | 2.17 E |
| Mongaup ≃ | 210 | 41.25 N | 74.45 W |
| Mongaup Valley | 210 | 41.40 N | 74.47 W |
| Mongbwalu | 154 | 1.57 N | 30.02 E |
| Mongbyŏn-ni | 271b | 37.40 N | 126.44 E |
| Mong Cai | 110 | 21.32 N | 107.58 E |
| Monge ∧ | 266c | 38.46 N | 9.26 W |
| Monger, Îles II | 186 | 51.05 N | 58.45 W |
| Mongeri | 150 | 8.19 N | 11.44 W |
| Mongers Lake ⊜ | 162 | 29.15 S | 117.05 E |
| Monggon Qulu | 89 | 48.35 N | 119.49 E |
| Monggŭmp'o | 98 | 38.09 N | 124.47 E |
| Möng Hai | 110 | 20.46 N | 99.49 E |
| Möng Hawm | 110 | 23.51 N | 98.20 E |
| Monghidoro | 66 | 44.13 N | 11.19 E |
| Möng Hpāyak | 110 | 20.53 N | 99.54 E |
| Möng Hsat | 110 | 20.32 N | 99.15 E |
| Monghyr → Munger | 124 | 25.23 N | 86.28 E |
| Mongi ≃ | 164 | 6.35 S | 147.35 E |
| Mongiana | 68 | 38.31 N | 16.19 E |
| Mongibello → Etna, Monte ∧1 | 70 | 37.46 N | 15.00 E |
| Mongiuffi | 70 | 37.55 N | 15.17 E |
| Möng Küng | 110 | 21.36 N | 97.32 E |
| Möng Ma | 110 | 21.37 N | 99.54 E |
| Möng Mit | 110 | 23.07 N | 96.41 E |
| Möng Nai | 110 | 20.31 N | 97.52 E |
| Möng Nawng | 110 | 21.39 N | 98.08 E |
| Mongo, Tchad | 146 | 12.11 N | 18.42 E |
| Mongo, In., U.S. | 216 | 41.41 N | 85.17 W |
| Mongo ≃ | 150 | 9.34 N | 12.11 W |
| Mongoj | 88 | 53.57 N | 113.50 E |
| Mongol Altajn nuruu ⋀ | 90 | 46.30 N | 93.00 E |
| Mongol Ard Uls → Mongolia □1 | 90 | 46.00 N | 105.00 E |
| Mongolei → Mongolia □1 | 90 | 46.00 N | 105.00 E |
| Mongol els ◆2 | 88 | 47.45 N | 94.30 E |
| Mongolia (Mongol Ard Uls) □1 | 90 | 46.00 N | 105.00 E |
| Mongolie → Mongolia □1 | 90 | 46.00 N | 105.00 E |
| Mongomo | 152 | 1.38 N | 11.19 E |
| Möngön Mor't | 88 | 48.11 N | 108.29 E |
| Mongororo | 146 | 12.01 N | 22.28 E |
| Mongoumba | 152 | 3.38 N | 18.36 E |
| Möng Pai | 110 | 19.44 N | 97.05 E |
| Möng Pan | 110 | 20.19 N | 98.22 E |
| Möng Pawn | 110 | 20.49 N | 97.28 E |
| Möng Ping | 110 | 22.22 N | 99.02 E |
| Mongpong ≃ | 116 | 12.44 N | 120.48 E |
| Mongrando | 62 | 45.31 N | 8.00 E |
| Möng Si | 110 | 23.40 N | 98.23 E |
| Mong Tung Hang | 271d | 22.20 N | 114.02 E |
| Mongu | 152 | 15.15 S | 23.09 E |
| Môngua | 152 | 16.43 S | 15.23 E |
| Monguelfo (Welsberg) | 64 | 46.45 N | 12.06 E |
| Monguno | 146 | 12.40 N | 13.38 E |
| Möng Yai | 110 | 22.25 N | 98.02 E |
| Möng Yawng | 110 | 21.11 N | 100.22 E |
| Monheim, Dtsch. | 56 | 48.50 N | 10.51 E |
| Monheim, Dtsch. | 56 | 51.05 N | 6.52 E |
| Moniaive | 44 | 55.12 N | 3.55 W |
| Mönichkirchen | 61 | 47.31 N | 16.02 E |
| Monico | 190 | 45.34 N | 89.09 W |
| Monida Pass )( | 202 | 44.33 N | 112.18 W |
| Mon Idée | 50 | 49.53 N | 4.23 E |
| Monie | 152 | 4.00 S | 17.22 E |
| Monie Bay c | 208 | 38.13 N | 75.51 W |
| Monie Creek ≃ | 208 | 38.14 N | 75.50 W |
| Monifieth | 46 | 56.29 N | 2.49 W |
| Monimail | 46 | 56.18 N | 3.08 W |
| Moninger | 214 | 40.14 N | 80.13 W |
| Monino | 82 | 55.50 N | 38.11 E |
| Moniquirá | 246 | 5.52 N | 73.36 W |
| Mõniste | 76 | 57.35 N | 26.33 E |
| Monistrol-d'Allier | 62 | 44.57 N | 3.38 E |
| Monistrol-sur-Loire | 62 | 45.17 N | 4.10 E |
| Monitor Range ⋀ | 204 | 38.45 N | 116.30 W |
| Monitor Valley V | 204 | 39.00 N | 116.40 W |
| Monívea | 48 | 53.23 N | 8.43 W |
| Monjolo | 256 | 22.49 S | 42.57 W |
| Monk, Pointe > | 275a | 45.29 N | 73.57 W |
| Monkayo | 116 | 7.50 N | 126.03 E |
| Mönkebude | 54 | 53.46 N | 13.57 E |
| Monken Hadley ◆8 | 260 | 51.40 N | 0.11 W |
| Monkey Bay | 154 | 14.05 S | 34.55 E |
| Monkey River | 236 | 16.22 N | 88.29 W |
| Mońki | 30 | 53.24 N | 22.49 E |
| Monkira | 166 | 24.49 S | 140.34 E |
| Monkoto | 152 | 1.38 S | 20.39 E |
| Monks Heath | 262 | 53.16 N | 2.14 W |
| Monkton | 212 | 43.35 N | 81.05 W |
| Monmouth, Wales, U.K. | 42 | 51.50 N | 2.43 W |
| Monmouth, Il., U.S. | 190 | 40.54 N | 90.38 W |
| Monmouth, In., U.S. | 216 | 40.52 N | 84.57 W |
| Monmouth, Or., U.S. | 202 | 44.50 N | 123.13 W |
| Monmouth □6 | 208 | 40.16 N | 74.17 W |
| Monmouth Beach | 276 | 40.19 N | 73.58 W |
| Monmouth Hills | 276 | 40.24 N | 74.00 W |
| Monmouth Junction | 208 | 40.22 N | 74.32 W |
| Monmouth Mountain ∧ | 182 | 51.00 N | 123.47 W |
| Monnickendam | 52 | 52.27 N | 5.02 E |
| Monnow ≃ | 42 | 51.48 N | 2.42 W |
| Mono □5 | 150 | 6.45 N | 1.50 E |
| Mono □6 | 226 | 38.18 N | 119.22 W |
| Mono ≃ | 150 | 6.17 N | 1.51 E |
| Mono, Caño ≃ | 246 | 4.25 N | 67.47 W |
| Mono, Punta > | 236 | 11.36 N | 83.39 W |
| Monobe | 96 | 33.42 N | 133.53 E |
| Monobe ≃ | 96 | 33.32 N | 133.41 E |
| Monocacy ≃ | 208 | 39.13 N | 77.27 W |
| Monocacy Station | 208 | 40.16 N | 75.46 W |
| Monogarovo | 82 | 54.42 N | 38.45 E |
| Mono Island I | 175e | 7.21 S | 155.34 E |
| Mono Lake ⊜ | 204 | 38.00 N | 119.00 W |
| Monomoy Island I | 207 | 41.35 N | 69.59 W |
| Monomoy Point > | 207 | 41.33 N | 70.02 W |
| Monon | 216 | 40.52 N | 86.52 W |
| Monona, Ia., U.S. | 190 | 43.03 N | 91.23 W |
| Monona, Wi., U.S. | 216 | 43.03 N | 89.20 W |
| Monona, Lake ⊜ | 216 | 43.03 N | 89.22 W |
| Monongahela | 214 | 40.12 N | 79.55 W |
| Monongahela ≃ | 188 | 40.27 N | 80.00 W |
| Monongahela Brook ≃ | 285 | 39.47 N | 75.09 W |
| Monopoli | 68 | 40.57 N | 17.19 E |
| Monor | 30 | 47.21 N | 19.27 E |
| Mono Road Station | 275b | 43.51 N | 79.51 W |
| Monòver | 34 | 38.26 N | 0.50 W |
| Monowai, Lake ⊜ | 172 | 45.52 S | 167.27 E |
| Monponsett | 207 | 42.01 N | 70.50 W |
| Monponsett Pond ⊜ | 283 | 42.01 N | 70.51 W |
| Monreal | 34 | 42.42 N | 1.30 W |
| Monreal del Campo | 34 | 40.47 N | 1.21 W |
| Monreale | 70 | 38.05 N | 13.17 E |
| Monreale, Castello di ⊥ | 71 | 39.38 N | 8.49 E |
| Monroe, Ct., U.S. | 207 | 41.19 N | 73.12 W |
| Monroe, Fl., U.S. | 220 | 25.52 N | 81.06 W |
| Monroe, Ga., U.S. | 192 | 33.47 N | 83.42 W |
| Monroe, In., U.S. | 216 | 40.44 N | 84.56 W |
| Monroe, Ia., U.S. | 190 | 41.31 N | 93.06 W |
| Monroe, La., U.S. | 194 | 32.30 N | 92.07 W |
| Monroe, Mi., U.S. | 214 | 41.54 N | 83.23 W |
| Monroe, Ne., U.S. | 198 | 41.28 N | 97.35 W |
| Monroe, N.J., U.S. | 276 | 41.06 N | 74.38 W |
| Monroe, N.Y., U.S. | 210 | 41.19 N | 74.11 W |
| Monroe, N.C., U.S. | 192 | 34.59 N | 80.32 W |
| Monroe, Oh., U.S. | 218 | 39.26 N | 84.21 W |
| Monroe, Or., U.S. | 202 | 44.18 N | 123.17 W |
| Monroe, Ut,. U.S. | 200 | 38.37 N | 112.07 W |
| Monroe, Va., U.S. | 192 | 37.30 N | 79.07 W |
| Monroe, Wa., U.S. | 224 | 47.51 N | 121.58 W |
| Monroe, Wi., U.S. | 190 | 42.36 N | 89.38 W |
| Monroe □6, Fl., U.S. | 220 | 25.10 N | 81.10 W |
| Monroe □6, Il., U.S. | 219 | 38.20 N | 90.09 W |
| Monroe □6, In., U.S. | 218 | 39.10 N | 86.26 W |
| Monroe □6, Mi., U.S. | 216 | 41.55 N | 83.26 W |
| Monroe □6, Mo., U.S. | 219 | 39.30 N | 92.00 W |
| Monroe □6, N.Y., U.S. | 210 | 43.10 N | 77.36 W |
| Monroe □6, Pa., U.S. | 210 | 40.59 N | 75.12 W |
| Monroe, Lake ⊜ | 220 | 28.52 N | 81.16 W |
| Monroe Bridge | 207 | 42.43 N | 72.56 W |
| Monroe Center, Ct., U.S. | 207 | 41.20 N | 73.12 W |
| Monroe Center, Il., U.S. | 216 | 42.06 N | 89.00 W |
| Monroe City, In., U.S. | 194 | 38.36 N | 87.21 W |
| Monroe City, Mo., U.S. | 219 | 39.39 N | 91.44 W |
| Monroe City, Tx., U.S. | 222 | 29.47 N | 94.35 W |
| Monroe Lake ⊜1 | 218 | 39.05 N | 86.25 W |
| Monroe Manor | 216 | 41.36 N | 86.40 W |
| Monroeton | 210 | 41.43 N | 76.30 W |
| Monroeville, Al., U.S. | 194 | 31.31 N | 87.19 W |
| Monroeville, In., U.S. | 216 | 40.58 N | 84.52 W |
| Monroeville, N.J., U.S. | 208 | 39.37 N | 75.09 W |
| Monroeville, Oh., U.S. | 214 | 41.14 N | 82.41 W |
| Monroeville, Pa., U.S. | 214 | 40.26 N | 79.47 W |
| Monroeville Mall ◆9 | 279b | 40.26 N | 79.48 W |
| Monrovia, Liber. | 150 | 6.18 N | 10.47 W |
| Monrovia, Ca., U.S. | 228 | 34.08 N | 117.59 W |
| Monrovia, In., U.S. | 218 | 39.34 N | 86.28 W |
| Monrovia Mountain Park ♠ | 280 | 34.10 N | 118.10 W |
| Monrovia Peak ∧ | 280 | 34.13 N | 117.58 W |
| Mons (Bergen), Bel. | 50 | 50.27 N | 3.56 E |
| Mons, Fr. | 62 | 43.41 N | 6.43 E |
| Monschau | 56 | 50.33 N | 6.14 E |
| Monse | 112 | 4.07 S | 123.15 E |
| Monsefú | 248 | 6.52 S | 79.52 W |
| Monselice | 64 | 45.14 N | 11.45 E |
| Monsenhor Hipólito | 250 | 6.59 S | 41.07 W |
| Monsenhor Paulo | 256 | 21.46 S | 45.33 W |
| Monsenhor Tabosa | 250 | 4.47 S | 40.04 W |
| Monsey | 210 | 41.06 N | 74.04 W |
| Monsheim | 56 | 49.38 N | 8.12 E |
| Møns Klint ✢4 | 41 | 54.58 N | 12.33 E |
| Monsols | 58 | 46.13 N | 4.31 E |
| Monson, Me., U.S. | 188 | 45.17 N | 69.30 W |
| Monson, Ma., U.S. | 207 | 42.06 N | 72.19 W |
| Monster | 52 | 52.02 N | 4.10 E |
| Mönsterås | 26 | 57.02 N | 16.26 E |
| Monsummano Terme | 66 | 43.52 N | 10.49 E |
| Montà | 62 | 44.48 N | 7.57 E |
| Montabaur | 56 | 50.26 N | 7.50 E |
| Montafon V | 58 | 47.02 N | 9.57 E |
| Montagano | 66 | 41.39 N | 14.40 E |
| Montagnana | 64 | 45.14 N | 11.28 E |
| Montagnareale | 70 | 38.07 N | 14.57 E |
| Montagne d'Ambre, Parque National de la ♠ | 157b | 12.40 S | 49.05 E |
| Montagnola ⋀ | 66 | 43.17 N | 11.11 E |
| Montagrier | 32 | 45.16 N | 0.29 E |
| Montagu | 158 | 33.45 S | 20.08 E |
| Montague, P.E., Can. | 186 | 46.10 N | 62.39 W |
| Montague, Ca., U.S. | 204 | 41.43 N | 122.31 W |
| Montague, Ma., U.S. | 207 | 42.32 N | 72.32 W |
| Montague, Mi., U.S. | 190 | 43.25 N | 86.21 W |
| Montague, Tx., U.S. | 196 | 33.40 N | 97.43 W |
| Montague, Isla I | 232 | 31.45 N | 114.48 W |
| Montague City | 207 | 42.35 N | 72.35 W |
| Montague Island I | 180 | 60.00 N | 147.30 W |
| Montague Peak ∧ | 180 | 60.15 N | 147.01 W |
| Montagu Island I | 18 | 58.25 S | 26.20 W |
| Montaigle, Château de ⊥ | 56 | 50.18 N | 4.49 E |
| Montaigu | 32 | 46.59 N | 1.19 W |
| Montaigut-en-Combraille | 32 | 46.11 N | 2.48 E |
| Montainville | 261 | 48.53 N | 1.52 E |
| Montaione | 66 | 43.33 N | 10.55 E |
| Montajtas | 85 | 42.06 N | 68.58 E |
| Montalba | 222 | 31.53 N | 95.38 W |
| Montalbán | 34 | 40.50 N | 0.48 W |
| Montalbancito | 286c | 10.28 N | 66.59 W |
| Montalbano Elicona | 70 | 38.02 N | 15.01 E |
| Montalbano Ionico | 68 | 40.17 N | 16.34 E |
| Montalcino | 66 | 43.03 N | 11.29 E |
| Montaldo di Cosola | 62 | 44.40 N | 9.11 E |
| Montale | 66 | 43.56 N | 11.01 E |
| Montalegre | 34 | 41.49 N | 7.48 W |
| Montalet-le-Bois | 261 | 49.03 N | 1.50 E |
| Montalieu-Vercieu | 62 | 45.49 N | 5.24 E |
| Montallegro | 70 | 37.23 N | 13.21 E |
| Mont Alto | 208 | 39.50 N | 77.33 W |
| Montalto ∧ | 68 | 38.10 N | 15.55 E |
| Montalto delle Marche | 66 | 42.59 N | 13.36 E |
| Montalto di Castro | 66 | 42.21 N | 11.37 E |
| Montalto Ligure | 62 | 43.56 N | 7.51 E |
| Montalto Uffugo | 68 | 39.25 N | 16.10 E |
| Montalvin Manor | 226 | 37.59 N | 122.21 W |
| Montana, Blg. | 38 | 43.25 N | 23.13 E |
| Montana, Schw. | 58 | 46.18 N | 7.29 E |
| Montana, Ak., U.S. | 180 | 62.05 N | 150.04 W |
| Montana □3, U.S. | 178 | 47.00 N | 110.00 W |
| Montana □3, U.S. | 202 | 47.00 N | 110.00 W |
| Montana de Oro State Park ♠ | 226 | 35.15 N | 120.50 W |
| Montana Indian Reserve ◆4 | 182 | 52.43 N | 113.25 W |
| Montanaro | 62 | 45.14 N | 7.51 E |
| Montánchez | 34 | 39.13 N | 6.09 W |
| Montandon | 210 | 40.58 N | 76.51 W |
| Montanha | 255 | 18.08 S | 40.21 W |
| Montano Antilia | 68 | 40.10 N | 15.22 E |
| Montara | 226 | 37.33 N | 122.31 W |
| Montara Beach ♠ | 282 | 37.33 N | 122.31 W |
| Montara Mountain ⋀ | 282 | 37.32 N | 122.27 W |
| Montargil | 34 | 39.05 N | 8.10 W |
| Montargis | 50 | 48.00 N | 2.45 E |
| Montataire | 50 | 49.16 N | 2.26 E |
| Montauban | 32 | 44.01 N | 1.21 E |
| Montauban, Lac ⊜ | 206 | 46.52 N | 72.10 W |
| Montauban-les-Mines | 206 | 46.50 N | 72.20 W |
| Montauk | 207 | 41.02 N | 71.57 W |
| Montauk, Lake ⊜ | 207 | 41.04 N | 71.55 W |
| Montauk Point > | 207 | 41.04 N | 71.52 W |
| Montauroux | 62 | 43.37 N | 6.46 E |
| Monta Vista | 282 | 37.19 N | 122.03 W |
| Montazzoli | 66 | 41.57 N | 14.26 E |
| Montbard | 50 | 47.37 N | 4.20 E |
| Montbarrey | 58 | 47.01 N | 5.39 E |
| Montbazon | 50 | 47.17 N | 0.43 E |
| Montbéliard | 58 | 47.31 N | 6.48 E |
| Mont Belvieu | 222 | 29.50 N | 94.53 W |
| Montbenoît | 58 | 46.59 N | 6.28 E |
| Montblanc | 34 | 41.22 N | 1.10 E |
| Mont Blanc, Tunnel du ◆5 | 58 | 45.50 N | 6.53 E |
| Mont-Bonvillers | 56 | 49.20 N | 5.51 E |
| Montbovon | 58 | 46.29 N | 7.03 E |
| Montbozon | 58 | 47.28 N | 6.16 E |
| Montbrison | 62 | 45.36 N | 4.03 E |
| Montbron | 32 | 45.40 N | 0.30 E |
| Montbronn | 56 | 48.59 N | 7.19 E |
| Montcada i Reixas | 266d | 41.29 N | 2.11 E |
| Montcalm □6 | 206 | 46.20 N | 74.20 W |
| Montceau-les-Mines | 58 | 46.40 N | 4.22 E |
| Montcenis | 58 | 46.47 N | 4.23 E |
| Mont Cenis, Col du )( | 62 | 45.15 N | 6.54 E |
| Mont Cenis, Lac du ⊜ | 62 | 45.14 N | 6.55 E |
| Montcevelles, Lac ⊜ | 186 | 51.07 N | 60.38 W |
| Montchanin, Fr. | 58 | 46.45 N | 4.27 E |
| Montchanin, De., U.S. | 285 | 39.47 N | 75.35 W |
| Montchauvet | 261 | 48.54 N | 1.38 E |
| Montclair, Ca., U.S. | 228 | 34.06 N | 117.41 W |
| Montclair, N.J., U.S. | 210 | 40.49 N | 74.12 W |
| Montclair State College ʊ2 | 276 | 40.51 N | 74.12 W |
| Mont Clare | 285 | 40.08 N | 75.30 W |
| Montcornet | 50 | 49.41 N | 4.01 E |
| Montdale | 210 | 41.32 N | 75.37 W |
| Mont-de-Marsan | 32 | 43.53 N | 0.30 W |
| Montdidier | 50 | 49.39 N | 2.34 E |
| Mont-Dore | 175f | 22.16 S | 166.34 E |
| Monte, Castel del ⊥ | 68 | 41.05 N | 16.16 E |
| Monte, Cima del ∧ | 66 | 42.47 N | 10.23 E |
| Monte, Laguna del ⊜, Arg. | 252 | 37.00 S | 62.28 W |
| Monte, Laguna del ⊜, Arg. | 258 | 35.28 S | 58.49 W |
| Montea ∧ | 68 | 39.40 N | 15.57 E |
| Monte Adone, Galleria di ◆5 | 64 | 44.21 N | 11.25 E |
| Monteagle | 194 | 35.15 N | 85.50 W |
| Monteagudo | 248 | 19.49 S | 63.59 W |
| Monte Albán ⊥ | 234 | 17.02 N | 96.45 W |
| Monte Alegre, Bra. | 250 | 2.01 S | 54.04 W |
| Monte Alegre, Bra. | 250 | 6.04 S | 35.20 W |
| Monte Alegre de Goiás | 255 | 13.14 S | 47.10 W |
| Monte Alegre de Minas | 255 | 18.52 S | 48.52 W |
| Monte Alegre de Sergipe | 250 | 10.02 S | 37.33 W |
| Monte Alegre do Piauí | 250 | 9.46 S | 45.18 W |
| Monte Alegre do Sul | 256 | 22.40 S | 46.41 W |
| Monte Azul | 255 | 15.09 S | 42.53 W |
| Monte Azul Paulista | 255 | 20.55 S | 48.38 W |
| Montebello, P.Q., Can. | 206 | 45.39 N | 74.56 W |
| Montebello, It. | 62 | 45.00 N | 9.06 E |
| Montebello, P.R. | 240m | 18.22 N | 66.31 W |
| Montebello, Ca., U.S. | 228 | 34.00 N | 118.06 W |
| Montebello Iónico | 68 | 37.59 N | 15.45 E |
| Monte Bello Islands II | 162 | 20.25 S | 115.32 E |
| Montebello Vicentino | 64 | 45.27 N | 11.23 E |
| Montebelluna | 64 | 45.47 N | 12.03 E |
| Monte Belo | 256 | 21.20 S | 46.23 W |
| Montebruno | 62 | 44.31 N | 9.15 E |
| Monte Buey | 252 | 32.55 S | 62.27 W |
| Montecalvo Irpino | 68 | 41.11 N | 15.02 E |
| Monte Campatri | 267a | 41.48 N | 12.44 E |
| Montecarlo | 252 | 26.34 S | 54.47 W |
| Monte Carlo ◆8 | 62 | 43.44 N | 7.25 E |
| Monte Carmelo | 255 | 18.43 S | 47.29 W |
| Montecarotto | 66 | 43.31 N | 13.04 E |
| Monte Caseros | 252 | 30.15 S | 57.39 W |
| Montecassiano | 66 | 43.21 N | 13.26 E |
| Montecassino, Abbazia di ʊ1 | 66 | 41.29 N | 13.48 E |
| Montecastrilli | 66 | 42.39 N | 12.29 E |
| Montecatini-Terme | 66 | 43.53 N | 10.46 E |
| Monte Cavallo | 66 | 42.59 N | 13.00 E |
| Montecchio | 66 | 43.51 N | 12.46 E |
| Montecchio Emilia | 64 | 44.42 N | 10.27 E |
| Montecchio Maggiore | 64 | 45.30 N | 11.24 E |
| Montecelio | 66 | 42.01 N | 12.44 E |
| Monte Ceneri, Passo )( | 58 | 46.08 N | 8.55 E |
| Montechiaro d'Asti | 62 | 45.01 N | 8.07 E |
| Montechiarugolo | 64 | 44.42 N | 10.25 E |
| Monte Chingolo ◆8 | 288 | 34.45 S | 58.20 W |
| Monteciccardo | 66 | 43.49 N | 12.48 E |
| Montecilfone | 66 | 41.54 N | 14.50 E |
| Montecillos, Cordillera de ⋀ | 236 | 14.25 N | 87.51 W |
| Montecito | 204 | 34.26 N | 119.37 W |
| Monte Comán | 252 | 34.36 S | 67.54 W |
| Montecorice | 68 | 40.14 N | 14.59 E |
| Montecorvino Pugliano | 68 | 40.41 N | 14.57 E |
| Montecorvino Rovella | 68 | 40.42 N | 14.59 E |
| Montecosaro | 66 | 43.19 N | 13.37 E |
| Monte Creek | 182 | 50.39 N | 119.57 W |
| Montecreto | 64 | 44.14 N | 10.41 E |
| Montecristi, Ec. | 246 | 1.03 S | 80.40 W |
| Monte Cristi, Rep. Dom. | 238 | 19.52 N | 71.39 W |
| Monte Cristo | 248 | 14.43 S | 61.14 W |
| Montecristo, Isola di I | 36 | 42.20 N | 10.19 E |
| Montecuccolo ʊ1 | 64 | 44.19 N | 10.50 E |
| Montedinove | 66 | 42.58 N | 13.35 E |
| Monte di Procida | 68 | 40.48 N | 14.03 E |
| Monte do Carmo | 250 | 10.45 S | 48.07 W |
| Montedoro | 70 | 37.27 N | 13.49 E |
| Monte Escobedo | 234 | 22.18 N | 103.35 W |
| Monte Estoril | 266c | 38.42 N | 9.24 W |
| Montefalcione | 68 | 40.58 N | 14.53 E |
| Montefalco | 66 | 42.54 N | 12.39 E |
| Montefalcone di Val Fortore | 68 | 41.20 N | 15.00 E |
| Montefano | 66 | 43.25 N | 13.26 E |
| Montefeltro ◆1 | 66 | 43.50 N | 12.15 E |
| Montefiascone | 66 | 42.32 N | 12.02 E |
| Montefiorino | 64 | 44.22 N | 10.37 E |
| Monteforte d'Alpone | 64 | 45.25 N | 11.17 E |
| Monteforte Irpino | 68 | 40.54 N | 14.42 E |
| Montefrío | 34 | 37.19 N | 4.01 W |
| Montegallo | 66 | 42.50 N | 13.19 E |
| Montegiordano | 68 | 40.02 N | 16.32 E |
| Montegiorgio | 66 | 43.08 N | 13.32 E |
| Monte Giovi, Passo di (Jaufen Pass) )( | 64 | 46.50 N | 11.19 E |
| Montego Bay | 241q | 18.28 N | 77.55 W |
| Montegranaro | 66 | 43.14 N | 13.38 E |
| Monte Grande | 252 | 30.06 S | 70.31 W |
| Monte Grimano | 66 | 43.52 N | 12.29 E |
| Montegrotto Terme | 64 | 45.19 N | 11.46 E |
| Montegut | 194 | 29.28 N | 90.33 W |
| Monteiasi | 68 | 40.30 N | 17.23 E |
| Monteiro | 250 | 7.53 S | 37.07 W |
| Monteiro Lobato | 256 | 22.58 S | 45.50 W |
| Monteith, Mount ∧ | 182 | 55.45 N | 122.30 W |
| Montejícar | 34 | 37.34 N | 3.30 W |
| Montejinni | 164 | 16.40 S | 131.45 E |
| Montelavar | 266c | 38.51 N | 9.20 W |
| Monteleone di Puglia | 68 | 41.10 N | 15.15 E |
| Monteleone di Spoleto | 66 | 42.39 N | 12.58 E |
| Monteleone Rocco Doria | 71 | 40.29 N | 8.34 E |
| Monteleone Sabino | 66 | 42.14 N | 12.51 E |
| Montelepre | 70 | 38.05 N | 13.10 E |
| Montelíbano | 246 | 8.05 N | 75.29 W |
| Montélimar | 62 | 44.34 N | 4.45 E |
| Montelindo ≃ | 252 | 23.56 S | 57.12 W |
| Montella | 68 | 40.51 N | 15.01 E |
| Montellano | 34 | 37.00 N | 5.34 W |
| Montello, Nv., U.S. | 204 | 41.15 N | 114.11 W |
| Montello, Wi., U.S. | 190 | 43.47 N | 89.19 W |
| Monteluco ʊ1 | 66 | 42.43 N | 12.45 E |
| Montelungo | 64 | 44.24 N | 9.54 E |
| Montelupo Fiorentino | 66 | 43.44 N | 11.01 E |
| Montemaggiore Belsito | 70 | 37.51 N | 13.46 E |
| Montemagno | 62 | 44.59 N | 8.20 E |
| Monte Maíz | 252 | 33.12 S | 62.36 W |
| Montemarano | 68 | 40.55 N | 15.00 E |
| Montemarciano | 66 | 43.38 N | 13.19 E |
| Montemayor, Meseta de ⋀1 | 254 | 44.20 S | 66.10 W |
| Montemesola | 68 | 40.34 N | 17.20 E |
| Montemiletto | 68 | 41.01 N | 14.54 E |
| Montemilone | 68 | 41.02 N | 15.58 E |
| Montemor | 266c | 38.49 N | 9.12 W |
| Montemor ∧ | 266c | 38.49 N | 9.12 W |
| Montemorelos | 232 | 25.12 N | 99.49 W |
| Montemor-o-Novo | 34 | 38.39 N | 8.13 W |
| Montemor-o-Velho | 34 | 40.10 N | 8.41 W |
| Montemurro | 68 | 40.18 N | 15.59 E |
| Montendre | 32 | 45.17 N | 0.24 W |
| Montenegro | 252 | 29.42 S | 51.28 W |
| Montenegro → Crna Gora □3 | 38 | 42.30 N | 19.18 E |
| Montenero | 66 | 43.30 N | 10.21 E |
| Montenero ∧ | 68 | 39.13 N | 16.35 E |
| Montenero di Bisaccia | 66 | 41.57 N | 14.47 E |
| Monteodorisio | 66 | 42.05 N | 14.39 E |
| Monte Oliveto Maggiore, Abbazia del ʊ1 | 66 | 43.12 N | 11.32 E |
| Monte Pascoal, Parque Nacional de ♠ | 255 | 16.54 S | 39.24 W |
| Monte Patria | 252 | 30.42 S | 70.58 W |
| Montepescali | 66 | 42.53 N | 11.05 E |
| Monte Porzio Catone | 267a | 41.49 N | 12.43 E |
| Monteprandone | 66 | 42.55 N | 13.50 E |
| Montepuez | 154 | 13.07 S | 39.00 E |
| Montepuez ≃ | 154 | 12.32 S | 40.27 E |
| Montepulciano | 66 | 43.05 N | 11.47 E |
| Monte Quemado | 252 | 25.48 S | 62.52 W |
| Monterado | 112 | 0.45 N | 109.08 E |
| Monterchi | 66 | 43.29 N | 12.07 E |
| Montereale | 66 | 42.31 N | 13.15 E |
| Montereale Valcellina | 64 | 46.10 N | 12.39 E |
| Montereau | 50 | 47.51 N | 2.34 E |
| Montereau-Faut-Yonne | 50 | 48.23 N | 2.57 E |
| Montereau-sur-le-Jard | 261 | 48.35 N | 2.40 E |
| Monterey, Ca., U.S. | 226 | 36.36 N | 121.53 W |
| Monterey, In., U.S. | 216 | 41.09 N | 86.28 W |
| Monterey, Ky., U.S. | 218 | 38.25 N | 84.52 W |
| Monterey, Ma., U.S. | 207 | 42.10 N | 73.12 W |
| Monterey, N.Y., U.S. | 210 | 42.18 N | 77.03 W |
| Monterey, Tn., U.S. | 194 | 36.08 N | 85.16 W |
| Monterey, Va., U.S. | 188 | 38.24 N | 79.34 W |
| Monterey □6 | 226 | 36.40 N | 121.38 W |
| Monterey Bay c | 226 | 36.45 N | 121.55 W |
| Monterey Park | 228 | 34.03 N | 118.07 W |
| Monterey Peninsula Airport ⊠ | 226 | 36.35 N | 121.51 W |
| Montería | 246 | 8.46 N | 75.53 W |
| Monteriggioni | 66 | 43.23 N | 11.13 E |
| Montero | 248 | 17.20 S | 63.15 W |
| Monte Romano | 66 | 42.16 N | 11.54 E |
| Monteroni d'Arbia | 66 | 43.14 N | 11.25 E |
| Monteroni di Lecce | 68 | 40.19 N | 18.06 E |
| Monteros | 252 | 27.10 S | 65.30 W |
| Monterosso al Mare | 62 | 44.09 N | 9.39 E |
| Monterosso Almo | 70 | 37.05 N | 14.46 E |
| Monterosso Calabro | 68 | 38.43 N | 16.17 E |
| Monterotondo | 66 | 42.03 N | 12.37 E |
| Monterotondo Marittimo | 66 | 43.09 N | 10.51 E |
| Monterrey, Méx. | 232 | 25.40 N | 100.19 W |
| Monterrey, Méx. | 234 | 16.05 N | 93.23 W |
| Monterrico, Hipódromo de ♠ | 286d | 12.06 S | 76.59 W |
| Monterubbiano | 66 | 43.05 N | 13.43 E |
| Montes Altos | 250 | 5.50 S | 47.04 W |
| Monte San Biagio | 66 | 41.21 N | 13.21 E |
| Monte San Giovanni Campano | 66 | 41.38 N | 13.31 E |
| Montesano | 224 | 46.58 N | 123.36 W |
| Montesano sulla Marcellana | 68 | 40.16 N | 15.42 E |
| Monte San Savino | 66 | 43.20 N | 11.43 E |
| Monte Santa Maria Tiberina | 66 | 43.26 N | 12.09 E |
| Monte Sant'Angelo | 68 | 41.42 N | 15.57 E |
| Monte Santo | 250 | 10.26 S | 39.20 W |
| Monte Santo de Minas | 256 | 21.12 S | 46.59 W |
| Monte Santu, Capo di > | 71 | 40.05 N | 9.44 E |
| Montesarchio | 68 | 41.04 N | 14.38 E |
| Montescaglioso | 68 | 40.33 N | 16.40 E |
| Montes Claros | 255 | 16.43 S | 43.52 W |
| Montescudaio | 66 | 43.18 N | 10.40 E |
| Montese | 64 | 44.16 N | 10.56 E |
| Monte Sereno | 226 | 37.15 N | 122.01 W |
| Monte Sião | 256 | 22.26 S | 46.34 W |
| Montesilvano Marina | 66 | 42.31 N | 14.09 E |
| Montespaccato ◆8 | 267a | 41.54 N | 12.23 E |
| Montespertoli | 66 | 43.38 N | 11.04 E |
| Montespluga | 58 | 46.30 N | 9.21 E |
| Montets, Col des )( | 58 | 46.00 N | 6.55 E |
| Monteux | 62 | 44.02 N | 5.00 E |
| Montevago | 70 | 37.42 N | 12.58 E |
| Montevallo | 194 | 33.06 N | 86.51 W |
| Montevarchi | 66 | 43.31 N | 11.34 E |
| Monteverde | 68 | 41.00 N | 15.32 E |
| Monte Verde ≃ | 256 | 21.55 S | 43.33 W |
| Monteverde Nuovo ◆8 | 267a | 41.51 N | 12.27 E |
| Montevergine, Santuario di ʊ1 | 68 | 40.55 N | 14.45 E |
| Montevideo, Mn., U.S. | 198 | 44.56 N | 95.43 W |
| Montevideo, Ur. | 258 | 34.53 S | 56.11 W |
| Montevideo □5 | 258 | 34.50 S | 56.12 W |
| Montevideo, Cerro de ∧2 | 258 | 33.54 S | 56.15 W |
| Monte Vista | 200 | 37.34 N | 106.08 W |
| Montévrain | 261 | 48.53 N | 2.45 E |
| Montezemolo | 62 | 44.22 N | 8.08 E |
| Montezuma, Ga., U.S. | 192 | 32.18 N | 84.01 W |
| Montezuma, In., U.S. | 194 | 39.47 N | 87.22 W |
| Montezuma, Ia., U.S. | 190 | 41.35 N | 92.31 W |
| Montezuma, Ks., U.S. | 198 | 37.35 N | 100.26 W |
| Montezuma, N.Y., U.S. | 210 | 43.00 N | 76.42 W |
| Montezuma, Oh., U.S. | 216 | 40.29 N | 84.33 W |
| Montezuma Castle National Monument ♠ | 200 | 34.38 N | 110.49 W |
| Montezuma Creek ≃ | 200 | 37.17 N | 109.20 W |
| Montezuma Hills ⋀2 | 282 | 38.07 N | 121.51 W |
| Montezuma Slough ≃ | 226 | 38.04 N | 121.52 W |
| Montfaucon, Fr. | 56 | 49.17 N | 5.08 E |
| Montfaucon, Fr. | 62 | 45.10 N | 4.18 E |
| Montfaucon, Schw. | 58 | 47.17 N | 7.03 E |
| Montfermeil | 261 | 48.54 N | 2.34 E |
| Montfleur | 58 | 46.19 N | 5.26 E |
| Montfort, Fr. | 32 | 48.08 N | 1.58 W |
| Montfort, Wi., U.S. | 190 | 42.58 N | 90.25 W |
| Montfort-l'Amaury | 50 | 48.47 N | 1.49 E |
| Montfort-le-Rotrou | 50 | 48.03 N | 0.25 E |
| Montfort-sur-Risle | 50 | 49.18 N | 0.40 E |
| Montfrin | 62 | 43.53 N | 4.36 E |
| Montgé | 261 | 49.02 N | 2.45 E |
| Montgenèvre | 62 | 44.56 N | 6.43 E |
| Montgenèvre, Col de )( | 62 | 44.56 N | 6.44 E |
| Montgeron | 261 | 48.42 N | 2.27 E |
| Montgeroult | 261 | 49.05 N | 2.00 E |
| Montgesoye | 58 | 47.05 N | 6.12 E |
| Montgomery → Sāhīwāl, Pāk. | 123 | 30.40 N | 73.06 E |
| Montgomery, Wales, U.K. | 42 | 52.33 N | 3.03 W |
| Montgomery, Al., U.S. | 194 | 32.23 N | 86.18 W |
| Montgomery, Il., U.S. | 216 | 41.43 N | 88.20 W |
| Montgomery, La., U.S. | 194 | 31.40 N | 92.53 W |
| Montgomery, Mi., U.S. | 216 | 41.46 N | 84.48 W |
| Montgomery, Mn., U.S. | 190 | 44.26 N | 93.34 W |
| Montgomery, N.Y., U.S. | 210 | 41.31 N | 74.14 W |
| Montgomery, Oh., U.S. | 218 | 39.13 N | 84.21 W |
| Montgomery, Pa., U.S. | 210 | 41.10 N | 76.52 W |
| Montgomery, Tx., U.S. | 222 | 30.23 N | 95.42 W |
| Montgomery, W.V., U.S. | 188 | 38.11 N | 81.19 W |
| Montgomery □6, Il., U.S. | 219 | 39.09 N | 89.29 W |
| Montgomery □6, Md., U.S. | 208 | 39.05 N | 77.09 W |
| Montgomery □6, Mo., U.S. | 219 | 38.57 N | 91.27 W |
| Montgomery □6, N.Y., U.S. | 210 | 42.57 N | 74.22 W |
| Montgomery □6, Oh., U.S. | 218 | 39.45 N | 84.15 W |
| Montgomery □6, Pa., U.S. | 208 | 40.07 N | 75.21 W |
| Montgomery □6, Tx., U.S. | 222 | 30.18 N | 95.30 W |
| Montgomery City | 219 | 38.58 N | 91.30 W |
| Montgomery Dam ◆6 | 214 | 40.39 N | 80.24 W |
| Montgomery Knolls | 284b | 39.14 N | 76.48 W |
| Montgomery Mall ◆9 | 284c | 39.01 N | 77.09 W |
| Montgomery Square | 284c | 39.04 N | 77.09 W |
| Montgomeryville | 285 | 40.15 N | 75.15 W |
| Montgomeryville Airport ⊠ | 285 | 40.15 N | 75.14 W |
| Montguyon | 32 | 45.13 N | 0.11 W |
| Monthermé | 56 | 49.53 N | 4.44 E |
| Monthey | 58 | 46.15 N | 6.57 E |
| Monthois | 56 | 49.19 N | 4.43 E |
| Monthureux-sur-Saône | 58 | 48.02 N | 5.58 E |
| Monthyon | 261 | 49.00 N | 2.50 E |
| Monti | 71 | 40.49 N | 9.19 E |
| Monticelli d'Ongina | 64 | 45.05 N | 9.56 E |
| Monticello, Ar., U.S. | 194 | 33.37 N | 91.47 W |
| Monticello, Fl., U.S. | 192 | 30.32 N | 83.52 W |
| Monticello, Ga., U.S. | 192 | 33.18 N | 83.41 W |
| Monticello, Il., U.S. | 194 | 40.01 N | 88.34 W |
| Monticello, In., U.S. | 216 | 40.44 N | 86.45 W |
| Monticello, Ia., U.S. | 190 | 42.14 N | 91.11 W |
| Monticello, Ky., U.S. | 194 | 36.49 N | 84.50 W |
| Monticello, Mn., U.S. | 190 | 45.18 N | 93.47 W |
| Monticello, Ms., U.S. | 194 | 31.33 N | 90.06 W |
| Monticello, Mo., U.S. | 219 | 40.07 N | 91.42 W |
| Monticello, N.Y., U.S. | 210 | 41.39 N | 74.41 W |
| Monticello, Ut,. U.S. | 200 | 37.52 N | 109.20 W |
| Monticello, Wi., U.S. | 190 | 42.44 N | 89.35 W |
| Monticello ⊥ | 188 | 38.00 N | 78.30 W |
| Monticello Conte Otto | 64 | 45.35 N | 11.35 E |
| Monticello Dam ◆6 | 226 | 38.30 N | 122.07 W |
| Monticello Woods | 284c | 38.47 N | 77.10 W |
| Montichiari | 64 | 45.25 N | 10.23 E |
| Monticiano | 66 | 43.08 N | 11.11 E |
| Montiel, Campo de ≡ | 34 | 38.46 N | 2.44 W |
| Montier-en-Der | 58 | 48.29 N | 4.46 E |
| Montieri | 66 | 43.08 N | 11.01 E |
| Montieri, Poggio di ∧ | 66 | 43.08 N | 11.00 E |
| Montiers-sur-Saulx | 58 | 48.32 N | 5.16 E |
| Montignac | 32 | 45.04 N | 1.10 E |
| Montigny | 58 | 48.31 N | 6.48 E |
| Montigny-Devant-Sassey | 56 | 49.26 N | 5.09 E |
| Montigny-le-Bretonneux | 261 | 48.46 N | 2.02 E |
| Montigny-le-Roi | 58 | 48.00 N | 5.30 E |
| Montigny-lès-Cormeilles | 261 | 48.59 N | 2.12 E |
| Montigny-lès-Metz | 56 | 49.06 N | 6.09 E |
| Montigny-sur-Aube | 58 | 47.57 N | 4.46 E |
| Montijo, Esp. | 34 | 38.55 N | 6.37 W |
| Montijo, Pan. | 236 | 7.59 N | 81.03 W |
| Montijo, Port. | 34 | 38.42 N | 8.58 W |
| Montijo, Aeroporto ⊠ | 266c | 38.42 N | 9.02 W |
| Montijo, Golfo de c | 246 | 7.40 N | 81.07 W |
| Montilla | 34 | 37.35 N | 4.38 W |
| Montividiu | 255 | 17.24 S | 51.14 W |
| Montivilliers | 50 | 49.33 N | 0.12 E |
| Montjay-la-Tour | 261 | 48.55 N | 2.40 E |
| Montjoie, Lac ⊜, P.Q., Can. | 206 | 46.17 N | 75.08 W |
| Montjoie, Lac ⊜, P.Q., Can. | 206 | 45.25 N | 72.06 W |
| Mont-Joli | 186 | 48.35 N | 68.11 W |
| Montjovet | 62 | 45.43 N | 7.40 E |
| Montjuich, Estadio de ♠ | 266d | 41.22 N | 2.09 E |
| Montjuich, Faro de ◆5 | 266d | 41.21 N | 2.11 E |
| Montjuich, Parque de ♠ | 266d | 41.21 N | 2.09 E |
| Mont-Laurier | 176 | 46.33 N | 75.30 W |
| Montlebon | 58 | 47.02 N | 6.37 E |
| Montlhéry | 50 | 48.38 N | 2.16 E |
| Montlhéry, Tour de ♠ | 261 | 48.38 N | 2.16 E |
| Montlignon | 261 | 49.01 N | 2.17 E |
| Montlouet | 261 | 48.31 N | 1.43 E |
| Mont-Louis | 32 | 42.31 N | 2.07 E |
| Montlouis-sur-Loire | 50 | 47.23 N | 0.50 E |
| Montluçon | 32 | 46.21 N | 2.36 E |
| Montluel | 62 | 45.51 N | 5.03 E |
| Montmagny, P.Q., Can. | 186 | 46.59 N | 70.33 W |
| Montmagny, Fr. | 261 | 48.58 N | 2.21 E |
| Montmajour, Abbaye de ʊ1 | 62 | 43.43 N | 4.40 E |
| Montmartre ◆8 | 261 | 48.53 N | 2.21 E |
| Montmédy | 56 | 49.31 N | 5.22 E |
| Montmélian | 62 | 45.30 N | 6.04 E |
| Montmeló | 266d | 41.33 N | 2.15 E |
| Montmerle-sur-Saône | 58 | 46.05 N | 4.46 E |
| Montmin | 62 | 45.48 N | 6.16 E |
| Montmirail, Fr. | 50 | 48.52 N | 3.32 E |
| Montmirail, Fr. | 50 | 48.06 N | 0.48 E |
| Montmirey-le-Château | 58 | 47.13 N | 5.32 E |
| Montmoreau-Saint-Cybard | 32 | 45.24 N | 0.08 E |
| Montmorenci | 216 | 40.28 N | 87.02 W |
| Montmorency, Austl. | 274b | 37.43 S | 145.07 E |
| Montmorency → Beauport, P.Q., Can. | 186 | 46.52 N | 71.11 W |
| Montmorency, Fr. | 261 | 49.00 N | 2.20 E |
| Montmorency ≃ | 186 | 46.53 N | 71.07 W |
| Montmorency, Forêt de ♠ | 261 | 49.02 N | 2.16 E |
| Montmorillon | 32 | 46.26 N | 0.52 E |
| Montmort | 50 | 48.55 N | 3.49 E |
| Monto | 166 | 24.52 S | 151.07 E |
| Montodine | 62 | 45.17 N | 9.42 E |
| Montoggio | 62 | 44.31 N | 9.03 E |
| Montoire-sur-le-Loir | 50 | 47.45 N | 0.52 E |
| Montone | 66 | 43.22 N | 12.20 E |
| Montone ≃ | 66 | 44.24 N | 12.14 E |
| Montopoli in Val d'Arno | 66 | 43.40 N | 10.45 E |
| Mont Orford, Parc du ♠ | 206 | 45.22 N | 72.05 W |
| Montorio al Vomano | 66 | 42.35 N | 13.38 E |
| Montorio nei Frentani | 66 | 41.46 N | 14.55 E |
| Montoro | 34 | 38.01 N | 4.23 W |
| Mont'Orso, Galleria di ◆5 | 66 | 41.20 N | 13.15 E |
| Montour □6 | 210 | 40.58 N | 76.37 W |
| Montour Falls | 210 | 42.20 N | 76.50 W |
| Montour Run ≃, Pa., U.S. | 279b | 40.36 N | 79.57 W |
| Montour Run ≃, Pa., U.S. | 279b | 40.31 N | 80.08 W |
| Montoursville | 210 | 41.15 N | 76.55 W |
| Mont Park | 274b | 37.43 S | 145.04 E |
| Montparnasse, Gare ◆5 | 261 | 48.51 N | 2.19 E |
| Mont Peko, Parc National du ♠ | 150 | 7.00 N | 7.15 W |
| Montpelier, Jam. | 241q | 18.22 N | 77.56 W |
| Montpelier, Id., U.S. | 202 | 42.19 N | 111.17 W |
| Montpelier, In., U.S. | 216 | 40.33 N | 85.16 W |
| Montpelier, Md., U.S. | 284c | 39.04 N | 76.51 W |
| Montpelier, Ms., U.S. | 194 | 33.43 N | 88.56 W |
| Montpelier, Oh., U.S. | 216 | 41.35 N | 84.36 W |
| Montpelier, Vt., U.S. | 188 | 44.15 N | 72.34 W |
| Montpellier | 62 | 43.36 N | 3.53 E |
| Montpellier-Fréjorgues, Aéroport de ⊠ | 62 | 43.33 N | 4.00 E |
| Montpezat-sous-Bauzon | 62 | 44.43 N | 4.12 E |
| Mont-Pichet | 261 | 48.53 N | 2.54 E |
| Montpon-Ménesterol | 32 | 45.00 N | 0.10 E |
| Montpont-en-Bresse | 58 | 46.33 N | 5.09 E |
| Montréal, P.Q., Can. | 206 | 45.31 N | 73.34 W |
| Montréal, P.Q., Can. | 275a | 45.31 N | 73.34 W |
| Montréal, Fr. | 50 | 47.32 N | 4.02 E |
| Montreal, Wi., U.S. | 190 | 46.25 N | 90.14 W |
| Montreal ≃, On., Can. | 190 | 47.14 N | 84.39 W |
| Montreal ≃, On., Can. | 190 | 47.08 N | 79.27 W |
| Montreal ≃, Sk., Can. | 184 | 55.06 N | 105.19 W |
| Montreal ≃, U.S. | 190 | 46.44 N | 90.25 W |
| Montréal, Base des Forces Canadiennes ■ | 275a | 45.31 N | 73.25 W |
| Montréal, Île de I | 206 | 45.30 N | 73.40 W |
| Montréal, Université de ʊ2 | 275a | 45.30 N | 73.37 W |
| Montréal-Est | 206 | 45.38 N | 73.31 W |
| Montreal International Airport ⊠ | 206 | 45.28 N | 73.45 W |
| Montreal Lake | 184 | 54.03 N | 105.46 W |
| Montreal Lake ⊜ | 184 | 54.20 N | 105.40 W |
| Montreal Lake Indian Reserve ◆4 | 184 | 54.00 N | 105.45 W |
| Montréal-Nord | 206 | 45.36 N | 73.38 W |
| Montréal-Ouest | 275a | 45.27 N | 73.39 W |
| Montreal Water Works Aqueduct ⩶1 | 275a | 45.26 N | 73.36 W |
| Montrésor | 50 | 47.09 N | 1.12 E |
| Montresta | 71 | 40.22 N | 8.30 E |
| Montret | 58 | 46.41 N | 5.07 E |
| Montreuil | 261 | 48.52 N | 2.26 E |
| Montreuil-Bellay | 32 | 47.08 N | 0.09 W |
| Montreuil-sous-Bois | 50 | 48.52 N | 2.26 E |
| Montreuil-sur-Mer | 50 | 50.28 N | 1.46 E |
| Montreux | 58 | 46.26 N | 6.55 E |
| Montrevel-en-Bresse | 58 | 46.20 N | 5.08 E |
| Montrichard | 50 | 47.21 N | 1.11 E |
| Montriond | 58 | 46.12 N | 6.41 E |
| Mont-Rolland | 206 | 45.57 N | 74.07 W |
| Montrond-les-Bains | 62 | 45.38 N | 4.14 E |
| Montrose, Austl. | 274b | 37.49 S | 145.21 E |
| Montrose, Scot., U.K. | 46 | 56.43 N | 2.29 W |
| Montrose, Ca., U.S. | 228 | 34.12 N | 118.13 W |
| Montrose, Co., U.S. | 200 | 38.28 N | 107.52 W |
| Montrose, Ia., U.S. | 190 | 40.31 N | 91.24 W |
| Montrose, Mi., U.S. | 190 | 43.10 N | 83.53 W |
| Montrose, N.Y., U.S. | 210 | 41.15 N | 73.56 W |
| Montrose, Oh., U.S. | 214 | 41.08 N | 81.37 W |
| Montrose, Pa., U.S. | 210 | 41.50 N | 75.52 W |
| Montrose, S.D., U.S. | 198 | 43.41 N | 97.11 W |
| Montrose Harbor c | 278 | 41.58 N | 87.38 W |
| Montrose Hill | 279b | 40.30 N | 79.51 W |
| Montross | 208 | 38.05 N | 76.49 W |
| Montrouge | 261 | 48.49 N | 2.19 E |
| Mont-Royal | 206 | 45.31 N | 73.39 W |
| Mont Royal, Parc ♠ | 275a | 45.31 N | 73.35 W |
| Mont Royal Tunnel ◆5 | 275a | 45.31 N | 73.38 W |
| Montry | 261 | 48.53 N | 2.50 E |
| Monts | 50 | 47.17 N | 0.37 E |
| Monts, Pointe des > | 186 | 49.20 N | 67.23 W |
| Mont-Saint-Aignan | 50 | 49.28 N | 1.05 E |
| Mont-Sainte-Anne, Parc du ♠ | 186 | 47.08 N | 70.55 W |
| Mont-Saint-Hilaire | 206 | 45.34 N | 73.11 W |
| Mont-Saint-Martin | 56 | 49.32 N | 5.47 E |
| Mont-Saint-Michel → Le Mont-Saint-Michel ʊ1 | 32 | 48.38 N | 1.32 W |
| Mont-Saint-Vincent | 58 | 46.38 N | 4.29 E |
| Montsauche | 50 | 47.13 N | 4.01 E |
| Montsec | 56 | 48.53 N | 5.43 E |
| Montserrat □2, N.A. | 230 | 16.45 N | 62.12 W |
| Montserrat □2, N.A. | 238 | 16.45 N | 62.12 W |
| Montserrat, Monasterio de ʊ1 | 34 | 41.36 N | 1.49 E |
| Montsoult | 261 | 49.04 N | 2.19 E |
| Montsûrs | 28 | 48.08 N | 0.33 W |
| Mont-sur-Vaudrey | 58 | 46.58 N | 5.36 E |
| Mont-Tremblant, Parc provincial du ♠ | 206 | 46.42 N | 74.20 W |
| Montuenga | 34 | 41.03 N | 4.37 W |
| Montvale, N.J., U.S. | 276 | 41.02 N | 74.01 W |
| Montvale, Va., U.S. | 192 | 37.23 N | 79.43 W |
| Montverde | 220 | 28.36 N | 81.41 W |
| Montville, Ct., U.S. | 207 | 41.27 N | 72.08 W |
| Montville, N.J., U.S. | 276 | 40.54 N | 74.23 W |
| Montville, Oh., U.S. | 214 | 41.36 N | 81.03 W |
| Montville Airpark ⊠ | 276 | 40.56 N | 74.20 W |
| Monument, S. Afr. | 273d | 26.06 S | 27.43 E |
| Monument, Or., U.S. | 202 | 44.49 N | 119.25 W |
| Monument, Pa., U.S. | 214 | 41.07 N | 77.42 W |
| Monument Beach | 207 | 41.43 N | 70.36 W |
| Monument Draw V, U.S. | 196 | 32.27 N | 102.20 W |
| Monument Draw V, Tx., U.S. | 196 | 30.51 N | 102.33 W |
| Monument Hill State Historic Site ⊥ | 222 | 29.53 N | 96.54 W |
| Monumento | 256 | 22.44 S | 43.51 W |
| Monument Peak ∧, Co., U.S. | 200 | 39.43 N | 107.55 W |
| Monument Peak ∧, Id., U.S. | 202 | 42.07 N | 114.14 W |
| Monument Valley V | 200 | 37.05 N | 110.20 W |

| | | | | | |
|---|---|---|---|---|---|
| ≃ | River | Fluß | Río | Rivière | Rio |
| ⩶ | Canal | Kanal | Canal | Canal | Canal |
| ∟ | Waterfall, Rapids | Wasserfall, Stromschnellen | Cascada, Rápidos | Chute d'eau, Rapides | Cascata, Rápidos |
| ꓤ | Strait | Meeresstraße | Estrecho | Détroit | Estreito |
| c | Bay, Gulf | Bucht, Golf | Bahía, Golfo | Baie, Golfe | Baía, Golfo |
| ⊜ | Lake, Lakes | See, Seen | Lago, Lagos | Lac, Lacs | Lago, Lagos |
| ≡ | Swamp | Sumpf | Pantano | Marais | Pântano |
| ⊓ | Ice Features, Glacier | Eis- und Gletscherformen | Accidentes Glaciales | Formes glaciaires | Acidentes glaciares |
| ⊤ | Other Hydrographic Features | Andere Hydrographische Objekte | Otros Elementos Hidrográficos | Autres données hydrographiques | Outros acidentes hidrográficos |
| ✢ | Submarine Features | Untermeerische Objekte | Accidentes Submarinos | Formes de relief sous-marin | Acidentes submarinos |
| □ | Political Unit | Politische Einheit | Unidad Politica | Entité politique | Unidade política |
| ʊ | Cultural Institution | Kulturelle Institution | Institución Cultural | Institution culturelle | Instituição cultural |
| ⊥ | Historical Site | Historische Stätte | Sitio Histórico | Site historique | Sitio histórico |
| ♠ | Recreational Site | Erholungs- und Ferienort | Sitio de Recreo | Centre de loisirs | Area de Lazer |
| ⊠ | Airport | Flughafen | Aeropuerto | Aéroport | Aeroporto |
| ■ | Military Installation | Militäranlage | Instalación Militar | Installation militaire | Instalação militar |
| ◆ | Miscellaneous | Verschiedenes | Misceláneo | Divers | Diversos |

Monundilla, Mount ∧ 170 32.45 S 150.29 E
Monveda 152 2.57 N 21.27 E
Monymusk 46 57.13 N 2.31 W
Monyo 110 17.59 N 95.30 E
Monywa 110 22.05 N 95.08 E
Monza 62 45.35 N 9.16 E
Monze 154 16.16 S 27.28 E
Monzen 92 37.17 N 136.46 E
Monzie 46 56.24 N 3.48 W
Monzón, Esp. 34 41.55 N 0.12 E
Monzón, Perú 248 9.10 S 76.23 W
Moóca ✦8 287b 23.33 S 46.35 W
Moóca, Ribeirão da ≃ 287b 23.36 S 46.35 W
Moodie Island I 176 64.37 N 65.30 W
Moodus 207 41.30 N 72.27 W
Moodus Reservoir ⊜1 207 41.30 N 72.24 W
Moody 222 31.18 N 97.21 W
Moody Air Force Base ■ 192 30.59 N 83.11 W
Moody Wood Dale Airport ✈ 278 41.59 N 87.58 W
Mooers 206 44.58 N 73.35 W
Mooi ≃, S. Afr. 158 26.53 S 26.56 E
Mooi ≃, S. Afr. 158 28.45 S 30.34 E
Mooirivier 158 29.13 S 29.50 E
Mook 52 51.45 N 5.54 E
Mookane 156 24.59 S 24.33 E
Mooketsi 156 23.35 S 30.05 E
Moolawatana 166 29.55 S 139.43 E
Moolman 158 27.10 S 30.53 E
Mooloogool 162 26.06 S 119.05 E
Moon 214 40.31 N 80.14 W
Moon ≃ 212 45.08 N 79.59 W
Moon, Mountains of the → Ruwenzori Range ⋏ 154 0.23 N 29.54 E
Moonachie 276 40.50 N 74.02 W
Moonah Creek ≃ 166 22.03 S 138.33 E
Moon Crest 279b 40.32 N 80.11 W
Moondarra Reservoir ⊜1 169 38.04 S 146.22 E
Moonee Valley Racecourse ♦ 274b 37.46 S 144.56 E
Moonie 166 27.43 S 150.22 E
Moonie ≃ 166 29.19 S 148.43 E
Moon Island I, On., Can. 212 45.09 N 80.01 W
Moon Island I, Ma., U.S. 283 42.18 N 71.00 W
Moon Run 214 40.27 N 80.06 W
Moonta 168b 34.04 S 137.35 E
Moor, Kepulauan II 164 2.57 S 135.45 E
Moora 162 30.39 S 116.00 E
Moorabbin 169 37.56 S 145.02 E
Moorabbin Airport ✈ 274b 37.59 S 145.09 E
Mooraberree 166 25.14 S 140.59 E
Moorabool ≃ 169 38.09 S 144.19 E
Moorarie 162 25.56 S 117.35 E
Moorbad Lobenstein 54 50.26 N 11.38 E
Moorburg 52 53.17 N 7.53 E
Moorcroft 198 44.15 N 104.56 W
Moordorf 52 53.28 N 7.23 E
Moordrecht 52 51.59 N 4.40 E
Moore, Austl. 171a 26.53 S 152.18 E
Moore, Eng., U.K. 262 53.21 N 2.38 W
Moore, Id., U.S. 202 43.44 N 113.21 W
Moore, Mt., U.S. 202 46.58 N 109.41 W
Moore, Ok., U.S. 196 35.20 N 97.29 W
Moore, Tx., U.S. 196 29.03 N 99.01 W
Moore ≃ 162 31.22 S 115.29 E
Moore, Lake ⊜ 162 29.50 S 117.35 E
Moorea I 174s 17.32 S 149.50 W
Moorebank 274a 33.56 S 150.56 E
Moore Creek ≃ 212 45.29 N 77.58 W
Moorefield, Ky., U.S. 218 38.16 N 83.55 W
Moorefield, Oh., U.S. 214 40.12 N 81.10 W
Moorefield, W.V., U.S. 188 39.03 N 78.58 W
Moore Haven 220 26.49 N 81.05 W
Moore Haven Lock ✦5 220 26.51 N 81.05 W
Moore Lake ⊜, On., Can. 212 45.26 N 78.01 W
Moore Lake ⊜, On., Can. 212 44.48 N 78.48 W
Moore Lake ⊜, Mi., U.S. 281 42.37 N 83.36 W
Mooreland, In., U.S. 218 39.59 N 85.15 W
Mooreland, Ok., U.S. 196 36.26 N 99.12 W
Moore Point ≻ 275b 43.48 N 79.03 W
Moore Reservoir ⊜1 188 44.25 N 71.50 W
Mooresburg 210 40.59 N 76.43 W
Moores Creek National Battlefield ♦ 192 34.24 N 78.08 W
Moores Hill 218 39.06 N 85.05 W
Moore Station 222 32.11 N 95.35 W
Moorestown 208 39.58 N 74.56 W
Moorestown Mall ✦9 285 39.56 N 74.58 W
Mooresville, In., U.S. 218 39.36 N 86.22 W
Mooresville, N.C., U.S. 192 35.35 N 80.48 W
Mooreville 281 42.06 N 83.44 W
Moorfoot Hills ⋏2 46 55.45 N 3.02 W
Moorhead, Mn., U.S. 198 46.52 N 96.46 W
Moorhead, Ms., U.S. 194 33.27 N 90.30 W
Mooring 222 30.41 N 96.33 W
Mooringsport 194 32.41 N 93.57 W
Moormerland 52 53.20 N 7.27 E
Moornanyah Lake ⊜ 166 33.02 S 143.58 E
Moorooka 171a 27.32 S 153.02 E
Mooroolbark 274b 37.47 S 145.19 E
Moorpark 228 34.17 N 118.53 W
Moorreesburg 158 33.08 S 18.40 E
Moorrege 52 53.40 N 9.39 E
Moorriem 52 53.15 N 8.19 E
Moorsel 50 50.57 N 4.06 E
Moorside 262 53.34 N 2.04 W
Moorslede 50 50.53 N 3.04 E
Moos → Moso, It. 64 46.41 N 12.23 E
Moos → Moso in Passiria, It. 64 46.50 N 11.10 E
Moosach ✦8 60 48.11 N 11.31 E
Moosbrunn 264b 48.01 N 16.28 E
Moosburg 61 46.39 N 14.10 E
Moosburg an der Isar 60 48.29 N 11.57 E
Moose ≃, Me., U.S. 188 45.40 N 69.42 W
Moose ≃, N.Y., U.S. 212 43.37 N 75.22 W
Moose Creek 206 45.15 N 74.58 W
Moose Creek ≃ 206 45.23 N 75.04 W
Moosehead Lake ⊜ 188 45.40 N 69.40 W
Mooseheart 216 41.49 N 88.20 W
Moose Heights 182 53.05 N 122.30 W
Moose Hill ∧2 283 42.07 N 71.13 W
Moose Island I 184 51.42 N 97.10 W
Moose Jaw 184 50.23 N 105.32 W
Moose Jaw ≃ 184 50.34 N 105.17 W
Moose Lake, Mb., Can. 184 53.43 N 100.20 W
Moose Lake, Mn., U.S. 190 46.27 N 92.45 W
Moose Lake ⊜, Ab., Can. 182 54.15 N 110.55 W
Moose Lake ⊜, Mb., Can. 184 53.55 N 99.45 W
Moose Lake ⊜, On., Can. 212 45.09 N 78.28 W
Mooselookmeguntic Lake ⊜ 188 44.53 N 70.48 W
Moose Mountain ∧ 184 49.45 N 102.37 W
Moose Mountain Creek ≃ 184 49.12 N 102.10 W
Moose Mountain Provincial Park ♦ 184 49.48 N 102.25 W
Moose Pass 180 60.29 N 149.22 W
Moosinning 60 48.17 N 11.51 E
Moosomin 184 50.07 N 101.40 W
Moosomin Indian Reserve ✦4 184 53.06 N 108.14 W
Moosonee 176 51.17 N 80.39 W
Moosup 207 41.42 N 71.52 W
Mooti 144 0.35 N 41.56 E
Moots Creek ≃ 216 40.32 N 86.47 W
Mootwingee National Park ♦ 166 31.07 S 142.23 E
Mopane 156 22.37 S 29.52 E
Mopeia Velha 156 17.59 S 35.44 E
Mopipi 156 21.07 S 24.55 E
Mopo 100 33.07 N 113.02 E
Moppo → Mokp'o 98 34.48 N 126.22 E
Mopti 150 14.30 N 4.12 W
Mopti □4 150 14.40 N 4.15 W
Moqokorei 144 4.04 N 46.08 E
Moquegua 248 17.12 S 70.56 W
Moquegua □5 248 16.50 S 70.55 W
Mór 30 47.23 N 18.12 E
Mor ≃ 126 24.01 N 88.03 E
Mòr, Glen V 46 57.10 N 4.40 W
Mor, Sgurr ∧ 46 57.42 N 5.03 W
Mora, Cam. 146 11.03 N 14.09 E
Mora, Esp. 34 39.41 N 3.46 W
Mora, India 272c 18.54 N 72.56 E
Mora, Port. 34 38.56 N 8.10 W
Mora, Sve. 26 61.00 N 14.33 E
Mora, Mn., U.S. 190 45.52 N 93.17 W
Mora, N.M., U.S. 200 35.58 N 105.19 W
Mora ≃ 196 35.44 N 104.23 W
Mora, Arroyo de la ≃ 196 34.05 N 104.18 W
Moraby 40 60.23 N 15.35 E
Morač ≃ 76 52.35 N 27.35 E
Morača, Manastir ✝1 38 42.44 N 19.20 E
Morada 226 38.01 N 121.15 W
Morādābād 124 28.50 N 78.47 E
Morada Nova 250 5.07 S 38.23 W
Morada Nova de Minas 255 18.37 S 45.22 W
Moradel, Montaña de ∧ 236 15.06 N 86.16 W
Mora de Rubielos 34 40.15 N 0.45 W
Moraduccio 66 44.10 N 11.29 E
Morafenobe 157b 17.49 S 44.55 E
Morąg 30 53.56 N 19.56 E
Moraga 226 37.50 N 122.08 W
Mórahalom 30 46.13 N 19.54 E
Moraine 218 39.42 N 84.13 W
Moraine Hills State Park ♦ 216 42.18 N 88.15 W
Moraine State Park ♦ 214 40.56 N 80.07 W
Morainvilliers 261 48.56 N 1.56 E
Morākhi ≃ 126 24.01 N 88.10 E
Morākhi Reservoir ⊜1 126 24.10 N 87.15 E
Mor'akovskij Zaton 86 56.45 N 84.41 E
Moral de Calatrava 34 38.50 N 3.35 W
Moraleda, Canal ⋃ 254 44.30 S 73.30 W
Morales, Guat. 236 15.29 N 88.49 W
Morales, Perú 248 6.28 S 76.28 W
Morales, Arroyo ≃ 258 34.48 S 58.36 W
Morales, Laguna ⊂ 234 23.35 N 97.47 W
Moramanga 157b 18.56 S 48.12 E
Moran, Ks., U.S. 198 37.54 N 95.10 W
Moran, Mi., U.S. 190 45.59 N 84.49 W
Moran, Tx., U.S. 196 32.33 N 99.10 W
Moran ≃ 164 15.16 S 125.33 E
Moranbah 166 22.00 S 148.02 E
Morangis 261 48.42 N 2.20 E
Morangup Hill ∧2 168a 31.41 S 116.19 E
Morann 214 40.48 N 78.21 W
Morano Calabro 68 39.50 N 16.08 E
Morano sul Po 62 45.10 N 8.22 E
Moran State Park ♦ 224 48.41 N 122.52 W
Morant Bay 241q 17.53 N 76.25 W
Morant Cays II 238 17.24 N 75.59 W
Morant Point ≻ 241q 17.55 N 76.10 W
Morar, Loch ⊜ 46 56.57 N 5.43 W
Mörarp 41 56.04 N 12.52 E
Morasverdes 34 40.36 N 6.16 W
Morat, Lac de (Murtensee) ⊜ 58 46.55 N 7.05 E
Moratalla 34 38.12 N 1.53 W
Morattico 208 37.47 N 76.37 W
Moratuwa 122 6.46 N 79.53 E
Morava □9 30 49.30 N 17.00 E
Morava (March) ≃ 30 48.10 N 16.59 E
Morāveh Tappeh 128 37.55 N 55.57 E
Moravia, C.R. 236 9.51 N 83.26 W
Moravia, Ia., U.S. 190 40.53 N 92.48 W
Moravia, N.Y., U.S. 210 42.42 N 76.25 W
Moravia → Morava □9 30 49.20 N 17.00 E
Moravian Indian Reserve ✦4 214 42.34 N 81.53 W
Moravská Dyje ≃ 61 48.51 N 15.30 E
Moravská Ostrava → Ostrava 30 49.50 N 18.17 E
Moravská Třebová 30 49.45 N 16.40 E
Moravské Budějovice 61 49.03 N 15.49 E
Moravský Krumlov 61 49.03 N 16.19 E
Morawa 162 29.13 S 116.00 E
Morawhanna 246 8.16 N 59.45 W
Moraya 248 21.45 S 65.32 W
Morayfield 171a 27.07 S 152.57 E
Moray Firth ⊂1 46 57.50 N 3.30 W
Morazán, Guat. 236 14.56 N 90.09 W
Morazán, Hond. 236 15.17 N 87.34 W
Morbach 56 49.48 N 7.07 E
Morbegno 58 46.08 N 9.34 E
Morbi 120 22.49 N 70.50 E
Morbihan □5 32 47.55 N 2.50 W
Mörbisch am See 61 47.45 N 16.40 E
Morbras ≃ 261 48.47 N 2.29 E
Mörbylånga 26 56.31 N 16.23 E
Morcenx 32 44.02 N 0.55 W
Morciano di Romagna 66 43.55 N 12.38 E
Morcone 68 41.20 N 14.40 E
Morcote 58 45.56 N 8.55 E
Morcy 80 51.18 N 47.51 E
Morden 184 49.11 N 98.05 W
Morden ✦8 260 51.24 N 0.12 W
Mordialloc 169 38.00 S 145.05 E
Mordino 24 61.21 N 51.52 E
Mordoğan 130 38.30 N 26.37 E
Mordovija □3, Ross. 72 54.30 N 44.00 E
Mordovija □3, Ross. 80 54.30 N 44.00 E
Mordovo, Ross. 80 51.07 N 45.48 E
Mordovo, Ross. 80 52.05 N 40.46 E
Mordovo-Adel'akovo 80 53.47 N 51.36 E
Mordovskij Buguruslan 80 53.48 N 52.31 E
Mordovskij zapovednik ✦4 80 54.48 N 43.20 E
Mordves 82 54.34 N 38.13 E
Mordvinia → Mordovija □3 80 54.30 N 44.00 E
Mordy 30 52.13 N 22.31 E
More, Ben ∧, Scot., U.K. 46 56.21 N 4.35 W
More, Ben ∧, Scot., U.K. 46 56.25 N 6.01 W
More, Loch ⊜ 46 58.17 N 4.52 W
More Assynt, Ben ∧ 46 58.08 N 4.53 W
Moreau ≃, Mo., U.S. 219 38.33 N 92.06 W
Moreau ≃, S.D., U.S. 198 45.18 N 100.43 W
Moreau, North Fork ≃ 198 45.09 N 102.50 W
Moreau, South Fork ≃ 198 45.09 N 102.50 W
Moreau Peak ∧ 198 45.21 N 103.43 W
Moreauville 194 31.02 N 91.58 W
Morec 80 51.03 N 44.03 E
Morecambe 44 54.04 N 2.53 W
Morecambe Bay ⊂ 44 54.07 N 3.00 W
Moree, Austl. 166 29.28 S 149.51 E
Morée, Fr. 50 47.54 N 1.14 E
Morehead, Pap. N. Gui. 164 8.40 S 141.35 E
Morehead, Ky., U.S. 218 38.11 N 83.25 W
Morehead ≃ 164 9.00 S 141.25 E
Morehead City 192 34.43 N 76.43 W
Morehouse 194 36.50 N 89.41 W
Moreira César 256 22.55 S 45.22 W
Moreland, Austl. 274b 37.45 S 144.58 E
Moreland, Ga., U.S. 192 33.17 N 84.46 W
Moreland, Ky., U.S. 194 37.30 N 84.48 W
Moreland Hills 279a 41.27 N 81.29 W
Morelia 234 19.42 N 101.07 W
Morell 186 46.25 N 62.42 W
Morella, Austl. 166 22.59 S 143.52 E
Morella, Esp. 34 40.37 N 0.06 W
Morello ≃ 70 37.29 N 14.08 E
Morelos, Méx. 196 28.25 N 100.53 W
Morelos, Méx. 232 26.42 N 107.40 W
Morelos, Méx. 234 22.53 N 102.37 W
Morelos □3 234 18.45 N 99.00 W
Moremi Wildlife Reserve ✦4 156 19.10 S 23.15 E
Morena 124 26.30 N 78.09 E
Morena, Sierra ∧ 282 37.25 N 122.18 W
Morena, Sierra ⋏ 34 38.00 N 5.00 W
Morenci, Az., U.S. 200 33.04 N 109.21 W
Morenci, Mi., U.S. 216 41.43 N 84.13 W
Moreni 38 45.00 N 25.39 E
Moreno 258 34.39 S 58.48 W
Moreno □5 288 34.36 S 58.48 W
Moreno, Bahía ⊂ 252 23.35 S 70.30 W
Moreno Valley 228 33.56 N 117.09 W
Møre og Romsdal □6 26 62.40 N 7.50 E
Mores 71 40.33 N 8.50 E
Moresby Island I, B.C., Can. 182 52.50 N 131.55 W
Moresby Island I, B.C., Can. 224 48.40 N 123.20 W
Mores Island I 238 26.18 N 77.33 W
Moresnet 56 50.43 N 5.59 E
Morestel 62 45.40 N 5.28 E
Moreton, Austl. 164 12.28 S 142.38 E
Moreton, Eng., U.K. 44 53.24 N 3.07 W
Moreton, Eng., U.K. 260 51.44 N 0.14 E
Moreton, Cape ≻ 171a 27.02 S 153.28 E
Moreton Bay ⊂ 171a 27.20 S 153.15 E
Moretonhampstead 42 50.40 N 3.45 W
Moreton-in-Marsh 42 51.59 N 1.42 W
Moreton Island I 171a 27.10 S 153.25 E
Moreton Island National Park ♦ 171a 27.09 S 153.25 E
Moret-sur-Loing 50 48.22 N 2.49 E
Moretta 62 44.46 N 7.32 E
Moreuil 50 49.46 N 2.29 E
Morey Park 210 42.33 N 73.43 W
Morey Peak ∧ 204 38.37 N 116.17 W
Morez 58 46.31 N 6.02 E
Morfa Nefyn 42 52.56 N 4.33 W
Mörfelden-Walldorf 56 49.58 N 8.34 E
Morga 80 54.26 N 46.29 E
Morgan, Austl. 166 34.02 S 139.40 E
Morgan, Ga., U.S. 192 31.32 N 84.35 W
Morgan, Ky., U.S. 218 38.36 N 84.23 W
Morgan, Mn., U.S. 198 44.25 N 94.55 W
Morgan, Pa., U.S. 279b 40.22 N 80.08 W
Morgan, Tx., U.S. 222 32.01 N 97.37 W
Morgan, Ut., U.S. 200 41.02 N 111.40 W
Morgan □6, Il., U.S. 219 39.44 N 90.14 W
Morgan □6, In., U.S. 218 39.30 N 86.25 W
Morgan, Mount ∧ 171b 35.44 S 148.47 E
Morgan City, Al., U.S. 194 34.28 N 86.34 W
Morgan City, La., U.S. 194 29.41 N 91.12 W
Morgan Creek ≃ 196 32.19 N 100.55 W
Morganfield 194 37.41 N 87.55 W
Morgan Hill 226 37.07 N 121.39 W
Morganito 246 5.04 N 67.44 W
Morgan Park ✦8 278 41.42 N 87.40 W
Morgan's Bay 158 32.43 S 28.20 E
Morgan's Point 222 29.41 N 94.59 W
Morgans Point ≻ 212 42.52 N 79.21 W
Morgan State College ✝2 284b 39.21 N 76.35 W
Morgantina ⊥ 70 37.25 N 14.29 E
Morganton 192 35.44 N 81.41 W
Morgantown, In., U.S. 218 39.22 N 86.15 W
Morgantown, Ky., U.S. 194 37.13 N 86.41 W
Morgantown, Md., U.S. 208 38.21 N 76.58 W
Morgantown, Ms., U.S. 194 31.18 N 89.54 W
Morgantown, Ms., U.S. 194 31.34 N 91.20 W
Morgantown, Oh., U.S. 218 39.08 N 83.13 W
Morgantown, Pa., U.S. 208 40.09 N 75.54 W
Morgantown, W.V., U.S. 188 39.37 N 79.57 W
Morganville 208 40.23 N 74.15 W
Morgan Whyalla Pipeline ≛1 168b 33.48 S 138.56 E
Morganza 194 30.44 N 91.35 W
Morgårdshammar 40 60.09 N 15.23 E
Morgauši 80 55.58 N 46.47 E
Morgenzon 158 26.45 S 29.36 E
Morges 58 46.31 N 6.30 E
Morgex 62 45.45 N 7.02 E
Morghāb (Murgab) ≃ 128 38.18 N 61.12 E
Morghar 126 23.40 N 89.37 E
Morghūm, Kūh-e ∧ 128 33.06 N 57.30 E
Morgongåva 40 59.56 N 16.57 E
Morgongiori 71 39.45 N 8.46 E
Morguilla, Punta ≻ 252 37.46 S 73.40 W
Morhange 56 48.55 N 6.38 E
Mori, It. 64 45.51 N 10.59 E
Mori, Nihon 92a 42.06 N 140.35 E
Mori, Nihon 94 34.50 N 137.56 E
Mori, Nihon 270 34.32 N 135.00 E
Mori ≃ 164 10.00 S 148.30 E
Moriah 241r 11.15 N 60.43 W
Moriah, Mount ∧ 204 39.17 N 114.12 W
Morialta Conservation Park ♦ 168b 34.55 S 138.40 E
Moriarty 200 34.59 N 106.02 W
Moriarty, Mount ∧ 224 49.08 N 124.26 W
Morib 114 2.45 N 101.26 E
Moribaya 150 9.53 N 9.33 W
Morice ≃ 182 54.24 N 126.45 W
Morice Lake ⊜ 182 54.00 N 127.37 W
Morichal Largo ≃ 246 9.27 N 62.25 W
Moricsala rezervāts ♦ 76 57.17 N 22.11 E
Morie, Loch ⊜ 46 57.44 N 4.28 W
Morienval 50 49.18 N 2.56 E
Morigerati 68 40.08 N 15.33 E
Moriguchi 96 34.44 N 135.34 E
Morija 158 29.34 S 27.31 E
Moriki 150 12.52 N 6.30 E
Morin Dawa 89 48.28 N 124.27 E
Moringen 52 51.42 N 9.52 E
Morino, It. 66 41.53 N 13.25 E
Morino, Ross. 76 57.54 N 30.22 E
Morinville 182 53.48 N 113.39 W
Morioka 92 39.42 N 141.09 E
Morīri, Tso ⊜ 120 32.54 N 78.20 E
Morisset 170 33.06 S 151.29 E
Moriston ≃ 46 57.12 N 4.36 W
Moritzburg ⊥ 54 51.09 N 13.40 E
Morivione ✦8 266b 45.26 N 9.12 E
Morivs'k 78 51.06 N 30.50 E
Moriya 94 35.56 N 140.00 E
Moriyama 94 35.04 N 135.59 E
Moriyama-chūtonchi, Rikujō-jieitai- ■ 94 35.12 N 136.57 E
Moriyoshi-zan ∧ 92 39.58 N 140.33 E
Morki 80 56.25 N 49.01 E
Morkill ≃ 182 53.42 N 120.30 W
Morkiny Gory 76 57.33 N 36.18 E
Mörkö I 40 58.59 N 17.40 E
Morkoka ≃ 74 65.10 N 115.52 E
Mørkøv 41 55.40 N 11.32 E
Morlaix 32 48.35 N 3.50 W
Morlanwelz 50 50.27 N 4.14 E
Morles 56 50.38 N 9.51 E
Morley, Eng., U.K. 44 53.46 N 1.36 W
Morley, Mi., U.S. 190 43.29 N 85.26 W
Morley, N.Y., U.S. 212 44.40 N 75.12 W
Morley Green 262 53.20 N 2.16 W
Mörlunda 26 57.19 N 15.51 E
Mormal' 76 52.45 N 29.53 E
Mormanno 68 39.53 N 16.00 E
Mormant 50 48.36 N 2.53 E
Mormoiron 62 44.04 N 5.11 E
Mormon Lake ⊜ 200 34.57 N 111.27 W
Mormon Peak ∧ 204 36.57 N 114.30 W
Mormon Reservoir ⊜1 202 43.16 N 114.49 W
Mormon Slough ≃ 226 37.57 N 121.18 W
Mormon Station Historical State Monument ♦ 226 39.00 N 119.50 W
Mormugao 122 15.24 N 73.48 E
Morna 272a 28.35 N 77.22 E
Mornant 62 45.37 N 4.40 E
Mornas 62 44.12 N 4.44 E
Morne-à-l'Eau 241o 16.21 N 61.31 W
Morne Trois Pitons National Park ♦ 240d 15.19 N 61.19 W
Morney 166 25.22 S 141.28 E
Morningdale 207 42.18 N 71.45 W
Morningside 284c 38.50 N 76.53 W
Morningside Park ♦ 275b 43.47 N 79.12 W
Morningstar ≃ 48 52.27 N 8.41 W
Morning Sun 190 41.05 N 91.15 W
Mornington 169 38.13 S 145.03 E
Mornington, Isla I 254 49.45 S 75.23 W
Mornington Island I 164 16.33 S 139.24 E
Mornington Island Aboriginal Land Trust ✦4 164 16.20 S 139.20 E
Mornington Peninsula ≻1 169 38.20 S 145.05 E
Morno 150 8.41 N 1.31 W
Morrou, Hadjer ∧ 146 17.12 N 23.08 E
Moro, Indon. 114 0.46 N 103.43 E
Moro, Or., U.S. 224 45.29 N 120.43 W
Moro ≃ 150 7.25 N 11.03 W
Morobe 164 7.45 S 147.35 E
Morobe □5 164 7.00 S 146.30 E
Morocco 216 40.56 N 87.27 W
Morocco (Al-Magreb) □1, Afr. 134 32.00 N 5.00 W
Morocco (Al-Magreb) □1, Afr. 148 32.00 N 5.00 W
Morococala 248 18.10 S 66.44 W
Morococha 248 11.37 S 76.09 W
Moro Creek ≃ 194 33.18 N 92.22 W
Morogoro 154 6.49 S 37.40 E
Morogoro □4 154 8.00 S 37.15 E
Moro Gulf ⊂ 116 6.51 N 123.00 E
Moroka 273d 26.16 S 27.52 E
Morokweng 158 26.12 S 23.45 E
Moroleón 234 20.08 N 101.12 W
Morombe 157b 21.45 S 43.22 E
Morón, Arg. 258 34.39 S 58.37 W
Morón, Cuba 240p 22.06 N 78.38 W
Mörön, Mong. 88 48.15 N 100.23 E
Mörön, Mong. 88 47.24 N 110.16 E
Mörön, Mong. 88 49.38 N 100.10 E
Morón, Ven. 246 10.29 N 68.11 W
Morón □5 288 34.37 S 58.37 W
Mörön ≃ 88 47.14 N 110.37 E
Morón, Aeródromo ✈ 288 34.41 S 58.38 W
Morón, Arroyo ≃ 288 34.33 S 58.37 W
Morona ≃ 246 4.45 S 77.04 W
Morona-Santiago □4 246 2.30 S 78.00 W
Morondava 157b 20.17 S 44.17 E
Morón de Almazán 34 41.25 N 2.25 W
Morón de la Frontera 34 37.08 N 5.27 W
Morones, Sierra ⋏ 234 21.45 N 103.10 W
Morong 116 14.41 N 120.16 E
Morongo Indian Reservation ✦4 204 33.59 N 116.50 W
Moroni, Comores 157a 11.41 S 43.16 E
Moroni, Ut., U.S. 200 39.31 N 111.35 W
Moron Us ≃, Zhg. 90 34.42 N 94.50 E
Moron Us ≃, Zhg. 120 34.42 N 94.50 E
Moros ≃ 34 41.03 N 4.15 W
Morošečnoje 74 56.24 N 156.12 E
Morotai I 108 2.20 N 128.25 E
Moroto 154 2.32 N 34.39 E
Moroto ∧ 154 2.32 N 34.46 E
Morouba 152 6.11 N 20.13 E
Morovis 240m 18.20 N 66.24 W
Morowali 112 1.52 S 121.30 E
Moroyama 94 35.56 N 139.19 E
Morozivka 83 49.28 N 39.54 E
Morozkovo 86 59.29 N 61.01 E
Morozovka 78 50.09 N 39.38 E
Morozovsk 80 48.22 N 41.50 E
Morozovskaja 24 61.10 N 50.18 E
Morpeth, On., Can. 214 42.23 N 81.51 W
Morpeth, Eng., U.K. 44 55.10 N 1.41 W
Morphett Vale 168b 35.07 S 138.31 E
Morra, Monte ∧ 267a 42.02 N 12.50 E
Morral 214 40.41 N 83.12 W
Morral, Arroyo del ≃ 266d 41.29 N 2.03 E
Morrelganj 126 22.28 N 89.51 E
Morrice 216 42.50 N 84.11 W
Morrill 198 41.57 N 103.55 W
Morrilton 194 35.09 N 92.44 W
Morrin 182 51.40 N 112.47 W
Morrinhos, Bra. 250 3.14 S 40.07 W
Morrinhos, Bra. 255 17.44 S 49.07 W
Morrinsville 172 37.39 S 175.32 E
Morris, Mb., Can. 184 49.21 N 97.22 W
Morris, Ct., U.S. 207 41.41 N 73.11 W
Morris, Il., U.S. 216 41.21 N 88.25 W
Morris, In., U.S. 218 39.16 N 85.10 W
Morris, Mn., U.S. 198 45.35 N 95.54 W
Morris, N.Y., U.S. 210 42.32 N 75.14 W
Morris, Ok., U.S. 196 35.36 N 95.51 W
Morris, Pa., U.S. 210 41.36 N 77.18 W
Morris □6, N.J., U.S. 210 40.48 N 74.29 W
Morris □6, Tx., U.S. 222 33.05 N 94.45 W
Morris ≃ 184 49.21 N 97.22 W
Morris, Mount ∧ 162 26.09 S 131.04 E
Morrisburg 212 44.54 N 75.11 W
Morrisdale 214 40.56 N 78.13 W
Morris Dam ✦6 280 34.11 N 117.53 W
Morris Jesup, Kap ≻ 16 83.38 N 33.52 W
Morris Lake ⊜ 276 41.03 N 74.37 W
Morrison, Arg. 252 32.36 S 62.50 W
Morrison, Il., U.S. 190 41.48 N 89.57 W
Morrison, Mo., U.S. 219 38.40 N 91.38 W
Morrison, Point ≻ 168b 35.44 S 137.47 E
Morrison Creek ≃ 275b 43.28 N 79.39 W
Morrison Lake ⊜, On., Can. 212 44.52 N 79.28 W
Morrison Lake ⊜, Mi., U.S. 216 42.53 N 85.13 W
Morrisonville 219 39.25 N 89.27 W
Morris Park ♦ 285 39.59 N 75.15 W
Morris Plains 210 40.49 N 74.28 W
Morris Reservoir ⊜1 228 34.12 N 117.52 W
Morris Run 210 41.40 N 77.01 W
Morristown, Az., U.S. 200 33.51 N 112.37 W
Morristown, Il., U.S. 216 42.10 N 89.03 W
Morristown, In., U.S. 218 39.40 N 85.41 W
Morristown, Mn., U.S. 190 44.14 N 93.26 W
Morristown, N.J., U.S. 210 40.47 N 74.28 W
Morristown, N.Y., U.S. 212 44.35 N 75.38 W
Morristown, Oh., U.S. 214 40.04 N 81.05 W
Morristown, S.D., U.S. 198 45.56 N 101.43 W
Morristown, Tn., U.S. 192 36.12 N 83.17 W
Morristown Airport ✈ 276 40.48 N 74.25 W
Morristown National Historical Park ♦ 210 40.46 N 74.32 W
Morrisville, N.Y., U.S. 210 42.53 N 75.38 W
Morrisville, Pa., U.S. 208 40.12 N 74.47 W
Morrisville, Vt., U.S. 188 44.33 N 72.35 W
Morrito 236 11.37 N 85.05 W
Morro 246 2.39 S 80.19 W
Morro, Castillo del (Morro Castle) ⊥ 286b 23.09 N 82.21 W
Morro, Punta ≻ 232 19.39 N 90.42 W
Morro Agudo 287a 22.45 S 43.29 W
Morro Bay 226 35.21 N 120.50 W
Morro Bay ⊂ 226 35.20 N 120.51 W
Morro Bay State Park ♦ 226 35.20 N 120.52 W
Morro Creek ≃ 226 35.23 N 120.52 W
Morro do Chapéu 250 11.33 S 41.09 W
Morro d'Oro 66 42.39 N 13.54 E
Morro Mazatán 234 16.07 N 95.27 W
Morrone del Sannio 66 41.43 N 14.47 E
Morropón 248 5.15 S 80.00 W
Morro Rock ∧ 226 35.22 N 120.52 W
Morros 250 2.52 S 44.03 W
Morrosquillo, Golfo de ⊂ 246 9.35 N 75.40 W
Morrow, La., U.S. 194 30.49 N 92.04 W
Morrow, Oh., U.S. 218 39.21 N 84.07 W
Morrow □6 214 40.33 N 82.50 W
Morrow Island I 282 38.07 N 122.05 W
Morrow Mountain State Park ♦ 192 35.23 N 80.05 W
Morrow Point Reservoir ⊜1 200 38.25 N 107.30 W
Mörrum 26 56.11 N 14.45 E
Morrumbala 154 17.22 S 35.36 E
Morrumbene 156 23.39 S 35.20 E
Mörrumsån ≃ 26 56.09 N 14.44 E
Mors I 26 56.50 N 8.45 E
Morsains 50 48.48 N 3.32 E
Morsang-sur-Orge 261 48.40 N 2.21 E
Moršansk 80 53.26 N 41.49 E
Morsbach 56 50.52 N 7.43 E
Morschwiller-le-Bas 58 47.45 N 7.16 E
Morščichino 265b 55.56 N 37.20 E
Morse, Sk., Can. 184 50.25 N 107.03 W
Morse, La., U.S. 194 30.07 N 92.29 W
Morse, Tx., U.S. 196 36.04 N 101.29 W
Morse Mill 219 38.17 N 90.40 W
Mörsenbroich ✦8 263 51.15 N 6.48 E
Morse Reservoir ⊜1 218 40.06 N 86.02 W
Morses Pond ⊜ 283 42.18 N 71.19 W
Morsi 120 21.21 N 78.00 E
Morskaja Masel'ga 24 63.06 N 34.54 E
Morskoj Bir'učok, ostrov I 84 44.42 N 47.02 E
Morson 184 49.03 N 94.18 W
Morsott 36 35.40 N 8.01 E
Morstein 285 40.01 N 75.35 W
Mort 272a 28.43 N 77.25 E
Morta 272a 28.44 N 77.27 E
Mortagne 32 48.31 N 0.33 E
Mortagne ≃ 58 48.33 N 6.27 E
Mortagne-au-Perche 50 48.31 N 0.33 E
Mortagne-sur-Sèvre 32 47.00 N 0.57 W
Mortain 32 48.39 N 0.56 W
Mortana 162 33.02 S 134.07 E
Mortara 62 45.15 N 8.44 E
Morteau 58 47.04 N 6.37 E
Mortefontaine 50 49.07 N 2.36 E
Mortegliano 64 45.57 N 13.10 E
Morte Point ≻ 42 51.11 N 4.13 W
Morteratsch, Piz ∧ 58 46.22 N 9.51 E
Morteros 252 30.42 S 62.00 W
Mortes, Rio das ≃, Bra. 255 11.45 S 50.44 W
Mortes, Rio das ≃, Bra. 256 21.18 S 43.58 W
Mortesoro 140 10.12 N 34.09 E
Mort-Homme, Forêt du ✦3 56 49.15 N 5.15 E
Mortimer 42 51.22 N 1.04 W
Mortlach 184 50.28 N 106.03 W
Mortlake, Austl. 166 38.05 S 142.48 E
Mortlake, Austl. 274a 33.51 S 151.07 E
Mortlake ✦8 260 51.28 N 0.16 W
Mortlock ≃ 168a 31.42 S 116.55 E
Mortlock Islands II 14 5.27 N 153.40 E
Mortlock North ≃ 168a 31.38 S 116.42 E
Mortola Inferiore 62 43.47 N 7.33 E
Morton, Il., U.S. 190 40.36 N 89.27 W
Morton, Mn., U.S. 198 44.33 N 94.59 W
Morton, Ms., U.S. 194 32.21 N 89.39 W
Morton, N.Y., U.S. 210 43.20 N 78.00 W
Morton, Pa., U.S. 285 39.55 N 75.20 W
Morton, Tx., U.S. 196 33.43 N 102.45 W
Morton, Wa., U.S. 224 46.33 N 122.16 W
Morton, Mount ∧2 274b 37.56 S 145.20 E
Morton Arboretum ♦ 278 41.49 N 88.04 W
Morton Craig Range ⋏ 162 28.12 S 124.41 E
Morton Grove 216 42.02 N 87.46 W
Morton National Park ♦ 170 35.00 S 150.10 E
Mortons Gap 194 37.14 N 87.28 W
Mortorio, Isola I 71 41.05 N 9.36 E
Mortornès del Vallès 266d 41.33 N 2.16 E
Mortrée 50 48.38 N 0.05 E
Mörtschach 64 46.55 N 12.55 E
Mortsel 50 51.10 N 4.28 E
M'ortvyj Donec ≃ 83 47.15 N 39.14 E
Morty 80 55.49 N 51.44 E
Morua 175f 16.54 S 168.32 E
Morumbi ✦8 287b 23.36 S 46.42 E
Morumbi, Estádio do ♦ 287b 23.37 S 46.43 W
Morungaba 256 22.52 S 46.48 W
Morungole ∧ 154 3.49 N 34.02 E
Moruya 166 35.55 S 150.05 E
Morvan ⋏ 32 47.05 N 4.00 E
Morvant 241r 10.39 N 61.28 W
Morven, Austl. 166 26.25 S 147.07 E
Morven, N.Z. 172 44.50 S 171.07 E
Morven, Ga., U.S. 192 30.56 N 83.29 W
Morven, N.C., U.S. 192 34.51 N 80.00 W
Morven ∧, Scot., U.K. 46 58.14 N 3.42 W
Morven ∧, Scot., U.K. 46 57.07 N 3.02 W
Morwell 169 38.14 S 146.24 E
Morwell ≃ 169 38.10 S 146.23 E
Morwenstow 42 50.54 N 4.33 W
Moryń 30 52.49 N 14.13 E
Morženga 76 59.37 N 40.12 E
Morzhovoi 180 54.55 N 163.18 W
Morzine 58 46.11 N 6.43 E
Moržovec, ostrov I 24 66.44 N 42.35 E
Moša ≃, Ross. 24 62.25 N 39.46 E
M'oša ≃, Ross. 80 55.25 N 49.22 E
Mosal'sk 76 54.29 N 34.59 E
Mosambik → Mozambique □1 138 18.15 S 35.00 E
Mošanicy 82 54.56 N 38.23 E
Mosås 40 59.12 N 15.08 E
Mosbach 56 49.21 N 9.08 E
Mosborough 44 53.19 N 1.22 W
Mosby 26 58.14 N 7.54 E
Mosby Woods 284c 38.52 N 77.18 W
Moscavide 266c 38.47 N 9.06 W
Mosciano Sant'Angelo 66 42.45 N 13.53 E
Moščnyj, ostrov I 76 60.01 N 27.50 E
Moscos Islands II 110 14.00 N 97.45 E
Moscou → Moskva 82 55.45 N 37.35 E
Moscow → Moskva, Ross. 82 55.45 N 37.35 E
Moscow, Id., U.S. 202 46.43 N 116.59 W
Moscow, In., U.S. 218 39.29 N 85.34 W
Moscow, Oh., U.S. 218 38.51 N 84.13 W
Moscow, Pa., U.S. 210 41.20 N 75.31 W
Moscow, Tx., U.S. 222 30.55 N 94.50 W
Moscow Air Terminal ✈ 265b 55.48 N 37.32 E
Moscow Circus ♦ 265b 55.43 N 37.33 E
Moscow Mills 219 38.56 N 90.55 W
Moscow Station ✦5 265a 59.56 N 30.22 E
Moscow Victory Park ♦ 265a 59.52 N 30.20 E
Moscow Zoo ♦ 265b 55.46 N 37.34 E
Moscú → Moskva 82 55.45 N 37.35 E
Moscufo 66 42.25 N 14.03 E
Mosel 54 50.47 N 12.28 E
Mosel (Moselle) ≃ 32 50.22 N 7.36 E
Moselebe ≃ 156 25.03 S 23.13 E
Moselle, Ms., U.S. 194 31.30 N 89.16 W
Moselle, Mo., U.S. 219 38.23 N 90.54 W
Moselle □5 56 49.00 N 6.30 E
Moselle (Mosel) ≃ 32 50.22 N 7.36 E
Moselotte ≃ 58 48.01 N 6.38 E
Mošenskoje 76 58.31 N 34.35 E
Möser 54 52.13 N 11.48 E
Mosermandl ∧ 64 47.12 N 13.24 E
Mosers River 186 44.59 N 62.15 W
Moses Lake 202 47.07 N 119.16 W
Moses Lake ⊜1 202 47.10 N 119.20 W
Moses Point 180 64.42 N 162.03 W
Moses Power Plant ✦6 284a 43.09 N 79.02 W
Mosetse 156 20.37 S 26.32 E
Mosgiel 172 45.53 S 170.21 E
Moshannon 214 41.02 N 78.00 W
Moshannon Creek ≃ 214 41.04 N 78.06 W
Moshanpu 100 29.34 N 112.41 E
Moshaweng ≃ 158 26.35 S 22.50 E
Mosheim, Tn., U.S. 192 36.11 N 82.57 W
Mosheim, Tx., U.S. 222 31.38 N 97.36 W
Moshi 154 3.21 S 37.20 E
Moshi ≃ 150 9.18 N 4.38 E
Moshiyu 104 41.15 N 124.05 E
Moshny 78 49.32 N 31.44 E
Mosier 224 45.41 N 121.23 W
Mosier Hill ∧2 214 40.06 N 80.24 W
Mosina 30 52.16 N 16.51 E
Mosinee 190 44.47 N 89.42 W
Mosjøen 24 65.50 N 13.10 E
Moskal'onki 86 54.59 N 71.54 E
Moskal'vo 89 53.35 N 142.30 E
Moskau → Moskva 82 55.45 N 37.35 E
Moskenesøya I 24 67.59 N 13.00 E
Moskháton 267c 37.57 N 23.41 E
Moškino 80 57.45 N 45.20 E
Moskito-Golf → Mosquitos, Golfo de los ⊂ 236 9.00 N 81.15 W
Moškovo 86 55.18 N 83.37 E
Moskovskaja Slav'anka 265a 59.45 N 30.30 E
Moskovskaja vozvyšennost' ⋏1 76 56.15 N 37.30 E
Moskva (Moscow), Ross. 82 55.45 N 37.35 E
Moskva (Moscow), Ross. 265b 55.45 N 37.35 E
Moskva ≃ 76 55.05 N 38.50 E
Moskva, Gorod □7 265b 55.45 N 37.35 E
Moskva, pik ∧ 85 38.57 N 71.49 E
Moskva Oblast' □4 76 55.30 N 37.30 E
Moskvy, kanal imeni ≛ 82 56.43 N 37.08 E
Mosman 170 33.49 S 151.14 E
Mosman Park 168a 32.01 S 115.46 E
Moso (Moos) 64 46.41 N 12.23 E
Moso in Passiria (Moos) 64 46.50 N 11.10 E
Mošok 80 55.48 N 41.17 E
Mosolovo 80 54.17 N 40.32 E
Mosomane 156 24.04 S 26.15 E
Mosoni-Duna ≃ 61 47.54 N 17.17 E
Mosonmagyaróvár 30 47.51 N 17.17 E
Mosonszolnok 61 47.51 N 17.11 E
Mosopa 156 24.50 S 25.31 E
Mospyne 83 47.53 N 38.03 E
Mosqueiro 250 1.10 S 48.28 W
Mosquera 246 2.30 N 78.29 W
Mosquero 196 35.46 N 103.57 W
Mosquic, Lac ⊜ 206 46.39 N 74.28 W
Mosquito, Punta ≻ 246 9.07 N 77.53 W
Mosquito, Riacho ≃ 252 22.02 S 57.57 W
Mosquito Brook ≃ 283 42.40 N 71.02 W
Mosquito Creek ≃, Ia., U.S. 198 41.11 N 95.50 W
Mosquito Creek ≃, Oh., U.S. 214 41.10 N 80.45 W
Mosquito Creek ≃, Pa., U.S. 214 41.07 N 78.07 W
Mosquito Creek Lake ⊜1 214 41.22 N 80.45 W
Mosquito Creek State Park ♦ 214 41.22 N 80.45 W
Mosquito Indian Reserve ✦4 184 52.30 N 108.15 W
Mosquito Lagoon ⊂ 220 28.45 N 80.45 W
Mosquitos, Costa de □9 236 13.00 N 83.45 W
Mosquitos, Golfo de los ⊂ 236 9.00 N 81.15 W
Moss 26 59.26 N 10.42 E
Mossaka 152 1.13 S 16.48 E
Mossâmedes 255 16.07 S 50.11 W
Mossbank, Sk., Can. 184 49.55 N 105.59 W
Moss Bank, Eng., U.K. 262 53.29 N 2.44 W
Mossbank, Scot., U.K. 46a 60.27 N 1.12 W
Moss Bank Park ♦ 262 53.36 N 2.28 W
Moss Beach 282 37.32 N 122.31 W
Mossburn 172 45.40 S 168.15 E
Mosselbaai (Mossel Bay) 158 34.11 S 22.08 E
Mosselbaai ⊂ 158 34.06 S 22.20 E
Mossendjo 152 2.57 S 12.44 E
Mosses, Col des )( 58 46.24 N 7.06 E
Mossgiel 166 33.15 S 144.34 E
Moss Hill 222 30.15 N 94.45 W
Mossig ≃ 58 48.33 N 7.30 E
Mössingen 58 48.24 N 9.03 E
Moss Landing 226 36.48 N 121.47 W
Mossleigh 182 50.43 N 113.20 W
Mossley 262 53.32 N 2.02 W
Mossley Hill ✦8 262 53.23 N 2.55 W
Mossman 164 16.28 S 145.22 E
Mossmans Brook ≃ 276 41.03 N 74.27 W
Moss Moor ✦3 262 53.37 N 2.00 W
Moss Mountain ∧ 194 34.50 N 92.40 W
Mossø ⊜ 41 56.02 N 9.48 E
Mosson ≃ 62 43.33 N 3.54 E
Mossoró 250 5.11 S 37.20 W
Mosso Santa Maria 62 45.38 N 8.08 E
Moss Point 194 30.24 N 88.32 W
Moss Point ≻ 279a 41.37 N 81.32 W
Moss Side 262 53.46 N 2.57 W
Mossuril 154 14.58 S 40.42 E
Moss Vale 170 34.33 S 150.22 E
Mossy ≃, Mb., Can. 184 51.39 N 99.55 W
Mossy ≃, Sk., Can. 184 54.05 N 103.00 W
Mossyrock 224 46.31 N 122.29 W
Mossyrock Dam ✦6 224 46.32 N 122.25 W
Most 54 50.32 N 13.39 E
Mosta 80 56.32 N 42.10 E
Mostar 36 43.20 N 17.49 E
Mostardas, Bra. 252 31.06 S 50.57 W
Mostardas, Bra. 256 23.44 S 46.38 W
Møsting, Kap ≻ 176 64.00 N 41.00 W
Mostiștea ≃ 38 44.15 N 27.10 E
Mostizzolo 64 46.24 N 11.01 E
Most na Soči 64 46.09 N 13.44 E
Móstoles 266a 40.19 N 3.51 W
Mostoos Hills ⋏2 184 55.00 N 109.15 W
Mostovaja 76 56.13 N 33.08 E
Mostove 78 47.24 N 30.59 E


**Symbols** in the index entries represent the broad categories identified in the key at the right. Symbols with superior numbers (⋏1) identify subcategories (see complete key on page *I · 1).*

**Symbole** im Register stellen die rechts im Schlüssel erklärten Kategorien dar. Symbole mit hochgestellten Ziffern (⋏1) bezeichnen Unterabteilungen einer Kategorie (vgl. vollständiger Schlüssel auf Seite *I · 1).*

**Los símbolos** incluídos en el texto del índice representan las grandes categorías identificadas con la clave a la derecha. Los símbolos con numeros en su parte superior (⋏1) identifican las subcategorías (véase la clave completa en la página *I · 1).*

**Les symboles** de l'index représentent les catégories indiquées dans la légende à droite. Les symboles suivis d'un indice (⋏1) représentent des sous-catégories (voir légende complète à la page *I · 1).*

**Os símbolos** incluídos no texto do índice representam as grandes categorias identificadas com a chave à direita. Os símbolos com números em sua parte superior (⋏1) identificam as subcategorias (veja-se a chave completa à página *I · 1).*

| | | | | |
|---|---|---|---|---|
| ∧ Mountain | Berg | Montaña | Montagne | Montanha |
| ⋏ Mountains | Gebirge | Montañas | Montagnes | Montanhas |
| )( Pass | Paß | Paso | Col | Passo |
| V Valley, Canyon | Tal, Cañon | Valle, Cañón | Vallée, Canyon | Vale, Canhão |
| ≃ Plain | Ebene | Llano | Plaine | Planície |
| ≻ Cape | Kap | Cabo | Cap | Cabo |
| I Island | Insel | Isla | Île | Ilha |
| II Islands | Inseln | Islas | Îles | Ilhas |
| ⊥ Other Topographic Features | Andere Topographische Objekte | Otros Elementos Topográficos | Autres données topographiques | Outros acidentes topográficos |

ESPAÑOL: Nombre | Página | Lat.°′ | Long.°′ W = Oeste
FRANÇAIS: Nom | Page | Lat.°′ | Long.°′ W = Ouest
PORTUGUÊS: Nome | Página | Lat.°′ | Long.°′ W = Oeste


| Nombre | Página | Lat.°′ | Long.°′ W = Oeste |
|---|---|---|---|
| Mostovka | 86 | 58.10 N | 65.31 E |
| Mostovskoj | 84 | 44.25 N | 40.48 E |
| Mostovskoje | 86 | 55.46 N | 66.22 E |
| Mostrim (Edgeworthstown) | 48 | 53.42 N | 7.36 W |
| Mostyn, Malay. | 112 | 4.40 N | 118.11 E |
| Mostyn, Wales, U.K. | 44 | 53.19 N | 3.16 W |
| Mostys'ka | 78 | 49.48 N | 23.09 E |
| Mosul → Al-Mawṣil | 128 | 36.20 N | 43.08 E |
| Møsvatnet ⊜ | 26 | 59.52 N | 8.05 E |
| Mota | 144 | 11.02 N | 37.52 E |
| Mota I | 175f | 13.49 S | 167.42 E |
| Motaba ≏ | 152 | 2.03 N | 18.03 E |
| Mota del Cuervo | 34 | 39.30 N | 2.52 W |
| Mota del Marqués | 34 | 41.38 N | 5.10 W |
| Motagua ≏ | 236 | 15.44 N | 88.14 W |
| Motal' | 76 | 52.19 N | 25.36 E |
| Motala | 26 | 58.33 N | 15.03 E |
| Motala ström ≏ | 40 | 58.38 N | 16.10 E |
| Mota Lava I | 175f | 13.40 S | 167.40 E |
| Motane I | 174x | 9.59 S | 138.49 W |
| Motatán | 246 | 9.24 N | 70.36 W |
| Motaze | 156 | 24.48 S | 32.52 E |
| Motegi | 94 | 36.32 N | 140.11 E |
| Mote Park ♦ | 260 | 51.17 N | 0.34 E |
| Moteve, Cap › | 174x | 9.58 S | 139.02 W |
| Moth | 124 | 25.43 N | 78.57 E |
| Mother Brook ≊ | 283 | 42.15 N | 71.10 W |
| Motherwell | 46 | 55.48 N | 4.00 W |
| Motihāri | 124 | 26.39 N | 84.55 E |
| Motilla del Palancar | 34 | 39.34 N | 1.53 W |
| Motiong | 116 | 11.47 N | 125.00 E |
| Motiti Island I | 172 | 37.38 S | 176.26 E |
| Motjärnshyttan | 40 | 59.56 N | 13.58 E |
| Motloutse | 156 | 21.28 S | 27.24 E |
| Motloutse ≏ | 156 | 22.15 S | 29.00 E |
| Moto-ara ≏ | 94 | 35.53 N | 139.50 E |
| Motobu | 174m | 26.39 N | 127.54 E |
| Motola, Monte ∧ | 68 | 40.22 N | 15.26 E |
| Motopu | 174x | 9.55 S | 139.03 W |
| Motor Island I | 284a | 42.58 N | 78.56 W |
| Motorki | 80 | 56.53 N | 51.29 E |
| Motorovo | 86 | 56.31 N | 71.10 E |
| Motosu | 94 | 35.29 N | 136.40 E |
| Motosu-ko ⊜ | 94 | 35.28 N | 138.35 E |
| Motou | 106 | 32.18 N | 120.34 E |
| Motovilovo | 80 | 55.36 N | 43.51 E |
| Motovun | 64 | 45.20 N | 13.50 E |
| Motoyama | 96 | 33.45 N | 133.35 E |
| Moto-yama ∧[2] | 174f | 24.48 N | 141.20 E |
| Motozintla de Mendoza | 232 | 15.22 N | 92.14 W |
| Motril | 34 | 36.45 N | 3.31 W |
| Motrone | 64 | 43.54 N | 10.12 E |
| Motru | 38 | 44.50 N | 23.00 E |
| Mott | 198 | 46.22 N | 102.19 W |
| Motta | 64 | 45.36 N | 11.29 E |
| Motta Camastra | 70 | 37.54 N | 15.10 E |
| Motta d'Affermo | 70 | 37.59 N | 14.18 E |
| Motta di Livenza | 64 | 45.47 N | 12.36 E |
| Mottafollone | 68 | 39.39 N | 16.04 E |
| Motta Montecorvino | 68 | 41.30 N | 15.07 E |
| Motta San Giovanni | 68 | 38.00 N | 15.41 E |
| Motta Sant'Anastasia | 70 | 37.31 N | 14.58 E |
| Motta Visconti | 62 | 45.17 N | 8.59 E |
| Motten | 56 | 50.24 N | 9.46 E |
| Möttingen | 56 | 48.48 N | 10.35 E |
| Mottingham ➛[8] | 260 | 51.26 N | 0.03 E |
| Mottisfont | 42 | 51.02 N | 1.32 W |
| Mottola | 68 | 40.38 N | 17.03 E |
| Mottram in Longdendale | 262 | 53.27 N | 2.01 W |
| Motts Creek ≏ | 276 | 40.38 N | 73.45 W |
| Mottville, Mi., U.S. | 216 | 41.48 N | 85.45 W |
| Mottville, N.Y., U.S. | 210 | 42.59 N | 76.27 W |
| Motu ≏ | 172 | 37.51 S | 177.35 E |
| Motueka | 172 | 41.07 S | 173.00 E |
| Motueka ≏ | 172 | 41.05 S | 173.01 E |
| Motul [de Felipe Carrillo Puerto] | 232 | 21.06 N | 89.17 W |
| Motu One I[1] | 14 | 15.48 S | 154.33 W |
| Motupe | 248 | 6.09 S | 79.44 W |
| Motupena Point › | 175e | 6.32 S | 155.09 E |
| Motutapu I | 174k | 21.14 S | 159.43 W |
| Motygino | 86 | 58.11 N | 94.40 E |
| Motyklejka | 74 | 59.26 N | 148.38 E |
| Motyzhyn | 78 | 50.23 N | 29.55 E |
| Motyzlej | 80 | 54.54 N | 42.54 E |
| Mou | 175f | 21.05 S | 165.26 E |
| Mouanko | 152 | 3.39 N | 9.49 E |
| Mouans-Sartoux | 62 | 43.37 N | 6.58 E |
| Mouaskar | 148 | 35.45 N | 0.01 E |
| Mouchard | 58 | 46.58 N | 5.48 E |
| Mouchoir Bank ✣[2] | 238 | 20.57 N | 70.42 W |
| Mouchoir Passage ʮ | 238 | 21.10 N | 71.00 W |
| Moúdhros | 38 | 39.52 N | 25.16 E |
| Mouding | 102 | 25.24 N | 101.35 E |
| Moudjéria | 150 | 17.53 N | 12.20 W |
| Moudon | 58 | 46.40 N | 6.48 E |
| Moudongouma ≏ | 152 | 1.36 N | 17.24 E |
| Mouila | 152 | 1.52 S | 11.01 E |
| Mouit | 150 | 16.35 N | 13.05 W |
| Mouka | 152 | 7.16 N | 21.52 E |
| Moukden → Shenyang | 104 | 41.48 N | 123.27 E |
| Moulamein | 166 | 35.05 S | 144.02 E |
| Moulay-bou-Selham | 34 | 34.53 N | 6.15 W |
| Moulay-Idriss | 148 | 34.02 N | 5.27 W |
| Mouldsworth | 262 | 53.14 N | 2.44 W |
| Moule à Chique, Cap › | 241f | 13.43 N | 60.57 W |
| Moulhoulé | 144 | 12.36 N | 43.12 E |
| Moulin, Île du I | 275a | 45.41 N | 73.32 W |
| Moulin-des-Ponts | 58 | 46.20 N | 5.19 E |
| Moulineaux | 50 | 49.21 N | 0.58 E |
| Moulinet | 62 | 43.57 N | 7.25 E |
| Moulins | 32 | 46.34 N | 3.20 E |
| Moulins-la-Marche | 50 | 48.39 N | 0.29 E |
| Moulmein → Mawlamyine | 110 | 16.30 N | 97.38 E |
| Moulmeingyun | 110 | 16.23 N | 95.16 E |
| Moulouya, Oued ≏ | 148 | 35.05 N | 2.25 W |
| Moulton, Eng., U.K. | 44 | 53.13 N | 2.31 W |
| Moulton, Al., U.S. | 194 | 34.28 N | 87.17 W |
| Moulton, Ia., U.S. | 190 | 40.41 N | 92.40 W |
| Moulton, Tx., U.S. | 222 | 29.34 N | 97.09 W |
| Moultrie | 192 | 31.10 N | 83.47 W |
| Moultrie □[6] | 219 | 39.36 N | 88.37 W |
| Moultrie, Lake ⊜[1] | 192 | 33.20 N | 80.05 W |
| Mouly | 175f | 20.42 S | 166.25 E |
| Mound | 222 | 31.21 N | 97.38 W |
| Mound Bayou | 194 | 33.52 N | 90.43 W |
| Mound City, Il., U.S. | 194 | 37.05 N | 89.09 W |
| Mound City, Ks., U.S. | 198 | 38.08 N | 94.48 W |
| Mound City, Mo., U.S. | 194 | 40.07 N | 95.13 W |
| Mound City, S.D., U.S. | 198 | 45.43 N | 100.04 W |
| Mound City Group National Monument ♦ | 218 | 39.23 N | 83.00 W |
| Mound Lake ⊜ | 219 | 40.05 N | 90.17 W |
| Moundou | 146 | 8.34 N | 16.05 E |
| Moundridge | 198 | 38.12 N | 97.31 W |
| Mounds, Il., U.S. | 194 | 37.06 N | 89.11 W |
| Mounds, Ok., U.S. | 196 | 35.52 N | 96.03 W |
| Mounds State Park ♦ | 218 | 40.07 N | 85.37 W |
| Mounds State Recreation Area ♦ | 218 | 39.30 N | 84.59 W |
| Moundsville | 188 | 39.55 N | 80.44 W |
| Moundville | 194 | 32.59 N | 87.37 W |
| Moungali ➛[8] | 273b | 4.15 S | 15.17 E |
| Moung Roessei | 110 | 12.46 N | 103.27 E |
| Mounianzé ≏ | 152 | 0.32 N | 12.52 E |
| Mounier, Mont ∧ | 62 | 44.09 N | 6.58 E |
| Mounlapamôk | 110 | 14.20 N | 105.52 E |
| Mount Aetna | 208 | 40.25 N | 76.18 W |
| Mountain | 190 | 45.11 N | 88.28 W |
| Mountain □[4] | 116 | 17.20 N | 121.10 E |
| Mountain ≏ | 180 | 65.41 N | 128.50 W |
| Mountainair | 200 | 34.31 N | 106.14 W |
| Mountainaire | 200 | 35.05 N | 111.39 W |
| Mountain Ash | 42 | 51.42 N | 3.24 W |
| Mountain Brook | 194 | 33.30 N | 86.45 W |
| Mountain Chute Dam ➛[6] | 212 | 45.11 N | 76.54 W |
| Mountain City, Ga., U.S. | 192 | 34.55 N | 83.23 W |
| Mountain City, Nv., U.S. | 204 | 41.50 N | 115.57 W |
| Mountain City, Tn., U.S. | 192 | 36.28 N | 81.48 W |
| Mountain Creek | 194 | 32.43 N | 86.29 W |
| Mountain Creek ≏, Pa., U.S. | 208 | 40.09 N | 77.11 W |
| Mountain Creek ≏, Tx., U.S. | 222 | 32.42 N | 96.58 W |
| Mountain Creek Lake ⊜[1] | 222 | 32.43 N | 96.58 W |
| Mountain Dale | 210 | 41.41 N | 74.31 W |
| Mountain Grove | 194 | 37.07 N | 92.15 W |
| Mountain Home, Ar., U.S. | 194 | 36.20 N | 92.23 W |
| Mountain Home, Id., U.S. | 202 | 43.07 N | 115.41 W |
| Mountainhome, Pa., U.S. | 210 | 41.11 N | 75.17 W |
| Mountain Home Air Force Base ■ | 202 | 43.03 N | 115.52 W |
| Mountain Iron | 190 | 47.31 N | 92.37 W |
| Mountain Lake, Fl., U.S. | 220 | 27.57 N | 81.36 W |
| Mountain Lake, Mn., U.S. | 198 | 43.56 N | 94.55 W |
| Mountain Lake ⊜, On., Can. | 212 | 44.42 N | 81.03 W |
| Mountain Lake ⊜, On., Can. | 212 | 44.59 N | 78.43 W |
| Mountain Lake ⊜, N.J., U.S. | 276 | 40.53 N | 74.27 W |
| Mountain Lakes | 210 | 40.53 N | 74.26 W |
| Mountain Lodge | 210 | 41.23 N | 74.09 W |
| Mountain Nile (Baḥr al-Jabal) ≏ | 136 | 9.30 N | 30.30 E |
| Mountain Park | 182 | 52.55 N | 117.14 W |
| Mountain Pine | 194 | 34.34 N | 93.10 W |
| Mountain Point | 182 | 55.18 N | 131.32 W |
| Mountain Ranch | 226 | 38.14 N | 120.33 W |
| Mountainside | 208 | 40.40 N | 74.21 W |
| Mountain Spring Lakes | 276 | 41.02 N | 74.23 W |
| Mountain Valley Lake ⊜ | 279b | 40.18 N | 79.35 W |
| Mountain View, Ar., U.S. | 194 | 35.52 N | 92.07 W |
| Mountain View, Ca., U.S. | 226 | 37.23 N | 122.04 W |
| Mountain View, Mo., U.S. | 194 | 36.59 N | 91.42 W |
| Mountain View, Ok., U.S. | 196 | 35.05 N | 98.44 W |
| Mountain View, Wy., U.S. | 200 | 41.16 N | 110.20 W |
| Mountain View, Wy., U.S. | 200 | 42.51 N | 106.23 W |
| Mountain View Acres | 228 | 34.31 N | 117.24 W |
| Mountain Village | 180 | 62.05 N | 163.44 W |
| Mountain Zebra National Park ♦ | 158 | 32.16 S | 25.29 E |
| Mount Airy, Md., U.S. | 208 | 39.22 N | 77.09 W |
| Mount Airy, N.C., U.S. | 192 | 36.29 N | 80.36 W |
| Mount Airy ➛[8] | 285 | 40.04 N | 75.12 W |
| Mount Albert | 212 | 44.08 N | 79.19 W |
| Mount Alford | 171a | 28.04 S | 152.36 E |
| Mount Alida | 158 | 29.09 S | 30.18 E |
| Mount Angel | 224 | 45.04 N | 122.47 W |
| Mount Ann Park ♦ | 283 | 42.37 N | 70.44 W |
| Mount Arlington | 210 | 40.55 N | 74.38 W |
| Mount Aspiring National Park ♦ | 172 | 44.20 S | 168.45 E |
| Mount Assiniboine Provincial Park ♦ | 182 | 50.54 N | 115.40 W |
| Mount Auburn | 219 | 39.46 N | 89.16 W |
| Mount Augustus | 162 | 24.19 S | 116.54 E |
| Mount Ayliff | 158 | 30.54 S | 29.20 E |
| Mount Ayr, In., U.S. | 216 | 40.57 N | 87.18 W |
| Mount Ayr, Ia., U.S. | 198 | 40.42 N | 94.14 W |
| Mount Baldy | 280 | 34.14 N | 117.40 W |
| Mount Barker, Austl. | 162 | 34.38 S | 117.40 E |
| Mount Barker, Austl. | 168b | 35.04 S | 138.52 E |
| Mount Bellew Bridge | 48 | 53.28 N | 8.29 W |
| Mount Berry | 194 | 34.17 N | 85.11 W |
| Mount Bethel | 210 | 40.54 N | 75.07 W |
| Mount Blanchard | 216 | 40.53 N | 83.33 W |
| Mount Bold Reservoir ⊜[1] | 168b | 35.07 S | 138.42 E |
| Mount Brydges | 214 | 42.54 N | 81.29 W |
| Mount Buffalo National Park ♦ | 166 | 36.45 S | 146.45 E |
| Mount Buller | 169 | 37.10 S | 146.27 E |
| Mount Calm | 222 | 31.45 N | 96.53 W |
| Mount Carleton Provincial Park ♦ | 186 | 47.23 N | 66.50 W |
| Mount Carmel, Nf., Can. | 186 | 47.09 N | 53.29 W |
| Mount Carmel, Il., U.S. | 194 | 38.24 N | 87.45 W |
| Mount Carmel, Ky., U.S. | 218 | 38.29 N | 83.38 W |
| Mount Carmel, Oh., U.S. | 218 | 39.06 N | 84.18 W |
| Mount Carmel, Pa., U.S. | 208 | 40.47 N | 76.24 W |
| Mount Carmel Heights | 218 | 39.07 N | 84.18 W |
| Mount Carroll | 190 | 42.05 N | 89.58 W |
| Mount Cavenagh | 162 | 25.58 S | 133.15 E |
| Mount Charles | 275b | 43.41 N | 79.40 W |
| Mount Clare | 188 | 39.13 N | 80.21 W |
| Mount Clemens | 214 | 42.35 N | 82.52 W |
| Mount Colah | 274a | 33.41 S | 151.07 E |
| Mount Compass | 168b | 35.22 S | 138.37 E |
| Mount Cook | 172 | 43.44 S | 170.06 E |
| Mount Cook National Park ♦ | 172 | 43.35 S | 170.15 E |
| Mount Coot-tha Park ♦ | 171a | 27.28 S | 152.56 E |
| Mount Cory | 216 | 40.56 N | 83.50 W |
| Mount Crawford | 168b | 34.40 S | 138.57 E |
| Mount Crosby | 171a | 27.32 S | 152.48 E |
| Mount Currie Indian Reserve ➛[4] | 182 | 50.19 N | 122.42 W |
| Mount Dandenong | 274b | 37.50 S | 145.22 E |
| Mount Dennis ➛[8] | 275b | 43.42 N | 79.30 W |
| Mount Desert Island I | 188 | 44.20 N | 68.20 W |
| Mount Diablo Creek ≏ | 282 | 38.02 N | 122.02 W |
| Mount Diablo State Park ♦ | 226 | 37.51 N | 121.55 W |
| Mount Dora | 220 | 28.48 N | 81.38 W |
| Mount Doreen | 162 | 22.03 S | 131.18 E |
| Mount Druitt | 274a | 33.46 S | 150.49 E |
| Mount Eaton | 214 | 40.42 N | 81.42 W |
| Mount Eba | 166 | 30.12 S | 135.40 E |
| Mount Edgecumbe | 180 | 57.03 N | 135.21 W |
| Mount Edwards | 171a | 28.01 S | 152.31 E |
| Mount Elgon National Park ♦ | 154 | 1.07 N | 34.44 E |
| Mount Elizabeth | 164 | 16.15 S | 126.12 E |
| Mount Emu Creek ≏ | 169 | 38.18 S | 142.55 E |
| Mount Enterprise | 222 | 31.55 N | 94.41 W |
| Mount Ephraim | 285 | 39.52 N | 75.05 W |
| Mount Evelyn | 274b | 37.47 S | 145.23 E |
| Mount Fern | 276 | 40.52 N | 74.34 W |
| Mount Field National Park ♦ | 166 | 42.40 S | 146.35 E |
| Mount Fletcher | 158 | 30.40 S | 28.30 E |
| Mount Forest | 212 | 43.59 N | 80.44 W |
| Mount Freedom | 210 | 40.49 N | 74.34 W |
| Mount Frere | 158 | 31.00 S | 28.58 E |
| Mount Gambier | 166 | 37.50 S | 140.46 E |
| Mount Garnet | 166 | 17.41 S | 145.07 E |
| Mount Gay | 188 | 37.51 N | 82.00 W |
| Mount Gilead, N.C., U.S. | 192 | 35.12 N | 80.00 W |
| Mount Gilead, Oh., U.S. | 214 | 40.32 N | 82.49 W |
| Mount Gravatt | 171a | 27.33 S | 153.06 E |
| Mount Greenwood ➛[8] | 278 | 41.42 N | 87.43 W |
| Mount Gunson | 162 | 31.27 S | 137.11 E |
| Mount Hagen | 164 | 5.50 S | 144.15 E |
| Mount Hawke | 42 | 50.17 N | 5.12 W |
| Mount Hawthorn | 168a | 31.55 S | 115.50 E |
| Mount Healthy | 218 | 39.14 N | 84.32 W |
| Mount Hebron | 284b | 39.18 N | 76.50 W |
| Mount Helena | 168a | 31.53 S | 116.13 E |
| Mount Hermon, Ca., U.S. | 226 | 37.03 N | 122.04 W |
| Mount Hermon, Ma., U.S. | 207 | 42.40 N | 72.29 W |
| Mount Holly, N.J., U.S. | 208 | 39.59 N | 74.47 W |
| Mount Holly, N.C., U.S. | 192 | 35.17 N | 81.00 W |
| Mount Holly Springs | 208 | 40.07 N | 77.11 W |
| Mount Hope, Austl. | 166 | 34.07 S | 135.23 E |
| Mount Hope, On., Can. | 212 | 43.09 N | 79.55 W |
| Mount Hope, Ks., U.S. | 198 | 37.52 N | 97.39 W |
| Mount Hope, N.J., U.S. | 276 | 40.56 N | 74.33 W |
| Mount Hope, Oh., U.S. | 214 | 40.38 N | 81.47 W |
| Mount Hope, W.V., U.S. | 188 | 37.53 N | 81.09 W |
| Mount Hope Lake ⊜ | 276 | 40.56 N | 74.32 W |
| Mount Horeb | 190 | 43.00 N | 89.44 W |
| Mount Houston | 222 | 29.54 N | 95.18 W |
| Mount Howitt | 166 | 26.31 S | 142.16 E |
| Mount Hunter Rivulet ≏ | 274a | 34.02 S | 150.40 E |
| Mount Ida | 194 | 34.33 N | 93.38 W |
| Mount Isa | 166 | 20.44 S | 139.30 E |
| Mount Jackson, Pa., U.S. | 214 | 40.58 N | 80.26 W |
| Mount Jackson, Va., U.S. | 188 | 38.44 N | 78.38 W |
| Mount Jewett | 214 | 41.43 N | 78.38 W |
| Mount Juliet | 194 | 36.12 N | 86.31 W |
| Mount Kaputar National Park ♦ | 166 | 30.16 S | 150.10 E |
| Mount Kenya National Park ♦ | 154 | 0.09 S | 37.19 E |
| Mount Kisco | 210 | 41.12 N | 73.43 W |
| Mount Kokeby | 168a | 32.13 S | 116.58 E |
| Mountlake Terrace | 224 | 47.47 N | 122.18 W |
| Mount Laurel | 285 | 39.56 N | 74.54 W |
| Mount Lebanon | 214 | 40.21 N | 80.02 W |
| Mount Liberty | 214 | 40.21 N | 82.38 W |
| Mount Lofty Ranges ⛰ | 168b | 34.45 S | 139.00 E |
| Mount Magnet | 162 | 28.04 S | 117.49 E |
| Mount Manara | 166 | 32.29 S | 143.56 E |
| Mount Margaret, Austl. | 162 | 28.47 S | 122.11 E |
| Mount Margaret, Austl. | 166 | 26.54 S | 143.21 E |
| Mount Marion | 210 | 42.02 N | 73.59 W |
| Mount Martha | 169 | 38.17 S | 145.01 E |
| Mount Maunganui | 172 | 37.37 S | 176.11 E |
| Mount McKinley National Park → Denali National Park ♦ | 180 | 63.15 N | 150.30 W |
| Mount Mee | 171a | 27.04 S | 152.46 E |
| Mountmellick | 48 | 53.07 N | 7.20 W |
| Mount Misery Point › | 276 | 40.58 N | 73.05 W |
| Mount Mistake National Park ♦ | 171a | 27.53 S | 152.20 E |
| Mount Molloy | 164 | 16.41 S | 145.20 E |
| Mount Monger | 162 | 30.59 S | 121.53 E |
| Mount Moorosi | 158 | 30.16 S | 27.53 E |
| Mount Morgan | 166 | 23.39 S | 150.23 E |
| Mount Morris, Il., U.S. | 190 | 42.03 N | 89.25 W |
| Mount Morris, Mi., U.S. | 190 | 43.07 N | 83.41 W |
| Mount Morris, N.Y., U.S. | 210 | 42.43 N | 77.52 W |
| Mount Morris Dam ➛[6] | 210 | 42.44 N | 77.53 W |
| Mount Mulligan | 166 | 16.51 S | 144.52 E |
| Mount Nebo | 279b | 40.33 N | 80.06 W |
| Mountnessing | 260 | 51.39 N | 0.21 E |
| Mount Olive, Il., U.S. | 219 | 39.04 N | 89.43 W |
| Mount Olive, Ms., U.S. | 194 | 31.45 N | 89.39 W |
| Mount Olive, N.C., U.S. | 192 | 35.11 N | 78.04 W |
| Mount Oliver | 279b | 40.23 N | 79.59 W |
| Mount Olivet | 218 | 38.31 N | 84.02 W |
| Mount Orab | 218 | 39.01 N | 83.55 W |
| Mount Penn | 208 | 40.20 N | 75.54 W |
| Mount Perry | 166 | 25.11 S | 151.39 E |
| Mount Pleasant, Austl. | 168b | 34.47 S | 139.02 E |
| Mount Pleasant, On., Can. | 212 | 43.05 N | 80.19 W |
| Mount Pleasant, In., U.S. | 218 | 38.07 N | 86.31 W |
| Mount Pleasant, Ia., U.S. | 190 | 40.57 N | 91.33 W |
| Mount Pleasant, Mi., U.S. | 190 | 43.35 N | 84.46 W |
| Mount Pleasant, N.C., U.S. | 192 | 35.23 N | 80.26 W |
| Mount Pleasant, Oh., U.S. | 214 | 40.11 N | 80.48 W |
| Mount Pleasant, Pa., U.S. | 214 | 40.08 N | 79.32 W |
| Mount Pleasant, S.C., U.S. | 192 | 32.47 N | 79.51 W |
| Mount Pleasant, Tn., U.S. | 194 | 35.32 N | 87.12 W |
| Mount Pleasant, Tx., U.S. | 222 | 33.09 N | 94.58 W |
| Mount Pleasant, Ut., U.S. | 200 | 39.32 N | 111.27 W |
| Mount Pleasant Mills | 208 | 40.43 N | 77.01 W |
| Mount Pleasant Park ♦ | 284b | 39.22 N | 76.35 W |
| Mount Pocono | 210 | 41.07 N | 75.21 W |
| Mount Pritchard | 274a | 33.54 S | 150.54 E |
| Mount Prospect, S. Afr. | 158 | 27.29 S | 29.53 E |
| Mount Prospect, Il., U.S. | 216 | 42.03 N | 87.56 W |
| Mount Pulaski | 219 | 40.00 N | 89.16 W |
| Mount Rainier | 284c | 38.56 N | 76.57 W |
| Mount Rainier National Park ♦ | 224 | 46.52 N | 121.43 W |
| Mountrath | 48 | 53.00 N | 7.27 W |
| Mount Repose | 218 | 39.10 N | 84.14 W |
| Mount Revelstoke National Park ♦ | 182 | 51.06 N | 118.00 W |
| Mount Riddock | 162 | 23.03 S | 134.40 E |
| Mount Robson Provincial Park ♦ | 182 | 52.58 N | 113.50 W |
| Mount Rogers National Recreation Area ♦ | 192 | 36.42 N | 81.30 W |
| Mount Roskill | 172 | 36.55 S | 174.45 E |
| Mount Royal | 285 | 39.49 N | 75.13 W |
| Mount Rushmore National Memorial ⊥ | 198 | 43.50 N | 103.24 W |
| Mount Saint Helens National Volcanic Monument ♦ | 224 | 46.12 N | 122.11 W |
| Mount Sandiman | 162 | 24.24 S | 115.23 E |
| Mount Sarah | 162 | 26.57 S | 135.22 E |
| Mount Savage | 188 | 39.41 N | 78.52 W |
| Mount's Bay c | 42 | 50.03 N | 5.25 W |
| Mount Selinda | 154 | 20.25 S | 32.43 E |
| Mount Selman | 222 | 32.04 N | 95.17 W |
| Mount Seymour Provincial Park ♦ | 182 | 49.23 N | 122.57 W |
| Mount Shasta | 204 | 41.18 N | 122.18 W |
| Mount Sinai | 276 | 40.57 N | 73.02 W |
| Mount Sinai Harbor c | 276 | 40.57 N | 73.02 W |
| Mount Sinai Ridge ∧ | 218 | 39.04 N | 84.58 W |
| Mount Somers | 172 | 43.43 S | 171.24 E |
| Mountsorrel | 42 | 52.44 N | 1.07 W |
| Mount Spokane State Park ♦ | 202 | 47.58 N | 117.13 W |
| Mount Sterling, Il., U.S. | 219 | 39.59 N | 90.45 W |
| Mount Sterling, Ky., U.S. | 192 | 38.03 N | 83.56 W |
| Mount Sterling, Mo., U.S. | 219 | 38.28 N | 91.38 W |
| Mount Sterling, Oh., U.S. | 218 | 39.43 N | 83.15 W |
| Mount Stewart, P.E., Can. | 186 | 46.22 N | 62.52 W |
| Mount Stewart, S. Afr. | 158 | 33.10 S | 24.26 E |
| Mount Stromlo Observatory ♖[3] | 171b | 35.20 S | 149.00 E |
| Mount Summit | 218 | 40.00 N | 85.23 W |
| Mount Surprise | 166 | 18.09 S | 144.19 E |
| Mount Sylvia | 171a | 27.44 S | 152.14 E |
| Mount Tamalpais State Park ♦ | 226 | 37.54 N | 122.34 W |
| Mount Torrens | 168b | 34.52 S | 138.57 E |
| Mount Tremper | 210 | 42.03 N | 74.17 W |
| Mount Uniacke | 186 | 44.54 N | 63.50 W |
| Mount Union | 214 | 40.23 N | 77.52 W |
| Mount Upton | 210 | 42.25 N | 75.23 W |
| Mount Vernon, Austl. | 162 | 24.13 S | 118.14 E |
| Mount Vernon, Al., U.S. | 194 | 31.05 N | 88.00 W |
| Mount Vernon, Ga., U.S. | 192 | 32.10 N | 82.35 W |
| Mount Vernon, Il., U.S. | 219 | 38.19 N | 88.54 W |
| Mount Vernon, In., U.S. | 194 | 37.55 N | 87.53 W |
| Mount Vernon, Ia., U.S. | 190 | 41.55 N | 91.25 W |
| Mount Vernon, Ky., U.S. | 192 | 37.21 N | 84.20 W |
| Mount Vernon, Md., U.S. | 208 | 38.14 N | 75.49 W |
| Mount Vernon, Mo., U.S. | 194 | 37.06 N | 93.49 W |
| Mount Vernon, N.Y., U.S. | 210 | 42.45 N | 78.53 W |
| Mount Vernon, N.Y., U.S. | 210 | 40.54 N | 73.50 W |
| Mount Vernon, Oh., U.S. | 214 | 40.23 N | 82.29 W |
| Mount Vernon, Or., U.S. | 202 | 44.25 N | 119.06 W |
| Mount Vernon, Pa., U.S. | 279b | 40.17 N | 79.48 W |
| Mount Vernon, S.D., U.S. | 198 | 43.42 N | 98.15 W |
| Mount Vernon, Tx., U.S. | 222 | 33.11 N | 95.13 W |
| Mount Vernon, Wa., U.S. | 224 | 48.25 N | 122.19 W |
| Mount Vernon ⊥ | 208 | 38.47 N | 77.06 W |
| Mount Victoria | 170 | 33.35 S | 150.15 E |
| Mount Victory | 216 | 40.32 N | 83.31 W |
| Mount View | 207 | 41.38 N | 71.24 W |
| Mountville | 208 | 40.02 N | 76.26 W |
| Mount Vision | 210 | 42.35 N | 75.04 W |
| Mount Washington | 284b | 39.23 N | 76.41 W |
| Mount Washington ➛[8] | 284b | 39.22 N | 76.40 W |
| Mount Waverley | 274b | 37.53 S | 145.08 E |
| Mount Wedge, Austl. | 162 | 22.45 S | 132.09 E |
| Mount Wedge, Austl. | 162 | 33.29 S | 135.10 E |
| Mount Wellington | 172 | 36.54 S | 174.51 E |
| Mount Wilhelm National Park ♦ | 164 | 5.45 S | 145.05 E |
| Mount William National Park ♦ | 166 | 40.56 S | 148.15 E |
| Mount Willoughby | 162 | 27.58 S | 134.08 E |
| Mount Wilson Observatory ♖[3] | 228 | 34.14 N | 118.03 W |
| Mount Wolf | 208 | 40.03 N | 76.42 W |
| Mount Zion | 219 | 39.46 N | 88.53 W |
| Mounyaz | 146 | 10.41 N | 21.18 E |
| Moura, Austl. | 166 | 24.35 S | 149.58 E |
| Moura, Bra. | 246 | 1.27 S | 61.38 W |
| Moura, Port. | 34 | 38.08 N | 7.27 W |
| Moura, Tchad | 146 | 13.47 N | 21.13 E |
| Moura Brasil | 256 | 22.07 S | 43.09 W |
| Mouraya | 146 | 11.27 N | 20.59 E |
| Mourdi, Dépression du ⊥[7] | 146 | 18.10 N | 23.00 E |
| Mourdiah | 150 | 14.28 N | 7.28 W |
| Mouriès | 62 | 43.41 N | 4.52 E |
| Mourindi | 152 | 2.32 S | 10.48 E |
| Mourmelon-le-Grand | 50 | 49.08 N | 4.22 E |
| Mourne ≏ | 48 | 54.49 N | 7.28 W |
| Mourne Beg ≏ | 48 | 54.41 N | 7.39 W |
| Mourne Mountains ⛰ | 48 | 54.10 N | 6.04 W |
| Mousa I | 46a | 60.00 N | 1.11 W |
| Mouscron | 50 | 50.44 N | 3.13 E |
| Mousgougou | 146 | 10.47 N | 16.09 E |
| Moussa Ali ∧ | 144 | 12.28 N | 42.24 E |
| Mousseaux-sur-Seine | 261 | 49.03 N | 1.39 E |
| Moussey | 58 | 48.40 N | 6.47 E |
| Moussoro | 146 | 13.39 N | 16.29 E |
| Moussy-le-Neuf | 261 | 49.04 N | 2.36 E |
| Moussy-le-Vieux | 261 | 49.03 N | 2.38 E |
| Moustiers-Sainte-Marie | 62 | 43.51 N | 6.13 E |
| Moustique, Morne ∧ | 241o | 16.06 N | 61.44 W |
| Mouthe | 58 | 46.43 N | 6.12 E |
| Mouthier-Haute-Pierre | 58 | 47.02 N | 6.16 E |
| Moutier | 58 | 47.17 N | 7.23 E |
| Moûtiers | 62 | 45.29 N | 6.32 E |
| Moutiers-au-Perche | 50 | 48.29 N | 0.51 E |
| Moutnice | 61 | 49.02 N | 16.46 E |
| Moutohora | 172 | 38.17 S | 177.32 E |
| Moutomoukadi | 152 | 4.41 S | 13.15 E |
| Moutong | 112 | 0.28 N | 121.13 E |
| Mouy | 50 | 49.19 N | 2.19 E |
| Mouydir ⛰ | 148 | 24.45 N | 4.05 E |
| Mouyondzi | 152 | 3.58 S | 13.57 E |
| Mouzákion | 38 | 39.26 N | 21.40 E |
| Mouzarak | 146 | 13.11 N | 15.58 E |
| Mouzon | 56 | 49.36 N | 5.05 E |
| Mouzon ≏ | 58 | 48.21 N | 5.41 E |
| Moville, Ire. | 48 | 55.11 N | 7.03 W |
| Moville, Ia., U.S. | 198 | 42.29 N | 96.04 W |
| Mowang | 100 | 30.31 N | 113.34 E |
| Moweaqua | 219 | 39.37 N | 89.01 W |
| Mowein | 140 | 7.36 N | 28.11 E |
| Mowry Slough ≏ | 282 | 37.29 N | 122.03 W |
| Mowrystown | 218 | 39.02 N | 83.44 W |
| Mowu | 100 | 26.50 N | 117.42 E |
| Moxhe | 56 | 50.38 N | 5.05 E |
| Moxi | 107 | 30.18 N | 105.41 E |
| Moxico □[5] | 152 | 13.00 S | 20.30 E |
| Moxotó ≏ | 250 | 9.19 S | 38.14 W |
| Moy | 48 | 54.27 N | 6.42 W |
| Moy ≏ | 48 | 54.12 N | 9.08 W |
| Moy, Cnoc ∧[2] | 46 | 55.22 N | 5.46 W |
| Moya, Comores | 157a | 12.18 S | 44.27 E |
| Moya, Perú | 248 | 12.24 S | 75.10 W |
| Moyagee | 162 | 27.45 S | 117.54 E |
| Moyahua | 234 | 21.16 N | 103.10 W |
| Moyale, Ityo. | 144 | 3.30 N | 39.07 E |
| Moyale, Kenya | 154 | 3.32 N | 39.03 E |
| Moyamba | 150 | 8.10 N | 12.26 W |
| Moycullen | 48 | 53.21 N | 9.09 W |
| Moydans | 62 | 44.24 N | 5.30 E |
| Moÿ-de-l'Aisne | 50 | 49.45 N | 3.22 E |
| Moye Dao I | 98 | 36.55 N | 122.32 E |
| Moyen Atlas ⛰ | 148 | 33.30 N | 5.00 W |
| Moyen-Chari □[5] | 146 | 9.00 N | 18.00 E |
| Moyenmoutier | 58 | 48.23 N | 6.55 E |
| Moyenne-Sido | 146 | 8.13 N | 18.43 E |
| Moyenneville | 50 | 50.04 N | 1.45 E |
| Moyen-Ogooué □[4] | 152 | 0.30 S | 10.30 E |
| Moyenvic | 56 | 48.47 N | 6.33 E |
| Moyeuvre-Grande | 56 | 49.15 N | 6.02 E |
| Moyie | 182 | 49.17 N | 115.50 W |
| Moyie ≏ | 202 | 48.42 N | 116.11 W |
| Moyie Springs | 202 | 48.43 N | 116.11 W |
| Moylan | 285 | 39.54 N | 75.23 W |
| Moyle ≏ | 48 | 52.24 N | 7.39 W |
| Moyo | 154 | 3.39 N | 31.43 E |
| Moyo ≏ | 115b | 8.26 S | 117.28 E |
| Moyo, Pulau I | 115b | 8.15 S | 117.34 E |
| Moyobamba | 248 | 6.03 S | 76.58 W |
| Moyock | 208 | 36.31 N | 76.10 W |
| Moyogalpa | 236 | 11.32 N | 85.42 W |
| Moyowosi ≏ | 154 | 4.50 S | 31.24 E |
| Moyseyyivka | 83 | 49.14 N | 39.51 E |
| Moyu | 120 | 37.17 N | 79.44 E |
| Moyuta, Volcán ∧[1] | 236 | 14.02 N | 90.06 W |
| M'oža ≏, Europe | 76 | 55.27 N | 30.43 E |
| M'oža ≏, Ross. | 80 | 58.23 N | 44.54 E |
| Možajevka | 83 | 48.44 N | 39.45 E |
| Možajsk | 82 | 55.30 N | 36.01 E |
| Možajskij | 265a | 59.43 N | 30.07 E |
| Možajskoje vodochranilišče ⊜[1] | 82 | 55.35 N | 35.50 E |
| Mozambique → Moçambique | 154 | 15.03 S | 40.42 E |
| Mozambique (Moçambique) □[1] | 138 | 18.15 S | 35.00 E |
| Mozambique Channel ʮ | 138 | 19.00 S | 41.00 E |
| Mozambique Plateau ✣[3] | 10 | 32.00 S | 35.00 E |
| Mozarlândia | 255 | 14.47 S | 50.35 W |
| Možarovka | 86 | 51.09 N | 59.05 E |
| Možarov Majdan | 80 | 55.37 N | 45.53 E |
| Možary | 80 | 53.53 N | 41.02 E |
| Mozdok | 84 | 43.44 N | 44.38 E |
| Možga | 80 | 56.23 N | 52.17 E |
| Mozhabong Lake ⊜ | 190 | 46.57 N | 82.05 W |
| Mozia ⊥ | 70 | 37.52 N | 12.28 E |
| Mozichang | 107 | 29.20 N | 103.53 E |
| Mozolevo | 76 | 59.19 N | 33.51 E |
| Mozu | 270 | 34.34 N | 135.29 E |
| Mozuli | 76 | 56.36 N | 28.11 E |
| Mozzanica | 62 | 45.29 N | 9.41 E |
| Mozzano | 66 | 42.50 N | 13.31 E |
| Mozzate | 266b | 45.41 N | 8.57 E |
| Mpaka | 158 | 26.26 S | 31.47 E |
| Mpala | 154 | 6.45 S | 29.31 E |
| Mpama ≏ | 152 | 0.57 S | 15.39 E |
| Mpanda | 154 | 6.22 S | 31.02 E |
| Mpé | 152 | 2.54 S | 14.43 E |
| Mpese | 152 | 5.14 S | 15.33 E |
| Mpessoba | 150 | 12.40 N | 5.43 W |
| Mphoengs | 154 | 21.10 S | 27.51 E |
| Mpigi | 154 | 0.13 N | 32.42 E |
| Mpika | 154 | 11.54 S | 31.26 E |
| Mpila ➛[8] | 273b | 4.14 S | 15.18 E |
| Mpoka | 152 | 1.26 S | 17.02 E |
| Mpoko ≏ | 152 | 4.19 N | 18.33 E |
| Mporokoso | 154 | 9.23 S | 30.05 E |
| Mpouya | 152 | 2.37 S | 16.13 E |
| Mpraeso | 150 | 6.35 N | 0.44 W |
| Mpui | 154 | 8.21 S | 31.50 E |
| Mpulungu | 154 | 8.46 S | 31.07 E |
| Mpumalanga □[4] | 156 | 26.00 S | 30.30 E |
| Mpwapwa | 154 | 6.21 S | 36.29 E |
| Mqanduli | 158 | 31.48 S | 28.46 E |
| Mrągowo | 30 | 53.52 N | 21.19 E |
| Mrakovo | 86 | 52.43 N | 56.38 E |
| M'Ramani | 157a | 12.21 S | 44.32 E |
| Mranggen | 115a | 7.01 S | 110.31 E |
| Mras-Su ≏ | 86 | 53.45 N | 87.49 E |
| Mrhila, Jebel ∧ | 36 | 35.25 N | 9.14 E |
| Mrijo | 154 | 5.10 S | 36.15 E |
| Mrkonjić Grad | 36 | 44.25 N | 17.05 E |
| Mrkopalj | 36 | 45.19 N | 14.51 E |
| Mrocza | 30 | 53.14 N | 17.36 E |
| Msagali | 154 | 6.21 S | 36.18 E |
| M'Saken | 148 | 35.44 N | 10.35 E |
| Msata | 154 | 6.20 S | 38.23 E |
| Mscislaŭ | 76 | 54.02 N | 31.42 E |
| Msciž | 76 | 54.34 N | 28.10 E |
| Mšec | 54 | 50.10 N | 13.54 E |
| Mšeno | 54 | 50.27 N | 14.38 E |
| M'Sila | 148 | 35.46 N | 4.31 E |
| M'Sila, Oued ≏ | 34 | 35.46 N | 4.34 E |
| Mšinskaja | 76 | 59.01 N | 29.57 E |
| Msoro | 154 | 13.36 S | 31.55 E |
| Msta | 76 | 57.55 N | 34.29 E |
| Msta ≏ | 76 | 58.25 N | 31.20 E |
| Mstera | 80 | 56.23 N | 41.56 E |
| Mszana Dolna | 30 | 49.42 N | 20.05 E |
| Mszczonów | 30 | 51.58 N | 20.31 E |
| Mtakataka | 154 | 14.12 S | 34.32 E |
| Mtakuja | 154 | 7.22 S | 30.37 E |
| Mtama | 154 | 10.18 S | 39.22 E |
| Mtamvuna ≏ | 158 | 31.06 S | 30.12 E |
| Mtarazi National Park ♦ | 154 | 18.36 S | 32.50 E |
| Mtata ≏ | 158 | 31.58 S | 29.10 E |
| Mtelo ∧ | 154 | 1.39 N | 35.23 E |
| Mtilikwe ≏ | 154 | 21.09 S | 31.30 E |
| Mtito Andei | 154 | 2.41 S | 38.10 E |
| Mtowabaga | 154 | 2.30 S | 35.53 E |
| Mtsensk → Mcensk | 76 | 53.17 N | 36.35 E |
| Mtubatuba | 158 | 28.30 S | 32.08 E |
| Mtunzini | 158 | 28.57 S | 31.46 E |
| Mtwara | 154 | 10.16 S | 40.11 E |
| Mtwara □[4] | 154 | 11.00 S | 39.00 E |
| Mtyangimbori | 154 | 10.16 S | 35.31 E |
| Mu ≏, Mya. | 110 | 21.56 N | 95.38 E |
| Mu ≏, Nihon | 92a | 42.33 N | 141.56 E |
| Mu, Cerro ∧ | 246 | 9.29 N | 73.07 W |
| Mu'a | 174w | 21.11 S | 175.07 W |
| Muacandala | 152 | 10.02 S | 19.40 E |
| Mualama | 154 | 16.53 S | 38.17 E |
| Mualang | 112 | 0.42 N | 111.18 E |
| Mu'allaqah, Lubnān | 132 | 33.50 N | 35.54 E |
| Mu 'Allaqah, Sūd. | 140 | 13.28 N | 23.57 E |
| Muan | 98 | 34.58 N | 126.26 E |
| Muaná | 250 | 1.32 S | 49.13 W |
| Muanda | 152 | 5.56 S | 12.21 E |
| Muangai | 152 | 12.32 S | 19.51 E |
| Muang Bèng | 110 | 20.22 N | 101.44 E |
| Muang Hay | 110 | 21.03 N | 101.49 E |
| Muang Hinboun | 110 | 17.35 N | 104.36 E |
| Muang Hôngsa | 110 | 19.43 N | 101.20 E |
| Muang Houn | 110 | 20.09 N | 101.27 E |
| Muang Hounxianghoung | 110 | 21.37 N | 102.18 E |
| Muang Huang | 110 | 18.45 N | 103.42 E |
| Muang Khammouan | 110 | 17.24 N | 104.48 E |
| Muang Khao | 110 | 19.47 N | 103.29 E |
| Muang Khi | 110 | 18.27 N | 101.46 E |
| Muang Không | 110 | 14.07 N | 105.51 E |
| Muang Khôngxédôn | 110 | 15.34 N | 105.49 E |
| Muang La | 110 | 20.52 N | 102.07 E |
| Muang Liap | 110 | 18.29 N | 101.40 E |
| Muang Long | 110 | 20.57 N | 100.48 E |
| Muang Meung | 110 | 20.43 N | 100.28 E |
| Muang Ngoy, Lao | 102 | 20.43 N | 102.41 E |
| Muang Ngoy, Lao | 110 | 20.43 N | 102.41 |
| Muang Nong | 110 | 16.22 N | 106.30 |
| Muang Ou Nua | 110 | 22.18 N | 101.48 |
| Muang Ou Tai | 110 | 22.07 N | 101.48 E |
| Muang Pakbèng | 110 | 19.54 N | 101.08 E |
| Muang Pak-Lay | 110 | 18.12 N | 101.25 E |
| Muang Paktha | 110 | 20.06 N | 100.36 E |
| Muang Pakxan | 110 | 18.22 N | 103.39 E |
| Muang Peun | 110 | 20.13 N | 103.52 E |
| Muang Phalan | 110 | 16.39 N | 105.34 E |
| Muang Phiang | 110 | 19.06 N | 101.32 E |
| Muang Phônthong | 110 | 15.05 N | 105.39 E |
| Muang Phoun | 110 | 19.07 N | 102.43 E |
| Muang Sam Sip | 110 | 15.31 N | 104.44 E |
| Muang Sing | 110 | 21.11 N | 101.09 E |
| Muang Soum | 110 | 18.45 N | 102.36 E |
| Muang Souvannakhili | 110 | 15.23 N | 105.49 E |
| Muang Souy | 110 | 19.33 N | 102.52 E |
| Muang Sung | 110 | 20.19 N | 102.27 E |
| Muang Thadua | 110 | 19.26 N | 101.50 E |
| Muang Thatèng | 110 | 15.26 N | 106.23 E |
| Muang Thathôm | 110 | 19.00 N | 103.36 E |
| Muang Va | 110 | 21.53 N | 102.19 E |
| Muang Vangviang | 110 | 18.56 N | 102.27 E |
| Muang Vapi | 110 | 15.40 N | 105.55 E |
| Muang Xaignabouri | 110 | 19.15 N | 101.45 E |
| Muang Xamtong | 110 | 19.51 N | 103.51 E |
| Muang Xay | 110 | 20.42 N | 101.59 E |
| Muang Xépôn | 110 | 16.41 N | 106.14 E |
| Muang Xon | 110 | 20.27 N | 103.19 E |
| Muang Yo | 110 | 21.31 N | 101.51 E |
| Muang You | 110 | 19.49 N | 102.50 E |
| Muanza | 156 | 18.59 S | 34.48 E |
| Muar (Bandar Maharani) | 114 | 2.02 N | 102.34 E |
| Muar ≏ | 114 | 2.03 N | 102.35 E |
| Muara | 112 | 5.02 N | 115.02 E |
| Muaraaman | 112 | 3.07 S | 102.12 E |
| Muaraancalung | 112 | 0.27 N | 116.41 E |
| Muarabeliti | 112 | 3.15 S | 103.02 E |
| Muarabenangin | 112 | 0.58 S | 115.19 E |
| Muarabinuangeun | 115a | 6.50 S | 105.53 E |
| Muarabulian | 112 | 1.43 S | 103.15 E |
| Muarabungo | 112 | 1.28 S | 102.07 E |
| Muaradua | 112 | 4.32 S | 104.05 E |
| Muaraenim | 112 | 3.39 S | 103.48 E |
| Muaragusung | 112 | 1.35 N | 117.17 E |
| Muarajuloi | 112 | 0.12 S | 114.03 E |
| Muarakaman | 112 | 0.09 S | 116.43 E |
| Muarakelingi | 112 | 3.05 S | 103.14 E |
| Muarakumpe | 112 | 1.24 S | 104.00 E |
| Muaralabuh | 112 | 1.29 S | 101.03 E |
| Muaralakitan | 112 | 2.51 S | 103.19 E |
| Muaralasan | 112 | 1.48 N | 117.12 E |
| Muaralembu | 112 | 0.24 S | 101.21 E |
| Muaramawai | 112 | 0.37 N | 116.49 E |
| Muarapangean | 112 | 2.38 N | 116.41 E |
| Muarapantai | 112 | 0.45 S | 101.43 E |
| Muarapayang | 112 | 1.32 S | 115.48 E |
| Muararupit | 112 | 2.44 S | 102.54 E |
| Muarasabak | 112 | 1.08 S | 103.51 E |
| Muarasiberut | 108 | 1.36 S | 99.11 E |
| Muarasipongi | 112 | 0.37 N | 99.51 E |
| Muaratais | 114 | 1.17 N | 99.21 E |
| Muaratebo | 112 | 1.30 S | 102.26 E |
| Muarateladang | 112 | 2.50 S | 103.58 E |
| Muaratembesi | 112 | 1.42 S | 103.07 E |
| Muaratewe | 112 | 0.57 S | 114.53 E |
| Muaratuhup | 112 | 0.37 S | 114.50 E |
| Muaratunan | 112 | 1.24 S | 116.39 E |
| Muarawahau | 112 | 1.02 N | 116.52 E |
| Muāri, Rās › | 120 | 24.49 N | 66.40 E |
| Muasdale | 46 | 55.36 N | 5.41 W |
| Muá Ximica | 152 | 9.50 S | 18.41 E |
| Mubārakpur | 124 | 26.05 N | 83.18 E |
| Mubārakpur Dabās ➛[8] | 272a | 28.43 N | 77.03 E |
| Mubayyad ⏚[4] | 142 | 30.55 N | 32.48 E |
| Mubende | 154 | 0.35 N | 31.23 E |
| Mubi | 146 | 10.18 N | 13.20 E |
| Mubur, Pulau I | 112 | 3.20 N | 106.12 E |
| Mucaitá ≏ | 250 | 6.59 S | 42.40 W |
| Mucajaí ≏ | 246 | 2.25 N | 60.52 W |
| Mucambo | 250 | 3.54 S | 40.44 W |
| Mucári | 152 | 9.30 S | 16.54 E |
| Muccan | 162 | 20.38 S | 120.04 E |
| Muccia | 66 | 43.05 N | 13.02 E |
| Much | 56 | 50.54 N | 7.25 E |
| Mucha | 269d | 24.59 N | 121.34 E |
| Muchangpu | 100 | 31.55 N | 116.35 E |
| Muchanovo | 82 | 56.31 N | 38.20 E |
| Much Dewchurch | 42 | 51.59 N | 2.46 W |
| Muchea | 168a | 31.35 S | 115.59 E |
| Mücheln | 54 | 51.18 N | 11.48 E |
| Muchen | 89 | 48.10 N | 136.13 E |
| Muchengzhen | 107 | 29.47 N | 103.29 E |
| Much Hoole | 262 | 53.42 N | 2.48 W |
| Muchinga Escarpment ⊥[4] | 154 | 14.45 S | 29.30 E |
| Muchinga Mountains ⛰ | 154 | 12.20 S | 31.00 E |
| Muchino, Ross. | 80 | 58.11 N | 51.02 E |
| Muchino, Ross. | 89 | 52.16 N | 127.14 E |
| Muchor-Konduj | 88 | 52.25 N | 113.16 E |
| Muchrani | 84 | 41.56 N | 44.35 E |
| Muchtolovo | 80 | 55.27 N | 43.13 E |
| Muchuan | 107 | 28.55 N | 103.58 E |
| Much Wenlock | 42 | 52.36 N | 2.34 W |
| Mucifal | 266c | 38.48 N | 9.26 W |
| Mučikan | 88 | 53.02 N | 120.27 E |
| Muck I | 46 | 56.50 N | 6.15 W |
| Mücka | 54 | 51.18 N | 14.40 E |
| Muckadilla | 166 | 26.35 S | 148.23 E |
| Muckalee Creek ≏ | 192 | 31.38 N | 84.09 W |
| Muckamore | 48 | 54.41 N | 6.10 W |
| Mučkapskij | 80 | 51.52 N | 42.28 E |
| Mučkas | 24 | 64.02 N | 48.27 E |
| Mücke | 56 | 50.38 N | 9.03 E |
| Muckendorf an der Donau | 264b | 48.20 N | 16.09 E |
| Mucking | 260 | 51.30 N | 0.26 E |
| Muckle Roe I | 46a | 60.22 N | 1.27 W |
| Muckleshoot Indian Reservation ➛[4] | 224 | 47.16 N | 122.09 W |
| Muckno Lough ⊜ | 48 | 54.07 N | 6.42 W |
| Mucojo | 154 | 12.04 S | 40.28 E |
| Mucoma | 152 | 15.18 S | 13.39 E |
| Muconda | 152 | 10.34 S | 21.17 E |
| Mucope, Ang. | 152 | 16.24 S | 14.53 E |
| Mucope, Ang. | 152 | 8.42 S | 21.43 E |
| Mucrone, Monte ∧ | 62 | 45.36 N | 7.56 E |
| Mucubela | 154 | 16.55 S | 37.52 E |
| Mucuchíes | 246 | 8.45 N | 70.55 W |
| Mucugê | 255 | 13.00 S | 41.23 W |
| Mucuim ≏ | 248 | 6.33 S | 64.18 W |
| Muculo | 152 | 16.47 S | 14.51 E |
| Muçum | 252 | 29.10 S | 51.53 W |
| Mucumbura | 154 | 16.09 S | 31.31 E |
| Mucun | 100 | 26.44 N | 114.00 E |
| Mucupia | 156 | 18.01 S | 36.48 E |
| Mucupina, Monte ∧ | 236 | 15.08 N | 86.38 W |
| Mucur | 130 | 39.04 N | 34.23 E |
| Mucuri | 255 | 18.05 S | 39.34 W |
| Mucuri ≏ | 255 | 18.05 S | 39.34 W |
| Mucusso | 152 | 18.01 S | 21.25 E |
| Mud ≏, Ky., U.S. | 194 | 37.13 N | 86.54 W |
| Mud ≏, W.V., U.S. | 188 | 38.25 N | 82.17 W |
| Muda ≏ | 114 | 5.33 N | 100.22 E |
| Mudan ≏ | 89 | 46.22 N | 129.33 E |
| Mudanjiang | 89 | 44.35 N | 129.36 E |
| Mudanya | 130 | 40.22 N | 28.52 E |
| Mudau | 56 | 49.32 N | 9.11 E |
| Mudaysīsāt, Jabal ∧ | 132 | 31.39 N | 36.14 E |
| Mud Creek ≏, N.A. | 206 | 45.01 N | 72.24 W |
| Mud Creek ≏, U.S. | 198 | 43.17 N | 96.15 W |
| Mud Creek ≏, Il., U.S. | 219 | 38.21 N | 89.48 W |
| Mud Creek ≏, In., U.S. | 216 | 41.06 N | 86.21 W |


| Symbol | English | Deutsch | Español | Français | Português |
|---|---|---|---|---|---|
| ≏ | River | Fluß | Río | Rivière | Rio |
| ≊ | Canal | Kanal | Canal | Canal | Canal |
| ʟ | Waterfall, Rapids | Wasserfall, Stromschnellen | Cascada, Rápidos | Chute d'eau, Rapides | Cascata, Rápidos |
| ʮ | Strait | Meeresstraße | Estrecho | Détroit | Estreito |
| c | Bay, Gulf | Bucht, Golf | Bahía, Golfo | Baie, Golfe | Baía, Golfo |
| ⊜ | Lake, Lakes | See, Seen | Lago, Lagos | Lac, Lacs | Lago, Lagos |
| ≣ | Swamp | Sumpf | Pantano | Marais | Pântano |
| ⍓ | Ice Features, Glacier | Eis- und Gletscherformen | Accidentes Glaciales | Formes glaciaires | Acidentes glaciares |
| ⏚ | Other Hydrographic Features | Andere Hydrographische Objekte | Otros Elementos Hidrográficos | Autres données hydrographiques | Outros acidentes hidrográficos |
| ✣ | Submarine Features | Untermeerische Objekte | Accidentes Submarinos | Formes de relief sous-marin | Acidentes submarinos |
| □ | Political Unit | Politische Einheit | Unidad Politica | Entité politique | Unidade política |
| ♖ | Cultural Institution | Kulturelle Institution | Institución Cultural | Institution culturelle | Institução cultural |
| ⊥ | Historical Site | Historische Stätte | Sitio Histórico | Site historique | Sitio histórico |
| ♦ | Recreational Site | Erholungs- und Ferienort | Sitio de Recreo | Centre de loisirs | Area de Lazer |
| ⊠ | Airport | Flughafen | Aeropuerto | Aéroport | Aeroporto |
| ■ | Military Installation | Militäranlage | Instalación Militar | Installation militaire | Instalação militar |
| ➛ | Miscellaneous | Verschiedenes | Misceláneo | Divers | Diversos |

Mud Creek ≃, In., U.S. 216 40.26 N 85.55 W
Mud Creek ≃, Ne., U.S. 198 41.01 N 98.54 W
Mud Creek ≃, N.Y., U.S. 210 42.17 N 77.13 W
Mud Creek ≃, N.Y., U.S. 210 42.59 N 77.23 W
Mud Creek ≃, N.Y., U.S. 210 43.05 N 78.43 W
Mud Creek ≃, Ok., U.S. 196 33.55 N 97.28 W
Mud Creek ≃, S.D., U.S. 198 45.11 N 98.24 W
Mud Creek ≃, Tx., U.S. 222 31.48 N 94.58 W
Muddus Nationalpark ♦ 24 67.00 N 20.16 E
Muddy ≃, Nv., U.S. 204 36.27 N 114.22 W
Muddy ≃, Wa., U.S. 224 46.04 N 122.01 W
Muddy Boggy Creek ≃ 196 34.03 N 95.47 W
Muddy Branch ≃ 284c 39.03 N 77.18 W
Muddy Brook ≃ 276 41.07 N 73.20 W
Muddy Creek ≃, U.S. 276 41.03 N 74.02 W
Muddy Creek ≃, Mo., U.S. 194 38.51 N 93.03 W
Muddy Creek ≃, Mt., U.S. 202 47.56 N 111.46 W
Muddy Creek ≃, Oh., U.S. 214 41.27 N 83.03 W
Muddy Creek ≃, Pa., U.S. 208 39.47 N 76.18 W
Muddy Creek ≃, Ut,. U.S. 200 38.24 N 110.42 W
Muddy Creek ≃, Wy., U.S. 198 42.35 N 104.57 W
Muddy Creek ≃, Wy., U.S. 200 41.59 N 106.08 W
Muddy Creek ≃, Wy., U.S. 200 41.32 N 110.13 W
Muddy Creek ≃, Wy., U.S. 200 41.01 N 107.42 W
Muddy Creek ≃, Wy., U.S. 202 43.17 N 108.14 W
Muddy Fork ≃ 224 46.22 N 121.34 W
Muddy Gut c 284b 39.17 N 76.26 W
Muddy Peak ∧ 204 36.18 N 114.42 W
Müden, Dtsch. 52 52.52 N 10.07 E
Müden, Dtsch. 54 52.31 N 10.22 E
Mudersbach 56 50.50 N 7.57 E
Mudgee 166 32.36 S 149.35 E
Mudgeeraba 171a 28.04 S 153.22 E
Mudhol 122 16.21 N 75.17 E
Mud Island I 171a 27.20 S 153.15 E
Mud Islands II 169 38.17 S 144.45 E
Mudjatik ≃ 184 56.02 N 107.36 W
Mudjuga 24 63.46 N 39.15 E
Mud Lake ⊜, Id., U.S. 202 43.53 N 112.24 W
Mud Lake ⊜, Nv., U.S. 204 37.52 N 117.04 W
Mud Lake ⊜, N.Y., U.S. 212 44.30 N 75.28 W
Mud Lake Reservoir ⊜1 198 45.50 N 98.10 W
Mudon 110 16.15 N 97.44 E
Mudongzhen 102 29.35 N 106.51 E
Mudu 106 31.15 N 120.30 E
Mudug □4 144 6.15 N 48.00 E
Mudurnu 130 40.28 N 31.13 E
Mudurnu ≃ 130 40.49 N 30.33 E
M'ud'ur'um ≃ 85 40.53 N 76.36 E
Mueda 154 11.39 S 39.33 E
Muelle de los Bueyes 236 12.04 N 84.32 W
Mueller, Mount ∧2 162 19.54 S 127.51 E
Muenster 196 33.39 N 97.23 W
Mu'er 107 29.48 N 106.37 E
Muerte, Valle de la → Death Valley V 204 36.30 N 117.00 W
Muerto ≃ 252 23.02 S 62.29 W
Muerto, Mar → Dead Sea ⊜ 132 31.30 N 35.30 E
Mufulira 154 12.33 S 28.14 E
Mufuma 152 9.04 S 17.06 E
Mufu Shan ∧ 100 29.02 N 113.54 E
Mufu Shan ⋀ 100 29.00 N 114.00 E
Muğan düzü ≚ 84 39.40 N 48.15 E
Mugang 100 29.44 N 115.14 E
Mugazine 158 26.07 S 32.30 E
Mugegawa 94 35.31 N 136.51 E
Mugello V 66 43.55 N 11.30 E
Mügeln 54 51.14 N 13.02 E
Muger ≃ 144 9.54 N 37.57 E
Müggelberge ∧2 264a 52.25 N 13.39 E
Müggelheim ◆8 264a 52.25 N 13.40 E
Muggia 64 45.36 N 13.46 E
Muggio 266b 45.36 N 9.14 E
Mughal Sarāi 124 25.18 N 83.07 E
Mugi, Nihon 94 35.34 N 137.01 E
Mugi, Nihon 96 33.40 N 134.25 E
Mu Gia, Deo )( 110 17.40 N 105.47 E
Muginga 152 8.20 S 17.37 E
Muğla 130 37.12 N 28.22 E
Muğla □4 130 37.10 N 28.30 E
Mugodžarskaja 86 48.36 N 58.27 E
Mugodžary, gory ⋀2 86 49.00 N 58.40 E
Mugombazi 154 5.50 S 30.14 E
Mugo-ri 98 38.58 N 126.31 E
Mugrejevskij 80 56.36 N 42.21 E
Mugron 32 43.45 N 0.45 W
Mugu Karnālī ≃ 124 29.38 N 81.52 E
Mugur-Aksy 86 50.21 N 90.30 E
Mūḥ, Sabkhat al- ⊜ 130 34.30 N 38.20 E
Muhala 154 5.40 S 28.43 E
Muhamdi 124 27.57 N 80.13 E
Muḥammad, Ra's ≻ 140 27.44 N 34.15 E
Muhammadābād 124 26.02 N 83.23 E
Muhammadpur 126 23.24 N 89.36 E
Muḥammad Qawl 140 20.54 N 37.05 E
Muḥavec ≃ 76 52.05 N 23.39 E
Muḥayshir, Birkat ⊜ 142 30.43 N 31.56 E
Muheza 154 5.10 S 38.47 E
Muḥīṭ, Maṣrif al- ≡ 273c 30.07 N 31.06 E
Mühlacker 56 48.57 N 8.50 E
Mühlau 54 50.54 N 12.45 E
Mühlbach am Hochkönig 64 47.22 N 13.08 E
Muhlbach-sur-Munster 58 48.02 N 7.05 E
Mühlberg 54 51.26 N 13.13 E
Mühldorf 61 48.22 N 15.21 E
Mühldorf am Inn 60 48.15 N 12.32 E
Mühlen → Molini di Tures 64 46.54 N 11.56 E
Mühlenbeck 54 52.40 N 13.22 E
Mühlenbecker See ⊜ 264a 52.41 N 13.24 E
Muhlenberg 210 41.14 N 76.09 W
Mühlen-Berg ∧2 264a 52.23 N 13.15 E
Mühlen Eichsen 54 53.45 N 11.15 E
Mühlenfliess ≃ 264a 52.26 N 13.41 E
Mühlenrahmede 263 51.16 N 7.40 E
Mühlhausen, Dtsch. 54 51.12 N 10.27 E
Mühlhausen, Dtsch. 60 49.10 N 11.27 E
Mühlhausen, Dtsch. 263 51.33 N 7.44 E
Mühlhausen im Täle 56 48.34 N 9.39 E
Mühlheim 56 50.07 N 8.50 E
Mühlheim an der Donau 58 48.01 N 8.53 E
Mühlig-Hofmann Mountains ⋀ 9 72.00 S 5.20 E
Mühlleiten 264b 48.10 N 16.34 E
Mühltroff 54 50.32 N 11.55 E
Mühlviertel ◆1 30 48.25 N 14.10 E
Muhola 26 63.20 N 25.05 E
Muhoro 154 1.01 S 34.07 E
Muhos 26 64.48 N 25.59 E
Muḥradah 130 35.15 N 36.35 E
Mühringen 58 48.25 N 8.46 E
Muhu I 76 58.38 N 23.15 E
Muhula 154 13.53 S 39.30 E
Muhulu 154 1.03 S 27.17 E
Muhutwe 154 1.33 S 31.42 E
Muhu väin ⊔ 76 58.45 N 23.20 E
Muhuwesi ≃ 154 11.16 S 37.58 E
Muick, Loch ⊜ 46 56.55 N 3.10 W
Muiden 52 52.19 N 5.04 E
Muiderslot ⊥ 52 52.20 N 5.10 E
Muides-sur-Loire 50 47.40 N 1.31 E
Muié 152 14.25 S 20.36 E
Mui Hopohoponga Point ≻ 174w 21.09 S 175.02 W
Muikaichi 96 34.21 N 131.56 E
Muikamachi 94 37.04 N 138.53 E
Muine Bheag (Bagenalstown) 48 52.41 N 6.58 W
Muir, Mi., U.S. 216 42.59 N 84.56 W
Muir, Pa., U.S. 208 40.36 N 76.31 W
Muir, Mount ∧ 180 61.06 N 148.24 W
Muir Beach 282 37.52 N 122.35 W
Muirdrum 46 56.31 N 2.42 W
Muirkirk, Scot., U.K. 46 55.31 N 4.04 W
Muirkirk, Md., U.S. 284c 39.03 N 76.53 W
Muir of Ord 46 57.31 N 4.27 W
Muiron Islands II 162 21.35 S 114.20 E
Muir Seamount ✦3 16 33.41 N 62.30 W
Muirtown 46 56.16 N 3.45 W
Muir Woods 282 37.53 N 122.34 W
Muir Woods National Monument ♦ 226 37.54 N 122.33 W
Muiskraal 158 33.56 S 21.13 E
Muisne 246 0.36 N 80.02 W
Muite 154 14.02 S 39.00 E
Mui Wo 271d 22.16 N 113.59 E
Muizen, Bel. 50 51.01 N 4.31 E
Muizen, Bel. 56 50.46 N 5.10 E
Muja, Ityo. 144 12.02 N 39.29 E
Muja, Ross. 88 56.24 N 115.39 E
Muja ≃ 88 56.24 N 115.39 E
Mujāhidpur ◆8 272a 28.34 N 77.13 E
Mujang-ni 98 35.26 N 126.32 E
Mujezerskij 24 63.57 N 31.55 E
Mujiapucun 104 41.06 N 122.48 E
Mujiayu 105 40.24 N 116.55 E
Mujimbeji Mission 154 12.11 S 24.57 E
Mujnak 86 43.48 N 59.02 E
Muju 98 36.02 N 127.40 E
Mukacheve 78 48.27 N 22.45 E
Mukah 112 2.54 N 112.06 E
Mukaishima 96 34.20 N 133.10 E
Mukalla → Al-Mukallā 144 14.32 N 49.08 E
Mukandpur ◆8 272a 28.44 N 77.11 E
Mukandwara 120 24.49 N 75.59 E
Mukawa 94 35.47 N 138.23 E
Mukāwir 132 31.34 N 35.38 E
Mukāwir ⊥ 132 31.34 N 35.38 E
Mukawwar I 140 20.48 N 37.13 E
Mukdahan 110 16.32 N 104.43 E
Mukden → Shenyang 104 41.48 N 123.27 E
Muke Arba 144 8.57 N 42.09 E
Mukebo 154 6.49 S 28.03 E
Mukeriān 123 31.57 N 75.37 E
Mukharram al-Fawqānī 130 34.49 N 37.04 E
Mukhmās 132 31.52 N 35.17 E
Mukho 98 37.33 N 129.06 E
Mukilteo 224 47.56 N 122.18 W
Mukinbudin 162 30.54 S 118.13 E
Mukinge Hill 154 13.29 S 25.52 E
Mukō 96 34.56 N 135.42 E
Muko ≃ 96 34.41 N 135.23 E
Mukomuko 112 2.35 S 101.07 E
Mukomwenze 154 6.52 S 27.16 E
Mukoshima-rettō II 14 27.37 N 142.10 E
Mukry 128 37.36 N 65.44 E
Muksi-ri 98 39.52 N 125.54 E
Muksu ≃ 85 39.15 N 71.23 E
Muksūdpur 126 23.18 N 89.51 E
Muktāgācha 124 24.46 N 90.14 E
Muktsar 123 30.29 N 74.31 E
Mukuku 154 12.09 S 29.49 E
Mukuleshi ≃ 154 10.21 S 24.30 E
Mukur 86 48.03 N 54.30 E
Mukusaki 115b 8.33 S 121.37 E
Mukutan 154 0.38 N 36.16 E
Mukutawa ≃ 184 53.10 N 97.28 W
Mukwela 154 17.02 S 26.39 E
Mukwonago 216 42.51 N 88.19 W
Mūl 122 20.04 N 79.40 E
Mula, Esp. 34 38.03 N 1.30 W
Mula, Zhg. 102 29.40 N 100.39 E
Mula ≃, India 122 19.32 N 74.50 E
Mula ≃, India 122 18.34 N 74.20 E
Mūla ≃, Pāk. 120 27.57 N 67.36 E
Mulādi 126 22.54 N 90.25 E
Muladu I 122 7.01 N 72.59 E
Mulaly 86 45.27 N 78.19 E
Mulan 89 45.57 N 128.03 E
Muland ◆8 272c 19.10 N 72.57 E
Mulanda 152 14.41 S 21.48 E
Mulanje, Malaŵi 154 16.03 S 35.31 E
Mulanje, Moç. 154 16.03 S 35.45 E
Mulargia, Lago ⊜1 71 39.37 N 9.14 E
Mulas, Punta ≻ 240m 18.09 N 65.27 W
Mulas, Punta de ≻ 240p 21.01 N 75.35 W
Mulatos 232 28.39 N 108.51 W
Mulayit Taung ∧ 110 16.11 N 98.32 E
Mulazzo 64 44.19 N 9.53 E
Mulbāgal 122 13.10 N 78.24 E
Mulben 46 57.31 N 3.06 W
Mulberry, Ar., U.S. 194 35.30 N 94.03 W
Mulberry, Fl., U.S. 220 27.53 N 81.58 W
Mulberry, In., U.S. 216 40.20 N 86.39 W
Mulberry, Oh., U.S. 218 39.11 N 84.14 W
Mulberry ≃ 194 35.28 N 94.03 W
Mulberry Creek ≃, Al., U.S. 194 32.27 N 86.52 W
Mulberry Creek ≃, Tx., U.S. 196 34.37 N 100.55 W
Mulberry Fork ≃ 194 33.33 N 87.11 W
Mulberry Grove 219 38.55 N 89.16 W
Mulberry Mountain ∧ 194 35.42 N 92.56 W
Mulchatna ≃ 180 59.39 N 157.08 W
Mulchén 252 37.43 S 72.14 W
Mulda, Dtsch. 54 50.48 N 13.25 E
Mul'da, Ross. 24 67.28 N 63.34 E
Mulde ≃ 54 51.52 N 12.15 E
Muldenstein 54 51.40 N 12.19 E
Muldersdrif se Loop ≃ 273d 26.06 S 27.51 E
Muldersvlei 158 30.41 S 22.13 E
Muldoon 222 29.49 N 97.04 W
Muldraugh 194 37.56 N 85.59 W
Muldrow 194 35.24 N 94.35 W
Mule, Lac la ⊜ 186 51.33 N 65.35 W
Muleba 154 1.49 S 31.40 E
Mule Creek ≃ 198 37.05 N 99.00 W
Mulegé 232 26.53 N 112.01 W
Mulegns 58 46.33 N 9.37 E
Mulei 86 43.49 N 90.11 E
Mules (Mauls) 64 46.51 N 11.31 E
Mules, Pulau I 115b 8.54 S 120.17 E
Muleshoe 196 34.13 N 102.43 W
Mulevala 154 16.30 S 37.30 E
Mulga Downs 162 22.08 S 118.26 E
Mulgathing 162 30.15 S 134.00 E
Mulgathing Rocks ∧ 162 30.14 S 133.58 E
Mulghar 126 22.46 N 89.45 E
Mulgoa 170 33.50 S 150.40 E
Mulgoa Creek ≃ 274a 33.46 S 150.39 E
Mulgowie 171a 27.43 S 152.22 E
Mulgrave, Austl. 274b 37.56 S 145.12 E
Mulgrave, N.S., Can. 186 45.37 N 61.23 W
Mulgrave Hills ⋀2 180 67.42 N 163.24 W
Mulgul 162 24.49 S 118.26 E
Mulhacén ∧ 34 37.03 N 3.19 W
Mulhall 196 36.03 N 97.24 W
Mülhausen → Mulhouse 58 47.45 N 7.20 E
Mülheim 56 49.54 N 7.01 E
Mülheim an der Ruhr 56 51.24 N 6.54 E
Mülheimer Ruhrtalbrüke ◆5 263 51.23 N 6.54 E
Mülheim-Karlich 56 50.21 N 7.28 E
Mulhouse (Mülhausen) 58 47.45 N 7.20 E
Muli 102 27.50 N 101.15 E
Muling, Zhg. 89 44.56 N 130.31 E
Muling, Zhg. 89 44.31 N 130.13 E
Muling ≃ 89 45.53 N 133.30 E
Mulini, Capo ≻ 70 37.34 N 15.10 E
Mulino 224 45.13 N 122.34 W
Mulinu'u, Cape ≻ 175a 13.26 S 172.43 W
Mulita ≃ 116 7.18 N 124.52 E
Mulkear ≃ 48 52.40 N 8.33 W
Mūlki 122 13.06 N 74.48 E
Mull, Island of I 46 56.27 N 6.00 W
Mull, Sound of ⊔ 46 56.32 N 5.50 W
Mullagh 48 53.49 N 6.57 W
Mullaghareirk Mountains ⋀ 48 52.20 N 9.10 W
Mullaghcleevaun ∧ 48 53.06 N 6.24 W
Mullaghmore ∧ 48 54.52 N 6.51 W
Mullaloo Point ≻ 168a 31.48 S 115.44 E
Mullan 202 47.28 N 115.48 W
Mullen 198 42.02 N 101.02 W
Müllenbach 56 50.19 N 6.55 E
Mullengudgery 166 31.41 S 147.26 E
Mullens 192 37.34 N 81.22 W
Muller, Pegunungan ⋀ 112 0.40 N 113.50 E
Muller Creek ≃ 162 22.29 S 134.30 E
Muller Range ⋀ 164 5.35 S 142.15 E
Mullerup 41 55.30 N 11.13 E
Mullet Key I 220 27.37 N 82.44 W
Mullet Peninsula ≻1 48 54.12 N 10.00 W
Mullett Lake ⊜ 190 45.30 N 84.30 W
Mullewa 162 28.33 S 115.31 E
Mull Head ≻, Scot., U.K. 46 59.23 N 2.54 W
Mull Head ≻, Scot., U.K. 46 58.58 N 2.43 W
Müllheim 58 47.48 N 7.38 E
Mullhyttan 40 59.09 N 14.41 E
Mullica ≃ 208 39.33 N 74.25 W
Mullica, Alquatka Branch ≃ 285 39.47 N 74.48 W
Mullica, Sleeper Branch ≃ 285 39.39 N 74.40 W
Mullica Hill 208 39.44 N 75.13 W
Mulligan ≃ 166 25.00 S 138.30 E
Mulliken 216 42.45 N 84.53 W
Mullin 196 31.33 N 98.40 W
Mullinahone 48 52.30 N 7.30 W
Mullinavat 48 52.21 N 7.10 W
Mullingar 48 53.32 N 7.20 W
Mullins 192 34.12 N 79.15 W
Mullinville 198 37.35 N 99.28 W
Mullion 42 50.01 N 5.15 W
Mulloon Creek ≃ 171b 35.12 S 149.38 E
Mullovka 80 54.13 N 49.25 E
Müllrose 54 52.14 N 14.25 E
Mullsjö 26 57.55 N 13.53 E
Mullumbimby 166 28.33 S 153.30 E
Mullum Mullum Creek ≃ 274b 37.44 S 145.10 E
Mulobezi 154 16.48 S 25.09 E
Mulonda Funda 154 11.06 S 25.28 E
Mulondo 152 15.39 S 15.14 E
Mulongo 154 7.50 S 27.00 E
Mulshi Lake ⊜1 122 18.30 N 73.30 E
Multai 120 21.46 N 78.15 E
Multān 123 30.11 N 71.29 E
Multen ⊜ 40 59.10 N 14.37 E
Multia 26 62.25 N 24.47 E
Multnomah □6 224 45.30 N 122.22 W
Multnomah Channel ≃1 224 45.51 N 122.52 W
Multnomah Falls ∟ 224 45.35 N 122.07 W
Mulu, Gunong ∧ 112 4.04 N 114.56 E
Mulumbe, Monts ⋀ 154 8.16 S 28.16 E
Mulungushi 154 14.40 S 28.50 E
Mulungushi Dam ◆6 154 14.40 S 28.50 E
Mulvane 198 37.28 N 97.14 W
Mulwad 140 18.39 N 30.35 E
Mulyah Mountain ∧ 166 30.37 S 144.31 E
Muma 152 3.24 N 23.15 E
Mumbles Head ≻ 42 51.35 N 3.59 W
Mumbondo 152 10.09 S 14.15 E
Mumbra 272c 19.11 N 73.01 E
Mumbwa 154 14.59 S 27.04 E
Mumcular 130 37.05 N 27.40 E
Mume 154 9.40 S 27.26 E
Mumen 102 32.09 N 106.28 E
Mumeng 164 7.00 S 146.35 E
Mumford, N.Y., U.S. 210 42.59 N 77.52 W
Mumford, Tx., U.S. 222 30.44 N 96.34 W
Mumias 154 0.20 N 34.29 E
Mümling ≃ 56 49.50 N 9.09 E
Mumoni ∧ 154 0.31 S 38.01 E
Mumra 80 45.47 N 47.41 E
Mumu 140 12.06 N 23.42 E
Mumungwe 156 21.59 S 26.24 E
Mun ≃ 110 15.19 N 105.30 E
Mun, Jabal ∧ 140 14.08 N 22.42 E
Munā, Ar. Su. 144 21.25 N 39.52 E
Muna, Méx. 232 20.29 N 89.43 W
Muna ≃ 74 67.52 N 123.06 E
Muna, Pulau I 112 5.00 S 122.30 E
Muna, Selat ⊔ 112 5.15 S 122.10 E
Munā al-Amīr 142 29.54 N 31.15 E
Munābāo 120 25.45 N 70.17 E
Munajly 86 46.47 N 54.31 E
Munakata 96 33.50 N 130.35 E
Munam-ni 98 38.41 N 126.54 E
Munam-san ∧ 98 40.26 N 127.22 E
Munbong-ni 271b 37.43 N 126.49 E
Muncar 115a 8.26 S 114.20 E
Münchberg 54 50.11 N 11.47 E
Müncheberg 54 52.30 N 14.08 E
Münchehofe 264a 52.30 N 13.40 E
München (Munich) 60 48.08 N 11.34 E
Münchenbernsdorf 54 50.49 N 11.56 E
Münchenbuchsee 58 47.01 N 7.27 E
Münchendorf 264b 48.02 N 16.23 E
München-Erding, Flughafen ⊠ 60 48.22 N 11.48 E
München-Gladbach → Mönchengladbach 56 51.12 N 6.28 E
München-Riem, Flughafen ⊠ 60 48.08 N 11.41 E
Münchenstein 58 47.31 N 7.37 E
Münchhausen 56 50.57 N 8.43 E
Munchique, Cerro ∧ 246 2.32 N 76.57 W
Munchique, Parque Nacional ♦ 246 2.30 N 77.10 W
Munch'ŏn 98 39.16 N 127.15 E
Muncie 216 40.11 N 85.23 W
Muncusun 130 38.54 N 35.33 E
Muncy 210 41.12 N 76.47 W
Muncy Creek ≃ 210 41.13 N 76.48 W
Muncy Valley 210 41.21 N 76.35 W
Mundare 182 53.36 N 112.20 W
Mundaring 168a 31.54 S 116.10 E
Munday 196 33.26 N 99.37 W
Mundelein 216 42.15 N 88.00 W
Mündelheim ◆8 263 51.21 N 6.41 E
Münden 56 51.25 N 9.39 E
Munderfing 60 48.05 N 13.11 E
Munderkingen 58 48.14 N 9.38 E
Munderoo ∧ 171b 35.48 S 147.47 E
Mundesley 42 52.53 N 1.26 E
Mundijong 168a 32.18 S 115.59 E
Mundiwindi 162 23.52 S 120.09 E
Mūndka ◆8 272a 28.41 N 77.02 E
Mundo ≃ 34 38.19 N 1.40 W
Mundolsheim 58 48.39 N 7.42 E
Mundon Hill 260 51.41 N 0.42 E
Mundo Novo 255 11.52 S 40.28 W
Mundra 120 22.51 N 69.44 E
Mundrabilla 162 31.52 S 127.51 E
Mundubbera 166 25.36 S 151.18 E
Mundybaš 86 53.14 N 87.19 E
Mundytau, gora ∧ 85 38.00 N 68.27 E
Munene 154 20.38 S 30.03 E
Munenga 152 10.02 S 14.41 E
Munera 34 39.02 N 2.28 W
Munford 194 35.26 N 89.48 W
Munfordville 194 37.16 N 85.53 W
Mungallala 166 26.27 S 147.33 E
Mungallala Creek ≃ 166 28.05 S 147.15 E
Mungana 166 17.07 S 144.24 E
Mungaoli 124 24.25 N 78.06 E
Mungári 154 17.12 S 33.31 E
Mungar Junction 166 25.36 S 152.36 E
Mungau 152 13.56 S 21.55 E
Mungbere 154 2.38 N 28.30 E
Mungeli 124 22.04 N 81.41 E
Munger 124 25.23 N 86.28 E
Mungeranie 162 28.00 S 138.36 E
Mungindi 166 28.58 S 148.59 E
Munglinup 162 33.43 S 120.51 E
Mungo 152 11.49 S 16.16 E
Mungo National Park ♦ 166 33.44 S 143.02 E
Mungra Badshāhpur 124 25.40 N 82.11 E
Mungun-Tajga, gora ∧ 86 50.16 N 90.05 E
Mun'gyŏng 98 36.44 N 128.07 E
Munhall 214 40.23 N 79.54 W
Munhamade 154 16.37 S 36.58 E
Munhango 152 12.12 S 18.42 E
Munhango ≃ 152 11.20 S 19.50 E
Munhoz 256 22.37 S 46.22 W
Munhye-ri 98 38.10 N 127.19 E
Munich → München 60 48.08 N 11.34 E
Muniesa 34 41.02 N 0.48 W
Munim ≃ 250 2.45 S 44.04 W
Munirka ◆8 272a 28.34 N 77.10 E
Munising 190 46.24 N 86.38 W
Munith 216 42.23 N 84.15 W
Muñiz 258 34.33 S 58.42 W
Muniz Freire 255 20.28 S 41.25 W
Munkács → Mukacheve 78 48.27 N 22.45 E
Munka-Ljungby 41 56.15 N 12.58 E
Munkebjerg ∧2 41 55.41 N 9.37 E
Munkebo 41 55.27 N 10.34 E
Munkedal 26 58.29 N 11.41 E
Munkerud 40 59.50 N 13.31 E
Munkfors 40 59.50 N 13.32 E
Munksund 26 65.17 N 21.29 E
Munktorp 40 59.32 N 16.08 E
Munku-Sardyk, gora ∧ 88 51.45 N 100.32 E
Munlochy 46 57.32 N 4.15 W
Münnerstadt 56 50.15 N 10.11 E
Munnsville 210 42.58 N 75.35 W
Muñoz 116 15.43 N 120.54 E
Munozero 24 67.05 N 34.12 E
Muñoz Gamero, Península ≻1 254 52.30 S 73.10 W
Munpal-li 271b 37.45 N 126.43 E
Munro ◆8 288 34.32 S 58.31 W
Munroe Falls 214 41.08 N 81.26 W
Munro Lake ⊜ 184 54.38 N 95.16 W
Munsan 98 37.51 N 126.48 E
Munsarpur 126 24.18 N 88.26 E
Munsey Park 276 40.48 N 73.41 W
Munshiganj 124 23.33 N 90.32 E
Münsing 64 47.54 N 11.22 E
Münsingen, Dtsch. 58 48.25 N 9.29 E
Münsingen, Schw. 58 46.53 N 7.34 E
Munsö I 40 59.23 N 17.35 E
Munson, Ab., Can. 182 51.34 N 112.45 W
Munson, Pa., U.S. 214 40.57 N 78.10 W
Munson Knob ∧2 214 40.40 N 81.54 W
Munsons Corners 210 42.35 N 76.13 W
Münster, Dtsch. 52 51.57 N 7.37 E
Munster, Dtsch. 52 52.59 N 10.05 E
Münster, Dtsch. 56 49.55 N 8.52 E
Munster, Fr. 56 48.55 N 6.54 E
Munster, Fr. 58 48.03 N 7.08 E
Münster, Schw. 58 46.29 N 8.16 E
Munster, In., U.S. 216 41.33 N 87.30 W
Münster □5 52 51.50 N 7.25 E
Munster □9 48 52.25 N 8.20 W
Munster ≃ 48 52.33 N 7.12 W
Münsterkirche ⊍1 263 51.27 N 7.01 E
Münsterland ◆1 52 52.00 N 7.30 E
Münsterlingen 58 47.38 N 9.14 E
Münstermaifeld 56 50.15 N 7.22 E
Münstertal 58 47.51 N 7.47 E
Muntadgin 162 31.45 S 118.34 E
Muntahak ∧ 114 1.52 N 103.47 E
Munte 112 0.30 N 119.55 E
Muntele Mare, Vârful ∧ 38 46.29 N 23.14 E
Muntendam 52 53.07 N 6.53 E
Muntok 112 2.04 S 105.11 E
Mununzi 154 0.36 N 29.15 E
Munuscong Lake ⊜ 190 46.10 N 84.08 W
Münzenberg 56 50.27 N 8.46 E
Münzkirchen 60 48.29 N 13.34 E
Munzur Dağları ⋀ 130 39.30 N 39.10 E
Munzur Vadisi Milli Parkı ♦ 130 39.25 N 39.30 E
Muolea Point ≻ 229a 20.41 N 156.01 W
Muong Het 110 20.49 N 104.01 E
Muong Hinh 110 19.49 N 105.03 E
Muong Khoua 110 21.05 N 102.31 E
Muong Saiapoun 110 18.24 N 101.31 E
Muong Te 110 22.28 N 102.37 E
Muonio 24 67.57 N 23.42 E
Muotathal 58 46.59 N 8.46 E
Mupa 152 16.10 S 15.44 E
Mupa, Parque Nacional da ♦ 152 16.00 S 15.35 E
Muping 98 37.24 N 121.35 E
Mupini 156 17.50 S 19.40 E
Mup'ungjang 98 35.58 N 127.49 E
Muqaddam, Wādī V 140 18.04 N 31.30 E
Muqaṭṭa' 140 14.40 N 35.51 E
Muqaybirah, Bi'r al- ⊤4 142 30.53 N 32.50 E
Muqayshiṭ I 128 24.10 N 53.45 E
Muqdisho (Mogadishu) 144 2.04 N 45.22 E
Muqi 98 41.46 N 124.39 E
Muqsam, Jabal ∧ 140 13.38 N 27.42 E
Müqtädir 84 41.41 N 48.46 E
Muquequete 152 14.50 S 14.16 E
Muqui 255 20.57 S 41.20 W
Mur (Mura) ≃ 30 46.18 N 16.53 E
Mura (Mur) ≃, Europe 30 46.18 N 16.53 E
Mura ≃, Ross. 88 58.27 N 98.34 E
Muradiye, Tür. 84 38.59 N 43.46 E
Muradiye, Tür. 130 38.39 N 27.21 E
Murādnagar 124 28.47 N 77.30 E
Murafa ≃ 78 48.13 N 28.14 E
Murāgācha 126 23.32 N 88.24 E
Muraglione, Passo del )( 66 43.56 N 11.39 E
Murai Reservoir ⊜1 271c 1.24 N 103.41 E
Murajá 250 0.47 S 47.57 W
Murakami 92 38.14 N 139.29 E
Murallón, Cerro ∧ 254 49.48 S 73.25 W
Murambi 154 1.46 S 30.23 E
Muramvya 154 3.16 S 29.37 E
Murana 164 3.33 S 133.49 E
Murang'a 154 0.43 S 37.09 E
Murano, Isola di I 64 45.28 N 12.21 E
Muranskij porog ∟ 88 58.02 N 112.16 E
Muraoka 96 35.28 N 134.35 E
Muraši 24 59.24 N 48.55 E
Muraški 265b 55.59 N 37.45 E
Murat 32 45.07 N 2.52 E
Murat ≃ 84 38.39 N 39.50 E
Murat Dağı ∧ 130 38.55 N 29.43 E
Muratkovo 86 58.26 N 62.23 E
Muratlı 130 41.10 N 27.30 E
Muratove 83 48.48 N 38.45 E
Muratpur 272b 22.59 N 88.27 E
Murau 61 47.07 N 14.10 E
Muravera 71 39.25 N 9.34 E
Muravjovka 89 49.50 N 127.44 E
Muravjovo 76 56.14 N 34.14 E
Murayama 92 38.28 N 140.22 E
Murayama-chosuichi ⊜1 268 35.45 N 139.25 E
Muraysah, Ra's al- ≻ 146 31.55 N 25.02 E
Murča 34 41.24 N 7.27 W
Murcanyo 144 11.41 N 50.27 E
Mūrcheh Khvort 128 33.06 N 51.30 E
Murchin 54 53.54 N 13.44 E
Murchison, Austl. 166 36.37 S 145.14 E
Murchison, N.Z. 172 41.48 S 172.20 E
Murchison, Tx., U.S. 222 32.17 N 95.45 W
Murchison ≃ 162 27.42 S 114.09 E
Murchison, Mount ∧, Austl. 162 26.46 S 116.25 E
Murchison, Mount ∧, N.Z. 172 43.01 S 171.22 E
Murchison Falls → Kabalega Falls ∟ 154 2.17 N 31.41 E
Murchison Range ⋀ 162 20.11 S 134.26 E
Murcia, Esp. 34 37.59 N 1.07 W
Murcia, Pil. 116 10.36 N 123.02 E
Murcia □3, Esp. 34 38.00 N 1.30 W
Murcia □3, Esp. 148 37.55 N 1.30 W
Murciélago, Islas II 236 10.51 N 85.57 W
Murcielagos Bay c 116 8.39 N 123.33 E
Mur-de-Barrez 32 44.51 N 2.39 E
Murdeduke, Lake ⊜ 169 38.11 S 143.53 E
Murder Creek ≃, Al., U.S. 194 31.04 N 87.06 W
Murder Creek ≃, N.Y., U.S. 210 43.05 N 78.31 W
Murderkill ≃ 208 39.03 N 75.24 W
Murdo 198 43.53 N 100.42 W
Murdock 220 27.00 N 82.08 W
Mure 94 36.45 N 138.14 E
Mureaux, Aérodrome des ⊠ 261 49.00 N 1.57 E
Mureck 61 46.42 N 15.46 E
Mürefte 130 40.40 N 27.14 E
Mureș □6 38 46.35 N 24.40 E
Mureș (Maros) ≃ 38 46.15 N 20.13 E
Muret 32 43.28 N 1.21 E
Murewa 154 17.39 S 31.47 E
Murfreesboro, Ar., U.S. 194 34.03 N 93.41 W
Murfreesboro, N.C., U.S. 192 36.26 N 77.05 W
Murfreesboro, Tn., U.S. 194 35.50 N 86.23 W
Murg 58 47.33 N 8.01 E
Murg ≃ 56 48.55 N 8.10 E
Murgab 85 38.10 N 73.59 E
Murgab (Morghāb) ≃, Asia 128 38.18 N 61.12 E
Murgab ≃, Taj. 120 38.20 N 72.30 E
Murgenella 164 11.33 S 132.55 E
Murgeni 38 46.12 N 28.01 E
Murgenthal 58 47.16 N 7.50 E
Murgha Faqīrzai 120 31.03 N 67.48 E
Murgha Kibzai 120 30.44 N 69.25 E
Murgon 166 26.15 S 151.57 E
Muri, Cook Is. 174k 21.14 S 159.43 W
Muri, Nig. 146 9.11 N 10.53 E
Muri, Schw. 58 46.56 N 7.29 E
Muri, Schw. 58 47.16 N 8.21 E
Muria, Gunung ∧ 115a 6.36 S 110.53 E
Muriaé 255 21.08 S 42.22 W
Muriaé ≃ 255 21.43 S 41.22 W
Murias de Paredes 34 42.51 N 6.11 W
Muribeca 250 10.26 S 36.59 W
Muribeca dos Guararapes 250 8.10 S 35.01 W
Murici 250 9.19 S 35.56 W
Muricizal ≃ 250 6.40 S 48.40 W
Murīdke 123 31.48 N 74.16 E
Muriége 152 9.58 S 21.11 E
Muriel Lake ⊜ 182 54.10 N 110.40 W
Murih, Pulau I 112 1.54 N 108.38 E
Murila 152 10.44 S 20.20 E
Murilo I1 14 8.40 N 152.11 E
Mūrinda 123 30.47 N 76.29 E
Murinja 88 54.47 N 107.21 E
Murino, Ross. 88 51.30 N 104.23 E
Murino, Ross. 265a 60.03 N 30.27 E
Murinskij ≃ 265a 60.01 N 30.28 E
Muriqui 256 22.56 S 43.57 W
Muriqui ≃ 287a 22.52 S 43.02 W
Murisengo 62 45.05 N 8.08 E
Mūrītāniyā → Mauritania □1 134 20.00 N 12.00 W
Müritz ⊜ 54 53.25 N 12.43 E
Muriwai 172 38.46 S 177.55 E
Murkong Selek 120 27.49 N 95.16 E
Murlīganj 124 25.54 N 86.59 E
Murlo 66 43.09 N 11.23 E
Murmansk 24 68.58 N 33.05 E
Murmansk Oblast' □4 24 68.00 N 35.00 E
Murmansk Rise ✦3 12 75.00 N 37.00 E
Murmerwoude 52 53.16 N 6.00 E
Murmino 80 54.36 N 40.03 E
Murnau 64 47.40 N 11.12 E
Murnei 140 12.57 N 22.52 E
Murō 94 34.34 N 136.02 E
Murō-Akame-Aoyama-kokutei-kōen ♦ 94 34.30 N 136.10 E
Muro Lucano 68 40.45 N 15.29 E
Murom 80 55.34 N 42.02 E
Muromcevo 86 56.23 N 75.14 E
Muroran 92a 42.18 N 140.59 E
Muros 34 42.47 N 9.02 W
Muros e Noia, Ría de c1 34 42.45 N 9.00 W
Muroto 96 33.18 N 134.09 E
Muroto-Anan-kaigan-kokutei-kōen ♦ 96 33.41 N 134.32 E
Muroto-zaki ≻ 96 33.15 N 134.11 E
Murovani Kurylivtsi 78 48.43 N 27.31 E
Murowana Goślina 30 52.35 N 17.01 E
Murphy, Id., U.S. 202 43.13 N 116.33 W
Murphy, Mo., U.S. 219 38.29 N 90.29 W
Murphy, N.C., U.S. 192 35.05 N 84.02 W
Murphy Lake ⊜ 182 52.03 N 121.14 W
Murphys 226 38.08 N 120.27 W
Murphysboro 194 37.45 N 89.20 W
Murphy Slough ≃ 226 36.28 N 120.00 W
Murr ≃ 56 48.57 N 9.16 E
Murr, Wādī V 142 28.27 N 32.18 E
Murrah, Qārat al- ∧2 142 30.00 N 32.41 E
Murrah al-Kubrā, Al-Buḥayrah al- (Great Bitter Lake) ⊜ 142 30.20 N 32.23 E
Murrah aṣ-Ṣughrā, Al-Buḥayrah al- (Little Bitter Lake) ⊜ 142 30.13 N 32.33 E
Murra Murra 166 28.16 S 146.48 E
Murrāt, Ābār ⊤4 140 21.03 N 32.55 E
Murray, Ia., U.S. 190 41.02 N 93.56 W
Murray, Ky., U.S. 194 36.36 N 88.18 W
Murray, Ut,. U.S. 200 40.40 N 111.53 W
Murray ≃, Austl. 166 35.22 S 139.22 E
Murray ≃, Austl. 168a 32.35 S 115.46 E
Murray ≃, B.C., Can. 182 55.40 N 121.10 W
Murray, Lake ⊜ 164 7.00 S 141.30 E
Murray, Lake ⊜1 192 34.04 N 81.23 W
Murray, Mount ∧, Yk., Can. 180 60.54 N 128.49 W
Murray, Mount ∧, Pap. N. Gui. 164 6.46 S 144.01 E
Murray Bay → La Malbaie 186 47.39 N 70.10 W
Murray Bridge 168b 35.07 S 139.17 E
Murray Canal ≡ 212 44.04 N 77.35 W
Murray City 188 39.30 N 82.09 W
Murray Downs 162 21.04 S 134.40 E
Murray Fracture Zone ✦ 16 34.00 N 135.00 W
Murray Harbour 186 46.00 N 62.31 W
Murray Head ≻ 186 46.00 N 62.28 W
Murray Maxwell Bay c 176 70.00 N 80.00 W
Murray Mouth ≃1 168b 35.34 S 138.54 E
Murray River 186 46.01 N 62.37 W
Murraysburg 158 31.58 S 23.47 E
Murrayville, B.C., Can. 224 49.10 N 122.36 W
Murrayville, Il., U.S. 194 39.35 N 90.15 W
Murrébuè 154 13.02 S 40.30 E
Murree 123 33.54 N 73.24 E
Mürren 58 46.34 N 7.54 E
Murrhardt 56 48.59 N 9.34 E
Murrí ≃ 246 6.33 N 76.52 W
Murrieta 228 33.33 N 117.12 W
Murro di Porca, Capo ≻ 70 37.00 N 15.20 E
Murrumbidgee ≃ 166 34.43 S 143.12 E
Murrumburrah 166 34.33 S 148.21 E
Murrupula 154 15.27 S 38.47 E
Murrurundi 166 31.46 S 150.50 E
Murry Hill 279b 40.17 N 80.09 W
Murrysville 279b 40.25 N 79.41 W
Mursal 130 39.11 N 37.59 E
Mursala, Pulau I 114 1.38 N 98.32 E
Murshidābād 126 24.11 N 88.16 E
Mürşitpınar 130 36.54 N 38.19 E
Murska Sobota 36 46.40 N 16.10 E
Murskij, porog ∟ 88 58.27 N 98.30 E
Mursko Središće 61 46.31 N 16.27 E
Murtajāpur 122 20.44 N 77.23 E
Murtal 266c 38.42 N 9.22 W
Murtee 166 31.35 S 143.30 E
Murten 58 46.56 N 7.07 E
Murtensee → Morat, Lac de ⊜ 58 46.55 N 7.05 E
Murter, Otok I 36 43.48 N 15.37 E
Murtle Lake ⊜ 182 52.08 N 119.38 W
Murtoa 166 36.37 S 142.28 E
Murton 44 54.49 N 1.24 W
Murtosa 34 40.44 N 8.38 W
Muru 140 6.36 N 29.15 E
Muru ≃ 248 8.09 S 70.45 W
Muru, Capu di ≻ 36 41.44 N 8.40 E
Murud 122 18.19 N 72.58 E
Murud, Gunong ∧ 112 3.52 N 115.30 E
Murukta 74 67.46 N 102.01 E
Murung ≃ 112 0.12 S 114.03 E
Murupara 172 38.28 S 176.42 E
Mururoa I1 6 21.52 S 138.55 W
Murutinga 246 3.26 S 59.12 W
Murvaul, Lake ⊜1 222 32.03 N 94.28 W
Murvaul Creek ≃ 194 32.05 N 94.12 W
Murwāra 124 23.51 N 80.24 E
Murwillumbah 166 28.19 S 153.24 E
Mürz ≃ 61 47.24 N 15.17 E
Mürzsteg 61 47.40 N 15.29 E
Mürzzuschlag 61 47.36 N 15.41 E
Muş 130 38.44 N 41.30 E
Muş □4 128 39.00 N 42.00 E
Musa 152 2.40 N 19.18 E
Mūša ≃, Europe 76 56.24 N 24.10 E
Musa ≃, Pap. N. Gui. 164 9.25 S 148.50 E
Mūsā, Jabal (Mount Sinai) ∧ 140 28.32 N 33.59 E
Mūsā, 'Uyūn (Springs of Moses) ⊤4 142 29.52 N 32.39 E
Musabeyli 130 39.51 N 34.37 E
Musadi 152 2.34 S 22.47 E
Musaid 146 31.35 N 25.03 E
Mūsa Khel 123 32.38 N 71.44 E
Mūsa Khel Bāzār 120 30.52 N 69.49 E
Musala ∧ 38 42.11 N 23.34 E
Musan 98 42.14 N 129.13 E
Musandam Peninsula ≻1 128 26.18 N 56.24 E
Musao 154 7.43 S 26.17 E
Mūsā Qal'eh 120 32.22 N 64.46 E
Mūsā Qal'eh ≃ 128 32.05 N 64.51 E
Musar 272b 22.54 N 88.14 E
Musasa 154 3.21 S 31.33 E
Musashi → Iruma, Nihon 94 35.50 N 139.24 E
Musashi, Nihon 96 33.30 N 131.43 E
Musashimurayama 268 35.45 N 139.23 E
Musashino 94 35.42 N 139.34 E
Musashino-daichi ⋀1 268 35.45 N 139.35 E
Musau 58 47.32 N 10.40 E
Musay'īd 128 24.59 N 51.32 E
Musaymīr 144 13.27 N 44.37 E
Mūsāzai 120 30.23 N 66.32 E
Muscat → Masqaṭ 128 23.37 N 58.35 E
Muscat and Oman → Oman □1 118 22.00 N 58.00 E
Muscatatuck ≃ 218 38.46 N 86.10 W
Muscatatuck, Grassy Fork ≃ 218 38.45 N 85.07 W
Muscatatuck, Vernon Fork ≃ 218 38.46 N 85.54 W
Muscatine 190 41.25 N 91.03 W
Müsch 56 50.23 N 6.49 E
Mus-Chaja, gora ∧ 74 62.35 N 140.50 E
Muschu Island I 164 3.25 S 143.35 E
Muschwitz 54 51.11 N 12.07 E
Muscle Shoals 194 34.44 N 87.40 W
Musclow, Mount ∧ 182 53.17 N 127.09 W
Musclow Lake ⊜ 184 51.25 N 94.56 W
Muscoda 190 43.11 N 90.26 W
Musconetcong ≃ 210 40.36 N 75.11 W
Musconetcong, Lake ⊜ 276 40.54 N 74.42 W
Muscongus Bay c 188 43.55 N 69.20 W
Muscote Bay c 212 44.06 N 77.18 W
Muscowpetung Indian Reserve ◆4 184 50.45 N 104.15 W
Muscoy 228 34.09 N 117.20 W
Muse 214 40.17 N 80.12 W
Musengezi ≃ 154 15.43 S 31.14 E
Musgrave, Austl. 164 14.47 S 143.30 E
Musgrave, B.C., Can. 224 48.45 N 123.32 W
Musgrave, Mount ∧ 172 43.48 S 170.43 E
Musgrave Ranges ⋀ 162 26.10 S 131.50 E
Musgravetown 186 48.24 N 53.53 W
Mūshā 142 27.08 N 31.18 E
Mushābani 126 22.31 N 86.27 E
Mushāsh, Jabal al- ∧2 142 28.54 N 31.11 E
Mushenge 152 4.32 S 21.21 E
Mushie 152 3.01 S 16.54 E
Mushima 154 14.13 S 25.05 E
Mushin 150 6.32 N 3.22 E
Mūsi ≃, India 122 16.41 N 79.40 E
Musi ≃, Indon. 112 2.20 S 104.56 E
Musicians Seamounts ✦3 6 31.00 N 162.00 W
Muskauer Heide ◆3 54 51.25 N 14.40 E
Muskeg ≃ 182 54.01 N 119.03 W
Muskeget Channel ⊔ 207 41.25 N 70.20 W
Muskeget Island I 207 41.20 N 70.18 W
Muskeg Lake Indian Reserve ◆4 184 52.58 N 106.57 W
Muskego 216 42.54 N 88.08 W
Muskego Lake ⊜ 216 42.53 N 88.07 W
Muskegon 216 43.14 N 86.14 W
Muskegon □6 216 43.12 N 86.08 W
Muskegon ≃ 190 43.14 N 86.20 W
Muskegon County Airport ⊠ 216 43.10 N 86.14 W
Muskegon Heights 216 43.12 N 86.14 W
Muskegon Lake ⊜ 216 43.14 N 86.17 W
Muskegon State Park ♦ 216 43.14 N 86.20 W
Mušketova, gora ∧ 88 53.35 N 113.32 E
Muskingum □6 214 40.06 N 81.51 W


**Symbols** in the index entries represent the broad categories identified in the key at the right. Symbols with superior numbers (⋀1) identify subcategories (see complete key on page *I · 1*).

**Symbole** im Register stellen die rechts im Schlüssel erklärten Kategorien dar. Symbole mit hochgestellten Ziffern (⋀1) bezeichnen Unterabteilungen einer Kategorie (vgl. vollständiger Schlüssel auf Seite *I · 1*).

**Los símbolos** incluídos en el texto del índice representan las grandes categorías identificadas con la clave a la derecha. Los símbolos con numeros en su parte superior (⋀1) identifican las subcategorías (véase la clave completa en la página *I · 1*).

**Les symboles** de l'index représentent les catégories indiquées dans la légende à droite. Les symboles suivis d'un indice (⋀1) représentent des sous-catégories (voir légende complète à la page *I · 1*).

**Os símbolos** incluídos no texto do índice representam as grandes categorias identificadas com a chave à direita. Os símbolos com números em sua parte superior (⋀1) identificam as subcategorias (veja-se a chave completa à página *I · 1*).

| | | | | | |
|---|---|---|---|---|---|
| ∧ | Mountain | Berg | Montaña | Montagne | Montanha |
| ⋀ | Mountains | Gebirge | Montañas | Montagnes | Montanhas |
| )( | Pass | Paß | Paso | Col | Passo |
| V | Valley, Canyon | Tal, Cañon | Valle, Cañón | Vallée, Canyon | Vale, Canhão |
| ≚ | Plain | Ebene | Llano | Plaine | Planície |
| ≻ | Cape | Kap | Cabo | Cap | Cabo |
| I | Island | Insel | Isla | Île | Ilha |
| II | Islands | Inseln | Islas | Îles | Ilhas |
| ⊥ | Other Topographic Features | Andere Topographische Objekte | Otros Elementos Topográficos | Autres données topographiques | Outros acidentes topográficos |

## ESPAÑOL

| Nombre | Página | Lat.°′ | Long.°′ W = Oeste |
|---|---|---|---|
| Muskingum ≐ | 188 | 39.27 N | 81.30 W |
| Muskingum Brook ≐ | 285 | 39.48 N | 74.44 W |
| Muskira | 124 | 25.40 N | 79.48 E |
| Muskö I | 40 | 59.00 N | 18.06 E |
| Muskoday Indian Reserve ◈[4] | 184 | 53.06 N | 105.30 W |
| Muskogee | 196 | 35.44 N | 95.22 W |
| Muskoka □[6] | 212 | 45.05 N | 79.03 W |
| Muskoka, Lake ⊜ | 212 | 45.00 N | 79.25 W |
| Muskoka, North Branch ≐ | 212 | 45.02 N | 79.19 W |
| Muskoka, South Branch ≐ | 212 | 45.02 N | 79.19 W |
| Muskosh Channel ⊔ | 212 | 44.55 N | 79.53 W |
| Muskowekwan Indian Reserve ◈[4] | 184 | 51.19 N | 104.06 W |
| Muskrat Creek ≐ | 202 | 43.09 N | 108.11 W |
| Muskrat Dam Lake ⊜ | 184 | 53.25 N | 91.40 W |
| Muskrat Lake ⊜ | 190 | 45.40 N | 76.55 W |
| Muskwa ≐ | 176 | 58.45 N | 122.35 W |
| Muskwa Lake ⊜ | 182 | 56.09 N | 114.38 W |
| Muslimbāgh | 120 | 30.49 N | 67.45 E |
| Musl'umovo | 80 | 55.18 N | 53.12 E |
| Muşmuş | 132 | 32.32 N | 35.09 E |
| Musocco ◈[8] | 266b | 45.30 N | 9.08 E |
| Musofu Mission | 154 | 13.31 S | 29.02 E |
| Musoma | 154 | 1.30 S | 33.48 E |
| Musone ≐, It. | 64 | 45.50 N | 11.55 E |
| Musone ≐, It. | 66 | 43.28 N | 13.38 E |
| Musoshi | 154 | 11.54 S | 27.46 E |
| Musquanousse, Lac ⊜ | 186 | 50.22 N | 61.05 W |
| Musquapsink Brook ≐ | 276 | 40.59 N | 74.01 W |
| Musquaro, Lac ⊜ | 186 | 50.38 N | 61.05 W |
| Musquash ≐ | 212 | 44.57 N | 79.52 W |
| Musquash Brook ≐ | 283 | 42.42 N | 71.26 W |
| Musquashcut Pond ⊜ | 283 | 42.13 N | 70.46 W |
| Musquodoboit Harbour | 186 | 44.47 N | 63.09 W |
| Mussau Island I | 164 | 1.30 S | 149.40 E |
| Musselburgh | 46 | 55.57 N | 3.04 W |
| Musselkanaal | 52 | 52.56 N | 7.00 E |
| Musselshell ≐ | 202 | 47.21 N | 107.58 W |
| Mussende | 152 | 10.32 S | 16.05 E |
| Mussidan | 32 | 45.02 N | 0.22 E |
| Mussolo | 152 | 9.59 S | 17.19 E |
| Mussomeli | 70 | 37.35 N | 13.45 E |
| Mussoorie | 124 | 30.27 N | 78.05 E |
| Mussuco | 152 | 17.08 S | 19.05 E |
| Mussum | 52 | 51.48 N | 6.34 E |
| Mussuma | 152 | 14.14 S | 21.59 E |
| Mussy-sur-Seine | 58 | 47.58 N | 4.30 E |
| Mustafakemalpaşa | 130 | 40.02 N | 28.24 E |
| Mustafa Kemal Paşa ≐ | 130 | 40.07 N | 28.33 E |
| Mustafino | 80 | 55.01 N | 53.38 E |
| Mustahil | 144 | 5.12 N | 44.17 E |
| Müstair | 58 | 46.37 N | 10.27 E |
| Mustajevo | 80 | 51.48 N | 53.25 E |
| Mustajõe | 76 | 57.59 N | 26.58 E |
| Mustāng | 124 | 29.11 N | 83.58 E |
| Mustang Draw V | 196 | 32.12 N | 101.36 W |
| Mustang Island I | 196 | 27.45 N | 97.10 W |
| Mustāy | 142 | 30.37 N | 31.09 E |
| Musters, Lago ⊜ | 254 | 45.27 S | 69.13 W |
| Mustinka ≐ | 198 | 45.45 N | 96.38 W |
| Mustjala | 76 | 58.28 N | 22.14 E |
| Mustla | 76 | 58.14 N | 25.52 E |
| Musṭurud | 273c | 30.08 N | 31.17 E |
| Mustvee | 76 | 58.51 N | 26.56 E |
| Musu-dan › | 98 | 40.50 N | 129.43 E |
| Musun | 84 | 39.42 N | 43.49 E |
| Müsuslü | 84 | 40.28 N | 47.55 E |
| Muswellbrook | 166 | 32.16 S | 150.53 E |
| Muszyna | 30 | 49.21 N | 20.54 E |
| Mūt, Misr | 140 | 25.29 N | 28.59 E |
| Mut, Tür. | 130 | 36.39 N | 33.27 E |
| Muta | 61 | 46.37 N | 15.10 E |
| Mutá, Ponta do › | 255 | 13.52 S | 38.56 W |
| Mu'tah | 132 | 31.06 N | 35.42 E |
| Mutalau | 174v | 18.56 S | 169.50 W |
| Mutambara | 154 | 19.36 S | 32.33 E |
| Mutanchiang → Mudanjiang | 89 | 44.35 N | 129.36 E |
| Mutanda, Moç. | 156 | 21.02 S | 33.31 E |
| Mutanda, Zaïre | 152 | 5.17 S | 16.34 E |
| Mutanda Mission | 154 | 12.24 S | 26.16 E |
| Mutankiang → Mudanjiang | 89 | 44.35 N | 129.36 E |
| Mutarammil, Jabal al- ∧ | 132 | 31.04 N | 36.06 E |
| Mutare | 154 | 18.58 S | 32.40 E |
| Mutbīn | 132 | 33.09 N | 36.15 E |
| Mutějovice | 54 | 50.09 N | 13.41 E |
| Mutha | 154 | 1.48 S | 38.26 E |
| Muthill | 46 | 56.19 N | 3.50 W |
| Mutiko | 154 | 1.39 S | 28.12 E |
| Muting | 164 | 7.23 S | 140.20 E |
| Mutis, Gunung ∧ | 112 | 9.34 S | 124.14 E |
| Mutlu (Rezovska) ≐ | 38 | 41.59 N | 28.01 E |
| Mutoko | 154 | 17.24 S | 32.13 E |
| Mutombo-Mukulu | 152 | 7.58 S | 24.00 E |
| Mutoraj | 74 | 61.20 N | 100.30 E |
| Mutoto | 152 | 5.42 S | 22.42 E |
| Mutouchengzi | 98 | 41.20 N | 119.59 E |
| Mutouhao | 107 | 28.49 N | 105.04 E |
| Mutsamudu | 157a | 12.09 S | 44.25 E |
| Mutshatsha | 152 | 10.39 S | 24.27 E |
| Mutsu | 92 | 41.17 N | 141.10 E |
| Mutsuai | 268 | 35.08 N | 139.38 E |
| Mutsumi | 96 | 34.26 N | 131.34 E |
| Mutsuura ◈[8] | 268 | 35.19 N | 139.37 E |
| Mutsu-wan ⊂ | 92 | 41.05 N | 140.55 E |
| Muttaburra | 166 | 22.36 S | 144.33 E |
| Muttekopf ∧ | 58 | 47.16 N | 10.39 E |
| Muttenz | 58 | 47.32 N | 7.39 E |
| Mutters | 64 | 47.14 N | 11.23 E |
| Mutterstadt | 56 | 49.26 N | 8.21 E |
| Muttonbird Islands II | 172 | 47.15 S | 167.24 E |
| Muttontown | 276 | 40.49 N | 73.33 W |
| Muttra → Mathura | 124 | 27.30 N | 77.41 E |
| Mutual, Oh., U.S. | 218 | 40.05 N | 83.38 W |
| Mutual, Pa., U.S. | 279b | 40.14 N | 79.30 W |
| Muṭūbis | 142 | 31.18 N | 30.31 E |
| Mutuca, Ribeirão da ≐ | 256 | 21.36 S | 45.39 W |
| Mutuco, Lago ⊜ | 250 | 1.21 N | 50.24 W |
| Mutuípe | 255 | 13.15 S | 39.31 W |
| Mutum | 255 | 19.49 S | 41.26 W |
| Mutum ≐ | 246 | 4.25 S | 68.03 W |
| Mutum Biyu | 146 | 8.38 N | 10.46 E |
| Mutumbo | 152 | 13.14 S | 17.17 E |
| Mutunópolis | 255 | 13.40 S | 49.15 W |
| Muturi | 164 | 2.06 S | 133.43 E |
| Muturi ≐ | 164 | 2.13 S | 133.40 E |
| Mututi, Ilha do I | 250 | 0.45 S | 51.00 W |
| Mutzig | 58 | 48.32 N | 7.28 E |
| Mutzschen | 54 | 51.16 N | 12.53 E |
| Mu Us Shamo ◈[2] | 102 | 38.45 N | 109.10 E |
| Mūvattupula | 122 | 9.58 N | 76.35 E |
| Muvukoni | 154 | 0.24 S | 38.14 E |
| Muwopu | 104 | 41.03 N | 121.12 E |
| Muxaluando | 152 | 8.07 S | 14.17 E |
| Muxihe | 100 | 31.03 N | 115.21 E |
| Muxima | 152 | 9.31 S | 13.56 E |
| Muyaga | 154 | 3.14 S | 30.33 E |
| Muyang | 100 | 27.06 N | 119.34 E |
| Muyang ≐ | 100 | 27.00 N | 119.41 E |
| Muyinga | 154 | 2.51 S | 30.20 E |
| Muymano ≐ | 248 | 11.27 S | 69.03 W |
| Muy Muy | 236 | 12.46 N | 85.38 W |
| Muyua Island I | 164 | 9.05 S | 152.50 E |
| Muyuka | 152 | 4.17 N | 9.25 E |
| Muyumba | 154 | 7.15 S | 26.59 E |
| Mužač | 82 | 54.22 N | 36.21 E |
| Muzaffarābād | 123 | 34.22 N | 73.28 E |
| Muzaffargarh | 123 | 30.04 N | 71.12 E |
| Muzaffarnagar | 124 | 29.28 N | 77.41 E |

## FRANÇAIS

| Nom | Page | Lat.°′ | Long.°′ W = Ouest |
|---|---|---|---|
| Muzaffarpur | 124 | 26.07 N | 85.24 E |
| Muzambinho | 256 | 21.22 S | 46.32 W |
| Muzambinho ≐ | 256 | 21.15 S | 46.26 W |
| Muzambo ≐ | 256 | 21.17 S | 46.16 W |
| Muzat ≐ | 90 | 41.15 N | 83.27 E |
| Muzayrīb | 132 | 32.42 N | 36.01 E |
| Muzbek, gora ∧ | 85 | 40.23 N | 69.39 E |
| Muzbel' ◈[1] | 86 | 50.15 N | 70.50 E |
| Muzeze | 152 | 15.03 S | 17.43 E |
| Muzhen | 100 | 30.43 N | 117.56 E |
| Muži | 74 | 65.22 N | 64.40 E |
| Mužiči | 84 | 43.03 N | 44.59 E |
| Mužiksu | 86 | 47.42 N | 84.58 E |
| Muzillac | 32 | 47.33 N | 2.29 W |
| Muzkol, chrebet ⋏ | 85 | 38.25 N | 73.30 E |
| Muzoka | 154 | 16.41 S | 27.19 E |
| Muzon, Cape › | 182 | 54.41 N | 132.44 W |
| Muztag ∧, Zhg. | 120 | 36.03 N | 80.07 E |
| Muztag ∧, Zhg. | 120 | 36.25 N | 87.25 E |
| Muztagata ∧ | 85 | 38.17 N | 75.11 E |
| Muz Tau ∧ | 86 | 43.50 N | 85.40 E |
| Muzūrah | 142 | 28.53 N | 30.48 E |
| Muzzana del Turgnano | 64 | 45.49 N | 13.08 E |
| Mvam | 152 | 0.13 S | 9.39 E |
| Mvangan | 152 | 2.38 N | 11.44 E |
| Mvela | 154 | 14.46 S | 35.16 E |
| Mvengué | 152 | 3.17 N | 11.01 E |
| Mvolo | 140 | 6.03 N | 29.56 E |
| Mvomero | 154 | 6.20 S | 37.25 E |
| Mvoti ≐ | 158 | 29.24 S | 31.22 E |
| Mvoung ≐ | 152 | 0.04 N | 12.18 E |
| Mvouti | 152 | 4.15 S | 12.29 E |
| Mvuha | 154 | 7.12 S | 37.51 E |
| Mvuma | 154 | 19.19 S | 30.35 E |
| Mwadi-Kalumba | 152 | 7.53 S | 18.46 E |
| Mwadui | 154 | 3.33 S | 33.36 E |
| Mwali (Mohéli) I | 157a | 12.15 S | 43.45 E |
| Mwami | 154 | 16.40 S | 29.46 E |
| Mwanangumune | 152 | 15.31 S | 23.30 E |
| Mwango | 152 | 6.51 S | 24.13 E |
| Mwanza, Malaŵi | 154 | 15.37 S | 34.31 E |
| Mwanza, Tan. | 154 | 2.31 S | 32.54 E |
| Mwanza, Zaïre | 154 | 7.54 S | 26.45 E |
| Mwanza, Zam. | 152 | 17.02 S | 24.27 E |
| Mwanza □[4] | 154 | 2.45 S | 32.45 E |
| Mwanza Gulf ⊂ | 154 | 2.35 S | 32.51 E |
| Mwaya, Tan. | 154 | 9.33 S | 33.57 E |
| Mwaya, Tan. | 154 | 8.55 S | 36.50 E |
| Mweelrea ∧ | 48 | 53.38 N | 9.50 W |
| Mwehu | 154 | 5.44 S | 26.40 E |
| Mweka | 152 | 4.51 S | 21.34 E |
| Mwemena | 154 | 10.19 S | 27.28 E |
| Mwenda | 154 | 12.01 S | 28.44 E |
| Mwendjila | 152 | 7.12 S | 18.51 E |
| Mwene-Ditu | 152 | 7.03 S | 23.27 E |
| Mwenezi | 154 | 21.22 S | 30.45 E |
| Mwenga | 154 | 3.02 S | 28.26 E |
| Mwepo | 154 | 11.56 S | 26.11 E |
| Mwerasandu | 154 | 0.59 S | 30.23 E |
| Mwereni | 154 | 4.20 S | 39.08 E |
| Mweru, Lake ⊜ | 154 | 9.00 S | 28.45 E |
| Mweru Wantipa, Lake ⊜ | 154 | 8.45 S | 29.40 E |
| Mweru Wantipa National Park ♠ | 154 | 8.45 S | 29.30 E |
| Mwetshi | 152 | 4.42 S | 22.39 E |
| Mwilambwe | 154 | 8.07 S | 25.00 E |
| Mwilitau Islands II | 164 | 2.50 S | 146.20 E |
| Mwimbi | 154 | 8.39 S | 31.40 E |
| Mwingi | 154 | 0.56 S | 38.04 E |
| Mwinilunga | 152 | 11.44 S | 24.26 E |
| Mwitikira | 154 | 6.31 S | 35.39 E |
| Mwombezhi ≐ | 154 | 12.52 S | 25.00 E |
| Myaing | 110 | 21.37 N | 94.51 E |
| Myājlār | 120 | 26.15 N | 70.23 E |
| Myakka ≐ | 220 | 26.56 N | 82.11 W |
| Myakka, Lake ⊜ | 220 | 27.16 N | 82.17 W |
| Myakka City | 220 | 27.20 N | 82.09 W |
| Myakka River State Park ♠ | 220 | 27.15 N | 82.17 W |
| Myall Lakes National Park ♠ | 166 | 32.28 S | 152.22 E |
| Myall Range ⋏ | 170 | 32.58 S | 151.22 E |
| Myanaung | 110 | 18.17 N | 95.19 E |
| Myanmar (Burma) □[1] | 110 | 22.00 N | 98.00 E |
| Myaungmya | 110 | 16.36 N | 94.56 E |
| Myawadi | 110 | 16.41 N | 98.31 E |
| Mybster | 46 | 58.27 N | 3.25 W |
| Myckelgensjö | 26 | 63.34 N | 17.37 E |
| Myebon | 110 | 20.03 N | 93.22 E |
| Myeik → Mergui | 110 | 12.26 N | 98.36 E |
| Myers, Ky., U.S. | 218 | 38.21 N | 83.57 W |
| Myers, N.Y., U.S. | 210 | 42.32 N | 76.32 W |
| Myerstown | 208 | 40.22 N | 76.19 W |
| Myingyan | 110 | 21.28 N | 95.23 E |
| Myinmoletkat Taung ∧ | 110 | 13.28 N | 98.48 E |
| Myitkyinā | 110 | 25.23 N | 97.24 E |
| Myitnge ≐ | 110 | 21.52 N | 95.59 E |
| Myitta | 110 | 14.10 N | 98.31 E |
| Myittha | 110 | 21.25 N | 96.08 E |
| Myittha ≐ | 110 | 23.12 N | 94.17 E |
| Myjava | 30 | 48.45 N | 17.34 E |
| Myjeldino | 24 | 61.46 N | 54.48 E |
| Mykhaylivka, Ukr. | 78 | 49.19 N | 36.28 E |
| Mykhaylivka, Ukr. | 78 | 47.16 N | 35.14 E |
| Mykhaylivka, Ukr. | 83 | 48.44 N | 37.16 E |
| Mykil's'ke-na-Dnipri | 78 | 48.12 N | 35.12 E |
| Mykolayiv, Ukr. | 78 | 49.32 N | 23.58 E |
| Mykolayiv, Ukr. | 78 | 46.58 N | 32.00 E |
| Mykolayiv □[4] | 78 | 47.15 N | 31.45 E |
| Mykolayivka, Ukr. | 78 | 47.38 N | 33.12 E |
| Mykolayivka, Ukr. | 78 | 47.06 N | 34.14 E |
| Mykolayivka, Ukr. | 78 | 44.58 N | 33.37 E |
| Mykolayivka, Ukr. | 78 | 46.23 N | 29.24 E |
| Mykolayivka, Ukr. | 78 | 47.33 N | 30.25 E |
| Mykolayivka, Ukr. | 78 | 51.04 N | 34.02 E |
| Mykolayivka, Ukr. | 83 | 47.39 N | 37.41 E |
| Mykolayivka, Ukr. | 83 | 48.51 N | 37.46 E |
| Mykulyntsi | 78 | 49.24 N | 25.38 E |
| Myla | 24 | 65.25 N | 50.48 E |
| Mylau | 54 | 50.37 N | 12.16 E |
| Myl'džino | 86 | 59.03 N | 78.29 E |
| Myllendonk, Schloss ⊥ | 263 | 51.13 N | 6.29 E |
| Myllykoski | 26 | 60.47 N | 26.48 E |
| Myllymäki | 26 | 62.32 N | 24.17 E |
| Mylor | 168b | 35.03 S | 138.45 E |
| Mymensingh | 124 | 24.45 N | 90.24 E |
| Mynämäki | 26 | 60.40 N | 22.00 E |
| Mynaral | 86 | 45.25 N | 73.41 E |
| Mynbulak, gora ∧ | 85 | 41.43 N | 69.49 E |
| Mynfontein | 158 | 30.55 S | 23.57 E |
| Mynydd Bach ∧[2] | 42 | 52.15 N | 4.05 W |
| Mynydd Eppynt ∧ | 42 | 52.05 N | 3.30 W |
| Mynydd Hiraethog ∧ | 44 | 53.05 N | 3.33 W |
| Mynydd Pencarreg ∧[2] | 42 | 52.04 N | 4.04 W |
| Mynydd Preseli ∧ | 42 | 51.58 N | 4.42 W |
| Myōgata | 94 | 35.51 N | 137.02 E |
| Myōgi | 94 | 36.17 N | 138.49 E |
| Myōgi-Arafune-Saku-kōgen-kokutei-kōen ♠ | 94 | 36.12 N | 138.10 E |
| Myōgi-san ∧ | 94 | 36.17 N | 138.44 E |
| Myo-gyi | 110 | 21.27 N | 96.22 E |
| Myohaung | 110 | 20.36 N | 93.10 E |
| Myohyang-san ∧ | 98 | 40.02 N | 126.17 E |
| Myohyang-sanmaek ⋏ | 98 | 40.30 N | 127.00 E |
| Myojin-dake ∧ | 270 | 34.57 N | 135.36 E |
| Myōjin-san ∧ | 96 | 33.34 N | 133.04 E |
| Myōken-san ∧ | 96 | 35.24 N | 134.39 E |
| Myōken-zan ∧ | 270 | 34.56 N | 135.28 E |
| Myōken-zan ∧[2] | 270 | 34.30 N | 134.57 E |
| Myōkō | 94 | 36.56 N | 138.13 E |
| Myōkō-kōgen | 94 | 36.52 N | 138.12 E |
| Myōkō-san ∧ | 94 | 36.52 N | 138.07 E |

## PORTUGUÊS

| Nome | Página | Lat.°′ | Long.°′ W = Oeste |
|---|---|---|---|
| Myŏnmong-ni ◈[8] | 271b | 37.35 N | 127.05 E |
| Myponga | 168b | 35.24 S | 138.28 E |
| Myponga Reservoir ⊜[1] | 168b | 35.24 S | 138.26 E |
| Myra ⊥ | 130 | 36.15 N | 29.54 E |
| Mýrdalsjökull ⊓ | 24a | 63.40 N | 19.05 W |
| Myrhorod | 78 | 49.58 N | 33.36 E |
| Myrivs'ke | 78 | 48.05 N | 33.23 E |
| Myrnam | 182 | 53.40 N | 111.14 W |
| Myrnyy | 78 | 50.57 N | 28.34 E |
| Myronivka | 78 | 49.39 N | 30.59 E |
| Myronivs'kyy | 83 | 48.29 N | 38.17 E |
| Myroodah | 162 | 18.08 S | 124.16 E |
| Myropil' | 78 | 50.07 N | 27.41 E |
| Myropillya | 78 | 51.02 N | 35.16 E |
| Myrskylä (Mörskom) | 26 | 60.40 N | 25.51 E |
| Myrtle Beach | 192 | 33.41 N | 78.53 W |
| Myrtle Beach Air Force Base ■ | 192 | 33.41 N | 78.56 W |
| Myrtle Beach State Park ♠ | 192 | 33.37 N | 78.58 W |
| Myrtle Creek | 202 | 43.01 N | 123.17 W |
| Myrtle Grove | 194 | 30.25 N | 87.18 W |
| Myrtle Point | 202 | 43.03 N | 124.08 W |
| Myrtle Springs | 222 | 32.37 N | 95.56 W |
| Myrtletowne | 204 | 40.47 N | 124.04 W |
| Myrtleville | 170 | 34.29 S | 149.49 E |
| Myšega | 82 | 54.31 N | 37.02 E |
| Mysen | 26 | 59.33 N | 11.20 E |
| Myshuryn Rih | 78 | 48.50 N | 33.58 E |
| Mysia □[9] | 130 | 39.15 N | 28.00 E |
| Mysingen ⊔ | 40 | 59.00 N | 18.15 E |
| Myski | 86 | 53.42 N | 87.48 E |
| Myškino | 76 | 57.47 N | 38.27 E |
| Myśla ≐ | 54 | 52.40 N | 14.29 E |
| Myślenice | 30 | 49.51 N | 19.56 E |
| Myślibórz | 30 | 52.55 N | 14.52 E |
| Mysłowice | 30 | 50.15 N | 19.07 E |
| Mysore | 122 | 12.18 N | 76.39 E |
| Mys Šmidta | 180 | 68.56 N | 179.26 W |
| Mystic, Ct., U.S. | 207 | 41.21 N | 71.58 W |
| Mystic, Ia., U.S. | 190 | 40.46 N | 92.56 W |
| Mystic ≐ | 283 | 42.23 N | 71.03 W |
| Mystic Seaport ♁ | 207 | 41.22 N | 71.58 W |
| Mys Vchodnoj | 74 | 73.53 N | 86.43 E |
| Mysy | 24 | 60.34 N | 53.57 E |
| Mys Želanija | 72 | 76.56 N | 68.35 E |
| Myszków | 30 | 50.36 N | 19.20 E |
| Myszyniec | 30 | 53.24 N | 21.21 E |
| Myt | 80 | 56.48 N | 42.21 E |
| My Tho | 110 | 10.21 N | 106.21 E |
| Mytholm | 262 | 53.44 N | 2.01 W |
| Mytholmroyd | 262 | 53.44 N | 1.59 W |
| Mytilene → Mitilíni | 38 | 39.06 N | 26.32 E |
| Mytišči | 82 | 55.55 N | 37.46 E |
| Mytishchi → Mytišči | 82 | 55.55 N | 37.46 E |
| Mytišino | 76 | 54.48 N | 34.01 E |
| Mýto | 60 | 49.47 N | 13.44 E |
| Myton | 200 | 40.11 N | 110.03 W |
| Mývatn ⊜ | 24a | 65.37 N | 16.58 W |
| Myzove | 78 | 51.22 N | 24.31 E |
| M'zab, Oued V | 148 | 32.19 N | 5.24 E |
| Mže ≐ | 60 | 49.46 N | 13.25 E |
| Mzenga | 154 | 6.56 S | 38.43 E |
| Mziha | 154 | 5.54 S | 37.47 E |
| Mzimba | 154 | 11.52 S | 33.34 E |
| Mzimkulu ≐ | 158 | 30.44 S | 30.28 E |
| Mzimvubu ≐ | 158 | 31.38 S | 29.32 E |
| Mzintlava ≐ | 158 | 31.12 S | 29.18 E |
| Mzuzu | 154 | 11.27 S | 33.55 E |
| Mzymta ≐ | 84 | 43.27 N | 39.56 E |

## N

| | | | |
|---|---|---|---|
| Na I | 174r | 6.52 N | 158.22 E |
| Na (Tengtiao) ≐ | 110 | 22.05 N | 103.09 E |
| Naab ≐ | 60 | 49.01 N | 12.02 E |
| Naach, Jbel ∧ | 34 | 34.53 N | 3.22 W |
| Naachtpunkt Brook ≐ | 276 | 40.54 N | 74.15 W |
| Naaldwijk | 52 | 52.00 N | 4.12 E |
| Naalehu | 229d | 19.03 N | 155.35 W |
| Na'ām | 140 | 9.42 N | 28.27 E |
| Na'âma, Sebkhet en ≡ | 148 | 33.20 N | 0.16 W |
| Naaman Creek ≐ | 285 | 39.48 N | 75.27 W |
| Naaman Creek, South Branch ≐ | 285 | 39.49 N | 75.27 W |
| Naamans Garden | 285 | 39.49 N | 75.31 W |
| Naantali | 26 | 60.27 N | 22.02 E |
| Naarden | 52 | 52.17 N | 5.09 E |
| Naarn ≐ | 61 | 48.11 N | 14.49 E |
| Naas | 48 | 53.13 N | 6.39 W |
| Naas ≐ | 171b | 35.36 S | 149.04 E |
| Naast, Bel. | 50 | 50.33 N | 4.05 E |
| Naast, Scot., U.K. | 46 | 57.47 N | 5.39 W |
| Na'azuz, Har ∧ | 132 | 30.01 N | 35.00 E |
| Nabā, Jabal an- (Mount Nebo) ∧ | 132 | 31.46 N | 35.45 E |
| Nababiep | 156 | 29.36 S | 17.46 E |
| Nabābpur | 272b | 22.42 N | 88.12 E |
| Nabaganga ≐[1] | 126 | 22.59 N | 89.34 E |
| Nabagram | 126 | 24.12 N | 88.06 E |
| Nabalat Al-Ḥajanah | 140 | 13.13 N | 29.02 E |
| Nabari | 94 | 34.37 N | 136.05 E |
| Nabari ≐ | 94 | 34.45 N | 136.01 E |
| Nabarūh | 142 | 31.06 N | 31.18 E |
| Nabas | 116 | 11.50 N | 122.05 E |
| Nabasta | 126 | 23.15 N | 88.01 E |
| Nabawa | 162 | 28.31 S | 114.47 E |
| Nabb | 218 | 38.36 N | 85.38 W |
| Nabberu, Lake ⊜ | 162 | 25.36 S | 120.30 E |
| Nabburg | 60 | 49.28 N | 12.11 E |
| Nabeba, Mont ∧ | 152 | 1.57 N | 13.50 E |
| Nabeina | 174t | 1.26 N | 173.05 E |
| Naberera | 154 | 4.12 S | 36.56 E |
| Naberežnoje | 265b | 55.57 N | 37.58 E |
| Naberežnyje Čelny | 80 | 55.42 N | 52.19 E |
| Nabesna | 180 | 62.22 N | 143.00 W |
| Nabesna ≐ | 180 | 63.03 N | 141.52 W |
| Nabeul | 148 | 36.27 N | 10.44 E |
| Nābha | 123 | 30.22 N | 76.09 E |
| Nab Hill ∧[2] | 262 | 53.47 N | 1.57 W |
| Nabigou | 152 | 1.12 S | 9.31 E |
| Nabī Hārūn, Jabal an- ∧ | 132 | 30.19 N | 35.24 E |
| Nabileque ≐ | 248 | 20.55 S | 57.49 W |
| Nabire | 164 | 3.22 S | 135.29 E |
| Nabī Shu'ayb, Jabal an- ∧ | 144 | 15.17 N | 43.59 E |
| Nabisipi ≐ | 186 | 50.14 N | 62.13 W |
| Nabiswera | 154 | 1.28 N | 32.16 E |
| Nabī Yūnus, Ra's an- › | 132 | 33.39 N | 35.24 E |
| Nabnasset | 207 | 42.36 N | 71.25 W |
| Nabnasset Pond ⊜ | 283 | 42.37 N | 71.26 W |
| Nabogame | 232 | 26.14 N | 106.57 W |
| Naboomspruit | 156 | 24.32 S | 28.36 E |
| Nabordo | 150 | 10.10 N | 9.20 E |
| Nabou | 150 | 11.27 N | 2.43 W |
| Nabq | 140 | 28.04 N | 34.25 E |
| Nabua | 116 | 13.24 N | 123.22 E |
| Nabula | 120 | 31.55 N | 80.10 E |
| Nābulus | 132 | 32.13 N | 35.16 E |
| Nabunturan | 116 | 7.35 N | 125.58 E |
| Nacajuca | 234 | 18.08 N | 93.01 W |
| Nacala | 154 | 14.34 S | 40.41 E |
| Nacala-Velha | 154 | 14.32 S | 40.37 E |
| Načalovo | 80 | 46.20 N | 48.11 E |
| Nacaome | 236 | 13.31 N | 87.30 W |
| Nacasio Reservoir ⊜[1] | 226 | 38.05 N | 122.44 W |
| Nacastillo | 234 | 19.35 N | 104.55 W |
| Nacchie | 144 | 7.23 N | 40.10 E |
| Nacereddine | 34 | 36.08 N | 3.26 E |
| Nachabinka ≐ | 265b | 55.51 N | 37.12 E |
| Nachabino | 82 | 55.51 N | 37.11 E |
| Naches | 224 | 46.43 N | 120.41 W |
| Naches ≐ | 202 | 46.38 N | 120.31 W |
| Nachi-katsuura | 92 | 33.30 N | 135.55 E |
| Nāchinda | 126 | 21.53 N | 87.46 E |
| Nachingwea | 154 | 10.23 S | 38.46 E |
| Nāchna | 120 | 27.30 N | 71.43 E |
| Náchod | 30 | 50.25 N | 16.10 E |
| Nachodka | 89 | 42.48 N | 132.52 E |
| Nachrodt-Wiblingwerde | 263 | 51.19 N | 7.37 E |
| Nächstebreck ◈[8] | 263 | 51.18 N | 7.14 E |
| Nachterstedt | 54 | 51.49 N | 11.20 E |
| Nachuge | 110 | 10.45 N | 92.22 E |
| Nachvak Fiord ⊂[2] | 176 | 59.03 N | 63.45 W |
| Naci, Pil. | 116 | 14.19 N | 120.46 E |
| Naci, Pil. | 116 | 6.19 N | 124.46 E |
| Nacimiento | 252 | 37.30 S | 72.40 W |
| Nacimiento ≐ | 226 | 35.49 N | 120.45 W |
| Nacimiento, Lake ⊜[1] | 226 | 35.45 N | 121.00 W |
| Načinskij Golec, gora ∧ | 89 | 52.24 N | 118.53 E |
| Nacka | 40 | 59.18 N | 18.10 E |
| Naco, Méx. | 232 | 31.20 N | 109.56 W |
| Naco, Az., U.S. | 200 | 31.20 N | 109.56 W |
| Nacogdoches | 222 | 31.36 N | 94.39 W |
| Nacogdoches □[6] | 222 | 31.40 N | 94.45 W |
| Nacogdoches, Lake ⊜[1] | 222 | 31.37 N | 94.50 W |
| Nácori Chico | 232 | 29.39 N | 109.01 W |
| Nacozari de García | 232 | 30.24 N | 109.39 W |
| Ñacunday | 252 | 26.01 S | 54.46 W |
| Nada | 222 | 29.24 N | 96.23 W |
| Nada ◈[8] | 270 | 34.44 N | 135.14 E |
| Nadābhānga | 272b | 22.24 N | 88.14 E |
| Nadachi | 94 | 37.09 N | 138.06 E |
| Nadaleen Mountain ∧ | 180 | 64.15 N | 133.04 W |
| Nadasaki | 96 | 34.32 N | 133.52 E |
| Nádasd | 61 | 46.58 N | 16.37 E |
| Nadbai | 124 | 27.14 N | 77.12 E |
| Nadder ≐ | 42 | 51.03 N | 1.48 W |
| Nadela | 34 | 42.58 N | 7.30 W |
| Nadelkap → Agulhas, Cape › | 158 | 34.52 S | 20.00 E |
| Naden Harbour ⊂ | 182 | 54.00 N | 132.35 W |
| Nadeždinskoje | 89 | 48.18 N | 133.11 E |
| Nadi, Fiji | 175g | 17.48 S | 177.25 E |
| Nadi, Sūd. | 140 | 18.40 N | 33.42 E |
| Nadiād | 120 | 22.42 N | 72.52 E |
| Nadi Bay ⊂ | 175g | 17.44 S | 177.25 E |
| Nādir, Misr | 142 | 30.33 N | 30.51 E |
| Nadir, Vir. Is., U.S. | 240m | 18.19 N | 64.53 W |
| Nădlac | 38 | 46.10 N | 20.45 E |
| Nador | 148 | 35.12 N | 2.55 W |
| Nador □[4] | 148 | 35.09 N | 3.04 W |
| Nadporožje | 75 | 60.28 N | 34.17 E |
| Nadrin | 56 | 50.10 N | 5.41 E |
| Nadterečnaja | 84 | 43.37 N | 45.22 E |
| Nadvirna | 78 | 48.38 N | 24.34 E |
| Nadvoicy | 24 | 63.52 N | 34.15 E |
| Nadym | 72 | 65.35 N | 72.42 E |
| Nadym ≐ | 74 | 66.12 N | 72.00 E |
| Nadyrovo | 80 | 54.53 N | 52.28 E |
| Naeba-san ∧ | 94 | 36.51 N | 138.41 E |
| Nae-dong | 98 | 37.16 N | 126.27 E |
| Naejang-san Kukrip Kongwŏn ♠ | 98 | 35.28 N | 126.52 E |
| Naenwa | 120 | 25.46 N | 75.51 E |
| Nærbø | 26 | 58.40 N | 5.39 E |
| Næsby | 41 | 55.25 N | 10.22 E |
| Næstved | 41 | 55.14 N | 11.46 E |
| Nafada | 146 | 11.08 N | 11.20 E |
| Nafadji | 150 | 12.37 N | 11.37 W |
| Nafarros | 266c | 38.49 N | 9.25 W |
| Nafāzah, 'Alam ∧[2] | 142 | 30.30 N | 29.42 E |
| Näfels | 58 | 47.06 N | 9.04 E |
| Nafī | 128 | 24.57 N | 43.42 E |
| Nafīshah | 142 | 30.34 N | 32.15 E |
| Naftalan | 84 | 40.31 N | 46.50 E |
| Naftan, Puntan I › | 174n | 15.05 N | 145.45 E |
| Nāfūrah | 146 | 29.20 N | 21.20 E |
| Nafūsah, Jabal ⋏[2] | 146 | 31.50 N | 12.00 E |
| Nāg | 120 | 27.24 N | 65.08 E |
| Naga, Nihon | 96 | 34.16 N | 135.26 E |
| Naga, Pil. | 116 | 13.37 N | 123.11 E |
| Naga, Pil. | 116 | 10.13 N | 123.45 E |
| Nâga, Kreb en ±[4] | 148 | 24.00 N | 6.00 W |
| Naga, Oued en V | 148 | 27.53 N | 7.10 W |
| Nagaga | 154 | 10.54 S | 39.07 E |
| Nagahama, Nihon | 94 | 35.23 N | 136.16 E |
| Nagahama, Nihon | 96 | 33.36 N | 132.29 E |
| Nagahama, Nihon | 174m | 26.25 N | 127.44 E |
| Naga Hills ⋏ | 110 | 26.00 N | 95.00 E |
| Nagai, Nihon | 92 | 38.06 N | 140.02 E |
| Nagai, Nihon | 268 | 35.12 N | 139.37 E |
| Nagai Island I | 180 | 55.11 N | 159.55 W |
| Nagai Park ♠ | 270 | 34.36 N | 135.31 E |
| Nagaizumi | 94 | 35.08 N | 138.54 E |
| Nāgāland □[3] | 120 | 26.00 N | 95.00 E |
| Nagambie | 169 | 36.47 S | 145.10 E |
| Nagannu-shima I | 174m | 26.16 N | 127.33 E |
| Nagano | 94 | 36.39 N | 138.11 E |
| Nagano □[5] | 94 | 36.00 N | 138.00 E |
| Nagano-dam ◈[6] | 94 | 35.50 N | 136.33 E |
| Naganohara | 94 | 36.33 N | 138.38 E |
| Nagao, Nihon | 96 | 34.16 N | 134.10 E |
| Nagao, Nihon | 270 | 34.50 N | 135.43 E |
| Nagao-hana › | 96 | 35.32 N | 134.01 E |
| Nagaoka | 92 | 37.27 N | 138.51 E |
| Nagaokakyō | 94 | 34.55 N | 135.42 E |
| Nagaon | 120 | 26.20 N | 92.40 E |
| Nāgappattinam | 122 | 10.46 N | 79.50 E |
| Nagar, India | 123 | 32.07 N | 77.10 E |
| Nagar, India | 124 | 27.26 N | 77.06 E |
| Nagara | 270 | 34.26 N | 135.44 E |
| Nagara ≐ | 94 | 35.01 N | 136.43 E |
| Nagareyama | 94 | 35.51 N | 139.54 E |
| Nāgārjuna Sāgar ⊜[1] | 122 | 16.35 N | 79.21 E |
| Nagarote | 236 | 12.16 N | 86.34 W |
| Nagar Pārkar | 120 | 24.22 N | 70.45 E |
| Nāgarpur | 124 | 24.03 N | 89.53 E |
| Nagar Untāri | 124 | 24.17 N | 83.30 E |
| Nagarzê | 124 | 28.59 N | 90.25 E |
| Nagas | 116 | 13.06 N | 123.18 E |
| Nagasaka | 94 | 35.49 N | 138.22 E |
| Nagasaki | 92 | 32.48 N | 129.55 E |
| Nagasawa | 268 | 35.12 N | 139.41 E |
| Nagashima | 94 | 35.05 N | 136.42 E |
| Naga-shima I, Nihon | 96 | 33.49 N | 132.05 E |
| Naga-shima I, Nihon | 96 | 34.41 N | 134.15 E |
| Nagashino ⊥ | 94 | 34.56 N | 137.32 E |
| Nagasin Lake ⊜ | 190 | 47.44 N | 83.37 W |
| Nagasu, Nihon | 96 | 32.56 N | 130.27 E |
| Nagasu → Usa, Nihon | 96 | 33.31 N | 131.22 E |
| Nagata ◈[8] | 270 | 34.40 N | 135.09 E |
| Nagataki | 270 | 34.23 N | 135.20 E |
| Nagatino ◈[8] | 265b | 55.41 N | 37.41 E |
| Nagato, Nihon | 94 | 36.15 N | 138.16 E |
| Nagato, Nihon | 96 | 34.21 N | 131.10 E |
| Nagatsuda ◈[8] | 268 | 35.32 N | 139.30 E |
| Nāgaur | 120 | 27.12 N | 73.44 E |
| Nāgāvali ≐ | 122 | 18.13 N | 83.56 E |
| Nagavskaja | 80 | 47.47 N | 42.50 E |
| Nagawa | 94 | 36.05 N | 137.41 E |
| Nagawicka Lake ⊜ | 216 | 43.05 N | 88.23 W |
| Nagcarlan | 116 | 14.08 N | 121.25 E |
| Nagda | 120 | 23.27 N | 75.25 E |
| Nagele | 52 | 52.37 N | 5.44 E |
| Nāgercoil | 122 | 8.10 N | 77.26 E |
| Nagi | 96 | 35.07 N | 134.11 E |
| Nagiba | 116 | 13.41 N | 120.53 E |
| Nagibino | 86 | 55.46 N | 72.43 E |
| Nagichot | 154 | 4.16 N | 33.34 E |
| Nagīna | 124 | 29.27 N | 78.27 E |
| Nāgirāt | 126 | 23.38 N | 89.18 E |
| Nagi-san ∧ | 96 | 35.10 N | 134.11 E |
| Nagiso | 94 | 35.36 N | 137.37 E |
| Nagla | 272a | 28.31 N | 77.22 E |
| Naglarby | 40 | 60.25 N | 15.34 E |
| Nagles Mountains ⋏ | 48 | 52.05 N | 8.30 W |
| Nagłowice | 30 | 50.41 N | 20.06 E |
| Nago | 174m | 26.35 N | 127.59 E |
| Nāgod | 124 | 24.34 N | 80.36 E |
| Nagog Pond ⊜ | 283 | 42.31 N | 71.26 W |
| Nagoja → Nagoya | 94 | 35.10 N | 136.55 E |
| Nagold | 56 | 48.33 N | 8.43 E |
| Nagold ≐ | 56 | 48.52 N | 8.42 E |
| Nagorje | 76 | 56.55 N | 38.16 E |
| Nagorno-Karabakh □[9] | 84 | 40.00 N | 46.40 E |
| Nagornyj, Ross. | 74 | 55.58 N | 124.57 E |
| Nagornyj, Ross. | 265a | 59.43 N | 30.16 E |
| Nagorsk | 24 | 59.18 N | 50.48 E |
| Nagorskoje | 82 | 56.54 N | 38.06 E |
| Nago-wan ⊂ | 174m | 26.34 N | 127.57 E |
| Nagoya | 94 | 35.10 N | 136.55 E |
| Nagoya-kūkō ⊠ | 94 | 35.15 N | 136.55 E |
| Nāgpur | 120 | 21.09 N | 79.06 E |
| Nagqu | 120 | 31.34 N | 92.00 E |
| Nagrai | 123 | 34.23 N | 72.41 E |
| Nāgrākāta | 124 | 26.54 N | 88.55 E |
| Nagrota | 123 | 32.03 N | 76.05 E |
| Nagu I | 26 | 60.10 N | 21.48 E |
| Nagua | 238 | 19.23 N | 69.50 W |
| Naguabo | 240m | 18.13 N | 65.44 W |
| Naguilian | 116 | 17.01 N | 121.50 E |
| Nagumbuaya Point › | 116 | 13.34 N | 124.21 E |
| Naguri | 94 | 35.53 N | 139.11 E |
| Naguri I | 122 | 6.39 N | 72.55 E |
| Nagyatád | 30 | 46.14 N | 17.22 E |
| Nagybajom | 30 | 46.23 N | 17.31 E |
| Nagybánya → Baia Mare | 38 | 47.40 N | 23.35 E |
| Nagycenk | 61 | 47.36 N | 16.42 E |
| Nagyecsed | 30 | 47.52 N | 22.24 E |
| Nagykálló | 30 | 47.53 N | 21.51 E |
| Nagykanizsa | 30 | 46.27 N | 17.00 E |
| Nagykáta | 30 | 47.25 N | 19.45 E |
| Nagy-Kevély ∧[2] | 264c | 47.37 N | 18.59 E |
| Nagykőrös | 30 | 47.02 N | 19.43 E |
| Nagy-Milic ∧ | 30 | 48.35 N | 21.28 E |
| Nagytarcsa | 264c | 47.32 N | 19.17 E |
| Nagytétény ◈[8] | 264c | 47.24 N | 18.58 E |
| Nagyvarad → Oradea | 38 | 47.03 N | 21.57 E |
| Naha | 174m | 26.13 N | 127.40 E |
| Naha Airfield ⊠ | 174m | 26.13 N | 127.40 E |
| Nahabuan | 112 | 0.49 N | 114.05 E |
| Nahakki | 123 | 34.25 N | 71.20 E |
| Nahalal | 132 | 32.41 N | 35.12 E |
| Naḥal 'Oz | 132 | 31.28 N | 34.30 E |
| Naḥam | 132 | 31.46 N | 35.00 E |
| Nāhan | 124 | 30.33 N | 77.18 E |
| Nahang (Nihing) ≐ | 128 | 26.00 N | 62.44 E |
| Nahanni National Park ♠ | 180 | 61.40 N | 126.00 W |
| Nahant | 207 | 42.25 N | 70.55 W |
| Nahant Bay ⊂ | 207 | 42.27 N | 70.55 W |
| Nahant Beach ±[2] | 283 | 42.27 N | 70.56 W |
| Nahari | 96 | 33.25 N | 134.01 E |
| Nahari ≐ | 96 | 33.25 N | 134.01 E |
| Nahariyya | 132 | 33.00 N | 35.05 E |
| Naharpur ◈[8] | 272a | 28.42 N | 77.07 E |
| Nahāta | 126 | 23.20 N | 89.31 E |
| Nahāvand | 128 | 34.12 N | 48.22 E |
| Nahcotta | 224 | 46.30 N | 124.02 W |
| Nahe | 89 | 48.28 N | 124.52 E |
| Nahe ≐ | 56 | 49.58 N | 7.57 E |
| Naḥf | 132 | 32.56 N | 35.19 E |
| Nahirne | 78 | 45.26 N | 28.27 E |
| Nahma | 190 | 45.50 N | 86.39 W |
| Nahmer ◈[8] | 263 | 51.20 N | 7.35 E |
| Nahmer ≐ | 263 | 51.21 N | 7.35 E |
| Nahoe | 174x | 9.45 S | 138.55 W |
| Nahoï, Cap › | 175f | 14.39 S | 166.37 E |
| Nahol'chyk | 83 | 48.01 N | 39.04 E |
| Nahol'na ≐ | 83 | 47.57 N | 38.58 E |
| Nahol'no-Tarasivka | 83 | 48.00 N | 39.29 E |
| Nahon ≐ | 50 | 47.14 N | 1.39 E |
| Nahrīn | 120 | 36.01 N | 69.06 E |
| Nahr Ouassel, Oued ≐ | 148 | 35.42 N | 2.33 E |
| Nahualate ≐ | 236 | 14.03 N | 91.32 W |
| Nahuatzén | 234 | 19.42 N | 101.50 W |
| Nahuel Huapi | 254 | 41.03 S | 71.09 W |
| Nahuel Huapi, Lago ⊜ | 254 | 40.58 S | 71.30 W |
| Nahuel Huapi, Parque Nacional ♠ | 254 | 41.00 S | 71.48 W |
| Nahuel Niyeu | 254 | 40.30 S | 66.33 W |
| Nahunta | 192 | 31.12 N | 81.58 W |
| Nāhyā | 142 | 30.03 N | 31.07 E |
| Naia ≐ | 66 | 42.46 N | 12.22 E |
| Naica | 232 | 27.53 N | 105.31 W |
| Naicam | 184 | 52.25 N | 104.30 W |
| Nai Ga | 102 | 27.48 N | 97.30 E |
| Naiguatá, Pico ∧ | 286c | 10.33 N | 66.46 W |
| Naihāti, Bngl. | 126 | 22.49 N | 89.37 E |
| Naihāti, India | 126 | 22.54 N | 88.25 E |
| Naij Gol ≐, Zhg. | 102 | 36.20 N | 94.49 E |
| Naij Gol ≐, Zhg. | 120 | 36.20 N | 94.49 E |
| Naikliu | 112 | 9.30 S | 123.50 E |
| Naikoon Provincial Park ♠ | 182 | 53.50 N | 131.50 W |
| Naila | 54 | 50.19 N | 11.42 E |
| Nailin | 98 | 41.53 N | 119.15 E |
| Nails Creek ≐ | 222 | 30.16 N | 96.44 W |
| Nailsea | 42 | 51.26 N | 2.43 W |
| Nailsworth | 42 | 51.42 N | 2.14 W |
| Nā'im, Jabal an- ∧ | 132 | 31.04 N | 35.55 E |
| Naiman Qi | 89 | 42.55 N | 120.43 E |
| Nain, Nf., Can. | 176 | 56.32 N | 61.41 W |
| Nā'īn, Īrān | 128 | 32.52 N | 53.05 E |
| Nain ⊜ | 40 | 60.14 N | 13.50 E |
| Naini Tāl | 124 | 29.23 N | 79.27 E |
| Nainpur | 124 | 22.26 N | 80.07 E |
| Nairai I | 175g | 17.49 S | 179.24 E |
| Nairn, Scot., U.K. | 46 | 57.35 N | 3.53 W |
| Nairn, La., U.S. | 194 | 29.27 N | 89.38 W |
| Nairn ≐ | 46 | 57.35 N | 3.52 W |
| Nairne | 168b | 35.02 S | 138.54 E |
| Nairobi | 154 | 1.17 S | 36.49 E |
| Nairobi Airport ⊠ | 276 | 41.08 N | 74.21 W |
| Nairobi National Park ♠ | 154 | 1.24 S | 36.50 E |
| Naissaar I | 76 | 59.33 N | 24.32 E |
| Naita ∧ | 144 | 5.30 N | 35.18 E |
| Naitamba Island I | 175g | 17.31 S | 179.17 W |
| Naivasha | 154 | 0.43 S | 36.26 E |
| Naivasha, Lake ⊜ | 154 | 0.46 S | 36.21 E |
| Naivos | 114 | 2.30 N | 96.10 E |
| Naizifang | 105 | 39.36 N | 116.47 E |
| N'aizishen | 89 | 43.41 N | 127.29 E |
| Najac | 32 | 44.13 N | 1.59 E |
| Najafābād | 128 | 32.37 N | 51.21 E |
| Najafgarh ◈[8] | 272a | 28.37 N | 76.59 E |
| Najafgarh Drain ≊ | 272a | 28.43 N | 77.14 E |
| Najasa ≐ | 240p | 20.42 N | 77.55 W |
| Najd □[9] | 118 | 25.00 N | 44.30 E |
| Nájera | 34 | 42.25 N | 2.44 W |
| Najhā | 132 | 33.23 N | 36.22 E |
| Naj' Ḥammādī | 140 | 26.03 N | 32.15 E |
| Najībābād | 124 | 29.38 N | 78.20 E |
| Najin | 98 | 42.15 N | 130.18 E |
| Najinkouzi | 89 | 50.23 N | 126.57 E |
| Najio | 270 | 34.50 N | 135.18 E |
| Najstenjarvi | 24 | 62.16 N | 32.38 E |
| Naju | 98 | 35.03 N | 126.43 E |
| Najza, gora ∧ | 86 | 49.24 N | 70.42 E |
| Naka, Nihon | 94 | 36.27 N | 140.30 E |
| Naka, Nihon | 96 | 35.02 N | 134.55 E |
| Naka, Nihon | 268 | 35.49 N | 140.03 E |
| Naka, Nihon | 270 | 34.50 N | 135.48 E |
| Naka, Nihon | 270 | 34.42 N | 135.45 E |
| Naka, Nihon | 270 | 34.50 N | 135.56 E |
| Naka ◈[8] | 268 | 35.27 N | 139.39 E |
| Naka ≐, Nihon | 94 | 36.20 N | 140.36 E |
| Naka ≐, Nihon | 96 | 33.56 N | 134.42 E |
| Naka ≐, Nihon | 268 | 35.39 N | 139.51 E |
| Nakadōri-shima I | 92 | 32.57 N | 129.04 E |
| Nakagami | 268 | 35.49 N | 139.21 E |
| Nakagawa | 94 | 35.38 N | 137.56 E |
| Nakagawa ◈[8] | 268 | 35.33 N | 139.35 E |
| Nakagō | 94 | 36.58 N | 138.14 E |
| Nakagusuku | 174m | 26.15 N | 127.49 E |
| Nakagusuku-wan ⊂ | 174m | 26.14 N | 127.53 E |
| Nakagyō ◈[8] | 270 | 35.01 N | 135.45 E |
| Nakaheji | 96 | 33.47 N | 135.31 E |
| Nakai | 94 | 35.20 N | 139.14 E |
| Nakaizu | 94 | 34.57 N | 139.00 E |
| Nakajima, Nihon | 94 | 37.07 N | 136.51 E |
| Nakajima, Nihon | 96 | 33.58 N | 132.07 E |
| Nakajima, Nihon | 268 | 35.26 N | 139.56 E |
| Nakajima, Nihon | 268 | 35.18 N | 139.58 E |
| Naka-jima I | 96 | 33.58 N | 132.37 E |
| Nakajō, Nihon | 92 | 38.03 N | 139.24 E |
| Nakajō, Nihon | 94 | 36.36 N | 138.02 E |
| Nakakawane | 94 | 35.03 N | 138.05 E |
| Nāka Khārari | 120 | 25.15 N | 66.44 E |
| Nakalele Point › | 229a | 21.02 N | 156.35 W |
| Nākālia | 126 | 24.02 N | 89.40 E |
| Nakama, Nihon | 96 | 33.50 N | 130.43 E |
| Nakama, Nihon | 174m | 26.16 N | 127.44 E |
| Nakaminato | 94 | 36.21 N | 140.36 E |
| Nakamura | 96 | 32.59 N | 132.56 E |
| Nakanai Mountains ⋏ | 164 | 5.35 S | 151.10 E |
| Nakano, Nihon | 94 | 36.45 N | 138.22 E |
| Nakano, Nihon | 268 | 35.20 N | 139.54 E |
| Nakano, Nihon | 270 | 34.58 N | 135.58 E |
| Nakano ◈[8] | 268 | 35.42 N | 139.42 E |
| Nakanobu ◈[8] | 268 | 35.36 N | 139.43 E |
| Nakanojō | 94 | 36.35 N | 138.51 E |
| Nakano-shima I | 93b | 29.49 N | 129.52 E |
| Nakanoshima-suidō ⊔ | 93b | 29.44 N | 129.49 E |
| Nakanougan-jima I | 175d | 24.11 N | 123.33 E |
| Nakaosu | 174m | 26.37 N | 128.02 E |
| Nakaōzō ◈[8] | 270 | 34.51 N | 135.11 E |
| Nakape | 140 | 5.47 N | 28.37 E |
| Nakashibetsu | 92a | 43.33 N | 144.59 E |
| Nākāsipāra | 126 | 23.35 N | 88.21 E |
| Nakasongola | 154 | 1.19 N | 32.28 E |
| Nakatō | 268 | 35.45 N | 139.24 E |
| Nakatomi, Nihon | 94 | 35.28 N | 138.26 E |
| Nakatomi, Nihon | 268 | 35.49 N | 139.30 E |
| Nakatosa | 96 | 33.20 N | 133.14 E |
| Nakatsu, Nihon | 96 | 33.34 N | 131.13 E |
| Nakatsu, Nihon | 96 | 33.57 N | 135.18 E |
| Nakatsu, Nihon | 268 | 35.30 N | 139.20 E |
| Nakatsu ≐ | 94 | 37.00 N | 138.39 E |
| Nakatsue | 96 | 33.08 N | 130.56 E |
| Nakatsugawa | 94 | 35.29 N | 137.30 E |
| Nakatsumine-yama ∧ | 96 | 33.58 N | 134.31 E |
| Nakauchigami | 270 | 34.56 N | 135.10 E |
| Naka-umi ⊂ | 96 | 35.28 N | 133.12 E |
| Nakayama, Nihon | 96 | 33.38 N | 132.42 E |
| Nakayama, Nihon | 96 | 35.31 N | 133.35 E |
| Nakayama ◈[8] | 268 | 35.31 N | 139.33 E |
| Nakayama ≐ | 96 | 33.55 N | 133.08 E |
| Nakazato, Nihon | 94 | 36.05 N | 138.50 E |
| Nakazato, Nihon | 94 | 37.03 N | 138.42 E |
| Nakazuma | 268 | 35.58 N | 139.35 E |
| Nakéty | 175f | 21.33 S | 166.03 E |
| Nakfa | 144 | 16.43 N | 38.32 E |
| Nakhichevan → Naxçıvan Muxtar Respublikası □[3] | 84 | 39.20 N | 45.30 E |
| Nakhola | 120 | 26.07 N | 92.11 E |
| Nakhon Nayok | 110 | 14.12 N | 101.13 E |
| Nakhon Pathom | 110 | 13.49 N | 100.03 E |
| Nakhon Phanom | 110 | 17.24 N | 104.47 E |
| Nakhon Ratchasima | 110 | 14.58 N | 102.07 E |
| Nakhon Sawan | 110 | 15.41 N | 100.07 E |
| Nakhon Si Thammarat | 110 | 8.26 N | 99.58 E |
| Nakhon Thai | 110 | 17.07 N | 100.50 E |
| Nakhtarana | 120 | 23.20 N | 69.15 E |
| Nakina | 176 | 50.10 N | 86.42 W |
| Nakkaş ≐ | 267b | 41.00 N | 28.45 E |
| Nakło nad Notecią | 30 | 53.08 N | 17.35 E |
| Naknek | 180 | 58.44 N | 157.02 W |
| Naknek Lake ⊜ | 180 | 58.40 N | 156.15 W |
| Nako | 150 | 10.38 N | 3.04 W |
| Nakodar | 123 | 31.07 N | 75.29 E |
| Nakonde | 154 | 9.20 S | 32.42 E |
| Nakoso-no-seki-ato ⊥ | 94 | 36.53 N | 140.46 E |
| Nakou | 100 | 27.09 N | 117.38 E |
| Nakskov | 41 | 54.50 N | 11.09 E |
| Nakskov Fjord ⊂ | 41 | 54.50 N | 11.02 E |
| Näkten ⊜ | 26 | 62.52 N | 14.38 E |
| Naktong-gang ≐ | 98 | 35.07 N | 128.57 E |
| Nakūr | 124 | 29.55 N | 77.18 E |
| Nakuru | 154 | 0.17 S | 36.04 E |
| Nakuru, Lake ⊜ | 154 | 0.22 S | 36.05 E |
| Nakusp | 182 | 50.15 N | 117.48 W |
| Nāl ≐ | 120 | 26.02 N | 65.19 E |
| Nālāgarh | 123 | 31.03 N | 76.43 E |
| Nalajch | 88 | 47.45 N | 107.16 E |
| Nālanda | 124 | 25.07 N | 85.25 E |
| Nalao | 102 | 24.22 N | 105.23 E |
| Nalázi | 156 | 24.03 S | 33.20 E |
| Nalbach | 56 | 49.23 N | 6.47 E |
| Nalbāri | 120 | 26.25 N | 91.26 E |
| Nalcayec, Isla I | 254 | 46.06 S | 73.49 W |
| Nalchik → Nal'čik | 84 | 43.29 N | 43.37 E |
| Nālchiti | 124 | 22.38 N | 90.17 E |
| Nal'čik | 84 | 43.29 N | 43.37 E |
| Naldānga | 126 | 23.26 N | 89.11 E |
| Nāldera | 123 | 31.11 N | 77.11 E |
| Näldsjön ⊜ | 26 | 63.23 N | 14.17 E |
| Nałęczów | 30 | 51.18 N | 22.11 E |
| Nalgonda | 122 | 17.03 N | 79.16 E |
| Nalgora | 126 | 22.52 N | 90.39 E |
| Nalhāti | 126 | 24.18 N | 87.49 E |
| Naliagrām | 126 | 23.36 N | 89.37 E |
| Naliang | 102 | 21.43 N | 107.51 E |
| Nālikul | 272b | 22.49 N | 88.11 E |
| Nalinnes | 50 | 50.19 N | 4.26 E |
| Nalisan | 104 | 42.06 N | 122.12 E |
| Nallamalla Hills ⋏ | 122 | 15.30 N | 78.45 E |
| Nalles (Nals) | 64 | 46.32 N | 11.12 E |
| Nallıhan | 130 | 40.11 N | 31.21 E |
| Na Logu | 64 | 46.23 N | 13.45 E |
| Nalolo | 152 | 15.35 S | 23.07 E |
| Nalón ≐ | 34 | 43.32 N | 6.04 W |
| Nalong | 102 | 23.35 N | 106.05 E |
| Nalusa | 152 | 14.55 S | 22.13 E |
| Nālūt | 146 | 31.52 N | 10.59 E |
| Nalžovské Hory | 60 | 49.20 N | 13.33 E |
| Nam ≐ | 110 | 21.33 N | 98.38 E |
| Namaacha | 156 | 25.58 S | 32.01 E |
| Namachire | 152 | 11.26 S | 22.43 E |
| Namacunde | 152 | 17.18 S | 15.50 E |
| Namacurra | 154 | 17.29 S | 37.01 E |
| Namadgi National Park ♠ | 171b | 35.45 S | 148.57 E |
| Namak, Daryācheh-ye ⊜ | 128 | 34.30 N | 51.50 E |
| Namak, Kavīr-e ◈[2] | 128 | 34.45 N | 57.45 E |
| Namakan Lake ⊜ | 190 | 48.27 N | 92.35 W |
| Nāmakkal | 122 | 11.14 N | 78.10 E |
| Namaksār, Kowl-e ⊜ | 128 | 34.00 N | 60.30 E |
| Namakula | 174v | 18.57 S | 169.54 W |
| Namamugi ◈[8] | 268 | 35.29 N | 139.41 E |
| Namanga | 154 | 2.33 S | 36.46 E |
| Namangan | 85 | 41.00 N | 71.40 E |
| Namangan □[4] | 85 | 41.00 N | 71.15 E |
| Namanyere | 154 | 7.31 S | 31.03 E |
| Namapa | 154 | 13.43 S | 39.50 E |
| Namarodu, Cape › | 164 | 3.38 S | 152.30 E |
| Namarrói | 154 | 15.58 S | 36.55 E |
| Namasagali | 154 | 1.01 N | 32.57 E |
| Namatanai | 164 | 3.40 S | 152.25 E |
| Nambe Indian Reservation ◈[4] | 200 | 35.52 N | 105.57 W |
| Namber | 164 | 1.04 S | 134.49 E |
| Nambi | 162 | 28.54 S | 121.41 E |
| Namborn | 56 | 49.31 N | 7.08 E |


| | | | | |
|---|---|---|---|---|
| ≐ River | Fluß | Río | Rivière | Rio |
| ≊ Canal | Kanal | Canal | Canal | Canal |
| ∟ Waterfall, Rapids | Wasserfall, Stromschnellen | Cascada, Rápidos | Chute d'eau, Rapides | Cascata, Rápidos |
| ⊔ Strait | Meeresstraße | Estrecho | Détroit | Estreito |
| ⊂ Bay, Gulf | Bucht, Golf | Bahía, Golfo | Baie, Golfe | Baía, Golfo |
| ⊜ Lake, Lakes | See, Seen | Lago, Lagos | Lac, Lacs | Lago, Lagos |
| ≡ Swamp | Sumpf | Pantano | Marais | Pântano |
| ⊓ Ice Features, Glacier | Eis- und Gletscherformen | Accidentes Glaciales | Formes glaciaires | Acidentes glaciares |
| ⊤ Other Hydrographic Features | Andere Hydrographische Objekte | Otros Elementos Hidrográficos | Autres données hydrographiques | Outros acidentes hidrográficos |

| | | | | |
|---|---|---|---|---|
| ⊹ Submarine Features | Untermeerische Objekte | Accidentes Submarinos | Formes de relief sous-marin | Acidentes submarinos |
| □ Political Unit | Politische Einheit | Unidad Politica | Entité politique | Unidade política |
| ♁ Cultural Institution | Kulturelle Institution | Institución Cultural | Institution culturelle | Instituição cultural |
| ⊥ Historical Site | Historische Stätte | Sitio Histórico | Site historique | Sitio histórico |
| ♠ Recreational Site | Erholungs- und Ferienort | Sitio de Recreo | Centre de loisirs | Area de Lazer |
| ⊠ Airport | Flughafen | Aeropuerto | Aéroport | Aeroporto |
| ■ Military Installation | Militäranlage | Instalación Militar | Installation militaire | Instalação militar |
| ◈ Miscellaneous | Verschiedenes | Misceláneo | Divers | Diversos |

ENGLISH | DEUTSCH


| Name | Page | Lat.°′ | Long.°′ |
|---|---|---|---|
| Nambour | 166 | 26.38 S | 152.58 E |
| Nambouwalu | 175g | 16.59 S | 178.42 E |
| Nambuangongo | 152 | 8.01 S | 14.12 E |
| Nambucca Heads | 166 | 30.39 S | 153.00 E |
| Nam Can | 110 | 8.46 N | 104.59 E |
| Namcha Barwa → Namjagbarwa Feng ∧ | 102 | 29.38 N | 95.04 E |
| Namch'ang | 98 | 35.26 N | 129.16 E |
| Nam Co ⊜ | 120 | 30.42 N | 90.30 E |
| Namdae-ch'ŏn ≃ | 98 | 40.26 N | 128.57 E |
| Namdanak | 85 | 41.11 N | 69.42 E |
| Nam Dinh | 110 | 20.25 N | 106.10 E |
| Nämdö I | 40 | 59.12 N | 18.41 E |
| Nämdöfjärden ʯ | 40 | 59.12 N | 18.34 E |
| Nam Du, Quan Dao II | 110 | 9.42 N | 104.22 E |
| Namegawa | 94 | 36.04 N | 139.22 E |
| Nameh | 112 | 2.34 N | 116.21 E |
| Nameigos Lake ⊜ | 190 | 48.46 N | 84.43 W |
| Namekagon ≃ | 190 | 46.05 N | 92.06 W |
| Namen → Namur | 56 | 50.28 N | 4.52 E |
| Namerikawa | 94 | 36.46 N | 137.20 E |
| Náměšť | 61 | 49.12 N | 16.10 E |
| Nametil | 154 | 15.43 S | 39.21 E |
| Namew Lake ⊜ | 184 | 54.13 N | 101.56 W |
| Nam-gang ≃ | 98 | 39.03 N | 125.52 E |
| Namhae | 98 | 34.50 N | 127.54 E |
| Namhae-do I | 98 | 34.48 N | 127.57 E |
| Namhan-gang ≃ | 98 | 37.31 N | 127.18 E |
| Namhkam | 110 | 23.50 N | 97.41 E |
| Namho-ri | 98 | 38.07 N | 125.10 E |
| Namhsan | 110 | 22.58 N | 97.10 E |
| Namiai | 94 | 35.22 N | 137.41 E |
| Namib Desert ◈[2] | 156 | 23.00 S | 15.00 E |
| Namibe | 152 | 15.10 S | 12.09 E |
| Namibe □[5] | 152 | 15.20 S | 12.30 E |
| Namibia □[1], Afr. | 138 | 22.00 S | 17.00 E |
| Namibia □[1], Afr. | 156 | 22.00 S | 17.00 E |
| Namibie → Namibia □[1] | 156 | 22.00 S | 17.00 E |
| Namib-Naukluft Park ♦ | 156 | 23.30 S | 15.30 E |
| Namie | 92 | 37.29 N | 141.00 E |
| Namies | 158 | 29.18 S | 19.13 E |
| Namīn | 128 | 38.25 N | 48.30 E |
| Naminga | 88 | 56.33 N | 118.41 E |
| Namjagbarwa Feng ∧ | 102 | 29.38 N | 95.04 E |
| Nāmja La )( | 124 | 29.27 N | 82.34 E |
| Namji-ri | 98 | 35.23 N | 128.29 E |
| Nāmkhāna | 126 | 21.46 N | 88.14 E |
| Nam Kwo Chau I | 271d | 22.15 N | 114.21 E |
| Namlan | 110 | 22.15 N | 97.24 E |
| Nāmlāng ≃ | 124 | 29.28 N | 82.50 E |
| Namlea | 164 | 3.18 S | 127.06 E |
| Namling | 120 | 29.41 N | 89.04 E |
| Namlos | 58 | 47.21 N | 10.40 E |
| Nam Ngum Reservoir ⊜[1] | 110 | 18.30 N | 102.40 E |
| Namnoi, Khao ∧ | 110 | 10.36 N | 98.38 E |
| Namo | 112 | 1.24 S | 119.57 E |
| Namoi ≃ | 166 | 30.00 S | 148.07 E |
| Namoluk I[1] | 14 | 5.55 N | 153.08 E |
| Namonuito I[1] | 14 | 8.46 N | 150.02 E |
| Namorik I[1] | 14 | 5.36 N | 168.07 E |
| Namoruputh | 154 | 4.34 N | 35.57 E |
| Namounou | 150 | 11.52 N | 1.42 E |
| Namous, Oued en V | 148 | 31.00 N | 0.15 W |
| Namoya | 154 | 4.01 S | 27.34 E |
| Nampa, Ab., Can. | 182 | 56.02 N | 117.08 W |
| Nampa, Id., U.S. | 202 | 43.32 N | 116.33 W |
| Nampala | 150 | 15.17 N | 5.33 W |
| Nam Pat | 110 | 17.43 N | 100.41 E |
| Nampawng | 110 | 22.45 N | 97.52 E |
| Nam Phan □[9] | 110 | 11.00 N | 107.00 E |
| Nam Phong | 110 | 16.42 N | 102.52 E |
| Nampicuan | 116 | 15.44 N | 120.38 E |
| Namp'o | 98 | 38.45 N | 125.23 E |
| Nampont-Saint-Martin | 50 | 50.21 N | 1.45 E |
| Namp'ot'ae-san ∧ | 98 | 41.44 N | 128.24 E |
| Nampuecha | 154 | 13.59 S | 40.18 E |
| Nampula | 154 | 15.07 S | 39.15 E |
| Nampula □[5] | 154 | 15.00 S | 39.00 E |
| Namsang | 110 | 20.53 N | 97.43 E |
| Namsan Park ♦ | 271b | 37.34 N | 126.59 E |
| Namsanyŏng-ni | 98 | 38.59 N | 127.26 E |
| Namsen ≃ | 24 | 64.27 N | 11.28 E |
| Namsi | 98 | 39.54 N | 124.36 E |
| Namsos | 24 | 64.29 N | 11.30 E |
| Nam Tok | 110 | 14.14 N | 99.04 E |
| Namtu | 110 | 23.05 N | 97.24 E |
| Namu | 182 | 51.49 N | 127.52 W |
| Namu I[1] | 14 | 8.00 N | 168.10 E |
| Namuka-I-Lau I | 175g | 18.51 S | 178.38 W |
| Namúli, Serra ∧∧ | 154 | 15.15 S | 37.08 E |
| Namur, Bel. | 56 | 50.28 N | 4.52 E |
| Namur, P.Q., Can. | 206 | 45.54 N | 74.56 W |
| Namur □[4] | 56 | 50.20 N | 4.50 E |
| Namuruputh | 154 | 4.34 N | 35.57 E |
| Namutoni | 156 | 18.49 S | 16.55 E |
| Namwala | 154 | 15.45 S | 26.26 E |
| Namwera | 154 | 14.22 S | 35.30 E |
| Namwŏn | 98 | 35.25 N | 127.21 E |
| Namyang, C.M.I.K. | 98 | 42.57 N | 129.53 E |
| Namyang, Taehan | 98 | 37.14 N | 126.44 E |
| Namyit Island I | 108 | 10.11 N | 114.22 E |
| Namysłów | 30 | 51.05 N | 17.42 E |
| Nan | 110 | 18.47 N | 100.47 E |
| Nan ≃, Thai | 110 | 15.42 N | 100.09 E |
| Nan ≃, Zhg. | 100 | 28.15 N | 120.43 E |
| Nana ≃ | 152 | 5.00 N | 15.50 E |
| Nana Barya ≃ | 146 | 7.59 N | 17.43 E |
| Nana Barya, Réserve de Faune de la ◈[4] | 146 | 7.30 N | 17.30 E |
| Nanacamilpa | 234 | 19.29 N | 98.33 W |
| Nanaimo | 224 | 49.10 N | 123.56 W |
| Nanaimo ≃ | 224 | 49.08 N | 123.54 W |
| Nanaimo Lakes ⊜ | 224 | 49.07 N | 124.11 W |
| Nānakheri ◈[8] | 272a | 28.31 N | 76.59 E |
| Nana Kru | 150 | 4.50 N | 8.44 W |
| Nanakuli | 229c | 21.23 N | 158.09 W |
| Nanam | 98 | 41.43 N | 129.41 E |
| Nana-Mambéré □[5] | 152 | 5.30 N | 15.30 E |
| Nan'an | 100 | 24.58 N | 118.23 E |
| Nan'anba | 107 | 28.46 N | 104.38 E |
| Nanango | 166 | 26.40 S | 152.00 E |
| Nanantun | 110 | 24.45 N | 95.41 E |
| Nanao, Nihon | 94 | 37.03 N | 136.58 E |
| Nanao, T'aiwan | 100 | 24.28 N | 121.48 E |
| Nan'ao, Zhg. | 100 | 23.27 N | 117.02 E |
| Nan'ao Dao I | 100 | 23.26 N | 117.03 E |
| Nanao-wan ⊂ | 94 | 37.06 N | 137.00 E |
| Nanas Channel ʯ | 271c | 1.25 N | 103.58 E |
| Nanatsu-jima II | 92 | 37.36 N | 136.53 E |
| Nanatsuka | 94 | 36.44 N | 136.41 E |
| Nanay ≃ | 246 | 3.42 S | 73.16 W |
| Nanba | 102 | 32.20 N | 104.58 E |
| Nanbaita | 105 | 38.58 N | 115.39 E |
| Nanbaixia | 98 | 35.45 N | 117.23 E |
| Nanbaozhen | 106 | 31.32 N | 121.37 E |
| Nanbu, Nihon | 94 | 35.17 N | 138.27 E |
| Nanbu, Zhg. | 102 | 31.23 N | 106.02 E |
| Nancaicun | 105 | 39.28 N | 117.01 E |
| Nancefield | 273d | 26.17 S | 27.53 E |
| Nancha | 89 | 47.08 N | 129.19 E |
| Nanchang, Zhg. | 100 | 28.41 N | 115.53 E |
| Nanchang (Liantang), Zhg. | 100 | 28.34 N | 115.56 E |
| Nancheng, Zhg. | 100 | 25.39 N | 118.26 E |
| Nancheng, Zhg. | 100 | 27.35 N | 116.40 E |
| Nancheng → Hanzhong, Zhg. | 102 | 33.08 N | 107.02 E |
| Nanching → Nanjing | 106 | 32.03 N | 118.47 E |
| Nanchital | 234 | 18.04 N | 94.24 W |
| Nanchong | 107 | 30.48 N | 106.04 E |
| Nanchuan | 102 | 29.08 N | 107.07 E |
| Nanchuang | 100 | 24.36 N | 120.59 E |
| Nanch'ung → Nanchong | 107 | 30.48 N | 106.04 E |
| Nancowry Island I | 110 | 7.59 N | 93.32 E |
| Nancroix | 62 | 45.32 N | 6.46 E |
| Nancun, Zhg. | 98 | 36.32 N | 120.06 E |
| Nancun, Zhg. | 98 | 39.46 N | 114.07 E |
| Nancy | 58 | 48.41 N | 6.12 E |
| Nanda Devi ∧ | 124 | 30.23 N | 79.59 E |
| Nāndāha | 272b | 22.50 N | 88.17 E |
| Nandaime | 236 | 11.46 N | 86.03 W |
| Nanda Kot ∧ | 124 | 30.17 N | 80.05 E |
| Nandan | 96 | 34.15 N | 134.43 E |
| Nandarivatu | 175g | 17.34 S | 177.58 E |
| Nandashan | 100 | 29.01 N | 112.43 E |
| Nānded | 122 | 19.09 N | 77.20 E |
| Nāndgaon, India | 122 | 20.19 N | 74.39 E |
| Nāndgaon, India | 272c | 18.58 N | 73.08 E |
| Nandi Drug ∧ | 122 | 13.25 N | 77.42 E |
| Nandigrām | 126 | 22.01 N | 87.58 E |
| Nandikotkūr | 122 | 15.52 N | 78.16 E |
| Nanding ≃, Asia | 102 | 23.25 N | 98.41 E |
| Nanding ≃, Asia | 110 | 23.25 N | 98.41 E |
| Nandlstadt | 60 | 48.32 N | 11.48 E |
| Nandom | 150 | 10.51 N | 2.45 W |
| N'andoma | 24 | 61.40 N | 40.12 E |
| Nandu | 106 | 31.27 N | 119.19 E |
| Nandu ≃ | 110 | 20.04 N | 110.22 E |
| Nanduluohe | 105 | 40.11 N | 117.13 E |
| Nāndūra | 122 | 20.50 N | 76.27 E |
| Nandurbār | 122 | 21.22 N | 74.15 E |
| Nanduri | 175g | 16.27 S | 179.09 E |
| Nandy | 261 | 48.35 N | 2.34 E |
| Nandyāl | 122 | 15.29 N | 78.29 E |
| Nanfangquan | 106 | 31.26 N | 120.16 E |
| Nanfen | 104 | 41.06 N | 123.44 E |
| Nanfeng, Zhg. | 100 | 27.15 N | 116.32 E |
| Nanfeng, Zhg. | 100 | 29.16 N | 116.32 E |
| Nangabadau | 112 | 1.02 N | 111.54 E |
| Nangade | 154 | 11.05 S | 39.36 E |
| Nanga Eboko | 152 | 4.41 N | 12.22 E |
| Nangahale | 115b | 8.34 S | 122.32 E |
| Nangakelawit | 112 | 0.23 N | 112.26 E |
| Nāngal | 123 | 31.24 N | 76.14 E |
| Nangalangki | 112 | 1.15 S | 111.40 E |
| Nangalao Island I | 116 | 11.27 N | 120.11 E |
| Nangal Dewat ◈[8] | 272a | 28.33 N | 77.06 E |
| Nangamau | 112 | 0.06 S | 111.55 E |
| Nangamesi, Teluk ⊂ | 115b | 9.37 S | 120.20 E |
| Nangamuntatai | 112 | 0.22 S | 112.23 E |
| Nangang | 100 | 31.22 N | 116.59 E |
| Nan Gang ⊂ | 100 | 23.30 N | 117.00 E |
| Nan'gangwa | 105 | 39.46 N | 116.09 E |
| Nangaobat | 112 | 0.57 N | 113.13 E |
| Nangaocun | 105 | 39.25 N | 115.58 E |
| Nanga Parbat ∧ | 123 | 35.15 N | 74.36 E |
| Nangapinoh | 112 | 0.20 S | 111.44 E |
| Nangaraun | 112 | 0.38 N | 113.11 E |
| Nangarhār □[4] | 120 | 34.15 N | 70.30 E |
| Nangatayap | 112 | 1.32 S | 110.34 E |
| Nangezhuang | 105 | 39.31 N | 116.23 E |
| Nanggala Hill ∧ | 175e | 8.16 S | 157.43 E |
| Nanggulan | 115a | 7.46 S | 110.12 E |
| Nangi | 272b | 22.31 N | 88.13 E |
| Nangin | 110 | 10.31 N | 98.31 E |
| Nangis | 50 | 48.33 N | 3.00 E |
| Nangka ≃ | 269f | 14.41 N | 121.06 E |
| Nanglal ≃ | 126 | 24.20 N | 90.04 E |
| Nangloi ◈[8], India | 272a | 28.41 N | 77.05 E |
| Nāngloi ◈[8], India | 272a | 28.40 N | 77.02 E |
| Nangloi Jat ◈[8] | 272a | 28.41 N | 77.04 E |
| Nangnim | 98 | 40.58 N | 127.08 E |
| Nangnim-sanmaek ∧∧ | 98 | 40.00 N | 127.00 E |
| Nangō, Nihon | 92 | 31.32 N | 131.23 E |
| Nangō, Nihon | 94 | 37.13 N | 139.33 E |
| Nangola | 150 | 12.40 N | 6.36 W |
| Nangoma | 152 | 15.30 S | 23.08 E |
| Nangong | 98 | 37.24 N | 115.22 E |
| Nangou | 89 | 43.17 N | 128.37 E |
| Nangō-yama-tunnel ◈[6] | 94 | 35.12 N | 139.10 E |
| Nangqên | 102 | 32.22 N | 96.21 E |
| Nang Rong | 110 | 14.38 N | 102.48 E |
| Nanguan | 102 | 37.00 N | 112.31 E |
| Nangweshi | 152 | 16.26 S | 23.17 E |
| Nanhai → Foshan | 100 | 23.03 N | 113.09 E |
| Nanhai → South China Sea ⫪[2] | 108 | 10.00 N | 113.00 E |
| Nanhe | 98 | 37.01 N | 114.41 E |
| Nanhedian | 100 | 33.23 N | 112.25 E |
| Nanhekan | 107 | 30.24 N | 103.27 E |
| Nanhezhao | 105 | 39.05 N | 115.56 E |
| Nanhsi | 100 | 23.11 N | 120.29 E |
| Nanhu | 102 | 39.57 N | 94.13 E |
| Nanhua | 102 | 25.14 N | 101.13 E |
| Nanhualou | 104 | 42.30 N | 123.53 E |
| Nanhuang | 98 | 36.58 N | 121.47 E |
| Nanhui | 106 | 31.03 N | 121.45 E |
| Nan Hulsan Hu ⊜ | 102 | 36.39 N | 96.20 E |
| Nanhuta Shan ∧ | 100 | 24.22 N | 121.26 E |
| Nanhutou | 89 | 43.44 N | 128.55 E |
| Nanika Lake ⊜ | 182 | 53.45 N | 127.40 W |
| Naniwa ◈[8] | 270 | 34.39 N | 135.30 E |
| Nanjangūd | 122 | 12.06 N | 76.42 E |
| Nanjemoy | 208 | 38.27 N | 77.13 W |
| Nanjemoy Creek ⊂ | 208 | 38.25 N | 77.07 W |
| Nanji I | 100 | 27.28 N | 121.04 E |
| Nanjiang, Zhg. | 100 | 32.44 N | 120.52 E |
| Nanjiang, Zhg. | 102 | 32.33 N | 107.30 E |
| Nanjiangqiao | 100 | 28.58 N | 113.44 E |
| Nanjie | 107 | 29.11 N | 105.00 E |
| Nanjing, Zhg. | 100 | 24.41 N | 114.25 E |
| Nanjing, Zhg. | 100 | 24.32 N | 117.22 E |
| Nanjing (Nanking), Zhg. | 106 | 32.03 N | 118.47 E |
| Nanjing, Zhg. | 107 | 28.49 N | 105.12 E |
| Nanjinyi | 107 | 30.02 N | 104.42 E |
| Nanjirinji | 154 | 9.39 S | 39.04 E |
| Nanjō | 94 | 35.50 N | 136.13 E |
| Nanjuma ≃ | 105 | 39.24 N | 115.43 E |
| Nankan | 96 | 33.03 N | 130.32 E |
| Nankāna Sāhib | 123 | 31.27 N | 73.42 E |
| Nankang | 100 | 25.42 N | 114.44 E |
| Nankang ◈[8] | 269d | 25.03 N | 121.36 E |
| Nankin | 214 | 40.55 N | 82.17 W |
| Nanking → Nanjing | 106 | 32.03 N | 118.47 E |
| Nanko-kōen ♦ | 94 | 37.05 N | 140.14 E |
| Nankoku | 96 | 33.39 N | 133.44 E |
| Nankou | 100 | 26.38 N | 117.24 E |
| Nankouzhen | 105 | 40.14 N | 116.07 E |
| Nanku | 106 | 31.06 N | 120.37 E |
| Nankye | 110 | 14.20 N | 98.11 E |
| Nanle | 98 | 36.04 N | 115.10 E |
| Nanling, Zhg. | 100 | 30.56 N | 118.20 E |
| Nanling, Zhg. | 100 | 23.21 N | 115.25 E |
| Nanling, Zhg. | 104 | 41.37 N | 120.56 E |
| Nan Ling ∧∧ | 90 | 25.00 N | 112.00 E |
| Nanlinqiao | 100 | 29.35 N | 114.19 E |
| Nanliu ≃ | 102 | 21.38 N | 109.00 E |
| Nanliucun | 105 | 40.10 N | 116.04 E |
| Nanlongba | 102 | 28.02 N | 107.31 E |
| Nanlou Shan ∧ | 89 | 43.27 N | 126.42 E |
| Nanma | 102 | 24.17 N | 101.03 E |
| Nanmatang | 106 | 32.18 N | 120.38 E |
| Nanmeng | 105 | 39.11 N | 116.22 E |
| Nanmoku | 94 | 36.10 N | 138.44 E |
| Nannerch | 262 | 53.13 N | 3.15 W |
| Nannine | 162 | 26.53 S | 118.20 E |
| Nanning | 102 | 22.48 N | 108.20 E |
| Nanniwan | 102 | 36.29 N | 109.40 E |
| Nannō | 94 | 35.13 N | 136.36 E |
| Nannup | 162 | 33.59 S | 115.45 E |
| Nanny ≃ | 48 | 53.40 N | 6.14 W |
| Na Noi | 110 | 18.19 N | 100.43 E |
| Nānole ◈[8] | 272c | 19.01 N | 72.55 E |
| Nanoose Bay | 224 | 49.16 N | 124.12 W |
| Nanoose Harbour ⊂ | 224 | 49.20 N | 124.10 W |
| Nanoshi | 272c | 18.56 N | 73.05 E |
| Nanowin ≃ | 184 | 53.13 N | 97.13 W |
| Nanpan ≃, Zhg. | 102 | 24.34 N | 103.04 E |
| Nanpan ≃, Zhg. | 102 | 25.07 N | 106.00 E |
| Nānpāra | 124 | 27.52 N | 81.30 E |
| Nanpengchang | 107 | 29.21 N | 106.38 E |
| Nanpi | 98 | 38.02 N | 116.42 E |
| Nanpiao | 104 | 41.12 N | 120.39 E |
| Nanping, Zhg. | 89 | 43.24 N | 129.05 E |
| Nanping, Zhg. | 98 | 42.16 N | 129.09 E |
| Nanping, Zhg. | 100 | 26.38 N | 118.10 E |
| Nanping, Zhg. | 102 | 21.50 N | 107.28 E |
| Nanping, Zhg. | 102 | 33.07 N | 104.20 E |
| Nanpingji | 100 | 33.30 N | 116.51 E |
| Nanpu | 105 | 39.16 N | 118.12 E |
| Nanpu ≃ | 100 | 27.02 N | 118.18 E |
| Nanqingtuo | 105 | 39.37 N | 117.53 E |
| Nanqu | 104 | 40.44 N | 122.08 E |
| Nanquan | 98 | 36.24 N | 120.17 E |
| Nanri Dao I | 100 | 25.13 N | 119.30 E |
| Nansa ≃ | 34 | 43.22 N | 4.29 W |
| Nansei | 92 | 34.22 N | 136.41 E |
| Nansei-shotō (Ryukyu Islands) II | 90 | 26.30 N | 128.00 E |
| Nansemond □[6] | 208 | 36.43 N | 76.40 W |
| Nansen, Lago ⊜ | 254 | 47.57 S | 72.21 W |
| Nan Sha I | 106 | 31.36 N | 121.22 E |
| Nanshahe | 98 | 35.03 N | 117.12 E |
| Nanshan, Zhg. | 100 | 26.38 N | 118.20 E |
| Nanshan, Zhg. | 105 | 39.21 N | 115.34 E |
| Nanshan → Qilian Shan ∧∧ | 102 | 39.06 N | 98.40 E |
| Nanshanba | 100 | 25.34 N | 116.32 E |
| Nanshanchengzi | 98 | 42.09 N | 125.19 E |
| Nanshan Island I | 108 | 10.45 N | 115.49 E |
| Nanshankou | 102 | 43.09 N | 93.41 E |
| Nanshanlingcun | 105 | 39.09 N | 117.26 E |
| Nanshuang Dao I | 100 | 26.35 N | 120.08 E |
| Nanshui | 100 | 22.02 N | 113.16 E |
| Nansifa | 105 | 39.27 N | 116.27 E |
| Nansio | 154 | 2.08 S | 33.03 E |
| Nans-les-Pins | 62 | 43.22 N | 5.47 E |
| Nansunzhai | 269b | 31.21 N | 121.27 E |
| Nant | 32 | 44.01 N | 3.18 E |
| Nant ≃ | 50 | 47.32 N | 1.41 E |
| Nantai | 104 | 40.55 N | 122.47 E |
| Nantais, Lac ⊜ | 176 | 60.59 N | 74.00 W |
| Nantai-san ∧ | 94 | 36.43 N | 140.26 E |
| Nantai-zan ∧ | 94 | 36.46 N | 139.29 E |
| Nantang | 100 | 26.08 N | 115.12 E |
| Nantangdun | 106 | 31.15 N | 120.56 E |
| Nantangmei | 105 | 38.51 N | 114.56 E |
| Nantasket Beach | 283 | 42.16 N | 70.52 W |
| Nantawarra | 168b | 34.00 S | 138.14 E |
| Nant Bran ≃ | 42 | 51.57 N | 3.28 W |
| Nanterre | 50 | 48.53 N | 2.12 E |
| Nantes | 32 | 47.13 N | 1.33 W |
| Nanteuil-le-Haudouin | 50 | 49.08 N | 2.48 E |
| Nanteuil-lès-Meaux | 261 | 48.56 N | 2.54 E |
| Nantian, Zhg. | 100 | 27.57 N | 119.56 E |
| Nantian, Zhg. | 100 | 29.08 N | 121.56 E |
| Nantianmen | 104 | 40.56 N | 123.04 E |
| Nanticoke, On., Can. | 212 | 42.47 N | 80.12 W |
| Nanticoke, Md., U.S. | 208 | 38.16 N | 75.54 W |
| Nanticoke, Pa., U.S. | 210 | 41.12 N | 76.00 W |
| Nanticoke ≃ | 208 | 38.16 N | 75.56 W |
| Nanticoke Creek ≃, On., Can. | 212 | 42.48 N | 80.04 W |
| Nanticoke Creek ≃, N.Y., U.S. | 210 | 42.05 N | 76.05 W |
| Nantmeal Village | 285 | 40.08 N | 75.42 W |
| Nanto | 92 | 34.20 N | 136.31 E |
| Nanton | 182 | 50.21 N | 113.46 W |
| Nantong | 106 | 32.02 N | 120.53 E |
| Nant'ou, T'aiwan | 100 | 23.55 N | 120.41 E |
| Nantou, Zhg. | 100 | 22.33 N | 113.55 E |
| Nantouillet | 261 | 49.00 N | 2.42 E |
| Nantschang → Nanchang | 100 | 28.41 N | 115.53 E |
| Nantua | 58 | 46.09 N | 5.37 E |
| Nantuantingzhuang | 105 | 40.17 N | 118.17 E |
| Nantucket | 207 | 41.17 N | 70.06 W |
| Nantucket □[6] | 207 | 41.17 N | 70.06 W |
| Nantucket Island I | 207 | 41.16 N | 70.03 W |
| Nantucket Sound ʯ | 207 | 41.30 N | 70.15 W |
| Nantuego | 154 | 11.21 S | 38.24 E |
| Nantulo | 154 | 12.17 S | 39.03 E |
| Nantung → Nantong | 106 | 32.02 N | 120.53 E |
| Nantwich | 44 | 53.04 N | 2.32 W |
| Nanty Glo | 214 | 40.28 N | 78.50 W |
| Nant-y-moch Reservoir ⊜[1] | 42 | 52.27 N | 3.50 W |
| Nanu | 164 | 8.50 S | 142.40 E |
| Nanuet | 210 | 41.05 N | 74.00 W |
| Nanuet Mall ◈[9] | 276 | 41.06 N | 74.01 W |
| Nanuku Passage ʯ | 175g | 16.45 S | 179.15 W |
| Nanumanga I | 14 | 6.18 S | 176.20 E |
| Nanumea I[1] | 14 | 5.39 S | 176.08 E |
| Nanuque | 255 | 17.50 S | 40.21 W |
| Nānūr | 126 | 23.42 N | 87.52 E |
| Nanusa, Kepulauan II | 108 | 4.42 N | 127.06 E |
| Nanushuk ≃ | 180 | 69.18 N | 151.00 W |
| Nanwan | 100 | 32.09 N | 113.57 E |
| Nan Wan ⊂ | 100 | 21.55 N | 120.47 E |
| Nanwengkouzi | 89 | 51.10 N | 125.25 E |
| Nanwenquan | 107 | 29.26 N | 106.35 E |
| Nanxi, Zhg. | 100 | 31.31 N | 115.38 E |
| Nanxi, Zhg. | 100 | 26.24 N | 118.24 E |
| Nanxi, Zhg. | 107 | 28.51 N | 104.58 E |
| Nanxian | 102 | 29.20 N | 112.19 E |
| Nanxiang | 106 | 31.17 N | 121.18 E |
| Nanxikou | 107 | 30.43 N | 106.07 E |
| Nanxin, Zhg. | 98 | 35.33 N | 117.12 E |
| Nanxin, Zhg. | 105 | 39.11 N | 115.38 E |
| Nanxing Hu ⊜ | 106 | 31.08 N | 120.48 E |
| Nanxinzhuang | 98 | 36.39 N | 115.15 E |
| Nanxiong | 100 | 25.10 N | 114.20 E |
| Nanxun | 106 | 30.53 N | 120.26 E |
| Nanya | 100 | 26.52 N | 118.19 E |
| Nanyandang Shan ∧ | 100 | 27.36 N | 120.04 E |
| Nanyang, Zhg. | 100 | 27.24 N | 119.39 E |
| Nanyang, Zhg. | 100 | 33.00 N | 112.32 E |
| Nanyang, Zhg. | 100 | 33.25 N | 120.13 E |
| Nanyangcun | 106 | 31.53 N | 121.43 E |
| Nanyanggangzi | 89 | 48.43 N | 125.27 E |
| Nanyang Hu ⊜ | 98 | 35.12 N | 116.41 E |
| Nanyang Shan ∧ | 106 | 31.20 N | 120.28 E |
| Nanyang Technological Institute ❦[2] | 271c | 1.21 N | 103.41 E |
| Nanyi Hu ⊜ | 106 | 31.07 N | 118.57 E |
| Nan-yō | 92 | 38.03 N | 140.10 E |
| Nanyu | 100 | 25.59 N | 119.14 E |
| Nanyuan | 105 | 39.48 N | 116.23 E |
| Nanyuan Airport ⊠ | 271a | 39.47 N | 116.23 E |
| Nanyue | 100 | 27.13 N | 112.43 E |
| Nanyuki | 154 | 0.01 N | 37.04 E |
| Nanyulin | 105 | 40.09 N | 115.23 E |
| Nanzamu | 98 | 41.56 N | 124.23 E |
| Nanzha | 106 | 31.51 N | 120.15 E |
| Nanzhai | 106 | 31.34 N | 120.02 E |
| Nanzhang, Zhg. | 102 | 31.50 N | 111.41 E |
| Nanzhang, Zhg. | 105 | 39.03 N | 115.46 E |
| Nanzhao | 100 | 33.30 N | 112.27 E |
| Nanzhaoji | 100 | 32.38 N | 115.58 E |
| Nanzhen | 100 | 26.59 N | 119.57 E |
| Nanzhenjie | 106 | 31.48 N | 119.17 E |
| Nanzhila | 154 | 16.05 S | 26.07 E |
| Nanzhuang, Zhg. | 105 | 40.22 N | 116.21 E |
| Nanzhuang, Zhg. | 105 | 40.43 N | 114.58 E |
| Nao | 152 | 4.35 N | 15.09 E |
| Naoābād | 272b | 22.28 N | 88.27 E |
| Naoāpāra | 126 | 22.45 N | 89.39 E |
| Naococane, Lac ⊜ | 176 | 52.52 N | 70.40 W |
| Naoetsu | 94 | 37.11 N | 138.15 E |
| Naogaon | 124 | 24.47 N | 88.56 E |
| Naoiri | 96 | 33.04 N | 131.23 E |
| Naokot | 120 | 24.51 N | 69.27 E |
| Naoli ≃ | 89 | 47.20 N | 134.10 E |
| Naolinco | 234 | 19.39 N | 96.51 W |
| Não-me-Toque | 252 | 28.28 S | 52.49 W |
| Naong, Bukit ∧ | 112 | 2.40 N | 112.45 E |
| Nāopāra | 126 | 24.09 N | 88.54 E |
| Naopukuria | 272b | 22.55 N | 88.16 E |
| Naosap Lake ⊜ | 184 | 54.51 N | 101.24 W |
| Naoshima | 96 | 34.27 N | 133.59 E |
| Naours | 50 | 50.02 N | 2.17 E |
| Náousa | 38 | 40.37 N | 22.05 E |
| Naozhou Dao I | 102 | 20.57 N | 110.34 E |
| Napa | 226 | 38.17 N | 122.17 W |
| Napa □[6] | 226 | 38.18 N | 122.17 W |
| Napa ≃ | 226 | 38.07 N | 122.18 W |
| Napacao Point › | 116 | 9.43 N | 124.31 E |
| Napajedla | 30 | 49.10 N | 17.31 E |
| Napakiak | 180 | 60.42 N | 161.57 W |
| Napaku | 112 | 2.32 N | 115.58 E |
| Na Pali Coast State Park ♦ | 229b | 22.09 N | 159.41 W |
| Napalkovo | 74 | 70.03 N | 73.47 E |
| Napamute | 180 | 61.33 N | 158.42 W |
| Napanee | 212 | 44.15 N | 76.57 W |
| Napanee ≃ | 212 | 44.12 N | 77.02 W |
| Napanoch | 210 | 41.44 N | 74.22 W |
| Napareuli | 84 | 42.03 N | 45.31 E |
| Napas | 86 | 59.53 N | 81.58 E |
| Napaskiak | 180 | 60.42 N | 161.45 W |
| Napa Valley V | 226 | 38.18 N | 122.18 W |
| Napavine | 224 | 46.34 N | 122.54 W |
| Napayauan Island I | 116 | 12.22 N | 123.14 E |
| Napè | 110 | 18.18 N | 105.06 E |
| Napenay | 252 | 26.44 S | 60.37 W |
| Naperville | 216 | 41.47 N | 88.08 W |
| Napetipi ≃ | 186 | 51.21 N | 58.08 W |
| Napf ∧ | 58 | 47.00 N | 7.56 E |
| Napido | 164 | 0.41 S | 135.23 E |
| Napiéolédougou | 150 | 9.18 N | 5.35 W |
| Napier, N.Z. | 172 | 39.29 S | 176.55 E |
| Napier, S. Afr. | 158 | 34.29 S | 19.53 E |
| Napier, Mount ∧[2] | 162 | 17.32 S | 129.10 E |
| Napier Mountains ∧∧ | 9 | 66.30 S | 53.40 E |
| Napierville | 206 | 45.11 N | 73.25 W |
| Napierville □[6] | 206 | 45.10 N | 73.35 W |
| Napinka | 184 | 49.17 N | 100.50 W |
| Naplate | 216 | 41.20 N | 88.54 W |
| Naples → Napoli, It. | 68 | 40.51 N | 14.17 E |
| Naples, Fl., U.S. | 220 | 26.08 N | 81.47 W |
| Naples, Id., U.S. | 202 | 48.34 N | 116.23 W |
| Naples, Il., U.S. | 219 | 39.45 N | 90.36 W |
| Naples, N.Y., U.S. | 210 | 42.36 N | 77.24 W |
| Naples, Tx., U.S. | 222 | 33.12 N | 94.40 W |
| Naples Park | 220 | 26.16 N | 81.48 W |
| Napo | 102 | 23.16 N | 105.54 E |
| Napo □[4] | 246 | 0.30 S | 77.00 W |
| Napo ≃ | 246 | 3.20 S | 72.40 W |
| Napola | 70 | 37.59 N | 12.38 E |
| Napoleon, In., U.S. | 218 | 39.12 N | 85.19 W |
| Napoleon, Ky., U.S. | 218 | 38.46 N | 84.47 W |
| Napoleon, Mi., U.S. | 216 | 42.10 N | 84.15 W |
| Napoleon, N.D., U.S. | 198 | 46.30 N | 99.46 W |
| Napoleon, Oh., U.S. | 216 | 41.23 N | 84.07 W |
| Napoleonville | 194 | 29.56 N | 91.01 W |
| Nápoles → Napoli | 68 | 40.51 N | 14.17 E |
| Napoli (Naples) | 68 | 40.51 N | 14.17 E |
| Napoli □[4] | 68 | 40.53 N | 14.25 E |
| Napoli, Golfo di ⊂ | 68 | 40.43 N | 14.10 E |
| Napopo | 154 | 4.12 N | 28.02 E |
| Nappamerry | 166 | 27.36 S | 141.07 E |
| Nappanee | 216 | 41.26 N | 86.00 W |
| Nappan Island I | 212 | 44.23 N | 77.49 W |
| Napton on the Hill | 42 | 52.15 N | 1.24 W |
| Napu | 115b | 9.24 S | 119.56 E |
| Napudalutai Shan ∧ | 89 | 51.06 N | 122.13 E |
| Naqādah | 140 | 25.54 N | 32.43 E |
| Naqadeh | 128 | 36.57 N | 45.23 E |
| Naqb, Ra's an- ∧ | 132 | 29.50 N | 35.40 E |
| Nar ≃ | 42 | 52.45 N | 0.24 E |
| Nara, Mali | 150 | 15.10 N | 7.17 W |
| Nara, Nihon | 96 | 34.41 N | 135.50 E |
| Nara □[5] | 96 | 34.30 N | 135.50 E |
| Nāra ≃, Pāk. | 120 | 24.07 N | 69.07 E |
| Nara ≃, Ross. | 82 | 54.53 N | 37.26 E |
| Nara-bonchi ≚[1] | 270 | 34.38 N | 135.50 E |
| Narač | 76 | 54.56 N | 26.45 E |
| Narač ≃ | 76 | 54.26 N | 26.39 E |
| Narač, vozero ⊜ | 76 | 54.52 N | 26.45 E |
| Naracoorte | 166 | 36.58 S | 140.44 E |
| Naradhan | 166 | 33.37 S | 146.19 E |
| Narai ≃ | 94 | 36.20 N | 137.55 E |
| Narāil | 126 | 23.10 N | 89.30 E |
| Naraina ◈[8] | 272a | 28.37 N | 77.08 E |
| Naraini | 124 | 25.11 N | 80.29 E |
| Narainpur | 126 | 24.03 N | 86.36 E |
| Narakawa | 94 | 35.59 N | 137.50 E |
| Naramata | 182 | 49.36 N | 119.35 W |
| Naran | 88 | 48.34 N | 98.17 E |
| Naran Bulag | 86 | 49.22 N | 92.33 E |
| Nārang | 123 | 31.54 N | 74.31 E |
| Narangba | 171a | 27.12 S | 152.58 E |
| Naranja | 220 | 25.31 N | 80.25 W |
| Naranjal, Ec. | 246 | 2.42 S | 79.37 W |
| Naranjal, Ven. | 286c | 10.28 N | 67.02 W |
| Naranjito, Hond. | 236 | 14.57 N | 88.41 W |
| Naranjito, P.R. | 240m | 18.18 N | 66.15 W |
| Naranjo | 236 | 10.06 N | 84.22 W |
| Naranjo ≃ | 236 | 14.30 N | 92.11 W |
| Naranjo Islands II | 116 | 12.23 N | 124.03 E |
| Naranjos | 234 | 21.21 N | 97.41 W |
| Narao | 92 | 32.50 N | 129.04 E |
| Nara Park ♦ | 270 | 34.41 N | 135.52 E |
| Narasannapeta | 122 | 18.25 N | 84.03 E |
| Narasapur | 122 | 16.27 N | 81.40 E |
| Narasaraopet | 122 | 16.15 N | 80.04 E |
| Narashino | 94 | 35.41 N | 140.02 E |
| Narasun | 88 | 50.06 N | 112.58 E |
| Narat | 86 | 43.28 N | 83.44 E |
| Narathiwat | 110 | 6.26 N | 101.50 E |
| Nara Visa | 196 | 35.36 N | 103.05 W |
| Nara Women's University ❦[2] | 270 | 34.42 N | 135.49 E |
| Nārāyanganj | 124 | 23.37 N | 90.30 E |
| Nārāyaṇī □[8] | 124 | 27.15 N | 85.00 E |
| Nārāyaṇi ≃ | 124 | 25.39 N | 85.13 E |
| Nārāyanpāra | 272b | 22.54 N | 88.19 E |
| Nārāyanpet | 122 | 16.44 N | 77.30 E |
| Nārāyanpur | 272b | 22.29 N | 88.34 E |
| Narazeni | 84 | 42.27 N | 41.57 E |
| Narberth, Wales, U.K. | 42 | 51.48 N | 4.45 W |
| Narberth, Pa., U.S. | 285 | 40.00 N | 75.15 W |
| Narbonne | 32 | 43.11 N | 3.00 E |
| Narcao | 71 | 39.10 N | 8.40 E |
| Narcea ≃ | 34 | 43.28 N | 6.06 W |
| Narcondam Island I | 110 | 13.20 N | 94.16 E |
| Narcosli Creek ≃ | 182 | 52.49 N | 122.28 W |
| Nardò | 68 | 40.11 N | 18.02 E |
| Nare ≃ | 246 | 6.12 N | 74.35 W |
| Narellan | 170 | 34.02 S | 150.44 E |
| Narembeen | 162 | 32.04 S | 118.24 E |
| Narenbulake | 89 | 49.52 N | 120.23 E |
| Narendranagar | 124 | 30.10 N | 78.18 E |
| Nares Strait ʯ | 16 | 80.30 N | 68.00 W |
| Naretha | 162 | 31.00 S | 124.50 E |
| Narew ≃ | 30 | 52.26 N | 20.42 E |
| Nargund | 122 | 15.43 N | 75.23 E |
| Narhan | 272c | 19.08 N | 73.07 E |
| Nāri ≃ | 120 | 28.35 N | 67.50 E |
| Naria | 124 | 23.18 N | 90.25 E |
| Nariai | 270 | 34.53 N | 135.38 E |
| Nariel | 171b | 36.26 S | 147.50 E |
| Narijn ≃ | 88 | 50.20 N | 93.24 E |
| Narijnteel | 102 | 45.57 N | 101.29 E |
| Nārikelbāria | 126 | 23.17 N | 89.21 E |
| Nariman | 85 | 40.34 N | 72.48 E |
| Närimanabad | 84 | 38.53 N | 48.52 E |
| Narimba, Her Majesty's Air Station (Royal Australian Navy Airfield) ■ | 274a | 33.43 S | 150.53 E |
| Narin ≃ | 120 | 36.54 N | 92.51 E |
| Narince | 130 | 37.52 N | 38.46 E |
| Narinda, Baie de ⊂ | 157b | 14.55 S | 47.30 E |
| Nariño □[5] | 246 | 1.30 N | 78.00 W |
| Narita | 94 | 35.47 N | 140.19 E |
| Nariwa | 96 | 34.47 N | 133.33 E |
| Nariwa ≃ | 96 | 34.46 N | 133.36 E |
| Nar'jan-Mar | 24 | 67.39 N | 53.00 E |
| Nārkanda | 123 | 31.16 N | 77.27 E |
| Narkatiāganj | 124 | 27.06 N | 84.28 E |
| Närke □[9] | 40 | 59.06 N | 15.03 E |
| Närkes Marieberg | 40 | 59.12 N | 15.10 E |
| Narlı | 130 | 37.27 N | 37.09 E |
| Narma | 80 | 54.46 N | 42.01 E |
| Narmada ≃ | 120 | 21.38 N | 72.36 E |
| Narmada Valley V | 124 | 22.30 N | 77.00 E |
| Narmak ◈[8] | 267d | 35.43 N | 51.29 E |
| Narman | 130 | 40.21 N | 41.52 E |
| Narmušad' | 80 | 54.40 N | 41.07 E |
| Nar-Nar-Goon | 169 | 38.05 S | 145.34 E |
| Nārnaul | 124 | 28.03 N | 76.07 E |
| Narni | 66 | 42.31 N | 12.31 E |
| Naro | 70 | 37.18 N | 13.47 E |
| Naro ≃ | 70 | 37.14 N | 13.37 E |
| Narodnaja, gora ∧ | 24 | 65.04 N | 60.09 E |
| Narodychi | 78 | 51.13 N | 29.03 E |
| Naro-Fominsk | 82 | 55.23 N | 36.43 E |
| Naro Island I | 116 | 11.53 N | 123.40 E |
| Narok | 154 | 1.05 S | 35.52 E |
| Narol | 30 | 50.22 N | 23.21 E |
| Narooma | 166 | 36.14 S | 150.03 E |
| Naro-Osakovo | 82 | 55.33 N | 36.33 E |
| Naroulja | 78 | 51.48 N | 29.29 E |
| Narovčat | 80 | 53.52 N | 43.41 E |
| Nārowāl | 123 | 32.06 N | 74.53 E |
| Närpes (Närpiö) | 26 | 62.28 N | 21.20 E |
| Närpiö → Närpes | 26 | 62.28 N | 21.20 E |
| Narrabeen | 170 | 33.43 S | 151.18 E |
| Narrabeen Lagoon ⊂ | 274a | 33.43 S | 151.17 E |
| Narrabri | 166 | 30.19 S | 149.47 E |
| Narragansett | 207 | 41.25 N | 71.27 W |
| Narragansett Bay ⊂ | 207 | 41.40 N | 71.20 W |
| Narran ≃ | 166 | 29.45 S | 147.20 E |
| Narra Narra ∧ | 171b | 35.50 S | 147.27 E |
| Narrandera | 166 | 34.45 S | 146.33 E |
| Narraway ≃ | 182 | 54.48 N | 119.56 W |
| Narraweena | 274a | 33.45 S | 151.16 E |
| Narre Warren | 274b | 38.02 S | 145.19 E |
| Narre Warren North | 274b | 37.59 S | 145.19 E |
| Narrogin | 162 | 32.56 S | 117.10 E |
| Narromine | 166 | 32.14 S | 148.15 E |
| Narrows, Md., U.S. | 208 | 38.58 N | 76.15 W |
| Narrows, Va., U.S. | 192 | 37.19 N | 80.48 W |
| Narrowsburg | 210 | 41.36 N | 75.03 W |
| Närsen ⊜ | 40 | 60.17 N | 14.23 E |
| Narsimhapur | 124 | 22.57 N | 79.12 E |
| Narsinghdi | 124 | 23.55 N | 90.43 E |
| Narsinghgarh | 124 | 23.42 N | 77.06 E |
| Narsīpatnam | 122 | 17.40 N | 82.37 E |
| Narskije Prudy, ozero ⊜[1] | 82 | 55.32 N | 36.36 E |
| Narssaq | 176 | 60.54 N | 46.00 W |
| Nartkala | 84 | 43.33 N | 43.50 E |
| Nartuby ≃ | 62 | 43.28 N | 6.34 E |
| Naru | 92 | 32.49 N | 128.56 E |
| Narubis, Namibia | 158 | 27.10 S | 19.05 E |
| Narubis, Namibia | 158 | 26.55 S | 18.35 E |
| Naruko | 92 | 38.44 N | 140.43 E |
| Naruksovo | 80 | 54.37 N | 44.33 E |
| Naruo | 270 | 34.43 N | 135.23 E |
| Narusawa | 94 | 35.29 N | 138.41 E |
| Narutō, Nihon | 94 | 35.36 N | 140.25 E |
| Naruto, Nihon | 96 | 34.11 N | 134.37 E |
| Naruto-kaikyō ʯ | 96 | 34.14 N | 134.39 E |
| Narva, Eesti | 76 | 59.23 N | 28.12 E |
| Narva, Ross. | 86 | 55.25 N | 93.39 E |
| Narva ≃ | 76 | 59.27 N | 28.02 E |
| Narvacan | 116 | 17.25 N | 120.28 E |
| Narva-Jõesuu | 76 | 59.27 N | 28.03 E |
| Narva laht (Narvskij zaliv) ⊂ | 76 | 59.30 N | 27.40 E |
| Narvan | 85 | 40.15 N | 67.12 E |
| Narvik | 24 | 68.26 N | 17.25 E |
| Narvskij zaliv (Narva laht) ⊂ | 76 | 59.30 N | 27.40 E |
| Narvskoje vodochranilišče ⊜[1] | 76 | 59.18 N | 28.14 E |
| Narwāna | 124 | 29.37 N | 76.07 E |
| Narwietooma | 162 | 23.15 S | 132.35 E |
| Narym | 86 | 58.58 N | 81.30 E |
| Naryn, Kyrg. | 85 | 41.26 N | 75.59 E |
| Naryn, Ross. | 88 | 50.13 N | 96.27 E |
| Naryn □[4] | 85 | 41.30 N | 76.00 E |
| Naryn ≃ | 85 | 40.54 N | 71.45 E |
| Narynkol | 72 | 42.43 N | 80.12 E |
| Naryntau, gory ∧∧ | 85 | 41.25 N | 76.50 E |
| Naryškino | 76 | 52.58 N | 35.44 E |
| Naryū-zaki › | 96 | 35.36 N | 135.28 E |
| Narzole | 62 | 44.35 N | 7.52 E |
| Nås, Sve. | 40 | 60.27 N | 14.29 E |
| Näs, Sve. | 40 | 58.41 N | 15.50 E |
| Nasadkino | 82 | 56.29 N | 37.21 E |
| Näsåker | 26 | 63.26 N | 16.54 E |
| Na San, Thai | 110 | 8.48 N | 99.22 E |
| Na San, Viet | 110 | 21.12 N | 104.02 E |
| Nasarawa | 150 | 8.30 N | 7.40 E |
| Năsăud | 38 | 47.17 N | 24.24 E |
| Nasawa | 175f | 15.13 S | 168.09 E |
| NASA Wallops Station ❦[3] | 208 | 37.52 N | 75.28 W |
| Nasbinals | 32 | 44.40 N | 3.03 E |
| Naschel | 252 | 32.55 S | 65.23 W |
| Nase → Naze | 93b | 28.23 N | 129.30 E |
| Naseby, N.Z. | 172 | 45.02 S | 170.09 E |
| Naseby, Eng., U.K. | 42 | 52.25 N | 0.58 W |
| Naselle | 224 | 46.21 N | 123.48 W |
| Naselle ≃ | 224 | 46.25 N | 123.55 W |
| Nash | 194 | 33.27 N | 94.08 W |
| Nashawena Island I | 207 | 41.26 N | 70.53 W |
| Nāshik | 122 | 19.59 N | 73.48 E |
| Nashoba Brook ≃ | 283 | 42.28 N | 71.24 W |
| Nashport | 214 | 40.04 N | 82.09 W |
| Nashū', Wādī an- V | 146 | 26.25 N | 14.15 E |
| Nashua, Ia., U.S. | 190 | 42.57 N | 92.32 W |
| Nashua, Mt., U.S. | 202 | 48.07 N | 106.21 W |
| Nashua, N.H., U.S. | 207 | 42.45 N | 71.28 W |
| Nashua ≃ | 207 | 42.46 N | 71.27 W |
| Nashuixi | 102 | 30.09 N | 108.40 E |
| Näshultasjön ⊜ | 40 | 59.14 N | 16.21 E |
| Nashville, On., Can. | 275b | 43.50 N | 79.40 W |
| Nashville, Ar., U.S. | 194 | 33.56 N | 93.50 W |
| Nashville, Ga., U.S. | 192 | 31.12 N | 83.15 W |
| Nashville, Il., U.S. | 219 | 38.20 N | 89.22 W |
| Nashville, In., U.S. | 218 | 39.12 N | 86.15 W |
| Nashville, Mi., U.S. | 216 | 42.36 N | 85.05 W |
| Nashville, N.C., U.S. | 192 | 35.58 N | 77.57 W |
| Nashville, Oh., U.S. | 214 | 40.36 N | 82.07 W |
| Nashville, Tn., U.S. | 194 | 36.09 N | 86.47 W |
| Nashwaak ≃ | 186 | 45.57 N | 66.37 W |
| Nashwaaksis | 186 | 45.59 N | 66.39 W |
| Nashwah | 142 | 30.30 N | 31.29 E |
| Nashwauk | 190 | 47.22 N | 93.10 W |
| Nasia | 150 | 10.09 N | 0.48 W |
| Naṣīb | 132 | 32.33 N | 36.11 E |
| Našice | 38 | 45.29 N | 18.06 E |
| Nasielsk | 30 | 52.36 N | 20.48 E |
| Näsijärvi ⊜ | 26 | 61.37 N | 23.42 E |
| Nāṣir | 140 | 8.36 N | 33.04 E |
| Nāṣir, Buḥayrat (Lake Nasser) ⊜[1] | 140 | 22.40 N | 32.00 E |
| Nasīrābād, India | 120 | 26.18 N | 74.44 E |
| Nasīrābād, Pāk. | 120 | 28.23 N | 68.24 E |
| Naskaftym | 80 | 52.57 N | 45.38 E |
| Naskaupi ≃ | 176 | 53.45 N | 60.50 W |
| Näsnaren ⊜ | 40 | 58.51 N | 16.18 E |
| Naso | 70 | 38.07 N | 14.47 E |
| Nasondoye | 154 | 10.22 S | 25.06 E |
| Naso Point › | 116 | 10.25 N | 121.57 E |
| Nasorolevu ∧ | 175g | 16.38 S | 178.42 E |
| Naṣr | 142 | 30.36 N | 30.23 E |
| Naṣrābād | 128 | 34.08 N | 51.26 E |
| Naṣrānī, Jabal an- ∧ | 130 | 34.06 N | 37.24 E |
| Nasriddinbek | 85 | 40.41 N | 71.55 E |
| Nāsriganj | 124 | 25.03 N | 84.20 E |
| Nass ≃ | 182 | 55.00 N | 129.50 W |



| Name | Seite | Breite°′ | Länge°′ E = Ost |
|---|---|---|---|
| Nassau, Ba. | 240b | 25.05 N | 77.21 W |
| Nassau, Dtsch. | 54 | 50.46 N | 13.32 E |
| Nassau, Dtsch. | 56 | 50.19 N | 7.47 E |
| Nassau, N.Y., U.S. | 210 | 42.30 N | 73.36 W |
| Nassau □[6] | 210 | 40.45 N | 73.38 W |
| Nassau, Bahía ⊂ | 254 | 55.25 S | 67.40 W |
| Nassau Bay | 222 | 29.32 N | 95.05 W |
| Nassau Coliseum ♦ | 276 | 40.43 N | 73.36 W |
| Nassau International Airport ⊠ | 240b | 25.02 N | 77.28 W |
| Nassau Island I | 14 | 11.33 S | 165.25 W |
| Nassau Shores | 276 | 40.39 N | 73.26 W |
| Nassawadox | 208 | 37.28 N | 75.51 W |
| Nassawango Creek ≃ | 208 | 38.10 N | 75.25 W |
| Nassenfels | 60 | 48.48 N | 11.16 E |
| Nassenheide | 54 | 52.49 N | 13.12 E |
| Nasser, Lake → Nāṣir, Buḥayrat ⊜[1] | 140 | 22.40 N | 32.00 E |
| Nassereith | 58 | 47.19 N | 10.50 E |
| Nassian | 150 | 8.27 N | 3.29 W |
| Nässjö | 26 | 57.39 N | 14.41 E |
| Nastapoca ≃ | 176 | 56.55 N | 76.33 W |
| Nastapoka Islands II | 176 | 57.00 N | 76.50 W |
| Nastashka | 78 | 49.39 N | 30.19 E |
| Nastasjino | 82 | 54.28 N | 38.16 E |
| Nastätten | 56 | 50.12 N | 7.51 E |
| Nastauli | 272a | 28.43 N | 77.22 E |
| Nastf, Bi'r ⫪[4] | 142 | 30.18 N | 30.28 E |
| Nasu | 94 | 37.01 N | 140.07 E |
| Nasu-dake ∧, Nihon | 92 | 37.07 N | 139.58 E |
| Nasu-dake ∧, Nihon | 94 | 37.09 N | 139.58 E |
| Nasugbu | 116 | 14.05 N | 120.38 E |
| Nasukoin Mountain ∧ | 202 | 48.48 N | 114.35 W |
| Nasva | 76 | 56.35 N | 30.10 E |
| Nat ≃ | 190 | 48.48 N | 82.07 W |
| Nata, Bots. | 156 | 20.12 S | 26.12 E |
| Natá, Pan. | 236 | 8.20 N | 80.31 W |
| Nata ≃ | 156 | 20.14 S | 26.10 E |
| Natagaima | 246 | 3.37 N | 75.06 W |
| Nātāgarh | 272b | 22.42 N | 88.25 E |
| Natal, Bra. | 250 | 5.47 S | 35.13 W |
| Natal, B.C., Can. | 182 | 49.44 N | 114.50 W |
| Natal, Indon. | 110 | 0.33 N | 99.07 E |
| Natal → KwaZulu-Natal □[4] | 158 | 28.40 S | 30.40 E |
| Natal Basin ✧[1] | 10 | 30.00 S | 40.00 E |
| Natalia | 196 | 29.11 N | 98.51 W |
| Nataljevka | 83 | 47.10 N | 38.29 E |
| Nataljin Jar | 80 | 51.46 N | 50.35 E |
| Nataljino | 80 | 52.56 N | 49.02 E |
| Natalkuz Lake ⊜ | 182 | 53.26 N | 125.20 W |
| Natalspruit ≃ | 273d | 26.19 S | 28.10 E |
| Natanes Plateau ∧∧[1] | 200 | 33.35 N | 110.15 W |
| Natash, Wādī V | 140 | 24.25 N | 33.26 E |
| Natashō | 96 | 35.24 N | 135.38 E |
| Natashquan | 186 | 50.12 N | 61.49 W |
| Natashquan ≃ | 176 | 50.06 N | 61.49 W |
| Natashquan, Pointe de › | 186 | 50.06 N | 61.44 W |
| Natashquan Est ≃ | 186 | 51.20 N | 61.40 W |
| Natchez | 194 | 31.33 N | 91.24 W |
| Natchez Trace Parkway ♦ | 194 | 32.00 N | 91.00 W |
| Natchitoches | 194 | 31.45 N | 93.05 W |
| Natco Lake ⊜ | 276 | 40.26 N | 74.09 W |
| Natércia | 256 | 22.07 S | 45.30 W |
| Naters | 58 | 46.20 N | 7.59 E |
| Natewa Bay ⊂ | 175g | 16.35 S | 179.40 E |
| Na Thawi | 110 | 6.45 N | 100.42 E |
| Nāthdwāra | 120 | 24.56 N | 73.49 E |
| Nathia Gali | 123 | 34.04 N | 73.24 E |
| Nathkaw | 102 | 26.53 N | 96.13 E |
| Nathula I | 175g | 16.53 S | 177.25 E |
| Natick | 207 | 42.17 N | 71.21 W |
| Natick Laboratories ■ | 283 | 42.17 N | 71.22 W |
| Natimuk | 166 | 36.45 S | 141.57 E |
| Nation ≃ | 182 | 55.28 N | 123.35 W |
| National Agricultural Research Center ❦[3] | 284c | 39.02 N | 76.52 W |
| National Airport ⊠ | 281 | 42.19 N | 83.25 W |
| National Arboretum ♦ | 284c | 38.54 N | 76.58 W |
| National Assembly ❦ | 269a | 13.46 N | 100.31 E |
| National Baseball Hall of Fame and Museum ❦ | 210 | 42.42 N | 74.57 W |
| National City | 228 | 32.40 N | 117.05 W |
| National Gallery ❦ | 260 | 51.31 N | 0.08 W |
| National Institute of Health ❦ | 284c | 39.00 N | 77.06 W |
| National Maritime Museum ❦ | 260 | 51.29 N | 0.00 |
| National Park | 285 | 39.51 N | 75.10 W |
| National Taiwan Normal University ❦[2] | 269d | 25.02 N | 121.31 E |
| National Taiwan University ❦[2] | 269d | 25.01 N | 121.32 E |
| National Zoological Park ♦ | 284c | 38.56 N | 77.03 W |
| Natipi, Lac ⊜ | 186 | 51.27 N | 71.23 W |
| Natisone ≃ | 64 | 45.57 N | 13.22 E |
| Natitingou | 150 | 10.19 N | 1.22 E |
| Native Bay ⊂ | 176 | 63.52 N | 82.30 W |
| Natividade | 250 | 11.43 S | 47.47 W |
| Natividade da Serra | 256 | 23.24 S | 45.26 W |
| Natívitas ◈[8] | 286a | 19.14 N | 99.05 W |
| Nativity, Church of the ❦[1] | 132 | 31.43 N | 35.12 E |
| Natkyizin | 110 | 14.55 N | 97.57 E |
| Natl | 132 | 31.39 N | 35.52 E |
| Natoma | 198 | 39.11 N | 99.01 W |
| Natong | 102 | 23.01 N | 107.50 E |
| Nator | 124 | 24.25 N | 88.59 E |
| Natori | 92 | 38.08 N | 140.55 E |
| Natorp | 263 | 51.30 N | 7.38 E |
| Natron, Lake ⊜ | 154 | 2.25 S | 36.00 E |
| Natrona Heights | 214 | 40.37 N | 79.43 W |
| Naṭrūn, Wādī an- ±[7] | 142 | 30.25 N | 30.13 E |
| Natsui ≃ | 94 | 37.03 N | 140.59 E |
| Nattai ≃ | 170 | 34.05 S | 150.25 E |
| Nattai River | 170 | 34.04 S | 150.27 E |
| Nattam | 122 | 10.14 N | 78.14 E |
| Nåttarö I | 40 | 58.52 N | 18.07 E |
| Nattaset ∧ | 24 | 68.12 N | 27.20 E |
| Nattaung ∧ | 110 | 18.48 N | 97.02 E |
| Natters | 64 | 47.14 N | 11.22 E |
| Nattwerder | 264a | 52.26 N | 12.56 E |
| Natuchajevskaja | 78 | 44.54 N | 37.34 E |
| Nātudaha | 126 | 23.39 N | 88.41 E |
| Natukanaoka Pan ≚ | 156 | 18.40 S | 15.45 E |
| Natuna Besar I | 112 | 4.00 N | 108.15 E |
| Natuna Besar, Kepulauan II | 112 | 4.40 N | 108.00 E |
| Natuna Selatan, Kepulauan II | 112 | 2.45 N | 109.00 E |
| Natural Bridge | 212 | 44.04 N | 75.29 W |
| Natural Bridge ♦ | 192 | 37.38 N | 79.33 W |
| Natural Bridges National Monument ♦ | 200 | 37.30 N | 110.08 W |
| Natural Bridge State Resort Park ♦ | 192 | 37.47 N | 83.42 W |
| Naturaliste, Cape › | 162 | 33.32 S | 115.01 E |
| Naturaliste Channel ʯ | 162 | 25.25 S | 113.00 E |
| Naturita | 200 | 38.13 N | 108.34 W |
| Naturita Creek ≃ | 200 | 38.13 N | 108.32 W |
| Naturno (Naturns) | 64 | 46.39 N | 11.00 E |
| Natzungen | 52 | 51.36 N | 9.14 E |
| Nau | 85 | 40.09 N | 69.22 E |
| Nau, Cap de la › | 34 | 38.44 N | 0.14 E |
| Naucalpan de Juárez | 286a | 19.28 N | 99.14 W |
| Naucelle | 32 | 44.12 N | 2.20 E |
| Nauchnyy | 78 | 44.44 N | 34.01 E |
| Naude | 272c | 19.03 N | 73.06 E |
| Nauders | 58 | 46.53 N | 10.30 E |
| Nauen | 54 | 52.36 N | 12.52 E |
| Nauener Luch ≋ | 264a | 52.37 N | 12.55 E |


**Symbols** in the index entries represent the broad categories identified in the key at the right. Symbols with superior numbers (∧∧[1]) identify subcategories (see complete key on page *I · 1).*

**Symbole** im Register stellen die rechts im Schlüssel erklärten Kategorien dar. Symbole mit hochgestellten Ziffern (∧∧[1]) bezeichnen Unterabteilungen einer Kategorie (vgl. vollständiger Schlüssel auf Seite *I · 1).*

**Los símbolos** incluídos en el texto del índice representan las grandes categorías identificadas con la clave a la derecha. Los símbolos con numeros en su parte superior (∧∧[1]) identifican las subcategorías (véase la clave completa en la página *I · 1).*

**Les symboles** de l'index représentent les catégories indiquées dans la légende à droite. Les symboles suivis d'un indice (∧∧[1]) représentent des sous-catégories (voir légende complète à la page *I · 1).*

**Os símbolos** incluídos no texto do índice representam as grandes categorias identificadas com a chave à direita. Os símbolos com números em sua parte superior (∧∧[1]) identificam as subcategorias (veja-se a chave completa à página *I · 1).*

| | | | | | |
|---|---|---|---|---|---|
| ∧ | Mountain | Berg | Montaña | Montagne | Montanha |
| ∧∧ | Mountains | Gebirge | Montañas | Montagnes | Montanhas |
| )( | Pass | Paß | Paso | Col | Passo |
| V | Valley, Canyon | Tal, Cañon | Valle, Cañón | Vallée, Canyon | Vale, Canhão |
| ≚ | Plain | Ebene | Llano | Plaine | Planície |
| › | Cape | Kap | Cabo | Cap | Cabo |
| I | Island | Insel | Isla | Île | Ilha |
| II | Islands | Inseln | Islas | Îles | Ilhas |
| ± | Other Topographic Features | Andere Topographische Objekte | Otros Elementos Topográficos | Autres données topographiques | Outros acidentes topográficos |

## ESPAÑOL

| Nombre | Página | Lat.°' | Long.°' W = Oeste |
|---|---|---|---|
| Nauener Stadtforst ♠ | 264a | 52.38 N | 12.58 E |
| Naugachhia | 124 | 25.24 N | 87.06 E |
| Naugatuck | 207 | 41.30 N | 73.05 W |
| Naugatuck ≏ | 207 | 41.19 N | 73.05 W |
| Naughton | 190 | 46.24 N | 81.12 W |
| Naugol'noje | 82 | 56.22 N | 38.11 E |
| Naui | 140 | 18.28 N | 30.43 E |
| Naujamiestis | 76 | 55.41 N | 24.04 E |
| Naujan | 116 | 13.20 N | 121.18 E |
| Naujan, Lake ⊜ | 116 | 13.10 N | 121.21 E |
| Naujoji Akmenė | 76 | 56.19 N | 22.55 E |
| Naukan | 180 | 66.01 N | 169.43 W |
| Naulavaara ʌ [2] | 26 | 63.53 N | 28.13 E |
| Nauliila | 152 | 17.12 S | 14.42 E |
| Naumburg, Dtsch. | 54 | 51.09 N | 11.48 E |
| Naumburg, Dtsch. | 56 | 51.15 N | 9.10 E |
| Naumovščina | 76 | 58.23 N | 28.20 E |
| Naunak | 86 | 59.00 N | 80.13 E |
| Naundorf | 54 | 50.56 N | 13.25 E |
| Naunglon | 110 | 16.48 N | 97.45 E |
| Naungpale | 110 | 19.33 N | 97.08 E |
| Naunhof | 54 | 51.16 N | 12.35 E |
| Naupada ◆ [8] | 272c | 19.04 N | 72.50 E |
| Nā'ūr | 132 | 31.53 N | 35.50 E |
| Nauraushaun Brook ≏ | 276 | 41.03 N | 73.59 W |
| Nauroth | 56 | 50.42 N | 7.52 E |
| Nauroz Kalāt | 128 | 28.47 N | 65.38 E |
| Naurskaja | 84 | 43.38 N | 45.19 E |
| Nauru □ [1], Oc. | 14 | 0.32 S | 166.55 E |
| Nauru □ [1], Oc. | 174b | 0.32 S | 166.55 E |
| Naurzumskij zapovednik ♠ | 86 | 51.30 N | 64.20 E |
| Naushahro Fīroz | 120 | 26.50 N | 68.07 E |
| Naushon Island I | 207 | 41.29 N | 70.45 W |
| Nauški | 88 | 50.28 N | 106.07 E |
| Nausori | 175g | 18.02 S | 178.32 E |
| Naussac, Barrage de ◆ [6] | 62 | 44.46 N | 3.49 E |
| Naustdal | 26 | 61.31 N | 5.43 E |
| Nauta | 246 | 4.32 S | 73.33 W |
| Nautanwa | 124 | 27.26 N | 83.25 E |
| Nautilus Park | 207 | 41.22 N | 72.05 W |
| Nautla | 234 | 20.13 N | 96.47 W |
| Nauvoo | 190 | 40.33 N | 91.23 W |
| Nava, It. | 62 | 44.06 N | 7.22 E |
| Nava, Méx. | 232 | 28.25 N | 100.46 W |
| Nava, Arroyo de la ≏ | 266a | 40.31 N | 3.46 W |
| Nava, Colle di )( | 62 | 44.05 N | 7.53 E |
| Nava del Rey | 34 | 41.20 N | 5.05 W |
| Navadwip | 126 | 23.25 N | 88.22 E |
| Navael'nja | 76 | 53.28 N | 25.35 E |
| Navahermosa | 34 | 39.38 N | 4.28 W |
| Navahrudak | 76 | 53.36 N | 25.50 E |
| Navajo | 200 | 35.55 N | 109.01 W |
| Navajo ≏ | 200 | 37.01 N | 107.10 W |
| Navajo Creek ≏ | 200 | 36.59 N | 111.24 W |
| Navajo Hopi Joint Use Area ◆ [4] | 200 | 36.15 N | 110.30 W |
| Navajo Indian Reservation ◆ [4] | 200 | 36.25 N | 110.00 W |
| Navajo Mountain ʌ | 200 | 37.02 N | 110.52 W |
| Navajo National Monument ♠ | 200 | 36.40 N | 110.33 W |
| Navajo Reservoir ⊜ [1] | 200 | 36.55 N | 107.30 W |
| Naval | 116 | 11.34 N | 124.23 E |
| Navalmoral de la Mata | 34 | 39.54 N | 5.32 W |
| Naval Ordnance Test Station ■ | 228 | 35.32 N | 117.05 W |
| Navalvillar de Pela | 34 | 39.06 N | 5.28 W |
| Navan | 48 | 53.39 N | 6.41 W |
| Navapolack | 76 | 55.31 N | 28.38 E |
| Navāpur | 122 | 21.09 N | 73.48 E |
| Navarin, mys ≻ | 180 | 62.16 N | 179.10 E |
| Navarino → Pílos | 38 | 36.55 N | 21.43 E |
| Navarino, Isla I | 254 | 55.05 S | 67.40 W |
| Navarra □ [4] | 34 | 42.40 N | 1.30 W |
| Navarre, Austl. | 169 | 36.54 S | 143.07 E |
| Navarre, Oh., U.S. | 214 | 40.43 N | 81.31 W |
| Navarro | 258 | 35.01 S | 59.16 W |
| Navarro □ [6] | 222 | 32.05 N | 96.30 W |
| Navarro ≏ | 204 | 39.11 N | 123.45 W |
| Navarro, Cañada ≏ | 258 | 35.00 S | 59.18 W |
| Navarro, Laguna ⊜ | 258 | 35.01 S | 59.18 W |
| Navarro Mills Lake ⊜ [1] | 222 | 31.56 N | 96.45 W |
| Navasëlki, Bela. | 76 | 52.02 N | 24.21 E |
| Navasèlki, Bela. | 76 | 52.24 N | 28.33 E |
| Navašino | 80 | 55.32 N | 42.12 E |
| Navasota | 222 | 30.23 N | 96.05 W |
| Navasota ≏ | 222 | 30.20 N | 96.09 W |
| Navassa | 192 | 34.15 N | 78.00 W |
| Navassa Island I | 238 | 18.24 N | 75.01 W |
| Nave | 64 | 45.35 N | 10.17 E |
| Nävekvarn | 40 | 58.38 N | 16.49 E |
| Navenne | 58 | 47.36 N | 6.10 E |
| Naver ≏ | 46 | 58.32 N | 4.15 W |
| Naver, Loch ⊜ | 46 | 58.17 N | 4.23 W |
| Navesink | 276 | 40.23 N | 74.02 W |
| Navesink River ⊂ | 276 | 40.23 N | 73.58 W |
| Navesnoje | 76 | 52.17 N | 37.57 E |
| Nâves-Parmelan | 58 | 45.56 N | 6.11 E |
| Navesti ≏ | 76 | 58.30 N | 24.54 E |
| Navestock | 260 | 51.39 N | 0.13 E |
| Navestock Side | 260 | 51.39 N | 0.16 E |
| Navia, Arg. | 252 | 34.47 S | 66.35 W |
| Navia, Esp. | 34 | 43.32 N | 6.43 W |
| Navia ≏ | 34 | 43.33 N | 6.44 W |
| Navidad | 252 | 33.57 S | 71.50 W |
| Navidad ≏ | 196 | 28.41 N | 96.35 W |
| Navidad, Bahía de ⊂ | 234 | 19.17 N | 104.50 W |
| Navidad Bank ✣ [3] | 238 | 20.00 N | 68.50 W |
| Navio, Riacho do ≏ | 250 | 8.39 S | 38.36 W |
| Naviraí | 255 | 23.08 S | 54.13 W |
| Navis | 64 | 47.07 N | 11.32 E |
| Naviti I | 175g | 17.07 S | 177.15 E |
| Navl'a | 76 | 52.51 N | 34.30 E |
| Navl'a ≏ | 76 | 52.42 N | 34.01 E |
| Năvodari | 38 | 44.19 N | 28.36 E |
| Navoi | 72 | 40.15 N | 65.15 E |
| Navojoa | 232 | 27.06 N | 109.26 W |
| Navolato | 232 | 24.47 N | 107.42 W |
| Navoloki | 80 | 57.28 N | 41.59 E |
| Navotas | 269f | 14.39 N | 120.57 E |
| Návpaktos | 38 | 38.23 N | 21.50 E |
| Návplion | 38 | 37.34 N | 22.48 E |
| Navrongo | 150 | 10.54 N | 1.06 W |
| Navsāri | 120 | 20.51 N | 72.55 E |
| Navua | 175g | 18.14 S | 178.10 E |
| Navy Island I | 284a | 43.04 N | 79.01 W |
| Navy Pier ◆ [5] | 278 | 41.53 N | 87.36 W |
| Navy Yard City | 224 | 47.32 N | 122.41 W |
| Nawa, Nihon | 96 | 35.30 N | 133.30 E |
| Nawa → Naha, Nihon | 174m | 26.13 N | 127.40 E |
| Nawá, Sūrīy. | 132 | 32.53 N | 36.03 E |
| Nawābganj, Bngl. | 124 | 24.36 N | 88.17 E |
| Nawābganj, Bngl. | 126 | 23.40 N | 90.10 E |
| Nawābganj, India | 124 | 28.33 N | 79.38 E |
| Nawābganj, India | 124 | 26.52 N | 82.08 E |
| Nawābganj, India | 124 | 26.56 N | 81.13 E |
| Nawābshāh | 120 | 26.15 N | 68.25 E |
| Nawāda | 124 | 24.53 N | 85.32 E |
| Nāwah | 120 | 32.19 N | 67.53 E |
| Nawa Kot | 120 | 28.20 N | 71.22 E |
| Nawalapitiya | 122 | 7.03 N | 80.32 E |
| Nawalgarh | 120 | 27.51 N | 75.16 E |
| Nawān Kot | 123 | 31.06 N | 71.32 E |
| Nawanshahr | 123 | 31.07 N | 76.08 E |
| Nawāpāra, Bngl. | 126 | 23.02 N | 89.23 E |
| Nawāpāra, India | 122 | 20.58 N | 81.51 E |
| Nawapārā, India | 126 | 23.29 N | 88.15 E |
| Nawasā al-Ghayṭ | 142 | 30.58 N | 31.19 E |
| Nawāshahr | 123 | 34.10 N | 73.16 E |
| Nawāṣīf, Ḥarrat ⩡ [9] | 144 | 21.20 N | 42.10 E |
| Nawāy | 142 | 27.47 N | 30.46 E |
| Nawiliwili Bay ⊂ | 229b | 21.57 N | 159.21 W |
| Nawinda Kuta | 152 | 16.25 S | 24.28 E |

## FRANÇAIS

| Nom | Page | Lat.°' | Long.°' W = Ouest |
|---|---|---|---|
| Nawŏn-ni | 98 | 36.25 N | 126.40 E |
| Naxçıvan | 84 | 39.13 N | 45.24 E |
| Naxçıvan Muxtar Respublikası □ [3] | 84 | 39.20 N | 45.30 E |
| Naxera | 208 | 37.20 N | 76.27 W |
| Naxi | 107 | 28.47 N | 105.22 E |
| Náxos | 38 | 37.06 N | 25.23 E |
| Náxos I | 38 | 37.02 N | 25.35 E |
| Naxos ⊥ | 70 | 37.49 N | 15.17 E |
| Nayābās | 272a | 28.35 N | 77.19 E |
| Nayāgaon | 126 | 23.32 N | 90.46 E |
| Nayāgarh | 120 | 20.08 N | 85.06 E |
| Nayāgrām | 126 | 22.02 N | 87.11 E |
| Nayak | 120 | 34.44 N | 66.57 E |
| Nayāpāra | 126 | 21.35 N | 87.01 E |
| Nayarit | 204 | 32.20 N | 115.19 W |
| Nayarit □ [3] | 234 | 22.00 N | 105.00 W |
| Nayau Island I | 175g | 17.58 S | 179.03 W |
| Nāy Band, Īrān | 128 | 32.20 N | 57.34 E |
| Nāy Band, Īrān | 128 | 27.23 N | 52.38 E |
| Nāy Band, Kūh-e ʌ | 128 | 32.26 N | 57.22 E |
| Nayland | 42 | 51.59 N | 0.52 E |
| Naylor | 194 | 36.34 N | 90.36 W |
| Nayong | 102 | 26.50 N | 105.13 E |
| Nayoro | 92a | 44.21 N | 142.28 E |
| Nazālī Ṭāhā' | 142 | 28.11 N | 30.42 E |
| Nazaré, Bra. | 250 | 6.23 S | 47.40 W |
| Nazaré, Bra. | 255 | 13.02 S | 39.00 W |
| Nazaré, Port. | 34 | 39.36 N | 9.04 W |
| Nazaré da Mata | 250 | 7.44 S | 35.14 W |
| Nazaré do Piauí | 250 | 6.59 S | 42.40 W |
| Nazareno | 256 | 21.13 S | 44.37 W |
| Nazaré Paulista | 256 | 23.11 S | 46.24 W |
| Nazareth, Bel. | 50 | 50.58 N | 3.36 E |
| Nazareth, Pa., U.S. | 208 | 40.44 N | 75.18 W |
| Nazareth, Vanuatu | 175f | 15.29 S | 168.10 E |
| Nazareth → Nazerat, Yis. | 132 | 32.42 N | 35.18 E |
| Nazareth Bank ✣ [4] | 12 | 14.30 S | 60.45 E |
| Nazário | 255 | 16.36 S | 49.54 W |
| Nazarjevo, Ross. | 82 | 55.22 N | 36.24 E |
| Nazarjevo, Ross. | 265b | 55.59 N | 37.16 E |
| Nazarovo | 86 | 56.01 N | 90.26 E |
| Nazarovskij | 78 | 49.33 N | 40.56 E |
| Nazas | 232 | 25.14 N | 104.08 W |
| Nazas ≏ | 232 | 25.35 N | 105.00 W |
| Nazca | 248 | 14.50 S | 74.57 W |
| Nazca Ridge ✣ [3] | 18 | 22.00 S | 82.00 W |
| Naze | 93b | 28.23 N | 129.30 E |
| Nazeing | 260 | 51.44 N | 0.03 E |
| N'azepetrovsk | 86 | 56.03 N | 59.36 E |
| Naẓerat (Nazareth) | 132 | 32.42 N | 35.18 E |
| Naẓerat 'Illit | 132 | 32.42 N | 35.19 E |
| Nazija | 76 | 59.50 N | 31.35 E |
| Nazik Gölü ⊜ | 130 | 38.50 N | 42.16 E |
| Nazilli | 130 | 37.55 N | 28.21 E |
| Nazimicha | 265b | 55.59 N | 38.08 E |
| Nazımiye | 130 | 39.11 N | 39.50 E |
| Nazimovo | 86 | 59.30 N | 90.58 E |
| Nazina | 86 | 60.07 N | 78.52 E |
| Nāzira | 120 | 26.55 N | 94.44 E |
| Nāzir Hāt | 120 | 22.38 N | 91.47 E |
| Nāzirpur | 126 | 22.43 N | 89.58 E |
| Nazko ≏ | 182 | 53.07 N | 123.34 W |
| Nazlat al-'Amūdayn | 142 | 28.14 N | 30.42 E |
| Nazlat al-Badramān | 142 | 27.40 N | 30.44 E |
| Nazlat as-Sammān | 273c | 29.59 N | 31.08 E |
| Nazlat Khalīfah | 273c | 30.01 N | 31.10 E |
| Nazlat Quftan Bāshā | 142 | 28.57 N | 30.49 E |
| Nazlat Thābit | 142 | 28.25 N | 30.47 E |
| Nazran' | 84 | 43.13 N | 44.46 E |
| Nazret | 144 | 8.33 N | 39.16 E |
| Nazyvajevsk | 86 | 55.34 N | 71.21 E |
| N. B. C. Studios ʋ [3] | 280 | 34.09 N | 118.20 W |
| Nchanga | 154 | 12.30 S | 27.53 E |
| Nchelenge | 154 | 9.20 S | 28.50 E |
| Ncue | 152 | 2.01 N | 10.28 E |
| Ndabala | 154 | 13.28 S | 29.50 E |
| Ndala | 154 | 4.46 S | 33.16 E |
| N'dalatando | 152 | 9.18 S | 14.54 E |
| Ndali | 150 | 9.51 N | 2.43 E |
| Ndanda | 152 | 5.12 N | 22.21 E |
| Ndande | 150 | 15.16 N | 16.30 W |
| Ndarassa | 152 | 6.49 N | 22.15 E |
| Ndélé | 146 | 8.24 N | 20.39 E |
| Ndélélé | 152 | 4.02 N | 14.56 E |
| Ndemba | 152 | 0.11 N | 14.19 E |
| Ndendé | 152 | 2.23 S | 11.23 E |
| Ndikiniméki | 152 | 4.46 N | 10.50 E |
| Ndindi | 152 | 3.46 S | 11.09 E |
| N'Djamena | 146 | 12.07 N | 15.03 E |
| Ndji ≏ | 152 | 6.47 N | 22.14 E |
| Ndjili ◆ [8] | 273b | 4.20 S | 15.22 E |
| Ndjili ≏ | 273b | 4.19 S | 15.24 E |
| Ndjili, Grande Île de la I | 273b | 4.19 S | 15.24 E |
| Ndjim ≏ | 152 | 4.38 N | 11.24 E |
| Ndjo | 152 | 1.15 S | 14.30 E |
| Ndjolé | 152 | 0.11 S | 10.45 E |
| Ndogo, Lagune ⊂ | 152 | 2.35 S | 10.00 E |
| Ndola | 154 | 12.58 S | 28.38 E |
| Ndolo ◆ [8] | 273b | 4.19 S | 15.19 E |
| Ndona | 115b | 8.46 S | 121.45 E |
| Ndongo | 152 | 2.19 S | 13.38 E |
| Ndouba | 152 | 0.11 S | 14.09 E |
| Ndougou | 152 | 1.39 S | 9.40 E |
| Ndu | 152 | 4.41 N | 22.49 E |
| Nduguti | 154 | 4.18 S | 34.42 E |
| Nduindui | 175f | 15.24 S | 167.46 E |
| Ndumbwe | 154 | 10.14 S | 39.58 E |
| Ndumu Game Reserve ◆ [4] | 158 | 26.53 S | 32.15 E |
| Nduye | 154 | 1.50 N | 29.01 E |
| Ne | 268 | 35.47 N | 140.03 E |
| Nea ≏ | 26 | 63.13 N | 11.02 E |
| Neabul Creek ≏ | 166 | 27.45 S | 147.32 E |
| Néa Erithraía | 267c | 38.05 N | 23.49 E |
| Néa Filadhélfia | 267c | 38.02 N | 23.44 E |
| Neagari | 94 | 36.27 N | 136.27 E |
| Neagh, Lough ⊜ | 48 | 54.38 N | 6.24 W |
| Neah Bay | 224 | 48.22 N | 124.37 W |
| Néa Ionía | 267c | 38.02 N | 23.45 E |
| Neajlov ≏ | 38 | 44.11 N | 26.12 E |
| Néa Khalkidhón | 267c | 38.02 N | 23.43 E |
| Neale, Lake ⊜ | 162 | 24.22 S | 130.00 E |
| Neales ≏ | 162 | 28.08 S | 136.47 E |
| Neales Flat | 168b | 34.15 S | 139.10 E |
| Néa Liósia | 267c | 38.02 N | 23.42 E |
| Neamț □ [6] | 38 | 47.00 N | 26.30 E |
| Neandertal, Naturschutzgebiet ♠ | 263 | 51.15 N | 7.00 E |
| Néa Páfos (Paphos) | 130 | 34.45 N | 32.25 E |
| Neapel → Napoli | 68 | 40.51 N | 14.17 E |
| Néa Pendéli | 267c | 38.04 N | 23.52 E |
| Néa Péramos | 267c | 38.00 N | 23.26 E |
| Neápolis, Ellás | 38 | 36.30 N | 23.04 E |
| Neápolis, Ellás | 38 | 35.15 N | 25.37 E |
| Neapolis, Oh., U.S. | 216 | 41.29 N | 83.52 W |
| Near Islands II | 181a | 52.40 N | 173.30 E |
| Near North Side ◆ [8] | 278 | 41.54 N | 87.38 W |
| Néa Smírni | 267c | 37.57 N | 23.43 E |
| Neasons Hill | 214 | 41.37 N | 80.08 W |
| Neatahwanta, Lake ⊜ | 210 | 43.18 N | 76.27 W |
| Neath | 42 | 51.40 N | 3.48 W |
| Neath ≏ | 42 | 51.37 N | 3.50 W |
| Neauphle-le-Château | 50 | 48.49 N | 1.54 E |
| Neauphle-le-Vieux | 261 | 48.49 N | 1.52 E |
| Neavitt | 208 | 38.43 N | 76.16 W |
| Neba | 94 | 35.15 N | 137.35 E |
| Nebaj | 236 | 15.24 N | 91.08 W |
| Nebbou | 150 | 11.18 N | 1.53 W |
| Nebelhorn ʌ | 58 | 47.25 N | 10.20 E |
| Nebesnaja, gora ʌ | 86 | 43.19 N | 80.44 E |
| Nebeur | 36 | 36.17 N | 8.47 E |
| Nebine Creek ≏ | 166 | 29.07 S | 146.56 E |
| Nebit-Dag | 128 | 39.30 N | 54.22 E |
| Neblina, Pico da ʌ | 246 | 0.48 N | 66.02 W |
| Nebo | 194 | 39.27 N | 90.47 W |

## PORTUGUÊS

| Nome | Página | Lat.°' | Long.°' W = Oeste |
|---|---|---|---|
| Nebo, Mount ʌ, Ut., U.S. | 200 | 39.49 N | 111.46 W |
| Nebo, Mount → Nabā, Jabal an- ʌ, Urd. | 132 | 31.46 N | 35.45 E |
| Nebolči | 76 | 59.08 N | 33.18 E |
| Nebra | 54 | 51.17 N | 11.34 E |
| Nebraska | 218 | 39.04 N | 85.28 W |
| Nebraska □ [3], U.S. | 178 | 41.30 N | 100.00 W |
| Nebraska □ [3], U.S. | 198 | 41.30 N | 100.00 W |
| Nebraska City | 198 | 40.40 N | 95.51 W |
| Nebrodi ʎ | 70 | 37.54 N | 14.35 E |
| Nebyloje | 80 | 56.22 N | 39.59 E |
| Nečajevka | 80 | 53.17 N | 44.27 E |
| Nečajevo | 82 | 54.42 N | 37.23 E |
| Necaxa ≏ | 234 | 20.16 N | 97.27 W |
| Necedah | 190 | 44.01 N | 90.04 W |
| Nechajevskij | 80 | 50.25 N | 41.44 E |
| Nechako ≏ | 182 | 53.56 N | 122.42 W |
| Nechako Plateau ʎ [1] | 182 | 54.00 N | 124.30 W |
| Nechako Range ʎ | 182 | 53.20 N | 124.30 W |
| Nechako Reservoir ⊜ [1] | 182 | 53.25 N | 125.10 W |
| Nechayane | 78 | 46.57 N | 31.33 E |
| Neche | 198 | 48.59 N | 97.33 W |
| Neches | 222 | 31.52 N | 95.30 W |
| Neches ≏ | 194 | 29.55 N | 93.52 W |
| Nechí | 246 | 8.07 N | 74.46 W |
| Nechí ≏ | 246 | 8.08 N | 74.46 W |
| Nechisar National Park ♠ | 144 | 6.00 N | 37.50 E |
| Nechmeya | 36 | 36.36 N | 7.31 E |
| Nechranice, vodní nádrž ⊜ [1] | 54 | 50.20 N | 13.20 E |
| Neckar ≏ | 30 | 49.31 N | 8.26 E |
| Neckarbischofsheim | 56 | 49.17 N | 8.57 E |
| Neckarelz | 56 | 49.20 N | 9.06 E |
| Neckargemünd | 56 | 49.23 N | 8.47 E |
| Neckarsteinach | 56 | 49.25 N | 8.53 E |
| Neckarsulm | 56 | 49.12 N | 9.13 E |
| Neckartailfingen | 56 | 48.36 N | 9.16 E |
| Neckartenzlingen | 56 | 48.35 N | 9.14 E |
| Neck Creek ≏ | 276 | 40.36 N | 74.12 W |
| Necker | 284b | 39.23 N | 76.29 W |
| Necker Island I, Br. Vir. Is. | 240m | 18.33 N | 64.21 W |
| Necker Island I, Hi., U.S. | 14 | 23.35 N | 164.42 W |
| Necker Ridge ✣ [3] | 14 | 22.00 N | 167.15 W |
| Necochea | 252 | 38.33 S | 58.45 W |
| Necrópolis ◆ | 266a | 40.25 N | 3.38 W |
| Nedalssjön ⊜ | 26 | 62.56 N | 12.11 E |
| Nedanchychi | 78 | 51.30 N | 30.37 E |
| Ned Brown Preserve ♠ | 278 | 42.02 N | 88.01 W |
| Nedel'noje | 82 | 54.50 N | 36.39 E |
| Nederland | 194 | 29.58 N | 93.59 W |
| Nederland → Netherlands □ [1] | 30 | 52.15 N | 5.30 E |
| Nederlandse Antillen → Netherlands Antilles □ [2] | 241s | 12.15 N | 69.00 W |
| Neder Rijn ≏ [1] | 52 | 51.58 N | 5.20 E |
| Nederweert | 52 | 51.17 N | 5.45 E |
| Nederzwalm-Hermelgem | 50 | 50.53 N | 3.41 E |
| Nedlands | 168a | 31.59 S | 115.49 E |
| Nedlitz | 54 | 52.04 N | 12.14 E |
| Nedlitz ◆ [8] | 264a | 52.26 N | 13.03 E |
| Nêdong | 120 | 29.14 N | 91.46 E |
| Nedre Soppero | 24 | 68.01 N | 21.44 E |
| Nedre Vättern ⊜ | 40 | 59.49 N | 15.40 E |
| Nédroma | 148 | 35.01 N | 1.45 W |
| Nedrow | 210 | 42.58 N | 76.08 W |
| Nedryhayliv | 78 | 50.50 N | 33.53 E |
| Nedstrand | 26 | 59.21 N | 5.51 E |
| Neebish Island I | 190 | 46.16 N | 84.09 W |
| Neede | 52 | 52.08 N | 6.36 E |
| Needham, In., U.S. | 218 | 39.32 N | 85.58 W |
| Needham, Ma., U.S. | 207 | 42.17 N | 71.14 W |
| Needham Market | 42 | 52.09 N | 1.03 E |
| Needhams Point ≻ | 241g | 13.05 N | 59.36 W |
| Needle Mountain ʌ | 202 | 44.05 N | 109.37 W |
| Needles | 204 | 34.50 N | 114.36 W |
| Needling Hill ʌ [2] | 168a | 31.53 S | 116.56 E |
| Needville | 222 | 29.23 N | 95.50 W |
| Neelyton | 214 | 40.10 N | 77.50 W |
| Ñeembucú □ [5] | 252 | 27.00 S | 58.00 W |
| Neenah | 190 | 44.11 N | 88.27 W |
| Neepawa | 184 | 50.13 N | 99.29 W |
| Neerabup National Park ♠ | 168a | 31.41 S | 115.43 E |
| Neerim South | 169 | 38.01 S | 145.58 E |
| Neermoor | 52 | 53.18 N | 7.26 E |
| Neeroeteren | 56 | 51.05 N | 5.42 E |
| Neerpelt | 56 | 51.13 N | 5.25 E |
| Neersen | 263 | 51.15 N | 6.29 E |
| Nee Soon | 271c | 1.24 N | 103.49 E |
| Neetze | 52 | 53.15 N | 10.39 E |
| Neetze ≏ | 54 | 53.20 N | 10.28 E |
| Nefedjevo, Ross. | 82 | 54.39 N | 37.56 E |
| Nefedjevo, Ross. | 265b | 55.54 N | 37.10 E |
| Neffs | 208 | 40.42 N | 75.37 W |
| Neffsville | 208 | 40.06 N | 76.18 W |
| Nef'odovo | 86 | 58.48 N | 72.34 E |
| Nefta | 148 | 33.52 N | 7.33 E |
| Neftçala | 84 | 39.23 N | 49.16 E |
| Nefteabad | 85 | 40.12 N | 70.34 E |
| Neftegorsk | 84 | 44.22 N | 39.42 E |
| Neftekumsk | 84 | 44.45 N | 44.48 E |
| Nefyn | 42 | 52.57 N | 4.31 W |
| Nefza | 36 | 36.58 N | 9.05 E |
| Negage | 152 | 7.45 S | 15.16 E |
| Négala | 150 | 12.52 N | 8.27 W |
| Negapatam → Nāgappattinam | 122 | 10.46 N | 79.50 E |
| Negara, Indon. | 112 | 2.37 S | 115.06 E |
| Negara, Indon. | 115a | 8.22 S | 114.37 E |
| Negara ≏ | 112 | 3.00 S | 114.45 E |
| Negast | 54 | 54.15 N | 13.01 E |
| Negaunee | 190 | 46.29 N | 87.36 W |
| Negba | 132 | 31.40 N | 34.41 E |
| Negele | 144 | 5.20 N | 39.36 E |
| Negenborn | 52 | 51.53 N | 9.34 E |
| Negeribatin | 112 | 4.35 S | 104.32 E |
| Negeri Sembilan □ [3] | 114 | 2.45 N | 102.10 E |
| Negev Desert → HaNegev ◆ [1] | 132 | 30.30 N | 34.55 E |
| Negishi | 268 | 35.51 N | 139.23 E |
| Negley | 214 | 40.47 N | 80.32 W |
| Negola | 152 | 14.10 S | 14.30 E |
| Negomano | 154 | 11.27 S | 38.31 E |
| Negombo | 122 | 7.13 N | 79.50 E |
| Negotin | 38 | 44.14 N | 22.32 E |
| Negra, Laguna ⊜ | 252 | 34.03 S | 53.40 W |
| Negra, Ponta ≻ | 256 | 22.58 S | 42.42 W |
| Negra, Punta ≻, Belize | 232 | 16.17 N | 88.34 W |
| Negra, Punta ≻, Perú | 248 | 6.06 S | 81.09 W |
| Negrais | 266c | 38.53 N | 9.17 W |
| Negras, Lomas ʌ [2] | 286d | 11.55 S | 77.06 W |
| Negreira | 34 | 42.54 N | 8.44 W |
| Nègres, Pointe des ≻ | 240e | 14.36 N | 61.06 W |
| Negrești | 38 | 46.50 N | 27.27 E |
| Negrești-Oaș | 38 | 47.52 N | 23.25 E |
| Negrine | 148 | 34.30 N | 7.30 E |
| Negritos | 246 | 4.38 S | 81.19 W |
| Negro ≏, Arg. | 254 | 41.02 S | 62.47 W |
| Negro ≏, Bol. | 248 | 9.49 S | 65.42 W |
| Negro ≏, Bol. | 248 | 14.11 S | 63.07 W |
| Negro ≏, Bra. | 248 | 5.15 S | 70.53 W |
| Negro ≏, Bra. | 248 | 19.13 S | 57.17 W |
| Negro ≏, Bra. | 250 | 9.15 S | 47.34 W |
| Negro ≏, Bra. | 252 | 26.01 S | 50.30 W |
| Negro ≏, Col. | 246 | 5.44 N | 74.39 W |
| Negro ≏, N.A. | 236 | 13.02 N | 87.17 W |
| Negro ≏, Para. | 252 | 24.23 S | 57.11 W |
| Negro ≏, S.A. | 246 | 3.08 S | 59.55 W |
| Negro ≏, S.A. | 252 | 33.24 S | 58.22 W |
| Negro, Baia del ⊂ | 144 | 7.55 N | 49.55 E |
| Negro, Cerro ʌ, Arg. | 254 | 46.55 S | 70.12 W |
| Negro, Cerro ʌ, Arg. | 254 | 44.09 S | 69.30 W |
| Negro, Cerro ʌ, Méx. | 234 | 17.19 N | 97.25 W |
| Negro, Mar → Black Sea ⫪ [2] | 22 | 43.00 N | 35.00 E |
| Negros I | 116 | 10.00 N | 123.00 E |
| Negros Occidental □ [4] | 116 | 10.20 N | 123.00 E |
| Negros Oriental □ [4] | 116 | 9.40 N | 123.00 E |
| Negru Vodă | 38 | 43.50 N | 28.12 E |
| Neguac | 186 | 47.15 N | 65.05 W |
| Nehalem | 224 | 45.43 N | 123.53 W |
| Nehalem ≏ | 224 | 45.40 N | 123.56 W |
| Neharèlae | 76 | 53.36 N | 27.04 E |
| Nehawka | 198 | 40.49 N | 95.59 W |
| Nehbandān | 128 | 31.32 N | 60.02 E |
| Neheim-Hüsten | 56 | 51.27 N | 7.57 E |
| Nehonsey Brook ≏ | 285 | 39.49 N | 75.18 W |
| Néhoué, Baie de ⊂ | 175f | 20.21 S | 164.09 E |
| Nehru Planetarium ʋ | 272c | 18.59 N | 72.49 E |
| Neiba | 238 | 18.28 N | 71.25 W |
| Neichiang → Neijiang | 107 | 29.35 N | 105.03 E |
| Neidpath | 184 | 50.13 N | 107.15 W |
| Neige, Crêt de la ʌ | 58 | 46.16 N | 5.56 E |
| Neiges, Piton des ʌ | 157c | 21.05 S | 55.29 E |
| Neihart | 202 | 46.56 N | 110.44 W |
| Neihe ≏ | 100 | 22.54 N | 115.38 E |
| Neihu | 269d | 25.05 N | 121.34 E |
| Neihuang | 98 | 35.59 N | 114.55 E |
| Neijiang | 107 | 29.35 N | 105.03 E |
| Neikiang → Neijiang | 107 | 29.35 N | 105.03 E |
| Neilburg | 184 | 52.50 N | 109.38 W |
| Neillsville | 190 | 44.33 N | 90.35 W |
| Neilston | 46 | 55.47 N | 4.27 W |
| Neimen | 263 | 51.29 N | 7.48 E |
| Nei Monggol Zizhiqu (Inner Mongolia) □ [4] | 90 | 43.00 N | 115.00 E |
| Nein | 132 | 32.38 N | 35.21 E |
| Neindorf | 54 | 52.20 N | 10.50 E |
| Neinstedt | 54 | 51.45 N | 11.05 E |
| Neiqiu | 98 | 37.17 N | 114.31 E |
| Neira | 246 | 5.10 N | 75.32 W |
| Neirone | 62 | 44.27 N | 9.11 E |
| Neishuishan | 269d | 25.09 N | 121.43 E |
| Neisse (Nysa Łużycka) ≏ | 30 | 52.04 N | 14.46 E |
| Neiva | 246 | 2.56 N | 75.18 W |
| Neiwufuquan | 105 | 40.11 N | 117.39 E |
| Neixiang | 102 | 33.12 N | 111.57 E |
| Neixpa ≏ | 234 | 18.05 N | 102.46 W |
| Neizeng Shan ʌ | 100 | 24.02 N | 117.32 E |
| Neja, Ross. | 80 | 58.24 N | 46.31 E |
| Neja, Ross. | 80 | 58.18 N | 43.54 E |
| Neja ≏ | 80 | 57.48 N | 43.42 E |
| Nejapa de Madero | 234 | 16.37 N | 95.59 W |
| Nejd → Najd □ [9] | 118 | 25.00 N | 44.30 E |
| Nejdek | 54 | 50.17 N | 12.42 E |
| Nejo | 144 | 9.30 N | 35.30 E |
| Nejva ≏ | 86 | 57.54 N | 62.18 E |
| Nejvo-Šajtanskij | 86 | 57.44 N | 61.15 E |
| Nekalagba | 154 | 2.50 N | 28.01 E |
| Nekemte | 144 | 9.02 N | 36.31 E |
| Nekhab ⊥ | 140 | 25.10 N | 32.48 E |
| Nekhvoroshcha | 78 | 49.09 N | 34.44 E |
| Nekoosa | 190 | 44.18 N | 89.54 W |
| Nekor, Oued ≏ | 34 | 35.14 N | 3.45 W |
| Neko-zaki ≻ | 96 | 35.40 N | 134.46 E |
| Nekrasino | 82 | 56.18 N | 36.33 E |
| Nekrasovka | 265b | 55.41 N | 37.56 E |
| Nekrasovo, Ross. | 80 | 51.10 N | 45.18 E |
| Nekrasovo, Ross. | 82 | 54.30 N | 38.57 E |
| Nekrasovskoje | 80 | 57.41 N | 40.22 E |
| Nekselø I | 41 | 55.47 N | 11.18 E |
| Neksø | 26 | 55.04 N | 15.09 E |
| Nela Park ♠ | 279a | 41.33 N | 81.33 W |
| Nel'aty | 88 | 56.29 N | 115.41 E |
| Nelichu ʌ | 140 | 6.08 N | 34.25 E |
| Nelidovo | 76 | 56.13 N | 32.46 E |
| Neligh | 198 | 42.07 N | 98.01 W |
| Nel'kan | 74 | 57.40 N | 136.13 E |
| Nellie | 214 | 40.20 N | 82.04 W |
| Nellikuppam | 122 | 11.46 N | 79.41 E |
| Nellingen | 56 | 48.33 N | 9.47 E |
| Nellis Air Force Base ■ | 204 | 36.14 N | 115.02 W |
| Nelliston | 210 | 42.56 N | 74.37 W |
| Nellis Weapons Range ■ | 204 | 37.15 N | 116.20 W |
| Nellore | 122 | 14.26 N | 79.58 E |
| Nel'ma | 89 | 47.39 N | 139.09 E |
| Nelson, B.C., Can. | 182 | 49.29 N | 117.17 W |
| Nelson, N.Z. | 172 | 41.17 S | 173.17 E |
| Nelson, Eng., U.K. | 44 | 53.51 N | 2.13 W |
| Nelson, Ne., U.S. | 198 | 40.12 N | 98.04 W |
| Nelson, Pa., U.S. | 210 | 41.59 N | 77.14 W |
| Nelson ≏ | 184 | 57.04 N | 92.30 W |
| Nelson, Cape ≻, Austl. | 166 | 38.26 S | 141.33 E |
| Nelson, Cape ≻, Pap. N. Gui. | 164 | 9.00 S | 149.15 E |
| Nelson, Estrecho ⋓ | 254 | 51.37 S | 75.00 W |
| Nelson Creek ≏ | 222 | 30.56 N | 95.31 W |
| Nelson House | 184 | 55.47 N | 98.51 W |
| Nelson Island I | 180 | 60.35 N | 164.45 W |
| Nelson-Kennedy Ledges State Park ♠ | 214 | 41.18 N | 81.04 W |
| Nelson Lake ⊜ | 184 | 55.44 N | 100.00 W |
| Nelson Lakes National Park ♠ | 172 | 41.50 S | 172.40 E |
| Nelson Reservoir ⊜ [1] | 202 | 48.30 N | 107.34 W |
| Nelson's Dockyard ⊥ | 240c | 17.00 N | 61.46 W |
| Nelsonville, N.Y., U.S. | 210 | 41.25 N | 73.57 W |
| Nelsonville, Oh., U.S. | 188 | 39.27 N | 82.14 W |
| Nelspoort | 158 | 32.07 S | 23.00 E |
| Nelspoortjie | 158 | 29.58 S | 22.25 E |
| Nelspruit | 156 | 25.30 S | 30.58 E |
| Néma, Maur. | 150 | 16.37 N | 7.15 W |
| Nema, Ross. | 80 | 57.31 N | 50.31 E |
| Néma, Dahr ⩡ [4] | 150 | 16.40 N | 7.13 W |
| Nemadji ≏ | 190 | 46.41 N | 92.02 W |
| Nemah | 224 | 46.31 N | 123.51 W |
| Nemaha | 198 | 40.20 N | 95.40 W |
| Neman | 76 | 55.02 N | 22.02 E |
| Nëman (Nemunas) ≏ | 76 | 55.18 N | 21.23 E |
| Nematābād ◆ [8] | 267d | 35.38 N | 51.21 E |
| Nembe | 150 | 4.35 N | 6.26 E |
| Nembrala | 112 | 10.53 S | 122.50 E |
| Nembro | 62 | 45.45 N | 9.45 E |
| Nemčinovka | 265b | 55.43 N | 37.23 E |
| Nemda ≏, Ross. | 80 | 57.35 N | 48.56 E |
| Nemda ≏, Ross. | 80 | 57.21 N | 43.08 E |
| Nemegosenda ≏ | 190 | 48.31 N | 82.53 W |
| Nemegt uul ʎ | 102 | 43.40 N | 101.10 E |
| Nemeiben Lake ⊜ | 184 | 55.20 N | 105.20 W |
| Nemenčinė | 76 | 54.51 N | 25.29 E |
| Nementcha, Monts de ʎ | 148 | 34.52 N | 7.05 E |
| Nemeriči | 76 | 53.51 N | 33.59 E |
| Nemi | 66 | 41.43 N | 12.43 E |
| Nemi, Lago di ⊜ | 267a | 41.43 N | 12.42 E |
| Nemira Mare, Vârful ʌ | 38 | 46.15 N | 26.19 E |
| Nemirovo | 82 | 55.54 N | 36.12 E |
| Nemo | 222 | 32.16 N | 97.39 W |
| Nemoli | 68 | 40.04 N | 15.48 E |
| Nemor ≏ | 89 | 48.23 N | 124.32 E |
| Nemours | 50 | 48.16 N | 2.42 E |
| Nemovychi | 78 | 51.16 N | 26.38 E |
| Nemrut Gölü ⊜ | 130 | 38.37 N | 42.12 E |
| Nemuna, Bjeshkët e ʎ | 38 | 42.27 N | 19.47 E |
| Nemunas (Nëman) ≏ | 76 | 55.18 N | 21.23 E |
| Nemuro | 92a | 43.20 N | 145.35 E |
| Nemuro-hantō ≻ [1] | 92a | 43.21 N | 145.42 E |
| Nemuro Strait ⋓ | 92a | 44.00 N | 145.20 E |
| Nemyriv, Ukr. | 78 | 50.07 N | 23.25 E |
| Nemyriv, Ukr. | 78 | 48.58 N | 28.50 E |
| Nemzeti Museum ʋ | 264c | 47.29 N | 19.05 E |
| Nen ≏ | 89 | 45.25 N | 124.40 E |
| Nena Creek ≏ | 224 | 45.07 N | 121.07 W |
| Nenagh | 48 | 52.52 N | 8.12 W |
| Nenagh ≏ | 48 | 52.56 N | 8.17 W |
| Nenana | 180 | 64.34 N | 149.07 W |
| Nenana ≏ | 180 | 64.30 N | 149.00 W |
| Nenaševo | 82 | 54.34 N | 37.28 E |
| Nenasi | 114 | 3.08 N | 103.27 E |
| Nendaz | 58 | 46.11 N | 7.18 E |
| Nendeln | 58 | 47.12 N | 9.32 E |
| Nendo I | 14 | 10.45 S | 165.54 E |
| Nene ≏ | 42 | 52.48 N | 0.13 E |
| Nenggiri ≏ | 114 | 4.53 N | 101.48 E |
| Nengjia | 104 | 41.38 N | 120.46 E |
| Nengo ≏ | 152 | 14.27 S | 22.09 E |
| Nengonengo I [1] | 14 | 18.47 S | 141.48 W |
| Nenneper Fleuth ≏ | 263 | 51.32 N | 6.26 E |
| Nennhausen | 54 | 52.36 N | 12.30 E |
| Neno | 154 | 15.24 S | 34.39 E |
| Nentershausen | 56 | 51.01 N | 9.56 E |
| Nentón ≏ | 236 | 15.48 N | 91.52 W |
| Nenzing | 58 | 47.11 N | 9.42 E |
| Neo | 94 | 35.38 N | 136.37 E |
| Neo ≏ | 94 | 35.24 N | 136.34 E |
| Neoch I [1] | 175c | 7.03 N | 151.56 E |
| Neodesha | 198 | 37.25 N | 95.40 W |
| Neoga | 194 | 39.19 N | 88.27 W |
| Neola, Ia., U.S. | 198 | 41.26 N | 95.36 W |
| Neola, Ut,. U.S. | 200 | 40.26 N | 110.01 W |
| Neoneli | 71 | 40.04 N | 8.57 E |
| Néon Fáliron | 267c | 37.57 N | 23.40 E |
| Néon Karlovásion | 38 | 37.48 N | 26.44 E |
| Néon Psikhikón | 267c | 38.00 N | 23.47 E |
| Neopit | 190 | 44.58 N | 88.49 W |
| Neópolis | 250 | 10.18 S | 36.35 W |
| Neoshera | 123 | 33.09 N | 74.14 E |
| Neosho | 194 | 36.52 N | 94.22 W |
| Neosho ≏ | 194 | 35.48 N | 95.18 W |
| Neotsu | 224 | 45.00 N | 123.58 W |
| Nepa ≏ | 88 | 59.16 N | 108.16 E |
| Nepal (Nepāl) □ [1], Asia | 118 | 28.00 N | 84.00 E |
| Nepal (Nepāl) □ [1], Asia | 124 | 28.00 N | 84.00 E |
| Nepālgañj | 124 | 28.03 N | 81.37 E |
| Nepa Nagar | 120 | 21.28 N | 76.23 E |
| Nepaug Reservoir ⊜ [1] | 207 | 41.48 N | 72.57 W |
| Nepean | 212 | 45.18 N | 75.47 W |
| Nepean ≏ | 170 | 33.27 S | 150.53 E |
| Nepean, Point ≻ | 169 | 38.18 S | 144.39 E |
| Nepean Bay ⊂ | 168b | 35.42 S | 137.44 E |
| Nepean Island I | 174c | 29.04 S | 167.58 E |
| Nepean Reservoir ⊜ [1] | 170 | 34.22 S | 150.35 E |
| Nepecino | 82 | 55.12 N | 38.37 E |
| Nepeña | 248 | 9.10 S | 78.23 W |
| Nepewassi Lake ⊜ | 190 | 46.20 N | 80.40 W |
| Nephi | 200 | 39.42 N | 111.50 W |
| Nephin ʌ | 48 | 54.01 N | 9.22 W |
| Nephin Beg Range ʎ | 48 | 54.00 N | 9.35 W |
| Nepi | 66 | 42.14 N | 12.21 E |
| Nepisiguit ≏ | 186 | 47.37 N | 65.38 W |
| Nepisiguit Bay ⊂ | 186 | 47.46 N | 65.32 W |
| Népliget ♠ | 264c | 47.29 N | 19.07 E |
| Nepoko ≏ | 154 | 1.40 N | 27.01 E |
| Nepomuceno | 256 | 21.14 S | 45.15 W |
| Nepomuk | 60 | 49.29 N | 13.36 E |
| Neponset ≏ | 283 | 42.17 N | 71.02 W |
| Neponset Reservoir ⊜ [1] | 283 | 42.05 N | 71.15 W |
| Neponset River Reservation ♠ | 283 | 42.13 N | 71.08 W |
| Neppermin | 54 | 53.56 N | 14.02 E |
| Nepr'adva ≏ | 76 | 53.40 N | 38.39 E |
| Nép-sziget I | 264c | 47.34 N | 19.05 E |
| Neptune, N.J., U.S. | 208 | 40.12 N | 74.02 W |
| Neptune, Oh., U.S. | 216 | 40.36 N | 84.30 W |
| Neptune Beach | 192 | 30.18 N | 81.23 W |
| Neptune City | 208 | 40.12 N | 74.02 W |
| Neqarot, Naḥal V | 132 | 30.40 N | 35.15 E |
| Nera ≏, Europe | 38 | 44.49 N | 21.22 E |
| Nera ≏, It. | 66 | 42.26 N | 12.24 E |
| Nérac | 32 | 44.08 N | 0.20 E |
| Nerákion | 267c | 38.01 N | 23.27 E |
| Nerang | 171a | 28.00 S | 153.20 E |
| Nerang ≏ | 171a | 28.03 S | 153.17 E |
| Neratovice | 54 | 50.14 N | 14.31 E |
| Nerča ≏ | 88 | 51.56 N | 116.40 E |
| Nerchau | 54 | 51.16 N | 12.47 E |
| Nerčinsk | 88 | 51.58 N | 116.35 E |
| Nerčinskij Zavod | 88 | 51.19 N | 119.36 E |
| Nère ≏ | 50 | 47.34 N | 2.18 E |
| Nerechta | 80 | 57.28 N | 40.34 E |
| Nerenstetten | 56 | 48.31 N | 10.06 E |
| Neresheim | 56 | 48.45 N | 10.15 E |
| Nereta | 76 | 56.13 N | 25.18 E |
| Nereto | 66 | 42.49 N | 13.49 E |
| Neretva ≏ | 36 | 43.01 N | 17.27 E |
| Nerevoznoje | 80 | 56.53 N | 53.54 E |
| Nerima ◆ [8] | 268 | 35.44 N | 139.39 E |
| Neris (Vilija) ≏ | 76 | 54.54 N | 23.53 E |
| Nerito | 66 | 42.32 N | 13.28 E |
| Nerja | 34 | 36.44 N | 3.52 W |
| Nerka, Lake ⊜ | 180 | 59.30 N | 158.45 W |
| Nerl', Ross. | 76 | 57.03 N | 37.59 E |
| Nerl', Ross. | 80 | 56.40 N | 40.24 E |
| Nerl' ≏, Ross. | 76 | 57.07 N | 37.39 E |
| Nerl' ≏, Ross. | 80 | 56.11 N | 40.34 E |
| Nero, ozero ⊜ | 80 | 57.07 N | 39.27 E |
| Neroj | 88 | 54.28 N | 97.49 E |
| Néronde | 62 | 45.50 N | 4.14 E |
| Nérondes | 32 | 47.00 N | 2.49 E |
| Nerópolis | 255 | 16.25 S | 49.14 W |
| Nerriga | 170 | 35.07 S | 150.05 E |
| Nerrima | 162 | 18.24 S | 124.29 E |
| Nerrimunga Creek ≏ | 170 | 34.57 S | 150.04 E |
| Nersingen | 58 | 48.25 N | 10.07 E |
| Nerskaja ≏ | 82 | 55.23 N | 38.35 E |
| Nerul | 272c | 19.02 N | 73.01 E |
| Nerus ≏ | 114 | 5.20 N | 103.05 E |
| Nerussa ≏ | 76 | 52.33 N | 33.47 E |
| Nerva | 34 | 37.42 N | 6.32 W |
| Nervi | 62 | 44.23 N | 9.02 E |
| Nervia ≏ | 62 | 43.47 N | 7.38 E |
| Nerviano | 266b | 45.33 N | 8.58 E |
| Nerville-la-Forêt | 261 | 49.05 N | 2.17 E |
| Nes, Ned. | 52 | 53.04 N | 5.51 E |
| Nes, Ned. | 52 | 53.26 N | 5.45 E |
| Nes, Nor. | 26 | 60.34 N | 9.59 E |
| Nes', Ross. | 24 | 66.37 N | 44.36 E |
| Nes, Har ʌ | 132 | 30.22 N | 34.37 E |
| Nesbyen | 26 | 60.34 N | 9.09 E |
| Neščarda, vozero ⊜ | 76 | 55.54 N | 29.04 E |
| Neschwitz | 54 | 51.16 N | 14.20 E |
| Nesco | 208 | 39.38 N | 74.41 W |
| Nescochague Creek ≏ | 285 | 39.39 N | 74.41 W |
| Nescochague Creek, Great Swamp Branch ≏ | 285 | 39.41 N | 74.43 W |
| Nesconset | 276 | 40.51 N | 73.09 W |
| Nescopeck | 210 | 41.03 N | 76.13 W |
| Nescopeck Creek ≏ | 210 | 41.03 N | 76.14 W |
| Nescopeck Mountain ʌ | 210 | 41.03 N | 76.05 W |
| Nesebăr | 38 | 42.39 N | 27.44 E |
| Neshaminy Creek ≏ | 208 | 40.04 N | 74.55 W |
| Neshaminy Hills | 285 | 40.10 N | 74.57 W |
| Neshaminy Mall ◆ [9] | 285 | 40.08 N | 74.57 W |
| Neshaminy State Park ♠ | 285 | 40.05 N | 74.55 W |
| Neshaminy Woods | 285 | 40.10 N | 74.57 W |
| Neshannock Creek ≏ | 214 | 40.59 N | 80.21 W |
| Neshcheretove | 83 | 49.24 N | 38.48 E |
| Nesher | 132 | 32.46 N | 35.03 E |
| Nesjøen ⊜ [1] | 26 | 63.02 N | 12.01 E |
| Neškan | 180 | 67.03 N | 173.01 W |
| Neskaupstaður | 24a | 65.10 N | 13.43 W |
| Neskowin | 224 | 45.06 N | 123.58 W |
| Neskynpil'gyn, laguna ⊂ | 180 | 66.57 N | 172.4- W |
| Nesle | 50 | 49.46 N | 2.5- E |
| Nesna | 24 | 66.12 N | 13.0- E |
| Nespelem | 182 | 48.10 N | 118.5- W |
| Nesque ≏ | 62 | 43.59 N | 4.5- E |
| Nesquehoning | 210 | 40.51 N | 75.4- W |
| Ness | 262 | 53.17 N | 3.0- W |
| Ness, Loch ⊜ | 46 | 57.15 N | 4.30 W |
| Ness City | 198 | 38.27 N | 99.5- W |
| Nesse ≏ | 54 | 50.59 N | 10.32 E |
| Nesselrode, Mount ʌ | 180 | 58.58 N | 134.18 W |
| Nesselwang | 58 | 47.37 N | 10.30 E |
| Nesselwängle | 58 | 47.29 N | 10.37 E |
| Nesslau | 58 | 47.13 N | 9.13 E |
| Nessmersiel | 52 | 53.40 N | 7.21 E |
| Nesso | 58 | 45.55 N | 9.08 E |
| Neštěmice | 54 | 50.40 N | 14.07 E |
| Nesterkovo | 76 | 59.10 N | 30.33 |
| Nesterov | 76 | 54.38 N | 22.34 |
| Nesterovka | 80 | 52.26 N | 53 42 |
| Nesterovo, Ross. | 80 | 54.31 N | 41.49 E |
| Nesterovo, Ross. | 82 | 56.45 N | 36.30 E |
| Nesterovo, Ross. | 88 | 52.22 N | 107.53 E |
| Nestiary | 80 | 56.34 N | 45.21 E |
| Neston | 44 | 53.18 N | 3.04 W |
| Nestore ≏ | 66 | 43.21 N | 12.15 E |
| Néstos (Mesta) ≏ | 38 | 40.41 N | 24.44 E |
| Nestoyita | 78 | 47.47 N | 29.21 E |
| Nesttun | 26 | 60.19 N | 5.20 E |
| Nestucca ≏ | 224 | 45.12 N | 123.57 W |
| Nesvetaj | 83 | 47.27 N | 39.40 E |
| Nes Ẕiyyona | 132 | 31.55 N | 34.48 E |
| Netanya | 132 | 32.20 N | 34.51 E |
| Netarhāt | 124 | 23.29 N | 84.16 E |
| Netarts | 224 | 45.26 N | 123.56 W |
| Netarts Bay ⊂ | 224 | 45.24 N | 123.56 W |
| Netcong | 210 | 40.53 N | 74.42 W |
| Nethan ≏ | 46 | 55.42 N | 3.52 W |
| Nether Alderley | 262 | 53.17 N | 2.14 W |
| Netherdale | 166 | 21.08 S | 148.32 E |
| Netherlands (Nederland) □ [1], Europe | 22 | 52.15 N | 5.30 E |
| Netherlands (Nederland) □ [1], Europe | 30 | 52.15 N | 5.30 E |
| Netherlands Antilles (Nederlandse Antillen) □ [2], N.A. | 230 | 12.15 N | 68.45 W |
| Netherlands Antilles (Nederlandse Antillen) □ [2], N.A. | 241s | 12.15 N | 68.45 W |
| Netherton | 262 | 53.30 N | 2.58 W |
| Nethy Bridge | 46 | 57.16 N | 3.38 W |
| Netia | 154 | 14.48 S | 39.59 E |
| Netley Marsh | 42 | 50.53 N | 1.32 W |
| Neto ≏ | 68 | 39.13 N | 17.08 E |
| Netolice | 61 | 49.03 N | 14.12 E |
| Netphen | 56 | 50.55 N | 8.06 E |
| Netra | 56 | 51.06 N | 10.05 E |
| Netrakona | 124 | 24.53 N | 90.43 E |
| Netstal | 58 | 47.03 N | 9.03 E |
| Nettancourt | 56 | 48.52 N | 4.57 E |
| Nette | 52 | 52.02 N | 10.05 E |
| Nette ◆ [8] | 263 | 51.33 N | 7.25 E |
| Nettelstedt | 52 | 52.18 N | 8.41 E |
| Nettersheim | 56 | 50.30 N | 6.38 E |
| Nettetal | 56 | 51.18 N | 6.16 E |
| Nettilling Fiord ⊂ [2] | 176 | 66.02 N | 68.12 W |
| Nettilling Lake ⊜ | 176 | 66.30 N | 70.40 W |
| Nett Lake ⊜ | 190 | 48.10 N | 93.10 W |
| Nett Lake Indian Reservation ◆ [4] | 190 | 48.06 N | 93.10 W |
| Nettlebed | 42 | 51.35 N | 1.00 W |
| Nettle Creek ≏ | 218 | 40.03 N | 83.48 W |
| Nettleden | 260 | 51.47 N | 0.32 W |
| Nettleham | 44 | 53.16 N | 0.29 W |
| Nettlestead | 260 | 51.15 N | 0.25 E |
| Nettlestead Green | 260 | 51.14 N | 0.25 E |
| Nettleton | 194 | 34.05 N | 88.37 W |
| Nettuno | 66 | 41.27 N | 12.39 E |
| Nettuno, Grotta di ⩡ [5] | 71 | 40.34 N | 8.09 E |
| Netzschkau | 54 | 50.36 N | 12.14 E |
| Neualbenreuth | 60 | 49.59 N | 12.27 E |
| Neu-Anspach | 56 | 50.17 N | 8.29 E |
| Neuastenberg | 56 | 51.10 N | 8.29 E |
| Neubeckum | 52 | 51.48 N | 8.01 E |
| Neubeuern | 64 | 47.47 N | 12.08 E |
| Neubrandenburg | 54 | 53.33 N | 13.15 E |
| Neubraunschweig → New Brunswick □ [4] | 186 | 46.30 N | 66.15 W |
| Neubritannien → New Britain I | 164 | 6.00 S | 150.00 E |
| Neubukow | 54 | 54.02 N | 11.40 E |
| Neuburg am Inn | 60 | 48.30 N | 13.27 E |
| Neuburg an der Donau | 60 | 48.44 N | 11.11 E |
| Neuburg-Steinhausen | 54 | 53.58 N | 11.38 E |
| Neuchâtel | 58 | 46.59 N | 6.56 E |
| Neuchâtel □ [3] | 58 | 47.00 N | 6.55 E |
| Neuchâtel, Lac de ⊜ | 58 | 46.52 N | 6.50 E |
| Neu Darchau | 54 | 53.14 N | 10.53 E |
| Neu-Delhi → New Delhi | 124 | 28.36 N | 77.12 E |
| Neudenau | 56 | 49.17 N | 9.16 E |
| Neudietendorf | 54 | 50.55 N | 10.55 E |
| Neudorf, Sk., Can. | 184 | 50.44 N | 102.59 W |
| Neudorf, Dtsch. | 54 | 50.29 N | 12.58 E |
| Neudorf ◆ [8] | 263 | 51.25 N | 6.47 E |
| Neudörfl | 61 | 47.48 N | 16.17 E |
| Neudrossenfeld | 60 | 50.01 N | 11.30 E |
| Neue Hebriden → Vanuatu □ [1] | 175f | 16.00 S | 167.00 E |
| Neuemühle | 264a | 52.18 N | 13.39 E |
| Neuenburg, Dtsch. | 52 | 53.23 N | 7.57 E |
| Neuenbürg, Dtsch. | 56 | 48.50 N | 8.35 E |
| Neuenburg, Dtsch. | 58 | 47.49 N | 7.35 E |
| Neuenburg → Neuchâtel, Schw. | 58 | 46.59 N | 6.56 E |
| Neuendettelsau | 56 | 49.17 N | 10.47 E |
| Neuendorf | 54 | 54.31 N | 13.05 E |
| Neuendorfer See ⊜ | 54 | 52.07 N | 13.55 E |
| Neuenegg | 58 | 46.54 N | 7.18 E |
| Neuenhagen bei Berlin | 54 | 52.32 N | 13.41 E |
| Neuenhaus | 52 | 52.30 N | 6.59 E |
| Neuenhof ◆ [8] | 263 | 51.10 N | 7.13 E |
| Neuenhoven | 263 | 51.08 N | 6.31 E |
| Neue Niers ≏ | 263 | 51.16 N | 6.26 E |
| Neuenkamp ◆ [8] | 263 | 51.26 N | 6.44 E |
| Neuenkirchen, Dtsch. | 52 | 52.30 N | 8.04 E |
| Neuenkirchen, Dtsch. | 52 | 51.50 N | 8.26 E |
| Neuenkirchen, Dtsch. | 52 | 53.14 N | 8.31 E |
| Neuenkirchen, Dtsch. | 52 | 53.02 N | 9.42 E |
| Neuenkirchen, Dtsch. | 52 | 52.14 N | 7.22 E |
| Neuenkirchen, Dtsch. | 52 | 53.46 N | 8.53 E |
| Neuenkirchen, Dtsch. | 54 | 54.32 N | 13.20 E |
| Neuenrade | 56 | 51.17 N | 7.47 E |
| Neuensalz | 54 | 50.30 N | 12.13 E |
| Neuenstadt am Kocher | 56 | 49.14 N | 9.20 E |
| Neuenstein | 56 | 49.12 N | 9.35 E |
| Neuenwalde | 52 | 53.40 N | 8.40 E |
| Neuerburg | 56 | 50.00 N | 6.17 E |
| Neu-Erlaa ◆ [8] | 264b | 48.08 N | 16.19 E |
| Neues Palais ⊥ | 264a | 52.24 N | 13.01 E |
| Neu Fahrland | 264a | 52.26 N | 13.03 E |
| Neufahrn bei Freising | 60 | 48.19 N | 11.40 E |
| Neufahrn in Niederbayern | 60 | 48.44 N | 12.11 E |
| Neuf-Brisach | 58 | 48.01 N | 7.32 E |
| Neufchâteau, Bel. | 56 | 49.50 N | 5.26 E |
| Neufchâteau, Fr. | 58 | 48.21 N | 5.42 E |
| Neufchâtel-en-Bray | 50 | 49.44 N | 1.27 E |
| Neufchâtel-sur-Aisne | 50 | 49.26 N | 4.02 E |
| Neufelden | 61 | 48.29 N | 14.00 E |
| Neuffen | 56 | 48.33 N | 9.22 E |

| | English | Deutsch | Español | Français | Português |
|---|---|---|---|---|---|
| ≏ | River | Fluß | Río | Rivière | Rio |
| ≍ | Canal | Kanal | Canal | Canal | Canal |
| ⌞ | Waterfall, Rapids | Wasserfall, Stromschnellen | Cascada, Rápidos | Chute d'eau, Rapides | Cascata, Rápidos |
| ⋓ | Strait | Meeresstraße | Estrecho | Détroit | Estreito |
| ⊂ | Bay, Gulf | Bucht, Golf | Bahía, Golfo | Baie, Golfe | Baía, Golfo |
| ⊜ | Lake, Lakes | See, Seen | Lago, Lagos | Lac, Lacs | Lago, Lagos |
| ☷ | Swamp | Sumpf | Pantano | Marais | Pântano |
| ⊼ | Ice Features, Glacier | Eis- und Gletscherformen | Accidentes Glaciales | Formes glaciaires | Acidentes glaciares |
| ⫪ | Other Hydrographic Features | Andere Hydrographische Objekte | Otros Elementos Hidrográficos | Autres données hydrographiques | Outros acidentes hidrográficos |
| ✣ | Submarine Features | Untermeerische Objekte | Accidentes Submarinos | Formes de relief sous-marin | Acidentes submarinos |
| □ | Political Unit | Politische Einheit | Unidad Politica | Entité politique | Unidade política |
| ʋ | Cultural Institution | Kulturelle Institution | Institución Cultural | Institution culturelle | Instituição cultural |
| ⊥ | Historical Site | Historische Stätte | Sitio Histórico | Site historique | Sitio histórico |
| ♠ | Recreational Site | Erholungs- und Ferienort | Sitio de Recreo | Centre de loisirs | Area de Lazer |
| ⊠ | Airport | Flughafen | Aeropuerto | Aéroport | Aeroporto |
| ■ | Military Installation | Militäranlage | Instalación Militar | Installation militaire | Instalação militar |
| ◆ | Miscellaneous | Verschiedenes | Misceláneo | Divers | Diversos |

ENGLISH: Name / Page / Lat.°′ / Long.°′ — DEUTSCH: Name / Seite / Breite°′ / Länge°′ E = Ost


| Name | Page | Lat.°′ | Long.°′ |
| --- | --- | --- | --- |
| Neuffossé, Canal de ≍ | 50 | 50.45 N | 2.15 E |
| Neufmanil | 56 | 49.49 N | 4.48 E |
| Neuf-Marché | 50 | 49.25 N | 1.43 E |
| Neufmontiers-lès-Meaux | 261 | 48.58 N | 2.50 E |
| Neufundland → Newfoundland □[4] | 176 | 52.00 N | 56.00 W |
| Neufvilles | 50 | 50.34 N | 4.00 E |
| Neugersdorf | 54 | 50.59 N | 14.36 E |
| Neuglobsow | 54 | 53.09 N | 13.02 E |
| Neugraben-Fischbek ◆[8] | 52 | 53.28 N | 9.52 E |
| Neuguinea → New Guinea I | 164 | 5.00 S | 140.00 E |
| Neuhardenburg | 54 | 52.36 N | 14.15 E |
| Neuharlingersiel | 52 | 53.42 N | 7.42 E |
| Neu-Hartmannsdorf | 264a | 52.22 N | 13.51 E |
| Neuhaus, Dtsch. | 54 | 50.30 N | 11.08 E |
| Neuhaus, Dtsch. | 54 | 53.17 N | 10.55 E |
| Neuhaus, Dtsch. | 58 | 47.48 N | 8.34 E |
| Neuhaus, Dtsch. | 60 | 49.38 N | 11.33 E |
| Neuhaus, Öst. | 61 | 47.47 N | 15.11 E |
| Neuhaus an der Oste | 52 | 53.48 N | 9.02 E |
| Neuhausen, Dtsch. | 54 | 50.41 N | 13.28 E |
| Neuhausen, Dtsch. | 58 | 47.58 N | 8.55 E |
| Neuhausen, Schw. | 58 | 47.41 N | 8.37 E |
| Neuhaus im Solling | 52 | 51.45 N | 9.31 E |
| Neuhaus-Schierschnitz | 54 | 50.19 N | 11.14 E |
| Neuheum | 114 | 5.34 N | 95.32 E |
| Neuhof | 56 | 50.27 N | 9.40 E |
| Neuhof an der Zenn | 56 | 49.27 N | 10.38 E |
| Neuhofen | 56 | 49.25 N | 8.26 E |
| Neuhofen an der Krems | 61 | 48.08 N | 14.14 E |
| Neuillé-Pont-Pierre | 50 | 47.33 N | 0.33 E |
| Neuilly-en-Thelle | 50 | 49.13 N | 2.17 E |
| Neuilly-L'Évêque | 58 | 47.55 N | 5.26 E |
| Neuilly-Saint-Front | 50 | 49.10 N | 3.16 E |
| Neuilly-sur-Marne | 261 | 48.51 N | 2.32 E |
| Neuilly-sur-Seine | 50 | 48.53 N | 2.16 E |
| Neuirland → New Ireland I | 164 | 3.20 S | 152.00 E |
| Neu-Isenburg | 56 | 50.03 N | 8.41 E |
| Neukagran ◆[8] | 264b | 48.14 N | 16.27 E |
| Neu-Kaledonien → New Caledonia □[2] | 175f | 21.30 S | 165.30 E |
| Neukalen | 54 | 53.49 N | 12.47 E |
| Neu Kaliss | 54 | 53.10 N | 11.17 E |
| Neukieritzsch | 54 | 51.10 N | 12.25 E |
| Neukirch, Dtsch. | 54 | 51.17 N | 13.58 E |
| Neukirch, Dtsch. | 54 | 51.05 N | 14.20 E |
| Neukirch, Dtsch. | 58 | 47.39 N | 9.41 E |
| Neukirchen, Dtsch. | 41 | 54.52 N | 8.44 E |
| Neukirchen, Dtsch. | 54 | 51.05 N | 12.32 E |
| Neukirchen, Dtsch. | 54 | 50.47 N | 12.22 E |
| Neukirchen, Dtsch. | 54 | 50.46 N | 12.52 E |
| Neukirchen, Dtsch. | 54 | 54.19 N | 11.01 E |
| Neukirchen, Dtsch. | 56 | 50.52 N | 9.20 E |
| Neukirchen, Dtsch. | 56 | 50.46 N | 9.41 E |
| Neukirchen, Dtsch. | 56 | 49.29 N | 6.50 E |
| Neukirchen, Dtsch. | 60 | 49.16 N | 12.58 E |
| Neukirchen, Dtsch. | 263 | 51.07 N | 6.41 E |
| Neukirchen, Öst. | 64 | 47.15 N | 12.17 E |
| Neukirchen am Walde | 60 | 48.24 N | 13.46 E |
| Neukirchen bei Sulzbach-Rosenberg | 60 | 49.32 N | 11.38 E |
| Neukirchen-Vluyn | 56 | 51.27 N | 6.33 E |
| Neukloster | 54 | 53.52 N | 11.41 E |
| Neukölln ◆[8] | 54 | 52.29 N | 13.27 E |
| Neu Kosenow | 54 | 53.47 N | 13.46 E |
| Neulangerwisch | 264a | 52.19 N | 13.04 E |
| Neulengbach | 61 | 48.12 N | 15.55 E |
| Neulienken | 54 | 53.27 N | 14.22 E |
| Neu Lübbenau | 54 | 52.04 N | 13.53 E |
| Neulussheim | 56 | 49.17 N | 8.31 E |
| Neumagen | 56 | 49.51 N | 6.53 E |
| Neuman Creek ≃ | 284a | 42.42 N | 78.48 W |
| Neumark, Dtsch. | 54 | 50.39 N | 12.21 E |
| Neumark, Dtsch. | 54 | 51.05 N | 11.16 E |
| Neumarkt → Târgu Secuiesc, Rom. | 38 | 46.00 N | 26.08 E |
| Neumarkt → Târgu Mureș, Rom. | 38 | 46.33 N | 24.33 E |
| Neumarkt am Wallersee | 64 | 47.57 N | 13.14 E |
| Neumarkt im Hausruckkreis | 60 | 48.16 N | 13.45 E |
| Neumarkt in der Oberpfalz | 60 | 49.16 N | 11.28 E |
| Neumarkt in Steiermark | 61 | 47.04 N | 14.25 E |
| Neumarkt-Sankt Veit | 60 | 48.22 N | 12.30 E |
| Neumayer ʋ[3] | 9 | 70.37 S | 8.22 W |
| Neu Mukran | 54 | 54.29 N | 13.33 W |
| Neumünster | 30 | 54.04 N | 9.59 E |
| Neun ≃ | 110 | 19.42 N | 104.03 E |
| Neunburg vorm Wald | 60 | 49.21 N | 12.24 E |
| Neundorf | 54 | 51.49 N | 11.34 E |
| Neung-sur-Beuvron | 50 | 47.32 N | 1.48 E |
| Neunkirchen, Dtsch. | 56 | 50.48 N | 8.00 E |
| Neunkirchen, Dtsch. | 56 | 50.32 N | 8.06 E |
| Neunkirchen, Dtsch. | 56 | 49.20 N | 7.10 E |
| Neunkirchen, Öst. | 61 | 47.43 N | 16.05 E |
| Neunkirchen am Brand | 60 | 49.37 N | 11.08 E |
| Neunkirchen am Potzberg | 56 | 49.30 N | 7.29 E |
| Neunkirchen-Seelscheid | 56 | 50.51 N | 7.20 E |
| Neuötting | 60 | 48.14 N | 12.42 E |
| Neupetershain | 54 | 51.36 N | 14.09 E |
| Neuquén | 252 | 38.57 S | 68.04 W |
| Neuquén □[4] | 254 | 39.00 S | 70.00 W |
| Neuquén ≃ | 252 | 38.59 S | 68.00 W |
| Neurara | 252 | 24.10 S | 68.29 W |
| Neuravensburg | 58 | 47.38 N | 9.46 E |
| Neureisenberg | 264b | 48.01 N | 16.30 E |
| Neurode → Nowa Ruda | 30 | 50.35 N | 16.31 E |
| Neuruppin | 54 | 52.55 N | 12.48 E |
| Neusalz → Nowa Sól | 30 | 51.48 N | 15.44 E |
| Neusalza-Spremberg | 54 | 51.02 N | 14.32 E |
| Neu Sankt Johann | 58 | 47.14 N | 9.12 E |
| Neusäss, Dtsch. | 58 | 48.24 N | 10.50 E |
| Neusäss, Dtsch. | 58 | 48.24 N | 10.50 E |
| Neusatz → Novi Sad | 38 | 45.15 N | 19.50 E |
| Neuschottland → Nova Scotia □[4] | 186 | 45.00 N | 63.00 W |
| Neuschwanstein, Schloss ʋ | 64 | 47.35 N | 10.44 E |
| Neuse ≃ | 192 | 35.06 N | 76.30 W |
| Neuseddin, Dtsch. | 54 | 52.17 N | 12.59 E |
| Neuseddin, Dtsch. | 264a | 52.18 N | 12.59 E |
| Neuseeland → New Zealand □[1] | 172 | 41.00 S | 174.00 E |
| Neusibirische Inseln → Novosibirskije ostrova II | 74 | 75.00 N | 142.00 E |
| Neusiedl am See | 61 | 47.57 N | 16.51 E |
| Neusiedler See (Fertő) ⊜ | 61 | 47.50 N | 16.45 E |
| Neusohl → Banská Bystrica | 30 | 48.44 N | 19.07 E |
| Neusorg | 60 | 49.56 N | 11.58 E |
| Neuss | 56 | 51.12 N | 6.41 E |
| Neusserweyhe | 263 | 51.13 N | 6.39 E |
| Neustadt, On., Can. | 212 | 44.05 N | 81.00 W |
| Neustadt, Dtsch. | 54 | 52.52 N | 12.25 E |
| Neustadt, Dtsch. | 54 | 51.01 N | 14.13 E |
| Neustadt, Dtsch. | 54 | 50.44 N | 11.44 E |
| Neustadt, Dtsch. | 56 | 50.37 N | 7.26 E |
| Neustadt, Dtsch. | 56 | 50.51 N | 9.07 E |
| Neustadt ◆[8] | 52 | 53.04 N | 8.47 E |
| Neustadt am Kulm | 60 | 49.50 N | 11.50 E |
| Neustadt am Rübenberge | 52 | 52.30 N | 9.28 E |
| Neustadt an der Aisch | 56 | 49.34 N | 10.37 E |
| Neustadt an der Donau | 60 | 48.48 N | 11.46 E |
| Neustadt an der Waldnaab | 60 | 49.44 N | 12.11 E |
| Neustadt an der Weinstrasse | 56 | 49.21 N | 8.08 E |
| Neustadt bei Coburg | 56 | 50.19 N | 11.07 E |
| Neustädter Bucht C | 54 | 54.02 N | 10.50 E |
| Neustadt-Glewe | 54 | 53.25 N | 11.36 E |
| Neustadt in Holstein | 54 | 54.06 N | 10.48 E |
| Neustettin → Szczecinek | 30 | 53.43 N | 16.42 E |
| Neustift am Walde ◆[8] | 264b | 48.15 N | 16.18 E |
| Neustift im Stubaital | 64 | 47.07 N | 11.19 E |
| Neustrelitz | 54 | 53.21 N | 13.04 E |
| Neu Töplitz | 264a | 52.27 N | 12.54 E |
| Neutral Hills ⋏[2] | 184 | 52.10 N | 110.50 W |
| Neutraubling | 60 | 48.59 N | 12.12 E |
| Neutrebbin | 54 | 52.40 N | 14.13 E |
| Neu-Ulm | 58 | 48.23 N | 10.01 E |
| Neuve-Chapelle | 50 | 50.35 N | 2.47 E |
| Neuves-Maisons | 58 | 48.37 N | 6.06 E |
| Neuvic | 32 | 45.23 N | 2.16 E |
| Neuville-aux-Bois | 50 | 48.04 N | 2.03 E |
| Neuville-de-Poitou | 32 | 46.41 N | 0.15 E |
| Neuville-en-Condroz | 56 | 50.32 N | 5.27 E |
| Neuville-lès-Dieppe | 50 | 49.55 N | 1.06 E |
| Neuville-sur-Oise | 261 | 49.01 N | 2.04 E |
| Neuville-sur-Saône | 62 | 45.52 N | 4.51 E |
| Neuvy-le-Roi | 50 | 47.36 N | 0.36 E |
| Neuvy-sur-Barangeon | 50 | 47.19 N | 2.15 E |
| Neuvy-sur-Loire | 50 | 47.31 N | 2.53 E |
| Neuwaldegg ◆[8] | 264b | 48.14 N | 16.17 E |
| Neuwerk ◆[8] | 263 | 51.13 N | 6.28 E |
| Neuwerk I | 52 | 53.55 N | 8.30 E |
| Neuwied | 56 | 50.25 N | 7.27 E |
| Neuwiller-lès-Saverne | 56 | 48.49 N | 7.24 E |
| Neu Wulmstorf | 52 | 53.28 N | 9.48 E |
| Neu Zauche | 54 | 51.55 N | 14.10 E |
| Neuzelle | 54 | 52.05 N | 14.38 E |
| Neu Zittau | 54 | 52.23 N | 13.44 E |
| Neva ≃ | 265a | 59.57 N | 30.20 E |
| Névache | 62 | 45.01 N | 6.37 E |
| Nevada, Ia., U.S. | 190 | 42.01 N | 93.27 W |
| Nevada, Mo., U.S. | 194 | 37.50 N | 94.21 W |
| Nevada, Oh., U.S. | 214 | 40.49 N | 83.07 W |
| Nevada, Tx., U.S. | 222 | 33.02 N | 96.22 W |
| Nevada □[6] | 226 | 39.16 N | 121.01 W |
| Nevada □[3], U.S. | 178 | 39.00 N | 117.00 W |
| Nevada □[3], U.S. | 204 | 39.00 N | 117.00 W |
| Nevada, Sierra ⋏, Esp. | 34 | 37.05 N | 3.10 W |
| Nevada, Sierra ⋏, Ca., U.S. | 204 | 38.00 N | 119.15 W |
| Nevada City | 226 | 39.15 N | 121.00 W |
| Nevada Creek ≃ | 202 | 46.54 N | 113.02 W |
| Nevado, Cerro ∧, Arg. | 252 | 35.35 S | 68.30 W |
| Nevado, Cerro ∧, Col. | 246 | 3.59 N | 74.04 W |
| Nevado de Colima, Parque Nacional del ♦ | 234 | 19.30 N | 103.35 W |
| Nevado de Toluca, Parque Nacional ♦ | 234 | 19.10 N | 99.44 W |
| Neval'cevo | 86 | 58.38 N | 81.53 E |
| Nevali | 272c | 19.01 N | 73.07 E |
| Nevanka | 88 | 56.30 N | 98.54 E |
| Neve, Serra da ⋏ | 152 | 13.52 S | 13.26 E |
| Nevel' | 76 | 56.02 N | 29.55 E |
| Nevel'sk | 89 | 46.40 N | 141.53 E |
| Nevel'skogo, proliv ꓵ | 89 | 52.05 N | 141.35 E |
| Nevendon | 260 | 51.36 N | 0.30 E |
| Never | 89 | 53.58 N | 124.05 E |
| Neverkino | 80 | 52.47 N | 46.44 E |
| Neverovo | 80 | 55.07 N | 44.24 E |
| Nevers | 32 | 47.00 N | 3.09 E |
| Neversink ≃ | 210 | 41.21 N | 74.42 W |
| Neversink Reservoir ⊜[1] | 210 | 41.48 N | 74.42 W |
| Nevertire | 166 | 31.52 S | 147.39 E |
| Neves | 256 | 22.51 S | 43.06 W |
| Nevesinje | 38 | 43.15 N | 18.07 E |
| Nevėžis ≃ | 76 | 54.56 N | 23.46 E |
| Nevežkino | 80 | 53.07 N | 43.19 E |
| Neviano | 68 | 40.06 N | 18.06 E |
| Neviano degli Arduini | 64 | 44.35 N | 10.19 E |
| Neviges | 56 | 51.19 N | 7.05 E |
| Neville Island | 279b | 40.31 N | 80.08 W |
| Neville Island I | 279b | 40.31 N | 80.08 W |
| Nevinnomyssk | 84 | 44.38 N | 41.56 E |
| Nevis I | 238 | 17.10 N | 62.34 W |
| Nevis ≃ | 46 | 56.50 N | 5.00 W |
| Nevis, Ben ∧ | 46 | 56.48 N | 5.01 W |
| Nevis, Loch C | 46 | 57.01 N | 5.43 W |
| Nevjansk | 86 | 57.32 N | 60.13 E |
| Nevlunghamn | 26 | 58.58 N | 9.52 E |
| Nevon | 88 | 58.07 N | 102.49 E |
| Nevşehir | 130 | 38.38 N | 34.43 E |
| Nevşehir □[4] | 130 | 38.50 N | 34.40 E |
| Nevs'ke | 83 | 49.09 N | 37.58 E |
| Nevskoje | 76 | 58.08 N | 30.26 E |
| New ≃, Belize | 232 | 18.22 N | 88.24 W |
| New ≃, Guy. | 246 | 3.23 N | 57.36 W |
| New ≃, N.A. | 204 | 33.08 N | 115.44 W |
| New ≃, Eng., U.K. | 260 | 51.40 N | 0.01 W |
| New ≃, U.S. | 192 | 38.10 N | 81.12 W |
| New ≃, Az., U.S. | 200 | 33.31 N | 112.18 W |
| New ≃, Fl., U.S. | 192 | 29.50 N | 84.40 W |
| New ≃, Fl., U.S. | 192 | 29.55 N | 82.25 W |
| New ≃, N.C., U.S. | 192 | 34.32 N | 77.20 W |
| New ≃, S.C., U.S. | 192 | 32.09 N | 80.50 W |
| New ≃, Tn., U.S. | 192 | 36.25 N | 84.38 W |
| New, North Fork ≃ | 192 | 36.33 N | 81.21 W |
| Newabāgam | 272b | 22.48 N | 88.24 E |
| New Abbey | 44 | 54.59 N | 3.38 W |
| New Addington ◆[8] | 260 | 51.21 N | 0.01 W |
| Newala | 154 | 10.56 S | 39.18 E |
| New Albany, In., U.S. | 218 | 38.17 N | 85.49 W |
| New Albany, Ms., U.S. | 194 | 34.29 N | 89.00 W |
| New Albany, Oh., U.S. | 214 | 40.05 N | 82.49 W |
| New Albany, Pa., U.S. | 210 | 41.36 N | 76.27 W |
| New Albin | 190 | 43.29 N | 91.17 W |
| New Alexandria, Oh., U.S. | 214 | 40.17 N | 80.40 W |
| New Alexandria, Pa., U.S. | 214 | 40.24 N | 79.25 W |
| New Alexandria, Va., U.S. | 284c | 38.47 N | 77.03 W |
| New Alfa | 140 | 15.10 N | 35.40 E |
| New Almaden | 226 | 37.11 N | 121.49 W |
| New Alresford | 42 | 51.06 N | 1.10 W |
| New Amsterdam | 246 | 6.15 N | 57.31 W |
| New Angledool | 166 | 29.07 S | 147.57 E |
| Newark, Ar., U.S. | 194 | 35.42 N | 91.26 W |
| Newark, Ca., U.S. | 226 | 37.31 N | 122.02 W |
| Newark, De., U.S. | 208 | 39.41 N | 75.45 W |
| Newark, Il., U.S. | 216 | 41.32 N | 88.35 W |
| Newark, Md., U.S. | 208 | 38.15 N | 75.17 W |
| Newark, Mo., U.S. | 219 | 39.59 N | 91.59 W |
| Newark, N.J., U.S. | 210 | 40.44 N | 74.10 W |
| Newark, N.Y., U.S. | 210 | 43.02 N | 77.05 W |
| Newark, Oh., U.S. | 214 | 40.04 N | 82.24 W |
| Newark, Tx., U.S. | 222 | 33.00 N | 97.29 W |
| Newark Bay C, U.S. | 276 | 40.39 N | 74.09 W |
| Newark Bay C, N.J., U.S. | 276 | 40.40 N | 74.08 W |
| Newark Bay Bridge ◆[5] | 276 | 40.42 N | 74.07 W |
| Newark International Airport ⊠ | 210 | 40.42 N | 74.10 W |
| Newark Lake ⊜ | 204 | 39.41 N | 115.44 W |
| Newark-on-Trent | 44 | 53.05 N | 0.49 W |
| Newark Slough ≃ | 282 | 37.31 N | 122.05 W |
| Newark Valley | 210 | 42.13 N | 76.11 W |
| New Athens, Il., U.S. | 219 | 38.19 N | 89.52 W |
| New Athens, Oh., U.S. | 214 | 40.11 N | 80.59 W |
| New Augusta | 194 | 31.12 N | 89.02 W |
| Newaukum, North Fork ≃ | 224 | 46.36 N | 122.51 W |
| Newaukum, South Fork ≃ | 224 | 46.36 N | 122.51 W |
| Newaygo | 190 | 43.25 N | 85.48 W |
| New Baden, Il., U.S. | 219 | 38.32 N | 89.42 W |
| New Baden, Tx., U.S. | 222 | 31.03 N | 96.26 W |
| New Baltimore, Mi., U.S. | 214 | 42.40 N | 82.44 W |
| New Baltimore, N.Y., U.S. | 210 | 42.26 N | 73.47 W |
| New Bavaria | 216 | 41.12 N | 84.10 W |
| New Bedford, Ma., U.S. | 207 | 41.38 N | 70.56 W |
| New Bedford, Pa., U.S. | 214 | 41.06 N | 80.30 W |
| New Bedford ≃ | 42 | 52.35 N | 0.20 E |
| Newberg | 224 | 45.18 N | 122.58 W |
| New Berlin, Il., U.S. | 219 | 39.43 N | 89.54 W |
| New Berlin, N.Y., U.S. | 210 | 42.37 N | 75.19 W |
| New Berlin, Pa., U.S. | 210 | 40.53 N | 76.59 W |
| New Berlin, Wi., U.S. | 216 | 42.58 N | 88.06 W |
| New Berlinville | 208 | 40.20 N | 75.38 W |
| Newbern, Al., U.S. | 194 | 32.35 N | 87.31 W |
| Newbern, Il., U.S. | 219 | 39.01 N | 90.20 W |
| New Bern, N.C., U.S. | 192 | 35.06 N | 77.02 W |
| Newbern, Tn., U.S. | 194 | 36.06 N | 89.15 W |
| Newberry, Fl., U.S. | 192 | 29.38 N | 82.36 W |
| Newberry, Mi., U.S. | 190 | 46.21 N | 85.30 W |
| Newberry, S.C., U.S. | 192 | 34.16 N | 81.37 W |
| Newbery, Aeroparque ⊠, Arg. | 258 | 34.35 S | 58.24 W |
| Newbery, Aeroparque ⊠, Arg. | 288 | 34.35 S | 58.24 W |
| New Bethlehem | 214 | 41.00 N | 79.19 W |
| Newbiggin-by-the-Sea | 44 | 55.11 N | 1.30 W |
| New Bight | 238 | 24.19 N | 75.24 W |
| New Bloomfield, Mo., U.S. | 219 | 38.43 N | 92.05 W |
| New Bloomfield, Pa., U.S. | 208 | 40.25 N | 77.11 W |
| New Bloomington | 214 | 40.35 N | 83.19 W |
| Newbold Island I | 285 | 40.08 N | 74.45 W |
| Newboro | 212 | 44.39 N | 76.19 W |
| Newboro Lake ⊜ | 212 | 44.38 N | 76.20 W |
| Newborough, Austl. | 169 | 38.11 S | 146.17 E |
| Newborough, Wales, U.K. | 44 | 53.09 N | 4.22 W |
| New Boston, Il., U.S. | 190 | 41.10 N | 90.59 W |
| New Boston, Mi., U.S. | 216 | 42.09 N | 83.24 W |
| New Boston, Oh., U.S. | 218 | 38.45 N | 82.56 W |
| New Boston, Tx., U.S. | 194 | 33.27 N | 94.24 W |
| New Braintree | 207 | 42.19 N | 72.07 W |
| New Braunfels | 196 | 29.42 N | 98.07 W |
| New Bremen | 216 | 40.26 N | 84.22 W |
| Newbridge → Droichead Nua | 48 | 53.11 N | 6.48 W |
| Newbridge on Wye | 42 | 52.13 N | 3.27 W |
| New Brighton, N.Z. | 172 | 43.31 S | 172.44 E |
| New Brighton, Eng., U.K. | 262 | 53.26 N | 3.03 W |
| New Brighton, Pa., U.S. | 214 | 40.43 N | 80.18 W |
| New Brighton ◆[8] | 276 | 40.38 N | 74.06 W |
| New Britain, Ct., U.S. | 207 | 41.39 N | 72.46 W |
| New Britain, Pa., U.S. | 208 | 40.18 N | 75.11 W |
| New Britain I | 164 | 6.00 S | 150.00 E |
| New Britain Trench ✢[1] | 14 | 6.00 S | 153.00 E |
| New Brockton | 194 | 31.23 N | 85.55 W |
| Newbrook | 182 | 54.19 N | 112.57 W |
| New Brooklyn County Park ♦ | 285 | 39.43 N | 74.57 W |
| New Brunswick, In., U.S. | 218 | 39.57 N | 86.31 W |
| New Brunswick, N.J., U.S. | 208 | 40.29 N | 74.27 W |
| New Brunswick □[4], Can. | 176 | 46.30 N | 66.15 W |
| New Brunswick □[4], Can. | 186 | 46.30 N | 66.15 W |
| New Buffalo, Mi., U.S. | 216 | 41.47 N | 86.44 W |
| New Buffalo, Pa., U.S. | 208 | 40.27 N | 76.58 W |
| New Buildings | 48 | 54.57 N | 7.21 W |
| New Bullards Bar Reservoir ⊜[1] | 226 | 39.25 N | 121.08 W |
| Newburg, Mo., U.S. | 194 | 37.54 N | 91.54 W |
| Newburg, Pa., U.S. | 208 | 40.08 N | 77.32 W |
| Newburg, Pa., U.S. | 214 | 40.31 N | 78.25 W |
| Newburgh, On., Can. | 212 | 44.19 N | 76.52 W |
| Newburgh, Eng., U.K. | 262 | 53.35 N | 2.47 W |
| Newburgh, Scot., U.K. | 46 | 56.20 N | 3.15 W |
| Newburgh, Scot., U.K. | 46 | 57.18 N | 2.00 W |
| Newburgh, In., U.S. | 194 | 37.56 N | 87.24 W |
| Newburgh, N.Y., U.S. | 210 | 41.30 N | 74.00 W |
| Newburgh Heights | 279a | 41.27 N | 81.39 W |
| Newburn | 44 | 54.59 N | 1.43 W |
| Newbury, On., Can. | 214 | 42.41 N | 81.48 W |
| Newbury, Eng., U.K. | 42 | 51.25 N | 1.20 W |
| Newbury, Ma., U.S. | 207 | 42.49 N | 70.53 W |
| Newbury Old Town | 207 | 42.46 N | 70.51 W |
| Newburyport | 207 | 42.48 N | 70.52 W |
| Newby | 44 | 54.20 N | 0.28 W |
| Newby Bridge | 44 | 54.16 N | 2.58 W |
| New Caledonia (Nouvelle-Calédonie) □[2], Oc. | 14 | 21.30 S | 165.30 E |
| New Caledonia (Nouvelle-Calédonie) □[2], Oc. | 175f | 21.30 S | 165.30 E |
| New Caledonia Basin ✢[1] | 14 | 30.00 S | 165.00 E |
| New Canaan | 207 | 41.08 N | 73.29 W |
| New Canada ◆[8] | 273d | 26.13 S | 27.57 E |
| New Caney | 222 | 30.09 N | 95.13 W |
| New Canton | 219 | 39.38 N | 91.06 W |
| New-Carlisle, P.Q., Can. | 186 | 48.01 N | 65.20 W |
| New Carlisle, In., U.S. | 216 | 41.42 N | 86.30 W |
| New Carlisle, Oh., U.S. | 218 | 39.56 N | 84.01 W |
| New Carrollton | 284c | 38.58 N | 76.52 W |
| New Cassel | 276 | 40.45 N | 73.34 W |
| Newcastle, Austl. | 170 | 32.56 S | 151.46 E |
| Newcastle, N.B., Can. | 186 | 47.00 N | 65.34 W |
| Newcastle, On., Can. | 212 | 43.55 N | 78.35 W |
| Newcastle, Ire. | 48 | 52.16 N | 7.48 W |
| Newcastle, S. Afr. | 158 | 27.49 S | 29.55 E |
| Newcastle, Eng., U.K. | 42 | 52.26 N | 3.06 W |
| Newcastle, N. Ire., U.K. | 48 | 54.12 N | 5.54 W |
| Newcastle, Ca., U.S. | 226 | 38.53 N | 121.08 W |
| New Castle, Co., U.S. | 200 | 39.34 N | 107.32 W |
| New Castle, De., U.S. | 208 | 39.39 N | 75.34 W |
| New Castle, In., U.S. | 218 | 39.55 N | 85.22 W |
| New Castle, Ky., U.S. | 218 | 38.26 N | 85.10 W |
| Newcastle, Ne., U.S. | 198 | 42.33 N | 96.42 W |
| Newcastle, Oh., U.S. | 214 | 40.20 N | 82.10 W |
| Newcastle, Ok., U.S. | 196 | 35.15 N | 97.36 W |
| New Castle, Pa., U.S. | 214 | 41.00 N | 80.20 W |
| Newcastle, Tx., U.S. | 196 | 33.11 N | 98.44 W |
| New Castle, Va., U.S. | 192 | 37.30 N | 80.06 W |
| Newcastle, Wy., U.S. | 198 | 43.51 N | 104.12 W |
| New Castle □[6] | 208 | 39.44 N | 75.33 W |
| Newcastle Airport ⊠ | 44 | 55.03 N | 1.43 W |
| Newcastle Bay C | 164 | 10.50 S | 142.37 E |
| Newcastle Bight C[3] | 170 | 32.51 S | 151.54 E |
| Newcastle Creek ≃ | 164 | 17.20 S | 133.23 E |
| Newcastle Emlyn | 42 | 52.02 N | 4.28 W |
| Newcastle Mine | 182 | 51.28 N | 112.46 W |
| Newcastleton | 44 | 55.11 N | 2.49 W |
| Newcastle-under-Lyme | 44 | 53.00 N | 2.14 W |
| Newcastle upon Tyne | 44 | 54.59 N | 1.35 W |
| Newcastle Waters | 162 | 17.24 S | 133.24 E |
| Newcastle West | 48 | 52.27 N | 9.03 W |
| Newcestown | 48 | 51.47 N | 8.51 W |
| New Chicago | 216 | 41.34 N | 87.16 W |
| Newchurch, Wales, U.K. | 42 | 52.09 N | 3.08 W |
| New Church, Va., U.S. | 208 | 37.59 N | 75.32 W |
| New City | 210 | 41.08 N | 73.59 W |
| Newclare ◆[8] | 273d | 26.11 S | 27.58 E |
| New Columbia | 210 | 41.02 N | 76.52 W |
| New Columbus | 210 | 41.10 N | 76.18 W |
| Newcomerstown | 214 | 40.16 N | 81.36 W |
| New Concord | 188 | 39.59 N | 81.44 W |
| New Corydon | 216 | 40.34 N | 84.51 W |
| New Croton Aqueduct ≍[1] | 276 | 41.11 N | 73.49 W |
| New Croton Reservoir ⊜[1] | 210 | 41.14 N | 73.46 W |
| New Cumberland, Pa., U.S. | 208 | 40.13 N | 76.53 W |
| New Cumberland, W.V., U.S. | 214 | 40.29 N | 80.36 W |
| New Cumberland Dam ◆[6] | 214 | 40.32 N | 80.37 W |
| New Cumnock | 44 | 55.24 N | 4.12 W |
| New Dayton | 182 | 49.25 N | 112.23 W |
| New Deer | 46 | 57.30 N | 2.12 W |
| Newdegate | 162 | 33.06 S | 119.01 E |
| New Delhi, India | 124 | 28.36 N | 77.12 E |
| New Delhi, India | 272a | 28.36 N | 77.12 E |
| New Delhi Railroad Station ◆[5] | 272a | 28.39 N | 77.13 E |
| New Denver | 182 | 49.59 N | 117.22 W |
| New Derry | 214 | 40.21 N | 79.19 W |
| New Don Pedro Reservoir ⊜[1] | 226 | 37.43 N | 120.23 W |
| New Dundee | 212 | 43.21 N | 80.31 W |
| New Eagle | 214 | 40.12 N | 79.56 W |
| New Edinburg | 194 | 33.45 N | 92.14 W |
| New Effington | 198 | 45.51 N | 96.55 W |
| New Egypt | 208 | 40.04 N | 74.31 W |
| Newell, Ia., U.S. | 198 | 42.36 N | 95.00 W |
| Newell, S.D., U.S. | 198 | 44.42 N | 103.25 W |
| Newell, W.V., U.S. | 214 | 40.37 N | 80.36 W |
| Newell, Lake ⊜, Austl. | 162 | 24.50 S | 126.10 E |
| Newell, Lake ⊜, Ab., Can. | 182 | 50.25 N | 111.56 W |
| New Ellenton | 192 | 33.25 N | 81.41 W |
| Newellton | 194 | 32.04 N | 91.14 W |
| New Eltham ◆[8] | 260 | 51.26 N | 0.04 E |
| New England | 198 | 46.32 N | 102.52 W |
| New England National Park ♦ | 166 | 30.30 S | 152.15 E |
| New England Range ⋏ | 166 | 30.00 S | 151.50 E |
| Newenham, Cape ⟩ | 180 | 58.37 N | 162.12 W |
| Newent | 42 | 51.56 N | 2.24 W |
| New Enterprise | 214 | 40.10 N | 78.25 W |
| New Ermelo | 158 | 26.32 S | 30.02 E |
| New Falconwood | 284a | 42.59 N | 78.58 W |
| Newfane, N.Y., U.S. | 210 | 43.17 N | 78.42 W |
| Newfane, Vt., U.S. | 188 | 42.59 N | 72.39 W |
| New Ferry | 262 | 53.22 N | 2.59 W |
| Newfield, N.J., U.S. | 208 | 39.32 N | 75.01 W |
| Newfield, N.Y., U.S. | 210 | 42.22 N | 76.35 W |
| Newfield Pond ⊜ | 283 | 42.38 N | 71.22 W |
| New Florence, Mo., U.S. | 219 | 38.54 N | 91.26 W |
| New Florence, Pa., U.S. | 214 | 40.22 N | 79.04 W |
| New Forest ◆[3] | 42 | 50.53 N | 1.35 W |
| New Fork ≃ | 200 | 42.33 N | 109.58 W |
| Newfound Gap )( | 192 | 35.37 N | 83.25 W |
| Newfoundland, N.J., U.S. | 276 | 40.44 N | 74.29 W |
| Newfoundland, Pa., U.S. | 210 | 41.19 N | 75.19 W |
| Newfoundland □[4] | 176 | 52.00 N | 56.00 W |
| Newfoundland I | 186 | 48.30 N | 56.00 W |
| Newfoundland Basin ✢[1] | 8 | 45.00 N | 40.00 W |
| Newfoundland Ridge ✢[3] | 8 | 40.30 N | 48.00 W |
| New Franklin | 194 | 39.01 N | 92.44 W |
| New Freedom | 208 | 39.44 N | 76.42 W |
| New Galilee | 214 | 40.50 N | 80.24 W |
| New Galloway | 44 | 55.05 N | 4.10 W |
| New Garden | 285 | 39.49 N | 75.45 W |
| Newgate | 182 | 49.00 N | 115.10 W |
| Newgate Street | 260 | 51.44 N | 0.07 W |
| New Georgia I | 175e | 8.15 S | 157.30 E |
| New Georgia Group II | 175e | 8.30 S | 157.20 E |
| New Georgia Sound ꓵ | 175e | 8.00 S | 158.10 E |
| New Germantown | 208 | 40.18 N | 77.34 W |
| New Germany | 186 | 44.33 N | 64.43 W |
| New Glarus | 190 | 42.48 N | 89.38 W |
| New Glasgow | 186 | 45.35 N | 62.39 W |
| New Gretna | 208 | 39.35 N | 74.27 W |
| New Guinea I | 164 | 5.00 S | 140.00 E |
| Newgulf | 222 | 29.16 N | 95.54 W |
| Newhalem | 224 | 48.40 N | 121.14 W |
| Newhalen | 180 | 59.43 N | 154.54 W |
| Newhall | 42 | 52.48 N | 1.34 W |
| Newham ◆[8] | 42 | 51.32 N | 0.03 E |
| New Hamburg, On., Can. | 212 | 43.23 N | 80.42 W |
| New Hamburg, N.Y., U.S. | 210 | 41.35 N | 73.57 W |
| New Hampshire | 216 | 40.33 N | 83.57 W |
| New Hampshire □[3], U.S. | 178 | 43.35 N | 71.40 W |
| New Hampshire □[3], U.S. | 188 | 43.35 N | 71.40 W |
| New Hampton, Ia., U.S. | 190 | 43.03 N | 92.19 W |
| New Hampton, N.Y., U.S. | 210 | 41.25 N | 74.24 W |
| New Hanover, S. Afr. | 158 | 29.28 S | 30.28 E |
| New Hanover, Il., U.S. | 219 | 38.23 N | 90.13 W |
| New Hanover I | 164 | 2.30 S | 150.15 E |
| New Harmony | 194 | 38.07 N | 87.56 W |
| New Hartford, Ct., U.S. | 207 | 41.52 N | 72.58 W |
| New Hartford, Ia., U.S. | 190 | 42.34 N | 92.37 W |
| New Hartford, Mo., U.S. | 219 | 39.12 N | 91.16 W |
| New Hartford, N.Y., U.S. | 210 | 43.04 N | 75.18 W |
| Newhaven, Eng., U.K. | 42 | 50.47 N | 0.03 E |
| New Haven, Ct., U.S. | 207 | 41.18 N | 72.56 W |
| New Haven, Il., U.S. | 194 | 37.54 N | 88.07 W |
| New Haven, In., U.S. | 216 | 41.04 N | 85.00 W |
| New Haven, Ky., U.S. | 194 | 37.39 N | 85.35 W |
| New Haven, Mi., U.S. | 214 | 42.43 N | 82.48 W |
| New Haven, Mo., U.S. | 219 | 38.36 N | 91.13 W |
| New Haven, N.Y., U.S. | 212 | 43.29 N | 76.19 W |
| New Haven, Oh., U.S. | 214 | 41.02 N | 82.41 W |
| New Haven, W.V., U.S. | 188 | 38.59 N | 81.58 W |
| New Haven □[6] | 207 | 41.18 N | 72.56 W |
| New Hazelton | 182 | 55.15 N | 127.35 W |
| New Hebrides → Vanuatu □[1] | 175f | 16.00 S | 167.00 E |
| New Hebrides II | 175f | 16.00 S | 167.00 E |
| New Hebrides Trench ✢[1] | 14 | 22.30 S | 170.00 E |
| Newhebron | 194 | 31.44 N | 89.58 W |
| New Hempstead | 276 | 41.08 N | 74.03 W |
| New Hey | 262 | 53.36 N | 2.06 W |
| New Hogan Lake ⊜[1] | 226 | 38.09 N | 120.48 W |
| New Holland, Eng., U.K. | 44 | 53.42 N | 0.22 W |
| New Holland, Il., U.S. | 219 | 40.11 N | 89.36 W |
| New Holland, Oh., U.S. | 218 | 39.33 N | 83.15 W |
| New Holland, Pa., U.S. | 208 | 40.06 N | 76.05 W |
| New Holstein | 190 | 43.57 N | 88.05 W |
| New Hope, Al., U.S. | 194 | 34.32 N | 86.23 W |
| New Hope, Pa., U.S. | 208 | 40.21 N | 74.57 W |
| New Hudson | 281 | 42.30 N | 83.36 W |
| New Hyde Park | 276 | 40.44 N | 73.41 W |
| New Hythe | 260 | 51.19 N | 0.27 E |
| New Iberia | 194 | 30.00 N | 91.49 W |
| Newick | 42 | 50.58 N | 0.01 E |
| Newington, On., Can. | 206 | 45.07 N | 75.01 W |
| Newington, Eng., U.K. | 42 | 51.05 N | 1.08 E |
| Newington, Eng., U.K. | 260 | 51.21 N | 0.40 E |
| Newington, Ct., U.S. | 207 | 41.42 N | 72.43 W |
| Newinn | 48 | 52.26 N | 7.53 W |
| New Ipswich | 207 | 42.44 N | 71.51 W |
| New Ireland □[5] | 164 | 3.00 S | 151.30 E |
| New Ireland I | 164 | 3.20 S | 152.00 E |
| New Island I | 126 | 21.31 N | 88.12 E |
| New Jersey □[3], U.S. | 178 | 40.15 N | 74.30 W |
| New Jersey □[3], U.S. | 188 | 40.15 N | 74.30 W |
| New Jersey Institute of Technology ʋ[2] | 276 | 40.45 N | 74.11 W |
| New Johnsonville | 194 | 36.01 N | 87.58 W |
| New Kensington | 214 | 40.34 N | 79.45 W |
| New Kent | 208 | 37.31 N | 76.58 W |
| New Kent □[6] | 208 | 37.30 N | 77.00 W |
| New Kingstown | 208 | 40.13 N | 77.07 W |
| Newkirk | 196 | 36.52 N | 97.03 W |
| Newkirk Estates | 285 | 39.42 N | 75.36 W |
| New Knoxville | 216 | 40.29 N | 84.18 W |
| New Kowloon (Xinjiulong) | 271d | 22.20 N | 114.10 E |
| New Lagos ◆[8] | 273a | 6.30 N | 3.22 E |
| New Lake ⊜ | 192 | 35.38 N | 76.20 W |
| Newland | 192 | 36.05 N | 81.55 W |
| Newland Head ⟩ | 168b | 35.39 S | 138.31 E |
| Newland Range ⋏ | 162 | 27.53 S | 123.58 E |
| Newlands | 166 | 21.11 S | 147.54 E |
| Newlands ◆[8] | 273d | 26.11 S | 27.58 E |
| New Lane | 262 | 53.37 N | 2.52 W |
| New Lebanon, N.Y., U.S. | 210 | 42.27 N | 73.23 W |
| New Lebanon, Oh., U.S. | 218 | 39.45 N | 84.23 W |
| New Lebanon, Pa., U.S. | 214 | 41.25 N | 80.04 W |
| New Lebanon Center | 210 | 42.28 N | 73.25 W |
| New Leipzig | 198 | 46.22 N | 101.56 W |
| New Lenox | 216 | 41.30 N | 87.57 W |
| New Lexington | 188 | 39.42 N | 82.12 W |
| New Liberty | 218 | 38.36 N | 84.54 W |
| New Lisbon | 190 | 43.52 N | 90.09 W |
| New Liskeard | 190 | 47.30 N | 79.40 W |
| Newllano | 194 | 31.06 N | 93.16 W |
| New London, Ct., U.S. | 207 | 41.21 N | 72.07 W |
| New London, Ia., U.S. | 190 | 40.55 N | 91.23 W |
| New London, Mn., U.S. | 198 | 45.18 N | 94.56 W |
| New London, Mo., U.S. | 219 | 39.35 N | 91.24 W |
| New London, N.H., U.S. | 188 | 43.24 N | 71.59 W |
| New London, Oh., U.S. | 214 | 41.05 N | 82.24 W |
| New London, Pa., U.S. | 208 | 39.47 N | 75.52 W |
| New London, Tx., U.S. | 222 | 32.15 N | 94.56 W |
| New London, Wi., U.S. | 190 | 44.23 N | 88.44 W |
| New London □[6] | 207 | 41.21 N | 72.07 W |
| New London Submarine Base ■ | 207 | 41.24 N | 72.05 W |
| New Longton | 262 | 53.44 N | 2.45 W |
| Newlonsburg | 279b | 40.25 N | 79.40 W |
| New Lyme | 214 | 41.36 N | 80.47 W |
| Newlyn, Austl. | 169 | 37.25 S | 143.59 E |
| Newlyn, Eng., U.K. | 42 | 50.06 N | 5.33 W |
| Newlyn East | 42 | 50.22 N | 5.03 W |
| Newmachar | 46 | 57.16 N | 2.11 W |
| New Machavie | 158 | 26.48 S | 26.57 E |
| New Madison | 218 | 39.58 N | 84.42 W |
| New Madrid | 194 | 36.35 N | 89.31 W |
| Newmains | 44 | 55.47 N | 3.53 W |
| Newman, Austl. | 162 | 23.20 S | 119.46 E |
| Newman, Ca., U.S. | 226 | 37.18 N | 121.01 W |
| Newman, Il., U.S. | 194 | 39.47 N | 87.59 W |
| Newman, Mount ∧ | 162 | 23.16 S | 119.33 E |
| New Manchester | 214 | 40.31 N | 80.34 W |
| Newman Grove | 198 | 41.45 N | 97.46 W |
| Newmanstown | 208 | 40.20 N | 76.12 W |
| Newmansville | 219 | 40.00 N | 90.01 W |
| New Marion | 218 | 39.00 N | 85.22 W |
| Newmarket, Austl. | 171a | 27.25 S | 153.01 E |
| Newmarket, On., Can. | 212 | 44.03 N | 79.28 W |
| Newmarket, Ire. | 48 | 52.13 N | 9.00 W |
| Newmarket, S. Afr. | 273d | 26.17 S | 28.08 E |
| Newmarket, Eng., U.K. | 42 | 52.15 N | 0.25 E |
| New Market, Al., U.S. | 194 | 34.54 N | 86.25 W |
| New Market, Ia., U.S. | 198 | 40.43 N | 94.53 W |
| New Market, Md., U.S. | 208 | 39.22 N | 77.16 W |
| Newmarket, N.H., U.S. | 188 | 43.04 N | 70.56 W |
| New Market, N.J., U.S. | 276 | 40.34 N | 74.27 W |
| New Market, Va., U.S. | 188 | 38.39 N | 78.40 W |
| Newmarket on Fergus | 48 | 52.45 N | 8.53 W |
| Newmarket Race Course ♦ | 273d | 26.17 S | 28.08 E |
| New Marske | 44 | 54.34 N | 1.02 W |
| New Martinsville | 188 | 39.38 N | 80.51 W |
| New Meadows | 202 | 44.58 N | 116.16 W |
| New Melle | 219 | 38.42 N | 90.52 W |
| New Melones Lake ⊜[1] | 226 | 38.00 N | 120.32 W |
| New Memphis | 219 | 38.29 N | 89.41 W |
| New Mexico □[3] | 178 | 34.30 N | 106.00 W |
| New Miami | 218 | 39.26 N | 84.32 W |
| New Middletown | 214 | 40.58 N | 80.34 W |
| New Milford, Ct., U.S. | 207 | 41.34 N | 73.24 W |
| New Milford, Il., U.S. | 216 | 42.11 N | 89.04 W |
| New Milford, N.J., U.S. | 276 | 40.56 N | 74.01 W |
| New Milford, Pa., U.S. | 210 | 41.52 N | 75.43 W |
| New Millpond ⊜ | 276 | 40.50 N | 73.13 W |
| New Millport | 214 | 40.54 N | 78.32 W |
| New Mills | 44 | 53.23 N | 2.00 W |
| Newmilns | 46 | 55.37 N | 4.20 W |
| New Milton | 42 | 50.44 N | 1.40 W |
| New Minden | 219 | 38.26 N | 89.22 W |
| New Munster | 216 | 42.34 N | 88.13 W |
| Newnan | 192 | 33.22 N | 84.47 W |
| Newnans Lake ⊜ | 192 | 29.39 N | 82.13 W |
| Newnham | 42 | 51.49 N | 2.27 W |
| New Norcia | 162 | 30.58 S | 116.13 E |
| New Norfolk | 166 | 42.47 S | 147.03 E |
| New Norway | 182 | 52.53 N | 112.58 W |
| New Orleans | 194 | 29.57 N | 90.04 W |
| New Orleans Naval Air Station ■ | 194 | 29.51 N | 90.01 W |
| New Oxford | 208 | 39.51 N | 77.03 W |
| New Palestine | 218 | 39.43 N | 85.53 W |
| New Paltz | 210 | 41.44 N | 74.05 W |
| New Paris, In., U.S. | 216 | 41.30 N | 85.49 W |
| New Paris, Oh., U.S. | 218 | 39.51 N | 84.47 W |
| New Paris, Pa., U.S. | 214 | 40.06 N | 78.39 W |
| New Philadelphia, Oh., U.S. | 214 | 40.30 N | 81.27 W |
| New Philadelphia, Pa., U.S. | 208 | 40.43 N | 76.06 W |
| New Pine Creek | 202 | 41.59 N | 120.17 W |
| New Pitsligo | 46 | 57.35 N | 2.11 W |
| New Pittsburg | 214 | 40.50 N | 82.06 W |
| New Plymouth, N.Z. | 172 | 39.04 S | 174.05 E |
| New Plymouth, Id., U.S. | 202 | 43.58 N | 116.49 W |
| New Point | 218 | 39.18 N | 85.19 W |
| New Point Comfort ⟩ | 208 | 37.18 N | 76.17 W |
| Newport, Austl. | 274a | 33.40 S | 151.19 E |
| Newport, Austl. | 274b | 37.51 S | 144.53 E |
| Newport, P.Q., Can. | 186 | 48.16 N | 64.45 W |
| Newport, Ire. | 48 | 53.53 N | 9.34 W |
| Newport, Ire. | 48 | 52.42 N | 8.24 W |
| Newport, Eng., U.K. | 42 | 50.42 N | 1.18 W |
| Newport, Eng., U.K. | 42 | 52.47 N | 2.22 W |
| Newport, Eng., U.K. | 42 | 51.59 N | 0.15 E |
| Newport, Wales, U.K. | 42 | 52.01 N | 4.51 W |
| Newport, Wales, U.K. | 42 | 51.35 N | 3.00 W |
| Newport, Ar., U.S. | 194 | 35.36 N | 91.16 W |
| Newport, De., U.S. | 208 | 39.42 N | 75.36 W |
| Newport, In., U.S. | 194 | 39.53 N | 87.24 W |
| Newport, Ky., U.S. | 218 | 39.05 N | 84.29 W |
| Newport, Me., U.S. | 188 | 44.50 N | 69.16 W |
| Newport, Md., U.S. | 208 | 38.25 N | 76.54 W |
| Newport, Mi., U.S. | 216 | 42.00 N | 83.18 W |
| Newport, N.H., U.S. | 188 | 43.21 N | 72.10 W |
| Newport, N.J., U.S. | 208 | 39.17 N | 75.10 W |
| Newport, N.Y., U.S. | 210 | 43.11 N | 75.00 W |
| Newport, N.C., U.S. | 192 | 34.47 N | 76.51 W |
| Newport, Oh., U.S. | 216 | 39.23 N | 81.13 W |
| Newport, Or., U.S. | 202 | 44.38 N | 124.03 W |
| Newport, Pa., U.S. | 208 | 40.28 N | 77.07 W |
| Newport, R.I., U.S. | 207 | 41.29 N | 71.18 W |
| Newport, Tn., U.S. | 192 | 35.58 N | 83.11 W |
| Newport, Vt., U.S. | 206 | 44.56 N | 72.12 W |
| Newport, Wa., U.S. | 202 | 48.11 N | 117.02 W |
| Newport □[6] | 207 | 41.35 N | 71.15 W |
| Newport Bay C | 208 | 38.14 N | 75.13 W |
| Newport Beach | 228 | 33.37 N | 117.55 W |
| Newport Center | 206 | 44.57 N | 72.18 W |
| Newport Hills | 224 | 47.32 N | 122.10 W |
| Newport News | 208 | 36.58 N | 76.25 W |
| Newport-on-Tay | 46 | 56.26 N | 2.55 W |
| Newport Pagnell | 42 | 52.05 N | 0.44 W |
| New Port Richey | 220 | 28.14 N | 82.43 W |
| Newportville | 285 | 40.09 N | 74.53 W |
| Newportville Terrace | 285 | 40.07 N | 74.54 W |
| New Prague | 190 | 44.32 N | 93.34 W |
| New Preston | 207 | 41.40 N | 73.21 W |
| New Providence, N.J., U.S. | 210 | 40.41 N | 74.24 W |
| New Providence, Pa., U.S. | 208 | 39.56 N | 76.12 W |
| New Providence, Tn., U.S. | 194 | 36.32 N | 87.23 W |
| New Providence I | 240b | 25.02 N | 77.24 W |
| Newquay, Eng., U.K. | 42 | 50.25 N | 5.05 W |
| New Quay, Wales, U.K. | 42 | 52.13 N | 4.22 W |
| New Redruth | 273d | 26.16 S | 28.07 E |
| New Richland | 190 | 43.53 N | 93.29 W |
| New-Richmond, P.Q., Can. | 186 | 48.10 N | 65.52 W |
| New Richmond, Oh., U.S. | 218 | 38.56 N | 84.16 W |
| New Richmond, Wi., U.S. | 190 | 45.07 N | 92.32 W |
| New Riegel | 214 | 41.03 N | 83.19 W |
| New Rim Ditch ≍ | 228 | 35.08 N | 118.58 W |
| New Ringgold | 208 | 40.41 N | 76.00 W |
| New Road | 186 | 44.45 N | 63.28 W |
| New Roads | 194 | 30.42 N | 91.26 W |
| New Rochelle | 210 | 40.54 N | 73.46 W |
| New Rockford | 198 | 47.40 N | 99.08 W |
| New Romney | 42 | 50.59 N | 0.57 E |
| New Ross, N.S., Can. | 186 | 44.44 N | 64.27 W |
| New Ross, Ire. | 48 | 52.24 N | 6.56 W |
| New Rossington | 44 | 53.29 N | 1.04 W |
| Newry, N. Ire., U.K. | 48 | 54.11 N | 6.20 W |
| Newry, Pa., U.S. | 214 | 40.24 N | 78.26 W |
| Newry, S.C., U.S. | 192 | 34.43 N | 82.54 W |
| New Salem, In., U.S. | 218 | 39.32 N | 85.22 W |
| New Salem, N.D., U.S. | 198 | 46.50 N | 101.24 W |
| New Salisbury | 218 | 38.19 N | 86.06 W |
| New Sarum → Salisbury | 42 | 51.05 N | 1.48 W |
| New Schwabenland ◆[1] | 9 | 72.30 S | 1.00 E |
| New Scone | 46 | 56.25 N | 3.24 W |
| Newsham Park ♦ | 262 | 53.25 N | 2.56 W |
| New Sharon | 190 | 41.28 N | 92.39 W |
| New Sheffield | 214 | 40.36 N | 80.17 W |
| New Siberian Islands → Novosibirskoje ostrova II | 74 | 75.00 N | 142.00 E |
| New Smyrna Beach | 220 | 29.01 N | 80.55 W |
| Newsome | 222 | 32.59 N | 95.08 W |
| Newsoms | 208 | 36.37 N | 77.07 W |
| New South Wales □[3] | 166 | 33.00 S | 146.00 E |
| New South Wales, University of ʋ[2] | 274a | 33.55 S | 151.14 E |
| New South Wales Lawn Tennis Association Courts ♦ | 274a | 33.53 S | 151.14 E |
| New Springfield | 214 | 40.55 N | 80.36 W |
| New Square | 276 | 41.08 N | 74.02 W |
| New Stanton | 214 | 40.13 N | 79.37 W |
| Newstead | 169 | 37.07 S | 144.04 E |
| New Stuyahok | 180 | 59.29 N | 157.20 W |
| New Suffolk | 207 | 41.00 N | 72.28 W |
| New Summerfield | 222 | 31.59 N | 95.06 W |
| New Tazewell | 192 | 36.27 N | 83.33 W |
| New Terrell City Lake ⊜[1] | 222 | 32.44 N | 96.14 W |
| New Territories □[8] | 271d | 22.24 N | 114.10 E |
| New Thunderchild Indian Reserve ◆[4] | 184 | 53.30 N | 108.50 W |
| Newtok | 180 | 60.56 N | 164.38 W |
| Newton, Eng., U.K. | 44 | 53.57 N | 2.27 W |
| Newton, Eng., U.K. | 262 | 53.16 N | 2.43 W |
| Newton, Ga., U.S. | 192 | 31.18 N | 84.20 W |
| Newton, Il., U.S. | 194 | 38.59 N | 88.09 W |
| Newton, Ia., U.S. | 190 | 41.41 N | 93.02 W |
| Newton, Ks., U.S. | 198 | 38.02 N | 97.20 W |
| Newton, Ma., U.S. | 207 | 42.20 N | 71.12 W |
| Newton, Ms., U.S. | 194 | 32.19 N | 89.09 W |
| Newton, N.J., U.S. | 210 | 41.03 N | 74.45 W |
| Newton, N.C., U.S. | 192 | 35.40 N | 81.13 W |


**Symbols** in the index entries represent the broad categories identified in the key at the right. Symbols with superior numbers (⋏[1]) identify subcategories (see complete key on page *I · 1).*

**Symbole** im Register stellen die rechts im Schlüssel erklärten Kategorien dar. Symbole mit hochgestellten Ziffern (⋏[1]) bezeichnen Unterabteilungen einer Kategorie (vgl. vollständiger Schlüssel auf Seite *I · 1).*

**Los símbolos** incluídos en el texto del índice representan las grandes categorías identificadas con la clave a la derecha. Los símbolos con numeros en su parte superior (⋏[1]) identifican las subcategorías (véase la clave completa en la página *I · 1).*

**Les symboles** de l'index représentent les catégories indiquées dans la légende à droite. Les symboles suivis d'un indice (⋏[1]) représentent des sous-catégories (voir légende complète à la page *I · 1).*

**Os símbolos** incluídos no texto do índice representam as grandes categorias identificadas com a chave à direita. Os símbolos com números em sua parte superior (⋏[1]) identificam as subcategorias (veja-se a chave completa à página *I · 1).*

| | English | Deutsch | Español | Français | Português |
| --- | --- | --- | --- | --- | --- |
| ∧ | Mountain | Berg | Montaña | Montagne | Montanha |
| ⋏ | Mountains | Gebirge | Montañas | Montagnes | Montanhas |
| )( | Pass | Paß | Paso | Col | Passo |
| V | Valley, Canyon | Tal, Cañon | Valle, Cañón | Vallée, Canyon | Vale, Canhão |
| ≚ | Plain | Ebene | Llano | Plaine | Planície |
| ⟩ | Cape | Kap | Cabo | Cap | Cabo |
| I | Island | Insel | Isla | Île | Ilha |
| II | Islands | Inseln | Islas | Îles | Ilhas |
| ± | Other Topographic Features | Andere Topographische Objekte | Otros Elementos Topográficos | Autres données topographiques | Outros acidentes topográficos |

ESPAÑOL — Nombre | Página | Lat.°′ | Long.°′ W = Oeste
FRANÇAIS — Nom | Page | Lat.°′ | Long.°′ W = Ouest
PORTUGUÊS — Nome | Página | Lat.°′ | Long.°′ W = Oeste


Newton, Tx., U.S. 194 30.50 N 93.45 W
Newton □[6] 216 40.46 N 87.27 W
Newton Abbot 42 50.32 N 3.36 W
Newton Arlosh 44 54.53 N 3.15 W
Newton Aycliffe 44 54.36 N 1.32 W
Newton Brook ◆[8] 275b 43.48 N 79.24 W
Newton Center 283 42.20 N 71.12 W
Newton Falls, N.Y., U.S. 188 44.12 N 74.59 W
Newton Falls, Oh., U.S. 214 41.11 N 80.58 W
Newton Ferrers 42 50.18 N 4.02 W
Newton Flotman 42 52.32 N 1.16 E
Newton Hamilton 214 40.24 N 77.51 W
Newton Highlands 283 42.19 N 71.13 W
Newton-le-Willows 44 53.28 N 2.37 W
Newton Longville 42 51.58 N 0.46 W
Newton Lower Falls 283 42.19 N 71.23 W
Newtonmore 46 57.04 N 4.08 W
Newton Stewart 44 54.57 N 4.29 W
Newtonsville 218 39.11 N 84.05 W
Newton Upper Falls 283 42.19 N 71.13 W
Newtonville, On., Can. 212 43.56 N 78.30 W
Newtonville, Ma., U.S. 283 42.21 N 71.13 W
Newtonville, N.J., U.S. 208 39.33 N 74.51 W
New Toronto ◆[8] 275b 43.36 N 79.30 W
Newtown, Austl. 169 38.09 S 144.20 E
Newtown, Nf., Can. 186 49.12 N 53.31 W
Newtown, Eng., U.K. 262 53.21 N 2.00 W
Newtown, Wales, U.K. 42 52.32 N 3.19 W
Newtown, Ct., U.S. 207 41.24 N 73.18 W
Newtown, In., U.S. 216 40.12 N 87.08 W
Newtown, Ky., U.S. 218 38.13 N 84.57 W
New Town, N.D., U.S. 198 47.58 N 102.29 W
Newtown, Pa., U.S. 208 40.14 N 74.56 W
Newtown ◆[8] 274a 33.54 S 151.11 E
Newtownabbey 48 54.42 N 5.54 W
Newtownards 48 54.36 N 5.41 W
Newtownbutler 48 54.12 N 7.23 W
Newtown Creek ≃, N.Y., U.S. 276 40.44 N 73.58 W
Newtown Creek ≃, Pa., U.S. 285 40.13 N 74.56 W
Newtown Crommelin 48 54.59 N 6.13 W
Newtown Forbes 48 53.46 N 7.50 W
Newtownhamilton 48 54.12 N 6.35 W
Newtown Mount Kennedy 48 53.05 N 6.07 W
Newtown Saint Boswells 46 55.34 N 2.40 W
Newtown Square 208 39.59 N 75.24 W
Newtownstewart 48 54.43 N 7.24 W
New Tredegar 42 51.43 N 3.14 W
New Tripoli 208 40.41 N 75.45 W
New Troy 216 41.53 N 86.33 W
New Truxton 219 38.58 N 91.15 W
New Ulm, Mn., U.S. 190 44.18 N 94.27 W
New Ulm, Tx., U.S. 222 29.53 N 96.29 W
New Utrecht ◆[8] 276 40.36 N 73.59 W
New Vernon 276 40.45 N 74.30 W
New Vienna 218 39.19 N 83.41 W
Newville, In., U.S. 216 41.21 N 84.51 W
Newville, Pa., U.S. 208 40.10 N 77.23 W
New Vineyard 188 44.48 N 70.07 W
New Waltham 44 53.32 N 0.04 W
New Washington, Pil. 116 11.39 N 122.26 E
New Washington, In., U.S. 218 38.33 N 85.32 W
New Washington, Oh., U.S. 214 40.57 N 82.51 W
New Waterford, N.S., Can. 186 46.15 N 60.05 W
New Waterford, Oh., U.S. 214 40.50 N 80.36 W
New Waverly, In., U.S. 216 40.46 N 86.12 W
New Waverly, Tx., U.S. 222 30.32 N 95.29 W
New Westminster 224 49.12 N 122.55 W
New Whiteland 218 39.33 N 86.05 W
New Wilmington 214 41.07 N 80.19 W
New Windsor → Windsor, Eng., U.K. 42 51.29 N 0.38 W
New Windsor, Md., U.S. 208 39.32 N 77.06 W
New Windsor, N.Y., U.S. 210 41.30 N 74.01 W
New Woodbine Racetrack ♦ 275b 43.43 N 79.36 W
New Woodstock 210 42.50 N 75.51 W
New World Island I 186 49.35 N 54.40 W
New Year Creek ≃ 222 30.08 N 96.12 W
New York, N.Y., U.S. 210 40.43 N 74.01 W
New York, N.Y., U.S. 276 40.43 N 74.01 W
New York □[6] 276 40.47 N 73.58 W
New York □[3], U.S. 178 43.00 N 75.00 W
New York □[3], U.S. 188 43.00 N 75.00 W
New York, City College of ᵿ[2] 276 40.49 N 73.57 W
New York, Polytechnic Institute of ᵿ[2] 276 40.42 N 73.59 W
New York, State University of (Stony Brook) ᵿ[2], N.Y., U.S. 276 40.55 N 73.08 W
New York, State University of (Buffalo) ᵿ[2], N.Y., U.S. 284a 42.57 N 78.49 W
New York, State University of, College at Buffalo ᵿ[2] 284a 42.56 N 78.53 W
New York at Buffalo, State University of ᵿ[2] 284a 42.56 N 78.49 W
New York Mills, Mn., U.S. 198 46.31 N 95.22 W
New York Mills, N.Y., U.S. 210 43.06 N 75.18 W
New York State Barge Canal ≅ 210 43.05 N 78.43 W
New York Stock Exchange ᵿ 276 40.42 N 74.01 W
New Zealand □[1] 172 41.00 S 174.00 E
Nexapa ≃ 234 18.07 N 98.46 W
Nexon 32 45.41 N 1.11 E
Ney 216 41.23 N 84.32 W
Neyagawa 96 34.46 N 135.38 E
Neye 263 51.07 N 7.22 E
Neyestausee ◎[1] 263 51.08 N 7.24 E
Ney Lake ◎ 184 54.38 N 92.25 W
Neyland 42 51.43 N 4.57 W
Neylandville 222 33.12 N 96.00 W
Neyrīz 128 29.12 N 54.19 E
Neyshābūr 128 36.12 N 58.50 E
Neyyāttinkara 122 8.24 N 77.05 E
Nezahualcóyotl 234 19.27 N 99.03 W
Nezahualcóyotl, Presa ◎[1] 234 17.10 N 93.40 W
Nezamajevskaja 78 46.09 N 40.16 E
Nezameno-toko ♦ 94 35.46 N 137.42 E
Nežárka ≃ 61 49.11 N 14.41 E
Nezavertailovca 38 46.37 N 29.56 E
Nezlobnaja 84 44.08 N 43.23 E
Neznanka ≃ 265b 55.34 N 37.21 E
Neznanovo 80 54.02 N 40.06 E
Nezperce 202 46.14 N 116.14 W
Nez Perce Indian Reservation ◆[4] 202 46.20 N 116.30 W
Nez Perce National Historical Park ♦ 202 45.50 N 116.15 W
Nezpique, Bayou ≃ 194 30.12 N 92.35 W

Nezvěstice 60 49.39 N 13.32 E
Ngabang 112 0.23 N 109.57 E
Ngabé 152 3.12 S 16.11 E
Ngabordamlu, Tanjung › 164 6.56 S 134.11 E
Ngadda ≃ 146 12.40 N 13.50 E
Ngadirojo 115a 8.13 S 111.19 E
Ngadza 152 5.10 N 20.12 E
Ngahere 172 42.24 S 171.27 E
Ngala 146 12.20 N 14.10 E
Ngale 152 2.56 N 21.20 E
Ngali 152 2.27 S 19.20 E
Ngaliema, Baie de ⊂ 273b 4.19 S 15.16 E
Ngalipaeng 112 3.24 N 125.37 E
Ngaloa Harbour ⊂ 175g 19.06 S 178.11 E
Ngamaba 273b 4.14 S 15.16 E
Ngamba ◆[8] 273b 4.15 S 15.18 E
Ngambé 152 4.14 N 10.37 E
Ngamdu 146 11.48 N 12.18 E
Ngami, Lake ◎ 156 20.37 S 22.40 E
Ngamiland □[5] 156 19.09 S 22.47 E
Ngamo 154 19.08 S 27.32 E
Ngamouéri 273b 4.14 S 15.14 E
Ngamring 124 29.14 N 87.10 E
Nganda ᴧ 154 10.25 S 33.50 E
Ngangala 154 4.42 N 31.55 E
Ngangla Ringco ◎ 120 31.40 N 83.00 E
Nganglong Kangri ᴧ 120 32.45 N 81.12 E
Nganglong Kangri ⋀ 120 32.00 N 83.00 E
Ngangzê Co ◎ 120 31.05 N 86.55 E
Nganjuk 115a 7.36 S 111.55 E
Ngao 110 18.46 N 99.59 E
Ngaoui, Mont ᴧ 152 6.40 N 14.57 E
Ngaoundéré 152 7.19 N 13.35 E
Ngapali 110 18.26 N 94.19 E
Ngapara 172 44.57 S 170.45 E
Ngape 110 20.04 N 94.38 E
Ngaputaw 110 16.32 N 94.42 E
Ngara 154 2.28 S 30.39 E
Ngaramasch 175b 6.54 N 134.08 E
Ngarimbi 154 8.28 S 38.36 E
Ngaruawahia 172 37.40 S 175.09 E
Ngaruroro ≃ 172 39.34 S 176.56 E
Ngasamo 154 2.33 S 33.53 E
Ngat ≃ 110 19.09 N 99.01 E
Ngatangiia 174k 21.14 S 159.43 W
Ngatangiia Harbour ⊂ 174k 21.14 S 159.45 W
Ngatea 172 37.17 S 175.30 E
Ngathainggyaung 110 17.24 N 95.05 E
Ngatik I[1] 14 5.51 N 157.16 E
Ngau I 175g 18.02 S 179.18 E
Ngauruhoe, Mount ᴧ 172 39.09 S 175.38 E
Ngau Tau Kok → Kwun Tong 271d 22.19 N 114.12 E
Ngawen 115a 7.00 S 111.18 E
Ngawi 115a 7.24 S 111.26 E
Ngay Nua 110 21.50 N 101.54 E
Ngebard ✣[2] 175b 7.50 N 134.32 E
Ngebel 115a 7.46 S 111.37 E
Ngele 152 0.29 S 20.25 E
Ngemlis II 175b 7.07 N 134.15 E
Ngerengere 154 6.45 S 38.07 E
Ngerkeel 175b 7.25 N 134.30 E
Ngermechau 175b 7.35 N 134.39 E
Ngeruktabel I 175b 7.15 N 134.24 E
Ngetbong 175b 7.37 N 134.35 E
Ngetera 146 12.31 N 12.38 E
Nggamea Island I 175g 16.46 S 179.46 W
Nggatokae Island I 175e 8.46 S 158.11 E
Nggela Pile I 175e 9.05 S 160.15 E
Nggela Sule I 175e 9.05 S 160.15 E
Nggelelevu I 175g 16.05 S 179.09 W
Nggwavuma ≃ 158 26.58 S 32.17 E
Nghia Dan 110 19.18 N 105.26 E
Nghia Hanh 110 15.03 N 108.47 E
Nghia Lo 110 21.36 N 104.31 E
Ngiap ≃ 110 18.24 N 103.36 E
Ngidinga 152 5.37 S 15.17 E
Ngimbang 115a 7.17 S 112.12 E
Ng'iro ᴧ 154 2.08 N 36.51 E
Ng'iro, Ewaso ≃, Kenya 154 0.28 N 39.55 E
Ngiro, Ewaso ≃, Kenya 154 2.04 S 36.07 E
Ngkesol ✣[2] 175b 7.57 N 134.41 E
Ngkesol, Toachel ⋓ 175b 7.52 N 134.36 E
Ngo 152 2.29 S 15.45 E
Ngoangoa ≃ 140 5.48 N 25.09 E
Ngoboli 154 4.57 N 32.37 E
Ngoko ≃, Afr. 152 1.40 N 16.03 E
Ngoko ≃, Congo 152 0.25 S 15.29 E
Ngol-Kedju Hill ᴧ[2] 152 6.20 N 9.45 E
Ngolo 146 9.56 N 22.16 E
Ngom ≃ 102 31.11 N 97.15 E
Ngomahuru 154 20.26 S 30.43 E
Ngomba 154 8.23 S 32.53 E
Ngomba ᴧ 154 5.43 S 35.52 E
Ngombe, Zaïre 152 6.35 S 20.42 E
Ngombe, Zaïre 273b 4.24 S 15.11 E
Ngome 158 27.46 S 31.28 E
Ngomedzap 152 3.15 N 11.12 E
Ngomeni, Ras › 154 2.59 S 40.14 E
Ngong 154 1.22 S 36.39 E
Ngongotaha 172 38.05 S 176.12 E
Ngono ≃ 154 1.08 S 31.35 E
Ngonye Falls ⌞ 152 16.40 S 23.35 E
Ngop 140 6.16 N 30.12 E
Ngora 154 1.27 N 33.46 E
Ngorengore 154 1.02 S 35.30 E
Ngoring Hu ◎ 102 34.50 N 97.35 E
Ngoro 115a 7.41 S 112.16 E
Ngorongoro Crater ⏊[6] 154 3.10 S 35.35 E
Ngote 154 2.14 N 30.48 E
Ngoto 152 4.00 N 17.21 E
Ngotwane ≃ 156 23.35 S 26.58 E
Ngoulémakong 152 3.07 N 11.25 E
Ngouma 150 15.38 N 3.22 W
Ngounié □[4] 152 1.30 S 11.00 E
Ngounié ≃ 152 0.37 S 10.18 E
Ngouri 146 13.38 N 15.22 E
Ngouroundou 152 6.27 N 22.37 E
Ngourti 146 15.19 N 13.12 E
Ngoywa 154 5.56 S 32.48 E
Ngozi 154 2.54 S 29.50 E
Ngqeleni 158 31.40 S 29.02 E
Ngudiabaka ≃ 273b 4.25 S 15.11 E
Nguélémendouka 152 4.23 N 12.55 E
Ngugha ≃ 156 19.21 S 23.15 E
Nguigmi 146 14.15 N 13.07 E
Nguila 152 4.43 N 11.41 E
Nguiu 164 11.45 S 130.38 E
Ngulu I[1] 108 8.27 N 137.29 E
Ngum ≃ 110 18.09 N 103.06 E
Nguna, Île I 175f 17.26 S 168.21 E
Ngunga 154 3.41 S 33.34 E
Ngunju, Tanjung › 115b 10.19 S 120.28 E
Ngunut 115a 8.06 S 112.01 E
Ngurore 146 9.18 N 12.14 E
Nguru 146 12.52 N 10.27 E
Ngwempisi ≃ 158 26.42 S 31.26 E
Ngweni 158 27.56 S 32.15 E
Ngwenya ᴧ 158 26.11 S 31.02 E
Ngwerere 154 15.18 S 28.20 E
Ngweze ≃ 154 17.40 S 25.07 E
Nha Be 269c 10.42 N 106.44 E
Nhabe ≃, Bots. 156 20.22 S 22.58 E
Nha Be ≃, Viet 269c 10.39 N 106.44 E
Nhacoongo 156 24.18 S 35.14 E
Nhamacolomo 156 18.05 S 34.26 E
Nhamundá 250 2.14 S 56.43 W
Nhamundá ≃ 246 2.12 S 56.41 W
Nha Nam 110 21.27 N 106.06 E
Nhandeara 255 20.40 S 50.02 W
Nhareia 152 11.25 S 17.03 E
Nha Trang 110 12.15 N 109.11 E
Nhia ≃ 152 10.15 S 14.12 E
Nhill 166 36.20 S 141.39 E
Nhlangano 158 27.06 S 31.12 E
Nhlazatshe 158 28.10 S 31.14 E

Nhoma ≃ 156 18.52 S 20.53 E
Nhon Trach 269c 10.43 N 106.51 E
Nhulunbuy 164 12.11 S 136.47 E
Nhundo 152 14.25 S 21.23 E
Nhunguaçu 256 22.21 S 42.53 W
Niabembe 154 2.14 S 27.44 E
Niafounké 150 15.56 N 4.00 W
Niagara 190 45.46 N 87.59 W
Niagara □[6], On., Can. 212 43.05 N 79.20 W
Niagara □[6], N.Y., U.S. 210 43.10 N 78.42 W
Niagara ≃ 212 43.15 N 79.04 W
Niagara County Historical Center ᵿ 284a 43.10 N 78.43 W
Niagara Falls, On., Can. 212 43.06 N 79.04 W
Niagara Falls, On., Can. 284a 43.06 N 79.04 W
Niagara Falls, N.Y., U.S. 210 43.05 N 79.03 W
Niagara Falls, N.Y., U.S. 284a 43.05 N 79.03 W
Niagara Falls ⌞ 212 43.05 N 79.04 W
Niagara Falls Airport ⊠ 284a 43.02 N 79.08 W
Niagara Falls International Airport ⊠ 284a 43.06 N 78.56 W
Niagara-on-the-Lake 212 43.15 N 79.04 W
Niagara University ᵿ[2] 284a 43.08 N 79.02 W
Niagassola 150 12.19 N 9.07 W
Niah 112 3.52 N 113.44 E
Niakaramandougou 150 8.40 N 5.17 W
Niamey 150 13.31 N 2.07 E
Niamey □[5] 150 14.00 N 2.00 E
Niamtougou 150 9.46 N 1.06 E
Nianbadu 100 28.17 N 118.28 E
Niandan ≃ 150 10.30 N 10.26 W
Niandan Koro 150 11.05 N 9.15 W
Nianforando 150 9.32 N 10.31 W
Niangara 154 3.42 N 27.52 E
Niangay, Lac ◎ 150 15.50 N 3.00 W
Niangmake 102 30.14 N 99.40 E
Niangniangqong 104 41.00 N 121.13 E
Niangniangmiao 98 42.34 N 118.05 E
Niangniangwa 105 40.33 N 117.30 E
Niangoloko 150 10.17 N 4.55 W
Niangua ≃ 194 37.58 N 92.48 W
Niangzizhuang 105 40.02 N 118.05 E
Nia-Nia 154 1.24 N 27.36 E
Nianpan 104 41.48 N 124.02 E
Niantic, Ct., U.S. 207 41.19 N 72.11 W
Niantic, Il., U.S. 219 39.51 N 89.10 W
Nianyugou 104 42.00 N 123.59 E
Nianyushan 100 29.11 N 117.04 E
Nianzhuang 98 34.19 N 117.47 E
Nianzigang 100 31.03 N 114.18 E
Nianzishan 89 47.32 N 122.52 E
Niapu 154 2.25 N 26.28 E
Niari □[5] 152 3.15 S 12.30 E
Niari ≃ 152 3.56 S 12.12 E
Niaro 140 10.38 N 31.31 E
Nias, Pulau I 114 1.05 N 97.35 E
Niassa □[5] 154 13.30 S 36.00 E
Niatupo 246 9.33 N 78.54 W
Nibbiano 62 44.54 N 9.19 E
Nibe 26 56.59 N 9.38 E
Nibong Tebal 114 5.10 N 100.29 E
Nibra 272b 22.36 N 88.16 E
Nic 84 40.56 N 47.41 E
Nīca 76 56.19 N 21.04 E
Nica ≃ 86 57.29 N 64.33 E
Nicaea → İznik 130 40.26 N 29.43 E
Nicaragua □[1], N.A. 230 13.00 N 85.00 W
Nicaragua □[1], N.A. 236 13.00 N 85.00 W
Nicaragua, Lago de ◎ 236 11.30 N 85.30 W
Nicaro 240p 20.42 N 75.33 W
Nicastro 68 38.59 N 16.20 E
Ničatka, ozero ◎ 88 57.45 N 117.30 E
Nice 62 43.42 N 7.15 E
Nice-Côte d'Azur, Aéroport de ⊠ 62 43.40 N 7.14 E
Niceville 194 30.31 N 86.28 W
Nichelino 62 44.59 N 7.38 E
Nicheng 106 30.55 N 121.49 E
Nichihara 96 34.33 N 131.50 E
Nichinan, Nihon 92 31.36 N 131.23 E
Nichinan, Nihon 96 35.09 N 133.16 E
Nicholas □[6] 218 38.20 N 84.02 W
Nicholas Channel ⋓ 238 23.25 N 80.05 W
Nicholasville 192 37.52 N 84.34 W
Nicholls 192 31.31 N 82.38 W
Nicholl's Town 238 25.08 N 78.00 W
Nichols, Ca., U.S. 282 38.02 N 121.59 W
Nichols, Fl., U.S. 220 27.54 N 82.02 W
Nichols, N.Y., U.S. 210 42.01 N 76.22 W
Nichols Brook ≃ 283 42.37 N 70.59 W
Nicholson, Austl. 162 18.02 S 128.54 E
Nicholson, Ky., U.S. 218 38.54 N 84.33 W
Nicholson, Ms., U.S. 194 30.28 N 89.41 W
Nicholson, Pa., U.S. 210 41.37 N 75.46 W
Nicholson ≃, Austl. 162 17.34 S 128.38 E
Nicholson ≃, Austl. 166 17.31 S 139.36 E
Nicholson Island I 212 43.56 N 77.31 W
Nicholson Range ⋀ 162 27.15 S 116.45 E
Nicholson River Aboriginal Reserve ◆[4] 162 18.00 S 137.30 E
Nichols Run ≃ 284b 39.03 N 77.18 W
Nickerie □[5] 250 5.40 N 56.50 W
Nickerie ≃ 250 5.59 N 57.00 W
Nickerson 198 38.08 N 98.05 W
Nickol Bay ⊂ 162 20.39 S 116.52 E
Nicktown 214 40.37 N 78.48 W
Nicobar Islands II 110 8.00 N 93.30 E
Nicola 182 50.10 N 120.40 W
Nicola ≃ 182 50.25 N 121.18 W
Nicolae Bălcescu 38 47.34 N 26.52 E
Nicolai Mountain ᴧ 224 46.05 N 123.28 W
Nicola Lake ◎ 182 50.10 N 120.25 W
Nicola Mameet Indian Reserve ◆[4] 182 50.11 N 120.49 W
Nicolaus 226 38.54 N 121.35 W
Nicolet 206 46.13 N 72.37 W
Nicolet □[6] 206 46.15 N 72.20 W
Nicolet ≃ 206 46.14 N 72.39 W
Nicolet, Lac ◎ 206 45.50 N 71.33 W
Nicolet, Lake ◎ 190 46.20 N 84.15 W
Nicolet Centre ≃ 206 45.46 N 71.50 W
Nicolet Sud-Ouest ≃ 206 46.13 N 72.36 W
Nicoll Bay ⊂ 276 40.43 N 73.07 W
Nicollet 190 44.16 N 94.11 W
Nicoll Point › 276 40.42 N 73.09 W
Nicolosi 70 37.37 N 15.01 E
Nicosia, It. 70 37.45 N 14.24 E
Nicosia (Levkosía), Kípros 130 35.10 N 33.22 E
Nicosia (Lefkoşa), Kıbrıs 130 35.10 N 33.22 E
Nicotera 68 38.34 N 15.57 E
Nicoya 236 10.09 N 85.27 W
Nicoya, Golfo de ⊂ 236 9.47 N 84.48 W
Nicoya, Península de ›[1] 236 10.00 N 85.25 W
Nictheroy → Niterói 256 22.53 S 43.07 W
Nida 76 55.18 N 21.01 E
Nida ≃ 30 50.18 N 20.52 E
Nidadavole 122 16.55 N 81.40 E
Nidau 58 47.07 N 7.14 E
Nidd ≃ 44 54.01 N 1.12 W
Nidda 56 50.24 N 9.00 E
Nidda ≃ 56 50.06 N 8.34 E
Nidder ≃ 56 50.12 N 8.47 E
Nidderau 56 50.14 N 8.52 E
Nide 102 31.51 N 96.19 E
Nideggen 56 50.47 N 6.29 E
Nidelva ≃ 26 58.24 N 8.48 E

Nidwalden □[3] 58 46.55 N 8.28 E
Nidzica 30 53.22 N 20.26 E
Niebüll 41 54.48 N 8.50 E
Nied ≃ 56 49.23 N 6.40 E
Nied Allemande ≃ 56 49.10 N 6.26 E
Nieddu, Monte ᴧ 71 40.45 N 9.34 E
Niedenstein 56 51.14 N 9.19 E
Niederanven 56 49.39 N 6.16 E
Niederau 54 51.10 N 13.32 E
Niederaula 56 50.48 N 9.36 E
Niederbayern □[5] 60 48.45 N 12.45 E
Niederbipp 58 47.16 N 7.39 E
Niederbobritzsch 54 50.54 N 13.26 E
Niederbonsfeld 263 51.23 N 7.08 E
Niederbronn-Les-Bains 56 48.57 N 7.38 E
Niederdonk 263 51.14 N 6.41 E
Niederelfringhausen 263 51.21 N 7.10 E
Niedereschach 58 48.08 N 8.32 E
Niedere Tauern ⋀ 30 47.18 N 14.00 E
Niederfinow 54 52.50 N 13.55 E
Niederfrohna 54 50.53 N 12.43 E
Niedergörsdorf 54 51.59 N 13.00 E
Niederhaverbeck 52 53.09 N 9.54 E
Niederheimbach 56 50.02 N 7.48 E
Niederhone 56 51.13 N 10.06 E
Niederkassel 56 50.49 N 7.02 E
Nieder-Kassel ◆[8] 263 51.14 N 6.45 E
Niederkrüchten 56 51.12 N 6.13 E
Niederlande → Netherlands □[1] 30 52.15 N 5.30 E
Niederländische Antillen → Netherlands Antilles □[2] 241s 12.15 N 69.00 W
Niederlausitz □[9] 54 51.40 N 14.15 E
Niederlehme 54 52.19 N 13.39 E
Niedermarschacht 52 53.25 N 10.21 E
Niederndodeleben 54 52.08 N 11.30 E
Nieder-Neuendorf 264a 52.37 N 13.12 E
Niedernhall 56 49.17 N 9.36 E
Niedernwöhren 52 52.21 N 9.08 E
Niederoderwitz 54 50.57 N 14.44 E
Nieder-Ohmen 56 50.38 N 9.02 E
Nieder-Olm 56 49.55 N 8.11 E
Niederorschel 54 51.22 N 10.25 E
Niederösterreich □[3] 61 48.20 N 15.50 E
Niedersachsen □[3] 30 52.40 N 9.00 E
Niedersachswerfen 54 51.33 N 10.46 E
Niederschöneweide ◆[8] 264a 52.27 N 13.31 E
Niederschönhausen ◆[8] 54 52.35 N 13.23 E
Niedersonthofen 58 47.38 N 10.13 E
Niederstetten 56 49.24 N 9.55 E
Niederstotzingen 56 48.32 N 10.14 E
Niedersulz 61 48.29 N 16.40 E
Niedertrebra 54 51.04 N 11.35 E
Niederurnen 58 47.07 N 9.03 E
Niederwald 58 46.26 N 8.12 E
Niederwalgern 56 50.44 N 8.41 E
Niederweningen 58 47.30 N 8.23 E
Niederwerrn 56 50.04 N 10.11 E
Niederwiesa 54 50.51 N 13.01 E
Niederwürschnitz 54 50.43 N 12.45 E
Niederzier 56 50.53 N 6.28 E
Nied Française ≃ 56 49.10 N 6.26 E
Niedu 100 25.28 N 114.08 E
Niefang 152 1.50 N 10.14 E
Niefern-Öschelbronn 56 48.55 N 8.47 E
Nieheim 52 51.48 N 9.06 E
Niekerkshoop 158 29.19 S 22.51 E
Niel 50 51.07 N 4.20 E
Niellé 150 10.12 N 5.38 W
Niellim 146 9.42 N 17.49 E
Niem 152 6.12 N 15.14 E
Niemba 154 5.57 S 28.26 E
Niemegk 54 52.04 N 12.41 E
Niemeyer ◆[8] 287a 23.00 S 43.15 W
Niemodlin 30 50.39 N 17.37 E
Niéna 150 11.26 N 6.21 W
Nienberge 52 52.00 N 7.34 E
Nienborg-Wigbold 52 52.08 N 7.06 E
Nienburg, Dtsch. 52 52.38 N 9.13 E
Nienburg, Dtsch. 54 51.50 N 11.46 E
Niendorf 54 53.59 N 10.50 E
Nienhagen, Dtsch. 52 52.33 N 10.05 E
Nienhagen, Dtsch. 54 51.57 N 11.09 E
Niénokoué, Mont ᴧ[2] 150 5.26 N 7.10 W
Niepars 54 54.19 N 12.56 E
Niepkuhlen ≃ 263 51.29 N 6.31 E
Niepołomice 30 50.03 N 20.13 E
Nieppe 50 50.42 N 2.50 E
Nier ≃ 48 52.17 N 7.48 W
Niéré 146 14.30 N 21.09 E
Niéré, Hadjer ᴧ 146 14.21 N 21.40 E
Niéri Ko ≃ 150 13.21 N 13.23 W
Niers ≃ 52 51.43 N 5.57 E
Nierst 263 51.19 N 6.43 E
Nierstein 56 49.52 N 8.20 E
Niesen ᴧ 58 46.39 N 7.39 E
Niesky 54 51.17 N 14.49 E
Nieszawa 30 52.50 N 18.55 E
Nieto, Cañada de ≃ 258 34.00 S 58.15 W
Nieu Bethesda 158 31.51 S 24.34 E
Nieuw-Amsterdam, Ned. 52 52.44 N 6.51 E
Nieuw Amsterdam, Sur. 250 5.53 N 55.05 W
Nieuw-Buinen 52 52.57 N 6.55 E
Nieuwefontein 158 28.01 S 19.06 E
Nieuwegein 52 52.03 N 5.05 E
Nieuwe-Niedorp 52 52.45 N 4.54 E
Nieuwe-Pekela 52 53.04 N 6.58 E
Nieuweschans 52 53.11 N 7.12 E
Nieuwkoop 52 52.08 N 4.47 E
Nieuw Nickerie 250 5.57 N 56.59 W
Nieuwolda 52 53.14 N 6.59 E
Nieuwoudtville 158 31.23 S 19.07 E
Nieuwpoort, Bel. 50 51.08 N 2.45 E
Nieuwpoort, Ned. Ant. 241s 12.03 N 68.49 W
Nieuwpoort-Bad 50 51.09 N 2.42 E
Nieuw-Schoonebeek 52 52.38 N 6.59 E
Nieuw-Vennep 52 52.16 N 4.38 E
Nieuw-Weerdinge 52 52.52 N 6.59 E
Nieva ≃ 246 4.35 S 77.53 W
Nievenheim 56 51.07 N 6.46 E
Nievería 286d 11.59 S 76.55 W
Nièvre □[5] 32 47.05 N 3.30 E
Nièvre ≃ 50 47.10 N 3.13 E
Niga 150 13.38 N 5.27 W
Nigan 126 23.30 N 87.59 E
Niğde 130 37.59 N 34.42 E
Niğde □[4] 130 38.15 N 34.15 E
Nigei Island I 182 50.55 N 127.50 W
Nigel 158 26.30 S 28.28 E
Niger □[1] 134 16.00 N 8.00 E
Niger ≃ 150 5.33 N 6.33 E
Niger Delta ⏊[2] 150 4.50 N 6.00 E
Nigeria □[1] 134 10.00 N 8.00 E
Nigerian Museum ᵿ 273a 6.20 N 3.24 E
Nigg 46 57.43 N 4.00 W
Nighāsan 124 28.14 N 80.52 E
Nightcaps 172 45.58 S 168.02 E
Nighthawk 182 48.58 N 119.38 W
Night Hawk Lake ◎ 190 48.28 N 81.00 W
Nightingale Island I 10 37.24 S 12.28 W
Nightmute 180 60.29 N 164.43 W
Nigríta 38 40.55 N 23.30 E
Nihe 104 41.27 N 121.13 E
Nihing (Nahang) ≃ 128 26.00 N 62.44 E
Nihoa I 14 23.06 N 161.58 W
Nihommatsu 92 37.35 N 140.26 E
Nihon → Japan □[1] 92 36.00 N 138.00 E
Nihonbashi ◆[8] 268 35.41 N 139.47 E
Nihon-kai → Japan, Sea of ⊤[2] 90 40.00 N 135.00 E

Nihon University ᵿ[2] 268 35.42 N 139.45 E
Nihtaur 124 29.20 N 78.23 E
Nihuil, Embalse del ◎[1] 252 35.05 S 68.45 W
Niida ≃ 96 33.11 N 132.58 E
Niigata 92 37.55 N 139.03 E
Niigata □[5] 94 37.08 N 138.30 E
Niihama 96 33.58 N 133.16 E
Niihari 94 36.07 N 140.09 E
Niiharu 94 36.41 N 138.55 E
Niihau I 229b 21.55 N 160.10 W
Nii-jima I 92 34.22 N 139.16 E
Niimi 96 34.59 N 133.28 E
Niinisalo 26 61.50 N 22.29 E
Niitsu 92 37.48 N 139.07 E
Niiza 94 35.48 N 139.34 E
Níjar 34 36.58 N 2.12 W
Nijiaqiao 269b 31.14 N 121.21 E
Nijil 132 30.31 N 35.33 E
Nijkerk 52 52.13 N 5.30 E
Nijlen 56 51.10 N 4.39 E
Nijmegen 52 51.50 N 5.50 E
Nijo Castle ⊥ 270 35.01 N 135.45 E
Nijvel → Nivelles 50 50.36 N 4.20 E
Nijverdal 52 52.22 N 6.27 E
Níkaia 267c 37.58 N 23.39 E
Nikel' 24 69.24 N 30.12 E
Nikel'tau 86 50.23 N 58.13 E
Nikiforovo 265b 55.50 N 38.05 E
Nikiniki 112 9.49 S 124.28 E
Nikip Lake ◎ 184 52.53 N 91.53 W
Nikitovka 78 50.23 N 38.25 E
Nikitsch 61 47.32 N 16.40 E
Nikitskoje, Ross. 82 55.18 N 38.28 E
Nikitskoje, Ross. 82 55.13 N 35.46 E
Nikki 150 9.56 N 3.12 E
Nikkō 94 36.45 N 139.37 E
Nikkō-kokuritsu-kōen ♦ 94 36.49 N 139.33 E
Niklā al-'Inab 142 30.55 N 30.46 E
Niklasdorf 61 47.24 N 15.10 E
Nikobaren → Nicobar Islands II 110 8.00 N 93.30 E
Nikolai 180 62.58 N 154.09 W
Nikolajevka, Kaz. 86 49.10 N 81.59 E
Nikolajevka, Ross. 80 46.21 N 47.44 E
Nikolajevka, Ross. 80 52.28 N 49.14 E
Nikolajevka, Ross. 80 52.11 N 48.04 E
Nikolajevka, Ross. 80 53.08 N 47.12 E
Nikolajevka, Ross. 83 47.18 N 38.50 E
Nikolajevka, Ross. 86 56.29 N 95.06 E
Nikolajevka, Ross. 86 54.57 N 75.44 E
Nikolajevka, Ross. 88 55.46 N 98.10 E
Nikolajevka, Ross. 89 48.34 N 134.47 E
Nikolajevo 76 58.16 N 29.29 E
Nikolajevo-Kozlovskij 83 47.13 N 38.21 E
Nikolajevsk 80 50.01 N 45.28 E
Nikolajevskaja 80 47.37 N 41.29 E
Nikolajevsk-Na-Amure 89 53.08 N 140.44 E
Nikolajevskoje, Ross. 78 45.08 N 39.36 E
Nikolajevskoje, Ross. 88 51.04 N 111.48 E
Nikolajevskoje, Ross. 88 52.21 N 117.00 E
Nikolassee ◆[8] 264a 52.26 N 13.12 E
Nikolayev → Mykolayiv 78 46.58 N 32.00 E
Nikolo-Berezovec 76 58.38 N 42.17 E
Nikolo-Berjozovka 80 56.06 N 54.17 E
Nikolo-Chovanskoje 265b 55.36 N 37.27 E
Nikologory 80 56.09 N 41.59 E
Nikolo-Kropotki 82 56.44 N 37.55 E
Nikolo-L'vovsk 89 43.54 N 131.23 E
Nikolo-Makarovo 80 57.38 N 43.34 E
Nikolsdorf 64 46.47 N 12.55 E
Nikol'sk, Ross. 24 59.30 N 45.27 E
Nikol'sk, Ross. 80 53.45 N 46.05 E
Nikolski 180 52.56 N 168.52 W
Nikol'skij, Ross. 24 60.55 N 34.00 E
Nikol'skij, Ross. 86 56.18 N 68.58 E
Nikol'skij Toržok 76 59.53 N 38.46 E
Nikol'skoje, Ross. 74 55.12 N 166.00 E
Nikol'skoje, Ross. 76 52.39 N 36.04 E
Nikol'skoje, Ross. 76 55.26 N 35.04 E
Nikol'skoje, Ross. 76 59.23 N 44.36 E
Nikol'skoje, Ross. 76 59.30 N 42.32 E
Nikol'skoje, Ross. 78 50.35 N 41.10 E
Nikol'skoje, Ross. 80 47.46 N 46.24 E
Nikol'skoje, Ross. 80 52.37 N 43.49 E
Nikol'skoje, Ross. 82 54.51 N 35.53 E
Nikol'skoje, Ross. 82 54.27 N 36.24 E
Nikol'skoje, Ross. 82 54.30 N 36.50 E
Nikol'skoje, Ross. 82 54.03 N 37.10 E
Nikol'skoje, Ross. 82 54.18 N 35.53 E
Nikol'skoje, Ross. 82 55.37 N 36.41 E
Nikol'skoje, Ross. 82 55.15 N 36.04 E
Nikol'skoje, Ross. 82 56.09 N 36.43 E
Nikol'skoje, Ross. 82 55.53 N 36.26 E
Nikol'skoje, Ross. 86 57.12 N 84.21 E
Nikol'skoje, Ross. 86 52.02 N 55.43 E
Nikol'skoje, Ross. 265a 59.41 N 30.47 E
Nikol'skoje, Ross. 265b 55.46 N 37.54 E
Nikol'skoje-na-Čeremšane 80 54.03 N 49.14 E
Nikol'skoje-Ur'upino 265b 55.48 N 37.13 E
Nikonga ≃ 154 4.40 S 31.28 E
Nikonorovka 83 49.07 N 39.59 E
Nikonova Gora 76 60.22 N 36.07 E
Nikonovskoje 82 55.17 N 38.10 E
Nikopol, Blg. 38 43.42 N 24.54 E
Nikopol', Ukr. 78 47.35 N 34.25 E
Niksar 130 40.36 N 36.58 E
Nīkshahr 128 26.13 N 60.12 E
Nikšić 38 42.46 N 18.56 E
Nikulino, Ross. 76 55.16 N 33.46 E
Nikulino, Ross. 80 58.05 N 44.14 E
Nikulino, Ross. 82 56.48 N 35.50 E
Nikulino ◆[8] 265b 55.40 N 37.28 E
Nikulkino 82 56.07 N 38.38 E
Nikul'skoje 82 55.10 N 38.41 E
Nikumaroro I[1] 14 4.40 S 174.32 W
Nikunau I 14 1.23 S 176.26 E
Nil → Nile ≃ 140 30.10 N 31.06 E
Nīl, Nahr an- → Nile ≃ 140 30.10 N 31.06 E
Nila, Pulau I 164 6.44 S 129.31 E
Nilakka ◎ 26 63.07 N 26.33 E
Niland 204 33.14 N 115.31 W
Nil Blanc → White Nile ≃ 140 15.38 N 32.31 E
Nile □[5] 154 3.00 N 31.30 E
Nile (Nahr an-Nīl) ≃ 140 30.10 N 31.06 E
Niles, Il., U.S. 216 42.01 N 87.48 W
Niles, Mi., U.S. 216 41.49 N 86.15 W
Niles, Oh., U.S. 214 41.10 N 80.45 W
Niles Canyon V 282 37.36 N 121.56 W
Niles Pond ◎ 283 42.35 N 70.40 W
Nilgani 272b 22.46 N 88.26 E
Nilgaut, Lac ◎ 190 46.36 N 77.15 W
Nīlgiri 126 21.28 N 86.46 E
Nilka 86 43.47 N 82.20 E
Nilkitkwa ≃ 182 55.27 N 126.43 W
Nillahcootie, Lake ◎[1] 169 36.54 S 146.00 E
Nilo → Nile ≃ 140 30.10 N 31.06 E
Nilo Azul → Blue Nile ≃ 140 15.38 N 32.31 E
Nilo Blanco → White Nile ≃ 140 15.38 N 32.31 E
Nilópolis 256 22.49 S 43.25 W
Nilópolis □[7] 287a 22.49 S 43.26 W
Nilphāmāri 124 25.56 N 88.51 E
Nilsiä 26 63.12 N 28.05 E
Niltepec 234 16.34 N 94.37 W
Nilüfer ≃ 130 40.18 N 28.27 E
Nīlwāl ◆[8] 272a 28.40 N 76.59 E
Nilwood 219 39.24 N 89.49 W
Nima 96 35.09 N 132.24 E

Nīmach 120 24.28 N 74.[illegible] E
Niman ≃ 89 51.24 N 132.[illegible] E
Nimančik 89 52.09 N 133.[illegible] E
Nimba, Mount ᴧ 150 7.37 N 8.[illegible] W
Nimbāhera 120 24.37 N 74.[illegible] E
Nimba Range ⋀ 150 7.30 N 8.[illegible] W
Nimboran, Pegunungan ⋀ 164 2.45 S 140.2[illegible] E
Nimelen ≃ 89 52.27 N 136.3[illegible] E
Nîmes 62 43.50 N 4.2[illegible] E
Nimis 64 46.12 N 13.1[illegible] E
Nimishillen Creek ≃ 214 40.38 N 81.2[illegible] W
Nimisila 214 40.56 N 81.3[illegible] W
Nimisila Reservoir ◎[1] 214 40.57 N 81.3[illegible] W
Nīm Ka Thāna 120 27.44 N 75.4[illegible] E
Nimmitabel 166 36.31 S 149.1[illegible] E
Nimmonsburg 210 42.09 N 75.55 W
Nimpkish Lake ◎ 182 50.25 N 126.59 W
Nimrod Lake ◎[1] 194 34.55 N 93.20 W
Nīmrūz □[4] 128 30.30 N 62.00 E
Nims ≃ 56 49.51 N 6.28 E
Nimta 272b 22.40 N 88.25 E
Nimule 154 3.36 N 32.03 E
Nimule National Park ♦ 154 3.50 N 31.35 E
Nimy 50 50.28 N 3.57 E
Niña Bonita, Presa ◎[1] 286b 23.02 N 82.29 W
Nīnah, Wādī V 146 30.02 N 15.22 [illegible]
Nīnawā □[4] 128 36.10 N 42.35 E
Nīnawá (Nineveh) ⊥ 128 36.25 N 43.10 E
Nin Bay ⊂ 116 12.13 N 123.15 E
Ninda 152 14.47 S 21.24 E
Nindigully 166 28.21 S 148.49 E
Nindirí 236 12.00 N 86.08 W
Nine Ashes 260 51.42 N 0.18 E
Nine Degree Channel ⋓ 122 9.00 N 73.00 E
Ninemile Creek ≃, N.Y., U.S. 210 43.11 N 75.20 W
Ninemile Creek ≃, N.Y., U.S. 210 43.06 N 76.14 W
Ninemile Creek ≃, N.Y., U.S. 210 43.24 N 76.38 W
Nine Mile Creek ≃, Ut,. U.S. 200 39.50 N 109.53 W
Ninemile Island I 279b 40.29 N 79.52 W
Nine Mile Lake ◎ 212 44.57 N 79.34 W
Nine Mile Point › 212 44.09 N 76.34 W
Ninepin Group II 271d 22.16 N 114.21 E
Nineteen Hundred Five Memorial Cemetery ◆ 265a 59.51 N 30.27 E
Ninette 184 49.24 N 99.38 W
Ninetyeast Ridge ✣[3] 6 4.00 S 90.00 E
Ninety Mile Beach ⏊[2], Austl. 166 38.13 S 147.23 E
Ninety Mile Beach ⏊[2], N.Z. 172 34.48 S 173.00 E
Ninety Six 192 34.10 N 82.01 W
Nineveh, In., U.S. 218 39.22 N 86.05 W
Nineveh, N.Y., U.S. 210 42.12 N 75.36 W
Nineveh → Nīnawá ⊥ 128 36.25 N 43.10 E
Ninfa ⊥ 66 41.36 N 12.58 E
Ninfas, Punta › 254 42.56 S 64.20 W
Ninfield 42 50.53 N 0.25 E
Ninga 184 49.13 N 99.51 W
Ningaloo 162 22.42 S 113.40 E
Ning'an 89 44.22 N 129.25 E
Ningari 150 14.40 N 3.16 W
Ningbo 100 29.52 N 121.31 E
Ningcheng (Tianyi) 98 41.33 N 119.20 E
Ningde 100 26.43 N 119.33 E
Ningdu 100 26.31 N 115.58 E
Ningerum 164 5.41 S 141.08 E
Ninggang 100 26.50 N 114.02 E
Ningguo 106 30.38 N 118.58 E
Ninghai 100 29.17 N 121.25 E
Ninghe (Lutai) 105 39.20 N 117.48 E
Ninghepu 105 40.43 N 116.07 E
Ninghua 100 26.15 N 116.38 E
Ningi 150 11.04 N 9.32 E
Ningjin, Zhg. 98 37.37 N 114.55 E
Ningjin, Zhg. 98 37.39 N 116.48 E
Ningjing Shan ⋀ 102 29.45 N 98.45 E
Ningling 98 34.27 N 115.21 E
Ningming 102 22.07 N 107.05 E
Ningnan 102 27.11 N 102.36 E
Ningpo → Ningbo 100 29.52 N 121.31 E
Ningqiang 102 32.44 N 106.19 E
Ningshan 102 33.04 N 108.39 E
Ningsia → Yinchuan 102 38.30 N 106.18 E
Ningsia Hui Autonomous Region → Ningxia Huizu Zizhiqu □[4] 102 37.00 N 106.00 E
Ningwu 102 39.01 N 112.21 E
Ningxi 100 28.35 N 121.00 E
Ningxia Huizu Zizhiqu (Ningsia Hui) □[4] 102 37.00 N 106.00 E
Ningxian 102 35.31 N 108.01 E
Ningxiang 100 28.15 N 112.33 E
Ningyang 98 35.47 N 116.47 E
Ningyō-tōge )( 96 35.19 N 133.56 E
Ningyuan 102 25.37 N 111.46 E
Ningyuanbao 102 38.38 N 102.30 E
Ningyuanpu 105 40.44 N 114.54 E
Ninh Binh 110 20.15 N 105.59 E
Ninh Hoa 110 12.29 N 109.08 E
Ninhue 252 36.24 S 72.24 W
Ninigo Group II 164 1.15 S 144.15 E
Ninilchik 180 60.03 N 151.41 W
Ninnescah ≃ 198 37.20 N 97.10 W
Ninnescah, North Fork ≃ 198 37.34 N 97.42 W
Ninnescah, South Fork ≃ 198 37.34 N 97.42 W
Ninnis Glacier Tongue ⊓ 9 68.12 S 147.12 E
Ninocminda 84 41.18 N 43.35 E
Ninohe 92 40.16 N 141.18 E
Ninomiya, Nihon 94 35.18 N 139.16 E
Ninomiya, Nihon 94 36.22 N 139.58 E
Ninove 50 50.50 N 4.01 E
Niny 84 44.29 N 43.57 E
Nio 96 34.12 N 133.39 E
Nioaque 248 21.08 S 55.48 W
Nioaque ≃ 248 20.46 S 56.04 W
Niobe 214 42.01 N 79.27 W
Niobrara 198 42.45 N 98.01 W
Niobrara ≃ 198 42.45 N 98.00 W
Nioka 154 2.10 N 30.39 E
Nioki 152 2.43 S 17.41 E
Niokolo Koba 150 13.04 N 12.43 W
Niokolo Koba, Parc National du ♦ 150 13.00 N 13.00 W
Niono 150 14.15 N 6.00 W
Nionsamoridougou 150 8.43 N 8.50 W
Nioro du Rip 150 13.45 N 15.48 W
Nioro du Sahel 150 15.15 N 9.35 W
Niort 32 46.19 N 0.27 W
Niota 192 35.30 N 84.32 W
Nioût ⊤[4] 150 16.03 N 6.52 W
Nipan 166 24.47 S 150.01 E
Nipāni 122 16.24 N 74.23 E
Nipawin 184 53.22 N 104.00 W
Nipawin Provincial Park ♦ 184 54.00 N 104.40 W
Nipe, Bahía de ⊂ 240p 20.47 N 75.42 W
Nipekamew ≃ 184 54.59 N 104.52 W
Nipekamew Lake ◎ 184 54.24 N 104.58 W
Nipepe 154 14.01 S 37.55 E
Nipigon 190 49.01 N 88.16 W
Nipigon, Lake ◎ 176 49.50 N 88.30 W
Nipigon Bay ⊂ 190 48.53 N 87.50 W
Nipin ≃ 184 55.45 N 109.02 W


| Symbol | English | Deutsch | Español | Français | Português |
| --- | --- | --- | --- | --- | --- |
| ≃ | River | Fluß | Río | Rivière | Rio |
| ≅ | Canal | Kanal | Canal | Canal | Canal |
| ⌞ | Waterfall, Rapids | Wasserfall, Stromschnellen | Cascada, Rápidos | Chute d'eau, Rapides | Cascata, Rápidos |
| ⋓ | Strait | Meeresstraße | Estrecho | Détroit | Estreito |
| ⊂ | Bay, Gulf | Bucht, Golf | Bahía, Golfo | Baie, Golfe | Baía, Golfo |
| ◎ | Lake, Lakes | See, Seen | Lago, Lagos | Lac, Lacs | Lago, Lagos |
| ⁝ | Swamp | Sumpf | Pantano | Marais | Pântano |
| ⊓ | Ice Features, Glacier | Eis- und Gletscherformen | Accidentes Glaciales | Formes glaciaires | Acidentes glaciares |
| ⊤ | Other Hydrographic Features | Andere Hydrographische Objekte | Otros Elementos Hidrográficos | Autres données hydrographiques | Outros acidentes hidrográficos |
| ✣ | Submarine Features | Untermeerische Objekte | Accidentes Submarinos | Formes de relief sous-marin | Acidentes submarinos |
| □ | Political Unit | Politische Einheit | Unidad Politica | Entité politique | Unidade política |
| ᵿ | Cultural Institution | Kulturelle Institution | Institución Cultural | Institution culturelle | Institução cultural |
| ⊥ | Historical Site | Historische Stätte | Sitio Histórico | Site historique | Sitio histórico |
| ♦ | Recreational Site | Erholungs- und Ferienort | Sitio de Recreo | Centre de loisirs | Area de Lazer |
| ⊠ | Airport | Flughafen | Aeropuerto | Aéroport | Aeroporto |
| ▪ | Military Installation | Militäranlage | Instalación Militar | Installation militaire | Instalação militar |
| ◆ | Miscellaneous | Verschiedenes | Misceláneo | Divers | Diversos |

| Name | Page | Lat.°′ | Long.°′ |
|---|---|---|---|
| Nipisi Lake ⊜ | 182 | 55.47 N | 114.57 W |
| Nipissing □[6] | 212 | 45.30 N | 78.50 W |
| Nipissing, Lake ⊜ | 190 | 46.17 N | 80.00 W |
| Nipissis, Lac ⊜ | 186 | 51.02 N | 66.10 W |
| Nipisso, Lac ⊜ | 186 | 50.52 N | 65.50 W |
| Nipomo | 204 | 35.02 N | 120.28 W |
| Nippenicket, Lake ⊜ | 283 | 41.58 N | 71.03 W |
| Nippers Harbour | 186 | 49.48 N | 55.52 W |
| Nippersink Creek ≃ | 216 | 42.23 N | 88.22 W |
| Niqiu | 100 | 33.25 N | 115.38 E |
| Niquelândia | 255 | 14.27 S | 48.27 W |
| Niquero | 240p | 20.03 N | 77.35 W |
| Niquivil | 252 | 30.25 S | 68.42 W |
| Nīr | 128 | 38.02 N | 47.59 E |
| Nīr, Jabal an- ⛰[2] | 128 | 24.10 N | 43.20 E |
| Nīra ≃ | 122 | 17.59 N | 75.07 E |
| Nir'am | 132 | 31.31 N | 34.35 E |
| Nirasaki | 94 | 35.42 N | 138.27 E |
| Nirayama | 94 | 35.03 N | 138.57 E |
| Nirgua | 246 | 10.09 N | 68.34 W |
| Nirim | 132 | 31.20 N | 34.24 E |
| Nirmal | 122 | 19.06 N | 78.21 E |
| Nirmāli | 124 | 26.19 N | 86.35 E |
| Nirsa | 126 | 23.47 N | 86.43 E |
| Niš | 38 | 43.19 N | 21.54 E |
| Nisa | 34 | 39.31 N | 7.39 W |
| Nisāb, Ar. Su. | 128 | 29.11 N | 44.43 E |
| Nisāb, Yaman | 144 | 14.31 N | 46.30 E |
| Nišava ≃ | 38 | 43.22 N | 21.46 E |
| Nisbet | 210 | 41.13 N | 77.07 W |
| Niscemi | 70 | 37.09 N | 14.23 E |
| Nischintāpur | 272b | 22.26 N | 88.22 E |
| Nisf Thānī Bashbīsh | 142 | 31.07 N | 31.11 E |
| Nish → Niš | 38 | 43.19 N | 21.54 E |
| Nishan | 120 | 33.35 N | 85.30 E |
| Nishi ◆[8], Nihon | 268 | 35.27 N | 139.38 E |
| Nishi ◆[8], Nihon | 270 | 34.41 N | 135.30 E |
| Nishiarai ◆[8] | 268 | 35.47 N | 139.47 E |
| Nishiazai | 94 | 35.31 N | 136.10 E |
| Nishibetsuin | 270 | 34.58 N | 135.31 E |
| Nishi-Chūgoku-sanchi-kokutei-kōen ♦ | 96 | 34.40 N | 132.10 E |
| Nishigō | 94 | 37.09 N | 140.10 E |
| Nishiiyayama | 96 | 33.53 N | 133.49 E |
| Nishiizu | 94 | 34.46 N | 138.47 E |
| Nishi-jima I | 96 | 34.39 N | 134.29 E |
| Nishikata | 94 | 36.28 N | 139.45 E |
| Nishikatsura | 94 | 35.31 N | 138.51 E |
| Nishiki | 96 | 34.16 N | 131.57 E |
| Nishiki ≃ | 96 | 34.09 N | 132.15 E |
| Nishikiori | 270 | 34.29 N | 135.34 E |
| Nishikyō ◆[8] | 270 | 34.59 N | 135.40 E |
| Nishimori ◆[8] | 270 | 34.45 N | 135.01 E |
| Nishinari ◆[8] | 270 | 34.38 N | 135.28 E |
| Nishinasuno | 94 | 36.53 N | 139.59 E |
| Nishinomiya | 96 | 34.43 N | 135.20 E |
| Nishinoomote | 93b | 30.44 N | 131.00 E |
| Nishio | 94 | 34.52 N | 137.03 E |
| Nishitoda ◆[8] | 270 | 34.43 N | 135.00 E |
| Nishitosa | 96 | 33.09 N | 132.47 E |
| Nishiwaki | 96 | 34.59 N | 134.58 E |
| Nishiyodogawa ◆[8] | 270 | 34.42 N | 135.27 E |
| Nisinomiya → Nishinomiya | 96 | 34.43 N | 135.20 E |
| Nísiros I | 38 | 36.35 N | 27.10 E |
| Niska Lake ⊜ | 184 | 55.35 N | 108.38 W |
| Niskayuna | 210 | 42.46 N | 73.50 W |
| Nisling ≃ | 180 | 62.27 N | 139.30 W |
| Nismes | 56 | 50.05 N | 4.33 E |
| Nispen | 52 | 51.29 N | 4.28 E |
| Nisporeni | 38 | 47.06 N | 28.11 E |
| Nisqually ≃ | 224 | 47.06 N | 122.42 W |
| Nisqually Indian Reservation ◆[4] | 224 | 47.02 N | 122.42 W |
| Nisqually Reach ⊂ | 224 | 47.07 N | 122.45 W |
| Nissan ≃ | 26 | 56.40 N | 12.51 E |
| Nissequogue | 276 | 40.54 N | 73.12 W |
| Nissequogue ≃ | 276 | 40.54 N | 73.13 W |
| Nissequogue, Northeast Branch ≃ | 276 | 40.50 N | 73.13 W |
| Nissequogue River State Park ♦ | 276 | 40.51 N | 73.13 W |
| Nisser ⊜ | 26 | 59.10 N | 8.30 E |
| Nisshin | 94 | 35.08 N | 137.02 E |
| Nissoria | 70 | 37.39 N | 14.27 E |
| Nissum Bredning ⊂ | 26 | 56.38 N | 8.22 E |
| Nissum Fjord ⊂[2] | 26 | 56.21 N | 8.14 E |
| Nisswa | 190 | 46.31 N | 94.17 W |
| Nistelrode | 52 | 51.43 N | 5.33 E |
| Nister ≃ | 56 | 50.47 N | 7.43 E |
| Nistru (Dnister) ≃ | 78 | 46.18 N | 30.17 E |
| Nisutlin ≃ | 180 | 60.10 N | 132.30 W |
| Nita, Indon. | 115b | 8.40 S | 122.11 E |
| Nita, Nihon | 96 | 35.12 N | 133.01 E |
| Nitalas | 272c | 19.06 N | 73.08 E |
| Nītaure | 76 | 57.10 N | 25.10 E |
| Niterói | 256 | 22.53 S | 43.07 W |
| Niterói □[7] | 287a | 22.56 S | 43.04 W |
| Nith ≃, On., Can. | 212 | 43.12 N | 80.22 W |
| Nith ≃, Scot., U.K. | 44 | 55.00 N | 3.35 W |
| Nithāri | 272a | 28.35 N | 77.21 E |
| Nithāri ◆[8] | 272a | 28.42 N | 77.03 E |
| Nithi River | 182 | 54.01 N | 125.01 W |
| Nithsdale V | 44 | 55.14 N | 3.46 W |
| Nitibe | 112 | 9.19 S | 124.12 E |
| Nitinat | 224 | 48.55 N | 124.29 W |
| Nitinat ≃ | 224 | 48.49 N | 124.37 W |
| Nitinat Lake ⊜ | 182 | 48.45 N | 124.45 W |
| Niton | 42 | 50.35 N | 1.16 W |
| Nitra | 30 | 48.20 N | 18.05 E |
| Nitra ≃ | 30 | 47.46 N | 18.10 E |
| Nitro | 188 | 38.24 N | 81.50 W |
| Nitry | 50 | 47.40 N | 3.53 E |
| Nitta | 94 | 36.17 N | 139.18 E |
| Nittälven ≃ | 40 | 59.51 N | 14.50 E |
| Nittany Mountain ∧ | 210 | 41.00 N | 77.25 W |
| Nittedal | 26 | 60.04 N | 10.53 E |
| Nittenau | 60 | 49.12 N | 12.16 E |
| Nittendorf | 60 | 49.02 N | 11.58 E |
| Niu Aunfo Point › | 174w | 21.04 S | 175.20 W |
| Niubaotun | 105 | 39.46 N | 116.41 E |
| Niubu | 100 | 31.02 N | 117.39 E |
| Niuchutuncun | 104 | 41.28 N | 122.58 E |
| Niudouguang | 100 | 24.51 N | 115.44 E |
| Niue □[2], Oc. | 14 | 19.02 S | 169.52 W |
| Niue □[2], Oc. | 174v | 19.02 S | 169.52 W |
| Niu'erhe | 89 | 51.30 N | 121.49 E |
| Niufentai | 89 | 47.05 N | 120.02 E |
| Niufozhen | 107 | 29.23 N | 105.02 E |
| Niuhang | 100 | 28.44 N | 115.51 E |
| Niuhuaxi | 107 | 29.29 N | 103.48 E |
| Niujie | 102 | 27.47 N | 104.16 E |
| Niujingjie | 110 | 25.46 N | 100.33 E |
| Niuke | 120 | 30.41 N | 82.01 E |
| Niulakita I | 14 | 10.45 S | 179.30 E |
| Niulan ≃ | 102 | 27.28 N | 103.10 E |
| Niulanshan | 105 | 40.13 N | 116.39 E |
| Niumaowu | 98 | 40.58 N | 124.59 E |
| Niupeng | 106 | 31.32 N | 121.50 E |
| Niupichang | 107 | 30.35 N | 103.40 E |
| Niushitun | 98 | 35.18 N | 114.24 E |
| Niut, Gunung ∧ | 112 | 1.00 N | 109.55 E |
| Niutan | 107 | 29.05 N | 105.21 E |
| Niutao I | 14 | 6.06 S | 177.17 E |
| Niuti | 100 | 32.58 N | 113.35 E |
| Niutian | 100 | 27.17 N | 115.44 E |
| Niutoushan | 89 | 45.09 N | 126.45 E |
| Niutou Shan I | 100 | 29.07 N | 121.56 E |
| Niutuo | 105 | 39.15 N | 116.20 E |
| Niutuoshan | 106 | 31.04 N | 119.37 E |
| Niuxichang | 107 | 28.47 N | 104.31 E |
| Niuxintai | 104 | 41.21 N | 123.53 E |
| Niuxintun | 104 | 41.56 N | 121.21 E |
| Niuyuanzi | 105 | 40.20 N | 117.47 E |
| Niuzhuang, Zhg. | 98 | 37.21 N | 118.29 E |
| Niuzhuang, Zhg. | 104 | 40.58 N | 122.32 E |
| Nivå | 41 | 55.56 N | 12.31 E |
| Nivala | 26 | 63.55 N | 24.58 E |
| Nive ≃, Austl. | 166 | 26.02 S | 146.25 E |
| Nive ≃, Fr. | 32 | 43.30 N | 1.29 W |
| Nivelles (Nijvel) | 50 | 50.36 N | 4.20 E |
| Nivernais □[9] | 32 | 47.00 N | 3.30 E |
| Nivernais, Canal du ≊ | 50 | 47.40 N | 3.40 E |
| Niverville, Mb., Can. | 184 | 49.37 N | 97.01 W |
| Niverville, N.Y., U.S. | 210 | 42.26 N | 73.40 W |
| Nivillers | 50 | 49.28 N | 2.10 E |
| Nivnoje | 76 | 53.11 N | 32.35 E |
| Nivskij | 24 | 67.16 N | 32.23 E |
| Niwāno | 128 | 26.22 N | 62.43 E |
| Nixa | 194 | 37.02 N | 93.17 W |
| Nixi | 102 | 27.58 N | 99.27 E |
| Nixis | 107 | 30.08 N | 106.19 E |
| Nixizhen | 107 | 29.02 N | 104.16 E |
| Nixon, Nv., U.S. | 204 | 39.49 N | 119.21 W |
| Nixon, Pa., U.S. | 214 | 40.45 N | 79.56 W |
| Nixon, Tx., U.S. | 222 | 29.16 N | 97.45 W |
| Niyodo | 96 | 33.32 N | 133.08 E |
| Niyodo ≃ | 96 | 33.27 N | 133.29 E |
| Niyor | 114 | 2.05 N | 103.17 E |
| Niyu Shan I | 100 | 27.51 N | 121.03 E |
| Niža | 24 | 66.20 N | 43.16 E |
| Nizāmābād | 122 | 18.40 N | 78.07 E |
| Nizamghāt | 120 | 28.16 N | 95.42 E |
| Nizām Sāgar ⊜[1] | 122 | 18.10 N | 77.55 E |
| Nīzgān ≃ | 128 | 33.13 N | 63.40 E |
| Nizhniy Tagil → Nižnij Tagil | 86 | 57.55 N | 59.57 E |
| Nizhyn | 78 | 51.03 N | 31.54 E |
| Nizino | 265a | 59.50 N | 29.53 E |
| Nizip | 130 | 37.01 N | 37.46 E |
| Nízke Tatry ⛰ | 30 | 48.54 N | 19.40 E |
| Nízke Tatry, národní park ♦ | 30 | 47.48 N | 19.35 E |
| Nižn'aja | 80 | 56.34 N | 49.07 E |
| Nižn'aja Čvorovaja | 86 | 59.11 N | 77.31 E |
| Nižnaja Dobrinka | 80 | 50.18 N | 45.42 E |
| Nižn'aja Grajvoronka | 78 | 51.47 N | 37.45 E |
| Nižn'aja Irga | 86 | 56.51 N | 57.26 E |
| Nižn'aja Karelina | 88 | 57.55 N | 107.44 E |
| Nižn'aja Keul'skaja, šivera ∟ | 88 | 58.25 N | 102.46 E |
| Nižnaja Matrenka | 80 | 52.16 N | 40.06 E |
| Nižn'aja Omka | 86 | 55.26 N | 74.55 E |
| Nižn'aja Omra | 24 | 62.46 N | 55.46 E |
| Nižn'aja Ošma | 80 | 55.44 N | 51.18 E |
| Nižn'aja Peša | 24 | 66.43 N | 47.36 E |
| Nižn'aja Pojma | 88 | 56.11 N | 97.13 E |
| Nižn'aja Pokrovka | 80 | 51.40 N | 50.07 E |
| Nižn'aja Šachtama | 88 | 51.24 N | 117.40 E |
| Nižn'aja Salda | 86 | 58.05 N | 60.43 E |
| Nižn'aja Syzran' | 80 | 53.04 N | 48.34 E |
| Nižn'aja Tavda | 86 | 57.40 N | 66.12 E |
| Nižn'aja Tunguska ≃ | 74 | 65.48 N | 88.04 E |
| Nižn'aja Tura | 86 | 58.37 N | 59.49 E |
| Nižn'aja Vol'dža | 86 | 58.19 N | 79.20 E |
| Nižn'aja Zaimka | 88 | 56.09 N | 98.14 E |
| Nižneangarsk | 88 | 55.47 N | 109.33 E |
| Nižnebakanskij | 78 | 44.52 N | 37.52 E |
| Nižnečujskij | 85 | 43.12 N | 74.21 E |
| Nižnedevick | 78 | 51.33 N | 38.20 E |
| Nižne-Gnilovskoj ◆[8] | 83 | 47.11 N | 39.36 E |
| Nižnegnutov | 80 | 48.02 N | 42.22 E |
| Nižneilimsk | 88 | 57.11 N | 103.16 E |
| Nižneje Al'kejevo | 80 | 54.46 N | 50.03 E |
| Nižn'eje Gir'unino | 88 | 51.12 N | 116.58 E |
| Nižneje Kučukovo | 80 | 56.13 N | 52.57 E |
| Nižneje Kujto, ozero ⊜ | 24 | 64.58 N | 31.38 E |
| Nižneje M'ačkovo | 82 | 55.33 N | 37.59 E |
| Nižneje Romanovo | 86 | 59.47 N | 69.35 E |
| Nižneje Sančelejevo | 80 | 53.40 N | 49.27 E |
| Nižnekamsk | 80 | 55.32 N | 51.58 E |
| Nižnekamskoje vodochranilišče ⊜[1] | 24 | 55.50 N | 53.00 E |
| Nižnekundr'učen-Skaja | 80 | 47.45 N | 40.57 E |
| Nižnelemskij | 24 | 64.01 N | 56.16 E |
| Nižne-Mit'akin Pervyj | 83 | 48.41 N | 40.02 E |
| Nižne-Nagol'naja | 83 | 49.00 N | 39.59 E |
| Nižneoz'ornoje | 80 | 51.37 N | 53.56 E |
| Nižne-Podpol'nyj | 83 | 47.12 N | 40.01 E |
| Nižnetambovskoje | 89 | 50.54 N | 138.13 E |
| Nižnetroickij | 80 | 54.20 N | 53.41 E |
| Nižneudinsk | 88 | 54.54 N | 99.03 E |
| Nižnevartovsk | 74 | 60.56 N | 76.31 E |
| Nižnij Baskunčak | 80 | 48.13 N | 46.50 E |
| Nižnij Časučej | 88 | 50.31 N | 115.08 E |
| Nižnij Čir | 80 | 48.22 N | 43.03 E |
| Nižnij Čulym | 86 | 54.37 N | 78.56 E |
| Nižnije Černi | 80 | 47.41 N | 43.26 E |
| Nižnije Čeršely | 80 | 54.40 N | 52.08 E |
| Nižnije Ostrovcy | 82 | 55.35 N | 38.01 E |
| Nižnije Sergi | 86 | 56.40 N | 59.18 E |
| Nižnije Timers'any | 80 | 54.34 N | 47.45 E |
| Nižnije V'azovyje | 80 | 55.49 N | 48.32 E |
| Nižnij Ingaš | 88 | 56.12 N | 96.31 E |
| Nižnij Kisl'aj | 78 | 50.50 N | 40.11 E |
| Nižnij Kuranach | 74 | 58.49 N | 125.32 E |
| Nižnij Lomov | 80 | 53.32 N | 43.41 E |
| Nižnij Mamon | 78 | 50.11 N | 40.30 E |
| Nižnij Novgorod (Gorky) | 80 | 56.20 N | 44.00 E |
| Nižnij Novgorod Oblast' □[4] | 80 | 56.30 N | 45.00 E |
| Nižnij Odes | 24 | 63.40 N | 54.52 E |
| Nižnij Ol'šan | 78 | 50.45 N | 38.55 E |
| Nižnij P'andž | 120 | 37.08 N | 68.32 E |
| Nižnij Paramonov | 80 | 47.57 N | 41.55 E |
| Nižnij Šerebr'akov | 80 | 47.58 N | 41.02 E |
| Nižnij Škaft | 80 | 53.36 N | 45.40 E |
| Nižnij Stan | 88 | 52.18 N | 115.44 E |
| Nižnij Tagil | 86 | 57.55 N | 59.57 E |
| Nižnij Takanyš | 80 | 55.57 N | 51.04 E |
| Nižnij Ufalej | 86 | 55.55 N | 59.59 E |
| Nižnij V'aloz'orskij | 24 | 66.44 N | 35.10 E |
| Nizwā | 128 | 22.56 N | 57.32 E |
| Nizy-le-Comte | 50 | 49.34 N | 4.03 E |
| Nizza Monferrato | 62 | 44.46 N | 8.21 E |
| Nizzana | 132 | 30.53 N | 34.27 E |
| Nizzana, Nahal V | 132 | 30.57 N | 34.23 E |
| Nizzanim | 132 | 31.43 N | 34.38 E |
| Njassa-See → Nyasa, Lake ⊜ | 154 | 12.00 S | 34.30 E |
| Njasviž | 76 | 53.13 N | 26.40 E |
| Njazidja (Grande Comore) I | 157a | 11.35 S | 43.20 E |
| Njinjo | 154 | 8.48 S | 38.54 E |
| Njoko ≃ | 152 | 17.10 S | 24.05 E |
| Njombe | 154 | 9.20 S | 34.46 E |
| Njombe ≃ | 154 | 6.56 S | 35.06 E |
| Njupeskär ∟ | 26 | 61.38 N | 12.41 E |
| Njurunda | 26 | 62.16 N | 17.22 E |
| Nkambe | 152 | 6.38 N | 10.40 E |
| Nkandla | 158 | 28.37 S | 31.05 E |
| Nkawkaw | 150 | 6.33 N | 0.47 W |
| Nkayi | 154 | 19.00 S | 28.54 E |
| Nkhata Bay | 154 | 11.33 S | 34.18 E |
| Nkhotakota | 154 | 12.57 S | 34.17 E |
| Nkolabona | 152 | 1.14 N | 11.43 E |
| Nkomi, Lagune ⊂ | 152 | 1.35 S | 9.17 E |
| Nkongsamba | 152 | 4.57 N | 9.56 E |
| Nkonko | 154 | 6.20 S | 34.58 E |
| Nkoso | 152 | 2.42 S | 22.39 E |
| Nkoto | 152 | 1.56 S | 19.41 E |
| Nkunga | 152 | 4.41 S | 18.34 E |
| Nkurenkuru | 152 | 17.38 S | 18.35 E |
| Nkwalini | 158 | 28.45 S | 31.33 E |
| Nmai ≃ | 102 | 25.42 N | 97.30 E |
| Nnewi | 150 | 6.00 N | 6.59 E |
| Nō | 94 | 37.06 N | 137.59 E |
| Noābād | 272b | 22.34 N | 88.31 E |
| Noailles | 50 | 49.20 N | 2.12 E |
| Noākhāli | 124 | 22.49 N | 91.06 E |
| Noak Hill ◆[8] | 260 | 51.37 N | 0.14 E |
| Noale | 64 | 45.32 N | 12.04 E |
| Noāmundi | 124 | 22.09 N | 85.32 E |
| Noank | 207 | 41.19 N | 71.59 W |
| Noarlunga | 168b | 35.11 S | 138.30 E |
| Noasca | 62 | 45.27 N | 7.19 E |
| Noatak | 180 | 67.34 N | 162.59 W |
| Noatak ≃ | 180 | 67.00 N | 162.30 W |
| Nobby | 171a | 27.51 S | 151.54 E |
| Nobel | 212 | 45.25 N | 80.06 W |
| Nobeoka | 92 | 32.35 N | 131.40 E |
| Nobidome | 268 | 35.48 N | 139.35 E |
| Nobidome-yōsui ≊[1] | 268 | 35.44 N | 139.27 E |
| Nōbi-heiya ≚ | 94 | 35.15 N | 136.45 E |
| Nobili | 150 | 11.33 N | 1.12 W |
| Nobitz | 54 | 50.58 N | 12.29 E |
| Noble, Il., U.S. | 194 | 38.41 N | 88.13 W |
| Noble, Ok., U.S. | 196 | 35.08 N | 97.23 W |
| Noble □[6] | 216 | 41.24 N | 85.25 W |
| Noble Park | 274b | 37.58 S | 145.10 E |
| Noblestown | 279b | 40.24 N | 80.12 W |
| Noblesville | 218 | 40.02 N | 86.00 W |
| Nobleton, On., Can. | 212 | 43.54 N | 79.40 W |
| Nobleton, Fl., U.S. | 220 | 28.38 N | 82.15 W |
| Noboribetsu | 92a | 42.27 N | 141.11 E |
| Noborito | 268 | 35.37 N | 139.34 E |
| Nobres | 248 | 14.44 S | 56.20 W |
| Nobsa | 246 | 5.46 N | 72.57 W |
| Nocatee | 220 | 27.09 N | 81.52 W |
| Noccundra | 166 | 27.50 S | 142.36 E |
| Nocé | 50 | 48.22 N | 0.42 E |
| Noce ≃ | 64 | 46.09 N | 11.04 E |
| Nocera Inferiore | 68 | 40.44 N | 14.38 E |
| Nocera Superiore | 68 | 40.44 N | 14.40 E |
| Nocera Tirinese | 68 | 39.02 N | 16.09 E |
| Nocera Umbra | 66 | 43.05 N | 12.47 E |
| Noceto | 64 | 44.48 N | 10.11 E |
| Nochistlán | 234 | 21.22 N | 102.51 W |
| Nochten | 54 | 51.26 N | 14.36 E |
| Noci | 68 | 40.48 N | 17.08 E |
| Nociglia | 68 | 40.02 N | 18.20 E |
| Nockamixon Lake ⊜[1] | 208 | 40.28 N | 75.14 W |
| Nockamixon State Park ♦ | 208 | 40.27 N | 75.16 W |
| Nockatunga | 166 | 27.43 S | 142.43 E |
| Nocona | 196 | 33.47 N | 97.43 W |
| Nocupétaro | 234 | 18.48 N | 101.04 W |
| Noda | 94 | 35.56 N | 139.52 E |
| Nodagawa | 96 | 35.31 N | 135.06 E |
| Nodaway ≃ | 194 | 39.54 N | 94.58 W |
| Nodera | 270 | 34.45 N | 134.56 E |
| Nods | 58 | 47.06 N | 6.20 E |
| Noé, Ouadi V | 146 | 15.39 N | 21.19 E |
| Noel | 194 | 36.32 N | 94.29 W |
| Noenieput | 158 | 27.29 S | 20.06 E |
| Noepoli | 68 | 40.05 N | 16.20 E |
| Noer | 41 | 54.27 N | 10.00 E |
| Noetinger | 252 | 32.22 S | 62.19 W |
| Nœux-les-Mines | 50 | 50.29 N | 2.40 E |
| Nofels | 58 | 47.15 N | 9.34 E |
| Nogah | 132 | 31.37 N | 34.42 E |
| Nogajskaja step' ≚ | 84 | 44.17 N | 46.05 E |
| Nogales, Chile | 252 | 32.44 S | 71.15 W |
| Nogales, Méx. | 232 | 31.20 N | 110.56 W |
| Nogales, Méx. | 234 | 18.49 N | 97.10 W |
| Nogales, Az., U.S. | 200 | 31.20 N | 110.56 W |
| Nogami | 94 | 36.07 N | 139.07 E |
| Nogangjin | 98 | 39.30 N | 125.23 E |
| Nogara, It. | 64 | 45.11 N | 11.04 E |
| Nogara, Ityo. | 144 | 13.53 N | 36.32 E |
| Nogaro | 32 | 43.46 N | 0.02 W |
| Nōgata | 96 | 33.44 N | 130.44 E |
| Nogent-en-Bassigny | 58 | 48.02 N | 5.21 E |
| Nogent-le-Roi | 50 | 48.39 N | 1.32 E |
| Nogent-le-Rotrou | 50 | 48.19 N | 0.50 E |
| Nogent-sur-Marne | 261 | 48.50 N | 2.29 E |
| Nogent-sur-Oise | 50 | 49.16 N | 2.28 E |
| Nogent-sur-Seine | 50 | 48.29 N | 3.30 E |
| Nogent-sur-Vernisson | 50 | 47.51 N | 2.45 E |
| Nogi | 94 | 36.14 N | 139.44 E |
| Nogies Creek ≃ | 212 | 44.35 N | 78.31 W |
| Noginsk | 82 | 55.51 N | 38.27 E |
| Nogisaki | 268 | 35.57 N | 139.58 E |
| Nogliki | 89 | 51.48 N | 143.10 E |
| Nogmung | 102 | 27.30 N | 97.49 E |
| Nogoa ≃ | 166 | 23.33 S | 148.32 E |
| Nōgohaku-san ∧ | 94 | 35.46 N | 136.31 E |
| Nogoon Nuur | 86 | 49.33 N | 90.17 E |
| Nogoyá | 252 | 32.24 S | 59.48 W |
| Nógrád □[6] | 30 | 48.00 N | 19.35 E |
| Noguera Pallaresa ≃ | 34 | 42.15 N | 0.54 E |
| Noguera Ribagorzana ≃ | 34 | 41.40 N | 0.43 E |
| Nohain ≃ | 50 | 47.24 N | 2.55 E |
| Nohar | 123 | 29.11 N | 74.46 E |
| Noheji | 92 | 40.52 N | 141.08 E |
| Nohfelden | 56 | 49.35 N | 7.09 E |
| Nohili Point › | 229b | 22.04 N | 159.47 W |
| Nohjhīl | 124 | 27.51 N | 77.39 E |
| Nohta | 124 | 23.40 N | 79.34 E |
| Nohwa-do I | 98 | 34.12 N | 126.35 E |
| Noia | 34 | 42.47 N | 8.53 W |
| Noicattaro | 68 | 41.02 N | 16.59 E |
| Noichi | 96 | 33.33 N | 133.42 E |
| Noir, Causse ⛰[1] | 32 | 44.10 N | 3.15 E |
| Noir, Isla I | 254 | 54.29 S | 73.02 W |
| Noire ≃, P.Q., Can. | 190 | 45.54 N | 76.57 W |
| Noire ≃, P.Q., Can. | 206 | 45.33 N | 72.58 W |
| Noire ≃, P.Q., Can. | 206 | 46.39 N | 72.08 W |
| Noire, Mer du → Black Sea ⊤[2] | 22 | 43.00 N | 35.00 E |
| Noire, Montagne ∧ | 206 | 46.14 N | 74.18 W |
| Noire, Montagne ⛰ | 32 | 43.28 N | 2.18 E |
| Noirétable | 62 | 45.49 N | 3.46 E |
| Noirmoutier | 32 | 47.00 N | 2.14 W |
| Noirmoutier, Île de I | 32 | 47.00 N | 2.15 W |
| Noiseau | 261 | 48.47 N | 2.33 E |
| Noisiel | 261 | 48.51 N | 2.37 E |
| Noisy ≃ | 212 | 44.19 N | 80.08 W |
| Noisy-le-Grand | 261 | 48.51 N | 2.33 E |
| Noisy-le-Roi | 261 | 48.51 N | 2.04 E |
| Noisy-le-Sec | 261 | 48.53 N | 2.28 E |
| Nojember'an | 84 | 41.12 N | 45.01 E |
| Nojima-zaki › | 94 | 34.56 N | 139.53 E |
| Nojiri-ko ⊜ | 94 | 36.49 N | 138.13 E |
| Nojon | 102 | 43.10 N | 102.07 E |
| Nojon uul ⛰ | 102 | 43.10 N | 101.30 E |
| Nokami | 96 | 34.15 N | 135.20 E |
| Nokaneng | 156 | 19.40 S | 22.16 E |
| Nōke | 270 | 34.26 N | 135.29 E |
| Nokha Mandi | 120 | 27.35 N | 73.29 E |
| Nokia | 26 | 61.28 N | 23.30 E |
| Nokilalaki, Bulu ∧ | 112 | 1.13 S | 120.08 E |
| Nok Kundi | 128 | 28.46 N | 62.46 E |
| Nokogiri-yama ∧[2] | 268 | 35.09 N | 139.51 E |
| Nokomis, Sk., Can. | 184 | 51.30 N | 105.00 W |
| Nokomis, Fl., U.S. | 220 | 27.07 N | 82.26 W |
| Nokomis, Il., U.S. | 219 | 39.18 N | 89.17 W |
| Nokomis Lake ⊜ | 184 | 56.58 N | 103.02 W |
| Nokou | 146 | 14.35 N | 14.47 E |
| Nokpan-ni ◆[8] | 271b | 37.36 N | 126.56 E |
| Nokrek ∧ | 124 | 25.27 N | 90.20 E |
| Nokuku | 175f | 14.53 S | 166.35 E |
| Nola, Centraf. | 152 | 3.32 N | 16.04 E |
| Nola, It. | 68 | 40.55 N | 14.33 E |
| Nolan ≃ | 222 | 32.07 N | 97.26 W |
| Nolan Creek ≃ | 222 | 31.02 N | 97.26 W |
| Nolands Fork ≃ | 218 | 39.41 N | 85.07 W |
| Nolanville | 222 | 31.05 N | 97.36 W |
| Nolay | 58 | 46.57 N | 4.38 E |
| Nole | 62 | 45.15 N | 7.35 E |
| Noli | 62 | 44.12 N | 8.26 E |
| Noli, Capo di › | 62 | 44.12 N | 8.25 E |
| Nolichucky ≃ | 192 | 36.07 N | 83.14 W |
| Nolin ≃ | 194 | 37.13 N | 86.15 W |
| Nolin Lake ⊜[1] | 194 | 37.20 N | 86.10 W |
| Nolinsk | 80 | 57.33 N | 49.57 E |
| Nomad | 164 | 6.18 S | 142.14 E |
| Nomahegan Brook ≃ | 276 | 40.41 N | 74.18 W |
| Nomans Land I | 207 | 41.15 N | 70.49 W |
| Nombre de Dios, Méx. | 234 | 23.51 N | 104.14 W |
| Nombre de Dios, Pan. | 236 | 9.35 N | 79.28 W |
| Nombre de Dios, Cordillera ⛰ | 236 | 15.35 N | 86.55 W |
| Nome | 180 | 64.30 N | 165.24 W |
| Nomény | 56 | 48.54 N | 6.14 E |
| Nomexy | 58 | 48.18 N | 6.23 E |
| Nomgon, Mong. | 102 | 45.26 N | 105.08 E |
| Nomgon, Mong. | 102 | 42.50 N | 105.07 E |
| Nomgon uul ⛰ | 102 | 42.50 N | 104.20 E |
| Nomingue, Petit lac ⊜ | 206 | 46.21 N | 75.00 W |
| Nomini Bay ⊂ | 208 | 38.09 N | 76.43 W |
| Nominingue | 206 | 46.24 N | 75.02 W |
| Nominingue, Lac ⊜ | 206 | 46.26 N | 74.59 W |
| Nomoneas II | 175c | 7.24 N | 151.53 E |
| Nomozaki | 92 | 32.35 N | 129.45 E |
| Nomtsas | 156 | 24.22 S | 16.47 E |
| Nomura | 96 | 33.22 N | 132.38 E |
| Nona, Lake ⊜ | 220 | 28.24 N | 81.15 W |
| Nonacho Lake ⊜ | 176 | 61.42 N | 109.40 W |
| Nonancourt | 50 | 48.46 N | 1.12 E |
| Nonant-le-Pin | 50 | 48.42 N | 0.13 E |
| Nonantola | 64 | 44.41 N | 11.02 E |
| Nonburg | 24 | 65.34 N | 50.32 E |
| Nonceveux | 56 | 50.28 N | 5.44 E |
| Nondalton | 180 | 60.00 N | 154.49 W |
| Nondwa | 154 | 6.26 S | 35.20 E |
| Nondweni | 158 | 28.11 S | 30.49 E |
| None | 62 | 44.56 N | 7.32 E |
| Nonette ≃ | 50 | 49.12 N | 2.24 E |
| None-yama ∧ | 96 | 33.29 N | 134.10 E |
| Nong'an | 89 | 44.25 N | 125.10 E |
| Nong Bua Lamphu | 110 | 17.11 N | 102.25 E |
| Nong Han | 110 | 17.21 N | 103.07 E |
| Nong Hèt | 110 | 19.29 N | 103.59 E |
| Nong Khai | 110 | 17.52 N | 102.44 E |
| Nongoma | 158 | 27.58 S | 31.35 E |
| Nongpoh | 120 | 25.54 N | 91.53 E |
| Nongstoin | 120 | 25.31 N | 91.16 E |
| Nonnenhorn | 58 | 47.34 N | 9.36 E |
| Nonnevitz | 54 | 54.39 N | 13.17 E |
| Nonning | 166 | 32.30 S | 136.30 E |
| Nonnweiler | 56 | 49.36 N | 6.58 E |
| Nono | 144 | 8.32 N | 37.26 E |
| Nonoai | 252 | 27.21 S | 52.47 W |
| Nonoava | 232 | 27.28 N | 106.44 W |
| Nonoc Island I | 116 | 9.51 N | 125.37 E |
| Nono de Julho, Túnel ◆[5] | 287b | 23.34 S | 46.39 W |
| Nonogasta | 252 | 29.18 S | 67.30 W |
| Nonoichi | 94 | 36.32 N | 136.37 E |
| Nonouti I[1] | 14 | 0.40 S | 174.21 E |
| Nonsan | 98 | 36.12 N | 127.05 E |
| Nonsuch Bay ⊂ | 240c | 17.03 N | 61.42 W |
| Non Sung | 110 | 15.11 N | 102.16 E |
| Nonthaburi | 110 | 13.50 N | 100.29 E |
| Nonthaburi □[4] | 269a | 13.52 N | 100.27 E |
| Nontron | 32 | 45.32 N | 0.40 E |
| Nonvianuk Lake ⊜ | 180 | 59.00 N | 155.15 W |
| Noojee | 169 | 37.55 S | 146.00 E |
| Nookawarra | 162 | 26.19 S | 116.52 E |
| Nooksack | 224 | 48.55 N | 122.19 W |
| Nooksack ≃ | 224 | 48.46 N | 122.35 W |
| Nooksack, Middle Fork ≃ | 224 | 48.50 N | 122.08 W |
| Nooksack, North Fork ≃ | 224 | 48.50 N | 122.11 W |
| Nooksack, South Fork ≃ | 224 | 48.50 N | 122.11 W |
| Noonamah | 164 | 12.38 S | 131.04 E |
| Noonan | 198 | 48.53 N | 103.00 W |
| Noon Hill ∧[2] | 283 | 42.09 N | 71.19 W |
| Noonkanbah | 162 | 18.30 S | 124.50 E |
| Noorat | 169 | 38.12 S | 142.56 E |
| Noord-Beveland I | 52 | 51.35 N | 3.45 E |
| Noord-Brabant □[4] | 52 | 51.30 N | 5.00 E |
| Noord-Holland □[4] | 52 | 52.40 N | 4.50 E |
| Noordhollands Kanaal ≊ | 52 | 52.33 N | 4.50 E |
| Noordhorn | 52 | 53.16 N | 6.24 E |
| Noordoewer | 156 | 28.45 S | 17.37 E |
| Noordoost Polder ◆[1] | 52 | 52.42 N | 5.45 E |
| Noordpunt › | 241s | 12.23 N | 69.10 W |
| Noord-Scharwoude | 52 | 52.43 N | 4.47 E |
| Noordwijk aan Zee | 52 | 52.14 N | 4.26 E |
| Noordwijk-Binnen | 52 | 52.13 N | 4.27 E |
| Noordwijkerhout | 52 | 52.15 N | 4.30 E |
| Noordwolde | 52 | 52.54 N | 6.09 E |
| Noormarkku | 26 | 61.35 N | 21.52 E |
| Noorvik | 180 | 66.50 N | 161.12 W |
| Noosaville | 166 | 26.24 S | 153.04 E |
| Nootka Island I | 182 | 49.32 N | 126.42 W |
| Nootka Sound Ʉ | 182 | 49.33 N | 126.38 W |
| Nopaltepec | 234 | 18.17 N | 95.59 W |
| No Point, Point › | 276 | 41.09 N | 73.08 W |
| Nóqui | 152 | 5.51 S | 13.25 E |
| Nora, Sve. | 40 | 59.31 N | 15.02 E |
| Nora, In., U.S. | 218 | 39.55 N | 86.08 W |
| Nora ≃ | 89 | 52.26 N | 129.58 E |
| Nora ⊥ | 71 | 39.00 N | 9.01 E |
| Nor Ačin | 84 | 40.19 N | 44.35 E |
| Norah Head › | 170 | 33.17 S | 151.35 E |
| Nora Islands II | 144 | 16.02 N | 40.03 E |
| Norala | 116 | 6.28 N | 124.38 E |
| Noralee | 182 | 53.59 N | 126.26 W |
| Noranda | 190 | 48.15 N | 79.02 W |
| Noraskög ⛰ | 40 | 59.39 N | 14.50 E |
| Nora Springs | 190 | 43.08 N | 93.00 W |
| Norberg | 40 | 60.04 N | 15.56 E |
| Norberto de la Riestra | 252 | 35.16 S | 59.46 W |
| Norborne | 194 | 39.18 N | 93.40 W |
| Norcan Lake ⊜ | 212 | 45.10 N | 76.53 W |
| Norcatur | 198 | 39.50 N | 100.11 W |
| Norchia ⊥ | 66 | 42.20 N | 11.57 E |
| Norcia | 66 | 42.48 N | 13.05 E |
| Norco | 228 | 33.56 N | 117.33 W |
| Norcott, Mount ∧ | 162 | 32.07 S | 121.59 E |
| Norcross | 192 | 33.56 N | 84.12 W |
| Nord □[4], Cam. | 146 | 9.00 N | 13.30 E |
| Nord □[4], N. Cal. | 175f | 21.00 S | 165.00 E |
| Nord □[5] | 50 | 50.20 N | 3.40 E |
| Nord, Canal du ≊ | 50 | 50.16 N | 3.05 E |
| Nord, Cap → Nordkapp › | 24 | 71.11 N | 25.48 E |
| Nord, Gare ◆[5] | 261 | 48.53 N | 2.21 E |
| Nord, Grand lac du ⊜ | 186 | 50.54 N | 67.06 W |
| Nord, Petit lac du ⊜ | 186 | 50.50 N | 67.10 W |
| Nord, Rivière du ≃ | 206 | 45.31 N | 74.20 W |
| Nordamerika → North America ⊥[1] | 16 | 45.00 N | 100.00 W |
| Nordanholen | 40 | 60.30 N | 14.57 E |
| Nordausques | 50 | 50.49 N | 2.05 E |
| Nordaustlandet I | 12 | 79.48 N | 22.24 E |
| Nordbögge | 263 | 51.37 N | 7.44 E |
| Nordborg | 41 | 55.03 N | 9.45 E |
| Nordby | 41 | 55.58 N | 10.34 E |
| Nord Dakota → North Dakota □[3] | 198 | 47.30 N | 100.15 W |
| Norddeich | 52 | 53.37 N | 7.09 E |
| Nordegg | 182 | 52.28 N | 116.04 W |
| Nordegg ≃ | 182 | 52.53 N | 115.18 W |
| Norden, Dtsch. | 52 | 53.36 N | 7.12 E |
| Norden, Eng., U.K. | 262 | 53.38 N | 2.13 W |
| Norden, Ca., U.S. | 226 | 39.20 N | 120.22 W |
| Nordendorf | 56 | 48.36 N | 10.50 E |
| Nordenham | 52 | 53.29 N | 8.28 E |
| Nordenšel'da, archipelag II | 74 | 76.45 N | 96.00 E |
| Nordenskiold ≃ | 180 | 62.05 N | 136.18 W |
| Norderney | 52 | 53.42 N | 7.08 E |
| Norderney I | 52 | 53.42 N | 7.10 E |
| Norderstapel | 41 | 54.21 N | 9.14 E |
| Norderstedt | 52 | 53.43 N | 10.00 E |
| Nordfjord ⊂[2] | 26 | 61.54 N | 5.12 E |
| Nordfjordeid | 26 | 61.54 N | 6.00 E |
| Nordfold | 24 | 67.46 N | 15.12 E |
| Nordfriesische Inseln → North Frisian Islands II | 24 | 54.50 N | 8.12 E |
| Nordfriesland ◆[1] | 41 | 54.40 N | 9.10 E |
| Nordhalben | 54 | 50.22 N | 11.30 E |
| Nordhausen | 54 | 51.30 N | 10.47 E |
| Nordheim, Dtsch. | 56 | 49.07 N | 9.08 E |


ENGLISH


| Name | Page | Lat.°′ | Long.°′ |
|---|---|---|---|
| Nordheim, Tx., U.S. | 222 | 28.55 N | 97.36 W |
| Nordheim von der Rhön | 56 | 50.28 N | 10.11 E |
| Nordhelle ∧[2] | 263 | 51.09 N | 7.46 E |
| Nordholz | 52 | 53.47 N | 8.36 E |
| Nordhorn | 52 | 52.27 N | 7.05 E |
| Nordic Park | 278 | 41.57 N | 88.02 W |
| Nordingrå | 26 | 62.56 N | 18.16 E |
| Nordirland → Northern Ireland □[8] | 48 | 54.40 N | 6.45 W |
| Nordiyya | 132 | 32.19 N | 34.54 E |
| Nordkanal ≊ | 263 | 51.10 N | 6.42 E |
| Nordkapp › | 24 | 71.11 N | 25.48 E |
| Nordkinnhalvøya ›[1] | 24 | 70.55 N | 27.45 E |
| Nordkirchen | 52 | 51.44 N | 7.31 E |
| Nord-Kivu □[4] | 154 | 0.30 S | 28.30 E |
| Nordkjosbotn | 24 | 69.13 N | 19.30 E |
| Nord-Korea → Korea, North □[1] | 98 | 40.00 N | 127.00 E |
| Nordland | 224 | 48.03 N | 122.41 W |
| Nordland □[6] | 24 | 67.00 N | 14.40 E |
| Nördliche Dwina → Severnaja Dvina ≃ | 24 | 64.32 N | 40.30 E |
| Nördliches Eismeer → Arctic Ocean ⊤[1] | 16 | 85.00 N | 170.00 E |
| Nördlingen | 56 | 48.51 N | 10.30 E |
| Nordmaling | 26 | 63.34 N | 19.30 E |
| Nordmark | 40 | 59.50 N | 14.06 E |
| Nordmarka ◆[1] | 26 | 60.00 N | 10.25 E |
| Nordostrundingen › | 16 | 81.36 N | 12.09 W |
| Nord-Ostsee-Kanal ≊ | 30 | 53.53 N | 9.08 E |
| Nord-Ouest □[4] | 152 | 6.30 N | 10.30 E |
| Nordpfälzer Bergland ⛰ | 56 | 49.40 N | 7.40 E |
| Nordradde ≃ | 52 | 52.43 N | 7.17 E |
| Nordreisa | 24 | 69.46 N | 21.03 E |
| Nordre Strømfjord ⊂[2] | 176 | 67.50 N | 52.00 W |
| Nordrhein-Westfalen □[3] | 30 | 51.30 N | 7.30 E |
| Nordsee → North Sea ⊤[2] | 22 | 55.20 N | 3.00 E |
| Nordstemmen | 52 | 52.09 N | 9.46 E |
| Nordstrand I | 41 | 54.30 N | 8.53 E |
| Nordstrandischmoor I | 41 | 54.33 N | 8.48 E |
| Nord-Trøndelag □[6] | 24 | 64.25 N | 12.00 E |
| Nordvik | 74 | 74.02 N | 111.32 E |
| Nordwalde | 52 | 52.05 N | 7.28 E |
| Nordwest-Kap → North West Cape › | 162 | 21.45 S | 114.10 E |
| Nore | 26 | 60.10 N | 9.01 E |
| Nore ≃ | 48 | 52.25 N | 6.58 W |
| Noremberg → Nürnberg | 60 | 49.27 N | 11.04 E |
| Norf | 263 | 51.09 N | 6.43 E |
| Norf ≃ | 263 | 51.11 N | 6.44 E |
| Norfolk, Ct., U.S. | 207 | 41.59 N | 73.12 W |
| Norfolk, Ma., U.S. | 283 | 42.07 N | 71.19 W |
| Norfolk, Ne., U.S. | 198 | 42.02 N | 97.25 W |
| Norfolk, Va., U.S. | 208 | 36.50 N | 76.17 W |
| Norfolk □[6], Eng., U.K. | 42 | 52.35 N | 1.00 E |
| Norfolk □[6], Ma., U.S. | 207 | 42.10 N | 71.15 W |
| Norfolk Broads ◆[1] | 42 | 52.40 N | 1.30 E |
| Norfolk-Insel → Norfolk Island □[2] | 174c | 29.02 S | 167.57 E |
| Norfolk International Airport ⊠ | 208 | 36.54 N | 76.12 W |
| Norfolk Island □[2], Oc. | 14 | 29.02 S | 167.57 E |
| Norfolk Island □[2], Oc. | 174c | 29.02 S | 167.57 E |
| Norfolk Island Aerodrome ⊠ | 174c | 29.03 S | 167.56 E |
| Norfolk Naval Shipyard ■ | 208 | 36.49 N | 76.18 W |
| Norfolk Naval Station ■ | 208 | 36.57 N | 76.18 W |
| Norfolk Ridge ✧[3] | 14 | 29.00 S | 168.00 E |
| Norfork Lake ⊜[1] | 194 | 36.25 N | 92.10 W |
| Norg | 52 | 53.04 N | 6.27 E |
| Norge | 208 | 37.22 N | 76.46 W |
| Norge → Norway □[1] | 24 | 62.00 N | 10.00 E |
| Norham | 44 | 55.43 N | 2.10 W |
| Norheimsund | 26 | 60.22 N | 6.08 E |
| Noria de Ángeles | 234 | 22.27 N | 101.56 W |
| Norikura-dake ∧ | 94 | 36.06 N | 137.33 E |
| Noril'sk | 74 | 69.20 N | 88.06 E |
| Noring, Gunong ∧ | 114 | 5.24 N | 101.44 E |
| Norland, On., Can. | 212 | 44.43 N | 78.49 W |
| Norland, Fl., U.S. | 220 | 25.57 N | 80.12 W |
| Norlane | 169 | 38.06 S | 144.21 E |
| Norley | 262 | 53.15 N | 2.39 W |
| Norlina | 192 | 36.26 N | 78.11 W |
| Norma, It. | 66 | 41.35 N | 12.58 E |
| Norma, N.J., U.S. | 208 | 39.29 N | 75.05 W |
| Normal, Al., U.S. | 194 | 34.47 N | 86.34 W |
| Normal, Il., U.S. | 216 | 40.30 N | 88.59 W |
| Norman, Ar., U.S. | 194 | 34.27 N | 93.40 W |
| Norman, In., U.S. | 218 | 38.57 N | 86.16 W |
| Norman, Ok., U.S. | 196 | 35.13 N | 97.26 W |
| Norman ≃ | 166 | 17.28 S | 140.49 E |
| Norman, Lake ⊜[1] | 192 | 35.35 N | 80.55 W |
| Normanby, Austl. | 171a | 27.28 S | 153.01 E |
| Normanby, N.Z. | 172 | 39.32 S | 174.17 E |
| Normanby ≃ | 164 | 14.25 S | 144.08 E |
| Normanby Island I | 164 | 10.05 S | 151.05 E |
| Norman Creek ⊂ | 284b | 39.18 N | 76.25 W |
| Normandie □[9] | 32 | 49.00 N | 0.05 W |
| Normandie, Collines de ⛰[2] | 32 | 48.40 N | 0.30 W |
| Normandien | 158 | 27.57 S | 29.47 E |
| Normandy → Normandie □[9] | 32 | 49.00 N | 0.05 W |
| Normandy Heights | 284b | 39.17 N | 76.48 W |
| Normandy Park | 224 | 47.27 N | 122.21 W |
| Normangee | 222 | 31.02 N | 96.07 W |
| Normanhurst | 274a | 33.43 S | 151.06 E |
| Normanhurst, Mount ∧ | 162 | 25.04 S | 122.32 E |
| Norman Island I | 240m | 18.20 N | 64.37 W |
| Normannische Inseln → Channel Islands II | 28 | 49.20 N | 2.20 W |
| Norman Park | 192 | 31.16 N | 83.41 W |
| Normans Kill ≃ | 210 | 42.36 N | 73.44 W |
| Normanton, Austl. | 166 | 17.40 S | 141.05 E |
| Normanton, Eng., U.K. | 44 | 53.41 N | 1.27 W |
| Normanville | 168b | 35.27 S | 138.19 E |
| Norman Wells | 180 | 65.17 N | 126.51 W |
| Nor Marsh ≡ | 260 | 51.24 N | 0.38 E |
| Nornalup | 162 | 35.00 S | 116.49 E |
| Norogachi | 232 | 27.15 N | 107.07 W |
| Noroton ≃ | 276 | 41.03 N | 73.31 W |
| Noroton Point › | 276 | 41.03 N | 73.26 W |
| Norovlin | 88 | 48.40 N | 112.00 E |
| Noroy-le-Bourg | 58 | 47.37 N | 6.18 E |
| Norphlet | 194 | 33.18 N | 92.39 W |
| Norquay | 184 | 51.53 N | 102.05 W |
| Ñorquinco | 254 | 41.51 S | 70.54 W |
| Norra Barken ⊜ | 40 | 60.07 N | 15.31 E |
| Norra Björkfjärden ⊂ | 40 | 59.27 N | 17.28 E |
| Norrahammar | 26 | 57.42 N | 14.06 E |
| Norra Hörken ⊜ | 40 | 60.04 N | 14.53 E |
| Norra Kvarken (Merenkurkku) Ʉ | 26 | 63.36 N | 20.43 E |
| Norra Kvills Nationalpark ♦ | 26 | 57.44 N | 15.37 E |
| Norrälgen ⊜ | 40 | 59.50 N | 14.34 E |
| Norra Rörum | 41 | 56.01 N | 13.30 E |
| Norra Storfjället ∧ | 24 | 65.52 N | 15.18 E |
| Norra Yngern ⊜ | 40 | 59.09 N | 17.22 E |
| Norrboda | 40 | 60.28 N | 18.25 E |
| Norrbotten □[9] | 26 | 66.45 N | 23.00 E |
| Norrbottens Län □[6] | 24 | 66.00 N | 20.00 E |
| Nørre Åby | 41 | 55.27 N | 9.54 E |
| Nørre Alslev | 41 | 54.54 N | 11.54 E |


DEUTSCH


| Name | Seite | Breite°′ | Länge°′ E = Ost |
|---|---|---|---|
| Nørre Broby | 41 | 55.15 N | 10.14 E |
| Nørre Nærå | 41 | 55.34 N | 10.17 E |
| Norrent-Fontes | 50 | 50.35 N | 2.24 E |
| Nørre Snede | 41 | 55.58 N | 9.25 E |
| Nørresundby | 26 | 57.04 N | 9.55 E |
| Nørre Vejrup | 41 | 55.31 N | 8.47 E |
| Norrfjärden | 26 | 65.25 N | 21.27 E |
| Norridge | 216 | 41.57 N | 87.49 W |
| Norridgewock | 188 | 44.42 N | 69.47 W |
| Norris | 192 | 36.11 N | 84.04 W |
| Norris, Lake ⊜ | 220 | 28.57 N | 81.32 W |
| Norris Arm | 186 | 49.05 N | 55.15 W |
| Norris Bridge ◆[5] | 208 | 37.37 N | 76.26 W |
| Norris City | 194 | 37.58 N | 88.19 W |
| Norris Dam State Park ♦ | 192 | 36.14 N | 84.07 W |
| Norrish Creek ≃ | 224 | 49.10 N | 122.08 W |
| Norris Lake ⊜[1] | 192 | 36.20 N | 83.55 W |
| Norris Point | 186 | 49.31 N | 57.53 W |
| Norristown | 208 | 40.07 N | 75.20 W |
| Norrköping | 40 | 58.36 N | 16.11 E |
| Norroway Brook ≃ | 283 | 42.11 N | 71.03 W |
| Norrskedika | 40 | 60.17 N | 18.17 E |
| Norrsundet | 26 | 60.56 N | 17.08 E |
| Norrtälje | 40 | 59.46 N | 18.42 E |
| Norrtäljeviken ⊂ | 40 | 59.47 N | 18.53 E |
| Norseman | 162 | 32.12 S | 121.46 E |
| Norsewood | 172 | 40.04 S | 176.13 E |
| Norsjå ⊜ | 26 | 59.18 N | 9.20 E |
| Norsjö | 26 | 64.55 N | 19.29 E |
| Norsk | 89 | 52.20 N | 129.55 E |
| Norsminde | 41 | 56.01 N | 10.16 E |
| Norsup | 175f | 16.05 S | 167.23 E |
| Norte, Cabo ›, Bra. | 250 | 1.40 N | 49.55 W |
| Norte, Cabo ›, Chile | 174z | 27.03 S | 109.24 W |
| Norte, Cabo → Nordkapp ›, Nor. | 24 | 71.11 N | 25.48 E |
| Norte, Canal Ʉ | 288 | 34.37 S | 58.15 W |
| Norte, Canal do Ʉ | 250 | 0.30 N | 50.30 W |
| Norte, Cayo I | 240m | 18.20 N | 65.15 W |
| Norte, Estación del ◆[5], Esp. | 266a | 40.25 N | 3.43 W |
| Norte, Estación del ◆[5], Esp. | 266d | 41.24 N | 2.02 E |
| Norte, Mar del → North Sea ⊤[2] | 22 | 55.20 N | 3.00 E |
| Norte, Punta › | 254 | 42.04 S | 63.45 W |
| Norte, Serra do ⛰[1] | 248 | 11.20 S | 59.00 W |
| Norte de Santander □[3] | 238 | 9.15 N | 73.00 W |
| Norte de Santander □[5] | 246 | 8.00 N | 73.00 W |
| Nortelândia | 248 | 14.25 S | 56.48 W |
| Nörten-Hardenberg | 52 | 51.38 N | 9.56 E |
| North, S.C., U.S. | 192 | 33.36 N | 81.06 W |
| North, Va., U.S. | 208 | 37.26 N | 76.24 W |
| North ≃, Nf., Can. | 176 | 57.30 N | 62.05 W |
| North ≃, On., Can. | 212 | 44.44 N | 79.39 W |
| North ≃, Al., U.S. | 194 | 33.15 N | 87.30 W |
| North ≃, Ia., U.S. | 194 | 41.31 N | 93.27 W |
| North ≃, Ma., U.S. | 283 | 42.10 N | 70.43 W |
| North ≃, Mo., U.S. | 219 | 39.52 N | 91.27 W |
| North ≃, Wa., U.S. | 224 | 46.45 N | 123.53 W |
| North, Cape › | 186 | 47.02 N | 60.25 W |
| North Abington | 207 | 42.07 N | 70.57 W |
| North Adams, Ma., U.S. | 207 | 42.42 N | 73.06 W |
| North Adams, Mi., U.S. | 216 | 41.58 N | 84.32 W |
| North Albany | 202 | 44.39 N | 123.06 W |
| Northallerton | 44 | 54.20 N | 1.26 W |
| Northam, Austl. | 168a | 31.39 S | 116.40 E |
| Northam, S. Afr. | 156 | 25.03 S | 27.11 E |
| Northam, Eng., U.K. | 42 | 51.02 N | 4.12 W |
| North America ⊥[1] | 4 | 45.00 N | 100.00 W |
| North America ⊥[1] | 16 | 45.00 N | 100.00 W |
| North American Basin ✧[1] | 8 | 30.00 N | 60.00 W |
| North Amherst | 207 | 42.24 N | 72.31 W |
| North Amityville | 276 | 40.41 N | 73.25 W |
| Northampton, Austl. | 162 | 28.21 S | 114.37 E |
| Northampton, Eng., U.K. | 42 | 52.14 N | 0.54 W |
| Northampton, Md., U.S. | 284c | 38.52 N | 76.49 W |
| Northampton, Ma., U.S. | 207 | 42.19 N | 72.38 W |
| Northampton, N.Y., U.S. | 207 | 40.54 N | 72.40 W |
| Northampton, Pa., U.S. | 208 | 40.41 N | 75.29 W |
| Northampton □[6], N.C., U.S. | 208 | 36.28 N | 77.21 W |
| Northampton □[6], Pa., U.S. | 210 | 40.45 N | 75.18 W |
| Northampton □[6], Va., U.S. | 208 | 37.20 N | 75.50 W |
| Northamptonshire □[6] | 42 | 52.20 N | 0.50 W |
| North Andaman I | 110 | 13.15 N | 92.55 E |
| North Andover | 207 | 42.41 N | 71.08 W |
| North Andrews Gardens | 220 | 26.12 N | 80.07 W |
| North Anna ≃ | 192 | 37.48 N | 77.25 W |
| North Anson | 188 | 44.51 N | 69.54 W |
| North Apollo | 214 | 40.35 N | 79.33 W |
| North Arlington | 276 | 40.47 N | 74.08 W |
| North Arm ≃[1] | 224 | 49.12 N | 123.10 W |
| North Asheboro | 192 | 35.44 N | 79.49 W |
| North Atlanta | 192 | 33.51 N | 84.20 W |
| North Attleboro | 207 | 41.59 N | 71.20 W |
| North Attleboro National Fish Hatchery ♦ | 283 | 42.00 N | 71.17 W |
| North Auburn | 274a | 33.50 S | 151.02 E |
| North Augusta | 192 | 33.30 N | 81.57 W |
| North Aulatsivik Island I | 176 | 59.50 N | 64.00 W |
| North Aurora | 216 | 41.48 N | 88.19 W |
| North Australian Basin ✧[1] | 14 | 14.30 S | 116.30 E |
| Northaw | 260 | 51.42 N | 0.09 W |
| North Babylon | 276 | 40.42 N | 73.19 W |
| North Balabac Strait Ʉ | 116 | 8.10 N | 117.04 E |
| North Baltimore | 216 | 41.10 N | 83.40 W |
| North Balwyn | 274b | 37.48 S | 145.05 E |
| North Bannister | 168a | 32.35 S | 116.26 E |
| North Bārākpur | 126 | 22.46 N | 88.22 E |
| North Bass Island I | 214 | 41.43 N | 82.49 W |
| North Battleford | 184 | 52.47 N | 108.17 W |
| North Bay, On., Can. | 190 | 46.19 N | 79.28 W |
| North Bay, N.Y., U.S. | 210 | 43.14 N | 75.45 W |
| North Bay, Wi., U.S. | 216 | 42.46 N | 87.47 W |
| North Bay ⊂, On., Can. | 212 | 44.53 N | 79.48 W |
| North Bay ⊂, Wa., U.S. | 224 | 46.59 N | 124.04 W |
| North Bay Shore | 276 | 40.45 N | 73.16 W |
| North Bay Village | 220 | 25.51 N | 80.08 W |
| North Beach | 168a | 31.52 S | 115.45 E |
| North Beach ◆[8] | 282 | 37.48 N | 122.25 W |
| North Beach Peninsula ›[1] | 224 | 46.30 N | 124.02 W |
| North Belle Vernon | 214 | 40.08 N | 79.52 W |
| North Bellmore | 276 | 40.41 N | 73.32 W |
| North Bend, B.C., Can. | 182 | 49.53 N | 121.27 W |
| North Bend, Ne., U.S. | 198 | 41.27 N | 96.46 W |
| North Bend, Oh., U.S. | 218 | 39.09 N | 84.44 W |
| North Bend, Or., U.S. | 202 | 43.24 N | 124.13 W |
| North Bend, Pa., U.S. | 214 | 41.21 N | 77.42 W |
| North Bend, Wa., U.S. | 224 | 47.29 N | 121.47 W |
| North Benfleet | 260 | 51.35 N | 0.32 E |
| North Bengal Plains ≚ | 124 | 26.20 N | 88.30 E |
| North Bennington | 210 | 42.55 N | 73.14 W |
| North Bergen | 276 | 40.47 N | 74.02 W |


**Symbols** in the index entries represent the broad categories identified in the key at the right. Symbols with superior numbers (⛰[1]) identify subcategories (see complete key on page *I · 1*).

**Symbole** im Register stellen die rechts im Schlüssel erklärten Kategorien dar. Symbole mit hochgestellten Ziffern (⛰[1]) bezeichnen Unterabteilungen einer Kategorie (vgl. vollständiger Schlüssel auf Seite *I · 1*).

**Los símbolos** incluídos en el texto del índice representan las grandes categorías identificadas con la clave a la derecha. Los símbolos con numeros en su parte superior (⛰[1]) identifican las subcategorías (véase la clave completa en la página *I · 1*).

**Les symboles** de l'index représentent les catégories indiquées dans la légende à droite. Les symboles suivis d'un indice (⛰[1]) représentent des sous-catégories (voir légende complète à la page *I · 1*).

**Os símbolos** incluídos no texto do índice representam as grandes categorias identificadas com a chave à direita. Os símbolos com números em sua parte superior (⛰[1]) identificam as subcategorias (veja-se a chave completa à página *I · 1*).

| | | | | |
|---|---|---|---|---|
| ∧ Mountain | Berg | Montaña | Montagne | Montanha |
| ⛰ Mountains | Gebirge | Montañas | Montagnes | Montanhas |
| )( Pass | Paß | Paso | Col | Passo |
| V Valley, Canyon | Tal, Cañon | Valle, Cañón | Vallée, Canyon | Vale, Canhão |
| ≚ Plain | Ebene | Llano | Plaine | Planície |
| › Cape | Kap | Cabo | Cap | Cabo |
| I Island | Insel | Isla | Île | Ilha |
| II Islands | Inseln | Islas | Îles | Ilhas |
| ⊥ Other Topographic Features | Andere Topographische Objekte | Otros Elementos Topográficos | Autres données topographiques | Outros acidentes topográficos |

ESPAÑOL

Nombre | Página | Lat.°′ | Long.°′ W = Oeste

North Berwick, Scot., U.K. 46 56.04 N 2.44 W
North Berwick, Me., U.S. 188 43.18 N 70.44 W
North Bethlehem 210 42.40 N 73.50 W
North Bihar Plains ≃ 124 26.20 N 86.00 E
North Billerica 207 42.35 N 71.17 W
North Bloomfield 214 41.27 N 80.52 W
North Boggy Creek ≃ 196 34.23 N 96.04 W
North Bonneville 224 45.38 N 121.58 W
Northborough 207 42.19 N 71.38 W
North Bosque ≃ 196 31.40 N 97.24 W
North Boston 210 42.41 N 78.47 W
North Bourke 166 30.03 S 145.57 E
North Box Hill 274b 37.48 S 145.07 E
North Braddock 279b 40.23 N 79.50 W
North Branch, Mi., U.S. 190 43.13 N 83.11 W
North Branch, Mn., U.S. 190 45.30 N 92.58 W
North Branch, N.J., U.S. 210 40.36 N 74.41 W
North Branch Canal ≡ 224 47.12 N 120.40 W
North Branford 207 41.19 N 72.46 W
North Breakers ✢[2] 174g 28.14 N 177.25 W
Northbridge, Austl. 274a 33.49 S 151.13 E
Northbridge, Ma., U.S. 207 42.09 N 71.39 W
North Bristol 214 41.24 N 80.52 W
Northbrook, On., Can. 212 44.44 N 77.10 W
Northbrook, Il., U.S. 216 42.07 N 87.49 W
Northbrook, Pa., U.S. 285 39.55 N 75.41 W
North Brookfield, Ma., U.S. 207 42.16 N 72.05 W
North Brookfield, N.Y., U.S. 210 42.51 N 75.24 W
North Brunswick 208 40.28 N 74.28 W
North Buganda □[5] 154 1.00 N 32.15 E
North Caicos I 238 21.56 N 71.59 W
North Caldwell 276 40.51 N 74.16 W
North Canadian ≃ 196 35.17 N 95.31 W
North Canton, Ct., U.S. 207 41.53 N 72.53 W
North Canton, Ga., U.S. 192 34.14 N 84.29 W
North Canton, Oh., U.S. 214 40.52 N 81.24 W
North Cape 216 42.47 N 88.05 W
North Cape ›, P.E., Can. 186 47.05 N 64.00 W
North Cape ›, N.Z. 172 34.25 S 173.02 E
North Cape → Nordkapp ›, Nor. 24 71.11 N 25.48 E
North Cape ›, Pap. N. Gui. 164 2.32 S 150.49 E
North Cape ›, Mi., U.S. 216 41.44 N 83.25 W
North Cape May 208 38.58 N 74.57 W
North Captiva Island I 220 26.35 N 82.13 W
North Caribou Lake ⊜ 176 52.50 N 90.40 W
North Carolina □[3], U.S. 178 35.30 N 80.00 W
North Carolina □[3], U.S. 192 35.30 N 80.00 W
North Carver 207 41.55 N 70.48 W
North Cascades National Park ♦ 224 48.30 N 121.00 W
North Castor ≃ 212 45.16 N 75.24 W
North Catasauqua 208 40.40 N 75.29 W
North Chagrin Reservation ♦ 279a 41.34 N 81.26 W
North Channel ⊔, On., Can. 190 46.02 N 82.50 W
North Channel ⊔, On., Can. 212 44.10 N 76.45 W
North Channel ⊔, U.K. 44 55.10 N 5.40 W
North Channel ⊔, N.Y., U.S. 276 40.36 N 73.53 W
North Channel ≃[1] 281 42.38 N 82.40 W
North Charleroi 214 40.09 N 79.54 W
North Charleston 192 32.51 N 79.58 W
North Chatham 210 42.29 N 73.38 W
North Chelmsford 207 42.38 N 71.23 W
North Chicago 216 42.19 N 87.50 W
North Chili 210 43.06 N 77.45 W
Northchurch 260 51.46 N 0.36 W
North City 224 47.45 N 122.18 W
North Cleveland 222 30.21 N 95.06 W
Northcliff ◂[8] 273d 26.09 S 27.58 E
Northcliffe 162 34.36 S 116.07 E
North Clymer 214 42.04 N 79.34 W
North Cohasset 283 42.15 N 70.50 W
North Cohocton 210 42.34 N 77.28 W
North College Hill 218 39.13 N 84.33 W
North Collins 210 42.35 N 78.56 W
North Commerce Lake ⊜ 281 42.35 N 83.30 W
North Concho ≃ 196 31.27 N 100.25 W
North Conway 188 44.03 N 71.07 W
North Cotabato □[4] 116 7.15 N 124.50 E
Northcote 274b 37.46 S 145.00 E
North Cray ◂[8] 260 51.26 N 0.08 E
North Creek 188 43.41 N 73.59 W
North Creek ≃ 278 41.33 N 87.37 W
Northcrest 222 31.38 N 97.06 W
North Crossett 194 33.09 N 91.56 W
North Crosswicks 285 40.10 N 74.39 W
North Croton Creek ≃ 196 33.24 N 100.00 W
North Dakota □[3], U.S. 178 47.30 N 100.15 W
North Dakota □[3], U.S. 198 47.30 N 100.15 W
North Dandalup 168a 32.31 S 115.58 E
North Dandalup ≃ 168a 32.36 S 115.53 E
North Dartmouth 207 41.38 N 70.58 W
North Dighton 207 41.51 N 71.07 W
North Dorset Downs ⋏[1] 42 50.47 N 2.30 W
North Downs ⋏[1] 42 51.20 N 0.10 E
North Dum Dum 126 22.38 N 88.23 E
North Eagle Butte 198 45.02 N 101.15 W
North East, Md., U.S. 208 39.36 N 75.56 W
North East, Pa., U.S. 214 42.12 N 79.50 W
North-East □[5] 156 21.00 S 27.30 E
Northeast Cape 180 63.18 N 168.42 W
Northeast Cape › 180 63.17 N 168.45 W
Northeast Cape Fear ≃ 192 34.11 N 77.57 W
Northeast Creek ≃ 284b 39.18 N 76.29 W
North Eastern □[4] 154 1.00 N 40.15 E
Northeastern University ʊ[2] 283 42.20 N 71.05 W
North Eastham 207 41.51 N 69.59 W
Northeast Henrietta 210 43.04 N 77.36 W
Northeast Islands II 175c 7.36 N 151.57 E
North Easton 207 42.04 N 71.06 W
Northeast Pass ⊔ 175c 7.30 N 151.59 E
North East Point ›, Ba. 238 21.20 N 73.01 W
North East Point ›, Ba. 238 22.43 N 73.50 W
North East Point ›, Kiribati 174o 1.57 N 157.16 W
Northeast Point ›, St. Vin. 241h 13.03 N 61.13 W
Northeast Providence Channel ⊔ 238 25.40 N 77.09 W
North Edwards 228 35.01 N 117.44 W
North Egremont 207 42.11 N 73.26 W
Northeim 52 51.42 N 10.00 E
North Elkhorn Creek ≃ 218 38.13 N 84.48 W
North Elm Creek ≃ 222 30.53 N 97.00 W

FRANÇAIS

Nom | Page | Lat.°′ | Long.°′ W = Ouest

North English 190 41.30 N 92.04 W
Northern □[4], Ghana 150 9.30 N 1.00 W
Northern □[4], Malaŵi 154 11.00 S 34.00 E
Northern □[4], S.L. 150 9.15 N 11.45 W
Northern □[4], S. Afr. 156 23.30 S 29.30 E
Northern □[4], Zam. 154 11.00 S 31.00 E
Northern □[5] 154 2.50 N 32.45 E
Northern Arm 186 49.10 N 55.23 W
Northern Cape □[4] 156 29.00 S 21.00 E
Northern Cheyenne Indian Reservation ◂[4] 202 45.31 N 106.45 W
Northern Circārs ⋏[2] 122 18.00 N 83.15 E
Northern Cook Islands II 14 10.00 S 161.00 W
Northern Division □[5] 175g 16.30 S 179.30 E
Northern Dvina → Severnaja Dvina ≃ 24 64.32 N 40.30 E
Northern Indian Lake ⊜ 176 57.20 N 97.20 W
Northern Ireland □[8] 48 54.40 N 6.45 W
Northern Light Lake ⊜ 190 48.15 N 90.38 W
Northern Mariana Islands □[2] 14 16.00 N 149.00 E
Northern Samar □[4] 116 12.30 N 124.30 E
Northern Territory □[8] 160 20.00 S 134.00 E
North Esk ≃, Scot., U.K. 46 56.44 N 2.28 W
North Esk ≃, Scot., U.K. 46 55.54 N 3.04 W
North Essendon 274b 37.45 S 144.54 E
North Evans 210 42.42 N 78.56 W
Northey Island I 260 51.44 N 0.43 E
North Fabius ≃ 194 39.54 N 91.30 W
North Fairfield 214 41.06 N 82.36 W
North Fair Oaks 282 37.28 N 122.12 W
North Falmouth 207 41.38 N 70.37 W
North Ferriby 44 53.43 N 0.30 W
Northfield, B.C., Can. 224 49.11 N 123.59 W
Northfield, Ct., U.S. 207 41.41 N 73.06 W
Northfield, Il., U.S. 278 42.05 N 87.46 W
Northfield, Ma., U.S. 207 42.41 N 72.27 W
Northfield, Mn., U.S. 190 44.27 N 93.09 W
Northfield, N.J., U.S. 208 39.22 N 74.33 W
Northfield, Oh., U.S. 214 41.20 N 81.32 W
Northfield, Vt., U.S. 188 44.09 N 72.39 W
Northfield Airport ⊠ 279a 41.17 N 81.31 W
Northfield Center 279a 41.19 N 81.32 W
Northfield Park Race Track ♦ 279a 41.21 N 81.31 W
Northfield Village 279a 41.21 N 81.31 W
Northfield Woods 278 42.05 N 87.52 W
North Fiji Basin ✢[1] 14 16.00 S 174.00 E
North Fitzroy 274b 37.47 S 144.59 E
Northfleet 42 51.27 N 0.21 E
North Flinders Range ⋏ 166 31.00 S 139.00 E
North Fond du Lac 190 43.48 N 88.29 W
Northford 207 41.23 N 72.47 W
North Foreland › 42 51.23 N 1.27 E
North Fork 226 37.13 N 119.30 W
North Fork ≃ 194 36.13 N 92.17 W
North Fork Lake ⊜[1] 226 38.56 N 121.00 W
North Fork Reservoir ⊜[1] 224 45.13 N 122.15 W
North Fork Village 218 39.21 N 83.02 W
North Fort Myers 220 26.40 N 81.52 W
North Freedom 190 43.27 N 89.52 W
North Frisian Islands II 24 54.50 N 8.12 E
Northgate 216 43.01 N 85.36 W
Northgate ◂[9] 282 38.00 N 122.33 W
North Georgetown 214 40.51 N 80.59 W
North Glanford 212 43.11 N 79.54 W
North Glen Ellyn 278 41.54 N 88.04 W
Northglenn 200 39.53 N 104.59 W
North Gower 212 45.08 N 75.43 W
North Grafton 207 42.14 N 71.42 W
North Granby 207 41.59 N 72.49 W
North Grand Island Bridge ◂[5] 284a 43.04 N 78.59 W
North Great River 276 40.44 N 73.10 W
North Greece 212 43.15 N 77.44 W
North Grosvenordale 207 41.59 N 71.53 W
North Grove 216 40.37 N 85.58 W
North Gulfport 194 30.24 N 89.06 W
North Hadley 207 42.23 N 72.36 W
North Haledon 276 40.57 N 74.11 W
North Hampton 218 39.59 N 83.56 W
North Hanover 283 42.08 N 70.52 W
North Harbor ⊂ 269f 14.36 N 120.57 E
North Harbour ⊂ 274a 33.49 S 151.17 E
North Haven 207 41.23 N 72.51 W
North Head ›, Austl. 274a 33.49 S 151.18 E
North Head ›, N.Z. 172 36.25 S 174.03 E
North Henderson 192 36.21 N 78.22 W
North Henik Lake ⊜ 176 61.45 N 97.40 W
North Hero 188 44.49 N 73.17 W
North Highlands 226 38.41 N 121.22 W
North Hill 42 50.34 N 4.25 W
North Hills, De., U.S. 285 39.46 N 75.30 W
North Hills, Il., U.S. 278 42.18 N 88.01 W
North Hills, N.Y., U.S. 276 40.47 N 73.41 W
North Hinksey 42 51.45 N 1.16 W
North Hogan Creek ≃ 218 39.03 N 84.54 W
North Hollywood ◂[8] 280 34.10 N 118.23 W
North Holmwood 260 51.13 N 0.20 W
North Honcut Creek ≃ 226 39.19 N 121.36 W
North Hoosick 210 42.56 N 73.21 W
North Hornell 210 42.21 N 77.40 W
North Horr 154 3.19 N 37.04 E
North Houston 222 29.54 N 95.31 W
Northiam 42 50.59 N 0.36 E
North Industry 214 40.44 N 81.22 W
North Irwin 279b 40.20 N 79.43 W
North Island I, India 122 10.08 N 72.20 E
North Island I, Kenya 154 4.04 N 36.03 E
North Island I, N.Z. 172 39.00 S 176.00 E
North Island Naval Air Station ■ 228 32.42 N 117.12 W
North Islet I 116 8.56 N 120.02 E
North Jackson 214 41.06 N 80.52 W
North Java 210 42.41 N 78.20 W
North Judson 216 41.12 N 86.46 W
North Kenai 180 60.44 N 151.19 W
North Kingstown 207 41.38 N 71.25 W
North Kingsville 214 41.54 N 80.42 W
North Knife Lake ⊜ 176 58.05 N 97.05 W
North Knob ʌ 210 41.43 N 75.33 W
North Korea → Korea, North □[1] 98 40.00 N 127.00 E
North La Junta 198 37.59 N 103.31 W
North Lake 216 43.09 N 88.22 W
North Lake ⊜, N.Y., U.S. 276 41.09 N 73.41 W
North Lake ⊜, Tx., U.S. 222 32.57 N 96.58 W
North Lakhimpur 120 27.14 N 94.07 E
Northland ◂[9] 281 42.27 N 83.13 W
North Landing ≃ 208 36.31 N 76.01 W
North Laramie ≃ 198 42.08 N 104.56 W
North Las Vegas 204 36.11 N 115.07 W
North La Veta Pass )( 200 37.37 N 105.11 W
North Lawrence 214 40.51 N 81.38 W
Northleach 42 51.51 N 1.50 W
North Lewisburg 216 40.13 N 83.33 W
North Liberty 216 41.32 N 86.25 W
North Lima 214 40.56 N 80.39 W
North Lindenhurst 276 40.42 N 73.22 W
North Line Island I 276 40.38 N 73.29 W
Northline Terrace 222 29.55 N 95.25 W
North Little Rock 194 34.46 N 92.16 W
North Llano ≃ 196 30.30 N 99.46 W
North Logan 202 41.46 N 111.48 W

PORTUGUÊS

Nome | Página | Lat.°′ | Long.°′ W = Oeste

North Loon Mountain ʌ 202 45.07 N 115.52 W
North Loup 198 41.29 N 98.46 W
North Loup ≃ 198 41.17 N 98.23 W
North Luangwa National Park ♦ 154 11.50 S 32.15 E
North Luconia Shoals ✢[2] 108 5.40 N 112.35 E
North Macmillan ≃ 180 63.03 N 133.18 W
North Madison 214 41.48 N 81.03 W
North Magnetic Pole ◂ 16 77.19 N 101.49 W
North Malosmadulu Atoll I[1] 122 5.35 N 72.55 E
North Mamm Peak ʌ 200 39.23 N 107.52 W
North Manchester 216 41.00 N 85.46 W
North Manitou Island I 190 45.06 N 86.01 W
North Mankato 190 44.10 N 94.02 W
North Manly 274a 33.46 S 151.16 E
North Maroota 170 33.29 S 150.56 E
North Marshfield 283 42.08 N 70.46 W
North Marysville 224 48.07 N 122.09 W
North Massapequa 276 40.42 N 73.27 W
Northmead, Austl. 274a 33.47 S 151.00 E
Northmead, S. Afr. 273d 26.10 S 28.20 E
North Merrick 276 40.41 N 73.33 W
North Miami 220 25.53 N 80.11 W
North Miami Beach 220 25.55 N 80.09 W
North Middleboro 207 41.56 N 70.58 W
North Milk ≃ 202 49.08 N 112.23 W
North Mokelumne ≃ 226 38.08 N 121.35 W
North Moose Lake ⊜ 184 54.08 N 100.13 W
North Moreau Creek ≃ 194 38.30 N 92.18 W
North Muskegon 216 43.15 N 86.16 W
North Myrtle Beach 192 33.49 N 78.40 W
North Nahanni ≃ 180 62.05 N 124.30 W
North Naples 220 26.13 N 81.47 W
North Narrabeen 274a 33.42 S 151.18 E
North Nemah ≃ 224 46.30 N 123.53 W
North New Hyde Park 276 40.44 N 73.41 W
North New River Canal ≡ 220 26.05 N 80.12 W
North Newton 198 38.04 N 97.21 W
North Niles 216 41.52 N 86.15 W
North Norwich 210 42.37 N 75.31 W
North Oaks 222 30.22 N 97.41 W
North Ockendon ◂[8] 260 51.32 N 0.18 E
North Ogden 200 41.18 N 111.57 W
North Olmsted 214 41.24 N 81.55 W
Northolt Aerodrome ⊠ 260 51.33 N 0.23 W
Northome 190 47.52 N 94.16 W
Northop 262 53.12 N 3.08 W
North Ore Creek ≃ 281 42.43 N 83.47 W
North Orwell 210 41.55 N 76.19 W
North Ossetia → Severnaja Osetija □[3] 84 43.00 N 44.15 E
Northowram 262 53.44 N 1.50 W
North Oxford 207 42.09 N 71.52 W
North Palisade ʌ 204 37.06 N 118.31 W
North Palm Beach 220 26.49 N 80.04 W
North Para ≃ 168b 34.36 S 138.45 E
North Park ◂[8] 278 41.59 N 87.43 W
North Park ♦ 279b 40.36 N 80.00 W
North Park Lake ⊜ 279b 40.36 N 80.00 W
North Parramatta 274a 33.48 S 151.00 E
North Patchogue 276 40.47 N 73.00 W
North Peak ʌ, Ak., U.S. 180 62.34 N 162.23 W
North Peak ʌ, Ca., U.S. 282 37.33 N 122.28 W
North Pease ≃ 196 34.15 N 100.07 W
North Pelham, N.H., U.S. 283 42.46 N 71.21 W
North Pelham, N.Y., U.S. 276 40.55 N 73.48 W
North Pembroke 207 42.05 N 70.47 W
North Pender Island I 224 48.49 N 123.17 W
North Perry 214 41.47 N 81.07 W
North Petherton 42 51.06 N 3.01 W
North Philadelphia ◂[8] 285 39.58 N 75.09 W
North Philadelphia Airport ⊠ 285 40.05 N 75.01 W
North Pine ≃ 171a 27.17 S 153.01 E
North Pine Grove 214 41.24 N 79.13 W
North Piney Creek ≃ 200 42.31 N 110.05 W
North Pitcher 210 42.37 N 75.49 W
North Plainfield 210 40.37 N 74.25 W
North Plains 224 45.35 N 122.59 W
North Plains ≃ 200 34.40 N 108.15 W
North Platte 198 41.07 N 100.45 W
North Platte ≃ 178 41.07 N 100.42 W
North Pleasureville 218 38.22 N 85.07 W
North Plympton 283 41.59 N 70.48 W
North Point, H.K. 271d 22.17 N 114.12 E
Northpoint, Pa., U.S. 214 40.54 N 79.08 W
North Point ›, Barb. 241g 13.20 N 59.36 W
North Point ›, Md., U.S. 284b 39.12 N 76.27 W
North Point ›, Mi., U.S. 190 45.02 N 83.16 W
North Pole 180 64.45 N 147.21 W
North Pole ◂ 16 90.00 N 0.00
Northport, Al., U.S. 194 33.13 N 87.34 W
North Port, Fl., U.S. 220 27.03 N 82.15 W
Northport, Mi., U.S. 190 45.07 N 85.37 W
Northport, N.Y., U.S. 210 40.53 N 73.20 W
Northport, Wa., U.S. 202 48.54 N 117.46 W
North Portal 184 49.00 N 102.33 W
Northport Bay ⊂ 276 40.55 N 73.23 W
Northport Harbor ⊂ 276 40.53 N 73.22 W
North Powder 202 45.01 N 117.55 W
North Pownal 207 42.47 N 73.15 W
North Prairie 216 42.56 N 88.24 W
North Providence 207 41.50 N 71.25 W
North Puyallup 224 47.12 N 122.17 W
North Queensferry 46 56.01 N 3.25 W
North Quincy 219 39.58 N 91.24 W
North Raccoon ≃ 198 41.50 N 94.08 W
North Raisin ≃ 206 45.09 N 74.43 W
North Ram ≃ 182 52.16 N 115.38 W
North Randall 279a 41.27 N 81.32 W
North Reading 207 42.34 N 71.04 W
North Reservoir ⊜[1] 283 42.28 N 71.07 W
North Rhine-Westphalia → Nordrhein-Westfalen □[3] 30 51.30 N 7.30 E
North Richland Hills 222 32.50 N 97.13 W
North Richmond 282 37.57 N 122.22 W
Northridge, Oh., U.S. 218 39.59 N 83.46 W
Northridge, Oh., U.S. 218 39.48 N 84.11 W
Northridge ◂[8] 280 34.14 N 118.33 W
Northridge Fashion Center ◂[9] 280 34.13 N 118.33 W
North Ridge Village 218 39.57 N 86.09 W
North Ridgeville 214 41.23 N 82.01 W
North Rim 200 36.12 N 112.03 W
North River ⊂ 208 37.25 N 76.25 W
North Riverside 278 41.50 N 87.49 W
North Riverside Park Mall ◂[9] 278 41.51 N 87.49 W
North Robinson 214 40.48 N 82.51 W
North Rocks 274a 33.46 S 151.02 E
North Ronaldsay I 46 59.22 N 2.26 W
North Ronaldsay Firth ⊔ 46 59.20 N 2.25 W
North Rose 210 43.11 N 76.53 W
North Royalton 214 41.18 N 81.43 W
North Rustico 186 46.27 N 63.19 W
North Ryde 274a 33.48 S 151.07 E
North Salem 214 40.09 N 81.33 W
North Salt Lake 200 40.50 N 111.54 W
North San Juan 226 39.22 N 121.06 W
North Santiam ≃ 202 44.41 N 123.00 W

North Saskatchewan ≃ 176 53.15 N 105.05 W
North Saugeen ≃ 212 44.19 N 81.17 W
North Scituate, Ma., U.S. 207 42.13 N 70.47 W
North Scituate, R.I., U.S. 207 41.49 N 71.35 W
North Sea ⫪[2] 22 56.00 N 3.00 E
North Seaton Colliery 44 55.11 N 1.32 W
North Sentinel Island I 110 11.33 N 92.15 E
North Shields 44 55.01 N 1.27 W
Norths Highland ⋏[1] 9 66.40 S 126.00 E
North Shoal Lake ⊜ 184 50.29 N 97.40 W
North Shore 216 42.16 N 88.23 W
Northshore ◂[9] 283 42.32 N 70.57 W
North Shore Channel ≡ 278 42.05 N 87.41 W
North Shores 216 41.50 N 83.25 W
North Shoshone Peak ʌ 204 39.09 N 117.29 W
North Siberian Lowland → Severo-Sibirskaja nizmennost' ≃ 74 73.00 N 100.00 E
Northside 174h 2.47 S 171.43 W
North Singa 126 23.16 N 89.30 E
North Sioux City 198 42.31 N 96.28 W
North Skunk ≃ 190 41.15 N 92.02 W
North Solomons □[5] 175e 6.00 S 155.00 E
North Somercotes 44 53.28 N 0.08 E
North Sound ⊔, Antig. 240c 17.07 N 61.45 W
North Sound ⊔, Ire. 48 53.11 N 9.43 W
North Sound ⊔, Scot., U.K. 46 59.18 N 2.46 W
North Spicer Island I 176 68.30 N 78.55 W
North Spirit Lake ⊜ 184 52.30 N 92.53 W
North Spot I 236 16.15 N 88.11 W
North Springfield, Pa., U.S. 214 41.59 N 80.26 W
North Springfield, Va., U.S. 284c 38.48 N 77.12 W
North Stamford Reservoir ⊜[1] 276 41.08 N 73.32 W
North Star, De., U.S. 285 39.46 N 75.43 W
North Star, Oh., U.S. 216 40.19 N 84.34 W
North Sterling Reservoir ⊜[1] 198 40.47 N 103.17 W
North Stradbroke Island I 171a 27.35 S 153.28 E
North Sudbury 283 42.24 N 71.24 W
North Sulphur ≃ 196 33.23 N 95.18 W
North Sunday Creek ≃ 202 46.27 N 105.54 W
North Sunderland 44 55.34 N 1.39 W
North Swansea 207 41.46 N 71.15 W
North Sydenham ≃ 214 42.35 N 82.23 W
North Sydney, Austl. 274a 33.50 S 151.13 E
North Sydney, N.S., Can. 186 46.13 N 60.15 W
North Syracuse 210 43.08 N 76.07 W
North Tamborine 171a 27.56 S 153.11 E
North Taranaki Bight ⊂[3] 172 38.42 S 174.15 E
North Tarrytown 276 41.05 N 73.51 W
North Tawton 42 50.48 N 3.53 W
North Tea Lake ⊜ 190 45.56 N 79.03 W
North Terre Haute 194 39.31 N 87.21 W
North Tewksbury 283 42.38 N 71.14 W
North Thames ≃ 212 42.59 N 81.16 W
North Thompson ≃ 182 50.41 N 120.21 W
North Thoresby 44 53.28 N 0.03 W
North Tidworth 42 51.16 N 1.40 W
North Toe ≃ 192 36.00 N 82.16 W
North Tolsta 46 58.20 N 6.13 W
North Tonawanda 210 43.02 N 78.51 W
North Towanda 210 41.47 N 76.28 W
North Troy 206 44.59 N 72.24 W
North Truro 207 42.02 N 70.05 W
North Tule Draw V 196 34.30 N 101.36 W
North Tunica 194 34.42 N 90.23 W
North Turramurra 274a 33.43 S 151.09 E
North Twin Lake ⊜ 186 49.16 N 55.56 W
North Tyne ≃ 44 54.59 N 2.08 W
North Ubian Island I 116 6.09 N 120.27 E
North Uist I 46 57.36 N 7.18 W
Northumberland 210 40.53 N 76.47 W
Northumberland □[6], On., Can. 212 44.10 N 78.00 W
Northumberland □[6], Eng., U.K. 44 55.15 N 2.05 W
Northumberland □[6], Pa., U.S. 210 40.49 N 76.39 W
Northumberland □[6], Va., U.S. 208 37.50 N 76.25 W
Northumberland Isles II 166 21.40 S 150.00 E
Northumberland National Park ♦ 44 55.15 N 2.20 W
Northumberland Strait ⊔ 186 46.00 N 63.30 W
North Umpqua ≃ 202 43.16 N 123.27 W
North Uxbridge 207 42.05 N 71.38 W
Northvale 276 41.00 N 73.56 W
North Valley Hills ⋏[2] 285 40.02 N 75.40 W
North Valley Stream 276 40.41 N 73.42 W
North Vancouver 224 49.19 N 123.04 W
North Vandergrift 279b 40.36 N 79.34 W
North Vernon 218 39.00 N 85.37 W
North Versailles 279b 40.22 N 79.48 W
North Vietnam → Vietnam □[1] 108 16.00 N 108.00 E
Northville, Mi., U.S. 216 42.25 N 83.29 W
Northville, N.Y., U.S. 210 43.13 N 74.10 W
Northville Downs ♦ 281 42.26 N 83.29 W
Northvue 214 40.54 N 79.56 W
North Wabasca Lake ⊜ 182 56.00 N 113.55 W
North Wales 208 40.12 N 75.16 W
Northwall 46 59.16 N 2.17 W
North Walsham 42 52.50 N 1.24 E
North Wantagh 276 40.41 N 73.30 W
North Warren 214 41.52 N 79.09 W
North Washington, Pa., U.S. 214 41.03 N 79.49 W
North Washington, Pa., U.S. 279b 40.32 N 79.36 W
North Watuppa Pond ⊜ 207 41.42 N 71.06 W
Northway 180 62.58 N 141.56 W
North Weald Bassett 42 51.43 N 0.10 E
North Webster 216 41.19 N 85.41 W
North Weissport 210 40.50 N 75.41 W
North-West □[4] 156 26.30 S 25.00 E
Northwest ≃ 208 36.31 N 76.05 W
North West Cape ›, Austl. 162 21.45 S 114.10 E
Northwest Cape ›, Ak., U.S. 180 63.46 N 171.45 W
Northwest Cape ›, Fl., U.S. 220 25.13 N 81.11 W
North Westchester 207 41.34 N 72.24 W
North Western 210 43.20 N 75.22 W
North-Western □[4] 154 13.00 S 25.00 E
Northwestern University ʊ[2], Il., U.S. 278 42.04 N 87.40 W
Northwestern University (Chicago Campus) ʊ[2], Il., U.S. 278 41.54 N 87.37 W
Northwest Frontier □[4] 120 34.30 N 72.00 E
Northwest Gander ≃ 186 48.50 N 55.00 W
Northwest Harbor ⊂ 284b 39.16 N 76.35 W
Northwest Head › 116 10.08 N 118.45 E
Northwest Miramichi ≃ 186 46.58 N 65.35 W

Northwest Pacific Basin ✢[1] 6 40.00 N 155.00 E
North West Point › 174o 2.02 N 157.29 W
Northwest Providence Channel ⊔ 238 26.10 N 78.20 W
North West River 176 53.32 N 60.08 W
Northwest Territories □[4] 176 70.00 N 100.00 W
North Weymouth 283 42.15 N 70.57 W
Northwich 44 53.16 N 2.32 W
North Wichita ≃ 196 33.43 N 99.29 W
North Wilbraham 207 42.09 N 72.25 W
North Wildwood 208 39.00 N 74.47 W
North Wilkesboro 192 36.09 N 81.08 W
North Willow Creek ≃ 202 46.51 N 107.54 W
North Wilmington 283 42.34 N 71.09 W
North Windham, Ct., U.S. 207 41.44 N 72.09 W
North Windham, Me., U.S. 188 43.50 N 70.26 W
Northwold 42 52.33 N 0.35 E
Northwood, Eng., U.K. 42 50.44 N 1.19 W
Northwood, Ia., U.S. 190 43.26 N 93.13 W
Northwood, Mi., U.S. 216 42.19 N 85.38 W
Northwood, N.D., U.S. 198 47.44 N 97.33 W
Northwood, Oh., U.S. 214 41.36 N 83.28 W
Northwood ◂[8] 260 51.37 N 0.25 W
North Woodslee 281 42.13 N 82.43 W
Northwood Village 284c 39.02 N 77.01 W
North Yamhill ≃ 224 45.13 N 123.08 W
North Yelta 168b 34.03 S 137.37 E
North York 212 43.46 N 79.25 W
North York Moors ⋏[2] 44 54.24 N 0.53 W
North York Moors National Park ♦ 44 54.23 N 0.50 W
North Yorkshire □[6] 44 54.15 N 1.30 W
North Yuba ≃ 226 39.22 N 121.08 W
North Zulch 222 30.55 N 96.07 W
Norton, N.B., Can. 186 45.38 N 65.42 W
Norton, Eng., U.K. 44 54.09 N 0.47 W
Norton, Eng., U.K. 262 53.20 N 2.40 W
Norton, Ks., U.S. 198 39.50 N 99.53 W
Norton, Ma., U.S. 207 41.58 N 71.11 W
Norton, Oh., U.S. 214 41.01 N 81.39 W
Norton, Vt., U.S. 206 45.00 N 71.47 W
Norton, Va., U.S. 192 36.56 N 82.37 W
Norton, Zimb. 154 17.53 S 30.42 E
Norton Air Force Base ■ 228 34.06 N 117.14 W
Norton Basin ⊂ 276 40.36 N 73.47 W
Norton Bay ⊂ 180 64.45 N 161.15 W
Norton Creek ≃ 281 42.34 N 83.34 W
Norton Fitzwarren 42 51.02 N 3.09 W
Norton Grove 207 42.00 N 71.12 W
Norton Heath 260 51.43 N 0.19 E
Norton Hill 210 42.25 N 74.04 W
Norton Pond ⊜ 206 44.56 N 71.51 W
Norton Reservoir ⊜[1] 283 41.59 N 71.12 W
Norton Shores 216 43.10 N 86.15 W
Norton Sound ⊔ 180 63.50 N 164.00 W
Nortonville, On., Can. 275b 43.43 N 79.44 W
Nortonville, Ks., U.S. 198 39.25 N 95.20 W
Nortorf, Dtsch. 30 54.10 N 9.50 E
Nortorf, Dtsch. 52 53.55 N 9.16 E
Nort-sur-Erdre 32 47.26 N 1.30 W
Noruega → Norway □[1] 24 62.00 N 10.00 E
Noruega, Mar de → Norwegian Sea ⫪[2] 10 70.00 N 2.00 E
Norumbega Reservoir ⊜[1] 283 42.20 N 71.18 W
Nørup 41 55.43 N 9.19 E
Norval 212 43.39 N 79.51 W
Norvalspont 158 30.38 S 25.27 E
Norvège → Norway □[1] 24 62.00 N 10.00 E
Norvegia, Cape › 9 71.25 S 12.18 W
Norvell 216 42.10 N 84.11 W
Norvelt 214 40.12 N 79.32 W
Nörvenich 56 50.49 N 6.39 E
Norvin Green State Forest ♦ 276 41.03 N 74.20 W
Norwalk, Ca., U.S. 228 33.54 N 118.04 W
Norwalk, Ct., U.S. 207 41.07 N 73.24 W
Norwalk, Ia., U.S. 190 41.28 N 93.40 W
Norwalk, Oh., U.S. 214 41.14 N 82.36 W
Norwalk ≃ 207 41.06 N 73.25 W
Norwalk Harbor ⊂ 276 41.06 N 73.24 W
Norwalk Islands II 276 41.03 N 73.23 W
Norway, In., U.S. 216 40.47 N 86.46 W
Norway, Ia., U.S. 190 41.54 N 91.55 W
Norway, Me., U.S. 188 44.12 N 70.32 W
Norway, Mi., U.S. 190 45.47 N 87.54 W
Norway (Norge) □[1], Europe 22 62.00 N 10.00 E
Norway (Norge) □[1], Europe 24 62.00 N 10.00 E
Norway Bay ⊂ 176 71.08 N 104.35 W
Norway House 184 53.59 N 97.50 W
Norway Lake ⊜ 212 45.20 N 76.43 W
Norwegen → Norway □[1] 24 62.00 N 10.00 E
Norwegian Basin ✢[1] 10 68.00 N 2.00 W
Norwegian Sea ⫪[2] 10 70.00 N 2.00 E
Norwegian Trench ✢[1] 10 59.00 N 4.30 E
Norwell 283 42.09 N 70.47 W
Norwich, On., Can. 212 42.59 N 80.36 W
Norwich, Eng., U.K. 42 52.38 N 1.18 E
Norwich, Ct., U.S. 207 41.32 N 72.05 W
Norwich, Ks., U.S. 198 37.27 N 97.50 W
Norwich, N.Y., U.S. 210 42.31 N 75.31 W
Norwich Airport ⊠ 42 52.41 N 1.15 E
Norwin Heights 279b 40.20 N 79.44 W
Norwood, On., Can. 212 44.23 N 77.59 W
Norwood, Co., U.S. 200 38.07 N 108.17 W
Norwood, Ma., U.S. 207 42.11 N 71.12 W
Norwood, Mn., U.S. 190 44.46 N 93.55 W
Norwood, N.J., U.S. 276 40.59 N 73.57 W
Norwood, N.Y., U.S. 188 44.45 N 74.59 W
Norwood, N.C., U.S. 192 35.13 N 80.07 W
Norwood, Oh., U.S. 218 39.10 N 84.27 W
Norwood, Pa., U.S. 285 39.53 N 75.17 W
Norwood ◂[8] 273d 26.10 S 28.04 E
Norwood Memorial Airport ⊠ 283 42.11 N 71.10 W
Norwood Park ◂[8] 278 41.59 N 87.48 W
Norwood Pond ⊜ 283 42.35 N 70.52 W
Norwoodville 190 41.39 N 93.33 W
Noryang 98 34.56 N 127.52 E
Nosaka 94 35.39 N 140.34 E
Nosappu-misaki › 92a 43.23 N 145.49 E
Nosate 266b 45.33 N 8.43 E
Nosbonsing, Lake ⊜ 190 46.12 N 79.13 W
Nose 96 34.58 N 135.24 E
Nose ◂[8] 270 34.49 N 135.09 E
Nose Creek ≃ 182 54.52 N 119.38 W
Noshiro 92 40.12 N 140.02 E
Nosivka 78 50.55 N 31.35 E
Noska ≃ 86 58.53 N 68.40 E
Nosop (Nossob) ≃ 156 26.55 S 20.37 E
Nosova 86 59.30 N 63.13 E
Nosovaja, Ross. 24 68.15 N 54.35 E
Nosovaja, Ross. 80 57.15 N 45.35 E
Nosovo, Ross. 76 57.07 N 27.50 E
Nosovo, Ross. 83 47.16 N 38.40 E
Nosovščina 24 62.56 N 37.03 E
Noșratābād 128 29.54 N 59.59 E
Noss, Isle of I 46a 60.09 N 1.01 W
Nossa Senhora da Aparecida 256 22.02 S 42.48 W
Nossa Senhora das Dores 250 10.29 S 37.13 W
Nossa Senhora do Amparo 256 22.22 S 44.05 W

Nossa Senhora do Livramento 248 15.48 S 56.[illegible] W
Nossa Senhora do Ó ◂[8] 287b 23.30 S 46.[illegible] W
Nossebro 26 58.11 N 12.[illegible] E
Nossen 54 51.03 N 13.[illegible] E
Nossentiner Heide ◂[3] 54 53.35 N 12.2[illegible] E
Noss Head › 46 58.28 N 3.0[illegible] W
Nossob 156 22.18 S 17.1[illegible] E
Nossob (Nosop) ≃ 156 26.55 S 20.3[illegible] E
Nossombougou 150 13.06 N 7.5[illegible] W
Nošul' 24 60.09 N 49.2[illegible] E
Nosy Varika 157b 20.35 S 48.3[illegible] E
Notasulga 194 32.33 N 85.4[illegible] W
Notch Cliff 284b 39.27 N 76.31 W
Notch Hill 182 50.52 N 119.26 W
Notch Peak ʌ 200 39.08 N 113.24 W
Noteć ≃ 30 52.44 N 15.26 E
Notigi Lake ⊜ 184 55.57 N 99.18 W
Notikewin ≃ 176 57.15 N 117.05 W
Nótion Aiyaíon □[4] 38 37.00 N 25.30 E
Noto, It. 70 36.53 N 15.04 E
Noto, Nihon 92 37.18 N 137.09 E
Noto, Golfo di ⊂ 70 36.50 N 15.12
Noto, Val di ◂[1] 70 37.05 N 14.35
Noto Antica ⊥ 70 36.56 N 15.02 E
Notodden 26 59.34 N 9.17 E
Notogawa 94 35.10 N 136.10 E
Noto-hantō ›[1] 92 37.20 N 137.00 E
Noto-hantō-kokutei-kōen ♦ 94 37.10 N 136.50 E
Noto-jima 94 37.08 N 137.00 E
Noto-jima I 94 37.07 N 137.00 E
Nōtori-dake ʌ 94 35.37 N 138.15 E
Notoro-ko ⊜ 92a 44.05 N 144.10 E
Notozero, ozero ⊜ 24 66.28 N 32.05 E
Notre-Dame 186 46.19 N 64.43 W
Notre-Dame ʊ[1] 261 48.51 N 2.21 E
Notre-Dame, Bois ♦ 261 48.45 N 2.35 E
Notre-Dame, Monts ⋏ 186 48.10 N 68.00 W
Notre-Dame, Ruisseau ≃ 275a 45.41 N 73.26 W
Notre Dame Bay ⊂ 186 49.45 N 55.15 W
Notre-Dame-de-Bellecombe 62 45.48 N 6.31 E
Notre-Dame-de-Lorette ʊ[1] 50 50.25 N 2.42 E
Notre-Dame-de-Lourdes 184 49.32 N 98.33 W
Notre-Dame-de-Pierreville 206 46.06 N 72.53 W
Notre-Dame-des-Victoires ◂[8] 275a 45.35 N 73.34 W
Notre-Dame-du-Haut ʊ[1] 58 47.43 N 6.37 E
Notre-Dame-du-Laus 188 46.05 N 75.37 W
Notre-Dame-du-Nord 190 47.36 N 79.30 W
Notrees 196 31.55 N 102.45 W
Notreure ≃ 50 47.41 N 2.36 E
Notsu 96 33.02 N 131.42 E
Notsuharu 96 33.09 N 131.32 E
Nottawa 216 41.55 N 85.27 W
Nottawa Creek ≃ 216 42.01 N 85.24 W
Nottawasaga ≃ 212 44.32 N 80.01 W
Nottawasaga Bay ⊂ 212 44.35 N 80.15 W
Nottaway ≃ 176 51.22 N 79.55 W
Nottingham, Eng., U.K. 42 52.58 N 1.10 W
Nottingham, Pa., U.S. 208 39.45 N 76.01 W
Nottingham, Pa., U.S. 285 40.07 N 74.58 W
Nottingham Island I 176 63.20 N 77.55 W
Nottingham Park 278 41.46 N 87.48 W
Nottingham Road 158 29.22 S 30.00 E
Nottinghamshire □[6] 44 53.00 N 1.00 W
Notting Hill 274b 37.54 S 145.08 E
Nottleben 54 50.58 N 10.50 E
Nottoway 192 37.08 N 78.05 W
Nottoway ≃ 192 36.33 N 76.55 W
Nottuln 52 51.55 N 7.22 E
Notukeu Creek ≃ 184 49.55 N 106.30 W
Nouâdhibou 148 20.54 N 17.04 W
Nouâdhibou, Râs › 148 20.46 N 17.03 W
Nouakchott 150 18.06 N 15.57 W
Nouâmghâr 150 19.22 N 16.31 W
Nouan-le-Fuzelier 50 47.32 N 2.02 E
Nouans-les-Fontaines 50 47.08 N 1.18 E
Nouméa 175f 22.16 S 166.27 E
Noun ≃ 152 4.55 N 11.06 E
Nouna 150 12.44 N 3.52 W
Nounsley 260 51.46 N 0.36 E
Noupoort 158 31.10 S 24.57 E
Nous 158 28.44 S 19.52 E
Nouveau Brunswick → New Brunswick □[4] 186 46.30 N 66.15 W
Nouveau Mexique → New Mexico □[3] 178 34.30 N 106.00 W
Nouveau-Québec, Cratère du ⊥[6] 176 61.17 N 73.40 W
Nouvelle 186 48.08 N 66.19 W
Nouvelle ≃ 186 48.07 N 66.18 W
Nouvelle-Calédonie → New Caledonia □[2] 175f 21.30 S 165.30 E
Nouvelle-Calédonie (New Caledonia) I 175f 21.30 S 165.30 E
Nouvelle Écosse → Nova Scotia □[4] 186 45.00 N 63.00 W
Nouvelle-France, Cap de › 176 62.27 N 73.42 W
Nouvelle Galles du Sud → New South Wales □[3] 166 33.00 S 146.00 E
Nouvelle-Orléans → New Orleans 194 29.58 N 90.07 W
Nouvelles-Hébrides → Vanuatu □[1] 175f 16.00 S 167.00 E
Nouvelle Zélande → New Zealand □[1] 172 41.00 S 174.00 E
Nouvelle Zemble → Novaja Zeml'a II 72 74.00 N 57.00 E
Nouvion-en-Ponthieu 50 50.12 N 1.47 E
Nouvion-sur-Meuse 56 49.42 N 4.48 E
Nouzonville 56 49.49 N 4.45 E
Nova, Magy. 61 46.41 N 16.41 E
Nova, Oh., U.S. 214 41.02 N 82.18 W
Nova América 255 15.01 S 49.56 W
Nova Andradina 255 22.10 S 53.15 W
Nova Astrakhan' 83 49.07 N 38.36 E
Novabad, Taj. 85 39.01 N 70.09 E
Novabad, Taj. 85 38.37 N 68.45 E
Nová Baňa 30 48.26 N 18.39 E
Nova Bila 78 49.46 N 39.11 E
Nova Borova 78 50.42 N 28.39 E
Nová Bystřice 61 49.01 N 15.06 E
Nova Cachoeirinha ◂[8] 287b 23.28 S 46.40 W
Nova Caipemba 152 7.26 S 14.38 E
Novacella ʊ[1] 64 46.44 N 11.39 E
Nova Era 255 19.45 S 43.03 W
Nova Esperança 255 23.08 S 52.13 W
Novafeltria 66 43.53 N 12.17 E
Nova Friburgo 256 22.16 S 42.32 W
Nova Goa → Panaji 122 15.29 N 73.50 E
Nova Gorica 64 45.57 N 13.39 E
Nova Gradiška 36 45.16 N 17.23 E
Nova Granada 255 20.29 S 49.19 W
Nova Iguaçu 256 22.45 S 43.27 W
Nova Iguaçu □[7] 287a 22.45 S 43.29 W
Nova Ivanivka 78 45.55 N 29.05 E
Novaja, Ross. 82 55.13 N 38.54 E
Novaja, Ross. 265b 55.48 N 38.03 E
Novaja ◂[8] 265a 60.02 N 30.28 E
Novaja Binaradka 80 53.48 N 49.56 E
Novaja Čigla 78 51.13 N 40.28 E
Novaja Derevn'a, Ross. 82 54.01 N 38.53 E


| English | Deutsch | Español | Français | Português |
|---|---|---|---|---|
| ≃ River | Fluß | Río | Rivière | Rio |
| ≡ Canal | Kanal | Canal | Canal | Canal |
| Waterfall, Rapids | Wasserfall, Stromschnellen | Cascada, Rápidos | Chute d'eau, Rapides | Cascata, Rápidos |
| ⊔ Strait | Meeresstraße | Estrecho | Détroit | Estreito |
| ⊂ Bay, Gulf | Bucht, Golf | Bahía, Golfo | Baie, Golfe | Baía, Golfo |
| ⊜ Lake, Lakes | See, Seen | Lago, Lagos | Lac, Lacs | Lago, Lagos |
| Swamp | Sumpf | Pantano | Marais | Pântano |
| Ice Features, Glacier | Eis- und Gletscherformen | Accidentes Glaciales | Formes glaciaires | Acidentes glaciares |
| ⫪ Other Hydrographic Features | Andere Hydrographische Objekte | Otros Elementos Hidrográficos | Autres données hydrographiques | Outros acidentes hidrográficos |
| ✢ Submarine Features | Untermeerische Objekte | Accidentes Submarinos | Formes de relief sous-marin | Acidentes submarinos |
| □ Political Unit | Politische Einheit | Unidad Politica | Entité politique | Unidade política |
| ʊ Cultural Institution | Kulturelle Institution | Institución Cultural | Institution culturelle | Institução cultural |
| ⊥ Historical Site | Historische Stätte | Sitio Histórico | Site historique | Sitio histórico |
| ♦ Recreational Site | Erholungs- und Ferienort | Sitio de Recreo | Centre de loisirs | Area de Lazer |
| ⊠ Airport | Flughafen | Aeropuerto | Aéroport | Aeroporto |
| ■ Military Installation | Militäranlage | Instalación Militar | Installation militaire | Instalação militar |
| ◂ Miscellaneous | Verschiedenes | Misceláneo | Divers | Diversos |

Novaja Derevn'a, Ross. 88 57.15 N 103.08 E
Novaja Kalitva 78 50.06 N 40.01 E
Novaja Kazanka 80 48.57 N 49.36 E
Novaja Kazmaska 80 56.49 N 53.31 E
Novaja Kriuša 78 50.16 N 41.16 E
Novaja Ladoga 76 60.05 N 32.16 E
Novaja L'al'a 86 59.03 N 60.36 E
Novaja Maluksa 76 59.39 N 31.21 E
Novaja Malykla 80 54.13 N 49.57 E
Novaja Mojgora 82 54.27 N 38.32 E
Novaja Porubežka 80 51.45 N 49.40 E
Novaja Ropša 265a 59.45 N 29.53 E
Novaja Sibir', ostrov I 74 75.00 N 149.00 E
Novaja Slobodka 82 54.56 N 36.47 E
Novaja Šul'ba 86 50.33 N 81.20 E
Novaja Uda 88 54.07 N 103.33 E
Novaja Usman' 78 51.37 N 39.24 E
Novaja Zeml'a II 72 74.00 N 57.00 E
Nova Kakhovka 78 46.45 N 33.23 E
Nováky 30 48.43 N 18.34 E
Nova Lamego 150 12.19 N 14.11 W
Novale (Rauth) 64 46.24 N 11.30 E
Novalesa 62 45.11 N 7.01 E
Novaliches Reservoir ⊜[1] 269f 14.43 N 121.05 E
Nova Lima 255 19.59 S 43.51 W
Nova Lisboa → Huambo 152 12.44 S 15.47 E
Novalukoml' 76 54.40 N 29.08 E
Nova Lusitânia 156 19.54 S 34.35 E
Nova Mambone 156 20.59 S 35.01 E
Nova Mayachka 78 46.36 N 33.14 E
Nova Milanese 266b 45.35 N 9.12 E
Nova Nabúri 154 16.46 S 38.57 E
Nova Odesa 78 47.19 N 31.47 E
Nova Odessa 256 23.09 S 46.51 W
Nova Olinda 250 7.06 S 39.40 W
Nova Olinda do Norte 246 3.45 S 59.03 W
Nová Paka 30 50.29 N 15.31 E
Nova Ponente (Deutschnofen) 64 46.25 N 11.25 E
Nova Ponte 255 19.08 S 47.41 W
Nova Praha 78 48.33 N 32.54 E
Nova Prata 252 28.47 S 51.36 W
Novar 212 45.27 N 79.15 W
Novara 62 45.28 N 8.38 E
Novara □[4] 62 45.35 N 8.35 E
Novara di Sicilia 70 38.01 N 15.08 E
Nová Role 54 50.15 N 12.47 E
Nova Roma 255 13.51 S 46.57 W
Nova Russas 250 4.42 S 40.34 W
Nova Scotia □[4], Can. 176 45.00 N 63.00 W
Nova Scotia □[4], Can. 186 45.00 N 63.00 W
Nova Siri 68 40.09 N 16.32 E
Nova Sloboda 78 51.23 N 34.08 E
Nova Sofala 156 20.09 S 34.42 E
Nova Soure 250 11.14 S 38.29 W
Novate Mezzola 58 46.15 N 9.27 E
Novate Milanese 266b 45.32 N 9.08 E
Nova Timboteua 250 1.12 S 47.24 W
Novato 226 38.06 N 122.34 W
Novato Creek ≃ 282 38.06 N 122.29 W
Nova Ushytsya 78 48.49 N 27.16 E
Nova Vandúzi 156 18.57 S 33.16 E
Nova Varoš 38 43.28 N 19.48 E
Nova Venécia 255 18.43 S 40.24 W
Nova Viçosa 255 17.53 S 39.22 W
Nova Vida 248 10.11 S 62.47 W
Nova Vida, Cachoeira ⌞ 248 9.25 S 63.36 W
Nova Vodolaha 78 49.43 N 35.52 E
Novayanysol' 83 47.17 N 37.16 E
Nova Zagora 38 42.29 N 26.01 E
Nova Zburivka 78 46.28 N 32.24 E
Nove 64 45.43 N 11.40 E
Nové Hrady 61 48.47 N 14.37 E
Novelda 34 38.23 N 0.46 W
Novellara 64 44.51 N 10.44 E
Novelty 219 40.00 N 92.12 W
Nové Město 30 50.21 N 16.09 E
Nové Město nad Váhom 30 48.46 N 17.49 E
Nové Město na Moravě 30 49.34 N 16.04 E
Nové Mlýny, údolní nádrž ⊜[1] 61 48.54 N 16.34 E
Noventa di Piave 64 45.39 N 12.31 E
Noventa Padovana 64 45.24 N 11.58 E
Noventa Vicentina 64 45.17 N 11.32 E
Noves 62 43.52 N 4.54 E
Nové Sedlo 54 50.10 N 12.42 E
Nové Strašecí 54 50.07 N 13.53 E
Nové Údolí 60 48.48 N 13.48 E
Nové Zámky 30 47.59 N 18.11 E
Novgorod 76 58.31 N 31.17 E
Novgorod Oblast' □[4] 76 58.15 N 33.00 E
Novhorodka 78 48.21 N 32.39 E
Novhorod-Sivers'kyy 78 51.59 N 33.16 E
Novhorods'ke 83 48.20 N 37.50 E
Novi 216 42.28 N 83.28 W
Novi Basy 78 50.53 N 34.51 E
Novi Bečej 38 45.36 N 20.08 E
Novi Beograd 38 44.49 N 20.27 E
Novi Bilokorovychi 78 51.07 N 28.02 E
Novice 196 31.59 N 99.37 W
Novičicha 86 52.13 N 81.24 E
Novi di Modena 64 44.54 N 10.54 E
Novigrad, Hrv. 36 45.19 N 13.34 E
Novigrad, Hrv. 36 44.11 N 15.33 E
Novikovo, Ross. 86 58.15 N 80.39 E
Novikovo, Ross. 89 46.23 N 143.20 E
Novi Ligure 62 44.46 N 8.47 E
Noville 56 50.40 N 5.23 E
Novi Lyon Drain ≖ 281 42.30 N 83.38 W
Novinger 194 40.13 N 92.42 W
Novinka 76 59.49 N 33.20 E
Novion-Porcien 50 49.36 N 4.25 E
Novi Pazar, Blg. 38 43.21 N 27.12 E
Novi Pazar, Jugo. 38 43.08 N 20.31 E
Novi Sad 38 45.15 N 19.50 E
Novi Sanzhary 78 49.21 N 34.19 E
Novi Vinodolski 36 45.08 N 14.48 E
Novki 80 56.22 N 41.06 E
Novl'anka 80 55.48 N 41.44 E
Novlenskoje 76 59.37 N 39.20 E
Novo ≃, Bra. 248 4.55 S 70.33 W
Novo ≃, Bra. 250 4.30 S 53.50 W
Novo ≃, Bra. 250 6.22 S 55.42 W
Novo ≃, Bra. 256 21.23 S 42.44 W
Novo, Lago ⊜ 250 1.30 N 50.40 W
Nôvo Acôrdo 255 13.10 S 46.48 W
Novoaleksandrovka, Kaz. 86 51.47 N 68.49 E
Novoaleksandrovka, Ross. 80 51.56 N 52.26 E
Novoaleksandrovo 265b 55.59 N 37.33 E
Novoaleksandrovsk 80 45.29 N 41.16 E
Novoaleksejevka, Kaz. 86 52.56 N 64.41 E
Novoaleksejevka, Kaz. 86 52.47 N 74.54 E
Novoaleksejevka, Kaz. 86 50.08 N 55.39 E
Novoaltajsk 86 53.24 N 83.58 E
Novoamvrosiyivs'ke 83 47.49 N 38.29 E
Novoanninskij 80 50.32 N 42.41 E
Novoarchangel'skoje 265b 55.55 N 37.33 E
Novo Aripuanã 246 5.08 S 60.22 W
Novoarkhanhel's'k 78 48.39 N 30.48 E
Novoasbest 86 57.44 N 60.45 E
Novoaydar 83 48.57 N 39.00 E
Novoazovs'k 83 47.08 N 38.05 E
Novobatajsk 83 46.54 N 39.47 E
Novobelaja 78 49.49 N 39.18 E
Novobessergenovka 83 47.11 N 38.51 E
Novobogatinskoje 80 47.22 N 51.11 E
Novobogordskoje 80 53.11 N 53.56 E
Novobohdanivka 78 47.06 N 35.29 E
Novoborove 83 49.15 N 38.33 E
Novo Brasil 255 16.11 S 50.38 W
Novobratcevskij 82 55.51 N 37.23 E
Novoburejskij 89 49.49 N 129.54 E
Novočeboksarsk 80 56.08 N 47.30 E
Novo Čeremšansk 80 54.21 N 50.10 E
Novočerkassk 83 47.25 N 40.06 E
Novočernorečenskij 86 56.16 N 91.06 E
Novocharitonovo 82 55.35 N 38.30 E
Novocherkassk → Novočerkassk 83 47.25 N 40.06 E
Novochop'orsk 80 51.07 N 41.37 E
Novochop'orskij 80 51.06 N 41.33 E
Novochovrino ◆[8] 265b 55.52 N 37.30 E
Novociml'anskaja 80 47.59 N 42.17 E
Novo Cruzeiro 255 17.29 S 41.53 W
Novodanylivka 78 46.38 N 35.00 E
Novoderev'ankov-Skaja 78 46.19 N 38.45 E
Novodevičje 80 53.37 N 48.52 E
Novodolinka 86 51.12 N 72.33 E
Novodolinskij 86 49.44 N 72.45 E
Novodoroninskoje 88 51.08 N 112.08 E
Novodruzhes'k 83 48.58 N 38.21 E
Novodubovoje 76 52.19 N 39.13 E
Novodugino 76 55.38 N 34.18 E
Novodvinsk 24 64.26 N 40.47 E
Novodžerelijevskaja 78 45.46 N 38.41 E
Novoekonomichne 83 48.18 N 37.15 E
Novofetinino 82 56.14 N 39.17 E
Novogaritovo 80 52.47 N 40.07 E
Novogirejevo ◆[8] 265b 55.45 N 37.49 E
Novogorbovo 82 55.43 N 36.29 E
Novogornyj 86 55.37 N 60.47 E
Novogrigorjevskaja 80 49.26 N 43.37 E
Novogroznenskij 84 43.15 N 46.15 E
Novo Hamburgo 252 29.41 S 51.08 W
Novo Horizonte 255 21.28 S 49.13 W
Novohrad-Volyns'kyy 78 50.36 N 27.36 E
Novohrodivka 83 48.13 N 37.20 E
Novohryhorivka, Ukr. 78 46.24 N 34.59 E
Novohryhorivka, Ukr. 83 48.34 N 37.25 E
Novohupalivka 78 48.02 N 35.26 E
Novoiljinsk 88 51.42 N 108.41 E
Novoiljinskij 86 57.54 N 55.30 E
Novoivanivka 78 49.44 N 33.28 E
Novoivanovka 85 43.08 N 71.26 E
Novoivanovskoje 265b 55.43 N 37.22 E
Novoizborsk 76 57.50 N 27.59 E
Novojampol' 89 52.55 N 127.38 E
Novojamskoje 76 52.14 N 34.28 E
Novoje, Ross. 82 55.38 N 38.55 E
Novoje, Ross. 86 58.53 N 68.40 E
Novoje Alechnovo 82 56.02 N 36.49 E
Novojegorjevskoje 86 51.46 N 80.53 E
Novoje Koval'ovo 265a 59.59 N 30.34 E
Novoje Leušino 80 56.48 N 40.32 E
Novojenisejsk 86 58.16 N 92.24 E
Novoje Pavšino 82 54.15 N 37.07 E
Novoje Zarečje 76 57.43 N 34.22 E
Novokačalinsk 89 45.06 N 132.01 E
Novokadinsk 88 54.46 N 101.24 E
Novokamala 88 55.58 N 94.58 E
Novokarasuk 86 56.16 N 71.46 E
Novokaširovo 80 54.58 N 52.32 E
Novokaširsk 82 54.51 N 38.15 E
Novokazalinsk 86 45.50 N 62.10 E
Novokijevskij 80 50.27 N 43.08 E
Novokorsunskaja 78 45.38 N 39.09 E
Novokrasne 78 48.01 N 31.21 E
Novokrasnyanka 83 49.08 N 38.18 E
Novokručininskij 88 51.46 N 113.48 E
Novokubanka 86 51.40 N 70.44 E
Novokujbyševsk 80 53.07 N 49.58 E
Novokurovka 89 48.51 N 134.20 E
Novokuzneck 86 53.45 N 87.06 E
Novokuznetsk → Novokuzneck 86 53.45 N 87.06 E
Novolakskoje 84 43.07 N 46.29 E
Novolazarevskaja ʋ[3] 9 70.45 S 11.50 E
Novoleuškovskaja 78 45.59 N 39.58 E
Novoli 68 40.23 N 18.03 E
Novol'vovsk 76 53.55 N 38.47 E
Novomalorossijskaja 78 45.38 N 39.53 E
Novomansurkino 80 53.52 N 51.52 E
Novomargaritovka 83 46.54 N 38.50 E
Novomariinka 88 55.27 N 96.01 E
Novomarkovka 86 51.44 N 72.17 E
Novomel'nikov 84 43.56 N 45.09 E
Novomelovatka 78 50.27 N 40.46 E
Novomelovoje 78 51.23 N 38.13 E
Novo Mesto 36 45.48 N 15.10 E
Novomichajlovka 86 55.13 N 81.57 E
Novomichajlovskij 78 44.15 N 38.51 E
Novomichajlovskoje 82 55.25 N 37.10 E
Novominskaja 78 46.19 N 38.57 E
Novomoskovsk, Ross. 82 54.05 N 38.13 E
Novomoskovs'k, Ukr. 78 48.37 N 35.12 E
Novomykhaylivka, Ukr. 78 47.19 N 36.04 E
Novomykhaylivka, Ukr. 83 47.51 N 37.29 E
Novomykil's'ke 83 49.21 N 39.51 E
Novomykolayivka, Ukr. 78 46.13 N 32.45 E
Novomykolayivka, Ukr. 78 47.59 N 35.55 E
Novomyrhorod 78 48.47 N 31.39 E
Novomyšastovskaja 78 45.12 N 38.35 E
Novonagajevo 80 55.56 N 54.15 E
Novonikolajevka, Kaz. 85 42.26 N 70.28 E
Novonikolajevka, Ross. 83 46.59 N 39.36 E
Novonikolajevskij 80 50.58 N 42.22 E
Novonikolayevsk → Novosibirsk 86 55.02 N 82.55 E
Novonikol'skoje, Ross. 76 59.25 N 33.13 E
Novonikol'skoje, Ross. 80 49.09 N 45.00 E
Novonikol'skoje, Ross. 86 59.46 N 79.12 E
Novonikol'skoje, Ross. 265b 55.50 N 37.15 E
Novookhtyrka 83 48.55 N 38.49 E
Novooleksandrivka, Ukr. 83 48.17 N 39.37 E
Novooleksandrivka, Ukr. 83 49.08 N 39.17 E
Novooleksiyivka, Ukr. 78 46.06 N 32.30 E
Novooleksiyivka, Ukr. 78 46.13 N 34.39 E
Novo Oriente 250 5.32 S 40.42 W
Novoorsk 86 51.23 N 58.58 E
Novopavlovka 88 51.13 N 109.14 E
Novopavlovskaja 84 43.58 N 43.38 E
Novopavlovskoje 88 50.56 N 111.35 E
Novopetrovo 86 57.11 N 69.10 E
Novopetrovskoje 82 55.59 N 36.28 E
Novopiscovo 76 57.19 N 41.54 E
Novopodrezkovo 82 55.57 N 37.21 E
Novopokrovka, Kaz. 86 53.43 N 67.45 E
Novopokrovka, Kaz. 86 50.41 N 80.28 E
Novopokrovka, Kyrg. 85 42.52 N 74.45 E
Novopokrovka, Ross. 89 45.52 N 134.28 E
Novopokrovka, Ukr. 78 48.03 N 34.37 E
Novopokrovskoje 80 51.35 N 43.36 E
Novopolevodino 80 51.46 N 47.29 E
Novopskov 83 49.33 N 39.05 E
Novorajčichinsk 89 49.47 N 129.38 E
Novor'ažsk 80 53.44 N 40.07 E
Novorepnoje 80 51.06 N 48.24 E
Novorossijka 85 42.44 N 76.07 E
Novorossijsk 78 44.45 N 37.45 E
Novorossijskoje 86 50.13 N 58.00 E
Novorossiysk → Novorossijsk 78 44.45 N 37.45 E
Novorozsosh 83 49.32 N 39.15 E
Novorudnyj 86 51.30 N 58.10 E
Novorybinka 86 51.51 N 71.14 E
Novorybnoje 74 72.50 N 105.50 E
Novoržev 76 57.02 N 29.20 E
Novošachtinsk 83 47.47 N 39.56 E
Novosaratovka 265a 59.50 N 30.32 E
Novoščerbinovskaja 78 46.28 N 38.38 E
Novosel'e 86 54.10 N 76.53 E
Novoselenginsk 88 51.06 N 106.37 E
Novoselickoje 84 44.45 N 43.26 E
Novoselivka 83 49.04 N 37.42 E
Novoselivs'ke 78 45.26 N 33.34 E
Novoselje 265a 59.48 N 30.05 E
Novoselki, Ross. 82 55.08 N 37.33 E
Novoselki, Ross. 82 54.49 N 38.55 E
Novosel'nyj 86 50.00 N 54.38 E
Novoselovo 82 56.04 N 39.04 E
Novoselytsya, Ukr. 78 48.14 N 26.17 E
Novoselytsya, Ukr. 78 49.48 N 25.03 E
Novosemejkino 80 53.23 N 50.22 E
Novosergijevka, Ross. 80 52.06 N 53.39 E
Novosergijevka, Ross. 265a 59.54 N 30.34 E
Novoseslavino 80 53.21 N 40.26 E
Novošešminsk 80 55.04 N 51.15 E
Novoshakhtinsk → Novošachtinsk 83 47.47 N 39.56 E
Novosibirsk 86 55.02 N 82.55 E
Novosibirskije ostrova II 74 75.00 N 142.00 E
Novosibirsk Oblast' □[4] 86 55.00 N 80.00 E
Novosibirskoje vodochranilišče ⊜[1] 86 54.35 N 82.35 E
Novosil' 76 52.58 N 37.03 E
Novosil's'ke 78 45.20 N 28.33 E
Novosil'skoje 78 51.56 N 38.31 E
Novosokol'niki 76 56.21 N 30.10 E
Novos'olki, Ross. 76 56.01 N 33.37 E
Novos'olki, Ross. 80 55.48 N 42.41 E
Novos'olki, Ross. 80 54.50 N 39.46 E
Novos'olki, Ross. 265a 59.42 N 30.17 E
Novos'olovo, Ross. 86 55.04 N 91.07 E
Novos'olovo, Ross. 88 56.04 N 107.42 E
Novospasovka 83 47.42 N 39.04 E
Novospasskoje 80 53.08 N 47.45 E
Novostril'tsivka 83 49.20 N 39.55 E
Novostrojevo 76 54.27 N 21.50 E
Novosvitlivka 83 48.30 N 39.30 E
Novosysojevka 89 44.14 N 133.22 E
Novotavolžanka 78 50.22 N 36.50 E
Novotitarovskaja 78 45.14 N 39.00 E
Novotroick, Ross. 86 56.11 N 78.41 E
Novotroick, Ross. 86 51.12 N 58.20 E
Novotroickoje, Kaz. 85 43.42 N 73.46 E
Novotroickoje, Ross. 80 58.28 N 47.06 E
Novo-Troitsk → Novotroick 86 51.12 N 58.20 E
Novotroyits'ke, Ukr. 78 46.22 N 34.20 E
Novotroyits'ke, Ukr. 83 47.43 N 37.35 E
Novotulka, Ross. 80 52.38 N 48.45 E
Novotulka, Ross. 80 50.50 N 47.34 E
Novotul'skij 82 54.10 N 37.43 E
Novoukolovo 78 51.02 N 38.25 E
Novoukrayinka 78 48.19 N 31.32 E
Novouljanovsk 80 54.08 N 48.24 E
Novoural'sk 86 51.15 N 57.16 E
Novouzensk 80 50.28 N 48.08 E
Novovaršavka 86 54.11 N 74.42 E
Novovasylivka, Ukr. 78 46.51 N 36.46 E
Novovasylivka, Ukr. 78 46.48 N 35.44 E
Novov'atsk 80 58.29 N 49.44 E
Novov'azniki 80 56.12 N 42.10 E
Novovolyns'k 78 50.50 N 24.05 E
Novovoronežskij 78 51.16 N 39.11 E
Novovorontsovka 78 47.29 N 33.54 E
Novovoskresenovka 85 42.50 N 73.32 E
Novovoskresens'ke 78 47.21 N 33.37 E
Novozacharkino 80 52.11 N 48.29 E
Novozagorje 82 55.39 N 38.38 E
Novozavidovskij 82 56.33 N 36.26 E
Novožilovskaja 24 64.50 N 51.20 E
Novozizevka 80 50.48 N 49.08 E
Novozybkov 76 52.32 N 31.56 E
Novska 36 45.21 N 16.59 E
Nový Bohumín 30 49.56 N 18.20 E
Nový Bor 54 50.45 N 14.33 E
Novy Dvor 76 52.50 N 24.21 E
Novyj 86 55.39 N 86.39 E
Novyja Dzjanisavičy 76 54.12 N 29.13 E
Novyj Afon 84 43.06 N 40.48 E
Novyja Valosavičy 76 54.46 N 28.50 E
Novyj Bor 24 66.43 N 52.16 E
Novyj Bujan 80 53.41 N 50.04 E
Novyje Ajbesi 80 54.49 N 47.02 E
Novyje Burasy 80 52.08 N 46.06 E
Novyje Gorki 80 56.42 N 41.06 E
Novyje Maty 80 55.15 N 54.04 E
Novyje Salty 80 54.06 N 53.26 E
Novyje Z'atcy 80 57.27 N 52.36 E
Nový Jičín 30 49.36 N 18.00 E
Novyj Jegorlyk 80 46.24 N 41.54 E
Novyj Karačaj 84 43.49 N 41.56 E
Novyj Karamass 80 56.11 N 48.58 E
Novyj Kiner 80 56.24 N 49.44 E
Novyj Multan 80 57.09 N 52.19 E
Novyj Nekouz 76 57.54 N 38.04 E
Novyj Oskol 78 50.46 N 37.53 E
Novyj Port 74 67.40 N 72.52 E
Novyj Put' 85 43.29 N 73.52 E
Novyj Ropsk 76 52.18 N 32.19 E
Novyj Stan 82 56.18 N 37.00 E
Novyj Tap 86 57.04 N 67.49 E
Novyj Terek ≃ 84 43.37 N 47.25 E
Novyj Tevriz 86 59.04 N 78.08 E
Novyj Uzen' 72 43.18 N 52.48 E
Novyj Vas'ugan 86 58.34 N 76.29 E
Novy Pahost 76 55.30 N 27.29 E
Novy Torjal 80 57.00 N 48.44 E
Novyy Buh 78 47.41 N 32.30 E
Novyy Bykiv 78 50.36 N 31.39 E
Novyy Svit 83 47.48 N 38.00 E
Novyy Yarychiv 78 49.55 N 24.18 E
Nowa Dęba 30 50.26 N 21.46 E
Nowaja Semlja → Novaja Zeml'a II 72 74.00 N 57.00 E
Nowa Ruda 30 50.35 N 16.31 E
Nowa Sól (Neusalz) 30 51.48 N 15.44 E
Nowata 196 36.42 N 95.38 W
Nowater Creek ≃ 202 43.57 N 108.00 W
Nowbarān 128 35.08 N 48.42 E
Nowe 30 53.40 N 18.43 E
Nowe Miasto Lubawskie 30 53.27 N 19.35 E
Nowe Miasto nad Pilicą 30 51.38 N 20.35 E
Nowendoc 166 31.32 S 151.43 E
Nowe Warpno 30 53.44 N 14.16 E
Nowfel low Shātow 128 34.23 N 50.32 E
Nowgong 124 25.04 N 79.27 E
Nowingi 166 34.36 S 142.14 E
Nowitna ≃ 180 65.55 N 154.17 W
Nowogard 30 53.40 N 15.08 E
Nowogród 30 53.15 N 21.53 E
Nowogrodziec 30 51.12 N 15.25 E
Nowokusnezk → Novokuzneck 86 53.45 N 87.06 E
Nowood ≃ 202 44.17 N 107.58 W
Nowosibirsk → Novosibirsk 86 55.02 N 82.55 E
Nowra 170 34.53 S 150.36 E
Nowrangapur 122 19.14 N 82.33 E
Nowshāk ∧ 123 36.26 N 71.50 E
Nowshera 123 34.01 N 71.59 E
Nowy Dwór Gdański 30 54.13 N 19.06 E
Nowy Dwór Mazowiecki 30 52.26 N 20.43 E
Nowy Sącz 30 49.38 N 20.42 E
Nowy Sącz □[4] 30 49.30 N 20.15 E
Nowy Staw 30 54.09 N 19.00 E
Nowy Targ 30 49.29 N 20.02 E
Nowy Tomyśl 30 52.20 N 16.07 E
Now Zād 120 32.24 N 64.28 E
Noxapater 194 32.59 N 89.03 W
Noxe ≃ 50 48.33 N 3.35 E
Noxen 210 41.25 N 76.03 W
Noxon 202 48.00 N 115.47 W
Noxon Reservoir ⊜[1] 202 47.54 N 115.40 W
Noxubee ≃ 194 32.50 N 88.10 W
Noy ≃ 110 17.05 N 105.02 E
Noya ≃ 152 0.58 N 9.48 E
Noyant 50 47.31 N 0.08 E
Noye ≃ 50 49.51 N 2.20 E
Noyelles-sur Mer 50 50.11 N 1.43 E
Noyers 50 47.42 N 4.00 E
Noyers, Ruisseau des ≃ 275a 45.21 N 73.22 W
Noyers-sur-Jabron 62 44.10 N 5.50 E
Noyes Island I 182 55.30 N 133.40 W
Noyon 50 49.35 N 3.00 E
Nožaj-Jurt 84 43.05 N 46.24 E
Nozawa-onsen 94 36.55 N 138.27 E
Nozay, Fr. 32 47.34 N 1.38 W
Nozay, Fr. 261 48.40 N 2.14 E
Nozeroy 58 46.47 N 6.02 E
Nozori-dam ◆[6] 94 36.43 N 138.39 E
Nozori-ko ⊜ 94 36.42 N 138.39 E
Nozuta 268 35.35 N 139.27 E
Nqamakwe 158 32.12 S 27.56 E
Nqutu 158 28.13 S 30.32 E
N'Riquinha 152 15.45 S 21.42 E
N'Rougas 158 29.07 S 21.09 E
Nsa, Oued en V 148 32.28 N 5.24 E
Nsaba 150 5.39 N 0.45 W
Nsah 152 2.22 S 15.19 E
Nsang 152 2.02 N 10.56 E
Nsanje 154 16.55 S 35.12 E
Nsawam 150 5.50 N 0.20 W
Nsefu Game Reserve ◆[4] 154 13.07 S 32.10 E
Nsele ≃ 152 4.14 S 15.33 E
Nseleni 158 28.33 S 31.39 E
Nsok 152 1.08 N 11.16 E
Nsoko 158 27.02 S 31.57 E
Nsontin 152 3.09 S 18.00 E
Nsouélé 273b 4.12 S 15.11 E
Nsukka 150 6.52 N 7.24 E
Nsuta 150 5.17 N 1.58 W
Ntakat 150 16.49 N 11.43 W
Ntambanana 158 28.36 S 31.45 E
Ntandembele 152 2.11 S 17.08 E
Ntcheu 154 14.49 S 34.38 E
Ntem ≃ 152 2.15 N 9.45 E
Ntoum 152 0.23 N 9.47 E
Ntsama 152 0.32 S 14.38 E
N'Tsaoueni 157a 11.27 S 43.18 E
Ntui 152 4.27 N 11.38 E
Ntumba 154 8.20 S 32.05 E
Ntusi 154 0.03 N 31.13 E
Ntwetwe Pan ≚ 156 20.30 S 25.20 E
Nuala 154 13.27 S 28.16 E
Nuanchitang 104 41.02 N 120.41 E
Nuanetsi ≃ 156 22.40 S 31.50 E
Nuangola 210 41.09 N 75.58 W
Nuanli 102 23.26 N 100.51 E
Nuannuan 269d 25.06 N 121.44 E
Nuanshui 100 28.53 N 117.51 E
Nuanzhouying 100 25.22 N 117.22 E
Nuasjärvi ⊜ 26 64.10 N 28.05 E
Nuatabu 174t 1.33 N 172.59 E
Nuatja 150 6.57 N 1.10 E
Nu'aymah 132 32.38 N 36.10 E
Nūbah 142 30.29 N 31.33 E
Nūbah, Jibāl an- ⋏ 140 11.00 N 30.45 E
Nūbārīyah, Tur'at an- ≖ 142 30.43 N 30.46 E
Nubian Desert ◆[2] 140 20.30 N 33.00 E
Ñuble ≃ 252 36.39 S 72.27 W
Nubra ≃ 123 34.39 N 77.36 E
Nucet 38 46.28 N 22.35 E
Nucetto 62 44.20 N 8.04 E
Nucha → Şeki 84 41.12 N 47.12 E
Nuchatlitz Inlet ⊂ 182 49.45 N 126.55 W
N'uchča 24 63.27 N 46.28 E
Nuch'ŏn-ni 98 38.14 N 126.16 E
Nucla 200 38.16 N 108.32 W
Núcleo Colonial São Bento 287a 22.44 S 43.18 W
N'učpas 24 60.51 N 51.18 E
Nucuray ≃ 246 5.02 S 75.34 W
Nuda, Monte la ∧ 64 44.17 N 10.15 E
Nudaybah 142 30.59 N 30.22 E
Nüdlingen 56 50.13 N 10.08 E
Nudol' ≃ 82 56.07 N 36.42 E
Nudol'-Šarino 82 56.06 N 36.31 E
Nudow 264a 52.20 N 13.10 E
Nueces ≃ 196 27.50 N 97.30 W
Nueces Plains ≚ 196 28.30 N 99.15 W
Nueltin Lake ⊜ 176 60.20 N 99.50 W
Nuenen 52 51.29 N 5.33 E
Nü'er ≃ 98 40.57 N 121.19 E
Nü'erhe 104 41.04 N 121.00 E
Nuestra Señora de Talavera 252 25.26 S 63.48 W
Nueva, Isla I 254 55.13 S 66.30 W
Nueva Antioquia 246 6.05 N 69.26 W
Nueva Asunción □[5] 248 21.00 S 61.00 W
Nueva Atzacoalco ◆[8] 286a 19.29 N 99.05 W
Nueva Brunswick → New Brunswick □[4] 186 46.30 N 66.15 W
Nueva Caledonia → New Caledonia □[2] 175f 21.30 S 165.30 E
Nueva Chicago ◆[8] 288 34.40 S 58.30 W
Nueva Ciudad Guerrero 232 26.35 N 99.15 W
Nueva Concepción 236 14.08 N 89.18 W
Nueva Cuadrilla 234 18.04 N 101.33 W
Nueva Ecija □[4] 116 15.35 N 121.00 E
Nueva Escocia → Nova Scotia □[4] 186 45.00 N 63.00 W
Nueva Esparta □[3] 246 11.00 N 64.00 W
Nueva Francia 252 28.11 S 64.12 W
Nueva Galia 252 35.07 S 65.15 W
Nueva Germania 252 23.54 S 56.45 W
Nueva Gerona 240p 21.53 N 82.48 W
Nueva Guinea, Isla → New Guinea I 164 5.00 S 140.00 E
Nueva Hébridas → Vanuatu □[1] 175f 16.00 S 167.00 E
Nueva Helvecia 258 34.19 S 57.13 W
Nueva Imperial 252 38.44 S 72.57 W
Nueva Italia de Ruiz 234 19.01 N 102.06 W
Nueva Loja 246 0.06 N 76.52 W
Nueva Lubecka 254 44.32 S 70.24 W
Nueva Ocotepeque 236 14.24 N 89.13 W
Nueva Palmira 258 33.53 S 58.25 W
Nueva Paz 240p 22.46 N 81.45 W
Nueva Pompeya ◆[8] 288 34.39 S 58.25 W
Nueva Rosita 232 27.57 N 101.13 W
Nueva San Salvador 236 13.41 N 89.17 W
Nueva Segovia □[5] 236 13.40 N 86.10 W
Nueva Siberia, Islas → Novosibirskije ostrova II 74 75.00 N 142.00 E
Nueva Venecia 236 14.03 N 91.33 W
Nueva Vizcaya □[4] 116 16.25 N 121.10 E
Nueva Zelandia → New Zealand □[1] 172 41.00 S 174.00 E
Nueva Zembla, Isla de → Novaja Zeml'a II 72 74.00 N 57.00 E
Nueve, Canal Numero ≖ 252 36.11 S 57.18 W
Nueve de Julio 252 35.27 S 60.52 W
Nuevitas 240p 21.33 N 77.16 W
Nuevitas, Bahía de ⊂ 240p 21.30 N 77.12 W
Nuevo 228 33.48 N 117.09 W
Nuevo, Bajo ✢[4] 238 15.55 N 78.30 W
Nuevo, Cayo I 232 21.51 N 92.05 W
Nuevo, Golfo ⊂ 254 42.42 S 64.36 W
Nuevo Berlín 252 32.59 S 58.03 W


**ENGLISH**


Name Page Lat.°′ Long.°′
Nuevo Camarón 196 27.05 N 99.55 W
Nuevo Casas Grandes 232 30.25 N 107.55 W
Nuevo Chagres 236 9.14 N 80.05 W
Nuevo Delicias 232 26.15 N 102.50 W
Nuevo Laredo 232 27.30 N 99.31 W
Nuevo Léon 204 32.20 N 115.12 W
Nuevo León □[3] 232 25.40 N 100.00 W
Nuevo Morelos 234 17.31 N 95.02 W
Nuevo Necaxa 234 20.13 N 98.00 W
Nuevo Poblado el Oro 196 26.50 N 101.19 W
Nuevo Primero de Mayo 196 26.01 N 98.02 W
Nuevo Progreso 232 18.38 N 92.18 W
Nuevo Rocafuerte 246 0.56 S 75.24 W
Nuevo Saucillo 196 27.20 N 104.54 W
Nufcor 273d 26.17 S 27.44 E
Nugaal □[4] 144 8.30 N 49.00 E
Nugaaleed, Dooxo V 144 8.35 N 48.35 E
Nugget Point › 172 46.27 S 169.49 E
Nûgssuaq ›[1] 176 70.25 N 52.30 W
Nugu ⊜[1] 122 11.58 N 76.28 E
Nuguria Islands II 14 3.20 S 154.45 E
Nūh 124 28.07 N 77.01 E
Nūh, Rās › 128 25.05 N 62.24 E
Nuhaka 172 39.03 S 177.45 E
Nuhaydāt as-Sūd, Jabal an- ∧ 142 28.01 N 32.21 E
Nuhūd, Jabal an- ∧ 140 14.50 N 29.53 E
Nui I[1] 14 7.15 S 177.10 E
Nuia 76 58.04 N 25.33 E
Nuits-Saint-Georges 58 47.08 N 4.57 E
Nuits-sur-Armançon 50 47.44 N 4.12 E
N'uja 74 60.32 N 116.14 E
N'uja ≃ 74 60.32 N 116.20 E
Nujiang 102 29.58 N 97.25 E
N'uk, ozero ⊜ 24 64.27 N 31.45 E
Nuka Island I 180 59.21 N 150.42 W
Nukan 175c 7.23 N 151.53 E
Nukata 94 34.55 N 137.17 E
Nukatl', chrebet ⋏ 84 42.15 N 46.35 E
Nukey Bluff ⊥[4] 166 32.33 S 135.40 E
Nukhayb 128 32.02 N 42.15 E
Nukhaylah ⫪[4] 140 19.03 N 26.19 E
Nukhaylah, Wādī an- V 132 31.27 N 35.49 E
N'uksenica 24 60.25 N 44.13 E
Nuku'alofa 174w 21.08 S 175.12 W
Nukufetau I[1] 14 8.00 S 178.22 E
Nukuhu 164 5.35 S 149.25 E
Nukulaelae I[1] 14 9.23 S 179.52 E
Nukumanu Islands II 14 4.30 S 159.30 E
Nukunonu I 14 9.12 S 171.54 W
Nukunuku 174w 21.08 S 175.18 W
Nukuoro I[1] 14 3.51 N 154.58 E
Nukus 72 42.50 N 59.29 E
Nul 175f 16.49 S 168.24 E
Nulato 180 64.43 N 158.06 W
Nullagine 162 21.53 S 120.06 E
Nullagine ≃ 162 20.43 S 120.33 E
Nullarbor 162 31.26 S 130.55 E
Nullarbor National Park ♠ 162 31.30 S 130.30 E
Nullarbor Plain ≚ 162 31.00 S 129.00 E
Nulltown 218 39.35 N 85.10 W
Nul'vand 85 38.16 N 70.32 E
Nulvi 71 40.47 N 8.45 E
Num, Mios I 164 1.30 S 135.13 E
Numabin Bay ⊂ 184 56.30 N 103.08 W
Numakuma 96 34.23 N 133.20 E
Numan 146 9.28 N 12.02 E
Numana 66 43.31 N 13.37 E
Numancia 116 9.52 N 125.58 E
Numancia ⊥ 34 41.48 N 2.25 W
Numansdorp 52 51.44 N 4.26 E
Numara I 122 6.26 N 73.03 E
Numata, Nihon 92a 43.48 N 141.57 E
Numata, Nihon 94 36.38 N 139.03 E
Numata, Nihon 96 34.27 N 132.24 E
Numatinna ≃ 140 7.14 N 27.37 E
Numazu 94 35.06 N 138.52 E
Numbargulme, Mount ∧ 164 14.56 S 145.03 E
Number 5 Mine 214 41.08 N 80.11 W
Nümbrecht 56 50.54 N 7.32 E
Numedal V 26 60.06 N 9.06 E
Numeralla 171b 36.11 S 149.20 E
Numeralla ≃ 171b 36.06 S 149.11 E
Numfoor, Pulau I 164 1.03 S 134.54 E
Numidia 210 40.53 N 76.24 W
Numila 229b 21.54 N 159.33 W
Nu Mine 214 40.48 N 79.18 W
Numto 74 63.40 N 71.20 E
Numurkah 166 36.06 S 145.26 E
Nun ≃[1] 150 4.20 N 6.00 E
Nun'amo 180 65.37 N 170.40 W
Nunapitchuk 180 60.54 N 162.29 W
Nunawading 169 37.49 S 145.10 E
Nünchritz 54 51.18 N 13.23 E
Nunda 210 42.34 N 77.56 W
Nundah 171a 27.24 S 153.04 E
Nundu 154 3.49 S 29.05 E
Nuneaton 42 52.32 N 1.28 W
Núñes, Isla I 254 53.31 S 73.48 W
Núñez ◆[8] 288 34.33 S 58.27 W
Nunez ≃ 150 10.36 N 14.40 W
Nungarin 162 31.11 S 118.06 E
Nungesser Lake ⊜ 184 51.28 N 93.35 W
Nungwe 154 2.46 S 32.01 E
Nunica 216 43.04 N 86.04 W
Nunivak Island I 180 60.00 N 166.30 W
Nunjiang 89 49.10 N 125.11 E
Nunjikompita 162 32.16 S 134.19 E
Nunkini 232 20.20 N 90.11 W
Nunkun ∧ 123 33.59 N 76.01 E
Nunligran 180 64.48 N 175.24 W
Nunnelly 194 35.51 N 87.28 W
Ñuñoa 286e 33.28 S 70.36 W
Nunshan 89 48.59 N 125.14 E
Nunspeet 52 52.23 N 5.46 E
Nuomin ≃ 89 48.06 N 124.26 E
Nuomin Dashan ∧ 89 50.15 N 122.46 E
Nuon ≃ 150 6.30 N 8.36 W
Nuoro 71 40.19 N 9.20 E
Nuoro □[4] 71 40.10 N 9.20 E
Nuqruș, Jabal ∧ 140 24.49 N 34.36 E
Nuquí 246 5.42 N 77.17 W
Nura 86 48.53 N 62.20 E
Nura ≃ 86 50.30 N 69.59 E
Nurallao 71 39.47 N 9.05 E
Nuraminis 71 39.26 N 9.01 E
Nuratau, chrebet ⋏ 85 40.20 N 67.15 E
Nuraxi, Nuraghe su ⊥ 71 39.42 N 9.00 E
N'urba 74 63.17 N 118.20 E
Nürburg 56 50.21 N 6.57 E
Nürburgring ♠ 56 50.21 N 6.58 E
Nur Dağları ⋏ 130 36.45 N 36.20 E
Nure ≃ 62 45.03 N 9.49 E
Nurek 85 38.23 N 69.19 E
Nurekskoje vodochranilišče ⊜[1] 85 38.30 N 69.30 E
Nuremberg → Nürnberg, Dtsch. 60 49.27 N 11.04 E
Nuremberg, Pa., U.S. 210 40.56 N 76.10 W
Nürenbei 107 30.11 N 106.04 E
Nūrestān □[9] 123 35.30 N 70.45 E
Nurettin 130 39.14 N 42.25 E
Nurhak 130 37.58 N 37.25 E
Nuria, Monte ∧ 66 42.21 N 13.05 E
Nuriootpa 168b 34.29 S 139.00 E
Nurlat 80 54.26 N 50.46 E
Nurlaty 80 55.37 N 48.18 E
Nūrmahal 123 31.06 N 75.36 E
Nurmes 26 63.33 N 29.07 E
Nurmijärvi 26 60.28 N 24.48 E
Nūrnagar 126 22.20 N 89.03 E
Nürnberg 60 49.27 N 11.04 E
Nürnberg, Flughafen ⊠ 60 49.30 N 11.06 E


**DEUTSCH**


Name Seite Breite°′ Länge°′ E = Ost
Nūrpur, India 123 31.10 N 76.29 E
Nūrpur, India 123 32.18 N 75.54 E
Nurpur, India 126 22.13 N 88.05 E
Nūrpur, Pāk. 123 31.53 N 71.54 E
Nurrari Lakes ⊜ 162 29.01 S 130.05 E
Nurri 71 39.43 N 9.14 E
Nurri, Mount ∧[2] 166 31.42 S 146.02 E
Nursery 222 28.56 N 97.06 W
Nürtingen 56 48.38 N 9.20 E
Nus 62 45.45 N 7.28 E
Nūsah 144 14.00 N 46.43 E
Nusa Tenggara Barat □[4] 115b 8.50 S 117.30 E
Nusa Tenggara Timur □[4] 112 9.30 S 122.00 E
Nusaybin 130 37.03 N 41.13 E
Nuṣayrīyah, Jabal an- ⋏ 130 35.30 N 36.12 E
Nusco 68 40.53 N 15.05 E
Nushagak ≃ 180 59.00 N 158.30 W
Nushagak Bay ⊂ 180 58.40 N 158.40 W
Nushagak Peninsula ›[1] 180 58.30 N 159.00 W
Nu Shan ⋏ 102 27.00 N 99.00 E
Nüshan Hu ⊜ 100 32.57 N 118.03 E
Nu-shima I 96 34.10 N 134.50 E
Nushki 120 29.33 N 66.01 E
Nusplingen 58 48.08 N 8.53 E
Nušpoly 82 56.39 N 37.44 E
Nussdorf ◆[8] 264b 48.15 N 16.22 E
Nussdorf am Attersee 64 47.53 N 13.31 E
Nuta ≃ 96 34.23 N 133.04 E
Nutauge, laguna ⊂ 180 67.55 N 176.45 W
Nutepel'men, Ross. 180 67.26 N 174.56 W
Nutepelmen, Ross. 180 65.31 N 178.30 W
Nutfield 260 51.14 N 0.07 W
Nuth 56 50.55 N 5.54 E
Nuthe ≃, Dtsch. 54 51.58 N 11.53 E
Nuthe ≃, Dtsch. 54 52.23 N 13.04 E
Nut Lake Indian Reserve ◆[4] 184 52.20 N 103.30 W
Nutley 210 40.49 N 74.09 W
Nutrioso 200 33.57 N 109.12 W
Nut Swamp Brook ≃ 276 40.21 N 74.06 W
Nuttby Mountain ∧[2] 186 45.33 N 63.13 W
Nutter Fort 188 39.15 N 80.19 W
Nutting Lake 207 42.32 N 71.16 W
Nutting Lake ⊜ 283 42.32 N 71.16 W
Nutwood 219 39.05 N 90.39 W
Nutwood Downs 164 15.49 S 134.10 E
Nutzotin Mountains ⋏ 180 62.10 N 141.40 W
Nu'ūmīyah, Wādī an- V 142 29.31 N 31.17 E
Nuupere, Pointe › 174s 17.36 S 149.47 W
Nu'uuli 174u 14.18 S 170.42 W
N'uvčim 24 61.22 N 50.42 E
Nuwākoṭ 124 28.08 N 83.53 E
Nuwaybi' al-Muzayyinah 140 28.58 N 34.39 E
Nuwerus 158 31.08 S 18.24 E
Nuweveldberge ⋏ 158 32.13 S 22.10 E
Nuxis 71 39.09 N 8.44 E
Nuyakuk Lake ⊜ 180 60.00 N 158.40 W
Nuyts, Point › 162 35.04 S 116.37 E
Nuyts Archipelago II 162 32.35 S 133.17 E
Nūzvīd 122 16.47 N 80.51 E
N'Vinda 152 13.04 S 18.57 E
Nwa 152 6.30 N 11.00 E
Nxainxai 156 19.50 S 21.13 E
Nxai Pan National Park ♠ 156 19.45 S 24.50 E
Nxaunxau 156 18.19 S 21.04 E
Nyaake 150 4.52 N 7.37 W
Nyabéssan 152 2.24 N 10.24 E
Nyabing 162 33.32 S 118.09 E
Nyac 180 61.01 N 159.57 W
Nyack 210 41.05 N 73.55 W
Nyack Beach State Park ♠ 276 41.07 N 73.55 W
Nyadiri ≃ 154 16.44 S 32.33 E
Nyahanga 154 2.23 S 33.33 E
Nyahua 154 5.24 S 33.19 E
Nyahururu Falls 154 0.02 N 36.22 E
Nyah West 166 35.11 S 143.22 E
Nyainqêntanglha Feng ∧ 124 30.22 N 90.35 E
Nyainqêntanglha Shan ⋏ 120 30.00 N 90.00 E
Nyainrong 120 32.09 N 92.11 E
Nyakabindi 154 2.38 S 33.59 E
Nyakakiri 154 2.15 S 31.28 E
Nyakanazi 154 3.00 S 31.15 E
Nyakrom 150 5.37 N 0.48 W
Nyakulenga 152 13.03 S 23.29 E
Nyala 140 12.03 N 24.53 E
Nyalam 120 28.11 N 85.58 E
Nyalas 114 2.26 N 102.28 E
Nyamandhlovu 154 19.50 S 28.16 E
Nyamina 150 13.19 N 6.59 W
Nyamlell 140 9.07 N 26.58 E
Nyamougo 154 1.29 S 34.33 E
Nyamtumbo 154 10.29 S 36.02 E
Nyamwage 154 8.08 S 39.00 E
Nyandekwa 154 3.55 S 32.30 E
Nyanding, Khawr V 140 8.40 N 32.41 E
Nyang ≃ 124 29.25 N 94.22 E
Nyanga □[4] 152 3.00 S 11.00 E
Nyanga ≃ 152 2.58 S 10.15 E
Nyanga, Lake ⊜ 162 29.57 S 126.10 E
Nyangana 156 18.00 S 20.41 E
Nyangui ∧ 154 17.53 S 32.44 E
Nyanji Mission 154 14.23 S 31.48 E
Nyanza 154 2.21 S 29.45 E
Nyanza □[4] 154 0.30 S 34.30 E
Nyanza-Lac 154 4.21 S 29.36 E
Nyasa, Lake (Lake Malawi) ⊜ 154 12.00 S 34.30 E
Nyaunglebin 110 17.57 N 96.44 E
Nyavikungu 154 11.26 S 25.54 E
Nyazura 154 18.43 S 32.10 E
Nyazvidzi ≃ 154 20.00 S 32.17 E
Nybergsund 26 61.15 N 12.19 E
Nyborg 41 55.19 N 10.48 E
Nybro 26 56.45 N 15.54 E
Nyda 74 66.36 N 72.54 E
Nyêmo 124 29.25 N 90.08 E
Nyengo Swamp ≡ 152 14.51 S 22.07 E
Nyeri 154 0.25 S 36.57 E
Nyerol 140 8.41 N 32.02 E
Nyfer ≃ 42 52.02 N 4.50 W
Nygčigen, mys › 180 65.05 N 172.06 W
Nyhammar 40 60.17 N 14.58 E
Nyhyttan 40 59.40 N 14.48 E
Nyiel 140 6.06 N 31.13 E
Nyika National Park ♠ 154 10.48 S 33.48 E
Nyika Plateau ⋏[1] 154 10.40 S 33.50 E
Nyimba 154 14.35 S 30.52 E
Nyingchi 120 29.32 N 94.25 E
Nyíradony 30 47.41 N 21.55 E
Nyírbátor 30 47.50 N 22.08 E
Nyíregyháza 30 47.59 N 21.43 E
Nykøbing, Dan. 26 56.48 N 8.52 E
Nykøbing, Dan. 41 55.55 N 11.41 E
Nykøbing, Dan. 41 54.46 N 11.53 E
Nyköping 40 58.45 N 17.00 E
Nykroppa 40 59.38 N 14.18 E
Nykvarn 40 59.11 N 17.26 E
Nyland 26 63.00 N 17.46 E
Nyland Acres 228 34.14 N 119.09 W
Nylga, Ross. 80 56.46 N 52.22 E
Nylga, Ross. 89 51.38 N 127.35 E
Nylstroom 156 24.42 S 28.20 E
Nymagee 166 32.04 S 146.20 E
Nymboida ≃ 166 29.39 S 152.30 E
Nymburk 30 50.11 N 15.03 E
Nynäshamn 40 58.54 N 17.57 E
Nyngan 166 31.34 S 147.11 E
Nyoma 120 33.11 N 78.38 E
Nyon 58 46.23 N 6.14 E
Nyong ≃ 152 3.17 N 9.54 E


**Symbols** in the index entries represent the broad categories identified in the key at the right. Symbols with superior numbers (⋏[1]) identify subcategories (see complete key on page *I · 1*).

**Symbole** im Register stellen die rechts im Schlüssel erklärten Kategorien dar. Symbole mit hochgestellten Ziffern (⋏[1]) bezeichnen Unterabteilungen einer Kategorie (vgl. vollständiger Schlüssel auf Seite *I · 1*).

**Los símbolos** incluídos en el texto del índice representan las grandes categorías identificadas con la clave a la derecha. Los símbolos con numeros en su parte superior (⋏[1]) identifican las subcategorías (véase la clave completa en la página *I · 1*).

**Les symboles** de l'index représentent les catégories indiquées dans la légende à droite. Les symboles suivis d'un indice (⋏[1]) représentent des sous-catégories (voir légende complète à la page *I · 1*).

**Os símbolos** incluídos no texto do índice representam as grandes categorias identificadas com a chave à direita. Os símbolos com números em sua parte superior (⋏[1]) identificam as subcategorias (veja-se a chave completa à página *I · 1*).

| | | | | |
|---|---|---|---|---|
| ∧ Mountain | Berg | Montaña | Montagne | Montanha |
| ⋏ Mountains | Gebirge | Montañas | Montagnes | Montanhas |
| )( Pass | Paß | Paso | Col | Passo |
| V Valley, Canyon | Tal, Cañon | Valle, Cañón | Vallée, Canyon | Vale, Canhão |
| ≚ Plain | Ebene | Llano | Plaine | Planície |
| › Cape | Kap | Cabo | Cap | Cabo |
| I Island | Insel | Isla | Île | Ilha |
| II Islands | Inseln | Islas | Îles | Ilhas |
| ⊥ Other Topographic Features | Andere Topographische Objekte | Otros Elementos Topográficos | Autres données topographiques | Outros acidentes topográficos |

**ESPAÑOL**

| Nombre | Página | Lat.°′ | Long.°′ W = Oeste |
|---|---|---|---|
| Nyons | 62 | 44.22 N | 5.08 E |
| Nyord I | 41 | 55.03 N | 12.13 E |
| Nyou | 150 | 12.46 N | 1.56 W |
| Nýřany | 60 | 49.43 N | 13.12 E |
| Nyrov | 24 | 60.42 N | 56.40 E |
| Nýrsko | 60 | 49.18 N | 13.09 E |
| Nyš | 89 | 51.31 N | 142.46 E |
| Nysa, Pol. | 30 | 50.29 N | 17.20 E |
| Nyša, Ross. | 80 | 56.23 N | 51.51 E |
| Nysa Kłodzka ≏ | 30 | 50.49 N | 17.50 E |
| Nysa Łużycka (Neisse) ≏ | 30 | 52.04 N | 14.46 E |
| Nyslott → Savonlinna | 26 | 61.52 N | 28.53 E |
| Nysø | 41 | 55.08 N | 12.02 E |
| Nyssa | 202 | 43.52 N | 116.59 W |
| Nysted | 41 | 54.40 N | 11.45 E |
| Nytva | 86 | 57.56 N | 55.20 E |
| Nyūdō-zaki ≻ | 92 | 40.00 N | 139.42 E |
| Nyugati Pályaudvar ◆[5] | 264c | 47.31 N | 19.04 E |
| Nyūkawa | 94 | 36.10 N | 137.19 E |
| Nyumba ya Mungu Dam ◆[6] | 154 | 3.51 S | 37.28 E |
| Nyungwe | 154 | 10.16 S | 34.07 E |
| Nyunzu | 154 | 5.57 S | 28.01 E |
| Nyuri | 120 | 27.42 N | 92.13 E |
| Nyūzen | 94 | 36.56 N | 137.30 E |
| Nyvång | 41 | 56.08 N | 12.54 E |
| Nyvrovo | 89 | 54.19 N | 142.36 E |
| Nyzhankovychi | 78 | 49.40 N | 22.47 E |
| Nyzhni Sirohozy | 78 | 46.50 N | 34.23 E |
| Nyzhniy Rohachyk | 78 | 47.21 N | 34.02 E |
| Nyzhn'obaranykivka | 83 | 49.05 N | 39.51 E |
| Nyzhn'ohirs'kyy | 78 | 45.27 N | 34.44 E |
| Nyzhn'oteple | 83 | 48.48 N | 39.23 E |
| Nyzhnya Duvanka | 83 | 49.35 N | 38.10 E |
| Nyzhnya Krynka | 83 | 48.07 N | 38.11 E |
| Nyzhnya Vil'khova | 83 | 48.44 N | 39.35 E |
| Nyzhnye | 83 | 48.46 N | 38.37 E |
| Nyzy | 78 | 50.47 N | 34.46 E |
| Nzaba | 273b | 4.06 S | 15.16 E |
| Nzébéla | 150 | 8.05 N | 9.06 W |
| Nzega | 154 | 4.13 S | 33.11 E |
| Nzéla | 152 | 1.25 S | 12.39 E |
| Nzérékoré | 150 | 7.45 N | 8.49 W |
| N'zeto | 152 | 7.14 S | 12.52 E |
| Nzheleledam ⊜[1] | 156 | 22.44 S | 30.06 E |
| Nzi ≏ | 150 | 5.57 N | 4.50 W |
| Nzima | 154 | 3.03 S | 32.48 E |
| Nziro | 152 | 3.17 N | 24.06 E |
| Nzo ≏ | 150 | 6.16 N | 7.03 W |
| Nzoia ≏ | 154 | 0.03 N | 33.57 E |
| Nzubuka | 154 | 4.45 S | 32.50 E |
| Nzwani (Anjouan) I | 157a | 12.15 S | 44.25 E |

## O

| Nombre | Página | Lat.°′ | Long.°′ W = Oeste |
|---|---|---|---|
| Oa, Mull of ≻ | 46 | 55.35 N | 6.20 W |
| Oacoma | 198 | 43.47 N | 99.23 W |
| Oadby | 42 | 52.36 N | 1.04 W |
| Oad Street | 260 | 51.20 N | 0.41 E |
| Oahe, Lake ⊜[1] | 198 | 45.30 N | 100.25 W |
| Oahe Dam ◆[6] | 198 | 44.21 N | 100.23 W |
| Oahu I | 229c | 21.30 N | 158.00 W |
| Oak ≏ | 184 | 49.51 N | 100.28 W |
| O-Akan-dake ∧ | 92a | 43.27 N | 144.10 E |
| Oakbank, Austl. | 162 | 33.03 S | 140.35 E |
| Oakbank, Austl. | 168b | 34.59 S | 138.51 E |
| Oak Bay | 224 | 48.27 N | 123.18 W |
| Oak Beach | 276 | 40.38 N | 73.17 W |
| Oak Bluffs | 207 | 41.27 N | 70.33 W |
| Oakboro | 192 | 35.13 N | 80.19 W |
| Oak Brook | 278 | 41.49 N | 87.55 W |
| Oakbrook Center ◆[9] | 278 | 41.52 N | 87.57 W |
| Oakbrook Terrace | 278 | 41.52 N | 87.58 W |
| Oakburn | 184 | 50.35 N | 100.32 W |
| Oak City, N.C., U.S. | 192 | 35.57 N | 77.18 W |
| Oak City, Ut,. U.S. | 200 | 39.22 N | 112.20 W |
| Oak Creek, Co., U.S. | 200 | 40.16 N | 106.57 W |
| Oak Creek, Wi., U.S. | 216 | 42.53 N | 87.55 W |
| Oak Creek ≏, U.S. | 198 | 45.39 N | 100.31 W |
| Oak Creek ≏, Az., U.S. | 200 | 34.41 N | 111.56 W |
| Oak Creek ≏, Co., U.S. | 200 | 40.25 N | 106.50 W |
| Oak Creek ≏, Ks., U.S. | 198 | 39.29 N | 98.28 W |
| Oak Creek ≏, N.D., U.S. | 198 | 48.38 N | 100.24 W |
| Oak Creek ≏, Tx., U.S. | 196 | 31.48 N | 100.13 W |
| Oakdale, Ca., U.S. | 226 | 37.46 N | 120.50 W |
| Oakdale, Ct., U.S. | 207 | 41.27 N | 72.09 W |
| Oakdale, Il., U.S. | 219 | 38.16 N | 89.30 W |
| Oakdale, La., U.S. | 194 | 30.48 N | 92.39 W |
| Oakdale, Ma., U.S. | 207 | 42.23 N | 71.47 W |
| Oakdale, Ne., U.S. | 198 | 42.04 N | 97.58 W |
| Oakdale, N.J., U.S. | 285 | 39.59 N | 74.49 W |
| Oakdale, N.Y., U.S. | 210 | 40.44 N | 73.08 W |
| Oakdale, Pa., U.S. | 214 | 40.23 N | 80.11 W |
| Oakdale, Tn., U.S. | 192 | 35.59 N | 84.33 W |
| Oakdale Woods | 278 | 41.56 N | 87.58 W |
| Oakengates | 42 | 52.42 N | 2.28 W |
| Oakes | 198 | 46.08 N | 98.05 W |
| Oakesdale | 202 | 47.07 N | 117.14 W |
| Oakey | 171a | 27.26 S | 151.43 E |
| Oakeys Brook ≏ | 276 | 40.25 N | 74.30 W |
| Oakfield, Me., U.S. | 188 | 46.05 N | 68.09 W |
| Oakfield, N.Y., U.S. | 210 | 43.03 N | 78.16 W |
| Oakfield, Wi., U.S. | 190 | 43.41 N | 88.32 W |
| Oakford, Il., U.S. | 219 | 40.06 N | 89.58 W |
| Oakford, In., U.S. | 216 | 40.25 N | 86.06 W |
| Oakford, Pa., U.S. | 208 | 40.09 N | 74.58 W |
| Oak Forest | 216 | 41.36 N | 87.44 W |
| Oakgrove, Eng., U.K. | 262 | 53.13 N | 2.07 W |
| Oak Grove, La., U.S. | 194 | 32.51 N | 91.23 W |
| Oak Grove, Or., U.S. | 224 | 45.25 N | 122.38 W |
| Oak Hall | 208 | 37.56 N | 75.33 W |
| Oakham | 42 | 52.40 N | 0.43 W |
| Oak Harbor, Oh., U.S. | 214 | 41.30 N | 83.09 W |
| Oak Harbor, Wa., U.S. | 224 | 48.17 N | 122.38 W |
| Oak Hill, De., U.S. | 285 | 39.44 N | 75.36 W |
| Oak Hill, Fl., U.S. | 220 | 28.51 N | 80.51 W |
| Oak Hill, Mi., U.S. | 190 | 44.13 N | 86.18 W |
| Oak Hill, N.Y., U.S. | 210 | 42.25 N | 74.09 W |
| Oak Hill, Oh., U.S. | 188 | 38.54 N | 82.34 W |
| Oak Hill, W.V., U.S. | 188 | 37.58 N | 81.08 W |
| Oakhurst, Ca., U.S. | 226 | 37.19 N | 119.40 W |
| Oakhurst, N.J., U.S. | 208 | 40.16 N | 74.01 W |
| Oakhurst, Tx., U.S. | 222 | 30.44 N | 95.19 W |
| Oak Island I, N.S., Can. | 186 | 44.31 N | 64.18 W |
| Oak Island I, N.Y., U.S. | 276 | 40.39 N | 73.18 W |
| Oak Knolls | 204 | 34.51 N | 120.27 W |
| Oak Lake | 184 | 49.47 N | 100.38 W |
| Oak Lake ⊜, Mb., Can. | 184 | 49.40 N | 100.45 W |
| Oak Lake ⊜, On., Can. | 184 | 50.26 N | 93.50 W |
| Oak Lake ⊜, On., Can. | 212 | 44.36 N | 77.55 W |
| Oakland, On., Can. | 214 | 42.09 N | 82.36 W |
| Oakland, Ca., U.S. | 226 | 37.48 N | 122.16 W |
| Oakland, Ca., U.S. | 282 | 37.48 N | 122.16 W |
| Oakland, Fl., U.S. | 220 | 28.33 N | 81.38 W |
| Oakland, Il., U.S. | 194 | 39.39 N | 88.01 W |
| Oakland, Ia., U.S. | 198 | 41.18 N | 95.23 W |
| Oakland, Me., U.S. | 188 | 44.32 N | 69.43 W |
| Oakland, Md., U.S. | 188 | 39.24 N | 79.24 W |
| Oakland, Md., U.S. | 284c | 38.51 N | 76.55 W |
| Oakland, Ms., U.S. | 194 | 34.03 N | 89.54 W |
| Oakland, Ne., U.S. | 198 | 41.50 N | 96.28 W |
| Oakland, N.J., U.S. | 210 | 41.00 N | 74.15 W |
| Oakland, Or., U.S. | 202 | 43.25 N | 123.17 W |

**FRANÇAIS**

| Nom | Page | Lat.°′ | Long.°′ W = Ouest |
|---|---|---|---|
| Oakland, Pa., U.S. | 210 | 41.57 N | 75.36 W |
| Oakland, Pa., U.S. | 214 | 40.59 N | 80.22 W |
| Oakland, Tx., U.S. | 222 | 29.36 N | 96.50 W |
| Oakland □[6] | 216 | 42.40 N | 83.23 W |
| Oakland ◆[8] | 279b | 40.26 N | 79.58 W |
| Oakland-Alameda County Coliseum ♠ | 282 | 37.45 N | 122.12 W |
| Oakland Army Base ■ | 282 | 37.49 N | 122.19 W |
| Oakland Beach | 214 | 41.37 N | 80.18 W |
| Oakland City | 194 | 38.20 N | 87.20 W |
| Oakland Gardens ◆[8] | 276 | 40.45 N | 73.45 W |
| Oakland Mall ◆[9] | 281 | 42.32 N | 83.07 W |
| Oakland Park | 220 | 26.10 N | 80.07 W |
| Oakland-Pontiac Airport ⊠ | 281 | 42.40 N | 83.24 W |
| Oaklands | 168b | 35.00 S | 137.41 E |
| Oaklands ◆[8] | 273d | 26.09 S | 28.04 E |
| Oakland Southwest Airport ⊠ | 281 | 42.30 N | 83.37 W |
| Oakland University ⊍[2] | 281 | 42.41 N | 83.13 W |
| Oak Lane Manor | 285 | 39.47 N | 75.32 W |
| Oak Lawn, Il., U.S. | 216 | 41.43 N | 87.45 W |
| Oaklawn, Ks., U.S. | 198 | 37.36 N | 97.17 W |
| Oaklawn, Md., U.S. | 284c | 38.47 N | 76.57 W |
| Oakleigh | 169 | 37.54 S | 145.06 E |
| Oakleigh South | 274b | 37.56 S | 145.05 E |
| Oakley, Eng., U.K. | 42 | 51.15 N | 1.11 W |
| Oakley, Scot., U.K. | 46 | 56.04 N | 3.33 W |
| Oakley, Ca., U.S. | 226 | 37.58 N | 121.43 W |
| Oakley, Id., U.S. | 202 | 42.14 N | 113.52 W |
| Oakley, Il., U.S. | 219 | 39.53 N | 88.48 W |
| Oakley, Ks., U.S. | 198 | 39.08 N | 100.51 W |
| Oakley Park | 216 | 42.34 N | 83.30 W |
| Oaklyn | 285 | 39.54 N | 75.05 W |
| Oakman | 194 | 33.42 N | 87.23 W |
| Oakmont | 214 | 40.31 N | 79.50 W |
| Oak Mountain State Park ♠ | 194 | 33.22 N | 86.41 W |
| Oakmulgee Creek ≏ | 194 | 32.28 N | 87.09 W |
| Oak Neck ≻[1] | 276 | 40.54 N | 73.34 W |
| Oak Neck Point ≻ | 276 | 40.55 N | 73.34 W |
| Oakohay Creek ≏ | 194 | 31.44 N | 89.25 W |
| Oak Orchard Creek ≏ | 210 | 43.22 N | 78.12 W |
| Oak Orchard Swamp ☷ | 210 | 43.07 N | 78.18 W |
| Oakover ≏ | 162 | 20.43 S | 120.33 E |
| Oak Park, Austl. | 274b | 37.43 S | 144.55 E |
| Oak Park, Ca., U.S. | 228 | 34.11 N | 118.45 W |
| Oak Park, Il., U.S. | 216 | 41.53 N | 87.47 W |
| Oak Park, Mi., U.S. | 216 | 42.27 N | 83.10 W |
| Oak Park, Pa., U.S. | 285 | 40.15 N | 75.18 W |
| Oak Point | 184 | 50.30 N | 98.00 W |
| Oak Ridge, N.J., U.S. | 210 | 41.03 N | 74.29 W |
| Oakridge, Or., U.S. | 202 | 43.44 N | 122.27 W |
| Oak Ridge, Pa., U.S. | 214 | 41.00 N | 79.18 W |
| Oak Ridge, Tn., U.S. | 192 | 36.00 N | 84.16 W |
| Oak Ridge Lake | 276 | 41.00 N | 74.32 W |
| Oak Ridge National Laboratory ⊍[3] | 192 | 36.00 N | 84.15 W |
| Oak Ridge Reservoir ⊜[1] | 276 | 41.03 N | 74.30 W |
| Oaks | 285 | 40.08 N | 81.28 W |
| Oaks Corners | 210 | 42.56 N | 77.01 W |
| Oak Shades | 276 | 40.26 N | 74.13 W |
| Oakton | 284c | 38.52 N | 77.18 W |
| Oaktown | 194 | 38.52 N | 87.26 W |
| Oakura | 172 | 39.07 S | 173.57 E |
| Oak Valley, N.J., U.S. | 208 | 39.48 N | 75.09 W |
| Oak Valley, Va., U.S. | 284c | 38.54 N | 77.18 W |
| Oak View, Ca., U.S. | 228 | 34.24 N | 119.18 W |
| Oak View, Md., U.S. | 284c | 39.01 N | 76.59 W |
| Oakview, N.J., U.S. | 285 | 39.51 N | 75.09 W |
| Oakview Beach | 212 | 44.29 N | 80.03 W |
| Oakville, Mb., Can. | 184 | 49.56 N | 97.58 W |
| Oakville, On., Can. | 212 | 43.27 N | 79.41 W |
| Oakville, Ct., U.S. | 207 | 41.35 N | 73.05 W |
| Oakville, In., U.S. | 218 | 40.05 N | 85.23 W |
| Oakville, Mo., U.S. | 219 | 38.28 N | 90.18 W |
| Oakville, Wa., U.S. | 224 | 46.50 N | 123.13 W |
| Oakwood, On., Can. | 212 | 44.20 N | 78.53 W |
| Oakwood, N.J., U.S. | 285 | 39.52 N | 74.50 W |
| Oakwood, Oh., U.S. | 214 | 41.23 N | 81.29 W |
| Oakwood, Oh., U.S. | 216 | 41.05 N | 84.22 W |
| Oakwood, Oh., U.S. | 218 | 39.44 N | 84.10 W |
| Oakwood, Tx., U.S. | 222 | 31.35 N | 95.50 W |
| Oakwood Beach | 208 | 39.33 N | 75.31 W |
| Oakwood Park ♠ | 279a | 41.26 N | 82.06 W |
| Oamaru | 172 | 45.06 S | 170.58 E |
| Ōamishirasato | 94 | 35.31 N | 140.19 E |
| Ōana | 268 | 35.45 N | 140.04 E |
| Oancea | 38 | 45.55 N | 28.06 E |
| Ōarai | 94 | 36.18 N | 140.34 E |
| Oaro | 172 | 42.31 S | 173.30 E |
| Ōasa | 96 | 34.46 N | 132.28 E |
| Oat Creek ≏ | 226 | 38.50 N | 121.56 W |
| Oates Coast ⊥[2] | 9 | 70.00 S | 160.00 E |
| Oatka Creek ≏ | 210 | 43.01 N | 77.44 W |
| Oatlands | 166 | 42.18 S | 147.21 E |
| Oatley | 274a | 33.59 S | 151.05 E |
| Oatley Park ♠ | 274a | 33.59 S | 151.04 E |
| Oatman | 200 | 35.01 N | 114.22 W |
| Oaxaca □[3] | 234 | 17.00 N | 96.30 W |
| Oaxaca de Juárez | 234 | 17.03 N | 96.43 W |
| Ob' ≏ | 72 | 66.45 N | 69.30 E |
| Oba ≏ | 190 | 48.55 N | 84.17 W |
| Obaba | 152 | 2.00 S | 16.10 E |
| Obabika Lake ⊜ | 190 | 47.05 N | 80.17 W |
| Obal' | 76 | 55.22 N | 29.17 E |
| Obal' ≏ | 76 | 55.24 N | 29.02 E |
| Obala | 152 | 4.10 N | 11.32 E |
| Oba Lake ⊜ | 190 | 48.38 N | 84.18 W |
| Obama, Nihon | 92 | 32.43 N | 130.13 E |
| Obama, Nihon | 94 | 35.30 N | 135.45 E |
| Obama-wan ⊂ | 94 | 35.30 N | 135.42 E |
| Oban, Austl. | 166 | 21.14 S | 139.03 E |
| Oban, Nig. | 150 | 5.17 N | 8.35 E |
| Oban, Scot., U.K. | 46 | 56.25 N | 5.29 W |
| Obanazawa | 92 | 38.36 N | 140.24 E |
| Obando | 269f | 14.43 N | 120.56 E |
| Oban Hills ⋀[2] | 150 | 5.35 N | 8.35 E |
| Obara | 94 | 35.15 N | 137.18 E |
| O Barco de Valdeorras | 34 | 42.25 N | 6.59 W |
| Obata | 94 | 34.30 N | 136.40 E |
| Ob' Bay ⊂ | 9 | 70.35 S | 163.22 E |
| Obbo | 144 | 3.36 N | 38.54 E |
| Obbola | 26 | 63.42 N | 20.19 E |
| Obdach | 61 | 47.04 N | 14.41 E |
| Obed | 182 | 53.33 N | 117.12 W |
| Obed ≏ | 192 | 36.04 N | 84.39 W |
| Obeliai | 76 | 55.56 N | 25.48 E |
| Obelisk ∧ | 172 | 45.20 S | 169.12 E |
| Oberá | 252 | 27.29 S | 55.08 W |
| Oberägeri | 58 | 47.08 N | 8.37 E |
| Oberalppass )( | 58 | 46.39 N | 8.40 E |
| Oberalpstock ∧ | 58 | 46.44 N | 8.46 E |
| Oberammergau | 64 | 47.35 N | 11.04 E |
| Oberasbach | 56 | 49.25 N | 10.58 E |
| Oberau | 64 | 47.33 N | 11.08 E |
| Oberaudorf | 64 | 47.39 N | 12.10 E |
| Oberbauer | 263 | 51.17 N | 7.26 E |
| Oberbayern □[5] | 60 | 48.15 N | 11.45 E |
| Oberbieber | 56 | 50.28 N | 7.29 E |
| Oberbonsfeld | 263 | 51.22 N | 7.08 E |
| Oberbrügge | 263 | 51.11 N | 7.34 E |
| Obercunnersdorf | 54 | 51.02 N | 14.40 E |
| Oberderdingen | 56 | 49.04 N | 8.48 E |
| Oberdiessbach | 58 | 46.51 N | 7.38 E |
| Oberding | 60 | 48.19 N | 11.51 E |
| Oberdolling | 60 | 48.50 N | 11.35 E |
| Oberdorla | 54 | 51.10 N | 10.25 E |
| Oberdrauburg | 64 | 46.45 N | 12.58 E |
| Oberelfringhausen | 263 | 51.20 N | 7.11 E |
| Ober Engadin V | 58 | 46.37 N | 9.58 E |
| Oberengstringen | 58 | 47.25 N | 8.28 E |
| Oberer See → Superior, Lake ⊜ | 190 | 48.00 N | 88.00 W |

**PORTUGUÊS**

| Nome | Página | Lat.°′ | Long.°′ W = Oeste |
|---|---|---|---|
| Obere Saaletalsperre ⊜[1] | 54 | 50.30 N | 11.42 E |
| Oberfranken □[5] | 60 | 49.50 N | 11.20 E |
| Obergeis | 56 | 50.54 N | 9.35 E |
| Ober-Grafendorf | 61 | 48.09 N | 15.33 E |
| Obergum | 52 | 53.20 N | 6.31 E |
| Obergünzburg | 58 | 47.51 N | 10.25 E |
| Obergurgl | 64 | 46.52 N | 11.01 E |
| Obergurig | 54 | 51.07 N | 14.24 E |
| Oberhaan | 263 | 51.13 N | 7.02 E |
| Oberhaching | 60 | 48.02 N | 11.37 E |
| Oberharmersbach | 58 | 48.22 N | 8.07 E |
| Oberhaslach | 58 | 48.33 N | 7.20 E |
| Oberhausen | 56 | 51.28 N | 6.50 E |
| Oberhof | 54 | 50.41 N | 10.44 E |
| Oberhofen | 58 | 46.44 N | 7.40 E |
| Oberinntal V | 64 | 47.13 N | 10.45 E |
| Oberjettingen | 56 | 48.34 N | 8.46 E |
| Oberjoch | 58 | 47.31 N | 10.23 E |
| Ober-Kassel ◆[8] | 263 | 51.14 N | 6.46 E |
| Oberkirch | 58 | 48.31 N | 8.05 E |
| Oberkirchbach | 264b | 48.17 N | 16.12 E |
| Oberkirchen | 56 | 51.09 N | 8.22 E |
| Oberkochen | 56 | 48.47 N | 10.06 E |
| Oberkotzau | 54 | 50.16 N | 11.56 E |
| Oberlaa ◆[8] | 264b | 48.08 N | 16.24 E |
| Oberlaapark ♠ | 264b | 48.08 N | 16.25 E |
| Oberlausitz □[9] | 54 | 51.15 N | 14.00 E |
| Oberlin, Ks., U.S. | 198 | 39.49 N | 100.31 W |
| Oberlin, La., U.S. | 194 | 30.37 N | 92.45 W |
| Oberlin, Oh., U.S. | 214 | 41.17 N | 82.13 W |
| Oberlin, Pa., U.S. | 208 | 40.14 N | 76.49 W |
| Oberloisdorf | 61 | 47.27 N | 16.30 E |
| Oberlungwitz | 54 | 50.47 N | 12.44 E |
| Obermarchtal | 58 | 48.14 N | 9.34 E |
| Obermassfeld-Grimmenthal, Dtsch. | 54 | 50.32 N | 10.26 E |
| Obermassfeld-Grimmenthal, Dtsch. | 54 | 50.32 N | 10.26 E |
| Obermeiser | 56 | 51.26 N | 9.19 E |
| Obermieming | 64 | 47.18 N | 10.59 E |
| Obermodern | 56 | 48.51 N | 7.32 E |
| Ober-Mörlen | 56 | 50.22 N | 8.42 E |
| Obermoschel | 56 | 49.44 N | 7.46 E |
| Obermühl | 61 | 48.27 N | 13.55 E |
| Obernai | 58 | 48.28 N | 7.29 E |
| Obernbeck | 52 | 52.12 N | 8.41 E |
| Obernberg am Inn | 60 | 48.19 N | 13.20 E |
| Obernburg am Main | 56 | 49.50 N | 9.08 E |
| Oberndorf | 52 | 53.45 N | 9.08 E |
| Oberndorf am Neckar | 58 | 48.18 N | 8.34 E |
| Oberndorf bei Salzburg | 64 | 47.57 N | 12.56 E |
| Oberndorf in Tirol | 64 | 47.30 N | 12.23 E |
| Oberne | 171b | 35.24 S | 147.50 E |
| Oberne Hill ∧[2] | 171b | 35.26 S | 147.53 E |
| Obernhausen | 56 | 50.29 N | 9.56 E |
| Obernkirchen | 52 | 52.16 N | 9.07 E |
| Obernzell | 60 | 48.34 N | 13.39 E |
| Oberoderwitz | 54 | 50.58 N | 14.42 E |
| Oberon | 170 | 33.43 S | 149.52 E |
| Oberösterreich □[3] | 30 | 48.15 N | 14.00 E |
| Oberpfalz □[5] | 60 | 49.30 N | 12.10 E |
| Oberpleis | 56 | 50.43 N | 7.16 E |
| Oberpullendorf | 61 | 47.31 N | 16.31 E |
| Ober-Ramstadt | 56 | 49.49 N | 8.44 E |
| Oberried | 58 | 46.44 N | 7.58 E |
| Oberriet | 58 | 47.19 N | 9.33 E |
| Oberrimsingen | 58 | 47.59 N | 7.40 E |
| Oberröblingen | 54 | 51.26 N | 11.18 E |
| Oberrot | 56 | 49.01 N | 9.40 E |
| Ober Sankt Veit ◆[8] | 264b | 48.11 N | 16.16 E |
| Oberscheidental | 56 | 49.30 N | 9.09 E |
| Oberscheinfeld | 56 | 49.42 N | 10.26 E |
| Oberscheld | 56 | 50.44 N | 8.20 E |
| Oberschleissheim | 60 | 48.15 N | 11.34 E |
| Oberschöneweide ◆[8] | 264a | 52.28 N | 13.31 E |
| Oberseebach | 56 | 48.58 N | 7.59 E |
| Oberspier | 54 | 51.19 N | 10.51 E |
| Oberstadtfeld | 56 | 50.10 N | 6.46 E |
| Oberstaufen | 58 | 47.33 N | 10.01 E |
| Oberstdorf | 58 | 47.24 N | 10.16 E |
| Obersteinbach | 56 | 49.02 N | 7.41 E |
| Oberstenfeld | 56 | 49.01 N | 9.19 E |
| Oberstreu | 56 | 50.24 N | 10.17 E |
| Obersuhl | 56 | 50.56 N | 10.02 E |
| Obersulm | 56 | 49.08 N | 9.27 E |
| Obertheres | 56 | 50.01 N | 10.26 E |
| Oberthulba | 56 | 50.12 N | 9.58 E |
| Obertilliach | 64 | 46.42 N | 12.37 E |
| Obertraubling | 60 | 48.58 N | 12.10 E |
| Obertraun | 64 | 47.33 N | 13.41 E |
| Obertrum | 64 | 47.56 N | 13.05 E |
| Obertrumer See ⊜ | 60 | 47.58 N | 13.06 E |
| Obertyn | 78 | 48.42 N | 25.11 E |
| Oberueckersee ⊜ | 54 | 53.12 N | 13.52 E |
| Oberursel | 56 | 50.11 N | 8.35 E |
| Oberuzwil | 58 | 47.26 N | 9.08 E |
| Obervellach | 64 | 46.56 N | 13.12 E |
| Oberviechtach | 60 | 49.28 N | 12.25 E |
| Obervolta → Burkina Faso □[1] | 150 | 13.00 N | 1.30 W |
| Oberwald | 58 | 46.32 N | 8.21 E |
| Oberwart | 61 | 47.17 N | 16.13 E |
| Oberweissbach | 54 | 50.35 N | 11.08 E |
| Oberwengern | 263 | 51.23 N | 7.22 E |
| Oberwesel | 56 | 50.06 N | 7.43 E |
| Oberwiesenthal | 54 | 50.25 N | 12.59 E |
| Oberwolfach | 58 | 48.19 N | 8.12 E |
| Oberwölz Stadt | 61 | 47.13 N | 14.17 E |
| Oberzeiring | 61 | 47.15 N | 14.29 E |
| Obetz | 218 | 39.52 N | 82.57 W |
| Obey, East Fork ≏ | 192 | 36.27 N | 85.07 W |
| Obey, West Fork ≏ | 192 | 36.27 N | 85.09 W |
| Obgruiten | 263 | 51.13 N | 7.01 E |
| Obhausen | 54 | 51.23 N | 11.39 E |
| Obi | 150 | 8.22 N | 8.46 E |
| Obi, Kepulauan II | 164 | 1.30 S | 127.45 E |
| Obi, Pulau I | 164 | 1.30 S | 127.45 E |
| Obi, Selat ʊ | 164 | 0.52 S | 127.33 E |
| Obiaruku | 150 | 5.51 N | 6.09 E |
| Obichingou ≏ | 85 | 38.53 N | 70.01 E |
| Óbidos | 250 | 1.55 S | 55.31 W |
| Obi-Garm | 85 | 38.43 N | 69.42 E |
| Obihiro | 92a | 42.55 N | 143.12 E |
| Obikanda | 85 | 39.10 N | 67.10 E |
| Obikhody | 78 | 51.02 N | 28.59 E |
| Obilatu, Pulau I | 108 | 1.25 S | 127.20 E |
| Obil'noje | 80 | 47.31 N | 44.25 E |
| Obing | 60 | 48.00 N | 12.24 E |
| Obion | 194 | 36.15 N | 89.11 W |
| Obion ≏ | 194 | 35.55 N | 89.39 W |
| Obion, Middle Fork ≏ | 194 | 36.13 N | 88.56 W |
| Obion, Rutherford Fork ≏ | 194 | 36.17 N | 89.01 W |
| Obion, South Fork ≏ | 194 | 36.17 N | 89.03 W |
| Obion Creek ≏ | 194 | 36.35 N | 89.11 W |
| Obiou, Grande Tête de l' ∧ | 62 | 44.46 N | 5.50 E |
| Obira | 92a | 44.00 N | 141.35 E |
| Obitsu ≏ | 94 | 35.24 N | 139.54 E |
| Objačevo | 24 | 60.20 N | 49.34 E |
| Oblačnaja, gora ∧ | 89 | 43.45 N | 134.10 E |
| Öblarn | 61 | 47.27 N | 13.59 E |
| Oblastnaja | 80 | 56.59 N | 52.37 E |
| Oblivskaja | 80 | 48.32 N | 42.30 E |
| Oblong | 194 | 39.00 N | 87.54 W |
| Oblučje | 89 | 49.03 N | 131.04 E |
| Obninsk | 82 | 55.05 N | 36.37 E |
| Obnora ≏ | 76 | 58.14 N | 40.58 E |
| Obnova | 38 | 43.26 N | 24.59 E |
| Obo | 154 | 5.24 N | 26.30 E |
| Obobogorap | 158 | 27.18 S | 20.04 E |
| Obock | 144 | 11.59 N | 43.16 E |
| Obojan' | 78 | 51.13 N | 36.16 E |
| Ō-boke ♠ | 96 | 33.55 N | 133.46 E |
| Obokote | 154 | 0.52 S | 26.19 E |
| Oboldino | 265b | 55.53 N | 37.56 E |
| Obolon' | 78 | 49.36 N | 32.52 E |
| Oborniki | 30 | 52.39 N | 16.51 E |
| Obot | 144 | 4.30 N | 37.20 E |
| Obouya | 152 | 0.56 S | 15.43 E |
| Oboz'orskij | 24 | 63.28 N | 40.18 E |
| Obra ≏ | 30 | 52.36 N | 15.28 E |
| Obrazcovo-Travino | 80 | 45.58 N | 48.02 E |
| Obree, Mount ∧ | 164 | 9.30 S | 148.05 E |
| Obrenovac | 38 | 44.39 N | 20.12 E |
| O'Brien | 202 | 42.04 N | 123.42 W |
| O'Brien Coulee V | 202 | 48.38 N | 110.22 W |
| Obrighoven-Lackhausen | 52 | 51.40 N | 6.38 E |
| Obrovac | 36 | 44.12 N | 15.41 E |
| Obručeva, gora ∧ | 88 | 53.36 N | 113.52 E |
| Obručevka | 85 | 42.30 N | 69.05 E |
| Obruk | 130 | 38.10 N | 33.12 E |
| Obryta | 54 | 53.13 N | 14.59 E |
| Obryvistoje | 89 | 48.46 N | 144.40 E |
| Obša ≏ | 76 | 55.55 N | 32.32 E |
| Obšarovka | 80 | 53.07 N | 48.52 E |
| Obščij Syrt ∧ | 80 | 52.00 N | 51.30 E |
| Observation Peak ∧ | 204 | 40.46 N | 120.10 W |
| Observatoire, Caye de l' I | 160 | 21.25 S | 158.50 E |
| Observatory Inlet ⊂ | 182 | 55.10 N | 129.54 W |
| Obskaja guba ⊂ | 72 | 69.00 N | 73.00 E |
| Obsteig | 64 | 47.18 N | 10.56 E |
| Obtove | 78 | 51.37 N | 33.13 E |
| Ob' Trench ⊹[1] | 14 | 33.00 S | 98.00 E |
| Ōbu | 94 | 35.00 N | 136.58 E |
| Obu ◆[8] | 270 | 34.44 N | 135.09 E |
| Obuasi | 150 | 6.14 N | 1.39 W |
| Obubra | 150 | 6.05 N | 8.21 E |
| Obuchova | 76 | 56.06 N | 32.22 E |
| Obuchovka | 86 | 46.13 N | 81.05 E |
| Obuchovo, Ross. | 82 | 55.50 N | 38.16 E |
| Obuchovo, Ross. | 82 | 56.09 N | 36.55 E |
| Óbuda ◆[8] | 264c | 47.33 N | 19.02 E |
| Óbudai-sziget I | 264c | 47.33 N | 19.04 E |
| Obudu | 150 | 6.40 N | 9.09 E |
| Obukhiv | 78 | 50.08 N | 30.37 E |
| Obukhovychi | 78 | 51.00 N | 29.46 E |
| Obuse | 94 | 36.42 N | 138.19 E |
| Obushkong Lake ⊜ | 190 | 47.42 N | 80.48 W |
| Obuškovo | 82 | 55.47 N | 37.02 E |
| Obu-tōge )( | 270 | 34.44 N | 135.10 E |
| Obva ≏ | 86 | 58.32 N | 55.18 E |
| Obvinsk | 86 | 58.29 N | 54.51 E |
| Obwalden □[3] | 58 | 46.50 N | 8.14 E |
| Obytichna kosa ≻[2] | 78 | 46.33 N | 36.13 E |
| Obytichna zatoka ⊂ | 78 | 46.35 N | 36.00 E |
| Obžericha | 80 | 57.11 N | 42.58 E |
| Očakovo ◆[8] | 265b | 55.41 N | 37.27 E |
| Ocala | 192 | 29.11 N | 82.08 W |
| Ocallí | 248 | 6.09 S | 78.18 W |
| Očamčira | 84 | 42.44 N | 41.28 E |
| Ocamo ≏ | 246 | 2.48 N | 65.14 W |
| Ocampo, Méx. | 232 | 28.11 N | 108.23 W |
| Ocampo, Méx. | 232 | 27.20 N | 102.21 W |
| Ocampo, Méx. | 234 | 22.50 N | 99.20 W |
| Ocampo, Méx. | 234 | 21.39 N | 101.30 W |
| Ocaña, Col. | 246 | 8.15 N | 73.20 W |
| Ocaña, Esp. | 34 | 39.56 N | 3.31 W |
| Ocate Creek ≏ | 196 | 36.17 N | 104.30 W |
| Occaquan ≏ | 208 | 38.40 N | 77.14 W |
| Occaquan Reservoir ⊜[1] | 208 | 38.43 N | 77.22 W |
| Očchamuri | 84 | 41.52 N | 41.50 E |
| Occhieppo Inferiore | 62 | 45.33 N | 8.01 E |
| Occhiobello | 64 | 44.55 N | 11.35 E |
| Occhito, Lago di ⊜[1] | 66 | 41.35 N | 14.54 E |
| Occidental, Cordillera ⋀, Col. | 246 | 5.00 N | 76.00 W |
| Occidental, Cordillera ⋀, Perú | 248 | 10.00 S | 77.00 W |
| Occidental College ⊍[2] | 280 | 34.08 N | 118.13 W |
| Occidental de Zapata, Ciénaga ☷ | 240p | 22.25 N | 81.20 W |
| Occimiano | 62 | 45.03 N | 8.30 E |
| Occoquan | 208 | 38.41 N | 77.15 W |
| Occoquan Bay ⊂ | 208 | 38.37 N | 77.13 W |
| Ocean □[6] | 208 | 39.58 N | 74.12 W |
| Oceana | 192 | 37.41 N | 81.37 W |
| Oceana Naval Air Station ■ | 208 | 36.50 N | 76.02 W |
| Ocean Bay Park | 276 | 40.39 N | 73.08 W |
| Ocean Beach | 276 | 40.38 N | 73.18 W |
| Ocean Bluff | 207 | 42.05 N | 70.39 W |
| Ocean Breeze Park | 220 | 27.15 N | 80.14 W |
| Ocean Cape ≻ | 180 | 59.30 N | 139.45 W |
| Ocean City, Md., U.S. | 208 | 38.20 N | 75.05 W |
| Ocean City, N.J., U.S. | 208 | 39.16 N | 74.34 W |
| Ocean City, Wa., U.S. | 224 | 47.04 N | 124.09 W |
| Ocean Falls | 182 | 52.21 N | 127.40 W |
| Ocean Gate | 208 | 39.55 N | 74.08 W |
| Ocean Grove, Austl. | 169 | 38.16 S | 144.32 E |
| Ocean Grove, Ma., U.S. | 207 | 41.43 N | 71.12 W |
| Ocean Heights | 207 | 41.24 N | 70.33 W |
| Ocean Island → Banaba I | 174d | 0.52 S | 169.35 E |
| Ocean Lake ⊜[1] | 202 | 43.11 N | 108.36 W |
| Oceano | 204 | 35.06 N | 120.37 W |
| Ocean Park, B.C., Can. | 224 | 49.02 N | 122.53 W |
| Ocean Park, Wa., U.S. | 224 | 46.29 N | 124.02 W |
| Ocean Park ♠ | 271d | 22.15 N | 114.09 E |
| Ocean Port | 276 | 40.19 N | 74.00 W |
| Ocean Shores | 224 | 47.01 N | 124.09 W |
| Oceanside, Ca., U.S. | 228 | 33.11 N | 117.22 W |
| Oceanside, N.Y., U.S. | 210 | 40.38 N | 73.38 W |
| Ocean Springs | 194 | 30.24 N | 88.49 W |
| Ocean View, De., U.S. | 208 | 38.32 N | 75.05 W |
| Ocean View, N.J., U.S. | 208 | 39.10 N | 74.44 W |
| Oceanville | 208 | 39.28 N | 74.27 W |
| Oceola | 214 | 40.51 N | 83.06 W |
| Očer | 80 | 57.53 N | 54.42 E |
| O. C. Fisher Lake ⊜[1] | 196 | 31.30 N | 100.30 W |
| Ocha | 89 | 53.34 N | 142.56 E |
| Ocha, Mochun ʊ | 175c | 7.09 N | 151.53 E |
| Ochagavía, Canal ≍ | 286e | 33.30 S | 70.49 W |
| Ochakiv | 78 | 46.37 N | 31.33 E |
| Ochanomizu Women's University ⊍[2] | 268 | 35.43 N | 139.44 E |
| Ochansk | 86 | 57.43 N | 55.23 E |
| Ochapowace Indian Reserve ◆[4] | 184 | 50.30 N | 102.24 W |
| Ocheretyne | 83 | 48.14 N | 37.36 E |
| Ocheyedan | 198 | 43.24 N | 95.32 W |
| Ocheyedan ≏ | 198 | 43.08 N | 95.09 W |
| Ochi, Nihon | 96 | 33.32 N | 133.15 E |
| Ōchi, Nihon | 96 | 35.04 N | 132.36 E |
| Ōchi, Nihon | 96 | 34.16 N | 134.18 E |
| Ochiai | 96 | 35.01 N | 133.45 E |
| Ochiai ◆[8] | 268 | 35.43 N | 139.42 E |
| O'Chiese Indian Reserve ◆[4] | 182 | 52.50 N | 115.28 W |
| Ochil Hills ⋀[2] | 46 | 56.14 N | 3.40 W |
| Ochiltree | 44 | 55.28 N | 4.23 W |
| Ōchise ≏ | 94 | 35.03 N | 137.46 E |
| Ochlocknee | 192 | 30.58 N | 84.03 W |
| Ochlockonee ≏ | 192 | 29.58 N | 84.21 W |
| Ochoco Creek ≏ | 202 | 44.19 N | 120.53 W |
| Ochoco Mountains ⋀ | 202 | 44.30 N | 120.35 W |
| Ochopee | 220 | 25.54 N | 81.18 W |
| Ocho Rios | 241q | 18.25 N | 77.07 W |
| Ochota ≏ | 74 | 59.20 N | 143.04 E |
| Ochotsk | 74 | 59.23 N | 143.18 E |
| Ochotskisches Meer → Okhotsk, Sea of ⊤[2] | 74 | 53.00 N | 150.00 E |
| Ochotskoje more → Okhotsk, Sea of ⊤[2] | 74 | 53.00 N | 150.00 E |
| Ochre River | 184 | 51.03 N | 99.47 W |
| Ochsenfurt | 56 | 49.40 N | 10.03 E |
| Ochsenhausen | 58 | 48.04 N | 9.56 E |
| Ochsenwerder ◆[8] | 52 | 53.28 N | 10.05 E |
| Ochta ≏ | 265a | 59.57 N | 30.24 E |
| Ochtrup | 52 | 52.13 N | 7.11 E |
| Ochvat | 76 | 56.46 N | 32.27 E |
| Oci ≏ | 152 | 15.14 S | 15.16 E |
| Ocilla | 192 | 31.35 N | 83.15 W |
| Ock ≏ | 42 | 51.39 N | 1.17 W |
| Ockelbo | 26 | 60.53 N | 16.43 E |
| Öckerö | 26 | 57.43 N | 11.39 E |
| Ockham | 260 | 51.18 N | 0.27 W |
| Ockholm | 41 | 54.40 N | 8.49 E |
| Ockies | 158 | 31.31 S | 21.41 E |
| Ocklawaha, Lake ⊜[1] | 192 | 29.30 N | 81.50 W |
| Ocmulgee ≏ | 192 | 31.58 N | 82.32 W |
| Ocmulgee National Monument ♠ | 192 | 32.43 N | 83.38 W |
| Ocna Mureș | 38 | 46.23 N | 23.51 E |
| Ocnița | 38 | 48.24 N | 27.29 E |
| Ocoa, Bahía de ⊂ | 238 | 18.22 N | 70.39 W |
| Ocoee | 220 | 28.34 N | 81.32 W |
| Ocoee (Toccoa) ≏ | 192 | 35.12 N | 84.40 W |
| Ocoña | 248 | 16.26 S | 73.07 W |
| Ocoña ≏ | 248 | 16.28 S | 73.07 W |
| Oconee | 219 | 39.17 N | 89.07 W |
| Oconee ≏ | 192 | 31.58 N | 82.32 W |
| Oconee, Lake ⊜[1] | 192 | 33.30 N | 83.15 W |
| Ocongate | 248 | 13.38 S | 71.24 W |
| O'Connell | 170 | 33.32 S | 149.44 E |
| Oconomowoc | 216 | 43.06 N | 88.29 W |
| Oconomowoc ≏ | 216 | 43.07 N | 88.37 W |
| Oconomowoc Lake | 216 | 42.37 N | 88.28 W |
| Oconomowoc Lake ⊜ | 216 | 43.06 N | 88.27 W |
| Oconto | 190 | 44.53 N | 87.51 W |
| Oconto ≏ | 190 | 44.53 N | 87.50 W |
| Oconto, North Branch ≏ | 190 | 45.00 N | 88.23 W |
| Oconto Falls | 190 | 44.52 N | 88.08 W |
| Ocós | 236 | 14.31 N | 92.11 W |
| Ocosingo | 232 | 16.54 N | 92.07 W |
| Ocotal | 236 | 13.38 N | 86.29 W |
| Ocotepec | 234 | 17.13 N | 93.09 W |
| Ocotepeque □[5] | 236 | 14.30 N | 89.00 W |
| Ocotlán | 234 | 20.21 N | 102.46 W |
| Ocotlán de Morelos | 234 | 16.48 N | 96.40 W |
| Ocoyoacac | 234 | 19.16 N | 99.26 W |
| Ocozocoautla [de Espinosa] | 234 | 16.46 N | 93.22 W |
| Ocracoke | 192 | 35.06 N | 75.58 W |
| Ocracoke Island I | 192 | 35.09 N | 75.53 W |
| Ocre, Monte ∧ | 66 | 42.15 N | 13.26 E |
| Ocros | 248 | 10.24 S | 77.24 W |
| Octoraro Creek ≏ | 208 | 39.39 N | 76.09 W |
| Octoraro Creek, East Branch ≏ | 208 | 39.49 N | 76.02 W |
| Octoraro Creek, West Branch ≏ | 208 | 39.49 N | 76.05 W |
| Octoraro Lake ⊜[1] | 208 | 39.48 N | 76.02 W |
| Ocú | 236 | 7.57 N | 80.47 W |
| Ocuilán de Arteaga | 234 | 18.58 N | 99.25 W |
| Ocumare del Tuy | 246 | 10.07 N | 66.46 W |
| Ocuri | 248 | 18.50 S | 65.50 W |
| Ocussi | 112 | 9.12 S | 124.21 E |
| Oda, Ghana | 150 | 5.55 N | 0.59 W |
| Oda, Nihon | 96 | 33.34 N | 132.48 E |
| Ōda, Nihon | 96 | 35.11 N | 132.30 E |
| Oda ≏ | 96 | 34.37 N | 133.44 E |
| Oda, Jabal ∧ | 140 | 20.21 N | 36.39 E |
| Ŏdaejin | 98 | 41.34 N | 129.40 E |
| Odae-san Kukrip Kongwŏn ♠ | 98 | 37.46 N | 128.37 E |
| Ōdai | 94 | 34.24 N | 136.25 E |
| Ōdaigahara-zan ∧ | 92 | 34.11 N | 136.05 E |
| Odaka | 92 | 37.34 N | 141.00 E |
| Ödåkra | 41 | 56.06 N | 12.44 E |
| Odanakumadona | 156 | 20.53 S | 24.45 E |
| Ōdate | 92 | 40.16 N | 140.34 E |
| Odawara | 94 | 35.15 N | 139.10 E |
| Odayeri ◆[8] | 267b | 41.14 N | 28.51 E |
| Odda | 26 | 60.04 N | 6.33 E |
| Odden | 41 | 55.58 N | 11.22 E |
| Odder | 41 | 55.58 N | 10.10 E |
| Oddville | 218 | 38.27 N | 84.15 W |
| Odebolt | 198 | 42.18 N | 95.15 W |
| Ödeby | 40 | 59.24 N | 15.25 E |
| Odei ≏ | 184 | 56.06 N | 96.55 W |
| Odeleite, Ribeira de ≏ | 34 | 37.21 N | 7.27 W |
| Odell, Il., U.S. | 216 | 41.00 N | 88.31 W |
| Odell, Ne., U.S. | 198 | 40.03 N | 96.48 W |
| Odell, Or., U.S. | 224 | 45.37 N | 121.32 W |
| Odell, Tx., U.S. | 196 | 34.21 N | 99.25 W |
| Odell Lake ⊜ | 202 | 43.34 N | 122.00 W |
| Odelzhausen | 60 | 48.19 N | 11.12 E |
| Odem | 196 | 27.57 N | 97.34 W |
| Odemira | 34 | 37.36 N | 8.38 W |
| Ödemiş | 130 | 38.13 N | 27.59 E |
| Ödenburg → Sopron | 30 | 47.41 N | 16.36 E |
| Odendaalsrus | 158 | 27.48 S | 26.45 E |
| Odensbacken | 40 | 59.10 N | 15.32 E |
| Odense | 41 | 55.24 N | 10.23 E |
| Odense ≏ | 41 | 55.26 N | 10.26 E |
| Odense Fjord ⊂ | 41 | 55.30 N | 10.34 E |
| Odenthal | 56 | 51.02 N | 7.07 E |
| Odenton | 208 | 39.05 N | 76.42 W |
| Odenwald ⋀ | 56 | 49.40 N | 9.00 E |
| Oder ≏, Dtsch. | 52 | 51.40 N | 10.06 E |
| Oder (Odra) ≏, Europe | 30 | 53.32 N | 14.38 E |
| Oderberg | 54 | 52.52 N | 14.02 E |
| Oderbruch ◆[1] | 54 | 52.40 N | 14.15 E |
| Oderen | 58 | 47.55 N | 6.59 E |
| Oder-Havel-Kanal ≍ | 54 | 52.52 N | 14.02 E |
| Oder-Spree-Kanal ≍ | 54 | 52.23 N | 13.41 E |
| Odertalsperre ◆[6] | 54 | 51.38 N | 10.30 E |
| Oderzo | 64 | 45.47 N | 12.29 E |
| Odesa | 78 | 46.28 N | 30.44 E |
| Odesa □[4] | 78 | 47.30 N | 30.00 E |
| Ödeshög | 26 | 58.14 N | 14.39 E |
| Odessa, On., Can. | 212 | 44.17 N | 76.43 W |
| Odessa → Odesa, Ukr. | 78 | 46.28 N | 30.44 E |
| Odessa, De., U.S. | 208 | 39.27 N | 75.39 W |
| Odessa, Fl., U.S. | 220 | 28.11 N | 82.35 W |
| Odessa, Mo., U.S. | 194 | 38.59 N | 93.57 W |
| Odessa, N.Y., U.S. | 210 | 42.20 N | 76.47 W |
| Odessa, Tx., U.S. | 196 | 31.50 N | 102.22 W |
| Odessa, Wa., U.S. | 202 | 47.20 N | 118.41 W |
| Odessa Lake ⊜ | 212 | 44.19 N | 76.41 W |
| Odesskoje | 86 | 54.13 N | 72.58 E |
| Odiakwe | 156 | 20.01 S | 25.17 E |
| Odib, Wādī V | 140 | 22.38 N | 36.06 E |
| Odiel ≏ | 34 | 37.10 N | 6.54 W |
| Odienné | 150 | 9.30 N | 7.34 W |
| Odiham | 42 | 51.15 N | 0.57 W |
| Odin | 219 | 38.37 N | 89.03 W |
| Odin, Mount ∧ | 182 | 50.33 N | 118.08 W |
| Odincovo, Ross. | 82 | 54.40 N | 38.00 E |
| Odincovo, Ross. | 82 | 55.41 N | 37.17 E |
| Odiongan | 116 | 12.24 N | 121.59 E |
| Odiongan Bay ⊂ | 116 | 12.25 N | 121.58 E |
| Odivelas | 266c | 38.47 N | 9.11 W |
| Odobești | 38 | 45.45 N | 27.04 E |
| Odojev | 76 | 53.56 N | 36.41 E |
| Odolanów | 30 | 51.35 N | 17.39 E |
| Ōdomari-chosuichi ⊜ | 96 | 34.43 N | 132.18 E |
| Odon | 194 | 38.50 N | 86.59 W |
| Ŏdŏngk | 110 | 11.48 N | 104.45 E |
| O'Donnell | 196 | 32.57 N | 101.49 W |
| O'Donnell ≏ | 162 | 18.22 S | 126.36 E |
| Odoorn | 52 | 52.51 N | 6.51 E |
| Odorheiu Secuiesc | 38 | 46.18 N | 25.18 E |
| Odra (Oder) ≏ | 30 | 53.32 N | 14.38 E |
| Odra Port | 54 | 53.52 N | 14.14 E |
| Odrinhas | 266c | 38.53 N | 9.2[illegible] W |
| Odrzywół | 30 | 51.32 N | 20.3[illegible] E |
| Ødsted | 41 | 55.39 N | 9.2[illegible] E |
| Odum | 192 | 31.39 N | 82.0[illegible] W |
| Odžaci | 38 | 45.30 N | 19.1[illegible] E |
| Odzala, Parc National d' ♠ | 152 | 1.00 N | 15.00 E |
| Odzi | 154 | 18.58 S | 32.23 E |
| Odzi ≏ | 154 | 19.45 S | 32.24 E |
| Odziba | 152 | 3.35 S | 15.31 E |
| Ōe | 96 | 35.23 N | 135.09 E |
| Oebisfelde | 54 | 52.25 N | 10.59 E |
| Oedelem | 50 | 51.10 N | 3.20 E |
| Oederan | 54 | 50.52 N | 13.09 E |
| Oeding | 52 | 51.56 N | 6.49 E |
| Oedt | 56 | 51.19 N | 6.22 E |
| Oegstgeest | 52 | 52.10 N | 4.29 E |
| Oeiras, Bra. | 250 | 7.01 S | 42.08 W |
| Oeiras, Port. | 266c | 38.41 N | 9.21 W |
| Oeiras do Pará | 250 | 1.58 S | 49.51 W |
| Oelde | 52 | 51.49 N | 8.08 E |
| Oelemari ≏ | 250 | 3.13 N | 54.09 W |
| Oella | 284b | 39.16 N | 76.47 W |
| Oels → Oleśnica | 30 | 51.13 N | 17.23 E |
| Oelsig | 54 | 51.41 N | 13.22 E |
| Oelsnitz, Dtsch. | 54 | 50.24 N | 12.10 E |
| Oelsnitz, Dtsch. | 54 | 50.43 N | 12.41 E |
| Oelwein | 190 | 42.40 N | 91.54 W |
| Oenpelli | 164 | 12.20 S | 133.04 E |
| Oensingen | 58 | 47.17 N | 7.44 E |
| Oepping | 60 | 48.36 N | 13.56 E |
| Oeraro-do I | 98 | 34.27 N | 127.30 E |
| Oer-Erkenschwick | 52 | 51.39 N | 7.15 E |
| Oerlenbach | 56 | 50.09 N | 10.08 E |
| Oerlinghausen | 52 | 51.57 N | 8.39 E |
| Oermten | 263 | 51.29 N | 6.27 E |
| Oesede | 52 | 52.12 N | 8.04 E |
| Oeslau | 54 | 50.17 N | 11.01 E |
| Oespel ◆[8] | 263 | 51.30 N | 7.23 E |
| Oeste, Canal del ≍ | 266a | 40.32 N | 3.42 W |
| Oeste, Parque del ♠ | 266a | 40.26 N | 3.44 W |
| Oesterdam ◆[5] | 52 | 51.29 N | 4.15 E |
| Oestrich | 263 | 51.22 N | 7.38 E |
| Oestrich ◆[8] | 263 | 51.34 N | 7.22 E |
| Oestrum ◆[8] | 263 | 51.25 N | 6.40 E |
| Ōetaka-yama ∧ | 96 | 35.04 N | 132.26 E |
| Oettingen in Bayern | 56 | 48.57 N | 10.36 E |
| Oetz | 64 | 47.12 N | 10.54 E |
| Oeuf ≏ | 50 | 48.11 N | 2.21 E |
| Oeventrop | 56 | 51.23 N | 8.08 E |
| Oeversee | 41 | 54.42 N | 9.26 E |
| Ōe-yama ∧ | 96 | 35.27 N | 135.07 E |
| Oeyŏn-do I | 98 | 36.14 N | 126.05 E |
| Of | 130 | 40.57 N | 40.18 E |
| O'Fallon, Il., U.S. | 219 | 38.35 N | 89.54 W |
| O'Fallon, Mo., U.S. | 219 | 38.48 N | 90.41 W |
| O'Fallon Creek ≏ | 198 | 46.50 N | 105.09 W |
| Ofanto ≏ | 68 | 41.22 N | 16.13 E |
| Ofaqim | 132 | 31.17 N | 34.37 E |
| Ofenpass → Fuorn, Pass dal )( | 58 | 46.37 N | 10.15 E |
| Offa | 150 | 8.09 N | 4.44 E |
| Offaly □[6] | 48 | 53.20 N | 7.30 W |
| Offanengo | 62 | 45.22 N | 9.44 E |
| Offemont | 58 | 47.40 N | 6.53 E |
| Offenbach | 56 | 50.08 N | 8.47 E |
| Offenburg | 58 | 48.28 N | 7.57 E |
| Offendorf | 58 | 48.43 N | 7.55 E |
| Offerdal | 26 | 63.28 N | 14.00 E |
| Offham | 260 | 51.17 N | 0.23 E |
| Officer | 274b | 38.04 S | 145.25 E |
| Officer Creek ≏ | 162 | 27.45 S | 132.24 E |
| Offida | 66 | 42.56 N | 13.41 E |
| Offingen | 58 | 48.29 N | 10.21 E |
| Offranville | 50 | 49.52 N | 1.03 E |
| Offutt Air Force Base ■ | 198 | 41.08 N | 95.56 W |
| Oficina Alemania | 252 | 25.10 S | 69.55 W |
| Oficina Alianza | 248 | 20.46 S | 69.42 W |
| Oficina Chile | 252 | 25.09 S | 69.54 W |
| Oficina Pedro de Valdivia | 252 | 22.36 S | 69.40 W |
| Oficina Victoria | 248 | 20.44 S | 69.42 W |
| Ofin | 273a | 6.33 N | 3.30 E |
| Öflingen | 58 | 47.35 N | 7.55 E |
| Ofotfjorden ⊂[2] | 24 | 68.23 N | 16.10 E |
| Oftringen | 58 | 47.19 N | 7.56 E |
| Ofu | 174y | 14.10 S | 169.42 W |
| Ofu I | 174y | 14.11 S | 169.42 W |
| Ōfukuroshinden | 268 | 35.53 N | 139.27 E |
| Ōfuna | 268 | 35.21 N | 139.32 E |
| Ōfunato | 92 | 39.04 N | 141.43 E |
| Oga | 92 | 39.53 N | 139.51 E |
| Ogaden ◆[1] | 144 | 8.00 N | 44.00 E |
| Oga-hantō ≻[1] | 92 | 39.55 N | 139.50 E |
| Ōgaki, Nihon | 94 | 35.21 N | 136.37 E |
| Ōgaki, Nihon | 96 | 34.06 N | 132.30 E |
| Ogallala | 198 | 41.07 N | 101.43 W |
| Ogan ≏ | 112 | 3.01 S | 104.44 E |
| Ogano | 94 | 36.01 N | 139.00 E |
| Ogasa | 94 | 34.41 N | 138.06 E |
| Ogasawara-guntō (Bonin Islands) II | 14 | 27.00 N | 142.10 E |
| Ōgata, Nihon | 94 | 37.13 N | 138.20 E |
| Ōgata, Nihon | 96 | 33.01 N | 133.01 E |
| Ogata, Nihon | 96 | 32.58 N | 131.29 E |
| Ōga-tō ∧ | 94 | 36.13 N | 138.06 E |
| Ogatsu | 92 | 38.31 N | 141.28 E |
| Ogawa, Nihon | 92 | 32.35 N | 130.43 E |
| Ogawa, Nihon | 94 | 36.10 N | 140.21 E |
| Ogawa, Nihon | 94 | 36.37 N | 137.58 E |
| Ogawa, Nihon | 94 | 36.03 N | 139.16 E |
| Ogawa, Nihon | 94 | 36.45 N | 140.08 E |
| Ogawa, Nihon | 268 | 35.44 N | 139.28 E |
| Ogawara-ko ⊜ | 92 | 40.47 N | 141.20 E |
| Ogbomosho | 150 | 8.08 N | 4.15 E |
| Ogden, Ia., U.S. | 190 | 42.02 N | 94.01 W |
| Ogden, Ks., U.S. | 198 | 39.06 N | 96.42 W |
| Ogden, Pa., U.S. | 208 | 39.49 N | 75.27 W |
| Ogden, Ut,. U.S. | 200 | 41.13 N | 111.58 W |
| Ogden, Mount ∧ | 180 | 58.26 N | 133.23 W |
| Ogden Dunes | 216 | 41.38 N | 87.12 W |
| Ogden Island I | 212 | 44.52 N | 75.12 W |
| Ogden Reservoir ⊜[1] | 262 | 53.42 N | 2.22 W |
| Ogdensburg, N.J., U.S. | 210 | 41.04 N | 74.35 W |
| Ogdensburg, N.Y., U.S. | 212 | 44.41 N | 75.29 W |
| Ogeechee ≏ | 192 | 31.51 N | 81.06 W |
| Ōge-jima I | 96 | 34.12 N | 134.38 E |
| Ogema | 184 | 49.35 N | 104.55 W |
| Oggersheim | 56 | 49.29 N | 8.22 E |
| Oghi Fort | 123 | 34.31 N | 73.01 E |
| Ogibalovo | 76 | 60.34 N | 39.40 E |
| Ogidaki Mountain ∧[2] | 190 | 46.58 N | 83.58 W |
| Ogies | 158 | 26.02 S | 29.04 E |
| Ogi-jima I | 96 | 34.26 N | 134.04 E |
| Ogijo | 273a | 6.42 N | 3.31 E |
| Ogilvie, Austl. | 162 | 28.09 S | 114.38 E |
| Ogilvie, Mn., U.S. | 190 | 45.49 N | 93.25 W |
| Ogilvie ≏ | 180 | 65.52 N | 137.16 W |
| Ogilvie Mountains ⋀ | 180 | 65.00 N | 139.30 W |
| Ogilville | 218 | 39.08 N | 86.01 W |
| Ōgimi | 174m | 26.42 N | 128.07 E |
| Ōgino-sen ∧ | 96 | 35.26 N | 134.26 E |
| Ogle □[6] | 216 | 42.01 N | 89.20 W |
| Oglesby, Il., U.S. | 216 | 41.17 N | 89.03 W |
| Oglesby, Tx., U.S. | 222 | 31.25 N | 97.31 W |
| Oglethorpe | 192 | 32.17 N | 84.03 W |
| Ogliastra ◆[1] | 71 | 39.56 N | 9.37 E |
| Ogliastro Cilento | 68 | 40.21 N | 15.03 E |
| Oglio ≏ | 64 | 45.02 N | 10.39 E |
| Ogmore | 166 | 22.37 S | 149.40 E |
| Ogmore ≏ | 42 | 51.28 N | 3.38 W |
| Ogmore Vale | 42 | 51.38 N | 3.31 W |
| Ogni | 86 | 51.54 N | 83.31 E |
| Ognica | 54 | 53.07 N | 14.27 E |
| Ognon ≏ | 58 | 47.20 N | 5.29 E |


| | | | | |
|---|---|---|---|---|
| ≏ River | Fluß | Río | Rivière | Rio |
| ≍ Canal | Kanal | Canal | Canal | Canal |
| ⌊ Waterfall, Rapids | Wasserfall, Stromschnellen | Cascada, Rápidos | Chute d'eau, Rapides | Cascata, Rápidos |
| ʊ Strait | Meeresstraße | Estrecho | Détroit | Estreito |
| ⊂ Bay, Gulf | Bucht, Golf | Bahía, Golfo | Baie, Golfe | Baía, Golfo |
| ⊜ Lake, Lakes | See, Seen | Lago, Lagos | Lac, Lacs | Lago, Lagos |
| ☷ Swamp | Sumpf | Pantano | Marais | Pântano |
| ⊓ Ice Features, Glacier | Eis- und Gletscherformen | Accidentes Glaciales | Formes glaciaires | Acidentes glaciares |
| ⊤ Other Hydrographic Features | Andere Hydrographische Objekte | Otros Elementos Hidrográficos | Autres données hydrographiques | Outros acidentes hidrográficos |

| | | | | |
|---|---|---|---|---|
| ⊹ Submarine Features | Untermeerische Objekte | Accidentes Submarinos | Formes de relief sous-marin | Acidentes submarinos |
| □ Political Unit | Politische Einheit | Unidad Politica | Entité politique | Unidade política |
| ⊍ Cultural Institution | Kulturelle Institution | Institución Cultural | Institution culturelle | Instituição cultural |
| ⊥ Historical Site | Historische Stätte | Sitio Histórico | Site historique | Sitio histórico |
| ♠ Recreational Site | Erholungs- und Ferienort | Sitio de Recreo | Centre de loisirs | Area de Lazer |
| ⊠ Airport | Flughafen | Aeropuerto | Aéroport | Aeroporto |
| ■ Military Installation | Militäranlage | Instalación Militar | Installation militaire | Instalação militar |
| ◆ Miscellaneous | Verschiedenes | Misceláneo | Divers | Diversos |

ENGLISH

| Name | Page | Lat.°′ | Long.°′ |
|---|---|---|---|
| Ogn'ov Jar | 86 | 58.23 N | 76.29 E |
| Ogn'ovka | 86 | 49.36 N | 83.25 E |
| Ōgo | 94 | 36.25 N | 139.10 E |
| Ōgo ◆[8] | 270 | 34.49 N | 135.06 E |
| Ōgo ≃ | 270 | 34.47 N | 135.04 E |
| Ogoamas, Bulu ∧ | 112 | 0.40 N | 120.12 E |
| Ogōchi-dam ◆[6] | 94 | 35.47 N | 139.04 E |
| Ogodža | 89 | 52.44 N | 132.31 E |
| Ogoja | 150 | 6.40 N | 8.48 E |
| Ogoki ≃ | 176 | 51.38 N | 85.57 W |
| 'Ogol, Khaṭṭ el V | 150 | 20.01 N | 15.29 W |
| Ogooué ≃ | 152 | 0.49 S | 9.00 E |
| Ogooué-Ivindo □[4] | 152 | 1.00 N | 13.00 E |
| Ogooué-Lolo □[4] | 152 | 1.00 S | 12.30 E |
| Ogooué-Maritime □[4] | 152 | 2.00 S | 9.30 E |
| Ogōri, Nihon | 96 | 33.22 N | 130.32 E |
| Ogōri, Nihon | 96 | 34.06 N | 131.24 E |
| Ogose | 94 | 35.58 N | 139.18 E |
| Ogosta ≃ | 38 | 43.45 N | 23.51 E |
| Ogou ≃ | 150 | 7.50 N | 1.19 E |
| Ogoyo | 273a | 6.26 N | 3.29 E |
| Ogr | 140 | 12.02 N | 27.06 E |
| Ogre | 76 | 56.51 N | 24.36 E |
| Ogre ≃ | 76 | 56.48 N | 24.36 E |
| Ogrodzieniec | 30 | 50.27 N | 19.31 E |
| Ogrosen | 54 | 51.42 N | 14.02 E |
| O Grove | 34 | 42.30 N | 8.52 W |
| Ōguchi | 94 | 35.20 N | 136.55 E |
| Ŏgu-dong | 98 | 38.57 N | 126.56 E |
| Ogudu | 273a | 6.34 N | 3.24 E |
| Ogulin | 36 | 45.16 N | 15.14 E |
| Ogun ≃ | 150 | 6.36 N | 3.27 E |
| Ogun Forest Reserve ♠ | 273a | 6.37 N | 3.26 E |
| Oguni, Nihon | 92 | 38.04 N | 139.45 E |
| Oguni, Nihon | 96 | 33.07 N | 131.04 E |
| Ogunlogun | 273a | 6.41 N | 3.28 E |
| Ogunquit | 188 | 43.14 N | 70.35 W |
| Ogura-san ∧ | 94 | 36.02 N | 138.37 E |
| Ogurčinskij, ostrov I | 128 | 38.55 N | 53.02 E |
| Oguta | 150 | 5.44 N | 6.44 E |
| Oğuz, Azer. | 84 | 41.06 N | 47.28 E |
| Oğuz, Tür. | 130 | 37.49 N | 41.22 E |
| Oğuz, Tür. | 130 | 39.32 N | 38.51 E |
| Oğuzeli | 130 | 36.59 N | 37.30 E |
| Ogwashi-Uku | 150 | 6.10 N | 6.31 E |
| Ohakune | 172 | 39.25 S | 175.24 E |
| Ohanapecosh ≃ | 224 | 46.38 N | 121.37 W |
| Ohanet | 148 | 28.45 N | 8.55 E |
| Ohangwena □[4] | 156 | 17.30 S | 16.30 E |
| Ohār | 124 | 27.21 N | 84.37 E |
| Ōhara, Nihon | 94 | 35.15 N | 140.23 E |
| Ōhara, Nihon | 96 | 35.07 N | 134.20 E |
| Ōharano ◆[8] | 270 | 34.58 N | 135.40 E |
| Ōhara-tunnel ◆[5] | 94 | 35.12 N | 137.50 E |
| Ōhata | 92 | 41.24 N | 141.10 E |
| Ōhatake | 268 | 35.57 N | 139.46 E |
| Ohau, Lake ⊜ | 172 | 44.15 S | 169.51 E |
| Ohaupo | 172 | 37.55 S | 175.19 E |
| Ohey | 56 | 50.26 N | 5.08 E |
| O'Higgins, Cabo › | 174z | 27.05 S | 109.15 W |
| O'Higgins, Cerro ∧ | 254 | 48.48 S | 73.11 W |
| O'Higgins, Lago (Lago San Martín) ⊜ | 254 | 49.00 S | 72.40 W |
| Ohingaiti | 172 | 39.52 S | 175.43 E |
| Ohio | 190 | 41.34 N | 89.28 W |
| Ohio □[6], In., U.S. | 218 | 38.57 N | 84.51 W |
| Ohio □[6], W.V., U.S. | 214 | 40.09 N | 80.35 W |
| Ohio □[3], U.S. | 178 | 40.15 N | 82.45 W |
| Ohio □[3], U.S. | 188 | 40.15 N | 82.45 W |
| Ohio ≃ | 178 | 36.59 N | 89.08 W |
| Ohio Brush Creek ≃ | 218 | 38.41 N | 83.27 W |
| Ohio Brush Creek, Baker Fork ≃ | 218 | 39.02 N | 83.26 W |
| Ohio Brush Creek, Little West Fork ≃ | 218 | 38.58 N | 83.34 W |
| Ohio Brush Creek, West Fork ≃ | 218 | 38.56 N | 83.28 W |
| Ohio Canal ≋ | 279a | 41.26 N | 81.40 W |
| Ohio Caverns ≗[5] | 216 | 40.14 N | 83.43 W |
| Ohio City | 216 | 40.46 N | 84.36 W |
| Ohio Peak ∧ | 200 | 38.49 N | 107.07 W |
| Ohiopyle State Park ♠ | 188 | 39.50 N | 79.31 W |
| Ohioville, N.Y., U.S. | 210 | 41.45 N | 74.03 W |
| Ohioville, Pa., U.S. | 214 | 40.40 N | 80.29 W |
| Ōhira | 94 | 36.20 N | 139.42 E |
| Ōhira-yama ∧ | 96 | 34.20 N | 133.57 E |
| Ōhito | 94 | 35.01 N | 138.56 E |
| Ohlau → Oława | 30 | 50.57 N | 17.17 E |
| Ohligs ◆[8] | 263 | 51.09 N | 7.00 E |
| Ohlman | 219 | 39.21 N | 89.13 W |
| Ohlsdorf | 64 | 47.57 N | 13.47 E |
| Ohlstadt | 64 | 47.38 N | 11.14 E |
| Ohm ≃ | 56 | 50.51 N | 8.48 E |
| Ōho | 94 | 36.08 N | 140.06 E |
| Ohoitom | 164 | 5.56 S | 132.41 E |
| 'Ohonua | 174w | 21.20 S | 174.57 W |
| Ohoopee ≃ | 192 | 31.54 N | 82.07 W |
| Ōhori | 268 | 35.20 N | 139.52 E |
| Ohorn | 54 | 51.10 N | 14.02 E |
| Ohra Stausee ⊜[1] | 54 | 50.46 N | 10.42 E |
| Ohrdruf | 54 | 50.50 N | 10.44 E |
| Ohre ≃, Dtsch. | 54 | 52.18 N | 11.47 E |
| Ohře (Eger) ≃, Europe | 54 | 50.32 N | 14.08 E |
| Ohrid | 38 | 41.07 N | 20.47 E |
| Ohrid, Lake ⊜ | 38 | 41.02 N | 20.43 E |
| Ohrigstad | 156 | 24.49 S | 30.33 E |
| Öhringen | 56 | 49.12 N | 9.29 E |
| Ohrnberg | 56 | 49.15 N | 9.27 E |
| Ohuira, Bahía ⊂ | 232 | 25.38 N | 108.58 W |
| Ohura | 172 | 38.50 S | 174.59 E |
| Ōi, Nihon | 96 | 35.28 N | 135.37 E |
| Ōi, Nihon | 268 | 35.51 N | 139.30 E |
| Oi ◆[8] | 268 | 35.35 N | 139.45 E |
| Ōi ≃, Nihon | 94 | 34.46 N | 138.18 E |
| Ōi ≃, Nihon | 96 | 35.01 N | 135.39 E |
| Oiapoque | 250 | 3.50 N | 51.50 W |
| Oiapoque (Oyapock) ≃ | 250 | 4.08 N | 51.40 W |
| Oies, Île aux I | 186 | 47.07 N | 70.30 W |
| Ōigawa | 94 | 34.48 N | 138.17 E |
| Oignies | 50 | 50.28 N | 2.59 E |
| Oil Center | 196 | 32.29 N | 103.15 W |
| Oil City, La., U.S. | 194 | 32.44 N | 93.58 W |
| Oil City, Pa., U.S. | 214 | 41.26 N | 79.42 W |
| Oil Creek ≃ | 214 | 41.26 N | 79.42 W |
| Oil Creek State Park ♠ | 214 | 41.33 N | 79.40 W |
| Oildale | 226 | 35.25 N | 119.01 W |
| Oilmont | 182 | 48.44 N | 111.50 W |
| Oil Springs | 214 | 42.47 N | 82.07 W |
| Oilton, Ok., U.S. | 196 | 36.05 N | 96.35 W |
| Oilton, Tx., U.S. | 196 | 27.33 N | 98.59 W |
| Oil Trough | 194 | 35.37 N | 91.27 W |
| Oinville-sur-Montcient | 261 | 49.02 N | 1.51 E |
| Oir, Beinn an ∧ | 46 | 55.54 N | 6.00 W |
| Oirschot | 52 | 51.30 N | 5.18 E |
| Oise □[5] | 50 | 49.30 N | 2.30 E |
| Oise ≃ | 50 | 49.00 N | 2.04 E |
| Oise à l'Aisne, Canal de l' ≋ | 50 | 49.36 N | 3.11 E |
| Oisemont | 50 | 49.57 N | 1.46 E |
| Ōiso, Nihon | 94 | 35.18 N | 139.19 E |
| Ōiso, Nihon | 270 | 34.33 N | 135.01 E |
| Oissel | 50 | 49.20 N | 1.06 E |
| Oissery | 261 | 49.04 N | 2.49 E |
| Oisterwijk | 52 | 51.35 N | 5.12 E |
| Oistins | 241g | 13.04 N | 59.32 W |
| Ōita | 96 | 33.14 N | 131.36 E |
| Ōita □[5] | 96 | 33.15 N | 131.30 E |
| Ōita ≃ | 96 | 33.15 N | 131.37 E |
| Oiticica | 250 | 5.03 S | 41.05 W |
| Oituz, Pasul )( | 38 | 46.03 N | 26.23 E |
| Ōiwa | 270 | 34.53 N | 135.33 E |
| Oiyung | 124 | 29.39 N | 89.46 E |
| Ōizumi, Nihon | 94 | 36.15 N | 139.25 E |
| Ōizumi, Nihon | 94 | 35.52 N | 138.23 E |
| Oizuruga-dake ∧ | 94 | 36.18 N | 136.47 E |
| Öja I | 40 | 58.45 N | 17.52 E |
| Oja ≃ | 86 | 53.26 N | 91.55 E |
| Ojai | 228 | 34.26 N | 119.14 W |
| Öjaren ⊜ | 40 | 60.43 N | 16.50 E |
| Ojat' ≃ | 76 | 60.31 N | 33.00 E |
| Ojcowski Park Narodowy ♠ | 30 | 50.15 N | 19.50 E |
| Öje | 26 | 60.49 N | 13.51 E |
| Ojgon nuur ⊜ | 88 | 49.10 N | 96.36 E |
| Ojgor | 86 | 49.10 N | 89.17 E |
| Ōji | 96 | 34.35 N | 135.42 E |
| Ōjima | 94 | 36.15 N | 139.20 E |
| Ojinaga | 232 | 29.34 N | 104.25 W |
| Ojiya | 92 | 37.18 N | 138.48 E |
| Ojm'akon | 74 | 63.28 N | 142.49 E |
| Ojocaliente | 234 | 22.34 N | 102.15 W |
| Ojo de la Casa | 200 | 31.23 N | 106.32 W |
| Ojo del Carrizo | 232 | 29.58 N | 105.16 W |
| Ojo de Liebre, Laguna ⊂ | 232 | 27.45 N | 114.15 W |
| Ojok | 88 | 52.35 N | 104.27 E |
| Ojos del Salado, Nevado ∧ | 252 | 27.06 S | 68.32 W |
| Ojos Negros | 232 | 31.52 N | 116.16 W |
| Ojota | 273a | 6.35 N | 3.23 E |
| Ojtal, Kaz. | 85 | 42.55 N | 73.17 E |
| Ojtal, Kyrg. | 85 | 40.24 N | 74.06 E |
| Oju | 150 | 6.53 N | 8.26 E |
| Ojuelos de Jalisco | 234 | 21.52 N | 101.35 W |
| Ojus | 220 | 25.57 N | 80.09 W |
| Oka | 150 | 7.29 N | 5.49 E |
| Oka ≃, Ross. | 80 | 56.20 N | 43.59 E |
| Oka ≃, Ross. | 88 | 55.15 N | 102.10 E |
| Okaba | 164 | 8.06 S | 139.42 E |
| Okabe, Nihon | 94 | 36.12 N | 139.15 E |
| Okabe, Nihon | 94 | 34.55 N | 138.17 E |
| Okagaki | 96 | 33.50 N | 130.38 E |
| Okahandja | 156 | 21.59 S | 16.58 E |
| Okahukura | 172 | 38.47 S | 175.13 E |
| Okahumpka | 220 | 28.45 N | 81.54 W |
| Okaihau | 172 | 35.19 S | 173.47 E |
| Okalataka | 152 | 0.20 S | 14.59 E |
| Okaloacoochee Slough ≃ | 220 | 26.16 N | 81.17 W |
| Okamoto | 270 | 34.59 N | 135.58 E |
| Okamoto ◆[8] | 270 | 34.44 N | 135.16 E |
| Okanagan (Okanogan) ≃ | 182 | 48.06 N | 119.43 W |
| Okanagan Centre | 182 | 50.03 N | 119.27 W |
| Okanagan Falls | 182 | 49.21 N | 119.34 W |
| Okanagan Indian Reserve ◆[4] | 182 | 50.21 N | 119.17 W |
| Okanagan Lake ⊜ | 182 | 50.00 N | 119.28 W |
| Okanagan Landing | 182 | 50.14 N | 119.22 W |
| Okanagan Mountain Provincial Park ♠ | 182 | 49.45 N | 119.40 W |
| Okanagan Range (Okanogan Range) ⋏ | 182 | 49.00 N | 120.00 W |
| Okanogan | 202 | 48.21 N | 119.34 W |
| Okanogan □[6] | 224 | 48.39 N | 120.41 W |
| Okanogan (Okanagan) ≃ | 182 | 48.06 N | 119.43 W |
| Okanogan Range (Okanagan Range) ⋏ | 182 | 49.00 N | 120.00 W |
| Okapilco Creek ≃ | 192 | 30.45 N | 83.30 W |
| Okaputa | 156 | 20.09 S | 16.56 E |
| Okāra | 123 | 30.49 N | 73.27 E |
| Okarche | 196 | 35.44 N | 97.58 W |
| Okarito | 172 | 43.14 S | 170.11 E |
| Okasaki | 270 | 34.46 N | 135.52 E |
| Okatibbee Reservoir ⊜[1] | 194 | 32.30 N | 88.47 W |
| Okato | 172 | 39.12 S | 173.53 E |
| Okauchee | 216 | 43.06 N | 88.26 W |
| Okauchee Lake ⊜ | 216 | 43.07 N | 88.26 W |
| Okaukuejo | 156 | 19.10 S | 15.54 E |
| Okavango □[4] | 156 | 18.30 S | 19.30 E |
| Okavango (Cubango) ≃ | 138 | 18.50 S | 22.25 E |
| Okavango Delta ≚[2] | 156 | 18.45 S | 22.45 E |
| Ōkawa, Nihon | 92 | 33.12 N | 130.23 E |
| Ōkawa, Nihon | 94 | 35.05 N | 138.15 E |
| Ōkawa, Nihon | 96 | 33.47 N | 133.26 E |
| Ōkawachi | 96 | 35.04 N | 134.45 E |
| Ōkawado | 268 | 35.56 N | 139.50 E |
| Okawville | 219 | 38.26 N | 89.33 W |
| Okaya | 94 | 36.03 N | 138.03 E |
| Okayama | 96 | 34.39 N | 133.55 E |
| Okayama □[5] | 96 | 35.00 N | 134.00 E |
| Okazaki | 94 | 34.57 N | 137.10 E |
| Okch'ŏn | 98 | 36.20 N | 127.34 E |
| Oke-Aro | 273a | 6.41 N | 3.19 E |
| Okeechobee | 220 | 27.14 N | 80.49 W |
| Okeechobee □[6] | 220 | 27.25 N | 80.52 W |
| Okeechobee, Lake ⊜ | 220 | 26.55 N | 80.45 W |
| O'Keefe Centre ᵿ | 275b | 43.37 N | 79.22 W |
| Okeene | 196 | 36.06 N | 98.19 W |
| Okefenokee Swamp ⩸ | 192 | 30.42 N | 82.20 W |
| Okegawa | 94 | 36.00 N | 139.35 E |
| Okehampton | 42 | 50.44 N | 4.00 W |
| Okeigbo | 150 | 7.09 N | 4.43 E |
| Okemah | 196 | 35.25 N | 96.18 W |
| Okement ≃ | 42 | 50.50 N | 4.01 W |
| Okemos | 216 | 42.43 N | 84.25 W |
| Okene | 150 | 7.33 N | 6.15 E |
| Oke-Ode | 150 | 8.33 N | 5.02 E |
| Oke Ogbe | 273a | 6.24 N | 3.23 E |
| Oker | 52 | 51.54 N | 10.29 E |
| Oker ≃ | 54 | 52.30 N | 10.22 E |
| Okere ≃ | 154 | 2.07 N | 33.55 E |
| Okertalsperre ◆[6] | 52 | 51.48 N | 10.27 E |
| Okhaldunggā | 124 | 27.19 N | 86.30 E |
| Okhla ◆[8] | 272a | 28.34 N | 77.18 E |
| Okhotsk, Sea of (Ochotskoje more) Ŧ[2] | 74 | 53.00 N | 150.00 E |
| Okhotsk Basin ⇟[1] | 12 | 53.00 N | 148.00 E |
| Okhtyrka | 78 | 50.19 N | 34.55 E |
| Okiep | 156 | 29.39 S | 17.53 E |
| Okinawa | 174m | 26.20 N | 127.50 E |
| Okinawa □[5] | 93b | 26.31 N | 127.59 E |
| Okinawa-jima I | 174m | 26.30 N | 128.00 E |
| Okinawa-shotō II | 93b | 26.40 N | 128.00 E |
| Okino-Daitō-jima I | 90 | 24.28 N | 131.11 E |
| Okino-Erabu-shima I | 93b | 27.22 N | 128.35 E |
| Okino-Kl'uči | 88 | 50.36 N | 107.06 E |
| Okino-shima I, Nihon | 94 | 35.12 N | 136.04 E |
| Okino-shima I, Nihon | 96 | 34.07 N | 135.06 E |
| Okino-Tori-shima (Parece Vela) I | 90 | 20.25 N | 136.00 E |
| Oki-shotō II | 92 | 36.15 N | 133.15 E |
| Okitipupa | 150 | 6.29 N | 4.46 E |
| Okitsu-zaki › | 96 | 33.09 N | 133.14 E |
| Okkang-ni | 98 | 40.18 N | 124.42 E |
| Okkerbil' ≃ | 265a | 59.56 N | 30.26 E |
| Okladnevo | 76 | 58.36 N | 33.39 E |
| Oklahoma, Pa., U.S. | 214 | 41.07 N | 78.44 W |
| Oklahoma, Pa., U.S. | 279b | 40.35 N | 79.35 W |
| Oklahoma □[3], U.S. | 178 | 35.30 N | 98.00 W |
| Oklahoma □[3], U.S. | 196 | 35.30 N | 98.00 W |
| Oklahoma City | 196 | 35.28 N | 97.30 W |
| Oklawaha | 220 | 29.02 N | 81.55 W |
| Oklawaha ≃, Fl., U.S. | 192 | 29.28 N | 81.41 W |
| Oklawaha ≃, Fl., U.S. | 220 | 29.03 N | 81.52 W |
| Oklee | 198 | 47.50 N | 95.51 W |
| Okmulgee | 196 | 35.37 N | 95.57 W |
| Oko, Wādī V | 140 | 21.15 N | 35.56 E |
| Okobojo Creek ≃ | 198 | 44.38 N | 100.28 W |
| Okok ≃ | 154 | 2.06 N | 33.53 E |
| Okoka | 152 | 2.57 S | 23.27 E |
| Okola | 152 | 4.01 N | 11.23 E |
| Okollo | 154 | 2.40 N | 31.08 E |
| Okolo | 152 | 3.46 S | 23.55 E |
| Okolona, Ar., U.S. | 194 | 33.59 N | 93.20 W |
| Okolona, Ky., U.S. | 194 | 38.08 N | 85.41 W |
| Okolona, Ms., U.S. | 194 | 34.00 N | 88.45 W |
| Okombahe | 156 | 21.23 S | 15.22 E |
| Okondja | 152 | 0.41 S | 13.47 E |
| Okonek | 30 | 53.33 N | 16.50 E |
| Okonešnikovo | 86 | 54.50 N | 75.05 E |
| Okotoks | 182 | 50.44 N | 113.59 W |
| Okoyo | 152 | 1.28 S | 15.04 E |
| Okpara ≃ | 150 | 7.40 N | 2.35 E |
| Okrika | 150 | 4.47 N | 7.04 E |
| Oksbøl | 26 | 55.38 N | 8.17 E |
| Okskij zapovednik ◆[4] | 80 | 54.45 N | 40.45 E |
| Oksko-Donskaja ravnina ≚ | 80 | 53.00 N | 40.30 E |
| Oksovskij | 24 | 62.37 N | 39.55 E |
| Oksskolten ∧ | 24 | 65.59 N | 14.15 E |
| Oksu ≃, Asia | 85 | 40.12 N | 69.16 E |
| Oksu ≃, Taj. | 120 | 38.09 N | 73.57 E |
| Okt'abr', Kaz. | 85 | 43.41 N | 77.12 E |
| Okt'abr', Kaz. | 86 | 45.45 N | 61.34 E |
| Okt'abr', Ross. | 76 | 57.50 N | 37.26 E |
| Okt'abr'sk, Kaz. | 86 | 49.28 N | 57.25 E |
| Okt'abr'sk, Ross. | 80 | 53.11 N | 48.40 E |
| Okt'abr'skij, Kaz. | 86 | 52.35 N | 62.40 E |
| Okt'abr'skij, Kaz. | 86 | 49.38 N | 83.35 E |
| Okt'abr'skij, Ross. | 24 | 61.04 N | 43.08 E |
| Okt'abr'skij, Ross. | 24 | 59.29 N | 48.50 E |
| Okt'abr'skij, Ross. | 76 | 53.47 N | 39.29 E |
| Okt'abr'skij, Ross. | 78 | 44.56 N | 39.00 E |
| Okt'abr'skij, Ross. | 78 | 50.26 N | 36.22 E |
| Okt'abr'skij, Ross. | 80 | 54.28 N | 53.28 E |
| Okt'abr'skij, Ross. | 80 | 56.17 N | 44.12 E |
| Okt'abr'skij, Ross. | 80 | 57.08 N | 40.20 E |
| Okt'abr'skij, Ross. | 80 | 58.19 N | 44.19 E |
| Okt'abr'skij, Ross. | 80 | 56.35 N | 53.58 E |
| Okt'abr'skij, Ross. | 80 | 47.58 N | 43.38 E |
| Okt'abr'skij, Ross. | 82 | 55.37 N | 37.58 E |
| Okt'abr'skij, Ross. | 82 | 54.14 N | 38.54 E |
| Okt'abr'skij, Ross. | 83 | 47.28 N | 40.04 E |
| Okt'abr'skij, Ross. | 86 | 56.31 N | 57.12 E |
| Okt'abr'skij, Ross. | 88 | 50.04 N | 118.04 E |
| Okt'abr'skij, Ross. | 88 | 56.05 N | 99.26 E |
| Okt'abr'skij, Ross. | 89 | 53.01 N | 128.37 E |
| Okt'abr'skij, Ross. | 89 | 49.02 N | 140.11 E |
| Okt'abr'skij, Taj. | 85 | 38.33 N | 68.22 E |
| Okt'abr'skoje, Kaz. | 86 | 52.07 N | 65.40 E |
| Okt'abr'skoje, Ross. | 74 | 62.28 N | 66.03 E |
| Okt'abr'skoje, Ross. | 76 | 52.18 N | 39.44 E |
| Okt'abr'skoje, Ross. | 80 | 45.37 N | 42.49 E |
| Okt'abr'skoje, Ross. | 80 | 52.54 N | 46.30 E |
| Okt'abr'skoje, Ross. | 86 | 52.20 N | 55.30 E |
| Okt'abr'skoje, Ross. | 86 | 54.26 N | 62.44 E |
| Okt'abr'skoj Revol'ucii, ostrov I | 74 | 79.30 N | 97.00 E |
| Ok Tedi | 164 | 5.44 S | 141.09 E |
| Oktember'an | 84 | 40.09 N | 44.02 E |
| Oktong-ni | 98 | 38.27 N | 127.07 E |
| Oktwin | 110 | 18.49 N | 96.26 E |
| Oktyabrs'ke, Ukr. | 78 | 45.18 N | 34.09 E |
| Oktyabrs'ke, Ukr. | 83 | 48.28 N | 37.22 E |
| Oktyabr'skiy → Okt'abr'skij | 80 | 54.28 N | 53.28 E |
| Oku, Nihon | 96 | 34.40 N | 134.05 E |
| Oku, Nihon | 174m | 26.50 N | 128.17 E |
| Ōkubo, Nihon | 268 | 35.21 N | 139.56 E |
| Ōkubo, Nihon | 270 | 34.41 N | 134.57 E |
| Ōkubo ◆[8] | 268 | 35.24 N | 139.35 E |
| Okučani | 36 | 45.16 N | 17.12 E |
| Ōkuchi, Nihon | 92 | 32.04 N | 130.37 E |
| Ōkuchi, Nihon | 94 | 36.17 N | 136.39 E |
| Okuku ≃ | 172 | 43.16 S | 172.28 E |
| Okulovka | 76 | 58.26 N | 33.18 E |
| Okumi | 84 | 42.43 N | 41.45 E |
| Okundi | 150 | 6.22 N | 8.44 E |
| Okun'ov Nos | 24 | 66.15 N | 52.28 E |
| Ōkura-yama ∧ | 96 | 35.08 N | 133.22 E |
| Okusawa ◆[8] | 268 | 35.36 N | 139.40 E |
| Okushiri | 92a | 42.10 N | 139.31 E |
| Okushiri-tō I | 92a | 42.10 N | 139.27 E |
| Ōkusu-yama ∧[2] | 268 | 35.15 N | 139.38 E |
| Okuta | 150 | 9.14 N | 3.15 E |
| Okutadami Dam ◆[6] | 94 | 37.09 N | 139.15 E |
| Okutama | 94 | 35.47 N | 139.02 E |
| Okutama-ko ⊜ | 94 | 35.47 N | 139.02 E |
| Okutsu | 96 | 35.14 N | 133.56 E |
| Ōkuwa | 94 | 35.41 N | 137.40 E |
| Okwa (Chapman's) ≃ | 156 | 22.30 S | 23.00 E |
| Okwoga | 150 | 7.01 N | 7.50 E |
| Olá, Pan. | 236 | 8.25 N | 80.39 W |
| Ola, Ross. | 74 | 59.35 N | 151.17 E |
| Ola, Ar., U.S. | 194 | 35.01 N | 93.13 W |
| Ólafsfjörður | 24a | 66.06 N | 18.38 W |
| Olambwe Valley Game Reserve ◆[4] | 154 | 0.37 S | 34.15 E |
| Olancha | 204 | 36.16 N | 118.00 W |
| Olancha Peak ∧ | 204 | 36.16 N | 118.07 W |
| Olanchito | 236 | 15.30 N | 86.35 W |
| Olancho □[5] | 236 | 14.45 N | 86.00 W |
| Öland I | 26 | 56.45 N | 16.38 E |
| Olandsån ≃ | 40 | 60.20 N | 18.14 E |
| Olango Island I | 116 | 10.16 N | 124.03 E |
| Olanta | 192 | 33.56 N | 79.55 W |
| Olar | 192 | 33.10 N | 81.11 W |
| Olarevo | 76 | 59.22 N | 40.04 E |
| Olaria, Bra. | 256 | 21.52 S | 43.56 W |
| Olaria, Bra. | 287a | 22.41 S | 43.08 W |
| Olaria ◆[8] | 287a | 22.52 S | 43.15 W |
| Olary | 166 | 32.17 S | 140.19 E |
| Olascoaga | 252 | 35.12 S | 60.36 W |
| Olasore | 273a | 6.40 N | 3.17 E |
| Olathe, Co., U.S. | 200 | 38.36 N | 107.58 W |
| Olathe, Ks., U.S. | 198 | 38.52 N | 94.49 W |
| Olavarría | 252 | 36.54 S | 60.17 W |
| Olavinlinna ⊥ | 26 | 61.52 N | 29.00 E |
| Oława | 30 | 50.57 N | 17.17 E |
| Olbernhau | 54 | 50.39 N | 13.20 E |
| Olbersdorf | 54 | 50.52 N | 14.46 E |
| Olbersleben | 54 | 51.09 N | 11.20 E |
| Olbia | 71 | 40.55 N | 9.31 E |
| Olbia, Golfo di ⊂ | 71 | 40.55 N | 9.39 E |
| Ølby Lyng | 41 | 55.29 N | 12.09 E |
| Olca, Volcán ∧[1] | 248 | 20.57 S | 68.30 W |
| Ol'chi | 80 | 53.53 N | 41.28 E |
| Olching | 60 | 48.12 N | 11.20 E |
| Ol'chon, ostrov I | 88 | 53.09 N | 107.24 E |
| Ol'chovaja ≃ | 80 | 48.47 N | 40.51 E |
| Ol'chovatka | 78 | 50.18 N | 39.17 E |
| Ol'chovka, Ross. | 80 | 49.52 N | 44.34 E |
| Ol'chovka, Ross. | 86 | 56.22 N | 63.46 E |
| Olcott | 210 | 43.20 N | 78.42 W |
| Old ≃, Ca., U.S. | 226 | 38.04 N | 121.35 W |
| Old ≃, Tx., U.S. | 222 | 30.25 N | 96.19 W |
| Old Bahama Channel ⋃ | 238 | 22.30 N | 78.50 W |
| Old Bedford ≃ | 42 | 52.35 N | 0.20 E |
| Old Bennington | 210 | 42.52 N | 73.12 W |
| Old Bethpage | 276 | 40.45 N | 73.27 W |
| Old Bethpage Village ⊥ | 276 | 40.47 N | 73.28 W |
| Old Brazoria | 222 | 29.04 N | 95.34 W |
| Old Bridge | 276 | 40.24 N | 74.21 W |
| Old Brookville | 276 | 40.49 N | 73.36 W |
| Oldbury | 42 | 52.30 N | 2.00 W |
| Old Cairo → Mişr al-Qadīmah ◆[8] | 273c | 30.00 N | 31.14 E |
| Oldcastle | 48 | 53.46 N | 7.10 W |
| Old Colwyn | 44 | 53.18 N | 3.43 W |
| Old Cork | 166 | 22.56 S | 141.52 E |
| Old Creek Estates | 284c | 38.50 N | 77.16 W |
| Old Crow | 180 | 67.35 N | 139.50 W |
| Old Crow ≃ | 180 | 67.35 N | 139.50 W |
| Oldeani | 154 | 3.21 S | 35.33 E |
| Oldebroek | 52 | 52.26 N | 5.54 E |
| Old Economy ⊥ | 279b | 40.36 N | 80.14 W |
| Olden, Nor. | 26 | 61.50 N | 6.49 E |
| Olden, Tx., U.S. | 196 | 32.25 N | 98.45 W |
| Oldenbrok | 52 | 53.17 N | 8.23 E |
| Oldenburg, Dtsch. | 52 | 53.08 N | 8.13 E |
| Oldenburg, In., U.S. | 218 | 39.20 N | 85.12 W |
| Oldenburg □[9] | 52 | 53.00 N | 8.00 E |
| Oldenburg in Holstein | 54 | 54.17 N | 10.52 E |
| Oldendorf | 52 | 53.35 N | 9.14 E |
| Oldenstadt | 52 | 52.58 N | 10.35 E |
| Oldenswort | 41 | 54.22 N | 8.56 E |
| Oldenzaal | 52 | 52.19 N | 6.56 E |
| Oldersum | 52 | 53.20 N | 7.20 E |
| Old Faithful Geyser Ŧ[4] | 202 | 44.30 N | 110.45 W |
| Old Farm | 284c | 39.03 N | 77.09 W |
| Old Field | 276 | 40.57 N | 73.08 W |
| Old Field Point › | 276 | 40.58 N | 73.07 W |
| Old Forge, N.Y., U.S. | 188 | 43.42 N | 74.58 W |
| Old Forge, Pa., U.S. | 210 | 41.22 N | 75.44 W |
| Old Forge Village | 276 | 40.49 N | 74.29 W |
| Old Fort | 214 | 41.15 N | 83.09 W |
| Old Fort Erie ⊥ | 284a | 42.53 N | 78.56 W |
| Old Fort Henry ⊥ | 212 | 44.14 N | 76.28 W |
| Old Fort Mountain ∧ | 182 | 55.05 N | 126.30 W |
| Old Fort Niagara ⊥ | 284a | 43.16 N | 79.03 W |
| Old Fort Parker State Historic Site ⊥ | 222 | 31.34 N | 96.34 W |
| Old Fort Point › | 240b | 25.03 N | 77.29 W |
| Old Greenwich | 276 | 41.02 N | 73.34 W |
| Oldham, Eng., U.K. | 44 | 53.33 N | 2.07 W |
| Oldham, S.D., U.S. | 198 | 44.13 N | 97.18 W |
| Oldham □[6] | 218 | 38.23 N | 85.27 W |
| Oldham □[8] | 262 | 53.34 N | 2.03 W |
| Oldham Pines | 283 | 42.05 N | 70.50 W |
| Oldham Pond ⊜ | 283 | 42.03 N | 70.51 W |
| Oldham Village | 207 | 42.04 N | 70.49 W |
| Old Harbor | 180 | 57.12 N | 153.19 W |
| Old Harbour | 241q | 17.56 N | 77.07 W |
| Old Hickory Lake ⊜[1] | 194 | 36.18 N | 86.30 W |
| Old Howe ≃ | 44 | 53.57 N | 0.21 W |
| Oldisleben | 54 | 51.18 N | 11.10 E |
| Old Lyme | 207 | 41.18 N | 72.19 W |
| Old Malden ◆[8] | 260 | 51.23 N | 0.15 W |
| Oldman ≃ | 182 | 49.56 N | 111.42 W |
| Old Man House ⊥ | 224 | 47.43 N | 122.34 W |
| Old Man Mountain ∧ | 186 | 49.08 N | 57.43 W |
| Old Manor | 276 | 40.24 N | 74.11 W |
| Oldmans Creek ≃ | 208 | 39.47 N | 75.27 W |
| Oldmeldrum | 46 | 57.20 N | 2.20 W |
| Old Mkushi | 154 | 14.22 S | 29.22 E |
| Old Monroe | 219 | 38.55 N | 90.44 W |
| Old Mystic | 207 | 41.23 N | 71.57 W |
| Old Nene ≃ | 42 | 52.40 N | 0.10 E |
| Old North Bridge ⊥ | 283 | 42.28 N | 71.21 W |
| Old North Church ᵿ[1] | 283 | 42.22 N | 71.03 W |
| Old Ocean | 222 | 29.05 N | 95.45 W |
| Ol Doinyo Sapuk National Park ♠ | 154 | 1.09 S | 37.12 E |
| Ol'doj ≃ | 89 | 53.33 N | 123.21 E |
| Old Orchard ◆[9] | 278 | 42.04 N | 87.45 W |
| Old Orchard Beach | 188 | 43.31 N | 70.22 W |
| Old Perlican | 186 | 48.05 N | 53.01 W |
| Old Place Creek ≃ | 276 | 40.38 N | 74.12 W |
| Old Point Comfort › | 208 | 37.00 N | 76.19 W |
| Old Rhodes Key I | 220 | 25.22 N | 80.14 W |
| Old Ripley | 219 | 38.54 N | 89.34 W |
| Old Road Bay ⊂ | 284b | 39.12 N | 76.27 W |
| Old Road Bluff › | 240c | 16.59 N | 61.50 W |
| Old Round Rock | 222 | 30.31 N | 97.42 W |
| Olds | 182 | 51.47 N | 114.06 W |
| Old Saybrook | 207 | 41.17 N | 72.22 W |
| Oldsmar | 220 | 28.02 N | 82.39 W |
| Old Speck Mountain ∧ | 188 | 44.34 N | 70.57 W |
| Old Sturbridge Village ⊥ | 207 | 42.07 N | 72.07 W |
| Old Swamp ≃ | 283 | 42.11 N | 70.57 W |
| Old Swedes Church ᵿ[1] | 285 | 39.44 N | 75.32 W |
| Old Tampa Bay ⊂ | 220 | 27.56 N | 82.35 W |
| Old Tappan | 276 | 41.00 N | 73.59 W |
| Old Tate | 156 | 21.22 S | 27.46 E |
| Old Town | 188 | 44.56 N | 68.38 W |
| Old Trafford Cricket Ground ♠ | 262 | 53.28 N | 2.17 W |
| Old Trap | 192 | 36.15 N | 76.02 W |
| Olduvai Gorge V | 154 | 2.58 S | 35.22 E |
| Old Westbury | 276 | 40.47 N | 73.37 W |
| Old Westbury Gardens ♠ | 276 | 40.46 N | 73.36 W |
| Oldwick | 210 | 40.40 N | 74.44 W |
| Old Windsor | 260 | 51.28 N | 0.35 W |
| Old Wives Lake ⊜ | 184 | 50.06 N | 106.00 W |
| Old Woman Creek ≃ | 198 | 43.19 N | 104.21 W |
| Öldzijt, Mong. | 88 | 48.07 N | 102.34 E |
| Öldzijt, Mong. | 102 | 45.18 N | 106.12 E |
| Old Zoinsville | 208 | 40.29 N | 75.31 W |
| Olean | 210 | 42.04 N | 78.25 W |
| Olean Creek ≃ | 210 | 42.04 N | 78.25 W |
| O'Leary | 186 | 46.42 N | 64.13 W |
| Olecko | 30 | 54.03 N | 22.30 E |
| Olegário Maciel | 256 | 22.19 S | 45.35 W |
| Oleggio | 62 | 45.36 N | 8.38 E |
| Olekma → Ol'okma ≃ | 74 | 60.22 N | 120.42 E |
| Oleksandrivka, Ukr. | 78 | 48.43 N | 36.55 E |
| Oleksandrivka, Ukr. | 78 | 48.57 N | 32.14 E |
| Oleksandrivka, Ukr. | 78 | 47.42 N | 31.16 E |
| Oleksandrivka, Ukr. | 78 | 46.32 N | 35.29 E |
| Oleksandrivka, Ukr. | 83 | 47.47 N | 37.41 E |
| Oleksandrivka, Ukr. | 83 | 47.55 N | 37.35 E |
| Oleksandrivs'k | 83 | 48.35 N | 39.12 E |
| Oleksandriya | 78 | 48.40 N | 33.07 E |
| Oleksandro-Kalynove | 83 | 48.25 N | 37.40 E |
| Oleksiyevo-Druzhkivka | 83 | 48.34 N | 37.36 E |
| Oleksiyivka, Ukr. | 78 | 47.14 N | 36.32 E |
| Oleksiyivka, Ukr. | 83 | 49.25 N | 38.46 E |
| Oleksiyivka, Ukr. | 83 | 49.01 N | 39.11 E |
| Olema | 24 | 64.30 N | 46.08 E |
| Olen, Bel. | 56 | 51.09 N | 4.51 E |
| Ølen, Nor. | 26 | 59.36 N | 5.48 E |
| Ölen ⊜ | 40 | 59.13 N | 14.31 E |
| Olenegorsk | 24 | 68.09 N | 33.15 E |
| Olenica | 24 | 66.29 N | 35.20 E |
| Olenij, ostrov I | 74 | 72.25 N | 77.45 E |
| Olenino | 76 | 56.12 N | 33.29 E |
| Olenivka | 78 | 45.23 N | 32.32 E |
| Olenja Rečka | 86 | 52.48 N | 93.14 E |
| Olen'kovo | 82 | 54.34 N | 38.06 E |
| Olen'ok | 74 | 68.33 N | 112.18 E |
| Olen'ok ≃ | 74 | 73.00 N | 119.55 E |
| Olen'okskij zaliv ⊂ | 74 | 73.20 N | 121.00 E |
| Olentangy ≃ | 214 | 39.58 N | 83.06 W |
| Olenti ≃ | 80 | 49.50 N | 52.03 E |
| Olenty | 80 | 50.02 N | 52.07 E |
| Oleopolis | 214 | 41.27 N | 79.37 W |
| Oléron, Île d' I | 32 | 45.56 N | 1.15 W |
| Oles'ko | 78 | 49.58 N | 24.53 E |
| Olešná | 60 | 49.46 N | 13.48 E |
| Oleśnica | 30 | 51.13 N | 17.23 E |
| Olesno | 30 | 50.53 N | 18.25 E |
| Olevano Romano | 66 | 41.52 N | 13.02 E |
| Olevano sul Tusciano | 68 | 40.40 N | 15.01 E |
| Olevsk | 78 | 51.13 N | 27.39 E |
| Oley | 208 | 40.23 N | 75.47 W |
| Olfen | 52 | 51.42 N | 7.23 E |
| Ol'ga, Ross. | 89 | 43.45 N | 135.18 E |
| Olga, Wa., U.S. | 224 | 48.37 N | 122.50 W |
| Olga, Mount ∧, Austl. | 162 | 25.19 S | 130.46 E |
| Olga, Mount ∧, Vt., U.S. | 207 | 42.51 N | 72.48 W |
| Olgiata | 267a | 42.02 N | 12.22 E |
| Olgiate Comasco | 62 | 45.48 N | 8.58 E |
| Olgiate Olona | 62 | 45.38 N | 8.53 E |
| Ölgij, Mong. | 86 | 48.56 N | 89.57 E |
| Ölgij, Mong. | 86 | 48.59 N | 92.01 E |
| Olginate | 62 | 45.48 N | 9.24 E |
| Ol'ginka | 78 | 44.14 N | 38.53 E |
| Ol'gino | 89 | 52.53 N | 125.47 E |
| Ol'gino ◆[8] | 265a | 60.00 N | 30.09 E |
| Ol'ginskaja, Ross. | 78 | 45.57 N | 38.34 E |
| Ol'ginskaja, Ross. | 83 | 47.11 N | 39.56 E |
| Ølgod | 26 | 55.49 N | 8.37 E |
| Ol'govo | 82 | 56.16 N | 37.21 E |
| Olhão | 34 | 37.02 N | 7.50 W |
| Olho d'Água das Cunhãs | 250 | 4.43 S | 44.34 W |
| Olho d'Água das Flores | 250 | 9.33 S | 37.17 W |
| Ol'hopil' | 78 | 48.12 N | 29.29 E |
| Ol'hynka | 83 | 47.42 N | 37.31 E |
| Oli ≃ | 150 | 9.45 N | 4.38 E |
| Olib, Otok I | 36 | 44.22 N | 14.48 E |
| Oliden | 258 | 35.11 S | 57.57 W |
| Oliena | 71 | 40.16 N | 9.24 E |
| Olifants (Rio dos Elefantes) ≃, Afr. | 156 | 24.10 S | 32.40 E |
| Olifants ≃, Namibia | 156 | 25.30 S | 19.30 E |
| Olifants ≃, S. Afr. | 158 | 33.41 S | 21.42 E |
| Olifants ≃, S. Afr. | 158 | 31.42 S | 18.12 E |
| Olifants ≃, S. Afr. | 158 | 29.39 S | 21.10 E |
| Olifantshoek | 158 | 27.57 S | 22.42 E |
| Olifantsrivierberge ⋏ | 158 | 32.40 S | 19.00 E |
| Oliki | 265a | 59.46 N | 29.55 E |
| Olimarao I[1] | 108 | 7.41 N | 145.52 E |
| Olimbía ⊥ | 38 | 37.38 N | 21.41 E |
| Ólimbos | 38 | 35.44 N | 27.11 E |
| Ólimbos ∧ | 130 | 34.56 N | 32.52 E |
| Ólimbos, Óros (Mount Olympus) ∧ | 38 | 40.05 N | 22.21 E |
| Olímpia | 255 | 20.44 S | 48.54 W |
| Olímpico, Estadio ♠ | 286a | 19.20 N | 99.12 W |
| Olimpico, Stadio ♠ | 267a | 41.56 N | 12.27 E |
| Olímpio Noronha | 256 | 22.04 S | 45.16 W |
| Olimpo → Ólimbos, Óros ∧ | 38 | 40.05 N | 22.21 E |
| Olin | 190 | 41.59 N | 91.08 W |
| Olinalá | 234 | 17.50 N | 98.51 W |
| Olinda, Austl. | 170 | 32.50 S | 150.08 E |
| Olinda, Austl. | 274b | 37.51 S | 145.22 E |
| Olinda, Bra. | 250 | 8.01 S | 34.51 W |
| Olinda, Bra. | 256 | 22.49 S | 43.25 W |
| Olinda, Mount ∧ | 274b | 37.52 S | 145.21 E |
| Olinda Creek ≃ | 274b | 37.41 S | 145.21 E |
| Olindina | 250 | 11.22 S | 38.21 W |
| Olinsk | 88 | 52.24 N | 116.13 E |
| Olio | 166 | 21.54 S | 143.13 E |
| Olite | 34 | 42.29 N | 1.39 W |
| Oliva, Arg. | 252 | 32.03 S | 63.34 W |
| Oliva, Esp. | 34 | 38.55 N | 0.07 W |
| Oliva de la Frontera | 34 | 38.16 N | 6.55 W |
| Olivais ◆[8] | 266c | 38.46 N | 9.06 E |
| Olival Basto | 266c | 38.47 N | 9.10 W |
| Olivares, Cerro de ∧ | 252 | 30.18 S | 69.55 W |
| Olive Branch | 194 | 34.57 N | 89.49 W |
| Olivebridge | 210 | 41.55 N | 74.13 W |
| Olive Hill | 218 | 38.18 N | 83.10 W |
| Olivehurst | 226 | 39.05 N | 121.33 W |
| Oliveira | 255 | 20.41 S | 44.49 W |
| Oliveira dos Brejinhos | 255 | 12.19 S | 42.54 W |
| Oliveira Fortes | 256 | 21.20 S | 43.27 W |
| Olivelifuri I | 122 | 5.17 N | 73.35 E |
| Olive Mount ◆[8] | 262 | 53.24 N | 2.55 W |
| Olivença | 154 | 11.47 S | 35.13 E |
| Olivenza | 34 | 38.41 N | 7.06 W |
| Oliver | 182 | 49.11 N | 119.33 W |
| Olivera | 258 | 34.38 S | 59.15 W |
| Oliver Creek ≃ | 222 | 33.06 N | 97.17 W |
| Oliver Ditch ≋ | 216 | 41.00 N | 87.10 W |
| Oliverea | 210 | 42.04 N | 74.28 W |
| Oliver Estates | 284c | 38.59 N | 77.18 W |
| Oliveri | 70 | 38.07 N | 15.03 E |
| Oliver Lake ⊜ | 184 | 56.56 N | 103.22 W |
| Oliver Springs | 192 | 36.02 N | 84.20 W |
| Olivet, Fr. | 50 | 47.52 N | 1.54 E |
| Olivet, Mi., U.S. | 216 | 42.26 N | 84.55 W |
| Olivet, S.D., U.S. | 198 | 43.14 N | 97.40 W |
| Oliveto Citra | 68 | 40.41 N | 15.14 E |
| Oliveto Lucano | 68 | 40.32 N | 16.11 E |
| Olivette | 219 | 38.39 N | 90.22 W |
| Olivia | 198 | 44.46 N | 94.59 W |
| Olivine Range ⋏ | 172 | 44.18 S | 168.30 E |
| Olivo | 116 | 10.52 N | 123.53 E |
| Olivo ≃ | 70 | 37.22 N | 14.15 E |
| Olivone | 58 | 46.32 N | 8.57 E |
| Olivos ◆[8] | 258 | 34.32 S | 58.29 W |
| Öljaren ⊜ | 40 | 59.08 N | 16.02 E |
| Olji Moron ≃ | 89 | 44.16 N | 121.42 E |
| Olla | 194 | 31.54 N | 92.14 W |
| Ollagüe | 248 | 21.14 S | 68.16 W |
| Ollagüe, Volcán ∧[1] | 248 | 21.18 S | 68.12 W |
| Ollainville | 261 | 48.35 N | 2.13 E |
| Ollantaitambo | 248 | 13.16 S | 72.16 W |
| Ollatrim ≃ | 48 | 52.52 N | 8.13 W |
| Ollei | 175b | 7.43 N | 134.37 E |
| Ollerton | 262 | 53.17 N | 2.20 W |
| Ollerup | 41 | 55.04 N | 10.30 E |
| Olliergues | 62 | 45.40 N | 3.38 E |
| Ollioules | 62 | 43.08 N | 5.51 E |
| Ollomont | 62 | 45.50 N | 7.22 E |
| Ollon | 58 | 46.18 N | 7.00 E |
| Olloua | 152 | 0.56 S | 14.34 E |
| Olmedillo de Roa | 34 | 41.47 N | 3.56 W |
| Olmedo, Esp. | 34 | 41.23 N | 4.41 W |
| Olmedo, It. | 71 | 40.39 N | 8.23 E |
| Olmo al Brembo | 58 | 45.58 N | 9.39 E |
| Olmos | 248 | 5.59 S | 79.46 W |
| Olmsted | 214 | 41.24 N | 81.44 W |
| Olmsted Falls | 279a | 41.22 N | 81.54 W |
| Olmütz → Olomouc | 30 | 49.36 N | 17.16 E |
| Olney, Eng., U.K. | 42 | 52.09 N | 0.42 W |
| Olney, Il., U.S. | 194 | 38.43 N | 88.05 W |
| Olney, Md., U.S. | 208 | 39.09 N | 77.04 W |
| Olney, Mo., U.S. | 219 | 39.05 N | 91.15 W |
| Olney, Mt., U.S. | 182 | 48.32 N | 114.34 W |
| Olney, Tx., U.S. | 196 | 33.22 N | 98.45 W |
| Olney ◆[8] | 285 | 40.02 N | 75.08 W |
| Oloči | 89 | 51.21 N | 119.55 E |
| Olofström | 26 | 56.16 N | 14.30 E |
| Oloj ≃ | 74 | 66.29 N | 159.29 E |
| Ol'okma ≃ | 74 | 60.22 N | 120.42 E |
| Ol'okminsk | 74 | 60.24 N | 120.24 E |
| Ol'okminskij Stanovik ⋏ | 88 | 54.30 N | 120.00 E |
| Olokui ∧ | 229a | 21.08 N | 156.51 W |
| Olomane ≃ | 186 | 50.14 N | 60.37 W |
| Olombo | 152 | 1.18 S | 15.53 E |
| Olomega, Laguna ⊜ | 236 | 13.19 N | 88.04 W |
| Olomouc | 30 | 49.36 N | 17.16 E |
| Olona ≃ | 62 | 45.06 N | 9.21 E |
| Olonec | 24 | 61.00 N | 32.57 E |
| Olongapo | 116 | 14.50 N | 120.16 E |
| Olonki | 88 | 52.54 N | 103.45 E |
| Olorgasailie National Monument ♠ | 154 | 1.40 S | 36.22 E |
| Oloron, Gave d' ≃ | 32 | 43.33 N | 1.05 W |
| Oloron-Sainte-Marie | 32 | 43.12 N | 0.36 W |
| Olosega | 174y | 14.11 S | 169.39 W |
| Olosega I | 174y | 14.11 S | 169.39 W |
| Olot | 34 | 42.11 N | 2.29 E |
| Olov'annaja, Ross. | 88 | 50.56 N | 115.35 E |
| Olov'annaja, Ross. | 180 | 66.10 N | 178.59 W |
| Oloví | 54 | 50.11 N | 12.33 E |
| Olpe, Dtsch. | 56 | 51.02 N | 7.52 E |
| Olpe, Ks., U.S. | 198 | 38.15 N | 96.10 W |
| Olperer ∧ | 64 | 47.03 N | 11.39 E |
| Olsabach ≃ | 61 | 46.56 N | 14.25 E |
| Ol'šanka | 78 | 51.46 N | 35.25 E |
| Olšany | 60 | 49.24 N | 13.38 E |
| Olsberg | 56 | 51.21 N | 8.29 E |
| Ølsemagle | 41 | 55.30 N | 12.10 E |
| Olshammar | 40 | 58.45 N | 14.48 E |
| Ol'shana | 78 | 50.48 N | 34.02 E |
| Olst | 52 | 52.20 N | 6.06 E |
| Ølstykke | 41 | 55.47 N | 12.11 E |
| Olsufjevo | 76 | 53.36 N | 33.40 E |
| Olsztyn (Allenstein) | 30 | 53.48 N | 20.29 E |
| Olsztyn □[4] | 30 | 53.50 N | 20.40 E |
| Olsztynek | 30 | 53.36 N | 20.17 E |
| Olt □[6] | 38 | 44.20 N | 24.30 E |
| Olt ≃ | 38 | 43.43 N | 24.51 E |
| Olta | 252 | 30.37 S | 66.16 W |
| Olten | 58 | 47.21 N | 7.54 E |
| Olteni | 38 | 44.10 N | 25.18 E |
| Oltenița | 38 | 44.05 N | 26.39 E |

DEUTSCH

| Name | Seite | Breite°′ | Länge°′ E = Ost |
|---|---|---|---|
| Olteț ≃ | 38 | 44.14 N | 24.27 E |
| Olton | 196 | 34.11 N | 102.08 W |
| Oltre il Colle | 64 | 45.54 N | 9.46 E |
| Oltu | 130 | 40.33 N | 41.59 E |
| Oltu ≃ | 130 | 40.49 N | 41.40 E |
| Oluan Pi › | 100 | 21.54 N | 120.51 E |
| Olukonda | 156 | 18.03 S | 16.00 E |
| Olur | 130 | 40.50 N | 42.08 E |
| Olustee, Fl., U.S. | 192 | 30.12 N | 82.26 W |
| Olustee, Ok., U.S. | 196 | 34.32 N | 99.25 W |
| Olustee Creek ≃ | 192 | 29.57 N | 82.32 W |
| Oluta | 234 | 17.55 N | 94.54 W |
| Olutanga (Suba Nipa) | 116 | 7.26 N | 122.54 E |
| Olutanga Island I | 116 | 7.22 N | 122.52 E |
| Olutayan Island I | 116 | 11.39 N | 122.50 E |
| Olute | 273a | 6.28 N | 3.16 E |
| Ol'utorskij, mys › | 74 | 59.55 N | 170.27 E |
| Ol'utorskij zaliv ⊂ | 74 | 60.15 N | 168.30 E |
| Oluwo | 273a | 6.42 N | 3.18 E |
| Olvenstedt | 54 | 52.09 N | 11.34 E |
| Olvera | 34 | 36.56 N | 5.16 W |
| Olyka | 78 | 50.42 N | 25.51 E |
| Olykhovatka | 78 | 50.12 N | 37.31 E |
| Olym | 78 | 51.42 N | 38.10 E |
| Olymp → Ólimbos, Óros ∧ | 38 | 40.05 N | 22.21 E |
| Olympe, Mont → Ólimbos, Óros ∧ | 38 | 40.05 N | 22.21 E |
| Olympia | 224 | 47.02 N | 122.53 W |
| Olympia → Olimbía ⊥ | 38 | 37.38 N | 21.41 E |
| Olympia Fields | 216 | 41.32 N | 87.42 W |
| Olympia Heights | 220 | 25.43 N | 80.21 W |
| Olympia Park ♠ | 273d | 26.15 S | 28.26 E |
| Olympia-Stadion ♠ | 264a | 52.31 N | 13.14 E |
| Olympic Mountains ⋏ | 224 | 47.50 N | 123.45 W |
| Olympic National Park ♠ | 224 | 47.48 N | 123.30 W |
| Olympic Valley | 226 | 39.13 N | 120.14 W |
| Olympic View | 224 | 47.43 N | 122.45 W |
| Olympieion ⊥ | 267c | 37.58 N | 23.44 E |
| Olympique, Stade ♠ | 275a | 45.33 N | 73.33 W |
| Olympus, Mount → Ólimbos, Óros ∧, Ellás | 38 | 40.05 N | 22.21 E |
| Olympus, Mount ∧, Wa., U.S. | 224 | 47.48 N | 123.43 W |
| Olympus, Mount ∧[2] | 192 | 38.03 N | 83.39 W |
| Olyphant | 210 | 41.28 N | 75.36 W |
| Olyshivka | 78 | 51.13 N | 31.18 E |
| Olzai | 71 | 40.11 N | 9.09 E |
| Ol'zony | 88 | 52.57 N | 105.15 E |
| Om ≃, Pap. N. Gui. | 164 | 5.09 S | 142.22 E |
| Om' ≃, Ross. | 86 | 54.59 N | 73.22 E |
| Ōma | 92 | 41.32 N | 140.55 E |
| Ōmachi, Nihon | 94 | 36.30 N | 137.52 E |
| Ōmachi, Nihon | 270 | 34.28 N | 135.25 E |
| Omaezaki | 94 | 34.35 N | 138.13 E |
| Omae-zaki › | 94 | 34.36 N | 138.14 E |
| Ōmagari | 92 | 39.27 N | 140.29 E |
| Omagh, On., Can. | 275b | 43.30 N | 79.49 W |
| Omagh, N. Ire., U.K. | 48 | 54.36 N | 7.18 W |
| Ōmagi | 268 | 35.52 N | 139.42 E |
| Omaguas | 246 | 4.08 S | 73.15 W |
| Omaha, Ne., U.S. | 198 | 41.15 N | 95.56 W |
| Omaha, Tx., U.S. | 222 | 33.11 N | 94.45 W |
| Omaha Indian Reservation ◆[4] | 198 | 42.08 N | 96.22 W |
| Omaheke □[4] | 156 | 22.00 S | 19.00 E |
| Omak | 202 | 48.24 N | 119.31 W |
| Omakau | 172 | 45.05 S | 169.36 E |
| Omak Lake ⊜ | 202 | 48.16 N | 119.23 W |
| Omalo | 84 | 42.23 N | 45.38 E |
| Ōmama | 94 | 36.26 N | 139.17 E |
| Oman ('Umān) □[1] | 118 | 22.00 N | 58.00 E |
| Oman, Gulf of ⊂ | 118 | 24.30 N | 58.30 E |
| Omapere, Lake ⊜ | 172 | 35.21 S | 173.47 E |
| Omar | 192 | 37.45 N | 81.59 W |
| Omarama | 172 | 44.29 S | 169.58 E |
| Omaruru | 156 | 21.28 S | 15.56 E |
| Omaruru ≃ | 156 | 22.07 S | 14.15 E |
| Omas | 248 | 12.31 S | 76.17 W |
| Omatako ∧ | 156 | 21.07 S | 16.43 E |
| Omatako ≃ | 156 | 17.59 S | 20.30 E |
| Omate | 248 | 16.41 S | 70.59 W |
| Omatena | 115b | 9.53 S | 119.47 E |
| Ōma-zaki › | 92 | 41.32 N | 140.55 E |
| Ombai, Selat ⋃ | 112 | 8.30 S | 125.00 E |
| Ombella-Mpoko □[5] | 152 | 5.00 N | 18.00 E |
| Omberg ∧[2] | 26 | 58.20 N | 14.39 E |
| Ombersley | 42 | 52.17 N | 2.13 W |
| Ombombo | 156 | 18.43 S | 13.53 E |
| Omboué | 152 | 1.34 S | 9.15 E |
| Ombrone ≃ | 66 | 42.39 N | 11.00 E |
| Ombúes de Lavalle | 258 | 33.55 S | 57.47 W |
| Ombutosu ∧ | 156 | 21.22 S | 16.50 E |
| Ombwe | 154 | 4.22 S | 25.35 E |
| Omčak | 74 | 61.38 N | 147.55 E |
| Omčaly | 128 | 40.47 N | 53.43 E |
| Omdraaisvlei | 158 | 30.08 S | 23.08 E |
| Omdurman → Umm Durmān | 140 | 15.38 N | 32.30 E |
| Ōme | 94 | 35.47 N | 139.15 E |
| Omega, Ga., U.S. | 192 | 31.20 N | 83.35 W |
| Omega, Oh., U.S. | 218 | 39.09 N | 82.55 W |
| Omegna | 62 | 45.53 N | 8.24 E |
| Omel'nyk | 78 | 49.12 N | 33.32 E |
| Omelyanivka | 78 | 45.32 N | 34.53 E |
| Omemee | 212 | 44.18 N | 78.33 W |
| Omeo | 166 | 37.06 S | 147.36 E |
| Ömerköy | 130 | 39.48 N | 28.03 E |
| Ömerli | 130 | 37.24 N | 40.58 E |
| Ömerli Barajı ⊜[1] | 130 | 41.00 N | 29.20 E |
| Omerville | 206 | 45.17 N | 72.07 W |
| Ometepe, Isla de I | 236 | 11.30 N | 85.35 W |
| Ometepec | 234 | 16.41 N | 98.25 W |
| Ometepec ≃ | 234 | 16.30 N | 98.45 W |
| Om Hajer | 144 | 14.24 N | 36.46 E |
| Omi, Nihon | 94 | 36.27 N | 138.03 E |
| Ōmi, Nihon | 94 | 37.01 N | 137.48 E |
| Ōmi, Nihon | 94 | 35.20 N | 136.24 E |
| Omigawa | 94 | 35.51 N | 140.37 E |
| Ōmi-hachiman | 94 | 35.08 N | 136.06 E |
| Ōminato → Mutsu | 92 | 41.17 N | 141.10 E |
| Omineca ≃ | 182 | 56.05 N | 124.30 W |
| Omineca Mountains ⋏ | 182 | 56.00 N | 125.00 W |
| Omin-ni ◆[8] | 271b | 37.27 N | 127.01 E |
| Ōmino | 270 | 34.32 N | 135.33 E |
| Omišalj | 36 | 45.13 N | 14.34 E |
| Ōmi-shima I, Nihon | 96 | 34.25 N | 131.13 E |
| Ōmi-shima I, Nihon | 96 | 34.15 N | 133.00 E |
| Omitara | 156 | 22.18 S | 18.01 E |
| Omitlán ≃ | 234 | 17.06 N | 99.34 W |
| Ōmiya, Nihon | 94 | 36.33 N | 140.25 E |
| Ōmiya, Nihon | 94 | 35.54 N | 139.38 E |
| Ōmiya, Nihon | 96 | 35.35 N | 135.06 E |
| Ōmiya-daichi ⋏[1] | 268 | 35.56 N | 139.38 E |
| Ōmiya Park Race Track ♠ | 268 | 35.55 N | 139.38 E |
| Øm Kloster ⊥ | 41 | 56.03 N | 9.45 E |
| Ommaney, Cape › | 180 | 56.10 N | 134.39 W |
| Ommanney Bay ⊂ | 176 | 73.07 N | 100.11 W |
| Omme ≃ | 41 | 55.53 N | 8.40 E |
| Ommen | 52 | 52.32 N | 6.25 E |
| Ömnödelger | 88 | 47.52 N | 109.55 E |
| Ömnögov' | 86 | 49.06 N | 91.43 E |
| Ömnögov' □[4] | 102 | 43.00 N | 104.00 E |
| Omø I | 41 | 55.09 N | 11.10 E |
| Omo ≃ | 144 | 4.31 N | 35.59 E |
| Omoa, Bahía de ⊂ | 236 | 15.45 N | 88.10 W |
| Omodeo, Lago ⊜ | 71 | 40.08 N | 8.55 E |
| Omogo | 96 | 33.41 N | 133.02 E |
| Omoi ≃ | 94 | 36.09 N | 139.41 E |
| Omoko | 150 | 5.20 N | 6.39 E |
| Omole | 273a | 6.38 N | 3.22 E |
| Omoloj ≃ | 74 | 71.10 N | 132.08 E |
| Omolon ≃ | 74 | 68.42 N | 158.36 E |
| Omo National Park ♠ | 144 | 6.00 N | 35.45 E |
| Omono ≃ | 92 | 39.46 N | 140.03 E |


**Symbols** in the index entries represent the broad categories identified in the key at the right. Symbols with superior numbers (⋏[1]) identify subcategories (see complete key on page *I · 1).*

**Symbole** im Register stellen die rechts im Schlüssel erklärten Kategorien dar. Symbole mit hochgestellten Ziffern (⋏[1]) bezeichnen Unterabteilungen einer Kategorie (vgl. vollständiger Schlüssel auf Seite *I · 1).*

**Los símbolos** incluídos en el texto del índice representan las grandes categorías identificadas con la clave a la derecha. Los símbolos con numeros en su parte superior (⋏[1]) identifican las subcategorías (véase la clave completa en la página *I · 1).*

**Les symboles** de l'index représentent les catégories indiquées dans la légende à droite. Les symboles suivis d'un indice (⋏[1]) représentent des sous-catégories (voir légende complète à la page *I · 1).*

**Os símbolos** incluídos no texto do índice representam as grandes categorias identificadas com a chave à direita. Os símbolos com números em sua parte superior (⋏[1]) identificam as subcategorias (veja-se a chave completa à página *I · 1).*

| | English | Deutsch | Español | Français | Português |
|---|---|---|---|---|---|
| ∧ | Mountain | Berg | Montaña | Montagne | Montanha |
| ⋏ | Mountains | Gebirge | Montañas | Montagnes | Montanhas |
| )( | Pass | Paß | Paso | Col | Passo |
| V | Valley, Canyon | Tal, Cañon | Valle, Cañón | Vallée, Canyon | Vale, Canhão |
| ≚ | Plain | Ebene | Llano | Plaine | Planície |
| › | Cape | Kap | Cabo | Cap | Cabo |
| I | Island | Insel | Isla | Île | Ilha |
| II | Islands | Inseln | Islas | Îles | Ilhas |
| ≗ | Other Topographic Features | Andere Topographische Objekte | Otros Elementos Topográficos | Autres données topographiques | Outros acidentes topográficos |

## ESPAÑOL

| Nombre | Página | Lat. °′ | Long. °′ W = Oeste |
|---|---|---|---|
| Omont | 56 | 49.36 N | 4.44 E |
| Ōmori ◆[8] | 268 | 35.34 N | 139.44 E |
| Omotegō | 94 | 37.03 N | 140.18 E |
| Omoy | 152 | 1.21 S | 13.09 E |
| Omrel'kaj ≃ | 180 | 68.34 N | 170.30 E |
| Omro | 190 | 44.02 N | 88.44 W |
| Omsino | 80 | 58.36 N | 50.28 E |
| Omsk | 86 | 55.00 N | 73.24 E |
| Omsk Oblast' □[4] | 86 | 56.00 N | 73.00 E |
| Omsukčan | 74 | 62.32 N | 155.48 E |
| O-mu, Mya. | 110 | 22.58 N | 99.18 E |
| Ōmu, Nihon | 92a | 44.34 N | 142.58 E |
| Omu-Aran | 150 | 8.09 N | 5.07 E |
| Ōmuda → Ōmuta | 96 | 33.02 N | 130.27 E |
| Omul, Vârful ∧ | 38 | 45.26 N | 25.26 E |
| Omulew ≃ | 30 | 53.05 N | 21.32 E |
| Ōmura | 92 | 32.54 N | 129.57 E |
| Ōmura-wan c | 92 | 32.57 N | 129.52 E |
| Ōmuro | 268 | 35.54 N | 139.58 E |
| Omurtag | 38 | 43.06 N | 26.25 E |
| Omusati □[4] | 156 | 18.00 S | 14.45 E |
| Ōmuta | 96 | 33.02 N | 130.27 E |
| Omutinskij | 86 | 56.31 N | 67.41 E |
| Omutninsk | 86 | 58.40 N | 52.12 E |
| Ŏmyŏnbo | 98 | 41.16 N | 127.36 E |
| On | 110 | 21.40 N | 106.35 E |
| Ona, Nor. | 26 | 62.52 N | 6.34 E |
| Ona, Fl., U.S. | 220 | 27.28 N | 81.55 W |
| Ona ≃, Ross. | 86 | 52.34 N | 89.50 E |
| Ona → Bir'usa ≃, Ross. | 88 | 57.43 N | 95.24 E |
| Onabas | 232 | 29.27 N | 109.32 W |
| Onadikondo | 152 | 3.52 S | 24.10 E |
| Onaga | 198 | 39.29 N | 96.10 W |
| Onagawa | 92 | 38.26 N | 141.27 E |
| Onahama | 94 | 36.57 N | 140.54 E |
| Onalaska, Tx., U.S. | 222 | 30.48 N | 95.07 W |
| Onalaska, Wa., U.S. | 224 | 46.34 N | 122.43 W |
| Onamia | 190 | 46.04 N | 93.40 W |
| Onancock | 208 | 37.42 N | 75.44 W |
| Onangué, Lac ⊜ | 152 | 0.57 S | 10.04 E |
| Onaping ≃ | 190 | 46.37 N | 81.18 W |
| Onaping Lake ⊜ | 190 | 47.00 N | 81.30 W |
| Onarga | 216 | 40.42 N | 88.00 W |
| Ōnari | 268 | 35.55 N | 139.37 E |
| Onatchiway, Lac ⊜ | 186 | 49.00 N | 71.03 W |
| Onawa | 198 | 42.01 N | 96.05 W |
| Onaway | 190 | 45.21 N | 84.13 W |
| Oncativo | 252 | 31.55 S | 63.40 W |
| Once, Canal Numero Ξ | 252 | 36.09 S | 58.36 W |
| Onchāi | 272b | 22.57 N | 88.19 E |
| Onchan | 44 | 54.11 N | 4.27 W |
| Onch'ŏn-dong | 98 | 40.51 N | 129.07 E |
| Oncócua | 152 | 16.34 S | 13.28 E |
| Onda, Esp. | 34 | 39.58 N | 0.15 W |
| Onda, India | 126 | 23.08 N | 87.12 E |
| Ondangwa | 156 | 17.55 S | 16.00 E |
| Ondas, Rio de ≃ | 255 | 12.08 S | 45.00 W |
| Ondava ≃ | 30 | 48.27 N | 21.48 E |
| Onderdijk | 52 | 52.45 N | 5.07 E |
| Onderstedorings | 158 | 30.13 S | 20.37 E |
| Ondjiva | 152 | 17.03 S | 15.47 E |
| Ondo, Nig. | 150 | 7.04 N | 4.47 E |
| Ondo, Nihon | 96 | 34.11 N | 132.32 E |
| Ondo-ōhashi ◆[5] | 96 | 34.12 N | 132.33 E |
| Öndörchaan | 88 | 47.19 N | 110.39 E |
| Öndörchangaj | 88 | 49.20 N | 94.50 E |
| Öndör-Önc | 102 | 45.51 N | 103.11 E |
| Öndöršireet | 88 | 47.27 N | 104.50 E |
| Öndör-Ulaan | 88 | 48.03 N | 100.30 E |
| Ondozero, ozero ⊜ | 24 | 63.48 N | 33.20 E |
| O'Neals | 226 | 37.08 N | 119.42 W |
| One Arrow Indian Reserve ◆[4] | 184 | 52.48 N | 106.03 W |
| Oneco, Ct., U.S. | 207 | 41.41 N | 71.48 W |
| Oneco, Fl., U.S. | 220 | 27.26 N | 82.32 W |
| Onega | 24 | 63.55 N | 38.05 E |
| Onega ≃ | 24 | 63.58 N | 37.55 E |
| Onega, Lake → Onežskoje ozero ⊜ | 24 | 61.30 N | 35.45 E |
| Oneglia | 62 | 43.53 N | 8.02 E |
| One Hundred and Two ≃ | 194 | 39.44 N | 94.43 W |
| One Hundred and Two, West Fork ≃ | 194 | 40.26 N | 94.49 W |
| One Hundred Fifty Mile House | 182 | 52.06 N | 121.55 W |
| One Hundred Mile House | 182 | 51.39 N | 121.18 W |
| Oneida, Il., U.S. | 190 | 41.04 N | 90.13 W |
| Oneida, Ky., U.S. | 192 | 37.16 N | 83.38 W |
| Oneida, N.Y., U.S. | 210 | 43.05 N | 75.39 W |
| Oneida, Oh., U.S. | 218 | 39.28 N | 84.23 W |
| Oneida, Pa., U.S. | 210 | 40.54 N | 76.08 W |
| Oneida, Tn., U.S. | 192 | 36.29 N | 84.30 W |
| Oneida □[6] | 210 | 43.10 N | 75.20 W |
| Oneida ≃ | 210 | 43.12 N | 76.17 W |
| Oneida Castle | 210 | 43.05 N | 75.40 W |
| Oneida County Airport ⊠ | 210 | 43.09 N | 75.23 W |
| Oneida Creek ≃ | 210 | 43.10 N | 75.44 W |
| Oneida Indian Reservation ◆[4] | 190 | 44.30 N | 88.10 W |
| Oneida Indian Reserve ◆[4] | 214 | 42.49 N | 81.24 W |
| Oneida Lake ⊜ | 210 | 43.13 N | 76.00 W |
| O'Neil Forebay ⊜[1] | 226 | 37.05 N | 121.03 W |
| O'Neill | 198 | 42.27 N | 98.38 W |
| Onekama | 190 | 44.21 N | 86.12 W |
| Onekotan, ostrov I | 74 | 49.25 N | 154.45 E |
| Onema | 152 | 4.33 S | 24.31 E |
| Onemen, zaliv c | 180 | 64.45 N | 176.35 E |
| Oneonta, Al., U.S. | 194 | 33.56 N | 86.28 W |
| Oneonta, N.Y., U.S. | 210 | 42.27 N | 75.03 W |
| Oneroa I | 174k | 21.15 S | 159.43 W |
| Onești | 38 | 46.14 N | 26.44 E |
| One Tree Hill | 168b | 34.43 S | 138.46 E |
| One Tree Hill ∧[2] | 274b | 37.52 S | 145.19 E |
| One Tree Hill Lookout ♠ | 169 | 36.48 S | 144.18 E |
| Onevai I | 174w | 21.05 S | 175.07 W |
| Onex | 58 | 46.10 N | 6.06 E |
| Onežskaja guba c | 24 | 64.20 N | 36.30 E |
| Onežskij poluostrov ≻[1] | 24 | 64.35 N | 38.00 E |
| Onežskoje ozero (Lake Onega) ⊜ | 24 | 61.30 N | 35.45 E |
| Onga ≃ | 96 | 33.54 N | 130.39 E |
| Ongandjera | 156 | 17.53 S | 15.04 E |
| Ongaonga | 172 | 39.55 S | 176.25 E |
| Ongarue | 172 | 38.43 S | 175.17 E |
| Ong Con, Cu Lao I | 269c | 10.45 N | 106.50 E |
| Ongea Levu I | 175g | 19.08 S | 178.24 W |
| Ongeluks ≃ | 158 | 32.24 S | 19.46 E |
| Ongers ≃ | 158 | 31.04 S | 23.13 E |
| Ongerup | 162 | 33.58 S | 118.29 E |
| Ongijn ≃ | 102 | 44.30 N | 103.40 E |
| Ongjin | 98 | 37.57 N | 125.21 E |
| Ongoka | 154 | 1.23 S | 26.02 E |
| Ongole | 122 | 15.31 N | 80.04 E |
| Ongon | 102 | 45.21 N | 113.09 E |
| Ongudaj | 86 | 50.45 N | 86.09 E |
| Oni | 84 | 42.34 N | 43.27 E |
| Onich | 46 | 56.42 N | 5.13 W |
| Onida | 198 | 44.42 N | 100.03 W |
| Onifai | 71 | 40.24 N | 9.39 E |
| Oniferi | 71 | 40.16 N | 9.10 E |
| Onigajō-yama ∧ | 96 | 33.07 N | 132.41 E |
| Onilahy ≃ | 157b | 23.34 S | 43.45 E |
| Onin, Jazirah ≻[1] | 164 | 2.50 S | 132.05 E |
| Onion Creek ≃ | 222 | 30.12 N | 97.35 W |
| Onion Peak ∧ | 224 | 45.49 N | 123.53 W |
| Onishi | 94 | 36.09 N | 139.04 E |
| Onistagane, Lac ⊜ | 186 | 50.42 N | 71.19 W |
| Onitsha | 150 | 6.09 N | 6.47 E |
| Onji | 270 | 34.37 N | 135.38 E |
| Onjuku | 94 | 35.11 N | 140.22 E |

## FRANÇAIS

| Nom | Page | Lat. °′ | Long. °′ W = Ouest |
|---|---|---|---|
| Onkaparinga ≃ | 168b | 35.10 S | 138.28 E |
| Onkivesi ⊜ | 26 | 63.18 N | 27.18 E |
| Onko | 152 | 4.07 S | 19.59 E |
| Onley | 208 | 37.41 N | 75.42 W |
| Onna | 174m | 26.30 N | 127.51 E |
| Onnaing | 50 | 50.23 N | 3.36 E |
| Onno | 58 | 45.55 N | 9.17 E |
| Onny ≃ | 42 | 52.23 N | 2.45 W |
| Ōno, Nihon | 94 | 35.59 N | 136.29 E |
| Ōno, Nihon | 94 | 35.28 N | 136.38 E |
| Ōno, Nihon | 96 | 34.18 N | 132.17 E |
| Ōno, Nihon | 96 | 34.51 N | 134.56 E |
| Ōno, Nihon | 96 | 33.02 N | 131.30 E |
| Ono, Nihon | 270 | 34.57 N | 135.14 E |
| Ono, Pa., U.S. | 208 | 40.24 N | 76.32 W |
| Ono I | 175g | 18.55 S | 178.29 E |
| Ōno ≃ | 96 | 33.15 N | 131.43 E |
| Onochoj | 88 | 51.58 N | 108.01 E |
| Onoda | 96 | 33.59 N | 131.11 E |
| Ōno-dam ◆[6] | 96 | 35.15 N | 135.27 E |
| Onogami | 94 | 36.33 N | 138.56 E |
| Ōnohara | 96 | 34.05 N | 133.40 E |
| Ono-I-Lau I | 14 | 20.39 S | 178.42 W |
| Ōnojō | 96 | 33.32 N | 130.28 E |
| Onolimbu | 114 | 1.03 N | 97.53 E |
| Ōnomi | 96 | 33.21 N | 133.09 E |
| Onomichi | 96 | 34.25 N | 133.12 E |
| Onon | 88 | 49.08 N | 112.38 E |
| Onon ≃ | 88 | 51.42 N | 115.50 E |
| Onondaga, Mi., U.S. | 216 | 42.26 N | 84.33 W |
| Onondaga, N.Y., U.S. | 210 | 43.00 N | 76.11 W |
| Onondaga □[6] | 210 | 43.03 N | 76.09 W |
| Onondaga Creek ≃ | 210 | 43.04 N | 76.11 W |
| Onondaga Indian Reservation ◆[4] | 210 | 42.55 N | 76.09 W |
| Onor | 89 | 50.11 N | 142.40 E |
| Onota Lake ⊜ | 207 | 42.28 N | 73.17 W |
| Onoto | 246 | 9.36 N | 65.12 W |
| Onotoa I[1] | 14 | 1.52 S | 175.34 E |
| Onoway | 182 | 53.42 N | 114.12 W |
| Ons, Illa de I | 34 | 42.23 N | 8.56 W |
| Onsbjerg | 41 | 55.51 N | 10.35 E |
| Onseepkans | 158 | 28.46 S | 19.14 E |
| Onsen | 96 | 35.33 N | 134.29 E |
| Onset | 207 | 41.44 N | 70.39 W |
| Onslow | 162 | 21.39 S | 115.06 E |
| Onslow Bay c | 192 | 34.20 N | 77.20 W |
| Onslow Village | 260 | 51.14 N | 0.36 W |
| Onsted | 216 | 42.00 N | 84.11 W |
| Onstmettingen | 58 | 48.17 N | 9.00 E |
| Onstwedde | 52 | 53.02 N | 7.02 E |
| On-take ∧ | 92 | 31.35 N | 130.39 E |
| Ontake-san ∧ | 94 | 35.53 N | 137.29 E |
| Ontario, Ca., U.S. | 228 | 34.03 N | 117.39 W |
| Ontario, In., U.S. | 216 | 41.43 N | 85.23 W |
| Ontario, N.Y., U.S. | 210 | 43.13 N | 77.17 W |
| Ontario, Oh., U.S. | 214 | 40.45 N | 82.35 W |
| Ontario, Or., U.S. | 202 | 44.01 N | 116.57 W |
| Ontario □[6] | 210 | 42.54 N | 77.17 W |
| Ontario □[4] | 176 | 51.00 N | 85.00 W |
| Ontario, Lake ⊜ | 212 | 43.45 N | 78.00 W |
| Ontario Agricultural Museum Ʊ | 212 | 43.30 N | 79.56 W |
| Ontario Center | 210 | 43.14 N | 77.19 W |
| Ontario International Airport ⊠ | 228 | 34.04 N | 117.36 W |
| Ontario Place ♠ | 275b | 43.38 N | 79.25 W |
| Ontario Science Centre Ʊ | 275b | 43.43 N | 79.21 W |
| Ontelaunee, Lake ⊜ | 208 | 40.27 N | 75.55 W |
| Ontinyent (Onteniente) | 34 | 38.49 N | 0.37 W |
| Ontojärvi ⊜ | 26 | 64.08 N | 29.09 E |
| Ontonagon | 190 | 46.52 N | 89.18 W |
| Ontonagon ≃ | 190 | 46.52 N | 89.20 W |
| Ontonagon, East Branch ≃ | 190 | 46.42 N | 89.11 W |
| Ontonagon, Middle Branch ≃ | 190 | 46.42 N | 89.10 W |
| Ontonagon, West Branch ≃ | 190 | 46.42 N | 89.11 W |
| Ontong Java I[1] | 175e | 5.20 S | 159.30 E |
| Onufrijevo | 82 | 55.51 N | 36.31 E |
| Onufriyivka | 78 | 48.54 N | 33.26 E |
| Ōnuma | 268 | 35.32 N | 139.25 E |
| Onverwacht | 250 | 5.36 N | 55.12 W |
| Onward | 216 | 40.42 N | 86.12 W |
| Ŏnyang, Taehan | 98 | 36.47 N | 127.00 E |
| Ŏnyang, Taehan | 98 | 35.34 N | 129.07 E |
| Onzain | 50 | 47.30 N | 1.11 E |
| Onzo ≃ | 152 | 8.12 S | 13.16 E |
| Oobagooma | 162 | 16.46 S | 123.59 E |
| Oodnadatta | 162 | 27.33 S | 135.28 E |
| Ood Weyne | 144 | 9.25 N | 45.04 E |
| Ōoka | 94 | 36.30 N | 137.59 E |
| Ooldea | 162 | 30.27 S | 131.50 E |
| Oolitic | 218 | 38.54 N | 86.31 W |
| Oologah | 196 | 36.26 N | 95.42 W |
| Oologah Lake ⊜[1] | 196 | 36.33 N | 95.36 W |
| Ooma | 174d | 0.53 S | 169.36 E |
| Oombergen | 50 | 50.54 N | 3.50 E |
| Oona River | 182 | 53.57 N | 130.18 W |
| Ooratippra | 162 | 22.00 S | 136.00 E |
| Ooratippra Creek ≃ | 162 | 21.55 S | 136.05 E |
| Oorlogskloof ≃ | 158 | 31.52 S | 19.01 E |
| Oos | 56 | 48.47 N | 8.11 E |
| Oos-Londen → East London | 158 | 33.00 S | 27.55 E |
| Oostakker | 50 | 51.06 N | 3.46 E |
| Oostburg, Ned. | 52 | 51.20 N | 3.30 E |
| Oostburg, Wi., U.S. | 190 | 43.37 N | 87.47 W |
| Oost-Cappel | 50 | 50.55 N | 2.36 E |
| Oostduinkerke | 50 | 51.07 N | 2.41 E |
| Oostelijk Flevoland ◆[1] | 52 | 52.30 N | 5.40 E |
| Oostende (Ostende) | 50 | 51.13 N | 2.55 E |
| Oosterbeek | 52 | 52.00 N | 5.50 E |
| Oosterend | 52 | 53.05 N | 4.52 E |
| Oosterhout | 52 | 51.38 N | 4.51 E |
| Oosterschelde c | 52 | 51.33 N | 4.00 E |
| Oosterscheldedam ◆[6] | 52 | 51.38 N | 3.42 E |
| Oosterwolde | 52 | 52.59 N | 6.17 E |
| Oosterzele | 50 | 50.57 N | 3.48 E |
| Oosthuizen | 52 | 52.35 N | 5.00 E |
| Oostkamp | 50 | 51.09 N | 3.14 E |
| Oostmahorn | 52 | 53.24 N | 6.09 E |
| Oostmalle | 56 | 51.18 N | 4.44 E |
| Oostpunt ≻ | 241s | 12.02 N | 68.45 W |
| Oostrozebeke | 50 | 50.55 N | 3.20 E |
| Oost-Souburg | 52 | 51.27 N | 3.35 E |
| Oost-Vlaanderen □[4] | 50 | 51.00 N | 3.45 E |
| Oostvleteren | 50 | 50.56 N | 2.44 E |
| Oost-Vlieland | 52 | 53.17 N | 5.04 E |
| Oostvoorne | 52 | 51.55 N | 4.06 E |
| Ootmarsum | 52 | 52.25 N | 6.54 E |
| Ootsa Lake | 182 | 53.47 N | 126.03 W |
| Ootsa Lake ⊜ | 182 | 53.49 N | 126.18 W |
| Ootsi | 156 | 25.02 S | 25.45 E |
| Ootua, Mont ∧ | 174x | 9.47 S | 138.58 W |
| Opaka | 38 | 43.27 N | 26.10 E |
| Opala | 152 | 0.37 S | 24.21 E |
| Opalaca, Cordillera ⋏ | 236 | 14.30 N | 88.20 W |
| Opal Cliffs | 226 | 36.57 N | 121.57 W |
| Opale, Côte d' ⊥[2] | 50 | 50.40 N | 1.35 E |
| Opalenica | 30 | 52.19 N | 16.23 E |
| Opalicha | 265b | 55.49 N | 37.15 E |
| Opa-Locka | 220 | 25.54 N | 80.15 W |
| Opari | 154 | 3.56 N | 32.03 E |
| Oparino | 24 | 59.52 N | 48.17 E |
| Opasatica, Lac ⊜ | 190 | 48.05 N | 79.18 W |
| Opasatika Lake ⊜ | 190 | 49.04 N | 83.08 W |
| Opasquia | 184 | 53.16 N | 93.35 W |
| Opasquia Lake ⊜ | 184 | 53.18 N | 93.34 W |
| Opatija | 36 | 45.21 N | 14.19 E |
| Opatów | 30 | 50.49 N | 21.26 E |
| Opava | 30 | 49.56 N | 17.54 E |
| Opava ≃ | 30 | 49.50 N | 18.13 E |
| Opečenskij Posad | 76 | 58.16 N | 34.07 E |
| Opeepeesway Lake ⊜ | 190 | 47.38 N | 82.14 W |

## PORTUGUÊS

| Nome | Página | Lat. °′ | Long. °′ W = Oeste |
|---|---|---|---|
| Opeilu | 273a | 6.42 N | 3.18 E |
| Opelika | 194 | 32.38 N | 85.22 W |
| Opelousas | 194 | 30.32 N | 92.04 W |
| Open Bay c | 164 | 4.50 S | 151.20 E |
| Open Door | 258 | 34.30 S | 59.05 W |
| Opeongo ≃ | 190 | 45.30 N | 77.57 W |
| Opeongo Lake ⊜ | 190 | 45.42 N | 78.23 W |
| Opequon Creek ≃ | 188 | 39.35 N | 77.52 W |
| Opfikon | 58 | 47.26 N | 8.35 E |
| Ophain-Bois-Seigneur-Isaac | 50 | 50.40 N | 4.21 E |
| Ophasselt | 50 | 50.49 N | 3.53 E |
| Opheim | 202 | 48.51 N | 106.24 W |
| Opherdicke | 263 | 51.29 N | 7.38 E |
| Opheusden | 52 | 51.56 N | 5.38 E |
| Ophir, Ak., U.S. | 180 | 63.10 N | 156.31 W |
| Ophir, Or., U.S. | 202 | 42.33 N | 124.22 W |
| Ophirton ◆[8] | 273d | 26.14 S | 28.01 E |
| Ophthalmia Range ⋏ | 162 | 23.17 S | 119.30 E |
| Opi | 66 | 41.47 N | 13.50 E |
| Opienge | 154 | 0.12 N | 27.30 E |
| Opihikao | 229d | 19.25 N | 154.53 W |
| Opinaca ≃ | 176 | 52.15 N | 78.02 W |
| Opinan | 46 | 57.43 N | 5.47 W |
| Opinicon Lake ⊜ | 212 | 44.33 N | 76.20 W |
| Opiscotéo, Lac ⊜ | 176 | 53.10 N | 68.10 W |
| Opishnya | 78 | 49.58 N | 34.37 E |
| Opladen | 56 | 51.04 N | 7.00 E |
| Opmeer | 52 | 52.43 N | 4.56 E |
| Opobo | 150 | 4.34 N | 7.27 E |
| Opobo Town | 150 | 4.30 N | 7.30 E |
| Opočka | 76 | 56.43 N | 28.38 E |
| Opoczno | 30 | 51.23 N | 20.17 E |
| Opol | 116 | 8.31 N | 124.34 E |
| Opole (Oppeln) | 30 | 50.41 N | 17.55 E |
| Opole □[4] | 30 | 50.30 N | 17.45 E |
| Opole Lubelskie | 30 | 51.09 N | 21.58 E |
| Opon → Lapu-Lapu | 116 | 10.19 N | 123.57 E |
| Opononо, Lake ⊜ | 156 | 18.08 S | 15.45 E |
| Opopeo | 234 | 19.24 N | 101.36 W |
| Oporto → Porto | 34 | 41.11 N | 8.36 W |
| Opotiki | 172 | 38.00 S | 177.17 E |
| Opp | 194 | 31.16 N | 86.15 W |
| Oppach | 54 | 51.03 N | 14.30 E |
| Oppdal | 26 | 62.36 N | 9.40 E |
| Oppelhain | 54 | 51.33 N | 13.35 E |
| Oppeln → Opole | 30 | 50.41 N | 17.55 E |
| Oppenau | 58 | 48.28 N | 8.10 E |
| Oppenberg | 61 | 47.29 N | 14.16 E |
| Oppenheim, Dtsch. | 56 | 49.51 N | 8.21 E |
| Oppenheim, N.Y., U.S. | 210 | 43.04 N | 74.42 W |
| Oppenheim Park ♠ | 284a | 43.06 N | 78.54 W |
| Oppenhuizen | 52 | 53.00 N | 5.42 E |
| Oppido Lucano | 68 | 40.47 N | 16.00 E |
| Oppido Mamertina | 68 | 38.16 N | 16.00 E |
| Oppio | 66 | 44.03 N | 10.50 E |
| Oppland □[6] | 26 | 61.10 N | 9.40 E |
| Opportunity, Mt., U.S. | 202 | 46.07 N | 112.49 W |
| Opportunity, Wa., U.S. | 202 | 47.39 N | 117.14 W |
| Oppum ◆[8] | 263 | 51.19 N | 6.37 E |
| Opsa | 76 | 55.32 N | 26.47 E |
| Opsaheden | 40 | 60.28 N | 13.59 E |
| Optic Lake | 184 | 54.46 N | 101.13 W |
| Optima Lake ⊜[1] | 196 | 36.40 N | 101.10 W |
| Opua | 172 | 35.19 S | 174.07 E |
| Opunake | 172 | 39.27 S | 173.51 E |
| Opunohu, Baie d' c | 174s | 17.30 S | 149.51 W |
| Opuwo | 152 | 18.03 S | 13.45 E |
| Opwijk | 50 | 50.58 N | 4.11 E |
| Oquawka | 190 | 40.55 N | 90.56 W |
| Oquendo, Perú | 286d | 11.58 S | 77.08 W |
| Oquendo, Pil. | 116 | 12.08 N | 124.32 E |
| O'Quinn | 222 | 29.50 N | 96.58 W |
| Or' ≃ | 86 | 51.12 N | 58.30 E |
| Or, Côte d' ∧ | 58 | 47.10 N | 4.50 E |
| Or, Étang d' ⊜ | 261 | 48.38 N | 1.51 E |
| Ora (Auer), It. | 64 | 46.21 N | 11.18 E |
| Ora, Lībiyā | 146 | 28.33 N | 19.24 E |
| Ōra, Nihon | 174m | 26.33 N | 128.02 E |
| Ora Banda | 162 | 30.22 S | 121.04 E |
| Oracle | 200 | 32.36 N | 110.46 W |
| Oradea | 38 | 47.03 N | 21.57 E |
| Oradell | 276 | 40.57 N | 74.02 W |
| Oradell Reservoir ⊜[1] | 276 | 40.58 N | 74.01 W |
| Öræfajökull ⊓ | 24a | 64.03 N | 16.38 W |
| Orahovica | 38 | 45.31 N | 17.53 E |
| Orai | 124 | 25.59 N | 79.28 E |
| Oraibi Wash V | 200 | 35.26 N | 110.49 W |
| Oraison | 62 | 43.55 N | 5.55 E |
| Oran → Wahran, Alg. | 148 | 35.43 N | 0.43 W |
| Oran, Mo., U.S. | 194 | 37.05 N | 89.39 W |
| Oran, Sebkha d' ⊜ | 34 | 35.32 N | 0.48 W |
| Orange, Austl. | 166 | 33.17 S | 149.06 E |
| Orange, Fr. | 62 | 44.08 N | 4.48 E |
| Orange, Ca., U.S. | 228 | 33.47 N | 117.51 W |
| Orange, Ct., U.S. | 207 | 41.16 N | 73.01 W |
| Orange, Ma., U.S. | 207 | 42.35 N | 72.18 W |
| Orange, N.J., U.S. | 276 | 40.46 N | 74.13 W |
| Orange, Oh., U.S. | 279a | 41.26 N | 81.29 W |
| Orange, Tx., U.S. | 194 | 30.05 N | 93.44 W |
| Orange, Va., U.S. | 188 | 38.14 N | 78.06 W |
| Orange □[6], Ca., U.S. | 228 | 33.43 N | 117.54 W |
| Orange □[6], Fl., U.S. | 220 | 28.32 N | 81.16 W |
| Orange □[6], In., U.S. | 218 | 38.33 N | 86.28 W |
| Orange □[6], N.Y., U.S. | 210 | 41.24 N | 74.20 W |
| Orange (Oranje) ≃ | 156 | 28.41 S | 16.28 E |
| Orange, Cabo ≻ | 250 | 4.24 N | 51.33 W |
| Orange Bowl ♠ | 220 | 25.46 N | 80.14 W |
| Orangeburg, Ky., U.S. | 218 | 38.35 N | 83.39 W |
| Orangeburg, N.Y., U.S. | 210 | 41.03 N | 73.57 W |
| Orangeburg, S.C., U.S. | 192 | 33.29 N | 80.51 W |
| Orange City, Fl., U.S. | 220 | 28.57 N | 81.17 W |
| Orange City, Ia., U.S. | 198 | 43.00 N | 96.03 W |
| Orange County Airport ⊠ | 228 | 33.40 N | 117.51 W |
| Orange Cove | 226 | 36.37 N | 119.19 W |
| Orange Free State □[4], S. Afr. | 158 | 28.30 S | 27.00 E |
| Orange Free State → Free State □[4], S. Afr. | 158 | 28.30 S | 27.00 E |
| Orange Grove | 196 | 27.57 N | 97.56 W |
| Orange Grove ◆[8] | 273d | 26.10 S | 28.05 E |
| Orange Lake, Fl., U.S. | 192 | 29.25 N | 82.13 W |
| Orange Lake, N.Y., U.S. | 210 | 41.33 N | 74.06 W |
| Orange Lake ⊜ | 192 | 29.29 N | 82.10 W |
| Orangemouth → Oranjemund | 156 | 28.38 S | 16.24 E |
| Orange Park | 192 | 30.09 N | 81.42 W |
| Orange Park Acres | 280 | 33.48 N | 117.47 W |
| Orange Reservoir ⊜[1] | 276 | 40.46 N | 74.17 W |
| Orangevale | 226 | 38.40 N | 121.13 W |
| Orangeville, On., Can. | 212 | 43.55 N | 80.06 W |
| Orangeville, Oh., U.S. | 214 | 41.20 N | 80.31 W |
| Orangeville, Pa., U.S. | 210 | 41.05 N | 76.25 W |
| Orangeville, Ut., U.S. | 200 | 39.13 N | 111.03 W |
| Orange Walk | 232 | 18.06 N | 88.33 W |
| Orango Grande I | 150 | 11.10 N | 16.08 W |
| Orani, It. | 71 | 40.15 N | 9.11 E |
| Orani, Pil. | 116 | 14.49 N | 120.32 E |
| Oranienbaum | 54 | 51.48 N | 12.24 E |
| Oranienburg | 54 | 52.45 N | 13.14 E |
| Oranje | 52 | 52.55 N | 6.28 E |
| Oranje → Orange ≃ | 156 | 28.41 S | 16.28 E |
| Oranjefontein | 156 | 23.25 S | 27.41 E |
| Oranje Gebergte ⋏ | 250 | 3.00 N | 55.05 W |
| Oranjemund | 156 | 28.38 S | 16.24 E |
| Oranjerivier | 158 | 29.40 S | 24.12 E |
| Oranjestad | 241s | 12.33 N | 70.06 W |
| Oranjeville | 158 | 27.00 S | 28.15 E |
| Oranki | 80 | 55.53 N | 43.44 E |
| Oranmore | 48 | 53.16 N | 8.54 W |
| Ŏran-ni | 98 | 34.22 N | 126.29 E |
| Oranžerei | 80 | 45.50 N | 47.36 E |
| Or 'Aqiva | 132 | 32.30 N | 34.55 E |
| Orarak | 140 | 6.15 N | 32.23 E |
| Orari ≃ | 172 | 44.15 S | 171.25 E |
| Oras | 116 | 12.09 N | 125.26 E |
| Oras ≃ | 116 | 12.08 N | 125.26 E |
| Oras Bay c | 116 | 12.07 N | 125.28 E |
| Orăștie | 38 | 45.50 N | 23.12 E |
| Orașul Stalin → Brașov | 38 | 45.39 N | 25.37 E |
| Orativ | 78 | 49.12 N | 29.32 E |
| Oratório, Ribeirão do ≃ | 287b | 23.37 S | 46.32 W |
| Oravais (Oravainen) | 26 | 63.18 N | 22.23 E |
| Oravița | 38 | 45.02 N | 21.41 E |
| Orawia | 172 | 46.03 S | 167.49 E |
| Orb ≃ | 32 | 43.15 N | 3.18 E |
| Orba ≃ | 62 | 44.53 N | 8.37 E |
| Orba Co ⊜ | 120 | 34.32 N | 81.03 E |
| Orbassano | 62 | 45.01 N | 7.32 E |
| Orbe | 58 | 46.43 N | 6.32 E |
| Orbe ≃ | 58 | 46.47 N | 6.39 E |
| Orbec-en-Auge | 50 | 49.01 N | 0.25 E |
| Orbetello | 66 | 42.27 N | 11.13 E |
| Orbetello, Laguna di c | 66 | 42.27 N | 11.14 E |
| Orbey | 58 | 48.08 N | 7.10 E |
| Orbieu ≃ | 32 | 43.14 N | 2.54 E |
| Orbigny | 50 | 47.12 N | 1.14 E |
| Órbigo ≃ | 34 | 41.58 N | 5.40 W |
| Orbiquet ≃ | 50 | 49.09 N | 0.14 E |
| Orbisonia | 214 | 40.15 N | 77.54 W |
| Orbost | 166 | 37.42 S | 148.27 E |
| Örbyhus | 40 | 60.14 N | 17.42 E |
| Orcadas Ʊ[3] | 9 | 60.45 S | 44.43 W |
| Orcadas, Islas → Orkney Islands II | 46 | 59.00 N | 3.00 W |
| Orcadas del Sur, Islas → South Orkney Islands II | 9 | 60.35 S | 45.30 W |
| Orcades du Sud, Îles → South Orkney Islands II | 9 | 60.35 S | 45.30 W |
| Orcas | 224 | 48.36 N | 122.57 W |
| Orcas Island I | 224 | 48.39 N | 122.55 W |
| Orcemont | 261 | 48.35 N | 1.49 E |
| Orcera | 34 | 38.19 N | 2.39 W |
| Orchamps | 58 | 47.09 N | 5.40 E |
| Orchard, Ne., U.S. | 198 | 42.20 N | 98.14 W |
| Orchard, Tx., U.S. | 222 | 29.36 N | 95.58 W |
| Orchard City | 200 | 38.49 N | 107.58 W |
| Orchard Hills, Austl. | 274a | 33.47 S | 150.43 E |
| Orchard Hills, Pa., U.S. | 279b | 40.35 N | 79.32 W |
| Orchard Homes | 202 | 46.51 N | 114.02 W |
| Orchard Island | 216 | 40.28 N | 83.53 W |
| Orchard Lake ⊜ | 281 | 42.35 N | 83.22 W |
| Orchard Lake Village | 281 | 42.35 N | 83.21 W |
| Orchard Mesa | 200 | 39.02 N | 108.33 W |
| Orchard Park | 210 | 42.46 N | 78.44 W |
| Orchard Park Airport ⊠ | 284a | 42.48 N | 78.45 W |
| Orchard Peak ∧ | 226 | 35.44 N | 120.08 W |
| Orchards | 224 | 45.40 N | 122.33 W |
| Orchard Valley | 200 | 41.05 N | 104.48 W |
| Orchard View | 285 | 40.04 N | 74.53 W |
| Orchha | 124 | 25.21 N | 78.39 E |
| Orchies | 50 | 50.28 N | 3.14 E |
| Orchon | 88 | 49.09 N | 105.21 E |
| Orchon ≃ | 88 | 50.21 N | 106.05 E |
| Orchon Tuul | 88 | 48.58 N | 104.59 E |
| Orchyk ≃ | 78 | 49.10 N | 35.04 E |
| Orcia ≃ | 66 | 42.58 N | 11.21 E |
| Orcières | 62 | 44.41 N | 6.20 E |
| Orco ≃ | 62 | 45.10 N | 7.52 E |
| Ord | 198 | 41.36 N | 98.55 W |
| Ord ≃ | 160 | 15.30 S | 128.21 E |
| Ord, Mount ∧ | 162 | 17.20 S | 125.34 E |
| Orda | 86 | 57.12 N | 56.54 E |
| Orderville | 200 | 37.16 N | 112.38 W |
| Ordes | 34 | 43.04 N | 8.24 W |
| Ordesa, Parque Nacional de ♠ | 34 | 42.39 N | 0.02 E |
| Ord Mountain ∧ | 204 | 34.40 N | 116.49 W |
| Ord Mountains ⋏ | 228 | 34.42 N | 117.10 W |
| Ordoqui | 252 | 35.54 S | 61.10 W |
| Ord River | 162 | 17.23 S | 128.51 E |
| Ordu | 130 | 41.00 N | 37.53 E |
| Ordu □[4] | 130 | 40.45 N | 37.30 E |
| Ordubad | 84 | 38.56 N | 46.02 E |
| Ordway | 198 | 38.13 N | 103.45 W |
| Ordynskoje | 86 | 54.22 N | 81.56 E |
| Ordzhonikidze → Vladikavkaz, Ross. | 84 | 43.03 N | 44.40 E |
| Ordžhonikidze → Vladikavkaz, Ross. | 84 | 43.03 N | 44.40 E |
| Ordzhonikidze, Ukr. | 78 | 47.40 N | 34.04 E |
| Ordzhonikidze → Yenakiyeve, Ukr. | 83 | 48.14 N | 38.13 E |
| Ordžonikidze | 86 | 52.28 N | 61.46 E |
| Ordžonikidzeabad | 85 | 38.34 N | 69.01 E |
| Ordžonikidzevskaja | 84 | 43.18 N | 45.03 E |
| Ordžonikidzevskij, Ross. | 84 | 43.51 N | 41.54 E |
| Ordžonikidzevskij, Ross. | 86 | 54.46 N | 88.59 E |
| Ore | 150 | 6.44 N | 4.52 E |
| Ore ≃ | 46 | 56.10 N | 3.15 W |
| Öreälven ≃ | 26 | 63.32 N | 19.44 E |
| Oreana | 219 | 39.56 N | 88.51 W |
| Örebro | 40 | 59.17 N | 15.13 E |
| Örebro Län □[6] | 40 | 59.30 N | 15.00 E |
| Orechovka | 80 | 52.56 N | 48.14 E |
| Orechovo | 80 | 58.28 N | 41.58 E |
| Orechovo-Zujevo | 82 | 55.49 N | 38.59 E |
| Ore City | 222 | 32.48 N | 94.43 W |
| Oredež | 76 | 58.49 N | 30.20 E |
| Oredež ≃ | 76 | 58.49 N | 30.00 E |
| Orefield | 208 | 40.38 N | 75.35 W |
| Oregon, Il., U.S. | 190 | 42.00 N | 89.19 W |
| Oregon, Mo., U.S. | 194 | 39.59 N | 95.08 W |
| Oregon, Oh., U.S. | 214 | 41.38 N | 83.29 W |
| Oregon, Wi., U.S. | 216 | 42.55 N | 89.23 W |
| Oregon □[3], U.S. | 178 | 44.00 N | 121.00 W |
| Oregon □[3], U.S. | 202 | 44.00 N | 121.00 W |
| Oregon Caves National Monument ♠ | 202 | 42.06 N | 123.24 W |
| Oregon City | 224 | 45.21 N | 122.36 W |
| Oregon Creek ≃ | 226 | 39.23 N | 121.05 W |
| Oregon Dunes National Recreation Area ♠ | 202 | 43.45 N | 124.12 W |
| Oregon House | 226 | 39.21 N | 121.17 W |
| Öregrund | 40 | 60.20 N | 18.26 E |
| Öregrundsgrepen c | 40 | 60.27 N | 18.18 E |
| Orehoved | 41 | 54.57 N | 11.52 E |
| Orekhovo-Zuyevo → Orechovo-Zujevo | 82 | 55.49 N | 38.59 E |
| Orel | 76 | 52.59 N | 36.05 E |
| Orel', ozero ⊜ | 89 | 53.30 N | 139.42 E |
| Oreland | 285 | 40.07 N | 75.10 W |
| Orellana | 248 | 6.54 S | 75.04 W |
| Orellana, Embalse de ⊜[1] | 34 | 39.00 N | 5.25 W |
| Orel Oblast' □[4] | 76 | 53.00 N | 36.20 E |
| Orem | 200 | 40.17 N | 111.41 W |
| Ören | 130 | 37.02 N | 27.57 E |
| Orenburg | 86 | 51.54 N | 55.06 E |
| Orenburg Oblast' □[4] | 86 | 52.30 N | 54.00 E |
| Örencik | 130 | 39.16 N | 29.33 E |
| Oreng, Indon. | 114 | 4.03 N | 97.28 E |
| Oreng, Indon. | 114 | 4.33 N | 96.49 E |
| Orense | 252 | 38.40 S | 59.47 W |
| Orense □[4] | 34 | 42.15 N | 7.30 W |
| Örenşehir | 130 | 39.00 N | 36.39 E |
| Orepuki | 172 | 46.17 S | 167.44 E |
| Oreški | 82 | 55.43 N | 36.21 E |
| Orestes | 216 | 40.16 N | 85.43 W |
| Orestes Pereyra | 232 | 26.31 N | 105.40 W |
| Orestiás | 38 | 41.30 N | 26.31 E |
| Orestimba Creek ≃ | 226 | 37.25 N | 121.00 W |
| Øresund → The Sound ʊ | 41 | 55.50 N | 12.40 E |
| Oreti ≃ | 172 | 46.28 S | 168.17 E |
| Oreto ≃ | 70 | 38.06 N | 13.24 E |
| Orewa | 172 | 36.34 S | 174.42 E |
| Oreye | 56 | 50.44 N | 5.22 E |
| Orfanoú, Kólpos c | 38 | 40.40 N | 23.50 E |
| Orford, Eng., U.K. | 42 | 52.06 N | 1.31 E |
| Orford, Eng., U.K. | 262 | 53.25 N | 2.35 W |
| Orford, Mont ∧ | 206 | 45.19 N | 72.15 W |
| Orford Ness ≻ | 42 | 52.05 N | 1.34 E |
| Orfordville | 190 | 42.37 N | 89.15 W |
| Organ Needle ∧ | 200 | 32.21 N | 106.33 W |
| Organ Pipe Cactus National Monument ♠ | 200 | 32.00 N | 112.55 W |
| Órgãos, Serra dos ⋏ | 256 | 22.22 S | 42.45 W |
| Orgaz | 34 | 39.39 N | 3.54 W |
| Orge ≃ | 50 | 48.42 N | 2.24 E |
| Orgelet | 58 | 46.31 N | 5.37 E |
| Orgères-en-Beauce | 50 | 48.09 N | 1.42 E |
| Orgerus | 261 | 48.50 N | 1.42 E |
| Orgeval | 50 | 48.55 N | 1.59 E |
| Orgeval ≃ | 261 | 49.00 N | 1.54 E |
| Orgiano | 64 | 45.21 N | 11.28 E |
| Órgiva | 34 | 36.54 N | 3.25 W |
| Orgnac, Aven d' ⊥[5] | 62 | 44.19 N | 4.27 E |
| Orgnac-l'Aven | 62 | 44.19 N | 4.27 E |
| Orgof | 144 | 3.03 N | 41.44 E |
| Orgon | 62 | 43.47 N | 5.02 E |
| Orgosolo | 71 | 40.12 N | 9.21 E |
| Orgtrud | 80 | 56.12 N | 40.37 E |
| Orgūn | 120 | 32.51 N | 69.07 E |
| Orhaneli | 130 | 39.54 N | 29.00 E |
| Orhangazi | 130 | 40.30 N | 29.18 E |
| Orhanlar | 130 | 39.54 N | 27.37 E |
| Orhei | 38 | 47.23 N | 28.48 E |
| Oria, It. | 68 | 40.30 N | 17.38 E |
| Oria, Zaïre | 154 | 3.17 N | 30.41 E |
| Orica | 236 | 14.41 N | 86.56 W |
| Oriçanga, Rio do ≃ | 256 | 22.18 S | 47.03 W |
| Orichuna ≃ | 246 | 7.25 N | 68.58 W |
| Oriči | 80 | 58.24 N | 49.05 E |
| Orick | 204 | 41.17 N | 124.03 W |
| Oricola | 66 | 42.02 N | 13.02 E |
| Orient, Ia., U.S. | 198 | 41.12 N | 94.24 W |
| Orient, N.Y., U.S. | 207 | 41.08 N | 72.18 W |
| Orient, Oh., U.S. | 218 | 39.48 N | 83.09 W |
| Orient, Wa., U.S. | 182 | 48.53 N | 118.13 W |
| Oriental, Méx. | 234 | 19.22 N | 97.37 W |
| Oriental, N.C., U.S. | 192 | 35.01 N | 76.41 W |
| Oriental, Cordillera ⋏, Col. | 246 | 6.00 N | 73.00 W |
| Oriental, Cordillera ⋏, Perú | 248 | 11.00 S | 74.00 W |
| Oriental, Pico ∧ | 286c | 10.32 N | 66.50 W |
| Oriental de Zapata, Ciénaga ≡ | 240p | 22.15 N | 80.50 W |
| Oriental Park | 214 | 42.09 N | 79.22 W |
| Oriente | 252 | 38.44 S | 60.37 W |
| Orientos | 166 | 28.05 S | 141.14 E |
| Origgio | 266b | 45.36 N | 9.01 E |
| Origny-en-Thiérache | 50 | 49.54 N | 4.01 E |
| Origny-Sainte-Benoite | 50 | 49.50 N | 3.30 E |
| Orikhiv | 78 | 47.34 N | 35.47 E |
| Orikhivka | 83 | 48.17 N | 39.13 E |
| Oril' ≃ | 78 | 48.30 N | 34.54 E |
| Orillia | 212 | 44.37 N | 79.25 W |
| Orimattila | 26 | 60.48 N | 25.45 E |
| Orinda | 226 | 37.52 N | 122.10 W |
| Orinduik | 246 | 4.42 N | 60.01 W |
| Orini | 172 | 37.34 S | 175.18 E |
| Orinoco ≃ | 246 | 8.37 N | 62.15 W |
| Orinoco, Delta del ⊻[2] | 246 | 9.15 N | 61.30 W |
| Oriola (Orihuela) | 34 | 38.05 N | 0.57 W |
| Oriole, Md., U.S. | 208 | 38.10 N | 75.48 W |
| Oriole, Pa., U.S. | 210 | 41.08 N | 77.13 W |
| Oriole Park ♠ | 284b | 39.18 N | 76.37 W |
| Oriolo | 68 | 40.03 N | 16.27 E |
| Oriomo | 164 | 8.50 S | 143.15 E |
| Orion, Pil. | 116 | 14.37 N | 120.34 E |
| Orion, Il., U.S. | 190 | 41.21 N | 90.22 W |
| Oripää | 26 | 60.51 N | 22.41 E |
| Oriskany | 210 | 43.09 N | 75.19 W |
| Oriskany Battlefield State Historic Site ⊥ | 210 | 43.11 N | 75.23 W |
| Oriskany Creek ≃ | 210 | 43.10 N | 75.20 W |
| Oriskany Falls | 210 | 42.56 N | 75.27 W |
| Orissa □[3] | 118 | 20.00 N | 84.00 E |
| Orissaare | 76 | 58.34 N | 23.05 E |
| Orissa Coast Canal Ξ | 126 | 21.51 N | 87.41 E |
| Oristano | 71 | 39.54 N | 8.36 E |
| Oristano □[4] | 71 | 39.55 N | 8.40 E |
| Oristano, Golfo di c | 71 | 39.50 N | 8.29 E |
| Öriszentpéter | 61 | 46.51 N | 16.25 E |
| Orituco ≃ | 246 | 8.45 N | 67.27 W |
| Orivesi | 26 | 61.41 N | 24.21 E |
| Orivesi ⊜ | 26 | 62.16 N | 29.24 E |
| Oriximiná | 250 | 1.45 S | 55.52 W |
| Orizaba | 234 | 18.51 N | 97.06 W |
| Orizaba, Pico de (Volcán Citlaltépetl) ∧[1] | 234 | 19.01 N | 97.16 W |
| Orizona | 255 | 17.03 S | 48.18 W |
| Orjahovo | 38 | 43.45 N | 23.57 E |
| Ørje | 26 | 59.29 N | 11.39 E |
| Orjen ∧ | 38 | 42.30 N | 18.38 E |
| Ork, Ness of ≻ | 46 | 59.05 N | 2.48 W |
| Orkanger | 26 | 63.19 N | 9.52 E |
| Örkelljunga | 41 | 56.17 N | 13.17 E |
| Orken | 263 | 51.06 N | 6.34 E |
| Orkla ≃ | 26 | 63.18 N | 9.50 E |
| Orkney, Sk., Can. | 184 | 49.08 N | 107.55 W |
| Orkney, S. Afr. | 158 | 27.00 S | 26.39 E |
| Orkney □[4] | 46 | 59.00 N | 3.00 W |
| Orkney Islands II | 46 | 59.00 N | 3.00 W |
| Orla ≃ | 54 | 50.46 N | 11.31 E |
| Orlamünde | 54 | 50.47 N | 11.31 E |
| Orland, Ca., U.S. | 204 | 39.44 N | 122.11 W |
| Orland, In., U.S. | 216 | 41.43 N | 85.10 W |
| Orlândia | 255 | 20.43 S | 47.53 W |
| Orland Lake ⊜ | 278 | 41.38 N | 87.52 W |
| Orlando, S. Afr. | 273d | 26.14 S | 27.55 E |
| Orlando, Fl., U.S. | 220 | 28.32 N | 81.22 W |
| Orlando, Capo d' ≻ | 70 | 38.10 N | 14.45 E |
| Orlando Dam ⊜[1] | 273d | 26.16 S | 27.56 E |
| Orlando International Airport ⊠ | 220 | 28.26 N | 81.19 W |
| Orlando Naval Training Center ■ | 220 | 28.34 N | 81.20 W |
| Orlando West Extension | 273d | 26.15 S | 27.54 E |
| Orland Park | 216 | 41.37 N | 87.51 W |
| Orland Square ◆[9] | 278 | 41.36 N | 87.51 W |
| Orléanais □[9] | 50 | 47.50 N | 2.00 E |
| Orléans, On., Can. | 212 | 45.28 N | 75.31 W |
| Orléans, Fr. | 50 | 47.55 N | 1.54 E |
| Orleans, Ca., U.S. | 204 | 41.18 N | 123.32 W |
| Orleans, In., U.S. | 218 | 38.39 N | 86.27 W |
| Orleans, Ma., U.S. | 207 | 41.47 N | 69.59 W |
| Orleans, Ne., U.S. | 198 | 40.07 N | 99.27 W |
| Orleans, Vt., U.S. | 188 | 44.48 N | 72.[illegible] W |
| Orleans □[6], N.Y., U.S. | 210 | 43.15 N | 78.[illegible] W |
| Orleans □[6], Vt., U.S. | 206 | 44.57 N | 72.1[illegible] W |
| Orléans, Canal d' Ξ | 50 | 47.54 N | 1.5[illegible] E |
| Orléans, Île d' I | 186 | 46.55 N | 70.5[illegible] W |
| Orléansville → Ech Cheliff | 148 | 36.10 N | 1.2[illegible] E |
| Orlik, Kaz. | 80 | 48.17 N | 51.3[illegible] E |
| Orlik, Ross. | 88 | 52.30 N | 99.5[illegible] E |
| Orlinaja, gora ∧ | 180 | 62.35 N | 178.30 E |
| Orlinga | 88 | 56.03 N | 105.5[illegible] E |
| Orlinga ≃ | 88 | 56.03 N | 105.5[illegible] E |
| Orlivka, Ukr. | 78 | 51.54 N | 32.47 E |
| Orlivka, Ukr. | 78 | 45.40 N | 33.21 E |
| Orlivka, Ukr. | 83 | 48.10 N | 37.39 E |
| Orlja | 76 | 53.30 N | 24.59 E |
| Orlov | 80 | 58.33 N | 48.50 E |
| Orlová | 30 | 49.50 N | 18.24 E |
| Orlov Gaj | 80 | 50.57 N | 48.12 E |
| Orlovista | 220 | 28.32 N | 81.28 W |
| Orlovka, Ross. | 78 | 51.02 N | 40.32 E |
| Orlovka, Ross. | 86 | 59.03 N | 85.59 E |
| Orlovka ≃ | 86 | 58.40 N | 86.08 E |
| Orlovo, Ross. | 78 | 51.45 N | 39.35 E |
| Orlovo, Ross. | 265b | 55.38 N | 37.23 [illegible] |
| Orlovskij | 80 | 46.52 N | 42.03 |
| Orlu | 150 | 5.47 N | 7.02 |
| Orly | 261 | 48.45 N | 2.24 E |
| Ormanlı | 130 | 41.10 N | 31.39 E |
| Ormāra | 128 | 25.12 N | 64.38 E |
| Ormāra, Rās ≻ | 128 | 25.09 N | 64.35 E |
| Orme, Rivière à l' ≃ | 275a | 45.27 N | 73.56 W |
| Ormea | 62 | 44.09 N | 7.54 E |
| Ormesby | 44 | 54.33 N | 1.11 W |
| Ormesby Saint Margaret | 42 | 52.40 N | 1.42 E |
| Ormiston | 184 | 49.45 N | 105.22 W |
| Ormoc | 116 | 11.00 N | 124.37 E |
| Ormoc Bay c | 116 | 10.58 N | 124.35 E |
| Ormond | 274b | 37.54 S | 145.03 E |
| Ormond Beach | 192 | 29.17 N | 81.03 W |
| Ormož | 36 | 46.25 N | 16.09 E |
| Ormsby | 214 | 41.48 N | 78.33 W |
| Ormsby □[6] | 226 | 39.11 N | 119.46 W |
| Ormsjön ⊜ | 26 | 64.23 N | 16.03 E |
| Ormskirk | 44 | 53.35 N | 2.54 W |
| Ormstown | 206 | 45.08 N | 74.00 W |
| Ormtjernkampen Nasjonalpark ♠ | 26 | 61.12 N | 9.48 E |
| Ornain ≃ | 56 | 48.46 N | 4.47 E |
| Ornans | 58 | 47.06 N | 6.09 E |
| Ornäs | 40 | 60.31 N | 15.32 E |
| Ornavasso | 58 | 45.58 N | 8.24 E |
| Ornbau | 56 | 49.11 N | 10.40 E |
| Orne □[5] | 32 | 48.40 N | 0.05 E |
| Orne ≃, Fr. | 32 | 49.19 N | 0.14 W |
| Orne ≃, Fr. | 50 | 48.08 N | 0.11 E |
| Orne ≃, Fr. | 56 | 49.17 N | 6.11 E |
| Ornes | 26 | 61.18 N | 7.22 E |
| Orneta | 30 | 54.08 N | 20.08 E |
| Ornö I | 40 | 59.04 N | 18.24 E |
| Örnsköldsvik | 26 | 63.18 N | 18.43 E |
| Oro | 98 | 40.02 N | 127.26 E |
| Oro □[5] | 164 | 9.00 S | 148.30 E |
| Orø I | 41 | 55.46 N | 11.49 E |
| Orobie, Alpi ⋏ | 64 | 46.00 N | 10.00 E |
| Oročanskij Golec, gora ∧ | 88 | 53.29 N | 114.18 E |
| Oročen | 74 | 58.28 N | 125.26 E |
| Orocovis | 240m | 18.14 N | 66.23 W |
| Orocué | 246 | 4.48 N | 71.20 W |
| Orocuina | 236 | 13.26 N | 87.06 W |
| Orodara | 150 | 10.59 N | 4.55 W |
| Orofino | 202 | 46.28 N | 116.15 W |
| Orogen Zizhiqi | 89 | 50.34 N | 123.40 E |
| Örög nuur ⊜, Mong. | 86 | 50.10 N | 91.00 E |
| Orog nuur ⊜, Mong. | 102 | 45.03 N | 100.42 E |
| Oro Grande | 228 | 34.35 N | 117.20 W |
| Orohena, Mont ∧ | 174s | 17.37 S | 149.28 W |
| Orok, Oldoinyo ∧ | 154 | 2.29 S | 36.46 E |
| Oroku | 174m | 26.12 N | 127.39 E |
| Or'ol | 86 | 59.21 N | 56.35 E |
| Oroluk I[1] | 14 | 7.32 N | 155.18 E |
| Oromocto | 186 | 45.51 N | 66.29 W |
| Oromocto Lake ⊜ | 186 | 45.36 N | 67.00 W |
| Oron, Nig. | 150 | 4.48 N | 8.14 E |
| Oron, Ross. | 88 | 57.11 N | 116.28 E |
| Oron ≃ | 62 | 45.18 N | 4.47 E |
| Oron, ozero ⊜ | 88 | 57.06 N | 116.30 E |
| Orona I[1] | 14 | 4.29 S | 172.10 W |
| Oron-la-Ville | 58 | 46.34 N | 6.50 E |
| Orono, On., Can. | 212 | 43.59 N | 78.37 W |
| Orono, Me., U.S. | 188 | 44.52 N | 68.40 W |
| Oronoque ≃ | 246 | 2.45 N | 57.25 W |
| Oronsay I | 46 | 56.01 N | 6.16 W |
| Orontes → Asi ≃ | 130 | 36.02 N | 35.58 E |
| Oropa, Santuario di Ʊ[1] | 62 | 45.38 N | 7.58 E |
| Oropeo | 234 | 18.50 N | 101.48 W |
| Oroquieta | 116 | 8.29 N | 123.48 E |
| Orós | 250 | 6.15 S | 38.55 W |
| Orós, Açude ⊜[1] | 250 | 6.15 S | 39.05 W |
| Orosei | 71 | 40.23 N | 9.42 E |
| Orosei, Golfo di c | 71 | 40.15 N | 9.44 E |
| Orosháza | 30 | 46.34 N | 20.40 E |
| Orosi | 226 | 36.33 N | 119.17 W |
| Orosí, Volcán ∧[1] | 236 | 10.59 N | 85.29 W |
| Oroszlány | 30 | 47.30 N | 18.19 E |
| Orotelli | 71 | 40.18 N | 9.07 E |
| Orote Peninsula ≻[1] | 174p | 13.26 N | 144.38 E |
| Oroville, Ca., U.S. | 226 | 39.30 N | 121.33 W |
| Oroville, Wa., U.S. | 202 | 48.56 N | 119.26 W |
| Oroville, Lake ⊜[1] | 204 | 39.32 N | 121.25 W |
| Orowoc Creek ≃ | 276 | 40.43 N | 73.13 W |
| Orpheus Island I | 166 | 18.37 S | 146.30 E |
| Orphin | 261 | 48.35 N | 1.47 E |
| Orpierre | 62 | 44.19 N | 5.41 E |
| Orpington ◆[8] | 260 | 51.23 N | 0.06 E |
| Orreagal | 34 | 43.01 N | 1.19 W |
| Orrefors | 26 | 56.50 N | 15.45 E |
| Orrell | 44 | 53.32 N | 2.42 W |
| Orrick | 194 | 39.12 N | 94.07 W |
| Orrin | 198 | 48.05 N | 100.09 W |
| Orrin, Glen V | 46 | 57.30 N | 4.46 W |
| Orrin Reservoir ⊜[1] | 46 | 57.30 N | 4.45 W |
| Òrrius | 266d | 41.33 N | 2.21 E |
| Orr Lake ⊜, Mb., Can. | 184 | 56.07 N | 97.11 W |
| Orr Lake ⊜, On., Can. | 212 | 44.37 N | 79.47 W |
| Orroroo | 166 | 32.44 S | 138.37 E |
| Orrs Island | 188 | 43.45 N | 69.58 W |
| Orrtanna | 208 | 39.51 N | 77.22 W |
| Orrville, Al., U.S. | 194 | 32.18 N | 87.14 W |
| Orrville, Oh., U.S. | 214 | 40.50 N | 81.45 W |
| Orrville, Pa., U.S. | 279b | 40.33 N | 79.47 W |
| Orša, Bela. | 76 | 54.30 N | 30.24 E |
| Orsa, Sve. | 26 | 61.07 N | 14.37 E |
| Orša ≃ | 82 | 56.48 N | 36.11 E |
| Orsago | 64 | 45.56 N | 12.25 E |
| Orsan | 62 | 44.08 N | 4.40 E |
| Oršanka | 80 | 56.55 N | 47.53 E |
| Orsara di Puglia | 68 | 41.17 N | 15.16 E |
| Orsasjön ⊜ | 26 | 61.07 N | 14.34 E |
| Orsay | 50 | 48.42 N | 2.11 E |
| Orsett | 260 | 51.31 N | 0.22 E |
| Orsières | 58 | 46.02 N | 7.09 E |
| Orsjön ⊜ | 26 | 61.35 N | 16.20 E |
| Orsk | 86 | 51.12 N | 58.34 E |
| Örskär I | 40 | 60.31 N | 18.23 E |
| Ørslev | 41 | 55.02 N | 11.59 E |
| Orsogna | 66 | 42.13 N | 14.17 E |
| Orsomarso | 68 | 39.48 N | 15.55 E |
| Orson | 210 | 41.49 N | 75.27 W |
| Orșova | 38 | 44.42 N | 22.24 E |
| Ørsta | 26 | 62.12 N | 6.09 E |
| Ørsted | 41 | 55.20 N | 10.04 E |


| | | | | |
|---|---|---|---|---|
| ≃ River | Fluß | Río | Rivière | Rio |
| Ξ Canal | Kanal | Canal | Canal | Canal |
| L Waterfall, Rapids | Wasserfall, Stromschnellen | Cascada, Rápidos | Chute d'eau, Rapides | Cascata, Rápidos |
| ʊ Strait | Meeresstraße | Estrecho | Détroit | Estreito |
| c Bay, Gulf | Bucht, Golf | Bahía, Golfo | Baie, Golfe | Baía, Golfo |
| ⊜ Lake, Lakes | See, Seen | Lago, Lagos | Lac, Lacs | Lago, Lagos |
| ≡ Swamp | Sumpf | Pantano | Marais | Pântano |
| ⊓ Ice Features, Glacier | Eis- und Gletscherformen | Accidentes Glaciales | Formes glaciaires | Acidentes glaciares |
| ⊻ Other Hydrographic Features | Andere Hydrographische Objekte | Otros Elementos Hidrográficos | Autres données hydrographiques | Outros acidentes hidrográficos |

| | | | | |
|---|---|---|---|---|
| ✢ Submarine Features | Untermeerische Objekte | Accidentes Submarinos | Formes de relief sous-marin | Acidentes submarinos |
| □ Political Unit | Politische Einheit | Unidad Politica | Entité politique | Unidade política |
| Ʊ Cultural Institution | Kulturelle Institution | Institución Cultural | Institution culturelle | Instituição cultural |
| ⊥ Historical Site | Historische Stätte | Sitio Histórico | Site historique | Sítio histórico |
| ♠ Recreational Site | Erholungs- und Ferienort | Sitio de Recreo | Centre de loisirs | Área de Lazer |
| ⊠ Airport | Flughafen | Aeropuerto | Aéroport | Aeroporto |
| ■ Military Installation | Militäranlage | Instalación Militar | Installation militaire | Instalação militar |
| ◆ Miscellaneous | Verschiedenes | Misceláneo | Divers | Diversos |

ENGLISH | DEUTSCH


| Name | Page | Lat.°′ | Long.°′ |
|---|---|---|---|
| Örsundaån ≃ | 40 | 59.44 N | 17.21 E |
| Örsundsbro | 40 | 59.44 N | 17.18 E |
| Orta | 130 | 40.38 N | 33.06 E |
| Orta, Lago d' ⊜ | 62 | 45.49 N | 8.24 E |
| Ortaca | 130 | 36.49 N | 28.47 E |
| Ortakent | 130 | 37.02 N | 27.21 E |
| Ortaklar | 130 | 37.53 N | 27.30 E |
| Ortaköy, Tür. | 130 | 40.17 N | 35.16 E |
| Ortaköy, Tür. | 130 | 38.44 N | 34.03 E |
| Ortaköy, Tür. | 130 | 38.00 N | 34.23 E |
| Ortaköy, Tür. | 130 | 40.27 N | 38.02 E |
| Ortaköy ◆[8] | 267b | 41.03 N | 29.01 E |
| Orta Nova | 68 | 41.19 N | 15.42 E |
| Orta San Giulio | 62 | 45.48 N | 8.25 E |
| Orte | 66 | 42.27 N | 12.23 E |
| Ortega | 246 | 3.56 N | 75.13 W |
| Ortegal, Cabo ≻ | 34 | 43.45 N | 7.53 W |
| Orteguaza ≃ | 246 | 0.43 N | 75.16 W |
| Ortelsburg → Szczytno | 30 | 53.34 N | 21.00 E |
| Ortenberg, Dtsch. | 56 | 50.21 N | 9.02 E |
| Ortenberg, Dtsch. | 58 | 48.27 N | 7.58 E |
| Ortenburg | 60 | 48.33 N | 13.14 E |
| Orth | 54 | 54.27 N | 11.03 E |
| Orthez | 32 | 43.29 N | 0.46 W |
| Orthon ≃ | 248 | 10.50 S | 66.04 W |
| Ortigalita Creek ≃ | 226 | 36.57 N | 120.52 W |
| Ortigalita Peak ∧ | 226 | 36.48 N | 120.55 W |
| Ortigara, Monte ∧ | 64 | 46.00 N | 11.29 E |
| Ortigueira | 34 | 43.41 N | 7.51 W |
| Orting | 224 | 47.05 N | 122.12 W |
| Ortisei (Sankt Ulrich) | 64 | 46.34 N | 11.40 E |
| Ortiz, Méx. | 232 | 28.17 N | 110.43 W |
| Ortiz, Ven. | 246 | 9.37 N | 67.17 W |
| Ortles (Otler) ∧ | 64 | 46.31 N | 10.33 E |
| Ortles ∧∧ | 64 | 46.30 N | 10.40 E |
| Örtofta | 41 | 55.47 N | 13.14 E |
| Ortolo ≃ | 71 | 41.30 N | 8.55 E |
| Ortona | 66 | 42.21 N | 14.24 E |
| Ortona Lock ◆[5] | 220 | 26.47 N | 81.18 W |
| Orton Park ◆ | 275b | 43.46 N | 79.12 W |
| Ortonura | 85 | 41.29 N | 76.12 E |
| Ortonville, Mi., U.S. | 216 | 42.51 N | 83.26 W |
| Ortonville, Mn., U.S. | 198 | 45.18 N | 96.26 W |
| Ortonville State Recreation Area ◆ | 216 | 42.52 N | 83.26 W |
| Ortoterek | 85 | 41.56 N | 71.21 E |
| Orto-Tokoj | 85 | 42.21 N | 76.01 E |
| Ortovero | 62 | 44.03 N | 8.07 E |
| Ortrand | 54 | 51.22 N | 13.45 E |
| Örträsk | 26 | 64.08 N | 18.59 E |
| Ortueri | 71 | 40.02 N | 8.59 E |
| Ortúzar, Canal ≍ | 286e | 33.33 S | 70.47 W |
| Örtze ≃ | 52 | 52.40 N | 9.57 E |
| Oruanui | 172 | 38.35 S | 176.02 E |
| Oruba | 273a | 6.35 N | 3.25 E |
| Orudjevo | 82 | 56.26 N | 37.32 E |
| Orūmīyeh (Reẓā'īyeh) | 128 | 37.33 N | 45.04 E |
| Orūmīyeh, Daryācheh-ye (Lake Urmia) ⊜ | 128 | 37.40 N | 45.30 E |
| Orune | 71 | 40.24 N | 9.22 E |
| Oruro | 248 | 17.59 S | 67.09 W |
| Oruro □[5] | 248 | 18.40 S | 67.30 W |
| Or'us-Mijele ≃ | 88 | 58.35 N | 121.30 E |
| Orust I | 26 | 58.10 N | 11.38 E |
| Orūzgān (Qala-i-Hazār Qadam) | 120 | 32.56 N | 66.38 E |
| Orūzgān □[4] | 120 | 33.15 N | 66.00 E |
| Orval, Abbaye d' ⊌[1] | 56 | 49.38 N | 5.22 E |
| Orvanne ≃ | 50 | 48.22 N | 2.50 E |
| Orvieto | 66 | 42.43 N | 12.07 E |
| Orvilla | 208 | 40.16 N | 75.17 W |
| Orvilliers | 261 | 48.52 N | 1.39 E |
| Orvin ≃ | 50 | 48.28 N | 3.23 E |
| Orvinio | 66 | 42.08 N | 12.56 E |
| Orviston | 214 | 41.06 N | 77.45 W |
| Orvyn, gora ∧ | 180 | 65.14 N | 175.20 W |
| Orwell, N.Y., U.S. | 212 | 43.35 N | 76.00 W |
| Orwell, Oh., U.S. | 214 | 41.32 N | 80.52 W |
| Orwell ≃ | 42 | 51.57 N | 1.17 E |
| Orwigsburg | 208 | 40.39 N | 76.06 W |
| Orwin | 208 | 40.35 N | 76.31 W |
| Orxon ≃ | 88 | 49.00 N | 117.41 E |
| Or Yehuda | 132 | 32.01 N | 34.51 E |
| Orynyn | 78 | 48.46 N | 26.24 E |
| Oryu-dong ◆[8] | 271b | 37.29 N | 126.51 E |
| Orževka | 80 | 52.43 N | 42.55 E |
| Orzhiv | 78 | 50.45 N | 26.07 E |
| Orzhytsya | 78 | 49.48 N | 32.42 E |
| Orzinuovi | 62 | 45.24 N | 9.55 E |
| Orzyc ≃ | 30 | 52.47 N | 21.13 E |
| Orzysz | 30 | 53.49 N | 21.56 E |
| Oš, Kyrg. | 85 | 40.33 N | 72.48 E |
| Os, Nor. | 26 | 62.30 N | 11.12 E |
| Oš □[4] | 85 | 40.00 N | 72.30 E |
| Ōsa, Nihon | 96 | 35.05 N | 133.34 E |
| Osa, Ross. | 86 | 57.17 N | 55.26 E |
| Osa, Ross. | 88 | 53.24 N | 103.53 E |
| Oša ≃ | 86 | 57.13 N | 73.41 E |
| Osa, Península de ≻[1] | 236 | 8.34 N | 83.31 W |
| Osage, Ia., U.S. | 190 | 43.17 N | 92.48 W |
| Osage, Mo., U.S. | 219 | 38.25 N | 92.02 W |
| Osage, N.J., U.S. | 285 | 39.51 N | 75.01 W |
| Osage, Wy., U.S. | 198 | 43.58 N | 104.25 W |
| Osage □[6] | 219 | 38.27 N | 91.50 W |
| Osage ≃ | 194 | 38.35 N | 91.57 W |
| Osage Beach | 194 | 38.09 N | 92.37 W |
| Osage City | 198 | 38.38 N | 95.49 W |
| Osaka, Nihon | 94 | 35.57 N | 137.16 E |
| Ōsaka, Nihon | 96 | 34.40 N | 135.30 E |
| Ōsaka, Nihon | 270 | 34.40 N | 135.30 E |
| Ōsaka □[5] | 96 | 34.30 N | 135.30 E |
| Osaka Castle ⊥ | 270 | 34.41 N | 135.32 E |
| Ōsaka-heiya ≚ | 270 | 34.43 N | 135.30 E |
| Ōsaka International Airport ⊠ | 270 | 34.47 N | 135.26 E |
| Ōsaka-kō ⊂ | 270 | 34.38 N | 135.26 E |
| Ōsaka-kokusai-kūkō ⊠ | 96 | 34.47 N | 135.26 E |
| Osakarovka | 86 | 50.32 N | 72.39 E |
| Ōsaka-tōge )( | 270 | 34.56 N | 135.18 E |
| Osaka University ⊌[2] | 270 | 34.42 N | 135.30 E |
| Ōsaka-wan ⊂ | 96 | 34.30 N | 135.18 E |
| Ōsakiga-hana ≻ | 96 | 35.11 N | 132.25 E |
| Ōsaki-Kami-jima I | 96 | 34.14 N | 132.54 E |
| Osakis | 198 | 45.52 N | 95.09 W |
| Ōsaki-Shimo-jima I | 96 | 34.10 N | 132.50 E |
| Osăm ≃ | 38 | 43.42 N | 24.51 E |
| Osan | 98 | 37.11 N | 127.04 E |
| Osanovo | 82 | 54.12 N | 38.41 E |
| Osasco | 256 | 23.32 S | 46.46 W |
| Osasco □[7] | 287b | 23.32 S | 46.46 W |
| Ōsawano | 94 | 36.34 N | 137.12 E |
| Osawatomie | 198 | 38.29 N | 94.57 W |
| Ōsa-yama ∧ | 96 | 34.45 N | 132.12 E |
| Osbaldeston | 262 | 53.47 N | 2.32 W |
| Osborne, Ks., U.S. | 198 | 39.26 N | 98.41 W |
| Osborne, Pa., U.S. | 279b | 40.32 N | 80.10 W |
| Osbourn Seamount ◆[3] | 14 | 26.00 S | 174.50 W |
| Osburger Hochwald ∧∧ | 56 | 49.40 N | 6.50 E |
| Osburn | 202 | 47.30 N | 115.59 W |
| Osby | 26 | 56.22 N | 13.59 E |
| Osbyholm | 41 | 55.51 N | 13.36 E |
| Oscar Peak ∧ | 182 | 54.51 N | 129.07 W |
| Oscarville | 180 | 60.43 N | 161.46 W |
| Oscawana Lake | 210 | 41.23 N | 73.52 W |
| Osceola, Ar., U.S. | 194 | 35.42 N | 89.58 W |
| Osceola, In., U.S. | 216 | 41.39 N | 86.04 W |
| Osceola, Ia., U.S. | 190 | 41.02 N | 93.45 W |
| Osceola, Mo., U.S. | 194 | 38.02 N | 93.42 W |
| Osceola, Ne., U.S. | 198 | 41.10 N | 97.32 W |
| Osceola, Pa., U.S. | 210 | 41.59 N | 77.21 W |
| Osceola, Tx., U.S. | 222 | 32.08 N | 97.14 W |
| Osceola, Wi., U.S. | 190 | 45.19 N | 92.42 W |
| Osceola □[6] | 220 | 28.00 N | 81.15 W |
| Osceola Mills | 214 | 40.51 N | 78.16 W |
| Oščepkovo | 86 | 56.29 N | 70.42 E |
| Oschatz | 54 | 51.17 N | 13.07 E |
| Oschersleben | 54 | 52.01 N | 11.13 E |
| Oschiri | 71 | 40.43 N | 9.06 E |
| Oscoda | 190 | 44.26 N | 83.20 W |
| Öse ≃ | 263 | 51.26 N | 7.49 E |
| Osečenka | 76 | 57.33 N | 34.48 E |
| Osečina | 38 | 44.23 N | 19.36 E |
| Osejevskaja | 82 | 55.53 N | 38.10 E |
| Ošejkino | 82 | 56.15 N | 35.54 E |
| Osek | 54 | 50.37 N | 13.40 E |
| Ösel → Saaremaa I | 76 | 58.25 N | 22.30 E |
| Osen | 24 | 64.17 N | 10.30 E |
| Osetrovo | 88 | 56.47 N | 105.47 E |
| Ōse-zaki ≻ | 94 | 35.02 N | 138.47 E |
| Osgood, In., U.S. | 218 | 39.07 N | 85.17 W |
| Osgood, Oh., U.S. | 216 | 40.20 N | 84.30 W |
| Osgoode | 212 | 45.08 N | 75.36 W |
| Osh → Oš | 85 | 40.33 N | 72.48 E |
| Oshakati | 156 | 17.47 S | 15.41 E |
| Oshamambe | 92a | 42.30 N | 140.22 E |
| Oshana □[4] | 156 | 18.00 S | 15.30 E |
| O'Shanassy ≃ | 166 | 18.59 S | 138.46 E |
| O'Shaughnessy Dam ◆[6] | 226 | 37.57 N | 119.47 W |
| O'Shaughnessy Reservoir ⊜[1] | 214 | 40.12 N | 83.09 W |
| Oshawa | 212 | 43.54 N | 78.51 W |
| Oshawa Creek ≃ | 212 | 43.52 N | 78.49 W |
| Oshibe ◆[8] | 270 | 34.45 N | 135.04 E |
| Oshigambo | 156 | 17.47 S | 16.05 E |
| Oshika, Nihon | 92 | 38.16 N | 141.32 E |
| Ōshika, Nihon | 94 | 35.34 N | 138.02 E |
| Oshika-hantō ≻[1] | 92 | 38.20 N | 141.30 E |
| Oshikango | 156 | 17.25 S | 15.56 E |
| Oshikoto □[4] | 156 | 18.30 S | 17.30 E |
| Ōshima, Nihon | 92 | 33.03 N | 129.33 E |
| Ōshima, Nihon | 94 | 37.07 N | 138.30 E |
| Ōshima, Nihon | 94 | 34.45 N | 139.22 E |
| Ōshima, Nihon | 96 | 33.55 N | 132.15 E |
| Ō-shima I, Nihon | 92a | 41.30 N | 139.22 E |
| Ō-shima I, Nihon | 94 | 34.43 N | 139.23 E |
| Ō-shima I, Nihon | 94 | 36.15 N | 136.07 E |
| Ō-shima I, Nihon | 96 | 33.54 N | 130.26 E |
| Ō-shima I, Nihon | 96 | 34.30 N | 131.25 E |
| Ō-shima I, Nihon | 96 | 34.00 N | 133.22 E |
| Ō-shima I, Nihon | 96 | 34.09 N | 133.04 E |
| Ō-shima I, Nihon | 96 | 33.38 N | 134.30 E |
| Oshima-hantō ≻[1] | 92a | 42.00 N | 140.30 E |
| Oshimizu | 94 | 36.49 N | 136.46 E |
| Oshino | 94 | 35.28 N | 138.51 E |
| Oshivre ◆[8] | 272c | 19.09 N | 72.51 E |
| Oshkosh, Ne., U.S. | 198 | 41.24 N | 102.20 W |
| Oshkosh, Wi., U.S. | 190 | 44.01 N | 88.32 W |
| Oshnovīyeh | 128 | 37.02 N | 45.06 E |
| Oshodi | 273a | 6.34 N | 3.21 E |
| Oshoek | 158 | 26.13 S | 30.59 E |
| Oshogbo | 150 | 7.47 N | 4.34 E |
| Oshtemo | 216 | 42.15 N | 85.41 W |
| Oshtorān Kūh ∧ | 128 | 33.20 N | 49.16 E |
| Oshtorīnān | 128 | 34.01 N | 48.38 E |
| Oshwe | 152 | 3.24 S | 19.30 E |
| Osi | 150 | 8.08 N | 5.14 E |
| Osica de Jos | 38 | 44.15 N | 24.17 E |
| Osich'ŏn-ni | 98 | 41.25 N | 128.16 E |
| Osiek | 30 | 50.31 N | 21.28 E |
| Osiglia | 62 | 44.17 N | 8.12 E |
| Osijek | 38 | 45.33 N | 18.41 E |
| Osilinka ≃ | 182 | 56.05 N | 124.29 W |
| Osilo | 71 | 40.45 N | 8.40 E |
| Osimo | 66 | 43.29 N | 13.29 E |
| Osini | 71 | 39.50 N | 9.29 E |
| Osinki | 80 | 52.51 N | 49.30 E |
| Osinniki, Ross. | 80 | 58.03 N | 47.02 E |
| Osinniki, Ross. | 86 | 53.37 N | 87.21 E |
| Osinovka, Ross. | 88 | 50.34 N | 109.27 E |
| Osinovka, Ross. | 88 | 56.19 N | 101.56 E |
| Osinovskij chrebet ∧∧ | 180 | 67.10 N | 175.00 E |
| Osinów Dolny | 54 | 52.48 N | 14.10 E |
| Osio Sotto | 62 | 45.36 N | 9.35 E |
| Osipaonica | 38 | 44.33 N | 21.04 E |
| Osipenko → Berdyans'k | 78 | 46.45 N | 36.49 E |
| Osipovo Selo | 76 | 56.51 N | 30.30 E |
| Osire | 156 | 20.59 S | 17.19 E |
| Osivān | 120 | 26.43 N | 72.55 E |
| Oskaloosa, Ia., U.S. | 190 | 41.17 N | 92.38 W |
| Oskaloosa, Ks., U.S. | 198 | 39.12 N | 95.18 W |
| Oskar-Fredriksborg | 40 | 59.24 N | 18.26 E |
| Oskarshamn | 26 | 57.16 N | 16.26 E |
| Oskarström | 26 | 56.48 N | 12.58 E |
| Oskil (Oskol) ≃ | 78 | 49.06 N | 37.25 E |
| Os'kino | 78 | 51.14 N | 39.02 E |
| Oskol (Oskil) ≃ | 78 | 49.06 N | 37.25 E |
| Oskolkovo | 24 | 67.58 N | 53.42 E |
| Oskū | 128 | 37.55 N | 46.06 E |
| Oskuj | 76 | 59.17 N | 32.05 E |
| Oskuja ≃ | 76 | 59.14 N | 31.54 E |
| Osl'anka, gora ∧ | 86 | 59.10 N | 58.33 E |
| Oslava ≃ | 61 | 49.05 N | 16.22 E |
| Ösling ◆[1] | 56 | 49.55 N | 6.00 E |
| Oslo | 26 | 59.55 N | 10.45 E |
| Oslob | 116 | 9.31 N | 123.26 E |
| Oslofjorden ⊂[2] | 26 | 59.20 N | 10.35 E |
| Os'ma ≃, Ross. | 76 | 54.55 N | 33.24 E |
| Ošma ≃, Ross. | 80 | 57.52 N | 47.45 E |
| Osmānābād | 122 | 18.10 N | 76.02 E |
| Osmancık | 130 | 40.59 N | 34.49 E |
| Osmaneli | 130 | 40.22 N | 30.01 E |
| Osmaniye | 130 | 37.05 N | 36.14 E |
| Osmanpaşa | 130 | 39.38 N | 34.58 E |
| Osmeña | 116 | 10.11 N | 125.31 E |
| Osmington | 42 | 50.38 N | 2.22 W |
| Os'mino | 76 | 59.01 N | 29.06 E |
| Osminog, gora ∧ | 180 | 67.54 N | 176.50 E |
| Ösmo | 40 | 58.59 N | 17.54 E |
| Osmond | 198 | 42.21 N | 97.35 W |
| Osmore ≃ | 248 | 17.33 S | 71.12 W |
| Osmoy | 261 | 48.52 N | 1.43 E |
| Osmussaar I | 76 | 59.18 N | 23.22 E |
| Osnabrück | 52 | 52.16 N | 8.02 E |
| Ośno | 30 | 52.28 N | 14.50 E |
| Osny | 261 | 49.04 N | 2.04 E |
| Oso | 224 | 48.16 N | 121.56 W |
| Oso ≃ | 154 | 1.09 S | 27.22 E |
| Oso, Gran Lago del → Great Bear Lake ⊜ | 176 | 66.00 N | 120.00 W |
| Ošoba | 85 | 40.44 N | 70.26 E |
| Osogna | 58 | 46.18 N | 9.00 E |
| Osoppo | 64 | 46.15 N | 13.05 E |
| Osorakan-zan ∧ | 96 | 34.36 N | 132.08 E |
| Osore-yama ∧ | 92 | 41.18 N | 141.05 E |
| Osorio, Quebrada ≃ | 286c | 10.36 N | 66.56 W |
| Osório Fonseca | 250 | 3.40 S | 58.13 W |
| Osorno, Chile | 254 | 40.34 S | 73.09 W |
| Osorno, Esp. | 34 | 42.24 N | 4.22 W |
| Osorno, Volcán ∧[1] | 254 | 41.06 S | 72.30 W |
| Osorun | 273a | 6.33 N | 3.29 E |
| Os'otr ≃ | 82 | 54.58 N | 38.46 E |
| Osoyoos | 182 | 49.02 N | 119.28 W |
| Osoyoos Indian Reserve ◆[4] | 182 | 49.08 N | 119.30 W |
| Osoyoos Lake ⊜ | 182 | 49.00 N | 119.26 W |
| Osøyra | 26 | 60.11 N | 5.28 E |
| Ospedaletti | 62 | 43.48 N | 7.43 E |
| Ospedaletto, It. | 64 | 46.03 N | 11.33 E |
| Ospedaletto, It. | 64 | 46.17 N | 13.07 E |
| Ospino | 246 | 9.18 N | 69.27 W |
| Ospitale di Cadore | 64 | 46.20 N | 12.19 E |
| Ospitaletto | 64 | 45.33 N | 10.04 E |
| Osprey | 220 | 27.11 N | 82.29 W |
| Osprey Reef ◆[2] | 164 | 13.55 S | 146.38 E |
| Ospwagan Lake ⊜ | 184 | 55.35 N | 98.03 W |
| Oss | 52 | 51.46 N | 5.31 E |
| Ossa, Mount ∧ | 166 | 41.54 S | 146.01 E |
| Ossabaw Island I | 192 | 31.47 N | 81.06 W |
| Osse ≃, Fr. | 32 | 44.07 N | 0.17 E |
| Osse ≃, Nig. | 150 | 6.10 N | 5.20 E |
| Ossenberg | 263 | 51.34 N | 6.35 E |
| Ossendrecht | 52 | 51.24 N | 4.19 E |
| Osseo, Mi., U.S. | 216 | 41.53 N | 84.33 W |
| Osseo, Wi., U.S. | 190 | 44.34 N | 91.13 W |
| Ossett | 44 | 53.41 N | 1.35 W |
| Ossi | 71 | 40.40 N | 8.35 E |
| Ossiacher See ⊜ | 64 | 46.40 N | 13.55 E |
| Ossian, In., U.S. | 216 | 40.52 N | 85.09 W |
| Ossian, Ia., U.S. | 190 | 43.08 N | 91.45 W |
| Ossian, Loch ⊜ | 46 | 56.46 N | 4.38 W |
| Ossining | 210 | 41.09 N | 73.51 W |
| Ossipee | 188 | 43.41 N | 71.07 W |
| Ossjøen ⊜ | 26 | 61.13 N | 11.53 E |
| Ossling | 54 | 51.21 N | 14.09 E |
| Ossmannstedt, Dtsch. | 54 | 51.01 N | 11.26 E |
| Ossmannstedt, Dtsch. | 54 | 51.01 N | 11.26 E |
| Ossona | 266b | 45.30 N | 8.54 E |
| Ossora | 74 | 59.20 N | 163.13 E |
| Ossum-Bösinghoven | 263 | 51.18 N | 6.39 E |
| Ošta | 24 | 60.49 N | 35.32 E |
| Ostaboningue, Lac ⊜ | 190 | 47.09 N | 78.53 W |
| Östanå, Sve. | 40 | 59.33 N | 18.35 E |
| Östanå, Sve. | 40 | 60.38 N | 16.48 E |
| Östanbyn | 40 | 60.39 N | 16.48 E |
| Ostankino ◆[8] | 265b | 55.49 N | 37.37 E |
| Östansjö | 40 | 59.03 N | 14.59 E |
| Ostap'ye | 78 | 49.33 N | 33.46 E |
| Ostaškov | 76 | 57.09 N | 33.06 E |
| Ostašovo | 82 | 55.52 N | 35.52 E |
| Ostbevern | 52 | 52.02 N | 7.50 E |
| Østbirk | 41 | 55.58 N | 9.46 E |
| Ostbüren | 263 | 51.31 N | 7.46 E |
| Østby | 26 | 61.15 N | 12.32 E |
| Ostchinesisches Meer → East China Sea ◆[2] | 90 | 30.00 N | 126.00 E |
| Oste ≃ | 52 | 53.51 N | 8.59 E |
| Osted | 41 | 55.34 N | 11.58 E |
| Osteen | 220 | 28.50 N | 81.09 W |
| Ostellato | 66 | 44.45 N | 11.56 E |
| Ostende → Oostende | 50 | 51.13 N | 2.55 E |
| Ostenfelde | 52 | 51.52 N | 8.04 E |
| Oster | 78 | 50.57 N | 30.53 E |
| Oster ≃, Dtsch. | 60 | 48.43 N | 13.29 E |
| Oster ≃, Ukr. | 78 | 50.56 N | 30.52 E |
| Osterath | 56 | 51.16 N | 6.37 E |
| Osterbönen | 263 | 51.37 N | 7.48 E |
| Osterburg, Dtsch. | 54 | 52.47 N | 11.44 E |
| Osterburg, Pa., U.S. | 214 | 40.16 N | 78.31 W |
| Osterburken | 56 | 49.26 N | 9.26 E |
| Österbybruk | 40 | 60.12 N | 17.54 E |
| Österbymo | 26 | 57.50 N | 15.16 E |
| Ostercappeln | 52 | 52.20 N | 8.13 E |
| Österdalälven ≃ | 26 | 60.33 N | 15.08 E |
| Østerdalen V | 26 | 61.15 N | 11.10 E |
| Österfärnebo | 40 | 60.18 N | 16.48 E |
| Osterfeld | 54 | 51.05 N | 11.56 E |
| Osterfeld ◆[8] | 263 | 51.30 N | 6.53 E |
| Östergötland □[9] | 26 | 58.24 N | 15.34 E |
| Östergötlands Län □[6] | 26 | 58.25 N | 15.45 E |
| Österhaninge | 40 | 59.08 N | 18.12 E |
| Osterhofen | 60 | 48.42 N | 13.01 E |
| Øster Højst | 41 | 55.00 N | 9.03 E |
| Osterholz-Scharmbeck | 52 | 53.14 N | 8.47 E |
| Osterley Park ◆ | 260 | 51.30 N | 0.21 W |
| Österlövsta | 40 | 60.26 N | 17.47 E |
| Ostermundigen | 58 | 46.58 N | 7.29 E |
| Osternienburg | 54 | 51.48 N | 12.01 E |
| Osterode, Dtsch. | 52 | 51.44 N | 10.11 E |
| Osterode → Ostróda, Pol. | 30 | 53.43 N | 19.59 E |
| Osterøya I | 26 | 60.33 N | 5.35 E |
| Österreich → Austria □[1] | 30 | 47.20 N | 13.20 E |
| Österreichisches Freilichtmuseum ⊌ | 61 | 47.10 N | 15.19 E |
| Osterrönfeld | 41 | 54.17 N | 9.41 E |
| Östersjön → Baltic Sea ◆[2] | 24 | 57.00 N | 19.00 E |
| Österskär | 40 | 59.28 N | 18.18 E |
| Östersund | 26 | 63.11 N | 14.39 E |
| Östervåla | 40 | 60.11 N | 17.11 E |
| Osterville | 207 | 41.37 N | 70.23 W |
| Osterwick | 52 | 52.01 N | 7.13 E |
| Osterwieck | 54 | 51.58 N | 10.42 E |
| Ostfeld ◆[8] | 263 | 51.40 N | 7.45 E |
| Ostfildern | 56 | 48.43 N | 9.16 E |
| Østfold □[6] | 26 | 59.20 N | 11.30 E |
| Ostfriesische Inseln II | 52 | 53.44 N | 7.25 E |
| Ostfriesland □[9] | 52 | 53.20 N | 7.40 E |
| Ost-Ghats → Eastern Ghāts ∧∧ | 122 | 14.00 N | 78.50 E |
| Östhammar | 40 | 60.16 N | 18.22 E |
| Ostheim vor der Rhön | 56 | 50.27 N | 10.14 E |
| Osthofen | 56 | 49.42 N | 8.19 E |
| Ostia, Bonifica di ◆[1] | 267a | 41.46 N | 12.18 E |
| Ostia Antica ⊥ | 66 | 41.45 N | 12.16 E |
| Ostiano | 64 | 45.13 N | 10.15 E |
| Ostiglia | 64 | 45.04 N | 11.08 E |
| Ostky | 78 | 51.16 N | 27.22 E |
| Östliche Sierra Madre → Madre Oriental, Sierra ∧∧ | 232 | 22.00 N | 99.30 W |
| Östmark | 26 | 60.17 N | 12.45 E |
| Ost'or | 76 | 54.01 N | 32.48 E |
| Ost'or ≃ | 76 | 53.47 N | 31.46 E |
| Ostpeene ≃ | 54 | 53.43 N | 12.46 E |
| Ostra | 66 | 43.37 N | 13.09 E |
| Östraby | 41 | 55.46 N | 13.41 E |
| Ostrach | 58 | 47.57 N | 9.23 E |
| Ostrach ≃ | 58 | 48.04 N | 9.24 E |
| Östra Grevie | 41 | 55.28 N | 13.08 E |
| Östra Husby | 40 | 58.35 N | 16.33 E |
| Östra Laxsjön ⊜ | 40 | 58.54 N | 14.42 E |
| Östra Ljungby | 41 | 56.11 N | 13.04 E |
| Ostrander | 214 | 40.15 N | 83.12 W |
| Östra Ringsjön ⊜ | 41 | 55.52 N | 13.32 E |
| Ostrau → Ostrava, Česká Rep. | 30 | 49.50 N | 18.17 E |
| Ostrau, Dtsch. | 54 | 51.12 N | 13.09 E |
| Ostrava | 30 | 49.50 N | 18.17 E |
| Ostra Vetere | 66 | 43.36 N | 13.03 E |
| Ostrhauderfehn | 52 | 53.08 N | 7.37 E |
| Östrich | 263 | 51.40 N | 6.55 E |
| Ostricourt | 50 | 50.27 N | 3.02 E |
| Östringen | 56 | 49.13 N | 8.43 E |
| Ostritz | 54 | 51.01 N | 14.56 E |
| Ostróda | 30 | 53.43 N | 19.59 E |
| Ostrogožsk | 78 | 50.52 N | 39.05 E |
| Ostroh | 78 | 50.20 N | 26.31 E |
| Ostrokonje | 76 | 59.52 N | 42.02 E |
| Ostrołęka | 30 | 53.06 N | 21.34 E |
| Ostrołęka □[4] | 30 | 53.00 N | 21.30 E |
| Ostroróg | 30 | 52.39 N | 16.27 E |
| Ostrov, Česká Rep. | 54 | 50.17 N | 12.57 E |
| Ostrov, Rom. | 38 | 44.06 N | 27.22 E |
| Ostrov, Ross. | 76 | 57.20 N | 28.22 E |
| Ostrov, Ross. | 76 | 60.34 N | 37.55 E |
| Ostrov, Ross. | 265b | 55.35 N | 37.51 E |
| Ostrov I | 30 | 47.55 N | 17.35 E |
| Ostrov'anskij | 80 | 46.45 N | 42.13 E |
| Ostrovki | 265a | 59.48 N | 30.50 E |
| Ostrovskaja | 80 | 50.26 N | 44.27 E |
| Ostrovskoje | 80 | 57.48 N | 42.15 E |
| Ostrov-Zalit | 76 | 58.01 N | 28.04 E |
| Ostrowiec Świętokrzyski | 30 | 50.57 N | 21.23 E |
| Ostrów Lubelski | 30 | 51.30 N | 22.52 E |
| Ostrów Mazowiecka | 30 | 52.49 N | 21.54 E |
| Ostrów Wielkopolski | 30 | 51.39 N | 17.49 E |
| Ostrzeszów | 30 | 51.25 N | 17.57 E |
| Ostsee → Baltic Sea ◆[2] | 24 | 57.00 N | 19.00 E |
| Ostseebad Ahrenshoop | 54 | 54.23 N | 12.25 E |
| Ostseebad Boltenhagen | 54 | 54.00 N | 11.12 E |
| Ostseebad Dierhagen | 54 | 54.18 N | 12.22 E |
| Ostseebad Graal-Müritz | 54 | 54.15 N | 12.12 E |
| Ostseebad Nienhagen | 54 | 54.09 N | 11.58 E |
| Ostseebad Rerik | 54 | 54.06 N | 11.37 E |
| Ostseebad Wustrow | 54 | 54.21 N | 12.23 E |
| Ost-Sümmern | 263 | 51.26 N | 7.44 E |
| Osttirol □[9] | 64 | 46.55 N | 12.30 E |
| Ostúa ≃ | 236 | 14.17 N | 89.33 W |
| Ostuacán | 234 | 17.25 N | 93.18 W |
| Ostula | 234 | 18.30 N | 103.28 W |
| Ostuni | 68 | 40.44 N | 17.35 E |
| Ostwald | 58 | 48.33 N | 7.43 E |
| Osu | 98 | 35.31 N | 127.18 E |
| Osuga | 76 | 56.02 N | 34.18 E |
| Osuga ≃ | 76 | 57.16 N | 34.49 E |
| Ōsuka | 94 | 34.41 N | 137.59 E |
| O'Sullivan, Lac ⊜ | 190 | 47.37 N | 76.05 W |
| Osum ≃ | 38 | 40.48 N | 19.52 E |
| Ōsumi | 270 | 34.50 N | 135.45 E |
| Ōsumi-hantō ≻[1] | 92 | 31.20 N | 130.55 E |
| Ōsumi-kaikyō ⊔ | 92 | 31.00 N | 131.00 E |
| Ōsumi-shotō II | 93b | 30.30 N | 130.00 E |
| Osuna | 34 | 37.14 N | 5.07 W |
| Osupugo ∧ | 154 | 1.40 S | 35.49 E |
| Osvaldo Cruz | 255 | 21.47 S | 50.50 W |
| Ošvor | 24 | 66.58 N | 62.53 E |
| Oswaldtwistle | 44 | 53.43 N | 2.26 W |
| Oswaldtwistle Moor ◆[3] | 262 | 53.43 N | 2.23 W |
| Oswald West State Park ◆ | 224 | 45.45 N | 123.58 W |
| Oswayo | 214 | 41.55 N | 78.01 W |
| Oswayo Creek ≃ | 210 | 42.02 N | 78.21 W |
| Oswegatchie ≃ | 188 | 44.42 N | 75.30 W |
| Oswegatchie, Middle Branch ≃ | 212 | 44.07 N | 75.19 W |
| Oswegatchie, West Branch ≃ | 188 | 44.18 N | 75.20 W |
| Oswego, Il., U.S. | 216 | 41.40 N | 88.21 W |
| Oswego, In., U.S. | 216 | 41.19 N | 85.47 W |
| Oswego, Ks., U.S. | 198 | 37.10 N | 95.06 W |
| Oswego, N.Y., U.S. | 212 | 43.27 N | 76.30 W |
| Oswego □[6] | 212 | 43.22 N | 76.15 W |
| Oswego ≃, N.J., U.S. | 208 | 39.40 N | 74.32 W |
| Oswego ≃, N.Y., U.S. | 212 | 43.28 N | 76.31 W |
| Oswestry | 42 | 52.52 N | 3.04 W |
| Oświęcim | 30 | 50.03 N | 19.12 E |
| Osyka | 194 | 31.00 N | 90.28 W |
| Osynyve | 83 | 49.34 N | 39.05 E |
| Osypenko | 78 | 46.54 N | 36.49 E |
| Ota, Nihon | 94 | 35.58 N | 136.04 E |
| Ōta, Nihon | 94 | 36.18 N | 139.22 E |
| Ōta, Nihon | 96 | 33.31 N | 131.33 E |
| Ōta ◆[8] | 268 | 35.34 N | 139.43 E |
| Ōta ≃, Nihon | 94 | 34.40 N | 137.54 E |
| Ōta ≃, Nihon | 96 | 34.22 N | 132.25 E |
| Otaci | 38 | 48.25 N | 27.47 E |
| Otago Peninsula ≻[1] | 172 | 45.52 S | 170.40 E |
| Otahuhu | 172 | 36.57 S | 174.51 E |
| Ōtake | 96 | 34.12 N | 132.13 E |
| Otaki, N.Z. | 172 | 40.45 S | 175.09 E |
| Ōtaki, Nihon | 94 | 35.17 N | 140.15 E |
| Ōtaki, Nihon | 94 | 35.48 N | 137.33 E |
| Ōtaki, Nihon | 94 | 35.57 N | 138.56 E |
| Ōtaki ≃ | 94 | 35.49 N | 137.40 E |
| Ōtaki-yama ∧ | 96 | 34.07 N | 134.08 E |
| Ōta-Koizumi-hikojō ◆ | 94 | 36.16 N | 139.24 E |
| Otane | 172 | 39.53 S | 176.38 E |
| Otanmäki | 26 | 64.07 N | 27.06 E |
| Otar | 85 | 43.33 N | 75.13 E |
| Otari | 94 | 36.46 N | 137.54 E |
| Otaru | 92a | 43.13 N | 141.00 E |
| Otatara | 172 | 46.26 S | 168.18 E |
| Otatitlán | 234 | 18.12 N | 96.02 W |
| Otautau | 172 | 46.09 S | 168.00 E |
| Otava | 26 | 61.39 N | 27.04 E |
| Otava ≃ | 30 | 49.27 N | 14.12 E |
| Otavalo | 246 | 0.14 N | 78.16 W |
| Otavi | 156 | 19.39 S | 17.20 E |
| Ōtawara | 94 | 36.52 N | 140.02 E |
| Otawa-yama ∧ | 270 | 34.28 N | 135.53 E |
| Otay | 228 | 32.35 N | 117.03 W |
| Otchinjau | 152 | 16.30 S | 13.57 E |
| Oteapan | 234 | 18.00 N | 94.39 W |
| Otego | 210 | 42.23 N | 75.10 W |
| Otego Creek ≃ | 210 | 42.25 N | 75.07 W |
| Otéle | 152 | 3.35 N | 11.15 E |
| Otematata | 172 | 44.37 S | 170.16 E |
| Oteotea | 175e | 9.05 S | 161.11 E |
| Otepää | 76 | 58.03 N | 26.30 E |
| Oteros ≃ | 232 | 26.55 N | 108.22 W |
| Otford, Austl. | 170 | 34.12 S | 151.01 E |
| Otford, Eng., U.K. | 42 | 51.19 N | 0.12 E |
| Otgon | 88 | 47.11 N | 97.33 E |
| Otgon Tenger uul ∧ | 88 | 47.36 N | 97.36 E |
| Otham | 260 | 51.15 N | 0.35 E |
| Othello | 202 | 46.49 N | 119.10 W |
| Othery | 42 | 51.05 N | 2.53 W |
| Othfresen | 52 | 52.00 N | 10.23 E |
| Óthiris, Óros ∧∧ | 38 | 39.02 N | 22.37 E |
| Othis | 261 | 49.04 N | 2.41 E |
| Othonoí I | 38 | 39.50 N | 19.26 E |
| Oti ≃ | 150 | 8.40 N | 0.13 E |
| Otibanda | 164 | 7.15 S | 146.30 E |
| Otinapa | 232 | 24.11 N | 105.02 W |
| Otira | 172 | 42.50 S | 171.33 E |
| Otis, Co., U.S. | 198 | 40.08 N | 102.57 W |
| Otis, In., U.S. | 216 | 41.36 N | 86.54 W |
| Otis, Ks., U.S. | 198 | 38.32 N | 99.03 W |
| Otis, Ma., U.S. | 207 | 42.11 N | 73.05 W |
| Otisco | 218 | 38.32 N | 85.40 W |
| Otisco Lake ⊜ | 210 | 42.52 N | 76.18 W |
| Otish, Monts ∧∧ | 176 | 52.22 N | 70.30 W |
| Otis Reservoir ⊜[1] | 207 | 42.09 N | 73.02 W |
| Otisville | 210 | 41.28 N | 74.32 W |
| Otjassy | 80 | 53.14 N | 41.39 E |
| Otjikondo | 156 | 19.50 S | 15.23 E |
| Otjimbingue | 156 | 22.19 S | 16.10 E |
| Otjinene | 156 | 21.13 S | 18.42 E |
| Otjiwarongo | 156 | 20.29 S | 16.36 E |
| Otjozondjou ≃ | 156 | 20.18 S | 20.50 E |
| Otjozondjupa □[4] | 156 | 20.00 S | 18.00 E |
| Otley | 44 | 53.54 N | 1.41 W |
| Otmanlı | 130 | 41.52 N | 34.37 E |
| Otm'ok, pereval )( | 85 | 42.20 N | 73.10 E |
| Otmuchów | 30 | 50.28 N | 17.10 E |
| Otnes | 26 | 61.45 N | 11.14 E |
| Otnice | 61 | 49.05 N | 16.49 E |
| Ōtō | 96 | 33.41 N | 135.35 E |
| Otočac | 36 | 44.52 N | 15.14 E |
| Otog Qi | 102 | 39.08 N | 108.00 E |
| Ōtomi | 175d | 24.19 N | 123.54 E |
| Oton | 116 | 10.42 N | 122.29 E |
| Otonabee ≃ | 212 | 44.08 N | 78.14 W |
| Otoque, Isla I | 236 | 8.36 N | 79.36 W |
| Ōtori-kita | 270 | 34.33 N | 135.27 E |
| Otorma | 80 | 53.32 N | 42.32 E |
| Otoro ≃ | 236 | 15.00 N | 88.16 W |
| Otorohanga | 172 | 38.11 S | 175.12 E |
| Otoskwin ≃ | 176 | 52.13 N | 88.06 W |
| Otowa | 94 | 34.51 N | 137.18 E |
| Otowa-yama ∧ | 270 | 34.58 N | 135.51 E |
| Otowa-yama-tunnel ◆[5] | 94 | 34.58 N | 135.51 E |
| Ōtoyo | 96 | 33.46 N | 133.40 E |
| Otra ≃ | 26 | 58.09 N | 8.00 E |
| Otradnaja | 84 | 44.23 N | 41.31 E |
| Otradnoje | 265a | 59.47 N | 30.49 E |
| Otradnyj | 80 | 53.22 N | 51.21 E |
| Otranto | 68 | 40.09 N | 18.30 E |
| Otranto, Capo d' ≻ | 68 | 40.06 N | 18.31 E |
| Otranto, Strait of ⊔ | 38 | 40.00 N | 19.00 E |
| Otricoli | 66 | 42.25 N | 12.29 E |
| Otrokovice | 30 | 49.13 N | 17.31 E |
| Ötscher ∧ | 61 | 47.52 N | 15.12 E |
| Otsego | 216 | 42.27 N | 85.41 W |
| Otsego □[6] | 210 | 42.42 N | 74.56 W |
| Otsego Lake ⊜ | 210 | 42.45 N | 74.52 W |
| Otselic ≃ | 210 | 42.20 N | 75.58 W |
| Ōtsu, Nihon | 96 | 35.00 N | 135.52 E |
| Ōtsu, Nihon | 268 | 35.16 N | 139.42 E |
| Ōtsu ≃ | 270 | 34.30 N | 135.24 E |
| Ōtsuchi | 92 | 39.21 N | 141.54 E |
| Ōtsuki | 94 | 35.36 N | 138.57 E |
| Ōtsu-shima I | 96 | 34.00 N | 131.42 E |
| Otta, Nig. | 150 | 6.42 N | 3.10 E |
| Otta, Nor. | 26 | 61.46 N | 9.32 E |
| Otta ≃ | 26 | 61.46 N | 9.31 E |
| Ottakring ◆[8] | 264b | 48.12 N | 16.19 E |
| Ottana | 71 | 40.14 N | 9.02 E |
| Ottarnic Pond ⊜ | 283 | 42.46 N | 71.25 W |
| Ottati | 68 | 40.28 N | 15.19 E |
| Ottavia ◆[8] | 267a | 41.58 N | 12.24 E |
| Ottaviano | 68 | 40.51 N | 14.28 E |
| Ottawa, On., Can. | 212 | 45.25 N | 75.42 W |
| Ottawa, Il., U.S. | 216 | 41.20 N | 88.50 W |
| Ottawa, Ks., U.S. | 198 | 38.36 N | 95.16 W |
| Ottawa, Oh., U.S. | 216 | 41.01 N | 84.02 W |
| Ottawa □[6], Mi., U.S. | 216 | 42.57 N | 86.02 W |
| Ottawa □[6], Oh., U.S. | 214 | 41.31 N | 82.56 W |
| Ottawa ≃, Can. | 176 | 45.20 N | 73.58 W |
| Ottawa ≃, Oh., U.S. | 214 | 41.44 N | 83.28 W |
| Ottawa ≃, Oh., U.S. | 216 | 41.00 N | 84.15 W |
| Ottawa-Carleton □[6] | 212 | 45.15 N | 75.45 W |
| Ottawa Hills | 214 | 41.39 N | 83.38 W |
| Ottawa International Airport ⊠ | 212 | 45.19 N | 75.40 W |
| Ottawa Islands II | 176 | 59.30 N | 80.10 W |
| Ottbergen | 52 | 51.42 N | 9.18 E |
| Ottenby | 26 | 56.14 N | 16.25 E |
| Ottendorf-Okrilla | 54 | 51.11 N | 13.50 E |
| Ottenhöfen | 58 | 48.34 N | 8.09 E |
| Ottenschlag | 61 | 48.25 N | 15.13 E |
| Ottensheim | 61 | 48.20 N | 14.11 E |
| Ottenstein Stausee ⊜[1] | 61 | 48.37 N | 15.17 E |
| Otter ≃ | 42 | 50.46 N | 3.17 W |
| Otterbach ≃ | 56 | 49.07 N | 8.21 E |
| Otterbäcken | 40 | 58.57 N | 14.02 E |
| Otterbein | 216 | 40.29 N | 87.06 W |
| Otterburn | 44 | 55.14 N | 2.10 W |
| Otterburne | 184 | 49.30 N | 97.03 W |
| Otterburn Park | 206 | 45.33 N | 73.13 W |
| Otter Creek | 192 | 29.19 N | 82.46 W |
| Otter Creek ≃, On., Can. | 212 | 44.06 N | 81.07 W |
| Otter Creek ≃, Il., U.S. | 219 | 39.18 N | 90.07 W |
| Otter Creek ≃, In., U.S. | 218 | 38.58 N | 85.37 W |
| Otter Creek ≃, Ia., U.S. | 190 | 41.20 N | 93.30 W |
| Otter Creek ≃, Mo., U.S. | 219 | 39.31 N | 91.51 W |
| Otter Creek ≃, Mt., U.S. | 202 | 45.36 N | 106.17 W |
| Otter Creek ≃, N.Y., U.S. | 212 | 43.43 N | 75.23 W |
| Otter Creek ≃, Ut., U.S. | 200 | 38.10 N | 112.02 W |
| Otter Creek ≃, Vt., U.S. | 188 | 44.13 N | 73.17 W |
| Otter Creek Reservoir ⊜[1] | 200 | 38.12 N | 111.59 W |
| Otterfing | 64 | 47.55 N | 11.41 E |
| Otterhöfen | 56 | 48.33 N | 8.12 E |
| Otter-Lake, P.Q., Can. | 188 | 45.51 N | 76.26 W |
| Otter Lake, Mi., U.S. | 190 | 43.13 N | 83.28 W |
| Otter Lake ⊜, On., Can. | 212 | 44.47 N | 76.07 W |
| Otter Lake ⊜, On., Can. | 212 | 45.17 N | 79.56 W |
| Otter Lake ⊜, Sk., Can. | 184 | 55.35 N | 104.39 W |
| Otter Lake ⊜[1] | 219 | 39.26 N | 89.54 W |
| Otterlo | 52 | 52.06 N | 5.45 E |
| Otterndorf | 52 | 53.48 N | 8.53 E |
| Otterøya I | 26 | 62.42 N | 6.48 E |
| Otter River | 207 | 42.35 N | 72.03 W |
| Ottersberg | 52 | 53.06 N | 9.08 E |
| Ottershaw | 260 | 51.22 N | 0.32 W |
| Ottersleben | 54 | 52.05 N | 11.34 E |
| Ottersweier | 58 | 48.40 N | 8.07 E |
| Otter Tail ≃ | 198 | 46.16 N | 96.36 W |
| Otter Tail Lake ⊜ | 198 | 46.23 N | 95.40 W |
| Otterup | 41 | 55.31 N | 10.24 E |
| Otterville, On., Can. | 212 | 42.55 N | 80.36 W |
| Otterville, Il., U.S. | 219 | 39.03 N | 90.24 W |
| Otterville, Mo., U.S. | 194 | 38.41 N | 93.00 W |
| Ottery ≃ | 42 | 50.39 N | 4.20 W |
| Ottery Saint Mary | 42 | 50.45 N | 3.17 W |
| Ottignies | 56 | 50.40 N | 4.34 E |
| Ottine | 222 | 29.36 N | 97.35 W |
| Ottmarsbocholt | 52 | 51.49 N | 7.32 E |
| Ottnang | 60 | 48.06 N | 13.40 E |
| Ottnaren ⊜ | 40 | 60.29 N | 16.37 E |
| Otto, N.Y., U.S. | 210 | 42.21 N | 78.50 W |
| Otto, Tx., U.S. | 222 | 31.27 N | 96.49 W |
| Ottobeuren | 58 | 47.56 N | 10.18 E |
| Ottobeuren, Klosterkirche ⊌[1] | 58 | 47.56 N | 10.18 E |
| Ottobiano | 62 | 45.09 N | 8.50 E |
| Ottobrunn | 60 | 48.04 N | 11.40 E |
| Ottone | 62 | 44.37 N | 9.20 E |
| Ottosdal | 158 | 26.58 S | 26.00 E |
| Ottoshoop | 156 | 25.45 S | 25.59 E |
| Ottoville | 216 | 40.55 N | 84.20 W |
| Ottuk, Kyrg. | 85 | 42.18 N | 76.18 E |
| Ottuk, Kyrg. | 85 | 41.38 N | 75.51 E |
| Ottumwa | 190 | 41.00 N | 92.22 W |
| Ottweiler | 56 | 49.24 N | 7.09 E |
| Otty Lake ⊜ | 212 | 44.50 N | 76.13 W |
| Otu, Nig. | 150 | 8.14 N | 3.24 E |
| Otu → Ōtsu, Nihon | 96 | 35.00 N | 135.52 E |
| Otukpa | 150 | 7.09 N | 7.41 E |
| Otumpa | 252 | 27.19 S | 62.13 W |
| Otun | 273a | 6.42 N | 3.22 E |
| Otuquis, Bañados de ⊞ | 248 | 19.20 S | 58.30 W |
| Oturkpo | 150 | 7.14 N | 8.08 E |
| Otway, Bahía ⊔ | 254 | 53.20 S | 74.00 W |
| Otway, Cape ≻ | 166 | 38.52 S | 143.31 E |
| Otway, Seno ⊂ | 254 | 53.05 S | 71.30 W |
| Otway Range ∧∧ | 169 | 38.30 S | 143.50 E |
| Otwock | 30 | 52.07 N | 21.16 E |
| Otyniya | 78 | 48.44 N | 24.51 E |
| Ötztal V | 64 | 47.05 N | 10.55 E |
| Ötztaler Ache ≃ | 64 | 47.14 N | 10.50 E |
| Ötztaler Alpen (Alpi Venoste) ∧∧ | 64 | 46.45 N | 10.55 E |
| Ou ≃, Lao | 110 | 20.04 N | 102.13 E |
| Ou ≃, Zhg. | 100 | 28.01 N | 120.44 E |
| Ou ≃, Zhg. | 100 | 26.02 N | 113.09 E |
| Oua ≃ | 152 | 0.43 N | 12.55 E |
| Ouachita ≃ | 194 | 31.38 N | 91.49 W |
| Ouachita, Lake ⊜[1] | 194 | 34.40 N | 93.25 W |
| Ouachita Mountains ∧∧ | 194 | 34.40 N | 94.25 W |
| Ouaco | 175f | 20.50 S | 164.29 E |
| Ouadâne | 148 | 20.56 N | 11.37 W |
| Ouadda | 152 | 8.04 N | 22.24 E |
| Ouaddaï □[5] | 146 | 13.00 N | 21.00 E |
| Ouadey, Ouadi el V | 146 | 13.34 N | 18.03 E |
| Ouagadougou | 150 | 12.22 N | 1.31 W |
| Ouahigouya | 150 | 13.35 N | 2.25 W |
| Ouahran → Wahran | 148 | 35.43 N | 0.43 W |
| Ouaka □[5] | 152 | 6.00 N | 21.00 E |
| Ouaka ≃ | 152 | 4.59 N | 19.56 E |
| Oualâta | 150 | 17.18 N | 7.02 W |
| Ouâlata, Ḑahr ◆[4] | 150 | 17.48 N | 7.24 W |
| Oualé ≃ | 150 | 10.52 N | 0.51 E |
| Oualidia | 148 | 32.44 N | 9.08 W |
| Ouallam | 150 | 14.19 N | 2.05 E |
| Ouallene | 148 | 24.37 N | 1.14 E |
| Oualto | 150 | 9.01 N | 10.06 W |
| Ouanary | 250 | 4.13 N | 51.40 W |
| Ouanda Djallé | 146 | 8.54 N | 22.48 E |
| Ouandago | 146 | 7.10 N | 18.42 E |
| Ouandja ≃ | 146 | 9.35 N | 21.43 E |
| Ouandja-Vakaga, Réserve de la ◆[4] | 146 | 9.00 N | 21.30 E |
| Ouango | 152 | 4.19 N | 22.33 E |
| Ouangolodougou | 150 | 9.58 N | 5.09 W |
| Ouaninou | 150 | 8.11 N | 7.51 W |
| Ouanne ≃ | 50 | 47.57 N | 2.47 E |
| Ouan Taredert | 148 | 27.33 N | 9.32 E |
| Ouaquaga | 210 | 42.08 N | 75.39 W |
| Ouara ≃ | 154 | 5.05 N | 24.26 E |
| Ouarâne ◆[1] | 134 | 21.00 N | 10.30 W |
| Ouararda, Passe de )( | 148 | 21.01 N | 13.03 W |
| Ouareau ≃ | 206 | 45.56 N | 73.25 W |
| Ouareau, Lac ⊜[1] | 206 | 46.17 N | 74.09 W |
| Ouargaye | 150 | 11.32 N | 0.01 E |
| Ouarkoye | 150 | 12.05 N | 3.40 W |
| Ouarkziz, Jbel ∧∧ | 148 | 28.50 N | 9.00 W |
| Ouarsenis, Djebel ∧ | 34 | 35.53 N | 1.38 E |
| Ouarville | 50 | 48.21 N | 1.46 E |
| Ouarzazate | 148 | 30.57 N | 6.50 W |
| Ouarzazate □[4] | 148 | 30.55 N | 6.45 W |
| Ouassoulou ≃ | 150 | 11.35 N | 8.11 W |
| Ouatcha | 150 | 13.22 N | 9.18 E |
| Oubangui (Ubangi) ≃ | 152 | 0.30 S | 17.42 E |
| Ouche ≃ | 58 | 47.06 N | 5.16 E |
| Oucques | 50 | 47.49 N | 1.18 E |
| Ōuda | 94 | 34.28 N | 135.56 E |
| Oudaze Lake ⊜ | 212 | 45.27 N | 79.11 W |
| Oud-Beijerland | 52 | 51.49 N | 4.25 E |
| Ouddorp | 52 | 51.48 N | 3.56 E |
| Oude IJssel (Issel) ≃ | 52 | 52.00 N | 6.10 E |
| Oudenaarde | 50 | 50.51 N | 3.36 E |
| Oudenbosch | 52 | 51.35 N | 4.31 E |
| Oudenburg | 50 | 51.11 N | 3.00 E |
| Oude-Pekela | 52 | 53.04 N | 6.58 E |
| Oude Rijn ≃ | 52 | 52.05 N | 4.20 E |
| Oudeschild | 52 | 53.02 N | 4.50 E |
| Oude-Tonge | 52 | 51.41 N | 4.12 E |
| Oudewater | 52 | 52.02 N | 4.52 E |
| Oud-Gastel | 52 | 51.35 N | 4.27 E |
| Oudjda → Oujda | 148 | 34.41 N | 1.45 W |
| Oud-Loosdrecht | 52 | 52.13 N | 5.04 E |
| Oudtshoorn | 158 | 33.35 S | 22.14 E |
| Oudyoumoudi | 150 | 14.04 N | 0.28 W |
| Oued Athmenia | 34 | 36.15 N | 6.17 E |
| Oued Cheham | 36 | 36.23 N | 7.46 E |
| Oued edh Dheheb, Khlij ⊂ | 148 | 23.45 N | 15.47 W |
| Oued Fodda | 34 | 36.11 N | 1.32 E |
| Oued Meliz | 36 | 36.27 N | 8.34 E |
| Oued Rhiou | 34 | 35.58 N | 0.55 E |
| Oued Tlelat | 34 | 35.34 N | 0.27 W |
| Oued Zarga | 36 | 36.40 N | 9.25 E |
| Oued-Zem | 148 | 32.55 N | 6.33 W |
| Ouellé | 150 | 7.18 N | 4.01 W |
| Ouémé □[5] | 150 | 7.00 N | 2.35 E |
| Ouémé ≃ | 150 | 6.29 N | 2.32 E |
| Ouen, Île I | 175f | 22.26 S | 166.49 E |
| Ouenkoro | 150 | 13.23 N | 3.50 W |
| Ouenza, Djebel ∧ | 36 | 35.57 N | 8.05 E |
| Ouenzé ◆[8] | 273b | 4.14 S | 15.17 E |
| Ouessa | 150 | 11.03 N | 2.47 W |
| Ouessant, Île d' (Ushant) I | 32 | 48.28 N | 5.05 W |
| Ouesso | 152 | 1.37 N | 16.04 E |
| Ouest □[4] | 152 | 5.23 N | 10.45 E |
| Ouest, Pointe de l' ≻ | 186 | 49.52 N | 64.31 W |
| Ouest, Rivière de l' ≃ | 206 | 45.39 N | 74.21 W |
| Ouezzane | 148 | 34.52 N | 5.35 W |
| Ouffet | 56 | 50.26 N | 5.28 E |
| Ouganda → Uganda □[1] | 154 | 1.00 N | 32.00 E |
| Ougarou | 150 | 12.09 N | 0.56 E |
| Oughter, Lough ⊜ | 48 | 54.00 N | 7.30 W |
| Oughterard | 48 | 53.25 N | 9.17 W |
| Oughtibridge | 44 | 53.26 N | 1.33 W |
| Ouham □[5] | 152 | 7.00 N | 18.00 E |
| Ouham ≃ | 136 | 9.18 N | 18.14 E |
| Ouham-Pendé □[5] | 152 | 7.00 N | 16.00 E |
| Ouidah | 150 | 6.22 N | 2.05 E |
| Ouidi | 146 | 14.07 N | 12.58 E |
| Ouimet Canyon V | 190 | 48.47 N | 88.40 W |
| Ouistreham | 32 | 49.17 N | 0.15 W |
| Oujda | 148 | 34.41 N | 1.45 W |
| Oujda □[4] | 148 | 34.05 N | 2.10 W |
| Oulad Naïl, Monts des ∧∧ | 148 | 34.33 N | 3.28 E |
| Oulainen | 26 | 64.16 N | 24.48 E |
| Oulangan kansallispuisto ◆ | 24 | 66.12 N | 29.30 E |
| Oulchy-le-Château | 50 | 49.12 N | 3.21 E |
| Oule ≃ | 62 | 44.25 N | 5.21 E |
| Ouled Agla | 34 | 35.58 N | 4.45 E |
| Ouleout Creek ≃ | 210 | 42.20 N | 75.18 W |
| Oulins | 50 | 48.52 N | 1.28 E |
| Oullins | 62 | 45.43 N | 4.48 E |
| Oulou, Bahr ≃ | 146 | 9.48 N | 21.32 E |
| Oulton Broad | 42 | 52.31 N | 1.42 E |
| Oulu | 26 | 65.01 N | 25.28 E |
| Oulujärvi ⊜ | 26 | 64.20 N | 27.15 E |
| Oulujoki ≃ | 26 | 65.01 N | 25.25 E |
| Oulun lääni □[4] | 24 | 65.00 N | 27.00 E |
| Oulx | 62 | 45.02 N | 6.50 E |
| Oumba | 152 | 4.55 N | 19.04 E |
| Oum-Chalouba | 146 | 15.48 N | 20.46 E |
| Oumé | 150 | 6.23 N | 5.25 W |
| Oum El Bouagui | 148 | 35.53 N | 7.07 E |
| Oum er Rbia, Oued ≃ | 148 | 33.19 N | 8.21 W |
| Oum-Hadjer | 146 | 13.18 N | 19.41 E |
| Oum Hadjer, Ouadi V | 146 | 16.38 N | 20.14 E |
| Oumiao | 102 | 31.55 N | 112.09 E |
| Oumm eḑ Droûs Guebli, Sebkhet ⊜ | 148 | 24.03 N | 11.45 W |
| Oumm eḑ Droûs Telli, Sebkhet ⊜ | 148 | 24.20 N | 11.30 W |
| Ounâne, Bîr ◆[4] | 148 | 21.28 N | 3.56 W |
| Ounara | 148 | 31.33 N | 9.28 W |
| Ounasjoki ≃ | 24 | 66.30 N | 25.45 E |
| Oundle | 42 | 52.29 N | 0.29 W |
| Ounianga Kébir | 146 | 19.04 N | 20.29 E |
| Ouolossébougou | 150 | 12.00 N | 7.55 W |
| Our ≃ | 56 | 49.53 N | 6.18 E |
| Ouragahio | 150 | 6.19 N | 5.56 W |
| Ōura-wan ⊂ | 174m | 26.32 N | 128.04 E |
| Ouray | 200 | 38.01 N | 107.40 W |
| Ouray, Mount ∧ | 200 | 38.25 N | 106.14 W |
| Ource ≃ | 58 | 48.06 N | 4.23 E |
| Ourcq ≃ | 50 | 49.01 N | 3.01 E |
| Ourcq, Canal de l' ≍ | 50 | 48.51 N | 2.22 E |
| Ourém | 250 | 1.33 S | 47.06 W |
| Ourense | 34 | 42.20 N | 7.51 W |
| Ouri | 146 | 21.34 N | 19.13 E |
| Ouri, Tarso ∧ | 146 | 21.25 N | 18.56 E |
| Ouricuri | 250 | 7.53 S | 40.05 W |
| Ourimbah | 170 | 33.22 S | 151.23 E |
| Ourinhos | 255 | 22.59 S | 49.52 W |
| Ourique | 34 | 37.39 N | 8.13 W |
| Ournie | 171b | 35.56 S | 147.51 E |
| Ouro, Paraná do ≃ | 248 | 8.29 S | 70.30 W |
| Ouro, Ponta do ≻ | 158 | 26.51 S | 32.54 E |
| Ouro Branco | 250 | 6.42 S | 36.57 W |
| Ouro Fino | 256 | 22.17 S | 46.22 W |
| Ouro Preto | 255 | 20.23 S | 43.30 W |
| Ouro Preto ≃ | 248 | 11.02 S | 65.13 W |
| Ouroufa, Vallée d' V | 150 | 14.42 N | 7.00 E |
| Ours, Grand Lac de l' → Great Bear Lake ⊜ | 176 | 66.00 N | 120.00 W |
| Oursi | 150 | 14.41 N | 0.27 W |
| Ourthe ≃ | 56 | 50.38 N | 5.35 E |


**Symbols** in the index entries represent the broad categories identified in the key at the right. Symbols with superior numbers (∧∧[1]) identify subcategories (see complete key on page *I · 1).*

**Symbole** im Register stellen die rechts im Schlüssel erklärten Kategorien dar. Symbole mit hochgestellten Ziffern (∧∧[1]) bezeichnen Unterabteilungen einer Kategorie (vgl. vollständiger Schlüssel auf Seite *I · 1).*

**Los símbolos** incluídos en el texto del índice representan las grandes categorías identificadas con la clave a la derecha. Los símbolos con numeros en su parte superior (∧∧[1]) identifican las subcategorías (véase la clave completa en la página *I · 1).*

**Les symboles** de l'index représentent les catégories indiquées dans la légende à droite. Les symboles suivis d'un indice (∧∧[1]) représentent des sous-catégories (voir légende complète à la page *I · 1).*

**Os símbolos** incluídos no texto do índice representam as grandes categorias identificadas com a chave à direita. Os símbolos com números em sua parte superior (∧∧[1]) identificam as subcategorias (veja-se a chave completa à página *I · 1).*

| | | | | | |
|---|---|---|---|---|---|
| ∧ | Mountain | Berg | Montaña | Montagne | Montanha |
| ∧∧ | Mountains | Gebirge | Montañas | Montagnes | Montanhas |
| )( | Pass | Paß | Paso | Col | Passo |
| V | Valley, Canyon | Tal, Cañon | Valle, Cañón | Vallée, Canyon | Vale, Canhão |
| ≚ | Plain | Ebene | Llano | Plaine | Planície |
| ≻ | Cape | Kap | Cabo | Cap | Cabo |
| I | Island | Insel | Isla | Île | Ilha |
| II | Islands | Inseln | Islas | Îles | Ilhas |
| ◆ | Other Topographic Features | Andere Topographische Objekte | Otros Elementos Topográficos | Autres données topographiques | Outros acidentes topográficos |

**ESPAÑOL**

| Nombre | Página | Lat.°' | Long.°' W = Oeste |
|---|---|---|---|
| Ourthe Occidentale ≃ | 56 | 50.08 N | 5.41 E |
| Ourthe Orientale ≃ | 56 | 50.08 N | 5.41 E |
| Ourville-en-Caux | 50 | 49.44 N | 0.36 E |
| Ōu-sammyaku ⩘ | 92 | 38.45 N | 140.50 E |
| Ouse ≃, On., Can. | 212 | 44.17 N | 78.03 W |
| Ouse ≃, Eng., U.K. | 42 | 50.47 N | 0.03 E |
| Ouse ≃, Eng., U.K. | 44 | 53.42 N | 0.41 W |
| Oust ≃ | 32 | 47.39 N | 2.06 W |
| Outaouais, Rivière des → Ottawa ≃ | 176 | 45.20 N | 73.58 W |
| Outardes, Baie aux ⊂ | 186 | 49.02 N | 68.30 W |
| Outardes, Rivière aux ≃ | 176 | 49.04 N | 68.28 W |
| Outardes Est, Rivière aux ≃ | 206 | 45.06 N | 74.04 W |
| Outardes Quatre, Réservoir ⊜[1] | 186 | 49.50 N | 68.58 W |
| Outardes Trois, Barrage ◆[6] | 186 | 49.34 N | 68.48 W |
| Outarville | 50 | 48.13 N | 2.01 E |
| Outcalt | 276 | 40.23 N | 74.24 W |
| Outeniekwaberge ⩘ | 158 | 33.53 S | 22.35 E |
| Outerbridge Crossing ◆[5] | 276 | 40.31 N | 74.15 W |
| Outer Harbour | 168b | 34.47 S | 138.30 E |
| Outer Hebrides II | 46 | 57.45 N | 7.00 W |
| Outer Island I | 190 | 47.03 N | 90.30 W |
| Outer Santa Barbara Passage ⋓ | 228 | 33.10 N | 118.30 W |
| Outer Sister Island I | 166 | 39.39 S | 148.00 E |
| Outjo | 156 | 20.08 S | 16.08 E |
| Outlane | 262 | 53.39 N | 1.53 W |
| Outlet Bay ⊂ | 208 | 37.22 N | 75.49 W |
| Outlook, Sk., Can. | 184 | 51.30 N | 107.03 W |
| Outlook, Mt., U.S. | 198 | 48.53 N | 104.46 W |
| Outokumpu | 26 | 62.44 N | 29.01 E |
| Outpost Mountain ∧ | 180 | 69.08 N | 151.12 W |
| Outreau | 50 | 50.42 N | 1.35 E |
| Outremont | 206 | 45.31 N | 73.38 W |
| Outside Canal ≊ | 226 | 37.13 N | 121.02 W |
| Out Skerries II | 46a | 60.25 N | 0.42 W |
| Outwell | 42 | 52.37 N | 0.14 E |
| Ouvéa I | 175f | 20.30 S | 166.35 E |
| Ouvéa, Lagon d' ⊂ | 175f | 20.33 S | 166.27 E |
| Ouvèze ≃ | 62 | 43.59 N | 4.51 E |
| Ouvidor | 255 | 18.14 S | 47.50 W |
| Ouye, Forêt de l' ♠ | 261 | 48.32 N | 2.00 E |
| Ouyen | 166 | 35.04 S | 142.20 E |
| Ouzinkie | 180 | 57.55 N | 152.30 W |
| Ouzouer-le-Marché | 50 | 47.55 N | 1.32 E |
| Ouzouer-sur-Loire | 50 | 47.46 N | 2.29 E |
| Ouzzal, Oued i-n- V | 148 | 21.35 N | 2.00 E |
| Ovabağ | 130 | 37.43 N | 39.59 E |
| Ovacık, Tür. | 130 | 39.22 N | 39.13 E |
| Ovacık, Tür. | 130 | 41.05 N | 32.55 E |
| Ovada | 62 | 44.38 N | 8.38 E |
| Ovakent | 130 | 38.06 N | 28.02 E |
| Oval | 210 | 41.09 N | 77.11 W |
| Ovalau I | 175g | 17.40 S | 178.48 E |
| Ovalle | 252 | 30.36 S | 71.12 W |
| Ovamboland □[9] | 156 | 17.45 S | 16.30 E |
| Ovana, Cerro ∧ | 246 | 4.38 N | 66.57 W |
| Ovar | 34 | 40.52 N | 8.38 W |
| Ovaro | 64 | 46.29 N | 12.52 E |
| Ovčinino | 82 | 56.02 N | 39.03 E |
| Ovcyno | 265a | 59.48 N | 30.37 E |
| Övedskloster | 41 | 55.41 N | 13.38 E |
| Ovejas | 246 | 9.32 N | 75.14 W |
| Ovelgönne | 52 | 53.20 N | 8.25 E |
| Ovenden | 262 | 53.44 N | 1.53 W |
| Oveng | 152 | 2.25 N | 12.16 E |
| Overath | 56 | 50.55 N | 7.14 E |
| Overberge | 263 | 51.37 N | 7.41 E |
| Overbrook | 198 | 38.46 N | 95.33 W |
| Overbrook ◆[8], Pa., U.S. | 279b | 40.24 N | 79.59 W |
| Overbrook ◆[8], Pa., U.S. | 285 | 39.58 N | 75.16 W |
| Overdinkel | 52 | 52.14 N | 7.01 E |
| Overflakkee I | 52 | 51.45 N | 4.10 E |
| Overflowing ≃ | 184 | 53.10 N | 101.05 W |
| Overhalla | 24 | 64.30 N | 11.57 E |
| Overijse | 56 | 50.46 N | 4.32 E |
| Overijssel □[4] | 52 | 52.25 N | 6.30 E |
| Over Jerstal | 41 | 55.12 N | 9.18 E |
| Överkalix | 24 | 66.21 N | 22.56 E |
| Overland | 219 | 38.42 N | 90.21 W |
| Overland Park | 198 | 38.58 N | 94.40 W |
| Overlea | 208 | 39.22 N | 76.31 W |
| Overloon | 52 | 51.35 N | 5.57 E |
| Övermark (Ylimarkku) | 26 | 62.38 N | 21.30 E |
| Overpeck Creek ≃ | 276 | 40.51 N | 74.02 W |
| Overpelt | 56 | 51.13 N | 5.25 E |
| Overseal | 42 | 52.44 N | 1.34 W |
| Overstrand | 42 | 52.56 N | 1.20 E |
| Overton, Eng., U.K. | 42 | 51.15 N | 1.15 W |
| Overton, Ne., U.S. | 198 | 40.44 N | 99.32 W |
| Overton, Nv., U.S. | 204 | 36.32 N | 114.26 W |
| Overton, Tx., U.S. | 222 | 32.16 N | 94.58 W |
| Overton Arm ⊂ | 204 | 36.20 N | 114.25 W |
| Övertorneå | 24 | 66.23 N | 23.40 E |
| Överum | 26 | 57.59 N | 16.19 E |
| Over Wallop | 42 | 51.09 N | 1.35 W |
| Ovett | 194 | 31.29 N | 89.01 W |
| Ovid, Mi., U.S. | 216 | 43.00 N | 84.22 W |
| Ovid, N.Y., U.S. | 210 | 42.40 N | 76.49 W |
| Ovidiopol' | 78 | 46.17 N | 30.27 E |
| Oviedo, Esp. | 34 | 43.22 N | 5.50 W |
| Oviedo, Fl., U.S. | 220 | 28.40 N | 81.13 W |
| Oviglio | 62 | 44.52 N | 8.29 E |
| Oviken | 26 | 62.59 N | 14.24 E |
| Oviksfjällen ⩘ | 26 | 63.02 N | 13.51 E |
| Ovilla | 222 | 32.32 N | 96.53 W |
| Ovindoli | 66 | 42.08 N | 13.31 E |
| Ovinišče | 76 | 58.22 N | 37.02 E |
| Ovino | 76 | 59.41 N | 33.11 E |
| Ovīši | 76 | 57.34 N | 21.45 E |
| Övörchangaj □[4] | 102 | 46.00 N | 102.30 E |
| Øvre Anarjokka Nasjonalpark ♠ | 24 | 69.00 N | 25.00 E |
| Øvre Ardal | 26 | 61.19 N | 7.48 E |
| Øvre Dividal Nasjonalpark ♠ | 24 | 68.39 N | 19.45 E |
| Øvre Pasvik Nasjonalpark ♠ | 24 | 69.06 N | 28.55 E |
| Øvre Rendal | 26 | 61.53 N | 11.05 E |
| Övre Vättern ⊜ | 40 | 59.52 N | 15.40 E |
| Ovruch | 78 | 51.21 N | 28.49 E |
| Ovs'anikovo | 76 | 60.09 N | 45.16 E |
| Ovs'anka, Ross. | 86 | 55.57 N | 92.33 E |
| Ovs'anka, Ross. | 89 | 53.35 N | 126.57 E |
| Ovs'annikovo | 82 | 56.54 N | 37.33 E |
| Ovstug | 76 | 53.24 N | 33.52 E |
| Ōwada | 268 | 35.49 N | 139.33 E |
| Owaka | 172 | 46.27 S | 169.40 E |
| Owambo ≃ | 156 | 18.45 S | 17.03 E |
| Owando | 152 | 0.29 S | 15.55 E |
| Owaneco | 219 | 39.29 N | 89.12 W |
| Owariashi | 94 | 35.12 N | 137.02 E |
| Owasco | 210 | 42.51 N | 76.28 W |
| Owasco Inlet ≃ | 210 | 42.45 N | 76.28 W |
| Owasco Lake ⊜ | 210 | 42.52 N | 76.32 W |
| Owasco Outlet ≃ | 210 | 43.04 N | 76.39 W |
| Owase | 92 | 34.04 N | 136.12 E |
| Owasso | 196 | 36.16 N | 95.51 W |
| Owatonna | 190 | 44.05 N | 93.13 W |
| Owbeh | 128 | 34.22 N | 63.10 E |
| Owe | 272c | 19.04 N | 73.04 E |
| Owego | 210 | 42.06 N | 76.15 W |
| Owego Creek, East Branch ≃ | 210 | 42.10 N | 76.15 W |
| Owego Creek, West Branch ≃ | 210 | 42.10 N | 76.15 W |
| Owel, Lough ⊜ | 48 | 53.34 N | 7.25 W |
| Owen, Austl. | 168b | 34.16 S | 138.33 E |
| Owen, Dtsch. | 56 | 48.35 N | 9.27 E |
| Owen, In., U.S. | 218 | 38.27 N | 85.34 W |
| Owen, Wi., U.S. | 190 | 44.57 N | 90.33 W |

**FRANÇAIS**

| Nom | Page | Lat.°' | Long.°' W = Ouest |
|---|---|---|---|
| Owen □[6] | 218 | 38.33 N | 84.49 W |
| Owen, Mount ∧ | 172 | 41.33 S | 172.32 E |
| Owenboy ≃ | 48 | 51.48 N | 8.18 W |
| Owendo | 152 | 0.17 N | 9.30 E |
| Owenea ≃ | 48 | 54.47 N | 8.26 W |
| Owen Falls Dam ◆[6] | 154 | 0.27 N | 33.11 E |
| Owen Fracture Zone ✢ | 12 | 12.00 N | 58.00 E |
| Owenkillew ≃ | 48 | 54.44 N | 7.18 W |
| Owenmore ≃ | 48 | 54.07 N | 9.50 W |
| Owen River | 172 | 41.39 S | 172.27 E |
| Owens ≃ | 204 | 36.31 N | 117.57 W |
| Owensboro | 194 | 37.46 N | 87.06 W |
| Owens Creek ≃, Ca., U.S. | 226 | 37.13 N | 120.42 W |
| Owens Creek ≃, Md., U.S. | 208 | 39.33 N | 77.20 W |
| Owens Lake ⊜ | 204 | 36.25 N | 117.56 W |
| Owen Sound | 212 | 44.34 N | 80.56 W |
| Owen Sound ⊂ | 212 | 44.40 N | 80.55 W |
| Owen Stanley Range ⩘ | 164 | 9.20 S | 147.55 E |
| Owensville, In., U.S. | 194 | 38.16 N | 87.41 W |
| Owensville, Mo., U.S. | 219 | 38.20 N | 91.30 W |
| Owensville, Oh., U.S. | 218 | 39.07 N | 84.08 W |
| Owenton, Ky., U.S. | 218 | 38.32 N | 84.50 W |
| Owenton, Va., U.S. | 208 | 37.53 N | 77.06 W |
| Owentown | 222 | 32.26 N | 95.12 W |
| Owerri | 150 | 5.29 N | 7.02 E |
| Owhango | 172 | 39.00 S | 175.23 E |
| Owikeno Lake ⊜ | 182 | 51.41 N | 127.00 W |
| Owings | 208 | 38.43 N | 76.36 W |
| Owings Mills | 284b | 39.25 N | 76.46 W |
| Owingsville | 188 | 38.08 N | 83.45 W |
| Owl ≃, Ab., Can. | 182 | 54.54 N | 111.57 W |
| Owl ≃, Mb., Can. | 176 | 57.51 N | 92.44 W |
| Owl Creek ≃, U.S. | 198 | 44.41 N | 103.29 W |
| Owl Creek ≃, Mt., U.S. | 202 | 45.18 N | 107.21 W |
| Owl Creek ≃, Wy., U.S. | 202 | 43.41 N | 108.11 W |
| Owl Creek, South Fork ≃ | 202 | 43.43 N | 108.32 W |
| Owl Creek Mountains ⩘ | 202 | 43.30 N | 108.35 W |
| Owo | 150 | 7.15 N | 5.37 E |
| Oworonsoki | 273a | 6.33 N | 3.24 E |
| Owosso | 216 | 42.59 N | 84.10 W |
| Owuru ≃ | 273a | 6.39 N | 3.27 E |
| Owyhee | 204 | 41.56 N | 116.05 W |
| Owyhee ≃ | 202 | 43.46 N | 117.02 W |
| Owyhee, Lake ⊜[1] | 202 | 43.28 N | 117.20 W |
| Owyhee, South Fork ≃ | 202 | 42.26 N | 116.53 W |
| Oxapampa | 248 | 10.34 S | 75.24 W |
| Öxarfjörður ⊂ | 24a | 66.15 N | 16.45 W |
| Oxbow, Sk., Can. | 184 | 49.14 N | 102.11 W |
| Oxbow, Mi., U.S. | 281 | 42.38 N | 83.28 W |
| Oxbow, N.Y., U.S. | 212 | 44.17 N | 75.37 W |
| Oxbow Lake ⊜ | 281 | 42.38 N | 83.28 W |
| Ox Creek ≃ | 198 | 48.37 N | 100.17 W |
| Oxelösund | 40 | 58.40 N | 17.06 E |
| Oxford, N.S., Can. | 186 | 45.44 N | 63.52 W |
| Oxford, N.Z. | 172 | 43.18 S | 172.11 E |
| Oxford, Eng., U.K. | 42 | 51.46 N | 1.15 W |
| Oxford, Al., U.S. | 194 | 33.36 N | 85.50 W |
| Oxford, Ct., U.S. | 207 | 41.26 N | 73.07 W |
| Oxford, Fl., U.S. | 220 | 28.55 N | 82.02 W |
| Oxford, In., U.S. | 216 | 40.31 N | 87.14 W |
| Oxford, Ia., U.S. | 190 | 41.43 N | 91.47 W |
| Oxford, Ks., U.S. | 198 | 37.16 N | 97.10 W |
| Oxford, Ky., U.S. | 218 | 38.16 N | 84.30 W |
| Oxford, Me., U.S. | 188 | 44.07 N | 70.29 W |
| Oxford, Md., U.S. | 208 | 38.41 N | 76.10 W |
| Oxford, Ma., U.S. | 207 | 42.07 N | 71.51 W |
| Oxford, Mi., U.S. | 216 | 42.49 N | 83.15 W |
| Oxford, Ms., U.S. | 194 | 34.21 N | 89.31 W |
| Oxford, Ne., U.S. | 198 | 40.15 N | 99.38 W |
| Oxford, N.J., U.S. | 210 | 40.48 N | 74.59 W |
| Oxford, N.Y., U.S. | 210 | 42.26 N | 75.35 W |
| Oxford, N.C., U.S. | 192 | 36.18 N | 78.35 W |
| Oxford, Oh., U.S. | 218 | 39.30 N | 84.44 W |
| Oxford, Pa., U.S. | 208 | 39.47 N | 75.58 W |
| Oxford, Wi., U.S. | 190 | 43.46 N | 89.34 W |
| Oxford □[6] | 212 | 43.08 N | 80.50 W |
| Oxford Falls | 274a | 33.44 S | 151.15 E |
| Oxford House | 184 | 54.56 N | 95.16 W |
| Oxford House Indian Reserve ◆[4] | 184 | 54.54 N | 95.15 W |
| Oxford Junction | 190 | 41.59 N | 90.57 W |
| Oxford Lake ⊜ | 184 | 54.51 N | 95.37 W |
| Oxford Peak ∧ | 202 | 42.16 N | 112.06 W |
| Oxfordshire □[6] | 42 | 51.50 N | 1.15 W |
| Oxford Valley Mall ◆[9] | 285 | 40.11 N | 74.53 W |
| Oxhey | 260 | 51.39 N | 0.23 W |
| Oxie | 41 | 55.33 N | 13.04 E |
| Oxkutzcab | 232 | 20.18 N | 89.25 W |
| Oxley | 166 | 34.12 S | 144.06 E |
| Oxley Creek ≃ | 171a | 27.32 S | 153.00 E |
| Oxnard | 228 | 34.11 N | 119.10 W |
| Oxon Hill | 284c | 38.48 N | 76.59 W |
| Oxon Run ≃ | 284b | 38.49 N | 77.00 W |
| Ox Pasture Brook ≃ | 283 | 42.45 N | 70.54 W |
| Oxshott | 260 | 51.20 N | 0.21 W |
| Oxted | 42 | 51.16 N | 0.01 W |
| Oxtongue ≃ | 212 | 45.19 N | 79.01 W |
| Oxtongue Lake ⊜ | 212 | 45.22 N | 78.55 W |
| Oxus → Amu Darya ≃ | 72 | 43.40 N | 59.01 E |
| Oya, Malay. | 112 | 2.52 N | 111.53 E |
| Ōya, Nihon | 96 | 35.20 N | 134.40 E |
| Oya ≃ | 112 | 2.52 N | 111.52 E |
| Oyabe | 94 | 36.40 N | 136.52 E |
| Oyabe ≃ | 94 | 36.48 N | 137.04 E |
| Ōya-ji ʊ[1] | 94 | 36.38 N | 139.48 E |
| Ōyake-yama ∧[2] | 270 | 34.48 N | 135.51 E |
| Oyalı | 130 | 37.14 N | 41.45 E |
| Oyama, B.C., Can. | 182 | 50.07 N | 119.22 W |
| Oyama, Nihon | 94 | 36.18 N | 139.48 E |
| Ōyama, Nihon | 94 | 36.36 N | 137.18 E |
| Ōyama, Nihon | 94 | 35.21 N | 139.00 E |
| Ōyama, Nihon | 268 | 35.36 N | 139.22 E |
| Ōyamada | 94 | 34.46 N | 136.13 E |
| Ōyamazaki | 270 | 34.54 N | 135.42 E |
| Oyameyo, Volcán ∧[1] | 286a | 19.10 N | 99.11 W |
| Oyan | 152 | 0.02 N | 10.17 E |
| Ōyano | 92 | 32.35 N | 130.26 E |
| Oyapock (Oiapoque) ≃ | 250 | 4.08 N | 51.40 W |
| Oyashirazu ♠ | 94 | 36.59 N | 137.40 E |
| Oybin | 54 | 50.50 N | 14.44 E |
| Oye-et-Pallet | 58 | 46.51 N | 6.20 E |
| Oyem | 152 | 1.37 N | 11.35 E |
| Oyen | 184 | 51.22 N | 110.28 W |
| Øyeren ⊜ | 26 | 59.48 N | 11.14 E |
| Oykel ≃ | 46 | 57.56 N | 4.25 W |
| Oykel Bridge | 46 | 57.58 N | 4.43 W |
| Oy-Mittelberg | 58 | 47.38 N | 10.28 E |
| Oymyakon → Ojm'akon | 74 | 63.28 N | 142.49 E |
| Oyo, Congo | 152 | 0.01 N | 15.54 E |
| Oyo, Nig. | 150 | 7.51 N | 3.56 E |
| Oyo ≃ | 115a | 7.57 S | 110.22 E |
| Ōyodo | 96 | 34.23 N | 135.48 E |
| Ōyodo ◆[8] | 270 | 34.43 N | 135.30 E |
| Ōyodo ≃ | 92 | 31.53 N | 131.28 E |
| Oyón | 248 | 10.39 S | 76.47 W |
| Oyonnax | 58 | 46.15 N | 5.40 E |
| Ōyorogi-san ∧ | 96 | 35.05 N | 132.51 E |
| Oyotún | 248 | 6.51 S | 79.19 W |
| Oyster | 208 | 37.17 N | 75.55 W |
| Oyster Bay | 210 | 40.51 N | 73.31 W |
| Oyster Bay ⊂ | 276 | 40.55 N | 73.30 W |
| Oyster Bay Cove | 276 | 40.52 N | 73.31 W |
| Oyster Bay Harbor ⊂ | 276 | 40.53 N | 73.32 W |
| Oyster Creek | 222 | 29.00 N | 95.20 W |
| Oyster Creek ≃ | 222 | 28.59 N | 95.18 W |
| Oyster Point ∧ | 282 | 37.50 N | 121.52 W |
| Oyster Point › | 168b | 34.55 S | 137.48 E |

**PORTUGUÊS**

| Nome | Página | Lat.°' | Long.°' W = Oeste |
|---|---|---|---|
| Oyster Rock I[2] | 272c | 18.54 N | 72.50 E |
| Oysterville | 224 | 46.33 N | 124.02 W |
| Øystese | 26 | 60.23 N | 6.13 E |
| Oyten | 52 | 53.04 N | 9.01 E |
| Ozaki | 268 | 35.59 N | 139.51 E |
| Ozamiz | 116 | 8.08 N | 123.50 E |
| Ozanne ≃ | 50 | 48.11 N | 1.22 E |
| Ozark, Al., U.S. | 194 | 31.27 N | 85.38 W |
| Ozark, Ar., U.S. | 194 | 35.29 N | 93.49 W |
| Ozark, Mo., U.S. | 194 | 37.01 N | 93.12 W |
| Ozark National Scenic Riverways ♠ | 194 | 37.10 N | 91.10 W |
| Ozark Plateau ⩘[1] | 194 | 37.00 N | 93.00 W |
| Ozark Reservoir ⊜[1] | 194 | 35.35 N | 94.00 W |
| Ozarks, Lake of the ⊜[1] | 194 | 38.10 N | 92.50 W |
| Ozaukee □[6] | 216 | 44.14 N | 88.00 W |
| Ózd | 30 | 48.14 N | 20.18 E |
| Oze ≃ | 96 | 34.12 N | 132.14 E |
| Ozeblin ∧ | 36 | 44.35 N | 15.53 E |
| Ozek | 86 | 46.35 N | 60.41 E |
| Ozereckoje | 82 | 56.04 N | 37.23 E |
| Oželelje | 82 | 54.48 N | 38.17 E |
| Oželelki | 82 | 55.51 N | 38.52 E |
| Ozeriščе | 76 | 54.48 N | 33.13 E |
| Ozerki, Ross. | 80 | 51.13 N | 53.56 E |
| Ozerki, Ross. | 80 | 51.32 N | 45.16 E |
| Ozerki, Ross. | 80 | 52.01 N | 45.29 E |
| Ozerki, Ross. | 86 | 53.38 N | 83.44 E |
| Ozerki, Ross. | 265a | 59.54 N | 30.44 E |
| Ozerna ≃ | 82 | 55.44 N | 36.08 E |
| Ozerne | 78 | 50.11 N | 28.42 E |
| Ozerninskoje vodochranilišče ⊜[1] | 82 | 55.45 N | 36.15 E |
| Ozernovskij | 74 | 51.30 N | 156.31 E |
| Ozernyj | 180 | 66.24 N | 179.06 W |
| Ozero | 80 | 56.58 N | 44.43 E |
| Ozery | 82 | 54.51 N | 38.34 E |
| Ozette Lake ⊜ | 224 | 48.06 N | 124.38 W |
| Ozgoryš | 85 | 41.15 N | 74.45 E |
| Ozieri | 71 | 40.35 N | 9.00 E |
| Ozimek | 30 | 50.41 N | 18.13 E |
| Ozinki | 80 | 51.12 N | 49.45 E |
| Ozirs'k | 78 | 51.43 N | 26.24 E |
| Ožogino, ozero ⊜ | 74 | 69.16 N | 146.36 E |
| Ozoir-la-Ferrière | 261 | 48.46 N | 2.40 E |
| Ozona, Fl., U.S. | 220 | 28.04 N | 82.46 W |
| Ozona, Tx., U.S. | 196 | 30.42 N | 101.12 W |
| Ozone Park ◆[8] | 276 | 40.40 N | 73.51 W |
| Ozorków | 30 | 51.58 N | 19.19 E |
| Oz'ornaja | 86 | 51.08 N | 60.50 E |
| Oz'ornoje, Kaz. | 86 | 53.25 N | 63.15 E |
| Oz'ornoje, Ross. | 80 | 51.41 N | 44.55 E |
| Oz'ornoje, Ross. | 80 | 51.46 N | 51.28 E |
| Oz'ornoje, Ross. | 86 | 56.48 N | 71.15 E |
| Oz'ornyj | 80 | 57.10 N | 40.59 E |
| Oz'orsk | 76 | 54.25 N | 22.01 E |
| Oz'orskij | 89 | 46.36 N | 143.08 E |
| Ozouer-le-Voulgis | 261 | 48.40 N | 2.47 E |
| Özpınar | 130 | 37.57 N | 42.16 E |
| Ōzu, Nihon | 92 | 32.52 N | 130.52 E |
| Ōzu, Nihon | 96 | 33.30 N | 132.33 E |
| Ozubulu | 150 | 5.57 N | 6.51 E |
| Ozuluama | 234 | 21.40 N | 97.51 W |
| Ozumba | 234 | 19.03 N | 98.48 W |
| Ozurgeti | 84 | 41.56 N | 42.00 E |

**P**

| Nome | Página | Lat.°' | Long.°' W = Oeste |
|---|---|---|---|
| Pâ | 150 | 11.33 N | 3.15 W |
| Paagoumène | 175f | 20.29 S | 164.11 E |
| Paal | 56 | 51.02 N | 5.11 E |
| Paama □[8] | 175f | 16.28 S | 168.18 E |
| Paama I | 175f | 16.28 S | 168.14 E |
| Paar ≃ | 60 | 48.45 N | 11.33 E |
| Paardekraal Monument ⊥ | 273d | 26.06 S | 27.47 E |
| Paaren | 264a | 52.39 N | 12.59 E |
| Paarl | 158 | 33.45 S | 18.56 E |
| Paasbach ≃ | 263 | 51.25 N | 7.11 E |
| Paauilo | 229d | 20.02 N | 155.22 W |
| Pabarabuk | 164 | 6.05 S | 144.05 E |
| Pabbay I, Scot., U.K. | 46 | 56.51 N | 7.35 W |
| Pabbay I, Scot., U.K. | 46 | 57.46 N | 7.15 W |
| Pabbi | 123 | 34.01 N | 71.47 E |
| Pabbiring, Kepulauan II | 112 | 4.55 S | 119.25 E |
| Pabean | 112 | 6.50 S | 115.19 E |
| Pabellón, Punta › | 254 | 43.14 S | 74.23 W |
| Pabellón de Arteaga | 234 | 22.10 N | 102.21 W |
| Pabellones, Ensenada ⊂ | 232 | 24.27 N | 107.36 W |
| Pabianice | 30 | 51.40 N | 19.22 E |
| Pabillonis | 71 | 39.35 N | 8.43 E |
| Pablo | 202 | 47.36 N | 114.07 W |
| Pābna | 124 | 24.00 N | 89.15 E |
| Pabo | 154 | 3.00 N | 32.09 E |
| Pabradė | 76 | 54.59 N | 25.44 E |
| Paca | 115b | 8.29 S | 120.11 E |
| Pacaás Novas, Parque Nacional ♠ | 248 | 11.10 S | 63.30 W |
| Pacaás Novos ≃ | 248 | 10.51 S | 65.20 W |
| Pacaás Novos, Serra dos ⩘ | 248 | 10.45 S | 64.15 W |
| Pacaembu | 255 | 21.34 S | 51.17 W |
| Pacaembú, Estádio do ♠ | 287b | 23.33 S | 46.39 W |
| Pacajá ≃ | 250 | 1.56 S | 50.50 W |
| Pacajus | 250 | 4.10 S | 38.28 W |
| Pacaltsdorp | 158 | 34.00 S | 22.28 E |
| Pacaraima, Sierra de → Pakaraima Mountains ⩘ | 246 | 5.30 N | 60.40 W |
| Pacarán | 248 | 12.52 S | 76.03 W |
| Pacaraos | 248 | 11.11 S | 76.44 W |
| Pacasmayo | 248 | 7.24 S | 79.34 W |
| Pacatuba | 250 | 3.58 S | 38.37 W |
| Pace, Fl., U.S. | 194 | 30.35 N | 87.09 W |
| Pace, Ms., U.S. | 194 | 33.47 N | 90.51 W |
| Paceco | 70 | 37.59 N | 12.33 E |
| Pačelma, Ross. | 80 | 53.15 N | 43.21 E |
| Pačelma, Ross. | 80 | 53.20 N | 43.20 E |
| Pacet | 115a | 6.45 S | 107.03 E |
| Pachača | 74 | 60.34 N | 169.03 E |
| Pachacamac ⊥ | 248 | 12.14 S | 76.52 W |
| Pachamba | 126 | 24.12 N | 86.16 E |
| Fachaug Pond ⊜ | 207 | 41.34 N | 71.54 W |
| Pacheco | 226 | 37.59 N | 122.04 W |
| Pacheco, Isla I | 254 | 52.17 S | 74.45 W |
| Pacheco Creek ≃ | 226 | 36.58 N | 121.28 W |
| Pacheco Pass )( | 226 | 37.03 N | 121.13 W |
| Pāchh Elāsin | 126 | 24.08 N | 89.54 E |
| Pachino | 70 | 36.43 N | 15.05 E |
| Pachitea ≃ | 248 | 8.46 S | 74.32 W |
| Pachiza | 248 | 7.16 S | 76.46 W |
| Pachkoli ◆[8] | 272c | 19.08 N | 72.54 E |
| Pachmarhi | 124 | 22.28 N | 78.26 E |
| Pacho | 246 | 5.08 N | 74.10 W |
| Pachomovo | 82 | 54.38 N | 37.33 E |
| Pachor | 124 | 23.42 N | 76.44 E |
| Pāchora | 122 | 20.40 N | 75.21 E |
| Pachotnyj Ugol | 80 | 52.58 N | 41.56 E |
| Pachra ≃ | 82 | 55.32 N | 37.59 E |
| Pachtaabad | 85 | 38.28 N | 68.10 E |
| Pachuca [de Soto] | 234 | 20.07 N | 98.44 W |
| Paciência ◆[8] | 256 | 22.55 S | 43.38 W |
| Pacific, B.C., Can. | 182 | 54.46 N | 128.17 W |
| Pacific, Mo., U.S. | 219 | 38.28 N | 90.44 W |
| Pacific, Wa., U.S. | 224 | 47.15 N | 122.14 W |
| Pacific □[6] | 224 | 46.30 N | 123.39 W |
| Pacifica | 226 | 37.37 N | 122.29 W |
| Pacific-Antarctic Ridge ✢[3] | 6 | 62.00 S | 157.00 W |
| Pacific Beach | 224 | 47.12 N | 124.12 W |
| Pacific City | 224 | 45.12 N | 123.57 W |
| Pacific Creek ≃ | 200 | 42.08 N | 109.24 W |
| Pacific Gardens | 226 | 37.58 N | 121.20 W |
| Pacific Grove | 226 | 36.38 N | 121.56 W |

| | | | |
|---|---|---|---|
| Pacific Missile Test Center ■ | 228 | 34.07 N | 119.07 W |
| Pacífico, Océano → Pacific Ocean ⍑[1] | 6 | 10.00 S | 150.00 W |
| Pacific Ocean ⍑[1] | 4 | 10.00 S | 150.00 W |
| Pacific Ocean ⍑[1] | 6 | 10.00 S | 150.00 W |
| Pacifico Mountain ∧ | 228 | 34.23 N | 118.02 W |
| Pacific Palisades ◆[8] | 280 | 34.03 N | 118.32 W |
| Pacific Ranges ⩘ | 182 | 50.45 N | 125.30 W |
| Pacific Rim National Park ♠ | 182 | 48.45 N | 125.40 W |
| Pacifique, Océan → Pacific Ocean ⍑[1] | 6 | 10.00 S | 150.00 W |
| Pacijan Island I | 116 | 10.39 N | 124.20 E |
| Pacinan, Tanjung › | 115a | 7.36 S | 114.02 E |
| Paciran | 115a | 6.52 S | 112.20 E |
| Pacitan | 115a | 8.12 S | 111.07 E |
| Pack | 61 | 46.58 N | 14.59 E |
| Packanack Lake ⊜ | 276 | 40.56 N | 74.15 W |
| Packard Mountain ∧[2] | 207 | 42.28 N | 72.21 W |
| Páckevei-Duna ≃[1] | 264c | 47.19 N | 19.02 E |
| Pack Monadnock Mountain ∧ | 207 | 42.52 N | 71.52 W |
| Packsattel )( | 61 | 46.58 N | 14.58 E |
| Packwood | 224 | 46.36 N | 121.40 W |
| Packwood Lake ⊜ | 224 | 46.35 N | 121.34 W |
| Paclión | 248 | 10.18 S | 77.07 W |
| Pacock Brook ≃ | 276 | 41.05 N | 74.31 W |
| Paço de Arcos | 266c | 38.42 N | 9.17 W |
| Paço do Lumiar | 250 | 2.31 S | 44.07 W |
| Pacohuaras ≃ | 248 | 10.04 S | 65.46 W |
| Pacoima ◆[8] | 280 | 34.16 N | 118.26 W |
| Pacolet ≃ | 192 | 34.50 N | 81.27 W |
| Pacolet Mills | 192 | 34.55 N | 81.44 W |
| Pacora | 246 | 9.05 N | 79.17 W |
| Pacov | 30 | 49.28 N | 15.00 E |
| Pacquet | 186 | 49.59 N | 55.53 W |
| Pacuare ≃ | 236 | 10.14 N | 83.17 W |
| Pacuí ≃ | 255 | 16.46 S | 45.01 W |
| Pacuneiro ≃ | 255 | 13.02 S | 53.25 W |
| Pacy-sur-Eure | 50 | 49.01 N | 1.23 E |
| Paczkow | 30 | 50.27 N | 17.00 E |
| Padada | 116 | 6.42 N | 125.22 E |
| Padada ≃ | 116 | 6.42 N | 125.23 E |
| Padaido, Kepulauan II | 164 | 1.15 S | 136.30 E |
| Padam | 123 | 33.28 N | 76.53 E |
| Padamarang, Pulau I | 112 | 4.07 S | 121.24 E |
| Padamo ≃ | 246 | 2.54 N | 65.17 W |
| Padampur | 120 | 20.59 N | 83.04 E |
| Padang, Indon. | 112 | 1.39 S | 108.55 E |
| Padang, Indon. | 112 | 2.59 N | 105.40 E |
| Padang, Indon. | 112 | 6.11 S | 120.26 E |
| Padang, Indon. | 112 | 0.57 S | 100.21 E |
| Padang, Pulau I | 114 | 1.10 N | 102.20 E |
| Padang Besar | 114 | 6.40 N | 100.19 E |
| Padangbetuah | 112 | 3.39 S | 102.13 E |
| Padang Endau | 114 | 2.40 N | 103.37 E |
| Padangpanjang | 112 | 0.27 S | 100.25 E |
| Padangsidempuan | 114 | 1.22 N | 99.16 E |
| Padangtiji | 114 | 5.22 N | 95.50 E |
| Padangtikar, Pulau I | 112 | 0.50 S | 109.30 E |
| Padang Tungku | 114 | 4.14 N | 101.59 E |
| Padany | 24 | 63.17 N | 33.22 E |
| Padas | 115a | 7.25 S | 111.32 E |
| Padas ≃ | 112 | 5.14 N | 115.34 E |
| Padasjoki | 26 | 61.21 N | 25.17 E |
| Padauari ≃ | 246 | 0.15 S | 64.05 W |
| Padborg | 41 | 54.49 N | 9.22 E |
| Padcaya | 248 | 21.52 S | 64.48 W |
| Paddington ◆[8] | 260 | 51.31 N | 0.10 W |
| Paddington Station ◆[5] | 260 | 51.31 N | 0.11 W |
| Paddle ≃ | 182 | 54.05 N | 114.15 W |
| Paddle Prairie | 176 | 57.57 N | 117.29 W |
| Paddock Lake | 216 | 42.34 N | 88.06 W |
| Paddock Wood | 42 | 51.11 N | 0.23 E |
| Padea | 38 | 44.01 N | 23.52 E |
| Padea-besar I | 112 | 3.30 S | 123.05 E |
| Padeghar | 272c | 18.58 N | 73.03 E |
| Paden City | 188 | 39.36 N | 80.56 W |
| Paderborn | 52 | 51.43 N | 8.45 E |
| Paderno Dugnano | 266b | 45.34 N | 9.10 E |
| Paderno Ponchielli | 64 | 45.14 N | 9.55 E |
| Padghe | 272c | 19.03 N | 73.07 E |
| Padibe | 154 | 3.28 N | 32.50 E |
| Padiham | 44 | 53.49 N | 2.19 W |
| Padilla | 248 | 19.19 S | 64.20 W |
| Padilla Bay ⊂ | 224 | 48.35 N | 122.32 W |
| Padjelanta Nationalpark ♠ | 24 | 67.28 N | 16.41 E |
| Padle | 272c | 19.09 N | 73.03 E |
| Padloping Island I | 176 | 67.07 N | 62.35 W |
| Padma → Ganges ≃ | 124 | 23.22 N | 90.32 E |
| Padola | 64 | 46.36 N | 12.28 E |
| Padoue → Padova | 64 | 45.25 N | 11.53 E |
| Padova | 64 | 45.25 N | 11.53 E |
| Padova □[4] | 64 | 45.21 N | 11.49 E |
| Padovka | 80 | 52.28 N | 49.31 E |
| Pādra | 120 | 22.14 N | 73.05 E |
| Padrão, Ponta do › | 152 | 6.03 S | 12.18 E |
| Padrauna | 124 | 26.55 N | 83.59 E |
| Padre Bernardo | 255 | 15.21 S | 48.30 W |
| Padre Brito | 256 | 21.18 S | 43.59 W |
| Padre Burgos | 116 | 10.02 N | 125.01 E |
| Padre Island I | 196 | 27.00 N | 97.15 W |
| Padre Island National Seashore ♠ | 196 | 27.00 N | 97.25 W |
| Padre Miguel ◆[8] | 287a | 22.53 S | 43.26 W |
| Padre Paraíso | 255 | 17.06 S | 41.31 W |
| Padria | 71 | 40.24 N | 8.38 E |
| Padrón | 34 | 42.44 N | 8.40 W |
| Padrone, Cape › | 158 | 33.46 S | 26.30 E |
| Padrt' | 60 | 49.40 N | 13.46 E |
| Padstow, Austl. | 274a | 33.57 S | 151.02 E |
| Padstow, Eng., U.K. | 42 | 50.33 N | 4.56 W |
| Padsville | 76 | 55.09 N | 27.58 E |
| Padua → Padova | 64 | 45.25 N | 11.53 E |
| Paducah, Ky., U.S. | 194 | 37.05 N | 88.36 W |
| Paducah, Tx., U.S. | 196 | 34.00 N | 100.18 W |
| Padula | 68 | 40.20 N | 15.39 E |
| Paduli | 68 | 41.10 N | 14.53 E |
| Padunskaja | 86 | 55.02 N | 85.02 E |
| Paea | 174s | 17.41 S | 149.35 W |
| Paedun | 98 | 35.03 N | 128.21 E |
| Paekakariki | 172 | 40.59 S | 174.57 E |
| Paektu-san ∧ | 98 | 42.00 N | 128.03 E |
| Paengaroa | 172 | 37.49 S | 176.25 E |
| Paengnyŏng-do I | 98 | 37.57 N | 124.40 E |
| Paerdegat Basin ⊂ | 276 | 40.37 N | 73.54 W |
| Paeroa | 172 | 37.23 S | 175.40 E |
| Paesana | 62 | 44.41 N | 7.16 E |
| Paese | 64 | 45.40 N | 12.10 E |
| Paestum ⊥ | 68 | 40.25 N | 15.00 E |
| Paete | 116 | 14.23 N | 121.29 E |
| Páez ≃ | 246 | 2.28 N | 75.34 W |
| Pafúri | 156 | 22.27 S | 31.21 E |
| Pag | 36 | 44.27 N | 15.04 E |
| Pag, Otok I | 36 | 44.30 N | 15.00 E |
| Paga | 150 | 10.58 N | 1.06 W |
| Pagadenbaru | 115a | 6.28 S | 107.48 E |
| Pagadian | 116 | 7.49 N | 123.25 E |
| Pagadian Bay ⊂ | 116 | 7.48 N | 123.31 E |
| Pagai Selatan, Pulau I | 112 | 3.00 S | 100.20 E |
| Pagai Utara, Pulau I | 112 | 2.42 S | 100.07 E |
| Pagalungan | 116 | 7.04 N | 124.41 E |
| Pagan | 110 | 21.10 N | 94.51 E |
| Pagan I | 108 | 18.07 N | 145.46 E |
| Pagancillo | 252 | 29.34 S | 68.03 W |
| Paganella ∧ | 64 | 46.08 N | 11.02 E |
| Pagani | 68 | 40.45 N | 14.37 E |
| Paganica | 66 | 42.21 N | 13.28 E |
| Paganico | 66 | 42.56 N | 11.16 E |
| Pagaralam | 112 | 4.01 S | 103.16 E |
| Pagasitikós Kólpos ⊂ | 38 | 39.15 N | 22.51 E |

| | | | |
|---|---|---|---|
| Pagatan | 112 | 3.36 S | 115.56 E |
| Pagato ≃ | 184 | 55.49 N | 102.05 W |
| Pagato Lake ⊜ | 184 | 56.08 N | 102.30 W |
| Pagbilao | 116 | 13.58 N | 121.41 E |
| Pagbilao Grande Island I | 116 | 13.55 N | 121.46 E |
| Pagdanan Bay ⊂ | 116 | 10.31 N | 119.15 E |
| Page, Az., U.S. | 200 | 36.54 N | 111.28 W |
| Page, N.D., U.S. | 198 | 47.09 N | 97.34 W |
| Page Field ⊠ | 220 | 26.35 N | 81.52 W |
| Pagėgiai | 76 | 55.09 N | 21.54 E |
| Pageland | 192 | 34.46 N | 80.23 W |
| Page Manor | 218 | 39.45 N | 84.06 W |
| Pager ≃ | 154 | 3.09 N | 32.30 E |
| Pagerdewa | 112 | 3.46 S | 105.18 E |
| Paget, Mount ∧ | 244 | 54.26 S | 36.33 W |
| Paghmān | 120 | 34.36 N | 68.57 E |
| Paglia ≃ | 66 | 42.42 N | 12.11 E |
| Pagliara | 70 | 37.59 N | 15.22 E |
| Paglieta | 66 | 42.10 N | 14.30 E |
| Pagliete, Bonifica delle ◆[1] | 267a | 41.53 N | 12.12 E |
| Pagny-sur-Moselle | 56 | 48.59 N | 6.01 E |
| Pago Bay ⊂ | 174p | 13.25 N | 144.48 E |
| Pagoda Peak ∧ | 200 | 40.10 N | 107.20 W |
| Pagoda Point › | 110 | 15.57 N | 94.15 E |
| Pagon, Bukit ∧ | 112 | 4.18 N | 115.19 E |
| Pago Pago | 174u | 14.16 S | 170.42 W |
| Pago Pago Harbor ⊂ | 174u | 14.17 S | 170.40 W |
| Pago Pago International Airport ⊠ | 174u | 14.20 S | 170.43 W |
| Pagosa Springs | 200 | 37.16 N | 107.00 W |
| Pagote | 272c | 18.54 N | 72.59 E |
| Pagouda | 150 | 9.45 N | 1.19 E |
| Pagri | 124 | 27.44 N | 89.09 E |
| Pagsangahan | 116 | 13.13 N | 122.33 E |
| Pagsanjan | 116 | 14.15 N | 121.25 E |
| Paguate | 200 | 35.08 N | 107.22 W |
| Pagudpud | 116 | 18.34 N | 120.47 E |
| Pagueras, Torrente de ≃ | 266d | 41.28 N | 1.58 E |
| Paguyaman ≃ | 112 | 0.31 N | 122.38 E |
| Pagwi | 164 | 4.03 S | 143.02 E |
| Pah | 84 | 39.08 N | 39.40 E |
| Pahādi ◆[8] | 272c | 19.10 N | 72.51 E |
| Pahala | 229d | 19.12 N | 155.28 W |
| Pahalgam | 123 | 34.02 N | 75.20 E |
| Pahang □[3] | 114 | 3.30 N | 102.45 E |
| Pahang ≃ | 114 | 3.32 N | 103.28 E |
| Páhara, Laguna ⊂ | 236 | 14.18 N | 83.15 W |
| Pahāsu | 124 | 28.11 N | 78.03 E |
| Pahau Point › | 229b | 21.49 N | 160.15 W |
| Pahi | 114 | 5.28 N | 102.13 E |
| Pahia Point › | 172 | 46.19 S | 167.41 E |
| Pahiatua | 172 | 40.27 S | 175.50 E |
| Pahlād Garhi | 272a | 28.40 N | 77.21 E |
| Pahlavī → Bandar-e Anzalī | 128 | 37.28 N | 49.27 E |
| Pahoa | 229d | 19.29 N | 154.57 W |
| Pahokee | 220 | 26.49 N | 80.39 W |
| Pahost, Bela. | 76 | 53.51 N | 29.09 E |
| Pahost, Bela. | 76 | 52.51 N | 27.39 E |
| Pahraničny | 76 | 53.07 N | 23.58 E |
| Pahrump | 204 | 36.12 N | 115.58 W |
| Pahsimeroi ≃ | 202 | 44.41 N | 114.03 W |
| Pahuatlán de Valle | 234 | 20.17 N | 98.09 W |
| Pahvant Range ⩘ | 200 | 38.45 N | 112.15 W |
| Pai | 110 | 19.19 N | 98.27 E |
| Pai ≃ | 110 | 19.09 N | 97.33 E |
| Pai, Ilha do I | 287a | 22.59 S | 43.05 W |
| Paia | 229a | 20.54 N | 156.22 W |
| Paianía | 267c | 37.57 N | 23.51 E |
| Paicines | 226 | 36.44 N | 121.17 W |
| Paico | 248 | 14.02 S | 73.39 W |
| Paide | 76 | 58.54 N | 25.33 E |
| Paidorzu, Monte ∧ | 71 | 40.30 N | 9.05 E |
| Paifangchang | 107 | 30.31 N | 106.38 E |
| Paige | 222 | 30.13 N | 97.07 W |
| Paignton | 42 | 50.26 N | 3.34 W |
| Paiguano | 252 | 30.01 S | 70.32 W |
| Paihia | 172 | 35.17 S | 174.05 E |
| Paiho | 100 | 23.21 N | 120.25 E |
| Paiján | 248 | 7.44 S | 79.19 W |
| Päijänne ⊜ | 26 | 61.35 N | 25.30 E |
| Pāikgācha | 126 | 22.35 N | 89.20 E |
| Paikü Co ⊜ | 124 | 28.48 N | 85.36 E |
| Pail | 123 | 32.38 N | 72.27 E |
| Paila ≃ | 248 | 16.02 S | 64.12 W |
| Paila, Sierra la ⩘ | 196 | 25.50 N | 101.30 W |
| Pailin | 110 | 12.51 N | 102.36 E |
| Pailitas | 246 | 8.58 N | 73.38 W |
| Paillaco | 254 | 40.04 S | 72.53 W |
| Pailolo Channel ⋓ | 229a | 21.05 N | 156.42 W |
| Pailoutou | 106 | 30.56 N | 121.16 E |
| Pailoutun | 104 | 40.44 N | 122.49 E |
| Paimboeuf | 32 | 47.17 N | 2.02 W |
| Paimio | 26 | 60.27 N | 22.42 E |
| Paimpol | 32 | 48.46 N | 3.03 W |
| Painan | 112 | 1.21 S | 100.34 E |
| Paincourt | 214 | 42.23 N | 82.17 W |
| Painesdale | 190 | 47.02 N | 88.40 W |
| Painesville | 214 | 41.43 N | 81.14 W |
| Painscastle | 42 | 52.07 N | 3.12 W |
| Painshawfield | 44 | 54.56 N | 1.54 W |
| Painswick | 42 | 51.48 N | 2.11 W |
| Paint ≃ | 190 | 45.58 N | 88.15 W |
| Paint Creek ≃, Mi., U.S. | 281 | 42.06 N | 83.36 W |
| Paint Creek ≃, Oh., U.S. | 218 | 39.18 N | 82.56 W |
| Paint Creek ≃, Pa., U.S. | 214 | 41.10 N | 79.28 W |
| Paint Creek ≃, Tx., U.S. | 196 | 30.18 N | 99.54 W |
| Paint Creek, East Fork ≃ | 218 | 39.32 N | 83.25 W |
| Paint Creek, North Fork ≃ | 218 | 39.18 N | 83.02 W |
| Paint Creek Lake ⊜[1] | 218 | 39.15 N | 83.22 W |
| Painted Desert ◆[2] | 200 | 36.00 N | 111.20 W |
| Painted Post | 210 | 42.09 N | 77.05 W |
| Painted Rock Reservoir ⊜[1] | 200 | 33.00 N | 112.50 W |
| Painten | 60 | 49.00 N | 11.49 E |
| Painter | 208 | 37.35 N | 75.47 W |
| Painter Creek ≃ | 218 | 40.05 N | 84.21 W |
| Paintertown | 279b | 40.21 N | 79.42 W |
| Paint Lake ⊜ | 184 | 55.28 N | 97.57 W |
| Paint Rock | 196 | 31.30 N | 99.55 W |
| Paint Rock ≃ | 194 | 34.28 N | 86.28 W |
| Paintsville | 192 | 37.48 N | 82.48 W |
| Paiolinho | 256 | 21.52 S | 45.54 W |
| Pai Pobre, Morro do ∧ | 287b | 23.40 S | 46.55 W |
| Paisco | 64 | 46.04 N | 10.17 E |
| Paisha | 100 | 23.40 N | 119.35 E |
| Paisley, Austl. | 274b | 37.51 S | 144.51 E |
| Paisley, On., Can. | 212 | 44.18 N | 81.16 W |
| Paisley, Scot., U.K. | 46 | 55.50 N | 4.26 W |
| Paisley, Fl., U.S. | 220 | 28.59 N | 81.32 W |
| Paisley, Or., U.S. | 202 | 42.41 N | 120.32 W |
| Païta, N. Cal. | 175f | 22.08 S | 166.22 E |
| Paita, Perú | 248 | 5.06 S | 81.07 W |
| Paita, Bahía de ⊂ | 248 | 5.04 S | 81.05 W |
| Paitan | 100 | 23.31 N | 113.46 E |
| Paitan ≃ | 116 | 6.30 N | 117.30 E |
| Paitan, Teluk ⊂ | 116 | 6.45 N | 117.20 E |
| Paiton | 115a | 7.43 S | 113.30 E |
| Paiva | 256 | 21.18 S | 43.25 W |
| Paiva ≃ | 34 | 41.04 N | 8.16 W |
| Paizhou | 100 | 30.13 N | 113.56 E |
| Paj | 24 | 61.13 N | 34.24 E |
| Pajala | 24 | 67.11 N | 23.22 E |
| Pajan | 246 | 1.34 S | 80.25 W |
| Pajapan | 234 | 18.15 N | 94.42 W |
| Pajares, Puerto de )( | 34 | 43.00 N | 5.46 W |
| Pajaro | 226 | 36.54 N | 121.39 W |
| Pajaro ≃ | 226 | 36.51 N | 121.48 W |
| Pajaros Point › | 240m | 18.31 N | 64.18 W |

| | | | |
|---|---|---|---|
| Paj-Choj ⩘[2] | 72 | 69.00 N | 63.00 [illegible] |
| Pajdugina ≃ | 86 | 58.50 N | 81.47 [illegible] |
| Pajęczno | 30 | 51.09 N | 19.00 [illegible] |
| Pajeú ≃ | 250 | 8.55 S | 38.42 W |
| Pajiangkou | 100 | 23.46 N | 113.14 [illegible] |
| Pajjer, gora ∧ | 24 | 66.42 N | 64.25 [illegible] |
| Pajtug | 85 | 40.53 N | 72.15 [illegible] |
| Pak ≃ | 110 | 21.05 N | 102.31 |
| Páka, Magy. | 61 | 46.36 N | 16.39 |
| Paka, Malay. | 114 | 4.39 N | 103.26 [illegible] |
| Paka ≃ | 114 | 4.40 N | 103.27 E |
| Pākāla | 122 | 13.28 N | 79.07 E |
| Pakaljubičy | 76 | 52.30 N | 31.02 E |
| Pakaraima Mountains ⩘ | 246 | 5.30 N | 60.40 W |
| Pākaur | 124 | 24.38 N | 87.51 E |
| Pak Ban | 110 | 21.14 N | 102.28 E |
| Pakch'ŏn | 98 | 39.45 N | 125.35 E |
| Pak Chong | 110 | 14.42 N | 101.25 E |
| Pakeng | 140 | 6.55 N | 30.40 E |
| Pakenham, Austl. | 169 | 38.04 S | 145.29 E |
| Pakenham, On., Can. | 212 | 45.20 N | 76.17 W |
| Pākhāl ⊜[1] | 122 | 17.57 N | 79.59 E |
| Pákhi | 267c | 37.59 N | 23.22 E |
| Pákhi I | 267c | 37.58 N | 23.22 E |
| Pákhna | 130 | 34.46 N | 32.48 E |
| Pakhoi → Beihai | 102 | 21.29 N | 109.05 E |
| Pakin I[1] | 14 | 7.04 N | 157.48 E |
| Pakipaki | 172 | 39.41 S | 176.48 E |
| Pakistan (Pākistān) □[1], Asia | 118 | 30.00 N | 70.00 E |
| Pakistan (Pākistān) □[1], Asia | 120 | 30.00 N | 70.00 E |
| Pakistan, East → Bangladesh □[1] | 120 | 24.00 N | 90.00 E |
| Pak Kong | 271d | 22.23 N | 114.15 E |
| Pak Kret | 269a | 13.55 N | 100.30 E |
| Pak Kwo Chau I | 271d | 22.16 N | 114.20 E |
| Paklenica Nacionalni Park ♠ | 36 | 44.21 N | 15.23 E |
| Pakokku | 110 | 21.20 N | 95.05 E |
| Pakość | 30 | 52.49 N | 18.05 E |
| Pakouabo | 150 | 7.10 N | 5.48 W |
| Pakowki Lake ⊜ | 184 | 49.22 N | 110.57 W |
| Pākpattan | 123 | 30.21 N | 73.24 E |
| Pak Phanang | 110 | 8.21 N | 100.12 E |
| Pak Phayun | 110 | 7.21 N | 100.19 E |
| Pak Phraek | 110 | 8.13 N | 100.12 E |
| Pakrac | 36 | 45.26 N | 17.12 E |
| Pākrāganj | 126 | 24.00 N | 90.41 E |
| Pakruojis | 76 | 55.58 N | 23.52 E |
| Paks | 30 | 46.39 N | 18.53 E |
| Pak Sane → Muang Pakxan | 110 | 18.22 N | 103.39 E |
| Pāksey | 126 | 24.05 N | 89.03 E |
| Pak Thong Chai | 110 | 14.43 N | 102.01 E |
| Paktīā □[4] | 120 | 33.30 N | 69.30 E |
| Paktīkā □[4] | 120 | 32.30 N | 68.45 E |
| Pākundia | 126 | 24.20 N | 90.42 E |
| P'akupur ≃ | 74 | 65.00 N | 77.48 E |
| Pakwach | 154 | 2.28 N | 31.30 E |
| Pakwash Lake ⊜ | 184 | 50.45 N | 93.30 W |
| Pakxé | 110 | 15.07 N | 105.47 E |
| Pala, Mya. | 110 | 12.51 N | 98.40 E |
| Pala, Tchad | 146 | 9.22 N | 14.54 E |
| Pala, Ca., U.S. | 228 | 33.22 N | 117.05 W |
| Palaau State Park ♠ | 229a | 21.11 N | 157.00 W |
| Palabek | 154 | 3.26 N | 32.34 E |
| Palacca Point › | 238 | 21.15 N | 73.26 W |
| Palacios | 196 | 28.42 N | 96.13 W |
| Palacios ≃ | 248 | 16.36 S | 64.18 W |
| Paladru | 62 | 45.28 N | 5.33 E |
| Palagano | 64 | 44.20 N | 10.39 E |
| Palagianello | 68 | 40.37 N | 16.58 E |
| Palagiano | 68 | 40.35 N | 17.02 E |
| Palagonia | 70 | 37.19 N | 14.45 E |
| Palagruža, Otoci II | 36 | 42.24 N | 16.15 E |
| Palai | 122 | 9.44 N | 76.41 E |
| Palai, Punta ∧ | 71 | 40.20 N | 8.55 E |
| Palaia | 66 | 43.36 N | 10.46 E |
| Palaiá Epídhavros | 38 | 37.38 N | 23.09 E |
| Palaiá Psará | 38 | 38.46 N | 25.36 E |
| Palaikhóri | 130 | 34.55 N | 33.05 E |
| Pala Indian Reservation ◆[4] | 228 | 33.21 N | 117.04 W |
| Palaiokhóra | 38 | 35.14 N | 23.41 E |
| Palaión Fáliron | 267c | 37.55 N | 23.41 E |
| Palaiseau | 50 | 48.43 N | 2.15 E |
| Pālakodu | 122 | 16.32 N | 81.44 E |
| Pālam ◆[8] | 272a | 28.35 N | 77.05 E |
| Palam Airport ⊠ | 123 | 28.35 N | 77.07 E |
| Palamás | 38 | 39.28 N | 22.05 E |
| Palamós | 34 | 41.51 N | 3.08 E |
| Pālampur | 123 | 32.07 N | 76.32 E |
| Palamuse | 76 | 58.41 N | 26.35 E |
| Palamut | 130 | 38.59 N | 27.41 E |
| Palana | 74 | 59.07 N | 159.58 E |
| Palanan, Mount ∧ | 116 | 17.03 N | 122.15 E |
| Palanan Bay ⊂ | 116 | 17.09 N | 122.27 E |
| Palanan Point › | 116 | 17.09 N | 122.30 E |
| Palanas | 116 | 12.09 N | 123.55 E |
| Palandöken Dağları ⩘ | 130 | 39.47 N | 41.15 E |
| Pālang | 126 | 23.13 N | 90.21 E |
| Pālang ≃[1] | 126 | 23.15 N | 90.21 E |
| Palanga | 76 | 55.55 N | 21.03 E |
| Palanganene | 152 | 6.26 S | 18.50 E |
| Palangkaraya | 112 | 2.16 S | 113.56 E |
| Palani | 122 | 10.28 N | 77.32 E |
| Pālanpur | 120 | 24.10 N | 72.26 E |
| Palanquinos | 34 | 42.27 N | 5.31 W |
| Palanzano | 64 | 44.26 N | 10.11 E |
| Palaoa Point › | 229a | 20.44 N | 156.58 W |
| Palapag | 116 | 12.33 N | 125.07 E |
| Palapye | 156 | 22.37 S | 27.06 E |
| Pālār ≃ | 122 | 12.28 N | 80.10 E |
| Palasan Island I | 116 | 14.52 N | 122.03 E |
| Palas de Rei | 34 | 42.52 N | 7.52 W |
| Palāshdānga | 126 | 23.24 N | 87.22 E |
| Palāspol | 126 | 22.43 N | 89.05 E |
| Palasthali | 126 | 23.51 N | 87.03 E |
| Palata | 66 | 41.53 N | 14.47 E |
| Palatcy | 86 | 49.09 N | 83.43 E |
| Palatine | 216 | 42.06 N | 88.02 W |
| Palatine Bridge | 210 | 42.55 N | 74.35 W |
| Palatka, Ross. | 74 | 60.06 N | 150.54 E |
| Palatka, Fl., U.S. | 192 | 29.38 N | 81.38 W |
| Palau, It. | 71 | 41.11 N | 9.23 E |
| Palau, Méx. | 196 | 27.54 N | 101.26 W |
| Palau □[1], Oc. | 14 | 5.00 N | 137.00 E |
| Palau (Belau) □[1], Oc. | 175b | 7.30 N | 134.30 E |
| Palauig | 116 | 15.26 N | 119.54 E |
| Palaui Island I | 116 | 18.33 N | 122.08 E |
| Palau Islands II | 175b | 7.30 N | 134.30 E |
| Palauk | 110 | 13.16 N | 98.38 E |
| Pal'avaam ≃ | 180 | 68.50 N | 170.45 E |
| Pal'avaamskij chrebet ⩘ | 180 | 68.20 N | 177.00 E |
| Palavas-les-Flots | 62 | 43.32 N | 3.56 E |
| Palaw | 110 | 12.58 N | 98.39 E |
| Palawai Basin ≡[1] | 229a | 20.47 N | 156.55 W |
| Palawan □[4] | 116 | 10.00 N | 118.50 E |
| Palawan I | 116 | 9.30 N | 118.30 E |
| Palawan Passage ⋓ | 116 | 10.00 N | 118.00 E |
| Palayan | 116 | 15.33 N | 121.06 E |
| Pālayankottai | 122 | 8.43 N | 77.44 E |
| Palazzo Adriano | 70 | 37.41 N | 13.23 E |
| Palazzolo Acreide | 70 | 37.04 N | 14.54 E |
| Palazzolo dello Stella | 64 | 45.48 N | 13.05 E |
| Palazzolo sull'Oglio | 62 | 45.36 N | 9.53 E |
| Palazzolo Vercellese | 62 | 45.11 N | 8.14 E |
| Palazzo San Gervasio | 68 | 40.56 N | 16.00 E |
| Palazzuolo sul Senio | 66 | 44.07 N | 11.33 E |
| P'albong-san ∧ | 98 | 40.16 N | 127.57 E |
| Palca, Bol. | 248 | 16.34 S | 67.59 W |
| Palca, Perú | 248 | 11.21 S | 75.31 W |
| Palcamayo | 248 | 11.18 S | 75.46 W |
| Pal'co | 76 | 53.17 N | 34.56 E |
| Paldi | 224 | 48.48 N | 123.51 W |


| | | | | |
|---|---|---|---|---|
| ≃ River | Fluß | Río | Rivière | Rio |
| ≊ Canal | Kanal | Canal | Canal | Canal |
| ∟ Waterfall, Rapids | Wasserfall, Stromschnellen | Cascada, Rápidos | Chute d'eau, Rapides | Cascata, Rápidos |
| ⋓ Strait | Meeresstraße | Estrecho | Détroit | Estreito |
| ⊂ Bay, Gulf | Bucht, Golf | Bahía, Golfo | Baie, Golfe | Baía, Golfo |
| ⊜ Lake, Lakes | See, Seen | Lago, Lagos | Lac, Lacs | Lago, Lagos |
| ≡ Swamp | Sumpf | Pantano | Marais | Pântano |
| ⍓ Ice Features, Glacier | Eis- und Gletscherformen | Accidentes Glaciales | Formes glaciaires | Acidentes glaciares |
| ⍑ Other Hydrographic Features | Andere Hydrographische Objekte | Otros Elementos Hidrográficos | Autres données hydrographiques | Outros acidentes hidrográficos |

| | | | | |
|---|---|---|---|---|
| ✢ Submarine Features | Untermeerische Objekte | Accidentes Submarinos | Formes de relief sous-marin | Acidentes submarinos |
| □ Political Unit | Politische Einheit | Unidad Politica | Entité politique | Unidade política |
| ʊ Cultural Institution | Kulturelle Institution | Institución Cultural | Institution culturelle | Institução cultural |
| ⊥ Historical Site | Historische Stätte | Sitio Histórico | Site historique | Sitio histórico |
| ♠ Recreational Site | Erholungs- und Ferienort | Sitio de Recreo | Centre de loisirs | Area de Lazer |
| ⊠ Airport | Flughafen | Aeropuerto | Aéroport | Aeroporto |
| ■ Military Installation | Militäranlage | Instalación Militar | Installation militaire | Instalação militar |
| ◆ Miscellaneous | Verschiedenes | Misceláneo | Divers | Diversos |

ENGLISH — DEUTSCH


| Name | Page | Lat.°′ | Long.°′ |
|---|---|---|---|
| Paldiski | 76 | 59.20 N | 24.06 E |
| Pāldor ∧ | 124 | 28.16 N | 85.11 E |
| Palech | 80 | 56.48 N | 41.51 E |
| Palel | 120 | 24.27 N | 94.02 E |
| Paleleh | 112 | 1.04 N | 121.57 E |
| Palembang | 112 | 2.55 S | 104.45 E |
| Palena | 66 | 41.59 N | 14.08 E |
| Palena ≃ | 254 | 43.50 S | 72.59 W |
| Palena, Lago (Lago General Vintter) ⊜ | 254 | 43.55 S | 71.40 W |
| Palencia | 34 | 42.01 N | 4.32 W |
| Palencia □[4] | 34 | 42.25 N | 4.35 W |
| Palen Lake ⊜ | 204 | 33.46 N | 115.12 W |
| Palenque | 232 | 17.31 N | 91.58 W |
| Palenque ⊥ | 232 | 17.30 N | 92.00 W |
| Palenque, Punta ≻ | 238 | 18.14 N | 70.09 W |
| Palenville | 210 | 42.10 N | 74.01 W |
| Paleparto, Monte ∧ | 68 | 39.28 N | 16.34 E |
| Palermo, Col. | 246 | 2.54 N | 75.26 W |
| Palermo, It. | 70 | 38.07 N | 13.21 E |
| Palermo, Ca., U.S. | 226 | 39.26 N | 121.33 W |
| Palermo, Ur. | 252 | 33.48 S | 55.59 W |
| Palermo □[4] | 70 | 37.49 N | 13.35 E |
| Palermo ◆[8] | 288 | 34.35 S | 58.25 W |
| Palermo, Golfo di ⊂ | 70 | 38.08 N | 13.26 E |
| Palese, Aeroporto di ⊠ | 68 | 41.10 N | 16.47 E |
| Palesse | 76 | 53.05 N | 31.17 E |
| Palestina, Bra. | 255 | 20.23 S | 49.25 W |
| Palestina, Méx. | 196 | 29.10 N | 100.55 W |
| Palestine, Ar., U.S. | 194 | 34.58 N | 90.54 W |
| Palestine, Il., U.S. | 194 | 39.00 N | 87.36 W |
| Palestine, Oh., U.S. | 218 | 40.03 N | 84.45 W |
| Palestine, Tx., U.S. | 222 | 31.45 N | 95.37 W |
| Palestine □[9] | 132 | 32.00 N | 35.15 E |
| Palestine, Lake ⊜[1] | 222 | 32.06 N | 95.27 W |
| Palestrina | 66 | 41.50 N | 12.53 E |
| Paletwa | 110 | 21.18 N | 92.51 E |
| Palézieux | 58 | 46.33 N | 6.50 E |
| Palfau | 61 | 47.42 N | 14.48 E |
| Pālghāt | 122 | 10.47 N | 76.39 E |
| Palgrave, Mount ∧ | 162 | 23.22 S | 115.58 E |
| Palgrave Point ≻ | 156 | 20.45 S | 13.20 E |
| Palhais | 266c | 38.37 N | 9.03 W |
| Palhano | 250 | 4.44 S | 37.57 W |
| Palhano ≃ | 250 | 4.33 S | 37.42 W |
| Pāli, India | 120 | 25.46 N | 73.20 E |
| Pali, India | 124 | 25.51 N | 76.33 E |
| Paliano | 66 | 41.48 N | 13.03 E |
| Palidoro ◆[8] | 66 | 41.56 N | 12.11 E |
| Palikea ∧ | 229c | 21.26 N | 158.06 W |
| Palima | 112 | 4.20 S | 120.22 E |
| Palimanan | 115a | 6.42 S | 108.26 E |
| Palimbang | 116 | 6.12 N | 124.12 E |
| Palimé | 150 | 6.54 N | 0.38 E |
| Palín | 236 | 14.24 N | 90.42 W |
| Palinges | 32 | 46.33 N | 4.13 E |
| Palinuro | 68 | 40.02 N | 15.17 E |
| Palinuro, Capo ≻ | 68 | 40.02 N | 15.16 E |
| Palisade, Co., U.S. | 200 | 39.06 N | 108.21 W |
| Palisade, Ne., U.S. | 198 | 40.20 N | 101.06 W |
| Palisades, Id., U.S. | 202 | 43.21 N | 111.13 W |
| Palisades, N.Y., U.S. | 276 | 41.01 N | 73.55 W |
| Palisades Amusement Park ♦ | 276 | 40.50 N | 73.59 W |
| Palisades Interstate Park ♦ | 210 | 40.56 N | 73.55 W |
| Palisades Park, Mi., U.S. | 216 | 42.18 N | 86.19 W |
| Palisades Park, N.J., U.S. | 276 | 40.50 N | 73.59 W |
| Palisades Reservoir ⊜[1] | 202 | 43.15 N | 111.05 W |
| Paliseul | 56 | 49.54 N | 5.08 E |
| Pālitāna | 120 | 21.31 N | 71.50 E |
| Palivere | 76 | 58.59 N | 23.52 E |
| Palizada | 232 | 18.15 N | 92.05 W |
| Palizzi | 68 | 37.58 N | 15.59 E |
| Paljakka ∧[2] | 26 | 64.41 N | 28.08 E |
| Pälkäne | 26 | 61.20 N | 24.16 E |
| Palk Bay ⊂ | 122 | 9.30 N | 79.15 E |
| Palkino, Ross. | 76 | 57.32 N | 28.01 E |
| Palkino, Ross. | 80 | 58.15 N | 42.56 E |
| Pālkonda | 122 | 18.36 N | 83.45 E |
| Pālkonda Range ⋌ | 122 | 14.05 N | 79.05 E |
| Palk Strait ⊔ | 122 | 10.00 N | 79.45 E |
| Palla Bianca (Weisskugel) ∧ | 64 | 46.48 N | 10.44 E |
| Pallagorio | 68 | 39.18 N | 16.54 E |
| Pallamana | 168b | 35.02 S | 139.12 E |
| Pallasca | 248 | 8.15 S | 78.01 W |
| Pallas Green | 48 | 52.33 N | 8.22 W |
| Pallaskenry | 48 | 52.39 N | 8.52 W |
| Pallas-Ounastunturin kansallispuisto ♦ | 24 | 68.06 N | 24.00 E |
| Pallasovka | 80 | 50.03 N | 46.53 E |
| Pallastunturi ∧ | 24 | 68.06 N | 24.00 E |
| Pallejà | 266d | 41.25 N | 2.00 E |
| Pallës, Bishti i ≻ | 38 | 41.24 N | 19.24 E |
| Palling | 182 | 54.21 N | 125.55 W |
| Pallíni | 267c | 38.00 N | 23.53 E |
| Pallinup ≃ | 162 | 34.29 S | 118.54 E |
| Pallisa | 154 | 1.10 N | 33.42 E |
| Palliser, Cape ≻ | 172 | 41.37 S | 175.17 E |
| Palliser Bay ⊂ | 172 | 41.25 S | 175.05 E |
| Pallu | 123 | 28.56 N | 74.13 E |
| Palluau | 32 | 46.48 N | 1.37 W |
| Palma, Bra. | 255 | 21.22 S | 42.19 W |
| Palma, Moç. | 154 | 10.46 S | 40.29 E |
| P'al'ma, Ross. | 24 | 62.26 N | 35.53 E |
| Palma ≃ | 255 | 12.33 S | 47.52 W |
| Palma, Badia de ⊂ | 34 | 39.27 N | 2.35 E |
| Palmácia | 250 | 4.08 S | 38.50 W |
| Palma del Río | 34 | 37.42 N | 5.17 W |
| Palma [de Mallorca] | 34 | 39.34 N | 2.39 E |
| Palma di Montechiaro | 70 | 37.11 N | 13.46 E |
| Palmaḥim | 132 | 31.56 N | 34.42 E |
| Palmanova | 64 | 45.54 N | 13.19 E |
| Palma Pegada | 234 | 22.42 N | 101.48 W |
| Palmar ≃ | 246 | 10.10 N | 71.50 W |
| Palmar, Lago Artificial del ⊜[1] | 252 | 33.05 S | 57.10 W |
| Palmar Camp | 232 | 16.26 N | 88.53 W |
| Palmar de Cariaco | 286c | 10.34 N | 66.55 W |
| Palmar de los Sepúlveda | 232 | 25.43 N | 107.55 W |
| Palmar de Varela | 246 | 10.45 N | 74.45 W |
| Palmarejo | 240m | 18.03 N | 67.05 W |
| Palmares, Bra. | 250 | 8.41 S | 35.36 W |
| Palmares, C.R. | 236 | 9.21 N | 83.40 W |
| Palmares, C.R. | 236 | 10.03 N | 84.26 W |
| Palmares do Sul | 252 | 30.16 S | 50.31 W |
| Palmaria, Isola I | 62 | 44.02 N | 9.51 E |
| Palmarito | 246 | 7.37 N | 70.10 W |
| Palmarola, Isola I | 66 | 40.56 N | 12.51 E |
| Palmar Sur | 236 | 8.58 N | 83.29 W |
| Palmas, Bra. | 250 | 10.08 S | 48.18 W |
| Palmas, Bra. | 252 | 26.30 S | 52.00 W |
| Palmas, Méx. | 234 | 22.49 N | 103.57 W |
| Palmas, Golfo di ⊂ | 71 | 39.02 N | 8.31 E |
| Palmas, Ilha das I, Bra. | 287a | 23.02 S | 43.12 W |
| Palmas, Ilha das I, Bra. | 287a | 23.04 S | 43.31 W |
| Palmas Bellas | 236 | 9.14 N | 80.05 W |
| Palmas de Monte Alto | 255 | 14.16 S | 43.10 W |
| Palma Sola | 220 | 27.31 N | 82.38 W |
| Palma Soriano | 240p | 20.13 N | 76.00 W |
| Palm Bay | 220 | 28.02 N | 80.35 W |
| Palm Beach, Austl. | 170 | 33.36 S | 151.19 E |
| Palm Beach, Austl. | 171a | 28.08 S | 153.28 E |
| Palm Beach, Fl., U.S. | 220 | 26.42 N | 80.02 W |
| Palm Beach □[6] | 220 | 26.38 N | 80.27 W |
| Palm Beach Gardens | 220 | 26.49 N | 80.06 W |
| Palm Beach International Airport ⊠ | 220 | 26.41 N | 80.05 W |
| Palm City | 220 | 27.09 N | 80.16 W |
| Palmdale, Ca., U.S. | 228 | 34.34 N | 118.06 W |
| Palmdale, Fl., U.S. | 220 | 26.56 N | 81.18 W |
| Palmdale, Pa., U.S. | 208 | 40.18 N | 76.37 W |
| Palmdale, Lake ⊜[1] | 228 | 34.33 N | 118.07 W |
| Palm Desert | 204 | 33.43 N | 116.23 W |
| Palmeira, Bra. | 252 | 25.25 S | 50.00 W |
| Palmeira, C.V. | 150a | 16.46 N | 22.59 W |
| Palmeira das Missões | 252 | 27.55 S | 53.17 W |
| Palmeira d'Oeste | 255 | 20.23 S | 50.47 W |
| Palmeira dos Índios | 250 | 9.25 S | 36.37 W |
| Palmeirais | 250 | 5.58 S | 43.04 W |
| Palmeiral | 256 | 21.38 S | 46.31 W |
| Palmeiras | 255 | 12.31 S | 41.34 W |
| Palmeiras ≃, Bra. | 250 | 12.22 S | 47.08 W |
| Palmeiras ≃, Bra. | 255 | 15.25 S | 51.10 W |
| Palmeirina | 250 | 8.56 S | 36.17 W |
| Palmeirinhas, Ponta das ≻ | 152 | 9.05 S | 13.00 E |
| Palmela ≃ | 256 | 21.38 S | 45.23 W |
| Palmelo | 255 | 17.20 S | 48.27 W |
| Palmer, Austl. | 168b | 34.51 S | 139.10 E |
| Palmer, P.R. | 240m | 18.22 N | 65.46 W |
| Palmer, Ak., U.S. | 180 | 61.36 N | 149.07 W |
| Palmer, Il., U.S. | 219 | 39.27 N | 89.24 W |
| Palmer, Ma., U.S. | 207 | 42.09 N | 72.19 W |
| Palmer, Ms., U.S. | 194 | 31.16 N | 89.15 W |
| Palmer, Ne., U.S. | 198 | 41.13 N | 98.15 W |
| Palmer, Tn., U.S. | 194 | 35.21 N | 85.34 W |
| Palmer, Tx., U.S. | 222 | 32.26 N | 96.40 W |
| Palmer ≃, Austl. | 162 | 24.46 S | 133.25 E |
| Palmer ≃, Austl. | 164 | 15.34 S | 142.26 E |
| Palmer ≃, P.Q., Can. | 206 | 46.19 N | 71.27 W |
| Palmer ⊕[3] | 9 | 64.46 S | 64.03 W |
| Palmerah ◆[8] | 269e | 6.12 S | 106.47 E |
| Palmer Heights | 208 | 40.42 N | 75.16 W |
| Palmer Lake | 200 | 38.52 N | 104.48 W |
| Palmer Land ◆[1] | 9 | 71.30 S | 65.00 W |
| Palmer Mill Brook ≃ | 283 | 41.58 N | 70.52 W |
| Palmer Park | 284c | 38.55 N | 76.52 W |
| Palmer Park ♦ | 281 | 42.26 N | 83.07 W |
| Palmerston, On., Can. | 212 | 43.50 N | 80.51 W |
| Palmerston, N.Z. | 172 | 45.29 S | 170.43 E |
| Palmerston I[1] | 14 | 18.04 S | 163.10 W |
| Palmerston, Cape ≻ | 166 | 21.32 S | 149.29 E |
| Palmerston Lake ⊜ | 212 | 45.01 N | 76.50 W |
| Palmerston North | 172 | 40.21 S | 175.37 E |
| Palmerton | 210 | 40.48 N | 75.36 W |
| Palmerville | 164 | 15.59 S | 144.05 E |
| Palmetto, Fl., U.S. | 220 | 27.31 N | 82.34 W |
| Palmetto, Ga., U.S. | 192 | 33.31 N | 84.40 W |
| Palmetto, La., U.S. | 194 | 30.43 N | 91.54 W |
| Palmford | 158 | 27.11 S | 29.42 E |
| Palm Harbor | 220 | 28.04 N | 82.45 W |
| Palmi | 68 | 38.21 N | 15.51 E |
| Palminópolis | 255 | 16.47 S | 50.08 W |
| Palmira, Arg. | 252 | 33.03 S | 68.34 W |
| Palmira, Col. | 246 | 3.32 N | 76.16 W |
| Palmira, Cuba | 240p | 22.14 N | 80.23 W |
| Palmira, Ec. | 246 | 2.05 S | 78.43 W |
| Palmira, Méx. | 196 | 28.58 N | 100.47 W |
| Palmitas | 252 | 33.31 S | 57.49 W |
| Palmitos | 252 | 27.05 S | 53.08 W |
| Palmnicken → Jantarnyj | 76 | 54.52 N | 19.57 E |
| Palmoli | 66 | 41.56 N | 14.32 E |
| Palm River | 220 | 27.56 N | 82.23 W |
| Palms ◆[8] | 280 | 34.02 N | 118.25 W |
| Palm Shores | 220 | 28.11 N | 80.35 W |
| Palm Springs, Ca., U.S. | 204 | 33.49 N | 116.32 W |
| Palm Springs, Fl., U.S. | 220 | 26.39 N | 80.06 W |
| Palmyra → Tudmur, Sūrīy. | 130 | 34.33 N | 38.17 E |
| Palmyra, Il., U.S. | 219 | 39.26 N | 89.59 W |
| Palmyra, In., U.S. | 218 | 38.24 N | 86.06 W |
| Palmyra, Mi., U.S. | 216 | 41.52 N | 83.56 W |
| Palmyra, Mo., U.S. | 219 | 39.47 N | 91.31 W |
| Palmyra, N.J., U.S. | 208 | 40.00 N | 75.01 W |
| Palmyra, N.Y., U.S. | 210 | 43.03 N | 77.14 W |
| Palmyra, Oh., U.S. | 214 | 41.07 N | 81.02 W |
| Palmyra, Pa., U.S. | 208 | 40.18 N | 76.35 W |
| Palmyra, Va., U.S. | 192 | 37.51 N | 78.15 W |
| Palmyra, Wi., U.S. | 216 | 42.52 N | 88.35 W |
| Palmyra ⊥ | 130 | 34.33 N | 38.17 E |
| Palmyra Atoll I[1] | 14 | 5.52 N | 162.06 W |
| Palo, It. | 66 | 41.56 N | 12.06 E |
| Palo, Pil. | 116 | 11.10 N | 124.59 E |
| Palo Alto, Méx. | 196 | 26.32 N | 99.45 W |
| Palo Alto, Ca., U.S. | 226 | 37.26 N | 122.08 W |
| Palo Alto, Pa., U.S. | 208 | 40.41 N | 76.11 W |
| Palo Alto Airport ⊠ | 282 | 37.28 N | 122.07 W |
| Palo Blanco, Méx. | 196 | 26.45 N | 101.32 W |
| Palo Blanco, P.R. | 240m | 18.26 N | 66.39 W |
| Palo Blanco Creek ≃ | 196 | 27.10 N | 97.52 W |
| Paločka | 86 | 58.25 N | 84.32 E |
| Palo del Colle | 68 | 41.03 N | 16.42 E |
| Palo Duro Canyon State Park ♦ | 196 | 34.55 N | 101.42 W |
| Palo Duro Creek ≃, U.S. | 196 | 36.39 N | 100.58 W |
| Palo Duro Creek ≃, Tx., U.S. | 196 | 35.00 N | 101.54 W |
| Paloe, Pulau I | 115b | 8.20 S | 121.43 E |
| Paloemeu ≃ | 250 | 3.21 N | 55.26 W |
| Palo Flechado Pass )( | 200 | 36.25 N | 105.20 W |
| Paloh, Indon. | 112 | 1.43 N | 109.18 E |
| Paloh, Malay. | 112 | 2.25 N | 111.15 E |
| Paloh, Malay. | 114 | 2.11 N | 103.12 E |
| Paloich, Sūd. | 140 | 6.45 N | 30.08 E |
| Paloich, Sūd. | 140 | 10.28 N | 32.32 E |
| Palojoensuu | 24 | 68.17 N | 23.05 E |
| Paloma Creek ≃ | 226 | 36.15 N | 121.26 W |
| Palomares Creek ≃ | 282 | 37.42 N | 122.02 W |
| Palomar Mountain ∧ | 204 | 33.22 N | 116.50 W |
| Palomar Mountain State Park ♦ | 228 | 33.19 N | 116.53 W |
| Palomar Park | 282 | 37.29 N | 122.16 W |
| Palomas | 196 | 28.43 N | 103.45 W |
| Palomas Viejo | 232 | 31.44 N | 107.37 W |
| Palombara Sabina | 66 | 42.04 N | 12.46 E |
| Palominos, Isla I | 240m | 18.21 N | 65.34 W |
| Palomonte | 68 | 40.40 N | 15.17 E |
| Palompon | 116 | 11.03 N | 124.23 E |
| Palo Negro | 246 | 10.11 N | 67.33 W |
| Palo Pinto | 196 | 32.46 N | 98.18 W |
| Palo Pinto Reservoir ⊜[1] | 196 | 32.38 N | 98.18 W |
| Palopo | 112 | 3.00 S | 120.12 E |
| Palora ≃ | 246 | 1.51 S | 77.49 W |
| Palos, Cuba | 240p | 22.48 N | 81.44 W |
| Palos → Palos de la Frontera, Esp. | 34 | 37.14 N | 6.53 W |
| Palos, Cabo de ≻ | 34 | 37.38 N | 0.41 W |
| Palo Santo | 252 | 25.34 S | 59.21 W |
| Palos de la Frontera | 34 | 37.14 N | 6.53 W |
| Palos Gardens | 278 | 41.40 N | 87.48 W |
| Palos Heights | 216 | 41.40 N | 87.47 W |
| Palos Hills | 278 | 41.41 N | 87.49 W |
| Palos Hills ♦ | 278 | 41.42 N | 87.53 W |
| Palos Park | 278 | 41.40 N | 87.49 W |
| Palos Verdes Estates | 228 | 33.48 N | 118.23 W |
| Palos Verdes Hills ⋌[2] | 280 | 33.46 N | 118.21 W |
| Palos Verdes Point ≻ | 228 | 33.47 N | 118.26 W |
| Palotai-sziget I | 264c | 47.35 N | 19.05 E |
| Paloúkia | 267c | 37.58 N | 23.31 E |
| Palouse | 202 | 46.54 N | 117.04 W |
| Palouse ≃ | 202 | 46.35 N | 118.13 W |
| Palouse, South Fork ≃ | 202 | 46.53 N | 117.22 W |
| Palo Verde | 204 | 33.25 N | 114.43 W |
| Palo Verde, Parque Nacional ♦ | 236 | 10.15 N | 85.10 W |
| P'alovskoje vodochranilišče ⊜[1] | 82 | 56.03 N | 37.40 E |
| Palpa | 248 | 14.32 S | 75.11 W |
| Palpalá | 252 | 24.15 S | 65.12 W |
| Pålsboda | 40 | 59.04 N | 15.20 E |
| Pālsit | 126 | 23.12 N | 88.03 E |
| Paltamo | 26 | 64.25 N | 27.50 E |
| Palten ≃ | 61 | 47.34 N | 14.20 E |
| Palu, Indon. | 112 | 0.53 S | 119.53 E |
| Palu, Tür. | 130 | 38.42 N | 39.57 E |
| Palu ≃ | 112 | 0.52 S | 119.51 E |
| Palu, Teluk ⊂ | 112 | 0.40 S | 119.45 E |
| Paluan | 116 | 13.25 N | 120.28 E |
| Paluan Bay ⊂ | 116 | 13.23 N | 120.25 E |
| Palù del Fersina | 64 | 46.08 N | 11.21 E |
| Paludi | 68 | 39.32 N | 16.41 E |
| Paluga | 24 | 65.16 N | 45.11 E |
| Paluke | 150 | 5.02 N | 8.06 W |
| Paluška ∧ | 61 | 48.45 N | 14.24 E |
| Paluxy ≃ | 196 | 32.15 N | 97.43 W |
| Paluzza | 64 | 46.32 N | 13.01 E |
| Palvantaš | 85 | 40.34 N | 72.12 E |
| Palvār, Kūh-e ∧ | 128 | 30.04 N | 57.28 E |
| Palvart | 128 | 38.11 N | 64.34 E |
| Palwal | 124 | 28.09 N | 77.20 E |
| Pal-Waukee Airport ⊠ | 278 | 42.07 N | 87.54 W |
| Pam | 175f | 20.16 S | 164.19 E |
| Pama | 150 | 11.15 N | 0.42 E |
| Pama ≃ | 152 | 4.23 N | 18.27 E |
| Pamaluan | 112 | 1.04 S | 116.39 E |
| Pamanukan | 115a | 6.16 S | 107.49 E |
| Pamarayan | 115a | 6.16 S | 106.17 E |
| Pam'ati 13 Borcov | 86 | 56.13 N | 92.20 E |
| Pam'atnaja | 86 | 56.01 N | 65.42 E |
| Pam'at' Parižskoj Kommuny | 80 | 56.06 N | 44.31 E |
| Pāmban Channel ⊔ | 122 | 9.17 N | 79.10 E |
| Pāmban Island I | 122 | 9.15 N | 79.20 E |
| Pambeguwa | 150 | 10.40 N | 8.19 E |
| Pambuhan | 116 | 13.59 N | 123.05 E |
| Pambuhan ≃ | 116 | 12.34 N | 124.55 E |
| Pambujan | 116 | 12.34 N | 124.56 E |
| Pamekasan | 115a | 7.10 S | 113.28 E |
| Pamenang | 112 | 2.07 S | 102.31 E |
| Pameungpeuk | 115a | 7.38 S | 107.43 E |
| Pamiers | 32 | 43.07 N | 1.36 E |
| Pamir ⋌ | 118 | 38.00 N | 73.00 E |
| Pamlico ≃ | 192 | 35.20 N | 76.30 W |
| Pamlico Sound ⊔ | 192 | 35.20 N | 75.55 W |
| Pamotan | 115a | 6.46 S | 111.29 E |
| Pampa | 196 | 35.32 N | 100.57 W |
| Pampã ≃ | 255 | 17.43 S | 40.36 W |
| Pampa ◆[1] | 252 | 35.00 S | 63.00 W |
| Pampa Almirón | 252 | 26.42 S | 59.08 W |
| Pampacolca | 248 | 15.43 S | 72.33 W |
| Pampa del Castillo | 254 | 45.48 S | 68.05 W |
| Pampa del Chañar | 252 | 30.11 S | 68.43 W |
| Pampa del Indio | 252 | 26.02 S | 59.55 W |
| Pampa del Infierno | 252 | 26.31 S | 61.10 W |
| Pampa de los Guanacos | 252 | 26.14 S | 61.51 W |
| Pampa Grande | 248 | 18.05 S | 64.06 W |
| Pampana ≃ | 150 | 8.24 N | 12.00 W |
| Pampanga □[4] | 116 | 15.05 N | 120.40 E |
| Pampanga ≃ | 116 | 14.47 N | 120.39 E |
| Pampanua | 112 | 4.14 S | 120.08 E |
| Pamparato | 62 | 44.17 N | 7.55 E |
| Pampas | 248 | 12.24 S | 74.54 W |
| Pampas ≃ | 248 | 13.23 S | 73.15 W |
| Pampas del Heath, Santuario Nacional ♦ | 248 | 12.40 S | 68.15 W |
| Pampeluna → Pamplona | 34 | 42.49 N | 1.38 W |
| Pamphylia □[9] | 130 | 37.00 N | 31.00 E |
| Pamplico | 192 | 33.59 N | 79.34 W |
| Pamplona, Col. | 246 | 7.23 N | 72.39 W |
| Pamplona, Esp. | 34 | 42.49 N | 1.38 W |
| Pampoenpoort | 158 | 31.03 S | 22.40 E |
| Pampow | 54 | 53.32 N | 14.15 E |
| Pāmpur | 123 | 34.01 N | 74.56 E |
| Pamukkale (Hierapolis) ⊥ | 130 | 37.58 N | 29.19 E |
| Pamukova | 130 | 40.31 N | 30.09 E |
| Pamunkey ≃ | 208 | 37.32 N | 76.48 W |
| Pana | 219 | 39.23 N | 89.04 W |
| Panabá | 232 | 21.17 N | 88.16 W |
| Panabo | 116 | 7.19 N | 125.42 E |
| Panaca | 204 | 37.47 N | 114.23 W |
| Panacan | 116 | 9.16 N | 118.25 E |
| Panacea | 192 | 30.02 N | 84.23 W |
| Panache, Lake ⊜ | 190 | 46.15 N | 81.20 W |
| Panadura | 122 | 6.43 N | 79.54 E |
| Panaeati Island I | 164 | 10.40 S | 152.20 E |
| Panāgar | 124 | 23.18 N | 79.59 E |
| Panagjurište | 38 | 42.30 N | 24.11 E |
| Panagtaran Point ≻ | 116 | 9.41 N | 118.45 E |
| Panahan | 112 | 1.44 S | 111.49 E |
| Panaitan, Pulau I | 115a | 6.36 S | 105.12 E |
| Panaitan, Selat ⊔ | 115a | 6.40 S | 105.16 E |
| Panaji (Panjim) | 122 | 15.29 N | 73.50 E |
| Pānākua | 272b | 22.23 N | 88.21 E |
| Panamá, Bra. | 255 | 18.11 S | 49.21 W |
| Panamá, Pan. | 236 | 8.58 N | 79.32 W |
| Panama, Il., U.S. | 219 | 39.02 N | 89.32 W |
| Panama, N.Y., U.S. | 214 | 42.04 N | 79.29 W |
| Panama, Ok., U.S. | 194 | 35.10 N | 94.40 W |
| Panamá □[4] | 236 | 8.48 N | 79.55 W |
| Panama (Panamá) □[1], N.A. | 230 | 9.00 N | 80.00 W |
| Panama (Panamá) □[1], N.A. | 246 | 9.00 N | 80.00 W |
| Panamá, Bahía de ⊂ | 246 | 8.50 N | 79.20 W |
| Panamá, Canal de ≋ | 236 | 9.20 N | 79.55 W |
| Panamá, Golfo de ⊂ | 246 | 8.00 N | 79.30 W |
| Panamá, Istmo de ⊥[3] | 246 | 9.00 N | 80.00 W |
| Panama Basin ◆[1] | 18 | 5.00 N | 83.30 W |
| Panama City | 194 | 30.09 N | 85.39 W |
| Panamá Vieja ⊥ | 236 | 9.00 N | 79.29 W |
| Panambi | 252 | 28.18 S | 53.30 W |
| Panamint Range ⋌ | 204 | 36.30 N | 117.20 W |
| Panamint Valley V | 204 | 36.15 N | 117.20 W |
| Pan'an | 100 | 29.06 N | 120.27 E |
| Panao, Perú | 248 | 9.49 S | 76.00 W |
| Pan'ao, Zhg. | 107 | 30.09 N | 103.37 E |
| Panaon Island I | 116 | 10.03 N | 125.13 E |
| Panarea, Isola I | 70 | 38.38 N | 15.04 E |
| Panaro ≃ | 64 | 44.55 N | 11.25 E |
| Panarukan | 115a | 7.42 S | 113.56 E |
| Panasoffkee, Lake ⊜ | 220 | 28.47 N | 82.08 W |
| Panatinane Island I | 164 | 11.15 S | 153.10 E |
| Panay I | 116 | 11.15 N | 122.30 E |
| Panay ≃ | 116 | 11.35 N | 122.43 E |
| Panay Gulf ⊂ | 116 | 10.15 N | 122.15 E |
| Panayía | 38 | 39.59 N | 25.24 E |
| Panay Island I | 116 | 13.58 N | 124.20 E |
| Pancalieri | 62 | 44.50 N | 7.35 E |
| Pancas | 266c | 38.48 N | 8.55 W |
| Pančevo | 38 | 44.52 N | 20.39 E |
| Panchagarh | 124 | 26.20 N | 88.34 E |
| Pānchāl | 126 | 23.15 N | 87.18 E |
| Pānchet Hill ∧[2] | 126 | 23.37 N | 86.47 E |
| Pānchet Reservoir ⊜[1] | 126 | 23.40 N | 86.45 E |
| Pancheve | 78 | 48.44 N | 31.51 E |
| Pānchghara | 272b | 22.44 N | 88.16 E |
| Panchgram | 126 | 24.12 N | 88.01 E |
| Panch'iao | 269d | 25.01 N | 121.27 E |
| Panchla | 126 | 22.32 N | 88.09 E |
| Panchor | 114 | 2.10 N | 102.43 E |
| Pancho Simón ≃ | 286b | 23.03 N | 82.21 W |
| Pānchur | 272b | 22.32 N | 88.16 E |
| Pānchuria | 272b | 22.33 N | 88.29 E |
| Panciu | 38 | 45.55 N | 27.05 E |
| Panda | 156 | 24.02 S | 34.45 E |
| Pandakan | 115a | 7.39 S | 112.41 E |
| Pandamatenga | 156 | 18.35 S | 25.42 E |
| Pandan, Malay. | 112 | 3.09 N | 113.22 E |
| Pandan, Pil. | 116 | 11.43 N | 122.06 E |
| Pandan, Pil. | 116 | 14.03 N | 124.10 E |
| Pandan, Selat ⊔ | 271c | 1.15 N | 103.44 E |
| Pandanan Island I | 116 | 8.17 N | 117.13 E |
| Pandan Bay ⊂ | 116 | 11.43 N | 122.04 E |
| Pandan Reservoir ⊜[1] | 271c | 1.19 N | 103.44 E |
| Pandaria | 124 | 22.14 N | 81.25 E |
| Pandarochan Bay ⊂ | 116 | 12.12 N | 121.10 E |
| Pandasan | 112 | 6.28 N | 116.32 E |
| Pan de Azúcar | 252 | 34.48 S | 55.14 W |
| Pan de Azucar, Cerro ∧ | 286e | 33.19 S | 70.42 W |
| Pan de Azucar Island I | 116 | 11.17 N | 123.10 E |
| Pandegelang | 115a | 6.18 S | 106.06 E |
| Pandėlys | 76 | 56.01 N | 25.13 E |
| Pāndharkawada | 122 | 20.01 N | 78.32 E |
| Pandharpur | 122 | 17.40 N | 75.20 E |
| Pāndhurna | 122 | 21.36 N | 78.31 E |
| Pandian | 98 | 36.38 N | 116.27 E |
| Pandino | 62 | 45.24 N | 9.33 E |
| Pando | 252 | 34.43 S | 55.57 W |
| Pando □[5] | 248 | 11.20 S | 67.40 W |
| Pando, Cerro ∧ | 236 | 8.55 N | 82.43 W |
| Pandora | 216 | 40.56 N | 83.57 W |
| Pandu | 152 | 5.01 N | 19.16 E |
| Pandua, India | 124 | 25.08 N | 88.10 E |
| Pāndua, India | 126 | 23.05 N | 88.17 E |
| P'andž (Panj) ≃ | 120 | 37.06 N | 68.20 E |
| Panebianco ≃ | 70 | 37.24 N | 15.04 E |
| Panelas | 250 | 8.40 S | 36.01 W |
| Paneveggio | 64 | 46.18 N | 11.44 E |
| Panevėžys | 76 | 55.44 N | 24.21 E |
| Panfang | 100 | 27.54 N | 115.57 E |
| Panfilov | 86 | 44.10 N | 80.01 E |
| Panfilovo | 80 | 50.26 N | 42.55 E |
| Pāng ≃ | 110 | 20.58 N | 98.30 E |
| Panga | 154 | 1.51 N | 26.25 E |
| Pangala | 152 | 3.19 S | 14.34 E |
| Pangalanes, Canal des ≋ | 157b | 22.40 S | 47.50 E |
| Pangandaran | 115a | 7.41 S | 108.39 E |
| Pangani | 154 | 5.26 S | 38.58 E |
| Pangani ≃ | 154 | 5.26 S | 38.58 E |
| Panganiran | 116 | 13.02 N | 123.26 E |
| Pangantocan | 116 | 7.50 N | 124.49 E |
| Panganuran | 116 | 7.24 N | 122.03 E |
| Pangasinan □[4] | 116 | 16.00 N | 120.20 E |
| Pangbourne | 42 | 51.29 N | 1.05 W |
| Pangburn | 194 | 35.25 N | 91.50 W |
| Pange | 56 | 49.05 N | 6.22 E |
| Pangfou → Bengbu | 100 | 32.58 N | 117.24 E |
| Pangga, Tanjung ≻ | 115b | 8.55 S | 116.02 E |
| Panggezhuang, Zhg. | 105 | 39.38 N | 116.19 E |
| Panggezhuang, Zhg. | 105 | 39.16 N | 115.49 E |
| Panghkam | 110 | 23.53 N | 97.37 E |
| Pangi | 154 | 3.11 S | 26.38 E |
| Pangian | 112 | 1.06 S | 119.24 E |
| Pangjiabu | 105 | 40.36 N | 115.27 E |
| Pangkah | 115a | 6.58 S | 109.10 E |
| Pangkajene | 112 | 4.50 S | 119.32 E |
| Pangkalanbrandan | 114 | 4.01 N | 98.17 E |
| Pangkalanbuun | 112 | 2.41 S | 111.37 E |
| Pangkalansusu | 114 | 4.06 N | 98.14 E |
| Pangkalaseang, Tanjung ≻ | 112 | 0.42 S | 123.26 E |
| Pangkalpinang | 112 | 2.08 S | 106.08 E |
| Pangkatan | 114 | 2.09 N | 100.00 E |
| Pangke | 114 | 1.01 N | 103.10 E |
| Pangkor, Pulau I | 114 | 4.13 N | 100.33 E |
| Panglao | 116 | 9.35 N | 123.45 E |
| Panglao Island I | 116 | 9.35 N | 123.48 E |
| Pangman | 184 | 49.39 N | 104.38 W |
| Pangnirtung | 176 | 66.08 N | 65.44 W |
| Pango Aluquém | 152 | 8.43 S | 14.27 E |
| Pangŏjin | 98 | 35.29 N | 129.26 E |
| Pangong Tso ⊜ | 120 | 33.45 N | 78.43 E |
| Pangp'u → Bengbu | 100 | 32.58 N | 117.24 E |
| Pāngsa | 126 | 23.47 N | 89.25 E |
| Pangtara | 110 | 20.57 N | 96.40 E |
| Pangubatan | 116 | 6.57 N | 125.47 E |
| Panguil Bay ⊂ | 116 | 8.01 N | 123.43 E |
| Panguipulli | 254 | 39.38 S | 72.20 W |
| Panguipulli, Lago ⊜ | 254 | 39.43 S | 72.13 W |
| Panguiranan | 116 | 12.04 N | 123.19 E |
| Panguitch | 200 | 37.49 N | 112.26 W |
| Pangururan | 114 | 2.37 N | 98.42 E |
| Pangutaran | 116 | 6.18 N | 120.35 E |
| Pangutaran Group II | 116 | 6.15 N | 120.30 E |
| Pangutaran Island I | 116 | 6.18 N | 120.34 E |
| Pangutaran Passage ⊔ | 116 | 6.13 N | 120.30 E |
| Pangzidian | 107 | 30.38 N | 105.04 E |
| Panhandle | 196 | 35.20 N | 101.22 W |
| Paniai, Danau ⊜ | 164 | 3.50 S | 136.15 E |
| Pania-Mutombo | 152 | 5.11 S | 23.51 E |
| Paniau ∧ | 229b | 21.57 N | 160.05 W |
| Panié, Mont ∧ | 175f | 20.36 S | 164.46 E |
| Pānihāti | 126 | 22.42 N | 88.22 E |
| Panika | 80 | 50.59 N | 50.11 E |
| Panindícuaro | 234 | 19.59 N | 101.46 W |
| Panino, Ross. | 76 | 56.25 N | 34.34 E |
| Panino, Ross. | 78 | 51.38 N | 40.08 E |
| Panino-Nesterovo | 82 | 55.23 N | 38.11 E |
| Panīpāt | 124 | 29.23 N | 76.58 E |
| Paniqui | 116 | 15.40 N | 120.35 E |
| Panissières | 62 | 45.47 N | 4.20 E |
| Panitan | 116 | 11.28 N | 122.46 E |
| Panitian | 116 | 9.05 N | 118.05 E |
| Panj (P'andž) ≃ | 120 | 37.06 N | 68.20 E |
| Panjāb | 120 | 34.22 N | 67.01 E |
| Panjang | 115a | 5.28 S | 105.18 E |
| Panjang, Pulau I | 112 | 2.44 N | 108.55 E |
| Panjang, Selat ⊔ | 114 | 0.40 N | 102.30 E |
| Panje | 272c | 18.54 N | 72.57 E |
| Panjgūr | 128 | 26.58 N | 64.06 E |
| Panji | 114 | 2.34 N | 97.50 E |
| Panjiapie | 100 | 32.54 N | 120.42 E |
| Panjiatun | 104 | 41.04 N | 121.38 E |
| Panjim → Panaji | 122 | 15.29 N | 73.50 E |
| Pānjkora ≃ | 123 | 34.39 N | 71.44 E |
| Panjnad ≃ | 123 | 28.57 N | 70.30 E |
| Panjpāi | 120 | 29.55 N | 66.30 E |
| Panjshār ≃ | 120 | 34.38 N | 69.42 E |
| Pankakoski | 26 | 63.19 N | 30.09 E |
| Panke ≃ | 264a | 52.32 N | 13.22 E |
| Panker | 54 | 54.20 N | 10.34 E |
| Pānkhāli | 126 | 22.37 N | 89.31 E |
| Pankof, Cape ≻ | 180 | 54.40 N | 163.04 W |
| Pankow ◆[8] | 54 | 52.34 N | 13.25 E |
| Pankratovo | 76 | 59.10 N | 43.30 E |
| Pankshin | 150 | 9.20 N | 9.24 E |
| Panlong, Zhg. | 100 | 25.52 N | 114.52 E |
| Panlong, Zhg. | 106 | 31.58 N | 121.35 E |
| Panlong, Zhg. | 106 | 31.11 N | 121.16 E |
| Panlong (Lo) ≃ | 110 | 21.18 N | 105.25 E |
| Panlongzhen | 107 | 29.31 N | 105.17 E |
| P'anmunjŏm | 98 | 37.57 N | 126.40 E |
| Panna | 124 | 24.43 N | 80.12 E |
| Pannawonica | 162 | 21.44 S | 116.22 E |
| Panni | 68 | 41.13 N | 15.16 E |
| Panningen | 52 | 51.20 N | 5.59 E |
| Pannonhalma ⊕[1] | 30 | 47.28 N | 17.50 E |
| Panoche Creek ≃ | 226 | 36.44 N | 120.31 W |
| Panola | 194 | 31.58 N | 86.23 W |
| Panola □[6] | 222 | 32.07 N | 94.30 W |
| Páno Lévkara | 130 | 34.52 N | 33.18 E |
| Panopah | 112 | 1.56 S | 111.11 E |
| Páno Panayiá | 130 | 34.55 N | 32.38 E |
| Páno Plátres | 130 | 34.53 N | 32.52 E |
| Panora | 198 | 41.41 N | 94.21 W |
| Panorama | 255 | 21.21 S | 51.51 W |
| Pánormos | 38 | 37.38 N | 25.02 E |
| Panovo, Ross. | 24 | 59.48 N | 46.27 E |
| Panovo, Ross. | 88 | 58.58 N | 101.58 E |
| P'anp'yŏng-ni | 98 | 40.28 N | 125.49 E |
| Panruti | 122 | 11.46 N | 79.33 E |
| Pansfelde | 54 | 51.39 N | 11.16 E |
| Panshan | 104 | 41.12 N | 122.04 E |
| Panshanger Aerodrome ⊠ | 260 | 51.48 N | 0.08 W |
| Pansik, Rápido ᒪ | 236 | 14.30 N | 85.15 W |
| Pansionat | 265b | 55.59 N | 37.41 E |
| Pānskura | 126 | 22.25 N | 87.42 E |
| Pantabañgan | 116 | 15.50 N | 121.09 E |
| Pantalica, Necropoli di ⊥ | 70 | 37.08 N | 15.01 E |
| Pantanal Matogrossense, Parque Nacional do ♦ | 248 | 17.35 S | 57.40 W |
| Pantanaw | 110 | 16.59 N | 95.28 E |
| Pântano | 256 | 22.23 S | 46.01 W |
| Pântano, Ribeirão do ≃ | 256 | 22.15 S | 45.59 W |
| Pantar, Pulau I | 112 | 8.25 S | 124.07 E |
| Pantayivka | 78 | 48.41 N | 32.53 E |
| Panteleymonivka | 83 | 48.12 N | 37.59 E |
| Pantelleria | 70 | 36.50 N | 11.57 E |
| Pantelleria, Isola di I | 70 | 36.47 N | 12.00 E |
| Panteón Nacional ⊥ | 286c | 10.31 N | 66.55 W |
| Pantepec ≃ | 234 | 20.56 N | 97.44 W |
| Pantha | 110 | 23.49 N | 94.33 E |
| Pantheon ⊥ | 267a | 41.55 N | 12.29 E |
| Panther Creek ≃, Id., U.S. | 202 | 45.19 N | 114.24 W |
| Panther Creek ≃, Ky., U.S. | 194 | 37.45 N | 87.19 W |
| Panther Creek, South Fork ≃ | 194 | 37.42 N | 87.05 W |
| Panther Lake | 210 | 43.19 N | 75.54 W |
| Pantin | 50 | 48.54 N | 2.24 E |
| Pantitlán ◆[8] | 286a | 19.25 N | 99.05 W |
| Panto, Tanjung ≻ | 115a | 6.51 S | 105.54 E |
| Panton, Mount ∧[2] | 162 | 17.21 S | 129.13 E |
| Pantonlabu | 114 | 5.08 N | 97.28 E |
| Pantry Brook ≃ | 283 | 42.24 N | 71.22 W |
| Panu | 152 | 3.48 S | 19.07 E |
| Pánuco | 234 | 22.03 N | 98.10 W |
| Pánuco ≃ | 234 | 22.16 N | 97.47 W |
| Panuke Lake ⊜ | 186 | 44.48 N | 64.07 W |
| Panukulan | 116 | 14.56 N | 121.49 E |
| Pānuria | 126 | 23.49 N | 86.58 E |
| Panvel | 122 | 18.59 N | 73.06 E |
| Panvel ≃ | 272c | 19.01 N | 73.04 W |
| Panvel Creek ≃ | 272c | 18.59 N | 73.00 E |
| Panwāri | 124 | 25.27 N | 79.29 E |
| Panxi | 106 | 30.35 N | 119.20 E |
| Panxian | 102 | 25.50 N | 104.36 E |
| Panxidu | 98 | 35.39 N | 115.52 E |
| Panyabungan | 114 | 0.51 N | 99.33 E |
| Panyam | 150 | 9.25 N | 9.13 E |
| Panyang | 140 | 10.04 N | 29.58 E |
| Panyčevo | 86 | 57.05 N | 81.49 E |
| Panyu | 100 | 22.57 N | 113.20 E |
| Panyutyne | 78 | 48.56 N | 36.17 E |
| Panzerstausee ⊜[1] | 263 | 51.11 N | 7.16 E |
| Panzhuang | 105 | 39.20 N | 117.28 E |
| Panzi | 152 | 7.13 S | 17.58 E |
| Panzós | 236 | 15.24 N | 89.40 W |
| Pao ≃, Thai | 110 | 16.13 N | 103.43 E |
| Pao ≃, Ven. | 246 | 8.33 N | 68.01 W |
| Pao ≃, Ven. | 246 | 8.06 N | 64.17 W |
| Paochi → Baoji | 102 | 34.23 N | 107.09 E |
| Pão de Açúcar | 250 | 9.45 S | 37.26 W |
| Pão de Açúcar (Sugar Loaf) ∧ | 287a | 22.57 S | 43.09 W |
| Paoki → Baoji | 102 | 34.23 N | 107.09 E |
| Paola, It. | 68 | 39.22 N | 16.03 E |
| Paola, Ks., U.S. | 198 | 38.34 N | 94.52 W |
| Paoli, In., U.S. | 218 | 38.33 N | 86.28 W |
| Paoli, Pa., U.S. | 208 | 40.02 N | 75.28 W |
| Paoli, Wi., U.S. | 216 | 42.56 N | 89.32 W |
| Paonia | 200 | 38.52 N | 107.35 W |
| Pāonta Sāhib | 124 | 30.27 N | 77.37 E |
| Paopao | 174s | 17.31 S | 149.49 W |
| Paoshenmiao | 98 | 41.12 N | 118.17 E |
| Paotai Yingzi | 98 | 41.48 N | 115.12 E |
| Paoting → Baoding | 105 | 38.52 N | 115.29 E |
| Paotow → Baotou | 102 | 40.40 N | 109.59 E |
| Paoua | 152 | 7.15 N | 16.26 E |
| Paoying → Baoying | 100 | 33.16 N | 119.20 E |
| P'aozero, ozero ⊜ | 24 | 66.05 N | 30.58 E |
| Paozi | 104 | 42.13 N | 122.19 E |
| Pap | 85 | 40.53 N | 71.07 E |
| Pápa | 30 | 47.19 N | 17.28 E |
| Papa, Sound of ⊔ | 46a | 60.18 N | 1.41 W |
| Papagaio | 250 | 6.01 S | 45.21 W |
| Papagaio ≃, Bra. | 246 | 1.53 S | 62.35 W |
| Papagaio ≃, Bra. | 248 | 12.56 S | 58.18 W |
| Papagayo ≃ | 234 | 16.46 N | 99.43 W |
| Papagayo, Golfo de ⊂ | 236 | 10.42 N | 85.50 W |
| Papago Indian Reservation ◆[4] | 200 | 32.20 N | 112.00 W |
| Papaikou | 229d | 19.47 N | 155.05 W |
| Papakating Creek ≃ | 276 | 41.11 N | 74.38 W |
| Papakura | 172 | 37.04 S | 174.57 E |
| Papalia | 112 | 5.58 S | 124.01 E |
| Papaloapan ≃ | 234 | 18.42 N | 95.38 W |
| Papanoa | 234 | 17.21 N | 101.02 W |
| Papantla de Olarte | 234 | 20.27 N | 97.19 W |
| Papar, Indon. | 115a | 7.41 S | 112.04 E |
| Papar, Malay. | 112 | 5.44 N | 115.56 E |
| Papara, Poly. fr. | 174s | 17.44 S | 149.21 W |
| Papara, Sol.Is. | 175e | 7.02 S | 156.48 E |
| Paparoa | 172 | 36.06 S | 174.14 E |
| Paparoa National Park ♦ | 172 | 42.05 S | 171.25 E |
| Paparoa Range ⋌ | 172 | 42.00 S | 171.35 E |
| Papasidero | 68 | 39.52 N | 15.54 E |
| Papa Stour I | 46a | 60.20 N | 1.42 W |
| Papatoetoe | 172 | 36.58 S | 174.52 E |
| Papawai Point ≻ | 229a | 20.47 N | 156.33 W |
| Papa Westray I | 46 | 59.21 N | 2.54 W |
| Papeari | 174s | 17.45 S | 149.21 W |
| Papeete | 174s | 17.32 S | 149.34 W |
| Papelón | 286c | 10.27 N | 66.47 W |
| Papenburg | 52 | 53.05 N | 7.23 E |
| Papendrecht | 52 | 51.50 N | 4.40 E |
| Papenoo | 174s | 17.30 S | 149.25 W |
| Papenoo ≃ | 174s | 17.30 S | 149.25 W |
| Papetoai | 174s | 17.29 S | 149.52 W |
| Papey I | 24a | 64.37 N | 14.11 W |
| Paphlagonia □[9] | 130 | 41.10 N | 32.45 E |
| Paphos → Néa Páfos | 130 | 34.45 N | 32.25 E |
| Papilė | 76 | 56.09 N | 22.48 E |
| Papillion | 198 | 41.09 N | 96.02 W |
| Papineau | 216 | 40.58 N | 87.43 W |
| Papineau □[6] | 206 | 45.50 N | 75.00 W |
| Papineau, Lac ⊜ | 206 | 45.48 N | 74.46 W |
| Papineau Creek ≃ | 212 | 45.13 N | 77.43 W |
| Papineau-Labelle, Réserve ♦ | 188 | 45.55 N | 75.20 W |
| Papineau Lake ⊜ | 212 | 45.20 N | 77.50 W |
| Papineauville | 206 | 45.37 N | 75.01 W |
| Paposo | 252 | 25.01 S | 70.28 W |
| Papouasie Nouvelle-Guinée → Papua New Guinea □[1] | 164 | 6.00 S | 150.00 E |
| Papozze | 64 | 44.59 N | 12.02 E |
| Pappenheim | 56 | 48.56 N | 10.58 E |
| Paps of Jura ⋌ | 46 | 55.55 N | 6.00 W |
| Papua, Gulf of ⊂ | 164 | 8.30 S | 145.00 E |
| Papua Neuguinea → Papua New Guinea □[1] | 164 | 6.00 S | 150.00 E |
| Papua New Guinea □[1] | 164 | 6.00 S | 147.00 E |
| Papuasia Nueva Guinea → Papua New Guinea □[1] | 164 | 6.00 S | 150.00 E |
| Papucaia | 256 | 22.37 S | 42.44 W |
| Papudo | 252 | 32.31 S | 71.27 W |
| Papulovo | 24 | 60.34 N | 48.00 E |
| Papun | 110 | 18.04 N | 97.27 E |
| Papunáua ≃ | 246 | 2.09 N | 70.32 W |
| Papunya | 162 | 23.16 S | 131.54 E |
| Papurí ≃ | 246 | 0.36 N | 69.11 W |
| Paquequer ≃ | 256 | 22.12 S | 42.54 W |
| Paquequer, Serra do ⋌ | 256 | 22.12 S | 42.40 W |
| Paquera | 236 | 9.50 N | 84.56 W |
| Paquetá, Ilha de I | 287a | 22.46 S | 43.06 W |
| Par | 42 | 50.21 N | 4.43 W |
| Pará → Belém | 250 | 1.27 S | 48.29 W |
| Pará □[3] | 250 | 4.00 S | 53.00 W |
| Para □[5] | 250 | 5.30 N | 55.15 W |
| Pará ≃, Bra. | 250 | 1.30 S | 48.55 W |
| Pará ≃, Bra. | 255 | 19.13 S | 45.07 W |
| Para ≃, Ross. | 80 | 54.23 N | 40.52 E |
| Pará, Ilha do I | 250 | 0.18 S | 51.15 W |
| Para, Pulau I | 112 | 3.05 N | 125.30 E |
| Parabel' | 86 | 58.43 N | 81.31 E |
| Parabel' ≃ | 86 | 58.44 N | 81.35 E |
| Parabiago | 62 | 45.33 N | 8.57 E |
| Parabita | 68 | 40.03 N | 18.08 E |
| Paraburdoo | 162 | 23.14 S | 117.48 E |
| Paracale | 116 | 14.17 N | 122.48 E |
| Paracambi | 256 | 22.37 S | 43.43 W |
| Paracari ≃ | 250 | 4.36 S | 57.47 W |
| Paracas, Bahía de ⊂ | 248 | 13.50 S | 76.17 W |
| Paracas, Península de ≻[1] | 248 | 13.48 S | 76.24 W |
| Paracatu | 255 | 17.13 S | 46.52 W |
| Paracatu ≃, Bra. | 255 | 16.30 S | 45.04 W |
| Paracatu ≃, Bra. | 255 | 16.35 S | 45.06 W |
| Paracel Islands → Xisha Qundao II | 108 | 16.30 N | 112.15 E |
| Parachilna | 166 | 31.08 S | 138.23 E |
| Pārachinār | 120 | 33.54 N | 70.06 E |
| Paracho de Verduzco | 234 | 19.39 N | 102.04 W |
| Parachute | 200 | 39.27 N | 108.03 W |
| Paraćin | 38 | 43.52 N | 21.24 E |
| Parácuaro | 234 | 20.09 N | 100.46 W |
| Paracuellos de Jarama | 266a | 40.30 N | 3.32 W |
| Paracuru | 250 | 3.24 S | 39.04 W |
| Parád | 30 | 47.55 N | 20.02 E |
| Parada, Punta ≻ | 248 | 15.22 S | 75.12 W |
| Paradas | 34 | 37.18 N | 5.30 W |
| Paradise, Guy. | 246 | 6.45 N | 58.00 W |
| Paradise, Ca., U.S. | 204 | 39.44 N | 121.38 W |
| Paradise, Mt., U.S. | 202 | 47.23 N | 114.48 W |
| Paradise, Nv., U.S. | 204 | 36.09 N | 115.10 W |
| Paradise, Pa., U.S. | 208 | 40.01 N | 76.08 W |
| Paradise, Tx., U.S. | 222 | 33.09 N | 97.41 W |
| Paradise Hill, Sk., Can. | 184 | 53.32 N | 109.28 W |
| Paradise Hill, Ak., U.S. | 180 | 62.25 N | 160.03 W |
| Paradise Island I | 240b | 25.05 N | 77.19 W |
| Paradise Mountain ∧ | 171a | 27.45 S | 152.02 E |
| Paradise Valley, Az., U.S. | 200 | 33.31 N | 111.56 W |
| Paradise Valley, Nv., U.S. | 204 | 41.29 N | 117.32 W |
| Parado | 115b | 8.45 S | 118.36 E |
| Parado ≃ | 250 | 10.17 S | 55.39 W |
| Pāradwīp | 120 | 20.16 N | 86.37 E |
| Parafield | 168b | 34.47 S | 138.38 E |
| Parafiyivka | 78 | 50.53 N | 32.38 E |
| Parağaçay | 84 | 39.07 N | 45.56 E |
| Paragon | 218 | 39.23 N | 86.33 W |
| Paragonah | 200 | 37.53 N | 112.46 W |
| Paragould | 194 | 36.03 N | 90.30 W |
| Paraguá ≃, Bol. | 248 | 13.34 S | 61.53 W |
| Paragua ≃, Ven. | 246 | 6.55 N | 62.55 W |
| Paraguaçu | 256 | 21.33 S | 45.44 W |
| Paraguaçu ≃ | 255 | 12.45 S | 38.54 W |
| Paraguaçu Paulista | 255 | 22.25 S | 50.34 W |
| Paraguaipoa | 246 | 11.21 N | 71.57 W |
| Paraguaná, Península de ≻[1] | 246 | 11.55 N | 70.00 W |
| Paraguarí | 252 | 25.38 S | 57.09 W |
| Paraguarí □[5] | 252 | 26.00 S | 57.10 W |
| Paraguay □[1], S.A. | 244 | 23.00 S | 58.00 W |
| Paraguay □[1], S.A. | 252 | 23.00 S | 58.00 W |
| Paraguay (Paraguai) ≃ | 18 | 27.18 S | 58.38 W |
| Parahyba → João Pessoa | 250 | 7.07 S | 34.52 W |
| Parai, Reprêsa do ⊜[1] | 256 | 23.20 S | 45.35 W |
| Paraíba □[3] | 250 | 7.15 S | 36.30 W |
| Paraíba do Sul | 256 | 22.09 S | 43.17 W |
| Paraíba do Sul ≃ | 255 | 21.37 S | 41.03 W |
| Paraibano | 250 | 6.30 S | 44.01 W |
| Paraibuna | 256 | 23.23 S | 45.39 W |
| Paraibuna ≃, Bra. | 256 | 22.06 S | 43.08 W |
| Paraibuna ≃, Bra. | 256 | 23.22 S | 45.40 W |
| Paraibuna, Reprêsa do ⊜[1] | 256 | 23.25 S | 45.30 W |
| Paraíso, Bra. | 255 | 19.03 S | 52.59 W |
| Paraíso, Bra. | 256 | 22.19 S | 45.42 W |
| Paraíso, C.R. | 236 | 9.50 N | 83.51 W |
| Paraíso, Méx. | 234 | 18.24 N | 93.14 W |
| Paraiso, Pan. | 236 | 9.02 N | 79.38 W |
| Paraíso do Norte | 255 | 23.13 S | 52.38 W |
| Paraíso Garcia | 256 | 21.32 S | 43.53 W |
| Paraíso Novillero | 234 | 18.16 N | 95.59 W |
| Paraisópolis | 256 | 22.33 S | 45.47 W |
| Paraitinga ≃, Bra. | 256 | 23.34 S | 46.02 W |
| Paraitinga ≃, Bra. | 256 | 23.22 S | 45.40 W |
| Parakan | 115a | 7.17 S | 110.06 E |
| Parakou | 150 | 9.21 N | 2.37 E |
| Paralía Asprópirgos | 267c | 38.02 N | 23.35 E |
| Paralímni | 130 | 35.02 N | 33.59 E |
| Parama Island I | 164 | 9.00 S | 143.25 E |
| Paramakkudi | 122 | 9.33 N | 78.36 E |
| Paramaribo | 250 | 5.50 N | 55.10 W |
| Parambu | 250 | 6.13 S | 40.43 W |
| Paramillo, Parque Nacional ♦ | 246 | 7.15 N | 76.15 W |
| Paramirim | 255 | 13.26 S | 42.15 W |
| Paramirim ≃ | 250 | 11.34 S | 43.18 W |
| Paramithiá | 38 | 39.28 N | 20.30 E |
| Paramonga | 248 | 10.40 S | 77.50 W |
| Paramoti | 250 | 4.06 S | 39.15 W |
| Paramount | 228 | 33.53 N | 118.09 W |
| Paramus | 210 | 40.56 N | 74.04 W |
| Paramušir, ostrov I | 74 | 50.25 N | 155.50 E |
| Paramus Park ◆[9] | 276 | 40.57 N | 74.04 W |
| Paran, Naḥal (Wādī al-Jirāfī) V | 132 | 30.24 N | 35.10 E |
| Paraná, Arg. | 252 | 31.44 S | 60.32 W |
| Paranã, Bra. | 255 | 12.33 S | 47.52 W |
| Paraná □[3] | 252 | 24.00 S | 51.00 W |
| Paranã ≃, Bra. | 255 | 12.30 S | 48.14 W |
| Paraná ≃, S.A. | 18 | 33.43 S | 59.15 W |
| Paraná, Pico ∧ | 252 | 25.16 S | 48.48 W |
| Paranabi | 256 | 23.54 S | 45.14 W |
| Paraná Bravo ≃[1] | 258 | 33.53 S | 58.27 W |
| Paranacito ≃ | 258 | 33.44 S | 58.33 W |
| Paraná de las Palmas ≃[1] | 258 | 34.18 S | 58.33 W |
| Paranaguá | 252 | 25.31 S | 48.30 W |
| Paranaguá, Baía de ⊂ | 252 | 25.29 S | 48.33 W |
| Paraná Guazú ≃[1] | 258 | 34.00 S | 58.25 W |
| Paranaíba | 255 | 19.40 S | 51.11 W |
| Paranaíba ≃ | 255 | 20.07 S | 51.05 W |
| Paranaidji | 250 | 6.33 S | 47.27 W |
| Paranaíta ≃ | 250 | 9.28 S | 56.43 W |
| Paranam | 250 | 5.37 N | 55.06 W |
| Paraná Miní ≃[1] | 258 | 34.13 S | 58.25 W |
| Paranapanema ≃ | 255 | 22.40 S | 53.09 W |
| Paranapiacaba | 256 | 23.47 S | 46.19 W |
| Paranapiacaba, Serra do ⋌ | 252 | 24.20 S | 49.00 W |
| Parañaque | 269f | 14.30 N | 120.59 E |
| Paranavaí | 255 | 23.04 S | 52.28 W |
| Parang, Pil. | 116 | 7.23 N | 124.16 E |
| Parang, Pil. | 116 | 5.55 N | 120.54 E |
| Parang, Pulau I | 115a | 5.45 S | 110.14 E |
| Paran'ga | 80 | 56.43 N | 49.24 E |
| Parângu Mare, Vârful ∧ | 38 | 45.22 N | 23.33 E |
| Paranhos | 255 | 23.55 S | 55.25 W |
| Paranjang | 98 | 37.08 N | 126.55 E |
| Paranoá, Lago do ⊜ | 255 | 15.48 S | 47.50 W |


**Symbols** in the index entries represent the broad categories identified in the key at the right. Symbols with superior numbers (⋌[1]) identify subcategories (see complete key on page *I · 1).*

**Symbole** im Register stellen die rechts im Schlüssel erklärten Kategorien dar. Symbole mit hochgestellten Ziffern (⋌[1]) bezeichnen Unterabteilungen einer Kategorie (vgl. vollständiger Schlüssel auf Seite *I · 1).*

**Los símbolos** incluídos en el texto del índice representan las grandes categorías identificadas con la clave a la derecha. Los símbolos con numeros en su parte superior (⋌[1]) identifican las subcategorías (véase la clave completa en la página *I · 1).*

**Les symboles** de l'index représentent les catégories indiquées dans la légende à droite. Les symboles suivis d'un indice (⋌[1]) représentent des sous-catégories (voir légende complète à la page *I · 1).*

**Os símbolos** incluídos no texto do índice representam as grandes categorias identificadas com a chave à direita. Os símbolos com números em sua parte superior (⋌[1]) identificam as subcategorias (veja-se a chave completa à página *I · 1).*

| | | | | |
|---|---|---|---|---|
| ∧ Mountain | Berg | Montaña | Montagne | Montanha |
| ⋌ Mountains | Gebirge | Montañas | Montagnes | Montanhas |
| )( Pass | Paß | Paso | Col | Passo |
| V Valley, Canyon | Tal, Cañon | Valle, Cañón | Vallée, Canyon | Vale, Canhão |
| ≚ Plain | Ebene | Llano | Plaine | Planície |
| ≻ Cape | Kap | Cabo | Cap | Cabo |
| I Island | Insel | Isla | Île | Ilha |
| II Islands | Inseln | Islas | Îles | Ilhas |
| ⊥ Other Topographic Features | Andere Topographische Objekte | Otros Elementos Topográficos | Autres données topographiques | Outros acidentes topográficos |

ESPAÑOL · FRANÇAIS · PORTUGUÊS


| Nombre / Nom / Nome | Página / Page | Lat.°′ | Long.°′ W = Oeste / Ouest |
|---|---|---|---|
| Párao de Masa, Puerto de )( | 34 | 42.38 N | 3.46 W |
| Paraopeba | 255 | 19.18 S | 44.25 W |
| Parapara | 246 | 9.44 N | 67.18 W |
| Paraparaumu | 172 | 40.55 S | 175.01 E |
| Paraparaumu Beach | 172 | 40.54 S | 174.59 E |
| Parapayè | 58 | 45.55 N | 7.32 E |
| Parapetí ≃ | 248 | 18.58 S | 62.21 W |
| Parara | 112 | 2.37 S | 120.07 E |
| Parás, Méx. | 196 | 26.30 N | 99.31 W |
| Paras, Perú | 248 | 13.30 S | 74.35 W |
| Parasan | 116 | 8.05 N | 123.33 E |
| Parāsī | 124 | 27.32 N | 83.40 E |
| Parāsia | 124 | 22.12 N | 78.46 E |
| Parasida | 126 | 23.46 N | 87.20 E |
| Parasnāth | 124 | 23.59 N | 86.02 E |
| Paratei | 256 | 23.14 S | 46.00 W |
| Parateí ≃ | 256 | 23.12 S | 46.00 W |
| Parati | 256 | 23.13 S | 44.43 W |
| Paratico | 64 | 45.39 N | 9.57 E |
| Parati-Mirim | 256 | 23.14 S | 44.38 W |
| Paratinga | 255 | 12.42 S | 43.10 W |
| Paratoo | 166 | 32.42 S | 139.22 E |
| Parauapebas ≃ | 250 | 5.35 S | 49.41 W |
| Parauari ≃ | 250 | 4.36 S | 57.47 W |
| Paraúna | 255 | 17.02 S | 50.26 W |
| Paravani, ozero ⊜ | 84 | 41.26 N | 43.48 E |
| Para Wirra Recreation Park ♠ | 168b | 34.43 S | 138.50 E |
| Paray-le-Monial | 32 | 46.27 N | 4.07 E |
| Parbakalan | 114 | 2.38 N | 98.27 E |
| Pārbati ≃ | 124 | 25.51 N | 76.36 E |
| Pārbatipur | 124 | 25.39 N | 88.55 E |
| Parbhani | 122 | 19.16 N | 76.47 E |
| Parbig | 86 | 57.14 N | 81.24 E |
| Parbig ≃ | 86 | 57.37 N | 82.18 E |
| Parbold | 262 | 53.36 N | 2.46 W |
| Parburuan | 114 | 1.52 N | 99.55 E |
| Parcani | 38 | 46.49 N | 29.31 E |
| Parchen | 54 | 52.21 N | 12.05 E |
| Parchim | 54 | 53.25 N | 11.51 E |
| Parchment | 216 | 42.19 N | 85.34 W |
| Parcines (Partschins) | 64 | 46.41 N | 11.04 E |
| Parczew | 30 | 51.39 N | 22.54 E |
| Pardee Reservoir ⊜[1] | 226 | 38.16 N | 120.51 W |
| Pardeeville | 190 | 43.32 N | 89.18 W |
| Pardes Hanna-Karkur | 132 | 32.28 N | 34.58 E |
| Pārdi | 122 | 20.31 N | 72.57 E |
| Parding | 120 | 32.52 N | 88.39 E |
| Pardo ≃, Bra. | 250 | 5.21 S | 52.53 W |
| Pardo ≃, Bra. | 252 | 29.59 S | 52.23 W |
| Pardo ≃, Bra. | 255 | 15.48 S | 44.48 W |
| Pardo ≃, Bra. | 255 | 20.10 S | 48.38 W |
| Pardo ≃, Bra. | 255 | 22.55 S | 49.58 W |
| Pardo ≃, Bra. | 255 | 15.39 S | 38.57 W |
| Pardo ≃, Bra. | 255 | 21.46 S | 52.09 W |
| Pardo ≃, Bra. | 256 | 23.32 S | 45.30 W |
| Pardo ≃, Bra. | 256 | 21.25 S | 42.39 W |
| Pardomuan | 114 | 2.06 N | 98.20 E |
| Pardubice | 30 | 50.02 N | 15.47 E |
| Pare | 115a | 7.46 S | 112.11 E |
| Parèčča | 76 | 53.55 N | 24.07 E |
| Parece Vela → Okino-Tori-shima I | 90 | 20.25 N | 136.00 E |
| Parecis | 248 | 14.09 S | 56.56 W |
| Parecis ≃ | 248 | 12.56 S | 56.43 W |
| Parecis, Chapada dos ⋏ | 248 | 13.00 S | 60.00 W |
| Parede | 266c | 38.41 N | 9.21 W |
| Paredes de Nava | 34 | 42.09 N | 4.41 W |
| Paredón | 232 | 25.56 N | 100.58 W |
| Parelhas | 250 | 6.41 S | 36.39 W |
| Parelheiros ◆[8] | 256 | 23.51 S | 46.44 W |
| Pareloup, Lac de ⊜ | 32 | 44.15 N | 2.45 E |
| Paremata | 172 | 41.07 S | 174.52 E |
| Parempei I | 174r | 7.01 N | 158.15 E |
| Paren' | 74 | 62.28 N | 163.05 E |
| Paren' ≃ | 74 | 62.25 N | 163.10 E |
| Parengarenga Harbour ⊂ | 172 | 34.31 S | 172.57 E |
| Parent | 176 | 47.55 N | 74.37 W |
| Parent, Lac ⊜ | 190 | 48.38 N | 77.03 W |
| Parentis-en-Born | 32 | 44.21 N | 1.05 W |
| Pareora | 172 | 44.30 S | 171.12 E |
| Parepare | 112 | 4.01 S | 119.38 E |
| Parera | 252 | 35.08 S | 64.32 W |
| Parets del Vallès | 266d | 41.34 N | 2.14 E |
| Parey | 54 | 52.22 N | 11.59 E |
| Parfenjevo, Ross. | 24 | 61.21 N | 42.43 E |
| Parfenjevo, Ross. | 80 | 58.29 N | 43.25 E |
| Parfentevo | 82 | 55.06 N | 38.49 E |
| Parfino | 76 | 57.58 N | 31.41 E |
| Parforce-Heide ◆[3] | 264a | 52.22 N | 13.10 E |
| Párga | 38 | 39.17 N | 20.23 E |
| Pārgaon | 272c | 18.59 N | 73.05 E |
| Pargarutan | 114 | 1.28 N | 99.20 E |
| Pargas (Parainen) | 26 | 60.18 N | 22.18 E |
| Pargey Creek ≃ | 285 | 39.49 N | 75.18 W |
| Pargny-sur-Saulx | 56 | 48.46 N | 4.50 E |
| Pargolovo ◆[8] | 265a | 60.04 N | 30.18 E |
| Parham | 240c | 17.05 N | 61.46 W |
| Parhebangan | 114 | 2.15 N | 98.45 E |
| Pari ◆[8] | 287b | 23.32 S | 46.37 W |
| Paria ≃ | 200 | 36.52 N | 111.36 W |
| Paria, Gulf of ⊂ | 246 | 10.20 N | 62.00 W |
| Paria, Península de >[1] | 241r | 10.40 N | 62.10 W |
| Pariaguán | 246 | 8.51 N | 64.43 W |
| Pariaman | 112 | 0.38 S | 100.08 E |
| Pariamanu ≃ | 248 | 12.26 S | 69.16 W |
| Paricutín ∧[1] | 234 | 19.28 N | 102.15 W |
| Parida, Isla I | 236 | 8.07 N | 82.20 W |
| Pariette Draw V | 200 | 40.02 N | 109.45 W |
| Parigi, Indon. | 112 | 0.48 S | 120.10 E |
| Parigi, Indon. | 115a | 6.12 S | 106.22 E |
| Parigné-L'Évêque | 50 | 47.56 N | 0.22 E |
| Parika | 246 | 6.52 N | 58.25 W |
| Parikkala | 26 | 61.33 N | 29.30 E |
| Parima ≃ | 246 | 3.34 N | 63.47 W |
| Parima, Sierra ⋏ | 246 | 2.30 N | 64.00 W |
| Pariñas, Punta > | 246 | 4.40 S | 81.20 W |
| Parintins | 250 | 2.36 S | 56.44 W |
| Paripiranga | 250 | 10.41 S | 37.52 W |
| Pariquera-Açu | 252 | 24.43 S | 47.53 W |
| Paris, On., Can. | 212 | 43.12 N | 80.23 W |
| Paris, Fr. | 50 | 48.52 N | 2.20 E |
| Paris, Fr. | 261 | 48.52 N | 2.20 E |
| Paris, Ar., U.S. | 194 | 35.17 N | 93.43 W |
| Paris, Id., U.S. | 202 | 42.13 N | 111.24 W |
| Paris, Il., U.S. | 194 | 39.36 N | 87.41 W |
| Paris, Ky., U.S. | 218 | 38.12 N | 84.15 W |
| Paris, Me., U.S. | 188 | 44.15 N | 70.30 W |
| Paris, Mo., U.S. | 219 | 39.28 N | 92.00 W |
| Paris, Oh., U.S. | 214 | 40.48 N | 81.10 W |
| Paris, Pa., U.S. | 214 | 40.24 N | 80.31 W |
| Paris, Tn., U.S. | 194 | 36.18 N | 88.19 W |
| Paris, Tx., U.S. | 196 | 33.39 N | 95.33 W |
| Paris □[5] | 261 | 48.52 N | 2.20 E |
| Paris, Port de ⊂ | 261 | 48.57 N | 2.17 E |
| Parish | 210 | 43.24 N | 76.07 W |
| Parisien de Pantin, Cimetière ◆ | 261 | 48.54 N | 2.23 E |
| Parisienne, Ile I | 190 | 46.41 N | 84.44 W |
| Paris-le-Bourget, Aéroport de ⊠ | 50 | 48.52 N | 2.25 E |
| Parismina | 236 | 10.12 N | 83.38 W |
| Parismina ≃ | 236 | 10.19 N | 83.21 W |
| Paris-Orly, Aéroport de ⊠ | 50 | 48.43 N | 2.22 E |
| Paris-Plage, Aéroport ⊠ | 50 | 50.31 N | 1.38 E |
| Parit | 112 | 3.10 S | 104.38 E |
| Parita, Bahía de ⊂ | 236 | 8.08 N | 80.24 W |
| Parit Bunga | 114 | 2.04 N | 102.33 E |
| Parit Buntar | 114 | 5.07 N | 100.30 E |
| Pariti | 112 | 10.01 S | 123.43 E |
| Parit Jawa | 114 | 1.57 N | 102.39 E |
| Park ≃ | 198 | 48.28 N | 97.09 W |
| Park, North Branch ≃ | 198 | 48.26 N | 97.27 W |
| Park, South Branch ≃ | 198 | 48.26 N | 97.27 W |
| Parka | 154 | 4.31 N | 27.20 E |
| Parkano | 26 | 62.01 N | 23.01 E |
| Parkchester | 285 | 40.00 N | 75.35 W |
| Park City, Il., U.S. | 216 | 42.21 N | 87.53 W |
| Park City, Ks., U.S. | 198 | 37.48 N | 97.19 W |
| Park City, Mt., U.S. | 202 | 45.37 N | 108.55 W |
| Park City, Ut,. U.S. | 200 | 40.38 N | 111.29 W |
| Park Creek ≃ | 285 | 40.13 N | 75.08 W |
| Parkdale, P.E., Can. | 186 | 46.15 N | 63.07 W |
| Parkdale, Mo., U.S. | 219 | 38.29 N | 90.32 W |
| Parkdale, Or., U.S. | 224 | 45.31 N | 121.35 W |
| Parkdene | 273d | 26.14 S | 28.16 E |
| Parkent | 85 | 41.18 N | 69.40 E |
| Parker, Az., U.S. | 200 | 34.09 N | 114.17 W |
| Parker, Co., U.S. | 198 | 39.31 N | 104.45 W |
| Parker, Fl., U.S. | 194 | 30.07 N | 85.36 W |
| Parker, Pa., U.S. | 214 | 41.05 N | 79.41 W |
| Parker, S.D., U.S. | 198 | 43.23 N | 97.08 W |
| Parker □[6] | 222 | 32.48 N | 97.42 W |
| Parker ≃ | 207 | 42.45 N | 70.49 W |
| Parker, Cape > | 176 | 75.04 N | 79.40 W |
| Parker, Lake ⊜ | 220 | 28.04 N | 81.56 W |
| Parker City | 218 | 40.11 N | 85.12 W |
| Parker Dam | 204 | 34.17 N | 114.08 W |
| Parker Dam ◆[6] | 200 | 34.18 N | 114.10 W |
| Parker Ford | 285 | 40.12 N | 75.35 W |
| Parker Peak ∧ | 198 | 43.24 N | 103.41 W |
| Parker Range | 162 | 31.38 S | 119.35 E |
| Parker River National Wildlife Refuge ◆[4] | 283 | 42.45 N | 70.48 W |
| Parkersburg, Il., U.S. | 194 | 38.36 N | 88.03 W |
| Parkersburg, Ia., U.S. | 190 | 42.34 N | 92.47 W |
| Parkersburg, W.V., U.S. | 188 | 39.16 N | 81.33 W |
| Parkers Creek ≃ | 285 | 40.00 N | 74.53 W |
| Parkers Prairie | 198 | 46.09 N | 95.19 W |
| Parkerville | 168a | 31.53 S | 116.09 E |
| Parker Volcano ∧[1] | 116 | 6.07 N | 124.54 E |
| Parkes | 166 | 33.08 S | 148.11 E |
| Parkesburg | 208 | 39.57 N | 75.55 W |
| Park Falls | 190 | 45.56 N | 90.26 W |
| Parkfield | 226 | 35.54 N | 120.25 W |
| Park Forest | 216 | 41.28 N | 87.38 W |
| Parkgate, Eng., U.K. | 262 | 53.18 N | 3.05 W |
| Parkgate, Eng., U.K. | 262 | 53.16 N | 2.20 W |
| Park Hall | 208 | 38.13 N | 76.25 W |
| Parkhill, On., Can. | 190 | 43.09 N | 81.41 W |
| Parkhill, Pa., U.S. | 214 | 40.22 N | 78.52 W |
| Parkhill Gardens | 273d | 26.14 S | 28.11 E |
| Parkhomenko | 83 | 48.34 N | 39.43 E |
| Parkhomivka | 78 | 50.08 N | 35.01 E |
| Parkin | 194 | 35.15 N | 90.34 W |
| Park Lake | 216 | 42.48 N | 84.27 W |
| Parkland, Pa., U.S. | 285 | 40.09 N | 74.56 W |
| Parkland, Wa., U.S. | 224 | 47.09 N | 122.25 W |
| Parklawn | 284c | 38.50 N | 77.09 W |
| Park Layne | 218 | 39.53 N | 84.03 W |
| Parklea | 274a | 33.44 S | 150.57 E |
| Parkman | 214 | 41.22 N | 81.03 W |
| Park Meadows | 279b | 40.18 N | 79.44 W |
| Park Orchards | 274b | 37.46 S | 145.13 E |
| Park Plateau ⋏[1] | 198 | 37.15 N | 104.45 W |
| Park Range ⋏ | 200 | 40.40 N | 106.40 W |
| Park Rapids | 198 | 46.55 N | 95.03 W |
| Park Ridge, Il., U.S. | 216 | 42.00 N | 87.50 W |
| Park Ridge, N.J., U.S. | 276 | 41.02 N | 74.02 W |
| Park Ridge Farms | 285 | 40.10 N | 74.42 W |
| Park River | 198 | 48.23 N | 97.44 W |
| Parkrose | 224 | 45.33 N | 122.33 W |
| Park Rynie | 158 | 30.25 S | 30.35 E |
| Parks | 180 | 57.38 N | 154.00 W |
| Parks Creek ≃ | 212 | 44.17 N | 77.21 W |
| Park Shore Resort | 216 | 41.55 N | 85.59 W |
| Parkside, Md., U.S. | 284c | 39.02 N | 77.06 W |
| Parkside, Pa., U.S. | 285 | 39.52 N | 75.23 W |
| Parksley | 208 | 37.46 N | 75.39 W |
| Park Station ◆[5] | 273d | 26.12 S | 28.03 E |
| Parkstein | 60 | 49.44 N | 12.04 E |
| Parkstetten | 60 | 48.55 N | 12.36 E |
| Parkston | 198 | 43.23 N | 97.59 W |
| Parksville, B.C., Can. | 182 | 49.19 N | 124.19 W |
| Parksville, N.Y., U.S. | 210 | 41.51 N | 74.45 W |
| Parktown ◆[8] | 273d | 26.11 S | 28.03 E |
| Parktown North ◆[8] | 273d | 26.09 S | 28.02 E |
| Parkview | 279b | 40.30 N | 79.56 W |
| Parkville, Md., U.S. | 208 | 39.22 N | 76.32 W |
| Parkville, Mo., U.S. | 194 | 39.11 N | 94.40 W |
| Parkwater | 202 | 47.40 N | 117.19 W |
| Parkway, Ca., U.S. | 226 | 38.29 N | 121.27 W |
| Parkway, Mo., U.S. | 219 | 38.20 N | 90.57 W |
| Parkwood | 284c | 39.01 N | 77.05 W |
| Parla | 34 | 40.14 N | 3.46 W |
| Parlākimidi | 122 | 18.47 N | 84.06 E |
| Parle, Lac qui ⊜ | 198 | 45.07 N | 96.00 W |
| Parli | 122 | 18.51 N | 76.32 E |
| Parliament, Houses of ♁ | 260 | 51.30 N | 0.07 W |
| Parlier | 226 | 36.36 N | 119.31 W |
| Parma, It. | 64 | 44.48 N | 10.20 E |
| Parma, Id., U.S. | 202 | 43.47 N | 116.56 W |
| Parma, Mi., U.S. | 216 | 42.15 N | 84.35 W |
| Parma, Mo., U.S. | 194 | 36.36 N | 89.48 W |
| Parma, Oh., U.S. | 214 | 41.24 N | 81.43 W |
| Parma □[4] | 64 | 44.40 N | 10.10 E |
| Parma ≃ | 64 | 44.56 N | 10.26 E |
| Parma Heights | 214 | 41.23 N | 81.45 W |
| Parmain | 261 | 49.07 N | 2.12 E |
| Parmatown Mall ◆[9] | 279a | 41.23 N | 81.44 W |
| Parnaguá | 250 | 10.13 S | 44.38 W |
| Parnahyba → Parnaíba | 250 | 2.54 S | 41.47 W |
| Parnaíba | 250 | 2.54 S | 41.47 W |
| Parnaíba ≃ | 250 | 3.00 S | 41.50 W |
| Parnaibinha ≃ | 250 | 9.17 S | 45.55 W |
| Parnamirim | 250 | 8.05 S | 39.34 W |
| Parnarama | 250 | 5.41 S | 43.06 W |
| Parnassós ∧ | 38 | 38.32 N | 22.35 E |
| Parnassus | 172 | 42.43 S | 173.18 E |
| Parndorf | 61 | 47.59 N | 16.51 E |
| Parnell | 216 | 40.14 N | 88.42 W |
| Párnis ∧ | 38 | 38.11 N | 23.42 E |
| Párnis Óros ⋏ | 267c | 38.07 N | 23.44 E |
| Parnon ⋏ | 38 | 37.05 N | 22.40 E |
| Pärnu | 76 | 58.24 N | 24.32 E |
| Pärnu ≃ | 76 | 58.23 N | 24.29 E |
| Pärnu-Jaagupi | 76 | 58.37 N | 24.30 E |
| Pärnu laht ⊂ | 76 | 58.15 N | 24.25 E |
| Paro | 124 | 27.26 N | 89.25 E |
| Pārola | 120 | 20.53 N | 75.07 E |
| Paromaj | 89 | 52.50 N | 143.02 E |
| Paroo | 162 | 26.16 S | 119.46 E |
| Paroo ≃ | 166 | 31.28 S | 143.32 E |
| Parorā | 272b | 22.48 N | 88.09 E |
| Páros | 38 | 37.04 N | 25.08 E |
| Páros I | 38 | 37.08 N | 25.12 E |
| Parow | 158 | 33.53 S | 18.37 E |
| Parowan | 200 | 37.50 N | 112.49 W |
| Parpaillon ⋏ | 62 | 44.30 N | 6.40 E |
| Parpan | 58 | 46.46 N | 9.33 E |
| Parr | 216 | 41.02 N | 87.13 W |
| Parral, Chile | 252 | 36.09 S | 71.50 W |
| Parral → Hidalgo del Parral, Méx. | 232 | 26.56 N | 105.40 W |
| Parral, Oh., U.S. | 214 | 40.33 N | 81.30 W |
| Parral ≃ | 232 | 27.39 N | 105.07 W |
| Parramatta | 170 | 33.49 S | 151.00 E |
| Parramatta ≃ | 274a | 33.51 S | 151.14 E |
| Parramatta Park ♠ | 274a | 33.49 S | 151.00 E |
| Parramore Island I | 208 | 37.32 N | 75.38 W |
| Parras de la Fuente | 232 | 25.25 N | 102.11 W |
| Parrett ≃ | 42 | 51.13 N | 3.01 W |
| Parrish, Al., U.S. | 194 | 33.43 N | 87.17 W |
| Parrish, Fl., U.S. | 220 | 27.35 N | 82.25 W |
| Parris Island Marine Corps Recruit Depot ■ | 192 | 32.21 N | 80.41 W |
| Parrita | 236 | 9.30 N | 84.19 W |
| Parrita ≃ | 236 | 9.29 N | 84.19 W |
| Parrsboro | 186 | 45.24 N | 64.20 W |
| Parry, Cape > | 176 | 70.08 N | 124.24 W |
| Parry, Mount ∧ | 182 | 52.53 N | 128.45 W |
| Parry Bay ⊂ | 176 | 68.07 N | 82.00 W |
| Parry Channel ɥ | 16 | 74.20 N | 98.00 W |
| Parry Island I | 212 | 45.18 N | 80.10 W |
| Parry Island Indian Reserve ◆[4] | 212 | 45.18 N | 80.10 W |
| Parry Peninsula >[1] | 180 | 69.45 N | 124.30 W |
| Parry Sound | 212 | 45.21 N | 80.02 W |
| Parry Sound □[6] | 212 | 45.25 N | 79.55 W |
| Parry Sound ɥ | 212 | 45.21 N | 80.06 W |
| Parryville | 208 | 40.49 N | 75.40 W |
| Parsberg | 60 | 49.09 N | 11.43 E |
| Parsdorf | 60 | 48.09 N | 11.47 E |
| Parseierspitze ∧ | 58 | 47.10 N | 10.28 E |
| Parsęta ≃ | 30 | 54.12 N | 15.33 E |
| Parshād | 120 | 24.11 N | 73.42 E |
| Parshall | 198 | 47.57 N | 102.08 W |
| Parshallville | 281 | 42.41 N | 83.46 W |
| Paršino | 88 | 59.10 N | 111.48 E |
| Parsippany | 210 | 40.51 N | 74.25 W |
| Parsippany, Lake ⊜ | 276 | 40.51 N | 74.26 W |
| Parsnāth ∧ | 124 | 23.53 N | 86.08 E |
| Parsnip ≃ | 182 | 55.10 N | 123.00 W |
| Parsoburan | 114 | 2.19 N | 99.20 E |
| Parsonage Island I | 276 | 40.37 N | 73.37 W |
| Parsons, Ks., U.S. | 198 | 37.20 N | 95.15 W |
| Parsons, Tn., U.S. | 194 | 35.38 N | 88.07 W |
| Parsons, W.V., U.S. | 188 | 39.05 N | 79.40 W |
| Parsons, Mount ∧[2] | 164 | 13.33 S | 135.09 E |
| Parson's Pond | 186 | 50.02 N | 57.43 W |
| Parsons Pond ⊜ | 186 | 50.00 N | 57.35 W |
| Parsons Range ⋏ | 164 | 13.30 S | 135.15 E |
| Parsteiner See ⊜ | 54 | 52.55 N | 13.59 E |
| Pärsti | 76 | 58.25 N | 25.32 E |
| Partābpur | 124 | 23.29 N | 83.13 E |
| Partanna | 70 | 37.43 N | 12.53 E |
| Partāppur | 126 | 21.48 N | 86.44 E |
| Partenen | 58 | 46.58 N | 10.03 E |
| Parthala | 272a | 28.36 N | 77.24 E |
| Parthe ≃ | 54 | 51.22 N | 12.21 E |
| Parthenay | 32 | 46.39 N | 0.15 W |
| Partington | 262 | 53.25 N | 2.26 W |
| Partinico | 70 | 38.03 N | 13.07 E |
| Partizansk | 89 | 43.08 N | 133.09 E |
| Partizánske | 30 | 48.39 N | 18.23 E |
| Partizanskoje | 86 | 55.30 N | 94.24 E |
| Parton | 44 | 54.34 N | 3.35 W |
| Partridge, Point > | 224 | 48.13 N | 122.46 W |
| Partridge Creek ≃ | 212 | 44.44 N | 77.13 W |
| Partridge Crop Lake ⊜ | 184 | 55.38 N | 97.27 W |
| Partridge Point > | 186 | 50.09 N | 56.10 W |
| Partry | 48 | 53.41 N | 9.19 W |
| Partschins → Parcines | 64 | 46.41 N | 11.04 E |
| Paru ≃, Bra. | 250 | 1.33 S | 52.38 W |
| Parú ≃, Ven. | 246 | 4.20 N | 66.27 W |
| Parubcan | 116 | 13.43 N | 123.45 E |
| Paru de Este ≃ | 250 | 1.10 N | 54.40 W |
| Paru de Oeste ≃ | 250 | 1.30 S | 56.00 W |
| Parung | 115a | 6.25 S | 106.42 E |
| Pårup, Dan. | 41 | 55.24 N | 10.20 E |
| Pårup, Dan. | 41 | 56.08 N | 9.21 E |
| Parūr | 122 | 10.09 N | 76.14 E |
| Paruro | 248 | 13.46 S | 71.51 W |
| Parutyne | 78 | 46.43 N | 31.53 E |
| Parvān □[4] | 120 | 35.15 N | 69.30 E |
| Pārvatīpuram | 122 | 18.47 N | 83.26 E |
| Parvin State Park ♠ | 208 | 39.30 N | 75.09 W |
| Pârvomaj | 38 | 42.06 N | 25.13 E |
| Paryang | 120 | 30.11 N | 83.09 E |
| Paryčy | 76 | 52.48 N | 29.25 E |
| Påryd | 26 | 56.34 N | 15.55 E |
| Parys | 158 | 27.04 S | 27.16 E |
| Paša ≃ | 76 | 60.29 N | 32.55 E |
| Paşabahçe ◆[8] | 267b | 41.06 N | 29.05 E |
| Pasacao | 116 | 13.31 N | 123.03 E |
| Pasaco | 236 | 13.59 N | 90.12 W |
| Pasadena, Nf., Can. | 186 | 49.01 N | 57.36 W |
| Pasadena, Ca., U.S. | 228 | 34.08 N | 118.08 W |
| Pasadena, Md., U.S. | 208 | 39.06 N | 76.34 W |
| Pasadena, Tx., U.S. | 222 | 29.41 N | 95.12 W |
| Pasado, Cabo > | 246 | 0.22 S | 80.30 W |
| Pasaje | 246 | 3.20 S | 79.49 W |
| Pasaje ≃ | 252 | 25.35 S | 63.57 W |
| Pasaje Talavera ≃[1] | 258 | 33.53 S | 58.55 W |
| Pa Sak ≃ | 110 | 14.21 N | 100.35 E |
| Paşaköy | 130 | 35.09 N | 33.36 E |
| Pasaleng Bay ⊂ | 116 | 18.36 N | 120.56 E |
| Paşalimanı Adası I | 130 | 40.28 N | 27.37 E |
| Pasān | 124 | 22.51 N | 82.12 E |
| Pasanauri | 84 | 42.21 N | 44.41 E |
| Pasangkayu | 112 | 1.10 S | 119.20 E |
| Pasarbantal | 112 | 2.45 S | 101.20 E |
| Pasarseluma | 112 | 4.09 S | 102.32 E |
| Pasar Senen Station ◆[5] | 269e | 6.10 S | 106.50 E |
| Pasarsorkam | 114 | 1.53 N | 98.34 E |
| Pasarwajo | 112 | 5.29 S | 122.50 E |
| Pasatiempo | 226 | 37.02 N | 122.02 W |
| Pasaunda | 272a | 28.42 N | 77.21 E |
| Pasawng | 110 | 18.52 N | 97.18 E |
| Pasay | 269f | 14.33 N | 121.00 E |
| Pasayten ≃ | 224 | 49.08 N | 120.35 W |
| Pasayten, Middle Fork ≃ | 224 | 48.53 N | 120.37 W |
| Pasayten, West Fork ≃ | 224 | 48.53 N | 120.37 W |
| Pascack Brook ≃ | 276 | 40.59 N | 73.59 W |
| Pascagama, Lac ⊜ | 190 | 48.34 N | 75.36 W |
| Pascagoula | 194 | 30.21 N | 88.33 W |
| Pascagoula ≃ | 194 | 30.21 N | 88.34 W |
| Pascalis, Lac ⊜ | 190 | 48.16 N | 77.24 W |
| Paşcani | 38 | 47.15 N | 26.44 E |
| Pasching | 61 | 48.15 N | 14.12 E |
| Pasco | 202 | 46.13 N | 119.05 W |
| Pasco □[5] | 248 | 10.30 S | 75.15 W |
| Pasco □[6] | 220 | 28.20 N | 82.27 W |
| Pascoag | 207 | 41.57 N | 71.42 W |
| Pascoe Vale | 274b | 37.44 S | 144.56 E |
| Pascua ≃ | 254 | 48.13 S | 73.22 W |
| Pascua, Isla de (Easter Island) (Rapa Nui) I | 174z | 27.07 S | 109.22 W |
| Pas-de-Calais □[5] | 50 | 50.30 N | 2.20 E |
| Pas-en-Artois | 50 | 50.09 N | 2.30 E |
| Pasewalk | 54 | 53.30 N | 14.00 E |
| Pashmāl | 123 | 35.26 N | 72.36 E |
| Pasian di Prato | 64 | 46.03 N | 13.11 E |
| Pasiano di Pordenone | 64 | 45.51 N | 12.37 E |
| Pasig | 116 | 14.33 N | 121.05 E |
| Pasig ≃ | 269f | 14.36 N | 120.58 E |
| Pāsighāt | 120 | 28.04 N | 95.20 E |
| Pašija | 86 | 58.26 N | 58.16 E |
| P'asina ≃ | 74 | 73.50 N | 87.10 E |
| Pasinler (Hasankale) | 130 | 39.59 N | 41.41 E |
| Pašino | 86 | 55.11 N | 83.00 E |
| P'asino, ozero ⊜ | 74 | 69.45 N | 87.45 E |
| P'asinskij zaliv ⊂ | 74 | 74.00 N | 86.00 E |
| Pasirganting | 112 | 2.02 S | 100.53 E |
| Pasir Gudang | 271c | 1.27 N | 103.53 E |
| Pasirian | 115a | 8.13 S | 113.06 E |
| Pasir Mas | 114 | 6.02 N | 102.08 E |
| Pasir Panjang | 271c | 1.17 N | 103.47 E |
| Pasirpengarayan | 114 | 0.51 N | 100.16 E |
| Pasir Puteh, Malay. | 114 | 5.50 N | 102.24 E |
| Pasir Puteh, Malay. | 271c | 1.26 N | 103.56 E |
| Paskallavik | 26 | 57.10 N | 16.27 E |
| Paskeville | 168b | 34.02 S | 137.54 E |
| Paškovo, Ross. | 80 | 53.39 N | 42.40 E |
| Paškovo, Ross. | 89 | 48.54 N | 130.42 E |
| Paškovskij | 78 | 45.02 N | 39.06 E |
| Pasłęk | 30 | 54.05 N | 19.39 E |
| Pasłęka ≃ | 30 | 54.26 N | 19.45 E |
| Pasley, Cape > | 162 | 33.57 S | 123.31 E |
| Pasley Bay ⊂ | 176 | 70.40 N | 96.27 W |
| Pašman, Otok I | 36 | 43.58 N | 15.21 E |
| Pasmore ≃ | 166 | 31.07 S | 139.48 E |
| Pašn'a | 24 | 63.21 N | 56.28 E |
| Pasni | 128 | 25.16 N | 63.28 E |
| Paso de Indios | 254 | 43.52 S | 69.06 W |
| Paso del Cerro | 252 | 31.29 S | 55.50 W |
| Paso del Macho | 234 | 18.58 N | 96.43 W |
| Paso de los Libres | 252 | 29.43 S | 57.05 W |
| Paso de los Toros | 252 | 32.49 S | 56.31 W |
| Paso del Rey | 288 | 34.39 S | 58.46 W |
| Paso del Toro | 234 | 19.02 N | 96.07 W |
| Paso de Ovejas | 234 | 19.17 N | 96.26 W |
| Paso de Patria | 252 | 27.13 S | 58.35 W |
| Paso de San Antonio | 196 | 29.05 N | 103.55 W |
| Paso Hondo | 232 | 15.49 N | 92.02 W |
| Paso Limay | 254 | 40.33 S | 70.26 W |
| Pasorapa | 248 | 18.16 S | 64.37 W |
| Paso Robles | 226 | 35.37 N | 120.41 W |
| Paso Seco | 240m | 17.59 N | 66.23 W |
| Paso Severino, Embalse ⊜[1] | 258 | 34.15 S | 56.18 W |
| Pašozero | 76 | 60.02 N | 34.37 E |
| Pasqua Indian Reserve ◆[4] | 184 | 50.45 N | 104.02 W |
| Pasque Island I | 207 | 41.27 N | 70.50 W |
| Pasquel, Punta > | 232 | 25.30 N | 111.01 W |
| Pasquia Hills ⋏[2] | 184 | 53.13 N | 102.37 W |
| Pasquotank □[6] | 208 | 36.26 N | 76.26 W |
| Pasquotank ≃ | 192 | 36.10 N | 76.03 W |
| Pasrūr | 123 | 32.16 N | 74.40 E |
| Passadumkeag | 188 | 45.11 N | 68.37 W |
| Passadumkeag Mountain ∧[2] | 188 | 45.10 N | 68.20 W |
| Passage East | 48 | 52.13 N | 6.59 W |
| Passagem Franca | 250 | 6.10 S | 43.47 W |
| Passage Point > | 176 | 73.29 N | 115.17 W |
| Passage West | 48 | 51.52 N | 8.20 W |
| Passaic | 210 | 40.51 N | 74.07 W |
| Passaic □[6] | 210 | 40.55 N | 74.10 W |
| Passaic ≃ | 276 | 40.43 N | 74.07 W |
| Passaic Falls ∟ | 276 | 40.55 N | 74.11 W |
| Passamaquoddy Bay ⊂ | 186 | 45.06 N | 66.59 W |
| Passa Quatro | 256 | 22.23 S | 44.58 W |
| Passa Três | 256 | 22.42 S | 44.00 W |
| Passau | 60 | 48.35 N | 13.28 E |
| Passa Vinte | 256 | 22.13 S | 44.15 W |
| Pass Creek ≃ | 198 | 43.45 N | 101.28 W |
| Passero, Capo > | 70 | 36.40 N | 15.09 E |
| Passignano sul Trasimeno | 66 | 43.11 N | 12.08 E |
| Passirio (Passer) ≃ | 64 | 46.41 N | 11.10 E |
| Pass Island | 186 | 47.29 N | 56.11 W |
| Paŝskij Perevoz | 76 | 60.24 N | 32.59 E |
| Passo Corese | 66 | 42.09 N | 12.39 E |
| Passo Fundo | 252 | 28.15 S | 52.24 W |
| Passopisciaro | 70 | 37.52 N | 15.02 E |
| Passo Real, Reprêsa do ⊜[1] | 252 | 28.55 S | 53.10 W |
| Passos | 255 | 20.43 S | 46.37 W |
| Passow | 54 | 53.08 N | 14.06 E |
| Passy | 58 | 45.55 N | 6.41 E |
| Passy ◆[8] | 261 | 48.52 N | 2.17 E |
| Pastavy | 76 | 55.07 N | 26.50 E |
| Pastaza □[4] | 246 | 1.45 S | 76.50 W |
| Pastaza ≃ | 246 | 4.50 S | 76.25 W |
| Pastecho ≃ | 182 | 56.07 N | 114.15 W |
| Pasteur, Lac ⊜ | 186 | 50.13 N | 66.58 W |
| Pastillo | 240m | 17.59 N | 66.29 W |
| Pasto | 246 | 1.13 N | 77.17 W |
| Pastol Bay ⊂ | 180 | 63.07 N | 163.15 W |
| Pastora Peak ∧ | 200 | 36.47 N | 109.10 W |
| Pastoria Creek ≃ | 228 | 35.01 N | 118.51 W |
| Pastos Bons | 250 | 6.36 S | 44.05 W |
| Pastrana | 34 | 40.25 N | 2.55 W |
| Pastrengo | 64 | 45.29 N | 10.48 E |
| Pašukovo | 82 | 55.55 N | 38.16 E |
| Pasuquin | 116 | 18.20 N | 120.37 E |
| Pasuruan | 115a | 7.38 S | 112.54 E |
| Pasvalys | 76 | 56.04 N | 24.24 E |
| Pásztó | 30 | 47.55 N | 19.42 E |
| Pata | 116 | 5.51 N | 121.10 E |
| Patacamaya | 248 | 17.14 S | 67.55 W |
| Pātāchārkuchi | 120 | 26.31 N | 91.16 E |
| Patagonia | 200 | 31.32 N | 110.45 W |
| Patagonia ◆[1] | 254 | 44.00 S | 68.00 W |
| Pataha Creek ≃ | 202 | 46.31 N | 117.59 W |
| Pata Island I | 116 | 5.49 N | 121.10 E |
| Pātan, India | 120 | 23.50 N | 72.07 E |
| Pātan, India | 124 | 23.18 N | 79.42 E |
| Patapsco | 208 | 39.32 N | 76.53 W |
| Patapsco ≃ | 208 | 39.09 N | 76.27 W |
| Patapsco, Cooks Branch ≃ | 284b | 39.27 N | 76.53 W |
| Patapsco, Davis Branch ≃ | 284b | 39.19 N | 76.51 W |
| Patapsco, North Branch ≃ | 208 | 39.21 N | 76.53 W |
| Patapsco, Rockburn Branch ≃ | 284b | 39.14 N | 76.43 W |
| Patapsco, Soapstone Branch ≃ | 284b | 39.13 N | 76.43 W |
| Patapsco, South Branch ≃ | 208 | 39.21 N | 76.53 W |
| Patapsco River Neck >[1] | 284b | 39.14 N | 76.27 W |
| Patapsco Valley State Park ♠ | 208 | 39.20 N | 76.55 W |
| Patargān, Daqq-e ≡ | 128 | 33.30 N | 60.40 E |
| Pătârlagele | 38 | 45.19 N | 26.22 E |
| Pataudi | 124 | 28.19 N | 76.47 E |
| Pataula Creek ≃ | 192 | 31.46 N | 85.02 W |
| Patay | 50 | 48.03 N | 1.42 E |
| Pataz | 248 | 7.44 S | 77.37 W |
| Patchewollock | 166 | 35.23 S | 142.11 E |
| Patchogue | 210 | 40.45 N | 73.00 W |
| Patchogue Bay ⊂ | 276 | 40.44 N | 73.01 W |
| Patchway | 42 | 51.32 N | 2.34 W |
| Pat Cleburne, Lake ⊜[1] | 222 | 32.25 N | 97.30 W |
| Pate | 154 | 2.08 S | 41.00 E |
| Patea | 172 | 39.45 S | 174.28 E |
| Patea ≃ | 172 | 39.46 S | 174.29 E |
| Patearoa | 172 | 45.16 S | 170.03 E |
| Pategi | 150 | 8.44 N | 5.44 E |
| Pate Island I | 154 | 2.07 S | 41.03 E |
| Pateley Bridge | 44 | 54.05 N | 1.45 W |
| Patel Nagar ◆[8] | 272a | 28.39 N | 77.10 E |
| Patensie | 158 | 33.46 S | 24.49 E |
| Patéras Óros ⋏ | 267c | 38.07 N | 23.25 E |
| Patergassen | 64 | 46.49 N | 13.52 E |
| Paterna | 34 | 39.30 N | 0.26 W |
| Paternal ◆[8] | 288 | 34.36 S | 58.28 W |
| Paternion | 64 | 46.43 N | 13.38 E |
| Paternò | 70 | 37.34 N | 14.54 E |
| Pateros, Pil. | 269f | 14.33 N | 121.04 E |
| Pateros, Wa., U.S. | 202 | 48.03 N | 119.54 W |
| Patersdorf | 60 | 49.01 N | 12.59 E |
| Paterson, Austl. | 170 | 32.36 S | 151.37 E |
| Paterson, S. Afr. | 158 | 33.26 S | 25.58 E |
| Paterson, N.J., U.S. | 210 | 40.55 N | 74.10 W |
| Paterson ≃ | 170 | 32.43 S | 151.39 E |
| Paterson, Cape > | 169 | 38.40 S | 145.36 E |
| Paterson Inlet ⊂ | 172 | 46.55 S | 168.03 E |
| Paterswolde | 52 | 53.08 N | 6.35 E |
| Pātghāti | 126 | 22.53 N | 89.55 E |
| Pathalgaon | 124 | 22.34 N | 83.28 E |
| Pathānkot | 123 | 32.17 N | 75.39 E |
| Pathānkot Airport ⊠ | 123 | 32.15 N | 75.35 E |
| Pātharghāra | 272b | 22.34 N | 88.35 E |
| Patharia | 124 | 23.53 N | 79.12 E |
| Pathein (Bassein) | 110 | 16.47 N | 94.44 E |
| Pathfinder Reservoir ⊜[1] | 200 | 42.30 N | 106.50 W |
| Pathfinder Seamount ✦[3] | 16 | 50.55 N | 143.15 W |
| Pathiong | 140 | 6.46 N | 30.54 E |
| Pathiu | 110 | 10.42 N | 99.19 E |
| Path of Condie | 46 | 56.15 N | 3.30 W |
| Pāthrāil | 126 | 24.12 N | 89.56 E |
| Pathro ≃ | 126 | 24.12 N | 86.48 E |
| Pathum Thani | 110 | 14.01 N | 100.32 E |
| Pati, Indon. | 112 | 0.33 S | 111.19 E |
| Pati, Indon. | 115a | 6.45 S | 111.01 E |
| Patía | 246 | 2.04 N | 77.04 W |
| Patía ≃ | 246 | 2.13 N | 78.40 W |
| Patiāla | 123 | 30.19 N | 76.24 E |
| Patiāla ∧ | 123 | 32.32 N | 72.11 E |
| Pati do Alferes | 256 | 22.25 S | 43.25 W |
| P'atigorsk | 84 | 44.03 N | 43.04 E |
| Pātihāl | 272b | 22.39 N | 88.08 E |
| Patikul | 116 | 6.04 N | 121.06 E |
| Patillas | 240m | 18.00 N | 66.01 W |
| P'atimarskoje | 80 | 49.31 N | 50.32 E |
| Patinti, Selat ɥ | 164 | 0.30 S | 127.45 E |
| Patipāda | 272c | 19.04 N | 73.05 E |
| Pati Point > | 174p | 13.36 N | 144.57 E |
| Pātiram | 124 | 25.19 N | 88.45 E |
| Patire, Convento del ♁[1] | 68 | 39.34 N | 16.35 E |
| Pativilca | 248 | 10.42 S | 77.47 W |
| Pativilca ≃ | 248 | 10.44 S | 77.48 W |
| Pātkai Range ⋏ | 120 | 27.00 N | 96.00 E |
| Pat Mayse Reservoir ⊜[1] | 196 | 33.40 N | 95.35 W |
| Pátmos I | 38 | 37.20 N | 26.33 E |
| Patna, India | 124 | 25.36 N | 85.07 E |
| Patna, India | 126 | 21.56 N | 87.52 E |
| Pātna, India | 272b | 22.59 N | 88.18 E |
| Patna, Scot., U.K. | 44 | 55.21 N | 4.30 W |
| Patnāgarh | 122 | 20.43 N | 83.09 E |
| Patnanongan Island I | 116 | 14.48 N | 122.11 E |
| P'atnica, Ross. | 82 | 54.46 N | 38.09 E |
| P'atnica, Ross. | 82 | 56.05 N | 36.48 E |
| P'atnickoje, Ross. | 78 | 50.25 N | 37.51 E |
| P'atnickoje, Ross. | 82 | 54.20 N | 35.53 E |
| Pātnoli | 272c | 18.57 N | 73.05 E |
| Patnoñgon | 116 | 10.55 N | 122.00 E |
| Patnos | 84 | 39.14 N | 42.52 E |
| Pato Branco | 252 | 26.13 S | 52.40 W |
| Patoka | 219 | 38.45 N | 89.05 W |
| Patoka ≃ | 194 | 38.25 N | 87.44 W |
| Patoka Lake ⊜[1] | 194 | 38.20 N | 86.40 W |
| Patokino | 82 | 56.27 N | 39.06 E |
| Patomskoje nagorje ⋏[1] | 88 | 59.00 N | 115.00 E |
| Paton, Île I | 275a | 45.31 N | 73.45 W |
| Patonga | 154 | 2.46 N | 33.18 E |
| Patos | 250 | 7.01 S | 37.16 W |
| Patos, Lagoa dos ⊂ | 252 | 31.06 S | 51.15 W |
| Patos, Río de los ≃ | 252 | 31.18 S | 69.25 W |
| Patos, Rio dos ≃ | 248 | 13.33 S | 56.29 W |
| Patos de Minas | 255 | 18.35 S | 46.32 W |
| Patos Island I | 224 | 48.47 N | 122.56 W |
| P'atovskij | 82 | 54.41 N | 36.04 E |
| Patquía | 252 | 30.03 S | 66.53 W |
| Pátrai | 38 | 38.15 N | 21.44 E |
| Patraïkós Kólpos ⊂ | 38 | 38.14 N | 21.15 E |
| Patras → Pátrai | 38 | 38.15 N | 21.44 E |
| Pātrasāer | 124 | 23.13 N | 87.31 E |
| Patricio Lynch, Isla I | 254 | 48.37 S | 75.26 W |
| Patrick Air Force Base ■ | 220 | 28.15 N | 80.36 W |
| Patrick Henry International Airport ⊠ | 208 | 37.08 N | 76.30 W |
| Patrick Point > | 214 | 42.35 N | 81.28 W |
| Patrington | 44 | 53.41 N | 0.02 W |
| Patriot | 218 | 38.50 N | 84.49 W |
| Patrocínio | 255 | 18.57 S | 46.59 W |
| Patrocínio Paulista | 255 | 20.38 S | 47.17 W |
| Patsaliga Creek ≃ | 194 | 31.22 N | 86.31 W |
| Patscherkofel ∧ | 64 | 47.13 N | 11.28 E |
| Pattada | 71 | 40.35 N | 9.06 E |
| Pattani | 110 | 6.52 N | 101.16 E |
| Pattani ≃ | 110 | 6.53 N | 101.16 E |
| Patten | 188 | 45.59 N | 68.26 W |
| Pattenburg | 210 | 40.38 N | 75.01 W |
| Pattensen | 52 | 52.15 N | 9.46 E |
| Pattenville | 283 | 42.35 N | 71.14 W |
| Patterdale | 44 | 54.32 N | 2.56 W |
| Patterson, Ca., U.S. | 226 | 37.28 N | 121.07 W |
| Patterson, Ga., U.S. | 192 | 31.23 N | 82.08 W |
| Patterson, Il., U.S. | 219 | 39.29 N | 90.29 W |
| Patterson, La., U.S. | 194 | 29.41 N | 91.18 W |
| Patterson, N.Y., U.S. | 210 | 41.30 N | 73.36 W |
| Patterson, Oh., U.S. | 216 | 40.47 N | 83.32 W |
| Patterson ≃ | 274b | 38.05 S | 145.07 E |
| Patterson, Mount ∧ | 180 | 64.04 N | 134.39 W |
| Patterson Creek ≃ | 188 | 39.34 N | 78.44 W |
| Patterson Gardens | 216 | 41.56 N | 83.25 W |
| Patterson Heights | 214 | 40.45 N | 80.19 W |
| Patterson Island I | 190 | 48.39 N | 87.00 W |
| Patterson Park ♠ | 284b | 39.17 N | 76.35 W |
| Pattersonville | 210 | 42.53 N | 74.05 W |
| Patti, India | 123 | 31.17 N | 74.51 E |
| Patti, India | 124 | 25.55 N | 82.12 E |
| Patti, It. | 70 | 38.08 N | 14.58 E |
| Patti, Golfo di ⊂ | 36 | 38.12 N | 15.05 E |
| Pattison, Ms., U.S. | 194 | 31.53 N | 90.53 W |
| Pattison, Tx., U.S. | 222 | 29.49 N | 95.60 W |
| Pattoki | 123 | 31.01 N | 73.51 E |
| Patton | 214 | 40.37 N | 78.39 W |
| Patton, Cape > | 169 | 38.42 S | 143.50 E |
| Patton Park ♠ | 281 | 42.19 N | 83.10 W |
| Pattonsburg | 194 | 40.02 N | 94.08 W |
| Patton Seamounts ✦[3] | 16 | 54.20 N | 149.30 W |
| Pattscheid ◆[8] | 263 | 51.05 N | 7.03 E |
| Pattukkottai | 122 | 10.26 N | 79.19 E |
| Pattullo, Mount ∧ | 180 | 56.14 N | 129.39 W |
| Patu | 250 | 6.06 S | 37.38 W |
| Pātua | 126 | 22.06 N | 90.23 E |
| Patuākhāli | 124 | 22.21 N | 90.21 E |
| Patuca ≃ | 236 | 15.50 N | 84.17 W |
| Patuca, Punta > | 236 | 15.51 N | 84.18 W |
| Patuha, Gunung ∧ | 115a | 7.10 S | 107.23 E |
| Pātul | 272b | 22.45 N | 88.10 E |
| Patul, Cerro ∧ | 246 | 2.40 S | 79.03 W |
| Pātuli | 126 | 23.33 N | 88.15 E |
| Patulul | 236 | 14.25 N | 91.10 W |
| Patumahoe | 172 | 37.11 S | 174.50 E |
| Pātūr | 122 | 20.27 N | 76.56 E |
| Patusi | 164 | 2.10 S | 147.10 E |
| Patutu ∧ | 172 | 39.15 S | 175.51 E |
| Patuxent ≃ | 208 | 38.18 N | 76.25 W |
| Patuxent, Western Branch ≃ | 208 | 38.47 N | 76.43 W |
| Patuxent River Naval Air Test Center ■ | 208 | 38.17 N | 76.25 W |
| Patuxent Wildlife Research Center ♁[3] | 284c | 39.03 N | 76.48 W |
| Patvinsuon kansallispuisto ♠ | 24 | 63.10 N | 30.55 E |
| Patwāri | 272a | 28.35 N | 77.27 E |
| Pátzcuaro | 234 | 19.31 N | 101.36 W |
| Pátzcuaro, Lago de ⊜ | 234 | 19.35 N | 101.35 W |
| Patzicía | 236 | 14.38 N | 90.56 W |
| Patzig | 54 | 54.28 N | 13.24 E |
| Patzún | 236 | 14.41 N | 91.01 W |
| Pau | 32 | 43.18 N | 0.22 W |
| Pau, Gave de ≃ | 32 | 43.33 N | 1.12 W |
| Pau Brasil | 255 | 15.27 S | 39.39 W |
| Paucarbamba | 248 | 12.25 S | 74.36 W |
| Paucarpata | 248 | 16.26 S | 71.30 W |
| Paucartambo | 248 | 13.18 S | 71.40 W |
| Paudash Lake ⊜ | 212 | 44.58 N | 78.04 W |
| Pau dos Ferros | 250 | 6.07 S | 38.10 W |
| Pauh | 112 | 2.08 S | 102.48 E |
| Paunurri ∧ | 248 | 27.58 S | 88.50 E |
| Pauini | 248 | 7.40 S | 66.58 W |
| Pauini ≃, Bra. | 246 | 1.42 S | 62.50 W |
| Pauini ≃, Bra. | 248 | 7.47 S | 67.05 W |
| Pauk | 110 | 21.27 N | 94.[illegible] E |
| Pauksa Taung ∧ | 110 | 19.55 N | 94.[illegible] E |
| Paul | 202 | 42.36 N | 113.[illegible] W |
| Paul, Lac à ⊜ | 186 | 49.52 N | 70.[illegible] W |
| Paula Lima | 256 | 21.35 S | 43.2[illegible] W |
| Paularo | 64 | 46.32 N | 13.0[illegible] E |
| Paulaya ≃ | 236 | 15.51 N | 85.0[illegible] W |
| Paulding, Ms., U.S. | 194 | 32.01 N | 89.0[illegible] W |
| Paulding, Oh., U.S. | 216 | 41.08 N | 84.3[illegible] W |
| Paulding □[6] | 216 | 41.08 N | 84.3[illegible] W |
| Paulhan | 32 | 43.32 N | 3.2[illegible] E |
| Paulicéia | 255 | 21.17 S | 51.5[illegible] W |
| Paulilatino | 71 | 40.05 N | 8.4[illegible] E |
| Paulina Peak ∧ | 202 | 43.41 N | 121.1[illegible] W |
| Pauline, Mount ∧ | 182 | 53.33 N | 119.5[illegible] W |
| Paulinenaue | 54 | 52.40 N | 12.43 E |
| Paulínia | 256 | 22.45 S | 47.10 W |
| Paulino Neves | 250 | 2.43 S | 42.33 W |
| Paulins Kill | 210 | 41.03 N | 74.49 W |
| Paulins Kill ≃ | 210 | 40.55 N | 75.05 W |
| Paulinzella ⊥ | 54 | 50.42 N | 11.06 E |
| Paulis → Isiro | 154 | 2.47 N | 27.37 E |
| Paulistana | 250 | 8.09 S | 41.09 W |
| Paulistas | 255 | 18.25 S | 42.52 W |
| Paullina | 198 | 42.58 N | 95.41 W |
| Paull Lake ⊜ | 184 | 56.08 N | 104.50 W |
| Paullo | 62 | 45.25 N | 9.24 E |
| Paulo Afonso | 250 | 9.21 S | 38.14 W |
| Paulo Afonso, Cachoeira de ∟ | 250 | 9.24 S | 38.13 W |
| Paulo de Faria | 255 | 20.02 S | 49.24 W |
| Pauloff Harbor (Pavlof Harbor) | 180 | 54.27 N | 162.42 W |
| Paulpietersburg | 158 | 27.30 S | 30.51 E |
| Paul Roux | 158 | 28.18 S | 27.59 E |
| Paul-Sauvé, Parc ♠ | 275a | 45.28 N | 74.02 W |
| Paulsboro | 208 | 39.49 N | 75.14 W |
| Pauls Cross Roads | 208 | 37.52 N | 76.53 W |
| Paul Seamount ✦[3] | 14 | 23.26 N | 172.36 W |
| Paulstown → Whitehall | 48 | 52.41 N | 7.01 W |
| Pauls Valley | 196 | 34.44 N | 97.13 W |
| Paulton, Eng., U.K. | 42 | 51.18 N | 2.30 W |
| Paulton, Pa., U.S. | 279b | 40.34 N | 79.34 W |
| Pauma Indian Reservation ◆[4] | 228 | 33.22 N | 116.58 W |
| Pāunān | 272b | 22.57 N | 88.17 E |
| Paung | 110 | 16.37 N | 97.28 E |
| Paungbyin | 110 | 24.16 N | 94.49 E |
| Paungde | 110 | 18.29 N | 95.30 E |
| Paunggyi | 110 | 17.19 N | 96.11 E |
| Paup | 164 | 3.15 S | 142.35 E |
| Paupack | 210 | 41.24 N | 75.14 W |
| Pauri | 124 | 30.09 N | 78.47 E |
| Pausa, Dtsch. | 54 | 50.35 N | 12.00 E |
| Pausa, Perú | 248 | 15.16 S | 73.20 W |
| Pausin | 264a | 52.38 N | 13.03 E |
| Paute | 246 | 2.47 S | 78.50 W |
| Paute ≃ | 246 | 2.46 S | 78.16 W |
| Pauto ≃ | 246 | 5.09 N | 70.55 W |
| Pautou → Baotou | 102 | 40.40 N | 109.59 E |
| Pauwalu Point > | 229a | 20.52 N | 156.08 W |
| Pauwela | 229a | 20.56 N | 156.19 W |
| Pauwela Point > | 229a | 20.57 N | 156.19 W |
| Pavai ◆[8] | 272c | 19.07 N | 72.55 E |
| Pavai Lake ⊜ | 272c | 19.07 N | 72.55 E |
| Pavda | 86 | 59.15 N | 59.30 E |
| Pāveh | 128 | 35.03 N | 46.22 E |
| Pavel'cevo | 82 | 56.15 N | 36.26 E |
| Pavelec | 76 | 53.50 N | 39.16 E |
| Pavelec Station ◆[5] | 265b | 55.44 N | 37.38 E |
| Pavia | 62 | 45.10 N | 9.10 E |
| Pavia □[4] | 62 | 45.07 N | 9.08 E |
| Pavia, Naviglio di ≊ | 266b | 45.27 N | 9.11 E |
| Pavia di Udine | 64 | 45.59 N | 13.17 E |
| Pavilion, B.C., Can. | 182 | 50.52 N | 121.50 W |
| Pavilion, N.Y., U.S. | 210 | 42.52 N | 78.01 W |
| Pavilion Key I | 220 | 25.42 N | 81.22 W |
| Pavillion | 200 | 43.14 N | 108.41 W |
| Pavilly | 50 | 49.34 N | 0.58 E |
| Pāvilosta | 76 | 56.53 N | 21.14 E |
| Pavino | 24 | 59.07 N | 46.07 E |
| Pavione, Monte ∧ | 64 | 46.07 N | 11.50 E |
| Pavlice | 61 | 48.59 N | 15.53 E |
| Pavlikeni | 38 | 43.14 N | 25.18 E |
| Pavliščevo, Ross. | 82 | 55.11 N | 35.59 E |
| Pavliščevo, Ross. | 82 | 55.34 N | 35.59 E |
| Pavlivka, Ukr. | 78 | 47.45 N | 37.14 E |
| Pavlivka, Ukr. | 83 | 48.08 N | 39.33 E |
| Pavlivka, Ukr. | 83 | 49.36 N | 38.42 E |
| Pavlodar | 86 | 52.18 N | 76.57 E |
| Pavlodar □[8] | 86 | 52.00 N | 76.00 E |
| Pavlof Bay ⊂ | 180 | 55.30 N | 161.32 W |
| Pavlof Volcano ∧[1] | 180 | 55.24 N | 161.52 W |
| Pavlogradka | 86 | 54.12 N | 73.33 E |
| Pavlohrad | 78 | 48.32 N | 35.53 E |
| Pavlopil' | 83 | 47.16 N | 37.47 E |
| Pavlovka, Kaz. | 86 | 52.32 N | 63.06 E |
| Pavlovka, Ross. | 80 | 52.41 N | 47.09 E |
| Pavlovka, Ross. | 86 | 55.25 N | 56.33 E |
| Pavlovka, Ross. | 86 | 51.55 N | 54.47 E |
| Pavlovo, Ross. | 76 | 60.05 N | 45.17 E |
| Pavlovo, Ross. | 80 | 55.58 N | 43.04 E |
| Pavlovo, Ross. | 265a | 59.56 N | 30.40 E |
| Pavlovo, Ross. | 265a | 59.49 N | 30.54 E |
| Pavlovsk, Ross. | 76 | 59.41 N | 30.27 E |
| Pavlovsk, Ross. | 78 | 50.27 N | 40.08 E |
| Pavlovsk, Ross. | 86 | 53.20 N | 82.59 E |
| Pavlovskaja | 78 | 46.08 N | 39.48 E |
| Pavlovskaja Sloboda | 82 | 55.49 N | 37.05 E |
| Pavlovskij | 80 | 57.50 N | 54.51 E |
| Pavlovskij Posad | 82 | 55.47 N | 38.40 E |
| Pavlysh | 78 | 48.55 N | 33.21 E |
| Pavne | 272c | 19.05 N | 73.01 E |
| Pavo | 192 | 31.02 N | 84.04 W |
| Pavón, Arg. | 258 | 34.23 S | 59.03 W |
| Pavón, Col. | 246 | 3.37 N | 72.15 W |
| Pavón, Arroyo ≃ | 258 | 34.30 S | 57.05 W |
| Pavona | 267a | 41.43 N | 12.37 E |
| Pavonia | 214 | 40.49 N | 82.26 W |
| Pavšino | 265b | 55.49 N | 37.21 E |
| Pavšozero | 76 | 60.38 N | 35.34 E |
| Pavullo nel Frignano | 64 | 44.20 N | 10.50 E |
| Pavuna, Arroio ≃ | 287a | 22.58 S | 43.23 W |
| Pavuvu Island I | 175e | 9.03 S | 159.06 E |
| Pavy | 76 | 58.03 N | 29.30 E |
| Pawai, Pulau I | 271c | 1.12 N | 103.43 E |
| Pawan ≃ | 112 | 1.51 S | 109.57 E |
| Pawāyān | 124 | 28.04 N | 80.06 E |
| Pawcatuck | 207 | 41.22 N | 71.50 W |
| Paw Creek | 192 | 35.16 N | 80.56 W |
| Päwesin | 54 | 52.31 N | 12.42 E |
| Pawhuska | 196 | 36.40 N | 96.20 W |
| Pawling | 210 | 41.33 N | 73.36 W |
| Pawn ≃ | 110 | 18.53 N | 97.19 E |
| Pawnee, Il., U.S. | 219 | 39.35 N | 89.34 W |
| Pawnee, Ok., U.S. | 196 | 36.20 N | 96.48 W |
| Pawnee ≃ | 198 | 38.10 N | 99.06 W |
| Pawnee City | 198 | 40.06 N | 96.09 W |
| Pawnee Creek ≃ | 198 | 40.34 N | 103.14 W |
| Pawnee Rock | 198 | 38.15 N | 98.58 W |
| Pawni | 122 | 20.47 N | 79.38 E |
| Pawota | 110 | 17.46 N | 97.17 E |
| Paw Paw, Il., U.S. | 216 | 41.41 N | 88.59 W |
| Paw Paw, Mi., U.S. | 216 | 42.13 N | 85.53 W |
| Paw Paw, W.V., U.S. | 188 | 39.31 N | 78.27 W |
| Paw Paw ≃ | 216 | 42.07 N | 86.29 W |
| Paw Paw Creek ≃ | 216 | 40.52 N | 85.58 W |
| Paw Paw Lake | 216 | 42.12 N | 86.15 W |
| Paw Paw Lake ⊜ | 216 | 42.12 N | 86.16 W |
| Pawtucket | 207 | 41.52 N | 71.22 W |
| Pawtucket Falls ∟ | 207 | 42.39 N | 71.20 W |
| Paxoí I | 38 | 39.12 N | 20.12 E |
| Paxson | 180 | 63.02 N | 145.30 W |
| Paxton, Austl. | 170 | 32.54 S | 151.16 E |
| Paxton, Il., U.S. | 216 | 40.27 N | 88.05 W |
| Paxton, Ma., U.S. | 207 | 42.18 N | 71.55 W |
| Paxton, Ne., U.S. | 198 | 41.07 N | 101.21 W |


| Symbol | English | Deutsch | Español | Français | Português |
|---|---|---|---|---|---|
| ≃ | River | Fluß | Río | Rivière | Rio |
| ≊ | Canal | Kanal | Canal | Canal | Canal |
| ∟ | Waterfall, Rapids | Wasserfall, Stromschnellen | Cascada, Rápidos | Chute d'eau, Rapides | Cascata, Rápidos |
| ɥ | Strait | Meeresstraße | Estrecho | Détroit | Estreito |
| ⊂ | Bay, Gulf | Bucht, Golf | Bahía, Golfo | Baie, Golfe | Baía, Golfo |
| ⊜ | Lake, Lakes | See, Seen | Lago, Lagos | Lac, Lacs | Lago, Lagos |
| ≡ | Swamp | Sumpf | Pantano | Marais | Pântano |
| | Ice Features, Glacier | Eis- und Gletscherformen | Accidentes Glaciales | Formes glaciaires | Acidentes glaciares |
| | Other Hydrographic Features | Andere Hydrographische Objekte | Otros Elementos Hidrográficos | Autres données hydrographiques | Outros acidentes hidrográficos |

| Symbol | English | Deutsch | Español | Français | Português |
|---|---|---|---|---|---|
| ✦ | Submarine Features | Untermeerische Objekte | Accidentes Submarinos | Formes de relief sous-marin | Acidentes submarinos |
| □ | Political Unit | Politische Einheit | Unidad Política | Entité politique | Unidade política |
| ♁ | Cultural Institution | Kulturelle Institution | Institución Cultural | Institution culturelle | Instituição cultural |
| ⊥ | Historical Site | Historische Stätte | Sitio Histórico | Site historique | Sitio histórico |
| ♠ | Recreational Site | Erholungs- und Ferienort | Sitio de Recreo | Centre de loisirs | Área de Lazer |
| ⊠ | Airport | Flughafen | Aeropuerto | Aéroport | Aeroporto |
| ■ | Military Installation | Militäranlage | Instalación Militar | Installation militaire | Instalação militar |
| ◆ | Miscellaneous | Verschiedenes | Misceláneo | Divers | Diversos |

| Name | Page | Lat.°′ | Long.°′ |
|---|---|---|---|
| Paxtonia | 208 | 40.19 N | 76.48 W |
| Paxtonville | 208 | 40.46 N | 77.05 W |
| Paya | 236 | 15.37 N | 85.17 W |
| Paya Besar | 114 | 3.47 N | 103.16 E |
| Payadapu | 114 | 3.05 N | 97.23 E |
| Payāgpur | 124 | 27.25 N | 81.48 E |
| Payagyi | 110 | 17.29 N | 96.32 E |
| Payakumbuh | 112 | 0.14 S | 100.38 E |
| Paya Lebar | 271c | 1.22 N | 103.53 E |
| Paya Lebar Airport ⊠ | 271c | 1.21 N | 103.54 E |
| Payamlı | 130 | 37.01 N | 38.35 E |
| Payangan | 115b | 8.26 S | 115.15 E |
| Payas, Cerro ∧ | 236 | 15.50 N | 85.00 W |
| Payerne | 58 | 46.49 N | 6.56 E |
| Payeti | 115b | 9.41 S | 120.20 E |
| Payette | 202 | 44.04 N | 116.55 W |
| Payette ≃ | 202 | 44.05 N | 116.57 W |
| Payette, Middle Fork ≃ | 202 | 44.05 N | 116.07 W |
| Payette, North Fork ≃ | 202 | 44.05 N | 116.07 W |
| Payette, South Fork ≃ | 202 | 44.06 N | 116.00 W |
| Payette Lake ⊜[1] | 202 | 44.57 N | 116.05 W |
| Paylampur | 272b | 22.47 N | 88.16 E |
| Payne | 216 | 41.04 N | 84.43 W |
| Payne ≃ | 206 | 45.14 N | 75.08 W |
| Payne, Lac ⊜ | 176 | 59.25 N | 74.00 W |
| Payne Bay ⊂ | 176 | 60.00 N | 70.00 W |
| Payneham | 168b | 34.53 S | 138.38 E |
| Paynes Creek ≃ | 204 | 40.16 N | 122.11 W |
| Paynes Find | 162 | 29.15 S | 117.41 E |
| Paynesville, S. Afr. | 273d | 26.14 S | 28.28 E |
| Paynesville, Mn., U.S. | 198 | 45.22 N | 94.42 W |
| Paynesville, Mo., U.S. | 219 | 39.16 N | 90.54 W |
| Paynetown State Recreation Area ♦ | 218 | 39.05 N | 86.27 W |
| Paynton | 184 | 53.01 N | 108.56 W |
| Paysandú | 252 | 32.19 S | 58.05 W |
| Pays-Bas → Netherlands □[1] | 30 | 52.15 N | 5.30 E |
| Payson, Az., U.S. | 200 | 34.13 N | 111.19 W |
| Payson, Il., U.S. | 219 | 39.49 N | 91.14 W |
| Payson, Ut,. U.S. | 200 | 40.02 N | 111.43 W |
| Payún, Cerro ∧ | 252 | 36.30 S | 69.18 W |
| Paz ≃ | 236 | 13.45 N | 90.08 W |
| Paz, Cañada de la ≃ | 288 | 34.53 S | 58.38 W |
| Paz, Rio da ≃ | 250 | 9.14 S | 52.01 W |
| Pazar, Tür. | 130 | 41.11 N | 40.53 E |
| Pazar, Tür. | 130 | 40.17 N | 36.18 E |
| Pazarbaşı Burnu › | 130 | 41.10 N | 30.11 E |
| Pazarcık | 130 | 37.31 N | 37.19 E |
| Pazardžik | 38 | 42.12 N | 24.20 E |
| Pazarköy, Tür. | 130 | 40.55 N | 32.11 E |
| Pazarköy, Tür. | 130 | 39.51 N | 27.24 E |
| Pazarören | 130 | 38.41 N | 36.11 E |
| Pazaryeri, Tür. | 130 | 38.05 N | 28.14 E |
| Pazaryeri, Tür. | 130 | 40.00 N | 29.54 E |
| Paz de Ariporo | 246 | 5.53 N | 71.54 W |
| Paz de Río | 246 | 5.59 N | 72.47 W |
| Pazifischer Ozean → Pacific Ocean ✢[1] | 6 | 10.00 S | 150.00 W |
| P'ažijeva Sel'ga | 24 | 61.29 N | 34.29 E |
| Pazin | 36 | 45.14 N | 13.56 E |
| Pazña | 248 | 18.36 S | 66.55 W |
| Paznauntal V | 58 | 47.03 N | 10.20 E |
| Pčevža | 76 | 59.23 N | 32.20 E |
| Pčevža ≃ | 76 | 59.21 N | 31.54 E |
| Pchery | 54 | 50.10 N | 14.08 E |
| Pcič | 76 | 52.09 N | 28.52 E |
| Pcič ≃ | 76 | 52.09 N | 28.52 E |
| Pe | 110 | 13.28 N | 98.31 E |
| Pea | 174w | 21.10 S | 175.14 W |
| Pea ≃ | 194 | 31.01 N | 85.51 W |
| Peabody, Ks., U.S. | 198 | 38.10 N | 97.06 W |
| Peabody, Ma., U.S. | 207 | 42.31 N | 70.55 W |
| Peace ≃, Can. | 176 | 59.00 N | 111.25 W |
| Peace ≃, Fl., U.S. | 220 | 26.55 N | 82.05 W |
| Peace Arch ⊥ | 224 | 49.00 N | 122.45 W |
| Peace Bridge ◆[5] | 284a | 42.54 N | 78.55 W |
| Peace Canyon Dam ◆[6] | 182 | 55.59 N | 121.59 W |
| Peace Dale | 207 | 41.27 N | 71.29 W |
| Peacehaven | 42 | 50.47 N | 0.01 E |
| Peace River | 182 | 56.14 N | 117.17 W |
| Peach Creek | 188 | 37.52 N | 81.59 W |
| Peach Creek ≃, Tx., U.S. | 222 | 30.07 N | 95.10 W |
| Peach Creek ≃, Tx., U.S. | 222 | 29.24 N | 97.19 W |
| Peach Creek, Sandy Fork ≃ | 222 | 29.34 N | 97.19 W |
| Peachdale | 158 | 26.30 S | 24.42 E |
| Peachland | 182 | 49.46 N | 119.44 W |
| Peach Orchard | 192 | 33.28 N | 82.04 W |
| Peach Springs | 200 | 35.31 N | 113.25 W |
| Peacock Hills ⋏[2] | 176 | 66.05 N | 110.45 W |
| Peacock Point ›, On., Can. | 212 | 42.47 N | 79.59 W |
| Peacock Point ›, Wake I. | 174a | 19.16 N | 166.37 E |
| Peacock Sound ʊ | 9 | 72.55 S | 100.00 W |
| Pea Hill Branch ≃ | 284c | 38.45 N | 76.57 W |
| Peak Charles National Park ♦ | 162 | 32.55 S | 121.06 E |
| Peak Crossing | 171a | 27.47 S | 152.44 E |
| Peak Dale | 262 | 53.17 N | 1.52 W |
| Peak District National Park ♦ | 44 | 53.17 N | 1.45 W |
| Peak Downs | 166 | 22.12 S | 148.10 E |
| Peake Creek ≃ | 162 | 28.05 S | 136.07 E |
| Peaked Mountain ∧ | 186 | 46.34 N | 68.49 W |
| Peak Forest | 262 | 53.19 N | 1.50 W |
| Peak Forest Canal ≅ | 262 | 53.29 N | 2.06 W |
| Peak Hill, Austl. | 162 | 25.38 S | 118.43 E |
| Peak Hill, Austl. | 166 | 32.44 S | 148.12 E |
| Peakhurst | 274a | 33.58 S | 151.04 E |
| Peakview | 171b | 36.04 S | 149.24 E |
| Peäldoajvi ∧ | 24 | 69.11 N | 26.36 E |
| Peale, Mount ∧ | 200 | 38.26 N | 109.14 W |
| Peale Island I | 174a | 19.19 N | 166.35 E |
| Peapack Brook ≃ | 276 | 40.41 N | 74.39 W |
| Pearblossom | 228 | 34.30 N | 117.55 W |
| Pearce | 200 | 31.54 N | 109.49 W |
| Pearce, Royal Australian Air Force Station ■ | 168a | 31.41 S | 116.01 E |
| Pearce Point › | 164 | 14.25 S | 129.21 E |
| Peard Bay ⊂ | 180 | 70.51 N | 159.10 W |
| Pea Ridge ∧ | 218 | 38.25 N | 83.36 W |
| Pea Ridge National Military Park ♦ | 194 | 36.29 N | 94.06 W |
| Pearisburg | 192 | 37.19 N | 80.44 W |
| Pearl, Il., U.S. | 194 | 39.28 N | 90.38 W |
| Pearl, Ms., U.S. | 194 | 32.16 N | 90.07 W |
| Pearl ≃ | 194 | 30.11 N | 89.32 W |
| Pearl, Lake ⊜ | 283 | 42.04 N | 71.21 W |
| Pearland | 222 | 29.33 N | 95.17 W |
| Pearl and Hermes Atoll I[1] | 14 | 27.55 N | 175.45 W |
| Pearl Bank ✢[4] | 116 | 5.49 N | 119.42 E |
| Pearl Beach | 214 | 42.37 N | 82.35 W |
| Pearl City | 229c | 21.23 N | 157.58 W |
| Pearl Creek ≃ | 198 | 44.15 N | 98.08 W |
| Pearl Harbor ⊂ | 229c | 21.22 N | 157.58 W |
| Pearl Harbor Naval Station ■ | 229c | 21.21 N | 157.57 W |
| Pearl Peak ∧ | 204 | 40.14 N | 115.32 W |
| Pearl River, La., U.S. | 194 | 30.22 N | 89.44 W |
| Pearl River, N.Y., U.S. | 210 | 41.03 N | 74.01 W |
| Pearns Point › | 240c | 17.05 N | 61.54 W |
| Pearsall | 196 | 28.53 N | 99.05 W |
| Pearse Island I | 182 | 54.51 N | 130.21 W |
| Pearsoll Peak ∧ | 202 | 42.18 N | 123.50 W |
| Pearson | 192 | 31.17 N | 82.51 W |
| Pearson Lake ⊜ | 184 | 56.15 N | 97.15 W |
| Pearston | 158 | 32.35 S | 25.08 E |
| Peary Land ◆[1] | 16 | 83.00 N | 35.00 W |
| Pease ≃ | 196 | 34.12 N | 99.07 W |
| Pease Air Force Base ■ | 188 | 43.06 N | 70.49 W |
| Peasedown Saint John | 42 | 51.19 N | 2.27 W |
| Peaster | 222 | 32.52 N | 97.52 W |
| Peat Inn | 46 | 56.17 N | 2.53 W |
| Pebane | 154 | 17.10 S | 38.08 E |
| Pebas | 246 | 3.20 S | 71.49 W |
| Pebble Beach | 226 | 36.34 N | 121.57 W |
| Pebble Island I | 254 | 51.18 S | 59.35 W |
| Peć | 38 | 42.40 N | 20.19 E |
| Pecan Bayou ≃ | 196 | 31.28 N | 98.43 W |
| Pecangakan | 115a | 6.41 S | 110.42 E |
| Pecan Gap | 196 | 33.26 N | 95.51 W |
| Peçanha | 255 | 18.33 S | 42.34 W |
| Peças, Ilha das I | 252 | 25.26 S | 48.19 W |
| Pecatonica | 190 | 42.18 N | 89.21 W |
| Pecatonica ≃ | 190 | 42.27 N | 89.05 W |
| Pecatu | 115b | 8.50 S | 115.07 E |
| Peccioli | 66 | 43.33 N | 10.43 E |
| Pécel | 264c | 47.29 N | 19.21 E |
| Peçenek | 130 | 40.25 N | 32.19 E |
| Pečenga | 24 | 69.33 N | 31.07 E |
| Pečerniki | 82 | 54.39 N | 39.14 E |
| Pečernikovskije Vyselki | 82 | 54.10 N | 39.10 E |
| Pechanga Indian Reservation ◆[4] | 228 | 33.27 N | 117.04 W |
| Peche Island I | 281 | 42.21 N | 82.56 W |
| Pechenihy | 78 | 49.52 N | 36.55 E |
| Pechenizhyn | 78 | 48.32 N | 24.54 E |
| Pecheniz'ke vodoskhovyshche ⊜[1] | 78 | 50.05 N | 36.47 E |
| Pechera | 78 | 48.52 N | 28.42 E |
| Pechincha ◆[8] | 287a | 22.56 S | 43.21 W |
| Pechora → Pečora ≃ | 24 | 68.13 N | 54.15 E |
| Pechorka ≃ | 265b | 55.35 N | 38.03 E |
| Pechra-Jakovlevskaja | 265b | 55.48 N | 37.58 E |
| Pechra-Pokrovskoje | 265b | 55.50 N | 37.57 E |
| Pechu | 84 | 43.24 N | 40.49 E |
| Peči | 80 | 54.48 N | 44.19 E |
| Pecica | 38 | 46.10 N | 21.05 E |
| Pečicy | 82 | 55.36 N | 38.27 E |
| Pecixe, Ilha de I | 150 | 11.50 N | 16.05 W |
| Peck | 190 | 43.15 N | 82.49 W |
| Peck Bay ⊂ | 208 | 39.16 N | 74.37 W |
| Peck-Berge ⋏[2] | 264a | 52.36 N | 13.34 E |
| Peckeloh | 52 | 52.01 N | 8.07 E |
| Peckelsheim | 52 | 51.36 N | 9.07 E |
| Pecket Well | 262 | 53.46 N | 2.00 W |
| Peck Lake ⊜ | 210 | 43.07 N | 74.25 W |
| Peckman ≃ | 276 | 40.53 N | 74.13 W |
| Peconic ≃ | 207 | 40.55 N | 72.37 W |
| Pečora | 24 | 65.10 N | 57.11 E |
| Pečora ≃ | 24 | 68.13 N | 54.15 E |
| Pecora, Capo › | 71 | 39.27 N | 8.23 E |
| Pecoraro, Monte ∧ | 68 | 38.32 N | 16.20 E |
| Pečoro-Ilyčskij zapovednik ◆[4] | 24 | 62.20 N | 59.00 E |
| Pečorskaja guba ⊂ | 24 | 68.40 N | 54.45 E |
| Pečorskoje more ✢[2] | 24 | 70.00 N | 54.00 E |
| Pečory | 76 | 57.49 N | 27.36 E |
| Pecos, N.M., U.S. | 200 | 35.34 N | 105.40 W |
| Pecos, Tx., U.S. | 196 | 31.25 N | 103.29 W |
| Pecos ≃ | 178 | 29.42 N | 101.22 W |
| Pecos National Monument ♦ | 200 | 35.26 N | 105.56 W |
| Pecos Plains ≚ | 196 | 33.20 N | 104.30 W |
| Pecq | 50 | 50.41 N | 3.20 E |
| Pecquencourt | 50 | 50.23 N | 3.13 E |
| Pecqueuse | 261 | 48.39 N | 2.03 E |
| Pécs | 30 | 46.05 N | 18.13 E |
| Pedana | 122 | 16.16 N | 81.10 E |
| Pedara | 70 | 37.38 N | 15.04 E |
| Pedas | 114 | 2.37 N | 102.04 E |
| Pedasí | 246 | 7.32 N | 80.02 W |
| Pedaso | 66 | 43.06 N | 13.50 E |
| Peddāpuram | 122 | 17.05 N | 82.08 E |
| Pedder, Lake ⊜[1] | 166 | 42.54 S | 146.12 E |
| Peddie | 158 | 33.12 S | 27.07 E |
| Peddocks Island I | 283 | 42.17 N | 70.56 W |
| Pededze ≃ | 76 | 56.56 N | 26.54 E |
| Pedernales, Arg. | 252 | 35.15 S | 59.39 W |
| Pedernales, Méx. | 234 | 19.08 N | 101.28 W |
| Pedernales, Rep. Dom. | 238 | 18.02 N | 71.45 W |
| Pedernales, Ven. | 246 | 9.58 N | 62.16 W |
| Pedernales ≃ | 196 | 30.26 N | 98.04 W |
| Pedernales, Salar de ≚ | 252 | 26.15 S | 69.10 W |
| Pedernales Falls State Park ♦ | 196 | 30.20 N | 98.14 W |
| Pederobba | 64 | 45.53 N | 11.58 E |
| Pedersborg | 41 | 55.27 N | 11.34 E |
| Pederstrup | 41 | 54.54 N | 11.16 E |
| Pedesina | 58 | 46.05 N | 9.33 E |
| Pedhoulás | 130 | 34.58 N | 32.50 E |
| Pedja ≃ | 76 | 58.25 N | 26.11 E |
| Pedley | 228 | 33.59 N | 117.28 W |
| Pé do Morro | 256 | 22.20 S | 44.57 W |
| Pedra | 250 | 8.30 S | 36.57 W |
| Pedra Azul | 255 | 16.01 S | 41.16 W |
| Pedra Bela | 256 | 22.47 S | 46.27 W |
| Pedra Branca | 250 | 5.27 S | 39.43 W |
| Pedra de Guaratiba ◆[8] | 256 | 23.00 S | 43.39 W |
| Pedra Grande, Recifes da ✢[2] | 255 | 17.45 S | 38.58 W |
| Pedra Lume | 150a | 16.46 N | 22.54 W |
| Pedralva | 256 | 22.14 S | 45.28 W |
| Pedras | 250 | 2.48 S | 57.16 W |
| Pedras, Rio das ≃ | 287a | 22.51 S | 43.01 W |
| Pedras de Fogo | 250 | 7.23 S | 35.07 W |
| Pedra Selada | 256 | 22.21 S | 44.26 W |
| Pedras Negras | 248 | 12.51 S | 62.54 W |
| Pedras Salgadas | 34 | 41.32 N | 7.36 W |
| Pedraza | 246 | 10.11 N | 74.55 W |
| Pedregal, Pan. | 236 | 8.22 N | 82.26 W |
| Pedregal, Ven. | 246 | 11.01 N | 70.08 W |
| Pedregulho | 255 | 20.16 S | 47.29 W |
| Pedreira | 256 | 22.43 S | 46.55 W |
| Pedreira ≃ | 250 | 0.12 N | 50.47 W |
| Pedreiras | 250 | 4.34 S | 44.39 W |
| Pedriceña | 232 | 25.06 N | 103.47 W |
| Pedricktown | 208 | 39.46 N | 75.24 W |
| Pedrinhas | 250 | 11.12 S | 37.41 W |
| Pedro, Point › | 122 | 9.50 N | 80.14 E |
| Pedro Afonso | 250 | 8.59 S | 48.11 W |
| Pedro Antonio de los Santos | 234 | 21.36 N | 98.58 W |
| Pedro Avelino | 250 | 5.31 S | 36.23 W |
| Pedro Bay | 180 | 59.47 N | 154.07 W |
| Pedro Betancourt | 240p | 22.44 N | 81.17 W |
| Pedro Cays II | 238 | 17.00 N | 77.50 W |
| Pedro de Olla, Cerro ∧ | 234 | 17.07 N | 97.40 W |
| Pedro do Rio | 256 | 22.20 S | 43.09 W |
| Pedrógão Grande | 34 | 39.55 N | 8.09 W |
| Pedro Gomes | 255 | 18.04 S | 54.32 W |
| Pedro II | 250 | 4.25 S | 41.28 W |
| Pedro II, Ilha I | 246 | 1.10 N | 66.40 W |
| Pedro Juan Caballero | 252 | 22.34 S | 55.37 W |
| Pedro Leopoldo | 255 | 19.38 S | 44.03 W |
| Pedro Luro | 252 | 39.29 S | 62.41 W |
| Pedro Muñoz | 34 | 39.24 N | 2.58 W |
| Pedro Osório | 252 | 31.51 S | 52.45 W |
| Pedro R. Fernández | 252 | 28.45 S | 58.39 W |
| Pedro Teixeira | 256 | 21.43 S | 43.44 W |
| Pedro Velho | 250 | 6.26 S | 35.14 W |
| Peebinga | 166 | 34.56 S | 140.55 E |
| Peebles, Scot., U.K. | 46 | 55.39 N | 3.12 W |
| Peebles, Oh., U.S. | 218 | 38.56 N | 83.24 W |
| Peedamullah | 162 | 21.50 S | 115.38 E |
| Pee Dee ≃ | 192 | 34.43 N | 79.52 W |
| Peekaboo Mountain ∧[2] | 188 | 45.45 N | 67.53 W |
| Peekskill | 210 | 41.17 N | 73.55 W |
| Peel, Austl. | 170 | 33.19 S | 149.38 E |
| Peel, I. of Man | 44 | 54.13 N | 4.40 W |
| Peel □[6] | 212 | 43.45 N | 79.47 W |
| Peel ≃ | 180 | 67.37 N | 134.40 W |
| Peel Channel ≃[1] | 180 | 68.13 N | 135.00 W |
| Peel Fell ∧ | 44 | 55.17 N | 2.35 W |
| Peel Inlet ⊂ | 168a | 32.35 S | 115.44 E |
| Peel Island I | 171a | 27.30 S | 153.22 E |
| Pe Ell | 224 | 46.34 N | 123.17 W |
| Peel Point › | 176 | 73.22 N | 114.35 W |
| Peel Sound ʊ | 176 | 73.15 N | 96.30 W |
| Peene ≃ | 54 | 54.09 N | 13.46 E |
| Peenemünde | 54 | 54.08 N | 13.46 E |
| Peepeekisis Indian Reserve ◆[4] | 184 | 50.52 N | 103.24 W |
| Peer | 56 | 51.08 N | 5.28 E |
| Peerless | 202 | 48.46 N | 105.49 W |
| Peers | 182 | 53.40 N | 116.00 W |
| Peesane | 184 | 52.52 N | 103.36 W |
| Peetz | 198 | 40.57 N | 103.06 W |
| Peetzsee ⊜ | 264a | 52.26 N | 13.50 E |
| Pefferlaw | 212 | 44.19 N | 79.12 W |
| Pefferlaw Brook ≃ | 212 | 44.15 N | 79.13 W |
| Pegasus, Port ⊂ | 172 | 47.12 S | 167.41 E |
| Pegasus Bay ⊂ | 172 | 43.20 S | 173.00 E |
| Pegau | 54 | 51.10 N | 12.14 E |
| Pegli | 62 | 44.26 N | 8.48 E |
| Peglia, Monte ∧ | 66 | 42.49 N | 12.13 E |
| Pegnitz | 60 | 49.45 N | 11.33 E |
| Pegnitz ≃ | 60 | 49.29 N | 11.00 E |
| Pego | 34 | 38.51 N | 0.07 W |
| Pegolotte | 64 | 45.12 N | 12.02 E |
| Pegswood | 44 | 55.11 N | 1.38 W |
| Pegtymel' ≃ | 180 | 69.25 N | 174.35 E |
| Pegtymel'skij chrebet ⋏ | 180 | 68.30 N | 177.00 E |
| Pegu → Bago | 110 | 17.20 N | 96.29 E |
| Pegu ≃ | 110 | 16.47 N | 96.13 E |
| Pegueros | 234 | 20.57 N | 102.40 W |
| Peguis Indian Reserve ◆[4] | 184 | 51.20 N | 97.35 W |
| Pegu Yoma ⋏ | 110 | 19.00 N | 95.50 E |
| Pegwell Bay ⊂ | 42 | 51.18 N | 1.26 E |
| Pegyš | 24 | 63.26 N | 50.30 E |
| Pehčevo | 38 | 41.46 N | 22.54 E |
| Pehladpur ◆[8] | 272a | 28.35 N | 77.06 E |
| Pehlivanköy | 130 | 41.21 N | 26.55 E |
| Pehowa | 124 | 29.59 N | 76.35 E |
| Pehuajó | 252 | 35.48 S | 61.53 W |
| Pehula | 26 | 61.17 N | 22.42 E |
| Peian → Bei'an | 89 | 48.16 N | 126.36 E |
| Peiching → Beijing | 105 | 39.55 N | 116.25 E |
| Peigan Indian Reserve ◆[4] | 182 | 49.35 N | 113.40 W |
| Peihai → Beihai | 102 | 21.29 N | 109.05 E |
| Peij | 52 | 51.06 N | 5.53 E |
| Peijiatun | 98 | 39.19 N | 121.41 E |
| Peikang | 100 | 23.34 N | 120.18 E |
| Peikang ≃ | 100 | 23.31 N | 120.08 E |
| Peikant'ang Tao I | 100 | 26.13 N | 119.59 E |
| Peilstein im Mühlviertel | 60 | 48.37 N | 13.53 E |
| Peinan | 100 | 22.47 N | 121.07 E |
| Peinan ≃ | 100 | 22.46 N | 121.10 E |
| Peine | 52 | 52.19 N | 10.13 E |
| Peine, Pointe à › | 240d | 15.23 N | 61.15 W |
| Peinnechaung I | 110 | 19.59 N | 93.04 E |
| Peio | 64 | 46.22 N | 10.40 E |
| Peip'ing → Beijing | 105 | 39.55 N | 116.25 E |
| Peipsi järv (Čudskoje ozero) ⊜ | 76 | 58.45 N | 27.25 E |
| Peipus, Lake → Čudskoje ozero ⊜ | 76 | 58.45 N | 27.25 E |
| Peïra-Cava | 62 | 43.56 N | 7.22 E |
| Peirce, Cape › | 180 | 58.35 N | 161.47 W |
| Peisey-Nancroix | 62 | 45.33 N | 6.45 E |
| Peissenberg | 64 | 47.48 N | 11.04 E |
| Peissenberg ∧, Dtsch. | 60 | 47.48 N | 11.01 E |
| Peissenberg ∧, Dtsch. | 64 | 47.48 N | 11.01 E |
| Peiting | 58 | 47.47 N | 10.55 E |
| Peit'ou ◆[8] | 269d | 25.08 N | 121.30 E |
| Peitz | 54 | 51.51 N | 14.24 E |
| Peixe | 255 | 12.03 S | 48.32 W |
| Peixe, Rio do ≃, Bra. | 255 | 21.31 S | 51.58 W |
| Peixe, Rio do ≃, Bra. | 255 | 14.06 S | 50.51 W |
| Peixe, Rio do ≃, Bra. | 256 | 23.24 S | 45.28 W |
| Peixe, Rio do ≃, Bra. | 256 | 21.55 S | 43.21 W |
| Peixe, Rio do ≃, Bra. | 256 | 22.23 S | 46.51 W |
| Peixe, Rio do ≃, Bra. | 256 | 23.12 S | 46.06 W |
| Peixe, Rio do ≃, Bra. | 256 | 21.38 S | 45.11 W |
| Peixe-Boi | 250 | 1.12 S | 47.18 W |
| Peixes, Rio dos ≃ | 250 | 10.42 S | 57.56 W |
| Peixian (Yunhe), Zhg. | 98 | 34.21 N | 117.59 E |
| Peixian, Zhg. | 98 | 34.44 N | 116.59 E |
| Peixoto, Représa de ⊜[1] | 255 | 20.10 S | 47.20 W |
| Peixoto de Azevedo ≃ | 250 | 10.06 S | 55.31 W |
| Peiziyan | 98 | 35.07 N | 115.01 E |
| Pejantan, Pulau I | 112 | 0.07 N | 107.14 E |
| Pejelagartero | 234 | 18.04 N | 93.45 W |
| Pek ≃ | 38 | 44.46 N | 21.33 E |
| Pekalongan | 115a | 6.53 S | 109.40 E |
| Pekan | 114 | 3.30 N | 103.25 E |
| Pekanbaru | 112 | 0.32 N | 101.27 E |
| Pekanheran | 112 | 0.21 S | 102.26 E |
| Pekin, Il., U.S. | 190 | 40.34 N | 89.38 W |
| Pekin, In., U.S. | 218 | 38.29 N | 86.01 W |
| Pekin, N.Y., U.S. | 284a | 43.10 N | 78.53 W |
| Pekin, Oh., U.S. | 214 | 40.43 N | 81.07 W |
| Pékin → Beijing, Zhg. | 105 | 39.55 N | 116.25 E |
| Peking → Beijing | 105 | 39.55 N | 116.25 E |
| Peking National Library ʋ | 271a | 39.56 N | 116.22 E |
| Peking Railway Station ◆[5] | 271a | 39.54 N | 116.26 E |
| Peking University ʋ[2] | 271a | 39.59 N | 116.18 E |
| Peking Zoo ♦ | 271a | 39.56 N | 116.19 E |
| Peklino | 76 | 53.33 N | 33.32 E |
| Pekša ≃ | 80 | 55.53 N | 39.40 E |
| Pektubajevo | 80 | 57.02 N | 48.23 E |
| Pekul'nej, chrebet ⋏ | 180 | 66.00 N | 175.00 E |
| Pekul'nejskoje, ozero ⊜ | 180 | 62.40 N | 177.00 E |
| Péla | 150 | 7.37 N | 9.07 W |
| Pelabuhandagang | 112 | 1.08 S | 103.05 E |
| Pelabuhan Kelang | 114 | 3.00 N | 101.24 E |
| Pelabuhanratu | 115a | 6.59 S | 106.33 E |
| Pelabuhanratu, Teluk ⊂ | 115a | 7.03 S | 106.27 E |
| Pel'a-Chovanskaja | 80 | 54.36 N | 44.56 E |
| Pelado, Volcán ∧[1] | 286a | 19.09 N | 99.13 W |
| Pelagie, Isole II | 70a | 35.40 N | 12.40 E |
| Pelago | 66 | 43.46 N | 11.30 E |
| Pelahatchie | 194 | 32.18 N | 89.47 W |
| Pelahiyivka | 83 | 48.06 N | 38.36 E |
| Pelaihari | 112 | 3.48 S | 114.45 E |
| Pelalawan | 112 | 0.27 N | 102.05 E |
| Pelat, Mont ∧ | 62 | 44.16 N | 6.42 E |
| Pelawan | 114 | 2.47 N | 102.55 E |
| Pełczyce | 30 | 53.03 N | 15.18 E |
| Pélé, Mont ∧ | 152 | 3.15 S | 11.14 E |
| Pelechuco | 248 | 14.48 S | 69.04 W |
| Peleduj | 74 | 59.36 N | 112.45 E |
| Pelée, Montagne ∧ | 240e | 14.48 N | 61.10 W |
| Pelee, Point › | 214 | 41.54 N | 82.30 W |
| Pelee Island I | 214 | 41.46 N | 82.39 W |
| Pelee Passage ʊ | 214 | 41.52 N | 82.37 W |
| Pelega, Vârful ∧ | 38 | 45.22 N | 22.54 E |
| Pelekech ∧ | 154 | 3.48 N | 35.04 E |
| Peleliu → Beliliou I | 175b | 7.01 N | 134.15 E |
| Peleng, Pulau I | 112 | 1.20 S | 123.10 E |
| Peleng, Selat ʊ | 112 | 1.10 S | 122.45 E |
| Pelf, Monte ∧ | 64 | 46.14 N | 12.12 E |
| Pelham, On., Can. | 212 | 43.02 N | 79.17 W |
| Pelham, Al., U.S. | 194 | 33.17 N | 86.48 W |
| Pelham, Ga., U.S. | 192 | 31.07 N | 84.09 W |
| Pelham, Ma., U.S. | 207 | 42.23 N | 72.24 W |
| Pelham, N.H., U.S. | 207 | 42.44 N | 71.19 W |
| Pelham, N.Y., U.S. | 276 | 40.54 N | 73.48 W |
| Pelham Bay ⊂ | 276 | 40.52 N | 73.47 W |
| Pelham Bay Park ♦ | 276 | 40.52 N | 73.49 W |
| Pelham Manor | 276 | 40.53 N | 73.48 W |
| Pelhřimov | 30 | 49.26 N | 15.13 E |
| Pelican | 180 | 57.57 N | 136.14 W |
| Pelican ≃ | 198 | 46.17 N | 96.08 W |
| Pelican, Punta › | 200 | 31.19 N | 113.43 W |
| Pelican Bay ⊂ | 184 | 52.45 N | 100.20 W |
| Pelican Island I, Mo., U.S. | 219 | 38.52 N | 90.18 W |
| Pelican Island I, Tx., U.S. | 222 | 29.20 N | 94.48 W |
| Pelican Lagoon ⊂ | 168b | 35.50 S | 137.47 E |
| Pelican Lake | 190 | 45.30 N | 89.10 W |
| Pelican Lake ⊜, Ab., Can. | 182 | 55.47 N | 113.15 W |
| Pelican Lake ⊜, Mb., Can. | 184 | 49.20 N | 99.35 W |
| Pelican Lake ⊜, Mb., Can. | 184 | 53.50 N | 96.08 W |
| Pelican Lake ⊜, Mb., Can. | 184 | 52.30 N | 100.20 W |
| Pelican Lake ⊜, Sk., Can. | 184 | 55.08 N | 103.00 W |
| Pelican Lake ⊜, Sk., Can. | 184 | 50.32 N | 106.00 W |
| Pelican Lake ⊜, Mn., U.S. | 190 | 48.05 N | 92.54 W |
| Pelican Lake ⊜, S.D., U.S. | 198 | 44.52 N | 97.11 W |
| Pelican Mountain ∧ | 182 | 55.35 N | 113.40 W |
| Pelican Narrows | 184 | 55.10 N | 102.56 W |
| Pelican Point › | 168b | 34.48 S | 138.29 E |
| Pelican Rapids, Mb., Can. | 184 | 52.45 N | 100.42 W |
| Pelican Rapids, Mn., U.S. | 198 | 46.34 N | 96.04 W |
| Pelileo | 246 | 1.19 S | 78.32 W |
| Pelinia | 38 | 47.53 N | 27.50 E |
| Pelister ∧ | 38 | 41.00 N | 21.12 E |
| Pelješac, Poluotok ›[1] | 36 | 42.58 N | 17.20 E |
| Pelkosenniemi | 24 | 67.07 N | 27.30 E |
| Pelkum, Dtsch. | 52 | 51.39 N | 7.46 E |
| Pelkum, Dtsch. | 263 | 51.40 N | 7.24 E |
| Pella, S. Afr. | 158 | 29.01 S | 19.06 E |
| Pella, Ia., U.S. | 190 | 41.24 N | 92.54 W |
| Pélla ⊥ | 38 | 40.45 N | 22.33 E |
| Pellaro | 68 | 38.01 N | 15.39 E |
| Pell City | 194 | 33.35 N | 86.17 W |
| Pellechia, Monte ∧ | 66 | 42.07 N | 12.52 E |
| Pellegrini | 252 | 36.16 S | 63.09 W |
| Pellegrini, Lago ⊜ | 252 | 38.40 S | 68.00 W |
| Pellegrino, Cozzo ∧ | 68 | 39.45 N | 16.03 E |
| Pellegrino, Monte ∧ | 70 | 38.10 N | 13.21 E |
| Pellegrino Parmense | 64 | 44.44 N | 9.55 E |
| Pellendorf | 264b | 48.06 N | 16.27 E |
| Peller, Monte ∧ | 64 | 46.18 N | 10.57 E |
| Pellestrina, Litorale di ±[2] | 64 | 45.16 N | 12.18 E |
| Pelletier Lake ⊜ | 184 | 56.30 N | 97.00 W |
| Pellice ≃ | 62 | 44.50 N | 7.38 E |
| Pellingen | 56 | 49.40 N | 6.40 E |
| Pell Lake | 216 | 42.32 N | 88.21 W |
| Pello | 24 | 66.47 N | 24.00 E |
| Pellston | 190 | 45.33 N | 84.47 W |
| Pellworm I | 30 | 54.31 N | 8.38 E |
| Pelly | 184 | 51.52 N | 101.55 W |
| Pelly ≃ | 180 | 62.47 N | 137.19 W |
| Pelly Bay ⊂ | 176 | 68.53 N | 89.51 W |
| Pelly Crossing | 180 | 62.50 N | 136.35 W |
| Pelly Lake ⊜ | 176 | 65.59 N | 101.12 W |
| Pelly Mountains ⋏ | 180 | 62.00 N | 133.00 W |
| Pelón, Cerro ∧ | 234 | 20.05 N | 99.55 W |
| Peloncillo Mountains ⋏ | 200 | 32.15 N | 109.00 W |
| Pelopónnisos □[4] | 38 | 37.30 N | 22.30 E |
| Pelopónnisos (Peloponnesus) ›[1] | 38 | 37.30 N | 22.00 E |
| Peloritani, Monti ⋏ | 70 | 38.03 N | 15.20 E |
| Pelotas | 252 | 31.46 S | 52.20 W |
| Pelotas ≃ | 252 | 27.28 S | 51.55 W |
| Pelplin | 30 | 53.56 N | 18.42 E |
| Pelque ≃ | 254 | 51.03 S | 70.58 W |
| Pelsin | 54 | 53.48 N | 13.40 E |
| Pelusium Bay → Tīnah, Khalīj aṭ- ⊂ | 140 | 31.08 N | 32.40 E |
| Pel'ušn'a | 76 | 58.56 N | 32.52 E |
| Pélussin | 62 | 45.25 N | 4.41 E |
| Pelvo d'Elva ∧ | 62 | 44.33 N | 7.02 E |
| Pelym | 86 | 59.38 N | 63.05 E |
| Pemadumcook Lake ⊜ | 188 | 45.40 N | 68.55 W |
| Pemalang | 115a | 6.54 S | 109.22 E |
| Pemalang, Ujung › | 115a | 6.47 S | 109.29 E |
| Pemali ≃ | 115a | 6.47 S | 109.01 E |
| Pemangkat | 112 | 1.10 N | 108.58 E |
| Pematang | 112 | 0.12 S | 102.04 E |
| Pematangsiantar | 114 | 2.57 N | 99.03 E |
| Pematangtanahjawa | 114 | 2.53 N | 99.12 E |
| Pemba, Moç. | 154 | 12.58 S | 40.30 E |
| Pemba, Zam. | 154 | 16.31 S | 27.22 E |
| Pemba I | 154 | 5.10 S | 39.48 E |
| Pemba Channel ʊ | 154 | 5.10 S | 39.20 E |
| Pembarisan, Pegunungan ⋏ | 115a | 7.13 S | 108.45 E |
| Pemberton, Austl. | 162 | 34.28 S | 116.01 E |
| Pemberton, B.C., Can. | 182 | 50.20 N | 122.48 W |
| Pemberton, Eng., U.K. | 262 | 53.32 N | 2.41 W |
| Pemberton, N.J., U.S. | 208 | 39.58 N | 74.41 W |
| Pemberton, Oh., U.S. | 216 | 40.18 N | 84.02 W |
| Pemberton Airport ⊠ | 285 | 39.59 N | 74.41 W |
| Pemberton Heights | 285 | 39.58 N | 74.41 W |
| Pemberville | 214 | 41.24 N | 83.27 W |
| Pembina | 198 | 48.57 N | 97.14 W |
| Pembina ≃, Ab., Can. | 182 | 54.45 N | 114.15 W |
| Pembina ≃, N.A. | 184 | 48.57 N | 97.14 W |
| Pembina Hills ⋏[2] | 198 | 49.10 N | 98.25 W |
| Pembine | 190 | 45.38 N | 87.59 W |
| Pembrey | 42 | 51.42 N | 4.16 W |
| Pembroke, On., Can. | 190 | 45.49 N | 77.07 W |
| Pembroke, Wales, U.K. | 42 | 51.41 N | 4.55 W |
| Pembroke, Ga., U.S. | 192 | 32.08 N | 81.37 W |
| Pembroke, Ky., U.S. | 194 | 36.46 N | 87.21 W |
| Pembroke, Me., U.S. | 188 | 44.57 N | 67.09 W |
| Pembroke, N.Y., U.S. | 210 | 43.00 N | 78.27 W |
| Pembroke, N.C., U.S. | 192 | 34.40 N | 79.11 W |
| Pembroke, Va., U.S. | 192 | 37.19 N | 80.38 W |
| Pembroke, Cape › | 176 | 62.56 N | 81.55 W |
| Pembroke Castle ⊥ | 42 | 51.41 N | 4.56 W |
| Pembroke Dock | 42 | 51.42 N | 4.56 W |
| Pembroke Pines | 220 | 26.00 N | 80.13 W |
| Pembrokeshire Coast National Park ♦ | 42 | 51.47 N | 5.06 W |
| Pembuang | 112 | 2.34 S | 112.19 E |
| Pembuang ≃ | 112 | 3.24 S | 112.33 E |
| Pembury | 42 | 51.09 N | 0.20 E |
| Pemfling | 60 | 49.16 N | 12.37 E |
| Pemichigamau Lake ⊜ | 184 | 56.16 N | 99.33 W |
| Pemigewasset ≃ | 188 | 43.26 N | 71.40 W |
| Pemmican Portage | 184 | 53.56 N | 102.17 W |
| Pemuco | 252 | 36.58 S | 72.06 W |
| Pemynoos Indian Reserve ◆[4] | 182 | 50.29 N | 121.15 W |
| Pemzašen | 84 | 40.35 N | 43.57 E |
| Pena, Parque de ♦ | 266c | 38.47 N | 9.23 W |
| Peña Barroza | 248 | 22.10 S | 67.25 W |
| Peña Blanca | 236 | 8.27 N | 81.40 W |
| Peñafiel, Esp. | 34 | 41.36 N | 4.07 W |
| Penafiel, Port. | 34 | 41.12 N | 8.17 W |
| Pen'agino | 265b | 55.50 N | 37.21 E |
| Peña Gorda, Cerro ∧ | 234 | 20.44 N | 104.50 W |
| Peña Grande ◆[8] | 266a | 40.29 N | 3.44 W |
| Pen'akša | 80 | 56.22 N | 44.56 E |
| Peñalara ∧ | 34 | 40.51 N | 3.57 W |
| Peñalolén | 286e | 33.29 S | 70.32 W |
| Pena-Lunanga | 154 | 4.16 S | 28.10 E |
| Penalva | 250 | 3.18 S | 45.10 W |
| Penambulai, Pulau I | 164 | 6.24 S | 134.48 E |
| Penang → George Town | 114 | 5.25 N | 100.20 E |
| Penanjung, Teluk ⊂ | 115a | 7.45 S | 108.37 E |
| Penápolis | 255 | 21.24 S | 50.04 W |
| Peñaranda de Bracamonte | 34 | 40.54 N | 5.12 W |
| Pen Argyl | 210 | 40.52 N | 75.15 W |
| Penaron | 114 | 4.38 N | 97.40 E |
| Peñarroya-Pueblonuevo | 34 | 38.18 N | 5.16 W |
| Penarth | 42 | 51.27 N | 3.11 W |
| Peñas, Cabo de › | 34 | 43.39 N | 5.51 W |
| Penas, Golfo de ⊂ | 254 | 47.22 S | 74.50 W |
| Penasco | 200 | 36.10 N | 105.41 W |
| Peñasco, Rio ≃ | 196 | 32.45 N | 104.19 W |
| Penataquit Creek ≃ | 276 | 40.43 N | 73.14 W |
| Penbrook | 208 | 40.16 N | 76.50 W |
| Pencader | 42 | 52.01 N | 4.16 W |
| Pencahue | 252 | 35.24 S | 71.49 W |
| Pence | 190 | 46.25 N | 90.16 W |
| Pen Centre ◆[9] | 284a | 43.08 N | 79.14 W |
| Penchard | 261 | 48.59 N | 2.52 E |
| Penck Trough V | 9 | 73.00 S | 2.45 W |
| Penco | 252 | 36.44 S | 72.59 W |
| Pencoed | 42 | 51.32 N | 3.30 W |
| Pendang, Indon. | 112 | 1.28 S | 114.51 E |
| Pendang, Malay. | 114 | 6.00 N | 100.28 E |
| Pendé ≃ | 146 | 7.55 N | 16.36 E |
| Pendéli | 267c | 38.03 N | 23.52 E |
| Pendelikón Óros ⋏ | 267c | 38.06 N | 23.54 E |
| Pendembu, S.L. | 150 | 8.06 N | 10.42 W |
| Pendembu, S.L. | 150 | 9.06 N | 12.12 W |
| Pendências | 250 | 5.15 S | 36.43 W |
| Pendeng | 114 | 4.06 N | 97.36 E |
| Pender | 198 | 42.06 N | 96.42 W |
| Pender Bay ⊂ | 162 | 16.45 S | 122.42 E |
| Pendhar | 272c | 19.04 N | 73.06 E |
| Pendjari ≃ | 150 | 10.54 N | 0.51 E |
| Pendjari, Parc National de la ♦ | 150 | 11.20 N | 1.15 E |
| Pendlebury | 262 | 53.31 N | 2.20 W |
| Pendle Hill | 274a | 33.48 S | 150.57 E |
| Pendle Hill ∧[2] | 44 | 53.52 N | 2.17 W |
| Pendleton, In., U.S. | 218 | 39.59 N | 85.44 W |
| Pendleton, N.Y., U.S. | 284a | 43.05 N | 78.44 W |
| Pendleton, Or., U.S. | 202 | 45.40 N | 118.47 W |
| Pendleton, S.C., U.S. | 192 | 34.39 N | 82.47 W |
| Pendleton □[6] | 218 | 38.42 N | 84.22 W |
| Pendolo | 112 | 2.05 S | 120.42 E |
| Pendopo | 112 | 3.17 S | 103.52 E |
| Pend Oreille ≃ | 202 | 49.04 N | 117.37 W |
| Pend Oreille, Lake ⊜ | 202 | 48.10 N | 116.11 W |
| Pend Oreille, Mount ∧ | 202 | 48.25 N | 116.10 W |
| Pendotiba ≃ | 287a | 22.53 S | 43.02 W |
| Pendžikent | 85 | 39.29 N | 67.35 E |
| Penebel | 115b | 8.25 S | 115.09 E |
| Penedo | 250 | 10.17 S | 36.36 W |
| Penedono | 34 | 40.59 N | 7.24 W |
| Penela | 34 | 40.02 N | 8.23 W |
| Penelope | 222 | 31.52 N | 96.56 W |
| Penetang Harbour ⊂ | 212 | 44.47 N | 79.57 W |
| Penetanguishene | 212 | 44.47 N | 79.55 W |
| Penfield, Il., U.S. | 216 | 40.18 N | 87.57 W |
| Penfield, N.Y., U.S. | 210 | 43.07 N | 77.28 W |
| Penfield, Oh., U.S. | 214 | 41.10 N | 82.08 W |
| Penfield, Pa., U.S. | 214 | 41.13 N | 78.34 W |
| Penganga ≃ | 122 | 19.53 N | 79.09 E |
| Pengastulan | 115b | 8.11 S | 114.55 E |
| Peng Chau I | 271d | 22.17 N | 114.02 E |
| P'engchia Yü I | 100 | 25.38 N | 122.04 E |
| Penge, S. Afr. | 156 | 24.22 S | 30.13 E |
| Penge, Zaïre | 154 | 5.31 S | 24.37 E |
| Penge ◆[8] | 260 | 51.25 N | 0.04 W |
| Penggong | 106 | 30.27 N | 119.57 E |
| Penggongmiao | 100 | 26.07 N | 113.34 E |
| Penghu | 100 | 25.24 N | 118.11 E |
| P'enghu Ch'üntao (Pescadores) II | 100 | 23.30 N | 119.30 E |
| P'enghu Shuitao ʊ | 100 | 23.30 N | 119.50 E |
| Pengiki, Pulau I | 112 | 0.15 N | 108.03 E |
| Pengjiachang | 107 | 30.36 N | 103.53 E |
| Pengjialouzi | 104 | 41.56 N | 123.40 E |
| Pengjiawan | 100 | 32.16 N | 114.04 E |
| Pengjiawu | 105 | 39.41 N | 117.10 E |
| Pengkalan Baharu | 114 | 4.28 N | 100.38 E |
| Pengkou | 100 | 25.32 N | 116.42 E |
| Penglai (Dengzhou) | 98 | 37.48 N | 120.42 E |
| Penglaizhen | 107 | 30.36 N | 105.14 E |
| Penglang | 106 | 31.23 N | 121.05 E |
| Pengnan | 107 | 30.25 N | 105.53 E |
| Pengpu → Bengbu | 100 | 32.58 N | 117.24 E |
| Pengshan | 107 | 30.13 N | 103.52 E |
| Pengshi | 100 | 30.28 N | 113.10 E |
| Pengshui | 102 | 29.18 N | 108.09 E |
| Penguin | 166 | 41.07 S | 146.04 E |
| Pengwaluote Shan ∧ | 120 | 33.30 N | 86.35 E |
| Pengxi | 102 | 30.49 N | 105.40 E |
| Pengxian | 102 | 31.00 N | 103.50 E |
| Pengze | 100 | 29.53 N | 116.33 E |
| Pengzhai | 100 | 24.23 N | 115.06 E |
| Pengzhuangzi | 105 | 40.06 N | 114.51 E |
| Penha | 252 | 26.46 S | 48.39 W |
| Penha ◆[8] | 287a | 22.49 S | 43.17 W |
| Penha de França ◆[8] | 287b | 23.32 S | 46.32 W |
| Penha Longa, Bra. | 256 | 22.04 S | 43.05 W |
| Penhalonga, Zimb. | 154 | 18.54 S | 32.40 E |
| Penhold | 182 | 52.08 N | 113.52 W |
| Penhold, Canadian Forces Base ■ | 182 | 52.12 N | 113.53 W |
| Penhorn Creek ≃ | 276 | 40.45 N | 74.05 W |
| Penhsi → Benxi | 104 | 41.18 N | 123.45 E |
| Penibética, Cordillera ⋏ | 34 | 37.00 N | 4.00 W |
| Peniche | 34 | 39.21 N | 9.23 W |
| Penicuik | 46 | 55.50 N | 3.14 W |
| Penida, Nusa I | 115b | 8.44 S | 115.32 E |
| Penig | 54 | 50.56 N | 12.41 E |
| Peningo Neck ›[1] | 276 | 40.57 N | 73.41 W |
| Peninjai | 112 | 1.26 S | 101.50 E |
| Peninsula Lake ⊜ | 212 | 45.20 N | 79.05 W |
| Peninsula State Park ♦ | 190 | 45.09 N | 87.14 W |
| Peníscola | 34 | 40.21 N | 0.25 E |
| Penistone | 44 | 53.32 N | 1.37 W |
| Penitas | 196 | 26.17 N | 98.27 W |
| Penitencia Creek ≃ | 282 | 37.27 N | 121.55 W |
| Penitente, Serra do ⋏[2] | 250 | 8.45 S | 46.20 W |
| Penjamillo [de Degollado] | 234 | 20.06 N | 101.54 W |
| Pénjamo | 234 | 20.26 N | 101.44 W |
| Penketh | 262 | 53.23 N | 2.40 W |
| Penki → Benxi | 104 | 41.18 N | 123.45 E |
| Penkino | 82 | 54.50 N | 38.53 E |
| Penkridge | 42 | 52.44 N | 2.07 W |
| Penkun | 54 | 53.17 N | 14.14 E |
| Pen Lake ⊜ | 212 | 45.28 N | 78.23 W |
| Penllyn | 285 | 40.10 N | 75.15 W |
| Penmaenmawr | 44 | 53.16 N | 3.54 W |
| Penmarc'h, Pointe de › | 32 | 47.48 N | 4.22 W |
| Penn | 279b | 40.20 N | 79.38 W |
| Penna, Punta della › | 66 | 42.10 N | 14.43 E |
| Pennabilli | 66 | 43.49 N | 12.16 E |
| Penn Acres | 285 | 39.40 N | 75.34 W |
| Pennant Hills | 274a | 33.44 S | 151.04 E |
| Pennant Hills Park ♦ | 274a | 33.45 S | 151.06 E |
| Pennant Point › | 186 | 44.26 N | 63.39 W |
| Pennant Station | 184 | 50.33 N | 108.12 W |
| Pennask Lake ⊜ | 182 | 50.00 N | 120.05 W |
| Pennask Mountain ∧ | 182 | 49.53 N | 120.07 W |
| Penn Brook ≃ | 283 | 42.44 N | 70.59 W |
| Penn Cove ⊂ | 224 | 48.14 N | 122.41 W |
| Penn Cove Park | 224 | 48.14 N | 122.41 W |
| Penndel | 285 | 40.09 N | 74.55 W |
| Penne | 66 | 42.27 N | 13.55 E |
| Penne, Punta › | 68 | 40.41 N | 17.56 E |
| Penne-d'Agenais | 32 | 44.23 N | 0.49 E |
| Pennedepie | 50 | 49.25 N | 0.11 E |
| Pennel Creek ≃ | 198 | 46.34 N | 104.52 W |
| Penneru ≃ | 122 | 14.35 N | 80.10 E |
| Pennes (Pens) | 64 | 46.47 N | 11.25 E |
| Pennes, Val di V | 64 | 46.47 N | 11.25 E |
| Penneshaw | 168b | 35.44 S | 137.56 E |
| Penngrove | 226 | 38.18 N | 122.40 W |
| Penn Hills | 214 | 40.28 N | 79.51 W |
| Penn Hills Center ◆[9] | 279b | 40.28 N | 79.50 W |
| Pennines ⋏ | 44 | 54.10 N | 2.05 W |
| Pennines, Alpes ⋏ | 58 | 46.05 N | 7.50 E |
| Penningby | 40 | 59.41 N | 18.40 E |
| Penningby slott ⊥ | 40 | 59.41 N | 18.40 E |
| Pennington, N.J., U.S. | 208 | 40.19 N | 74.47 W |
| Pennington, Tx., U.S. | 222 | 31.11 N | 95.14 W |
| Pennington ≃[1] | 150 | 4.45 N | 5.35 E |
| Pennington Gap | 192 | 36.45 N | 83.01 W |
| Pennino, Monte ∧ | 66 | 43.06 N | 12.53 E |
| Penn Run | 214 | 40.37 N | 79.01 W |
| Pennsauken | 208 | 39.58 N | 75.04 W |
| Pennsauken Creek ≃ | 285 | 39.59 N | 75.03 W |
| Pennsauken Creek, North Branch ≃ | 285 | 39.58 N | 75.01 W |
| Pennsauken Creek, South Branch ≃ | 285 | 39.58 N | 75.01 W |
| Pennsboro | 188 | 39.17 N | 80.58 W |
| Penns Brook ≃ | 276 | 40.43 N | 74.32 W |
| Pennsburg | 208 | 40.23 N | 75.29 W |
| Pennsbury Heights | 285 | 40.12 N | 74.49 W |
| Pennsbury Manor ⊥ | 285 | 40.08 N | 74.46 W |
| Penn's Cave ±[5] | 210 | 40.53 N | 77.36 W |
| Penns Creek | 210 | 40.52 N | 77.04 W |
| Penns Creek ≃ | 210 | 40.48 N | 76.51 W |
| Pennsdale | 210 | 41.15 N | 76.48 W |
| Penns Grove | 208 | 39.43 N | 75.28 W |
| Pennside | 208 | 40.20 N | 75.53 W |
| Penns Neck | 276 | 40.20 N | 74.38 W |
| Pennsuco | 220 | 25.53 N | 80.22 W |
| Pennsville | 208 | 39.39 N | 75.31 W |
| Penns Woods | 279b | 40.21 N | 79.46 W |
| Pennsylvania □[3], U.S. | 178 | 40.45 N | 77.30 W |
| Pennsylvania □[3], U.S. | 188 | 40.45 N | 77.30 W |
| Pennsylvania, University of ʋ[2] | 285 | 39.57 N | 75.12 W |
| Pennsylvania Canal ≅ | 285 | 40.13 N | 74.47 W |
| Pennsylvania Station ◆[5] | 276 | 40.45 N | 74.00 W |
| Penn Valley, Ca., U.S. | 226 | 39.12 N | 121.11 W |
| Penn Valley, Pa., U.S. | 285 | 40.01 N | 75.16 W |
| Penn Valley Terrace | 285 | 40.11 N | 74.47 W |
| Pennville | 216 | 40.29 N | 85.08 W |
| Penn Wynne | 285 | 39.59 N | 75.16 W |
| Penny | 182 | 53.50 N | 121.17 W |
| Penn Yan | 210 | 42.39 N | 77.03 W |
| Pennycutaway ≃ | 184 | 56.43 N | 92.44 W |
| Penny Hill | 285 | 39.46 N | 75.30 W |
| Penny Ice Cap ◘ | 176 | 67.10 N | 66.00 W |
| Pennypack Creek ≃ | 285 | 40.02 N | 75.00 W |
| Pennypack Park ♦ | 285 | 40.04 N | 75.03 W |
| Penny Strait ʊ | 176 | 76.30 N | 97.00 W |
| Peno | 76 | 56.55 N | 32.45 E |
| Penobscot | 210 | 41.10 N | 75.52 W |
| Penobscot ≃ | 188 | 44.30 N | 68.50 W |
| Penobscot, East Branch ≃ | 186 | 45.35 N | 68.32 W |
| Penobscot, West Branch ≃ | 188 | 45.35 N | 68.32 W |
| Penobscot Bay ⊂ | 188 | 44.15 N | 68.52 W |
| Peno Creek ≃ | 219 | 39.32 N | 91.16 W |
| Pen'ok | 86 | 55.30 N | 81.34 E |
| Penola | 166 | 37.23 S | 140.50 E |
| Peñoles | 196 | 25.39 N | 104.30 W |
| Peñón Blanco | 232 | 24.47 N | 104.02 W |
| Penong | 162 | 31.55 S | 133.01 E |
| Penonomé | 236 | 8.31 N | 80.22 W |
| Penrhyn I[1] | 14 | 9.00 S | 158.00 W |
| Penrhyn Bay | 44 | 53.19 N | 3.45 W |
| Penrhyndeudraeth | 42 | 52.56 N | 4.04 W |
| Penrith, Austl. | 170 | 33.45 S | 150.42 E |
| Penrith, Eng., U.K. | 44 | 54.40 N | 2.44 W |
| Penryn, Eng., U.K. | 42 | 50.09 N | 5.06 W |
| Penryn, Ca., U.S. | 226 | 38.51 N | 121.10 W |
| Penryn, Pa., U.S. | 208 | 40.12 N | 76.22 W |
| Pens → Pennes | 64 | 46.47 N | 11.25 E |
| Pensacola | 194 | 30.25 N | 87.13 W |
| Pensacola Bay ⊂ | 194 | 30.25 N | 87.06 W |
| Pensacola Mountains ⋏ | 9 | 83.45 S | 55.00 W |
| Pensacola Naval Air Station ■ | 194 | 30.21 N | 87.19 W |
| Pensacola Seamount ✢[3] | 14 | 18.17 N | 157.20 W |
| Pensaukee ≃ | 190 | 44.49 N | 87.55 W |
| Pensby | 262 | 53.21 N | 3.06 W |
| Pense | 184 | 50.25 N | 105.00 W |
| Penshaw | 44 | 54.53 N | 1.29 W |
| Pensiangan | 112 | 4.33 N | 116.19 E |
| Pensilva | 42 | 50.30 N | 4.25 W |
| Pensilvania | 246 | 5.31 N | 75.05 W |
| Pentagna | 256 | 22.09 S | 43.45 W |
| Pentagon ʋ | 284c | 38.52 N | 77.03 W |
| Pentagon Mountain ∧ | 202 | 47.56 N | 113.07 W |
| Pentecost □[8] | 175f | 15.45 S | 168.12 E |
| Pentecoste | 250 | 3.48 S | 39.17 W |
| Pentecôte I | 175f | 15.42 S | 168.10 E |
| Pentecôte ≃ | 186 | 49.47 N | 67.10 W |
| Pentecôte, Lac ⊜ | 186 | 49.53 N | 67.20 W |
| Penticton | 182 | 49.30 N | 119.35 W |
| Penticton Indian Reserve ◆[4] | 182 | 49.30 N | 119.40 W |
| Pentire Point › | 42 | 50.36 N | 4.55 W |
| Pentland | 166 | 20.32 S | 145.24 E |
| Pentland Firth ʊ | 46 | 58.44 N | 3.07 W |
| Pentland Hills ⋏[2] | 46 | 55.48 N | 3.23 W |
| Pentling | 60 | 48.59 N | 12.04 E |
| Pentraeth | 44 | 53.17 N | 4.12 W |
| Pentre Halkyn | 262 | 53.15 N | 3.12 W |
| Pentucket, Lake ⊜ | 283 | 42.47 N | 71.05 W |
| Pentucket Pond ⊜ | 283 | 42.44 N | 71.00 W |
| Pentwater | 190 | 43.46 N | 86.25 W |
| Penuba | 112 | 0.20 S | 104.28 E |
| Peñuelas | 240m | 18.03 N | 66.43 W |
| Penuguan | 112 | 2.27 S | 104.31 E |
| Penukonda | 122 | 14.05 N | 77.35 E |
| Penunjok, Tanjong › | 114 | 4.22 N | 103.29 E |
| Pènwègon | 110 | 18.13 N | 96.34 E |
| Penwell | 196 | 31.44 N | 102.35 W |
| Peny | 78 | 51.04 N | 35.54 E |
| Penyagolosa ∧ | 34 | 40.13 N | 0.21 W |
| Penyal d'Ifac ♦ | 34 | 38.38 N | 0.05 E |
| Penyengat | 114 | 0.54 N | 102.20 E |
| Pen-y-Ghent ∧ | 44 | 54.09 N | 2.14 W |
| Penygroes, Wales, U.K. | 42 | 51.49 N | 4.02 W |
| Penygroes, Wales, U.K. | 44 | 53.04 N | 4.17 W |
| Penyu, Kepulauan II | 164 | 5.22 S | 127.46 E |
| Penyu, Teluk ⊂ | 115a | 7.45 S | 109.15 E |
| Penza | 80 | 53.13 N | 45.00 E |
| Penzance | 42 | 50.07 N | 5.33 W |
| Penza Oblast' □[4] | 80 | 53.00 N | 45.00 E |
| Penzberg | 64 | 47.45 N | 11.23 E |
| Penžina ≃ | 74 | 62.28 N | 165.18 E |
| Penzing ◆[8] | 264b | 48.12 N | 16.18 E |


**Symbols** in the index entries represent the broad categories identified in the key at the right. Symbols with superior numbers (⋏[1]) identify subcategories (see complete key on page *I · 1).*

**Symbole** im Register stellen die rechts im Schlüssel erklärten Kategorien dar. Symbole mit hochgestellten Ziffern (⋏[1]) bezeichnen Unterabteilungen einer Kategorie (vgl. vollständiger Schlüssel auf Seite *I · 1).*

**Los símbolos** incluídos en el texto del índice representan las grandes categorías identificadas con la clave a la derecha. Los símbolos con numeros en su parte superior (⋏[1]) identifican las subcategorías (véase la clave completa en la página *I · 1).*

**Les symboles** de l'index représentent les catégories indiquées dans la légende à droite. Les symboles suivis d'un indice (⋏[1]) représentent des sous-catégories (voir légende complète à la page *I · 1).*

**Os símbolos** incluídos no texto do índice representam as grandes categorias identificadas com a chave à direita. Os símbolos com números em sua parte superior (⋏[1]) identificam as subcategorias (veja-se a chave completa à página *I · 1).*

| English | Deutsch | Español | Français | Português |
|---|---|---|---|---|
| ∧ Mountain | Berg | Montaña | Montagne | Montanha |
| ⋏ Mountains | Gebirge | Montañas | Montagnes | Montanhas |
| ϰ Pass | Paß | Paso | Col | Passo |
| V Valley, Canyon | Tal, Cañon | Valle, Cañón | Vallée, Canyon | Vale, Canhão |
| ≚ Plain | Ebene | Llano | Plaine | Planície |
| › Cape | Kap | Cabo | Cap | Cabo |
| I Island | Insel | Isla | Île | Ilha |
| II Islands | Inseln | Islas | Îles | Ilhas |
| ± Other Topographic Features | Andere Topographische Objekte | Otros Elementos Topográficos | Autres données topographiques | Outros acidentes topográficos |

ESPAÑOL — Nombre | Página | Lat.°′ | Long.°′ W = Oeste
FRANÇAIS — Nom | Page | Lat.°′ | Long.°′ W = Ouest
PORTUGUÊS — Nome | Página | Lat.°′ | Long.°′ W = Oeste

| Nombre | Página | Lat.°′ | Long.°′ W = Oeste |
|---|---|---|---|
| Penzino | 80 | 52.07 N | 50.27 E |
| Penžinskaja guba c | 74 | 61.00 N | 162.00 E |
| Penžinskij chrebet ⋏ | 74 | 62.30 N | 167.00 E |
| Penzlin | 54 | 53.30 N | 13.05 E |
| Péone | 62 | 44.07 N | 6.54 E |
| Peoples Creek ≃ | 202 | 48.24 N | 108.19 W |
| Peoples Ditch ≅ | 226 | 36.15 N | 119.41 W |
| Peoria, Az., U.S. | 200 | 33.34 N | 112.14 W |
| Peoria, Il., U.S. | 190 | 40.41 N | 89.35 W |
| Peoria, Oh., U.S. | 216 | 40.19 N | 83.27 W |
| Peoria Heights | 190 | 40.44 N | 89.34 W |
| Peotillos | 234 | 22.30 N | 100.37 W |
| Peotone | 216 | 41.19 N | 87.47 W |
| Peover Eye ≃ | 262 | 53.15 N | 2.31 W |
| Peover Heath | 262 | 53.15 N | 2.19 W |
| Pepa | 154 | 7.42 S | 29.47 E |
| Pepacton Reservoir ⊜[1] | 210 | 42.06 N | 74.54 W |
| Pepaw ≃ | 184 | 52.40 N | 102.23 W |
| Pepel | 150 | 8.35 N | 13.03 W |
| Peper | 140 | 7.04 N | 33.00 E |
| Pepin | 190 | 44.26 N | 92.08 W |
| Pepin, Lake ⊜ | 190 | 44.30 N | 92.15 W |
| Pepinster | 56 | 50.34 N | 5.49 E |
| Pepperell | 207 | 42.40 N | 71.35 W |
| Pepper Park State Recreation Area ♦ | 220 | 27.30 N | 80.18 W |
| Pepper Pike | 279a | 41.28 N | 81.27 W |
| Peqi'in Ḥadasha | 132 | 32.59 N | 35.20 E |
| Peqin | 38 | 41.03 N | 19.45 E |
| Pequannock | 210 | 40.57 N | 74.17 W |
| Pequannock ≃ | 276 | 40.58 N | 74.17 W |
| Pequanticut Brook ≃ | 283 | 42.01 N | 71.08 W |
| Pequea Creek ≃ | 208 | 39.53 N | 76.22 W |
| Pequeno ≃ | 287a | 22.55 S | 43.25 W |
| Pequeri | 256 | 21.50 S | 43.06 W |
| Pequest ≃ | 210 | 40.50 N | 75.05 W |
| Pequez | 208 | 39.53 N | 76.22 W |
| Pequizeiro | 250 | 8.32 S | 48.58 W |
| Pequop Mountains ⋏ | 204 | 40.45 N | 114.40 W |
| Pequot Lakes | 190 | 46.36 N | 94.18 W |
| Perabumulih | 112 | 3.27 S | 104.15 E |
| Perak □[3] | 114 | 5.00 N | 101.00 E |
| Perak ≃ | 114 | 3.58 N | 100.53 E |
| Perak, Kuala c | 114 | 4.00 N | 100.47 E |
| Peralba, Monte ∧ | 64 | 46.37 N | 12.43 E |
| Perales de Alfambra | 34 | 40.38 N | 1.00 W |
| Perales del Rio | 266a | 40.19 N | 3.38 W |
| Peralillo | 252 | 34.29 S | 71.29 W |
| Peralta | 200 | 34.50 N | 106.41 W |
| Pérama | 267c | 37.58 N | 23.34 E |
| Perambalur | 122 | 11.14 N | 78.53 E |
| Perämeri (Bottenviken) c | 26 | 65.00 N | 23.00 E |
| Peranāmbattu | 122 | 12.56 N | 78.43 E |
| Peraní, Ákra › | 267c | 37.54 N | 23.31 E |
| Perarolo di Cadore | 64 | 46.24 N | 12.21 E |
| Peräseinäjoki | 26 | 62.34 N | 23.04 E |
| Percé | 186 | 48.31 N | 64.13 W |
| Percée, Pointe ∧ | 58 | 45.57 N | 6.33 E |
| Perch ≃ | 212 | 44.00 N | 76.05 W |
| Perchas | 240m | 18.19 N | 66.59 W |
| Perchau | 61 | 47.06 N | 14.27 E |
| Perchauer Sattel )( | 61 | 47.07 N | 14.27 E |
| Perche, Collines du ⋏[2] | 50 | 48.25 N | 0.40 E |
| Perche Creek ≃ | 194 | 38.49 N | 92.24 W |
| Perch Lake ⊜ | 212 | 44.07 N | 75.54 W |
| Perchtoldsdorf | 61 | 48.07 N | 16.17 E |
| Perchuškovo | 265b | 55.41 N | 37.10 E |
| Percival Lakes ⊜ | 162 | 21.25 S | 125.00 E |
| Percy Creek ≃ | 212 | 44.15 N | 77.49 W |
| Percy Isles II | 166 | 21.39 S | 150.16 E |
| Percy Lake ⊜ | 212 | 45.13 N | 78.22 W |
| Percy Reach ⊜ | 212 | 44.15 N | 77.45 W |
| Perdagangan-tomuon | 114 | 3.09 N | 99.20 E |
| Perdasdefogu | 71 | 39.41 N | 9.26 E |
| Perdeberg | 158 | 28.59 S | 25.05 E |
| Perdekop | 158 | 27.13 S | 29.38 E |
| Perdices, Arroyo de las ≃ | 288 | 34.41 S | 58.22 W |
| Perdida ≃ | 250 | 9.13 S | 47.59 W |
| Perdido | 194 | 31.00 N | 87.37 W |
| Perdido ≃, Bra. | 248 | 22.10 S | 57.33 W |
| Perdido ≃, U.S. | 194 | 30.29 N | 87.26 W |
| Perdido, Arroyo ≃ | 254 | 42.55 S | 67.00 W |
| Perdido, Arroyo del ≃ | 258 | 33.37 S | 57.23 W |
| Perdido, Cuchilla del ⋏[2] | 258 | 33.43 S | 57.17 W |
| Perdido, Monte ∧ | 34 | 42.40 N | 0.05 E |
| Perdido Bay c | 194 | 30.21 N | 87.27 W |
| Perdifumo | 68 | 40.16 N | 15.01 E |
| Perdix | 208 | 40.22 N | 76.57 W |
| Perdizes | 255 | 19.21 S | 47.17 W |
| Perdreauville | 261 | 48.58 N | 1.38 E |
| Perdu, Lac ⊜ | 186 | 50.44 N | 70.14 W |
| Perdue | 184 | 52.04 N | 107.32 W |
| Perebrody | 78 | 51.43 N | 27.00 E |
| Perechyn | 78 | 48.44 N | 22.26 E |
| Peredel | 76 | 55.12 N | 35.41 E |
| Peredel'cy | 82 | 55.36 N | 37.21 E |
| Peredelkino | 265b | 55.39 N | 37.21 E |
| Peredmistne | 78 | 45.57 N | 34.37 E |
| Peregino | 76 | 57.27 N | 31.21 E |
| Perehins'ke | 78 | 48.49 N | 24.12 E |
| Perehonivka | 78 | 48.32 N | 30.31 E |
| Pereira | 246 | 4.49 N | 75.43 W |
| Pereira Barreto | 255 | 20.38 S | 51.07 W |
| Pereiro | 250 | 6.03 S | 38.28 W |
| Perejaslavka | 89 | 47.58 N | 135.06 E |
| Perejaslavskaja | 78 | 45.51 N | 39.02 E |
| Perejež'na | 24 | 59.43 N | 48.12 E |
| Perekopivka | 78 | 50.37 N | 33.25 E |
| Perekopnoje | 80 | 51.13 N | 48.04 E |
| Perekopskaja | 80 | 49.21 N | 43.20 E |
| Père-Lachaise, Cimetière du ◆ | 261 | 48.51 N | 2.25 E |
| Perelazovskij | 80 | 49.09 N | 42.33 E |
| Perelazy | 76 | 53.02 N | 31.28 E |
| Perelesinskij | 78 | 51.44 N | 40.07 E |
| Perel'ub | 80 | 51.52 N | 50.22 E |
| Pere Marquette ≃ | 190 | 43.57 N | 86.27 W |
| Pere Marquette, Big South Branch ≃ | 190 | 43.56 N | 86.10 W |
| Pere Marquette State Park ♦ | 219 | 39.00 N | 90.30 W |
| Perem'otnoje | 80 | 51.11 N | 50.49 E |
| Peremyshlyany | 78 | 49.41 N | 24.33 E |
| Peremyšl' | 82 | 54.16 N | 36.10 E |
| Perené ≃ | 248 | 11.09 S | 74.18 W |
| Perenjori | 162 | 29.26 S | 116.17 E |
| Pereputje | 92a | 46.17 N | 141.54 E |
| Pererov | 78 | 52.04 N | 28.00 E |
| Pereščepnoje | 80 | 50.32 N | 45.06 E |
| Pereshchepyne | 78 | 49.01 N | 35.22 E |
| Pereslavl'-Zalesskij | 82 | 56.44 N | 38.51 E |
| Peresypkino Pervoje | 80 | 52.55 N | 42.55 E |
| Peretrusovo | 82 | 56.51 N | 36.53 E |
| Perevals'k | 83 | 48.26 N | 38.47 E |
| Perevoz, Ross. | 80 | 55.36 N | 44.32 E |
| Perevoz, Ross. | 88 | 59.00 N | 116.57 E |
| Perevoz, Ross. | 265a | 59.43 N | 30.47 E |
| Pereyaslav-Khmel'nyts'kyy | 78 | 50.06 N | 31.30 E |
| Pereyra, Arroyo ≃ | 288 | 34.47 S | 58.08 W |
| Pereyra, Punta › | 258 | 34.14 S | 58.04 W |
| Pérez | 252 | 33.00 S | 60.46 W |
| Perfugas | 71 | 40.50 N | 8.53 E |
| Perg | 61 | 48.15 N | 14.37 E |
| Pergamino | 252 | 33.53 S | 60.35 W |
| Pergamum ⊥ | 130 | 39.10 N | 27.13 E |
| Pergau ≃ | 114 | 5.23 N | 102.02 E |
| Pergine Valdarno | 66 | 43.28 N | 11.41 E |
| Pergine Valsugana | 64 | 46.04 N | 11.14 E |
| Pergola | 66 | 43.34 N | 12.50 E |
| Pergusa, Lago di ⊜ | 70 | 37.31 N | 14.18 E |
| Perham | 198 | 46.35 N | 95.34 W |
| Perho | 26 | 63.13 N | 24.25 E |
| Peri | 64 | 45.39 N | 10.54 E |
| Peri ≃ | 130 | 38.50 N | 39.35 E |
| Peribán de Ramos | 234 | 19.32 N | 102.28 W |
| Péribonca ≃ | 176 | 48.45 N | 72.05 W |
| Péribonca, Lac ⊜ | 186 | 50.04 N | 71.15 W |
| Perico, Arg. | 252 | 24.23 S | 65.06 W |
| Perico, Cuba | 240p | 22.46 N | 81.01 W |
| Pericos | 232 | 25.03 N | 107.42 W |
| Pericumã ≃ | 250 | 2.17 S | 44.42 W |
| Peridot | 200 | 33.18 N | 110.27 W |
| Périers | 32 | 49.11 N | 1.25 W |
| Perigiraja | 112 | 0.16 S | 103.30 E |
| Périgord □[9] | 32 | 45.20 N | 1.00 E |
| Perigoso, Canal ʉ | 250 | 0.05 N | 49.40 W |
| Périgueux | 32 | 45.11 N | 0.43 E |
| Perijá, Serranía De ⋏ | 246 | 10.00 N | 73.00 W |
| Perim → Barīm I | 144 | 12.39 N | 43.25 E |
| Peri-Mirim | 250 | 2.38 S | 44.54 W |
| Perinaldo | 62 | 43.52 N | 7.40 E |
| Peringat | 114 | 6.02 N | 102.17 E |
| Periprava | 38 | 45.24 N | 29.32 E |
| Perisher Valley ♦ | 171b | 36.23 S | 145.24 E |
| Peristérion | 267c | 38.01 N | 23.42 E |
| Perito | 68 | 40.18 N | 15.09 E |
| Perito Moreno | 254 | 46.36 S | 70.56 W |
| Peritoró | 250 | 4.20 S | 44.18 W |
| Perivale ◆[8] | 260 | 51.32 N | 0.19 W |
| Periyakulam | 122 | 10.07 N | 77.33 E |
| Periyār ≃ | 122 | 10.11 N | 76.13 E |
| Perkasie | 208 | 40.22 N | 75.17 W |
| Perkins | 196 | 35.58 N | 97.02 W |
| Perkinsfield | 212 | 44.42 N | 79.57 W |
| Perkins Observatory ʊ[3] | 214 | 40.14 N | 83.02 W |
| Perkinston | 194 | 30.46 N | 89.08 W |
| Perkinsville, In., U.S. | 218 | 40.09 N | 85.52 W |
| Perkinsville, N.Y., U.S. | 210 | 42.32 N | 77.38 W |
| Perkiomen Creek ≃ | 208 | 40.07 N | 75.28 W |
| Perkiomen Creek, East Branch ≃ | 208 | 40.15 N | 75.27 W |
| Perkiomen Junction | 285 | 40.06 N | 75.28 W |
| Perkiomen Valley Airport ⊠ | 285 | 40.12 N | 75.25 W |
| Perl | 56 | 49.28 N | 6.23 E |
| Perlas, Archipiélago de las II | 246 | 8.25 N | 79.00 W |
| Perlas, Laguna de c | 236 | 12.30 N | 83.40 W |
| Perlas, Punta de › | 236 | 12.23 N | 83.30 W |
| Perleberg | 54 | 53.04 N | 11.51 E |
| Perlesreut | 60 | 48.47 N | 13.27 E |
| Perlez | 38 | 45.12 N | 20.24 E |
| Perlis □[3] | 114 | 6.30 N | 100.15 E |
| Perl'ovka | 78 | 51.51 N | 38.51 E |
| Perm' | 86 | 58.00 N | 56.15 E |
| Permanente Creek ≃ | 282 | 37.25 N | 122.05 W |
| Permas | 24 | 59.20 N | 45.34 E |
| Përmet | 38 | 40.14 N | 20.21 E |
| Permisi | 80 | 54.06 N | 45.48 E |
| Perm' Oblast' □[4] | 86 | 58.00 N | 58.00 E |
| Pernambuco → Recife | 250 | 8.03 S | 34.54 W |
| Pernambuco □[3] | 250 | 8.00 S | 37.00 W |
| Pernate | 266b | 45.27 N | 8.41 E |
| Pernatty Lagoon ⊜ | 166 | 31.31 S | 137.14 E |
| Pernay | 50 | 47.27 N | 0.30 E |
| Pernegg an der Mur | 61 | 47.22 N | 15.21 E |
| Pernes-les-Fontaines | 62 | 44.00 N | 5.03 E |
| Pernik | 38 | 42.36 N | 23.02 E |
| Pernink | 54 | 50.20 N | 12.45 E |
| Perniö | 26 | 60.12 N | 23.08 E |
| Pernitz | 61 | 47.54 N | 15.58 E |
| Pernovo | 82 | 55.58 N | 39.10 E |
| Pero | 266b | 45.31 N | 9.05 E |
| Peroba, Ribeirão do ≃ | 287b | 23.27 S | 46.22 W |
| Pérols, Étang de c | 62 | 43.33 N | 3.56 E |
| Peron, Cape › | 168a | 32.17 S | 115.41 E |
| Péronne | 50 | 49.56 N | 2.56 E |
| Peron Peninsula ›[1] | 162 | 25.55 S | 113.30 E |
| Pero Pinheiro | 266c | 38.51 N | 9.20 W |
| Perosa Argentina | 62 | 44.58 N | 7.10 E |
| Perote | 234 | 19.34 N | 97.14 W |
| Peroto | 248 | 14.50 S | 64.31 W |
| Pérou → Peru □[1] | 242 | 10.00 S | 76.00 W |
| Pérouges | 58 | 45.54 N | 5.11 E |
| Peroulaz | 62 | 45.42 N | 7.19 E |
| Perovo ◆[8] | 265b | 55.44 N | 37.46 E |
| Perow | 182 | 54.31 N | 126.26 W |
| Perpendicular, Point › | 170 | 35.06 S | 150.48 E |
| Perpignan | 32 | 42.41 N | 2.53 E |
| Perranporth | 42 | 50.20 N | 5.09 W |
| Perrault Falls | 184 | 50.19 N | 93.11 W |
| Perray ≃ | 261 | 48.31 N | 1.42 E |
| Perrero | 62 | 44.56 N | 7.05 E |
| Perriers-sur-Andelle | 50 | 49.25 N | 1.22 E |
| Perrignier | 58 | 46.18 N | 6.27 E |
| Perrigny | 58 | 46.40 N | 5.35 E |
| Perrin | 196 | 33.02 N | 98.04 W |
| Perrine | 220 | 25.36 N | 80.21 W |
| Perrineville | 208 | 40.13 N | 74.26 W |
| Perris | 228 | 33.46 N | 117.13 W |
| Perris, Lake ⊜[1] | 228 | 33.50 N | 117.10 W |
| Perro, Laguna del ⊜ | 200 | 34.40 N | 105.57 W |
| Perro, Punta del › | 34 | 36.45 N | 6.25 W |
| Perros, Bahía de c | 240p | 22.25 N | 78.30 W |
| Perros-Guirec | 32 | 48.49 N | 3.27 W |
| Perrot, Île I | 206 | 45.22 N | 73.57 W |
| Perry, Fl., U.S. | 192 | 30.07 N | 83.34 W |
| Perry, Ga., U.S. | 192 | 32.27 N | 83.43 W |
| Perry, Il., U.S. | 219 | 39.47 N | 90.45 W |
| Perry, Ia., U.S. | 190 | 41.50 N | 94.06 W |
| Perry, Ks., U.S. | 198 | 39.04 N | 95.23 W |
| Perry, Me., U.S. | 186 | 44.58 N | 67.04 W |
| Perry, Mi., U.S. | 216 | 42.49 N | 84.13 W |
| Perry, Mo., U.S. | 219 | 39.25 N | 91.40 W |
| Perry, N.Y., U.S. | 210 | 42.42 N | 78.00 W |
| Perry, Oh., U.S. | 214 | 41.45 N | 81.08 W |
| Perry, Ok., U.S. | 196 | 36.17 N | 97.17 W |
| Perry, Tx., U.S. | 222 | 31.25 N | 96.55 W |
| Perry, Ut,. U.S. | 200 | 41.27 N | 112.02 W |
| Perry □[6] | 208 | 40.25 N | 77.11 W |
| Perrydale | 224 | 45.02 N | 123.15 W |
| Perry Hall | 208 | 39.24 N | 76.27 W |
| Perry Heights | 214 | 40.47 N | 81.28 W |
| Perry-Jōriku-kinenhi ⊥ | 94 | 35.14 N | 139.43 E |
| Perry Lake ⊜[1] | 198 | 39.20 N | 95.30 W |
| Perryman | 208 | 39.28 N | 76.12 W |
| Perrymont | 279b | 40.33 N | 80.02 W |
| Perryopolis | 214 | 40.05 N | 79.45 W |
| Perry Park | 218 | 38.33 N | 85.00 W |
| Perry Point | 208 | 39.33 N | 76.04 W |
| Perrysburg, N.Y., U.S. | 210 | 42.27 N | 79.00 W |
| Perrysburg, Oh., U.S. | 214 | 41.33 N | 83.37 W |
| Perry's Landing Monument ⊥ | 268 | 35.13 N | 139.43 E |
| Perry's Victory and International Peace Memorial ⊥ | 214 | 41.33 N | 82.50 W |
| Perrysville | 214 | 40.39 N | 82.18 W |
| Perryton | 196 | 36.24 N | 100.48 W |
| Perryville, Ak., U.S. | 180 | 55.54 N | 159.10 W |
| Perryville, Ar., U.S. | 194 | 35.00 N | 92.48 W |
| Perryville, Ky., U.S. | 192 | 37.39 N | 84.57 W |
| Perryville, Md., U.S. | 208 | 39.33 N | 76.04 W |
| Perryville, Mo., U.S. | 194 | 37.43 N | 89.51 W |
| Perryville, N.Y., U.S. | 210 | 43.01 N | 75.48 W |
| Peršamajski | 76 | 53.54 N | 25.23 E |
| Persan | 50 | 49.09 N | 2.16 E |
| Perșani, Munții ⋏ | 38 | 45.40 N | 25.15 E |
| Persberg | 40 | 59.45 N | 14.15 E |
| Perschling ≃ | 61 | 48.20 N | 15.58 E |
| Perşembe | 130 | 41.04 N | 37.46 E |
| Persepolis → Takht-e Jamshīd ⊥ | 128 | 29.57 N | 52.52 E |
| Perseverance, Mount ∧ | 171a | 27.25 S | 152.10 E |
| Perseverancia | 248 | 14.44 S | 62.48 W |
| Pershagen | 40 | 59.10 N | 17.39 E |
| Pershing | 218 | 39.49 N | 84.53 W |
| Pershore | 42 | 52.07 N | 2.05 W |
| Pershotravens'k, Ukr. | 78 | 50.12 N | 27.39 E |
| Pershotravens'k, Ukr. | 78 | 48.22 N | 36.24 E |
| Pershotravneve, Ukr. | 78 | 51.24 N | 28.53 E |
| Pershotravneve, Ukr. | 83 | 47.03 N | 37.18 E |
| Pershyttan | 40 | 59.30 N | 15.00 E |
| Persia | 198 | 41.34 N | 95.34 W |
| Persia → Iran □[1] | 128 | 32.00 N | 53.00 E |
| Persian Gulf (Arabian Gulf) c | 128 | 27.00 N | 51.00 E |
| Pérsico, Golfo → Persian Gulf c | 128 | 27.00 N | 51.00 E |
| Persimmon Creek ≃ | 194 | 31.31 N | 86.50 W |
| Persique, Golfe → Persian Gulf c | 128 | 27.00 N | 51.00 E |
| Persischer Golf → Persian Gulf c | 128 | 27.00 N | 51.00 E |
| Perštejn | 54 | 50.23 N | 13.08 E |
| Perstorp | 41 | 56.08 N | 13.23 E |
| Pertandangan, Tanjung › | 114 | 2.41 N | 100.14 E |
| Pertek | 130 | 38.50 N | 39.22 E |
| Perth, Austl. | 168a | 31.56 S | 115.50 E |
| Perth, On., Can. | 212 | 44.54 N | 76.15 W |
| Perth, Scot., U.K. | 46 | 56.24 N | 3.28 W |
| Perth, N.Y., U.S. | 210 | 43.03 N | 74.12 W |
| Perth □[6] | 212 | 43.30 N | 81.05 W |
| Perth Amboy | 210 | 40.30 N | 74.15 W |
| Perth-Andover | 186 | 46.45 N | 67.42 W |
| Perth Basin ✦[1] | 14 | 28.30 S | 110.00 E |
| Perthes | 58 | 48.39 N | 4.49 E |
| Perth International Airport ⊠ | 168a | 31.57 S | 115.58 E |
| Perthois ◆[1] | 58 | 48.40 N | 4.45 E |
| Pertokar | 144 | 16.59 N | 37.28 E |
| Pertominsk | 24 | 64.47 N | 38.25 E |
| Pertovo | 80 | 54.22 N | 41.31 E |
| Pertuis | 62 | 43.41 N | 5.30 E |
| Pertusato, Capo › | 71 | 41.21 N | 9.10 E |
| Peru, Il., U.S. | 216 | 41.19 N | 89.07 W |
| Peru, In., U.S. | 216 | 40.45 N | 86.04 W |
| Peru, Ne., U.S. | 198 | 40.28 N | 95.44 W |
| Peru, N.Y., U.S. | 188 | 44.34 N | 73.31 W |
| Peru (Perú) □[1], S.A. | 242 | 10.00 S | 76.00 W |
| Peru (Perú) □[1], S.A. | 248 | 10.00 S | 76.00 W |
| Peruaçu ≃ | 255 | 15.11 S | 44.07 W |
| Peru Basin ✦[1] | 18 | 15.00 S | 85.00 W |
| Peruc | 54 | 50.19 N | 13.59 E |
| Perućac, Jezero ⊜[1] | 38 | 43.55 N | 19.10 E |
| Peru-Chile Trench ✦[1] | 18 | 20.00 S | 73.00 W |
| Perugia | 66 | 43.08 N | 12.22 E |
| Perugia □[4] | 66 | 43.03 N | 12.33 E |
| Perugorría | 252 | 29.20 S | 58.37 W |
| Peruíbe | 252 | 24.19 S | 47.00 W |
| Peruípe ≃ | 255 | 17.43 S | 39.16 W |
| Perumalpār I[1] | 122 | 11.10 N | 72.04 E |
| Peruque Creek ≃ | 219 | 38.53 N | 90.39 W |
| Perus ◆[8] | 256 | 23.25 S | 46.45 W |
| Perušić | 36 | 44.39 N | 15.23 E |
| Péruwelz | 50 | 50.31 N | 3.35 E |
| Pervaja Maja | 86 | 48.55 N | 67.25 E |
| Pervari | 128 | 37.54 N | 42.36 E |
| Pervenchères | 50 | 48.26 N | 0.26 E |
| Pervesinka | 80 | 52.13 N | 43.15 E |
| Pervijze | 50 | 51.05 N | 2.47 E |
| Pervoavgustovskij | 76 | 52.14 N | 35.03 E |
| Pervoje Pole | 180 | 63.05 N | 179.19 E |
| Pervomajevka | 85 | 42.05 N | 69.53 E |
| Pervomajka | 86 | 51.17 N | 70.08 E |
| Pervomajsk, Ross. | 80 | 54.53 N | 43.49 E |
| Pervomajsk, Ross. | 88 | 58.02 N | 94.05 E |
| Pervomajskij, Kyrg. | 85 | 42.51 N | 74.04 E |
| Pervomajskij, Ross. | 76 | 54.04 N | 32.29 E |
| Pervomajskij, Ross. | 80 | 53.22 N | 51.38 E |
| Pervomajskij, Ross. | 80 | 51.22 N | 48.54 E |
| Pervomajskij, Ross. | 80 | 53.15 N | 40.18 E |
| Pervomajskij, Ross. | 82 | 55.57 N | 37.52 E |
| Pervomajskij, Ross. | 82 | 54.03 N | 37.32 E |
| Pervomajskij, Ross. | 82 | 55.32 N | 37.09 E |
| Pervomajskij, Ross. | 86 | 53.41 N | 55.57 E |
| Pervomajskij, Ross. | 86 | 51.32 N | 55.06 E |
| Pervomajskij, Ross. | 86 | 59.29 N | 61.24 E |
| Pervomajskij, Ross. | 86 | 54.52 N | 61.08 E |
| Pervomajskij, Ross. | 88 | 51.44 N | 115.39 E |
| Pervomajskoje, Ross. | 76 | 52.56 N | 33.36 E |
| Pervomajskoje, Ross. | 80 | 55.05 N | 47.22 E |
| Pervomajskoje, Ross. | 80 | 46.03 N | 42.13 E |
| Pervomajskoje, Ross. | 80 | 46.21 N | 43.37 E |
| Pervomajskoje, Ross. | 80 | 48.50 N | 41.14 E |
| Pervomajskoje, Ross. | 80 | 51.28 N | 47.37 E |
| Pervomajskoje, Ross. | 80 | 50.56 N | 46.46 E |
| Pervomajskoje, Ross. | 86 | 53.45 N | 84.08 E |
| Pervomajskoje, Ross. | 86 | 57.06 N | 86.12 E |
| Pervomays'k, Ukr. | 78 | 48.04 N | 30.52 E |
| Pervomays'k, Ukr. | 83 | 48.37 N | 38.35 E |
| Pervomays'ke | 78 | 45.43 N | 33.51 E |
| Pervomays'kyy, Ukr. | 78 | 49.24 N | 36.12 E |
| Pervomays'kyy, Ukr. | 83 | 47.58 N | 38.47 E |
| Pervoural'sk | 86 | 56.54 N | 59.58 E |
| Pervušino | 80 | 58.02 N | 41.56 E |
| Pervyj Kuril'skij proliv ʉ | 74 | 50.50 N | 156.36 E |
| Perwenitz | 264a | 52.40 N | 13.01 E |
| Pes' | 76 | 58.55 N | 34.19 E |
| Pes' ≃ | 76 | 59.08 N | 35.18 E |
| Pesa ≃ | 66 | 43.44 N | 11.01 E |
| Pes'akov, ostrov I | 24 | 68.47 N | 57.35 E |
| Pesangrohan ≃ | 269e | 6.11 S | 106.45 E |
| Pesaro | 66 | 43.54 N | 12.55 E |
| Pesaro e Urbino □[4] | 66 | 43.40 N | 12.38 E |
| Pesca | 246 | 5.33 N | 73.03 W |
| Pescadero | 226 | 37.15 N | 122.22 W |
| Pescadero Creek ≃, Ca., U.S. | 226 | 37.16 N | 122.25 W |
| Pescadero Creek ≃, Ca., U.S. | 226 | 36.42 N | 121.17 W |
| Pescadores → P'enghu Ch'üntao II | 100 | 23.30 N | 119.30 E |
| Pescadores, Punta ›, Méx. | 232 | 23.46 N | 109.43 W |
| Pescadores, Punta ›, Perú | 248 | 16.21 S | 73.15 W |
| Pescaglia | 66 | 43.58 N | 10.25 E |
| Pesčanka | 80 | 51.18 N | 43.40 E |
| Pesčanoje, Kaz. | 86 | 53.01 N | 76.19 E |
| Pesčanoje, Ross. | 24 | 62.09 N | 35.48 E |
| Pesčanokopskoje | 80 | 46.12 N | 41.04 E |
| Pescantina | 64 | 45.29 N | 10.51 E |
| Pesčanyje, ostrova II | 83 | 46.52 N | 38.17 E |
| Pescara | 66 | 42.28 N | 14.13 E |
| Pescara □[4] | 66 | 42.20 N | 13.57 E |
| Pescara ≃ | 66 | 42.28 N | 14.13 E |
| Pescasseroli | 66 | 41.48 N | 13.47 E |
| Pesch | 263 | 51.11 N | 6.32 E |
| Pesch, Schloss ⊥ | 263 | 51.18 N | 6.39 E |
| Peschici | 68 | 41.57 N | 16.01 E |
| Peschiera del Garda | 64 | 45.26 N | 10.42 E |
| Peschio, Monte ∧ | 267a | 41.43 N | 12.46 E |
| Pescia | 66 | 43.54 N | 10.41 E |
| Pescina | 66 | 42.02 N | 13.39 E |
| Pescocostanzo | 66 | 41.53 N | 14.04 E |
| Pescolanciano | 66 | 41.41 N | 14.20 E |
| Pescopagano | 68 | 40.50 N | 15.24 E |
| Pescorocchiano | 66 | 42.12 N | 13.09 E |
| Pesco Sannita | 68 | 41.14 N | 14.49 E |
| Pesé | 236 | 7.54 N | 80.37 W |
| Pesek, Pulau I | 271c | 1.17 N | 103.41 E |
| Peseux | 58 | 46.59 N | 6.53 E |
| Peshastin | 224 | 47.34 N | 120.36 W |
| Peshastin Creek ≃ | 224 | 47.33 N | 120.35 W |
| Peshāwar | 123 | 34.01 N | 71.33 E |
| Peshīn Jān | 128 | 33.25 N | 61.28 E |
| Peshkopi | 38 | 41.41 N | 20.26 E |
| Peshtigo | 190 | 45.03 N | 87.44 W |
| Peshtigo ≃ | 190 | 44.58 N | 87.40 W |
| Pesio ≃ | 62 | 44.28 N | 7.53 E |
| Pesjane | 82 | 56.01 N | 38.48 E |
| Peski, Bela. | 76 | 53.21 N | 24.38 E |
| Peski, Ross. | 80 | 51.16 N | 42.27 E |
| Peski, Ross. | 82 | 55.13 N | 38.46 E |
| Peški, Ross. | 82 | 56.08 N | 37.04 E |
| Peskovatskoje | 82 | 54.03 N | 36.16 E |
| Peškovka, Kaz. | 86 | 53.45 N | 62.23 E |
| Peskovka, Ross. | 86 | 59.04 N | 52.22 E |
| Peškovo | 83 | 47.02 N | 39.24 E |
| Peškovo Grecovo | 82 | 54.26 N | 37.36 E |
| Pesmes | 58 | 47.17 N | 5.34 E |
| Pesnica | 61 | 46.36 N | 15.41 E |
| Pesnica ≃ | 61 | 46.24 N | 16.05 E |
| Pešnoj, poluostrov ›[2] | 80 | 46.52 N | 51.42 E |
| Pesočenskij | 82 | 54.10 N | 36.06 E |
| Pesočn'a | 80 | 54.07 N | 40.50 E |
| Pesočnoje | 80 | 58.01 N | 39.10 E |
| Pesočnyj | 76 | 60.07 N | 30.08 E |
| Peso da Régua | 34 | 41.10 N | 7.47 W |
| Pespire | 236 | 13.35 N | 87.22 W |
| Pesqueira | 250 | 8.22 S | 36.42 W |
| Pesquería | 196 | 25.47 N | 100.03 W |
| Pesquería ≃ | 196 | 25.54 N | 99.11 W |
| Pessac | 32 | 44.48 N | 0.38 W |
| Pessin | 54 | 52.38 N | 12.40 E |
| Pessinetto | 62 | 45.17 N | 7.24 E |
| Pest □[6] | 30 | 47.25 N | 19.20 E |
| Pest ◆[8] | 264c | 47.30 N | 19.04 E |
| Pest'aki | 80 | 56.43 N | 42.40 E |
| Peštera | 38 | 42.02 N | 24.18 E |
| Pesterzsébet ◆[8] | 264c | 47.26 N | 19.07 E |
| Pesthidegkút ◆[8] | 264c | 47.34 N | 18.58 E |
| Pestimre ◆[8] | 264c | 47.24 N | 19.12 E |
| Pestlőrinc ◆[8] | 264c | 47.26 N | 19.12 E |
| Pestovo, Ross. | 76 | 58.36 N | 35.48 E |
| Pestovo, Ross. | 80 | 57.12 N | 46.44 E |
| Pestovskoje vodochranilišče ⊜[1] | 82 | 56.06 N | 37.40 E |
| Pestravka | 80 | 52.24 N | 49.58 E |
| Pestrecy | 80 | 55.46 N | 49.39 E |
| Pestrikovo | 82 | 55.05 N | 38.53 E |
| Pestújhely ◆[8] | 264c | 47.32 N | 19.07 E |
| Petacalco, Bahía c | 234 | 17.57 N | 102.05 W |
| Petaḥ Tiqwa | 132 | 32.05 N | 34.53 E |
| Petäjävesi | 26 | 62.15 N | 25.12 E |
| Petal | 194 | 31.20 N | 89.15 W |
| Petalcingo | 232 | 17.17 N | 92.27 W |
| Petaling Jaya | 114 | 3.05 N | 101.39 E |
| Petalión, Kólpos c | 38 | 37.59 N | 24.02 E |
| Petaluma | 226 | 38.13 N | 122.38 W |
| Petaluma ≃ | 226 | 38.06 N | 122.30 W |
| Pétange | 56 | 49.34 N | 5.52 E |
| Petare | 246 | 10.29 N | 66.49 W |
| Petatlán | 234 | 17.31 N | 101.16 W |
| Petauke | 154 | 14.15 S | 31.20 E |
| Petawawa | 190 | 45.54 N | 77.17 W |
| Petawawa ≃ | 190 | 45.55 N | 77.15 W |
| Pété | 146 | 10.58 N | 14.30 E |
| Petegem | 50 | 50.58 N | 3.32 E |
| Petén □[5] | 236 | 16.15 N | 89.50 W |
| Petén Itzá, Lago ⊜ | 232 | 16.59 N | 89.50 W |
| Petenwell Lake ⊜[1] | 190 | 44.10 N | 89.57 W |
| Peter and Paul Fortress ⊥ | 265a | 59.57 N | 30.19 E |
| Peterboro | 210 | 42.58 N | 75.41 W |
| Peterborough, Austl. | 166 | 32.58 S | 138.50 E |
| Peterborough, On., Can. | 212 | 44.18 N | 78.19 W |
| Peterborough, Eng., U.K. | 42 | 52.35 N | 0.15 W |
| Peterborough, N.H., U.S. | 188 | 42.52 N | 71.57 W |
| Peterborough □[6] | 212 | 44.33 N | 78.15 W |
| Peterculter | 46 | 57.05 N | 2.16 W |
| Peterhead | 46 | 57.30 N | 1.49 W |
| Peter Hill ∧ | 46 | 56.58 N | 2.42 W |
| Peter I Island I | 9 | 68.47 S | 90.35 W |
| Peter Island I | 240m | 18.22 N | 64.35 W |
| Peter Lake ⊜, N.T., Can. | 176 | 63.08 N | 92.48 W |
| Peter Lake ⊜, Sk., Can. | 184 | 57.15 N | 103.53 W |
| Peterlee | 44 | 54.46 N | 1.19 W |
| Peter Lougheed Provincial Park ♦ | 182 | 50.45 N | 115.15 W |
| Peterman | 194 | 31.35 N | 87.15 W |
| Petermann Ranges ⋏ | 162 | 25.00 S | 129.46 E |
| Petermann Reserve ◆[4] | 162 | 25.00 S | 130.15 E |
| Peter Pond Lake ⊜ | 184 | 55.55 N | 108.44 W |
| Peter Pond Lake Indian Reserve ◆[4] | 184 | 55.55 N | 109.00 W |
| Petersberg | 56 | 50.33 N | 9.43 E |
| Peters Brook ≃ | 276 | 40.33 N | 74.37 W |
| Petersburg, Ak., U.S. | 180 | 56.49 N | 132.57 W |
| Petersburg, Il., U.S. | 219 | 40.00 N | 89.50 W |
| Petersburg, In., U.S. | 194 | 38.29 N | 87.16 W |
| Petersburg, Mi., U.S. | 216 | 41.54 N | 83.42 W |
| Petersburg, Ne., U.S. | 198 | 41.51 N | 98.04 W |
| Petersburg, N.J., U.S. | 208 | 39.15 N | 74.43 W |
| Petersburg, N.Y., U.S. | 210 | 42.44 N | 73.20 W |
| Petersburg, Oh., U.S. | 214 | 40.54 N | 80.31 W |
| Petersburg, Pa., U.S. | 214 | 40.34 N | 78.03 W |
| Petersburg, Tn., U.S. | 194 | 35.19 N | 86.38 W |
| Petersburg, Tx., U.S. | 196 | 33.52 N | 101.36 W |
| Petersburg, Va., U.S. | 208 | 37.13 N | 77.24 W |
| Petersburg, W.V., U.S. | 188 | 38.59 N | 79.07 W |
| Petersburg National Battlefield ♦ | 208 | 37.14 N | 77.22 W |
| Peters Canyon Reservoir ⊜[1] | 280 | 33.47 N | 117.45 W |
| Peters Creek ≃, Ca., U.S. | 282 | 37.15 N | 122.13 W |
| Peters Creek ≃, Pa., U.S. | 279b | 40.18 N | 79.52 W |
| Peters Creek, Piney Fork ≃ | 279b | 40.16 N | 79.58 W |
| Petersdorf | 54 | 54.29 N | 11.04 E |
| Petersfield, S. Afr. | 273d | 26.14 S | 28.26 E |
| Petersfield, Eng., U.K. | 42 | 51.00 N | 0.56 W |
| Petershagen, Dtsch. | 52 | 52.23 N | 8.58 E |
| Petershagen, Dtsch. | 54 | 52.24 N | 14.20 E |
| Petershagen, Dtsch. | 54 | 52.31 N | 13.46 E |
| Petersham, Austl. | 274a | 33.54 S | 151.09 E |
| Petersham, Ma., U.S. | 207 | 42.29 N | 72.11 W |
| Petershausen | 60 | 48.25 N | 11.28 E |
| Peters Hill ∧[2] | 168b | 34.11 S | 138.50 E |
| Peterson | 198 | 42.55 N | 95.20 W |
| Peterson Air Force Base ■ | 198 | 38.49 N | 104.42 W |
| Peters Pond ⊜ | 283 | 42.43 N | 71.16 W |
| Peterswald Hill ∧[2] | 162 | 26.43 S | 123.39 E |
| Peter the Great Bay → Petra Velikogo, zaliv c | 89 | 42.40 N | 132.00 E |
| Peter the Great Monument ⊥ | 265a | 59.56 N | 30.18 E |
| Pétervására | 30 | 48.01 N | 20.06 E |
| Petilia Policastro | 68 | 39.07 N | 16.47 E |
| Pétionville | 238 | 18.31 N | 72.17 W |
| Petit | 273d | 26.06 S | 28.22 E |
| Petit Bois Island I | 194 | 30.12 N | 88.26 W |
| Petit-Bourg | 241o | 16.12 N | 61.36 W |
| Petit-Canal | 241o | 16.23 N | 61.29 W |
| Petitcodiac | 186 | 45.56 N | 65.10 W |
| Petitcodiac ≃ | 186 | 45.50 N | 64.33 W |
| Petit Cul-de-Sac Marin c | 241o | 16.12 N | 61.33 W |
| Petite Nation, Rivière de la ≃ | 206 | 45.35 N | 75.06 W |
| Petite Rivière du Chêne ≃ | 206 | 46.34 N | 72.02 W |
| Petite Rivière Noire, Piton de la ∧ | 157c | 20.24 S | 57.24 E |
| Petite Rivière Rouge ≃ | 206 | 45.45 N | 75.00 W |
| Petites-Anses | 241o | 15.51 N | 61.39 W |
| Petite Sauldre ≃ | 50 | 47.26 N | 2.05 E |
| Petite Terre, Îles de la II | 241o | 16.10 N | 61.07 W |
| Petit Forte | 186 | 47.24 N | 54.40 W |
| Petit-Fort-Philippe | 50 | 51.00 N | 2.07 E |
| Petit-Goâve | 238 | 18.26 N | 72.52 W |
| Petit Jean ≃ | 194 | 35.10 N | 92.56 W |
| Petit Jean State Park ♦ | 194 | 35.06 N | 92.57 W |
| Petit Loango | 152 | 2.16 S | 9.35 E |
| Petit Loango, Parc National du ♦ | 152 | 2.15 S | 9.36 E |
| Petit Mécatina, Île du I | 186 | 50.33 N | 59.20 W |
| Petit Morin ≃ | 50 | 48.56 N | 3.07 E |
| Petitot ≃ | 176 | 60.14 N | 123.29 W |
| Petit Piton ∧ | 241f | 13.50 N | 61.04 W |
| Petit Rhône ≃ | 62 | 43.27 N | 4.24 E |
| Petit-Saint-Bernard, Col du )( | 62 | 45.41 N | 6.53 E |
| Petitsikapau Lake ⊜ | 176 | 54.45 N | 66.25 W |
| Petkeljärven kansallispuisto ♦ | 24 | 62.35 N | 31.12 E |
| Petkus | 54 | 51.59 N | 13.21 E |
| Petlād | 120 | 22.28 N | 72.48 E |
| Petlalcingo | 234 | 18.05 N | 97.54 W |
| Peto | 232 | 20.08 N | 88.55 W |
| Petoh | 114 | 2.53 N | 103.15 E |
| Petone | 172 | 41.13 S | 174.52 E |
| Petorca | 252 | 32.15 S | 70.56 W |
| Petoskey | 190 | 45.22 N | 84.57 W |
| Petownikip Lake ⊜ | 184 | 52.56 N | 92.02 W |
| Petra → Batrā ⊥ | 132 | 30.20 N | 35.26 E |
| Petralia Soprana | 70 | 37.47 N | 14.06 E |
| Petralia Sottana | 70 | 37.48 N | 14.05 E |
| Petras, Mount ∧ | 9 | 75.52 S | 128.38 W |
| Petra Velikogo, zaliv (Peter the Great Bay) c | 89 | 42.40 N | 132.00 E |
| Petre, Point › | 212 | 43.50 N | 77.09 W |
| Petrecovo | 24 | 61.18 N | 57.07 E |
| Petrella, Monte ∧ | 66 | 41.18 N | 13.40 E |
| Petrella Salto | 66 | 42.18 N | 13.04 E |
| Petrella Tifernina | 66 | 41.41 N | 14.42 E |
| Petrič | 38 | 41.24 N | 23.13 E |
| Petrie | 171a | 27.16 S | 152.59 E |
| Petrified Forest National Park ♦ | 200 | 34.55 N | 109.49 W |
| Petrila | 38 | 45.27 N | 23.25 E |
| Petrinja | 36 | 45.26 N | 16.17 E |
| Petriščevo, Ross. | 82 | 54.37 N | 36.57 E |
| Petriščevo, Ross. | 82 | 55.30 N | 36.18 E |
| Petrítis, Ákra › | 267c | 37.56 N | 23.24 E |
| Petrivka, Ukr. | 78 | 46.54 N | 30.44 E |
| Petrivka, Ukr. | 83 | 48.53 N | 39.52 E |
| Petrivka, Ukr. | 83 | 48.48 N | 39.16 E |
| Petrivs'ke | 78 | 49.10 N | 36.54 E |
| Petrodvorec | 76 | 59.53 N | 29.54 E |
| Petroglyphs Provincial Park ♦ | 212 | 44.33 N | 77.53 W |
| Petrograd → Sankt-Peterburg | 76 | 59.55 N | 30.15 E |
| Petrohué | 254 | 41.08 S | 72.25 W |
| Petrolândia | 250 | 9.05 S | 38.18 W |
| Petrólea | 246 | 8.30 N | 72.35 W |
| Petroleum | 216 | 40.36 N | 85.09 W |
| Petrolia, On., Can. | 214 | 42.52 N | 82.09 W |
| Petrolia, Pa., U.S. | 214 | 41.01 N | 79.43 W |
| Petrolia, Tx., U.S. | 196 | 34.01 N | 98.14 W |
| Petrolina | 250 | 9.24 S | 40.30 W |
| Petrolina de Goiás | 255 | 16.06 S | 49.20 W |
| Petronà | 68 | 39.03 N | 16.45 E |
| Petrona, Punta › | 240m | 17.56 N | 66.23 W |
| Petronila Creek ≃ | 196 | 27.32 N | 97.32 W |
| Petropavlivka, Ukr. | 78 | 48.27 N | 36.26 E |
| Petropavlivka, Ukr. | 83 | 49.43 N | 37.42 E |
| Petropavlovka, Ross. | 78 | 50.06 N | 40.54 E |
| Petropavlovka, Ross. | 88 | 50.38 N | 105.19 E |
| Petropavlovsk, Kaz. | 86 | 54.54 N | 69.06 E |
| Petropavlovsk, Ross. | 86 | 56.20 N | 57.09 E |
| Petropavlovsk-Kamčatskij | 74 | 53.01 N | 158.39 E |
| Petropavlovskoje, Ross. | 86 | 52.04 N | 84.08 E |
| Petropavlovskoje, Ross. | 88 | 58.13 N | 108.59 E |
| Petrópolis | 256 | 22.31 S | 43.10 W |
| Petros | 192 | 36.05 N | 84.26 W |
| Petroșani | 38 | 45.25 N | 23.22 E |
| Petrosino | 70 | 37.43 N | 12.29 E |
| Petro-Slav'anka | 265a | 59.48 N | 30.31 E |
| Petroso, Monte ∧ | 66 | 41.44 N | 13.55 E |
| Petroúpolis | 267c | 38.03 N | 23.41 E |
| Petrovac | 38 | 44.22 N | 21.27 E |
| Petrove | 78 | 48.20 N | 33.16 E |
| Petrovgrad → Zrenjanin | 38 | 45.23 N | 20.24 E |
| Petrovka | 80 | 53.13 N | 51.58 E |
| Petrovo, Ross. | 76 | 58.22 N | 35.09 E |
| Petrovo, Ross. | 82 | 55.00 N | 38.08 E |
| Petrovo, Ross. | 88 | 54.30 N | 105.15 E |
| Petrovo-Dal'neje | 265b | 55.45 N | 37.11 E |
| Petrovsk | 80 | 52.19 N | 45.23 E |
| Petrovskaja | 78 | 45.25 N | 37.57 E |
| Petrovs'ke | 83 | 48.18 N | 38.52 E |
| Petrovskij, Ross. | 80 | 56.39 N | 40.19 E |
| Petrovskij, Ross. | 80 | 50.45 N | 41.59 E |
| Petrovskij, Ross. | 82 | 54.29 N | 36.59 E |
| Petrovskoje, Ross. | 80 | 52.39 N | 40.15 E |
| Petrovskoje, Ross. | 80 | 57.01 N | 39.16 E |
| Petrovskoje, Ross. | 82 | 55.27 N | 38.21 E |
| Petrovskoje, Ross. | 82 | 55.32 N | 36.59 E |
| Petrovskoje, Ross. | 265b | 55.36 N | 37.53 E |
| Petrovsko-Razumovskoje ◆[8] | 265b | 55.50 N | 37.34 E |
| Petrovsk-Zabajkal'skij | 88 | 51.17 N | 108.50 E |
| Petrov Val | 80 | 50.09 N | 45.12 E |
| Petrozavodsk | 24 | 61.47 N | 34.20 E |
| Petrozsény → Petroșani | 38 | 45.25 N | 23.22 E |
| Petrun' | 24 | 66.28 N | 60.43 E |
| Petrusburg | 158 | 29.08 S | 25.27 E |
| Petrušino | 265a | 59.48 N | 30.50 E |
| Petrus Steyn | 158 | 27.38 S | 28.08 E |
| Petrusville | 158 | 30.05 S | 24.41 E |
| Petrykaŭ | 76 | 52.08 N | 28.30 E |
| Petrykivka | 78 | 48.43 N | 34.37 E |
| Petschora → Pečora ≃ | 24 | 68.13 N | 54.15 E |
| Petten | 52 | 52.45 N | 4.39 E |
| Pettenbach | 61 | 47.57 N | 14.01 E |
| Petteril ≃ | 44 | 54.54 N | 2.55 W |
| Petticoat Creek ≃ | 275b | 43.48 N | 79.06 W |
| Pettigoe | 48 | 54.33 N | 7.50 W |
| Pettinascura, Monte ∧ | 68 | 39.22 N | 16.37 E |
| Pettineo | 70 | 37.58 N | 14.17 E |
| Pettisville | 216 | 41.31 N | 84.13 W |
| Pettnau | 64 | 47.18 N | 11.08 E |
| Pettneu am Arlberg | 58 | 47.09 N | 10.20 E |
| Pettus | 196 | 28.37 N | 97.48 W |
| Petty Harbour | 186 | 47.28 N | 52.43 W |
| Petty Island I | 285 | 39.58 N | 75.07 W |
| Petua | 272b | 22.25 N | 88.27 E |
| Petuchovo | 86 | 55.06 N | 67.58 E |
| Petuški | 80 | 55.55 N | 39.28 E |
| Petworth | 42 | 50.59 N | 0.38 W |
| Petzow | 264a | 52.21 N | 12.56 E |
| Peudada | 114 | 5.12 N | 96.35 E |
| Peuerbach | 60 | 48.20 N | 13.46 E |
| Peuetsagoe, Gunung ∧ | 114 | 4.55 N | 96.20 E |
| Peureulak | 114 | 4.48 N | 97.53 E |
| Peureulak ≃ | 114 | 4.54 N | 97.53 E |
| Peureulak, Ujung › | 114 | 4.54 N | 97.54 E |
| Peusangan ≃ | 114 | 5.16 N | 96.51 E |
| Peusangan, Ujung › | 114 | 5.16 N | 96.5[illegible] E |
| Pevek | 74 | 69.42 N | 170.1[illegible] E |
| Pevely | 219 | 38.17 N | 90.2[illegible] W |
| Pevensey | 42 | 50.49 N | 0.2[illegible] E |
| Pevensey Levels ≋ | 42 | 50.50 N | 0.2[illegible] E |
| Peveragno | 62 | 44.20 N | 7.3[illegible] E |
| Pewamo | 216 | 43.00 N | 84.5[illegible] W |
| Pewaukee | 216 | 43.04 N | 88.1[illegible] W |
| Pewaukee Lake ⊜ | 216 | 43.04 N | 88.1[illegible] W |
| Pewee Valley | 218 | 38.18 N | 85.29 W |
| Pews Creek ≃ | 276 | 40.27 N | 74.06 W |
| Pewsey | 42 | 51.21 N | 1.46 W |
| Pewsey, Vale of V | 42 | 51.20 N | 1.48 W |
| Péyia | 130 | 34.53 N | 32.23 E |
| Peyrolles-en-Provence | 62 | 43.39 N | 5.35 E |
| Peyruis | 62 | 44.02 N | 5.56 E |
| Peza ≃ | 24 | 65.36 N | 44.35 E |
| Pezas | 86 | 54.39 N | 87.46 |
| Pezawa Taung ∧ | 110 | 19.33 N | 94.31 |
| Pézenas | 32 | 43.27 N | 3.25 E |
| Peženga | 76 | 59.10 N | 44.16 E |
| Pezinok | 30 | 48.18 N | 17.17 E |
| Pezu | 123 | 32.19 N | 70.44 E |
| Pezzana | 62 | 45.16 N | 8.29 E |
| Pfäfers | 58 | 46.59 N | 9.30 E |
| Pfaffenhausen | 58 | 48.07 N | 10.27 E |
| Pfaffenhofen an der Ilm | 60 | 48.31 N | 11.30 E |
| Pfaffenhofen an der Roth | 58 | 48.21 N | 10.10 E |
| Pfaffenhoffen | 56 | 48.51 N | 7.37 E |
| Pfaffenöden ∧[2] | 264b | 48.04 N | 16.33 E |
| Pfäffikersee ⊜ | 58 | 47.21 N | 8.48 E |
| Pfäffikon | 58 | 47.22 N | 8.47 E |
| Pfaffing | 64 | 48.03 N | 12.07 E |
| Pfaffnau | 58 | 47.14 N | 7.54 E |
| Pfaffstätten | 264b | 48.01 N | 16.16 E |
| Pfalzdorf | 52 | 51.42 N | 6.11 E |
| Pfänder ∧ | 58 | 47.30 N | 9.47 E |
| Pfarrkirchen | 60 | 48.27 N | 12.56 E |
| Pfarrweisach | 56 | 50.09 N | 10.44 E |
| Pfastatt | 58 | 47.47 N | 7.18 E |
| Pfatter | 60 | 48.58 N | 12.23 E |
| Pfaueninsel, Schloss ⊥ | 264a | 52.26 N | 13.07 E |
| Pfeddersheim | 56 | 49.38 N | 8.16 E |
| Pfeffenhausen | 60 | 48.40 N | 11.58 E |
| Pfeiffer-Big Sur State Park ♦ | 226 | 36.15 N | 121.47 W |
| Pferderennbahn ♦ | 263 | 51.31 N | 7.32 E |
| Pfinztal | 56 | 48.59 N | 8.33 E |
| Pflugerville | 222 | 30.26 N | 97.37 W |
| Pförring | 60 | 48.49 N | 11.41 E |
| Pforzen | 58 | 47.55 N | 10.37 E |
| Pforzheim | 56 | 48.54 N | 8.42 E |
| Pfreimd | 60 | 49.30 N | 12.11 E |
| Pfreimd ≃ | 60 | 49.29 N | 12.11 E |
| Pfrimm ≃ | 56 | 49.39 N | 8.22 E |
| Pfronten | 58 | 47.34 N | 10.33 E |
| Pfuhl | 58 | 48.24 N | 10.02 E |
| Pfullendorf | 58 | 47.55 N | 9.15 E |
| Pfullingen | 58 | 48.28 N | 9.13 E |
| Pfunds | 58 | 46.58 N | 10.33 E |
| Pfungstadt | 56 | 49.48 N | 8.36 E |
| Pfyn | 58 | 47.36 N | 8.57 E |
| Pha-an | 110 | 16.53 N | 97.38 E |
| Phachi ≃ | 110 | 13.56 N | 99.24 E |
| Phaéton, Port c | 174s | 17.44 S | 149.21 W |
| Phagwāra | 123 | 31.14 N | 75.46 E |
| Phala | 156 | 23.45 S | 26.57 E |
| Phalaborwa | 156 | 23.55 S | 31.13 E |
| Phalanx | 214 | 41.15 N | 80.58 W |
| Phalempin | 50 | 50.31 N | 3.01 E |
| Phālia | 123 | 32.26 N | 73.35 E |
| Phalodi | 120 | 27.08 N | 72.22 E |
| Phalsbourg | 56 | 48.46 N | 7.16 E |
| Phalta | 126 | 22.17 N | 88.07 E |
| Phaltan | 122 | 17.59 N | 74.26 E |
| Phalti | 272b | 22.46 N | 88.34 E |
| Phan | 110 | 19.28 N | 99.43 E |
| Phanat Nikhom | 110 | 13.27 N | 101.11 E |
| Phangan, Ko I | 110 | 9.45 N | 100.04 E |
| Phang Hoei, Khao ∧ | 110 | 15.15 N | 101.23 E |
| Phangnga | 110 | 8.28 N | 98.32 E |
| Phaniang ≃ | 110 | 16.49 N | 102.24 E |
| Phanom Dongrak, Thiu Khao ⋏ | 110 | 14.25 N | 103.30 E |
| Phanom Thuan | 110 | 14.07 N | 99.42 E |
| Phan Rang | 110 | 11.34 N | 108.59 E |
| Phan Thiet | 110 | 10.56 N | 108.06 E |
| Phan Thong | 110 | 13.28 N | 101.06 E |
| Phantom Lake | 216 | 42.52 N | 88.21 W |
| Pharenda | 124 | 27.06 N | 83.17 E |
| Phariāro | 120 | 27.12 N | 68.59 E |
| Pharr | 196 | 26.11 N | 98.11 W |
| Phasi Charoen | 269a | 13.43 N | 100.26 E |
| Phasi Charoen, Khlong ≅ | 269a | 13.44 N | 100.30 E |
| Phat Diem | 110 | 20.06 N | 106.06 E |
| Phato | 110 | 9.48 N | 98.48 E |
| Phatthalung | 110 | 7.37 N | 100.05 E |
| Phayao | 110 | 19.10 N | 99.55 E |
| Pheasant Creek ≃ | 184 | 50.35 N | 103.28 W |
| Pheba | 194 | 33.35 N | 88.56 W |
| Phelan | 228 | 34.25 N | 117.34 W |
| Phelps, N.Y., U.S. | 210 | 42.57 N | 77.03 W |
| Phelps, Tx., U.S. | 222 | 30.42 N | 95.27 W |
| Phelps, Wi., U.S. | 190 | 46.03 N | 89.05 W |
| Phelps Lake ⊜ | 192 | 35.46 N | 76.27 W |
| Phenix City | 192 | 32.28 N | 85.00 W |
| Phepane ≃ | 156 | 25.50 S | 22.45 E |
| Phet Buri ≃ | 110 | 13.13 N | 99.59 E |
| Phetchabun | 110 | 16.25 N | 101.08 E |
| Phetchabun, Thiu Khao ⋏ | 110 | 16.20 N | 100.55 E |
| Phetchaburi | 110 | 13.06 N | 99.57 E |
| Phibun Mangsahan | 110 | 15.14 N | 105.14 E |
| Phichai | 110 | 17.17 N | 100.05 E |
| Phichit | 110 | 16.26 N | 100.22 E |
| Philadelphia, S. Afr. | 158 | 33.40 S | 18.36 E |
| Philadelphia, Il., U.S. | 219 | 39.58 N | 90.07 W |
| Philadelphia, Ms., U.S. | 194 | 32.46 N | 89.07 W |
| Philadelphia, Mo., U.S. | 219 | 39.50 N | 91.44 W |
| Philadelphia, N.Y., U.S. | 212 | 44.09 N | 75.42 W |
| Philadelphia, Pa., U.S. | 208 | 39.57 N | 75.09 W |
| Philadelphia, Pa., U.S. | 285 | 39.57 N | 75.09 W |
| Philadelphia, Tn., U.S. | 192 | 35.40 N | 84.24 W |
| Philadelphia □[6] | 285 | 39.57 N | 75.07 W |
| Philadelphia International Airport ⊠ | 208 | 39.53 N | 75.14 W |
| Philadelphia Museum of Art ʊ | 285 | 39.58 N | 75.11 W |
| Philadelphia Naval Shipyard ■ | 285 | 39.53 N | 75.11 W |
| Philadelphia Park Race Track ♦ | 285 | 40.07 N | 74.57 W |
| Philae ⊥ | 140 | 24.01 N | 32.53 E |
| Phil Campbell | 194 | 34.21 N | 87.42 W |
| Philip | 198 | 44.02 N | 101.39 W |
| Philipp | 194 | 33.45 N | 90.12 W |
| Philippeville → Skikda, Alg. | 148 | 36.50 N | 6.58 E |
| Philippeville, Bel. | 50 | 50.12 N | 4.32 E |
| Philippi | 188 | 39.09 N | 80.02 W |
| Philippi, Lake ⊜ | 166 | 24.22 S | 139.00 E |
| Philippine Basin ✦[1] | 14 | 17.00 N | 132.00 E |
| Philippine International Convention Center ♦ | 269f | 14.32 N | 120.59 E |
| Philippinen → Philippines □[1] | 116 | 13.00 N | 122.00 E |

| | English | Deutsch | Español | Français | Português |
|---|---|---|---|---|---|
| ≃ | River | Fluß | Río | Rivière | Rio |
| ≅ | Canal | Kanal | Canal | Canal | Canal |
| ʟ | Waterfall, Rapids | Wasserfall, Stromschnellen | Cascada, Rápidos | Chute d'eau, Rapides | Cascata, Rápidos |
| ʉ | Strait | Meeresstraße | Estrecho | Détroit | Estreito |
| c | Bay, Gulf | Bucht, Golf | Bahía, Golfo | Baie, Golfe | Baía, Golfo |
| ⊜ | Lake, Lakes | See, Seen | Lago, Lagos | Lac, Lacs | Lago, Lagos |
| ≋ | Swamp | Sumpf | Pantano | Marais | Pântano |
| ⍓ | Ice Features, Glacier | Eis- und Gletscherformen | Accidentes Glaciales | Formes glaciaires | Acidentes glaciares |
| ⍑ | Other Hydrographic Features | Andere Hydrographische Objekte | Otros Elementos Hidrográficos | Autres données hydrographiques | Outros acidentes hidrográficos |
| ✦ | Submarine Features | Untermeerische Objekte | Accidentes Submarinos | Formes de relief sous-marin | Acidentes submarinos |
| □ | Political Unit | Politische Einheit | Unidad Politica | Entité politique | Unidade política |
| ʊ | Cultural Institution | Kulturelle Institution | Institución Cultural | Institution culturelle | Instituição cultural |
| ⊥ | Historical Site | Historische Stätte | Sitio Histórico | Site historique | Sitio histórico |
| ♦ | Recreational Site | Erholungs- und Ferienort | Sitio de Recreo | Centre de loisirs | Area de Lazer |
| ⊠ | Airport | Flughafen | Aeropuerto | Aéroport | Aeroporto |
| ■ | Military Installation | Militäranlage | Instalación Militar | Installation militaire | Instalação militar |
| ◆ | Miscellaneous | Verschiedenes | Misceláneo | Divers | Diversos |

Philippines (Pilipinas) □[1], Asia 108 13.00 N 122.00 E
Philippines (Pilipinas) □[1], Asia 116 13.00 N 122.00 E
Philippines, University of the ʋ[2] 269f 14.39 N 121.04 E
Philippine Sea ⊤[2] 14 20.00 N 135.00 E
Philippine Trench ◆[1] 14 9.00 N 127.00 E
Philippolis 158 30.19 S 25.13 E
Philippopolis → Plovdiv 38 42.09 N 24.45 E
Philippsburg 56 49.14 N 8.27 E
Philippsreut 60 48.52 N 13.41 E
Philippsthal, Dtsch. 56 50.51 N 10.00 E
Philippsthal, Dtsch. 264a 52.20 N 13.09 E
Philipsburg, P.Q., Can. 206 45.02 N 73.05 W
Philipsburg, Ned. Ant. 238 17.59 N 63.10 W
Philipsburg, Mt., U.S. 202 46.19 N 113.17 W
Philipsburg, Pa., U.S. 214 40.53 N 78.13 W
Philipsburg Manor ⊥ 276 41.05 N 73.52 W
Philipse Manor Hall State Historic Site ⊥ 276 40.56 N 73.54 W
Philip Smith Mountains ⋏ 180 68.30 N 148.00 W
Philipstown 158 30.26 S 24.29 E
Phillaur 123 31.01 N 75.47 E
Phillip Island I 169 38.29 S 145.14 E
Phillips, Me., U.S. 188 44.49 N 70.20 W
Phillips, Tx., U.S. 196 35.41 N 101.21 W
Phillips, Wi., U.S. 190 45.41 N 90.24 W
Phillipsburg, Ga., U.S. 192 31.34 N 83.31 W
Phillipsburg, Ks., U.S. 198 39.45 N 99.19 W
Phillipsburg, N.J., U.S. 210 40.41 N 75.11 W
Philmont 210 42.14 N 73.39 W
Philo, Il., U.S. 194 40.01 N 88.09 W
Philo, Oh., U.S. 188 39.51 N 81.54 W
Philomath 202 44.32 N 123.21 W
Philpots Island I 176 74.48 N 80.00 W
Phimai 110 15.13 N 102.30 E
Phinga 272b 22.41 N 88.25 E
Phitsanulok 110 16.50 N 100.15 E
Phnom Penh → Phnum Pénh 110 11.33 N 104.55 E
Phnum Pénh 110 11.33 N 104.55 E
Phnum Tbêng Méanchey 110 13.49 N 104.58 E
Pho ≃ 124 27.41 N 89.53 E
Phoenicia 210 42.05 N 74.18 W
Phoenix, Az., U.S. 200 33.26 N 112.04 W
Phoenix, Il., U.S. 278 41.36 N 87.38 W
Phoenix, Md., U.S. 208 39.30 N 76.36 W
Phoenix, N.Y., U.S. 210 43.13 N 76.18 W
Phoenix Islands II 14 4.00 S 172.00 W
Phoenix Lake ⊘[1] 282 37.57 N 122.35 W
Phoenix Park ♦ 281 42.24 N 83.27 W
Phoenixville 208 40.07 N 75.30 W
Phon 110 15.49 N 102.36 E
Phong ≃ 110 16.23 N 102.56 E
Phôngsali 110 21.41 N 102.06 E
Phong Tho 110 22.32 N 103.21 E
Phon Phisai 110 18.01 N 103.05 E
Phosphate Hill 166 21.52 S 139.51 E
Phrae 110 18.09 N 100.08 E
Phra Khanong ◆[8] 269a 13.42 N 100.35 E
Phra Nakhon → Krung Thep 110 13.45 N 100.31 E
Phra Nakhon Si Ayutthaya 110 14.21 N 100.33 E
Phran Kratai 110 16.40 N 99.36 E
Phrao 110 19.22 N 99.13 E
Phra Pradaeng 269a 13.40 N 100.32 E
Phra Rop, Khao ∧ 110 13.11 N 99.31 E
Phrom Phiram 110 17.02 N 100.12 E
Phrygia □[9] 130 39.00 N 30.00 E
Phsar Réam 110 10.30 N 103.37 E
Phu Cat 110 14.01 N 109.03 E
Phu Huu, Viet 110 18.58 N 105.31 E
Phu Huu, Viet 269c 10.43 N 106.47 E
Phuket 110 7.53 N 98.24 E
Phuket, Ko I 110 8.00 N 98.22 E
Phularwān 123 32.22 N 73.00 E
Phulbari 126 21.52 N 88.08 E
Phulbāria 126 23.22 N 89.50 E
Phuljhuri 126 22.12 N 90.04 E
Phulkusma 126 22.43 N 86.52 E
Phu Loc 110 16.16 N 107.53 E
Phūlpur 124 25.33 N 82.06 E
Phulra 123 34.20 N 73.03 E
Phultala 126 22.59 N 89.28 E
Phu Ly 110 20.32 N 105.56 E
Phum Duang ≃ 110 9.10 N 99.20 E
Phumĭ Bâ Khăm 110 13.51 N 107.22 E
Phumĭ Banam 110 11.19 N 105.18 E
Phumĭ Béng 110 13.05 N 104.18 E
Phumĭ Châmbák 110 11.14 N 104.49 E
Phumĭ Chângho Ândêng 110 12.39 N 104.35 E
Phumĭ Chhuk 110 10.50 N 104.28 E
Phumĭ Chruŏy Slêng 110 13.14 N 105.57 E
Phumĭ Dăk Dăm 110 12.20 N 107.21 E
Phumĭ Kâmpóng Srâlau 110 14.05 N 105.46 E
Phumĭ Kâmpóng Trâbâk 110 13.06 N 105.14 E
Phumĭ Kântuŏt Sâmraông 110 14.12 N 104.37 E
Phumĭ Kaôh Kért 110 13.47 N 104.32 E
Phumĭ Kaôh Kŏng 110 11.26 N 103.11 E
Phumĭ Khpôb 110 11.02 N 105.12 E
Phumĭ Krêk 110 11.46 N 105.56 E
Phumĭ Lvéa Kraôm 110 13.21 N 102.54 E
Phumĭ Moŭng 110 13.45 N 103.33 E
Phumĭ Narŭng 110 13.53 N 105.34 E
Phumĭ Phnum Srâlau 110 11.03 N 103.42 E
Phumĭ Prêk Kák 110 12.15 N 105.32 E
Phumĭ Prêk Sândêk 110 11.51 N 105.22 E
Phumĭ Prey Toch 110 12.54 N 103.23 E
Phumĭ Puŏk Chăs 110 13.26 N 103.44 E
Phumĭ Rôluŏs Chăs 110 13.19 N 104.00 E
Phumĭ Sâmraông 110 14.11 N 103.31 E
Phumĭ Spœ Tbong 110 12.20 N 105.19 E
Phumĭ Srê Kôkir 110 13.08 N 106.04 E
Phumĭ Srê Rônéam 110 12.16 N 106.25 E
Phumĭ Tbêng 110 13.35 N 104.55 E
Phumĭ Thalabârĭvăt 110 13.33 N 105.57 E
Phumĭ Thmâ Pôk 110 13.57 N 103.04 E
Phumĭ Tnaôt 110 12.56 N 104.34 E
Phumĭ Tœk Choŭ 110 13.36 N 103.24 E
Phu My 110 14.10 N 109.03 E
Phung Hiep 110 9.49 N 105.50 E
Phuntsholing 124 26.53 N 89.23 E
Phuoc Binh 110 11.50 N 106.58 E
Phuoc Khanh 269c 10.40 N 106.48 E
Phuoc Long 110 9.26 N 105.28 E
Phuoc Long Xa 269c 10.49 N 106.46 E
Phuoc Luong 269c 10.45 N 106.48 E
Phu Quoc 110 10.13 N 103.58 E
Phu Quoc, Dao I 110 10.12 N 104.00 E
Phurphura 272b 22.44 N 88.08 E
Phu Tho 110 21.24 N 105.13 E
Phu Tho Hoa 269c 10.46 N 106.38 E
Phu Tho Race Track ♦ 269c 10.46 N 106.40 E
Phutthaisong 110 15.32 N 103.01 E
Phu Vang 110 16.31 N 107.37 E
Phu Yen 110 21.16 N 104.39 E
Pi ≃ 100 32.26 N 116.34 E
Pia 154 4.00 N 26.17 E
Piabas 250 1.12 S 46.54 W
Piabetá 256 22.37 S 43.10 W
Piabonha ≃ 256 22.07 S 43.08 W
Piaçabuçu 250 10.24 S 36.25 W
Piacatuba 256 21.29 S 42.47 W
Piacenza 62 45.01 N 9.40 E
Piacenza □[4] 62 44.53 N 9.35 E
Piacouadie, Lac ⊘ 186 51.16 N 70.54 W
Piadena 64 45.08 N 10.22 E
Piaggine 68 40.21 N 15.23 E
Piako ≃ 172 37.12 S 175.30 E
Pialba 166 25.17 S 152.51 E
Piāli ≃ 272b 22.23 N 88.35 E
Piana 36 42.14 N 8.38 E
Piana, Isola I 71 40.58 N 8.13 E
Piana Crixia 62 44.29 N 8.18 E
Piana degli Albanesi 70 38.00 N 13.17 E
Piana degli Albanesi, Lago di ⊘ 70 37.58 N 13.18 E
Piana Mwanga 154 7.40 S 28.10 E
Piancastagnaio 66 42.51 N 11.41 E
Piancó 250 7.12 S 37.57 W
Pian Creek ≃ 166 30.02 S 148.12 E
Pian di Sco 66 43.38 N 11.33 E
Pianella 66 42.24 N 14.02 E
Pianello Val Tidone 62 44.57 N 9.24 E
Pianezza 62 45.06 N 7.33 E
Pianguan 102 39.24 N 111.30 E
Pianjiaojie 102 26.01 N 100.32 E
Piankatank ≃ 208 37.32 N 76.18 W
Pianling 104 41.24 N 123.58 E
Piano 64 45.46 N 11.08 E
Piano d'Arta 64 46.29 N 13.01 E
Piano del Voglio 66 44.10 N 11.13 E
Pianoro 64 44.22 N 11.20 E
Pianosa, Isola I, It. 36 42.35 N 10.04 E
Pianosa, Isola I, It. 66 42.13 N 15.45 E
Pianosinatico 66 44.07 N 10.44 E
Pianottoli-Caldarello 71 41.29 N 9.03 E
Pians 58 47.08 N 10.30 E
Pianu, Mochun ʮ 175c 7.20 N 151.26 E
Piapot 184 49.59 N 109.07 W
Piapot Indian Reserve ◆[4] 184 50.45 N 104.26 W
Piasa 219 39.07 N 90.07 W
Piasa Creek ≃ 219 38.56 N 90.17 W
Piaseczno 30 52.05 N 21.01 E
Piashti, Lac ⊘ 186 50.29 N 62.52 W
Piaski 30 51.08 N 22.51 E
Piat 116 17.48 N 121.29 E
Piatã 255 13.09 S 41.48 W
Piatra-Neamț 38 46.56 N 26.22 E
Piatra-Olt 38 44.24 N 24.16 E
Piatt □[6] 219 40.00 N 88.35 W
Piau 256 21.31 S 43.19 W
Piauí □[3] 250 7.00 S 43.00 W
Piauí ≃, Bra. 250 6.38 S 42.42 W
Piauí ≃, Bra. 255 16.41 S 41.53 W
Piauí, Morro do ∧ 255 14.59 S 47.31 W
Piaus ≃ 255 12.27 S 49.32 W
Piave ≃ 64 45.32 N 12.44 E
Piawaning 162 30.51 S 116.22 E
Piaxtla ≃ 232 23.42 N 106.49 W
Piazza Armerina 70 37.23 N 14.22 E
Piazzi, Isla I 254 51.45 S 74.05 W
Piazzola sul Brenta 64 45.32 N 11.47 E
Piberegg 61 47.05 N 15.05 E
Pibor ≃ 140 8.26 N 33.13 E
Pibor Post 140 6.48 N 33.08 E
Pibroch 182 54.16 N 113.52 W
Pic ≃ 190 48.36 N 86.18 W
Pica 248 20.30 S 69.21 W
Picacho 200 32.42 N 111.29 W
Picacho, Cerro del ∧ 286a 19.35 N 99.08 W
Pičajevo 80 53.15 N 42.12 E
Picanoc ≃ 190 46.05 N 76.03 W
Picardie □[9] 50 49.45 N 2.50 E
Picatinny Arsenal ■ 276 40.57 N 74.33 W
Picatinny Lake ⊘ 276 40.57 N 74.33 W
Picayune 194 30.31 N 89.40 W
Piccadilly 186 48.34 N 58.55 W
Piccadilly Station ◆[5] 262 53.28 N 2.14 W
Piccione 66 43.11 N 12.31 E
Piccolo, Mar ⊤[2] 68 40.29 N 17.16 E
Piccotts End 260 51.46 N 0.28 W
Pic de Tio ∧ 150 8.52 N 8.54 W
Piceance Creek ≃ 200 40.05 N 108.14 W
Picentini, Monti ⋏ 68 40.45 N 15.00 E
Picerno 68 40.38 N 15.38 E
Pičeury 80 54.19 N 45.50 E
Pīch ≃ 123 34.52 N 71.09 E
Pichana ≃ 246 3.31 S 71.43 W
Pichanal 252 23.19 S 64.13 W
Picheng 106 32.07 N 119.42 E
Picher 196 36.59 N 94.49 W
Pichhor 124 25.58 N 78.24 E
Pichilemu 252 34.23 S 72.00 W
Pichileufú, Arroyo ≃ 254 40.35 S 70.39 W
Pichimá 246 4.24 N 77.21 W
Pichi-Mahuida 252 38.50 S 64.57 W
Pichincha □[4] 246 0.10 S 78.40 W
Pichis ≃ 248 9.59 S 74.59 W
Pichl bei Wels 60 48.11 N 13.54 E
Pichor 124 25.11 N 78.11 E
Pichtovka 86 56.00 N 82.42 E
Pichucalco 234 17.31 N 93.09 W
Picinguaba 256 23.22 S 44.50 W
Picinisco 66 41.39 N 13.52 E
Pic Island I 190 48.43 N 86.38 W
Pickardville 182 54.03 N 113.53 W
Pickaway □[6] 218 39.36 N 82.57 W
Pickens, Ms., U.S. 194 32.53 N 89.58 W
Pickens, S.C., U.S. 192 34.53 N 82.42 W
Pickens, W.V., U.S. 188 38.39 N 80.12 W
Pickensville 194 33.14 N 88.16 W
Pickerel ≃ 190 45.55 N 80.50 W
Pickerel Lake ⊘ 184 52.36 N 99.30 W
Pickering, On., Can. 212 43.52 N 79.02 W
Pickering, Eng., U.K. 44 54.14 N 0.46 W
Pickering, Vale of V 44 54.12 N 0.45 W
Pickering Beach 212 43.50 N 78.59 W
Pickering Brook 168a 32.03 S 116.08 E
Pickering Creek ≃ 285 40.08 N 75.30 W
Pickering Creek Reservoir ⊘[1] 285 40.07 N 75.30 W
Pickett, Lake ⊘ 220 28.36 N 81.07 W
Pickford 190 46.09 N 84.21 W
Pičkir'ajevo 80 54.12 N 42.27 E
Pickle Crow 176 51.30 N 90.04 W
Pickmere 262 53.17 N 2.28 W
Pick Mere ⊘ 262 53.17 N 2.29 W
Pickstown 198 43.04 N 98.31 W
Pickton 222 33.02 N 95.24 W
Pickwick Lake ⊘[1] 194 34.55 N 88.10 W
Pickwick Landing Dam ◆[6] 194 35.00 N 88.21 W
Picnic Point > 274b 37.57 S 145.00 E
Pico 66 41.27 N 13.34 E
Pico ∧ 150a 14.56 N 24.21 W
Pico I 148a 38.28 N 28.20 W
Pico, Ponta do ∧ 148a 38.28 N 28.25 W
Pico da Neblina, Parque Nacional ♦ 246 0.30 N 66.00 W
Pico de Orizaba, Parque Nacional ♦ 234 19.05 N 97.16 W
Pico Rivera 228 33.58 N 118.05 W
Picos 250 7.05 S 41.28 W
Picota 248 6.55 S 76.20 W
Pico Truncado 254 46.48 S 67.58 W
Picquigny 50 49.57 N 2.09 E
Picton, Austl. 170 34.11 S 150.36 E
Picton, On., Can. 212 44.00 N 77.08 W
Picton, N.Z. 172 41.18 S 174.01 E
Picton, Eng., U.K. 262 53.14 N 2.51 W
Picton, Isla I 254 55.02 S 66.57 W
Picton Bay c 212 44.03 N 77.08 W
Picton Junction 168a 33.21 S 115.41 E
Pictou 186 45.41 N 62.43 W
Pictou Island I 186 45.50 N 62.34 W
Picture Butte 182 49.53 N 112.47 W
Pictured Rocks National Lakeshore ♦ 190 46.35 N 86.20 W
Picture Rocks 210 41.17 N 76.43 W
Picúa, Punta > 240m 18.25 N 65.46 W
Picuí 250 6.31 S 36.21 W
Picunda 84 43.12 N 40.21 E
Picún Leufú 254 39.31 S 69.15 W
Picún Leufú, Arroyo ≃ 254 39.31 S 69.08 W
Picuris Indian Reservation ◆[4] 200 36.12 N 105.42 W
Pidálion, Akrotírion > 130 34.56 N 34.05 E
Pidarak 128 25.51 N 63.14 E
Pidbyzh 78 49.22 N 23.15 E
Piddle ≃ 42 50.42 N 2.04 W
Piddletrenthide 42 50.48 N 2.25 W
Pide Adası I 267b 40.53 N 29.04 E
Pidhaytsi 78 49.16 N 25.08 E
Pidhorodna 78 48.07 N 30.51 E
Pidhorodne 78 48.34 N 35.08 E
Pidie, Ujung > 114 5.30 N 95.53 E
Piding 64 47.46 N 12.55 E
Pidkamin' 78 49.57 N 25.19 E
Pidlisne 78 48.47 N 32.15 E
Pidurutalagala ∧ 122 7.00 N 80.46 E
Pidvolochys'k 78 49.33 N 26.09 E
Piedade 287a 22.41 S 43.05 W
Piedade ◆[8] 287a 22.53 S 43.19 W
Piedade do Baruel 287b 23.37 S 46.18 W
Piedade do Rio Grande 256 21.28 S 44.12 W
Piedecuesta 246 6.59 N 73.03 W
Piedicavallo 62 45.42 N 7.57 E
Piedicroce 36 42.23 N 9.23 E
Piediluco 66 42.32 N 12.45 E
Piedimonte Etneo 70 37.48 N 15.12 E
Piedimonte Matese 68 41.21 N 14.22 E
Piedimonte San Germano 66 41.30 N 13.45 E
Piedimulera 58 46.01 N 8.16 E
Piè di Ripa 66 43.15 N 13.29 E
Piedmont, Al., U.S. 194 33.55 N 85.36 W
Piedmont, Ca., U.S. 226 37.49 N 122.13 W
Piedmont, Mo., U.S. 194 37.09 N 90.41 W
Piedmont, Oh., U.S. 214 40.11 N 81.12 W
Piedmont, S.C., U.S. 192 34.54 N 82.21 W
Piedmont Lake ⊘[1] 214 40.08 N 81.11 W
Piedra, C.R. 236 9.29 N 83.40 W
Piedra, Ca., U.S. 226 36.48 N 119.22 W
Piedra ≃ 200 37.01 N 107.24 W
Piedra, Cerro ∧ 252 37.41 S 73.07 W
Piedra Azul, Quebrada ≃ 286c 10.36 N 66.57 W
Piedrabuena 34 39.02 N 4.10 W
Piedra del Águila 254 40.03 S 70.05 W
Piedra del Águila, Embalse ⊘[1] 254 40.30 S 70.20 W
Piedrafita, Puerto de )( 34 42.40 N 7.01 W
Piedrahita 34 40.28 N 5.19 W
Piedra Roja 236 8.38 N 81.48 W
Piedras, Arroyo de las ≃ 288 34.43 S 58.19 W
Piedras, Punta >, Arg. 258 35.25 S 57.08 W
Piedras, Punta >, Ven. 246 10.40 N 61.40 W
Piedras Blancas 252 31.11 S 59.56 W
Piedras Blancas, Point > 226 35.40 N 121.17 W
Piedras Coloradas 252 32.23 S 57.36 W
Piedras Negras, Guat. 232 17.11 N 91.15 W
Piedras Negras, Méx. 232 28.42 N 100.31 W
Piedras Negras ⊥ 232 17.12 N 91.15 W
Piedra Sola 252 32.04 S 56.21 W
Piegaro 66 42.58 N 12.05 E
Pie Island I 190 48.15 N 89.05 W
Pieksämäki 26 62.18 N 27.08 E
Piéla 150 12.42 N 0.08 W
Pielach ≃ 61 48.15 N 15.22 E
Pielavesi 26 63.14 N 26.45 E
Pielavesi ⊘ 26 63.18 N 26.35 E
Pielinen ⊘ 26 63.15 N 29.40 E
Pieljekaise Nationalpark ♦ 24 66.18 N 16.58 E
Piemonte □[4] 36 45.00 N 8.00 E
Pienaarsrivier 156 25.15 S 28.18 E
Piendamó 246 2.38 N 76.30 W
Pieniężno 30 54.15 N 20.08 E
Pieniński Park Narodowy ♦ 30 49.25 N 20.25 E
Pieni-Salpausselkä ∧ 26 61.08 N 27.20 E
Piennes 56 49.19 N 5.47 E
Pieńsk 30 51.15 N 15.03 E
Pienza 66 43.04 N 11.41 E
Pierce, Co., U.S. 200 40.38 N 104.45 W
Pierce, Fl., U.S. 220 27.50 N 81.58 W
Pierce, Id., U.S. 202 46.29 N 115.47 W
Pierce, Ne., U.S. 198 42.11 N 97.31 W
Pierce, Tx., U.S. 222 29.14 N 96.12 W
Pierce □[6] 224 47.04 N 122.07 W
Pierce, Lake ⊘ 220 27.58 N 81.31 W
Pierce City 194 36.56 N 94.00 W
Pierce Lake ⊘, Can. 184 54.10 N 92.56 W
Pierce Lake ⊘, Sk., Can. 184 54.30 N 109.42 W
Pierceton 216 41.12 N 85.42 W
Piermont 210 41.03 N 73.55 W
Pierowall 46 59.20 N 2.59 W
Pierpont, Oh., U.S. 214 41.45 N 80.34 W
Pierpont, S.D., U.S. 198 45.29 N 97.49 W
Pierre 198 44.22 N 100.21 W
Pierre, Bayou ≃, La., U.S. 194 31.51 N 93.06 W
Pierre, Bayou ≃, Ms., U.S. 194 31.55 N 91.11 W
Pierre-Buffière 32 45.42 N 1.21 E
Pierreclos 58 46.20 N 4.41 E
Pierre-de-Bresse 58 46.53 N 5.15 E
Pierrefeu-du-Var 62 43.13 N 6.08 E
Pierrefitte-sur-Aire 56 48.54 N 5.20 E
Pierrefitte-sur-Sauldre 50 47.30 N 2.09 E
Pierrefitte-sur-Seine 261 48.58 N 2.22 E
Pierrefonds, P.Q., Can. 206 45.29 N 73.52 W
Pierrefonds, Fr. 50 49.21 N 2.59 E
Pierrefontaine-les-Varans 58 47.13 N 6.33 E
Pierrelatte 62 44.23 N 4.42 E
Pierrelaye 261 49.01 N 2.09 E
Pierre Part 194 29.57 N 91.12 W
Pierre Pertuis, Col de )( 58 47.12 N 7.11 E
Pierrepont Manor 212 43.44 N 76.04 W
Pierre-sur-Haute ∧ 62 45.39 N 3.49 E
Pierreville, P.Q., Can. 206 46.04 N 72.49 W
Pierreville, Trin. 241r 10.18 N 61.01 W
Pierron 219 38.47 N 89.36 W
Pierron, Lac ⊘ 206 46.53 N 74.20 W
Pierry 50 49.01 N 3.56 E
Pierson 192 29.14 N 81.27 W
Piersonville 285 40.10 N 74.42 W
Pierz 190 45.58 N 94.06 W
Piesendorf 64 47.17 N 12.43 E
Pieskow 54 52.16 N 14.04 E
Piesport 56 49.53 N 6.55 E
Piešt'any 30 48.36 N 17.50 E
Piesting ≃ 61 48.02 N 16.30 E
Pietarsaari → Jakobstad 26 63.40 N 22.42 E
Pieterburen 52 53.24 N 6.27 E
Pieterlen 58 47.11 N 7.20 E
Pietermaritzburg 158 29.37 S 30.16 E
Pietersburg 156 23.54 S 29.25 E
Pietrabbondante 66 41.45 N 14.23 E
Pietracamela 66 42.31 N 13.33 E
Pietracatella 66 41.35 N 14.52 E
Pietra del Pertusillo, Lago di ⊘ 68 40.17 N 15.58 E
Pietragalla 68 40.45 N 15.53 E
Pietra Ligure 62 44.09 N 8.17 E
Pietralunga 66 43.26 N 12.26 E
Pietramala 66 44.10 N 11.20 E
Pietramelara 68 41.16 N 14.11 E
Pietramontecorvino 68 41.32 N 15.07 E
Pietrapaola 68 39.29 N 16.49 E
Pietrapertosa 68 40.31 N 16.04 E
Pietraperzia 70 37.25 N 14.08 E
Pietrasanta 64 43.57 N 10.14 E
Pietrelcina 68 41.12 N 14.51 E
Piet Retief 158 27.01 S 30.50 E
Pietrosu, Vârful ∧, Rom. 38 47.36 N 24.38 E
Pietrosu, Vârful ∧, Rom. 38 47.08 N 25.11 E
Pieve 64 45.46 N 10.45 E
Pieve d'Alpago 64 46.10 N 12.21 E
Pieve del Cairo 62 45.03 N 8.48 E
Pieve di Cadore 64 46.26 N 12.22 E
Pieve di Cento 64 44.43 N 11.18 E
Pieve di Soligo 64 45.53 N 12.10 E
Pieve di Teco 62 44.03 N 7.56 E
Pieve Fosciana 64 44.08 N 10.25 E
Pievepelago 64 44.12 N 10.37 E
Pieve Porto Morone 62 45.07 N 9.26 E
Pieve Santo Stefano 66 43.40 N 12.02 E
Piffard 210 42.50 N 77.51 W
Pigari 80 51.24 N 49.42 E
Pigeon, Mi., U.S. 190 43.49 N 83.16 W
Pigeon, Pa., U.S. 214 41.32 N 79.03 W
Pigeon ≃, Mb., Can. 184 52.15 N 97.00 W
Pigeon ≃, On., Can. 212 44.22 N 78.31 W
Pigeon ≃, N.A. 190 48.00 N 89.34 W
Pigeon ≃, U.S. 192 36.00 N 83.11 W
Pigeon ≃, U.S. 216 41.46 N 85.47 W
Pigeon ≃, Mi., U.S. 190 43.56 N 83.17 W
Pigeon ≃, Mi., U.S. 190 45.27 N 84.33 W
Pigeon ≃, Mi., U.S. 216 42.54 N 86.11 W
Pigeon Bay c 214 42.01 N 82.40 W
Pigeon Cove 207 42.40 N 70.38 W
Pigeon Creek ≃, Al., U.S. 194 31.20 N 86.42 W
Pigeon Creek ≃, In., U.S. 194 37.59 N 87.35 W
Pigeon Creek ≃, In., U.S. 216 41.41 N 85.17 W
Pigeon Creek ≃, Pa., U.S. 279b 40.12 N 79.55 W
Pigeon Creek ≃, Pa., U.S. 285 40.12 N 75.35 W
Pigeon Forge 192 35.47 N 83.33 W
Pigeon Lake ⊘, Ab., Can. 182 53.00 N 114.00 W
Pigeon Lake ⊘, On., Can. 212 44.30 N 78.30 W
Pigeon Run ≃ 285 40.06 N 75.35 W
Pigeon Swamp ≡ 276 40.23 N 74.29 W
Pigezhuang 105 39.39 N 116.15 E
Pigg ≃ 192 37.00 N 79.29 W
Piggott 194 36.22 N 90.11 W
Piggs Peak 158 25.38 S 31.15 E
Pigkawagan 116 7.12 N 124.32 E
Piglio 66 41.49 N 13.08 E
Pigna 62 43.56 N 7.40 E
Pignans 62 43.18 N 6.13 E
Pignataro Maggiore 68 41.11 N 14.10 E
Pignola 68 40.34 N 15.47 E
Pigs, Bay of → Cochinos, Bahía de c 240p 22.07 N 81.10 W
Pigüé 252 37.37 S 62.25 W
Pigŭm-do I 98 34.45 N 125.55 E
Pihama 172 39.30 S 173.56 E
Piha Passage ʮ 174w 21.07 S 175.05 W
Pihāri 124 27.38 N 80.12 E
Pihlajavesi ⊘ 26 61.45 N 28.50 E
Pihlava 26 61.33 N 21.36 E
Pihtipudas 26 63.23 N 25.34 E
Pihuamo 234 19.15 N 103.23 W
P'ihyŏn 98 40.01 N 124.37 E
Piikkiö 26 60.26 N 22.31 E
Piippola 26 64.10 N 25.58 E
Pijijiapan 234 15.42 N 93.14 W
Pijnacker 52 52.02 N 4.27 E
Pijol, Pico ∧ 236 15.06 N 87.35 W
Pikal'ovo 76 59.31 N 34.06 E
Pikangikum 184 51.49 N 94.00 W
Pikangikum Lake ⊘ 184 51.48 N 94.00 W
Pike 210 42.33 N 78.09 W
Pike □[6], Il., U.S. 219 39.36 N 90.48 W
Pike □[6], Mo., U.S. 219 39.21 N 91.10 W
Pike □[6], Oh., U.S. 218 39.05 N 83.06 W
Pike □[6], Pa., U.S. 210 41.19 N 74.48 W
Pike ≃, N.A. 206 45.04 N 73.06 W
Pike ≃, Wi., U.S. 190 45.26 N 87.52 W
Pike, North Branch ≃ 190 45.30 N 88.01 W
Pike, South Branch ≃ 190 45.30 N 88.01 W
Pike Creek ≃, On., Can. 281 42.19 N 82.51 W
Pike Creek ≃, De., U.S. 285 39.42 N 75.42 W
Pike Lake ⊘ 212 44.46 N 76.21 W
Pikelot I 14 8.05 N 147.38 E
Pike Lowe ∧[2] 262 53.42 N 2.34 W
Pike Run ≃ 276 40.25 N 74.38 W
Pikes Peak 218 39.08 N 86.09 W
Pikes Peak ∧ 200 38.51 N 105.03 W
Pikes Rocks ∧[2] 214 41.56 N 79.24 W
Pikesville 208 39.22 N 76.43 W
Piketberg 158 32.54 S 18.46 E
Piketon 218 39.04 N 83.00 W
Piketown 208 40.23 N 76.45 W
Pikeville, Ky., U.S. 192 37.28 N 82.31 W
Pikeville, Tn., U.S. 194 35.36 N 85.11 W
Pikkola 265a 59.42 N 30.08 E
Pikou 98 39.24 N 122.20 E
Pikounda 152 0.33 N 16.42 E
Pikwitonei 184 55.35 N 97.09 W
Pila, Arg. 252 36.01 S 58.08 W
Pila, It. 62 45.41 N 7.18 E
Piła (Schneidemühl), Pol. 30 53.10 N 16.44 E
Piła □[4] 30 53.15 N 16.30 E
Pilanesberg ∧ 156 25.14 S 27.04 E
Pilanesberg Game Reserve ◆[4] 156 25.15 S 27.05 E
Pilão Arcado 250 9.56 S 42.29 W
Pilar, Arg. 252 31.41 S 63.54 W
Pilar, Arg. 252 31.27 S 61.15 W
Pilar, Arg. 258 34.27 S 58.54 W
Pilar, Bra. 250 9.36 S 35.56 W
Pilar, Bra. 287a 22.42 S 43.19 W
Pilar, Para. 252 26.52 S 58.23 W
Pilar, Pil. 116 11.29 N 123.00 E
Pilar, Pil. 116 9.52 N 126.06 E
Pilar □[5] 288 34.28 S 58.52 W
Pilar Bay c 116 11.34 N 123.00 E
Pilarcitos Creek ≃ 282 37.28 N 122.27 W
Pilarcitos Lake ⊘ 282 37.33 N 122.25 W
Pilar de Goiás 255 14.41 S 49.27 W
Pilar do Sul 255 23.49 S 47.42 W
Pilares 196 30.24 N 104.52 W
Pilas Group II 116 6.45 N 121.35 E
Pilas Island I 116 6.38 N 121.37 E
Pilatus ∧ 58 46.59 N 8.15 E
Pilawa 30 51.58 N 21.31 E
Pilaya ≃ 248 20.55 S 64.04 W
Pilcher Park ♦ 278 41.32 N 88.01 W
Pilchuck ≃ 224 47.55 N 122.02 W
Pilchuck Creek ≃ 224 48.12 N 122.13 W
Pilcomayo ≃ 18 25.21 S 57.42 W
Pilcomayo, Brazo Norte ≃ 252 24.56 S 58.16 W
Pilcomayo, Brazo Sur ≃ 252 24.56 S 58.16 W
Pil'dozero 24 65.43 N 33.28 E
Piles Creek ≃ 276 40.37 N 74.12 W
Pilga 162 21.29 S 119.25 E
Pilger 198 42.00 N 97.03 W
Pilgrim Gardens 285 39.57 N 75.19 W
Pilgrim Memorial Monument ⊥ 207 42.04 N 70.12 W
Pilgrims Hatch 260 51.38 N 0.17 E
Pilgrim's Rest 156 24.55 S 30.44 E
Pil'gyn 180 69.18 N 179.08 E
Pili 116 13.33 N 123.16 E
Pīlībhīt 124 28.38 N 79.48 E
Pilica ≃ 30 51.52 N 21.17 E
Pilipinas → Philippines □[1] 116 13.00 N 122.00 E
Pilis ⋏ 264c 47.37 N 18.59 E
Pilisborosjenő 264c 47.36 N 19.00 E
Pilkhua 124 28.43 N 77.39 E
Pillaro 246 1.10 S 78.32 W
Pillar Point > 282 37.30 N 122.30 W
Pillar Point >[1] 212 43.59 N 76.09 W
Pillau → Baltijsk 76 54.39 N 19.55 E
Pilley's Island 186 49.31 N 55.44 W
Pilliga 166 30.21 S 148.54 E
Pillings Pond ⊘ 283 42.32 N 71.02 W
Pillon, Col du )( 58 46.22 N 7.13 E
Pillow 208 40.38 N 76.48 W
Pillsbury Sound ʮ 240m 18.20 N 64.49 W
Pil'na 80 55.33 N 45.55 E
Pílos 38 36.55 N 21.43 E
Pilot ∧ 166 36.45 S 148.13 E
Pilot Butte 184 50.28 N 104.25 W
Pilot Grove 194 38.52 N 92.54 W
Pilot Hill 226 38.50 N 121.02 W
Pilot Knob 194 37.37 N 90.38 W
Pilot Knob ∧, Ar., U.S. 194 35.42 N 93.57 W
Pilot Knob ∧, Id., U.S. 202 45.54 N 115.42 W
Pilot Mound 184 49.16 N 98.55 W
Pilot Mountain 192 36.23 N 80.28 W
Pilot Peak ∧, Nv., U.S. 204 41.02 N 114.06 W
Pilot Peak ∧, Nv., U.S. 204 38.21 N 117.58 W
Pilot Peak ∧, Wy., U.S. 202 44.58 N 109.53 W
Pilot Point, Ak., U.S. 180 57.34 N 157.35 W
Pilot Point, Tx., U.S. 196 33.23 N 96.57 W
Pilot Rock 202 45.29 N 118.49 W
Pilot Rock ∧ 200 35.09 N 109.53 W
Pilot Station 180 61.56 N 162.54 W
Pilottown 194 29.10 N 89.15 W
Pilpah Range ⋏ 166 20.23 S 138.34 E
Pilsen → Plzeň 60 49.45 N 13.23 E
Pilsensee ⊘ 60 48.01 N 11.11 E
Pilsting 60 48.42 N 12.39 E
Pilsum 52 53.29 N 7.04 E
Piltene 76 57.13 N 21.40 E
Pilu ≃ 110 19.33 N 97.24 E
Piluchang 107 29.13 N 105.37 E
Pil'ugino 80 53.25 N 52.26 E
Pilusi 106 32.05 N 120.05 E
Pilzno 30 49.59 N 21.17 E
Pim ≃ 74 61.18 N 71.57 E
Pima 200 32.53 N 109.49 W
Pimah 110 15.36 N 107.25 E
Pimba 166 31.15 S 136.47 E
Pimelles 50 47.50 N 4.10 E
Pimenta Bueno ≃ 248 11.39 S 61.11 W
Pimenteira, Vereda ≃ 250 9.58 S 42.46 W
Pimenteiras 250 6.14 S 41.25 W
Pimentel, Bra. 250 3.43 S 45.30 W
Pimentel, Perú 248 6.50 S 79.57 W
Pimlico Race Course ♦ 284b 39.21 N 76.40 W
Pimmit Hills 284c 38.54 N 77.12 W
Pimmit Run ≃ 284c 38.55 N 77.07 W
Pimu-Lendo 152 1.46 N 20.54 E
Pimville ◆[8] 273d 26.16 S 27.54 E
Pina 34 41.29 N 0.32 W
Pina ≃ 76 52.10 N 26.14 E
Pinacanauan ≃ 116 17.37 N 121.44 E
Pináculo, Cerro ∧ 254 50.45 S 72.16 W
Pinalón, Cerro ∧ 236 15.05 N 89.55 W
Pinamalayan 116 13.02 N 121.29 E
Pinang → George Town 114 5.25 N 100.20 E
Pinang □[3] 114 5.20 N 100.20 E
Pinang, Pulau I 114 5.23 N 100.15 E
Pinangah 112 5.12 N 116.50 E
Pınarbaşı, Tür. 130 41.36 N 33.07 E
Pınarbaşı, Tür. 130 38.44 N 36.24 E
Pinar del Río 240p 22.25 N 83.42 W
Pinar del Río □[4] 240p 22.30 N 83.45 W
Pinardville 188 42.59 N 71.30 W
Pınarhisar 130 41.37 N 27.30 E
Pınarlar 130 38.53 N 39.29 E
Pinas, Arg. 252 31.09 S 65.29 W
Piñas, Ec. 246 3.42 S 79.42 W
Piñas, Cerro ∧ 236 15.25 N 85.47 W
Pinatubo, Mount ∧ 116 15.08 N 120.21 E
Pinazo, Arroyo ≃ 288 34.24 S 58.48 W
Pinchbeck 42 52.48 N 0.09 W
Pincher Creek 182 49.29 N 113.57 W
Pinchi Lake ⊘ 182 54.35 N 124.20 W
Pinckney 216 42.27 N 83.56 W
Pinckney State Recreation Area ♦ 216 42.25 N 84.04 W
Pinckneyville 194 38.04 N 89.22 W
Pinconning 190 43.51 N 83.57 W
Pincourt 206 45.23 N 74.00 W
Pinčuga 86 58.23 N 96.59 E
Pińczów 30 50.32 N 20.35 E
Pindaíba, Ribeirão ≃ 255 14.18 S 51.45 W
Pindale 110 21.11 N 95.51 E
Pindamonhangaba 256 22.55 S 45.28 W
Pindar 162 28.29 S 115.48 E
Pindaré ≃ 250 3.17 S 44.47 W
Pindaré-Mirim 250 3.37 S 45.21 W
Pind Dādan Khān 123 32.35 N 73.03 E
Pinde → Píndhos Óros ⋏ 38 39.49 N 21.14 E
Pinder Point > 192 26.28 N 78.39 W
Píndhos Óros (Pindus Mountains) ⋏ 38 39.49 N 21.14 E
Pindi Bhattiān 123 31.54 N 73.16 E
Pindiga 146 9.59 N 10.54 E
Pindi Gheb 123 33.14 N 72.16 E
Pindo → Píndhos Óros ⋏ 38 39.49 N 21.14 E
Pindobaçu 250 10.44 S 40.21 W
Pindorama de Goiás 250 10.55 S 47.40 W
Pinduši 24 62.56 N 34.35 E
Pindus Mountains → Píndhos Óros ⋏ 38 39.49 N 21.14 E
Pindwāra 120 24.48 N 73.04 E
Pine ≃, B.C., Can. 182 56.08 N 120.41 W
Pine ≃, Mb., Can. 184 52.00 N 100.09 W
Pine ≃, On., Can. 212 44.20 N 79.52 W
Pine ≃, Mi., U.S. 190 44.15 N 85.55 W
Pine ≃, Mi., U.S. 190 43.35 N 84.08 W
Pine ≃, Mi., U.S. 190 46.03 N 84.40 W
Pine ≃, Mi., U.S. 190 44.26 N 83.21 W
Pine ≃, Mi., U.S. 214 42.49 N 82.29 W
Pine ≃, Wi., U.S. 190 44.08 N 88.54 W
Pine ≃, Wi., U.S. 190 45.50 N 88.08 W
Pine ≃, Wi., U.S. 190 43.12 N 90.18 W
Pine Apple 194 31.52 N 86.59 W
Pine Banks Park ♦ 283 42.26 N 71.04 W
Pine Barrens ◆[1] 208 39.48 N 74.35 W
Pine Beach 206 45.32 N 73.57 W
Pine Bluff 194 34.13 N 92.00 W
Pine Bluffs 198 41.10 N 104.04 W
Pine Brook 276 40.52 N 74.20 W
Pine Brook ≃, U.S. 276 41.04 N 74.05 W
Pine Brook ≃, Ma., U.S. 283 42.00 N 70.47 W
Pine Brook ≃, N.J., U.S. 276 40.19 N 74.20 W
Pine Bush 210 41.36 N 74.17 W
Pine Castle 220 28.28 N 81.22 W
Pine City, Mn., U.S. 190 45.49 N 92.58 W
Pine City, N.Y., U.S. 210 42.02 N 76.52 W
Pinecliff Lake ⊘ 276 41.08 N 74.23 W
Pinecraft 220 27.19 N 82.30 W
Pine Creek 164 13.49 S 131.49 E
Pine Creek ≃, Ab., Can. 182 54.56 N 112.31 W
Pine Creek ≃, Ca., U.S. 204 40.40 N 120.46 W
Pine Creek ≃, Ca., U.S. 282 37.58 N 122.02 W
Pine Creek ≃, Nv., U.S. 204 40.36 N 116.10 W
Pine Creek ≃, Pa., U.S. 210 41.10 N 77.16 W
Pine Creek ≃, Pa., U.S. 279b 40.30 N 79.57 W
Pine Creek ≃, Pa., U.S. 285 40.05 N 75.37 W
Pine Creek, West Branch ≃ 210 41.43 N 77.38 W
Pine Creek Indian Reserve ◆[4] 184 52.03 N 100.14 W
Pine Creek Lake ⊘[1] 196 34.05 N 95.05 W
Pine Creek Point > 276 41.07 N 73.16 W
Pine Crest, Fl., U.S. 220 28.01 N 82.32 W
Pinecrest, Va., U.S. 208 38.50 N 77.09 W
Pinecrest Lake ⊘ 226 38.12 N 119.58 W
Pine Crest Point > 284a 42.52 N 79.11 W
Pinedale 200 42.52 N 109.51 W
Pine Falls 184 50.35 N 96.15 W
Pine Flat Lake ⊘[1] 226 36.52 N 119.18 W
Pinega 24 64.42 N 43.19 E
Pinega ≃ 24 64.08 N 41.54 E
Pine Glen 212 45.19 N 75.43 W
Pine Grove, On., Can. 275b 43.48 N 79.35 W
Pine Grove, Ca., U.S. 226 38.25 N 120.39 W
Pine Grove, Fl., U.S. 220 28.16 N 81.11 W
Pine Grove, N.J., U.S. 285 39.53 N 74.52 W
Pine Grove, Pa., U.S. 208 40.32 N 76.23 W
Pine Grove, W.V., U.S. 188 39.33 N 80.40 W
Pine Grove Mills 214 40.44 N 77.53 W
Pine Hill, Austl. 166 23.39 S 146.58 E
Pine Hill, Al., U.S. 194 31.58 N 87.35 W
Pine Hill, N.J., U.S. 208 39.47 N 74.59 W
Pine Hill, N.Y., U.S. 210 42.08 N 74.29 W
Pinehill, Tx., U.S. 222 32.06 N 94.36 W
Pine Hills 220 28.33 N 81.27 W
Pinehouse Lake 184 55.31 N 106.36 W
Pinehouse Lake ⊘ 184 55.32 N 106.35 W
Pinehurst, Ga., U.S. 192 32.11 N 83.45 W
Pinehurst, Id., U.S. 202 45.15 N 116.20 W
Pinehurst, Ma., U.S. 207 42.31 N 71.13 W
Pinehurst, N.Y., U.S. 284a 42.44 N 78.57 W
Pinehurst, N.C., U.S. 192 35.11 N 79.28 W
Pinehurst, Tx., U.S. 222 30.10 N 95.41 W
Pinehurst Lake ⊘ 182 54.39 N 111.25 W
Pine Island, Mn., U.S. 190 44.12 N 92.38 W
Pine Island, N.Y., U.S. 210 41.17 N 74.27 W
Pine Island I 220 26.35 N 82.06 W
Pine Island Bay c 9 74.50 S 102.05 W
Pine Island Bayou ≃ 194 30.10 N 94.07 W
Pine Island Creek ≃ 283 42.47 N 70.48 W
Pine Island Dam ◆[6] 214 40.08 N 80.43 W
Pine Island Sound ʮ 220 26.33 N 82.10 W
Pine Lake, In., U.S. 216 41.38 N 86.45 W
Pine Lake, Ma., U.S. 283 42.23 N 71.27 W
Pine Lake ⊘, On., Can. 212 44.57 N 79.27 W
Pine Lake ⊘, Mi., U.S. 281 42.35 N 83.20 W
Pine Lake ⊘, N.Y., U.S. 210 43.12 N 74.31 W
Pineland 194 31.14 N 93.58 W
Pine Lawn 219 38.41 N 90.16 W
Pinellas □[6] 220 27.53 N 82.43 W
Pinellas, Point > 220 27.42 N 82.38 W
Pinellas Park 220 27.50 N 82.41 W
Pine Marsh ≡ 276 40.37 N 73.34 W
Pine Meadow Lake ⊘ 276 41.11 N 74.07 W
Pine Mountain ∧, U.S. 192 36.55 N 83.20 W
Pine Mountain ∧, Ca., U.S. 226 35.41 N 121.05 W
Pine Mountain ∧, Ca., U.S. 280 34.13 N 117.54 W
Pine Mountain ∧, Ct., U.S. 207 41.58 N 72.56 W
Pine Mountain ∧, Ga., U.S. 192 32.51 N 84.47 W
Pine Mountain ∧, Or., U.S. 202 43.47 N 120.54 W
Pine Mountain ∧, Wy., U.S. 200 41.02 N 109.01 W
Pine Nut Mountains ⋏ 226 39.00 N 119.25 W
Pine Orchard Meadows 284b 39.17 N 76.52 W
Pine Pass )( 182 55.22 N 122.40 W
Pine Plains 210 41.59 N 73.40 W
Pine Point, Austl. 168b 34.34 S 137.52 E
Pine Point, N.T., Can. 176 61.01 N 114.15 W
Pine Point Park ♦ 275b 43.43 N 79.33 W
Pine Portage Dam ◆[6] 176 49.18 N 88.19 W
Pine Prairie 194 30.47 N 92.25 W
Piner 218 38.50 N 84.32 W
Pine Rest 283 42.23 N 71.26 W
Pine Ridge, Pa., U.S. 285 39.55 N 75.22 W
Pine Ridge, S.D., U.S. 198 43.01 N 102.33 W
Pine Ridge, Va., U.S. 284c 38.52 N 77.14 W
Pine Ridge ∧ 198 42.40 N 103.00 W
Pine Ridge Estates 276 41.02 N 73.41 W
Pine Ridge Indian Reservation ◆[4] 198 43.25 N 102.21 W
Pine River, Mb., Can. 184 51.47 N 100.32 W
Pine River, Mn., U.S. 190 46.43 N 94.24 W
Piñero 258 34.32 S 58.45 W
Pinerolo 62 44.53 N 7.21 E
Piñeros, Isla I 240m 18.15 N 65.35 W
Pinerovka 80 51.34 N 43.04 E
Pine Run ≃ 279b 40.37 N 79.35 W
Pines ≃ 283 42.27 N 70.58 W
Pines, Isle of → Juventud, Isla de la I 240p 21.40 N 82.50 W
Pines, Lake O' The ⊘[1] 222 32.46 N 94.35 W
Pines, Point of > 283 42.26 N 70.58 W
Pine Shores 220 27.17 N 82.32 W
Pines Lake ⊘ 276 41.00 N 74.16 W
Pines Run ≃ 285 39.50 N 75.05 W
Pine Swamp Knob ∧ 188 39.33 N 79.31 W
Pineto 66 42.36 N 14.04 E
Pinetop 200 34.07 N 109.56 W
Pinetops 192 35.47 N 77.38 W
Pinetown 158 29.52 S 30.46 E
Pine Tree Hill ∧ 114 3.43 N 101.42 E
Pine Valley, Md., U.S. 284b 39.26 N 76.39 W
Pine Valley, N.Y., U.S. 210 42.14 N 76.51 W
Pine Valley V 204 38.25 N 113.40 W
Pine Village 216 40.27 N 87.15 W
Pineville, Ky., U.S. 192 36.45 N 83.41 W
Pineville, La., U.S. 194 31.19 N 92.26 W
Pineville, Mo., U.S. 194 36.35 N 94.23 W
Pineville, N.C., U.S. 192 35.04 N 80.53 W
Pineville, Pa., U.S. 208 40.18 N 75.00 W
Pineville, W.V., U.S. 192 37.34 N 81.32 W
Pinewood, Fl., U.S. 220 25.53 N 80.14 W
Pinewood, S.C., U.S. 192 33.44 N 80.27 W
Piney 50 48.22 N 4.20 E
Piney ≃ 194 35.49 N 87.33 W
Piney Branch ≃ 284c 38.56 N 77.18 W
Piney Creek ≃, Tx., U.S. 222 31.03 N 94.34 W
Piney Creek ≃, Wy., U.S. 202 44.34 N 106.32 W
Piney Fork 214 40.15 N 80.50 W
Piney Point 222 29.46 N 95.31 W
Piney Point > 208 38.08 N 76.32 W
Piney Run ≃ 284c 38.58 N 77.17 W
Piney Woods 194 32.03 N 89.59 W
Pinfold 262 53.36 N 2.55 W
Ping ≃, Thai 110 15.42 N 100.09 E
Ping ≃, Zhg. 100 25.59 N 115.07 E


**Symbols** in the index entries represent the broad categories identified in the key at the right. Symbols with superior numbers (⋏[1]) identify subcategories (see complete key on page I · 1).

**Symbole** im Register stellen die rechts im Schlüssel erklärten Kategorien dar. Symbole mit hochgestellten Ziffern (⋏[1]) bezeichnen Unterabteilungen einer Kategorie (vgl. vollständiger Schlüssel auf Seite I · 1).

**Los símbolos** incluídos en el texto del índice representan las grandes categorías identificadas con la clave a la derecha. Los símbolos con numeros en su parte superior (⋏[1]) identifican las subcategorías (véase la clave completa en la página I · 1).

**Les symboles** de l'index représentent les catégories indiquées dans la légende à droite. Les symboles suivis d'un indice (⋏[1]) représentent des sous-catégories (voir légende complète à la page I · 1).

**Os símbolos** incluídos no texto do índice representam as grandes categorias identificadas com a chave à direita. Os símbolos com números em sua parte superior (⋏[1]) identificam as subcategorias (veja-se a chave completa à página I · 1).

| | English | Deutsch | Español | Français | Português |
|---|---|---|---|---|---|
| ∧ | Mountain | Berg | Montaña | Montagne | Montanha |
| ⋏ | Mountains | Gebirge | Montañas | Montagnes | Montanhas |
| )( | Pass | Paß | Paso | Col | Passo |
| V | Valley, Canyon | Tal, Cañon | Valle, Cañón | Vallée, Canyon | Vale, Canhão |
| ≚ | Plain | Ebene | Llano | Plaine | Planície |
| > | Cape | Kap | Cabo | Cap | Cabo |
| I | Island | Insel | Isla | Île | Ilha |
| II | Islands | Inseln | Islas | Îles | Ilhas |
| ⊥ | Other Topographic Features | Andere Topographische Objekte | Otros Elementos Topográficos | Autres données topographiques | Outros acidentes topográficos |

| Nombre / Nom / Nome | Página / Page | Lat.°′ | Long.°′ W = Oeste / W = Ouest |
|---|---|---|---|
| Pinga | 154 | 1.01 S | 28.42 E |
| Ping'an, Zhg. | 89 | 45.20 N | 123.42 E |
| Ping'an, Zhg. | 104 | 41.11 N | 123.26 E |
| Ping'an, Zhg. | 107 | 30.36 N | 104.42 E |
| Ping'anbu | 98 | 41.45 N | 116.13 E |
| Ping'ancheng | 105 | 40.03 N | 117.48 E |
| Ping'andi | 104 | 42.34 N | 121.52 E |
| Pingaring | 162 | 32.45 S | 118.37 E |
| Pingba, Zhg. | 100 | 31.19 N | 113.18 E |
| Pingba, Zhg. | 102 | 26.22 N | 106.09 E |
| Pingchang | 102 | 31.35 N | 107.03 E |
| Pingchao | 106 | 32.07 N | 120.45 E |
| Pingding | 98 | 37.48 N | 113.37 E |
| Pingdingpu | 104 | 42.22 N | 123.55 E |
| Pingdingshan, Zhg. | 98 | 41.26 N | 124.45 E |
| Pingdingshan, Zhg. | 100 | 33.45 N | 113.17 E |
| Pingding Shan ∧ | 89 | 46.38 N | 128.27 E |
| Pingdu | 98 | 36.47 N | 119.54 E |
| Pingelap I[1] | 14 | 6.13 N | 160.42 E |
| Pingelly | 162 | 32.32 S | 117.05 E |
| Pingfang, Zhg. | 100 | 30.07 N | 113.48 E |
| Pingfang, Zhg. | 104 | 41.17 N | 120.40 E |
| Pingfang, Zhg. | 104 | 41.28 N | 120.48 E |
| Pingfang, Zhg. | 104 | 42.14 N | 120.38 E |
| Pingfang, Zhg. | 104 | 42.27 N | 120.38 E |
| Pingfang, Zhg. | 271a | 39.56 N | 116.33 E |
| Pingfangdu | 104 | 41.45 N | 121.12 E |
| Pingfangzi | 104 | 41.31 N | 121.21 E |
| Pinggau | 61 | 47.27 N | 16.04 E |
| Pinggu | 105 | 40.09 N | 117.07 E |
| Pingguo | 102 | 23.19 N | 107.39 E |
| Pinghai, Zhg. | 100 | 25.14 N | 119.15 E |
| Pinghai, Zhg. | 100 | 22.39 N | 114.53 E |
| Pinghe, Zhg. | 100 | 24.25 N | 117.22 E |
| Pinghe, Zhg. | 102 | 22.51 N | 102.30 E |
| Pinghe ≃ | 100 | 24.25 N | 116.36 E |
| P'inghsiang → Pingxiang | 102 | 22.09 N | 106.43 E |
| Pinghu, Zhg. | 100 | 26.46 N | 118.48 E |
| Pinghu, Zhg. | 100 | 30.56 N | 115.22 E |
| Pinghu, Zhg. | 100 | 22.42 N | 114.08 E |
| Pinghu, Zhg. | 106 | 30.42 N | 121.01 E |
| Pingjiang | 100 | 28.44 N | 113.34 E |
| Pingjing | 105 | 39.20 N | 116.06 E |
| Pinglan | 100 | 22.22 N | 113.27 E |
| Pingle, Zhg. | 102 | 24.37 N | 110.40 E |
| Pingle, Zhg. | 102 | 24.31 N | 106.59 E |
| Pingli | 102 | 32.19 N | 109.21 E |
| Pingliang | 102 | 35.32 N | 106.41 E |
| Pinglidian | 98 | 37.17 N | 119.59 E |
| Pingling | 100 | 23.39 N | 114.23 E |
| Pinglucheng | 102 | 39.50 N | 112.19 E |
| Pingluo | 102 | 38.57 N | 106.35 E |
| Pingluopu | 104 | 41.56 N | 123.20 E |
| Pingnan, Zhg. | 100 | 26.56 N | 119.02 E |
| Pingnan, Zhg. | 102 | 23.30 N | 110.30 E |
| Pingqiao | 100 | 33.24 N | 119.13 E |
| Pingquan | 98 | 40.59 N | 118.34 E |
| Pingrup | 162 | 33.32 S | 118.31 E |
| Ping Shan, H.K. | 271d | 22.27 N | 114.00 E |
| Pingshan, Zhg. | 100 | 25.36 N | 117.52 E |
| Pingshan, Zhg. | 100 | 23.26 N | 113.15 E |
| Pingshan, Zhg. | 100 | 22.43 N | 114.22 E |
| Pingshan, Zhg. | 102 | 38.15 N | 114.10 E |
| Pingshang | 98 | 35.11 N | 119.07 E |
| Pingshi, Zhg. | 100 | 32.32 N | 113.03 E |
| Pingshi, Zhg. | 100 | 25.20 N | 113.02 E |
| Pingshui | 100 | 29.53 N | 120.38 E |
| Pingtaizi | 105 | 40.44 N | 116.25 E |
| Pingtan, Zhg. | 100 | 25.31 N | 119.47 E |
| Pingtan, Zhg. | 100 | 23.04 N | 114.38 E |
| Pingtan, Zhg. | 107 | 29.50 N | 105.56 E |
| Pingtan, Zhg. | 107 | 29.38 N | 105.16 E |
| Pingtan Dao I | 100 | 25.33 N | 119.48 E |
| Pingtang | 102 | 25.50 N | 107.19 E |
| Pingtian | 100 | 25.19 N | 113.31 E |
| P'ingtung | 100 | 22.40 N | 120.29 E |
| Pingües, Cayos II | 240p | 20.47 N | 78.15 W |
| Pingwang | 106 | 30.59 N | 120.38 E |
| Pingwu | 102 | 32.29 N | 104.37 E |
| Pingxiang, Zhg. | 100 | 27.38 N | 113.50 E |
| Pingxiang, Zhg. | 102 | 22.09 N | 106.43 E |
| Pingyang, Zhg. | 89 | 48.13 N | 124.23 E |
| Pingyang, Zhg. | 100 | 27.41 N | 120.33 E |
| Pingyao, Zhg. | 102 | 37.16 N | 112.09 E |
| Pingyao, Zhg. | 106 | 30.24 N | 119.58 E |
| Pingyi | 98 | 35.34 N | 117.37 E |
| Pingyin | 98 | 36.19 N | 116.22 E |
| Pingyu | 100 | 32.57 N | 114.41 E |
| Pingyuan, Zhg. | 98 | 37.11 N | 116.25 E |
| Pingyuan, Zhg. | 100 | 24.36 N | 115.54 E |
| Pingzhai | 102 | 24.07 N | 104.22 E |
| Pingzhuang | 98 | 42.03 N | 119.22 E |
| Pinhal | 256 | 22.12 S | 46.45 W |
| Pinhal, Ribeirão do ≃ | 256 | 22.42 S | 46.42 W |
| Pinhal Novo | 34 | 38.38 N | 8.55 W |
| Pinhalzinho | 256 | 22.46 S | 46.36 W |
| Pinhão | 250 | 10.34 S | 37.44 W |
| Pinheiral | 256 | 22.31 S | 43.59 W |
| Pinheirinhos | 256 | 22.26 S | 44.59 W |
| Pinheiro | 250 | 2.31 S | 45.05 W |
| Pinheiro de Loures | 266c | 38.50 N | 9.12 W |
| Pinheiro Machado | 252 | 31.34 S | 53.23 W |
| Pinheiros, Bra. | 255 | 18.21 S | 40.14 W |
| Pinheiros, Bra. | 256 | 22.32 S | 44.54 W |
| Pinheiros ≃ | 287b | 23.32 S | 46.44 W |
| Pinhel | 34 | 40.46 N | 7.04 W |
| Pinhoe | 42 | 50.44 N | 3.27 W |
| Pinhuã ≃ | 248 | 6.21 S | 65.00 W |
| Pini, Pulau I | 110 | 0.08 N | 98.40 E |
| Pinillos | 246 | 8.55 N | 74.28 W |
| Piniós ≃ | 38 | 39.54 N | 22.45 E |
| Pinitos, Sierra de ⋏ | 200 | 31.08 N | 110.50 W |
| Pinjar, Lake ⊜ | 168a | 31.38 S | 115.49 E |
| Pinjarra | 168a | 32.37 S | 115.53 E |
| Pinjor Garden ♦ | 123 | 30.47 N | 76.47 E |
| Pinka ≃ | 61 | 47.00 N | 16.35 E |
| Pinkafeld | 61 | 47.22 N | 16.07 E |
| Pinkiang → Harbin | 89 | 45.45 N | 126.41 E |
| Pinlaung | 110 | 20.08 N | 96.47 E |
| Pinlebu | 110 | 24.05 N | 95.21 E |
| Pinn ≃ | 260 | 51.31 N | 0.29 W |
| Pinnacle ∧, N.Z. | 172 | 41.49 S | 173.17 E |
| Pinnacle ∧, N.Y., U.S. | 188 | 43.13 N | 74.23 W |
| Pinnacle ∧, Va., U.S. | 188 | 39.08 N | 78.26 W |
| Pinnacle Buttes ∧ | 202 | 43.44 N | 109.57 W |
| Pinnacle Island I | 180 | 60.12 N | 172.46 W |
| Pinnacle Peak ∧ | 224 | 46.45 N | 121.43 W |
| Pinnacles National Monument ♦ | 226 | 36.28 N | 121.19 W |
| Pinnaroo | 166 | 35.16 S | 140.55 E |
| Pinneberg | 52 | 53.40 N | 9.47 E |
| Pinner ◆[8] | 260 | 51.36 N | 0.23 W |
| Pino, Sierra del ⋏ | 196 | 28.15 N | 103.03 W |
| Pin Oak Creek ≃ | 222 | 31.57 N | 96.28 W |
| Pinocchio | 66 | 43.35 N | 13.30 E |
| Pinochle Peak ∧ | 224 | 45.43 N | 123.36 W |
| Pinole | 226 | 38.00 N | 122.17 W |
| Pinole Creek ≃ | 282 | 38.01 N | 122.18 W |
| Pinole Point › | 282 | 38.01 N | 122.22 W |
| Pinole Ridge ∧ | 282 | 37.59 N | 122.15 W |
| Pinos | 234 | 22.18 N | 101.34 W |
| Pinos, Mount ∧ | 228 | 34.50 N | 119.09 W |
| Pinos, Point › | 226 | 36.38 N | 121.56 W |
| Pinos Puente | 34 | 37.15 N | 3.45 W |
| Pinotepa de Don Luis | 234 | 16.25 N | 97.55 W |
| Pinrang | 112 | 3.48 S | 119.38 E |
| Pins, Île de → Juventud, Isla de la I | 240p | 21.40 N | 82.50 W |
| Pins, Île des I | 175f | 22.37 S | 167.30 E |
| Pins, Pointe aux › | 214 | 42.15 N | 81.51 W |
| Pins, Rivière des ≃ | 206 | 46.01 N | 72.03 W |
| Pinsk | 76 | 52.07 N | 26.04 E |
| Pinson | 194 | 33.41 N | 86.41 W |
| Pinsot | 62 | 45.21 N | 6.06 E |
| Pinta, Isla I | 246a | 0.35 N | 90.44 W |
| Pintada Arroyo V | 196 | 34.53 N | 104.39 W |
| Pintado | 258 | 33.50 S | 56.18 W |
| Pintado ≃ | 255 | 13.33 S | 50.16 W |
| Pintado, Arroyo de ≃ | 258 | 34.08 S | 56.14 W |
| Pintado, Cuchilla del ⋏[2] | 258 | 34.12 S | 56.25 W |
| Pintados | 248 | 20.37 S | 69.38 W |
| Pintados, Salar de ≃ | 248 | 20.30 S | 69.42 W |
| Pintasan | 112 | 5.26 N | 117.43 E |
| Pinteus | 266c | 38.52 N | 9.09 W |
| Pintlala Creek ≃ | 194 | 32.21 N | 86.30 W |
| Pinto Butte ∧ | 184 | 49.22 N | 107.25 W |
| Pinto Creek ≃, Ab., Can. | 182 | 53.51 N | 117.35 W |
| Pinto Creek ≃, Sk., Can. | 184 | 49.40 N | 106.42 W |
| Pintos, Arroyo de ≃ | 258 | 33.55 S | 56.51 W |
| Pintos Negreiros | 256 | 22.18 S | 45.13 W |
| Pintoyacu ≃, Ec. | 246 | 2.07 S | 76.03 W |
| Pintoyacu ≃, Perú | 246 | 3.35 S | 73.55 W |
| Pinturas ≃ | 254 | 46.35 S | 70.18 W |
| Pintuyan | 116 | 9.57 N | 125.15 E |
| Pin'ug | 24 | 60.15 N | 47.48 E |
| Pinukpuk | 116 | 17.35 N | 121.22 E |
| Pinwherry | 44 | 55.09 N | 4.50 W |
| Pinxton | 44 | 53.06 N | 1.19 W |
| Pinzano al Tagliamento | 64 | 46.11 N | 12.57 E |
| Pinzgau V | 64 | 47.15 N | 12.40 E |
| Pinzón, Isla I | 246a | 0.36 S | 90.40 W |
| Piobbico | 66 | 43.35 N | 12.31 E |
| Pioche | 204 | 37.55 N | 114.27 W |
| Pio IX | 250 | 6.50 S | 40.37 W |
| Piolenc | 62 | 44.11 N | 4.46 E |
| Piombino | 66 | 42.55 N | 10.32 E |
| Piombino, Canale di ⋓ | 66 | 42.53 N | 10.30 E |
| Pioneer, Austl. | 162 | 31.48 S | 121.43 E |
| Pioneer, Ca., U.S. | 226 | 38.25 N | 120.33 W |
| Pioneer, Oh., U.S. | 216 | 41.40 N | 84.33 W |
| Pioneer Mine | 182 | 50.46 N | 122.46 W |
| Pioneer Mountains ⋏ | 202 | 45.40 N | 113.00 W |
| Pioneer Park ♦ | 273d | 26.14 S | 28.04 E |
| Pioner, ostrov I | 74 | 79.50 N | 92.30 E |
| Pionerskij | 76 | 54.57 N | 20.20 E |
| Pionierbivak | 164 | 2.16 S | 138.02 E |
| Pionki | 30 | 51.30 N | 21.27 E |
| Pio Pico State Historical Monument ♦ | 280 | 33.59 N | 118.04 W |
| Piopio | 172 | 38.28 S | 175.01 E |
| Pioppo | 70 | 38.03 N | 13.14 E |
| Piora, Mount ∧ | 164 | 6.45 S | 146.00 E |
| Pioraco | 66 | 43.11 N | 12.59 E |
| Piorini ≃ | 246 | 3.23 S | 63.30 W |
| Piorini, Lago ⊜ | 246 | 3.34 S | 63.15 W |
| Piotrków Trybunalski | 30 | 51.25 N | 19.42 E |
| Piotrków Trybunalski □[4] | 30 | 51.30 N | 19.45 E |
| Piotta | 58 | 46.31 N | 8.40 E |
| Pio V. Corpus (Limbujan) | 116 | 11.53 N | 124.03 E |
| Piove di Sacco | 64 | 45.18 N | 12.02 E |
| Piovene-Rocchette | 64 | 45.45 N | 11.25 E |
| Pio XII | 250 | 3.53 S | 45.17 W |
| Pipa | 107 | 29.07 N | 105.05 E |
| Pipalkoti | 124 | 30.26 N | 79.27 E |
| Pipanaco, Salar de ≃ | 252 | 28.07 S | 66.25 W |
| Pīpār | 120 | 26.23 N | 73.32 E |
| Piparia | 124 | 22.45 N | 78.21 E |
| Pīpār Road | 120 | 26.27 N | 73.27 E |
| Pipas | 152 | 14.56 S | 12.12 E |
| Pipe Creek ≃, In., U.S. | 194 | 40.08 N | 85.52 W |
| Pipe Creek ≃, In., U.S. | 216 | 40.45 N | 86.13 W |
| Pipe Creek ≃, In., U.S. | 218 | 39.26 N | 85.06 W |
| Piper City | 216 | 40.45 N | 88.11 W |
| Pipe Spring National Monument ♦ | 200 | 36.43 N | 112.33 W |
| Pipestem Creek ≃ | 198 | 46.54 N | 98.43 W |
| Pipestem State Park ♦ | 192 | 37.32 N | 81.00 W |
| Pipestone | 198 | 44.00 N | 96.19 W |
| Pipestone ≃ | 176 | 52.53 N | 89.23 W |
| Pipestone Creek ≃, Can. | 184 | 49.42 N | 100.45 W |
| Pipestone Creek ≃, Mi., U.S. | 216 | 42.04 N | 86.24 W |
| Pipestone National Monument ♦ | 198 | 44.00 N | 96.18 W |
| Pipi ≃ | 146 | 7.27 N | 22.48 E |
| Pipinas | 258 | 35.32 S | 57.20 W |
| Piping Brook ≃ | 276 | 41.08 N | 73.37 W |
| Pipiriki | 172 | 39.29 S | 175.03 E |
| Piplān | 123 | 32.17 N | 71.21 E |
| Piplūn | 126 | 23.21 N | 88.07 E |
| Pipmuacan, Réservoir ⊜[1] | 186 | 49.35 N | 70.30 W |
| Pipri | 124 | 23.58 N | 82.40 E |
| Pipriac | 28 | 47.49 N | 1.57 W |
| Piqiang | 85 | 40.20 N | 77.38 E |
| Piqiao | 106 | 31.34 N | 119.27 E |
| Piqua | 218 | 40.08 N | 84.14 W |
| Piquet Carneiro | 250 | 5.48 S | 39.25 W |
| Piquete | 256 | 22.36 S | 45.11 W |
| Piquete, Ribeirão ≃ | 256 | 22.36 S | 45.01 W |
| Piquiri ≃, Bra. | 248 | 17.39 S | 55.09 W |
| Piquiri ≃, Bra. | 248 | 17.18 S | 56.44 W |
| Piquiri ≃, Bra. | 252 | 24.03 S | 54.14 W |
| Pira | 150 | 8.30 N | 1.44 E |
| Piracaia | 256 | 23.03 S | 46.21 W |
| Piracanjuba | 255 | 17.18 S | 49.01 W |
| Piracanjuba ≃ | 255 | 18.14 S | 48.48 W |
| Piracão ≃ | 287a | 23.02 S | 43.36 W |
| Piracicaba | 255 | 22.43 S | 47.38 W |
| Piracicaba ≃ | 255 | 22.36 S | 48.19 W |
| Piraçununga | 255 | 21.59 S | 47.25 W |
| Piracuruca | 250 | 3.56 S | 41.42 W |
| Pirae | 174s | 17.32 S | 149.33 W |
| Piraeus → Piraiévs | 38 | 37.57 N | 23.38 E |
| Pirahmet | 130 | 38.11 N | 39.51 E |
| Piraí | 256 | 22.38 S | 43.54 W |
| Piraí ≃ | 256 | 22.28 S | 43.50 W |
| Piraí do Sul | 252 | 24.31 S | 49.56 W |
| Piraiévs (Piraeus) | 38 | 37.57 N | 23.38 E |
| Piraino | 70 | 38.10 N | 14.52 E |
| Piraju | 255 | 23.12 S | 49.23 W |
| Pirajuba | 255 | 19.54 S | 48.42 W |
| Pirajucara, Ribeirão ≃ | 287b | 23.34 S | 46.43 W |
| Pirajuí | 255 | 21.59 S | 49.29 W |
| Pirakata | 126 | 22.34 N | 87.11 E |
| Piramida, gora ∧ | 88 | 54.15 N | 95.45 E |
| Piramidal'nyj, pik ∧ | 85 | 39.34 N | 69.57 E |
| Pirámide de Cuicuilco ⊥ | 286a | 19.18 N | 99.11 W |
| Pirámide de Santa Cecilia ⊥ | 286a | 19.33 N | 99.09 W |
| Pirámide de Tenayuca ⊥ | 286a | 19.32 N | 99.11 W |
| Piram Island I | 120 | 21.36 N | 72.41 E |
| Piran | 36 | 45.32 N | 13.34 E |
| Piraña, Arroyo ≃ | 288 | 34.24 S | 58.30 W |
| Pirané | 252 | 25.43 S | 59.06 W |
| Piranga | 255 | 20.41 S | 43.18 W |
| Pirangaí | 256 | 22.34 S | 44.37 W |
| Piranguçu | 256 | 22.31 S | 45.30 W |
| Piranguinho | 256 | 22.24 S | 45.32 W |
| Piranhas | 255 | 16.31 S | 51.51 W |
| Piranhas ≃, Bra. | 250 | 5.15 S | 36.45 W |
| Piranhas ≃, Bra. | 250 | 8.40 S | 49.28 W |
| Piranhas ≃, Bra. | 250 | 5.56 S | 48.15 W |
| Piranji ≃ | 250 | 4.23 S | 37.48 W |
| Pīrān Shahr | 128 | 36.41 N | 45.08 E |
| Pirapemas | 250 | 3.43 S | 44.14 W |
| Pirapetinga ≃ | 256 | 21.37 S | 42.32 W |
| Pirapetinga, Ribeirão ≃ | 256 | 21.49 S | 43.36 W |
| Pirapó ≃ | 255 | 22.30 S | 52.01 W |
| Pirapora | 255 | 17.21 S | 44.56 W |
| Pirapora do Bom Jesus | 256 | 23.24 S | 47.00 W |
| Pirapora do Bom Jesus □[7] | 287b | 23.24 S | 46.56 W |
| Piraputanga | 255 | 20.26 S | 55.32 W |
| Piraquara | 252 | 25.26 S | 49.04 W |
| Piraquê ≃ | 287a | 23.01 S | 43.37 W |
| Pirarajá | 252 | 33.44 S | 54.45 W |
| Pirata, Monte ∧[2] | 240m | 18.06 N | 65.33 W |
| Pirate Creek ≃ | 282 | 37.33 N | 121.52 W |
| Piratinga ≃ | 255 | 15.41 S | 46.07 W |
| Piratini | 252 | 31.27 S | 53.06 W |
| Piratini ≃ | 252 | 28.06 S | 55.27 W |
| Piratininga | 287a | 22.57 S | 43.04 W |
| Piratininga, Lagoa ⊂ | 256 | 22.57 S | 43.05 W |
| Piratuba | 252 | 27.27 S | 51.48 W |
| Piratuba, Lago ⊂ | 250 | 1.37 N | 50.10 W |
| Piratucu ≃ | 250 | 1.59 S | 56.58 W |
| Piraúba | 256 | 21.17 S | 43.02 W |
| Piraube, Lac ⊜ | 186 | 50.33 N | 71.42 W |
| Piray ≃ | 248 | 16.32 S | 63.45 W |
| Piraziz | 130 | 40.58 N | 38.08 E |
| Pirbright | 260 | 51.18 N | 0.39 W |
| Pirdop | 38 | 42.42 N | 24.11 E |
| Pirenópolis | 255 | 15.51 S | 48.57 W |
| Pires, Ribeirão ≃ | 287b | 23.43 S | 46.25 W |
| Pires do Rio | 255 | 17.18 S | 48.17 W |
| Pírgos | 38 | 37.41 N | 21.28 E |
| Piriá | 250 | 1.40 S | 50.02 W |
| Piriápolis | 252 | 34.54 S | 55.17 W |
| Piribebuy | 252 | 25.29 S | 57.03 W |
| Pirin ⋏ | 38 | 41.40 N | 23.30 E |
| Pirinççi ◆[8] | 267b | 41.10 N | 28.50 E |
| Pirineos → Pyrenees ⋏ | 34 | 42.40 N | 1.00 E |
| Piripiri | 250 | 4.16 S | 41.47 W |
| Piritiba | 250 | 11.44 S | 40.34 W |
| Píritu, Ven. | 246 | 11.22 N | 69.08 W |
| Píritu, Ven. | 246 | 9.23 N | 69.12 W |
| Pirituba ◆[8] | 287b | 23.29 S | 46.43 W |
| Pīr Mahal | 123 | 30.46 N | 72.26 E |
| Pirmasens | 56 | 49.12 N | 7.36 E |
| Pirna | 54 | 50.58 N | 13.56 E |
| Piroči | 82 | 55.04 N | 38.57 E |
| Pirogovskij | 265b | 55.59 N | 37.44 E |
| Pirogovskoje vodochranilišče ⊜[1] | 82 | 55.58 N | 37.40 E |
| Pirojpur | 126 | 22.34 N | 89.59 E |
| Pirón ≃ | 34 | 41.23 N | 4.31 W |
| Pirongia | 172 | 38.00 S | 175.12 E |
| Pirot | 38 | 43.09 N | 22.35 E |
| Pirovano | 252 | 36.30 S | 61.34 W |
| Pirovskoje | 86 | 57.37 N | 92.16 E |
| Pīr Panjāl Range ⋏ | 123 | 33.37 N | 74.32 E |
| Pirpirituba | 250 | 6.46 S | 35.30 W |
| Pirreşit Tepe ∧ | 84 | 38.56 N | 43.55 E |
| Pirsaat | 84 | 39.54 N | 49.24 E |
| Pirsaatçay ≃ | 84 | 39.53 N | 49.19 E |
| Pirtleville | 200 | 31.22 N | 109.34 W |
| Piru, Indon. | 164 | 3.04 S | 128.12 E |
| Piru, Ca., U.S. | 228 | 34.25 N | 118.48 W |
| Piru, Lake ⊜[1] | 228 | 34.30 N | 118.45 W |
| Piru, Teluk ⊂ | 164 | 3.10 S | 128.08 E |
| Piru Creek ≃ | 228 | 34.23 N | 118.47 W |
| Pisa | 66 | 43.43 N | 10.23 E |
| Pisa □[4] | 66 | 43.25 N | 10.43 E |
| Pisa ∧[2] | 26 | 63.13 N | 28.18 E |
| Pisa ≃ | 30 | 53.15 N | 21.52 E |
| Pisa, Certosa di ʊ[1] | 66 | 43.45 N | 10.31 E |
| Pisa, Mount ∧ | 172 | 44.52 S | 169.11 E |
| Pisagua | 248 | 19.36 S | 70.13 W |
| Pisam-bong ∧ | 98 | 40.41 N | 126.34 E |
| Pisang, Pulau I | 164 | 1.23 S | 128.55 E |
| Pisarevka | 78 | 49.53 N | 40.12 E |
| Pisarve | 272c | 19.06 N | 73.05 E |
| Pisau, Tanjong › | 116 | 6.04 N | 118.03 E |
| Piščalje | 80 | 58.14 N | 48.42 E |
| Piscasaw Creek ≃ | 216 | 42.16 N | 88.49 W |
| Piscataway | 210 | 40.29 N | 74.23 W |
| Piscataway Creek ≃, Md., U.S. | 208 | 38.42 N | 77.02 W |
| Piscataway Creek ≃, Va., U.S. | 208 | 37.54 N | 76.50 W |
| Pişchia | 38 | 45.55 N | 21.20 E |
| Pisciotta | 68 | 40.06 N | 15.14 E |
| Pisco | 248 | 13.42 S | 76.13 W |
| Pisco ≃ | 248 | 13.42 S | 76.15 W |
| Pişcolt | 38 | 47.35 N | 22.18 E |
| Piscovo | 80 | 57.11 N | 40.32 E |
| Piseco Lake ⊜ | 210 | 43.23 N | 74.36 W |
| Písek | 30 | 49.19 N | 14.10 E |
| Pisgah, Md., U.S. | 208 | 38.32 N | 77.08 W |
| Pisgah, Oh., U.S. | 218 | 39.19 N | 84.22 W |
| Pisgah Forest | 192 | 35.15 N | 82.42 W |
| Pishan | 120 | 37.37 N | 78.18 E |
| Pishchana | 78 | 48.08 N | 29.44 E |
| Pishchane, Ukr. | 78 | 49.44 N | 31.50 E |
| Pishchane, Ukr. | 83 | 49.34 N | 37.51 E |
| Pishchanka | 78 | 48.12 N | 28.53 E |
| Pishīn | 120 | 30.35 N | 67.00 E |
| Pishīn Lora (Lowrah) ≃ | 120 | 29.09 N | 64.55 E |
| Pısıdıa □[9] | 130 | 37.30 N | 31.00 E |
| Pisinemo | 200 | 32.02 N | 112.18 W |
| Pising | 112 | 5.05 S | 121.54 E |
| Piskivka | 78 | 50.42 N | 29.38 E |
| Pisky, Ukr. | 78 | 50.23 N | 33.27 E |
| Pisky, Ukr. | 83 | 49.26 N | 38.59 E |
| Pisky-Rad'kivs'ki | 83 | 49.17 N | 37.36 E |
| Pismo Beach | 226 | 35.08 N | 120.38 W |
| Pišnur | 80 | 57.47 N | 47.58 E |
| Piso, Lake ⊜ | 150 | 6.48 N | 11.17 W |
| Pisogne | 64 | 45.48 N | 10.06 E |
| Pisqui ≃ | 248 | 7.45 S | 75.01 W |
| Pissila | 150 | 13.10 N | 0.49 W |
| Pissos | 32 | 44.19 N | 0.47 W |
| Pistakee Highlands | 216 | 42.25 N | 88.11 W |
| Pistakee Lake ⊜ | 216 | 42.23 N | 88.12 W |
| Pisticci | 68 | 40.23 N | 16.34 E |
| Pistoia | 66 | 43.55 N | 10.54 E |
| Pistoia □[4] | 64 | 43.58 N | 10.50 E |
| Pistolet Bay ⊂ | 186 | 51.32 N | 55.50 W |
| Pistuk Peak ∧ | 180 | 59.43 N | 159.42 W |
| Pisuerga ≃ | 34 | 41.33 N | 4.52 W |
| Pisz | 30 | 53.38 N | 21.49 E |
| Pit ≃ | 204 | 40.45 N | 122.22 W |
| Pit, North Fork ≃ | 204 | 41.28 N | 120.33 W |
| Pit, South Fork ≃ | 204 | 41.28 N | 120.33 W |
| Pita | 150 | 11.05 N | 12.24 W |
| Pital | 246 | 2.16 N | 75.49 W |
| Pitalito | 246 | 1.51 N | 76.02 W |
| Pitampura Kālan ◆[8] | 272a | 28.42 N | 77.08 E |
| Pitanga | 252 | 24.46 S | 51.44 W |
| Pitangueiras | 255 | 21.02 S | 48.13 W |
| Pitangueiras, Ribeirão das ≃ | 256 | 21.27 S | 44.27 W |
| Pitangui | 255 | 19.40 S | 44.54 W |
| Pitcairn | 279b | 40.24 N | 79.46 W |
| Pitcairn □[2], Oc. | 6 | 25.04 S | 130.05 W |
| Pitcairn □[2], Oc. | 174e | 25.04 S | 130.05 W |
| Pitcher | 210 | 42.35 N | 75.52 W |
| Pitch Place | 260 | 51.16 N | 0.36 W |
| Piteå | 26 | 65.20 N | 21.30 E |
| Piteälven ≃ | 24 | 65.14 N | 21.32 E |
| Piteglio | 66 | 44.01 N | 10.46 E |
| Pitelino | 80 | 54.34 N | 41.49 E |
| Piterka | 80 | 50.42 N | 47.27 E |
| Piteşti | 38 | 44.52 N | 24.52 E |
| Pithapuram | 122 | 17.07 N | 82.16 E |
| Pithara | 162 | 30.24 S | 116.40 E |
| Pithiviers | 50 | 48.10 N | 2.15 E |
| Pithorāgarh | 124 | 29.35 N | 80.13 E |
| Piti, Lagoa ⊜ | 158 | 26.34 S | 32.53 E |
| Pitigliano | 66 | 42.38 N | 11.40 E |
| Fitim | 80 | 53.12 N | 42.21 E |
| Pitinga ≃ | 246 | 1.32 S | 59.49 W |
| Pitiquito | 232 | 30.42 N | 112.02 W |
| Pitjantjatjara Lands ◆[4] | 162 | 27.00 S | 130.30 E |
| Pitk'aranta | 24 | 61.34 N | 31.27 E |
| Pitkas Point | 180 | 62.02 N | 163.17 W |
| Pitlochry | 46 | 56.43 N | 3.45 W |
| Pitman | 208 | 39.43 N | 75.07 W |
| Pitman Airport ⊠ | 285 | 39.45 N | 75.08 W |
| Pitmedden | 46 | 57.20 N | 2.11 W |
| Pitner Ditch ≊ | 216 | 41.14 N | 86.53 W |
| Pitogo | 116 | 10.08 N | 124.33 E |
| Pitomača | 36 | 45.57 N | 17.14 E |
| Pitou, Zhg. | 100 | 25.01 N | 114.35 E |
| Pitou, Zhg. | 100 | 23.34 N | 116.05 E |
| Pitou, Zhg. | 100 | 24.26 N | 114.22 E |
| Pitrufquén | 254 | 38.59 S | 72.39 W |
| Pitsea | 260 | 51.34 N | 0.31 E |
| Pitseng | 158 | 28.58 S | 28.16 E |
| Pitsford Reservoir ⊜[1] | 42 | 52.20 N | 0.52 W |
| Pitt ≃ | 224 | 49.12 N | 122.47 W |
| Pitt, Mount ∧ | 174c | 29.01 S | 167.56 E |
| Pittem | 50 | 51.00 N | 3.16 E |
| Pitten ≃ | 61 | 47.44 N | 16.14 E |
| Pittenweem | 46 | 56.12 N | 2.44 W |
| Pitti Island I | 122 | 10.50 N | 72.38 E |
| Pitt Island I | 182 | 53.35 N | 129.45 W |
| Pitt Lake ⊜ | 182 | 49.25 N | 122.32 W |
| Pitt Meadows | 224 | 49.13 N | 122.39 W |
| Pittsboro, In., U.S. | 218 | 39.51 N | 86.28 W |
| Pittsboro, Ms., U.S. | 194 | 33.56 N | 89.20 W |
| Pittsboro, N.C., U.S. | 192 | 35.43 N | 79.10 W |
| Pittsburg, Ca., U.S. | 226 | 38.01 N | 121.53 W |
| Pittsburg, In., U.S. | 216 | 40.37 N | 86.42 W |
| Pittsburg, Ks., U.S. | 198 | 37.24 N | 94.42 W |
| Pittsburg, N.H., U.S. | 206 | 45.03 N | 71.23 W |
| Pittsburg, Tx., U.S. | 222 | 32.59 N | 94.57 W |
| Pittsburgh, Pa., U.S. | 214 | 40.26 N | 79.59 W |
| Pittsburgh, Pa., U.S. | 279b | 40.26 N | 79.59 W |
| Pittsburgh, University of ʊ[2] | 279b | 40.27 N | 79.58 W |
| Pittsburgh-Monroeville Airport ⊠ | 279b | 40.27 N | 79.46 W |
| Pittsfield, Il., U.S. | 219 | 39.36 N | 90.48 W |
| Pittsfield, Me., U.S. | 188 | 44.46 N | 69.23 W |
| Pittsfield, Ma., U.S. | 207 | 42.27 N | 73.14 W |
| Pittsfield, N.H., U.S. | 188 | 43.18 N | 71.19 W |
| Pittsfield, Pa., U.S. | 214 | 41.50 N | 79.23 W |
| Pittsford, Mi., U.S. | 216 | 41.52 N | 84.28 W |
| Pittsford, N.Y., U.S. | 210 | 43.05 N | 77.31 W |
| Pitt Stadium ♦ | 279b | 40.27 N | 79.58 W |
| Pittston | 210 | 41.19 N | 75.47 W |
| Pittsview | 194 | 32.11 N | 85.09 W |
| Pittsville | 208 | 38.23 N | 75.24 W |
| Pittsworth | 166 | 27.43 S | 151.38 E |
| Pitt Water ⊂ | 170 | 33.37 S | 151.18 E |
| Pituil | 252 | 28.34 S | 67.27 W |
| Pitumarca | 248 | 13.59 S | 71.25 W |
| Pituri Creek ≃ | 166 | 22.58 S | 138.50 E |
| Pitzbach ≃ | 64 | 47.13 N | 10.46 E |
| Pitztal V | 64 | 47.07 N | 10.47 E |
| Pium | 250 | 10.27 S | 49.11 W |
| Pium ≃ | 250 | 10.12 S | 49.57 W |
| Piura | 248 | 5.12 S | 80.38 W |
| Piura □[5] | 248 | 5.10 S | 80.00 W |
| Piura ≃ | 248 | 5.32 S | 80.53 W |
| Piute Peak ∧ | 204 | 35.27 N | 118.24 W |
| Piute Reservoir ⊜[1] | 200 | 38.17 N | 112.12 W |
| Piva ≃ | 38 | 43.21 N | 18.51 E |
| Pivan' | 89 | 50.29 N | 137.06 E |
| Pivdennyy Buh ≃ | 78 | 46.59 N | 31.58 E |
| Piverone | 62 | 45.27 N | 8.00 E |
| Pivijay | 246 | 10.28 N | 74.37 W |
| Piwniczna | 30 | 49.27 N | 20.42 E |
| Pixian | 102 | 30.49 N | 103.49 E |
| Pixley | 226 | 35.58 N | 119.17 W |
| Pižanka | 80 | 57.28 N | 48.33 E |
| Pižma | 80 | 57.52 N | 47.06 E |
| Pižma ≃ | 80 | 57.37 N | 48.58 E |
| Pizzighettone | 62 | 45.11 N | 9.47 E |
| Pizzillo, Monte ∧ | 70 | 37.48 N | 15.01 E |
| Pizzo | 68 | 38.44 N | 16.10 E |
| Pizzoferrato | 66 | 41.55 N | 14.14 E |
| Pizzoli | 66 | 42.26 N | 13.18 E |
| Pizzone | 66 | 41.40 N | 14.02 E |
| Pjalka | 24 | 66.43 N | 40.59 E |
| Pjana ≃ | 80 | 55.40 N | 45.57 E |
| Pjaršai | 76 | 54.02 N | 26.41 E |
| Pjöngjang → P'yŏngyang | 98 | 39.01 N | 125.45 E |
| P. K. le Rouxdam ⊜[1] | 158 | 30.12 S | 24.54 E |
| Placanica | 68 | 38.25 N | 16.27 E |
| Place Bonaventure ◆[9] | 275a | 45.30 N | 73.34 W |
| Placentia, Nf., Can. | 186 | 47.14 N | 53.58 W |
| Placentia, Ca., U.S. | 228 | 33.52 N | 117.52 W |
| Placentia Bay ⊂ | 186 | 47.15 N | 54.30 W |
| Placer, Pil. | 116 | 11.52 N | 123.55 E |
| Placer, Pil. | 116 | 9.39 N | 125.36 E |
| Placer □[6] | 226 | 38.54 N | 121.04 W |
| Placeres del Oro ≃ | 234 | 18.27 N | 100.57 W |
| Placeres de Picacho | 234 | 23.11 N | 105.42 W |
| Placerville | 226 | 38.43 N | 120.47 W |
| Placetas | 240p | 22.19 N | 79.40 W |
| Place Versailles ◆[9] | 275a | 45.35 N | 73.32 W |
| Plachino | 76 | 54.28 N | 39.20 E |
| Placid, Lake ⊜ | 220 | 27.14 N | 81.22 W |
| Placida | 220 | 26.49 N | 82.15 W |
| Plácido de Castro | 248 | 10.20 S | 67.11 W |
| Plácido Rosas | 252 | 32.45 S | 53.44 W |
| Placita de Morelos | 234 | 18.31 N | 103.42 W |
| Plačkovica ⋏ | 38 | 41.45 N | 22.35 E |
| Plaffeien | 58 | 46.44 N | 7.17 E |
| Plages, Lac des ⊜ | 206 | 45.59 N | 74.54 W |
| Plage-Sainte-Cécile | 50 | 50.34 N | 1.35 E |
| Plailly | 261 | 49.06 N | 2.35 E |
| Plai Mat ≃ | 110 | 15.22 N | 102.45 E |
| Plain | 224 | 47.46 N | 120.39 W |
| Plain City, Oh., U.S. | 214 | 40.06 N | 83.16 W |
| Plain City, Ut., U.S. | 200 | 41.17 N | 112.05 W |
| Plain Dealing | 194 | 32.54 N | 93.41 W |
| Plaines, Île aux I | 275a | 45.21 N | 73.50 W |
| Plainfield, Ct., U.S. | 207 | 41.40 N | 71.54 W |
| Plainfield, Il., U.S. | 216 | 41.37 N | 88.12 W |
| Plainfield, In., U.S. | 218 | 39.42 N | 86.23 W |
| Plainfield, Ma., U.S. | 207 | 42.30 N | 72.55 W |
| Plainfield, N.J., U.S. | 210 | 40.37 N | 74.26 W |
| Plainfield, Oh., U.S. | 214 | 40.13 N | 81.43 W |
| Plainfield, Pa., U.S. | 208 | 40.12 N | 77.17 W |
| Plainfield, Wi., U.S. | 190 | 44.12 N | 89.29 W |
| Plains, Ga., U.S. | 192 | 32.02 N | 84.23 W |
| Plains, Ks., U.S. | 198 | 37.15 N | 100.35 W |
| Plains, Mt., U.S. | 202 | 47.27 N | 114.52 W |
| Plains, Tx., U.S. | 196 | 33.11 N | 102.50 W |
| Plainsboro | 208 | 40.20 N | 74.36 W |
| Plainview, Ca., U.S. | 226 | 36.08 N | 119.08 W |
| Plainview, Il., U.S. | 219 | 39.10 N | 89.59 W |
| Plainview, Mn., U.S. | 190 | 44.09 N | 92.10 W |
| Plainview, Ne., U.S. | 198 | 42.20 N | 97.47 W |
| Plainview, N.Y., U.S. | 210 | 40.46 N | 73.28 W |
| Plainview, Tx., U.S. | 196 | 34.11 N | 101.42 W |
| Plainville, Ct., U.S. | 207 | 41.40 N | 72.51 W |
| Plainville, Il., U.S. | 219 | 39.47 N | 91.11 W |
| Plainville, In., U.S. | 194 | 38.48 N | 87.09 W |
| Plainville, Ks., U.S. | 198 | 39.14 N | 99.17 W |
| Plainville, Ma., U.S. | 207 | 42.00 N | 71.20 W |
| Plainville, N.Y., U.S. | 210 | 43.10 N | 76.27 W |
| Plainwell | 216 | 42.26 N | 85.38 W |
| Plaisance, Baie de ⊂ | 186 | 47.18 N | 61.53 W |
| Plaisir | 261 | 48.49 N | 1.57 E |
| Plaistow | 207 | 42.50 N | 71.05 W |
| Plakhtiyivka | 78 | 46.07 N | 29.43 E |
| Plaksino | 76 | 56.11 N | 30.42 E |
| Plamondon | 182 | 54.51 N | 112.19 W |
| Plampang | 115b | 8.48 S | 117.48 E |
| Planá | 60 | 49.52 N | 12.44 E |
| Plana, Illa I | 34 | 38.10 N | 0.28 W |
| Planada | 226 | 37.18 N | 120.19 W |
| Planalto, Bra. | 252 | 27.20 S | 53.03 W |
| Planalto, Bra. | 255 | 14.39 S | 40.29 W |
| Planches | 50 | 48.42 N | 0.22 E |
| Plandome | 276 | 40.48 N | 73.42 W |
| Plandome Heights | 276 | 40 48 N | 73.42 W |
| Plandome Manor | 276 | 40.49 N | 73.42 W |
| Plan-d'Orgon | 62 | 43.48 N | 5.00 E |
| Plane ≃ | 54 | 52.23 N | 12.30 E |
| Planegg | 60 | 48.06 N | 11.25 E |
| Planers'ke | 78 | 44.57 N | 35.14 E |
| Planeta Rica | 246 | 8.25 N | 75.36 W |
| Plangeross | 64 | 46.59 N | 10.52 E |
| Plankenfels | 60 | 49.53 N | 11.20 E |
| Plankinton | 198 | 43.42 N | 98.29 W |
| Plano, Il., U.S. | 216 | 41.39 N | 88.32 W |
| Plano, Tx., U.S. | 222 | 33.01 N | 96.41 W |
| Plansee ⊜ | 64 | 47.28 N | 10.48 E |
| Plantagenet | 206 | 45.32 N | 75.00 W |
| Plantation, Fl., U.S. | 220 | 24.59 N | 80.33 W |
| Plantation, Fl., U.S. | 220 | 26.07 N | 80.14 W |
| Plantation, Ky., U.S. | 218 | 38.17 N | 85.36 W |
| Plantation Key I | 220 | 24.58 N | 80.33 W |
| Plant City | 220 | 28.01 N | 82.06 W |
| Plantersville, Al., U.S. | 194 | 32.39 N | 86.55 W |
| Plantersville, Ms., U.S. | 194 | 34.12 N | 88.39 W |
| Plantersville, Tx., U.S. | 222 | 30.20 N | 95.52 W |
| Planting Fields Arboretum State Park ♦ | 276 | 40.52 N | 73.33 W |
| Plantsite | 200 | 33.03 N | 109.19 W |
| Plantsville | 207 | 41.35 N | 72.53 W |
| Plaquemine | 194 | 30.17 N | 91.14 W |
| Plaridel, Pil. | 116 | 10.32 N | 124.46 E |
| Plaridel, Pil. | 116 | 8.37 N | 123.43 E |
| Plasencia | 34 | 40.02 N | 6.05 W |
| Plaški | 36 | 45.05 N | 15.22 E |
| Plassenburg ⊥ | 60 | 50.06 N | 11.28 E |
| Plassey | 126 | 23.47 N | 88.15 E |
| Plast | 86 | 54.22 N | 60.50 E |
| Plaster Rock | 186 | 46.54 N | 67.24 W |
| Plastovo | 82 | 54.17 N | 37.03 E |
| Plastun | 89 | 44.45 N | 136.19 E |
| Plastunovskaja | 78 | 45.18 N | 39.16 E |
| Plasy | 60 | 49.56 N | 13.24 E |
| Plata | 54 | 53.33 N | 11.30 E |
| Plata, Isla de la I | 246 | 1.16 S | 81.06 W |
| Plata, Río de la ⊂[1] | 258 | 35.00 S | 57.00 W |
| Plata, Río de la ≃ | 240m | 18.29 N | 66.15 W |
| Platani ≃ | 70 | 37.24 N | 13.16 E |
| Platania | 68 | 39.00 N | 16.19 E |
| Plátanos | 288 | 34.47 S | 58.11 W |
| Plátanos, Arroyo ≃ | 288 | 34.45 S | 58.08 W |
| Plate, Île I | 275a | 45.22 N | 73.48 W |
| Platea | 214 | 41.57 N | 80.20 W |
| Plateau Creek ≃ | 200 | 39.11 N | 108.18 W |
| Plateaux □[5] | 152 | 2.15 S | 15.30 E |
| Platì | 68 | 38.13 N | 16.03 E |
| Platinum | 180 | 59.01 N | 161.49 W |
| Platnirovskaja | 78 | 45.23 N | 39.23 E |
| Plato | 246 | 9.47 N | 74.47 W |
| Platono-Petrovka | 83 | 46.59 N | 39.28 E |
| Platonovka | 80 | 52.43 N | 41.57 E |
| Platón Sánchez | 234 | 21.17 N | 98.22 W |
| Platovo | 83 | 48.05 N | 39.53 E |
| Platrand | 158 | 27.08 S | 29.29 E |
| Platt | 260 | 51.17 N | 0.20 E |
| Platta | 58 | 46.40 N | 8.51 E |
| Platte | 198 | 43.23 N | 98.50 W |
| Platte ≃, U.S. | 194 | 39.16 N | 94.50 W |
| Platte ≃, Mn., U.S. | 190 | 45.47 N | 94.17 W |
| Platte ≃, Ne., U.S. | 198 | 41.04 N | 95.53 W |
| Platte ≃, Wi., U.S. | 190 | 42.37 N | 90.40 W |
| Platte Center | 198 | 41.32 N | 97.29 W |
| Platte City | 194 | 39.22 N | 94.46 W |
| Platte Creek ≃ | 198 | 43.19 N | 99.00 W |
| Platte Island I | 138 | 5.52 S | 55.23 E |
| Plattekill | 210 | 41.37 N | 74.05 W |
| Platteville, Co., U.S. | 200 | 40.12 N | 104.49 W |
| Platteville, Wi., U.S. | 190 | 42.44 N | 90.28 W |
| Platt Hall ⊥ | 262 | 53.27 N | 2.13 W |
| Plattling | 60 | 48.47 N | 12.53 E |
| Plattsburg | 194 | 39.33 N | 94.26 W |
| Plattsburgh | 188 | 44.41 N | 73.27 W |
| Plattsburgh Air Force Base ■ | 188 | 44.40 N | 73.28 W |
| Plattsmouth | 198 | 41.00 N | 95.52 W |
| Plattsville | 212 | 43.18 N | 80.37 W |
| Platveld | 156 | 19.58 S | 17.07 E |
| Plau | 54 | 53.27 N | 12.16 E |
| Plaue, Dtsch. | 54 | 52.24 N | 12.25 E |
| Plaue, Dtsch. | 54 | 50.47 N | 10.54 E |
| Plauen | 54 | 50.30 N | 12.08 E |
| Plauer See ⊜ | 54 | 53.30 N | 12.20 E |
| Plav | 38 | 42.36 N | 19.56 E |
| Plave | 64 | 46.02 N | 13.36 E |
| Plaviņas | 76 | 56.37 N | 25.43 E |
| Plavsk | 76 | 53.43 N | 37.18 E |
| Plaxtol | 260 | 51.15 N | 0.18 E |
| Playa Azul | 234 | 17.59 N | 102.24 W |
| Playa Baracoa | 286b | 23.03 N | 82.34 W |
| Playa Bonita | 236 | 9.39 N | 84.27 W |
| Playa de Fajardo | 240m | 18.20 N | 65.38 W |
| Playa de Guayanés | 240m | 18.04 N | 65.49 W |
| Playa de Guayanilla | 240m | 18.01 N | 66.46 W |
| Playa del Carmen | 232 | 20.36 N | 87.06 W |
| Playa del Rey ◆[8] | 280 | 33.58 N | 118.26 W |
| Playa de Naguabo | 240m | 18.12 N | 65.43 W |
| Playa de Ponce | 240m | 17.59 N | 66.37 W |
| Playa Noriega, Laguna ⊜ | 232 | 29.10 N | 111.50 W |
| Playas Lake ⊜ | 200 | 31.50 N | 108.34 W |
| Playa Vicente | 234 | 17.50 N | 95.49 W |
| Play Cu | 110 | 13.59 N | 108.00 E |
| Playford ≃ | 162 | 19.03 S | 135.35 E |
| Playgreen Lake ⊜ | 184 | 54.00 N | 98.10 W |
| Playland ♦ | 276 | 40.58 N | 73.41 W |
| Plaza | 198 | 48.01 N | 101.57 W |
| Plaza at Mid Island ◆[9] | 276 | 40.46 N | 73.32 W |
| Plaza de Caisán | 236 | 8.46 N | 82.45 W |
| Plaza de Mayo ♦ | 288 | 34.36 S | 58.23 W |
| Plaza de Toros ♦ | 266a | 40.26 N | 3.39 W |
| Plaza de Toros Las Arenas ♦ | 266d | 41.23 N | 2.09 W |
| Plaza de Toros Monumental ♦ | 266d | 41.24 N | 2.11 E |
| Plaza Huincul | 252 | 38.55 S | 69.09 W |
| Plaza Park | 285 | 40.04 N | 74.53 W |
| Plazas de Soberanía en el Norte de África → Spanish North Africa □[2] | 34 | 35.53 N | 5.19 W |
| Pleasant | 275b | 43.41 N | 79.49 W |
| Pleasant, Lake ⊜[1] | 200 | 33.53 N | 112.16 W |
| Pleasant, Mount ∧ | 192 | 37.44 N | 79.10 W |
| Pleasant, Mount ∧[2] | 186 | 45.26 N | 66.49 W |
| Pleasant Bay | 186 | 46.49 N | 60.48 W |
| Pleasantdale, Sk., Can. | 184 | 52.35 N | 104.30 W |
| Pleasantdale, N.Y., U.S. | 210 | 42.47 N | 73.40 W |
| Pleasant Gap | 214 | 40.52 N | 77.44 W |
| Pleasant Garden | 192 | 35.57 N | 79.45 W |
| Pleasant Grove, Ca., U.S. | 226 | 38.49 N | 121.29 W |
| Pleasant Grove, Ut., U.S. | 200 | 40.21 N | 111.44 W |
| Pleasant Grove Creek ≃ | 226 | 38.48 N | 121.32 W |
| Pleasant Hill, Ca., U.S. | 226 | 37.56 N | 122.03 W |
| Pleasant Hill, Il., U.S. | 219 | 39.26 N | 90.52 W |
| Pleasant Hill, La., U.S. | 194 | 31.49 N | 93.31 W |
| Pleasant Hill, Mo., U.S. | 194 | 38.47 N | 94.16 W |
| Pleasant Hill, N.C., U.S. | 208 | 36.32 N | 77.32 W |
| Pleasant Hill, Oh., U.S. | 218 | 40.03 N | 84.20 W |
| Pleasant Hill Lake ⊜[1] | 214 | 40.38 N | 82.21 W |
| Pleasant Hills | 214 | 40.20 N | 79.57 W |
| Pleasant Lake, In., U.S. | 216 | 41.34 N | 85.00 W |
| Pleasant Lake, Mi., U.S. | 216 | 42.23 N | 84.22 W |
| Pleasant Lake ⊜ | 216 | 42.13 N | 83.56 W |
| Pleasant Mills | 216 | 40.47 N | [illegible]4.51 W |
| Pleasant Mount | 210 | 41.44 N | 75.26 W |
| Pleasanton, Ca., U.S. | 226 | 37.39 N | 121.52 W |
| Pleasanton, Ks., U.S. | 198 | 38.10 N | 94.42 W |
| Pleasanton, Tx., U.S. | 196 | 28.58 N | 98.28 W |
| Pleasanton Ridge ∧ | 282 | 37.40 N | 1[illegible]1.55 W |
| Pleasant Plains, Il., U.S. | 219 | 39.52 N | [illegible]9.55 W |
| Pleasant Plains, N.J., U.S. | 208 | 40.00 N | 7[illegible].13 W |
| Pleasant Point | 172 | 44.16 S | 17[illegible].08 E |
| Pleasant Prairie | 216 | 42.33 N | 8[illegible].57 W |
| Pleasant Ridge | 281 | 42.31 N | 8[illegible].10 W |
| Pleasant Unity | 214 | 40.15 N | 7[illegible].28 W |
| Pleasant Valley, N.Y., U.S. | 210 | 41.44 N | 7[illegible].49 W |
| Pleasant Valley, Oh., U.S. | 218 | 39.22 N | 8[illegible].03 W |
| Pleasant Valley, Pa., U.S. | 279b | 40.31 N | 75.18 W |
| Pleasantville, Ia., U.S. | 190 | 41.23 N | 93.[illegible]6 W |
| Pleasantville, Md., U.S. | 284b | 39.11 N | 76.[illegible]8 W |
| Pleasantville, N.J., U.S. | 208 | 39.23 N | 74.[illegible]1 W |
| Pleasantville, N.Y., U.S. | 210 | 41.07 N | 73.[illegible]7 W |
| Pleasantville, Pa., U.S. | 214 | 41.35 N | 79.[illegible]4 W |
| Pleasington | 262 | 53.44 N | 2.[illegible] W |
| Pleasure Beach | 207 | 41.18 N | 72.[illegible] W |
| Pleasure Ridge Park | 218 | 38.09 N | 85.[illegible] W |
| Pleasureville | 218 | 38.33 N | 85.[illegible] W |
| Pléaux | 32 | 45.08 N | 2.1[illegible] E |
| Plechanovo | 82 | 54.14 N | 37.3[illegible] E |
| Plechanovskoje | 76 | 52.39 N | 39.5[illegible] E |
| Plechovo | 78 | 51.07 N | 35.1[illegible] E |
| Plechý (Plöckenstein) ∧ | 60 | 48.46 N | 13.5[illegible] E |
| Pledger | 222 | 29.11 N | 95.5[illegible] W |
| Pleebo | 150 | 4.35 N | 7.4[illegible] W |
| Pleiku → Play Cu | 110 | 13.59 N | 108.00 E |
| Pleinfeld | 56 | 49.06 N | 10.59 E |
| Pleissa | 54 | 50.50 N | 12.46 E |
| Pleisse ≃ | 54 | 51.20 N | 12.22 E |
| Pléneuf | 32 | 48.36 N | 2.33 W |
| Plenty | 184 | 51.47 N | 108.36 W |
| Plenty ≃, Austl. | 162 | 23.25 S | 136.31 E |
| Plenty ≃, Austl. | 274b | 37.45 S | 145.07 E |
| Plenty, Bay of ⊂ | 172 | 37.40 S | 177.00 E |
| Plentywood | 198 | 48.46 N | 104.33 W |
| Plered | 115a | 6.38 S | 107.23 E |
| Pleščanicy | 76 | 54.25 N | 27.50 E |
| Pleščejevo, ozero ⊜ | 82 | 56.46 N | 38.47 E |
| Pleseck | 24 | 62.43 N | 40.20 E |
| Plešivka | 82 | 54.23 N | 37.09 E |
| Plesná ≃ | 54 | 50.07 N | 12.28 E |
| Pless, Dtsch. | 58 | 48.05 N | 10.08 E |
| Pless → Pszczyna, Pol. | 30 | 49.59 N | 18.57 E |
| Plessa | 54 | 51.28 N | 13.37 E |
| Plessisville | 206 | 46.14 N | 71.47 W |
| Pleszew | 30 | 51.54 N | 17.48 E |
| Pletenevka | 82 | 54.31 N | 36.06 E |
| Pletenyy Tashlyk | 78 | 48.29 N | 31.40 E |
| Pleternica | 38 | 45.17 N | 17.48 E |
| Plétipi, Lac ⊜ | 176 | 51.44 N | 70.06 W |
| Plettenberg | 56 | 51.13 N | 7.52 E |
| Plettenbergbaai | 158 | 34.04 S | 23.22 E |
| Pleurs | 50 | 48.41 N | 3.52 E |
| Pleven | 38 | 43.25 N | 24.37 E |
| Plevna, Mo., U.S. | 219 | 39.58 N | 92.05 W |
| Plevna, Mt., U.S. | 198 | 46.25 N | 104.31 W |
| Pleyben | 32 | 48.14 N | 3.58 W |
| Pleystein | 60 | 49.39 N | 12.25 E |
| Pliening | 60 | 48.12 N | 11.48 E |
| Pliezhausen | 56 | 48.33 N | 9.12 E |
| Plimmerton | 172 | 41.05 S | 174.52 E |
| Plimoth Plantation ⊥ | 207 | 41.57 N | 70.38 W |
| Plintovka | 265a | 60.01 N | 30.46 E |
| Pliszka ≃ | 54 | 52.14 N | 14.42 E |
| Plitvička Jezera Nacionalni Park ♦ | 36 | 44.53 N | 15.38 E |
| Plješevica ⋏ | 36 | 44.40 N | 15.45 E |
| Pljevlja | 38 | 43.21 N | 19.21 E |
| Ploaghe | 71 | 40.40 N | 8.45 E |
| Plochingen | 56 | 48.42 N | 9.25 E |
| Płock | 30 | 52.33 N | 19.43 E |
| Płock □[4] | 30 | 52.25 N | 19.45 E |
| Plöckenpass )( | 64 | 46.36 N | 12.58 E |
| Plöckenstein (Plechý) ∧ | 60 | 48.46 N | 13.51 E |
| Plockton | 46 | 57.20 N | 5.39 W |
| Pločno ∧ | 36 | 43.36 N | 17.34 E |
| Plodorodnoje | 80 | 46.44 N | 41.06 E |
| Ploegsteert | 50 | 50.43 N | 2.53 E |
| Ploërmel | 32 | 47.56 N | 2.24 W |
| Ploeşti → Ploieşti | 38 | 44.56 N | 26.02 E |
| Plogastel-Saint-Germain | 28 | 47.59 N | 4.16 W |
| Ploieşti | 38 | 44.56 N | 26.02 E |
| Plomárion | 38 | 38.59 N | 26.22 E |
| Plomb du Cantal ∧ | 32 | 45.03 N | 2.46 E |
| Plombières-les-Bains | 58 | 47.58 N | 6.29 E |
| Plombières-lès-Dijon | 58 | 47.20 N | 4.58 E |
| Plomer | 258 | 34.48 S | 59.02 W |
| Plomer, Point › | 166 | 31.19 S | 152.58 E |
| Plön | 54 | 54.09 N | 10.25 E |
| Plonge, Lac la ⊜ | 184 | 55.08 N | 107.25 W |
| Płońsk | 30 | 52.38 N | 20.23 E |
| Pl'os | 80 | 57.27 N | 41.31 E |
| Plose, Cima delle ∧ | 64 | 46.42 N | 11.44 E |
| Ploskij | 78 | 46.17 N | 40.15 E |
| Ploskoje | 76 | 52.45 N | 38.21 E |
| Ploskoš' | 76 | 56.46 N | 31.16 E |
| Pl'oso | 76 | 59.47 N | 35.43 E |
| Plössberg, Dtsch. | 60 | 49.47 N | 12.19 E |
| Plössberg, Dtsch. | 60 | 49.47 N | 12.19 E |
| Plotbišče | 80 | 56.50 N | 50.35 E |
| Plotina | 83 | 48.33 N | 40.05 E |
| Plotnica | 76 | 52.03 N | 26.39 E |
| Plottier | 252 | 38.58 S | 68.14 W |
| Płoty | 30 | 53.49 N | 15.16 E |
| Plötz | 54 | 51.38 N | 11.56 E |
| Plouay | 32 | 47.55 N | 3.20 W |
| Ploučnice ≃ | 54 | 50.47 N | 14.13 E |
| Ploudalmézeau | 32 | 48.32 N | 4.39 W |
| Plouguenast | 32 | 48.17 N | 2.43 W |
| Plouha | 32 | 48.41 N | 2.56 W |
| Plovdiv | 38 | 42.09 N | 24.45 E |
| Plovdiv □[4] | 38 | 42.08 N | 24.32 E |
| Plover ≃ | 190 | 44.29 N | 89.35 W |
| Plover Islands II | 180 | 71.15 N | 155.30 W |
| Pluckemin | 276 | 40.39 N | 74.39 W |
| Plum, Pa., U.S. | 214 | 40.31 N | 79.45 W |
| Plum, Pa., U.S. | 214 | 41.35 N | 79.51 W |
| Plum, Tx., U.S. | 222 | 29.56 N | 96.58 W |
| Pluma Hidalgo | 234 | 15.55 N | 96.25 W |
| Plumas | 184 | 50.25 N | 99.02 W |
| Plumbridge | 48 | 54.46 N | 7.15 W |
| Plum Brook ≃ | 281 | 42.34 N | 82.58 W |
| Plum Creek ≃, Il., U.S. | 278 | 41.33 N | 87.29 W |
| Plum Creek ≃, Ne., U.S. | 198 | 41.52 N | 96.44 W |
| Plum Creek ≃, Oh., U.S. | 279a | 41.18 N | 82.09 W |
| Plum Creek ≃, Pa., U.S. | 279b | 40.31 N | 79.51 W |
| Plum Creek ≃, S.D., U.S. | 198 | 44.13 N | 100.43 W |
| Plum Creek ≃, Tx., U.S. | 196 | 29.38 N | 97.36 W |


| Symbol | English | Deutsch | Español | Français | Português |
|---|---|---|---|---|---|
| ≃ | River | Fluß | Río | Rivière | Rio |
| ≊ | Canal | Kanal | Canal | Canal | Canal |
| ⌊ | Waterfall, Rapids | Wasserfall, Stromschnellen | Cascada, Rápidos | Chute d'eau, Rapides | Cascata, Rápidos |
| ⋓ | Strait | Meeresstraße | Estrecho | Détroit | Estreito |
| ⊂ | Bay, Gulf | Bucht, Golf | Bahía, Golfo | Baie, Golfe | Baía, Golfo |
| ⊜ | Lake, Lakes | See, Seen | Lago, Lagos | Lac, Lacs | Lago, Lagos |
| ⁝ | Swamp | Sumpf | Pantano | Marais | Pântano |
| ⩍ | Ice Features, Glacier | Eis- und Gletscherformen | Accidentes Glaciales | Formes glaciaires | Acidentes glaciares |
| ⫪ | Other Hydrographic Features | Andere Hydrographische Objekte | Otros Elementos Hidrográficos | Autres données hydrographiques | Outros acidentes hidrográficos |
| ✣ | Submarine Features | Untermeerische Objekte | Accidentes Submarinos | Formes de relief sous-marin | Acidentes submarinos |
| □ | Political Unit | Politische Einheit | Unidad Politica | Entité politique | Unidade política |
| ʊ | Cultural Institution | Kulturelle Institution | Institución Cultural | Institution culturelle | Instituição cultural |
| ⊥ | Historical Site | Historische Stätte | Sitio Histórico | Site historique | Sitio histórico |
| ♦ | Recreational Site | Erholungs- und Ferienort | Sitio de Recreo | Centre de loisirs | Area de Lazer |
| ⊠ | Airport | Flughafen | Aeropuerto | Aéroport | Aeroporto |
| ■ | Military Installation | Militäranlage | Instalación Militar | Installation militaire | Instalação militar |
| ◆ | Miscellaneous | Verschiedenes | Misceláneo | Divers | Diversos |

ENGLISH: Name | Page | Lat.°′ | Long.°′
DEUTSCH: Name | Seite | Breite°′ | Länge°′ E = Ost


| Name | Page | Lat.°′ | Long.°′ |
|---|---|---|---|
| Plum Creek, Clear Fork ≃ | 222 | 29.45 N | 97.37 W |
| Plumerville | 194 | 35.09 N | 92.38 W |
| Plum Grove | 222 | 30.15 N | 95.05 W |
| Plum Grove Estates | 278 | 42.04 N | 88.02 W |
| Plum Island | 283 | 42.49 N | 70.59 W |
| Plum Island I, Ma., U.S. | 207 | 42.45 N | 70.48 W |
| Plum Island I, N.Y., U.S. | 207 | 41.11 N | 72.12 W |
| Plum Island Airport ⊠ | 283 | 42.48 N | 70.50 W |
| Plum Island Sound ʯ | 283 | 42.45 N | 70.48 W |
| Plum Island State Park ♦ | 283 | 42.42 N | 70.47 W |
| Plumley | 262 | 53.17 N | 2.25 W |
| Plummer | 202 | 47.20 N | 116.53 W |
| Plummers Landing | 218 | 38.19 N | 83.33 W |
| Plumper Sound ʯ | 224 | 48.47 N | 123.13 W |
| Plum Point > | 276 | 40.50 N | 40.43 W |
| Plumpton | 274a | 33.45 S | 150.50 E |
| Plumridge Lakes ⊜ | 162 | 29.30 S | 125.25 E |
| Plum Run ≃ | 279b | 40.15 N | 80.13 W |
| Plumsteadville | 208 | 40.23 N | 75.09 W |
| Plumtree | 154 | 20.30 S | 27.50 E |
| Plumville | 214 | 40.48 N | 79.11 W |
| Plumwood | 218 | 40.01 N | 83.23 W |
| Plungė | 76 | 55.55 N | 21.51 E |
| Pl'uskovo | 76 | 52.46 N | 33.49 E |
| Pl'ussa | 76 | 58.26 N | 29.21 E |
| Pl'ussa ≃ | 76 | 59.19 N | 28.11 E |
| Plutarco Elías Calles, Presa ⊜1 | 232 | 29.10 N | 109.40 W |
| Pluvigner | 32 | 47.46 N | 3.01 E |
| Plym ≃ | 42 | 50.22 N | 4.07 W |
| Plymouth, Monts. | 238 | 16.42 N | 62.13 W |
| Plymouth, Trin. | 241r | 11.13 N | 60.47 W |
| Plymouth, Eng., U.K. | 42 | 50.23 N | 4.10 W |
| Plymouth, Ca., U.S. | 226 | 38.29 N | 120.51 W |
| Plymouth, Ct., U.S. | 207 | 41.40 N | 73.03 W |
| Plymouth, Il., U.S. | 194 | 40.17 N | 90.55 W |
| Plymouth, In., U.S. | 216 | 41.20 N | 86.18 W |
| Plymouth, Ma., U.S. | 207 | 41.57 N | 70.40 W |
| Plymouth, Mi., U.S. | 216 | 42.22 N | 83.28 W |
| Plymouth, Ne., U.S. | 198 | 40.18 N | 96.59 W |
| Plymouth, N.H., U.S. | 188 | 43.45 N | 71.41 W |
| Plymouth, N.Y., U.S. | 210 | 42.37 N | 75.36 W |
| Plymouth, N.C., U.S. | 192 | 35.52 N | 76.44 W |
| Plymouth, Oh., U.S. | 214 | 41.00 N | 82.40 W |
| Plymouth, Pa., U.S. | 210 | 41.14 N | 75.56 W |
| Plymouth, Wi., U.S. | 190 | 43.44 N | 87.58 W |
| Plymouth □6 | 207 | 41.58 N | 70.41 W |
| Plymouth ≃ | 283 | 42.12 N | 70.54 W |
| Plymouth Airport ⊠ | 42 | 50.25 N | 4.06 W |
| Plymouth Bay c | 207 | 41.57 N | 70.37 W |
| Plymouth Harbor c | 283 | 41.58 N | 70.39 W |
| Plymouth Meeting | 285 | 40.06 N | 75.16 W |
| Plymouth Meeting Mall ⊕9 | 285 | 40.07 N | 75.17 W |
| Plymouth Rock ⊥ | 207 | 41.57 N | 70.39 W |
| Plymouth Valley | 285 | 40.07 N | 75.23 W |
| Plympton, Eng., U.K. | 42 | 50.23 N | 4.03 W |
| Plympton, Ma., U.S. | 207 | 41.57 N | 70.48 W |
| Plymptonville | 214 | 41.03 N | 78.28 W |
| Plymstock | 42 | 50.22 N | 4.04 W |
| Plynlimon ∧ | 42 | 52.28 N | 3.47 W |
| Plyskiv | 78 | 49.23 N | 29.18 E |
| Plysky | 78 | 51.07 N | 32.24 E |
| Plzeň | 60 | 49.45 N | 13.23 E |
| Pniewy | 30 | 52.31 N | 16.15 E |
| Pô | 150 | 11.10 N | 1.09 W |
| Po ≃, It. | 36 | 44.57 N | 12.04 E |
| Po ≃, Zhg. | 100 | 28.57 N | 116.39 E |
| Po, Foci del (Mouths of the Po) ≃1 | 64 | 44.52 N | 12.30 E |
| Pô, Parc National de ♦ | 150 | 11.30 N | 1.15 W |
| Poá | 256 | 23.32 S | 46.20 W |
| Poá ≃ | 287b | 23.37 S | 46.45 W |
| Poana ≃ | 250 | 0.56 N | 57.03 W |
| Poarta Orientală, Pasul )( | 38 | 45.06 N | 22.18 E |
| Poás, Volcán ∧1 | 236 | 10.11 N | 84.13 W |
| Pobé, Bénin | 150 | 6.58 N | 2.41 E |
| Pobé, Burkina | 150 | 13.53 N | 1.45 W |
| Pobeda, gora ∧ | 74 | 65.12 N | 146.12 E |
| Pobeda Ice Island I | 9 | 64.30 S | 97.00 E |
| Pobedino | 74 | 49.51 N | 142.49 E |
| Pobedy, pik ∧ | 72 | 42.02 N | 80.05 E |
| Pobershau | 54 | 50.38 N | 13.13 E |
| Poběžovice | 60 | 49.31 N | 12.48 E |
| Poblado Cerro Gordo | 240m | 18.29 N | 66.20 W |
| Poblado Jacaguas | 240m | 18.03 N | 66.32 W |
| Poblado Medianía Alta | 240m | 18.26 N | 65.50 W |
| Poblado Sábalos | 240m | 18.11 N | 67.09 W |
| Poblado Santana | 240m | 18.27 N | 66.40 W |
| Poblet | 258 | 35.04 S | 57.57 W |
| Pobra de Trives | 34 | 42.20 N | 7.15 W |
| Pocahontas, Ar., U.S. | 194 | 36.15 N | 90.58 W |
| Pocahontas, Il., U.S. | 219 | 38.49 N | 89.32 W |
| Pocahontas, Ia., U.S. | 198 | 42.44 N | 94.40 W |
| Pocahontas State Park ♦ | 208 | 37.23 N | 77.34 W |
| Pocantico Hills | 276 | 41.06 N | 73.50 W |
| Pocantico Lake ⊜ | 276 | 41.07 N | 73.50 W |
| Poção | 250 | 8.11 S | 36.42 W |
| Pocasset | 207 | 41.41 N | 70.37 W |
| Pocatalico ≃ | 188 | 38.29 N | 81.49 W |
| Pocatello | 202 | 42.52 N | 112.26 W |
| Počep | 76 | 52.56 N | 33.27 E |
| Pocé-sur-Cisse | 50 | 47.26 N | 0.59 E |
| Pochayiv | 78 | 50.01 N | 25.31 E |
| Pöchlarn | 61 | 48.12 N | 15.13 E |
| Pochvistnevo | 80 | 53.38 N | 52.08 E |
| Pocinhos, Bra. | 250 | 7.04 S | 36.03 W |
| Pocinhos, Bra. | 256 | 21.56 S | 46.25 W |
| Počinki | 80 | 54.42 N | 44.51 E |
| Počinnaja Sopka | 76 | 58.25 N | 34.22 E |
| Počinok | 76 | 54.25 N | 32.27 E |
| Pocitos, Salar ≚ | 252 | 24.30 S | 67.03 W |
| Pockau | 54 | 50.42 N | 13.14 E |
| Pocking, Dtsch. | 60 | 48.24 N | 13.19 E |
| Pöcking, Dtsch. | 64 | 47.58 N | 11.18 E |
| Pocklington | 44 | 53.56 N | 0.46 W |
| Pocoata | 248 | 18.41 S | 66.11 W |
| Poço da Cruz, Açude ⊜1 | 250 | 8.30 S | 37.35 W |
| Poço do Bispo ⊕8 | 266c | 38.44 N | 9.06 W |
| Poções | 255 | 14.31 S | 40.21 W |
| Poço Fundo | 256 | 21.48 S | 45.58 W |
| Poço Fundo, Cachoeira do ⌊ | 256 | 22.10 S | 44.13 W |
| Pocol | 64 | 46.31 N | 12.07 E |
| Pocola | 194 | 35.13 N | 94.28 W |
| Pocomoke ≃ | 208 | 37.58 N | 75.39 W |
| Pocomoke City | 208 | 38.04 N | 75.34 W |
| Pocomoke Sound ʯ | 208 | 37.52 N | 75.49 W |
| Pocona | 248 | 17.39 S | 65.24 W |
| Poconé | 248 | 16.15 S | 56.37 W |
| Pocono International Raceway ♦ | 210 | 41.03 N | 75.31 W |
| Pocono Lake | 210 | 41.06 N | 75.31 W |
| Pocono Manor | 210 | 41.06 N | 75.22 W |
| Pocono Mountains ⋏2 | 210 | 41.10 N | 75.20 W |
| Pocono Pines | 210 | 41.05 N | 75.29 W |
| Pocono Summit | 210 | 41.07 N | 75.25 W |
| Pocopson | 285 | 39.54 N | 75.37 W |
| Pocopson Creek ≃ | 285 | 39.54 N | 75.37 W |
| Poço Redondo | 250 | 9.49 S | 37.41 W |
| Poços de Caldas | 256 | 21.48 S | 46.34 W |
| Poço Verde | 250 | 10.42 S | 38.11 W |
| Pocrane | 255 | 19.37 S | 41.37 W |
| Pocrí | 236 | 8.16 N | 80.33 W |
| Podbel'skaja | 80 | 53.37 N | 51.50 E |
| Podberezje, Ross. | 76 | 56.57 N | 30.38 E |
| Podberezje, Ross. | 82 | 56.46 N | 37.10 E |
| Podbořany | 54 | 50.11 N | 13.25 E |
| Podborki | 82 | 54.11 N | 35.56 E |
| Podborovje | 76 | 59.30 N | 35.02 E |
| Podbužje | 76 | 53.30 N | 34.56 E |
| Podčerje | 24 | 63.57 N | 57.34 E |
| Podchožeje | 82 | 54.19 N | 38.34 E |
| Podčinnyj | 80 | 50.52 N | 45.13 E |
| Poddębice | 30 | 51.53 N | 18.58 E |
| Poddemjur | 24 | 64.05 N | 53.26 E |
| Poddolgoje | 76 | 53.12 N | 38.04 E |
| Poddorje | 76 | 57.28 N | 31.07 E |
| Poděbrady | 30 | 50.08 N | 15.07 E |
| Po della Donzella ≃ | 64 | 44.48 N | 12.25 E |
| Po delle Tolle ≃ | 64 | 44.50 N | 12.28 E |
| Podensac | 32 | 44.39 N | 0.22 W |
| Podenzano | 62 | 44.57 N | 9.41 E |
| Podersdorf am See | 61 | 47.51 N | 16.50 E |
| Podgorenskij | 78 | 50.24 N | 39.39 E |
| Podgorica | 38 | 42.26 N | 19.14 E |
| Podgornaja | 78 | 50.28 N | 41.10 E |
| Podgornoje, Kaz. | 85 | 42.55 N | 72.25 E |
| Podgornoje, Ross. | 78 | 51.43 N | 39.07 E |
| Podgornoje, Ross. | 78 | 50.27 N | 39.37 E |
| Podgornoje, Ross. | 80 | 46.33 N | 43.07 E |
| Podgornoje, Ross. | 86 | 57.47 N | 82.36 E |
| Podhůří | 60 | 49.28 N | 13.40 E |
| Podi | 112 | 1.08 S | 121.16 E |
| Po di Goro ≃ | 64 | 44.48 N | 12.27 E |
| Podillya □9 | 78 | 48.50 N | 27.30 E |
| Podil's'ka vysochyna ⋏1 | 78 | 49.00 N | 27.00 E |
| Po di Volano ≃ | 64 | 44.49 N | 12.15 E |
| Podjom-Michajlovka | 80 | 52.49 N | 50.32 E |
| Podjuchy ⊕8 | 54 | 53.20 N | 14.36 E |
| Podkamennaja Tunguska | 74 | 61.36 N | 90.09 E |
| Podkamennaja Tunguska ≃ | 74 | 61.36 N | 90.18 E |
| Podkoren | 64 | 46.30 N | 13.45 E |
| Podkumok ≃ | 84 | 44.14 N | 43.36 E |
| Podlasie ⊕1 | 30 | 52.30 N | 23.00 E |
| Podlesnoje | 80 | 51.50 N | 47.03 E |
| Podlopatki | 88 | 50.55 N | 107.05 E |
| Podmošje | 82 | 56.23 N | 37.24 E |
| Podol'sk | 82 | 55.26 N | 37.33 E |
| Podor, Maur. | 150 | 16.40 N | 15.00 W |
| Podor, Sén. | 150 | 16.40 N | 14.57 W |
| Podora | 24 | 62.22 N | 54.19 E |
| Podosinovec | 24 | 60.17 N | 47.04 E |
| Podoz'orskij | 80 | 57.14 N | 40.20 E |
| Podporožje | 24 | 60.53 N | 34.07 E |
| Podravina ⊕1 | 36 | 45.40 N | 17.40 E |
| Podravska Slatina | 38 | 45.42 N | 17.42 E |
| Podrezčicha | 24 | 59.22 N | 51.28 E |
| Podstepnoje | 80 | 51.08 N | 51.28 E |
| Podt'osovo | 88 | 58.36 N | 92.06 E |
| Pod'uga | 24 | 61.06 N | 40.53 E |
| Podujevo | 38 | 42.55 N | 21.11 E |
| Poduškino | 265b | 55.43 N | 37.17 E |
| Podu Turcului | 38 | 46.12 N | 27.23 E |
| Podymachino | 88 | 56.59 N | 106.11 E |
| Podyvotje | 78 | 52.03 N | 34.08 E |
| Poe | 216 | 40.56 N | 85.05 W |
| Poechos, Embalse ⊜1 | 246 | 4.40 S | 80.30 W |
| Poel I | 54 | 54.00 N | 11.26 E |
| Poeldijk | 52 | 52.01 N | 4.12 E |
| Poelela, Lagoa ⊜ | 156 | 24.38 S | 35.00 E |
| Poelkapelle | 50 | 50.55 N | 2.57 E |
| Poestenkill | 210 | 42.41 N | 73.34 W |
| Poesten Kill ≃ | 210 | 42.43 N | 73.42 W |
| Poetto | 71 | 39.12 N | 9.10 E |
| Pofadder | 158 | 29.10 S | 19.22 E |
| Pogamasing Lake ⊜ | 190 | 46.57 N | 81.50 W |
| Pogan, Zhg. | 100 | 28.18 N | 116.46 E |
| Pogan, Zhg. | 100 | 27.40 N | 116.46 E |
| Pogăniș ≃ | 38 | 45.41 N | 21.22 E |
| Pogar | 76 | 52.33 N | 33.16 E |
| Poge, Cape > | 207 | 41.25 N | 70.27 W |
| Poggendorf | 54 | 54.03 N | 13.07 E |
| Poggiardo | 68 | 40.03 N | 18.23 E |
| Poggibonsi | 66 | 43.28 N | 11.09 E |
| Poggio | 64 | 44.30 N | 10.00 E |
| Poggio Berni | 66 | 44.02 N | 12.24 E |
| Poggio Bustone | 66 | 42.30 N | 12.53 E |
| Poggio Imperiale | 68 | 41.49 N | 15.22 E |
| Poggiomarino | 68 | 40.48 N | 14.32 E |
| Poggio Mirteto | 66 | 42.16 N | 12.41 E |
| Poggio Moiano | 66 | 42.12 N | 12.53 E |
| Poggioreale | 70 | 37.47 N | 13.01 E |
| Poggio Renatico | 64 | 44.46 N | 11.29 E |
| Poggiorsini | 68 | 40.55 N | 16.15 E |
| Poggio Rusco | 64 | 44.59 N | 11.07 E |
| Poggio Sannita | 66 | 41.47 N | 14.25 E |
| Pöggstall | 61 | 48.19 N | 15.12 E |
| Pogibi | 89 | 52.12 N | 141.42 E |
| Pogil-to I | 98 | 34.09 N | 126.33 E |
| Pogliano | 266b | 45.32 N | 8.59 E |
| Pogny | 56 | 48.52 N | 4.29 E |
| Pogoanele | 38 | 44.54 N | 27.00 E |
| Pogodajevo | 80 | 51.37 N | 51.04 E |
| Pogoniani | 38 | 40.00 N | 20.25 E |
| Pogoreloje Gorodišče | 76 | 56.08 N | 34.56 E |
| Pogoso | 152 | 6.46 S | 17.12 E |
| Pogost, Ross. | 80 | 57.39 N | 42.33 E |
| Pogost, Ross. | 82 | 56.52 N | 39.04 E |
| Pogožeje | 78 | 51.36 N | 37.16 E |
| Pogradec | 38 | 40.54 N | 20.39 E |
| Po Grande ≃ | 64 | 44.57 N | 12.26 E |
| Pograničnoje | 80 | 50.32 N | 48.38 E |
| Pograničnyj, Ross. | 80 | 46.57 N | 45.46 E |
| Pograničnyj, Ross. | 89 | 44.25 N | 131.24 E |
| Pogromni Volcano ∧1 | 180 | 54.33 N | 164.45 W |
| Pogromnoje | 80 | 52.35 N | 52.32 E |
| Pogruznaja | 80 | 54.14 N | 50.29 E |
| Poh | 112 | 0.46 S | 122.49 E |
| P'ohang | 98 | 36.03 N | 129.20 E |
| Pohatcong Creek ≃ | 210 | 40.37 N | 75.11 W |
| Pohénégamook | 186 | 47.31 N | 69.16 W |
| Pohick Creek ≃ | 284c | 38.46 N | 77.14 W |
| Pohick Creek, Rabbit Branch ≃ | 284c | 38.48 N | 77.17 W |
| Pohick Creek, Sideburn Branch ≃ | 284c | 38.48 N | 77.17 W |
| Pohjanmaa ⊕1 | 26 | 64.00 N | 25.00 E |
| Pohjois-Karjalan lääni □4 | 24 | 63.00 N | 30.00 E |
| Pöhl, Talsperre ⊕6 | 54 | 50.33 N | 12.12 E |
| Pöhla | 54 | 50.31 N | 12.49 E |
| Pöhlde | 52 | 51.37 N | 10.18 E |
| Pohl-Göns | 56 | 50.28 N | 8.39 E |
| Pohlheim | 56 | 50.34 N | 8.45 E |
| Pohnpei I | 174r | 6.55 N | 158.15 E |
| Pohořelice | 61 | 48.59 N | 16.32 E |
| Pohorje ⋏ | 61 | 46.30 N | 15.20 E |
| Pohrebyshche | 78 | 49.29 N | 29.16 E |
| Pohri | 124 | 25.32 N | 77.21 E |
| Pohsien → Boxian | 100 | 33.53 N | 115.45 E |
| Pohue Bay c | 229d | 19.00 N | 155.48 W |
| Poiana Mare | 38 | 43.55 N | 23.04 E |
| Poiana Ruscă, Munții ⋏ | 38 | 45.41 N | 22.30 E |
| Pöide | 76 | 58.31 N | 23.03 E |
| Poigny-la-Forêt | 261 | 48.41 N | 1.45 E |
| Poim | 80 | 53.01 N | 43.11 E |
| Poing | 64 | 48.10 N | 11.49 E |
| Poinsett, Cape > | 9 | 65.42 S | 113.18 E |
| Poinsett, Lake ⊜, Fl., U.S. | 220 | 28.20 N | 80.50 W |
| Poinsett, Lake ⊜, S.D., U.S. | 198 | 44.34 N | 97.05 W |
| Point | 222 | 32.56 N | 95.52 W |
| Point Arena | 204 | 38.54 N | 123.41 W |
| Point Au Fer Island I | 194 | 29.15 N | 91.15 W |
| Point Baker | 180 | 56.21 N | 133.37 W |
| Pointblank | 222 | 30.45 N | 95.13 W |
| Point Chautauqua | 214 | 42.14 N | 79.28 W |
| Point Comfort | 196 | 28.41 N | 96.33 W |
| Point Cook | 274b | 37.56 S | 144.45 E |
| Point Cook Royal Australian Air Force Station ■ | 169 | 37.56 S | 144.45 E |
| Point du Jour, Ruisseau du ≃ | 206 | 45.50 N | 73.25 W |
| Pointe-à-la-Frégate | 186 | 49.12 N | 64.55 W |
| Pointe-à-la-Garde | 186 | 48.05 N | 66.32 W |
| Pointe a la Hache | 194 | 29.34 N | 89.47 W |
| Pointe-à-Maurier | 186 | 50.20 N | 59.48 W |
| Pointe-à-Pitre | 241o | 16.14 N | 61.32 W |
| Pointe-à-Pitre-le Raizet, Aéroport de ⊠ | 241o | 16.17 N | 61.32 W |
| Pointe-au-Chêne | 206 | 45.38 N | 74.45 W |
| Pointe Aux Peaux Farms | 216 | 41.57 N | 83.16 W |
| Pointe-aux-Trembles | 206 | 45.39 N | 73.30 W |
| Pointe-Calumet | 275a | 45.30 N | 73.58 W |
| Pointe-Claire | 206 | 45.26 N | 73.50 W |
| Pointe-des-Cascades | 275a | 45.20 N | 73.58 W |
| Pointe-des-Galets → Le Port | 157c | 20.55 S | 55.18 E |
| Pointe-du-Moulin | 275a | 45.22 N | 73.52 W |
| Point Edward | 214 | 43.00 N | 82.24 W |
| Pointe-Noire, Congo | 152 | 4.48 S | 11.51 E |
| Pointe-Noire, Guad. | 241o | 16.14 N | 61.47 W |
| Point Enterprise | 222 | 31.40 N | 96.26 W |
| Pointers | 208 | 39.35 N | 75.26 W |
| Point Fortin | 241r | 10.11 N | 61.41 W |
| Point Hope | 180 | 68.21 N | 166.41 W |
| Point Imperial ∧ | 200 | 36.16 N | 111.58 W |
| Point Independence | 207 | 41.44 N | 70.39 W |
| Point Lake ⊜ | 176 | 65.15 N | 113.04 W |
| Point Leamington | 186 | 49.20 N | 55.24 W |
| Point Lookout, Md., U.S. | 208 | 38.02 N | 76.19 W |
| Point Lookout, N.Y., U.S. | 276 | 40.35 N | 73.35 W |
| Point Marion | 188 | 39.44 N | 79.53 W |
| Point McLeay | 168b | 35.32 S | 139.06 E |
| Point Nepean National Park ♦ | 169 | 38.25 S | 144.45 E |
| Point of Rocks | 208 | 39.16 N | 77.32 W |
| Point O'Woods | 276 | 40.39 N | 73.08 W |
| Point Pass | 168b | 34.05 S | 139.03 E |
| Point Pelee National Park ♦ | 214 | 41.57 N | 82.30 W |
| Point Peninsula >1 | 212 | 44.01 N | 76.15 W |
| Point Pleasant, Md., U.S. | 284b | 39.11 N | 76.35 W |
| Point Pleasant, N.J., U.S. | 208 | 40.04 N | 74.04 W |
| Point Pleasant, Oh., U.S. | 218 | 38.54 N | 84.14 W |
| Point Pleasant, Pa., U.S. | 208 | 40.25 N | 75.04 W |
| Point Pleasant, W.V., U.S. | 188 | 38.50 N | 82.08 W |
| Point Pleasant Beach | 208 | 40.05 N | 74.02 W |
| Point Reyes National Seashore ♦ | 204 | 38.00 N | 122.58 W |
| Point Roberts | 224 | 48.59 N | 123.04 W |
| Point Salines International Airport ⊠ | 241k | 12.01 N | 61.47 W |
| Point Samson | 162 | 20.36 S | 117.12 E |
| Point Sapin | 186 | 46.58 N | 64.50 W |
| Point View Reservoir ⊜1 | 276 | 40.58 N | 74.15 W |
| Point Whiteshed | 180 | 60.28 N | 145.57 W |
| Poirino | 62 | 44.55 N | 7.51 E |
| Poisevo | 80 | 55.32 N | 53.30 E |
| Poison Creek ≃ | 202 | 43.15 N | 108.09 W |
| Poison Spider Creek ≃ | 200 | 42.46 N | 106.31 W |
| Poisson Blanc, Réservoir du ⊜1 | 188 | 46.00 N | 75.45 W |
| Poissonnier Point > | 162 | 19.57 S | 119.11 E |
| Poissons | 58 | 48.25 N | 5.13 E |
| Poissy | 50 | 48.56 N | 2.03 E |
| Poitiers | 32 | 46.35 N | 0.20 E |
| Poitou □9 | 32 | 46.20 N | 0.30 W |
| Poix | 50 | 49.47 N | 1.59 E |
| Poix-Terron | 56 | 49.39 N | 4.39 E |
| Pojarkovo | 89 | 49.38 N | 128.38 E |
| Pojma ≃ | 88 | 56.54 N | 97.48 E |
| Pojo | 248 | 17.45 S | 64.49 W |
| Pojoaque Valley | 200 | 35.59 N | 106.00 W |
| Pojuca | 255 | 12.21 S | 38.20 W |
| Pojuca ≃ | 255 | 12.34 S | 38.03 W |
| Pokagon State Park ♦ | 216 | 41.43 N | 85.01 W |
| Pokaran | 120 | 26.55 N | 71.55 E |
| Pokataroo | 166 | 29.35 S | 148.42 E |
| Pokatejeva | 88 | 56.59 N | 97.25 E |
| Pokatilovka, Kaz. | 80 | 51.06 N | 51.53 E |
| Pokatilovka, Kaz. | 86 | 45.23 N | 80.10 E |
| Poke Run ≃ | 279b | 40.30 N | 79.33 W |
| Pokharā | 124 | 28.14 N | 83.59 E |
| Pokharia | 126 | 23.55 N | 86.37 E |
| Poko, Sūd. | 140 | 5.38 N | 31.50 E |
| Poko, Zaïre | 154 | 3.09 N | 26.53 E |
| Pokoinu | 174k | 21.12 S | 159.49 W |
| Pokojnoje | 84 | 44.48 N | 44.16 E |
| Pokok Sena | 114 | 6.10 N | 100.32 E |
| Pokrov | 82 | 55.55 N | 39.10 E |
| Pokrovka, Kaz. | 86 | 54.17 N | 68.15 E |
| Pokrovka, Kaz. | 86 | 49.28 N | 81.28 E |
| Pokrovka, Kyrg. | 85 | 42.20 N | 78.01 E |
| Pokrovka, Kyrg. | 85 | 42.45 N | 71.36 E |
| Pokrovka, Ross. | 80 | 48.22 N | 46.04 E |
| Pokrovka, Ross. | 80 | 53.47 N | 53.19 E |
| Pokrovka, Ross. | 89 | 43.57 N | 131.39 E |
| Pokrovsk | 74 | 61.29 N | 129.06 E |
| Pokrovskaja Arčada | 80 | 52.56 N | 44.13 E |
| Pokrovs'ke, Ukr. | 78 | 47.59 N | 36.14 E |
| Pokrovs'ke, Ukr. | 78 | 46.32 N | 31.38 E |
| Pokrovs'ke, Ukr. | 78 | 49.44 N | 38.13 E |
| Pokrovs'ke, Ukr. | 83 | 48.37 N | 38.09 E |
| Pokrovskoje, Ross. | 76 | 52.38 N | 36.51 E |
| Pokrovskoje, Ross. | 80 | 54.04 N | 43.37 E |
| Pokrovskoje, Ross. | 80 | 53.54 N | 40.26 E |
| Pokrovskoje, Ross. | 82 | 56.25 N | 37.03 E |
| Pokrovskoje, Ross. | 82 | 55.53 N | 36.19 E |
| Pokrovskoje, Ross. | 83 | 47.25 N | 38.54 E |
| Pokrovskoje, Ross. | 86 | 57.14 N | 66.48 E |
| Pokrovskoje, Ross. | 265a | 59.44 N | 30.46 E |
| Pokrovskoje ⊕8 | 265b | 55.37 N | 37.37 E |
| Pokrovsko-Strešnevo ⊕8 | 265b | 55.49 N | 37.29 E |
| Pokrovsk-Ural'skij | 86 | 60.10 N | 59.49 E |
| Pokur | 74 | 61.02 N | 75.26 E |
| Pola → Pula, Hrv. | 64 | 44.52 N | 13.50 E |
| Pola, Pil. | 116 | 13.09 N | 121.26 E |
| Pola, Ross. | 76 | 57.56 N | 31.50 E |
| Pola ≃ | 76 | 58.04 N | 31.37 E |
| Pola Bay c | 116 | 13.10 N | 121.28 E |
| Polacca | 200 | 35.50 N | 110.22 W |
| Polacca Wash V | 200 | 35.22 N | 110.50 W |
| Polack | 76 | 55.31 N | 28.46 E |
| Pola de Laviana | 34 | 43.15 N | 5.34 W |
| Pola de Lena | 34 | 43.10 N | 5.49 W |
| Pola de Siero | 34 | 43.23 N | 5.40 W |
| Polān | 128 | 25.35 N | 61.12 E |
| Polanco | 252 | 33.54 S | 55.09 W |
| Poland, Kiribati | 174o | 1.59 N | 157.32 W |
| Poland, N.Y., U.S. | 210 | 43.13 N | 75.03 W |
| Poland, Oh., U.S. | 214 | 41.01 N | 80.37 W |
| Poland (Polska) □1, Europe | 22 | 52.00 N | 19.00 E |
| Poland (Polska) □1, Europe | 30 | 52.00 N | 19.00 E |
| Polangui | 116 | 13.17 N | 123.29 E |
| Polanów | 30 | 54.08 N | 16.39 E |
| Polapare ≃ | 115b | 9.43 S | 119.06 E |
| Pol'arnik | 180 | 67.03 N | 178.53 W |
| Pol'arnyj, Ross. | 24 | 69.12 N | 33.22 E |
| Pol'arnyj, Ross. | 74 | 69.10 N | 178.48 E |
| Pol'arnyj Ural ⋏ | 24 | 66.55 N | 64.30 E |
| Polatlı | 130 | 39.36 N | 32.09 E |
| Polba | 272b | 22.57 N | 88.18 E |
| Polbain | 46 | 58.02 N | 5.23 W |
| Polbeth | 46 | 55.52 N | 3.33 W |
| Polch | 56 | 50.18 N | 7.18 E |
| Polcirkeln | 24 | 66.34 N | 21.05 E |
| Polcura | 252 | 37.17 S | 71.43 W |
| Połczyn Zdrój | 30 | 53.46 N | 16.06 E |
| Polden Hills ⋏2 | 42 | 51.08 N | 2.50 W |
| Poldnevica | 80 | 58.37 N | 46.38 E |
| Pol'dorak | 85 | 39.25 N | 69.56 E |
| Poleang | 112 | 4.42 S | 121.46 E |
| Polebridge | 182 | 48.45 N | 114.17 W |
| Polecat Creek ≃ | 196 | 36.00 N | 95.57 W |
| Poledník ∧ | 60 | 49.04 N | 13.24 E |
| Polee, Pulau I | 164 | 2.12 S | 130.15 E |
| Polegate | 42 | 50.49 N | 0.15 E |
| Pol-e Khomrī | 120 | 35.56 N | 68.43 E |
| Pole Moor | 262 | 53.39 N | 1.54 W |
| Polen → Poland □1 | 30 | 52.00 N | 19.00 E |
| Polenezköy ⊕8 | 267b | 41.07 N | 29.12 E |
| Pol-e Safīd | 128 | 36.06 N | 53.01 E |
| Polesden Lacey ⊥ | 260 | 51.15 N | 0.22 W |
| Polesella | 64 | 44.58 N | 11.45 E |
| Polesine ⊕1 | 64 | 45.00 N | 11.45 E |
| Polesine Parmense | 64 | 45.01 N | 10.04 E |
| Polessk [Labiau] | 76 | 54.52 N | 21.05 E |
| Polesworth | 42 | 52.37 N | 1.36 W |
| Polesye ⊕1 | 72 | 52.00 N | 27.00 E |
| Polevaja | 78 | 51.37 N | 36.30 E |
| Polevskoj | 86 | 56.26 N | 60.11 E |
| Polewali | 112 | 3.25 S | 119.20 E |
| Pol-e Žahāb | 128 | 34.28 N | 45.52 E |
| Polgár | 30 | 47.52 N | 21.08 E |
| Polgooth | 42 | 50.19 N | 4.48 W |
| Pŏlgyo | 98 | 34.52 N | 127.21 E |
| Poli, Cam. | 146 | 8.29 N | 13.15 E |
| Poli, Zhg. | 98 | 35.43 N | 119.47 E |
| Poli, Zhg. | 98 | 35.57 N | 118.17 E |
| Polia | 68 | 38.45 N | 16.19 E |
| Políaigos I | 38 | 36.46 N | 24.38 E |
| Policastro, Golfo di c | 68 | 40.00 N | 15.30 E |
| Policastro Bussentino | 68 | 40.09 N | 15.32 E |
| Police | 30 | 53.35 N | 14.33 E |
| Polička | 30 | 49.43 N | 16.16 E |
| Policoro | 68 | 40.13 N | 16.41 E |
| Polignac | 62 | 45.04 N | 3.52 E |
| Polignano a Mare | 68 | 41.00 N | 17.13 E |
| Poligny | 58 | 46.50 N | 5.43 E |
| Polihale State Park ♦ | 229b | 22.05 N | 159.45 W |
| Políkastron | 38 | 41.00 N | 22.34 E |
| Polikhnítos | 38 | 39.05 N | 26.11 E |
| Polillo | 116 | 14.43 N | 121.56 E |
| Polillo Island I | 116 | 14.50 N | 121.57 E |
| Polillo Islands II | 116 | 14.50 N | 122.05 E |
| Polillo Strait ʯ | 116 | 14.44 N | 121.51 E |
| Polinesia Francesa → French Polynesia □2 | 14 | 15.00 S | 140.00 W |
| Polinik ∧ | 64 | 46.54 N | 13.09 E |
| Polinyà de Vallès | 266d | 41.33 N | 2.10 E |
| Pólis | 130 | 35.02 N | 32.25 E |
| Polis'ke | 78 | 51.14 N | 29.22 E |
| Polist' ≃ | 76 | 58.06 N | 31.31 E |
| Polistena | 68 | 38.25 N | 16.05 E |
| Politécnico Nacional, Instituto ʋ2 | 286a | 19.30 N | 99.08 W |
| Politotdel'skoje | 83 | 47.33 N | 39.05 E |
| Pölitz → Police | 30 | 53.35 N | 14.33 E |
| Polivanovo | 80 | 53.36 N | 47.23 E |
| Políyiros | 38 | 40.23 N | 23.27 E |
| Polizzi Generosa | 70 | 37.49 N | 14.00 E |
| Polizzo, Monte ∧ | 70 | 37.52 N | 12.47 E |
| Polk, Ne., U.S. | 198 | 41.04 N | 97.47 W |
| Polk, Oh., U.S. | 214 | 40.57 N | 82.13 W |
| Polk, Pa. U.S. | 214 | 41.22 N | 79.55 W |
| Polk □6, Fl., U.S. | 220 | 28.01 N | 81.37 W |
| Polk □6, Or., U.S. | 224 | 45.00 N | 123.23 W |
| Polk □6, Tx., U.S. | 222 | 30.45 N | 94.48 W |
| Polk City | 220 | 28.10 N | 81.49 W |
| Pol'kino | 74 | 71.10 N | 99.13 E |
| Polkton | 192 | 35.00 N | 80.12 W |
| Polla | 68 | 40.30 N | 15.30 E |
| Pollāchi | 122 | 10.40 N | 77.01 E |
| Pöllau | 61 | 47.18 N | 15.51 E |
| Pöllauberg | 61 | 47.19 N | 15.52 E |
| Polleben | 54 | 51.34 N | 11.36 E |
| Pollenfeld | 60 | 48.57 N | 11.12 E |
| Pollenza | 66 | 43.16 N | 13.21 E |
| Pollica | 68 | 40.11 N | 15.03 E |
| Pollina | 70 | 37.59 N | 14.09 E |
| Polling | 64 | 47.48 N | 11.09 E |
| Pollino, Monte ∧ | 68 | 39.55 N | 16.11 E |
| Polloc Harbor c | 116 | 7.23 N | 124.12 E |
| Pollock, La., U.S. | 194 | 31.31 N | 92.24 W |
| Pollock, S.D., U.S. | 198 | 45.54 N | 100.17 W |
| Pollock Pines | 226 | 38.46 N | 120.34 W |
| Pollock Run ≃ | 279b | 40.14 N | 79.47 W |
| Pollok | 222 | 31.27 N | 94.52 W |
| Pollutri | 66 | 42.08 N | 14.35 E |
| Pollux ∧ | 172 | 44.14 S | 168.53 E |
| Polmak | 24 | 70.04 N | 28.00 E |
| Polmont | 46 | 55.59 N | 3.42 W |
| Polná | 30 | 49.29 N | 15.43 E |
| Polnaja ≃ | 83 | 48.54 N | 39.50 E |
| Pol'noje-Jaltunovo | 80 | 53.59 N | 41.52 E |
| Polnovo-Seliger | 76 | 57.32 N | 32.55 E |
| Polo, Il., U.S. | 190 | 41.59 N | 89.34 W |
| Polo, Mo., U.S. | 194 | 39.33 N | 94.02 W |
| Polochic ≃ | 236 | 15.28 N | 89.22 W |
| Polock | 86 | 52.46 N | 59.42 E |
| Pologne → Poland □1 | 30 | 52.00 N | 19.00 E |
| Pologoje Zajmišče | 80 | 48.29 N | 45.57 E |
| Pologrudovo | 86 | 57.07 N | 74.13 E |
| Polohy | 78 | 47.29 N | 36.15 E |
| Polom, Ross. | 24 | 59.13 N | 50.50 E |
| Polom, Ross. | 80 | 57.47 N | 53.29 E |
| Polo Magnético del Sur → South Magnetic Pole ⊕ | 9 | 65.18 S | 139.30 E |
| Pölömäki ∧2 | 26 | 63.21 N | 27.03 E |
| Polomet' ≃ | 76 | 57.41 N | 32.12 E |
| Polomolok | 116 | 6.14 N | 125.03 E |
| Polonia → Poland □1 | 30 | 52.00 N | 19.00 E |
| Polonia, Arroyo ≃ | 258 | 34.10 S | 57.15 W |
| Polonio, Cabo > | 252 | 34.24 S | 53.46 W |
| Polonnaruwa | 122 | 7.56 N | 81.00 E |
| Polonnaruwa ⊥ | 122 | 7.56 N | 81.00 E |
| Polonne | 78 | 50.07 N | 27.30 E |
| Pološkovo | 82 | 54.08 N | 35.53 E |
| Polo Sur → South Pole ⊕ | 9 | 90.00 S | 0.00 |
| Polotn'anyj | 82 | 54.45 N | 36.00 E |
| Polotsk → Polock | 76 | 55.31 N | 28.46 E |
| Polovinnoje, Ross. | 86 | 54.43 N | 63.50 E |
| Polovinnoje, Ross. | 86 | 53.46 N | 79.15 E |
| Polovo | 76 | 57.03 N | 32.27 E |
| Polovynkyne | 83 | 49.14 N | 38.55 E |
| Polperro | 42 | 50.19 N | 4.31 W |
| Polruan | 42 | 50.19 N | 4.36 W |
| Pöls | 61 | 47.13 N | 14.35 E |
| Pölsbach ≃ | 61 | 47.11 N | 14.45 E |
| Polska → Poland □1 | 30 | 52.00 N | 19.00 E |
| Polski Trămbeš | 38 | 43.22 N | 25.38 E |
| Polson | 202 | 47.41 N | 114.09 W |
| Polster ∧ | 61 | 47.32 N | 14.58 E |
| Polsum | 52 | 51.37 N | 7.03 E |
| Poltava | 78 | 49.35 N | 34.34 E |
| Poltava □4 | 78 | 49.45 N | 34.00 E |
| Poltavka | 86 | 54.22 N | 71.45 E |
| Poltevy Pen'ki | 80 | 54.35 N | 42.06 E |
| Poltimore | 188 | 45.47 N | 75.43 W |
| Põltsamaa | 76 | 58.38 N | 25.58 E |
| Põltsamaa ≃ | 76 | 58.27 N | 26.09 E |
| Poludino | 86 | 54.51 N | 69.55 E |
| Poluj ≃ | 74 | 66.31 N | 66.33 E |
| Polunočnoje | 74 | 60.52 N | 60.25 E |
| Polur | 82 | [illegible] | [illegible] |
| Polur'adinki | 82 | 54.51 N | 38.41 E |
| Poluškino | 265b | 55.41 N | 38.05 E |
| Pol'ustrovo ⊕8 | 265a | 59.58 N | 30.25 E |
| Põlva | 76 | 58.03 N | 27.03 E |
| Polvaredas | 258 | 35.35 S | 59.30 W |
| Polverigi | 66 | 43.31 N | 13.23 E |
| Polvijärvi | 26 | 62.51 N | 29.22 E |
| Polvilho | 287b | 23.23 S | 46.50 W |
| Polvoranca | 266a | 40.19 N | 3.48 W |
| Polynesia II | 14 | 4.00 S | 156.00 W |
| Polynesian Cultural Center ʋ | 229c | 21.39 N | 157.55 W |
| Polynésie française → French Polynesia □2 | 14 | 15.00 S | 140.00 W |
| Polynnoje | 80 | 46.51 N | 46.56 E |
| Polysajevo | 86 | 54.35 N | 86.14 E |
| Pölzig | 54 | 50.57 N | 12.11 E |
| Poma, Lago ⊜1 | 70 | 37.55 N | 13.06 E |
| Pomabamba | 248 | 8.50 S | 77.28 W |
| Pomacanchi | 248 | 14.02 S | 71.34 W |
| Pomahaka ≃ | 172 | 46.09 S | 169.34 E |
| Pomarance | 66 | 43.18 N | 10.52 E |
| Pomarico | 68 | 40.31 N | 16.33 E |
| Pomarkku | 26 | 61.42 N | 22.00 E |
| Pomata | 248 | 16.16 S | 69.18 W |
| Pomáz | 264c | 47.39 N | 19.02 E |
| Pomba ≃ | 256 | 21.24 S | 42.32 W |
| Pombais, Ribeira de ≃ | 266c | 38.48 N | 9.07 W |
| Pombal, Bra. | 250 | 6.46 S | 37.47 W |
| Pombal, Port. | 34 | 39.55 N | 8.38 W |
| Pombia | 266b | 45.39 N | 8.38 E |
| Pomellen | 54 | 53.20 N | 14.23 E |
| Pomene | 156 | 22.53 S | 35.33 E |
| Pomerania □9 | 30 | 54.00 N | 16.00 E |
| Pomeranian Bay c | 54 | 54.00 N | 14.15 E |
| Pomerene | 200 | 31.59 N | 110.17 W |
| Pomerode | 252 | 26.45 S | 49.11 W |
| Pomeroon ≃ | 246 | 7.37 N | 58.45 W |
| Pomeroon-Supenaam □4 | 246 | 7.20 N | 58.50 W |
| Pomeroy, S. Afr. | 158 | 28.33 S | 30.26 E |
| Pomeroy, N. Ire., U.K. | 48 | 54.36 N | 6.55 W |
| Pomeroy, Ia., U.S. | 198 | 42.33 N | 94.41 W |
| Pomeroy, Oh., U.S. | 188 | 39.01 N | 82.02 W |
| Pomeroy, Pa., U.S. | 208 | 39.58 N | 75.53 W |
| Pomeroy, Wa., U.S. | 202 | 46.28 N | 117.36 W |
| Pomezia | 66 | 41.40 N | 12.30 E |
| Pomfret, S. Afr. | 156 | 25.50 S | 23.32 E |
| Pomfret, Ct., U.S. | 207 | 41.53 N | 71.57 W |
| Pomfret, Md., U.S. | 208 | 38.34 N | 77.01 W |
| Pomi | 38 | 47.42 N | 23.19 E |
| Pomichna | 78 | 48.14 N | 31.26 E |
| Pomigliano | 68 | 40.54 N | 14.23 E |
| Pominovo | 82 | 55.26 N | 39.11 E |
| Pomio | 164 | 5.30 S | 151.30 E |
| Pommard | 58 | 47.01 N | 4.47 E |
| Pomme de Terre ≃, Mn., U.S. | 198 | 45.10 N | 96.05 W |
| Pomme de Terre ≃, Mo., U.S. | 194 | 38.11 N | 93.24 W |
| Pomme de Terre Lake ⊜1 | 194 | 37.51 N | 93.19 W |
| Pommelsbrunn | 60 | 49.30 N | 11.31 E |
| Pommera | 50 | 50.10 N | 2.26 E |
| Pommern → Pomerania □9 | 30 | 54.00 N | 16.00 E |
| Pommersche Bucht → Pomeranian Bay c | 54 | 54.00 N | 14.15 E |
| Pommersfelden | 56 | 49.46 N | 10.49 E |
| Pomona, Namibia | 156 | 27.09 S | 15.18 E |
| Pomona, Ca., U.S. | 228 | 34.03 N | 117.45 W |
| Pomona, Ks., U.S. | 198 | 38.36 N | 95.27 W |
| Pomona, N.J., U.S. | 208 | 39.28 N | 74.34 W |
| Pomona, N.Y., U.S. | 276 | 41.10 N | 74.02 W |
| Pomona College ʋ2 | 280 | 34.06 N | 117.44 W |
| Pomona Estates | 273d | 26.06 S | 28.15 E |
| Pomona Lake ⊜1 | 198 | 38.40 N | 95.35 W |
| Pomona Park | 192 | 29.30 N | 81.35 W |
| Pomongo | 152 | 5.00 S | 19.08 E |
| Pomorie | 38 | 42.33 N | 27.39 E |
| Pomorskij proliv ʯ | 24 | 68.30 N | 50.00 E |
| Pomoryany | 78 | 49.38 N | 24.56 E |
| Pomorze → Pomerania □9 | 30 | 54.00 N | 16.00 E |
| Pomozdino | 24 | 62.12 N | 54.06 E |
| Pompano Beach | 220 | 26.14 N | 80.07 W |
| Pompano Beach Highlands | 220 | 26.16 N | 80.06 W |
| Pompei | 68 | 40.45 N | 14.30 E |
| Pompei ⊥ | 68 | 40.45 N | 14.30 E |
| Pompéia | 255 | 22.08 S | 50.10 W |
| Pompejevka | 89 | 48.23 N | 130.46 E |
| Pompeston Creek ≃ | 285 | 40.01 N | 75.01 W |
| Pompéu | 255 | 19.12 S | 44.59 W |
| Pompey, Fr. | 56 | 48.46 N | 6.07 E |
| Pompey, N.Y., U.S. | 210 | 42.54 N | 76.01 W |
| Pomponio Creek ≃ | 282 | 37.18 N | 122.25 W |
| Pomponio State Beach ♦ | 282 | 37.17 N | 122.24 W |
| Pomponne | 261 | 48.53 N | 2.41 E |
| Pompon-yama ∧ | 270 | 34.56 N | 135.37 E |
| Pomposa | 66 | 44.49 N | 12.11 E |
| Pomposa, Abbazia di ʋ1 | 64 | 44.49 N | 12.11 E |
| Pompton ≃ | 276 | 40.54 N | 74.16 W |
| Pompton Lakes | 210 | 41.00 N | 74.17 W |
| Pompton Lakes ⊜ | 276 | 41.00 N | 74.17 W |
| Pomquet | 186 | 45.38 N | 61.51 W |
| Pomssen | 54 | 51.14 N | 12.37 E |
| Ponape → Pohnpei I | 174r | 6.55 N | 158.15 E |
| Ponask Lake ⊜ | 184 | 54.00 N | 92.41 W |
| Ponass Lakes ⊜ | 184 | 52.18 N | 103.58 W |
| Ponazyrevo | 80 | 58.21 N | 46.19 E |
| Ponca | 198 | 42.33 N | 96.42 W |
| Ponca City | 196 | 36.42 N | 97.05 W |
| Ponca Creek ≃ | 198 | 42.48 N | 98.05 W |
| Ponce | 240m | 18.01 N | 66.37 W |
| Ponce, Aeropuerto ⊠ | 240m | 18.01 N | 66.34 W |
| Ponce de Leon | 194 | 30.43 N | 85.56 W |
| Ponce de Leon Bay c | 220 | 25.21 N | 81.07 W |
| Ponce de Leon Inlet c | 192 | 29.04 N | 80.55 W |
| Poncé-sur-le-Loir | 50 | 47.46 N | 0.40 E |
| Poncha Pass )( | 200 | 38.25 N | 106.05 W |
| Ponchatoula | 194 | 30.26 N | 90.26 W |
| Poncin | 58 | 46.05 N | 5.24 E |
| Poncitlán | 234 | 20.22 N | 102.55 W |
| Pond ≃ | 194 | 37.32 N | 87.21 W |
| Pond Brook ≃, N.J., U.S. | 276 | 41.02 N | 74.15 W |
| Pond Brook ≃, Oh., U.S. | 279a | 41.17 N | 81.24 W |
| Pondcreek | 196 | 36.40 N | 97.48 W |
| Pond Creek ≃, U.S. | 196 | 36.40 N | 97.33 W |
| Pond Creek ≃, Tx., U.S. | 222 | 31.02 N | 96.46 W |
| Pond Eddy | 210 | 41.27 N | 74.49 W |
| Ponder | 222 | 33.11 N | 97.17 W |
| Pondera Coulee V | 202 | 48.16 N | 111.03 W |
| Ponders End ⊕8 | 260 | 51.39 N | 0.03 W |
| Pondicherry | 122 | 11.56 N | 79.53 E |
| Pondicherry □8 | 122 | 11.56 N | 79.50 E |
| Pond Inlet | 176 | 72.41 N | 78.00 W |
| Pond Inlet c | 176 | 72.46 N | 77.00 W |
| Pondok Tanjong | 114 | 5.00 N | 100.44 E |
| Pondoland □9 | 158 | 31.10 S | 29.30 E |
| Pondosa | 204 | 41.12 N | 121.41 W |
| Pond Run ≃ | 208 | 40.13 N | 74.44 W |
| Poneas Island I | 116 | 9.55 N | 125.57 E |
| Ponente, Capo > | 70a | 35.31 N | 12.31 E |
| Ponente, Riviera di ⋏2 | 62 | 44.10 N | 8.20 E |
| Ponérihouen | 175f | 21.05 S | 165.24 E |
| Poneto | 216 | 40.39 N | 85.13 W |
| Ponežukaj | 78 | 45.03 N | 39.22 E |
| Ponferrada | 34 | 42.33 N | 6.35 W |
| Pong | 110 | 19.10 N | 100.17 E |
| Pongani | 164 | 9.05 S | 148.35 E |
| Pongara, Pointe > | 152 | 0.21 N | 9.21 E |
| Pongaroa | 172 | 40.33 S | 176.11 E |
| Pongau V | 64 | 47.21 N | 13.14 E |
| Pong Dam ⊕6 | 123 | 31.59 N | 75.57 E |
| Ponghyŏn | 98 | 37.49 N | 125.36 E |
| Pongo ≃ | 140 | 8.42 N | 27.40 E |
| Pongolo ≃ | 158 | 26.57 S | 32.17 E |
| Pon'goma | 24 | 65.21 N | 34.25 E |
| Pong Tamale | 150 | 9.41 N | 0.49 W |
| Ponhook Lake ⊜ | 186 | 44.19 N | 64.53 W |
| Poni ≃ | 208 | 38.07 N | 77.26 W |
| Poniatowa | 30 | 51.11 N | 22.05 E |
| Poniec | 30 | 51.47 N | 16.50 E |
| Ponil Creek ≃ | 196 | 36.29 N | 104.48 W |
| Poninka | 78 | 50.12 N | 27.32 E |
| Ponino | 80 | 58.16 N | 52.49 E |
| Ponitz, Dtsch. | 54 | 50.51 N | 12.25 E |
| Pönitz, Dtsch. | 54 | 54.03 N | 10.40 E |
| Ponizovje | 76 | 55.17 N | 31.04 E |
| Ponkapoag Pond ⊜ | 283 | 42.12 N | 71.06 W |
| Pônley | 110 | 12.26 N | 104.27 E |
| Ponnaiyār ≃ | 122 | 11.46 N | 79.47 E |
| Ponnāni | 122 | 10.46 N | 75.54 E |
| Ponnūru Nidubrolu | 122 | 16.04 N | 80.34 E |
| Pono | 164 | 6.22 S | 134.36 E |
| Ponoj | 24 | 67.05 N | 41.07 E |
| Ponoj ≃ | 24 | 66.59 N | 41.17 E |
| Ponoka | 182 | 52.42 N | 113.35 W |
| Ponomar'ovka, Ross. | 80 | 53.19 N | 54.08 E |
| Ponomar'ovka, Ross. | 86 | 56.08 N | 82.23 E |
| Ponornytsya | 78 | 51.43 N | 32.49 E |
| Ponorogo | 115a | 7.52 S | 111.27 E |
| Ponpāj | 272b | 22.56 N | 88.15 E |
| Pons | 32 | 45.35 N | 0.33 W |
| Ponsacco | 66 | 43.37 N | 10.38 E |
| Ponson Island I | 116 | 10.46 N | 124.32 E |
| Ponsul ≃ | 34 | 39.40 N | 7.31 W |
| Pont | 62 | 45.34 N | 7.07 E |
| Pont-à-Celles | 50 | 50.30 N | 4.21 E |
| Ponta Delgada | 148a | 37.44 N | 25.40 W |
| Ponta Delgada □5 | 148a | 37.40 N | 25.30 W |
| Ponta de Pedras | 250 | 1.23 S | 48.52 W |
| Ponta Grossa | 252 | 25.05 S | 50.09 W |
| Pontalete | 256 | 21.27 S | 45.40 W |
| Pontalina | 255 | 17.31 S | 49.27 W |
| Pontallier-sur-Saône | 58 | 47.18 N | 5.25 E |
| Pont-à-Marcq | 50 | 50.31 N | 3.07 E |
| Pont-à-Mousson | 56 | 48.54 N | 6.04 E |
| Ponta Negra | 256 | 22.57 S | 35.10 W |
| Pontão | 34 | 39.55 N | 8.22 W |
| Ponta Porã | 255 | 22.32 S | 55.43 W |
| Pontardawe | 42 | 51.44 N | 3.51 W |
| Pontardulais | 42 | 51.43 N | 4.03 W |
| Pontarlier | 58 | 46.54 N | 6.22 E |
| Pontas de Pedra | 250 | 7.38 S | 34.48 W |
| Pontassieve | 66 | 43.46 N | 11.26 E |
| Pontaubert | 50 | 47.29 N | 3.52 E |
| Pont-Audemer | 50 | 49.21 N | 0.31 E |
| Pontault-Combault | 261 | 48.47 N | 2.36 E |
| Pontaumur | 32 | 45.52 N | 2.40 E |
| Pont-Aven | 32 | 47.51 N | 3.45 W |
| Pontbriand | 206 | 46.09 N | 71.15 W |
| Pont Canavese | 62 | 45.25 N | 7.36 E |
| Pontcarré | 261 | 48.48 N | 2.42 E |
| Pontcharra | 62 | 45.26 N | 6.01 E |
| Pontchartrain | 261 | 48.48 N | 1.54 E |
| Pontchartrain, Lake ⊜ | 194 | 30.10 N | 90.10 W |
| Pontchâteau | 32 | 47.26 N | 2.05 W |
| Pont-Croix | 32 | 48.02 N | 4.29 W |
| Pont-d'Ain | 58 | 46.03 N | 5.20 E |
| Pont d'Arc ♦ | 62 | 44.23 N | 4.26 E |
| Pont-de-Bonne | 56 | 50.27 N | 5.17 E |
| Pont-de-Chéruy | 62 | 45.45 N | 5.11 E |
| Pont-de-l'Arche | 50 | 49.18 N | 1.10 E |
| Pont-de-Pany | 58 | 47.18 N | 4.49 E |
| Pont-de-Poitte | 58 | 46.35 N | 5.41 E |
| Pont-de-Roide | 58 | 47.23 N | 6.46 E |
| Pont-de-Ruan | 50 | 47.15 N | 0.35 E |
| Pont-de-Salars | 32 | 44.17 N | 2.44 E |
| Pont-de-Vaux | 58 | 46.26 N | 4.56 E |
| Pont-de-Veyle | 58 | 46.16 N | 4.53 E |
| Ponte a Elsa | 66 | 43.41 N | 10.54 E |
| Ponte Alta do Bom Jesus | 255 | 12.06 S | 46.29 W |
| Ponte Alta do Norte | 250 | 10.45 S | 47.34 W |
| Ponte a Moriano | 66 | 43.54 N | 10.31 E |
| Ponteareas | 34 | 42.11 N | 8.30 W |
| Pontebba | 64 | 46.30 N | 13.18 E |
| Ponte Branca | 255 | 16.27 S | 52.40 W |
| Ponte Caffaro | 64 | 45.50 N | 10.32 E |
| Pontecagnano | 68 | 40.39 N | 14.52 E |
| Ponte-Caldelas | 34 | 42.23 N | 8.30 W |
| Pontecchio Marconi | 64 | 44.25 N | 11.15 E |
| Pontecchio Polesine | 64 | 45.01 N | 11.49 E |
| Pontecorvo | 66 | 41.27 N | 13.40 E |
| Pontecurone | 62 | 44.57 N | 8.56 E |
| Ponte da Barca | 34 | 41.48 N | 8.25 W |
| Ponte d'Arbia | 66 | 43.10 N | 11.28 E |
| Ponte delle Arche | 64 | 46.02 N | 10.52 E |
| Ponte dell'Olio | 62 | 44.52 N | 9.39 E |
| Pontedera | 66 | 43.40 N | 10.38 E |
| Ponte de Sor | 34 | 39.15 N | 8.01 W |
| Pontedeume | 34 | 43.24 N | 8.10 W |
| Ponte di Barbarano | 64 | 45.23 N | 11.34 E |
| Ponte di Legno | 64 | 46.16 N | 10.31 E |
| Ponte di Nava | 62 | 44.08 N | 7.53 E |
| Ponte di Piave | 64 | 45.43 N | 12.28 E |
| Ponte do Lima | 34 | 41.46 N | 8.35 W |
| Ponte do Púngoè | 156 | 19.30 S | 34.32 E |
| Pontefract | 44 | 53.42 N | 1.18 W |
| Ponte Galeria ⊕8 | 267a | 41.49 N | 12.21 E |
| Ponte Gardena (Waidbruck) | 64 | 46.36 N | 11.32 E |
| Ponte Ghiereto | 66 | 43.59 N | 11.15 E |
| Pontegrande | 58 | 45.59 N | 8.09 E |
| Ponte in Valtellina | 64 | 46.12 N | 9.59 E |
| Ponteix | 184 | 49.45 N | 107.29 W |
| Pontelagoscuro | 64 | 44.53 N | 11.36 E |
| Ponteland | 44 | 55.03 N | 1.44 W |
| Pontelandolfo | 68 | 41.17 N | 14.41 E |
| Pontelongo | 64 | 45.15 N | 12.02 E |
| Ponte nell'Alpi | 64 | 46.11 N | 12.16 E |
| Ponte Nova | 255 | 20.24 S | 42.54 W |
| Pont-en-Royans | 62 | 45.04 N | 5.21 E |
| Ponte Nuovo | 66 | 43.01 N | 12.28 E |
| Pontenure | 62 | 44.59 N | 9.47 E |
| Pontepetri | 66 | 44.02 N | 10.53 E |
| Pontericcioli | 66 | 43.26 N | 12.38 E |
| Ponte Rocchetta | 64 | 46.14 N | 11.04 E |
| Ponterwyd | 42 | 52.25 N | 3.50 W |
| Ponte San Giovanni | 66 | 43.05 N | 12.26 E |
| Ponte San Pietro | 62 | 45.42 N | 9.35 E |
| Pontesbury | 42 | 52.39 N | 2.54 W |
| Ponte Selva | 64 | 45.52 N | 9.54 E |
| Ponte Serrada | 252 | 26.52 S | 51.58 W |
| Pontestura | 62 | 45.08 N | 8.20 E |
| Ponte Tresa | 58 | 45.58 N | 8.52 E |
| Pontevedra, Arg. | 258 | 34.45 S | 58.42 W |
| Pontevedra, Esp. | 34 | 42.26 N | 8.38 W |
| Pontevedra, Pil. | 116 | 10.22 N | 122.52 E |
| Pontevedra □4 | 34 | 42.30 N | 8.40 W |
| Pontevedra, Ría de c | 34 | 42.22 N | 8.45 W |
| Ponte Vedra Beach | 192 | 30.14 N | 81.23 W |
| Pont-Évêque | 62 | 45.32 N | 4.55 E |
| Pontevico | 64 | 45.16 N | 10.05 E |
| Pontfaverger-Moronvilliers | 50 | 49.18 N | 4.19 E |
| Pontgibaud | 32 | 45.50 N | 2.52 E |
| Ponthévrard | 261 | 48.33 N | 1.55 E |
| Ponthierry | 261 | 48.32 N | 2.33 E |
| Ponthierville → Ubundu | 154 | 0.21 S | 25.29 E |
| Pontiac, Il., U.S. | 216 | 40.52 N | 88.37 W |
| Pontiac, Mi., U.S. | 216 | 42.38 N | 83.17 W |
| Pontiac □6 | 212 | 46.30 N | 77.00 W |
| Pontiac Lake ⊜ | 281 | 42.40 N | 83.28 W |
| Pontiac Lake State Recreation Area ♦ | 216 | 42.41 N | 83.28 W |


**Symbols** in the index entries represent the broad categories identified in the key at the right. Symbols with superior numbers (⋏1) identify subcategories (see complete key on page *I · 1*).

**Symbole** im Register stellen die rechts im Schlüssel erklärten Kategorien dar. Symbole mit hochgestellten Ziffern (⋏1) bezeichnen Unterabteilungen einer Kategorie (vgl. vollständiger Schlüssel auf Seite *I · 1*).

**Los símbolos** incluidos en el texto del índice representan las grandes categorías identificadas con la clave a la derecha. Los símbolos con números en su parte superior (⋏1) identifican las subcategorías (véase la clave completa en la página *I · 1*).

**Les symboles** de l'index représentent les catégories indiquées dans la légende à droite. Les symboles suivis d'un indice (⋏1) représentent des sous-catégories (voir légende complète à la page *I · 1*).

**Os símbolos** incluídos no texto do índice representam as grandes categorias identificadas com a chave à direita. Os símbolos com números em sua parte superior (⋏1) identificam as subcategorias (veja-se a chave completa à página *I · 1*).

| | | | | |
|---|---|---|---|---|
| ∧ Mountain | Berg | Montaña | Montagne | Montanha |
| ⋏ Mountains | Gebirge | Montañas | Montagnes | Montanhas |
| )( Pass | Paß | Paso | Col | Passo |
| V Valley, Canyon | Tal, Cañon | Valle, Cañón | Vallée, Canyon | Vale, Canhão |
| ≃ Plain | Ebene | Llano | Plaine | Planície |
| > Cape | Kap | Cabo | Cap | Cabo |
| I Island | Insel | Isla | Île | Ilha |
| II Islands | Inseln | Islas | Îles | Ilhas |
| ⊥ Other Topographic Features | Andere Topographische Objekte | Otros Elementos Topográficos | Autres données topographiques | Outros acidentes topográficos |

| ESPAÑOL Nombre | Página | Lat.°′ | Long.°′ W = Oeste |
|---|---|---|---|
| Pontiac Mall ➔[9] | 281 | 42.39 N | 83.20 W |
| Pontiac State Recreation Area ♠ | 281 | 42.41 N | 83.28 W |
| Pontianak | 112 | 0.02 S | 109.20 E |
| Pontian Kechil | 114 | 1.29 N | 103.23 E |
| Pontida | 62 | 45.43 N | 9.30 E |
| Pontigny | 50 | 47.55 N | 3.43 E |
| Pontinha ➔[8] | 266c | 38.46 N | 9.11 W |
| Pontinia | 66 | 41.24 N | 13.02 E |
| Pontivy | 32 | 48.04 N | 2.59 W |
| Pont-l'Abbé | 32 | 47.52 N | 4.13 W |
| Pont-lès-Moulins | 58 | 47.19 N | 6.22 E |
| Pont-l'Évêque | 50 | 49.18 N | 0.11 E |
| Pontlevoy | 50 | 47.23 N | 1.15 E |
| Pontoise | 50 | 49.03 N | 2.06 E |
| Pontoise-Cormeilles-en-Vexin, Aérodrome ⊠ | 261 | 49.06 N | 2.02 E |
| Ponton Creek ≏ | 162 | 31.10 S | 124.25 E |
| Pontonnyj | 265a | 59.47 N | 30.38 E |
| Pontoon Beach | 219 | 38.43 N | 90.04 W |
| Pontorson | 32 | 48.33 N | 1.31 W |
| Pontotoc, Ms., U.S. | 194 | 34.14 N | 88.59 W |
| Pontotoc, Tx., U.S. | 196 | 30.54 N | 98.59 W |
| Pontremoli | 62 | 44.22 N | 9.53 E |
| Pont-Remy | 50 | 50.03 N | 1.55 E |
| Pontresina | 58 | 46.28 N | 9.53 E |
| Pontrhydfendigaid | 42 | 52.17 N | 3.51 W |
| Pont-Rouge | 206 | 46.45 N | 71.42 W |
| Pont-Royal | 62 | 43.43 N | 5.11 E |
| Ponts | 34 | 41.55 N | 1.12 E |
| Pont-Sainte-Marie | 50 | 48.19 N | 4.06 E |
| Pont-Sainte-Maxence | 50 | 49.18 N | 2.36 E |
| Pont-Saint-Esprit | 62 | 44.15 N | 4.39 E |
| Pont-Saint-Martin | 62 | 45.36 N | 7.48 E |
| Pont-Scorff | 28 | 47.50 N | 3.24 W |
| Ponts Quentin, Ruisseau des ≏ | 261 | 48.44 N | 1.48 E |
| Pont-sur-Yonne | 50 | 48.17 N | 3.12 E |
| Pontuda, Ilha I | 287a | 23.02 S | 43.18 W |
| Pontus □[9] | 130 | 40.15 N | 38.00 E |
| Pontvallain | 50 | 47.45 N | 0.12 E |
| Pont-Viau ➔[8] | 275a | 45.34 N | 73.41 W |
| Pontyberem | 42 | 51.17 N | 4.09 W |
| Pontycymer | 42 | 51.37 N | 3.34 W |
| Pontypool | 42 | 51.43 N | 3.02 W |
| Pontypridd | 42 | 51.37 N | 3.22 W |
| Pony | 202 | 45.39 N | 111.53 W |
| Ponyri | 76 | 52.19 N | 36.20 E |
| Ponza | 66 | 40.54 N | 12.58 E |
| Ponza, Isola di I | 66 | 40.55 N | 12.57 E |
| Ponziane, Isole II | 66 | 40.55 N | 12.57 E |
| Ponzone | 62 | 44.35 N | 8.27 E |
| Poochera | 162 | 32.43 S | 134.51 E |
| Pool □[5] | 152 | 3.30 S | 15.00 E |
| Poole | 42 | 50.43 N | 1.59 W |
| Poole, Mount ʌ | 166 | 29.37 S | 141.46 E |
| Poole Bay c | 42 | 50.42 N | 1.52 W |
| Pooler | 192 | 32.06 N | 81.14 W |
| Poole's Cavern ±[5] | 262 | 53.14 N | 1.56 W |
| Pooles Island I | 208 | 39.17 N | 76.16 W |
| Poolesville | 208 | 39.08 N | 77.25 W |
| Poolewe | 46 | 57.45 N | 5.37 W |
| Pooley Island I | 182 | 52.44 N | 128.16 W |
| Pool's Cove | 186 | 47.41 N | 55.26 W |
| Poolville | 222 | 32.58 N | 97.52 W |
| Poona → Pune | 122 | 18.32 N | 73.52 E |
| Pooncarie | 166 | 33.23 S | 142.34 E |
| Poondinna, Mount ʌ | 162 | 27.20 S | 129.59 E |
| Poopo | 248 | 18.23 S | 66.59 W |
| Poopó, Lago ⊜ | 248 | 18.45 S | 67.07 W |
| Pooraka | 168b | 34.50 S | 138.37 E |
| Poor Knights Islands II | 172 | 35.30 S | 174.45 E |
| Poor Man Indian Reserve ➔[4] | 184 | 51.30 N | 104.23 W |
| Poor Meadow Brook ≏ | 283 | 42.01 N | 70.55 W |
| Poortjie | 158 | 30.13 S | 22.44 E |
| Poowong | 169 | 38.21 S | 145.46 E |
| Popa, Isla I | 236 | 9.11 N | 82.07 W |
| Popasna | 83 | 48.37 N | 38.20 E |
| Popasne | 78 | 48.48 N | 35.31 E |
| Popayán | 246 | 2.27 N | 76.36 W |
| Pope | 194 | 34.12 N | 89.56 W |
| Pope Creek ≏ | 226 | 38.37 N | 122.17 W |
| Popelnaste | 78 | 48.39 N | 33.43 E |
| Poperečnoje | 88 | 52.23 N | 110.42 E |
| Poperinge | 50 | 50.51 N | 2.43 E |
| Popești | 38 | 47.14 N | 22.25 E |
| Popești-Leordeni | 38 | 44.23 N | 26.10 E |
| Pope Valley | 226 | 38.37 N | 122.26 W |
| Popham Bay c | 176 | 64.10 N | 65.10 W |
| Popigaj | 74 | 71.55 N | 110.47 E |
| Popigaj ≏ | 74 | 72.54 N | 106.36 E |
| Popil'nya | 78 | 49.57 N | 29.27 E |
| Popiltah Lake ⊜ | 166 | 33.10 S | 141.43 E |
| Popinci | 38 | 42.25 N | 24.17 E |
| Popki | 80 | 50.11 N | 44.30 E |
| Popkum | 224 | 49.12 N | 121.44 W |
| Poplar, Ca., U.S. | 226 | 36.03 N | 119.08 W |
| Poplar, Mt., U.S. | 198 | 48.06 N | 105.11 W |
| Poplar, Wi., U.S. | 190 | 46.35 N | 91.47 W |
| Poplar ➔[8] | 260 | 51.31 N | 0.01 W |
| Poplar ≏, Can. | 184 | 53.00 N | 97.24 W |
| Poplar ≏, N.A. | 198 | 48.05 N | 105.11 W |
| Poplar ≏, Mn., U.S. | 198 | 47.51 N | 96.04 W |
| Poplar, West Fork ≏ | 198 | 48.31 N | 105.22 W |
| Poplar Bluff | 194 | 36.45 N | 90.23 W |
| Poplar Grove | 216 | 42.22 N | 88.49 W |
| Poplar Heights | 284c | 38.53 N | 77.12 W |
| Poplar Hill | 184 | 52.05 N | 94.18 W |
| Poplar Mountain ʌ | 194 | 36.43 N | 85.03 W |
| Poplar Point | 184 | 50.04 N | 97.57 W |
| Poplar Ridge | 210 | 42.44 N | 76.37 W |
| Poplar Springs | 208 | 39.21 N | 77.06 W |
| Poplarville | 194 | 30.50 N | 89.32 W |
| Poplevinskij | 76 | 53.41 N | 39.33 E |
| Popocatépetl, Volcán ʌ[1] | 234 | 19.02 N | 98.38 W |
| Popof Island I | 180 | 55.17 N | 160.25 W |
| Popoh | 115a | 8.15 S | 111.48 E |
| Popokabaka | 152 | 5.42 S | 16.35 E |
| Popoli | 66 | 42.10 N | 13.50 E |
| Popondetta | 164 | 8.46 S | 148.14 E |
| Popova | 89 | 42.58 N | 131.42 E |
| Popovka, Ross. | 76 | 60.08 N | 39.21 E |
| Popovka, Ross. | 80 | 49.14 N | 41.12 E |
| Popovkino | 82 | 56.07 N | 36.01 E |
| Popovo | 38 | 43.21 N | 26.13 E |
| Poppberg ʌ | 60 | 49.25 N | 11.35 E |
| Poppel | 56 | 51.27 N | 5.02 E |
| Poppenhausen | 56 | 50.06 N | 10.08 E |
| Poppenricht | 60 | 49.29 N | 11.48 E |
| Poppi | 66 | 43.43 N | 11.46 E |
| Popple ≏ | 190 | 45.50 N | 88.21 W |
| Poprad | 30 | 49.03 N | 20.18 E |
| Poprad ≏ | 30 | 49.38 N | 20.42 E |
| Popricani | 38 | 47.18 N | 27.31 E |
| Pŏpsŏng | 98 | 35.22 N | 126.27 E |
| Pŏptong | 98 | 38.59 N | 127.05 E |
| Poptún | 236 | 16.21 N | 89.26 W |
| Populonia | 66 | 42.59 N | 10.29 E |
| Poputnaja | 84 | 44.31 N | 41.27 E |
| Poquessing Creek ≏ | 285 | 40.03 N | 74.58 W |
| Poquetanuck | 207 | 41.29 N | 72.02 W |
| Poquonock | 207 | 41.54 N | 72.40 W |
| Poquonock Bridge | 207 | 41.20 N | 72.01 W |
| Poquoson | 208 | 37.07 N | 76.21 W |
| Poquoson ≏ | 208 | 37.10 N | 76.24 W |
| Poquott | 276 | 40.57 N | 73.05 W |
| Porādaha | 126 | 23.51 N | 89.01 E |
| Porādiha | 126 | 21.33 N | 86.26 E |
| Porāli Nai ≏ | 120 | 25.58 N | 66.26 E |
| Poranga | 250 | 4.44 S | 40.55 W |
| Porangahau | 172 | 40.18 S | 176.37 E |
| Porangatu | 255 | 13.26 S | 49.10 W |
| Porazava | 76 | 52.56 N | 24.22 E |
| Porbandar | 120 | 21.38 N | 69.36 E |

| FRANÇAIS Nom | Page | Lat.°′ | Long.°′ W = Ouest |
|---|---|---|---|
| Porce ≏ | 246 | 7.28 N | 74.53 W |
| Porchaman | 128 | 33.08 N | 63.51 E |
| Porcher Island I | 182 | 53.57 N | 130.30 W |
| Porcheville | 261 | 48.58 N | 1.47 E |
| Porchov | 76 | 57.46 N | 29.34 E |
| Porcia | 64 | 45.57 N | 12.36 E |
| Porciúncula | 255 | 20.58 S | 42.02 W |
| Porco | 248 | 19.50 S | 65.59 W |
| Porcos, Rio dos ≏ | 255 | 12.42 S | 45.07 W |
| Porcuna | 34 | 37.52 N | 4.11 W |
| Porcupine ≏ | 180 | 66.35 N | 145.15 W |
| Porcupine Brook ≏ | 283 | 42.46 N | 71.13 W |
| Porcupine Creek ≏ | 202 | 48.07 N | 106.20 W |
| Porcupine Creek, Middle Fork ≏ | 202 | 48.31 N | 106.30 W |
| Porcupine Creek, West Fork ≏ | 202 | 48.31 N | 106.30 W |
| Porcupine Dome ʌ | 180 | 65.31 N | 145.31 W |
| Porcupine Hills ⋏[2] | 184 | 52.30 N | 101.45 W |
| Porcupine Mountains State Park ♠ | 190 | 46.47 N | 89.50 W |
| Pordenone | 64 | 45.57 N | 12.39 E |
| Pordenone □[4] | 64 | 46.00 N | 12.45 E |
| Pordim | 38 | 43.23 N | 24.51 E |
| Poreč | 36 | 45.13 N | 13.37 E |
| Porecatu | 255 | 22.43 S | 51.24 W |
| Porečje, Ross. | 76 | 55.43 N | 35.33 E |
| Porečje, Ross. | 76 | 56.06 N | 30.29 E |
| Porečje-Rybnoje | 80 | 57.06 N | 39.23 E |
| Poreckoje | 80 | 55.12 N | 46.20 E |
| Porez | 80 | 57.40 N | 51.10 E |
| Porgera | 164 | 5.28 S | 143.12 E |
| Pori | 26 | 61.29 N | 21.47 E |
| Poricy Brook ≏ | 276 | 40.21 N | 74.05 W |
| Poringland | 42 | 52.33 N | 1.21 E |
| Porirua | 172 | 41.08 S | 174.51 E |
| Porjaguba | 24 | 66.47 N | 33.45 E |
| Porkkala | 26 | 59.59 N | 24.26 E |
| Porlamar | 246 | 10.57 N | 63.51 W |
| Porlezza | 58 | 46.03 N | 9.07 E |
| Porlock | 42 | 51.14 N | 3.36 W |
| Porma ≏ | 34 | 42.29 N | 5.28 W |
| Pornassio | 62 | 44.04 N | 7.52 E |
| Pörnbach | 60 | 48.37 N | 11.28 E |
| Pornic | 32 | 47.07 N | 2.06 W |
| Poro ʌ | 154 | 1.14 N | 36.37 E |
| Porog, Ross. | 24 | 63.50 N | 38.29 E |
| Porog, Ross. | 76 | 59.16 N | 33.24 E |
| Porogi | 265a | 59.46 N | 30.47 E |
| Poro Island I | 116 | 10.40 N | 124.27 E |
| Porokylä | 26 | 63.33 N | 29.06 E |
| Poroma | 248 | 18.29 S | 65.30 W |
| Poronaj ≏ | 89 | 49.14 N | 143.06 E |
| Poronajsk | 89 | 49.14 N | 143.04 E |
| Porong | 115a | 7.32 S | 112.41 E |
| Porong ≏ | 115a | 7.32 S | 112.51 E |
| Poropotank ≏ | 208 | 37.27 N | 76.42 W |
| Poroshkove | 78 | 48.41 N | 22.45 E |
| Porosozero | 24 | 62.43 N | 32.42 E |
| Poroto Mountains ⋏ | 154 | 9.00 S | 33.45 E |
| Porožskij | 88 | 56.04 N | 101.46 E |
| Porpoise Bay c | 9 | 66.30 S | 128.30 E |
| Porpoise Channel ʉ | 276 | 40.55 N | 73.09 W |
| Porquerolles | 62 | 43.00 N | 6.12 E |
| Porquerolles, Île de I | 62 | 43.00 N | 6.13 E |
| Porrentruy | 58 | 47.25 N | 7.05 E |
| Porretta Terme | 64 | 44.09 N | 10.59 E |
| Porsangen c[2] | 24 | 70.58 N | 27.00 E |
| Porsangerhalvøya ›[1] | 24 | 70.50 N | 25.00 E |
| Porsea | 114 | 2.27 N | 99.09 E |
| Porsgrunn | 26 | 59.09 N | 9.40 E |
| Porsuk ≏ | 130 | 39.42 N | 31.59 E |
| Port → Le Port | 157c | 20.55 S | 55.18 E |
| Portachuelo | 248 | 17.21 S | 63.24 W |
| Portacloy | 48 | 54.19 N | 9.48 W |
| Port Adelaide | 168b | 34.51 S | 138.30 E |
| Portadown | 48 | 54.26 N | 6.27 W |
| Portaferry | 48 | 54.23 N | 5.33 W |
| Portage, In., U.S. | 216 | 41.34 N | 87.10 W |
| Portage, Mi., U.S. | 216 | 42.12 N | 85.34 W |
| Portage, Oh., U.S. | 216 | 41.20 N | 83.39 W |
| Portage, Pa., U.S. | 214 | 40.23 N | 78.40 W |
| Portage, Ut,. U.S. | 200 | 41.58 N | 112.14 W |
| Portage, Wi., U.S. | 190 | 43.32 N | 89.27 W |
| Portage □[6] | 214 | 41.09 N | 81.15 W |
| Portage ≏, Mi., U.S. | 216 | 41.57 N | 85.38 W |
| Portage ≏, Oh., U.S. | 214 | 41.31 N | 83.05 W |
| Portage, East Branch ≏ | 216 | 41.17 N | 83.31 W |
| Portage, Middle Branch ≏ | 216 | 41.22 N | 83.28 W |
| Portage, North Branch ≏ | 216 | 41.25 N | 83.27 W |
| Portage, South Branch ≏ | 216 | 41.22 N | 83.30 W |
| Portage Bay c | 184 | 51.33 N | 98.50 W |
| Portage Des Sioux | 219 | 38.55 N | 90.20 W |
| Portage Lake ⊜, Mi., U.S. | 190 | 47.04 N | 88.30 W |
| Portage Lake ⊜, Mi., U.S. | 216 | 42.03 N | 85.31 W |
| Portage Lake ⊜, Mi., U.S. | 216 | 42.25 N | 83.54 W |
| Portage Lakes | 214 | 40.59 N | 81.32 W |
| Portage Lakes ⊜ | 214 | 40.59 N | 81.32 W |
| Portage Lakes State Park ♠ | 214 | 40.57 N | 81.32 W |
| Portage-la-Prairie | 184 | 49.59 N | 98.18 W |
| Portage Park ➔[8] | 278 | 41.57 N | 87.46 W |
| Portageville, Mo., U.S. | 194 | 36.25 N | 89.41 W |
| Portageville, N.Y., U.S. | 210 | 42.34 N | 78.02 W |
| Portal, Ga., U.S. | 192 | 32.32 N | 81.55 W |
| Portal, N.D., U.S. | 198 | 48.59 N | 102.32 W |
| Port Alberni | 224 | 49.14 N | 124.48 W |
| Portal del Infierno ∟ | 236 | 14.22 N | 85.38 W |
| Portalegre, Bra. | 250 | 6.02 S | 38.00 W |
| Portalegre, Port. | 34 | 39.17 N | 7.26 W |
| Portales | 196 | 34.11 N | 103.20 W |
| Port Alexander | 180 | 56.15 N | 134.39 W |
| Port Alfred (Kowie) | 158 | 33.36 S | 26.55 E |
| Port Alice | 182 | 50.23 N | 127.27 W |
| Port Allegany | 214 | 41.48 N | 78.16 W |
| Port Allen | 194 | 30.27 N | 91.12 W |
| Port Alma, Austl. | 166 | 23.35 S | 150.51 E |
| Port Alma, On., Can. | 214 | 42.11 N | 82.15 W |
| Port Alsworth | 180 | 60.12 N | 154.20 W |
| Port Angeles | 224 | 48.07 N | 123.25 W |
| Port Angeles Harbor c | 224 | 48.07 N | 123.24 W |
| Port Anson | 186 | 49.32 N | 55.50 W |
| Port Antonio | 241q | 18.11 N | 76.28 W |
| Port Aransas | 196 | 27.50 N | 97.04 W |
| Portarlington, Austl. | 169 | 38.07 S | 144.39 E |
| Portarlington, Ire. | 48 | 53.10 N | 7.11 W |
| Port Arthur, Austl. | 166 | 43.09 S | 147.51 E |
| Port Arthur → Thunder Bay, On., Can. | 190 | 48.23 N | 89.15 W |
| Port Arthur, Tx., U.S. | 194 | 29.53 N | 93.55 W |
| Port Arthur → Lüshun, Zhg. | 98 | 38.48 N | 121.16 E |
| Port Ashton | 180 | 60.04 N | 148.01 W |
| Port Askaig | 46 | 55.51 N | 6.07 W |
| Port Augusta | 166 | 32.30 S | 137.46 E |
| Port au Port | 186 | 48.33 N | 58.44 W |
| Port au Port Bay c | 186 | 48.40 N | 58.45 W |
| Port au Port Peninsula ›[1] | 186 | 48.35 N | 59.00 W |
| Port-au-Prince | 238 | 18.32 N | 72.20 W |
| Port-au-Prince, Baie de c | 238 | 18.40 N | 72.30 W |
| Port Austin | 190 | 44.02 N | 82.59 W |
| Port-aux-Basques → Channel-Port-aux-Basques | 186 | 47.34 N | 59.09 W |
| Portavogie | 48 | 54.27 N | 5.27 W |
| Porta Westfalica | 52 | 52.14 N | 8.55 E |

| PORTUGUÊS Nome | Página | Lat.°′ | Long.°′ W = Oeste |
|---|---|---|---|
| Porta Westfalica ♠ | 52 | 52.14 N | 8.55 E |
| Port Bannatyne | 46 | 55.52 N | 5.05 W |
| Port Barre | 194 | 30.33 N | 91.57 W |
| Port Bell | 154 | 0.17 N | 32.39 E |
| Port-Bergé | 157b | 15.33 S | 47.40 E |
| Port Blair | 110 | 11.40 N | 92.45 E |
| Port Blakely | 224 | 47.37 N | 122.28 W |
| Port Blandford | 186 | 48.21 N | 54.10 W |
| Port Bolivar | 222 | 29.23 N | 94.46 W |
| Port Borden | 186 | 46.15 N | 63.42 W |
| Port-Bouët | 150 | 5.15 N | 3.58 W |
| Port Broughton | 166 | 33.36 S | 137.56 E |
| Port Burwell | 212 | 42.39 N | 80.49 W |
| Port Byron, Il., U.S. | 190 | 41.36 N | 90.20 W |
| Port Byron, N.Y., U.S. | 210 | 43.02 N | 76.37 W |
| Port Campbell | 169 | 38.37 S | 143.00 E |
| Port Campbell National Park ♠ | 169 | 38.38 S | 142.55 E |
| Port Canning | 126 | 22.18 N | 88.40 E |
| Port Carbon | 208 | 40.42 N | 76.10 W |
| Port Carling | 212 | 45.07 N | 79.35 W |
| Port-Cartier | 186 | 50.01 N | 66.52 W |
| Port-Cartier Sept-Îles, Réserve ♠ | 186 | 50.35 N | 67.10 W |
| Port Chalmers | 172 | 45.49 S | 170.37 E |
| Port Charlotte | 220 | 26.58 N | 82.05 W |
| Port Chester | 210 | 41.00 N | 73.39 W |
| Port Chester Harbor c | 276 | 40.59 N | 73.40 W |
| Port Clements | 182 | 53.42 N | 132.11 W |
| Port Clinton, Austl. | 168b | 34.14 S | 138.01 E |
| Port Clinton, Oh., U.S. | 214 | 41.30 N | 82.56 W |
| Port Clinton, Pa., U.S. | 208 | 40.35 N | 76.02 W |
| Port Clyde | 188 | 43.55 N | 69.15 W |
| Port Colborne | 212 | 42.53 N | 79.14 W |
| Port Colden | 210 | 40.45 N | 74.57 W |
| Port Columbus International Airport ⊠ | 218 | 40.00 N | 82.53 W |
| Port Coquitlam | 224 | 49.16 N | 122.46 W |
| Port Costa | 282 | 38.03 N | 122.11 W |
| Port Crane | 210 | 42.10 N | 75.50 W |
| Port Credit | 212 | 43.33 N | 79.35 W |
| Port-Cros | 62 | 43.00 N | 6.23 E |
| Port-Cros, Île de I | 62 | 43.00 N | 6.24 E |
| Port-Cros, Parc National de ♠ | 62 | 43.01 N | 6.24 E |
| Port-Daniel, Réserve ♠ | 186 | 48.18 N | 64.55 W |
| Port-de-Bouc | 62 | 43.24 N | 4.59 E |
| Port-de-Paix | 238 | 19.57 N | 72.50 W |
| Port Deposit | 208 | 39.36 N | 76.06 W |
| Port Dickinson | 210 | 42.08 N | 75.53 W |
| Port Dickson | 114 | 2.31 N | 101.48 E |
| Porte Crayon, Mount ʌ | 188 | 38.56 N | 79.27 W |
| Port Edward, B.C., Can. | 182 | 54.14 N | 130.18 W |
| Port Edward, S. Afr. | 158 | 31.02 S | 30.13 E |
| Port Edward → Weihai, Zhg. | 98 | 37.28 N | 122.07 E |
| Port Edwards | 190 | 44.21 N | 89.51 W |
| Portegolpe | 236 | 10.20 N | 85.46 W |
| Porteiras | 250 | 7.31 S | 39.07 W |
| Porteirinha | 255 | 15.44 S | 43.02 W |
| Portel, Bra. | 250 | 1.57 S | 50.49 W |
| Portel, Port. | 34 | 38.18 N | 7.42 W |
| Portela, Aeroporto da ⊠ | 266c | 38.46 N | 9.08 W |
| Port Elgin, N.B., Can. | 186 | 46.03 N | 64.05 W |
| Port Elgin, On., Can. | 190 | 44.26 N | 81.24 W |
| Port Elizabeth, St. Vin. | 241h | 13.03 N | 61.13 W |
| Port Elizabeth, S. Afr. | 158 | 33.58 S | 25.40 E |
| Port Elizabeth, N.J., U.S. | 208 | 39.18 N | 74.58 W |
| Port Ellen | 46 | 55.39 N | 6.12 W |
| Port Elliot | 168b | 35.32 S | 138.41 E |
| Port-en-Bessin | 32 | 49.21 N | 0.45 W |
| Porter, In., U.S. | 216 | 41.36 N | 87.04 W |
| Porter, Ok., U.S. | 196 | 35.52 N | 95.31 W |
| Porter, Tx., U.S. | 222 | 30.06 N | 95.14 W |
| Porter, Wa., U.S. | 224 | 46.56 N | 123.18 W |
| Porter □[6] | 216 | 41.28 N | 87.04 W |
| Port'Ercole | 66 | 42.23 N | 11.12 E |
| Porter Corners | 210 | 43.09 N | 73.53 W |
| Porter Creek ≏ | 279a | 41.41 N | 81.56 W |
| Port Erin | 44 | 54.06 N | 4.44 W |
| Porter Lake ⊜ | 184 | 56.21 N | 107.20 W |
| Porter Point › | 241h | 13.23 N | 61.11 W |
| Porter Springs | 222 | 31.16 N | 95.36 W |
| Porters Retreat | 170 | 34.00 S | 149.48 E |
| Porters Run ≏ | 279b | 40.27 N | 79.33 W |
| Portersville | 214 | 40.56 N | 80.09 W |
| Porterville, S. Afr. | 158 | 33.00 S | 19.00 E |
| Porterville, Ca., U.S. | 204 | 36.03 N | 119.00 W |
| Porterville, Ms., U.S. | 194 | 32.41 N | 88.28 W |
| Portes-lés-Valence | 62 | 44.52 N | 4.53 E |
| Port Essington | 182 | 54.09 N | 129.57 W |
| Portete, Bahía c | 246 | 12.13 N | 71.55 W |
| Port-Étienne → Nouâdhibou | 148 | 20.54 N | 17.04 W |
| Port Ewen | 210 | 41.54 N | 73.58 W |
| Port-Eynon | 42 | 51.33 N | 4.13 W |
| Port-Eynon Point › | 42 | 51.32 N | 4.12 W |
| Portezuelo | 234 | 20.25 N | 102.31 W |
| Port Fairy | 166 | 38.23 S | 142.14 E |
| Port Fitzroy | 172 | 36.10 S | 175.21 E |
| Port Gamble | 224 | 47.51 N | 122.34 W |
| Port Gamble Indian Reservation ➔[4] | 224 | 47.53 N | 122.34 W |
| Port Gentil | 152 | 0.43 S | 8.47 E |
| Port Germein | 166 | 33.01 S | 138.00 E |
| Port Gibson, Ms., U.S. | 194 | 31.57 N | 90.59 W |
| Port Gibson, N.Y., U.S. | 210 | 43.02 N | 77.09 W |
| Port Glasgow | 46 | 55.57 N | 4.41 W |
| Portglenone | 48 | 54.52 N | 6.29 W |
| Port Graham | 180 | 59.21 N | 151.50 W |
| Port Greville | 186 | 45.24 N | 64.33 W |
| Porth | 42 | 51.38 N | 3.25 W |
| Port Hacking | 274a | 34.04 S | 151.08 E |
| Port Hacking Point › | 170 | 34.05 S | 151.10 E |
| Port Harcourt | 150 | 4.43 N | 7.05 E |
| Port Hardy | 182 | 50.43 N | 127.29 W |
| Port Hawkesbury | 186 | 45.37 N | 61.21 W |
| Porthcawl | 42 | 51.29 N | 3.43 W |
| Port Hedland | 162 | 20.19 S | 118.34 E |
| Port Heiden | 180 | 56.55 N | 158.41 W |
| Port Henry | 188 | 44.02 N | 73.27 W |
| Port Hill | 186 | 46.35 N | 63.53 W |
| Porthleven | 42 | 50.05 N | 5.19 W |
| Porthmadog | 42 | 52.55 N | 4.08 W |
| Porth Neigwl c | 42 | 52.48 N | 4.34 W |
| Port Hood | 186 | 46.01 N | 61.32 W |
| Port Hope, On., Can. | 212 | 43.57 N | 78.18 W |
| Port Hope, Mi., U.S. | 190 | 43.56 N | 82.42 W |
| Port Howe | 238 | 24.15 N | 75.21 W |
| Port Hueneme | 228 | 34.08 N | 119.11 W |
| Port Hughes | 168b | 34.04 S | 137.32 E |
| Port Huron | 214 | 42.58 N | 82.25 W |
| Portici | 68 | 40.49 N | 14.20 E |
| Portico di Romagna | 66 | 44.01 N | 11.47 E |
| Portigliola | 68 | 38.14 N | 16.13 E |
| Port-Iliç | 84 | 38.53 N | 48.48 E |
| Portimão | 34 | 37.08 N | 8.32 W |
| Portinho, Rio do ≏ | 287a | 23.03 S | 43.35 W |
| Port Isaac | 42 | 50.35 N | 4.49 W |
| Port Isabel | 196 | 26.04 N | 97.12 W |
| Portishead | 42 | 51.30 N | 2.46 W |
| Port Jefferson, N.Y., U.S. | 210 | 40.56 N | 73.03 W |
| Port Jefferson, Oh., U.S. | 216 | 40.19 N | 84.05 W |

| | | | |
|---|---|---|---|
| Port Jefferson Harbor c | 276 | 40.58 N | 73.05 W |
| Port Jefferson Station | 210 | 40.55 N | 73.02 W |
| Port Jervis | 210 | 41.22 N | 74.41 W |
| Port Julia | 168b | 34.40 S | 137.52 E |
| Port-Katon | 83 | 46.52 N | 38.46 E |
| Port Kembla | 170 | 34.29 S | 150.54 E |
| Port Kennedy | 285 | 40.06 N | 75.25 W |
| Port Kenny | 162 | 33.10 S | 134.42 E |
| Portknockie | 46 | 57.41 N | 2.51 W |
| Port Láirge → Waterford | 48 | 52.15 N | 7.06 W |
| Port Lambton | 214 | 42.39 N | 82.30 W |
| Portland, Austl. | 166 | 38.21 S | 141.36 E |
| Portland, Austl. | 170 | 33.22 S | 150.00 E |
| Portland, N.Z. | 172 | 35.48 S | 174.19 E |
| Portland, Ar., U.S. | 194 | 33.14 N | 91.30 W |
| Portland, Ct., U.S. | 207 | 41.34 N | 72.38 W |
| Portland, In., U.S. | 216 | 40.26 N | 84.58 W |
| Portland, Me., U.S. | 188 | 43.39 N | 70.15 W |
| Portland, Mi. U.S. | 216 | 42.52 N | 84.54 W |
| Portland, Mo., U.S. | 219 | 38.42 N | 91.43 W |
| Portland, N.Y., U.S. | 214 | 42.22 N | 79.28 W |
| Portland, N.D., U.S. | 198 | 47.29 N | 97.22 W |
| Portland, Or., U.S. | 224 | 45.31 N | 122.40 W |
| Portland, Pa., U.S. | 210 | 40.55 N | 75.06 W |
| Portland, Tn., U.S. | 194 | 36.34 N | 86.30 W |
| Portland, Tx., U.S. | 196 | 27.52 N | 97.19 W |
| Portland, Wi., U.S. | 216 | 43.12 N | 88.58 W |
| Portland, Bill of › | 42 | 50.31 N | 2.27 W |
| Portland, Cape › | 166 | 40.45 S | 147.57 E |
| Portland, Isle of I | 42 | 50.33 N | 2.27 W |
| Portland Bay c | 166 | 38.19 S | 141.47 E |
| Portland Bight c[3] | 241q | 17.53 N | 77.08 W |
| Portland Canal c | 182 | 55.10 N | 130.08 W |
| Portland Creek Pond ⊜ | 186 | 50.12 N | 57.34 W |
| Portland Inlet c | 182 | 54.50 N | 130.15 W |
| Portland International Airport ⊠ | 224 | 45.35 N | 122.36 W |
| Portland Island I | 172 | 39.17 S | 177.52 E |
| Portland Mills | 214 | 41.23 N | 78.50 W |
| Portland Point › | 241q | 17.42 N | 77.11 W |
| Portlandville | 210 | 42.32 N | 74.58 W |
| Port Laoise (Maryborough) | 48 | 53.02 N | 7.17 W |
| Port Lavaca | 196 | 28.36 N | 96.37 W |
| Portlaw | 48 | 52.17 N | 7.19 W |
| Port-Lesney | 58 | 47.00 N | 5.49 E |
| Portlethen | 46 | 57.03 N | 2.06 W |
| Port Leyden | 212 | 43.35 N | 75.21 W |
| Port Lincoln | 166 | 34.44 S | 135.52 E |
| Port Lions | 180 | 57.52 N | 152.53 W |
| Portlock Reefs ✣[2] | 164 | 9.30 S | 144.45 E |
| Port Logan | 44 | 54.43 N | 4.56 W |
| Port Loko | 150 | 8.46 N | 12.47 W |
| Port-Louis, Fr. | 32 | 47.43 N | 3.21 W |
| Port-Louis, Guad. | 241o | 16.25 N | 61.32 W |
| Port Louis, Maus. | 157c | 20.10 S | 57.30 E |
| Port Ludlow | 224 | 47.55 N | 122.40 W |
| Port-Lyautey → Kenitra | 148 | 34.16 N | 6.40 W |
| Port MacDonnell | 166 | 38.03 S | 140.42 E |
| Port Macquarie | 166 | 31.26 S | 152.55 E |
| Port Madison Indian Reservation ➔[4] | 224 | 47.45 N | 122.35 W |
| Portmahomack | 46 | 57.49 N | 3.50 W |
| Port Maitland | 186 | 43.59 N | 66.09 W |
| Port Maria | 241q | 18.22 N | 76.54 W |
| Portmarnock | 48 | 53.25 N | 6.08 W |
| Port Matilda | 214 | 40.48 N | 78.03 W |
| Port Mayaca | 220 | 27.08 N | 80.12 W |
| Port McNeill | 182 | 50.35 N | 127.06 W |
| Port McNicoll | 212 | 44.45 N | 79.49 W |
| Port Melbourne | 274b | 37.51 S | 144.56 E |
| Port Mellon | 182 | 49.32 N | 123.29 W |
| Port-Menier | 186 | 49.48 N | 64.20 W |
| Port Moller | 180 | 55.59 N | 160.34 W |
| Port Monmouth | 276 | 40.25 N | 74.05 W |
| Port Moody | 224 | 49.17 N | 122.51 W |
| Port Morant | 241q | 17.54 N | 76.19 W |
| Portmore | 241q | 17.58 N | 76.53 W |
| Port Moresby | 164 | 9.30 S | 147.10 E |
| Port Moresby □[5] | 164 | 9.30 S | 147.10 E |
| Port Morien | 186 | 46.08 N | 59.52 W |
| Port Morris | 276 | 40.54 N | 74.41 W |
| Port Mouton | 186 | 43.56 N | 64.51 W |
| Port Murray | 210 | 40.47 N | 74.54 W |
| Portnaguran | 46 | 58.17 N | 6.13 W |
| Portnahaven | 46 | 55.41 N | 6.31 W |
| Port Neches | 194 | 29.59 N | 93.57 W |
| Port Neill | 166 | 34.07 S | 136.20 E |
| Port Nelson | 184 | 57.03 N | 92.36 W |
| Portneuf | 206 | 46.42 N | 71.53 W |
| Portneuf □[6] | 206 | 46.45 N | 72.00 W |
| Portneuf ≏, P.Q., Can. | 186 | 48.38 N | 69.05 W |
| Portneuf ≏, P.Q., Can. | 206 | 46.42 N | 71.53 W |
| Portneuf ≏, Id., U.S. | 202 | 42.58 N | 112.35 W |
| Portneuf, Lac ⊜ | 186 | 49.08 N | 70.18 W |
| Portneuf-Station | 206 | 46.43 N | 71.54 W |
| Portneuf-sur-Mer | 186 | 48.37 N | 69.06 W |
| Port Neville | 182 | 50.29 N | 126.05 W |
| Port Noarlunga | 168b | 35.09 S | 138.28 E |
| Port Nolloth | 156 | 29.17 S | 16.51 E |
| Port Norris | 208 | 39.14 N | 75.02 W |
| Porto, Bra. | 250 | 3.54 S | 42.42 W |
| Porto, Port. | 34 | 41.11 N | 8.36 W |
| Porto, Bonifica di ➔[1] | 267a | 41.48 N | 12.16 E |
| Porto Acre | 248 | 9.34 S | 67.31 W |
| Porto Alegre, Bra. | 252 | 30.04 S | 51.11 W |
| Porto Alegre, S. Tom./P. | 152 | 0.02 N | 6.32 E |
| Porto Amboim | 152 | 10.44 S | 13.44 E |
| Porto Azzurro | 66 | 42.46 N | 10.24 E |
| Portobello | 46 | 55.58 N | 3.07 W |
| Porto Belo, Bra. | 252 | 27.10 S | 48.33 W |
| Portobelo, Pan. | 236 | 9.33 N | 79.39 W |
| Porto Calvo | 250 | 9.04 S | 35.24 W |
| Porto Ceresio | 58 | 45.54 N | 8.55 E |
| Port O'Connor | 196 | 28.27 N | 96.24 W |
| Porto das Caixas | 256 | 22.42 S | 42.53 W |
| Porto d'Ascoli | 66 | 42.55 N | 13.53 E |
| Porto das Flôres | 256 | 22.05 S | 43.34 W |
| Porto das Gabarras | 250 | 3.07 S | 44.34 W |
| Pôrto de Mós | 34 | 39.36 N | 8.39 W |
| Porto de Moz | 250 | 1.45 S | 52.14 W |
| Porto de Pedras | 250 | 9.10 S | 35.17 W |
| Porto di Potenza Picena | 66 | 43.21 N | 13.42 E |
| Porto di Traiano, Necropoli del ⊥ | 267a | 41.46 N | 12.16 E |
| Porto dos Gaúchos | 250 | 11.29 S | 57.22 W |
| Porto Empedocle | 70 | 37.17 N | 13.32 E |
| Porto Esperança | 248 | 19.37 S | 57.27 W |
| Porto Esperidião | 248 | 15.51 S | 58.28 W |
| Porto Farina | 36 | 37.10 N | 10.12 E |
| Porto Feliz | 255 | 23.13 S | 47.32 W |
| Portoferraio | 66 | 42.49 N | 10.19 E |
| Porto Ferreira | 255 | 21.51 S | 47.28 W |
| Portofino | 62 | 44.18 N | 9.12 E |
| Port of Ness | 46 | 58.29 N | 6.13 W |
| Porto Franco | 250 | 6.20 S | 47.24 W |
| Port of Spain | 241r | 10.39 N | 61.31 W |
| Porto Garibaldi | 66 | 44.41 N | 12.14 E |
| Porto Grande | 250 | 0.42 N | 51.24 W |
| Portogruaro | 64 | 45.47 N | 12.50 E |
| Porto Inglês | 150a | 15.08 N | 23.13 W |
| Portola | 204 | 39.48 N | 120.28 W |
| Portola State Park ♠ | 226 | 37.15 N | 122.13 W |
| Portola Valley | 226 | 37.23 N | 122.13 W |
| Porto Lucena | 252 | 27.51 S | 55.01 W |
| Pörtom (Pirttikylä) | 26 | 62.42 N | 21.37 E |
| Portomaggiore | 64 | 44.42 N | 11.48 E |
| Porto Maurizio | 62 | 43.52 N | 8.01 E |
| Porto Mendes | 252 | 24.30 S | 54.20 W |
| Porto Murtinho | 248 | 21.42 S | 57.52 W |
| Porto Nacional | 250 | 10.42 S | 48.25 W |

| | | | |
|---|---|---|---|
| Porto-Novo, Bénin | 150 | 6.29 N | 2.37 E |
| Porto Novo, Bra. | 256 | 23.40 S | 45.28 W |
| Porto Novo, India | 122 | 11.29 N | 79.46 E |
| Porto Novo Creek c | 273a | 6.26 N | 3.20 E |
| Portopalo, It. | 70 | 36.41 N | 15.08 E |
| Porto Palo, It. | 70 | 37.34 N | 12.54 E |
| Port Orange | 192 | 29.06 N | 80.59 W |
| Port Orchard | 224 | 47.32 N | 122.38 W |
| Porto Real | 256 | 22.25 S | 44.20 W |
| Porto Real do Colégio | 250 | 10.11 S | 36.49 W |
| Porto Recanati | 66 | 43.26 N | 13.40 E |
| Port Orford | 202 | 42.44 N | 124.29 W |
| Porto Rico | 152 | 6.08 S | 12.30 E |
| Porto Rico → Puerto Rico □[2] | 240m | 18.15 N | 66.30 W |
| Portorož | 64 | 45.31 N | 13.36 E |
| Porto Salvo | 266c | 38.43 N | 9.18 W |
| Porto San Giorgio | 66 | 43.11 N | 13.48 E |
| Porto Santana | 250 | 0.03 S | 51.11 W |
| Porto Sant'Elpidio | 66 | 43.15 N | 13.45 E |
| Porto Santo I | 148 | 33.04 N | 16.20 W |
| Porto Santo Stefano | 66 | 42.26 N | 11.07 E |
| Porto São José | 255 | 22.43 S | 53.10 W |
| Portoscuso | 71 | 39.12 N | 8.23 E |
| Porto Seguro, Bra. | 255 | 16.26 S | 39.05 W |
| Porto-Séguro, Togo | 150 | 6.12 N | 1.29 E |
| Porto Torres | 71 | 40.50 N | 8.24 E |
| Porto União | 252 | 26.15 S | 51.05 W |
| Porto Válter | 248 | 8.15 S | 72.45 W |
| Porto Valtravaglia | 58 | 45.58 N | 8.41 E |
| Porto-Vecchio | 36 | 41.35 N | 9.16 E |
| Porto Velho | 248 | 8.46 S | 63.54 W |
| Porto Velho do Cunha | 256 | 21.50 S | 42.32 W |
| Portovenere | 62 | 44.03 N | 9.51 E |
| Portoviejo | 246 | 1.03 S | 80.27 W |
| Portpatrick, Scot., U.K. | 44 | 54.51 N | 5.07 W |
| Port Patrick, Vanuatu | 175f | 20.08 S | 169.47 E |
| Port Penn | 208 | 39.31 N | 75.34 W |
| Port Perry | 212 | 44.06 N | 78.57 W |
| Port Phillip Bay c | 169 | 38.07 S | 144.48 E |
| Port Pirie | 166 | 33.11 S | 138.01 E |
| Port Providence | 285 | 40.08 N | 75.30 W |
| Portraine | 48 | 53.30 N | 6.07 W |
| Port Reading | 276 | 40.33 N | 74.15 W |
| Portree | 46 | 57.24 N | 6.12 W |
| Port Renfrew | 224 | 48.33 N | 124.25 W |
| Port Republic | 208 | 39.31 N | 74.29 W |
| Port Rexton | 186 | 48.23 N | 53.20 W |
| Port Richey | 220 | 28.16 N | 82.43 W |
| Port Richmond | 208 | 37.33 N | 76.49 W |
| Port Robinson | 284a | 43.02 N | 79.13 W |
| Port Rowan | 214 | 42.37 N | 80.28 W |
| Port Royal, Jam. | 241q | 17.56 N | 76.51 W |
| Port Royal, Ky., U.S. | 218 | 38.33 N | 85.04 W |
| Port Royal, Pa., U.S. | 208 | 40.32 N | 77.23 W |
| Port Royal, S.C., U.S. | 192 | 32.22 N | 80.41 W |
| Port Royal, Va., U.S. | 208 | 38.10 N | 77.11 W |
| Port-Royal-des-Champs, Abbaye de ʋ[1] | 261 | 48.45 N | 2.01 E |
| Port Royal National Historic Park ♠ | 186 | 44.44 N | 65.40 W |
| Portrush | 48 | 55.12 N | 6.40 W |
| Port Said → Būr Sa'īd | 142 | 31.16 N | 32.18 E |
| Port-Sainte-Marie | 32 | 44.15 N | 0.24 E |
| Port Saint Joe | 192 | 29.49 N | 85.18 W |
| Port Saint Johns | 158 | 31.38 S | 29.33 E |
| Port-Saint-Louis | 62 | 43.23 N | 4.48 E |
| Port Saint Lucie | 220 | 27.20 N | 80.20 W |
| Port Saint Mary | 44 | 54.05 N | 4.43 W |
| Port-Saint-Servan | 186 | 51.19 N | 58.02 W |
| Port Salerno | 220 | 27.08 N | 80.12 W |
| Portsalon | 48 | 55.13 N | 7.37 W |
| Port Sanilac | 190 | 43.25 N | 82.32 W |
| Port Saunders | 186 | 50.39 N | 57.18 W |
| Pörtschach | 61 | 46.37 N | 14.08 E |
| Portsea | 169 | 38.19 S | 144.43 E |
| Port Seton | 46 | 55.58 N | 2.57 W |
| Port Shepstone | 158 | 30.46 S | 30.22 E |
| Portslade | 42 | 50.50 N | 0.11 W |
| Portsmouth, Dom. | 240d | 15.35 N | 61.28 W |
| Portsmouth, Eng., U.K. | 42 | 50.48 N | 1.05 W |
| Portsmouth, N.H., U.S. | 188 | 43.04 N | 70.45 W |
| Portsmouth, Oh., U.S. | 218 | 38.43 N | 82.59 W |
| Portsmouth, R.I., U.S. | 207 | 41.36 N | 71.15 W |
| Portsmouth, Va., U.S. | 208 | 36.50 N | 76.17 W |
| Portsmouth Naval Shipyard ▪ | 188 | 43.05 N | 70.45 W |
| Portsoy | 46 | 57.41 N | 2.41 W |
| Port Stanley, On., Can. | 214 | 42.40 N | 81.13 W |
| Port Stanley → Stanley, Falk. Is. | 254 | 51.42 S | 57.51 W |
| Portstewart | 48 | 55.11 N | 6.43 W |
| Port Sudan → Būr Sūdān | 140 | 19.37 N | 37.14 E |
| Port Sulphur | 194 | 29.28 N | 89.41 W |
| Port Sunlight | 262 | 53.21 N | 2.59 W |
| Port-sur-Saône | 58 | 47.41 N | 6.03 E |
| Port Talbot | 42 | 51.36 N | 3.47 W |
| Port Taufiq → Būr Tawfīq | 128 | 29.57 N | 32.34 E |
| Porttipahdan tekojärvi ⊜[1] | 24 | 68.08 N | 26.40 E |
| Port Tobacco River c | 208 | 38.27 N | 77.02 W |
| Port Townsend | 224 | 48.07 N | 122.45 W |
| Port Trevorton | 208 | 40.42 N | 76.52 W |
| Portugal □[1], Europe | 22 | 39.30 N | 8.00 W |
| Portugal □[1], Europe | 34 | 39.30 N | 8.00 W |
| Portugal, Cachoeira ∟ | 248 | 9.55 S | 64.16 W |
| Portugal Cove South | 186 | 46.42 N | 53.15 W |
| Portugalete | 34 | 43.19 N | 3.01 W |
| Portuguesa □[3] | 246 | 9.10 N | 69.15 W |
| Portuguesa ≏ | 246 | 7.57 N | 67.32 W |
| Portuguese Guinea → Guinea-Bissau □[1] | 150 | 12.00 N | 15.00 W |
| Portumna | 48 | 53.06 N | 8.13 W |
| Port Union, Nf., Can. | 186 | 48.30 N | 53.05 W |
| Port Union, On., Can. | 275b | 43.47 N | 79.08 W |
| Port-Vendres | 32 | 42.31 N | 3.07 E |
| Port Victoria → Victoria | 138 | 4.38 S | 55.27 E |
| Port Vila | 175f | 17.44 S | 168.19 E |
| Portville | 210 | 42.02 N | 78.20 W |
| Port Vincent | 168b | 34.47 S | 137.51 E |
| Port-Vladimir | 24 | 69.25 N | 33.06 E |
| Port Vue | 279b | 40.20 N | 79.52 W |
| Port Waikato | 172 | 37.23 S | 174.44 E |
| Port Wakefield, Austl. | 168b | 34.11 S | 138.09 E |
| Port Wakefield, Ak., U.S. | 180 | 58.03 N | 153.03 W |
| Port Washington, B.C., Can. | 224 | 48.49 N | 123.19 W |
| Port Washington, N.Y., U.S. | 210 | 40.49 N | 73.41 W |
| Port Washington, Oh., U.S. | 214 | 40.27 N | 81.37 W |
| Port Washington, Wi., U.S. | 190 | 43.23 N | 87.52 W |
| Port Weld | 114 | 4.50 N | 100.38 E |
| Port Welshpool | 169 | 38.42 S | 146.28 E |
| Port Wentworth | 192 | 32.08 N | 81.09 W |
| Port William, Scot., U.K. | 44 | 54.46 N | 4.35 W |
| Port William, Oh., U.S. | 218 | 39.33 N | 83.47 W |
| Port Wing | 190 | 46.46 N | 91.23 W |
| Porum | 196 | 35.21 N | 95.15 W |

| | | | |
|---|---|---|---|
| Porus | 241q | 18.02 N | 77.25 W |
| Porvenir, Chile | 254 | 53.18 S | 70.22 W |
| Porvenir, Méx. | 232 | 31.15 N | 105.51 W |
| Porvoo (Borgå) | 26 | 60.24 N | 25.40 E |
| Porvoonjoki ≏ | 26 | 60.23 N | 25.40 E |
| Porz | 56 | 50.53 N | 7.03 E |
| Porzdni | 80 | 57.00 N | 2.33 E |
| Porzuna | 34 | 39.09 N | 4.09 W |
| Posada | 71 | 40.38 N | 9.43 E |
| Posada ≏ | 71 | 40.39 N | 9.45 E |
| Posadas, Arg. | 252 | 27.23 S | 55.53 W |
| Posadas, Esp. | 34 | 37.48 N | 5.06 W |
| Posavina V | 36 | 45.10 N | [illegible].20 E |
| Poščharv | 85 | 38.24 N | 7[illegible].10 E |
| Poschiavino ≏ | 58 | 46.12 N | 1[illegible].10 E |
| Poschiavo | 58 | 46.18 N | 1[illegible].04 E |
| Pošechon'e | 76 | 58.30 N | 3[illegible].07 E |
| Posen → Poznań, Pol. | 30 | 52.25 N | 16.55 E |
| Posen, Il., U.S. | 278 | 41.37 N | 87.40 W |
| Posen, Mi., U.S. | 190 | 45.15 N | 83.41 W |
| Poseritz | 54 | 54.18 N | 13.16 E |
| Posesión, Bahía c | 254 | 52.17 S | 69.14 W |
| Posevnaja | 86 | 54.18 N | 83.20 E |
| Poshan → Boshan | 98 | 36.29 N | 117.50 E |
| Poshiwu | 106 | 30.22 N | 119.[illegible]6 E |
| Posieux | 58 | 46.46 N | 7.[illegible]6 E |
| Posina | 64 | 45.47 N | 11.[illegible]5 E |
| Pösing | 60 | 49.14 N | 12.[illegible]3 E |
| Posio | 26 | 66.06 N | 28.[illegible]9 E |
| Positano | 68 | 40.38 N | 14.[illegible] E |
| Posjet | 89 | 42.39 N | 130.[illegible] E |
| Poso | 112 | 1.23 S | 120.[illegible]4 E |
| Poso, Danau ⊜ | 112 | 1.52 S | 120.[illegible] E |
| Poso, Teluk c | 112 | 1.15 S | 120.5[illegible] E |
| Poso Creek ≏ | 226 | 35.41 N | 119.2[illegible] W |
| Posof | 130 | 41.31 N | 42.4[illegible] E |
| Pos'olki | 80 | 53.08 N | 46.2[illegible] E |
| Pos'olok | 265a | 59.43 N | 30.1[illegible] E |
| Posŏng | 98 | 34.47 N | 127.0[illegible] E |
| Posooy, Mount ʌ | 116 | 17.21 N | 120.4[illegible] E |
| Pospelicha | 86 | 51.57 N | 81.4[illegible] E |
| Possagno | 64 | 45.51 N | 11.5[illegible] E |
| Posse, Bra. | 255 | 14.05 S | 46.22 W |
| Posse, Bra. | 256 | 22.16 S | 43.06 W |
| Possel | 152 | 5.01 N | 19.15 E |
| Possendorf | 54 | 50.57 N | 13.42 E |
| Posses | 256 | 21.43 S | 46.08 W |
| Possession Islands II | 9 | 71.27 S | 171.08 E |
| Possession Sound ʉ | 224 | 48.00 N | 122.20 W |
| Possidhonia ⊥ | 38 | 37.40 N | 24.00 E |
| Pössneck | 54 | 50.42 N | 11.37 E |
| Possruck (Kozjak) ⋏ | 61 | 46.37 N | 15.28 E |
| Possum Kingdom Lake ⊜[1] | 196 | 32.55 N | 98.28 W |
| Post | 196 | 33.11 N | 101.22 W |
| Posta | 66 | 42.31 N | 13.06 E |
| Postal (Burgstall) | 64 | 46.36 N | 11.11 E |
| Postau | 60 | 48.39 N | 12.20 E |
| Postbauer | 60 | 49.19 N | 11.21 E |
| Post Creek ≏ | 210 | 42.09 N | 77.02 W |
| Poste-de-la-Baleine | 176 | 55.17 N | 77.45 W |
| Postelle | 192 | 35.02 N | 84.22 W |
| Poste Ramartina | 157b | 19.38 S | 45.58 E |
| Posterholt | 52 | 51.07 N | 6.03 E |
| Post Falls | 202 | 47.43 N | 116.57 W |
| Postiglione | 68 | 40.33 N | 15.13 E |
| Postmasburg | 158 | 28.18 S | 23.05 E |
| Postojna | 36 | 45.47 N | 14.13 E |
| Postojnska jama ±[7] | 36 | 45.47 N | 14.12 E |
| Postoloprty | 54 | 50.20 N | 13.40 E |
| P'ostraja Dresva | 74 | 61.34 N | 156.41 E |
| Postrevalle | 248 | 18.29 S | 63.51 W |
| Postsee ⊜ | 54 | 54.13 N | 10.13 E |
| Poststadion ♠ | 264a | 52.32 N | 13.21 E |
| Postville | 190 | 43.05 N | 91.34 W |
| Pota | 115b | 8.20 S | 120.46 E |
| Potaizi | 104 | 41.34 N | 121.08 E |
| Potake Pond ⊜ | 276 | 41.08 N | 74.13 W |
| Pótam | 232 | 27.36 N | 110.23 W |
| Potanino | 76 | 60.16 N | 32.47 E |
| Potaro ≏ | 246 | 5.22 N | 58.54 W |
| Potaro Landing | 246 | 5.23 N | 59.08 W |
| Potaro-Siparuni □[4] | 246 | 5.00 N | 59.30 W |
| Potato Creek ≏, Ga., U.S. | 192 | 32.47 N | 84.21 W |
| Potato Creek ≏, Pa., U.S. | 214 | 41.53 N | 78.23 W |
| Potawatomie Woods ♠ | 278 | 42.08 N | 87.53 W |
| Potchefstroom | 158 | 26.46 S | 27.01 E |
| Poté | 255 | 17.49 S | 41.49 W |
| Poteau | 194 | 35.03 N | 94.37 W |
| Poteau ≏ | 194 | 35.23 N | 94.26 W |
| Poteet | 196 | 29.02 N | 98.34 W |
| Potengi ≏ | 250 | 5.47 S | 35.16 W |
| Pötenitz | 54 | 53.57 N | 10.58 E |
| Pötenitzer Wiek c | 54 | 53.55 N | 10.55 E |
| Potenji | 250 | 7.06 S | 40.00 W |
| Potenza | 68 | 40.38 N | 15.49 E |
| Potenza □[4] | 68 | 40.30 N | 15.50 E |
| Potenza ≏ | 66 | 43.25 N | 13.40 E |
| Potenza Picena | 66 | 43.22 N | 13.37 E |
| Poteriteri, Lake ⊜ | 172 | 46.06 S | 167.08 E |
| Potes | 34 | 43.09 N | 4.37 W |
| Potfontein | 158 | 30.12 S | 24.08 E |
| Potgietersrus | 156 | 24.15 S | 28.55 E |
| Poth | 196 | 29.04 N | 98.05 W |
| Potholes Reservoir ⊜[1] | 202 | 47.01 N | 119.19 W |
| Poti | 84 | 42.09 N | 41.40 E |
| Poti ≏ | 250 | 5.02 S | 42.50 W |
| Potic Creek ≏ | 210 | 42.16 N | 73.55 W |
| Potiraguá | 255 | 15.36 S | 39.53 W |
| Potirendaba | 255 | 21.08 S | 49.08 W |
| Potiskum | 146 | 11.43 N | 11.05 E |
| Potiyivka | 78 | 50.37 N | 28.58 E |
| Potlatch | 202 | 46.55 N | 116.53 W |
| Potlatch ≏ | 202 | 46.28 N | 116.46 W |
| Po Toi Island I | 271d | 22.10 N | 114.15 E |
| Po Toi Island Group II | 271d | 22.11 N | 114.16 E |
| Potol Point › | 116 | 11.56 N | 121.57 E |
| Potomac, Il., U.S. | 216 | 40.18 N | 87.48 W |
| Potomac, Md., U.S. | 284c | 39.01 N | 77.12 W |
| Potomac ≏ | 188 | 38.00 N | 76.18 W |
| Potomac, South Branch ≏ | 188 | 39.31 N | 78.35 W |
| Potomac, South Branch, North Fork ≏ | 188 | 38.59 N | 79.11 W |
| Potomac, South Branch, South Fork ≏ | 188 | 39.04 N | 78.59 W |
| Potomac Creek ≏ | 208 | 38.21 N | 77.18 W |
| Potomac Creek, Long Branch ≏ | 208 | 38.23 N | 77.29 W |
| Potomac Heights | 208 | 38.36 N | 77.08 W |
| Poto-Poto ➔[8] | 273b | 4.15 S | 15.18 E |
| Potosí, Bol. | 248 | 19.35 S | 65.45 W |
| Potosi, Mo., U.S. | 194 | 37.56 N | 90.47 W |
| Potosí □[5] | 248 | 20.40 S | 67.00 W |
| Pototan | 116 | 10.55 N | 122.40 E |
| Potrerillos, Chile | 252 | 26.26 S | 69.29 W |
| Potrerillos, Hond. | 236 | 15.11 N | 87.58 W |
| Potrerillos Arriba | 236 | 8.41 N | 82.30 W |
| Potrero | 236 | 10.28 N | 85.47 W |
| Potrero ➔[8] | 282 | 37.48 N | 122.24 W |
| Potrero de Gallegos | 234 | 22.38 N | 103.41 W |
| Potrero del Llano | 196 | 29.12 N | 104.28 W |
| Potrero Grande | 236 | 9.00 N | 83.11 W |
| Potrite | 248 | 61.32 S | 16.10 W |
| Potro, Cerro del ʌ | 252 | 28.24 S | 69.39 W |
| Potsdam, Dtsch. | 54 | 52.24 N | 13.04 E |
| Potsdam, N.Y., U.S. | 188 | 44.40 N | 74.58 W |
| Potsdam, Oh., U.S. | 218 | 39.58 N | 84.25 W |
| Potsdam, Staatsforst ♠ | 264a | 52.26 N | 13.04 E |
| Potshausen | 52 | 53.11 N | 7.37 E |


| Symbol | English | Deutsch | Español | Français | Português |
|---|---|---|---|---|---|
| ≏ | River | Fluß | Río | Rivière | Rio |
| ≅ | Canal | Kanal | Canal | Canal | Canal |
| ∟ | Waterfall, Rapids | Wasserfall, Stromschnellen | Cascada, Rápidos | Chute d'eau, Rapides | Cascata, Rápidos |
| ʉ | Strait | Meeresstraße | Estrecho | Détroit | Estreito |
| c | Bay, Gulf | Bucht, Golf | Bahía, Golfo | Baie, Golfe | Baía, Golfo |
| ⊜ | Lake, Lakes | See, Seen | Lago, Lagos | Lac, Lacs | Lago, Lagos |
| ≡ | Swamp | Sumpf | Pantano | Marais | Pântano |
| ⊓ | Ice Features, Glacier | Eis- und Gletscherformen | Accidentes Glaciales | Formes glaciaires | Acidentes glaciares |
| ⍑ | Other Hydrographic Features | Andere Hydrographische Objekte | Otros Elementos Hidrográficos | Autres données hydrographiques | Outros acidentes hidrográficos |
| ✣ | Submarine Features | Untermeerische Objekte | Accidentes Submarinos | Formes de relief sous-marin | Acidentes submarinos |
| □ | Political Unit | Politische Einheit | Unidad Politica | Entité politique | Unidade política |
| ʋ | Cultural Institution | Kulturelle Institution | Institución Cultural | Institution culturelle | Institução cultural |
| ⊥ | Historical Site | Historische Stätte | Sitio Histórico | Site historique | Sitio histórico |
| ♠ | Recreational Site | Erholungs- und Ferienort | Sitio de Recreo | Centre de loisirs | Area de Lazer |
| ⊠ | Airport | Flughafen | Aeropuerto | Aéroport | Aeroporto |
| ▪ | Military Installation | Militäranlage | Instalación Militar | Installation militaire | Instalação militar |
| ➔ | Miscellaneous | Verschiedenes | Misceláneo | Divers | Diversos |

ENGLISH / DEUTSCH


| Name | Page | Lat. °′ | Long. °′ |
|---|---|---|---|
| Pott, Île I | **175f** | 19.35 S | 163.36 E |
| Pottawatomie Creek ≃ | **198** | 38.29 N | 94.55 W |
| Pottawatomi Indian Reservation ◆[4] | **198** | 39.20 N | 95.50 W |
| Pottendorf | **61** | 47.55 N | 16.23 E |
| Potten End | **260** | 51.46 N | 0.31 W |
| Pottenhofen | **61** | 48.46 N | 16.33 E |
| Pottenstein | **60** | 49.46 N | 11.25 E |
| Potter | **198** | 41.13 N | 103.18 W |
| Potter □[6] | **214** | 41.47 N | 78.01 W |
| Potter Hollow | **210** | 42.25 N | 74.13 W |
| Potter Lake | **216** | 42.50 N | 88.21 W |
| Potter Point › | **274a** | 34.03 S | 151.13 E |
| Potters Bar | **42** | 51.42 N | 0.11 W |
| Potters Mills | **208** | 40.48 N | 77.32 W |
| Potter Street | **260** | 51.46 N | 0.08 E |
| Pottersville | **276** | 40.42 N | 74.43 W |
| Potterville | **216** | 42.38 N | 84.45 W |
| Pöttmes | **60** | 48.35 N | 11.06 E |
| Potton | **42** | 52.08 N | 0.14 W |
| Potts Camp | **194** | 34.38 N | 89.18 W |
| Potts Creek ≃ | **192** | 37.45 N | 80.00 W |
| Potts Grove | **210** | 41.00 N | 76.48 W |
| Potts Hill Reservoirs ⊜[1] | **274a** | 33.54 S | 151.02 E |
| Pott Shrigley | **262** | 53.19 N | 2.05 W |
| Pottstown | **208** | 40.14 N | 75.39 W |
| Pottstown Landing | **285** | 40.14 N | 75.40 W |
| Pottstown Limerick Airport ⊠ | **285** | 40.14 N | 75.34 W |
| Pottstown Municipal Airport ⊠ | **285** | 40.16 N | 75.40 W |
| Pottsville | **208** | 40.41 N | 76.11 W |
| Potwin | **198** | 37.56 N | 97.01 W |
| Pötzleinsdorf ◆[8] | **264b** | 48.15 N | 16.19 E |
| Pötzleinsdorfer Park ♦ | **264b** | 48.14 N | 16.18 E |
| P'otzu | **100** | 23.28 N | 120.14 E |
| Pouancé | **32** | 47.44 N | 1.11 W |
| Pouce-Coupe | **182** | 55.43 N | 120.08 W |
| Pouce Coupé ≃ | **182** | 56.08 N | 119.52 W |
| Pouch | **54** | 51.37 N | 12.24 E |
| Pouch Cove | **186** | 47.46 N | 52.46 W |
| Pouembout | **175f** | 21.08 S | 164.53 E |
| Poughkeepsie | **210** | 41.42 N | 73.55 W |
| Poughquag | **210** | 41.37 N | 73.41 W |
| Pouilly-en-Auxois | **58** | 47.16 N | 4.33 E |
| Pouilly-sur-Loire | **50** | 47.17 N | 2.57 E |
| Pouilly-sur-Meuse | **56** | 49.32 N | 5.07 E |
| Poulain, Étang ⊜ | **261** | 48.43 N | 1.44 E |
| Poulan | **192** | 31.30 N | 83.47 W |
| Poulaphouca Reservoir ⊜[1] | **48** | 53.08 N | 6.31 W |
| Poulin-de-Courval, Lac ⊜ | **186** | 48.52 N | 70.27 W |
| Poulsbo | **224** | 47.44 N | 122.38 W |
| Poulter, Lac ⊜ | **190** | 47.07 N | 76.45 W |
| Poultney | **188** | 43.31 N | 73.14 W |
| Poulton-le-Fylde | **44** | 53.51 N | 2.59 W |
| Poum | **175f** | 20.14 S | 164.02 E |
| Poŭn | **98** | 36.29 N | 127.43 E |
| Pound | **192** | 37.07 N | 82.36 W |
| Poundmaker Indian Reserve ◆[4] | **184** | 52.51 N | 109.00 W |
| Poundstock | **42** | 50.46 N | 4.33 W |
| Pouoanuu, Mont ∧ | **174x** | 9.49 S | 139.07 W |
| Pourri, Mont ∧ | **62** | 45.32 N | 6.52 E |
| Pouru-Saint-Rémy | **56** | 49.41 N | 5.05 E |
| Pourville-sur-Mer | **50** | 49.55 N | 1.02 E |
| Pouso Alegre | **256** | 22.13 S | 45.56 W |
| Pouso Alto | **256** | 22.11 S | 44.58 W |
| Pouso Redondo | **252** | 27.15 S | 49.57 W |
| Pouso Sêco | **256** | 22.41 S | 44.10 W |
| Pouss | **146** | 10.51 N | 15.03 E |
| Poutasi | **175a** | 14.01 S | 171.41 W |
| Poŭthĭsăt | **110** | 12.32 N | 103.55 E |
| Poŭthĭsăt ≃ | **110** | 12.41 N | 104.09 E |
| Pouxeux | **58** | 48.06 N | 6.34 E |
| Pouzauges | **32** | 46.47 N | 0.50 W |
| Považská Bystrica | **30** | 49.08 N | 18.27 E |
| Povenec | **24** | 62.51 N | 34.45 E |
| Poverello, Monte ∧ | **70** | 38.05 N | 15.22 E |
| Poverennyj | **80** | 46.45 N | 43.12 E |
| Poverty Bay ⊂ | **172** | 38.42 S | 177.58 E |
| Povetkino | **82** | 54.20 N | 38.23 E |
| Poviglio | **64** | 44.51 N | 10.32 E |
| Povljen ⩓ | **38** | 43.55 N | 19.30 E |
| Póvoa, Mouchão da I | **266c** | 38.51 N | 9.03 W |
| Povoação | **148a** | 37.45 N | 25.15 W |
| Póvoa de Santa Iria | **266c** | 38.52 N | 9.04 W |
| Póvoa de Santo Adrião | **266c** | 38.48 N | 9.10 W |
| Póvoa de Varzim | **34** | 41.23 N | 8.46 W |
| Povorino | **80** | 51.12 N | 42.14 E |
| Povorotnyj, mys › | **89** | 42.42 N | 133.04 E |
| Povorsk | **78** | 51.16 N | 25.07 E |
| Povrly | **54** | 50.40 N | 14.10 E |
| Povungnituk | **176** | 60.02 N | 77.10 W |
| Povungnituk, Rivière de ≃ | **176** | 60.03 N | 77.15 W |
| Powassan | **190** | 46.05 N | 79.22 W |
| Poway | **228** | 32.57 N | 117.02 W |
| Powder ≃, U.S. | **178** | 46.44 N | 105.26 W |
| Powder ≃, Or., U.S. | **202** | 44.45 N | 117.03 W |
| Powder, Dry Fork ≃ | **200** | 43.47 N | 106.15 W |
| Powder, Middle Fork ≃ | **200** | 43.42 N | 106.33 W |
| Powder, North Fork ≃ | **202** | 43.42 N | 106.33 W |
| Powder, Red Fork ≃ | **202** | 43.39 N | 106.47 W |
| Powder, South Fork ≃ | **202** | 43.40 N | 106.30 W |
| Powder Horn Lake ⊜ | **278** | 41.38 N | 87.32 W |
| Powderly, Ky., U.S. | **194** | 37.09 N | 87.10 W |
| Powderly, Tx., U.S. | **196** | 33.49 N | 95.31 W |
| Powdermaker Ditch ≅ | **279a** | 41.30 N | 82.02 W |
| Powder Mill Village | **284c** | 39.03 N | 76.57 W |
| Powder River Pass )( | **202** | 44.09 N | 107.04 W |
| Powell, Oh., U.S. | **214** | 40.09 N | 83.05 W |
| Powell, Pa., U.S. | **210** | 41.42 N | 76.31 W |
| Powell, Tx., U.S. | **222** | 32.07 N | 96.20 W |
| Powell, Wy., U.S. | **202** | 44.45 N | 108.45 W |
| Powell ≃ | **192** | 36.29 N | 83.42 W |
| Powell, Lake ⊜[1] | **200** | 37.25 N | 110.45 W |
| Powell, Mount ∧ | **200** | 39.46 N | 106.20 W |
| Powell Creek ≃, Austl. | **166** | 25.02 S | 143.40 E |
| Powell Creek ≃, Oh., U.S. | **216** | 41.17 N | 84.21 W |
| Powellhurst | **224** | 45.30 N | 122.32 W |
| Powell Lake ⊜ | **182** | 50.11 N | 124.24 W |
| Powell River | **182** | 49.52 N | 124.33 W |
| Powells Valley | **208** | 40.26 N | 76.56 W |
| Powellton | **188** | 38.05 N | 81.19 W |
| Powellville | **208** | 38.19 N | 75.22 W |
| Powers, Mi., U.S. | **190** | 45.41 N | 87.31 W |
| Powers, Or., U.S. | **202** | 42.53 N | 124.04 W |
| Powers Lake, N.D., U.S. | **198** | 48.33 N | 102.38 W |
| Powers Lake, Wi., U.S. | **216** | 42.33 N | 88.17 W |
| Powers Lookout ♦ | **169** | 36.50 S | 146.22 E |
| Powhatan, La., U.S. | **194** | 31.52 N | 93.12 W |
| Powhatan, Va., U.S. | **192** | 37.32 N | 77.55 W |
| Powhatan Mill | **284b** | 39.20 N | 76.43 W |
| Powhatan Point | **188** | 39.51 N | 80.48 W |
| Powis, Vale of V | **42** | 52.38 N | 3.08 W |
| Powissett Brook ≃ | **283** | 42.16 N | 71.14 W |
| Powlett ≃ | **169** | 38.35 S | 145.32 E |
| Pownal | **210** | 42.45 N | 73.14 W |
| Powys □[6] | **42** | 52.17 N | 3.20 W |
| Poxoréo | **255** | 15.50 S | 54.23 W |
| Poya | **175f** | 21.19 S | 165.07 E |
| Poyang Hu ⊜ | **100** | 29.00 N | 116.25 E |
| Poyan Reservoir ⊜[1] | **271c** | 1.23 N | 103.40 E |
| Poyen | **194** | 34.19 N | 92.38 W |
| Poygan, Lake ⊜ | **190** | 44.09 N | 88.50 W |
| Poyle | **260** | 51.28 N | 0.31 W |
| Poynette | **190** | 43.23 N | 89.24 W |
| Poynor | **222** | 32.04 N | 95.36 W |
| Poynton | **44** | 53.21 N | 2.07 W |
| Poyntz Pass | **48** | 54.18 N | 6.23 W |
| Poyraz ◆[8] | **267b** | 41.12 N | 29.07 E |
| Poyraz Burnu › | **267b** | 41.12 N | 29.08 E |
| Poysdorf | **61** | 48.40 N | 16.38 E |
| Pozantı | **130** | 37.25 N | 34.52 E |
| Požarevac | **38** | 44.37 N | 21.11 E |
| Poza Rica | **234** | 20.33 N | 97.27 W |
| Požarskoje | **89** | 46.16 N | 134.04 E |
| Pozdejevka | **89** | 50.36 N | 128.56 E |
| Požega | **38** | 43.50 N | 20.02 E |
| Poznań | **30** | 52.25 N | 16.55 E |
| Poznań □[4] | **30** | 52.20 N | 16.55 E |
| Pozo Alcón | **34** | 37.42 N | 2.56 W |
| Pozo Almonte | **248** | 20.16 S | 69.48 W |
| Pozoblanco | **34** | 38.22 N | 4.51 W |
| Pozo-Cañada | **34** | 38.48 N | 1.45 W |
| Pozo Colorado | **252** | 23.28 S | 58.51 W |
| Pozo del Molle | **252** | 32.02 S | 62.55 W |
| Pozo del Tigre | **252** | 24.54 S | 60.19 W |
| Pozo Hondo | **252** | 27.10 S | 64.30 W |
| Pozos, Punta › | **254** | 47.57 S | 65.47 W |
| Pozsony → Bratislava | **30** | 48.09 N | 17.07 E |
| Pozuelo de Alarcón, Esp. | **34** | 40.26 N | 3.49 W |
| Pozuelo de Alarcón, Esp. | **266a** | 40.26 N | 3.49 W |
| Pozuelos | **246** | 10.11 N | 64.39 W |
| Pozuelos, Laguna ⊜ | **252** | 22.22 S | 66.01 W |
| Pozuzo | **248** | 10.04 S | 75.32 W |
| Pozuzo ≃ | **248** | 9.52 S | 75.12 W |
| Požva | **86** | 59.05 N | 56.05 E |
| Pozzallo | **70** | 36.43 N | 14.51 E |
| Pozzillo, Lago di ⊜ | **70** | 37.40 N | 14.35 E |
| Pozzolo Formigaro | **62** | 44.48 N | 8.47 E |
| Pozzomaggiore | **71** | 40.24 N | 8.39 E |
| Pozzuoli | **68** | 40.49 N | 14.07 E |
| Pozzuolo del Friuli | **64** | 45.59 N | 13.12 E |
| Pra ≃, Ghana | **150** | 5.01 N | 1.37 W |
| Pra ≃, Ross. | **80** | 54.45 N | 41.01 E |
| Prabuty | **30** | 53.46 N | 19.10 E |
| Praça Cruzeiro | **256** | 22.43 S | 42.38 W |
| Praça Sêca ◆[8] | **287a** | 22.54 S | 43.21 W |
| Prachatice | **30** | 49.01 N | 14.00 E |
| Prachin Buri | **110** | 14.03 N | 101.22 E |
| Prachuap Khiri Khan | **110** | 11.49 N | 99.48 E |
| Prackenbach | **60** | 49.06 N | 12.50 E |
| Pracuí ≃ | **250** | 2.26 S | 51.19 W |
| Pracupi ≃ | **250** | 2.06 S | 51.30 W |
| Pradelles | **62** | 44.46 N | 3.53 E |
| Pradera | **246** | 3.25 N | 76.15 W |
| Prades | **32** | 42.37 N | 2.26 E |
| Pradleves | **62** | 44.25 N | 7.17 E |
| Prado | **255** | 17.21 S | 39.13 W |
| Prado, Museo del ♁ | **266a** | 40.25 N | 3.41 W |
| Prado Dam ◆[6] | **280** | 33.54 N | 117.39 W |
| Prado Flood Control Basin ≚[1] | **280** | 33.54 N | 117.38 W |
| Prados | **255** | 21.03 S | 44.05 W |
| Prads | **62** | 44.13 N | 6.27 E |
| Præstø | **41** | 55.07 N | 12.03 E |
| Prag → Praha | **54** | 50.05 N | 14.26 E |
| Praga → Praha | **54** | 50.05 N | 14.26 E |
| Pragelato | **62** | 45.01 N | 6.57 E |
| Pragersko | **61** | 46.23 N | 15.40 E |
| Praglia, Monastero di ♁[1] | **64** | 45.23 N | 11.45 E |
| Prägraten | **64** | 47.01 N | 12.23 E |
| Prague → Praha, Česká Rep. | **54** | 50.05 N | 14.26 E |
| Prague, Ne., U.S. | **198** | 41.18 N | 96.48 W |
| Prague, Ok., U.S. | **196** | 35.29 N | 96.41 W |
| Praha (Prague) | **54** | 50.05 N | 14.26 E |
| Praha ∧ | **60** | 49.40 N | 13.49 E |
| Prahova □[6] | **38** | 45.00 N | 26.00 E |
| Prahova ≃ | **38** | 44.43 N | 26.27 E |
| Prahran | **274b** | 37.51 S | 144.59 E |
| Praia | **150a** | 14.55 N | 23.31 W |
| Praia a Mare | **68** | 39.54 N | 15.47 E |
| Praia da Cruz Quebrada | **266c** | 38.42 N | 9.14 W |
| Praia da Enseada | **256** | 23.29 S | 45.05 W |
| Praia das Maçãs | **266c** | 38.50 N | 9.28 W |
| Praia da Vitória | **148a** | 38.44 N | 27.04 W |
| Praia de Araçatiba | **256** | 23.15 S | 44.21 W |
| Praia Funda, Ponta da › | **287a** | 23.05 S | 43.33 W |
| Praia Grande, Bra. | **252** | 29.12 S | 49.57 W |
| Praia Grande, Bra. | **256** | 24.01 S | 46.25 W |
| Praiano | **68** | 40.37 N | 14.32 E |
| Praikalogu | **115b** | 9.45 S | 119.25 E |
| Prainha | **250** | 1.48 S | 53.29 W |
| Prainha Nova | **248** | 7.16 S | 60.23 W |
| Prairie | **166** | 20.52 S | 144.36 E |
| Prairie ≃, Mi., U.S. | **216** | 41.55 N | 85.38 W |
| Prairie ≃, Mn., U.S. | **190** | 47.18 N | 93.29 W |
| Prairie ≃, Wi., U.S. | **190** | 45.10 N | 89.42 W |
| Prairie City, Il., U.S. | **190** | 40.37 N | 90.28 W |
| Prairie City, Ia., U.S. | **190** | 41.35 N | 93.14 W |
| Prairie City, Or., U.S. | **202** | 44.27 N | 118.42 W |
| Prairie Creek ≃, Fl., U.S. | **220** | 26.59 N | 81.56 W |
| Prairie Creek ≃, Il., U.S. | **216** | 41.21 N | 88.12 W |
| Prairie Creek ≃, Il., U.S. | **216** | 40.55 N | 87.49 W |
| Prairie Creek ≃, Il., U.S. | **278** | 41.36 N | 87.40 W |
| Prairie Creek ≃, Mi., U.S. | **216** | 42.59 N | 85.01 W |
| Prairie Creek ≃, Ne., U.S. | **198** | 41.22 N | 97.32 W |
| Prairie Creek Reservoir ⊜[1] | **218** | 40.08 N | 85.17 W |
| Prairie Dog Creek ≃ | **198** | 40.00 N | 99.23 W |
| Prairie du Chien | **190** | 43.03 N | 91.08 W |
| Prairie du Sac | **190** | 43.17 N | 89.43 W |
| Prairie Elk Creek ≃ | **198** | 48.00 N | 105.51 W |
| Prairie Grove | **194** | 35.58 N | 94.19 W |
| Prairie Hill | **222** | 31.39 N | 96.47 W |
| Prairie Lea | **222** | 29.44 N | 97.45 W |
| Prairie River | **184** | 52.52 N | 103.00 W |
| Prairies, Coteau des ⩓[2] | **198** | 44.30 N | 96.45 W |
| Prairies, Lake of the ⊜[1] | **184** | 51.05 N | 101.25 W |
| Prairies, Rivière des ≃ | **275a** | 45.42 N | 73.29 W |
| Prairie View, Il., U.S. | **278** | 42.12 N | 87.57 W |
| Prairie View, Tx., U.S. | **222** | 30.05 N | 95.59 W |
| Prairie Village | **198** | 38.59 N | 94.38 W |
| Prajekan | **115a** | 7.47 S | 113.59 E |
| Prakhon Chai | **110** | 14.37 N | 103.05 E |
| Pralboino | **64** | 45.16 N | 10.13 E |
| Prali | **62** | 44.54 N | 7.03 E |
| Pralls Island I | **276** | 40.37 N | 74.12 W |
| Pralognan-la-Vanoise | **62** | 45.23 N | 6.43 E |
| Pram | **60** | 48.14 N | 13.37 E |
| Pram ≃ | **60** | 48.28 N | 13.26 E |
| Pramaggiore, Monte ∧ | **64** | 46.22 N | 12.33 E |
| Prambachkirchen | **60** | 48.19 N | 13.55 E |
| Prambanan | **115a** | 7.45 S | 110.30 E |
| Pr'amicyno | **78** | 51.39 N | 35.56 E |
| Pramort | **54** | 54.26 N | 12.55 E |
| Prampram | **150** | 5.42 N | 0.07 E |
| Pran Buri | **110** | 12.23 N | 99.55 E |
| Pran Buri ≃ | **110** | 12.24 N | 100.00 E |
| Prang | **150** | 7.59 N | 0.53 W |
| Prangli I | **76** | 59.38 N | 25.02 E |
| Prānhita ≃ | **122** | 18.49 N | 79.55 E |
| Pranzo | **64** | 45.55 N | 10.48 E |
| Prapa, Khlong ≅ | **269a** | 13.46 N | 100.32 E |
| Prapat | **114** | 2.40 N | 98.56 E |
| Praraye | **58** | 45.55 N | 7.32 E |
| Prärien → Great Plains ≚ | **16** | 42.00 N | 100.00 W |
| Praskoveja | **84** | 44.43 N | 44.12 E |
| Praslin, Lac ⊜ | **186** | 50.03 N | 69.48 W |
| Praslin Island I | **138** | 4.19 S | 55.44 E |
| Prasonísi, Ákra › | **38** | 35.52 N | 27.46 E |
| Praszka | **30** | 51.04 N | 18.26 E |
| Prat, Isla I | **254** | 48.15 S | 75.00 W |
| Prata, Bra. | **250** | 7.41 S | 37.06 W |
| Prata, Bra. | **255** | 19.18 S | 48.55 W |
| Prata, Bra. | **287a** | 22.45 S | 43.25 W |
| Prata, Rio da ≃, Bra. | **255** | 17.28 S | 46.35 W |
| Prata, Rio da ≃, Bra. | **255** | 18.49 S | 49.54 W |
| Prata, Rio da ≃, Bra. | **287a** | 22.56 S | 43.34 W |
| Pratāpgarh, India | **120** | 24.02 N | 74.47 E |
| Pratāpgarh, India | **124** | 25.54 N | 81.58 E |
| Pratāpnagar | **126** | 22.23 N | 89.13 E |
| Pratápolis | **255** | 20.45 S | 46.52 W |
| Pratas Island → Tungsha Tao I | **90** | 20.42 N | 116.43 E |
| Pratau | **54** | 51.50 N | 12.38 E |
| Pratella | **68** | 41.24 N | 14.11 E |
| Prater ♦ | **264b** | 48.12 N | 16.25 E |
| Prathet Thai → Thailand □[1] | **110** | 15.00 N | 100.00 E |
| Pratinha | **255** | 19.46 S | 46.24 W |
| Prato | **66** | 43.53 N | 11.06 E |
| Prato □[4] | **64** | 44.00 N | 11.05 E |
| Prato allo Stelvio | **64** | 46.37 N | 10.35 E |
| Pratola Peligna | **66** | 42.06 N | 13.52 E |
| Pratola Serra | **68** | 40.59 N | 14.51 E |
| Pratolino | **66** | 43.52 N | 11.18 E |
| Pratomagno ⩓ | **66** | 43.39 N | 11.39 E |
| Pratt | **198** | 37.38 N | 98.44 W |
| Pratteln | **58** | 47.31 N | 7.42 E |
| Prättigau V | **58** | 46.55 N | 9.45 E |
| Pratt's Bottom ◆[8] | **260** | 51.20 N | 0.07 E |
| Prattsburg | **210** | 42.31 N | 77.17 W |
| Prattsville | **210** | 42.18 N | 74.26 W |
| Prattville | **194** | 32.27 N | 86.27 W |
| Pratudão ≃ | **255** | 13.56 S | 44.55 W |
| Prauthoy | **58** | 47.40 N | 5.17 E |
| Pravaja Mama ≃ | **88** | 57.10 N | 111.54 E |
| Pravda | **89** | 47.00 N | 142.01 E |
| Pravdinsk, Ross. | **76** | 54.27 N | 21.01 E |
| Pravdinsk, Ross. | **80** | 56.32 N | 43.34 E |
| Pravdinskij | **82** | 56.04 N | 37.51 E |
| Pravia | **34** | 43.29 N | 6.07 W |
| Prawet Buri Rom, Khlong ≅ | **269a** | 13.42 N | 100.35 E |
| Prawle Point › | **42** | 50.13 N | 3.42 W |
| Praya | **115b** | 8.42 S | 116.17 E |
| Pr'aža | **24** | 61.42 N | 33.35 E |
| Praz-sur-Arly | **62** | 45.50 N | 6.34 E |
| Prazzo | **62** | 44.29 N | 7.03 E |
| Preakness Brook ≃ | **276** | 40.54 N | 74.15 W |
| Preakness Mountain ∧ | **276** | 40.58 N | 74.13 W |
| Preakness Valley Park ♦ | **276** | 40.55 N | 74.14 W |
| Preble, In., U.S. | **216** | 40.50 N | 85.01 W |
| Preble, N.Y., U.S. | **210** | 42.44 N | 76.09 W |
| Preble □[6] | **218** | 39.45 N | 84.38 W |
| Preci | **66** | 42.53 N | 13.02 E |
| Prečistoje, Ross. | **76** | 55.41 N | 34.56 E |
| Prečistoje, Ross. | **76** | 55.31 N | 32.22 E |
| Prečistoje, Ross. | **80** | 58.27 N | 40.19 E |
| Précy-sous-Thil | **50** | 47.23 N | 4.19 E |
| Précy-sur-Marne | **261** | 48.56 N | 2.47 E |
| Précy-sur-Oise | **50** | 49.12 N | 2.22 E |
| Preda | **58** | 46.36 N | 9.46 E |
| Predappio | **66** | 44.06 N | 11.58 E |
| Predazzo | **64** | 46.19 N | 11.36 E |
| Predeal | **38** | 45.30 N | 25.35 E |
| Prédecelle ≃ | **261** | 48.35 N | 2.07 E |
| Předenice | **60** | 49.37 N | 13.24 E |
| Predești | **38** | 44.21 N | 23.36 E |
| Predgornoje | **86** | 47.10 N | 81.02 E |
| Predigtstuhl ∧ | **61** | 48.48 N | 15.22 E |
| Předin | **61** | 49.12 N | 15.40 E |
| Predivinsk | **86** | 57.04 N | 93.27 E |
| Predlitz [-Turrach] | **64** | 47.04 N | 13.55 E |
| Predoi (Prettau) | **64** | 47.02 N | 12.06 E |
| Predore | **64** | 45.40 N | 10.01 E |
| Preeceville | **184** | 51.58 N | 102.40 W |
| Pré-en-Pail | **32** | 48.27 N | 0.12 W |
| Preesall | **44** | 53.55 N | 2.58 W |
| Preetz | **54** | 54.14 N | 10.16 E |
| Pregarten | **61** | 48.21 N | 14.32 E |
| Pregel → Pregol'a ≃ | **76** | 54.41 N | 20.22 E |
| Pregnana | **266b** | 45.31 N | 9.00 E |
| Pregol'a ≃ | **76** | 54.41 N | 20.22 E |
| Pregonero | **246** | 8.01 N | 71.46 W |
| Pregos | **256** | 21.46 S | 42.54 W |
| Pregradnaja | **84** | 43.58 N | 41.12 E |
| Pregradnoje | **80** | 45.49 N | 41.45 E |
| Preguiças ≃ | **250** | 2.34 S | 42.44 W |
| Preila | **76** | 55.22 N | 21.04 E |
| Preiļi | **76** | 56.18 N | 26.43 E |
| Preissac, Lac ⊜ | **190** | 48.20 N | 78.20 W |
| Prekestolen ♦ | **26** | 59.00 N | 6.01 E |
| Preko | **36** | 44.05 N | 15.11 E |
| Prekomurje ◆[1] | **61** | 46.40 N | 16.10 E |
| Prĕk Poŭthĭ | **110** | 11.51 N | 105.07 E |
| Prelate | **184** | 50.51 N | 109.23 W |
| Přelouč | **30** | 50.02 N | 15.34 E |
| Premana | **58** | 46.03 N | 9.25 E |
| Prembun | **115a** | 7.43 S | 109.48 E |
| Prémery | **50** | 47.10 N | 3.20 E |
| Premià de Dalt | **266d** | 41.31 N | 2.21 E |
| Premià de Mar | **266d** | 41.29 N | 2.21 E |
| Premnitz | **54** | 52.32 N | 12.19 E |
| Prémont, P.Q., Can. | **206** | 46.22 N | 73.03 W |
| Premont, Tx., U.S. | **196** | 27.21 N | 98.07 W |
| Prémontré | **50** | 49.33 N | 3.24 E |
| Premuda, Otok I | **36** | 44.20 N | 14.37 E |
| Prenestini, Monti ⩓ | **66** | 41.50 N | 12.55 E |
| Prenjas | **38** | 41.04 N | 20.32 E |
| Prentice | **190** | 45.32 N | 90.17 W |
| Prentiss | **194** | 31.35 N | 89.52 W |
| Prenton | **262** | 53.22 N | 3.03 W |
| Prenzlau | **54** | 53.19 N | 13.52 E |
| Prenzlauer Berg ◆[8] | **264a** | 52.32 N | 13.26 E |
| Preobraženije | **89** | 42.57 N | 133.55 E |
| Preobraženovka | **89** | 48.04 N | 131.55 E |
| Preobrazhenne | **83** | 49.32 N | 38.10 E |
| Preparis Island I | **110** | 14.52 N | 93.41 E |
| Preparis North Channel ʉ | **110** | 15.27 N | 94.05 E |
| Preparis South Channel ʉ | **110** | 14.40 N | 94.00 E |
| Přerov | **30** | 49.27 N | 17.27 E |
| Prerow | **54** | 54.26 N | 12.35 E |
| Pré-Saint-Didier | **62** | 45.46 N | 6.59 E |
| Presanella, Cima ∧ | **64** | 46.13 N | 10.40 E |
| Prescot | **44** | 53.26 N | 2.48 W |
| Prescott, On., Can. | **212** | 44.43 N | 75.31 W |
| Prescott, Az., U.S. | **200** | 34.32 N | 112.28 W |
| Prescott, Ar., U.S. | **194** | 33.48 N | 93.22 W |
| Prescott, Or., U.S. | **224** | 46.02 N | 122.53 W |
| Prescott, Wi., U.S. | **190** | 44.44 N | 92.48 W |
| Prescott and Russell □[6] | **206** | 45.25 N | 75.00 W |
| Prescott Island I | **176** | 73.01 N | 96.50 W |
| Preševo | **38** | 42.18 N | 21.39 E |
| Presho | **198** | 43.54 N | 100.03 W |
| Presicce | **68** | 39.54 N | 18.16 E |
| Presidencia de la Plaza | **252** | 27.01 S | 59.51 W |
| Presidencia Roca | **252** | 26.08 S | 59.36 W |
| Presidencia Roque Sáenz Peña | **252** | 26.47 S | 60.27 W |
| Presidente Costa e Silva, Ponte ◆[5] | **287a** | 22.53 S | 43.10 W |
| Presidente Derqui | **258** | 34.29 S | 58.51 W |
| Presidente Dutra | **250** | 5.15 S | 44.30 W |
| Presidente Epitácio | **255** | 21.46 S | 52.06 W |
| Presidente Getúlio | **252** | 27.03 S | 49.37 W |
| Presidente Hayes □[5] | **252** | 24.00 S | 59.00 W |
| Presidente Nicolás Avellaneda, Parque ♦ | **288** | 34.39 S | 58.29 W |
| Presidente Olegário | **255** | 18.25 S | 46.25 W |
| Presidente Prudente | **255** | 22.07 S | 51.22 W |
| Presidente Ríos, Lago ⊜ | **254** | 46.28 S | 74.25 W |
| Presidente Roosevelt, Estação ◆[5] | **287b** | 23.33 S | 46.36 W |
| Presidente Venceslau | **255** | 21.52 S | 51.50 W |
| Presidential Heights | **279b** | 40.34 N | 80.03 W |
| President Roxas | **116** | 11.26 N | 122.56 E |
| Presidio | **196** | 29.33 N | 104.22 W |
| Presidio ≃ | **234** | 23.06 N | 106.17 W |
| Presidio of San Francisco ■ | **226** | 37.48 N | 122.28 W |
| Presles | **56** | 50.23 N | 4.35 E |
| Presles-en-Brie | **261** | 48.43 N | 2.45 E |
| Presnogor'kovka | **86** | 54.30 N | 65.45 E |
| Presnovka | **86** | 54.40 N | 67.09 E |
| Presolana, Passo della )( | **64** | 45.55 N | 10.06 E |
| Prešov | **30** | 49.00 N | 21.15 E |
| Prespa, Lake ⊜ | **38** | 40.55 N | 21.00 E |
| Prespansko Jezero → Prespa, Lake ⊜ | **38** | 40.55 N | 21.00 E |
| Presque Isle | **186** | 46.40 N | 68.00 W |
| Presque Isle ›[1] | **214** | 42.09 N | 80.06 W |
| Presque Isle ≃ | **190** | 46.43 N | 89.59 W |
| Presque Isle State Park ♦ | **214** | 42.09 N | 80.06 W |
| Presqu'ile Bay ⊂ | **212** | 44.01 N | 77.43 W |
| Presqu'ile Peninsula ›[1] | **212** | 44.00 N | 77.41 W |
| Presqu'ile Provincial Park ♦ | **212** | 44.00 N | 77.42 W |
| Pressana | **64** | 45.17 N | 11.24 E |
| Pressath | **60** | 49.46 N | 11.56 E |
| Pressbaum | **61** | 48.11 N | 16.05 E |
| Pressburg → Bratislava | **30** | 48.09 N | 17.07 E |
| Pressel | **54** | 51.34 N | 12.41 E |
| Pressig | **54** | 50.21 N | 11.19 E |
| Prestatyn | **44** | 53.20 N | 3.24 W |
| Prestbury | **262** | 53.17 N | 2.09 W |
| Prestea | **150** | 5.27 N | 2.08 W |
| Presteigne | **42** | 52.17 N | 3.00 W |
| Přeštice | **60** | 49.34 N | 13.20 E |
| Presto | **279b** | 40.23 N | 80.07 W |
| Preston, Austl. | **169** | 37.45 S | 145.01 E |
| Preston, Eng., U.K. | **42** | 50.39 N | 2.25 W |
| Preston, Eng., U.K. | **44** | 53.46 N | 0.12 W |
| Preston, Eng., U.K. | **44** | 53.46 N | 2.42 W |
| Preston, Ga., U.S. | **192** | 32.03 N | 84.32 W |
| Preston, Id., U.S. | **202** | 42.05 N | 111.52 W |
| Preston, Ia., U.S. | **190** | 42.03 N | 90.24 W |
| Preston, Ks., U.S. | **198** | 37.45 N | 98.33 W |
| Preston, Md., U.S. | **208** | 38.42 N | 75.54 W |
| Preston, Mn., U.S. | **190** | 43.40 N | 92.04 W |
| Preston, Wa., U.S. | **224** | 47.31 N | 121.55 W |
| Preston □[8] | **262** | 53.48 N | 2.42 W |
| Preston ≃, Austl. | **168a** | 33.20 S | 115.40 E |
| Preston ≃, P.Q., Can. | **206** | 46.05 N | 75.04 W |
| Preston, Cape › | **162** | 20.51 S | 116.12 E |
| Preston, Lac ⊜ | **206** | 46.05 N | 75.04 W |
| Preston, Lake ⊜, Austl. | **168a** | 32.59 S | 115.42 E |
| Preston, Lake ⊜, Fl., U.S. | **220** | 28.18 N | 81.08 W |
| Preston Airport ⊠ | **276** | 40.22 N | 74.15 W |
| Preston Brook | **262** | 53.19 N | 2.39 W |
| Preston Brook Canal Tunnel ◆[5] | **262** | 53.19 N | 2.38 W |
| Preston Heights | **216** | 41.28 N | 88.08 W |
| Preston Hollow | **210** | 42.27 N | 74.13 W |
| Preston North End Football Ground ♦ | **262** | 53.47 N | 2.42 W |
| Prestonpans | **46** | 55.57 N | 3.00 W |
| Preston Peak ∧ | **204** | 41.50 N | 123.37 W |
| Prestonsburg | **192** | 37.39 N | 82.46 W |
| Prestrud Inlet ⊂ | **9** | 78.18 S | 156.00 W |
| Preststranda | **26** | 59.06 N | 9.04 E |
| Prestville | **182** | 55.44 N | 118.37 W |
| Prestwich | **44** | 53.32 N | 2.17 W |
| Prestwick | **46** | 55.29 N | 4.37 W |
| Prestwick Airport ⊠ | **46** | 55.30 N | 4.36 W |
| Preto ≃, Bra. | **246** | 1.41 S | 63.48 W |
| Preto ≃, Bra. | **248** | 8.03 S | 62.54 W |
| Preto ≃, Bra. | **250** | 11.21 S | 43.52 W |
| Preto ≃, Bra. | **250** | 3.32 S | 43.46 W |
| Preto ≃, Bra. | **255** | 13.37 S | 48.06 W |
| Preto ≃, Bra. | **255** | 17.00 S | 46.12 W |
| Preto ≃, Bra. | **255** | 18.44 S | 50.23 W |
| Preto ≃, Bra. | **255** | 20.08 S | 49.38 W |
| Preto ≃, Bra. | **256** | 22.14 S | 43.07 W |
| Preto ≃, Bra. | **256** | 22.01 S | 43.20 W |
| Preto do Igapó-açu ≃ | **246** | 4.26 S | 59.48 W |
| Pretoria | **158** | 25.45 S | 28.10 E |
| Pretoriusvlei | **158** | 28.30 S | 22.59 E |
| Prettau → Predoi | **64** | 47.02 N | 12.06 E |
| Prettin | **54** | 51.39 N | 12.55 E |
| Prettyboy Reservoir ⊜[1] | **208** | 39.38 N | 76.45 W |
| Pretty Prairie | **198** | 37.46 N | 98.01 W |
| Pretzfeld | **60** | 49.45 N | 11.11 E |
| Pretzier | **54** | 52.49 N | 11.15 E |
| Pretzsch | **54** | 51.42 N | 12.48 E |
| Preussisch Eylau → Bagrationovsk | **76** | 54.23 N | 20.39 E |
| Preussisch-Oldendorf | **52** | 52.18 N | 8.30 E |
| Preussisch-Ströhen | **52** | 52.29 N | 8.40 E |
| Prevalje | **61** | 46.32 N | 14.55 E |
| Préveza | **38** | 38.57 N | 20.44 E |
| Prévost | **206** | 45.52 N | 74.05 W |
| Prevost Island I | **224** | 48.50 N | 123.22 W |
| Prey Lvéa | **110** | 11.10 N | 104.57 E |
| Prey Nób | **110** | 10.38 N | 103.47 E |
| Prey Vêng | **110** | 11.29 N | 105.19 E |
| Prezza, Monte ∧ | **66** | 42.02 N | 13.49 E |
| Priaral'skije Karakumy, peski ◆[2] | **86** | 47.00 N | 63.30 E |
| Priargunsk | **88** | 50.27 N | 119.00 E |
| Priay | **58** | 46.00 N | 5.17 E |
| Pribilof Islands II | **180** | 57.00 N | 170.00 W |
| Priboj | **38** | 43.35 N | 19.31 E |
| Příbram | **30** | 49.42 N | 14.01 E |
| Pribylovo | **76** | 60.26 N | 28.40 E |
| Priccio, Cozzo ∧ | **70** | 37.01 N | 14.46 E |
| Price, Austl. | **168b** | 34.17 S | 138.00 E |
| Price, Tx., U.S. | **222** | 32.08 N | 94.57 W |
| Price, Ut,. U.S. | **200** | 39.35 N | 110.48 W |
| Price ≃ | **200** | 39.10 N | 110.06 W |
| Price, Cape › | **110** | 13.34 N | 93.03 E |
| Price Bend ⊂ | **276** | 40.55 N | 73.24 W |
| Price Island I | **182** | 52.23 N | 128.36 W |
| Prichard | **194** | 30.44 N | 88.04 W |
| Prichsenstadt | **56** | 49.49 N | 10.21 E |
| Prickly Point › | **241k** | 11.59 N | 61.45 W |
| Priddy | **196** | 31.40 N | 98.31 W |
| Priego | **34** | 40.27 N | 2.18 W |
| Priego de Córdoba | **34** | 37.26 N | 4.11 W |
| Priekule, Lat. | **76** | 56.26 N | 21.35 E |
| Priekule, Liet. | **76** | 55.33 N | 21.19 E |
| Prienai | **76** | 54.38 N | 23.57 E |
| Prien am Chiemsee | **64** | 47.51 N | 12.20 E |
| Prieros | **54** | 52.13 N | 13.46 E |
| Prieska | **158** | 29.40 S | 22.42 E |
| Priest ≃ | **202** | 48.11 N | 116.53 W |
| Priestewitz | **54** | 51.15 N | 13.30 E |
| Priest Island I | **46** | 57.58 N | 5.30 W |
| Priest Lake ⊜ | **202** | 48.34 N | 116.52 W |
| Priestley, Mount ∧ | **182** | 55.13 N | 128.53 W |
| Priest Rapids Lake ⊜[1] | **202** | 46.45 N | 119.55 W |
| Priest River | **202** | 48.10 N | 116.54 W |
| Prieta, Loma ∧ | **226** | 37.07 N | 121.51 W |
| Prieta, Peña ∧ | **34** | 43.01 N | 4.44 W |
| Prieto ≃ | **240m** | 18.15 N | 66.54 W |
| Prieto Diaz | **116** | 13.02 N | 124.12 E |
| Prievidza | **30** | 48.47 N | 18.37 E |
| Prignitz ◆[1] | **54** | 53.05 N | 12.15 E |
| Priiskovyj, Ross. | **86** | 54.39 N | 88.42 E |
| Priiskovyj, Ross. | **88** | 51.57 N | 116.39 E |
| Prijedor | **36** | 44.59 N | 16.43 E |
| Prijepolje | **38** | 43.23 N | 19.39 E |
| Prijutnoje | **80** | 46.06 N | 43.31 E |
| Prijutovo | **80** | 53.54 N | 53.56 E |
| Prikaspijskaja nizmennost' ≚ | **80** | 48.00 N | 52.00 E |
| Prikro | **150** | 7.39 N | 3.59 W |
| Prilep | **38** | 41.20 N | 21.33 E |
| Prilepy | **82** | 54.03 N | 37.42 E |
| Prilly | **58** | 46.32 N | 6.36 E |
| Priluki, Ross. | **76** | 59.16 N | 39.53 E |
| Priluki, Ross. | **82** | 54.51 N | 37.53 E |
| Prima Porta ◆[8] | **267a** | 42.00 N | 12.29 E |
| Primavera | **250** | 0.56 S | 47.06 W |
| Přimda | **60** | 49.41 N | 12.41 E |
| Primeira Cruz | **250** | 2.30 S | 43.26 W |
| Primeiro de Maio | **255** | 22.48 S | 51.01 W |
| Primera | **196** | 26.14 N | 97.43 W |
| Primero ≃ | **252** | 31.00 S | 63.12 W |
| Primero de Mayo | **196** | 27.12 N | 101.15 W |
| Primghar | **198** | 43.05 N | 95.37 W |
| Primolano | **64** | 45.58 N | 11.42 E |
| Primorje [Warnicken] | **76** | 54.57 N | 20.02 E |
| Primorka | **83** | 47.16 N | 39.03 E |
| Primorsk, Ross. | **76** | 54.44 N | 20.01 E |
| Primorsk, Ross. | **76** | 60.22 N | 28.36 E |
| Primorsk, Ross. | **80** | 49.16 N | 45.03 E |
| Primorskij | **89** | 43.07 N | 131.38 E |
| Primorskij chrebet ⩓ | **88** | 52.30 N | 106.00 E |
| Primorskij Kraj □[8] | **89** | 45.25 N | 135.25 E |
| Primorsko | **38** | 42.10 N | 27.51 E |
| Primorsko-Achtarsk | **78** | 46.03 N | 38.11 E |
| Primos | **285** | 39.55 N | 75.18 W |
| Primrose, S. Afr. | **273d** | 26.12 S | 28.10 E |
| Primrose, Pa., U.S. | **210** | 40.42 N | 76.17 W |
| Primrose, Pa., U.S. | **279b** | 40.21 N | 80.16 W |
| Primrose Brook ≃ | **276** | 40.43 N | 74.31 W |
| Primrose Lake ⊜ | **184** | 54.55 N | 109.45 W |
| Prims ≃ | **56** | 49.20 N | 6.44 E |
| Primstal | **56** | 49.32 N | 6.58 E |
| Prince, Lake ⊜[1] | **208** | 36.48 N | 76.38 W |
| Prince Albert, On., Can. | **212** | 44.05 N | 78.58 W |
| Prince Albert, Sk., Can. | **184** | 53.12 N | 105.46 W |
| Prince Albert, S. Afr. | **158** | 33.13 S | 22.02 E |
| Prince Albert Mountains ⩓ | **9** | 76.00 S | 161.30 E |
| Prince Albert National Park ♦ | **184** | 54.00 N | 106.25 W |
| Prince Albert Road | **158** | 33.01 S | 21.40 E |
| Prince Albert Sound ʉ | **176** | 70.25 N | 115.00 W |
| Prince Alexander Mountains ⩓ | **164** | 3.30 S | 142.50 E |
| Prince Alfred Hamlet | **158** | 33.18 S | 19.20 E |
| Prince Charles Island I | **176** | 67.50 N | 76.00 W |
| Prince Charles Mountains ⩓ | **9** | 72.00 S | 67.00 E |
| Prince-de-Galles, Île du → Prince of Wales Island I, Austl. | **164** | 10.40 S | 142.10 E |
| Prince-de-Galles, Île du → Prince of Wales Island I, N.T., Can. | **176** | 72.40 N | 99.00 W |
| Prince Edward □[6] | **212** | 44.00 N | 77.15 W |
| Prince Edward Bay ⊂ | **212** | 43.57 N | 76.57 W |
| Prince Edward Island □[4], Can. | **176** | 46.20 N | 63.20 W |
| Prince Edward Island □[4], Can. | **186** | 46.20 N | 63.20 W |
| Prince Edward Island National Park ♦ | **186** | 46.31 N | 63.26 W |
| Prince Edward Islands II | **6** | 46.35 S | 37.56 E |
| Prince Edward Park ♦ | **274a** | 34.02 S | 151.03 E |
| Prince Edward Point › | **212** | 43.56 N | 76.52 W |
| Prince Frederick | **208** | 38.32 N | 76.35 W |
| Prince Gallitzin State Park ♦ | **214** | 40.40 N | 78.32 W |
| Prince George, B.C., Can. | **182** | 53.55 N | 122.45 W |
| Prince George, Va., U.S. | **208** | 37.13 N | 77.17 W |
| Prince George □[6] | **208** | 37.13 N | 77.10 W |
| Prince Georges □[6] | **208** | 38.49 N | 76.45 W |
| Prince Georges Plaza ◆[9] | **284c** | 38.58 N | 76.57 W |
| Prince Leopold Island I | **176** | 74.02 N | 89.55 W |
| Prince of Wales, Cape › | **180** | 65.40 N | 168.05 W |
| Prince of Wales Island I, Austl. | **164** | 10.40 S | 142.10 E |
| Prince of Wales Island I, N.T., Can. | **176** | 72.40 N | 99.00 W |
| Prince of Wales Island I, Ak., U.S. | **180** | 55.47 N | 132.50 W |
| Prince of Wales Strait ʉ | **176** | 73.00 N | 117.00 W |
| Prince Olav Coast ⊥[2] | **9** | 68.30 S | 42.30 E |
| Prince Patrick Island I | **16** | 76.45 N | 119.30 W |
| Prince Regent ≃ | **164** | 15.28 S | 125.05 E |
| Prince Regent Inlet ⊂ | **176** | 73.00 N | 90.30 W |
| Prince Regent Nature Reserve ♦ | **164** | 15.30 S | 125.30 E |
| Prince Rupert | **182** | 54.19 N | 130.19 W |
| Prince Rupert Bay ⊂ | **240d** | 15.34 N | 61.29 W |
| Prince Rupert Bluff Point › | **240d** | 15.35 N | 61.29 W |
| Princesa, Puerto ⊂ | **116** | 9.45 N | 118.43 E |
| Princesa Astrid, Costa → Princess Astrid Coast ⊥[2] | **9** | 70.45 S | 12.30 E |
| Princesa Carlota, Bahía → Princess Charlotte Bay ⊂ | **164** | 14.25 S | 144.00 E |
| Princesa Isabel | **250** | 7.44 S | 38.00 W |
| Princesa Marta, Costa → Princess Martha Coast ⊥[2] | **9** | 72.00 S | 7.30 W |
| Princesa Ragnhild, Costa → Princess Ragnhild Coast ⊥[2] | **9** | 70.15 S | 27.30 E |
| Princes Bay ⊂ | **276** | 40.31 N | 74.12 W |
| Princes Risborough | **42** | 51.44 N | 0.51 W |
| Princess Anne | **208** | 38.12 N | 75.41 W |
| Princess Astrid Coast ⊥[2] | **9** | 70.45 S | 12.30 E |
| Princess Charlotte Bay ⊂ | **164** | 14.25 S | 144.00 E |
| Princess Martha Coast ⊥[2] | **9** | 72.00 S | 7.30 W |
| Princess Ragnhild Coast ⊥[2] | **9** | 70.15 S | 27.30 E |
| Princess Ranges ⩓ | **162** | 26.08 S | 121.55 E |
| Princess Royal Channel ʉ | **182** | 53.10 N | 128.37 W |
| Princess Royal Island I | **182** | 52.57 N | 128.49 W |
| Princes Town | **241r** | 10.16 N | 61.23 W |
| Princeton, B.C., Can. | **182** | 49.27 N | 120.31 W |
| Princeton, Nf., Can. | **186** | 48.25 N | 53.36 W |
| Princeton, On., Can. | **212** | 43.10 N | 80.32 W |
| Princeton, Ca., U.S. | **226** | 39.24 N | 122.00 W |
| Princeton, Fl., U.S. | **220** | 25.32 N | 80.24 W |
| Princeton, Il., U.S. | **190** | 41.22 N | 89.27 W |
| Princeton, In., U.S. | **194** | 38.21 N | 87.34 W |
| Princeton, Ky., U.S. | **194** | 37.06 N | 87.52 W |
| Princeton, Me., U.S. | **188** | 45.13 N | 67.34 W |
| Princeton, Mi., U.S. | **190** | 46.17 N | 87.28 W |
| Princeton, Mn., U.S. | **190** | 45.34 N | 93.34 W |
| Princeton, Mo., U.S. | **194** | 40.24 N | 93.34 W |
| Princeton, N.J., U.S. | **208** | 40.20 N | 74.39 W |
| Princeton, N.C., U.S. | **192** | 35.27 N | 78.09 W |
| Princeton, Tx., U.S. | **222** | 33.11 N | 96.30 W |
| Princeton, W.V., U.S. | **192** | 37.21 N | 81.06 W |
| Princeton, Wi., U.S. | **190** | 43.51 N | 89.07 W |
| Princeton Airfield ⊠ | **276** | 40.24 N | 74.39 W |
| Princeton Battlefield Park ⊥ | **276** | 40.20 N | 74.41 W |
| Princeton Junction | **208** | 40.19 N | 74.37 W |
| Princeton Township | **276** | 40.22 N | 74.40 W |
| Princeton University ♁[2] | **276** | 40.21 N | 74.39 W |
| Princetown | **42** | 50.33 N | 4.00 W |
| Princeville, P.Q., Can. | **206** | 46.10 N | 71.53 W |
| Princeville, Il., U.S. | **190** | 40.56 N | 89.45 W |
| Princeville, N.C., U.S. | **192** | 35.53 N | 77.31 W |
| Prince William □[6] | **208** | 38.42 N | 77.27 W |
| Prince William Forest Park ♦ | **208** | 38.36 N | 77.23 W |
| Prince William Sound ʉ | **180** | 60.40 N | 147.00 W |
| Príncipe I | **152** | 1.37 N | 7.25 E |
| Príncipe Alberto, Montes → Prince Albert Mountains ⩓ | **9** | 76.00 S | 161.30 E |
| Príncipe Carlos, Montes → Prince Charles Mountains ⩓ | **9** | 72.00 S | 67.00 E |
| Principe Channel ʉ | **182** | 53.28 N | 130.00 W |
| Príncipe da Beira | **248** | 12.25 S | 64.25 W |
| Príncipe de Gales, Isla → Prince of Wales Island I, Austl. | **164** | 10.40 S | 142.10 E |
| Príncipe de Gales, Isla → Prince of Wales Island I, N.T., Can. | **176** | 72.40 N | 99.00 W |
| Príncipe Eduardo, Isla → Prince Edward Island □[4] | **186** | 46.20 N | 63.20 W |
| Príncipe Olav, Costa → Prince Olav Coast ⊥[2] | **9** | 68.30 S | 42.30 E |
| Príncipe Patricio, Isla → Prince Patrick Island I | **16** | 76.45 N | 119.30 W |
| Prineville | **202** | 44.18 N | 120.51 W |
| Prineville Reservoir ⊜[1] | **202** | 44.08 N | 120.42 W |
| Prineville Southeast | **202** | 44.17 N | 120.53 W |
| Pringgabaja | **115b** | 8.34 S | 116.37 E |
| Pringsewu | **112** | 5.24 S | 104.55 E |
| Pringy | **261** | 48.31 N | 2.34 E |
| Prinsenbeek | **52** | 51.36 N | 4.42 E |
| Prinses Margrietkanaal ≅ | **52** | 53.10 N | 5.55 E |
| Prinshof | **158** | 32.06 S | 20.53 E |
| Prinzapolka | **236** | 13.24 N | 83.34 W |
| Prinzapolka ≃ | **236** | 13.24 N | 83.34 W |
| Prinzessin Astrid-Küste → Princess Astrid Coast ⊥[2] | **9** | 70.45 S | 12.30 E |
| Prinzessin Charlotte Bucht → Princess Charlotte Bay ⊂ | **164** | 14.25 S | 144.00 E |
| Prinzessin Martha-Küste → Princess Martha Coast ⊥[2] | **9** | 72.00 S | 7.30 W |
| Prinzessin Ragnhild-Küste → Princess Ragnhild Coast ⊥[2] | **9** | 70.15 S | 27.30 E |
| Priobskoje plato ⩓[1] | **86** | 52.40 N | 83.00 E |
| Priioksko-Terrasnyj zapovednik ◆[4] | **82** | 54.51 N | 37.36 E |
| Priolo Gargallo | **70** | 37.09 N | 15.11 E |
| Prior, Cabo › | **34** | 43.34 N | 8.19 W |
| Priort | **264a** | 52.31 N | 12.58 E |
| Priozernyj | **80** | 47.23 N | 45.14 E |
| Prioz'ornyj | **86** | 47.50 N | 84.13 E |
| Prioz'orsk | **24** | 61.02 N | 30.04 E |
| Pripet → Prypjac' ≃ | **78** | 51.21 N | 30.09 E |
| Pripet Marshes → Polesje ◆[1] | **72** | 52.00 N | 27.00 E |
| Pripol'arnyj Ural ⩓ | **24** | 65.00 N | 60.00 E |
| Prirečje | **88** | 55.07 N | 101.03 E |
| Prirečnoje | **80** | 51.03 N | 52.26 E |
| Přísečnice | **54** | 50.27 N | 13.06 E |
| Priselje | **76** | 55.09 N | 32.49 E |
| Prislon | **82** | 56.48 N | 37.16 E |
| Pristan'-Prževal'sk | **85** | 42.34 N | 78.18 E |
| Pristen' | **78** | 51.15 N | 36.41 E |
| Priština | **38** | 42.39 N | 21.10 E |
| Pritchett | **198** | 37.22 N | 102.51 W |
| Přitluky | **61** | 48.51 N | 16.46 E |
| Pritzerbe | **54** | 52.30 N | 12.27 E |
| Pritzier | **54** | 53.22 N | 11.04 E |
| Pritzwalk | **54** | 53.09 N | 12.10 E |
| Priural'nyj | **80** | 51.29 N | 53.06 E |
| Privas | **62** | 44.44 N | 4.36 E |
| Priverno | **66** | 41.28 N | 13.11 E |
| Privodino | **24** | 61.05 N | 46.28 E |
| Privokzal'nyj, Ross. | **82** | 55.59 N | 35.56 E |
| Privokzal'nyj, Ross. | **86** | 58.53 N | 60.43 E |
| Privol'naja | **78** | 46.09 N | 38.42 E |
| Privol'noje | **80** | 50.57 N | 46.06 E |
| Privolžje | **80** | 52.52 N | 48.37 E |
| Privolžsk | **80** | 57.23 N | 41.17 E |
| Privolžskaja vozvyšennost' ⩓[1] | **80** | 52.00 N | 46.00 E |
| Privolžskij, Ross. | **80** | 46.24 N | 48.00 E |
| Privolžskij, Ross. | **80** | 51.24 N | 46.02 E |
| Privolžskoje | **80** | 51.06 N | 45.57 E |
| Prizren | **38** | 42.12 N | 20.44 E |
| Prizzi | **70** | 37.43 N | 13.26 E |
| Prizzi, Lago di ⊜ | **70** | 37.44 N | 13.25 E |
| Prnjavor | **36** | 44.52 N | 17.40 E |
| Probolinggo | **115a** | 7.45 S | 113.13 E |
| Proboštov | **54** | 50.39 N | 13.50 E |
| Probstzella | **54** | 50.32 N | 11.22 E |
| Probus | **42** | 50.17 N | 4.57 W |
| Procchio | **66** | 42.47 N | 10.15 E |
| Prochladnoje | **86** | 48.30 N | 82.41 E |
| Prochladnyj | **84** | 43.46 N | 44.00 E |
| Prochorkino | **86** | 59.34 N | 79.26 E |
| Prochorovka | **82** | 54.07 N | 38.11 E |
| Prochowice | **30** | 51.17 N | 16.22 E |
| Procida | **68** | 40.46 N | 14.02 E |
| Procida, Isola di I | **68** | 40.45 N | 14.01 E |
| Procter | **182** | 49.37 N | 116.57 W |
| Proctor, Mn., U.S. | **190** | 46.44 N | 92.13 W |
| Proctor, Vt., U.S. | **188** | 43.39 N | 73.02 W |
| Proctor Brook ≃ | **283** | 42.32 N | 70.54 W |
| Proctor Lake ⊜ | **228** | 35.07 N | 118.21 W |
| Proctor Lake ⊜[1] | **196** | 32.02 N | 98.32 W |
| Proddatūr | **122** | 14.44 N | 78.33 E |
| Proença-a-Nova | **34** | 39.45 N | 7.55 W |
| Profen | **54** | 51.07 N | 12.13 E |
| Pro Football Hall of Fame ♁ | **214** | 40.49 N | 81.25 W |
| Prognoj | **83** | 48.45 N | 39.51 E |
| Progreso, Méx. | **196** | 27.28 N | 100.59 W |
| Progreso, Méx. | **232** | 21.17 N | 89.40 W |
| Progreso, Méx. | **234** | 23.48 N | 103.18 W |
| Progreso, Méx. | **234** | 20.15 N | 99.12 W |
| Progreso, Ur. | **258** | 34.40 S | 56.13 W |
| Progress, Ross. | **89** | 49.42 N | 129.39 E |
| Progress, Or., U.S. | **224** | 45.28 N | 122.47 W |


**Symbols** in the index entries represent the broad categories identified in the key at the right. Symbols with superior numbers (⩓[1]) identify subcategories (see complete key on page *I · 1).*

**Symbole** im Register stellen die rechts im Schlüssel erklärten Kategorien dar. Symbole mit hochgestellten Ziffern (⩓[1]) bezeichnen Unterabteilungen einer Kategorie (vgl. vollständiger Schlüssel auf Seite *I · 1).*

**Los símbolos** incluídos en el texto del índice representan las grandes categorías identificadas con la clave a la derecha. Los símbolos con numeros en su parte superior (⩓[1]) identifican las subcategorías (véase la clave completa en la página *I · 1).*

**Les symboles** de l'index représentent les catégories indiquées dans la légende à droite. Les symboles suivis d'un indice (⩓[1]) représentent des sous-catégories (voir légende complète à la page *I · 1).*

**Os símbolos** incluídos no texto do índice representam as grandes categorias identificadas com a chave à direita. Os símbolos com números em sua parte superior (⩓[1]) identificam as subcategorias (veja-se a chave completa à página *I · 1).*

| | | | | | |
|---|---|---|---|---|---|
| ∧ | Mountain | Berg | Montaña | Montagne | Montanha |
| ⩓ | Mountains | Gebirge | Montañas | Montagnes | Montanhas |
| )( | Pass | Paß | Paso | Col | Passo |
| V | Valley, Canyon | Tal, Cañon | Valle, Cañón | Vallée, Canyon | Vale, Canhão |
| ≚ | Plain | Ebene | Llano | Plaine | Planície |
| › | Cape | Kap | Cabo | Cap | Cabo |
| I | Island | Insel | Isla | Île | Ilha |
| II | Islands | Inseln | Islas | Îles | Ilhas |
| ⊥ | Other Topographic Features | Andere Topographische Objekte | Otros Elementos Topográficos | Autres données topographiques | Outros acidentes topográficos |

**ESPAÑOL** | **FRANÇAIS** | **PORTUGUÊS**

| Nombre / Nom / Nome | Página / Page | Lat.°′ | Long.°′ W = Oeste / Ouest |
|---|---|---|---|
| Progress, Pa., U.S. | 208 | 40.08 N | 76.34 W |
| Project City | 204 | 40.41 N | 122.21 W |
| Prokopjeva | 88 | 58.03 N | 100.39 E |
| Prokopjevsk | 86 | 53.53 N | 86.45 E |
| Prokopyevsk → Prokopjevsk | 86 | 53.53 N | 86.45 E |
| Prokuplje | 38 | 43.14 N | 21.36 E |
| Prokuševo | 76 | 59.55 N | 34.56 E |
| Prokutkino | 86 | 56.19 N | 69.46 E |
| Proletarij | 76 | 58.26 N | 31.44 E |
| Proletarsk, Ross. | 80 | 46.42 N | 41.44 E |
| Proletarsk, Taj. | 85 | 40.10 N | 69.30 E |
| Proletarskij, Ross. | 78 | 50.47 N | 35.47 E |
| Proletarskij, Ross. | 82 | 55.01 N | 37.23 E |
| Prolysovo | 76 | 52.54 N | 34.09 E |
| Prome (Pyè) | 110 | 18.49 N | 95.13 E |
| Promised Land State Park ♠ | 210 | 41.18 N | 75.11 W |
| Promissão | 255 | 21.32 S | 49.52 W |
| Promontogno | 58 | 46.21 N | 9.34 E |
| Prompton | 210 | 41.35 N | 75.19 W |
| Prompton Lake ⊜[1] | 210 | 41.36 N | 75.20 W |
| Prompton Lake State Park ♠ | 210 | 41.37 N | 75.22 W |
| Promyšlennaja | 86 | 54.55 N | 85.40 E |
| Promyšlennovskij | 86 | 55.29 N | 86.12 E |
| Promyšlennyj | 24 | 67.35 N | 63.55 E |
| Promyslovka | 80 | 45.44 N | 47.10 E |
| Pron'a ≃ | 80 | 54.21 N | 40.24 E |
| Pron'a Gorodišče | 82 | 54.15 N | 38.43 E |
| Pronin | 80 | 49.12 N | 42.11 E |
| Pronja ≃ | 76 | 53.25 N | 31.01 E |
| Pronsfeld | 56 | 50.10 N | 6.20 E |
| Pronsk | 76 | 54.07 N | 39.37 E |
| Prony, Baie du ⊂ | 175f | 22.22 S | 166.53 E |
| Prophet ≃ | 176 | 58.45 N | 122.45 W |
| Prophetstown | 190 | 41.40 N | 89.56 W |
| Propriá | 250 | 10.13 S | 36.51 W |
| Propriano | 36 | 41.40 N | 8.55 E |
| Prorer Wiek ⊂ | 54 | 54.27 N | 13.38 E |
| Prorva | 86 | 46.03 N | 53.15 E |
| Proryvnoje | 86 | 54.23 N | 64.26 E |
| Prösen | 54 | 51.25 N | 13.30 E |
| Proserpine | 166 | 20.24 S | 148.34 E |
| Prosigk | 54 | 51.42 N | 12.03 E |
| Proskurov → Khmel'nyts'kyy | 78 | 49.25 N | 27.00 E |
| Prosna ≃ | 30 | 52.10 N | 17.39 E |
| Prosnica | 80 | 58.26 N | 50.15 E |
| Prosotsáni | 38 | 41.10 N | 23.59 E |
| Prospect, Austl. | 168b | 34.54 S | 138.35 E |
| Prospect, Austl. | 274a | 33.48 S | 150.56 E |
| Prospect, Ct., U.S. | 207 | 41.30 N | 72.58 W |
| Prospect, N.Y., U.S. | 210 | 43.18 N | 75.09 W |
| Prospect, Oh., U.S. | 214 | 40.27 N | 83.11 W |
| Prospect, Pa., U.S. | 214 | 40.54 N | 80.03 W |
| Prospect Bay ⊂ | 208 | 38.56 N | 76.14 W |
| Prospect Creek ≃ | 274a | 33.55 S | 150.59 E |
| Prospect Heights | 278 | 42.05 N | 87.56 W |
| Prospect Hill | 168b | 35.13 S | 138.44 E |
| Prospect Hill ∧[2], Ma., U.S. | 207 | 41.21 N | 70.45 W |
| Prospect Hill ∧[2], Ma., U.S. | 283 | 42.23 N | 71.15 W |
| Prospect Hill Park ♠ | 283 | 42.23 N | 71.15 W |
| Prospect Park, N.J., U.S. | 276 | 40.56 N | 74.10 W |
| Prospect Park, Pa., U.S. | 214 | 41.31 N | 78.13 W |
| Prospect Park, Pa., U.S. | 285 | 39.53 N | 75.18 W |
| Prospect Park ♠ | 276 | 40.40 N | 73.58 W |
| Prospect Park Lake ⊜ | 276 | 40.39 N | 73.57 W |
| Prospect Plains | 276 | 40.19 N | 74.28 W |
| Prospect Point | 276 | 40.58 N | 74.38 W |
| Prospect Point > | 276 | 40.52 N | 73.43 W |
| Prospect Reservoir ⊜[1] | 274a | 33.49 S | 150.54 E |
| Prospectville | 285 | 40.13 N | 75.11 W |
| Prosper | 222 | 33.14 N | 96.48 W |
| Prosperi Airport ⊠ | 278 | 41.33 N | 87.47 W |
| Prosperidad | 116 | 8.34 N | 125.52 E |
| Prosser | 202 | 46.12 N | 119.46 W |
| Prosser Creek Reservoir ⊜[1] | 226 | 39.22 N | 120.08 W |
| Prostějov | 30 | 49.29 N | 17.07 E |
| Prostki | 30 | 53.43 N | 22.26 E |
| Proston | 166 | 26.10 S | 151.36 E |
| Prosyana | 78 | 48.07 N | 36.23 E |
| Prosyane | 78 | 49.42 N | 35.47 E |
| Prošyka | 76 | 54.29 N | 29.08 E |
| Proszowice | 30 | 50.12 N | 20.18 E |
| Protasovo, Ross. | 82 | 54.48 N | 38.35 E |
| Protasovo, Ross. | 82 | 54.11 N | 37.00 E |
| Protasovo, Ross. | 82 | 56.08 N | 37.36 E |
| Protea | 273d | 26.17 S | 27.51 E |
| Protection | 198 | 37.12 N | 99.29 W |
| Protection Island I | 224 | 48.07 N | 122.55 W |
| Protem | 158 | 34.16 S | 20.05 E |
| Protivín | 61 | 49.12 N | 14.13 E |
| Protoka ≃ | 78 | 45.43 N | 37.46 E |
| Protva | 82 | 55.01 N | 36.41 E |
| Protva ≃ | 82 | 54.51 N | 37.16 E |
| Protville | 36 | 36.54 N | 10.01 E |
| Prötzel | 54 | 52.38 N | 13.59 E |
| Proud Lake State Recreation Area ♠ | 281 | 42.34 N | 83.33 W |
| Proulxville | 206 | 46.40 N | 72.30 W |
| Provadija | 38 | 43.11 N | 27.26 E |
| Provencal | 194 | 31.39 N | 93.12 W |
| Provence □[9] | 62 | 44.00 N | 6.00 E |
| Provence, Alpes de ⩘ | 62 | 43.40 N | 6.00 E |
| Provenchères-sur-Fave | 58 | 48.19 N | 7.05 E |
| Providence, Ky., U.S. | 194 | 37.23 N | 87.45 W |
| Providence, R.I., U.S. | 207 | 41.49 N | 71.24 W |
| Providence, Ut,. U.S. | 200 | 41.42 N | 111.48 W |
| Providence □[6] | 207 | 41.52 N | 71.36 W |
| Providence ≃ | 207 | 41.43 N | 71.21 W |
| Providence Forge | 208 | 37.26 N | 77.02 W |
| Providence Island I | 138 | 9.14 S | 51.02 E |
| Providência, Bra. | 256 | 21.40 S | 42.35 W |
| Providencia, Chile | 286e | 33.26 S | 70.37 W |
| Providencia, Méx. | 196 | 27.06 N | 103.32 W |
| Providencia, Isla de I | 236 | 13.21 N | 81.22 W |
| Providenciales I | 238 | 21.47 N | 72.17 W |
| Providenija | 180 | 64.23 N | 173.18 W |
| Providenija, buchta ⊂ | 180 | 64.30 N | 173.20 W |
| Provincetown | 207 | 42.03 N | 70.10 W |
| Provins | 50 | 48.33 N | 3.18 E |
| Provo | 200 | 40.14 N | 111.39 W |
| Provo ≃ | 200 | 40.14 N | 111.44 W |
| Provost | 184 | 52.21 N | 110.16 W |
| Provost, Lac ⊜ | 206 | 46.22 N | 74.00 W |
| Proyizhdzhe | 83 | 49.25 N | 38.58 E |
| Prozor | 36 | 43.49 N | 17.37 E |
| Pru ≃ | 150 | 7.58 N | 0.53 W |
| Prudence Island I | 207 | 41.37 N | 71.19 W |
| Prudentópolis | 252 | 25.12 S | 50.57 W |
| Prudentov | 80 | 49.39 N | 46.19 E |
| Prudhoe | 44 | 54.58 N | 1.51 W |
| Prudhoe Bay ⊂ | 180 | 70.20 N | 148.20 W |
| Prudhoe Island I | 166 | 21.19 S | 149.40 E |
| Prudišči | 82 | 54.24 N | 38.26 E |
| Prudki | 82 | 54.46 N | 36.29 E |
| Prudnik | 30 | 50.19 N | 17.34 E |
| Prudyanka | 78 | 50.14 N | 36.09 E |
| Pruggern | 64 | 47.25 N | 13.52 E |
| Prüm | 56 | 50.12 N | 6.25 E |
| Prüm ≃ | 56 | 49.49 N | 6.28 E |
| Pruna, Punta sa ∧ | 71 | 40.11 N | 9.26 E |
| Prunay-le-Temple | 261 | 48.52 N | 1.40 E |
| Prunay-sous-Ablis | 261 | 48.32 N | 1.48 E |
| Prunedale | 226 | 36.47 N | 121.40 W |
| Prunéřov | 54 | 50.25 N | 13.16 E |
| Prunières | 62 | 44.33 N | 6.20 E |
| Prunn, Schloss ⊥ | 60 | 48.57 N | 11.44 E |
| Pruszków | 30 | 52.11 N | 20.48 E |
| Prut ≃ | 78 | 45.30 N | 28.12 E |
| Pruth → Prut ≃ | 78 | 45.30 N | 28.12 E |
| Prutz | 58 | 47.05 N | 10.40 E |
| Pružany | 76 | 52.33 N | 24.28 E |
| Pryadivka | 78 | 48.55 N | 34.41 E |
| Pryazovs'ka vysochyna ⩘[1] | 83 | 47.30 N | 37.30 E |
| Pryazovs'ke | 78 | 46.43 N | 35.38 E |
| Prychornomors'ka nyzovyna ≚ | 78 | 47.00 N | 33.00 E |
| Prydniprovs'ka nyzovyna ≚ | 78 | 50.00 N | 32.00 E |
| Prydniprovs'ka vysochyna ⩘[1] | 78 | 49.00 N | 32.00 E |
| Prydz Bay ⊂ | 9 | 69.00 S | 76.00 E |
| Prykolotne | 78 | 50.09 N | 37.21 E |
| Pryluky | 78 | 50.36 N | 32.24 E |
| Prymors'k | 78 | 46.44 N | 36.20 E |
| Prymors'ke | 83 | 47.11 N | 37.42 E |
| Prymors'kyy | 78 | 45.07 N | 35.29 E |
| Pryor | 196 | 36.19 N | 95.19 W |
| Pryor Creek ≃ | 202 | 45.54 N | 108.19 W |
| Pryor Mountain ∧[2] | 222 | 31.43 N | 95.12 W |
| Prypjac' (Pryp'yat') ≃ | 78 | 51.21 N | 30.09 E |
| Pryputni | 78 | 50.57 N | 32.14 E |
| Pryp'yat' | 78 | 51.26 N | 30.10 E |
| Pryp'yat' (Prypjac') ≃ | 78 | 51.21 N | 30.09 E |
| Pryshyb | 78 | 47.16 N | 35.21 E |
| Prysor ≃ | 42 | 52.56 N | 4.00 W |
| Prystin | 83 | 49.36 N | 37.38 E |
| Pryvillya, Ukr. | 83 | 49.01 N | 38.18 E |
| Pryvillya, Ukr. | 83 | 48.52 N | 37.16 E |
| Pryvil'ne | 78 | 47.29 N | 32.17 E |
| Pryvitne | 78 | 44.50 N | 34.41 E |
| Przasnysz | 30 | 53.01 N | 20.55 E |
| Przedbórz | 30 | 51.06 N | 19.53 E |
| Przemków | 30 | 51.32 N | 15.48 E |
| Przemocze | 54 | 53.27 N | 14.55 E |
| Przemyśl | 30 | 49.47 N | 22.47 E |
| Przemyśl □[4] | 30 | 50.00 N | 22.40 E |
| Przeworsk | 30 | 50.05 N | 22.29 E |
| Przewóz | 54 | 51.29 N | 14.59 E |
| Przybiernów | 54 | 53.46 N | 14.46 E |
| Przysucha | 30 | 51.22 N | 20.38 E |
| Pšagar | 85 | 39.58 N | 68.08 E |
| Psakhná | 38 | 38.35 N | 23.38 E |
| Psará I | 38 | 38.35 N | 25.37 E |
| Psárion | 38 | 37.20 N | 21.51 E |
| Psebaj | 84 | 44.07 N | 40.47 E |
| Pšecha ≃ | 78 | 44.47 N | 39.48 E |
| Psekups ≃ | 78 | 45.00 N | 39.09 E |
| Pselec | 78 | 51.17 N | 36.32 E |
| Psikhikón | 267c | 38.01 N | 23.46 E |
| Pšiš ≃ | 78 | 45.01 N | 39.18 E |
| Pšiš, gora ∧ | 84 | 43.24 N | 41.12 E |
| Psittália I | 267c | 37.56 N | 23.35 E |
| Pskem | 85 | 41.56 N | 70.22 E |
| Pskem ≃ | 85 | 41.38 N | 70.01 E |
| Pskent | 85 | 40.54 N | 69.20 E |
| Pskov | 76 | 57.50 N | 28.20 E |
| Pskov Oblast' □[4] | 76 | 57.00 N | 29.00 E |
| Pskovskoje ozero ⊜ | 76 | 58.00 N | 28.00 E |
| Pskowsee → Pskovskoje ozero ⊜ | 76 | 58.00 N | 28.00 E |
| Ps'ol ≃ | 78 | 49.02 N | 33.33 E |
| Pšov | 54 | 50.10 N | 13.29 E |
| Pszczyna | 30 | 49.59 N | 18.57 E |
| Ptarmigan, Cape > | 176 | 71.04 N | 118.07 W |
| Ptolemaís | 38 | 40.31 N | 21.41 E |
| Ptolemais ⊥ | 146 | 32.43 N | 20.57 E |
| Ptuj | 36 | 46.25 N | 15.52 E |
| Pu ≃, Zhg. | 104 | 41.21 N | 122.47 E |
| Pu ≃, Zhg. | 107 | 30.25 N | 103.49 E |
| Puah, Pulau I | 112 | 0.30 S | 122.34 E |
| Puakonikai | 174d | 0.52 S | 169.36 E |
| Puamau, Baie ⊂ | 174x | 9.46 S | 138.52 W |
| Puán, Arg. | 252 | 37.33 S | 62.43 W |
| Puan, Taehan | 98 | 35.45 N | 126.44 E |
| Pubāil | 126 | 23.56 N | 90.29 E |
| Pubnico | 186 | 43.42 N | 65.47 W |
| Pucallpa | 248 | 8.23 S | 74.32 W |
| Pucara | 248 | 18.43 S | 64.11 W |
| Pucarani | 248 | 16.23 S | 68.30 W |
| Puccha ≃ | 248 | 9.05 S | 76.54 W |
| Puccia, Serra di ∧ | 70 | 37.44 N | 13.56 E |
| Puce | 214 | 42.18 N | 82.47 W |
| Puces ≃ | 281 | 42.18 N | 82.47 W |
| Pučevejem ≃ | 180 | 68.48 N | 170.30 E |
| Pučež | 80 | 56.59 N | 43.11 E |
| Puchberg am Schneeberg | 61 | 47.47 N | 15.54 E |
| Pucheng, Zhg. | 100 | 27.55 N | 118.31 E |
| Pucheng, Zhg. | 102 | 34.59 N | 109.29 E |
| Pucheta | 252 | 29.54 S | 57.34 W |
| Puchheim | 60 | 48.09 N | 11.20 E |
| Púchov | 30 | 49.08 N | 18.20 E |
| Pucioasa | 38 | 45.04 N | 25.26 E |
| Pucio Point > | 116 | 11.46 N | 121.51 E |
| Pučišća | 36 | 43.21 N | 16.44 E |
| Puck | 30 | 54.44 N | 18.27 E |
| Puckapunyal | 169 | 37.01 S | 145.03 E |
| Pucketa Creek ≃ | 279b | 40.33 N | 79.45 W |
| Pudahuel | 286e | 33.26 S | 70.46 W |
| Pudding ≃ | 224 | 45.18 N | 122.43 W |
| Puddingstone Reservoir ⊜[1] | 280 | 34.05 N | 117.48 W |
| Puddington | 262 | 53.15 N | 3.00 W |
| Puddletown | 42 | 50.45 N | 2.21 W |
| Pūdeh Tal ≃ | 128 | 31.03 N | 62.15 E |
| Pudem | 80 | 58.18 N | 52.10 E |
| Pudi | 102 | 27.58 N | 99.05 E |
| Pudimoe | 158 | 27.26 S | 24.44 E |
| Puding | 102 | 26.21 N | 105.40 E |
| Pudino | 86 | 57.34 N | 79.24 E |
| Pudops Dam ◆[6] | 186 | 48.09 N | 56.50 W |
| Pudož | 24 | 61.48 N | 36.32 E |
| Pudsey | 44 | 53.48 N | 1.40 W |
| Pudu ≃ | 102 | 26.19 N | 102.45 E |
| Puduari ≃ | 246 | 2.08 S | 61.15 W |
| Puduhe | 102 | 25.39 N | 102.39 E |
| Pudukkottai | 122 | 10.23 N | 78.49 E |
| Puebla □[3] | 234 | 18.50 N | 98.00 W |
| Puebla de Alcocer | 34 | 38.59 N | 5.15 W |
| Puebla de Don Fadrique | 34 | 37.58 N | 2.26 W |
| Puebla de Don Rodrigo | 34 | 39.05 N | 4.37 W |
| Puebla de Sanabria | 34 | 42.03 N | 6.38 W |
| Puebla [de Zaragoza] | 234 | 19.03 N | 98.12 W |
| Pueblito de Ponce | 240m | 18.26 N | 66.58 W |
| Pueblo | 198 | 38.15 N | 104.36 W |
| Pueblo Libertador | 252 | 30.13 S | 59.23 W |
| Pueblo Libre | 286d | 12.05 S | 77.04 W |
| Pueblo Mountain ∧ | 202 | 42.06 N | 118.39 W |
| Pueblo Nuevo, Col. | 246 | 8.31 N | 75.15 W |
| Pueblo Nuevo, Méx. | 234 | 20.31 N | 101.22 W |
| Pueblo Nuevo, Nic. | 236 | 13.23 N | 86.29 W |
| Pueblo Nuevo, P.R. | 240m | 18.28 N | 66.51 W |
| Pueblo Nuevo, Ur. | 258 | 34.26 S | 56.29 W |
| Pueblo Nuevo, Ven. | 246 | 11.58 N | 69.55 W |
| Pueblo Nuevo ◆[8] | 266a | 40.26 N | 3.39 W |
| Pueblo Nuevo Tiquisate | 236 | 14.17 N | 91.22 W |
| Pueblo of Acoma | 200 | 35.03 N | 107.35 W |
| Pueblo Reservoir ⊜[1] | 198 | 38.15 N | 104.45 W |
| Puebloviejo, Ec. | 246 | 1.34 S | 79.30 W |
| Pueblo Viejo, Méx. | 234 | 17.33 N | 100.05 W |
| Pueblo Viejo, Méx. | 234 | 16.14 N | 94.39 W |
| Pueblo Viejo, Laguna ⊂ | 234 | 22.10 N | 97.53 W |
| Pueblo Yaqui | 232 | 27.19 N | 110.01 W |
| Puelches | 252 | 38.09 S | 65.55 W |
| Puente Alto | 252 | 33.37 S | 70.35 W |
| Puente de Arganda | 266a | 40.19 N | 3.31 W |
| Puente de Ixtla | 234 | 18.37 N | 99.20 W |
| Puente del Arzobispo | 34 | 39.48 N | 5.10 W |
| Puente Genil | 34 | 37.23 N | 4.47 W |
| Puente Hills ⩘[2] | 280 | 34.00 N | 117.55 W |
| Puente Hills Mall ◆[9] | 280 | 33.59 N | 117.56 W |
| Puente la Reina | 34 | 42.40 N | 1.49 W |
| Puente Negro | 196 | 27.55 N | 101.01 W |
| Puente Nuevo, Embalse de ⊜[1] | 34 | 38.00 N | 5.00 W |
| Puente Piedra | 286d | 11.57 S | 77.05 W |
| Pueo Point > | 229b | 21.54 N | 160.04 W |
| Pu'er | 102 | 23.07 N | 101.00 E |
| Puerca, Punta > | 240m | 18.14 N | 65.36 W |
| Puerco ≃ | 200 | 34.53 N | 110.07 W |
| Puerco, Rio ≃ | 200 | 34.22 N | 106.50 W |
| Pu'erdu | 102 | 28.08 N | 104.24 E |
| Puerto Acosta | 248 | 15.32 S | 69.15 W |
| Puerto Adela | 252 | 24.33 S | 54.22 W |
| Puerto Aisén | 254 | 45.24 S | 72.42 W |
| Puerto Alegre | 248 | 13.53 S | 61.36 W |
| Puerto Ángel | 234 | 15.40 N | 96.29 W |
| Puerto Arista | 234 | 15.56 N | 93.48 W |
| Puerto Armuelles | 236 | 8.17 N | 82.52 W |
| Puerto Asís | 246 | 0.30 N | 76.31 W |
| Puerto Ayacucho | 246 | 5.40 N | 67.35 W |
| Puerto Ayora, Ec. | 246a | 0.45 S | 90.19 W |
| Puerto Ayora, Ec. | 246a | 0.45 S | 90.19 W |
| Puerto Bahía Negra | 248 | 20.15 S | 58.12 W |
| Puerto Baquerizo Moreno | 246a | 0.54 S | 89.36 W |
| Puerto Barrios | 236 | 15.43 N | 88.36 W |
| Puerto Bermejo | 252 | 26.56 S | 58.30 W |
| Puerto Bermúdez | 248 | 10.20 S | 74.54 W |
| Puerto Berrío | 246 | 6.29 N | 74.24 W |
| Puerto Bolívar, Col. | 246 | 12.15 N | 71.58 W |
| Puerto Bolívar, Ec. | 246 | 3.16 S | 79.59 W |
| Puerto Boyacá | 246 | 5.45 N | 74.39 W |
| Puerto Busch | 248 | 20.02 S | 57.55 W |
| Puerto Cabello | 246 | 10.28 N | 68.01 W |
| Puerto Cabezas | 236 | 14.02 N | 83.23 W |
| Puerto Carreño | 246 | 6.12 N | 67.22 W |
| Puerto Casado | 252 | 22.20 S | 57.55 W |
| Puerto Castilla | 236 | 16.01 N | 86.01 W |
| Puerto Chicama | 248 | 7.42 S | 79.27 W |
| Puerto Colombia | 246 | 10.59 N | 74.58 W |
| Puerto Constanza | 258 | 33.50 S | 59.03 W |
| Puerto Cortés | 236 | 15.48 N | 87.56 W |
| Puerto Cumarebo | 246 | 11.29 N | 69.21 W |
| Puerto de Eten | 248 | 6.54 S | 79.52 W |
| Puerto Delicia | 252 | 26.12 S | 54.35 W |
| Puerto de Lomas | 248 | 15.34 S | 74.50 W |
| Puerto Delón | 236 | 14.22 N | 85.53 W |
| Puerto del Rosario | 148 | 28.30 N | 13.52 W |
| Puerto Deseado | 254 | 47.45 S | 65.54 W |
| Puerto El Triunfo | 236 | 13.17 N | 88.33 W |
| Puerto Escondido | 234 | 15.50 N | 97.10 W |
| Puerto Espãna → Port of Spain | 241r | 10.39 N | 61.31 W |
| Puerto Esperanza | 252 | 26.01 S | 54.39 W |
| Puerto Felipe, Bahía → Port Phillip Bay ⊂ | 169 | 38.07 S | 144.48 E |
| Puerto Fonciere | 252 | 22.29 S | 57.48 W |
| Puerto Francisco de Orellana | 246 | 0.28 S | 76.58 W |
| Puerto Gonzalo Moreno | 248 | 11.06 S | 66.10 W |
| Puerto Guaraní | 248 | 21.18 S | 57.55 W |
| Puerto Heath | 248 | 12.30 S | 68.40 W |
| Puerto Iguazú | 252 | 25.34 S | 54.34 W |
| Puerto Inca | 248 | 9.22 S | 74.58 W |
| Puerto Ingeniero Ibáñez | 254 | 46.18 S | 71.56 W |
| Puerto Inírida | 246 | 3.53 N | 67.52 W |
| Puerto Jiménez | 236 | 8.33 N | 83.19 W |
| Puerto Juárez | 232 | 21.11 N | 86.49 W |
| Puerto la Cruz | 246 | 10.13 N | 64.38 W |
| Puerto la Plata, Zona Nacional □[5] | 288 | 34.52 S | 57.52 W |
| Puerto Leda | 248 | 20.41 S | 58.02 W |
| Puerto Leguízamo | 246 | 0.12 S | 74.46 W |
| Puerto Lempira | 236 | 15.13 N | 83.47 W |
| Puerto Libertad, Arg. | 252 | 25.55 S | 54.36 W |
| Puerto Libertad, Méx. | 232 | 29.55 N | 112.43 W |
| Puerto Limón, Col. | 246 | 3.23 N | 73.30 W |
| Puerto Limón, C.R. | 236 | 10.00 N | 83.02 W |
| Puertollano | 34 | 38.41 N | 4.07 W |
| Puerto Lobos | 254 | 42.00 S | 65.06 W |
| Puerto López | 246 | 4.05 N | 72.58 W |
| Puerto Madero | 236 | 14.44 N | 92.25 W |
| Puerto Madryn | 254 | 42.46 S | 65.03 W |
| Puerto Maldonado | 248 | 12.36 S | 69.11 W |
| Puerto Manatí | 240p | 21.22 N | 76.50 W |
| Puerto Mihanovich | 248 | 20.52 S | 57.59 W |
| Puerto Montt | 254 | 41.28 S | 72.57 W |
| Puerto Morazán | 236 | 12.51 N | 87.11 W |
| Puerto Morelos | 232 | 20.50 N | 86.52 W |
| Puerto Nariño | 246 | 4.56 N | 67.48 W |
| Puerto Natales | 254 | 51.44 S | 72.31 W |
| Puerto Nuevo, Punta > | 240m | 18.30 N | 66.24 W |
| Puerto Octay | 254 | 40.58 S | 72.54 W |
| Puerto Ordaz → Ciudad Guayana | 246 | 8.22 N | 62.40 W |
| Puerto Padre | 240p | 21.12 N | 76.36 W |
| Puerto Páez | 246 | 6.13 N | 67.28 W |
| Puerto Palmer, Pico ∧ | 196 | 27.08 N | 101.47 W |
| Puerto Peñasco | 232 | 31.20 N | 113.33 W |
| Puerto Pilón | 236 | 9.22 N | 79.48 W |
| Puerto Pinasco | 252 | 22.43 S | 57.50 W |
| Puerto Pirámide | 254 | 42.34 S | 64.17 W |
| Puerto Piray | 252 | 26.28 S | 54.42 W |
| Puerto Píritu | 246 | 10.04 N | 65.03 W |
| Puerto Plata | 238 | 19.48 N | 70.41 W |
| Puerto Portillo | 248 | 9.46 S | 72.45 W |
| Puerto Princesa, Pil. | 116 | 9.44 N | 118.44 E |
| Puerto Princesa, Pil. | 116 | 10.06 N | 125.29 E |
| Puerto Real, Esp. | 34 | 36.32 N | 6.11 W |
| Puerto Real, P.R. | 240m | 18.05 N | 67.11 W |
| Puerto Rico, Arg. | 252 | 26.48 S | 55.02 W |
| Puerto Rico, Bol. | 248 | 11.05 S | 67.38 W |
| Puerto Rico, Col. | 246 | 1.54 N | 75.10 W |
| Puerto Rico □[2], N.A. | 230 | 18.15 N | 66.30 W |
| Puerto Rico □[2], N.A. | 240m | 18.15 N | 66.30 W |
| Puerto Rico Trench ✢[1] | 16 | 20.00 N | 66.00 W |
| Puerto Rondón | 246 | 6.17 N | 71.06 W |
| Puerto Saavedra | 252 | 38.47 S | 73.24 W |
| Puerto Salgar | 246 | 5.28 N | 74.39 W |
| Puerto Sandino | 236 | 12.12 N | 86.46 W |
| Puerto San José | 236 | 13.55 N | 90.49 W |
| Puerto San Julián | 254 | 49.18 S | 67.43 W |
| Puerto Santa Cruz | 254 | 50.01 S | 68.31 W |
| Puerto Sastre | 252 | 22.06 S | 57.59 W |
| Puerto Siles | 248 | 12.48 S | 65.05 W |
| Puerto Suarez | 248 | 18.57 S | 57.51 W |
| Puerto Supe | 248 | 10.49 S | 77.45 W |
| Puerto Tejada | 246 | 3.14 N | 76.24 W |
| Puerto Tolosa | 246 | 0.59 S | 74.09 W |
| Puerto Umbría | 246 | 0.52 N | 76.33 W |
| Puerto Vallarta | 234 | 20.37 N | 105.15 W |
| Puerto Varas | 254 | 41.19 S | 72.59 W |
| Puerto Victoria, Arg. | 252 | 26.20 S | 54.39 W |
| Puerto Victoria, Perú | 248 | 9.54 S | 74.58 W |
| Puerto Viejo, C.R. | 236 | 10.26 N | 83.59 W |
| Puerto Viejo, C.R. | 236 | 9.39 N | 82.45 W |
| Puerto Villamil | 246a | 0.56 S | 91.01 W |
| Puerto Villamizar | 246 | 8.19 N | 72.26 W |
| Puerto Villarroel | 248 | 16.50 S | 64.47 W |
| Puerto Visser | 254 | 45.24 S | 67.08 W |
| Puerto Wilches | 246 | 7.21 N | 73.54 W |
| Puerto Williams | 254 | 54.56 S | 67.37 W |
| Puerto Ybapobó | 252 | 23.42 S | 57.12 W |
| Pueyrredón, Lago (Lago Cochrane) ⊜ | 254 | 47.20 S | 72.00 W |
| Puffendorf | 56 | 50.56 N | 6.13 E |
| Puffing Billy Railroad Station ◆[5] | 274b | 37.55 S | 145.21 E |
| Pugačov | 80 | 52.01 N | 48.50 E |
| Pugač'ovo | 80 | 56.35 N | 53.02 E |
| Puge, Tan. | 154 | 4.45 S | 33.07 E |
| Puge, Zhg. | 102 | 27.28 N | 102.31 E |
| Puget, Cape > | 180 | 59.52 N | 148.26 W |
| Puget Island I | 224 | 46.10 N | 123.23 W |
| Puget Sound ⊔ | 224 | 47.50 N | 122.30 W |
| Puget Sound Naval Shipyard ■ | 224 | 47.33 N | 122.38 W |
| Puget-sur-Argens | 62 | 43.27 N | 6.41 E |
| Puget-Théniers | 62 | 43.57 N | 6.54 E |
| Puget-Ville | 62 | 43.17 N | 6.08 E |
| Pugh, Mount ∧ | 224 | 48.08 N | 121.22 W |
| Pughtown | 285 | 40.10 N | 75.40 W |
| Puglia □[4] | 68 | 41.15 N | 16.15 E |
| Pugong-ni | 271b | 37.43 N | 126.58 E |
| Pugŏ-ri | 98 | 42.01 N | 129.59 E |
| Pugwash | 186 | 45.51 N | 63.40 W |
| Puḫavičy | 76 | 53.32 N | 28.15 E |
| Puhe | 104 | 41.57 N | 123.36 E |
| Puhi | 229b | 21.58 N | 159.23 W |
| Puhja | 76 | 58.20 N | 26.19 E |
| Puhos | 26 | 62.05 N | 29.54 E |
| Puhosjärvi ⊜ | 26 | 65.19 N | 27.55 E |
| Puica | 248 | 15.04 S | 72.42 W |
| Puiești | 38 | 46.25 N | 27.33 E |
| Puigcerdá | 34 | 42.26 N | 1.56 E |
| Puigmal ∧ | 34 | 42.23 N | 2.07 E |
| Puimoisson | 62 | 43.52 N | 6.08 E |
| Puinahua, Canal de ≅[1] | 248 | 5.20 S | 74.13 W |
| Puināń | 272b | 22.56 N | 88.13 E |
| Puir | 89 | 53.10 N | 141.25 E |
| Puisaye, Collines de la ⩘[2] | 50 | 47.40 N | 3.15 E |
| Puiseaux | 50 | 48.12 N | 2.28 E |
| Puiseaux ≃ | 50 | 48.00 N | 2.44 E |
| Puiseux-en-France | 261 | 49.04 N | 2.29 E |
| Puiseux-Pontoise | 261 | 49.03 N | 2.01 E |
| Puisieux | 50 | 50.07 N | 2.42 E |
| Puits ≃ | 50 | 48.31 N | 4.15 E |
| Pujada Bay ⊂ | 116 | 6.51 N | 126.14 E |
| Pujehun | 150 | 7.21 N | 11.42 W |
| Puji, Zhg. | 100 | 27.59 N | 113.25 E |
| Puji, Zhg. | 100 | 29.58 N | 112.32 E |
| Pujiang, Zhg. | 100 | 29.28 N | 119.53 E |
| Pujiang, Zhg. | 107 | 30.12 N | 103.30 E |
| Pujilí | 246 | 0.57 S | 78.41 W |
| Pujon | 115a | 7.50 S | 112.28 E |
| Pujun | 112 | 1.20 S | 114.20 E |
| Pujut | 114 | 1.25 N | 100.39 E |
| Pujut, Tanjung > | 115a | 5.52 S | 106.02 E |
| Pukaki, Lake ⊜ | 172 | 44.07 S | 170.10 E |
| Pukalani | 229a | 20.50 N | 156.20 W |
| Pukaskwa ≃ | 190 | 48.00 N | 85.53 W |
| Pukaskwa National Park ♠ | 190 | 48.20 N | 85.50 W |
| Pukch'ang | 98 | 39.36 N | 126.17 E |
| Pukchin | 98 | 40.10 N | 125.43 E |
| Pukch'ŏn | 98 | 36.13 N | 126.45 E |
| Pukch'ŏng | 98 | 40.15 N | 128.20 E |
| Pukë | 38 | 42.03 N | 19.54 E |
| Pukeashun Mountain ∧ | 182 | 51.12 N | 119.14 W |
| Pukekohe | 172 | 37.12 S | 174.55 E |
| Puketeraki Range ⩘ | 172 | 42.58 S | 172.12 E |
| Puketoi Range ⩘ | 172 | 40.30 S | 176.05 E |
| Pukeuri Junction | 172 | 45.02 S | 171.02 E |
| Pukhan-gang ≃ | 98 | 37.31 N | 127.18 E |
| Pŭkhan-san ∧ | 271b | 37.41 N | 127.00 E |
| Pukhrāyān | 124 | 26.14 N | 79.51 E |
| Pukoo | 229d | 21.04 N | 156.48 W |
| Pukou, Zhg. | 100 | 26.16 N | 119.35 E |
| Pukou, Zhg. | 106 | 32.07 N | 118.43 E |
| Puksoozero | 24 | 62.38 N | 40.36 E |
| Puksubaek-san ∧ | 98 | 40.42 N | 127.44 E |
| Puktae-ch'ŏn ≃ | 98 | 40.28 N | 129.00 E |
| Pula, Hrv. | 36 | 44.52 N | 13.50 E |
| Pula, It. | 71 | 39.01 N | 9.00 E |
| Pulacayo | 248 | 20.25 S | 66.41 W |
| Pulandian Wan ⊂ | 98 | 39.18 N | 121.35 E |
| Pulanduta Point > | 116 | 11.54 N | 123.10 E |
| Pulangi ≃ | 116 | 7.18 N | 124.50 E |
| Pulangpisau | 112 | 2.46 S | 114.14 E |
| Pulap I[1] | 14 | 7.35 N | 149.24 E |
| Púlar, Cerro ∧ | 252 | 24.11 S | 68.04 W |
| Pulaski, In., U.S. | 216 | 40.59 N | 86.40 W |
| Pulaski, Mi., U.S. | 216 | 42.07 N | 84.40 W |
| Pulaski, N.Y., U.S. | 212 | 43.34 N | 76.07 W |
| Pulaski, Oh., U.S. | 216 | 41.30 N | 84.26 W |
| Pulaski, Pa., U.S. | 214 | 41.07 N | 80.26 W |
| Pulaski, Tn., U.S. | 194 | 35.11 N | 87.01 W |
| Pulaski, Va., U.S. | 192 | 37.02 N | 80.46 W |
| Pulaski, Wi., U.S. | 190 | 44.40 N | 88.14 W |
| Pulaski □[6] | 216 | 41.03 N | 86.36 W |
| Pulau ≃ | 164 | 5.50 S | 138.15 E |
| Pulaukida | 112 | 2.44 S | 102.34 E |
| Pulaukijang | 112 | 0.42 S | 103.12 E |
| Pulaumerak, Indon. | 115a | 5.56 S | 106.00 E |
| Pulaumerak, Indon. | 115a | 5.56 S | 106.00 E |
| Pulauraja | 114 | 2.42 N | 99.37 E |
| Puławy | 30 | 51.25 N | 21.57 E |
| Pulborough | 42 | 50.58 N | 0.30 W |
| Pul'chakim | 85 | 38.10 N | 67.21 E |
| Pulehu Gulch V | 229a | 20.50 N | 156.28 W |
| Pulfero | 64 | 46.11 N | 13.29 E |
| Pulga | 123 | 31.59 N | 77.26 E |
| Pulgaon | 122 | 20.44 N | 78.20 E |
| Pulham Market | 42 | 52.26 N | 1.14 E |
| Pulheim | 56 | 51.00 N | 6.47 E |
| Puli | 100 | 23.58 N | 120.57 E |
| Pulicat | 122 | 13.25 N | 80.19 E |
| Pulicat Lake ⊂ | 122 | 13.40 N | 80.10 E |
| Pulichatum | 128 | 35.57 N | 61.07 E |
| Puliciano | 66 | 43.23 N | 11.51 E |
| Puliyangudi | 122 | 9.10 N | 77.25 E |
| Pulj → Pula | 64 | 44.52 N | 13.50 E |
| Pulkau | 61 | 48.42 N | 15.51 E |
| Pulkau ≃ | 61 | 48.43 N | 16.21 E |
| Pulkkila | 26 | 64.16 N | 25.52 E |
| Pulkovo ◆[8] | 265a | 59.46 N | 30.20 E |
| Pullman, Mi., U.S. | 216 | 42.29 N | 86.05 W |
| Pullman, Wa., U.S. | 202 | 46.43 N | 117.10 W |
| Pullman ◆[8] | 278 | 41.43 N | 87.36 W |
| Púllo | 248 | 15.14 S | 73.50 W |
| Pully | 58 | 46.31 N | 6.39 E |
| Pul'mo | 78 | 51.31 N | 23.47 E |
| Pulo ⊥ | 68 | 41.12 N | 16.34 E |
| Pulo Anna I | 108 | 4.40 N | 131.58 E |
| Pulog, Mount ∧ | 116 | 16.36 N | 120.54 E |
| Pulogadung ◆[8] | 269e | 6.11 S | 106.54 E |
| Pulon'ga | 24 | 66.17 N | 40.02 E |
| Púlpito do Sul | 152 | 15.46 S | 12.00 E |
| Pulsano | 68 | 40.23 N | 17.22 E |
| Pulsen | 54 | 51.23 N | 13.26 E |
| Pulsnitz | 54 | 51.11 N | 14.01 E |
| Pulsnitz ≃ | 54 | 51.27 N | 13.30 E |
| Pulteney | 210 | 42.31 N | 77.10 W |
| Pultneyville | 210 | 43.17 N | 77.11 W |
| Pułtusk | 30 | 52.43 N | 21.05 E |
| Pulü, Zhg. | 107 | 29.50 N | 106.11 E |
| Pulu, Zhg. | 120 | 36.11 N | 81.30 E |
| Pulupandan | 116 | 10.31 N | 122.48 E |
| Pulur | 130 | 40.10 N | 39.53 E |
| Pulusuk I | 14 | 6.42 N | 149.19 E |
| Pulversheim | 58 | 47.51 N | 7.18 E |
| Puma Yumco ⊜ | 124 | 28.35 N | 90.20 E |
| Pumbi | 152 | 3.26 N | 22.11 E |
| Pumei | 102 | 23.28 N | 105.15 E |
| Pumphrey | 284b | 39.13 N | 76.38 W |
| Pumpkin Buttes ∧ | 200 | 43.44 N | 105.54 W |
| Pumpkin Center | 228 | 35.18 N | 119.05 W |
| Pumpkin Creek ≃, Mt., U.S. | 198 | 46.15 N | 105.45 W |
| Pumpkin Creek ≃, Ne., U.S. | 198 | 41.38 N | 103.01 W |
| Pumsaint | 42 | 52.03 N | 3.58 W |
| Pumsi | 80 | 57.12 N | 51.39 E |
| Puná, Isla I | 246 | 2.50 S | 80.08 W |
| Punaauia | 174s | 17.38 S | 149.36 W |
| Punaauia, Pointe de > | 174s | 17.38 S | 149.36 W |
| Punakha | 124 | 27.37 N | 89.52 E |
| Punaluu | 229c | 21.35 N | 157.53 W |
| Punan, Indon. | 112 | 1.20 N | 115.34 E |
| Punan, Indon. | 112 | 3.24 N | 116.16 E |
| Punan, Zhg. | 100 | 24.39 N | 117.41 E |
| Punata | 248 | 17.32 S | 65.50 W |
| Pūnch | 123 | 33.46 N | 74.06 E |
| Pūnch ≃ | 123 | 33.12 N | 73.40 E |
| Puncha | 126 | 23.10 N | 86.39 E |
| Punchaw | 182 | 53.28 N | 123.13 W |
| Punchbowl | 274a | 33.56 S | 151.03 E |
| Pundaguitan | 116 | 6.22 N | 126.10 E |
| Punda Maria | 156 | 22.40 S | 31.05 E |
| Pünderich | 56 | 50.02 N | 7.08 E |
| Pūndri | 124 | 29.45 N | 76.33 E |
| Punduga | 76 | 60.08 N | 40.12 E |
| Pune (Poona) | 122 | 18.32 N | 73.52 E |
| P'ungam-ni | 98 | 37.43 N | 128.11 E |
| Pungan | 85 | 40.45 N | 70.49 E |
| Punganūru | 122 | 13.22 N | 78.35 E |
| Pungarancho ≃ | 234 | 18.47 N | 100.41 W |
| Pungești | 38 | 46.42 N | 27.20 E |
| Punggol | 271c | 1.25 N | 103.55 E |
| Punggol ≃ | 271c | 1.25 N | 103.54 E |
| Pungki | 114 | 4.17 N | 96.13 E |
| Pungo ≃ | 192 | 35.23 N | 76.33 W |
| Pungo Andongo | 152 | 9.40 S | 15.35 E |
| Púngoè ≃ | 154 | 19.50 S | 34.48 E |
| P'ungsan, C.M.I.K. | 98 | 40.47 N | 128.10 E |
| P'ungsan, C.M.I.K. | 98 | 38.28 N | 125.01 E |
| P'ungsong-ni | 98 | 39.56 N | 127.11 E |
| Punia | 154 | 1.28 S | 26.27 E |
| Punilla, Sierra de la ⩘ | 252 | 28.55 S | 69.00 W |
| Puning | 100 | 23.18 N | 116.12 E |
| Punitaqui | 252 | 30.50 S | 71.16 W |
| Punjab □[3] | 123 | 31.00 N | 75.30 E |
| Punjab □[4] | 120 | 31.00 N | 72.00 E |
| Punkaharju ♠ | 26 | 61.47 N | 29.20 E |
| Punkalaidun | 26 | 61.07 N | 23.06 E |
| Punnichy | 184 | 51.23 N | 104.18 W |
| Puno | 248 | 15.50 S | 70.02 W |
| Puno □[5] | 248 | 15.00 S | 70.00 W |
| Punta, Castillo de la ⊥ | 286b | 23.09 N | 82.21 W |
| Punta, Cerro de ∧ | 240m | 18.10 N | 66.36 W |
| Punta Alegre | 240p | 22.23 N | 78.49 W |
| Punta Alta | 254 | 38.53 S | 62.05 W |
| Punta Arenas | 254 | 53.09 S | 70.55 W |
| Punta Banda, Cabo > | 232 | 31.45 N | 116.45 W |
| Punta Brava ◆[8] | 286b | 23.01 N | 82.30 W |
| Punta Cardón | 246 | 11.38 N | 70.14 W |
| Punta Colnett | 232 | 31.05 N | 116.05 W |
| Punta de Agua Creek (Tramperos Creek) ≃ | 196 | 35.32 N | 102.27 W |
| Punta de Bombón | 248 | 17.11 S | 71.48 W |
| Punta de Díaz | 252 | 28.03 S | 70.37 W |
| Punta del Cobre | 252 | 27.30 S | 70.16 W |
| Punta del Este | 252 | 34.58 S | 54.57 W |
| Punta Delgada | 254 | 42.46 S | 63.38 W |
| Punta de los Llanos | 252 | 30.09 S | 66.33 W |
| Punta de Mata | 246 | 9.43 N | 63.38 W |
| Punta de Piedras | 246 | 10.54 N | 64.06 W |
| Punta Flecha | 116 | 7.23 N | 123.25 E |
| Punta Gorda, Belize | 232 | 16.07 N | 88.48 W |
| Punta Gorda, Nic. | 236 | 11.31 N | 83.47 W |
| Punta Gorda, Fl., U.S. | 220 | 26.55 N | 82.02 W |
| Punta Gorda ≃ | 236 | 11.30 N | 83.47 W |
| Punta Gorda, Bahía de ⊂ | 236 | 11.15 N | 83.45 W |
| Punta Negra, Salar de ≚ | 252 | 24.35 S | 69.00 W |
| Punta Prieta | 232 | 28.58 N | 114.17 W |
| Punta Raisi, Aeroporto di ⊠ | 70 | 38.11 N | 13.06 E |
| Puntarenas | 236 | 9.58 N | 84.50 W |
| Puntarenas □[4] | 236 | 9.00 N | 83.15 W |
| Punta Santiago | 240m | 18.10 N | 65.45 W |
| Puntas del Sauce | 258 | 33.51 S | 57.01 W |
| Punto Fijo | 246 | 11.42 N | 70.13 W |
| Puntzi Lake ⊜ | 182 | 52.12 N | 124.02 W |
| Punung | 115a | 8.08 S | 111.01 E |
| Punxsutawney | 214 | 40.56 N | 78.58 W |
| Puolanka | 26 | 64.52 N | 27.40 E |
| Puolo Point > | 229b | 21.54 N | 159.36 W |
| Puper | 164 | 0.10 S | 131.18 E |
| Pup'yŏng | 271b | 37.30 N | 126.43 E |
| Puqi, Zhg. | 100 | 28.11 N | 121.01 E |
| Puqi, Zhg. | 100 | 29.43 N | 113.53 E |
| Puqian, Zhg. | 100 | 23.34 N | 114.38 E |
| Puqian, Zhg. | 102 | 20.03 N | 110.36 E |
| Puquio | 248 | 14.42 S | 74.08 W |
| Pur ≃ | 74 | 67.31 N | 77.55 E |
| Purabiya Plain ≚ | 124 | 25.50 N | 82.30 E |
| Puracé, Volcán ∧[1] | 246 | 2.21 N | 76.23 W |
| Purandarpur | 126 | 23.51 N | 87.36 E |
| Pūranpur | 124 | 28.31 N | 80.09 E |
| Purari ≃ | 164 | 7.25 S | 145.05 E |
| Purba | 114 | 2.54 N | 98.42 E |
| Purbashthāli | 126 | 23.28 N | 88.21 E |
| Purbeck, Isle of I | 42 | 50.38 N | 2.00 W |
| Purbolinggo | 115a | 7.24 S | 109.22 E |
| Purcell | 196 | 35.00 N | 97.21 W |
| Purcell Mountains ⩘ | 182 | 50.00 N | 116.30 W |
| Purcellville | 188 | 39.08 N | 77.42 W |
| Purchase | 276 | 41.02 N | 73.43 W |
| Purchena | 34 | 37.21 N | 2.22 W |
| Purdon | 222 | 31.57 N | 96.37 W |
| Purdoški | 80 | 54.40 N | 43.32 E |
| Purdy | 194 | 36.49 N | 93.55 W |
| Purech | 80 | 56.39 N | 43.05 E |
| Pureora ∧ | 172 | 38.33 S | 175.38 E |
| Purépero | 234 | 19.55 N | 102.01 W |
| Purfleet | 42 | 51.29 N | 0.15 E |
| Purga | 171a | 27.43 S | 152.44 E |
| Purga Creek ≃ | 171a | 27.42 S | 152.45 E |
| Purgatoire ≃ | 198 | 38.04 N | 103.10 W |
| Purgatory Brook ≃ | 283 | 42.11 N | 71.11 W |
| Pürgg | 61 | 47.32 N | 14.04 E |
| Purgstall an der Erlauf | 61 | 48.03 N | 15.08 E |
| Puri | 120 | 19.48 N | 85.51 E |
| Purial, Sierra del ⩘ | 240p | 20.12 N | 74.42 W |
| Purificación, Col. | 246 | 3.51 N | 74.55 W |
| Purificación, Méx. | 234 | 19.43 N | 104.38 W |
| Purificación ≃, Méx. | 232 | 23.58 N | 98.42 W |
| Purificación ≃, Méx. | 234 | 19.18 N | 104.54 W |
| Purikari neem > | 76 | 59.40 N | 25.43 E |
| Purísima | 196 | 29.09 N | 100.46 W |
| Purísima, Sierra de la ⩘ | 196 | 26.30 N | 101.44 W |
| Purisima Creek ≃ | 282 | 37.24 N | 122.26 W |
| Purísima de Bustos | 234 | 21.02 N | 101.52 W |
| Purkersdorf | 61 | 48.12 N | 16.11 E |
| Purleigh | 260 | 51.41 N | 0.40 E |
| Purley | 222 | 33.05 N | 95.16 W |
| Purley ◆[8] | 260 | 51.20 N | 0.07 W |
| Purling | 210 | 42.17 N | 74.00 W |
| Purmerend | 52 | 52.31 N | 4.57 E |
| Pūrna ≃, India | 122 | 19.07 N | 77.02 E |
| Pūrna ≃, India | 122 | 21.05 N | 76.00 E |
| Pūrnia | 124 | 25.47 N | 87.31 E |
| Puronga | 76 | 60.09 N | 40.54 E |
| Purranque | 254 | 40.55 S | 73.10 W |
| Purrorumba Hill ∧ | 171b | 35.10 S | 149.23 E |
| Purros | 156 | 18.38 S | 12.59 E |
| Purrumbete, Lake ⊜ | 169 | 38.17 S | 143.14 E |
| Pursat → Poŭthĭsăt | 110 | 12.32 N | 103.55 E |
| Purton | 42 | 51.36 N | 1.52 W |
| Puruándiro | 234 | 20.05 N | 101.30 W |
| Puruarán | 234 | 19.06 N | 101.32 W |
| Puruí ≃ | 246 | 1.40 S | 68.08 W |
| Purukcahu | 112 | 0.35 S | 114.35 E |
| Puruliya | 126 | 23.20 N | 86.22 E |
| Puruni ≃ | 246 | 6.00 N | 59.12 W |
| Purus (Purús) ≃ | 242 | 3.42 S | 61.28 W |
| Puruvesi ⊜ | 26 | 61.50 N | 29.27 E |
| Purvis | 194 | 31.08 N | 89.24 W |
| Purwakarta | 115a | 6.34 S | 107.26 E |
| Purwantoro | 115a | 7.51 S | 111.15 E |
| Purwareja | 115a | 7.28 S | 109.25 E |
| Purwodadi, Indon. | 115a | 7.49 S | 110.00 E |
| Purwodadi, Indon. | 115a | 7.05 S | 110.54 E |
| Purwokerto | 115a | 7.25 S | 109.14 E |
| Purworejo | 115a | 7.43 S | 110.01 E |
| Pusa | 112 | 1.36 N | 111.17 E |
| Pusad | 122 | 19.54 N | 77.35 E |
| Pusan | 98 | 35.06 N | 129.03 E |
| Pusan □[4] | 98 | 35.10 N | 129.05 E |
| Pūsa Road | 124 | 25.59 N | 85.41 E |
| Pusat Gayo, Pegunungan ⩘ | 114 | 4.15 N | 97.05 E |
| Puščino | 82 | 54.50 N | 37.36 E |
| Pusgo Point > | 116 | 13.31 N | 122.38 E |
| Pushang | 98 | 36.08 N | 119.42 E |
| Pushkar | 120 | 26.30 N | 74.33 E |
| Pushkarivka | 78 | 48.40 N | 34.16 E |
| Pushkin → Puškin | 76 | 59.43 N | 30.25 E |
| Pushkin Airport ⊠ | 265a | 59.41 N | 30.21 E |
| Pushkin Drama Theatre ⚲ | 265a | 59.56 N | 30.21 E |
| Pushthrough | 186 | 47.39 N | 56.10 W |
| Puskiakiwenin Indian Reserve ◆[4] | 184 | 53.57 N | 110.26 W |
| Puškin | 76 | 59.43 N | 30.25 E |
| Puškino, Ross. | 80 | 51.14 N | 4[illegible].59 E |
| Puškino, Ross. | 82 | 56.01 N | 37.51 E |
| Puškino, Ross. | 82 | 56.36 N | 3[illegible].46 E |
| Puškinskij | 265a | 59.43 N | 3[illegible].18 E |
| Puškinskije Gory | 76 | 57.01 N | 28.54 E |
| Puskwaskau ≃ | 182 | 55.29 N | 118.10 W |
| Puslinch Lake ⊜ | 212 | 43.25 N | 80.16 W |
| Pusŏng-ni | 98 | 40.19 N | 127.19 E |
| Püspökladány | 30 | 47.19 N | 21.07 E |
| Pussay | 50 | 48.21 N | [illegible]0 E |
| Püssi | 76 | 59.24 N | 27.01 E |
| Pustertal V | 64 | 46.45 N | 12.[illegible]0 E |
| Pustin' | 76 | 59.54 N | 35.[illegible]2 E |
| Pustomyty | 78 | 49.42 N | 23.[illegible]6 E |
| Pustoš' | 76 | 60.07 N | 42.[illegible]5 E |
| Pustoška | 76 | 56.20 N | 29.[illegible]2 E |
| Pustozersk | 24 | 67.33 N | 52.[illegible]7 E |
| Pusur ≃[1] | 126 | 21.45 N | 89.[illegible]0 E |
| Puszczykowo | 30 | 52.17 N | 16.[illegible]2 E |
| Putaendo | 252 | 32.38 S | 70.4[illegible] W |
| Putah Creek ≃ | 226 | 38.33 N | 121.[illegible] W |
| Putai | 100 | 23.23 N | 120.[illegible] E |
| Putana, Volcán ∧[1] | 252 | 22.43 S | 67.5[illegible] W |
| Putang ≃ | 269e | 6.13 S | 106.5[illegible] E |
| Putangqiao | 106 | 31.34 N | 118.5[illegible] E |
| Putao | 102 | 27.21 N | 97.2[illegible] E |
| Putaruru | 172 | 38.03 S | 175.4[illegible] E |
| Put'atin | 89 | 42.52 N | 132.2[illegible] E |
| Put'atino | 80 | 54.10 N | 41.0[illegible] E |
| Putbus | 54 | 54.21 N | 13.28 E |
| Puteaux | 261 | 48.53 N | 2.14 E |
| Puteran, Pulau I | 115a | 7.05 S | 114.0[illegible] E |
| Putfontein Landbouhoewes | 273d | 26.08 S | 28.24 E |
| Putgarten | 54 | 54.40 N | 13.25 E |
| Puth Kalān ◆[8] | 272a | 28.43 N | 77.05 E |
| Putian, Zhg. | 100 | 25.26 N | 119.01 E |
| Putian, Zhg. | 100 | 29.16 N | 114.58 E |
| Putifigari | 71 | 40.34 N | 8.27 E |
| Putignano | 68 | 40.51 N | 17.07 E |
| Putilkovo | 265b | 55.52 N | 37.23 E |
| Putina | 248 | 14.55 S | 69.52 W |
| Put-in-Bay | 214 | 41.39 N | 82.49 W |
| Putincevo | 86 | 49.50 N | 84.22 |
| Puting, Tanjung > | 112 | 3.31 S | 111.46 E |
| Putla de Guerrero | 234 | 17.02 N | 97.56 W |
| Putlitz | 54 | 53.15 N | 12.02 E |
| Putnam, Ct., U.S. | 207 | 41.54 N | 71.54 W |
| Putnam, Tx., U.S. | 196 | 32.22 N | 99.12 W |
| Putnam □[6], N.Y., U.S. | 210 | 41.26 N | 73.41 W |
| Putnam □[6], Oh., U.S. | 216 | 41.01 N | 84.03 W |
| Putnam Lake | 210 | 41.28 N | 73.35 W |
| Putnam Lake ⊜ | 276 | 41.05 N | 73.38 W |
| Putnam Valley | 210 | 41.20 N | 73.52 W |
| Putnamville Reservoir ⊜[1] | 283 | 42.36 N | 70.57 W |
| Putney, Ga., U.S. | 192 | 31.29 N | 84.07 W |
| Putney, Vt., U.S. | 188 | 42.58 N | 72.31 W |
| Putney ◆[8] | 260 | 51.28 N | 0.13 W |
| Putney Island I | 126 | 21.42 N | 89.20 E |
| Puto | 175e | 5.41 S | 154.43 E |
| Putorana, plato ⩘[1] | 74 | 69.00 N | 95.00 E |
| Putorino | 172 | 39.08 S | 177.00 E |
| Putre | 248 | 18.12 S | 69.35 W |
| Putri Narrows ⊔ | 271c | 1.27 N | 103.42 E |
| Putsonderwater | 158 | 29.09 S | 21.51 E |
| Pütt | 263 | 51.11 N | 6.59 E |
| Puttalam | 122 | 8.02 N | 79.49 E |
| Puttalam Lagoon ⊂ | 122 | 8.07 N | 79.47 E |
| Putte, Bel. | 56 | 51.04 N | 4.38 E |
| Putte, Ned. | 52 | 51.22 N | 4.23 E |
| Puttelange-lès-Farschviller | 56 | 49.03 N | 6.56 E |
| Putten | 52 | 52.15 N | 5.36 E |
| Putten I | 52 | 51.50 N | 4.15 E |
| Puttgarden | 54 | 54.30 N | 11.13 E |
| Püttlingen | 56 | 49.17 N | 6.53 E |
| Puttūr | 122 | 13.27 N | 79.33 E |
| Putty | 170 | 32.57 S | 150.40 E |
| Putty Creek ≃ | 170 | 33.05 S | 150.37 E |
| Putú | 252 | 35.13 S | 72.17 W |
| Putumayo □[8] | 246 | 0.30 N | 76.00 W |
| Putumayo (Içá) ≃ | 246 | 3.07 S | 67.58 W |
| Putuo | 100 | 29.58 N | 122.17 E |
| Putu Range ⩘ | 150 | 5.30 N | 8.10 W |
| Pütürge | 130 | 38.12 N | 38.53 E |
| Putussibau | 112 | 0.50 N | 112.56 E |
| Putyla | 78 | 48.01 N | 25.03 E |
| Putyvl' | 78 | 51.21 N | 33.52 E |
| Putzkau | 54 | 51.06 N | 14.13 E |
| Putzu Idu | 71 | 40.02 N | 8.25 E |
| Pu'uhonua o Honaunau National Historical Park ♠ | 229d | 19.25 N | 155.54 W |
| Puu Kaaumakua ∧ | 229c | 21.30 N | 157.54 W |
| Puu Keahiakahoe ∧ | 229c | 21.23 N | 157.49 W |
| Puukohola Heiau National Historic Site ⊥ | 229d | 20.00 N | 155.46 W |
| Puukolii | 229a | 20.56 N | 156.40 W |
| Puu Kukui ∧ | 229a | 20.52 N | 156.35 W |
| Puula ⊜ | 26 | 61.50 N | 26.42 E |
| Puumala | 26 | 61.32 N | 28.11 E |
| Puunene | 229a | 20.51 N | 156.27 W |
| Pu'upu'a | 175a | 13.34 S | 172.09 W |
| Puurmani | 76 | 58.34 N | 26.17 E |
| Puurs | 50 | 51.05 N | 4.17 E |
| Puuwai | 229b | 21.54 N | 160.12 W |
| Puxi | 100 | 25.10 N | 119.08 E |
| Puxian | 102 | 36.30 N | 111.02 E |
| Puxico | 194 | 36.56 N | 90.09 W |
| Puxingchang | 107 | 30.41 N | 105.06 E |
| Puyallup | 224 | 47.11 N | 122.17 W |
| Puyallup ≃ | 224 | 47.15 N | 122.24 W |
| Puyang | 98 | 35.42 N | 114.59 E |
| Puyang ≃ | 100 | 30.05 N | 120.11 E |
| Puyango (Tumbes) ≃ | 246 | 3.30 S | 80.27 W |
| Puy-de-Dôme □[5] | 32 | 45.45 N | 3.05 E |
| Puyehue | 254 | 40.40 S | 72.37 W |
| Puyehue, Volcán ∧[1] | 254 | 40.35 S | 72.08 W |
| Puylaurens | 32 | 43.34 N | 2.01 E |
| Puy-l'Évêque | 32 | 44.30 N | 1.08 E |
| Puyloubier | 62 | 43.31 N | 5.41 E |
| Puymorens, Col de )( | 32 | 42.30 N | 1.50 E |
| Puyo, Ec. | 246 | 1.28 S | 77.59 W |
| Puyŏ, Taehan | 98 | 36.18 N | 126.54 E |
| Puysegur Point > | 172 | 46.09 S | 166.36 E |
| Puyuan | 106 | 30.41 N | 120.38 E |
| Puyuguapi, Canal ⊔ | 254 | 44.45 S | 72.48 W |
| Puyun-dong | 98 | 41.55 N | 129.30 E |
| Pūzak, Hāmūn-e ⊜ | 128 | 31.30 N | 61.45 E |
| Puzhen | 106 | 32.09 N | 118.41 E |
| Puzzle Creek ≃ | 162 | 17.58 S | 135.41 E |
| Puzzle Lake ⊜, On., Can. | 212 | 44.36 N | 76.58 W |


| | | | | |
|---|---|---|---|---|
| ≃ River | Fluß | Río | Rivière | Rio |
| ≅ Canal | Kanal | Canal | Canal | Canal |
| ⌊ Waterfall, Rapids | Wasserfall, Stromschnellen | Cascada, Rápidos | Chute d'eau, Rapides | Cascata, Rápidos |
| ⊔ Strait | Meeresstraße | Estrecho | Détroit | Estreito |
| ⊂ Bay, Gulf | Bucht, Golf | Bahía, Golfo | Baie, Golfe | Baía, Golfo |
| ⊜ Lake, Lakes | See, Seen | Lago, Lagos | Lac, Lacs | Lago, Lagos |
| ≡ Swamp | Sumpf | Pantano | Marais | Pântano |
| ⊼ Ice Features, Glacier | Eis- und Gletscherformen | Accidentes Glaciales | Formes glaciaires | Acidentes glaciares |
| ⊤ Other Hydrographic Features | Andere Hydrographische Objekte | Otros Elementos Hidrográficos | Autres données hydrographiques | Outros acidentes hidrográficos |

| | | | | |
|---|---|---|---|---|
| ✢ Submarine Features | Untermeerische Objekte | Accidentes Submarinos | Formes de relief sous-marin | Acidentes submarinos |
| □ Political Unit | Politische Einheit | Unidad Politica | Entité politique | Unidade política |
| ⚲ Cultural Institution | Kulturelle Institution | Institución Cultural | Institution culturelle | Instituição cultural |
| ⊥ Historical Site | Historische Stätte | Sitio Histórico | Site historique | Sitio histórico |
| ♠ Recreational Site | Erholungs- und Ferienort | Sitio de Recreo | Centre de loisirs | Area de Lazer |
| ⊠ Airport | Flughafen | Aeropuerto | Aéroport | Aeroporto |
| ■ Military Installation | Militäranlage | Instalación Militar | Installation militaire | Instalação militar |
| ◆ Miscellaneous | Verschiedenes | Misceláneo | Divers | Diversos |

Puzzle Lake ⊜, Fl., U.S. 220 28.41 N 81.02 W
Pwalagu 150 10.35 N 0.50 W
Pwani □[4] 154 7.00 S 39.00 E
Pweto 154 8.28 S 28.54 E
Pwinbyu 110 20.22 N 94.40 E
Pwllheli 42 52.53 N 4.25 W
Pyalo 110 19.09 N 95.11 E
Pyalong 169 37.07 S 144.54 E
Pyamalaw ≃[1] 110 15.49 N 94.42 E
Pyapon ′ 110 16.17 N 95.41 E
Pyatigorsk → P'atigorsk 84 44.03 N 43.04 E
P'yatykhatky 78 48.24 N 33.42 E
Pyawbwe 110 20.35 N 96.04 E
Pyaye 110 19.15 N 95.06 E
Pyčas 80 56.29 N 52.28 E
Pye Islands II 180 59.22 N 150.25 W
Pygmalion Point › 110 6.45 N 93.49 E
Pyhäjärvi ⊜, Europe 26 61.53 N 30.00 E
Pyhäjärvi ⊜, Suomi 26 62.46 N 25.30 E
Pyhäjärvi ⊜, Suomi 26 63.35 N 25.57 E
Pyhäjärvi ⊜, Suomi 26 61.28 N 23.35 E
Pyhäjärvi ⊜, Suomi 26 61.00 N 22.18 E
Pyhäjoki 26 64.28 N 24.14 E
Pyhäjoki ≃ 26 64.28 N 24.13 E
Pyhämaa I 26 60.57 N 21.20 E
Pyhän-Häkin kansallispuisto ♦ 26 62.52 N 25.30 E
Pyhäsalmi 26 63.41 N 25.59 E
Pyhäselkä 26 62.26 N 29.58 E
Pyhäselkä ⊜ 26 62.26 N 29.58 E
Pyhätunturi ∧ 24 67.01 N 27.09 E
Pyhätunturin kansallispuisto ♦ 24 67.01 N 27.10 E
Pyhra 61 48.10 N 15.41 E
Pyhtää (Pyttis) 26 60.29 N 26.32 E
Pyinbongyi 110 17.34 N 96.34 E
Pyingaing 110 23.09 N 94.51 E
Pyinkayaing 110 15.58 N 94.24 E
Pyinmana 110 19.44 N 96.13 E
Pyle 42 51.32 N 3.42 W
Pylos → Pílos 38 36.55 N 21.43 E
Pymatuning Creek ≃ 214 41.18 N 80.27 W
Pymatuning Reservoir ⊜[1] 214 41.37 N 80.30 W
Pymatuning State Park ♦, Oh., U.S. 214 41.38 N 80.33 W
Pymatuning State Park ♦, Pa., U.S. 214 41.30 N 80.27 W
Pymble 274a 33.45 S 151.09 E
Pyngopil'gyn, laguna ⊂ 180 67.24 N 175.10 W
Pyŏktong 98 40.35 N 125.20 E
Pyŏlch'ang-ni 98 39.17 N 126.26 E
P'yŏngan Namdo □[4] 98 39.20 N 126.00 E
P'yŏngan Pukdo □[4] 98 40.10 N 125.20 E
P'yŏngch'ang 98 37.23 N 128.22 E
P'yŏngdong-ni 98 37.10 N 128.02 E
P'yŏnggang 98 38.26 N 127.16 E
P'yonghae 98 36.46 N 129.28 E
P'yŏngsan 98 38.19 N 126.23 E
P'yŏngt'aek 98 37.00 N 127.05 E
P'yŏngyang 98 39.01 N 125.45 E
P'yŏngyang □[4] 98 39.05 N 125.50 E
Pyŏrha-ri 98 40.48 N 126.32 E
Pyote 196 31.32 N 103.08 W
Pyramid Head › 228 32.49 N 118.21 W
Pyramid Lake ⊜ 204 40.00 N 119.35 W
Pyramid Lake ⊜[1] 228 34.39 N 118.47 W
Pyramid Lake Indian Reservation ⟜[4] 204 40.20 N 119.35 W
Pyramid Peak ∧, Ca., U.S. 226 38.50 N 120.19 W
Pyramid Peak ∧, Wa., U.S. 224 47.07 N 121.24 W
Pyramid Peak ∧, Wy., U.S. 200 43.27 N 110.28 W
Pyramid Point › 174h 2.52 S 171.37 W
Pyramids of Giza → Jīzah, Ahrāmāt al- ⊥ 142 29.59 N 31.08 E
Pyrenäen → Pyrenees ⋀ 34 42.40 N 1.00 E
Pyrenees ⋀ 34 42.40 N 1.00 E
Pyrénées-Atlantiques □[5] 32 43.15 N 0.50 W
Pyrénées Occident, Parc National des ♦ 32 42.48 N 0.08 W
Pyrénées-Orientales □[5] 32 42.30 N 2.20 E
Pyre Peak ∧ 180 52.20 N 172.31 W
Pyrford 260 51.19 N 0.30 W
Pyrgi ⊥ 66 42.01 N 11.58 E
Pyrgos → Pírgos 38 37.41 N 21.28 E
Pyrkanajjan, gora ∧ 180 69.14 N 175.50 E
Pyrkino 80 53.29 N 45.07 E
Pyrmont 216 40.28 N 86.41 W
Pyrohivka 78 51.54 N 33.18 E
Pyryatyn 78 50.15 N 32.30 E
Pyrzyce 30 53.10 N 14.55 E
Pyšma 86 56.56 N 63.13 E
Pyšma ≃ 86 57.08 N 66.18 E
Pys'menne 78 48.13 N 35.48 E
Pytalovo 76 57.04 N 27.56 E
Pythonga, Lac ⊜ 190 46.23 N 76.25 W
Pyu 110 18.29 N 96.26 E
Pyuntaza 110 17.52 N 96.44 E
Pyūthān 124 28.06 N 82.54 E
Pyvėsa ≃ 76 56.06 N 24.27 E
Pyzdry 30 52.11 N 17.41 E


## Q


Qäbälä 84 40.59 N 47.50 E
Qabāṭīyah 132 32.25 N 35.17 E
Qabbāsīn 130 36.25 N 37.34 E
Qabb Ilyās 132 33.48 N 35.49 E
Qabırrı (Iori) ≃ 84 41.03 N 46.17 E
Qabr Hūd 144 16.08 N 49.37 E
Qacentina (Constantine) 148 36.22 N 6.37 E
Qaddīs Anṭūn, Dayr al- (Monastery of Saint Anthony) ☸[1] 142 28.55 N 32.21 E
Qaddīs Būlus, Dayr al- (Monastery of Saint Paul) ☸[1] 142 28.52 N 32.33 E
Qāderābād 128 30.17 N 53.16 E
Qādiān 123 31.49 N 75.23 E
Qā'emshahr 128 36.28 N 52.53 E
Qā'en 128 33.44 N 59.11 E
Qāfilah 142 31.04 N 30.16 E
Qagan 88 49.14 N 118.08 E
Qagan Nur ⊜, Zhg. 98 41.23 N 113.55 E
Qagan Nur ⊜, Zhg. 102 43.37 N 114.40 E
Qahā 142 30.17 N 31.12 E
Qahar Youyi Zhongqi 102 41.09 N 112.38 E
Qahbûna 142 30.48 N 31.54 E
Qaidam ≃ 102 36.39 N 96.20 E
Qaidam Pendi ≍[1] 120 37.00 N 95.00 E
Qakar 120 36.32 N 80.43 E
Qala' an-Naḥl 140 13.38 N 34.57 E
Qalabshū 142 31.26 N 31.19 E
Qalamshāh 142 29.10 N 30.50 E
Qalandīyah 132 31.50 N 35.14 E
Qalandūl 142 27.49 N 30.50 E
Qalāt 120 32.07 N 66.54 E
Qal'at ash-Shaqīf (Beaufort Castle) ⊥ 132 33.19 N 35.32 E
Qal'at Bīshah 144 20.01 N 42.36 E
Qal'at Ṣāliḥ 128 31.31 N 47.16 E
Qal'at Sukkar 128 31.51 N 46.05 E
Qal'eh Shahr 120 35.33 N 65.34 E
Qal'eh-ye Deh-e Bārez 128 27.26 N 57.12 E
Qal'eh-ye Now, Afg. 120 35.27 N 67.08 E
Qal'eh-ye Now, Afg. 128 34.59 N 63.08 E
Qal'eh-ye Panjeh 123 37.00 N 72.36 E
Qal'eh-ye Sarkārī 120 35.54 N 67.17 E
Qallābāt, Sūd. 140 12.43 N 23.26 E
Qallābāt, Sūd. 140 12.58 N 36.09 E
Qallīn 142 31.03 N 30.51 E
Qalqilīya 132 32.11 N 34.58 E
Qalyūb 142 30.11 N 31.12 E
Qamar, Ghubbat al- ⊂ 118 16.00 N 52.30 E
Qamata 158 32.00 S 27.21 E
Qamdo 102 31.11 N 97.15 E
Qamīnis 146 31.39 N 20.03 E
Qamr-ud-dīn Kārez 120 31.39 N 68.25 E
Qamṣar 128 33.45 N 51.26 E
Qanā, Ar. Su. 128 27.47 N 41.25 E
Qānā, Lubnān 132 33.13 N 35.18 E
Qanāyah 132 33.01 N 36.11 E
Qandahār 120 31.32 N 65.30 E
Qandahār □[4] 120 31.00 N 65.45 E
Qandala 144 11.28 N 49.52 E
Qanṭarah, Jabal ∧[2] 142 30.09 N 30.15 E
Qantur 140 9.45 N 25.52 E
Qarabağlar 84 39.26 N 45.12 E
Qarabağ silsiläsi ⋀ 84 39.42 N 46.36 E
Qaraçala 84 39.48 N 48.57 E
Qaraçay ≃ 84 41.28 N 49.00 E
Qaracinar 84 40.26 N 46.34 E
Qārah, Ar. Su. 128 29.52 N 40.15 E
Qārah, Sūrīy. 130 34.09 N 36.44 E
Qarah Bāgh 128 34.56 N 61.46 E
Qarak 85 38.23 N 76.58 E
Qarasu 84 40.11 N 48.41 E
Qarāvol 120 37.14 N 68.46 E
Qardho 144 9.30 N 49.05 E
Qareh ≃ 128 34.52 N 51.25 E
Qareh Sū ≃ 128 39.27 N 47.23 E
Qareh Ẕīā' od Dīn 84 38.54 N 45.02 E
Qarqan ≃ 90 39.25 N 88.20 E
Qarqīn 120 37.25 N 66.03 E
Qarṭabā 130 34.06 N 35.51 E
Qārūn, Birkat (Lake Moeris) ⊜ 142 29.28 N 30.40 E
Qaryat al-Qaddāhīyah 146 31.22 N 15.14 E
Qaryat al-Zuwaytīnah 146 30.58 N 20.07 E
Qaṣa-e Qand 128 26.12 N 60.45 E
Qāsh, Nahr al- (Gash) ≃ 140 16.48 N 35.51 E
Qashqeh, Kūh-e ∧ 128 28.23 N 55.18 E
Qāsim 132 32.59 N 36.05 E
Qāsimwāla 123 30.09 N 73.50 E
Qaṣr ad-Dayr, Jabal ∧ 132 30.48 N 35.34 E
Qaṣr al-Azraq ⊥ 132 31.53 N 36.49 E
Qaṣr al-Dubārā (Garden City) ⟜[8] 273c 30.02 N 31.14 E
Qaṣr al-Farāfirah 140 27.03 N 27.58 E
Qaṣr al-Jibālī 142 29.20 N 30.38 E
Qaṣr al-Kharānah ⊥ 132 31.44 N 36.28 E
Qaṣr al-Mushāsh ⊥ 132 31.49 N 36.19 E
Qaṣr al-Mushattā ⊥ 132 31.44 N 36.01 E
Qaṣr al Qarābūllī 146 32.45 N 13.43 E
Qaṣr 'Amrah ⊥ 132 31.48 N 36.35 E
Qaṣr aṭ-Ṭūbah ⊥ 132 31.20 N 36.34 E
Qaṣr Baghdād 142 30.44 N 30.53 E
Qaṣr Bū-Hādī 146 31.03 N 16.40 E
Qaṣr Ḍab'ah ⊥ 132 31.36 N 36.03 E
Qaṣr-e Fīrūzeh 267d 35.40 N 51.32 E
Qasr el-Boukhari 148 35.51 N 2.52 E
Qaṣr-e Shīrīn 128 34.31 N 45.35 E
Qaṣr Qārūn 142 29.25 N 30.25 E
Qa'ṭabah 144 13.51 N 44.42 E
Qaṭanā 132 33.26 N 36.05 E
Qatar (Qaṭar) □[1], Asia 118 25.00 N 51.10 E
Qatar (Qaṭar) □[1], Asia 128 25.00 N 51.10 E
Qaṭia, Bi'r ⊤[4] 142 30.58 N 32.45 E
Qaṭmah 130 36.36 N 36.57 E
Qaṭrānī, Jabal ∧[2] 142 29.41 N 30.35 E
Qattāntyah, Ghurd al- ≐[8] 142 29.50 N 30.17 E
Qattara Depression → Qaṭṭārah, Munkhafaḍ al- ≐[7] 140 30.00 N 27.30 E
Qaṭṭārah, Munkhafaḍ al- (Qattara Depression) ≐[7] 140 30.00 N 27.30 E
Qaṭṭīnah, Buḥayrat ⊜[1] 130 34.39 N 36.34 E
Qawz Rajab 140 16.04 N 35.34 E
Qax 84 41.26 N 46.56 E
Qāy 142 29.09 N 30.57 E
Qayṭah 132 33.04 N 36.08 E
Qazanbulag 84 40.38 N 46.41 E
Qazangöldağ ∧ 84 39.13 N 46.00 E
Qazax 84 41.06 N 45.22 E
Qāzigund 123 33.38 N 75.09 E
Qazımämmäd 84 40.03 N 48.56 E
Qazvīn 128 36.16 N 50.00 E
Qeh 102 42.18 N 100.59 E
Qena → Qinā 140 26.10 N 32.43 E
Qeqertaq I 176 71.55 N 55.30 W
Qesari, Ḥorbat (Cæsarea) ⊥ 132 32.30 N 34.53 E
Qeshm 128 26.58 N 56.16 E
Qeshm, Jazīreh-ye I 128 26.45 N 55.45 E
Qetura 132 29.58 N 35.03 E
Qeydār 128 36.07 N 48.35 E
Qeyṣār 120 35.41 N 64.17 E
Qezel Owzan ≃ 128 36.45 N 49.22 E
Qezel Qeshlāq 84 39.08 N 45.21 E
Qi ≃, Zhg. 98 35.30 N 114.17 E
Qi ≃, Zhg. 100 30.09 N 115.20 E
Qi ≃, Zhg. 107 30.38 N 105.26 E
Qi ≃, Zhg. 107 29.15 N 106.24 E
Qiakemake 85 40.05 N 75.24 E
Qian ≃ 102 23.25 N 110.10 E
Qian'an, Zhg. 89 45.00 N 124.01 E
Qian'an, Zhg. 98 39.59 N 118.40 E
Qiancaijiatun 104 41.14 N 121.38 E
Qiandiwu 105 39.16 N 116.38 E
Qiandong 100 23.41 N 116.55 E
Qiandun 106 31.16 N 121.00 E
Qianertaizi 104 42.04 N 122.42 E
Qianfang 100 28.32 N 116.13 E
Qian Gorlos 89 45.08 N 124.47 E
Qiangzilu 105 40.26 N 117.13 E
Qianhonghepu 104 41.23 N 123.07 E
Qianhuang 106 31.36 N 119.58 E
Qianji 100 33.55 N 118.56 E
Qianjiadian 89 43.42 N 122.35 E
Qianjiang, Zhg. 100 30.25 N 112.51 E
Qianjiang, Zhg. 102 23.37 N 109.00 E
Qianjian'gangzi 104 41.34 N 122.26 E
Qianjiangtai 104 41.46 N 122.03 E
Qianjiaqiao 106 30.53 N 121.31 E
Qianjiaying 105 39.35 N 118.21 E
Qianjiazhuang 106 32.16 N 120.17 E
Qianjing 106 31.33 N 121.15 E
Qianjinmiao 100 25.09 N 118.20 E
Qiankeng 106 30.43 N 119.47 E
Qiankoutou 105 39.42 N 117.01 E
Qianlijiazhuang 105 39.25 N 118.17 E
Qianluanshanzi 104 42.17 N 122.27 E
Qianmajiagushanzi 104 42.23 N 123.33 E
Qianmintun 104 41.49 N 123.15 E
Qianning 102 30.30 N 101.31 E
Qianpai 102 22.22 N 111.11 E
Qianqi 100 27.20 N 120.20 E
Qianqianjianglugou 104 41.59 N 120.58 E
Qiansandaoliangzi 104 42.06 N 120.44 E
Qianshahezi 104 41.46 N 123.01 E
Qianshan, Zhg. 100 30.38 N 116.33 E
Qianshan, Zhg. 106 31.06 N 120.24 E
Qian Shan ⋀ 104 40.52 N 123.25 E
Qianshuangshanzi 104 41.22 N 121.13 E
Qiansuo 100 28.44 N 121.27 E
Qiantang ≃ 106 30.23 N 120.33 E
Qiantangzhen 107 30.12 N 106.18 E
Qianwei, Zhg. 98 40.12 N 120.06 E
Qianwei, Zhg. 107 29.12 N 103.57 E
Qianxi, Zhg. 102 26.57 N 106.00 E
Qianxi, Zhg. 105 40.09 N 118.19 E
Qianxiatazi 104 42.23 N 123.53 E
Qianyamen 104 42.04 N 121.26 E
Qianyang 102 27.11 N 110.04 E
Qianyaopu 104 42.02 N 123.37 E
Qi'anzhen 106 32.11 N 121.03 E
Qianzhou 106 31.42 N 120.13 E
Qiaodun 100 27.29 N 120.18 E
Qiaoershan ⋀ 102 31.48 N 99.10 E
Qiaogou 100 32.26 N 115.45 E
Qiaohengjin 102 29.30 N 99.50 E
Qiaojia 102 26.57 N 102.52 E
Qiaojiang 269b 31.15 N 121.19 E
Qiaokou 100 25.55 N 113.10 E
Qiaolima 120 34.35 N 81.00 E
Qiaolin 100 31.57 N 118.32 E
Qiaomu 98 39.34 N 114.27 E
Qiaopurikebazha 85 38.48 N 76.19 E
Qiaoqi 106 31.49 N 120.18 E
Qiaoshe 100 28.48 N 115.58 E
Qiaosi 106 30.21 N 120.18 E
Qiaotou, Zhg. 100 33.05 N 112.46 E
Qiaotou, Zhg. 102 28.17 N 99.22 E
Qiaotou, Zhg. 104 41.13 N 123.44 E
Qiaotou, Zhg. 106 32.11 N 119.14 E
Qiaotou, Zhg. 107 29.18 N 104.39 E
Qiaotoucun 106 30.36 N 119.08 E
Qiaotouji 100 31.45 N 117.34 E
Qiaotoupu 106 30.33 N 118.50 E
Qiaotouyi 100 28.24 N 112.58 E
Qiaotouzhen 106 30.49 N 119.13 E
Qiaowan 102 40.36 N 96.55 E
Qiaowei 102 22.51 N 109.50 E
Qiaoxia 106 31.09 N 119.35 E
Qiaoxiajie 100 28.10 N 120.34 E
Qiaozhen 106 31.39 N 121.24 E
Qibao 106 31.09 N 121.20 E
Qibyā 132 31.59 N 35.01 E
Qichun 100 30.17 N 115.26 E
Qiddīsah Kātrīnā, Dayr al- (Monastery of Saint Catherine) ☸[1] 140 28.29 N 34.01 E
Qidong, Zhg. 102 26.44 N 112.04 E
Qidong, Zhg. 106 31.49 N 121.40 E
Qidu 100 30.16 N 117.46 E
Qiemo 120 38.08 N 85.32 E
Qiesanglinzi 104 41.42 N 123.30 E
Qieshikou 271a 39.59 N 116.24 E
Qiezixi 107 29.25 N 106.30 E
Qifosi 107 29.27 N 105.58 E
Qifṭ (Coptos) 140 26.00 N 32.49 E
Qigong 102 28.38 N 100.38 E
Qigongtai 104 41.50 N 123.08 E
Qihe (Yancheng) 98 36.48 N 116.44 E
Qiji 98 37.16 N 115.21 E
Qijiadian 89 46.48 N 125.36 E
Qijian 107 30.14 N 106.09 E
Qijiang 107 29.02 N 106.39 E
Qijiapuzi 104 40.54 N 122.31 E
Qijiawan 100 30.53 N 114.13 E
Qijiawopeng 104 41.02 N 121.26 E
Qijiazi 104 41.54 N 122.58 E
Qika 89 50.35 N 119.16 E
Qikou 98 38.35 N 117.31 E
Qila Abdullāh 120 30.43 N 66.38 E
Qila Dīdār Singh 123 32.08 N 74.01 E
Qilaguganni Shan ∧ 124 28.46 N 87.38 E
Qila Lādgasht 128 27.54 N 62.57 E
Qila Saifullāh 120 30.43 N 68.21 E
Qila Sobha Singh 123 32.14 N 74.46 E
Qilian 102 38.05 N 100.12 E
Qilian Shan ∧ 102 39.12 N 98.35 E
Qilian Shan ⋀ 102 39.06 N 98.40 E
Qili Hai ≡ 105 39.19 N 117.33 E
Qilihe, Zhg. 104 41.21 N 121.16 E
Qilihe, Zhg. 104 41.30 N 121.15 E
Qilihezi 104 40.56 N 121.02 E
Qiling 100 24.05 N 115.27 E
Qilingzicun 104 41.05 N 123.06 E
Qilinmen 106 32.04 N 118.55 E
Qilinzhen 106 31.56 N 121.21 E
Qiliping 100 31.27 N 114.39 E
Qiliqiao 106 31.35 N 120.48 E
Qilizhen, Zhg. 102 35.43 N 108.59 E
Qilizhen, Zhg. 106 32.19 N 121.05 E
Qilṭ, 'Ayn al- ⊤[4] 132 31.50 N 35.23 E
Qimafang 98 40.08 N 114.31 E
Qiman al-'Arūs 142 29.18 N 31.10 E
Qimen, Zhg. 100 29.52 N 117.42 E
Qimen, Zhg. 100 25.18 N 113.15 E
Qimoudi 105 39.35 N 115.32 E
Qimu Jiao › 98 37.46 N 120.12 E
Qin ≃, Zhg. 100 23.58 N 115.47 E
Qin ≃, Zhg. 100 26.16 N 115.52 E
Qin ≃, Zhg. 102 35.01 N 113.25 E
Qinā 140 26.10 N 32.43 E
Qinā, Wādī V, Miṣr 140 26.12 N 32.44 E
Qinā, Wādī V, Miṣr 142 29.39 N 31.53 E
Qincaigou 104 40.38 N 120.37 E
Qing ≃, Zhg. 98 42.26 N 123.50 E
Qing ≃, Zhg. 102 30.22 N 111.20 E
Qing'an 89 46.52 N 127.30 E
Qingbaikou 105 40.01 N 115.50 E
Qingcaoge 100 30.50 N 116.46 E
Qingcheng 98 37.12 N 117.40 E
Qingchengzi 104 40.44 N 123.36 E
Qingchuan 102 32.36 N 105.09 E
Qingcungang 106 30.56 N 121.34 E
Qingdao (Tsingtao) 98 36.06 N 120.19 E
Qingdian 105 39.51 N 117.22 E
Qingduizi, Zhg. 98 39.50 N 123.18 E
Qingduizi, Zhg. 104 41.28 N 121.53 E
Qingfeng 98 35.54 N 115.07 E
Qingfengtuo 98 40.59 N 116.04 E
Qingfu 102 28.29 N 104.35 E
Qinggang 89 46.43 N 126.07 E
Qingguang 105 39.11 N 117.02 E
Qingguji 98 34.45 N 115.47 E
Qinghai (Tsinghai) □[4] 90 36.00 N 96.00 E
Qinghai Hu ⊜ 102 36.50 N 100.20 E
Qinghai Nanshan ⋀ 102 37.06 N 99.05 E
Qinghe, Zhg. 86 46.36 N 90.39 E
Qinghe, Zhg. 98 40.02 N 122.35 E
Qinghe, Zhg. 104 42.32 N 124.09 E
Qinghe, Zhg. 105 40.01 N 116.20 E
Qinghecheng 104 41.28 N 124.15 E
Qinghechengzi 104 41.44 N 121.25 E
Qinghemen 104 41.45 N 121.25 E
Qinghezhen 98 37.16 N 117.39 E
Qinghu 100 28.40 N 118.34 E
Qinghua 100 29.24 N 117.46 E
Qinghuayuan 105 40.00 N 116.19 E
Qinghuazhen 100 32.55 N 112.19 E
Qingjian 102 37.10 N 110.00 E
Qingjiang, Zhg. 100 28.05 N 115.29 E
Qingjiang, Zhg. 100 28.16 N 121.06 E
Qingjiang, Zhg. 100 33.35 N 119.02 E
Qingjiang, Zhg. 107 29.17 N 105.34 E
Qingjujie 107 30.42 N 106.07 E
Qinglian 100 24.27 N 112.45 E
Qingliu 100 26.12 N 116.52 E
Qingliuzhen 107 29.56 N 105.19 E
Qinglong, Zhg. 98 40.24 N 118.54 E
Qinglong, Zhg. 100 25.28 N 114.28 E
Qinglong, Zhg. 102 25.50 N 105.10 E
Qinglong ≃, Zhg. 98 39.51 N 118.51 E
Qinglong ≃, Zhg. 105 39.35 N 117.46 E
Qinglongchang, Zhg. 107 28.50 N 106.31 E
Qinglongchang, Zhg. 107 29.51 N 105.40 E
Qinglongchang, Zhg. 107 30.20 N 103.51 E
Qinglonggang 106 31.51 N 121.15 E
Qinglongguan 107 30.25 N 104.48 E
Qinglongji 98 34.05 N 116.37 E
Qinglongwan ≃ 105 39.19 N 117.32 E
Qingmuguan 107 29.41 N 106.18 E
Qingningsi 106 31.16 N 121.33 E
Qingping, Zhg. 98 36.47 N 116.06 E
Qingping, Zhg. 107 29.00 N 106.21 E
Qingping, Zhg. 107 30.14 N 106.12 E
Qingpu 106 31.09 N 121.06 E
Qingshan, Zhg. 100 31.33 N 116.22 E
Qingshan, Zhg. 100 30.38 N 114.23 E
Qingshan, Zhg. 106 30.15 N 119.52 E
Qingshan, Zhg. 106 30.36 N 119.41 E
Qingshan, Zhg. 106 30.43 N 120.03 E
Qingshanpu 100 29.27 N 114.01 E
Qingshen 107 29.50 N 103.50 E
Qingshui, Zhg. 102 34.42 N 106.21 E
Qingshui, Zhg. 102 39.23 N 99.09 E
Qingshui, Zhg. 107 30.10 N 104.03 E
Qingshui ≃, Zhg. 102 37.30 N 105.30 E
Qingshui ≃, Zhg. 102 27.08 N 109.36 E
Qingshuihe 86 44.12 N 80.45 E
Qingshuijian 105 39.59 N 115.58 E
Qingshuilang Shan ⋀ 102 26.15 N 99.35 E
Qingshuixi 102 29.09 N 103.55 E
Qingtan 100 31.48 N 112.48 E
Qingtang, Zhg. 100 26.28 N 115.48 E
Qingtang, Zhg. 100 24.14 N 113.51 E
Qingtian 100 28.10 N 120.17 E
Qingtong 107 29.28 N 103.27 E
Qingtongxia 102 37.53 N 105.54 E
Qingtuosi 98 35.29 N 118.20 E
Qingtuozi, Zhg. 104 41.05 N 121.28 E
Qingtuozi, Zhg. 105 39.08 N 117.45 E
Qingxi, Zhg. 89 49.19 N 127.10 E
Qingxi, Zhg. 100 31.40 N 118.00 E
Qingxi, Zhg. 107 30.40 N 106.14 E
Qingxian 98 38.34 N 116.46 E
Qingxizhen 107 29.09 N 103.55 E
Qingyang, Zhg. 89 45.20 N 128.47 E
Qingyang, Zhg. 100 30.38 N 117.48 E
Qingyang, Zhg. 102 36.06 N 107.47 E
Qingyangzhen 106 31.46 N 120.15 E
Qingyi ≃ 107 29.34 N 103.42 E
Qingyuan, Zhg. 98 42.13 N 124.56 E
Qingyuan, Zhg. 100 27.38 N 119.04 E
Qingyuan, Zhg. 100 23.42 N 113.02 E
Qingyuan → Baoding, Zhg. 105 38.52 N 115.29 E
Qingyun (Xiejiaji) 98 37.52 N 117.21 E
Qingyunbao 104 42.34 N 123.50 E
Qingyundian 105 39.38 N 116.29 E
Qing Zang Gaoyuan ⋀[1] 12 33.00 N 92.00 E
Qingzhen, Zhg. 102 26.29 N 106.22 E
Qingzhen, Zhg. 106 30.45 N 120.30 E
Qingzhou 100 23.39 N 116.57 E
Qinhuai ≃ 106 32.01 N 118.50 E
Qinhuangdao (Chinwangtao) 98 39.56 N 119.36 E
Qinjia 89 46.47 N 127.00 E
Qinlan 100 32.37 N 119.08 E
Qin Ling (Tsinlingshan) ⋀ 102 34.00 N 108.00 E
Qinnan 100 33.16 N 119.55 E
Qinshui 102 35.41 N 112.11 E
Qintong 100 32.39 N 120.08 E
Qinxian 102 36.48 N 112.41 E
Qinyang 102 35.06 N 112.57 E
Qinyuan 102 36.30 N 112.15 E
Qinzhou 102 21.59 N 108.36 E
Qionghai (Jiaji) 110 19.20 N 110.30 E
Qionglai 107 30.25 N 103.27 E
Qionglaishan ⋀ 102 31.21 N 102.50 E
Qionglong Shan ∧ 106 31.15 N 120.25 E
Qiongzhong, Zhg. 90 19.02 N 109.49 E
Qiongzhong, Zhg. 110 19.04 N 109.48 E
Qiongzhou Haixia ⊔ 102 20.10 N 110.15 E
Qipandi 105 39.46 N 115.12 E
Qipanshan 98 42.05 N 117.30 E
Qiqian 89 52.12 N 120.49 E
Qiqihar (Tsitsihar) 89 47.19 N 123.55 E
Qira 120 37.00 N 80.47 E
Qir'awn, Buḥayrat al- ⊜[1] 132 33.34 N 35.42 E
Qırmızı Bazar 84 39.41 N 46.58 E
Qiryat 132 32.49 N 35.06 E
Qiryat 'Anavim 132 31.48 N 35.07 E
Qiryat Ata 132 32.48 N 35.06 E
Qiryat Bialik 132 32.50 N 35.05 E
Qiryat Gat 132 31.36 N 34.46 E
Qiryat Ḥayyim 132 32.49 N 35.04 E
Qiryat Mal'akhi 132 31.44 N 34.44 E
Qiryat Motzkin 132 32.50 N 35.04 E
Qiryat Ono 132 32.04 N 34.51 E
Qiryat Shemona 132 33.13 N 35.34 E
Qiryat Tiv'on 132 32.43 N 35.08 E
Qiryat Yam 132 32.51 N 35.04 E
Qirzah, Wādī V 146 30.56 N 14.31 E
Qiseqi Shan ∧ 89 48.37 N 122.32 E
Qishn 144 15.26 N 51.40 E
Qishon ≃ 132 32.49 N 35.02 E
Qishrān I 144 20.14 N 40.05 E
Qishudang 107 29.13 N 104.39 E
Qishuyan 106 31.44 N 120.04 E
Qiṣrāyā 130 34.53 N 36.26 E
Qitai 86 44.01 N 89.28 E
Qitaihe 89 45.48 N 130.53 E
Qitaizi 104 41.33 N 122.11 E
Qitamu 89 44.22 N 126.20 E
Qitangzhen 107 29.47 N 106.16 E
Qiting 100 31.02 N 114.44 E
Qitingqiao 106 31.26 N 119.52 E
Qitou 100 24.54 N 117.29 E
Qiubei 102 24.07 N 104.12 E
Qiuchang 107 28.59 N 104.42 E
Qiuji 100 33.51 N 118.01 E
Qiujia 106 31.49 N 121.51 E
Qiujiatun 104 41.20 N 121.00 E
Qiujin 100 29.10 N 115.42 E
Qiuxi ≃ 107 29.58 N 104.40 E
Qiuxizhen 107 29.56 N 104.41 E
Qiweigang 106 32.01 N 119.59 E
Qixia 98 37.17 N 120.48 E
Qixian (Zhaoge), Zhg. 98 35.38 N 114.11 E
Qixian, Zhg. 100 34.33 N 114.47 E
Qixianji 100 33.28 N 117.01 E
Qixiashan 106 32.10 N 118.57 E
Qi Xia Si ☸[1] 106 32.12 N 118.58 E
Qixingqiao 106 30.49 N 120.51 E
Qiyahe 89 53.02 N 120.33 E
Qiyang 102 26.29 N 111.43 E
Qiyi 100 32.30 N 112.54 E
Qiying 102 36.38 N 106.25 E
Qizhou 100 30.04 N 115.20 E
Qızılağac körfäzi ⊂ 84 39.09 N 49.03 E
Qizil Jilga 120 35.21 N 78.52 E
Qizil Langar 120 35.13 N 77.59 E
Qnadsa 148 31.48 N 2.26 W
Qobustan 84 40.06 N 49.24 E
Qogir Feng (K2) ∧ 123 35.53 N 76.30 E
Qolhak ⟜[8] 267d 35.47 N 51.26 E
Qom 128 34.39 N 50.54 E
Qom ≃ 128 34.48 N 51.02 E
Qomolangma Feng → Everest, Mount ∧ 124 27.59 N 86.56 E
Qomsheh 128 32.01 N 51.52 E
Qonaqkänd 84 41.04 N 48.37 E
Qondūz ≃ 120 37.00 N 68.16 E
Qorveh 128 35.10 N 47.48 E
Qoṭbābād 128 28.42 N 53.34 E
Qoṭūr 128 38.28 N 44.25 E
Qu ≃, Zhg. 100 29.12 N 119.27 E
Qu ≃, Zhg. 102 30.01 N 106.24 E
Quabbin Reservoir ⊜[1] 207 42.22 N 72.18 W
Quaddick Reservoir ⊜[1] 207 41.57 N 71.49 W
Quadra Island I 182 50.08 N 125.16 W
Quadraro ⟜[8] 267a 41.51 N 12.33 E
Quadrath-Ichendorf 56 50.56 N 6.41 E
Quadros, Lagoa dos ⊂ 252 29.42 S 50.05 W
Quāidābād 123 32.20 N 71.52 E
Quail Lake ⊜[1] 228 34.47 N 118.45 W


**ENGLISH**

Name / Page / Lat.°′ / Long.°′


Quail Valley 228 33.43 N 117.15 W
Quairading 162 32.01 S 117.25 E
Quakake 210 40.51 N 76.02 W
Quakenbrück 52 52.40 N 7.57 E
Quaker Hill, Ct., U.S. 207 41.22 N 72.06 W
Quaker Hill, N.Y., U.S. 210 41.35 N 73.33 W
Quakers Hill 170 33.43 S 150.53 E
Quakers Knob ∧[2] 214 40.21 N 80.24 W
Quaker Street 210 42.44 N 74.11 W
Quakertown, N.J., U.S. 210 40.33 N 74.56 W
Quakertown, Pa., U.S. 208 40.26 N 75.20 W
Qualicum Beach 182 49.21 N 124.27 W
Quambatook 166 35.51 S 143.31 E
Quanah 196 34.17 N 99.44 W
Quanbao Shan ∧ 102 34.09 N 111.29 E
Quangang 100 28.10 N 115.34 E
Quang Ngai 110 15.07 N 108.48 E
Quang Trach 110 17.45 N 106.27 E
Quanjiang 100 27.43 N 113.59 E
Quanjiao 100 32.06 N 118.16 E
Quan Long → Ca Mau 110 9.11 N 105.08 E
Quanmian 104 42.02 N 122.13 E
Quannan 100 24.44 N 114.31 E
Quannapowitt, Lake ⊜ 283 42.31 N 71.05 W
Quanshang 100 26.25 N 116.55 E
Quanshengpu 104 41.59 N 123.22 E
Quanshui 104 41.18 N 124.11 E
Quanshuitou 105 40.24 N 116.39 E
Quantico, Md., U.S. 208 38.22 N 75.44 W
Quantico, Va., U.S. 208 38.31 N 77.17 W
Quantico Marine Corps Air Station ■ 208 38.31 N 77.19 W
Quantock Hills ⋀[2] 42 51.07 N 3.10 W
Quantou 89 42.52 N 124.07 E
Quanxishi 100 26.51 N 112.45 E
Quanyanhezi 104 40.52 N 123.26 E
Quanzhou (Chuanchou) 100 24.54 N 118.35 E
Quanzhou Gang ⊂ 100 24.52 N 118.37 E
Qu'Appelle 184 50.33 N 103.52 W
Qu'Appelle ≃ 184 50.25 N 101.20 W
Qu'Appelle Dam ⟜[6] 184 51.00 N 106.25 W
Quaraí 252 30.23 S 56.27 W
Quaraí ≃ 252 30.12 S 57.36 W
Quaregnon 50 50.26 N 3.51 E
Quarles, Pegunungan ⋀ 112 2.55 S 119.30 E
Quarrata 66 43.51 N 10.58 E
Quarré-les-Tombes 50 47.22 N 3.59 E
Quarry 222 30.18 N 96.30 W
Quarry Heights 276 41.04 N 73.45 W
Quarryville, Ct., U.S. 207 41.51 N 72.25 W
Quarryville, Pa., U.S. 208 39.53 N 76.09 W
Quartu Sant'Elena 71 39.14 N 9.11 E
Quartz Hill 228 34.39 N 118.13 W
Quartz Lake ⊜ 176 70.55 N 80.33 W
Quartz Mountain ∧ 202 43.10 N 122.40 W
Quartzsite 200 33.39 N 114.13 W
Quatis 256 22.25 S 44.16 W
Quatre, Isle à I 241h 12.57 N 61.15 W
Quatsino Sound ⊔ 182 50.25 N 127.55 W
Quba 84 41.22 N 48.31 E
Qubadlı 84 39.22 N 46.34 E
Qubei 124 28.18 N 86.53 E
Qūchān 128 37.06 N 58.30 E
Quchijie 102 28.03 N 111.53 E
Qudaym 130 35.03 N 38.25 E
Qudi 98 37.06 N 117.15 E
Qudsia Gardens ♦ 272a 28.40 N 77.13 E
Quê ≃ 152 14.45 S 14.45 E
Queanbeyan 171b 35.21 S 149.14 E
Queanbeyan ≃ 171b 35.20 S 149.14 E
Québec 206 46.49 N 71.14 W
Québec □[6] 206 46.50 N 71.20 W
Québec □[4] 176 52.00 N 72.00 W
Quebec Airport ⊠ 206 46.47 N 71.23 W
Quebec House ⊥ 260 51.14 N 0.05 E
Quebeck 194 35.49 N 85.34 W
Quebra-Anzol ≃ 255 19.09 S 47.38 W
Quebra-Cangalha, Serra do ⋀ 256 22.55 S 45.10 W
Quebracho 252 31.57 S 57.53 W
Quebrada Seca 240m 18.14 N 65.40 W
Quebradillas 240m 18.29 N 66.56 W
Quebrangulo 250 9.20 S 36.29 W
Quecholac 234 18.57 N 97.40 W
Quechultenango 234 17.25 N 99.13 W
Quecreek 214 40.06 N 79.05 W
Quedal, Cabo › 254 40.59 S 73.59 W
Quedas 156 19.30 S 33.29 E
Quedlinburg 54 51.48 N 11.09 E
Queen 214 40.16 N 78.31 W
Queen Alexandra Range ⋀ 9 84.00 S 168.00 E
Queen Alia International Airport ⊠ 132 31.44 N 35.59 E
Queen Anne 208 38.55 N 75.57 W
Queen Anne Creek ≃ 285 40.08 N 74.53 W
Queen Annes □[6] 208 39.03 N 76.04 W
Queen Bess, Mount ∧ 182 51.16 N 124.34 W
Queenborough 42 51.26 N 0.45 E
Queen Charlotte 182 53.16 N 132.05 W
Queen Charlotte Bay ⊂ 254 51.50 S 60.40 W
Queen Charlotte Islands II 182 53.00 N 132.00 W
Queen Charlotte Mountains ⋀ 182 53.00 N 132.00 W
Queen Charlotte Sound ⊔ 182 51.30 N 129.30 W
Queen Charlotte Strait ⊔ 182 50.50 N 127.25 W
Queen City, Mo., U.S. 194 40.24 N 92.34 W
Queen City, Tx., U.S. 194 33.08 N 94.09 W
Queen Elizabeth II Reservoir ⊜[1] 260 51.23 N 0.24 W
Queen Elizabeth Islands II 16 78.00 N 95.00 W
Queen Fabiola Mountains ⋀ 9 71.30 S 35.40 E
Queen Mary ☸ 280 33.45 N 118.12 W
Queen Mary Coast ≐[2] 9 67.00 S 96.00 E
Queen Mary Reservoir ⊜[1] 260 51.25 N 0.28 W
Queen Maud Gulf ⊂ 176 68.25 N 102.30 W
Queen Maud Land ⟜[1] 9 72.30 S 12.00 E
Queen Maud Mountains ⋀ 9 86.00 S 160.00 W
Queens □[6] 210 40.34 N 73.52 W
Queensbury 44 53.46 N 1.50 W
Queens Channel ⊔, Austl. 164 14.46 S 129.24 E
Queens Channel ⊔, N.T., Can. 176 76.11 N 96.00 W
Queenscliff 169 38.16 S 144.40 E
Queensferry, Scot., U.K. 46 55.59 N 3.25 W
Queensferry, Wales, U.K. 44 53.12 N 3.01 W
Queensland □[3] 160 22.00 S 145.00 E
Queensland Plateau ✢[3] 14 17.00 S 150.00 E
Queens Park ♦, Austl. 274a 33.54 S 151.16 E
Queens Park ♦, On., Can. 275b 43.40 N 79.24 W
Queens Park ♦, Eng., U.K. 262 53.35 N 2.27 W
Queen's Park ♦, Eng., U.K. 262 53.44 N 2.28 W
Queensport 186 45.20 N 61.16 W


**DEUTSCH**

Name / Seite / Breite°′ / Länge°′ E = Ost


Queens Sound ⊔ 182 51.55 N 128.11 W
Queenston 284a 43.10 N 79.03 W
Queenston Chippawa Power Canal ≊ 284a 43.08 N 79.03 W
Queenstown, Austl. 166 42.05 S 145.33 E
Queenstown, Guy. 246 7.12 N 58.29 W
Queenstown → Cobh, Ire. 48 51.51 N 8.17 W
Queenstown, N.Z. 172 45.02 S 168.40 E
Queenstown, S. Afr. 158 31.52 S 26.52 E
Queenstown, Md., U.S. 208 38.59 N 76.09 W
Queensville 212 44.08 N 79.28 W
Queen Victoria Park ♦ 284a 43.05 N 79.05 W
Que'er'ao I 100 28.48 N 121.51 E
Queerhe 104 40.57 N 121.35 E
Queets 224 47.32 N 124.19 W
Queets ≃ 224 47.33 N 124.21 W
Queguay Grande ≃ 252 32.09 S 58.09 W
Queich ≃ 56 49.14 N 8.23 E
Queige 62 45.43 N 6.28 E
Queimada, Ilha I 250 0.10 S 50.50 W
Queimada Nova 250 8.35 S 41.25 W
Queimadas 250 10.58 S 39.38 W
Queimados 256 22.42 S 43.34 W
Queiros, Cap › 175f 14.55 S 167.01 E
Quela 152 9.16 S 17.02 E
Quelimane 156 17.53 S 36.51 E
Quelizhen 106 30.54 N 121.26 E
Quelle 52 52.00 N 8.29 E
Quellendorf 54 51.45 N 12.07 E
Quellón 254 43.07 S 73.37 W
Quelo 152 6.27 S 12.48 E
Quelpart Island → Cheju-do I 90 33.20 N 126.30 E
Queluz → Conselheiro Lafaiete, Bra. 255 20.40 S 43.48 W
Queluz, Bra. 256 22.32 S 44.46 W
Queluz, Port. 266c 38.45 N 9.15 W
Quemado, N.M., U.S. 200 34.20 N 108.29 W
Quemado, Tx., U.S. 196 28.56 N 100.38 W
Quemado, Punta de › 240p 20.13 N 74.08 W
Quemado de Güines 240p 22.48 N 80.15 W
Quemahoning Reservoir ⊜[1] 214 40.09 N 78.57 W
Quembo ≃ 152 14.57 S 20.22 E
Quemchi 254 42.09 S 73.29 W
Quemoy → Chinmen Tao I 100 24.27 N 118.23 E
Quemú Quemú 252 36.03 S 63.33 W
Quend 50 50.19 N 1.38 E
Quend Plage 50 50.19 N 1.33 E
Queñi, Nevado de ∧ 254 40.14 S 71.49 W
Quenouilles, Lac aux ⊜ 206 46.10 N 74.23 W
Quentin 208 40.17 N 76.26 W
Quepos 236 9.27 N 84.09 W
Quepos, Punta › 236 9.23 N 84.10 W
Quequén 252 38.32 S 58.42 W
Querary ≃ 246 1.04 N 69.51 W
Quercianella 66 43.27 N 10.22 E
Quercy □[9] 32 44.30 N 1.25 E
Querecotillo 248 4.50 S 80.40 W
Querenburg ⟜[8] 263 51.27 N 7.16 E
Querenhorst 54 52.20 N 10.57 E
Querétaro 234 20.36 N 100.23 W
Querétaro □[3] 234 21.00 N 99.55 W
Querfurt 54 51.23 N 11.36 E
Quero 64 45.55 N 11.56 E
Querobabi 232 30.03 N 111.01 W
Quesada, C.R. 236 10.19 N 84.26 W
Quesada, Esp. 34 37.51 N 3.04 W
Queset Brook ≃ 283 42.02 N 71.04 W
Queshan 100 32.48 N 114.01 E
Quesnel 182 52.59 N 122.30 W
Quesnel ≃ 182 53.00 N 122.30 W
Quesnel Lake ⊜ 182 52.32 N 121.05 W
Quesnoy 50 50.43 N 3.00 E
Que Son 110 15.40 N 108.14 E
Questa 200 36.42 N 105.35 W
Questembert 32 47.40 N 2.27 W
Quetico Lake ⊜ 190 48.34 N 91.52 W
Quetico Provincial Park ♦ 190 48.30 N 91.30 W
Quetta 120 30.12 N 67.00 E
Quettehou 32 49.36 N 1.18 W
Quetzala ≃ 234 16.35 N 98.30 W
Quetzaltenango 236 14.50 N 91.31 W
Quetzaltenango □[5] 236 14.45 N 91.40 W
Quevedo 246 1.02 S 79.29 W
Quezaltepeque, El Sal. 236 13.50 N 89.17 W
Quezaltepeque, Guat. 236 14.38 N 89.27 W
Quezon, Pil. 116 15.34 N 120.49 E
Quezon, Pil. 116 14.01 N 122.11 E
Quezon □[4] 116 13.58 N 122.02 E
Quezon City 116 14.38 N 121.03 E
Quezon Memorial ⊥ 269f 14.39 N 121.03 E
Qufu 98 35.36 N 117.02 E
Qugou, Zhg. 102 36.10 N 100.56 E
Qugou, Zhg. 105 39.17 N 116.15 E
Quibala 152 10.46 S 14.59 E
Quibaxi 152 8.29 S 14.36 E
Quibdó 246 5.42 N 76.40 W
Quiberon 32 47.29 N 3.07 W
Quiberville 50 49.54 N 0.55 E
Quíbor 246 9.56 N 69.37 W
Quibray Bay ⊂ 274a 34.01 S 151.11 E
Quibú ≃ 286b 23.05 N 82.27 W
Quiçama, Parque Nacional de ♦ 152 9.45 S 13.30 E
Qui Chau 110 19.33 N 105.06 E
Quiches 248 8.25 S 77.27 W
Quickborn 52 53.44 N 9.53 E
Quiculungo 152 8.31 S 15.19 E
Quidapil Point › 116 6.49 N 123.57 E
Quidnessett 207 41.37 N 71.27 W
Quidnick 207 41.41 N 71.32 W
Quiechapa ≃ 234 16.37 N 95.59 W
Quien Sabe Creek ≃ 226 36.43 N 121.09 W
Quiévrain 50 50.24 N 3.41 E
Quiévy 50 50.10 N 3.25 E
Quiindy 252 25.58 S 57.16 W
Quila 232 24.23 N 107.13 W
Quilalí 236 13.34 N 86.02 W
Quilates, Cap › 34 35.20 N 3.45 W
Quilcene 224 47.49 N 122.52 W
Quilenda 152 10.33 S 14.22 E
Quilengues 152 14.05 S 14.04 E
Quileute Indian Reservation ⟜[4] 224 47.55 N 124.38 W
Quilicura 286e 33.22 S 70.45 W
Quilimarí 252 32.07 S 71.30 W
Quilino 252 30.12 S 64.29 W
Quillabamba 248 12.49 S 72.43 W
Quillacollo 248 17.26 S 66.17 W
Quillagua 248 21.39 S 69.33 W
Quillan 32 42.52 N 2.11 E
Quillebeuf-sur-Seine 50 49.29 N 0.31 E
Quill Lake 184 52.05 N 104.15 W
Quillota 252 32.53 S 71.16 W
Quilmes 258 34.44 S 58.16 W
Quilmes □[5] 288 34.44 S 58.16 W
Quilmes, Aeródromo ⊠ 288 34.42 S 58.15 W
Quilombo ≃ 256 23.52 S 46.21 W
Quilon 122 8.53 N 76.36 E
Quilotosa Wash V 200 32.56 N 112.46 W
Quilpie 166 26.37 S 144.15 E
Quilpué 252 33.03 S 71.27 W
Quilty 48 52.47 N 9.26 W
Quimarí, Alto de ∧ 246 8.07 N 76.23 W
Quimbango 152 11.01 S 17.26 E
Quimbaya 246 4.38 N 75.47 W
Quimbele 152 6.28 S 16.13 E
Quimbo 152 13.59 S 16.05 E
Quimbonge 152 8.36 S 18.30 E
Quimbumbe 152 7.50 S 14.03 E


**Symbols** in the index entries represent the broad categories identified in the key at the right. Symbols with superior numbers (⋀[1]) identify subcategories (see complete key on page *I · 1).*

**Symbole** im Register stellen die rechts im Schlüssel erklärten Kategorien dar. Symbole mit hochgestellten Ziffern (⋀[1]) bezeichnen Unterabteilungen einer Kategorie (vgl. vollständiger Schlüssel auf Seite *I · 1).*

**Los símbolos** incluídos en el texto del índice representan las grandes categorías identificadas con la clave a la derecha. Los símbolos con numeros en su parte superior (⋀[1]) identifican las subcategorías (véase la clave completa en la página *I · 1).*

**Les symboles** de l'index représentent les catégories indiquées dans la légende à droite. Les symboles suivis d'un indice (⋀[1]) représentent des sous-catégories (voir légende complète à la page *I · 1).*

**Os símbolos** incluídos no texto do índice representam as grandes categorias identificadas com a chave à direita. Os símbolos com números em sua parte superior (⋀[1]) identificam as subcategorias (veja-se a chave completa à página *I · 1).*

| | English | Deutsch | Español | Français | Português |
|---|---|---|---|---|---|
| ∧ | Mountain | Berg | Montaña | Montagne | Montanha |
| ⋀ | Mountains | Gebirge | Montañas | Montagnes | Montanhas |
| )( | Pass | Paß | Paso | Col | Passo |
| V | Valley, Canyon | Tal, Cañon | Valle, Cañón | Vallée, Canyon | Vale, Canhão |
| ≍ | Plain | Ebene | Llano | Plaine | Planície |
| › | Cape | Kap | Cabo | Cap | Cabo |
| I | Island | Insel | Isla | Île | Ilha |
| II | Islands | Inseln | Islas | Îles | Ilhas |
| ✢ | Other Topographic Features | Andere Topographische Objekte | Otros Elementos Topográficos | Autres données topographiques | Outros acidentes topográficos |

**ESPAÑOL**

| Nombre | Página | Lat.°′ | Long.°′ W = Oeste |
|---|---|---|---|
| Quimby | 198 | 42.37 N | 95.38 W |
| Quime | 248 | 17.02 S | 67.15 W |
| Quimichis | 234 | 22.21 N | 105.32 W |
| Quimilí | 252 | 27.38 S | 62.25 W |
| Quimper | 32 | 48.00 N | 4.06 W |
| Quimperlé | 32 | 47.52 N | 3.33 W |
| Quinalasag Island I | 116 | 13.56 N | 123.38 E |
| Quinault | 224 | 47.28 N | 123.50 W |
| Quinault ≃ | 224 | 47.23 N | 124.18 W |
| Quinault, Lake ⊜ | 224 | 47.28 N | 123.52 W |
| Quinault, North Fork ≃ | 224 | 47.32 N | 123.40 W |
| Quinault Indian Reservation ◆[4] | 224 | 47.24 N | 124.10 W |
| Quinby Inlet ⊂ | 208 | 37.28 N | 75.40 W |
| Quincampoix | 50 | 49.32 N | 1.11 E |
| Quince Mil | 248 | 13.16 S | 70.38 W |
| Quinches | 248 | 12.13 S | 76.05 W |
| Quincy, Ca., U.S. | 204 | 39.56 N | 120.56 W |
| Quincy, Fl., U.S. | 192 | 30.35 N | 84.35 W |
| Quincy, Il., U.S. | 219 | 39.56 N | 91.24 W |
| Quincy, Ky., U.S. | 218 | 38.37 N | 83.07 W |
| Quincy, Ma., U.S. | 207 | 42.15 N | 71.00 W |
| Quincy, Mi., U.S. | 216 | 41.56 N | 84.53 W |
| Quincy, Oh., U.S. | 216 | 40.17 N | 83.58 W |
| Quincy, Or., U.S. | 224 | 46.08 N | 123.09 W |
| Quincy, Pa., U.S. | 208 | 39.48 N | 77.35 W |
| Quincy, Wa., U.S. | 202 | 47.14 N | 119.51 W |
| Quincy Bay ⊂ | 283 | 42.17 N | 70.58 W |
| Quincy-sous-Sénart | 261 | 48.40 N | 2.33 E |
| Quincy-Voisins | 261 | 48.54 N | 2.53 E |
| Quindanning | 168a | 33.03 S | 116.34 E |
| Quindío □[5] | 246 | 4.30 N | 75.40 W |
| Quinebaug | 207 | 42.01 N | 71.57 W |
| Quinebaug ≃ | 207 | 41.33 N | 72.03 W |
| Quines | 252 | 32.13 S | 65.48 W |
| Quinga | 154 | 15.49 S | 40.15 E |
| Quingey | 58 | 47.06 N | 5.53 E |
| Quingyi ≃ | 100 | 31.12 N | 118.29 E |
| Quinhagak | 180 | 59.45 N | 161.43 W |
| Qui Nhon | 110 | 13.46 N | 109.14 E |
| Quiniluban Islands II | 116 | 11.27 N | 120.48 E |
| Quinjenje | 152 | 12.49 S | 14.55 E |
| Quinlan | 222 | 32.55 N | 96.08 W |
| Quinn ≃ | 204 | 40.52 N | 119.03 W |
| Quiñones, Arroyo de los ≃ | 266a | 40.33 N | 3.34 W |
| Quinson | 62 | 43.42 N | 6.02 E |
| Quinta da Boa Vista ♠ | 287a | 22.54 S | 43.15 W |
| Quintanar de la Orden | 34 | 39.34 N | 3.03 W |
| Quintana Roo □[3] | 232 | 19.40 N | 88.30 W |
| Quinta Normal | 286e | 33.27 S | 70.42 W |
| Quinta Normal de Agricultura ʊ[2] | 286e | 33.27 S | 70.42 W |
| Quinte, Bay of ⊂ | 212 | 44.07 N | 77.15 W |
| Quinter | 198 | 39.04 N | 100.13 W |
| Quintero | 252 | 32.47 S | 71.32 W |
| Quintette Mountain ∧ | 182 | 54.52 N | 120.53 W |
| Quintin | 32 | 48.24 N | 2.55 W |
| Quintino Sella, Canale ≊ | 266b | 45.29 N | 8.38 E |
| Quinto | 34 | 41.25 N | 0.29 W |
| Quinto ≃ | 252 | 34.14 S | 64.10 W |
| Quinto Creek ≃ | 226 | 37.11 N | 121.02 W |
| Quinto de Noviembre, Presa ◆[6] | 236 | 13.59 N | 88.44 W |
| Quinton, Sk., Can. | 184 | 51.23 N | 104.24 W |
| Quinton, N.J., U.S. | 208 | 39.32 N | 75.24 W |
| Quinton, Ok., U.S. | 196 | 35.07 N | 95.22 W |
| Quinto Romano ◆[8] | 266b | 45.29 N | 9.05 E |
| Quinzano d'Oglio | 64 | 45.19 N | 10.00 E |
| Quinzáu | 152 | 6.51 S | 12.46 E |
| Quinze, Lac des ⊜ | 190 | 47.35 N | 79.05 W |
| Quionga | 154 | 10.37 S | 40.30 E |
| Quipapá | 250 | 8.50 S | 36.02 W |
| Quipeio | 152 | 12.26 S | 15.30 E |
| Quipemba | 152 | 7.12 S | 15.06 E |
| Quipit ≃ | 116 | 8.04 N | 122.29 E |
| Quipungo | 152 | 14.51 S | 14.30 E |
| Quiquive ≃ | 248 | 14.39 S | 67.38 W |
| Quirauk Mountain ∧ | 208 | 39.42 N | 77.31 W |
| Quiriguá ⊥ | 236 | 15.17 N | 89.04 W |
| Quirihue | 252 | 36.17 S | 72.32 W |
| Quirima | 152 | 10.48 S | 18.09 E |
| Quirimba, Ilha I | 154 | 12.20 S | 40.36 E |
| Quirimbo | 152 | 10.36 S | 14.12 E |
| Quirindi | 166 | 31.31 S | 150.41 E |
| Quirino □[4] | 116 | 16.25 N | 121.35 E |
| Quirinópolis | 255 | 18.32 S | 50.30 W |
| Quiriquire | 246 | 9.59 N | 63.13 W |
| Quiriri ≃ | 152 | 15.13 S | 18.47 E |
| Quiririm | 256 | 23.02 S | 45.38 W |
| Quirke Lake ⊜ | 190 | 46.28 N | 82.33 W |
| Quiroga, Esp. | 34 | 42.29 N | 7.16 W |
| Quiroga, Méx. | 234 | 19.40 N | 101.32 W |
| Quirós | 252 | 28.47 S | 65.07 W |
| Quirpon Island I | 186 | 51.35 N | 55.25 W |
| Quirra, Salto di ◆[1] | 71 | 39.35 N | 9.33 E |
| Quissac | 62 | 43.55 N | 4.00 E |
| Quissanga | 154 | 12.25 S | 40.29 E |
| Quissico | 156 | 24.42 S | 34.44 E |
| Quissongo | 152 | 10.01 S | 15.07 E |
| Quistello | 64 | 45.00 N | 10.59 E |
| Quitapa | 152 | 10.23 S | 18.14 E |
| Quitaque | 196 | 34.22 N | 101.04 W |
| Quitasueño ✣[4] | 236 | 14.20 N | 81.15 W |
| Quiterajo | 154 | 11.48 S | 40.25 E |
| Quitilipi | 252 | 26.52 S | 60.13 W |
| Quitman, Ga., U.S. | 192 | 30.47 N | 83.33 W |
| Quitman, Ms., U.S. | 194 | 32.02 N | 88.43 W |
| Quitman, Tx., U.S. | 222 | 32.47 N | 95.27 W |
| Quitman, Lake ⊜[1] | 222 | 32.52 N | 95.27 W |
| Quito | 246 | 0.13 S | 78.30 W |
| Quitzdorf, Speicherbecken ⊜[1] | 54 | 51.17 N | 14.45 E |
| Quivilla | 248 | 9.32 S | 76.41 W |
| Quixadá | 250 | 4.58 S | 39.01 W |
| Quixeramobim | 250 | 5.12 S | 39.17 W |
| Quixeré | 250 | 5.05 S | 37.59 W |
| Quixico | 152 | 7.59 S | 14.25 E |
| Quixinge | 152 | 9.52 S | 14.23 E |
| Quixito ≃ | 246 | 4.29 S | 70.18 W |
| Quizenga | 152 | 9.21 S | 15.28 E |
| Qujiadian | 89 | 43.13 N | 123.53 E |
| Qujiang, Zhg. | 100 | 28.15 N | 115.45 E |
| Qujiang, Zhg. | 100 | 24.48 N | 113.17 E |
| Qujiang, Zhg. | 100 | 24.41 N | 113.35 E |
| Qujing | 102 | 25.32 N | 103.41 E |
| Qujiu | 102 | 22.28 N | 107.40 E |
| Qukou | 105 | 39.46 N | 117.07 E |
| Qulay'ah, Ra's al- › | 128 | 28.53 N | 48.18 E |
| Qulin | 194 | 36.35 N | 90.14 W |
| Qulubbā | 142 | 27.45 N | 30.50 E |
| Qulūd, Jabal ∧[2] | 140 | 11.41 N | 29.31 E |
| Qulūṣanā | 142 | 28.21 N | 30.44 E |
| Qulzum, Baḥr al- ⊂ | 142 | 29.55 N | 32.31 E |
| Qumar ≃, Zhg. | 90 | 34.42 N | 94.50 E |
| Qumar ≃, Zhg. | 120 | 34.39 N | 95.00 E |
| Qumarlêb | 102 | 34.35 N | 95.27 E |
| Qumbu | 158 | 31.10 S | 28.48 E |
| Qumrān, Khirbat ⊥ | 132 | 31.44 N | 35.27 E |
| Qunayfidhah, Nafūd ⍊[8] | 128 | 24.45 N | 45.30 E |
| Qunbush Al-Ḥamrā' | 142 | 29.00 N | 30.59 E |
| Qungtag | 120 | 29.59 N | 87.33 E |
| Qunshen'guan | 105 | 39.49 N | 117.59 E |
| Quobba, Point › | 162 | 24.23 S | 113.24 E |
| Quoich ≃ | 176 | 64.00 N | 93.30 W |
| Quoich, Loch ⊜ | 46 | 57.04 N | 5.17 W |
| Quoile ≃ | 48 | 54.21 N | 5.42 W |
| Quoin Point › | 158 | 34.46 S | 19.37 E |
| Quonochontaug | 207 | 41.21 N | 71.43 W |
| Quorn | 166 | 32.21 S | 138.03 E |
| Quorndon | 42 | 52.45 N | 1.09 W |
| Quoxo ≃ | 156 | 22.16 S | 24.02 E |
| Qurayyah, Wādī V | 132 | 30.26 N | 34.01 E |
| Qurayyāt | 128 | 23.17 N | 58.55 E |

**FRANÇAIS**

| Nom | Page | Lat.°′ | Long.°′ W = Ouest |
|---|---|---|---|
| Qurdūd | 140 | 10.17 N | 29.56 E |
| Qurrāṣah | 140 | 14.38 N | 32.12 E |
| Qurūn Harhash ∧[2] | 142 | 28.09 N | 31.42 E |
| Qūṣ | 140 | 25.55 N | 32.45 E |
| Qusar | 84 | 41.25 N | 48.26 E |
| Quṣayr ad-Daffah ⊥ | 146 | 30.20 N | 23.57 E |
| Qūshchī | 128 | 37.59 N | 45.03 E |
| Qushui | 107 | 30.41 N | 106.02 E |
| Qutang | 100 | 32.30 N | 120.21 E |
| Qutbapur ◆[8] | 272a | 28.35 N | 77.01 E |
| Qutb Minar ʊ[1] | 272a | 28.32 N | 77.11 E |
| Qutdligssat | 176 | 70.04 N | 53.01 W |
| Quthing | 158 | 30.30 S | 27.36 E |
| Quṭūr | 142 | 30.59 N | 30.57 E |
| Quwaysinā | 142 | 30.34 N | 31.09 E |
| Quxi, Zhg. | 100 | 28.00 N | 120.31 E |
| Quxi, Zhg. | 100 | 23.36 N | 116.26 E |
| Quxia | 106 | 32.06 N | 120.09 E |
| Quxian, Zhg. | 100 | 28.58 N | 118.52 E |
| Quxian, Zhg. | 102 | 30.51 N | 106.59 E |
| Quxingji | 98 | 34.52 N | 114.39 E |
| Quxiong | 102 | 31.09 N | 96.00 E |
| Qüxü | 120 | 29.22 N | 90.43 E |
| Quyang | 98 | 38.34 N | 114.42 E |
| Qūyjāq-e-Bālā | 84 | 39.16 N | 47.07 E |
| Quyon | 188 | 45.31 N | 76.14 W |
| Quyquyó | 252 | 26.14 S | 57.01 W |
| Quzaymah, Jabal ∧ | 132 | 30.34 N | 36.21 E |
| Quzhou | 98 | 36.46 N | 114.57 E |
| Quzong | 102 | 30.08 N | 96.00 E |
| **R** | | | |
| Råå | 41 | 56.00 N | 12.44 E |
| Raab → Győr, Magy. | 30 | 47.42 N | 17.38 E |
| Raab, Öst. | 60 | 48.21 N | 13.39 E |
| Raab (Rába) ≃ | 30 | 47.42 N | 17.38 E |
| Raabs an der Thaya | 61 | 48.51 N | 15.30 E |
| Raadt ◆[8] | 263 | 51.24 N | 6.56 E |
| Raahe | 26 | 64.41 N | 24.29 E |
| Rääkkylä | 26 | 62.19 N | 29.37 E |
| Raalte | 52 | 52.24 N | 6.16 E |
| Raamsdonksveer | 52 | 51.42 N | 4.56 E |
| Ra'anana | 132 | 32.11 N | 34.53 E |
| Raas, Pulau I | 115a | 7.09 S | 114.32 E |
| Raasay I | 46 | 57.23 N | 6.04 W |
| Raasay, Sound of ⊌ | 46 | 57.27 N | 6.06 W |
| Raasdorf | 264b | 48.15 N | 16.34 E |
| Raasiku | 76 | 59.22 N | 25.11 E |
| Rab | 36 | 44.46 N | 14.46 E |
| Rab, Otok I | 36 | 44.47 N | 14.45 E |
| Raba | 115b | 8.27 S | 118.46 E |
| Rába (Raab) ≃, Europe | 30 | 47.42 N | 17.38 E |
| Raba ≃, Pol. | 30 | 50.09 N | 20.30 E |
| Rabaable | 144 | 8.17 N | 48.18 E |
| Rabaçal ≃ | 34 | 41.30 N | 7.12 W |
| Rábade | 34 | 43.07 N | 7.37 W |
| Rábahidvég | 61 | 47.04 N | 16.45 E |
| Rabai | 154 | 3.58 S | 39.37 E |
| Rabak | 140 | 13.09 N | 32.44 E |
| Rabal | 164 | 6.22 S | 134.52 E |
| Rabaraba | 164 | 10.00 S | 149.50 E |
| Rabat, Magreb | 148 | 34.02 N | 6.51 W |
| Rabat, Malta | 36 | 35.52 N | 14.25 E |
| Rabat (Victoria), Malta | 36 | 36.02 N | 14.14 E |
| Rabat □[4] | 148 | 33.57 N | 6.50 W |
| Rabaul | 164 | 4.12 S | 152.12 E |
| Rabbit ≃ | 216 | 42.38 N | 86.06 W |
| Rabbit, Lac ⊜ | 190 | 47.30 N | 78.22 W |
| Rabbit Creek ≃, S.D., U.S. | 198 | 45.13 N | 102.10 W |
| Rabbit Creek ≃, Tx., U.S. | 222 | 32.26 N | 94.47 W |
| Rabbit Ears Pass )( | 200 | 40.23 N | 106.37 W |
| Rabbit Lake ⊜, On., Can. | 190 | 47.00 N | 79.37 W |
| Rabbit Lake ⊜, Ca., U.S. | 228 | 34.27 N | 117.01 W |
| Rabbs Creek ≃ | 222 | 29.59 N | 96.55 W |
| Rábca ≃ | 61 | 47.43 N | 17.17 E |
| R'abcevo | 76 | 54.39 N | 32.19 E |
| Rabeira, Ponta da › | 287a | 22.49 S | 43.10 W |
| Rabenau | 54 | 50.57 N | 13.38 E |
| Rabette, Ruisseau la ≃ | 261 | 48.35 N | 2.00 E |
| Rābi', Ash-Shallāl ar- (Fourth Cataract) ∟ | 140 | 18.47 N | 32.03 E |
| Rābigh | 128 | 22.48 N | 39.01 E |
| Rabinal | 236 | 15.06 N | 90.27 W |
| Rabiusa ≃ | 58 | 46.48 N | 9.20 E |
| Rabka | 30 | 49.36 N | 19.56 E |
| Rabkavi Banhatti | 122 | 16.28 N | 75.06 E |
| Rabnābād Channel ⊌ | 126 | 21.50 N | 90.19 E |
| Rabnābād Islands II | 126 | 21.58 N | 90.24 E |
| Râbnița (Rybnica) | 38 | 47.45 N | 29.01 E |
| Raboċeostrovsk | 24 | 64.59 N | 34.48 E |
| Rabočij | 86 | 59.07 N | 79.00 E |
| Rabong, Gunong ∧ | 114 | 4.48 N | 102.07 E |
| Rabotki | 80 | 56.03 N | 44.38 E |
| R'abovskij | 80 | 50.01 N | 41.53 E |
| Rabun Bald ∧ | 192 | 34.58 N | 83.18 W |
| Rabwāh | 123 | 31.44 N | 72.50 E |
| Raby | 262 | 53.19 N | 3.02 W |
| Rabyānah ⍑[4] | 146 | 24.15 N | 22.00 E |
| Rabyānah, Ṣaḥrā' ◆[2] | 146 | 24.30 N | 21.00 E |
| Racale | 68 | 39.57 N | 18.06 E |
| Racalmuto | 70 | 37.24 N | 13.44 E |
| Răcari | 38 | 44.38 N | 25.45 E |
| Raccoon ≃ | 194 | 41.35 N | 93.37 W |
| Raccoon Creek ≃, N.J., U.S. | 208 | 39.48 N | 75.23 W |
| Raccoon Creek ≃, Oh., U.S. | 188 | 38.43 N | 82.11 W |
| Raccoon Creek ≃, Oh., U.S. | 214 | 40.02 N | 82.24 W |
| Raccoon Creek ≃, Pa., U.S. | 214 | 40.38 N | 80.22 W |
| Raccoon Creek ≃, Pa., U.S. | 285 | 39.48 N | 75.23 W |
| Raccoon Creek ≃, Va., U.S. | 208 | 36.48 N | 77.10 W |
| Raccoon Creek, South Branch ≃ | 285 | 39.44 N | 75.15 W |
| Raccoon Creek State Park ♠ | 214 | 40.30 N | 80.27 W |
| Raccoon Island I | 285 | 39.49 N | 75.22 W |
| Raccuia | 70 | 38.03 N | 14.54 E |
| Race, Cape › | 186 | 46.40 N | 53.10 W |
| Raceland | 194 | 29.43 N | 90.35 W |
| Race Point › | 207 | 42.04 N | 70.14 W |
| Racette, Lac ⊜ | 206 | 46.34 N | 74.03 W |
| Racette, Ruisseau ≃ | 206 | 46.36 N | 74.04 W |
| Raceview | 273d | 26.17 S | 28.08 E |
| Rach'a | 76 | 60.05 N | 30.49 E |
| Rach Gia | 110 | 10.01 N | 105.05 E |
| Rach Gia, Vinh ⊂ | 110 | 10.00 N | 105.00 E |
| Rachmanovka | 80 | 51.57 N | 49.29 E |
| Rachmanovo | 82 | 55.44 N | 38.37 E |
| Raciąż | 30 | 52.47 N | 20.06 E |
| Racibórz (Ratibor) | 30 | 50.06 N | 18.13 E |
| Racine, Pa., U.S. | 214 | 40.49 N | 80.20 W |
| Racine, Wi., U.S. | 216 | 42.43 N | 87.46 W |
| Racine □[6] | 216 | 42.45 N | 88.05 W |
| Racines | 64 | 46.52 N | 11.18 E |
| Račinskij chrebet ⋏ | 84 | 42.30 N | 43.30 E |
| Rackerby | 226 | 39.26 N | 121.20 W |
| Ráckeve | 30 | 47.10 N | 18.56 E |
| Rackwick | 46 | 58.52 N | 3.23 W |
| Rackwitz | 54 | 51.26 N | 12.23 E |
| R'ad | 76 | 57.56 N | 35.04 E |
| Råda | 40 | 60.00 N | 13.36 E |
| Radama, Nosy II | 157b | 14.00 S | 47.47 E |
| Radama, Presqu'île ›[1] | 157b | 14.16 S | 47.53 E |

**PORTUGUÊS**

| Nome | Página | Lat.°′ | Long.°′ W = Oeste |
|---|---|---|---|
| Rådasjön ⊜ | 40 | 59.58 N | 13.38 E |
| Radaškovičy | 76 | 54.09 N | 27.14 E |
| Radaur | 124 | 30.02 N | 77.09 E |
| Rădăuți | 38 | 47.51 N | 25.55 E |
| Radbuza ≃ | 60 | 49.45 N | 13.23 E |
| Radčenskoje | 78 | 49.48 N | 40.32 E |
| Radcliff | 194 | 37.50 N | 85.56 W |
| Radcliffe | 44 | 53.34 N | 2.20 W |
| Radcliffe on Trent | 42 | 52.57 N | 1.03 W |
| Radda in Chianti | 66 | 43.29 N | 11.22 E |
| Raddusa | 70 | 37.28 N | 14.32 E |
| Råde | 26 | 59.21 N | 10.51 E |
| Radebaugh | 279b | 40.19 N | 79.35 W |
| Radeberg | 54 | 51.07 N | 13.55 E |
| Radebeul | 54 | 51.06 N | 13.40 E |
| Radeburg | 54 | 51.13 N | 13.43 E |
| Radeče | 36 | 46.04 N | 15.11 E |
| Radegast | 54 | 51.39 N | 12.05 E |
| Radekhiv | 78 | 50.18 N | 24.37 E |
| Radenci | 61 | 46.38 N | 16.03 E |
| Radenthein | 64 | 46.48 N | 13.43 E |
| Radevormwald | 56 | 51.12 N | 7.21 E |
| Radford | 192 | 37.07 N | 80.34 W |
| Rādhānagar, India | 126 | 23.09 N | 87.19 E |
| Rādhānagar, India | 272b | 22.27 N | 88.28 E |
| Rādhanpur | 120 | 23.50 N | 71.36 E |
| Radici, Foce delle )( | 64 | 44.12 N | 10.31 E |
| Radicofani | 66 | 42.54 N | 11.46 E |
| Radicondoli | 66 | 43.16 N | 11.02 E |
| Rădinești | 38 | 44.48 N | 23.46 E |
| Radiščevo | 80 | 52.51 N | 47.53 E |
| Radisson | 184 | 52.27 N | 107.23 W |
| Radium Hot Springs | 182 | 50.38 N | 116.03 W |
| Rad'kovka | 78 | 51.06 N | 36.58 E |
| Radlett | 42 | 51.42 N | 0.20 W |
| Radlett Aerodrome ⊠ | 260 | 51.43 N | 0.19 W |
| Radley Run ≃ | 285 | 39.54 N | 75.37 W |
| Radlje ob Dravi | 61 | 46.37 N | 15.13 E |
| Rådmansö ›[1] | 40 | 59.45 N | 18.55 E |
| Radnevo | 38 | 42.18 N | 25.56 E |
| Radnice | 60 | 49.51 N | 13.37 E |
| Radnor, Oh., U.S. | 214 | 40.23 N | 83.09 W |
| Radnor, Pa., U.S. | 285 | 40.02 N | 75.21 W |
| Radnor Forest ∧ | 42 | 52.18 N | 3.10 W |
| Radnor Mere ⊜ | 262 | 53.17 N | 2.14 W |
| Rădoaia | 38 | 47.44 N | 28.09 E |
| Radofinnikovo | 76 | 59.09 N | 30.55 E |
| Radogošča | 76 | 59.47 N | 34.51 E |
| Radolfzell | 58 | 47.44 N | 8.58 E |
| Radom, Pol. | 30 | 51.25 N | 21.10 E |
| Radom, Il., U.S. | 219 | 38.17 N | 89.12 W |
| Radom □[4] | 30 | 51.25 N | 21.15 E |
| Radomicko | 54 | 52.10 N | 14.58 E |
| Radomir | 38 | 42.33 N | 22.58 E |
| Radomka | 78 | 51.56 N | 32.32 E |
| Radomka ≃ | 30 | 51.43 N | 21.26 E |
| Radomsko | 30 | 51.05 N | 19.25 E |
| Radomyshl' | 78 | 50.30 N | 29.14 E |
| Radomyśl Wielki | 30 | 50.12 N | 21.16 E |
| Radošice | 60 | 49.33 N | 13.39 E |
| Radotin | 30 | 50.00 N | 14.22 E |
| Radovicy | 80 | 55.06 N | 39.32 E |
| Radoviš | 38 | 41.38 N | 22.28 E |
| Radovljica | 36 | 46.21 N | 14.11 E |
| Radstadt | 64 | 47.23 N | 13.27 E |
| Radstädter Tauern )( | 64 | 47.15 N | 13.34 E |
| Radstock | 42 | 51.18 N | 2.28 W |
| Radstock, Cape › | 162 | 33.12 S | 134.20 E |
| Raduha ∧ | 61 | 46.25 N | 14.45 E |
| Radul' | 78 | 51.49 N | 30.42 E |
| Radun' | 76 | 54.03 N | 25.00 E |
| Radushne | 78 | 47.49 N | 33.29 E |
| Radutino | 76 | 52.39 N | 33.57 E |
| Radviliškis | 76 | 55.50 N | 23.31 E |
| Radville | 184 | 49.27 N | 104.17 W |
| Radway | 182 | 54.04 N | 112.57 W |
| Radykovskoje | 80 | 45.56 N | 41.57 E |
| Radymno | 30 | 49.57 N | 22.48 E |
| Radyr | 42 | 51.31 N | 3.15 W |
| Radziejów | 30 | 52.38 N | 18.32 E |
| Radzyń Chełmiński | 30 | 53.24 N | 18.56 E |
| Radzyń Podlaski | 30 | 51.48 N | 22.38 E |
| Rae | 176 | 62.50 N | 116.03 W |
| Rae ≃ | 176 | 67.55 N | 115.30 W |
| Rāe Bareli | 124 | 26.13 N | 81.14 E |
| Raeford | 192 | 34.58 N | 79.13 W |
| Rae Isthmus ⍊[3] | 176 | 66.55 N | 86.10 W |
| Rāenda | 126 | 22.18 N | 89.51 E |
| Raeren | 56 | 50.41 N | 6.07 E |
| Raesfeld | 52 | 51.46 N | 6.50 E |
| Raeside, Lake ⊜ | 162 | 29.30 S | 122.00 E |
| Rae Strait ⊌ | 176 | 68.45 N | 95.00 W |
| Raetihi | 172 | 39.26 S | 175.17 E |
| Rafaela | 252 | 31.16 S | 61.29 W |
| Rafael Calzada | 258 | 34.48 S | 58.22 W |
| Rafael Castillo | 288 | 34.43 S | 58.37 W |
| Rafael Perazza | 258 | 34.32 S | 56.47 W |
| Rafaḥ | 132 | 31.18 N | 34.15 E |
| Rafaï | 152 | 4.58 N | 23.56 E |
| Rafalivka | 78 | 51.19 N | 25.59 E |
| Raffadali | 70 | 37.24 N | 13.32 E |
| Raffelberg, Rennbahn ♠ | 263 | 51.26 N | 6.50 E |
| Raffili Mission | 140 | 6.53 N | 27.58 E |
| Rafḥā' | 128 | 29.42 N | 43.30 E |
| Rafinesque, Mount ∧[2] | 210 | 42.47 N | 73.37 W |
| Rafsanjān | 128 | 30.24 N | 56.01 E |
| Raft ≃ | 202 | 42.37 N | 113.15 W |
| Raft River Mountains ⋏ | 200 | 41.55 N | 113.25 W |
| Rafz | 58 | 47.37 N | 8.32 E |
| Raga | 140 | 8.28 N | 25.41 E |
| Ragada | 64 | 46.10 N | 10.38 E |
| Ragang, Mount ∧ | 116 | 7.43 N | 124.32 E |
| Ragay | 116 | 13.49 N | 122.47 E |
| Ragay Gulf ⊂ | 116 | 13.30 N | 122.45 E |
| Rågeleje | 41 | 56.06 N | 12.10 E |
| Rägelin | 54 | 53.01 N | 12.38 E |
| Ragewitz | 54 | 51.14 N | 12.51 E |
| Ragged, Mount ∧ | 162 | 33.27 S | 123.25 E |
| Ragged Island I | 238 | 22.12 N | 75.44 W |
| Ragged Island Range II | 238 | 22.40 N | 75.54 W |
| Ragged Lake ⊜ | 212 | 45.28 N | 78.38 W |
| Ragged Top Mountain ∧ | 200 | 41.27 N | 105.20 W |
| Raghabpur | 272b | 22.25 N | 88.21 E |
| Rāghogarh | 124 | 24.27 N | 77.12 E |
| Raghumāthbāri | 126 | 22.22 N | 87.47 E |
| Raghunāthpur, Bngl. | 126 | 23.12 N | 89.31 E |
| Raghunāthpur, India | 126 | 23.33 N | 86.40 E |
| Raglan, Austl. | 170 | 33.26 S | 149.36 E |
| Raglan, N.Z. | 172 | 37.48 S | 174.53 E |
| Raglan, Wales, U.K. | 42 | 51.47 N | 2.51 W |
| Ragland | 194 | 33.44 N | 86.09 W |
| Ragnitz | 61 | 46.50 N | 15.35 E |
| Rago Nasjonalpark ♠ | 24 | 67.26 N | 16.00 E |
| Ragow | 264a | 52.17 N | 13.33 E |
| Ragozino | 86 | 59.15 N | 77.52 E |
| Rågsveden | 40 | 60.29 N | 14.05 E |
| Raguda, Ghubbet ⊂ | 144 | 10.45 N | 46.34 E |
| Raguhn | 54 | 51.42 N | 12.17 E |
| Raguli | 80 | 45.38 N | 43.42 E |
| Ragusa → Dubrovnik, Hrv. | 38 | 42.38 N | 18.07 E |
| Ragusa, It. | 70 | 36.55 N | 14.44 E |
| Ragusa □[4] | 70 | 36.55 N | 14.36 E |
| Raguva | 76 | 55.34 N | 24.36 E |
| Raha | 112 | 4.51 S | 122.43 E |
| Rahačou | 76 | 53.05 N | 30.03 E |
| Rahad, Nahr ar- (Rahad) ≃ | 140 | 14.28 N | 33.31 E |
| Rahad al-Bardī | 140 | 11.18 N | 23.53 E |
| Rahad Game Reserve ◆[4] | 140 | 13.06 N | 35.05 E |
| Rahaṭ, Ḥarrat ⍊[9] | 144 | 22.20 N | 40.05 E |
| Rahatgaon | 124 | 22.15 N | 77.14 E |
| Rāhatgarh | 124 | 23.47 N | 78.22 E |
| Raḥbah | 130 | 34.30 N | 36.09 E |

| | | | |
|---|---|---|---|
| Rahden | 52 | 52.26 N | 8.36 E |
| Rahimatpur | 122 | 17.36 N | 74.12 E |
| Rahīm Ki Bāzār | 120 | 24.19 N | 69.09 E |
| Rahīmyār Khān | 120 | 28.25 N | 70.18 E |
| Rahm | 263 | 51.26 N | 6.26 E |
| Rahm ◆[8], Dtsch. | 263 | 51.32 N | 7.23 E |
| Rahm ◆[8], Dtsch. | 263 | 51.21 N | 6.47 E |
| Rahmede ≃ | 263 | 51.17 N | 7.41 E |
| Rahmer See ⊜ | 264a | 52.45 N | 13.25 E |
| Rahns | 285 | 40.12 N | 75.27 W |
| Rahnsdorf ◆[8] | 264a | 52.26 N | 13.42 E |
| Rāhon | 123 | 31.03 N | 76.07 E |
| Rahotu | 172 | 39.20 S | 173.48 E |
| Rahouia | 34 | 35.32 N | 1.01 E |
| Rāhwāli | 123 | 32.15 N | 74.10 E |
| Rahway | 210 | 40.36 N | 74.16 W |
| Rahway ≃ | 276 | 40.35 N | 74.12 W |
| Rahway, East Branch ≃ | 276 | 40.42 N | 74.18 W |
| Rahway, Robinsons Branch ≃ | 276 | 40.37 N | 74.17 W |
| Rahway, South Branch ≃ | 276 | 40.36 N | 74.17 W |
| Rahway, West Branch ≃ | 276 | 40.42 N | 74.18 W |
| Rahway River Parkway ♠ | 276 | 40.41 N | 74.19 W |
| Raiano | 66 | 42.06 N | 13.49 E |
| Raiatea I | 14 | 16.50 S | 151.25 W |
| Rāichūr | 122 | 16.12 N | 77.22 E |
| Raidak ≃ | 124 | 26.22 N | 89.45 E |
| Rāidighi | 126 | 22.00 N | 88.26 E |
| Raiding | 61 | 47.34 N | 16.32 E |
| Raiford | 192 | 30.03 N | 82.14 W |
| Raiganj | 124 | 25.37 N | 88.07 E |
| Raigarh | 122 | 21.54 N | 83.24 E |
| Raijua, Pulau I | 112 | 10.37 S | 121.36 E |
| Rāikot | 123 | 30.39 N | 75.36 E |
| Railroad | 208 | 39.46 N | 76.42 W |
| Railroad Canyon Reservoir ⊜[1] | 228 | 33.42 N | 117.16 W |
| Railroad Creek ≃ | 224 | 48.12 N | 120.36 W |
| Rail Road Flat | 226 | 38.20 N | 120.30 W |
| Railroad Valley V | 204 | 38.25 N | 115.40 W |
| Railton | 166 | 41.21 S | 146.25 E |
| Raimangal ≃ | 126 | 21.47 N | 89.08 E |
| Rain, Dtsch. | 56 | 48.41 N | 10.55 E |
| Rain → Riva di Tures, It. | 64 | 46.57 N | 12.04 E |
| Rainbach im Innkreis | 60 | 48.27 N | 13.32 E |
| Rainbow | 228 | 33.24 N | 117.10 W |
| Rainbow Bridge ◆[5] | 284a | 43.05 N | 79.04 W |
| Rainbow Bridge National Monument ♠ | 200 | 37.06 N | 110.57 W |
| Rainbow Falls ∟ | 182 | 52.23 N | 119.59 W |
| Rainbow Lakes | 276 | 40.52 N | 74.28 W |
| Rainbow Park ♠ | 278 | 41.46 N | 87.33 W |
| Rainbow Shores | 212 | 43.37 N | 76.12 W |
| Rainelle | 188 | 37.58 N | 80.46 W |
| Rainford | 44 | 53.30 N | 2.48 W |
| Rainham | 42 | 51.23 N | 0.36 E |
| Rainham ◆[8] | 260 | 51.31 N | 0.12 E |
| Rainhill | 262 | 53.26 N | 2.46 W |
| Rainhill Stoops | 262 | 53.24 N | 2.45 W |
| Rainier, Or., U.S. | 224 | 46.05 N | 122.56 W |
| Rainier, Wa., U.S. | 224 | 46.53 N | 122.41 W |
| Rainier, Mount ∧ | 224 | 46.52 N | 121.46 W |
| Rainow | 262 | 53.17 N | 2.04 W |
| Rains □[6] | 222 | 32.50 N | 95.47 W |
| Rainsboro | 218 | 39.13 N | 83.25 W |
| Rainsford Island I | 283 | 42.18 N | 70.57 W |
| Rainworth | 44 | 53.07 N | 1.08 W |
| Rainy ≃, N.A. | 184 | 48.50 N | 94.41 W |
| Rainy ≃, Mi., U.S. | 190 | 45.27 N | 84.13 W |
| Rainy Lake ⊜, On., Can. | 212 | 45.32 N | 79.30 W |
| Rainy Lake ⊜, N.A. | 184 | 48.42 N | 93.10 W |
| Rainy Pass )( | 224 | 48.32 N | 120.39 W |
| Rainy River | 190 | 48.43 N | 94.34 W |
| Rāipur, Bngl. | 126 | 23.03 N | 90.46 E |
| Raipur, India | 122 | 21.14 N | 81.38 E |
| Raipur, India | 124 | 30.19 N | 78.06 E |
| Raipur, India | 126 | 22.48 N | 86.57 E |
| Raipur, India | 272a | 28.32 N | 77.20 E |
| Raipur, India | 272b | 22.24 N | 88.09 E |
| Rāipura | 126 | 23.59 N | 90.53 E |
| Raipur Uplands ⋏[1] | 122 | 21.00 N | 82.20 E |
| Rairākhol | 120 | 21.04 N | 84.21 E |
| Ra'īs | 128 | 23.34 N | 38.36 E |
| Raisdorf | 54 | 54.17 N | 10.16 E |
| Raisen | 124 | 23.20 N | 77.48 E |
| Ráisi, Punta › | 70 | 38.11 N | 13.06 E |
| Raisin | 226 | 36.36 N | 119.54 W |
| Raisin ≃, On., Can. | 206 | 45.08 N | 74.29 W |
| Raisin ≃, Mi., U.S. | 216 | 41.53 N | 83.20 W |
| Rāisinghnagar | 123 | 29.32 N | 73.27 E |
| Raismes | 50 | 50.23 N | 3.29 E |
| Raisting | 64 | 47.55 N | 11.07 E |
| Raita | 126 | 24.07 N | 88.57 E |
| Raitenbuch | 60 | 49.01 N | 11.08 E |
| Raití | 236 | 14.35 N | 85.02 W |
| Raivavae I | 14 | 23.52 S | 147.40 W |
| Rāiwind | 123 | 31.15 N | 74.13 E |
| Raizeux | 261 | 48.37 N | 1.41 E |
| Raja, Gili I | 115a | 7.14 S | 113.47 E |
| Raja, Ujung › | 114 | 3.45 N | 96.33 E |
| Rājābāri | 126 | 23.23 N | 90.28 E |
| Rajabasa | 112 | 5.25 S | 104.24 E |
| Rājābhāt Khāwa | 124 | 26.37 N | 89.32 E |
| Rājābhita | 126 | 23.52 N | 86.20 E |
| Rājahmundry | 122 | 16.59 N | 81.47 E |
| Rajāj | 140 | 10.55 N | 24.43 E |
| Rāja Jang | 123 | 31.13 N | 74.16 E |
| Raja-Jooseppi | 24 | 68.28 N | 28.21 E |
| Rājākhera | 124 | 26.55 N | 78.11 E |
| Rājaldesar | 120 | 28.02 N | 74.28 E |
| Rājāluka | 126 | 22.09 N | 86.38 E |
| Rajamäki | 26 | 60.32 N | 24.45 E |
| Rājampet | 122 | 14.11 N | 79.10 E |
| Rajang ≃ | 112 | 2.04 N | 111.12 E |
| Rājanpur | 120 | 29.06 N | 70.19 E |
| Rājapālaiyam | 122 | 9.27 N | 77.34 E |
| Rājāpur, Bngl. | 126 | 22.34 N | 90.09 E |
| Rājāpur, India | 122 | 16.40 N | 73.31 E |
| Rājāpur, India | 124 | 25.23 N | 81.09 E |
| Rājāpur, India | 272b | 22.39 N | 88.11 E |
| Rājapur Canal ≊ | 272b | 22.30 N | 88.07 E |
| Rājasthān □[3] | 120 | 27.00 N | 74.00 E |
| Rājauri | 123 | 33.23 N | 74.18 E |
| Rājbāri, Bngl. | 124 | 23.46 N | 89.39 E |
| Rājbāri, India | 126 | 22.25 N | 88.48 E |
| Raj Bhavan ʊ | 272b | 22.34 N | 88.21 E |
| Rājbirāj | 124 | 26.32 N | 86.44 E |
| Rajčichinsk | 89 | 49.46 N | 129.25 E |
| Rājendrapur | 126 | 24.06 N | 90.27 E |
| Rajevskij | 86 | 54.04 N | 54.56 E |
| Rāj Gangpur | 124 | 22.11 N | 84.36 E |
| Rājganj ≃[1] | 126 | 22.21 N | 90.16 E |
| Rājgarh, India | 123 | 28.38 N | 75.23 E |
| Rājgarh, India | 124 | 23.56 N | 76.58 E |
| Rājgarh, India | 124 | 27.14 N | 76.38 E |
| Rajghat ʊ[1] | 272a | 28.39 N | 77.15 E |
| Rājgīr | 124 | 25.02 N | 85.25 E |
| Rajgorod | 80 | 48.26 N | 44.55 E |
| Rajgorodok | 80 | 48.48 N | 52.53 E |
| Rajgród | 30 | 53.44 N | 22.42 E |
| Rājhāt | 272b | 22.56 N | 88.21 E |
| Rajhrad | 61 | 49.05 N | 16.37 E |
| Rājibpur | 272b | 22.49 N | 88.34 E |
| Rajik | 112 | 2.36 S | 105.56 E |
| Rajka | 30 | 48.00 N | 17.12 E |
| Rājkot | 120 | 22.18 N | 70.47 E |
| Rajkuzi | 265a | 59.47 N | 29.57 E |
| Rājmahāl | 124 | 25.03 N | 87.50 E |
| Rājmahāl Hills ⋏[2] | 124 | 24.40 N | 87.25 E |
| Rājnagar | 126 | 23.57 N | 87.19 E |
| Rāj Nāndgaon | 120 | 21.06 N | 81.02 E |
| Rajokri ◆[8] | 272a | 28.31 N | 77.07 E |

| | | | |
|---|---|---|---|
| Raj-Oleksandrivka | 83 | 48.48 N | 37.51 E |
| Rājpipla | 120 | 21.47 N | 73.34 E |
| Rājpur, India | 120 | 21.56 N | 75.08 E |
| Rājpur, India | 126 | 22.25 N | 88.25 E |
| Rājpur, India | 272a | 28.44 N | 77.22 E |
| Rājpur ◆[8] | 272a | 28.41 N | 77.12 E |
| Rājpura | 124 | 30.29 N | 76.36 E |
| Rājshāhi | 124 | 24.22 N | 88.36 E |
| Rājshāhi □[5] | 124 | 25.15 N | 89.15 E |
| Rājula | 122 | 21.03 N | 71.26 E |
| Raka | 124 | 29.26 N | 85.50 E |
| Raka ≃ | 124 | 29.24 N | 87.58 E |
| Rakaia | 172 | 43.45 S | 172.01 E |
| Rakaia ≃ | 172 | 43.56 S | 172.13 E |
| Rakamaz | 30 | 48.08 N | 21.30 E |
| Rakaposhi ∧ | 123 | 36.10 N | 74.30 E |
| Rakata, Pulau I | 115a | 6.10 S | 105.26 E |
| Rakha La )( | 124 | 27.53 N | 87.34 E |
| Rakhawt, Wādī V | 144 | 17.40 N | 51.40 E |
| Rakhine □[8] | 110 | 19.00 N | 94.15 E |
| Rakhiv | 78 | 48.03 N | 24.12 E |
| Rakhmanivka | 78 | 47.48 N | 33.13 E |
| Rakhneh | 128 | 31.39 N | 59.13 E |
| Rakhni | 120 | 30.03 N | 69.55 E |
| Rakhny-Lisovi | 78 | 48.47 N | 28.29 E |
| Rakhshān ≃ | 128 | 27.10 N | 63.25 E |
| Rākīn | 132 | 31.14 N | 35.42 E |
| Rakitnoje, Ross. | 78 | 50.51 N | 35.50 E |
| Rakitnoje, Ross. | 89 | 45.36 N | 134.17 E |
| Rakke | 76 | 58.59 N | 26.15 E |
| Rakkestad | 26 | 59.26 N | 11.21 E |
| Rakoniewice | 30 | 52.10 N | 16.16 E |
| Rakops | 156 | 21.00 S | 24.32 E |
| Rákoscsaba ◆[8] | 264c | 47.29 N | 19.17 E |
| Rákoshegy ◆[8] | 264c | 47.28 N | 19.14 E |
| Rákoskeresztúr ◆[8] | 264c | 47.29 N | 19.15 E |
| Rákoskert ◆[8] | 264c | 47.28 N | 19.19 E |
| Rákosliget ◆[8] | 264c | 47.30 N | 19.16 E |
| Rákospalota ◆[8] | 264c | 47.34 N | 19.08 E |
| Rákos-patak ≃ | 264c | 47.33 N | 19.04 E |
| Rákosszentmihály ◆[8] | 264c | 47.32 N | 19.11 E |
| Rakovnická plošina ⋏[1] | 54 | 50.08 N | 13.47 E |
| Rakovník | 54 | 50.05 N | 13.43 E |
| Rakovski | 38 | 42.18 N | 24.58 E |
| Rakša | 80 | 53.33 N | 41.37 E |
| Raksakiny | 86 | 60.37 N | 73.52 E |
| Rakuša | 80 | 47.03 N | 52.47 E |
| Råkvåg | 26 | 63.46 N | 10.05 E |
| Rakvere | 76 | 59.22 N | 26.20 E |
| Rakwa | 164 | 2.42 S | 134.30 E |
| Raleigh, Nf., Can. | 186 | 51.34 N | 55.44 W |
| Raleigh, Ms., U.S. | 194 | 32.02 N | 89.31 W |
| Raleigh, N.C., U.S. | 192 | 35.46 N | 78.38 W |
| Raleigh Hills | 224 | 45.29 N | 122.45 W |
| Raleighvallen Voltz Berg, Natuurreservaat ♠, Sur. | 246 | 4.45 N | 56.05 W |
| Raleighvallen Voltz Berg, Natuurreservaat ♠, Sur. | 250 | 4.50 N | 55.10 W |
| Ralik Chain II | 14 | 8.00 N | 167.00 E |
| Ralls | 196 | 33.40 N | 101.23 W |
| Ralls □[6] | 219 | 39.34 N | 91.30 W |
| Ralsko ∧ | 54 | 50.42 N | 14.47 E |
| Ralston, Ne., U.S. | 198 | 41.12 N | 96.02 W |
| Ralston, Pa., U.S. | 210 | 41.31 N | 76.57 W |
| Ram ≃ | 182 | 52.23 N | 115.25 W |
| Rama, Nic. | 236 | 12.09 N | 84.15 W |
| Rama, Yis. | 132 | 32.56 N | 35.22 E |
| Rama ≃ | 236 | 12.08 N | 84.13 W |
| Ramacca | 70 | 37.23 N | 14.42 E |
| Rāmachandrapuram | 122 | 16.51 N | 82.01 E |
| Ramādah | 144 | 13.38 N | 43.56 E |
| Ramah | 200 | 35.07 N | 108.29 W |
| Ramah Indian Reservation ◆[4] | 200 | 34.50 N | 108.25 W |
| Rama Indian Reserve ◆[4] | 212 | 44.41 N | 79.15 W |
| Ramales de la Victoria | 34 | 43.15 N | 3.27 W |
| Rām Allāh | 132 | 31.54 N | 35.12 E |
| Rāman | 123 | 29.58 N | 74.58 E |
| Rāmanagaram | 122 | 12.43 N | 77.18 E |
| Rāmanāthapuram | 122 | 9.23 N | 78.50 E |
| Ramānāthpur | 272b | 22.41 N | 88.14 E |
| Ramanbāti | 272b | 22.47 N | 88.08 E |
| Rāmānuj Ganj | 124 | 23.48 N | 83.42 E |
| Ramapo | 276 | 41.08 N | 74.10 W |
| Ramapo ≃ | 276 | 40.58 N | 74.17 W |
| Ramapo Lake ⊜ | 276 | 41.02 N | 74.16 W |
| Ramapo Mountains ⋏ | 276 | 41.08 N | 74.12 W |
| Ramas, Cape › | 122 | 15.07 N | 73.55 E |
| Ramasaig | 46 | 57.24 N | 6.44 W |
| Ramasucha | 76 | 52.46 N | 33.33 E |
| Ramat Gan | 132 | 32.05 N | 34.49 E |
| Ramat HaSharon | 132 | 32.09 N | 34.50 E |
| Ramat HaShofét | 132 | 32.37 N | 35.06 E |
| Ramathlabama | 156 | 25.40 S | 25.35 E |
| Ramatuelle | 62 | 43.13 N | 6.37 E |
| Rama VI Bridge ◆[5] | 269a | 13.48 N | 100.31 E |
| Rāmban | 123 | 33.15 N | 75.15 E |
| Rambervillers | 58 | 48.21 N | 6.38 E |
| Rambi I | 175g | 16.30 S | 179.59 E |
| Rambipuji | 115a | 8.13 S | 113.36 E |
| Rambleton Acres | 208 | 39.39 N | 75.38 W |
| Ramblewood | 285 | 39.55 N | 74.56 W |
| Rambouillet | 50 | 48.39 N | 1.50 E |
| Rambouillet, Château de ⊥ | 261 | 48.39 N | 1.49 E |
| Rambouillet, Forêt de ♠ | 261 | 48.40 N | 1.50 E |
| Rambutyo Island I | 164 | 2.20 S | 147.50 E |
| Rām Dās | 123 | 31.58 N | 74.54 E |
| Rāmdia | 126 | 23.42 N | 89.32 E |
| Rāmdurg | 122 | 15.57 N | 75.18 E |
| Ramea | 186 | 47.31 N | 57.23 W |
| Ramea Islands II | 186 | 47.31 N | 57.21 W |
| Rāmechhāp | 124 | 27.20 N | 86.05 E |
| Rame Head ›, S. Afr. | 158 | 31.48 S | 29.22 E |
| Rame Head ›, Eng., U.K. | 42 | 50.19 N | 4.13 W |
| Rämen ⊜ | 40 | 60.18 N | 15.10 E |
| Ramenje, Ross. | 76 | 60.17 N | 43.46 E |
| Ramenje, Ross. | 82 | 56.34 N | 37.13 E |
| Ramenka ◆[8] | 265b | 55.41 N | 37.30 E |
| Ramenskoje | 82 | 55.34 N | 38.14 E |
| Ramer | 194 | 32.03 N | 86.13 W |
| Ramerupt | 50 | 48.31 N | 4.18 E |
| Rameški | 76 | 57.21 N | 36.03 E |
| Rāmeswaram | 122 | 9.17 N | 79.18 E |
| Ramey | 214 | 40.48 N | 78.24 W |
| Rāmganj | 126 | 23.06 N | 90.51 E |
| Rāmgarh, Bngl. | 120 | 22.59 N | 91.44 E |
| Rāmgarh, India | 120 | 27.22 N | 70.30 E |
| Rāmgarh, India | 120 | 27.15 N | 75.11 E |
| Rāmgarh, India | 124 | 23.38 N | 85.31 E |
| Rāmgarh, India | 124 | 24.34 N | 87.15 E |
| Rāmgarh, India | 126 | 22.42 N | 87.04 E |
| Rāmgarh Hills ⋏[2] | 124 | 22.50 N | 83.10 E |
| Ram Head › | 240m | 18.18 N | 64.42 W |
| Rāmhormoz | 128 | 31.16 N | 49.36 E |
| Ramingining | 164 | 12.19 S | 135.03 E |
| Ramingstein | 64 | 47.04 N | 13.50 E |
| Ramírez, Méx. | 196 | 27.20 N | 100.58 W |
| Ramírez, Méx. | 196 | 25.57 N | 97.46 W |
| Ramiriquí | 246 | 5.24 N | 73.20 W |
| Ramis ≃ | 144 | 7.59 N | 41.34 E |
| Rāmjībanpur | 126 | 22.50 N | 87.37 E |
| Rāmkānāli | 126 | 23.35 N | 86.45 E |
| Raml, Qārat ar- ∧[2] | 142 | 30.02 N | 30.39 E |
| Ramla | 132 | 31.55 N | 34.52 E |
| Ramlu ∧ | 144 | 13.24 N | 41.51 E |
| Ramm, Jabal ∧ | 132 | 29.35 N | 35.24 E |
| Rämmen | 40 | 60.07 N | 14.08 E |
| Râmna ≃ | 38 | 45.39 N | 27.19 E |
| Rāmnagar, India | 123 | 32.49 N | 75.19 E |

| | | | |
|---|---|---|---|
| Rāmnagar, India | 124 | 25.17 N | [illegible]3.02 E |
| Rāmnagar, India | 124 | 29.24 N | [illegible]9.07 E |
| Rāmnagar, India | 126 | 21.41 N | 7.33 E |
| Rāmnagar, India | 272b | 22.23 N | [illegible]8.19 E |
| Ramnäs | 40 | 59.46 N | [illegible]6.12 E |
| Râmnicu Sărat | 38 | 45.23 N | 7.03 E |
| Râmnicu Vâlcea | 38 | 45.06 N | [illegible]4.22 E |
| Ramo | 144 | 6.42 N | [illegible]1.23 E |
| Ramon' | 78 | 51.54 N | [illegible].20 E |
| Ramon, Har ∧ | 132 | 30.30 N | [illegible].38 E |
| Ramon, Makhtésh ⍊[7] | 132 | 30.36 N | [illegible].49 E |
| Ramon, Naḥal V | 132 | 30.36 N | [illegible].55 E |
| Ramona, Ca., U.S. | 228 | 33.02 N | 11[illegible].52 W |
| Ramona, Ok., U.S. | 196 | 36.31 N | 9[illegible].55 W |
| Ramona, S.D., U.S. | 198 | 44.07 N | 9[illegible].12 W |
| Ramor, Lough ⊜ | 48 | 53.49 N | [illegible].05 W |
| Ramos | 234 | 22.50 N | 10[illegible].55 W |
| Ramos ◆[8] | 287a | 22.51 S | 4[illegible].15 W |
| Ramos ≃[1] | 150 | 5.08 N | [illegible]22 E |
| Ramosch | 58 | 46.50 N | 1[illegible].22 E |
| Ramos Island I | 116 | 8.06 N | 11[illegible].02 E |
| Ramos Mejía | 258 | 34.38 S | 5[illegible].34 W |
| Ramot | 132 | 32.46 N | 3[illegible].40 E |
| Ramotswa | 156 | 24.56 S | 2[illegible].50 E |
| Rāmpāl | 126 | 22.34 N | 8[illegible].39 E |
| Rampart | 180 | 65.30 N | 150[illegible]1 W |
| Ramparts ≃ | 180 | 66.11 N | 129[illegible]3 W |
| Rampillon | 50 | 48.33 N | 3[illegible]4 E |
| Rampside | 44 | 54.05 N | 3[illegible]0 W |
| Rāmpur, India | 120 | 31.27 N | 77[illegible]8 E |
| Rāmpur, India | 123 | 29.49 N | 77[illegible]7 E |
| Rāmpur, India | 124 | 28.49 N | 79[illegible]2 E |
| Rāmpura | 120 | 24.28 N | 75[illegible]6 E |
| Rāmpura Phūl | 123 | 30.17 N | 75[illegible]4 E |
| Rampur Boalia → Rājshāhi | 124 | 24.22 N | 88[illegible]6 E |
| Rāmpur Hāt | 126 | 24.10 N | 87[illegible]7 E |
| Ramrath | 263 | 51.06 N | 6[illegible]1 E |
| Ramree Island I | 110 | 19.06 N | 93[illegible]3 E |
| Rāmsāgar | 126 | 23.05 N | 87[illegible]7 E |
| Ramsau | 64 | 47.36 N | 12[illegible] E |
| Ramsay Range ⋏ | 162 | 18.31 S | 127[illegible] E |
| Ramsbeck | 56 | 51.18 N | 8[illegible] E |
| Ramsberg | 40 | 59.46 N | 15.1[illegible] E |
| Ramsbottom | 44 | 53.40 N | 2.1[illegible] W |
| Ramsden Bellhouse | 260 | 51.37 N | 0.2[illegible] E |
| Ramsden Heath | 260 | 51.38 N | 0.2[illegible] E |
| Ramsdorf | 52 | 51.54 N | 6.5[illegible] E |
| Ramsele | 26 | 63.33 N | 16.2[illegible] E |
| Ramseur | 192 | 35.44 N | 79.3[illegible] W |
| Ramsey, I. of Man | 44 | 54.20 N | 4.2[illegible] W |
| Ramsey, Eng., U.K. | 42 | 51.56 N | 1.1[illegible] E |
| Ramsey, Eng., U.K. | 42 | 52.27 N | 0.0[illegible] W |
| Ramsey, Il., U.S. | 219 | 39.08 N | 89.0[illegible] W |
| Ramsey, N.J., U.S. | 210 | 41.03 N | 74.0[illegible] W |
| Ramsey Bay ⊂ | 44 | 54.20 N | 4.2[illegible] W |
| Ramsey Brook ≃ | 276 | 41.02 N | 74.0[illegible] W |
| Ramsey Creek ≃ | 219 | 39.03 N | 89.04 W |
| Ramsey Island I | 42 | 51.52 N | 5.1[illegible] W |
| Ramsey Lake ⊜ | 190 | 47.15 N | 82.16 W |
| Ramsey Lake State Park ♠ | 219 | 39.10 N | 89.08 W |
| Ramsgate, Austl. | 274a | 33.59 S | 151.08 [illegible] |
| Ramsgate, S. Afr. | 158 | 30.55 S | 30.20 [illegible] |
| Ramsgate, Eng., U.K. | 42 | 51.20 N | 1.25 [illegible] |
| Rāmshai | 124 | 26.44 N | 88.51 [illegible] |
| Rāmshīr | 128 | 30.54 N | 49.24 [illegible] |
| Ramshorn Peak ∧ | 202 | 45.09 N | 111.06 W |
| Rämshyttan | 40 | 60.18 N | 15.13 [illegible] |
| Ramsjö | 26 | 62.11 N | 15.39 [illegible] |
| Ramsloh | 52 | 53.06 N | 7.40 [illegible] |
| Ramstein | 56 | 49.27 N | 7.33 [illegible] |
| Ramstein-Miesenbach | 56 | 50.21 N | 8.59 [illegible] |
| Rāmtek | 120 | 21.24 N | 79.20 [illegible] |
| Rāmu, Bngl. | 120 | 21.25 N | 92.07 [illegible] |
| Ramu, Kenya | 154 | 3.56 N | 41.13 [illegible] |
| Ramu ≃ | 164 | 4.02 S | 144.41 E |
| Ramuševo | 76 | 57.50 N | 31.37 E |
| Ramvik | 26 | 62.49 N | 17.51 E |
| Ramville, Îlet I | 240e | 14.42 N | 60.53 W |
| Ramygala | 76 | 55.31 N | 24.18 E |
| Ramzaj | 80 | 53.18 N | 44.44 E |
| Rānāghāt | 126 | 23.11 N | 88.35 E |
| Rana Kao, Volcán ∧[1] | 174z | 27.11 S | 109.27 W |
| Ranalt | 64 | 47.02 N | 11.13 E |
| Rāna Pratāp Sāgar ⊜[1] | 120 | 24.50 N | 75.35 E |
| Rånäs | 40 | 59.48 N | 18.17 E |
| Ranau | 112 | 5.58 N | 116.41 E |
| Ranau, Danau ⊜ | 112 | 4.50 S | 103.55 E |
| Ranbīrsinghpura | 123 | 32.38 N | 74.44 E |
| Ranburne | 194 | 33.31 N | 85.20 W |
| Rancabali | 115a | 7.08 S | 107.21 E |
| Rancagua | 252 | 34.10 S | 70.45 W |
| Rancah | 115a | 7.12 S | 108.30 E |
| Rance ≃ | 32 | 48.31 N | 1.59 W |
| Rancevo, Ross. | 76 | 56.56 N | 34.03 E |
| Rancevo, Ross. | 76 | 56.40 N | 33.02 E |
| Rancharia | 255 | 22.15 S | 50.55 W |
| Rancheria | 180 | 60.05 N | 130.40 W |
| Ranchería ≃ | 246 | 11.34 N | 72.54 W |
| Rancheria Rock ∧ | 202 | 44.53 N | 120.08 W |
| Ranches of Taos | 200 | 36.22 N | 105.37 W |
| Ranchester | 202 | 44.54 N | 107.09 W |
| Rānchi | 124 | 23.21 N | 85.20 E |
| Ranchillos | 252 | 26.57 S | 65.03 W |
| Rānchi Plateau ⋏[1] | 124 | 23.20 N | 84.50 E |
| Ranch Lake ⊜ | 184 | 52.30 N | 104.46 W |
| Rancho Colorado, Presa de ⊜[1] | 286a | 19.29 N | 99.17 W |
| Rancho Cordova | 226 | 38.35 N | 121.18 W |
| Rancho Nuevo, Méx. | 196 | 26.22 N | 99.54 W |
| Rancho Nuevo, Méx. | 234 | 23.12 N | 97.48 W |
| Rancho Palos Verdes | 228 | 33.45 N | 118.24 W |
| Rancho Rinconado | 226 | 37.18 N | 122.01 W |
| Rancho Santa Fe | 228 | 33.01 N | 117.12 W |
| Rancho Veloz | 240p | 22.53 N | 80.23 W |
| Ranchuelo | 240p | 22.23 N | 80.09 W |
| Ranco, Lago ⊜ | 254 | 40.14 S | 72.24 W |
| Rancocas | 208 | 40.00 N | 74.52 W |
| Rancocas Creek ≃ | 285 | 40.02 N | 74.59 W |
| Rancocas Creek, North Branch ≃ | 208 | 40.00 N | 74.52 W |
| Rancocas Creek, South Branch ≃ | 208 | 40.00 N | 74.52 W |
| Rancocas Creek, Southwest Branch ≃ | 285 | 39.57 N | 74.48 W |
| Rancocas Heights | 285 | 39.59 N | 74.51 W |
| Rancocas State Park ♠ | 285 | 40.00 N | 74.50 W |
| Rancocas Woods | 285 | 39.59 N | 74.51 W |
| Rancul | 252 | 35.03 S | 64.42 W |
| Rand | 166 | 35.36 S | 146.35 E |
| Rand (Germiston) Airport ⊠ | 273d | 26.15 S | 28.09 E |
| Randa | 58 | 46.07 N | 7.47 E |
| Randall Lake ⊜ | 216 | 41.57 N | 85.02 W |
| Randall Park Mall ◆[9] | 279a | 41.26 N | 81.32 W |
| Randalls Island I | 276 | 40.48 N | 73.55 W |
| Randallstown | 284b | 39.22 N | 76.48 W |
| Randalstown | 48 | 54.45 N | 6.19 W |
| Randan | 32 | 46.01 N | 3.21 E |
| Rāndaveswar | 126 | 23.43 N | 87.17 E |
| Randazzo | 70 | 37.53 N | 14.57 E |
| Randbøl | 41 | 55.42 N | 9.16 E |
| Randburg | 273d | 26.06 S | 27.59 E |
| Randers | 26 | 56.28 N | 10.03 E |
| Randfontein | 158 | 26.11 S | 27.42 E |
| Randfontein □[5] | 273d | 26.13 S | 27.40 E |
| Randgate | 273d | 26.11 S | 27.41 E |
| Randhurst ◆[9] | 278 | 42.05 N | 87.56 W |
| Randle | 224 | 46.32 N | 121.57 W |
| Randleman | 192 | 35.49 N | 79.48 W |
| Randlett | 196 | 34.10 N | 98.27 W |
| Randolph, Az., U.S. | 200 | 32.55 N | 111.30 W |
| Randolph, Me., U.S. | 188 | 44.13 N | 69.46 W |
| Randolph, Ma., U.S. | 207 | 42.09 N | 71.02 W |


| Symbol | English | Deutsch | Español | Français | Português |
|---|---|---|---|---|---|
| ≃ | River | Fluß | Río | Rivière | Rio |
| ≊ | Canal | Kanal | Canal | Canal | Canal |
| ∟ | Waterfall, Rapids | Wasserfall, Stromschnellen | Cascada, Rápidos | Chute d'eau, Rapides | Cascata, Rápidos |
| ⊌ | Strait | Meeresstraße | Estrecho | Détroit | Estreito |
| ⊂ | Bay, Gulf | Bucht, Golf | Bahía, Golfo | Baie, Golfe | Baía, Golfo |
| ⊜ | Lake, Lakes | See, Seen | Lago, Lagos | Lac, Lacs | Lago, Lagos |
| ⁝ | Swamp | Sumpf | Pantano | Marais | Pântano |
| ⊼ | Ice Features, Glacier | Eis- und Gletscherformen | Accidentes Glaciales | Formes glaciaires | Acidentes glaciares |
| ⍑ | Other Hydrographic Features | Andere Hydrographische Objekte | Otros Elementos Hidrográficos | Autres données hydrographiques | Outros acidentes hidrográficos |
| ✣ | Submarine Features | Untermeerische Objekte | Accidentes Submarinos | Formes de relief sous-marin | Acidentes submarinos |
| □ | Political Unit | Politische Einheit | Unidad Politica | Entité politique | Unidade política |
| ʊ | Cultural Institution | Kulturelle Institution | Institución Cultural | Institution culturelle | Instituição cultural |
| ⊥ | Historical Site | Historische Stätte | Sitio Histórico | Site historique | Sitio histórico |
| ♠ | Recreational Site | Erholungs- und Ferienort | Sitio de Recreo | Centre de loisirs | Area de Lazer |
| ⊠ | Airport | Flughafen | Aeropuerto | Aéroport | Aeroporto |
| ■ | Military Installation | Militäranlage | Instalación Militar | Installation militaire | Instalação militar |
| ◆ | Miscellaneous | Verschiedenes | Misceláneo | Divers | Diversos |

| Name | Page | Lat.°′ | Long.°′ |
|---|---|---|---|
| Randolph, Ne., U.S. | 198 | 42.22 N | 97.21 W |
| Randolph, N.Y., U.S. | 210 | 42.09 N | 78.58 W |
| Randolph, Oh., U.S. | 214 | 41.01 N | 81.14 W |
| Randolph, Ut,. U.S. | 200 | 41.39 N | 111.10 W |
| Randolph, Vt., U.S. | 188 | 43.55 N | 72.39 W |
| Randolph, Wi., U.S. | 190 | 43.32 N | 89.00 W |
| Randolph □[6], In., U.S. | 218 | 40.10 N | 85.00 W |
| Randolph □[6], Mo., U.S. | 219 | 39.22 N | 92.20 W |
| Randolph Air Force Base ■ | 196 | 29.32 N | 98.16 W |
| Randolph Hills | 284c | 39.03 N | 77.05 W |
| Randolph Village | 284c | 38.53 N | 76.52 W |
| Random Island I | 186 | 48.08 N | 53.45 W |
| Random Lake | 190 | 43.33 N | 87.57 W |
| Randow ≃ | 54 | 53.41 N | 14.04 E |
| Randowaya | 164 | 1.52 S | 136.31 E |
| Randowbruch ⩸ | 54 | 53.15 N | 14.10 E |
| Randsburg | 228 | 35.22 N | 117.39 W |
| Randse Afrikaanse Universiteit ʋ[2] | 273d | 26.11 S | 27.50 E |
| Randsfjorden ⊜ | 26 | 60.25 N | 10.24 E |
| Rand Stadium ♦ | 273d | 26.14 S | 28.03 E |
| Randublatung | 115a | 7.12 S | 111.23 E |
| Randudongkal | 115a | 7.06 S | 109.19 E |
| Randwick | 170 | 33.55 S | 151.15 E |
| Randwick Racecourse ♦ | 274a | 33.54 S | 151.14 E |
| Råneå | 26 | 65.52 N | 22.18 E |
| Ranelagh | 258 | 34.48 S | 58.12 W |
| Rāner | 123 | 28.53 N | 73.17 E |
| Ranérou | 150 | 15.18 N | 13.58 W |
| Rāneswar | 126 | 24.02 N | 87.25 E |
| Raneue | 114 | 5.03 N | 95.20 E |
| Ranford | 168a | 32.48 S | 116.31 E |
| Ranfurly, N.Z. | 172 | 45.08 S | 170.06 E |
| Ranfurly, Scot., U.K. | 46 | 55.52 N | 4.33 W |
| Rangae | 114 | 6.17 N | 101.44 E |
| Rāngāmāti | 120 | 22.38 N | 92.12 E |
| Rangantemiang | 112 | 0.35 S | 113.19 E |
| Rangas, Tanjung ≻ | 112 | 2.38 S | 118.49 E |
| Rangasa, Tanjung ≻ | 112 | 3.33 S | 118.56 E |
| Rangaunu Bay c | 172 | 34.50 S | 173.15 E |
| Range Creek ≃ | 200 | 39.18 N | 110.04 W |
| Range Indian Reserve ◆[4] | 182 | 49.09 N | 119.50 W |
| Rangeley | 188 | 44.57 N | 70.38 W |
| Rangely | 200 | 40.05 N | 108.48 W |
| Ranger | 196 | 32.28 N | 98.40 W |
| Ranger Lake ⊜ | 190 | 46.54 N | 83.35 W |
| Rangersdorf | 64 | 46.51 N | 12.58 E |
| Ranghe | 100 | 33.43 N | 112.51 E |
| Rangia | 120 | 26.28 N | 91.38 E |
| Rangiora | 172 | 43.18 S | 172.36 E |
| Rangitaiki ≃ | 172 | 37.54 S | 176.53 E |
| Rangitata ≃ | 172 | 44.12 S | 171.30 E |
| Rangitikei ≃ | 172 | 40.18 S | 175.14 E |
| Rangitukia | 172 | 37.46 S | 178.27 E |
| Rangkasbitung | 115a | 6.21 S | 106.15 E |
| Rangkul' | 85 | 38.29 N | 74.22 E |
| Rangoon → Yangon | 110 | 16.47 N | 96.10 E |
| Rangoon ≃ | 110 | 16.29 N | 96.21 E |
| Rangpo | 124 | 27.11 N | 88.32 E |
| Rangpur, Bngl. | 124 | 25.45 N | 89.15 E |
| Rangpur, Pāk. | 123 | 30.31 N | 71.34 E |
| Rangpuri ⊥ | 272a | 28.33 N | 77.08 E |
| Rangsang, Pulau I | 114 | 1.00 N | 102.55 E |
| Rangsdorf | 54 | 52.17 N | 13.25 E |
| Rangsdorfer See ⊜ | 264a | 52.17 N | 13.24 E |
| Ranguana Cay I | 236 | 16.20 N | 88.09 W |
| Ranguana Entrance ⩌ | 236 | 16.19 N | 88.09 W |
| Rangun → Yangon | 110 | 16.47 N | 96.10 E |
| Ranholas | 266c | 38.47 N | 9.22 W |
| Rānibāndh | 126 | 22.52 N | 86.47 E |
| Rānībennur | 122 | 14.37 N | 75.37 E |
| Rānīganj | 126 | 23.37 N | 87.08 E |
| Rānikhet | 124 | 29.39 N | 79.25 E |
| Ranino | 80 | 52.58 N | 40.15 E |
| Ranis | 54 | 50.39 N | 11.34 E |
| Rānīwāra | 120 | 24.45 N | 72.13 E |
| Rāniyah | 128 | 36.15 N | 44.53 E |
| Rankamhaeng National Park ♦ | 110 | 17.10 N | 99.58 E |
| Ranken ≃ | 166 | 20.31 S | 137.36 E |
| Ranken Store | 166 | 19.35 S | 136.55 E |
| Rankin, Il., U.S. | 216 | 40.27 N | 87.53 W |
| Rankin, Mi., U.S. | 216 | 42.55 N | 83.46 W |
| Rankin, Pa., U.S. | 279b | 40.24 N | 79.52 W |
| Rankin, Tx., U.S. | 196 | 31.13 N | 101.56 W |
| Rankin Inlet | 176 | 62.45 N | 92.10 W |
| Rankins Springs | 166 | 33.50 S | 146.16 E |
| Rankūs | 132 | 33.45 N | 36.23 E |
| Rankweil | 58 | 47.17 N | 9.39 E |
| Ranlo | 192 | 35.17 N | 81.07 W |
| Ranneje | 80 | 51.29 N | 52.37 E |
| Rannersdorf | 264b | 48.08 N | 16.28 E |
| Rannoch, Loch ⊜ | 46 | 56.41 N | 4.20 W |
| Rannoch Moor ◆[3] | 46 | 56.38 N | 4.40 W |
| Rann of Kutch → Kutch, Rann of ◆[1] | 120 | 24.05 N | 70.10 E |
| Ranobe ≃ | 157b | 17.10 S | 44.08 E |
| Ranohira | 157b | 22.29 S | 45.24 E |
| Ranomafana, Madag. | 157b | 18.57 S | 48.50 E |
| Ranomafana, Madag. | 157b | 24.36 S | 46.58 E |
| Ranomena | 157b | 23.25 S | 47.17 E |
| Ranong | 110 | 9.58 N | 98.38 E |
| Ranongga Island I | 175e | 8.05 S | 156.34 E |
| Ranopiso | 157b | 25.03 S | 46.40 E |
| Ranot | 110 | 7.46 N | 100.19 E |
| Ranotsara Nord | 157b | 22.48 S | 46.36 E |
| Rānsai | 272c | 18.53 N | 73.05 E |
| Ransäter | 40 | 59.46 N | 13.26 E |
| Ransiki | 164 | 1.30 S | 134.10 E |
| Ransom, Il., U.S. | 216 | 41.09 N | 88.39 W |
| Ransom, Ks., U.S. | 198 | 38.38 N | 99.56 W |
| Ransom, Pa., U.S. | 210 | 41.24 N | 75.50 W |
| Ransom Creek ≃ | 284a | 43.04 N | 78.45 W |
| Ransomville | 210 | 43.14 N | 78.54 W |
| Ranson | 188 | 39.17 N | 77.51 W |
| Ransta | 40 | 59.48 N | 16.38 E |
| Rantabe | 157b | 15.42 S | 49.39 E |
| Rantasalmi | 26 | 62.04 N | 28.18 E |
| Rantau, Indon. | 112 | 2.56 S | 115.09 E |
| Rantau, Malay. | 114 | 2.35 N | 101.58 E |
| Rantaukampar | 114 | 1.24 N | 100.59 E |
| Rantaupanjang, Indon. | 112 | 1.51 S | 102.19 E |
| Rantaupanjang, Indon. | 112 | 1.16 S | 101.49 E |
| Rantaupanjang, Indon. | 114 | 0.58 N | 99.13 E |
| Rantauprapat | 114 | 2.06 N | 99.50 E |
| Rantekombola, Bulu ∧ | 112 | 3.21 S | 120.01 E |
| Ranten | 61 | 47.09 N | 14.05 E |
| Rantepao | 112 | 2.59 S | 119.54 E |
| Rantigny | 50 | 49.20 N | 2.26 E |
| Rantoul | 216 | 40.09 N | 88.20 W |
| Rantsila | 26 | 64.31 N | 25.39 E |
| Rantzau | 54 | 54.15 N | 10.30 E |
| Ranua | 26 | 65.55 N | 26.32 E |
| Rānvād | 272c | 18.53 N | 72.55 E |
| Ranwanalenaus | 156 | 19.35 S | 22.47 E |
| Råö | 26 | 57.24 N | 11.56 E |
| Rao'er | 100 | 28.48 N | 117.40 E |
| Raohe | 89 | 46.47 N | 134.00 E |
| Raon-L'Étape | 58 | 48.24 N | 6.51 E |
| Raon-sur-Plaine | 58 | 48.31 N | 7.06 E |
| Raoping | 100 | 23.43 N | 117.01 E |
| Raoui, 'Erg er ◆[2] | 148 | 29.17 N | 2.20 W |
| Raoul | 192 | 34.27 N | 83.36 W |
| Raoul Island I | 14 | 29.16 S | 177.54 W |
| Raoyang | 98 | 38.16 N | 115.44 E |
| Raoyang ≃ | 104 | 41.50 N | 122.35 E |
| Raoyanghe | 104 | 41.46 N | 122.26 E |
| Rapa I | 14 | 27.36 S | 144.20 W |
| Rapa, Ponta do ≻ | 252 | 27.22 S | 48.26 W |
| Rapallo | 62 | 44.21 N | 9.14 E |
| Rapang | 112 | 3.50 S | 119.48 E |
| Rāpar | 120 | 23.34 N | 70.38 E |
| Raparo, Monte ∧ | 68 | 40.12 N | 15.59 E |
| Rapatovo | 80 | 55.04 N | 54.37 E |
| Rāpch ≃ | 128 | 25.28 N | 59.21 E |
| Rapel ≃ | 252 | 33.55 S | 71.51 W |
| Rapel, Embalse ⊜[1] | 252 | 34.12 S | 71.30 W |
| Rapelli | 252 | 26.24 S | 64.29 W |
| Raphoe | 48 | 54.52 N | 7.36 W |
| Rapid ≃, Mi., U.S. | 190 | 45.55 N | 86.58 W |
| Rapid ≃, Mn., U.S. | 198 | 48.42 N | 94.26 W |
| Rapid ≃, Wa., U.S. | 224 | 47.48 N | 121.18 W |
| Rapidan ≃ | 188 | 38.22 N | 77.37 W |
| Rapid Bay | 168b | 35.32 S | 138.12 E |
| Rapid City, Mb., Can. | 184 | 50.08 N | 100.02 W |
| Rapid City, Mi., U.S. | 190 | 44.50 N | 85.16 W |
| Rapid City, S.D., U.S. | 198 | 44.04 N | 103.13 W |
| Rapid Creek ≃ | 198 | 43.54 N | 102.37 W |
| Rapide Taureau, Barrage du ◆[6] | 206 | 46.52 N | 73.39 W |
| Rapid River | 190 | 45.55 N | 86.58 W |
| Räpina | 76 | 58.06 N | 27.27 E |
| Rapkan | 85 | 40.22 N | 70.40 E |
| Rapla | 76 | 59.01 N | 24.47 E |
| Rapness | 46 | 59.14 N | 2.51 W |
| Rapolano Terme | 66 | 43.17 N | 11.36 E |
| Rapolla | 68 | 40.58 N | 15.41 E |
| Rapone | 68 | 40.51 N | 15.30 E |
| Raposo ∧[2] | 266c | 38.40 N | 9.11 W |
| Rappahannock ≃ | 208 | 37.34 N | 76.18 W |
| Rappbodestausee ⊜[1] | 54 | 51.44 N | 10.53 E |
| Rappenlochschlucht ⌞ | 58 | 47.23 N | 9.47 E |
| Rappottenstein | 61 | 48.31 N | 15.05 E |
| Rāptī □[8] | 124 | 28.15 N | 82.30 E |
| Rāpti (Rāptī) ≃, Asia | 124 | 26.18 N | 83.41 E |
| Rāptī ≃, Nepāl | 124 | 27.33 N | 84.07 E |
| Rapulo ≃ | 248 | 13.43 S | 65.32 W |
| Rapu-Rapu | 116 | 13.11 N | 124.08 E |
| Rapu Rapu Island I | 116 | 13.12 N | 124.09 E |
| Raqabah, Khashm ar- ∧[2] | 142 | 28.18 N | 31.43 E |
| Raquette ≃ | 206 | 45.00 N | 74.42 W |
| Raraka I[1] | 14 | 16.10 S | 144.54 W |
| Rara National Park ♦ | 124 | 29.35 N | 82.05 E |
| Rārh Plains ≃ | 126 | 23.13 N | 87.20 E |
| Rāribahāl | 126 | 24.05 N | 87.21 E |
| Raritan | 210 | 40.34 N | 74.38 W |
| Raritan ≃ | 208 | 40.29 N | 74.17 W |
| Raritan, North Branch ≃ | 210 | 40.33 N | 74.41 W |
| Raritan, South Branch ≃ | 210 | 40.33 N | 74.41 W |
| Raritan Bay c | 208 | 40.28 N | 74.12 W |
| Raroïa I | 14 | 16.01 S | 142.27 W |
| Raron | 58 | 46.19 N | 7.48 E |
| Rarotonga I | 174k | 21.14 S | 159.46 W |
| Rarotonga International Airport ⊠ | 174k | 21.12 S | 159.49 W |
| Rarz | 85 | 39.23 N | 68.44 E |
| Rasa, Ilha I | 287a | 23.04 S | 43.09 W |
| Rasa, Punta ≻, Arg. | 252 | 36.17 S | 56.47 W |
| Rasa, Punta ≻, Arg. | 254 | 40.51 S | 62.19 W |
| Rašaant | 88 | 49.07 N | 101.25 E |
| Rasa de Guaratiba, Ilha I | 256 | 23.05 S | 43.34 W |
| Rasa Island I | 116 | 9.14 N | 118.27 E |
| Ra's al-'Ayn | 130 | 36.51 N | 40.04 E |
| Ra's al-Barr | 142 | 31.31 N | 31.50 E |
| Ra's al-Khalīj | 142 | 31.15 N | 31.39 E |
| Ra's al-Khaymah | 128 | 25.47 N | 55.57 E |
| Ra's al-Unūf | 146 | 30.31 N | 18.34 E |
| Ra's al-Ushsh ◆[8] | 142 | 31.08 N | 32.18 E |
| Ra's an-Naqb, Miṣr | 132 | 29.36 N | 34.51 E |
| Ra's an-Naqb, Urd. | 132 | 30.00 N | 35.29 E |
| Rasawi | 164 | 2.04 S | 134.01 E |
| Ra's Ba'labakk | 130 | 34.15 N | 36.25 E |
| Rasbo | 40 | 59.57 N | 17.53 E |
| Râşcani | 38 | 47.58 N | 27.32 E |
| Raschau | 54 | 50.32 N | 12.50 E |
| Raşcov | 38 | 47.57 N | 28.50 E |
| Ras Dashen Terara ∧ | 144 | 13.16 N | 38.24 E |
| Rasdorf | 56 | 50.43 N | 9.53 E |
| Raseborg | 26 | 59.59 N | 23.39 E |
| Raseiniai | 76 | 55.24 N | 23.07 E |
| Râs el Aïoun | 36 | 35.30 N | 8.18 E |
| Ras el Ma, Alg. | 148 | 34.31 N | 0.46 W |
| Râs el Mâ, Mali | 150 | 16.37 N | 4.28 W |
| Ras el Oued | 34 | 35.57 N | 5.03 E |
| Rashād | 140 | 11.51 N | 31.04 E |
| Rāshayyā | 132 | 33.30 N | 35.51 E |
| Rashīd (Rosetta) | 142 | 31.24 N | 30.25 E |
| Rashīd, Far' (Rosetta Branch) ≃ | 142 | 31.30 N | 30.21 E |
| Rashīd, Maṣabb (Rosetta Mouth) ≃[1] | 142 | 31.30 N | 30.20 E |
| Rashīd Qal'eh | 120 | 31.31 N | 67.31 E |
| Rashin → Najin | 98 | 42.15 N | 130.18 E |
| Rashivka | 78 | 50.14 N | 33.54 E |
| Rasht | 128 | 37.16 N | 49.36 E |
| Rashtrapati Bhawan ʋ | 272a | 28.37 N | 77.12 E |
| Rasina ≃ | 38 | 43.37 N | 21.22 E |
| Rāsipuram | 122 | 11.28 N | 78.10 E |
| Rasi Salai | 110 | 15.20 N | 104.09 E |
| Rāsk | 128 | 26.13 N | 61.25 E |
| Raška | 38 | 43.17 N | 20.37 E |
| Rask Mølle | 41 | 55.52 N | 9.37 E |
| Rās Koh ∧ | 128 | 28.50 N | 65.12 E |
| Raskunda | 126 | 22.48 N | 87.26 E |
| Rasm al-Arwām, Sabkhat ⊜ | 130 | 35.53 N | 37.40 E |
| Rasna | 76 | 54.01 N | 31.12 E |
| Râşnov | 38 | 45.36 N | 25.28 E |
| Raso, Cabo ≻ | 266c | 38.43 N | 9.29 W |
| Raso, Ilhéu I | 150a | 16.37 N | 24.36 W |
| Rasocolmo, Capo ≻ | 70 | 38.18 N | 15.31 E |
| Rason Lake ⊜ | 162 | 28.46 S | 124.20 E |
| Rasony | 76 | 55.53 N | 28.49 E |
| Raspberry Peak ∧ | 194 | 34.23 N | 94.01 W |
| Raspopinskaja | 80 | 49.24 N | 42.52 E |
| Rasra | 124 | 25.51 N | 83.51 E |
| Rass Jebel | 36 | 37.13 N | 10.09 E |
| Rasskazovka | 265b | 55.38 N | 37.20 E |
| Rasskazovo | 80 | 52.40 N | 41.53 E |
| Rassua, ostrov I | 74 | 47.45 N | 153.01 E |
| Rassudovo | 82 | 55.29 N | 36.54 E |
| Rassvet, Ross. | 84 | 43.58 N | 46.44 E |
| Rassvet, Ross. | 84 | 43.58 N | 46.44 E |
| Rassvet, Ross. | 86 | 57.02 N | 91.34 E |
| Rassvet, Ross. | 88 | 57.02 N | 91.34 E |
| Rassypnaja | 80 | 51.35 N | 53.37 E |
| Rast | 38 | 43.53 N | 23.17 E |
| Rasta ≃ | 76 | 53.36 N | 30.56 E |
| Rastälven ≃ | 40 | 59.37 N | 14.56 E |
| Ra's Tannūrah | 128 | 26.42 N | 50.06 E |
| Rastatt | 56 | 48.51 N | 8.12 E |
| Rastede | 52 | 53.15 N | 8.11 E |
| Rastegai'sa ∧ | 24 | 70.00 N | 26.18 E |
| Rastenberg | 54 | 51.10 N | 11.25 E |
| Rastenburg → Kętrzyn | 30 | 54.06 N | 21.23 E |
| Rastorf | 54 | 54.16 N | 10.19 E |
| Rastorgujevo | 82 | 55.33 N | 37.41 E |
| Rastovcy | 82 | 56.39 N | 37.35 E |
| Rastow | 54 | 53.27 N | 11.26 E |
| Rastunovo | 82 | 55.16 N | 37.50 E |
| Rasu, Monte ∧ | 71 | 40.25 N | 9.00 E |
| Rasūl | 123 | 32.42 N | 73.34 E |
| Rasūlnagar | 123 | 32.20 N | 73.47 E |
| Rasulpur | 272a | 28.37 N | 77.22 E |
| Rasulpur ◆[8] | 272a | 28.42 N | 77.01 E |
| Rasun di sopra | 64 | 46.48 N | 12.03 E |
| Rasun di sotto | 64 | 46.47 N | 12.02 E |
| Rasura | 58 | 46.06 N | 9.33 E |
| Råsvalen ⊜ | 40 | 59.40 N | 15.10 E |
| Rat ≃, Mb., Can. | 184 | 49.35 N | 97.08 W |
| Rat ≃, Mb., Can. | 184 | 55.41 N | 99.04 W |
| Ratahan | 112 | 1.04 N | 124.48 E |
| Ratak Chain II | 14 | 9.00 N | 171.00 E |
| Ratamka | 76 | 53.56 N | 27.21 E |
| Ratangarh | 120 | 28.05 N | 74.36 E |
| Ratanpur, India | 126 | 23.07 N | 87.04 E |
| Ratanpur, India | 272b | 22.50 N | 88.14 E |
| Rätansbyn | 26 | 62.29 N | 14.32 E |
| Rat Burana | 269a | 13.41 N | 100.30 E |
| Ratčino, Ross. | 80 | 53.02 N | 39.55 E |
| Ratčino, Ross. | 82 | 55.16 N | 38.39 E |
| Ratcliff | 222 | 31.24 N | 95.08 W |
| Rateče | 64 | 46.30 N | 13.43 E |
| Ratekau | 54 | 53.57 N | 10.44 E |
| Rāth | 124 | 25.35 N | 79.34 E |
| Rath ◆[8] | 263 | 51.17 N | 6.49 E |
| Rathangan | 48 | 53.12 N | 6.59 W |
| Rathbone | 210 | 42.08 N | 77.19 W |
| Rathbun Lake ⊜ | 212 | 44.47 N | 78.12 W |
| Rathbun Lake ⊜[1] | 190 | 40.54 N | 93.05 W |
| Rathcoole | 48 | 53.16 N | 6.28 W |
| Rathcormack | 48 | 52.05 N | 8.17 W |
| Rathdowney, Austl. | 171a | 28.12 S | 152.52 E |
| Rathdowney, Ire. | 48 | 52.50 N | 7.34 W |
| Rathdrum, Ire. | 48 | 52.56 N | 6.13 W |
| Rathdrum, Id., U.S. | 202 | 47.48 N | 116.53 W |
| Rathebur | 54 | 53.44 N | 13.46 E |
| Ratheim | 52 | 51.04 N | 6.10 E |
| Rathen | 46 | 57.38 N | 2.02 W |
| Rathenow | 54 | 52.36 N | 12.20 E |
| Rathfriland | 48 | 54.14 N | 6.10 W |
| Rathkeale | 48 | 52.32 N | 8.56 W |
| Rathlin Island I | 48 | 55.18 N | 6.13 W |
| Rathlin Sound ⩌ | 48 | 55.15 N | 6.15 W |
| Ráth Luirc (Charleville) | 48 | 52.21 N | 8.41 W |
| Rathmecke | 263 | 51.15 N | 7.38 E |
| Rathmelton | 48 | 55.02 N | 7.38 W |
| Rathmore | 48 | 52.03 N | 9.13 W |
| Rathmullan | 48 | 55.06 N | 7.33 W |
| Rathnew | 48 | 53.00 N | 6.05 W |
| Ratho | 46 | 55.55 N | 3.22 W |
| Rathowen | 48 | 53.40 N | 7.31 W |
| Rathstock | 54 | 52.31 N | 14.32 E |
| Rathwell | 184 | 49.40 N | 98.32 W |
| Ratibor → Racibórz | 30 | 50.06 N | 18.13 E |
| Raticosa, Passo della )( | 66 | 44.10 N | 11.20 E |
| Rätikon ⋏ | 58 | 47.03 N | 9.40 E |
| Ratingen | 56 | 51.18 N | 6.51 E |
| Ratisbon → Regensburg | 60 | 49.01 N | 12.06 E |
| Rätische Alpen → Rhaetian Alps ⋏ | 58 | 46.30 N | 10.00 E |
| Rat Island I | 181a | 51.55 N | 178.20 E |
| Rat Islands II | 181a | 51.40 N | 178.30 E |
| Rat'kovo | 82 | 56.01 N | 38.38 E |
| Rat Lake ⊜ | 184 | 56.10 N | 99.40 W |
| Ratlām | 120 | 23.19 N | 75.04 E |
| Ratmanova, ostrov I | 180 | 65.46 N | 169.02 W |
| Ratnāgiri | 122 | 16.59 N | 73.18 E |
| Ratnapura | 122 | 6.41 N | 80.24 E |
| Ratne | 78 | 51.40 N | 24.31 E |
| Ratodero | 120 | 27.48 N | 68.18 E |
| Raton | 196 | 36.54 N | 104.26 W |
| Raton Pass )( | 196 | 36.59 N | 104.29 W |
| Ratqah, Wādī ar- V | 130 | 34.25 N | 40.55 E |
| Ratt ≃ | 224 | 47.27 N | 124.21 W |
| Rattanaburi | 110 | 15.19 N | 103.51 E |
| Rattaphum | 110 | 7.08 N | 100.16 E |
| Rattelsdorf | 56 | 50.01 N | 10.53 E |
| Ratten | 61 | 47.29 N | 15.43 E |
| Rattlesnake | 202 | 46.56 N | 113.59 W |
| Rattlesnake Creek ≃, Ks., U.S. | 198 | 38.13 N | 98.22 W |
| Rattlesnake Creek ≃, Oh., U.S. | 218 | 39.16 N | 83.23 W |
| Rattlesnake Creek ≃, Or., U.S. | 202 | 42.44 N | 117.47 W |
| Rattlesnake Creek ≃, Wa., U.S. | 224 | 46.45 N | 120.55 W |
| Rattlesnake Creek ≃, Wa., U.S. | 224 | 45.48 N | 121.29 W |
| Rattlesnake Mountain ∧ | 207 | 41.42 N | 72.50 W |
| Rattlesnake Peak ∧ | 280 | 34.16 N | 117.47 W |
| Rattling Brook | 186 | 49.38 N | 56.10 W |
| Rattling Run ≃ | 279b | 40.33 N | 79.32 W |
| Rattray | 46 | 56.35 N | 3.19 W |
| Rattray Head ≻ | 46 | 57.37 N | 1.49 W |
| Rattu | 123 | 35.08 N | 74.48 E |
| Rättvik | 26 | 60.53 N | 15.06 E |
| Ratz, Mount ∧ | 180 | 57.23 N | 132.19 W |
| Ratzeburg | 54 | 53.42 N | 10.46 E |
| Ratzeburger See ⊜ | 54 | 53.45 N | 10.47 E |
| Rätzlingen | 54 | 52.23 N | 11.08 E |
| Rau | 112 | 0.34 N | 100.01 E |
| Raub, Malay. | 114 | 3.48 N | 101.52 E |
| Raub, In., U.S. | 216 | 40.44 N | 87.29 W |
| Raubling | 64 | 47.48 N | 12.07 E |
| Raubsville | 208 | 40.38 N | 75.12 W |
| Rauch | 252 | 36.46 S | 59.06 W |
| Raucheck ∧ | 64 | 47.30 N | 13.14 E |
| Rauchenwarth | 264b | 48.05 N | 16.32 E |
| Rauchtown | 210 | 41.07 N | 77.14 W |
| Raucourt-et-Flaba | 56 | 49.36 N | 4.57 E |
| Rauen | 54 | 52.20 N | 14.01 E |
| Rauenstein | 54 | 50.24 N | 11.03 E |
| Raufarhöfn | 24a | 66.30 N | 15.57 W |
| Raufoss | 26 | 60.43 N | 10.37 E |
| Rauhe Ebrach ≃ | 56 | 49.50 N | 10.56 E |
| Raukumara Range ⋏ | 172 | 37.47 S | 178.02 E |
| Raul Soares | 255 | 20.05 S | 42.22 W |
| Rauma | 26 | 61.08 N | 21.30 E |
| Rauma ≃ | 26 | 62.33 N | 7.43 E |
| Raumünzach | 56 | 48.38 N | 8.21 E |
| Rauna | 76 | 57.20 N | 25.43 E |
| Raunds | 42 | 52.21 N | 0.33 W |
| Raung, Gunung ∧ | 115a | 8.08 S | 114.03 E |
| Raunheim | 56 | 50.01 N | 8.28 E |
| Raupal'an | 180 | 65.28 N | 171.59 W |
| Raurimu | 172 | 39.07 S | 175.24 E |
| Rauris | 64 | 47.13 N | 13.00 E |
| Raurkela | 124 | 22.13 N | 84.53 E |
| Rauschenberg | 56 | 50.53 N | 8.55 E |
| Rausu | 92a | 44.01 N | 145.12 E |
| Răut ≃ | 38 | 47.15 N | 29.09 E |
| Rautalampi | 26 | 62.38 N | 26.50 E |
| Rāutara | 272b | 22.51 N | 88.28 E |
| Rautavaara | 26 | 63.29 N | 28.18 E |
| Ravahere I[1] | 14 | 18.14 S | 142.09 W |
| Ravalgaon | 122 | 20.38 N | 74.25 E |
| Ravanica, Manastir ʋ[1] | 38 | 43.58 N | 21.26 E |
| Ravānsar | 128 | 34.43 N | 46.40 E |
| Ravanusa | 70 | 37.16 N | 13.58 E |
| Rāvar | 128 | 31.15 N | 56.53 E |
| Ravarano | 64 | 44.35 N | 10.04 E |
| Ravarino | 64 | 44.44 N | 11.06 E |
| Rava-Rus'ka | 78 | 50.14 N | 23.37 E |
| Ravascletto | 64 | 46.32 N | 12.57 E |
| Ravat | 85 | 39.54 N | 70.12 E |
| Ravello | 68 | 40.39 N | 14.37 E |
| Ravelo | 248 | 18.48 S | 65.32 W |
| Raven | 192 | 37.05 N | 81.51 W |
| Ravena | 210 | 42.28 N | 73.49 W |
| Ravenglass | 44 | 54.21 N | 3.24 W |
| Raven Lake ⊜ | 212 | 45.13 N | 78.51 W |
| Ravenna, It. | 66 | 44.25 N | 12.12 E |
| Ravenna, Ky., U.S. | 192 | 37.41 N | 83.57 W |
| Ravenna, Mi., U.S. | 216 | 43.11 N | 85.56 W |
| Ravenna, Ne., U.S. | 198 | 41.01 N | 98.54 W |
| Ravenna, Oh., U.S. | 214 | 41.09 N | 81.14 W |
| Ravenna □[4] | 66 | 44.25 N | 11.59 E |
| Ravensbourne | 171a | 27.22 S | 152.10 E |
| Ravensbourne National Park ♦ | 171a | 27.21 S | 152.15 E |
| Ravensburg | 58 | 47.47 N | 9.37 E |
| Ravenscrag | 184 | 49.30 N | 109.05 W |
| Ravensdale | 224 | 47.21 N | 121.58 W |
| Ravenshoe | 166 | 17.37 S | 145.29 E |
| Ravenstein | 56 | 49.24 N | 9.30 E |
| Ravensthorpe | 162 | 33.35 S | 120.02 E |
| Ravenswood, S. Afr. | 273d | 26.11 S | 28.15 E |
| Ravenswood, Mi., U.S. | 216 | 42.45 N | 84.36 W |
| Ravenswood, W.V., U.S. | 188 | 38.56 N | 81.45 W |
| Ravenswood Park ♦ | 283 | 42.36 N | 70.42 W |
| Ravenswood Point ≻ | 282 | 37.30 N | 122.08 W |
| Ravensworth | 284c | 38.48 N | 77.13 W |
| Rāver | 120 | 21.15 N | 76.02 E |
| Ravernet ≃ | 48 | 54.30 N | 6.04 W |
| Rāvi ≃ | 123 | 30.35 N | 71.49 E |
| Ravières | 50 | 47.45 N | 4.17 E |
| Ravine | 208 | 40.34 N | 76.24 W |
| Ravine Lake ⊜[1] | 276 | 40.43 N | 74.38 W |
| Ravinia Park ♦ | 278 | 42.09 N | 87.46 W |
| Ravna Gora | 36 | 45.23 N | 14.57 E |
| Ravne | 61 | 46.33 N | 14.58 E |
| Ravnina | 128 | 37.57 N | 62.40 E |
| Ravsted | 41 | 55.01 N | 9.08 E |
| Rāwah | 128 | 34.28 N | 41.55 E |
| Rawaki I[1] | 14 | 3.43 S | 170.43 W |
| Rāwala Kot | 123 | 33.52 N | 73.46 E |
| Rāwalpindi | 123 | 33.36 N | 73.04 E |
| Rawa Mazowiecka | 30 | 51.46 N | 20.16 E |
| Rāwāndūz | 128 | 36.37 N | 44.31 E |
| Rawang | 114 | 3.19 N | 101.35 E |
| Rawas ≃ | 112 | 2.42 S | 103.24 E |
| Rāwatsar | 123 | 29.17 N | 74.23 E |
| Rawāwiṣ, Wādī V | 146 | 30.26 N | 15.24 E |
| Rawḍah ⊜ | 130 | 35.15 N | 41.05 E |
| Rawḍah, Wādī ar- V | 130 | 34.22 N | 37.21 E |
| Rawd al-Faraj ◆[8] | 273c | 30.05 N | 31.14 E |
| Rawḍaw, Jazīrat ar- I | 273c | 30.01 N | 31.13 E |
| Rawdon | 206 | 46.03 N | 73.43 W |
| Rawene | 172 | 35.24 S | 173.30 E |
| Rawḥah | 144 | 19.28 N | 41.48 E |
| Rawhide Creek ≃ | 198 | 42.06 N | 104.20 W |
| Rawhide Lake ⊜ | 190 | 46.39 N | 82.37 W |
| Rawhide Mountain ∧ | 204 | 38.17 N | 116.25 W |
| Rawi | 112 | 2.07 S | 113.56 E |
| Rawi, Ko I | 114 | 6.33 N | 99.14 E |
| Rawicz | 30 | 51.37 N | 16.52 E |
| Rawlinna | 162 | 31.01 S | 125.20 E |
| Rawlins | 200 | 41.47 N | 107.14 W |
| Rawlinson, Mount ∧ | 162 | 25.58 S | 127.28 E |
| Rawlinson Range ⋏ | 162 | 24.51 S | 128.00 E |
| Rawmarsh | 44 | 53.27 N | 1.21 W |
| Rawreth | 260 | 51.37 N | 0.35 E |
| Rawson, Arg. | 252 | 34.36 S | 60.04 W |
| Rawson, Arg. | 254 | 43.18 S | 65.06 W |
| Rawson, Oh., U.S. | 216 | 40.57 N | 83.47 W |
| Rawsonville | 158 | 33.41 S | 19.20 E |
| Rawtenstall | 44 | 53.42 N | 2.18 W |
| Rawu | 102 | 29.30 N | 96.45 E |
| Rax ⋏ | 61 | 47.42 N | 15.43 E |
| Raxāul | 124 | 26.59 N | 84.51 E |
| Ray, Il., U.S. | 219 | 40.12 N | 90.29 W |
| Ray, In., U.S. | 216 | 41.45 N | 84.53 W |
| Ray, N.D., U.S. | 198 | 48.20 N | 103.09 W |
| Ray ≃ | 42 | 51.48 N | 1.15 W |
| Ray, Cape ≻ | 186 | 47.40 N | 59.18 W |
| Raya | 112 | 1.05 N | 118.32 E |
| Raya, Bukit ∧ | 112 | 0.40 S | 112.41 E |
| Raya, Gunong ∧ | 114 | 6.22 N | 99.49 E |
| Raya, Pulau I | 114 | 4.52 N | 95.22 E |
| Rāyachoti | 122 | 14.03 N | 78.45 E |
| Rāyadurg | 122 | 14.42 N | 76.52 E |
| Rāyagarha | 122 | 19.10 N | 83.25 E |
| Rayburn | 222 | 30.25 N | 94.56 W |
| Rayen, Dtsch. | 263 | 51.28 N | 6.32 E |
| Rāyen, Īrān | 128 | 29.34 N | 57.26 E |
| Rayhorodka | 83 | 48.50 N | 39.04 E |
| Rayhorodok | 83 | 48.54 N | 37.43 E |
| Ray Hubbard, Lake ⊜[1] | 222 | 32.53 N | 96.35 W |
| Rāyikhah I | 128 | 26.12 N | 36.21 E |
| Rayland | 214 | 40.11 N | 80.41 W |
| Rayleigh | 42 | 51.36 N | 0.36 E |
| Raymond, Ab., Can. | 182 | 49.27 N | 112.39 W |
| Raymond, Ca., U.S. | 226 | 37.13 N | 119.54 W |
| Raymond, Il., U.S. | 219 | 39.19 N | 89.34 W |
| Raymond, Mn., U.S. | 198 | 45.00 N | 95.14 W |
| Raymond, Ms., U.S. | 194 | 32.15 N | 90.25 W |
| Raymond, Oh., U.S. | 216 | 40.20 N | 83.28 W |
| Raymond, Wa., U.S. | 224 | 46.41 N | 123.43 W |
| Raymond Terrace | 170 | 32.46 S | 151.44 E |
| Raymondville | 196 | 26.29 N | 97.47 W |
| Raymore | 184 | 51.25 N | 104.31 W |
| Ray Mountains ⋏ | 180 | 65.45 N | 151.30 W |
| Rāyna | 126 | 23.05 N | 87.54 E |
| Rayne | 194 | 30.14 N | 92.16 W |
| Raynham | 207 | 41.56 N | 71.04 W |
| Raynham Greyhound Park ♦ | 283 | 41.59 N | 71.04 W |
| Rayón, Méx. | 232 | 29.43 N | 110.35 W |
| Rayón, Méx. | 234 | 17.12 N | 93.00 W |
| Rayón, Méx. | 234 | 21.51 N | 99.40 W |
| Rayones | 232 | 25.01 N | 100.05 W |
| Rayong | 110 | 12.40 N | 101.17 E |
| Rāypur | 272b | 22.25 N | 88.31 E |
| Rayrah ≖[4] | 140 | 15.21 N | 34.41 E |
| Rayse Creek ≃ | 219 | 38.13 N | 89.00 W |
| Raystown Lake ⊜[1] | 214 | 40.20 N | 78.05 W |
| Rayton | 158 | 25.45 S | 28.32 E |
| Raytown | 194 | 39.00 N | 94.27 W |
| Rayville | 194 | 32.28 N | 91.45 W |
| Raywood | 222 | 30.02 N | 94.40 W |
| Raz, Pointe du ≻ | 32 | 48.02 N | 4.44 W |
| Raza, Punta ≻ | 234 | 21.02 N | 105.20 W |
| Razan, Īrān | 128 | 35.23 N | 49.02 E |
| R'azan', Ross. | 80 | 54.38 N | 39.44 E |
| R'azancevo | 82 | 56.42 N | 39.12 E |
| Ražanj | 38 | 43.40 N | 21.33 E |
| R'azan' Oblast' □[4] | 76 | 54.30 N | 40.30 E |
| R'azanovo | 82 | 55.29 N | 37.31 E |
| Razbegaj | 265a | 59.47 N | 29.56 E |
| Războieni | 38 | 47.05 N | 26.32 E |
| Razdan | 84 | 40.30 N | 44.46 E |
| Razdan ≃ | 84 | 39.58 N | 44.27 E |
| Razdolinsk | 86 | 58.25 N | 94.38 E |
| Razdolje | 88 | 52.27 N | 103.13 E |
| Razdol'noje | 89 | 43.30 N | 131.52 E |
| Razdol'nyj | 80 | 46.38 N | 42.57 E |
| Razdorskaja | 78 | 47.33 N | 40.38 E |
| Razdory | 265b | 55.45 N | 37.18 E |
| Răzeni | 38 | 46.46 N | 28.54 E |
| R'aženoje | 83 | 47.31 N | 38.52 E |
| Raževo | 86 | 56.09 N | 68.25 E |
| Razgrad | 38 | 43.32 N | 26.31 E |
| Razgrad □[4] | 38 | 43.32 N | 26.31 E |
| Razim, Lacul ⊜ | 38 | 44.54 N | 28.57 E |
| Razlog | 38 | 41.53 N | 23.28 E |
| Razmachnino | 88 | 51.47 N | 115.28 E |
| Razmitelevo | 265a | 59.54 N | 30.41 E |
| Rāznas ezers ⊜ | 76 | 56.20 N | 27.27 E |
| Raznočinovka | 80 | 46.37 N | 47.57 E |
| Raznomojka | 86 | 52.29 N | 55.52 E |
| Razorback Mountain ∧ | 182 | 51.35 N | 124.42 W |
| R'ažsk | 80 | 53.43 N | 40.04 E |
| Răzvani | 38 | 44.25 N | 26.53 E |
| Razvil'noje | 80 | 46.14 N | 41.18 E |
| Razzoli, Isola I | 71 | 41.18 N | 9.21 E |
| Ré, Île de I | 32 | 46.12 N | 1.25 W |
| Rea ≃ | 42 | 52.18 N | 2.32 W |
| Read | 262 | 53.49 N | 2.21 W |
| Reading, Eng., U.K. | 42 | 51.28 N | 0.59 W |
| Reading, Il., U.S. | 216 | 41.05 N | 88.51 W |
| Reading, Ks., U.S. | 198 | 38.31 N | 95.57 W |
| Reading, Ma., U.S. | 207 | 42.31 N | 71.05 W |
| Reading, Mi., U.S. | 216 | 41.50 N | 84.44 W |
| Reading, Oh., U.S. | 218 | 39.13 N | 84.26 W |
| Reading, Pa., U.S. | 208 | 40.20 N | 75.55 W |
| Reading Center | 210 | 42.26 N | 76.56 W |
| Reading Station ◆[5] | 285 | 39.57 N | 75.10 W |
| Readington | 210 | 40.34 N | 74.44 W |
| Readlyn | 190 | 42.42 N | 92.13 W |


| ENGLISH Name | Page | Lat.°′ | Long.°′ |
|---|---|---|---|
| Readsboro | 207 | 42.46 N | 72.56 W |
| Readstown | 190 | 43.26 N | 90.45 W |
| Reagan | 222 | 31.13 N | 96.47 W |
| Real | 116 | 14.40 N | 121.36 E |
| Real ≃ | 250 | 11.27 S | 37.22 W |
| Real, Cordillera ⋏ | 248 | 19.00 S | 66.30 W |
| Real, Estero ≃ | 236 | 12.55 N | 87.23 W |
| Real del Padre | 252 | 34.50 S | 67.46 W |
| Real de San Carlos | 258 | 34.26 S | 57.53 W |
| Realengo ◆[8] | 256 | 22.53 S | 43.25 W |
| Real Felipe, Museo Histórico del ⊥ | 286d | 12.04 S | 77.09 W |
| Realicó | 252 | 35.02 S | 64.15 W |
| Realitos | 196 | 27.27 N | 98.32 W |
| Realmonte | 70 | 37.18 N | 13.28 E |
| Reamstown | 208 | 40.12 N | 76.07 W |
| Reana del Roiale | 64 | 46.12 N | 13.13 E |
| Reardan | 202 | 47.40 N | 117.52 W |
| Reata | 232 | 26.08 N | 101.05 W |
| Reatini, Monti ⋏ | 66 | 42.28 N | 13.00 E |
| Réau | 261 | 48.37 N | 2.38 E |
| Reay | 46 | 58.33 N | 3.47 W |
| Reay Forest ◆[3] | 46 | 58.19 N | 4.47 W |
| Rebecca, Lake ⊜ | 162 | 29.53 S | 122.10 E |
| Rebecq-Rognon | 50 | 50.40 N | 4.08 E |
| Rebeida, Wādī V | 140 | 20.45 N | 34.06 E |
| Rebel Hill | 285 | 40.04 N | 75.20 W |
| Rebersburg | 210 | 40.57 N | 77.27 W |
| Rebi | 164 | 6.23 S | 134.06 E |
| Rebiana Sand Sea → Rabyānah, Ṣaḥrā' ◆[2] | 146 | 24.20 N | 20.37 E |
| Rebild Bakker ♦ | 26 | 56.50 N | 9.51 E |
| Reboly | 24 | 63.50 N | 30.47 E |
| Rebouças | 252 | 25.36 S | 50.42 W |
| Reboucas, Túnel ◆[5] | 287a | 22.56 S | 43.14 W |
| Rebricha | 86 | 53.05 N | 82.20 E |
| Rebun-tō I | 92a | 45.23 N | 141.02 E |
| Recalde | 252 | 36.39 S | 61.05 W |
| Recanati | 66 | 43.24 N | 13.32 E |
| Rečane | 76 | 56.25 N | 31.39 E |
| Recco | 62 | 44.22 N | 9.09 E |
| Recey-sur-Ource | 58 | 47.47 N | 4.52 E |
| Rēchah Lām | 120 | 34.58 N | 70.51 E |
| Rechberghausen | 56 | 48.44 N | 9.38 E |
| Recherche, Archipelago of the II | 162 | 34.05 S | 122.45 E |
| Recherche, Cape ≻ | 175e | 10.11 S | 161.19 E |
| Réchicourt-le-Château | 58 | 48.40 N | 6.51 E |
| Rechlin | 54 | 53.21 N | 12.43 E |
| Rechna Doāb ⋏[1] | 123 | 31.35 N | 73.30 E |
| Rechnitz | 61 | 47.18 N | 16.27 E |
| Recife | 250 | 8.03 S | 34.54 W |
| Recife, Kaap ≻ | 158 | 34.02 S | 25.44 E |
| Recinto | 252 | 36.48 S | 71.44 W |
| Recke | 52 | 52.22 N | 7.43 E |
| Recklinghausen | 52 | 51.36 N | 7.13 E |
| Recknitz ≃ | 54 | 54.14 N | 12.28 E |
| Recoaro Terme | 64 | 45.42 N | 11.13 E |
| Recogne | 56 | 49.55 N | 5.22 E |
| Recoleta | 286e | 33.23 S | 70.38 W |
| Recologne | 58 | 47.16 N | 5.50 E |
| Reconquista | 252 | 29.09 S | 59.39 W |
| Reconquista, Río de la ≃ | 288 | 34.25 S | 58.35 W |
| Recovery Glacier ⊓ | 9 | 81.10 S | 28.00 W |
| Recreio | 255 | 21.32 S | 42.28 W |
| Recreo | 252 | 29.16 S | 65.04 W |
| Rector | 194 | 36.15 N | 90.17 W |
| Rectorville | 218 | 38.34 N | 83.39 W |
| Recuay | 248 | 9.43 S | 77.28 W |
| Rěčyca, Bela. | 76 | 52.22 N | 30.25 E |
| Rěčyca, Bela. | 78 | 51.52 N | 26.48 E |
| Recz | 30 | 53.16 N | 15.33 E |
| Red (Hong) (Yuan) ≃, Asia | 110 | 20.17 N | 106.34 E |
| Red ≃, N.A. | 178 | 50.24 N | 96.48 W |
| Red ≃, U.S. | 178 | 31.00 N | 91.40 W |
| Red ≃, U.S. | 194 | 36.32 N | 87.22 W |
| Red ≃, Ky., U.S. | 192 | 37.51 N | 84.05 W |
| Red ≃, N.M., U.S. | 200 | 36.39 N | 105.42 W |
| Red ≃, Wi., U.S. | 190 | 44.49 N | 88.38 W |
| Red, Elm Fork ≃ | 196 | 34.53 N | 99.19 W |
| Red, North Fork ≃ | 196 | 34.24 N | 99.14 W |
| Red, Prairie Dog Town Fork ≃ | 196 | 34.35 N | 99.58 W |
| Red, Salt Fork ≃ | 196 | 34.27 N | 99.22 W |
| Red, South Fork ≃ | 194 | 36.41 N | 86.56 W |
| Red, West Fork ≃ | 194 | 36.32 N | 87.21 W |
| Reda | 30 | 54.37 N | 18.21 E |
| Redang, Pulau I | 114 | 5.47 N | 103.00 E |
| Redange | 56 | 49.46 N | 5.54 E |
| Redang Panjang | 114 | 5.07 N | 100.47 E |
| Red Bank, N.J., U.S. | 208 | 40.20 N | 74.03 W |
| Red Bank, Tn., U.S. | 194 | 35.07 N | 85.17 W |
| Red Bank Battle Monument ⊥ | 285 | 39.52 N | 75.11 W |
| Redbank Creek ≃ | 214 | 40.58 N | 79.33 W |
| Red Banks | 194 | 34.49 N | 89.33 W |
| Red Bay, Nf., Can. | 186 | 51.44 N | 56.25 W |
| Red Bay, Al., U.S. | 194 | 34.26 N | 88.08 W |
| Redbay, Fl., U.S. | 194 | 30.35 N | 85.56 W |
| Red Bay c | 48 | 55.04 N | 6.02 W |
| Redberry Lake ⊜ | 184 | 52.40 N | 107.10 W |
| Redbird | 214 | 41.48 N | 81.06 W |
| Red Bluff | 204 | 40.10 N | 122.14 W |
| Red Bluff Reservoir ⊜[1] | 196 | 31.57 N | 103.56 W |
| Red Boiling Springs | 194 | 36.31 N | 85.50 W |
| Redbourn | 42 | 51.48 N | 0.24 W |
| Redbridge ◆[8] | 42 | 51.34 N | 0.05 E |
| Red Bud | 219 | 38.12 N | 89.59 W |
| Red Canyon V | 198 | 43.18 N | 103.49 W |
| Redcar | 44 | 54.37 N | 1.04 W |
| Red Cedar ≃, Mi., U.S. | 216 | 42.43 N | 84.33 W |
| Red Cedar ≃, Wi., U.S. | 190 | 44.42 N | 91.53 W |
| Red Cedar Lake ⊜ | 190 | 46.45 N | 79.54 W |
| Red Clay Creek ≃ | 285 | 39.43 N | 75.39 W |
| Red Clay Creek, East Branch ≃ | 285 | 39.49 N | 75.42 W |
| Red Clay Creek, West Branch ≃ | 285 | 39.49 N | 75.42 W |
| Redcliff, Ab., Can. | 184 | 50.05 N | 110.47 W |
| Red Cliff, Co., U.S. | 200 | 39.31 N | 106.22 W |
| Redcliff, Zimb. | 154 | 19.02 S | 29.50 E |
| Redcliffe | 171a | 27.14 S | 153.07 E |
| Redcliffe, Mount ∧ | 162 | 28.25 S | 121.32 E |
| Red Cliff Indian Reservation ◆[4] | 190 | 46.50 N | 90.47 W |
| Red Cliffs | 166 | 34.19 S | 142.11 E |
| Red Cloud | 198 | 40.05 N | 98.31 W |
| Red Creek | 210 | 43.14 N | 76.43 W |
| Red Creek ≃ | 194 | 30.41 N | 88.40 W |
| Red Cross Lake ⊜ | 184 | 55.05 N | 92.55 W |
| Red Deer | 182 | 52.16 N | 113.48 W |
| Red Deer ≃, Can. | 176 | 50.56 N | 109.54 W |
| Red Deer ≃, Can. | 184 | 52.53 N | 101.01 W |
| Red Deer Creek ≃ | 196 | 35.56 N | 100.24 W |
| Red Deer Lake ⊜, Ab., Can. | 182 | 52.43 N | 113.02 W |
| Red Deer Lake ⊜, Mb., Can. | 184 | 52.56 N | 101.20 W |
| Reddersburg | 158 | 29.38 S | 26.07 E |
| Red Devil | 180 | 61.46 N | 157.18 W |
| Red Dial | 44 | 54.48 N | 3.10 W |
| Reddick | 216 | 41.06 N | 88.15 W |
| Redding, Ca., U.S. | 204 | 40.35 N | 122.23 W |
| Redding, Ct., U.S. | 207 | 41.18 N | 73.23 W |
| Redding Ridge | 207 | 41.18 N | 73.21 W |
| Reddish | 262 | 53.26 N | 2.09 W |
| Redditch | 42 | 52.19 N | 1.56 W |
| Rede ≃ | 44 | 55.08 N | 2.13 W |
| Redefin | 54 | 53.21 N | 11.11 E |
| Redelinghuys | 158 | 32.30 S | 18.33 E |
| Redenção | 250 | 4.13 S | 38.43 W |
| Redenção da Serra | 256 | 23.16 S | 45.33 W |
| Redesdale V | 44 | 55.17 N | 2.16 W |

| DEUTSCH Name | Seite | Breite°′ | Länge°′ E = Ost |
|---|---|---|---|
| Redes Mere ⊜ | 262 | 53.15 N | 2.14 W |
| Redeye ≃ | 198 | 46.26 N | 94.49 W |
| Redfield, Ia., U.S. | 198 | 41.35 N | 94.11 W |
| Redfield, N.Y., U.S. | 212 | 43.32 N | 75.49 W |
| Redfield, S.D., U.S. | 198 | 44.52 N | 98.31 W |
| Redfish Lake ⊜ | 202 | 44.07 N | 114.56 W |
| Redford | 196 | 29.47 N | 104.10 W |
| Redford ◆[8] | 281 | 42.25 N | 83.16 W |
| Redford Township | 216 | 42.25 N | 83.16 W |
| Red Fox Forest | 284c | 38.49 N | 77.15 W |
| Redhead | 241r | 10.47 N | 60.57 W |
| Red Hill, Austl. | 162 | 21.59 S | 116.03 E |
| Redhill, Eng., U.K. | 42 | 51.14 N | 0.11 W |
| Red Hill, Ca., U.S. | 280 | 33.45 N | 117.48 W |
| Red Hill, Pa., U.S. | 208 | 40.22 N | 75.29 W |
| Red Hill ∧ | 172 | 41.38 S | 173.04 E |
| Redhill Aerodrome ⊠ | 260 | 51.12 N | 0.07 W |
| Red Hill Branch ≃ | 284b | 39.14 N | 76.51 W |
| Red Hook | 210 | 41.59 N | 73.52 W |
| Redhouse Creek ≃ | 284b | 39.18 N | 76.31 W |
| Rédics | 61 | 46.36 N | 16.30 E |
| Red Indian Lake ⊜ | 186 | 48.40 N | 56.50 W |
| Redinger Lake ⊜[1] | 226 | 37.09 N | 119.26 W |
| Redington Beach | 220 | 27.49 N | 82.49 W |
| Redington Shores | 220 | 27.50 N | 82.50 W |
| Red Island I | 186 | 47.23 N | 54.11 W |
| Redja ≃ | 76 | 58.05 N | 31.33 E |
| Redkey | 216 | 40.21 N | 85.09 W |
| Redkino | 82 | 56.38 N | 36.17 E |
| Red Lake, On., Can. | 184 | 51.03 N | 93.49 W |
| Redlake, Mn., U.S. | 198 | 47.53 N | 95.01 W |
| Red Lake ⊜, On., Can. | 184 | 51.01 N | 94.05 W |
| Red Lake ⊜, Az., U.S. | 200 | 35.40 N | 114.04 W |
| Red Lake ⊜, S.D., U.S. | 198 | 43.44 N | 99.13 W |
| Red Lake ⊜[1] | 222 | 31.40 N | 95.58 W |
| Red Lake ≃ | 198 | 47.55 N | 97.01 W |
| Red Lake Falls | 198 | 47.52 N | 96.16 W |
| Red Lake Indian Reservation ◆[4] | 198 | 48.05 N | 95.05 W |
| Red Lake Road | 184 | 49.58 N | 93.22 W |
| Redland, Scot., U.K. | 46 | 59.05 N | 3.05 W |
| Redland, Tx., U.S. | 222 | 31.25 N | 94.43 W |
| Redland Bay | 171a | 27.37 S | 153.18 E |
| Redlands, S. Afr. | 158 | 29.52 S | 22.57 E |
| Redlands, Ca., U.S. | 228 | 34.01 N | 117.12 W |
| Redlands, Co., U.S. | 200 | 39.04 N | 108.38 W |
| Red Level | 194 | 31.24 N | 86.36 W |
| Red Lick | 194 | 31.47 N | 90.58 W |
| Redlin | 54 | 53.22 N | 12.01 E |
| Red Lion, Pa., U.S. | 208 | 39.54 N | 76.36 W |
| Red Lion, Pa., U.S. | 285 | 39.53 N | 75.41 W |
| Red Lion Airport ⊠ | 285 | 39.54 N | 74.45 W |
| Red Lodge | 202 | 45.11 N | 109.14 W |
| Red Mill | 206 | 46.25 N | 72.28 W |
| Redmond, Or., U.S. | 202 | 44.16 N | 121.10 W |
| Redmond, Ut,. U.S. | 200 | 39.00 N | 111.51 W |
| Redmond, Wa., U.S. | 224 | 47.40 N | 122.07 W |
| Red Mountain | 228 | 35.21 N | 117.36 W |
| Red Mountain ∧, Ca., U.S. | 204 | 41.35 N | 123.06 W |
| Red Mountain ∧, Ca., U.S. | 228 | 35.21 N | 117.36 W |
| Red Mountain ∧, Mt., U.S. | 202 | 47.07 N | 112.44 W |
| Red Mountain Pass )( | 200 | 37.54 N | 107.43 W |
| Rednitz ≃ | 56 | 49.28 N | 10.59 E |
| Red Oak, Ia., U.S. | 198 | 41.00 N | 95.13 W |
| Red Oak, Ok., U.S. | 196 | 34.57 N | 95.04 W |
| Red Oak, Tx., U.S. | 222 | 32.31 N | 96.48 W |
| Red Oak Creek ≃ | 222 | 32.28 N | 96.30 W |
| Red Oaks Mill | 210 | 41.40 N | 73.53 W |
| Redon | 32 | 47.39 N | 2.05 W |
| Redonda I | 238 | 16.55 N | 62.19 W |
| Redonda, Ilha I | 256 | 23.04 S | 43.12 W |
| Redonda, Isla I | 241r | 9.52 N | 61.35 W |
| Redonda Islands II | 182 | 50.13 N | 124.48 W |
| Redondela | 34 | 42.17 N | 8.36 W |
| Redondo, Port. | 34 | 38.39 N | 7.33 W |
| Redondo, Wa., U.S. | 224 | 47.20 N | 122.19 W |
| Redondo, Mount ∧ | 116 | 10.21 N | 125.38 E |
| Redondo Beach | 228 | 33.50 N | 118.23 W |
| Redondo Beach State Park ♦ | 280 | 33.50 N | 118.24 W |
| Redoubt, Mount ∧ | 224 | 48.57 N | 121.18 W |
| Redoubt Volcano ∧[1] | 180 | 60.29 N | 152.45 W |
| Red Pass | 182 | 52.59 N | 118.59 W |
| Red Pheasant Indian Reserve ◆[4] | 184 | 52.30 N | 108.07 W |
| Red Pine Lake ⊜ | 212 | 45.12 N | 78.42 W |
| Red Point ≻ | 170 | 34.29 S | 150.55 E |
| Red Rock, B.C., Can. | 182 | 53.39 N | 122.41 W |
| Red Rock, On., Can. | 190 | 48.58 N | 88.15 W |
| Red Rock, Tx., U.S. | 222 | 29.58 N | 97.27 W |
| Red Rock I | 282 | 37.56 N | 122.26 W |
| Red Rock ≃ | 202 | 44.59 N | 112.52 W |
| Red Rock, Lake ⊜[1] | 190 | 41.30 N | 93.02 W |
| Red Rock Canyon State Park ♦ | 228 | 35.23 N | 118.00 W |
| Red Rock Creek ≃ | 196 | 36.36 N | 97.03 W |
| Red Rocks Point ≻ | 162 | 32.13 S | 127.32 E |
| Red Root Creek ≃ | 276 | 40.30 N | 74.19 W |
| Red Run ≃, Md., U.S. | 284b | 39.24 N | 76.47 W |
| Red Run ≃, Mi., U.S. | 281 | 42.34 N | 82.58 W |
| Redruth | 42 | 50.13 N | 5.14 W |
| Red Sea ≖[2] | 136 | 20.00 N | 38.00 E |
| Red Springs | 192 | 34.48 N | 79.11 W |
| Redstone | 182 | 52.08 N | 123.42 W |
| Redstone ≃, N.T., Can. | 180 | 64.17 N | 124.33 W |
| Redstone ≃, On., Can. | 190 | 48.27 N | 81.03 W |
| Redstone Arsenal ■ | 194 | 34.38 N | 86.38 W |
| Redstone Creek ≃ | 198 | 44.04 N | 98.05 W |
| Redstone Lake ⊜ | 212 | 45.11 N | 78.32 W |
| Red Sucker ≃ | 184 | 55.19 N | 92.31 W |
| Red Sucker Lake ⊜ | 184 | 54.09 N | 93.40 W |
| Reduction | 279b | 40.11 N | 79.46 W |
| Redut | 80 | 47.22 N | 51.53 E |
| Redvers | 184 | 49.33 N | 101.39 W |
| Redwater | 182 | 53.57 N | 113.06 W |
| Redwater ≃ | 198 | 48.03 N | 105.13 W |
| Red Wharf Bay c | 44 | 53.18 N | 4.10 W |
| Redwillow ≃ | 182 | 55.04 N | 119.21 W |
| Red Willow Creek ≃ | 198 | 40.13 N | 100.29 W |
| Red Wing | 190 | 44.33 N | 92.32 W |
| Redwood | 212 | 44.18 N | 75.48 W |
| Redwood ≃ | 198 | 44.34 N | 95.05 W |
| Redwood City | 226 | 37.29 N | 122.14 W |
| Redwood Creek ≃, Ca., U.S. | 204 | 41.18 N | 124.05 W |
| Redwood Creek ≃, Ca., U.S. | 226 | 38.18 N | 122.18 W |
| Redwood Creek ≃, Ca., U.S. | 282 | 37.31 N | 122.12 W |
| Redwood Creek ≃, Ca., U.S. | 282 | 37.52 N | 122.35 W |
| Redwood Estates | 226 | 37.10 N | 121.59 W |
| Redwood Falls | 198 | 44.32 N | 95.07 W |
| Redwood National Park ♦ | 204 | 41.30 N | 124.05 W |
| Redwood Point ≻ | 282 | 37.32 N | 122.12 W |
| Redwood Regional Park ♦ | 282 | 37.38 N | 122.10 W |
| Redwood Terrace | 282 | 37.19 N | 122.18 W |
| Redwood Valley | 204 | 39.15 N | 123.12 W |
| Ree, Lough ⊜ | 48 | 53.35 N | 8.00 W |
| Reed City | 190 | 43.52 N | 85.30 W |
| Reeder | 198 | 46.06 N | 102.56 W |
| Reeders | 210 | 41.01 N | 75.20 W |
| Reed Lake ⊜, Mb., Can. | 184 | 54.37 N | 100.30 W |
| Reed Lake ⊜, Sk., Can. | 184 | 50.24 N | 107.05 W |
| Reedley | 226 | 36.35 N | 119.26 W |
| Reedsburg, Oh., U.S. | 214 | 40.49 N | 82.07 W |
| Reedsburg, Wi., U.S. | 190 | 43.31 N | 90.00 W |

**Symbols** in the index entries represent the broad categories identified in the key at the right. Symbols with superior numbers (⋏[1]) identify subcategories (see complete key on page *I · 1).*

**Symbole** im Register stellen die rechts im Schlüssel erklärten Kategorien dar. Symbole mit hochgestellten Ziffern (⋏[1]) bezeichnen Unterabteilungen einer Kategorie (vgl. vollständiger Schlüssel auf Seite *I · 1).*

**Los símbolos** incluídos en el texto del índice representan las grandes categorías identificadas con la clave a la derecha. Los símbolos con numeros en su parte superior (⋏[1]) identifican las subcategorías (véase la clave completa en la página *I · 1).*

**Les symboles** de l'index représentent les catégories indiquées dans la légende à droite. Les symboles suivis d'un indice (⋏[1]) représentent des sous-catégories (voir légende complète à la page *I · 1).*

**Os símbolos** incluídos no texto do índice representam as grandes categorias identificadas com a chave à direita. Os símbolos com números em sua parte superior (⋏[1]) identificam as subcategorias (veja-se a chave completa à página *I · 1).*

| | English | Deutsch | Español | Français | Português |
|---|---|---|---|---|---|
| ∧ | Mountain | Berg | Montaña | Montagne | Montanha |
| ⋏ | Mountains | Gebirge | Montañas | Montagnes | Montanhas |
| )( | Pass | Paß | Paso | Col | Passo |
| V | Valley, Canyon | Tal, Cañon | Valle, Cañón | Vallée, Canyon | Vale, Canhão |
| ≃ | Plain | Ebene | Llano | Plaine | Planície |
| ≻ | Cape | Kap | Cabo | Cap | Cabo |
| I | Island | Insel | Isla | Île | Ilha |
| II | Islands | Inseln | Islas | Îles | Ilhas |
| ⊥ | Other Topographic Features | Andere Topographische Objekte | Otros Elementos Topográficos | Autres données topographiques | Outros acidentes topográficos |

ESPAÑOL

| Nombre | Página | Lat.°′ | Long.°′ W = Oeste |
|---|---|---|---|
| Reeds Peak ʌ | 200 | 33.09 N | 107.51 W |
| Reedsport | 202 | 43.42 N | 124.05 W |
| Reedsville, Pa., U.S. | 208 | 40.39 N | 77.35 W |
| Reedsville, Wi., U.S. | 190 | 44.09 N | 87.57 W |
| Reedurban | 214 | 40.47 N | 81.26 W |
| Reedville | 208 | 37.50 N | 76.16 W |
| Reedy Creek ≃ | 220 | 28.04 N | 81.21 W |
| Reedy Creek Swamp ≋ | 220 | 28.17 N | 81.31 W |
| Reedy Lake ⊜ | 220 | 27.44 N | 81.22 W |
| Reefton | 172 | 42.07 S | 171.52 E |
| Reelfoot Lake ⊜ | 194 | 36.25 N | 89.22 W |
| Reepham | 42 | 52.46 N | 1.07 E |
| Reersø › [1] | 41 | 55.31 N | 11.06 E |
| Rees | 52 | 51.45 N | 6.23 E |
| Reese | 190 | 43.27 N | 83.41 W |
| Reese ≃ | 204 | 40.39 N | 116.54 W |
| Reese Air Force Base ■ | 196 | 33.36 N | 102.02 W |
| Reeseville | 190 | 43.18 N | 88.50 W |
| Reesville | 218 | 39.29 N | 83.41 W |
| Reetz | 54 | 53.11 N | 11.52 E |
| Refaa, Djebel ʌ | 34 | 35.34 N | 5.52 E |
| Refahiye | 130 | 39.54 N | 38.46 E |
| Reform | 194 | 33.22 N | 88.00 W |
| Reforma de Pineda | 234 | 16.24 N | 94.28 W |
| Refton | 208 | 39.57 N | 76.14 W |
| Refuge Cove | 182 | 50.07 N | 124.50 W |
| Refugio | 196 | 28.18 N | 97.16 W |
| Refugio, Isla I | 254 | 43.58 S | 73.12 W |
| Refugio Creek ≃ | 282 | 38.01 N | 122.17 W |
| Rega ≃ | 30 | 54.10 N | 15.18 E |
| Regaïa | 34 | 35.38 N | 5.46 W |
| Regalbuto | 70 | 37.39 N | 14.38 E |
| Regau | 64 | 47.59 N | 13.41 E |
| Regen | 60 | 48.59 N | 13.07 E |
| Regen ≃ | 60 | 49.01 N | 12.06 E |
| Regência | 255 | 19.36 S | 39.49 W |
| Regency Estates | 284c | 39.03 N | 77.10 W |
| Regeneração | 250 | 6.15 S | 42.41 W |
| Regensburg | 60 | 49.01 N | 12.06 E |
| Regensdorf | 58 | 47.26 N | 8.28 E |
| Regenstauf | 60 | 49.08 N | 12.08 E |
| Regent, Austl. | 274b | 37.44 S | 145.00 E |
| Regent, N.D., U.S. | 198 | 46.25 N | 102.33 W |
| Regent Park | 284c | 39.03 N | 77.10 W |
| Regents Park | 274a | 33.53 S | 151.02 E |
| Regents Park ⬥ [8] | 273d | 26.15 S | 28.04 E |
| Regent's Park ♦ | 260 | 51.32 N | 0.09 W |
| Regentville | 274a | 33.47 S | 150.40 E |
| Reggâne | 148 | 26.42 N | 0.10 E |
| Regge ≃ | 52 | 52.31 N | 6.22 E |
| Reggello | 66 | 43.41 N | 11.32 E |
| Reggio di Calabria | 68 | 38.07 N | 15.39 E |
| Reggio di Calabria □ [4] | 68 | 38.10 N | 16.00 E |
| Reggiolo | 64 | 44.55 N | 10.48 E |
| Reggio nell'Emilia | 64 | 44.43 N | 10.36 E |
| Reggio nell'Emilia □ [4] | 64 | 44.37 N | 10.37 E |
| Regharen ⊜ | 40 | 58.54 N | 15.46 E |
| Reghin | 38 | 46.47 N | 24.42 E |
| Regina, Sk., Can. | 184 | 50.25 N | 104.39 W |
| Régina, Guy. fr. | 250 | 4.19 N | 52.08 W |
| Regina, S. Afr. | 158 | 27.02 S | 26.30 E |
| Regina Beach | 184 | 50.47 N | 105.00 W |
| Regina Elena, Canale ≊ | 266b | 45.41 N | 8.39 E |
| Región Metropolitana □ [4] | 252 | 33.30 S | 70.30 W |
| Regis-Breitingen | 54 | 51.05 N | 12.26 E |
| Registro | 252 | 24.30 S | 47.50 W |
| Registro do Araguaia | 255 | 15.44 S | 51.50 W |
| Regiwar | 120 | 25.57 N | 65.44 E |
| Regla ⬥ [8] | 286b | 23.08 N | 82.20 W |
| Regnéville | 32 | 49.01 N | 1.33 W |
| Regnitz ≃ | 56 | 49.54 N | 10.49 E |
| Rego Park ⬥ [8] | 276 | 40.44 N | 73.52 W |
| Regozero | 24 | 65.28 N | 31.10 E |
| Regresso, Cachoeira do ʟ | 250 | 0.58 S | 54.51 W |
| Regstrup | 41 | 55.40 N | 11.37 E |
| Reguengos de Monsaraz | 34 | 38.25 N | 7.32 W |
| Rehau | 54 | 50.15 N | 12.02 E |
| Rehbach ≃ | 56 | 49.27 N | 8.27 E |
| Rehberge ʌ [2] | 264a | 52.35 N | 13.11 E |
| Rehberge, Volkspark ♦ | 264a | 52.33 N | 13.20 E |
| Rehburg | 52 | 52.28 N | 9.13 E |
| Rehden | 52 | 52.37 N | 8.29 E |
| Rehe | 56 | 50.38 N | 8.07 E |
| Rehefeld-Zaunhaus | 54 | 50.43 N | 13.42 E |
| Rehfelde | 54 | 52.30 N | 13.54 E |
| Rehli | 124 | 23.38 N | 79.05 E |
| Rehme | 52 | 52.12 N | 8.49 E |
| Rehna | 54 | 53.47 N | 11.03 E |
| Rehoboth | 156 | 23.18 S | 17.03 E |
| Rehoboth Bay ᑕ | 208 | 38.40 N | 75.06 W |
| Rehoboth Beach | 208 | 38.43 N | 75.04 W |
| Rehoboth Seamount ✥ [3] | 16 | 37.30 N | 59.50 W |
| Réhon | 56 | 49.30 N | 5.45 E |
| Reḥovot | 132 | 31.54 N | 34.49 E |
| Rehti | 124 | 22.44 N | 77.26 E |
| Reiche Ebrach ≃ | 56 | 49.49 N | 10.58 E |
| Reiche Liesing ≃ | 264b | 48.08 N | 16.16 E |
| Reichelsheim | 56 | 49.43 N | 8.50 E |
| Reichenau, Dtsch. | 58 | 47.41 N | 9.03 E |
| Reichenau, Schw. | 58 | 46.49 N | 9.24 E |
| Reichenau an der Rax | 61 | 47.42 N | 15.50 E |
| Reichenbach, Dtsch. | 54 | 51.08 N | 14.48 E |
| Reichenbach, Dtsch. | 54 | 50.37 N | 12.18 E |
| Reichenbach → Dzierżoniów, Pol. | 30 | 50.44 N | 16.39 E |
| Reichenbach, Schw. | 58 | 46.38 N | 7.42 E |
| Reichenberg → Liberec | 30 | 50.46 N | 15.03 E |
| Reichenhofen | 58 | 47.50 N | 9.58 E |
| Reichensachsen | 56 | 51.09 N | 9.59 E |
| Reichen Spitze ʌ | 64 | 47.09 N | 12.07 E |
| Reichertshausen | 60 | 48.28 N | 11.31 E |
| Reichertsheim | 60 | 48.12 N | 12.17 E |
| Reichertshofen | 60 | 48.40 N | 11.28 E |
| Reichraming | 61 | 47.53 N | 14.27 E |
| Reichsbrücke ⬥ [5] | 264b | 48.14 N | 16.25 E |
| Reichshoffen | 56 | 48.56 N | 7.40 E |
| Reichstädt | 54 | 50.52 N | 13.38 E |
| Reid | 162 | 30.49 S | 128.26 E |
| Reid, Mount ʌ, Austl. | 162 | 17.58 S | 130.38 E |
| Reid, Mount ʌ, Ak., U.S. | 182 | 55.42 N | 131.15 W |
| Reid Lake ⊜ [1] | 184 | 50.02 N | 108.05 W |
| Reidsville, Ga., U.S. | 192 | 32.05 N | 82.07 W |
| Reidsville, N.C., U.S. | 192 | 36.21 N | 79.39 W |
| Reiffton | 208 | 40.19 N | 75.53 W |
| Reigate | 42 | 51.14 N | 0.13 W |
| Reigate and Banstead □ [8] | 260 | 51.17 N | 0.12 W |
| Reignac-sur-Indre | 50 | 47.13 N | 0.55 E |
| Reignier | 58 | 46.08 N | 6.16 E |
| Reigoldswil | 58 | 47.24 N | 7.41 E |
| Reihoku | 92 | 32.31 N | 130.02 E |
| Reillanne | 62 | 43.53 N | 5.40 E |
| Reims | 50 | 49.15 N | 4.02 E |
| Reims, Montagne de ⋏ [2] | 50 | 49.08 N | 4.00 E |
| Reina Alejandra → Queen Alexandra Range ⋏ | 9 | 84.00 S | 168.00 E |
| Reina Carlota, Estrecho de la → Queen Charlotte Sound ʊ | 182 | 51.30 N | 129.30 W |
| Reinach, Schw. | 58 | 47.30 N | 7.35 E |
| Reinach, Schw. | 58 | 47.15 N | 8.11 E |
| Reina Fabiola → Queen Fabiola Mountains ⋏ | 9 | 71.30 S | 35.40 E |

FRANÇAIS

| Nom | Page | Lat.°′ | Long.°′ W = Ouest |
|---|---|---|---|
| Reina Maria, Costa de la → Queen Mary Coast ⏊ [2] | 9 | 67.00 S | 96.00 E |
| Reina Maud, Tierras de la → Queen Maud Land ⬥ [1] | 9 | 72.30 S | 12.00 E |
| Reinbeck | 190 | 42.19 N | 92.35 W |
| Reinbek | 52 | 53.31 N | 10.14 E |
| Reinberg | 54 | 54.12 N | 13.15 E |
| Reindeer ≃ | 184 | 55.36 N | 103.11 W |
| Reindeer Island I | 184 | 52.25 N | 98.00 W |
| Reindeer Lake ⊜ | 176 | 57.15 N | 102.40 W |
| Reindeer Station | 180 | 68.42 N | 134.06 W |
| Reine Charlotte, Détroit de la → Queen Charlotte Sound ʊ | 182 | 51.30 N | 129.30 W |
| Reinerton | 208 | 40.36 N | 76.34 W |
| Reinfeld | 52 | 53.49 N | 10.28 E |
| Reinga, Cape › | 172 | 34.25 S | 172.41 E |
| Reinhardswald ⋏ | 52 | 51.30 N | 9.30 E |
| Reinhardtsdorf | 54 | 50.53 N | 14.11 E |
| Reinheim | 56 | 49.49 N | 8.50 E |
| Reinickendorf ⬥ [8] | 264a | 52.35 N | 13.21 E |
| Reinosa | 34 | 43.00 N | 4.08 W |
| Reino Unido → United Kingdom □ [1] | 28 | 54.00 N | 2.00 W |
| Reinsdorf, Dtsch. | 54 | 50.42 N | 12.33 E |
| Reinsdorf, Dtsch. | 54 | 51.54 N | 12.37 E |
| Reinshagen ⬥ [8] | 263 | 51.10 N | 7.09 E |
| Reinstorf | 54 | 53.50 N | 11.38 E |
| Reis | 130 | 38.16 N | 31.35 E |
| Reisach | 64 | 46.39 N | 13.09 E |
| Reisaelva ≃ | 24 | 69.48 N | 21.00 E |
| Reisbach | 60 | 48.34 N | 12.38 E |
| Reischach | 60 | 48.17 N | 12.44 E |
| Reisdorf | 56 | 49.53 N | 6.15 E |
| Reisdorf, Camp ■ | 273b | 4.21 S | 15.15 E |
| Reisholz ⬥ [8] | 263 | 51.11 N | 6.52 E |
| Reisjärvi | 26 | 63.37 N | 24.54 E |
| Reiss | 46 | 58.28 N | 3.10 W |
| Reisterstown | 208 | 39.28 N | 76.49 W |
| Reisterstown Road Plaza ⬥ [9] | 284b | 39.02 N | 76.42 W |
| Reitano | 70 | 37.58 N | 14.20 E |
| Reitdiep ≊ | 52 | 53.20 N | 6.18 E |
| Reith bei Seefeld | 64 | 47.18 N | 11.12 E |
| Reit im Winkl | 64 | 47.40 N | 12.28 E |
| Reitz | 158 | 27.53 S | 28.31 E |
| Reitzenhain | 54 | 50.33 N | 13.13 E |
| Reivilo | 158 | 27.36 S | 24.08 E |
| Rejinagar | 126 | 23.53 N | 88.15 E |
| Rejmyra | 40 | 58.50 N | 15.55 E |
| Rejowiec Fabryczny | 30 | 51.08 N | 23.13 E |
| Rejštejn | 60 | 49.09 N | 13.31 E |
| Rekarne | 40 | 59.26 N | 16.20 E |
| Rekarne □ [9] | 40 | 59.17 N | 16.25 E |
| Reken | 52 | 51.50 N | 7.02 E |
| Rekjoāti | 272b | 22.37 N | 88.28 E |
| Reliance, N.T., Can. | 176 | 62.42 N | 109.08 W |
| Reliance, Wy., U.S. | 200 | 41.40 N | 109.11 W |
| Relief Reservoir ⊜ [1] | 226 | 38.16 N | 119.44 W |
| Religione, Punta › | 70 | 36.42 N | 14.46 E |
| Reliz Creek ≃ | 226 | 36.19 N | 121.18 W |
| Rellingen | 52 | 53.39 N | 9.49 E |
| Rellinghausen ⬥ [8] | 263 | 51.25 N | 7.04 E |
| Reloncaví, Seno ᑕ | 254 | 41.40 S | 72.35 W |
| Remada | 148 | 32.19 N | 10.24 E |
| Remagen, Dtsch. | 30 | 50.34 N | 7.13 E |
| Remagen, Dtsch. | 56 | 50.34 N | 7.13 E |
| Rémalard | 50 | 48.26 N | 0.47 E |
| Remanso | 250 | 9.37 S | 42.07 W |
| Remarde ≃ | 261 | 48.35 N | 2.15 E |
| Remarkable, Mount ʌ | 162 | 32.48 S | 138.10 E |
| Rembang | 115a | 6.42 S | 111.20 E |
| Rembau | 114 | 2.35 N | 102.06 E |
| Rembia | 114 | 2.20 N | 102.13 E |
| Remchi | 34 | 35.04 N | 1.26 W |
| Remchingen | 56 | 48.57 N | 8.35 E |
| Remda | 54 | 50.46 N | 11.13 E |
| Remecó | 252 | 37.38 S | 63.39 W |
| Remedios, Col. | 246 | 7.02 N | 74.41 W |
| Remedios, Cuba | 240p | 22.30 N | 79.33 W |
| Remedios, Pan. | 236 | 8.14 N | 81.51 W |
| Remedios, Punta › | 236 | 13.31 N | 89.49 W |
| Remedios, Santuario de los ʋ [1] | 286a | 19.28 N | 99.15 W |
| Remedios de Escalada ⬥ [8] | 258 | 34.43 S | 58.23 W |
| Remels | 52 | 53.18 N | 7.44 E |
| Remennicy | 82 | 56.43 N | 36.36 E |
| Remer | 190 | 47.03 N | 93.54 W |
| Remeshk | 128 | 26.50 N | 58.49 E |
| Remhoogte | 158 | 29.33 S | 23.01 E |
| Remich | 56 | 49.33 N | 6.22 E |
| Remich Airport ⊠ | 279b | 40.36 N | 79.49 W |
| Rémigny, Lac ⊜ | 190 | 47.51 N | 79.12 W |
| Rémilly | 56 | 49.01 N | 6.24 E |
| Reminderville | 214 | 41.20 N | 81.23 W |
| Remington, In., U.S. | 216 | 40.45 N | 87.09 W |
| Remington, Va., U.S. | 188 | 38.32 N | 77.48 W |
| Rémire | 250 | 4.53 N | 52.17 W |
| Remiremont | 58 | 48.01 N | 6.35 E |
| Remolá, Estany del ᑕ | 266d | 41.17 N | 2.04 E |
| Remollon | 62 | 44.28 N | 6.10 E |
| Remontnoje | 80 | 46.33 N | 43.39 E |
| Remoray | 58 | 46.46 N | 6.14 E |
| Remoulins | 62 | 43.56 N | 4.34 E |
| Rempang, Pulau I | 114 | 0.51 N | 104.10 E |
| Remptendorf | 54 | 50.31 N | 11.39 E |
| Rems ≃ | 56 | 48.52 N | 9.16 E |
| Remscheid | 56 | 51.11 N | 7.11 E |
| Remscheider-Stausee ⊜ [1] | 263 | 51.10 N | 7.14 E |
| Remsen, Ia., U.S. | 198 | 42.48 N | 95.58 W |
| Remsen, N.Y., U.S. | 210 | 43.19 N | 75.11 W |
| Remsfeld | 56 | 51.00 N | 9.29 E |
| Remuna | 126 | 21.33 N | 86.54 E |
| Remus | 190 | 43.36 N | 85.09 W |
| Rémuzat | 62 | 44.24 N | 5.21 E |
| Rena | 26 | 61.08 N | 11.22 E |
| Renaix → Ronse | 50 | 50.45 N | 3.36 E |
| Renāla Khurd | 123 | 30.53 N | 73.36 E |
| Rena Point › | 116 | 16.10 N | 119.45 E |
| Renard Islands II | 164 | 10.50 S | 153.05 E |
| Renata | 182 | 49.26 N | 118.06 W |
| Renaud Island I | 9 | 65.40 S | 66.00 W |
| Renca | 286e | 33.24 S | 70.44 W |
| Renca, Cerro ʌ | 286e | 33.23 S | 70.43 W |
| Rencēni | 76 | 57.44 N | 25.26 E |
| Renchen | 56 | 48.35 N | 8.01 E |
| Rencontre East | 186 | 47.38 N | 55.12 W |
| Rencun | 98 | 36.19 N | 113.50 E |
| Renda, Ityo. | 144 | 14.30 N | 39.53 E |
| Renda, Lat. | 76 | 57.09 N | 22.22 E |
| Rende | 68 | 39.19 N | 16.11 E |
| Rendena, Valle V | 64 | 46.08 N | 10.42 E |
| Rend Lake ⊜ [1] | 194 | 38.05 N | 88.58 W |
| Rendova Island I | 175e | 8.32 S | 157.20 E |
| Rendsburg | 41 | 54.18 N | 9.40 E |
| Renens | 58 | 46.32 N | 6.35 E |
| Renesse | 52 | 51.44 N | 3.46 E |
| Renews | 186 | 46.56 N | 52.56 W |
| Renfrew, On., Can. | 212 | 45.28 N | 76.41 W |
| Renfrew, Scot., U.K. | 46 | 55.53 N | 4.24 W |
| Renfrew, Pa., U.S. | 214 | 40.46 N | 79.58 W |
| Renfrew □ [6] | 212 | 45.25 N | 77.05 W |
| Rengam | 114 | 1.53 N | 103.24 E |
| Ren'gang | 106 | 32.01 N | 120.50 E |
| Rengasdengklok | 115a | 6.09 S | 107.17 E |
| Rengat | 112 | 0.24 S | 102.33 E |
| Rengel | 115a | 7.04 S | 112.00 E |
| Rengen ⊜ | 26 | 64.05 N | 14.03 E |
| Rengezhuang | 105 | 39.45 N | 118.10 E |
| Rengit | 114 | 1.41 N | 103.09 E |
| Rengkang | 112 | 1.07 N | 112.10 E |

PORTUGUÊS

| Nome | Página | Lat.°′ | Long.°′ W = Oeste |
|---|---|---|---|
| Rengo | 252 | 34.25 S | 70.52 W |
| Rengsdorf | 56 | 50.30 N | 7.29 E |
| Reng Tlāng ʌ | 120 | 21.59 N | 92.36 E |
| Renhe, Zhg. | 100 | 33.32 N | 114.02 E |
| Renhe, Zhg. | 100 | 27.41 N | 115.15 E |
| Renhechang | 107 | 30.30 N | 105.56 E |
| Renheji | 100 | 31.56 N | 115.07 E |
| Renhua | 100 | 25.06 N | 113.44 E |
| Renhuai | 102 | 27.48 N | 106.18 E |
| Reni | 78 | 45.27 N | 28.17 E |
| Renick | 188 | 37.59 N | 80.21 W |
| Renish Point › | 46 | 57.44 N | 6.59 W |
| Renjiawopeng | 104 | 41.27 N | 122.18 E |
| Renjiaxu | 106 | 30.49 N | 121.00 E |
| Renju | 100 | 24.51 N | 115.54 E |
| Renko | 26 | 60.54 N | 24.17 E |
| Renkum | 52 | 51.58 N | 5.45 E |
| Renliuchang | 107 | 29.13 N | 106.39 E |
| Renlong | 107 | 30.32 N | 105.47 E |
| Renmark | 166 | 34.11 S | 140.45 E |
| Renmei | 100 | 25.50 N | 117.56 E |
| Renmin | 89 | 46.37 N | 125.32 E |
| Renna, Monte ʌ | 70 | 36.52 N | 14.41 E |
| Rennau | 54 | 52.17 N | 10.55 E |
| Renne, Lac du → Reindeer Lake ⊜ | 176 | 57.15 N | 102.40 W |
| Renne, Rivière le ≃ | 206 | 45.41 N | 72.39 W |
| Rennell I | 160 | 11.40 S | 160.10 E |
| Rennell, Islas II | 254 | 52.00 S | 74.00 W |
| Rennell and Bellona □ [4] | 175e | 10.45 S | 160.00 E |
| Rennell Sound ʊ | 182 | 53.25 N | 132.40 W |
| Renner | 222 | 32.59 N | 96.47 W |
| Rennerdale | 279b | 40.24 N | 80.08 W |
| Rennerod | 56 | 50.36 N | 8.04 E |
| Renner Springs | 162 | 18.20 S | 133.48 E |
| Rennertshofen | 60 | 48.45 N | 11.02 E |
| Rennes | 32 | 48.05 N | 1.41 W |
| Rennick Bay ᑕ | 9 | 70.18 S | 161.45 E |
| Rennick Glacier ⊓ | 9 | 70.30 S | 161.45 E |
| Rennie | 184 | 49.51 N | 95.33 W |
| Rennie's Mill | 271d | 22.18 N | 114.15 E |
| Renningen | 56 | 48.46 N | 8.56 E |
| Renntier-See → Reindeer Lake ⊜ | 176 | 57.15 N | 102.40 W |
| Rennweg | 64 | 47.01 N | 13.37 E |
| Reno, Nv., U.S. | 226 | 39.31 N | 119.48 W |
| Reno, Pa., U.S. | 214 | 41.25 N | 79.45 W |
| Reno, Tx., U.S. | 222 | 32.56 N | 97.05 W |
| Reno ≃ | 64 | 44.37 N | 12.16 E |
| Reno Beach | 214 | 41.40 N | 83.15 W |
| Reno Hill ʌ | 200 | 42.35 N | 106.03 W |
| Reno International Airport ⊠ | 226 | 39.30 N | 119.46 W |
| Renoster ≃ | 158 | 31.37 S | 20.37 E |
| Renous | 186 | 46.49 N | 65.48 W |
| Renous ≃ | 186 | 46.50 N | 65.50 W |
| Renovo | 214 | 41.19 N | 77.45 W |
| Renqiao | 100 | 33.27 N | 117.16 E |
| Renqiu | 98 | 38.43 N | 116.05 E |
| Rens | 41 | 54.54 N | 9.06 E |
| Renshan | 100 | 22.50 N | 114.48 E |
| Renshou, Zhg. | 100 | 27.08 N | 117.51 E |
| Renshou, Zhg. | 107 | 30.00 N | 104.08 E |
| Rensjön | 24 | 68.05 N | 19.49 E |
| Rensselaer, In., U.S. | 216 | 40.56 N | 87.09 W |
| Rensselaer, Mo., U.S. | 219 | 39.40 N | 91.33 W |
| Rensselaer, N.Y., U.S. | 210 | 42.38 N | 73.44 W |
| Rensselaer □ [6] | 210 | 42.43 N | 73.40 W |
| Rensselaer Falls | 212 | 44.35 N | 75.19 W |
| Rensselaerville | 210 | 42.30 N | 74.08 W |
| Rentería | 34 | 43.19 N | 1.54 W |
| Rentfort ⬥ [8] | 263 | 51.35 N | 6.57 E |
| Renton | 224 | 47.28 N | 122.12 W |
| Rentuo | 107 | 29.14 N | 106.23 E |
| Rentweinsdorf | 56 | 50.04 N | 10.47 E |
| Renun ≃ | 114 | 3.05 N | 97.55 E |
| Renville | 198 | 44.47 N | 95.12 W |
| Renwez | 56 | 49.50 N | 4.36 E |
| Renwick, N.Z. | 172 | 41.30 S | 173.50 E |
| Renwick, Ia., U.S. | 190 | 42.49 N | 93.58 W |
| Renyichang | 107 | 29.29 N | 105.28 E |
| Renziehalusen Park ♦ | 279b | 40.21 N | 79.50 W |
| Réo, Burkina | 150 | 12.19 N | 2.28 W |
| Reo, Indon. | 115b | 8.19 S | 120.30 E |
| Reola ⬥ [8] | 272a | 28.34 N | 76.59 E |
| Repaupo | 235 | 39.48 N | 75.18 W |
| Repbäcken | 40 | 60.31 N | 15.20 E |
| Répce ≃ | 30 | 47.41 N | 17.03 E |
| Repentigny | 206 | 45.44 N | 73.28 W |
| Repetek | 128 | 38.34 N | 63.11 E |
| Repino | 76 | 60.10 N | 29.52 E |
| Repjovka, Ross. | 78 | 51.05 N | 38.39 E |
| Repjovka, Ross. | 80 | 53.09 N | 48.06 E |
| Repolka | 76 | 59.16 N | 29.34 E |
| Repolovo | 86 | 60.40 N | 69.50 E |
| Reporoa | 172 | 38.26 S | 176.21 E |
| Reposaari | 26 | 61.37 N | 21.27 E |
| Reppenstedt | 52 | 53.15 N | 10.21 E |
| Repton | 194 | 31.24 N | 87.14 W |
| Republic, Ks., U.S. | 198 | 39.55 N | 97.49 W |
| Republic, Mi., U.S. | 190 | 46.24 N | 87.58 W |
| Republic, Mo., U.S. | 194 | 37.07 N | 93.28 W |
| Republic, Oh., U.S. | 214 | 41.07 N | 83.00 W |
| Republic, Wa., U.S. | 202 | 48.38 N | 118.44 W |
| República Centroafricana → Central African Republic □ [1] | 136 | 7.00 N | 21.00 E |
| Republic Airport ⊠ | 276 | 40.44 N | 73.25 W |
| Republican ≃ | 198 | 39.03 N | 96.48 W |
| Republican, North Fork ≃ | 198 | 40.01 N | 101.59 W |
| Republican, South Fork ≃ | 198 | 40.03 N | 101.31 W |
| Republic Observatory ʋ [3] | 273d | 26.11 S | 28.05 E |
| Republic Steel Corporation ʋ [3] | 279a | 41.28 N | 81.40 W |
| République centrafricaine → Central African Republic □ [1] | 136 | 7.00 N | 21.00 E |
| Repueblo de Oriente | 196 | 25.51 N | 99.39 W |
| Repulse Bay | 176 | 66.32 N | 86.15 W |
| Repulse Bay ᑕ | 166 | 20.36 S | 148.43 E |
| Repvåg | 24 | 70.45 N | 25.41 E |
| Requena, Esp. | 34 | 39.29 N | 1.06 W |
| Requena, Perú | 248 | 4.58 S | 73.50 W |
| Réquista | 32 | 44.02 N | 2.32 E |
| Rère ≃ | 50 | 47.22 N | 1.50 E |
| Reriutaba | 250 | 4.10 S | 40.35 W |
| Reşadiye | 130 | 40.24 N | 37.21 E |
| Reşadiye ⬥ [8] | 267b | 41.05 N | 29.15 E |
| Reşadiye Yarımadası › [1] | 130 | 36.40 N | 27.45 E |
| Resang, Tanjong › | 114 | 2.35 N | 103.51 E |
| Resarö | 40 | 59.26 N | 18.20 E |
| Rescalda | 266b | 45.38 N | 8.56 E |
| Rescaldina | 266b | 45.37 N | 8.57 E |
| Reschenpass (Passo di Resia) )( | 64 | 46.50 N | 10.30 E |
| Rescue | 208 | 36.59 N | 76.33 W |
| Research | 274b | 37.42 S | 145.11 E |
| Reseda ⬥ [8] | 280 | 34.12 N | 118.31 W |
| Resen | 38 | 41.05 N | 21.00 E |
| Resende | 256 | 22.28 S | 44.27 W |
| Reserva | 252 | 24.38 S | 50.52 W |
| Reserva, Parque de la ♦ | 286d | 12.04 S | 77.02 W |
| Reserve, La., U.S. | 194 | 30.03 N | 90.33 W |
| Reserve, N.M., U.S. | 200 | 33.42 N | 108.45 W |
| Reserve Township | 279b | 40.29 N | 79.59 W |
| Reservoir | 274b | 37.43 S | 145.00 E |
| Reservoir Pond ⊜ | 283 | 42.10 N | 71.07 W |
| Rešetnikovo | 82 | 56.27 N | 36.34 E |

| | | | |
|---|---|---|---|
| Reshetylivka | 78 | 49.34 N | 34.04 E |
| Reshui | 98 | 42.09 N | 119.18 E |
| Reshuitang | 102 | 24.10 N | 103.09 E |
| Resia, Lago di ⊜ | 64 | 46.47 N | 10.32 E |
| Resia, Passo di (Reschenpass) )( | 64 | 46.50 N | 10.30 E |
| Resipol, Beinn ʌ | 46 | 56.43 N | 5.39 W |
| Resistencia | 252 | 27.27 S | 58.59 W |
| Reşiţa | 38 | 45.17 N | 21.53 E |
| Resiutta | 64 | 46.23 N | 13.13 E |
| Resko | 30 | 53.47 N | 15.25 E |
| Rešma | 80 | 57.24 N | 42.34 E |
| Resolute | 176 | 74.41 N | 94.54 W |
| Resolution Island I, N.T., Can. | 176 | 61.30 N | 65.00 W |
| Resolution Island I, N.Z. | 172 | 45.40 S | 166.40 E |
| Resolven | 42 | 51.42 N | 3.42 W |
| Resort, Loch ᑕ | 46 | 58.03 N | 7.06 W |
| Rešoty | 76 | 57.09 N | 28.30 E |
| Resplandes | 250 | 6.17 S | 45.13 W |
| Resplendor | 255 | 19.20 S | 41.15 W |
| Ressa ≃ | 76 | 54.45 N | 35.10 E |
| Ressaca, Ribeirão da ≃ | 287b | 23.38 S | 46.51 W |
| Resse ⬥ [8] | 263 | 51.34 N | 7.07 E |
| Resseta ≃ | 76 | 53.49 N | 35.15 E |
| Ressons-sur-Matz | 50 | 49.33 N | 2.45 E |
| Resthaven | 216 | 41.16 N | 88.09 W |
| Restigouche (Ristigouche) ≃ | 186 | 48.04 N | 66.20 W |
| Restín, Punta › | 246 | 4.17 S | 81.15 W |
| Restinga Seca | 252 | 29.49 S | 53.23 W |
| Reston, Mb., Can. | 184 | 49.35 N | 101.02 W |
| Reston, Scot., U.K. | 46 | 55.51 N | 2.11 W |
| Reston, Va., U.S. | 208 | 38.58 N | 77.20 W |
| Restoule Lake ⊜ | 190 | 46.03 N | 79.47 W |
| Restrepo, Col. | 246 | 4.15 N | 73.33 W |
| Restrepo, Col. | 246 | 3.48 N | 76.31 W |
| Resuttano | 70 | 37.41 N | 14.02 E |
| Retalhuleu | 236 | 14.32 N | 91.41 W |
| Retalhuleu □ [5] | 236 | 14.20 N | 91.50 W |
| Retamosa | 252 | 33.35 S | 54.44 W |
| Retem, Oued er V | 148 | 33.30 N | 5.45 E |
| Řetenice | 54 | 50.38 N | 13.46 E |
| Retezat, Munţii ⋏ | 38 | 45.25 N | 23.00 E |
| Retezat, Parcul Naţional ♦ | 38 | 45.20 N | 22.50 E |
| Rethel | 50 | 49.31 N | 4.22 E |
| Rethem | 52 | 52.45 N | 9.23 E |
| Réthimnon | 38 | 35.22 N | 24.29 E |
| Retiche, Alpi → Rhaetian Alps ⋏ | 58 | 46.30 N | 10.00 E |
| Retie | 56 | 51.16 N | 5.04 E |
| Retiers | 28 | 47.55 N | 1.23 W |
| Retiro, Estacion ⬥ [5] | 288 | 34.36 S | 58.22 W |
| Retiro, Parque del ♦ | 266a | 40.25 N | 3.41 W |
| Retournac | 62 | 45.12 N | 4.02 E |
| Retreat | 222 | 32.03 N | 96.29 W |
| Retreat ≃ | 170 | 34.07 S | 149.38 E |
| Retsof | 210 | 42.50 N | 77.53 W |
| Rettenberg | 58 | 47.35 N | 10.17 E |
| Rettendon | 260 | 51.39 N | 0.33 E |
| Rettendon Place | 260 | 51.38 N | 0.34 E |
| Rettichovka | 89 | 44.10 N | 132.47 E |
| Rettin | 54 | 54.06 N | 10.53 E |
| Return Creek ≃ | 226 | 37.56 N | 119.28 W |
| Retz | 61 | 48.45 N | 15.57 E |
| Retzow | 54 | 52.37 N | 12.41 E |
| Reuden | 54 | 52.04 N | 12.18 E |
| Reungeut | 114 | 4.34 N | 96.22 E |
| Reunion (Réunion) □ [2], Afr. | 138 | 21.06 S | 55.36 E |
| Reunion (Réunion) □ [2], Afr. | 157c | 21.06 S | 55.36 E |
| Reus | 34 | 41.09 N | 1.07 E |
| Reuschenberg | 263 | 51.10 N | 6.42 E |
| Reusel | 52 | 51.21 N | 5.22 E |
| Reuss ≃ | 58 | 47.28 N | 8.14 E |
| Reuterstadt Stavenhagen | 54 | 53.42 N | 12.53 E |
| Reutlingen | 58 | 48.29 N | 9.11 E |
| Reutov | 82 | 55.46 N | 37.52 E |
| Reutte | 58 | 47.29 N | 10.43 E |
| Reuver | 52 | 51.17 N | 6.05 E |
| Revadim | 132 | 31.46 N | 34.48 E |
| Rev'akino | 82 | 54.22 N | 37.40 E |
| Reval → Tallinn | 76 | 59.25 N | 24.45 E |
| Revda, Ross. | 24 | 67.58 N | 34.32 E |
| Revda, Ross. | 86 | 56.48 N | 59.57 E |
| Réveillon, Ruisseau le ≃ | 261 | 48.42 N | 2.30 E |
| Revel | 62 | 45.11 N | 5.52 E |
| Revelganj | 124 | 25.47 N | 84.40 E |
| Revelstoke | 182 | 50.59 N | 118.12 W |
| Revelstoke, Lake ⊜ [1] | 202 | 51.30 N | 119.25 W |
| Reventazón | 248 | 6.10 S | 80.58 W |
| Reventazón ≃ | 236 | 10.17 N | 83.24 W |
| Revere, It. | 64 | 45.03 N | 11.08 E |
| Revere, Ma., U.S. | 207 | 42.24 N | 71.00 W |
| Revere, Pa., U.S. | 208 | 40.31 N | 75.10 W |
| Revere Beach ⏊ [2] | 283 | 42.25 N | 70.59 W |
| Revermont ⋏ [2] | 58 | 46.27 N | 5.25 E |
| Revesby | 274a | 33.57 S | 151.01 E |
| Revest-du-Bion | 62 | 44.05 N | 5.33 E |
| Révia | 154 | 13.23 S | 36.31 E |
| Reviga | 38 | 44.42 N | 27.06 E |
| Revigny-sur-Ornain | 56 | 48.50 N | 4.59 E |
| Revilla del Campo | 34 | 42.13 N | 3.32 W |
| Revillagigedo, Islas II | 232 | 19.00 N | 111.30 W |
| Revillagigedo Channel ʊ | 182 | 55.10 N | 131.13 W |
| Revillagigedo Island I | 182 | 55.35 N | 131.23 W |
| Revillo | 198 | 45.01 N | 96.34 W |
| Revin | 56 | 49.56 N | 4.38 E |
| Revloc | 214 | 40.29 N | 78.45 W |
| Řevničov | 54 | 50.08 N | 13.45 E |
| Revò | 64 | 46.23 N | 11.03 E |
| Revol'ucii, pik ʌ | 85 | 38.31 N | 72.21 E |
| Revolución Mexicana | 234 | 16.03 N | 93.04 W |
| Revolution, Museum of the ʋ | 265b | 55.46 N | 37.36 E |
| Revsundssjön ⊜ | 26 | 62.49 N | 15.17 E |
| Revúboè ≃ | 154 | 16.13 S | 33.37 E |
| Revuè ≃ | 156 | 19.49 S | 34.00 E |
| Rew | 214 | 41.54 N | 78.32 W |
| Rewa | 124 | 24.32 N | 81.18 E |
| Rewa ≃ | 246 | 3.53 N | 58.45 W |
| Rewāri | 124 | 28.11 N | 76.37 E |
| Rewataya, Taka ✥ [2] | 112 | 6.05 S | 118.55 E |
| Rex, Mount ʌ | 9 | 74.57 S | 76.00 W |
| Rexburg | 202 | 43.49 N | 111.47 W |
| Rexdale ⬥ [8] | 275b | 43.43 N | 79.35 W |
| Rexford, Ks., U.S. | 198 | 39.28 N | 100.44 W |
| Rexford, Mt., U.S. | 202 | 48.52 N | 115.13 W |
| Rexhame | 283 | 42.06 N | 70.40 W |
| Rexton | 186 | 46.39 N | 64.52 W |
| Rexville | 210 | 42.05 N | 77.40 W |
| Rey, Arroyo del ≃ | 288 | 34.46 S | 58.27 W |
| Rey, Embalse del ⊜ [1] | 266a | 40.18 N | 3.32 W |
| Rey, Estrecho del → King Sound ʊ | 162 | 17.00 S | 123.30 E |
| Rey, Isla del I | 246 | 8.22 N | 78.55 W |
| Rey, Laguna del ⊜ | 196 | 27.01 N | 103.26 W |
| Rey Bouba | 146 | 8.40 N | 14.11 E |
| Reyes | 248 | 14.19 S | 67.23 W |
| Reyes, Point › | 204 | 38.00 N | 123.01 W |
| Reyes Peak ʌ | 228 | 34.38 N | 119.17 W |
| Reyhanlı | 130 | 36.18 N | 36.32 E |
| Rey Jorge, Estrecho → King George Sound ʊ | 162 | 35.03 S | 117.57 E |
| Rey Jorge, Isla → King George Island I | 9 | 62.00 S | 58.15 W |
| Reykjanes › [1] | 24a | 63.49 N | 22.43 W |
| Reykjanes Ridge ✥ [3] | 10 | 62.00 N | 27.00 W |
| Reykjavík | 24a | 64.09 N | 21.51 W |
| Reynella | 168b | 35.06 S | 138.32 E |

| | | | |
|---|---|---|---|
| Reyno | 194 | 36.21 N | 90.45 W |
| Reynolds, Ga., U.S. | 192 | 32.33 N | 84.05 W |
| Reynolds, In., U.S. | 216 | 40.44 N | 86.52 W |
| Reynolds, N.D., U.S. | 198 | 47.57 N | 97.45 W |
| Reynolds Channel ʊ | 276 | 40.36 N | 73.40 W |
| Reynolds Creek ≃, Austl. | 171a | 27.56 S | 152.36 E |
| Reynolds Creek ≃, On., Can. | 212 | 43.00 N | 80.58 W |
| Reynoldsville | 214 | 41.05 N | 78.53 W |
| Reynosa | 232 | 26.07 N | 98.18 W |
| Reyssouze ≃ | 58 | 46.27 N | 4.54 E |
| Rež | 86 | 57.23 N | 61.24 E |
| Rež ≃ | 86 | 57.54 N | 62.18 E |
| Reza, gora (Kūh-e Rīzeh) ʌ | 128 | 37.47 N | 58.05 E |
| Rezé | 32 | 47.12 N | 1.34 W |
| Rēzekne | 76 | 56.30 N | 27.19 E |
| Rēzekne ≃ | 76 | 56.46 N | 26.58 E |
| Rezina | 38 | 47.44 N | 28.58 E |
| Rezino | 86 | 55.51 N | 75.18 E |
| Rezovo | 38 | 41.59 N | 28.02 E |
| Rezovska (Mutlu) ≃ | 38 | 41.59 N | 28.01 E |
| Rezvānshahr | 128 | 37.33 N | 49.09 E |
| Rezzato | 64 | 45.31 N | 10.19 E |
| Rezzoaglio | 62 | 44.32 N | 9.23 E |
| Rezzonico | 58 | 46.04 N | 9.16 E |
| Rhade | 52 | 53.19 N | 9.07 E |
| Rhadeswood Reservoir ⊜ [1] | 262 | 53.29 N | 1.56 W |
| Rhaetian Alps (Rätische Alpen) (Alpi Retiche) ⋏ | 58 | 46.30 N | 10.00 E |
| Rhallamane, Sebkha de ≃ | 148 | 23.41 N | 9.50 W |
| Rhame | 198 | 46.13 N | 103.39 W |
| Rharbi, Île I | 148 | 34.39 N | 11.03 E |
| Rharbi, Zahrez ⊜ | 148 | 34.50 N | 2.50 E |
| Rhauderfehn | 52 | 53.08 N | 7.35 E |
| Rhaunen | 56 | 49.52 N | 7.20 E |
| Rhayader | 42 | 52.18 N | 3.30 W |
| Rhea Creek ≃ | 202 | 45.30 N | 119.46 W |
| Rheda-Wiedenbrück | 52 | 51.50 N | 8.18 E |
| Rhede, Dtsch. | 52 | 53.03 N | 7.16 E |
| Rhede, Dtsch. | 52 | 51.51 N | 7.16 E |
| Rheden | 52 | 52.01 N | 6.02 E |
| Rheems | 208 | 40.08 N | 76.34 W |
| Rheidol ≃ | 42 | 52.25 N | 4.05 W |
| Rheims → Reims | 50 | 49.15 N | 4.02 E |
| Rhein | 184 | 51.22 N | 102.10 W |
| Rhein → Rhine ≃ | 30 | 51.52 N | 6.02 E |
| Rheinau | 56 | 48.41 N | 7.56 E |
| Rheinbach | 56 | 50.37 N | 6.57 E |
| Rheinberg | 52 | 51.33 N | 6.35 E |
| Rheinböllen | 56 | 50.00 N | 7.40 E |
| Rheinbreitbach | 56 | 50.37 N | 7.14 E |
| Rheinbrohl | 56 | 50.30 N | 7.19 E |
| Rheinbrücke ⬥ [5] | 263 | 51.12 N | 6.44 E |
| Rheindürkheim | 56 | 49.42 N | 8.21 E |
| Rheine | 52 | 52.17 N | 7.26 E |
| Rheineck | 58 | 47.28 N | 9.35 E |
| Rheinen | 263 | 51.27 N | 7.38 E |
| Rheinfall ʟ | 58 | 47.41 N | 8.38 E |
| Rheinfelden, Dtsch. | 58 | 47.33 N | 7.47 E |
| Rheinfelden, Schw. | 58 | 47.33 N | 7.48 E |
| Rheinhausen | 56 | 51.24 N | 6.44 E |
| Rhein-Herne-Kanal ≊ | 263 | 51.27 N | 6.47 E |
| Rheinhessen-Pfalz □ [5] | 56 | 49.30 N | 8.00 E |
| Rheinkamp | 52 | 51.30 N | 6.37 E |
| Rheinland-Pfalz □ [3] | 56 | 50.00 N | 7.00 E |
| Rheinsberg | 54 | 53.06 N | 12.53 E |
| Rheinstadion ♦ | 263 | 51.16 N | 6.44 E |
| Rheinstein, Burg ⊥ | 56 | 50.00 N | 7.50 E |
| Rheinstetten | 56 | 48.58 N | 8.18 E |
| Rheinwald V | 58 | 46.32 N | 9.17 E |
| Rheinwaldhorn ʌ | 58 | 46.30 N | 9.02 E |
| Rheirs, Oued V | 148 | 30.39 N | 4.26 W |
| Rhêmes-Notre-Dame | 62 | 45.34 N | 7.07 E |
| Rhenen | 52 | 51.57 N | 5.34 E |
| Rhens | 56 | 50.17 N | 7.37 E |
| Rheurdt | 56 | 51.27 N | 6.28 E |
| Rheydt | 56 | 51.10 N | 6.25 E |
| Rheydt, Schloss ⊥ | 263 | 51.11 N | 6.29 E |
| Rhin ≃, Dtsch. | 54 | 52.59 N | 12.55 E |
| Rhin → Rhine ≃, Europe | 30 | 51.52 N | 6.02 E |
| Rhinau | 58 | 48.19 N | 7.42 E |
| Rhine | 192 | 31.59 N | 83.12 W |
| Rhine (Rhein) (Rhin) ≃ | 30 | 51.52 N | 6.02 E |
| Rhinebeck | 210 | 41.55 N | 73.54 W |
| Rhinecliff | 210 | 41.55 N | 73.57 W |
| Rhineland | 219 | 38.43 N | 91.31 W |
| Rhinelander | 190 | 45.38 N | 89.24 W |
| Rhin Kanal ≊ | 54 | 52.47 N | 12.24 E |
| Rhinluch ≋ | 54 | 52.50 N | 12.50 E |
| Rhinns of Kells ⋏ | 44 | 55.07 N | 4.22 W |
| Rhinns Point › | 46 | 55.40 N | 6.30 W |
| Rhino Camp | 154 | 2.58 N | 31.24 E |
| Rhinow | 54 | 52.45 N | 12.20 E |
| Rhiou, Oued ≃ | 34 | 36.00 N | 0.55 E |
| Rhir, Cap › | 148 | 30.38 N | 9.55 W |
| Rhis, Oued ≃ | 34 | 35.14 N | 3.57 W |
| Rhiw ≃ | 42 | 52.36 N | 3.11 W |
| Rho | 62 | 45.32 N | 9.02 E |
| Rhode Island □ [3], U.S. | 178 | 41.40 N | 71.30 W |
| Rhode Island □ [3], U.S. | 207 | 41.40 N | 71.30 W |
| Rhode Island I | 207 | 41.33 N | 71.15 W |
| Rhode Island Sound ʊ | 207 | 41.25 N | 71.15 W |
| Rhodes, Austl. | 274a | 33.50 S | 151.05 E |
| Rhodes → Ródhos, Ellás | 38 | 36.26 N | 28.13 E |
| Rhodes, S. Afr. | 158 | 30.47 S | 27.59 E |
| Rhodes, Eng., U.K. | 262 | 53.33 N | 2.14 W |
| Rhodes → Ródhos I | 38 | 36.10 N | 28.00 E |
| Rhodesia → Zimbabwe □ [1] | 154 | 20.00 S | 30.00 E |
| Rhodes Inyanga National Park ♦ | 154 | 18.12 S | 32.45 E |
| Rhodes Matopos National Park ♦ | 154 | 20.33 S | 28.20 E |
| Rhodes Park ♦ | 273d | 26.12 S | 28.06 E |
| Rhodes Peak ʌ | 202 | 46.41 N | 114.47 W |
| Rhodes' Tomb ⊥ | 154 | 20.30 S | 28.30 E |
| Rhododendron | 224 | 45.20 N | 121.55 W |
| Rhododendron State Park ♦ | 207 | 42.47 N | 72.12 W |
| Rhodon | 261 | 48.43 N | 2.04 E |
| Rhodon, Ruisseau le ≃ | 261 | 48.42 N | 2.04 E |
| Rhodope Mountains (Rodopi) (Orosirá Rodhópis) ⋏ | 38 | 41.30 N | 24.30 E |
| Rhodt | 56 | 49.16 N | 8.07 E |
| Rhome | 222 | 33.03 N | 97.28 W |
| Rhön ⋏ | 56 | 50.30 N | 9.50 E |
| Rhondda | 42 | 51.40 N | 3.27 W |
| Rhône □ [5] | 32 | 45.55 N | 4.40 E |
| Rhône ≃ | 32 | 43.20 N | 4.50 E |
| Rhône à Sète, Canal du ≊ | 62 | 43.25 N | 3.42 E |
| Rhône au Rhin, Canal du ≊ | 58 | 47.06 N | 5.19 E |
| Rhoose | 42 | 51.24 N | 3.20 W |
| Rhosesmor | 262 | 53.12 N | 3.10 W |
| Rhosllanerchrugog | 44 | 53.00 N | 3.03 W |
| Rhosneigr | 44 | 53.14 N | 4.31 W |
| Rhos-on-Sea | 44 | 53.19 N | 3.45 W |
| Rhossili | 42 | 51.34 N | 4.17 W |
| Rhourde-el-Baguel | 148 | 31.24 N | 6.57 E |
| Rhuddlan | 44 | 53.18 N | 3.27 W |
| Rhüden | 52 | 51.56 N | 10.07 E |
| Rhue ≃ | 32 | 45.23 N | 2.29 E |

| | | | |
|---|---|---|---|
| Rhyl | 44 | 53.19 N | 3.29 W |
| Rhymney | 42 | 51.46 N | 3.18 W |
| Rhymney ≃ | 42 | 51.28 N | 3.10 W |
| Rhynie | 46 | 57.19 N | 2.50 W |
| Riaba | 152 | 3.23 N | 8.46 E |
| Riace | 68 | 38.25 N | 16.29 E |
| Riachão | 250 | 7.22 S | 46.37 W |
| Riachão do Dantas | 250 | 11.04 S | 37.44 W |
| Riachão do Jacuípe | 250 | 11.48 S | 39.21 W |
| Riacho de Santana | 255 | 13.37 S | 42.57 W |
| Riacho Grande | 256 | 23.48 S | 46.35 W |
| Riachos, Islas de los II | 254 | 40.10 S | 62.08 W |
| Riachuelo, Bra. | 250 | 10.44 S | 37.11 W |
| Riachuelo, Chile | 254 | 40.49 S | 73.21 W |
| Riachuelo, Ur. | 258 | 34.28 S | 57.43 W |
| Riachuelo ≃ | 288 | 34.38 S | 58.22 W |
| Riachuelo, Arroyo ≃ | 258 | 34.27 S | 57.44 W |
| Rialma | 255 | 15.18 S | 49.34 W |
| Rialto, Bra. | 256 | 22.35 S | 44.[illegible]6 W |
| Rialto, Ca., U.S. | 228 | 34.06 N | 117.22 W |
| Riamkanan, Waduk ⊜ [1] | 112 | 3.30 S | 115.05 E |
| Rianápolis | 255 | 15.29 S | 49.23 W |
| Riāng | 120 | 27.32 N | 92.55 E |
| Riangnom | 140 | 9.55 N | 30.0[illegible] E |
| Riaño | 34 | 42.58 N | 5.0[illegible] W |
| Rians | 62 | 43.37 N | 5.45 E |
| Riánsares ≃ | 34 | 39.32 N | 3.1[illegible] W |
| Riāsi | 123 | 33.05 N | 74.5[illegible] E |
| Riau □ [4] | 112 | 1.00 N | 102.0[illegible] E |
| Riau, Kepulauan II | 112 | 1.00 N | 104.3[illegible] E |
| Riaz | 58 | 46.38 N | 7.0[illegible] E |
| Riaza | 34 | 41.17 N | 3.28 W |
| Riaza ≃ | 34 | 41.42 N | 3.55 W |
| Ribadavia | 34 | 42.17 N | 8.08 W |
| Ribadeo | 34 | 43.32 N | 7.02 W |
| Ribadesella | 34 | 43.28 N | 5.04 W |
| Ribas de Jarama | 266a | 40.23 N | 3.31 W |
| Ribas do Rio Pardo | 255 | 20.27 S | 53.46 W |
| Ribauè | 154 | 14.57 S | 38.17 E |
| Ribble ≃ | 44 | 53.44 N | 2.50 W |
| Ribbleton | 262 | 53.46 N | 2.40 W |
| Ribble Valley □ [8] | 262 | 53.48 N | 2.31 W |
| Ribbon Fall ʟ | 226 | 37.44 N | 119.39 W |
| Ribchester | 262 | 53.49 N | 2.32 W |
| Ribe | 41 | 55.21 N | 8.46 E |
| Ribe □ [6] | 41 | 55.35 N | 8.50 E |
| Ribe ≃ | 41 | 55.21 N | 8.40 E |
| Ribeauvillé | 58 | 48.12 N | 7.19 |
| Ribécourt | 50 | 49.31 N | 2.55 |
| Ribeira | 252 | 24.40 S | 49.01 W |
| Ribeira do Iguape ≃ | 252 | 24.40 S | 47.24 W |
| Ribeira do Pombal | 250 | 10.50 S | 38.32 W |
| Ribeira Grande, C.V. | 150a | 17.11 N | 25.04 W |
| Ribeira Grande, Port. | 148a | 37.49 N | 25.31 W |
| Ribeirão | 250 | 8.31 S | 35.23 W |
| Ribeirão das Lajes, Represa do ⊜ [1] | 256 | 22.45 S | 43.55 W |
| Ribeirão de São Joaquim | 256 | 22.17 S | 44.11 W |
| Ribeirão do Pinhal | 255 | 23.24 S | 50.18 W |
| Ribeirão Pires | 256 | 23.43 S | 46.25 W |
| Ribeirão Preto | 255 | 21.10 S | 47.48 W |
| Ribeirão Vermelho | 255 | 21.11 S | 45.03 W |
| Ribeirãozinho | 255 | 16.27 S | 52.35 W |
| Ribeiro Gonçalves | 250 | 7.32 S | 45.14 W |
| Ribeiro Junqueira | 256 | 21.28 S | 42.31 W |
| Ribeiros | 256 | 21.59 S | 45.35 W |
| Ribemont | 50 | 49.48 N | 3.28 E |
| Ribera | 70 | 37.30 N | 13.16 E |
| Riberalta | 248 | 10.59 S | 66.06 W |
| Riberão Pires □ [7] | 287b | 23.43 S | 46.21 W |
| Ribiers | 62 | 44.14 N | 5.52 E |
| Rib Lake | 190 | 45.19 N | 90.12 W |
| Ribnica, Slvn. | 36 | 45.44 N | 14.44 E |
| Ribnica, Slvn. | 61 | 46.32 N | 15.16 E |
| Ribnitz-Damgarten | 54 | 54.15 N | 12.28 E |
| Ribstone Creek ≃ | 184 | 52.51 N | 110.05 W |
| Ricadi | 68 | 38.37 N | 15.52 E |
| Ricarda, Estany de la ᑕ | 266d | 41.18 N | 2.07 E |
| Ricardo Flores Magón | 232 | 29.58 N | 106.58 W |
| Ricaurte | 246 | 1.13 N | 77.59 W |
| Riccall | 44 | 53.50 N | 1.04 W |
| Riccarton | 172 | 43.32 S | 172.36 E |
| Riccia | 66 | 41.29 N | 14.50 E |
| Riccione | 66 | 43.59 N | 12.39 E |
| Rice | 222 | 32.15 N | 96.30 W |
| Rice Creek ≃ | 216 | 42.16 N | 84.57 W |
| Rice Lake | 190 | 45.30 N | 91.44 W |
| Rice Lake ⊜, On., Can. | 190 | 47.42 N | 82.08 W |
| Rice Lake ⊜, On., Can. | 212 | 44.08 N | 78.13 W |
| Rice Lake Indian Reserve ⬥ [4] | 212 | 44.10 N | 78.12 W |
| Riceville, Ia., U.S. | 190 | 43.22 N | 92.33 W |
| Riceville, Pa., U.S. | 214 | 41.47 N | 79.48 W |
| Riceville, Tn., U.S. | 192 | 35.23 N | 84.41 W |
| Rich, Cape › | 212 | 44.43 N | 80.38 W |
| Richan | 184 | 49.59 N | 92.49 W |
| Richard B. Russell Lake ⊜ [1] | 192 | 34.05 N | 82.39 W |
| Richard Collinson Inlet ᑕ | 176 | 72.45 N | 113.45 W |
| Richards | 222 | 30.32 N | 95.51 W |
| Richard's Bay | 158 | 28.47 S | 32.06 E |
| Richard's Bay ᑕ | 158 | 28.50 S | 32.02 E |
| Richards-Gebaur Air Force Base ■ | 194 | 38.51 N | 94.33 W |
| Richard's Harbour | 186 | 47.37 N | 56.24 W |
| Richards Island I | 180 | 69.20 N | 134.30 W |
| Richardson | 222 | 32.56 N | 96.43 W |
| Richardson ≃ | 176 | 58.30 N | 111.30 W |
| Richardson, Mount ʌ | 162 | 28.49 S | 119.59 E |
| Richardson Bay ᑕ | 282 | 37.52 N | 122.29 W |
| Richardson Mountains ⋏, Can. | 180 | 67.15 N | 136.30 W |
| Richardson Mountains ⋏, N.Z. | 172 | 44.45 S | 168.31 E |
| Richardson Park | 285 | 39.44 N | 75.35 W |
| Richardsville | 214 | 41.14 N | 79.01 W |
| Richard-Toll | 150 | 16.28 N | 15.41 W |
| Richardton | 198 | 46.53 N | 102.18 W |
| Rîchât, Guelb er ʌ [2] | 148 | 21.07 N | 11.24 W |
| Richboro | 208 | 40.13 N | 75.01 W |
| Richburg | 210 | 42.05 N | 78.09 W |
| Riche, Pointe › | 186 | 50.42 N | 57.25 W |
| Richebourg | 261 | 48.49 N | 1.38 E |
| Richelieu, P.Q., Can. | 206 | 45.27 N | 73.15 W |
| Richelieu, Fr. | 32 | 47.01 N | 0.19 E |
| Richelieu □ [6] | 206 | 45.55 N | 73.00 W |
| Richelieu ≃ | 206 | 46.03 N | 73.07 W |
| Richer | 184 | 49.39 N | 96.28 W |
| Richey | 198 | 47.38 N | 105.04 W |
| Richfield, Id., U.S. | 202 | 43.02 N | 114.09 W |
| Richfield, Mn., U.S. | 190 | 44.53 N | 93.16 W |
| Richfield, Oh., U.S. | 214 | 41.14 N | 81.39 W |
| Richfield, Pa., U.S. | 208 | 40.41 N | 77.07 W |
| Richfield, Ut,. U.S. | 200 | 38.46 N | 112.05 W |
| Richfield Springs | 210 | 42.51 N | 74.59 W |
| Richford, N.Y., U.S. | 210 | 42.21 N | 76.12 W |
| Richford, Vt., U.S. | 206 | 44.59 N | 72.40 W |
| Rich Fountain | 219 | 38.24 N | 91.53 W |
| Richgrove | 226 | 35.48 N | 119.07 W |
| Richhill, N. Ire., U.K. | 48 | 54.23 N | 6.33 W |
| Rich Hill, Mo., U.S. | 194 | 38.05 N | 94.12 W |
| Richibucto | 186 | 46.41 N | 64.52 W |
| Richisau | 58 | 47.02 N | 8.54 E |
| Richky | 78 | 51.07 N | 34.30 E |
| Richland, Ga., U.S. | 192 | 32.05 N | 84.40 W |
| Richland, Mi., U.S. | 216 | 42.22 N | 85.27 W |
| Richland, Mo., U.S. | 194 | 37.51 N | 92.24 W |
| Richland, N.J., U.S. | 208 | 39.29 N | 74.52 W |
| Richland, N.Y., U.S. | 212 | 43.34 N | 76.03 W |
| Richland, Pa., U.S. | 208 | 40.21 N | 76.16 W |
| Richland, Tx., U.S. | 222 | 31.56 N | 96.26 W |
| Richland, Tx., U.S. | 222 | 32.57 N | 95.49 W |


| | | | | |
|---|---|---|---|---|
| ≃ River | Fluß | Río | Rivière | Rio |
| ≊ Canal | Kanal | Canal | Canal | Canal |
| ʟ Waterfall, Rapids | Wasserfall, Stromschnellen | Cascada, Rápidos | Chute d'eau, Rapides | Cascata, Rápidos |
| ʊ Strait | Meeresstraße | Estrecho | Détroit | Estreito |
| ᑕ Bay, Gulf | Bucht, Golf | Bahía, Golfo | Baie, Golfe | Baía, Golfo |
| ⊜ Lake, Lakes | See, Seen | Lago, Lagos | Lac, Lacs | Lago, Lagos |
| ≋ Swamp | Sumpf | Pantano | Marais | Pântano |
| ⊓ Ice Features, Glacier | Eis- und Gletscherformen | Accidentes Glaciales | Formes glaciaires | Acidentes glaciares |
| ⊤ Other Hydrographic Features | Andere Hydrographische Objekte | Otros Elementos Hidrográficos | Autres données hydrographiques | Outros acidentes hidrográficos |

| | | | | |
|---|---|---|---|---|
| ✥ Submarine Features | Untermeerische Objekte | Accidentes Submarinos | Formes de relief sous-marin | Acidentes submarinos |
| □ Political Unit | Politische Einheit | Unidad Politica | Entité politique | Unidade política |
| ʋ Cultural Institution | Kulturelle Institution | Institución Cultural | Institution culturelle | Institução cultural |
| ⊥ Historical Site | Historische Stätte | Sitio Histórico | Site historique | Sitio histórico |
| ♦ Recreational Site | Erholungs- und Ferienort | Sitio de Recreo | Centre de loisirs | Area de Lazer |
| ⊠ Airport | Flughafen | Aeropuerto | Aéroport | Aeroporto |
| ■ Military Installation | Militäranlage | Instalación Militar | Installation militaire | Instalação militar |
| ⬥ Miscellaneous | Verschiedenes | Misceláneo | Divers | Diversos |

| Name | Page | Lat.°′ | Long.°′ |
|---|---|---|---|
| Richland, Wa., U.S. | 202 | 46.17 N | 119.17 W |
| Richland □[6] | 214 | 40.46 N | 82.31 W |
| Richland Center | 190 | 43.20 N | 90.23 W |
| Richland Creek ≃, Il., U.S. | 219 | 38.14 N | 89.54 W |
| Richland Creek ≃, Tn., U.S. | 194 | 35.02 N | 86.55 W |
| Richland Creek ≃, Tx., U.S. | 222 | 31.58 N | 96.03 W |
| Richland Creek Lake ⊜[1] | 222 | 32.00 N | 96.13 W |
| Richlands, N.C., U.S. | 192 | 34.53 N | 77.32 W |
| Richlands, Va., U.S. | 192 | 37.05 N | 81.47 W |
| Richland Springs | 196 | 31.16 N | 98.57 W |
| Richmond, Austl. | 166 | 20.44 S | 143.08 E |
| Richmond, Austl. | 170 | 33.36 S | 150.46 E |
| Richmond, Austl. | 274b | 37.49 S | 145.00 E |
| Richmond, B.C., Can. | 224 | 49.09 N | 123.06 W |
| Richmond, On., Can. | 212 | 45.11 N | 75.50 W |
| Richmond, P.Q., Can. | 206 | 45.40 N | 72.09 W |
| Richmond, N.Z. | 172 | 41.20 S | 173.11 E |
| Richmond, S. Afr. | 158 | 31.23 S | 23.56 E |
| Richmond, S. Afr. | 158 | 29.54 S | 30.08 E |
| Richmond, Eng., U.K. | 44 | 54.24 N | 1.44 W |
| Richmond, Ca., U.S. | 226 | 37.56 N | 122.20 W |
| Richmond, Il., U.S. | 216 | 42.28 N | 88.18 W |
| Richmond, In., U.S. | 218 | 39.49 N | 84.53 W |
| Richmond, Ks., U.S. | 198 | 38.24 N | 95.15 W |
| Richmond, Ky., U.S. | 192 | 37.44 N | 84.17 W |
| Richmond, Me., U.S. | 188 | 44.05 N | 69.47 W |
| Richmond, Ma., U.S. | 207 | 42.22 N | 73.22 W |
| Richmond, Mi., U.S. | 214 | 42.48 N | 82.45 W |
| Richmond, Mn., U.S. | 190 | 45.27 N | 94.31 W |
| Richmond, Mo., U.S. | 194 | 39.16 N | 93.58 W |
| Richmond, Oh., U.S. | 214 | 40.26 N | 80.46 W |
| Richmond, Tx., U.S. | 222 | 29.34 N | 95.45 W |
| Richmond, Ut,. U.S. | 200 | 41.55 N | 111.48 W |
| Richmond, Vt., U.S. | 188 | 44.24 N | 72.59 W |
| Richmond, Va., U.S. | 208 | 37.33 N | 77.27 W |
| Richmond □[6], P.Q., Can. | 206 | 45.40 N | 72.00 W |
| Richmond □[6], N.Y., U.S. | 210 | 40.38 N | 74.05 W |
| Richmond □[6], Va., U.S. | 208 | 37.32 N | 77.28 W |
| Richmond ⇾[8], Eng., U.K. | 42 | 51.28 N | 0.18 W |
| Richmond ⇾[8], Ca., U.S. | 282 | 37.46 N | 122.29 W |
| Richmond ⇾[8], Pa., U.S. | 285 | 39.59 N | 75.06 W |
| Richmond, Mount ∧ | 172 | 41.29 S | 173.24 E |
| Richmond, Point > | 282 | 37.55 N | 122.23 W |
| Richmond Beach | 224 | 47.46 N | 122.23 W |
| Richmond Creek ≃ | 276 | 40.34 N | 74.11 W |
| Richmond Heights, Fl., U.S. | 220 | 25.37 N | 80.22 W |
| Richmond Heights, Mo., U.S. | 219 | 38.37 N | 90.19 W |
| Richmond Heights, Oh., U.S. | 214 | 41.33 N | 81.30 W |
| Richmond Highlands | 224 | 47.45 N | 122.20 W |
| Richmond Hill, On., Can. | 212 | 43.52 N | 79.27 W |
| Richmond Hill, Ga., U.S. | 192 | 31.56 N | 81.18 W |
| Richmond Hill ⇾[8] | 276 | 40.42 N | 73.49 W |
| Richmond International Airport ⊠ | 208 | 37.30 N | 77.19 W |
| Richmond Mall ⇾[9] | 279a | 41.32 N | 81.30 W |
| Richmond National Battlefield Park ♦ | 208 | 37.25 N | 77.23 W |
| Richmond Park ♦ | 260 | 51.26 N | 0.16 W |
| Richmond Peak ∧ | 241h | 13.17 N | 61.13 W |
| Richmond Range ⋏ | 172 | 41.27 S | 173.30 E |
| Richmond Royal Australian Air Force Base ■ | 170 | 33.37 S | 150.48 E |
| Richmond-San Rafael Bridge ⇾[5] | 282 | 37.56 N | 122.27 W |
| Richmondtown Restoration ⊥ | 276 | 40.34 N | 74.09 W |
| Richmond Valley ⇾[8] | 276 | 40.31 N | 74.13 W |
| Richmondville | 210 | 42.38 N | 74.33 W |
| Richrath | 263 | 51.08 N | 6.56 E |
| Rich Square | 192 | 36.16 N | 77.17 W |
| Rich Stadium ♦ | 284a | 42.57 N | 78.47 W |
| Richtenberg | 54 | 54.12 N | 12.53 E |
| Richterswil | 58 | 47.13 N | 8.42 E |
| Richton | 194 | 31.20 N | 88.56 W |
| Richton Park | 216 | 41.29 N | 87.42 W |
| Richvale, On., Can. | 212 | 43.51 N | 79.26 W |
| Richvale, Ca., U.S. | 226 | 39.30 N | 121.45 W |
| Richview | 219 | 38.23 N | 89.11 W |
| Richville, N.Y., U.S. | 212 | 44.25 N | 75.23 E |
| Richville, Oh., U.S. | 214 | 40.45 N | 81.27 W |
| Richwood, N.J., U.S. | 285 | 39.43 N | 75.10 W |
| Richwood, Oh., U.S. | 214 | 40.25 N | 83.17 W |
| Richwood, W.V., U.S. | 188 | 38.13 N | 80.32 W |
| Richwood Village | 222 | 29.04 N | 95.25 W |
| Ricinskij zapovednik ♦ | 84 | 43.25 N | 40.30 E |
| Rickenbacker Air Force Base ■ | 218 | 39.48 N | 82.56 W |
| Rickenpass )( | 58 | 47.14 N | 9.02 E |
| Ricken Tunnel ⇾[5] | 58 | 47.12 N | 9.05 E |
| Ricketts Glen State Park ♦ | 210 | 41.20 N | 76.18 W |
| Ricketts Point > | 274b | 38.00 S | 145.02 E |
| Rickleån ≃ | 26 | 64.05 N | 20.56 E |
| Rickling | 54 | 54.01 N | 10.13 E |
| Rickmansworth | 42 | 51.39 N | 0.29 W |
| Rico | 200 | 37.41 N | 108.01 W |
| Ricoa ≃ | 241s | 11.30 N | 69.12 W |
| Ricobayo, Embalse de ⊜[1] | 34 | 41.30 N | 5.55 W |
| Ricupe | 152 | 14.37 S | 21.25 E |
| Ridāʻ | 144 | 14.38 N | 44.54 E |
| Ridanna (Ridnaun) | 64 | 46.55 N | 11.15 E |
| Riddarhyttan | 40 | 59.48 N | 15.33 E |
| Ridderkerk | 52 | 51.52 N | 4.36 E |
| Riddes | 58 | 46.10 N | 7.13 E |
| Riddle | 202 | 42.57 N | 123.21 W |
| Riddle Mountain ∧ | 202 | 43.07 N | 118.30 W |
| Riddlesburg | 214 | 40.10 N | 78.15 W |
| Riddlewood | 285 | 39.54 N | 75.26 W |
| Riddon, Loch ⊂ | 46 | 55.58 N | 5.12 W |
| Rideau ≃ | 212 | 45.27 N | 75.42 W |
| Ridge, Eng., U.K. | 260 | 51.41 N | 0.15 W |
| Ridge, N.Y., U.S. | 207 | 40.54 N | 72.53 W |
| Ridge, Tx., U.S. | 222 | 31.09 N | 96.19 W |
| Ridge Acres | 276 | 40.41 N | 74.32 W |
| Ridgecrest, Ca., U.S. | 204 | 35.37 N | 117.40 W |
| Ridgecrest, Wa., U.S. | 224 | 47.45 N | 122.21 W |
| Ridgedale | 184 | 53.04 N | 104.09 W |
| Ridge Farm | 194 | 39.53 N | 87.39 W |
| Ridgefield, Ct., U.S. | 207 | 41.16 N | 73.29 W |
| Ridgefield, Il., U.S. | 216 | 42.16 N | 88.22 W |
| Ridgefield, N.J., U.S. | 210 | 40.50 N | 74.00 W |
| Ridgefield, Wa., U.S. | 224 | 45.48 N | 122.44 W |
| Ridgefield Park | 276 | 40.51 N | 74.01 W |
| Ridgeland, Ms., U.S. | 194 | 32.25 N | 90.07 W |
| Ridgeland, S.C., U.S. | 192 | 32.28 N | 80.58 W |
| Ridgely, Md., U.S. | 208 | 38.56 N | 75.53 W |
| Ridgely, Tn., U.S. | 194 | 36.15 N | 89.29 W |
| Ridge Manor | 220 | 28.31 N | 82.10 W |
| Ridgemont | 210 | 43.13 N | 77.43 W |
| Ridgetown | 214 | 42.26 N | 81.54 W |
| Ridgeville, Mb., Can. | 184 | 49.04 N | 97.01 W |
| Ridgeville, In., U.S. | 216 | 40.17 N | 85.01 W |
| Ridgeville, S.C., U.S. | 192 | 33.05 N | 80.18 W |
| Ridgeville Corners | 216 | 41.26 N | 84.15 W |
| Ridgeway, On., Can. | 284a | 42.53 N | 79.03 W |
| Ridgeway, Mi., U.S. | 216 | 41.59 N | 83.51 W |
| Ridgeway, Mo., U.S. | 194 | 40.22 N | 93.56 W |
| Ridgeway, N.J., U.S. | 208 | 40.01 N | 74.17 W |
| Ridgeway, Oh., U.S. | 216 | 40.30 N | 83.34 W |
| Ridgeway, Tx., U.S. | 222 | 33.11 N | 95.46 W |
| Ridgeway, Wi., U.S. | 190 | 43.00 N | 89.59 W |
| Ridgeway Ditch ≅ | 279a | 41.25 N | 82.05 W |
| Ridgewood | 210 | 40.58 N | 74.07 W |
| Ridgewood ⇾[8] | 276 | 40.42 N | 73.53 W |
| Ridgewood Farm | 285 | 39.57 N | 75.34 W |
| Ridgewood Reservoir ⊜[1] | 276 | 40.41 N | 73.53 W |
| Ridgway, Co., U.S. | 200 | 38.09 N | 107.46 W |
| Ridgway, Il., U.S. | 194 | 37.47 N | 88.15 W |
| Ridgway, Pa., U.S. | 214 | 41.25 N | 78.43 W |
| Riding Mountain ∧ | 184 | 50.37 N | 99.37 W |
| Riding Mountain National Park ♦ | 184 | 50.55 N | 100.25 W |
| Ridīwajār | 124 | 27.57 N | 83.26 E |
| Ridley Creek ≃ | 285 | 39.51 N | 75.21 W |
| Ridley Creek State Park ♦ | 285 | 39.57 N | 75.27 W |
| Ridley Park | 285 | 39.52 N | 75.19 W |
| Ridnaun → Ridanna | 64 | 46.55 N | 11.15 E |
| Riebeek-Kasteel | 158 | 33.23 S | 18.53 E |
| Riebeek-Oos | 158 | 33.10 S | 26.10 E |
| Riebeek-Wes | 158 | 33.21 S | 18.52 E |
| Riecawr, Loch ⊜ | 44 | 55.13 N | 4.27 W |
| Riedau | 60 | 48.18 N | 13.38 E |
| Riedelbach | 56 | 50.18 N | 8.23 E |
| Rieden | 60 | 49.19 N | 11.57 E |
| Riedenburg | 60 | 48.58 N | 11.41 E |
| Rieder | 54 | 51.44 N | 11.10 E |
| Riederalp | 58 | 46.23 N | 8.01 E |
| Riedern | 56 | 49.40 N | 9.23 E |
| Ried im Innkreis | 60 | 48.13 N | 13.30 E |
| Ried im Oberinntal | 58 | 47.03 N | 10.39 E |
| Riedisheim | 58 | 47.45 N | 7.22 E |
| Riedlingen | 58 | 48.09 N | 9.28 E |
| Riedstadt | 56 | 49.50 N | 8.30 E |
| Riegel | 58 | 48.09 N | 7.45 E |
| Riegelsville, N.J., U.S. | 210 | 40.49 N | 74.52 W |
| Riegelsville, Pa., U.S. | 208 | 40.36 N | 75.12 W |
| Riegelwood | 192 | 34.20 N | 78.15 W |
| Riegersburg | 61 | 47.00 N | 15.56 E |
| Riegersburg, Schloss ⊥ | 61 | 47.01 N | 15.56 E |
| Riegersdorf | 64 | 46.33 N | 13.47 E |
| Riehen | 58 | 47.35 N | 7.39 E |
| Rieka → Rijeka | 36 | 45.20 N | 14.27 E |
| Rielasingen-Worblingen | 58 | 47.44 N | 8.50 E |
| Riemke ⇾[8] | 263 | 51.30 N | 7.13 E |
| Riemst | 56 | 50.48 N | 5.36 E |
| Rieneck | 56 | 50.05 N | 9.38 E |
| Rienza (Rienz) ≃ | 64 | 46.43 N | 11.39 E |
| Rienzi | 194 | 34.45 N | 88.31 W |
| Riesa | 54 | 51.18 N | 13.17 E |
| Riesco, Isla I | 254 | 53.00 S | 72.30 W |
| Rieseby | 41 | 54.32 N | 9.48 E |
| Riesel | 222 | 31.28 N | 96.56 W |
| Riesenbeck | 52 | 52.16 N | 7.37 E |
| Riese Pio X | 64 | 45.44 N | 11.55 E |
| Riesi | 70 | 37.17 N | 14.05 E |
| Riestedt | 54 | 51.29 N | 11.21 E |
| Riet ≃, S. Afr. | 158 | 31.20 S | 20.17 E |
| Riet ≃, S. Afr. | 158 | 29.00 S | 23.54 E |
| Rietavas | 76 | 55.44 N | 21.56 E |
| Rietberg | 52 | 51.47 N | 8.25 E |
| Rietbron | 158 | 32.54 S | 23.10 E |
| Rietfontein | 156 | 21.58 S | 20.58 E |
| Riethuiskraal | 158 | 34.20 S | 21.22 E |
| Rieti | 66 | 42.24 N | 12.51 E |
| Rieti □[4] | 66 | 42.18 N | 12.52 E |
| Rietschen | 54 | 51.23 N | 14.47 E |
| Rietspruit ≃, S. Afr. | 273d | 26.19 S | 28.18 E |
| Rietspruit ≃, S. Afr. | 273d | 26.06 S | 27.39 E |
| Rietvlei | 158 | 30.29 S | 29.51 E |
| Rietzer See ⊜ | 54 | 52.22 N | 12.39 E |
| Rievaulx Abbey ʋ[1] | 44 | 54.16 N | 1.07 W |
| Riez | 62 | 43.49 N | 6.06 E |
| Riezlern | 58 | 47.21 N | 10.11 E |
| Rif ⋏ | 148 | 35.00 N | 4.00 W |
| Riffe Lake ⊜[1] | 224 | 46.30 N | 122.20 W |
| Rifflart | 273b | 4.25 S | 15.21 E |
| Rifiano (Riffian) | 64 | 46.42 N | 11.11 E |
| Rifle | 200 | 39.32 N | 107.46 W |
| Rifle ≃ | 190 | 44.00 N | 83.49 W |
| Rifstangi > | 24a | 66.35 N | 16.10 W |
| Rifton | 210 | 41.50 N | 74.03 W |
| Rift Valley □[4] | 154 | 0.30 N | 36.00 E |
| Rift Valley V | 10 | 3.00 S | 29.00 E |
| Rift Valley Lakes National Park ♦ | 144 | 7.30 N | 38.30 E |
| Rīga, Lat. | 76 | 56.57 N | 24.06 E |
| Riga, Ross. | 88 | 56.36 N | 106.17 E |
| Riga, Mi., U.S. | 216 | 41.49 N | 83.50 W |
| Riga, Gulf of (Rīgas jūras līcis) (Riia laht) ⊂ | 76 | 57.30 N | 23.35 E |
| Riga, Mount ∧ | 162 | 21.59 S | 116.25 E |
| Rigacikun | 150 | 10.40 N | 7.28 E |
| Rigaih | 114 | 4.40 N | 95.34 E |
| Rīgān | 128 | 28.37 N | 58.58 E |
| Rīgas jūras līcis → Riga, Gulf of ⊂ | 76 | 57.30 N | 23.35 E |
| Rīga Station ⇾[5] | 265b | 55.48 N | 37.38 E |
| Rigaud | 206 | 45.29 N | 74.18 W |
| Rigaud ≃ | 206 | 45.29 N | 74.18 W |
| Rigby | 202 | 43.40 N | 111.54 W |
| Rīgestān ⇾[1] | 128 | 31.00 N | 65.00 E |
| Riggins | 202 | 45.25 N | 116.18 W |
| Riggisberg | 58 | 46.48 N | 7.29 E |
| Riggston | 219 | 39.42 N | 90.25 W |
| Rigi ∧ | 58 | 47.05 N | 8.30 E |
| Rignano Flaminio | 66 | 42.12 N | 12.29 E |
| Rignano Garganico | 68 | 41.40 N | 15.35 E |
| Rignano sull'Arno | 66 | 43.43 N | 11.27 E |
| Rigney | 58 | 47.23 N | 6.11 E |
| Rigney Bluff | 210 | 43.19 N | 77.38 W |
| Rigny-Ussé | 50 | 47.15 N | 0.18 E |
| Rigo | 164 | 9.47 S | 147.34 E |
| Rigolet | 176 | 54.20 N | 58.35 W |
| Rig-Rig | 146 | 14.16 N | 14.21 E |
| Rigside | 46 | 55.36 N | 3.47 W |
| Riguldi | 76 | 59.08 N | 23.33 E |
| Rīh, Jazīrat ar- I | 140 | 18.10 N | 38.27 E |
| Rihāb | 132 | 32.19 N | 36.06 E |
| Rihand ≃ | 124 | 24.33 N | 82.59 E |
| Rihand Dam ⇾[6] | 124 | 24.05 N | 82.45 E |
| Riihimäki | 26 | 60.45 N | 24.46 E |
| Riiser-Larsen Peninsula >[1] | 9 | 68.55 S | 34.00 E |
| Rijau | 150 | 11.07 N | 5.14 E |
| Riječki Zaljev ⊂ | 36 | 45.15 N | 14.25 E |
| Rijeka | 36 | 45.20 N | 14.27 E |
| Rijen | 52 | 51.35 N | 4.55 E |
| Rijkevorsel | 56 | 51.21 N | 4.46 E |
| Rijksdorp | 52 | 52.09 N | 4.25 E |
| Rijn → Rhine ≃ | 30 | 51.52 N | 6.02 E |
| Rijnsburg | 52 | 52.12 N | 4.27 E |
| Rijssel → Lille | 50 | 50.38 N | 3.04 E |
| Rijssen | 52 | 52.18 N | 6.30 E |
| Rijswijk | 52 | 52.04 N | 4.20 E |
| Rikers Island I | 276 | 40.47 N | 73.53 W |
| Rikers Island Channel µ | 276 | 40.47 N | 73.52 W |
| Rikkavesi ⊜ | 26 | 62.50 N | 28.44 E |
| Riksgränsen | 24 | 68.24 N | 18.12 E |
| Rikuchū-kaigan-kokuritsu-kōen ♦ | 92 | 39.25 N | 141.57 E |
| Rikuzen-takata | 92 | 39.01 N | 141.38 E |
| Rila ⋏ | 38 | 42.08 N | 23.33 E |
| Riley | 198 | 39.17 N | 96.49 W |
| Riley, Mount ∧ | 200 | 31.55 N | 107.07 W |
| Riley, Point > | 168b | 33.53 S | 137.36 E |
| Riley Creek ≃ | 216 | 41.02 N | 84.00 W |
| Riley Lake ⊜ | 212 | 44.50 N | 79.11 W |
| Rileys Range ⋏ | 170 | 34.21 S | 150.10 E |
| Rilievo | 70 | 37.55 N | 12.33 E |
| Rillieux | 62 | 45.49 N | 4.54 E |
| Rillington | 44 | 54.09 N | 0.42 W |
| Rillito | 200 | 32.24 N | 111.09 W |
| Rillton | 214 | 40.17 N | 79.44 W |
| Rilly-la-Montagne | 50 | 49.10 N | 4.03 E |
| Rilski manastir ʋ[1] | 38 | 42.08 N | 23.20 E |
| Rima ≃ | 150 | 13.04 N | 5.10 E |
| Rímac | 286d | 12.03 S | 77.03 W |
| Rímac ≃ | 248 | 12.02 S | 77.09 W |
| Rimachi, Laguna ⊜ | 246 | 4.25 S | 76.43 W |
| Rimāh, Jabal ar- ∧ | 132 | 32.19 N | 36.52 E |
| Rima San Giuseppe | 62 | 45.52 N | 8.00 E |
| Rimatara I | 14 | 22.38 S | 152.51 W |
| Rimavská Sobota | 30 | 48.23 N | 20.02 E |
| Rimbey | 182 | 52.38 N | 114.14 W |
| Rimbo | 40 | 59.45 N | 18.22 E |
| Rimé, Ouadi V | 146 | 14.02 N | 18.03 E |
| Rimersburg | 214 | 41.02 N | 79.30 W |
| Rimforsa | 26 | 58.08 N | 15.40 E |
| Rimi | 150 | 12.58 N | 7.43 E |
| Rimini | 66 | 44.04 N | 12.34 E |
| Rimini □[4] | 66 | 44.00 N | 12.35 E |
| Rimo Glacier ⊓ | 123 | 35.25 N | 77.30 E |
| Rimogne | 56 | 49.50 N | 4.33 E |
| Rimouski | 186 | 48.26 N | 68.33 W |
| Rimouski ≃ | 186 | 48.27 N | 68.32 W |
| Rimouski, Réserve ♦ | 186 | 48.03 N | 68.15 W |
| Rimpar | 56 | 49.51 N | 9.57 E |
| Rimrock Lake ⊜[1] | 224 | 46.38 N | 121.12 W |
| Rimsko-Korsakovka | 80 | 51.34 N | 48.31 E |
| Rín → Rhine ≃ | 30 | 51.52 N | 6.02 E |
| Rinbung | 124 | 29.21 N | 89.57 E |
| Rinca | 115b | 8.37 S | 119.48 E |
| Rinca, Pulau I | 115b | 8.41 S | 119.42 E |
| Rinchnach | 60 | 48.57 N | 13.12 E |
| Rinčin Lchumbe | 88 | 51.07 N | 99.40 E |
| Rincón, C.R. | 236 | 8.42 N | 83.29 W |
| Rincón, P.R. | 240m | 18.20 N | 67.15 W |
| Rincon, Ga., U.S. | 192 | 32.17 N | 81.14 W |
| Rincon, N.M., U.S. | 200 | 32.40 N | 107.03 W |
| Rincón, Bahía de ⊂ | 240m | 17.58 N | 66.20 W |
| Rinconada | 252 | 22.26 S | 66.10 W |
| Rinconada, Hipódromo de la ♦ | 286c | 10.26 N | 66.56 W |
| Rincón de la Vieja, Parque Nacional ♦ | 236 | 10.48 N | 85.18 W |
| Rincón del Bonete, Lago Artificial de ⊜[1] | 252 | 32.45 S | 56.00 W |
| Rincón del Ocote, Cerro ∧ | 236 | 13.36 N | 87.10 W |
| Rincón de Romos | 234 | 22.14 N | 102.18 W |
| Rincon Indian Reservation ⇾[4] | 228 | 33.15 N | 116.57 W |
| Rindal | 26 | 63.03 N | 9.13 E |
| Rindown Castle ⊥ | 48 | 53.32 N | 7.59 W |
| Rīngas | 120 | 27.21 N | 75.34 E |
| Ringdove | 175f | 16.38 S | 168.09 E |
| Ringe | 41 | 55.14 N | 10.29 E |
| Ringebu | 26 | 61.31 N | 10.10 E |
| Ringenwalde | 54 | 53.03 N | 13.42 E |
| Ringertown | 279b | 40.25 N | 79.36 W |
| Ringford | 44 | 54.54 N | 4.03 W |
| Ringgau ⇾[1] | 56 | 51.04 N | 10.04 E |
| Ringgit, Gunung ∧ | 115a | 7.43 S | 113.50 E |
| Ringgold, Ga., U.S. | 192 | 34.54 N | 85.06 W |
| Ringgold, La., U.S. | 194 | 32.19 N | 93.16 W |
| Ringgold, Pa., U.S. | 214 | 41.00 N | 79.10 W |
| Ringgold Isles II | 175g | 16.15 S | 179.25 W |
| Ringim | 150 | 12.08 N | 9.10 E |
| Ringkøbing | 26 | 56.05 N | 8.15 E |
| Ringkøbing □[6] | 41 | 56.10 N | 8.50 E |
| Ringkøbing Fjord ⊂[2] | 26 | 56.00 N | 8.15 E |
| Ringlet | 114 | 4.25 N | 101.23 E |
| Ringling | 196 | 34.10 N | 97.35 W |
| Ringling Museums ʋ | 220 | 27.23 N | 82.34 W |
| Ringmer | 42 | 50.53 N | 0.04 E |
| Ringoes | 208 | 40.26 N | 74.52 W |
| Rings Island | 283 | 42.49 N | 70.52 W |
| Ringsted, Dan. | 41 | 55.27 N | 11.49 E |
| Ringsted, Ia., U.S. | 198 | 43.17 N | 94.30 W |
| Ringtown | 210 | 40.51 N | 76.14 W |
| Ringvassøy I | 24 | 69.55 N | 19.15 E |
| Ringville | 48 | 52.02 N | 7.34 W |
| Ringwood, Austl. | 169 | 37.49 S | 145.14 E |
| Ringwood, Eng., U.K. | 42 | 50.51 N | 1.47 W |
| Ringwood, N.J., U.S. | 210 | 41.06 N | 74.14 W |
| Ringwood Manor ⊥ | 276 | 41.08 N | 74.15 W |
| Ringwood North | 274b | 37.48 S | 145.14 E |
| Ringwood State Park ♦ | 210 | 41.08 N | 74.16 W |
| Riñihue | 254 | 39.49 S | 72.27 W |
| Riñihue, Lago ⊜ | 254 | 39.50 S | 72.18 W |
| Rinjani, Gunung ∧ | 115b | 8.24 S | 116.28 E |
| Rinkenæs | 41 | 54.54 N | 9.34 E |
| Rinkerode | 52 | 51.50 N | 7.41 E |
| Rinnes, Ben ∧ | 46 | 57.23 N | 3.15 W |
| Rinnthal | 56 | 49.13 N | 7.55 E |
| Rinsumageest | 52 | 53.18 N | 5.57 E |
| Rinteln | 52 | 52.11 N | 9.04 E |
| Rinxent | 50 | 50.48 N | 1.44 E |
| Rio, Fl., U.S. | 220 | 27.13 N | 80.14 W |
| Rio, Wi., U.S. | 190 | 43.26 N | 89.14 W |
| Rio Azul | 252 | 25.43 S | 50.47 W |
| Riobamba | 246 | 1.40 S | 78.38 W |
| Río Blanco, Chile | 252 | 32.55 S | 70.19 W |
| Río Blanco (Tenango de Rio Blanco), Méx. | 234 | 18.50 N | 97.09 W |
| Rio Bonito | 256 | 22.43 S | 42.37 W |
| Rio Bonito ⇾[8] | 287b | 23.43 S | 46.41 W |
| Rio Branco, Bra. | 248 | 9.58 S | 67.48 W |
| Río Branco, Ur. | 252 | 32.34 S | 53.25 W |
| Río Bravo, Méx. | 196 | 28.17 N | 100.55 W |
| Río Bravo, Méx. | 232 | 25.59 N | 98.06 W |
| Rio Brilhante | 255 | 21.48 S | 54.33 W |
| Río Bueno | 254 | 40.19 S | 72.58 W |
| Río Caribe | 246 | 10.42 N | 63.07 W |
| Rio Casca | 255 | 20.13 S | 42.39 W |
| Río Cauto | 240p | 20.33 N | 76.55 W |
| Río Ceballos | 252 | 31.10 S | 64.20 W |
| Río Chico, Arg. | 254 | 41.43 S | 70.30 W |
| Río Chico, Ven. | 246 | 10.18 N | 65.59 W |
| Rio Claro, Bra. | 255 | 22.24 S | 47.33 W |
| Rio Claro, Bra. | 256 | 22.43 S | 44.09 W |
| Rio Claro, Trin. | 241r | 10.18 N | 61.11 W |
| Rio Claro, Reprêsa do ⊜[1] | 256 | 23.39 S | 45.54 W |
| Río Colorado | 252 | 39.01 S | 64.05 W |
| Rio Comprido ⇾[8] | 287a | 22.55 S | 43.12 W |
| Río Cuarto | 252 | 33.08 S | 64.21 W |
| Rio das Flores | 256 | 22.10 S | 43.35 W |
| Rio das Pedras | 156 | 23.12 S | 35.23 E |
| Rio de Contas | 255 | 13.36 S | 41.48 W |
| Rio de Janeiro, Bra. | 256 | 22.54 S | 43.14 W |
| Rio de Janeiro, Bra. | 287a | 22.54 S | 43.14 W |
| Rio de Janeiro □[3] | 255 | 22.00 S | 42.30 W |
| Rio de Janeiro □[7] | 287a | 22.55 S | 43.30 W |
| Río de Jesús | 236 | 7.59 N | 81.10 W |
| Rio Dell | 204 | 40.29 N | 124.06 W |
| Rio de Mouro | 266c | 38.46 N | 9.20 W |
| Río de Oro | 246 | 8.17 N | 73.23 W |
| Rio do Prado | 255 | 16.35 S | 40.34 W |
| Rio do Sul | 252 | 27.13 S | 49.39 W |
| Rio Douro | 287a | 22.39 S | 43.32 W |
| Rio Espera | 255 | 20.51 S | 43.29 W |
| Río Gallegos | 254 | 51.38 S | 69.13 W |
| Río Grande, Arg. | 254 | 53.47 S | 67.42 W |
| Rio Grande, Bra. | 252 | 32.02 S | 52.05 W |
| Río Grande, Méx. | 234 | 15.59 N | 97.27 W |
| Río Grande, Méx. | 234 | 23.50 N | 103.02 W |
| Río Grande, Nic. | 236 | 12.53 N | 86.32 W |
| Río Grande, P.R. | 240m | 18.23 N | 65.50 W |
| Rio Grande, N.J., U.S. | 208 | 39.00 N | 74.52 W |
| Río Grande, Ven. | 286c | 10.35 N | 66.57 W |
| Rio Grande → Grande, Rio ≃ | 178 | 25.57 N | 97.09 W |
| Rio Grande, Ponte do ⇾[5] | 287b | 23.46 S | 46.31 W |
| Rio Grande City | 196 | 26.22 N | 98.49 W |
| Rio Grande Da Serra, Bra. | 256 | 23.44 S | 46.24 W |
| Rio Grande da Serra, Bra. | 287b | 23.44 S | 46.24 W |
| Rio Grande da Serra □[7] | 287b | 23.45 S | 46.23 W |
| Rio Grande do Norte □[3] | 250 | 5.45 S | 36.00 W |
| Rio Grande do Sul → Rio Grande | 252 | 32.02 S | 52.05 W |
| Rio Grande do Sul □[3] | 252 | 30.00 S | 54.00 W |
| Riograndina | 256 | 22.11 S | 42.30 W |
| Ríohacha | 246 | 11.33 N | 72.55 W |
| Río Hato | 236 | 8.23 N | 80.10 W |
| Río Hondo, Méx. | 286a | 19.25 N | 99.16 W |
| Rio Hondo, Tx., U.S. | 196 | 26.14 N | 97.34 W |
| Rioja | 248 | 6.05 S | 77.09 W |
| Rio Jaguari, Reservatório do ⊜[1] | 256 | 22.55 S | 46.25 W |
| Río Jueyes | 240m | 18.01 N | 66.20 W |
| Riola | 64 | 44.16 N | 11.04 E |
| Río Lagartos | 232 | 21.36 N | 88.10 W |
| Riolândia | 255 | 19.59 S | 49.40 W |
| Rio Largo | 250 | 9.29 S | 35.51 W |
| Riola Sardo | 71 | 39.59 N | 8.32 E |
| Rio Linda | 226 | 38.41 N | 121.26 W |
| Riolo Terme | 66 | 44.16 N | 11.43 E |
| Río Luján | 258 | 34.17 S | 58.54 W |
| Riom | 32 | 45.54 N | 3.07 E |
| Riomaggiore | 62 | 44.06 N | 9.44 E |
| Rio Marina | 66 | 42.49 N | 10.25 E |
| Río Mayo | 254 | 45.41 S | 70.16 W |
| Rio Mulatos | 248 | 19.42 S | 66.47 W |
| Río Muni □[4] | 152 | 1.30 N | 10.30 E |
| Riondel | 182 | 49.46 N | 116.52 W |
| Rio Negro, Bra. | 252 | 26.06 S | 49.48 W |
| Rio Negro, Bra. | 255 | 19.27 S | 54.58 W |
| Río Negro, Chile | 254 | 40.47 S | 73.14 W |
| Ríonegro, Col. | 246 | 6.09 N | 75.22 W |
| Rionegro, Col. | 246 | 7.16 N | 73.09 W |
| Río Negro □[4] | 254 | 40.00 S | 67.00 W |
| Rio Negro, Pantanal do ≡ | 248 | 19.00 S | 56.00 W |
| Rionero in Vulture | 68 | 40.56 N | 15.41 E |
| Rionero Sannitico | 66 | 41.42 N | 14.08 E |
| Rioni ≃ | 84 | 42.08 N | 41.39 E |
| Rio Novo | 256 | 21.29 S | 43.08 W |
| Rio Novo do Sul | 255 | 20.52 S | 40.56 W |
| Riópar | 34 | 38.30 N | 2.27 W |
| Rio Pardo | 252 | 29.59 S | 52.22 W |
| Rio Pardo de Minas | 255 | 15.37 S | 42.33 W |
| Río Pico | 254 | 44.13 S | 71.21 W |
| Río Piedras, Arg. | 252 | 25.18 S | 64.54 W |
| Río Piedras, P.R. | 240m | 18.24 N | 66.03 W |
| Río Pilcomayo, Parque Nacional ♦ | 252 | 25.10 S | 58.00 W |
| Rio Piracicaba | 255 | 19.55 S | 43.11 W |
| Rio Pomba | 256 | 21.17 S | 43.11 W |
| Rio Prêto, Bra. | 256 | 22.06 S | 43.50 W |
| Rio Prêto → São José do Rio Prêto, Bra. | 256 | 22.10 S | 42.57 W |
| Rio Rancho | 200 | 35.14 N | 106.38 W |
| Rio Real | 250 | 11.28 S | 37.56 W |
| Rio Saliceto | 64 | 44.49 N | 10.49 E |
| Río San Juan □[5] | 236 | 11.10 N | 84.30 W |
| Río Segundo | 252 | 31.40 S | 63.55 W |
| Ríosucio, Col. | 246 | 5.25 N | 75.42 W |
| Ríosucio, Col. | 246 | 7.27 N | 77.07 W |
| Río Tercero | 252 | 32.11 S | 64.06 W |
| Rio Tinto | 250 | 6.48 S | 35.05 W |
| Riotord | 62 | 45.14 N | 4.24 E |
| Rio Tuba | 116 | 8.30 N | 117.25 E |
| Riou, Île de I | 62 | 43.11 N | 5.24 E |
| Rioveggio | 64 | 44.17 N | 11.14 E |
| Rio Verde, Bra. | 255 | 17.43 S | 50.56 W |
| Ríoverde, Méx. | 234 | 21.56 N | 99.59 W |
| Rio Verde de Mato Grosso | 255 | 18.56 S | 54.52 W |
| Rio Vermelho | 255 | 18.18 S | 43.00 W |
| Rio Vista, Ca., U.S. | 226 | 38.09 N | 121.41 W |
| Rio Vista, Tx., U.S. | 222 | 32.14 N | 97.23 W |
| Rioz | 58 | 47.25 N | 6.04 E |
| Riozinho ≃, Bra. | 246 | 2.55 S | 67.07 W |
| Riozinho ≃, Bra. | 250 | 7.06 S | 51.40 W |
| Riozinho ≃, Bra. | 250 | 10.22 S | 49.50 W |
| Riozinho ≃, Bra. | 250 | 8.25 S | 45.43 W |
| Říp ∧ | 54 | 50.24 N | 14.18 E |
| Ripacandida | 68 | 40.55 N | 15.43 E |
| Ripalti, Punta dei > | 66 | 42.42 N | 10.25 E |
| Ripatransone | 66 | 43.00 N | 13.46 E |
| Ripky | 78 | 51.48 N | 31.05 E |
| Ripley, Eng., U.K. | 44 | 53.03 N | 1.24 W |
| Ripley, Eng., U.K. | 260 | 51.18 N | 0.29 W |
| Ripley, Il., U.S. | 219 | 40.01 N | 90.38 W |
| Ripley, In., U.S. | 216 | 41.06 N | 86.39 W |
| Ripley, Ms., U.S. | 194 | 34.43 N | 88.57 W |
| Ripley, N.Y., U.S. | 214 | 42.16 N | 79.42 W |
| Ripley, Oh., U.S. | 218 | 38.44 N | 83.50 W |
| Ripley, Tn., U.S. | 194 | 35.44 N | 89.31 W |
| Ripley, W.V., U.S. | 188 | 38.49 N | 81.42 W |
| Ripley □[6] | 218 | 39.04 N | 85.15 W |
| Ripoll | 34 | 42.12 N | 2.12 E |
| Ripoll ≃ | 266d | 41.29 N | 2.12 E |
| Ripollet | 266d | 41.30 N | 2.10 E |
| Ripon, P.Q., Can. | 206 | 45.47 N | 75.06 W |
| Ripon, Eng., U.K. | 44 | 54.08 N | 1.31 W |
| Ripon, Ca., U.S. | 226 | 37.44 N | 121.07 W |
| Ripon, Wi., U.S. | 190 | 43.50 N | 88.50 W |
| Riposto | 70 | 37.44 N | 15.12 E |
| Rippling Ridge | 284b | 39.11 N | 76.37 W |
| Ripponden | 44 | 53.41 N | 1.57 W |
| Rippowam ≃ | 276 | 41.03 N | 73.33 W |
| Riquewihr | 58 | 48.10 N | 7.18 E |
| Ririba, Laga ≃ | 154 | 3.34 N | 37.15 E |
| Ririe | 202 | 43.37 N | 111.46 W |
| Risālpur Cantonment | 123 | 34.04 N | 72.00 E |
| Risaralda □[5] | 246 | 5.00 N | 76.00 W |
| Risasi | 154 | 0.25 S | 25.44 E |
| Risbäck | 26 | 64.42 N | 15.32 E |
| Risca | 42 | 51.37 N | 3.07 W |
| Rischenau | 52 | 51.53 N | 9.17 E |
| Riscle | 32 | 43.40 N | 0.05 W |
| Risco, Ilha do I | 246 | 3.07 S | 58.19 W |
| Rishāʼ, Wādī ar- V | 128 | 25.33 N | 44.05 E |
| Rīshahr | 128 | 28.55 N | 50.50 E |
| Rishīkesh | 124 | 30.07 N | 78.19 E |
| Rishiri-Rebun-Sarobetsu-kokuritsu-kōen ♦ | 92a | 45.10 N | 141.35 E |
| Rishiri-suidō µ | 92a | 45.10 N | 141.25 E |
| Rishiri-tō I | 92a | 45.11 N | 141.15 E |
| Rishiri-zan ∧ | 92a | 45.11 N | 141.15 E |
| Rishmayyā | 132 | 33.44 N | 35.36 E |
| Rishon LeẔiyyon | 132 | 31.58 N | 34.48 E |
| Rishpon | 132 | 32.12 N | 34.49 E |
| Rishra | 272b | 22.43 N | 88.21 E |
| Rishrāsh, Wādī V | 142 | 29.29 N | 31.16 E |
| Rishton | 262 | 53.46 N | 2.25 W |
| Rishworth | 262 | 53.40 N | 1.57 W |
| Rishworth Moor ⇾[3] | 262 | 53.39 N | 2.01 W |
| Risinge | 40 | 58.42 N | 15.51 E |
| Rising Star | 196 | 32.05 N | 98.57 W |
| Rising Sun, In., U.S. | 218 | 38.56 N | 84.51 W |
| Rising Sun, Md., U.S. | 208 | 39.41 N | 76.03 W |
| Risingsun, Oh., U.S. | 214 | 41.16 N | 83.25 W |
| Risle ≃ | 50 | 49.26 N | 0.23 E |
| Risnjak ∧ | 36 | 45.26 N | 14.37 E |
| Risø | 41 | 55.42 N | 12.06 E |
| Rison, Ar., U.S. | 194 | 33.57 N | 92.11 W |
| Rison, Md., U.S. | 208 | 38.32 N | 77.10 W |
| Risør | 26 | 58.43 N | 9.14 E |
| Ris-Orangis | 50 | 48.39 N | 2.25 E |
| Riss ≃ | 58 | 48.17 N | 9.49 E |
| Rissani | 148 | 31.23 N | 4.09 W |
| Risskov ⇾[8] | 41 | 56.11 N | 10.14 E |
| Risstissen | 58 | 48.16 N | 9.49 E |
| Risti | 76 | 58.59 N | 24.03 E |
| Ristigouche (Restigouche) ≃ | 186 | 48.04 N | 66.20 W |
| Ristiina | 26 | 61.30 N | 27.16 E |
| Ristijärvi | 26 | 64.30 N | 28.13 E |
| Ristinge | 41 | 54.50 N | 10.38 E |
| Ristna | 76 | 58.56 N | 22.05 E |
| Risum-Lindholm | 41 | 54.45 N | 8.53 E |
| Rita Blanca Creek ≃ | 196 | 35.40 N | 102.29 W |
| Ritchie, S. Afr. | 158 | 29.02 S | 24.38 E |
| Ritchie, Md., U.S. | 284c | 38.52 N | 76.52 W |
| Ritchie Branch ≃ | 284c | 38.53 N | 76.52 W |
| Rithāla ⇾[8] | 272a | 28.43 N | 77.06 E |
| Ritidian Point > | 174p | 13.39 N | 144.51 E |
| Ritscher Upland ⋏[1] | 9 | 73.20 S | 9.30 W |
| Ritsumeikan University ʋ[2] | 270 | 35.01 N | 135.46 E |
| Ritsurin-kōen ♦ | 96 | 34.21 N | 134.02 E |
| Ritta Island I | 220 | 26.44 N | 80.48 W |
| Ritter, Mount ∧ | 226 | 37.42 N | 119.12 W |
| Ritterhude | 52 | 53.11 N | 8.45 E |
| Rittersgrün | 54 | 50.29 N | 12.47 E |
| Rittman | 214 | 40.58 N | 81.46 W |
| Rittō | 94 | 35.01 N | 136.00 E |
| Ritzville | 202 | 47.07 N | 118.22 W |
| Riu | 120 | 28.19 N | 95.03 E |
| Riva | 208 | 38.57 N | 76.35 W |
| Rivadavia, Arg. | 252 | 35.28 S | 62.57 W |
| Rivadavia, Arg. | 252 | 33.11 S | 68.28 W |
| Rivadavia, Arg. | 252 | 24.11 S | 62.53 W |
| Rivadavia, Arg. | 252 | 31.33 S | 68.37 W |
| Rivadavia, Chile | 252 | 29.58 S | 70.34 W |
| Riva del Garda | 64 | 45.53 N | 10.50 E |
| Riva del Sole | 66 | 42.46 N | 10.52 E |
| Riva di Tures (Rain) | 64 | 46.57 N | 12.04 E |
| Rivanazzano | 62 | 44.56 N | 9.01 E |
| Rivanna ≃ | 192 | 37.45 N | 78.10 W |
| Rivare | 216 | 40.49 N | 84.50 W |
| Rivarolo Canavese | 62 | 45.19 N | 7.43 E |
| Rivarolo Mantovano | 64 | 45.04 N | 10.26 E |
| Rivas | 236 | 11.26 N | 85.50 W |
| Rivas □[5] | 236 | 11.25 N | 85.50 W |
| Rivasdale | 273d | 26.17 S | 27.56 E |
| Rīvash | 128 | 35.26 N | 58.26 E |
| Rivas-Vaciamadrid | 266a | 40.20 N | 3.31 W |
| Riva Trigoso | 62 | 44.16 N | 9.26 E |
| Rive, Île de la I | 273b | 4.21 S | 15.26 E |
| Rive d'Arcano | 64 | 46.08 N | 13.02 E |
| Rive-de-Gier | 62 | 45.32 N | 4.37 E |
| Rivello | 68 | 40.04 N | 15.45 E |
| Rivera, Arg. | 252 | 37.12 S | 63.14 W |
| Rivera, Col. | 246 | 2.47 N | 75.15 W |
| Rivera, Ur. | 252 | 30.54 S | 55.31 W |
| Riverbank | 226 | 37.44 N | 120.56 W |
| River Cess | 150 | 5.28 N | 9.32 W |
| Riverdale, Ca., U.S. | 226 | 36.25 N | 119.51 W |
| Riverdale, Il., U.S. | 278 | 41.38 N | 87.37 W |
| Riverdale, Md., U.S. | 284c | 38.57 N | 76.55 W |
| Riverdale, N.J., U.S. | 276 | 40.59 N | 74.18 W |
| Riverdale, N.D., U.S. | 198 | 47.29 N | 101.22 W |
| Riverdale ⇾[8] | 276 | 40.54 N | 73.54 W |
| Riverdale Heights | 284c | 38.58 N | 76.55 W |
| Riverdale Park ♦ | 275b | 43.40 N | 79.21 W |
| River Drive Park | 212 | 44.08 N | 79.31 W |
| River Edge, N.J., U.S. | 276 | 40.55 N | 74.02 W |
| River Edge, Oh., U.S. | 279a | 41.25 N | 81.51 W |
| River Falls, Al., U.S. | 194 | 31.21 N | 86.32 W |
| River Falls, Wi., U.S. | 190 | 44.51 N | 92.37 W |
| River Forest | 278 | 41.53 N | 87.48 W |
| Rivergaro | 62 | 44.55 N | 9.36 E |
| River Grove | 278 | 41.55 N | 87.50 W |
| Riverhaven | 216 | 41.05 N | 85.02 W |
| Riverhead, Eng., U.K. | 260 | 51.17 N | 0.10 E |
| Riverhead, N.Y., U.S. | 207 | 40.55 N | 72.39 W |
| River Hébert | 186 | 45.42 N | 64.23 W |
| River Hill | 279b | 40.12 N | 79.54 W |
| River Hills | 216 | 43.10 N | 87.55 W |
| Riverhurst | 184 | 50.53 N | 106.52 W |
| Riverina ⇾[1] | 166 | 35.30 S | 145.30 E |
| River John | 186 | 45.45 N | 63.03 W |
| River Jordan | 224 | 48.25 N | 124.03 W |
| Riverlea | 214 | 40.05 N | 83.02 W |
| River Lea Navigation ≅ | 260 | 51.32 N | 0.02 W |
| River Meadow Brook ≃ | 283 | 42.38 N | 71.17 W |
| Rivermont | 192 | 35.13 N | 77.38 W |
| Rivero, Isla I | 254 | 45.37 S | 74.20 W |
| River Oaks | 284c | 38.57 N | 77.11 W |
| River of Ponds | 186 | 50.32 N | 57.24 W |
| River Pines, Ca., U.S. | 226 | 38.33 N | 120.45 W |
| River Pines, Ma., U.S. | 207 | 42.33 N | 71.17 W |
| River Plaza | 208 | 40.21 N | 74.05 W |
| River Ridge Estates | 284c | 38.47 N | 77.00 W |
| River Road | 202 | 44.03 N | 123.05 W |
| River Rouge | 216 | 42.16 N | 83.08 W |
| River Rouge Park ♦ | 281 | 42.22 N | 83.15 W |
| Rivers | 184 | 50.02 N | 100.12 W |
| Rivers, Lake of the ⊜ | 184 | 49.45 N | 105.45 W |
| Riversdale, N.Z. | 172 | 45.54 S | 168.45 E |
| Riversdale, S. Afr. | 158 | 34.07 S | 21.15 E |
| Riverside, Ca., U.S. | 228 | 33.57 N | 117.23 W |
| Riverside, Ct., U.S. | 276 | 41.02 N | 73.35 W |
| Riverside, Il., U.S. | 278 | 41.50 N | 87.49 W |
| Riverside, Ia., U.S. | 190 | 41.28 N | 91.34 W |
| Riverside, Mi., U.S. | 216 | 42.11 N | 86.23 W |
| Riverside, Mi., U.S. | 216 | 42.17 N | 84.29 W |
| Riverside, N.J., U.S. | 208 | 40.01 N | 74.57 W |
| Riverside, N.Y., U.S. | 210 | 42.55 N | 73.40 W |
| Riverside, N.Y., U.S. | 210 | 42.08 N | 77.01 W |
| Riverside, Pa., U.S. | 210 | 40.57 N | 76.38 W |
| Riverside, Tx., U.S. | 222 | 30.57 N | 95.24 W |
| Riverside, Wa., U.S. | 182 | 48.30 N | 119.30 W |
| Riverside □[6] | 228 | 33.45 N | 117.10 W |
| Riverside ⇾[8] | 281 | 42.20 N | 82.57 W |
| Riverside International Raceway ♦ | 228 | 33.57 N | 117.17 W |
| Riverside Manors | 284a | 43.11 N | 79.03 W |
| Riverside Park ♦, Mi., U.S. | 281 | 42.22 N | 83.26 W |
| Riverside Park ♦, N.Y., U.S. | 284a | 42.57 N | 78.54 W |
| Rivers Inlet | 182 | 51.41 N | 127.15 W |
| Rivers Inlet ⊂ | 182 | 51.39 N | 127.30 W |
| Riversleigh | 166 | 19.02 S | 138.44 E |
| Riverstone | 170 | 33.40 S | 150.52 E |
| Riverton, Austl. | 168b | 34.09 S | 138.45 E |
| Riverton, Mb., Can. | 184 | 50.59 N | 96.59 W |
| Riverton, N.Z. | 172 | 46.21 S | 168.01 E |
| Riverton, Il., U.S. | 219 | 39.51 N | 89.33 W |
| Riverton, Ne., U.S. | 198 | 40.05 N | 98.45 W |
| Riverton, N.J., U.S. | 208 | 40.00 N | 75.00 W |
| Riverton, Ut,. U.S. | 200 | 40.31 N | 111.56 W |
| Riverton, Va., U.S. | 188 | 38.56 N | 78.11 W |
| Riverton, Wy., U.S. | 200 | 43.01 N | 108.22 W |
| Riverton Heights | 224 | 47.28 N | 122.18 W |
| River Vale | 276 | 40.59 N | 74.00 W |
| Riverview, S. Afr. | 158 | 28.27 S | 32.10 E |
| River View, Al., U.S. | 194 | 32.47 N | 85.08 W |
| Riverview, Fl., U.S. | 220 | 27.51 N | 82.19 W |
| Riverview, Ks., U.S. | 198 | 37.47 N | 97.22 W |
| Riverview, Mi., U.S. | 216 | 42.10 N | 83.10 W |
| Riverview Park ♦ | 279b | 40.29 N | 80.01 W |
| Riverwood, Austl. | 274a | 33.57 S | 151.03 E |
| Riverwood, In., U.S. | 218 | 40.06 N | 85.58 W |
| Riverwoods | 278 | 42.10 N | 87.54 W |
| Rives, Fr. | 62 | 45.21 N | 5.30 E |
| Rives, Tn., U.S. | 194 | 36.21 N | 89.02 W |
| Rivesaltes | 32 | 42.46 N | 2.52 E |
| Rives Junction | 216 | 42.23 N | 84.27 W |
| Rive Sud, Canal de la ≅ | 275a | 45.25 N | 73.41 W |
| Rivesville | 188 | 39.31 N | 80.07 W |
| Riviera, Az., U.S. | 204 | 35.04 N | 114.35 W |
| Riviera, Tx., U.S. | 196 | 27.18 N | 97.49 W |
| Riviera V | 58 | 46.15 N | 8.58 E |
| Riviera Beach, Fl., U.S. | 220 | 26.46 N | 80.03 W |
| Riviera Beach, Md., U.S. | 208 | 39.10 N | 76.30 W |
| Rivière-à-Claude | 186 | 49.13 N | 65.54 W |
| Rivière-au-Tonnerre | 186 | 50.16 N | 64.47 W |
| Rivière-Bleue | 186 | 47.26 N | 69.03 W |
| Rivière-Bois-Clair | 206 | 46.34 N | 71.50 W |
| Rivière-de-la-Chaloupe | 186 | 49.08 N | 62.32 W |
| Rivière-des-Prairies ⇾[8] | 275a | 45.39 N | 73.33 W |
| Rivière-du-Loup | 186 | 47.50 N | 69.32 W |
| Rivière du Rempart | 157c | 20.06 S | 57.41 E |
| Rivière-Matane | 186 | 48.39 N | 67.20 W |
| Rivière-Mékinac | 206 | 46.47 N | 72.48 W |
| Rivière-Pentecôte | 186 | 49.47 N | 67.10 W |
| Rivière-Pilote | 240e | 14.29 N | 60.54 W |
| Rivière-Salée | 240e | 14.32 N | 60.59 W |
| Rivière-Verte | 186 | 47.19 N | 68.09 W |
| Riviersonderend | 158 | 34.09 S | 19.55 E |
| Rivignano | 64 | 45.52 N | 13.03 E |
| Rivington | 262 | 53.37 N | 2.34 W |
| Rivington Reservoirs ⊜[1] | 262 | 53.37 N | 2.34 W |
| Rivisondoli | 66 | 41.52 N | 14.04 E |
| Rivne, Ukr. | 78 | 50.37 N | 26.15 E |
| Rivne, Ukr. | 78 | 48.15 N | 31.45 E |
| Rivne □[4] | 78 | 51.00 N | 26.30 E |
| Rivoli | 62 | 45.04 N | 7.31 E |
| Rivoli Bay ⊂ | 166 | 37.32 S | 140.04 E |
| Rivolta d'Adda | 62 | 45.28 N | 9.31 E |
| Rivoltella | 64 | 45.27 N | 10.33 E |
| Riwaka | 172 | 41.05 S | 173.00 E |
| Rixford | 214 | 41.55 N | 78.30 W |
| Rixheim | 58 | 47.46 N | 7.24 E |
| Riyadh → Ar-Riyāḍ | 128 | 24.38 N | 46.43 E |
| Rīyāq | 132 | 33.51 N | 36.00 E |
| Rizal, Pil. | 116 | 15.43 N | 121.06 E |
| Rizal → Pasay, Pil. | 269f | 14.33 N | 121.00 E |
| Rizal □[4] | 116 | 14.35 N | 121.10 E |
| Rizal Memorial Stadium ♦ | 269f | 14.34 N | 120.59 E |
| Rize | 130 | 41.02 N | 40.31 E |
| Rize □[4] | 130 | 40.55 N | 40.55 E |
| Rīzeh, Kūh-e (gora Reza) ∧ | 128 | 37.47 N | 58.05 E |
| Rizhao | 98 | 35.27 N | 119.29 E |
| Rizziconi | 68 | 38.25 N | 15.57 E |
| Rizzuto, Capo > | 68 | 38.54 N | 17.06 E |
| Rjukan | 26 | 59.52 N | 8.34 E |
| Rkîz, Lac ⊜ | 150 | 16.50 N | 15.19 W |
| Rô | 175f | 21.22 S | 167.50 E |
| Roa, Esp. | 34 | 41.42 N | 3.55 W |
| Roa, Nor. | 26 | 60.17 N | 10.37 E |
| Roa, Zaïre | 154 | 3.49 N | 24.56 E |
| Roachdale | 194 | 39.50 N | 86.48 W |
| Roade | 42 | 52.09 N | 0.53 W |
| Roadford Reservoir ⊜[1] | 42 | 50.43 N | 4.13 W |
| Roadhead | 44 | 55.04 N | 2.46 W |
| Roadknight, Point > | 169 | 38.26 S | 144.11 E |
| Roadside | 158 | 27.31 S | 28.52 E |
| Road Town | 240m | 18.27 N | 64.37 W |
| Roag, East Loch ⊂ | 46 | 58.14 N | 6.48 W |
| Roag, West Loch ⊂ | 46 | 58.13 N | 6.53 W |
| Roaming Rock, Lake ⊜[1] | 214 | 41.38 N | 80.49 W |
| Roaming Shores | 214 | 41.39 N | 80.49 W |
| Roana | 64 | 45.52 N | 11.28 E |
| Roan Cliffs ⊥[4] | 200 | 39.20 N | 109.40 W |
| Roan Creek ≃ | 200 | 39.20 N | 108.13 W |
| Roan Fell ∧ | 44 | 55.13 N | 2.52 W |
| Roan Mountain | 192 | 36.11 N | 82.04 W |
| Roann | 216 | 40.54 N | 85.55 W |
| Roanne | 32 | 46.02 N | 4.04 E |
| Roanoke, Al., U.S. | 194 | 33.09 N | 85.22 W |
| Roanoke, Il., U.S. | 190 | 40.47 N | 89.11 W |
| Roanoke, In., U.S. | 216 | 40.57 N | 85.22 W |
| Roanoke, Tx., U.S. | 222 | 33.01 N | 97.14 W |
| Roanoke, Va., U.S. | 192 | 37.16 N | 79.56 W |
| Roanoke (Staunton) ≃ | 192 | 35.56 N | 76.43 W |
| Roanoke Island I | 192 | 35.53 N | 75.39 W |
| Roanoke Rapids | 192 | 36.27 N | 77.39 W |
| Roanoke Rapids Dam ⇾[6] | 192 | 36.24 N | 77.40 W |
| Roan Plateau ⋏[1] | 200 | 39.30 N | 109.40 W |
| Roans Prairie | 222 | 30.35 N | 95.57 W |
| Roaring ≃ | 224 | 45.13 N | 122.12 W |
| Roaring Branch | 210 | 41.34 N | 76.57 W |
| Roaring Brook ≃ | 212 | 43.44 N | 75.24 W |
| Roaring Fork ≃ | 200 | 39.33 N | 107.20 W |
| Roaring River Slough ≃ | 282 | 38.05 N | 121.55 W |
| Roaring Run ≃ | 279b | 40.33 N | 79.32 W |
| Roaring Spring | 214 | 40.20 N | 78.23 W |
| Roaring Springs | 196 | 33.54 N | 100.52 W |
| Roaringwater Bay ⊂ | 48 | 51.31 N | 9.26 W |
| Roatán | 236 | 16.18 N | 86.35 W |
| Roatán, Isla de I | 236 | 16.23 N | 86.30 W |
| Robâa Oued Yahia | 36 | 36.05 N | 9.35 E |
| Robāṭ Karīm | 128 | 35.28 N | 51.05 E |
| Robbeneiland I | 158 | 33.49 S | 18.22 E |
| Robbers Cave State Park ♦ | 196 | 35.01 N | 95.27 W |
| Robbins, Ca., U.S. | 226 | 38.53 N | 121.42 W |
| Robbins, Il., U.S. | 216 | 41.38 N | 87.42 W |
| Robbins, N.C., U.S. | 192 | 35.26 N | 79.35 W |
| Robbins, Tn., U.S. | 192 | 36.21 N | 84.35 W |
| Robbins Airport ⊠ | 283 | 42.34 N | 70.58 W |
| Robbins Ditch ≅ | 216 | 41.21 N | 86.43 W |
| Robbins Island I | 166 | 40.41 S | 144.57 E |
| Robbins Pond ⊜ | 283 | 42.00 N | 70.55 W |
| Robbins Rest | 276 | 40.39 N | 73.10 W |
| Robbinsville, N.J., U.S. | 208 | 40.13 N | 74.37 W |
| Robbinsville, N.C., U.S. | 192 | 35.19 N | 83.48 W |
| Robbio | 62 | 45.17 N | 8.35 E |
| Robe, Austl. | 166 | 37.11 S | 139.45 E |
| Robe, Ityo. | 144 | 7.52 N | 39.38 E |
| Robe ≃, Austl. | 162 | 21.19 S | 115.40 E |
| Robe ≃, Ire. | 48 | 53.37 N | 9.16 W |
| Robe, Mount ∧[2] | 166 | 31.40 S | 141.20 E |
| Robecchetto con Induno | 266b | 45.32 N | 8.46 E |
| Robecco d'Oglio | 64 | 45.15 N | 10.04 E |
| Robecco sul Naviglio | 266b | 45.26 N | 8.53 E |
| Röbel | 54 | 53.23 N | 12.35 E |
| Robeline | 194 | 31.41 N | 93.18 W |
| Röberget ∧[2] | 40 | 59.45 N | 14.54 E |
| Robersonville | 192 | 35.49 N | 77.15 W |
| Robert, Havre du ⊂ | 240e | 14.40 N | 60.55 W |
| Roberta | 192 | 32.43 N | 84.00 W |
| Roberta Mills | 192 | 35.22 N | 80.38 W |
| Robert E. Lee Memorial Park ♦ | 284b | 39.23 N | 76.39 W |
| Robert E. Lee's Birthplace ⊥ | 208 | 38.10 N | 76.49 W |
| Robert-Espagne | 56 | 48.45 N | 5.02 E |
| Robert F. Kennedy Memorial Stadium ♦ | 284c | 38.53 N | 76.58 W |
| Robert H. Treman State Park ♦ | 210 | 42.24 N | 76.35 W |
| Robert Lee | 196 | 31.54 N | 100.29 W |
| Robert Louis Stevenson Memorial State Park ♦ | 226 | 38.40 N | 122.36 W |
| Robert Louis Stevenson's Tomb ⊥ | 175a | 13.50 S | 171.44 W |
| Robert Morse College ʋ[2] | 279b | 40.31 N | 80.12 W |
| Robert Moses State Park ♦ | 210 | 40.37 N | 73.16 W |
| Robert Mueller Municipal Airport ⊠ | 222 | 30.18 N | 97.42 W |
| Roberto Payró | 258 | 35.10 S | 57.39 W |
| Robert Point > | 168a | 32.31 S | 115.42 E |
| Roberts, Id., U.S. | 202 | 43.43 N | 112.07 W |
| Roberts, Il., U.S. | 216 | 40.37 N | 88.11 W |
| Roberts, Mt., U.S. | 202 | 45.21 N | 109.10 W |
| Roberts, Mount ∧ | 171a | 28.13 S | 152.28 E |
| Roberts, Point > | 224 | 49.00 N | 123.06 W |


**Symbols** in the index entries represent the broad categories identified in the key at the right. Symbols with superior numbers (⋏[1]) identify subcategories (see complete key on page *I · 1).*

**Symbole** im Register stellen die rechts im Schlüssel erklärten Kategorien dar. Symbole mit hochgestellten Ziffern (⋏[1]) bezeichnen Unterabteilungen einer Kategorie (vgl. vollständiger Schlüssel auf Seite *I · 1).*

**Los símbolos** incluídos en el texto del índice representan las grandes categorías identificadas con la clave a la derecha. Los símbolos con numeros en su parte superior (⋏[1]) identifican las subcategorías (véase la clave completa en la página *I · 1).*

**Les symboles** de l'index représentent les catégories indiquées dans la légende à droite. Les symboles suivis d'un indice (⋏[1]) représentent des sous-catégories (voir légende complète à la page *I · 1).*

**Os símbolos** incluídos no texto do índice representam as grandes categorias identificadas com a chave à direita. Os símbolos com números em sua parte superior (⋏[1]) identificam as subcategorias (veja-se a chave completa à página *I · 1).*

| English | Deutsch | Español | Français | Português |
|---|---|---|---|---|
| ∧ Mountain | Berg | Montaña | Montagne | Montanha |
| ⋏ Mountains | Gebirge | Montañas | Montagnes | Montanhas |
| )( Pass | Paß | Paso | Col | Passo |
| V Valley, Canyon | Tal, Cañon | Valle, Cañón | Vallée, Canyon | Vale, Canhão |
| ≚ Plain | Ebene | Llano | Plaine | Planície |
| > Cape | Kap | Cabo | Cap | Cabo |
| I Island | Insel | Isla | Île | Ilha |
| II Islands | Inseln | Islas | Îles | Ilhas |
| ⊥ Other Topographic Features | Andere Topographische Objekte | Otros Elementos Topográficos | Autres données topographiques | Outros acidentes topográficos |

ESPAÑOL / FRANÇAIS / PORTUGUÊS


| Nombre / Nom / Nome | Página / Page | Lat.°′ | Long.°′ W = Oeste / W = Ouest |
|---|---|---|---|
| Robert's Arm | 186 | 49.29 N | 55.49 W |
| Robertsbridge | 42 | 50.59 N | 0.29 E |
| Roberts Canyon V | 280 | 34.11 N | 117.54 W |
| Roberts Creek Mountain ∧ | 204 | 39.52 N | 116.18 W |
| Robertsdale, Al., U.S. | 194 | 30.33 N | 87.42 W |
| Robertsdale, Pa., U.S. | 214 | 40.11 N | 78.06 W |
| Robertsfield | 150 | 6.15 N | 10.24 W |
| Robertsfors | 26 | 64.11 N | 20.51 E |
| Robertsganj | 124 | 24.42 N | 83.04 E |
| Robertsham ◆[8] | 273d | 26.15 S | 28.00 E |
| Robertsholm | 40 | 60.35 N | 76.16 E |
| Robert S. Kerr Lake ⊜[1] | 194 | 35.25 N | 95.00 W |
| Roberts Mountain ∧ | 180 | 60.03 N | 166.16 W |
| Robertson, Austl. | 170 | 34.35 S | 150.35 E |
| Robertson, S. Afr. | 158 | 33.46 S | 19.50 E |
| Robertson □[6], Ky., U.S. | 218 | 38.32 N | 84.04 W |
| Robertson □[6], Tx., U.S. | 222 | 31.00 N | 96.30 W |
| Robertson, Lac ⊜ | 186 | 51.00 N | 59.10 W |
| Robertson Bay ⊂ | 9 | 71.25 S | 170.00 E |
| Robertson Range ⋏ | 162 | 23.10 S | 121.00 E |
| Robertsonville | 206 | 46.09 N | 71.13 W |
| Roberts Park | 278 | 41.44 N | 87.49 W |
| Roberts Peak ∧ | 182 | 52.57 N | 120.32 W |
| Robertsport | 150 | 6.45 N | 11.22 W |
| Robertstown | 168b | 34.00 S | 139.05 E |
| Robertsville | 214 | 40.46 N | 81.11 W |
| Robertville | 56 | 50.27 N | 6.07 E |
| Roberval | 176 | 48.31 N | 72.13 W |
| Robin Hood's Bay | 44 | 54.25 N | 0.33 W |
| Robins Air Force Base ▪ | 192 | 32.38 N | 83.35 W |
| Robins Island I | 207 | 40.58 N | 72.28 W |
| Robinson, Il., U.S. | 194 | 39.00 N | 87.44 W |
| Robinson, Tx., U.S. | 222 | 31.28 N | 97.06 W |
| Robinson ≃ | 164 | 16.03 S | 137.16 E |
| Robinson, Lake ⊜[1] | 192 | 34.26 N | 80.10 W |
| Robinson Brook ≃ | 283 | 43.02 N | 71.13 W |
| Robinson Creek ≃ | 226 | 38.16 N | 119.15 W |
| Róbinson Crusoe, Isla (Isla Más a Tierra) I | 244 | 33.38 S | 78.52 W |
| Robinson Gorge National Park ♠ | 166 | 25.15 S | 149.10 E |
| Robinson Lake ⊜ | 222 | 29.35 N | 94.36 W |
| Robinson Lake Aerodrome ⊠ | 273d | 26.08 S | 27.42 E |
| Robinson Pond ⊜ | 283 | 42.48 N | 71.23 W |
| Robinson Range ⋏ | 162 | 25.45 S | 119.00 E |
| Robinson Run ≃ | 279b | 40.23 N | 80.06 W |
| Robinson Run, North Branch ≃ | 279b | 40.23 N | 80.11 W |
| Robinsons | 186 | 48.15 N | 58.48 W |
| Robinvale | 166 | 34.36 S | 142.46 E |
| Robleda | 34 | 40.23 N | 6.36 W |
| Robledo | 34 | 38.46 N | 2.26 W |
| Roblin | 184 | 51.14 N | 101.21 W |
| Roboré | 248 | 18.20 S | 59.45 W |
| Röbrinken | 40 | 58.36 N | 15.53 E |
| Rob Roy Island I | 175e | 7.25 S | 157.35 E |
| Robson, Mount ∧ | 182 | 53.07 N | 119.09 W |
| Robstown | 196 | 27.47 N | 97.40 W |
| Roby, Eng., U.K. | 262 | 53.25 N | 2.51 W |
| Roby, Il., U.S. | 219 | 39.44 N | 89.24 W |
| Roby, Tx., U.S. | 196 | 32.44 N | 100.22 W |
| Roby Mill | 262 | 53.34 N | 2.44 W |
| Roca, Cabo da › | 34 | 38.47 N | 9.30 W |
| Roçado | 250 | 6.40 S | 44.19 W |
| Rocafuerte | 246 | 0.55 S | 80.28 W |
| Roça Grande | 256 | 21.36 S | 42.58 W |
| Rocanville | 184 | 50.24 N | 101.43 W |
| Roca Partida, Isla I | 232 | 19.01 N | 112.02 W |
| Roca Partida, Punta › | 234 | 18.42 N | 95.10 W |
| Rocas, Atol das I[1] | 250 | 3.52 S | 33.59 W |
| Roccabernarda | 68 | 39.08 N | 16.52 E |
| Roccacasale | 66 | 42.07 N | 13.53 E |
| Roccadaspide | 68 | 40.26 N | 15.12 E |
| Rocca di Cambio | 66 | 42.14 N | 13.29 E |
| Rocca di Mezzo | 66 | 42.12 N | 13.31 E |
| Rocca di Neto | 68 | 39.11 N | 17.00 E |
| Rocca di Papa | 66 | 41.46 N | 12.42 E |
| Roccafluvione | 66 | 42.51 N | 13.29 E |
| Roccagloriosa | 68 | 40.06 N | 15.26 E |
| Roccalbegna | 66 | 42.47 N | 11.30 E |
| Roccalumera | 70 | 37.58 N | 15.24 E |
| Rocca Massima | 66 | 41.41 N | 12.55 E |
| Roccamena | 70 | 37.50 N | 13.09 E |
| Roccamonfina | 68 | 41.17 N | 13.59 E |
| Roccanova | 68 | 40.13 N | 16.12 E |
| Roccapalumba | 70 | 37.48 N | 13.39 E |
| Rocca Pia | 66 | 41.56 N | 13.59 E |
| Rocca Pietore | 64 | 46.26 N | 11.59 E |
| Roccaprebalza | 64 | 44.31 N | 9.57 E |
| Rocca Priora | 267a | 41.48 N | 12.45 E |
| Roccaraso | 66 | 41.51 N | 14.05 E |
| Rocca San Casciano | 66 | 44.03 N | 11.50 E |
| Rocca Santa Maria | 66 | 42.41 N | 13.30 E |
| Roccasecca | 66 | 41.33 N | 13.40 E |
| Roccasecca dei Volsci | 66 | 41.29 N | 13.13 E |
| Roccastrada | 66 | 43.00 N | 11.10 E |
| Roccavione | 62 | 44.19 N | 7.29 E |
| Roccavivara | 66 | 41.50 N | 14.36 E |
| Roccelito, Monte ∧ | 70 | 37.50 N | 13.47 E |
| Roccella Ionica | 68 | 38.19 N | 16.24 E |
| Roccella Valdemone | 70 | 37.56 N | 15.00 E |
| Rocchetta Sant'Antonio | 68 | 41.06 N | 15.27 E |
| Rocciamelone ∧ | 62 | 45.12 N | 7.05 E |
| Ročegda | 24 | 62.42 N | 43.23 E |
| Roch ≃ | 44 | 53.34 N | 2.18 W |
| Rocha, Bra. | 256 | 21.28 S | 45.49 W |
| Rocha, Ur. | 252 | 34.29 S | 54.20 W |
| Rocha Miranda ◆[8] | 287a | 22.52 S | 43.22 W |
| Rocha Sobrinho | 287a | 22.47 S | 43.25 W |
| Rochdale, Eng., U.K. | 44 | 53.38 N | 2.09 W |
| Rochdale, Ma., U.S. | 207 | 42.11 N | 71.54 W |
| Rochdale, N.Y., U.S. | 210 | 41.43 N | 73.50 W |
| Rochdale □[8] | 262 | 53.37 N | 2.08 W |
| Rochdale Canal ≊ | 262 | 53.43 N | 1.54 W |
| Roche | 42 | 50.24 N | 4.48 W |
| Rochebrune, Grand Pic de ∧ | 62 | 44.49 N | 6.51 E |
| Rochechouart | 32 | 45.50 N | 0.50 E |
| Rochedinho | 255 | 20.14 S | 54.33 W |
| Rochedo | 255 | 19.57 S | 54.52 W |
| Rochedo de Minas | 256 | 21.38 S | 43.01 W |
| Rochefort, Bel. | 56 | 50.10 N | 5.13 E |
| Rochefort, Fr. | 32 | 45.57 N | 0.58 W |
| Rochefort-en-Yvelines | 50 | 48.35 N | 1.59 E |
| Rochefort-Montagne | 32 | 45.41 N | 2.48 E |
| Rochefort-sur-Nenon | 58 | 47.07 N | 5.34 E |
| Roche Harbor | 224 | 48.36 N | 123.08 W |
| Rochehaut | 56 | 49.51 N | 5.00 E |
| Roche-la-Molière | 62 | 45.26 N | 4.19 E |
| Roche-lez-Beaupré | 58 | 47.17 N | 6.07 E |
| Rochelle, Ga., U.S. | 192 | 31.57 N | 83.27 W |
| Rochelle, Il., U.S. | 216 | 41.55 N | 89.04 W |
| Rochelle, Tx., U.S. | 196 | 31.13 N | 99.13 W |
| Rochelle Park | 276 | 40.54 N | 74.04 W |
| Rochemaure | 62 | 44.35 N | 4.42 E |
| Roche-Percée | 184 | 49.03 N | 102.45 W |
| Rochepot, Château de la ⊥ | 58 | 46.57 N | 4.40 E |
| Rocher Fendu, Rapides du ∟ | 275a | 45.19 N | 73.57 W |
| Rochester, Austl. | 166 | 36.22 S | 144.42 E |
| Rochester, Eng., U.K. | 42 | 51.24 N | 0.30 E |
| Rochester, Eng., U.K. | 44 | 55.16 N | 2.16 W |
| Rochester, Il., U.S. | 219 | 39.45 N | 89.32 W |
| Rochester, In., U.S. | 216 | 41.03 N | 86.12 W |
| Rochester, Ma., U.S. | 207 | 41.43 N | 70.49 W |
| Rochester, Mi., U.S. | 214 | 42.40 N | 83.08 W |
| Rochester, Mn., U.S. | 190 | 44.01 N | 92.28 W |
| Rochester, N.H., U.S. | 188 | 43.18 N | 70.58 W |
| Rochester, N.Y., U.S. | 210 | 43.09 N | 77.36 W |
| Rochester, Oh., U.S. | 214 | 41.07 N | 82.18 W |
| Rochester, Pa., U.S. | 214 | 40.42 N | 80.17 W |
| Rochester, Tx., U.S. | 196 | 33.19 N | 99.51 W |
| Rochester, Wa., U.S. | 224 | 46.49 N | 123.05 W |
| Rochester, Wi., U.S. | 216 | 42.44 N | 88.13 W |
| Rochester City Airport ⊠ | 260 | 51.21 N | 0.30 E |
| Rochester Hills | 214 | 42.40 N | 83.09 W |
| Rochester Mills | 214 | 40.49 N | 78.59 W |
| Rochester-Monroe County Airport ⊠ | 210 | 43.07 N | 77.40 W |
| Rochester-Utica State Recreation Area ♠ | 214 | 42.39 N | 83.04 W |
| Rochetaillée | 62 | 45.25 N | 4.27 E |
| Rocheuses → Rocky Mountains ⋏ | 16 | 48.00 N | 116.00 W |
| Rochford | 42 | 51.36 N | 0.43 E |
| Rochford □[8] | 260 | 51.36 N | 0.39 E |
| Rochfortbridge | 48 | 53.23 N | 7.17 W |
| Rochlitz | 54 | 51.03 N | 12.47 E |
| Rochon, Lac ⊜ | 206 | 46.43 N | 75.14 W |
| Rock | 190 | 46.04 N | 87.09 W |
| Rock □[6] | 216 | 42.41 N | 89.05 W |
| Rock ≃, U.S. | 190 | 41.29 N | 90.37 W |
| Rock ≃, U.S. | 198 | 43.05 N | 96.27 W |
| Rockall I | 22 | 57.35 N | 13.48 W |
| Rockall Rise ✣[3] | 10 | 59.00 N | 14.00 W |
| Rockanje | 52 | 51.53 N | 4.05 E |
| Rockaway, N.J., U.S. | 210 | 40.54 N | 74.30 W |
| Rockaway, Or., U.S. | 224 | 45.36 N | 123.56 W |
| Rockaway ≃ | 210 | 40.51 N | 74.21 W |
| Rockaway Inlet ⊂ | 276 | 40.34 N | 73.55 W |
| Rockaway Neck | 276 | 40.51 N | 74.21 W |
| Rockaway Park ◆[8] | 276 | 40.35 N | 73.50 W |
| Rockaway Point ◆[8] | 276 | 40.33 N | 73.55 W |
| Rockaway Point › | 276 | 40.33 N | 73.56 W |
| Rockaways' Playland ♠ | 276 | 40.35 N | 73.49 W |
| Rockbank | 274b | 37.43 S | 144.39 E |
| Rock Bay | 182 | 50.20 N | 125.29 W |
| Rockbridge | 219 | 39.16 N | 90.12 W |
| Rock Bridge State Park ♠ | 219 | 38.53 N | 92.19 W |
| Rock Brook ≃ | 276 | 40.25 N | 74.40 W |
| Rock Candy Mountain ∧ | 224 | 47.01 N | 123.07 W |
| Rockcastle ≃ | 192 | 36.58 N | 84.21 W |
| Rock City Falls | 210 | 43.04 N | 73.55 W |
| Rockcliffe Park | 212 | 45.27 N | 75.41 W |
| Rockcorry | 48 | 54.07 N | 7.01 W |
| Rock Creek, B.C., Can. | 182 | 49.06 N | 118.58 W |
| Rock Creek, Oh., U.S. | 214 | 41.39 N | 80.51 W |
| Rock Creek ≃, N.A. | 202 | 48.25 N | 107.05 W |
| Rock Creek ≃, U.S. | 208 | 39.43 N | 77.13 W |
| Rock Creek ≃, U.S. | 284c | 38.54 N | 77.04 W |
| Rock Creek ≃, Ca., U.S. | 226 | 37.55 N | 120.58 W |
| Rock Creek ≃, Co., U.S. | 198 | 40.20 N | 102.31 W |
| Rock Creek ≃, Il., U.S. | 216 | 41.12 N | 87.59 W |
| Rock Creek ≃, In., U.S. | 216 | 40.42 N | 86.35 W |
| Rock Creek ≃, In., U.S. | 216 | 40.49 N | 85.23 W |
| Rock Creek ≃, Mt., U.S. | 202 | 45.31 N | 108.49 W |
| Rock Creek ≃, Mt., U.S. | 202 | 46.43 N | 113.40 W |
| Rock Creek ≃, Nv., U.S. | 204 | 40.39 N | 116.54 W |
| Rock Creek ≃, Or., U.S. | 202 | 45.34 N | 120.25 W |
| Rock Creek ≃, Or., U.S. | 202 | 42.39 N | 119.08 W |
| Rock Creek ≃, Or., U.S. | 224 | 45.51 N | 123.12 W |
| Rock Creek ≃, S.D., U.S. | 198 | 43.44 N | 97.58 W |
| Rock Creek ≃, Ut., U.S. | 200 | 40.17 N | 110.30 W |
| Rock Creek ≃, Wa., U.S. | 202 | 46.55 N | 117.56 W |
| Rock Creek ≃, Wa., U.S. | 202 | 45.42 N | 120.29 W |
| Rock Creek ≃, Wy., U.S. | 200 | 41.54 N | 106.08 W |
| Rock Creek Butte ∧ | 202 | 44.49 N | 118.07 W |
| Rock Creek Hills | 284c | 39.01 N | 77.04 W |
| Rock Creek Park ♠ | 284c | 38.58 N | 77.03 W |
| Rock Cut State Park ♠ | 216 | 42.20 N | 89.00 W |
| Rockdale, Austl. | 170 | 33.57 S | 151.08 E |
| Rockdale, Il., U.S. | 216 | 41.30 N | 88.06 W |
| Rockdale, Md., U.S. | 284b | 39.21 N | 76.45 W |
| Rockdale, Pa., U.S. | 285 | 39.53 N | 75.26 W |
| Rockdale, Tx., U.S. | 222 | 30.39 N | 97.00 W |
| Rockdale, W.V., U.S. | 214 | 40.18 N | 80.35 W |
| Rockefeller Center ʋ | 276 | 40.45 N | 74.00 W |
| Rockefeller Park ♠ | 279a | 41.32 N | 81.38 W |
| Rockefeller Plateau ⋏[1] | 9 | 80.00 S | 135.00 W |
| Rockenhausen | 56 | 49.38 N | 7.49 E |
| Rockensüss | 56 | 51.03 N | 9.50 E |
| Rockfall | 207 | 41.31 N | 72.41 W |
| Rock Falls | 190 | 41.46 N | 89.41 W |
| Rock Ferry | 262 | 53.22 N | 3.00 W |
| Rockfield | 216 | 40.38 N | 86.34 W |
| Rock Flat | 171b | 36.21 S | 149.12 E |
| Rock Flat Creek ≃ | 171b | 36.07 S | 149.12 E |
| Rockford, Al., U.S. | 194 | 32.53 N | 86.13 W |
| Rockford, Il., U.S. | 216 | 42.16 N | 89.05 W |
| Rockford, In., U.S. | 218 | 38.59 N | 85.54 W |
| Rockford, Ia., U.S. | 190 | 43.03 N | 92.56 W |
| Rockford, Mi., U.S. | 190 | 43.07 N | 85.33 W |
| Rockford, Oh., U.S. | 216 | 40.41 N | 84.38 W |
| Rockford, Tn., U.S. | 192 | 35.49 N | 83.56 W |
| Rock Forest | 206 | 45.20 N | 71.59 W |
| Rockglen, Sk., Can. | 184 | 49.10 N | 105.57 W |
| Rock Glen, N.Y., U.S. | 210 | 42.41 N | 78.07 W |
| Rock Hall | 208 | 39.08 N | 76.14 W |
| Rockhammar | 40 | 59.32 N | 15.26 E |
| Rockhampton | 166 | 23.23 S | 150.31 E |
| Rockhampton Downs | 162 | 18.57 S | 135.01 E |
| Rock Hill, N.Y., U.S. | 210 | 41.38 N | 74.36 W |
| Rock Hill, S.C., U.S. | 192 | 34.55 N | 81.01 W |
| Rockhill Furnace | 214 | 40.15 N | 77.54 W |
| Rockingham, Austl. | 168a | 32.17 S | 115.44 E |
| Rockingham, N.C., U.S. | 192 | 34.56 N | 79.46 W |
| Rockingham □[6] | 207 | 42.50 N | 71.15 W |
| Rockingham Bay ⊂ | 166 | 18.10 S | 146.05 E |
| Rockingham Forest ◆[3] | 42 | 52.30 N | 0.37 W |
| Rockingham Park ♠ | 283 | 42.47 N | 71.14 W |
| Rockingham State Historic Site ⊥ | 276 | 40.24 N | 74.37 W |
| Rock Island, P.Q., Can. | 206 | 45.01 N | 72.06 W |
| Rock Island, Il., U.S. | 190 | 41.30 N | 90.34 W |
| Rock Island, Tx., U.S. | 222 | 29.32 N | 96.35 W |
| Rocklake | 198 | 48.47 N | 99.15 W |
| Rock Lake ⊜, Mb., Can. | 184 | 49.11 N | 99.12 W |
| Rock Lake ⊜, On., Can. | 212 | 45.30 N | 78.23 W |
| Rock Lake ⊜, Il., U.S. | 278 | 41.40 N | 88.03 W |
| Rock Lake ⊜, N.D., U.S. | 198 | 48.50 N | 99.10 W |
| Rock Lake ⊜, Wi., U.S. | 216 | 43.04 N | 88.56 W |
| Rockland, On., Can. | 188 | 45.33 N | 75.17 W |
| Rockland, De., U.S. | 285 | 39.47 N | 75.34 W |
| Rockland, Id., U.S. | 202 | 42.34 N | 112.52 W |
| Rockland, Me., U.S. | 188 | 44.06 N | 69.06 W |
| Rockland, Ma., U.S. | 207 | 42.07 N | 70.55 W |
| Rockland, Mi., U.S. | 190 | 46.44 N | 89.10 W |
| Rockland, N.Y., U.S. | 210 | 41.58 N | 74.54 W |
| Rockland □[6] | 210 | 41.09 N | 73.59 W |
| Rockland Lake | 276 | 41.09 N | 73.55 W |
| Rockland Lake ⊜ | 276 | 41.08 N | 73.55 W |
| Rockland Lake State Park ♠ | 276 | 41.08 N | 73.55 W |
| Rocklands Reservoir ⊜[1] | 166 | 37.15 S | 142.00 E |
| Rockledge, Fl., U.S. | 220 | 28.21 N | 80.43 W |
| Rockledge, Pa., U.S. | 285 | 40.03 N | 75.05 W |
| Rockleigh | 276 | 41.00 N | 73.55 W |
| Rocklin | 226 | 38.47 N | 121.14 W |
| Rockmart | 192 | 34.00 N | 85.02 W |
| Rock Meadow Brook ≃ | 283 | 42.16 N | 71.13 W |
| Rock of Cashel ⊥ | 48 | 52.31 N | 7.53 W |
| Rock Point | 208 | 38.16 N | 76.50 W |
| Rock Point Provincial Park ♠ | 212 | 42.51 N | 79.33 W |
| Rock Pond ⊜ | 283 | 42.44 N | 71.00 W |
| Rockport, Il., U.S. | 219 | 39.32 N | 91.00 W |
| Rockport, Ky., U.S. | 194 | 37.20 N | 86.59 W |
| Rockport, Me., U.S. | 188 | 44.11 N | 69.04 W |
| Rockport, Ma., U.S. | 207 | 42.39 N | 70.37 W |
| Rock Port, Mo., U.S. | 194 | 40.24 N | 95.30 W |
| Rockport, Tx., U.S. | 196 | 28.01 N | 97.03 W |
| Rock Rapids | 198 | 43.25 N | 96.10 W |
| Rock River | 200 | 41.44 N | 105.58 W |
| Rock Run | 208 | 39.59 N | 75.50 W |
| Rock Run ≃ | 284c | 38.58 N | 77.11 W |
| Rock Sound | 238 | 24.54 N | 76.12 W |
| Rocksprings, Tx., U.S. | 196 | 30.00 N | 100.12 W |
| Rock Springs, Wy., U.S. | 200 | 41.35 N | 109.12 W |
| Rockstone | 246 | 5.59 N | 58.33 W |
| Rock Stream | 210 | 42.28 N | 76.56 W |
| Rockton, Il., U.S. | 216 | 42.27 N | 89.04 W |
| Rockton, Pa., U.S. | 214 | 41.05 N | 78.39 W |
| Rock Valley | 198 | 43.12 N | 96.17 W |
| Rockville, N.Z. | 172 | 40.44 S | 172.38 E |
| Rockville, Ct., U.S. | 207 | 41.52 N | 72.27 W |
| Rockville, In., U.S. | 194 | 39.45 N | 87.13 W |
| Rockville, Md., U.S. | 208 | 39.05 N | 77.09 W |
| Rockville, Ma., U.S. | 283 | 42.08 N | 71.21 W |
| Rockville, Pa., U.S. | 208 | 40.20 N | 76.54 W |
| Rockville, R.I., U.S. | 207 | 41.27 N | 71.30 W |
| Rockville Centre | 210 | 40.39 N | 73.38 W |
| Rockwall | 222 | 32.55 N | 96.27 W |
| Rockwall □[6] | 222 | 32.55 N | 96.23 W |
| Rockwell, Ia., U.S. | 190 | 42.59 N | 93.11 W |
| Rockwell, N.C., U.S. | 192 | 35.33 N | 80.24 W |
| Rockwell, Lake ⊜ | 214 | 41.12 N | 81.19 W |
| Rockwell City | 198 | 42.23 N | 94.38 W |
| Rockwell International Corporation ʋ[3] | 280 | 33.52 N | 117.51 W |
| Rockwood, On., Can. | 212 | 43.37 N | 80.08 W |
| Rockwood, Me., U.S. | 188 | 45.41 N | 69.44 W |
| Rockwood, Mi., U.S. | 216 | 42.04 N | 83.14 W |
| Rockwood, Or., U.S. | 224 | 45.31 N | 122.28 W |
| Rockwood, Pa., U.S. | 188 | 39.54 N | 79.09 W |
| Rockwood, Tn., U.S. | 192 | 35.51 N | 84.41 W |
| Rockwood Lake ⊜ | 276 | 41.06 N | 73.38 W |
| Rockwood Lake Brook ≃ | 276 | 41.03 N | 73.36 W |
| Rocky | 196 | 35.09 N | 99.03 W |
| Rocky ≃, Ab., Can. | 182 | 53.08 N | 117.59 W |
| Rocky ≃, Mi., U.S. | 216 | 41.57 N | 85.39 W |
| Rocky ≃, N.C., U.S. | 192 | 35.37 N | 79.09 W |
| Rocky ≃, Oh., U.S. | 214 | 41.30 N | 81.49 W |
| Rocky, East Branch ≃ | 279a | 41.24 N | 81.53 W |
| Rocky, West Branch ≃ | 214 | 41.24 N | 81.53 W |
| Rocky Arroyo V | 196 | 32.32 N | 104.21 W |
| Rocky Boy's Indian Reservation ◆[4] | 202 | 48.18 N | 109.45 W |
| Rocky Branch ≃ | 284c | 38.53 N | 77.19 W |
| Rocky Cape National Park ♠ | 166 | 40.56 S | 145.35 E |
| Rocky Comfort Creek ≃ | 192 | 32.59 N | 82.25 W |
| Rocky Coulee V | 202 | 47.10 N | 119.16 W |
| Rocky Creek ≃ | 192 | 35.53 N | 80.47 W |
| Rockyford, Ab., Can. | 182 | 51.13 N | 113.08 W |
| Rocky Ford, Co., U.S. | 198 | 38.06 N | 103.43 W |
| Rocky Ford Creek ≃ | 216 | 41.19 N | 83.37 W |
| Rocky Fork Lake ⊜ | 218 | 39.11 N | 83.28 W |
| Rocky Fork State Park ♠ | 218 | 39.11 N | 83.30 W |
| Rocky Gorge Reservoir ⊜[1] | 208 | 39.07 N | 76.54 W |
| Rocky Grove | 214 | 41.25 N | 79.49 W |
| Rocky Gully | 162 | 34.30 S | 116.48 E |
| Rocky Harbour | 186 | 49.36 N | 57.55 W |
| Rocky Harbour ⊂ | 271d | 22.20 N | 114.19 E |
| Rocky Hill, Ct., U.S. | 207 | 41.40 N | 72.39 W |
| Rocky Hill, N.J., U.S. | 276 | 40.24 N | 74.38 W |
| Rocky Island Lake ⊜[1] | 190 | 46.56 N | 83.04 W |
| Rocky Lake ⊜ | 184 | 54.08 N | 101.30 W |
| Rocky Mount, N.C., U.S. | 192 | 35.57 N | 77.48 W |
| Rocky Mount, Va., U.S. | 192 | 36.59 N | 79.53 W |
| Rocky Mountain ∧ | 202 | 47.49 N | 112.49 W |
| Rocky Mountain House | 182 | 52.22 N | 114.55 W |
| Rocky Mountain National Park ♠ | 200 | 40.19 N | 105.42 W |
| Rocky Mountains ⋏ | 16 | 48.00 N | 116.00 W |
| Rocky Point, N.Y., U.S. | 207 | 40.57 N | 72.56 W |
| Rocky Point, Wa., U.S. | 224 | 47.35 N | 122.41 W |
| Rocky Point ›, Ba. | 192 | 26.00 N | 77.25 W |
| Rocky Point ›, Ire. | 48 | 54.42 N | 8.48 W |
| Rocky Point ›, Namibia | 156 | 19.03 S | 12.30 E |
| Rocky Point ›, Norf. I. | 174c | 29.03 S | 167.55 E |
| Rocky Point ›, Ak., U.S. | 180 | 64.25 N | 163.10 W |
| Rocky Point ›, Ma., U.S. | 207 | 41.57 N | 70.35 W |
| Rocky Point ›, N.Y., U.S. | 276 | 40.55 N | 73.32 W |
| Rocky Ridge | 214 | 41.32 N | 83.13 W |
| Rocky Ridge ∧ | 282 | 37.48 N | 122.03 W |
| Rocky River | 214 | 41.28 N | 81.50 W |
| Rocky River Reservation ♠ | 279a | 41.27 N | 81.50 W |
| Rocky Run ≃, N.D., U.S. | 198 | 47.38 N | 99.02 W |
| Rocky Run ≃, Pa., U.S. | 285 | 39.54 N | 75.28 W |
| Rocky Run ≃, Va., U.S. | 284c | 38.58 N | 77.15 W |
| Rocky Saugeen ≃ | 212 | 44.13 N | 80.53 W |
| Rocky Top ∧ | 202 | 44.47 N | 122.17 W |
| Roclenge-sur-Geer | 56 | 50.45 N | 5.36 E |
| Rocosas, Montañas → Rocky Mountains ⋏ | 16 | 48.00 N | 116.00 W |
| Rocquencourt | 261 | 48.50 N | 2.07 E |
| Rocroi | 50 | 49.55 N | 4.31 E |
| Roda | 192 | 36.58 N | 82.49 W |
| Roda ≃ | 54 | 50.52 N | 11.44 E |
| Rodach | 56 | 50.20 N | 10.46 E |
| Rodach ≃, Dtsch. | 54 | 50.09 N | 11.10 E |
| Rodach ≃, Dtsch. | 56 | 50.08 N | 10.52 E |
| Rodakove | 83 | 48.33 N | 39.02 E |
| Rodalben | 56 | 49.14 N | 7.38 E |
| Rodalquilar | 34 | 37.40 N | 2.08 W |
| Rodas | 240p | 22.20 N | 80.33 W |
| Rodas → Ródhos I | 38 | 36.10 N | 28.00 E |
| Rodaun ◆[8] | 264b | 48.08 N | 16.16 E |
| Rødberg | 26 | 60.16 N | 8.58 E |
| Rødby | 41 | 54.42 N | 11.24 E |
| Rødbyhavn | 41 | 54.39 N | 11.21 E |
| Roddickton | 186 | 50.52 N | 56.08 W |
| Rødding | 41 | 55.23 N | 9.06 E |
| Rodeiro | 256 | 21.12 S | 42.52 W |
| Rødekro | 41 | 55.04 N | 9.21 E |
| Rodel | 46 | 57.41 N | 7.05 W |
| Roden | 52 | 53.07 N | 6.26 E |
| Roden ≃ | 42 | 52.43 N | 2.36 W |
| Rodenberg | 52 | 52.18 N | 9.21 E |
| Rodenkirchen, Dtsch. | 52 | 53.24 N | 8.26 E |
| Rodenkirchen, Dtsch. | 56 | 50.54 N | 6.59 E |
| Rödentel | 54 | 50.17 N | 11.01 E |
| Rodeo, Arg. | 252 | 30.12 S | 69.06 W |
| Rodeo, Méx. | 232 | 25.11 N | 104.34 W |
| Rodeo, Ca., U.S. | 226 | 38.01 N | 122.15 W |
| Rodeo, N.M., U.S. | 200 | 31.50 N | 109.01 W |
| Rodeo Lagoon ⊂ | 282 | 37.50 N | 122.31 W |
| Röderau | 54 | 51.19 N | 13.19 E |
| Roderick ≃ | 162 | 26.57 S | 116.13 E |
| Roderick Island I | 182 | 52.40 N | 128.22 W |
| Rödermark | 56 | 49.59 N | 8.50 E |
| Rodewisch | 54 | 50.32 N | 12.24 E |
| Rodez | 32 | 44.21 N | 2.35 E |
| Rodgau | 56 | 50.02 N | 8.54 E |
| Rodheim-Bieber | 56 | 50.37 N | 8.35 E |
| Rodhópis, Orosirá → Rhodope Mountains ⋏ | 38 | 41.30 N | 24.30 E |
| Ródhos (Rhodes) | 38 | 36.26 N | 28.13 E |
| Ródhos (Rhodes) I | 38 | 36.10 N | 28.00 E |
| Rodi Garganico | 68 | 41.55 N | 15.53 E |
| Roding | 60 | 49.12 N | 12.32 E |
| Roding ≃ | 42 | 51.31 N | 0.06 E |
| Rodinka | 80 | 57.24 N | 43.34 E |
| Rodino, Ross. | 76 | 58.57 N | 44.59 E |
| Rodino, Ross. | 86 | 52.30 N | 80.15 E |
| Rodionovo-Nesvetajskaja | 83 | 47.36 N | 39.42 E |
| Rodleben | 54 | 51.54 N | 12.12 E |
| Rodman | 180 | 57.28 N | 135.21 W |
| Rodman Naval Station ▪ | 236 | 8.56 N | 79.36 W |
| Rodn'a | 76 | 56.22 N | 34.55 E |
| Rodnei, Munții ⋏ | 38 | 47.35 N | 24.40 E |
| Rodney, On., Can. | 214 | 42.34 N | 81.41 W |
| Rodney, Ms., U.S. | 194 | 31.51 N | 91.11 W |
| Rodney, Cape ›, N.Z. | 172 | 36.17 S | 174.49 E |
| Rodney, Cape ›, Ak., U.S. | 180 | 64.39 N | 166.24 W |
| Rodney Bay ⊂ | 241f | 14.05 N | 60.58 W |
| Rodney Village | 208 | 39.07 N | 75.31 W |
| Rodničok | 80 | 51.26 N | 42.54 E |
| Rodniki, Ross. | 80 | 57.06 N | 41.44 E |
| Rodniki, Ross. | 265b | 55.39 N | 38.04 E |
| Rodnikovka | 86 | 50.39 N | 57.12 E |
| Rodolfo, Lago → Rudolf, Lake ⊜ | 144 | 3.30 N | 36.05 E |
| Rodonit, Kep i › | 38 | 41.35 N | 19.27 E |
| Rødovre | 41 | 55.41 N | 12.29 E |
| Rodrigo de Freitas Lagoa ⊂ | 287a | 22.58 S | 43.13 W |
| Rodrigues I | 12 | 19.42 S | 63.25 E |
| Rodríguez, Méx. | 196 | 27.10 N | 100.01 W |
| Rodríguez, Ur. | 258 | 34.23 S | 56.33 W |
| Rodríguez, Arroyo ≃ | 288 | 34.52 S | 58.02 W |
| Roduco | 208 | 36.27 N | 76.48 W |
| Rødven | 26 | 62.38 N | 7.33 E |
| Rødvig | 41 | 55.15 N | 12.23 E |
| Rodyns'ke | 83 | 48.25 N | 37.19 E |
| Roe ≃ | 48 | 55.07 N | 6.59 W |
| Roebling | 208 | 40.06 N | 74.47 W |
| Roebourne | 162 | 20.47 S | 117.09 E |
| Roebuck Bay ⊂ | 162 | 18.04 S | 122.17 E |
| Roehampton ◆[8] | 260 | 51.27 N | 0.14 W |
| Roe Island I | 282 | 38.04 N | 122.02 W |
| Roeland Park | 198 | 39.02 N | 94.37 W |
| Roelands | 168a | 33.18 S | 115.50 E |
| Roeliff Jansen Kill ≃ | 210 | 42.11 N | 73.52 W |
| Roelofarendsveen | 52 | 52.12 N | 4.38 E |
| Roelofskamp | 158 | 26.10 S | 24.24 E |
| Roen, Monte ∧ | 64 | 46.22 N | 11.11 E |
| Roer (Rur) ≃ | 56 | 51.12 N | 5.59 E |
| Roermond | 52 | 51.12 N | 6.00 E |
| Roesbrugge-Haringe | 50 | 50.55 N | 2.37 E |
| Roeselare (Roulers) | 50 | 50.57 N | 3.08 E |
| Roesinger, Lake ⊜ | 224 | 47.58 N | 121.55 W |
| Roessleville | 210 | 42.41 N | 73.48 W |
| Roes Welcome Sound ʉ | 176 | 64.00 N | 88.00 W |
| Roetgen | 56 | 50.39 N | 6.12 E |
| Rœulx | 50 | 50.30 N | 4.06 E |
| Roff | 196 | 34.37 N | 96.50 W |
| Röfors | 40 | 58.57 N | 14.37 E |
| Rofrano | 68 | 40.12 N | 15.25 E |
| Rogačevo | 82 | 56.26 N | 37.10 E |
| Rogačovka | 78 | 51.30 N | 39.34 E |
| Rogagua, Laguna ⊜ | 248 | 13.43 S | 66.54 W |
| Rogaguado, Laguna ⊜ | 248 | 12.52 S | 65.43 W |
| Rogaland □[6] | 26 | 59.00 N | 6.15 E |
| Rogalik | 83 | 48.56 N | 40.03 E |
| Rogans Hill | 274a | 33.44 S | 151.01 E |
| Rogan's Seat ∧ | 44 | 54.25 N | 2.07 W |
| Rogart | 46 | 58.00 N | 4.08 W |
| Rogäsen | 54 | 52.19 N | 12.20 E |
| Rogaška Slatina | 36 | 46.14 N | 15.38 E |
| Rogatica | 38 | 43.48 N | 19.00 E |
| Rogätz | 54 | 52.19 N | 11.46 E |
| Rogen ⊜ | 26 | 62.19 N | 12.23 E |
| Roger, Lac ⊜ | 190 | 47.50 N | 78.51 W |
| Roger Island I | 283 | 42.43 N | 70.50 W |
| Rogers, Ar., U.S. | 194 | 36.19 N | 94.07 W |
| Rogers, Ct., U.S. | 207 | 41.50 N | 71.54 W |
| Rogers, Oh., U.S. | 214 | 40.48 N | 80.38 W |
| Rogers, Tx., U.S. | 222 | 30.55 N | 97.13 W |
| Rogers, Mount ∧ | 192 | 36.39 N | 81.33 W |
| Rogers City | 190 | 45.25 N | 83.49 W |
| Rogers Lake ⊜ | 228 | 34.52 N | 117.51 W |
| Rogers Park ◆[8] | 278 | 42.01 N | 87.40 W |
| Rogers Pass )( | 182 | 51.17 N | 117.31 W |
| Rogersville, N.B., Can. | 186 | 46.44 N | 65.26 W |
| Rogersville, Al., U.S. | 194 | 34.49 N | 87.17 W |
| Rogersville, Tn., U.S. | 192 | 36.24 N | 83.00 W |
| Roggenburg | 58 | 48.17 N | 10.14 E |
| Roggeveldberge ⋏ | 158 | 32.17 S | 20.08 E |
| Roggewein, Cabo › | 174z | 27.07 S | 109.15 W |
| Roggiano Gravina | 68 | 39.37 N | 16.09 E |
| Roghudi | 68 | 38.03 N | 15.55 E |
| Rogliano, Fr. | 36 | 42.57 N | 9.25 E |
| Rogliano, It. | 68 | 39.11 N | 16.20 E |
| Rognac | 62 | 43.29 N | 5.14 E |
| Rognedino | 76 | 53.48 N | 33.33 E |
| Rögnitz ≃ | 54 | 53.19 N | 10.57 E |
| Rognon ≃ | 58 | 48.23 N | 5.10 E |
| Rogny | 50 | 47.45 N | 2.53 E |
| Rogojampi | 115a | 8.19 S | 114.17 E |
| Rogovatoje | 78 | 51.14 N | 38.22 E |
| Rogovo | 82 | 55.13 N | 37.05 E |
| Rogovskaja | 78 | 45.44 N | 38.44 E |
| Rogovskoje | 80 | 58.33 N | 50.43 E |
| Rogožkino | 83 | 47.10 N | 39.21 E |
| Rogoźno | 30 | 52.46 N | 17.00 E |
| Rogue ≃, Mi., U.S. | 190 | 43.04 N | 85.35 W |
| Rogue ≃, Or., U.S. | 202 | 42.26 N | 124.25 W |
| Rogue River | 202 | 42.26 N | 123.10 W |
| Rohan' | 78 | 49.54 N | 36.29 E |
| Rohatyn | 78 | 49.25 N | 24.37 E |
| Rohdenhaus | 263 | 51.18 N | 7.01 E |
| Rohilkhand Plains ≌ | 124 | 28.20 N | 79.30 E |
| Rohinjan | 272c | 19.06 N | 73.04 E |
| Rohitpur | 126 | 23.42 N | 90.19 E |
| Rohl ≃ | 140 | 6.22 N | 29.46 E |
| Röhlinghausen ◆[8] | 263 | 51.30 N | 7.10 E |
| Rohnert Park | 226 | 38.20 N | 122.42 W |
| Rohoziv | 78 | 50.14 N | 31.03 E |
| Rohrbach in Oberösterreich | 60 | 48.34 N | 13.59 E |
| Rohrbach-lès-Bitche | 56 | 49.03 N | 7.16 E |
| Rohrbeck | 264a | 52.32 N | 13.02 E |
| Rohrberg | 54 | 52.42 N | 11.02 E |
| Röhrenfurth | 56 | 51.09 N | 9.32 E |
| Rohri | 120 | 27.41 N | 68.54 E |
| Rohr in Niederbayern | 60 | 48.46 N | 11.58 E |
| Röhrmoos | 60 | 48.20 N | 11.28 E |
| Röhrnbach | 60 | 48.44 N | 13.32 E |
| Röhrsdorf | 54 | 50.51 N | 12.50 E |
| Rohtak | 123 | 28.54 N | 76.34 E |
| Rohunta, Laguna ⊂ | 236 | 15.12 N | 83.30 W |
| Roi, Île du → King Island I | 166 | 39.50 S | 144.00 E |
| Roia (Roya) ≃ | 62 | 43.48 N | 7.35 E |
| Roi Et | 110 | 16.03 N | 103.40 E |
| Roi Georges, Îles du II | 14 | 14.32 S | 145.08 W |
| Roi Léopold, Monts du → King Leopold Ranges ⋏ | 160 | 17.30 S | 125.45 E |
| Roine ⊜ | 26 | 61.24 N | 24.06 E |
| Roinville | 261 | 48.32 N | 2.03 E |
| Roisel | 50 | 49.57 N | 3.06 E |
| Roissy | 261 | 48.47 N | 2.39 E |
| Roissy-en-France | 261 | 49.00 N | 2.31 E |
| Roitzsch | 54 | 51.34 N | 12.16 E |
| Roja | 76 | 57.30 N | 22.49 E |
| Rojas | 252 | 34.12 S | 60.44 W |
| Rojo → Red ≃ | 178 | 31.00 N | 91.40 W |
| Rojo, Cabo ›, Méx. | 234 | 21.33 N | 97.20 W |
| Rojo, Cabo ›, P.R. | 240m | 17.56 N | 67.11 W |
| Rojo, Mar → Red Sea ⊤[2] | 136 | 20.00 N | 38.00 E |
| Rokan | 112 | 0.34 N | 100.25 E |
| Rokan ≃ | 114 | 2.00 N | 100.52 E |
| Rokan-kanan ≃ | 114 | 1.23 N | 100.56 E |
| Rokan-kiri ≃ | 114 | 1.23 N | 100.56 E |
| Röke | 41 | 56.14 N | 13.30 E |
| Rokeby National Park ♠ | 164 | 13.40 S | 142.55 E |
| Rokel ≃ | 150 | 8.33 N | 12.48 W |
| Rokewood | 169 | 37.54 S | 143.43 E |
| Rokewood Junction | 169 | 37.51 S | 143.41 E |
| Rokhah | 120 | 35.16 N | 69.28 E |
| Rokiškis | 76 | 55.58 N | 25.35 E |
| Rokkō-san ∧ | 96 | 34.46 N | 135.16 E |
| Rokkō-sanchi ⋏ | 270 | 34.45 N | 135.13 E |
| Roklum | 54 | 52.04 N | 10.44 E |
| Rokuan kansallispuisto ♠ | 26 | 64.32 N | 26.33 E |
| Rokugō | 94 | 35.29 N | 138.27 E |
| Rokugō ◆[8] | 268 | 35.33 N | 139.43 E |
| Rokusei | 94 | 36.58 N | 136.52 E |
| Rokycany | 60 | 49.45 N | 13.36 E |
| Rokytná ≃ | 61 | 49.05 N | 16.22 E |
| Rokytne, Ukr. | 78 | 49.42 N | 30.27 E |
| Rokytne, Ukr. | 78 | 51.17 N | 27.14 E |
| Rolampont | 58 | 47.57 N | 5.16 E |
| Roland, Mb., Can. | 184 | 49.25 N | 97.55 W |
| Roland, Ar., U.S. | 194 | 34.54 N | 92.29 W |
| Roland, Ia., U.S. | 190 | 42.09 N | 93.30 W |
| Roland, Lake ⊜[1] | 284b | 39.23 N | 76.38 W |
| Roland C. Nickerson State Park ♠ | 207 | 41.46 N | 70.03 W |
| Rolândia | 255 | 23.18 S | 51.22 W |
| Roland Park ◆[8] | 284b | 39.22 N | 76.39 W |
| Roland Run ≃ | 284b | 39.23 N | 76.39 W |
| Rolava ≃ | 54 | 50.15 N | 12.51 E |
| Røldal | 26 | 59.49 N | 6.48 E |
| Roldán | 252 | 32.54 S | 60.54 W |
| Roldanillo | 246 | 4.24 N | 76.09 W |
| Rolde | 52 | 52.58 N | 6.38 E |
| Roldskov ◆[3] | 26 | 56.48 N | 9.50 E |
| Rolette | 198 | 48.39 N | 99.50 W |
| Roleystone | 168a | 32.08 S | 116.04 E |
| Rolfe | 198 | 42.48 N | 94.31 W |
| Roll, Az., U.S. | 200 | 32.45 N | 113.59 W |
| Roll, In., U.S. | 216 | 40.33 N | 85.23 W |
| Rolla, B.C., Can. | 182 | 55.54 N | 120.09 W |
| Rolla, Ks., U.S. | 198 | 37.07 N | 101.07 W |
| Rolla, Mo., U.S. | 194 | 37.57 N | 91.46 W |
| Rolla, N.D., U.S. | 198 | 48.51 N | 99.37 W |
| Rolle | 58 | 46.28 N | 6.20 E |
| Rolle, Passo di )( | 64 | 46.18 N | 11.47 E |
| Rolleboise | 261 | 49.01 N | 1.36 E |
| Rolleston, Austl. | 166 | 24.28 S | 148.37 E |
| Rolleston, N.Z. | 172 | 43.35 S | 172.23 E |
| Rolling Acres | 284b | 39.17 N | 76.52 W |
| Rollingbay | 224 | 47.39 N | 122.30 W |
| Rolling Fork | 194 | 32.54 N | 90.52 W |
| Rolling Fork ≃ | 194 | 37.55 N | 85.50 W |
| Rolling Hills | 280 | 33.46 N | 118.21 W |
| Rolling Hills Estates | 280 | 33.47 N | 118.21 W |
| Rolling Meadows | 216 | 42.05 N | 88.00 W |
| Rolling Prairie | 216 | 41.40 N | 86.37 W |
| Rolling River Indian Reserve ◆[4] | 184 | 50.27 N | 100.00 W |
| Rollingstone | 166 | 19.03 S | 146.24 E |
| Rollingwood | 282 | 37.57 N | 122.20 W |
| Rollins | 182 | 47.54 N | 114.11 W |
| Rollins Reservoir ⊜[1] | 226 | 39.08 N | 120.57 W |
| Rolvsøya I | 24 | 71.00 N | 24.00 E |
| Rom → Roma | 66 | 41.54 N | 12.29 E |
| Roma, Austl. | 166 | 26.35 S | 148.47 E |
| Roma (Rome), It. | 66 | 41.54 N | 12.29 E |
| Roma (Rome), It. | 267a | 41.54 N | 12.29 E |
| Roma, Leso. | 158 | 29.27 S | 27.45 E |
| Roma, Tx., U.S. | 196 | 26.25 N | 99.01 W |
| Roma □[4] | 66 | 41.58 N | 12.40 E |
| Romagna □[9] | 64 | 44.30 N | 12.15 E |
| Romagnano Sesia | 62 | 45.38 N | 8.23 E |
| Romagne-sous-Montfaucon | 56 | 49.20 N | 5.05 E |
| Romain, Cape › | 192 | 33.00 N | 79.22 W |
| Romaine ≃ | 176 | 50.18 N | 63.47 W |
| Romainmôtier | 58 | 46.42 N | 6.29 E |
| Romainville | 261 | 48.53 N | 2.26 E |
| Romakloster | 26 | 57.31 N | 18.27 E |
| Roman | 38 | 46.55 N | 26.56 E |
| Roman ≃ | 42 | 51.51 N | 0.57 E |
| Romanche ≃ | 62 | 45.05 N | 5.43 E |
| Romanche Gap ✣[1] | 10 | 0.10 S | 18.15 W |
| Romang, Pulau I | 164 | 7.35 S | 127.26 E |
| Romang, Selat ʉ | 164 | 7.30 S | 127.00 E |
| Romania (România) □[1], Europe | 22 | 46.00 N | 25.30 E |
| Romania (România) □[1], Europe | 38 | 46.00 N | 25.30 E |
| Romankivtsi | 78 | 48.29 N | 27.13 E |
| Roman-Kosh, hora ∧ | 78 | 44.37 N | 34.15 E |
| Roman Nose Mountain ∧ | 202 | 43.55 N | 123.44 W |
| Romano, Cape › | 220 | 25.50 N | 81.41 W |
| Romano, Cayo I | 240p | 22.04 N | 77.50 W |
| Romano Banco | 266b | 45.25 N | 9.06 E |
| Romano di Lombardia | 62 | 45.31 N | 9.45 E |
| Romanova | 88 | 57.04 N | 103.24 E |
| Romanovka, Ross. | 80 | 51.24 N | 47.23 E |
| Romanovka, Ross. | 80 | 51.45 N | 42.45 E |
| Romanovka, Ross. | 80 | 49.47 N | 45.05 E |
| Romanovka, Ross. | 86 | 54.38 N | 76.03 E |
| Romanovka, Ross. | 88 | 53.14 N | 112.46 E |
| Romanovka, Ross. | 265a | 60.03 N | 30.42 E |
| Romanovo, Ross. | 82 | 56.39 N | 39.14 E |
| Romanovo, Ross. | 86 | 52.37 N | 81.14 E |
| Romanovo, Ross. | 86 | 59.09 N | 61.30 E |
| Romanovo, Ross. | 86 | 53.58 N | 80.30 E |
| Romans d'Isonzo | 64 | 45.53 N | 13.26 E |
| Romanshorn | 58 | 47.34 N | 9.22 E |
| Romans-sur-Isère | 62 | 45.03 N | 5.03 E |
| Romansville | 285 | 39.57 N | 75.45 W |
| Romanzof Mountains ⋏ | 180 | 69.00 N | 1[illegible]4.00 W |
| Romaški | 80 | 50.13 N | [illegible].41 E |
| Romaškino | 80 | 52.29 N | [illegible].48 E |
| Romaškovo | 265b | 55.44 N | [illegible].20 E |
| Romayor | 222 | 30.27 N | [illegible].50 W |
| Rombari | 154 | 4.33 N | 3[illegible].02 E |
| Romblon | 116 | 12.35 N | 12[illegible].15 E |
| Romblon □[4] | 116 | 12.30 N | 12[illegible].10 E |
| Romblon Island I | 116 | 12.33 N | 12[illegible].17 E |
| Romblon Passage ʉ | 116 | 12.27 N | 12[illegible].12 E |
| Rombo, Ilhéus do II | 150a | 14.58 N | 2[illegible].40 W |
| Rome → Roma, It. | 66 | 41.54 N | 12.29 E |
| Rome, Ga., U.S. | 192 | 34.15 N | 85.09 W |
| Rome, Il., U.S. | 190 | 40.53 N | 89.30 W |
| Rome, Ms., U.S. | 194 | 33.57 N | 90.28 W |
| Rome, N.Y., U.S. | 210 | 43.12 N | 75.27 W |
| Rome, Oh., U.S. | 214 | 41.36 N | 80.52 W |
| Rome, Pa., U.S. | 210 | 41.51 N | 76.[illegible]1 W |
| Rome, Wi., U.S. | 216 | 42.58 N | 88.[illegible]8 W |
| Rome City | 216 | 41.29 N | 85.[illegible]2 W |
| Romeleåsen ⋏[2] | 41 | 55.34 N | 13.[illegible]3 E |
| Romenay | 58 | 46.30 N | 5.[illegible]4 E |
| Romeno | 64 | 46.24 N | 11.[illegible]7 E |
| Romentino | 62 | 45.28 N | 8.[illegible]2 E |
| Romeo | 214 | 42.48 N | 83.[illegible] W |
| Romeoville | 216 | 41.38 N | 88.[illegible] W |
| Römerberg | 56 | 49.17 N | 8.[illegible] E |
| Romero, Isla I | 258 | 33.48 S | 59.[illegible] W |
| Römerstein | 58 | 48.30 N | 9.[illegible] E |
| Rometan | 128 | 39.56 N | 64.2[illegible] E |
| Rometta | 70 | 38.10 N | 15.2[illegible] E |
| Romfartuna | 40 | 59.44 N | 16.3[illegible] E |
| Romford ◆[8] | 260 | 51.35 N | 0.1[illegible] E |
| Römhild | 54 | 50.24 N | 10.3[illegible] E |
| Romiley | 262 | 53.25 N | 2.0[illegible] W |
| Romilly, Mount ∧[2] | 162 | 20.27 S | 126.3[illegible] E |
| Romilly-sur-Seine | 50 | 48.31 N | 3.4[illegible] E |
| Romit | 85 | 38.44 N | 69.1[illegible] E |
| Romit, zapovednik ♠ | 85 | 38.52 N | 69.2[illegible] E |
| Romita | 234 | 20.52 N | 101.31 W |
| Romitorio | 267a | 42.01 N | 12.39 E |
| Rommani | 148 | 34.34 N | 6.37 W |
| Romme | 40 | 60.26 N | 15.30 E |
| Rommerskirchen | 56 | 51.02 N | 6.40 E |
| Romney, In., U.S. | 216 | 40.14 N | 86.54 W |
| Romney, W.V., U.S. | 188 | 39.20 N | 78.45 W |
| Romney Marsh ≚ | 42 | 51.03 N | 0.55 E |
| Romny, Ross. | 89 | 50.44 N | 129.15 E |
| Romny, Ukr. | 78 | 50.45 N | 33.30 E |
| Rømø I | 26 | 55.08 N | 8.31 E |
| Romodan | 78 | 49.59 N | 33.19 E |
| Romodanovo | 80 | 54.26 N | 45.20 E |
| Romoland | 228 | 33.45 N | 117.10 W |
| Romont | 58 | 46.42 N | 6.55 E |
| Romorantin-Lanthenay | 50 | 47.22 N | 1.45 E |
| Rompin, Malay. | 114 | 2.42 N | 102.31 E |
| Rompin, Malay. | 114 | 2.48 N | 103.29 E |
| Rompin ≃ | 114 | 2.49 N | 103.29 E |
| Romrod | 56 | 50.43 N | 9.13 E |
| Romsdalen V | 26 | 62.15 N | 8.05 E |
| Romsdalsfjorden ⊂[2] | 26 | 62.39 N | 7.15 E |
| Romsey, Austl. | 169 | 37.21 S | 144.45 E |
| Romsey, Eng., U.K. | 42 | 50.59 N | 1.30 W |
| Romsø I | 41 | 55.31 N | 10.48 E |
| Romulus, Mi., U.S. | 216 | 42.13 N | 83.23 W |
| Romulus, N.Y., U.S. | 210 | 42.45 N | 76.50 W |
| Røn, Nor. | 26 | 61.03 N | 9.03 E |
| Ron, Viet | 110 | 17.53 N | 106.27 E |
| Ron, Mui › | 110 | 18.07 N | 106.27 E |
| Rona, Schw. | 58 | 46.34 N | 9.38 E |
| Rona, Zaïre | 154 | 2.14 N | 30.52 E |
| Rona I, Scot., U.K. | 46 | 57.34 N | 5.59 W |
| Rona I, Scot., U.K. | 46 | 59.07 N | 5.49 W |
| Ronald | 224 | 47.14 N | 121.01 W |
| Ronan | 202 | 47.31 N | 114.06 W |
| Ronas Hill ∧[2] | 46a | 60.31 N | 1.28 W |
| Ronas Voe ⊂ | 46a | 60.32 N | 1.29 W |
| Ronay I | 46 | 57.29 N | 7.11 W |
| Roncade | 64 | 45.38 N | 12.22 E |
| Roncador, Cayos de ✣[4] | 236 | 13.32 N | 80.03 W |
| Roncador, Serra do ⋏[1] | 242 | 12.00 S | 52.00 W |
| Roncador Reef ✣[2] | 175e | 6.13 S | 159.22 E |
| Roncegno | 64 | 46.03 N | 11.25 E |
| Ronceverte | 192 | 37.44 N | 80.27 W |
| Ronchamp | 58 | 47.42 N | 6.39 E |
| Ronchi dei Legionari | 64 | 45.50 N | 13.30 E |
| Ronchin | 50 | 50.36 N | 3.06 E |
| Ronchis | 64 | 45.49 N | 13.00 E |
| Ronciglione | 66 | 42.17 N | 12.13 E |
| Ronco | 58 | 46.08 N | 8.44 E |
| Ronco Canavese | 62 | 45.30 N | 7.32 E |
| Roncofreddo | 66 | 44.02 N | 12.20 E |
| Roncone | 64 | 45.59 N | 10.40 E |
| Ronco Scrivia | 62 | 44.37 N | 8.59 E |
| Roncq | 50 | 50.45 N | 3.07 E |
| Rond, Sommet ∧ | 206 | 45.05 N | 72.33 W |
| Ronda | 34 | 36.44 N | 5.10 W |
| Rondane ∧ | 26 | 61.55 N | 9.45 E |
| Rondane Nasjonal Park ♠ | 26 | 61.50 N | 9.50 E |
| Rønde | 41 | 56.18 N | 10.29 E |
| Ronde, Pointe › | 240d | 15.33 N | 61.29 W |
| Rondeau Harbour ⊂ | 214 | 42.18 N | 81.53 W |
| Rondeau Provincial Park ♠ | 214 | 42.16 N | 81.51 W |
| Rondebult | 273d | 26.18 S | 28.14 E |
| Ronde Island I | 241k | 12.18 N | 61.35 W |
| Rondissone | 62 | 45.15 N | 7.58 E |
| Rondon | 255 | 23.23 S | 52.48 W |
| Rondônia □[3] | 248 | 11.00 S | 63.00 W |
| Rondonópolis | 255 | 16.28 S | 54.38 W |
| Rondout | 278 | 42.17 N | 87.53 W |
| Rondout Creek ≃ | 210 | 41.55 N | 73.53 W |
| Rondout Reservoir ⊜[1] | 210 | 41.50 N | 74.29 W |
| Rone ≃ | 50 | 50.46 N | 3.27 E |
| Ronehamn | 26 | 57.10 N | 18.29 E |
| Rong ≃ | 102 | 24.32 N | 109.15 E |
| Ronga | 80 | 56.43 N | 48.32 E |
| Rongai | 154 | 0.10 S | 35.51 E |
| Rong'an | 102 | 25.10 N | 109.20 E |
| Rongbaca | 102 | 31.48 N | 99.40 E |
| Rongchang | 107 | 29.24 N | 105.36 E |
| Rongcheng, Zhg. | 98 | 37.08 N | 122.23 E |
| Rongcheng, Zhg. | 105 | 39.03 N | 115.52 E |
| Rongding | 107 | 28.57 N | 103.40 E |
| Ronge, Lac la ⊜ | 184 | 55.10 N | 105.00 W |
| Rongelap I[1] | 14 | 11.20 N | 166.50 E |
| Rongjiang | 102 | 25.52 N | 108.37 E |
| Rongkop | 115a | 8.10 S | 110.45 E |
| Rongola | 158 | 27.22 S | 31.37 E |
| Rongotea | 172 | 40.18 S | 175.25 E |
| Rõngu | 76 | 58.09 N | 26.15 E |
| Rongui, Ilha I | 154 | 10.50 S | 40.40 E |
| Rongwanshi | 100 | 28.10 N | 112.57 E |
| Rongxian, Zhg. | 102 | 22.50 N | 110.38 E |
| Rongxian, Zhg. | 107 | 29.28 N | 104.25 E |
| Ronkiti Harbor ⊂ | 174r | 6.48 N | 158.10 E |
| Ronkonkoma | 276 | 40.48 N | 73.06 W |
| Ronkonkoma, Lake ⊜ | 276 | 40.50 N | 73.07 W |
| Rønne | 26 | 55.06 N | 14.42 E |
| Rönne ≃ | 41 | 56.16 N | 12.50 E |
| Ronneburg | 54 | 50.51 N | 12.10 E |
| Ronneby | 26 | 56.12 N | 15.18 E |
| Ronne Entrance ⊂ | 9 | 72.30 S | 74.00 W |
| Ronne Ice Shelf ⊓ | 9 | 78.30 S | 61.00 W |
| Ronnenberg | 52 | 52.20 N | 9.40 E |
| Rönneshytta | 40 | 58.56 N | 15.02 E |
| Rönninge | 40 | 59.12 N | 17.44 E |
| Ronroni | 175e | 9.37 S | 159.58 E |
| Rönsahl | 263 | 51.07 N | 7.30 E |
| Ronsdorf ◆[8] | 263 | 51.14 N | 7.12 E |
| Ronse (Renaix-Gleiche) | 50 | 50.45 N | 3.36 E |
| Röntgenmuseum ʋ | 263 | 51.12 N | 7.16 E |


| English | Deutsch | Español | Français | Português |
|---|---|---|---|---|
| ≃ River | Fluß | Río | Rivière | Rio |
| ≊ Canal | Kanal | Canal | Canal | Canal |
| ∟ Waterfall, Rapids | Wasserfall, Stromschnellen | Cascada, Rápidos | Chute d'eau, Rapides | Cascata, Rápidos |
| ʉ Strait | Meeresstraße | Estrecho | Détroit | Estreito |
| ⊂ Bay, Gulf | Bucht, Golf | Bahía, Golfo | Baie, Golfe | Baía, Golfo |
| ⊜ Lake, Lakes | See, Seen | Lago, Lagos | Lac, Lacs | Lago, Lagos |
| ≚ Swamp | Sumpf | Pantano | Marais | Pântano |
| ⊓ Ice Features, Glacier | Eis- und Gletscherformen | Accidentes Glaciales | Formes glaciaires | Acidentes glaciares |
| ⊤ Other Hydrographic Features | Andere Hydrographische Objekte | Otros Elementos Hidrográficos | Autres données hydrographiques | Outros acidentes hidrográficos |
| ✣ Submarine Features | Untermeerische Objekte | Accidentes Submarinos | Formes de relief sous-marin | Acidentes submarinos |
| □ Political Unit | Politische Einheit | Unidad Politica | Entité politique | Unidade política |
| ʋ Cultural Institution | Kulturelle Institution | Institución Cultural | Institution culturelle | Instituição cultural |
| ⊥ Historical Site | Historische Stätte | Sitio Histórico | Site historique | Sitio histórico |
| ♠ Recreational Site | Erholungs- und Ferienort | Sitio de Recreo | Centre de loisirs | Area de Lazer |
| ⊠ Airport | Flughafen | Aeropuerto | Aéroport | Aeroporto |
| ▪ Military Installation | Militäranlage | Instalación Militar | Installation militaire | Instalação militar |
| ◆ Miscellaneous | Verschiedenes | Misceláneo | Divers | Diversos |

ENGLISH — Name | Page | Lat.°′ | Long.°′
DEUTSCH — Name | Seite | Breite°′ | Länge°′ E = Ost


Ronuro ≃ 255 11.56 S 53.33 W
Roodepoort □[5] 273d 26.10 S 27.52 E
Roodepoort-Maraisburg 158 26.11 S 27.54 E
Roodeschool 52 53.25 N 6.45 E
Roodhouse 219 39.29 N 90.22 W
Roof Butte ∧ 200 36.28 N 109.05 W
Rooiberge ∧ 158 28.27 S 28.26 E
Rooiboklaagte ≃ 156 20.50 S 21.00 E
Rooidam 158 28.07 S 21.15 E
Rooilyf 158 28.49 S 21.57 E
Rooiwal 158 27.18 S 27.32 E
Rooks Creek ≃ 216 40.57 N 88.44 W
Rookwood Cemetery ◆ 274a 33.53 S 151.04 E
Roon, Pulau I 164 2.23 S 134.33 E
Rooniu, Mont ∧ 174s 17.49 S 149.12 W
Roordahuizum 52 53.06 N 5.46 E
Roorkee 124 29.52 N 77.53 E
Roosboom 158 28.36 S 29.44 E
Roosendaal 52 51.32 N 4.28 E
Roosevelt, Az., U.S. 200 33.40 N 111.08 W
Roosevelt, Mn., U.S. 198 48.48 N 95.05 W
Roosevelt, N.J., U.S. 208 40.13 N 74.28 W
Roosevelt, N.Y., U.S. 276 40.40 N 73.35 W
Roosevelt, Ok., U.S. 196 34.50 N 99.01 W
Roosevelt, Ut,. U.S. 200 40.17 N 109.59 W
Roosevelt ≃ 248 7.35 S 60.20 W
Roosevelt Beach 210 43.19 N 78.52 W
Roosevelt Campobello International Park ♦ 186 44.52 N 66.58 W
Roosevelt Field ◆[9] 276 40.45 N 73.37 W
Roosevelt Island I 9 79.30 S 162.00 W
Roosevelt Park 216 43.11 N 86.15 W
Roosevelt Park ♦ 276 40.33 N 74.21 W
Roosevelt Roads Naval Station ■ 240m 18.15 N 65.38 W
Roosevelt Terrace 226 38.08 N 122.16 W
Root 58 47.07 N 8.23 E
Root ≃, N.T., Can. 180 62.50 N 123.40 W
Root ≃, Mn., U.S. 190 43.46 N 91.15 W
Root ≃, Wi., U.S. 216 42.44 N 87.47 W
Root, North Branch ≃ 190 43.49 N 92.10 W
Root, South Branch ≃ 190 43.44 N 91.58 W
Root Lake ⊜ 184 54.04 N 101.24 W
Rootstown 214 41.05 N 81.14 W
Rooty Hill 170 33.46 S 150.50 E
Ropang 115b 8.52 S 117.29 E
Ropaži 76 57.08 N 24.30 E
Ropča 24 63.02 N 52.16 E
Ropczyce 30 50.03 N 21.37 E
Roper 192 35.52 N 76.36 W
Roper ≃ 164 14.43 S 135.27 E
Roper Bar 164 14.44 S 134.44 E
Roper Valley 164 14.56 S 134.00 E
Ropes Creek ≃ 274a 33.43 S 150.47 E
Ropesville 196 33.26 N 102.09 W
Roppe 58 47.40 N 6.55 E
Ropša 265a 59.44 N 29.52 E
Roque 250 3.01 S 45.23 W
Roquebillière 62 44.01 N 7.18 E
Roquebrune-Cap-Martin 62 43.46 N 7.28 E
Roquebrune-sur-Argens 62 43.26 N 6.38 E
Roquefavour, Aqueduc de ≊[1] 62 43.31 N 5.19 E
Roquefort 32 44.02 N 0.19 W
Roquemaure 62 44.03 N 4.47 E
Roque Pérez 258 35.25 S 59.20 W
Roquestéron 62 43.52 N 7.00 E
Roquevaire 62 43.21 N 5.36 E
Rora Head › 46 58.52 N 3.25 W
Roraima □[3] 246 1.00 N 61.00 W
Roraima, Mount ∧ 246 5.12 N 60.44 W
Rörbäcksnäs 26 61.08 N 12.49 E
Roreto Chisone 62 44.59 N 7.06 E
Rorey Lake ⊜ 180 66.55 N 128.25 W
Rorke Lake ⊜ 184 54.33 N 92.30 W
Rorke's Drift ⊥ 158 28.20 S 30.32 E
Rorketon 184 51.26 N 99.32 W
Røros 26 62.35 N 11.20 E
Rorschach 58 47.29 N 9.30 E
Rørvig 41 55.57 N 11.46 E
Rørvik 24 64.51 N 11.14 E
Ros' 76 53.17 N 24.24 E
Ros' ≃ 78 49.39 N 31.35 E
Rosà, It. 64 45.43 N 11.45 E
Rosa, Zam. 154 9.38 S 31.21 E
Rosa, Cap › 36 36.58 N 8.14 E
Rosa, Lake ⊜ 238 21.00 N 73.30 W
Rosa, Monte ∧ 58 45.55 N 7.53 E
Rosairinho 266c 38.40 N 9.01 W
Rošal' 80 55.40 N 39.51 E
Rosales, Méx. 232 28.12 N 105.33 W
Rosales, Pil. 116 15.54 N 120.38 E
Rosalia 202 47.14 N 117.22 W
Rosalie, Lake ⊜ 220 27.58 N 81.28 W
Rosalind Bank ✦[4] 238 16.30 N 80.30 W
Rosamond, Ca., U.S. 228 34.51 N 118.09 W
Rosamond, Il., U.S. 219 39.23 N 89.10 W
Rosamond Lake ⊜ 228 34.50 N 118.04 W
Rosamorada 234 22.08 N 105.12 W
Rosana 255 22.33 S 53.00 W
Rosander, Mount ∧ 224 48.46 N 124.42 W
Rosanky 222 29.56 N 97.18 W
Rosanna 274b 37.45 S 145.04 E
Rosans 62 44.23 N 5.28 E
Rosario, Arg. 252 32.57 S 60.40 W
Rosário, Bra. 250 2.57 S 44.14 W
Rosario, Méx. 232 27.37 N 109.16 W
Rosario, Méx. 234 23.00 N 105.52 W
Rosario, Para. 252 24.27 S 57.03 W
Rosario, Pil. 116 13.51 N 121.12 E
Rosario, Pil. 116 16.14 N 120.29 E
Rosario, Ur. 258 34.19 S 57.21 W
Rosario, Ven. 246 10.19 N 72.19 W
Rosario ≃, Arg. 252 24.50 S 65.43 W
Rosario ≃, Ur. 258 34.26 S 57.21 W
Rosario, Bahía ⊂ 232 29.52 N 115.45 W
Rosario, Cayo el I 240p 21.38 N 81.53 W
Rosario, Islas del II 246 10.10 N 75.46 W
Rosario Bank ✦[2] 238 18.30 N 84.05 W
Rosario de Arriba 232 30.01 N 115.40 W
Rosario de la Frontera 252 25.48 S 64.58 W
Rosario de Lerma 252 24.59 S 65.35 W
Rosario del Tala 252 32.18 S 59.09 W
Rosário de Minas 256 21.43 S 43.38 W
Rosário do Sul 252 30.15 S 54.55 W
Rosário Oeste 248 14.50 S 56.25 W
Rosario Strait ⊔ 224 48.30 N 122.45 W
Rosarito, Méx. 204 32.20 N 117.02 W
Rosarito, Méx. 232 26.27 N 111.38 W
Rosarito, Embalse de ⊜[1] 34 40.05 N 5.15 W
Rosarno 68 38.29 N 15.59 E
Rosas 196 26.09 N 103.27 W
Rosazza 62 45.41 N 7.58 E
Rošča 82 54.47 N 36.51 E
Rosche 54 52.59 N 10.45 E
Roščino 76 60.15 N 29.37 E
Rosciolo 66 42.07 N 13.20 E
Roscoe, Il., U.S. 216 42.25 N 89.01 W
Roscoe, N.Y., U.S. 210 41.55 N 74.54 W
Roscoe, Pa., U.S. 214 40.04 N 79.51 W
Roscoe, S.D., U.S. 198 45.26 N 99.20 W
Roscoe, Tx., U.S. 196 32.26 N 100.32 W
Roscoe ≃ 180 69.40 N 120.57 W
Roscoe Village ⊥ 214 40.18 N 81.54 W
Roscoff 32 48.44 N 3.59 E
Roscommon, Ire. 48 53.38 N 8.11 W
Roscommon, Mi., U.S. 190 44.29 N 84.35 W
Roscommon □[6] 48 53.45 N 8.15 W
Roscrea 48 52.57 N 7.47 W
Rosdorf 52 51.30 N 9.53 E
Rose, It. 68 39.24 N 16.17 E
Rose, N.Y., U.S. 210 43.09 N 76.53 W
Rose, Monte ∧ 70 37.39 N 13.25 E
Rose, Mount ∧ 226 39.21 N 119.55 W
Rose, Pointe de la › 240e 14.40 N 60.53 W
Roseau, Dom. 240d 15.18 N 61.24 W
Roseau, Mn., U.S. 198 48.50 N 95.45 W
Roseau ≃, Dom. 240d 15.18 N 61.24 W
Roseau ≃, N.A. 198 49.08 N 97.15 W
Roseau ≃, St. Luc. 241f 13.58 N 61.02 W
Rosebank ◆[8] 273d 26.09 S 28.02 E
Rosebank Station 275b 43.47 N 79.07 W
Roseberry Lakes ⊜ 184 52.40 N 92.30 W
Roseberth 166 25.47 S 139.37 E
Rosebery 166 41.46 S 145.32 E
Rosebery ◆[8] 274a 33.55 S 151.12 E
Rose-Blanche 186 47.37 N 58.41 W
Roseboom 210 42.45 N 74.47 W
Roseboro 192 34.57 N 78.30 W
Rose Bowl ♦ 280 34.10 N 118.09 W
Rosebud, Austl. 169 38.21 S 144.54 E
Rosebud, Mo., U.S. 219 38.23 N 91.24 W
Rosebud, Mt., U.S. 202 46.16 N 106.26 W
Rose Bud, Pa., U.S. 214 40.45 N 78.33 W
Rosebud, S.D., U.S. 198 43.13 N 100.51 W
Rosebud, Tx., U.S. 222 31.04 N 96.58 W
Rosebud ≃ 182 51.25 N 112.37 W
Rosebud Creek ≃ 202 46.16 N 106.28 W
Rosebud Indian Reservation ◆[4] 198 43.25 N 100.28 W
Roseburg 202 43.13 N 123.20 W
Rosebush 190 43.41 N 84.46 W
Rose City 190 44.25 N 84.07 W
Rose Creek ≃, U.S. 198 40.04 N 97.07 W
Rose Creek ≃, Ca., U.S. 226 38.07 N 120.24 W
Rosecroft Raceway ♦ 284c 38.48 N 76.58 W
Rosedale, Austl. 166 24.38 S 151.55 E
Rosedale, Ab., Can. 182 51.25 N 112.38 W
Rosedale, B.C., Can. 224 49.11 N 121.48 W
Rosedale, In., U.S. 194 39.37 N 87.17 W
Rosedale, La., U.S. 194 30.27 N 91.27 W
Rosedale, Md., U.S. 284b 39.19 N 76.30 W
Rosedale, Ms., U.S. 194 33.51 N 91.01 W
Rosedale ◆[8], On., Can. 275b 43.41 N 79.22 W
Rosedale ◆[8], N.Y., U.S. 276 40.39 N 73.45 W
Rosedale Estates 284c 38.47 N 76.58 W
Rosedale Hills 218 39.42 N 86.07 W
Rosedene 158 32.01 S 22.07 E
Rosehall 246 6.16 N 57.21 W
Rosehearty 46 57.42 N 2.07 W
Rose-Hill, Maus. 157c 20.14 S 57.27 E
Rose Hill, N.C., U.S. 192 34.49 N 78.01 W
Rose Hill, Va., U.S. 192 36.40 N 83.22 W
Rosehill Cemetery ◆ 278 41.59 N 87.41 W
Rosehill Racecourse ♦ 274a 33.49 S 151.02 E
Rose Hills Memorial Park ◆ 280 34.01 N 118.02 W
Roseira 256 22.54 S 45.18 W
Rose Island I, Am. Sam. 14 14.32 S 168.08 W
Rose Island I, Ba. 192 25.06 N 77.14 W
Rose Lake 182 54.24 N 126.02 W
Roseland, Ca., U.S. 226 38.30 N 122.55 W
Roseland, In., U.S. 216 41.42 N 86.15 W
Roseland, La., U.S. 194 30.45 N 90.30 W
Roseland, N.J., U.S. 276 40.49 N 74.17 W
Roseland, Oh., U.S. 214 40.47 N 82.32 W
Roseland ◆[8] 278 41.42 N 87.38 W
Roselawn 216 41.09 N 87.19 W
Roselle, Il., U.S. 216 41.59 N 88.04 W
Roselle, N.J., U.S. 276 40.39 N 74.15 W
Roselle Field ⊠ 278 41.59 N 88.06 W
Rosellen 263 51.08 N 6.43 E
Roselle Park 276 40.39 N 74.15 W
Rosellerheide 263 51.07 N 6.44 E
Rose Lodge 224 45.01 N 123.52 W
Rosemary 182 50.46 N 112.05 W
Rosemary Brook ≃ 283 42.19 N 71.15 W
Rosemead 280 34.04 N 118.04 W
Rosemère 206 45.38 N 73.48 W
Rosemont, Ca., U.S. 226 38.34 N 121.20 W
Rosemont, Il., U.S. 278 41.59 N 87.52 W
Rosemont, Ky., U.S. 218 38.01 N 84.32 W
Rosemont, Oh., U.S. 214 41.03 N 80.53 W
Rosemont, Pa., U.S. 285 40.01 N 75.19 W
Rosemont Horizon ♦ 278 42.00 N 87.53 W
Rosenberg 222 29.33 N 95.48 W
Rosendaël 50 51.02 N 2.24 E
Rosendal, Nor. 26 59.59 N 6.01 E
Rosendal, S. Afr. 158 28.30 S 27.55 E
Rosendale 210 41.51 N 74.05 W
Roseneath 273d 26.17 S 28.11 E
Rosenfeld 58 48.17 N 8.43 E
Rosengarten, Dtsch. 52 53.23 N 9.54 E
Rosengarten, Dtsch. 56 49.04 N 9.44 E
Rosenhayn 208 39.28 N 75.07 W
Rosenheim 64 47.51 N 12.07 E
Rosenhügel ◆[8] 263 51.10 N 7.12 E
Rosenow 54 53.38 N 13.02 E
Rosenthal, Dtsch. 54 50.51 N 14.04 E
Rosenthal, Dtsch. 56 50.58 N 8.52 E
Rosenthal ◆[8] 264a 52.36 N 13.23 E
Rose Peak ∧ 200 33.26 N 109.22 W
Rosepine 194 30.55 N 93.17 W
Rose Point › 182 54.13 N 131.35 W
Rosersberg 40 59.35 N 17.53 E
Rosersberg ⊥ 40 59.34 N 17.50 E
Roses, Golf de ⊂ 34 42.10 N 3.15 E
Roseto 210 40.52 N 75.12 W
Roseto Capo Spulico 68 39.59 N 16.36 E
Roseto degli Abruzzi 66 42.41 N 14.01 E
Roseto Valfortore 68 41.22 N 15.06 E
Rosetown 184 51.33 N 108.00 W
Rose Tree 285 39.56 N 75.23 W
Rose Tree Park ♦ 285 39.56 N 75.24 W
Rosetta → Rashīd 142 31.24 N 30.25 E
Rosetta Branch → Rashīd, Far' ≃ 142 31.30 N 30.21 E
Rosetta Mouth → Rashīd, Maṣabb ≃[1] 142 31.30 N 30.20 E
Rosettenville ◆[8] 273d 26.15 S 28.03 E
Rosevale 171a 27.51 S 152.29 E
Rose Valley, Sk., Can. 184 52.18 N 103.50 W
Rose Valley, Pa., U.S. 285 39.53 N 75.23 W
Rose Valley, Pa., U.S. 285 40.10 N 75.13 W
Rose Valley, Wa., U.S. 224 46.06 N 122.50 W
Roseville, Austl. 274a 33.47 S 151.11 E
Roseville, Ca., U.S. 226 38.45 N 121.17 W
Roseville, Il., U.S. 190 40.43 N 90.39 W
Roseville, Mi., U.S. 214 42.29 N 82.56 W
Roseville, Mn., U.S. 190 45.00 N 93.09 W
Roseville, Oh., U.S. 188 39.48 N 82.04 W
Roseville, Pa., U.S. 210 41.51 N 76.57 W
Roseville Park 285 39.42 N 75.43 W
Rosewood, Austl. 171a 27.39 S 152.35 E
Rosewood, Austl. 171b 35.41 S 147.52 E
Rosewood, Oh., U.S. 216 40.13 N 83.58 W
Rosewood Heights 219 38.53 N 90.05 W
Roseworthy 168b 34.32 S 138.44 E
Roshage › 26 57.07 N 8.38 E
Roshanara Gardens ♦ 272a 28.40 N 77.12 E
Rosharon 222 29.21 N 95.28 W
Rosheim 58 48.30 N 7.28 E
Rosherville Dam ⊜[1] 273d 26.14 S 28.07 E
Rosh Ha'Ayin 132 32.06 N 34.57 E
Rosholt, S.D., U.S. 198 45.52 N 96.43 W
Rosholt, Wi., U.S. 190 44.37 N 89.18 W
Rosh Pinna 132 32.58 N 35.32 E
Rosica ≃ 38 43.15 N 25.42 E
Rosice 30 49.11 N 16.23 E
Rosiclare 194 37.25 N 88.20 W
Rosières-aux-Salines 58 48.36 N 6.20 E
Rosières-en-Santerre 50 49.49 N 2.43 E
Rosiers, Rivière des ≃ 206 45.59 N 72.07 W
Rosignano Marittimo 66 43.24 N 10.28 E
Rosignano Solvay 66 43.23 N 10.26 E
Rosignol 246 6.17 N 57.32 W
Roșiori de Vede 38 44.07 N 25.00 E
Rositz 54 51.01 N 12.22 E
Roskilde 41 55.39 N 12.05 E
Roskilde □[6] 41 55.30 N 12.05 E
Roskilde Fjord ⊂ 41 55.56 N 12.00 E
Roskow 54 52.28 N 12.42 E
Roslagen □[9] 40 59.30 N 18.40 E
Roslags-Bro 40 59.50 N 18.44 E
Rosl'akovo 24 69.03 N 33.09 E
Rosl'atino 76 59.46 N 44.15 E
Roslavl' 76 53.57 N 32.52 E
Roslev 26 56.42 N 8.59 E
Roslindale ◆[8] 283 42.18 N 71.07 W
Roslyn, N.Y., U.S. 276 40.48 N 73.39 W
Roslyn, Pa., U.S. 208 40.07 N 75.08 W
Roslyn, Pa., U.S. 285 39.57 N 75.36 W
Roslyn, Wa., U.S. 224 47.13 N 120.59 W
Roslyn Estates 276 40.47 N 73.40 W
Roslyn Harbor 276 40.49 N 73.38 W
Roslyn Heights 276 40.47 N 73.38 W
Rosmalen 52 51.43 N 5.22 E
Rosman 192 35.08 N 82.49 W
Rosmead 158 31.29 S 25.08 E
Ros Mhic Thriúin → New Ross 48 52.24 N 6.56 W
Røsnæs ›[1] 41 55.44 N 10.59 E
Rosne, Ruisseau le ≃ 261 48.58 N 2.25 E
Rosneath 46 56.01 N 4.49 W
Rosny-sous-Bois 261 48.53 N 2.29 E
Rosny-sur-Seine 50 49.00 N 1.38 E
Rosolina 64 45.05 N 12.15 E
Rosolini 70 36.49 N 14.57 E
Rošore 85 38.20 N 72.19 E
Rosporden 32 47.58 N 3.50 W
Rösrath 56 50.54 N 7.11 E
Ross, Austl. 166 42.02 S 147.29 E
Ross, N.Z. 172 42.54 S 170.49 E
Ross, Ca., U.S. 226 37.55 N 122.32 W
Ross, In., U.S. 278 41.32 N 87.23 W
Ross, Oh., U.S. 218 39.19 N 84.39 W
Ross □[6] 218 39.20 N 83.06 W
Ross ≃ 180 61.59 N 132.26 W
Ross, Cape › 116 10.56 N 119.13 E
Ross, Mount ∧ 172 41.28 S 175.21 E
Ross, Point › 174c 29.04 S 167.56 E
Ross, Pointe › 275a 45.21 N 73.48 W
Rossa 58 46.22 N 9.08 E
Rossach 56 50.09 N 10.56 E
Rossano 68 39.35 N 16.39 E
Rossasna 76 54.39 N 30.53 E
Rossau 54 52.47 N 11.38 E
Rossbach 54 51.15 N 11.53 E
Ross Behy 48 52.02 N 9.58 W
Ross-Béthio 150 16.16 N 16.08 W
Rossburg 216 40.17 N 84.38 W
Rossburn 184 50.40 N 100.52 W
Ross Carbery 48 51.35 N 9.01 W
Rosscott Manor 285 39.39 N 75.44 W
Ross Dam ◆[6] 224 48.44 N 121.04 W
Rossdorf 56 49.51 N 8.45 E
Rosseau 212 45.16 N 79.39 W
Rosseau, Lake ⊜ 212 45.10 N 79.35 W
Rossel, Cap › 175f 20.23 S 166.36 E
Rossell y Rius 252 33.11 S 55.42 W
Rossen ⊜ 40 60.19 N 16.26 E
Rossendale □[8] 262 53.43 N 2.14 W
Rosser 222 32.28 N 96.27 W
Rosses Bay ⊂ 48 55.02 N 8.27 W
Rosses Point 48 54.18 N 8.33 W
Rossford 214 41.37 N 83.33 W
Ross Fork Creek ≃ 202 47.05 N 109.43 W
Rosshaupten 58 47.39 N 10.43 E
Rosshyttan 40 60.04 N 16.21 E
Ross Ice Shelf ⊓ 9 81.30 S 175.00 W
Rossiglione 62 44.34 N 8.40 E
Rossignol, Lake ⊜ 186 44.10 N 65.10 W
Rossija → Russia □[1] 72 60.00 N 80.00 E
Rössing 156 22.31 S 14.52 E
Rossio, Estação do ◆[5] 266c 38.43 N 9.09 W
Ross Island I, Ant. 9 77.30 S 168.00 E
Ross Island I, Mb., Can. 184 54.14 N 97.45 W
Rossiter 214 40.53 N 78.55 W
Rossitten → Rybačij 76 55.09 N 20.51 E
Rossla 54 51.28 N 11.04 E
Ross Lake ⊜[1] 224 48.53 N 121.04 W
Ross Lake National Recreation Area ♦ 224 48.45 N 121.00 W
Rossland 182 49.05 N 117.48 W
Rosslare 48 52.17 N 6.23 W
Rosslare Harbour 48 52.15 N 6.22 W
Rosslau 54 51.53 N 12.14 E
Rosslea 48 54.14 N 7.11 W
Rossleben, Dtsch. 54 51.18 N 11.26 E
Rossleben, Dtsch. 54 51.18 N 11.26 E
Rosslyn Farms 279b 40.26 N 80.05 W
Rossmoor 280 33.47 N 118.05 W
Rossmore 274a 33.57 S 150.46 E
Rossmoyne 208 40.13 N 76.57 W
Rosso 150 16.30 N 15.49 W
Rossön 26 63.55 N 16.21 E
Ross-on-Wye 42 51.55 N 2.35 W
Rossoš', Ross. 78 50.12 N 39.34 E
Rossoš', Ross. 78 51.08 N 38.29 E
Rossouw 158 31.09 S 27.18 E
Ross R. Barnett Reservoir ⊜[1] 194 32.30 N 90.00 W
Ross River 180 61.59 N 132.27 W
Ross-Schelfeis → Ross Ice Shelf ⊓ 9 81.30 S 175.00 W
Ross Sea ⊤[2] 9 76.00 S 175.00 W
Rosstal 56 49.25 N 10.52 E
Rosston 218 40.03 N 86.17 W
Ross Township 279b 40.32 N 80.01 W
Rossu, Capu › 36 42.14 N 8.33 E
Røssvatnet ⊜ 24 65.45 N 14.00 E
Rossville, Ga., U.S. 192 34.58 N 85.17 W
Rossville, Il., U.S. 216 40.22 N 87.40 W
Rossville, In., U.S. 216 40.25 N 86.35 W
Rossville, Ks., U.S. 198 39.08 N 95.57 W
Rossville, Md., U.S. 284b 39.20 N 76.29 W
Rosswein 54 51.03 N 13.10 E
Røst II 24 67.28 N 11.59 E
Rostāq 120 37.07 N 69.49 E
Röstånga 41 56.00 N 13.17 E
Rostavytsya ≃ 78 49.44 N 30.01 E
Rosthern 184 52.40 N 106.17 W
Rostherne 262 53.21 N 2.23 W
Rostherne Mere ⊜ 262 53.21 N 2.23 W
Roštkala 120 37.16 N 71.49 E
Rostock 54 54.05 N 12.07 E
Rostov 80 57.11 N 39.25 E
Rostov-na-Donu 83 47.14 N 39.42 E
Rostov Oblast' □[4] 78 48.00 N 40.00 E
Rostrataville 158 26.49 S 25.39 E
Rostraver Airport ⊠ 279b 40.13 N 79.50 W
Rostrevor 48 54.06 N 6.12 W
Rosvinskoje 24 66.32 N 52.26 E
Roswell, Ga., U.S. 192 34.01 N 84.21 W
Roswell, N.M., U.S. 196 33.23 N 104.31 W
Roswell, Oh., U.S. 214 40.28 N 81.21 W
Rosyth 46 56.03 N 3.26 W
Rot ≃ 58 48.19 N 9.54 E
Rota 34 36.37 N 6.21 W
Rota I 108 14.10 N 145.12 E
Rot am See 56 49.15 N 10.01 E
Rotan 196 32.51 N 100.27 W
Rotanda 156 19.33 S 32.50 E
Rot an der Rot 58 48.01 N 10.02 E
Rotary Island I 285 40.14 N 74.49 W
Rotbach ≃ 263 51.34 N 6.41 E
Rotberg 264a 52.21 N 13.31 E
Rote-Erde, Stadion ♦ 263 51.30 N 7.27 E
Rotenburg 52 53.06 N 9.24 E
Rotenburg an der Fulda 56 51.00 N 9.45 E
Roter Main ≃ 60 50.04 N 11.24 E
Rotes Meer → Red Sea ⊤[2] 136 20.00 N 38.00 E
Roth, Dtsch. 56 50.46 N 7.42 E
Roth, Dtsch. 60 49.15 N 11.06 E
Roth ≃ 58 48.27 N 10.10 E
Rötha 54 51.12 N 12.25 E
Rothaargebirge ⋏ 56 51.05 N 8.15 E
Rothbury 44 55.19 N 1.55 W
Rothbury Forest ◆[3] 44 55.18 N 1.54 W
Rothemühl 54 53.36 N 13.49 E
Röthenbach, Dtsch. 58 47.37 N 9.59 E
Röthenbach, Schw. 58 46.51 N 7.45 E
Röthenbach an der Pegnitz 60 49.29 N 11.15 E
Rothenburg 54 51.20 N 14.58 E
Rothenburg ob der Tauber 56 49.23 N 10.10 E
Rothenfels 56 49.54 N 9.35 E
Rothenkirchen 54 50.33 N 12.30 E
Rothenschirmbach 54 51.27 N 11.33 E
Rothenstein ∧[2] 263 51.07 N 7.41 E
Rother ≃, Eng., U.K. 42 50.54 N 0.42 E
Rother ≃, Eng., U.K. 42 50.57 N 0.32 W
Rothera ⊎[3] 9 67.34 S 68.08 W
Rotherham, N.Z. 172 42.42 S 172.57 E
Rotherham, Eng., U.K. 44 53.26 N 1.20 W
Rothes 46 57.31 N 3.13 W
Rothesay, N.B., Can. 186 45.23 N 66.00 W
Rothesay, Scot., U.K. 46 55.51 N 5.03 W
Röthlein 56 49.59 N 10.13 E
Rothneusiedl ◆[8] 264b 48.08 N 16.23 E
Rothrist 58 47.19 N 7.53 E
Rothsay, Austl. 162 29.17 S 116.53 E
Rothsay, Mn., U.S. 198 46.28 N 96.16 W
Rothschild 190 44.53 N 89.37 W
Rothsville 208 40.09 N 76.15 W
Rothwell, N.B., Can. 186 46.04 N 66.04 W
Rothwell, Eng., U.K. 42 52.25 N 0.48 W
Rothwell, Eng., U.K. 44 53.46 N 1.29 W
Roti, Pulau I 112 10.45 S 123.10 E
Roti, Selat ⊔ 112 10.25 S 123.25 E
Roto 166 33.03 S 145.28 E
Rotoiti, Lake ⊜, N.Z. 172 38.02 S 176.25 E
Rotoiti, Lake ⊜, N.Z. 172 41.50 S 172.50 E
Rotomanu 172 42.39 S 171.32 E
Rotonda 68 39.57 N 16.02 E
Rotondella 68 40.10 N 16.32 E
Rotondo, Monte ∧ 36 42.13 N 9.03 E
Rotoroa, Lake ⊜ 172 41.52 S 172.38 E
Rotorua 172 38.09 S 176.15 E
Rotorua, Lake ⊜ 172 38.05 S 176.16 E
Rotowaro 172 37.36 S 175.05 E
Rott 64 47.54 N 10.59 E
Rott ≃ 60 48.27 N 13.26 E
Rottach-Egern 64 47.41 N 11.46 E
Rott am Inn 64 47.59 N 12.07 E
Röttenbach 60 49.09 N 11.02 E
Rottenbach-Tremersdorf 56 50.21 N 10.56 E
Rottenbuch 64 47.44 N 10.58 E
Rottenburg am Neckar 58 48.28 N 8.56 E
Rottenburg an der Laaber 60 48.42 N 12.02 E
Rottenmann 61 47.31 N 14.22 E
Rotterdam, Ned. 52 51.55 N 4.28 E
Rotterdam, N.Y., U.S. 210 42.48 N 73.59 W
Rotterdam, Luchthaven ⊠ 52 51.58 N 4.30 E
Rotterdam Junction 210 42.52 N 74.03 W
Rotthalmünster 60 48.21 N 13.12 E
Rotthausen ◆[8] 263 51.30 N 7.05 E
Rottingdean 42 50.48 N 0.04 W
Röttingen 56 49.31 N 9.58 E
Rottleberode 54 51.31 N 10.57 E
Rottnest Island I 168a 32.00 S 115.30 E
Rottofreno 62 45.03 N 9.34 E
Rottum 263 51.36 N 7.42 E
Rottumeroog I 52 53.33 N 6.35 E
Rottumerplaat I 52 53.32 N 6.30 E
Rottweil 58 48.10 N 8.37 E
Rotuma I 14 12.30 S 177.05 E
Rotwand ∧ 64 47.39 N 11.56 E
Rötz 60 49.21 N 12.32 E
Roubaix 50 50.42 N 3.10 E
Roubideau Creek ≃ 200 38.44 N 108.10 W
Roubidoux Creek ≃ 194 37.51 N 92.13 W
Roubion ≃ 62 44.31 N 4.42 E
Rouceux 58 48.22 N 5.41 E
Roudnice [nad Labem] 54 50.22 N 14.16 E
Rouen 50 49.26 N 1.05 E
Rougé 32 47.47 N 1.27 W
Rouge ≃, On., Can. 212 43.48 N 79.07 W
Rouge ≃, P.Q., Can. 206 45.39 N 74.42 W
Rouge ≃, P.Q., Can. 206 45.33 N 74.20 W
Rouge → Red ≃, U.S. 178 31.00 N 91.40 W
Rouge, Bell Branch ≃ 281 42.23 N 83.16 W
Rouge, Lac ⊜ 206 46.56 N 74.38 W
Rouge, Mer → Red Sea ⊤[2] 136 20.00 N 38.00 E
Rouge, River ≃ 281 42.17 N 83.06 W
Rougeau, Forêt de ♦ 261 48.35 N 2.30 E
Rougemont, Fr. 58 47.29 N 6.21 E
Rougemont, Schw. 58 46.29 N 7.12 E
Rougemont-le-Château 58 47.44 N 6.58 E
Rough ≃ 194 37.29 N 87.08 W
Rough And Ready 226 39.14 N 121.08 W
Rough River Lake ⊜[1] 194 37.40 N 86.25 W
Rouiba 34 36.44 N 3.17 E
Rouillac 32 45.47 N 0.04 W
Rouillon 261 48.33 N 2.00 E
Roulans 58 47.19 N 6.14 E
Rouleau 184 50.11 N 104.55 W
Roulers → Roeselare 50 50.57 N 3.08 E
Roulette 214 41.46 N 78.09 W
Roumanie → Romania □[1] 38 46.00 N 25.30 E
Round Harbour 186 49.51 N 55.40 W
Roundhead 216 40.34 N 83.50 W
Round Hill Head › 166 24.10 S 151.53 E
Round Hill Regional Park ♦ 279b 40.15 N 79.51 W
Round Knowe ∧[2] 48 55.08 N 6.55 W
Round Lake, Il., U.S. 278 42.21 N 88.05 W
Round Lake, Mn., U.S. 198 43.32 N 95.28 W
Round Lake, N.Y., U.S. 210 42.56 N 73.47 W
Round Lake ⊜, Nf., Can. 186 51.08 N 56.33 W
Round Lake ⊜, On., Can. 190 45.38 N 77.32 W
Round Lake ⊜, On., Can. 212 44.30 N 77.52 W
Round Lake ⊜, On., Can. 212 45.28 N 79.24 W
Round Lake ⊜, Sk., Can. 184 50.33 N 102.23 W
Round Lake ⊜, Il., U.S. 278 42.22 N 88.05 W
Round Lake ⊜, Mi., U.S. 216 41.58 N 84.17 W
Round Lake Beach 216 42.22 N 88.05 W
Round Lake Park 216 42.21 N 88.04 W
Round Mound ∧[2] 198 38.55 N 99.39 W
Round Mountain 204 38.42 N 117.04 W
Round Mountain ∧, Austl. 166 30.27 S 152.14 E
Round Mountain ∧, Austl. 171b 36.15 S 148.34 E
Round Pond ⊜, Nf., Can. 186 48.10 N 56.00 W
Round Pond ⊜, Ma., U.S. 283 42.36 N 70.49 W
Round Rock 222 30.30 N 97.40 W
Roundstone 48 53.23 N 9.53 W
Round Top 210 42.16 N 74.02 W
Round Top ∧[2] 208 40.30 N 76.42 W
Round Top Regional Park ♦ 282 37.51 N 122.12 W
Roundup 202 46.26 N 108.32 W
Round Valley Indian Reservation ◆[4] 204 39.50 N 123.20 W
Round Valley Reservoir ⊜[1] 210 40.36 N 74.50 W
Roundwood 48 53.04 N 6.13 W
Roura 250 4.44 N 52.20 W
Rourkela → Raurkela 124 22.13 N 84.53 E
Rousay I 46 59.10 N 3.02 W
Rouse Hill 274a 33.41 S 150.56 E
Rouses Point 206 45.00 N 73.22 W
Rouseville 214 41.28 N 79.41 W
Rousies 50 50.16 N 4.00 E
Rousseau, Lake ⊜[1] 220 29.02 N 82.32 W
Rousset, Col de )( 62 44.50 N 5.24 E
Roussigny 261 48.39 N 2.06 E
Roussillon, Fr. 62 45.22 N 4.49 E
Roussillon, Fr. 62 43.54 N 5.17 E
Roussillon □[9] 32 42.30 N 2.30 E
Roussy-le-Village 56 49.27 N 6.10 E
Routhierville 186 48.11 N 67.09 W
Routot 50 49.23 N 0.44 E
Rouveen 52 52.36 N 6.11 E
Rouvignies 50 50.20 N 3.26 E
Rouville □[6] 206 45.23 N 73.04 W
Rouvray 50 47.25 N 4.06 E
Rouvray, Lac ⊜ 186 49.18 N 70.49 W
Rouxville 158 30.29 S 26.46 E
Rouyn 190 48.15 N 79.01 W
Rouzerville 208 39.44 N 77.32 W
Rovaniemi 24 66.34 N 25.48 E
Rovasenda 62 45.32 N 8.19 E
Rovato 64 45.34 N 10.00 E
Rove, Tunnel du ◆[5] 62 43.22 N 5.17 E
Rovegno 62 44.35 N 9.17 E
Rovellasca 62 45.40 N 9.03 E
Rovello Porro 62 45.39 N 9.02 E
Roven'ki 78 49.56 N 38.54 E
Roven'ky 83 48.05 N 39.21 E
Rovenskaja Slabada 76 52.13 N 30.19 E
Roverbella 64 45.16 N 10.46 E
Rovere 66 42.10 N 13.31 E
Roverè della Luna 64 46.15 N 11.10 E
Roveredo 58 46.14 N 9.08 E
Rovereto 64 45.53 N 11.02 E
Roverè Veronese 64 45.36 N 11.03 E
Rövershagen 54 54.10 N 12.15 E
Roversi 252 27.35 S 61.57 W
Roverud 26 60.15 N 12.03 E
Roviano 66 42.01 N 13.00 E
Rovigo 64 45.04 N 11.47 E
Rovigo □[4] 64 45.02 N 11.50 E
Rovinj 36 45.05 N 13.38 E
Rovira 246 4.14 N 75.14 W
Rovnoje, Kyrg. 85 42.53 N 73.32 E
Rovnoje, Ross. 80 50.47 N 46.05 E
Rovubu (Ruvubu) ≃ 154 2.23 S 30.47 E
Rovuma (Ruvuma) ≃ 154 10.29 S 40.28 E
Rów 54 52.58 N 14.45 E
Rowan □[6] 218 38.17 N 83.26 W
Rowan Lake ⊜ 184 49.18 N 93.32 W
Rowanty Creek ≃ 208 36.58 N 77.21 W
Rowena, Austl. 166 29.49 S 148.54 E
Rowena, Tx., U.S. 196 31.39 N 100.03 W
Rowe Park ♦ 273a 6.30 N 3.23 E
Rowhill 273d 26.14 S 28.26 E
Rowland, N.C., U.S. 192 34.32 N 79.17 W
Rowland, Pa., U.S. 210 41.28 N 75.03 W
Rowland Flat 168b 34.35 S 138.56 E
Rowland Heights 280 33.58 N 117.54 W
Rowlands Gill 44 54.54 N 1.45 W
Rowlesburg 188 39.20 N 79.40 W
Rowlett 222 32.54 N 96.33 W
Rowlett, Isla I 254 44.48 S 74.25 W
Rowlett Creek ≃ 222 32.49 N 96.31 W
Rowley 207 42.43 N 70.52 W
Rowley ≃, N.T., Can. 176 70.16 N 77.45 W
Rowley ≃, Ma., U.S. 283 42.43 N 70.49 W
Rowley Island I 176 69.08 N 78.50 W
Rowley Shoals ✦[2] 162 17.30 S 119.00 E
Rowntree Mill Park ♦ 275b 43.45 N 79.35 W
Rowsburg 214 40.52 N 82.10 W
Rowville 274b 37.56 S 145.14 E
Roxa, Ilha I 150 11.15 N 15.40 W
Roxana 219 38.50 N 90.04 W
Roxas, Pil. 108 11.35 N 122.45 E
Roxas, Pil. 116 17.08 N 121.36 E
Roxas, Pil. 116 12.35 N 121.31 E
Roxas, Pil. 116 10.20 N 119.21 E
Roxas (Capiz), Pil. 116 11.35 N 122.45 E
Roxboro, P.Q., Can. 275a 45.31 N 73.48 W
Roxboro, N.C., U.S. 192 36.23 N 78.58 W
Roxborough 241r 11.15 N 60.35 W
Roxborough ◆[8] 285 40.02 N 75.13 W
Roxburgh, N.Z. 172 45.32 S 169.19 E
Roxburgh, Scot., U.K. 46 55.34 N 2.30 W
Roxbury, Ct., U.S. 207 41.33 N 73.18 W
Roxbury, N.Y., U.S. 210 42.17 N 74.33 W
Roxbury, Pa., U.S. 214 40.07 N 77.40 W
Roxbury, Va., U.S. 208 37.28 N 77.09 W
Roxbury ◆[8], Ma., U.S. 283 42.20 N 71.06 W
Roxbury ◆[8], N.Y., U.S. 276 40.34 N 73.54 W
Roxby Downs 162 30.43 S 136.46 E
Roxel 52 51.57 N 7.32 E
Roxen ⊜ 26 58.30 N 15.41 E
Roxie 194 31.30 N 91.04 W
Roxo, Cap › 150 12.20 N 16.43 W
Roxton 196 33.33 N 95.44 W
Roxton Pond (Sainte-Pudentienne) 206 45.29 N 72.40 W
Roxwell 260 51.45 N 0.23 E
Roy, N.M., U.S. 196 35.56 N 104.11 W
Roy, Ut., U.S. 200 41.09 N 112.01 W
Roy, Wa., U.S. 224 47.00 N 122.32 W
Roya (Roia) ≃ 62 43.48 N 7.35 E
Royal 198 43.03 N 95.17 W
Royal Albert Hall ⊎ 260 51.30 N 0.11 W
Royal Australian Naval College ⊎[2] 170 35.07 S 150.42 E
Royal Bangkok Sports Club ♦ 269a 13.44 N 100.33 E
Royal Botanic Gardens ♦, Austl. 274a 33.52 S 151.13 E
Royal Botanic Gardens ♦, Austl. 274b 37.50 S 144.59 E
Royal Canal ≊ 48 53.21 N 6.15 W
Royal Center 216 40.51 N 86.29 W
Royal Chitwan National Park ♦ 124 27.30 N 84.30 E
Royal City 202 46.54 N 119.38 W
Royale, Isle I 190 48.00 N 89.00 W
Royal Gorge V 200 38.17 N 105.45 W
Royal Island I 192 25.31 N 76.51 W
Royalla 171b 35.31 S 149.09 E
Royal Leamington Spa 42 52.18 N 1.31 W
Royal Natal National Park ♦ 158 28.45 S 28.57 E
Royal National Park ♦ 170 34.10 S 151.05 E
Royal Naval College ■ 260 51.29 N 0.01 W
Royal Oak, B.C., Can. 224 48.30 N 123.23 W
Royal Oak, Md., U.S. 208 38.44 N 76.10 W
Royal Oak, Mi., U.S. 216 42.29 N 83.08 W
Royal Oak Township 281 42.27 N 83.10 W
Royal Ontario Museum ⊎ 275b 43.40 N 79.24 W
Royal Palms State Beach ♦ 280 33.44 N 118.19 W
Royal Park ♦ 274b 37.47 S 144.57 E
Royal Roads ⊂ 224 48.26 N 123.26 W
Royalton, In., U.S. 218 39.56 N 86.21 W
Royalton, Mn., U.S. 190 45.49 N 94.17 W
Royalton, Pa., U.S. 208 40.11 N 76.44 W
Royal Tunbridge Wells 42 51.08 N 0.16 E
Royal Turf Club ♦ 269a 13.46 N 100.32 E
Royan 32 45.37 N 1.01 W
Royaume-Uni → United Kingdom □[1] 28 54.00 N 2.00 W
Roybon 62 45.15 N 5.15 E
Royce Brook ≃ 276 40.32 N 70.35 W
Roydon, Eng., U.K. 42 51.46 N 0.03 E
Roydon, Eng., U.K. 42 52.50 N 0.32 E
Roye 50 49.42 N 2.48 E
Royersford 208 40.11 N 75.32 W
Royerton 216 40.15 N 85.21 W
Roy Hill 162 22.38 S 119.57 E
Roylyanka 78 46.17 N 29.46 E
Royse City 222 32.58 N 96.19 W
Royston, Eng., U.K. 42 52.03 N 0.01 W
Royston, Eng., U.K. 44 53.37 N 1.27 W
Royston, Ga., U.S. 192 34.17 N 83.06 W
Royton 44 53.34 N 2.08 W
Rožaj 38 42.50 N 20.10 E
Różan 30 52.53 N 21.25 E
Rozay-en-Brie 50 48.41 N 2.58 E
Roždestvenka, Kaz. 86 50.52 N 71.22 E
Roždestvenka, Ross. 86 55.21 N 77.29 E
Roždestvenka, Ross. 86 55.42 N 70.00 E
Roždestveno, Ross. 76 57.44 N 37.57 E
Roždestveno, Ross. 80 53.15 N 50.04 E
Roždestveno, Ross. 82 56.51 N 36.33 E
Roždestveno, Ross. 82 55.57 N 36.23 E
Roždestvenskaja Chava 78 51.38 N 39.40 E
Roždestvenskoje, Ross. 80 58.09 N 45.35 E
Roždestvenskoje, Ross. 80 52.47 N 42.10 E
Roždestvenskoje, Ross. 80 51.14 N 42.10 E
Roždestvo 76 57.36 N 33.48 E
Rozdil'na 78 46.51 N 30.05 E
Rozdol'ne, Ukr. 78 45.47 N 33.29 E
Rozdol'ne, Ukr. 83 47.37 N 38.01 E
Rozdory 78 48.21 N 35.42 E
Rozel 43b 49.14 N 2.03 W
Rozelle 274a 33.52 S 151.10 E
Roželov 60 49.33 N 13.48 E
Rozewie, Przylądek › 30 54.51 N 18.21 E
Rozhnof, Cape › 180 55.58 N 160.58 W
Rozhnyativ 78 48.56 N 24.09 E
Rozhyshche 78 50.54 N 25.15 E
Rozivka 78 47.23 N 37.04 E
Rožki 80 56.41 N 50.31 E
Rozkishne 83 48.30 N 39.18 E
Rožkov 80 51.39 N 52.19 E
Rožmberk ⊜ 61 49.04 N 14.47 E
Rožmberk nad Vltavou 61 48.39 N 14.22 E
Rožmitál pod Třemšínem 60 49.36 N 13.52 E
Rožňava 30 48.40 N 20.32 E
Roznov 38 46.50 N 26.31 E
Rožnov pod Radhoštěm 30 49.28 N 18.10 E
Rożnów 30 49.46 N 20.42 E
Rozoy-sur-Serre 50 49.43 N 4.08 E
Rozsypne 83 48.08 N 38.34 E
Roztocze ⋏[2] 30 50.30 N 23.20 E
Roztoky 54 50.09 N 14.22 E
Rozzano 62 45.20 N 9.06 E
Rrëshen 38 41.47 N 19.54 E
Rrogozhinë 38 41.05 N 19.40 E
Rtiščevo 80 52.16 N 43.47 E
Ru ≃ 100 32.43 N 115.01 E
Ru, Tanjong › 114 2.50 N 101.17 E
Ruabon 42 52.59 N 3.02 W
Ruacaná 152 17.25 S 14.12 E
Ruacana Falls ⊾ 152 17.22 S 14.12 E
Ruaha National Park ♦ 154 7.30 S 34.40 E
Ruahine Range ⋏ 172 40.00 S 176.06 E
Ruahmi, Ra's › 142 28.44 N 32.50 E
Ruanda 154 10.33 S 34.57 E
Ruanda → Rwanda □[1] 154 2.00 S 30.00 E
Ruango 164 5.35 S 150.10 E
Ruapehu, Mount ∧ 172 39.17 S 175.34 E
Ruapuke Island I 172 46.47 S 168.30 E
Ruatahuna 172 38.33 S 176.57 E
Ruatapu 172 42.48 S 170.53 E
Ruathair, Loch an ⊜ 46 58.18 N 3.56 W
Ruatoria 172 37.53 S 178.20 E
Ruawai 172 36.08 S 174.02 E
Rub' al Khali → Ar-Rub' al-Khālī ◆[2] 118 20.00 N 51.00 E
Rubanivka 78 47.00 N 34.10 E
Rubbestadneset 26 59.49 N 5.17 E
Rubcovsk 86 51.33 N 81.10 E
Rubeho Mountains ⋏ 154 6.55 S 36.30 E
Rubel' 78 51.58 N 27.04 E
Rübeland 54 51.45 N 10.50 E
Rubelles 261 48.34 N 2.41 E
Rubery ◆[8] 42 52.24 N 2.00 W
Rubeshibe 92a 43.47 N 143.38 E
Rubežinskoje 80 51.26 N 51.59 E
Rubí, Esp. 266d 41.29 N 2.02 E
Rubi, Zaïre 154 2.49 N 25.14 E
Rubí ≃, Esp. 266d 41.26 N 2.00 E
Rubi ≃, Zaïre 152 2.48 N 23.54 E
Rubiana 62 45.08 N 7.23 E
Rubiataba 255 15.08 S 49.48 W
Rubicon ≃ 226 39.00 N 120.44 W
Rubicone ≃ 66 44.08 N 12.28 E
Rubidoux 228 33.59 N 117.24 W
Rubiera 64 44.39 N 10.45 E
Rubim 255 16.23 S 40.32 W
Rubino 150 6.04 N 4.18 W
Rubio 246 7.43 N 72.22 W
Rubio Woods ♦ 278 41.38 N 87.46 W
Rubizhne 83 49.01 N 38.23 E
Rubl'ovo 82 55.47 N 37.21 E
Rublyivka 78 49.15 N 33.19 E
Ruboani 140 8.06 N 30.45 E
Rubona 154 0.33 N 30.10 E
Rubondo Island I 154 2.20 S 31.52 E
Rubondo Island National Park ♦ 154 2.20 S 31.52 E
Rubtsi 83 49.12 N 37.33 E
Rubtsovsk → Rubcovsk 86 51.33 N 81.10 E
Ruby, Ak., U.S. 180 64.44 N 155.30 W
Ruby, N.Y., U.S. 210 42.01 N 74.01 W
Ruby ≃ 202 45.34 N 112.21 W
Ruby Creek ≃ 224 48.43 N 120.59 W
Ruby Dome ∧ 204 40.37 N 115.28 W
Ruby Lake ⊜ 204 40.10 N 115.30 W
Ruby Mountains ⋏ 204 40.25 N 115.35 W
Ruby Valley V 204 40.30 N 115.15 W
Rucava 76 56.09 N 21.10 E
Ruchan' 76 53.33 N 32.48 E
Ruche 261 49.02 N 2.27 E
Rucheng 100 25.34 N 113.41 E
Ruciane-Nida 30 53.39 N 21.35 E
Ručji ◆[8] 265a 60.01 N 30.24 E
Ručjuvom 24 66.42 N 61.08 E
Rucphen 52 51.32 N 4.34 E
Ruda 64 45.50 N 13.24 E
Rudall 166 33.41 S 136.16 E


**Symbols** in the index entries represent the broad categories identified in the key at the right. Symbols with superior numbers (⋏[1]) identify subcategories (see complete key on page *I · 1*).

**Symbole** im Register stellen die rechts im Schlüssel erklärten Kategorien dar. Symbole mit hochgestellten Ziffern (⋏[1]) bezeichnen Unterabteilungen einer Kategorie (vgl. vollständiger Schlüssel auf Seite *I · 1*).

**Los símbolos** incluídos en el texto del índice representan las grandes categorías identificadas con la clave a la derecha. Los símbolos con numeros en su parte superior (⋏[1]) identifican las subcategorías (véase la clave completa en la página *I · 1*).

**Les symboles** de l'index représentent les catégories indiquées dans la légende à droite. Les symboles suivis d'un indice (⋏[1]) représentent des sous-catégories (voir légende complète à la page *I · 1*).

**Os símbolos** incluídos no texto do índice representam as grandes categorias identificadas com a chave à direita. Os símbolos com números em sua parte superior (⋏[1]) identificam as subcategorias (veja-se a chave completa à página *I · 1*).

| | English | Deutsch | Español | Français | Português |
|---|---|---|---|---|---|
| ∧ | Mountain | Berg | Montaña | Montagne | Montanha |
| ⋏ | Mountains | Gebirge | Montañas | Montagnes | Montanhas |
| )( | Pass | Paß | Paso | Col | Passo |
| V | Valley, Canyon | Tal, Cañon | Valle, Cañón | Vallée, Canyon | Vale, Canhão |
| ≚ | Plain | Ebene | Llano | Plaine | Planície |
| › | Cape | Kap | Cabo | Cap | Cabo |
| I | Island | Insel | Isla | Île | Ilha |
| II | Islands | Inseln | Islas | Îles | Ilhas |
| ⊥ | Other Topographic Features | Andere Topographische Objekte | Otros Elementos Topográficos | Autres données topographiques | Outros acidentes topográficos |

ESPAÑOL — Nombre | Página | Lat.°' | Long.°' W = Oeste
FRANÇAIS — Nom | Page | Lat.°' | Long.°' W = Ouest
PORTUGUÊS — Nome | Página | Lat.°' | Long.°' W = Oeste


Rudall ≃ 162 22.16 S 122.47 E
Rudall River National Park ♦ 162 22.25 S 122.40 E
Ruda Śląska 30 50.18 N 18.51 E
Rudauli 124 26.45 N 81.45 E
Ruḍaymat al-Liwā' 132 33.01 N 36.35 E
Rūdbār, Afg. 128 30.09 N 62.36 E
Rūdbār, Īrān 128 36.48 N 49.24 E
Rudbøl 41 54.54 N 8.45 E
Ruddervoorde 50 51.06 N 3.12 E
Ruddiman Terrace 216 43.12 N 86.17 W
Rudelsburg ⊥ 54 51.07 N 11.43 E
Ruden I 54 54.12 N 13.46 E
Rudersberg 56 48.53 N 9.32 E
Rüdersdorf, Dtsch. 54 52.29 N 13.47 E
Rudersdorf, Öst. 61 47.03 N 16.07 E
Rüdersdorf, Forst ✦3 264a 52.26 N 13.50 E
Rüdesheim am Rhein 56 49.59 N 7.56 E
Rudeville 276 41.09 N 74.33 W
Rudewa 154 10.06 S 34.39 E
Rudge Ramos 287b 23.41 S 46.34 W
Rūdiškės 76 54.31 N 24.50 E
Rudivka 83 49.24 N 38.27 E
Rudkino 78 51.27 N 39.01 E
Rudkøbing 41 54.56 N 10.43 E
Rudky 78 49.39 N 23.29 E
Rudn'a, Ross. 76 54.57 N 31.06 E
Rudn'a, Ross. 80 50.48 N 44.33 E
Rudnaja Pristan' 89 44.22 N 135.48 E
Rudnevka ≃ 265b 55.43 N 37.56 E
Rudnevo 82 54.44 N 38.09 E
Rudničnyj, Kaz. 86 44.40 N 78.55 E
Rudničnyj, Ross. 24 59.38 N 52.27 E
Rudničnyj, Ross. 86 56.08 N 86.12 E
Rudničnyj, Ross. 86 59.42 N 60.18 E
Rudnik 30 50.28 N 22.15 E
Rüdnitz 54 52.43 N 13.37 E
Rudnyj, Kaz. 86 52.57 N 63.07 E
Rudnyj, Ross. 89 44.21 N 134.58 E
Rudnytsya 78 48.15 N 28.55 E
Rudo 38 43.37 N 19.22 E
Rudolf, Lake (Lake Turkana) ⊜ 144 3.30 N 36.00 E
Rudolfov 61 48.59 N 14.34 E
Rudolph 216 41.17 N 83.40 W
Rudolstadt 54 50.43 N 11.20 E
Rudong, Zhg. 102 21.39 N 111.23 E
Rudong, Zhg. 106 32.19 N 121.12 E
Rudovka 80 53.07 N 42.23 E
Rudow ✦8 54 52.25 N 13.30 E
Rūdsar 128 37.08 N 50.18 E
Ruds Vedby 41 55.33 N 11.23 E
Rudyard, Mi., U.S. 190 46.13 N 84.36 W
Rudyard, Mt., U.S. 202 48.33 N 110.33 W
Rudyerd Bay c 182 55.35 N 130.44 W
Rudzensk 76 53.36 N 27.52 E
Rue, Fr. 50 50.16 N 1.40 E
Rue, Schw. 58 46.37 N 6.50 E
Ruecas ≃ 34 39.00 N 5.55 W
Rueil-Malmaison 261 48.53 N 2.11 E
Ruen ʌ 38 42.10 N 22.31 E
Ruenya (Luenha) ≃ 154 16.24 S 33.48 E
Rufā'ah 140 14.46 N 33.22 E
Ruffano 68 39.59 N 18.15 E
Ruffec 32 46.01 N 0.12 E
Ruffieu 58 46.00 N 5.40 E
Ruffieux 62 45.51 N 5.50 E
Ruffin 192 33.00 N 80.48 W
Ruffle Bar I 276 40.36 N 46.51 W
Rufford 262 53.38 N 2.49 W
Rufford Old Hall ⊥ 262 53.38 N 2.49 W
Ruffs Dale 279b 40.10 N 79.37 W
Rufidschi → Rufiji ≃ 154 8.00 S 39.20 E
Rufiji ≃ 154 8.00 S 39.20 E
Rufina 66 43.49 N 11.29 E
Rufino 252 34.16 S 62.42 W
Rufisque 150 14.43 N 17.17 W
Rufunsa 154 15.05 S 29.40 E
Rufus 224 45.41 N 120.44 W
Rufus, Mount ʌ 168b 34.20 S 139.07 E
Rugāji 76 57.00 N 27.08 E
Rugao 100 32.25 N 120.36 E
Rugby, Eng., U.K. 42 52.23 N 1.15 W
Rugby, N.D., U.S. 198 48.22 N 99.59 W
Rugeley 42 52.46 N 1.55 W
Rügen I 54 54.25 N 13.24 E
Rüggeberg 263 51.16 N 7.22 E
Rugged Mountain ʌ 182 50.02 N 126.41 W
Ruggles Beach 214 41.22 N 82.29 W
Rugles 50 48.49 N 0.42 E
Rugufu ≃ 154 5.10 S 30.14 E
Ruguj 76 59.28 N 32.50 E
Ruhama 132 31.30 N 34.42 E
Ruhea 124 26.10 N 88.25 E
Rühen 54 52.29 N 10.53 E
Ruhengeri 154 1.30 S 29.38 E
Ruhla 54 50.53 N 10.22 E
Ruhland 54 51.27 N 13.52 E
Ruhlsdorf 264a 52.23 N 13.16 E
Ruhmannsfelden 60 48.59 N 12.59 E
Ruhner Berge ʌ2 54 53.17 N 11.55 E
Ruhnu saar I 76 57.48 N 23.15 E
Ruhpolding 64 47.45 N 12.38 E
Ruhr ≃ 52 51.27 N 6.44 E
Ruhrort ✦8 263 51.26 N 6.45 E
Ruhr-Universität ♥2 263 51.27 N 7.16 E
Ruhstorf an der Rott 60 48.26 N 13.20 E
Ruhudji ≃ 154 8.52 S 36.01 E
Ruhuhu ≃ 154 10.31 S 34.34 E
Ruhunu National Park ♦ 122 6.30 N 81.30 E
Rui'an 100 27.49 N 120.38 E
Ruichang 100 29.41 N 115.40 E
Ruicheng 102 34.45 N 110.45 E
Ruidoso 200 33.19 N 105.40 W
Ruidoso, Rio ≃ 200 33.23 N 105.16 W
Ruidoso Downs 200 33.19 N 105.36 W
Ruifeng Sha I 106 31.25 N 121.36 E
Ruihong 100 28.45 N 116.23 E
Ruijin 100 25.50 N 116.00 E
Ruinen 52 52.46 N 6.22 E
Ruiselede 50 51.03 N 3.24 E
Ruislip ✦8 260 51.34 N 0.25 W
Ruivo, Pico ʌ 148 32.45 N 16.56 W
Ruiz 234 21.57 N 105.09 W
Ruiz, Nevado del ʌ1 246 4.54 N 75.18 W
Ruiz de Montoya 252 26.59 S 55.03 W
Rūjiena 76 57.54 N 25.21 E
Rujm ar-Rashīd, Jabal ʌ 132 31.53 N 36.18 E
Rujm aṣ-Ṣakhrī 132 31.02 N 35.43 E
Rukan-shō ✢2 174m 26.06 N 127.32 E
Ruki ≃ 152 0.05 N 18.17 E
Rukni 126 23.33 N 86.33 E
Rukungiri 154 0.48 S 29.55 E
Rukwa □4 154 7.00 S 31.30 E
Rukwa, Lake ⊜ 154 8.00 S 32.25 E
Rule 196 33.11 N 99.53 W
Rule Creek ≃ 198 38.02 N 103.02 W
Ruleville 194 33.43 N 90.33 W
Rulle 52 52.20 N 8.04 E
Rully 58 46.52 N 4.45 E
Rulo 198 40.03 N 95.25 W
Rülzheim 56 49.09 N 8.16 E
Rum 61 47.08 N 16.51 E
Rum I 46 57.00 N 6.20 W
Rum ≃ 190 45.11 N 93.23 W
Rum, Sound of ʯ 46 56.56 N 6.14 W
Ruma 38 45.00 N 19.49 E
Rumaat 164 5.49 S 132.48 E
Rumāh 128 25.34 N 47.09 E
Rumahtinggih 164 6.23 S 140.17 E
Rum'ancevo, Ross. 82 55.38 N 37.26 E
Rum'ancevo, Ross. 82 55.58 N 36.32 E
Rumänien → Romania □1 38 46.00 N 25.30 E
Rumaysh 132 33.05 N 35.22 E
Rumbek 140 6.48 N 29.41 E
Rumbeke 50 50.56 N 3.10 E
Rumberpon, Pulau I 164 1.50 S 134.15 E
Rumbling Bridge 46 56.10 N 3.35 W
Rumburk 54 50.57 N 14.32 E
Rum Cay I 238 23.40 N 74.53 W
Rumelange 56 49.28 N 6.02 E
Rumelifeneri ✦8 267b 41.14 N 29.06 E
Rumelihisarı ✦8 267b 41.05 N 29.03 E
Rumelihisarı ⊥ 267b 41.05 N 29.02 E
Rumelikavağı ✦8 267b 41.11 N 29.04 E
Rumford 188 44.33 N 70.33 W
Rumford ≃ 283 41.58 N 71.11 W
Rumia 30 54.35 N 18.25 E
Rumigny 50 49.48 N 4.16 E
Rumilly 62 45.52 N 5.57 E
R'uminskoje 82 56.31 N 38.47 E
Rum Jungle 164 13.01 S 131.00 E
R'umki 265a 59.47 N 30.02 E
Rümlang 58 47.27 N 8.32 E
Rummah, Wādī ar- V 128 26.12 N 44.04 E
Rummānah 142 31.01 N 32.40 E
Rummānah, Bi'r ar- ⊤4 142 31.00 N 32.40 E
Rummel 214 40.13 N 78.48 W
Rummelsburg ✦8 264a 52.30 N 13.29 E
Rummenohl ✦8 263 51.17 N 7.32 E
Rumney 42 51.31 N 3.07 W
Rumoi 92a 43.56 N 141.39 E
Rumont 56 48.50 N 5.17 E
Rumphi 154 11.01 S 33.52 E
Rump Mountain ʌ 188 45.12 N 71.04 W
Rumson 208 40.22 N 73.59 W
Rumst 50 51.05 N 4.25 E
Rumula 164 16.35 S 145.20 E
Rumung I 174q 9.37 N 138.10 E
Rumuruti 154 0.16 N 36.32 E
Runan 100 33.01 N 114.22 E
Runanga 172 42.24 S 171.16 E
Runaway, Cape › 172 37.32 S 177.59 E
Runazi 154 2.47 S 31.28 E
Runcorn ✦8 44 53.20 N 2.44 W
Rundeng 114 2.39 N 97.52 E
Rundēni 76 56.16 N 27.50 E
Rundu 156 17.52 S 19.43 E
Rundvik 26 63.32 N 19.26 E
Runere 154 3.06 S 33.16 E
Rŭng, Kaôh I 110 10.44 N 103.14 E
Rungāni 120 26.38 N 65.43 E
Runge 222 28.52 N 97.42 W
Rungis 261 48.45 N 2.21 E
Rungis-Halles, Marché de ♥ 261 48.46 N 2.21 E
Rungsted 41 55.53 N 12.33 E
Rungus Point › 116 13.43 N 123.58 E
Rungwa, Tan. 154 7.21 S 31.40 E
Rungwa, Tan. 154 6.57 S 33.31 E
Rungwa ≃ 154 7.36 S 31.50 E
Rungwa Game Reserve ✦4 154 7.00 S 34.10 E
Rungwe 154 9.10 S 33.36 E
Runhällen 40 60.02 N 16.49 E
Runheji 100 32.30 N 116.05 E
Runkel 56 50.24 N 8.10 E
Runmarö I 40 59.17 N 18.46 E
Runn ⊜ 40 60.33 N 15.40 E
Runnemede 285 39.51 N 75.04 W
Running Springs 228 34.12 N 117.07 W
Running Water Draw V 196 33.58 N 101.30 W
Runnymede □8 260 51.24 N 0.32 W
Runnymede ⊥ 42 51.26 N 0.34 W
Rünthe 263 51.39 N 7.39 E
Runwell 260 51.37 N 0.32 E
Ruo ≃, Afr. 154 16.33 S 35.09 E
Ruo ≃, Zhg. 102 41.00 N 100.10 E
Ruo'ergai 102 33.16 N 102.55 E
Ruoheng 100 28.24 N 121.31 E
Ruokolahti 26 61.17 N 28.50 E
Ruoms 62 44.27 N 4.21 E
Ruoqiang 90 38.30 N 88.05 E
Ruoti 68 40.43 N 15.41 E
Ruovesi 26 61.59 N 24.05 E
Ruoxi 100 29.18 N 115.20 E
Rupanco 254 40.46 S 72.42 W
Rupanco, Lago ⊜ 254 40.49 S 72.28 W
Rupari 168b 35.37 S 139.09 E
Rupat, Pulau I 114 1.50 N 101.35 E
Rupat, Selat ʯ 114 1.50 N 101.25 E
Rupdia 126 23.08 N 89.13 E
Rupea 38 46.02 N 25.13 E
Rupert, Id., U.S. 202 42.37 N 113.40 W
Rupert, Vt., U.S. 210 43.15 N 73.13 W
Rupert, W.V., U.S. 188 37.57 N 80.41 W
Rupert, Rivière de ≃ 176 51.29 N 78.45 W
Rupert Creek ≃ 166 20.53 S 142.23 E
Rupganj 126 23.48 N 90.31 E
Rūpnagar 123 30.59 N 76.31 E
Rūpnārāyan ≃ 126 22.13 N 88.03 E
Ruponda 154 10.15 S 38.42 E
Ruppertenrod 56 50.37 N 9.05 E
Ruppiner See ⊜ 54 52.48 N 12.50 E
Rupprechtseck ʌ 61 47.14 N 14.00 E
Rupt de Mad ≃ 56 49.01 N 6.02 E
Rupt-sur-Moselle 58 47.56 N 6.40 E
Rupununi ≃ 246 4.03 N 58.34 W
Ruqqād, Wādī ar- V 132 32.44 N 35.46 E
Rur (Roer) ≃ 56 51.12 N 5.59 E
Rural Hall 192 36.14 N 80.17 W
Rural Retreat 192 36.53 N 81.16 W
Rural Ridge 279b 40.35 N 79.50 W
Rural Valley 214 40.48 N 79.18 W
Rurberg 56 50.37 N 6.22 E
Ruri-kei ♦ 96 35.03 N 135.26 E
Rurrenabaque 248 14.28 S 67.34 W
Rurstausee ⊜1 56 50.36 N 6.22 E
Rurutu I 14 22.26 S 151.20 W
Rusambo 154 16.35 S 32.12 E
Rušan 120 37.58 N 71.30 E
Rusaniv 78 50.29 N 31.09 E
Rusanivka 78 50.32 N 33.44 E
Rusape 154 18.32 S 32.07 E
Rusavkina-Popovščina 265b 55.42 N 38.04 E
Ruṣayriṣ, Khazzān ar- ⊜1 140 11.40 N 34.20 E
Ruschuk → Ruse 38 43.50 N 25.57 E
Ruscom ≃ 214 42.18 N 82.38 W
Ruscom Station 214 42.13 N 82.39 W
Ruse, Blg. 38 43.50 N 25.57 E
Ruše, Slvn. 61 46.32 N 15.31 E
Rusera 124 25.45 N 86.02 E
Rush, Ire. 48 53.32 N 6.06 W
Rush, N.Y., U.S. 210 42.59 N 77.39 W
Rush, Pa., U.S. 210 41.47 N 76.03 W
Rush □6 218 39.37 N 85.27 W
Rush ≃, N.D., U.S. 198 47.00 N 96.54 W
Rush ≃, Wi., U.S. 190 44.34 N 92.19 W
Rushan (Xiacun) 98 36.54 N 121.29 E
Rush Center 198 38.27 N 99.18 W
Rush City 190 45.41 N 92.57 W
Rush Creek ≃, Co., U.S. 198 38.22 N 102.32 W
Rush Creek ≃, Ne., U.S. 198 41.27 N 102.32 W
Rush Creek ≃, N.Y., U.S. 284a 42.00 N 78.52 W
Rush Creek ≃, Oh., U.S. 188 39.38 N 82.33 W
Rush Creek ≃, Oh., U.S. 214 40.34 N 83.20 W
Rush Creek ≃, Ok., U.S. 196 34.42 N 97.10 W
Rushden 42 52.17 N 0.36 W
Rushford, Mn., U.S. 190 43.48 N 91.45 W
Rushford, N.Y., U.S. 210 42.23 N 78.15 W
Rushford Lake ⊜1 214 42.23 N 78.12 W
Rush Hill 219 39.13 N 91.43 W
Rush Lake ⊜, On., Can. 190 47.48 N 82.12 W
Rush Lake ⊜, Wi., U.S. 190 43.56 N 88.49 W
Rushland 285 40.15 N 75.02 W
Rushmore 198 43.37 N 95.48 W
Rusholme ✦8 262 53.27 N 2.12 W
Rush Springs 196 34.46 N 97.57 W
Rushsylvania 216 40.27 N 83.40 W
Rushville, Il., U.S. 219 40.07 N 90.33 W
Rushville, In., U.S. 218 39.36 N 85.26 W
Rushville, Ne., U.S. 198 42.43 N 102.27 W
Rushville, N.Y., U.S. 210 42.45 N 77.13 W
Rusinga Island I 154 0.24 S 34.10 E
Rusizi (Ruzizi) ≃ 154 3.16 S 29.14 E
Rusk 222 31.47 N 95.09 W
Rusk □6 222 32.10 N 94.50 W
Rusken ⊜ 26 57.17 N 14.20 E
Ruskin, B.C., Can. 224 49.12 N 122.28 W
Ruskin, Fl., U.S. 220 27.43 N 82.26 W
Ruskington 44 53.02 N 0.23 W
Rusnė 76 55.18 N 21.22 E
Rušons ⊜ 76 56.11 N 27.02 E
Rusovce 61 48.04 N 17.10 E
Russa 272b 22.29 N 88.21 E
Russas 250 4.56 S 37.58 W
Russbach ≃ 61 48.10 N 16.58 E
Russee 41 54.18 N 10.04 E
Russell, Mb., Can. 184 50.47 N 101.15 W
Russell, On., Can. 212 45.15 N 75.22 W
Russell, N.Z. 172 35.16 S 174.07 E
Russell, Ia., U.S. 190 40.58 N 93.11 W
Russell, Ks., U.S. 198 38.53 N 98.51 W
Russell, Ky., U.S. 188 38.31 N 82.41 W
Russell, Ma., U.S. 207 42.11 N 72.51 W
Russell, Mn., U.S. 198 44.19 N 95.57 W
Russell, Pa., U.S. 214 41.56 N 79.08 W
Russell, Cape › 176 75.15 N 117.35 W
Russell, Mount ʌ 180 62.48 N 151.52 W
Russell Cave National Monument ♦ 194 34.54 N 85.48 W
Russell Creek ≃ 194 37.14 N 85.30 W
Russell Gardens 276 40.47 N 73.43 W
Russell Island I 176 73.55 N 98.25 W
Russell Islands II 175e 9.04 S 159.12 E
Russellkonda 120 19.56 N 84.35 E
Russell Lake ⊜ 184 56.15 N 101.30 W
Russell Range ⋏ 162 33.24 S 123.28 E
Russells Point 216 40.28 N 83.54 W
Russell Springs 194 37.03 N 85.05 W
Russellton 214 40.37 N 79.50 W
Russellville, Al., U.S. 194 34.30 N 87.43 W
Russellville, Ar., U.S. 194 35.16 N 93.08 W
Russellville, Ky., U.S. 194 36.50 N 86.53 W
Russellville, Mo., U.S. 194 38.30 N 92.26 W
Russellville, Oh., U.S. 218 38.51 N 83.47 W
Russellville, Or., U.S. 224 45.31 N 122.33 W
Rüsselsheim 56 50.00 N 8.25 E
Russi 66 44.22 N 12.02 E
Russia 216 40.14 N 84.24 W
Russia □1, Europe 72 60.00 N 80.00 E
Russia □1, Europe 74 60.00 N 100.00 E
Russian ≃ 204 38.27 N 123.08 W
Russian Mission 180 61.47 N 161.19 W
Russiaville 216 40.25 N 86.16 W
Russka 76 58.59 N 28.30 E
Russkaja Bujlovka 78 50.22 N 40.03 E
Russkaja Gavan' 74 76.10 N 62.35 E
Russkaja Pol'ana 86 53.47 N 73.53 E
Russkaja Talovka 80 49.59 N 49.05 E
Russkaja Žuravka 80 50.21 N 40.33 E
Russkij 89 43.03 N 131.50 E
Russkij, ostrov I 74 77.00 N 96.00 E
Russkij Aktaš 80 55.02 N 52.07 E
Russkij Brod 76 52.36 N 37.22 E
Russkij Kameškir 80 52.52 N 46.06 E
Russkij Turek 80 57.03 N 50.13 E
Russkij Vožoj 80 56.57 N 53.22 E
Russkij Zavorot, mys › 24 68.58 N 54.34 E
Russkoje 83 47.45 N 38.56 E
Russkoje-Dobrino 80 54.22 N 52.28 E
Russko-Vysockoje 265a 59.42 N 29.56 E
Rust, Dtsch. 58 48.16 N 7.43 E
Rust, Öst. 61 47.48 N 16.41 E
Rustajskij 80 56.31 N 44.49 E
Rustam 123 34.21 N 72.17 E
Rustavi 84 41.33 N 45.02 E
Rustburg 192 37.16 N 79.06 W
Rustenburg 158 25.37 S 27.08 E
Rustfontein 158 30.28 S 29.17 E
Rustic Canyon V 280 34.04 N 118.31 W
Rustig 158 27.22 S 27.09 E
Rustington 42 50.48 N 0.31 W
Ruston, La., U.S. 194 32.31 N 92.38 W
Ruston, Wa., U.S. 224 47.17 N 122.30 W
Rusville 273d 26.10 S 28.18 E
Rutana 154 3.55 S 30.00 E
Rute 34 37.19 N 4.22 W
Rütenbrock 52 52.50 N 7.10 E
Ruteng 115b 8.36 S 120.27 E
Rutenga 154 21.08 S 30.45 E
Rutersville 222 29.57 N 96.48 W
Rutgers University ♥2, N.J., U.S. 276 40.30 N 74.27 W
Rutgers University (Newark) ♥2, N.J., U.S. 276 40.44 N 74.10 W
Rutgers University (Camden) ♥2, N.J., U.S. 285 39.56 N 75.07 W
Ruth, Ms., U.S. 194 31.22 N 90.18 W
Ruth, Nv., U.S. 204 39.16 N 114.59 W
Rüthen 52 51.29 N 8.25 E
Rutherford, Ca., U.S. 226 38.28 N 122.25 W
Rutherford, N.J., U.S. 210 40.49 N 74.06 W
Rutherford, Tn., U.S. 194 36.07 N 88.59 W
Rutherfordton 192 35.22 N 81.57 W
Rutherglen, Scot., U.K. 46 55.50 N 4.12 W
Ruther Glen, Va., U.S. 208 37.56 N 77.27 W
Ruthin 44 53.07 N 3.18 W
Ruthton 198 44.10 N 96.06 W
Ruthven, On., Can. 214 42.03 N 82.40 W
Ruthven, Ia., U.S. 198 43.07 N 94.53 W
Rüti 58 47.16 N 8.51 E
Rutigliano 68 41.01 N 17.00 E
Rutino 68 40.18 N 15.04 E
Rutka ≃ 80 56.22 N 46.38 E
Rutland, B.C., Can. 182 49.53 N 119.24 W
Rutland, Fl., U.S. 220 28.51 N 82.13 W
Rutland, Il., U.S. 216 40.59 N 89.03 W
Rutland, Ma., U.S. 207 42.22 N 71.56 W
Rutland, N.D., U.S. 198 46.03 N 97.30 W
Rutland, Vt., U.S. 188 43.36 N 72.58 W
Rutland □6 210 43.21 N 73.15 W
Rutland Island I 110 11.25 N 92.40 E
Rutland State Park ♦ 207 42.23 N 72.01 W
Rutland Water ⊜1 42 52.39 N 0.38 W
Rutledge, Ga., U.S. 192 33.37 N 83.36 W
Rutledge, Pa., U.S. 285 39.54 N 75.20 W
Rutledge, Tn., U.S. 192 36.16 N 83.30 W
Rutog 120 33.27 N 79.42 E
Rutshuru 154 1.11 S 29.27 E
Rüttenscheid ✦8 263 51.26 N 7.00 E
Rutter 190 46.06 N 80.40 W
Rutul 84 41.33 N 47.25 E
Ruukki 26 64.40 N 25.06 E
Ruurlo 52 52.05 N 6.26 E
Ruvo del Monte 68 40.51 N 15.32 E
Ruvo di Puglia 68 41.07 N 16.29 E
Ruvu 154 6.48 S 38.39 E
Ruvu ≃ 154 6.23 S 38.52 E
Ruvubu (Rovubu) ≃ 154 2.23 S 30.47 E
Ruvuma □4 154 11.00 S 36.00 E
Ruvuma (Rovuma) ≃ 154 10.29 S 40.28 E
Ruwayān, Wādī ar- ∸7 142 29.07 N 30.10 E
Ruwaybah ⊤4 140 15.39 N 28.45 E
Ruwayfī, Jabal ar- ʌ 132 31.12 N 36.00 E
Ruwenzori National Park ♦ 154 0.15 S 30.00 E
Ruwenzori Range ⋏ 154 0.23 N 29.54 E
Ruwer 56 49.47 N 6.43 E
Ruwer ≃ 56 49.47 N 6.42 E
Ruya (Luia) ≃ 154 16.34 S 33.12 E
Ruyang 100 34.10 N 112.26 E
Ruy Barbosa 255 12.18 S 40.27 W
Ruyigi 154 3.29 S 30.15 E
Ruyton-Eleven-Towns 42 52.48 N 2.54 W
Ruza 82 55.42 N 36.12 E
Ruza ≃ 82 55.38 N 36.17 E
Ruzajevka, Kaz. 86 52.49 N 66.57 E
Ruzajevka, Ross. 80 54.04 N 44.57 E
Ružany 76 52.52 N 24.53 E
Ruzhyn 78 49.43 N 29.14 E
Ruzizi (Rusizi) ≃ 154 3.16 S 29.14 E
Ružomberok 30 49.06 N 19.18 E
Ruzskoje vodochranilišče ⊜1 82 55.47 N 36.00 E
Ruzychna 78 49.24 N 26.58 E
Ruzyně ⊠ 54 50.06 N 14.17 E
Ruzzah, Jabal ʌ2 142 30.01 N 30.26 E
Rwamagana 154 1.57 S 30.34 E
Rwanda □1, Afr. 138 2.00 S 30.00 E
Rwanda □1, Afr. 154 2.00 S 30.00 E
Rwashamaire 154 0.49 S 30.08 E
Ry 41 56.05 N 9.46 E
Ryal Fold 262 53.41 N 2.30 W
Ryan 196 34.01 N 97.57 W
Ryan ≃ 182 50.25 N 122.43 W
Ryan, Loch c 44 54.58 N 5.02 W
Ryan Peak ʌ 202 43.54 N 114.25 W
Ryans Creek ≃ 169 36.43 S 146.12 E
Ryarsh 260 51.19 N 0.24 E
Ryasnopil' 78 47.04 N 31.12 E
Ryazan' → R'azan' 80 54.38 N 39.44 E
Rybačij 76 55.09 N 20.51 E
Rybačij, poluostrov ›1 24 69.42 N 32.36 E
Rybačje 86 46.27 N 81.32 E
Rybackaja ✦8 265a 60.00 N 30.30 E
Rybackoje ✦8 265a 59.50 N 30.30 E
Rybakivka 78 46.37 N 31.20 E
Rybinsk 76 58.03 N 38.52 E
Rybinsker Stausee → Rybinskoje vodochranilišče ⊜1 76 58.30 N 38.25 E
Rybinskije Budy 78 51.13 N 35.57 E
Rybinskoje 86 55.47 N 94.47 E
Rybinskoje vodochranilišče ⊜1 76 58.30 N 38.25 E
Rybkino 80 54.15 N 43.46 E
Rybnaja Sloboda 80 55.28 N 50.09 E
Rybnik 30 50.06 N 18.32 E
Rybnoje, Ross. 76 54.44 N 39.30 E
Rybnoje, Ross. 86 58.08 N 94.30 E
Rybnovsk 89 53.12 N 141.50 E
Ryburn ≃ 262 53.43 N 1.54 W
Rybuška 80 51.17 N 45.26 E
Rychwał 30 52.05 N 18.09 E
Ryčkovo 86 58.09 N 61.43 E
Rycroft 182 55.45 N 118.43 W
Ryd 26 56.28 N 14.41 E
Rydaholm 26 56.59 N 14.16 E
Rydal, Austl. 170 33.29 S 150.02 E
Rydal, Pa., U.S. 285 40.06 N 75.06 W
Rydalmere 274a 33.49 S 151.02 E
Rydbo 40 59.28 N 18.11 E
Ryde, Austl. 170 33.49 S 151.06 E
Ryde, Eng., U.K. 42 50.44 N 1.10 W
Ryder 198 47.55 N 101.40 W
Ryder's Hill ʌ2 42 50.31 N 3.53 W
Ryderwood 224 46.22 N 123.02 W
Rydsgård 41 55.28 N 13.35 E
Rydzyna 30 51.48 N 16.40 E
Rye, Austl. 169 38.23 S 144.49 E
Rye, Eng., U.K. 42 50.57 N 0.44 E
Rye, N.Y., U.S. 210 40.58 N 73.41 W
Rye, Tx., U.S. 222 30.27 N 94.46 W
Rye ≃ 44 54.10 N 0.45 W
Ryegate 202 46.17 N 109.15 W
Rye Hills-Rye Brook 276 41.00 N 73.41 W
Rye Lake ⊜ 276 41.04 N 73.43 W
Ryeosu → Yŏsu 98 34.46 N 127.44 E
Rye Patch Reservoir ⊜1 204 40.38 N 118.18 W
Ryer Island I 282 38.05 N 122.01 W
Ryes 32 49.19 N 0.37 W
Ryfoss 26 61.09 N 8.49 E
Ryfylke ✦1 26 59.30 N 5.30 E
Rygge 26 59.23 N 10.43 E
Rygnestad 26 59.16 N 7.29 E
Ryhope 44 54.52 N 1.21 W
Rykaartspos 158 26.32 S 26.39 E
Ryker Lake ⊜ 276 41.03 N 74.33 W
Rykerts 182 49.00 N 116.35 W
Ryki 30 51.39 N 21.56 E
Rykonec 76 59.33 N 36.34 E
Ryley 182 53.17 N 112.26 W
Ryloviči 76 52.31 N 32.04 E
Ryl'sk 78 51.36 N 34.43 E
Rylstone 170 32.48 S 149.58 E
Rymanów 30 49.34 N 21.53 E
Rýmařov 30 49.56 N 17.16 E
Ryn 30 53.56 N 21.33 E
Rynfield 273d 26.09 S 28.20 E
Rynok 80 45.39 N 47.34 E
Ryn-Peski ✦2 80 48.24 N 49.00 E
Ryō 270 34.44 N 135.55 E
Ryōhaku-sanchi ⋏ 94 36.09 N 136.45 E
Ryojun → Lüshun 98 38.48 N 121.16 E
Ryōkami 94 36.00 N 138.58 E
Ryōke 268 35.58 N 139.33 E
Ryōnan 96 33.15 N 133.55 E
Ryōtsu 92 38.05 N 138.26 E
Rypin 30 53.05 N 19.25 E
Ryshnivka 78 49.47 N 27.25 E
Ryslinge 41 55.15 N 10.33 E
Rysy ʌ 30 49.12 N 20.04 E
Ryton 44 54.59 N 1.46 W
Ryton ≃ 44 53.25 N 1.00 W
Ryton-on-Dunsmore 42 52.22 N 1.26 W
Ryūga-do ∸5 96 33.39 N 133.45 E
Ryūgasaki 94 35.54 N 140.11 E
Ryūjin 96 33.53 N 135.29 E
Ryukyu Islands → Nansei-shotō II 90 26.30 N 128.00 E
Ryukyu Trench ✢1 12 24.45 N 128.00 E
Ryūmon-dake ʌ 270 34.26 N 135.53 E
Ryūō, Nihon 94 35.04 N 136.07 E
Ryūō, Nihon 94 35.39 N 138.30 E
Ryūsen 270 34.28 N 135.37 E
Ryūyō 94 34.40 N 137.48 E
Ržaksa 80 52.09 N 42.02 E
Ržanica 76 53.26 N 33.55 E
Ržava 78 51.14 N 36.43 E
Rzepin 30 52.22 N 14.50 E
Rzeszów 30 50.03 N 22.00 E
Rzeszów □4 30 50.00 N 22.00 E
Ržev 76 56.16 N 34.20 E
Rzhyshchiv 78 49.58 N 31.03 E
Ržovka ✦8 265a 59.58 N 30.30 E

S

Sa 110 18.34 N 100.45 E
Sa ≃ 105 40.22 N 117.58 E
Saa 152 4.22 N 11.27 E
Sa'ad 132 31.28 N 34.32 E
Sa'ādatābād 128 30.06 N 53.08 E
Sääksjärvi ⊜ 26 61.24 N 22.24 E
Saal 54 54.19 N 12.29 E
Saalach ≃ 64 47.51 N 13.00 E
Saal an der Donau 60 48.54 N 11.56 E
Saal an der Saale 56 50.19 N 10.21 E
Saalbach 64 47.23 N 12.38 E
Saalburg 54 50.30 N 11.43 E
Saaldorf, Dtsch. 54 50.27 N 11.41 E
Saaldorf, Dtsch. 64 47.52 N 12.56 E
Saale ≃ 54 51.57 N 11.55 E
Saaler Bodden c 54 54.20 N 12.28 E
Saales 58 48.21 N 7.07 E
Saaletalsperre ✦6 54 50.30 N 11.43 E
Saalfeld 54 50.39 N 11.22 E
Saalfelden 64 47.25 N 12.51 E
Šaamar 88 50.08 N 106.10 E
Saâne ≃, Fr. 50 49.54 N 0.56 E
Saane (Sarine) ≃, Schw. 58 46.59 N 7.15 E
Saanen 58 46.29 N 7.16 E
Saanenmöser 58 46.31 N 7.18 E
Saanich Inlet c 224 48.38 N 123.30 W
Saar → Saarland □3 56 49.20 N 7.00 E
Saar (Sarre) ≃ 56 49.42 N 6.34 E
Saarbrücken 56 49.14 N 6.59 E
Saarburg 56 49.36 N 6.33 E
Sääre 76 57.56 N 22.02 E
Saarelouis → Saarlouis 56 49.21 N 6.45 E
Saaremaa I 76 58.25 N 22.30 E
Saarijärvi 26 62.43 N 25.16 E
Saaristomeren kansallispuisto ♦ 26 59.50 N 21.50 E
Saarland □3 56 49.20 N 7.00 E
Saarlautern → Saarlouis 56 49.21 N 6.45 E
Saarlouis 56 49.21 N 6.45 E
Saarmund 264a 52.19 N 13.07 E
Saarn ✦8 263 51.24 N 6.53 E
Saarnberg ✦8 263 51.25 N 6.53 E
Saas Almagell 58 46.07 N 7.58 E
Saas Fee 58 46.07 N 7.55 E
Saas Grund 58 46.08 N 7.56 E
Saastal V 58 46.10 N 7.56 E
Saatlı 84 39.56 N 48.23 E
Saavedra 252 37.45 S 62.22 W
Saba I 238 17.38 N 63.10 W
Saba ≃, Nihon 96 34.02 N 131.30 E
Saba ≃, Ross. 76 59.08 N 29.00 E
Sabā', Wādī al- V 128 28.35 N 36.35 E
Saba Bank ✢2 238 17.30 N 63.30 W
Šabac 38 44.45 N 19.42 E
Sabadell 34 41.33 N 2.06 E
Sabae 94 35.57 N 136.11 E
Sab'ah 142 30.15 N 32.33 E
Sabah □3 112 5.20 N 117.10 E
Sabajevo 80 53.59 N 45.43 E
Sabak, Cape › 181a 52.20 N 173.45 E
Sabak Bernam 114 3.46 N 100.59 E
Sabal 112 0.59 S 123.14 E
Sabalān ʌ 128 38.15 N 47.48 E
Sabalana, Kepulauan II 112 6.45 S 118.50 E
Sabalgarh 124 26.15 N 77.24 E
Sabaluka Game Reserve ✦4 140 16.18 N 32.40 E
Sabana 240m 18.20 N 65.44 W
Sabana, Archipiélago de II 240p 23.00 N 80.00 W
Sabana de La Mar 238 19.04 N 69.23 W
Sabana de Mendoza 246 9.26 N 70.46 W
Sabanagrande, Hond. 236 13.50 N 87.15 W
Sabana Grande, P.R. 240m 18.05 N 66.58 W
Sabanalamar, Ensenada c 240p 21.36 N 78.44 W
Sabanalarga 246 10.38 N 74.55 W
Sabana Llana 240m 18.02 N 66.15 W
Sabancuy 232 18.58 N 91.11 W
Sabaneta, Rep. Dom. 238 19.30 N 71.21 W
Sabaneta, Ven. 246 8.46 N 69.56 W
Sabaneta, Puntan › 174n 15.17 N 145.49 E
Sābang, India 126 22.11 N 87.36 E
Sabang (Dampelas), Indon. 112 0.11 N 119.51 E
Sabang, Indon. 114 5.55 N 95.19 E
Sabanillas 232 25.08 N 101.44 W
Šabanovo 82 55.38 N 38.43 E
Şabanözü 130 40.29 N 33.18 E
Sabará 255 19.54 S 43.48 W
Sabarei 154 4.20 N 36.55 E
Sābari ≃ 122 17.34 N 81.15 E
Sābarmati ≃ 120 22.18 N 72.22 E
Sabasṭīyah (Samaria) 132 32.17 N 35.12 E
Sab'atayn, Ramlat as- ∸8 144 15.30 N 46.10 E
Sabathu 123 30.59 N 76.59 E
Sabatini, Monti ⋏ 66 42.10 N 12.15 E
Sabato ≃ 66 41.08 N 14.45 E
Sabaudia 66 41.18 N 13.01 E
Sabaudia, Lago di c 66 41.16 N 13.02 E
Sabaúna 256 23.29 S 46.05 W
Saba Wanak 144 10.33 N 44.08 E
Sabaya 248 19.01 S 68.23 W
Ṣabāyā, Jabal I 144 18.35 N 41.03 E
Sabažo 84 42.14 N 41.48 E
Sabbioneta 64 45.00 N 10.29 E
Sabe 272c 19.11 N 73.02 E
Šabel'sk 83 46.51 N 38.29 E
Ṣāberī, Hāmūn-e ⊜ 128 31.30 N 61.20 E
Sabetha 198 39.54 N 95.48 W
Sabhā, Lībiyā 146 27.03 N 14.26 E
Ṣabḥā, Urd. 132 32.20 N 36.30 E
Sābhār 126 23.51 N 90.15 E
Sabi (Save) ≃, Afr. 156 21.00 S 35.02 E
Sabi ≃, Nihon 94 36.48 N 140.04 E
Sabicy 76 58.50 N 29.18 E
Sabidana, Jabal ʌ 140 18.04 N 36.50 E
Sabie 156 25.10 S 30.48 E
Sábiè ≃ 156 25.19 S 32.18 E
Sabile 76 57.03 N 22.35 E
Sabillasville 208 39.42 N 77.27 W
Sabina 218 39.29 N 83.38 W
Sabina □9 66 42.15 N 12.42 E
Sabinal 196 29.19 N 99.27 W
Sabinal ≃ 196 29.06 N 99.27 W
Sabinal, Cayo I 240p 21.40 N 77.18 W
Sabiñánigo 34 42.31 N 0.22 W
Sabinas 232 27.51 N 101.07 W
Sabinas ≃, Méx. 232 27.37 N 100.42 W
Sabinas ≃, Méx. 232 26.51 N 99.34 W
Sabinas ≃, Méx. 234 22.59 N 98.58 W
Sabinas Hidalgo 232 26.30 N 100.10 W
Sabine ≃ 178 30.00 N 93.45 W
Sabine, Cowleech Fork ≃ 222 33.03 N 95.59 W
Sabine, Mount ʌ, Ant. 9 71.55 S 169.33 E
Sabine, Mount ʌ, Austl. 169 38.38 S 143.44 E
Sabine, South Fork ≃ 222 32.52 N 96.10 W
Sabine Bay c 176 75.35 N 109.30 W
Sabine Lake ⊜ 194 29.50 N 93.50 W
Sabine Pass c 194 29.44 N 93.52 W
Sabine Peninsula ›1 176 76.20 N 109.30 W
Sabini, Monti ⋏ 66 42.13 N 12.50 E
Sabinópolis 255 18.40 S 43.06 W
Sabinov 30 49.06 N 21.06 E
Sabinsville 210 41.52 N 77.31 W
Sabir, Jabal ʌ 144 13.30 N 44.03 E
Sabirabad 84 40.01 N 48.29 E
Šabla 38 43.32 N 28.32 E
Sabl'a, gora ʌ 24 64.48 N 58.50 E
Sablayan 116 12.50 N 120.46 E
Sable, Anse au c 275a 45.21 N 73.56 W
Sable, Cape › 186 43.25 N 65.35 W
Sable, Cape ›1 220 25.12 N 81.05 W
Sable, Île de I 160 19.15 S 159.56 E
Sable, Rivière du ≃ 176 55.30 N 68.21 W
Sable Island I 186 43.55 N 59.50 W
Sables, Lac aux ⊜ 206 46.53 N 72.22 W
Sables, River aux ≃ 190 46.13 N 82.04 W
Sablé-sur-Sarthe 32 47.50 N 0.20 W
Sablinskoje 84 44.31 N [illegible]3.14 E
Sablūkah, Ash-Shallāl as- (Sixth Cataract) ⌞ 140 16.20 N [illegible]2.42 E
Šablykino 76 52.51 N [illegible]5.12 E
Sabo 152 7.50 N 7.49 E
Saboeiro 250 6.32 S [illegible]9.54 W
Sabogal ≃ 236 10.55 N [illegible]4.43 W
Sāboli ✦8 272a 28.43 N [illegible]7.18 E
Sabonkafi 150 14.38 N [illegible]3.45 E
Sabor ≃ 34 41.10 N [illegible].07 W
Sabou 150 12.04 N [illegible].14 W
Sabourin, Lac ⊜ 190 47.58 N 7[illegible].41 W
Sabra, Tanjung › 164 2.17 S 13[illegible].19 E
Ṣabrātah 146 32.47 N 1[illegible].29 E
Sabres 32 44.09 N [illegible].44 W
Sabrevois 206 45.12 N 7[illegible].14 W
Sabrina Coast ∸2 9 67.00 S 11[illegible].30 E
Sabuda, Pulau I 164 2.38 S 13[illegible].36 E
Sabugal 34 40.21 N 7[illegible]5 W
Sabugo 266c 38.49 N 9[illegible]18 W
Sabuka 273b 4.27 S 15[illegible]10 E
Sabula 190 42.04 N 90[illegible]0 W
Sabunçu, Azer. 84 40.26 N 49[illegible]6 E
Sabuncu, Tür. 130 39.33 N 30[illegible]2 E
Saburovo 265b 55.53 N 37.[illegible]6 E
Saburovo ✦8 265b 55.38 N 37.[illegible]2 E
Ṣabyā 144 17.09 N 42.[illegible]7 E
Sabyin 110 19.06 N 94.[illegible]1 E
Sabyndy 86 50.53 N 70.[illegible]3 E
Sabzevār 128 36.13 N 57.[illegible] E
Sac ≃ 194 38.01 N 93.[illegible]3 W
Sacaba 248 17.23 S 66.[illegible] W
Sacaca 248 18.05 S 66.[illegible] W
Sacacomie, Lac ⊜ 206 46.31 N 73.1[illegible] W
Sacagawea ≃ 202 47.27 N 107.5[illegible] W
Sacajawea Peak ʌ 202 45.15 N 117.1[illegible] W
Sacanche 248 7.05 S 76.4[illegible] W
Sacandaga ≃ 210 43.19 N 73.5[illegible] W
Sacandaga, West Branch ≃ 210 43.22 N 74.1[illegible] W
Sacandica 152 5.58 S 15.5[illegible] E
Sacaola 152 12.57 S 22.25 E
Sacariúna ≃ 248 12.52 S 57.22 W
Sacaton 200 33.04 N 111.44 W
Sacavém 266c 38.47 N 9.06 W
Sačchere 84 42.21 N 43.23 E
Sac City 198 42.25 N 94.59 W
Sacco ≃ 66 41.31 N 13.32 E
Sacedón 34 40.29 N 2.43 W
Săcele 38 45.37 N 25.42 E
Şaç Geçidi )( 130 39.54 N 42.22
Šacha ≃ 82 56.45 N 39.10
Sachalin, ostrov (Sakhalin) I 89 51.00 N 143.00 E
Sachalin Oblast' □4 89 51.00 N 143.00 E
Sachalinskij zaliv c 89 53.45 N 141.30 E
Šachand 85 40.54 N 71.28 E
Sachayoj 252 26.41 S 61.50 W
Saché 50 47.14 N 0.33 E
Šache ≃ 84 43.47 N 39.27 E
Sachicapa 152 10.21 S 19.59 E
Sachigo ≃ 176 55.06 N 88.58 W
Sachigo Lake ⊜ 184 53.49 N 92.08 W
Sachimbo 152 9.14 S 20.16 E
Šachovskaja 76 56.02 N 35.29 E
Šachrichan 85 40.44 N 72.03 E
Šachrinau 85 38.34 N 68.20 E
Šachrisabz 72 39.03 N 66.50 E
Šachristan 85 39.47 N 68.49 E
Šachristan, pereval )( 85 39.33 N 68.33 E
Šachrovka 80 58.34 N 52.12 E
Sachse 222 32.59 N 96.36 W
Sachseln 58 46.52 N 8.15 E
Sachsen □3 30 51.00 N 13.00 E
Sachsen □9 30 52.45 N 9.30 E
Sachsen-Anhalt □3 54 52.00 N 11.30 E
Sachsenbrunn 54 50.27 N 10.56 E
Sachsenburg 64 46.50 N 13.21 E
Sachsenhagen 52 52.24 N 9.16 E
Sachsenhausen, Dtsch. 54 52.47 N 13.14 E
Sachsenhausen, Dtsch. 56 51.15 N 9.00 E
Sachs Harbour 176 72.00 N 125.00 W
Sächsische Schweiz ✦1 54 50.55 N 14.10 E
Šachterskij 180 64.42 N 177.40 E
Šachtinsk 86 49.40 N 72.37 E
Šacht'orsk 89 49.11 N 142.07 E
Šachty 83 47.42 N 40.13 E
Šachunja 80 57.40 N 46.37 E
Sachy 56 49.40 N 5.08 E
Sacile 64 45.57 N 12.30 E
Šack, Bela. 76 53.25 N 27.41 E
Šack, Ross. 80 54.01 N 41.43 E
Sackets Harbor 212 43.56 N 76.07 W
Sackville 186 45.54 N 64.22 W
Saclay 261 48.44 N 2.10 E
Saclay, Étang de ⊜ 261 48.45 N 2.10 E
Saco, Me., U.S. 188 43.30 N 70.26 W
Saco, Mt., U.S. 202 48.27 N 107.20 W
Saco ≃ 188 43.27 N 70.22 W
Saco Bay c 188 43.30 N 70.15 W
Sacol Island I 116 6.58 N 122.13 E
Sacotes 266c 38.48 N 9.20 W
Sacra, Isola I 267a 41.45 N 12.15 E
Sacra Família do Tinguá 256 22.29 S 43.36 W
Sacramento, Bra. 255 19.53 S 47.27 W
Sacramento, Ca., U.S. 226 38.34 N 121.29 W
Sacramento □6 226 38.35 N 121.30 W
Sacramento ≃, Ca., U.S. 204 38.03 N 121.56 W
Sacramento ≃, N.M., U.S. 200 32.16 N 105.31 W
Sacramento, Pampa del ⁝ 248 8.00 S 75.50 W
Sacramento Metropolitan Airport ⊠ 226 38.42 N 121.37 W
Sacramento Mountains ⋏ 200 32.45 N 105.30 W
Sacramento River Deep Water Ship Channel ≍ 226 38.15 N 121.40 W
Sacramento South 226 38.32 N 121.26 W
Sacramento Valley V 204 39.15 N 122.00 W
Sacramento Wash V 200 34.43 N 114.28 W
Sacre ≃ 248 12.56 S 58.18 W
Sacré-Cœur ♥1 261 48.53 N 2.21 E
Sacred Heart 198 44.47 N 95.21 W
Sacriston 44 54.49 N 1.37 W
Sacro, Monte ʌ 68 40.13 N 15.20 E
Sacro Monte ♥1 62 45.49 N 8.15 E
Sacrow ✦8 264a 52.26 N 13.06 E
Sacrower-Paretzer Kanal ≍ 264a 52.28 N 12.55 E
Sacrower See ⊜ 264a 52.27 N 13.06 E
Săcueni 38 47.21 N 22.06 E
Sacul 222 31.50 N 94.56 W
Sacupana 246 8.35 N 61.39 W
Sada, Esp. 34 43.21 N 8.15 W
Sada, Nihon 96 35.15 N 132.43 E
Sádaba 34 42.17 N 1.16 W
Sadābād, India 124 27.27 N 78.03 E
Sa'dābād, Īrān 128 29.23 N 51.07 E
Sa'dābād, Īrān 128 34.51 N 50.36 E
Ṣadad 130 34.18 N 36.56 E
Ṣa'dah 144 16.52 N 43.37 E
Sadaik Taung ʌ 110 15.09 N 98.12 E
Sadali 71 39.49 N 9.16 E
Sada-misaki › 96 33.20 N 132.01 E
Sada-misaki-hantō ›1 96 33.26 N 132.13 E
Sadamitsu 96 34.02 N 134.04 E
Sadane ≃ 115a 6.01 S 106.37 E
Sadang ≃ 112 3.43 S 119.27 E
Sadanga 116 17.09 N 121.02 E
Sadani 154 6.03 S 38.47 E


| | | | | |
|---|---|---|---|---|
| ≃ River | Fluß | Río | Rivière | Rio |
| ≍ Canal | Kanal | Canal | Canal | Canal |
| ⌞ Waterfall, Rapids | Wasserfall, Stromschnellen | Cascada, Rápidos | Chute d'eau, Rapides | Cascata, Rápidos |
| ʯ Strait | Meeresstraße | Estrecho | Détroit | Estreito |
| c Bay, Gulf | Bucht, Golf | Bahía, Golfo | Baie, Golfe | Baía, Golfo |
| ⊜ Lake, Lakes | See, Seen | Lago, Lagos | Lac, Lacs | Lago, Lagos |
| ⁝ Swamp | Sumpf | Pantano | Marais | Pântano |
| ⊓ Ice Features, Glacier | Eis- und Gletscherformen | Accidentes Glaciales | Formes glaciaires | Acidentes glaciares |
| ⊤ Other Hydrographic Features | Andere Hydrographische Objekte | Otros Elementos Hidrográficos | Autres données hydrographiques | Outros acidentes hidrográficos |

| | | | | |
|---|---|---|---|---|
| ✢ Submarine Features | Untermeerische Objekte | Accidentes Submarinos | Formes de relief sous-marin | Acidentes submarinos |
| □ Political Unit | Politische Einheit | Unidad Política | Entité politique | Unidade política |
| ♥ Cultural Institution | Kulturelle Institution | Institución Cultural | Institution culturelle | Instituição cultural |
| ⊥ Historical Site | Historische Stätte | Sitio Histórico | Site historique | Sitio histórico |
| ♦ Recreational Site | Erholungs- und Ferienort | Sitio de Recreo | Centre de loisirs | Area de Lazer |
| ⊠ Airport | Flughafen | Aeropuerto | Aéroport | Aeroporto |
| ■ Military Installation | Militäranlage | Instalación Militar | Installation militaire | Instalação militar |
| ✦ Miscellaneous | Verschiedenes | Misceláneo | Divers | Diversos |

| Name | Page | Lat.°′ | Long.°′ |
|---|---|---|---|
| Sadao | 110 | 6.38 N | 100.26 E |
| Sadarpur, Bngl. | 126 | 23.28 N | 90.02 E |
| Sādarpur, India | 272a | 28.33 N | 77.21 E |
| Sadčikovka | 86 | 53.01 N | 63.27 E |
| Sadda | 120 | 33.42 N | 70.20 E |
| Saddle ≃ | 276 | 40.52 N | 74.07 W |
| Saddleback, Mount ∧ | 168a | 32.58 S | 116.28 E |
| Saddle Brook | 276 | 40.54 N | 74.06 W |
| Saddlebunch Keys II | 220 | 24.37 N | 81.37 W |
| Saddle Lake Indian Reserve ◆[4] | 182 | 54.00 N | 111.40 W |
| Saddle Mountain ∧, Co., U.S. | 200 | 38.50 N | 105.28 W |
| Saddle Mountain ∧, Or., U.S. | 224 | 45.58 N | 123.41 W |
| Saddle Mountains ⋏ | 202 | 46.50 N | 119.55 W |
| Saddle Mountain State Park ♠ | 224 | 45.58 N | 123.41 W |
| Saddle Peak ∧ | 110 | 13.09 N | 93.01 E |
| Saddle River | 276 | 40.54 N | 74.05 W |
| Saddle Rock | 276 | 40.48 N | 73.45 W |
| Saddleworth, Austl. | 168b | 34.05 S | 138.47 E |
| Saddleworth, Eng., U.K. | 262 | 53.33 N | 1.59 W |
| Saddleworth Moor ◆[3] | 262 | 53.33 N | 1.57 W |
| Sa Dec | 110 | 10.18 N | 105.46 E |
| Sadelkow | 54 | 53.36 N | 13.26 E |
| Sādhaura | 124 | 30.23 N | 77.13 E |
| Sādhuhāti | 126 | 23.34 N | 89.01 E |
| Sadieville | 218 | 38.23 N | 84.32 W |
| Sadiola | 150 | 13.53 N | 11.42 W |
| Sādiqābād | 120 | 28.18 N | 70.08 E |
| Sadiya | 120 | 27.50 N | 95.40 E |
| Sa'dīyah, Wādī V | 144 | 20.35 N | 39.38 E |
| Sa'dīyāt, Ra's as- › | 132 | 33.41 N | 35.25 E |
| Sadler Lake ◎ | 184 | 55.17 N | 103.45 W |
| Sado I | 92 | 38.00 N | 138.25 E |
| Sado ≃ | 34 | 38.29 N | 8.55 W |
| Sado-kaikyō ʮ | 92 | 37.50 N | 138.40 E |
| Sadon | 84 | 42.51 N | 44.00 E |
| Sadovoje, Ross. | 80 | 46.56 N | 44.23 E |
| Sadovoje, Ross. | 80 | 47.46 N | 44.30 E |
| Sadovoje Pervoje | 78 | 51.33 N | 40.29 E |
| Sadowara | 92 | 32.02 N | 131.26 E |
| Šādri | 120 | 25.11 N | 73.26 E |
| Šadrina | 89 | 51.33 N | 130.22 E |
| Šadrino | 86 | 55.52 N | 91.06 E |
| Šadrinsk | 86 | 56.05 N | 63.38 E |
| Sadsburyville | 208 | 39.59 N | 75.53 W |
| Sādulpur | 123 | 28.38 N | 75.24 E |
| Sädvaluspen | 24 | 66.24 N | 16.51 E |
| Sæby, Dan. | 26 | 57.20 N | 10.32 E |
| Sæby, Dan. | 41 | 55.33 N | 11.19 E |
| Saegertown | 214 | 41.43 N | 80.09 W |
| Sae Islands II | 164 | 0.45 S | 145.15 E |
| Saeki → Saiki, Nihon | 96 | 32.57 N | 131.54 E |
| Saeki, Nihon | 96 | 34.22 N | 132.11 E |
| Saeki, Nihon | 96 | 34.51 N | 134.06 E |
| Saengil-to I | 98 | 34.19 N | 126.59 E |
| Saerbeck | 52 | 52.10 N | 7.38 E |
| Saerluojia Hu ◎ | 120 | 33.55 N | 86.55 E |
| Særslev, Dan. | 41 | 55.31 N | 10.11 E |
| Særslev, Dan. | 41 | 55.43 N | 11.23 E |
| Saeul | 56 | 49.44 N | 5.59 E |
| Ṣafā, Tulūl aṣ- ∧[1] | 132 | 33.02 N | 37.12 E |
| Safad → Ẕefat | 132 | 32.58 N | 35.30 E |
| Safājah, Jazīrat I | 140 | 26.45 N | 33.59 E |
| Safakulevo | 86 | 54.59 N | 62.33 E |
| Ṣafānīyah | 142 | 28.49 N | 30.48 E |
| Safdar Jang Airport ⊠ | 272a | 28.37 N | 77.13 E |
| Safdar Jang's Tomb ⊥ | 272a | 28.36 N | 77.13 E |
| Safed Koh Range ⋏ | 123 | 33.58 N | 70.25 E |
| Safe Harbor Dam ◆[6] | 208 | 39.59 N | 76.28 W |
| Safenbach ≃ | 61 | 47.06 N | 16.05 E |
| Safety Bay | 168a | 32.18 S | 115.43 E |
| Safety Harbor | 220 | 27.59 N | 82.41 W |
| Säffle | 26 | 59.08 N | 12.56 E |
| Safford | 200 | 32.50 N | 109.42 W |
| Saffron Walden | 42 | 52.01 N | 0.15 E |
| Safi | 148 | 32.20 N | 9.17 W |
| Safi □[4] | 148 | 32.05 N | 9.00 W |
| Safia | 164 | 9.35 S | 148.40 E |
| Ṣafīābād | 128 | 36.45 N | 57.58 E |
| Ṣafīd ≃ | 120 | 36.44 N | 65.38 E |
| Ṣafīd Kūh, Selseleh-ye ⋏ | 128 | 34.30 N | 63.30 E |
| Safidon | 124 | 29.25 N | 76.40 E |
| Safiental V | 58 | 46.40 N | 9.18 E |
| Safioune, Sebkhet ≡ | 148 | 32.16 N | 5.27 E |
| Safipur | 126 | 23.01 N | 90.22 E |
| Ṣāfītā | 130 | 34.49 N | 36.07 E |
| Safonovo, Ross. | 24 | 65.42 N | 47.39 E |
| Safonovo, Ross. | 76 | 55.06 N | 33.15 E |
| Safonovo, Ross. | 82 | 55.33 N | 38.17 E |
| Safrakköyü ◆[8] | 267b | 41.00 N | 28.47 E |
| Safranbolu | 130 | 41.15 N | 32.45 E |
| Ṣaft al-'Inab | 142 | 30.49 N | 30.41 E |
| Ṣaft al-Khammār | 142 | 28.02 N | 30.42 E |
| Ṣaft al-Laban | 273c | 30.02 N | 31.10 E |
| Ṣaft al-Mulūk | 142 | 30.49 N | 30.41 E |
| Ṣaft Rāshīn | 142 | 28.58 N | 30.55 E |
| Ṣaft Turāb | 142 | 30.54 N | 31.07 E |
| Ṣafwān | 128 | 30.07 N | 47.43 E |
| Saga, Kaz. | 86 | 50.23 N | 64.15 E |
| Saga, Kaz. | 86 | 49.25 N | 55.17 E |
| Saga, Nihon | 92 | 33.15 N | 130.18 E |
| Saga, Nihon | 96 | 33.05 N | 133.06 E |
| Saga, Zhg. | 120 | 29.30 N | 85.22 E |
| Saga □[5] | 96 | 33.21 N | 130.28 E |
| Sagaba | 152 | 11.17 S | 23.07 E |
| Sagae | 92 | 38.22 N | 140.17 E |
| Sagaing | 110 | 21.52 N | 95.59 E |
| Sagaing □[8] | 110 | 24.00 N | 95.00 E |
| Sagak, Cape › | 180 | 52.48 N | 169.08 W |
| Šagalaherang | 115a | 6.40 S | 107.39 E |
| Šagalakasa | 80 | 46.54 N | 50.43 E |
| Sagamāthā □[8] | 124 | 27.15 N | 86.45 E |
| Sagami ≃ | 94 | 35.19 N | 139.22 E |
| Sagamihara | 94 | 35.34 N | 139.23 E |
| Sagamihara-daichi ⋏[1] | 268 | 35.27 N | 139.27 E |
| Sagamiko | 94 | 35.37 N | 139.12 E |
| Sagami-ko ◎ | 94 | 35.35 N | 139.16 E |
| Sagami-nada ⊂ | 94 | 35.00 N | 139.30 E |
| Sagami-wan ⊂ | 94 | 35.15 N | 139.25 E |
| Sagamore, Ma., U.S. | 207 | 41.46 N | 70.31 W |
| Sagamore, Pa., U.S. | 214 | 40.46 N | 79.13 W |
| Sagamore Beach | 207 | 41.47 N | 70.31 W |
| Sagamore Hill National Historic Site ⊥ | 276 | 40.53 N | 73.30 W |
| Sagamore Hills | 279a | 41.02 N | 81.26 W |
| Sagan → Żagań | 30 | 51.37 N | 15.19 E |
| Šagan ≃, Kaz. | 86 | 50.37 N | 79.15 E |
| Sagån ≃, Sve. | 40 | 59.35 N | 16.54 E |
| Saganaga Lake ◎ | 190 | 48.14 N | 90.52 W |
| Saganashkee Slough ≃ | 278 | 41.41 N | 87.53 W |
| Saganash Lake ◎ | 190 | 49.04 N | 82.35 W |
| Saganoseki | 96 | 33.15 N | 131.53 E |
| Saganthit Kyun I | 110 | 11.56 N | 98.29 E |
| Sagaon | 272c | 19.12 N | 73.06 E |
| Sāgar, India | 122 | 14.10 N | 75.02 E |
| Sāgar, India | 124 | 23.50 N | 78.43 E |
| Sagara | 94 | 34.41 N | 138.12 E |
| Sagaranten | 115a | 7.13 S | 106.52 E |
| Sagard | 54 | 54.31 N | 13.33 E |
| Sāgardīghi | 126 | 24.17 N | 88.06 E |
| Sagaredžo | 84 | 41.44 N | 45.20 E |
| Sāgar Island I | 126 | 21.43 N | 88.06 E |
| Sagarmatha → Everest, Mount ∧ | 124 | 27.59 N | 86.56 E |
| Sagarmatha National Park ♠ | 124 | 27.50 N | 86.45 E |
| Sāgar Plateau ⋏[1] | 124 | 23.30 N | 78.30 E |
| Sagavanirktok ≃ | 180 | 70.20 N | 148.00 W |
| Sagay | 116 | 10.57 N | 123.25 E |
| Sage, Mount ∧ | 240m | 18.25 N | 64.39 W |
| Sage Creek ≃, N.A. | 202 | 48.58 N | 110.06 W |
| Sage Creek ≃, U.S. | 202 | 44.50 N | 108.26 W |
| Sage Creek ≃, Mt., U.S. | 202 | 47.16 N | 109.43 W |
| Sage Creek ≃, Mt., U.S. | 202 | 48.20 N | 110.03 W |
| Sagemace Bay ⊂ | 184 | 51.49 N | 100.03 W |
| Sagerton | 196 | 33.05 N | 99.58 W |
| Saggaubach ≃ | 61 | 46.43 N | 15.24 E |
| Sag Harbor | 207 | 40.59 N | 72.17 W |
| Ṣaghbīn | 132 | 33.37 N | 35.42 E |
| Ṣaghīr, Al-Baḥr aṣ- ≡ | 142 | 31.09 N | 31.56 E |
| Sagil | 86 | 50.20 N | 91.40 E |
| Saginaw, Mi., U.S. | 190 | 43.25 N | 83.56 W |
| Saginaw, Tx., U.S. | 222 | 32.52 N | 97.22 W |
| Saginaw ≃ | 190 | 43.39 N | 83.51 W |
| Saginaw Bay ⊂ | 190 | 43.50 N | 83.40 W |
| Sagiz, Kaz. | 80 | 47.31 N | 53.16 E |
| Sagiz, Kaz. | 86 | 48.12 N | 54.56 E |
| Sağkaya | 130 | 37.11 N | 35.41 E |
| Sagleipie | 150 | 7.00 N | 8.52 W |
| Saglek Bay ⊂ | 176 | 58.35 N | 63.00 W |
| Šaglyteniz, ozero ◎ | 86 | 54.08 N | 69.52 E |
| Šagonar | 86 | 51.32 N | 92.48 E |
| Sagrado | 64 | 45.52 N | 13.29 E |
| Sagres | 34 | 37.00 N | 8.56 W |
| Sag Sag | 164 | 5.35 S | 148.20 E |
| Sagsaj | 86 | 48.54 N | 89.37 E |
| Sagsajn ≃ | 102 | 44.50 N | 96.26 E |
| Sagu, Indon. | 112 | 8.15 S | 123.13 E |
| Şagu, Rom. | 38 | 46.03 N | 21.17 E |
| Saguache | 200 | 38.05 N | 106.05 W |
| Saguache Creek ≃ | 200 | 37.52 N | 105.51 W |
| Sagua de Tánamo | 240p | 20.35 N | 75.14 W |
| Sagua la Chica ≃ | 240p | 22.45 N | 79.39 W |
| Sagua la Grande | 240p | 22.49 N | 80.05 W |
| Saguaro National Park ♠ | 200 | 32.12 N | 110.38 W |
| Saguenay ≃ | 176 | 48.08 N | 69.44 W |
| Saguna | 272b | 22.59 N | 88.29 E |
| Sagunay Lake | 216 | 41.43 N | 86.34 W |
| Sagunt | 34 | 39.41 N | 0.16 W |
| Saguny | 78 | 50.36 N | 39.43 E |
| Sagutjevo | 76 | 52.28 N | 33.28 E |
| Sāgwāra | 120 | 23.41 N | 74.01 E |
| Sagy | 261 | 49.03 N | 1.57 E |
| Sa'gya | 120 | 28.55 N | 88.05 E |
| Sagyndyk, mys › | 84 | 44.02 N | 50.52 E |
| Sagyz ≃ | 86 | 47.32 N | 53.20 E |
| Sah | 150 | 15.38 N | 4.03 W |
| Saḥāb | 132 | 31.53 N | 36.00 E |
| Sahaba | 140 | 18.55 N | 30.28 E |
| Sahagún, Col. | 246 | 8.57 N | 75.27 W |
| Sahagún, Esp. | 34 | 42.22 N | 5.02 W |
| Saḥam | 132 | 32.42 N | 35.47 E |
| Saḥam al-Jawlān | 132 | 32.46 N | 35.56 E |
| Sahana Ambodipont | 157b | 14.37 S | 50.11 E |
| Sahand, Kūh-e ∧ | 128 | 37.44 N | 46.27 E |
| Sahara ◆[2] | 10 | 26.00 N | 13.00 E |
| Sahāranpur | 124 | 29.58 N | 77.33 E |
| Sahara Occidental → Western Sahara □[2] | 148 | 24.30 N | 13.00 W |
| Sahara Occidentale → Western Sahara □[2] | 148 | 24.30 N | 13.00 W |
| Saharsa | 124 | 25.53 N | 86.36 E |
| Sahasinaka | 157b | 21.49 S | 47.49 E |
| Sahasrail | 126 | 23.19 N | 89.43 E |
| Sahaswān | 124 | 28.05 N | 78.45 E |
| Şahbuz | 84 | 39.25 N | 45.34 E |
| Sahel ◆[1] | 134 | 17.00 N | 2.00 E |
| Sahel, Canal du ≋ | 150 | 13.44 N | 6.05 W |
| Sahel, Oued ≃ | 34 | 36.26 N | 4.33 E |
| Sāhibabad | 272a | 28.40 N | 77.22 E |
| Sahibābad ◆[8] | 272a | 28.45 N | 77.05 E |
| Sāhibganj | 124 | 25.15 N | 87.39 E |
| Sāhibi ≃ | 124 | 28.29 N | 76.44 E |
| Şahin | 130 | 41.01 N | 26.50 E |
| Sāhīwāl, Pāk. | 123 | 30.40 N | 73.06 E |
| Sāhīwāl, Pāk. | 123 | 31.58 N | 72.20 E |
| Sahlenburg | 52 | 53.52 N | 8.38 E |
| Ṣaḥneh | 128 | 34.29 N | 47.41 E |
| Ṣaḥrā', Bi'r ⊤[4] | 140 | 22.52 N | 28.37 E |
| Ṣahrajat al-Kubrā wa Kafr Jirjis Yūsuf | 142 | 30.38 N | 31.17 E |
| Sahtlam | 224 | 48.48 N | 123.54 W |
| Sahuaripa | 232 | 29.03 N | 109.14 W |
| Sahuarita | 200 | 31.57 N | 110.58 W |
| Sahuayo de José María Morelos | 234 | 20.04 N | 102.43 W |
| Sahul Shelf ✚[4] | 14 | 12.30 S | 125.00 E |
| Sahunivka | 78 | 49.17 N | 32.23 E |
| Sa Huynh | 110 | 14.40 N | 109.04 E |
| Ṣahwat al-Qamḥ | 132 | 32.36 N | 36.23 E |
| Šahy | 30 | 48.05 N | 18.57 E |
| Saï | 150 | 13.50 N | 5.00 W |
| Sai ≃, India | 124 | 25.39 N | 82.47 E |
| Sai ≃, Nihon | 94 | 36.36 N | 136.35 E |
| Sai ≃, Nihon | 94 | 36.37 N | 138.14 E |
| Saibai Island I | 164 | 9.24 S | 142.40 E |
| Sai Buri | 110 | 6.42 N | 101.37 E |
| Sai Buri ≃ | 110 | 6.43 N | 101.39 E |
| Saïda | 148 | 34.50 N | 0.09 E |
| Saidābād, Bngl. | 126 | 24.18 N | 89.43 E |
| Sa'īdābād, Īrān | 267d | 35.40 N | 51.11 E |
| Saidaiji | 96 | 34.39 N | 134.02 E |
| Saïdia | 148 | 35.04 N | 2.15 W |
| Sa'īdīyeh | 128 | 36.26 N | 48.48 E |
| Saido | 268 | 35.52 N | 139.41 E |
| Saidor | 164 | 5.35 S | 146.30 E |
| Saidpur, Bngl. | 124 | 25.47 N | 88.54 E |
| Saidpur, India | 124 | 25.33 N | 83.11 E |
| Saidu | 123 | 34.45 N | 72.21 E |
| Saigawa | 96 | 33.39 N | 130.57 E |
| Saignelégier | 58 | 47.15 N | 7.00 E |
| Saignon | 62 | 43.52 N | 5.26 E |
| Saigō | 92 | 36.12 N | 133.20 E |
| Saigon → Thanh Pho Ho Chi Minh | 269c | 10.45 N | 106.40 E |
| Sai Gon ≃ | 269c | 10.45 N | 106.45 E |
| Saihaku | 96 | 35.20 N | 133.20 E |
| Saihan Toroi | 102 | 41.41 N | 100.26 E |
| Saijō, Nihon | 96 | 33.55 N | 133.11 E |
| Saijō, Nihon | 96 | 34.56 N | 133.07 E |
| Saijō ≃ | 96 | 34.48 N | 132.51 E |
| Saikai-kokuritsu-kōen ♠ | 92 | 33.12 N | 129.22 E |
| Sai Keng | 271d | 22.26 N | 114.16 E |
| Saiki | 96 | 32.57 N | 131.54 E |
| Saiki-wan ⊂ | 96 | 33.00 N | 131.58 E |
| Sai Kung | 271d | 22.23 N | 114.15 E |
| Saileati | 85 | 38.57 N | 74.45 E |
| Sailkupa | 126 | 23.41 N | 89.15 E |
| Saillans | 62 | 44.42 N | 5.11 E |
| Sailly | 261 | 49.02 N | 1.48 E |
| Sailmouille, Ruisseau ≃ | 261 | 48.37 N | 2.17 E |
| Sailolof | 164 | 1.15 S | 130.46 E |
| Sailor Creek ≃ | 202 | 42.56 N | 115.29 W |
| Sail-sous-Couzan | 62 | 45.44 N | 3.57 E |
| Šaim | 86 | 60.21 N | 64.14 E |
| Saima | 98 | 41.00 N | 124.14 E |
| Saimaa ◎ | 26 | 61.15 N | 28.15 E |
| Saimaa Canal ≋ | 26 | 61.05 N | 28.18 E |
| Saimbeyli | 130 | 38.00 N | 36.06 E |
| Saín Alto | 234 | 23.35 N | 103.15 W |
| Saindak | 128 | 29.17 N | 61.34 E |
| Şā'īn Dezh | 128 | 36.40 N | 46.33 E |
| Sainghin-en-Weppes | 50 | 50.33 N | 2.54 E |
| Sainjang | 98 | 39.15 N | 125.51 E |
| Sainō-ha'iji ⊥ | 96 | 35.29 N | 133.39 E |
| Sains-du-Nord | 50 | 50.06 N | 4.00 E |
| Sains-en-Gohelle | 50 | 50.27 N | 2.41 E |
| Sains-Richaumont | 50 | 49.49 N | 3.42 E |
| Saint Abb's Head › | 46 | 55.54 N | 2.09 W |
| Sainte-Adèle | 206 | 45.57 N | 74.07 W |
| Sainte-Adresse | 50 | 49.30 N | 0.05 E |
| Saint-Adrien | 206 | 45.49 N | 71.43 W |
| Saint-Affrique | 32 | 43.57 N | 2.53 E |
| Saint-Agapit | 206 | 46.34 N | 71.27 W |
| Saint Agatha | 212 | 43.26 N | 80.36 W |
| Sainte-Agathe, Mb., Can. | 184 | 49.34 N | 97.10 W |
| Sainte-Agathe, Fr. | 62 | 45.49 N | 3.37 E |
| Sainte-Agathe [-de-Lotbinière] | 206 | 46.23 N | 71.24 W |
| Sainte-Agathe-des-Monts | 206 | 46.03 N | 74.17 W |
| Sainte-Agnès, Fr. | 62 | 43.48 N | 7.28 E |
| Saint Agnes, Eng., U.K. | 42 | 50.18 N | 5.13 W |
| Saint Agnes I | 42a | 49.54 N | 6.20 W |
| Saint-Agrève | 62 | 45.01 N | 4.24 E |
| Saint-Aignan | 50 | 47.16 N | 1.23 E |
| Saint-Aimé (Massueville) | 206 | 45.55 N | 72.56 W |
| Saint Albans, Austl. | 169 | 37.44 S | 144.48 E |
| Saint Albans, Austl. | 170 | 33.17 S | 150.59 E |
| Saint Alban's, Nf., Can. | 186 | 47.52 N | 55.51 W |
| Saint Albans, Eng., U.K. | 42 | 51.46 N | 0.21 W |
| Saint Albans, Mo., U.S. | 219 | 38.35 N | 90.46 W |
| Saint Albans, Vt., U.S. | 188 | 44.48 N | 73.05 W |
| Saint Albans, W.V., U.S. | 188 | 38.23 N | 81.50 W |
| Saint Albans □[8] | 260 | 51.45 N | 0.20 W |
| Saint Albans ◆[8] | 276 | 40.42 N | 73.46 W |
| Saint Albans, Cape › | 168b | 35.49 S | 138.07 E |
| Saint Albans Cathedral ✝[1] | 260 | 51.45 N | 0.20 W |
| Saint Albert, Ab., Can. | 182 | 53.38 N | 113.38 W |
| Saint-Albert, P.Q., Can. | 206 | 46.00 N | 72.05 W |
| Saint Aldhelm's Head › | 42 | 50.34 N | 2.04 W |
| Saint-Alexandre-de-Kamouraska | 186 | 47.41 N | 69.38 W |
| Saint-Alexis-des-Monts | 206 | 46.28 N | 73.08 W |
| Saint-Amable | 275a | 45.39 N | 73.18 W |
| Saint-Amand | 56 | 48.49 N | 4.36 E |
| Saint-Amand-en-Puisaye | 50 | 47.31 N | 3.04 E |
| Saint-Amand-les-Eaux | 50 | 50.26 N | 3.26 E |
| Saint-Amand-Longpré | 50 | 47.41 N | 1.01 E |
| Saint-Amand-Montrond | 32 | 46.44 N | 2.30 E |
| Saint-Amant-Roche-Savine | 62 | 45.34 N | 3.38 E |
| Saint-Amarin | 58 | 47.53 N | 7.01 E |
| Saint-Ambroix | 62 | 44.15 N | 4.11 E |
| Sainte-Amélie | 184 | 50.59 N | 99.21 W |
| Saint-Amour | 58 | 46.26 N | 5.21 E |
| Saint-André | 157c | 20.57 S | 55.39 E |
| Saint-André, Cap › | 157b | 16.11 S | 44.27 E |
| Saint-André, Ruisseau ≃ | 275a | 45.22 N | 73.29 W |
| Saint-André-Avellin | 206 | 45.43 N | 75.03 W |
| Saint-André-de-l'Eure | 50 | 48.54 N | 1.17 E |
| Saint-André-de-Valborgne | 62 | 44.09 N | 3.41 E |
| St.-André-Est | 206 | 45.34 N | 74.20 W |
| Saint-André-les-Alpes | 62 | 43.58 N | 6.30 E |
| Saint-André-les-Vergers | 50 | 48.17 N | 4.03 E |
| Saint Andrew | 241g | 13.15 N | 59.33 W |
| Saint Andrew, Mount ∧ | 241h | 13.11 N | 61.13 W |
| Saint Andrew Lakes ◎ | 212 | 44.36 N | 76.40 W |
| Saint Andrews, N.B., Can. | 186 | 45.05 N | 67.03 W |
| Saint Andrews, Scot., U.K. | 46 | 56.20 N | 2.48 W |
| Saint Andrews, S.C., U.S. | 192 | 32.46 N | 79.59 W |
| Saint Andrews Bay ⊂ | 46 | 56.22 N | 2.50 W |
| Saint Andrew's Cathedral ✝[1] | 271c | 1.18 N | 103.51 E |
| Saint Andrews Channel ʮ | 186 | 46.03 N | 60.38 W |
| Saint Ann | 219 | 38.43 N | 90.22 W |
| Sainte-Anne, Guad. | 241o | 16.14 N | 61.23 W |
| Saint Anne, Guernsey | 43b | 49.42 N | 2.12 W |
| Sainte-Anne, Mart. | 240e | 14.26 N | 60.53 W |
| Saint Anne, Il., U.S. | 216 | 41.01 N | 87.42 W |
| Sainte-Anne ≃ | 206 | 46.33 N | 72.12 W |
| Saint Anne, Cathedral of ✝[1] | 273b | 4.18 S | 15.19 E |
| Sainte Anne, Lac ◎, Ab., Can. | 182 | 53.43 N | 114.27 W |
| Sainte-Anne, Lac ◎, P.Q., Can. | 186 | 50.05 N | 67.50 W |
| Sainte-Anne-de-Beaupré | 186 | 47.02 N | 70.56 W |
| Sainte-Anne-de-Bellevue | 275a | 45.24 N | 73.57 W |
| Sainte-Anne-de-la-Pérade | 206 | 46.35 N | 72.12 W |
| Sainte-Anne-de-Madawaska | 186 | 47.15 N | 68.02 W |
| Sainte-Anne-des-Chênes | 184 | 49.40 N | 96.40 W |
| Sainte-Anne-des-Monts | 186 | 49.08 N | 66.30 W |
| Sainte-Anne-des-Plaines | 206 | 46.46 N | 73.48 W |
| Saint Anne of the Congo ✝[1] | 273b | 4.16 S | 15.17 E |
| Saint Anne's | 44 | 53.45 N | 3.02 W |
| Saint Ann's Bay | 241q | 18.26 N | 77.08 W |
| Saint Anns Bay ⊂ | 186 | 46.20 N | 60.30 W |
| Saint Ann's Head › | 42 | 51.41 N | 5.10 W |
| Saint-Anselme | 186 | 46.37 N | 70.58 W |
| Saint Ansgar | 190 | 43.22 N | 92.55 W |
| Saint-Anthème | 62 | 45.31 N | 3.55 E |
| Saint Anthony, N.B., Can. | 186 | 46.22 N | 64.45 W |
| Saint Anthony, Nf., Can. | 186 | 51.22 N | 55.35 W |
| Saint Anthony, Id., U.S. | 202 | 43.57 N | 111.40 W |
| Saint-Antoine, P.Q., Can. | 206 | 45.46 N | 73.59 W |
| Saint-Antoine, Fr. | 62 | 45.10 N | 5.13 E |
| Saint-Antonin | 32 | 44.09 N | 1.45 E |
| Saint-Apollinaire (Francoeur) | 206 | 46.37 N | 71.31 W |
| Saint Arnaud, Austl. | 166 | 36.37 S | 143.15 E |
| Saint Arnaud, N.Z. | 172 | 41.48 S | 172.50 E |
| Saint-Arnoult, Forêt de ♠ | 261 | 48.35 N | 1.55 E |
| Saint-Arnoult-en-Yvelines | 50 | 48.34 N | 1.56 E |
| Saint Arvans | 42 | 51.40 N | 2.41 W |
| Saint Asaph | 44 | 53.16 N | 3.26 W |
| Saint-Astier | 32 | 45.09 N | 0.32 E |
| Saint Athan | 42 | 51.24 N | 3.25 W |
| Saint-Auban | 62 | 43.51 N | 6.44 E |
| Saint-Aubert, Mont ∧[2] | 50 | 50.39 N | 3.24 E |
| Saint Aubert Island I | 219 | 38.40 N | 91.52 W |
| Saint-Aubin, Fr. | 50 | 49.53 N | 0.53 E |
| Saint-Aubin, Fr. | 58 | 47.02 N | 5.20 E |
| Saint Aubin, Jersey | 43b | 49.11 N | 2.10 W |
| Saint-Aubin, Schw. | 58 | 46.54 N | 6.47 E |
| Saint-Aubin-lès-Elbeuf | 50 | 49.18 N | 1.01 E |
| Saint-Aubin-sur-Aire | 58 | 48.42 N | 5.27 E |
| Saint-Augustin | 157b | 23.33 S | 43.46 E |
| Saint-Augustin ≃ | 176 | 51.14 N | 58.41 W |
| Saint-Augustin-Deux-Montagnes | 275a | 45.38 N | 73.59 W |
| Saint Augustine | 192 | 29.53 N | 81.18 W |
| Saint-Augustin Nord-Ouest ≃ | 186 | 51.16 N | 58.42 W |
| Saint-Augustin-Saguenay | 186 | 51.14 N | 58.39 W |
| Saint-Aulaye | 32 | 45.12 N | 0.08 E |
| Saint Austell | 42 | 50.20 N | 4.48 W |
| Saint-Avertin | 50 | 47.22 N | 0.44 E |
| Saint-Avold | 56 | 49.06 N | 6.42 E |
| Saint-Ay | 50 | 47.51 N | 1.45 E |
| Saint-Aygulf | 62 | 43.23 N | 6.44 E |
| Saint Barbe | 186 | 51.12 N | 56.46 W |
| Saint Barnabas Chapel ✝[1] | 174c | 29.02 S | 167.55 E |
| Saint-Barthélemy I | 238 | 17.54 N | 62.50 W |
| Saint-Basile | 186 | 47.21 N | 68.14 W |
| Saint-Basile-de-Portneuf | 206 | 46.45 N | 71.49 W |
| Saint-Basile-le-Grand | 206 | 45.32 N | 73.17 W |
| Saint Bathans, Mount ∧ | 172 | 44.44 S | 169.46 E |
| Sainte-Baume, Chaîne de la ⋏ | 62 | 43.20 N | 5.45 E |
| Saint-Béat | 32 | 42.55 N | 0.42 E |
| Saint Bees | 44 | 54.30 N | 3.37 W |
| Saint Bees Head › | 44 | 54.32 N | 3.38 W |
| Saint Benedict | 214 | 40.38 N | 78.44 W |
| Saint-Benoît, Fr. | 261 | 48.40 N | 1.55 E |
| Saint-Benoît, Réu. | 157c | 21.02 S | 55.43 E |
| Saint-Benoît-du-Sault | 32 | 46.27 N | 1.23 E |
| Saint-Benoît-en-Woëvre | 56 | 48.59 N | 5.47 E |
| Saint Bernard | 218 | 39.10 N | 84.29 W |
| Saint-Bernard, Île I | 275a | 45.23 N | 73.45 W |
| Saint-Bernard-de-Dorchester | 206 | 46.30 N | 71.08 W |
| Saint-Béron | 62 | 45.30 N | 5.43 E |
| Saint-Blaise, P.Q., Can. | 206 | 45.13 N | 73.17 W |
| Saint-Blaise, Schw. | 58 | 47.01 N | 6.59 E |
| Saint-Blaise-la-Roche | 58 | 48.24 N | 7.10 E |
| Saint Blaize, Cape › | 158 | 34.11 S | 22.10 E |
| Saint Blazey | 42 | 50.22 N | 4.43 W |
| Saint-Blin | 58 | 48.16 N | 5.25 E |
| Saint-Bonaventure, P.Q., Can. | 206 | 45.58 N | 72.41 W |
| Saint Bonaventure, N.Y., U.S. | 210 | 42.05 N | 78.28 W |
| Saint-Boniface-de-Shawinigan | 206 | 46.30 N | 72.49 W |
| Saint-Bonnet | 62 | 44.41 N | 6.05 E |
| Saint-Bonnet-de-Joux | 58 | 46.29 N | 4.27 E |
| Saint-Bonnet-le-Château | 62 | 45.25 N | 4.04 E |
| Saint-Bonnet-le-Froid | 62 | 45.09 N | 4.27 E |
| Saint Boswells | 46 | 55.34 N | 2.39 W |
| Saint Brendan's | 186 | 48.52 N | 53.40 W |
| Saint-Brice-sous-Forêt | 261 | 49.00 N | 2.21 E |
| Saint Bride, Mount ∧ | 182 | 51.30 N | 115.57 W |
| Saint Bride's | 186 | 46.55 N | 54.10 W |
| Saint Brides Bay ⊂ | 42 | 51.48 N | 5.15 W |
| Saint Bride's Major | 42 | 51.28 N | 3.38 W |
| Saint-Brieuc | 32 | 48.31 N | 2.47 W |
| Saint-Brieux | 184 | 52.38 N | 104.52 W |
| Saint-Broing-les-Moines | 58 | 47.41 N | 4.50 E |
| Saint-Bruno | 206 | 45.32 N | 73.21 W |
| Saint-Bruno, Mont ∧[2] | 275a | 45.33 N | 73.19 W |
| Saint-Calais | 50 | 47.55 N | 0.45 E |
| Saint-Calixte-de-Kilkenny | 206 | 45.57 N | 73.51 W |
| Saint-Cannat | 62 | 43.37 N | 5.18 E |
| Saint-Casimir | 206 | 46.40 N | 72.08 W |
| Saint-Cassien, Lac de ◎[1] | 62 | 43.35 N | 6.48 E |
| Saint Catharines | 212 | 43.10 N | 79.15 W |
| Saint Catharines Airport ⊠ | 284a | 43.11 N | 79.10 W |
| Saint Catherine | 220 | 28.37 N | 82.08 W |
| Saint Catherine, Monastery of → Qiddīsah Kātrīnā, Dayr al- ✝[1] | 140 | 28.29 N | 34.01 E |
| Saint Catherine, Mount ∧ | 241k | 12.10 N | 61.40 W |
| Sainte-Catherine-de-Fierbois | 50 | 47.09 N | 0.39 E |
| Saint Catherines Island I | 192 | 31.38 N | 81.10 W |
| Saint Catherine's Point › | 42 | 50.34 N | 1.15 W |
| Saint-Célestin (Annaville) | 206 | 46.13 N | 72.26 W |
| Saint-Céré | 32 | 44.52 N | 1.53 E |
| Saint-Cergue | 58 | 46.27 N | 6.09 E |
| Saint-Césaire | 206 | 45.25 N | 73.00 W |
| Saint-Cézaire-sur-Siagne | 62 | 43.39 N | 6.48 E |
| Saint-Chamas | 62 | 43.33 N | 5.02 E |
| Saint-Chamond | 62 | 45.28 N | 4.30 E |
| Saint-Chaptes | 62 | 43.58 N | 4.17 E |
| Saint Charles, Ar., U.S. | 194 | 34.22 N | 91.08 W |
| Saint Charles, Id., U.S. | 202 | 42.06 N | 111.23 W |
| Saint Charles, Il., U.S. | 216 | 41.54 N | 88.18 W |
| Saint Charles, Md., U.S. | 208 | 38.36 N | 76.56 W |
| Saint Charles, Mi., U.S. | 190 | 43.17 N | 84.08 W |
| Saint Charles, Mn., U.S. | 190 | 43.58 N | 92.03 W |
| Saint Charles, Mo., U.S. | 219 | 38.47 N | 90.28 W |
| Saint Charles □[6] | 219 | 38.47 N | 90.43 W |
| Saint-Charles ≃ | 275a | 45.40 N | 73.27 W |
| Saint-Charles, Lac ◎ | 206 | 46.55 N | 71.23 W |
| Saint-Charles-de-Drummond | 206 | 45.54 N | 72.28 W |
| Saint Charles Mesa | 198 | 38.15 N | 104.32 W |
| Saint-Charles-sur-Richelieu | 206 | 45.41 N | 73.11 W |
| Saint-Chef | 62 | 45.38 N | 5.22 E |
| Saint-Chély-d'Apcher | 32 | 44.48 N | 3.17 E |
| Saint-Chéron | 261 | 48.33 N | 2.07 E |
| Saint-Christophe-en-Bazelle | 50 | 47.11 N | 1.43 E |
| Saint-Christophe-Nevis → Saint Kitts and Nevis □[1] | 238 | 17.20 N | 62.45 W |
| Saint Christopher (Saint Kitts) I | 238 | 17.20 N | 62.45 W |
| Saint Christopher-Nevis → Saint Kitts y Nevis □[1] | 238 | 17.20 N | 62.45 W |
| Saint-Chrysostome | 206 | 45.06 N | 73.46 W |
| Saint-Ciers-sur-Gironde | 32 | 45.18 N | 0.37 W |
| Saint Clair, Mi., U.S. | 214 | 42.48 N | 82.29 W |
| Saint Clair, Mo., U.S. | 219 | 38.20 N | 90.58 W |
| Saint Clair, Pa., U.S. | 208 | 40.43 N | 76.11 W |
| Saint Clair, Pa., U.S. | 279b | 40.16 N | 79.33 W |
| Saint Clair □[6], Il., U.S. | 219 | 38.31 N | 90.00 W |
| Saint Clair □[6], Mi., U.S. | 214 | 42.50 N | 82.42 W |
| Saint Clair ≃ | 214 | 42.37 N | 82.31 W |
| Saint Clair, Lake ◎ | 214 | 42.25 N | 82.41 W |
| Saint Clair Beach | 281 | 42.19 N | 82.51 W |
| Saint Clair Flats | 214 | 42.32 N | 82.37 W |
| Saint Clair Flats ≚ | 281 | 42.35 N | 82.36 W |
| Saint Clair Flats Canal ≋ | 214 | 42.20 N | 82.58 W |
| Saint Clair Flats State Wildlife Area ◆[4] | 281 | 42.36 N | 82.40 W |
| Saint Clair Haven | 214 | 42.34 N | 82.47 W |
| Saint Clair Shores | 214 | 42.29 N | 82.53 W |
| Saint-Clair-sur-Epte | 50 | 49.12 N | 1.41 E |
| Saint Clairsville, Oh., U.S. | 214 | 40.04 N | 80.54 W |
| Saint Clairsville, Pa., U.S. | 214 | 40.09 N | 78.31 W |
| Saint Clair Tunnel ◆[5] | 214 | 42.57 N | 82.25 W |
| Saint-Claud | 32 | 45.53 N | 0.23 E |
| Saint-Claude, Mb., Can. | 184 | 49.40 N | 98.22 W |
| Saint-Claude, Fr. | 58 | 46.23 N | 5.52 E |
| Saint-Claude, Guad. | 241o | 16.02 N | 61.42 W |
| Saint-Claude, Ruisseau ≃ | 275a | 45.25 N | 73.28 W |
| Saint Clears | 42 | 51.50 N | 4.30 W |
| Saint-Clément | 58 | 48.32 N | 6.36 E |
| Saint Clements | 212 | 43.31 N | 80.39 W |
| Saint Clements Bay ⊂ | 208 | 38.17 N | 76.42 W |
| Sainte-Clothilde | 206 | 45.59 N | 72.14 W |
| Sainte-Clotilde-de-Châteauguay | 206 | 45.10 N | 73.41 W |
| Saint-Cloud, Fr. | 50 | 48.50 N | 2.11 E |
| Saint Cloud, Fl., U.S. | 220 | 28.14 N | 81.16 W |
| Saint Cloud, Mn., U.S. | 190 | 45.33 N | 94.09 W |
| Saint-Cloud, Parc de ♠ | 261 | 48.50 N | 2.13 E |
| Saint-Colomban-des-Villards | 62 | 45.18 N | 6.14 E |
| Sainte-Colombe | 58 | 47.52 N | 4.32 E |
| Saint Columb Major | 42 | 50.26 N | 4.56 W |
| Saint Combs | 46 | 57.39 N | 1.54 W |
| Saint-Constant | 206 | 45.22 N | 73.37 W |
| Saint-Cosme-en-Vairais | 50 | 48.16 N | 0.28 E |
| Sainte-Croix, P.Q., Can. | 206 | 46.38 N | 71.44 W |
| Sainte-Croix, Schw. | 58 | 46.49 N | 6.31 E |
| Saint Croix I | 241n | 17.45 N | 64.45 W |
| Saint Croix ≃, N.A. | 186 | 45.10 N | 67.10 W |
| Saint Croix ≃, U.S. | 190 | 44.45 N | 92.49 W |
| Sainte-Croix, Barrage de ◆[6] | 62 | 43.45 N | 6.08 E |
| Sainte-Croix-aux-Mines | 58 | 48.16 N | 7.13 E |
| Saint Croix Falls | 190 | 45.24 N | 92.38 W |
| Saint Croix Island I | 158 | 33.48 S | 25.45 E |
| Saint Croix Island National Monument ♠ | 188 | 45.08 N | 67.08 W |
| Saint Croix National Scenic Riverway ♠ | 190 | 46.00 N | 92.25 W |
| Saint Croix State Park ♠ | 190 | 46.00 N | 92.40 W |
| Sainte-Croix-Vallée-Francaise | 62 | 44.11 N | 3.44 E |
| Saint-Cuthbert | 206 | 46.09 N | 73.14 W |
| Saint-Cyprien | 32 | 44.52 N | 1.02 E |
| Saint-Cyrille-de-Wendover | 206 | 45.56 N | 72.26 W |
| Saint-Cyr-l'École | 50 | 48.48 N | 2.04 E |
| Saint-Cyr-l'École, Aérodrome de ⊠ | 261 | 48.49 N | 2.04 E |
| Saint Cyr Range ⋏ | 180 | 61.10 N | 131.10 W |
| Sainte-Cyr-sous-Dourdan | 261 | 48.34 N | 2.02 E |
| Saint-Cyr-sur-Loire | 50 | 47.24 N | 0.40 E |
| Saint-Cyr-sur-Mer | 62 | 43.11 N | 5.43 E |
| Saint-Dalmas-de-Tende | 62 | 44.03 N | 7.35 E |
| Saint-Damien-de-Brandon | 206 | 46.20 N | 73.29 W |
| Saint David, Az., U.S. | 200 | 31.54 N | 110.12 W |
| Saint David, Il., U.S. | 190 | 40.29 N | 90.02 W |
| Saint David's, Nf., Can. | 186 | 48.12 N | 58.52 W |
| Saint Davids, On., Can. | 284a | 43.10 N | 79.06 W |
| Saint David's, Wales, U.K. | 42 | 51.54 N | 5.16 W |
| Saint Davids, Pa., U.S. | 285 | 40.02 N | 75.22 W |
| Saint David's Cathedral ✝[1] | 42 | 51.54 N | 5.16 W |
| Saint David's Head › | 42 | 51.55 N | 5.19 W |
| Saint David's Island I | 240a | 32.22 N | 64.39 W |
| Saint Day | 42 | 50.14 N | 5.11 W |
| Saint-Denis, Fr. | 50 | 48.56 N | 2.22 E |
| Saint-Denis, Réu. | 157c | 20.52 S | 55.28 E |
| Saint-Denis, Basilique ✝[1] | 261 | 48.56 N | 2.22 E |
| Saint-Denis-de-l'Hôtel | 50 | 47.52 N | 2.07 E |
| Saint-Denis-en-Bugey | 58 | 45.57 N | 5.20 E |
| Saint-Denis-Rivière-Richelieu | 206 | 45.47 N | 73.09 W |
| Saint Dennis | 42 | 50.23 N | 4.53 W |
| Saint-Didier-en-Velay | 62 | 45.18 N | 4.17 E |
| Saint-Didier-les-Bains | 62 | 44.00 N | 5.07 E |
| Saint-Dié | 58 | 48.17 N | 6.57 E |
| Saint-Disdier | 62 | 44.44 N | 5.54 E |
| Saint-Dizier | 58 | 48.38 N | 4.57 E |
| Saint Dogmaels | 42 | 52.05 N | 4.40 W |
| Saint-Donat-de-Montcalm | 206 | 46.19 N | 74.13 W |
| Saint-Donat-sur-l'Herbasse | 62 | 45.07 N | 5.00 E |
| Sainte-Dorothée ◆[8] | 275a | 45.32 N | 73.49 W |
| Saint-Dyé-sur-Loire | 50 | 47.39 N | 1.29 E |
| Saint-Édouard-de-Maskinongé | 206 | 46.20 N | 73.09 W |
| Saint Edward | 198 | 41.34 N | 97.52 W |
| Saint-Égrève | 62 | 45.14 N | 5.41 E |
| Saint Eleanor's | 186 | 46.25 N | 63.49 W |
| Saint Elias, Cape › | 180 | 59.52 N | 144.30 W |
| Saint Elias, Mount ∧ | 180 | 60.18 N | 140.55 W |
| Saint Elias Mountains ⋏ | 180 | 60.30 N | 139.30 W |
| Saint-Élie | 250 | 4.50 N | 53.17 W |
| Saint Elmo | 219 | 39.01 N | 88.50 W |
| Saint-Éloi | 186 | 48.02 N | 69.14 W |
| Saint-Émile-de-Montcalm | 206 | 46.06 N | 74.00 W |
| Saint-Émile-de-Québec | 206 | 46.52 N | 71.20 W |
| Saint-Émile-de-Suffolk | 206 | 45.56 N | 74.55 W |
| Sainte-Enimie | 32 | 44.22 N | 3.26 E |
| Saint-Épain | 50 | 47.08 N | 0.32 E |
| Saint-Esprit ≃ | 206 | 45.52 N | 73.27 W |
| Saint-Étienne | 62 | 45.26 N | 4.24 E |
| Saint-Étienne-de-Lugdarès | 62 | 44.39 N | 3.57 E |
| Saint-Étienne-de-Saint-Geoirs | 62 | 45.20 N | 5.21 E |
| Saint-Étienne-des-Grès | 206 | 46.26 N | 72.46 W |
| Saint-Étienne-de-Tinée | 62 | 44.15 N | 6.55 E |
| Saint-Étienne-du-Rouvray | 50 | 49.23 N | 1.06 E |
| Saint-Étienne-en-Dévoluy | 62 | 44.42 N | 5.56 E |
| Saint-Étienne-le-Laus | 62 | 44.30 N | 6.10 E |
| Saint-Étienne-les-Orgues | 62 | 44.03 N | 5.47 E |
| Saint-Étienne-lès-Remiremont | 58 | 48.02 N | 6.37 E |
| Saint-Eugène | 206 | 45.30 N | 74.28 W |
| Saint-Eustache | 206 | 45.34 N | 73.54 W |
| Saint-Evroult-Notre-Dame-du-Bois | 50 | 48.48 N | 0.28 E |
| Saint-Fabien | 186 | 48.18 N | 68.52 W |
| Saint Faith's | 158 | 30.30 S | 30.12 E |
| Saint-Fargeau | 50 | 47.38 N | 3.04 E |
| Saint-Fargeau-Ponthierry | 261 | 48.33 N | 2.32 E |
| Saint-Félicien, P.Q., Can. | 176 | 48.39 N | 72.26 W |
| Saint-Félicien, Fr. | 62 | 45.05 N | 4.38 E |
| Sainte-Félicité | 186 | 48.54 N | 67.20 W |
| Saint-Félix | 62 | 45.48 N | 5.58 E |
| Saint-Félix-de-Kingsey | 206 | 45.48 N | 72.12 W |
| Saint-Félix-de-Valois | 206 | 46.10 N | 73.26 W |
| Saint-Ferdinand (Bernierville) | 206 | 46.06 N | 71.34 W |
| Saintfield | 48 | 54.28 N | 5.50 W |
| Saint Fillans | 46 | 56.23 N | 4.07 W |
| Saint-Firmin | 62 | 44.47 N | 6.02 E |
| Saint-Firmin-sur-Loire | 50 | 47.37 N | 2.44 E |
| Saint-Flavien | 206 | 46.31 N | 71.36 W |
| Saint-Florent | 36 | 42.41 N | 9.18 E |
| Saint-Florentin | 50 | 48.00 N | 3.44 E |
| Saint-Florent-sur-Cher | 32 | 46.59 N | 2.15 E |
| Saint-Floris, Parc National ♠ | 146 | 9.40 N | 21.35 E |
| Saint-Flour | 32 | 45.02 N | 3.05 E |
| Saint-Fons | 62 | 45.42 N | 4.52 E |
| Saint-Fortunat | 206 | 45.58 N | 71.36 W |
| Sainte-Foy | 206 | 46.47 N | 71.17 W |
| Sainte-Foy-la-Grande | 32 | 44.50 N | 0.13 E |
| Sainte-Foy-l'Argentière | 62 | 45.42 N | 4.28 E |
| Sainte-Foy-lès-Lyon | 62 | 45.44 N | 4.48 E |
| Sainte-Foy-Tarentaise | 62 | 45.35 N | 6.53 E |
| Saint Francis, Ks., U.S. | 198 | 39.46 N | 101.47 W |
| Saint Francis, S.D., U.S. | 198 | 43.08 N | 100.54 W |
| Saint Francis, Wi., U.S. | 216 | 42.58 N | 87.52 W |
| Saint Francis ≃, N.A. | 186 | 47.10 N | 68.57 W |
| Saint Francis ≃, U.S. | 194 | 34.38 N | 90.35 W |
| Saint Francis, Cape ›, Nf., Can. | 186 | 47.50 N | 52.47 W |
| Saint Francis, Cape ›, S. Afr. | 158 | 34.14 S | 24.49 E |
| Saint Francis, Lake ◎ | 206 | 45.08 N | 74.25 W |
| Saint Francis Bay ⊂ | 158 | 34.35 S | 25.10 E |
| Saint Francisville | 194 | 30.46 N | 91.22 W |
| Saint-François | 241o | 16.15 N | 61.17 W |
| Saint-François ≃ | 206 | 46.07 N | 72.55 W |
| Saint-François, Lac ◎ | 206 | 45.55 N | 71.10 W |
| Saint-François de Boundji | 152 | 1.03 S | 15.22 E |
| Saint-François-de-Laval ◆[8] | 275a | 45.40 N | 73.34 W |
| Saint-François-du-Lac | 206 | 46.04 N | 72.50 W |
| Saint Francois Mountains ⋏[2] | 194 | 37.30 N | 90.35 W |
| Saint-François-sur-Bugeon | 62 | 45.24 N | 6.21 E |
| Saint-Front | 62 | 44.59 N | 4.08 E |
| Saint-Gabriel | 206 | 46.17 N | 73.23 W |
| Saint-Gabriel-de-Gaspé | 186 | 48.31 N | 64.32 W |
| Saint-Gabriel-de-Rimouski | 186 | 48.25 N | 68.10 W |
| Saint-Gall → Sankt Gallen | 58 | 47.25 N | 9.23 E |
| Saint-Galmier | 62 | 45.35 N | 4.19 E |
| Sainte-Gauburge-Sainte-Colombe | 50 | 48.42 N | 0.26 E |
| Saint-Gaudens | 32 | 43.07 N | 0.44 E |
| Saint-Gaudens National Historic Site ⊥ | 188 | 43.29 N | 72.19 W |
| Saint-Gaultier | 32 | 46.38 N | 1.25 E |
| Saint-Gély-du-Fesc | 62 | 43.42 N | 3.48 E |
| Saint-Genest-Lerpt | 62 | 45.27 N | 4.20 E |
| Saint-Genest-Malifaux | 62 | 45.20 N | 4.25 E |
| Sainte-Geneviève, P.Q., Can. | 275a | 45.29 N | 73.52 W |
| Sainte Genevieve, Mo., U.S. | 194 | 37.59 N | 90.03 W |
| Sainte-Geneviève-de-Batiscan | 206 | 46.32 N | 72.20 W |
| Sainte-Geneviève-des-Bois | 50 | 48.38 N | 2.20 E |
| Saint-Gengoux-le-National | 58 | 46.37 N | 4.39 E |
| Saint-Genis-de-Saintonge | 32 | 45.29 N | 0.34 W |
| Saint-Genis-Laval | 62 | 45.41 N | 4.48 E |
| Saint-Genis-Pouilly | 58 | 46.15 N | 6.01 E |
| Saint-Genix-sur-Guiers | 62 | 45.36 N | 5.38 E |
| Saint-Geoire-en-Valdaine | 62 | 45.27 N | 5.38 E |
| Saint George, Austl. | 166 | 28.02 S | 148.35 E |
| Saint George, Ber. | 240a | 32.22 N | 64.40 W |
| Saint George, N.B., Can. | 186 | 45.08 N | 66.49 W |
| Saint George, On., Can. | 212 | 43.15 N | 80.15 W |
| Saint George, Pa., U.S. | 214 | 41.15 N | 79.47 W |
| Saint George, S.C., U.S. | 192 | 33.11 N | 80.34 W |
| Saint George, Ut., U.S. | 200 | 37.06 N | 113.34 W |
| Saint George ◆[8] | 276 | 40.39 N | 74.05 W |
| Saint George, Cape ›, Nf., Can. | 186 | 48.27 N | 59.15 W |
| Saint George, Cape ›, Pap. N. Gui. | 164 | 4.52 S | 152.52 E |
| Saint George, Cape ›, Fl., U.S. | 192 | 29.35 N | 85.04 W |
| Saint George, Point › | 204 | 41.47 N | 124.15 W |
| Saint George Island, Ak., U.S. | 180 | 56.36 N | 169.32 W |
| Saint George Island, Md., U.S. | 208 | 38.07 N | 76.29 W |
| Saint George Island I, Ak., U.S. | 180 | 56.35 N | 169.35 W |
| Saint George Island I, Fl., U.S. | 192 | 29.39 N | 84.55 W |
| Saint George's, Nf., Can. | 186 | 48.26 N | 58.29 W |
| Saint-Georges, P.Q., Can. | 188 | 46.07 N | 70.40 W |
| Saint-Georges, P.Q., Can. | 206 | 46.37 N | 72.40 W |
| Saint-Georges, Fr. | 58 | 48.40 N | 6.56 E |
| Saint George's, Gren. | 241k | 12.03 N | 61.45 W |
| Saint-Georges, Guy. fr. | 250 | 3.54 N | 51.48 W |
| Saint Georges, De., U.S. | 208 | 39.33 N | 75.39 W |
| Saint Georges Basin ⊂ | 170 | 35.07 S | 150.36 E |
| Saint George's Bay ⊂, Nf., Can. | 186 | 48.20 N | 59.00 W |
| Saint Georges Bay ⊂, N.S., Can. | 186 | 45.50 N | 61.45 W |
| Saint George's Channel ʮ, Europe | 28 | 52.00 N | 6.00 W |
| Saint George's Channel ʮ, Pap. N. Gui. | 164 | 4.30 S | 152.30 E |
| Saint-Georges-de-Reneins | 58 | 46.04 N | 4.43 E |
| Saint-Georges-de-Windsor | 206 | 45.42 N | 71.50 W |
| Saint-Georges-en-Couzan | 62 | 45.42 N | 3.56 E |
| Saint Georges Head › | 170 | 35.12 S | 150.42 E |
| Saint George's Island I | 240a | 32.22 N | 64.40 W |
| Saint George Sound ʮ | 192 | 29.47 N | 84.42 W |
| Saint-Gérard, Bel. | 56 | 50.21 N | 4.45 E |
| Saint-Gérard, P.Q., Can. | 206 | 45.46 N | 71.25 W |
| Saint-Germain ≃ | 206 | 45.55 N | 72.30 W |
| Saint-Germain, Forêt de ♠ | 261 | 48.55 N | 2.05 E |


**Symbols** in the index entries represent the broad categories identified in the key at the right. Symbols with superior numbers (⋏[1]) identify subcategories (see complete key on page *I · 1).*

**Symbole** im Register stellen die rechts im Schlüssel erklärten Kategorien dar. Symbole mit hochgestellten Ziffern (⋏[1]) bezeichnen Unterabteilungen einer Kategorie (vgl. vollständiger Schlüssel auf Seite *I · 1).*

**Los símbolos** incluídos en el texto del índice representan las grandes categorías identificadas con la clave a la derecha. Los símbolos con numeros en su parte superior (⋏[1]) identifican las subcategorías (véase la clave completa en la página *I · 1).*

**Les symboles** de l'index représentent les catégories indiquées dans la légende à droite. Les symboles suivis d'un indice (⋏[1]) représentent des sous-catégories (voir légende complète à la page *I · 1).*

**Os símbolos** incluídos no texto do índice representam as grandes categorias identificadas com a chave à direita. Os símbolos com números em sua parte superior (⋏[1]) identificam as subcategorias (veja-se a chave completa à página *I · 1).*

| | ENGLISH | DEUTSCH | ESPAÑOL | FRANÇAIS | PORTUGUÊS |
|---|---|---|---|---|---|
| ∧ | Mountain | Berg | Montaña | Montagne | Montanha |
| ⋏ | Mountains | Gebirge | Montañas | Montagnes | Montanhas |
| )( | Pass | Paß | Paso | Col | Passo |
| V | Valley, Canyon | Tal, Cañon | Valle, Cañón | Vallée, Canyon | Vale, Canhão |
| ≚ | Plain | Ebene | Llano | Plaine | Planície |
| › | Cape | Kap | Cabo | Cap | Cabo |
| I | Island | Insel | Isla | Île | Ilha |
| II | Islands | Inseln | Islas | Îles | Ilhas |
| ≗ | Other Topographic Features | Andere Topographische Objekte | Otros Elementos Topográficos | Autres données topographiques | Outros acidentes topográficos |

ESPAÑOL — FRANÇAIS — PORTUGUÊS


| Nombre / Nom / Nome | Página / Page / Página | Lat.°′ | Long.°′ W = Oeste / W = Ouest / W = Oeste |
|---|---|---|---|
| Saint-Germain-de-Calberte | 62 | 44.13 N | 3.48 E |
| Saint-Germain-de-Grantham | 206 | 45.50 N | 72.34 W |
| Saint-Germain-de-Joux | 58 | 46.11 N | 5.44 E |
| Saint-Germain-des-Champs | 50 | 47.25 N | 3.55 E |
| Saint-Germain-du-Bois | 58 | 46.45 N | 5.15 E |
| Saint-Germain-du-Plain | 58 | 46.42 N | 4.58 E |
| Saint-Germain-en-Laye | 50 | 48.54 N | 2.05 E |
| Saint-Germain-en-Laye, Château de ⊥ | 261 | 48.54 N | 2.06 E |
| Saint-Germain-Laval | 62 | 45.50 N | 4.01 E |
| Saint-Germain-Laxis | 261 | 48.35 N | 2.43 E |
| Saint-Germain-Lembron | 32 | 45.28 N | 3.14 E |
| Saint-Germain-lès-Arlay | 58 | 46.46 N | 5.34 E |
| Saint-Germain-lès-Corbeil | 261 | 48.37 N | 2.29 E |
| Saint-Germain-l'Herm | 32 | 45.28 N | 3.33 E |
| Saint-Germain-sur-Morin | 261 | 48.53 N | 2.51 E |
| Saint Germans | 42 | 50.24 N | 4.18 W |
| Saint-Germer-de-Fly | 50 | 49.27 N | 1.47 E |
| Saint-Gervais-d'Auvergne | 32 | 46.02 N | 2.49 E |
| Saint-Gervais-les-Bains | 62 | 45.54 N | 6.43 E |
| Saint-Gervasy | 62 | 43.53 N | 4.29 E |
| Saint-Géry | 32 | 44.29 N | 1.35 E |
| Saint-Gilles, Bel. | 50 | 50.49 N | 4.20 E |
| Saint-Gilles, P.Q., Can. | 206 | 46.31 N | 71.22 W |
| Saint-Gilles, Fr. | 62 | 43.41 N | 4.26 E |
| Saint-Gilles-Croix-de-Vie | 32 | 46.42 N | 1.57 W |
| Saint-Gingolph | 58 | 46.24 N | 6.52 E |
| Saint-Girons | 32 | 42.59 N | 1.09 E |
| Saint-Gobain | 50 | 49.36 N | 3.23 E |
| Saint Gotthard Pass → San Gottardo, Passo del )( | 58 | 46.33 N | 8.34 E |
| Saint Govan's Head › | 42 | 51.36 N | 4.55 W |
| Saint-Gratien | 261 | 48.58 N | 2.17 E |
| Saint-Grégoire (Larochelle) | 206 | 46.16 N | 72.30 W |
| Saint Gregory, Mount ∧ | 186 | 49.19 N | 58.13 W |
| Saint-Guénolé | 32 | 47.49 N | 4.20 W |
| Saint-Guillaume-d'Upton | 206 | 45.53 N | 72.46 W |
| Saint-Héand | 62 | 45.31 N | 4.22 E |
| Saint Helena | 226 | 38.30 N | 122.28 W |
| Saint Helena □[2] | 10 | 15.57 S | 5.42 W |
| Saint Helena, Mount ∧ | 226 | 38.40 N | 122.38 W |
| Saint Helena Sound ʊ | 192 | 32.27 N | 80.25 W |
| Sainte-Hélène, Île I | 275a | 45.31 N | 73.32 W |
| Sainte-Hélène-de-Bagot | 206 | 45.44 N | 72.44 W |
| Saint Helens, Austl. | 166 | 41.20 S | 148.15 E |
| Saint Helens, Eng., U.K. | 42 | 50.42 N | 1.06 W |
| Saint Helens, Eng., U.K. | 44 | 53.28 N | 2.44 W |
| Saint Helens, Or., U.S. | 224 | 45.51 N | 122.48 W |
| Saint Helens □[8] | 262 | 53.28 N | 2.45 W |
| Saint Helens, Mount ∧[1] | 224 | 46.12 N | 122.11 W |
| Saint Helens Canal ≊ | 262 | 53.27 N | 2.42 W |
| Saint Helier | 43b | 49.11 N | 2.06 W |
| Saint Henry | 216 | 40.25 N | 84.38 W |
| Sainte-Hermine | 32 | 46.33 N | 1.04 W |
| Saint-Hilaire-du-Harcouët | 32 | 48.35 N | 1.06 W |
| Saint-Hilarion | 261 | 48.37 N | 1.44 E |
| Saint-Hippolyte, Fr. | 58 | 47.19 N | 6.49 E |
| Saint-Hippolyte, Fr. | 62 | 43.38 N | 4.45 E |
| Saint-Hippolyte-de-Kilkenny | 206 | 45.56 N | 74.01 W |
| Saint-Hippolyte-du-Fort | 62 | 43.58 N | 3.51 E |
| Saint-Honorat, Mont ∧ | 62 | 44.05 N | 6.46 E |
| Saint-Hubert, Bel. | 56 | 50.01 N | 5.23 E |
| Saint-Hubert, P.Q., Can. | 206 | 45.30 N | 73.25 W |
| Saint-Hubert, Étang de ⊜ | 261 | 48.43 N | 1.51 E |
| Saint-Hubert-le-Roi | 261 | 48.43 N | 1.52 E |
| Saint-Hugues | 206 | 45.48 N | 72.52 W |
| Saint-Hyacinthe | 206 | 45.37 N | 72.57 W |
| Saint-Hyacinthe □[6] | 206 | 45.40 N | 73.05 W |
| Saint-Ignace, N.B., Can. | 186 | 46.42 N | 65.05 W |
| Saint Ignace, Mi., U.S. | 190 | 45.52 N | 84.43 W |
| Saint Ignace Island I | 190 | 48.48 N | 87.55 W |
| Saint Ignatius, Guy. | 246 | 3.20 N | 59.47 W |
| Saint Ignatius, Mt., U.S. | 202 | 47.19 N | 114.05 W |
| Saint-Imier | 58 | 47.09 N | 7.00 E |
| Saint-Imier, Vallon de V | 58 | 47.10 N | 7.00 E |
| Saint-Isidore | 186 | 47.33 N | 65.03 W |
| Saint-Isidore-d'Auckland | 206 | 45.16 N | 71.31 W |
| Saint-Isidore-de-Laprairie | 275a | 45.18 N | 73.41 W |
| Saint Ives, Austl. | 274a | 33.44 S | 151.10 E |
| Saint Ives, Eng., U.K. | 32 | 50.12 N | 5.29 W |
| Saint Ives, Eng., U.K. | 42 | 52.20 N | 0.05 W |
| Saint Ives Bay c | 42 | 50.14 N | 5.28 W |
| Saint Jacob | 219 | 38.43 N | 89.46 W |
| Saint Jacobs | 212 | 43.32 N | 80.33 W |
| Saint-Jacques | 206 | 45.57 N | 73.34 W |
| Saint-Jacques ≃ | 275a | 45.26 N | 73.29 W |
| Saint James, Il., U.S. | 219 | 38.57 N | 88.51 W |
| Saint James, Mi., U.S. | 190 | 45.45 N | 85.30 W |
| Saint James, Mn., U.S. | 198 | 43.58 N | 94.37 W |
| Saint James, Mo., U.S. | 194 | 37.59 N | 91.36 W |
| Saint James, N.Y., U.S. | 210 | 40.52 N | 73.09 W |
| Saint James, Cape › | 182 | 51.56 N | 131.01 W |
| Saint James City | 220 | 26.29 N | 82.04 W |
| Saint James Islands II | 240m | 18.19 N | 64.50 W |
| Saint-Janvier | 275a | 45.43 N | 73.56 W |
| Saint-Jean □[6] | 206 | 45.15 N | 73.20 W |
| Saint-Jean ≃, P.Q., Can. | 186 | 48.46 N | 64.26 W |
| Saint-Jean ≃, P.Q., Can. | 186 | 50.17 N | 64.20 W |
| Saint-Jean, Île I | 275a | 45.41 N | 73.39 W |
| Saint-Jean, Lac ⊜ | 176 | 48.35 N | 72.05 W |
| Saint-Jean, Rapides de ʟ | 275a | 45.19 N | 73.15 W |
| Saint-Jean Airport ⊠ | 275a | 45.18 N | 73.17 W |
| Saint-Jean-aux-Bois | 50 | 49.21 N | 2.55 E |
| Saint-Jean-Baptiste | 184 | 49.16 N | 97.21 W |
| Saint-Jean-Baptiste-de-Rouville | 206 | 45.31 N | 73.07 W |
| Saint-Jean-Cap-Ferrat | 62 | 43.41 N | 7.20 E |
| Saint-Jean-d'Angély | 32 | 45.57 N | 0.31 W |
| Saint-Jean-d'Assé | 50 | 48.09 N | 0.07 E |
| Saint-Jean-de-Bournay | 62 | 45.29 N | 5.08 E |
| Saint-Jean-de-Braye | 50 | 47.54 N | 1.58 E |
| Saint-Jean-de-la-Roulle | 50 | 47.55 N | 1.52 E |
| Saint-Jean-de-Losne | 58 | 47.06 N | 5.15 E |
| Saint-Jean-de-Luz | 32 | 43.23 N | 1.40 W |
| Saint-Jean-de-Maurienne | 62 | 45.17 N | 6.21 E |
| Saint-Jean-de-Monts | 32 | 46.48 N | 2.03 W |
| Saint-Jean-des-Piles | 206 | 46.41 N | 72.45 W |
| Saint-Jean-du-Gard | 62 | 44.06 N | 3.53 E |
| Saint-Jean-en-Royans | 62 | 45.01 N | 5.18 E |
| Saint-Jean-Pied-de-Port | 32 | 43.10 N | 1.14 W |
| Saint-Jean-Port-Joli | 186 | 47.13 N | 70.16 W |
| Saint-Jean-Soleymieux | 62 | 45.30 N | 4.02 E |
| Saint-Jean-sur-Richelieu | 206 | 45.19 N | 73.16 W |
| Saint-Jeoire | 58 | 46.09 N | 6.28 E |
| Saint-Jérôme | 206 | 45.47 N | 74.00 W |
| Saint Jo | 196 | 33.41 N | 97.31 W |
| Saint Joachim | 214 | 42.16 N | 82.38 W |
| Saint Joe | 216 | 41.18 N | 84.54 W |
| Saint Joe ≃ | 202 | 47.21 N | 116.42 W |
| Saint John, N.B., Can. | 186 | 45.16 N | 66.03 W |
| Saint John, Jersey | 43b | 49.15 N | 2.08 W |
| Saint John, In., U.S. | 216 | 41.27 N | 87.28 W |
| Saint John, Ks., U.S. | 198 | 38.00 N | 98.45 W |
| Saint John, N.D., U.S. | 198 | 48.56 N | 99.42 W |
| Saint John, Wa., U.S. | 202 | 47.05 N | 117.34 W |
| Saint John I | 240m | 18.20 N | 64.45 W |
| Saint John ≃, Liber. | 150 | 6.40 N | 9.10 W |
| Saint John ≃, N.A. | 186 | 45.15 N | 66.04 W |
| Saint John, Cape › | 186 | 50.00 N | 55.32 W |
| Saint John, Lake ⊜, Nf., Can. | 186 | 48.23 N | 54.41 W |
| Saint John, Lake ⊜, On., Can. | 212 | 44.41 N | 79.20 W |
| Saint John Bay c | 186 | 50.54 N | 57.08 W |
| Saint John Island I | 186 | 50.49 N | 57.14 W |
| Saint John's, Antig. | 240c | 17.06 N | 61.51 W |
| Saint John's, Nf., Can. | 186 | 47.34 N | 52.43 W |
| Saint Johns → Saint-Jean-sur-Richelieu, P.Q., Can. | 206 | 45.19 N | 73.16 W |
| Saint John's, I. of Man | 44 | 54.13 N | 4.38 W |
| Saint Johns, Az., U.S. | 200 | 34.30 N | 109.21 W |
| Saint Johns, Mi., U.S. | 216 | 43.00 N | 84.33 W |
| Saint Johns, Mo., U.S. | 219 | 38.42 N | 90.20 W |
| Saint Johns, Oh., U.S. | 216 | 40.33 N | 84.05 W |
| Saint Johns ≃, Ca., U.S. | 226 | 36.25 N | 119.25 W |
| Saint Johns ≃, Fl., U.S. | 192 | 30.24 N | 81.24 W |
| Saint Johnsburg | 210 | 43.05 N | 78.53 W |
| Saint Johnsbury | 188 | 44.25 N | 72.00 W |
| Saint Johns Creek ≃ | 219 | 38.34 N | 91.01 W |
| Saint John's Jerusalem ⊥ | 260 | 51.25 N | 0.14 E |
| Saint Johns Marsh ≡ | 220 | 27.45 N | 80.40 W |
| Saint John's Point › | 48 | 54.13 N | 5.40 W |
| Saint John's University ȣ[2] | 276 | 40.43 N | 73.48 W |
| Saint Johnsville | 210 | 42.59 N | 74.41 W |
| Saint Joseph, N.B., Can. | 186 | 45.59 N | 64.34 W |
| Saint Joseph, Dom. | 240d | 15.26 N | 61.26 W |
| Saint-Joseph, Mart. | 240e | 14.40 N | 61.03 W |
| Saint-Joseph, N. Cal. | 175f | 20.27 S | 166.36 E |
| Saint-Joseph, Réu. | 157c | 21.22 S | 55.36 E |
| Saint Joseph, Il., U.S. | 194 | 40.06 N | 88.02 W |
| Saint Joseph, La., U.S. | 194 | 31.55 N | 91.14 W |
| Saint Joseph, Mi., U.S. | 216 | 42.05 N | 86.29 W |
| Saint Joseph, Mn., U.S. | 190 | 45.33 N | 94.19 W |
| Saint Joseph, Mo., U.S. | 194 | 39.46 N | 94.50 W |
| Saint Joseph, Tn., U.S. | 194 | 35.02 N | 87.30 W |
| Saint Joseph □[6], In., U.S. | 216 | 41.41 N | 86.15 W |
| Saint Joseph □[6], Mi., U.S. | 216 | 41.55 N | 85.31 W |
| Saint Joseph ≃, U.S. | 216 | 42.07 N | 86.29 W |
| Saint Joseph ≃, U.S. | 216 | 41.05 N | 85.08 W |
| Saint Joseph, East Branch ≃ | 216 | 41.39 N | 84.34 W |
| Saint-Joseph, Île I | 275a | 45.41 N | 73.42 W |
| Saint-Joseph, Lac ⊜ | 206 | 46.54 N | 71.38 W |
| Saint Joseph, Lake ⊜ | 176 | 51.05 N | 90.35 W |
| Saint Joseph, West Branch ≃ | 216 | 41.39 N | 84.34 W |
| Saint Joseph Bay c | 192 | 29.47 N | 85.21 W |
| Saint Joseph Channel ʊ | 190 | 46.19 N | 84.04 W |
| Saint-Joseph-d'Alma → Alma | 186 | 48.33 N | 71.39 W |
| Saint-Joseph-de-Beauce | 186 | 46.18 N | 70.53 W |
| Saint-Joseph-de-Mékinac | 206 | 46.55 N | 72.42 W |
| Saint-Joseph-de-Sorel | 206 | 46.02 N | 73.07 W |
| Saint-Joseph-du-Lac | 275a | 45.32 N | 74.00 W |
| Saint Joseph Island I | 190 | 46.13 N | 83.57 W |
| Saint Joseph's University ȣ[2] | 285 | 40.00 N | 75.14 W |
| Saint-Jouin-Bruneval | 50 | 49.39 N | 0.10 E |
| Saint-Jovite | 206 | 46.07 N | 74.36 W |
| Sainte-Julie | 206 | 45.35 N | 73.19 W |
| Saint-Julien | 58 | 46.23 N | 5.27 E |
| Saint-Julien-Chapteuil | 62 | 45.02 N | 4.04 E |
| Saint-Julien-du-Sault | 50 | 48.02 N | 3.18 E |
| Saint-Julien-du-Verdon | 62 | 43.55 N | 6.32 E |
| Saint-Julien-en-Beauchêne | 62 | 44.37 N | 5.42 E |
| Saint-Julien-en-Born | 32 | 44.04 N | 1.14 W |
| Saint-Julien-en-Genevois | 58 | 46.08 N | 6.05 E |
| Saint-Julien-en-Jarez | 62 | 45.28 N | 4.31 E |
| Saint-Julien-les-Villas | 50 | 48.16 N | 4.06 E |
| Saint-Julien-Molin-Molette | 62 | 45.19 N | 4.37 E |
| Sainte-Julienne | 206 | 45.58 N | 73.43 W |
| Saint-Junien | 32 | 45.53 N | 0.54 E |
| Saint Just, P.R. | 240m | 18.23 N | 66.00 W |
| Saint Just, Eng., U.K. | 42 | 50.07 N | 5.42 W |
| Saint-Just-en-Chaussée | 50 | 49.30 N | 2.26 E |
| Saint-Just-en-Chevalet | 32 | 45.55 N | 3.50 E |
| Saint-Justin | 206 | 46.15 N | 73.05 W |
| Saint-Just-Malmont | 62 | 45.20 N | 4.19 E |
| Saint-Just-sur-Loire | 62 | 45.29 N | 4.16 E |
| Saint Keverne | 42 | 50.03 N | 5.06 W |
| Saint Kilda, Austl. | 168b | 34.44 S | 138.32 E |
| Saint Kilda, Austl. | 169 | 37.52 S | 144.59 E |
| Saint Kilda, N.Z. | 172 | 45.54 S | 170.30 E |
| Saint Kilda I | 28 | 57.49 N | 8.36 W |
| Saint Kitts | 168b | 34.21 S | 139.04 E |
| Saint Kitts → Saint Christopher I | 238 | 17.20 N | 62.45 W |
| Saint Kitts and Nevis □[1], N.A. | 230 | 17.20 N | 62.45 W |
| Saint Kitts and Nevis □[1], N.A. | 238 | 17.20 N | 62.45 W |
| Saint-Lambert, P.Q., Can. | 206 | 45.30 N | 73.30 W |
| Saint-Lambert, Fr. | 261 | 48.44 N | 2.01 E |
| Saint Landry | 194 | 30.50 N | 92.15 W |
| Saint-Laurent, Mb., Can. | 184 | 50.24 N | 97.56 W |
| Saint-Laurent, P.Q., Can. | 206 | 45.30 N | 73.40 W |
| Saint-Laurent, Fr. | 58 | 48.09 N | 6.27 E |
| Saint-Laurent → Saint Lawrence ≃ | 176 | 49.30 N | 67.00 W |
| Saint-Laurent-Blangy | 50 | 50.18 N | 2.48 E |
| Saint-Laurent-de-Chamousset | 62 | 45.44 N | 4.28 E |
| Saint-Laurent-du-Maroni | 250 | 5.30 N | 54.02 W |
| Saint-Laurent-du-Maroni □[8] | 250 | 4.00 N | 53.30 W |
| Saint-Laurent-du-Pont | 62 | 45.23 N | 5.44 E |
| Saint-Laurent-du-Var | 62 | 43.40 N | 7.11 E |
| Saint-Laurent-en-Caux | 50 | 49.45 N | 0.53 E |
| Saint-Laurent-en-Grandvaux | 58 | 46.35 N | 5.57 E |
| Saint-Laurent-et-Benon | 32 | 45.09 N | 0.49 W |
| Saint-Laurent-les-Bains | 62 | 44.37 N | 3.58 E |
| Saint-Laurent-sur-Saône | 58 | 46.18 N | 4.50 E |
| Saint Lawrence, Austl. | 166 | 22.21 S | 149.31 E |
| Saint Lawrence, Nf., Can. | 186 | 46.55 N | 55.24 W |
| Saint Lawrence □[6] | 212 | 44.30 N | 75.27 W |
| Saint Lawrence ≃ | 176 | 49.30 N | 67.00 W |
| Saint Lawrence, Cape › | 186 | 47.03 N | 60.37 W |
| Saint Lawrence, Gulf of c | 186 | 48.00 N | 62.00 W |
| Saint Lawrence, Lake ⊜ | 206 | 44.56 N | 75.04 W |
| Saint Lawrence Island I | 180 | 63.30 N | 170.30 W |
| Saint Lawrence Islands National Park ♠ | 212 | 44.18 N | 76.08 W |
| Saint-Lawrence Seaway ≊ | 275a | 45.43 N | 73.25 W |
| Saint-Lazare | 184 | 50.26 N | 101.16 W |
| Saint-Lazare, Gare ◆[5] | 261 | 48.53 N | 2.20 E |
| Saint-Léandre | 186 | 48.44 N | 67.36 W |
| Saint-Léger-en-Yvelines | 50 | 48.43 N | 1.46 E |
| Saint-Léger-sur-Dheune | 58 | 46.51 N | 4.38 E |
| Saint Leo | 220 | 28.20 N | 82.15 W |
| Saint Leon | 218 | 39.17 N | 84.57 W |
| Saint-Léonard, N.B. Can. | 186 | 47.10 N | 67.56 W |
| Saint-Léonard, P.Q., Can. | 206 | 45.35 N | 73.35 W |
| Saint Leonard, Md., U.S. | 208 | 38.28 N | 76.30 W |
| Saint-Léonard-d'Aston | 206 | 46.06 N | 72.22 W |
| Saint Leonards, Eng., U.K. | 42 | 50.49 N | 1.51 W |
| Saint Leonards, Eng. U.K. | 42 | 50.51 N | 0.34 E |
| Saint-Leu-d'Esserent | 50 | 49.13 N | 2.25 E |
| Saint-Leu-la-Forêt | 50 | 49.01 N | 2.15 E |
| Saint-Liboire | 206 | 45.39 N | 72.46 W |
| Saint-Lô | 32 | 49.07 N | 1.05 W |
| Saint-Louis, Sk., Can. | 184 | 52.56 N | 105.49 W |
| Saint-Louis, Fr. | 58 | 47.35 N | 7.34 E |
| Saint-Louis, Guad. | 241o | 15.57 N | 61.19 W |
| Saint-Louis, Réu. | 157c | 21.16 S | 55.25 E |
| Saint-Louis, Sén. | 150 | 16.02 N | 16.30 W |
| Saint Louis, Mi., U.S. | 190 | 43.24 N | 84.36 W |
| Saint Louis, Mo., U.S. | 219 | 38.37 N | 90.11 W |
| Saint Louis, Tx., U.S. | 222 | 32.18 N | 95.20 W |
| Saint-Louis □[4] | 150 | 16.00 N | 14.30 W |
| Saint Louis □[6] | 219 | 38.39 N | 90.25 W |
| Saint-Louis ≃, P.Q., Can. | 275a | 45.19 N | 73.53 W |
| Saint Louis ≃, U.S. | 190 | 46.45 N | 92.06 W |
| Saint-Louis, Lac ⊜ | 206 | 45.24 N | 73.48 W |
| Saint-Louis, Pointe › | 275a | 45.19 N | 73.53 W |
| Saint Louis Crossing | 218 | 39.19 N | 85.51 W |
| Saint-Louis-de-Champlain | 206 | 46.25 N | 72.36 W |
| Saint-Louis-de-Kent | 186 | 46.44 N | 64.58 W |
| Saint Louis Park | 190 | 44.56 N | 93.20 W |
| Saint Louisville | 214 | 40.10 N | 82.25 W |
| Saint-Loup-sur-Aujon | 58 | 47.53 N | 5.05 E |
| Saint-Loup-sur-Semouse | 58 | 47.53 N | 6.16 E |
| Saint-Luc, P.Q., Can. | 206 | 45.22 N | 73.18 W |
| Saint-Luc, Schw. | 58 | 46.13 N | 7.36 E |
| Sainte-Luce | 240e | 14.28 N | 60.56 W |
| Saint Lucia □[1], N.A. | 230 | 13.53 N | 60.58 W |
| Saint Lucia □[1], N.A. | 241f | 13.53 N | 60.58 W |
| Saint Lucia, Cape › | 158 | 28.25 S | 32.25 E |
| Saint Lucia, Lake ⊜ | 158 | 28.05 S | 32.26 E |
| Saint Lucia Channel ʊ | 238 | 14.09 N | 60.57 W |
| Saint Lucia Estuary | 158 | 28.22 S | 32.25 E |
| Saint Lucia Game Reserve ◆[4] | 158 | 28.10 S | 32.28 E |
| Sainte-Lucie, Fr. | 36 | 41.42 N | 9.22 E |
| Saint Lucie, Fl., U.S. | 220 | 27.29 N | 80.20 W |
| Saint Lucie □[6] | 220 | 27.23 N | 80.26 W |
| Saint Lucie Canal ≊ | 220 | 27.10 N | 80.15 W |
| Saint Lucie Inlet c | 220 | 27.10 N | 80.10 W |
| Saint Lucie Lock ◆[5] | 220 | 27.07 N | 80.17 W |
| Saint-Lucien | 261 | 48.39 N | 1.38 E |
| Saint-Lupicin | 58 | 46.24 N | 5.47 E |
| Sainte-Magnance | 50 | 47.27 N | 4.04 E |
| Saint Magnus Bay c | 46a | 60.24 N | 1.34 W |
| Saint Magnus Cathedral ȣ[1] | 46 | 58.58 N | 2.57 W |
| Saint-Malo, P.Q., Can. | 206 | 45.12 N | 71.30 W |
| Saint-Malo, Fr. | 32 | 48.39 N | 2.01 W |
| Saint-Malo, Golfe de c | 32 | 48.45 N | 2.00 W |
| Saint-Mamert-du-Gard | 62 | 43.53 N | 4.12 E |
| Saint-Mammès | 50 | 48.23 N | 2.49 E |
| Saint-Mandé | 261 | 48.50 N | 2.25 E |
| Saint-Mandrier-sur-Mer | 62 | 43.04 N | 5.56 E |
| Saint-Marc | 238 | 19.07 N | 72.42 W |
| Saint-Marc, Canal de ʊ | 238 | 18.50 N | 72.45 W |
| Saint-Marc-des-Carrières | 206 | 46.41 N | 72.03 W |
| Saint-Marcel | 58 | 46.47 N | 4.54 E |
| Saint-Marcellin | 62 | 45.09 N | 5.19 E |
| Saint-Marcelline-de-Kildare | 206 | 46.07 N | 73.36 W |
| Saint-Marc-sur-Richelieu | 275a | 45.41 N | 73.12 W |
| Saint-Mard | 261 | 49.02 N | 2.42 E |
| Saint Margaret Bay c | 186 | 51.01 N | 56.58 W |
| Saint Margaret's at Cliffe | 42 | 51.09 N | 1.24 E |
| Saint Margarets Bay c | 186 | 44.35 N | 64.00 W |
| Saint Margaret's Hope | 46 | 58.49 N | 2.57 W |
| Sainte-Marguerite ≃ | 176 | 50.09 N | 66.36 W |
| Sainte-Marguerite, Baie c | 186 | 50.06 N | 66.36 W |
| Sainte-Marguerite-sur-Mer | 50 | 49.55 N | 0.57 E |
| Sainte-Marie | 240e | 14.47 N | 61.00 W |
| Sainte-Marie, Cap › | 157b | 25.36 S | 45.08 E |
| Sainte-Marie-aux-Mines (Markirch) | 58 | 48.15 N | 7.11 E |
| Saint Maries | 202 | 47.18 N | 116.33 W |
| Saint Maries ≃ | 202 | 47.19 N | 116.33 W |
| Saint-Marin → San Marino □[1] | 66 | 43.56 N | 12.25 E |
| Saint Marks, S. Afr. | 158 | 32.01 S | 27.22 E |
| Saint Marks, Fl., U.S. | 192 | 30.09 N | 84.12 W |
| Saint Marks ≃ | 192 | 30.08 N | 84.12 W |
| Sainte-Marthe-de-Gaspé | 186 | 49.12 N | 66.10 W |
| Sainte-Marthe-sur-le-Lac | 275a | 45.32 N | 73.56 W |
| Saint-Martin (Sint Maarten) I | 238 | 18.04 N | 63.04 W |
| Saint-Martin, Cap › | 240e | 14.52 N | 61.13 W |
| Saint Martin, Lake ⊜ | 184 | 51.37 N | 98.29 W |
| Saint-Martin-Boulogne | 50 | 50.43 N | 1.38 E |
| Saint-Martin-d'Ardèche | 62 | 44.18 N | 4.35 E |
| Saint-Martin-d'Auxigny | 50 | 47.12 N | 2.25 E |
| Saint-Martin-de-Belleville | 62 | 45.23 N | 6.30 E |
| Saint-Martin-de-Bossenay | 50 | 48.26 N | 3.41 E |
| Saint-Martin-de-Bréthencourt | 261 | 48.31 N | 1.56 E |
| Saint-Martin-de-Crau | 62 | 43.38 N | 4.49 E |
| Saint-Martin-de-Londres | 62 | 43.47 N | 3.44 E |
| Saint-Martin-de-Nigelles | 261 | 48.37 N | 1.37 E |
| Saint-Martin-d'Entraunes | 62 | 44.08 N | 6.46 E |
| Saint-Martin-des-Champs | 261 | 48.53 N | 1.43 E |
| Saint-Martin-de-Valamas | 62 | 44.56 N | 4.22 E |
| Saint-Martin-d'Hères | 62 | 45.10 N | 5.46 E |
| Saint-Martin-du-Puy | 50 | 47.20 N | 3.52 E |
| Saint-Martin-du-Tertre | 261 | 49.06 N | 2.21 E |
| Saint-Martin-du-Var | 62 | 43.49 N | 7.12 E |
| Sainte-Martine | 206 | 45.15 N | 73.48 W |
| Saint-Martin-en-Bresse | 58 | 46.49 N | 5.04 E |
| Saint-Martin-la-Garenne | 261 | 49.02 N | 1.41 E |
| Saint-Martin-la-Plaine | 62 | 45.32 N | 4.36 E |
| Saint Martins, N.B., Can. | 186 | 45.21 N | 65.32 W |
| Saint Martin's, Eng., U.K. | 42 | 52.55 N | 2.59 W |
| Saint Martin's I | 42a | 49.58 N | 6.20 W |
| Saint Martins Keys II | 220 | 28.47 N | 82.44 W |
| Saint-Martin-Vésubie | 62 | 44.04 N | 7.15 E |
| Saint Martinville | 194 | 30.07 N | 91.49 W |
| Saint Mary | 194 | 37.52 N | 89.58 W |
| Saint Mary ≃, B.C., Can. | 182 | 49.37 N | 115.38 W |
| Saint Mary ≃, N.A. | 182 | 49.37 N | 112.52 W |
| Saint Mary, Cape › | 150 | 13.28 N | 16.40 W |
| Saint Mary, Mount ∧ | 164 | 8.10 S | 147.00 E |
| Saint Mary Bourne | 42 | 51.16 N | 1.24 W |
| Saint Mary Cray ◆[8] | 260 | 51.23 N | 0.07 E |
| Saint Mary Lake ⊜ | 202 | 48.40 N | 113.30 W |
| Saint Marylebone ◆[8] | 260 | 51.31 N | 0.10 W |
| Saint Mary of the Lake Seminary ȣ[2] | 278 | 42.17 N | 88.00 W |
| Saint Mary Peak ∧ | 166 | 31.30 S | 138.33 E |
| Saint Mary Reservoir ⊜[1] | 182 | 49.19 N | 113.12 W |
| Saint Marys, Austl. | 166 | 41.35 S | 148.10 E |
| Saint Marys, Austl. | 170 | 33.47 S | 150.47 E |
| Saint Mary's, Nf., Can. | 186 | 46.55 N | 53.34 W |
| Saint Mary's, On., Can. | 212 | 43.16 N | 81.08 W |
| Saint Marys, Ak., U.S. | 180 | 62.04 N | 163.10 W |
| Saint Marys, Ga., U.S. | 192 | 30.43 N | 81.32 W |
| Saint Marys, Ks., U.S. | 198 | 39.11 N | 96.04 W |
| Saint Marys, Oh., U.S. | 216 | 40.32 N | 84.23 W |
| Saint Marys, Pa., U.S. | 214 | 41.25 N | 78.33 W |
| Saint Marys, W.V., U.S. | 188 | 39.23 N | 81.12 W |
| Saint Marys □[6] | 208 | 38.17 N | 76.38 W |
| Saint Mary's I | 42a | 49.55 N | 6.18 W |
| Saint Marys ≃, N.S., Can. | 186 | 45.02 N | 61.54 W |
| Saint Marys ≃, N.A. | 190 | 45.58 N | 83.54 W |
| Saint Marys ≃, U.S. | 192 | 30.43 N | 81.27 W |
| Saint Marys ≃, U.S. | 216 | 41.05 N | 85.08 W |
| Saint Marys ≃, Md., U.S. | 208 | 38.06 N | 76.26 W |
| Saint Mary's, Cape ›, Nf., Can. | 186 | 46.49 N | 54.12 W |
| Saint Marys, Cape ›, N.S., Can. | 186 | 44.05 N | 66.13 W |
| Saint Marys, North Prong ≃ | 192 | 30.22 N | 82.06 W |
| Saint Marys, South Prong ≃ | 192 | 30.22 N | 82.06 W |
| Saint Mary's Bay | 42 | 51.00 N | 0.58 E |
| Saint Mary's Bay c, Nf., Can. | 186 | 46.50 N | 53.47 W |
| Saint Marys Bay c, N.S., Can. | 186 | 44.25 N | 66.10 W |
| Saint Marys City | 208 | 38.11 N | 76.26 W |
| Saint Mary's Hoo | 260 | 51.28 N | 0.36 E |
| Saint Marys Lake ⊜ | 278 | 42.17 N | 87.59 W |
| Saint Mary's Marshes ≡ | 260 | 51.28 N | 0.35 E |
| Saint-Mathieu | 32 | 45.42 N | 0.46 E |
| Saint-Mathieu, Pointe de › | 32 | 48.20 N | 4.46 W |
| Saint-Mathieu-de-Laprairie | 275a | 45.19 N | 73.31 W |
| Saint Matthew Island I | 180 | 60.30 N | 172.45 W |
| Saint Matthews, Ky., U.S. | 218 | 38.15 N | 85.39 W |
| Saint Matthews, S.C., U.S. | 192 | 33.39 N | 80.46 W |
| Saint Matthias Group II | 164 | 1.30 S | 149.40 E |
| Saint-Maur-des-Fossés | 50 | 48.48 N | 2.30 E |
| Sainte-Maure-de-Touraine | 32 | 47.07 N | 0.37 E |
| Saint-Maurice, Fr. | 261 | 48.49 N | 2.25 E |
| Saint-Maurice, Schw. | 58 | 46.13 N | 7.00 E |
| Saint-Maurice □[6] | 206 | 46.35 N | 73.00 W |
| Saint-Maurice ≃ | 176 | 46.21 N | 72.31 W |
| Saint-Maurice, Parc de ♠ | 206 | 46.52 N | 73.10 W |
| Saint-Maurice-en-Montagne | 58 | 46.34 N | 5.50 E |
| Saint-Maurice-Montcouronne | 261 | 48.35 N | 2.07 E |
| Saint Mawes | 42 | 50.09 N | 5.01 W |
| Saint Mawgan | 42 | 50.28 N | 4.58 W |
| Saint-Max | 58 | 48.42 N | 6.13 E |
| Sainte-Maxime | 62 | 43.18 N | 6.38 E |
| Saint-Maximin-la-Sainte-Baume | 62 | 43.27 N | 5.52 E |
| Saint-Méen-le-Grand | 32 | 48.11 N | 2.12 W |
| Saint Meinrad | 194 | 38.10 N | 86.48 W |
| Sainte-Menehould | 56 | 49.05 N | 4.54 E |
| Saint-Menges | 56 | 49.44 N | 4.56 E |
| Sainte-Mère-Église | 32 | 49.25 N | 1.19 W |
| Saint Merryn | 42 | 50.31 N | 4.58 W |
| Saint-Méry | 261 | 48.35 N | 2.50 E |
| Sainte-Mesme | 261 | 48.32 N | 1.58 E |
| Saint-Mesmes | 261 | 48.59 N | 2.42 E |
| Saint Michael, Ak., U.S. | 180 | 63.29 N | 162.02 W |
| Saint Michael, Pa., U.S. | 214 | 40.20 N | 78.46 W |
| Saint Michaels | 208 | 38.47 N | 76.13 W |
| Saint-Michel, Fr. | 50 | 49.55 N | 4.08 E |
| Saint-Michel, Fr. | 62 | 45.13 N | 6.28 E |
| Saint-Michel ◆[8] | 275a | 45.35 N | 73.35 W |
| Saint-Michel-de-Napierville | 206 | 45.14 N | 73.34 W |
| Saint-Michel-des-Saints | 206 | 46.41 N | 73.55 W |
| Saint-Michel-sur-Meurthe | 58 | 48.19 N | 6.54 E |
| Saint-Michel-sur-Orge | 261 | 48.38 N | 2.18 E |
| Saint-Mihiel | 56 | 48.54 N | 5.33 E |
| Saint Monance | 46 | 56.12 N | 2.46 W |
| Sainte-Monique-des-Deux-Montagnes | 275a | 45.40 N | 74.00 W |
| Sainte-Montaine | 50 | 47.29 N | 2.19 E |
| Saint-Moritz → Sankt Moritz | 58 | 46.30 N | 9.50 E |
| Saint-Narcisse | 206 | 46.34 N | 72.28 W |
| Saint-Nazaire | 32 | 47.17 N | 2.12 W |
| Saint-Nazaire-en-Royans | 62 | 45.04 N | 5.15 E |
| Saint-Nazaire-le-Désert | 62 | 44.34 N | 5.17 E |
| Saint Nazianz | 190 | 44.00 N | 87.55 W |
| Saint Neots | 42 | 52.14 N | 0.17 W |
| Saint-Nicéphore | 206 | 45.50 N | 72.25 W |
| Saint-Nicolas → Sint-Niklaas, Bel. | 50 | 51.10 N | 4.08 E |
| Saint-Nicolas, Bel. | 56 | 50.38 N | 5.32 E |
| Saint-Nicolas, P.Q., Can. | 206 | 46.42 N | 71.24 W |
| Saint-Nicolas-aux-Bois | 50 | 49.36 N | 3.25 E |
| Saint-Nicolas-d'Aliermont | 50 | 49.53 N | 1.13 E |
| Saint-Nizier-du-Moucherotte | 62 | 45.10 N | 5.38 E |
| Saint-Nom-la-Bretèche | 261 | 48.51 N | 2.01 E |
| Saint Nora Lake ⊜ | 212 | 45.08 N | 78.49 W |
| Saint-Norbert-d'Arthabaska | 206 | 46.07 N | 71.50 W |
| Sainte-Odile ȣ[1] | 58 | 48.26 N | 7.24 E |
| Saint-Omer | 50 | 50.45 N | 2.15 E |
| Saintonge □[9] | 32 | 45.30 N | 0.30 W |
| Saint-Ouen, Fr. | 50 | 50.02 N | 2.03 E |
| Saint-Ouen, Fr. | 261 | 48.54 N | 2.20 E |
| Saint-Ouen-l'Aumône | 50 | 49.03 N | 2.06 E |
| Saint-Pacôme | 186 | 47.24 N | 69.57 W |
| Saint-Pamphile | 186 | 46.58 N | 69.47 W |
| Saint Pancras ◆[8] | 260 | 51.32 N | 0.07 W |
| Saint Paris | 218 | 40.07 N | 83.57 W |
| Saint-Pascal | 186 | 47.32 N | 69.49 W |
| Saint-Paterne | 50 | 48.24 N | 0.07 E |
| Saint-Pathus | 261 | 49.04 N | 2.48 E |
| Saint-Patrice, Lac ⊜ | 190 | 46.22 N | 77.20 W |
| Saint Paul, Ab., Can. | 182 | 53.59 N | 111.17 W |
| Saint-Paul, Fr. | 62 | 43.42 N | 7.07 E |
| Saint-Paul, Fr. | 62 | 44.31 N | 6.45 E |
| Saint-Paul, Réu. | 157c | 21.00 S | 55.16 E |
| Saint Paul, In., U.S. | 218 | 39.25 N | 85.28 W |
| Saint Paul, Ks., U.S. | 198 | 37.31 N | 95.10 W |
| Saint Paul, Mn., U.S. | 190 | 44.57 N | 93.05 W |
| Saint Paul, Ne., U.S. | 198 | 41.13 N | 98.27 W |
| Saint Paul, Or., U.S. | 224 | 45.12 N | 122.58 W |
| Saint Paul, Va., U.S. | 192 | 36.54 N | 82.18 W |
| Saint-Paul ≃, Can. | 176 | 51.26 N | 57.40 W |
| Saint Paul ≃, Liber. | 150 | 6.23 N | 10.48 W |
| Saint Paul, Cape › | 150 | 5.49 N | 0.57 E |
| Saint-Paul, Île I | 6 | 38.43 S | 77.29 E |
| Saint-Paul, Lac ⊜ | 206 | 46.18 N | 72.29 W |
| Saint Paul Bay c | 116 | 10.14 N | 118.54 E |
| Saint-Paul-de-Chester (Chesterville) | 206 | 45.57 N | 71.49 W |
| Saint-Paul-en-Jarez | 62 | 45.29 N | 4.35 E |
| Saint-Paul-et-Valmalle | 62 | 43.38 N | 3.40 E |
| Saint-Paulien | 62 | 45.08 N | 3.49 E |
| Saint-Paulin | 206 | 46.25 N | 73.01 W |
| Saint Paul Island | 180 | 57.07 N | 170.17 W |
| Saint Paul Island I, N.S., Can. | 186 | 47.15 N | 60.10 W |
| Saint Paul Island I, Ak., U.S. | 180 | 57.10 N | 170.15 W |
| Saint Pauls | 192 | 34.48 N | 78.58 W |
| Saint Paul's Cathedral ȣ[1] | 260 | 51.31 N | 0.06 W |
| Saint Paul's Cray ◆[8] | 260 | 51.24 N | 0.07 E |
| Saint Pauls Inlet c | 186 | 49.50 N | 57.45 W |
| Saint Paul's Point › | 174e | 25.04 S | 130.05 W |
| Saint-Paul-Trois-Châteaux | 62 | 44.21 N | 4.46 E |
| Saint-Péravy-la-Colombe | 50 | 48.00 N | 1.42 E |
| Saint-Péray | 62 | 44.57 N | 4.50 E |
| Saint-Père | 50 | 47.28 N | 3.46 E |
| Saint Peter, Il., U.S. | 219 | 38.52 N | 88.51 W |
| Saint Peter, Mn., U.S. | 190 | 44.19 N | 93.57 W |
| Saint Peter, Lake ⊜ | 212 | 45.18 N | 78.02 W |
| Saint Peter Island I | 162 | 32.17 S | 133.35 E |
| Saint Peter Port | 43b | 49.27 N | 2.32 W |
| Saint Peters, N.S., Can. | 186 | 45.40 N | 60.52 W |
| Saint Peters, Mo., U.S. | 219 | 38.48 N | 90.37 W |
| Saint Peters, Pa., U.S. | 285 | 40.11 N | 75.44 W |
| Saint Peters Bay | 186 | 46.25 N | 62.35 W |
| Saint Petersburg → Sankt-Peterburg, Ross. | 76 | 59.55 N | 30.15 E |
| Saint Petersburg, Fl., U.S. | 220 | 27.46 N | 82.40 W |
| Saint Petersburg, Pa., U.S. | 214 | 41.10 N | 79.37 W |
| Saint Petersburg Beach | 220 | 27.43 N | 82.44 W |
| Saint Peter's College ȣ[2] | 276 | 40.44 N | 74.05 W |
| Saint-Philippe-d'Argenteuil | 206 | 45.37 N | 74.25 W |
| Saint-Philippe-de-Laprairie | 275a | 45.21 N | 73.28 W |
| Saint-Pie | 206 | 45.30 N | 72.54 W |
| Saint-Pierre, P.Q., Can. | 275a | 45.27 N | 73.39 W |
| Saint-Pierre, Fr. | 62 | 45.40 N | 3.45 E |
| Saint-Pierre, It. | 62 | 45.42 N | 7.14 E |
| Saint-Pierre, Mart. | 240e | 14.45 N | 61.11 W |
| Saint-Pierre, Réu. | 157c | 21.19 S | 55.29 E |
| Saint-Pierre, St. P./M. | 186 | 46.47 N | 56.11 W |
| Saint-Pierre I | 186 | 46.47 N | 56.11 W |
| Saint-Pierre ≃ | 275a | 45.23 N | 73.34 W |
| Saint-Pierre, Lac ⊜, P.Q., Can. | 186 | 50.08 N | 68.26 W |
| Saint-Pierre, Lac ⊜, P.Q., Can. | 206 | 46.12 N | 72.52 W |
| Saint Pierre and Miquelon (Saint-Pierre-et-Miquelon) □[2], N.A. | 176 | 46.55 N | 56.20 W |
| Saint Pierre and Miquelon (Saint-Pierre-et-Miquelon) □[2], N.A. | 186 | 46.55 N | 56.20 W |
| Saint-Pierre-d'Albigny | 62 | 45.34 N | 6.09 E |
| Saint-Pierre-de-Bœuf | 62 | 45.22 N | 4.45 E |
| Saint-Pierre-de-Broughton | 206 | 46.15 N | 71.12 W |
| Saint-Pierre-de-Chartreuse | 62 | 45.20 N | 5.49 E |
| Saint-Pierre-des-Corps | 50 | 47.23 N | 0.44 E |
| Saint-Pierre-de-Vacquière | 62 | 43.52 N | 4.13 E |
| Saint-Pierre-du-Vauvray | 50 | 49.14 N | 1.13 E |
| Saint-Pierre-Église | 32 | 49.40 N | 1.24 W |
| Saint-Pierre-en-Port | 50 | 49.48 N | 0.29 E |
| Saint-Pierre-et-Miquelon → Saint Pierre and Miquelon □[2] | 186 | 46.55 N | 56.20 W |
| Saint Pierre Island I | 138 | 9.19 S | 50.43 E |
| Saint Pierre-Jolys | 184 | 49.26 N | 96.59 W |
| Saint Pierre-le-Moûtier | 32 | 46.48 N | 3.07 E |
| Saint-Pierre-lès-Elbeuf | 50 | 49.16 N | 1.03 E |
| Saint-Pierre-sur-Dives | 28 | 49.01 N | 0.02 W |
| Saint-Pierreville | 62 | 44.49 N | 4.29 E |
| Saint-Point, Lac de ⊜ | 58 | 46.49 N | 6.19 E |
| Saint-Pol-de-Léon | 32 | 48.41 N | 3.59 W |
| Saint-Pol-sur-Mer | 50 | 51.02 N | 2.21 E |
| Saint-Pol-sur-Ternoise | 50 | 50.23 N | 2.20 E |
| Saint-Polycarpe | 206 | 45.18 N | 74.18 W |
| Saint-Pons | 32 | 43.29 N | 2.46 E |
| Saint-Pourçain-sur-Sioule | 32 | 46.19 N | 3.17 E |
| Saint-Prex | 58 | 46.29 N | 6.28 E |
| Saint-Priest | 62 | 45.42 N | 4.57 E |
| Saint-Priest-en-Jarez | 62 | 45.28 N | 4.22 E |
| Saint-Prix | 261 | 49.01 N | 2.16 E |
| Saint-Prosper-de-Dorchester | 188 | 46.13 N | 70.29 W |
| Saint-Quentin, N.B., Can. | 186 | 47.30 N | 67.2[illegible] W |
| Saint-Quentin, Fr. | 50 | 49.51 N | 3.1[illegible] E |
| Saint-Quentin, Canal de ≊ | 50 | 49.36 N | 3.1[illegible] E |
| Saint-Quentin, Étang de ⊜ | 261 | 48.47 N | 2.0[illegible] E |
| Saint-Rambert-d'Albon | 62 | 45.17 N | 4.49 E |
| Saint-Rambert-en-Bugey | 58 | 45.57 N | 5.26 E |
| Saint-Rambert-sur-Loire | 62 | 45.30 N | 4.15 E |
| Saint-Raphaël | 62 | 43.25 N | 6.46 E |
| Saint-Raymond | 206 | 46.54 N | 71.50 W |
| Saint-Rédempter-de-Lévis | 206 | 46.42 N | 71.17 W |
| Saint Regis | 202 | 47.17 N | 115.06 W |
| Saint-Régis ≃, P.Q., Can. | 275a | 45.24 N | 73.34 W |
| Saint Regis ≃, N.A. | 188 | 45.00 N | 74.39 W |
| Saint Regis ≃, Mt., U.S. | 202 | 47.18 N | 115.05 W |
| Saint Regis, West Branch ≃ | 188 | 44.47 N | 74.46 W |
| Saint Regis Falls | 188 | 44.40 N | 74.32 W |
| Saint Regis Indian Reservation ◆[4] | 206 | 44.58 N | 74.39 W |
| Saint-Rémi | 206 | 45.16 N | 73.37 W |
| Saint-Rémi-d'Amherst | 206 | 46.01 N | 74.46 W |
| Saint-Rémy (lès-Chevreuse), Fr. | 50 | 48.42 N | 2.05 E |
| Saint-Rémy, Fr. | 58 | 46.46 N | 4.50 E |
| Saint Remy, N.Y., U.S. | 210 | 41.54 N | 74.01 W |
| Saint-Rémy-de-Provence | 62 | 43.47 N | 4.50 E |
| Saint-Rémy-en-Bouzemont | 58 | 48.38 N | 4.39 E |
| Saint-Rémy-l'Honoré | 261 | 48.45 N | 1.53 E |
| Saint-Rémy-sur-Avre | 50 | 48.46 N | 1.15 E |
| Saint-Renan | 32 | 48.26 N | 4.37 W |
| Saint-Révérien | 50 | 47.13 N | 3.30 E |
| Saint-Rhémy | 62 | 45.50 N | 7.11 E |
| Saint-Riquier | 50 | 50.08 N | 1.57 E |
| Saint Robert | 194 | 37.50 N | 92.09 W |
| Saint-Roch-de-l'Achigan | 206 | 45.51 N | 73.36 W |
| Saint-Romain-de-Colbosc | 50 | 49.32 N | 0.22 E |
| Saint-Romain-le-Puy | 62 | 45.33 N | 4.07 E |
| Saint-Romans | 62 | 45.07 N | 5.19 E |
| Saint-Romuald | 206 | 46.45 N | 71.14 W |
| Sainte-Rosalie | 206 | 45.38 N | 72.54 W |
| Sainte-Rose | 241o | 16.20 N | 61.42 W |
| Sainte-Rose ◆[8] | 275a | 45.36 N | 73.47 W |
| Sainte-Rose-du-Lac | 184 | 51.03 N | 99.32 W |
| Saintry-sur-Seine | 261 | 48.36 N | 2.30 E |
| Saintes, Bel. | 50 | 50.42 N | 4.10 E |
| Saintes, Fr. | 32 | 45.45 N | 0.38 W |
| Saint-Saëns | 50 | 49.40 N | 1.17 E |
| Saint Sampson | 43b | 49.29 N | 2.31 W |
| Saint-Satur | 50 | 47.20 N | 2.51 E |
| Saint-Saturnin-d'Apt | 62 | 43.56 N | 5.23 E |
| Saint-Sauveur, Fr. | 50 | 47.37 N | 3.12 E |
| Saint-Sauveur, Fr. | 58 | 47.48 N | 6.23 E |
| Saint-Sauveur-des-Monts | 206 | 45.52 N | 74.10 W |
| Saint-Sauveur-sur-Tinée | 62 | 44.05 N | 7.06 E |
| Saint-Savin | 32 | 46.34 N | 0.52 E |
| Saint-Savinien | 32 | 45.53 N | 0.41 W |
| Saint Saviour | 43b | 49.11 N | 2.06 W |
| Saint Sebastian Bay c | 158 | 34.25 S | 21.00 E |
| Saint-Sébastien | 206 | 45.07 N | 73.09 W |
| Saint-Sébastien, Cap › | 157b | 12.26 S | 48.44 E |
| Saint-Seine-l'Abbaye | 58 | 47.26 N | 4.47 E |
| Saint Séverin | 56 | 50.32 N | 5.25 E |
| Saint Shotts | 186 | 46.38 N | 53.35 W |
| Sainte-Sigolène | 62 | 45.14 N | 4.15 E |
| Saint-Siméon | 186 | 47.50 N | 69.53 W |
| Saint-Simon | 50 | 49.45 N | 3.10 E |
| Saint Simons Island | 192 | 31.09 N | 81.22 W |
| Saint Simons Island I | 192 | 31.14 N | 81.21 W |
| Saint-Sixte ≃ | 206 | 45.39 N | 75.08 W |
| Saintes-Maries, Golfe des c | 62 | 43.25 N | 4.31 E |
| Saintes-Maries-de-la-Mer | 62 | 43.27 N | 4.26 E |
| Sainte-Sophie-de-Mégantic | 206 | 46.09 N | 71.42 W |
| Saint-Soupplets | 261 | 49.02 N | 2.48 E |
| Saint Stanislas Bay c | 174o | 1.53 N | 157.30 W |
| Saint-Stanislas-de-Kosta | 206 | 45.11 N | 74.08 W |
| Saint Stephen, N.B., Can. | 186 | 45.12 N | 67.17 W |
| Saint Stephen, S.C., U.S. | 192 | 33.24 N | 79.55 W |
| Saint-Sulpice-de-Favières | 261 | 48.33 N | 2.11 E |
| Saint-Sulpice-les-Feuilles | 32 | 46.19 N | 1.22 E |
| Sainte-Suzanne | 58 | 47.30 N | 6.46 E |
| Saint-Sylvestre | 206 | 46.22 N | 71.14 W |
| Saint-Symphorien, Fr. | 32 | 44.26 N | 0.30 W |
| Saint-Symphorien, Fr. | 261 | 48.31 N | 1.46 E |
| Saint-Symphorien-d'Ozon | 62 | 45.38 N | 4.52 E |
| Saint-Symphorien-sur-Coise | 62 | 45.38 N | 4.27 E |
| Sainte-Thècle | 206 | 46.49 N | 72.31 W |
| Saint-Théodore-d'Acton | 206 | 45.41 N | 72.35 W |
| Sainte-Thérèse | 206 | 45.38 N | 73.51 W |
| Sainte-Thérèse, Île I, P.Q., Can. | 275a | 45.41 N | 73.28 W |
| Sainte-Thérèse, Île I, P.Q., Can. | 275a | 45.22 N | 73.15 W |
| Saint-Thibault-des-Vignes | 261 | 48.52 N | 2.41 E |
| Saint Thomas, On., Can. | 212 | 42.47 N | 81.12 W |
| Saint Thomas, Mo., U.S. | 219 | 38.22 N | 92.13 W |


| | English | Deutsch | Español | Français | Português |
|---|---|---|---|---|---|
| ≃ | River | Fluß | Río | Rivière | Rio |
| ≊ | Canal | Kanal | Canal | Canal | Canal |
| ʟ | Waterfall, Rapids | Wasserfall, Stromschnellen | Cascada, Rápidos | Chute d'eau, Rapides | Cascata, Rápidos |
| ʊ | Strait | Meeresstraße | Estrecho | Détroit | Estreito |
| c | Bay, Gulf | Bucht, Golf | Bahía, Golfo | Baie, Golfe | Baía, Golfo |
| ⊜ | Lake, Lakes | See, Seen | Lago, Lagos | Lac, Lacs | Lago, Lagos |
| ≡ | Swamp | Sumpf | Pantano | Marais | Pântano |
| ⍓ | Ice Features, Glacier | Eis- und Gletscherformen | Accidentes Glaciales | Formes glaciaires | Acidentes glaciares |
| ⊤ | Other Hydrographic Features | Andere Hydrographische Objekte | Otros Elementos Hidrográficos | Autres données hydrographiques | Outros acidentes hidrográficos |

| | English | Deutsch | Español | Français | Português |
|---|---|---|---|---|---|
| ✢ | Submarine Features | Untermeerische Objekte | Accidentes Submarinos | Formes de relief sous-marin | Acidentes submarinos |
| □ | Political Unit | Politische Einheit | Unidad Politica | Entité politique | Unidade política |
| ȣ | Cultural Institution | Kulturelle Institution | Institución Cultural | Institution culturelle | Institução cultural |
| ⊥ | Historical Site | Historische Stätte | Sitio Histórico | Site historique | Sitio histórico |
| ♠ | Recreational Site | Erholungs- und Ferienort | Sitio de Recreo | Centre de loisirs | Area de Lazer |
| ⊠ | Airport | Flughafen | Aeropuerto | Aéroport | Aeroporto |
| ■ | Military Installation | Militäranlage | Instalación Militar | Installation militaire | Instalação militar |
| ◆ | Miscellaneous | Verschiedenes | Misceláneo | Divers | Diversos |

| Name | Page | Lat.°′ | Long.°′ |
|---|---|---|---|
| Saint Thomas, N.D., U.S. | 198 | 48.37 N | 97.26 W |
| Saint Thomas → Charlotte Amalie, Vir. Is., U.S. | 240m | 18.21 N | 64.56 W |
| Saint Thomas I | 240m | 18.21 N | 64.55 W |
| Saint-Timothée | 206 | 45.18 N | 74.02 W |
| Saint-Tite | 206 | 46.44 N | 72.34 W |
| Saint-Tite-des-Caps | 186 | 47.08 N | 70.47 W |
| Saint-Trivier-de-Courtes | 58 | 46.28 N | 5.05 E |
| Saint-Trivier-sur-Moignans | 58 | 46.04 N | 4.54 E |
| Saint-Tropez | 62 | 43.16 N | 6.38 E |
| Saint Tudy | 42 | 50.33 N | 4.43 W |
| Sainte-Tulle | 62 | 43.47 N | 5.46 E |
| Saint-Ubald | 206 | 46.45 N | 72.16 W |
| Saint-Urbain-de-Charlevoix | 186 | 47.33 N | 70.32 W |
| Saint-Ursanne | 58 | 47.22 N | 7.10 E |
| Saint-Uze | 62 | 45.11 N | 4.52 E |
| Saint-Valérien | 50 | 48.11 N | 3.06 E |
| Saint-Valéry-en-Caux | 50 | 49.52 N | 0.44 E |
| Saint-Valéry-sur-Somme | 50 | 50.11 N | 1.38 E |
| Saint-Vallier, Fr. | 58 | 46.38 N | 4.22 E |
| Saint-Vallier, Fr. | 62 | 45.10 N | 4.49 E |
| Saint-Vallier-de-Thiey | 62 | 43.42 N | 6.51 E |
| Saint-Varent | 32 | 46.53 N | 0.14 W |
| Saint-Venant | 50 | 50.37 N | 2.33 E |
| Saint-Véran | 62 | 44.42 N | 6.52 E |
| Sainte-Victoire, Montagne ∧ | 62 | 43.32 N | 5.39 E |
| Saint-Victoret | 62 | 43.25 N | 5.14 E |
| Saint-Vincent, It. | 62 | 45.45 N | 7.39 E |
| Saint Vincent, Mn., U.S. | 198 | 48.58 N | 97.13 W |
| Saint Vincent I | 241h | 13.15 N | 61.12 W |
| Saint-Vincent, Baie de ⊂ | 175f | 22.00 S | 166.05 E |
| Saint-Vincent, Cap › | 157b | 21.57 S | 43.16 E |
| Saint Vincent, Cape ›, Austl. | 166 | 43.18 S | 145.50 E |
| Saint Vincent, Cape → São Vicente, Cabo de ›, Port. | 34 | 37.01 N | 9.00 W |
| Saint Vincent, Gulf ⊂ | 168b | 35.00 S | 138.05 E |
| Saint Vincent and the Grenadines □[1], N.A. | 230 | 13.15 N | 61.12 W |
| Saint Vincent and the Grenadines □[1], N.A. | 241h | 13.15 N | 61.12 W |
| Saint-Vincent-de-Paul ◆[8] | 275a | 45.37 N | 73.39 W |
| Saint-Vincent-de-Tyrosse | 32 | 43.40 N | 1.18 W |
| Saint Vincent Passage ʮ | 238 | 13.30 N | 61.00 W |
| Saint Vincent's | 186 | 46.48 N | 53.38 W |
| Saint-Vit | 58 | 47.11 N | 5.49 E |
| Saint-Vith | 56 | 50.17 N | 6.08 E |
| Saint-Vivien-de-Médoc | 32 | 45.26 N | 1.02 W |
| Saint-Vrain | 261 | 48.33 N | 2.20 E |
| Saint Walburg | 184 | 53.39 N | 109.12 W |
| Saint-Wandrille-Rançon | 50 | 49.32 N | 0.46 E |
| Saint-Wenceslas ≃ | 206 | 46.18 N | 72.23 W |
| Saint Williams | 212 | 42.40 N | 80.25 W |
| Saint-Witz | 261 | 49.05 N | 2.34 E |
| Saint-Yrieix-la-Perche | 32 | 45.31 N | 1.12 E |
| Saint-Yvon | 186 | 49.10 N | 64.48 W |
| Saint-Zacharie | 62 | 43.23 N | 5.43 E |
| Saint-Zénon | 206 | 46.33 N | 73.49 W |
| Sāinthiya | 126 | 23.57 N | 87.40 E |
| Saipan I | 174n | 15.12 N | 145.45 E |
| Saipan Channel ʮ | 174n | 15.05 N | 145.41 E |
| Saipan International Airport ⊠ | 174n | 15.07 N | 145.43 E |
| Saiqi | 100 | 27.00 N | 119.43 E |
| Saishu-to → Cheju-do I | 90 | 33.20 N | 126.30 E |
| Saita | 96 | 34.08 N | 133.49 E |
| Saita ≃ | 96 | 34.08 N | 133.38 E |
| Saitama □[5] | 94 | 36.00 N | 139.30 E |
| Saitama University υ[2] | 268 | 35.52 N | 139.36 E |
| Saito | 92 | 32.06 N | 131.24 E |
| Saiwai ◆[8] | 268 | 35.33 N | 139.41 E |
| Saiwa Swamp National Park ♦ | 154 | 1.06 N | 35.12 E |
| Saiyidān ◆[8] | 272a | 28.40 N | 77.05 E |
| Sai Yok | 110 | 14.07 N | 99.08 E |
| Sajak | 86 | 47.02 N | 77.22 E |
| Sajam | 164 | 0.53 S | 132.41 E |
| Sajama | 248 | 18.07 S | 69.00 W |
| Sajama, Nevado ∧ | 248 | 18.06 S | 68.54 W |
| Sajan → Sayan Mountains ⋏ | 88 | 52.45 N | 96.00 E |
| Sajanogorsk | 86 | 53.08 N | 91.29 E |
| Sajano-Šušenskoje vodochranilišče ⊜[1] | 86 | 52.20 N | 92.25 E |
| Sajantuj | 88 | 51.44 N | 107.30 E |
| Sajasan | 84 | 43.03 N | 46.17 E |
| Sajat | 128 | 38.47 N | 63.53 E |
| Sajchan | 88 | 48.40 N | 102.39 E |
| Sajchandulaan | 102 | 44.40 N | 109.01 E |
| Sajchan-Ovoo | 102 | 45.27 N | 103.54 E |
| Sajchin | 80 | 48.50 N | 46.47 E |
| Sajen | 115a | 7.40 S | 112.31 E |
| Šajgino | 80 | 57.46 N | 46.51 E |
| Şajīd I | 144 | 16.52 N | 41.50 E |
| Šajmak' | 120 | 37.27 N | 74.44 E |
| Sajnšand | 102 | 44.52 N | 110.09 E |
| Sajó (Slaná) ≃ | 30 | 47.56 N | 21.08 E |
| Sajószentpéter | 30 | 48.13 N | 20.44 E |
| Sajram | 85 | 42.18 N | 69.45 E |
| Sajukino | 80 | 52.47 N | 41.59 E |
| Sājūr (Bağırsak) ≃ | 130 | 36.40 N | 38.05 E |
| Sak ≃ | 158 | 30.02 S | 20.40 E |
| Saka, Kenya | 154 | 0.09 S | 39.20 E |
| Saka, Nihon | 96 | 34.20 N | 132.31 E |
| Sakado | 94 | 35.57 N | 139.24 E |
| Sakae, Nihon | 94 | 35.50 N | 140.15 E |
| Sakae, Nihon | 94 | 36.58 N | 138.35 E |
| Sa Kaeo | 110 | 13.49 N | 102.04 E |
| Sakahogi | 94 | 35.26 N | 136.59 E |
| Sakai, Nihon | 94 | 36.10 N | 136.14 E |
| Sakai, Nihon | 94 | 36.16 N | 139.15 E |
| Sakai, Nihon | 94 | 36.06 N | 139.48 E |
| Sakai, Nihon | 96 | 34.35 N | 135.28 E |
| Sakai, Nihon | 268 | 35.25 N | 139.22 E |
| Sakai ≃ | 94 | 35.18 N | 139.29 E |
| Sakaide | 96 | 34.19 N | 133.52 E |
| Sakaigawa | 94 | 35.35 N | 138.37 E |
| Sakaiminato | 96 | 35.33 N | 133.15 E |
| Sakākah | 128 | 29.59 N | 40.06 E |
| Sakakawea, Lake ⊜[1] | 198 | 47.50 N | 102.20 W |
| Sakaki | 94 | 36.28 N | 138.11 E |
| Sakakita | 94 | 36.25 N | 138.01 E |
| Sakala, Pulau I | 112 | 6.54 S | 116.15 E |
| Sakami ≃ | 176 | 53.40 N | 76.40 W |
| Sakami, Lac ⊜ | 176 | 53.15 N | 76.45 W |
| Sakania | 154 | 12.45 S | 28.34 E |
| Sakar | 128 | 38.56 N | 63.45 E |
| Sakar ⋏ | 38 | 41.59 N | 26.16 E |
| Sakaraha | 157b | 22.55 S | 44.32 E |
| Sakar-Čaga | 128 | 37.38 N | 61.40 E |
| Sakar Island I | 164 | 5.25 S | 148.05 E |
| Sakartvelo → Georgia □[1] | 22 | 42.00 N | 44.00 E |
| Sakarya | 130 | 40.46 N | 30.24 E |
| Sakarya □[4] | 130 | 40.45 N | 30.35 E |
| Sakarya ≃ | 130 | 41.07 N | 30.39 E |
| Sakashita | 94 | 35.34 N | 137.32 E |
| Sakassou | 150 | 7.27 N | 5.18 W |
| Sakata | 92 | 38.55 N | 139.50 E |
| Sakauchi | 94 | 35.36 N | 136.25 E |
| Sakawa | 96 | 33.30 N | 133.17 E |
| Sakawa ≃ | 94 | 35.15 N | 139.11 E |
| Sakchu | 98 | 40.23 N | 125.01 E |
| Sakesar | 123 | 32.33 N | 71.56 E |
| Sakété | 150 | 6.43 N | 2.40 E |
| Sakhā | 142 | 31.05 N | 30.57 E |
| Sakhalin → Sachalin, ostrov I | 89 | 51.00 N | 143.00 E |
| Sākhar | 120 | 32.57 N | 65.32 E |
| Sakhi Sarwar | 120 | 29.59 N | 70.18 E |
| Sakhnin | 132 | 32.52 N | 35.17 E |
| Sakhnovshchyna | 78 | 49.08 N | 35.53 E |
| Şakhrīyāt, Jabal aş- ∧ | 132 | 31.01 N | 36.21 E |
| Sakht Sar | 128 | 36.53 N | 50.41 E |
| Şāki ◆[8] | 272c | 19.06 N | 72.53 E |
| Šakiai | 76 | 54.57 N | 23.03 E |
| Sākib | 132 | 32.17 N | 35.49 E |
| Sakiet Sidi Youssef | 36 | 36.13 N | 8.22 E |
| Sakijang Bendera, Pulau I | 271c | 1.13 N | 103.51 E |
| Sakijang Pelepah, Pulau I | 271c | 1.13 N | 103.52 E |
| Sakishima-shotō II | 175d | 24.46 N | 124.00 E |
| Sakito | 92 | 33.02 N | 129.32 E |
| Sakkara → Şaqqārah | 142 | 29.51 N | 31.13 E |
| Sakmara ≃ | 86 | 51.46 N | 55.01 E |
| Sako | 270 | 34.53 N | 135.47 E |
| Sakon Nakhon | 110 | 17.10 N | 104.09 E |
| Sakonnet | 207 | 41.28 N | 71.12 W |
| Sakonnet Point › | 207 | 41.27 N | 71.12 W |
| Sakoyra | 150 | 14.17 N | 1.24 E |
| Sakra, Pulau I | 271c | 1.16 N | 103.42 E |
| Sakrand | 120 | 26.08 N | 68.16 E |
| Sakrivier | 158 | 30.54 S | 20.28 E |
| Saks | 194 | 33.42 N | 85.52 W |
| Saksahan' ≃ | 78 | 47.53 N | 33.18 E |
| Saksauldala ◆[2] | 86 | 44.30 N | 73.00 E |
| Sakskøbing | 41 | 54.48 N | 11.39 E |
| Sakti | 124 | 22.02 N | 82.58 E |
| Saku, Nihon | 94 | 36.09 N | 138.30 E |
| Saku, Nihon | 94 | 36.13 N | 138.29 E |
| Sakubva | 154 | 19.00 S | 32.10 E |
| Sakugi | 96 | 34.52 N | 132.43 E |
| Sakuma | 94 | 35.05 N | 137.48 E |
| Sakuma-dam ◆[6] | 94 | 35.05 N | 137.47 E |
| Sakuma-ko ⊜[1] | 94 | 35.08 N | 137.47 E |
| Sakura | 94 | 35.43 N | 140.14 E |
| Sakura ≃ | 94 | 36.05 N | 140.14 E |
| Sakurae | 96 | 34.57 N | 132.20 E |
| Sakurai | 96 | 34.30 N | 135.51 E |
| Sakura-tōge )( | 270 | 34.36 N | 135.53 E |
| Saku-shima I | 94 | 34.43 N | 137.03 E |
| Sakutō | 96 | 35.01 N | 134.14 E |
| Sakwaso Lake ⊜ | 184 | 53.01 N | 91.55 W |
| Saky | 78 | 45.09 N | 33.35 E |
| Säkylä | 26 | 61.02 N | 22.20 E |
| Sakyō ◆[8] | 270 | 35.02 N | 135.48 E |
| Sal I | 150a | 16.45 N | 22.55 W |
| Sal ≃ | 80 | 47.31 N | 40.45 E |
| Sal, Cay I | 238 | 23.42 N | 80.24 W |
| Sal, Ponta do › | 266c | 38.41 N | 9.22 W |
| Şal, Punta › | 236 | 15.53 N | 87.37 W |
| Šal'a, Ross. | 86 | 57.15 N | 58.43 E |
| Šal'a, Slvk. | 30 | 48.09 N | 17.52 E |
| Sala, Sve. | 40 | 59.55 N | 16.36 E |
| Sala, Ouadi V | 146 | 17.00 N | 20.53 E |
| Sala Baganza | 64 | 44.43 N | 10.14 E |
| Salabangka, Kepulauan II | 112 | 3.02 S | 122.25 E |
| Salaberry, Île de I | 206 | 45.17 N | 74.07 W |
| Salaberry-de-Valleyfield | 206 | 45.15 N | 74.08 W |
| Salaca ≃ | 76 | 57.45 N | 24.21 E |
| Salacgrīva | 76 | 57.45 N | 24.21 E |
| Sala Consilina | 68 | 40.24 N | 15.36 E |
| Salada, Laguna ⊜, Arg. | 258 | 35.17 S | 59.24 W |
| Salada, Laguna ⊜, Méx. | 232 | 32.20 N | 115.40 W |
| Saladas | 252 | 28.15 S | 58.38 W |
| Saladillo | 252 | 35.38 S | 59.46 W |
| Saladillo ≃, Arg. | 252 | 33.25 S | 63.02 W |
| Saladillo ≃, Arg. | 252 | 29.05 S | 63.25 W |
| Saladillo, Arroyo ≃ | 258 | 35.33 S | 59.04 W |
| Saladillo de Rodríguez, Arroyo ≃ | 258 | 35.29 S | 59.01 W |
| Saladillo Dulce, Arroyo ≃ | 252 | 31.25 S | 60.33 W |
| Salado, Arg. | 252 | 28.18 S | 67.15 W |
| Salado, Tx., U.S. | 222 | 30.57 N | 97.32 W |
| Salado ≃, Arg. | 252 | 38.49 S | 64.57 W |
| Salado ≃, Arg. | 252 | 31.42 S | 60.44 W |
| Salado ≃, Arg. | 252 | 35.44 S | 57.21 W |
| Salado ≃, Arg. | 252 | 29.13 S | 66.34 W |
| Salado ≃, Cuba | 240p | 20.36 N | 76.56 W |
| Salado ≃, Méx. | 232 | 26.52 N | 99.19 W |
| Salado ≃, Méx. | 234 | 18.44 N | 103.36 W |
| Salado ≃, Méx. | 234 | 17.55 N | 96.58 W |
| Salado, Arroyo ≃, Arg. | 254 | 41.37 S | 65.02 W |
| Salado, Arroyo ≃, Arg. | 254 | 40.35 S | 66.33 W |
| Salado, Rio ≃ | 200 | 34.16 N | 106.52 W |
| Salado Creek ≃, Tx., U.S. | 196 | 29.14 N | 98.25 W |
| Salado Creek ≃, Tx., U.S. | 222 | 30.59 N | 97.25 W |
| Salaga | 150 | 8.33 N | 0.31 W |
| Salagle | 144 | 1.50 N | 42.17 E |
| Sālah | 132 | 32.38 N | 36.46 E |
| Şalāh ad-Dīn □[4] | 128 | 34.15 N | 43.55 E |
| Şalahin | 144 | 2.57 N | 46.26 E |
| Sala'ilua | 175a | 13.41 S | 172.34 W |
| Salair | 86 | 54.13 N | 85.47 E |
| Salairskij kr'až ∧ | 86 | 54.15 N | 85.30 E |
| Sălaj □[6] | 38 | 47.15 N | 23.00 E |
| Salak | 114 | 2.34 N | 98.20 E |
| Salak, Gunung ∧ | 115a | 6.42 S | 106.44 E |
| Şalakas | 76 | 55.35 N | 26.08 E |
| Šalakuša | 24 | 62.15 N | 40.17 E |
| Salal | 146 | 14.51 N | 17.13 E |
| Salala, Chile | 252 | 30.41 S | 71.32 W |
| Salala, Liber. | 150 | 6.40 N | 10.05 W |
| Salālah, Sūd. | 140 | 21.19 N | 36.13 E |
| Şalālah, 'Umān | 118 | 17.00 N | 54.06 E |
| Salamá, Guat. | 236 | 15.06 N | 90.16 W |
| Salamá, Hond. | 236 | 14.50 N | 86.36 W |
| Salamajärven kansallispuisto ♦ | 26 | 63.20 N | 24.40 E |
| Salaman | 115a | 7.35 S | 110.08 E |
| Salamanca, Chile | 252 | 31.47 S | 70.58 W |
| Salamanca, Esp. | 34 | 40.58 N | 5.39 W |
| Salamanca, Méx. | 234 | 20.34 N | 101.12 W |
| Salamanca, Perú | 248 | 15.31 S | 72.50 W |
| Salamanca, Perú | 286d | 12.05 S | 77.00 W |
| Salamanca, N.Y., U.S. | 210 | 42.09 N | 78.42 W |
| Salamanca □[4] | 34 | 40.45 N | 6.00 W |
| Salamanga | 158 | 26.28 S | 32.39 E |
| Salamat □[5] | 146 | 11.00 N | 20.30 E |
| Salamat, Bahr ≃ | 146 | 9.27 N | 18.06 E |
| Salāmbek | 120 | 28.18 N | 65.09 E |
| Salamina | 246 | 5.25 N | 75.29 W |
| Salamínos, Órmos ⊂ | 267c | 37.56 N | 23.27 E |
| Salamís | 38 | 37.58 N | 23.29 E |
| Salamís I | 38 | 37.54 N | 23.26 E |
| Salamis ⊥ | 130 | 35.10 N | 33.54 E |
| Salamīyah | 130 | 35.01 N | 37.03 E |
| Salām Khān | 120 | 31.47 N | 66.45 E |
| Salamonia | 216 | 40.23 N | 84.52 W |
| Salamonie ≃ | 216 | 40.50 N | 85.43 W |
| Salamonie Lake ⊜[1] | 216 | 40.46 N | 85.37 W |
| Salāmūn | 142 | 31.04 N | 31.28 E |
| Salandra | 68 | 40.31 N | 16.19 E |
| Sālang, Tūnel-e ◆[5] | 120 | 35.19 N | 69.02 E |
| Salani | 175a | 14.00 S | 171.33 W |
| Salantai | 76 | 56.04 N | 21.32 E |
| Salaparuta | 70 | 37.47 N | 13.00 E |
| Salaquí | 246 | 7.18 N | 77.33 W |
| Salaquí ≃ | 246 | 7.27 N | 77.07 W |
| Salāqūs | 142 | 28.44 N | 30.50 E |
| Salar | 85 | 41.21 N | 69.22 E |
| Salara | 64 | 44.59 N | 11.25 E |
| Sălard | 38 | 47.13 N | 22.03 E |
| Salarjovo | 265b | 55.37 N | 37.26 E |
| Salas | 248 | 6.16 S | 79.37 W |
| Salas de los Infantes | 34 | 42.01 N | 3.17 W |
| Salat ≃ | 32 | 43.10 N | 0.58 E |
| Salatiga | 115a | 7.19 S | 110.30 E |
| Salauš | 80 | 55.59 N | 52.53 E |
| Salavat | 86 | 53.21 N | 55.55 E |
| Salavaux | 58 | 46.55 N | 7.02 E |
| Salaverry | 248 | 8.14 S | 78.58 W |
| Salavina | 252 | 28.48 S | 63.25 W |
| Salawati I | 164 | 1.07 S | 130.52 E |
| Salawe | 154 | 3.19 S | 32.52 E |
| Salay | 116 | 8.52 N | 124.47 E |
| Salāya | 120 | 22.19 N | 69.35 E |
| Sala y Gómez, Isla I | 18 | 26.28 S | 105.28 W |
| Sala y Gomez Ridge ✣[3] | 18 | 25.00 S | 98.00 W |
| Salazgor' | 80 | 54.07 N | 43.09 E |
| Salba | 88 | 53.14 N | 92.36 E |
| Salbani | 126 | 22.38 N | 87.20 E |
| Salbohed | 40 | 59.55 N | 16.19 E |
| Salbosjön ⊜ | 40 | 59.50 N | 14.54 E |
| Şalbris | 50 | 47.26 N | 2.03 E |
| Šalbuzdag, gora ∧ | 84 | 41.19 N | 47.48 E |
| Salcajá | 236 | 14.53 N | 91.27 W |
| Salccantay, Nevado ∧ | 248 | 13.20 S | 72.33 W |
| Salcedo, Pil. | 116 | 11.09 N | 125.40 E |
| Salcedo, Rep. Dom. | 238 | 19.23 N | 70.25 W |
| Salcha ≃ | 180 | 64.29 N | 147.00 W |
| Salching | 60 | 48.49 N | 12.34 E |
| Şalcia | 38 | 43.57 N | 24.56 E |
| Šalčininkai | 76 | 54.18 N | 25.23 E |
| Salcombe | 42 | 50.13 N | 3.47 W |
| Şalda ≃ | 86 | 58.48 N | 61.20 E |
| Šaldaj | 86 | 51.56 N | 78.48 E |
| Saldaña | 34 | 42.31 N | 4.44 W |
| Saldaña ≃ | 246 | 4.01 N | 74.52 W |
| Saldanha | 158 | 33.00 S | 17.56 E |
| Şaldanhabaai ⊂ | 158 | 33.04 S | 18.00 E |
| Šaldež | 80 | 56.52 N | 44.46 E |
| Saldungaray | 252 | 38.12 S | 61.47 W |
| Saldus | 76 | 56.40 N | 22.30 E |
| Sale, Austl. | 166 | 38.06 S | 147.04 E |
| Sale, It. | 62 | 44.59 N | 8.48 E |
| Salé, Magreb | 148 | 34.04 N | 6.50 W |
| Sale, Eng., U.K. | 44 | 53.26 N | 2.19 W |
| Salebabu, Pulau I | 108 | 3.55 N | 126.40 E |
| Salechard | 74 | 66.33 N | 66.40 E |
| Sale Creek | 194 | 35.22 N | 85.06 W |
| Salée, Rivière ʮ | 241o | 16.17 N | 61.33 W |
| Saleh, Teluk ⊂ | 115b | 8.34 S | 117.57 E |
| Salelologa | 175a | 13.44 S | 172.10 W |
| Salem, On., Can. | 212 | 43.42 N | 80.27 W |
| Salem, Dtsch. | 58 | 47.46 N | 9.16 E |
| Salem, India | 122 | 11.39 N | 78.10 E |
| Salem, S. Afr. | 158 | 33.28 S | 26.29 E |
| Salem, Sve. | 40 | 59.13 N | 17.44 E |
| Salem, Ar., U.S. | 194 | 36.22 N | 91.49 W |
| Salem, Il., U.S. | 219 | 38.37 N | 88.56 W |
| Salem, In., U.S. | 218 | 38.03 N | 86.15 W |
| Salem, Ia., U.S. | 190 | 40.51 N | 91.37 W |
| Salem, Ky., U.S. | 194 | 37.15 N | 88.14 W |
| Salem, Ma., U.S. | 207 | 42.31 N | 70.53 W |
| Salem, Mi., U.S. | 281 | 42.24 N | 83.34 W |
| Salem, Mo., U.S. | 194 | 37.38 N | 91.32 W |
| Salem, N.H., U.S. | 207 | 42.47 N | 71.12 W |
| Salem, N.J., U.S. | 208 | 39.34 N | 75.28 W |
| Salem, N.Y., U.S. | 210 | 43.10 N | 73.19 W |
| Salem, Oh., U.S. | 214 | 40.54 N | 80.51 W |
| Salem, Or., U.S. | 224 | 44.56 N | 123.02 W |
| Salem, S.D., U.S. | 198 | 43.43 N | 97.23 W |
| Salem, Ut,. U.S. | 200 | 40.03 N | 111.40 W |
| Salem, Va., U.S. | 192 | 37.17 N | 80.03 W |
| Salem, W.V., U.S. | 188 | 39.16 N | 80.33 W |
| Salem, Wi., U.S. | 216 | 42.33 N | 88.06 W |
| Salem □[6] | 208 | 39.34 N | 75.20 W |
| Salem ≃ | 208 | 39.34 N | 75.31 W |
| Salem Airfield ⊠ | 281 | 42.25 N | 83.34 W |
| Sale Marasino | 64 | 45.43 N | 10.06 E |
| Salem Canal ≅ | 285 | 39.41 N | 75.31 W |
| Salem Depot | 283 | 42.47 N | 71.12 W |
| Salem Harbor ⊂ | 283 | 42.31 N | 70.53 W |
| Salem Heights | 214 | 40.54 N | 80.53 W |
| Salemi | 70 | 37.49 N | 12.48 E |
| Salem Maritime National Historic Site ⊥ | 207 | 42.31 N | 70.53 W |
| Salem State College υ[2] | 283 | 42.30 N | 70.54 W |
| Salem Upland ⋏[1] | 194 | 37.25 N | 91.30 W |
| Sälen, Sve. | 26 | 61.10 N | 13.16 E |
| Salen, Scot., U.K. | 46 | 56.43 N | 5.47 W |
| Salen, Scot., U.K. | 46 | 56.31 N | 5.57 W |
| Salentina, Penisola ›[1] | 68 | 40.25 N | 18.00 E |
| Salentine, Murge ◆[1] | 68 | 40.02 N | 18.13 E |
| Salento | 68 | 40.15 N | 15.11 E |
| Salernes | 62 | 43.33 N | 6.14 E |
| Salerno | 68 | 40.41 N | 14.47 E |
| Salerno □[4] | 68 | 40.27 N | 15.16 E |
| Salerno, Golfo di ⊂ | 68 | 40.32 N | 14.42 E |
| Salers | 32 | 45.08 N | 2.30 E |
| Salesbury | 262 | 53.47 N | 2.30 W |
| Salesópolis | 256 | 23.32 S | 45.51 W |
| Salève, Mont ∧ | 58 | 46.07 N | 6.10 E |
| Salford | 44 | 53.28 N | 2.18 W |
| Salford □[8] | 262 | 53.28 N | 2.23 W |
| Şalfords | 260 | 51.12 N | 0.10 W |
| Šalgačova | 24 | 62.19 N | 39.35 E |
| Salgado | 250 | 11.02 S | 37.28 W |
| Salgan | 80 | 55.14 N | 45.30 E |
| Şalgar | 246 | 5.58 N | 75.59 W |
| Šalgija | 86 | 47.35 N | 70.36 E |
| Salgótarján | 30 | 48.07 N | 19.48 E |
| Salgueiro | 250 | 8.04 S | 39.06 W |
| Salher ∧ | 122 | 20.43 N | 73.56 E |
| Salhyr ≃ | 78 | 45.38 N | 35.01 E |
| Sali, Alg. | 148 | 26.58 N | 0.01 W |
| Şali, Hrv. | 36 | 43.56 N | 15.10 E |
| Šali, Ross. | 80 | 55.41 N | 49.40 E |
| Šali, Ross. | 84 | 43.08 N | 45.54 E |
| Salí ≃ | 252 | 27.33 S | 64.57 W |
| Salice Salentino | 68 | 40.23 N | 17.58 E |
| Salice Terme | 62 | 44.55 N | 9.01 E |
| Salici, Monte ∧ | 70 | 37.44 N | 14.38 E |
| Salida, Ca., U.S. | 226 | 37.42 N | 121.05 W |
| Salida, Co., U.S. | 200 | 38.32 N | 105.59 W |
| Salies-de-Béarn | 32 | 43.29 N | 0.55 W |
| Şalīf | 144 | 15.18 N | 42.40 E |
| Salignac-Eyvignes | 32 | 44.59 N | 1.19 E |
| Salihli | 130 | 38.29 N | 28.09 E |
| Salihorsk | 76 | 52.48 N | 27.32 E |
| Şālikha | 126 | 23.18 N | 89.22 E |
| Šalikovo | 82 | 55.30 N | 36.13 E |
| Salim | 140 | 12.52 N | 28.40 E |
| Salima | 154 | 13.47 S | 34.26 E |
| Salīmah, Wāḥat ⫧[4] | 140 | 21.22 N | 29.19 E |
| Salimani | 157a | 11.47 S | 43.17 E |
| Salimbatu | 112 | 2.57 N | 117.21 E |
| Salimgarh Fort ⊥ | 272a | 28.40 N | 77.14 E |
| Salimi | 152 | 9.24 S | 23.35 E |
| Salin | 110 | 20.35 N | 94.39 E |
| Salina, Ks., U.S. | 198 | 38.50 N | 97.36 W |
| Salina, Ok., U.S. | 196 | 36.17 N | 95.09 W |
| Salina, Pa., U.S. | 214 | 40.31 N | 79.30 W |
| Salina, Ut,. U.S. | 200 | 38.57 N | 111.51 W |
| Salina, Canale di ʮ | 70 | 38.32 N | 14.54 E |
| Salina, Isola I | 70 | 38.34 N | 14.50 E |
| Salina Cruz | 234 | 16.10 N | 95.12 W |
| Salina Point › | 238 | 22.13 N | 74.18 W |
| Salinas, Bra. | 255 | 16.10 S | 42.17 W |
| Salinas, Ec. | 246 | 2.13 S | 80.58 W |
| Salinas, P.R. | 240m | 17.59 N | 66.18 W |
| Salinas, Ca., U.S. | 226 | 36.40 N | 121.39 W |
| Salinas ≃, Bra. | 255 | 16.37 S | 42.18 W |
| Salinas (Chixoy) ≃, N.A. | 232 | 16.28 N | 90.33 W |
| Salinas ≃, Ca., U.S. | 226 | 36.45 N | 121.48 W |
| Salinas, Pampa de las ≚ | 252 | 31.58 S | 66.42 W |
| Salinas, Ponta das › | 152 | 12.50 S | 12.56 E |
| Salinas, Sierra de ⋏ | 226 | 36.18 N | 121.20 W |
| Salinas de Garci Mendoza | 248 | 19.38 S | 67.43 W |
| Salinas de Hidalgo | 234 | 22.38 N | 101.43 W |
| Salinas del Rey | 196 | 27.38 N | 102.24 W |
| Salinas Municipal Airport ⊠ | 226 | 36.40 N | 121.40 W |
| Salinas National Monument ♦ | 200 | 34.05 N | 106.14 W |
| Salinas Valley V | 226 | 36.15 N | 121.15 W |
| Salinas Victoria | 196 | 25.53 N | 100.19 W |
| Salin-de-Giraud | 62 | 43.25 N | 4.44 E |
| Salindres | 62 | 44.10 N | 4.10 E |
| Saline, La., U.S. | 194 | 32.09 N | 92.58 W |
| Saline, Mi., U.S. | 216 | 42.10 N | 83.46 W |
| Saline ≃, Ar., U.S. | 194 | 33.44 N | 93.58 W |
| Saline ≃, Ar., U.S. | 194 | 33.10 N | 92.08 W |
| Saline ≃, Il., U.S. | 194 | 37.35 N | 88.08 W |
| Saline ≃, Ks., U.S. | 198 | 38.51 N | 97.30 W |
| Saline ≃, Mi., U.S. | 216 | 41.59 N | 83.37 W |
| Saline, North Fork ≃ | 194 | 37.44 N | 88.19 W |
| Saline Bayou ≃ | 194 | 31.45 N | 92.58 W |
| Saline di Volterra | 66 | 43.22 N | 10.49 E |
| Saline Lake ⊜[1] | 194 | 31.55 N | 92.55 W |
| Salines, Point › | 241k | 12.00 N | 61.48 W |
| Salines, Pointe des › | 240e | 14.24 N | 60.53 W |
| Salineville | 214 | 40.37 N | 80.51 W |
| Salingyi | 110 | 21.58 N | 95.03 E |
| Şalinópolis | 250 | 0.37 S | 47.20 W |
| Šalinskoje | 86 | 55.43 N | 93.46 E |
| Salins-les-Bains | 58 | 46.57 N | 5.53 E |
| Salins-les-Thermes | 62 | 45.28 N | 6.32 E |
| Salipolo | 112 | 3.45 S | 119.29 E |
| Salisbury, Austl. | 168b | 34.46 S | 138.38 E |
| Salisbury, Dom. | 240d | 15.26 N | 61.27 W |
| Salisbury, Eng., U.K. | 42 | 51.05 N | 1.48 W |
| Salisbury, Ct., U.S. | 207 | 41.59 N | 73.25 W |
| Salisbury, Md., U.S. | 208 | 38.21 N | 75.35 W |
| Salisbury, Ma., U.S. | 207 | 42.50 N | 70.51 W |
| Salisbury, Mo., U.S. | 194 | 39.25 N | 92.48 W |
| Salisbury, N.C., U.S. | 192 | 35.40 N | 80.28 W |
| Salisbury, Pa., U.S. | 188 | 39.45 N | 79.04 W |
| Salisbury → Harare, Zimb. | 154 | 17.50 S | 31.03 E |
| Salisbury Cathedral υ[1] | 42 | 51.05 N | 1.48 W |
| Salisbury Center | 210 | 43.09 N | 74.47 W |
| Salisbury Hall ⊥ | 260 | 51.43 N | 0.16 W |
| Salisbury Island I, Austl. | 162 | 34.21 S | 123.32 E |
| Salisbury Island I, N.T., Can. | 176 | 63.30 N | 77.00 W |
| Salisbury Mills | 210 | 41.26 N | 74.08 W |
| Salisbury Plain ≚ | 42 | 51.12 N | 1.55 W |
| Salisbury Plain ≚ | 283 | 42.02 N | 70.58 W |
| Salish Mountains ⋏ | 202 | 48.15 N | 114.45 W |
| Salito ≃ | 70 | 37.29 N | 13.46 E |
| Salitpa | 194 | 31.37 N | 88.01 W |
| Salitre ≃ | 250 | 9.29 S | 40.39 W |
| Şalix | 214 | 40.18 N | 78.46 W |
| Šalkar | 80 | 48.03 N | 48.56 E |
| Šalkar, ozero ⊜ | 80 | 50.33 N | 51.40 E |
| Šalkar-Jega-Kara, ozero ⊜ | 86 | 50.45 N | 60.54 E |
| Salkehatchie ≃ | 192 | 32.37 N | 80.53 W |
| Şalkhad | 132 | 32.29 N | 36.43 E |
| Salkhia | 272b | 22.35 N | 88.21 E |
| Salkum | 224 | 46.31 N | 122.37 W |
| Salla | 24 | 66.50 N | 28.40 E |
| Salladasburg | 210 | 41.17 N | 77.14 W |
| Sallagriffon | 62 | 43.53 N | 6.54 E |
| Sallanches | 58 | 45.56 N | 6.38 E |
| Salland ◆[1] | 52 | 52.20 N | 6.20 E |
| Salles-Curan | 32 | 44.11 N | 2.47 E |
| Salles-sous-Bois | 62 | 44.27 N | 4.56 E |
| Sallgast | 54 | 51.35 N | 13.51 E |
| Salling ◆[1] | 26 | 56.40 N | 9.00 E |
| Salliqueló | 252 | 36.45 S | 62.56 W |
| Sallisaw | 196 | 35.27 N | 94.47 W |
| Sallisaw Creek ≃ | 194 | 35.23 N | 94.52 W |
| Salluit | 176 | 62.14 N | 75.38 W |
| Sallūm | 140 | 19.23 N | 37.06 E |
| Sallūm, Khalīj as- ⊂ | 146 | 31.41 N | 25.21 E |
| Salm ≃ | 56 | 49.51 N | 6.51 E |
| Salmās | 128 | 38.11 N | 44.47 E |
| Salmchâteau | 56 | 50.16 N | 5.54 E |
| Salme | 76 | 58.10 N | 22.15 E |
| Salmi | 24 | 61.22 N | 31.53 E |
| Salmo | 182 | 49.12 N | 117.17 W |
| Salmon | 202 | 45.10 N | 113.53 W |
| Salmon ≃, B.C., Can. | 182 | 54.05 N | 122.34 W |
| Salmon ≃, N.B., Can. | 186 | 46.06 N | 65.56 W |
| Salmon ≃, On., Can. | 212 | 44.11 N | 77.15 W |
| Salmon ≃, N.A. | 188 | 45.02 N | 74.31 W |
| Salmon ≃, Ct., U.S. | 207 | 41.29 N | 72.29 W |
| Salmon ≃, Id., U.S. | 202 | 45.51 N | 116.46 W |
| Salmon ≃, N.Y., U.S. | 212 | 43.35 N | 76.12 W |
| Salmon ≃, Or., U.S. | 224 | 45.03 N | 124.00 W |
| Salmon ≃, Or., U.S. | 224 | 45.22 N | 122.02 W |
| Salmon, East Fork ≃ | 202 | 44.16 N | 114.19 W |
| Salmon, Middle Fork ≃ | 202 | 45.18 N | 114.36 W |
| Salmon, North Branch ≃ | 212 | 43.32 N | 75.48 W |
| Salmon, South Fork ≃ | 202 | 45.23 N | 115.31 W |
| Salmon Arm | 182 | 50.42 N | 119.16 W |
| Salmon-Bay | 186 | 51.26 N | 57.36 W |
| Salmon Creek ≃, N.Y., U.S. | 210 | 43.16 N | 77.02 W |
| Salmon Creek ≃, N.Y., U.S. | 210 | 43.19 N | 77.43 W |
| Salmon Creek ≃, Wa., U.S. | 224 | 46.26 N | 122.52 W |
| Salmon Creek ≃, Wa., U.S. | 224 | 45.44 N | 122.45 W |
| Salmon Falls Creek ≃ | 202 | 42.43 N | 114.51 W |
| Salmon Falls Creek Reservoir ⊜[1] | 202 | 42.08 N | 114.45 W |
| Salmon Gums | 162 | 32.59 S | 121.38 E |
| Salmon Lake ⊜ | 212 | 44.49 N | 78.28 W |
| Salmon Mountain ∧ | 188 | 45.14 N | 71.08 W |
| Salmon Mountains ⋏ | 204 | 41.00 N | 123.00 W |
| Salmon Peak ∧ | 196 | 29.28 N | 100.10 W |
| Salmon Point › | 212 | 43.52 N | 77.14 W |
| Salmon River Mountains ⋏ | 202 | 44.45 N | 115.30 W |
| Salmon River Reservoir ⊜[1] | 212 | 43.32 N | 75.52 W |
| Salmon Valley | 182 | 54.05 N | 122.41 W |
| Salmyš ≃ | 86 | 52.01 N | 55.21 E |
| Sal'nytsya | 78 | 49.44 N | 28.02 E |
| Salo, Centraf. | 152 | 3.12 N | 16.07 E |
| Salò, It. | 64 | 45.36 N | 10.31 E |
| Salo, Suomi | 26 | 60.23 N | 23.08 E |
| Salobel'ak | 80 | 57.07 N | 48.05 E |
| Salobra ≃ | 248 | 20.12 S | 56.29 W |
| Salomatino | 80 | 50.01 N | 44.50 E |
| Salome | 200 | 33.46 N | 113.36 W |
| Salomon, Cap › | 240e | 14.30 N | 61.06 W |
| Salomon, Îles → Solomon Islands □[1] | 175e | 8.00 S | 159.00 E |
| Salomón, Islas → Solomon Islands □[1] | 175e | 8.00 S | 159.00 E |
| Salomone, Monte ∧ | 267a | 41.47 N | 12.44 E |
| Salomon-Inseln → Solomon Islands □[1] | 175e | 8.00 S | 159.00 E |
| Salon ≃ | 58 | 47.32 N | 5.41 E |



| ENGLISH Name | Page | Lat.°′ | Long.°′ |
|---|---|---|---|
| Salona | 210 | 41.05 N | 77.28 W |
| Salon-de-Provence | 62 | 43.38 N | 5.06 E |
| Salonga ≃ | 152 | 0.10 S | 19.50 E |
| Salonga, Parc National de la ♦ | 152 | 1.45 S | 21.20 E |
| Salonika → Thessaloníki | 38 | 40.38 N | 22.56 E |
| Salonta | 38 | 46.48 N | 21.40 E |
| Salor ≃ | 34 | 39.39 N | 7.03 W |
| Salorno (Salurn) | 64 | 46.14 N | 11.13 E |
| Saloslovo | 265b | 55.42 N | 37.09 E |
| Şaloum ≃ | 150 | 13.50 N | 16.45 W |
| Šalovka ≃ | 265b | 55.47 N | 38.12 E |
| Salpausselkä ∧ | 26 | 61.00 N | 26.30 E |
| Şalpazarı | 130 | 40.59 N | 39.10 E |
| Şalqīn | 130 | 36.08 N | 36.27 E |
| Sal Rei | 150a | 16.11 N | 22.55 W |
| Salsacate | 252 | 31.19 S | 65.05 W |
| Salsette Island I | 272c | 19.10 N | 72.53 E |
| Salsilgo, Qawz ±[8] | 140 | 10.49 N | 22.54 E |
| Salsipuedes, Canal ʮ | 232 | 28.37 N | 113.00 W |
| Salsipuedes, Punta ›, C.R. | 236 | 8.28 N | 83.37 W |
| Salsipuedes, Punta ›, Méx. | 232 | 32.05 N | 116.53 W |
| Şal'sk | 80 | 46.28 N | 41.33 E |
| Šal'skij | 24 | 61.48 N | 35.58 E |
| Sal'sko-Manyčskaja gr'ada ∧ | 80 | 46.40 N | 42.30 E |
| Salso ≃ | 70 | 37.06 N | 13.57 E |
| Salsomaggiore Terme | 64 | 44.49 N | 9.59 E |
| Salt ≃, U.S. | 202 | 43.08 N | 111.02 W |
| Salt ≃, Az., U.S. | 200 | 33.23 N | 112.18 W |
| Salt ≃, Ky., U.S. | 194 | 38.00 N | 85.57 W |
| Salt ≃, Mi., U.S. | 281 | 42.39 N | 82.47 W |
| Salt ≃, Mo., U.S. | 219 | 39.28 N | 91.04 W |
| Salt, Elk Fork ≃ | 219 | 39.28 N | 91.53 W |
| Salt, Middle Fork ≃ | 219 | 39.28 N | 91.49 W |
| Salt, North Fork ≃ | 219 | 39.30 N | 91.47 W |
| Salt, South Fork ≃ | 219 | 39.28 N | 91.49 W |
| Salta | 252 | 24.47 S | 65.25 W |
| Salta □[4] | 252 | 25.00 S | 64.30 W |
| Saltaim, ozero ⊜ | 86 | 56.10 N | 71.45 E |
| Saltair | 224 | 48.57 N | 123.46 W |
| Saltaire | 276 | 40.39 N | 73.12 W |
| Saltanovka | 76 | 52.47 N | 34.17 E |
| Saltara | 66 | 43.45 N | 12.54 E |
| Salt Ash, Austl. | 170 | 32.47 S | 151.55 E |
| Saltash, Eng., U.K. | 42 | 50.24 N | 4.12 W |
| Saltbæk Vig ⊂ | 41 | 55.43 N | 11.12 E |
| Salt Basin ⊜ | 196 | 31.50 N | 105.00 W |
| Saltburn-by-the-Sea | 44 | 54.35 N | 0.58 W |
| Salt Cay I | 240b | 25.06 N | 77.18 W |
| Saltcoats, Sk., Can. | 184 | 51.03 N | 102.12 W |
| Saltcoats, Scot., U.K. | 46 | 55.38 N | 4.47 W |
| Salt Creek ≃, On., Can. | 275b | 43.48 N | 79.42 W |
| Salt Creek ≃, Ca., U.S. | 204 | 36.15 N | 116.49 W |
| Salt Creek ≃, Il., U.S. | 194 | 40.08 N | 89.50 W |
| Salt Creek ≃, Il., U.S. | 278 | 41.49 N | 87.50 W |
| Salt Creek ≃, In., U.S. | 216 | 41.37 N | 87.09 W |
| Salt Creek ≃, In., U.S. | 218 | 38.50 N | 86.32 W |
| Salt Creek ≃, In., U.S. | 218 | 39.27 N | 85.09 W |
| Salt Creek ≃, Ks., U.S. | 198 | 39.06 N | 97.44 W |
| Salt Creek ≃, N.M., U.S. | 196 | 33.35 N | 104.23 W |
| Salt Creek ≃, Ok., U.S. | 196 | 36.32 N | 96.43 W |
| Salt Creek ≃, Or., U.S. | 202 | 43.43 N | 122.26 W |
| Salt Creek ≃, Or., U.S. | 224 | 45.09 N | 123.13 W |
| Salt Creek ≃, Wy., U.S. | 202 | 43.41 N | 106.20 W |
| Salt Creek, Middle Fork ≃ | 218 | 39.04 N | 86.15 W |
| Salt Creek, North Fork ≃, Il., U.S. | 216 | 40.13 N | 88.50 W |
| Salt Creek, North Fork ≃, In., U.S. | 218 | 39.08 N | 86.21 W |
| Salt Creek, West Branch ≃ | 278 | 42.02 N | 88.01 W |
| Salt Creek South Fork ≃ | 218 | 39.02 N | 86.16 W |
| Salt Draw V | 196 | 31.19 N | 103.28 W |
| Saltee Islands II | 48 | 52.07 N | 6.36 W |
| Salten | 41 | 56.05 N | 9.35 E |
| Saltfleet | 44 | 53.25 N | 0.11 E |
| Saltford | 42 | 51.24 N | 2.27 W |
| Salt Fork Lake ⊜[1] | 214 | 41.07 N | 81.30 W |
| Salt Fork State Park ♦ | 214 | 40.06 N | 81.29 W |
| Saltholm I | 41 | 55.38 N | 12.46 E |
| Saltillo, Méx. | 232 | 25.25 N | 101.00 W |
| Saltillo, Ms., U.S. | 194 | 34.22 N | 88.40 W |
| Saltillo, Pa., U.S. | 214 | 40.13 N | 78.01 W |
| Saltillo, Tn., U.S. | 194 | 35.22 N | 88.12 W |
| Saltillo, Tx., U.S. | 222 | 33.11 N | 95.20 W |
| Salt Island I | 240m | 18.23 N | 64.31 W |
| Salt Lake | 158 | 29.16 S | 24.00 E |
| Salt Lake ⊜ | 196 | 34.05 N | 103.05 W |
| Salt Lake City | 200 | 40.45 N | 111.53 W |
| Salto, Arg. | 252 | 34.17 S | 60.15 W |
| Salto, Ur. | 252 | 31.23 S | 57.58 W |
| Salto ≃ | 66 | 42.23 N | 12.54 E |
| Salto, Lago del ⊜ | 66 | 42.15 N | 13.02 E |
| Salto da Divisa | 255 | 16.00 S | 39.57 W |
| Salto de las Rosas | 252 | 34.43 S | 68.14 W |
| Salto del Fraile › | 286d | 12.11 S | 77.03 W |
| Salto del Guairá | 252 | 24.03 S | 54.17 W |
| Salto Grande | 255 | 22.54 S | 49.59 W |
| Salto Grande, Embalse ⊜[1] | 252 | 31.00 S | 57.55 W |
| Salton City | 204 | 33.19 N | 115.59 W |
| Salton Sea ⊜ | 204 | 33.19 N | 115.50 W |
| Salton Sea State Recreation Area ♦ | 204 | 33.29 N | 115.53 W |
| Saltonstall, Lake ⊜ | 283 | 42.47 N | 71.04 W |
| Sāltora | 126 | 23.32 N | 86.56 E |
| Saltoro Range ⋏ | 123 | 35.17 N | 77.03 E |
| Salto Santiago, Represa de ⊜[1] | 252 | 25.40 S | 52.30 W |
| Salt Pan Creek ≃ | 274a | 33.59 S | 151.02 E |
| Saltpeter Creek ⊂ | 284b | 39.20 N | 76.22 W |
| Salt Point | 210 | 41.44 N | 73.42 W |
| Saltpond | 150 | 5.12 N | 1.04 W |
| Salt Range ⋏ | 123 | 32.40 N | 72.35 E |
| Salt River Indian Reservation ◆[4] | 200 | 33.31 N | 111.48 W |
| Saltsburg | 214 | 40.29 N | 79.27 W |
| Saltsjöbaden | 40 | 59.17 N | 18.18 E |
| Salt Slough ≃ | 226 | 37.18 N | 120.54 W |
| Saltspring Island I | 224 | 48.47 N | 123.30 W |
| Salt Springs Reservoir ⊜[1] | 226 | 38.30 N | 120.11 W |
| Saltville | 192 | 36.52 N | 81.45 W |
| Salt Wells Creek ≃ | 200 | 41.39 N | 108.59 W |
| Saltykovka, Ross. | 80 | 52.07 N | 44.05 E |
| Saltykovka, Ross. | 265b | 55.46 N | 37.55 E |
| Saluda, S.C., U.S. | 192 | 34.00 N | 81.46 W |
| Saluda, Va., U.S. | 208 | 37.36 N | 76.35 W |
| Saluda ≃ | 192 | 34.00 N | 81.04 W |
| Saludecio | 66 | 43.52 N | 12.40 E |
| Saluën → Salween ≃ | 12 | 16.31 N | 97.37 E |
| Salue Timpaus, Selat ʮ | 112 | 1.55 S | 124.00 E |
| Salug | 116 | 8.07 N | 122.47 E |
| Saluggia | 62 | 45.14 N | 8.00 E |
| Sālūmbar | 120 | 24.08 N | 74.03 E |
| Salunga | 208 | 40.06 N | 76.26 W |
| Saluping Island I | 116 | 6.20 N | 122.02 E |
| Salūq 'Atīq | 130 | 36.36 N | 39.07 E |
| Sālūr | 122 | 18.32 N | 83.13 E |



| DEUTSCH Name | Seite | Breite°′ | Länge°′ E = Ost |
|---|---|---|---|
| Salurn → Salorno | 64 | 46.14 N | 11.13 E |
| Salussola | 62 | 45.27 N | 8.07 E |
| Salutaris | 256 | 22.10 S | 43.17 W |
| Saluzzo | 62 | 44.39 N | 7.29 E |
| Salvación, Bahía ⊂ | 254 | 50.55 S | 75.05 W |
| Salvado, Mount ∧ | 162 | 25.15 S | 121.01 E |
| Salvador, Bra. | 255 | 12.59 S | 38.31 W |
| Salvador, Pil. | 116 | 7.54 N | 123.50 E |
| Salvador, El → El Salvador □[1] | 236 | 13.50 N | 88.55 W |
| Salvador, Lake ⊜ | 194 | 29.45 N | 90.15 W |
| Salvador Island I | 116 | 15.31 N | 119.55 E |
| Salvador María | 258 | 35.18 S | 59.10 W |
| Salvador Mazza | 252 | 22.04 S | 63.43 W |
| Salvage | 186 | 48.41 N | 53.38 W |
| Salvail ≃ | 206 | 45.49 N | 72.58 W |
| Salvaterra | 250 | 0.46 S | 48.31 W |
| Salvaterra de Magos | 34 | 39.01 N | 8.48 W |
| Salvatierra | 234 | 20.13 N | 100.53 W |
| Salve | 68 | 39.51 N | 18.17 E |
| Salviac | 32 | 44.41 N | 1.16 E |
| Salwā, Dawḥat ⊂ | 128 | 25.30 N | 50.40 E |
| Salwā Baḥrī | 140 | 24.44 N | 32.56 E |
| Salween ≃ | 12 | 16.31 N | 97.37 E |
| Salyan, Azer. | 84 | 39.34 N | 48.58 E |
| Salyān, Nepāl | 124 | 28.22 N | 82.10 E |
| Salyer | 204 | 40.53 N | 123.35 W |
| Salyersville | 192 | 37.45 N | 83.04 W |
| Salza ≃, Dtsch. | 54 | 51.32 N | 11.50 E |
| Salza ≃, Öst. | 61 | 47.40 N | 14.43 E |
| Salzach ≃ | 30 | 48.12 N | 12.56 E |
| Salza Irpina | 68 | 40.55 N | 14.53 E |
| Salzbergen | 52 | 52.19 N | 7.20 E |
| Salzböde ≃ | 56 | 50.40 N | 8.42 E |
| Salzbrunn | 156 | 24.23 S | 18.00 E |
| Salzburg | 64 | 47.48 N | 13.02 E |
| Salzburg □[3] | 64 | 47.25 N | 13.15 E |
| Salzgitter | 52 | 52.10 N | 10.25 E |
| Salzgitter-Bad ◆[8] | 52 | 52.04 N | 10.23 E |
| Salzgitter-Barum ◆[8] | 52 | 52.07 N | 10.25 E |
| Salzgitter-Immendorf ◆[8] | 52 | 52.09 N | 10.26 E |
| Salzgitter-Lebenstedt ◆[8] | 52 | 52.09 N | 10.20 E |
| Salzgitter-Thiede ◆[8] | 52 | 52.11 N | 10.29 E |
| Salzgitter-Watenstedt ◆[8] | 54 | 52.06 N | 10.22 E |
| Salzhaff ⊂ | 54 | 54.06 N | 11.36 E |
| Salzhausen | 52 | 53.13 N | 10.09 E |
| Salzhemmendorf | 52 | 52.04 N | 9.35 E |
| Salzkammergut ◆[1] | 64 | 47.45 N | 13.30 E |
| Salzkotten | 52 | 51.40 N | 8.36 E |
| Salzmünde | 54 | 51.31 N | 11.49 E |
| Salzwedel | 54 | 52.51 N | 11.09 E |
| Salzweg | 60 | 48.37 N | 13.29 E |
| Sam, Gabon | 152 | 0.58 N | 11.16 E |
| Sām, India | 120 | 26.50 N | 70.31 E |
| Samā | 132 | 32.28 N | 36.14 E |
| Sama ≃ | 248 | 18.10 S | 70.40 W |
| Sam A. Baker State Park ♦ | 194 | 37.16 N | 90.34 W |
| Samacá | 246 | 5.29 N | 73.29 W |
| Samacèvičy | 76 | 53.13 N | 31.50 E |
| Samacimbo | 152 | 13.33 S | 16.59 E |
| Samādūn | 142 | 30.20 N | 30.57 E |
| Samagaltaj | 88 | 50.36 N | 95.03 E |
| Samah | 146 | 28.12 N | 19.09 E |
| Samāika ◆[8] | 272a | 28.32 N | 77.05 E |
| Samaipata | 248 | 18.09 S | 63.52 W |
| Samal (Peñaplata) | 116 | 7.05 N | 125.42 E |
| Samalá ≃ | 236 | 14.11 N | 91.47 W |
| Samalanga | 114 | 5.13 N | 96.22 E |
| Şamalayuca | 200 | 31.21 N | 106.28 W |
| Šamaldy-Saj | 85 | 41.12 N | 72.11 E |
| Samales Group II | 116 | 6.00 N | 121.45 E |
| Samalga Pass ʮ | 180 | 52.48 N | 169.25 W |
| Samal Island I | 116 | 7.03 N | 125.44 E |
| Sāmalkot | 122 | 17.03 N | 82.11 E |
| Samālūt | 142 | 28.18 N | 30.42 E |
| Samambaia ≃ | 255 | 22.45 S | 53.21 W |
| Samāna, India | 124 | 30.09 N | 76.12 E |
| Samaná, Rep. Dom. | 238 | 19.13 N | 69.19 W |
| Samaná, Bahía de ⊂ | 238 | 19.10 N | 69.25 W |
| Samaná, Cabo › | 238 | 19.18 N | 69.09 W |
| Samana Cay I | 238 | 23.06 N | 73.42 W |
| Samandağı | 130 | 36.07 N | 35.56 E |
| Samandıra | 130 | 40.59 N | 29.13 E |
| Samandıra ≃ | 267b | 40.59 N | 29.15 E |
| Samangān | 120 | 36.16 N | 68.01 E |
| Samangān □[4] | 120 | 36.15 N | 67.40 E |
| Samangwa | 152 | 4.24 S | 24.10 E |
| Samani | 92a | 42.07 N | 142.56 E |
| Samaniego | 246 | 1.20 N | 77.35 W |
| Samanlı Dağları ⋏ | 130 | 40.36 N | 29.30 E |
| Samannūd | 142 | 30.58 N | 31.15 E |
| Samar | 132 | 29.49 N | 35.01 E |
| Samar □[4] | 116 | 11.50 N | 125.00 E |
| Samar I | 116 | 12.00 N | 125.00 E |
| Samara | 80 | 53.12 N | 50.09 E |
| Samara ≃, Ross. | 80 | 53.10 N | 50.04 E |
| Samara ≃, Ukr. | 78 | 48.27 N | 35.07 E |
| Samarai | 164 | 10.37 S | 150.40 E |
| Samara Oblast' □[4] | 80 | 53.30 N | 50.30 E |
| Samarate | 62 | 45.38 N | 8.47 E |
| Samarga | 89 | 47.17 N | 138.48 E |
| Samarga ≃ | 89 | 47.15 N | 138.46 E |
| Samaria, Id., U.S. | 202 | 42.07 N | 112.20 W |
| Samaria, Mi., U.S. | 216 | 41.48 N | 83.35 W |
| Samaria (As-Sāmirah) □[9] | 132 | 32.15 N | 35.10 E |
| Samaria, Mount ∧ | 169 | 36.52 S | 146.03 E |
| Samaria Gorge → Farángi Samariás V | 38 | 35.18 N | 24.00 E |
| Samariapo | 246 | 5.15 N | 67.48 W |
| Samarinda | 112 | 0.30 S | 117.09 E |
| Samarka | 89 | 44.44 N | 134.13 E |
| Samarkand | 85 | 39.40 N | 66.48 E |
| Samarkand □[4] | 85 | 39.40 N | 67.15 E |
| Sāmarrā' | 128 | 34.12 N | 43.52 E |
| Samar Sea ⫧[2] | 116 | 12.15 N | 124.15 E |
| Samarskoje, Kaz. | 86 | 49.00 N | 83.23 E |
| Samarskoje, Ross. | 83 | 46.56 N | 39.41 E |
| Şamarskoje, Ross. | 86 | 52.02 N | 58.10 E |
| Šamary | 86 | 57.21 N | 58.14 E |
| Samasata | 123 | 29.21 N | 71.33 E |
| Samassi | 71 | 39.29 N | 8.54 E |
| Samastīpur | 124 | 25.51 N | 85.47 E |
| Samatya ◆[8] | 267b | 41.00 N | 28.56 E |
| Samaúna | 248 | 7.50 S | 60.02 W |
| Samawāri | 120 | 28.34 N | 66.46 E |
| Şamaxı | 84 | 40.38 N | 48.39 E |
| Šamba, Centraf. | 152 | 6.49 N | 21.12 E |
| Samba, India | 123 | 32.34 N | 75.07 E |
| Samba, Zaïre | 152 | 0.14 N | 21.19 E |
| Samba, Zaïre | 154 | 4.38 S | 26.22 E |
| Samba Caju | 152 | 8.46 S | 15.24 E |
| Sambaetiba | 256 | 22.41 S | 42.48 W |
| Sambaíba | 250 | 7.08 S | 45.21 W |
| Sambalpur | 120 | 21.27 N | 83.58 E |
| Sambar, Tanjung › | 112 | 2.59 S | 110.19 E |
| Sambas | 112 | 1.20 N | 109.15 E |
| Sambava | 157b | 14.16 S | 50.10 E |
| Sambawizi | 154 | 18.21 S | 26.16 E |
| Şambayat | 130 | 37.41 N | 38.03 E |
| Šambāza | 120 | 31.49 N | 69.20 E |
| Sambek, Ross. | 83 | 47.20 N | 39.01 E |
| Sambek, Ross. | 83 | 47.45 N | 39.48 E |
| Sambek ≃ | 83 | 47.16 N | 39.01 E |
| Sambesi → Zambezi ≃ | 138 | 18.55 S | 36.04 E |
| Sambhal | 124 | 28.35 N | 78.33 E |
| Sāmbhar | 120 | 26.55 N | 75.12 E |
| Sāmbhar Lake ⊜ | 120 | 26.58 N | 75.05 E |
| Sambia → Zambia □[1] | 154 | 14.30 S | 27.30 E |
| Sambiase | 68 | 38.58 N | 16.17 E |
| Sambir | 78 | 49.32 N | 23.11 E |
| Sambit, Pulau I | 112 | 1.46 N | 119.03 E |
| Sambito ≃ | 250 | 5.40 S | 42.10 W |


**Symbols** in the index entries represent the broad categories identified in the key at the right. Symbols with superior numbers (⋏[1]) identify subcategories (see complete key on page I · 1).

**Symbole** im Register stellen die rechts im Schlüssel erklärten Kategorien dar. Symbole mit hochgestellten Ziffern (⋏[1]) bezeichnen Unterabteilungen einer Kategorie (vgl. vollständiger Schlüssel auf Seite I · 1).

**Los símbolos** incluídos en el texto del índice representan las grandes categorías identificadas con la clave a la derecha. Los símbolos con numeros en su parte superior (⋏[1]) identifican las subcategorías (véase la clave completa en la página I · 1).

**Les symboles** de l'index représentent les catégories indiquées dans la légende à droite. Les symboles suivis d'un indice (⋏[1]) représentent des sous-catégories (voir légende complète à la page I · 1).

**Os símbolos** incluídos no texto do índice representam as grandes categorias identificadas com a chave à direita. Os símbolos com números em sua parte superior (⋏[1]) identificam as subcategorias (veja-se a chave completa à página I · 1).

| | | | | | |
|---|---|---|---|---|---|
| ∧ | Mountain | Berg | Montaña | Montagne | Montanha |
| ⋏ | Mountains | Gebirge | Montañas | Montagnes | Montanhas |
| )( | Pass | Paß | Paso | Col | Passo |
| V | Valley, Canyon | Tal, Cañon | Valle, Cañón | Vallée, Canyon | Vale, Canhão |
| ≚ | Plain | Ebene | Llano | Plaine | Planície |
| › | Cape | Kap | Cabo | Cap | Cabo |
| I | Island | Insel | Isla | Île | Ilha |
| II | Islands | Inseln | Islas | Îles | Ilhas |
| ± | Other Topographic Features | Andere Topographische Objekte | Otros Elementos Topográficos | Autres données topographiques | Outros acidentes topográficos |

ESPAÑOL — Nombre | Página | Lat.°′ | Long.°′ W = Oeste
FRANÇAIS — Nom | Page | Lat.°′ | Long.°′ W = Ouest
PORTUGUÊS — Nome | Página | Lat.°′ | Long.°′ W = Oeste


| Nombre / Nom / Nome | Página / Page | Lat.°′ | Long.°′ |
|---|---|---|---|
| Sambo | 152 | 12.57 S | 16.05 E |
| Samboan | 116 | 9.32 N | 123.18 E |
| Samboja | 112 | 1.02 S | 117.02 E |
| Sambolabbo | 152 | 7.05 N | 11.59 E |
| Sâmbor | 110 | 12.46 N | 105.58 E |
| Samborombón ≃ | 252 | 35.43 S | 57.20 W |
| Samborombón, Bahía c | 252 | 36.00 S | 57.12 W |
| Samborondón | 246 | 1.57 S | 79.44 W |
| Sambre ≃ | 32 | 50.28 N | 4.52 E |
| Sambre à l'Oise, Canal de la ≊ | 50 | 49.39 N | 3.20 E |
| Sambreville | 56 | 50.26 N | 4.37 E |
| Sambriāl | 123 | 32.28 N | 74.21 E |
| Sambú ≃ | 246 | 8.05 N | 78.18 W |
| Sambuca di Sicilia | 70 | 37.39 N | 13.07 E |
| Sambuca Pistoiese | 66 | 44.06 N | 11.00 E |
| Sambughetti, Monte ∧ | 70 | 37.50 N | 14.22 E |
| Sambungo | 152 | 8.39 S | 20.43 E |
| Sambusu | 156 | 17.50 S | 19.20 E |
| Samch'ŏk | 98 | 37.27 N | 129.10 E |
| Sam Chom, Khao ∧ | 110 | 8.07 N | 99.26 E |
| Samch'ŏnp'o | 98 | 34.57 N | 128.03 E |
| Samdžir, gora ∧ | 88 | 52.32 N | 93.53 E |
| Same | 154 | 4.04 S | 37.44 E |
| Same ≃ | 94 | 36.54 N | 140.49 E |
| Samedan | 58 | 46.33 N | 9.52 E |
| Samegawa | 94 | 37.02 N | 140.31 E |
| Sāmen | 128 | 34.12 N | 48.42 E |
| Samene, Oued ∨ | 148 | 26.49 N | 7.08 E |
| Samer | 50 | 50.38 N | 1.45 E |
| Sameru Dando ∧ | 124 | 27.02 N | 90.20 E |
| Samet' | 80 | 57.49 N | 40.44 E |
| Samford | 171a | 27.23 S | 152.53 E |
| Samfya | 154 | 11.21 S | 29.32 E |
| Samga | 98 | 35.25 N | 128.05 E |
| Samho | 98 | 39.56 N | 127.53 E |
| Saminka ≃ | 265b | 55.45 N | 37.17 E |
| Samiria ≃ | 246 | 4.42 S | 74.13 W |
| Samish | 224 | 48.35 N | 122.33 W |
| Samish ≃ | 224 | 48.38 N | 122.29 W |
| Samish, Lake ⊜ | 224 | 48.39 N | 122.24 W |
| Samish Bay c | 224 | 48.36 N | 122.28 W |
| Samj | 132 | 32.27 N | 36.30 E |
| Samka | 110 | 20.09 N | 96.57 E |
| Šämkir | 84 | 40.50 N | 46.02 E |
| Samlesbury | 262 | 53.46 N | 2.38 W |
| Samlesbury Aerodrome ⊠ | 262 | 53.47 N | 2.34 W |
| Samlesbury Bottoms | 262 | 53.45 N | 2.34 W |
| Samlesbury Higher Hall ⊥ | 262 | 53.46 N | 2.34 W |
| Şamlı | 130 | 39.48 N | 27.51 E |
| Sammamish, Lake ⊜ | 224 | 47.36 N | 122.06 W |
| Sammichele di Bari | 68 | 40.53 N | 16.57 E |
| Samnangjin | 98 | 35.23 N | 128.50 E |
| Samnaun | 58 | 46.56 N | 10.22 E |
| Samnaungruppe ⋏ | 58 | 47.00 N | 10.25 E |
| Sam Ngao | 110 | 17.15 N | 99.01 E |
| Samnū | 146 | 27.17 N | 14.53 E |
| Samnye | 98 | 35.55 N | 127.05 E |
| Samo | 164 | 3.58 S | 152.51 E |
| Samoa → Western Samoa □[1] | 175a | 13.55 S | 172.00 W |
| Samoa → American Samoa □[2] | 175a | 14.20 S | 170.00 W |
| Samoa americane → American Samoa □[2] | 175a | 14.20 S | 170.00 W |
| Samoa Basin ✥[1] | 14 | 16.00 S | 166.00 W |
| Samoa i Sisifo → Western Samoa □[1] | 175a | 13.55 S | 172.00 W |
| Samoa Islands II | 175a | 14.00 S | 171.00 W |
| Samo Alto | 252 | 30.25 S | 70.58 W |
| Samoa Occidental → Western Samoa □[1] | 175a | 13.55 S | 172.00 W |
| Samoa Occidentales → Western Samoa □[1] | 175a | 13.55 S | 172.00 W |
| Samobor | 36 | 45.48 N | 15.43 E |
| Samoded | 24 | 63.38 N | 40.29 E |
| Samoëns | 58 | 46.05 N | 6.44 E |
| Samofalovka | 80 | 48.57 N | 44.13 E |
| Samoggia ≃ | 64 | 44.41 N | 11.15 E |
| Samojlovka | 80 | 51.12 N | 43.43 E |
| Samokov | 38 | 42.20 N | 23.33 E |
| Samolaco | 58 | 46.15 N | 9.21 E |
| Samora ≃ | 266c | 38.50 N | 8.57 W |
| Sámos | 38 | 37.45 N | 27.00 E |
| Sámos I | 38 | 37.48 N | 26.44 E |
| Samosdelka | 80 | 46.02 N | 47.53 E |
| Samoset | 220 | 27.28 N | 82.32 W |
| Samosir, Pulau I | 114 | 2.35 N | 98.50 E |
| Samothrace → Samothráki I | 38 | 40.30 N | 25.32 E |
| Samothráki | 38 | 40.28 N | 25.31 E |
| Samothráki (Samothrace) I | 38 | 40.30 N | 25.32 E |
| Samouco | 266c | 38.43 N | 9.00 W |
| Samovol'no-Ivanovka | 80 | 52.33 N | 50.53 E |
| S'amozero | 24 | 61.54 N | 33.18 E |
| Sampacho | 252 | 33.23 S | 64.43 W |
| Sampaga | 112 | 2.19 S | 119.07 E |
| Sampaio Correia | 256 | 22.52 S | 42.36 W |
| Sampalan | 115b | 8.41 S | 115.34 E |
| Sampanahan | 112 | 2.38 S | 116.11 E |
| Sampang | 115a | 7.12 S | 113.14 E |
| Sampara ≃ | 112 | 3.49 S | 122.28 E |
| Sampawams Creek ≃ | 276 | 40.41 N | 73.19 W |
| Sam Pervyj | 86 | 45.28 N | 56.06 E |
| Sampéyre | 62 | 44.34 N | 7.11 E |
| Sampford Peverell | 42 | 50.56 N | 3.22 W |
| Sampieri | 70 | 36.43 N | 14.44 E |
| Sampit | 112 | 2.32 S | 112.57 E |
| Sampit ≃ | 112 | 2.44 S | 112.54 E |
| Sampit, Teluk c | 112 | 3.05 S | 113.03 E |
| Sampolawa | 112 | 5.36 S | 122.43 E |
| Sampson | 279b | 40.10 N | 79.53 W |
| Sampson State Park ♠ | 210 | 42.44 N | 76.55 W |
| Sampués | 246 | 9.11 N | 75.23 W |
| Sampur | 80 | 52.19 N | 41.37 E |
| Sampwe | 154 | 9.20 S | 27.26 E |
| Samrāla | 123 | 30.51 N | 76.11 E |
| Sam Rayburn Reservoir ⊜[1] | 194 | 31.27 N | 94.37 W |
| Samre | 144 | 13.07 N | 39.10 E |
| Samreboi | 150 | 5.36 N | 2.34 W |
| Samro, ozero ⊜ | 76 | 58.57 N | 28.49 E |
| Samrong, Khlong ≊ | 269a | 13.39 N | 100.34 E |
| Sams ≃ | 224 | 47.38 N | 124.01 W |
| Samsang | 120 | 30.31 N | 82.37 E |
| Samsø I | 41 | 55.52 N | 10.37 E |
| Samsø Bælt ʊ | 41 | 55.48 N | 10.47 E |
| Samson, Al., U.S. | 194 | 31.06 N | 86.02 W |
| Sam Son, Viet | 110 | 19.44 N | 105.54 E |
| Samson I | 42a | 49.56 N | 6.22 W |
| Samson Indian Reserve ◆[4] | 182 | 52.48 N | 113.10 W |
| Samsonovka | 85 | 42.44 N | 70.32 E |
| Samsonvale, Lake ⊜[1] | 171a | 27.15 S | 152.55 E |
| Samsonville | 210 | 41.53 N | 74.18 W |
| Sams Point ∧ | 210 | 41.40 N | 74.22 W |
| Samsu | 98 | 41.19 N | 127.59 E |
| Samsun | 130 | 41.17 N | 36.20 E |
| Samsun □[4] | 130 | 41.15 N | 36.00 E |
| Samsun Körfezi c | 130 | 41.18 N | 36.21 E |
| Samtens | 54 | 54.21 N | 13.17 E |
| Samthar | 124 | 25.51 N | 78.55 E |
| Samtown | 194 | 31.16 N | 92.26 W |
| Samtredia | 84 | 42.10 N | 42.20 E |
| Samu | 112 | 2.01 S | 115.57 E |
| Samūdragarh | 126 | 23.21 N | 88.20 E |
| Samuel, Mount ∧ | 162 | 19.41 S | 134.09 E |
| Samuel P. Taylor State Park ♠ | 226 | 38.01 N | 122.44 W |
| Samugheo | 71 | 39.57 N | 8.56 E |
| Samuhú | 252 | 27.31 S | 60.24 W |
| Samui, Ko I | 110 | 9.30 N | 100.00 E |
| Samukawa | 94 | 35.22 N | 139.23 E |
| Samundri | 123 | 31.04 N | 72.58 E |
| Samur ≃ | 84 | 41.53 N | 48.32 E |
| Samur-Abşeron kanalı ≊ | 84 | 41.38 N | 48.25 E |
| Samus' | 86 | 56.46 N | 84.44 E |
| Samusele | 152 | 10.06 S | 24.05 E |
| Samut Prakan | 110 | 13.36 N | 100.36 E |
| Samut Prakan □[4] | 269a | 13.35 N | 100.35 E |
| Samut Sakhon | 110 | 13.32 N | 100.17 E |
| Samut Songkhram | 110 | 13.24 N | 100.00 E |
| Samuyi Shankou )( | 124 | 29.55 N | 84.46 E |
| S'amža | 76 | 60.01 N | 41.02 E |
| San | 150 | 13.18 N | 4.54 W |
| San (Xan) ≃, Asia | 110 | 13.32 N | 105.58 E |
| San ≃, Europe | 30 | 50.44 N | 21.50 E |
| San ≃, Zhg. | 100 | 33.02 N | 119.21 E |
| Saña, Perú | 248 | 6.55 S | 79.35 W |
| Şan'ā', Yaman | 144 | 15.23 N | 44.12 E |
| Sana ≃, Bos. | 36 | 45.03 N | 16.23 E |
| San'a ≃, Ross. | 82 | 54.41 N | 35.55 E |
| Sanaag □[4] | 144 | 10.30 N | 47.45 E |
| Sanaba | 150 | 12.25 N | 3.49 W |
| Sanaba ≃ | 150 | 15.06 N | 10.55 W |
| Şanabū | 142 | 27.30 N | 30.47 E |
| Sanada | 94 | 36.27 N | 138.20 E |
| Sanae ♆[3] | 9 | 70.30 S | 2.30 W |
| Sanafā | 142 | 30.47 N | 31.21 E |
| Şanāfīr I | 128 | 27.55 N | 34.40 E |
| Sanaga ≃ | 152 | 3.35 N | 9.38 E |
| Sanage-yama ∧ | 94 | 35.12 N | 137.10 E |
| Sanagōchi | 96 | 33.59 N | 134.28 E |
| San Agustín, Arg. | 252 | 38.01 S | 58.21 W |
| San Agustín, Arg. | 252 | 31.59 S | 64.23 W |
| San Agustín, Bol. | 248 | 21.05 S | 67.45 W |
| San Agustín, Col. | 246 | 1.53 N | 76.16 W |
| San Agustín, Méx. | 200 | 31.31 N | 106.15 W |
| San Agustin, Pil. | 116 | 16.30 N | 121.45 E |
| San Agustin, Pil. | 116 | 12.25 N | 120.59 E |
| San Agustin, Cape › | 116 | 6.16 N | 126.11 E |
| San Agustin, Plains of ≃ | 200 | 33.50 N | 108.00 W |
| San Agustín Atenango | 234 | 17.38 N | 97.59 W |
| San Agustín de Valle Fértil | 252 | 30.38 S | 67.27 W |
| San Agustín Loxicha | 234 | 16.01 N | 96.38 W |
| San Agustín Tlaxiaca | 234 | 20.07 N | 98.53 W |
| Sanak Islands II | 180 | 54.25 N | 162.35 W |
| San Alberto | 196 | 27.30 N | 101.20 W |
| San Alejo | 236 | 13.26 N | 87.58 W |
| Şān al-Ḥajar, Birkat ⊜ | 142 | 31.03 N | 31.54 E |
| Şān al-Ḥajar al-Qiblīyah | 142 | 30.58 N | 31.52 E |
| Sanalona, Presa ⊜[1] | 232 | 24.53 N | 107.00 W |
| San Ambrosio, Isla I | 244 | 26.21 S | 79.52 W |
| Sanam Chai, Khlong ≊ | 269a | 13.38 N | 100.27 E |
| Sanana | 112 | 2.04 S | 125.58 E |
| Sanana, Pulau I | 112 | 2.12 S | 125.55 E |
| Sānand | 120 | 22.59 N | 72.23 E |
| Sanandaj | 128 | 35.19 N | 47.00 E |
| Sanandita | 248 | 21.40 S | 63.35 W |
| San Andreas | 226 | 38.11 N | 120.40 W |
| San Andreas Fault ∨ | 226 | 36.20 N | 121.00 W |
| San Andreas Lake ⊜ | 282 | 37.36 N | 122.26 W |
| San Andrés, Col. | 236 | 12.35 N | 81.42 W |
| San Andrés, Col. | 246 | 6.49 N | 72.52 W |
| San Andrés, Méx. | 232 | 27.14 N | 114.14 W |
| San Andrés, Pan. | 236 | 8.36 N | 82.44 W |
| San Andrés, Isla de I | 236 | 12.32 N | 81.42 W |
| San Andrés, Laguna c | 234 | 22.40 N | 97.52 W |
| San Andrés Calpan | 234 | 19.06 N | 98.27 W |
| San Andrés Cohamiata | 234 | 22.12 N | 104.03 W |
| San Andrés de Giles | 258 | 34.27 S | 59.27 W |
| San Andres Mountains ⋏ | 200 | 32.55 N | 106.45 W |
| San Andres Point › | 116 | 13.34 N | 121.52 E |
| San Andrés Sajcabajá | 236 | 15.13 N | 90.55 W |
| San Andrés Timilpan | 234 | 19.52 N | 99.45 W |
| San Andrés Totoltepec ◆[8] | 286a | 19.15 N | 99.10 W |
| San Andrés Tuxtla | 234 | 18.27 N | 95.13 W |
| San Andrés y Providencia □[8] | 238 | 12.30 N | 81.45 W |
| Sananduva | 252 | 27.57 S | 51.48 W |
| San Angel → Álvaro Obregón ◆[8] | 286a | 19.21 N | 99.12 W |
| San Angelo | 196 | 31.27 N | 100.26 W |
| San Anselmo | 226 | 37.58 N | 122.33 W |
| San Antero | 246 | 9.23 N | 75.46 W |
| San Antonio, Arg. | 252 | 28.57 S | 65.20 W |
| San Antonio, Arg. | 252 | 28.56 S | 65.06 W |
| San Antonio, Belize | 236 | 16.15 N | 89.02 W |
| San Antonio, Chile | 252 | 27.53 S | 70.03 W |
| San Antonio, Chile | 252 | 33.35 S | 71.38 W |
| San Antonio, Col. | 246 | 3.55 N | 75.28 W |
| San Antonio, C.R. | 236 | 10.12 N | 85.26 W |
| San Antonio, N. Mar. Is. | 174n | 15.08 N | 145.43 E |
| San Antonio, Perú | 248 | 6.22 S | 76.21 W |
| San Antonio, Pil. | 116 | 12.25 N | 124.17 E |
| San Antonio, Pil. | 116 | 14.57 N | 120.05 E |
| San Antonio, P.R. | 240m | 18.30 N | 67.07 W |
| San Antonio, Fl., U.S. | 220 | 28.20 N | 82.16 W |
| San Antonio, N.M., U.S. | 200 | 35.06 N | 106.22 W |
| San Antonio, Tx., U.S. | 196 | 29.25 N | 98.29 W |
| San Antonio, Ur. | 252 | 31.22 S | 57.48 W |
| San Antonio, Ur. | 258 | 34.27 S | 56.05 W |
| San Antonio □[7] | 286b | 22.55 N | 82.29 W |
| San Antonio ≃, Méx. | 196 | 29.13 N | 103.47 W |
| San Antonio ≃, Méx. | 232 | 31.00 N | 116.15 W |
| San Antonio ≃, Ca., U.S. | 226 | 35.52 N | 120.48 W |
| San Antonio ≃, Tx., U.S. | 196 | 28.30 N | 96.50 W |
| San Antonio ≃[1] | 288 | 34.24 S | 58.31 W |
| San Antonio, Cabo › | 252 | 36.40 S | 56.42 W |
| San Antonio, Cabo de › | 240p | 21.52 N | 84.57 W |
| San Antonio, Lake ⊜[1] | 226 | 35.55 N | 121.00 W |
| San Antonio, Mount ∧ | 228 | 34.17 N | 117.39 W |
| San Antonio, Punta ›, Méx. | 232 | 26.31 N | 111.28 W |
| San Antonio, Punta ›, Méx. | 232 | 29.46 N | 115.42 W |
| San Antonio, Rio ≃ | 200 | 37.11 N | 105.55 W |
| San Antonio Bay c, Pil. | 116 | 8.38 N | 117.35 E |
| San Antonio Bay c, Tx., U.S. | 196 | 28.20 N | 96.45 W |
| San Antonio Canyon ∨ | 280 | 34.12 N | 117.40 W |
| San Antonio Creek ≃ | 226 | 38.09 N | 122.33 W |
| San Antonio Dam ◆[6] | 280 | 34.09 N | 117.41 W |
| San Antonio de Areco | 258 | 34.15 S | 59.28 W |
| San Antonio de Galipán | 286c | 10.33 N | 66.53 W |
| San Antonio de los Baños | 240p | 22.53 N | 82.30 W |
| San Antonio de los Cobres | 252 | 24.11 S | 66.21 W |
| San Antonio del Táchira | 246 | 7.50 N | 72.27 W |
| San Antonio de Padua, Arg. | 258 | 34.40 S | 58.42 W |
| San Antonio de Padua, Méx. | 234 | 22.35 N | 104.30 W |
| San Antonio de Padua, Mission ♆[1] | 226 | 36.01 N | 121.15 W |
| San Antonio de Tamanaco | 246 | 9.41 N | 66.03 W |
| San Antonio El Bravo | 232 | 30.10 N | 104.42 W |
| San Antonio Eloxochitlán | 234 | 18.11 N | 96.52 W |
| San Antonio Heights | 228 | 34.10 N | 117.40 W |
| San Antonio Mountain ∧ | 200 | 36.52 N | 106.02 W |
| San Antonio Nogalar | 234 | 23.04 N | 98.22 W |
| San Antonio Oeste | 254 | 40.44 S | 64.56 W |
| San Antonio Reservoir ⊜[1] | 226 | 37.35 N | 121.50 W |
| San Antonio Someyucan | 286a | 19.27 N | 99.16 W |
| San Antonio Suchitepéquez | 236 | 14.32 N | 91.25 W |
| San Antonio Tecómitl ◆[8] | 286a | 19.13 N | 98.59 W |
| San Antonio Ticino | 266b | 45.35 N | 8.46 E |
| San Ardo | 226 | 36.01 N | 120.54 W |
| Sanaroa Island I | 164 | 9.35 S | 151.00 E |
| Sanary-sur-Mer | 62 | 43.07 N | 5.48 E |
| Sanatoga | 285 | 40.15 N | 75.36 W |
| Sanatoga Creek ≃ | 285 | 40.14 N | 75.36 W |
| Sanatorium | 194 | 31.53 N | 89.46 W |
| San Augustine | 194 | 31.31 N | 94.06 W |
| San Augustin Pass )( | 200 | 32.26 N | 106.34 W |
| Sanaur | 124 | 30.18 N | 76.27 E |
| Sanāw | 144 | 17.50 N | 51.00 E |
| Sanāwad | 120 | 22.11 N | 76.04 E |
| Sanāwān | 123 | 30.19 N | 70.59 E |
| Sanbao, Zhg. | 102 | 43.00 N | 93.19 E |
| Sanbao, Zhg. | 105 | 40.20 N | 116.02 E |
| Sanbaoyingzi | 104 | 41.34 N | 120.56 E |
| San Bartolomeo in Galdo | 68 | 41.24 N | 15.01 E |
| San Basilio | 71 | 39.32 N | 9.11 E |
| San Benedetto, Alpe di ⋏ | 66 | 43.53 N | 11.43 E |
| San Benedetto del Tronto | 66 | 42.57 N | 13.53 E |
| San Benedetto in Alpe | 66 | 43.59 N | 11.41 E |
| San Benedetto Po | 64 | 45.02 N | 10.55 E |
| San Benedicto, Isla I | 232 | 19.18 N | 110.49 W |
| San Benigno Canavese | 62 | 45.13 N | 7.46 E |
| San Benito, Bol. | 248 | 17.31 S | 65.55 W |
| San Benito, Guat. | 232 | 16.55 N | 89.54 W |
| San Benito, Perú | 248 | 7.26 S | 78.56 W |
| San Benito, Tx., U.S. | 196 | 26.07 N | 97.37 W |
| San Benito □[6] | 226 | 36.51 N | 121.24 W |
| San Benito ≃ | 226 | 36.53 N | 121.34 W |
| San Benito Mountain ∧ | 226 | 36.22 N | 120.38 W |
| San Bernard ≃ | 222 | 28.52 N | 95.27 W |
| San Bernardino, Schw. | 58 | 46.28 N | 9.12 E |
| San Bernardino, Ca., U.S. | 228 | 34.07 N | 117.18 W |
| San Bernardino □[6] | 228 | 34.40 N | 117.17 W |
| San Bernardino, Passo del )( | 58 | 46.30 N | 9.11 E |
| San Bernardino Mountains ⋏ | 204 | 34.10 N | 116.45 W |
| San Bernardino National Forest ♠ | 280 | 34.12 N | 117.38 W |
| San Bernardino Strait ʊ | 116 | 12.32 N | 124.10 E |
| San Bernardo, Arg. | 252 | 27.17 S | 60.42 W |
| San Bernardo, Chile | 252 | 33.36 S | 70.43 W |
| San Bernardo, Méx. | 232 | 25.59 N | 105.33 W |
| San Bernardo, Isla I | 236 | 11.32 N | 85.06 W |
| San Bernardo, Islas de II | 246 | 9.45 N | 75.50 W |
| San Bernardo del Viento | 246 | 9.21 N | 75.57 W |
| Sanbe-yama ∧ | 96 | 35.08 N | 132.37 E |
| San Biagio | 66 | 44.35 N | 11.52 E |
| San Biagio di Callalta | 64 | 45.41 N | 12.22 E |
| San Biagio Platani | 70 | 37.31 N | 13.32 E |
| San Biagio Saracinisco | 66 | 41.37 N | 13.55 E |
| San Blas, Méx. | 232 | 26.05 N | 108.46 W |
| San Blas, Méx. | 234 | 21.31 N | 105.16 W |
| San Blas, Cape › | 192 | 29.40 N | 85.22 W |
| San Blas, Golfo de c | 246 | 9.30 N | 79.00 W |
| San Blas, Serranía De ⋏ | 246 | 9.18 N | 79.00 W |
| San Blas de los Sauces | 252 | 28.24 S | 67.05 W |
| San Bonifacio | 64 | 45.24 N | 11.16 E |
| San Borja | 248 | 14.49 S | 66.51 W |
| Sanborn, Ia., U.S. | 198 | 43.10 N | 95.39 W |
| Sanborn, Mn., U.S. | 198 | 44.12 N | 95.07 W |
| Sanborn, N.Y., U.S. | 210 | 43.08 N | 78.53 W |
| Sanborn, N.D., U.S. | 198 | 46.56 N | 98.13 W |
| San Bovio | 266b | 45.28 N | 9.19 E |
| San Bruno | 226 | 37.37 N | 122.24 W |
| San Bruno, Point › | 282 | 37.39 N | 122.22 W |
| San Bruno Mountain ∧ | 282 | 37.42 N | 122.25 W |
| Sanbu | 94 | 35.39 N | 140.23 E |
| San Buenaventura, Bol. | 248 | 14.28 S | 67.35 W |
| San Buenaventura, Méx. | 232 | 27.05 N | 101.32 W |
| San Buenaventura → Ventura, Ca., U.S. | 228 | 34.17 N | 119.18 W |
| San Buono | 66 | 41.59 N | 14.34 E |
| San Calogero | 68 | 38.34 N | 16.01 E |
| San Calogero, Monte ∧ | 70 | 37.57 N | 13.44 E |
| San Candido (Innichen) | 64 | 46.44 N | 12.17 E |
| Sancang | 100 | 32.45 N | 120.43 E |
| San Carlo | 58 | 46.25 N | 8.32 E |
| San Carlos, Arg. | 252 | 27.45 S | 55.54 W |
| San Carlos, Arg. | 252 | 33.46 S | 69.02 W |
| San Carlos, Arg. | 252 | 25.56 S | 65.56 W |
| San Carlos, Chile | 252 | 36.25 S | 71.58 W |
| San Carlos, Chile | 286e | 33.36 S | 70.35 W |
| San Carlos, Méx. | 232 | 29.01 N | 100.51 W |
| San Carlos, Méx. | 232 | 24.35 N | 98.56 W |
| San Carlos, Nic. | 236 | 11.07 N | 84.47 W |
| San Carlos, Pan. | 236 | 8.29 N | 79.57 W |
| San Carlos, Para. | 252 | 22.16 S | 57.18 W |
| San Carlos, Pil. | 116 | 10.30 N | 123.25 E |
| San Carlos, Pil. | 116 | 15.55 N | 120.20 E |
| San Carlos, Az., U.S. | 200 | 33.20 N | 110.27 W |
| San Carlos, Ca., U.S. | 226 | 37.29 N | 122.15 W |
| San Carlos, Ur. | 252 | 34.48 S | 54.55 W |
| San Carlos, Ven. | 246 | 9.40 N | 68.36 W |
| San Carlos ≃, C.R. | 236 | 10.47 N | 84.12 W |
| San Carlos ≃, Az., U.S. | 200 | 33.16 N | 110.27 W |
| San Carlos ≃, Ven. | 246 | 9.07 N | 68.25 W |
| San Carlos, Riacho ≃ | 252 | 22.51 S | 57.51 W |
| San Carlos Airport ⊠ | 282 | 37.31 N | 122.15 W |
| San Carlos Bay c | 220 | 26.28 N | 82.03 W |
| San Carlos Borromeo, Mission ♆[1] | 226 | 36.34 N | 121.55 W |
| San Carlos Centro | 252 | 31.44 S | 61.06 W |
| San Carlos de Bariloche | 254 | 41.09 S | 71.18 W |
| San Carlos de Bolívar | 252 | 36.15 S | 61.06 W |
| San Carlos de Chena | 286e | 33.35 S | 70.44 W |
| San Carlos de Guaroa | 246 | 3.44 N | 73.14 W |
| San Carlos del Zulia | 246 | 9.01 N | 71.55 W |
| San Carlos de Río Negro | 246 | 1.55 N | 67.04 W |
| San Carlos Indian Reservation ◆[4] | 200 | 33.23 N | 110.09 W |
| San Carlos Reservoir ⊜[1] | 200 | 33.13 N | 110.24 W |
| San Carlos Viejo, Canal ≊ | 286e | 33.25 S | 70.38 W |
| San Carpoforo Creek ≃ | 226 | 35.47 N | 121.19 W |
| San Casciano dei Bagni | 66 | 42.52 N | 11.53 E |
| San Casciano in Val di Pesa | 66 | 43.39 N | 11.11 E |
| San Cataldo, It. | 68 | 40.23 N | 18.17 E |
| San Cataldo, It. | 70 | 37.29 N | 13.59 E |
| San Cayetano | 252 | 38.20 S | 59.37 W |
| Sancergues | 50 | 47.09 N | 2.55 E |
| Sancerre | 50 | 47.20 N | 2.51 E |
| Sancerrois, Collines du ⋏[2] | 50 | 47.25 N | 2.45 E |
| San Cesario di Lecce | 68 | 40.18 N | 18.10 E |
| San Cesario sul Panaro | 64 | 44.34 N | 11.02 E |
| Sancey-le-Grand | 58 | 47.18 N | 6.35 E |
| Sancha, Zhg. | 105 | 40.27 N | 116.26 E |
| Sancha, Zhg. | 106 | 31.52 N | 119.06 E |
| Sancha ≃ | 102 | 26.55 N | 106.06 E |
| Sanchaba | 107 | 30.19 N | 104.14 E |
| Sanchahe | 89 | 44.59 N | 126.04 E |
| Sanchakou | 105 | 39.47 N | 117.19 E |
| Sanchang | 106 | 31.54 N | 121.15 E |
| Sanchazi | 104 | 41.07 N | 124.15 E |
| Sanchazicun | 104 | 42.03 N | 123.59 E |
| Sanchenglong | 89 | 44.02 N | 120.58 E |
| Sánchez | 238 | 19.14 N | 69.36 W |
| Sanchez Creek ≃ | 222 | 32.36 N | 97.50 W |
| Sánchez Magallanes | 234 | 18.14 N | 93.52 W |
| Sānchi | 124 | 23.29 N | 77.44 E |
| Sanchih | 100 | 25.16 N | 121.30 E |
| San Chirico Raparo | 68 | 40.11 N | 16.05 E |
| Sanch'ŏng | 98 | 35.26 N | 127.54 E |
| Sanchung | 269d | 25.04 N | 121.30 E |
| Sanch'ungch'iao | 269d | 25.12 N | 121.35 E |
| San Cipirello | 70 | 37.58 N | 13.10 E |
| San Ciro de Acosta | 234 | 21.38 N | 99.49 W |
| San Clemente, Esp. | 34 | 39.24 N | 2.26 W |
| San Clemente, Ca., U.S. | 228 | 33.25 N | 117.36 W |
| San Clemente, Arroyo de ≃ | 266d | 41.20 N | 2.00 E |
| San Clemente, Cerro ∧ | 254 | 46.36 S | 73.20 W |
| San Clemente a Casauria ♆[1] | 66 | 42.14 N | 13.55 E |
| San Clemente Island I | 228 | 32.54 N | 118.29 W |
| Sancoins | 32 | 46.50 N | 2.55 E |
| San Colombano al Lambro | 62 | 45.11 N | 9.29 E |
| San Cono | 70 | 37.17 N | 14.22 E |
| Sanco Point › | 116 | 8.15 N | 126.27 E |
| San Cosme | 252 | 27.22 S | 58.31 W |
| San Cosmo Albanese | 68 | 39.35 N | 16.25 E |
| San Costantino Albanese | 68 | 40.02 N | 16.18 E |
| San Cristóbal, Arg. | 252 | 30.19 S | 61.14 W |
| San Cristóbal, Cuba | 240p | 22.43 N | 83.03 W |
| San Cristóbal, Rep. Dom. | 238 | 18.25 N | 70.06 W |
| San Cristóbal, Ven. | 246 | 7.46 N | 72.14 W |
| San Cristobal I | 175e | 10.36 S | 161.45 E |
| San Cristóbal, Bahía c | 232 | 27.23 N | 114.38 W |
| San Cristóbal, Cerro ∧, Chile | 286e | 33.25 S | 70.39 W |
| San Cristóbal, Cerro ∧, Perú | 286d | 12.02 S | 77.01 W |
| San Cristóbal, Isla I | 246a | 0.50 S | 89.26 W |
| San Cristóbal, Nevis → Saint Kitts and Nevis □[1] | 238 | 17.20 N | 62.45 W |
| San Cristóbal, Volcán ∧[1] | 236 | 12.42 N | 87.01 W |
| San Cristóbal de la Barranca | 234 | 21.03 N | 103.26 W |
| San Cristóbal de la Laguna | 148 | 28.29 N | 16.19 W |
| San Cristóbal de las Casas | 234 | 16.45 N | 92.38 W |
| San Cristóbal Totonicapán | 236 | 14.55 N | 91.26 W |
| San Cristobal Trench ✥[1] | 14 | 11.15 S | 162.45 E |
| San Cristóbal Verapaz | 236 | 15.23 N | 90.24 W |
| San Cristobal Wash ∨ | 200 | 32.47 N | 113.44 W |
| San Croce, Monte ∧ | 66 | 41.17 N | 13.58 E |
| Sancti Spíritus | 240p | 21.56 N | 79.27 W |
| Sancti Spíritus □[4] | 240p | 22.00 N | 79.20 W |
| San Cugat, Riera de ≃ | 266d | 41.29 N | 2.11 E |
| Sančursk | 80 | 56.57 N | 47.15 E |
| Sancy, Puy de ∧ | 32 | 45.32 N | 2.49 E |
| Sand, Dtsch. | 56 | 48.32 N | 7.55 E |
| Sand, Nor. | 26 | 59.29 N | 6.15 E |
| Sand ≃, Ab., Can. | 184 | 54.22 N | 111.05 W |
| Sand ≃, S. Afr. | 156 | 22.25 S | 30.05 E |
| Sand ≃, S. Afr. | 158 | 28.05 S | 26.25 E |
| Sanda, Nihon | 96 | 34.53 N | 135.14 E |
| Sanda, Nihon | 268 | 35.28 N | 139.21 E |
| Sandafā al-Fa'r | 142 | 28.32 N | 30.40 E |
| Sandai | 112 | 1.15 S | 110.31 E |
| Sanda Island I | 44 | 55.18 N | 5.34 W |
| Sandakan | 112 | 5.50 N | 118.07 E |
| Sandakan, Pelabuhan c | 116 | 5.45 N | 118.05 E |
| San Damián | 248 | 12.02 S | 76.24 W |
| San Damiano d'Asti | 62 | 44.50 N | 8.04 E |
| San Damiano Macra | 62 | 44.29 N | 7.16 E |
| Sândăn | 110 | 12.42 N | 106.01 E |
| Sandan, Chāh ⫧[4] | 128 | 28.59 N | 63.27 E |
| Sandane | 26 | 61.46 N | 6.13 E |
| San Daniele del Friuli | 64 | 46.09 N | 13.00 E |
| Sandan-kyō ♠ | 96 | 34.38 N | 132.13 E |
| Sandanski | 38 | 41.34 N | 23.17 E |
| Sandaogang | 89 | 46.08 N | 130.05 E |
| Sandaogou, Zhg. | 104 | 41.39 N | 121.45 E |
| Sandaogou, Zhg. | 105 | 39.33 N | 115.27 E |
| Sandaohe | 86 | 44.21 N | 85.37 E |
| Sandaoliangzi | 104 | 41.20 N | 122.07 E |
| Sandaolingzi | 104 | 40.58 N | 124.08 E |
| Sandaozhen | 89 | 47.25 N | 126.25 E |
| Sandaré | 150 | 14.42 N | 10.18 W |
| Sandared | 26 | 57.43 N | 12.47 E |
| Sandarne | 26 | 61.16 N | 17.10 E |
| Sand Arroyo ∨ | 196 | 37.29 N | 101.29 W |
| Sandata | 80 | 46.16 N | 41.46 E |
| Sandau | 54 | 52.47 N | 12.02 E |
| Sandaun □[5] | 164 | 4.00 S | 141.30 E |
| Sanday I | 46 | 59.15 N | 2.35 W |
| Sanday Sound c | 46 | 59.11 N | 2.31 W |
| Sandbach | 44 | 53.09 N | 2.22 W |
| Sandbank | 46 | 55.59 N | 4.58 W |
| Sandbanks Provincial Park ♠ | 212 | 43.55 N | 77.17 W |
| Sandbochum ◆[8] | 263 | 51.40 N | 7.41 E |
| Sand City | 226 | 36.37 N | 121.51 W |
| Sand Coulee | 202 | 47.23 N | 111.10 W |
| Sand Coulee Creek ≃ | 202 | 47.27 N | 111.18 W |
| Sand Creek ≃, U.S. | 200 | 41.13 N | 105.43 W |
| Sand Creek ≃, In., U.S. | 218 | 39.03 N | 85.51 W |
| Sand Creek ≃, Ks., U.S. | 198 | 37.26 N | 98.12 W |
| Sand Creek ≃, Mn., U.S. | 190 | 45.56 N | 92.39 W |
| Sand Creek ≃, Mt., U.S. | 202 | 47.18 N | 106.45 W |
| Sand Creek ≃, S.D., U.S. | 198 | 44.02 N | 98.05 W |
| Sand Creek ≃, Wy., U.S. | 200 | 43.27 N | 105.26 W |
| Sand Creek ≃, Wy., U.S. | 200 | 41.02 N | 107.52 W |
| Sand Creek ≃, Wy., U.S. | 202 | 44.16 N | 107.55 W |
| Sand Cut | 220 | 26.56 N | 80.35 W |
| Sande, Dtsch. | 52 | 51.45 N | 8.39 E |
| Sande, Dtsch. | 52 | 53.30 N | 8.01 E |
| Sandefjord | 26 | 59.08 N | 10.14 E |
| San Demetrio Corone | 68 | 39.34 N | 16.22 E |
| San Demetrio ne'Vestini | 66 | 42.17 N | 13.34 E |
| Sanders, Az., U.S. | 200 | 35.12 N | 109.19 W |
| Sanders, Ky., U.S. | 218 | 38.39 N | 84.56 W |
| Sandersdorf, Dtsch. | 54 | 51.37 N | 12.15 E |
| Sandersdorf, Dtsch. | 60 | 48.54 N | 11.37 E |
| Sandersleben | 54 | 51.40 N | 11.34 E |
| Sanderson | 196 | 30.08 N | 102.23 W |
| Sanderstead ◆[8] | 260 | 51.20 N | 0.05 W |
| Sanderston | 168b | 34.46 S | 139.13 E |
| Sandersville, Ga., U.S. | 192 | 32.58 N | 82.48 W |
| Sandersville, Ms., U.S. | 194 | 31.47 N | 89.01 W |
| Sandeshkhali | 126 | 22.22 N | 88.53 E |
| Sandesneben | 52 | 53.41 N | 10.30 E |
| Sandfly Lake ⊜ | 184 | 55.45 N | 106.05 W |
| Sand Fork | 188 | 38.54 N | 80.45 W |
| Sandgate, Austl. | 171a | 27.20 S | 153.05 E |
| Sandgate, Eng., U.K. | 42 | 51.05 N | 1.08 E |
| Sandhammaren › | 26 | 55.23 N | 14.12 E |
| Sandhamn | 40 | 59.17 N | 18.55 E |
| Sandhead | 44 | 54.48 N | 4.58 W |
| Sandheuwel | 158 | 31.46 S | 20.48 E |
| Sandhill, On., Can. | 275b | 43.50 N | 79.49 W |
| Sand Hill, Ma., U.S. | 207 | 42.13 N | 70.44 W |
| Sand Hill ∧[2] | 210 | 42.31 N | 77.37 W |
| Sand Hill ≃ | 198 | 47.36 N | 96.52 W |
| Sand Hills ⋏[2] | 198 | 42.00 N | 101.00 W |
| Sandhorst | 52 | 53.29 N | 7.29 E |
| Sandhurst | 42 | 51.19 N | 0.48 W |
| Sāndi | 124 | 27.18 N | 79.57 E |
| Sandia | 248 | 14.17 S | 69.26 W |
| Sandia Crest ∧ | 200 | 35.13 N | 106.27 W |
| Sandia Indian Reservation ◆[4] | 200 | 35.15 N | 106.30 W |
| Sandian | 100 | 30.56 N | 114.48 E |
| San Diego, Ca., U.S. | 228 | 32.42 N | 117.09 W |
| San Diego, Tx., U.S. | 196 | 27.45 N | 98.14 W |
| San Diego □[6] | 228 | 33.00 N | 117.05 W |
| San Diego ≃, Cuba | 240p | 22.20 N | 83.16 W |
| San Diego ≃, Ca., U.S. | 204 | 32.46 N | 117.13 W |
| San Diego, Cabo › | 254 | 54.38 S | 65.07 W |
| San Diego Aqueduct ≊[1] | 228 | 32.55 N | 116.55 W |
| San Diego Bay c | 228 | 32.37 N | 117.07 W |
| San Diego Creek ≃ | 196 | 27.47 N | 98.03 W |
| San Diego de Alcala, Mission ♆[1] | 228 | 32.48 N | 117.06 W |
| San Diego de la Unión | 234 | 21.28 N | 100.52 W |
| San Diego Naval Training Center ■ | 228 | 32.44 N | 117.13 W |
| San Dieguito ≃ | 228 | 32.58 N | 117.16 W |
| Sandies Creek ≃ | 222 | 29.06 N | 97.20 W |
| Sandıklı | 130 | 38.28 N | 30.17 E |
| Sandīla | 124 | 27.05 N | 80.31 E |
| Sandilands | 168b | 34.31 S | 137.46 E |
| Sandilands Village | 240b | 25.02 N | 77.18 W |
| San Dimas | 228 | 34.06 N | 117.48 W |
| San Dimas Canyon ∨ | 280 | 34.10 N | 117.46 W |
| San Dimas Reservoir ⊜[1] | 280 | 34.09 N | 117.43 W |
| San Dionisio, Nic. | 236 | 12.45 N | 85.51 W |
| San Dionisio, Pil. | 116 | 11.16 N | 123.06 E |
| Sand Island I, Mid. Is. | 174g | 28.12 N | 177.23 W |
| Sand Island I, Hi., U.S. | 229c | 21.18 N | 157.53 W |
| Sand Islet I | 174g | 28.16 N | 177.23 W |
| Sandiway | 262 | 53.14 N | 2.36 W |
| Sand Key I | 220 | 27.53 N | 82.51 W |
| Sandkrug | 54 | 52.53 N | 13.52 E |
| Sandl | 61 | 48.33 N | 14.38 E |
| Sand Lake | 210 | 42.38 N | 73.32 W |
| Sand Lake ⊜, On., Can. | 184 | 50.05 N | 94.39 W |
| Sand Lake ⊜, On., Can. | 212 | 44.56 N | 77.02 W |
| Sand Lake ⊜, On., Can. | 212 | 44.34 N | 76.15 W |
| Sandling ∧ | 64 | 47.39 N | 13.43 E |
| Sandnes | 26 | 58.51 N | 5.44 E |
| Sandness | 46a | 60.17 N | 1.38 W |
| Sandoa | 152 | 9.41 S | 22.52 E |
| Sandogora | 80 | 58.12 N | 40.59 E |
| Sandomierz | 30 | 50.41 N | 21.45 E |
| San Domingo Creek ≃ | 226 | 38.07 N | 120.40 W |
| San Domino, Isola I | 66 | 42.07 N | 15.29 E |
| Sandon | 260 | 51.43 N | 0.32 E |
| Sandoná | 246 | 1.17 N | 77.28 W |
| San Donaci | 68 | 40.27 N | 17.55 E |
| San Donà di Piave | 64 | 45.38 N | 12.34 E |
| San Donato di Lecce | 68 | 40.15 N | 18.10 E |
| San Donato di Ninea | 68 | 39.42 N | 16.03 E |
| San Donato Milanese | 62 | 45.24 N | 9.16 E |
| San Donato Val di Comino | 66 | 41.42 N | 13.49 E |
| Sandongo | 152 | 15.30 S | 21.28 E |
| San Dorligo della Valle | 64 | 45.36 N | 13.51 E |
| Sandouping | 102 | 30.48 N | 110.49 E |
| Sandoval | 219 | 38.36 N | 89.06 W |
| Sandovalina | 255 | 22.27 S | 51.44 W |
| Sandover ≃ | 162 | 21.43 S | 136.32 E |
| Sandovo | 76 | 58.28 N | 36.25 E |
| Sandoway | 110 | 18.28 N | 94.22 E |
| Sandown | 42 | 50.39 N | 1.09 W |
| Sandown Park Racecourse ♠, Austl. | 274b | 37.57 S | 145.10 E |
| Sandown Park Race Course ♠, Eng., U.K. | 260 | 51.22 N | 0.22 W |
| Sand Point, Ak., U.S. | 180 | 55.20 N | 160.30 W |
| Sandpoint, Id., U.S. | 202 | 48.16 N | 116.33 W |
| Sandrancourt | 261 | 49.02 N | 1.39 E |
| Sandray I | 46 | 56.53 N | 7.30 W |
| Sandridge, Eng., U.K. | 260 | 51.47 N | 0.18 W |
| Sand Ridge, N.Y., U.S. | 210 | 43.15 N | 76.14 W |
| Sandrigo | 64 | 45.39 N | 11.36 E |
| Sandringham, Austl. | 166 | 24.05 S | 139.04 E |
| Sandringham, Austl. | 169 | 37.57 S | 145.00 E |
| Sandringham, Eng., U.K. | 42 | 52.50 N | 0.30 E |
| Sandringham ◆[8] | 273d | 26.09 S | 28.07 E |
| Sandringham House ⊥ | 42 | 52.50 N | 0.30 E |
| Sand River Valley | 158 | 28.28 S | 29.33 E |
| Sands Key I | 220 | 25.30 N | 80.11 W |
| Sandslån | 26 | 63.01 N | 17.47 E |
| Sandspit | 182 | 53.14 N | 131.50 W |
| Sands Point | 276 | 40.51 N | 73.43 W |
| Sands Point › | 276 | 40.52 N | 73.44 W |
| Sand Springs, Ok., U.S. | 196 | 36.08 N | 96.06 W |
| Sand Springs, Tx., U.S. | 196 | 32.15 N | 101.22 W |
| Sandspruit | 158 | 27.18 S | 29.48 E |
| Sandspruit ≃ | 273d | 26.07 S | 28.04 E |
| Sandstedt | 52 | 53.21 N | 8.31 E |
| Sandston | 208 | 37.31 N | 77.18 W |
| Sandstone, Austl. | 162 | 27.59 S | 1[illegible]9.17 E |
| Sandstone, Mn., U.S. | 190 | 46.07 N | [illegible]2.52 W |
| Sandstone Creek ≃ | 216 | 42.23 N | [illegible]4.33 W |
| Sandu, Zhg. | 100 | 29.46 N | 1[illegible].12 E |
| Sandu, Zhg. | 100 | 26.02 N | 1[illegible].16 E |
| Sandu, Zhg. | 100 | 29.12 N | 1[illegible].40 E |
| Sandu, Zhg. | 102 | 25.59 N | 1[illegible].52 E |
| Sanduan | 104 | 41.10 N | 12[illegible].27 E |
| Sandu Ao c | 100 | 26.35 N | 11[illegible].50 E |
| Sandugan Point › | 116 | 9.18 N | 12[illegible].36 E |
| Sandumba | 152 | 13.45 S | 1[illegible]29 E |
| Sandun, Zhg. | 106 | 31.52 N | 12[illegible]50 E |
| Sandun, Zhg. | 106 | 30.19 N | 12[illegible].05 E |
| Sanduo | 100 | 32.49 N | 11[illegible]42 E |
| Sandusky, In., U.S. | 218 | 39.25 N | 8[illegible]29 W |
| Sandusky, Mi., U.S. | 190 | 43.25 N | 8[illegible]49 W |
| Sandusky, N.Y., U.S. | 210 | 42.30 N | 78[illegible]23 W |
| Sandusky, Oh., U.S. | 214 | 41.26 N | 82[illegible]12 W |
| Sandusky □[6] | 214 | 41.21 N | 83[illegible]07 W |
| Sandusky ≃ | 214 | 41.27 N | 83[illegible]10 W |
| Sandusky Bay c | 214 | 41.27 N | 82[illegible]2 W |
| Sand uul ∧ | 102 | 43.27 N | 104.[illegible]4 E |
| Sandvig | 26 | 55.17 N | 14.[illegible]7 E |
| Sandvika | 26 | 59.54 N | 10.[illegible]1 E |
| Sandviken | 40 | 60.37 N | 16.[illegible]6 E |
| Sandweiler | 56 | 49.37 N | 6.[illegible]3 E |
| Sandwich, Eng., U.K. | 42 | 51.17 N | 1.[illegible] E |
| Sandwich, Il., U.S. | 216 | 41.38 N | 88.[illegible] W |
| Sandwich, Ma., U.S. | 207 | 41.45 N | 70.[illegible] W |
| Sandwich Bay c, Nf., Can. | 176 | 53.35 N | 57.1[illegible] W |
| Sandwich Bay c, Namibia | 156 | 23.22 S | 14.3[illegible] E |
| Sandwich del Sur, Islas → South Sandwich Islands II | 18 | 57.45 S | 26.3[illegible] W |
| Sandwick, B.C., Can. | 182 | 49.42 N | 124.5[illegible] W |
| Sandwick, Scot., U.K. | 46a | 60.00 N | 1.1[illegible] W |
| Sand Wick c | 46a | 60.42 N | 0.5[illegible] W |
| Sandwīp | 124 | 22.29 N | 91.2[illegible] E |
| Sandwīp Channel ʊ | 124 | 22.30 N | 91.3[illegible] E |
| Sandwīp Island I | 124 | 22.30 N | 91.2[illegible] E |
| Sandy, Eng., U.K. | 42 | 52.08 N | 0.18 W |
| Sandy, Or., U.S. | 224 | 45.23 N | 122.15 W |
| Sandy, Pa., U.S. | 214 | 41.07 N | 78.47 W |
| Sandy, Ut., U.S. | 200 | 40.35 N | 111.53 W |
| Sandy ≃, Me., U.S. | 188 | 44.45 N | 69.52 W |
| Sandy ≃, Or., U.S. | 224 | 45.34 N | 122.24 W |
| Sandy ≃, Va., U.S. | 192 | 36.35 N | 79.25 W |
| Sandy Bay c, Nic. | 236 | 14.28 N | 83.16 W |
| Sandy Bay c, Ma., U.S. | 283 | 42.40 N | 70.37 W |
| Sandy Bay Indian Reserve ◆[4] | 184 | 50.33 N | 98.40 W |
| Sandy Bay Mountain ∧ | 188 | 45.47 N | 70.25 W |
| Sandy Beach | 210 | 43.04 N | 78.55 W |
| Sandy Branch ≃ | 284c | 39.03 N | 77.16 W |
| Sandy Cape ›, Austl. | 166 | 41.25 S | 144.45 E |
| Sandy Cape ›, Austl. | 166 | 24.42 S | 153.17 E |
| Sandy Creek | 212 | 43.38 N | 76.05 W |
| Sandy Creek ≃, Austl. | 166 | 32.10 S | 144.39 E |
| Sandy Creek ≃, U.S. | 196 | 34.25 N | 99.35 W |
| Sandy Creek ≃, U.S. | 196 | 36.50 N | 98.10 W |
| Sandy Creek ≃, Il., U.S. | 219 | 39.34 N | 90.35 W |
| Sandy Creek ≃, N.Y., U.S. | 212 | 43.44 N | 76.15 W |
| Sandy Creek ≃, N.Y., U.S. | 212 | 43.20 N | 77.55 W |
| Sandy Creek ≃, N.C., U.S. | 192 | 36.08 N | 78.02 W |
| Sandy Creek ≃, Oh., U.S. | 214 | 40.38 N | 81.26 W |
| Sandy Creek ≃, Pa., U.S. | 214 | 41.18 N | 79.51 W |
| Sandy Creek ≃, Tx., U.S. | 196 | 30.34 N | 98.26 W |
| Sandy Creek ≃, Tx., U.S. | 222 | 29.02 N | 96.33 W |
| Sandy Creek, East Branch ≃ | 210 | 43.17 N | 78.03 W |
| Sandy Creek, North Branch ≃ | 212 | 43.51 N | 75.58 W |
| Sandy Creek, West Branch ≃ | 210 | 43.17 N | 78.03 W |
| Sandy Desert ◆[2] | 128 | 28.40 N | 62.30 E |
| Sandy Hook, Ct., U.S. | 207 | 41.25 N | 73.16 W |
| Sandy Hook, Ky., U.S. | 192 | 38.05 N | 83.07 W |
| Sandy Hook, Ms., U.S. | 194 | 31.02 N | 89.48 W |
| Sandy Hook ›[2] | 208 | 40.27 N | 74.00 W |
| Sandy Hook Bay c | 276 | 40.26 N | 74.03 W |
| Sandykači | 128 | 36.33 N | 62.34 E |
| Sandy Key I | 220 | 25.02 N | 81.01 W |
| Sandy Lake | 214 | 41.20 N | 80.04 W |
| Sandy Lake ⊜, Nf., Can. | 186 | 49.16 N | 57.00 W |
| Sandy Lake ⊜, On., Can. | 184 | 53.02 N | 93.00 W |
| Sandy Lake ⊜, On., Can. | 212 | 44.33 N | 78.24 W |
| Sandy Lick Creek ≃ | 214 | 41.09 N | 79.05 W |
| Sandy Point ›, Austl. | 168b | 34.16 S | 138.09 E |
| Sandy Point ›, Trin. | 241r | 11.09 N | 60.50 W |
| Sandy Point ›, R.I., U.S. | 207 | 41.14 N | 71.35 W |
| Sandy Point Town | 238 | 17.22 N | 62.50 W |
| Sandy Ridge | 214 | 40.49 N | 78.14 W |
| Sandy Springs | 192 | 33.55 N | 84.22 W |
| Sandyville, Md., U.S. | 208 | 39.31 N | 76.55 W |
| Sandyville, Oh., U.S. | 214 | 40.38 N | 81.23 W |
| Sandžak ◆[1] | 38 | 43.10 N | 19.30 E |
| San Eladio | 258 | 34.46 S | 59.11 W |
| San Elizario | 200 | 31.35 N | 106.16 W |
| San Emigdio Creek ≃ | 228 | 35.02 N | 119.11 W |
| San Emilio | 116 | 17.14 N | 120.37 E |
| Sanen ≃ | 115a | 8.23 S | 113.37 E |
| San Enrique | 252 | 35.47 S | 60.22 W |
| San Estanislao | 252 | 24.39 S | 56.26 W |
| San Esteban | 236 | 15.17 N | 85.52 W |
| San Esteban, Isla I | 232 | 28.42 N | 112.36 W |
| San Esteban de Gormaz | 34 | 41.35 N | 3.12 W |
| San Fele | 68 | 40.49 N | 15.32 E |
| San Felice (Sankt Felix) | 64 | 46.30 N | 11.08 E |
| San Felice Circeo | 66 | 41.14 N | 13.05 E |
| San Felice sul Panaro | 64 | 44.50 N | 11.08 E |
| San Felipe, Chile | 252 | 32.45 S | 70.44 W |
| San Felipe, Col. | 246 | 1.55 N | 67.06 W |
| San Felípe, Méx. | 232 | 31.00 N | 114.52 W |
| San Felipe, Méx. | 234 | 21.29 N | 101.13 W |
| San Felipe, Pil. | 116 | 15.04 N | 120.04 E |
| San Felipe, Tx., U.S. | 222 | 29.48 N | 96.06 W |
| San Felipe, Ven. | 246 | 10.20 N | 68.44 W |
| San Felipe, Castillo de ⊥ | 236 | 15.39 N | 89.01 W |
| San Felipe, Cayos de II | 240p | 21.58 N | 83.30 W |
| San Felipe Aztatán | 234 | 22.23 N | 105.24 W |
| San Felipe Creek ≃ | 204 | 33.09 N | 115.46 W |
| San Felipe de Vichayal | 248 | 4.52 S | 81.05 W |
| San Felipe Indian Reservation ◆[4] | 200 | 35.26 N | 106.26 W |
| San Felipe Jalapa de Díaz | 234 | 18.04 N | 96.32 W |
| San Felipe Nuevo Mercurio | 232 | 24.22 N | 102.06 W |
| San Felipe Pueblo | 200 | 35.27 N | 106.28 W |
| San Félix ≃ | 236 | 8.10 N | 81.51 W |
| San Félix, Isla I | 244 | 26.17 S | 80.05 W |


| Symbol | English | Deutsch | Español | Français | Português |
|---|---|---|---|---|---|
| ≃ | River | Fluß | Río | Rivière | Rio |
| ≊ | Canal | Kanal | Canal | Canal | Canal |
| ⌞ | Waterfall, Rapids | Wasserfall, Stromschnellen | Cascada, Rápidos | Chute d'eau, Rapides | Cascata, Rápidos |
| ʊ | Strait | Meeresstraße | Estrecho | Détroit | Estreito |
| c | Bay, Gulf | Bucht, Golf | Bahía, Golfo | Baie, Golfe | Baía, Golfo |
| ⊜ | Lake, Lakes | See, Seen | Lago, Lagos | Lac, Lacs | Lago, Lagos |
| ≡ | Swamp | Sumpf | Pantano | Marais | Pântano |
| ⁂ | Ice Features, Glacier | Eis- und Gletscherformen | Accidentes Glaciales | Formes glaciaires | Acidentes glaciares |
| ⫧ | Other Hydrographic Features | Andere Hydrographische Objekte | Otros Elementos Hidrográficos | Autres données hydrographiques | Outros acidentes hidrográficos |
| ✥ | Submarine Features | Untermeerische Objekte | Accidentes Submarinos | Formes de relief sous-marin | Acidentes submarinos |
| □ | Political Unit | Politische Einheit | Unidad Politica | Entité politique | Unidade política |
| ♆ | Cultural Institution | Kulturelle Institution | Institución Cultural | Institution culturelle | Instituição cultural |
| ⊥ | Historical Site | Historische Stätte | Sitio Histórico | Site historique | Sitio histórico |
| ♠ | Recreational Site | Erholungs- und Ferienort | Sitio de Recreo | Centre de loisirs | Sitio de Lazer |
| ⊠ | Airport | Flughafen | Aeropuerto | Aéroport | Aeroporto |
| ■ | Military Installation | Militäranlage | Instalación Militar | Installation militaire | Instalação militar |
| ◆ | Miscellaneous | Verschiedenes | Misceláneo | Divers | Diversos |

**ENGLISH** — Name | Page | Lat.°′ | Long.°′

**DEUTSCH** — Name | Seite | Breite°′ | Länge°′ E = Ost


| Name | Page | Lat.°′ | Long.°′ |
|---|---|---|---|
| San Ferdinando di Puglia | **68** | 41.18 N | 16.04 E |
| San Fermín | **196** | 26.20 N | 104.49 W |
| San Fernando, Arg. | **258** | 34.26 S | 58.34 W |
| San Fernando, Chile | **252** | 34.35 S | 71.00 W |
| San Fernando, Esp. | **34** | 36.28 N | 6.12 W |
| San Fernando, Méx. | **196** | 28.32 N | 100.54 W |
| San Fernando, Méx. | **200** | 31.16 N | 110.36 W |
| San Fernando, Méx. | **232** | 24.50 N | 98.10 W |
| San Fernando, Méx. | **234** | 16.52 N | 93.13 W |
| San Fernando, Pil. | **116** | 16.37 N | 120.19 E |
| San Fernando, Pil. | **116** | 12.30 N | 123.46 E |
| San Fernando, Pil. | **116** | 15.01 N | 120.41 E |
| San Fernando, Trin. | **241r** | 10.17 N | 61.28 W |
| San Fernando, Ca., U.S. | **228** | 34.16 N | 118.26 W |
| San Fernando, Ven. | **246** | 7.54 N | 67.28 W |
| San Fernando □5 | **288** | 34.28 S | 58.34 W |
| San Fernando, Aeródromo ⊠ | **288** | 34.27 S | 58.35 W |
| San Fernando Airport ⊠ | **280** | 34.17 N | 118.25 W |
| San Fernando Creek ≃ | **196** | 27.28 N | 97.46 W |
| San Fernando de Atabapo | **246** | 4.03 N | 67.42 W |
| San Fernando de Henares | **266a** | 40.26 N | 3.32 W |
| San Fernando del Valle de Catamarca | **252** | 28.28 S | 65.47 W |
| San Fernando Mission ʋ1 | **280** | 34.16 N | 118.28 W |
| San Fernando Point > | **116** | 16.38 N | 120.17 E |
| San Fernando Valley V | **280** | 34.13 N | 118.27 W |
| San Fili | **68** | 39.20 N | 16.09 E |
| San Filippo del Mela, It. | **70** | 38.10 N | 15.17 E |
| San Filippo del Mela, It. | **70** | 38.10 N | 15.17 E |
| Sånfjället ∧ | **26** | 62.17 N | 13.32 E |
| Sånfjällets Nationalpark ♦ | **26** | 62.20 N | 13.40 E |
| San Floriano | **64** | 46.02 N | 12.18 E |
| Sanford, Co., U.S. | **200** | 37.15 N | 105.54 W |
| Sanford, Fl., U.S. | **220** | 28.48 N | 81.16 W |
| Sanford, Me., U.S. | **188** | 43.26 N | 70.46 W |
| Sanford, Mi., U.S. | **190** | 43.40 N | 84.22 W |
| Sanford, N.C., U.S. | **192** | 35.28 N | 79.10 W |
| Sanford, Tx., U.S. | **196** | 35.42 N | 101.32 W |
| Sanford ≃ | **162** | 27.22 S | 115.53 E |
| Sanford, Mount ∧ | **180** | 62.13 N | 144.09 W |
| San Francesco, Convento ʋ1, It. | **66** | 42.28 N | 12.45 E |
| San Francesco, Convento ʋ1, It. | **267a** | 42.03 N | 12.46 E |
| San Francisco, Arg. | **252** | 31.26 S | 62.05 W |
| San Francisco, Col. | **246** | 1.11 N | 76.53 W |
| San Francisco, C.R. | **236** | 9.49 N | 85.15 W |
| San Francisco, El Sal. | **236** | 13.42 N | 88.06 W |
| San Francisco, Pan. | **236** | 8.15 N | 80.58 W |
| San Francisco, Pil. | **116** | 8.30 N | 125.56 E |
| San Francisco, Pil. | **116** | 10.04 N | 125.09 E |
| San Francisco, Ca., U.S. | **226** | 37.46 N | 122.25 W |
| San Francisco, Ca., U.S. | **282** | 37.46 N | 122.25 W |
| San Francisco □6 | **226** | 37.45 N | 122.22 W |
| San Francisco ≃, Arg. | **252** | 23.16 S | 64.03 W |
| San Francisco → São Francisco ≃, Bra. | **242** | 10.30 S | 36.24 W |
| San Francisco ≃, U.S. | **200** | 32.59 N | 109.22 W |
| San Francisco, Arroyo ≃ | **288** | 34.43 S | 58.19 W |
| San Francisco, Paso de )( | **252** | 26.53 S | 68.19 W |
| San Francisco, University of ʋ2 | **282** | 37.46 N | 122.26 W |
| San Francisco Bay c | **226** | 37.43 N | 122.17 W |
| San Francisco Creek ≃ | **196** | 29.53 N | 102.19 W |
| San Francisco Culhuacán ◆8 | **286a** | 19.20 N | 99.08 W |
| San Francisco de Borja | **232** | 27.53 N | 106.41 W |
| San Francisco de Horizonte | **196** | 25.56 N | 103.26 W |
| San Francisco de Lajas | **234** | 23.07 N | 105.07 W |
| San Francisco de la Paz | **236** | 14.55 N | 86.14 W |
| San Francisco del Chañar | **252** | 29.47 S | 63.56 W |
| San Francisco del Monte de Oro | **252** | 32.36 S | 66.08 W |
| San Francisco del Oro | **232** | 26.52 N | 105.51 W |
| San Francisco del Rincón | **234** | 21.01 N | 101.51 W |
| San Francisco de Macoris | **238** | 19.18 N | 70.15 W |
| San Francisco de Mostazal | **252** | 33.59 S | 70.43 W |
| San Francisco el Grande, Iglesia de ʋ1 | **266a** | 40.25 N | 3.43 W |
| San Francisco International Airport ⊠ | **226** | 37.37 N | 122.23 W |
| San Francisco Ixhuatán | **234** | 16.22 N | 94.29 W |
| San Francisco Libre | **236** | 12.30 N | 86.18 W |
| San Francisco Maritime National Historical Park ♦ | **282** | 37.48 N | 122.27 W |
| San Francisco-Oakland Bay Bridge ◆5 | **282** | 37.48 N | 122.22 W |
| San Francisco State Fish and Game Refuge ◆4 | **282** | 37.35 N | 122.25 W |
| San Francisco State University ʋ2 | **282** | 37.43 N | 122.28 W |
| San Francisco Tlalcilalcalpa | **234** | 19.18 N | 99.46 W |
| San Francisco Tlaltenco ◆8 | **286a** | 19.17 N | 99.01 W |
| San Francisco Zoological Gardens ♦ | **282** | 37.44 N | 122.30 W |
| San Francisquito Creek ≃ | **282** | 37.28 N | 122.07 W |
| San Franco, Cerro ∧ | **236** | 15.25 N | 87.18 W |
| San Fratello | **70** | 38.01 N | 14.36 E |
| San Fratello ≃ | **70** | 38.02 N | 14.34 E |
| Sanga, Ang. | **152** | 11.07 S | 15.22 E |
| Sanga, Burkina | **150** | 11.10 N | 0.10 E |
| Sanga, Mali | **150** | 14.28 N | 3.19 W |
| Sanga, Zaïre | **154** | 7.02 S | 28.21 E |
| San Gabriel, Ec. | **246** | 0.36 N | 77.49 W |
| San Gabriel, Ca., U.S. | **228** | 34.05 N | 118.06 W |
| San Gabriel ≃, Ca., U.S. | **280** | 33.45 N | 118.07 W |
| San Gabriel ≃, Tx., U.S. | **222** | 30.46 N | 97.01 W |
| San Gabriel, Isla I | **258** | 34.28 S | 57.54 W |
| San Gabriel, North Fork ≃, Ca., U.S. | **280** | 34.15 N | 117.52 W |
| San Gabriel, North Fork ≃, Tx., U.S. | **196** | 30.38 N | 97.41 W |
| San Gabriel, South Fork ≃ | **196** | 30.38 N | 97.41 W |
| San Gabriel Arcangel, Mission ʋ1 | **280** | 34.06 N | 118.06 W |
| San Gabriel Chilac | **234** | 18.19 N | 97.21 W |
| San Gabriel Dam ◆6 | **280** | 34.13 N | 117.52 W |
| San Gabriel Mountains ⁂ | **228** | 34.20 N | 118.00 W |
| San Gabriel Peak ∧ | **280** | 34.15 N | 118.06 W |
| San Gabriel Reservoir ◎1 | **228** | 34.13 N | 117.51 W |
| Săngăçal burnu > | **84** | 40.07 N | 49.30 E |
| San Galgano, Abbazia di ʋ1 | **66** | 43.10 N | 11.10 E |
| Šangaly | **24** | 61.08 N | 43.19 E |
| Sangamankanda Point > | **122** | 7.01 N | 81.52 E |
| Sangamner | **122** | 19.34 N | 74.13 E |
| Sangamon □6 | **219** | 39.47 N | 89.40 W |
| Sangamon ≃ | **194** | 40.07 N | 90.20 W |
| Sangamon, South Fork ≃ | **219** | 39.48 N | 89.32 W |
| Sanga Puitã | **255** | 22.40 S | 55.36 W |
| Sangar | **74** | 63.55 N | 127.31 E |
| Sangar Sarāy | **120** | 34.24 N | 70.38 E |
| Sangasanga-dalam | **112** | 0.40 S | 117.14 E |
| Sanga Sanga Island I | **116** | 5.04 N | 119.47 E |
| Sangat | **123** | 30.05 N | 74.50 E |
| Sangatte | **50** | 50.56 N | 1.45 E |
| San Gavino Monreale | **71** | 39.33 N | 8.47 E |
| Sangay ∧1 | **246** | 2.00 S | 78.20 W |
| Sangay, Parque Nacional ♦ | **246** | 1.50 S | 78.20 W |
| Sangayán, Isla I | **248** | 13.51 S | 76.28 W |
| Sang Bast | **128** | 35.59 N | 59.46 E |
| Sangbé | **152** | 6.03 N | 12.28 E |
| Sangchris Lake ◎1 | **219** | 39.35 N | 89.30 W |
| Sangchris Lake State Park ♦ | **219** | 39.38 N | 89.28 W |
| Sangchungshih | **100** | 25.04 N | 121.29 E |
| Sangeang, Pulau I | **115b** | 8.12 S | 119.04 E |
| Sang-e Māsheh | **120** | 33.08 N | 67.27 E |
| San Gemini | **66** | 42.37 N | 12.33 E |
| San Genesio Atesino | **64** | 46.32 N | 11.20 E |
| Sangenjaya ◆8 | **268** | 35.38 N | 139.40 E |
| Sanger, Ca., U.S. | **226** | 36.42 N | 119.33 W |
| Sanger, Tx., U.S. | **196** | 33.21 N | 97.10 W |
| Sângera | **38** | 47.38 N | 28.09 E |
| Sangerhausen | **54** | 51.28 N | 11.17 E |
| San Germán | **240m** | 18.05 N | 67.03 W |
| San Germano Vercellese | **62** | 45.21 N | 8.15 E |
| San Geronimo | **226** | 38.01 N | 122.39 W |
| San Gerónimo, Arroyo ≃ | **258** | 33.57 S | 56.05 W |
| Sangerville | **188** | 45.09 N | 69.21 W |
| Sanggan ≃ | **90** | 40.21 N | 115.21 E |
| Sanggar, Teluk c | **115b** | 8.20 S | 118.18 E |
| Sanggau | **112** | 0.08 N | 110.36 E |
| Sangge-ri ◆8 | **271b** | 37.41 N | 127.05 E |
| Sanggin Dalai | **102** | 38.11 N | 105.17 E |
| Sanggona | **112** | 3.52 S | 121.46 E |
| Sangha □5, Centraf. | **152** | 3.35 N | 16.20 E |
| Sangha □5, Congo | **152** | 1.00 N | 15.30 E |
| Sangha ≃ | **152** | 1.13 S | 16.49 E |
| Sanghar | **120** | 26.02 N | 68.57 E |
| San Giacomo (Sankt Jakob in Pfitsch) | **64** | 46.57 N | 11.36 E |
| San Giacomo Filippo | **58** | 46.20 N | 9.21 E |
| Sangihe, Kepulauan II | **112** | 3.00 N | 125.30 E |
| Sangihe, Pulau I | **112** | 3.35 N | 125.32 E |
| Sangijn dalaj nuur ◎ | **88** | 49.17 N | 99.00 E |
| San Gil | **246** | 6.33 N | 73.08 W |
| Sangilen, chrebet ⁂ | **88** | 50.18 N | 96.30 E |
| San Gimignano | **66** | 43.28 N | 11.02 E |
| San Ginesio | **66** | 43.06 N | 13.19 E |
| San Gion | **58** | 46.38 N | 8.50 E |
| San Giorgio | **68** | 40.51 N | 14.23 E |
| San Giorgio Canavese | **62** | 45.20 N | 7.48 E |
| San Giorgio della Richinvelda | **64** | 46.03 N | 12.52 E |
| San Giorgio del Sannio | **68** | 41.04 N | 14.51 E |
| San Giorgio di Lomellina | **62** | 45.10 N | 8.47 E |
| San Giorgio di Nogaro | **64** | 45.50 N | 13.13 E |
| San Giorgio di Piano | **64** | 44.39 N | 11.22 E |
| San Giorgio Ionico | **68** | 40.27 N | 17.23 E |
| San Giorgio la Molara | **68** | 41.16 N | 14.55 E |
| San Giorgio Lucano | **68** | 40.07 N | 16.23 E |
| San Giorgio Monferrato | **62** | 45.07 N | 8.23 E |
| San Giorgio Morgeto | **68** | 38.23 N | 16.06 E |
| San Giorgio Piacentino | **62** | 44.57 N | 9.44 E |
| San Giorgio su Legnano | **266b** | 45.34 N | 8.55 E |
| San Giovanni (Sankt Johann) | **64** | 46.38 N | 11.44 E |
| San Giovanni al Timavo (Sankt Johann in Ahrn) | **64** | 46.58 N | 11.57 E |
| San Giovanni a Piro | **68** | 40.03 N | 15.27 E |
| San Giovanni-Bianco | **58** | 45.52 N | 9.39 E |
| San Giovanni d'Asso | **66** | 43.09 N | 11.35 E |
| San Giovanni Gemini | **70** | 37.38 N | 13.39 E |
| San Giovanni Ilarione | **64** | 45.30 N | 11.15 E |
| San Giovanni in Croce | **64** | 45.05 N | 10.22 E |
| San Giovanni in Fiore | **68** | 39.15 N | 16.42 E |
| San Giovanni in Laterano ʋ1 | **267a** | 41.53 N | 12.30 E |
| San Giovanni in Persiceto | **64** | 44.38 N | 11.11 E |
| San Giovanni la Punta | **70** | 37.35 N | 15.07 E |
| San Giovanni Lupatoto | **64** | 45.23 N | 11.03 E |
| San Giovanni Rotondo | **68** | 41.42 N | 15.44 E |
| San Giovanni Suergiu | **71** | 39.07 N | 8.31 E |
| San Giovanni Valdarno | **66** | 43.34 N | 11.32 E |
| San Giuliano, Lago di ◎ | **68** | 40.37 N | 16.30 E |
| San Giuliano Milanese | **266b** | 45.24 N | 9.17 E |
| San Giuliano Terme | **66** | 43.46 N | 10.26 E |
| San Giuseppe, It. | **62** | 44.22 N | 8.18 E |
| San Giuseppe, It. | **70** | 37.58 N | 13.11 E |
| San Giuseppe Vesuviano | **68** | 40.50 N | 14.30 E |
| San Giustino | **66** | 43.33 N | 12.10 E |
| San Giusto, Aeroporto di ⊠ | **66** | 43.41 N | 10.21 E |
| San Giusto Canavese | **62** | 45.19 N | 7.49 E |
| Sangju | **98** | 36.26 N | 128.09 E |
| Sangkapura | **115a** | 5.52 S | 112.40 E |
| Sângkê ≃ | **110** | 13.13 N | 103.41 E |
| Sangkhai | **110** | 14.39 N | 103.52 E |
| Sangkulirang | **112** | 0.59 N | 117.58 E |
| Sāngla | **123** | 31.43 N | 73.23 E |
| Sangley Point > | **269f** | 14.30 N | 120.55 E |
| Sāngli | **122** | 16.52 N | 74.34 E |
| Sanglin | **100** | 27.54 N | 114.46 E |
| Sangluoshu | **98** | 37.31 N | 117.43 E |
| Sangmélima | **152** | 2.56 N | 11.59 E |
| Sangngagqoiling | **120** | 28.33 N | 93.00 E |
| Sangnyŏng-ni | **98** | 38.14 N | 126.54 E |
| Sango | **270** | 34.36 N | 135.42 E |
| San Godenzo | **66** | 43.55 N | 11.37 E |
| Sāngole | **122** | 17.26 N | 75.12 E |
| Sangolquí | **246** | 0.19 S | 78.27 W |
| San Gorgonio Mountain ∧ | **204** | 34.06 N | 116.50 W |
| San Gottardo, Passo del )( | **58** | 46.33 N | 8.34 E |
| Sangou | **98** | 41.02 N | 118.11 E |
| Sangre de Cristo Mountains ⁂ | **200** | 37.30 N | 105.15 W |
| San Gregorio, Arg. | **252** | 34.19 S | 62.02 W |
| San Gregorio, It. | **66** | 42.19 N | 13.29 E |
| San Gregorio, Ca., U.S. | **226** | 37.19 N | 122.23 W |
| San Gregorio, Ur. | **252** | 32.37 S | 55.40 W |
| San Gregorio, Ur. | **258** | 33.57 S | 56.45 W |
| San Gregorio ◆8 | **286a** | 19.15 N | 99.03 W |
| San Gregorio, Arroyo ≃ | **258** | 33.59 S | 56.50 W |
| San Gregorio Creek ≃ | **282** | 37.19 N | 122.25 W |
| San Gregorio Magno | **68** | 40.39 N | 15.24 E |
| San Gregorio State Beach ♦ | **282** | 37.19 N | 122.24 W |
| Sangre Grande | **241r** | 10.35 N | 61.07 W |
| Sangro ≃ | **66** | 42.14 N | 14.32 E |
| Sangrūr | **123** | 30.14 N | 75.50 E |
| Sangsang | **120** | 29.25 N | 86.40 E |
| Sangshuyuan | **86** | 42.23 N | 88.30 E |
| Sangsues, Lac aux ◎ | **190** | 46.29 N | 77.57 W |
| Sangtuda | **85** | 38.04 N | 69.04 E |
| Sanguandian | **100** | 31.19 N | 118.05 E |
| Sanguang | **106** | 31.47 N | 121.16 E |
| Sanguanmiao | **100** | 32.25 N | 114.04 E |
| Sanguanyingzi | **104** | 41.39 N | 120.44 E |
| Sangudo | **182** | 53.53 N | 114.54 W |
| Sangue, Rio do ≃ | **248** | 11.01 S | 58.39 W |
| Sangüesa | **34** | 42.35 N | 1.17 W |
| Sanguinetto | **64** | 45.11 N | 11.09 E |
| Sanguliu | **104** | 40.45 N | 124.14 E |
| Sāngurli | **272c** | 18.56 N | 73.07 E |
| Sangutane ≃ | **156** | 24.07 S | 33.47 E |
| Sangvor, Taj. | **85** | 38.47 N | 71.12 E |
| Sangvor, Taj. | **85** | 38.53 N | 71.06 E |
| Sangwa | **154** | 5.30 S | 26.00 E |
| Sangya | **120** | 30.52 N | 91.40 E |
| Sangyuanbao | **105** | 40.15 N | 115.32 E |
| Sangyuanbu | **106** | 31.37 N | 118.53 E |
| Sangyuanzhen | **107** | 30.30 N | 103.26 E |
| Sangzhi | **102** | 29.18 N | 110.02 E |
| Sangzidian | **98** | 36.46 N | 116.55 E |
| Sanhe, Zhg. | **100** | 24.24 N | 116.34 E |
| Sanhe, Zhg. | **105** | 39.59 N | 117.04 E |
| Sanhechang, Zhg. | **102** | 31.22 N | 106.48 E |
| Sanhechang, Zhg. | **107** | 30.04 N | 105.01 E |
| Sanhecun | **98** | 42.28 N | 129.39 E |
| Sanheji | **100** | 32.42 N | 117.55 E |
| Sanhekou | **106** | 31.50 N | 120.08 E |
| Sanhetun | **104** | 42.38 N | 123.38 E |
| Sanhezhan | **89** | 52.34 N | 126.02 E |
| Sanhezhen | **100** | 31.30 N | 117.14 E |
| Sanhezhuang | **105** | 40.04 N | 116.18 E |
| San Hipólito, Punta > | **232** | 26.59 N | 113.59 W |
| Sanhsient'ai I | **100** | 23.08 N | 121.25 E |
| Sanhsing | **100** | 24.40 N | 121.39 E |
| Sanhu | **100** | 27.55 N | 115.24 E |
| Sanhui, Zhg. | **107** | 30.06 N | 106.36 E |
| Sanhui, Zhg. | **107** | 29.57 N | 105.53 E |
| Sanhūr | **142** | 29.25 N | 30.46 E |
| Sanhūr al-Madīnah | **142** | 31.07 N | 30.44 E |
| Sani | **100** | 24.25 N | 120.46 E |
| Sanibel | **220** | 26.26 N | 82.01 W |
| Sanibel Island I | **220** | 26.27 N | 82.06 W |
| Sānī Bherī ≃ | **124** | 28.42 N | 82.16 E |
| San Ignacio, Arg. | **252** | 27.16 S | 55.32 W |
| San Ignacio, C.R. | **236** | 9.48 N | 84.09 W |
| San Ignacio, Hond. | **236** | 14.38 N | 87.02 W |
| San Ignacio, Méx. | **232** | 27.27 N | 112.51 W |
| San Ignacio, Méx. | **234** | 23.12 N | 100.12 W |
| San Ignacio, Méx. | **234** | 23.55 N | 106.25 W |
| San Ignacio, Para. | **252** | 26.52 S | 57.03 W |
| San Ignacio, Perú | **248** | 5.08 S | 78.59 W |
| San Ignacio, Isla I | **232** | 25.25 N | 108.54 W |
| San Ignacio, Laguna ◎ | **232** | 26.54 N | 113.13 W |
| San Ignacio de Moxo | **248** | 14.53 S | 65.36 W |
| San Ignacio de Velasco | **248** | 16.23 S | 60.59 W |
| San Ildefonso, Cape > | **116** | 16.02 N | 121.59 E |
| San Ildefonso, Cerro ∧ | **236** | 15.31 N | 88.17 W |
| San Ildefonso Indian Reservation ◆4 | **200** | 35.53 N | 106.08 W |
| San Ildefonso la Granja | **34** | 40.54 N | 4.00 W |
| San Ildefonso Peninsula >1 | **116** | 16.10 N | 122.05 E |
| San Ildefonso Villa Alta | **234** | 17.21 N | 96.09 W |
| San'in-kaigan-kokuritsu-kōen ♦ | **96** | 35.38 N | 134.38 E |
| Sanino | **265a** | 59.50 N | 29.54 E |
| Sani Pass )( | **158** | 29.34 S | 29.19 E |
| San Isidro, Arg. | **252** | 28.27 S | 65.44 W |
| San Isidro, Arg. | **258** | 34.27 S | 58.30 W |
| San Isidro, C.R. | **236** | 9.22 N | 83.42 W |
| San Isidro, Méx. | **200** | 31.31 N | 106.18 W |
| San Isidro, Nic. | **236** | 12.56 N | 86.12 W |
| San Isidro, Perú | **286d** | 12.07 S | 77.03 W |
| San Isidro, Pil. | **116** | 11.24 N | 124.21 E |
| San Isidro, Tx., U.S. | **196** | 26.42 N | 98.27 W |
| San Isidro □5 | **288** | 34.29 S | 58.33 W |
| San Isidro el Real, Catedral de ʋ1 | **266a** | 40.25 N | 3.42 W |
| Sanitaria Springs | **210** | 42.09 N | 75.46 W |
| Sanitatas | **156** | 18.11 S | 12.47 E |
| Sanitz | **54** | 54.04 N | 12.22 E |
| San Jacinto, Col. | **246** | 9.50 N | 75.08 W |
| San Jacinto, Méx. | **196** | 25.29 N | 103.44 W |
| San Jacinto, Pil. | **116** | 12.34 N | 123.44 E |
| San Jacinto, Ca., U.S. | **228** | 33.47 N | 116.57 W |
| San Jacinto □6 | **222** | 30.35 N | 95.10 W |
| San Jacinto ≃, Ca., U.S. | **228** | 33.43 N | 117.16 W |
| San Jacinto ≃, Tx., U.S. | **222** | 29.46 N | 95.05 W |
| San Jacinto, East Fork ≃ | **222** | 30.05 N | 95.09 W |
| San Jacinto, West Fork ≃ | **222** | 30.02 N | 95.15 W |
| San Jacinto Monument ⊥ | **222** | 29.45 N | 95.01 W |
| San Jacinto Peak ∧ | **204** | 33.49 N | 116.41 W |
| San Jacinto Valley V | **228** | 33.50 N | 117.05 W |
| Sanjahā | **142** | 30.50 N | 31.38 E |
| San Javier, Arg. | **252** | 27.53 S | 55.08 W |
| San Javier, Arg. | **252** | 30.35 S | 59.57 W |
| San Javier, Bol. | **248** | 14.34 S | 64.42 W |
| San Javier, Bol. | **248** | 16.20 S | 62.38 W |
| San Javier, Méx. | **196** | 26.16 N | 99.27 W |
| San Javier, Ur. | **252** | 32.41 S | 58.08 W |
| San Javier ≃ | **252** | 31.30 S | 60.20 W |
| San Javier de Loncomilla | **252** | 35.35 S | 71.45 W |
| Sanjāwi | **120** | 30.17 N | 68.21 E |
| Sanje | **154** | 0.46 S | 31.30 E |
| San Jeronimito | **234** | 17.33 N | 101.20 W |
| San Jerónimo, Guat. | **236** | 15.03 N | 90.12 W |
| San Jerónimo, Méx. | **234** | 17.08 N | 100.28 W |
| San Jerónimo Norte | **252** | 31.33 S | 61.05 W |
| Sanjiadian, Zhg. | **105** | 40.09 N | 116.36 E |
| Sanjiadian, Zhg. | **105** | 39.58 N | 116.06 E |
| Sanjiadian, Zhg. | **105** | 39.22 N | 115.58 E |
| Sanjiang, Zhg. | **102** | 25.42 N | 109.23 E |
| Sanjiang, Zhg. | **107** | 29.33 N | 104.03 E |
| Sanjiangzhen | **107** | 30.31 N | 103.48 E |
| Sanjiaocheng | **102** | 36.47 N | 104.40 E |
| Sanjiaopao | **104** | 41.22 N | 122.17 E |
| Sanjiaoshancun | **104** | 40.42 N | 122.49 E |
| Sanjiazhen | **107** | 30.17 N | 105.32 E |
| Sanjiazi, Zhg. | **104** | 41.53 N | 121.42 E |
| Sanjiazi, Zhg. | **104** | 40.42 N | 123.16 E |
| Sanjiazi, Zhg. | **104** | 40.54 N | 121.59 E |
| Sanjiazi, Zhg. | **104** | 42.33 N | 121.38 E |
| Sanjiazi, Zhg. | **104** | 42.02 N | 122.20 E |
| Sanjiaziyingzi | **104** | 41.52 N | 120.49 E |
| Sanjie, Zhg. | **100** | 32.35 N | 118.08 E |
| Sanjie, Zhg. | **102** | 25.01 N | 101.02 E |
| Sanjō | **92** | 37.37 N | 138.57 E |
| San Joaquín, Bol. | **248** | 13.04 S | 64.49 W |
| San Joaquín, Chile | **286e** | 33.30 S | 70.37 W |
| San Joaquín, Para. | **252** | 24.57 S | 56.07 W |
| San Joaquin, Pil. | **116** | 10.35 N | 122.08 E |
| San Joaquin, Ca., U.S. | **226** | 36.36 N | 120.11 W |
| San Joaquin □6 | **226** | 37.57 N | 121.17 W |
| San Joaquín ≃, Bol. | **248** | 13.08 S | 63.41 W |
| San Joaquin ≃, Ca., U.S. | **226** | 38.03 N | 121.50 W |
| San Joaquin, Middle Fork ≃ | **226** | 37.32 N | 119.11 W |
| San Joaquin, North Fork ≃ | **226** | 37.32 N | 119.11 W |
| San Joaquin, South Fork ≃ | **226** | 37.26 N | 119.14 W |
| San Joaquin Valley V | **204** | 36.50 N | 120.10 W |
| San Jon | **196** | 35.06 N | 103.19 W |
| San Jorge, Arg. | **252** | 31.54 S | 61.52 W |
| San Jorge, El Sal. | **236** | 13.25 N | 88.21 W |
| San Jorge, Nic. | **236** | 11.27 N | 85.48 W |
| San Jorge ≃ | **246** | 9.07 N | 74.44 W |
| San Jorge, Bahía de c | **200** | 31.12 N | 113.15 W |
| San Jorge, Cabo > | **254** | 45.47 S | 67.21 W |
| San Jorge, Canal de → Saint George's Channel ⊔ | **28** | 52.00 N | 6.00 W |
| San Jorge, Golfo c | **254** | 46.00 S | 67.00 W |
| San Jorge Island I | **175e** | 8.27 S | 159.35 E |
| San José, Arg. | **252** | 27.46 S | 55.47 W |
| San José, C.R. | **236** | 9.56 N | 84.05 W |
| San José, Méx. | **196** | 28.16 N | 100.15 W |
| San Jose, N. Mar. Is. | **174n** | 15.09 N | 145.43 E |
| San José, Para. | **252** | 25.33 S | 56.45 W |
| San Jose, Pil. | **116** | 10.45 N | 121.56 E |
| San Jose, Pil. | **116** | 15.48 N | 121.00 E |
| San Jose, Pil. | **116** | 12.27 N | 121.03 E |
| San Jose, Ca., U.S. | **226** | 37.20 N | 121.53 W |
| San Jose, Ca., U.S. | **282** | 37.20 N | 121.53 W |
| San Jose, Il., U.S. | **194** | 40.18 N | 89.36 W |
| San Jose, N.M., U.S. | **200** | 35.23 N | 105.28 W |
| San José, Ven. | **286c** | 10.34 N | 66.57 W |
| San José □4 | **236** | 9.40 N | 84.00 W |
| San José □5 | **258** | 34.15 S | 56.45 W |
| San José □7 | **286b** | 22.57 N | 82.14 W |
| San Jose ≃, B.C., Can. | **182** | 52.14 N | 122.15 W |
| San José ≃, Ur. | **258** | 34.38 S | 56.29 W |
| San Jose, Arroyo ≃ | **282** | 38.03 N | 122.30 W |
| San José, Golfo c | **254** | 42.20 S | 64.18 W |
| San José, Isla I, Méx. | **232** | 25.00 N | 110.38 W |
| San José, Isla I, Pan. | **246** | 8.15 N | 79.07 W |
| San José, Laguna c | **240m** | 18.25 N | 66.01 W |
| San Jose, Mission ʋ1 | **282** | 37.32 N | 121.55 W |
| San Jose, Rio ≃ | **200** | 34.52 N | 107.01 W |
| San Jose Arena ♦ | **282** | 37.20 N | 121.54 W |
| San José Ayuquila | **234** | 17.58 N | 97.57 W |
| San José Batuc | **232** | 29.15 N | 109.44 W |
| San José Buena Vista | **236** | 13.49 N | 90.19 W |
| San Jose Creek ≃ | **280** | 34.01 N | 118.03 W |
| San José de Aura | **196** | 27.34 N | 101.23 W |
| San José de Bácum | **232** | 27.32 N | 110.09 W |
| San Jose de Buan | **116** | 12.02 N | 125.01 E |
| San José de Chiquitos | **248** | 17.51 S | 60.47 W |
| San José de Copán | **236** | 14.54 N | 88.44 W |
| San José de Feliciano | **252** | 30.23 S | 58.45 W |
| San José de Galipán | **286c** | 10.35 N | 66.54 W |
| San José de Galipán, Quebrada ≃ | **286c** | 10.37 N | 66.54 W |
| San José de Gracia | **234** | 20.40 N | 102.35 W |
| San José de Guanipa | **246** | 8.54 N | 64.09 W |
| San José de Guaribe | **246** | 9.52 N | 65.48 W |
| San José de Iturbide | **234** | 21.00 N | 100.23 W |
| San José de Jáchal | **252** | 30.14 S | 68.45 W |
| San José de la Esquina | **252** | 33.06 S | 61.42 W |
| San José de la Parilla | **234** | 23.44 N | 104.07 W |
| San José de la Popa | **196** | 26.10 N | 100.47 W |
| San José de las Flores | **234** | 17.20 N | 95.24 W |
| San José de las Lajas | **240p** | 22.58 N | 82.09 W |
| San José de las Raíces | **232** | 24.35 N | 100.14 W |
| San José del Cabo | **232** | 23.03 N | 109.41 W |
| San José del Guaviare | **246** | 2.35 N | 72.38 W |
| San José de Llanetes | **234** | 22.55 N | 103.16 W |
| San José de los Molinos | **248** | 13.57 S | 75.41 W |
| San José de Lourdes | **234** | 23.18 N | 103.01 W |
| San José del Valle | **234** | 23.20 N | 98.24 W |
| San José de Mayo | **258** | 34.20 S | 56.42 W |
| San José de Ocuné | **246** | 4.15 N | 70.20 W |
| San José de Sisa | **248** | 6.37 S | 76.39 W |
| San José de Tiznados | **246** | 9.23 N | 67.33 W |
| San Jose Hills ⁂2 | **280** | 34.04 N | 117.49 W |
| San Jose Island I | **196** | 28.10 N | 96.45 W |
| San Jose Municipal Airport ⊠ | **226** | 37.22 N | 121.56 W |
| San Jose State University ʋ2 | **282** | 37.20 N | 121.53 W |
| San Juan, Arg. | **252** | 31.32 S | 68.31 W |
| San Juan, Guat. | **236** | 15.52 N | 88.53 W |
| San Juan, Méx. | **196** | 29.34 N | 104.36 W |
| San Juan, Perú | **248** | 15.21 S | 75.10 W |
| San Juan, Pil. | **116** | 13.50 N | 121.24 E |
| San Juan, Pil. | **116** | 16.40 N | 120.20 E |
| San Juan, Pil. | **116** | 8.25 N | 126.20 E |
| San Juan, P.R. | **240m** | 18.28 N | 66.07 W |
| San Juan □4 | **252** | 31.00 S | 69.00 W |
| San Juan □6 | **224** | 48.34 N | 122.59 W |
| San Juan ≃, Arg. | **252** | 32.17 S | 67.22 W |
| San Juan ≃, B.C., Can. | **224** | 48.34 N | 124.24 W |
| San Juan ≃, Col. | **246** | 4.03 N | 77.27 W |
| San Juan ≃, Méx. | **232** | 26.22 N | 98.51 W |
| San Juan ≃, Méx. | **234** | 18.36 N | 95.40 W |
| San Juan ≃, Méx. | **234** | 17.59 N | 99.47 W |
| San Juan ≃, N.A. | **236** | 10.56 N | 83.42 W |
| San Juan ≃, Perú | **248** | 13.27 S | 76.11 W |
| San Juan ≃, Pil. | **269f** | 14.35 N | 121.01 E |
| San Juan ≃, S.A. | **246** | 1.11 N | 78.33 W |
| San Juan ≃, U.S. | **200** | 37.18 N | 110.28 W |
| San Juan ≃, Ur. | **258** | 34.17 S | 57.58 W |
| San Juan ≃, Ven. | **246** | 10.14 N | 62.38 W |
| San Juan, Bahía de c | **240m** | 18.27 N | 66.07 W |
| San Juan, Cabezas de > | **240m** | 18.23 N | 65.37 W |
| San Juan, Cabo >, Arg. | **254** | 54.44 S | 63.44 W |
| San Juan, Cabo >, Gui. Ecu. | **152** | 1.08 N | 9.23 E |
| San Juan, Embalse de ◎1 | **34** | 40.30 N | 4.15 W |
| San Juan, Pasaje de ⊔ | **240m** | 18.24 N | 65.37 W |
| San Juan, Pico ∧ | **240p** | 21.59 N | 80.09 W |
| San Juan, Port c | **224** | 48.34 N | 124.27 W |
| San Juan, Punta > | **174z** | 27.03 S | 109.22 W |
| San Juan Basin ≚1 | **200** | 36.15 N | 108.20 W |
| San Juan Bautista, Méx. | **196** | 26.58 N | 101.24 W |
| San Juan Bautista, Para. | **252** | 26.38 S | 57.10 W |
| San Juan Bautista, Ca., U.S. | **226** | 36.51 N | 121.32 W |
| San Juan Bautista State Historical Park ♦ | **226** | 36.51 N | 121.31 W |
| San Juan Capistrano | **228** | 33.30 N | 117.39 W |
| San Juan Capistrano Mission ʋ1 | **228** | 33.31 N | 117.40 W |
| San Juan Cotzal | **236** | 15.26 N | 91.01 W |
| San Juan Creek ≃, Ca., U.S. | **226** | 35.40 N | 120.22 W |
| San Juan Creek ≃, Ca., U.S. | **228** | 33.28 N | 117.41 W |
| San Juan de Abajo | **234** | 20.48 N | 105 13 W |
| San Juan de Aragón, Bosque ♦ | **286a** | 19.28 N | 99.04 W |
| San Juan de Aragón, Zoológico de ♦ | **286a** | 19.28 N | 99.05 W |
| San Juan de Colón | **246** | 8.02 N | 72.16 W |
| San Juan de Dios | **286c** | 10.35 N | 66.55 W |
| San Juan de Guadalupe | **232** | 24.38 N | 102.44 W |
| San Juan de la Maguana | **238** | 18.48 N | 71.14 W |
| San Juan de la Vega | **234** | 20.38 N | 100.46 W |
| San Juan del César | **246** | 10.46 N | 73.01 W |
| San Juan del Monte | **269f** | 14.36 N | 121.02 E |
| San Juan del Norte | **236** | 10.55 N | 83.42 W |
| San Juan del Oro ≃ | **248** | 21.02 S | 65.19 W |
| San Juan de los Cayos | **246** | 11.10 N | 68.25 W |
| San Juan de los Lagos | **234** | 21.15 N | 102.18 W |
| San Juan de los Lagos ≃ | **234** | 21.18 N | 102.33 W |
| San Juan de los Morros | **246** | 9.55 N | 67.21 W |
| San Juan del Río, Méx. | **232** | 24.47 N | 104.27 W |
| San Juan del Río, Méx. | **234** | 20.23 N | 100.00 W |
| San Juan del Salado | **234** | 23.18 N | 101.56 W |
| San Juan del Sur | **236** | 11.15 N | 85.52 W |
| San Juan de Lurigancho | **286d** | 11.59 S | 77.01 W |
| San Juan de Micay ≃ | **246** | 3.05 N | 77.32 W |
| San Juan de Miraflores | **286d** | 12.11 S | 76.57 W |
| San Juan de Payara | **246** | 7.39 N | 67.36 W |
| San Juan de Sabinas | **196** | 27.55 N | 101.18 W |
| San Juan Evangelista | **234** | 17.54 N | 95.08 W |
| San Juan Guichicovi | **234** | 16.58 N | 95.06 W |
| San Juanico | **232** | 26.15 N | 112.24 W |
| San Juanillo | **236** | 10.02 N | 85.44 W |
| San Juan Indian Reservation ◆4 | **200** | 36.03 N | 106.04 W |
| San Juan Island I | **224** | 48.32 N | 123.05 W |
| San Juan Island National Historical Park ♦ | **224** | 48.28 N | 123.00 W |
| San Juan Islands II | **224** | 48.36 N | 122.50 W |
| San Juanito, Isla I | **234** | 21.43 N | 106.38 W |
| San Juan Ixcaquixtla | **234** | 18.27 N | 97.49 W |
| San Juan Ixtayopan ◆8 | **286a** | 19.14 N | 99.00 W |
| San Juan Lachao | **234** | 16.14 N | 97.09 W |
| San Juan Mazatlán | **234** | 17.02 N | 95.25 W |
| San Juan Mountains ⁂ | **200** | 37.35 N | 107.10 W |
| San Juan Nepomuceno, Col. | **246** | 9.57 N | 75.05 W |
| San Juan Nepomuceno, Para. | **252** | 26.06 S | 55.58 W |
| San Juan Peyotán | **234** | 22.24 N | 104.21 W |
| San Juan Quiahije | **234** | 16.17 N | 97.20 W |
| San Juan Sacatepéquez | **236** | 14.43 N | 90.39 W |
| San Juan Teita | **234** | 17.05 N | 97.25 W |
| San Juan y Martínez | **240p** | 22.16 N | 83.50 W |
| San Julián, Méx. | **234** | 21.01 N | 102.10 W |
| San Julian, Pil. | **116** | 11.45 N | 125.27 E |
| San Julian, Quebrada ≃ | **286c** | 10.37 N | 66.51 W |
| San Justo, Arg. | **252** | 30.47 S | 60.35 W |
| San Justo, Arg. | **258** | 34.40 S | 58.33 W |
| San Justo, Aeródromo ⊠ | **288** | 34.44 S | 58.36 W |
| Sankanbiaiwa ∧ | **150** | 8.56 N | 10.48 W |
| Sankarani ≃ | **150** | 12.01 N | 8.19 W |
| Sankarankovil | **122** | 9.10 N | 77.33 E |
| Sankarpur | **272b** | 22.51 N | 88.27 E |
| Sānkdaha | **126** | 22.46 N | 89.10 E |
| Sankeng | **100** | 23.36 N | 112.48 E |
| Sankertown | **214** | 40.28 N | 78.35 W |
| Sankeshu | **104** | 42.38 N | 122.25 E |
| Sankeshwar | **122** | 16.16 N | 74.29 E |
| Sankey Brook ≃ | **262** | 53.22 N | 2.38 W |
| Sankh ≃ | **124** | 22.15 N | 84.48 E |
| Sankheda | **120** | 22.10 N | 73.35 E |
| Sankosh ≃ | **124** | 26.48 N | 89.56 E |
| Sānkra | **120** | 21.18 N | 82.39 E |
| Sānkrāil | **272b** | 22.34 N | 88.14 E |
| Sankt Aegyd am Neuwalde | **61** | 47.52 N | 15.35 E |
| Sankt Andrä | **61** | 46.46 N | 14.49 E |
| Sankt Andrä [-vor dem Hagenthale] | **61** | 48.19 N | 16.13 E |
| Sankt Andreasberg | **54** | 51.43 N | 10.31 E |
| Sankt Anton am Arlberg | **58** | 47.08 N | 10.16 E |
| Sankt Antönien | **58** | 46.58 N | 9.49 E |
| Sankt Augustin | **56** | 50.40 N | 7.16 E |
| Sankt Bartholomä ʋ1 | **64** | 47.32 N | 12.58 E |
| Sankt Blasien | **58** | 47.46 N | 8.07 E |
| Sankt Christopher-Nevis → Saint Kitts and Nevis □1 | **238** | 17.20 N | 62.45 W |
| Sankt Florian ʋ1 | **61** | 48.12 N | 14.23 E |
| Sankt Gallen, Öst. | **61** | 47.41 N | 14.37 E |
| Sankt Gallen, Schw. | **58** | 47.25 N | 9.23 E |
| Sankt Gallen □3 | **58** | 47.10 N | 9.08 E |
| Sankt Gallenkirch | **58** | 47.01 N | 9.59 E |
| Sankt Georgen, Dtsch. | **58** | 47.59 N | 7.47 E |
| Sankt Georgen, Öst. | **61** | 46.43 N | 14.55 E |
| Sankt Georgen im Attergau | **64** | 47.56 N | 13.29 E |
| Sankt Gertraud → Santa Gertrude | **64** | 46.29 N | 10.53 E |
| Sankt Gertrud ◆8 | **54** | 53.52 N | 10.47 E |
| Sankt Gilgen | **64** | 47.46 N | 13.22 E |
| Sankt Goar | **56** | 50.09 N | 7.43 E |
| Sankt Goarshausen | **56** | 50.09 N | 7.44 E |
| Sankt Helena → Saint Helena □2 | **8** | 15.57 S | 5.42 W |
| Sankt Hubert | **56** | 51.23 N | 6.26 E |
| Sankt Ingbert | **56** | 49.17 N | 7.06 E |
| Sankt Jakob → San Giacomo | **64** | 46.57 N | 11.36 E |
| Sankt Jakob im Lesachtal | **64** | 46.41 N | 12.56 E |
| Sankt Jakob im Rosental | **61** | 46.33 N | 14.03 E |
| Sankt Jakob in Defereggen | **64** | 46.55 N | 12.20 E |
| Sankt Johann → San Giovanni | **64** | 46.38 N | 11.44 E |
| Sankt Johann am Tauern | **61** | 47.22 N | 14.29 E |
| Sankt Johann im Pongau | **64** | 47.21 N | 13.12 E |
| Sankt Johann im Walde | **64** | 46.54 N | 12.37 E |
| Sankt Johann in Tirol | **64** | 47.31 N | 12.26 E |
| Sankt Kanzian | **61** | 46.37 N | 14.34 E |
| Sankt Leonhard → San Leonardo | **64** | 46.49 N | 11.15 E |
| Sankt Leonhard am Forst | **61** | 48.09 N | 15.17 E |
| Sankt Leonhard im Pitztal | **64** | 47.04 N | 10.51 E |
| Sankt Lorenz ◆8 | **54** | 53.51 N | 10.40 E |
| Sankt Lorenz → Saint Lawrence ≃ | **176** | 49.30 N | 67.00 W |
| Sankt Lorenzen → San Lorenzo di Sebato | **64** | 46.47 N | 11.54 E |
| Sankt Lorenzen im Lesachtal | **64** | 46.42 N | 12.47 E |
| Sankt Lorenz-Golf → Saint Lawrence, Gulf of c | **186** | 48.00 N | 62.00 W |
| Sankt Lorenz-Insel → Saint Lawrence Island I | **180** | 63.30 N | 170.30 W |
| Sankt Margarethen an der Raab | **61** | 47.03 N | 15.45 E |
| Sankt Märgen | **58** | 48.00 N | 8.05 E |
| Sankt Margrethen | **58** | 47.27 N | 9.36 E |
| Sankt Martin | **64** | 47.28 N | 13.23 E |
| Sankt Martin an der Raab | **61** | 46.55 N | 16.08 E |
| Sankt Martin in Gsies → San Martino in Casies | **64** | 46.49 N | 12.14 E |
| Sankt Mauritz | **52** | 51.57 N | 7.39 E |
| Sankt Michael im Lungau | **64** | 47.06 N | 13.38 E |
| Sankt Michael in Obersteiermark | **61** | 47.20 N | 15.01 E |
| Sankt Michel → Mikkeli | **26** | 61.41 N | 27.15 E |
| Sankt Moritz | **58** | 46.30 N | 9.50 E |
| Sankt Niklaus | **58** | 46.11 N | 7.48 E |
| Sankt Nikolaus → San Nicolò d'Ultima | **64** | 46.30 N | 10.55 E |
| Sankt Oswald | **60** | 48.54 N | 13.25 E |
| Sankt Paul im Lavanttal | **61** | 46.42 N | 14.52 E |
| Sankt Peter | **58** | 48.01 N | 8.01 E |
| Sankt Peter ʋ1 | **263** | 51.37 N | 7.12 E |
| Sankt Peter am Kammersberg | **61** | 47.11 N | 14.11 E |
| Sankt Peter am Ottersbach | **61** | 46.48 N | 15.45 E |
| Sankt-Peterburg (Saint Petersburg), Ross. | **76** | 59.55 N | 30.15 E |
| Sankt-Peterburg (Saint Petersburg), Ross. | **265a** | 59.55 N | 30.15 E |
| Sankt-Peterburg, Gorod □7 | **265a** | 59.55 N | 30.15 E |
| Sankt Peter in der Au | **61** | 48.03 N | 14.37 E |
| Sankt Peter-Ording | **30** | 54.18 N | 8.38 E |
| Sankt Pölten | **61** | 48.12 N | 15.37 E |
| Sankt-Quirinus-Dom ʋ1 | **263** | 51.12 N | 6.42 E |
| Sankt Stefan an der Gail | **64** | 46.37 N | 13.31 E |
| Sankt Stefan im Rosental | **61** | 46.54 N | 15.42 E |
| Sankt Ulrich → Ortisei | **64** | 46.34 N | 11.40 E |
| Sankt Valentin | **61** | 48.10 N | 14.32 E |
| Sankt Veit an der Glan | **61** | 46.46 N | 14.21 E |
| Sankt Veit an der Gölsen | **61** | 48.03 N | 15.40 E |
| Sankt Veit im Pongau | **64** | 47.20 N | 13.09 E |
| Sankt-Viktors-Dom ʋ1 | **263** | 51.40 N | 6.27 E |
| Sankt Vincent → Saint Vincent and the Grenadines □1 | **241h** | 13.15 N | 61.12 W |
| Sankt Wallburg → Santa Valburga | **64** | 46.33 N | 11.00 E |
| Sankt Wendel | **56** | 49.28 N | 7.10 E |
| Sankt-Willibrodi-Dom ʋ1 | **263** | 51.40 N | 6.37 E |
| Sankt Wolfgang, Dtsch. | **60** | 48.13 N | 12.08 E |
| Sankt Wolfgang, Dtsch. | **60** | 48.13 N | 12.08 E |
| Sankt Wolfgang im Salzkammergut | **64** | 47.44 N | 13.27 E |
| Sankuru ≃ | **152** | 4.17 S | 20.25 E |
| San Lázaro | **252** | 22.10 S | 57.55 W |
| San Lázaro, Cabo > | **232** | 24.48 N | 112.19 W |
| San Lazaro Race Track ♦ | **269f** | 14.37 N | 120.59 E |
| San Lazzaro di Savena | **64** | 44.28 N | 11.25 E |
| San Leandro | **226** | 37.43 N | 122.09 W |
| San Leandro Creek ≃ | **282** | 37.45 N | 122.12 W |
| San Leo | **66** | 43.54 N | 12.21 E |
| San Leon | **222** | 29.29 N | 94.55 W |
| San Leonardo (Sankt Leonhard), It. | **64** | 46.49 N | 11.15 E |
| San Leonardo, Méx. | **196** | 27.28 N | 104.55 W |
| San Leonardo ≃ | **70** | 37.59 N | 13.41 E |
| San Leone | **70** | 37.16 N | 13.35 E |
| Sanlicheng | **100** | 31.48 N | 114.12 E |
| Sanlidian | **100** | 30.48 N | 118.15 E |
| Sanlifan | **100** | 30.51 N | 115.15 E |
| Sanlintang | **106** | 31.08 N | 121.29 E |
| Sanlipu | **106** | 31.46 N | 119.03 E |
| Sanliuji | **100** | 32.08 N | 116.19 E |
| Şanlıurfa | **130** | 37.08 N | 38.46 E |
| Şanlıurfa □4 | **130** | 37.20 N | 39.15 E |
| San Lope | **246** | 6.12 N | 71.56 W |
| San Lorenzo, Arg. | **252** | 28.08 S | 58.46 W |
| San Lorenzo, Arg. | **252** | 32.45 S | 60.44 W |
| San Lorenzo, Bol. | **248** | 21.26 S | 64.47 W |
| San Lorenzo, Ec. | **246** | 1.17 N | 78.50 W |
| San Lorenzo, Hond. | **236** | 13.25 N | 87.27 W |
| San Lorenzo, It. | **68** | 38.01 N | 15.50 E |
| San Lorenzo, Méx. | **196** | 25.37 N | 97.35 W |
| San Lorenzo, Méx. | **232** | 25.32 N | 102.11 W |
| San Lorenzo, Nic. | **236** | 12.23 N | 85.40 W |
| San Lorenzo, P.R. | **240m** | 18.11 N | 65.58 W |
| San Lorenzo, Ca., U.S. | **226** | 37.40 N | 122.07 W |
| San Lorenzo, Ven. | **246** | 9.47 N | 71.04 W |
| San Lorenzo ≃, Méx. | **232** | 24.15 N | 107.24 W |
| San Lorenzo → Saint Lawrence ≃, N.A. | **176** | 49.30 N | 67.00 W |
| San Lorenzo ≃, Ca., U.S. | **226** | 36.58 N | 122.01 W |
| San Lorenzo, Bahía de c | **236** | 13.19 N | 87.30 W |
| San Lorenzo, Cabo > | **246** | 1.04 S | 80.56 W |
| San Lorenzo, Golfo del → Saint Lawrence, Gulf of c | **186** | 48.00 N | 62.00 W |
| San Lorenzo, Isla I, Méx. | **232** | 28.38 N | 112.51 W |
| San Lorenzo, Isla I, Perú | **248** | 12.05 S | 77.15 W |
| San Lorenzo, Monte (Cerro Cochrane) ∧ | **254** | 47.37 S | 72.19 W |
| San Lorenzo Bellizzi | **68** | 39.53 N | 16.20 E |
| San Lorenzo Creek ≃, Ca., U.S. | **226** | 36.12 N | 120.38 W |
| San Lorenzo Creek ≃, Ca., U.S. | **282** | 37.39 N | 122.09 W |
| San Lorenzo de El Escorial | **34** | 40.35 N | 4.09 W |
| San Lorenzo de la Parrilla | **34** | 39.51 N | 2.22 W |
| San Lorenzo del Vallo | **68** | 39.40 N | 16.18 E |
| San Lorenzo di Sebato (Sankt Lorenzen) | **64** | 46.47 N | 11.54 E |
| San Lorenzo in Campo | **66** | 43.36 N | 12.56 E |
| San Lorenzo Nuovo | **66** | 42.41 N | 11.54 E |
| San Lorenzo Tezonco ◆8 | **286a** | 19.18 N | 99.04 W |
| San Luca | **68** | 38.09 N | 16.04 E |
| Sanlúcar de Barrameda | **34** | 36.47 N | 6.21 W |
| Sanlúcar la Mayor | **34** | 37.23 N | 6.12 W |
| San Lucas, Bol. | **248** | 20.06 S | 65.07 W |


**Symbols** in the index entries represent the broad categories identified in the key at the right. Symbols with superior numbers (⁂1) identify subcategories (see complete key on page *I · 1).*

**Symbole** im Register stellen die rechts im Schlüssel erklärten Kategorien dar. Symbole mit hochgestellten Ziffern (⁂1) bezeichnen Unterabteilungen einer Kategorie (vgl. vollständiger Schlüssel auf Seite *I · 1).*

**Los símbolos** incluídos en el texto del índice representan las grandes categorías identificadas con la clave a la derecha. Los símbolos con numeros en su parte superior (⁂1) identifican las subcategorías (véase la clave completa en la página *I · 1).*

**Les symboles** de l'index représentent les catégories indiquées dans la légende à droite. Les symboles suivis d'un indice (⁂1) représentent des sous-catégories (voir légende complète à la page *I · 1).*

**Os símbolos** incluídos no texto do índice representam as grandes categorias identificadas com a chave à direita. Os símbolos com números em sua parte superior (⁂1) identificam as subcategorias (veja-se a chave completa à página *I · 1).*

| Symbol | English | Deutsch | Español | Français | Português |
|---|---|---|---|---|---|
| ∧ | Mountain | Berg | Montaña | Montagne | Montanha |
| ⁂ | Mountains | Gebirge | Montañas | Montagnes | Montanhas |
| )( | Pass | Paß | Paso | Col | Passo |
| V | Valley, Canyon | Tal, Cañon | Valle, Cañón | Vallée, Canyon | Vale, Canhão |
| ≚ | Plain | Ebene | Llano | Plaine | Planície |
| > | Cape | Kap | Cabo | Cap | Cabo |
| I | Island | Insel | Isla | Île | Ilha |
| II | Islands | Inseln | Islas | Îles | Ilhas |
| ⊥ | Other Topographic Features | Andere Topographische Objekte | Otros Elementos Topográficos | Autres données topographiques | Outros acidentes topográficos |

ESPAÑOL · FRANÇAIS · PORTUGUÊS

| Nombre / Nom / Nome | Página / Page | Lat.°′ | Long.°′ W = Oeste / W = Ouest |
|---|---|---|---|
| San Lucas, Ec. | 246 | 3.45 S | 79.15 W |
| San Lucas, Méx. | 232 | 22.53 N | 109.54 W |
| San Lucas, Ca., U.S. | 226 | 36.08 N | 121.01 W |
| San Lucas, Cabo › | 232 | 22.52 N | 109.53 W |
| San Luis, Arg. | 252 | 33.18 S | 66.21 W |
| San Luis, Cuba | 240p | 20.12 N | 75.51 W |
| San Luis, Cuba | 240p | 22.17 N | 83.46 W |
| San Luis, Guat. | 236 | 16.14 N | 89.27 W |
| San Luis, Perú | 286d | 12.04 S | 77.00 W |
| San Luis, Az., U.S. | 200 | 32.04 N | 111.57 W |
| San Luis, Co., U.S. | 200 | 37.12 N | 105.25 W |
| San Luis, Ven. | 246 | 11.07 N | 69.42 W |
| San Luis □[4] | 252 | 34.00 S | 66.00 W |
| San Luis ✦[8] | 286b | 23.05 N | 82.20 W |
| San Luis ≃ | 234 | 17.13 N | 100.55 W |
| San Luis, Arroyo ≃ | 258 | 34.10 S | 57.44 W |
| San Luís, Laguna ⊜ | 248 | 13.45 S | 64.00 W |
| San Luis, Sierra de ⋏ | 252 | 32.40 S | 65.50 W |
| San Luis Acatlán | 234 | 16.48 N | 98.45 W |
| San Luis Creek ≃ | 200 | 37.42 N | 105.44 W |
| San Luis de la Loma | 234 | 17.18 N | 100.55 W |
| San Luis de la Paz | 234 | 21.18 N | 100.31 W |
| San Luis del Cordero | 232 | 25.26 N | 104.18 W |
| San Luis del Palmar | 252 | 27.31 S | 58.34 W |
| San Luis Gonzaga | 232 | 24.55 N | 111.16 W |
| San Luis Gonzaga, Bahía c | 232 | 29.48 N | 114.22 W |
| San Luis Jilotepeque | 236 | 14.39 N | 89.44 W |
| San Luis Obispo | 226 | 35.16 N | 120.39 W |
| San Luis Obispo □[6] | 226 | 35.30 N | 120.30 W |
| San Luis Pass c | 222 | 29.05 N | 95.08 W |
| San Luis Peak ∧ | 200 | 37.59 N | 106.56 W |
| San Luis Potosí | 234 | 22.09 N | 100.59 W |
| San Luis Potosí □[3] | 234 | 22.30 N | 100.30 W |
| San Luis Reservoir ⊜[1] | 226 | 37.07 N | 121.05 W |
| San Luis Rey | 228 | 33.14 N | 117.20 W |
| San Luis Rey ≃ | 204 | 33.12 N | 117.24 W |
| San Luis Rey, Mission ʋ[1] | 228 | 33.14 N | 117.20 W |
| San Luis Río Colorado | 232 | 32.29 N | 114.48 W |
| San Luis Soyatlán | 234 | 20.12 N | 103.18 W |
| San Luis State Recreation Area ♠ | 226 | 37.04 N | 121.05 W |
| San Luis Valley V | 200 | 37.25 N | 106.00 W |
| Sanluri | 71 | 39.34 N | 8.54 E |
| San Macario | 266b | 45.36 N | 8.47 E |
| Sanmaiden | 270 | 34.34 N | 135.51 E |
| San Mamete | 58 | 46.02 N | 9.04 E |
| San Mango d'Aquino | 68 | 39.03 N | 16.11 E |
| San Manuel, Arg. | 252 | 37.47 S | 58.50 W |
| San Manuel, Méx. | 234 | 17.37 N | 93.24 W |
| San Manuel, Az., U.S. | 200 | 32.35 N | 110.37 W |
| San Marcelino | 116 | 14.58 N | 120.09 E |
| San Marcello Pistoiese | 66 | 44.03 N | 10.47 E |
| San Marcial ≃ | 232 | 28.04 N | 110.44 W |
| San Marco, Capo ›, It. | 70 | 37.30 N | 13.01 E |
| San Marco, Capo ›, It. | 71 | 39.51 N | 8.26 E |
| San Marco Argentano | 68 | 39.33 N | 16.07 E |
| San Marco dei Cavoti | 68 | 41.18 N | 14.53 E |
| San Marco in Lamis | 68 | 41.43 N | 15.38 E |
| San Marco la Catola | 68 | 41.31 N | 15.00 E |
| San Marcos, Chile | 252 | 30.56 S | 71.03 W |
| San Marcos, Col. | 246 | 8.39 N | 75.08 W |
| San Marcos, C.R. | 236 | 9.40 N | 84.01 W |
| San Marcos, El Sal. | 236 | 13.39 N | 89.11 W |
| San Marcos, Guat. | 236 | 14.58 N | 91.48 W |
| San Marcos, Hond. | 236 | 14.24 N | 88.56 W |
| San Marcos, Hond. | 236 | 15.17 N | 88.23 W |
| San Marcos, Méx. | 234 | 16.48 N | 99.21 W |
| San Marcos, Méx. | 234 | 20.02 N | 99.20 W |
| San Marcos, Méx. | 234 | 20.47 N | 104.11 W |
| San Marcos, Ca., U.S. | 228 | 33.08 N | 117.09 W |
| San Marcos, Tx., U.S. | 196 | 29.52 N | 97.56 W |
| San Marcos □[5] | 236 | 15.00 N | 91.55 W |
| San Marcos ≃ | 196 | 29.29 N | 97.28 W |
| San Marcos, Isla I | 232 | 27.13 N | 112.06 W |
| San Marcos, Laguna ⊜ | 234 | 20.17 N | 103.33 W |
| San Marcos, Universidad Nacional de ʋ[2] | 286d | 12.04 S | 77.05 W |
| San Marcos Arteaga | 234 | 17.45 N | 97.58 W |
| San Marcos de Colón | 236 | 13.26 N | 86.48 W |
| San Marino, S. Mar. | 66 | 43.55 N | 12.28 E |
| San Marino, Ca., U.S. | 280 | 34.07 N | 118.06 W |
| San Marino □[1], Europe | 22 | 43.56 N | 12.25 E |
| San Marino □[1], Europe | 66 | 43.56 N | 12.25 E |
| San Martín, Arg. | 252 | 29.14 S | 65.46 W |
| San Martín, Arg. | 252 | 33.04 S | 68.28 W |
| San Martín → General San Martín, Arg. | 258 | 34.34 S | 58.32 W |
| San Martín, Col. | 246 | 3.42 N | 73.42 W |
| San Martin, Ca., U.S. | 226 | 37.05 N | 121.37 W |
| San Martín, Ur. | 258 | 33.45 S | 57.37 W |
| San Martín □[5] | 248 | 7.00 S | 76.50 W |
| San Martín ≃, Bol. | 248 | 11.50 S | 67.16 W |
| San Martín ≃, Bol. | 248 | 13.08 S | 63.43 W |
| San Martín ʋ[3] | 9 | 68.07 S | 67.08 W |
| San Martín, Arroyo ≃ | 258 | 33.49 S | 57.44 W |
| San Martín, Cuchilla ⋏[2] | 258 | 33.45 S | 57.54 W |
| San Martín, Lago (Lago O'Higgins) ⊜ | 254 | 49.00 S | 72.40 W |
| San Martín, Volcán ∧[1] | 234 | 18.33 N | 95.12 W |
| San Martín de Bolaños | 234 | 21.29 N | 103.58 W |
| San Martín de las Vacas | 196 | 25.30 N | 101.20 W |
| San Martín de los Andes | 254 | 40.10 S | 71.21 W |
| San Martin de Porras | 286d | 12.04 S | 77.04 W |
| San Martín de Valdeiglesias | 34 | 40.21 N | 4.24 W |
| San Martín Hidalgo | 234 | 20.27 N | 103.57 W |
| San Martino, It. | 62 | 45.27 N | 8.47 E |
| San Martino (Sankt Martin), It. | 64 | 46.47 N | 11.13 E |
| San Martino, It. | 64 | 45.25 N | 10.35 E |
| San Martino Buon Albergo | 64 | 45.25 N | 11.05 E |
| San Martino d'Agri | 68 | 40.14 N | 16.04 E |
| San Martino di Castrozza | 64 | 46.16 N | 11.48 E |
| San Martino di Lupari | 64 | 45.39 N | 11.51 E |
| San Martino in Badia (Sankt Martin) | 64 | 46.41 N | 11.52 E |
| San Martino in Casies (Sankt Martin in Gsies) | 64 | 46.49 N | 12.14 E |
| San Martino in Rio | 64 | 44.44 N | 10.48 E |
| San Martino Valle Caudina | 68 | 41.01 N | 14.39 E |
| San Martín Peras | 234 | 17.19 N | 98.15 W |
| San Marzano di San Giuseppe | 68 | 40.27 N | 17.30 E |
| San Mateo, Méx. | 234 | 22.59 N | 103.30 W |
| San Mateo, Pil. | 269f | 14.42 N | 121.07 E |
| San Mateo, Ca., U.S. | 226 | 37.33 N | 122.19 W |
| San Mateo, Fl., U.S. | 192 | 29.36 N | 81.35 W |
| San Mateo, N.M., U.S. | 200 | 35.19 N | 107.38 W |
| San Mateo, Ven. | 246 | 9.45 N | 64.33 W |
| San Mateo □[6] | 226 | 37.25 N | 122.20 W |
| San Mateo Atenco | 234 | 19.16 N | 99.32 W |
| San Mateo Bridge ✦[5] | 282 | 37.36 N | 122.13 W |
| San Mateo Canyon V | 228 | 33.23 N | 117.36 W |
| San Mateo Creek ≃ | 282 | 37.34 N | 122.18 W |
| San Mateo del Mar | 234 | 16.12 N | 95.00 W |
| San Mateo Ixtatán | 236 | 15.50 N | 91.29 W |
| San Mateo Memorial Park ♠ | 282 | 37.17 N | 122.18 W |
| San Mateo Point › | 228 | 33.23 N | 117.36 W |
| San Mateo Tecoloapan | 286a | 19.34 N | 99.14 W |
| San Matías | 248 | 16.22 S | 58.24 W |
| San Matías, Golfo c | 254 | 41.30 S | 64.15 W |
| San Mauro Castelverde | 70 | 37.55 N | 14.11 E |
| San Mauro Forte | 68 | 40.29 N | 16.15 E |
| San Mauro la Bruca | 68 | 40.07 N | 15.17 E |
| San Mauro Marchesato | 68 | 39.06 N | 16.56 E |
| San Mauro Torinese | 62 | 45.06 N | 7.46 E |
| San Medi, Arroyo de ≃ | 266d | 41.28 N | 2.06 E |
| Sanmen | 100 | 29.06 N | 121.24 E |
| San Menaio | 68 | 41.56 N | 15.58 E |
| Sanmen Wan c | 100 | 29.08 N | 121.44 E |
| Sanmenxia (Shanxian) | 102 | 34.45 N | 111.05 E |
| San Michele, Sacra di ʋ[1] | 62 | 45.11 N | 7.21 E |
| San Michele all'Adige | 64 | 46.12 N | 11.08 E |
| San Michele al Tagliamento | 64 | 45.46 N | 12.59 E |
| San Michele di Ganzaria | 70 | 37.17 N | 14.26 E |
| San Michele Mondovì | 62 | 44.23 N | 7.54 E |
| San Michele Salentino | 68 | 40.38 N | 17.37 E |
| San Miguel, Arg. | 252 | 28.00 S | 57.36 W |
| San Miguel → General Sarmiento, Arg. | 258 | 34.33 S | 58.43 W |
| San Miguel, Bol. | 248 | 16.42 S | 61.01 W |
| San Miguel, Chile | 286e | 33.30 S | 70.40 W |
| San Miguel, Ec. | 246 | 1.44 S | 79.01 W |
| San Miguel, El Sal. | 236 | 13.29 N | 88.11 W |
| San Miguel, Esp. | 148 | 28.05 N | 16.37 W |
| San Miguel, Méx. | 232 | 29.10 N | 101.28 W |
| San Miguel, Méx. | 234 | 23.23 N | 98.10 W |
| San Miguel, Pan. | 246 | 8.27 N | 78.56 W |
| San Miguel, Perú | 248 | 13.01 S | 73.58 W |
| San Miguel, Perú | 286d | 12.06 S | 77.07 W |
| San Miguel, Pil. | 116 | 15.09 N | 120.59 E |
| San Miguel, Ca., U.S. | 226 | 35.45 N | 120.41 W |
| San Miguel ≃, Bol. | 248 | 13.52 S | 63.56 W |
| San Miguel (Cuilco) ≃, N.A. | 236 | 15.56 N | 92.10 W |
| San Miguel ≃, S.A. | 246 | 0.08 N | 75.51 W |
| San Miguel ≃, S.A. | 248 | 19.15 S | 59.20 W |
| San Miguel ≃, Co., U.S. | 200 | 38.23 N | 108.48 W |
| San Miguel, Cerro ∧[2] | 248 | 19.19 S | 60.36 W |
| San Miguel, Golfo de c | 246 | 8.22 N | 78.17 W |
| San Miguel, Volcán de ∧[1] | 236 | 13.26 N | 88.16 W |
| San Miguel Arcángel, Mission ʋ[1] | 226 | 35.44 N | 120.42 W |
| San Miguel Bay c | 116 | 13.50 N | 123.10 E |
| San Miguel Chimalapa | 234 | 16.43 N | 94.41 W |
| San Miguel Creek ≃ | 196 | 28.30 N | 98.25 W |
| San Miguel de Allende | 234 | 20.55 N | 100.45 W |
| San Miguel de Cruces | 232 | 24.25 N | 105.51 W |
| San Miguel del Monte | 258 | 35.27 S | 58.48 W |
| San Miguel de Pallaques | 248 | 7.00 S | 78.51 W |
| San Miguel de Salcedo | 246 | 1.02 S | 78.34 W |
| San Miguel de Tucumán | 252 | 26.49 S | 65.13 W |
| San Miguel El Alto | 234 | 21.01 N | 102.21 W |
| San Miguel El Grande | 234 | 17.02 N | 97.37 W |
| San Miguel Island I, Pil. | 116 | 13.23 N | 123.48 E |
| San Miguel Island I, Ca., U.S. | 204 | 34.02 N | 120.22 W |
| San Miguel Islands II | 116 | 7.45 N | 118.28 E |
| San Miguelito | 236 | 11.24 N | 84.54 W |
| San Miguel Ixtahuacán | 236 | 15.15 N | 91.45 W |
| San Miguel Mountain ∧ | 228 | 32.42 N | 116.56 W |
| San Miguel Sola de Vega | 234 | 16.31 N | 96.59 W |
| San Miguel Talea de Castro | 234 | 17.22 N | 96.15 W |
| San Miguel Tecuixiapan | 234 | 17.58 N | 99.27 W |
| San Miguel Tenango | 234 | 16.16 N | 95.36 W |
| San Miguel Totolapan | 234 | 18.08 N | 100.23 W |
| Sanming | 100 | 26.14 N | 117.36 E |
| San Miniato | 66 | 43.41 N | 10.51 E |
| San Murezzan → Sankt Moritz | 58 | 46.30 N | 9.50 E |
| Sannahed | 40 | 59.06 N | 15.09 E |
| Sannan | 96 | 35.04 N | 135.02 E |
| Sannār | 140 | 13.33 N | 33.38 E |
| San Narciso, Pil. | 116 | 13.34 N | 122.34 E |
| San Narciso, Pil. | 116 | 15.01 N | 120.05 E |
| Sannazzaro de'Burgondi | 62 | 45.06 N | 8.54 E |
| Sannicandro di Bari | 68 | 41.00 N | 16.48 E |
| Sannicandro Garganico | 68 | 41.50 N | 15.34 E |
| Sannicola | 68 | 40.05 N | 18.04 E |
| San Nicola, Isola I | 66 | 42.07 N | 15.30 E |
| San Nicola, Monte ∧ | 68 | 38.35 N | 16.24 E |
| San Nicola Arcella | 68 | 39.51 N | 15.48 E |
| San Nicola da Crissa | 68 | 38.40 N | 16.17 E |
| San Nicolás, Cuba | 240p | 22.47 N | 81.55 W |
| San Nicolás, Esp. | 148 | 27.59 N | 15.46 W |
| San Nicolás, Hond. | 236 | 15.00 N | 88.45 W |
| San Nicolás, Méx. | 234 | 16.26 N | 98.32 W |
| San Nicolás, Perú | 248 | 15.13 S | 75.12 W |
| San Nicolas, Pil. | 116 | 18.09 N | 120.38 E |
| San Nicolás ≃ | 234 | 19.40 N | 105.14 W |
| San Nicolás de los Arroyos | 252 | 33.20 S | 60.13 W |
| San Nicolás de los Garza | 196 | 25.45 N | 100.18 W |
| San Nicolas Island I | 204 | 33.15 N | 119.31 W |
| Sânnicolau Mare | 38 | 46.05 N | 20.38 E |
| San Nicolò di Comelico | 64 | 46.35 N | 12.31 E |
| San Nicolò d'Ultimo (Sankt Nikolaus) | 64 | 46.30 N | 10.55 E |
| San Nicolò Ferrarese | 64 | 44.42 N | 11.42 E |
| San Nicolò Gerrei | 71 | 39.30 N | 9.18 E |
| Sannieshof | 158 | 26.30 S | 25.47 E |
| Sannikova, proliv Ш | 74 | 74.30 N | 140.00 E |
| Şannīn, Jabal ∧ | 132 | 33.57 N | 35.52 E |
| Sannio, Monti del ⋏ | 66 | 41.30 N | 14.45 E |
| Sanniquellie | 150 | 7.22 N | 8.43 W |
| Sannohe | 92 | 40.22 N | 141.15 E |
| Sannois | 261 | 48.58 N | 2.15 E |
| Sannūr, Wādī V | 142 | 28.58 N | 31.03 E |
| Sano | 94 | 36.19 N | 139.35 E |
| Sañogasta | 252 | 29.18 S | 67.36 W |
| Sanok | 30 | 49.34 N | 22.13 E |
| Sânon ≃ | 58 | 48.38 N | 6.20 E |
| San Onofre | 246 | 9.44 N | 75.32 W |
| San Onofre Mountain ∧ | 228 | 33.22 N | 117.30 W |
| San Pablo, Chile | 254 | 40.24 S | 73.01 W |
| San Pablo, Col. | 246 | 1.40 N | 77.00 W |
| San Pablo, Pil. | 116 | 14.04 N | 121.19 E |
| San Pablo, Pil. | 116 | 7.40 N | 123.27 E |
| San Pablo, Ca., U.S. | 226 | 37.57 N | 122.20 W |
| San Pablo ✦[3] | 286a | 19.11 N | 99.04 W |
| San Pablo ≃, Bol. | 248 | 14.52 S | 63.42 W |
| San Pablo ≃, Méx. | 234 | 18.32 N | 96.01 W |
| San Pablo ≃, Pan. | 236 | 7.51 N | 81.10 W |
| San Pablo, Point › | 282 | 37.58 N | 122.26 W |
| San Pablo Autopan | 234 | 19.21 N | 99.40 W |
| San Pablo Bay c | 226 | 38.06 N | 122.22 W |
| San Pablo Creek ≃ | 282 | 37.58 N | 122.30 W |
| San Pablo Huixtepec | 234 | 16.50 N | 96.46 W |
| San Pablo Reservoir ⊜[1] | 282 | 37.56 N | 122.15 W |
| San Pablo Ridge ∧ | 282 | 37.55 N | 122.15 W |
| San Pablo Strait Ш | 282 | 37.58 N | 122.26 W |
| San Pablo Villa de Mitla | 234 | 16.55 N | 96.24 W |
| Sanpāda | 272c | 19.04 N | 73.01 E |
| San Pancrazio Salentino | 68 | 40.25 N | 17.50 E |
| San Paolo | 64 | 46.29 N | 11.15 E |
| San Paolo di Civitate | 68 | 41.44 N | 15.15 E |
| San Pascual | 116 | 13.08 N | 122.59 E |
| San Pasqual Indian Reservation ✦[4] | 228 | 33.12 N | 116.58 W |
| San Pedro, Arg. | 252 | 33.40 S | 59.40 W |
| San Pedro, Arg. | 252 | 24.14 S | 64.52 W |
| San Pedro, Arg. | 252 | 27.57 S | 65.10 W |
| San Pedro, Chile | 252 | 21.57 S | 68.34 W |
| San Pedro, Chile | 252 | 33.54 S | 71.28 W |
| San Pedro, Col. | 246 | 9.24 N | 75.04 W |
| San Pedro, C.R. | 236 | 9.56 N | 84.03 W |
| San Pédro, C. Iv. | 150 | 4.44 N | 6.37 W |
| San Pedro, Para. | 252 | 24.07 S | 56.59 W |
| San Pedro, Tx., U.S. | 196 | 27.47 N | 97.40 W |
| San Pedro, Ur. | 258 | 34.21 S | 57.51 W |
| San Pedro, Ven. | 246 | 8.50 N | 71.58 W |
| San Pedro □[5] | 252 | 24.15 S | 56.30 W |
| San Pedro ✦[8] | 228 | 33.44 N | 118.18 W |
| San Pedro ≃, Cuba | 240p | 21.09 N | 78.30 W |
| San Pedro ≃, Méx. | 232 | 30.56 N | 108.08 W |
| San Pedro ≃, Méx. | 234 | 21.45 N | 105.30 W |
| San Pedro ≃, N.A. | 200 | 32.59 N | 110.47 W |
| San Pedro ≃, N.A. | 232 | 17.45 N | 91.25 W |
| San Pedro ≃, Ven. | 286c | 10.35 N | 66.48 W |
| San Pedro, Arroyo ≃ | 258 | 34.21 S | 57.56 W |
| San Pedro, Point ›, Ca., U.S. | 282 | 37.35 N | 122.31 W |
| San Pedro, Point ›, Ca., U.S. | 282 | 37.59 N | 122.27 W |
| San Pedro, Punta › | 252 | 25.30 S | 70.38 W |
| San Pedro, Volcán ∧[1] | 252 | 21.53 S | 68.25 W |
| San Pedro Amuzgos | 234 | 16.39 N | 98.06 W |
| San Pedro Apóstol | 234 | 16.44 N | 96.44 W |
| San Pedro Ayampuc | 236 | 14.47 N | 90.27 W |
| San Pedro Bay c, Pil. | 116 | 11.11 N | 125.05 E |
| San Pedro Bay c, Ca., U.S. | 228 | 33.45 N | 118.11 W |
| San Pedro Breakwater ✦[5] | 280 | 33.42 N | 118.16 W |
| San Pedro Carchá | 236 | 15.29 N | 90.16 W |
| San Pedro Channel Ш | 228 | 33.35 N | 118.25 W |
| San Pedro Creek ≃, Ca., U.S. | 282 | 37.36 N | 122.30 W |
| San Pedro Creek ≃, Tx., U.S. | 222 | 31.34 N | 95.14 W |
| San Pedro de Arriba | 258 | 34.18 S | 57.47 W |
| San Pedro de Atacama | 252 | 22.55 S | 68.13 W |
| San Pedro de Buena Vista | 248 | 18.13 S | 65.59 W |
| San Pedro de Curahuara | 248 | 17.40 S | 68.02 W |
| San Pedro de la Cueva | 232 | 29.18 N | 109.44 W |
| San Pedro de las Colonias | 232 | 25.45 N | 102.59 W |
| San Pedro del Gallo | 232 | 25.33 N | 104.18 W |
| San Pedro de Lloc | 248 | 7.26 S | 79.31 W |
| San Pedro del Norte | 236 | 13.04 N | 84.33 W |
| San Pedro del Paraná | 252 | 26.46 S | 56.15 W |
| San Pedro de Macorís | 238 | 18.27 N | 69.18 W |
| San Pedro El Alto | 234 | 16.01 N | 96.28 W |
| San Pedro Huamelula | 234 | 16.02 N | 95.40 W |
| San Pedro Jicayán | 234 | 16.25 N | 97.59 W |
| San Pedro Juchatengo | 234 | 16.21 N | 97.06 W |
| San Pedro Mártir ✦[8] | 286a | 19.16 N | 99.10 W |
| San Pedro Mixtepec | 234 | 16.00 N | 97.07 W |
| San Pedro Peaks ⋏ | 200 | 36.07 N | 106.49 W |
| San Pedro Pinula | 236 | 14.40 N | 89.51 W |
| San Pedro Pochutla | 234 | 15.44 N | 96.28 W |
| San Pedro Sacatepéquez | 236 | 14.58 N | 91.46 W |
| San Pedro Sula | 236 | 15.27 N | 88.02 W |
| San Pedro Tabasco | 232 | 17.47 N | 91.10 W |
| San Pedro Tapanatepec | 234 | 16.21 N | 94.12 W |
| San Pedro Tututepec | 234 | 16.09 N | 97.38 W |
| San Pedro Xalostoc | 286a | 19.32 N | 99.05 W |
| San Pedro y Miquelón → Saint Pierre and Miquelon □[2] | 186 | 46.55 N | 56.20 W |
| San Pelayo | 246 | 8.58 N | 75.51 W |
| San Pellegrino | 62 | 45.50 N | 9.40 E |
| San Piero a Grado | 66 | 43.41 N | 10.21 E |
| San Piero in Bagno | 66 | 43.51 N | 11.58 E |
| San Pierre | 216 | 41.12 N | 86.53 W |
| San Pietro (Sankt Peter) | 64 | 47.01 N | 12.03 E |
| San Pietro, Isola di I | 71 | 39.08 N | 8.17 E |
| San Pietro a Maida | 68 | 38.50 N | 16.20 E |
| San Pietro di Cadore | 64 | 46.34 N | 12.35 E |
| San Pietro in Casale | 64 | 44.42 N | 11.24 E |
| San Pietro in Gu | 64 | 45.37 N | 11.40 E |
| San Pietro in Guarano | 68 | 39.20 N | 16.19 E |
| San Pietro in Palazzi | 66 | 43.20 N | 10.30 E |
| San Pietro in Vaticano ʋ[1] | 267a | 41.54 N | 12.28 E |
| San Pietro Vara | 62 | 44.20 N | 9.35 E |
| San Pietro Vernotico | 68 | 40.29 N | 18.00 E |
| San Pitch ≃ | 200 | 39.03 N | 111.51 W |
| Sanpoil ≃ | 202 | 47.53 N | 118.41 W |
| San Policarpio | 116 | 12.11 N | 125.30 E |
| San Polo d'Enza | 64 | 44.38 N | 10.26 E |
| Sanpu | 98 | 34.09 N | 117.10 E |
| Sanqiao | 106 | 30.35 N | 119.58 E |
| San Quentin | 282 | 37.56 N | 122.29 W |
| San Quentin State Prison ʋ | 282 | 37.56 N | 122.28 W |
| Sanquhar | 44 | 55.22 N | 3.56 W |
| Sanquianga, Parque Nacional ♠ | 246 | 2.30 N | 78.15 W |
| San Quintin | 116 | 16.00 N | 120.50 E |
| San Quintín, Cabo › | 232 | 30.21 N | 116.00 W |
| San Quirico d'Orcia | 66 | 43.03 N | 11.36 E |
| Sanqutan | 100 | 27.17 N | 115.04 E |
| Sanquzhen | 107 | 29.39 N | 105.37 E |
| San Rafael, Arg. | 252 | 34.36 S | 68.20 W |
| San Rafael, Chile | 252 | 35.19 S | 71.32 W |
| San Rafael, Méx. | 232 | 25.01 N | 100.33 W |
| San Rafael, Méx. | 234 | 20.12 N | 96.51 W |
| San Rafael, Ca., U.S. | 226 | 37.58 N | 122.31 W |
| San Rafael, N.M., U.S. | 200 | 35.06 N | 107.52 W |
| San Rafael, Ven. | 246 | 10.58 N | 71.44 W |
| San Rafael ≃, Bol. | 248 | 18.38 S | 58.55 W |
| San Rafael ≃, Ut,. U.S. | 200 | 38.47 N | 110.07 W |
| San Rafael Bay c | 282 | 37.58 N | 122.28 W |
| San Rafael de las Tortillas | 196 | 26.49 N | 99.32 W |
| San Rafael del Norte | 236 | 13.12 N | 86.06 W |
| San Rafael del Sur | 236 | 11.51 N | 86.27 W |
| San Rafael Desert ✦[2] | 200 | 38.40 N | 110.30 W |
| San Rafael Hills ⋏[2] | 280 | 34.10 N | 118.12 W |
| San Rafael Mountains ⋏ | 204 | 34.45 N | 119.50 W |
| San Rafael Oriente | 236 | 13.23 N | 88.21 W |
| San Rafael Swell ⋏[1] | 200 | 38.40 N | 110.45 W |
| San Rafael Tasajera | 236 | 13.16 N | 88.52 W |
| San Ramón, Arg. | 252 | 27.42 S | 64.17 W |
| San Ramón, Bol. | 248 | 13.17 S | 64.43 W |
| San Ramón, C.R. | 236 | 10.06 N | 84.28 W |
| San Ramón, Hond. | 236 | 14.41 N | 84.43 W |
| San Ramón, Perú | 248 | 11.08 S | 75.20 W |
| San Ramon, Pil. | 116 | 13.16 N | 124.05 E |
| San Ramon, Ca., U.S. | 282 | 37.47 N | 121.59 W |
| San Ramón, Ur. | 252 | 34.18 S | 55.58 W |
| San Ramon Creek ≃ | 282 | 37.54 N | 122.03 W |
| San Ramón de la Nueva Orán | 252 | 23.08 S | 64.20 W |
| San Ramon Valley V | 282 | 37.46 N | 121.58 W |
| Sanrao | 100 | 23.59 N | 116.50 E |
| San-rei ∧ | 96 | 33.50 N | 133.59 E |
| San Remigio | 116 | 11.05 N | 123.56 E |
| San Remo, Austl. | 169 | 38.31 S | 145.22 E |
| San Remo, It. | 62 | 43.49 N | 7.46 E |
| San Remo, N.Y., U.S. | 210 | 40.52 N | 73.13 W |
| San Roberto | 68 | 38.18 N | 15.44 E |
| San Rodrigo ≃ | 196 | 28.54 N | 100.37 W |
| San Román ≃ | 236 | 16.21 N | 90.22 W |
| San Román, Cabo › | 246 | 12.12 N | 70.00 W |
| San Roque, Arg. | 252 | 28.34 S | 58.43 W |
| San Roque, Arg. | 252 | 30.17 S | 68.41 W |
| San Roque, Esp. | 34 | 36.13 N | 5.24 W |
| San Roque, N. Mar. Is. | 174n | 15.15 N | 145.47 E |
| San Roque, Pil. | 269f | 14.29 N | 120.54 E |
| San Roque, Cabo → São Roque, Cabo de › | 250 | 5.29 S | 35.16 W |
| San Roque, Punta › | 232 | 27.11 N | 114.26 W |
| San Rosendo | 252 | 37.16 S | 72.43 W |
| San Rufo | 68 | 40.26 N | 15.28 E |
| San Saba | 196 | 31.11 N | 98.43 W |
| San Saba ≃ | 196 | 31.15 N | 98.35 W |
| San Saep, Khlong ≍ | 269a | 13.45 N | 100.36 E |
| San Salvador, Arg. | 252 | 29.16 S | 57.31 W |
| San Salvador, Arg. | 252 | 31.37 S | 58.30 W |
| San Salvador, El Sal. | 236 | 13.42 N | 89.12 W |
| San Salvador (Watling Island) I | 238 | 24.02 N | 74.28 W |
| San Salvador ≃ | 258 | 33.37 S | 58.06 W |
| San Salvador, Cuchilla ⋏[2] | 258 | 33.56 S | 57.45 W |
| San Salvador, Volcán de ∧[1] | 236 | 13.44 N | 89.17 W |
| San Salvador de Jujuy | 252 | 24.11 S | 65.18 W |
| San Salvador el Seco | 234 | 19.08 N | 97.39 W |
| San Salvatore, Monte ∧ | 70 | 37.50 N | 14.03 E |
| San Salvatore Monferrato | 62 | 44.59 N | 8.34 E |
| San Salvatore Telesino | 68 | 41.14 N | 14.30 E |
| San Salvo | 66 | 42.03 N | 14.44 E |
| Sansanné-Mango | 150 | 10.21 N | 0.28 E |
| Sans Bois Creek ≃ | 196 | 35.20 N | 94.50 W |
| San Sebastián, El Sal. | 236 | 13.44 N | 88.50 W |
| San Sebastián → Donostia, Esp. | 34 | 43.19 N | 1.59 W |
| San Sebastián, Guat. | 236 | 14.34 N | 91.39 W |
| San Sebastián, Hond. | 236 | 14.24 N | 88.42 W |
| San Sebastián, Méx. | 234 | 20.47 N | 104.51 W |
| San Sebastián, P.R. | 240m | 18.20 N | 66.59 W |
| San Sebastián, Bahía c | 254 | 53.12 S | 68.20 W |
| San Sebastián de la Gomera | 148 | 28.06 N | 17.06 W |
| San Sebastián del Álamo | 234 | 21.26 N | 102.21 W |
| San Sebastián de los Reyes | 266a | 40.33 N | 3.38 W |
| San Sebastián de Yalí | 236 | 13.18 N | 86.11 W |
| San Sebastiano | 64 | 45.38 N | 10.16 E |
| San Sebastiano Curone | 62 | 44.47 N | 9.04 E |
| San Sebastián Tecomaxtlahuaca | 234 | 17.21 N | 98.02 W |
| San Sebastián Zinacatepec | 234 | 18.20 N | 97.15 W |
| San Secondo Parmense | 64 | 44.55 N | 10.14 E |
| Sansepolcro | 66 | 43.34 N | 12.08 E |
| San Severino Lucano | 68 | 40.01 N | 16.08 E |
| San Severino Marche | 66 | 43.13 N | 13.10 E |
| San Severo | 68 | 41.41 N | 15.23 E |
| Sansha | 100 | 26.58 N | 120.12 E |
| Sanshengchang | 89 | 44.51 N | 120.21 E |
| Sanshierzhan | 89 | 53.16 N | 121.49 E |
| Sanshijia, Zhg. | 98 | 41.44 N | 119.15 E |
| Sanshijia, Zhg. | 98 | 41.05 N | 119.03 E |
| Sanshilibao | 98 | 39.15 N | 121.48 E |
| Sanshiling | 106 | 30.51 N | 119.29 E |
| Sanshisanzhan | 89 | 53.10 N | 121.27 E |
| Sanshui | 100 | 23.11 N | 112.53 E |
| San Sigismondo (Sankt Sigmund) | 64 | 46.49 N | 11.46 E |
| San Simeon | 226 | 35.39 N | 121.11 W |
| San Simon, Méx. | 204 | 30.30 N | 115.58 W |
| San Simon, Az., U.S. | 200 | 32.16 N | 109.13 W |
| San Simón ≃, Bol. | 248 | 13.13 S | 63.31 W |
| San Simon ≃, Az., U.S. | 200 | 32.50 N | 109.39 W |
| San Simon Wash V | 200 | 31.45 N | 112.25 W |
| San Siro ✦[8] | 266b | 45.29 N | 9.07 E |
| Sanski Most | 36 | 44.46 N | 16.40 E |
| Sanso | 150 | 11.43 N | 6.51 W |
| San Solano | 252 | 31.29 S | 65.55 W |
| Sansom Park Village | 222 | 32.48 N | 97.24 W |
| Sanson | 172 | 40.13 S | 175.25 E |
| San Sosti | 68 | 39.40 N | 16.02 E |
| San Sperate | 71 | 39.21 N | 9.00 E |
| Sans Souci | 274a | 33.59 S | 151.08 E |
| Sans-Souci ⊥ | 238 | 19.37 N | 72.12 W |
| Sanssouci, Schloss ʋ | 54 | 52.24 N | 13.02 E |
| San Stefano Ticino | 266b | 45.29 N | 8.55 E |
| Santa, Perú | 248 | 8.59 S | 78.36 W |
| Santa, Pil. | 116 | 17.29 N | 120.26 E |
| Santa ≃ | 248 | 8.58 S | 78.39 W |
| Santa, Isla del I | 248 | 9.02 S | 78.40 W |
| Santa Adélia | 255 | 21.16 S | 48.48 W |
| Santa Albertina | 255 | 20.02 S | 50.44 W |
| Santa Amalia | 34 | 39.01 N | 6.01 W |
| Santa Ana, Arg. | 252 | 27.22 S | 55.34 W |
| Santa Ana, Bol. | 248 | 13.45 S | 65.35 W |
| Santa Ana, Bol. | 248 | 18.43 S | 58.44 W |
| Santa Ana, Col. | 246 | 9.19 N | 74.35 W |
| Santa Ana, Ec. | 246 | 1.13 S | 80.23 W |
| Santa Ana, El Sal. | 236 | 13.59 N | 89.34 W |
| Santa Ana, Méx. | 232 | 24.04 N | 100.30 W |
| Santa Ana, Méx. | 232 | 30.33 N | 111.07 W |
| Santa Ana, Ca., U.S. | 228 | 33.44 N | 117.52 W |
| Santa Ana, Ven. | 246 | 9.19 N | 64.39 W |
| Santa Ana ≃, Cuba | 286b | 23.04 N | 82.32 W |
| Santa Ana ≃, Ca., U.S. | 228 | 33.38 N | 117.57 W |
| Santa Ana, Volcán de ∧[1] | 236 | 13.50 N | 89.38 W |
| Santa Ana Canyon V | 280 | 33.53 N | 117.43 W |
| Santa Ana de Chena | 286e | 33.34 S | 70.47 W |
| Santa Ana del Alto Beni | 248 | 15.31 S | 67.30 W |
| Santa Ana Heights | 228 | 33.39 N | 117.54 W |
| Santa Ana Indian Reservation ✦[4] | 200 | 35.28 N | 106.37 W |
| Santa Ana Island I | 175e | 10.50 S | 162.28 E |
| Santa Ana Maya | 234 | 20.00 N | 101.01 W |
| Santa Ana Mountains ⋏ | 228 | 33 45 N | 117.35 W |
| Santa Ana Race Track ♠ | 269f | 14.35 N | 121.01 E |
| Santa Ana Tlacotenco ✦[8] | 286a | 19.10 N | 98.59 W |
| Santa Anita | 234 | 20.33 N | 103.27 W |
| Santa Anita Canyon V | 280 | 34.12 N | 118.01 W |
| Santa Anita Park ♠ | 280 | 34.08 N | 118.03 W |
| Santa Anna | 196 | 31.44 N | 99.19 W |
| Santa Apolonia | 196 | 25.38 N | 97.59 W |
| Santa Bárbara, Chile | 252 | 37.40 S | 72.01 W |
| Santa Barbara, Col. | 246 | 5.53 N | 75.35 W |
| Santa Bárbara, Hond. | 236 | 14.53 N | 88.14 W |
| Santa Bárbara, Méx. | 232 | 26.48 N | 105.49 W |
| Santa Bárbara, Méx. | 234 | 18.52 N | 101.07 W |
| Santa Barbara, Ca., U.S. | 204 | 34.25 N | 119.42 W |
| Santa Bárbara, Ven. | 246 | 3.57 N | 67.06 W |
| Santa Bárbara, Ven. | 246 | 7.47 N | 71.10 W |
| Santa Bárbara □[5] | 236 | 15.10 N | 88.20 W |
| Santa Barbara □[6] | 228 | 33.28 N | 119.02 W |
| Santa Bárbara ≃ | 248 | 16.58 S | 61.39 W |
| Santa Bárbara, Morro de ∧ | 287a | 22.57 S | 43.28 W |
| Santa Bárbara, Túnel ✦[5] | 287a | 22.56 S | 43.12 W |
| Santa Barbara Channel Ш | 204 | 34.15 N | 119.55 W |
| Santa Bárbara do Monte Verde | 256 | 21.58 S | 43.42 W |
| Santa Bárbara do Sul | 252 | 28.22 S | 53.15 W |
| Santa Barbara do Tugúrio | 256 | 21.15 S | 43.35 W |
| Santa Barbara Island I | 228 | 33.28 N | 119.02 W |
| Santa Branca | 256 | 23.24 S | 45.53 W |
| Santa Branca, Represa ⊜[1] | 256 | 23.20 S | 45.50 W |
| Santaca | 158 | 26.36 S | 32.32 E |
| Santa Catalina, Arg. | 252 | 21.57 S | 66.04 W |
| Santa Catalina, Pil. | 116 | 9.20 N | 122.51 E |
| Santa Catalina, Ur. | 258 | 33.49 S | 57.29 W |
| Santa Catalina, Arroyo ≃ | 288 | 34.46 S | 58.27 W |
| Santa Catalina, Gulf of c | 228 | 33.20 N | 117.45 W |
| Santa Catalina, Isla I | 232 | 25.40 N | 110.47 W |
| Santa Catalina, Laguna ⊜ | 288 | 34.46 S | 58.27 W |
| Santa Catalina Island I | 228 | 33.23 N | 118.24 W |
| Santa Catalina o Calovébora | 236 | 8.47 N | 81.20 W |
| Santa Catarina, Méx. | 204 | 31.37 N | 115.48 W |
| Santa Catarina, Méx. | 232 | 25.41 N | 100.28 W |
| Santa Catarina □[3] | 252 | 27.00 S | 50.00 W |
| Santa Catarina, Ilha de I | 252 | 27.36 S | 48.30 W |
| Santa Catarina Juquila | 234 | 16.14 N | 97.18 W |
| Santa Caterina di Pittinuri | 71 | 40.06 N | 8.30 E |
| Santa Caterina Valfurva | 64 | 46.25 N | 10.29 E |
| Santa Caterina Villarmosa | 70 | 37.35 N | 14.02 E |
| Santa Cecília | 252 | 26.56 S | 50.27 W |
| Santa Cesarea Terme | 68 | 40.02 N | 18.29 E |
| Santa Clara, Col. | 246 | 2.43 S | 69.43 W |
| Santa Clara, Cuba | 240p | 22.24 N | 79.58 W |
| Santa Clara, Méx. | 232 | 29.17 N | 107.01 W |
| Santa Clara, Méx. | 234 | 19.41 N | 102.30 W |
| Santa Clara, Méx. | 286a | 19.34 N | 99.04 W |
| Santa Clara, Ca., U.S. | 226 | 37.20 N | 121.56 W |
| Santa Clara, Ut,. U.S. | 200 | 37.07 N | 113.39 W |
| Santa Clara □[6] | 226 | 37.20 N | 121.53 W |
| Santa Clara ≃, Ca., U.S. | 228 | 34.14 N | 119.16 W |
| Santa Clara ≃, Ut,. U.S. | 200 | 37.05 N | 113.36 W |
| Santa Clara, Bahía de c | 240p | 23.05 N | 80.30 W |
| Santa Clara, University of ʋ[2] | 282 | 37.21 N | 121.56 W |
| Santa Clara de Olimar | 252 | 32.55 S | 54.58 W |
| Santa Clara Indian Reservation ✦[4] | 200 | 35.59 N | 106.10 W |
| Santa Clara Valley V | 226 | 37.10 N | 121.40 W |
| Santa Clarita, Perú | 286d | 12.00 S | 77.01 W |
| Santa Clarita, Ca., U.S. | 228 | 34.23 N | 118.32 E |
| Santa Clotilde | 246 | 2.34 S | 73.44 W |
| Santa Coloma de Cervelló | 266d | 41.22 N | 2.01 E |
| Santa Coloma de Farners | 34 | 41.52 N | 2.40 E |
| Santa Coloma de Gramanet | 266d | 41.27 N | 2.13 E |
| Santa Comba | 34 | 43.02 N | 8.49 W |
| Santa Comba Dão | 34 | 40.24 N | 8.08 W |
| Santa Cristina | 64 | 46.34 N | 11.43 E |
| Santa Cristina d'Aspromonte | 68 | 38.15 N | 15.58 E |
| Santa Croce | 64 | 46.05 N | 12.18 E |
| Santa Croce, Capo › | 70 | 37.14 N | 15.15 E |
| Santa Croce, Lago di ⊜ | 64 | 46.10 N | 12.20 E |
| Santa Croce Camerina | 70 | 36.50 N | 14.31 E |
| Santa Croce del Sannio | 68 | 41.23 N | 14.43 E |
| Santa Croce di Magliano | 66 | 41.42 N | 14.59 E |
| Santa Croce Sull'Arno | 66 | 43.42 N | 10.47 E |
| Santa Cruz, Bra. | 250 | 6.13 S | 36.01 W |
| Santa Cruz, Bra. | 255 | 19.56 S | 40.09 W |
| Santa Cruz, Chile | 252 | 34.38 S | 71.22 W |
| Santa Cruz, C.R. | 236 | 10.16 N | 85.36 W |
| Santa Cruz, Méx. | 200 | 31.14 N | 110.35 W |
| Santa Cruz, Perú | 248 | 6.37 S | 78.57 W |
| Santa Cruz, Pil. | 116 | 6.50 N | 125.25 E |
| Santa Cruz, Pil. | 116 | 14.17 N | 121.25 E |
| Santa Cruz, Pil. | 116 | 13.29 N | 122.02 E |
| Santa Cruz, Pil. | 116 | 13.04 N | 120.43 E |
| Santa Cruz, Pil. | 116 | 15.46 N | 119.55 E |
| Santa Cruz (Tubajon), Pil. | 116 | 10.19 N | 125.33 E |
| Santa Cruz, Ca., U.S. | 226 | 36.58 N | 122.01 W |
| Santa Cruz, Ven. | 246 | 8.25 N | 71.39 W |
| Santa Cruz, Ven. | 286c | 10.26 N | 67.01 W |
| Santa Cruz □[4] | 254 | 49.00 S | 70.00 W |
| Santa Cruz □[5] | 248 | 17.30 S | 61.30 W |
| Santa Cruz □[6] | 226 | 36.58 N | 122.01 W |
| Santa Cruz ✦[8], Bra. | 256 | 22.56 S | 43.41 W |
| Santa Cruz ✦[8], India | 272c | 19.05 N | 72.50 E |
| Santa Cruz ≃, Arg. | 254 | 50.08 S | 68.20 W |
| Santa Cruz ≃, Cuba | 286b | 23.04 N | 82.29 W |
| Santa Cruz ≃, N.A. | 200 | 32.42 N | 111.33 W |
| Santa Cruz, Ilha I | 287a | 22.52 S | 43.07 W |
| Santa Cruz, Isla I | 246a | 0.38 S | 90.23 W |
| Santa Cruz, Sierra de ⋏ | 236 | 15.40 N | 89.15 W |
| Santa Cruz Basin ✢[1] | 14 | 12.00 S | 163.00 E |
| Santa Cruz Cabrália | 255 | 16.17 S | 39.02 W |
| Santa Cruz da Graciosa | 148a | 39.05 N | 28.01 W |
| Santa Cruz das Flores | 148a | 39.27 N | 31.07 W |
| Santa Cruz de Goiás | 255 | 17.19 S | 48.30 W |
| Santa Cruz de Juventino Rosas | 234 | 20.39 N | 101.00 W |
| Santa Cruz de la Palma | 148 | 28.41 N | 17.45 W |
| Santa Cruz de la Sierra | 248 | 17.48 S | 63.10 W |
| Santa Cruz de la Zarza | 34 | 39.58 N | [illegible].10 W |
| Santa Cruz del Quiché | 236 | 15.02 N | 9[illegible].08 W |
| Santa Cruz del Sur | 240p | 20.43 N | 7[illegible].00 W |
| Santa Cruz de Mudela | 34 | 38.38 N | [illegible]28 W |
| Santa Cruz de Tenerife | 148 | 28.27 N | 1[illegible]14 W |
| Santa Cruz de Tenerife □[4], Esp. | 34 | 28.20 N | 1[illegible]50 W |
| Santa Cruz de Tenerife □[4], Esp. | 148 | 28.15 N | 17[illegible]0 W |
| Santa Cruz do Capibaribe | 250 | 7.57 S | 36 [illegible]2 W |
| Santa Cruz do Piauí | 250 | 7.09 S | 41.[illegible]8 W |
| Santa Cruz do Prata | 256 | 21.12 S | 46.[illegible]5 W |
| Santa Cruz do Rio Pardo | 255 | 22.55 S | 49.[illegible]7 W |
| Santa Cruz do Sul | 252 | 29.43 S | 52.[illegible] W |
| Santa Cruz International Airport ⊠ | 272c | 19.05 N | 72.[illegible] E |
| Santa Cruz Island I | 204 | 34.01 N | 119.[illegible] W |
| Santa Cruz Islands II | 14 | 11.00 S | 166.1[illegible] E |
| Santa Cruz Meyehualco ✦[8] | 286a | 19.20 N | 99.0[illegible] W |
| Santa Cruz Mountains ⋏ | 226 | 37.15 N | 122.0[illegible] W |
| Santa Cruz Point › | 116 | 15.44 N | 119.5[illegible] E |
| Santa Cruz Tacache de Mina | 234 | 17.51 N | 98.0[illegible] W |
| Santadi | 71 | 39.05 N | 8.4[illegible] E |
| Santa Domenica Talao | 68 | 39.49 N | 15.51 E |
| Santa Domenica Vittoria | 70 | 37.55 N | 14.58 E |
| Sant Adrià de Besòs | 266d | 41.25 N | 2.14 E |
| Santa Elena, Arg. | 252 | 30.57 S | 59.48 W |
| Santa Elena, Ec. | 246 | 2.14 S | 80.51 W |
| Santa Elena, El Sal. | 236 | 13.22 N | 88.25 W |
| Santa Elena, Méx. | 196 | 27.59 N | 103.56 W |
| Santa Elena, Méx. | 232 | 27.28 N | 102.33 W |
| Santa Elena, Méx. | 234 | 18.39 N | 101.34 W |
| Santa Elena ≃ | 248 | 15.42 S | 67.13 W |
| Santa Elena, Bahía de c | 246 | 2.06 S | 80.53 W |
| Santa Elena, Cabo › | 236 | 10.54 N | 85.57 W |
| Santa Elena, Golfo de c | 236 | 10.59 N | 85.50 W |
| Santa Elena, Punta › | 246 | 2.11 S | 81.00 W |
| Santa Elena del Gomero | 286e | 33.29 S | 70.46 W |
| Santa Elena de Uairén | 246 | 4.37 N | 61.08 W |
| Santa Elisabetta | 70 | 37.26 N | 13.33 E |
| Santa Eufemia | 34 | 38.36 N | 4.54 W |
| Santa Eulalia, Esp. | 34 | 40.34 N | 1.19 W |
| Santa Eulalia, Guat. | 236 | 15.45 N | 91.29 W |
| Santa Eulària del Riu | 34 | 38.59 N | 1.31 E |
| Santa Fe, Arg. | 252 | 31.38 S | 60.42 W |
| Santa Fé, Bra. | 255 | 15.40 S | 51.16 W |
| Santa Fé, Bra. | 255 | 23.01 S | 51.48 W |
| Santa Fe, Esp. | 34 | 37.11 N | 3.43 W |
| Santa Fe, Hond. | 236 | 15.55 N | 86.05 W |
| Santa Fé, Pan. | 236 | 8.31 N | 81.05 W |
| Santa Fe, Pil. | 116 | 11.09 N | 123.47 E |
| Santa Fe, Pil. | 116 | 16.10 N | 120.57 E |
| Santa Fe, Pil. | 116 | 12.10 N | 122.00 E |
| Santa Fe, Mo., U.S. | 219 | 39.22 N | 91.49 W |
| Santa Fe, N.M., U.S. | 200 | 35.41 N | 105.56 W |
| Santa Fe □[4] | 252 | 31.00 S | 61.00 W |
| Santa Fé ✦[8] | 286b | 23.05 N | 82.31 W |
| Santa Fe ≃, Fl., U.S. | 192 | 29.53 N | 82.53 W |
| Santa Fe ≃, N.M., U.S. | 200 | 35.36 N | 106.20 W |
| Santa Fé, Aeropuerto ⊠ | 286b | 23.04 N | 82.28 W |
| Santa Fe, Isla I | 246a | 0.49 S | 90.04 W |
| Santa Fé, Ribeirão ≃ | 287b | 23.24 S | 46.48 W |
| Santa Fe Baldy ∧ | 200 | 35.50 N | 105.46 W |
| Santa Fe Dam ✦[6] | 280 | 34.07 N | 117.58 W |
| Santa Fe de Bogotá | 246 | 4.36 N | 74.05 W |
| Santa Fe de Minas | 255 | 16.42 S | 45.26 W |
| Santa Fé do Sul | 255 | 20.13 S | 50.56 W |
| Santa Fe Flood Control Basin ≚[1] | 280 | 34.07 N | 117.58 W |
| Santa Fe Springs | 280 | 33.56 N | 118.04 W |
| Santa Filomena | 250 | 9.07 S | 45.56 W |
| Santa Fiora | 66 | 42.50 N | 11.35 E |
| Santa Flavia | 70 | 38.05 N | 13.31 E |
| Sant'Agata Bolognese | 64 | 44.40 N | 11.08 E |
| Sant'Agata de'Goti | 68 | 41.05 N | 14.30 E |
| Sant'Agata del Bianco | 68 | 38.05 N | 16.05 E |
| Sant'Agata di Militello | 70 | 38.04 N | 14.38 E |
| Sant'Agata di Puglia | 68 | 41.09 N | 15.23 E |
| Sant'Agata Feltria | 66 | 43.52 N | 12.12 E |
| Sant'Agata sul Santerno | 66 | 44.26 N | 11.51 E |
| Santa Gertrude (Sankt Gertraud) | 64 | 46.29 N | 10.53 E |
| Santa Gertrudis | 196 | 26.09 N | 98.44 W |
| Santa Giusta, Stagno di ⊜ | 71 | 39.52 N | 8.35 E |
| Sant'Agostino | 64 | 44.48 N | 11.23 E |
| Sāntāhār | 124 | 24.48 N | 88.59 E |
| Santa Helena | 250 | 2.14 S | 45.18 W |
| Santa Helena de Goiás | 255 | 17.43 S | 50.35 W |
| Santai, Zhg. | 85 | 39.14 N | 77.42 E |
| Santai, Zhg. | 86 | 44.35 N | 81.18 E |
| Santai, Zhg. | 102 | 31.10 N | 105.02 E |
| Santai, Zhg. | 104 | 41.48 N | 121.53 E |
| Santai, Zhg. | 104 | 41.56 N | 123.11 E |
| Santai, Zhg. | 105 | 38.58 N | 115.49 E |
| Santa Inês | 255 | 13.17 S | 39.48 W |
| Santa Inés, Bahía c | 232 | 26.59 N | 111.59 W |
| Santa Inés, Isla I | 254 | 53.45 S | 72.45 W |
| Santa Inés Ahuatempan | 234 | 18.25 N | 98.01 W |
| Santa Iria de Azóia | 266c | 38.51 N | 9.05 W |
| Santa Isabel, Arg. | 252 | 36.15 S | 66.56 W |
| Santa Isabel, Arg. | 252 | 33.54 S | 61.42 W |
| Santa Isabel, Bra. | 256 | 23.19 S | 46.14 W |
| Santa Isabel, Ec. | 246 | 3.21 S | 79.19 W |
| Santa Isabel → Malabo, Gui. Ecu. | 152 | 3.45 N | 8.47 E |
| Santa Isabel, Méx. | 234 | 23.15 N | 100.52 W |
| Santa Isabel, P.R. | 240m | 17.58 N | 66.24 W |
| Santa Isabel I | 175e | 8.00 S | 159.00 E |
| Santa Isabel ≃ | 236 | 15.59 N | 90.00 W |
| Santa Isabel, Pico de ∧ | 152 | 3.35 N | 8.46 E |
| Santa Isabel Creek ≃ | 196 | 27.39 N | 99.38 W |
| Santa Isabel de Sihuas | 248 | 16.20 S | 72.06 W |
| Santa Isabel do Araguaia | 250 | 6.07 S | 48.19 W |
| Santa Isabel do Rio Prêto | 256 | 22.14 S | 44.05 W |
| Santaizi | 104 | 41.21 N | 121.36 E |
| Santa Josefa | 116 | 8.02 N | 125.57 E |
| Santa Julia | 286e | 33.30 S | 70.38 W |
| Santa Juliana | 255 | 19.19 S | 47.32 W |
| Santal, Baie du c | 175f | 20.50 S | 167.05 E |
| Sant'Alberto | 66 | 44.32 N | 12.09 E |
| Sant'Alfio | 70 | 37.44 N | 15.08 E |
| Sāntalpur | 120 | 23.45 N | 71.10 E |
| Santa Luce | 66 | 43.28 N | 10.34 E |
| Santa Lucía, Arg. | 252 | 28.59 S | 59.06 W |
| Santa Lucía, Arg. | 252 | 31.32 S | 68.29 W |
| Santa Lucía, Cuba | 240p | 21.02 N | 76.00 W |
| Santa Lucía, Cuba | 240p | 22.40 N | 83.58 W |
| Santa Lucia, It. | 64 | 46.28 N | 10.21 E |
| Santa Lucia, It. | 64 | 45.26 N | 10.57 E |
| Santa Lucía, Ur. | 258 | 34.27 S | 56.24 W |
| Santa Lucía, Ven. | 246 | 8.07 N | 69.46 W |

| | | | | | | | | | |
|---|---|---|---|---|---|---|---|---|---|
| ≃ River | Fluß | Río | Rivière | Rio | ✢ Submarine Features | Untermeerische Objekte | Accidentes Submarinos | Formes de relief sous-marin | Acidentes submarinos |
| ≍ Canal | Kanal | Canal | Canal | Canal | □ Political Unit | Politische Einheit | Unidad Politica | Entité politique | Unidade política |
| ⌞ Waterfall, Rapids | Wasserfall, Stromschnellen | Cascada, Rápidos | Chute d'eau, Rapides | Cascata, Rápidos | ʋ Cultural Institution | Kulturelle Institution | Institución Cultural | Institution culturelle | Institução cultural |
| Ш Strait | Meeresstraße | Estrecho | Détroit | Estreito | ⊥ Historical Site | Historische Stätte | Sitio Histórico | Site historique | Sitio histórico |
| c Bay, Gulf | Bucht, Golf | Bahía, Golfo | Baie, Golfe | Baía, Golfo | ♠ Recreational Site | Erholungs- und Ferienort | Sitio de Recreo | Centre de loisirs | Area de Lazer |
| ⊜ Lake, Lakes | See, Seen | Lago, Lagos | Lac, Lacs | Lago, Lagos | ⊠ Airport | Flughafen | Aeropuerto | Aéroport | Aeroporto |
| ≡ Swamp | Sumpf | Pantano | Marais | Pântano | ■ Military Installation | Militäranlage | Instalación Militar | Installation militaire | Instalação militar |
| Ᾱ Ice Features, Glacier | Eis- und Gletscherformen | Accidentes Glaciales | Formes glaciaires | Acidentes glaciares | ✦ Miscellaneous | Verschiedenes | Misceláneo | Divers | Diversos |
| ≚ Other Hydrographic Features | Andere Hydrographische Objekte | Otros Elementos Hidrográficos | Autres données hydrographiques | Outros acidentes hidrográficos | | | | | |

ENGLISH: Name — Page — Lat.°′ — Long.°′
DEUTSCH: Name — Seite — Breite°′ — Länge°′ E = Ost


Santa Lucía → Saint Lucia □[1] 241f 13.53 N 60.58 W
Santa Lucía ≚ 258 34.48 S 56.22 W
Santa Lucía, Cabo → Saint Lucia, Cape › 158 28.25 S 32.25 E
Santa Lucía, Cuchilla ⋏[2] 258 34.09 S 56.11 W
Santa Lucía Chico ≚ 258 34.21 S 56.20 W
Santa Lucía Cotzumalguapa 236 14.20 N 91.01 W
Santa Lucia Creek ≚ 226 36.13 N 121.30 W
Santa Lucia del Mela 70 38.09 N 15.17 E
Santa Lucia di Piave 64 45.51 N 12.17 E
Santa Lucia Range ⋏ 226 36.00 N 121.20 W
Santaluz 250 11.15 S 39.22 W
Santa Luzia, Bra. 250 6.53 S 36.56 W
Santa Luzia, Port. 34 37.44 N 8.24 W
Santa Luzia I 150a 16.46 N 24.45 W
Santa Magdalena 252 34.30 S 63.56 W
Santa-Manza, Golfu di ⊂ 71 41.37 N 9.22 E
Santa Margarita 226 35.23 N 120.36 W
Santa Margarita ≚ 228 33.14 N 117.25 W
Santa Margarita, Isla I 232 24.27 N 111.50 W
Santa Margarita Lake ⊛[1] 226 35.20 N 120.28 W
Santa Margarita Mountains ⋏ 228 33.30 N 117.25 W
Santa Margherita di Belice 70 37.41 N 13.01 E
Santa Margherita Ligure 62 44.20 N 9.12 E
Santa María, Arg. 252 26.41 S 66.02 W
Santa Maria, Bra. 252 29.41 S 53.48 W
Santa Maria, C.V. 150a 16.36 N 22.54 W
Santa María, C.R. 236 9.39 N 83.57 W
Santa María, Méx. 196 28.02 N 101.38 W
Santa María, Pan. 236 8.07 N 80.40 W
Santa Maria, Pil. 116 17.22 N 120.29 E
Santa María, P.R. 240m 18.09 N 65.26 W
Santa Maria, Schw. 58 46.16 N 9.09 E
Santa Maria, Schw. 58 46.36 N 10.24 E
Santa Maria, Ca., U.S. 204 34.57 N 120.26 W
Santa Maria I, Port. 148a 36.58 N 25.06 W
Santa Maria I, Vanuatu 175f 14.15 S 167.30 E
Santa Maria ≚, Bra. 252 29.48 S 54.56 W
Santa Maria ≚, Bra. 252 21.50 S 54.53 W
Santa María ≚, Méx. 232 31.00 N 107.14 W
Santa María ≚, Méx. 234 21.48 N 99.10 W
Santa María ≚, Pan. 236 8.06 N 80.29 W
Santa Maria ≚, Az., U.S. 200 34.19 N 113.31 W
Santa María, Bahía ⊂ 232 25.04 N 108.06 W
Santa María, Cabo → Sainte-Marie, Cap ›, Madag. 157b 25.36 S 45.08 E
Santa María, Cabo ›, Ur. 252 34.40 S 54.10 W
Santa Maria, Cabo de ›, Ang. 152 13.25 S 12.32 E
Santa Maria, Cabo de ›, Moç. 158 26.05 S 32.58 E
Santa Maria, Cabo de ›, Port. 34 36.58 N 7.54 W
Santa María, Cape › 238 23.41 N 75.19 W
Santa María, Cayo I 240p 22.40 N 79.00 W
Santa María, Cerro ∧ 286d 11.56 S 76.57 W
Santa Maria, Giogo di (Pass Umbrail) )( 64 46.34 N 10.25 E
Santa María, Isla I, Chile 252 37.02 S 73.33 W
Santa María, Isla I, Ec. 246a 1.17 S 90.26 W
Santa Maria, Isola I 71 41.17 N 9.22 E
Santa María, Laguna de ⊛ 200 31.07 N 107.16 W
Santa Maria, Ribeirão ≚ 250 7.10 S 49.13 W
Santa María, Volcán ∧[1] 236 14.45 N 91.33 W
Santa María Ajoloapan 234 19.58 N 99.03 W
Santa Maria a Monte 66 43.42 N 10.42 E
Santa María Asunción Tlaxiaco 234 17.16 N 97.41 W
Santa Maria a Vico 68 41.02 N 14.29 E
Santa María Ayoquezco 234 16.41 N 96.50 W
Santa Maria Capua Vetere 68 41.05 N 14.15 E
Santa María Chimalapa 234 16.55 N 94.41 W
Santa María Colotepec 234 15.53 N 96.55 W
Santa Maria da Boa Vista 250 8.49 S 39.49 W
Santa Maria da Vitória 255 13.24 S 44.12 W
Santa Maria degli Angeli 66 43.03 N 12.34 E
Santa María de Huazamoto 234 22.30 N 104.30 W
Santa María de Ipire 246 8.49 N 65.19 W
Santa Maria de Itabira 255 19.27 S 43.08 W
Santa Maria del Cedro 68 39.45 N 15.50 E
Santa Maria della Versa 62 44.59 N 9.18 E
Santa Maria delle Grazie ʋ[1] 266b 45.27 N 9.10 E
Santa María del Oro 232 25.56 N 105.22 W
Santa María de los Ángeles 234 22.11 N 103.14 W
Santa María del Refugio 234 23.44 N 101.14 W
Santa María del Río 234 21.48 N 100.45 W
Santa María del Valle 234 20.54 N 102.22 W
Santa Mariá de Mohovano 232 26.42 N 103.39 W
Santa Maria di Galeria ⊸[8] 267a 42.01 N 12.19 E
Santa Maria di Leuca, Capo › 68 39.47 N 18.22 E
Santa Maria di Licodia 70 37.37 N 14.53 E
Santa Maria di Siponto ʋ[1] 68 41.40 N 15.51 E
Santa Maria do Suaçuí 255 18.12 S 42.25 W
Santa María Huazolotitlán 234 16.17 N 97.56 W
Santa María Jalapa del Marqués 234 16.30 N 95.28 W
Santa María la Real de Nieva 34 41.04 N 4.24 W
Santa Maria Madalena 255 21.57 S 42.01 W
Santa Maria Maggiore 58 46.08 N 8.28 E
Santa Maria Maggiore ʋ[1] 267a 41.53 N 12.30 E
Santa Maria Nuova 66 43.29 N 13.18 E
Santa-Maria-Siché 36 41.52 N 8.59 E
Santa María Tulpetlac 286a 19.34 N 99.03 W
Santa María Xadani 234 15.56 N 96.04 W
Santa María Zoquitlán 234 16.33 N 96.23 W
Santa Marinella 66 42.02 N 11.51 E
Santa Marta, Col. 246 11.15 N 74.13 W
Santa Marta, Guat. 236 13.58 N 91.18 W
Santa Marta, Cabo de › 152 13.52 S 12.25 E
Santa Marta, Cerro ∧ 234 18.19 N 94.48 W
Santa Marta, Ciénaga Grande ⊂ 246 10.50 N 74.25 W
Santa Marta Grande, Cabo de › 252 28.38 S 48.45 W
Sant'Ambrogio 64 45.31 N 10.50 E
Santa Mónica, Méx. 196 28.12 N 100.37 W
Santa Monica, Ca., U.S. 228 34.01 N 118.29 W
Santa Mónica ⊸[8] 286c 10.29 N 66.53 W
Santa Monica Bay ⊂ 228 33.54 N 118.25 W
Santa Monica Beach State Park ◆ 280 34.01 N 118.30 W
Santa Monica Mountains ⋏ 228 34.05 N 118.40 W
Santa Monica Mountains National Recreation Area ◆ 228 34.05 N 118.45 W
Santa Monica Municipal Airport ⊠ 280 34.01 N 118.27 W
Santan 112 0.03 S 117.28 E
Santana, Bra. 255 12.59 S 44.03 W
Sântana, Rom. 38 46.21 N 21.30 E
Santana ⊸[8] 287b 23.29 S 46.38 W
Santana ≚ 255 19.43 S 51.02 W
Santana, Coxilha de ⋏[2] 252 31.15 S 55.15 W
Santana, Ilha de I 250 2.18 S 43.41 W
Santana, Ribeirão ≚ 250 9.47 S 50.13 W
Santana da Boa Vista 252 30.52 S 53.07 W
Santana da Vargem 256 21.15 S 45.30 W
Santana de Caldas 256 21.50 S 46.24 W
Santana de Cataguases 256 21.17 S 42.33 W
Santana de Parnáiba 256 23.27 S 46.55 W
Santana de Parnaíba □[7] 287b 23.27 S 46.54 W
Santana do Campestre 256 21.16 S 42.56 W
Santana do Capivari 256 22.14 S 44.56 W
Santana do Cariri 250 7.11 S 39.44 W
Santana do Deserto 256 21.57 S 43.11 W
Santana do Garambéu 256 21.36 S 44.06 W
Santana do Ipanema 250 9.22 S 37.14 W
Santana do Livramento 252 30.53 S 55.31 W
Santana do Matos 250 5.57 S 36.39 W
Santander, Col. 246 3.01 N 76.28 W
Santander, Esp. 34 43.28 N 3.48 W
Santander, Pil. 116 9.25 N 123.20 E
Santander □[5] 246 7.00 N 73.15 W
Santander Jiménez 232 24.13 N 98.28 W
Sant'Andrea, Isola I 68 40.03 N 17.57 E
Sant'Andrea Frius 71 39.29 N 9.10 E
Sant Andreu de la Barca 266d 41.27 N 1.59 E
Santa Nella 226 37.03 N 121.02 W
Santanésia 256 22.30 S 43.49 W
Santang 100 28.44 N 116.32 E
Sant'Angelo, Castel ⊥ 267a 41.55 N 12.28 E
Sant'Angelo, Monte ∧ 267a 41.56 N 12.49 E
Sant'Angelo dei Lombardi 68 40.56 N 15.11 E
Sant'Angelo in Vado 66 43.40 N 12.25 E
Sant'Angelo Lodigiano 62 45.14 N 9.24 E
Sant'Angelo Muxard 70 37.28 N 13.32 E
Sant'Angelo Romano 267a 42.02 N 12.42 E
Santanghu 102 44.13 N 93.22 E
Santanilla, Islas II 238 17.25 N 83.55 W
Santa Ninfa 70 37.46 N 12.53 E
Sant'Antimo 68 40.56 N 14.14 E
Sant'Antine, Nuraghe ⊥ 71 40.29 N 8.46 E
Sant'Antioco 71 39.04 N 8.27 E
Sant'Antioco, Isola di I 71 39.02 N 8.25 E
Sant Antoni de Portmany 34 38.58 N 1.18 E
Sant'Antonio Abate 68 40.43 N 14.32 E
Sant'Antonio di Santadi 71 39.43 N 8.29 E
Sant'Antonio Morignone 64 46.24 N 10.21 E
Santanyi 34 39.22 N 3.07 E
Santa Panagia, Capo › 70 37.07 N 15.18 E
Santa Paula 228 34.21 N 119.03 W
Santa Paula Creek ≚ 228 34.21 N 119.03 W
Santa Perpètua de Mogoda 266d 41.32 N 2.11 E
Santapogue Creek ≚ 276 40.40 N 73.21 W
Santa Pola, Cap de › 34 38.12 N 0.31 W
Sant'Apollinare in Classe ʋ[1] 66 44.22 N 12.15 E
Santaquin 200 39.58 N 111.47 W
Santa Quitéria 250 4.20 S 40.10 W
Santa Quitéria do Maranhão 250 3.31 S 42.32 W
Sant'Arcangelo 68 40.15 N 16.17 E
Santarcangelo di Romagna 66 44.04 N 12.27 E
Sant'Arcangelo Trimonte 68 41.10 N 14.56 E
Santarém, Bra. 250 2.26 S 54.42 W
Santarém, Port. 34 39.14 N 8.41 W
Santarém □[5] 266c 38.50 N 8.56 W
Santaren Channel ⊔ 238 24.00 N 79.30 W
Santa Rita, Bra. 250 7.08 S 34.58 W
Santa Rita, Bra. 287a 22.41 S 43.28 W
Santa Rita, Col. 246 0.33 N 73.58 W
Santa Rita, Hond. 236 15.09 N 87.53 W
Santa Rita, Méx. 196 27.29 N 100.33 W
Santa Rita, Méx. 232 28.34 N 111.42 W
Santa Rita, Pil. 116 11.27 N 124.56 E
Santa Rita, Mt., U.S. 182 48.42 N 112.19 W
Santa Rita, Ven. 246 10.32 N 71.32 W
Santa Rita, Punta › 258 34.28 S 57.52 W
Santa Rita de Caldas 256 22.02 S 46.20 W
Santa Rita de Catuna 252 30.57 S 66.13 W
Santa Rita de Jacutinga 256 22.09 S 44.06 W
Santa Rita del Rucio 234 23.04 N 100.19 W
Santa Rita do Araguaia 255 17.20 S 53.12 W
Santa Rita do Ibitipoca 256 21.33 S 43.55 W
Santa Rita do Sapucaí 256 22.15 S 45.42 W
Santa Rita do Weil 246 3.29 S 69.19 W
Santa Rita Park 226 37.02 N 120.35 W
Santa Rosa, Arg. 252 36.37 S 64.17 W
Santa Rosa, Arg. 252 23.22 S 64.30 W
Santa Rosa, Bol. 248 14.10 S 66.53 W
Santa Rosa, Bol. 248 10.36 S 67.25 W
Santa Rosa, Bol. 248 17.07 S 63.35 W
Santa Rosa, Bra. 252 27.52 S 54.29 W
Santa Rosa, Bra. 255 15.01 S 47.13 W
Santa Rosa, Col. 246 2.31 N 68.13 W
Santa Rosa, C.R. 236 10.51 N 85.38 W
Santa Rosa, Ec. 246 3.27 S 79.58 W
Santa Rosa, Méx. 204 31.59 N 116.45 W
Santa Rosa, Méx. 234 22.18 N 104.24 W
Santa Rosa, Para. 248 21.46 S 61.43 W
Santa Rosa, Para. 252 26.52 S 56.49 W
Santa Rosa, Ca., U.S. 226 38.26 N 122.42 W
Santa Rosa, N.M., U.S. 196 34.56 N 104.40 W
Santa Rosa, Tx., U.S. 196 26.15 N 97.50 W
Santa Rosa, Ur. 258 34.30 S 56.03 W
Santa Rosa, Ven. 246 8.26 N 69.24 W
Santa Rosa, Ven. 246 7.03 N 68.28 W
Santa Rosa, Ven. 286c 10.30 N 66.46 W
Santa Rosa □[5] 236 14.10 N 90.18 W
Santa Rosa, Mount ∧[2] 174p 13.32 N 144.55 E
Santa Rosa, Parque Nacional ◆ 236 10.50 N 85.45 W
Santa Rosa, Presa ⊛[1] 234 20.58 N 103.35 W
Santa Rosa Beach 194 30.23 N 86.13 W
Santa Rosa Creek ≚ 226 35.34 N 121.06 W
Santa Rosa de Aguán 236 15.57 N 85.43 W
Santa Rosa de Amanadona 246 1.29 N 66.55 W
Santa Rosa [de Copán] 236 14.47 N 88.46 W
Santa Rosa de Huechuraba 286e 33.21 S 70.41 W
Santa Rosa del Conlara 252 32.20 S 65.12 W
Santa Rosa de Leales 252 27.09 S 65.15 W
Santa Rosa de Lima 236 13.37 N 87.53 W
Santa Rosa de Locobe 286e 33.26 S 70.33 W
Santa Rosa del Palmar 248 16.54 S 62.24 W
Santa Rosa de Osos 246 6.39 N 75.28 W
Santa Rosa de Río Primero 252 31.09 S 63.23 W
Santa Rosa de Sucumbíos 246 0.22 N 77.10 W
Santa Rosa de Viterbo 246 5.53 N 72.59 W
Santa Rosa Indian Reservation ⊸[4] 204 33.35 N 116.35 W
Santa Rosa Island I, Ca., U.S. 204 33.58 N 120.06 W
Santa Rosa Island I, Fl., U.S. 194 30.22 N 86.55 W
Santa Rosa Jáuregui 234 20.44 N 100.27 W
Santa Rosalía, Méx. 196 26.08 N 98.59 W
Santa Rosalía, Méx. 232 27.19 N 112.17 W
Santa Rosalía, Ven. 246 9.02 N 69.01 W
Santa Rosa Range ⋏ 204 41.35 N 117.40 W
Santa Rosa Wash V 200 33.00 N 112.00 W
Santa Rosita 286d 12.03 S 76.59 W
Sant'Arsenio 68 40.28 N 15.29 E
Šantarskije ostrova II 74 55.00 N 137.36 E
Santa Severa 66 42.02 N 11.57 E
Santa Severina 68 39.09 N 16.55 E
Santa Sofia 66 43.57 N 11.54 E
Santa Susana Mountains ⋏ 228 34.20 N 118.42 W
Santa Sylvina 252 27.49 S 61.09 W
Santa Tecla → Nueva San Salvador 236 13.41 N 89.17 W
Santa Teresa, Bra. 255 19.55 S 40.36 W
Santa Teresa, Méx. 196 29.34 N 104.39 W
Santa Teresa, Méx. 200 30.52 N 111.33 W
Santa Teresa, Méx. 232 25.17 N 97.51 W
Santa Teresa, Méx. 234 22.28 N 104.44 W
Santa Teresa ≚ 255 11.47 S 48.37 W
Santa Teresa, Embalse de ⊛[1] 34 40.40 N 5.30 W
Santa Teresa de lo Ovalle 286e 33.23 S 70.47 W
Santa Teresa di Riva 70 37.57 N 15.22 E
Santa Teresa Gallura 71 41.14 N 9.11 E
Santa Tereza de Goiás 255 13.38 S 49.01 W
Santa Terezinha 250 10.28 S 50.31 W
Santa Uxia 34 42.33 N 9.00 W
Santa Valburga (Sankt Wallburg) 64 46.33 N 11.00 E
Santa Venerina 70 37.41 N 15.08 E
Santa Venetia 226 38.01 N 122.31 W
Santa Vitória 255 18.50 S 50.08 W
Santa Vitória do Palmar 252 33.31 S 53.21 W
Santa Vittoria, Monte ∧ 71 39.45 N 9.18 E
Santa Vittoria in Matenano 66 43.01 N 13.29 E
Santa Ynez ≚ 204 34.41 N 120.36 W
Santa Ynez Canyon V 280 34.04 N 118.34 W
Santa Ysabel Indian Reservation ⊸[4] 204 33.11 N 116.41 W
Sant Bartomeu de la Quadra 266d 41.26 N 2.02 E
Sant Boi de Llobregat 266d 41.21 N 2.03 E
Sant Carles de la Ràpita 34 40.37 N 0.36 E
Sant Climent de Llobregat 266d 41.20 N 2.00 E
Sant Cugat del Vallès 266d 41.28 N 2.05 E
Santee 228 32.50 N 116.58 W
Santee ≚ 192 33.14 N 79.28 W
Santee Dam ⊸[6] 192 33.24 N 80.12 W
Santee Indian Reservation ⊸[4] 198 42.45 N 97.50 W
Sant'Egidio alla Vibrata 66 42.49 N 13.42 E
Sant'Elena 64 45.12 N 11.43 E
Sant'Elia a Pianisi 66 41.38 N 14.52 E
Sant'Elia Fiumerapido 66 41.32 N 13.52 E
Sant'Elpidio a Mare 66 43.14 N 13.41 E
Santena 62 44.57 N 7.45 E
Santenay 58 46.55 N 4.41 E
Santeny 261 48.43 N 2.34 E
San Teodoro, It. 70 37.51 N 14.42 E
San Teodoro, It. 71 40.46 N 9.39 E
Santermo in Colle 68 40.48 N 16.45 E
Santerno ≚ 64 44.34 N 11.58 E
Santerre □[9] 50 49.40 N 2.40 E
Sant'Eufemia, Golfo di ⊂ 68 38.50 N 16.00 E
Sant'Eufemia a Maiella 66 42.07 N 14.02 E
Sant'Eufemia d'Aspromonte 68 38.16 N 15.52 E
Sant'Eufemia Lamezia 68 38.55 N 16.15 E
Sant Feliu de Guíxols 34 41.47 N 3.02 E
Sant Feliu de Llobregat 266d 41.23 N 2.03 E
Sant Fost de Campsentelles 266d 41.31 N 2.14 E
Sānthia, Bngl. 126 24.03 N 89.33 E
Santhià, It. 62 45.22 N 8.10 E
Santiago, Bol. 248 18.19 S 59.34 W
Santiago, Bra. 252 29.11 S 54.53 W
Santiago, Chile 252 33.27 S 70.40 W
Santiago, Chile 286e 33.27 S 70.40 W
Santiago → Santiago de Compostela, Esp. 34 42.53 N 8.33 W
Santiago, Méx. 232 23.28 N 109.43 W
Santiago, Pan. 236 8.06 N 80.59 W
Santiago, Para. 252 27.09 S 56.47 W
Santiago, Perú 248 14.11 S 75.44 W
Santiago, Pil. 116 16.41 N 121.33 E
Santiago I 150a 15.05 N 23.40 W
Santiago ≚, Arg. 288 34.50 S 57.57 W
Santiago ≚, Méx. 232 25.11 N 105.26 W
Santiago ≚, S.A. 246 4.27 S 77.38 W
Santiago, Cape › 116 13.46 N 120.39 E
Santiago, Cerro ∧ 236 8.33 N 81.44 W
Santiago, Isla I, Arg. 288 34.50 S 57.53 W
Santiago, Isla I, Ec. 246a 0.14 S 90.45 W
Santiago, Serranía de ⋏ 248 18.25 S 59.25 W
Santiago Atitlán 236 14.38 N 91.14 W
Santiago Chazumba 234 18.12 N 97.40 W
Santiago Choapan 234 17.20 N 95.57 W
Santiago Creek ≚, Ca., U.S. 228 35.06 N 119.17 W
Santiago Creek ≚, Ca., U.S. 228 33.46 N 117.54 W
Santiago Dam ⊸[6] 280 33.47 N 117.43 W
Santiago de Cao 248 7.58 S 79.15 W
Santiago de Chocorvos 248 13.50 S 75.16 W
Santiago de Chuco 248 8.09 S 78.11 W
Santiago de Compostela 34 42.53 N 8.33 W
Santiago de Cuba 240p 20.01 N 75.49 W
Santiago de Cuba □[4] 240p 20.10 N 75.55 W
Santiago de Huari 248 19.00 S 66.48 W
Santiago de Huata 248 16.06 S 68.53 W
Santiago de la Peña 234 20.57 N 97.24 W
Santiago de las Vegas ⊸[8] 286b 22.58 N 82.23 W
Santiago del Estero 252 27.47 S 64.16 W
Santiago del Estero □[4] 252 28.00 S 63.30 W
Santiago de los Caballeros 238 19.27 N 70.42 W
Santiago de Machaca 248 17.05 S 69.16 W
Santiago de Méndez 246 2.43 S 78.19 W
Santiago de Surco 286d 12.09 S 77.01 W
Santiago do Cacém 34 38.01 N 8.42 W
Santiago Island I 116 16.24 N 119.56 E
Santiago Ixcuintla 234 21.49 N 105.13 W
Santiago Ixtayutla 234 16.33 N 97.39 W
Santiago Jamiltepec 234 16.17 N 97.49 W
Santiago Juxtlahuaca 234 17.20 N 98.01 W
Santiago Lachiguirí 234 16.41 N 95.32 W
Santiago Larre 258 35.34 S 59.10 W
Santiago Maravatío 234 20.10 N 101.00 W
Santiago Papasquiaro 232 25.03 N 105.25 W
Santiago Peak ∧, Ca., U.S. 228 33.42 N 117.32 W
Santiago Peak ∧, Tx., U.S. 196 29.47 N 103.25 W
Santiago Pinotepa Nacional 234 16.19 N 98.01 W
Santiago Reservoir ⊛[1] 228 33.47 N 117.43 W
Santiago Tepalcatlapan ⊸[8] 286a 19.15 N 99.08 W
Santiago Tulantepec 234 20.02 N 98.22 W
Santiago Tutla 234 17.10 N 95.26 W
Santiago Tuxtla 234 18.28 N 95.18 W
Santiago Vázquez 258 34.48 S 56.21 W
Santiago Yaveo 234 17.19 N 95.42 W
Santiago Zacatepec 234 17.11 N 95.51 W
Santiaguillo, Laguna ⊛ 232 24.48 N 104.48 W
Santiam Pass )( 202 44.25 N 121.51 W
San Tian Zhu (Three Indian Temples) ʋ[1] 106 30.15 N 120.08 E
Santiao Chiao › 100 25.02 N 121.59 E
Santiaoqiao 106 31.36 N 121.22 E
Santi Filippo e Giacomo 70 37.51 N 12.31 E
Santiguila 150 12.42 N 7.26 W
Sant'Ilario d'Enza 64 44.46 N 10.27 E
San Timoteo 246 9.48 N 71.04 W
San Timoteo Canyon V 228 34.04 N 117.17 W
Säntis ∧ 58 47.15 N 9.21 E
Santissima Trinita di Saccargia ʋ[1] 71 40.41 N 8.42 E
Santissimo ⊸[8] 287a 22.53 S 43.31 W
Santisteban del Puerto 34 38.15 N 3.12 W
Sant Joan de Labritja 34 39.05 N 1.30 E
Sant Joan Despí 266d 41.22 N 2.04 E
Sant Jordi, Golf de ⊂ 34 40.53 N 1.00 E
Sant Just Desvern 266d 41.23 N 2.05 E
Sant Mateu 34 40.28 N 0.11 E
Santō, Nihon 94 35.21 N 136.22 E
Santō, Nihon 96 35.19 N 134.53 E
Santo, Tx., U.S. 196 32.36 N 98.13 W
Santo, Vanuatu 175f 15.32 S 167.08 E
Santo Aleixo 256 22.34 S 43.04 W
Santo Amaro, Bra. 250 2.33 S 43.14 W
Santo Amaro, Bra. 255 12.32 S 38.43 W
Santo Amaro ⊸[8] 287b 23.39 S 46.42 W
Santo Amaro, Ilha de I 256 23.57 S 46.14 W
Santo Amaro das Brotas 250 10.47 S 37.04 W
Santo Anastácio 255 21.58 S 51.39 W
Santo André 256 23.40 S 46.31 W
Santo Ângelo 252 28.18 S 54.16 W
Santo Antão I 150a 17.05 N 25.10 W
Santo Antônio, Bra. 250 6.18 S 35.27 W
Santo António, S. Tom./P. 152 1.39 N 7.26 E
Santo Antônio ≚, Bra. 250 11.31 S 48.37 W
Santo Antônio ≚, Bra. 255 17.30 S 45.37 W
Santo Antônio ≚, Bra. 287a 22.42 S 43.37 W
Santo Antônio, Ilha de I 156 21.58 S 35.28 E
Santo Antônio da Charneca 266c 38.37 N 9.02 W
Santo Antônio da Patrulha 252 29.50 S 50.32 W
Santo Antônio de Jesus 255 12.58 S 39.16 W
Santo Antônio de Pádua 255 21.32 S 42.11 W
Santo Antonio de Posse 256 22.36 S 46.55 W
Santo Antônio do Amparo 255 20.57 S 44.55 W
Santo Antônio do Aventureiro 256 21.45 S 42.49 W
Santo Antônio do Içá 246 3.05 S 67.57 W
Santo Antônio do Jardim 256 22.07 S 46.41 W
Santo Antônio do Leverger 248 15.52 S 56.05 W
Santo Antônio do Pinhal 256 22.47 S 45.41 W
Santo Antônio do Rio Verde 255 17.57 S 47.27 W
Santo Antônio do Sudoeste 252 26.02 S 53.44 W
Santo Augusto 252 27.51 S 53.47 W
Santo Corazón 248 17.59 S 58.51 W
Santo Domingo, Cuba 240p 22.35 N 80.15 W
Santo Domingo, Méx. 196 25.38 N 101.05 W
Santo Domingo, Méx. 196 25.48 N 104.28 W
Santo Domingo, Méx. 232 25.32 N 112.02 W
Santo Domingo, Nic. 236 12.16 N 85.05 W
Santo Domingo, Rep. Dom. 238 18.28 N 69.54 W
Santo Domingo ≚, Méx. 234 16.41 N 93.00 W
Santo Domingo ≚, Méx. 234 17.40 N 98.07 W
Santo Domingo ≚, Méx. 234 18.10 N 96.08 W
Santo Domingo ≚, Méx. 236 16.15 N 91.17 W
Santo Domingo, Arroyo ≚ 204 30.43 N 116.03 W
Santo Domingo, Isla → Hispaniola I 238 19.00 N 71.00 W
Santo Domingo de la Calzada 34 42.26 N 2.57 W
Santo Domingo de los Colorados 246 0.15 S 79.09 W
Santo Domingo Indian Reservation ⊸[4] 200 35.30 N 106.25 W
Santo Domingo Nuxaá 234 17.08 N 97.02 W
Santo Domingo Pueblo 200 35.30 N 106.21 W
Santo Domingo Tehuantepec 234 16.20 N 95.14 W
Santo Domingo Teojomulco 234 16.36 N 97.14 W
Santo Domingo Zanatepec 234 16.29 N 94.21 W
Santo Estêvão 255 12.26 S 39.13 W
Sant'Olcese 62 44.30 N 8.58 E
Santolea, Embalse de ⊛[1] 34 40.47 N 0.19 W
Santo / Malo □[8] 175f 15.20 S 166.55 E
San Tomé 246 8.58 N 64.08 W
San Tommaso 66 42.11 N 13.58 E
Sant'Omobono Imagna 62 45.48 N 9.32 E
Santoña 34 43.27 N 3.27 W
Santong ≚ 98 42.39 N 126.03 E
Santo Nino Island I 116 11.55 N 124.27 E
Sant' Onofrio ⊸[8] 267a 41.56 N 12.25 E
Santo Onofre ≚ 255 12.34 S 43.12 W
Santop, Pic ∧ 175f 18.39 S 169.03 E
Sant'Oreste 66 42.14 N 12.32 E
Santorini → Thíra I 38 36.24 N 25.29 E
Santorso 64 45.44 N 11.23 E
Santos 256 23.57 S 46.20 W
Santos, Arroyo de los ≚ 258 35.28 S 57.29 W
Santos, Baía de ⊂ 256 24.00 S 46.21 W
Santos Dumont 256 21.28 S 43.34 W
Santos Dumont, Aeroporto ⊠ 256 22.55 S 43.10 W
Santoshpur 272b 22.40 N 88.10 E
Santo Stefano, Isola I 66 40.47 N 13.27 E
Santo Stefano Belbo 62 44.43 N 8.14 E
Santo Stefano d'Aveto 62 44.35 N 9.27 E
Santo Stefano di Cadore 64 46.33 N 12.32 E
Santo Stefano di Camastra 70 38.01 N 14.21 E
Santo Stefano di Magra 64 44.10 N 9.55 E
Santo Stefano Quisquina 70 37.37 N 13.29 E
Santo Stino di Livenza 64 45.44 N 12.41 E
Santos Tomás del Norte 236 13.11 N 86.56 W
Santo Tirso 34 41.21 N 8.28 W
Santo Tomás, Col. 246 10.46 N 74.45 W
Santo Tomás, Méx. 232 31.33 N 116.24 W
Santo Tomás, Nic. 236 12.04 N 85.05 W
Santo Tomás, Perú 248 6.36 S 77.48 W
Santo Tomás, Perú 248 14.29 S 72.06 W
Santo Tomas, Pil. 116 7.29 N 125.38 E
Santo Tomás ≚, Méx. 204 31.32 N 116.40 W
Santo Tomás ≚, Perú 248 13.47 S 72.09 W
Santo Tomás, Punta › 232 31.34 N 116.42 W
Santo Tomas, University of ʋ[2] 269f 14.37 N 120.59 E
Santo Tomás, Volcán ∧[1] 246a 0.48 S 91.07 W
Santo Tomás y Principe → Sao Tome and Principe □[1] 152 1.00 N 7.00 E
Santo Tomé, Arg. 252 28.33 S 56.03 W
Santo Tomé, Arg. 252 31.40 S 60.46 W
Santo Tomé de Guayana → Ciudad Guayana 246 8.22 N 62.40 W
Sant'pietro, Lago di ⊛ 68 41.01 N 15.30 E
Santpoort 52 52.25 N 4.38 E
Sant Quirze de la Serra 266d 41.32 N 2.05 E
Santuanjiang 106 30.54 N 121.43 E
Santuario de Quillacas 248 19.14 S 66.58 W
Santu Lussurgiu 71 40.08 N 8.39 E
Santunying 105 40.14 N 118.12 E
Sant Vicenç dels Horts 266d 41.24 N 2.01 E
San Ubaldo 236 11.51 N 85.20 W
Sanuki 268 35.16 N 139.53 E
Sanuki-sammyaku ⋏ 96 34.09 N 134.11 E
Şānūr 132 32.21 N 35.15 E
San Valentino in Abruzzo Citeriore 66 42.14 N 13.59 E
San Valentino Torio 68 40.48 N 14.36 E
San Venanzo 66 42.52 N 12.16 E
San Vendemiano 64 45.54 N 12.20 E
San Vicente, Arg. 252 28.30 S 64.09 W
San Vicente, Arg. 258 34.58 S 58.22 W
San Vicente, El Sal. 236 13.38 N 88.48 W
San Vicente □[5] 288 34.56 S 58.24 W
San Vicente → Saint Vincent and the Grenadines □[1] 241h 13.15 N 61.12 W
San Vicente, Cabo → São Vicente, Cabo de › 34 37.01 N 9.00 W
San Vicente, Volcán de ∧[1] 236 13.36 N 88.51 W
San Vicente Creek ≚ 282 37.32 N 122.31 W
San Vicente de Alcántara 34 39.21 N 7.08 W
San Vicente de Cañete 248 13.05 S 76.24 W
San Vicente de Chucurí 246 6.54 N 73.25 W
San Vicente de la Barquera 34 43.26 N 4.24 W
San Vicente del Caguán 246 2.07 N 74.46 W
San Vicente de Tagua-Tagua 252 34.26 S 71.05 W
San Vicente Mountain ∧ 280 34.08 N 118.31 W
San Vicente Reservoir ⊛[1] 228 32.55 N 116.55 W
San Vicente Tancuayalab 234 21.44 N 98.34 W
San Vigilio 64 45.34 N 10.41 E
San Vigilio ʋ[1] 64 46.37 N 11.07 E
San Vincenzo 66 43.06 N 10.32 E
San Vito, C.R. 236 8.50 N 82.58 W
San Vito, It. 71 39.26 N 9.32 E
San Vito, Capo › 70 38.11 N 12.44 E
San Vito, Serralta di ∧ 68 38.46 N 16.22 E
San Vito al Tagliamento 64 45.54 N 12.52 E
San Vito Chietino 66 42.18 N 14.27 E
San Vito dei Normanni 68 40.39 N 17.42 E
San Vito lo Capo 70 38.10 N 12.45 E
San Vito Romano 66 41.53 N 12.59 E
San Vito sullo Ionio 68 38.43 N 16.25 E
Sanwa, Nihon 94 37.07 N 138.21 E
Sanwa, Nihon 94 36.12 N 139.49 E
Sanwa, Nihon 96 34.42 N 133.15 E
San Xavier Indian Reservation ⊸[4] 200 32.05 N 111.08 W
Sanxi, Zhg. 100 30.22 N 118.25 E
Sanxi, Zhg. 100 27.42 N 120.04 E
Sanxing, Zhg. 106 31.47 N 121.35 E
Sanxing, Zhg. 106 31.58 N 121.07 E
Sanxingchang, Zhg. 107 30.19 N 104.09 E
Sanxingchang, Zhg. 107 30.32 N 104.38 E
Sanxingjie 106 32.06 N 121.01 E
Sanyang, Zhg. 100 28.37 N 116.15 E
Sanyang, Zhg. 100 31.20 N 113.10 E
Sanyang, Zhg. 100 27.57 N 114.22 E
Sanyangzhen 106 31.55 N 121.29 E
Sanyanjing 104 41.28 N 122.27 E
Sanyanqiao 100 28.39 N 113.43 E
Sanyati ≚ 154 16.49 S 28.45 E
San Ygnacio 196 27.03 N 99.27 W
Sanyō, Nihon 96 34.45 N 134.01 E
Sanyō, Nihon 96 34.02 N 131.10 E
Sanyuan 102 34.35 N 108.54 E
Sanyuanpu 98 42.02 N 125.44 E
Sanyuhao 98 42.30 N 117.34 E
Sanyuzhen 106 32.08 N 121.19 E
Sanza 68 40.15 N 15.33 E
Sanzao Dao I 100 22.03 N 113.21 E
Sanza Pombo 152 7.19 S 15.59 E
Sanzar ≚ 85 40.00 N 67.40 E
San Zeno di Montagna 64 45.37 N 10.43 E
Sanzha 98 41.44 N 114.39 E
Sanzhan, Zhg. 89 49.42 N 125.20 E
Sanzhan, Zhg. 89 49.36 N 126.38 E
Sanzuodian 98 41.36 N 118.49 E
São Benedito 250 4.03 S 40.53 W
São Benedito ≚ 250 9.11 S 57.02 W
São Benedito das Areias 256 21.19 S 47.02 W
São Benedito do Rio Preto 250 3.20 S 43.35 W
São Bento 250 2.42 S 44.50 W
São Bento ≚ 256 21.42 S 45.18 W
São Bento, Mosteiro de ʋ[1] 287a 22.54 S 43.11 W
São Bento Abade 256 21.35 S 45.04 W
São Bento de Caldas 256 22.08 S 46.18 W
São Bento do Norte 250 5.04 S 36.02 W
São Bento do Sapucaí 256 22.42 S 45.43 W
São Bento do Sul 252 26.15 S 49.23 W
São Bento do Una 250 8.32 S 36.22 W
São Bernardino 287a 22.40 S 43.26 W
São Bernardo 250 3.22 S 42.24 W
São Bernardo do Campo 256 23.42 S 46.33 W
São Bernardo do Campo □[7] 287b 23.44 S 46.33 W
São Borja 252 28.39 S 56.00 W
São Brás 250 10.05 S 36.55 W
São Brás de Alportel 34 37.09 N 7.53 W
São Braz, Cabo de › 152 9.59 S 13.19 E
São Caetano de Odivelas 250 0.45 S 48.02 W
São Caetano do Sul 256 23.36 S 46.34 W
São Caetano do Sul □[7] 287b 23.37 S 46.33 W
São Carlos 255 22.01 S 47.54 W
São Cristóvão 250 11.01 S 37.12 W
São Cristóvão ⊸[8] 287a 22.54 S 43.14 W
Saodatun 104 42.02 N 123.31 E
São Domingos, Bra. 252 26.34 S 52.32 W
São Domingos, Bra. 255 13.24 S 46.19 W
São Domingos, Bra. 256 21.41 S 42.47 W
São Domingos, Gui.-B. 150 12.22 N 16.08 W
São Domingos ≚, Bra. 248 12.28 S 64.13 W
São Domingos ≚, Bra. 255 13.24 S 47.12 W
São Domingos ≚, Bra. 255 19.13 S 50.44 W
São Domingos ≚, Bra. 255 20.03 S 53.13 W
São Domingos da Bocaina 256 21.50 S 44.01 W
São Domingos do Capim 250 1.41 S 47.47 W
São Domingos do Maranhão 250 5.42 S 44.22 W
São Felipe 255 14.49 S 41.23 W
São Félix de Balsas 250 7.08 S 44.52 W
São Félix do Araguaia 250 11.36 S 50.39 W
São Félix do Piauí 250 5.56 S 42.07 W
São Filipe 150a 14.54 N 24.31 W
São Francisco 255 15.57 S 44.52 W
São Francisco ≚, Bra. 242 10.30 S 36.24 W
São Francisco ≚, Bra. 255 16.09 S 40.39 W
São Francisco ≚, Bra. 256 21.50 S 42.42 W
São Francisco ≚, Bra. 287a 22.57 S 43.20 W
São Francisco, Baía de ⊂ 252 26.10 S 48.34 W
São Francisco, Ilha de I 252 26.18 S 48.37 W
São Francisco de Assis 252 29.33 S 55.08 W
São Francisco de Goiás 255 15.55 S 49.16 W
São Francisco de Paula 252 29.27 S 50.35 W
São Francisco do Croará 287a 22.42 S 43.08 W
São Francisco do Maranhão 250 6.15 S 42.52 W
São Francisco do Piauí 250 7.15 S 42.32 W
São Francisco do Sul 252 26.14 S 48.39 W
São Francisco Xavier 256 22.54 S 45.58 W
São Gabriel 252 30.20 S 54.19 W
São Gabriel da Palha 255 19.01 S 40.32 W
São Gabriel de Goiás 255 15.12 S 47.34 W
São Gonçalo, Bra. 256 21.36 S 46.19 W
São Gonçalo, Bra. 256 22.51 S 43.04 W
São Gonçalo □[7] 287a 22.48 S 43.01 W
São Gonçalo do Abaeté 255 18.20 S 45.49 W
São Gonçalo do Sapucaí 256 21.54 S 45.36 W
São Gonçalo dos Campos 255 12.25 S 38.58 W
Sao Hill 154 8.20 S 35.12 E
São Jerônimo 252 29.58 S 51.43 W
São Jerônimo, Serra de ⋏[1] 255 16.30 S 54.50 W
São Jerônimo da Serra 255 23.43 S 50.44 W
São João 150 11.32 N 15.26 W
São João ≚, Bra. 255 12.27 S 51.07 W
São João ≚, Bra. 256 22.33 S 42.29 W
São João da Barra 255 21.38 S 41.03 W
São João da Boa Vista 256 21.58 S 46.47 W
São João D'Aliança 255 14.42 S 47.32 W
São João da Madeira 34 40.54 N 8.30 W
São João da Mata 256 21.56 S 45.56 W
São João da Ponte 255 15.56 S 44.01 W
São João da Serra 256 21.28 S 43.27 W
São João das Lampas 266c 38.52 N 9.24 W
São João de Côrtes 250 2.12 S 44.32 W
São João del-Rei 255 21.09 S 44.16 W
São João de Meriti 256 22.48 S 43.22 W
São João de Meriti □[7] 287a 22.48 S 43.21 W
São João de Meriti ≚ 287a 22.48 S 43.18 W
São João do Araguaia 250 5.23 S 48.46 W
São João do Jaguaribe 250 5.16 S 38.16 W
São João do Paraíso 255 15.19 S 42.01 W
São João do Piauí 250 8.21 S 42.15 W
São João do Sabugi 250 6.43 S 37.12 W
São João dos Patos 250 6.30 S 43.42 W
São João Evangelista 255 18.32 S 42.45 W
São João Nepomuceno 256 21.33 S 43.01 W
São João Novo 256 23.33 S 47.01 W
São Joaquim 252 28.18 S 49.56 W
São Joaquim, Parque Nacional de ◆ 252 28.15 S 49.57 W
São Joaquim da Barra 255 20.35 S 47.53 W
São Jorge I 148a 38.38 N 28.03 W
São Jorge, Castelo de ⊥ 266c 38.43 N 9.08 W
São José, Bra. 252 27.38 S 48.39 W
São José, Bra. 256 22.43 S 42.36 W
São José ≚, Bra. 255 19.10 S 40.12 W
São José ≚, Bra. 287a 22.39 S 43.27 W
São José, Ponta de › 152 12.36 S 13.12 E


**Symbols** in the index entries represent the broad categories identified in the key at the right. Symbols with superior numbers (⋏[1]) identify subcategories (see complete key on page *I · 1).*

**Symbole** im Register stellen die rechts im Schlüssel erklärten Kategorien dar. Symbole mit hochgestellten Ziffern (⋏[1]) bezeichnen Unterabteilungen einer Kategorie (vgl. vollständiger Schlüssel auf Seite *I · 1).*

**Los símbolos** incluídos en el texto del índice representan las grandes categorías identificadas con la clave a la derecha. Los símbolos con numeros en su parte superior (⋏[1]) identifican las subcategorías (véase la clave completa en la página *I · 1).*

**Les symboles** de l'index représentent les catégories indiquées dans la légende à droite. Les symboles suivis d'un indice (⋏[1]) représentent des sous-catégories (voir légende complète à la page *I · 1).*

**Os símbolos** incluídos no texto do índice representam as grandes categorias identificadas com a chave à direita. Os símbolos com números em sua parte superior (⋏[1]) identificam as subcategorias (veja-se a chave completa à página *I · 1).*

| Symbol | English | Deutsch | Español | Français | Português |
|---|---|---|---|---|---|
| ∧ | Mountain | Berg | Montaña | Montagne | Montanha |
| ⋏ | Mountains | Gebirge | Montañas | Montagnes | Montanhas |
| )( | Pass | Paß | Paso | Col | Passo |
| V | Valley, Canyon | Tal, Cañon | Valle, Cañón | Vallée, Canyon | Vale, Canhão |
| ≚ | Plain | Ebene | Llano | Plaine | Planície |
| › | Cape | Kap | Cabo | Cap | Cabo |
| I | Island | Insel | Isla | Île | Ilha |
| II | Islands | Inseln | Islas | Îles | Ilhas |
| ⊥ | Other Topographic Features | Andere Topographische Objekte | Otros Elementos Topográficos | Autres données topographiques | Outros acidentes topográficos |

ESPAÑOL

| Nombre | Página | Lat.°′ | Long.°′ W = Oeste |
|---|---|---|---|
| São José da Laje | 250 | 9.01 S | 36.03 W |
| São José de Anauá | 246 | 1.00 N | 61.23 W |
| São José de Encoge | 152 | 7.38 S | 14.41 E |
| São José de Mipibu | 250 | 6.05 S | 35.15 W |
| São José de Piranhas | 250 | 7.07 S | 38.30 W |
| São José do Alegre | 256 | 22.19 S | 45.32 W |
| São José do Barreiro | 256 | 22.38 S | 44.35 W |
| São José do Belmonte | 250 | 7.52 S | 38.46 W |
| São José do Campestre | 250 | 6.18 S | 35.42 W |
| São José do Cedro | 252 | 26.30 S | 53.30 W |
| São José do Egito | 250 | 7.28 S | 37.16 W |
| São José do Gurupi | 250 | 1.36 S | 46.13 W |
| São José do Norte | 252 | 32.01 S | 52.03 W |
| São José do Peixe | 250 | 7.24 S | 42.34 W |
| São José do Piriá | 250 | 1.17 S | 46.18 W |
| São José do Rio Pardo | 256 | 21.36 S | 46.54 W |
| São José do Rio Preto, Bra. | 255 | 20.48 S | 49.23 W |
| São José do Rio Prêto, Bra. | 256 | 22.10 S | 42.57 W |
| São José dos Campos | 256 | 23.11 S | 45.53 W |
| São José dos Lopes | 256 | 21.48 S | 43.53 W |
| São José dos Pinhais | 252 | 25.31 S | 49.13 W |
| São José do Turvo | 256 | 22.21 S | 43.59 W |
| São Julião da Barra | 266c | 38.40 N | 9.21 W |
| São Julião do Tojal | 266c | 38.51 N | 9.08 W |
| São Leopoldo | 252 | 29.46 S | 51.09 W |
| São Lourenço | 256 | 22.07 S | 45.03 W |
| São Lourenço, Pantanal de ≡ | 248 | 17.30 S | 56.30 W |
| São Lourenço da Serra | 256 | 23.52 S | 46.57 W |
| São Lourenço do Oeste | 252 | 26.24 S | 52.46 W |
| São Lourenço do Sul | 252 | 31.22 S | 51.58 W |
| São Luís | 250 | 2.31 S | 44.16 W |
| São Luís de Montes Belos | 255 | 16.32 S | 50.20 W |
| São Luís do Curu | 250 | 3.40 S | 39.14 W |
| São Luís Do Paraitinga | 256 | 23.14 S | 45.20 W |
| São Luís do Quitunde | 250 | 9.20 S | 35.33 W |
| São Luís Gonzaga | 252 | 28.24 S | 54.58 W |
| São Mamede | 250 | 6.56 S | 37.06 W |
| São Manuel | 255 | 22.44 S | 48.34 W |
| São Manuel ≃ | 242 | 7.21 S | 58.03 W |
| São Manuel do Guaiaçu | 256 | 21.20 S | 42.51 W |
| São Marcos ≃ | 255 | 18.15 S | 47.37 W |
| São Mateus, Bra. | 255 | 18.44 S | 39.51 W |
| São Mateus, Bra. | 256 | 22.49 S | 43.23 W |
| São Mateus, Port. | 148a | 38.26 N | 28.27 W |
| São Mateus, Braço Norte ≃ | 255 | 18.37 S | 40.05 W |
| São Mateus de Minas | 256 | 22.42 S | 46.03 W |
| São Mateus do Sul | 252 | 25.52 S | 50.23 W |
| São Miguel | 250 | 6.13 S | 38.30 W |
| São Miguel I | 148a | 37.47 N | 25.30 W |
| São Miguel ≃ | 255 | 16.26 S | 41.00 W |
| São Miguel do Araguaia | 255 | 13.19 S | 50.13 W |
| São Miguel d'Oeste | 252 | 26.45 S | 53.34 W |
| São Miguel do Guamá | 250 | 1.37 S | 47.27 W |
| São Miguel dos Campos | 250 | 9.47 S | 36.05 W |
| São Miguel dos Macacos | 250 | 1.11 S | 50.28 W |
| São Miguel do Tapuio | 250 | 5.30 S | 41.20 W |
| São Miguel Paulista (Baquiriru) ◆[8] | 256 | 23.30 S | 46.26 W |
| Saona, Isla I | 238 | 18.09 N | 68.40 W |
| Saonara | 64 | 45.22 N | 11.59 E |
| Saône ≃ | 58 | 45.44 N | 4.50 E |
| Saône-et-Loire □[5] | 32 | 46.42 N | 4.45 E |
| Saonek | 164 | 0.28 S | 130.47 E |
| Saoner | 120 | 21.23 N | 78.54 E |
| São Nicolau I | 150a | 16.35 N | 24.15 W |
| São Nicolau ≃ | 250 | 5.45 S | 42.02 W |
| São Paulo, Bra. | 256 | 23.32 S | 46.37 W |
| São Paulo, Bra. | 287b | 23.32 S | 46.37 W |
| São Paulo □[3] | 255 | 22.00 S | 49.00 W |
| São Paulo □[7] | 287b | 23.33 S | 46.38 W |
| São Paulo, Ribeirão de ≃ | 256 | 22.16 S | 46.37 W |
| São Paulo de Olivença | 246 | 3.27 S | 68.48 W |
| São Paulo do Potengi | 250 | 5.55 S | 35.45 W |
| São Pedro | 255 | 19.53 S | 51.55 W |
| São Pedro ≃ | 255 | 16.30 S | 41.17 W |
| São Pedro de Caldas | 256 | 21.49 S | 46.16 W |
| São Pedro de Viseu | 250 | 2.33 S | 49.33 W |
| São Pedro do Estoril | 266c | 38.42 N | 9.22 W |
| São Pedro do Piauí | 250 | 5.56 S | 42.43 W |
| São Pedro do Sul, Bra. | 252 | 29.37 S | 54.10 W |
| São Pedro do Sul, Port. | 34 | 40.45 N | 8.04 W |
| São Rafael | 250 | 5.47 S | 36.55 W |
| São Raimundo das Mangabeiras | 250 | 7.01 S | 45.29 W |
| São Raimundo Nonato | 250 | 9.01 S | 42.42 W |
| Saorge | 62 | 43.59 N | 7.33 E |
| Saori | 94 | 35.11 N | 136.44 E |
| São Romão | 255 | 16.22 S | 45.04 W |
| São Roque, Bra. | 256 | 23.06 S | 44.42 W |
| São Roque, Bra. | 256 | 23.32 S | 47.08 W |
| São Roque, Cabo de › | 250 | 5.29 S | 35.16 W |
| São Roque da Fartura | 256 | 21.51 S | 46.45 W |
| São Salvador → Salvador | 255 | 12.59 S | 38.31 W |
| São Sebastião | 256 | 23.48 S | 45.25 W |
| São Sebastião, Canal de ʮ | 256 | 23.48 S | 45.23 W |
| São Sebastião, Ilha de I | 256 | 23.50 S | 45.18 W |
| São Sebastião, Pico de ∧ | 256 | 23.52 S | 45.23 W |
| São Sebastião, Ponta › | 156 | 22.07 S | 35.30 E |
| São Sebastião da Bela Vista | 256 | 22.10 S | 45.45 W |
| São Sebastião da Boa Vista | 250 | 1.42 S | 49.31 W |
| São Sebastião da Grama | 256 | 21.43 S | 46.49 W |
| São Sebastião da Vitória | 256 | 21.14 S | 44.25 W |
| São Sebastião do Barreado | 256 | 22.04 S | 43.38 W |
| São Sebastião do Maranhão | 255 | 18.05 S | 42.35 W |
| São Sebastião do Paraíso | 255 | 20.55 S | 47.00 W |
| São Sebastião do Rio Claro | 255 | 15.45 S | 51.30 W |
| São Sebastião do Rio Verde | 256 | 22.13 S | 44.58 W |
| São Sebastião dos Robertos | 256 | 22.13 S | 46.32 W |
| São Sebastião do Umbuzeiro | 250 | 8.09 S | 37.01 W |
| São Sepé | 252 | 30.10 S | 53.34 W |
| São Silvestre do Jacareí | 256 | 23.23 S | 46.01 W |
| São Simão, Bra. | 255 | 18.56 S | 50.30 W |
| São Simão, Bra. | 255 | 21.30 S | 47.33 W |
| São Simão, Represa de ⊜[1] | 255 | 18.40 S | 50.00 W |

FRANÇAIS

| Nom | Page | Lat.°′ | Long.°′ W = Ouest |
|---|---|---|---|
| São Tiago | 255 | 20.55 S | 44.30 W |
| São Timóteo | 255 | 13.51 S | 42.11 W |
| São Tomé, Bra. | 250 | 5.58 S | 36.04 W |
| São Tomé, S. Tom./P. | 152 | 0.20 N | 6.44 E |
| São Tomé I | 152 | 0.12 N | 6.39 E |
| São Tomé ≃, Bra. | 250 | 8.10 S | 58.13 W |
| São Tomé ≃, Bra. | 256 | 21.26 S | 46.02 W |
| São Tomé, Cabo de › | 255 | 21.59 S | 40.59 W |
| São Tomé, Pico de ∧ | 152 | 0.16 N | 6.33 E |
| Sao Tome and Principe (São Tomé e Principe) □[1], Afr. | 138 | 1.00 N | 7.00 E |
| Sao Tome and Principe (São Tomé e Principe) □[1], Afr. | 152 | 1.00 N | 7.00 E |
| São Tomé das Letras | 256 | 21.43 S | 44.59 W |
| Sao Tomé-et-Principe → Sao Tome and Principe □[1] | 152 | 1.00 N | 7.00 E |
| Saou | 62 | 44.39 N | 5.04 E |
| Saoura, Oued V | 148 | 29.00 N | 0.55 W |
| São Valério ≃ | 250 | 11.20 S | 48.28 W |
| São Vicente | 256 | 23.58 S | 46.23 W |
| São Vicente I | 150a | 16.50 N | 25.00 W |
| São Vicente, Cabo de (Cape Saint Vincent) › | 34 | 37.01 N | 9.00 W |
| São Vicente, Ribeirão ≃ | 256 | 21.59 S | 45.40 W |
| São Vicente de Minas | 256 | 21.42 S | 44.27 W |
| São Vicente Ferrer | 250 | 7.35 S | 35.30 W |
| Sa Pa | 110 | 22.21 N | 103.50 E |
| Sápai | 38 | 41.02 N | 25.41 E |
| Sapanca | 130 | 40.41 N | 30.16 E |
| Sapang Baho ≃ | 269f | 14.33 N | 121.06 E |
| Sapao | 116 | 10.01 N | 126.02 E |
| Sapão ≃ | 250 | 11.01 S | 45.32 W |
| Saparua, Pulau I | 164 | 3.34 S | 128.40 E |
| Sapatgrām | 124 | 26.20 N | 90.08 E |
| Sapé, Bra. | 250 | 7.06 S | 35.13 W |
| Sape, Indon. | 115b | 8.34 S | 118.59 E |
| Sapé ≃ | 287a | 22.52 S | 43.02 W |
| Sape, Selat ʮ | 115b | 8.39 S | 119.18 E |
| Sapele | 150 | 5.54 N | 5.41 E |
| Sapello ≃ | 200 | 35.47 N | 104.59 W |
| Sapelo Island I | 192 | 31.28 N | 81.15 W |
| Saperkino | 80 | 54.05 N | 51.38 E |
| Şaphane | 130 | 39.01 N | 29.14 E |
| Sapian Bay ⊂ | 116 | 11.33 N | 122.37 E |
| Sapindji | 152 | 9.39 S | 23.12 E |
| Sapitwa ∧ | 154 | 15.57 S | 35.36 E |
| Šapki | 76 | 59.36 N | 31.14 E |
| Šapkina ≃ | 24 | 66.44 N | 52.25 E |
| Šapkino | 80 | 51.42 N | 42.24 E |
| Šapkovo, Ross. | 76 | 55.47 N | 33.20 E |
| Sapkovo, Ross. | 82 | 54.34 N | 39.10 E |
| Sa Pobla | 34 | 39.46 N | 3.01 E |
| Sapockin | 76 | 53.50 N | 23.39 E |
| Sapodilla Cays I | 236 | 16.08 N | 88.15 W |
| Saponara | 70 | 38.11 N | 15.26 E |
| Saponé | 150 | 12.03 N | 1.36 W |
| Sap'o-ri | 98 | 40.49 N | 129.31 E |
| Sap'ornaja | 265a | 59.46 N | 30.41 E |
| Saporoschje → Zaporizhzhya | 78 | 47.50 N | 35.10 E |
| Saposoa | 248 | 6.56 S | 76.48 W |
| Sapou | 175c | 7.18 N | 151.53 E |
| Sapožok | 80 | 53.56 N | 40.41 E |
| Sappa Creek ≃ | 198 | 40.07 N | 99.38 W |
| Sappa Creek, Middle Fork ≃ | 198 | 39.40 N | 100.53 W |
| Sappa Creek, North Fork ≃ | 198 | 39.47 N | 100.35 W |
| Sappa Creek, South Fork ≃ | 198 | 39.47 N | 100.35 W |
| Sappada | 64 | 46.34 N | 12.41 E |
| Sapphire Mountains ⋏ | 202 | 46.20 N | 113.45 W |
| Sappho | 224 | 48.04 N | 124.16 W |
| Sappington | 219 | 38.32 N | 90.22 W |
| Sapporo | 92a | 43.03 N | 141.21 E |
| Sapri | 68 | 40.04 N | 15.38 E |
| Šapša | 76 | 60.34 N | 34.01 E |
| Sap Songkhla, Thale ⊂ | 110 | 7.13 N | 100.30 E |
| Šapsugskaja | 78 | 44.45 N | 38.05 E |
| Saptakośī ≃ | 124 | 26.31 N | 86.58 E |
| Sapta-ri | 271b | 37.43 N | 126.44 E |
| Sapu | 152 | 12.29 S | 19.26 E |
| Sapucaí | 256 | 22.19 S | 46.42 W |
| Sapucaí ≃ | 256 | 21.33 S | 45.40 W |
| Sapucaia | 256 | 22.00 S | 42.54 W |
| Sapucaí-Mirim | 256 | 22.44 S | 45.45 W |
| Sapucaí-Mirim ≃ | 256 | 22.12 S | 45.53 W |
| Sapudi, Pulau I | 115a | 7.06 S | 114.20 E |
| Sapulpa | 196 | 35.59 N | 96.06 W |
| Sapulu | 115a | 6.54 S | 112.57 E |
| Sapuran | 115a | 7.28 S | 109.58 E |
| Sapwe | 154 | 10.57 S | 28.10 E |
| Sāq, Jabal ∧[2] | 128 | 26.17 N | 43.16 E |
| Sāqiat al-ʻAbd | 140 | 20.48 N | 30.19 E |
| Sāqiyat Makkī | 142 | 30.00 N | 31.13 E |
| Şaqqārah | 142 | 29.51 N | 31.13 E |
| Şaqqārah (Step Pyramid) ⊥ | 142 | 29.52 N | 31.13 E |
| Saqqez | 128 | 36.14 N | 46.16 E |
| Saquarema | 256 | 22.56 S | 42.30 W |
| Saquarema, Lagoa de ⊂ | 256 | 22.55 S | 42.33 W |
| Saquena | 248 | 4.40 S | 73.31 W |
| Saquish Neck ›[1] | 283 | 42.00 N | 70.37 W |
| Saquisilí | 246 | 0.51 S | 78.40 W |
| Sāra, Bngl. | 126 | 24.07 N | 89.02 E |
| Sara, Burkina | 150 | 11.43 N | 3.50 W |
| Sara, Pil. | 116 | 11.16 N | 123.01 E |
| Sara, Ross. | 80 | 54.38 N | 46.46 E |
| Sarāb | 128 | 37.56 N | 47.32 E |
| Sarabia, Méx. | 234 | 20.31 N | 101.05 W |
| Sarabia, Méx. | 234 | 17.03 N | 95.01 W |
| Sarabia ≃ | 234 | 17.11 N | 94.56 W |
| Sarābiyūm | 142 | 30.23 N | 32.17 E |
| Saraburi | 110 | 14.32 N | 100.55 E |
| Saracena | 68 | 39.46 N | 16.09 E |
| Saraceno, Monte ∧ | 66 | 41.27 N | 14.44 E |
| Saracura ≃ | 255 | 12.18 S | 40.07 W |
| Saracuruna ≃ | 287a | 22.41 S | 43.13 W |
| Saraféré | 150 | 15.50 N | 3.42 W |
| Saragosa | 196 | 31.01 N | 103.39 W |
| Saragossa → Zaragoza | 34 | 41.38 N | 0.53 W |
| Saraguay ◆[8] | 275a | 45.31 N | 73.45 W |
| Saraguro | 246 | 3.36 S | 79.13 W |
| Sarai | 80 | 53.44 N | 41.00 E |
| Sarāi Alamgir | 123 | 32.54 N | 73.45 E |
| Saraikela | 124 | 22.43 N | 85.57 E |
| Sarāi Naurang | 123 | 32.50 N | 70.47 E |
| Saraipāli | 120 | 21.20 N | 83.00 E |
| Säräisniemi | 26 | 64.27 N | 26.47 E |
| Sarajas de Madrid ◆[8] | 266a | 40.28 N | 3.35 W |
| Sarajčik | 80 | 47.30 N | 51.43 E |
| Sarajevo | 38 | 43.52 N | 18.25 E |
| Saraj-Gir | 80 | 53.36 N | 53.24 E |
| Saraji | 166 | 22.21 S | 148.18 E |
| Sarajskij | 80 | 47.19 N | 40.45 E |
| Sarakhs | 128 | 36.32 N | 61.11 E |
| Saraktaš | 86 | 51.50 N | 56.22 E |
| Sarala | 86 | 54.52 N | 89.14 E |
| Saraland | 194 | 30.49 N | 88.04 W |
| Šaraldaj | 88 | 51.01 N | 107.38 E |
| Saralžin | 80 | 49.12 N | 48.55 E |
| Saramacca □[5] | 250 | 5.40 N | 55.40 W |
| Saramacca ≃ | 250 | 5.51 N | 55.53 W |
| Saramaguacán ≃ | 240p | 21.30 N | 77.17 W |
| Saran, Fr. | 50 | 47.57 N | 1.53 E |
| Şaran', Kaz. | 86 | 49.46 N | 72.52 E |
| Šaran, Ross. | 80 | 54.49 N | 54.00 E |

PORTUGUÊS

| Nome | Página | Lat.°′ | Long.°′ W = Oeste |
|---|---|---|---|
| Saran, Gunung ∧ | 112 | 0.25 S | 111.18 E |
| Saranac | 216 | 42.55 N | 85.12 W |
| Saranac ≃ | 188 | 44.42 N | 73.27 W |
| Saranac Lake | 188 | 44.19 N | 74.07 W |
| Saranakan, gora ∧ | 88 | 52.35 N | 113.50 E |
| Şaranap | 282 | 37.53 N | 122.06 W |
| Šaranbaš-Kn'azevo | 80 | 54.58 N | 54.09 E |
| Saranda | 154 | 5.43 S | 34.59 E |
| Sarandapótamos ≃ | 267c | 38.03 N | 23.34 E |
| Sarandë | 38 | 39.52 N | 20.00 E |
| Sarandi | 252 | 27.56 S | 52.55 W |
| Sarandí ◆[8] | 258 | 34.40 S | 58.21 W |
| Sarandí del Yi | 252 | 33.21 S | 55.38 W |
| Sarandí Grande | 258 | 33.44 S | 56.20 W |
| Şarandira | 256 | 21.50 S | 43.11 W |
| Šaranga | 80 | 57.11 N | 46.34 E |
| Sarangani Bay ⊂ | 116 | 5.57 N | 125.11 E |
| Sarangani Island I | 116 | 5.27 N | 125.28 E |
| Sarangani Islands II | 116 | 5.25 N | 125.26 E |
| Sarangani Strait ʮ | 116 | 5.31 N | 125.23 E |
| Sārangarh | 120 | 21.36 N | 83.05 E |
| Sārangpur | 124 | 23.34 N | 76.28 E |
| Sārankhola | 126 | 22.18 N | 89.47 E |
| Saranley | 144 | 2.22 N | 42.17 E |
| Saranpaul' | 24 | 64.14 N | 60.53 E |
| Saransk | 80 | 54.11 N | 45.11 E |
| Sara Peak ∧ | 150 | 9.41 N | 9.17 E |
| Saraphi | 110 | 18.43 N | 99.03 E |
| Sarapiquí ≃ | 236 | 10.43 N | 83.56 W |
| Şarapó ≃ | 287a | 22.46 S | 43.37 W |
| Šarapovo, Ross. | 80 | 55.17 N | 44.42 E |
| Šarapovo, Ross. | 82 | 55.11 N | 37.16 E |
| Sarapuí ≃ | 287a | 22.46 S | 43.24 W |
| Sarapuí, Canal de ≊ | 287a | 22.44 S | 43.16 W |
| Sarapul | 80 | 56.28 N | 53.48 E |
| Sarapul'skaja vozvyšennost' ⋏[1] | 80 | 56.15 N | 53.30 E |
| Sarapul'skoje | 89 | 48.52 N | 135.59 E |
| Sarāqib | 130 | 35.52 N | 36.48 E |
| Sarare | 246 | 9.47 N | 69.10 W |
| Sarare ≃ | 246 | 7.18 N | 70.41 W |
| Sarar Plain ≃ | 144 | 9.25 N | 46.17 E |
| Sara Sara, Nevado ∧ | 248 | 15.19 S | 73.27 W |
| Sarasota | 220 | 27.20 N | 82.31 W |
| Sarasota □[6] | 220 | 27.10 N | 82.21 W |
| Sarasota Bay ⊂ | 220 | 27.23 N | 82.39 W |
| Sarasota-Bradenton Airport ⊠ | 220 | 27.24 N | 82.33 W |
| Şarasota Springs | 220 | 27.17 N | 82.28 W |
| Sarašova | 76 | 52.33 N | 24.13 E |
| Saraswati ≃ | 272b | 22.59 N | 88.22 E |
| Sarata | 78 | 46.02 N | 29.38 E |
| Sarath | 126 | 24.14 N | 86.50 E |
| Saratoga, Austl. | 170 | 33.28 S | 151.21 E |
| Saratoga, Ca., U.S. | 226 | 37.15 N | 122.01 W |
| Saratoga, In., U.S. | 216 | 40.14 N | 84.55 W |
| Saratoga, Tx., U.S. | 222 | 30.17 N | 94.31 W |
| Saratoga, Wy., U.S. | 200 | 41.27 N | 106.48 W |
| Saratoga □[6] | 210 | 43.00 N | 73.51 W |
| Saratoga Battlefield Monument ⊥ | 210 | 43.05 N | 73.35 W |
| Saratoga Creek ≃ | 282 | 37.25 N | 121.58 W |
| Saratoga Lake ⊜ | 210 | 43.01 N | 73.39 W |
| Saratoga National Historical Park ♠ | 210 | 43.00 N | 73.38 W |
| Saratoga Passage ʮ | 224 | 48.10 N | 122.30 W |
| Saratoga Spa State Park ♠ | 210 | 43.03 N | 73.50 W |
| Şaratoga Springs | 210 | 43.04 N | 73.47 W |
| Šara-Togot | 88 | 53.01 N | 106.43 E |
| Saratok | 112 | 1.44 N | 111.20 E |
| Saratov | 80 | 51.34 N | 46.02 E |
| Saratovka | 86 | 51.12 N | 54.54 E |
| Saratov Oblast' □[4] | 80 | 51.30 N | 47.00 E |
| Saratovskoje vodochranilišče ⊜[1] | 80 | 52.45 N | 48.30 E |
| Saraurcu ∧ | 246 | 0.06 S | 77.55 W |
| Sarāvān, Īrān | 128 | 27.15 N | 62.40 E |
| Saravan, Lao | 110 | 15.43 N | 106.25 E |
| Sarawak □[3] | 112 | 2.30 N | 113.30 E |
| Saray | 130 | 41.26 N | 27.55 E |
| Saraya, Guinée | 150 | 10.46 N | 10.24 W |
| Saraya, Sén. | 150 | 12.50 N | 11.45 W |
| Sarāyān | 128 | 33.51 N | 58.31 E |
| Saraycık | 130 | 40.57 N | 35.08 E |
| Saraydüzü | 130 | 41.20 N | 34.52 E |
| Sarā-ye Aḥmadī | 128 | 27.56 N | 56.42 E |
| Sarayevo → Sarajevo | 38 | 43.52 N | 18.25 E |
| Sarayköy | 130 | 37.55 N | 28.58 E |
| Sarayönü | 130 | 38.17 N | 32.25 E |
| Sarbaj | 80 | 53.39 N | 51.34 E |
| Sarbāz | 128 | 26.39 N | 61.15 E |
| Sarbinowo | 54 | 52.40 N | 14.40 E |
| Sárbogárd | 30 | 46.53 N | 18.38 E |
| Sarca ≃ | 64 | 45.52 N | 10.52 E |
| Sarce ≃ | 50 | 48.09 N | 4.18 E |
| Sarcee Indian Reserve ◆[4] | 182 | 50.58 N | 114.06 W |
| Sarcelle, Passe de la ʮ | 175f | 22.29 S | 167.12 E |
| Sarcelles | 50 | 49.00 N | 2.23 E |
| Sarche di Calavino | 64 | 46.03 N | 10.57 E |
| Şarcidano ◆[1] | 71 | 39.49 N | 9.10 E |
| Šarčino | 86 | 53.09 N | 81.45 E |
| Sarclet | 46 | 58.22 N | 3.07 W |
| Sarcoxie | 194 | 37.04 N | 94.06 W |
| Sārda (Mahākālī) ≃ | 124 | 27.22 N | 81.23 E |
| Sard āb )( | 123 | 36.40 N | 71.32 E |
| Sārda Canal ≊ | 124 | 28.08 N | 80.24 E |
| Sardagna | 64 | 46.03 N | 11.06 E |
| Sardah | 124 | 24.18 N | 88.44 E |
| Sardaq | 128 | 34.48 N | 58.07 E |
| Sardara | 71 | 39.37 N | 8.49 E |
| Sardār Chāh | 128 | 27.58 N | 64.50 E |
| Sardārpur | 120 | 22.39 N | 74.59 E |
| Sardārshahr | 120 | 28.26 N | 74.29 E |
| Sar Dasht, Īrān | 128 | 36.09 N | 45.28 E |
| Sar Dasht, Īrān | 128 | 32.32 N | 48.52 E |
| Sardegna □[4] | 71 | 40.00 N | 9.00 E |
| Sardegna (Sardinia) I | 71 | 40.00 N | 9.00 E |
| Sardeh Band | 120 | 33.17 N | 68.39 E |
| Sardhana | 124 | 29.09 N | 77.37 E |
| Sardiha | 126 | 22.22 N | 87.09 E |
| Sardinal | 236 | 10.31 N | 85.39 W |
| Sardinata | 246 | 8.05 N | 72.48 W |
| Sardinia, N.Y., U.S. | 210 | 42.32 N | 78.31 W |
| Sardinia, Oh., U.S. | 218 | 39.00 N | 83.48 W |
| Sardinia → Sardegna I | 71 | 40.00 N | 9.00 E |
| Sardinien → Sardegna I | 71 | 40.00 N | 9.00 E |
| Sardis, B.C., Can. | 224 | 49.08 N | 121.57 W |
| Sardis, Al., U.S. | 194 | 32.17 N | 86.59 W |
| Sardis, Ga., U.S. | 192 | 32.58 N | 81.45 W |
| Sardis, Ky., U.S. | 218 | 38.31 N | 83.57 W |
| Sardis, Ms., U.S. | 194 | 34.26 N | 89.55 W |
| Sardis, Pa., U.S. | 279b | 40.29 N | 79.42 W |
| Sardis, Tn., U.S. | 194 | 35.27 N | 88.18 W |
| Sardis Lake ⊜[1] | 194 | 34.27 N | 89.43 W |
| Şardona, Piz ∧ | 58 | 46.55 N | 9.15 E |
| Šardonem' | 24 | 63.56 N | 44.37 E |
| Sarek ∧ | 24 | 67.25 N | 17.46 E |
| Sareks Nationalpark ♠ | 24 | 67.15 N | 17.30 E |
| Sārenga, India | 126 | 22.46 N | 87.02 E |
| Sārenga, India | 272b | 22.31 N | 88.13 E |
| Sarentina, Valle V | 64 | 46.35 N | 11.25 E |
| Sarentino (Sarnthein) | 64 | 46.38 N | 11.21 E |
| Sar-e Pol | 120 | 36.14 N | 65.55 E |
| Sarepta | 194 | 32.53 N | 93.26 W |
| Sarezskoje, ozero ⊜ | 85 | 38.13 N | 72.45 E |
| Sarezzo | 64 | 45.39 N | 10.12 E |
| Sargans | 58 | 47.03 N | 9.26 E |
| Sargasso Sea ∓[2] | 8 | 30.00 N | 50.00 W |
| Sargasso Sea ∓[2] | 8 | 30.00 N | 50.00 W |
| Sargatskoje | 86 | 55.37 N | 73.30 E |
| Sargau ≃ | 85 | 43.25 N | 73.50 E |
| Sargé-lès-le-Mans | 50 | 48.02 N | 0.14 E |
| Sargent, Ga., U.S. | 192 | 33.25 N | 84.52 W |

| | | | |
|---|---|---|---|
| Sargent, Ne., U.S. | 198 | 41.38 N | 99.22 W |
| Sargent Creek ≃ | 226 | 35.57 N | 120.52 W |
| Şargodha | 123 | 32.05 N | 72.40 E |
| Šargol'džin | 88 | 52.21 N | 114.42 E |
| Şargul', ozero ⊜ | 86 | 54.35 N | 78.51 E |
| Šargun | 85 | 38.37 N | 67.53 E |
| Sarh | 146 | 9.09 N | 18.23 E |
| Sarhli, Djebel ∧ | 34 | 36.06 N | 0.40 E |
| Sārī | 128 | 36.34 N | 53.04 E |
| Saría I | 38 | 35.50 N | 27.15 E |
| Saribi, Tanjung › | 164 | 1.36 S | 135.25 E |
| Sarıbuğday | 130 | 40.35 N | 35.35 E |
| Saric | 232 | 31.08 N | 111.23 W |
| Saricumbe | 152 | 12.12 S | 19.46 E |
| Sarigan I | 108 | 16.42 N | 145.47 E |
| Sarıgazi ◆[8] | 267b | 41.01 N | 29.12 E |
| Sarıgöl | 130 | 38.14 N | 28.43 E |
| Sarıkamış | 130 | 40.20 N | 42.35 E |
| Sarıkaya, Tür. | 130 | 38.47 N | 32.15 E |
| Sarıkaya, Tür. | 130 | 39.30 N | 35.24 E |
| Sarikei | 112 | 2.07 N | 111.31 E |
| Sarıköy | 130 | 40.12 N | 27.36 E |
| Sarilhos Grandes | 266c | 38.41 N | 8.58 W |
| Sarilhos Pequenos | 266c | 38.41 N | 8.59 W |
| Sarim | 154 | 0.23 S | 40.58 E |
| Sarimbun, Pulau I | 271c | 1.26 N | 103.41 E |
| Sarina | 166 | 21.26 S | 149.13 E |
| Sarine (Saane) ≃ | 58 | 46.59 N | 7.15 E |
| Sariñena | 34 | 41.48 N | 0.10 W |
| Sarıoğlan | 130 | 39.05 N | 35.59 E |
| Saripul' | 85 | 38.26 N | 70.08 E |
| Sarīr | 146 | 27.36 N | 22.32 E |
| Sarısu | 84 | 39.01 N | 42.55 E |
| Sarita | 196 | 27.13 N | 97.47 W |
| Sariwŏn | 98 | 38.31 N | 125.44 E |
| Sarıyar Barajı ⊜[1] | 130 | 40.02 N | 31.40 E |
| Şarız | 130 | 38.30 N | 36.30 E |
| Šarja | 80 | 58.24 N | 45.30 E |
| Sarju (Babaī) ≃ | 124 | 27.42 N | 81.16 E |
| Sark I | 43b | 49.26 N | 2.21 W |
| Sark ≃ | 44 | 54.58 N | 3.04 W |
| Şarkad | 30 | 46.44 N | 21.23 E |
| Šarkan | 80 | 57.18 N | 53.53 E |
| Şarkand | 86 | 45.26 N | 79.54 E |
| Šarkauščyna | 76 | 55.22 N | 27.28 E |
| Şarkikaraağaç | 130 | 38.04 N | 31.23 E |
| Şarkışla | 130 | 39.21 N | 36.26 E |
| Şarköy | 130 | 40.37 N | 27.06 E |
| Şarlat-la-Canéda | 32 | 44.53 N | 1.13 E |
| Šarlauk | 128 | 38.13 N | 55.38 E |
| Şarles | 198 | 48.56 N | 98.59 W |
| Šarlyk | 86 | 52.55 N | 54.35 E |
| Sarmakovo | 84 | 43.43 N | 43.12 E |
| Sarmanovo | 80 | 55.15 N | 52.36 E |
| Sărmaşu | 38 | 46.46 N | 24.11 E |
| Sarmathura | 124 | 26.31 N | 77.22 E |
| Sarmatskaja ≃ | 83 | 47.20 N | 38.48 E |
| Sármellék | 30 | 46.44 N | 17.10 E |
| Sarmi | 164 | 1.51 S | 138.44 E |
| Sarmiento | 254 | 45.36 S | 69.05 W |
| Sarmiento ≃ | 288 | 34.25 S | 58.35 W |
| Sarmiento de Gambia, Cerro ∧ | 254 | 54.27 S | 70.50 W |
| Sarmiento de Gamboa, Lago ⊜ | 254 | 51.04 S | 72.45 W |
| Särna | 26 | 61.41 N | 13.08 E |
| Sarna, ozero ⊜ | 80 | 48.24 N | 44.38 E |
| Sarnano | 66 | 43.02 N | 13.18 E |
| Sārnāth ⊥ | 124 | 25.24 N | 83.01 E |
| Sarnen | 58 | 46.54 N | 8.15 E |
| Sărnena Gora ⋏ | 38 | 42.35 N | 25.10 E |
| Sarner See ⊜ | 58 | 46.52 N | 8.13 E |
| Sarnia | 214 | 42.58 N | 82.23 W |
| Sarnico | 64 | 45.40 N | 9.57 E |
| Sarno | 68 | 40.49 N | 14.37 E |
| Sarnow | 54 | 53.45 N | 13.37 E |
| Sarnowa | 30 | 51.38 N | 16.54 E |
| Sarnthein → Sarentino | 64 | 46.38 N | 11.21 E |
| Šarnutovskij | 80 | 47.40 N | 43.46 E |
| Sarny | 78 | 51.21 N | 26.36 E |
| Şaroako | 112 | 2.31 S | 121.22 E |
| Šaroargun ≃ | 84 | 43.02 N | 45.44 E |
| Sarolangun | 112 | 2.18 S | 102.42 E |
| Saroma-ko ⊜ | 92a | 44.08 N | 143.50 E |
| Saron | 158 | 33.11 S | 19.01 E |
| Saronikós Kólpos ⊂ | 38 | 37.45 N | 23.30 E |
| Saronno | 62 | 45.38 N | 9.02 E |
| Saros Körfezi ⊂ | 130 | 40.30 N | 26.20 E |
| Sárospatak | 30 | 48.19 N | 21.34 E |
| Sarowbī | 120 | 34.36 N | 69.43 E |
| Sarpa | 80 | 47.07 N | 45.29 E |
| Şarpa, ozero ⊜ | 80 | 47.18 N | 45.20 E |
| Šarpajevka | 78 | 48.34 N | 40.59 E |
| Sar Passage ʮ | 175b | 7.12 N | 134.23 E |
| Şarpinskije ozera ⊜ | 80 | 47.30 N | 45.00 E |
| Šar Planina ⋏ | 38 | 42.05 N | 20.50 E |
| Sarpsborg | 26 | 59.17 N | 11.07 E |
| Sarpy Creek ≃ | 202 | 46.15 N | 107.09 W |
| Sárrabus ◆[1] | 71 | 39.23 N | 9.21 E |
| Sarralbe | 56 | 49.00 N | 7.01 E |
| Sarras | 62 | 45.11 N | 4.48 E |
| Sarrath, Oued V | 36 | 35.59 N | 8.23 E |
| Sarratt | 260 | 51.41 N | 0.29 W |
| Sarre | 62 | 45.43 N | 7.15 E |
| Sarre (Saar) ≃ | 56 | 49.42 N | 6.34 E |
| Sarre Blanche ≃ | 56 | 48.41 N | 7.01 E |
| Sarrebourg | 58 | 48.44 N | 7.03 E |
| Sarrebruck → Saarbrücken | 56 | 49.14 N | 6.59 E |
| Sarreguemines | 56 | 49.06 N | 7.03 E |
| Sarre Rouge ≃ | 56 | 48.41 N | 7.01 E |
| Sarre-Union | 56 | 48.56 N | 7.05 E |
| Sarria | 34 | 42.47 N | 7.24 W |
| Sarriá ◆[8] | 266d | 41.24 N | 2.08 E |
| Sarro | 150 | 13.43 N | 5.15 W |
| Sarroch | 71 | 39.04 N | 9.00 E |
| Şars | 86 | 56.33 N | 57.07 E |
| Šarscin | 76 | 52.39 N | 31.03 E |
| Sarsfield | 212 | 45.27 N | 75.21 W |
| Sarsina | 66 | 43.55 N | 12.08 E |
| Sarsol | 272c | 19.02 N | 73.01 E |
| Sarstedt | 52 | 52.14 N | 9.51 E |
| Sarstein ∧ | 64 | 47.36 N | 13.41 E |
| Sarstoon (Sarstún) ≃ | 236 | 15.53 N | 88.55 W |
| Sarstún (Sarstoon) ≃ | 236 | 15.53 N | 88.55 W |
| Sarsuna | 272b | 22.28 N | 88.18 E |
| Sart | 56 | 50.31 N | 5.56 E |
| Sartang ≃ | 74 | 67.44 N | 133.12 E |
| Sarteano | 66 | 42.59 N | 11.52 E |
| Sartell | 190 | 45.37 N | 94.12 W |
| Sartène | 36 | 41.36 N | 8.59 E |
| Sarthe □[5] | 32 | 48.00 N | 0.05 E |
| Sarthe ≃ | 32 | 47.30 N | 0.32 W |
| Sartičala | 84 | 41.43 N | 45.10 E |
| Sartilly | 32 | 48.45 N | 1.27 W |
| Sartirana Lomellina | 62 | 45.07 N | 8.39 E |
| Sartlan, ozero ⊜ | 86 | 55.00 N | 78.35 E |
| Sartol'gen | 80 | 48.57 N | 47.03 E |
| Sartrouville | 261 | 48.57 N | 2.10 E |
| Saru | 85 | 42.20 N | 77.55 E |
| Sarufutsu | 92a | 45.16 N | 142.12 E |
| Saruhanlı | 130 | 38.44 N | 27.34 E |
| Şärur, Azer. | 84 | 39.33 N | 44.58 E |
| Şarūr, ʻUmān | 128 | 23.22 N | 58.07 E |
| Šar Us ≃ | 88 | 47.08 N | 97.38 E |
| Saru-shima I | 268 | 35.17 N | 139.42 E |
| Sarvadyk | 80 | 46.07 N | 44.07 E |
| Sárvár | 30 | 47.15 N | 16.57 E |
| Sarver | 214 | 40.44 N | 79.45 W |
| Sarvestān | 128 | 29.16 N | 53.13 E |
| Sárvíz ≃ | 30 | 46.24 N | 18.41 E |
| Saryagač | 85 | 41.27 N | 69.10 E |
| Saryassija | 85 | 38.25 N | 67.57 E |
| Sarybasat | 86 | 46.38 N | 60.27 E |
| Sarybulak, Kaz. | 85 | 43.24 N | 71.30 E |
| Sarybulak, Kaz. | 86 | 49.27 N | 76.27 E |
| Sarybulak, Kyrg. | 85 | 40.54 N | 73.49 E |
| Sarych, mys › | 78 | 44.23 N | 33.45 E |
| Sarychosor | 85 | 38.32 N | 69.49 E |

| | | | |
|---|---|---|---|
| Sarydala | 85 | 41.11 N | 70.27 E |
| Saryesik-Atyrau, peski ◆[2] | 86 | 45.30 N | 76.00 E |
| Saryg-Sep | 88 | 51.30 N | 95.36 E |
| Sarykamskoje ozero ⊜ | 72 | 41.56 N | 57.25 E |
| Sarykoby | 85 | 43.44 N | 72.35 E |
| Sarykol'skij chrebet ⋏ | 120 | 38.00 N | 74.30 E |
| Sarykomej | 86 | 45.12 N | 74.11 E |
| Sarykopa, ozero ⊜ | 86 | 50.22 N | 64.08 E |
| Sarymogol | 85 | 39.55 N | 72.47 E |
| Şaryozek | 86 | 44.22 N | 77.59 E |
| Šarypovo | 86 | 55.33 N | 89.12 E |
| Saryšagan | 86 | 46.07 N | 73.38 E |
| Sarysu | 86 | 48.23 N | 69.59 E |
| Sarysu ≃ | 86 | 45.12 N | 66.36 E |
| Sary-Taš | 85 | 39.44 N | 73.15 E |
| Sarytau | 86 | 49.54 N | 76.41 E |
| Saryžaz | 72 | 42.55 N | 79.38 E |
| Sarzana | 64 | 44.07 N | 9.58 E |
| Sarzanello, Fortezza di ⊥ | 64 | 44.08 N | 9.58 E |
| Sarzeau | 32 | 47.32 N | 2.46 W |
| S'as' ≃ | 76 | 60.09 N | 32.30 E |
| Saʻsaʻ, Sūrīy. | 132 | 33.17 N | 36.02 E |
| Sasa, Yis. | 132 | 33.02 N | 35.24 E |
| Sasabe | 200 | 31.27 N | 111.31 W |
| Sasabe ≃ | 200 | 30.41 N | 111.56 W |
| Sasabeneh | 144 | 7.55 N | 43.39 E |
| Sasaga-mine ∧ | 96 | 33.49 N | 133.17 E |
| Sasaginnigak Lake ⊜ | 184 | 51.36 N | 95.40 W |
| Sasago-tunnel ◆[5] | 94 | 35.38 N | 138.47 E |
| Sasaguri | 96 | 33.37 N | 130.32 E |
| Sasak | 110 | 0.01 S | 99.42 E |
| Sasakwa | 196 | 34.56 N | 96.31 W |
| Sasamungga | 175e | 7.02 S | 156.47 E |
| Sasao | 270 | 34.57 N | 135.20 E |
| Sasar, Tanjung › | 115b | 9.17 S | 119.56 E |
| Sāsarām | 124 | 24.57 N | 84.02 E |
| Sasayama | 96 | 35.04 N | 135.13 E |
| Sasa-yama ∧ | 96 | 33.03 N | 132.40 E |
| Sasbach, Dtsch. | 56 | 48.38 N | 8.06 E |
| Sasbach, Dtsch. | 58 | 48.08 N | 7.37 E |
| Sasco Brook ≃ | 276 | 41.07 N | 73.18 W |
| Sásd | 30 | 46.15 N | 18.06 E |
| Sasebo | 92 | 33.10 N | 129.43 E |
| Sasebo Naval Base ■ | 92 | 33.09 N | 129.45 E |
| Saseenos | 224 | 48.24 N | 123.40 W |
| Saseginaga, Lac ⊜ | 190 | 47.06 N | 78.35 W |
| Sashalom ◆[8] | 264c | 47.31 N | 19.11 E |
| Sas-hegy ∧[2] | 264c | 47.23 N | 19.18 E |
| Sashiki | 174m | 26.10 N | 127.47 E |
| Sashima | 94 | 36.08 N | 139.51 E |
| Saskatchewan □[4], Can. | 176 | 54.00 N | 105.00 W |
| Saskatchewan □[4], Can. | 184 | 54.00 N | 105.00 W |
| Saskatchewan ≃ | 184 | 53.12 N | 99.16 W |
| Saskatoon | 184 | 52.07 N | 106.38 W |
| Saskylach | 74 | 71.55 N | 114.01 E |
| Saslaya, Cerro ∧ | 238 | 13.45 N | 85.03 W |
| Sasmik, Cape › | 180 | 51.36 N | 177.55 W |
| Sāsni | 124 | 27.43 N | 78.05 E |
| Sasnovy Bor | 76 | 52.32 N | 29.36 E |
| Sasolburg | 158 | 26.48 S | 27.45 E |
| Sason | 130 | 38.20 N | 41.25 E |
| Sasovo | 80 | 54.21 N | 41.54 E |
| Saspamco | 196 | 29.14 N | 98.18 W |
| Saspul Gompa | 123 | 34.15 N | 77.09 E |
| Sassafras, Austl. | 274b | 37.52 S | 145.21 E |
| Sassafras, Ky., U.S. | 192 | 37.14 N | 83.06 W |
| Sassafras ≃ | 208 | 39.23 N | 76.02 W |
| Sassafras Mountain ∧ | 192 | 35.03 N | 82.48 W |
| Sassafras Neck ›[1] | 208 | 39.25 N | 75.55 W |
| Sassandra | 150 | 4.58 N | 6.05 W |
| Sassandra ≃ | 150 | 4.58 N | 6.05 W |
| Sassano | 68 | 40.20 N | 15.33 E |
| Sassari | 71 | 40.44 N | 8.33 E |
| Sassari □[4] | 71 | 40.40 N | 9.00 E |
| Sassbach ≃ | 61 | 46.43 N | 15.48 E |
| Sasse ≃ | 62 | 44.15 N | 5.55 E |
| Sassello | 62 | 44.29 N | 8.30 E |
| Sassenage | 62 | 45.12 N | 5.40 E |
| Sassenberg | 52 | 51.59 N | 8.02 E |
| Sassenheim | 52 | 52.13 N | 4.31 E |
| Sassnitz | 54 | 54.31 N | 13.38 E |
| Sassocorvaro | 66 | 43.47 N | 12.30 E |
| Sasso di Castalda | 68 | 40.30 N | 15.40 E |
| Sassoferrato | 66 | 43.26 N | 12.51 E |
| Sasso Marconi | 64 | 44.24 N | 11.15 E |
| S'as'stroj | 76 | 60.08 N | 32.34 E |
| Sassuolo | 64 | 44.33 N | 10.47 E |
| Sastobe | 85 | 42.34 N | 70.00 E |
| Sastown | 150 | 4.40 N | 8.26 W |
| Sastre | 252 | 31.45 S | 61.50 W |
| Sas van Gent | 52 | 51.14 N | 3.47 E |
| Sasyk, ozero ⊜ | 78 | 45.12 N | 33.31 E |
| Sasykkol', ozero ⊜ | 86 | 46.35 N | 81.00 E |
| Şasykoli | 80 | 47.33 N | 47.00 E |
| Šat ≃ | 82 | 54.08 N | 37.47 E |
| Satadougou | 150 | 12.21 N | 10.07 W |
| Satah Mountain ∧ | 182 | 52.29 N | 124.41 W |
| Şatakunta ◆[1] | 26 | 61.30 N | 23.00 E |
| Šatalovka | 78 | 51.09 N | 38.16 E |
| Šatalovo | 76 | 54.20 N | 32.27 E |
| Sata-misaki › | 92 | 30.59 N | 130.40 E |
| Satāna | 122 | 20.35 N | 74.12 E |
| Sataniv | 78 | 49.15 N | 26.16 E |
| Satanta | 198 | 37.26 N | 100.59 W |
| Sátão | 34 | 40.44 N | 7.44 W |
| Sātāra, India | 122 | 17.41 N | 73.59 E |
| Satara, S. Afr. | 156 | 24.29 S | 31.47 E |
| Sataua | 175a | 13.28 S | 172.40 W |
| Sātbāria, Bngl. | 126 | 23.52 N | 89.26 E |
| Sātbāria, India | 272b | 22.25 N | 88.33 E |
| Satélite | 232 | 31.43 N | 106.23 W |
| Satellite Beach | 220 | 28.10 N | 80.35 W |
| Satellite Channel ʮ | 224 | 48.43 N | 123.30 W |
| Satema | 152 | 4.18 N | 21.42 E |
| Satengar, Pulau I | 112 | 7.31 S | 117.17 E |
| Säter | 40 | 60.21 N | 15.45 E |
| Sātgāchia | 126 | 23.16 N | 88.08 E |
| Sātghara | 272b | 22.44 N | 88.21 E |
| Satilla ≃ | 192 | 30.59 N | 81.28 W |
| Satilpa Creek ≃ | 194 | 31.39 N | 88.05 W |
| Satin | 222 | 31.21 N | 97.02 W |
| Satipo | 248 | 11.16 S | 74.37 W |
| Sátiro Dias | 250 | 11.36 S | 38.36 W |
| Satis | 80 | 55.02 N | 43.48 E |
| Satīt (Tekeze) ≃ | 140 | 14.20 N | 35.50 E |
| Satka | 86 | 55.03 N | 59.01 E |
| Satkānia | 120 | 22.04 N | 92.03 E |
| Şātkhira | 124 | 22.43 N | 89.06 E |
| Šatki | 80 | 55.11 N | 44.08 E |
| Satla Bīl ≡ | 126 | 22.54 N | 90.04 E |
| Satluj → Sutlej ≃ | 120 | 29.23 N | 71.02 E |
| Satna | 124 | 24.35 N | 80.50 E |
| Sato, Cañada de ≃ | 288 | 34.35 S | 58.38 W |
| Satomi | 94 | 36.43 N | 140.30 E |
| Sátoraljaújhely | 30 | 48.24 N | 21.39 E |
| Šatov | 61 | 48.48 N | 16.01 E |
| Šatovo | 82 | 54.56 N | 37.14 E |
| Şatow | 54 | 53.59 N | 11.51 E |
| Šatpajev | 86 | 47.55 N | 67.28 E |
| Sātpura Range ⋏ | 122 | 22.00 N | 78.00 E |
| Sätrabrunn | 40 | 59.51 N | 16.27 E |
| Şatriano di Lucania | 68 | 40.33 N | 15.33 E |
| Šatrovo | 86 | 56.31 N | 64.38 E |
| Satrup | 41 | 54.41 N | 9.35 E |
| Satsop ≃ | 224 | 47.03 N | 123.30 W |
| Satsop, East Fork ≃ | 224 | 47.02 N | 123.32 W |
| Satsop, Middle Fork ≃ | 224 | 47.05 N | 123.30 W |
| Satsop, West Fork ≃ | 224 | 47.02 N | 123.32 W |
| Satsuma | 194 | 30.51 N | 88.03 W |
| Satsuma-hantō ›[1] | 92 | 31.25 N | 130.25 E |
| Satsunan-shotō II | 93b | 29.00 N | 130.00 E |
| Sattahip | 110 | 12.40 N | 100.54 E |

| | | | |
|---|---|---|---|
| Sāttānkulam | 122 | 8.27 N | [illegible].56 E |
| Satte | 94 | 36.04 N | 13[illegible].43 E |
| Sattel | 58 | 47.05 N | [illegible].42 E |
| Sattenapalle | 122 | 16.24 N | 8[illegible].11 E |
| Satthwa | 110 | 17.46 N | 9[illegible].30 E |
| Sattledt | 61 | 48.04 N | 1[illegible].03 E |
| Satui | 112 | 3.47 S | 11[illegible].27 E |
| Sātuli | 272b | 22.33 N | 8[illegible].34 E |
| Satu Mare | 38 | 47.48 N | 2[illegible].53 E |
| Satu Mare □[6] | 38 | 47.40 N | 2[illegible].00 E |
| Şatun | 110 | 6.37 N | 100.[illegible]4 E |
| Šatura | 80 | 55.34 N | 39.[illegible]2 E |
| Saturna | 224 | 48.43 N | 123.[illegible]1 W |
| Saturna Island I | 224 | 48.47 N | 123.[illegible]8 W |
| Şaturnino M. Laspiur | 252 | 31.42 S | 62.[illegible]9 W |
| Šaturtorf | 76 | 55.34 N | 39.[illegible]6 E |
| Satus Creek ≃ | 202 | 46.16 N | 120.[illegible]7 W |
| Satus Peak ∧ | 224 | 46.15 N | 120.[illegible]5 W |
| Satyamangalam | 122 | 11.31 N | 77.[illegible]5 E |
| Satzkorn | 264a | 52.29 N | 12.[illegible] E |
| Sau ≃ | 269c | 10.46 N | 106.[illegible] E |
| Saualpe ⋏ | 61 | 46.55 N | 14.[illegible] E |
| Sauble ≃ | 212 | 44.40 N | 81.1[illegible] W |
| Sauce, Arg. | 252 | 30.05 S | 58.4[illegible] W |
| Sauce, Perú | 248 | 6.44 S | 76.1[illegible] W |
| Sauce, Ur. | 258 | 34.39 S | 56.0[illegible] W |
| Sauce, Arroyo ≃ | 258 | 34.26 S | 57.2[illegible] W |
| Sauce, Arroyo del ≃ | 288 | 34.41 S | 58.5[illegible] W |
| Sauce Corto, Arroyo ≃ | 252 | 36.55 S | 61.4[illegible] W |
| Saucier | 194 | 30.38 N | 89.0[illegible] W |
| Saucillo | 232 | 28.01 N | 105.1[illegible] W |
| Sauda | 26 | 59.39 N | 6.2[illegible] E |
| Saudade | 256 | 21.56 S | 43.03 W |
| Sauđárkrókur | 24a | 65.46 N | 19.41 W |
| Saúde | 250 | 10.56 S | 40.24 W |
| Saúde ◆[8] | 287b | 23.37 S | 46.37 W |
| Saudi Arabia (Al-ʻArabīyah as-Suʻūdīyah) □[1] | 118 | 25.00 N | 45.00 [illegible] |
| Saudi-Arabien → Saudi Arabia □[1] | 118 | 25.00 N | 45.00 [illegible] |
| Saudron | 58 | 48.30 N | 5.20 [illegible] |
| Sauer ≃, Europe | 56 | 48.55 N | 8.10 [illegible] |
| Sauer (Sûre) ≃, Europe | 56 | 49.44 N | 6.31 E |
| Sauerkohl-Berge ∧[2] | 264a | 52.20 N | 13.45 E |
| Sauerlach | 64 | 47.58 N | 11.38 E |
| Sauerland ◆[1] | 52 | 51.10 N | 8.00 E |
| Saueruiná ≃ | 248 | 12.00 S | 58.43 W |
| Sauê-Uiná ≃ | 248 | 12.24 S | 58.40 W |
| Saug ≃ | 116 | 7.27 N | 125.44 E |
| Saugatuck, Ct., U.S. | 276 | 41.08 N | 73.23 W |
| Saugatuck, Mi., U.S. | 216 | 42.39 N | 86.12 W |
| Saugatuck ≃ | 276 | 41.07 N | 73.22 W |
| Saugatuck Reservoir ⊜[1] | 207 | 41.16 N | 73.22 W |
| Saugeen ≃ | 190 | 44.30 N | 81.22 W |
| Saugeen Indian Reserve ◆[4] | 212 | 44.33 N | 81.18 W |
| Saugerties | 210 | 42.04 N | 73.57 W |
| Saughall | 262 | 53.13 N | 2.58 W |
| Saugor → Sāgar | 124 | 23.50 N | 78.43 E |
| Saugstad, Mount ∧ | 182 | 52.15 N | 126.31 W |
| Saugus | 207 | 42.27 N | 71.00 W |
| Saugus ≃ | 283 | 42.28 N | 70.58 W |
| Saugus Iron Works National Historic Site ⊥ | 283 | 42.28 N | 71.01 W |
| Sauh, Tanjong › | 114 | 3.46 N | 100.49 E |
| Saujil | 252 | 28.11 S | 66.14 W |
| Saujon | 32 | 45.40 N | 0.56 W |
| Sauk ≃, Mn., U.S. | 198 | 45.36 N | 94.10 W |
| Sauk ≃, Wa., U.S. | 224 | 48.30 N | 121.37 W |
| Sauk Centre | 198 | 45.44 N | 94.57 W |
| Sauk City | 190 | 43.16 N | 89.43 W |
| Sauk Rapids | 190 | 45.35 N | 94.09 W |
| Sauksaj ≃ | 85 | 39.11 N | 72.15 E |
| Sauk Village | 216 | 41.29 N | 87.34 W |
| Saukville | 190 | 43.22 N | 87.56 W |
| Şaül | 250 | 3.37 N | 53.12 W |
| Šaul'der | 85 | 42.47 N | 68.24 E |
| Sauldre ≃ | 50 | 47.16 N | 1.30 E |
| Sauldre, Canal de la ≊ | 50 | 47.36 N | 2.06 E |
| Saulgau | 58 | 48.01 N | 9.30 E |
| Saulgrub | 64 | 47.40 N | 11.01 E |
| Saulheim | 56 | 49.51 N | 8.09 E |
| Saulieu | 50 | 47.16 N | 4.14 E |
| Saulkrasti | 76 | 57.17 N | 24.25 E |
| Saulnot | 58 | 47.34 N | 6.38 E |
| Sault-au-Mouton | 186 | 48.33 N | 69.15 W |
| Sault au Récollet ◆[8] | 275a | 45.34 N | 73.39 W |
| Sault aux Cochons, Rivière du ≃ | 186 | 48.44 N | 69.04 W |
| Sault-de-Vaucluse | 62 | 44.05 N | 5.25 E |
| Saulteaux ≃ | 182 | 55.16 N | 114.25 W |
| Saulteaux Indian Reserve ◆[4] | 184 | 53.08 N | 108.18 W |
| Sault-lès-Rethel | 50 | 49.30 N | 4.22 E |
| Sault Sainte Marie, On., Can. | 190 | 46.31 N | 84.20 W |
| Sault Sainte Marie, Mi., U.S. | 190 | 46.29 N | 84.20 W |
| Saulx ≃, Fr. | 56 | 48.45 N | 4.35 E |
| Saulx ≃, Fr. | 261 | 48.41 N | 2.19 E |
| Saulx-de-Vesoul | 58 | 47.42 N | 6.17 E |
| Saulx-les-Chartreux | 261 | 48.42 N | 2.16 E |
| Saulxures-sur-Moselotte | 58 | 47.57 N | 6.46 E |
| Šaum'ani | 84 | 41.21 N | 44.46 E |
| Saumarez Reef ✦[2] | 166 | 21.50 S | 153.40 E |
| Saumlaki | 164 | 7.57 S | 131.19 E |
| Saumon, Rivière au ≃ | 206 | 45.41 N | 71.27 W |
| Saumons, Rivíere aux ≃ | 186 | 49.25 N | 62.15 W |
| Saumur | 32 | 47.16 N | 0.05 W |
| Saundatti | 122 | 15.47 N | 75.07 E |
| Saundersfoot | 42 | 51.43 N | 4.43 W |
| Saunders Island I, Falk. Is. | 254 | 51.20 S | 60.10 W |
| Saunders Island I, S. Geor. | 9 | 57.47 S | 26.27 W |
| Saunders Point ∧[2] | 162 | 27.52 S | 125.38 E |
| Saunderstown | 207 | 41.30 N | 71.25 W |
| Saunemin | 216 | 40.54 N | 88.24 W |
| Saupite | 152 | 13.54 S | 17.43 E |
| Sauquoit | 210 | 43.00 N | 75.16 W |
| Sauquoit Creek ≃ | 210 | 43.08 N | 75.16 W |
| Saura | 84 | 44.14 N | 50.50 E |
| Sauran | 85 | 43.29 N | 67.50 E |
| Saurimo | 152 | 9.39 S | 20.24 E |
| Sausalito | 226 | 37.51 N | 122.29 W |
| Sausar | 120 | 21.39 N | 78.47 E |
| Sauškin | 80 | 49.30 N | 43.32 E |
| Sausset-les-Pins | 62 | 43.20 N | 5.07 E |
| Saussy | 58 | 47.28 N | 4.57 E |
| Sausu | 112 | 1.00 S | 120.30 E |
| Saútar | 152 | 11.06 S | 18.27 E |
| Sauteurs | 241k | 12.14 N | 61.38 W |
| Sauvas | 62 | 44.19 N | 4.09 E |
| Sauve | 62 | 43.56 N | 3.57 E |
| Sauveterre | 62 | 44.02 N | 4.48 E |
| Sauveterre-de-Béarn | 32 | 43.24 N | 0.56 W |
| Sauveterre-de-Guyenne | 32 | 44.42 N | 0.05 W |
| Sauvie Island I | 224 | 45.41 N | 122.49 W |
| Sauvo | 26 | 60.21 N | 22.42 E |
| Sauwald ◆[3] | 60 | 48.32 N | 13.40 E |
| Sauzal | 200 | 31.37 N | 106.18 W |
| Sauze di Cesana | 62 | 44.56 N | 6.51 E |
| Sauze d'Oulx | 62 | 45.02 N | 6.52 E |
| Sava, It. | 68 | 40.24 N | 17.34 E |
| S'ava, Ross. | 80 | 58.01 N | 46.22 E |
| Sava ≃ | 38 | 44.50 N | 20.26 E |
| Sävaån ≃ | 40 | 59.45 N | 17.24 E |
| Savage, Md., U.S. | 208 | 39.08 N | 76.49 W |
| Savage, Mt., U.S. | 198 | 47.27 N | 104.20 W |

| | | | | | |
|---|---|---|---|---|---|
| ≃ | River | Fluß | Río | Rivière | Rio |
| ≊ | Canal | Kanal | Canal | Canal | Canal |
| L | Waterfall, Rapids | Wasserfall, Stromschnellen | Cascada, Rápidos | Chute d'eau, Rapides | Cascata, Rápidos |
| ʮ | Strait | Meeresstraße | Estrecho | Détroit | Estreito |
| ⊂ | Bay, Gulf | Bucht, Golf | Bahía, Golfo | Baie, Golfe | Baía, Golfo |
| ⊜ | Lake, Lakes | See, Seen | Lago, Lagos | Lac, Lacs | Lago, Lagos |
| ≡ | Swamp | Sumpf | Pantano | Marais | Pântano |
| ⊓ | Ice Features, Glacier | Eis- und Gletscherformen | Accidentes Glaciales | Formes glaciaires | Acidentes glaciares |
| ∓ | Other Hydrographic Features | Andere Hydrographische Objekte | Otros Elementos Hidrográficos | Autres données hydrographiques | Outros acidentes hidrográficos |

| | | | | | |
|---|---|---|---|---|---|
| ✦ | Submarine Features | Untermeerische Objekte | Accidentes Submarinos | Formes de relief sous-marin | Acidentes submarinos |
| □ | Political Unit | Politische Einheit | Unidad Politica | Entité politique | Unidade política |
| ʊ | Cultural Institution | Kulturelle Institution | Institución Cultural | Institution culturelle | Institução cultural |
| ⊥ | Historical Site | Historische Stätte | Sitio Histórico | Site historique | Sitio histórico |
| ♠ | Recreational Site | Erholungs- und Ferienort | Sitio de Recreo | Centre de loisirs | Area de Lazer |
| ⊠ | Airport | Flughafen | Aeropuerto | Aéroport | Aeroporto |
| ■ | Military Installation | Militäranlage | Instalación Militar | Installation militaire | Instalação militar |
| ◆ | Miscellaneous | Verschiedenes | Misceláneo | Divers | Diversos |

| Name | Page | Lat.°′ | Long.°′ |
|---|---|---|---|
| Savai'i I | 175a | 13.35 S | 172.25 W |
| Savala ≃ | 80 | 51.03 N | 41.30 E |
| Savalen ⊜ | 26 | 62.15 N | 10.29 E |
| Savalou | 150 | 7.56 N | 1.58 E |
| Savana Island I | 240m | 18.20 N | 65.05 W |
| Savana Passage ⊍ | 240m | 18.21 N | 65.04 W |
| Savane ≃ | 186 | 51.08 N | 71.26 W |
| Savanna, Il., U.S. | 190 | 42.05 N | 90.09 W |
| Savanna, Ok., U.S. | 196 | 34.49 N | 95.50 W |
| Savannah, Ga., U.S. | 192 | 32.05 N | 81.06 W |
| Savannah, Mo., U.S. | 194 | 39.56 N | 94.49 W |
| Savannah, N.Y., U.S. | 210 | 43.04 N | 76.45 W |
| Savannah, Oh., U.S. | 214 | 40.57 N | 82.21 W |
| Savannah, Tn., U.S. | 194 | 35.13 N | 88.14 W |
| Savannah ≃ | 192 | 32.02 N | 80.53 W |
| Savannah River Plant ʊ[3] | 192 | 33.15 N | 81.40 W |
| Savannah Sound | 192 | 25.06 N | 76.09 W |
| Savannakhét | 110 | 16.33 N | 104.45 E |
| Savanna-la-Mar | 241q | 18.13 N | 78.08 W |
| Savanna Portage State Park ♦ | 190 | 46.51 N | 93.10 W |
| Sāvantvādi | 122 | 15.54 N | 73.49 E |
| Savanūr | 122 | 14.58 N | 75.21 E |
| Sävar | 26 | 63.54 N | 20.34 E |
| Savara ≃ | 62 | 45.42 N | 7.12 E |
| Săvârșin | 38 | 46.01 N | 22.14 E |
| Savasse ≃ | 62 | 45.03 N | 5.02 E |
| Savaştepe | 130 | 39.22 N | 27.40 E |
| Savat | 130 | 38.21 N | 40.38 E |
| Savcılıbüyükoba | 130 | 39.14 N | 33.41 E |
| Savé | 150 | 8.02 N | 2.29 E |
| Save (Sabi) ≃, Afr. | 156 | 21.00 S | 35.02 E |
| Save ≃, Fr. | 32 | 43.47 N | 1.17 E |
| Sāveh | 128 | 35.01 N | 50.20 E |
| Savelli | 68 | 39.19 N | 16.47 E |
| Savelugu | 150 | 9.37 N | 0.49 W |
| Savenay | 32 | 47.22 N | 1.57 W |
| Săveni | 38 | 47.57 N | 26.52 E |
| Saverdun | 32 | 43.14 N | 1.35 E |
| Savernake Forest ◆[3] | 42 | 51.24 N | 1.38 W |
| Saverne | 56 | 48.44 N | 7.22 E |
| Savery Creek ≃ | 200 | 41.01 N | 107.27 W |
| Savick Brook ≃ | 262 | 53.45 N | 2.47 W |
| Savičy | 76 | 52.25 N | 29.03 E |
| Savièse | 58 | 46.16 N | 7.20 E |
| Savigliano | 62 | 44.38 N | 7.40 E |
| Savignano Irpino | 68 | 41.14 N | 15.11 E |
| Savignano sul Panaro | 64 | 44.29 N | 11.02 E |
| Savignano sul Rubicone | 66 | 44.05 N | 12.24 E |
| Savignone | 62 | 44.34 N | 8.58 E |
| Savigny-lès-Beaune | 58 | 47.04 N | 4.49 E |
| Savigny-le-Temple | 261 | 48.35 N | 2.35 E |
| Savigny-sur-Braye | 50 | 47.53 N | 0.49 E |
| Savigny-sur-Orge | 50 | 48.40 N | 2.21 E |
| Savill Gardens ♦ | 260 | 51.27 N | 0.36 W |
| Savines | 62 | 44.32 N | 6.24 E |
| Savinjske Alpe ⋀ | 61 | 46.23 N | 14.35 E |
| Savinka, Ross. | 80 | 50.06 N | 47.06 E |
| Savinka, Ross. | 82 | 54.27 N | 38.52 E |
| Savino | 80 | 56.35 N | 41.13 E |
| Savino-Borisovskaja | 24 | 62.38 N | 44.34 E |
| Savinsk | 89 | 52.10 N | 140.23 E |
| Savinskij | 24 | 62.58 N | 40.08 E |
| Savio | 66 | 44.18 N | 12.18 E |
| Savio ≃ | 66 | 44.19 N | 12.20 E |
| Saviore dell'Adamello | 64 | 46.05 N | 10.24 E |
| Şavitaipale | 26 | 61.12 N | 27.42 E |
| Šavnik | 38 | 42.57 N | 19.05 E |
| Savognin | 58 | 46.36 N | 9.36 E |
| Savoie □[5] | 32 | 45.30 N | 6.25 E |
| Savoie □[9] | 58 | 45.55 N | 6.30 E |
| Savo Island I | 175e | 9.08 S | 159.49 E |
| Savolaks ◆[1] | 26 | 62.00 N | 28.00 E |
| Sav'olovo | 82 | 56.52 N | 37.22 E |
| Sav'olovo Station ◆[5] | 265b | 55.48 N | 37.35 E |
| Savona, B.C., Can. | 182 | 50.45 N | 120.50 W |
| Savona, It. | 62 | 44.17 N | 8.30 E |
| Savona, N.Y., U.S. | 210 | 42.17 N | 77.13 W |
| Savona □[4] | 62 | 44.18 N | 8.16 E |
| Savonlinna | 26 | 61.52 N | 28.53 E |
| Savonnières | 50 | 47.21 N | 0.33 E |
| Savonranta | 26 | 62.11 N | 29.12 E |
| Savoonga | 180 | 63.42 N | 170.27 W |
| Savory Creek ≃ | 162 | 23.22 S | 122.37 E |
| Savoureuse ≃ | 58 | 47.31 N | 6.51 E |
| Savoy | 196 | 33.34 N | 96.21 W |
| Savran' | 78 | 48.09 N | 30.04 E |
| Savruši | 80 | 55.02 N | 50.40 E |
| Sävsjö | 26 | 57.25 N | 14.40 E |
| S'avta | 24 | 67.08 N | 61.45 E |
| Savu Basin ✢[1] | 14 | 9.15 S | 123.15 E |
| Savudrija | 64 | 45.30 N | 13.30 E |
| Savur | 130 | 37.33 N | 40.53 E |
| Savur-Mohyla ⊥ | 83 | 47.56 N | 38.46 E |
| Savusavu | 175g | 16.16 S | 179.21 E |
| Savusavu Bay ⊂ | 175g | 16.45 S | 179.15 E |
| Savu Sea → Sawu, Laut ∓[2] | 112 | 9.40 S | 122.00 E |
| Savuto ≃ | 68 | 39.02 N | 16.06 E |
| Savvatejevka | 88 | 52.20 N | 103.39 E |
| Savvino, Ross. | 82 | 56.33 N | 37.47 E |
| Savvino, Ross. | 82 | 55.43 N | 36.48 E |
| Savvo-Borz'a | 88 | 50.46 N | 118.18 E |
| Savyntsi | 78 | 49.24 N | 37.04 E |
| Şawāb, Wādī aş- V | 130 | 34.36 N | 40.25 E |
| Sawabala Point > | 164 | 10.10 S | 151.15 E |
| Sawah | 112 | 2.23 N | 115.14 E |
| Sawahlunto | 112 | 0.40 S | 100.47 E |
| Sawai | 164 | 2.58 S | 129.09 E |
| Sawai, Teluk ⊂ | 164 | 2.52 S | 129.12 E |
| Sawāi Mādhopur | 124 | 25.59 N | 76.22 E |
| Sawākin | 140 | 19.07 N | 37.20 E |
| Sawal, Gunung ∧ | 115a | 7.12 S | 108.16 E |
| Sawan, Indon. | 115b | 8.08 S | 115.11 E |
| Sawan, Mya. | 110 | 24.30 N | 96.19 E |
| Sawang | 114 | 0.45 N | 103.21 E |
| Sawankhalok | 110 | 17.19 N | 99.50 E |
| Sawara | 94 | 35.53 N | 140.30 E |
| Sawata | 92 | 38.00 N | 138.16 E |
| Sawatch Range ⋀ | 200 | 39.10 N | 106.25 W |
| Sawbridgeworth | 42 | 51.50 N | 0.09 E |
| Sawdā', Jabal as- ⋀[2] | 146 | 28.40 N | 15.30 E |
| Sawdā', Qurnat as- ∧ | 130 | 34.18 N | 36.07 E |
| Sawdirī | 140 | 14.25 N | 29.05 E |
| Sawel Mountain ∧ | 48 | 54.49 N | 7.02 W |
| Sawhāj | 140 | 26.33 N | 31.42 E |
| Sawi | 110 | 10.14 N | 99.07 E |
| Sawin, Lac ⊜ | 206 | 46.32 N | 73.54 W |
| Sawknah | 146 | 29.04 N | 15.47 E |
| Şawl | 142 | 29.21 N | 31.14 E |
| Sawla | 150 | 9.17 N | 2.25 W |
| Saw Log Creek ≃ | 198 | 38.07 N | 99.42 W |
| Saw Mill ≃ | 276 | 40.56 N | 73.53 W |
| Sawmill Brook ≃, Ma., U.S. | 283 | 42.34 N | 70.46 W |
| Sawmill Brook ≃, N.J., U.S. | 276 | 40.28 N | 74.26 W |
| Sawmill Creek ≃, N.J., U.S. | 276 | 40.46 N | 74.05 W |
| Sawmill Creek ≃, Pa., U.S. | 279b | 40.10 N | 79.58 W |
| Sawmill Pond Brook ≃ | 276 | 41.10 N | 74.23 W |
| Sawmill Run ≃ | 285 | 40.07 N | 75.21 W |
| Sawmills | 154 | 19.31 S | 28.02 E |
| Şawqirah, Ghubbat ⊂ | 118 | 18.35 N | 57.00 E |
| Sawston | 42 | 52.07 N | 0.10 E |
| Sawtayr ∓[4] | 140 | 17.03 N | 30.24 E |
| Sawtooth National Recreation Area ♦ | 202 | 44.00 N | 114.55 W |
| Sawtry | 42 | 52.27 N | 0.17 W |
| Sawu, Laut (Savu Sea) ∓[2] | 112 | 9.40 S | 122.00 E |
| Sawu, Pulau I | 112 | 10.30 S | 121.54 E |
| Sawyer, Mi., U.S. | 216 | 41.53 N | 86.35 W |
| Sawyer, N.D., U.S. | 198 | 48.05 N | 101.03 W |
| Sawyers Hill ∧[2] | 186 | 47.11 N | 53.52 W |
| Sawyers Valley | 168a | 31.54 S | 116.13 E |
| Sawyerville, P.Q., Can. | 206 | 45.20 N | 71.34 W |
| Sawyerville, Il., U.S. | 219 | 39.05 N | 89.48 W |
| Sawyerwood | 214 | 41.02 N | 81.27 W |
| Saxby ≃ | 166 | 18.25 S | 140.53 E |
| Saxdalen | 40 | 60.09 N | 14.57 E |
| Saxen ⊜ | 40 | 59.46 N | 14.25 E |
| Saxike | 120 | 30.44 N | 86.22 E |
| Saxilby | 44 | 53.17 N | 0.40 W |
| Saxis | 208 | 37.55 N | 75.43 W |
| Saxmundham | 42 | 52.13 N | 1.29 E |
| Saxon, Schw. | 58 | 46.09 N | 7.11 E |
| Saxon, Wi., U.S. | 190 | 46.29 N | 90.24 W |
| Saxonburg | 214 | 40.45 N | 79.49 W |
| Saxon Woods Park ♦ | 276 | 40.59 N | 73.45 W |
| Saxony → Sachsen □[3] | 30 | 51.00 N | 13.00 E |
| Saxony → Sachsen □[9] | 30 | 52.45 N | 9.30 E |
| Saxton | 214 | 40.12 N | 78.14 W |
| Say | 150 | 13.07 N | 2.21 E |
| Sāy, Jazīrat I | 140 | 20.42 N | 30.20 E |
| Saya de Malha Bank ✢[4] | 12 | 10.30 S | 61.30 E |
| Sayama, Nihon | 94 | 35.51 N | 139.24 E |
| Sayama, Nihon | 270 | 34.31 N | 135.34 E |
| Sayama-kyūryō ⋀[2] | 268 | 35.47 N | 139.24 E |
| Sayán | 248 | 11.08 S | 77.12 W |
| Sayan Mountains (Sajany) ⋀ | 88 | 52.45 N | 96.00 E |
| Sayansk | 88 | 54.02 N | 102.06 E |
| Sayaxché | 232 | 16.31 N | 90.10 W |
| Saybrook, Il., U.S. | 216 | 40.25 N | 88.31 W |
| Saybrook, Oh., U.S. | 214 | 41.50 N | 80.51 W |
| Saybrook Manor | 207 | 41.17 N | 72.23 W |
| Sayda, Dtsch. | 54 | 50.43 N | 13.25 E |
| Şaydā (Sidon), Lubnān | 132 | 33.33 N | 35.22 E |
| Şaydā □[4] | 132 | 33.15 N | 35.15 E |
| Şaydnāyā | 132 | 33.42 N | 36.22 E |
| Sayghān | 120 | 35.11 N | 67.42 E |
| Sayḥūt | 144 | 15.12 N | 51.14 E |
| Sayil ⊥ | 232 | 20.16 N | 89.42 W |
| Saylah | 142 | 29.21 N | 30.58 E |
| Saylorsburg | 210 | 40.54 N | 75.19 W |
| Saylorville Lake ⊜[1] | 190 | 41.48 N | 93.46 W |
| Saylūn, Khirbat (Shiloh) ⊥ | 132 | 32.03 N | 35.17 E |
| Säynätsalo | 26 | 62.08 N | 25.46 E |
| Sayō | 96 | 35.00 N | 134.22 E |
| Şayqal, Baḥr ⊜ | 132 | 33.40 N | 37.06 E |
| Sayram Hu ⊜ | 86 | 44.36 N | 81.13 E |
| Sayre, Ok., U.S. | 196 | 35.17 N | 99.38 W |
| Sayre, Pa., U.S. | 210 | 41.58 N | 76.30 W |
| Sayreville | 208 | 40.27 N | 74.21 W |
| Sayula | 234 | 19.52 N | 103.37 W |
| Sayula, Laguna de ⊜ | 234 | 20.03 N | 103.31 W |
| Sayula de Alemán | 234 | 17.52 N | 94.57 W |
| Sayultepec | 234 | 17.27 N | 97.17 W |
| Sayville | 210 | 40.44 N | 73.04 W |
| Sayward | 182 | 50.22 N | 125.55 W |
| Saywūn | 144 | 15.56 N | 48.47 E |
| Saza | 92 | 33.14 N | 129.39 E |
| Sazanit I | 38 | 40.30 N | 19.16 E |
| Sazdy, Kaz. | 80 | 46.57 N | 49.19 E |
| Sazdy, Kaz. | 86 | 47.22 N | 61.48 E |
| Saze | 62 | 43.56 N | 4.41 E |
| Sažino | 86 | 56.20 N | 58.11 E |
| Sazlijka ≃ | 38 | 42.02 N | 25.52 E |
| Şazonovo | 76 | 59.04 N | 35.14 E |
| Šazud | 120 | 37.43 N | 72.11 E |
| Sazykul', ozero ⊜ | 86 | 55.22 N | 67.34 E |
| Sba | 148 | 28.13 N | 0.08 W |
| Sbeïtla | 148 | 35.14 N | 9.08 E |
| Sbiba | 36 | 35.33 N | 9.05 E |
| Şcaddan | 162 | 33.27 S | 121.43 E |
| Ščadryn | 76 | 52.53 N | 29.33 E |
| Scaër | 32 | 48.02 N | 3.42 W |
| Scafati | 68 | 40.45 N | 14.31 E |
| Scafell Pikes ∧ | 44 | 54.27 N | 3.12 W |
| Scaggsville | 208 | 39.09 N | 76.54 W |
| Scajaquada Creek ≃ | 284a | 42.56 N | 78.53 W |
| Scala, Teatro alla ʊ | 266b | 45.28 N | 9.11 E |
| Scala Coeli | 68 | 39.27 N | 16.53 E |
| Scalasaig | 46 | 56.04 N | 6.11 W |
| Scalby | 44 | 54.18 N | 0.27 W |
| Scalea | 68 | 39.49 N | 15.48 E |
| Scaletta Zanclea | 70 | 38.03 N | 15.28 E |
| Scalloway | 46a | 60.08 N | 1.18 W |
| Scalpay I, Scot., U.K. | 46 | 57.52 N | 6.40 W |
| Scalpay I, Scot., U.K. | 46 | 57.17 N | 5.59 W |
| Scalp Level | 214 | 40.14 N | 78.50 W |
| Scalp Mountain ∧[2] | 48 | 55.04 N | 7.24 W |
| Scammon | 198 | 37.16 N | 94.49 W |
| Scammon Bay | 180 | 61.53 N | 165.38 W |
| Scammon Bay ⊂ | 180 | 61.53 N | 165.54 W |
| Scammonden Water ⊜[1] | 262 | 53.38 N | 1.56 W |
| Scampton | 44 | 53.18 N | 0.34 W |
| Scandale | 68 | 39.07 N | 16.57 E |
| Scandia | 198 | 39.47 N | 97.47 W |
| Scandiano | 64 | 44.36 N | 10.43 E |
| Scandicci | 66 | 43.45 N | 11.11 E |
| Scanlon | 190 | 46.42 N | 92.25 W |
| Scanno | 66 | 41.54 N | 13.53 E |
| Scansano | 66 | 42.41 N | 11.20 E |
| Scantic ≃ | 207 | 41.52 N | 72.38 W |
| Scapa | 182 | 51.52 N | 111.59 W |
| Scapa Flow ⊂ | 46 | 58.55 N | 3.06 W |
| Scapegoat Mountain ∧ | 202 | 47.19 N | 112.50 W |
| Ščapino | 74 | 55.19 N | 159.25 E |
| Ščapov | 80 | 51.01 N | 51.11 E |
| Ščapovo | 82 | 55.09 N | 38.11 E |
| Scappoose | 224 | 45.45 N | 122.52 W |
| Şcar ≃ | 44 | 55.13 N | 3.46 W |
| Ščara ≃ | 76 | 53.27 N | 24.45 E |
| Scaramia, Capo > | 70 | 36.47 N | 14.29 E |
| Scarba I | 46 | 56.11 N | 5.43 W |
| Scarborough, Austl. | 168a | 31.54 S | 115.45 E |
| Scarborough, On., Can. | 212 | 43.47 N | 79.15 W |
| Scarborough, Trin. | 241r | 11.11 N | 60.44 W |
| Scarborough, Eng., U.K. | 44 | 54.17 N | 0.24 W |
| Scarborough Centre ◆[9] | 275b | 43.47 N | 79.16 W |
| Scarborough Point > | 171a | 27.12 S | 153.07 E |
| Scarborough Reef ✢[2] | 116 | 15.08 N | 117.46 E |
| Scardroy | 46 | 57.31 N | 4.59 W |
| Scargill | 172 | 42.56 S | 172.57 E |
| Scarinish | 46 | 56.29 N | 6.48 W |
| Scarisbrick | 262 | 53.37 N | 2.56 W |
| Scărișoara | 38 | 44.00 N | 24.35 E |
| Scarlino | 66 | 42.54 N | 10.51 E |
| Scarp I | 46 | 58.02 N | 7.08 W |
| Scarpe ≃ | 50 | 50.30 N | 3.27 E |
| Scarperia | 66 | 44.00 N | 11.21 E |
| Scarper Peak ∧ | 282 | 37.32 N | 122.26 W |
| Scarriff | 48 | 52.55 N | 8.31 W |
| Scarsdale, Austl. | 169 | 37.40 S | 143.40 E |
| Scarsdale, N.Y., U.S. | 210 | 40.59 N | 73.49 W |
| Scartaglin | 48 | 52.10 N | 9.26 W |
| Scarth Hill | 262 | 53.33 N | 2.52 W |
| Scatarie Island I | 186 | 46.00 N | 59.44 W |
| Scatter Creek ≃ | 224 | 46.48 N | 123.06 W |
| Scauri, It. | 66 | 41.15 N | 13.42 E |
| Scauri, It. | 70 | 36.45 N | 11.58 E |
| Scavaig, Loch ⊂ | 46 | 57.09 N | 6.10 W |
| Scawfell Island I | 166 | 20.52 S | 149.36 E |
| Sceaux | 50 | 48.47 N | 2.17 E |
| Sceaux, Château de ⊥ | 261 | 48.46 N | 2.18 E |
| Ščedrovka | 83 | 49.30 N | 40.17 E |
| Ščeglovo | 265a | 60.02 N | 30.46 E |
| Ščeljajur | 24 | 65.21 N | 53.21 E |
| Ščelkan ≃ | 80 | 50.47 N | 43.33 E |
| Ščelkovo | 76 | 55.55 N | 38.00 E |
| Ščemilovo | 265b | 55.48 N | 38.05 E |
| Scena | 64 | 46.41 N | 11.12 E |
| Scenery Hill | 214 | 40.05 N | 80.04 W |
| Sceptre | 184 | 50.51 N | 109.15 W |
| Ščerbakovo, Ross. | 74 | 65.15 N | 160.30 E |
| Ščerbakovo, Ross. | 86 | 56.01 N | 73.29 E |
| Ščerbakty | 86 | 52.29 N | 78.09 E |
| Ščerbinka | 82 | 55.31 N | 37.35 E |
| Scerni | 66 | 42.07 N | 14.34 E |
| Scey-sur-Saône-et-Saint-Albin | 58 | 47.40 N | 5.58 E |
| Schaale ≃ | 54 | 53.21 N | 10.49 E |
| Schaalsee ⊜ | 54 | 53.35 N | 10.57 E |
| Schaan | 58 | 47.10 N | 9.31 E |
| Schabs → Sciaves | 64 | 46.46 N | 11.40 E |
| Schachendorf | 61 | 47.16 N | 16.26 E |
| Schaefferstown | 208 | 40.17 N | 76.17 W |
| Schaephuysen | 263 | 51.26 N | 6.29 E |
| Schaerbeek | 50 | 50.51 N | 4.23 E |
| Schafberg ∧ | 64 | 47.47 N | 13.27 E |
| Schäferberg ∧[2] | 264a | 52.25 N | 13.08 E |
| Schaffhausen | 58 | 47.42 N | 8.38 E |
| Schaffhausen □[3] | 58 | 47.40 N | 8.35 E |
| Schafstädt | 54 | 51.23 N | 11.46 E |
| Schäftlarn | 64 | 47.59 N | 11.28 E |
| Schagen | 52 | 52.46 N | 4.47 E |
| Schaghticoke | 210 | 42.54 N | 73.35 W |
| Schalchen | 60 | 48.07 N | 13.10 E |
| Schale | 52 | 52.26 N | 7.37 E |
| Schalkau | 54 | 50.24 N | 11.00 E |
| Schalke ◆[8] | 263 | 51.31 N | 7.05 E |
| Schälker Heide ◆[3] | 263 | 51.24 N | 7.36 E |
| Schalksmühle | 56 | 51.14 N | 7.31 E |
| Schaller | 198 | 42.30 N | 95.18 W |
| Schanck, Cape > | 169 | 38.30 S | 144.53 E |
| S-Chanf | 58 | 46.36 N | 9.59 E |
| Schanfigg V | 58 | 46.51 N | 9.38 E |
| Schanghai → Shanghai | 106 | 31.14 N | 121.28 E |
| Schangnau | 58 | 46.50 N | 7.52 E |
| Schapbach | 58 | 48.22 N | 8.17 E |
| Schapen | 52 | 52.24 N | 7.33 E |
| Şchaprode | 54 | 54.31 N | 13.10 E |
| Šchara, gora ∧ | 84 | 43.00 N | 43.06 E |
| Scharbeutz | 54 | 54.03 N | 10.44 E |
| Schardenberg | 60 | 48.32 N | 13.30 E |
| Schardenberg ∧[2] | 263 | 51.27 N | 6.28 E |
| Schärding | 60 | 48.27 N | 13.26 E |
| Scharhörn I | 52 | 53.57 N | 8.25 E |
| Schari → Chari ≃ | 146 | 12.58 N | 14.31 E |
| Scharmützelsee ⊜ | 54 | 52.15 N | 14.03 E |
| Scharnhorst ◆[8] | 263 | 51.32 N | 7.32 E |
| Scharnitz | 60 | 47.23 N | 11.17 E |
| Scharnitzer Klause )( | 64 | 47.24 N | 11.16 E |
| Scharrel | 52 | 53.04 N | 7.42 E |
| Scharzfeld | 52 | 51.37 N | 10.22 E |
| Schässburg → Sighișoara | 38 | 46.13 N | 24.48 E |
| Schauinsland ∧ | 58 | 47.55 N | 7.54 E |
| Schaumburg | 216 | 42.02 N | 88.05 W |
| Schaut | 84 | 43.43 N | 42.32 E |
| Schebeli → Shabeelle ≃ | 144 | 0.12 S | 42.45 E |
| Schechen | 64 | 47.56 N | 12.08 E |
| Scheessel | 52 | 53.10 N | 9.29 E |
| Schefferville | 176 | 54.48 N | 66.50 W |
| Scheggia | 66 | 43.24 N | 12.40 E |
| Scheggino | 66 | 42.43 N | 12.50 E |
| Scheibbs | 61 | 48.00 N | 15.10 E |
| Scheiblingstein | 264b | 48.16 N | 16.13 E |
| Scheidegg | 58 | 47.35 N | 9.51 E |
| Scheifling | 61 | 47.09 N | 14.24 E |
| Scheinfeld | 56 | 49.40 N | 10.27 E |
| Schelde (Escaut) ≃ | 50 | 51.22 N | 4.15 E |
| Schelklingen | 58 | 48.22 N | 9.44 E |
| Schell Creek Range ⋀ | 204 | 39.10 N | 114.40 W |
| Schellenberg ∧ | 60 | 48.18 N | 13.03 E |
| Schellerten | 52 | 52.11 N | 10.06 E |
| Schellsburg | 214 | 40.03 N | 78.39 W |
| Schelsen ◆[8] | 263 | 51.09 N | 6.31 E |
| Schemmerhofen | 58 | 48.11 N | 9.47 E |
| Schenectady | 210 | 42.48 N | 73.56 W |
| Schenectady □[6] | 210 | 42.47 N | 73.53 W |
| Schenefeld | 52 | 53.36 N | 9.49 E |
| Schenevus | 210 | 42.32 N | 74.49 W |
| Schenevus Creek ≃ | 210 | 42.29 N | 74.59 W |
| Schenkendorf | 264a | 52.16 N | 13.35 E |
| Schenkenhorst | 264a | 52.20 N | 13.12 E |
| Schenklengsfeld | 56 | 50.49 N | 9.50 E |
| Schenley | 214 | 40.41 N | 79.40 W |
| Schenley Park ♦ | 279b | 40.26 N | 79.56 W |
| Scheppach | 58 | 48.25 N | 10.27 E |
| Schepsdorf-Lohne | 52 | 52.30 N | 7.16 E |
| Schererville | 216 | 41.30 N | 87.27 W |
| Scherfede | 52 | 51.32 N | 9.02 E |
| Scherlebeck | 263 | 51.37 N | 7.08 E |
| Schermbeck | 52 | 51.41 N | 6.52 E |
| Schermerhorn | 52 | 52.36 N | 4.52 E |
| Schermützelsee ⊜ | 54 | 52.34 N | 14.04 E |
| Scherpenheuvel | 56 | 50.59 N | 4.59 E |
| Scherpenzeel | 52 | 52.05 N | 5.30 E |
| Schertz | 196 | 29.33 N | 98.16 W |
| Schesch, Erg → Chech, Erg ◆[2] | 148 | 25.00 N | 2.15 W |
| Schesslitz | 60 | 49.59 N | 11.01 E |
| Schevelinger-Stausee ⊜[1] | 263 | 51.08 N | 7.26 E |
| Scheveningen ◆[8] | 52 | 52.06 N | 4.18 E |
| Schiedam | 52 | 51.55 N | 4.24 E |
| Schieder | 52 | 51.55 N | 9.09 E |
| Schiefbahn | 56 | 51.14 N | 6.31 E |
| Schiehallion ∧ | 46 | 56.40 N | 4.06 W |
| Schierke | 54 | 51.46 N | 10.40 E |
| Schierling | 60 | 48.50 N | 12.08 E |
| Schiermonnikoog | 52 | 53.24 N | 6.10 E |
| Schiermonnikoog I | 52 | 53.28 N | 6.15 E |
| Schiers | 58 | 46.59 N | 9.41 E |
| Schiessen | 58 | 48.18 N | 10.14 E |
| Schiffdorf | 52 | 53.32 N | 8.39 E |
| Schiffenensee ⊜ | 58 | 46.50 N | 7.10 E |
| Schifferstadt | 56 | 49.23 N | 8.22 E |
| Schiffshebewerk ◆[5] | 263 | 51.37 N | 7.19 E |
| Schihkiatschwang → Shijiazhuang | 98 | 38.03 N | 114.28 E |
| Schijndel | 52 | 51.37 N | 5.25 E |
| Schikoku → Shikoku I | 92 | 33.45 N | 133.30 E |
| Schilde | 56 | 51.14 N | 4.34 E |
| Schilde ≃ | 54 | 53.26 N | 10.53 E |
| Schildow | 54 | 52.38 N | 13.23 E |
| Schildwolde | 52 | 53.14 N | 6.49 E |
| Schiller Park | 216 | 41.57 N | 87.52 W |
| Schillingsfürst | 56 | 49.17 N | 10.15 E |
| Schillingstedt | 54 | 51.14 N | 11.11 E |
| Schilpario | 64 | 46.01 N | 10.09 E |
| Schiltach | 58 | 48.17 N | 8.20 E |
| Schiltigheim | 58 | 48.36 N | 7.45 E |
| Schimborn | 56 | 50.03 N | 9.11 E |
| Schimmert | 56 | 50.55 N | 5.50 E |
| Schinveld | 56 | 50.57 N | 5.59 E |
| Schinznach Bad | 58 | 47.27 N | 8.10 E |
| Schio | 64 | 45.43 N | 11.21 E |
| Schipbeek ≃ | 52 | 52.14 N | 6.09 E |
| Schiphol, Luchthaven ⊠ | 52 | 52.17 N | 4.40 E |
| Schipkau | 54 | 51.31 N | 13.53 E |
| Schirgiswalde | 54 | 51.05 N | 14.27 E |
| Schirmeck | 58 | 48.29 N | 7.13 E |
| Schirnding | 54 | 50.05 N | 12.13 E |
| Schisuoka → Shizuoka | 94 | 34.58 N | 138.23 E |
| Schjetman Reef ✢[2] | 14 | 15.10 N | 178.40 W |
| Schkeuditz | 54 | 51.24 N | 12.13 E |
| Schkoder-See → Scutari, Lake ⊜ | 38 | 42.12 N | 19.18 E |
| Schkölen | 54 | 51.02 N | 11.49 E |
| Schkopau | 54 | 51.23 N | 11.59 E |
| Schladen | 54 | 52.01 N | 10.32 E |
| Schladming | 64 | 47.23 N | 13.41 E |
| Schlanders → Silandro | 64 | 46.38 N | 10.46 E |
| Schlangen | 52 | 51.49 N | 8.50 E |
| Schlangenbad | 56 | 50.05 N | 8.05 E |
| Schlänitz-See ⊜ | 264a | 52.27 N | 12.57 E |
| Schlanstedt | 54 | 52.00 N | 11.02 E |
| Schlater | 194 | 33.38 N | 90.20 W |
| Schlegel Lake ⊜ | 276 | 40.59 N | 74.03 W |
| Schlei ⊂ | 41 | 54.36 N | 9.51 E |
| Schleiden | 56 | 50.31 N | 6.28 E |
| Schleife | 54 | 51.32 N | 14.32 E |
| Schleinitz Range ⋀ | 164 | 3.10 S | 151.40 E |
| Schleithal | 56 | 48.59 N | 8.02 E |
| Schleitheim | 58 | 47.45 N | 8.29 E |
| Schleiz | 54 | 50.34 N | 11.49 E |
| Schlema | 54 | 50.40 N | 12.40 E |
| Schlepzig | 54 | 52.01 N | 13.53 E |
| Schlesien → Silesia □[9] | 30 | 51.00 N | 16.45 E |
| Schlesischer (Ost) Bahnhof ◆[5] | 264a | 52.30 N | 13.26 E |
| Schleswig, Dtsch. | 41 | 54.31 N | 9.33 E |
| Schleswig, Ia., U.S. | 198 | 42.09 N | 95.26 W |
| Schleswig-Holstein □[3] | 30 | 54.20 N | 9.40 E |
| Schlettau | 54 | 50.33 N | 12.56 E |
| Schlettstadt → Sélestat | 58 | 48.16 N | 7.27 E |
| Schleusingen | 54 | 50.31 N | 10.45 E |
| Schlicke ∧ | 58 | 47.31 N | 10.37 E |
| Schlieben | 54 | 51.43 N | 13.23 E |
| Schliengen | 58 | 47.46 N | 7.35 E |
| Schlieren | 58 | 47.24 N | 8.27 E |
| Schliersee | 64 | 47.44 N | 11.51 E |
| Schlitz | 56 | 50.40 N | 9.33 E |
| Schloss Holte-Stukenbrock | 52 | 51.54 N | 8.39 E |
| Schloss Neuhaus | 52 | 51.44 N | 8.43 E |
| Schlossvippach | 54 | 51.06 N | 11.08 E |
| Schlotheim | 54 | 51.14 N | 10.39 E |
| Schluchsee | 58 | 47.49 N | 8.10 E |
| Schluchsee ⊜ | 58 | 47.49 N | 8.10 E |
| Schlucht, Col de la )( | 58 | 48.04 N | 7.02 E |
| Schlüchtern | 56 | 50.20 N | 9.31 E |
| Schluderns → Sluderno | 64 | 46.40 N | 10.35 E |
| Schlüsselburg | 52 | 52.29 N | 9.04 E |
| Schlüsselfeld | 56 | 49.45 N | 10.37 E |
| Schlutup ◆[8] | 54 | 53.53 N | 10.48 E |
| Schmachtendorf ◆[8] | 263 | 51.32 N | 6.49 E |
| Schmalfeld | 52 | 53.52 N | 9.58 E |
| Schmallenberg | 56 | 51.09 N | 8.17 E |
| Schmalnau | 56 | 50.27 N | 9.47 E |
| Schmannewitz | 54 | 51.24 N | 12.58 E |
| Schmarsau | 54 | 52.54 N | 11.21 E |
| Schmelz | 56 | 49.27 N | 6.51 E |
| Schmida ≃ | 61 | 48.21 N | 16.09 E |
| Schmidmühlen | 60 | 49.16 N | 11.56 E |
| Schmidt | 56 | 50.39 N | 6.25 E |
| Schmidtsdrif | 158 | 28.41 S | 24.02 E |
| Schmiedeberg | 54 | 50.50 N | 13.40 E |
| Schmiedefeld | 54 | 50.37 N | 10.49 E |
| Schmöckwitz ◆[8] | 264a | 52.23 N | 13.39 E |
| Schmölln | 54 | 50.53 N | 12.20 E |
| Schmutter ≃ | 58 | 48.42 N | 10.46 E |
| Schnabelwaid | 60 | 49.49 N | 11.35 E |
| Schnackenburg | 54 | 53.02 N | 11.32 E |
| Schnaitsee | 60 | 48.04 N | 12.22 E |
| Schnaittach | 60 | 49.31 N | 11.19 E |
| Schnaittenbach | 60 | 49.33 N | 12.01 E |
| Schnakenbek | 52 | 53.23 N | 10.30 E |
| Schnecksville | 208 | 40.41 N | 75.36 W |
| Schneeberg | 54 | 50.36 N | 12.38 E |
| Schneeberg ∧, Dtsch. | 54 | 50.03 N | 11.51 E |
| Schneeberg ∧, Öst. | 61 | 47.47 N | 15.47 E |
| Schneidemühl → Piła | 30 | 53.10 N | 16.44 E |
| Schneider | 216 | 41.11 N | 87.26 W |
| Schneifel ⋀[1] | 56 | 50.15 N | 6.25 E |
| Schnelldorf | 56 | 49.12 N | 10.11 E |
| Schneverdingen | 52 | 53.07 N | 9.47 E |
| Schney | 56 | 50.10 N | 11.04 E |
| Schober Gruppe ⋀ | 64 | 46.55 N | 12.42 E |
| Schobüll | 41 | 54.30 N | 9.00 E |
| Schöckl ∧ | 61 | 47.11 N | 15.28 E |
| Schodn'a | 82 | 55.57 N | 37.18 E |
| Schodn'a ≃ | 265b | 55.50 N | 37.25 E |
| Schœlcher | 240e | 14.37 N | 61.06 W |
| Schoenbrunn Village State Memorial ⊥ | 214 | 40.27 N | 81.24 W |
| Schofield | 190 | 44.54 N | 89.36 W |
| Schofield Barracks ■ | 229c | 21.30 N | 158.04 W |
| Schofields | 274a | 33.42 S | 150.52 E |
| Schöftland | 58 | 47.18 N | 8.03 E |
| Schoharie | 210 | 42.39 N | 74.18 W |
| Schoharie □[6] | 210 | 42.40 N | 74.19 W |
| Schoharie Creek ≃ | 210 | 42.57 N | 74.18 W |
| Schoharie Reservoir ⊜[1] | 210 | 42.22 N | 74.26 W |
| Scholen | 52 | 52.44 N | 8.46 E |
| Scholes | 44 | 53.49 N | 1.25 W |
| Schollene | 54 | 52.41 N | 12.13 E |
| Schöllenen V | 58 | 46.40 N | 8.35 E |
| Schöller ◆[8] | 263 | 51.14 N | 7.01 E |
| Schöllkrippen | 56 | 50.05 N | 9.14 E |
| Schöllnach | 60 | 48.45 N | 13.11 E |
| Scholls | 224 | 45.24 N | 122.55 W |
| Scholven ◆[8] | 263 | 51.36 N | 7.01 E |
| Schomberg, On., Can. | 212 | 44.00 N | 79.41 W |
| Schömberg, Dtsch. | 56 | 48.47 N | 8.38 E |
| Schömberg, Dtsch. | 58 | 48.13 N | 8.46 E |
| Schonach | 58 | 48.08 N | 8.11 E |
| Schönaich | 56 | 48.39 N | 9.03 E |
| Schönau, Dtsch. | 56 | 49.26 N | 8.49 E |
| Schönau, Dtsch. | 58 | 47.47 N | 7.53 E |
| Schönau, Dtsch. | 64 | 47.37 N | 12.59 E |
| Schönbeck | 54 | 53.34 N | 13.34 E |
| Schönberg, Dtsch. | 54 | 50.31 N | 11.57 E |
| Schönberg, Dtsch. | 54 | 50.11 N | 12.19 E |
| Schönberg, Dtsch. | 54 | 53.51 N | 10.56 E |
| Schönberg, Dtsch. | 54 | 54.23 N | 10.22 E |
| Schönberg, Dtsch. | 60 | 48.50 N | 13.20 E |
| Schönberger Strand | 54 | 54.25 N | 10.24 E |
| Schönberg im Stubaital | 64 | 47.11 N | 11.25 E |
| Schönborn | 54 | 51.36 N | 13.30 E |
| Schönbrunn | 54 | 50.32 N | 10.53 E |
| Schönbrunn, Schloss ʊ | 264b | 48.11 N | 16.19 E |
| Schönbrunner Schlosspark ♦ | 264b | 48.11 N | 16.19 E |
| Schondorf | 64 | 48.04 N | 11.07 E |
| Schondra ≃ | 56 | 50.07 N | 9.44 E |
| Schönebeck, Dtsch. | 54 | 53.03 N | 12.13 E |
| Schönebeck, Dtsch. | 54 | 52.01 N | 11.44 E |
| Schönebeck ◆[8] | 263 | 51.28 N | 6.56 E |
| Schöneberg ◆[8] | 264a | 52.29 N | 13.21 E |
| Schöneck, Dtsch. | 54 | 50.23 N | 12.20 E |
| Schöneck, Dtsch. | 56 | 50.13 N | 8.52 E |
| Schönecken | 56 | 50.09 N | 6.27 E |
| Schönefeld | 264a | 52.23 N | 13.30 E |
| Schöneiche | 54 | 52.28 N | 13.41 E |
| Schönenwerd | 58 | 47.22 N | 8.00 E |
| Schönerlinde | 264a | 52.39 N | 13.27 E |
| Schönewalde | 54 | 51.49 N | 13.13 E |
| Schönfeld | 264a | 52.41 N | 13.44 E |
| Schönfliess | 264a | 52.39 N | 13.20 E |
| Schongau | 58 | 47.49 N | 10.54 E |
| Schönhagen, Dtsch. | 41 | 54.38 N | 10.01 E |
| Schönhagen, Dtsch. | 52 | 51.41 N | 9.33 E |
| Schönhausen, Dtsch. | 54 | 52.35 N | 12.02 E |
| Schönhausen, Dtsch. | 263 | 51.37 N | 7.38 E |
| Schönheide | 54 | 50.30 N | 12.31 E |
| Schönholthausen | 56 | 51.11 N | 8.00 E |
| Schöningen | 54 | 52.08 N | 10.58 E |
| Schönkirchen | 54 | 54.20 N | 10.15 E |
| Schönmünzach | 56 | 48.36 N | 8.22 E |
| Schonnebeck ◆[8] | 263 | 51.29 N | 7.04 E |
| Schönningstedt | 52 | 53.32 N | 10.15 E |
| Schönow | 54 | 52.40 N | 13.32 E |
| Schönsee | 60 | 49.31 N | 12.33 E |
| Schönthal | 60 | 49.21 N | 12.36 E |
| Schonungen | 56 | 50.03 N | 10.18 E |
| Schönwald, Dtsch. | 54 | 50.12 N | 12.05 E |
| Schönwald, Dtsch. | 58 | 48.06 N | 8.11 E |
| Schönwalde, Dtsch. | 54 | 54.11 N | 10.45 E |
| Schönwalde, Dtsch. | 54 | 52.40 N | 13.26 E |
| Schönwalde, Dtsch. | 54 | 52.37 N | 13.07 E |
| Schönwalde, Dtsch. | 54 | 51.59 N | 13.45 E |
| Schönwies | 58 | 47.11 N | 10.39 E |
| Schoodic Lake ⊜ | 188 | 45.21 N | 68.54 W |
| Schoolcraft | 216 | 42.06 N | 85.38 W |
| Schoolhouse Run ≃ | 285 | 40.13 N | 75.27 W |
| Schoombee | 158 | 31.28 S | 25.30 E |
| Schoondijke | 52 | 51.21 N | 3.32 E |
| Schoonebeek | 52 | 52.40 N | 6.53 E |
| Schoonhoven | 52 | 51.56 N | 4.51 E |
| Schoorl | 52 | 52.42 N | 4.41 E |
| Schopfheim | 58 | 47.39 N | 7.49 E |
| Schopfloch | 56 | 49.07 N | 10.18 E |
| Schopp | 56 | 49.21 N | 7.41 E |
| Schöppenstedt | 54 | 52.08 N | 10.46 E |
| Schöppingen | 52 | 52.05 N | 7.14 E |
| Schorfheide | 54 | 52.56 N | 13.43 E |
| Schorfheide ◆[3] | 54 | 52.55 N | 13.35 E |
| Schörfling | 64 | 47.56 N | 13.36 E |
| Schorndorf | 56 | 48.48 N | 9.31 E |
| Schortens | 52 | 53.31 N | 7.56 E |
| Schoten | 50 | 51.15 N | 4.30 E |
| Schötmar | 52 | 52.04 N | 8.45 E |
| Schotten | 56 | 50.30 N | 9.07 E |
| Schottland → Scotland □[8] | 28 | 57.00 N | 4.00 W |
| Schouten, Kepulauan II | 164 | 0.55 S | 135.55 E |
| Schouten Island I | 166 | 42.19 S | 148.17 E |
| Schouten Islands II | 164 | 3.30 S | 144.40 E |
| Schouwen I | 52 | 51.43 N | 3.50 E |
| Schrader Creek ≃ | 210 | 41.43 N | 76.30 W |
| Schrader Range ⋀ | 164 | 5.05 S | 144.15 E |
| Schramberg | 58 | 48.13 N | 8.23 E |
| Schram City | 219 | 39.09 N | 89.27 W |
| Schrankogel ∧ | 64 | 47.02 N | 11.06 E |
| Schraplau | 54 | 51.26 N | 11.40 E |
| Schreiber | 190 | 48.48 N | 87.15 W |
| Schrems | 61 | 48.47 N | 15.04 E |
| Schrick | 61 | 48.30 N | 16.37 E |
| Schriesheim | 56 | 49.29 N | 8.40 E |
| Schriever | 194 | 29.44 N | 90.48 W |
| Schrobenhausen | 60 | 48.33 N | 11.17 E |
| Schröcken | 58 | 47.15 N | 10.05 E |
| Schroffenstein ∧ | 158 | 27.11 S | 18.42 E |
| Schroon ≃ | 188 | 43.29 N | 73.49 W |
| Schroon Lake ⊜ | 188 | 43.47 N | 73.46 W |
| Schrozberg | 56 | 49.20 N | 9.59 E |
| Schruns | 58 | 47.04 N | 9.55 E |
| Schulenburg | 222 | 29.40 N | 96.54 W |
| Schuls → Scuol | 58 | 46.48 N | 10.18 E |
| Schultz Lake ⊜ | 176 | 64.45 N | 97.30 W |
| Schulzendorf | 54 | 52.22 N | 13.35 E |
| Schulzenhöhe | 264a | 52.29 N | 13.47 E |
| Schumacher | 190 | 48.28 N | 81.18 W |
| Schüpfheim | 58 | 46.57 N | 8.01 E |
| Schüren ◆[8] | 263 | 51.30 N | 7.32 E |
| Schurwald ⋀ | 56 | 48.46 N | 9.29 E |
| Schussen ≃ | 58 | 47.37 N | 9.32 E |
| Schussenried | 58 | 48.00 N | 9.40 E |
| Schüttenberg ∧[2] | 61 | 48.05 N | 16.44 E |
| Schutter ≃ | 58 | 48.34 N | 7.50 E |
| Schüttorf | 52 | 52.19 N | 7.13 E |
| Schuyler, Ne., U.S. | 198 | 41.26 N | 97.03 W |
| Schuyler, Va., U.S. | 192 | 37.47 N | 78.41 W |
| Schuyler □[6], Il., U.S. | 219 | 40.07 N | 90.34 W |
| Schuyler □[6], N.Y., U.S. | 210 | 42.23 N | 76.52 W |
| Schuyler Lake | 210 | 42.47 N | 75.02 W |
| Schuylerville | 210 | 43.06 N | 73.34 W |
| Schuylkill □[6] | 210 | 40.41 N | 76.12 W |
| Schuylkill ≃ | 208 | 39.53 N | 75.12 W |
| Schuylkill Canal ≊ | 285 | 40.14 N | 75.42 W |
| Schuylkill Haven | 208 | 40.37 N | 76.10 W |
| Schwaan | 54 | 53.56 N | 12.06 E |
| Schwabach | 60 | 49.20 N | 11.01 E |
| Schwaben □[5] | 58 | 48.15 N | 10.30 E |
| Schwaben □[9] | 30 | 48.10 N | 9.25 E |
| Schwabhausen | 60 | 48.18 N | 11.21 E |
| Schwäbische Alb ⋀ | 58 | 48.25 N | 9.30 E |
| Schwäbisch Gmünd | 56 | 48.48 N | 9.47 E |
| Schwäbisch Hall | 56 | 49.07 N | 9.44 E |
| Schwabmünchen | 58 | 48.11 N | 10.45 E |
| Schwabstedt | 41 | 54.23 N | 9.11 E |
| Schwadorf | 61 | 48.04 N | 16.35 E |
| Schwafheim | 263 | 51.25 N | 6.39 E |
| Schwagstorf | 52 | 52.31 N | 7.45 E |
| Schwaig | 60 | 49.28 N | 11.12 E |
| Schwaigern | 56 | 49.08 N | 9.03 E |
| Schwalenberg | 52 | 51.52 N | 9.11 E |
| Schwalm ≃ | 56 | 51.10 N | 9.25 E |
| Schwalmstadt | 56 | 50.55 N | 9.11 E |
| Schwalmtal | 56 | 51.13 N | 6.16 E |
| Schwanau | 58 | 48.21 N | 7.46 E |
| Schwanden | 58 | 47.00 N | 9.04 E |
| Schwandorf | 60 | 49.20 N | 12.08 E |
| Schwanebeck, Dtsch. | 54 | 52.37 N | 13.32 E |
| Schwanebeck, Dtsch. | 54 | 51.58 N | 11.07 E |
| Schwanenstadt | 60 | 48.03 N | 13.46 E |
| Schwanenwerder ◆[8] | 264a | 52.27 N | 13.10 E |
| Schwaner, Pegunungan ⋀ | 112 | 0.40 S | 112.40 E |
| Schwanewede | 52 | 53.14 N | 8.35 E |
| Schwangau | 58 | 47.35 N | 10.44 E |
| Schwansen ◆[1] | 41 | 54.35 N | 9.50 E |
| Schwante | 264a | 52.44 N | 13.05 E |
| Schwarme | 52 | 52.54 N | 9.01 E |
| Schwarmstedt | 52 | 52.40 N | 9.37 E |
| Schwartau ≃ | 54 | 53.56 N | 10.41 E |
| Schwarza | 54 | 50.38 N | 10.32 E |
| Schwarza ≃, Dtsch. | 54 | 50.41 N | 11.19 E |
| Schwarza ≃, Öst. | 61 | 47.43 N | 16.13 E |
| Schwarzach, Dtsch. | 60 | 48.55 N | 12.49 E |
| Schwarzach, Öst. | 58 | 47.27 N | 9.45 E |
| Schwarzach ≃ | 60 | 49.36 N | 12.08 E |
| Schwarzach im Pongau | 64 | 47.19 N | 13.09 E |
| Schwarzbach ≃, Dtsch. | 56 | 49.16 N | 7.18 E |
| Schwarzbach ≃, Dtsch. | 263 | 51.19 N | 6.44 E |
| Schwarzburg | 54 | 50.38 N | 11.12 E |
| Schwarze Elster ≃ | 54 | 51.49 N | 12.51 E |
| Schwarze Laber ≃ | 60 | 49.00 N | 12.03 E |
| Schwarzenbach am Wald | 54 | 50.17 N | 11.37 E |
| Schwarzenbach an der Saale | 54 | 50.13 N | 11.56 E |
| Schwarzenbek | 52 | 53.30 N | 10.29 E |
| Schwarzenberg | 54 | 50.32 N | 12.47 E |
| Schwarzenberg ◆[8] | 263 | 51.24 N | 6.42 E |
| Schwarzenberg Park ♦ | 264b | 48.14 N | 16.15 E |
| Schwarzenborn | 56 | 50.55 N | 9.27 E |
| Schwarzenbruck | 60 | 49.21 N | 11.14 E |
| Schwarzenburg | 58 | 46.49 N | 7.21 E |
| Schwarzenfeld | 60 | 49.23 N | 12.08 E |
| Schwarze Pumpe | 54 | 51.32 N | 14.20 E |
| Schwarzer Berg ∧[2] | 263 | 51.41 N | 7.12 E |
| Schwarzer Mann ∧ | 56 | 50.15 N | 6.21 E |
| Schwarzer Regen ≃ | 60 | 49.10 N | 12.50 E |
| Schwarzes Meer → Black Sea ∓[2] | 22 | 43.00 N | 35.00 E |
| Schwarzheide | 54 | 51.29 N | 13.51 E |
| Schwarzhofen | 60 | 49.22 N | 12.20 E |
| Schwarzkogel ∧ | 61 | 47.25 N | 15.25 E |
| Schwarzrand ⋀ | 156 | 25.37 S | 16.50 E |
| Schwarzriegel ∧ | 60 | 49.14 N | 12.56 E |
| Schwarzsee | 58 | 46.40 N | 7.20 E |
| Schwarzwald (Black Forest) ⋀ | 58 | 48.00 N | 8.15 E |
| Schwarzwälder Hochwald ◆[3] | 56 | 49.39 N | 6.55 E |
| Schwatka Mountains ⋀ | 180 | 67.25 N | 157.00 W |
| Schwaz | 64 | 47.20 N | 11.42 E |
| Schwechat | 61 | 48.08 N | 16.29 E |
| Schwechat ≃ | 61 | 48.08 N | 16.34 E |
| Schweden → Sweden □[1] | 24 | 62.00 N | 15.00 E |
| Schwedeneck | 41 | 54.27 N | 10.05 E |
| Schwedt | 54 | 53.03 N | 14.17 E |
| Schweez | 54 | 53.53 N | 12.24 E |
| Schweflinghausen | 263 | 51.16 N | 7.25 E |
| Schwegenheim | 56 | 49.16 N | 8.20 E |
| Schwei | 52 | 53.24 N | 8.21 E |
| Schweich | 56 | 49.49 N | 6.45 E |
| Schweidnitz → Świdnica | 30 | 50.51 N | 16.29 E |
| Schweighausen | 58 | 48.13 N | 7.57 E |
| Schweighouse-sur-Moder | 56 | 48.49 N | 7.44 E |
| Schweinfurt | 56 | 50.03 N | 10.14 E |
| Schweinitz | 54 | 51.48 N | 13.01 E |
| Schweinrich | 54 | 53.10 N | 12.37 E |
| Schweitenkirchen | 60 | 48.30 N | 11.36 E |
| Schweiz → Switzerland □[1] | 58 | 47.00 N | 8.00 E |
| Schweizer Nationalpark ♦ | 58 | 46.38 N | 10.11 E |
| Schweizer-Reneke | 158 | 27.11 S | 25.18 E |
| Schwelm | 56 | 51.17 N | 7.17 E |
| Schwendi | 58 | 48.10 N | 9.58 E |
| Schwenke | 263 | 51.11 N | 7.26 E |
| Schwenksville | 285 | 40.16 N | 75.28 W |
| Schwepnitz | 54 | 51.20 N | 13.57 E |
| Schwerin, Dtsch. | 54 | 53.38 N | 11.25 E |
| Schwerin, Dtsch. | 263 | 51.33 N | 7.20 E |
| Schweriner See ⊜ | 54 | 53.45 N | 11.28 E |
| Schwertberg | 61 | 48.16 N | 14.35 E |
| Schwerte | 56 | 51.26 N | 7.34 E |
| Schwetzingen | 56 | 49.23 N | 8.34 E |
| Schweyen | 56 | 49.10 N | 7.24 E |
| Schwieberdingen | 56 | 48.52 N | 9.04 E |
| Schwielochsee ⊜ | 54 | 52.03 N | 14.12 E |
| Schwielowsee ⊜ | 54 | 52.20 N | 12.57 E |
| Schwindegg | 60 | 48.16 N | 12.15 E |
| Schwitten | 263 | 51.27 N | 7.48 E |
| Schwyz | 58 | 47.02 N | 8.40 E |
| Schwyz □[3] | 58 | 47.05 N | 8.40 E |
| Sciacca | 70 | 37.31 N | 13.03 E |
| Sciara | 70 | 37.55 N | 13.45 E |
| Sciaves (Schabs) | 64 | 46.46 N | 11.40 E |
| Scicli | 70 | 36.47 N | 14.42 E |
| Scie ≃ | 50 | 49.55 N | 1.02 E |
| Science and Industry, Museum of ʊ | 278 | 41.47 N | 87.35 W |
| Sciez | 58 | 46.20 N | 6.23 E |
| Scigliano | 68 | 39.08 N | 16.19 E |
| Ščigry | 78 | 51.53 N | 36.55 E |
| Scilla | 68 | 38.15 N | 15.44 E |
| Scilly, Isles of II | 42a | 49.55 N | 6.20 W |
| Ścinawa | 30 | 51.25 N | 16.27 E |
| Scio, N.Y., U.S. | 210 | 42.10 N | 77.59 W |
| Scio, Oh., U.S. | 214 | 40.23 N | 81.05 W |
| Scio, Or., U.S. | 202 | 44.42 N | 122.50 W |
| Scionzier | 58 | 46.03 N | 6.34 E |
| Sciota | 210 | 40.56 N | 75.19 W |
| Scioto □[6] | 218 | 38.48 N | 83.01 W |
| Scioto ≃ | 188 | 38.44 N | 83.01 W |
| Scioto Brush Creek ≃ | 218 | 38.50 N | 83.01 W |
| Scipio, In., U.S. | 218 | 39.05 N | 85.43 W |
| Scipio, Ut,. U.S. | 200 | 39.14 N | 112.06 W |
| Scipio Center | 210 | 42.47 N | 76.34 W |
| Şcippo Creek ≃ | 218 | 39.31 N | 82.59 W |
| Šćit ∧ | 36 | 44.02 N | 17.47 E |
| Scituate | 207 | 42.11 N | 70.43 W |
| Scituate Reservoir ⊜[1] | 207 | 41.47 N | 71.36 W |
| Sclafani Bagni | 70 | 37.49 N | 13.51 E |
| Scobey | 202 | 48.47 N | 105.25 W |
| Scoffera, Passo della )( | 62 | 44.29 N | 9.07 E |
| Scofield Reservoir ⊜[1] | 200 | 39.47 N | 111.09 W |
| Şcoglitti ◆[8] | 70 | 36.53 N | 14.26 E |
| Ščokino | 76 | 54.01 N | 37.31 E |
| Şcole | 42 | 52.22 N | 1.10 E |
| Ščolkovo | 82 | 55.55 N | 38.00 E |
| Scoltenna ≃ | 64 | 44.15 N | 10.50 E |
| Scolt Head > | 42 | 52.58 N | 0.42 E |
| Scone | 166 | 32.03 S | 150.52 E |
| Scooba | 194 | 32.49 N | 88.28 W |
| Scopello | 62 | 45.46 N | 8.06 E |
| Scordia | 70 | 37.18 N | 14.51 E |
| Scoresby | 274b | 37.54 S | 145.14 E |
| Scorrano, It. | 66 | 42.35 N | 13.49 E |
| Scorrano, It. | 68 | 40.05 N | 18.18 E |
| Scorzè | 64 | 45.34 N | 12.06 E |
| Scotch ≃ | 206 | 45.27 N | 74.59 W |
| Scotch Plains | 210 | 40.39 N | 74.23 W |
| Scotchtown | 210 | 41.29 N | 74.21 W |
| Scotia, Ne., U.S. | 198 | 41.27 N | 98.42 W |
| Scotia, N.Y., U.S. | 210 | 42.49 N | 73.57 W |
| Scotia Lake ⊜ | 190 | 47.05 N | 81.23 W |
| Scotian Shelf ✢[4] | 16 | 44.00 N | 62.00 W |
| Scotia Ridge ✢[3] | 18 | 54.00 S | 50.00 W |
| Scotia Sea ∓[2] | 9 | 56.00 S | 40.00 W |
| Scotland, On., Can. | 212 | 43.01 N | 80.22 W |
| Scotland, Pa., U.S. | 208 | 39.58 N | 77.35 W |
| Scotland, S.D., U.S. | 198 | 43.08 N | 97.43 W |
| Scotland, Tx., U.S. | 196 | 33.40 N | 98.28 W |
| Scotland □[8] | 28 | 57.00 N | 4.00 W |
| Scotland Neck | 192 | 36.07 N | 77.25 W |
| Scotland Run ≃ | 285 | 39.39 N | 75.03 W |
| Scotlandville | 194 | 30.31 N | 91.10 W |
| Scotrun | 210 | 41.04 N | 75.19 W |
| Scotsburn | 186 | 45.39 N | 62.51 W |
| Scotstown | 206 | 45.32 N | 71.17 W |
| Scott, Sk., Can. | 184 | 52.23 N | 108.50 W |
| Scott, Ms., U.S. | 194 | 33.35 N | 91.04 W |
| Scott, Oh., U.S. | 216 | 40.59 N | 84.35 W |
| Scott □[6], Il., U.S. | 219 | 39.38 N | 90.27 W |
| Scott □[6], In., U.S. | 218 | 38.41 N | 85.46 W |
| Scott □[6], Ky., U.S. | 218 | 38.18 N | 84.35 W |
| Scott ≃ | 204 | 41.48 N | 123.02 W |
| Scott, Cape > | 182 | 50.47 N | 128.26 W |
| Scott, Mount ∧, Ok., U.S. | 196 | 34.44 N | 98.32 W |
| Scott, Mount ∧, Or., U.S. | 202 | 42.56 N | 122.01 W |
| Scott Air Force Base ■ | 219 | 38.32 N | 89.52 W |
| Scott Base ʊ[3] | 9 | 77.50 S | 166.25 E |
| Scottburgh | 158 | 30.19 S | 30.40 E |
| Scott City, Ks., U.S. | 198 | 38.28 N | 100.54 W |
| Scott City, Mo., U.S. | 194 | 37.13 N | 89.31 W |
| Scott Cove ⊂ | 276 | 41.03 N | 73.28 W |
| Scott Creek ≃ | 226 | 37.02 N | 122.13 W |
| Scottdale, Mi., U.S. | 216 | 42.03 N | 86.27 W |
| Scottdale, Pa., U.S. | 214 | 40.06 N | 79.35 W |
| Scotter | 44 | 53.29 N | 0.40 W |
| Scott Haven | 279b | 40.15 N | 79.47 W |
| Scott Island I, Ant. | 9 | 67.24 S | 179.55 W |
| Scott Island I, On., Can. | 212 | 44.36 N | 76.20 W |
| Scott Islands II | 182 | 50.48 N | 128.40 W |
| Scott Lake | 220 | 25.56 N | 80.13 W |
| Scott Mountain ∧ | 202 | 44.11 N | 115.47 W |
| Scott Peak ∧ | 202 | 44.21 N | 112.50 W |
| Scott Reef ✢[2] | 160 | 14.00 S | 121.50 E |
| Scott Run ≃ | 284c | 38.58 N | 77.12 W |
| Scotts | 216 | 42.11 N | 85.24 W |
| Scottsbluff | 198 | 41.52 N | 103.40 W |
| Scotts Bluff National Monument ♦ | 198 | 41.49 N | 103.41 W |
| Scottsboro | 194 | 34.40 N | 86.02 W |
| Scottsburg, In., U.S. | 218 | 38.41 N | 85.46 W |
| Scottsburg, N.Y., U.S. | 210 | 42.40 N | 77.43 W |
| Scottsdale, Austl. | 166 | 41.10 S | 147.31 E |
| Scottsdale, Az., U.S. | 200 | 33.30 N | 111.53 W |
| Scotts Flat Reservoir ⊜[1] | 226 | 39.17 N | 120.55 W |


**Symbols** in the index entries represent the broad categories identified in the key at the right. Symbols with superior numbers (⋀[1]) identify subcategories (see complete key on page *I · 1).*

**Symbole** im Register stellen die rechts im Schlüssel erklärten Kategorien dar. Symbole mit hochgestellten Ziffern (⋀[1]) bezeichnen Unterabteilungen einer Kategorie (vgl. vollständiger Schlüssel auf Seite *I · 1).*

**Los símbolos** incluídos en el texto del índice representan las grandes categorías identificadas con la clave a la derecha. Los símbolos con numeros en su parte superior (⋀[1]) identifican las subcategorías (véase la clave completa en la página *I · 1).*

**Les symboles** de l'index représentent les catégories indiquées dans la légende à droite. Les symboles suivis d'un indice (⋀[1]) représentent des sous-catégories (voir légende complète à la page *I · 1).*

**Os símbolos** incluídos no texto do índice representam as grandes categorias identificadas com a chave à direita. Os símbolos com números em sua parte superior (⋀[1]) identificam as subcategorias (veja-se a chave completa à página *I · 1).*

| | | | | |
|---|---|---|---|---|
| ∧ Mountain | Berg | Montaña | Montagne | Montanha |
| ⋀ Mountains | Gebirge | Montañas | Montagnes | Montanhas |
| )( Pass | Paß | Paso | Col | Passo |
| V Valley, Canyon | Tal, Cañon | Valle, Cañón | Vallée, Canyon | Vale, Canhão |
| ≃ Plain | Ebene | Llano | Plaine | Planície |
| > Cape | Kap | Cabo | Cap | Cabo |
| I Island | Insel | Isla | Île | Ilha |
| II Islands | Inseln | Islas | Îles | Ilhas |
| ≗ Other Topographic Features | Andere Topographische Objekte | Otros Elementos Topográficos | Autres données topographiques | Outros acidentes topográficos |

**ESPAÑOL**

| Nombre | Página | Lat.°′ | Long.°′ W = Oeste |
|---|---|---|---|
| Scotts Head › | 240d | 15.13 N | 61.23 W |
| Scotts Hill | 194 | 35.31 N | 88.15 W |
| Scotts Level Branch ≏ | 284b | 39.22 N | 76.45 W |
| Scottsmoor | 220 | 28.46 N | 80.53 W |
| Scotts Valley | 226 | 37.03 N | 122.00 W |
| Scottsville, Ky., U.S. | 194 | 36.45 N | 86.11 W |
| Scottsville, N.Y., U.S. | 210 | 43.01 N | 77.44 W |
| Scott Township | 279b | 40.32 N | 80.11 W |
| Scottville, Il., U.S. | 219 | 39.29 N | 90.06 W |
| Scottville, Mi., U.S. | 190 | 43.57 N | 86.16 W |
| Scourie | 46 | 58.20 N | 5.08 W |
| Scout Lake | 184 | 49.22 N | 106.00 W |
| Scrabster | 46 | 58.37 N | 3.32 W |
| Scranton, Ia., U.S. | 198 | 42.01 N | 94.32 W |
| Scranton, N.Y., U.S. | 210 | 42.44 N | 78.50 W |
| Scranton, N.D., U.S. | 198 | 46.08 N | 103.08 W |
| Scranton, Pa., U.S. | 210 | 41.24 N | 75.39 W |
| Scremerston | 44 | 55.44 N | 1.59 W |
| Screven | 192 | 31.29 N | 82.01 W |
| Screw ≏ | 164 | 3.55 S | 142.50 E |
| Scribner | 198 | 41.40 N | 96.39 W |
| Scridain, Loch ⊂ | 46 | 56.21 N | 6.07 W |
| Scripps Institution of Oceanography ⊽[3] | 228 | 32.52 N | 117.15 W |
| Scrivia ≏ | 62 | 45.03 N | 8.54 E |
| Scroggins | 222 | 32.58 N | 95.11 W |
| Scrooby | 44 | 53.25 N | 1.01 W |
| Scrub Island I | 240m | 18.28 N | 64.31 W |
| Ščučinsk | 86 | 52.56 N | 70.12 E |
| Ščučje, Ross. | 78 | 51.45 N | 40.29 E |
| Ščučje, Ross. | 80 | 51.46 N | 40.29 E |
| Ščučje, Ross. | 86 | 55.17 N | 63.59 E |
| Ščučje Ozero | 86 | 56.28 N | 56.38 E |
| Ščučyn | 76 | 53.36 N | 24.45 E |
| Scugog ≏ | 212 | 44.24 N | 78.45 W |
| Scugog, Lake ⊜ | 212 | 44.10 N | 78.51 W |
| Scugog Indian Reserve ◆[4] | 212 | 44.11 N | 78.54 W |
| Scugog Island I | 212 | 44.10 N | 78.53 W |
| Ščukino | 82 | 54.28 N | 37.01 E |
| Scunthorpe | 44 | 53.36 N | 0.38 W |
| Scuol (Schuls) | 58 | 46.48 N | 10.18 E |
| Scuppernong ≏ | 216 | 42.54 N | 88.42 W |
| Scurcola Marsicana | 66 | 42.03 N | 13.20 E |
| Ščurovo | 82 | 55.03 N | 38.49 E |
| Scurrival Point › | 46 | 57.04 N | 7.31 W |
| Scurry | 222 | 32.31 N | 96.23 W |
| Scutari → Shkodër | 38 | 42.05 N | 19.30 E |
| Scutari, Lake ⊜ | 38 | 42.12 N | 19.18 E |
| Ščviha ≏ | 78 | 52.04 N | 27.54 E |
| Ščytkavičy | 76 | 53.13 N | 27.59 E |
| Sé ◆[8] | 287b | 23.33 S | 46.37 W |
| Seabeck | 224 | 47.38 N | 122.51 W |
| Sea Bird Island I | 224 | 49.15 N | 121.45 W |
| Seabird Island Indian Reserve ◆[4] | 182 | 49.17 N | 121.42 W |
| Seaboard | 192 | 36.29 N | 77.26 W |
| Sea Bright | 276 | 40.21 N | 73.58 W |
| Seabrook, Md., U.S. | 284c | 38.58 N | 76.50 W |
| Seabrook, N.J., U.S. | 208 | 39.30 N | 75.13 W |
| Seabrook, Tx., U.S. | 222 | 29.33 N | 95.01 W |
| Seabrook, Lake ⊜ | 162 | 30.56 S | 119.40 E |
| Sea Cliff | 210 | 40.50 N | 73.38 W |
| Seacock Swamp ≏ | 208 | 36.48 N | 76.51 W |
| Seacombe | 262 | 53.25 N | 3.01 W |
| Sea Dog Island I | 276 | 40.36 N | 73.35 W |
| Seadrift | 196 | 28.30 N | 96.47 W |
| Seaford, Eng., U.K. | 42 | 50.46 N | 0.06 E |
| Seaford, De., U.S. | 208 | 38.38 N | 75.36 W |
| Seaford, N.Y., U.S. | 276 | 40.39 N | 73.29 W |
| Seaford, Va., U.S. | 208 | 37.11 N | 76.26 W |
| Seaford Creek ≏ | 276 | 40.38 N | 73.29 W |
| Seaforth, Austl. | 274a | 33.48 S | 151.15 E |
| Seaforth, On., Can. | 190 | 43.33 N | 81.24 W |
| Seaforth, Eng., U.K. | 262 | 53.28 N | 3.01 W |
| Seaforth, Loch ⊂ | 46 | 57.54 N | 6.40 W |
| Seafox Seamount ✦[3] | 14 | 30.30 S | 172.45 W |
| Seager Wheeler Lake ⊜ | 184 | 54.27 N | 103.30 W |
| Seagoville | 222 | 32.38 N | 96.32 W |
| Seagraves | 196 | 32.56 N | 102.33 W |
| Seaham | 44 | 54.52 N | 1.21 W |
| Seaholme | 274b | 37.52 S | 144.50 E |
| Seahorse Breakers ✦[2] | 112 | 5.30 N | 112.37 E |
| Seahorse Point › | 176 | 63.47 N | 80.09 W |
| Seahouses | 44 | 55.35 N | 1.38 W |
| Sea Island I | 224 | 49.12 N | 123.10 W |
| Sea Islands II | 192 | 31.20 N | 81.20 W |
| Sea Isle City | 208 | 39.09 N | 74.41 W |
| Seal | 260 | 51.17 N | 0.14 E |
| Seal ≏ | 176 | 59.04 N | 94.48 W |
| Seal, Cape › | 158 | 34.07 S | 23.25 E |
| Sea Lake | 166 | 35.30 S | 142.51 E |
| Sealand | 262 | 53.12 N | 2.58 W |
| Sealark Channel ʉ | 175e | 9.18 S | 160.20 E |
| Seal Bay ⊂ | 9 | 71.40 S | 12.25 W |
| Seal Beach | 228 | 33.44 N | 118.06 W |
| Seal Beach National Wildlife Refuge ◆[4] | 280 | 33.45 N | 118.03 W |
| Seal Cays II | 238 | 21.10 N | 71.38 W |
| Seal Cove, N.B., Can. | 186 | 44.39 N | 66.51 W |
| Seal Cove, Nf., Can. | 186 | 49.56 N | 56.23 W |
| Sealdah Railroad Station ◆[5] | 272b | 22.34 N | 88.23 E |
| Seale | 194 | 32.17 N | 85.10 W |
| Sealevel | 192 | 34.51 N | 76.23 W |
| Seal Island I | 186 | 43.25 N | 66.01 W |
| Seal Islands II | 282 | 38.03 N | 122.03 W |
| Seal Lake ⊜ | 176 | 54.18 N | 61.40 W |
| Seal Rocks II[1] | 282 | 37.47 N | 122.31 W |
| Sealston | 208 | 38.15 N | 77.19 W |
| Sealy | 222 | 29.46 N | 96.09 W |
| Seaman | 218 | 38.56 N | 83.34 W |
| Seamer | 44 | 54.14 N | 0.26 W |
| Seanor | 214 | 40.13 N | 78.54 W |
| Seara | 252 | 27.07 S | 52.17 W |
| Searchlight | 204 | 35.27 N | 114.55 W |
| Searcy | 194 | 35.15 N | 91.44 W |
| Searles Lake ⊜ | 204 | 35.43 N | 117.20 W |
| Sears Lake ⊜ | 281 | 42.35 N | 83.39 W |
| Searsport | 188 | 44.27 N | 68.55 W |
| Sears Tower ⊽ | 278 | 41.53 N | 87.38 W |
| Searsville Lake ⊜ | 282 | 37.24 N | 122.14 W |
| Seascale | 44 | 54.24 N | 3.29 W |
| Seashore State Park ♠ | 208 | 36.54 N | 76.02 W |
| Seaside, Ca., U.S. | 226 | 36.36 N | 121.51 W |
| Seaside, Or., U.S. | 224 | 45.59 N | 123.55 W |
| Seaside Park | 208 | 39.55 N | 74.04 W |
| Seaside Park ♠ | 276 | 41.10 N | 73.12 W |
| SeaTac | 224 | 47.25 N | 122.19 W |
| Seaton, Eng., U.K. | 42 | 50.43 N | 3.05 W |
| Seaton, Eng., U.K. | 44 | 54.41 N | 3.33 W |
| Seaton, Eng., U.K. | 44 | 53.54 N | 0.14 W |
| Seaton ≏ | 42 | 50.22 N | 4.22 W |
| Seaton Delaval | 44 | 55.04 N | 1.31 W |
| Seaton Sluice | 44 | 55.05 N | 1.28 W |
| Seat Pleasant | 284c | 38.53 N | 76.54 W |
| Seattle | 224 | 47.36 N | 122.19 W |
| Seattle, Mount ʌ | 180 | 60.06 N | 139.11 W |
| Seattle Heights | 224 | 47.48 N | 122.20 W |
| Seattle-Tacoma International Airport ⊠ | 224 | 47.27 N | 122.18 W |
| Seatuck National Wildlife Refuge ◆[4] | 276 | 40.43 N | 73.13 W |
| Seaview, Eng., U.K. | 42 | 50.43 N | 1.06 W |
| Sea View, Ma., U.S. | 283 | 42.08 N | 70.42 W |
| Seaview, N.Y., U.S. | 276 | 40.39 N | 73.09 W |
| Seaview, Wa., U.S. | 224 | 46.20 N | 124.03 W |
| Seaward Kaikoura Range ⋏ | 172 | 42.14 S | 173.39 E |
| Seaward Roads ʉ | 174g | 28.13 N | 177.25 W |
| Sea World ♠, Fl., U.S. | 220 | 28.25 N | 81.28 W |

**FRANÇAIS**

| Nom | Page | Lat.°′ | Long.°′ W = Ouest |
|---|---|---|---|
| Sea World ♠, Oh., U.S. | 214 | 41.21 N | 81.23 W |
| Seba | 112 | 10.29 S | 121.50 E |
| Sébaco | 236 | 12.51 N | 86.06 W |
| Sebago Lake ⊜ | 188 | 43.50 N | 70.35 W |
| Se Bai ≏ | 110 | 15.13 N | 104.47 E |
| Sebakor, Teluk ⊂ | 164 | 3.35 S | 132.50 E |
| Sebakung | 112 | 1.37 S | 116.26 E |
| Šebalin | 80 | 47.22 N | 43.36 E |
| Šebalino, Ross. | 80 | 48.16 N | 43.21 E |
| Šebalino, Ross. | 86 | 51.17 N | 85.40 E |
| Sebanga | 114 | 1.24 N | 101.10 E |
| Sebangan, Teluk ⊂ | 112 | 3.15 S | 113.30 E |
| Sebangka, Pulau I | 112 | 0.07 N | 104.36 E |
| Sébaou, Oued ≏ | 34 | 36.55 N | 3.55 E |
| Sebarok, Pulau I | 271c | 1.13 N | 103.48 E |
| Sebastian, Fl., U.S. | 220 | 27.46 N | 80.29 W |
| Sebastian, Tx., U.S. | 196 | 26.20 N | 97.47 W |
| Sebastian, Cape › | 202 | 42.19 N | 124.26 W |
| Sebastian Inlet ⊂ | 220 | 27.51 N | 80.26 W |
| Sebastián Vizcaíno, Bahía ⊂ | 232 | 28.00 N | 114.30 W |
| Sebastião de Lacerda | 256 | 22.17 S | 43.35 W |
| Sebastopol, Austl. | 169 | 37.36 S | 143.51 E |
| Sebastopol, Ca., U.S. | 204 | 38.24 N | 122.49 W |
| Sebastopol, Ms., U.S. | 194 | 32.34 N | 89.20 W |
| Sebatik, Pulau I | 112 | 4.10 N | 117.45 E |
| Sebba | 150 | 13.26 N | 0.32 E |
| Sebderat | 144 | 15.26 N | 36.40 E |
| Sébé ≏ | 152 | 1.02 S | 13.06 E |
| Sebec Lake ⊜ | 188 | 45.18 N | 69.18 W |
| Sebeka | 198 | 46.38 N | 95.05 W |
| Šebekino | 78 | 50.25 N | 36.56 E |
| Sébékoro | 150 | 12.57 N | 8.59 W |
| Seben | 130 | 40.24 N | 31.34 E |
| Sebenico → Šibenik | 36 | 43.44 N | 15.54 E |
| Sebera, Punta ʌ | 71 | 39.03 N | 8.50 E |
| Seberi | 252 | 27.29 S | 53.24 W |
| Seberida | 112 | 0.43 S | 102.31 E |
| Šeberta | 88 | 54.40 N | 99.54 E |
| Sebeş | 38 | 45.58 N | 23.34 E |
| Sebesi, Pulau I | 115a | 5.57 S | 105.30 E |
| Sebes Körös (Crişul Repede) ≏ | 38 | 46.55 N | 20.59 E |
| Sebewaing | 190 | 43.43 N | 83.27 W |
| Sebež | 76 | 56.17 N | 28.29 E |
| Sebille Manor | 281 | 42.39 N | 82.49 W |
| Şebinkarahisar | 130 | 40.18 N | 38.26 E |
| Sebiş | 38 | 46.23 N | 22.08 E |
| Sebnitz | 54 | 50.58 N | 14.16 E |
| Sebou, Oued ≏ | 148 | 34.15 N | 6.40 W |
| Sebree | 194 | 37.36 N | 87.31 W |
| Sebrell | 208 | 36.47 N | 77.07 W |
| Sebring, Fl., U.S. | 220 | 27.29 N | 81.26 W |
| Sebring, Oh., U.S. | 214 | 40.55 N | 81.01 W |
| Sebringville | 212 | 43.24 N | 81.04 W |
| Sebuku | 112 | 4.03 N | 116.56 E |
| Sebuku, Pulau I, Indon. | 112 | 3.30 S | 116.22 E |
| Sebuku, Pulau I, Indon. | 115a | 5.53 S | 105.31 E |
| Sebuku, Teluk ⊂ | 112 | 4.00 N | 118.26 E |
| Šebunino | 89 | 46.27 N | 141.51 E |
| Seč | 60 | 49.36 N | 13.30 E |
| Seca, Ilha I | 287a | 22.50 S | 43.11 W |
| Secane | 285 | 39.55 N | 75.18 W |
| Secang | 115a | 7.23 S | 110.15 E |
| Secas, Islas II | 236 | 7.58 N | 82.02 W |
| Secaucus | 276 | 40.47 N | 74.03 W |
| Secchia ≏ | 64 | 45.04 N | 11.00 E |
| Sečenovo | 80 | 55.13 N | 45.54 E |
| Secesh ≏ | 202 | 45.02 N | 115.43 W |
| Séchault | 56 | 49.16 N | 4.44 E |
| Sechelt | 182 | 49.28 N | 123.45 W |
| Šechman' | 76 | 52.32 N | 40.29 E |
| Sechura | 248 | 5.33 S | 80.51 W |
| Sechura, Bahía de ⊂ | 248 | 5.42 S | 81.00 W |
| Sechura, Desierto de ◆[2] | 248 | 5.50 S | 80.40 W |
| Seckach | 56 | 49.26 N | 9.20 E |
| Seckau | 61 | 47.16 N | 14.47 E |
| Seckau ⊽[1] | 61 | 47.16 N | 14.47 E |
| Seckauer Alpen ⋏ | 61 | 47.20 N | 14.40 E |
| Seckauer Zinken ʌ | 61 | 47.20 N | 14.44 E |
| Seclantas | 252 | 25.18 S | 66.15 W |
| Seclin | 50 | 50.33 N | 3.02 E |
| Seco ≏, Arg. | 252 | 23.08 S | 63.57 W |
| Seco ≏, Arg. | 254 | 48.34 S | 67.02 W |
| Seco ≏, Esp. | 266d | 41.30 N | 2.09 E |
| Seco, Arroyo ≏, Ca., U.S. | 226 | 36.25 N | 121.20 W |
| Seco, Arroyo ≏, Ca., U.S. | 280 | 34.05 N | 118.13 W |
| Seco Creek ≏, N.M., U.S. | 200 | 32.59 N | 107.18 W |
| Seco Creek ≏, Tx., U.S. | 196 | 29.02 N | 99.08 W |
| Seco Island I | 116 | 11.19 N | 121.40 E |
| Second ≏ | 276 | 40.47 N | 74.09 W |
| Second Cliff ±[4] | 283 | 42.12 N | 70.43 W |
| Second Han-gang Bridge ◆[5] | 271b | 37.34 N | 126.54 E |
| Second Herring Brook ≏ | 283 | 42.09 N | 70.47 W |
| Second Lake ⊜ | 206 | 45.09 N | 71.10 W |
| Second Mountain ʌ | 208 | 40.33 N | 76.30 W |
| Second San Diego Aqueduct ≊[1] | 228 | 32.41 N | 117.01 W |
| Second Swamp ≏ | 208 | 37.08 N | 77.12 W |
| Second Valley | 168b | 35.33 S | 138.14 E |
| Second Watchung Mountain ʌ | 276 | 40.55 N | 74.13 W |
| Sečovce | 30 | 48.43 N | 21.40 E |
| Sečovská Polianka | 30 | 48.47 N | 21.42 E |
| Secretário, Ribeirão do ≏ | 256 | 22.14 S | 43.25 W |
| Secretary | 208 | 38.36 N | 75.56 W |
| Secretary Island I | 172 | 45.15 S | 166.55 E |
| Section | 194 | 34.34 N | 85.59 W |
| Secubun Island I | 116 | 5.06 N | 120.18 E |
| Sécure ≏ | 248 | 15.10 S | 64.52 W |
| Security | 198 | 38.45 N | 104.44 W |
| Security Square ◆[9] | 284b | 39.19 N | 76.45 W |
| Séd ≏ | 30 | 47.00 N | 18.31 E |
| Seda, Lat. | 76 | 57.40 N | 25.46 E |
| Seda, Liet. | 76 | 56.10 N | 22.04 E |
| Seda, Zhg. | 102 | 32.20 N | 100.41 E |
| Seda ≏ | 76 | 57.47 N | 25.15 E |
| Sedah | 112 | 10.46 S | 123.12 E |
| Sedalia, Ab., Can. | 184 | 51.41 N | 110.40 W |
| Sedalia, In., U.S. | 216 | 40.25 N | 86.31 W |
| Sedalia, Mo., U.S. | 194 | 38.42 N | 93.13 W |
| Sedalia, Oh., U.S. | 218 | 39.44 N | 83.29 W |
| Sedan, Austl. | 168b | 34.35 S | 139.18 E |
| Sedan, Fr. | 56 | 49.42 N | 4.57 E |
| Sedan, Ks., U.S. | 198 | 37.07 N | 96.11 W |
| Sedanka, Cape › | 180 | 53.49 N | 166.06 W |
| Sedanka Island I | 180 | 53.50 N | 166.10 W |
| Sedano | 34 | 42.43 N | 3.45 W |
| Sedano, Tanjung › | 115a | 7.49 S | 114.27 E |
| Sedanovo | 88 | 56.58 N | 101.22 E |
| Sedari, Tanjung › | 115a | 5.57 S | 107.18 E |
| Sedayu | 115a | 6.59 S | 112.33 E |
| Sedbergh | 44 | 54.20 N | 2.31 W |
| Sedco Hills | 228 | 33.39 N | 117.24 W |
| Seddin-Berg ʌ[2] | 264a | 52.24 N | 13.40 E |
| Seddinsee ⊜ | 264a | 52.23 N | 13.41 E |
| Seddon | 172 | 41.40 S | 174.05 E |
| Seddonville | 172 | 41.33 S | 171.59 E |
| Sedé Boqér | 132 | 30.52 N | 34.47 E |
| Sedel'nikovo | 86 | 56.57 N | 75.18 E |
| Séderon | 62 | 44.12 N | 5.32 E |
| Sederot | 132 | 31.31 N | 34.35 E |
| Sedgefield, Eng., U.K. | 44 | 54.39 N | 1.26 W |
| Sedgefield, N.J., U.S. | 276 | 40.51 N | 74.28 W |
| Sedgefield, N.C., U.S. | 192 | 35.10 N | 80.51 W |

**PORTUGUÊS**

| Nome | Página | Lat.°′ | Long.°′ W = Oeste |
|---|---|---|---|
| Sedge Island I | 276 | 40.21 N | 73.59 W |
| Sedgewick | 182 | 52.46 N | 111.41 W |
| Sedgwick, Co., U.S. | 198 | 40.56 N | 102.31 W |
| Sedgwick, Ks., U.S. | 198 | 37.55 N | 97.25 W |
| Sedgwick, Mount ʌ | 200 | 35.11 N | 108.06 W |
| Sédhiou | 150 | 12.44 N | 15.33 W |
| Sedico | 64 | 46.06 N | 12.06 E |
| Sedilo | 71 | 40.10 N | 8.55 E |
| Sedini | 71 | 40.51 N | 8.49 E |
| Sedlčany | 30 | 49.40 N | 14.26 E |
| Sedley | 208 | 36.46 N | 76.59 W |
| Sedlice | 60 | 49.23 N | 13.56 E |
| Sedlitz | 54 | 51.33 N | 14.03 E |
| Sedlo ʌ | 54 | 50.36 N | 14.17 E |
| Sedniv | 78 | 51.39 N | 31.34 E |
| Šedok | 84 | 44.13 N | 40.52 E |
| Sedom (Sodom) ⊥ | 132 | 31.04 N | 35.23 E |
| Sedona | 200 | 34.52 N | 111.45 W |
| Sedot Yam | 132 | 32.29 N | 34.53 E |
| Sedova, pik ʌ | 72 | 73.29 N | 54.58 E |
| Sedrata | 36 | 36.08 N | 7.32 E |
| Sedriano | 62 | 45.29 N | 8.58 E |
| Sedrina | 62 | 45.47 N | 9.38 E |
| Sedro Woolley | 224 | 48.30 N | 122.14 W |
| Sedrun | 58 | 46.41 N | 8.46 E |
| Šedtim | 24 | 66.25 N | 56.20 E |
| Šeduva | 76 | 55.46 N | 23.46 E |
| Sędziszów | 30 | 50.04 N | 21.41 E |
| See | 58 | 47.05 N | 10.28 E |
| Seeberg, Dtsch. | 264a | 52.33 N | 13.41 E |
| Seeberg, Schw. | 58 | 47.09 N | 7.40 E |
| Seebergsattel )( | 61 | 47.38 N | 15.18 E |
| Seeber Lake ⊜ | 184 | 53.52 N | 93.03 W |
| Seeboden | 64 | 46.49 N | 13.30 E |
| Seebruck | 64 | 47.56 N | 12.28 E |
| Seeburg | 264a | 52.31 N | 13.07 E |
| Seefeld, Dtsch. | 52 | 53.27 N | 8.21 E |
| Seefeld, Dtsch. | 54 | 52.37 N | 13.40 E |
| Seefeld in Tirol | 64 | 47.20 N | 11.11 E |
| Seefin ʌ[2] | 48 | 52.18 N | 8.32 W |
| Seeg | 58 | 47.38 N | 10.36 E |
| Seege ≏ | 54 | 53.04 N | 11.23 E |
| Seegefeld | 264a | 52.33 N | 13.05 E |
| Seehausen, Dtsch. | 54 | 51.57 N | 12.55 E |
| Seehausen, Dtsch. | 54 | 52.06 N | 11.17 E |
| Seehausen, Dtsch. | 54 | 52.53 N | 11.45 E |
| Seeheim | 156 | 26.50 S | 17.45 E |
| Seeheim-Jugenheim | 56 | 49.45 N | 8.38 E |
| Seehof | 264a | 52.24 N | 13.17 E |
| Seeis | 156 | 22.29 S | 17.39 E |
| Seekaskootch Indian Reserve ◆[4] | 184 | 53.43 N | 109.55 W |
| Seekoegat | 158 | 33.03 S | 22.31 E |
| Seekoei ≏ | 158 | 30.18 S | 25.01 E |
| Seekonk | 207 | 41.48 N | 71.20 W |
| Seelbach | 58 | 48.18 N | 7.56 E |
| Seeley Lake | 202 | 47.10 N | 113.29 W |
| Seeleys Bay | 212 | 44.29 N | 76.14 W |
| Seelingstädt | 54 | 50.46 N | 12.14 E |
| Seelow | 54 | 52.32 N | 14.23 E |
| Seelyville, In., U.S. | 194 | 39.29 N | 87.16 W |
| Seelyville, Pa., U.S. | 210 | 41.35 N | 75.17 W |
| Seelze | 52 | 52.24 N | 9.35 E |
| Seemade | 144 | 7.10 N | 48.36 E |
| Seemalik Butte ʌ | 180 | 60.09 N | 167.08 W |
| Seemenbach ≏ | 56 | 50.17 N | 8.59 E |
| Seemore Downs | 162 | 30.42 S | 125.15 E |
| Seen | 58 | 47.29 N | 8.46 E |
| Seengen | 58 | 47.19 N | 8.13 E |
| Seeon | 64 | 47.58 N | 12.26 E |
| Seer Green | 260 | 51.37 N | 0.36 W |
| Seergu | 102 | 32.00 N | 103.33 E |
| Seerhausen | 54 | 51.16 N | 13.15 E |
| Sées | 50 | 48.36 N | 0.10 E |
| Seesen | 52 | 51.53 N | 10.10 E |
| Seeshaupt | 64 | 47.49 N | 11.18 E |
| Seest | 41 | 55.29 N | 9.27 E |
| Seetal | 61 | 47.09 N | 13.57 E |
| Seetaler Alpen ⋏ | 61 | 47.05 N | 14.35 E |
| Seevetal | 52 | 53.23 N | 9.59 E |
| Seewalchen am Attersee | 64 | 47.57 N | 13.35 E |
| Seewiesen | 61 | 47.37 N | 15.16 E |
| Seewinkel ◆[1] | 61 | 47.48 N | 16.49 E |
| Seewis | 58 | 47.00 N | 9.32 E |
| Séez | 62 | 45.37 N | 6.48 E |
| Seez ≏ | 58 | 47.07 N | 9.18 E |
| Şefaatli | 130 | 39.31 N | 34.46 E |
| Sefadu | 150 | 8.39 N | 10.59 W |
| Sefar ⊥ | 148 | 24.27 N | 9.16 E |
| Sefare | 156 | 23.02 S | 27.28 E |
| Seferihisar | 130 | 38.11 N | 26.51 E |
| Séféto | 150 | 14.08 N | 9.49 W |
| Seffern | 56 | 50.04 N | 6.30 E |
| Seffner | 220 | 27.59 N | 82.17 W |
| Sefīd ≏ | 128 | 37.26 N | 49.55 E |
| Sefīd Ābeh | 128 | 30.56 N | 60.35 E |
| Sefrou | 148 | 33.50 N | 4.50 W |
| Sefton, N.Z. | 172 | 43.15 S | 172.40 E |
| Sefton, Eng., U.K. | 262 | 53.30 N | 2.58 W |
| Sefton □[8] | 262 | 53.34 N | 3.14 W |
| Sefton, Mount ʌ | 172 | 43.41 S | 170.03 E |
| Sefton Park ♠ | 262 | 53.23 N | 2.56 W |
| Segag | 144 | 7.40 N | 42.50 E |
| Segaliud ≏ | 116 | 5.43 N | 117.55 E |
| Segama ≏ | 112 | 5.27 N | 118.48 E |
| Segamat | 114 | 2.30 N | 102.49 E |
| Segang | 100 | 31.58 N | 114.18 E |
| Segangane | 34 | 35.09 N | 3.00 W |
| Segarcea | 38 | 44.06 N | 23.45 E |
| Šegarka ≏ | 86 | 57.16 N | 84.05 E |
| Segbana | 150 | 10.56 N | 3.42 E |
| Segbwema | 150 | 8.00 N | 10.57 W |
| Segen ≏ | 144 | 4.49 N | 36.57 E |
| Segera | 164 | 8.15 S | 143.30 E |
| Segeri | 112 | 4.39 S | 119.33 E |
| Segesta ⊥ | 70 | 37.56 N | 12.50 E |
| Segesvár → Sighişoara | 38 | 46.13 N | 24.48 E |
| Segeža | 24 | 63.44 N | 34.19 E |
| Seggiano | 66 | 42.56 N | 11.33 E |
| Seggueur, Oued es ∨ | 148 | 31.39 N | 2.26 E |
| Šegmas | 24 | 64.43 N | 49.14 E |
| Segni | 66 | 41.41 N | 13.01 E |
| Segno | 222 | 30.35 N | 94.41 W |
| Segorbe | 34 | 39.51 N | 0.29 W |
| Ségou | 150 | 13.27 N | 6.16 W |
| Ségou □[4] | 150 | 14.00 N | 5.40 E |
| Šegovary | 24 | 62.23 N | 42.57 E |
| Segovia, Col. | 246 | 7.07 N | 74.42 W |
| Segovia, Esp. | 34 | 40.57 N | 4.07 W |
| Segovia □[4] | 34 | 41.15 N | 4.00 W |
| Segozero, ozero ⊜ | 24 | 63.18 N | 33.45 E |
| Segrate | 266b | 45.29 N | 9.19 E |
| Segré | 32 | 47.41 N | 0.53 W |
| Segre ≏ | 34 | 41.22 N | 0.20 E |
| Seguam Island I | 180 | 52.17 N | 172.30 W |
| Seguam Pass ʉ | 180 | 52.08 N | 172.45 W |
| Séguédine | 146 | 20.12 N | 12.59 E |
| Séguéla, C. Iv. | 150 | 7.57 N | 6.40 W |
| Séguéla, Mali | 150 | 14.07 N | 6.44 W |
| Séguélon | 150 | 9.25 N | 7.09 W |
| Séguénéga | 150 | 13.27 N | 1.58 W |
| Seguí | 252 | 31.57 S | 60.08 W |
| Seguin | 196 | 29.34 N | 97.57 W |
| Seguin ≏ | 212 | 45.21 N | 80.01 W |
| Seguine Point › | 276 | 40.31 N | 74.12 W |
| Segula Island I | 181a | 52.01 N | 178.07 E |
| Segundo | 198 | 37.07 N | 104.45 W |
| Segundo ≏ | 252 | 31.21 S | 62.59 W |
| Seguntur | 112 | 1.54 N | 117.47 E |
| Segura | 34 | 39.50 N | 6.59 W |
| Segura ≏ | 34 | 38.06 N | 0.38 W |
| Segura, Sierra de ⋏ | 34 | 38.00 N | 2.43 W |
| Sehāni Kalān | 272a | 28.41 N | 77.25 E |
| Sehāni Khurd | 272a | 28.42 N | 77.25 E |
| Sehāra Bāzār | 126 | 23.06 N | 87.49 E |
| Sehithwa | 156 | 20.23 S | 22.45 E |
| Sehlabathebe | 158 | 29.53 S | 29.05 E |

| Nome | Página | Lat.°′ | Long.°′ |
|---|---|---|---|
| Sehlabathebe National Park ♠ | 158 | 29.53 S | 29.06 E |
| Sehma | 54 | 50.32 N | 13.00 E |
| Sehnde | 52 | 52.18 N | 9.57 E |
| Sehnkwehn | 150 | 5.13 N | 9.12 W |
| Sehnkwehn ≏ | 150 | 5.12 N | 9.21 W |
| Sehore | 124 | 23.12 N | 77.05 E |
| Sehwān | 120 | 26.26 N | 67.52 E |
| Sehyŏn-ni | 98 | 38.20 N | 127.41 E |
| Seia | 34 | 40.25 N | 7.42 W |
| Seibert | 198 | 39.18 N | 102.52 W |
| Seibu | 268 | 35.50 N | 139.22 E |
| Seiches-sur-le-Loir | 32 | 47.35 N | 0.22 W |
| Seidan | 96 | 34.19 N | 134.45 E |
| Seidersville | 210 | 40.35 N | 75.23 W |
| Seiersberg | 61 | 47.01 N | 15.24 E |
| Seiffen | 54 | 50.39 N | 13.26 E |
| Seifhennersdorf | 54 | 50.56 N | 14.36 E |
| Seignelay | 50 | 47.54 N | 3.36 E |
| Seigneurial, Lac ⊜ | 275a | 45.33 N | 73.20 W |
| Seika | 270 | 34.46 N | 135.48 E |
| Seikpyu | 110 | 20.55 N | 94.47 E |
| Seil I | 46 | 56.18 N | 5.39 W |
| Seiland I | 24 | 70.25 N | 23.15 E |
| Seilhac | 32 | 45.22 N | 1.42 E |
| Seiling | 196 | 36.08 N | 98.55 W |
| Seillans | 62 | 43.38 N | 6.38 E |
| Seille ≏, Fr. | 56 | 49.07 N | 6.11 E |
| Seille ≏, Fr. | 58 | 46.31 N | 4.56 E |
| Seilo | 140 | 12.20 N | 23.50 E |
| Seim → Sejm ≏ | 78 | 51.27 N | 32.34 E |
| Sein, Île de I | 32 | 48.02 N | 4.51 W |
| Seinaiji | 94 | 35.30 N | 137.42 E |
| Seinäjoki | 26 | 62.47 N | 22.50 E |
| Seine ≏, Mb., Can. | 184 | 49.54 N | 97.07 W |
| Seine ≏, On., Can. | 190 | 48.40 N | 92.49 W |
| Seine ≏, Fr. | 32 | 49.26 N | 0.26 E |
| Seine, Baie de la ⊂ | 32 | 49.30 N | 0.30 W |
| Seine-et-Marne □[5] | 50 | 48.30 N | 3.00 E |
| Seine-Maritime □[5] | 50 | 49.45 N | 1.00 E |
| Seine-Port | 50 | 48.33 N | 2.33 E |
| Seine-Saint-Denis □[5] | 261 | 48.55 N | 2.30 E |
| Seip Mound State Memorial ⊥ | 218 | 39.15 N | 83.13 W |
| Seipstown | 208 | 40.35 N | 75.40 W |
| Seis de Septiembre → Morón | 258 | 34.39 S | 58.37 W |
| Seishin → Ch'ŏngjin | 98 | 41.47 N | 129.50 E |
| Seitenstetten | 61 | 48.02 N | 14.39 E |
| Seitovka | 80 | 46.43 N | 48.03 E |
| Seitsemisen kansallispuisto ♠ | 26 | 61.58 N | 23.20 E |
| Seiwa | 94 | 34.29 N | 136.30 E |
| Seixal | 34 | 38.38 N | 9.06 W |
| Seixas, Ponta do › | 250 | 7.09 S | 34.47 W |
| Seiz | 61 | 47.23 N | 14.55 E |
| Seize Îles, Lac des ⊜ | 206 | 45.54 N | 74.28 W |
| Sejaka | 112 | 3.34 S | 116.12 E |
| Sejerø I | 41 | 55.53 N | 11.09 E |
| Sejerø Bugt ⊂ | 41 | 55.50 N | 11.15 E |
| Sejm (Seym) ≏ | 78 | 51.27 N | 32.34 E |
| Sejmčan | 74 | 62.53 N | 152.26 E |
| Šejno | 80 | 53.22 N | 43.12 E |
| Sejny | 30 | 54.07 N | 23.20 E |
| Sejorong | 115b | 9.02 S | 116.48 E |
| Sejs | 41 | 56.09 N | 9.36 E |
| Sekači | 80 | 50.30 N | 43.37 E |
| Sekadau | 112 | 0.01 S | 110.54 E |
| Sekake | 158 | 29.58 S | 28.27 E |
| Sekampung ≏ | 115a | 5.36 S | 105.50 E |
| Sekayam ≏ | 112 | 0.07 N | 110.38 E |
| Sekayu | 112 | 2.51 S | 103.51 E |
| Seke, Ityo. | 144 | 9.56 N | 38.19 E |
| Seke, Tan. | 154 | 3.20 S | 33.31 E |
| Seke-Banza | 152 | 5.20 S | 13.16 E |
| Sekeladi | 112 | 2.38 S | 102.14 E |
| Sekenke | 154 | 4.16 S | 34.10 E |
| Şekerli | 130 | 37.33 N | 39.22 E |
| Šeki, Azer. | 84 | 41.12 N | 47.12 E |
| Seki, Nihon | 94 | 35.29 N | 136.55 E |
| Seki, Nihon | 94 | 34.51 N | 136.24 E |
| Seki, Tür. | 130 | 36.24 N | 29.13 E |
| Sekidō-san ʌ | 94 | 36.58 N | 136.59 E |
| Sekigahara | 94 | 35.22 N | 136.28 E |
| Sekigane | 96 | 35.22 N | 133.46 E |
| Sekijō | 94 | 36.14 N | 139.55 E |
| Sekima | 112 | 1.41 S | 111.31 E |
| Sekinomiya | 96 | 35.22 N | 134.38 E |
| Sekiu | 224 | 48.15 N | 124.18 W |
| Sekiya | 270 | 34.27 N | 135.42 E |
| Sekiyado | 94 | 36.06 N | 139.47 E |
| Seki-zaki › | 96 | 33.15 N | 131.54 E |
| Sekoma | 156 | 24.41 S | 23.50 E |
| Sekondi-Takoradi | 150 | 4.59 N | 1.43 W |
| Sekota | 144 | 12.38 N | 39.03 E |
| Sekpiegu | 150 | 9.33 N | 0.02 W |
| Sekretaris ≏ | 269e | 6.10 S | 106.47 E |
| Sekretarka | 80 | 52.36 N | 44.11 E |
| Šekšema | 80 | 58.22 N | 45.11 E |
| Šeksna | 76 | 59.13 N | 38.30 E |
| Sekudai | 114 | 1.32 N | 103.40 E |
| Sela ≏[1] | 126 | 21.54 N | 89.39 E |
| Sela, Ponta da › | 256 | 23.54 S | 45.27 W |
| Šelabolicha | 86 | 53.25 N | 82.37 E |
| Sela Dingay | 144 | 9.59 N | 39.33 E |
| Šelagskij, mys › | 74 | 70.06 N | 170.26 E |
| Selah | 202 | 46.39 N | 120.31 W |
| Selai ≏ | 114 | 2.13 N | 103.26 E |
| Šelajevo | 88 | 56.56 N | 97.42 E |
| Selama | 114 | 5.13 N | 100.42 E |
| Šelanger | 80 | 56.13 N | 48.16 E |
| Selangor □[3] | 114 | 3.20 N | 101.30 E |
| Selangor ≏ | 114 | 3.20 N | 101.15 E |
| Selaön I | 40 | 59.24 N | 17.12 E |
| Selaphum | 110 | 16.02 N | 103.57 E |
| Selargius | 71 | 39.16 N | 9.10 E |
| Selaru, Pulau I | 164 | 8.09 S | 131.00 E |
| Selatan, Tanjung › | 112 | 4.10 S | 114.38 E |
| Selatpanjang | 114 | 1.00 N | 102.43 E |
| Selawik | 180 | 66.37 N | 160.03 W |
| Selawik ≏ | 180 | 66.36 N | 160.20 W |
| Selawik Lake ⊜ | 180 | 66.30 N | 160.40 W |
| Selayar, Pulau I | 112 | 6.05 S | 120.30 E |
| Selayar, Selat ʉ | 112 | 5.42 S | 120.28 E |
| Selb | 54 | 50.10 N | 12.08 E |
| Selbeck ◆[8] | 263 | 51.22 N | 6.52 E |
| Selbecke ◆[8] | 263 | 51.20 N | 7.28 E |
| Selbitz | 54 | 50.19 N | 11.44 E |
| Selborne | 42 | 51.06 N | 0.56 W |
| Selbu | 26 | 63.13 N | 11.02 E |
| Selbusjøen ⊜ | 26 | 63.14 N | 10.54 E |
| Selby, Austl. | 274b | 37.55 S | 145.22 E |
| Selby, Eng., U.K. | 44 | 53.48 N | 1.04 W |
| Selby, S.D., U.S. | 198 | 45.30 N | 100.01 W |
| Selby ◆[8] | 273d | 26.13 S | 28.02 E |
| Selbyville | 208 | 38.27 N | 75.13 W |
| Selchow | 264a | 52.21 N | 13.28 E |
| Sel'co, Ross. | 24 | 63.18 N | 41.22 E |
| Sel'co, Ross. | 76 | 53.22 N | 34.06 E |
| Selcourt | 273d | 26.18 S | 28.27 E |
| Selčuga ≏ | 89 | 49.42 N | 133.20 E |
| Selçuk | 130 | 37.56 N | 27.22 E |
| Sel'cy, Ross. | 76 | 57.57 N | 35.59 E |
| Sel'cy, Ross. | 265a | 59.57 N | 30.43 E |
| Selden, Ks., U.S. | 198 | 39.32 N | 100.34 W |
| Selden, N.Y., U.S. | 210 | 40.51 N | 73.02 W |
| Seldovia | 180 | 59.27 N | 151.43 W |
| Sele ≏ | 68 | 40.29 N | 14.56 E |
| Sele, Piana del ≡ | 68 | 40.33 N | 14.57 E |
| Sele, Selat ʉ | 164 | 1.10 S | 131.05 E |
| Sele, Tanjung › | 164 | 1.26 S | 130.55 E |
| Selebi Phikwe | 156 | 22.00 S | 27.50 E |
| Šelec | 76 | 52.33 N | 33.35 E |
| Šelechov | 88 | 52.13 N | 104.08 E |
| Selečn'a | 76 | 52.23 N | 34.23 E |
| Selection Park | 273d | 26.18 S | 28.27 E |
| Selegas | 71 | 39.34 N | 9.06 E |
| Selemadeg | 115b | 8.29 S | 115.02 E |

| Nome | Página | Lat.°′ | Long.°′ |
|---|---|---|---|
| Selembao | 273b | 4.22 S | 15.17 E |
| Selemdža ≏ | 89 | 51.42 N | 128.53 E |
| Selemdžinsk | 89 | 52.36 N | 131.08 E |
| Šelemeti | 80 | 57.27 N | 48.07 E |
| Selendi | 130 | 38.45 N | 28.53 E |
| Selenduma | 88 | 50.55 N | 106.10 E |
| Selenga (Selenge) ≏ | 88 | 52.16 N | 106.16 E |
| Selenge, Mong. | 88 | 49.25 N | 103.59 E |
| Selenge, Zaïre | 152 | 1.58 S | 18.11 E |
| Selenge □[4] | 88 | 49.30 N | 106.30 E |
| Selenge (Selenga) ≏ | 88 | 52.16 N | 106.16 E |
| Selenginsk | 88 | 52.06 N | 107.01 E |
| Selenicë | 38 | 40.32 N | 19.38 E |
| Selenn'ach ≏ | 74 | 67.48 N | 144.54 E |
| Selent | 54 | 54.17 N | 10.26 E |
| Selenter See ⊜ | 54 | 54.17 N | 10.28 E |
| Sélestat (Schlettstadt) | 58 | 48.16 N | 7.27 E |
| Seletar ≏ | 271c | 1.25 N | 103.52 E |
| Seletar, Pulau I | 271c | 1.27 N | 103.52 E |
| Seletar Airport ⊠ | 271c | 1.16 N | 103.53 E |
| Seletar Hills | 271c | 1.23 N | 103.53 E |
| Seletar Reservoir ⊜[1] | 271c | 1.24 N | 103.48 E |
| Selezen'ovo, Ross. | 26 | 60.45 N | 28.39 E |
| Selezen'ovo, Ross. | 76 | 59.12 N | 42.18 E |
| Selezni, Ross. | 76 | 55.39 N | 31.29 E |
| Selezni, Ross. | 80 | 52.48 N | 41.15 E |
| Selezn'ovo | 76 | 60.45 N | 28.39 E |
| Self Defense Fleet Headquarters ■ | 268 | 35.18 N | 139.38 E |
| Selfoss | 24a | 63.56 N | 20.57 W |
| Selfridge | 198 | 46.02 N | 100.55 W |
| Selfridge Air National Guard Base ■ | 281 | 42.36 N | 82.49 W |
| Selghar | 272c | 18.57 N | 73.02 E |
| Sel'gon | 89 | 49.36 N | 135.26 E |
| Sélibaby | 150 | 15.10 N | 12.11 W |
| Šelichino | 89 | 50.22 N | 137.38 E |
| Šelichova, zaliv ⊂ | 74 | 60.00 N | 158.00 E |
| Šelichovo | 88 | 55.42 N | 97.41 E |
| Seligenthal | 54 | 50.45 N | 10.28 E |
| Seliger, ozero ⊜ | 76 | 57.13 N | 33.05 E |
| Seligman, Az., U.S. | 200 | 35.19 N | 112.52 W |
| Seligman, Mo., U.S. | 194 | 36.31 N | 93.56 W |
| Selim | 114 | 3.51 N | 101.29 E |
| Selimbau | 112 | 0.37 N | 112.08 E |
| Selimiye | 130 | 37.24 N | 27.40 E |
| Selim River | 114 | 3.50 N | 101.24 E |
| Selínia | 267c | 37.56 N | 23.32 E |
| Selinsgrove | 208 | 40.47 N | 76.51 W |
| Selinunte ⊥ | 70 | 37.35 N | 12.49 E |
| Selišče, Ross. | 24 | 64.58 N | 46.18 E |
| Selišče, Ross. | 76 | 56.53 N | 33.16 E |
| Selitrennoje | 80 | 47.11 N | 47.27 E |
| Selivanovskaja | 80 | 48.52 N | 41.42 E |
| Seližarovo | 76 | 56.51 N | 33.27 E |
| Selje | 26 | 62.03 N | 5.22 E |
| Seljord | 26 | 59.29 N | 8.37 E |
| Selkämeri (Bottenhavet) ⊂ | 26 | 62.00 N | 20.00 E |
| Selke ≏ | 54 | 51.52 N | 11.14 E |
| Selkirk, Mb., Can. | 184 | 50.09 N | 96.52 W |
| Selkirk, On., Can. | 212 | 42.49 N | 79.56 W |
| Selkirk, Scot., U.K. | 46 | 55.33 N | 2.50 W |
| Selkirk, N.Y., U.S. | 210 | 42.32 N | 73.48 W |
| Selkirk Mountains ⋏ | 182 | 51.00 N | 117.40 W |
| Selkirk Provincial Park ♠ | 212 | 42.49 N | 79.58 W |
| Selkirk Shores State Park ♠ | 212 | 43.33 N | 76.12 W |
| Šelkovka | 82 | 55.32 N | 36.22 E |
| Šelkovskaja | 84 | 43.30 N | 46.22 E |
| Sella | 64 | 46.00 N | 11.25 E |
| Sella, Monte ʌ | 64 | 46.40 N | 12.02 E |
| Sella, Passo di (Sellajoch) )( | 64 | 46.30 N | 11.45 E |
| Sella di Corno | 66 | 42.21 N | 13.14 E |
| Sellano | 66 | 42.54 N | 12.55 E |
| Selle ≏ | 50 | 49.54 N | 2.17 E |
| Seller Lake ⊜ | 184 | 55.00 N | 94.32 W |
| Sellero | 64 | 46.03 N | 10.20 E |
| Sellers | 192 | 34.17 N | 79.28 W |
| Sellersburg | 218 | 38.23 N | 85.45 W |
| Sellersville | 208 | 40.21 N | 75.18 W |
| Selles-sur-Cher | 50 | 47.16 N | 1.33 E |
| Sellia Marina | 68 | 38.55 N | 16.45 E |
| Sellières | 58 | 46.50 N | 5.34 E |
| Sellin | 54 | 54.22 N | 13.41 E |
| Sells | 200 | 31.54 N | 111.52 W |
| Selly Oak ◆[8] | 42 | 52.25 N | 1.52 W |
| Selm | 52 | 51.42 N | 7.28 E |
| Selma, Al., U.S. | 194 | 32.24 N | 87.01 W |
| Selma, Ca., U.S. | 226 | 36.34 N | 119.36 W |
| Selma, In., U.S. | 218 | 40.11 N | 85.16 W |
| Selma, N.C., U.S. | 192 | 35.32 N | 78.17 W |
| Selman City | 222 | 32.11 N | 94.58 W |
| Selmer | 194 | 35.10 N | 88.35 W |
| Selmigerheide ◆[8] | 263 | 51.38 N | 7.47 E |
| Selmont | 194 | 32.23 N | 87.01 W |
| Selmsdorf | 54 | 53.48 N | 10.50 E |
| Selommes | 50 | 47.45 N | 1.12 E |
| Šelon' ≏ | 76 | 58.14 N | 30.50 E |
| Seloncourt | 58 | 47.28 N | 6.52 E |
| Selong | 115b | 8.39 S | 116.32 E |
| Selongey | 58 | 47.35 N | 5.10 E |
| Šelopugino | 88 | 51.39 N | 117.33 E |
| Selouane | 34 | 35.04 N | 2.58 W |
| Selous, Mount ʌ | 180 | 62.57 N | 132.31 W |
| Selous Game Reserve ◆[4] | 154 | 9.10 S | 37.10 E |
| Selsdon ◆[8] | 260 | 51.21 N | 0.04 W |
| Selsey | 42 | 50.44 N | 0.48 W |
| Selsey Bill › | 42 | 50.43 N | 0.48 W |
| Selsingen | 52 | 53.22 N | 9.13 E |
| Selston | 44 | 53.04 N | 1.20 W |
| Selters | 56 | 50.32 N | 7.44 E |
| Selty | 80 | 57.19 N | 52.10 E |
| Seltz | 56 | 48.53 N | 8.06 E |
| Selu, Pulau I | 164 | 7.32 S | 130.54 E |
| Selva, Arg. | 252 | 29.46 S | 62.03 W |
| Selva, It. | 64 | 46.33 N | 11.46 E |
| Sel'vačevo | 82 | 55.25 N | 37.57 E |
| Selva di Cadore | 64 | 46.27 N | 12.02 E |
| Selvagens, Ilhas II | 148 | 30.05 N | 15.55 W |
| Selvas ◆[3] | 242 | 5.00 S | 68.00 W |
| Selvino | 62 | 45.48 N | 9.45 E |
| Selway ≏ | 202 | 46.08 N | 115.36 W |
| Selwyn | 166 | 21.32 S | 140.30 E |
| Selwyn, Mount ʌ | 182 | 55.59 N | 123.36 W |
| Selwyn, Passage ʉ | 175f | 16.03 S | 168.12 E |
| Selwyn Lake ⊜ | 176 | 59.55 N | 104.35 W |
| Selwyn Mountains ⋏ | 180 | 63.10 N | 130.20 W |
| Selwyn Range ⋏ | 166 | 21.35 S | 140.35 E |
| Selyatyn | 78 | 47.53 N | 25.12 E |
| Selydove | 83 | 48.08 N | 37.18 E |
| Selz ≏ | 56 | 49.59 N | 8.02 E |
| Šemacha | 86 | 56.15 N | 59.16 E |
| Semai, Pulau I | 164 | 3.08 S | 132.30 E |
| Semakau, Pulau I | 271c | 1.12 N | 103.46 E |
| Seman ≏ | 38 | 40.56 N | 19.24 E |
| Semanggol | 114 | 4.57 N | 100.38 E |
| Semangka, Teluk ⊂ | 112 | 5.36 S | 104.42 E |
| Šemanicha | 80 | 57.18 N | 45.24 E |
| Semans | 184 | 51.25 N | 104.44 W |
| Semanu | 115a | 8.00 S | 110.39 E |
| Semarang | 115a | 6.58 S | 110.25 E |
| Semaria | 124 | 24.16 N | 79.54 E |
| Sematan | 112 | 1.48 N | 109.46 E |
| Semau, Pulau I | 112 | 10.13 S | 123.22 E |
| Semayang, Kenohan ⊜ | 112 | 0.14 S | 116.28 E |
| Sembabule | 154 | 0.05 S | 31.27 E |
| Sembadel | 62 | 45.16 N | 3.41 E |
| Sembakung ≏ | 112 | 3.47 N | 117.30 E |
| Sembawang | 271c | 1.27 N | 103.50 E |
| Sembé | 152 | 1.39 N | 14.36 E |
| Semberong ≏ | 114 | 2.27 N | 103.37 E |
| Semblançay | 50 | 47.30 N | 0.35 E |
| Sembo ≏ | 152 | 7.42 S | 13.01 E |
| Semcy | 76 | 52.51 N | 33.28 E |

| Nome | Página | Lat.°′ | Long.°′ |
|---|---|---|---|
| Şemdinli | 128 | 37.18 N | 4[illegible].35 E |
| Šemeliškės | 76 | 54.40 N | 2[illegible].40 E |
| Semenanjung Malaysia □[9] | 114 | 4.00 N | 10[illegible].00 E |
| Semendua | 152 | 3.11 S | 1[illegible].05 E |
| Semène ≏ | 62 | 45.23 N | [illegible].13 E |
| Semenicului, Munţii ⋏ | 38 | 45.05 N | 2[illegible].05 E |
| Semenivka, Ukr. | 78 | 49.36 N | 3[illegible].10 E |
| Semenivka, Ukr. | 78 | 52.10 N | 3[illegible].35 E |
| Semenyih | 114 | 2.57 N | 10[illegible].51 E |
| Semertak | 89 | 52.57 N | 13[illegible].34 E |
| Semeru, Gunung ʌ | 115a | 8.06 S | 11[illegible].55 E |
| Šemetovo | 82 | 54.28 N | 38.30 E |
| Semežava | 76 | 52.58 N | 27.[illegible]0 E |
| Semiahmoo Bay ⊂ | 224 | 48.58 N | 122.[illegible]8 W |
| Semibalki | 83 | 47.00 N | 39.[illegible]3 E |
| Semibratovo | 80 | 57.18 N | 39.[illegible]2 E |
| Semibugry | 80 | 46.11 N | 48.[illegible]6 E |
| Semichi Islands II | 181a | 52.42 N | 174.[illegible]0 E |
| Semides'atnoje | 78 | 51.21 N | 38.[illegible]4 E |
| Semidi Islands II | 180 | 56.07 N | 156.[illegible]4 W |
| Semigorsk | 88 | 56.42 N | 104.[illegible]1 E |
| Semijarka | 86 | 50.54 N | 78.[illegible] E |
| Semikarakorsk | 80 | 47.31 N | 40.[illegible] E |
| Semilej | 80 | 53.57 N | 45.[illegible] E |
| Semilovo | 80 | 55.04 N | 42.[illegible] E |
| Semiluki | 78 | 51.41 N | 39.[illegible] E |
| Semily | 30 | 50.36 N | 15.[illegible] E |
| Seminara | 68 | 38.20 N | 15.[illegible] E |
| Seminary | 194 | 31.33 N | 89.[illegible] W |
| Seminoe Reservoir ⊜[1] | 200 | 42.00 N | 106.5[illegible] W |
| Seminoe State Park ♠ | 202 | 42.05 N | 106.5[illegible] W |
| Seminole, Fl., U.S. | 220 | 27.50 N | 82.4[illegible] W |
| Seminole, Ok., U.S. | 196 | 35.13 N | 96.4[illegible] W |
| Seminole, Tx., U.S. | 196 | 32.43 N | 102.3[illegible] W |
| Seminole □[6] | 220 | 28.45 N | 81.1[illegible] W |
| Seminole, Lake ⊜[1] | 192 | 30.46 N | 84.5[illegible] W |
| Seminole Draw ∨ | 196 | 32.27 N | 102.2[illegible] W |
| Seminole Park | 220 | 27.52 N | 82.4[illegible] W |
| Seminskij chrebet ⋏ | 86 | 51.05 N | 85.5[illegible] E |
| Semiozerje | 88 | 49.52 N | 110.2[illegible] E |
| Semioz'ornoje | 86 | 52.22 N | 64.08 E |
| Semioz'ornyj | 88 | 53.44 N | 120.25 E |
| Semipalatinsk | 86 | 50.28 N | 80.13 E |
| Semipalatinsk □[8] | 86 | 49.00 N | 80.00 E |
| Semipolka | 86 | 54.07 N | 67.16 E |
| Semirara Island I | 116 | 12.04 N | 121.23 E |
| Semisopochnoi Island I | 181a | 52.00 N | 179.35 E |
| Semitau | 112 | 0.33 N | 111.58 E |
| Semizbuga | 86 | 50.12 N | 74.48 E |
| Semizbugy, gora ʌ | 86 | 50.10 N | 74.56 E |
| Semjany | 80 | 56.02 N | 45.59 E |
| Semli Kalān | 124 | 24.10 N | 76.39 |
| Seml'ovo | 76 | 55.03 N | 33.58 |
| Semmens Lake ⊜ | 184 | 55.03 N | 94.11 W |
| Semmering | 61 | 47.38 N | 15.49 E |
| Semnān | 128 | 35.33 N | 53.24 E |
| Semnān □[4] | 128 | 35.30 N | 54.00 E |
| Semois ≏ | 56 | 49.53 N | 4.45 E |
| Šemonaicha | 86 | 50.39 N | 81.54 E |
| Sem'ono-Aleksandrovka | 78 | 51.03 N | 40.12 E |
| Sem'onov | 24 | 56.48 N | 44.30 E |
| Sem'onovka, Kaz. | 86 | 51.20 N | 70.46 E |
| Sem'onovka, Kyrg. | 85 | 42.43 N | 77.32 E |
| Sem'onovskoje, Ross. | 82 | 55.03 N | 37.46 E |
| Sem'onovskoje, Ross. | 82 | 55.18 N | 38.21 E |
| Šemordan | 80 | 56.11 N | 50.26 E |
| Sempach | 58 | 47.08 N | 8.11 E |
| Sempacher See ⊜ | 58 | 47.09 N | 8.09 E |
| Sempang Mangayau, Tanjong › | 112 | 7.02 N | 116.45 E |
| Semple Lake ⊜ | 184 | 55.02 N | 95.33 W |
| Sempol | 115a | 8.01 S | 114.03 E |
| Semporna | 112 | 4.28 N | 118.36 E |
| Sempu, Pulau I | 115a | 8.26 S | 112.42 E |
| Semuda | 112 | 2.51 S | 112.58 E |
| Semuliki ≏ | 154 | 1.14 N | 30.28 E |
| Semur-en-Auxois | 50 | 47.29 N | 4.20 E |
| Šemurša | 80 | 54.53 N | 47.32 E |
| Šemypolky | 78 | 50.43 N | 30.56 E |
| Šemyšejka | 80 | 52.54 N | 45.24 E |
| Semža | 24 | 66.09 N | 44.08 E |
| Sên ≏ | 110 | 12.32 N | 104.28 E |
| Sena, Bol. | 248 | 11.32 S | 67.11 W |
| Sena, Moç. | 154 | 17.27 S | 35.00 E |
| Sena → Seine ≏ | 32 | 49.26 N | 0.26 E |
| Senador Amaral | 256 | 22.35 S | 46.11 W |
| Senador Canedo | 255 | 16.43 S | 49.05 W |
| Senador Côrtes | 256 | 21.48 S | 42.56 W |
| Senador Firmino | 255 | 20.55 S | 43.06 W |
| Senador Guiomard | 248 | 10.14 S | 67.36 W |
| Senador José Bento | 256 | 22.10 S | 46.10 W |
| Senador José Porfirio | 250 | 2.39 S | 51.55 W |
| Senador Pompeu | 250 | 5.35 S | 39.22 W |
| Senago | 266b | 45.35 N | 9.07 E |
| Senahú | 236 | 15.24 N | 89.50 W |
| Senai | 114 | 1.36 N | 103.39 E |
| Senainville | 261 | 48.30 N | 1.37 E |
| Senaja | 112 | 6.45 N | 117.03 E |
| Senaki | 84 | 42.17 N | 42.04 E |
| Senale | 64 | 46.31 N | 11.06 E |
| Senales, Val di ∨ | 64 | 46.45 N | 10.50 E |
| Sena Madureira | 248 | 9.04 S | 68.40 W |
| Senamaninik | 114 | 0.45 N | 100.47 E |
| Senanayake Samudra ⊜[1] | 122 | 7.11 N | 81.29 E |
| Senang, Pulau I | 271c | 1.11 N | 103.44 E |
| Senanga | 152 | 16.06 S | 23.16 E |
| Sénart, Forêt de ♠ | 261 | 48.40 N | 2.30 E |
| Sénas | 62 | 43.45 N | 5.05 E |
| Senate | 184 | 49.18 N | 109.41 W |
| Senath | 194 | 36.08 N | 90.09 W |
| Senatobia | 194 | 34.37 N | 89.58 W |
| Šenber | 86 | 49.46 N | 66.09 E |
| Šenbertal | 86 | 48.43 N | 60.20 E |
| Sencha | 78 | 50.16 N | 33.20 E |
| Send | 260 | 51.17 N | 0.31 W |
| Sendafa | 144 | 9.07 N | 39.00 E |
| Sendai, Nihon | 92 | 31.49 N | 130.18 E |
| Sendai, Nihon | 92 | 38.15 N | 140.53 E |
| Sendai ≏, Nihon | 92 | 31.51 N | 130.12 E |
| Sendai ≏, Nihon | 96 | 35.32 N | 134.11 E |
| Sendai-heiya ≡ | 92 | 38.15 N | 141.00 E |
| Sendelingsdrif | 156 | 28.12 S | 16.53 E |
| Senden, Dtsch. | 52 | 51.51 N | 7.29 E |
| Senden, Dtsch. | 58 | 48.19 N | 10.03 E |
| Sendenhorst | 52 | 51.50 N | 7.49 E |
| Sendhwa | 120 | 21.41 N | 75.06 E |
| Sêndo | 102 | 31.42 N | 95.16 E |
| Sendurjana | 120 | 21.32 N | 78.17 E |
| Senduruhan | 112 | 1.00 S | 110.46 E |
| Sene ≏ | 150 | 7.30 N | 0.33 W |
| Senebui, Tanjung › | 114 | 2.17 N | 101.03 E |
| Senec | 30 | 48.14 N | 17.24 E |
| Seneca, Il., U.S. | 216 | 41.18 N | 88.36 W |
| Seneca, Ks., U.S. | 198 | 39.50 N | 96.03 W |
| Seneca, Md., U.S. | 284c | 39.04 N | 77.17 W |
| Seneca, Mo., U.S. | 194 | 36.50 N | 94.36 W |
| Seneca, Or., U.S. | 202 | 44.08 N | 118.58 W |
| Seneca, Pa., U.S. | 214 | 41.23 N | 79.42 W |
| Seneca, S.C., U.S. | 192 | 34.41 N | 82.57 W |
| Seneca □[6], N.Y., U.S. | 210 | 42.54 N | 76.52 W |
| Seneca □[6], Oh., U.S. | 214 | 41.07 N | 83.11 W |
| Seneca ≏ | 210 | 43.12 N | 76.17 W |
| Seneca, Mount ʌ | 210 | 42.01 N | 78.49 W |
| Seneca Castle | 210 | 42.53 N | 77.06 W |
| Seneca Caverns ±[5] | 214 | 41.11 N | 82.53 W |
| Seneca Creek ⊂ | 284b | 39.19 N | 76.22 W |
| Seneca Creek ≏ | 196 | 36.36 N | 102.52 W |
| Seneca Falls | 210 | 42.54 N | 76.47 W |
| Seneca Lake ⊜ | 210 | 42.40 N | 76.57 W |
| Seneca Mall ◆[9] | 284a | 42.50 N | 78.47 W |

| | | | | |
|---|---|---|---|---|
| ≏ River | Fluß | Río | Rivière | Rio |
| ≊ Canal | Kanal | Canal | Canal | Canal |
| ⌞ Waterfall, Rapids | Wasserfall, Stromschnellen | Cascada, Rápidos | Chute d'eau, Rapides | Cascata, Rápidos |
| ʉ Strait | Meeresstraße | Estrecho | Détroit | Estreito |
| ⊂ Bay, Gulf | Bucht, Golf | Bahía, Golfo | Baie, Golfe | Baía, Golfo |
| ⊜ Lake, Lakes | See, Seen | Lago, Lagos | Lac, Lacs | Lago, Lagos |
| ≡ Swamp | Sumpf | Pantano | Marais | Pântano |
| ⊓ Ice Features, Glacier | Eis- und Gletscherformen | Accidentes Glaciales | Formes glaciaires | Acidentes glaciares |
| ⍑ Other Hydrographic Features | Andere Hydrographische Objekte | Otros Elementos Hidrográficos | Autres données hydrographiques | Outros acidentes hidrográficos |
| ✦ Submarine Features | Untermeerische Objekte | Accidentes Submarinos | Formes de relief sous-marin | Acidentes submarinos |
| □ Political Unit | Politische Einheit | Unidad Politica | Entité politique | Unidade política |
| ⊽ Cultural Institution | Kulturelle Institution | Institución Cultural | Institution culturelle | Institução cultural |
| ⊥ Historical Site | Historische Stätte | Sitio Histórico | Site historique | Sitio histórico |
| ♠ Recreational Site | Erholungs- und Ferienort | Sitio de Recreo | Centre de loisirs | Area de Lazer |
| ⊠ Airport | Flughafen | Aeropuerto | Aéroport | Aeroporto |
| ■ Military Installation | Militäranlage | Instalación Militar | Installation militaire | Instalação militar |
| ◆ Miscellaneous | Verschiedenes | Misceláneo | Divers | Diversos |

ENGLISH — Name | Page | Lat.°′ | Long.°′
DEUTSCH — Name | Seite | Breite°′ | Länge°′ E = Ost


Seneca State Park ♠ 208 39.08 N 77.15 W
Senecaville Lake ⊜[1] 188 39.55 N 81.25 W
Seneffe 50 50.31 N 4.15 E
Senegal (Sénégal) □[1], Afr. 134 14.00 N 14.00 W
Senegal (Sénégal) □[1], Afr. 150 14.00 N 14.00 W
Sénégal ≃ 150 15.48 N 16.32 W
Seneghe 71 40.05 N 8.36 E
Senekal 158 28.19 S 27.36 E
Senerchia 68 40.44 N 15.12 E
Senetosa, Capu di › 71 41.33 N 8.47 E
Sénez 62 43.55 N 6.24 E
Senežskoje, ozero ⊜ 82 56.12 N 37.00 E
Senftenberg 54 51.31 N 14.00 E
Senga Hill 154 9.22 S 31.12 E
Sengbachstausee ⊜[1] 263 51.08 N 7.09 E
Şengejskij, ostrov I 24 68.27 N 51.05 E
Şengel'dy 85 43.59 N 77.26 E
Šengel'šij 86 48.33 N 57.28 E
Sengés 255 24.06 S 49.29 W
Senggarang 114 1.45 N 103.03 E
Sênggê ≃ 120 32.28 N 79.44 E
Senghenydd 42 51.36 N 3.16 W
Sengilej 80 53.58 N 48.46 E
Sengkamang 114 0.42 N 101.55 E
Sengsengebirge ⩘ 61 47.47 N 14.15 E
Senguer ≃ 254 45.32 S 68.54 W
Sengwa ≃ 154 17.07 S 28.05 E
Sengwarden 52 53.35 N 8.02 E
Senhāti 126 22.53 N 89.33 E
Senhor do Bonfim 250 10.27 S 40.11 W
Senica 30 48.41 N 17.22 E
Senigallia 66 43.43 N 13.13 E
Senirkent 130 38.07 N 30.33 E
Senise 68 40.09 N 16.18 E
Senj 36 44.59 N 14.54 E
Senja I 24 69.20 N 17.30 E
Senjitu 98 41.56 N 116.25 E
Senjō-san ∧ 96 35.26 N 133.36 E
Senkaku-shotō II 90 25.45 N 124.00 E
Senkevychivka 78 50.32 N 25.02 E
Senkobo 154 17.38 S 25.58 E
Sen'kove 83 49.31 N 37.43 E
Şenköy 130 36.05 N 36.05 E
Šenkursk 24 62.08 N 42.53 E
Senlac 184 52.29 N 109.41 W
Şenlikköy ◆[8] 267b 40.59 N 28.47 E
Senlis 50 49.12 N 2.35 E
Senlisse 261 48.41 N 1.59 E
Senmonorom 110 12.27 N 107.12 E
Senn, Ḍahr ou ±[4] 150 18.30 N 11.00 W
Sennaja 78 45.15 N 37.01 E
Sennan 96 34.22 N 135.17 E
Senne (Zenne) ≃ 50 51.04 N 4.26 E
Sennecey-le-Grand 58 46.39 N 4.52 E
Senne II → Sennestadt 52 51.59 N 8.37 E
Sennen 42 50.04 N 5.42 W
Sennestadt 52 51.59 N 8.37 E
Senneterre 190 48.23 N 77.15 W
Senneville 275a 45.27 N 73.57 W
Sennevoy-le-Bas 50 47.48 N 4.17 E
Sennoj, Ross. 80 52.11 N 46.57 E
Sennoj, Ross. 80 50.16 N 43.37 E
Sennokura-yama ∧ 94 36.49 N 138.50 E
Sennori 71 40.47 N 8.35 E
Sennwald 58 47.16 N 9.30 E
Sennybridge 42 51.57 N 3.34 W
Senoia 192 33.18 N 84.33 W
Senonches 50 48.33 N 1.02 E
Senones 58 48.24 N 6.59 E
Senorbì 71 39.32 N 9.08 E
Sénou 150 12.31 N 6.56 W
Sénouire ≃ 62 45.11 N 3.34 E
Şenpazar 130 41.48 N 33.16 E
Šenqu → Orange ≃ 156 28.41 S 16.28 E
Senqunyane ≃ 158 30.03 S 28.10 E
Senriyama 270 34.47 N 135.30 E
Sens 50 48.12 N 3.17 E
Sense ≃ 58 46.54 N 7.14 E
Sensée ≃ 50 50.16 N 3.06 E
Sensée, Canal de la ≊ 50 50.14 N 3.17 E
Sensuntepeque 236 13.52 N 88.38 W
Şenta 38 45.56 N 20.04 E
Šentala 80 54.27 N 51.29 E
Sentani, Danau ⊜ 164 2.36 S 140.34 E
Sentarum, Danau ⊜ 112 0.51 N 112.06 E
Sentas 86 49.19 N 82.28 E
Sentelek 86 51.13 N 83.44 E
Şentery 154 5.22 S 25.45 E
Šentilj 61 46.41 N 15.40 E
Sentinel 196 35.09 N 99.10 W
Sentinel Butte ∧ 198 46.53 N 103.50 W
Sentinel Peak ∧ 182 54.54 N 121.57 W
Sentinel Range ⩘ 9 78.10 S 85.30 W
Şentino ≃ 66 43.24 N 12.59 E
Šentjur 36 46.13 N 15.24 E
Sentolo 115a 7.50 S 110.13 E
Sentosa I 271c 1.15 N 103.50 E
Sento Sé 250 9.51 S 41.51 W
Sentsū-zan ∧ 96 35.09 N 133.11 E
Senyavin Islands II 14 6.55 N 158.00 E
Senye 152 1.34 N 9.50 E
Şenyurt 130 37.06 N 40.40 E
Šenzaki-wan ⊂ 96 34.24 N 131.15 E
Sen-zan ∧ 96 34.21 N 134.51 E
Senzig 54 52.17 N 13.39 E
Senzu-dake ∧ 270 34.57 N 135.52 E
Seo de Urgel 34 42.21 N 1.28 E
Seohāra 124 29.13 N 78.35 E
Seolag-san Kukrip Kongwŏn ♠ 98 38.09 N 128.24 E
Seon 58 47.21 N 8.10 E
Seonāth ≃ 122 21.44 N 82.28 E
Seoni 124 22.05 N 79.32 E
Seoni Mālwa 124 22.27 N 77.28 E
Seorīnārāyan 120 21.44 N 82.35 E
Seoul → Sŏul 98 37.33 N 126.58 E
Seoul Bridge ◆[5] 271b 37.32 N 126.56 E
Seoul National University ⊍[2] 271b 37.28 N 126.57 E
Seoul Stadium ♠ 271b 37.35 N 127.02 E
Seoul Station ◆[5] 271b 37.34 N 126.58 E
Sepahat 114 1.34 N 101.53 E
Sepang 114 2.42 N 101.45 E
Sepanjang, Pulau I 112 7.10 S 115.50 E
Separation Creek ≃ 200 41.59 N 107.28 W
Separation Point › 172 40.47 S 173.00 E
Sepasu 112 0.43 N 117.35 E
Sepatini ≃ 248 7.36 S 65.24 W
Sépeaux 50 47.57 N 3.14 E
Sepetiba ◆[8] 256 22.58 S 43.42 W
Sepetiba, Baía de ⊂ 256 23.00 S 43.48 W
Sepi 175e 8.33 S 159.50 E
Sepik ≃ 164 3.51 S 144.34 E
Sepino 66 41.24 N 14.37 E
Sep'o 98 38.39 N 127.22 E
Sępólno Krajeńskie 30 53.28 N 17.32 E
Sépone → Muang Xépôn 110 16.41 N 106.14 E
Sepopa 156 18.13 S 22.13 E
Sępopol 30 54.15 N 21.00 E
Sepoti ≃ 248 6.43 S 61.38 W
Sepotuba ≃ 248 15.56 S 57.39 W
Seppeltsfield 168b 34.30 S 138.54 E
Seppenrade 52 51.46 N 7.23 E
Sepphoris → Ẓippori 132 32.45 N 35.17 E
Seppois-le-Bas 58 47.33 N 7.10 E
Septeuil 261 48.54 N 1.41 E
Sept Frères, Lac des ⊜ 206 46.20 N 75.10 W
Sept-Îles (Seven Islands) 186 50.12 N 66.23 W
Septvaux 50 49.34 N 3.23 E
Sepulga ≃ 194 31.11 N 86.46 W
Sepúlveda 34 41.18 N 3.45 W
Sepulveda ◆[8] 280 34.13 N 118.28 W
Sepulveda Dam ◆[6] 280 34.10 N 118.29 W
Sepulveda Flood Control Basin ≚[1] 228 34.11 N 118.29 W
Seputih ≃ 112 4.42 S 105.54 E
Sepyč 80 58.11 N 54.08 E
Sequals 64 46.10 N 12.50 E
Sequatchie ≃ 192 35.02 N 85.38 W
Sequeros 34 40.31 N 6.01 W
Sequillo ≃ 34 41.45 N 5.30 W
Sequim 224 48.04 N 123.06 W
Sequim Bay ⊂ 224 48.03 N 123.02 W
Sequoia National Park ♠ 204 36.30 N 118.30 W
Sera 96 34.36 N 133.03 E
Şera, Pulau I 164 7.40 S 131.05 E
Šerabad 128 37.40 N 67.01 E
Serachs 128 36.32 N 61.13 E
Şerafettin Dağları ⩘ 130 39.05 N 41.10 E
Şerafimovič 80 49.36 N 42.43 E
Šeragul 88 54.29 N 100.56 E
Seraidi 36 36.55 N 7.41 E
Seraing 56 50.36 N 5.29 E
Seraja ≃ 82 56.15 N 38.45 E
Serakhovychi 78 51.25 N 24.40 E
Seram (Ceram) I 164 3.00 S 129.00 E
Seram, Laut (Ceram Sea) ⊤[2] 108 2.30 S 128.00 E
Serampore 126 22.45 N 88.21 E
Serang 115a 6.07 S 106.09 E
Serang ≃ 115a 6.43 S 110.35 E
Serangoon 271c 1.22 N 103.54 E
Serangoon ≃ 271c 1.24 N 103.56 E
Serangoon, Pulau I 271c 1.25 N 103.56 E
Serangoon Harbour ⊂ 271c 1.23 N 103.57 E
Serapo 66 41.13 N 13.34 E
Serasan, Pulau I 112 2.30 N 109.03 E
Serasan, Selat ⊔ 112 2.20 N 109.00 E
Seravalle Sesia 62 45.41 N 8.19 E
Seravezza 64 43.59 N 10.13 E
Seraya, Pulau I 271c 1.16 N 103.43 E
Serayevo → Sarajevo 38 43.52 N 18.25 E
Şerayu ≃ 115a 7.41 S 109.06 E
Šerbakul' 86 54.38 N 72.24 E
Serbeulangit, Pegunungan ⩘ 114 3.45 N 97.50 E
Serbia → Srbija □[3] 38 44.00 N 21.00 E
Serchio ≃ 64 43.47 N 10.16 E
Serdce-Kamen', mys › 180 66.57 N 171.40 W
Serdež 80 57.17 N 48.17 E
Serdo 144 11.58 N 41.18 E
Serdoba ≃ 80 52.34 N 44.01 E
Serdobsk 80 52.28 N 44.13 E
Serdyte 83 48.02 N 38.24 E
Séré'ama, Mont ∧ 175f 13.47 S 167.29 E
Serebr'anka, Ross. 86 57.13 N 70.42 E
Serebr'anka, Ross. 265b 55.45 N 37.55 E
Serebr'anka ≃ 265b 55.47 N 37.42 E
Serebr'ansk 86 49.43 N 83.20 E
Serebr'anyj Bor ◆[8] 265b 55.48 N 37.25 E
Serebr'anyje Prudy 82 54.28 N 38.44 E
Serebrovo 88 55.24 N 97.52 E
Serebryans'kyy lis ♠ 83 48.55 N 38.00 E
Sered' 30 48.17 N 17.44 E
Sereda, Ross. 76 55.54 N 35.31 E
Şereda, Ross. 80 58.00 N 40.27 E
Šeredar' ≃ 82 55.56 N 39.04 E
Seredejskij 76 54.03 N 35.14 E
Seredīči 76 53.35 N 35.51 E
Serednikovo, Ross. 80 55.15 N 39.40 E
Serednikovo, Ross. 265b 55.56 N 37.14 E
Seredn'ovo 265b 55.35 N 37.18 E
Seredyna-Buda 78 52.11 N 34.01 E
Seredžius 76 55.05 N 23.25 E
Şereflikoçhisar 130 38.56 N 33.33 E
Šeregeš 86 52.57 N 88.02 E
Seregno 62 45.39 N 9.12 E
Serein ≃ 50 47.55 N 3.31 E
Şeremban 114 2.43 N 101.56 E
Šeremetjevka 80 55.23 N 51.32 E
Šeremetjevo, Aeroport ⊠ 82 55.59 N 37.24 E
Šeremetjevskij 82 55.59 N 37.30 E
Seremuk ≃ 164 1.36 S 131.46 E
Serena 216 41.29 N 88.44 W
Seren del Grappa 64 45.59 N 11.51 E
Serengeti National Park ♠ 154 2.20 S 34.50 E
Serengeti Plain ≚ 154 2.50 S 35.00 E
Serengka 112 1.40 S 110.40 E
Serenje 154 13.15 S 30.14 E
Sereno 256 21.19 S 42.39 W
Seret (Siret) ≃, Europe 38 45.24 N 28.01 E
Seret ≃, Ukr. 78 48.38 N 25.52 E
Serfaus 58 47.02 N 10.36 E
Ser'ga 86 57.46 N 56.52 E
Sergač 80 55.32 N 45.28 E
Sergeant 214 41.38 N 78.45 W
Sergeant Bluff 198 42.24 N 96.21 W
Sergeja Kirova, ostrova II 74 77.12 N 89.30 E
Sergejevka, Kaz. 86 53.51 N 67.25 E
Sergejevka, Kaz. 86 51.39 N 68.13 E
Sergejevka, Ross. 89 44.22 N 131.39 E
Sergejevka, Ross. 89 43.21 N 133.22 E
Sergejevo 86 57.18 N 86.02 E
Sergen 130 41.42 N 27.42 E
Sergijevka 78 51.46 N 41.05 E
Sergijev Posad (Zagorsk) 82 56.18 N 38.08 E
Sergijevskaja, Ross. 76 60.16 N 43.54 E
Sergijevskaja, Ross. 80 50.16 N 43.47 E
Sergijevskij 80 51.56 N 51.54 E
Sergili 85 41.13 N 69.14 E
Sergines 50 48.20 N 3.15 E
Serginskij 72 62.30 N 65.38 E
Sergipe □[3] 250 10.30 S 37.30 W
Sergokala 84 42.27 N 47.40 E
Sergozero, ozero ⊜ 24 66.47 N 36.42 E
Serhiyivka 83 48.40 N 37.22 E
Seria 112 4.39 N 114.23 E
Serian 112 1.10 N 110.34 E
Seriana, Valle V 64 45.55 N 9.55 E
Seriate 62 45.41 N 9.43 E
Seribu, Kepulauan II 115a 5.36 S 106.33 E
Seribudolok, Indon. 114 2.56 N 98.37 E
Seribudolok, Indon. 114 2.51 N 99.04 E
Sericho 154 1.05 N 39.05 E
Seridó ≃ 250 6.12 S 37.10 W
Sérifontaine 50 49.21 N 1.46 E
Sérifos 38 37.09 N 24.31 E
Sérifos I 38 37.11 N 24.31 E
Sérignan-du-Comtat 62 44.11 N 4.51 E
Sérigny ≃ 176 56.47 N 66.00 W
Serik 130 36.55 N 31.06 E
Seringat, Pulau I 271c 1.14 N 103.51 E
Serino 68 40.51 N 14.52 E
Serinyol 130 36.24 N 36.11 E
Serio ≃ 62 45.16 N 9.45 E
Seritinga 256 21.54 S 44.30 W
Serjol 24 60.02 N 48.58 E
Serkhe, Cerro ∧ 248 17.22 S 69.22 W
Serkout, Djebel ∧ 148 23.30 N 6.48 E
Serkovo 82 54.28 N 38.46 E
Şerles ∧ 64 47.08 N 11.23 E
Šerlovaja Gora 88 50.34 N 116.15 E
Serm ◆[8] 263 51.21 N 6.42 E
Sermaise 261 48.32 N 2.05 E
Sermaises 50 48.18 N 2.12 E
Sermaize-les-Bains 56 48.47 N 4.55 E
Serman 80 53.34 N 46.22 E
Sermata, Pulau I 164 8.13 S 128.55 E
Sermide 64 45.00 N 11.18 E
Sermilik ⊂[2] 176 65.37 N 38.03 W
Sermizelles 50 47.32 N 3.48 E
Şermoneta 66 41.33 N 12.59 E
Šerna ≃ 82 55.51 N 38.34 E
Sernambetiba, Pontal de › 287a 23.02 S 43.27 W
Sernambitiba 287a 22.41 S 42.59 W
Sernovodsk 80 53.56 N 51.17 E
Sernur 80 56.56 N 49.09 E
Sernyky 78 51.49 N 26.14 E
Sernyy Zavod 128 39.59 N 58.50 E
Séro 150 14.48 N 11.04 W
Serodino 252 32.37 S 60.57 W
Ser'odka 76 58.10 N 28.12 E
Seroglazka 80 47.01 N 47.29 E
Ser'ogovo 24 62.20 N 50.36 E
Serooskerke 52 51.42 N 3.50 E
Seropédica 256 22.44 S 43.43 W
Serov 86 59.29 N 60.31 E
Serovo 85 40.27 N 71.12 E
Serowe 156 22.25 S 26.44 E
Ser'oža ≃ 80 55.34 N 42.29 E
Serpa 34 37.56 N 7.36 W
Serpeddì, Punta ∧ 71 39.22 N 9.18 E
Serpejsk 76 54.20 N 34.59 E
Serpent, Rivière au ≃ 186 49.33 N 71.14 W
Serpentine 168a 32.22 S 115.59 E
Serpentine ≃ 168a 32.33 S 115.46 E
Serpentine Lakes ⊜ 162 28.32 S 129.09 E
Serpentine National Park ♠ 168a 32.22 S 116.01 E
Serpentine Reservoir ⊜[1] 168a 32.25 S 116.08 E
Serpent Mound State Memorial ⊥ 218 39.02 N 83.26 W
Serpents Mouth ⊔ 241r 10.00 N 62.00 W
Serpneve 78 46.18 N 29.02 E
Serpuchov 82 54.55 N 37.25 E
Serpukhov → Serpuchov 82 54.55 N 37.25 E
Serqo → Sark I 43b 49.26 N 2.21 W
Serra 255 20.07 S 40.18 W
Serra, Monte ∧ 66 43.46 N 10.33 E
Serra Branca 250 7.29 S 36.40 W
Serracapriola 68 41.48 N 15.09 E
Serrada 64 45.53 N 11.09 E
Serra da Canastra, Parque Nacional da ♠ 255 20.10 S 46.40 W
Serra da Capivara, Parque Nacionl da ♠ 250 8.40 S 42.15 W
Serra d'Aiello 68 39.05 N 16.08 E
Serra de'Conti 66 43.33 N 13.02 E
Serra de Outes 34 42.51 N 8.54 W
Serra di Corvo, Lago di ⊜[1] 68 40.51 N 16.14 E
Serradifalco 70 37.27 N 13.53 E
Serra do Navio 250 0.59 N 52.03 W
Serra dos Aimorés 255 17.46 S 40.15 W
Serra do Salitre 255 19.06 S 46.41 W
Serra dos Órgãos, Parque Nacional da ♠ 256 22.26 S 43.02 W
Sérrai 38 41.05 N 23.32 E
Serramanna 71 39.25 N 8.55 E
Serramazzoni 64 44.25 N 10.47 E
Serramonte Center ◆[9] 282 37.40 N 122.28 W
Serrana 255 21.14 S 47.36 W
Serrana, Cayo de ✦[4] 236 14.23 N 80.12 W
Serra Negra 256 22.36 S 46.42 W
Serra Negra do Norte 250 6.40 S 37.24 W
Serrânia 255 21.33 S 46.03 W
Serranilla, Cayo de ✦[4] 236 15.50 N 79.50 W
Serranópolis 255 18.16 S 52.00 W
Serranos 256 21.51 S 44.30 W
Serrara 68 40.42 N 13.54 E
Serra San Bruno 68 38.35 N 16.20 E
Serra San Quirico 66 43.27 N 13.01 E
Serrastretta 68 39.01 N 16.25 E
Serrat, Cap › 36 37.14 N 9.13 E
Serra Talhada 250 7.59 S 38.18 W
Serravalle, It. 66 42.47 N 13.01 E
Serravalle, S. Mar. 66 43.57 N 12.30 E
Serravalle all'Adige 64 45.49 N 11.01 E
Serravalle Scrivia 62 44.43 N 8.51 E
Serre 68 40.35 N 15.11 E
Serre ≃ 50 49.41 N 3.23 E
Serrenti 71 39.29 N 8.58 E
Serre-Ponçon, Barrage de ◆[6] 62 44.33 N 6.30 E
Serre-Ponçon, Lac de ⊜[1] 62 44.30 N 6.17 E
Serres 62 44.26 N 5.43 E
Serrezuela 252 30.38 S 65.23 W
Serri 71 39.42 N 9.08 E
Serrières 62 45.19 N 4.45 E
Serrinha 250 11.39 S 39.00 W
Serriola, Bocca )( 66 43.31 N 12.21 E
Serris 261 48.51 N 2.47 E
Serrita 250 7.56 S 39.19 W
Serro 255 18.37 S 43.23 W
Şersale 68 39.01 N 16.44 E
Šerstobitovo 86 57.16 N 78.52 E
Sertã 34 39.48 N 8.06 W
Sertânia 250 8.05 S 37.16 W
Sertãozinho 256 22.19 S 46.03 W
Sertig-Dörfli 58 46.44 N 9.51 E
Sertung, Pulau I 115a 6.06 S 105.24 E
Seru 144 7.50 N 40.28 E
Şerua, Pulau I 164 6.18 S 130.01 E
Šerubaj-Nura ≃ 86 49.54 N 72.31 E
Serui 164 1.53 S 136.14 E
Seruini ≃ 248 7.42 S 66.42 W
Serule 156 21.58 S 27.20 E
Serutu, Pulau I 112 1.42 S 108.45 E
Seruwai 114 4.21 N 98.10 E
Sérvia 38 40.11 N 22.00 E
Servi Burnu › 130 41.40 N 28.06 E
Servigliano 66 43.05 N 13.29 E
Servon 261 48.43 N 2.35 E
Servoz 58 45.56 N 6.46 E
Serwaru 112 8.10 S 127.42 E
Sêrxü 102 33.04 N 97.45 E
Seryševo 89 51.08 N 128.20 E
ses, Munții ⩘ 38 47.05 N 22.30 E
Šešan 180 66.46 N 171.26 W
Sesayap ≃ 112 3.36 N 117.15 E
Sesayap Lama 112 3.36 N 117.03 E
Seščа 76 53.45 N 33.23 E
Sese Islands II 154 0.20 S 32.20 E
Seseke ≃ 263 51.37 N 7.32 E
Sesfontein 156 19.07 S 13.39 E
Sesheke 152 17.28 S 24.18 E
Seshu 105 39.33 N 115.37 E
Sesia ≃ 62 45.05 N 8.37 E
Sesia, Val V 62 45.47 N 8.05 E
Sesibu 112 4.02 N 116.33 E
Sesimbra 34 38.26 N 9.06 W
Seskar, ostrov I 76 60.02 N 28.23 E
Şeskarö 26 65.44 N 23.44 E
Šešma ≃ 80 55.27 N 51.05 E
Sesmarias ≃ 256 22.28 S 44.27 W
Sesoko-jima I 174m 26.38 N 127.52 E
Sespe 228 34.23 N 118.58 W
Sespe Creek ≃ 204 34.23 N 118.57 W
Sessa 152 13.56 S 20.38 E
Sessa Aurunca 68 41.14 N 13.56 E
Ses Salines, Cap de › 34 39.16 N 3.03 E
Séssé 146 11.30 N 17.34 E
Sessenheim 56 48.48 N 7.59 E
Sesslach 56 50.11 N 10.51 E
Şesta Godano 62 44.17 N 9.40 E
Şestakovo, Ross. 82 56.21 N 35.49 E
Šestakovo, Ross. 88 56.29 N 103.59 E
Sestao 34 43.18 N 3.00 W
Sestino 66 43.42 N 12.18 E
Sesto (Sexten) 64 46.42 N 12.21 E
Sesto Calende 62 45.44 N 8.38 E
Sesto Fiorentino 66 43.50 N 11.12 E
Sestola 64 44.14 N 10.46 E
Sesto San Giovanni 62 45.32 N 9.14 E
Sestra ≃, Ross. 80 52.11 N 49.36 E
Sestra ≃, Ross. 82 56.43 N 37.14 E
Sestriere 62 44.57 N 6.53 E
Sestri Levante 62 44.16 N 9.24 E
Sestri Ponente 62 44.25 N 8.51 E
Sestroreck 76 60.06 N 29.58 E
Sestroreckij Razliv, ozero ⊜ 265a 60.04 N 30.00 E
Şestu 71 39.18 N 9.05 E
Šešupe ≃ 76 55.03 N 22.12 E
Šešurga 80 57.29 N 47.35 E
Šešuvis ≃ 76 55.13 N 22.15 E
Šeta, Liet. 76 55.17 N 24.15 E
Seta, Nihon 270 34.58 N 135.55 E
Seta ≃ 270 34.56 N 135.54 E
Setagaya ◆[8] 268 35.39 N 139.40 E
Setail ≃ 115a 8.30 S 114.21 E
Setaka 96 33.09 N 130.28 E
Setana 92a 42.26 N 139.51 E
Setapak 114 3.11 N 101.42 E
Setauket 210 40.57 N 73.07 W
Sète 62 43.24 N 3.41 E
Sete Barras 252 24.23 S 47.55 W
Sete Cidades, Parque Nacional de ♠ 250 3.50 S 41.40 W
Sete de Setembro ≃ 255 12.56 S 52.51 W
Sete Lagoas 255 19.27 S 44.14 W
Sete Pontes 256 22.51 S 43.05 W
Sete Quedas, Cachoeira das ∟ 250 9.27 S 56.41 W
Sete Quedas, Parque Nacional de ♠ 252 24.02 S 54.12 W
Sete Rios ◆[8] 266c 38.45 N 9.10 W
Setesdal V 26 59.25 N 7.25 E
Seth Ward 196 34.13 N 101.42 W
Setī □[8] 124 29.15 N 81.00 E
Setī ≃ 124 28.58 N 81.06 E
Setlagodi 158 26.16 S 25.06 E
Set Net, Punta › 236 12.28 N 83.30 W
Seto, Nihon 94 35.14 N 137.06 E
Seto, Nihon 96 33.27 N 132.15 E
Seto, Nihon 96 34.44 N 134.02 E
Setoda 96 34.18 N 133.05 E
Seto-naikai ⊤[2] 96 34.20 N 133.30 E
Seto-naikai-kokuritsu-kōen ♠ 96 34.15 N 133.28 E
Seton Hall University ⊍[2] 276 40.45 N 74.15 W
Seton Lake ⊜ 182 50.45 N 122.05 W
Seton Portage 182 50.43 N 122.18 W
Seto-saki › 174m 26.51 N 128.18 E
Setouchi 93b 28.10 N 129.15 E
Seto-zaki › 96 33.40 N 135.20 E
Setraki 78 49.23 N 40.49 E
Setta ≃ 64 44.22 N 11.14 E
Settat 148 33.04 N 7.37 W
Settat □[4] 148 33.05 N 7.30 W
Setté Cama 152 2.32 S 9.45 E
Settecamini ◆[8] 267a 41.56 N 12.37 E
Sette-Daban, chrebet ⩘ 74 62.00 N 138.00 E
Settee Lake ⊜ 184 57.03 N 96.55 W
Settepani, Monte ∧ 62 44.15 N 8.12 E
Settimo Milanese 266b 45.29 N 9.03 E
Settimo San Pietro 71 39.17 N 9.11 E
Settimo Torinese 62 45.09 N 7.46 E
Settimo Vittone 62 45.33 N 7.50 E
Settingiano 68 38.55 N 16.31 E
Setting Lake ⊜ 184 55.00 N 98.38 W
Settle 44 54.04 N 2.16 W
Settlement Point › 169 38.25 S 145.25 E
Settlers 156 25.02 S 28.30 E
Settlers Cabin Regional Park ♠ 279b 40.26 N 80.10 W
Settons, Lac des ⊜ 50 47.11 N 4.04 E
Settsu 96 34.46 N 135.33 E
Setúbal 34 38.32 N 8.54 W
Setúbal ⊏[5] 266c 38.37 N 9.00 W
Setúbal, Baía de ⊂ 34 38.27 N 8.53 W
Setun' ≃ 265b 55.44 N 37.33 E
Seubersdorf 60 49.10 N 11.38 E
Seui 71 39.50 N 9.19 E
Seúl → Sŏul 98 37.33 N 126.58 E
Seul, Lac ⊜ 184 50.20 N 92.30 W
Seul Choix Point › 190 45.56 N 85.52 W
Seulimeum 114 5.22 N 95.35 E
Seulo 71 39.52 N 9.14 E
Seumanyam 114 3.45 N 96.38 E
Seurre 58 47.00 N 5.09 E
Seuzach 58 47.32 N 8.44 E
Sev ≃ 76 52.24 N 34.10 E
Sevan 84 40.34 N 44.57 E
Sevan, ozero ⊜ 84 40.20 N 45.20 E
Sévaré 150 14.32 N 4.06 W
Sevastopol', Kaz. 86 53.08 N 65.44 E
Sevastopol', Ukr. 78 44.36 N 33.32 E
Sevelen, Dtsch. 52 51.29 N 6.25 E
Şevelen, Schw. 58 47.07 N 9.29 E
Ševelevskaja 24 60.52 N 44.12 E
Ševelevskij Majdan 80 54.25 N 42.15 E
Seven ≃ 44 54.11 N 0.52 W
Seven Caves ±[5] 218 39.13 N 83.23 W
Seven Creeks ≃ 169 36.43 S 145.34 E
Seven Harbors 216 42.40 N 83.34 W
Sevenhill 168b 33.53 S 138.38 E
Seven Hills, Austl. 274a 33.46 S 150.57 E
Seven Hills, Oh., U.S. 214 41.23 N 81.40 W
Seven Islands → Sept-Îles 186 50.12 N 66.23 W
Seven Kings ◆[8] 260 51.34 N 0.05 E
Seven Mile 218 39.28 N 84.33 W
Seven Mile Beach National Park ♠ 170 34.49 S 150.46 E
Sevenmile Bridge ◆[5] 220 24.41 N 81.11 W
Sevenmile Creek ≃ 218 39.28 N 84.33 W
Sevenoaks, Eng., U.K. 42 51.16 N 0.12 E
Seven Oaks, Tx., U.S. 222 30.51 N 94.51 W
Sevenoaks □[8] 260 51.18 N 0.10 E
Sevenoaks Weald 260 51.14 N 0.12 E
Seven Palm Lake ⊜ 220 25.12 N 80.44 W
Seven Persons 184 49.52 N 110.54 W
Seven Sisters 42 51.46 N 3.43 W
Seven Sisters Peaks ⩘ 182 54.58 N 128.10 W
Seventy Mile House 182 51.18 N 121.24 W
Seven Valleys 208 39.51 N 76.46 W
Sévérac-le-Château 32 44.19 N 3.04 E
Severance Center ◆[9] 279a 41.31 N 81.33 W
Severka ≃ 82 55.10 N 38.45 E
Severn, S. Afr. 158 26.36 S 22.52 E
Severn, Md., U.S. 208 39.08 N 76.41 W
Severn, N.C., U.S. 208 36.30 N 77.11 W
Severn, Va., U.S. 208 37.17 N 76.24 W
Severn ≃, On., Can. 176 56.02 N 87.36 W
Severn ≃, On., Can. 212 44.52 N 79.41 W
Severn ≃, U.K. 42 51.35 N 2.40 W
Severn, Mouth of the ≃ 42 51.25 N 3.00 W
Severnaja Dvina ≃ 24 64.32 N 40.30 E
Severnaja Osetija □[3], Ross. 72 43.00 N 44.15 E
Severnaja Osetija □[3], Ross. 84 43.00 N 44.15 E
Severnaja Sos'va ≃ 72 64.10 N 65.28 E
Severnaja Zeml'a II 74 79.30 N 98.00 E
Severna Park 208 39.04 N 76.32 W
Severn Bridge ◆[5] 42 51.39 N 2.42 W
Severne 83 48.04 N 38.44 E
Severn Lake ⊜ 184 53.54 N 90.48 W
Severnoje, Ross. 80 58.02 N 41.26 E
Severnoje, Ross. 80 54.06 N 52.32 E
Severnoje, Ross. 84 44.49 N 42.51 E
Severnoje, Ross. 86 56.21 N 78.23 E
Severn River ⊂, Md., U.S. 208 38.58 N 76.23 W
Severn River ⊂, Va., U.S. 208 37.19 N 76.25 W
Severn Tunnel ◆[5] 42 51.35 N 2.44 W
Severnyj, Ross. 24 67.38 N 64.06 E
Severnyj, Ross. 265b 55.56 N 37.33 E
Severnyje uvaly ⩘[2] 24 59.30 N 49.00 E
Severnyj Kommunar 80 58.23 N 54.02 E
Severnyj Prijut 84 43.16 N 41.51 E
Severnyj Ural ⩘ 24 63.00 N 59.00 E
Severo-Bajkal'skoje nagorje ⩘[1] 88 57.00 N 111.00 E
Severočeský Kraj □[4] 30 50.30 N 14.00 E
Severodvinsk 24 64.34 N 39.50 E
Severo-Dvinskij kanal ≊ 76 59.45 N 38.22 E
Severo-Jenisejskij 74 60.22 N 93.01 E
Severo-Kazachstan □[8] 86 54.30 N 69.00 E
Severo-Kuril'sk 74 50.40 N 156.08 E
Severomoravský Kraj □[4] 30 49.45 N 17.50 E
Severomorsk 24 69.05 N 33.24 E
Severo-Mujskij chrebet ⩘ 88 56.30 N 114.00 E
Severo-Sibirskaja nizmennost' ≚ 74 73.00 N 100.00 E
Severoural'sk 86 60.09 N 59.57 E
Severo-Zadonsk 82 54.02 N 38.24 E
Severskaja 78 44.51 N 38.42 E
Severucha 86 58.28 N 63.25 E
Severy 198 37.37 N 96.13 W
Seveso 62 45.39 N 9.09 E
Şeveso ≃ 266b 45.30 N 9.12 E
Ševětin 61 49.06 N 14.35 E
Sevettijärvi 24 69.26 N 28.38 E
Sevier ≃ 200 39.04 N 113.06 W
Sevier, East Fork ≃ 200 38.14 N 112.12 W
Sevier Bridge Reservoir ⊜[1] 200 39.21 N 111.57 W
Sevier Desert ◆[2] 200 39.25 N 112.50 W
Sevier Lake ⊜ 200 38.55 N 113.09 W
Sevierville 192 35.52 N 83.33 W
Sevilla, Col. 246 4.16 N 75.57 W
Sevilla (Seville), Esp. 34 37.23 N 5.59 W
Sevilla □[4] 34 37.25 N 5.35 W
Sevilla, Isla I 236 8.14 N 82.24 W
Seville → Sevilla, Esp. 34 37.23 N 5.59 W
Seville, Fl., U.S. 192 29.19 N 81.29 W
Seville, Oh., U.S. 214 41.00 N 81.51 W
Sevir 130 39.12 N 38.13 E
Şevketiye 130 40.05 N 27.51 E
Ševli ≃ 89 54.08 N 133.04 E
Sevlievo 38 43.01 N 25.06 E
Sevran 50 48.56 N 2.32 E
Sevrej 102 43.35 N 102.12 E
Sèvres 50 48.49 N 2.12 E
Sévrier 58 45.52 N 6.08 E
Şevsk 78 52.09 N 34.30 E
Ševykan 88 54.20 N 106.49 E
Sewa ≃ 150 7.18 N 12.08 W
Sewanee 194 35.04 N 85.55 W
Sewāni 123 28.55 N 75.37 E
Seward, Ak., U.S. 180 60.06 N 149.26 W
Seward, Ne., U.S. 198 40.54 N 97.05 W
Seward, N.Y., U.S. 210 42.43 N 74.37 W
Seward, Pa., U.S. 214 40.25 N 79.01 W
Seward Glacier ⊓ 180 60.22 N 140.15 W
Seward Peninsula ›[1] 180 65.00 N 164.00 W
Sewaren 276 40.33 N 74.15 W
Sewekow 54 53.15 N 12.39 E
Sewell, Chile 252 34.05 S 70.23 W
Sewell, N.J., U.S. 208 39.45 N 75.08 W
Sewen 58 47.48 N 6.54 E
Sewernaja-Semlja → Severnaja Zeml'a II 74 79.30 N 98.00 E
Seweweekspoort 158 33.22 S 21.25 E
Sewickley 214 40.32 N 80.11 W
Sewickley Creek ≃ 279b 40.14 N 79.47 W
Sewickley Heights 279b 40.33 N 80.09 W
Sewickley Hills 279b 40.34 N 80.08 W
Sewri ◆[8] 272c 19.00 N 72.51 E
Sexcello 152 3.58 S 11.38 E
Sexsmith 182 55.21 N 118.47 W
Sexten → Sesto 64 46.42 N 12.21 E
Sextin ≃ 232 25.44 N 105.14 W
Sexton 218 39.42 N 85.27 W
Sexton Island I 276 40.39 N 73.14 W
Seya ◆[8], Nihon 268 35.29 N 139.29 E
Seya ◆[8], Nihon 268 35.27 N 139.30 E
Seybaplaya 232 19.39 N 90.40 W
Seybothenreuth 60 49.54 N 11.43 E
Seybouse, Oued ≃ 148 36.54 N 7.47 E
Seychellen → Seychelles □[1] 138 4.35 S 55.40 E
Seychelles □[1] 138 4.35 S 55.40 E
Seychelles Bank ✦[4] 12 4.45 S 55.30 E
Seyches 32 44.33 N 0.18 E
Seyda 54 51.53 N 12.53 E
Seydim 130 40.33 N 34.45 E
Seydişehir 130 37.25 N 31.51 E
Seyðisfjörður 24a 65.16 N 14.00 W
Seyfe Gölü ⊜ 130 39.13 N 34.23 E
Seyhan ≃ 130 36.43 N 34.53 E
Seyhan Barajı ⊜[1] 130 37.05 N 35.15 E
Seyitgazi 130 39.27 N 30.43 E
Seylac 144 11.21 N 43.29 E
Seym (Sejm) ≃ 78 51.27 N 32.34 E
Seymour, Austl. 169 37.02 S 145.08 E
Seymour, S. Afr. 158 32.33 S 26.46 E
Seymour, Ct., U.S. 207 41.23 N 73.04 W
Seymour, In., U.S. 218 38.57 N 85.53 W
Seymour, Ia., U.S. 190 40.40 N 93.07 W
Seymour, Mo., U.S. 194 37.08 N 92.46 W
Seymour, Tx., U.S. 196 33.35 N 99.15 W
Seymour, Wi., U.S. 190 44.30 N 88.19 W
Seymour ≃ 182 51.05 N 126.50 W
Seymour Inlet ⊂ 182 51.03 N 127.10 W
Seymour Johnson Air Force Base ■ 192 35.21 N 77.58 W
Seymour Range ⩘ 224 48.40 N 124.00 W
Seymourville 194 30.27 N 91.29 W
Seyne 62 44.21 N 6.21 E
Seynod 58 45.53 N 6.05 E
Seyring 264b 48.20 N 16.29 E
Seyssel 58 45.57 N 5.49 E
Şeytan ≃ 267b 41.06 N 28.59 E
Sežana 36 45.42 N 13.52 E
Sézanne 50 48.43 N 3.43 E
Şezela 158 30.24 S 30.42 E
Šežim 24 62.07 N 58.21 E
Sezimovo Ústí 30 49.23 N 14.42 E
Sezze 66 41.30 N 13.03 E
Sfântu Gheorghe 38 45.52 N 25.47 E
Sfântu Gheorghe, Brațul ≃[1] 38 44.53 N 29.36 E
Sfântu Gheorghe, Ostrovul I 38 45.07 N 29.22 E
Sfax 148 34.44 N 10.46 E
Sferracavallo ◆[8] 70 38.12 N 13.17 E
Sfizef 148 35.14 N 0.15 W
Sforzesco, Castello ⊥ 266b 45.28 N 9.11 E
's-Gravendeel 52 51.46 N 4.37 E
's-Gravenhage (The Hague) 52 52.06 N 4.18 E
's-Gravenzande 52 52.00 N 4.10 E
Sgritheall, Beinn ∧ 46 57.08 N 5.35 W
Sgurgola 66 41.40 N 13.09 E
Sha ≃, Zhg. 98 37.31 N 117.50 E
Sha ≃, Zhg. 100 33.39 N 114.38 E
Sha ≃, Zhg. 100 26.35 N 118.02 E
Sha ≃, Zhg. 104 41.21 N 123.07 E
Sha'alav, Har ∧ 132 30.04 N 35.06 E
Sha'alvim 132 31.52 N 34.59 E
Shaanxi (Shensi) □[4] 102 35.00 N 109.00 E
Sha'ar HaGolan 132 32.41 N 35.36 E
Sha'ar Menashe 132 32.27 N 35.01 E
Shab'ā 132 33.21 N 35.45 E
Shaba □[4] 154 8.00 S 27.00 E
Shābah 142 31.11 N 30.46 E
Shabakunk Creek ≃ 285 40.15 N 74.43 W
Shabās al-Milḥ 142 31.12 N 30.39 E
Shabās ash-Shuhadā' 142 31.05 N 30.45 E
Shabās 'Umayr 142 31.06 N 30.48 E
Shabbona 216 41.46 N 88.52 W
Shabeellaha Dhexe □[4] 144 3.00 N 46.00 E
Shabeellaha Hoose □[4] 144 1.30 N 44.15 E
Shabeelle (Shebele) ≃ 144 0.12 S 42.45 E
Shabel'kivka 83 48.45 N 37.29 E
Shabestar 128 38.11 N 45.42 E
Shabo 78 46.08 N 30.23 E
Shabomeka Lake ⊜ 212 44.54 N 77.09 W
Shabotik ≃ 190 48.50 N 85.34 W
Shabqadar 123 34.13 N 71.34 E
Shabrāmant 142 29.56 N 31.12 E
Shabshīr al-Ḥiṣṣah 142 30.52 N 31.04 E
Shabunda 154 2.42 S 27.20 E
Shabwah 144 15.22 N 47.01 E
Shache (Yarkand) 120 38.25 N 77.16 E
Shacheng 105 40.25 N 115.31 E
Shacheng Gang ⊂ 100 27.10 N 120.24 E
Shackan Indian Reserve ◆[4] 182 50.17 N 121.12 W
Shackleton Ice Shelf ⊓ 9 66.00 S 100.00 E
Shackleton Range ⩘ 9 80.40 S 26.00 W
Shādegān 128 30.40 N 48.38 E
Shade Gap 214 40.11 N 77.52 W
Shadehill Reservoir ⊜[1] 198 45.45 N 102.15 W
Shade Mountain ∧ 208 40.34 N 77.30 W
Shades Glen 210 41.11 N 75.42 W
Shadi 100 26.08 N 114.49 E
Shadian 98 35.30 N 114.26 E
Shading 102 31.20 N 94.40 E
Shadow Lake ⊜, On., Can. 212 44.43 N 78.48 W
Shadow Lake ⊜, Ma., U.S. 283 42.50 N 71.14 W
Shadow Lake ⊜, N.J., U.S. 276 40.21 N 74.06 W
Shado-Wood Village 214 40.35 N 79.12 W
Shadrinsk → Šadrinsk 86 56.05 N 63.38 E
Shadui 102 31.30 N 100.10 E
Shady Cove 202 42.04 N 122.36 W
Shady Grove, Fl., U.S. 192 30.17 N 83.37 W
Shady Grove, Tx., U.S. 222 32.48 N 97.01 W
Shady Hills 216 40.36 N 85.41 W
Shady Shores 222 33.10 N 97.02 W
Shadyside 188 39.58 N 80.45 W
Sha'f 132 32.38 N 36.51 E
Shafer, Lake ⊜ 216 40.47 N 86.46 W
Shafer Butte ∧ 202 43.47 N 116.05 W
Shafir 132 31.42 N 34.44 E
Shaft 128 37.12 N 49.24 E
Shafter 226 35.30 N 119.16 W
Shaftesbury 42 51.01 N 2.12 W
Shafton 279b 40.20 N 79.42 W
Shaftsburg 216 42.48 N 84.18 W
Shaftsbury 210 43.00 N 73.11 W
Shafu 100 22.25 N 113.01 E
Shag ≃ 172 45.29 S 170.49 E
Shagamu 150 6.51 N 3.39 E
Shageluk 180 62.36 N 159.32 W
Shag Rocks II[1] 244 53.33 S 42.02 W
Shaguotun 104 41.10 N 120.38 E
Shāhābād, India 122 17.08 N 76.56 E
Shāhābād, India 123 30.10 N 76.53 E
Shāhābād, India 124 27.39 N 79.57 E
Shāhābād, India 272c 19.01 N 73.02 E
Shāhābād, Īrān 128 37.32 N 56.54 E
Shāhābād, Īrān 267d 35.47 N 51.31 E
Shāhāda 120 21.28 N 74.18 E
Shah Alam 114 3.04 N 101.33 E
Shahany, ozero ⊜ 78 45.43 N 29.53 E
Shahbā' 132 32.51 N 36.37 E
Shāhbandar 120 24.10 N 67.54 E
Shāhbāz Kalāt 128 26.42 N 63.58 E
Shāhbāzpur ⊔ 124 22.05 N 90.50 E
Shahdād, Namakzār-e ≚ 128 30.30 N 58.30 E
Shāhdādkot 120 27.51 N 67.54 E
Shāhdādpur 120 25.56 N 68.37 E
Shāhdara, India 272a 28.30 N 77.25 E
Shāhdara, Pāk. 123 31.38 N 74.18 E
Shāhdara ◆[8] 272a 28.40 N 77.18 E
Shahdol 124 23.20 N 81.21 E
Shahe, Zhg. 98 36.56 N 114.30 E
Shahe, Zhg. 98 34.44 N 118.58 E
Shahe, Zhg. 98 37.01 N 119.43 E
Shahe, Zhg. 102 22.06 N 109.43 E
Shahedian 100 33.01 N 113.44 E
Shaheji 100 32.26 N 118.14 E
Shahepu 104 41.08 N 121.01 E
Shaheyi 98 39.53 N 118.31 E
Shaheying 104 40.50 N 120.46 E
Shahezhan 98 35.49 N 116.23 E
Shahezhen 105 40.08 N 116.15 E
Shahezi 89 46.05 N 129.20 E
Shāhganj 124 26.03 N 82.41 E
Shāhgarh, India 120 27.07 N 69.54 E
Shāhgarh, India 124 24.19 N 79.08 E
Shaḥḥāt 146 32.49 N 21.52 E
Shāhī Kowt 123 34.16 N 70.34 E
Shāhjahānpur 124 27.53 N 79.55 E
Shāh Jūy 120 32.31 N 67.25 E
Shāh Kot 123 31.34 N 73.29 E
Shāh Kūh ∧ 128 31.37 N 59.16 E
Shāhpur, India 122 16.42 N 76.50 E
Shāhpur, Pāk. 120 28.43 N 68.25 E
Shāhpur, Pāk. 123 32.17 N 72.26 E
Shāhpura, India 120 27.23 N 75.58 E
Shāhpura, India 120 25.38 N 74.56 E
Shāhpura, India 124 23.11 N 80.42 E
Shāhpur Chākar 120 26.09 N 68.39 E
Shahrak 120 34.06 N 64.18 E
Shahr-e Bābak 128 30.07 N 55.09 E
Shahr-e Kord 128 32.19 N 50.50 E
Shahr-e Monjān 120 36.02 N 70.46 E
Shahr-e Ṣafā 128 31.50 N 66.22 E
Shahrestān 120 34.22 N 66.47 E
Shāhrūd ≃ 128 36.40 N 49.26 E
Shahryār 128 35.28 N 51.05 E
Shahu 100 30.11 N 113.39 E
Shāhzādpur 126 24.10 N 89.36 E
Shā'ib al-Banāt, Jabal ∧ 140 26.59 N 33.29 E
Shaighālu 120 31.11 N 68.49 E
Shaikou 100 27.19 N 117.35 E
Sha'īrah, Jabal ∧[2] 132 30.06 N 34.17 E
Sha'īrah, Jabal ash- ⩘ 132 29.31 N 34.29 E
Shājāpur 124 23.26 N 76.16 E
Shajian 100 24.46 N 117.38 E
Shajianzi 98 41.01 N 125.26 E
Shajiazhuang 106 32.13 N 120.53 E
Shajing 100 23.36 N 114.06 E
Shajingzi 102 37.42 N 105.09 E
Shakaga-dake ∧ 96 33.11 N 130.53 E
Shakaga-hana › 96 34.25 N 134.14 E
Shakaga-take-tunnel ◆[5] 96 33.27 N 130.52 E
Shakardarra 123 33.14 N 71.30 E
Shakargarh 123 32.16 N 75.10 E
Shakarpura 272a 28.46 N 77.21 E
Shakarpur Khās ◆[8] 272a 28.38 N 77.17 E
Shakaskraal 158 29.26 S 31.14 E
Shakawe 156 18.23 S 21.50 E
Shakeng 98 42.13 N 116.35 E
Shaker Heights 214 41.28 N 81.32 W
Shaker Heights Park ♠ 279a 41.29 N 81.33 W
Shakespeare 212 43.22 N 80.49 W
Shākhen 128 33.22 N 59.32 E


**Symbols** in the index entries represent the broad categories identified in the key at the right. Symbols with superior numbers (⩘[1]) identify subcategories (see complete key on page *I · 1).*

**Symbole** im Register stellen die rechts im Schlüssel erklärten Kategorien dar. Symbole mit hochgestellten Ziffern (⩘[1]) bezeichnen Unterabteilungen einer Kategorie (vgl. vollständiger Schlüssel auf Seite *I · 1).*

**Los símbolos** incluídos en el texto del índice representan las grandes categorías identificadas con la clave a la derecha. Los símbolos con numeros en su parte superior (⩘[1]) identifican las subcategorías (véase la clave completa en la página *I · 1).*

**Les symboles** de l'index représentent les catégories indiquées dans la légende à droite. Les symboles suivis d'un indice (⩘[1]) représentent des sous-catégories (voir légende complète à la page *I · 1).*

**Os símbolos** incluídos no texto do índice representam as grandes categorias identificadas com a chave à direita. Os símbolos com números em sua parte superior (⩘[1]) identificam as subcategorias (veja-se a chave completa à página *I · 1).*

| | | | | | |
|---|---|---|---|---|---|
| ∧ | Mountain | Berg | Montaña | Montagne | Montanha |
| ⩘ | Mountains | Gebirge | Montañas | Montagnes | Montanhas |
| )( | Pass | Paß | Paso | Col | Passo |
| V | Valley, Canyon | Tal, Cañon | Valle, Cañón | Vallée, Canyon | Vale, Canhão |
| ≚ | Plain | Ebene | Llano | Plaine | Planície |
| › | Cape | Kap | Cabo | Cap | Cabo |
| I | Island | Insel | Isla | Île | Ilha |
| II | Islands | Inseln | Islas | Îles | Ilhas |
| ± | Other Topographic Features | Andere Topographische Objekte | Otros Elementos Topográficos | Autres données topographiques | Outros acidentes topográficos |

ESPAÑOL — Nombre, Página, Lat.°′, Long.°′ W = Oeste · FRANÇAIS — Nom, Page, Lat.°′, Long.°′ W = Ouest · PORTUGUÊS — Nome, Página, Lat.°′, Long.°′ W = Oeste


| Nombre / Nom / Nome | Página / Page | Lat.°′ | Long.°′ |
|---|---|---|---|
| Shakhtars'k | 83 | 48.03 N | 38.28 E |
| Shakhtne | 83 | 47.57 N | 38.17 E |
| Shakhty → Šachty | 83 | 47.42 N | 40.13 E |
| Shaki | 150 | 8.39 N | 3.25 E |
| Shākir, Jazīrat I | 140 | 27.30 N | 33.59 E |
| Shakopee | 190 | 44.47 N | 93.31 W |
| Shakotan-hantō ≻1 | 92a | 43.20 N | 140.30 E |
| Shakou | 100 | 24.25 N | 113.32 E |
| Shakshūk | 142 | 29.28 N | 30.42 E |
| Shaktoolik | 180 | 64.20 N | 161.09 W |
| Shakujii ◆8 | 268 | 35.45 N | 139.37 E |
| Shakūrpur ◆8 | 272a | 28.41 N | 77.09 E |
| Shala, Lake ⊜ | 144 | 7.25 N | 38.30 E |
| Shalalth | 182 | 50.44 N | 122.13 W |
| Shalatayn, Bi'r ⍑4 | 140 | 23.08 N | 35.36 E |
| Shaleitian Dao I | 98 | 39.03 N | 118.44 E |
| Shaler Mountains ⋏ | 176 | 72.35 N | 110.45 W |
| Shaleshanto | 156 | 19.09 S | 23.58 E |
| Shalford | 260 | 51.13 N | 0.34 W |
| Shālimah | 142 | 31.14 N | 30.52 E |
| Shalimar Railroad Station ◆5 | 272b | 22.33 N | 88.19 E |
| Shaling, Zhg. | 104 | 41.09 N | 122.22 E |
| Shaling, Zhg. | 104 | 41.20 N | 123.01 E |
| Shalingpu | 104 | 41.47 N | 123.11 E |
| Shalingzi | 105 | 40.42 N | 114.55 E |
| Shaliuhe, Zhg. | 102 | 36.28 N | 98.57 E |
| Shaliuhe, Zhg. | 105 | 39.53 N | 117.56 E |
| Shallotte | 192 | 33.58 N | 78.23 W |
| Shallowater | 196 | 33.41 N | 101.59 W |
| Shallow Brook ≃ | 276 | 40.21 N | 74.35 W |
| Shallow Lake | 212 | 44.36 N | 81.05 W |
| Shaluhe | 89 | 51.08 N | 126.00 E |
| Shaluli Shan ⋏ | 102 | 30.45 N | 99.45 E |
| Shalyhyne | 78 | 51.34 N | 34.07 E |
| Shām, Bādiyat ash- (Syrian Desert) ◆2 | 128 | 32.00 N | 40.00 E |
| Shām, Jabal ash- ∧ | 128 | 23.13 N | 57.16 E |
| Shama ≃ | 154 | 6.16 S | 32.27 E |
| Shaman | 85 | 38.50 N | 75.36 E |
| Shamattawa | 184 | 55.52 N | 92.05 W |
| Shambe | 140 | 7.07 N | 30.46 E |
| Shambi | 152 | 1.49 S | 22.39 E |
| Shambu | 144 | 9.40 N | 37.03 E |
| Shambuanda | 152 | 6.38 S | 20.13 E |
| Shām Churasi | 123 | 31.30 N | 75.45 E |
| Shamei | 100 | 24.32 N | 118.25 E |
| Shamepūr ◆8 | 272a | 28.45 N | 77.09 E |
| Shamīl | 128 | 27.30 N | 56.53 E |
| Shāmli | 124 | 29.27 N | 77.19 E |
| Shammākh | 132 | 30.30 N | 35.30 E |
| Shamokin | 208 | 40.47 N | 76.33 W |
| Shamona Creek ≃ | 285 | 40.02 N | 75.43 W |
| Shamrayivka | 78 | 49.46 N | 29.49 E |
| Shamrock, Fl., U.S. | 192 | 29.38 N | 83.08 W |
| Shamrock, Tx., U.S. | 196 | 35.12 N | 100.14 W |
| Shamsābād | 124 | 27.01 N | 78.08 E |
| Shamsher | 272a | 28.44 N | 77.24 E |
| Shamva | 154 | 17.18 S | 31.34 E |
| Shan □3 | 110 | 22.00 N | 98.00 E |
| Shanbiao | 98 | 35.28 N | 113.57 E |
| Shancheng | 102 | 37.01 N | 107.00 E |
| Shanchengzhen | 98 | 42.23 N | 125.26 E |
| Shandaken | 210 | 42.07 N | 74.23 W |
| Shandan | 102 | 38.45 N | 101.15 E |
| Shandatgyi | 110 | 19.37 N | 94.43 E |
| Shandī | 140 | 16.42 N | 33.26 E |
| Shandian ≃ | 98 | 42.23 N | 116.21 E |
| Shandianhe | 98 | 42.22 N | 116.15 E |
| Shandīd | 142 | 30.55 N | 30.40 E |
| Shandon | 226 | 35.39 N | 120.22 W |
| Shandong | 107 | 29.31 N | 106.25 E |
| Shandong (Shantung) □4 | 98 | 36.00 N | 118.00 E |
| Shandong Bandao (Shantung Peninsula) ≻1 | 98 | 37.00 N | 121.00 E |
| Shandrivka | 78 | 48.57 N | 35.46 E |
| Shaner | 279b | 40.17 N | 79.47 W |
| Shanesville | 214 | 40.31 N | 81.39 W |
| Shangalume | 154 | 10.49 S | 26.34 E |
| Shangani | 154 | 19.47 S | 29.22 E |
| Shangani ≃ | 154 | 18.41 S | 27.10 E |
| Shang'ao | 106 | 30.41 N | 119.25 E |
| Shangba | 106 | 32.11 N | 118.46 E |
| Shangbahe | 100 | 30.40 N | 115.05 E |
| Shangbai | 106 | 30.29 N | 119.58 E |
| Shangbancheng | 105 | 40.50 N | 118.03 E |
| Shangbatang | 102 | 32.46 N | 96.20 E |
| Shangcai | 100 | 33.16 N | 114.15 E |
| Shangcang | 105 | 39.54 N | 117.23 E |
| Shangchen | 106 | 30.07 N | 119.53 E |
| Shangcheng | 100 | 31.48 N | 115.24 E |
| Shangchewan | 100 | 29.48 N | 113.01 E |
| Shangch'iu → Shangqiu | 98 | 34.27 N | 115.42 E |
| Shangchuan Dao I | 102 | 21.42 N | 112.47 E |
| Shangdang | 106 | 32.06 N | 119.24 E |
| Shangdayangqi | 89 | 51.09 N | 124.02 E |
| Shangdian | 100 | 34.07 N | 112.23 E |
| Shangdianmiao | 106 | 30.56 N | 120.51 E |
| Shangdouying | 105 | 40.36 N | 115.33 E |
| Shangdu | 98 | 41.29 N | 113.34 E |
| Shangduichunshi | 104 | 41.00 N | 123.02 E |
| Shangdundu | 100 | 27.56 N | 116.15 E |
| Shangfu | 100 | 28.40 N | 114.59 E |
| Shanggaixin | 102 | 23.25 N | 100.02 E |
| Shanggan | 100 | 25.56 N | 119.22 E |
| Shanggang | 100 | 33.30 N | 120.04 E |
| Shanggangzi | 104 | 42.26 N | 123.03 E |
| Shanggao | 100 | 28.18 N | 114.54 E |
| Shanggecun | 106 | 31.49 N | 119.07 E |
| Shanggu | 98 | 40.47 N | 118.28 E |
| Shangguanying | 98 | 41.18 N | 117.07 E |
| Shanghai, Va., U.S. | 208 | 37.37 N | 76.47 W |
| Shanghai, Zhg. | 106 | 31.07 N | 121.22 E |
| Shanghai, Zhg. | 106 | 31.14 N | 121.28 E |
| Shanghai, Zhg. | 269b | 31.14 N | 121.28 E |
| Shanghailingao | 104 | 41.57 N | 120.55 E |
| Shanghai Museum ⊍ | 269b | 31.13 N | 121.28 E |
| Shanghai Shi (Shanghai Shih) □7 | 106 | 31.10 N | 121.30 E |
| Shanghai Station ◆5 | 269b | 31.15 N | 121.28 E |
| Shanghang | 100 | 25.06 N | 116.25 E |
| Shanghe | 98 | 37.19 N | 117.07 E |
| Shanghekou | 98 | 40.26 N | 124.47 E |
| Shanghetou | 105 | 39.12 N | 116.59 E |
| Shanghewantun | 104 | 41.42 N | 123.23 E |
| Shang Hu ⊜ | 106 | 31.39 N | 120.41 E |
| Shanghuang | 106 | 31.33 N | 119.34 E |
| Shanghuangqi | 98 | 41.29 N | 116.31 E |
| Shanghucun | 105 | 40.45 N | 115.45 E |
| Shangjao → Shangrao | 100 | 28.26 N | 117.58 E |
| Shangjiafen | 104 | 41.18 N | 121.10 E |
| Shangjiahe | 98 | 41.51 N | 124.28 E |
| Shangjiaodao | 100 | 29.00 N | 119.54 E |
| Shangjiatai | 104 | 40.53 N | 123.35 E |
| Shangjie | 100 | 27.06 N | 116.06 E |
| Shangjin | 102 | 33.09 N | 110.03 E |
| Shangjiuwu | 100 | 33.59 N | 113.01 E |
| Shangkasa | 120 | 33.45 N | 80.12 E |
| Shangkou | 98 | 36.59 N | 118.53 E |
| Shanglanjiagou | 104 | 40.52 N | 120.37 E |
| Shanglin, Zhg. | 98 | 38.19 N | 116.05 E |
| Shanglin, Zhg. | 102 | 23.28 N | 108.33 E |
| Shanglin, Zhg. | 104 | 41.31 N | 122.14 E |
| Shanglishi | 100 | 27.52 N | 113.46 E |
| Shangliuhezicun | 104 | 41.28 N | 123.32 E |
| Shangliulinzi | 104 | 41.02 N | 123.13 E |
| Shangmagushan | 104 | 41.41 N | 124.10 E |
| Shangmatai | 105 | 39.22 N | 117.15 E |
| Shangmatun | 104 | 40.57 N | 123.22 E |
| Shangmingdian | 106 | 31.12 N | 120.57 E |
| Shangmingju | 105 | 39.41 N | 115.12 E |
| Shangnan | 102 | 33.31 N | 110.45 E |
| Shangpandaoling | 104 | 41.42 N | 121.14 E |
| Shangpeibu | 106 | 31.28 N | 119.13 E |
| Shangping, Zhg. | 100 | 25.57 N | 117.33 E |
| Shangping, Zhg. | 100 | 24.43 N | 115.27 E |
| Shangping, Zhg. | 100 | 24.29 N | 114.38 E |
| Shangpuzi | 104 | 41.37 N | 121.35 E |
| Shangqianbu | 106 | 30.27 N | 120.04 E |
| Shangqiao | 100 | 31.02 N | 117.42 E |
| Shangqing, Zhg. | 100 | 25.53 N | 118.36 E |
| Shangqing, Zhg. | 100 | 28.02 N | 117.00 E |
| Shangqingshuicun | 105 | 39.56 N | 115.38 E |
| Shangqiu (Zhuji), Zhg. | 98 | 34.27 N | 115.42 E |
| Shangqiu, Zhg. | 98 | 34.23 N | 115.37 E |
| Shangrao | 100 | 28.26 N | 117.58 E |
| Shangshe | 102 | 38.15 N | 113.20 E |
| Shangshibatai | 104 | 42.02 N | 120.51 E |
| Shangshui | 100 | 33.33 N | 114.34 E |
| Shangsi | 102 | 22.09 N | 107.57 E |
| Shangtan | 106 | 30.27 N | 118.42 E |
| Shangtang | 100 | 33.23 N | 118.02 E |
| Shan Guan )( | 100 | 27.30 N | 117.06 E |
| Shangweiniuchang | 104 | 40.54 N | 120.44 E |
| Shangxian | 102 | 33.51 N | 109.54 E |
| Shangxingzhen | 106 | 31.32 N | 119.15 E |
| Shangxinhe | 106 | 32.02 N | 118.43 E |
| Shangxinqiu | 104 | 42.27 N | 121.37 E |
| Shangyangbao | 98 | 42.30 N | 124.14 E |
| Shangyangcun | 106 | 30.48 N | 118.40 E |
| Shangye | 98 | 35.26 N | 117.59 E |
| Shangyi (Nanhaoqian) | 98 | 41.04 N | 114.03 E |
| Shangying | 89 | 44.10 N | 127.17 E |
| Shangyinkou | 102 | 32.52 N | 103.04 E |
| Shangyou | 100 | 25.51 N | 114.30 E |
| Shangyou ≃ | 100 | 25.49 N | 114.50 E |
| Shangyou Shuiku ⊜1 | 100 | 25.52 N | 114.21 E |
| Shangyu | 100 | 30.02 N | 120.54 E |
| Shangyuan | 104 | 41.39 N | 120.55 E |
| Shangyun | 102 | 23.01 N | 99.50 E |
| Shangzhai | 98 | 39.13 N | 114.17 E |
| Shangzhaoshugou | 104 | 42.12 N | 121.58 E |
| Shangzhazi | 105 | 40.52 N | 117.42 E |
| Shangzhenzhuang | 105 | 40.20 N | 117.06 E |
| Shangzhi | 89 | 45.13 N | 127.59 E |
| Shangzhuangtai | 105 | 39.41 N | 115.25 E |
| Shanhaiguan | 98 | 40.01 N | 119.44 E |
| Shanhaikwan → Shanhaiguan | 98 | 40.01 N | 119.44 E |
| Shanhecun | 89 | 45.38 N | 128.27 E |
| Shanhetun | 89 | 44.44 N | 127.12 E |
| Shanjiazhuang | 105 | 38.52 N | 115.45 E |
| Shanklin | 42 | 50.38 N | 1.10 W |
| Shankou, Zhg. | 100 | 26.40 N | 117.46 E |
| Shankou, Zhg. | 100 | 28.58 N | 115.12 E |
| Shankou, Zhg. | 100 | 28.48 N | 114.29 E |
| Shankou, Zhg. | 102 | 21.38 N | 109.43 E |
| Shanlenggang | 102 | 28.33 N | 103.23 E |
| Shanli | 100 | 29.52 N | 117.21 E |
| Shanlian | 106 | 30.42 N | 120.19 E |
| Shanmenjie | 106 | 30.40 N | 118.52 E |
| Shanmulong | 102 | 24.39 N | 98.05 E |
| Shannanguan | 100 | 31.36 N | 116.52 E |
| Shannock | 207 | 41.26 N | 71.38 W |
| Shannon, Ire. | 48 | 52.43 N | 8.53 W |
| Shannon, N.Z. | 172 | 40.33 S | 175.25 E |
| Shannon, S. Afr. | 158 | 29.08 S | 26.18 E |
| Shannon, Ga., U.S. | 192 | 34.20 N | 85.04 W |
| Shannon, Il., U.S. | 190 | 42.09 N | 89.44 W |
| Shannon, Ms., U.S. | 194 | 34.06 N | 88.42 W |
| Shannon ≃ | 48 | 52.36 N | 9.41 W |
| Shannon, Lake ⊜ | 224 | 48.37 N | 121.42 W |
| Shannon, Mouth of the ≃1 | 48 | 52.30 N | 9.50 W |
| Shannon Airport ⊠ | 48 | 52.41 N | 8.55 W |
| Shannons Flat | 171b | 35.54 S | 148.58 E |
| Shannontown | 192 | 33.53 N | 80.21 W |
| Shannonville | 212 | 44.12 N | 77.13 W |
| Shanpo | 100 | 30.06 N | 114.20 E |
| Shanrendong | 89 | 46.50 N | 123.08 E |
| Shanrenqiao | 106 | 31.16 N | 120.27 E |
| Shanshan | 86 | 42.52 N | 90.10 E |
| Shanshenmiao | 105 | 40.45 N | 117.11 E |
| Shanshūr | 142 | 30.21 N | 31.00 E |
| Shansi → Shanxi □4 | 102 | 37.00 N | 112.00 E |
| Shanting | 98 | 35.09 N | 117.29 E |
| Shāntipur | 126 | 23.15 N | 88.26 E |
| Shantou (Swatow) | 100 | 23.23 N | 116.41 E |
| Shantung → Shandong □4 | 98 | 36.00 N | 118.00 E |
| Shantung Peninsula → Shandong Bandao ≻1 | 98 | 37.00 N | 121.00 E |
| Shanty Bay | 212 | 44.25 N | 79.36 W |
| Shanwa | 154 | 3.10 S | 33.46 E |
| Shanwei | 100 | 22.47 N | 115.21 E |
| Shanxi (Shansi) □4 | 102 | 37.00 N | 112.00 E |
| Shanxian, Zhg. | 98 | 34.48 N | 116.03 E |
| Shanxian → Sanmenxia, Zhg. | 102 | 34.45 N | 111.05 E |
| Shanxiawu | 100 | 28.52 N | 113.52 E |
| Shanxu | 102 | 22.21 N | 107.58 E |
| Shanyang, Zhg. | 100 | 26.43 N | 119.13 E |
| Shanyang, Zhg. | 102 | 33.35 N | 109.49 E |
| Shanyang, Zhg. | 106 | 31.19 N | 120.16 E |
| Shanyao | 100 | 25.13 N | 118.55 E |
| Shanyaqiao | 106 | 31.15 N | 119.25 E |
| Shanyin | 102 | 39.33 N | 112.50 E |
| Shanzhangjiafen | 105 | 40.37 N | 116.44 E |
| Shanzui | 105 | 40.48 N | 118.13 E |
| Shanzuizi | 104 | 41.55 N | 120.30 E |
| Shaobo | 100 | 32.30 N | 119.32 E |
| Shaodenggao | 104 | 42.13 N | 121.47 E |
| Shaodian, Zhg. | 98 | 34.08 N | 118.25 E |
| Shaodian, Zhg. | 100 | 33.10 N | 114.18 E |
| Shaoguan | 100 | 24.50 N | 113.37 E |
| Shaogudian | 98 | 36.57 N | 115.32 E |
| Shaoguyingzi | 104 | 41.33 N | 120.27 E |
| Shaohing → Shaoxing | 100 | 30.00 N | 120.35 E |
| Shaohsing → Shaoxing | 100 | 30.00 N | 120.35 E |
| Shaojiaolou | 106 | 31.05 N | 121.32 E |
| Shaokuan → Shaoguan | 100 | 24.50 N | 113.37 E |
| Shaowu | 100 | 27.20 N | 117.28 E |
| Shaoxing | 100 | 30.00 N | 120.35 E |
| Shaoyang, Zhg. | 102 | 27.15 N | 111.28 E |
| Shaoyang, Zhg. | 102 | 27.00 N | 111.18 E |
| Shaoyun | 107 | 29.30 N | 105.57 E |
| Shaozihe | 98 | 40.13 N | 123.33 E |
| Shap | 44 | 54.32 N | 2.41 W |
| Shapinsay I | 46 | 59.03 N | 2.53 W |
| Shāpūr ≃ | 128 | 29.39 N | 51.03 E |
| Shaq'ah, Ra's ash- ≻ | 130 | 34.19 N | 35.41 E |
| Shaqqā | 132 | 32.53 N | 36.42 E |
| Shaqq al-Ju'ayfir, Wādī ∨ | 140 | 15.16 N | 26.00 E |
| Shaqrā', Ar. Su. | 128 | 25.15 N | 45.15 E |
| Shaqrā, Lubnān | 132 | 33.12 N | 35.28 E |
| Shaqrā', Sūrīy. | 132 | 32.54 N | 36.14 E |
| Shaqrā', Yaman | 144 | 13.21 N | 45.42 E |
| Shaquan | 86 | 44.33 N | 83.25 E |
| Shaquzhen | 107 | 30.33 N | 103.45 E |
| Sharafābād | 272a | 28.36 N | 77.23 E |
| Sharafkhāneh | 128 | 38.11 N | 45.29 E |
| Sharan Jogīzai | 120 | 31.02 N | 68.33 E |
| Sharatin Mountain ∧ | 180 | 57.49 N | 152.41 W |
| Sharbatāt, Ra's ash- ≻ | 118 | 17.56 N | 56.21 E |
| Sharbīn, Jabal ∧ | 132 | 33.43 N | 36.21 E |
| Sharbot Lake | 212 | 44.46 N | 76.41 W |
| Sharbot Lake ⊜ | 212 | 44.46 N | 76.41 W |
| Share | 150 | 8.50 N | 4.56 E |
| Sharhorod | 78 | 48.44 N | 28.05 E |
| Shari | 92a | 43.55 N | 144.50 E |
| Shari-dake ∧ | 92a | 43.46 N | 144.43 E |
| Sharīṭah, Ra's ≻ | 128 | 26.23 N | 56.23 E |
| Sharivka | 78 | 50.01 N | 35.27 E |
| Shark ≃ | 220 | 25.21 N | 81.05 W |
| Shark Bay ⊂ | 162 | 25.30 S | 113.30 E |
| Shark Point ≻, Austl. | 274a | 33.55 S | 151.17 E |
| Shark Point ≻, Fl., U.S. | 220 | 25.23 N | 81.09 W |
| Shark River Hills | 208 | 40.12 N | 74.03 W |
| Sharktooth Mountain ∧ | 180 | 58.35 N | 127.57 W |
| Sharm ash-Shaykh | 140 | 27.51 N | 34.17 E |
| Sharnbrook | 42 | 52.13 N | 0.32 W |
| Sharnūb | 142 | 31.01 N | 30.35 E |
| Sharon, On., Can. | 214 | 42.53 N | 81.22 W |
| Sharon, Ct., U.S. | 207 | 41.52 N | 73.28 W |
| Sharon, Ma., U.S. | 207 | 42.07 N | 71.10 W |
| Sharon, N.D., U.S. | 198 | 47.35 N | 97.53 W |
| Sharon, Pa., U.S. | 214 | 41.13 N | 80.29 W |
| Sharon, Tn., U.S. | 194 | 36.14 N | 88.49 W |
| Sharon, Wi., U.S. | 216 | 42.30 N | 88.43 W |
| Sharon Center | 214 | 41.06 N | 81.44 W |
| Sharon Hill | 285 | 39.54 N | 75.16 W |
| Sharon Park | 218 | 39.23 N | 84.35 W |
| Sharon Springs, Ks., U.S. | 198 | 38.53 N | 101.45 W |
| Sharon Springs, N.Y., U.S. | 210 | 42.48 N | 74.37 W |
| Sharon Valley | 207 | 41.53 N | 73.29 W |
| Sharonville | 218 | 39.16 N | 84.24 W |
| Sharpe, Lake ⊜1 | 198 | 44.05 N | 99.55 W |
| Sharpe Lake ⊜ | 184 | 54.24 N | 93.30 W |
| Sharpes | 220 | 28.25 N | 80.45 W |
| Sharp Island I | 271d | 22.22 N | 114.17 E |
| Sharpley | 285 | 39.48 N | 75.33 W |
| Sharp Park ♠ | 282 | 37.37 N | 122.29 W |
| Sharp Peak ∧ | 116 | 5.58 N | 125.31 E |
| Sharpsburg, Il., U.S. | 219 | 39.37 N | 89.21 W |
| Sharpsburg, Ky., U.S. | 218 | 38.12 N | 83.55 W |
| Sharpsburg, Pa., U.S. | 279b | 40.29 N | 79.55 W |
| Sharps Hill | 279b | 40.30 N | 79.56 W |
| Sharps Run ≃ | 285 | 39.54 N | 74.49 W |
| Sharpsville, In., U.S. | 216 | 40.22 N | 86.05 W |
| Sharpsville, Pa., U.S. | 214 | 41.15 N | 80.28 W |
| Sharptown, Md., U.S. | 208 | 38.32 N | 75.43 W |
| Sharptown, N.J., U.S. | 285 | 39.39 N | 75.21 W |
| Sharqī, Al-Jabal ash- (Anti-Lebanon) ⋏ | 132 | 33.35 N | 36.00 E |
| Sharqīyah, Aṣ-Ṣaḥrā' ash- (Arabian Desert) ◆2 | 140 | 28.00 N | 32.00 E |
| Sharqpur | 123 | 31.28 N | 74.06 E |
| Sharshar, Jabal ∧2 | 140 | 23.52 N | 30.20 E |
| Shartlesville | 208 | 40.31 N | 76.06 W |
| Shārūnah | 142 | 28.36 N | 30.51 E |
| Shārūnah, Wādī ∨ | 142 | 28.36 N | 30.52 E |
| Shasha | 144 | 6.20 N | 35.57 E |
| Shashe ≃ | 156 | 22.14 S | 29.20 E |
| Shashemene | 144 | 7.12 N | 38.43 E |
| Shashi | 102 | 30.19 N | 112.14 E |
| Shashibu | 100 | 25.48 N | 114.54 E |
| Shasi → Shashi | 102 | 30.19 N | 112.14 E |
| Shasta | 204 | 40.36 N | 122.29 W |
| Shasta ≃ | 204 | 41.50 N | 122.35 W |
| Shasta, Mount ∧1 | 204 | 41.20 N | 122.20 W |
| Shasta Lake ⊜1 | 204 | 40.50 N | 122.25 W |
| Shatangjiang | 106 | 31.25 N | 120.01 E |
| Shaṭānūf | 142 | 30.14 N | 31.04 E |
| Shatawī | 140 | 14.39 N | 32.06 E |
| Shāṭi', Wādī ash- ∨ | 146 | 27.30 N | 13.15 E |
| Shatian, Zhg. | 100 | 25.53 N | 113.44 E |
| Shatian, Zhg. | 100 | 23.59 N | 113.56 E |
| Shatila | 132 | 33.51 N | 35.30 E |
| Sha Tin | 271d | 22.23 N | 114.11 E |
| Shats'k | 78 | 51.31 N | 23.57 E |
| Shats'kyy Pryrodnyy Natsional'nyy Park ♠ | 78 | 51.30 N | 23.55 E |
| Shatt al-Arab → Arab, Shatt al- ≃ | 128 | 29.57 N | 48.34 E |
| Shattuck | 196 | 36.16 N | 99.52 W |
| Shatuji | 98 | 35.18 N | 115.45 E |
| Shatuosi | 102 | 31.20 N | 108.51 E |
| Shauck | 214 | 40.37 N | 82.40 W |
| Shaunavon | 184 | 49.40 N | 108.25 W |
| Shaver Lake | 226 | 37.09 N | 119.18 W |
| Shaver Lake ⊜1 | 226 | 37.08 N | 119.17 W |
| Shavertown | 210 | 41.19 N | 75.55 W |
| Shavé Ẕiyyon | 132 | 32.59 N | 35.05 E |
| Shavington | 44 | 53.04 N | 2.27 W |
| Shaw, Eng., U.K. | 44 | 53.34 N | 2.05 W |
| Shaw, Ms., U.S. | 194 | 33.36 N | 90.46 W |
| Shaw ≃ | 162 | 20.20 S | 119.17 E |
| Shaw Air Force Base ■ | 192 | 33.58 N | 80.29 W |
| Shawan, Zhg. | 86 | 44.34 N | 85.48 E |
| Shawan, Zhg. | 100 | 27.52 N | 119.28 E |
| Shawan, Zhg. | 107 | 29.25 N | 103.33 E |
| Shawanaga Inlet ⊂ | 190 | 45.32 N | 80.24 W |
| Shawangunk Kill ≃ | 210 | 41.41 N | 74.10 W |
| Shawangunk Mountains ⋏ | 210 | 41.35 N | 74.30 W |
| Shawano | 190 | 44.46 N | 88.36 W |
| Shawbury | 42 | 52.47 N | 2.39 W |
| Shaw Creek ≃ | 192 | 33.34 N | 81.30 W |
| Shawforth | 262 | 53.41 N | 2.10 W |
| Shawhan | 218 | 38.18 N | 84.16 W |
| Shawinigan | 206 | 46.33 N | 72.45 W |
| Shawinigan ≃ | 206 | 46.32 N | 72.46 W |
| Shawinigan, Lac ⊜ | 206 | 46.41 N | 73.10 W |
| Shawinigan Falls → Shawinigan | 206 | 46.33 N | 72.45 W |
| Shawinigan-Sud | 206 | 46 31 N | 72.45 W |
| Shaw Island I | 224 | 48.34 N | 122.57 W |
| Shawmarī, Wādī ash- ∨ | 132 | 30.21 N | 36.25 E |
| Shawmere ≃ | 190 | 48.20 N | 82.28 W |
| Shawnee, Ks., U.S. | 198 | 39.02 N | 94.43 W |
| Shawnee, Oh., U.S. | 188 | 39.36 N | 82.12 W |
| Shawnee, Ok., U.S. | 196 | 35.19 N | 96.55 W |
| Shawnee, Lake ⊜ | 276 | 40.58 N | 74.35 W |
| Shawnee Hills | 214 | 40.07 N | 83.09 W |
| Shawnee On Delaware | 210 | 41.01 N | 75.07 W |
| Shawnee State Park ♠ | 218 | 38.43 N | 83.10 W |
| Shawneetown | 194 | 37.42 N | 88.11 W |
| Shawnī | 142 | 30.45 N | 30.55 E |
| Shawnigan Lake | 224 | 48.38 N | 123.35 W |
| Shawnigan Lake ⊜ | 224 | 48.37 N | 123.37 W |
| Shawo, Som. | 144 | 3.26 N | 45.21 E |
| Shawo, Zhg. | 98 | 34.28 N | 114.37 E |
| Shawo, Zhg. | 100 | 31.44 N | 115.08 E |
| Shawo, Zhg. | 100 | 28.52 N | 114.47 E |
| Shawsheen ≃ | 283 | 42.42 N | 71.08 W |
| Shawsheen Village | 283 | 42.40 N | 71.09 W |
| Shawtown | 279b | 40.20 N | 79.42 W |
| Shawville | 188 | 45.36 N | 76.30 W |
| Shaxi, Zhg. | 100 | 28.34 N | 118.06 E |
| Shaxi, Zhg. | 100 | 26.53 N | 115.34 E |
| Shaxi, Zhg. | 100 | 24.38 N | 113.42 E |
| Shaxi, Zhg. | 106 | 31.34 N | 121.04 E |
| Shaxian | 100 | 26.24 N | 117.47 E |
| Shaxikou | 100 | 26.33 N | 118.02 E |
| Shaximiao | 107 | 29.57 N | 106.19 E |
| Shayang | 100 | 30.42 N | 112.33 E |
| Shaybārā I | 128 | 25.27 N | 36.48 E |
| Shay Gap | 162 | 20.25 S | 120.03 E |
| Shaykh, Jabal ash- (Mount Hermon) ∧ | 132 | 33.26 N | 35.51 E |
| Shaykh, Wādī ash- ∨ | 142 | 28.48 N | 30.55 E |
| Shaykh Al-Ḥadīd | 130 | 36.30 N | 36.35 E |
| Shaykh Miskīn | 132 | 32.49 N | 36.09 E |
| Shaykh Sa'd | 128 | 32.34 N | 46.17 E |
| Shaykh 'Uthmān | 144 | 12.52 N | 44.59 E |
| Shayuan | 100 | 27.45 N | 120.38 E |
| Shazhen | 98 | 36.23 N | 115.47 E |
| Shazhou | 106 | 31.52 N | 120.32 E |
| Shazihe | 102 | 32.12 N | 106.42 E |
| Shchastya | 83 | 48.44 N | 39.14 E |
| Shchekino → Ščokino | 76 | 54.01 N | 37.31 E |
| Shchelkovo → Ščolkovo | 76 | 55.55 N | 38.00 E |
| Shcherbakov → Rybinsk | 76 | 58.03 N | 38.52 E |
| Shchors | 78 | 51.49 N | 31.59 E |
| Shchors'k | 78 | 48.22 N | 34.06 E |
| Shchotove | 83 | 48.09 N | 39.04 E |
| She ≃ | 100 | 30.41 N | 114.32 E |
| Sheaf ≃ | 44 | 53.23 N | 1.26 W |
| Shea Island I | 276 | 41.03 N | 73.24 W |
| Sheakleyville | 214 | 41.27 N | 80.13 W |
| Shea Stadium ♠ | 276 | 40.45 N | 73.51 W |
| Shebele | 144 | 9.43 N | 42.43 E |
| Shebele (Shabeelle) ≃ | 144 | 0.12 S | 42.45 E |
| Shebelynka | 78 | 49.27 N | 36.30 E |
| Sheberghān | 120 | 36.41 N | 65.45 E |
| Shebeshekong ≃ | 212 | 45.26 N | 80.19 W |
| Sheboygan | 190 | 43.45 N | 87.42 W |
| Sheboygan ≃ | 190 | 43.45 N | 87.42 W |
| Sheboygan Falls | 190 | 43.43 N | 87.48 W |
| Shebu | 100 | 27.40 N | 112.48 E |
| Shechem → Nābulus | 132 | 32.13 N | 35.16 E |
| Shechem ⊥ | 132 | 32.13 N | 35.15 E |
| Shecheng | 102 | 37.14 N | 113.05 E |
| Shedd Canyon ∨ | 226 | 35.39 N | 120.26 W |
| Shedden | 214 | 42.44 N | 81.21 W |
| Shediac | 186 | 46.13 N | 64.32 W |
| Shedin Peak ∧ | 182 | 55.55 N | 127.32 W |
| Sheekh | 144 | 9.56 N | 45.11 E |
| Sheelin, Lough ⊜ | 48 | 53.48 N | 7.22 W |
| Sheenjek ≃ | 180 | 66.45 N | 144.33 W |
| Sheep ≃ | 182 | 50.44 N | 113.51 W |
| Sheep Creek ≃, Ab., Can. | 182 | 54.04 N | 119.00 W |
| Sheep Creek ≃, U.S. | 202 | 42.27 N | 115.36 W |
| Sheep Creek ≃, Ut., U.S. | 200 | 40.55 N | 109.39 W |
| Sheep Creek ≃, Wy., U.S. | 200 | 42.03 N | 106.04 W |
| Sheep Haven ⊂ | 48 | 55.10 N | 7.52 W |
| Sheepmoor | 158 | 26.42 S | 30.13 E |
| Sheep Mountain ∧, Az., U.S. | 200 | 32.32 N | 114.14 W |
| Sheep Mountain ∧, Wy., U.S. | 200 | 43.33 N | 110.32 W |
| Sheep Peak ∧ | 196 | 31.14 N | 104.59 W |
| Sheepranch | 226 | 38.13 N | 120.28 W |
| Sheep Range ⋏ | 204 | 36.45 N | 115.05 W |
| Sheepshead Bay ◆8 | 276 | 40.35 N | 73.56 W |
| 's-Heerenberg | 52 | 51.53 N | 6.15 E |
| 's-Heerenhoek | 52 | 51.27 N | 3.46 E |
| Sheerness | 42 | 51.27 N | 0.45 E |
| Sheet Harbour | 186 | 44.55 N | 62.32 W |
| Shefar'am | 132 | 32.48 N | 35.10 E |
| Sheffield, N.Z. | 172 | 43.23 S | 172.01 E |
| Sheffield, Eng., U.K. | 44 | 53.23 N | 1.28 W |
| Sheffield, Al., U.S. | 194 | 34.45 N | 87.41 W |
| Sheffield, Il., U.S. | 190 | 41.21 N | 89.44 W |
| Sheffield, Ia., U.S. | 190 | 42.53 N | 93.12 W |
| Sheffield, Ma., U.S. | 207 | 42.06 N | 73.21 W |
| Sheffield, Oh., U.S. | 214 | 41.25 N | 82.05 W |
| Sheffield, Pa., U.S. | 214 | 41.42 N | 79.02 W |
| Sheffield, Tx., U.S. | 196 | 30.41 N | 101.49 W |
| Sheffield Island I | 276 | 41.03 N | 73.25 W |
| Sheffield Island Harbor ⊂ | 276 | 41.03 N | 73.25 W |
| Sheffield Lake | 214 | 41.29 N | 82.06 W |
| Sheffield Lake ⊜ | 186 | 49.20 N | 56.35 W |
| Shefford | 42 | 52.02 N | 0.20 W |
| Shefford □6 | 206 | 45.25 N | 72.30 W |
| Shefu | 100 | 26.11 N | 115.22 E |
| Shegangshi | 100 | 28.32 N | 113.36 E |
| Shegaon | 122 | 20.47 N | 76.41 E |
| Sheho | 184 | 51.38 N | 103.12 W |
| Shehong | 102 | 30.56 N | 105.22 E |
| Shehongmiao | 107 | 30.44 N | 106.03 E |
| Shehy Mountains ⋏ | 48 | 51.48 N | 9.15 W |
| Sheikh Hasan | 144 | 12.04 N | 35.53 E |
| Sheikhpura | 124 | 25.09 N | 85.51 E |
| Shekatika | 186 | 51.17 N | 58.20 W |
| Shekhūpura | 123 | 31.42 N | 73.59 E |
| Sheki → Şeki | 84 | 41.12 N | 47.12 E |
| Shekki → Zhongshan | 100 | 22.31 N | 113.22 E |
| Shek Kong | 271d | 22.26 N | 114.06 E |
| Shek Kong Airfield ⊠ | 271d | 22.27 N | 114.05 E |
| Shek Kwu Chau I | 271d | 22.12 N | 113.59 E |
| Shekou | 100 | 30.44 N | 114.20 E |
| Shek Uk Shan ∧ | 271d | 22.27 N | 114.18 E |
| Shelagyote Peak ∧ | 182 | 55.58 N | 127.12 W |
| Shelbina | 219 | 39.41 N | 92.02 W |
| Shelbourne | 169 | 36.52 S | 144.01 E |
| Shelburn | 194 | 39.11 N | 87.24 W |
| Shelburne, N.S., Can. | 186 | 43.46 N | 65.19 W |
| Shelburne, On., Can. | 212 | 44.04 N | 80.12 W |
| Shelburne Bay ⊂ | 164 | 11.49 S | 143.00 E |
| Shelburne Falls | 207 | 42.36 N | 72.44 W |
| Shelby, In., U.S. | 216 | 41.11 N | 87.20 W |
| Shelby, Ia., U.S. | 198 | 41.30 N | 95.27 W |
| Shelby, Mi., U.S. | 190 | 43.36 N | 86.21 W |
| Shelby, Ms., U.S. | 194 | 33.57 N | 90.46 W |
| Shelby, Mt., U.S. | 202 | 48.30 N | 111.51 W |
| Shelby, Ne., U.S. | 198 | 41.11 N | 97.25 W |
| Shelby, N.C., U.S. | 192 | 35.17 N | 81.32 W |
| Shelby, Oh., U.S. | 214 | 40.52 N | 82.39 W |
| Shelby □6, Il., U.S. | 219 | 39.24 N | 88.48 W |
| Shelby □6, In., U.S. | 218 | 39.31 N | 85.47 W |
| Shelby □6, Ky., U.S. | 218 | 38.15 N | 85.13 W |
| Shelby □6, Mo., U.S. | 219 | 39.49 N | 92.03 W |
| Shelby □6, Oh., U.S. | 216 | 40.17 N | 84.09 W |
| Shelby Village | 281 | 42.38 N | 83.04 W |
| Shelbyville, Il., U.S. | 219 | 39.24 N | 88.47 W |
| Shelbyville, In., U.S. | 218 | 39.31 N | 85.46 W |
| Shelbyville, Ky., U.S. | 218 | 38.12 N | 85.13 W |
| Shelbyville, Mo., U.S. | 219 | 39.48 N | 92.02 W |
| Shelbyville, Tn., U.S. | 194 | 35.29 N | 86.27 W |
| Shelbyville, Lake ⊜1 | 219 | 39.30 N | 88.40 W |
| Sheldon, Il., U.S. | 216 | 40.46 N | 87.33 W |
| Sheldon, Ia., U.S. | 198 | 43.10 N | 95.51 W |
| Sheldon, Mi., U.S. | 216 | 42.17 N | 83.28 W |
| Sheldon, Mo., U.S. | 194 | 37.39 N | 94.17 W |
| Sheldon, Tx., U.S. | 222 | 29.52 N | 95.08 W |
| Sheldon Brook ≃ | 276 | 41.03 N | 73.52 W |
| Sheldon Creek ≃ | 212 | 44.07 N | 79.53 W |
| Sheldon Point | 180 | 62.32 N | 164.52 W |
| Sheldon Reservoir ⊜1 | 222 | 29.52 N | 95.10 W |
| Sheldonville | 283 | 42.02 N | 71.23 W |
| Sheldrake ≃ | 276 | 40.57 N | 73.44 W |
| Sheldrake Lake ⊜, On., Can. | 212 | 44.49 N | 77.16 W |
| Sheldrake Lake ⊜, N.Y., U.S. | 276 | 40.57 N | 73.46 W |
| Shelikof Strait ʮ | 180 | 57.30 N | 155.00 W |
| Shell ≃ | 184 | 50.58 N | 101.24 W |
| Shell, Loch ⊂ | 46 | 58.00 N | 6.30 W |
| Shellbrook | 184 | 53.13 N | 106.24 W |
| Shell Brook ≃ | 184 | 53.21 N | 106.00 W |
| Shell Creek ≃, U.S. | 200 | 40.56 N | 108.37 W |
| Shell Creek ≃, Ne., U.S. | 198 | 41.27 N | 96.58 W |
| Shell Creek ≃, N.D., U.S. | 198 | 47.59 N | 102.17 W |
| Shell Creek ≃, Wy., U.S. | 202 | 44.31 N | 108.03 W |
| Shellen | 146 | 9.54 N | 12.00 E |
| Shelley, B.C., Can. | 182 | 54.00 N | 122.37 W |
| Shelley, Id., U.S. | 202 | 43.22 N | 112.07 W |
| Shellharbour | 170 | 34.35 S | 150.52 E |
| Shell Lake, Sk., Can. | 184 | 53.18 N | 107.04 W |
| Shell Lake, Wi., U.S. | 190 | 45.44 N | 91.55 W |
| Shell Lakes ⊜ | 162 | 29.21 S | 127.25 E |
| Shellman | 192 | 31.45 N | 84.36 W |
| Shellmouth Dam ◆6 | 184 | 50.58 N | 101.25 W |
| Shellow Bowells | 260 | 51.45 N | 0.20 E |
| Shell Rock | 190 | 42.42 N | 92.34 W |
| Shell Rock ≃ | 190 | 42.38 N | 92.30 W |
| Shellrock Peak ∧ | 224 | 46.43 N | 121.14 W |
| Shellsburg | 190 | 42.05 N | 91.52 W |
| Shelocta | 214 | 40.39 N | 79.18 W |
| Shelter, Port ⊂ | 271d | 22.21 N | 114.17 E |
| Shelter Island | 207 | 41.04 N | 72.20 W |
| Shelter Island I, H.K. | 271d | 22.20 N | 114.17 E |
| Shelter Island I, N.Y., U.S. | 207 | 41.04 N | 72.20 W |
| Shelter Island Heights | 207 | 41.05 N | 72.21 W |
| Shelter Island Sound ʮ | 207 | 41.03 N | 72.22 W |
| Shelton, Ct., U.S. | 207 | 41.18 N | 73.05 W |
| Shelton, Ne., U.S. | 198 | 40.47 N | 98.44 W |
| Shelton, Wa., U.S. | 224 | 47.13 N | 123.06 W |
| Shemanker ≃ | 150 | 8.12 N | 9.45 E |
| Shemogue | 186 | 46.09 N | 64.11 W |
| Shemya Station | 181a | 52.43 N | 174.05 E |
| Shenandoah, Ia., U.S. | 198 | 40.45 N | 95.22 W |
| Shenandoah, Pa., U.S. | 208 | 40.49 N | 76.12 W |
| Shenandoah, Va., U.S. | 188 | 38.29 N | 78.37 W |
| Shenandoah ≃ | 188 | 39.19 N | 77.44 W |
| Shenandoah, North Fork ≃ | 188 | 38.57 N | 78.12 W |
| Shenandoah, South Fork ≃ | 188 | 38.57 N | 78.12 W |
| Shenandoah Heights | 210 | 40.49 N | 76.12 W |
| Shenandoah National Park ♠ | 188 | 38.48 N | 78.12 W |
| Shenango | 214 | 41.23 N | 80.24 W |
| Shenango ≃ | 214 | 40.57 N | 80.23 W |
| Shenango River Lake ⊜1 | 214 | 41.22 N | 80.28 W |
| Shenchi | 102 | 39.09 N | 112.19 E |
| Shencottah | 122 | 8.58 N | 77.16 E |
| Shencun | 106 | 31.04 N | 118.51 E |
| Shendam | 150 | 8.53 N | 9.32 E |
| Shendang | 106 | 30.34 N | 120.49 E |
| Shending Shan ∧ | 89 | 46.38 N | 133.28 E |
| Shenduncun | 106 | 30.48 N | 120.25 E |
| Shenfield | 260 | 51.38 N | 0.19 E |
| Shengang, Zhg. | 100 | 27.20 N | 116.18 E |
| Shengang, Zhg. | 106 | 31.54 N | 120.08 E |
| Shenge | 150 | 7.55 N | 12.57 W |
| Shengfang | 105 | 39.04 N | 116.42 E |
| Shenggongjing | 106 | 31.07 N | 119.48 E |
| Shenghongqing | 100 | 30.12 N | 114.56 E |
| Shengjiachi | 107 | 30.28 N | 105.03 E |
| Shengjiaqiao | 106 | 31.27 N | 121.24 E |
| Shengjiatun | 104 | 41.14 N | 121.22 E |
| Shengjin'gao | 104 | 42.04 N | 120.43 E |
| Shengou | 100 | 34.08 N | 113.13 E |
| Shengqing | 104 | 41.34 N | 121.36 E |
| Shengshan | 106 | 30.50 N | 120.15 E |
| Shengshui | 98 | 35.45 N | 119.39 E |
| Shengshuihezi | 98 | 42.27 N | 125.59 E |
| Shengsi Liedao II | 100 | 30.42 N | 122.20 E |
| Shengtian | 100 | 27.14 N | 113.06 E |
| Shengxian | 100 | 29.36 N | 120.48 E |
| Shengze | 106 | 30.55 N | 120.39 E |
| Shengzigou | 104 | 41.35 N | 124.04 E |
| Shenhu | 100 | 24.38 N | 118.39 E |
| Shenipsit Lake ⊜ | 207 | 41.53 N | 72.26 W |
| Shenji | 98 | 34.47 N | 115.09 E |
| Shenjia | 89 | 46.06 N | 126.46 E |
| Shenjiadian | 89 | 46.35 N | 130.38 E |
| Shenjiatai | 104 | 41.22 N | 120.50 E |
| Shenjiawan | 106 | 31.43 N | 121.19 E |
| Shenjiazhuang | 106 | 32.18 N | 120.26 E |
| Shenjing, Zhg. | 102 | 21.59 N | 112.28 E |
| Shenjing, Zhg. | 105 | 40.24 N | 114.49 E |
| Shenjingzi | 104 | 41.47 N | 123.41 E |
| Shenk'eng | 269d | 25.00 N | 121.36 E |
| Shenkou | 100 | 28.42 N | 116.02 E |
| Shenley | 260 | 51.41 N | 0.17 W |
| Shenmu | 102 | 38.56 N | 110.19 E |
| Shennan | 105 | 38.59 N | 114.56 E |
| Shenorock | 210 | 41.20 N | 73.44 W |
| Shenqiu | 100 | 33.24 N | 115.02 E |
| Shenquan | 100 | 22.59 N | 116.20 E |
| Shenquan Gang ⊂ | 100 | 22.54 N | 116.18 E |
| Shensi → Shaanxi □4 | 102 | 35.00 N | 109.00 E |
| Shenton, Mount ∧ | 162 | 28.00 S | 123.22 E |
| Shentuan | 98 | 35.30 N | 119.17 E |
| Shenxian, Zhg. | 98 | 38.01 N | 115.33 E |
| Shenxian, Zhg. | 98 | 36.15 N | 115.41 E |
| Shenxing | 105 | 39.02 N | 115.19 E |
| Shenyang (Mukden) | 104 | 41.48 N | 123.27 E |
| Shenze | 98 | 38.11 N | 115.11 E |
| Shenzhen | 100 | 22.32 N | 114.08 E |
| Sheoganj | 120 | 25.09 N | 73.04 E |
| Sheokhāla | 126 | 22.46 N | 88.10 E |
| Sheopur | 124 | 25.40 N | 76.42 E |
| Shepard | 182 | 50.57 N | 113.55 W |
| Shepard Island I | 9 | 74.25 S | 132.30 W |
| Shepards Brook ≃ | 283 | 42.08 N | 71.25 W |
| Shepaug ≃ | 207 | 41.28 N | 73.19 W |
| Shepetivka | 78 | 50.11 N | 27.04 E |
| Shepherd, Mi., U.S. | 190 | 43.31 N | 84.41 W |
| Shepherd, Tx., U.S. | 222 | 30.30 N | 95.01 W |
| Shepherd □8 | 175f | 17.05 S | 168.25 E |
| Shepherd, Îles II | 175f | 16.55 S | 168.36 E |
| Shepherdstown | 188 | 39.25 N | 77.48 W |
| Shepherdsville | 194 | 37.59 N | 85.42 W |
| Sheppard Air Force Base ■ | 196 | 33.58 N | 98.30 W |
| Sheppard Peak ∧ | 180 | 57.41 N | 132.37 W |
| Sheppard Pond ⊜ | 276 | 41.08 N | 74.13 W |
| Shepparton | 166 | 36.23 S | 145.25 E |
| Shepperd, Lake ⊜ | 162 | 29.55 S | 123.09 E |
| Shepperton | 260 | 51.24 N | 0.27 W |
| Sheppey, Isle of I | 42 | 51.24 N | 0.50 E |
| Sheppler Hill ∧2 | 279b | 40.09 N | 79.49 W |
| Sheppton | 210 | 40.53 N | 76.07 W |
| Shepshed | 42 | 52.47 N | 1.18 W |
| Shepton Mallet | 42 | 51.12 N | 2.33 W |
| Shepway | 260 | 51.15 N | 0.33 E |
| Sheqi | 100 | 33.03 N | 112.57 E |
| Sherab | 140 | 10.43 N | 24.47 E |
| Sherada | 144 | 7.21 N | 36.32 E |
| Sheraden ◆8 | 279b | 40.28 N | 80.05 W |
| Sherard, Cape ≻ | 176 | 74.36 N | 80.25 W |
| Sherborn | 283 | 42.14 N | 71.22 W |
| Sherborne | 42 | 50.57 N | 2.31 W |
| Sherborne Lake ⊜ | 212 | 45.11 N | 78.47 W |
| Sherborne Saint John | 42 | 51.18 N | 1.07 W |
| Sherbro ≃ | 150 | 7.45 N | 12.55 W |
| Sherbro Island I | 150 | 7.45 N | 12.55 W |
| Sherbrooke, N.S., Can. | 186 | 45.08 N | 61.59 W |
| Sherbrooke, P.Q., Can. | 206 | 45.25 N | 71.54 W |
| Sherbrooke □6 | 206 | 45.25 N | 71.55 W |
| Sherbrooke Lake ⊜ | 186 | 44.40 N | 64.35 W |
| Sherburn | 198 | 43.39 N | 94.43 W |
| Sherburne | 210 | 42.40 N | 75.29 W |
| Sherburne Reef ✢2 | 164 | 3.20 S | 148.00 E |
| Sherburn in Elmet | 44 | 53.48 N | 1.15 W |
| Shercock | 48 | 54.00 N | 6.54 W |
| Shere | 260 | 51.13 N | 0.28 W |
| Sheridan, Ar., U.S. | 194 | 34.18 N | 92.24 W |
| Sheridan, Ca., U.S. | 226 | 38.59 N | 121.22 W |
| Sheridan, Il., U.S. | 216 | 41.32 N | 88.41 W |
| Sheridan, In., U.S. | 218 | 40.08 N | 86.13 W |
| Sheridan, Mt., U.S. | 202 | 45.27 N | 112.11 W |
| Sheridan, Or., U.S. | 202 | 45.05 N | 123.23 W |
| Sheridan, Pa., U.S. | 208 | 40.21 N | 76.14 W |
| Sheridan, Tx., U.S. | 222 | 29.29 N | 96.40 W |
| Sheridan, Wy., U.S. | 202 | 44.47 N | 106.57 W |
| Sheridan, Mount ∧ | 202 | 44.16 N | 110.32 W |
| Sheridan Park ♠ | 284a | 42.59 N | 78.54 W |
| Sheringa | 162 | 33.51 S | 135.15 E |
| Sheringham | 42 | 52.57 N | 1.12 E |
| Sherkston | 284a | 42.53 N | 79.08 W |
| Sherlock ≃ | 162 | 20.44 S | 117.35 E |
| Sherman, Ct., U.S. | 207 | 41.34 N | 73.29 W |
| Sherman, Il., U.S. | 219 | 39.54 N | 89.36 W |
| Sherman, Ky., U.S. | 218 | 38.44 N | 84.36 W |
| Sherman, Ms., U.S. | 194 | 34.21 N | [illegible]8.50 W |
| Sherman, N.Y., U.S. | 214 | 42.09 N | [illegible]9.35 W |
| Sherman, Tx., U.S. | 196 | 33.38 N | [illegible]6.36 W |
| Sherman □6 | 224 | 45.25 N | 1[illegible]0.49 W |
| Sherman Creek ≃ | 208 | 40.23 N | [illegible]7.02 W |
| Sherman Mills | 188 | 45.52 N | [illegible]8.23 W |
| Sherman Mountain ∧ | 194 | 36.01 N | [illegible]3.17 W |
| Sherman Oaks ◆8 | 280 | 34.09 N | 1[illegible]8.26 W |
| Sherman Reservoir ⊜1 | 198 | 41.20 N | [illegible].55 W |
| Sherman Station | 188 | 45.53 N | [illegible].25 W |
| Sherpur, Bngl. | 124 | 24.41 N | [illegible].25 E |
| Sherpur, Bngl. | 124 | 25.01 N | [illegible].01 E |
| Sher Qila | 123 | 36.06 N | 7[illegible].03 E |
| Sherrard | 190 | 41.19 N | 9[illegible].31 W |
| Sherridon | 184 | 55.07 N | 10[illegible].05 W |
| Sherrill | 210 | 43.04 N | 7[illegible]35 W |
| Sherrodsville | 214 | 40.29 N | 8[illegible]14 W |
| Sher Shāh | 123 | 30.06 N | 7[illegible]21 E |
| Shertallai | 122 | 9.42 N | 7[illegible]20 E |
| 's-Hertogenbosch | 52 | 51.41 N | [illegible]19 E |
| Sherway Centre ◆9 | 275b | 43.37 N | 79[illegible]33 W |
| Sherwood, On., Can. | 275b | 43.50 N | 79[illegible]31 W |
| Sherwood, P.E., Can. | 186 | 46.17 N | 63[illegible]08 W |
| Sherwood, Ar., U.S. | 194 | 34.48 N | 92[illegible]3 W |
| Sherwood, Md., U.S. | 208 | 38.36 N | 76[illegible]9 W |
| Sherwood, Mi., U.S. | 216 | 42.00 N | 85[illegible]4 W |
| Sherwood, N.D., U.S. | 198 | 48.57 N | 101.[illegible]7 W |
| Sherwood, Oh., U.S. | 216 | 41.17 N | 84.[illegible]3 W |
| Sherwood, Or., U.S. | 224 | 45.21 N | 122.[illegible]0 W |
| Sherwood, Tn., U.S. | 194 | 35.04 N | 85.[illegible] W |
| Sherwood, Lake ⊜ | 281 | 42.36 N | 83.[illegible] W |
| Sherwood Forest, Ca., U.S. | 226 | 37.57 N | 122.[illegible] W |
| Sherwood Forest, Md., U.S. | 284c | 39.05 N | 77.0[illegible] W |
| Sherwood Forest ◆3 | 44 | 53.08 N | 1.0[illegible] W |
| Sherwood Island State Park ♠ | 276 | 41.07 N | 73.2[illegible] W |
| Sherwood Manor | 207 | 42.01 N | 72.3[illegible] W |
| Sherwood Park, Ab., Can. | 182 | 53.31 N | 113.1[illegible] W |
| Sherwood Park, De., U.S. | 285 | 39.44 N | 75.3[illegible] W |
| Sherwood Park, N.Y., U.S. | 210 | 42.36 N | 73.43 [illegible] |
| Sherwood Park ♠ | 275b | 43.43 N | 79.24 [illegible] |
| Sherwood Point ≻ | 276 | 41.07 N | 73.20 [illegible] |
| Sherwood Shores | 196 | 30.36 N | 98.22 [illegible] |
| She Shan ∧2 | 106 | 31.06 N | 121.11 [illegible] |
| Sheshea ≃ | 248 | 9.36 S | 74.10 [illegible] |
| Shesh Gāv | 120 | 33.45 N | 68.33 [illegible] |
| Shestakivka | 78 | 48.32 N | 31.58 [illegible] |
| Shesternya | 78 | 47.33 N | 33.16 [illegible] |
| Shet Bandar | 272c | 18.58 N | 72.56 [illegible] |
| Shetek, Lake ⊜ | 198 | 44.08 N | 95.42 [illegible] |
| Shetland □4 | 46a | 60.30 N | 1.15 [illegible] |
| Shetland del Sur, Islas → South Shetland Islands II | 9 | 62.00 S | 58.00 [illegible] |
| Shetland Islands II | 46a | 60.30 N | 1.15 [illegible] |
| Shetou | 106 | 31.39 N | 119.27 E |
| Shetrunji ≃ | 120 | 21.19 N | 72.07 E |
| Shetucket ≃ | 207 | 41.31 N | 72.05 W |
| Sheva | 272c | 18.56 N | 72.57 E |
| Sheva Nhava | 272c | 18.58 N | 72.58 E |
| Shevaroy Hills ⋏2 | 122 | 11.50 N | 78.16 E |
| Shevchenkove, Ukr. | 78 | 45.33 N | 29.20 E |
| Shevchenkove, Ukr. | 78 | 51.40 N | 33.39 E |
| Shevchenkove, Ukr. | 78 | 49.41 N | 37.10 E |
| Shevchenkove Druhe | 78 | 47.29 N | 36.08 E |
| Shevington | 262 | 53.34 N | 2.42 W |
| Shevington Moor | 262 | 53.35 N | 2.41 W |
| Shewa □4 | 144 | 9.00 N | 39.00 E |
| Shewa Gimira | 144 | 7.00 N | 35.50 E |
| Shexian, Zhg. | 98 | 36.33 N | 113.40 E |
| Shexian, Zhg. | 100 | 29.53 N | 118.26 E |
| Sheyang, Zhg. | 100 | 33.20 N | 119.38 E |
| Sheyang, Zhg. | 100 | 33.46 N | 120.18 E |
| Sheyenne | 198 | 47.49 N | 99.07 W |
| Sheyenne ≃ | 198 | 47.05 N | 96.50 W |
| Sheykhābād | 120 | 34.05 N | 68.45 E |
| Shey-Phoksundo National Park ♠ | 124 | 29.30 N | 82.45 E |
| Shezhu | 106 | 31.19 N | 119.16 E |
| Shiḥīm | 132 | 33.37 N | 35.29 E |
| Shi ≃, Zhg. | 100 | 32.18 N | 114.31 E |
| Shi ≃, Zhg. | 100 | 32.32 N | 115.52 E |
| Shiant, Sound of ʮ | 46 | 57.55 N | 6.25 W |
| Shiant Islands II | 46 | 57.53 N | 6.21 W |
| Shiawassee □6 | 216 | 42.56 N | 84.09 W |
| Shiawassee ≃ | 216 | 43.06 N | 84.10 W |
| Shiawassee, South Branch ≃ | 216 | 42.49 N | 83.56 W |
| Shiba | 100 | 32.45 N | 118.07 E |
| Shiba ≃ | 268 | 35.47 N | 139.44 E |
| Shibadu | 102 | 28.01 N | 110.51 E |
| Shibakawa | 94 | 35.13 N | 138.33 E |
| Shibām | 144 | 15.56 N | 48.38 E |
| Shiban | 107 | 30.18 N | 104.28 E |
| Shibanxi | 107 | 29.17 N | 103.51 E |
| Shibaocheng | 102 | 39.48 N | 96.10 E |
| Shibarni | 140 | 14.50 N | 24.25 E |
| Shibasaki | 268 | 35.39 N | 139.34 E |
| Shibata | 92 | 37.57 N | 139.20 E |
| Shibayama | 94 | 35.41 N | 140.25 E |
| Shibayama-gata ⊜ | 94 | 36.21 N | 136.23 E |
| Shibden Hall ⊥ | 262 | 53.44 N | 1.51 W |
| Shibecha | 92a | 43.17 N | 144.36 E |
| Shibetsu, Nihon | 92a | 43.40 N | 145.08 E |
| Shibetsu, Nihon | 92a | 44.10 N | 142.23 E |
| Shibi | 100 | 26.43 N | 120.02 E |
| Shibīn al-Kawm | 142 | 30.33 N | 31.01 E |
| Shibīn al-Qanāṭir | 142 | 30.19 N | 31.19 E |
| Shibing | 102 | 26.50 N | 108.04 E |
| Shibishan | 100 | 29.21 N | 116.45 E |
| Shiblanjah | 142 | 30.28 N | 31.16 E |
| Shibu | 98 | 36.45 N | 119.27 E |
| Shibukawa | 94 | 36.29 N | 139.00 E |
| Shibure-yama ∧ | 270 | 34.45 N | 135.05 E |
| Shibushi | 92 | 31.28 N | 131.07 E |
| Shibutsu-san ∧ | 94 | 36.54 N | 139.11 E |
| Shibuya ◆8 | 268 | 35.40 N | 139.42 E |
| Shibuzi | 98 | 36.09 N | 119.06 E |
| Shicha | 100 | 28.24 N | 115.50 E |
| Shichangyu | 104 | 41.12 N | 123.14 E |
| Shicheng, Zhg. | 98 | 40.39 N | 124.17 E |
| Shicheng, Zhg. | 100 | 25.18 N | 119.21 E |
| Shicheng, Zhg. | 100 | 26.22 N | 116.22 E |
| Shicheng Dao I | 98 | 39.31 N | 123.02 E |
| Shichisō | 94 | 35.33 N | 137.07 E |
| Shickley | 198 | 40.25 N | 97.43 W |
| Shickshinny | 210 | 41.09 N | 76.09 W |
| Shidai | 100 | 30.20 N | 117.56 E |
| Shidao | 98 | 36.53 N | 122.23 E |
| Shideng | 102 | 26.44 N | 99.11 E |
| Shidler | 196 | 36.46 N | 96.39 W |
| Shido | 96 | 34.19 N | 134.10 E |
| Shidong, Zhg. | 107 | 28.59 N | 105.27 E |
| Shidong, Zhg. | 107 | 30.25 N | 105.20 E |
| Shidongzigou | 105 | 40.41 N | 118.23 E |
| Shiel, Loch ⊜ | 46 | 56.47 N | 5.35 W |
| Shiel Bridge | 46 | 57.12 N | 5.25 W |
| Shieldaig | 46 | 57.31 N | 5.39 W |
| Shieldhill | 46 | 55.58 N | 3.46 W |
| Shields ≃ | 202 | 45.43 N | 110.28 W |
| Shiercun | 106 | 30.31 N | 119.34 E |
| Shi'er Shan ∧ | 100 | 29.18 N | 118.08 E |
| Shi'erwei | 106 | 32.15 N | 119.14 E |
| Shifang | 100 | 25.01 N | 116.14 E |
| Shifnal | 42 | 52.40 N | 2.21 W |
| Shifo | 107 | 29.58 N | 103.50 E |
| Shifobao | 104 | 41.28 N | 121.27 E |
| Shifochang | 107 | 30.19 N | 105.07 E |
| Shifodian | 100 | 32.06 N | 115.46 E |
| Shifosi | 104 | 42.08 N | 123.20 E |
| Shifoya | 98 | 40.12 N | 123.10 E |
| Shiga, Nihon | 94 | 36.20 N | 137.59 E |
| Shiga, Nihon | 94 | 35.09 N | 135.55 E |


| English | Deutsch | Español | Français | Português |
|---|---|---|---|---|
| ≃ River | Fluß | Río | Rivière | Rio |
| ≅ Canal | Kanal | Canal | Canal | Canal |
| ʟ Waterfall, Rapids | Wasserfall, Stromschnellen | Cascada, Rápidos | Chute d'eau, Rapides | Cascata, Rápidos |
| ʮ Strait | Meeresstraße | Estrecho | Détroit | Estreito |
| ⊂ Bay, Gulf | Bucht, Golf | Bahía, Golfo | Baie, Golfe | Baía, Golfo |
| ⊜ Lake, Lakes | See, Seen | Lago, Lagos | Lac, Lacs | Lago, Lagos |
| ≡ Swamp | Sumpf | Pantano | Marais | Pântano |
| ⊓ Ice Features, Glacier | Eis- und Gletscherformen | Accidentes Glaciales | Formes glaciaires | Acidentes glaciares |
| ⍑ Other Hydrographic Features | Andere Hydrographische Objekte | Otros Elementos Hidrográficos | Autres données hydrographiques | Outros acidentes hidrográficos |
| ✢ Submarine Features | Untermeerische Objekte | Accidentes Submarinos | Formes de relief sous-marin | Acidentes submarinos |
| □ Political Unit | Politische Einheit | Unidad Politica | Entité politique | Unidade política |
| ⊍ Cultural Institution | Kulturelle Institution | Institución Cultural | Institution culturelle | Instituição cultural |
| ⊥ Historical Site | Historische Stätte | Sitio Histórico | Site historique | Sitio histórico |
| ♠ Recreational Site | Erholungs- und Ferienort | Sitio de Recreo | Centre de loisirs | Area de Lazer |
| ⊠ Airport | Flughafen | Aeropuerto | Aéroport | Aeroporto |
| ■ Military Installation | Militäranlage | Instalación Militar | Installation militaire | Instalação militar |
| ◆ Miscellaneous | Verschiedenes | Misceláneo | Divers | Diversos |

**ENGLISH** / **DEUTSCH**


| Name / Name | Page / Seite | Lat.°′ / Breite°′ | Long.°′ / Länge°′ E = Ost |
|---|---|---|---|
| Shiga ◻[5] | 96 | 35.15 N | 136.00 E |
| Shigaib | 140 | 15.01 N | 23.36 E |
| Shigang, Zhg. | 100 | 32.13 N | 120.58 E |
| Shigang, Zhg. | 106 | 32.14 N | 121.00 E |
| Shigangmen | 269b | 31.21 N | 121.17 E |
| Shigaopu | 107 | 30.16 N | 104.01 E |
| Shigar ≃, Asia | 123 | 34.39 N | 75.51 E |
| Shigar ≃, Pāk. | 123 | 34.39 N | 75.51 E |
| Shigaraki | 94 | 34.52 N | 136.03 E |
| Shigaraki-gū ▼[1] | 94 | 34.54 N | 136.04 E |
| Shigenobu | 96 | 33.48 N | 132.50 E |
| Shigenobu ≃ | 96 | 33.48 N | 132.41 E |
| Shigezhuang, Zhg. | 105 | 38.57 N | 116.19 E |
| Shigezhuang, Zhg. | 105 | 38.59 N | 115.36 E |
| Shigezhuang, Zhg. | 105 | 39.18 N | 116.53 E |
| Shigouyi | 102 | 37.44 N | 106.26 E |
| Shigu, Zhg. | 100 | 29.27 N | 117.14 E |
| Shigu, Zhg. | 102 | 26.50 N | 99.55 E |
| Shiguaigou | 102 | 40.42 N | 110.20 E |
| Shiguantun | 104 | 41.38 N | 123.39 E |
| Shigulingyu | 105 | 40.38 N | 116.54 E |
| Shīḥān ∧ | 132 | 31.23 N | 35.44 E |
| Shihch'i → Zhongshan | 100 | 22.31 N | 113.22 E |
| Shihchiachuang → Shijiazhuang | 98 | 38.03 N | 114.28 E |
| Shihe | 98 | 39.19 N | 121.52 E |
| Shihengyuanyu | 106 | 31.50 N | 121.45 E |
| Shihezi | 86 | 44.18 N | 86.02 E |
| Shihkiachwang → Shijiazhuang | 98 | 38.03 N | 114.28 E |
| Shihlin ◆[8] | 269d | 25.06 N | 121.31 E |
| Shihti | 269d | 25.02 N | 121.44 E |
| Shihting | 269d | 24.59 N | 121.39 E |
| Shihu, Zhg. | 98 | 41.29 N | 126.18 E |
| Shihu, Zhg. | 105 | 40.04 N | 117.17 E |
| Shihuajie | 102 | 32.20 N | 111.25 E |
| Shihudang | 106 | 30.58 N | 121.07 E |
| Shihuixi | 107 | 29.02 N | 105.04 E |
| Shihuiyaozi | 104 | 42.08 N | 123.47 E |
| Shihuxia | 105 | 40.48 N | 117.22 E |
| Shiida | 96 | 33.39 N | 131.04 E |
| Shijiaba | 107 | 30.18 N | 104.46 E |
| Shijiagangzi | 104 | 42.19 N | 123.34 E |
| Shijiagou | 104 | 42.27 N | 123.28 E |
| Shijiao | 100 | 23.36 N | 112.59 E |
| Shijiaqiao, Zhg. | 106 | 30.46 N | 120.06 E |
| Shijiaqiao, Zhg. | 106 | 32.18 N | 119.26 E |
| Shijiawu | 105 | 39.21 N | 116.15 E |
| Shijiaxiang | 107 | 29.38 N | 104.59 E |
| Shijiayaozhuang | 106 | 32.13 N | 120.29 E |
| Shijiazhai, Zhg. | 98 | 38.56 N | 114.18 E |
| Shijiazhai, Zhg. | 269b | 31.23 N | 121.30 E |
| Shijiazhen | 106 | 31.51 N | 121.10 E |
| Shijiazhuang | 98 | 38.03 N | 114.28 E |
| Shijiazi, Zhg. | 104 | 42.07 N | 122.18 E |
| Shijiazi, Zhg. | 104 | 42.39 N | 122.06 E |
| Shijiedu | 106 | 30.57 N | 119.13 E |
| Shijing, Zhg. | 98 | 35.30 N | 118.57 E |
| Shijing, Zhg. | 100 | 24.40 N | 118.24 E |
| Shijing, Zhg. | 105 | 39.54 N | 114.58 E |
| Shijingshan | 105 | 39.56 N | 116.07 E |
| Shijiu Hu ◎ | 106 | 31.28 N | 118.53 E |
| Shijiusuo | 98 | 35.24 N | 119.29 E |
| Shijiu Tuo I | 98 | 39.11 N | 118.56 E |
| Shijōnawate | 270 | 34.45 N | 135.39 E |
| Shijūmagari-tōge )( | 96 | 35.11 N | 133.32 E |
| Shika | 94 | 37.01 N | 136.47 E |
| Shikami-yama ∧ | 270 | 34.47 N | 135.10 E |
| Shikano | 96 | 35.28 N | 134.04 E |
| Shikārpur, India | 122 | 14.16 N | 75.21 E |
| Shikārpur, India | 124 | 28.17 N | 78.01 E |
| Shikārpur, Pāk. | 120 | 27.57 N | 68.38 E |
| Shikatsu | 94 | 35.14 N | 136.53 E |
| Shikengkong ∧ | 100 | 24.56 N | 113.00 E |
| Shikewusumiao | 102 | 40.13 N | 108.52 E |
| Shiki | 94 | 35.50 N | 139.35 E |
| Shikishima | 94 | 35.41 N | 138.32 E |
| Shikohābād | 124 | 27.06 N | 78.36 E |
| Shikoku I | 92 | 33.45 N | 133.30 E |
| Shikoku-sanchi ⩓ | 96 | 33.47 N | 133.30 E |
| Shikoma | 268 | 35.11 N | 139.56 E |
| Shikotsu-ko ◎ | 92a | 42.45 N | 141.20 E |
| Shikotsu-Tōya-kokuritsu-kōen ♦ | 92a | 42.47 N | 141.00 E |
| Shikuang | 106 | 31.54 N | 121.24 E |
| Shil | 272c | 19.09 N | 73.03 E |
| Shilabo | 144 | 6.05 N | 44.48 E |
| Shilbottle | 44 | 55.23 N | 1.42 W |
| Shildon | 44 | 54.38 N | 1.39 W |
| Shiliangji | 100 | 33.54 N | 115.14 E |
| Shilibao | 105 | 39.55 N | 116.29 E |
| Shiliguri | 124 | 26.42 N | 88.26 E |
| Shilihe | 104 | 41.31 N | 123.22 E |
| Shiling | 106 | 30.26 N | 119.35 E |
| Shilipeng | 106 | 31.14 N | 119.35 E |
| Shilipu, Zhg. | 105 | 39.29 N | 116.18 E |
| Shilipu, Zhg. | 105 | 39.11 N | 115.59 E |
| Shilipu, Zhg. | 105 | 40.15 N | 117.58 E |
| Shiliuban | 100 | 24.08 N | 117.33 E |
| Shillelagh | 48 | 52.45 N | 6.32 W |
| Shillingstone | 42 | 50.54 N | 2.14 W |
| Shillington | 208 | 40.18 N | 75.57 W |
| Shillong | 120 | 25.34 N | 91.53 E |
| Shilo, Canadian Forces Base ■ | 184 | 49.49 N | 99.38 W |
| Shiloh, Il., U.S. | 219 | 38.34 N | 89.54 W |
| Shiloh, N.J., U.S. | 208 | 39.27 N | 75.17 W |
| Shiloh, Oh., U.S. | 214 | 40.58 N | 82.36 W |
| Shiloh, Oh., U.S. | 218 | 39.49 N | 84.13 W |
| Shiloh, Oh., U.S. | 218 | 39.49 N | 84.13 W |
| Shiloh, Pa., U.S. | 208 | 39.59 N | 76.49 W |
| Shiloh → Saylūn, Khirbat ⊥ | 132 | 32.03 N | 35.17 E |
| Shiloh National Military Park ♦ | 194 | 35.06 N | 88.21 W |
| Shilong, Zhg. | 100 | 23.07 N | 113.48 E |
| Shilong, Zhg. | 102 | 23.54 N | 109.40 E |
| Shilong, Zhg. | 107 | 30.15 N | 106.34 E |
| Shilou | 100 | 22.58 N | 113.29 E |
| Shima, Nihon | 92 | 34.13 N | 136.51 E |
| Shima, Nihon | 270 | 34.59 N | 135.20 E |
| Shima, Zhg. | 100 | 24.27 N | 117.49 E |
| Shima, Zhg. | 107 | 29.38 N | 105.50 E |
| Shimabara | 92 | 32.47 N | 130.22 E |
| Shimachang, Zhg. | 107 | 28.59 N | 105.55 E |
| Shimachang, Zhg. | 107 | 29.03 N | 105.36 E |
| Shimada, Nihon | 94 | 34.49 N | 138.11 E |
| Shimada, Nihon | 268 | 35.59 N | 139.25 E |
| Shimagahara | 94 | 34.46 N | 136.03 E |
| Shima-hantō ›[1] | 94 | 34.26 N | 136.33 E |
| Shimamiao | 106 | 32.08 N | 119.20 E |
| Shimamoto | 96 | 34.53 N | 135.40 E |
| Shimane ◻[5] | 96 | 35.00 N | 132.30 E |
| Shimane-hantō ›[1] | 96 | 35.30 N | 133.00 E |
| Shimantan | 100 | 33.17 N | 113.28 E |
| Shimanto ≃ | 96 | 32.56 N | 133.00 E |
| Shimata ≃ | 96 | 33.57 N | 131.55 E |
| Shimbiris ∧ | 144 | 10.44 N | 47.15 E |
| Shimei | 106 | 32.14 N | 120.10 E |
| Shimen, Zhg. | 98 | 39.44 N | 118.52 E |
| Shimen, Zhg. | 102 | 29.28 N | 111.17 E |
| Shimen, Zhg. | 105 | 40.06 N | 117.42 E |
| Shimen, Zhg. | 106 | 30.37 N | 120.26 E |
| Shimen, Zhg. | 107 | 29.36 N | 106.27 E |
| Shimen, Zhg. | 107 | 29.09 N | 106.02 E |
| Shimencun, Zhg. | 106 | 31.21 N | 119.34 E |
| Shimencun, Zhg. | 106 | 30.23 N | 119.41 E |
| Shimendong | 100 | 28.16 N | 120.07 E |
| Shimengou | 104 | 40.40 N | 123.43 E |
| Shimenjie | 100 | 29.34 N | 116.44 E |
| Shimenlou | 100 | 28.58 N | 114.51 E |
| Shimenying | 105 | 39.54 N | 116.05 E |
| Shimenzi | 89 | 48.30 N | 121.31 E |
| Shimian | 102 | 29.18 N | 102.22 E |
| Shimiaozi | 104 | 40.39 N | 123.31 E |
| Shimizu, Nihon | 92 | 35.01 N | 138.29 E |
| Shimizu → Tosa-shimizu, Nihon | 92 | 32.46 N | 132.57 E |
| Shimizu, Nihon | 92a | 43.01 N | 142.53 E |
| Shimizu, Nihon | 94 | 36.02 N | 136.09 E |
| Shimizu, Nihon | 94 | 35.01 N | 138.29 E |
| Shimizu, Nihon | 96 | 34.05 N | 135.26 E |
| Shimizu-tunnel ◆[5] | 94 | 36.52 N | 138.55 E |
| Shimla | 123 | 31.06 N | 77.10 E |
| Shimminato | 94 | 36.47 N | 137.04 E |
| Shimobe | 94 | 35.27 N | 138.29 E |
| Shimoda | 94 | 34.40 N | 138.57 E |
| Shimodate | 94 | 36.18 N | 139.59 E |
| Shimofusa | 94 | 35.52 N | 140.21 E |
| Shimofusa-daichi ⩓[1] | 268 | 35.45 N | 139.58 E |
| Shimofusa-kōkūkichi, Kaijō-jieitai- ■ | 94 | 35.50 N | 140.05 E |
| Shimofusa Naval Air Base ■ | 268 | 35.48 N | 140.01 E |
| Shimoga | 122 | 13.55 N | 75.34 E |
| Shimogawara | 268 | 35.56 N | 139.21 E |
| Shimogōri | 268 | 35.21 N | 140.03 E |
| Shimogyō ◆[8] | 270 | 34.59 N | 135.45 E |
| Shimohōya | 268 | 35.45 N | 139.34 E |
| Shimoichi | 96 | 34.22 N | 135.47 E |
| Shimoigusa ◆[8] | 268 | 35.43 N | 139.37 E |
| Shimoji | 175d | 24.45 N | 125.16 E |
| Shimoji-jima I | 175d | 24.49 N | 125.09 E |
| Shimojō | 94 | 35.24 N | 137.47 E |
| Shimokawa | 92a | 44.18 N | 142.39 E |
| Shimokita-hantō ›[1] | 92 | 41.15 N | 141.00 E |
| Shimomatsu | 270 | 34.27 N | 135.23 E |
| Shimomizo | 268 | 35.31 N | 139.23 E |
| Shimoni | 154 | 4.39 S | 39.23 E |
| Shimoniikura | 268 | 35.47 N | 139.38 E |
| Shimonita | 94 | 36.13 N | 138.47 E |
| Shimonoseki | 96 | 33.57 N | 130.57 E |
| Shimookudomi | 268 | 35.53 N | 139.26 E |
| Shimoryūzu-zaki › | 96 | 33.30 N | 133.34 E |
| Shimosakamoto | 270 | 35.03 N | 135.53 E |
| Shimosuwa | 94 | 36.04 N | 138.05 E |
| Shimotajiri | 270 | 34.57 N | 135.28 E |
| Shimotomi | 268 | 35.50 N | 139.29 E |
| Shimotsu | 96 | 34.10 N | 135.08 E |
| Shimotsuchidana | 268 | 35.24 N | 139.27 E |
| Shimotsui | 96 | 34.26 N | 133.47 E |
| Shimotsuma | 94 | 36.11 N | 139.58 E |
| Shimotsuruma | 268 | 35.29 N | 139.28 E |
| Shimoya | 268 | 35.23 N | 139.21 E |
| Shimoyama | 94 | 35.02 N | 137.19 E |
| Shimoyugi | 268 | 35.38 N | 139.23 E |
| Shimura ◆[8] | 268 | 35.46 N | 139.41 E |
| Shin, Loch ◎ | 46 | 58.06 N | 4.34 W |
| Shinagawa ◆[8] | 268 | 35.37 N | 139.45 E |
| Shinan | 102 | 22.43 N | 109.54 E |
| Shinano | 94 | 36.48 N | 138.13 E |
| Shinano ≃ | 92 | 37.56 N | 139.03 E |
| Shinarā | 142 | 28.47 N | 30.46 E |
| Shināṣ | 128 | 24.46 N | 56.28 E |
| Shinawari | 123 | 33.32 N | 70.48 E |
| Shinbārī | 273c | 30.07 N | 31.09 E |
| Shīndand | 128 | 33.18 N | 62.08 E |
| Shindenbaru-kichi, Kōkū-jieitai- ■ | 92 | 32.04 N | 131.30 E |
| Shindo | 268 | 35.21 N | 139.21 E |
| Shiner | 222 | 29.25 N | 97.10 W |
| Shingbwiyang | 110 | 26.41 N | 96.13 E |
| Shingishū → Sinŭiju | 98 | 40.05 N | 124.24 E |
| Shinglehouse | 214 | 41.57 N | 78.11 W |
| Shingle Springs | 226 | 38.40 N | 120.56 W |
| Shing Mun Reservoir ◎[1] | 271d | 22.23 N | 114.08 E |
| Shingo | 96 | 34.59 N | 133.23 E |
| Shingū, Nihon | 92 | 33.44 N | 135.59 E |
| Shingū, Nihon | 96 | 34.55 N | 134.33 E |
| Shingū, Nihon | 96 | 33.56 N | 133.38 E |
| Shingwidzi | 156 | 23.05 S | 31.25 E |
| Shingwidzi (Singuédeze) ≃ | 156 | 23.53 S | 32.17 E |
| Shinichi | 96 | 34.33 N | 133.16 E |
| Shining Tor ∧ | 262 | 53.16 N | 2.01 W |
| Shinīrah | 132 | 32.22 N | 36.45 E |
| Shinji | 96 | 35.24 N | 132.54 E |
| Shinji-ko ◎ | 96 | 35.27 N | 132.58 E |
| Shinjō, Nihon | 92 | 38.46 N | 140.18 E |
| Shinjō, Nihon | 270 | 34.30 N | 135.44 E |
| Shinjuku ◆[8] | 268 | 35.41 N | 139.42 E |
| Shinkawa | 94 | 35.09 N | 136.50 E |
| Shīnkay | 120 | 31.57 N | 67.26 E |
| Shinkolobwe | 154 | 11.02 S | 26.35 E |
| Shinmachi | 94 | 36.16 N | 139.07 E |
| Shinminato ≃ | 270 | 34.38 N | 135.09 E |
| Shinnārah, Minqār ⍊[4] | 142 | 28.52 N | 30.38 E |
| Shinnayō | 96 | 34.04 N | 131.47 E |
| Shinnecock Bay ⊂ | 207 | 40.52 N | 72.28 W |
| Shinnel Water ≃ | 44 | 55.13 N | 3.49 W |
| Shinness | 46 | 58.05 N | 4.28 W |
| Shinnston | 188 | 39.23 N | 80.18 W |
| Shino-jima I | 94 | 34.39 N | 137.00 E |
| Shinsai-bashi ◆[8] | 270 | 34.40 N | 135.31 E |
| Shinshār | 130 | 34.36 N | 36.44 E |
| Shinshiro | 94 | 34.54 N | 137.30 E |
| Shinshū-shinmachi | 94 | 36.34 N | 138.01 E |
| Shintone | 94 | 35.50 N | 140.20 E |
| Shinyanga | 154 | 3.40 S | 33.26 E |
| Shinyanga ◻[4] | 154 | 3.45 S | 33.00 E |
| Shin-yōdo ≃[1] | 270 | 34.41 N | 135.26 E |
| Shio | 94 | 36.52 N | 136.48 E |
| Shiobara | 94 | 36.58 N | 139.49 E |
| Shiocton | 190 | 44.26 N | 88.34 W |
| Shiogama | 92 | 38.19 N | 141.01 E |
| Shiojiri | 94 | 36.06 N | 137.58 E |
| Shiojiri-tōge )( | 94 | 36.05 N | 138.02 E |
| Shiomi-dake ∧ | 94 | 35.34 N | 138.12 E |
| Shionoe | 96 | 34.10 N | 134.05 E |
| Shiono-misaki › | 92 | 33.26 N | 135.45 E |
| Shioya | 94 | 36.46 N | 139.51 E |
| Shioya ◆[8] | 270 | 34.38 N | 135.06 E |
| Shioya-zaki ›, Nihon | 92 | 33.26 N | 135.45 E |
| Shioya-zaki ›, Nihon | 94 | 36.59 N | 140.59 E |
| Shiozawa | 94 | 37.02 N | 138.51 E |
| Shipai, Zhg. | 100 | 23.08 N | 113.21 E |
| Shipai, Zhg. | 106 | 31.30 N | 120.55 E |
| Shipanpu | 107 | 30.28 N | 104.23 E |
| Shipantuo | 107 | 30.25 N | 106.13 E |
| Ship Bottom | 208 | 39.38 N | 74.10 W |
| Shipbourne | 260 | 51.15 N | 0.17 E |
| Ship Cove | 186 | 47.06 N | 54.05 W |
| Shipdham | 42 | 52.37 N | 0.53 E |
| Shiping, Zhg. | 102 | 28.20 N | 107.42 E |
| Shiping, Zhg. | 102 | 23.47 N | 102.30 E |
| Shipley | 44 | 53.50 N | 1.47 W |
| Shipman, Il., U.S. | 219 | 39.07 N | 90.03 W |
| Shipman, Va., U.S. | 192 | 37.43 N | 78.50 W |
| Shippan Point › | 276 | 41.01 N | 73.32 W |
| Shippegan | 186 | 47.45 N | 64.42 W |
| Shippensburg | 208 | 40.03 N | 77.31 W |
| Shippenville | 214 | 41.15 N | 79.28 W |
| Shippingport | 214 | 40.38 N | 80.25 W |
| Shippō | 94 | 35.10 N | 136.48 E |
| Shiprock | 200 | 36.47 N | 108.41 W |
| Ship Rock ∧ | 200 | 36.42 N | 108.50 W |
| Shipshaw ≃ | 186 | 48.27 N | 71.12 W |
| Shipshewana | 216 | 41.40 N | 85.34 W |
| Shipston-on-Stour | 42 | 52.04 N | 1.37 W |
| Shipton-under-Wychwood | 42 | 51.51 N | 1.35 W |
| Shipu, Zhg. | 100 | 29.13 N | 121.55 E |
| Shipu, Zhg. | 106 | 31.15 N | 121.03 E |
| Shiqi → Zhongshan | 100 | 22.31 N | 113.22 E |
| Shiqian | 102 | 27.31 N | 108.20 E |
| Shiqiao, Zhg. | 100 | 33.12 N | 112.36 E |
| Shiqiao, Zhg. | 100 | 26.58 N | 114.23 E |
| Shiqiao, Zhg. | 106 | 30.30 N | 119.11 E |
| Shiqiao, Zhg. | 107 | 30.25 N | 104.31 E |
| Shiqiaopu | 107 | 30.05 N | 105.23 E |
| Shiqiaozi | 104 | 41.27 N | 123.43 E |
| Shiqma ≃ | 132 | 31.36 N | 34.30 E |
| Shiquan, Zhg. | 102 | 33.03 N | 108.17 E |
| Shiquan, Zhg. | 106 | 30.30 N | 120.48 E |
| Shirahama, Nihon | 94 | 34.54 N | 139.54 E |
| Shirahama, Nihon | 96 | 33.40 N | 135.20 E |
| Shirahata-yama ∧ | 96 | 34.54 N | 134.23 E |
| Shiraitono-taki ⌞ | 94 | 35.18 N | 138.38 E |
| Shirakami-misaki › | 92a | 41.24 N | 140.12 E |
| Shirakawa, Nihon | 94 | 37.07 N | 140.13 E |
| Shirakawa, Nihon | 94 | 35.35 N | 137.12 E |
| Shirakawa, Nihon | 94 | 36.16 N | 136.54 E |
| Shirakawa-no-seki-ato ⊥ | 94 | 37.03 N | 140.15 E |
| Shirakawa-tōge ∧[2] | 270 | 34.42 N | 135.07 E |
| Shirako | 94 | 35.26 N | 140.23 E |
| Shirākol | 126 | 22.18 N | 88.16 E |
| Shirakura-yama ∧ | 94 | 35.00 N | 137.46 E |
| Shirama-yama ∧ | 96 | 34.01 N | 135.23 E |
| Shiramine | 94 | 36.10 N | 136.37 E |
| Shirane | 94 | 35.38 N | 138.28 E |
| Shirane-san ∧, Nihon | 94 | 36.38 N | 138.32 E |
| Shirane-san ∧, Nihon | 94 | 36.48 N | 139.22 E |
| Shirane-san (Kita-dake) ∧, Nihon | 94 | 35.40 N | 138.15 E |
| Shiranuka | 92a | 42.57 N | 144.05 E |
| Shiraoi | 92a | 42.33 N | 141.21 E |
| Shiraoka | 94 | 36.01 N | 139.40 E |
| Shiraone | 272c | 19.03 N | 73.01 E |
| Shirasawa | 94 | 36.40 N | 139.08 E |
| Shirati | 154 | 1.08 S | 33.59 E |
| Shīrāz | 128 | 29.36 N | 52.32 E |
| Shirbīn | 142 | 31.11 N | 31.32 E |
| Shirdley Hill | 262 | 53.36 N | 2.58 W |
| Shire (Chire) ≃ | 154 | 17.42 S | 35.19 E |
| Shirebrook | 44 | 53.12 N | 1.13 W |
| Shiremanstown | 208 | 40.13 N | 76.57 W |
| Shiretoko-hantō ›[1] | 92a | 44.00 N | 145.00 E |
| Shiretoko-kokuritsu-kōen ♦ | 92a | 44.08 N | 145.10 E |
| Shiretoko-misaki › | 92a | 44.14 N | 145.17 E |
| Shīrīn ≃ | 120 | 36.49 N | 65.01 E |
| Shīr Kūh ∧ | 128 | 31.34 N | 54.04 E |
| Shirland | 216 | 42.27 N | 89.12 W |
| Shirley, B.C., Can. | 224 | 48.23 N | 123.54 W |
| Shirley, Il., U.S. | 216 | 40.24 N | 89.04 W |
| Shirley, In., U.S. | 218 | 39.53 N | 85.34 W |
| Shirley, Ma., U.S. | 207 | 42.32 N | 71.39 W |
| Shirley Plantation ⊥ | 208 | 37.21 N | 77.15 W |
| Shirleysburg | 214 | 40.18 N | 77.53 W |
| Shiro | 222 | 30.37 N | 95.53 W |
| Shiroi | 94 | 35.48 N | 140.04 E |
| Shiroishi | 92 | 38.00 N | 140.37 E |
| Shirokawa | 96 | 33.23 N | 132.46 E |
| Shirone | 92 | 37.46 N | 139.01 E |
| Shirotori, Nihon | 94 | 35.53 N | 136.52 E |
| Shirotori, Nihon | 96 | 34.15 N | 134.20 E |
| Shirouma-dake ∧ | 94 | 36.45 N | 137.46 E |
| Shiroyama | 94 | 35.35 N | 139.19 E |
| Shiro-yama ∧ | 270 | 34.38 N | 135.53 E |
| Shirpur | 120 | 21.21 N | 74.53 E |
| Shirrell Heath | 42 | 50.55 N | 1.12 W |
| Shirshābah | 142 | 30.47 N | 31.10 E |
| Shīrvān | 128 | 37.24 N | 57.55 E |
| Shisaka-jima I | 96 | 34.07 N | 133.11 E |
| Shisanling | 105 | 40.19 N | 116.16 E |
| Shi San Ling (Ming Tombs) ⊥ | 105 | 40.19 N | 116.13 E |
| Shisanzhan | 89 | 51.21 N | 125.43 E |
| Shisha Hai ◎ | 271a | 39.57 N | 116.22 E |
| Shishaldin Volcano ∧[1] | 180 | 54.45 N | 163.57 W |
| Shishan | 104 | 41.16 N | 121.30 E |
| Shishi | 100 | 24.48 N | 118.38 E |
| Shishikui | 96 | 33.34 N | 134.18 E |
| Shishi Shan ∧ | 100 | 24.44 N | 117.54 E |
| Shishmaref | 180 | 66.14 N | 166.09 W |
| Shishmaref Inlet ⊂ | 180 | 66.07 N | 165.50 W |
| Shishou | 102 | 29.43 N | 112.19 E |
| Shisht al-An'ām | 142 | 30.52 N | 30.44 E |
| Shisiazhan | 89 | 51.36 N | 125.42 E |
| Shisixian | 104 | 40.53 N | 122.59 E |
| Shisler Point › | 284a | 42.52 N | 79.08 W |
| Shisui | 94 | 35.43 N | 140.16 E |
| Shitai | 100 | 30.13 N | 117.27 E |
| Shitan, Zhg. | 100 | 27.44 N | 112.42 E |
| Shitan, Zhg. | 100 | 23.10 N | 113.47 E |
| Shitang, Zhg. | 100 | 28.16 N | 121.36 E |
| Shitang, Zhg. | 102 | 25.38 N | 110.50 E |
| Shitangwan | 106 | 31.40 N | 120.13 E |
| Shitara | 94 | 35.05 N | 137.35 E |
| Shithāthah | 128 | 32.33 N | 43.29 E |
| Shiting, Zhg. | 100 | 27.36 N | 113.16 E |
| Shiting, Zhg. | 105 | 39.31 N | 115.41 E |
| Shitoufangzi | 89 | 48.38 N | 126.08 E |
| Shitougouzi | 89 | 49.19 N | 125.55 E |
| Shitoumiao | 102 | 41.41 N | 106.50 E |
| Shitoumiaozi | 104 | 41.38 N | 121.26 E |
| Shitoushan | 105 | 40.27 N | 116.13 E |
| Shitoushuangmiao | 98 | 41.28 N | 118.55 E |
| Shituan | 107 | 30.09 N | 105.01 E |
| Shitunwei | 104 | 41.07 N | 121.31 E |
| Shiv | 120 | 26.11 N | 71.15 E |
| Shivalya | 126 | 23.50 N | 89.47 E |
| Shively | 218 | 38.12 N | 85.49 W |
| Shivering, Mount ∧ | 170 | 34.08 S | 150.02 E |
| Shivpuri | 124 | 25.26 N | 77.39 E |
| Shivta, Horvot (Subeita) ⊥ | 132 | 30.53 N | 34.38 E |
| Shivwits Plateau ⩓[1] | 200 | 36.15 N | 113.40 W |
| Shiwaku-shotō II | 96 | 34.20 N | 133.45 E |
| Shiwan, Zhg. | 100 | 27.17 N | 112.57 E |
| Shiwan, Zhg. | 100 | 28.12 N | 113.49 E |
| Shiwan, Zhg. | 100 | 23.01 N | 113.04 E |
| Shiwan, Zhg. | 102 | 37.35 N | 109.01 E |
| Shiwenchang | 104 | 41.43 N | 123.54 E |
| Shiwu | 89 | 43.48 N | 124.13 E |
| Shixi, Zhg. | 100 | 28.16 N | 117.45 E |
| Shixi, Zhg. | 100 | 28.16 N | 115.36 E |
| Shixia | 105 | 40.20 N | 114.59 E |
| Shixian | 89 | 43.05 N | 129.47 E |
| Shixiancun | 106 | 31.12 N | 120.29 E |
| Shixiechang | 107 | 29.51 N | 106.41 E |
| Shixing | 100 | 24.58 N | 114.03 E |
| Shixun | 100 | 24.44 N | 118.11 E |
| Shiyachang | 107 | 30.27 N | 106.31 E |
| Shiyan, Zhg. | 102 | 32.38 N | 110.44 E |
| Shiyan, Zhg. | 107 | 30.22 N | 104.27 E |
| Shiyangchang, Zhg. | 107 | 29.56 N | 105.37 E |
| Shiyangchang, Zhg. | 107 | 30.42 N | 105.57 E |
| Shiyanqiao | 107 | 29.19 N | 105.22 E |
| Shiyiwei | 106 | 31.59 N | 120.43 E |
| Shiyizhan | 89 | 51.13 N | 125.52 E |
| Shiyu | 107 | 29.46 N | 106.06 E |
| Shizhangzi | 98 | 40.24 N | 119.48 E |
| Shizheng | 100 | 24.32 N | 115.50 E |
| Shizhenjie | 100 | 28.51 N | 116.56 E |
| Shizhong, Zhg. | 100 | 24.57 N | 117.06 E |
| Shizhong, Zhg. | 106 | 30.44 N | 120.16 E |
| Shizhongtan | 107 | 30.26 N | 104.35 E |
| Shizhu, Zhg. | 100 | 28.48 N | 120.06 E |
| Shizhu, Zhg. | 102 | 29.56 N | 108.09 E |
| Shizhuang | 106 | 32.08 N | 120.31 E |
| Shizhuangzi, Zhg. | 104 | 42.24 N | 122.53 E |
| Shizhuangzi, Zhg. | 105 | 40.38 N | 116.59 E |
| Shizhuzi | 104 | 41.18 N | 121.35 E |
| Shizichang | 107 | 29.32 N | 106.14 E |
| Shizigu | 105 | 39.23 N | 118.08 E |
| Shizikou | 100 | 24.12 N | 113.38 E |
| Shizilin | 106 | 31.26 N | 121.25 E |
| Shizipo | 105 | 40.21 N | 115.07 E |
| Shizipu | 106 | 30.59 N | 119.07 E |
| Shizuchi-kokutei-kōen ♦ | 96 | 33.45 N | 133.08 E |
| Shizugawa | 92 | 38.40 N | 141.27 E |
| Shizui, Zhg. | 89 | 43.08 N | 126.06 E |
| Shizui, Zhg. | 98 | 38.52 N | 113.42 E |
| Shizuma ≃ | 96 | 35.12 N | 132.28 E |
| Shizunai | 92a | 42.20 N | 142.22 E |
| Shizuoka | 94 | 34.58 N | 138.23 E |
| Shizuoka ◻[5] | 94 | 35.00 N | 138.00 E |
| Shkodër | 38 | 42.05 N | 19.30 E |
| Shkumbin ≃ | 38 | 41.01 N | 19.26 E |
| Shō ≃ | 94 | 36.47 N | 137.04 E |
| Shoal ≃ | 194 | 30.41 N | 86.39 W |
| Shoal Cape › | 162 | 33.53 S | 121.07 E |
| Shoal Creek ≃, U.S. | 194 | 40.28 N | 92.42 W |
| Shoal Creek ≃, U.S. | 194 | 34.50 N | 87.33 W |
| Shoal Creek ≃, U.S. | 194 | 37.05 N | 94.42 W |
| Shoal Creek ≃, Il., U.S. | 219 | 38.28 N | 89.35 W |
| Shoal Creek ≃, Mo., U.S. | 194 | 39.44 N | 93.32 W |
| Shoal Creek, East Fork ≃ | 219 | 38.51 N | 89.30 W |
| Shoal Creek, Middle Fork ≃ | 219 | 39.05 N | 89.33 W |
| Shoal Creek, West Fork ≃ | 219 | 39.05 N | 89.33 W |
| Shoal Harbour | 186 | 48.11 N | 53.59 W |
| Shoalhaven ≃ | 170 | 34.52 S | 150.44 E |
| Shoalhaven Bight ⊂[3] | 170 | 34.52 S | 150.47 E |
| Shoal Lake | 184 | 50.26 N | 100.34 W |
| Shoal Lake ◎ | 184 | 49.32 N | 95.00 W |
| Shoal Point › | 276 | 41.08 N | 73.15 W |
| Shoals | 194 | 38.39 N | 86.47 W |
| Shoals, Bay of ⊂ | 168b | 35.37 S | 137.37 E |
| Shoalwater, Cape › | 224 | 46.44 N | 124.06 W |
| Shoalwater Bay ⊂ | 166 | 22.02 S | 150.25 E |
| Shōbara | 96 | 34.51 N | 133.01 E |
| Shōboku | 96 | 35.06 N | 134.07 E |
| Shobonier | 219 | 38.52 N | 89.05 W |
| Shōbu | 94 | 36.04 N | 139.36 E |
| Shōdai | 270 | 34.51 N | 135.42 E |
| Shōdo-shima I | 96 | 34.30 N | 134.17 E |
| Shoeburyness | 42 | 51.32 N | 0.48 E |
| Shoe Cove | 186 | 49.55 N | 55.33 W |
| Shoemakersville | 208 | 40.30 N | 75.58 W |
| Shōgawa | 94 | 36.34 N | 136.59 E |
| Shogunle | 273a | 6.35 N | 3.21 E |
| Shohola | 210 | 41.28 N | 74.55 W |
| Shohola Creek ≃ | 210 | 41.28 N | 74.55 W |
| Shokambetsu-dake ∧ | 92a | 43.43 N | 141.31 E |
| Shokan | 210 | 41.58 N | 74.13 W |
| Shōkawa | 94 | 36.02 N | 136.57 E |
| Sholingnur | 122 | 13.07 N | 79.25 E |
| Shomera | 132 | 33.05 N | 35.17 E |
| Shomolu | 273a | 6.32 N | 3.23 E |
| Shōmyō-no-taki ⌞ | 94 | 36.35 N | 137.24 E |
| Shona, Eilean I | 46 | 56.47 N | 5.52 W |
| Shōnai | 96 | 33.11 N | 131.26 E |
| Shōnai ≃ | 94 | 35.04 N | 136.50 E |
| Shōnan | 268 | 35.50 N | 140.02 E |
| Shongum | 276 | 40.50 N | 74.33 W |
| Shongum Lake ◎ | 276 | 40.51 N | 74.32 W |
| Shongwe | 158 | 27.24 S | 32.25 E |
| Shōō | 96 | 35.02 N | 134.08 E |
| Shooters Hill | 170 | 33.54 S | 149.52 E |
| Shooters Island I | 276 | 40.39 N | 74.10 W |
| Shopiere | 216 | 42.34 N | 88.57 W |
| Shoranūr | 122 | 10.46 N | 76.17 E |
| Shorāpur | 122 | 16.31 N | 76.45 E |
| Shoreacres, B.C., Can. | 182 | 49.26 N | 117.32 W |
| Shore Acres, Ca., U.S. | 226 | 38.02 N | 121.58 W |
| Shore Acres, Ma., U.S. | 207 | 42.12 N | 70.44 W |
| Shore Acres, N.J., U.S. | 208 | 40.01 N | 74.06 W |
| Shoreacres, Tx., U.S. | 222 | 29.37 N | 95.01 W |
| Shoreditch ◆[8] | 260 | 51.32 N | 0.05 W |
| Shoreham, Austl. | 169 | 38.25 S | 145.03 E |
| Shoreham, Eng., U.K. | 260 | 51.20 N | 0.11 E |
| Shoreham, Mi., U.S. | 216 | 42.03 N | 86.30 W |
| Shoreham-by-Sea | 42 | 50.49 N | 0.16 W |
| Shorewood, Il., U.S. | 216 | 41.32 N | 88.12 W |
| Shorewood, Wi., U.S. | 216 | 43.05 N | 87.53 W |
| Shorewood Hills | 216 | 43.04 N | 89.26 W |
| Shorkot | 123 | 30.50 N | 72.04 E |
| Shorkot Road | 123 | 30.47 N | 72.15 E |
| Shorne | 260 | 51.25 N | 0.26 E |
| Short Beach | 207 | 41.15 N | 72.50 W |
| Short Creek | 214 | 40.11 N | 80.55 W |
| Shortland Islands II | 175e | 6.55 S | 155.53 E |
| Short Mountain ∧ | 192 | 36.23 N | 83.10 W |
| Shortsville | 210 | 42.57 N | 77.13 W |
| Shoshone | 202 | 42.56 N | 114.24 W |
| Shoshone ≃ | 202 | 44.52 N | 108.11 W |
| Shoshone, North Fork ≃ | 202 | 44.29 N | 109.18 W |
| Shoshone, South Fork ≃ | 202 | 44.27 N | 109.14 W |
| Shoshone Basin ≚[1] | 202 | 43.05 N | 108.05 W |
| Shoshone Lake ◎ | 202 | 44.22 N | 110.43 W |
| Shoshone Mountains ⩓ | 204 | 39.00 N | 117.30 W |
| Shoshone Peak ∧ | 204 | 36.56 N | 116.16 W |
| Shoshone Range ⩓ | 204 | 40.20 N | 116.50 W |
| Shoshong | 156 | 22.59 S | 26.30 E |
| Shoshoni | 200 | 43.14 N | 108.06 W |
| Shostka | 78 | 51.52 N | 33.30 E |
| Shotley Gate | 42 | 51.58 N | 1.15 E |
| Shotton | 262 | 53.12 N | 3.02 W |
| Shotton Colliery | 44 | 54.44 N | 1.20 W |
| Shotts | 46 | 55.49 N | 3.48 W |
| Shotwick | 262 | 53.14 N | 2.59 W |
| Shou'anzhen | 107 | 30.16 N | 103.37 E |
| Shouchang | 100 | 29.22 N | 119.13 E |
| Shoufeng | 100 | 23.52 N | 121.30 E |
| Shouguang | 98 | 36.53 N | 118.42 E |
| Shouning | 100 | 27.27 N | 119.30 E |
| Shournagh ≃ | 48 | 51.53 N | 8.35 W |
| Shoushan | 104 | 41.12 N | 123.03 E |
| Shouwangfen | 105 | 40.35 N | 117.48 E |
| Shouxian | 100 | 32.35 N | 116.47 E |
| Shouyang | 102 | 37.59 N | 113.09 E |
| Shōwa, Nihon | 94 | 36.37 N | 139.04 E |
| Shōwa, Nihon | 96 | 34.43 N | 133.39 E |
| Showell | 208 | 38.23 N | 75.12 W |
| Show Low | 200 | 34.15 N | 110.01 W |
| Shpola | 78 | 49.01 N | 31.24 E |
| Shpykiv | 78 | 48.46 N | 28.35 E |
| Shqipëri → Albania ◻[1] | 38 | 41.00 N | 20.00 E |
| Shramkivka | 78 | 50.10 N | 32.05 E |
| Shreve | 214 | 40.40 N | 82.01 W |
| Shreveport | 194 | 32.30 N | 93.44 W |
| Shrevewood | 284c | 38.53 N | 77.13 W |
| Shrewsbury, Eng., U.K. | 42 | 52.43 N | 2.45 W |
| Shrewsbury, Ma., U.S. | 207 | 42.17 N | 71.42 W |
| Shrewsbury, N.J., U.S. | 208 | 40.19 N | 74.03 W |
| Shrewsbury, Pa., U.S. | 208 | 39.46 N | 76.40 W |
| Shrewsbury River ⊂ | 276 | 40.21 N | 74.00 W |
| Shrewton | 42 | 51.12 N | 1.55 W |
| Shri Dūngargarh | 120 | 28.05 N | 74.00 E |
| Shri Mohangarh | 120 | 27.17 N | 71.14 E |
| Shriner Mountain ∧ | 210 | 40.56 N | 77.20 W |
| Shrīrangapattana | 122 | 12.25 N | 76.42 E |
| Shrivenham | 42 | 51.36 N | 1.39 W |
| Shropshire ◻[6] | 42 | 52.40 N | 2.40 W |
| Shropshire Union Canal ≡ | 262 | 53.17 N | 2.53 W |
| Shrub Oak | 210 | 41.20 N | 73.49 W |
| Shrule | 48 | 53.30 N | 9.08 W |
| Shtormove | 83 | 49.06 N | 38.55 E |
| Shu ≃ | 98 | 34.07 N | 118.30 E |
| Shuajingsi | 102 | 32.00 N | 103.05 E |
| Shuanfeng Shan ∧ | 107 | 29.26 N | 105.47 E |
| Shuang ≃ | 269d | 25.00 N | 121.31 E |
| Shuangbai | 102 | 24.54 N | 101.32 E |
| Shuangcheng | 89 | 45.21 N | 126.17 E |
| Shuangchengzi | 105 | 40.11 N | 118.03 E |
| Shuangdian | 100 | 32.23 N | 120.51 E |
| Shuangdun | 106 | 32.13 N | 121.08 E |
| Shuangfeng, Zhg. | 102 | 27.24 N | 112.05 E |
| Shuangfeng, Zhg. | 106 | 31.31 N | 121.01 E |
| Shuangfeng, Zhg. | 106 | 31.31 N | 121.02 E |
| Shuangfeng Shan ∧ | 100 | 24.28 N | 114.43 E |
| Shuangfengyi | 107 | 29.27 N | 105.09 E |
| Shuangfu | 105 | 39.48 N | 117.44 E |
| Shuangfuchang, Zhg. | 107 | 29.41 N | 103.31 E |
| Shuangfuchang, Zhg. | 107 | 30.08 N | 103.32 E |
| Shuanggang, Zhg. | 89 | 45.07 N | 122.59 E |
| Shuanggang, Zhg. | 100 | 28.11 N | 117.30 E |
| Shuanggetun | 89 | 48.58 N | 129.57 E |
| Shuanggou, Zhg. | 98 | 34.03 N | 117.37 E |
| Shuanggou, Zhg. | 100 | 32.12 N | 112.21 E |
| Shuanggou, Zhg. | 100 | 33.16 N | 118.10 E |
| Shuanggufen | 107 | 29.38 N | 104.11 E |
| Shuanghe, Zhg. | 100 | 31.33 N | 116.46 E |
| Shuanghe, Zhg. | 100 | 31.41 N | 112.46 E |
| Shuanghe, Zhg. | 107 | 29.40 N | 104.48 E |
| Shuanghe, Zhg. | 107 | 30.07 N | 105.10 E |
| Shuanghe, Zhg. | 107 | 30.15 N | 104.44 E |
| Shuanghechang, Zhg. | 107 | 28.51 N | 104.51 E |
| Shuanghechang, Zhg. | 107 | 29.25 N | 106.17 E |
| Shuanghechang, Zhg. | 107 | 29.12 N | 105.43 E |
| Shuanghechang, Zhg. | 107 | 29.18 N | 105.36 E |
| Shuang-hsi | 269d | 25.01 N | 121.39 E |
| Shuangji ≃ | 100 | 34.05 N | 114.24 E |
| Shuangjiang, Zhg. | 100 | 26.48 N | 116.28 E |
| Shuangjiang, Zhg. | 102 | 23.37 N | 99.41 E |
| Shuangjiang, Zhg. | 107 | 30.13 N | 105.45 E |
| Shuangjiangqiao | 102 | 25.19 N | 98.51 E |
| Shuangjianji | 100 | 33.12 N | 116.40 E |
| Shuangjingzi | 104 | 42.28 N | 123.42 E |
| Shuangkou | 105 | 39.15 N | 117.02 E |
| Shuangliao | 89 | 43.31 N | 123.30 E |
| Shuanglin | 106 | 30.47 N | 120.19 E |
| Shuanglingzi, Zhg. | 104 | 40.54 N | 124.10 E |
| Shuanglingzi, Zhg. | 104 | 40.50 N | 123.06 E |
| Shuangliu | 107 | 30.34 N | 103.55 E |
| Shuangliushu | 100 | 31.56 N | 115.12 E |
| Shuanglongtai | 104 | 40.56 N | 122.39 E |
| Shuangmiao, Zhg. | 100 | 28.24 N | 120.45 E |
| Shuangmiao, Zhg. | 100 | 32.09 N | 116.52 E |
| Shuangmiaozi, Zhg. | 104 | 42.25 N | 122.17 E |
| Shuangmiaozi, Zhg. | 104 | 42.02 N | 121.52 E |
| Shuangpai | 110 | 25.57 N | 111.32 E |
| Shuangpaishi | 106 | 31.24 N | 118.59 E |
| Shuangqiao, Zhg. | 100 | 32.29 N | 116.41 E |
| Shuangqiao, Zhg. | 105 | 39.54 N | 116.37 E |
| Shuangqiao, Zhg. | 106 | 30.59 N | 118.47 E |
| Shuangshanzi | 98 | 40.21 N | 119.08 E |
| Shuangshipu | 107 | 29.14 N | 104.42 E |
| Shuangshiqiao, Zhg. | 107 | 29.22 N | 105.51 E |
| Shuangshiqiao, Zhg. | 107 | 29.23 N | 104.29 E |
| Shuangshu | 105 | 39.34 N | 117.01 E |
| Shuangshutai | 89 | 43.50 N | 121.15 E |
| Shuangtaizi, Zhg. | 104 | 41.34 N | 121.12 E |
| Shuangtaizi, Zhg. | 104 | 42.21 N | 124.10 E |
| Shuangtaizi, Zhg. | 104 | 42.25 N | 123.11 E |
| Shuangtaizi, Zhg. | 104 | 41.00 N | 122.34 E |
| Shuangtaizi, Zhg. | 104 | 41.11 N | 121.14 E |
| Shuangtaizi ≃ | 104 | 40.59 N | 121.51 E |
| Shuangtaizihe Kou ≃[1] | 104 | 40.55 N | 121.50 E |
| Shuangtang, Zhg. | 100 | 28.01 N | 116.44 E |
| Shuangtang, Zhg. | 105 | 39.03 N | 116.17 E |
| Shuangtang, Zhg. | 105 | 38.53 N | 116.54 E |
| Shuangtangdian | 106 | 30.59 N | 118.51 E |
| Shuangtuo | 105 | 39.14 N | 117.20 E |
| Shuangtuozhen | 105 | 39.29 N | 118.23 E |
| Shuangxi, Zhg. | 100 | 27.01 N | 119.03 E |
| Shuangxi, Zhg. | 106 | 30.24 N | 119.50 E |
| Shuangyang | 89 | 43.32 N | 125.42 E |
| Shuangyangdian | 104 | 41.07 N | 121.16 E |
| Shuangyaocun | 105 | 38.55 N | 117.03 E |
| Shuangyashan | 89 | 46.37 N | 131.22 E |
| Shu'ayb, Wādī V | 132 | 31.54 N | 35.38 E |
| Shu'ayt, Wādī V | 144 | 18.15 N | 52.00 E |
| Shubenacadie ≃ | 186 | 45.20 N | 63.30 W |
| Shublik Mountains ⩓ | 180 | 69.31 N | 145.40 W |
| Shubrā al-Khaymah | 142 | 30.06 N | 31.15 E |
| Shubrā Bābil | 142 | 30.54 N | 31.11 E |
| Shubrā Khalfūn | 142 | 30.29 N | 31.05 E |
| Shubrā Khīt | 142 | 31.02 N | 30.43 E |
| Shubuta | 194 | 31.51 N | 88.41 W |
| Shucheng | 100 | 31.27 N | 116.57 E |
| Shufu | 85 | 39.27 N | 75.52 E |
| Shufuka Shan ∧ | 89 | 50.28 N | 123.10 E |
| Shugudali | 89 | 52.47 N | 124.02 E |
| Shuheyingzi | 104 | 42.18 N | 122.16 E |
| Shuhezhen | 106 | 31.35 N | 121.35 E |
| Shūhō | 96 | 34.13 N | 131.18 E |
| Shuhong | 100 | 28.39 N | 120.09 E |
| Shuibatang | 102 | 28.39 N | 107.03 E |
| Shuibei, Zhg. | 100 | 28.04 N | 115.01 E |
| Shuibei, Zhg. | 106 | 31.40 N | 119.39 E |
| Shuichaoyang | 100 | 26.22 N | 117.57 E |
| Shuicheng | 102 | 26.41 N | 104.50 E |
| Shuidao | 98 | 37.10 N | 121.33 E |
| Shuidiangou | 89 | 47.43 N | 122.40 E |
| Shuidong, Zhg. | 106 | 31.23 N | 119.37 E |
| Shuidong, Zhg. | 106 | 30.47 N | 118.57 E |
| Shuidongjie | 106 | 31.07 N | 119.33 E |
| Shuiduixia | 106 | 30.17 N | 118.50 E |
| Shuihai | 100 | 33.02 N | 120.26 E |
| Shuihouling | 100 | 30.43 N | 116.26 E |
| Shuiji | 100 | 27.26 N | 118.20 E |
| Shuijiahuangdi | 104 | 42.14 N | 123.28 E |
| Shuijian | 105 | 40.09 N | 115.58 E |
| Shuijing | 102 | 26.10 N | 99.09 E |
| Shuijingtang | 102 | 28.50 N | 108.11 E |
| Shuikou, Zhg. | 100 | 26.59 N | 117.41 E |
| Shuikou, Zhg. | 100 | 26.22 N | 118.44 E |
| Shuikou, Zhg. | 100 | 24.00 N | 115.55 E |
| Shuikou, Zhg. | 100 | 26.18 N | 113.46 E |
| Shuikou, Zhg. | 102 | 25.54 N | 109.06 E |
| Shuikou, Zhg. | 107 | 29.29 N | 103.42 E |
| Shuikouchang | 107 | 29.33 N | 103.40 E |
| Shuikouguan | 102 | 22.30 N | 106.34 E |
| Shuikoushan | 102 | 26.30 N | 112.30 E |
| Shuikouxu | 100 | 25.09 N | 114.28 E |
| Shuiliandong | 98 | 42.12 N | 125.09 E |
| Shuimenzi | 98 | 39.36 N | 122.19 E |
| Shuimingqiao | 106 | 31.03 N | 119.09 E |
| Shuimoqipan | 85 | 39.51 N | 76.42 E |
| Shuiquan'gou | 104 | 41.58 N | 121.50 E |
| Shuiquanzi, Zhg. | 104 | 42.15 N | 121.32 E |
| Shuiquanzi, Zhg. | 104 | 40.53 N | 121.05 E |
| Shuitangzi | 102 | 29.18 N | 101.10 E |
| Shuiting | 100 | 29.10 N | 119.14 E |
| Shuitou, Zhg. | 100 | 24.43 N | 118.25 E |
| Shuitou, Zhg. | 100 | 23.53 N | 113.37 E |
| Shuitou, Zhg. | 100 | 27.38 N | 120.16 E |
| Shuitouwei | 100 | 26.06 N | 115.28 E |
| Shuituzhen | 107 | 29.47 N | 106.31 E |
| Shuiyang | 106 | 31.14 N | 118.47 E |
| Shuiyang ≃ | 106 | 31.14 N | 118.48 E |
| Shuiye | 98 | 36.08 N | 114.07 E |
| Shuizhai | 98 | 36.54 N | 117.24 E |
| Shuizhuyang | 100 | 26.59 N | 119.13 E |
| Shujāābād | 123 | 29.53 N | 71.18 E |
| Shujālpur | 124 | 23.24 N | 76.43 E |
| Shujiawazi | 104 | 42.20 N | 121.57 E |
| Shuksan, Mount ∧ | 224 | 48.50 N | 121.36 W |
| Shulan | 89 | 44.27 N | 126.57 E |
| Shulaps Peak ∧ | 182 | 50.57 N | 122.31 W |
| Shule | 85 | 39.23 N | 76.06 E |
| Shule ≃ | 102 | 40.50 N | 94.10 E |
| Shūlgareh | 120 | 36.19 N | 66.53 E |
| Shul'hynka | 83 | 49.08 N | 38.56 E |
| Shullsburg | 190 | 42.34 N | 90.13 W |
| Shulu (Xinji) | 98 | 37.54 N | 115.13 E |
| Shumagin Islands II | 180 | 55.07 N | 159.45 W |
| Shumatuscacant ≃ | 283 | 42.03 N | 70.51 W |
| Shumen → Šumen | 38 | 43.16 N | 26.55 E |
| Shums'k | 78 | 50.07 N | 26.07 E |
| Shūnah, Wādī ash- V | 142 | 29.38 N | 32.13 E |
| Shun'an | 100 | 30.57 N | 117.57 E |
| Shūnat Nimrīn | 132 | 31.54 N | 35.37 E |
| Shunayn, Sabkhat ◎ | 146 | 30.30 N | 21.00 E |
| Shunchang | 100 | 26.50 N | 117.48 E |
| Shunde | 100 | 22.50 N | 113.14 E |
| Shundian | 100 | 34.15 N | 113.20 E |
| Shundianqiao | 106 | 31.24 N | 120.41 E |
| Shunge | 102 | 37.25 N | 95.27 E |
| Shungnak | 180 | 66.53 N | 157.02 W |
| Shunhechang | 107 | 29.57 N | 104.42 E |
| Shunlongchang | 107 | 30.04 N | 103.27 E |
| Shunshanpu | 104 | 42.08 N | 122.21 E |
| Shuntianhu | 100 | 24.08 N | 114.48 E |
| Shunyi | 105 | 40.08 N | 116.38 E |
| Shuoduzong | 102 | 30.48 N | 95.47 E |
| Shuojiaji | 100 | 33.42 N | 119.44 E |
| Shuping | 107 | 29.19 N | 104.43 E |
| Shupiyan | 123 | 33.43 N | 74.50 E |
| Shuqayyiqah, Nafūd ⍊[8] | 128 | 25.45 N | 43.55 E |
| Shuqualak | 194 | 32.58 N | 88.34 W |
| Shūr ≃, Īrān | 128 | 31.45 N | 55.15 E |
| Shūr ≃, Īrān | 128 | 34.38 N | 51.46 E |
| Shūr ≃, Īrān | 128 | 30.57 N | 57.42 E |
| Shūr ≃, Īrān | 128 | 35.57 N | 56.24 E |
| Shuri | 174m | 26.13 N | 127.43 E |
| Shurkhua | 110 | 22.15 N | 93.38 E |
| Shurugwi | 154 | 19.40 S | 30.00 E |
| Shūsf | 128 | 31.48 N | 60.01 E |
| Shūsh | 128 | 32.11 N | 48.15 E |
| Shushan | 210 | 43.05 N | 73.21 W |
| Shushan Hu ◎ | 98 | 35.36 N | 116.27 E |
| Shūshtar | 128 | 32.03 N | 48.51 E |
| Shuswap ≃ | 182 | 50.50 N | 119.00 W |
| Shuswap Lake ◎ | 182 | 50.57 N | 119.15 W |
| Shuṭab | 142 | 27.08 N | 31.14 E |
| Shutendōji-yama ∧ | 96 | 33.06 N | 130.54 E |
| Shuteye Peak ∧ | 226 | 37.21 N | 119.25 W |
| Shutlingsloe ∧ | 262 | 53.13 N | 2.02 W |
| Shūtō | 96 | 34.05 N | 132.05 E |
| Shuwak | 140 | 14.23 N | 35.52 E |
| Shuwaykah | 132 | 32.20 N | 35.02 E |
| Shuya, Nihon | 174m | 26.40 N | 128.06 E |
| Shuya → Šuja, Ross. | 24 | 61.55 N | 34.12 E |
| Shuyak Island I | 180 | 58.35 N | 152.30 W |
| Shuyang | 98 | 34.08 N | 118.47 E |
| Shuyūkh Fawqānī | 130 | 36.46 N | 38.03 E |
| Shuzenji | 94 | 34.58 N | 138.56 E |
| Shwangliao → Liaoyuan | 89 | 42.54 N | 125.07 E |
| Shwebo | 110 | 22.34 N | 95.42 E |
| Shwegun | 110 | 17.09 N | 97.39 E |
| Shwegyin | 110 | 17.55 N | 96.53 E |
| Shweli (Longchuan) ≃ | 102 | 23.56 N | 96.17 E |
| Shwenyaung | 110 | 20.46 N | 96.57 E |
| Shyamdih | 126 | 23.47 N | 86.56 E |
| Shyok | 120 | 34.11 N | 78.08 E |
| Shyok ≃ | 120 | 35.13 N | 75.53 E |
| Shypuvate | 78 | 49.56 N | 37.24 E |
| Shyrmivka | 78 | 49.34 N | 29.06 E |
| Shyroke, Ukr. | 78 | 47.41 N | 33.14 E |
| Shyroke, Ukr. | 78 | 48.08 N | 34.49 E |
| Shyrokolanivka | 78 | 47.10 N | 31.24 E |
| Shyrokyne | 83 | 47.06 N | 37.49 E |
| Shyryaeve | 78 | 47.23 N | 30.13 E |
| Shyshaky | 78 | 49.53 N | 34.00 E |
| Si ≃ | 98 | 35.11 N | 116.42 E |
| Sia | 164 | 6.49 S | 134.19 E |
| Siabu | 114 | 1.01 N | 99.29 E |
| Siachen Glacier ⊓ | 123 | 35.30 N | 77.00 E |
| Siagne ≃ | 62 | 43.32 N | 6.57 E |
| Siāhān Range ⩓ | 128 | 27.25 N | 64.30 E |
| Sīāh Kūh, Kavīr-e ≚ | 128 | 32.40 N | 53.52 E |
| Sīāh Kūh, Selseleh-ye ⩓ | 128 | 34.00 N | 64.00 E |
| Siak ≃ | 114 | 1.13 N | 102.09 E |
| Siak Kecil ≃ | 114 | 1.16 N | 102.08 E |
| Siak Sri Indrapura | 114 | 0.46 N | 102.04 E |
| Sialang | 114 | 1.31 N | 99.27 E |
| Sialejevskaja P'atina | 80 | 53.49 N | 44.32 E |
| Siālkot | 123 | 32.30 N | 74.31 E |
| Sialsūk | 120 | 23.24 N | 92.45 E |
| Siam → Thailand ◻[1] | 110 | 15.00 N | 100.00 E |
| Siam, Gulf of → Thailand, Gulf of ⊂ | 110 | 10.00 N | 101.00 E |
| Siamanna | 71 | 39.55 N | 8.46 E |
| Sian → Xi'an, Zhg. | 102 | 34.15 N | 108.52 E |
| Si'an, Zhg. | 106 | 30.54 N | 119.39 E |
| Siangtan → Xiangtan | 100 | 27.51 N | 112.54 E |
| Sianhala | 150 | 10.03 N | 6.51 W |
| Sianów | 30 | 54.15 N | 16.16 E |
| Siantan, Pulau I | 112 | 3.10 N | 106.15 E |
| Sianzhuang | 100 | 33.05 N | 119.13 E |
| Siapa ≃ | 246 | 2.07 N | 66.28 W |
| Siargao Island I | 116 | 9.53 N | 126.02 E |
| Siari | 123 | 34.56 N | 76.44 E |
| Siasconset | 207 | 41.15 N | 69.58 W |
| Siasi | 116 | 5.33 N | 120.49 E |
| Siasi Island I | 116 | 5.33 N | 120.51 E |
| Šiaškotan, ostrov I | 74 | 48.49 N | 154.06 E |
| Siátista | 38 | 40.16 N | 21.33 E |
| Siaton | 116 | 9.04 N | 123.02 E |
| Siaton ≃ | 116 | 9.02 N | 123.02 E |
| Siaton Point › | 116 | 9.03 N | 123.01 E |
| Siau, Pulau I | 112 | 2.42 N | 125.24 E |
| Siaugues-Saint-Romain | 62 | 45.06 N | 3.38 E |
| Šiauliai | 76 | 55.56 N | 23.19 E |
| Sibago Island I | 116 | 6.45 N | 122.24 E |
| Sibā'ī, Jabal as- ∧ | 140 | 25.43 N | 34.09 E |
| Sibaj | 86 | 52.42 N | 58.39 E |
| Sibalom | 116 | 10.47 N | 122.01 E |
| Sibanicú | 240p | 21.14 N | 77.31 W |
| Sibao | 100 | 25.55 N | 116.42 E |
| Sibari | 68 | 39.45 N | 16.27 E |
| Sibari, Piana di ≚ | 68 | 39.45 N | 16.25 E |
| Sibasa | 156 | 22.53 S | 30.33 E |
| Sibati | 86 | 47.12 N | 88.15 E |
| Sibayi ◎ | 158 | 27.20 S | 32.40 E |
| Sibay Island I | 116 | 11.51 N | 121.29 E |
| Sibbald | 184 | 51.23 N | 110.09 W |
| Sibbald Point Provincial Park ♦ | 212 | 44.19 N | 79.19 W |
| Šibbe | 85 | 39.53 N | 72.05 E |
| Sibbo | 26 | 60.22 N | 25.16 E |
| Sibchar | 126 | 23.21 N | 90.09 E |
| Šibenik | 36 | 43.44 N | 15.54 E |
| Siberia → Sibir' ◆[1] | 74 | 65.00 N | 110.00 E |
| Siberia Occidental, Llanura de → Zapadno-Sibirskaja ravnina ≚ | 72 | 60.00 N | 75.00 E |
| Sibérie Occidental, Dépression de la → Zapadno-Sibirskaja ravnina ≚ | 72 | 60.00 N | 75.00 E |
| Siberut, Pulau I | 108 | 1.20 S | 98.55 E |
| Sibi | 120 | 29.33 N | 67.53 E |
| Sibiči | 89 | 46.04 N | 135.22 E |
| Sibidiri | 164 | 9.00 S | 142.15 E |
| Sibigo | 114 | 2.51 N | 95.55 E |
| Sibillini, Monti ⩓ | 66 | 42.54 N | 13.13 E |
| Sibir' (Siberia) ◆[1] | 74 | 65.00 N | 110.00 E |
| Sibir'akova, ostrov I | 74 | 72.50 N | 79.00 E |
| Sibircevo | 89 | 44.12 N | 132.26 E |
| Sibiti | 152 | 3.41 S | 13.21 E |
| Sibiti ≃ | 154 | 3.49 S | 34.46 E |
| Sibiu | 38 | 45.48 N | 24.09 E |
| Sibiu ◻[6] | 38 | 46.00 N | 24.15 E |
| Sible Hedingham | 42 | 51.58 N | 0.35 E |
| Sibley, Il., U.S. | 216 | 40.35 N | 88.23 W |
| Sibley, Ia., U.S. | 198 | 43.23 N | 95.45 W |
| Sibley, La., U.S. | 194 | 32.33 N | 93.18 W |
| Sibley, Ms., U.S. | 194 | 31.22 N | 91.23 W |
| Sibley Peninsula ›[1] | 190 | 48.25 N | 88.45 W |
| Sibley Provincial Park ♦ | 190 | 48.25 N | 88.49 W |
| Siboa | 112 | 0.30 N | 120.02 E |
| Sibochi | 107 | 28.50 N | 104.32 E |
| Sibolga | 114 | 1.45 N | 98.48 E |


**Symbols** in the index entries represent the broad categories identified in the key at the right. Symbols with superior numbers (⩓[1]) identify subcategories (see complete key on page *I · 1).*

**Symbole** im Register stellen die rechts im Schlüssel erklärten Kategorien dar. Symbole mit hochgestellten Ziffern (⩓[1]) bezeichnen Unterabteilungen einer Kategorie (vgl. vollständiger Schlüssel auf Seite *I · 1).*

**Los símbolos** incluídos en el texto del índice representan las grandes categorías identificadas con la clave a la derecha. Los símbolos con numeros en su parte superior (⩓[1]) identifican las subcategorías (véase la clave completa en la página *I · 1).*

**Les symboles** de l'index représentent les catégories indiquées dans la légende à droite. Les symboles suivis d'un indice (⩓[1]) représentent des sous-catégories (voir légende complète à la page *I · 1).*

**Os símbolos** incluídos no texto do índice representam as grandes categorias identificadas com a chave à direita. Os símbolos com números em sua parte superior (⩓[1]) identificam as subcategorias (veja-se a chave completa à página *I · 1).*

| | | | | |
|---|---|---|---|---|
| ∧ Mountain | Berg | Montaña | Montagne | Montanha |
| ⩓ Mountains | Gebirge | Montañas | Montagnes | Montanhas |
| )( Pass | Paß | Paso | Col | Passo |
| V Valley, Canyon | Tal, Cañon | Valle, Cañón | Vallée, Canyon | Vale, Canhão |
| ≚ Plain | Ebene | Llano | Plaine | Planície |
| › Cape | Kap | Cabo | Cap | Cabo |
| I Island | Insel | Isla | Île | Ilha |
| II Islands | Inseln | Islas | Îles | Ilhas |
| ⍊ Other Topographic Features | Andere Topographische Objekte | Otros Elementos Topográficos | Autres données topographiques | Outros acidentes topográficos |

**ESPAÑOL**

| Nombre | Página | Lat.°′ | Long.°′ W = Oeste |
|---|---|---|---|
| Siborang | 114 | 1.08 N | 99.26 E |
| Siborongborong | 114 | 2.13 N | 98.59 E |
| Sibpur, Bngl. | 124 | 24.02 N | 90.44 E |
| Sibpur, India | 272b | 22.24 N | 88.33 E |
| Sibpur, India | 272b | 22.34 N | 88.19 E |
| Sibsa ≃[1] | 126 | 22.01 N | 89.30 E |
| Sibsāgar | 120 | 26.59 N | 94.39 E |
| Sibu | 112 | 2.18 N | 111.49 E |
| Sibu, Pulau I | 114 | 2.13 N | 104.04 E |
| Sibuatan, Gunung ∧ | 114 | 2.56 N | 98.24 E |
| Sibuguey ≃ | 116 | 7.38 N | 122.48 E |
| Sibuguey Bay c | 116 | 7.30 N | 122.40 E |
| Sibut | 152 | 5.44 N | 19.05 E |
| Sibuti | 112 | 4.03 N | 113.48 E |
| Sibutu Island I | 112 | 4.46 N | 119.29 E |
| Sibutu Passage ⋓ | 112 | 4.50 N | 119.35 E |
| Sibuyan Island I | 116 | 12.25 N | 122.34 E |
| Sibuyan Sea ∓[2] | 116 | 12.50 N | 122.40 E |
| Siby | 150 | 12.23 N | 8.20 W |
| Sibyŏn | 98 | 38.19 N | 126.41 E |
| Sicamous | 182 | 50.50 N | 119.00 W |
| Sicapoo, Mount ∧ | 116 | 18.01 N | 120.56 E |
| Siccus ≃ | 166 | 31.26 S | 139.30 E |
| Sichakou | 98 | 41.39 N | 116.26 E |
| Šichany | 80 | 52.07 N | 47.13 E |
| Sichifulo ≃ | 154 | 17.26 S | 25.02 E |
| Si Chon | 110 | 9.00 N | 99.54 E |
| Sichote-Alin' ⩘ | 89 | 48.00 N | 138.00 E |
| Sichote-Alinskij zapovednik ♦ | 89 | 45.15 N | 136.15 E |
| Šichtovo | 76 | 55.43 N | 32.18 E |
| Sichuan (Szechwan) □[4] | 102 | 31.00 N | 105.00 E |
| Sichuan Pendi ≌[1] | 102 | 30.00 N | 105.00 E |
| Sichuanzhai | 102 | 23.02 N | 101.44 E |
| Sicié, Cap › | 62 | 43.03 N | 5.51 E |
| Sicignano degli Alburni | 68 | 40.34 N | 15.18 E |
| Sicilia □[4] | 70 | 37.30 N | 14.00 E |
| Sicilia (Sicily) I | 70 | 37.30 N | 14.00 E |
| Sicilia, Isla de → Sicilia I | 70 | 37.30 N | 14.00 E |
| Sicily → Sicilia I | 70 | 37.30 N | 14.00 E |
| Sicily, Strait of ⋓ | 36 | 37.20 N | 11.20 E |
| Sicily Island | 194 | 31.50 N | 91.39 W |
| Sicklerville | 208 | 39.43 N | 74.58 W |
| Sickte | 54 | 52.13 N | 10.38 E |
| Sicogon Island I | 116 | 11.27 N | 123.16 E |
| Sico Tinto ≃ | 236 | 15.58 N | 84.58 W |
| Sicuani | 248 | 14.16 S | 71.13 W |
| Siculiana | 70 | 37.20 N | 13.25 E |
| Şicun | 106 | 31.55 N | 119.18 E |
| Šid | 38 | 45.08 N | 19.13 E |
| Sīdah, Qārat ∧[2] | 142 | 30.16 N | 29.58 E |
| Sidamo □[4] | 144 | 5.00 N | 39.00 E |
| Sidao | 271a | 39.51 N | 116.26 E |
| Sidaohe | 105 | 40.24 N | 117.17 E |
| Sidareja | 115a | 7.29 S | 108.47 E |
| Sidas | 112 | 0.24 N | 109.46 E |
| Sidcup ⊸[8] | 260 | 51.25 N | 0.06 E |
| Siddeburen | 52 | 53.15 N | 6.52 E |
| Siddhapur | 120 | 23.55 N | 72.23 E |
| Siddinghausen | 263 | 51.32 N | 7.48 E |
| Siddington | 262 | 53.14 N | 2.14 W |
| Siddipet | 122 | 18.06 N | 78.51 E |
| Sideia Island I | 164 | 10.35 S | 150.50 E |
| Sidel'kino | 80 | 54.32 N | 51.08 E |
| Sidéradougou | 150 | 10.40 N | 4.15 W |
| Siderno | 68 | 38.16 N | 16.18 E |
| Siderópolis | 252 | 28.35 S | 49.26 W |
| Šiderti ≃, Kaz. | 80 | 50.10 N | 52.20 E |
| Šiderti ≃, Kaz. | 86 | 52.32 N | 74.50 E |
| Sidhauli | 124 | 27.17 N | 80.50 E |
| Sídheros, Ákra › | 38 | 35.19 N | 26.19 E |
| Sidhi | 124 | 24.25 N | 81.53 E |
| Sidhirókastron | 38 | 41.14 N | 23.22 E |
| Sīdī 'Abd ar-Raḥmān | 140 | 30.58 N | 29.44 E |
| Sidi Aïch | 34 | 36.37 N | 4.42 E |
| Sidi Aïssa | 148 | 35.53 N | 3.48 E |
| Sidi Akacha | 34 | 36.28 N | 1.18 E |
| Sidi Ali | 34 | 36.06 N | 0.25 E |
| Sidi Ali, Oued V | 148 | 34.07 N | 2.05 W |
| Sidi Ali Ben Nasrallah | 36 | 35.15 N | 9.50 E |
| Sīdī Barrānī | 140 | 31.36 N | 25.55 E |
| Sidi bel Abbès | 148 | 35.13 N | 0.10 W |
| Sidi Bennour | 148 | 32.30 N | 8.30 W |
| Sidi Bou Zid | 148 | 35.02 N | 9.30 E |
| Sidi Daoud | 36 | 37.00 N | 10.55 E |
| Sidi el Hani, Sebkhet ⊜ | 36 | 35.33 N | 10.25 E |
| Sīdī Ghāzī | 142 | 31.12 N | 31.03 E |
| Sīdī Ḥunaysh | 140 | 31.10 N | 27.37 E |
| Sidi Ifni | 148 | 29.24 N | 10.12 W |
| Sidi Kacem | 148 | 34.15 N | 5.39 W |
| Sidikalang | 114 | 2.45 N | 98.19 E |
| Sidimo | 144 | 2.27 N | 41.58 E |
| Sidi Mohammed Ben Ali | 34 | 36.09 N | 0.51 E |
| Sidi Moussa, Oued V | 148 | 26.58 N | 3.54 E |
| Sidi Okba | 148 | 34.48 N | 5.54 E |
| Sīdī Sālim | 142 | 31.17 N | 30.48 E |
| Sidi Slimane | 148 | 34.15 N | 5.49 W |
| Sidi Smaïl | 148 | 32.49 N | 8.30 W |
| Sidlaghatta | 122 | 13.23 N | 77.52 E |
| Sidlaw Hills ⩘[2] | 46 | 56.30 N | 3.10 W |
| Sidley, Mount ∧ | 9 | 77.02 S | 126.00 W |
| Sidli | 124 | 26.33 N | 90.28 E |
| Sidman | 214 | 40.20 N | 78.45 W |
| Sidmouth | 42 | 50.41 N | 3.15 W |
| Sidnaw | 190 | 46.30 N | 88.42 W |
| Sidney, B.C., Can. | 224 | 48.39 N | 123.24 W |
| Sidney, Il., U.S. | 194 | 40.01 N | 88.04 W |
| Sidney, In., U.S. | 216 | 41.06 N | 85.45 W |
| Sidney, Ia., U.S. | 198 | 40.44 N | 95.38 W |
| Sidney, Mt., U.S. | 198 | 47.43 N | 104.09 W |
| Sidney, Ne., U.S. | 198 | 41.08 N | 102.58 W |
| Sidney, N.Y., U.S. | 210 | 42.18 N | 75.23 W |
| Sidney, Oh., U.S. | 216 | 40.17 N | 84.09 W |
| Sidney Center | 210 | 42.17 N | 75.15 W |
| Sidney Island I | 224 | 48.37 N | 123.18 W |
| Sidney Lanier, Lake ⊜[1] | 192 | 34.15 N | 83.57 W |
| Sido | 150 | 11.40 N | 7.36 W |
| Sidoan | 112 | 0.16 N | 120.12 E |
| Sidoarjo | 115a | 7.27 S | 112.43 E |
| Sidon → Şaydā, Lubnān | 132 | 33.33 N | 35.22 E |
| Sidon, Ms., U.S. | 194 | 33.24 N | 90.12 W |
| Sidorovo | 76 | 58.48 N | 40.58 E |
| Sidory | 80 | 50.08 N | 43.19 E |
| Sidr, Ra's as- › | 142 | 29.36 N | 32.40 E |
| Sidr, Wādī V | 142 | 29.40 N | 32.41 E |
| Sidra, Gulf of → Surt, Khalīj c | 146 | 31.30 N | 18.00 E |
| Sidrolândia | 255 | 20.55 S | 54.58 W |
| Sidu, Zhg. | 100 | 23.48 N | 117.18 E |
| Sidu, Zhg. | 100 | 24.12 N | 115.15 E |
| Siduan | 106 | 30.59 N | 121.48 E |
| Siebengebirge ⩘[2] | 56 | 50.40 N | 7.14 E |
| Siebenlehn | 54 | 51.01 N | 13.18 E |
| Sieber | 52 | 51.42 N | 10.25 E |
| Siebnen | 58 | 47.11 N | 8.54 E |
| Siedenbollentin | 54 | 53.44 N | 13.23 E |
| Siedenburg | 52 | 52.41 N | 8.56 E |
| Siedlce | 30 | 52.11 N | 22.16 E |
| Siedlce □[4] | 30 | 52.15 N | 22.00 E |
| Sieg ≃ | 56 | 50.45 N | 7.05 E |
| Siegburg | 56 | 50.47 N | 7.12 E |
| Siegen | 56 | 50.52 N | 8.02 E |
| Siegenburg | 60 | 48.45 N | 11.51 E |
| Siegendorf im Burgenland | 61 | 47.47 N | 16.33 E |
| Siegenfeld | 264b | 48.02 N | 16.10 E |
| Sieghartskirchen | 61 | 48.15 N | 16.01 E |
| Siegsdorf | 64 | 47.46 N | 12.39 E |
| Sielbeck | 54 | 54.11 N | 10.37 E |
| Sielenbach | 60 | 48.24 N | 11.10 E |
| Sielow | 54 | 51.50 N | 14.22 E |

**FRANÇAIS**

| Nom | Page | Lat.°′ | Long.°′ W = Ouest |
|---|---|---|---|
| Siemens, Cape › | 164 | 1.21 S | 149.34 E |
| Siemensstadt ⊸[8] | 264a | 52.32 N | 13.17 E |
| Siemianowice Śląskie | 30 | 50.19 N | 19.01 E |
| Siemiatycze | 30 | 52.26 N | 22.53 E |
| Siĕmpang | 110 | 14.07 N | 106.23 E |
| Siĕmréab | 110 | 13.22 N | 103.51 E |
| Siems-Dänischburg ⊸[8] | 54 | 53.55 N | 10.44 E |
| Siena | 66 | 43.19 N | 11.21 E |
| Siena □[4] | 66 | 43.13 N | 11.24 E |
| Sieniawa | 30 | 50.11 N | 22.36 E |
| Sienna → Siena | 66 | 43.19 N | 11.21 E |
| Sienyang → Xianyang | 102 | 34.22 N | 108.42 E |
| Sieradz | 30 | 51.36 N | 18.45 E |
| Sieradz □[4] | 30 | 51.40 N | 18.45 E |
| Sieraków | 30 | 52.39 N | 16.04 E |
| Sierck-les-Bains | 56 | 49.26 N | 6.21 E |
| Sierksdorf | 54 | 54.04 N | 10.46 E |
| Sierning | 61 | 48.03 N | 14.19 E |
| Sierpc | 30 | 52.52 N | 19.41 E |
| Si'erpu | 104 | 40.47 N | 120.41 E |
| Sierra □[6] | 226 | 39.30 N | 120.30 W |
| Sierra Blanca | 200 | 31.11 N | 105.21 W |
| Sierra Blanca Peak ∧ | 200 | 33.23 N | 105.48 W |
| Sierra-Bullones | 116 | 9.51 N | 124.20 E |
| Sierra Chica | 252 | 36.50 S | 60.13 W |
| Sierra City | 226 | 39.33 N | 120.37 W |
| Sierra Colorada | 254 | 40.35 S | 67.48 W |
| Sierra de Agua | 232 | 17.32 N | 88.54 W |
| Sierra Gorda | 252 | 22.54 S | 69.19 W |
| Sierra Leona → Sierra Leone □[1] | 150 | 8.30 N | 11.30 W |
| Sierra Leone □[1], Afr. | 134 | 8.30 N | 11.30 W |
| Sierra Leone □[1], Afr. | 150 | 8.30 N | 11.30 W |
| Sierra Leone Basin ✣[1] | 10 | 5.00 N | 17.00 W |
| Sierra Leone Rise ✣[3] | 10 | 5.30 N | 21.00 W |
| Sierra Madre | 228 | 34.09 N | 118.03 W |
| Sierra Mojada | 196 | 27.17 N | 103.42 W |
| Sierra Nevada, Parque Nacional ♦ | 246 | 8.36 N | 70.50 W |
| Sierra Peak ∧ | 280 | 33.51 N | 117.39 W |
| Sierra San Pedro Mártir, Parque Nacional ♦ | 204 | 31.00 N | 115.30 W |
| Sierras Bayas | 252 | 36.57 S | 60.09 W |
| Sierraville | 226 | 39.35 N | 120.21 W |
| Sierra Vista | 200 | 31.33 N | 110.18 W |
| Sierre | 58 | 46.18 N | 7.32 E |
| Siersleben | 54 | 51.36 N | 11.32 E |
| Siesta Key | 220 | 27.19 N | 82.34 W |
| Siesta Key I | 220 | 27.16 N | 82.33 W |
| Siete Puntas ≃ | 252 | 23.34 S | 57.20 W |
| Siethen | 264a | 52.17 N | 13.13 E |
| Siethener See ⊜ | 264a | 52.17 N | 13.12 E |
| Sietow | 54 | 53.26 N | 12.35 E |
| Sieve ≃ | 66 | 43.46 N | 11.26 E |
| Sievering ⊸[8] | 264b | 48.15 N | 16.20 E |
| Siezenheim | 64 | 47.48 N | 12.59 E |
| Sifahandra | 114 | 1.30 N | 97.21 E |
| Sifangtai, Zhg. | 89 | 46.55 N | 127.00 E |
| Sifangtai, Zhg. | 104 | 41.33 N | 121.19 E |
| Sifangtai, Zhg. | 104 | 41.02 N | 122.46 E |
| Sifangtai, Zhg. | 104 | 41.35 N | 122.57 E |
| Sifen | 100 | 27.32 N | 113.30 E |
| Sifeni | 144 | 12.16 N | 40.21 E |
| Sifentoudun | 106 | 32.18 N | 121.21 E |
| Siffu ≃ | 116 | 17.12 N | 121.48 E |
| Sifié | 150 | 7.59 N | 6.55 W |
| Sífnos I | 38 | 36.59 N | 24.40 E |
| Sifón Villanueva | 196 | 27.17 N | 100.17 W |
| Sifton | 184 | 51.21 N | 100.07 W |
| Sig, Alg. | 34 | 35.32 N | 0.11 W |
| Sig, Ross. | 24 | 65.35 N | 34.13 E |
| Şi Galangang | 114 | 1.15 N | 99.20 E |
| Šigali | 80 | 55.33 N | 48.02 E |
| Sigean | 32 | 43.02 N | 2.59 E |
| Sigel | 214 | 41.17 N | 79.07 W |
| Sigep | 110 | 1.02 S | 98.49 E |
| Siggebohyttan | 40 | 59.37 N | 15.01 E |
| Siggelkow | 54 | 53.23 N | 11.56 E |
| Sighetu Marmației | 38 | 47.56 N | 23.54 E |
| Sighișoara | 38 | 46.13 N | 24.48 E |
| Sighty Crag ∧ | 44 | 55.07 N | 2.37 W |
| Sigillo | 66 | 43.20 N | 12.44 E |
| Sigiriya | 122 | 7.57 N | 80.45 E |
| Siglan | 74 | 59.02 N | 152.25 E |
| Siglerville | 208 | 40.44 N | 77.31 W |
| Sigli | 114 | 5.23 N | 95.57 E |
| Sigli, Cap › | 34 | 36.54 N | 4.46 E |
| Sigloy | 50 | 47.50 N | 2.14 E |
| Siglufjörður | 24a | 66.10 N | 18.56 W |
| Sigmaringen | 58 | 48.05 N | 9.13 E |
| Sigmaringendorf | 58 | 48.04 N | 9.15 E |
| Signa | 66 | 43.47 N | 11.05 E |
| Signachi | 84 | 41.37 N | 45.54 E |
| Signalberg ∧ | 60 | 49.28 N | 12.32 E |
| Signal Hill, Ca., U.S. | 280 | 33.47 N | 118.09 W |
| Signal Hill, Il., U.S. | 219 | 38.34 N | 90.05 W |
| Signal Hill National Historic Park ♦ | 186 | 47.35 N | 52.40 W |
| Signal Mountain | 194 | 35.07 N | 85.20 W |
| Signal Mountain ∧ | 188 | 44.12 N | 72.20 W |
| Signal Peak ∧ | 200 | 37.19 N | 113.29 W |
| Signau | 58 | 46.55 N | 7.43 E |
| Signes | 62 | 43.18 N | 5.52 E |
| Signy ᵾ[3] | 9 | 60.43 S | 45.36 W |
| Signy-l'Abbaye | 50 | 49.42 N | 4.25 E |
| Signy-Le-Petit | 50 | 49.54 N | 4.17 E |
| Šigony | 80 | 53.23 N | 48.42 E |
| Sigourney | 190 | 41.20 N | 92.12 W |
| Sigre ≃ | 236 | 15.49 N | 84.38 W |
| Sigriswil | 58 | 46.43 N | 7.42 E |
| Sígsig | 246 | 3.01 S | 78.45 W |
| Sigtuna | 40 | 59.37 N | 17.43 E |
| Siguanea, Ensenada de la c | 240p | 21.38 N | 83.05 W |
| Siguatepeque | 236 | 14.32 N | 87.49 W |
| Siguel ≃ | 116 | 5.58 N | 125.06 E |
| Sigüenza | 34 | 41.04 N | 2.38 W |
| Sigües | 34 | 42.38 N | 1.00 W |
| Siguiri | 150 | 11.25 N | 9.10 W |
| Sigulda | 76 | 57.09 N | 24.51 E |
| Sigurd | 200 | 38.50 N | 111.58 W |
| Siguri Falls ʟ | 154 | 8.31 S | 37.23 E |
| Sihabuhabu, Dolok ∧ | 114 | 2.10 N | 99.21 E |
| Sihai | 105 | 40.33 N | 116.24 E |
| Sihala → Sri Lanka □[1] | 122 | 7.00 N | 81.00 E |
| Sihanoukville → Kâmpóng Saôm | 110 | 10.38 N | 103.30 E |
| Sihecun | 105 | 39.56 N | 117.07 E |
| Sihepeng | 114 | 1.06 N | 99.27 E |
| Sihl ≃ | 58 | 47.23 N | 8.32 E |
| Sihlepu | 158 | 27.42 S | 32.06 E |
| Sihlsee ⊜ | 58 | 47.07 N | 8.47 E |
| Sihong | 100 | 33.28 N | 118.11 E |
| Sihor | 120 | 21.42 N | 71.58 E |
| Sihorā | 124 | 23.29 N | 80.07 E |
| Sihu | 98 | 34.38 N | 117.59 E |
| Sihuas | 248 | 8.34 S | 77.37 W |
| Sihuas ≃ | 248 | 16.37 S | 72.19 W |
| Sihui | 102 | 23.19 N | 112.40 E |
| Sihŭng ⊸[8] | 271b | 37.28 N | 126.54 E |
| Siikajoki ≃ | 26 | 64.50 N | 24.44 E |
| Siilinjärvi | 26 | 63.05 N | 27.40 E |
| Si'Īr | 132 | 31.35 N | 35.09 E |
| Siirt | 130 | 37.56 N | 41.57 E |
| Siirt □[4] | 128 | 38.00 N | 42.00 E |
| Sija | 24 | 63.38 N | 41.38 E |
| Sijā ≃ | 124 | 29.08 N | 81.35 E |
| Sijbekarspel | 52 | 52.43 N | 4.59 E |
| Sijiaba | 106 | 32.02 N | 121.18 E |
| Sijianfang | 104 | 42.29 N | 122.17 E |
| Sijiao Shan I | 100 | 30.41 N | 122.28 E |
| Sijiazi | 98 | 41.47 N | 120.06 E |
| Sijing | 106 | 31.07 N | 121.16 E |

**PORTUGUÊS**

| Nome | Página | Lat.°′ | Long.°′ W = Oeste |
|---|---|---|---|
| Sijunjung | 112 | 0.42 S | 100.58 E |
| Sijupu | 107 | 30.02 N | 106.18 E |
| Sik | 114 | 5.49 N | 100.44 E |
| Sika | 115b | 8.45 S | 122.12 E |
| Sikalongo | 154 | 16.46 S | 27.07 E |
| Sikandarābād | 124 | 28.27 N | 77.42 E |
| Sikandarpur, India | 272a | 28.42 N | 77.21 E |
| Sikandarpur, India | 272b | 22.57 N | 88.12 E |
| Sikandra | 124 | 24.57 N | 86.02 E |
| Sikandra Rao | 124 | 27.42 N | 78.24 E |
| Sikanni Chief ≃ | 176 | 58.20 N | 121.50 W |
| Sikao | 110 | 7.34 N | 99.21 E |
| Sīkar | 120 | 27.37 N | 75.09 E |
| Sikarpur | 272b | 22.36 N | 88.32 E |
| Sikasso | 150 | 11.19 N | 5.40 W |
| Sikasso □[4] | 150 | 10.55 N | 7.00 W |
| Sikelenge | 152 | 14.50 S | 24.14 E |
| Sikeli | 112 | 5.16 S | 121.48 E |
| Sikensi | 150 | 5.40 N | 4.34 W |
| Sikeshu | 86 | 44.25 N | 84.14 E |
| Sikeston | 194 | 36.52 N | 89.35 W |
| Sikfors | 40 | 59.48 N | 14.35 E |
| Si Khiu | 110 | 14.53 N | 101.44 E |
| Sikiá | 38 | 40.02 N | 23.56 E |
| Sikiang → Xi ≃ | 102 | 22.25 N | 113.23 E |
| Sikijang | 114 | 4.22 N | 98.02 E |
| Siking → Xi'an | 102 | 34.15 N | 108.52 E |
| Síkinos | 38 | 36.39 N | 25.06 E |
| Síkinos I | 38 | 36.39 N | 25.06 E |
| Sikión ⊥ | 38 | 37.59 N | 22.44 E |
| Sikkim □[3] | 124 | 27.35 N | 88.35 E |
| Siklós ⊥ | 30 | 45.55 N | 18.25 E |
| Sikonge | 154 | 5.38 S | 32.46 E |
| Sikosi | 156 | 17.59 S | 23.19 E |
| Šikotan, ostrov (Shikotan-tō) I | 92a | 43.47 N | 146.45 E |
| Sikrod | 272a | 28.43 N | 77.11 E |
| Sikt'ach | 74 | 69.55 N | 125.02 E |
| Sikuati | 112 | 6.53 N | 116.40 E |
| Sikutu | 112 | 0.53 N | 120.37 E |
| Sil' | 83 | 48.43 N | 38.02 E |
| Sil ≃ | 34 | 42.27 N | 7.43 W |
| Šila | 86 | 56.33 N | 93.02 E |
| Silacayoapan | 234 | 17.30 N | 98.09 W |
| Sila Grande ⩘ | 68 | 39.22 N | 16.30 E |
| Sila Greca ⩘ | 68 | 39.30 N | 16.30 E |
| Silai ≃ | 126 | 22.41 N | 87.46 E |
| Silalahi | 114 | 2.48 N | 98.32 E |
| Šilalė | 76 | 55.28 N | 22.12 E |
| Silam, Gunong ∧ | 116 | 4.58 N | 118.10 E |
| Silāmpur ⊸[8] | 272a | 28.40 N | 77.16 E |
| Silandro (Schlanders) | 64 | 46.38 N | 10.46 E |
| Silang | 116 | 14.14 N | 120.58 E |
| Silangcheng | 98 | 42.19 N | 115.43 E |
| Silanus | 71 | 40.17 N | 8.53 E |
| Silao | 234 | 20.56 N | 101.26 W |
| Sila Piccola ⩘ | 68 | 39.05 N | 16.35 E |
| Silas | 194 | 31.45 N | 88.19 W |
| Silat | 112 | 0.21 N | 111.47 E |
| Sīlat az-Ẓahr | 132 | 32.19 N | 35.11 E |
| Silau ≃ | 114 | 2.58 N | 99.48 E |
| Silaut | 112 | 2.22 S | 101.08 E |
| Silaw Aihagam, Gunung ∧ | 114 | 5.25 N | 95.40 E |
| Silay | 116 | 10.48 N | 122.58 E |
| Silay, Mount ∧ | 116 | 10.47 N | 123.14 E |
| Silba | 36 | 44.23 N | 14.42 E |
| Silbertal | 58 | 47.05 N | 9.59 E |
| Silchar | 120 | 24.49 N | 92.48 E |
| Şilda, India | 126 | 22.37 N | 86.49 E |
| Šil'da, Ross. | 86 | 51.46 N | 59.45 E |
| Şile | 130 | 41.11 N | 29.36 E |
| Sile ≃ | 64 | 45.33 N | 12.27 E |
| Sileby | 42 | 52.43 N | 1.06 W |
| Šilega | 24 | 64.03 N | 44.01 E |
| Silenrieux | 50 | 50.14 N | 4.24 E |
| Silent Lake ⊜ | 212 | 44.55 N | 78.04 W |
| Silent Lake Provincial Park ♦ | 212 | 44.54 N | 78.05 W |
| Siler City | 192 | 35.43 N | 79.27 W |
| Sileru ≃ | 122 | 17.47 N | 81.24 E |
| Silesia □[9] | 30 | 51.00 N | 16.45 E |
| Silet | 148 | 22.44 N | 4.37 E |
| Sileti ≃ | 86 | 53.06 N | 73.22 E |
| Siletiteniz, ozero ⊜ | 86 | 53.15 N | 73.15 E |
| Siletz | 202 | 44.43 N | 123.55 W |
| Siletz ≃ | 202 | 44.54 N | 124.00 W |
| Silex | 219 | 39.07 N | 91.03 W |
| Silgaḍhī | 124 | 29.16 N | 80.59 E |
| Silghāt | 120 | 26.37 N | 92.56 E |
| Silhouette I | 138 | 4.29 S | 55.14 E |
| Siliana | 148 | 36.05 N | 9.22 E |
| Siliana, Oued ≃ | 36 | 36.33 N | 9.25 E |
| Silifke | 130 | 36.22 N | 33.56 E |
| Şilijiang | 105 | 39.43 N | 117.28 E |
| Šilikti | 86 | 47.10 N | 84.32 E |
| Silingan, Mount ∧ | 116 | 7.46 N | 122.30 E |
| Siling Co ⊜ | 120 | 31.50 N | 89.00 E |
| Siliqua | 71 | 39.18 N | 8.48 E |
| Silistra | 38 | 44.07 N | 27.16 E |
| Şilivri | 130 | 41.04 N | 28.15 E |
| Šiljak ∧ | 38 | 43.45 N | 21.50 E |
| Siljan ⊜ | 26 | 60.50 N | 14.45 E |
| Siljansnäs | 26 | 60.45 N | 14.42 E |
| Šilka | 88 | 51.51 N | 116.02 E |
| Šilka ≃ | 74 | 53.22 N | 121.32 E |
| Silkāripāra | 126 | 24.14 N | 87.28 E |
| Silkeborg | 41 | 56.10 N | 9.34 E |
| Silkworth | 210 | 41.16 N | 76.05 W |
| Sill ≃ | 64 | 47.16 N | 11.25 E |
| Sillamäe | 76 | 59.24 N | 27.45 E |
| Sillānwāli | 123 | 31.50 N | 72.33 E |
| Sillaro ≃ | 64 | 44.34 N | 11.51 E |
| Sille | 130 | 37.56 N | 32.26 E |
| Sillem Island I | 176 | 70.55 N | 71.30 W |
| Sillen ⊜ | 40 | 58.59 N | 17.22 E |
| Sillenstede | 52 | 53.34 N | 7.59 E |
| Sillery, P.Q., Can. | 206 | 46.46 N | 71.15 W |
| Sillery, Fr. | 50 | 49.12 N | 4.08 E |
| Silli | 150 | 11.36 N | 2.30 W |
| Sillian | 64 | 46.45 N | 12.25 E |
| Sillil | 144 | 10.59 N | 43.26 E |
| Sillon de Talbert ›[1] | 32 | 48.53 N | 3.05 W |
| Silloth | 44 | 54.52 N | 3.23 W |
| Sillustani ⊥ | 248 | 15.45 S | 70.05 W |
| Silly-le-Long | 261 | 49.06 N | 2.48 E |
| Šil'naja Balka | 80 | 50.34 N | 49.01 E |
| Silnice | 60 | 48.54 N | 13.44 E |
| Siloam Springs | 194 | 36.11 N | 94.32 W |
| Siloam Springs State Park ♦ | 219 | 39.53 N | 90.54 W |
| Şilogui | 110 | 1.14 S | 99.00 E |
| Šiloviči | 76 | 55.24 N | 32.33 E |
| Šilovka | 80 | 54.03 N | 48.40 E |
| Šilovo, Ross. | 76 | 55.00 N | 33.46 E |
| Šilovo, Ross. | 80 | 54.19 N | 40.53 E |
| Silowana Plains ≌ | 152 | 17.00 S | 23.15 E |
| Silphuh | 126 | 23.44 N | 86.22 E |
| Silsbee | 194 | 30.20 N | 94.10 W |
| Silsby Lake ⊜ | 184 | 55.29 N | 95.46 W |
| Silschede | 263 | 51.21 N | 7.19 E |
| Silsden | 44 | 53.55 N | 1.55 W |
| Sils im Engadin | 58 | 46.22 N | 9.46 E |
| Silton | 184 | 50.48 N | 104.55 W |
| Siluas | 112 | 1.17 N | 109.51 E |
| Şiluko | 150 | 6.31 N | 5.09 E |
| Šilute | 76 | 55.21 N | 21.29 E |
| Silvacane, Abbaye de ᵾ[1] | 62 | 43.44 N | 5.20 E |
| Silvan (Miyafarkin) | 130 | 38.08 N | 41.01 E |
| Silvana | 224 | 48.12 N | 122.15 W |
| Silvāneh | 128 | 37.25 N | 44.51 E |
| Silvânia | 255 | 16.42 S | 48.38 W |
| Silvano d'Orba | 62 | 44.41 N | 8.40 E |
| Silvan Reservoir ⊜[1] | 169 | 37.50 S | 145.25 E |
| Silvaplana | 58 | 46.26 N | 9.47 E |
| Silvassa | 122 | 20.17 N | 73.00 E |
| Silveiras | 256 | 22.40 S | 44.52 W |

| | | | |
|---|---|---|---|
| Silver | 196 | 32.04 N | 100.40 W |
| Silverado | 228 | 33.45 N | 117.35 W |
| Silver Bank ✣[2] | 238 | 20.30 N | 69.45 W |
| Silver Bank Passage ⋓ | 238 | 20.45 N | 70.15 W |
| Silver Bay | 190 | 47.17 N | 91.15 W |
| Silver Bell | 200 | 32.23 N | 111.29 W |
| Silver City, N.M., U.S. | 200 | 32.46 N | 108.16 W |
| Silver City, N.C., U.S. | 192 | 35.00 N | 79.12 W |
| Silver Creek, Ms., U.S. | 194 | 31.36 N | 89.59 W |
| Silver Creek, Ne., U.S. | 198 | 41.18 N | 97.39 W |
| Silver Creek, N.Y., U.S. | 214 | 42.32 N | 79.10 W |
| Silver Creek ≃, Az., U.S. | 200 | 34.44 N | 110.02 W |
| Silver Creek ≃, Ca., U.S. | 226 | 38.47 N | 120.35 W |
| Silver Creek ≃, Ca., U.S. | 226 | 36.36 N | 120.41 W |
| Silver Creek ≃, Il., U.S. | 219 | 38.20 N | 89.52 W |
| Silver Creek ≃, Il., U.S. | 278 | 41.54 N | 87.50 W |
| Silver Creek ≃, In., U.S. | 218 | 39.36 N | 84.59 W |
| Silver Creek ≃, In., U.S. | 218 | 38.17 N | 85.47 W |
| Silver Creek ≃, Ky., U.S. | 192 | 37.48 N | 84.30 W |
| Silver Creek ≃, Mi., U.S. | 281 | 42.06 N | 83.17 E |
| Silver Creek ≃, Or., U.S. | 202 | 43.16 N | 119.13 W |
| Silver Creek ≃, Wa., U.S. | 224 | 46.32 N | 121.55 W |
| Silver Creek, Muddy Fork ≃ | 218 | 38.25 N | 86.44 W |
| Silver Creek, South Fork ≃ | 226 | 38.49 N | 120.27 W |
| Silverdale, B.C., Can. | 224 | 49.09 N | 122.24 W |
| Silverdale, N.Z. | 172 | 36.37 S | 174.40 E |
| Silverdale, Eng., U.K. | 44 | 54.10 N | 2.49 W |
| Silverdale, Pa., U.S. | 208 | 40.21 N | 75.16 W |
| Silverdale, Wa., U.S. | 224 | 47.38 N | 122.41 W |
| Silverdalen | 26 | 57.32 N | 15.44 E |
| Silverdome ♦ | 281 | 42.39 N | 83.15 W |
| Silver End | 42 | 51.51 N | 0.37 E |
| Silver Falls State Park ♦ | 202 | 44.48 N | 122.50 W |
| Silverfields | 273d | 26.07 S | 27.49 E |
| Silver Fork ≃ | 219 | 39.06 N | 92.21 W |
| Silver Grove | 218 | 39.02 N | 84.23 W |
| Silver Hill | 284c | 38.50 N | 76.56 W |
| Silverhope Creek ≃ | 224 | 49.18 N | 121.27 W |
| Silver Lake, Ca., U.S. | 226 | 38.38 N | 120.07 W |
| Silver Lake, In., U.S. | 216 | 41.04 N | 85.53 W |
| Silver Lake, Ks., U.S. | 198 | 39.06 N | 95.51 W |
| Silver Lake, Ma., U.S. | 207 | 42.34 N | 71.11 W |
| Silver Lake, Mn., U.S. | 190 | 44.54 N | 94.11 W |
| Silver Lake, Oh., U.S. | 214 | 41.09 N | 81.27 W |
| Silver Lake, Or., U.S. | 202 | 43.07 N | 121.02 W |
| Silverlake, Wa., U.S. | 224 | 46.17 N | 122.48 W |
| Silver Lake, Wi., U.S. | 216 | 42.32 N | 88.09 W |
| Silver Lake ⊜, Ca., U.S. | 226 | 38.39 N | 120.07 W |
| Silver Lake ⊜, De., U.S. | 208 | 39.11 N | 75.32 W |
| Silver Lake ⊜, Ma., U.S. | 283 | 42.01 N | 70.48 W |
| Silver Lake ⊜, N.Y., U.S. | 210 | 42.42 N | 78.02 W |
| Silver Lake ⊜, N.Y., U.S. | 276 | 41.03 N | 73.45 W |
| Silver Lake ⊜, Or., U.S. | 202 | 43.06 N | 120.53 W |
| Silver Lake ⊜, Or., U.S. | 202 | 43.22 N | 119.24 W |
| Silver Lake ⊜, Wa., U.S. | 224 | 46.17 N | 122.47 W |
| Silver Lake ⊜, Wa., U.S. | 224 | 48.58 N | 122.04 W |
| Silver Lake Park ♦ | 276 | 41.03 N | 73.45 W |
| Silver Lake Reservoir ⊜[1], Ca., U.S. | 280 | 34.06 N | 118.16 W |
| Silver Lake Reservoir ⊜[1], N.Y., U.S. | 276 | 40.37 N | 74.06 W |
| Silvermine ≃ | 276 | 41.08 N | 73.26 W |
| Silver Mine Bay c | 271d | 22.16 N | 114.00 E |
| Silvermine Brook ≃ | 276 | 41.08 N | 73.27 W |
| Silvermine Mountains ⩘ | 48 | 52.45 N | 8.15 W |
| Silvermines | 48 | 52.47 N | 8.13 W |
| Silver Mountain ∧ | 280 | 34.12 N | 117.52 W |
| Silver Peak ∧ | 228 | 33.28 N | 118.35 W |
| Silver Peak Range ⩘ | 204 | 37.35 N | 117.45 W |
| Silver Spring, Md., U.S. | 208 | 38.59 N | 77.01 W |
| Silver Spring, Pa., U.S. | 208 | 40.04 N | 76.26 W |
| Silver Springs, Nv., U.S. | 226 | 39.24 N | 119.13 W |
| Silver Springs, N.Y., U.S. | 210 | 42.39 N | 78.05 W |
| Silver Springs State Park ♦ | 216 | 41.38 N | 88.32 W |
| Silver Star Mountain ∧ | 224 | 48.33 N | 120.35 W |
| Silver Star Provincial Park ♦ | 182 | 50.22 N | 119.05 W |
| Silverstone | 42 | 52.05 N | 1.02 W |
| Silver Streams | 158 | 28.20 S | 23.33 E |
| Silverthrone Mountain ∧ | 182 | 51.31 N | 126.06 W |
| Silvertip Mountain ∧ | 202 | 47.47 N | 113.15 W |
| Silverton, Austl. | 166 | 31.53 S | 141.13 E |
| Silverton, B.C., Can. | 182 | 49.57 N | 117.21 W |
| Silverton, Eng., U.K. | 42 | 50.48 N | 3.28 W |
| Silverton, Co., U.S. | 200 | 37.48 N | 107.39 W |
| Silverton, N.J., U.S. | 208 | 40.00 N | 74.08 W |
| Silverton, Oh., U.S. | 218 | 39.12 N | 84.24 W |
| Silverton, Or., U.S. | 224 | 45.00 N | 122.46 W |
| Silverton, Tx., U.S. | 196 | 34.28 N | 101.19 W |
| Silverwood Lake ⊜[1] | 228 | 34.18 N | 117.19 W |
| Silves | 34 | 37.11 N | 8.26 W |
| Silvi | 66 | 42.34 N | 14.05 E |
| Silvia | 246 | 2.37 N | 76.21 W |
| Silvianópolis | 256 | 22.02 S | 45.50 W |
| Silvícola | 164 | 8.39 S | 126.59 E |
| Silvies ≃ | 202 | 43.22 N | 118.48 W |
| Silview | 285 | 39.42 N | 75.37 W |
| Silvolde | 52 | 51.55 N | 6.23 E |
| Silvretta Gruppe ⩘ | 58 | 46.50 N | 10.10 E |
| Sim | 86 | 54.59 N | 57.41 E |
| Sim, Cap › | 148 | 31.23 N | 9.51 W |
| Sima, Comores | 157a | 12.11 S | 44.17 E |
| Sima, Ross. | 80 | 56.41 N | 39.33 E |
| Simaltala | 124 | 24.43 N | 86.33 E |
| Simanavičy | 76 | 53.05 N | 28.38 E |
| Simanggang | 112 | 1.15 N | 111.26 E |
| Simangumban | 114 | 1.42 N | 99.10 E |
| Šimaničy | 78 | 51.53 N | 28.04 E |
| Šimanovsk | 89 | 52.00 N | 127.42 E |
| Simao | 102 | 22.50 N | 101.00 E |
| Simão Dias | 250 | 10.44 S | 37.49 W |
| Simão Pereira | 256 | 21.58 S | 43.19 W |
| Simara Island I | 116 | 12.48 N | 122.03 E |
| Simard, Lac ⊜ | 190 | 47.37 N | 78.41 W |
| Simaria Kalān | 124 | 24.04 N | 84.56 E |
| Simatang, Pulau I | 112 | 1.04 N | 120.23 E |
| Simav | 130 | 39.05 N | 28.59 E |
| Simav ≃ | 130 | 40.23 N | 28.31 E |
| Simav Gölü ⊜ | 130 | 39.09 N | 28.55 E |
| Simaxis | 71 | 39.56 N | 8.41 E |
| Simba, Kenya | 154 | 2.10 S | 37.36 E |
| Simba, Tan. | 154 | 1.44 S | 34.13 E |

| | | | |
|---|---|---|---|
| Simba, Zaïre | 152 | 0.36 N | 22.55 E |
| Simbach | 60 | 48.34 N | 12.45 E |
| Simbach am Inn | 60 | 48.16 N | 13.01 E |
| Simbario | 68 | 38.37 N | 16.20 E |
| Simberi Island I | 164 | 2.40 S | 152.00 E |
| Simbirsk → Uljanovsk | 80 | 54.20 N | 48.24 E |
| Simbo, Tan. | 154 | 4.53 S | 29.44 E |
| Simbo, Tan. | 154 | 4.40 S | 33.27 E |
| Simbo Island I | 175e | 8.17 S | 156.33 E |
| Simbruini, Monti ⩘ | 66 | 41.55 N | 13.15 E |
| Simbu □[5] | 164 | 6.05 S | 145.00 E |
| Simcoe | 212 | 42.50 N | 80.18 W |
| Simcoe □[6] | 212 | 44.25 N | 79.50 W |
| Simcoe, Lake ⊜ | 212 | 44.20 N | 79.20 W |
| Simcoe Creek ≃ | 224 | 46.22 N | 120.36 W |
| Simcoe Island I | 212 | 44.10 N | 76.31 W |
| Simcoe Point › | 275b | 43.49 N | 79.01 W |
| Simdega | 124 | 22.37 N | 84.31 E |
| Simen | 104 | 40.44 N | 123.49 E |
| Simeng | 107 | 29.56 N | 103.44 E |
| Simen Mountains National Park ♦ | 144 | 13.08 N | 38.15 E |
| Simenti | 150 | 13.00 N | 13.25 W |
| Simeonovgrad | 38 | 42.02 N | 25.50 E |
| Simeri ≃ | 68 | 38.52 N | 16.43 E |
| Simeria | 38 | 45.51 N | 23.01 E |
| Simeto ≃ | 70 | 37.24 N | 15.06 E |
| Simeulue, Pulau I | 114 | 2.33 N | 96.05 E |
| Simeyiz | 78 | 44.26 N | 34.01 E |
| Simeykyne | 83 | 48.19 N | 39.32 E |
| Simferopol' | 78 | 44.57 N | 34.06 E |
| Sími | 38 | 36.36 N | 27.50 E |
| Sími I | 38 | 36.35 N | 27.52 E |
| Simi, Arroyo ≃ | 228 | 34.16 N | 118.39 W |
| Simiane | 62 | 43.25 N | 5.26 E |
| Simianshan | 107 | 28.49 N | 105.09 E |
| Simikoṭ | 124 | 29.58 N | 81.50 E |
| Similaun ∧ | 64 | 46.46 N | 10.53 E |
| Similkameen ≃ | 182 | 48.56 N | 119.26 W |
| Simingchang | 107 | 29.02 N | 105.45 E |
| Simiri | 150 | 14.08 N | 2.08 E |
| Simisa Island I | 116 | 5.57 N | 121.35 E |
| Simití | 246 | 7.58 N | 73.57 W |
| Simi Valley | 228 | 34.16 N | 118.47 W |
| Simiyu ≃ | 154 | 2.33 S | 33.25 E |
| Simizu → Shimizu | 94 | 35.01 N | 138.29 E |
| Simla, India | 272b | 22.54 N | 88.22 E |
| Simla, India | 272b | 22.47 N | 88.16 E |
| Simla, Co., U.S. | 198 | 39.08 N | 104.05 W |
| Simla ⊸[8] | 272b | 22.35 N | 88.22 E |
| Simlāpāl | 126 | 22.55 N | 87.05 E |
| Şimleu Silvaniei | 38 | 47.14 N | 22.48 E |
| Simlipālgarh | 126 | 21.51 N | 86.23 E |
| Simme ≃ | 58 | 46.41 N | 7.38 E |
| Simmelsdorf | 60 | 49.36 N | 11.21 E |
| Simmental V | 58 | 46.37 N | 7.25 E |
| Simmerath | 56 | 50.36 N | 6.18 E |
| Simmerberg | 58 | 47.35 N | 9.56 E |
| Simmering ⊸[8] | 264b | 48.11 N | 16.25 E |
| Simmern | 56 | 49.59 N | 7.31 E |
| Simmesport | 194 | 30.59 N | 91.48 W |
| Simmie | 184 | 49.57 N | 108.06 W |
| Simmons Island I | 282 | 38.06 N | 121.58 W |
| Simmons Point › | 282 | 38.03 N | 121.56 W |
| Simmonswood Moss ⊸[3] | 262 | 53.30 N | 2.50 W |
| Simms | 202 | 47.29 N | 111.55 W |
| Simnas | 76 | 54.24 N | 23.39 E |
| Simoca | 252 | 27.16 S | 65.21 W |
| Simões | 250 | 7.36 S | 40.49 W |
| Simojärvi ⊜ | 26 | 66.06 N | 27.03 E |
| Simojoki ≃ | 26 | 65.37 N | 25.03 E |
| Simojovel | 234 | 17.12 N | 92.38 W |
| Simon, Lac ⊜, P.Q., Can. | 206 | 46.10 N | 74.45 W |
| Simon, Lac ⊜, P.Q., Can. | 206 | 45.58 N | 75.05 W |
| Simón Bolívar, Aeropuerto Internacional ⊠ | 286c | 10.37 N | 66.59 W |
| Simoneti | 84 | 42.14 N | 42.52 E |
| Simonette ≃ | 182 | 55.07 N | 118.00 W |
| Simonhouse Lake ⊜ | 184 | 54.30 N | 101.10 W |
| Simonicha | 80 | 56.31 N | 53.50 E |
| Simonoseki → Shimonoseki | 96 | 33.57 N | 130.57 E |
| Simonsbath | 42 | 51.09 N | 3.45 W |
| Simonson Brook ≃ | 276 | 40.26 N | 74.37 W |
| Simonstone | 262 | 53.48 N | 2.20 W |
| Simonstorp | 40 | 58.47 N | 16.09 E |
| Simon's Town | 158 | 34.14 S | 18.26 E |
| Simonton Lake | 216 | 41.44 N | 85.59 W |
| Şimoom Sound | 182 | 50.45 N | 126.29 W |
| Šimorskoje | 80 | 55.19 N | 42.02 E |
| Simpang, Indon. | 112 | 1.16 S | 104.05 E |
| Simpang, Indon. | 112 | 1.03 S | 110.06 E |
| Simpang, Indon. | 112 | 0.09 N | 103.15 E |
| Simpangampat | 114 | 2.55 N | 99.43 E |
| Simpang Empat | 114 | 6.20 N | 100.11 E |
| Simpang-kanan ≃ | 114 | 2.21 N | 97.51 E |
| Simpang-kiri ≃ | 114 | 2.21 N | 97.51 E |
| Simpang Rengam | 114 | 1.50 N | 103.19 E |
| Simpangtiga | 114 | 2.23 N | 99.47 E |
| Simpangulim | 114 | 5.06 N | 97.32 E |
| Simpele | 26 | 61.26 N | 29.22 E |
| Simplício Mendes | 250 | 7.51 S | 41.54 W |
| Simplon Pass )( | 58 | 46.15 N | 8.02 E |
| Simplon Tunnel ⊸[5] | 58 | 46.15 N | 8.05 E |
| Simpnäs | 40 | 59.52 N | 19.04 E |
| Simp'o-ri | 98 | 38.36 N | 127.41 E |
| Simpson, La., U.S. | 194 | 31.14 N | 93.00 W |
| Simpson, Pa., U.S. | 210 | 41.35 N | 75.29 W |
| Simpson ≃ | 254 | 45.25 S | 72.32 W |
| Simpson, Isla I | 254 | 45.53 S | 73.48 W |
| Simpson Desert ⊸[2] | 162 | 25.00 S | 137.00 E |
| Simpson Desert National Park ♦ | 162 | 25.40 S | 138.15 E |
| Simpson Island I | 190 | 48.48 N | 87.40 W |
| Simpson Lake ⊜ | 180 | 68.10 N | 126.35 W |
| Simpson Peak ∧ | 180 | 59.44 N | 131.27 W |
| Simpson Peninsula ›[1] | 176 | 68.34 N | 88.45 W |
| Simpsons Gap National Park ♦ | 162 | 23.40 S | 133.45 E |
| Simpson Strait ⋓ | 176 | 68.27 N | 97.45 W |
| Simpsonville, Ky., U.S. | 218 | 38.13 N | 85.21 W |
| Simpsonville, Md., U.S. | 208 | 39.11 N | 76.52 W |
| Simpsonville, S.C., U.S. | 192 | 34.44 N | 82.15 W |
| Simrishamn | 26 | 55.33 N | 14.20 E |
| Sims | 216 | 40.30 N | 85.51 W |
| Şimsbury | 207 | 41.52 N | 72.48 W |
| Šimsk | 76 | 58.13 N | 30.43 E |
| Simssee ⊜ | 64 | 47.52 N | 12.14 E |
| Simunjan | 112 | 1.23 N | 110.45 E |
| Simurāli | 126 | 23.03 N | 88.30 E |
| Simušir, ostrov I | 74 | 46.58 N | 152.02 E |
| Sīnā' □[4] | 142 | 30.15 N | 32.40 E |
| Sīna ≃ | 122 | 17.22 N | 75.54 E |
| Sīnā', Shibh Jazīrat (Sinai Peninsula) ›[1] | 140 | 29.30 N | 34.00 E |
| Sinabang | 114 | 2.29 N | 96.23 E |
| Sinabelkirchen | 61 | 47.06 N | 15.50 E |
| Sinabung, Gunung ∧ | 114 | 3.10 N | 98.24 E |
| Sinadhago | 144 | 5.22 N | 46.20 E |
| Sinagra | 70 | 38.05 N | 14.51 E |
| Sinai, Mount ∧, Gren. | 241k | 12.04 N | 61.42 W |
| Sinai, Mount → Mūsā, Jabal ∧, Mişr | 140 | 28.32 N | 33.59 E |
| Sinaia | 38 | 45.21 N | 25.33 E |
| Sinai Peninsula → Sīnā', Shibh Jazīrat ›[1] | 140 | 29.30 N | 34.00 E |
| Sin'aja ≃, Europe | 76 | 57.10 N | 28.31 E |
| Sin'aja ≃, Ross. | 74 | 61.06 N | 126.50 E |

| | | | |
|---|---|---|---|
| Sinajana | 174p | 13.28 N | 144.45 E |
| Sinako, Mount ∧ | 116 | 7.30 N | 125.17 E |
| Sinaloa □[3] | 232 | 25.00 N | 107.30 W |
| Sinaloa ≃ | 232 | 25.18 N | 108.30 W |
| Sinalunga | 66 | 43.12 N | 11.44 E |
| Sinamaica | 246 | 11.05 N | 71.51 W |
| Sinamary ≃ | 250 | 5.27 N | 53.00 W |
| Sinan, Tür. | 130 | 37.52 N | 41.00 E |
| Sinan, Zhg. | 102 | 27.54 N | 108.18 E |
| Sinanju | 98 | 39.36 N | 125.36 E |
| Sinanpaşa | 130 | 38.45 N | 30.15 E |
| Sīnarū | 142 | 29.22 N | 30.45 E |
| Sinatle | 84 | 42.28 N | 43.04 E |
| Sin'avka | 83 | 47.17 N | 39.17 E |
| Sīnāwin | 146 | 31.02 N | 10.36 E |
| Sinbad Creek ≃ | 282 | 37.35 N | 121.53 W |
| Sinbaungwe | 110 | 19.43 N | 95.[illegible] E |
| Sinbo | 110 | 24.46 N | 97.[illegible]3 E |
| Sinbokchang | 98 | 41.01 N | 128.[illegible]4 E |
| Sincan, Tür. | 130 | 39.28 N | 37.[illegible]4 E |
| Sincan, Tür. | 130 | 39.59 N | 32.[illegible] E |
| Sincé | 246 | 9.15 N | 75.[illegible] W |
| Sincelejo | 246 | 9.18 N | 75.2[illegible] W |
| Sinch'ang, C.M.I.K. | 98 | 40.07 N | 128.2[illegible] E |
| Sinch'ang, C.M.I.K. | 98 | 40.19 N | 125.2[illegible] E |
| Sinch'ŏn | 98 | 38.22 N | 125.2[illegible] E |
| Sinch'ŏn-ni | 271b | 37.27 N | 126.4[illegible] E |
| Sinclair | 200 | 41.46 N | 107.0[illegible] W |
| Sinclair, Lake ⊜[1] | 192 | 33.11 N | 83.16 W |
| Sinclair, Point › | 162 | 32.06 S | 133.00 E |
| Sinclair Island I | 224 | 48.37 N | 122.40 W |
| Sinclair Mills | 182 | 54.02 N | 121.41 W |
| Sinclair's Bay c | 46 | 58.30 N | 3.07 W |
| Sinclairville | 214 | 42.15 N | 79.15 W |
| Sind □[4] | 120 | 25.30 N | 69.00 E |
| Sind ≃ | 124 | 26.26 N | 79.13 E |
| Sinda | 89 | 48.57 N | 136.18 E |
| Sindal | 26 | 57.28 N | 10.13 E |
| Sindangan | 116 | 8.14 N | 123.00 E |
| Sindangan ≃ | 116 | 8.13 N | 123.00 E |
| Sindangan Bay c | 116 | 8.11 N | 122.50 E |
| Sindangan Point › | 116 | 8.10 N | 122.40 E |
| Sindangbarang | 115a | 7.27 S | 107.08 E |
| Sindara | 152 | 1.02 S | 10.40 E |
| Sindari | 120 | 25.35 N | 71.55 E |
| Sindelfingen | 56 | 48.42 N | 9.00 E |
| Sindèr | 150 | 14.29 N | 1.22 E |
| Sindhnūr | 122 | 15.47 N | 76.46 E |
| Sindhulī Māḍhi | 124 | 27.16 N | 85.58 E |
| Sindi | 76 | 58.24 N | 24.40 E |
| Sindia | 71 | 40.18 N | 8.39 E |
| Sindingale | 110 | 18.17 N | 94.25 E |
| Sındıran | 130 | 39.17 N | 32.41 E |
| Sındırgı | 130 | 39.14 N | 28.10 E |
| Sindiyūn | 142 | 30.15 N | 31.12 E |
| Sin-do I | 98 | 39.48 N | 124.14 E |
| Sindŏk | 98 | 36.47 N | 126.10 E |
| Sindor | 24 | 62.50 N | 51.57 E |
| Sindou | 150 | 10.40 N | 5.10 W |
| Sindri | 126 | 23.45 N | 86.42 E |
| Sind Sāgar Doāb ⩘[1] | 123 | 31.30 N | 71.30 E |
| Sine V | 150 | 14.10 N | 16.28 W |
| Sinegorje | 24 | 59.42 N | 50.40 E |
| Sinegorsk | 89 | 47.10 N | 142.30 E |
| Şinegorskij | 78 | 48.00 N | 40.53 E |
| Šine-Ider | 88 | 48.56 N | 99.33 E |
| Sinekçi | 130 | 40.16 N | 27.24 E |
| Sinekli | 130 | 41.14 N | 28.12 E |
| Sinendé | 150 | 10.21 N | 2.23 E |
| Sinen'kije | 80 | 51.15 N | 45.46 E |
| Sinepuxent Bay c | 208 | 38.16 N | 75.09 W |
| Sines | 34 | 37.57 N | 8.52 W |
| Sines, Cabo de › | 34 | 37.57 N | 8.53 W |
| Sinewit, Mount ∧ | 164 | 4.40 S | 152.00 E |
| Sinez'orki | 76 | 53.02 N | 34.26 E |
| Sinfra | 150 | 6.37 N | 5.55 W |
| Singair | 126 | 23.49 N | 90.08 E |
| Singako | 146 | 9.50 N | 19.29 E |
| Singal | 123 | 36.06 N | 73.53 E |
| Singalamwe | 156 | 17.41 S | 23.23 E |
| Singālila ∧ | 124 | 27.13 N | 88.01 E |
| Singālila Range ⩘ | 124 | 27.25 N | 88.05 E |
| Singaparna | 115a | 7.21 S | 108.06 E |
| Singapore, Sing. | 114 | 1.17 N | 103.51 E |
| Singapore, Sing. | 271c | 1.17 N | 103.51 E |
| Singapore □[1], Asia | 108 | 1.22 N | 103.48 E |
| Singapore □[1], Asia | 114 | 1.22 N | 103.48 E |
| Singapore I | 271c | 1.23 N | 103.48 E |
| Singapore ≃ | 271c | 1.17 N | 103.51 E |
| Singapore, National University of ᵾ[2] | 271c | 1.18 N | 103.46 E |
| Singapore Station ⊸[5] | 271c | 1.17 N | 103.50 E |
| Singapore Strait ⋓ | 112 | 1.15 N | 104.00 E |
| Singapour → Singapore □[1] | 114 | 1.22 N | 103.48 E |
| Singapur → Singapore | 114 | 1.17 N | 103.51 E |
| Singapur → Singapore □[1] | 114 | 1.22 N | 103.48 E |
| Singaraja | 115b | 8.07 S | 115.06 E |
| Singarka ≃ | 265a | 59.53 N | 29.54 E |
| Singāti | 126 | 22.44 N | 89.43 E |
| Singatoka | 175g | 18.08 S | 177.30 E |
| Sing Buri | 110 | 14.53 N | 100.25 E |
| Singe | 272b | 22.57 N | 88.26 E |
| Singen (Hohentwiel) | 58 | 47.46 N | 8.50 E |
| Singer | 194 | 30.39 N | 93.24 W |
| Singhi | 126 | 23.37 N | 87.48 E |
| Singida | 154 | 4.49 S | 34.45 E |
| Singida □[4] | 154 | 5.30 S | 34.30 E |
| Singing, India | 102 | 28.59 N | 94.50 E |
| Singing, India | 120 | 28.53 N | 94.47 E |
| Singing Tower ♦ | 220 | 27.57 N | 81.34 W |
| Singkaling Hkāmti | 110 | 26.00 N | 95.42 E |
| Singkang | 112 | 4.08 S | 120.01 E |
| Singkawang | 112 | 0.54 N | 109.00 E |
| Singkep, Pulau I | 112 | 0.30 S | 104.25 E |
| Singkil | 114 | 2.17 N | 97.49 E |
| Singkuang | 114 | 1.03 N | 98.56 E |
| Singleton, Austl. | 170 | 32.34 S | 151.10 E |
| Singleton, Eng., U.K. | 42 | 50.55 N | 0.46 W |
| Singleton, Mount ∧, Austl. | 162 | 29.28 S | 117.18 E |
| Singleton, Mount ∧, Austl. | 162 | 22.00 S | 130.49 E |
| Singleton Ditch ≍ | 216 | 41.10 N | 87.37 W |
| Singlewell or Ifield | 260 | 51.25 N | 0.23 E |
| Singö | 40 | 60.10 N | 18.44 E |
| Singö I | 40 | 60.11 N | 18.46 E |
| Singora → Songkhla | 110 | 7.12 N | 100.36 E |
| Şingorkai | 164 | 5.55 S | 146.55 E |
| Şingoža | 86 | 47.45 N | 80.40 E |
| Singpāra | 272b | 22.40 N | 88.31 E |
| Singrāmau | 124 | 25.57 N | 82.23 E |
| Singuédeze (Shingwidzi) ≃ | 156 | 23.53 S | 32.17 E |
| Singur | 126 | 22.49 N | 88.14 E |
| Sin'gye | 98 | 38.36 N | 126.30 E |
| Sinhai → Lianyungang | 98 | 34.39 N | 119.16 E |
| Sinh Ho | 110 | 22.22 N | 103.14 E |
| Sinhŭng | 98 | 40.11 N | 127.34 E |
| Siniaka-Minia, Réserve de ■ | 146 | 10.30 N | 18.00 E |
| Sinička ≃ | 265b | 55.50 N | 37.19 E |
| Sinije gory ⩘[2] | 80 | 51.10 N | 49.25 E |
| Sinije Lip'agi | 78 | 51.23 N | 38.29 E |
| Siniloan | 116 | 14.25 N | 121.27 E |
| Sining → Xining | 102 | 36.38 N | 101.55 E |
| Siniscola | 71 | 40.34 N | 9.41 E |
| Sinj | 36 | 43.42 N | 16.38 E |
| Sinjah | 140 | 13.09 N | 33.56 E |
| Sinjai | 112 | 5.07 S | 120.15 E |
| Sinjang-ni | 98 | 39.04 N | 127.46 E |
| Sinjār | 128 | 36.19 N | 41.52 E |
| Sinjār, Jabal ⩘ | 130 | 36.25 N | 41.40 E |
| Sinjauka | 76 | 52.58 N | 26.29 E |


| | | | | | |
|---|---|---|---|---|---|
| ≃ River | Fluß | Río | Rivière | Rio | |
| ≍ Canal | Kanal | Canal | Canal | Canal | |
| ʟ Waterfall, Rapids | Wasserfall, Stromschnellen | Cascada, Rápidos | Chute d'eau, Rapides | Cascata, Rápidos | |
| ⋓ Strait | Meeresstraße | Estrecho | Détroit | Estreito | |
| c Bay, Gulf | Bucht, Golf | Bahía, Golfo | Baie, Golfe | Baía, Golfo | |
| ⊜ Lake, Lakes | See, Seen | Lago, Lagos | Lac, Lacs | Lago, Lagos | |
| ≌ Swamp | Sumpf | Pantano | Marais | Pântano | |
| ⊓ Ice Features, Glacier | Eis- und Gletscherformen | Accidentes Glaciales | Formes glaciaires | Acidentes glaciares | |
| ∓ Other Hydrographic Features | Andere Hydrographische Objekte | Otros Elementos Hidrográficos | Autres données hydrographiques | Outros acidentes hidrográficos | |

| | | | | |
|---|---|---|---|---|
| ✣ Submarine Features | Untermeerische Objekte | Accidentes Submarinos | Formes de relief sous-marin | Acidentes submarinos |
| □ Political Unit | Politische Einheit | Unidad Politica | Entité politique | Unidade política |
| ᵾ Cultural Institution | Kulturelle Institution | Institución Cultural | Institution culturelle | Instituição cultural |
| ⊥ Historical Site | Historische Stätte | Sitio Histórico | Site historique | Sitio histórico |
| ♦ Recreational Site | Erholungs- und Ferienort | Sitio de Recreo | Centre de loisirs | Area de Lazer |
| ⊠ Airport | Flughafen | Aeropuerto | Aéroport | Aeroporto |
| ■ Military Installation | Militäranlage | Instalación Militar | Installation militaire | Instalação militar |
| ⊸ Miscellaneous | Verschiedenes | Misceláneo | Divers | Diversos |

Sinji-do I 98 34.20 N 126.50 E
Sinkan 110 24.08 N 97.01 E
Sinkāt 140 18.50 N 36.50 E
Sinkiang → Xinjiang Uygur Zizhiqu □[4] 90 40.00 N 85.00 E
Sinking ≃ 48 53.37 N 8.52 W
Sinking Creek ≃ 210 40.51 N 77.34 W
Sinking Spring, Oh., U.S. 218 39.04 N 83.23 W
Sinking Spring, Pa., U.S. 208 40.19 N 76.02 W
Şin'kok-ni 271b 37.37 N 126.46 E
Šinkovo, Ross. 76 56.03 N 31.31 E
Sin'kovo, Ross. 82 56.26 N 36.04 E
Sin'kovo, Ross. 82 54.37 N 38.56 E
Sin'kovo, Ross. 82 56.23 N 37.19 E
Sinks Canyon State Park ♦ 200 42.45 N 108.50 W
Sin-le-Noble 50 50.22 N 3.07 E
Sinmak 98 38.25 N 126.14 E
Sinmi-do I 98 39.33 N 124.53 E
Sinn ≃ 56 50.03 N 9.42 E
Sinnahwā 142 30.25 N 31.21 E
Sinnai 71 39.18 N 9.12 E
Sinnamahoning 214 41.19 N 78.06 W
Sinnamary 250 5.23 N 52.57 W
Sinnar 122 19.51 N 74.00 E
Sinnemahoning Creek ≃ 210 41.15 N 77.54 W
Sinnemahoning Creek, Bennett Branch ≃ 210 41.20 N 78.08 W
Sinnemahoning Creek, Driftwood Branch ≃ 210 41.20 N 78.08 W
Sinnemahoning Creek, First Fork ≃ 210 41.19 N 78.05 W
Sinnersdorf 56 51.01 N 6.49 E
Sinnes 26 58.56 N 6.50 E
Sinni ≃ 68 40.09 N 16.42 E
Sinntal 56 50.18 N 9.38 E
Sinnūris 142 29.25 N 30.52 E
Sinnyŏng 98 36.04 N 128.46 E
Sino, Pedra do ∧ 256 22.30 S 43.03 W
Sinoie, Lacul ⊜ 38 44.38 N 28.53 E
Sinop, Bra. 250 11.55 S 55.35 W
Sinop, Tür. 130 42.01 N 35.09 E
Sinop □[4] 130 41.40 N 34.50 E
Sinop Burnu > 130 42.02 N 35.12 E
Sinp'a 98 41.24 N 127.46 E
Sinp'o 98 40.03 N 128.12 E
Sins 58 47.11 N 8.23 E
Sinsang 98 39.38 N 127.25 E
Sinsen 263 51.40 N 7.11 E
Sinsheim 56 49.15 N 8.53 E
Sinsiang → Xinxiang 98 35.20 N 113.51 E
Sinsin 56 50.17 N 5.15 E
Sinsi-ri 98 39.59 N 124.58 E
Sinskoje 74 61.08 N 126.48 E
Sinspelt 56 49.58 N 6.19 E
Sint-Amandsberg 50 51.04 N 3.45 E
Sint-Andries 50 51.12 N 3.10 E
Sintang 112 0.04 N 111.30 E
Sint Annaland 52 51.36 N 4.06 E
Sint Annaparochie 52 53.16 N 5.39 E
Sint Anthonis 52 51.37 N 5.52 E
Sint Christoffelberg ∧[2] 241s 12.20 N 69.08 W
Sint-Denijs-Westrem 50 51.01 N 3.40 E
Sint Eustatius I 238 17.30 N 62.59 W
Sint-Gillis-Waas 50 51.13 N 4.08 E
Sint Helenabaai c 158 32.43 S 18.05 E
Sint-Joris-Weert 56 50.48 N 4.39 E
Sint-Joris-Winge 56 50.55 N 4.52 E
Sint-Katelijne-Waver 56 51.04 N 4.32 E
Sint-Kruis, Bel. 50 51.13 N 3.15 E
Sint Kruis, Ned. Ant. 241s 12.18 N 69.08 W
Sint-Lenaarts 56 51.21 N 4.41 E
Sint Maarten 52 52.46 N 4.44 E
Sint Maarten (Saint-Martin) I 238 18.04 N 63.04 W
Sint Maartensdijk 52 51.33 N 4.05 E
Sint-Michiels 50 51.11 N 3.12 E
Sint Michielsgestel 52 51.38 N 5.21 E
Sint Nicolaas 241s 12.27 N 69.52 W
Sint-Niklaas (Saint-Nicolas) 50 51.10 N 4.08 E
Sint-Oedenrode 52 51.34 N 5.27 E
Sinton 196 28.02 N 97.30 W
Sintong 114 1.31 N 100.58 E
Sint Pancras 52 52.39 N 4.46 E
Sint-Pieters-Leeuw 50 50.47 N 4.14 E
Sintra 34 38.48 N 9.23 W
Sintra, Serra de ⋏[2] 266c 38.47 N 9.25 W
Sintra Granjo do Marquez, Aeroporto ⊠ 266c 38.49 N 9.20 W
Sint-Truiden 56 50.48 N 5.12 E
Sint Willebrord 52 51.33 N 4.35 E
Sinú ≃ 246 9.24 N 75.49 W
Sin'ucha ≃ 84 44.45 N 40.58 E
Sin'uga 88 57.45 N 115.13 E
Sinŭiju 98 40.05 N 124.24 E
Sinujif 144 8.33 N 48.59 E
Sinŭp, C.M.I.K. 98 39.54 N 126.47 E
Sinŭp, Taehan 98 37.54 N 127.12 E
Sinwŏn-ni 98 38.13 N 125.44 E
Sinzig 56 50.32 N 7.15 E
Sinzing 60 49.00 N 12.02 E
Sió ≃, Magy. 30 46.20 N 18.55 E
Sio ≃, Togo 150 6.17 N 1.13 E
Siocon 116 7.42 N 122.08 E
Siófok 30 46.54 N 18.04 E
Sioma 152 16.39 S 23.30 E
Sioma Ngweze National Park ♦ 152 17.15 S 23.20 E
Sion (Sitten) 58 46.14 N 7.21 E
Sionascaig, Loch ⊜ 46 58.04 N 5.11 W
Sion Mills 48 54.47 N 7.29 W
Sioule ≃ 32 46.22 N 3.19 E
Sioux Center 198 43.04 N 96.10 W
Sioux City 198 42.30 N 96.24 W
Sioux Falls 198 43.33 N 96.42 W
Sioux Lookout 184 50.06 N 91.55 W
Sioux Narrows 184 49.25 N 94.06 W
Sioux Rapids 198 42.53 N 95.09 W
Sipalay 116 9.45 N 122.24 E
Sipalay ≃ 116 9.46 N 122.24 E
Sipaliwini □[5] 250 4.00 N 56.00 W
Sipaliwini ≃ 250 2.22 N 56.50 W
Sipaozi 104 41.26 N 122.13 E
Sipapo ≃ 246 5.03 N 67.48 W
Siparia 241r 10.08 N 61.30 W
Šipčenski Prohod )( 38 42.46 N 25.19 E
Şipek 130 40.14 N 41.29 E
Sipes 220 28.48 N 81.14 W
Sipesville 214 40.06 N 79.06 W
Šipicyno, Ross. 24 61.17 N 46.28 E
Šipicyno, Ross. 86 56.04 N 77.18 E
Šipilovo 82 54.49 N 37.32 E
Siping 89 43.12 N 124.20 E
Sipingjie 98 42.31 N 125.08 E
Sipirok 114 1.37 N 99.16 E
Sipitang 112 5.05 N 115.33 E
Sipiwesk 184 55.27 N 97.24 W
Sipiwesk Lake ⊜ 184 55.05 N 97.35 W
Siple, Mount ∧ 9 73.15 S 126.06 W
Siple Coast ⊥[2] 9 82.00 S 153.00 W
Sipocot 116 13.46 N 122.58 E
Sipofaneni 158 26.41 S 31.41 E
Sipot 114 4.31 N 96.02 E
Şipoteni 38 47.18 N 28.11 E
Sipplingen 58 47.47 N 9.05 E
Si Prachan 110 14.37 N 100.09 E
Sipsey ≃ 194 33.00 N 88.10 W
Sipsey Creek ≃ 194 33.53 N 88.17 W
Sipu 98 40.48 N 113.43 E
Sipul 164 5.50 S 148.45 E
Šipunovo 86 52.13 N 82.17 E
Šipunskij, mys > 74 53.06 N 160.02 E
Sipupus 114 1.25 N 99.31 E
Sipura, Pulau I 112 2.12 S 99.40 E
Siqian, Zhg. 100 22.31 N 112.52 E
Siqian, Zhg. 100 24.40 N 114.06 E
Siqueira Campos 255 23.42 S 49.50 W
Siquia ≃ 236 12.09 N 84.13 W
Siquijor 116 9.13 N 123.30 E
Siquijor □[4] 116 9.11 N 123.34 E
Siquijor Island I 116 9.11 N 123.34 E
Siquirres 236 10.06 N 83.30 W
Siquisique 246 10.34 N 69.42 W
Sīra, India 122 13.45 N 76.54 E
Sira, Nor. 26 58.25 N 6.38 E
Šira, Ross. 86 54.29 N 89.56 E
Sira ≃ 26 58.17 N 6.24 E
Si Racha 110 13.10 N 100.56 E
Siracuas 248 21.03 S 61.46 W
Siracusa (Syracuse) 70 37.04 N 15.17 E
Siracusa □[4] 70 37.03 N 15.00 E
Sir Adam Beck II Reservoir ⊜[1] 284a 43.08 N 79.04 W
Şirāhā 124 26.39 N 86.12 E
Šir'aj 80 49.34 N 44.07 E
Sirājganj 124 24.27 N 89.43 E
Sir Alexander, Mount ∧ 182 53.56 N 120.23 W
Sirāmpur 126 24.08 N 86.20 E
Şiran 130 40.12 N 39.08 E
Sirasso 150 9.16 N 6.06 W
Sirault 50 50.30 N 3.47 E
Siraway 116 7.34 N 122.08 E
Sirba ≃ 150 13.46 N 1.40 E
Şīr Banī Yās I 128 24.19 N 52.37 E
Sir Colin Mackenzie Wildlife Sanctuary ◂[4] 169 37.40 S 145.32 E
Sirdalsvatn ⊜ 26 58.33 N 6.41 E
Sīrdān 128 36.39 N 49.12 E
Sirdar 182 49.15 N 116.37 W
Sir Douglas, Mount ∧ 182 50.44 N 115.20 W
Sire 144 9.00 N 36.55 E
Sir Edward Pellew Group II 164 15.40 S 136.48 E
Širega 76 60.10 N 41.15 E
Sireniki 180 64.25 N 173.57 W
Sirente, Monte ∧ 66 42.09 N 13.36 E
Siret 38 47.57 N 26.04 E
Siret (Seret) ≃ 38 45.24 N 28.01 E
Sirevåg 26 58.30 N 5.47 E
Sir Francis Drake, Mount ∧ 182 50.48 N 124.47 W
Sir Francis Drake Channel ʊ 240m 18.25 N 64.30 W
Sirghāyā 132 33.48 N 36.09 E
Sirḥān, Wādī as- V 128 30.30 N 38.00 E
Sirhind 124 30.39 N 76.23 E
Sirhind Canal ≊ 123 30.47 N 76.01 E
Siria → Syria □[1] 128 35.00 N 38.00 E
Sirik, Tanjong > 112 2.46 N 111.19 E
Sirikit Reservoir ⊜[1] 110 17.50 N 100.30 E
Şirina I 130 36.21 N 26.42 E
Širinguši 80 53.51 N 42.46 E
Sirino, Monte ∧ 68 40.08 N 15.50 E
Siriya-zaki > 92 41.26 N 141.28 E
Sir James MacBrien, Mount ∧ 180 62.07 N 127.41 W
Sīrjān 128 29.27 N 55.40 E
Sir Joseph Banks Group II 166 34.32 S 136.17 E
Sirkābād 126 23.16 N 86.12 E
Sirkeli 130 40.09 N 32.52 E
Sirmaur 124 24.51 N 81.23 E
Sirmione 64 45.30 N 10.36 E
Sirnach 58 47.28 N 9.00 E
Şirnak 128 37.32 N 42.28 E
Şirnak □[4] 128 37.30 N 42.30 E
Širo, Jabal ∧ 140 14.23 N 24.23 E
Sirocina 76 55.23 N 29.37 E
Şirohi 120 24.54 N 72.51 E
Širokaja Pad' 89 50.14 N 142.09 E
Širokij 89 49.45 N 129.30 E
Širokij Bujerak 80 52.07 N 47.46 E
Širokovo 88 55.27 N 99.23 E
Sirolo 66 43.32 N 13.37 E
Sirombu 114 0.57 N 97.25 E
Sironj 124 24.06 N 77.42 E
Síros → Ermoúpolis 38 37.26 N 24.56 E
Síros I 38 37.26 N 24.54 E
Sirotinskaja 80 49.16 N 43.39 E
Siroua, Jebel ∧ 148 30.41 N 7.37 W
Sırpsındığı 130 41.46 N 26.29 E
Sirrah, Nafūd as- ⊥[8] 128 23.05 N 44.25 E
Sīrrī, Jazīreh-ye I 128 25.55 N 54.32 E
Sirsa, India 123 29.32 N 75.01 E
Sirsa, India 126 22.14 N 86.38 E
Sirsāganj 124 27.03 N 78.42 E
Sirs al-Layyānah 142 30.26 N 30.58 E
Sir Sandford, Mount ∧ 182 51.40 N 117.52 W
Sirsi 122 14.37 N 74.51 E
Sirsilla 122 18.23 N 78.50 E
Sirsinā, Mişr 142 30.36 N 30.54 E
Sirsinā, Mişr 142 29.24 N 30.58 E
Sirsiri 154 4.24 N 31.53 E
Sir Thomas, Mount ∧ 162 27.10 S 129.45 E
Siruma 116 14.00 N 123.15 E
Sirupa ≃ 232 29.10 N 108.35 W
Şirvan 130 38.02 N 42.00 E
Šīrvān (Diyālā) ≃ 128 33.14 N 44.31 E
Şirvan düzü ≚ 84 40.15 N 48.00 E
Širvintos 76 55.03 N 24.57 E
Sir Wilfrid Laurier, Mount ∧ 182 52.47 N 119.45 W
Sir Wilfrid Laurier's Birthplace National Historic Site ⊥ 206 45.51 N 73.45 W
Sirykrabet ⊥ 86 44.07 N 62.35 E
Šís ≃, Guat. 236 14.09 N 91.39 W
Šiš ≃, Ross. 86 57.19 N 73.23 E
Sisa, Mount ∧ 164 6.08 S 142.45 E
Sisaba ∧ 154 6.09 S 29.48 E
Sisaiya Thāna 124 27.35 N 81.20 E
Sisak 36 45.29 N 16.23 E
Si Sa Ket 110 15.07 N 104.20 E
Šišakovo 76 60.02 N 41.30 E
Si Satchanalai 110 17.31 N 99.46 E
Šišchid (Kyzyl-Chem) ≃ 88 51.21 N 96.58 E
Šiševka 76 58.52 N 38.52 E
Sishangcun 105 40.16 N 116.33 E
Sishen 158 27.55 S 22.59 E
Sishili 106 32.09 N 120.45 E
Sishilijie 100 29.08 N 116.44 E
Sishilipu 105 40.12 N 118.08 E
Sishuang Liedao II 100 26.42 N 120.24 E
Sishui 98 35.39 N 117.15 E
Sisian 84 39.32 N 46.02 E
Sisib Lake ⊜ 184 52.35 N 99.22 W
Sisikon 58 46.57 N 8.42 E
Sisim ≃ 88 55.09 N 91.54 E
Sisipuk Lake ⊜ 184 55.45 N 101.50 W
Šiškejevo 80 54.12 N 44.45 E
Šiškino 88 52.18 N 113.35 E
Siskiyou Mountains ⋏ 204 41.55 N 123.15 W
Siskiyou Pass )( 202 42.03 N 122.36 W
Şişli ◂[8] 267b 41.04 N 28.59 E
Šišlovo 82 54.14 N 38.33 E
Sison 116 9.40 N 125.31 E
Sisŏphŏn 110 13.35 N 102.59 E
Sisquoc ≃ 204 34.54 N 120.18 W
Sissa ≃ 115b 8.29 S 121.18 E
Sissach 58 47.28 N 7.49 E
Sissano 164 3.00 S 142.05 E
Sisséla 150 10.49 N 10.37 W
Sisseton 198 45.39 N 97.02 W
Sisseton Indian Reservation ◂[4] 198 45.40 N 97.02 W
Sissili ≃ 150 10.16 N 1.15 W
Sisson Branch Reservoir ⊜[1] 186 47.16 N 67.20 W
Sissonne 50 49.34 N 3.54 E
Sissonville 188 38.31 N 81.37 W
Sīstān ◂[1] 128 30.30 N 62.00 E
Sīstān va Balūchestān □[4] 128 28.30 N 60.30 E
Sister Bay 190 45.11 N 87.07 W
Sister Lakes 216 42.05 N 86.12 W
Sisteron 62 44.12 N 5.56 E
Sisters 202 44.17 N 121.32 W
Sistersville 188 39.33 N 80.59 W
Sistig 56 50.29 N 6.30 E
Sisto ≃ 66 41.18 N 13.10 E
Sistranda 26 63.43 N 8.50 E
Sit' ≃, Ross. 76 58.16 N 37.54 E
Sit' ≃, Ross. 76 59.59 N 40.10 E
Sitabamba 248 8.02 S 77.44 W
Sitai, Zhg. 85 39.23 N 77.56 E
Sitai, Zhg. 98 41.16 N 114.23 E
Sitaizi, Zhg. 104 42.29 N 123.20 E
Sitaizi, Zhg. 104 41.17 N 122.16 E
Sitaizui 105 40.49 N 115.20 E
Sitakili 150 13.07 N 11.14 W
Sitalike 154 6.38 S 31.08 E
Sitalkuchi 124 26.10 N 89.11 E
Sītāmarhi 124 26.36 N 85.29 E
Sitampiky 157b 16.41 S 46.06 E
Si Tangkay 112 4.40 N 119.24 E
Sītāpur 124 27.34 N 80.41 E
Sītāpur Branch ≊ 124 28.10 N 80.25 E
Sitārāmpur 126 23.43 N 86.53 E
Siteki 158 26.32 S 31.58 E
Si Thep ⊥ 110 15.30 N 101.10 E
Sithoniá 38 35.12 N 26.07 E
Sithoniá >[1] 38 40.10 N 23.47 E
Sitidgi Lake ⊜ 180 68.32 N 132.42 W
Sítio D'Abadia 255 14.48 S 46.16 W
Sítio Novo 250 5.51 S 46.43 W
Sitka 180 57.03 N 135.02 W
Sitkalidak Island I 180 57.10 N 153.14 W
Sitka National Historical Park ♦ 180 57.05 N 135.15 W
Sitka Point > 180 57.00 N 135.49 W
Sitka Sound ʊ 180 57.00 N 135.30 W
Sitkinak Island I 180 56.35 N 154.12 W
Sitkinak Strait ʊ 180 56.39 N 154.06 W
Sitkino 88 56.23 N 98.21 E
Sitna ≃ 38 47.37 N 27.08 E
Sitn'a-Ščelkanovo 82 54.58 N 37.59 E
Sitnica ≃ 38 42.45 N 21.01 E
Sitniki 80 56.27 N 44.06 E
Sitnikovo 86 56.23 N 67.53 E
Sitobela 158 26.53 S 31.36 E
Sitona 144 14.28 N 37.27 E
Sitrah 128 26.09 N 50.38 E
Sitrah ⍑[4] 140 28.42 N 26.54 E
Sittard 56 51.00 N 5.53 E
Sitten → Sion 58 46.14 N 7.21 E
Sittendorf 264b 48.05 N 16.10 E
Sittensen 52 53.17 N 9.30 E
Sitter ≃ 58 47.29 N 9.14 E
Sittingbourne 42 51.21 N 0.44 E
Sittoung ≃ 110 17.10 N 96.58 E
Sittwe (Akyab) 110 20.09 N 92.54 E
Situ 105 39.20 N 115.39 E
Situbondo 115a 7.42 S 114.00 E
Siufaalele Point > 174y 14.17 S 169.29 W
Si'ufage 174y 14.14 S 169.32 W
Siulakderas 112 1.55 S 101.18 E
Siu Lek Yuen 271d 22.23 N 114.12 E
Siumbatu 112 2.45 S 122.03 E
Siumpu, Pulau I 112 5.40 S 122.31 E
Siuna 236 13.44 N 84.46 W
Siurgus Donigala 71 39.35 N 9.12 E
Siuri 126 23.55 N 87.32 E
Siusi (Seis) 64 46.32 N 11.34 E
Siuslaw ≃ 202 44.01 N 124.08 W
Siva ≃ 80 56.48 N 53.55 E
Sivaganga 122 9.52 N 78.29 E
Sivakāsi 122 9.27 N 77.49 E
Sivaki 89 52.39 N 126.45 E
Sīvand ≃ 128 29.51 N 52.46 E
Sivas 130 39.45 N 37.02 E
Sivas □[4] 130 39.30 N 37.15 E
Sivaslı 130 38.30 N 29.42 E
Sivé 150 15.42 N 13.12 W
Ševeluč, vulkan ∧[1] 74 56.39 N 161.18 E
Siverek 130 37.45 N 39.19 E
Siverskij 76 59.21 N 30.05 E
Sivers'kyy Donets' ≃ 72 47.35 N 40.54 E
Sivers'kyy Donets'-Donbas, kanal ≊ 83 48.55 N 37.45 E
Sivkovo 82 55.26 N 35.53 E
Sivomaskinskij 24 66.40 N 62.35 E
Sivri Ada I 267b 40.54 N 28.59 E
Sivrice 130 38.27 N 39.19 E
Sivrihisar 130 39.27 N 31.34 E
Sivry-Courtry 261 48.32 N 2.45 E
Sivry-sur-Meuse 56 49.19 N 5.16 E
Sīwah 140 29.12 N 25.31 E
Sīwah, Wāḥat ⍑[4] 140 29.12 N 25.31 E
Siwalik Range ⋏ 120 31.00 N 78.00 E
Siwān 124 26.13 N 84.22 E
Siwang ≃ 107 29.25 N 103.50 E
Sixaola ≃ 236 9.34 N 82.34 W
Six Flags Great America ♦ 216 42.21 N 87.55 W
Six Flags over Mid-America ♦ 219 38.31 N 90.40 W
Six Flags Over Texas ♦ 222 32.45 N 97.05 W
Six-Fours-la-Plage 62 43.06 N 5.51 E
Sixian 100 33.30 N 117.56 E
Sixitou 100 27.31 N 119.57 E
Six Mile Creek ≃, On., Can. 284a 43.15 N 79.10 W
Sixmile Creek ≃, Ky., U.S. 218 38.26 N 84.58 W
Sixmile Creek ≃, N.Y., U.S. 284a 43.17 N 78.58 W
Sixmilecross 48 54.34 N 7.08 W
Six Mile Lake ⊜ 212 44.55 N 79.45 W
Sixmile Run ≃ 276 40.28 N 74.35 W
Six Mile Water ≃ 48 54.42 N 6.14 W
Six Nations Indian Reserve ◂[4] 212 43.03 N 80.07 W
Sixshooter Draw V 196 30.51 N 102.33 W
Sixteen Mile Creek ≃, On., Can. 275b 43.27 N 79.40 W
Sixteenmile Creek ≃, Mt., U.S. 202 46.06 N 111.23 W
Sixth Cataract → Sablūkah, Ash-Shallāl as- ⌊ 140 16.20 N 32.42 E
Siyāl, Jazā'ir II 140 22.47 N 36.12 E
Siyāna 124 28.38 N 78.03 E
Siyang 100 33.43 N 118.41 E
Si Yat ≃ 110 13.42 N 101.26 E
Siyäzän 84 41.05 N 49.06 E
Siyeteb 140 18.00 N 35.01 E
Siz'absk 24 65.05 N 53.49 E
Sizaja 88 58.07 N 100.38 E
Sizhijian 98 42.25 N 114.36 E
Siziano 62 45.20 N 9.12 E
Sizilien → Sicilia I 70 37.30 N 14.00 E
Siziman 89 50.43 N 140.26 E
Siziwang Qi 102 41.33 N 111.31 E
Sizun 32 48.24 N 4.05 W
Sizuoka → Shizuoka 94 34.58 N 138.23 E
Sjælland I 41 55.30 N 11.45 E
Sjællands Odde >[1] 41 55.58 N 11.22 E
Sjalec 76 53.23 N 30.24 E
Själevad 26 63.18 N 18.36 E
Sjanno 76 54.49 N 29.43 E
Sjanovo 82 54.59 N 37.25 E
Sjarheevičy 76 53.30 N 27.45 E
Sjenica 38 43.16 N 20.00 E
Sjeništa ∧ 38 43.42 N 18.37 E
Sjoa ≃ 26 61.41 N 9.33 E
Sjöbo 41 55.38 N 13.42 E
Sjøholt 26 62.29 N 6.48 E
Sjösa 40 58.46 N 17.04 E
Sjötorp 40 58.50 N 13.59 E
Skaby 264a 52.19 N 13.51 E
Skaby-Berge ∧[2] 264a 52.19 N 13.49 E
Skåde 41 56.06 N 10.13 E
Skadovs'k 78 46.08 N 32.54 E
Skælskør 41 55.15 N 11.19 E
Skærbæk, Dan. 41 55.31 N 9.38 E
Skærbæk, Dan 41 55.09 N 8.46 E
Skævinge 41 55.55 N 12.10 E
Skaftafell National Park ♦ 24a 64.15 N 17.00 W
Skaftung 26 62.07 N 21.22 E
Skagafjörður c 24a 65.55 N 19.35 W
Skagen 26 57.44 N 10.36 E
Skagern ⊜ 40 58.59 N 14.17 E
Skagerrak ʊ 26 57.45 N 9.00 E
Skagersvik 40 58.58 N 14.06 E
Skaggs Creek ≃ 194 36.54 N 86.04 W
Skagit □[6] 224 48.29 N 121.45 W
Skagit ≃ 224 48.20 N 122.25 W
Skagit Bay c 224 48.19 N 122.24 W
Skagway 180 59.28 N 135.19 W
Skaidi 24 70.25 N 24.30 E
Skaistkalne 76 56.23 N 24.39 E
Skála Oropoú 38 38.20 N 23.46 E
Skala-Podil's'ka 78 48.51 N 26.12 E
Skalat 78 49.26 N 25.59 E
Skalbmierz 30 50.19 N 20.25 E
Skälderviken 41 56.17 N 12.50 E
Skälderviken c 41 56.18 N 12.38 E
Skalica 30 48.51 N 17.14 E
Skalino 76 58.32 N 40.13 E
Skalistaja, gora ∧ 84 42.48 N 45.08 E
Skalistyj, gora ∧ 180 68.12 N 178.10 E
Skalistyj chrebet ⋏ 84 43.15 N 43.00 E
Skalistyj Golec, gora ∧ 88 56.24 N 119.12 E
Skalka ⊜ 24 66.50 N 18.46 E
Skalka, vodní Nádrž ⊜[1] 54 50.06 N 12.19 E
Skalná 54 50.07 N 12.23 E
Skal'nyj 86 58.22 N 57.59 E
Skamania 224 45.37 N 122.02 W
Skamania □[6] 224 45.58 N 121.53 W
Skamlingsbanke ∧[2] 41 55.25 N 9.34 E
Skamokawa 224 46.16 N 123.27 W
Skanderborg 41 56.02 N 9.56 E
Skanderborg Sø ⊜ 41 56.01 N 9.56 E
Skåne □[9] 41 55.59 N 13.30 E
Skaneateles 210 42.56 N 76.25 W
Skaneateles Falls 210 43.00 N 76.27 W
Skaneateles Lake ⊜ 210 42.53 N 76.24 W
Skånevik 26 59.44 N 5.59 E
Skänninge 26 58.24 N 15.05 E
Skanör 26 55.25 N 12.52 E
Skara 26 58.22 N 13.25 E
Skaraborgs Län □[6] 26 58.20 N 13.30 E
Skaramagás 267c 38.01 N 23.36 E
Skärblacka 40 58.34 N 15.54 E
Skarð 24a 64.03 N 19.50 W
Skardhø ∧ 26 62.30 N 8.45 E
Skārdu 123 35.18 N 75.37 E
Skärhamn 26 58.00 N 11.33 E
Skarhult 41 55.49 N 13.23 E
Skarnes 26 60.15 N 11.41 E
Skarodnae 78 51.38 N 28.49 E
Skärplinge 40 60.28 N 17.46 E
Skarszewy 30 54.05 N 18.27 E
Skårup 41 55.05 N 10.42 E
Skaryszew 30 51.19 N 21.15 E
Skarżysko-Kamienna 30 51.08 N 20.53 E
Skášov 60 49.31 N 13.26 E
Skate Creek ≃ 224 46.37 N 121.41 W
Skattkärr 40 59.25 N 13.41 E
Skaudvilė 76 55.24 N 22.35 E
Skaugum 26 59.51 N 10.26 E
Skawina 30 49.59 N 19.49 E
Skebobruk 40 59.58 N 18.36 E
Skebokvarn 40 59.04 N 16.42 E
Skedviken ⊜ 40 59.46 N 18.16 E
Skedvisjön ⊜ 40 59.35 N 15.40 E
Skeena ≃ 182 54.09 N 130.02 W
Skeena Crossing 182 55.06 N 127.49 W
Skeena Mountains ⋏ 176 57.00 N 128.30 W
Skeen Peak ∧ 222 32.59 N 97.48 W
Skegness 44 53.10 N 0.21 E
Skegrie 41 55.24 N 13.04 E
Skei 26 61.38 N 6.30 E
Skeikampen 26 61.20 N 10.07 E
Skelde 41 54.51 N 9.44 E
Skeleton Coast ⊥[2] 156 19.15 S 12.30 E
Skeleton Coast Park ♦ 156 19.25 S 12.55 E
Skeleton Creek ≃ 196 35.58 N 97.25 W
Skeleton Lake ⊜ 212 45.15 N 79.27 W
Skellefteå 26 64.46 N 20.57 E
Skellefteälven ≃ 26 64.42 N 21.06 E
Skelleftehamn 26 64.41 N 21.14 E
Skellig Rocks II[1] 48 51.48 N 10.31 W
Skellytown 196 35.34 N 101.11 W
Skelmersdale 44 53.33 N 2.48 W
Skelmorlie 46 55.51 N 4.53 W
Skelton, Eng., U.K. 44 54.33 N 0.59 W
Skelton, Eng., U.K. 44 54.43 N 2.51 W
Skene 26 57.29 N 12.38 E
Skene, Mount ∧ 169 37.25 S 146.23 E
Skepptuna 40 59.43 N 18.05 E
Skerne ≃ 44 54.29 N 1.34 W
Skerpioensdrif 158 31.05 S 21.33 E
Skerries 48 53.35 N 6.07 W
Skerryvore I[2] 46 56.19 N 7.07 W
Skewen 42 51.40 N 3.51 W
Skhíza I 38 36.44 N 21.46 E
Ski 26 59.43 N 10.50 E
Skíathos 38 39.10 N 23.29 E
Skíathos I 38 39.10 N 23.28 E
Skiatook 196 36.22 N 96.00 W
Skibbereen 48 51.33 N 9.15 W
Skibby 41 55.45 N 11.58 E
Skibotn 24 69.24 N 20.16 E
Skidal' 76 53.34 N 24.15 E
Skiddaw ∧ 44 54.38 N 3.08 W
Skidegate 182 53.15 N 132.00 W
Skidegate Inlet c 182 53.14 N 132.00 W
Skidmore 196 28.15 N 97.41 W
Skien 26 59.12 N 9.36 E
Skierniewice 30 51.58 N 20.08 E
Skierniewice □[4] 30 52.10 N 20.15 E
Skiftet ʊ 26 60.15 N 21.05 E
Skihist Mountain ∧ 182 50.11 N 121.54 W
Skikda (Philippeville) 148 36.50 N 6.58 E
Skilak Lake ⊜ 180 60.25 N 150.25 W
Skillet Fork ≃ 194 38.08 N 88.07 W
Skillingaryd 26 57.26 N 14.05 E
Skillman 276 40.25 N 74.42 W
Škin' 82 55.11 N 38.30 E
Skinnastaður 24a 66.07 N 16.24 W
Skinner Reservoir ⊜[1] 228 33.35 N 117.03 W
Skinnskatteberg 40 59.50 N 15.41 E
Skippack 285 40.14 N 75.24 W
Skippack Creek ≃ 285 40.09 N 75.27 W
Skippack Creek, West Branch ≃ 285 40.14 N 75.23 W
Skippers 208 36.37 N 77.38 W
Skipskop 158 34.33 S 20.25 E
Skipton, Austl. 169 37.41 S 143.22 E
Skipton, Eng., U.K. 44 53.58 N 2.01 W
Skirfare ≃ 44 54.07 N 2.01 W
Skirmish Point > 171a 27.05 S 153.13 E
Skíros 38 38.53 N 24.33 E
Skíros I 38 38.53 N 24.32 E
Skivarp 41 55.25 N 13.34 E
Skive 26 56.34 N 9.02 E
Skjálfandafljót ≃ 24a 65.57 N 17.38 W
Skjálfandi c 24a 66.08 N 17.38 W

| ENGLISH Name | Page | Lat.°′ | Long.°′ |
|---|---|---|---|

Skjeberg 26 59.14 N 11.12 E
Skjern 26 55.57 N 8.30 E
Skjern ≃ 41 55.57 N 8.40 E
Sklad 74 71.55 N 123.33 E
Škloŭ 76 54.13 N 30.18 E
Skniga ≃ 82 54.53 N 37.24 E
Skobeleva, pik ∧ 85 39.49 N 72.44 E
Skoby 40 60.02 N 18.01 E
Škocjanske jame ⊥[7] 36 45.40 N 14.00 E
Skodborg 41 55.25 N 9.09 E
Skodsborg 41 55.49 N 12.34 E
Skoenmakerskop 158 34.02 S 25.33 E
Škofije 64 45.34 N 13.48 E
Škofja Loka 36 46.10 N 14.18 E
Skoganvarre 24 69.47 N 25.06 E
Skoghall 40 59.19 N 13.26 E
Skogstorp 40 59.20 N 16.28 E
Skokholm Island I 42 51.42 N 5.16 W
Skoki 30 52.41 N 17.10 E
Skokie 216 42.02 N 87.44 W
Skokie ≃ 216 42.05 N 87.46 W
Skokie Lagoons c 278 42.07 N 87.47 W
Skokloster ⊥ 40 59.42 N 17.37 E
Skokomish, North Fork ≃ 224 47.18 N 123.14 W
Skokomish, South Fork ≃ 224 47.18 N 123.14 W
Skokomish Indian Reservation ◂[4] 224 47.21 N 123.12 W
Sköldinge 40 59.02 N 16.26 E
Skole 78 49.02 N 23.29 E
Sköllersta 40 59.09 N 15.20 E
Skolsta 40 59.40 N 17.14 E
Skolwin 54 53.32 N 14.35 E
Skomer Island I 42 51.44 N 5.17 W
Skomoroshky 78 49.20 N 29.26 E
Skomoroški 82 54.05 N 36.57 E
Skón 110 12.04 N 105.04 E
Skookumchuck ≃ 224 46.41 N 123.00 W
Skookumchuck Reservoir ⊜[1] 224 47.47 N 122.42 W
Skoonspruit ≃ 158 27.00 S 26.38 E
Skootamatta ≃ 212 44.32 N 77.20 W
Skootamatta Lake ⊜ 212 44.50 N 77.15 W
Skópelos, Ellás 38 39.07 N 23.43 E
Skópelos, Ellás 38 39.02 N 26.26 E
Skópelos I 38 39.10 N 23.40 E
Skopin 76 53.51 N 39.33 E
Skopje 38 41.59 N 21.26 E
Skórcz 30 53.48 N 18.32 E
Skorodnoje 78 51.05 N 37.14 E
Skørping 26 56.50 N 9.53 E
Skotfoss 26 59.12 N 9.30 E
Škotovo 89 43.20 N 132.21 E
Skotterud 26 59.59 N 12.07 E
Skovby 41 54.53 N 10.00 E
Skövde 26 58.24 N 13.50 E
Skovlund 41 55.44 N 8.43 E
Skovorodino 89 53.59 N 123.55 E
Skowhegan 188 44.45 N 69.43 W
Skownan 184 51.57 N 99.36 W
Skradin 36 43.49 N 15.56 E
Skreen 48 54.15 N 8.45 W
Skreia 26 60.39 N 10.56 E
Skriplivka 76 57.32 N 30.38 E
Skrīveri 76 56.39 N 25.08 E
Skromberga 41 56.00 N 12.58 E
Skrudaliena 76 55.49 N 26.43 E
Skrunda 76 56.41 N 22.01 E
Skruv 26 56.41 N 15.22 E
Skrydstrup 41 55.14 N 9.15 E
Skudeneshavn 26 59.09 N 5.17 E
Skukuza 156 25.01 S 31.38 E
Skuleberget ∧[2] 26 63.05 N 18.21 E
Skulforp 26 58.21 N 13.49 E
Skull 48 51.32 N 9.33 W
Skull Creek ≃ 222 29.32 N 96.24 W
Skull Valley 200 34.30 N 112.41 W
Skull Valley Indian Reservation ◂[4] 200 40.24 N 112.45 W
Skultuna 40 59.43 N 16.25 E
Skuna ≃ 194 33.54 N 89.41 W
Skunk ≃ 190 40.42 N 91.07 W
Škunovka 86 50.45 N 55.27 E
Skuodas 76 56.16 N 21.32 E
Škuratovskij 82 54.07 N 37.36 E
Škurinskaja 78 46.35 N 39.22 E
Skurišenskaja 80 49.52 N 42.57 E
Skurup 41 55.28 N 13.30 E
Skutskär 40 60.38 N 17.25 E
Skvyra 78 49.44 N 29.40 E
Skwentna 180 61.58 N 151.11 W
Skwentna ≃ 180 62.00 N 151.08 W
Skwierzyna 30 52.36 N 15.30 E
Skye, Island of I 46 57.18 N 6.15 W
Sky Harbor Airport ⊠ 278 42.09 N 87.51 W
Skykomish 224 47.42 N 121.21 W
Skykomish ≃ 224 47.50 N 122.03 W
Skykomish, North Fork ≃ 224 47.47 N 121.33 W
Skykomish, South Fork ≃ 224 47.47 N 121.33 W
Sky Lake 220 28.28 N 81.24 W
Sky Lake ⊜ 212 44.48 N 81.15 W
Skyland, Nv., U.S. 226 39.01 N 119.56 W
Skyland, N.C., U.S. 192 35.29 N 82.31 W
Skylight 218 38.25 N 85.31 W
Skyline 284c 38.50 N 76.54 W
Skyline Lakes ⊜ 276 41.04 N 74.16 W
Skyllberg 40 58.57 N 14.59 E
Skyring, Península >[1] 254 45.58 S 74.53 W
Skyring, Seno ʊ 254 52.35 S 72.00 W
Sky Sailing Airport ⊠ 282 37.30 N 121.58 W
Skytop 210 41.14 N 75.15 W
Skyttorp 40 60.05 N 17.44 E
Skyway 224 47.29 N 122.14 W
Slabada 76 53.58 N 28.08 E
Slabodka 76 55.41 N 27.11 E
Slackhall 262 53.20 N 1.53 W
Slackwood 208 40.15 N 74.44 W
Slade Green ◂[8] 260 51.28 N 0.12 E
Sladkij 80 46.10 N 42.17 E
Sladkovo 86 55.32 N 70.20 E
Slagelse 41 55.24 N 11.22 E
Slagnäs 24 65.34 N 18.05 E
Slagovišči 76 53.57 N 35.54 E
Slaithwaite 262 53.37 N 1.53 W
Slamannan 46 55.56 N 3.50 W
Slamet, Gunung ∧ 115a 7.14 S 109.12 E
Slaná (Sajó) ≃ 30 47.56 N 21.08 E
Slancy 76 59.06 N 28.04 E
Slaney ≃ 48 52.21 N 6.30 W
Slangerup 41 55.51 N 12.11 E
Slănic 38 45.15 N 25.57 E
Slănic Moldova 38 46.13 N 26.26 E
Slano 36 42.47 N 17.54 E
Slanské vrchy ⋏ 30 48.50 N 21.30 E
Slaný 54 50.11 N 14.04 E
Šlapanice 30 49.10 N 16.44 E
Slaščevskaja 80 49.52 N 42.21 E
Śląsk → Silesia □[9] 30 51.00 N 16.45 E
Slastucha 80 51.57 N 44.32 E
Slate Bottom Creek ≃ 284a 42.53 N 78.45 W
Slate Creek ≃, Ks., U.S. 198 37.08 N 97.09 W
Slate Creek ≃, Pa., U.S. 279b 40.28 N 79.32 W
Slatedale 208 40.45 N 75.40 W
Slate Hill 210 41.23 N 74.29 W
Slater, Ia., U.S. 190 41.52 N 93.40 W
Slater, Mo., U.S. 194 39.13 N 93.04 W
Slater Creek ≃ 200 40.59 N 107.23 W
Slatersville 207 42.00 N 71.34 W
Slaterville Springs 210 42.24 N 76.21 W
Slatina 38 44.26 N 24.22 E
Slatington 208 40.44 N 75.36 W
Slaton 196 33.26 N 101.38 W
Slattocks 262 53.35 N 2.10 W
Slatyne 78 50.12 N 36.11 E

| DEUTSCH Name | Seite | Breite°′ | Länge°′ E = Ost |
|---|---|---|---|

Slaughter 194 30.43 N 91.08 W
Slauharad 76 53.27 N 31.00 E
Slaunae 76 54.18 N 29.27 E
Slaung 115a 8.02 S 111.24 E
Slautnoje 74 63.00 N 167.59 E
Slava 89 52.08 N 129.24 E
Slav'anka, Ross. 89 42.53 N 131.21 E
Slav'anka, Uzb. 85 40.40 N 68.32 E
Slav'anka ≃ 265a 59.50 N 30.32 E
Slav'ansk-na-Kubani 78 45.15 N 38.08 E
Slave ≃ 176 61.18 N 113.39 W
Slavečna ≃ 78 51.41 N 29.41 E
Slave Coast ⊥[2] 150 6.25 N 3.00 E
Slave Lake 182 55.17 N 114.46 W
Slavgorod 86 53.00 N 78.40 E
Slavhorod, Ukr. 78 48.06 N 35.31 E
Slavhorod, Ukr. 78 50.36 N 35.21 E
Slavitino 82 56.41 N 39.13 E
Slavkino 80 52.58 N 47.11 E
Slavkoviči 76 57.39 N 29.05 E
Slavkovský les ⋏ 54 50.07 N 12.45 E
Slavkov u Brna 61 49.09 N 16.52 E
Slavonia → Slavonija □[9] 36 45.00 N 18.00 E
Slavonice 61 49.00 N 15.21 E
Slavonija □[9] 36 45.00 N 18.00 E
Slavonska Požega 36 45.20 N 17.41 E
Slavonski Brod 38 45.10 N 18.01 E
Slavsk 76 55.03 N 21.41 E
Slavs'ke 78 48.49 N 23.24 E
Slavuta 78 50.18 N 26.52 E
Sława 30 51.53 N 16.04 E
Slawi 115a 6.59 S 109.08 E
Sławno 30 54.22 N 16.40 E
Slayton 198 43.59 N 95.45 W
Slea ≃ 44 53.03 N 0.12 W
Sleaford 42 53.00 N 0.24 W
Slea Head > 48 52.06 N 10.27 W
Sleat, Point of > 46 57.01 N 6.02 W
Sleat, Sound of ʊ 46 57.06 N 5.49 W
Sledge 194 34.25 N 90.13 W
Sledge Island I 180 64.29 N 166.13 W
Sled Lake ⊜ 184 54.27 N 107.25 W
Sledmere 44 54.04 N 0.35 W
Slednevo 82 56.25 N 38.36 E
Sledzjuki 76 53.35 N 30.22 E
Sleen 52 52.46 N 6.48 E
Sleeping Bear Dunes National Lakeshore ♦ 190 44.50 N 86.08 W
Sleeping Giant State Park ♦ 207 41.25 N 72.53 W
Sleepy Eye 198 44.17 N 94.43 W
Sleepy Hollow, Ca., U.S. 226 38.00 N 122.34 W
Sleepy Hollow, Ca., U.S. 280 33.57 N 117.47 W
Sleetmute 180 61.42 N 157.11 W
Sleidinge 50 51.08 N 3.41 E
Sleights 44 54.27 N 0.40 W
Sleman 115a 7.42 S 110.20 E
Slepino 76 59.11 N 29.02 E
Ślesin 30 52.23 N 18.19 E
Slessor Glacier ⌂ 9 79.50 S 28.30 W
Slickville 214 40.27 N 79.31 W
Slidell 194 30.16 N 89.46 W
Slide Mountain ∧ 210 42.00 N 74.23 W
Sliderock Mountain ∧ 202 46.35 N 113.33 W
Sliedrecht 52 51.49 N 4.45 E
Slieve Aughty Mountains ⋏ 48 53.05 N 8.35 W
Slieve Bloom Mountains ⋏ 48 53.05 N 7.35 W
Slievekimalta ∧ 48 52.45 N 8.16 W
Slievenamon ∧ 48 52.25 N 7.34 W
Sligeach → Sligo 48 54.17 N 8.28 W
Sligo (Sligeach), Ire. 48 54.17 N 8.28 W
Sligo, Pa., U.S. 214 41.06 N 79.29 W
Sligo □[6] 48 54.10 N 8.40 W
Sligo Bay c 48 54.20 N 8.40 W
Sligo Creek ≃ 284c 38.57 N 76.58 W
Slikkerveer 52 51.53 N 4.37 E
Slingebeek ≃ 52 51.56 N 6.17 E
Slinger 190 43.20 N 88.17 W
Šlino, ozero ⊜ 76 57.40 N 33.23 E
Slioch ∧ 46 57.41 N 5.22 W
Slippery Rock 214 41.03 N 80.03 W
Slippery Rock Creek ≃ 214 40.51 N 80.15 W
Šlissel'burg 265a 59.57 N 31.02 E
Slite 26 57.43 N 18.48 E
Slīteres Rezervāts ♦ 76 57.38 N 22.25 E
Sliven 38 42.40 N 26.19 E
Slivnica 38 42.51 N 23.02 E
Sloan, Ia., U.S. 198 42.13 N 96.13 W
Sloan, Nv., U.S. 204 35.56 N 115.12 W
Sloan, N.Y., U.S. 210 42.53 N 78.47 W
Sloan Peak ∧ 224 48.03 N 121.20 W
Sloansville 210 42.46 N 74.20 W
Sloatsburg 210 41.09 N 74.11 W
Slobidka 78 47.53 N 29.21 E
Sloboda, Ross. 76 55.30 N 31.51 E
Sloboda, Ross. 78 51.09 N 40.17 E
Sloboda, Ukr. 78 51.11 N 33.37 E
Slobodka 82 54.22 N 37.33 E
Slobodskoj 86 58.42 N 50.12 E
Slobozia, Mol. 38 46.44 N 29.43 E
Slobozia, Rom. 38 44.34 N 27.23 E
Slobozia, Rom. 38 43.51 N 25.54 E
Slobozia Mare 38 45.34 N 28.12 E
Slocan 182 49.46 N 117.28 W
Slocan Lake ⊜ 182 49.56 N 117.22 W
Slochteren 52 53.12 N 6.47 E
Slocomb 194 31.06 N 85.35 W
Slocum 207 41.32 N 71.31 W
Slocum Mountain ∧ 228 35.18 N 117.13 W
Słomniki 30 50.15 N 20.06 E
Slonim 76 53.06 N 25.19 E
Slonovka 78 50.39 N 37.45 E
Słońsk 54 52.35 N 14.50 E
Sloop Channel ʊ 276 40.36 N 73.31 W
Sloping Hills 276 40.42 N 74.34 W
Slosh Indian Reserve ◂[4] 182 50.44 N 122.13 W
Sloten 52 52.54 N 5.38 E
Sloten ◂[8] 52 52.21 N 4.48 E
Slotermeer ⊜ 52 52.55 N 5.40 E
Slough 42 51.31 N 0.36 W
Slough □[8] 260 51.32 N 0.35 W
Slough Brook ≃ 276 40.45 N 74.21 W
Sloughhouse 226 38.30 N 121.12 W
Slovakia □[1] 22 48.30 N 20.00 E
Slovan 214 40.21 N 80.23 W
Slovechne 78 51.23 N 28.21 E
Slovenia □[1], Europe 22 46.15 N 15.10 E
Slovenia (Slovenija) □[1], Europe 36 46.15 N 15.10 E
Slovenj Gradec 61 46.31 N 15.05 E
Slovenska Bistrica, Slvn. 36 46.23 N 15.34 E
Slovenska Bistrica, Slvn. 61 46.23 N 15.34 E
Slovenske Gorice ⋏[2] 61 46.35 N 15.55 E
Slovenské rudohorie ⋏ 30 48.45 N 20.00 E
Slovinka 80 58.02 N 43.07 E
Slov'yanhirs'k 83 49.02 N 37.31 E
Slov'yanka 78 48.24 N 36.43 E
Slov'yanoserbs'k 83 48.42 N 38.59 E
Slov'yans'k 83 48.52 N 37.37 E
Słowiński Park Narodowy ♦ 30 54.40 N 17.25 E
Słubice 54 52.20 N 14.32 E
Sluč ≃ 76 52.08 N 27.31 E
Sluch ≃ 78 51.37 N 26.38 E
Sluck 76 53.01 N 27.33 E
Sl'ud'anka 88 51.38 N 103.42 E
Sluderno (Schluderns) 64 46.40 N 10.35 E
Sludy 76 58.52 N 36.52 E
Sluis 52 51.18 N 3.24 E

**Symbols** in the index entries represent the broad categories identified in the key at the right. Symbols with superior numbers (⋏[1]) identify subcategories (see complete key on page *I · 1).*

**Symbole** im Register stellen die rechts im Schlüssel erklärten Kategorien dar. Symbole mit hochgestellten Ziffern (⋏[1]) bezeichnen Unterabteilungen einer Kategorie (vgl. vollständiger Schlüssel auf Seite *I · 1).*

**Los símbolos** incluídos en el texto del índice representan las grandes categorías identificadas con la clave a la derecha. Los símbolos con numeros en su parte superior (⋏[1]) identifican las subcategorías (véase la clave completa en la página *I · 1).*

**Les symboles** de l'index représentent les catégories indiquées dans la légende à droite. Les symboles suivis d'un indice (⋏[1]) représentent des sous-catégories (voir légende complète à la page *I · 1).*

**Os símbolos** incluídos no texto do índice representam as grandes categorias identificadas com a chave à direita. Os símbolos com números em sua parte superior (⋏[1]) identificam as subcategorias (veja-se a chave completa à página *I · 1).*

| | | | | | |
|---|---|---|---|---|---|
| ∧ Mountain | Berg | Montaña | Montagne | Montanha |
| ⋏ Mountains | Gebirge | Montañas | Montagnes | Montanhas |
| )( Pass | Paß | Paso | Col | Passo |
| V Valley, Canyon | Tal, Cañon | Valle, Cañón | Vallée, Canyon | Vale, Canhão |
| ≚ Plain | Ebene | Llano | Plaine | Planície |
| > Cape | Kap | Cabo | Cap | Cabo |
| I Island | Insel | Isla | Île | Ilha |
| II Islands | Inseln | Islas | Îles | Ilhas |
| ⊥ Other Topographic Features | Andere Topographische Objekte | Otros Elementos Topográficos | Autres données topographiques | Outros acidentes topográficos |

ESPAÑOL — Nombre | Página | Lat.°' | Long.°' W = Oeste
FRANÇAIS — Nom | Page | Lat.°' | Long.°' W = Ouest
PORTUGUÊS — Nome | Página | Lat.°' | Long.°' W = Oeste


| | | | |
|---|---|---|---|
| Sluiskil | 52 | 51.16 N | 3.50 E |
| Šluknov | 54 | 51.00 N | 14.27 E |
| Slunj | 36 | 45.07 N | 15.35 E |
| Słupca | 30 | 52.19 N | 17.52 E |
| Słupia ≃ | 30 | 54.35 N | 16.50 E |
| Słupsk (Stolp) | 30 | 54.28 N | 17.01 E |
| Słupsk □[4] | 30 | 54.10 N | 17.15 E |
| Slurry | 156 | 25.49 S | 25.52 E |
| Šl'uz-Mokr'aki | 86 | 59.17 N | 88.50 E |
| Sly, Oued ≃ | 34 | 36.04 N | 1.08 E |
| Smachtino | 82 | 54.51 N | 36.25 E |
| Smackover | 194 | 33.21 N | 92.43 W |
| Smackover Creek ≃ | 194 | 33.22 N | 92.24 W |
| Småland □[9] | 26 | 57.20 N | 15.00 E |
| Smålandsfarvandet ʊ | 41 | 55.05 N | 11.20 E |
| Smålandsstenar | 26 | 57.10 N | 13.24 E |
| Smalininkai | 76 | 55.05 N | 22.35 E |
| Smaljany | 76 | 54.36 N | 30.04 E |
| Smaljavičy | 76 | 54.02 N | 28.05 E |
| Smallbridge | 262 | 53.38 N | 2.08 W |
| Smalleytown | 276 | 40.39 N | 74.28 W |
| Smallwood | 210 | 41.40 N | 74.49 W |
| Smallwood Reservoir ⊜[1] | 176 | 54.05 N | 64.30 W |
| Smallwood State Park ♠ | 208 | 38.33 N | 77.12 W |
| Smara | 148 | 26.44 N | 11.41 W |
| Smarhon' | 76 | 54.29 N | 26.24 E |
| Smartt Syndicate Dam ⊜[1] | 158 | 30.40 S | 23.18 E |
| Smartville | 226 | 39.12 N | 121.18 W |
| Smeaton | 184 | 53.30 N | 104.49 W |
| Smeaton Bay c | 182 | 55.20 N | 130.50 W |
| Smečno | 54 | 50.10 N | 14.03 E |
| Smedby | 40 | 58.33 N | 16.16 E |
| Smědeč | 61 | 48.56 N | 14.09 E |
| Smederevo | 38 | 44.40 N | 20.56 E |
| Smederevska Palanka | 38 | 44.22 N | 20.58 E |
| Smedjebacken | 40 | 60.08 N | 15.25 E |
| Šmel'ovka | 80 | 54.47 N | 49.11 E |
| Smelt Brook ≃, Ma., U.S. | 283 | 42.13 N | 70.58 W |
| Smelt Brook ≃, Ma., U.S. | 283 | 42.00 N | 70.43 W |
| Smelt Pond ⊜ | 283 | 41.58 N | 70.43 W |
| Smeralda, Costa ⊻[2] | 71 | 41.04 N | 9.30 E |
| Smerwick Harbour c | 48 | 52.12 N | 10.24 W |
| Smethport | 214 | 41.48 N | 78.26 W |
| Smethwick | 42 | 52.30 N | 1.58 W |
| Smicksburg | 214 | 40.52 N | 79.10 W |
| Smidovič | 89 | 48.36 N | 133.49 E |
| Šmidta → Mys Šmidta | 180 | 68.56 N | 179.26 W |
| Šmidta, mys › | 180 | 68.56 N | 179.30 W |
| Šmidta, ostrov I | 74 | 81.08 N | 90.48 E |
| Šmidta, poluostrov ›[1] | 89 | 54.10 N | 142.40 E |
| Śmigiel | 30 | 52.01 N | 16.32 E |
| Smila | 78 | 49.14 N | 31.53 E |
| Smilavičy | 76 | 53.45 N | 28.01 E |
| Smilde | 52 | 52.57 N | 6.27 E |
| Smile, Ukr. | 78 | 50.55 N | 33.36 E |
| Smile, Ky., U.S. | 218 | 38.15 N | 83.29 W |
| Smiley, Sk., Can. | 184 | 51.37 N | 109.29 W |
| Smiley, Tx., U.S. | 222 | 29.16 N | 97.38 W |
| Smiltene | 76 | 57.26 N | 25.56 E |
| Smirnovo | 86 | 54.31 N | 69.25 E |
| Smirnych | 89 | 49.43 N | 142.38 E |
| Smir-Restinga | 34 | 35.42 N | 5.23 W |
| Smite ≃ | 44 | 53.04 N | 0.48 W |
| Smith | 182 | 55.10 N | 114.02 W |
| Smith □[6] | 222 | 32.20 N | 95.15 W |
| Smith ≃, U.S. | 192 | 36.29 N | 79.45 W |
| Smith ≃, Ca., U.S. | 204 | 41.56 N | 124.12 W |
| Smith ≃, Mt., U.S. | 202 | 47.25 N | 111.29 W |
| Smith ≃, Or., U.S. | 202 | 43.43 N | 124.05 W |
| Smith, Cape › | 190 | 45.48 N | 81.35 W |
| Smith Arm c | 180 | 66.15 N | 124.00 W |
| Smith Bay c | 180 | 70.51 N | 154.25 W |
| Smithboro, Il., U.S. | 219 | 38.54 N | 89.20 W |
| Smithboro, N.Y., U.S. | 210 | 42.02 N | 76.24 W |
| Smith Canyon V | 198 | 37.46 N | 103.26 W |
| Smith Center | 198 | 39.46 N | 98.47 W |
| Smith Creek ≃, S.D., U.S. | 198 | 43.58 N | 99.20 W |
| Smith Creek ≃, Wa., U.S. | 224 | 46.45 N | 123.53 W |
| Smithdale | 279b | 40.14 N | 79.48 W |
| Smithers, B.C., Can. | 182 | 54.47 N | 127.10 W |
| Smithers, W.V., U.S. | 188 | 38.10 N | 81.18 W |
| Smithers Lake ⊜[1] | 222 | 29.29 N | 95.38 W |
| Smithfield, Austl. | 168b | 34.41 S | 138.41 E |
| Smithfield, Austl. | 274a | 33.51 S | 150.57 E |
| Smithfield, On., Can. | 212 | 44.04 N | 77.41 W |
| Smithfield, S. Afr. | 158 | 30.09 S | 26.30 E |
| Smithfield, Eng., U.K. | 44 | 54.59 N | 2.52 W |
| Smithfield, N.C., U.S. | 192 | 35.30 N | 78.20 W |
| Smithfield, Oh., U.S. | 214 | 40.16 N | 80.46 W |
| Smithfield, Pa., U.S. | 214 | 39.48 N | 79.48 W |
| Smithfield, Ut,. U.S. | 200 | 41.50 N | 111.49 W |
| Smithfield, Va., U.S. | 208 | 36.58 N | 76.37 W |
| Smithflat | 226 | 38.44 N | 120.45 W |
| Smith Haven Mall ◆[9] | 276 | 40.52 N | 73.08 W |
| Smithills Hall ⊥ | 262 | 53.36 N | 2.27 W |
| Smith Island I, Ant. | 9 | 62.59 S | 62.32 W |
| Smith Island I, N.C., U.S. | 192 | 33.52 N | 77.59 W |
| Smith Island I, Va., U.S. | 208 | 37.10 N | 75.51 W |
| Smith Island I, Wa., U.S. | 224 | 48.19 N | 122.50 W |
| Smith Island II | 208 | 38.01 N | 76.02 W |
| Smithland | 194 | 37.08 N | 88.24 W |
| Smithmill | 214 | 40.46 N | 78.25 W |
| Smith Mountain ʌ | 280 | 34.17 N | 117.52 W |
| Smith Mountain Lake ⊜[1] | 192 | 37.10 N | 79.40 W |
| Smith Peak ʌ | 202 | 48.50 N | 116.39 W |
| Smith Peninsula ›[1] | 9 | 74.25 S | 61.15 W |
| Smith Point | 222 | 29.27 N | 94.45 W |
| Smith Point ›, N.S., Can. | 186 | 45.51 N | 63.25 W |
| Smith Point ›, Tx., U.S. | 222 | 29.32 N | 94.46 W |
| Smith Point ›, Va., U.S. | 208 | 37.53 N | 76.14 W |
| Smithport | 214 | 40.50 N | 78.52 W |
| Smith River | 204 | 41.55 N | 124.08 W |
| Smiths | 194 | 32.32 N | 85.05 W |
| Smithsburg | 208 | 39.39 N | 77.34 W |
| Smiths Creek | 214 | 42.55 N | 82.36 W |
| Smiths Falls | 212 | 44.54 N | 76.01 W |
| Smiths Fork ≃ | 202 | 41.23 N | 110.12 W |
| Smiths Grove | 194 | 37.03 N | 86.12 W |
| Smiths Mills | 276 | 41.01 N | 74.22 W |
| Smith Sound ʊ | 182 | 51.18 N | 127.48 W |
| Smithton, Austl. | 166 | 40.51 S | 145.07 E |
| Smithton, Il., U.S. | 219 | 38.24 N | 89.59 W |
| Smithton, Mo., U.S. | 194 | 38.40 N | 93.05 W |
| Smithton, Pa., U.S. | 279b | 40.09 N | 79.44 W |
| Smithtown | 210 | 40.52 N | 73.13 W |
| Smithtown Bay c | 276 | 40.57 N | 73.12 W |
| Smith Valley | 218 | 39.36 N | 86.12 W |
| Smithville, On., Can. | 212 | 43.06 N | 79.33 W |
| Smithville, Ga., U.S. | 192 | 31.54 N | 84.15 W |
| Smithville, In., U.S. | 218 | 39.04 N | 86.30 W |
| Smithville, Ms., U.S. | 194 | 34.04 N | 88.23 W |
| Smithville, Mo., U.S. | 194 | 39.23 N | 94.34 W |
| Smithville, N.J., U.S. | 208 | 39.59 N | 74.44 W |
| Smithville, N.J., U.S. | 285 | 39.29 N | 74.27 W |
| Smithville, Oh., U.S. | 214 | 40.51 N | 81.51 W |
| Smithville, Tn., U.S. | 194 | 35.57 N | 85.48 W |
| Smithville, Tx., U.S. | 222 | 30.00 N | 97.09 W |
| Smithville Flats | 210 | 42.24 N | 75.49 W |
| Smithville Lake ⊜[1] | 194 | 39.25 N | 94.30 W |
| Smögen | 26 | 58.21 N | 11.13 E |
| Smoke Creek ≃, Mt., U.S. | 198 | 48.18 N | 104.41 W |
| Smoke Creek ≃, N.Y., U.S. | 284a | 42.49 N | 78.52 W |
| Smoke Creek, South Branch ≃ | 284a | 42.49 N | 78.49 W |
| Smoke Creek Desert ◆[2] | 204 | 40.30 N | 119.40 W |
| Smoke Lake ⊜ | 212 | 45.32 N | 78.41 W |
| Smokeless | 214 | 40.24 N | 76.02 W |
| Smokerun | 214 | 40.48 N | 78.26 W |
| Smoketown | 208 | 40.02 N | 76.12 W |
| Smokey, Cape › | 186 | 46.38 N | 60.21 W |
| Smokey Dome ʌ | 202 | 43.29 N | 114.56 W |
| Smoky ≃ | 182 | 56.10 N | 117.21 W |
| Smoky Bay | 162 | 32.22 S | 133.56 E |
| Smoky Cape › | 166 | 30.56 S | 153.05 E |
| Smoky Hill ≃ | 198 | 39.03 N | 96.48 W |
| Smoky Hill, North Fork ≃ | 198 | 38.55 N | 101.17 W |
| Smoky Lake | 182 | 54.07 N | 112.28 W |
| Smøla I | 24 | 63.24 N | 8.00 E |
| Smol'aninovo | 89 | 43.19 N | 132.28 E |
| Smolensk | 76 | 54.47 N | 32.03 E |
| Smolenskaja vozvyšennost' ⩘[1] | 76 | 54.30 N | 33.00 E |
| Smolensk Oblast' □[4] | 76 | 55.00 N | 33.00 E |
| Smolenskoje | 86 | 52.20 N | 85.05 E |
| Smólikas ʌ | 38 | 40.06 N | 20.52 E |
| Smoljan | 38 | 41.35 N | 24.41 E |
| Smolny ᵾ | 265a | 59.57 N | 30.24 E |
| Smoot | 200 | 42.37 N | 110.54 W |
| Smoothstone ≃ | 184 | 55.20 N | 106.39 W |
| Smoothstone Lake ⊜ | 184 | 54.40 N | 106.50 W |
| Smorodovka | 76 | 57.08 N | 29.52 E |
| Smotrych | 78 | 48.56 N | 26.34 E |
| Smotrych ≃ | 78 | 48.34 N | 26.38 E |
| Smuškovoje | 80 | 47.20 N | 45.55 E |
| Smyčka | 82 | 56.04 N | 35.56 E |
| Smygehamn | 41 | 55.21 N | 13.22 E |
| Smygehuk › | 41 | 55.21 N | 13.23 E |
| Smyley Island I | 9 | 72.55 S | 78.00 W |
| Smyrna → İzmir, Tür. | 130 | 38.25 N | 27.09 E |
| Smyrna, De., U.S. | 208 | 39.17 N | 75.36 W |
| Smyrna, Ga., U.S. | 192 | 33.53 N | 84.30 W |
| Smyrna, N.Y., U.S. | 210 | 42.41 N | 75.34 W |
| Smyrna, Tn., U.S. | 194 | 35.58 N | 86.31 W |
| Smyrna ≃ | 208 | 39.22 N | 75.31 W |
| Smyšl'ajevka | 80 | 53.15 N | 50.22 E |
| Smyth, Canal ʊ | 254 | 52.15 S | 73.40 W |
| Smythe, Mount ʌ | 176 | 57.54 N | 124.53 W |
| Smythe Park ♠ | 275b | 43.41 N | 79.30 W |
| Smythesdale | 169 | 37.38 S | 143.41 E |
| Sn'adin | 78 | 52.04 N | 28.19 E |
| Snæfell ʌ, Ísland | 24a | 64.48 N | 15.32 W |
| Snaefell ʌ, I. of Man | 44 | 54.16 N | 4.27 W |
| Snæfellsness ›[1] | 24a | 64.50 N | 23.00 W |
| Snag | 180 | 62.24 N | 140.22 W |
| Snaght, Slieve ʌ | 48 | 55.12 N | 7.20 W |
| Snagost' | 78 | 51.21 N | 34.54 E |
| Snahapish ≃ | 224 | 47.38 N | 124.11 W |
| Snaith | 44 | 53.41 N | 1.02 W |
| Šn'ajevo | 80 | 52.34 N | 46.11 E |
| Snake ≃, Yk., Can. | 180 | 65.58 N | 134.10 W |
| Snake ≃, U.S. | 202 | 46.12 N | 119.02 W |
| Snake ≃, Ca., U.S. | 226 | 39.07 N | 121.43 W |
| Snake ≃, Mn., U.S. | 190 | 45.49 N | 92.46 W |
| Snake ≃, Mn., U.S. | 198 | 48.26 N | 97.07 W |
| Snake ≃, Ne., U.S. | 198 | 42.47 N | 100.48 W |
| Snake Bight c[3] | 220 | 25.10 N | 80.50 W |
| Snake Brook ≃ | 283 | 42.18 N | 71.22 W |
| Snake Creek ≃, Mt., U.S. | 202 | 48.32 N | 108.53 W |
| Snake Creek ≃, Ne., U.S. | 198 | 42.01 N | 102.45 W |
| Snake Creek ≃, S.D., U.S. | 198 | 44.58 N | 98.29 W |
| Snake Creek, South Fork ≃ | 198 | 45.02 N | 98.36 W |
| Snake Creek Canal ≋ | 220 | 25.57 N | 80.11 W |
| Snake Indian ≃ | 182 | 53.11 N | 118.00 W |
| Snake Range ⩘ | 204 | 39.00 N | 114.15 W |
| Snake Rapids ⌞ | 212 | 45.14 N | 77.20 W |
| Snake River Plain ≚ | 202 | 43.00 N | 113.00 W |
| Snake Valley | 169 | 37.37 S | 143.35 E |
| Snake Valley V | 204 | 39.20 N | 113.55 W |
| Snape | 42 | 52.11 N | 1.30 E |
| Snaptun | 41 | 55.49 N | 10.04 E |
| Snares Islands II | 9 | 48.00 S | 166.30 E |
| Snasahögarna ʌ | 26 | 63.13 N | 12.21 E |
| Snay Pôl | 110 | 11.40 N | 105.13 E |
| Sneads | 192 | 30.42 N | 84.55 W |
| Snedsted | 26 | 56.54 N | 8.32 E |
| Sneedville | 192 | 36.31 N | 83.13 W |
| Sneek | 52 | 53.02 N | 5.40 E |
| Sneekermeer ⊜ | 52 | 53.02 N | 5.45 E |
| Snee-osh-Beach | 224 | 48.24 N | 122.33 W |
| Sneeuberg ʌ | 158 | 32.25 S | 19.12 E |
| Sneeuberg ⩘ | 158 | 31.46 S | 24.20 E |
| Snekkersten | 41 | 56.00 N | 12.36 E |
| Snelgrove | 275b | 43.44 N | 79.49 W |
| Snelling | 204 | 37.31 N | 120.26 W |
| Snettisham | 42 | 52.53 N | 0.30 E |
| Sněžka ʌ | 30 | 50.44 N | 15.44 E |
| Snežnaja ≃ | 88 | 51.28 N | 104.38 E |
| Snežnik ʌ | 36 | 45.35 N | 14.27 E |
| Śniardwy, Jezioro ⊜ | 30 | 53.46 N | 21.44 E |
| Snicarte | 219 | 40.07 N | 90.14 W |
| Snicarte Island I | 219 | 40.08 N | 90.12 W |
| Snihurivka | 78 | 47.06 N | 32.47 E |
| Snina | 30 | 48.59 N | 22.07 E |
| Snipe Keys II | 220 | 24.40 N | 81.38 W |
| Snipe Lake ⊜ | 182 | 55.07 N | 116.46 W |
| Snizhne | 83 | 48.01 N | 38.46 E |
| Snizort, Loch c | 46 | 57.34 N | 6.28 W |
| Snøde | 41 | 55.05 N | 10.55 E |
| Snodland | 42 | 51.20 N | 0.27 E |
| Snoghøj | 41 | 55.31 N | 9.43 E |
| Snøhetta ʌ | 26 | 62.20 N | 9.17 E |
| Snohomish | 224 | 47.54 N | 122.05 W |
| Snohomish □[6] | 224 | 48.02 N | 121.41 W |
| Snohomish ≃ | 224 | 48.01 N | 122.13 W |
| Snønipa ʌ | 26 | 61.42 N | 6.41 E |
| Snook | 222 | 30.29 N | 96.28 W |
| Snoqualmie | 224 | 47.31 N | 121.49 W |
| Snoqualmie ≃ | 224 | 47.50 N | 122.03 W |
| Snoqualmie, Middle Fork ≃ | 224 | 47.31 N | 121.46 W |
| Snoqualmie, North Fork ≃ | 224 | 47.31 N | 121.46 W |
| Snoqualmie, South Fork ≃ | 224 | 47.31 N | 121.46 W |
| Snoqualmie Falls | 224 | 47.32 N | 121.49 W |
| Snoqualmie Mountain ʌ | 224 | 47.27 N | 121.25 W |
| Snoqualmie Pass )( | 224 | 47.25 N | 121.25 W |
| Snøtinden ʌ | 24 | 66.38 N | 14.00 E |
| Snoụ | 76 | 53.13 N | 26.24 E |
| Snov ≃ | 78 | 51.45 N | 31.45 E |
| Snover | 190 | 43.27 N | 82.58 W |
| Snowbird Lake ⊜ | 176 | 60.41 N | 103.00 W |
| Snow Canyon State Park ♠ | 200 | 37.11 N | 113.42 W |
| Snow Creek ≃ | 224 | 47.59 N | 122.53 W |
| Snowden, Sk., Can. | 184 | 53.30 N | 104.41 W |
| Snowden, Pa., U.S. | 279b | 40.16 N | 79.58 W |
| Snowden Oaks | 284c | 39.04 N | 76.52 W |
| Snowdenville | 285 | 40.11 N | 75.36 W |
| Snowdon ʌ | 44 | 53.04 N | 4.05 W |
| Snowdonia National Park ♠ | 28 | 53.00 N | 3.57 W |
| Snowdoun | 194 | 32.14 N | 86.17 W |
| Snowdrift | 176 | 62.23 N | 110.47 W |
| Snowflake | 200 | 34.30 N | 110.04 W |
| Snow Hill, Md., U.S. | 208 | 38.10 N | 75.23 W |
| Snow Hill, N.C., U.S. | 192 | 35.27 N | 77.40 W |
| Snowking Mountain ʌ | 224 | 48.24 N | 121.17 W |
| Snow Lake | 184 | 54.53 N | 100.02 W |
| Snow Lakes ⊜ | 224 | 47.29 N | 120.45 W |
| Snowmass Mountain ʌ | 200 | 39.07 N | 107.04 W |
| Snow Mountain ʌ | 226 | 39.23 N | 122.45 W |
| Snow Peak ʌ | 202 | 48.35 N | 118.29 W |
| Snows Brook ≃ | 283 | 42.47 N | 71.06 W |
| Snow Shoe | 214 | 41.02 N | 77.57 W |
| Snowshoe Butte ʌ | 224 | 47.13 N | 121.22 W |
| Snowshoe Peak ʌ | 202 | 48.13 N | 115.41 W |
| Snowtown | 166 | 33.47 S | 138.13 E |
| Snow Water Lake ⊜ | 204 | 41.07 N | 115.00 W |
| Snowy ≃ | 166 | 37.48 S | 148.32 E |
| Snowy Mountain ʌ | 188 | 43.42 N | 74.23 W |
| Snowy Mountains ⩘ | 166 | 36.30 S | 148.20 E |
| Snowyside Peak ʌ | 202 | 43.57 N | 114.58 W |
| Snubba Range ⩘ | 171b | 35.40 S | 148.10 E |
| Snuöl | 110 | 12.04 N | 106.26 E |
| Snyatyn | 78 | 48.28 N | 25.34 E |
| Snyder, Ok., U.S. | 196 | 34.39 N | 98.57 W |
| Snyder, Tx., U.S. | 196 | 32.43 N | 100.55 W |
| Snyder □[6] | 210 | 40.47 N | 77.03 W |
| Snydertown | 210 | 40.53 N | 76.40 W |
| Soacha | 246 | 4.35 N | 74.13 W |
| Soahany | 157b | 18.42 S | 44.13 E |
| Soaker, Mount ʌ | 172 | 45.23 S | 167.15 E |
| Soalala | 157b | 16.06 S | 45.20 E |
| Soalara | 157b | 23.36 S | 43.44 E |
| Soaloka | 157b | 18.32 S | 45.15 E |
| Sŏam | 98 | 38.01 N | 126.43 E |
| Soamanonga | 157b | 23.52 S | 44.47 E |
| Soān ≃ | 123 | 33.01 N | 71.44 E |
| Soan-do I | 98 | 34.09 N | 126.39 E |
| Soanierana Ivongo | 157b | 16.55 S | 49.35 E |
| Soanindrariny | 157b | 19.54 S | 47.14 E |
| Soap Creek ≃ | 190 | 40.55 N | 92.14 W |
| Soap Lake | 202 | 47.23 N | 119.29 W |
| Soasiu → Tidore | 108 | 0.40 N | 127.26 E |
| Soatá | 246 | 6.20 N | 72.41 W |
| Soavina | 157b | 20.23 S | 46.56 E |
| Soavinandriana | 157b | 19.09 S | 46.45 E |
| Soay I | 46 | 57.08 N | 6.14 W |
| Soazza | 58 | 46.22 N | 9.13 E |
| Sob ≃ | 78 | 48.42 N | 29.17 E |
| Sobaek-sanmaek ⩘ | 98 | 36.00 N | 128.00 E |
| Sobat ≃ | 140 | 9.22 N | 31.33 E |
| Sobernheim | 56 | 49.47 N | 7.38 E |
| Soběšice | 60 | 49.12 N | 13.41 E |
| Soběslav | 30 | 49.15 N | 14.44 E |
| Sobger ≃ | 164 | 3.44 S | 140.20 E |
| Sobinka | 80 | 55.59 N | 40.01 E |
| Soboba Indian Reservation ◆[4] | 228 | 33.47 N | 116.54 W |
| Soboko | 140 | 6.49 N | 24.50 E |
| Sobolekovo | 80 | 55.39 N | 51.53 E |
| Sobolev | 80 | 51.56 N | 51.43 E |
| Sobolevo | 82 | 55.31 N | 38.43 E |
| Sobolino | 88 | 53.23 N | 119.42 E |
| Sobolivka | 78 | 48.36 N | 29.30 E |
| Sobótka | 30 | 50.55 N | 16.45 E |
| Sobradinho | 252 | 29.24 S | 53.03 W |
| Sobradinho, Reprêsa de ⊜[1] | 250 | 9.40 S | 42.00 W |
| Sobrado | 34 | 41.02 N | 8.16 W |
| Sobral | 250 | 3.42 S | 40.21 W |
| Sobrance | 30 | 48.45 N | 22.11 E |
| Sobrante Ridge ʌ | 282 | 37.58 N | 122.15 W |
| Sobrarbe ◆[1] | 34 | 42.22 N | 0.10 E |
| Sobue | 94 | 35.15 N | 136.43 E |
| Søby | 41 | 54.56 N | 10.16 E |
| Sobych | 78 | 51.52 N | 33.14 E |
| Soča | 64 | 46.20 N | 13.39 E |
| Soča (Isonzo) ≃ | 64 | 45.47 N | 13.32 E |
| Socaire | 252 | 23.36 S | 67.51 W |
| Socchieve | 64 | 46.25 N | 12.52 E |
| Soc Giang | 110 | 22.54 N | 106.01 E |
| Socgorodok | 78 | 50.11 N | 38.09 E |
| Soch | 85 | 39.57 N | 71.08 E |
| Soch ≃ | 85 | 40.20 N | 71.02 E |
| Sochaczew | 30 | 52.14 N | 20.14 E |
| Sochaux | 58 | 47.31 N | 6.50 E |
| Soch'e → Shache | 120 | 38.25 N | 77.16 E |
| Sochi → Soči | 84 | 43.35 N | 39.45 E |
| Sŏch'ŏn | 98 | 36.05 N | 126.41 E |
| Sochondo | 88 | 51.49 N | 112.32 E |
| Sochondo, gora ʌ | 88 | 49.44 N | 111.05 E |
| Soch'ŏng-do I | 98 | 37.46 N | 124.45 E |
| Sochor, gora ʌ | 88 | 51.18 N | 105.15 E |
| Soči | 84 | 43.35 N | 39.45 E |
| Social Circle | 192 | 33.39 N | 83.43 W |
| Social Security Administration ᵾ | 284b | 39.19 N | 76.44 W |
| Sociedade Hípica Paulista ♠ | 287b | 23.36 S | 46.41 W |
| Société, Archipel de la (Society Islands) II | 14 | 17.00 S | 150.00 W |
| Society Hill | 192 | 34.30 N | 79.51 W |
| Society Islands → Société, Archipel de la II | 14 | 17.00 S | 150.00 W |
| Society Ridge ✣[3] | 14 | 17.00 S | 151.00 W |
| Soco ≃ | 238 | 18.27 N | 69.12 W |
| Socoltenango | 232 | 16.13 N | 92.15 W |
| Socompa, Paso )( | 252 | 24.27 S | 68.18 W |
| Soconusco, Sierra de → Madre, Sierra ⩘ | 236 | 15.20 N | 92.20 W |
| Socorro, Bra. | 256 | 22.36 S | 46.32 W |
| Socorro, Col. | 246 | 6.29 N | 73.16 W |
| Socorro, Pil. | 116 | 9.37 N | 125.58 E |
| Socorro, N.M., U.S. | 200 | 34.03 N | 106.53 W |
| Socorro, Tx., U.S. | 200 | 31.39 N | 106.18 W |
| Socorro ◆[8] | 287b | 23.39 S | 46.42 W |
| Socorro, Isla I | 232 | 18.45 N | 110.58 W |
| Socota | 248 | 6.18 S | 78.44 W |
| Socotora, Isla → Suquṭrā I | 118 | 12.30 N | 54.00 E |
| Socotra → Suquṭrā I | 118 | 12.30 N | 54.00 E |
| Soc Trang | 110 | 9.36 N | 105.58 E |
| Socuéllamos | 34 | 39.17 N | 2.48 W |
| Soda Creek | 182 | 52.21 N | 122.18 W |
| Soda Creek ≃ | 226 | 38.48 N | 122.29 W |
| Soda Lake ⊜, Ca., U.S. | 204 | 35.08 N | 116.04 W |
| Soda Lake ⊜, Ca., U.S. | 226 | 35.15 N | 119.53 W |
| Sodankylä | 24 | 67.29 N | 26.32 E |
| Soda Springs | 202 | 42.39 N | 111.36 W |
| Soddy-Daisy | 194 | 35.16 N | 85.10 W |
| Sodegaura | 94 | 35.26 N | 139.57 E |
| Söderälgen ⊜ | 40 | 59.43 N | 14.35 E |
| Söderåsen ⩘[2] | 41 | 56.04 N | 13.05 E |
| Söderbärke | 40 | 60.05 N | 15.33 E |
| Söderby-Karl | 40 | 59.53 N | 18.41 E |
| Söderfors | 40 | 60.23 N | 17.14 E |
| Söderhamn | 26 | 61.18 N | 17.03 E |
| Söderköping | 26 | 58.29 N | 16.18 E |
| Södermanland □[9] | 41 | 59.12 N | 16.49 E |
| Södermanlands Län □[6] | 40 | 59.15 N | 16.40 E |
| Södernmanland □[9] | 40 | 59.12 N | 16.49 E |
| Söderslätt □[9] | 41 | 55.29 N | 13.15 E |
| Södertälje | 40 | 59.12 N | 17.37 E |
| Södertörn ›[1] | 40 | 59.05 N | 18.00 E |
| Sodhra | 123 | 32.28 N | 74.11 E |
| Sodingen ◆[8] | 263 | 51.32 N | 7.15 E |
| Sodium | 158 | 30.11 S | 23.09 E |
| Sodo | 144 | 6.52 N | 37.47 E |
| Sodom → Sedom ⊥ | 132 | 31.04 N | 35.23 E |
| Sodpur | 272b | 22.39 N | 88.23 E |
| Södra Björkfjärden c | 40 | 59.18 N | 17.32 E |
| Södra Hörken ⊜ | 40 | 60.02 N | 15.02 E |
| Södra Kvarken ʊ | 26 | 60.15 N | 19.05 E |
| Södra Råda | 40 | 59.01 N | 14.10 E |
| Södra Sandby | 41 | 55.43 N | 13.20 E |
| Södra Vi | 26 | 57.45 N | 15.48 E |
| Sodražica | 36 | 45.46 N | 14.38 E |
| Sodus | 210 | 43.14 N | 77.03 W |
| Sodus Bay c | 210 | 43.15 N | 76.58 W |
| Sodus Creek ≃ | 210 | 43.13 N | 76.56 W |
| Sodus Point | 210 | 43.16 N | 76.59 W |
| Sŏdu-su ≃ | 98 | 42.05 N | 129.00 E |
| Sodwalls | 170 | 33.31 S | 149.59 E |
| Sodwana Bay National Park ♠ | 158 | 27.30 S | 32.39 E |
| Soe | 112 | 9.52 S | 124.17 E |
| Soeda | 96 | 33.34 N | 130.52 E |
| Soekmekaar | 156 | 23.28 S | 29.58 E |
| Soela väin ʊ | 76 | 58.40 N | 22.35 E |
| Soerabaja → Surabaya | 115a | 7.15 S | 112.45 E |
| Soest, Dtsch. | 52 | 51.34 N | 8.07 E |
| Soest, Ned. | 52 | 52.09 N | 5.18 E |
| Soestdijk | 52 | 52.11 N | 5.18 E |
| Soestdijk, Paleis ᵾ | 52 | 52.12 N | 5.15 E |
| Soeste ≃ | 52 | 53.10 N | 7.44 E |
| Soesterberg | 52 | 52.07 N | 5.17 E |
| Soeurs, Île des I | 275a | 45.28 N | 73.33 W |
| Sofádhes | 38 | 39.20 N | 22.06 E |
| Sofala | 170 | 33.05 S | 149.42 E |
| Sofala □[5] | 156 | 19.00 S | 35.00 E |
| Sofia → Sofija | 38 | 42.41 N | 23.19 E |
| Sofia ≃ | 157b | 15.27 S | 47.23 E |
| Sofiero | 41 | 56.05 N | 12.39 E |
| Sofija (Sofia) | 38 | 42.41 N | 23.19 E |
| Sofija □[4] | 38 | 42.17 N | 23.16 E |
| Sofijsk, Ross. | 89 | 51.34 N | 139.52 E |
| Sofijsk, Ross. | 89 | 52.15 N | 133.58 E |
| Sofiyivka, Ukr. | 78 | 46.33 N | 34.03 E |
| Sofiyivka, Ukr. | 78 | 48.04 N | 33.52 E |
| Sofiyivs'kyy | 83 | 48.12 N | 38.52 E |
| Sofjanga | 24 | 65.52 N | 31.15 E |
| Sofjino | 82 | 55.30 N | 38.11 E |
| Sofrino | 82 | 56.09 N | 37.56 E |
| Sofronovo | 76 | 59.48 N | 36.54 E |
| Sogakofe | 150 | 6.00 N | 0.36 E |
| Sogamoso | 246 | 5.43 N | 72.56 W |
| Sogamoso ≃ | 246 | 7.13 N | 73.56 W |
| Soğanlı ≃ | 130 | 41.11 N | 32.38 E |
| Soğanlı Geçidi )( | 130 | 40.33 N | 40.16 E |
| Soğanlıköy ◆[8] | 267b | 40.55 N | 29.12 E |
| Sogcho → Sokch'o | 98 | 38.12 N | 128.36 E |
| Sogda | 89 | 50.24 N | 132.12 E |
| Sögel | 52 | 52.50 N | 7.31 E |
| Sogen | 164 | 9.25 S | 147.25 E |
| Sogindy | 85 | 43.27 N | 74.38 E |
| Sogliano al Rubicone | 66 | 44.00 N | 12.18 E |
| Sognafjorden c[2] | 26 | 61.06 N | 5.10 E |
| Søgne | 26 | 58.05 N | 7.49 E |
| Sogne Fjord → Sognafjorden c[2] | 26 | 61.06 N | 5.10 E |
| Sogn og Fjordane □[6] | 26 | 61.30 N | 6.50 E |
| Sogod, Pil. | 116 | 10.45 N | 124.00 E |
| Sogod, Pil. | 116 | 10.23 N | 124.59 E |
| Sogod Bay c | 116 | 10.15 N | 125.02 E |
| Sogo Nur ⊜ | 102 | 42.18 N | 101.08 E |
| Sogoža ≃ | 76 | 58.28 N | 39.06 E |
| Sogri-san Kukrip Kongwŏn ♠ | 98 | 36.33 N | 127.52 E |
| Soğuksu Milli Parkı ♠ | 130 | 40.25 N | 32.35 E |
| Söğüt | 130 | 40.00 N | 30.11 E |
| Söğütalan | 130 | 40.03 N | 28.34 E |
| Söğüt Gölü ⊜ | 130 | 37.03 N | 29.53 E |
| Söğütlü | 130 | 40.54 N | 30.29 E |
| Sog Xian | 120 | 31.50 N | 93.45 E |
| Sohāg → Sawhāj | 140 | 26.33 N | 31.42 E |
| Sohāgpur, India | 124 | 23.19 N | 81.21 E |
| Sohāgpur, India | 124 | 22.42 N | 78.12 E |
| Soham | 42 | 52.20 N | 0.20 E |
| Sohano | 175e | 5.27 S | 154.40 E |
| Soharkha | 272a | 28.35 N | 77.24 E |
| Soheit-Tinlot | 56 | 50.29 N | 5.22 E |
| Sohland | 54 | 51.02 N | 14.25 E |
| Söhlde | 52 | 52.11 N | 10.14 E |
| Sohna | 124 | 28.15 N | 77.04 E |
| Sŏhŭng | 98 | 38.27 N | 126.10 E |
| Sŏhwa-ri | 98 | 38.15 N | 128.13 E |
| Soignies (Zinnik) | 50 | 50.35 N | 4.04 E |
| Soignolles-en-Brie | 261 | 48.39 N | 2.42 E |
| Soin | 150 | 12.47 N | 3.49 W |
| Soindres | 261 | 48.57 N | 1.40 E |
| Soini | 26 | 62.52 N | 24.13 E |
| Sointula | 182 | 50.38 N | 127.01 W |
| Soira ʌ | 144 | 14.45 N | 39.32 E |
| Soisalo ʌ | 26 | 62.40 N | 28.10 E |
| Soissons | 50 | 49.22 N | 3.20 E |
| Soisy-sous-Montmorency | 261 | 48.59 N | 2.18 E |
| Soisy-sur-Seine | 261 | 48.39 N | 2.27 E |
| Sōja | 96 | 34.40 N | 133.45 E |
| Sojana | 24 | 65.48 N | 43.20 E |
| Sojat | 120 | 25.55 N | 73.40 E |
| Šojda | 24 | 61.11 N | 37.40 E |
| Sojiji Temple ᵾ[1] | 268 | 35.31 N | 139.41 E |
| Sojītra | 120 | 22.33 N | 72.43 E |
| Šojna | 24 | 67.52 N | 44.08 E |
| Sŏjosŏn-man c | 98 | 39.20 N | 124.50 E |
| Sojoton Point › | 116 | 9.58 N | 122.27 E |
| Sok ≃ | 80 | 53.24 N | 50.08 E |
| Sōka, Nihon | 94 | 35.49 N | 139.48 E |
| Soka, Taehan | 271b | 37.30 N | 126.48 E |
| Sokal' | 78 | 50.29 N | 24.17 E |
| Šokal'skogo, proliv ʊ | 74 | 79.00 N | 100.25 E |
| Sokch'o | 98 | 38.12 N | 128.36 E |
| Söke | 130 | 37.45 N | 27.24 E |
| Sokehs Passage ʊ | 174r | 7.01 N | 158.11 E |
| Sokele | 154 | 9.55 S | 24.36 E |
| Sokhós | 38 | 40.49 N | 23.21 E |
| Sokna | 26 | 60.14 N | 9.54 E |
| Sokodé | 150 | 8.59 N | 1.08 E |
| Sokol, Ross. | 74 | 72.24 N | 126.48 E |
| Sokol, Ross. | 76 | 59.28 N | 40.10 E |
| Sokol, Ross. | 89 | 47.14 N | 142.45 E |
| Sokol ʌ | 60 | 49.03 N | 13.31 E |
| Sokółka, Pol. | 30 | 53.25 N | 23.31 E |
| Sokolka, Ross. | 80 | 55.34 N | 51.30 E |
| Sokol'niki ◆[8] | 265b | 55.48 N | 37.41 E |
| Sokolniki Park ♠ | 265b | 55.48 N | 37.41 E |
| Sokol'nikovo | 82 | 55.21 N | 35.49 E |
| Sokolo | 150 | 14.44 N | 6.08 W |
| Sokolohirne | 78 | 46.29 N | 34.58 E |
| Sokolov | 54 | 50.09 N | 12.40 E |
| Sokolova Hora | 78 | 50.19 N | 28.36 E |
| Sokolova Pustyn' | 82 | 54.51 N | 38.03 E |
| Sokolovka | 86 | 55.06 N | 69.12 E |
| Sokolovo, Ross. | 24 | 65.21 N | 56.57 E |
| Sokolovo, Ross. | 76 | 52.55 N | 34.39 E |
| Sokolovo, Ross. | 80 | 52.49 N | 42.26 E |
| Sokolovo, Ross. | 82 | 56.02 N | 36.55 E |
| Sokolovo, Ross. | 86 | 52.33 N | 84.46 E |
| Sokolovo-Kundr'učenskij | 83 | 47.50 N | 39.57 E |
| Sokołów | 30 | 50.14 N | 22.07 E |
| Sokołów Podlaski | 30 | 52.25 N | 22.15 E |
| Sokol'skoje | 80 | 57.08 N | 43.13 E |
| Sokone | 150 | 13.53 N | 16.22 W |
| Sokoto | 150 | 13.04 N | 5.16 E |
| Sokoto ≃ | 150 | 11.20 N | 4.10 E |
| Sŏkp'o-ri | 98 | 37.46 N | 125.27 E |
| Sokrutovka | 80 | 47.54 N | 46.33 E |
| Šokša | 76 | 58.24 N | 42.27 E |
| Soksa-ri | 98 | 40.40 N | 127.17 E |
| Sokskije jary ⩘[2] | 80 | 54.10 N | 51.30 E |
| Sŏk-to I | 98 | 38.40 N | 125.00 E |
| Sokuluk | 85 | 42.52 N | 74.18 E |
| Sokur, Ross. | 80 | 52.01 N | 45.48 E |
| Sokur, Ross. | 86 | 55.13 N | 83.13 E |
| Sokyryany | 78 | 48.27 N | 27.25 E |
| Sokyryntsi | 78 | 50.42 N | 32.46 E |
| Sol' | 30 | 48.56 N | 21.36 E |
| Sol, Costa del ⊻[2] | 34 | 36.40 N | 4.00 W |
| Sola, Nor. | 26 | 58.53 N | 5.36 E |
| Sola, Vanuatu | 175f | 13.53 S | 167.33 E |
| Sola, Zaïre | 154 | 5.09 S | 27.06 E |
| Soła ≃ | 30 | 50.04 N | 19.13 E |
| Solacolu | 38 | 44.23 N | 26.34 E |
| Solai | 154 | 0.02 N | 36.09 E |
| Šolaksaj | 86 | 51.45 N | 64.48 E |
| Solan | 123 | 30.55 N | 77.07 E |
| Solana | 220 | 26.56 N | 82.01 W |
| Solana Beach | 228 | 32.59 N | 117.16 W |
| Solander, Cape › | 274a | 34.01 S | 151.14 E |
| Solander Island I | 172 | 46.34 S | 166.53 E |
| Solânea | 250 | 6.45 S | 35.39 W |
| Solangāri | 272b | 22.36 N | 88.27 E |
| Sol'anka ≃ | 80 | 50.10 N | 51.20 E |
| Solano | 116 | 16.31 N | 121.11 E |
| Solano □[6] | 226 | 38.15 N | 121.52 W |
| Solāpur | 122 | 17.41 N | 75.55 E |
| Solar, Morro ʌ[2] | 286d | 12.11 S | 77.02 W |
| Solarino | 70 | 37.06 N | 15.07 E |
| Solaro | 266b | 45.37 N | 9.05 E |
| Solaro, Monte ʌ | 68 | 40.33 N | 14.13 E |
| Solberg | 26 | 63.47 N | 17.38 E |
| Solbiate Arno | 62 | 45.42 N | 8.48 E |
| Solbiate Olona | 266b | 45.39 N | 8.53 E |
| Solca, Arg. | 252 | 30.46 S | 66.28 W |
| Solca, Rom. | 38 | 47.42 N | 25.50 E |
| Solčava | 61 | 46.25 N | 14.41 E |
| Sol'cy | 76 | 58.08 N | 30.20 E |
| Solda Gölü ⊜ | 130 | 37.33 N | 29.42 E |
| Soldatskaja | 84 | 43.48 N | 43.49 E |
| Soldatskoje | 85 | 40.52 N | 68.56 E |
| Soldatsko-Stepnoje | 80 | 49.32 N | 45.30 E |
| Sölde ◆[8] | 263 | 51.31 N | 7.35 E |
| Sol de Julio | 252 | 29.33 S | 63.27 W |
| Sölden | 64 | 46.58 N | 11.00 E |
| Sölderholz ◆[8] | 263 | 51.29 N | 7.35 E |
| Soldier Creek ≃ | 198 | 39.04 N | 95.39 W |
| Soldier Field ♠ | 278 | 41.52 N | 87.37 W |
| Soldier Key I | 220 | 25.35 N | 80.10 W |
| Soldier Point › | 240c | 17.02 N | 61.41 W |
| Soldier Pond | 186 | 47.09 N | 68.34 W |
| Soldiers Grove | 190 | 43.23 N | 90.46 W |
| Soldotna | 180 | 60.29 N | 151.04 W |
| Sole, Val di V | 64 | 46.20 N | 10.45 E |
| Solebury | 208 | 40.23 N | 75.02 W |
| Solec Kujawski | 30 | 53.06 N | 18.14 E |
| Soledad, Col. | 246 | 10.55 N | 74.46 W |
| Soledad, Ca., U.S. | 226 | 36.25 N | 121.19 W |
| Soledad, Ven. | 246 | 8.10 N | 63.34 W |
| Soledad, Cerro ʌ | 196 | 26.29 N | 103.23 W |
| Soledad de Doblado | 234 | 19.03 N | 96.25 W |
| Soledad Díez Gutiérrez | 234 | 22.12 N | 100.57 W |
| Soledade | 252 | 28.50 S | 52.30 W |
| Soledade de Minas | 256 | 22.04 S | 45.03 W |
| Soledad Pass )( | 228 | 34.30 N | 118.07 W |
| Soleduck ≃ | 224 | 47.55 N | 124.35 W |
| Solemar | 256 | 24.05 S | 46.36 W |
| Solen | 198 | 46.23 N | 100.47 W |
| Sølen ʌ | 26 | 61.55 N | 11.30 E |
| Solenoje | 80 | 46.14 N | 42.32 E |
| Solentiname, Archipiélago de II | 236 | 11.10 N | 85.00 W |
| Solenzara | 36 | 41.51 N | 9.23 E |
| Solenzo | 150 | 12.11 N | 4.05 W |
| Solero | 62 | 44.55 N | 8.30 E |
| Solers | 261 | 48.40 N | 2.43 E |
| Solesmes | 50 | 50.11 N | 3.30 E |
| Soleure → Solothurn | 58 | 47.13 N | 7.32 E |
| Solferino | 64 | 45.23 N | 10.34 E |
| Solginskij | 24 | 61.05 N | 41.19 E |
| Solgne | 56 | 48.58 N | 6.18 E |
| Solgonskij kr'až ʌ | 86 | 55.30 N | 91.00 E |
| Solhan | 130 | 38.58 N | 41.03 E |
| Solheim, Nor. | 26 | 60.53 N | 5.27 E |
| Solheim, S. Afr. | 273d | 26.11 S | 28.10 E |
| Soliera | 64 | 44.45 N | 10.55 E |
| Soligalič | 76 | 59.05 N | 42.17 E |
| Solignac-sur-Loire | 62 | 44.58 N | 3.53 E |
| Soligny-la-Trappe | 50 | 48.37 N | 0.32 E |
| Solihull | 42 | 52.25 N | 1.45 W |
| Solikamsk | 86 | 59.39 N | 56.47 E |
| Solila | 157b | 21.25 S | 46.37 E |
| Sol'-Ileck | 86 | 51.10 N | 54.59 E |
| Soliman | 148 | 36.42 N | 10.30 E |
| Solimões → Amazon ≃ | 242 | 0.10 S | 49.00 W |
| Solin ≃ | 50 | 48.02 N | 2.43 E |
| Solingen | 56 | 51.10 N | 7.05 E |
| Solís, Arg. | 258 | 34.18 S | 59.20 W |
| Solís, Ur. | 252 | 34.36 S | 55.29 W |
| Solís, Presa ⊜[1] | 234 | 20.05 N | 100.36 W |
| Soliseño | 196 | 26.01 N | 97.48 W |
| Söll | 64 | 47.30 N | 12.11 E |
| Sollar | 84 | 41.40 N | 48.38 E |
| Sollas | 46 | 57.39 N | 7.21 W |
| Sollefteå | 26 | 63.10 N | 17.16 E |
| Sollenau | 61 | 47.53 N | 16.15 E |
| Sollentuna | 40 | 59.28 N | 17.54 E |
| Sóller | 34 | 39.46 N | 2.42 E |
| Søllerød | 41 | 55.49 N | 12.31 E |
| Sollerön I | 26 | 60.55 N | 14.37 E |
| Søllested | 41 | 54.49 N | 11.17 E |
| Solliès-Pont | 62 | 43.11 N | 6.03 E |
| Solling ⩘ | 52 | 51.45 N | 9.35 E |
| Söllingen | 54 | 52.05 N | 10.55 E |
| Sollom | 262 | 53.40 N | 2.50 W |
| Sollstedt | 54 | 51.25 N | 10.31 E |
| Solms | 56 | 50.32 N | 8.24 E |
| Solna | 40 | 59.22 N | 18.01 E |
| Solncedar | 78 | 44.34 N | 38.01 E |
| Solncevo | 265b | 55.39 N | 37.24 E |
| Solnečnogorsk | 82 | 56.11 N | 36.59 E |
| Solnhofen | 56 | 48.53 N | 10.59 E |
| Solo → Surakarta | 115a | 7.35 S | 110.50 E |
| Solo ≃ | 115a | 6.47 S | 112.33 E |
| Šolochovskij | 80 | 48.18 N | 41.03 E |
| Solodča | 80 | 49.39 N | 44.17 E |
| Solodniki | 80 | 48.25 N | 45.16 E |
| Solofra | 68 | 40.50 N | 14.51 E |
| Sologne ◆[1] | 50 | 47.20 N | 2.00 E |
| Sologoncy | 74 | 66.13 N | 114.14 E |
| Solok | 112 | 0.48 S | 100.39 E |
| Sololá, Guat. | 236 | 14.46 N | 91.11 W |
| Solola, Som. | 144 | 0.07 N | 41.31 E |
| Sololá □[5] | 236 | 14.40 N | 91.15 W |
| Solomennikova | 86 | 58.20 N | 89.02 E |
| Solomennoje | 24 | 61.51 N | 34.19 E |
| Solomon, Az., U.S. | 200 | 32.48 N | 109.37 W |
| Solomon, Ks., U.S. | 198 | 38.55 N | 97.22 W |
| Solomon ≃ | 198 | 38.54 N | 97.22 W |
| Solomon, North Fork ≃ | 198 | 39.29 N | 98.26 W |
| Solomon, South Fork ≃ | 198 | 39.29 N | 98.26 W |
| Solomon Basin ✣[1] | 14 | 7.00 S | 152.00 E |
| Solomon Islands □[1] | 175e | 8.00 S | 159.00 E |
| Solomon Islands II | 175e | 8.00 S | 159.00 E |
| Solomons | 208 | 38.20 N | 76.28 W |
| Solomon Sea ⊤[2] | 14 | 8.00 S | 155.00 E |
| Solomon's Pools → Sulaymān, Birak ⊥ | 132 | 31.41 N | 35.10 E |
| Solon, Ia., U.S. | 190 | 41.48 N | 91.29 W |
| Solon, Me., U.S. | 188 | 44.56 N | 69.51 W |
| Solon, Oh., U.S. | 214 | 41.23 N | 81.26 W |
| Solon, Zhg. | 89 | 46.36 N | 121.13 E |
| Solone, Ukr. | 78 | 48.13 N | 34.52 E |
| Solone, Ukr. | 83 | 49.18 N | 37.39 E |
| Solone Ozero | 78 | 45.53 N | 34.27 E |
| Solonešnoje | 86 | 51.40 N | 84.21 E |
| Solonka | 80 | 50.13 N | 41.28 E |
| Sol'onoje | 84 | 44.03 N | 40.53 E |
| Sol'onoje, ozero ⊜ | 86 | 55.20 N | 70.05 E |
| Sol'onoje Zajmišče | 80 | 47.56 N | 46.07 E |
| Solonópole | 250 | 5.44 S | 39.01 W |
| Solon Springs | 190 | 46.21 N | 91.49 W |
| Solopaca | 68 | 41.11 N | 14.33 E |
| Solor, Kepulauan II | 112 | 8.25 S | 123.30 E |
| Solor, Pulau I | 112 | 8.27 S | 123.05 E |
| Solotča | 80 | 54.48 N | 39.51 E |
| Solothurn | 58 | 47.13 N | 7.32 E |
| Solothurn □[3] | 58 | 47.25 N | 7.35 E |
| Solotvyn | 78 | 48.42 N | 24.25 E |
| Solotvyna | 78 | 47.57 N | 23.52 E |
| Soloveckije ostrova II | 24 | 65.07 N | 35.53 E |
| Solovjovka | 76 | 60.46 N | 30.09 E |
| Solovjovsk, Ross. | 88 | 49.55 N | [illegible]5.42 E |
| Solovjovsk, Ross. | 89 | 54.14 N | 1[illegible]4.26 E |
| Solre-le-Château | 50 | 50.10 N | 4.05 E |
| Solre-sur-Sambre | 50 | 50.18 N | 4.08 E |
| Solrød Strand | 41 | 55.32 N | [illegible]2.14 E |
| Solsona | 34 | 41.59 N | 1.31 E |
| Solt | 30 | 46.48 N | [illegible]9.00 E |
| Šolta, Otok I | 36 | 43.23 N | [illegible]6.15 E |
| Solṭānābād | 128 | 36.23 N | [illegible].02 E |
| Soltau | 52 | 52.59 N | [illegible].49 E |
| Solton | 86 | 52.50 N | 8[illegible].28 E |
| Solunto ⊥ | 70 | 38.06 N | 1[illegible].32 E |
| Solus, Mount ʌ | 168a | 32.28 S | 11[illegible].13 E |
| Solutré-Pouilly | 58 | 46.18 N | [illegible].43 E |
| Solva | 42 | 51.52 N | [illegible].11 W |
| Solva ≃ | 42 | 51.52 N | [illegible].17 W |
| Solvang | 204 | 34.36 N | 12[illegible]8 W |
| Solvarbo | 40 | 60.24 N | 15.40 E |
| Solvay | 210 | 43.03 N | 76.12 W |
| Sölvesborg | 26 | 56.03 N | 14.[illegible]3 E |
| Sol'vyčegodsk | 24 | 61.21 N | 46.[illegible]2 E |
| Solway Firth c[1] | 44 | 54.50 N | 3.[illegible]5 W |
| Solwezi | 154 | 12.11 S | 26.[illegible]5 E |
| Soly | 76 | 54.31 N | 26.[illegible]1 E |
| Solymár | 264c | 47.36 N | 18.5[illegible] E |
| Solza | 24 | 64.33 N | 39.[illegible] E |
| Sōma, Nihon | 92 | 37.48 N | 140.[illegible] E |
| Soma, Tür. | 130 | 39.10 N | 27.[illegible] E |
| Somabula | 154 | 19.41 S | 29.4[illegible] E |
| Sōmahara-chūtonchi, Rikujō-jieitai- ■ | 94 | 36.23 N | 138.5[illegible] E |
| Somain | 50 | 50.22 N | 3.1[illegible] E |
| Somalia (Somaliya) □[1], Afr. | 136 | 6.00 N | 48.00 E |
| Somalia (Somaliya) □[1], Afr. | 144 | 6.00 N | 48.00 E |
| Somali Basin ✣[1] | 12 | 0.00 | 52.00 E |
| Somalie → Somalia □[1] | 144 | 6.00 N | 48.00 E |
| Somaliland → Somalia □[1] | 144 | 6.00 N | 48.00 E |
| Somali Republic → Somalia □[1] | 144 | 6.00 N | 48.00 E |
| Somaliya → Somalia □[1] | 144 | 6.00 N | 48.00 |
| Somalomo | 152 | 3.23 N | 12.44 [illegible] |
| Sŏman | 98 | 41.20 N | 128.54 E |
| Somanga | 154 | 8.24 S | 39.17 E |
| Sombernon | 58 | 47.18 N | 4.42 E |
| Sombo | 152 | 8.42 S | 20.57 E |
| Sombor | 38 | 45.46 N | 19.07 E |
| Sombra | 214 | 42.43 N | 82.29 W |
| Sombrerete | 234 | 23.38 N | 103.39 W |
| Sombreretillo | 196 | 26.19 N | 99.58 W |
| Sombrero I | 238 | 18.36 N | 63.26 W |
| Sombrero Channel ʊ | 110 | 7.41 N | 93.35 E |
| Sombrio | 252 | 29.07 S | 49.40 W |
| Sombrio, Lagoa do c | 252 | 29.12 S | 49.42 W |
| Şomcuta Mare | 38 | 47.31 N | 23.29 E |
| Somdari | 120 | 25.49 N | 72.35 E |
| Somenos | 224 | 48.49 N | 123.44 W |
| Somercotes | 44 | 53.04 N | 1.22 W |
| Somerdale, N.J., U.S. | 208 | 39.50 N | 75.01 W |
| Somerdale, Oh., U.S. | 214 | 40.34 N | 81.22 W |
| Someren | 52 | 51.24 N | 5.44 E |
| Somero | 26 | 60.37 N | 23.32 E |
| Sõmerpalu | 76 | 57.51 N | 26.48 E |
| Somers, Austl. | 169 | 38.24 S | 145.10 E |
| Somers, Ct., U.S. | 207 | 41.59 N | 72.26 W |
| Somers, Mt., U.S. | 202 | 48.04 N | 114.13 W |
| Somers, Wi., U.S. | 216 | 42.38 N | 87.54 W |
| Somersby | 170 | 33.25 S | 151.17 E |
| Somerset, Austl. | 166 | 41.03 S | 145.49 E |
| Somerset, Mb., Can. | 184 | 49.24 N | 98.39 W |
| Somerset, Co., U.S. | 200 | 38.55 N | 107.28 W |
| Somerset, Ky., U.S. | 192 | 37.05 N | 84.36 W |
| Somerset, Md., U.S. | 284c | 38.58 N | 77.05 W |
| Somerset, Ma., U.S. | 207 | 41.46 N | 71.07 W |
| Somerset, N.J., U.S. | 208 | 40.44 N | 74.34 W |
| Somerset, Oh., U.S. | 188 | 39.48 N | 82.17 W |
| Somerset, Pa., U.S. | 188 | 40.00 N | 79.04 W |
| Somerset, Tx., U.S. | 196 | 29.13 N | 98.40 W |
| Somerset, Wi., U.S. | 190 | 45.07 N | 92.40 W |
| Somerset □[6], Eng., U.K. | 42 | 51.08 N | 3.00 W |
| Somerset □[6], Md., U.S. | 208 | 38.12 N | 75.41 W |
| Somerset □[6], N.J., U.S. | 208 | 40.34 N | 74.37 W |
| Somerset □[6], Pa., U.S. | 214 | 40.09 N | 79.00 W |
| Somerset Airport ⊠ | 276 | 40.37 N | 74.40 W |
| Somerset Center | 216 | 42.03 N | 84.25 W |
| Somerset East | 158 | 32.42 S | 25.35 E |
| Somerset Hills Airport ⊠ | 276 | 40.41 N | 74.32 W |
| Somerset Island I, Ber. | 240a | 32.17 N | 64.52 W |
| Somerset Island I, N.T., Can. | 176 | 73.15 N | 93.30 W |
| Somerset Reservoir ⊜[1] | 171a | 27.03 S | 152.35 E |
| Somerset West | 158 | 34.08 S | 18.50 E |
| Somersham | 42 | 52.23 N | 0.01 E |
| Somers Point | 208 | 39.19 N | 74.35 W |
| Somersworth | 188 | 43.15 N | 70.51 W |
| Somerton, Eng., U.K. | 42 | 51.03 N | 2.44 W |
| Somerton, Az., U.S. | 200 | 32.35 N | 114.42 W |
| Somerton ◆[8] | 285 | 40.06 N | 75.01 W |
| Somerton Creek ≃ | 208 | 36.32 N | 76.55 W |
| Somervell □[6] | 222 | 32.15 N | 97.45 W |
| Somerville, Austl. | 169 | 38.13 S | 145.10 E |
| Somerville, Ma., U.S. | 207 | 42.23 N | 71.06 W |
| Somerville, N.J., U.S. | 210 | 40.34 N | 74.36 W |
| Somerville, Oh., U.S. | 218 | 39.33 N | 84.38 W |
| Somerville, Tn., U.S. | 194 | 35.14 N | 89.21 W |
| Somerville, Tx., U.S. | 222 | 30.20 N | 96.31 W |
| Somerville Lake ⊜[1] | 222 | 30.18 N | 96.40 W |
| Someş (Szamos) ≃ | 38 | 48.07 N | 22.22 E |
| Someşu Cald ≃ | 38 | 46.44 N | 23.22 E |
| Someşu Mare ≃ | 38 | 47.12 N | 24.12 E |
| Someşu Mic ≃ | 38 | 47.09 N | 23.55 E |
| Someşu Rece ≃ | 38 | 46.44 N | 23.22 E |
| Somino | 76 | 59.21 N | 34.52 E |
| Somis | 228 | 34.16 N | 119.00 W |
| Sŏmjin-gang ≃ | 98 | 34.58 N | 127.46 E |
| Somma | 66 | 42.40 N | 12.44 E |
| Sommacampagna | 64 | 45.24 N | 10.50 E |
| Somma Lombardo, It. | 62 | 45.41 N | 8.42 E |
| Somma Lombardo, It. | 266b | 45.41 N | 8.42 E |
| Sommariva | 166 | 26.24 S | 146.36 E |
| Sommariva del Bosco | 62 | 44.46 N | 7.47 E |
| Sommatino | 70 | 37.20 N | 13.59 E |
| Somme □[5] | 50 | 49.55 N | 2.30 E |
| Somme ≃, Fr. | 50 | 49.01 N | 4.12 E |
| Somme ≃, Fr. | 50 | 50.11 N | 1.39 E |
| Somme, Baie de la c | 50 | 50.14 N | 1.33 E |
| Somme, Canal de la ≋ | 50 | 49.55 N | 2.43 E |
| Sommedieue | 56 | 49.05 N | 5.28 E |
| Sommelsdijk | 52 | 51.45 N | 4.09 E |
| Sommen ⊜ | 26 | 58.01 N | 15.15 E |
| Sommepy-Tahure | 56 | 49.15 N | 4.33 E |
| Sommerberg ◆[8] | 263 | 51.27 N | 7.32 E |
| Sömmerda | 54 | 51.10 N | 11.07 E |
| Sommersdorf | 54 | 53.17 N | 14.11 E |
| Sommersted | 41 | 55.19 N | 9.19 E |
| Sommesous | 50 | 48.44 N | 4.12 E |
| Somme Woods ♠ | 278 | 42.09 N | 87.49 W |
| Somnitel'nyj | 89 | 52.12 N | 139.04 E |
| Somo ≃ | 190 | 45.29 N | 89.48 W |


| Symbol | English | Deutsch | Español | Français | Português |
|---|---|---|---|---|---|
| ≃ | River | Fluß | Río | Rivière | Rio |
| ≋ | Canal | Kanal | Canal | Canal | Canal |
| ⌞ | Waterfall, Rapids | Wasserfall, Stromschnellen | Cascada, Rápidos | Chute d'eau, Rapides | Cascata, Rápidos |
| ʊ | Strait | Meeresstraße | Estrecho | Détroit | Estreito |
| c | Bay, Gulf | Bucht, Golf | Bahía, Golfo | Baie, Golfe | Baía, Golfo |
| ⊜ | Lake, Lakes | See, Seen | Lago, Lagos | Lac, Lacs | Lago, Lagos |
| ≣ | Swamp | Sumpf | Pantano | Marais | Pântano |
| ⊓ | Ice Features, Glacier | Eis- und Gletscherformen | Accidentes Glaciales | Formes glaciaires | Acidentes glaciares |
| ⊤ | Other Hydrographic Features | Andere Hydrographische Objekte | Otros Elementos Hidrográficos | Autres données hydrographiques | Outros acidentes hidrográficos |
| ✣ | Submarine Features | Untermeerische Objekte | Accidentes Submarinos | Formes de relief sous-marin | Acidentes submarinos |
| □ | Political Unit | Politische Einheit | Unidad Politica | Entité politique | Unidade política |
| ᵾ | Cultural Institution | Kulturelle Institution | Institución Cultural | Institution culturelle | Institução cultural |
| ⊥ | Historical Site | Historische Stätte | Sitio Histórico | Site historique | Sitio histórico |
| ♠ | Recreational Site | Erholungs- und Ferienort | Sitio de Recreo | Centre de loisirs | Area de Lazer |
| ⊠ | Airport | Flughafen | Aeropuerto | Aéroport | Aeroporto |
| ■ | Military Installation | Militäranlage | Instalación Militar | Installation militaire | Instalação militar |
| ◆ | Miscellaneous | Verschiedenes | Misceláneo | Divers | Diversos |

ENGLISH — DEUTSCH


| Name | Page / Seite | Lat.°′ / Breite°′ | Long.°′ / Länge°′ E = Ost |
|---|---|---|---|
| Somogy □[6] | 30 | 46.25 N | 17.35 E |
| Somonauk | 216 | 41.38 N | 88.40 W |
| Somonauk Creek ≃ | 216 | 41.32 N | 88.41 W |
| Somosierra, Puerto de )( | 34 | 41.09 N | 3.35 W |
| Somosomo | 175g | 16.46 S | 179.58 W |
| Somosomo Strait ⊔ | 175g | 16.47 S | 179.58 E |
| Somotillo | 236 | 13.02 N | 86.55 W |
| Somoto | 236 | 13.28 N | 86.35 W |
| Somovo, Ross. | 76 | 52.53 N | 34.58 E |
| Somovo, Ross. | 78 | 51.44 N | 39.23 E |
| Sompeta | 122 | 18.56 N | 84.36 E |
| Somplago | 64 | 46.21 N | 13.04 E |
| Sompolno | 30 | 52.24 N | 18.31 E |
| Somport, Puerto de )( | 34 | 42.48 N | 0.31 W |
| Sompuis | 50 | 48.41 N | 4.23 E |
| Somuncurá, Meseta de ⋏[1] | 254 | 41.30 S | 67.15 W |
| Somvix | 58 | 46.44 N | 8.56 E |
| Šomyškol' | 86 | 46.30 N | 59.53 E |
| Son, Ned. | 52 | 51.31 N | 5.30 E |
| Son, Nor. | 26 | 59.31 N | 10.42 E |
| Son ≃ | 124 | 25.42 N | 84.52 E |
| Soná | 236 | 8.01 N | 81.19 W |
| Sona-Bata | 152 | 4.54 S | 15.09 E |
| Sonādugi | 126 | 22.47 N | 90.40 E |
| Sonaguera | 236 | 15.38 N | 86.20 W |
| Sonahula | 124 | 25.05 N | 87.09 E |
| Sonāmarg | 123 | 34.18 N | 75.18 E |
| Sonāmukhi | 126 | 23.18 N | 87.25 E |
| Sonāpur | 126 | 23.42 N | 89.30 E |
| Sonar | 164 | 2.33 S | 133.00 E |
| Sonār ≃ | 124 | 24.24 N | 79.56 E |
| Sonari | 272c | 18.52 N | 72.59 E |
| Sonarpur | 272b | 22.26 N | 88.25 E |
| Sonātikri | 272b | 22.57 N | 88.20 E |
| Sonceboz | 58 | 47.11 N | 7.11 E |
| Sonchamp | 261 | 48.35 N | 1.53 E |
| Sŏnch'ŏn | 98 | 39.48 N | 124.55 E |
| Soncino | 62 | 45.24 N | 9.52 E |
| Sondags ≃, S. Afr. | 158 | 33.44 S | 25.51 E |
| Sondags ≃, S. Afr. | 158 | 28.43 S | 30.16 E |
| Sondalo | 64 | 46.20 N | 10.19 E |
| Sønderå ≃ | 41 | 54.53 N | 8.59 E |
| Sønderborg | 41 | 54.55 N | 9.47 E |
| Sønderby | 41 | 55.47 N | 10.01 E |
| Sønder Felding | 41 | 55.57 N | 8.47 E |
| Sønderhav | 41 | 54.51 N | 9.30 E |
| Sønderjylland □[6] | 41 | 55.10 N | 9.15 E |
| Sønder Nærå | 41 | 55.18 N | 10.30 E |
| Sønder Omme | 41 | 55.50 N | 8.54 E |
| Sondershausen | 54 | 51.22 N | 10.52 E |
| Søndersø | 41 | 55.29 N | 10.16 E |
| Sondi | 114 | 2.58 N | 98.52 E |
| Søndre Strømfjord | 176 | 66.59 N | 50.40 W |
| Søndre Strømfjord c[2] | 176 | 66.30 N | 52.15 W |
| Sondrio | 64 | 46.10 N | 9.52 E |
| Sondrio □[4] | 58 | 46.10 N | 10.03 E |
| Sonduga | 76 | 60.08 N | 41.55 E |
| Sone ≃ | 126 | 21.34 N | 86.54 E |
| Sonepur | 120 | 20.50 N | 83.55 E |
| Sonestown | 210 | 41.21 N | 76.33 W |
| Song, Malay. | 112 | 2.01 N | 112.33 E |
| Song, Nig. | 146 | 9.50 N | 12.38 E |
| Song, Thai | 110 | 18.28 N | 100.11 E |
| Song ≃ | 100 | 27.02 N | 118.18 E |
| Song'ao | 100 | 29.36 N | 121.41 E |
| Songbahutun | 104 | 41.28 N | 121.11 E |
| Song Bay Hap, Cua c | 110 | 8.46 N | 104.52 E |
| Songbu | 100 | 31.05 N | 114.48 E |
| Sŏngbyŏn-ni | 98 | 38.03 N | 125.18 E |
| Song Cau | 110 | 13.27 N | 109.13 E |
| Sŏng-ch'ŏn-gang ≃ | 98 | 39.48 N | 127.35 E |
| Songcun | 106 | 30.26 N | 119.43 E |
| Songe | 26 | 58.41 N | 9.00 E |
| Songea | 154 | 10.41 S | 35.39 E |
| Songeons | 50 | 49.33 N | 1.52 E |
| Songgaizhen | 107 | 29.03 N | 105.54 E |
| Songgang | 100 | 22.49 N | 113.51 E |
| Songgato ≃ | 164 | 3.26 S | 140.22 E |
| Songhe | 100 | 31.10 N | 113.20 E |
| Songhua ≃ | 89 | 47.44 N | 132.32 E |
| Songhuahu ⊜[1] | 89 | 43.20 N | 127.07 E |
| Songhuajiang | 89 | 44.46 N | 125.54 E |
| Songhwa | 98 | 38.21 N | 125.08 E |
| Songino | 88 | 48.54 N | 95.54 E |
| Sŏngjang-ni | 98 | 41.02 N | 126.50 E |
| Songjiachang | 107 | 28.47 N | 104.55 E |
| Songjiang | 106 | 31.01 N | 121.14 E |
| Songjiangzhen | 98 | 42.12 N | 126.56 E |
| Songjiapu | 107 | 29.38 N | 104.44 E |
| Songjiaying | 105 | 40.38 N | 115.14 E |
| Sŏngjin → Kimch'aek | 98 | 40.41 N | 129.12 E |
| Songjŏng | 98 | 35.10 N | 126.46 E |
| Sŏngju | 98 | 35.55 N | 128.16 E |
| Songkan | 102 | 28.27 N | 106.50 E |
| Songkhla | 110 | 7.12 N | 100.36 E |
| Songkhram ≃ | 110 | 17.39 N | 104.28 E |
| Songkou, Zhg. | 100 | 25.48 N | 118.36 E |
| Songkou, Zhg. | 100 | 24.32 N | 116.24 E |
| Songlinba | 100 | 24.00 N | 115.59 E |
| Songlindian | 105 | 39.25 N | 115.54 E |
| Songling | 89 | 48.02 N | 121.12 E |
| Song Ling ⋏ | 98 | 41.10 N | 120.09 E |
| Songmen | 100 | 28.19 N | 121.34 E |
| Songming | 102 | 25.24 N | 102.59 E |
| Sŏngmo-do I | 98 | 37.42 N | 126.18 E |
| Sŏngnae-ri | 98 | 39.28 N | 126.59 E |
| Sŏngnam | 98 | 37.26 N | 127.08 E |
| Sŏng-ni | 98 | 39.38 N | 127.06 E |
| Songnim | 98 | 38.44 N | 125.38 E |
| Songo | 152 | 7.22 S | 14.51 E |
| Songololo | 152 | 5.42 S | 14.02 E |
| Songot ∧ | 154 | 3.59 N | 34.28 E |
| Songpan | 102 | 32.40 N | 103.24 E |
| Song Phi Nong | 110 | 14.13 N | 100.03 E |
| Sŏngsa-ri | 271b | 37.38 N | 126.52 E |
| Songshancun | 104 | 41.02 N | 121.09 E |
| Songshu | 98 | 39.50 N | 122.06 E |
| Songshugou | 105 | 41.02 N | 117.49 E |
| Songtangmiao | 106 | 31.08 N | 119.16 E |
| Songtao | 102 | 28.06 N | 109.05 E |
| Songtun | 98 | 39.54 N | 123.56 E |
| Šonguj | 24 | 68.47 N | 33.00 E |
| Songu-ri | 98 | 37.49 N | 127.09 E |
| Songwe, Zaïre | 154 | 3.24 S | 26.16 E |
| Songwe, Zaïre | 154 | 12.25 S | 29.40 E |
| Songwe ≃ | 154 | 9.43 S | 33.56 E |
| Songxi, Zhg. | 100 | 27.33 N | 118.46 E |
| Songxi, Zhg. | 100 | 26.16 N | 116.59 E |
| Songxia, Zhg. | 100 | 25.44 N | 119.36 E |
| Songxia, Zhg. | 100 | 30.07 N | 120.51 E |
| Songxian | 102 | 34.10 N | 112.05 E |
| Songyan | 98 | 37.13 N | 113.43 E |
| Songyin | 106 | 30.54 N | 121.13 E |
| Songyin ≃ | 100 | 28.18 N | 119.44 E |
| Songzhangzi | 98 | 41.13 N | 119.08 E |
| Songzhuang | 106 | 32.06 N | 121.17 E |
| Son Ha | 110 | 15.03 N | 108.34 E |
| Soni, Ehi ∧ | 146 | 20.49 N | 17.23 E |
| Sonico | 64 | 46.10 N | 10.21 E |
| Sonid Youqi | 102 | 42.44 N | 112.40 E |
| Sonid Zuoqi | 102 | 43.58 N | 113.59 E |
| Sonīpat | 124 | 28.59 N | 77.01 E |
| Sonkach | 124 | 22.59 N | 76.21 E |
| Sonk'ol', ozero ⊜ | 85 | 41.50 N | 75.08 E |
| Sonkovo | 76 | 57.47 N | 37.09 E |
| Son La | 110 | 21.19 N | 103.54 E |
| Sonmiāni | 120 | 25.26 N | 66.36 E |
| Sonmiāni Bay c | 120 | 25.15 N | 66.30 E |
| Sonnberg ∧ | 264b | 48.20 N | 16.15 E |
| Sonneberg | 54 | 50.22 N | 11.10 E |
| Sonnefeld | 56 | 50.13 N | 11.08 E |
| Sonnen | 60 | 48.41 N | 13.43 E |
| Sonnenberg ∧[2] | 61 | 47.52 N | 16.28 E |
| Sonnenbühl | 58 | 48.24 N | 9.12 E |
| Sonnewalde | 54 | 51.42 N | 13.38 E |
| Sonning Common | 42 | 51.31 N | 0.59 W |
| Sonningdale | 184 | 52.24 N | 107.40 W |
| Sonnino | 66 | 41.25 N | 13.14 E |
| Sonntagberg | 61 | 47.59 N | 14.45 E |
| Sono | 270 | 34.48 N | 135.55 E |
| Sono, Rio do ≃, Bra. | 250 | 8.58 S | 48.11 W |
| Sono, Rio do ≃, Bra. | 255 | 17.02 S | 45.32 W |
| Sonobe | 96 | 35.06 N | 135.28 E |
| Sonogno | 58 | 46.21 N | 8.47 E |
| Sonoita Creek ≃ | 200 | 31.30 N | 110.58 W |
| Sonoma | 226 | 38.17 N | 122.27 W |
| Sonoma □[6] | 226 | 38.26 N | 122.35 W |
| Sonoma Creek ≃ | 226 | 38.10 N | 122.24 W |
| Sonoma Mountains ⋏ | 226 | 38.17 N | 122.35 W |
| Sonoma Peak ∧ | 204 | 40.52 N | 117.36 W |
| Sonoma State Historical Park ♦ | 226 | 38.18 N | 122.28 W |
| Sononder | 158 | 29.43 S | 21.51 E |
| Sonop | 158 | 25.39 S | 27.42 E |
| Sonora, Ca., U.S. | 226 | 37.59 N | 120.22 W |
| Sonora, Tx., U.S. | 196 | 30.34 N | 100.38 W |
| Sonora □[3] | 232 | 29.20 N | 110.40 W |
| Sonora ≃ | 232 | 28.48 N | 111.33 W |
| Sonoran Desert ◆[2] | 16 | 30.00 N | 113.00 W |
| Sonora Pass )( | 226 | 38.19 N | 119.37 W |
| Sonostrov | 24 | 66.09 N | 34.10 E |
| Sonoyta | 232 | 31.51 N | 112.50 W |
| Sonoyta ≃ | 200 | 31.16 N | 113.26 W |
| Sonpār Hills ⋏[2] | 124 | 24.20 N | 82.15 E |
| Sonqor | 128 | 34.47 N | 47.36 E |
| Sŏnsan | 98 | 36.16 N | 128.17 E |
| Sonsbeck | 52 | 51.37 N | 6.22 E |
| Sonseca | 34 | 39.42 N | 3.57 W |
| Sonskyn | 158 | 30.47 S | 26.28 E |
| Sonsón | 246 | 5.42 N | 75.18 W |
| Sonsonate | 236 | 13.43 N | 89.44 W |
| Sonsorol Islands II | 108 | 5.20 N | 132.13 E |
| Sonstorp | 40 | 58.45 N | 15.36 E |
| Sonstraal | 158 | 27.07 S | 22.28 E |
| Sontag | 194 | 31.39 N | 90.12 W |
| Son Tay | 110 | 21.08 N | 105.30 E |
| Sonthofen | 58 | 47.31 N | 10.17 E |
| Sontra | 56 | 51.04 N | 9.56 E |
| Sonwān | 124 | 27.40 N | 81.45 E |
| Sonyea | 210 | 42.41 N | 77.50 W |
| Soo → Sault Sainte Marie | 190 | 46.29 N | 84.20 W |
| Soochow → Suzhou | 106 | 31.18 N | 120.37 E |
| Sooke | 224 | 48.23 N | 123.43 W |
| Sooke ≃ | 224 | 48.23 N | 123.42 W |
| Sooke Basin c | 224 | 48.23 N | 123.40 W |
| Sooke Lake ⊜ | 224 | 48.33 N | 123.42 W |
| Sooner Lake ⊜[1] | 196 | 36.26 N | 97.02 W |
| Soonwald ⋏ | 56 | 49.55 N | 7.40 E |
| Sooyaac | 144 | 0.03 N | 42.17 E |
| Sopa Sopa Head › | 164 | 1.58 S | 146.35 E |
| Sopchoppy | 192 | 30.03 N | 84.29 W |
| Soperton | 192 | 32.22 N | 82.35 W |
| Sop Hao | 110 | 20.33 N | 104.27 E |
| Sophia | 192 | 37.42 N | 81.15 W |
| Sopki | 76 | 57.06 N | 30.55 E |
| Sopot | 30 | 54.28 N | 18.34 E |
| Sop Pong | 110 | 22.04 N | 102.03 E |
| Sop Prap | 110 | 17.53 N | 99.20 E |
| Soprabolzano | 64 | 46.32 N | 11.24 E |
| Sopron | 30 | 47.41 N | 16.36 E |
| Sopronhorpács | 61 | 47.29 N | 16.44 E |
| Sopronkövesd | 61 | 47.33 N | 16.45 E |
| Šoptykol' | 86 | 51.16 N | 75.45 E |
| Sopur | 123 | 34.18 N | 74.28 E |
| Sŏp'yŏng-ni | 98 | 35.01 N | 127.24 E |
| Soquel | 226 | 36.59 N | 121.57 W |
| Soquel Creek ≃ | 226 | 36.58 N | 121.57 W |
| Sor, Ribeira de ≃ | 34 | 39.00 N | 8.17 W |
| Sora | 66 | 41.43 N | 13.37 E |
| Sorada | 122 | 19.45 N | 84.26 E |
| Sorae-san ∧ | 271b | 37.27 N | 126.47 E |
| Soraga | 64 | 46.22 N | 11.39 E |
| Soragna | 64 | 44.56 N | 10.07 E |
| Söråker | 26 | 62.31 N | 17.30 E |
| Sorano | 66 | 42.41 N | 11.43 E |
| Šorapani | 84 | 42.05 N | 43.05 E |
| Soras | 248 | 14.07 S | 73.37 W |
| Sorata | 248 | 15.47 S | 68.40 W |
| Soratte, Monte ∧ | 66 | 42.15 N | 12.30 E |
| Sorau → Żary | 30 | 51.38 N | 15.09 E |
| Soraya | 248 | 14.10 S | 73.19 W |
| Sorbas | 34 | 37.07 N | 2.07 W |
| Šorbas, gora ∧ | 86 | 47.25 N | 84.12 E |
| Sorbhog | 120 | 26.30 N | 90.52 E |
| Sorbie | 44 | 54.48 N | 4.26 W |
| Sorbo ≃ | 85 | 38.45 N | 69.20 E |
| Sorbolo | 64 | 44.51 N | 10.28 E |
| Sorbonne ʋ[2] | 261 | 48.51 N | 2.21 E |
| Sorcier, Lac au ⊜ | 206 | 46.42 N | 73.24 W |
| Sordevolo | 62 | 45.34 N | 7.59 E |
| Sore | 32 | 44.20 N | 0.35 W |
| Sorel | 206 | 46.02 N | 73.07 W |
| Sorell | 166 | 42.47 S | 147.33 E |
| Sorell, Cape › | 166 | 42.12 S | 145.10 E |
| Sorel Point › | 43b | 49.16 N | 2.10 W |
| Sörenberg | 58 | 46.50 N | 8.03 E |
| Sorento | 219 | 39.00 N | 89.34 W |
| Soreq ≃ | 132 | 31.56 N | 34.42 E |
| Soresina | 64 | 45.17 N | 9.51 E |
| Sörfjärden c | 40 | 59.24 N | 16.50 E |
| Sørfjorden c[2] | 26 | 60.24 N | 6.40 E |
| Sørfold | 24 | 67.28 N | 15.22 E |
| Sörforsa | 26 | 61.40 N | 17.00 E |
| Sorge ≃ | 41 | 54.21 N | 9.25 E |
| Sorgono | 71 | 40.01 N | 9.06 E |
| Sorgues | 62 | 44.00 N | 4.52 E |
| Sorgun | 130 | 39.49 N | 35.11 E |
| Sori | 62 | 44.22 N | 9.06 E |
| Soria | 34 | 41.46 N | 2.28 W |
| Soria □[4] | 34 | 41.35 N | 2.35 W |
| Soriano | 252 | 33.24 S | 58.19 W |
| Soriano □[5] | 258 | 33.45 S | 57.45 W |
| Soriano Calabro | 68 | 38.36 N | 16.14 E |
| Soriano nel Cimino | 66 | 42.25 N | 12.14 E |
| Sorico | 58 | 46.10 N | 9.22 E |
| Sorido | 164 | 1.09 S | 136.03 E |
| Sori-do I | 98 | 34.26 N | 127.48 E |
| Sørli | 26 | 64.15 N | 13.45 E |
| Sormonne ≃ | 56 | 49.46 N | 4.40 E |
| Sorn | 46 | 55.30 N | 4.18 W |
| Sorne ≃ | 58 | 47.22 N | 7.22 E |
| Sorø, Dan. | 41 | 55.26 N | 11.34 E |
| Soro, India | 120 | 21.17 N | 86.40 E |
| Soro, Monte ∧ | 70 | 37.56 N | 14.42 E |
| Soroca | 38 | 48.09 N | 28.17 E |
| Sorocaba | 255 | 23.29 S | 47.27 W |
| Sorocabuçu ≃ | 256 | 23.38 S | 47.13 W |
| Soročinka | 80 | 47.30 N | 51.44 E |
| Soročinsk | 80 | 52.26 N | 53.10 E |
| Soročkino | 86 | 57.02 N | 68.52 E |
| Soroco | 240m | 18.22 N | 65.38 W |
| Sorok | 88 | 52.20 N | 100.12 E |
| Sorok ≃ | 61 | 47.07 N | 16.50 E |
| Sorokino, Ross. | 86 | 53.45 N | 84.58 E |
| Sorokino, Ross. | 86 | 54.13 N | 91.31 E |
| Sorokoshychi | 78 | 51.12 N | 30.35 E |
| Soroksár ◆[8] | 264c | 47.24 N | 19.07 E |
| Sorol I[1] | 108 | 8.08 N | 140.23 E |
| Soron | 124 | 27.53 N | 78.45 E |
| Sorong | 164 | 0.53 S | 131.15 E |
| Sororó ≃ | 250 | 5.24 S | 49.07 W |
| Sorot' ≃ | 76 | 57.04 N | 28.50 E |
| Soroti | 154 | 1.43 N | 33.37 E |
| Sorovskije | 86 | 59.53 N | 71.34 E |
| Sørøya I | 24 | 70.36 N | 22.46 E |
| Sorpestausee ⊜[1] | 56 | 51.20 N | 7.56 E |
| Sorraia ≃ | 34 | 38.56 N | 8.53 W |
| Sorrento, Austl. | 169 | 38.20 S | 144.45 E |
| Sorrento, It. | 68 | 40.37 N | 14.22 E |
| Sorrento, Fl., U.S. | 220 | 28.48 N | 81.33 W |
| Sorrento, La., U.S. | 194 | 30.11 N | 90.51 W |
| Sorris Sorris | 156 | 20.57 S | 14.50 E |
| Sør Rondane Mountains ⋏ | 9 | 72.00 S | 25.00 E |
| Sorsakoski | 26 | 62.27 N | 27.39 E |
| Sorsatunturi ∧ | 24 | 67.24 N | 29.38 E |
| Sorsele | 24 | 65.30 N | 17.30 E |
| Sorsk | 86 | 54.01 N | 90.12 E |
| Sorso | 71 | 40.48 N | 8.34 E |
| Sorsogon | 116 | 12.58 N | 124.00 E |
| Sorsogon □[4] | 116 | 12.50 N | 123.55 E |
| Sorsogon Bay c | 116 | 12.55 N | 123.55 E |
| Sörstafors | 40 | 59.35 N | 16.13 E |
| Šorsu | 85 | 40.17 N | 70.48 E |
| Sort | 34 | 42.24 N | 1.08 E |
| Šortandy | 86 | 51.42 N | 71.00 E |
| Sortat | 46 | 58.33 N | 3.13 W |
| Sortavala | 24 | 61.42 N | 30.41 E |
| Sortino | 70 | 37.09 N | 15.02 E |
| Sortland | 24 | 68.40 N | 15.20 E |
| Sør-Trøndelag □[6] | 26 | 63.00 N | 10.40 E |
| Sorunda | 40 | 59.01 N | 17.48 E |
| Sörup | 41 | 54.43 N | 9.40 E |
| Sõrve neem › | 76 | 57.54 N | 22.03 E |
| Sörvik | 40 | 60.11 N | 15.09 E |
| Sorviži | 80 | 57.52 N | 48.32 E |
| Sosa, Dtsch. | 54 | 50.30 N | 12.39 E |
| Sosa, Taehan | 271b | 37.29 N | 126.47 E |
| Šoša ≃ | 82 | 56.31 N | 36.05 E |
| Sŏsan | 98 | 36.47 N | 126.26 E |
| Sösdala | 41 | 56.02 N | 13.40 E |
| Sos del Rey Católico | 34 | 42.30 N | 1.13 W |
| Sosedka | 80 | 53.15 N | 42.40 E |
| Sosedno | 76 | 58.14 N | 28.42 E |
| Sosenka ≃, Ross. | 265b | 55.35 N | 37.23 E |
| Sosenka ≃, Ross. | 265b | 55.47 N | 37.42 E |
| Sosenki | 82 | 55.34 N | 37.26 E |
| Sösetalsperre ◆[6] | 52 | 51.44 N | 10.20 E |
| Soshigaya ◆[8] | 268 | 35.39 N | 139.36 E |
| Sösjöfjällen ⋏ | 26 | 63.53 N | 13.15 E |
| Šoška | 24 | 62.42 N | 50.40 E |
| Soskovo | 76 | 52.45 N | 35.23 E |
| Sosna ≃ | 76 | 52.42 N | 38.55 E |
| Sosneado, Cerro ∧ | 252 | 34.45 S | 69.59 W |
| Sosnicy | 76 | 57.38 N | 30.25 E |
| Sosnogorsk | 24 | 63.37 N | 53.51 E |
| Sosnovaja Maza | 80 | 52.30 N | 47.53 E |
| Sosnovaja Pol'ana ◆[8] | 265a | 59.50 N | 30.09 E |
| Sosnove | 78 | 50.49 N | 27.00 E |
| Sosnovec | 24 | 64.26 N | 34.27 E |
| Sosnovica | 76 | 60.21 N | 40.50 E |
| Sosnovka, Kaz. | 86 | 51.26 N | 79.28 E |
| Sosnovka, Kyrg. | 85 | 42.40 N | 73.55 E |
| Sosnovka, Ross. | 24 | 66.30 N | 40.32 E |
| Sosnovka, Ross. | 80 | 56.13 N | 47.13 E |
| Sosnovka, Ross. | 80 | 57.48 N | 51.43 E |
| Sosnovka, Ross. | 80 | 56.17 N | 51.17 E |
| Sosnovka, Ross. | 80 | 53.14 N | 41.22 E |
| Sosnovka, Ross. | 80 | 57.16 N | 53.31 E |
| Sosnovka, Ross. | 80 | 54.06 N | 46.38 E |
| Sosnovka, Ross. | 80 | 52.26 N | 43.29 E |
| Sosnovka, Ross. | 82 | 54.31 N | 38.08 E |
| Sosnovka, Ross. | 82 | 54.54 N | 38.41 E |
| Sosnovka, Ross. | 86 | 59.10 N | 81.18 E |
| Sosnovka, Ross. | 88 | 54.09 N | 109.35 E |
| Sosnovo, Ross. | 76 | 60.33 N | 30.15 E |
| Sosnovo, Ross. | 80 | 56.42 N | 54.35 E |
| Sosnovoborsk | 80 | 53.18 N | 46.16 E |
| Sosnovo-Oz'orskoje | 88 | 52.31 N | 111.30 E |
| Sosnovskij | 86 | 54.36 N | 73.10 E |
| Sosnovskoje | 80 | 55.48 N | 43.10 E |
| Sosnovyj Bor, Ross. | 76 | 59.55 N | 29.07 E |
| Sosnovyj Bor, Ross. | 86 | 57.07 N | 55.03 E |
| Sosnovyj Solonec | 80 | 53.17 N | 49.33 E |
| Sosnowiec | 30 | 50.18 N | 19.08 E |
| Sosnytsya | 78 | 51.32 N | 32.28 E |
| Soso | 194 | 31.45 N | 89.16 W |
| Sosok | 112 | 0.17 N | 110.14 E |
| Sospel | 62 | 43.53 N | 7.27 E |
| Sospirolo | 64 | 46.09 N | 12.04 E |
| Sossusvlei ⊜ | 156 | 24.40 S | 15.23 E |
| Šoštanj | 36 | 46.23 N | 15.03 E |
| Sŏsura | 98 | 42.16 N | 130.37 E |
| Sos'va, Ross. | 72 | 63.40 N | 62.06 E |
| Sos'va, Ross. | 86 | 59.10 N | 61.50 E |
| Sos'va ≃ | 86 | 59.32 N | 62.20 E |
| Sosyka ≃ | 78 | 46.35 N | 39.05 E |
| Sot' ≃ | 80 | 58.00 N | 40.39 E |
| Sota ≃ | 150 | 11.52 N | 3.24 E |
| Sotik | 154 | 0.41 S | 35.21 E |
| Sotkamo | 26 | 64.08 N | 28.25 E |
| Sotnicyno | 80 | 54.17 N | 41.49 E |
| Soto de Aldovea | 266a | 40.26 N | 3.27 W |
| Soto de Pajares | 266a | 40.17 N | 3.32 W |
| Soto la Marina | 234 | 23.46 N | 98.13 W |
| Soto La Marina ≃ | 234 | 23.45 N | 97.45 W |
| Soto la Marina, Barra I | 232 | 24.10 N | 97.43 W |
| Sotomayor | 248 | 19.18 S | 65.03 W |
| Sotonera, Embalse de ⊜[1] | 34 | 42.05 N | 0.48 W |
| Sotouboua | 150 | 8.34 N | 0.59 E |
| Sotta | 71 | 41.32 N | 9.12 E |
| Sottens | 58 | 46.39 N | 6.44 E |
| Sottern ⊜ | 40 | 59.02 N | 15.29 E |
| Sotteville | 50 | 49.25 N | 1.06 E |
| Sottile, Punta › | 70a | 35.30 N | 12.38 E |
| Sotto il Monte | 62 | 45.43 N | 9.30 E |
| Sottomarina | 64 | 45.13 N | 12.17 E |
| Sottrum | 52 | 53.06 N | 9.14 E |
| Sottunga I | 26 | 60.08 N | 20.40 E |
| Souain-Perthes-lès-Hurlus | 56 | 49.11 N | 4.32 E |
| Souanké | 152 | 2.05 N | 14.03 E |
| Soubakaniédougou | 150 | 10.28 N | 5.01 W |
| Soubré | 150 | 5.47 N | 6.36 W |
| Soudan | 166 | 20.05 S | 137.00 E |
| Soudan → Sudan □[1] | 140 | 15.00 N | 30.00 E |
| Soude ≃ | 50 | 48.52 N | 4.10 E |
| Soudersburg | 208 | 40.01 N | 76.09 W |
| Souderton | 208 | 40.18 N | 75.19 W |
| Souesmes | 50 | 47.27 N | 2.10 E |
| Soufflay | 152 | 2.01 N | 14.54 E |
| Soufflenheim | 56 | 48.50 N | 7.58 E |
| Soufflot, Lac ⊜ | 190 | 47.24 N | 78.31 W |
| Souflíon | 38 | 41.12 N | 26.18 E |
| Soufrière | 241f | 13.52 N | 61.04 W |
| Soufrière ∧, Guad. | 241o | 16.03 N | 61.40 W |
| Soufrière ∧, St. Vin. | 241h | 13.20 N | 61.11 W |
| Soufrière Bay c, Dom. | 240d | 15.14 N | 61.22 W |
| Soufrière Bay c, St. Luc. | 241f | 13.51 N | 61.04 W |
| Sougahatchee Creek ≃ | 194 | 32.38 N | 85.50 W |
| Sougne-Remouchamps | 56 | 50.29 N | 5.40 E |
| Souguer | 148 | 35.12 N | 1.30 E |
| Souhegan ≃ | 188 | 42.51 N | 71.29 W |
| Souillac | 32 | 44.54 N | 1.29 E |
| Souilly | 56 | 49.01 N | 5.17 E |
| Souk-el-Arba-des-Beni-Hassan | 34 | 35.16 N | 5.20 W |
| Souk-Khemis-du-Sahel | 34 | 35.17 N | 6.05 W |
| Souk Larbat Gharb | 148 | 34.43 N | 6.01 W |
| Sŏul (Seoul), Taehan | 98 | 37.33 N | 126.58 E |
| Sŏul (Seoul), Taehan | 271b | 37.33 N | 126.58 E |
| Sŏul □[4] | 98 | 37.34 N | 127.00 E |
| Soulac-sur-Mer | 32 | 45.31 N | 1.07 W |
| Soulaines-Dhuys | 58 | 48.22 N | 4.44 E |
| Soulanges □[6] | 206 | 45.20 N | 74.15 W |
| Soulanges, Canal de ≍ | 275a | 45.20 N | 73.58 W |
| Souloougou | 150 | 13.01 N | 0.23 E |
| Soulsbyville | 226 | 37.59 N | 120.16 W |
| Soultzeren | 58 | 48.04 N | 7.06 E |
| Soultz-Haut-Rhin | 58 | 47.53 N | 7.14 E |
| Soultzmatt | 58 | 47.58 N | 7.14 E |
| Soultz-sous-Forêts | 56 | 48.56 N | 7.53 E |
| Soummam, Oued ≃ | 34 | 36.45 N | 5.04 E |
| Sound Beach | 210 | 40.57 N | 72.58 W |
| Sounding Creek ≃ | 184 | 52.06 N | 110.28 W |
| Sounding Lake ⊜ | 184 | 52.08 N | 110.29 W |
| Sound View Park ♦ | 276 | 40.49 N | 73.52 W |
| Soúnion, Ákra › | 38 | 37.39 N | 24.02 E |
| Soup Harbour c | 212 | 43.51 N | 77.11 W |
| Souppes-sur-Loing | 50 | 48.11 N | 2.44 E |
| Souq Ahras | 148 | 36.23 N | 8.00 E |
| Sources, Mont-aux- ∧ | 158 | 28.46 S | 28.52 E |
| Soure, Bra. | 250 | 0.44 S | 48.31 W |
| Soure, Port. | 34 | 40.03 N | 8.38 W |
| Sour el Ghozlane | 148 | 36.10 N | 3.45 E |
| Souris, Mb., Can. | 184 | 49.38 N | 100.15 W |
| Souris, P.E., Can. | 186 | 46.21 N | 62.15 W |
| Souris ≃ | 198 | 49.39 N | 99.34 W |
| Sourlake | 194 | 30.09 N | 94.25 W |
| Sourland Mountain ∧[2] | 208 | 40.29 N | 74.43 W |
| Sourou ≃ | 150 | 12.45 N | 3.25 W |
| Souroukaha | 150 | 8.13 N | 5.08 W |
| Souš | 54 | 50.32 N | 13.34 E |
| Sous, Oued V | 148 | 30.27 N | 9.31 W |
| Sousa | 250 | 6.45 S | 38.14 W |
| Sousânia | 255 | 16.11 S | 49.05 W |
| Sousas | 256 | 22.52 S | 46.59 W |
| Sousel | 34 | 38.57 N | 7.40 W |
| Sous-le-Vent, Îles → Leeward Islands II | 238 | 17.00 N | 63.00 W |
| Sousse | 148 | 35.49 N | 10.38 E |
| Sout ≃, S. Afr. | 158 | 28.56 S | 20.40 E |
| Sout ≃, S. Afr. | 158 | 31.35 S | 18.24 E |
| Sout ≃, S. Afr. | 158 | 33.03 S | 23.28 E |
| South ≃, Ia., U.S. | 190 | 41.29 N | 93.20 W |
| South ≃, Ma., U.S. | 283 | 42.10 N | 70.43 W |
| South ≃, Mo., U.S. | 219 | 39.52 N | 91.26 W |
| South ≃, N.J., U.S. | 208 | 40.29 N | 74.23 W |
| South ≃, N.C., U.S. | 192 | 34.20 N | 78.03 W |
| South ≃, Va., U.S. | 192 | 37.46 N | 79.23 W |
| South ≃, Va., U.S. | 208 | 38.02 N | 77.23 W |
| South Acton | 207 | 42.27 N | 71.27 W |
| South Africa (Suid-Afrika) □[1], Afr. | 138 | 30.00 S | 26.00 E |
| South Africa (Suid-Afrika) □[1], Afr. | 156 | 30.00 S | 26.00 E |
| Southall ◆[8] | 260 | 51.31 N | 0.23 W |
| South Alligator ≃ | 164 | 12.15 S | 132.24 E |
| Southam | 42 | 52.15 N | 1.23 W |
| South Amboy | 208 | 40.28 N | 74.17 W |
| South America ⚲[1] | 4 | 15.00 S | 60.00 W |
| South America ⚲[1] | 18 | 15.00 S | 60.00 W |
| South Amherst, Ma., U.S. | 207 | 42.20 N | 72.30 W |
| South Amherst, Oh., U.S. | 214 | 41.22 N | 82.14 W |
| Southampton, N.S., Can. | 186 | 45.35 N | 64.15 W |
| Southampton, On., Can. | 212 | 44.29 N | 81.23 W |
| Southampton, Eng., U.K. | 42 | 50.55 N | 1.25 W |
| Southampton, Ma., U.S. | 207 | 42.13 N | 72.43 W |
| Southampton, N.Y., U.S. | 207 | 40.53 N | 72.23 W |
| Southampton, Pa., U.S. | 285 | 40.10 N | 75.02 W |
| Southampton □[6] | 208 | 36.42 N | 77.05 W |
| Southampton (Eastleigh) Airport ⊠ | 42 | 50.57 N | 1.21 W |
| Southampton, Cape › | 176 | 62.09 N | 83.40 W |
| Southampton Island I | 176 | 64.20 N | 84.40 W |
| South Andaman I | 110 | 11.45 N | 92.45 E |
| South Anna ≃ | 192 | 37.48 N | 77.25 W |
| South Apopka | 220 | 28.39 N | 81.31 W |
| Southard | 208 | 40.08 N | 74.14 W |
| Southards Pond ⊜ | 276 | 40.43 N | 73.20 W |
| South Ashburnham | 207 | 42.36 N | 71.56 W |
| South Aulatsivik Island I | 176 | 56.45 N | 61.30 W |
| South Australia □[3] | 162 | 30.00 S | 135.00 E |
| South Australian Basin ✧[1] | 14 | 38.00 S | 126.00 E |
| Southaven | 194 | 34.59 N | 90.02 W |
| South Bald Mountain ∧ | 200 | 40.45 N | 105.41 W |
| South Baldy ∧ | 200 | 33.59 N | 107.11 W |
| South Banda Basin ✧[1] | 14 | 6.30 S | 127.30 E |
| Southbank | 182 | 54.02 N | 125.46 W |
| South Barre | 207 | 42.23 N | 72.05 W |
| South Barrington | 278 | 42.06 N | 88.07 W |
| South Barrule ∧[2] | 44 | 54.12 N | 4.40 W |
| South Bass Island I | 214 | 41.39 N | 82.49 W |
| South Bay | 220 | 26.39 N | 80.42 W |
| South Bay c, Mb., Can. | 184 | 56.43 N | 99.00 W |
| South Bay c, N.T., Can. | 176 | 63.58 N | 83.30 W |
| South Bay c, On., Can. | 190 | 45.38 N | 81.50 W |
| South Bay c, On., Can. | 212 | 43.55 N | 77.03 W |
| South Bay c, On., Can. | 212 | 44.52 N | 79.47 W |
| South Bay c, Fl., U.S. | 220 | 26.42 N | 80.45 W |
| South Bay c, Va., U.S. | 208 | 37.14 N | 75.52 W |
| South Bay c, Wa., U.S. | 224 | 46.53 N | 124.04 W |
| South Baymouth | 190 | 45.33 N | 82.01 W |
| South Beach ♦ | 276 | 40.35 N | 74.05 W |
| South Beacon Mountain ∧ | 210 | 41.29 N | 73.57 W |
| South Bedias Creek ≃ | 222 | 30.54 N | 95.42 W |
| South Bellingham | 207 | 42.03 N | 71.28 W |
| South Belmar | 208 | 40.10 N | 74.02 W |
| South Beloit | 216 | 42.29 N | 89.02 W |
| South Bend, In., U.S. | 216 | 41.41 N | 86.15 W |
| South Bend, Wa., U.S. | 224 | 46.40 N | 123.48 W |
| South Benfleet | 42 | 51.33 N | 0.34 E |
| South Bentinck Arm c | 182 | 52.15 N | 126.50 W |
| South Bethlehem | 214 | 41.00 N | 79.20 W |
| South Bihar Plains ≚ | 124 | 25.15 N | 84.30 E |
| South Bloomfield | 218 | 39.43 N | 82.59 W |
| Southborough, Eng., U.K. | 42 | 51.10 N | 0.15 E |
| Southborough, Ma., U.S. | 207 | 42.18 N | 71.31 W |
| South Bosque ≃ | 222 | 31.29 N | 97.16 W |
| South Boston | 192 | 36.41 N | 78.54 W |
| South Boston ◆[8] | 283 | 42.20 N | 71.03 W |
| South Bound Brook | 276 | 40.33 N | 74.32 W |
| South Bradenton | 220 | 27.27 N | 82.35 W |
| South Branch, Nf., Can. | 186 | 47.55 N | 59.02 W |
| South Branch, N.J., U.S. | 276 | 40.33 N | 74.42 W |
| South Brent | 42 | 50.25 N | 3.50 W |
| Southbridge, N.Z. | 172 | 43.49 S | 172.15 E |
| Southbridge, Ma., U.S. | 207 | 42.04 N | 72.02 W |
| South Britain | 207 | 41.28 N | 73.15 W |
| Southbrook, Austl. | 171a | 27.41 S | 151.43 E |
| Southbrook, N.Z. | 172 | 43.20 S | 172.36 E |
| South Brook ≃ | 285 | 39.52 N | 75.44 W |
| South Brookfield | 186 | 44.23 N | 64.58 W |
| South Brooklyn ◆[8] | 276 | 40.41 N | 73.59 W |
| South Bruny Island I | 166 | 43.23 S | 147.17 E |
| South Buganda □[5] | 154 | 0.30 S | 31.35 E |
| South Burlington | 188 | 44.28 N | 73.10 W |
| Southbury | 207 | 41.28 N | 73.12 W |
| South Butler | 210 | 43.08 N | 76.46 W |
| South Byfield | 283 | 42.44 N | 70.54 W |
| South Byron | 210 | 43.03 N | 78.04 W |
| South Cairo | 210 | 42.17 N | 73.57 W |
| South Canaan | 210 | 41.30 N | 75.25 W |
| South Cape › | 175g | 17.01 S | 179.55 E |
| South Carolina □[3], U.S. | 178 | 34.00 N | 81.00 W |
| South Carolina □[3], U.S. | 192 | 34.00 N | 81.00 W |
| South Carver | 207 | 41.50 N | 70.44 W |
| South Castor ≃ | 212 | 45.15 N | 75.23 W |
| South Cave | 44 | 53.46 N | 0.35 W |
| South Cerney | 42 | 51.40 N | 1.56 W |
| South Chagrin Reservation ♦ | 279a | 41.25 N | 81.25 W |
| South Channel ⊔, Pil. | 116 | 14.20 N | 120.37 E |
| South Channel ⊔, Mi., U.S. | 190 | 45.38 N | 84.32 W |
| South Channel ≃[1] | 281 | 42.32 N | 82.40 W |
| South Chaplin | 207 | 41.46 N | 72.07 W |
| South Charleston, Oh., U.S. | 218 | 39.49 N | 83.38 W |
| South Charleston, W.V., U.S. | 188 | 38.22 N | 81.41 W |
| South Chatham | 207 | 41.40 N | 70.01 W |
| South Chelmsford | 283 | 42.34 N | 71.23 W |
| South Chicago ◆[8] | 278 | 41.44 N | 87.33 W |
| South China Basin ✧[1] | 12 | 15.00 N | 115.00 E |
| South China Sea ⩪[2] | 108 | 10.00 N | 113.00 E |
| South Cle Elum | 224 | 47.11 N | 120.56 W |
| South Coast Botanic Garden ♦ | 280 | 33.47 N | 118.21 W |
| South Coatesville | 208 | 39.58 N | 75.49 W |
| South Coffeyville | 196 | 36.59 N | 95.37 W |
| South Concho ≃ | 196 | 31.21 N | 100.28 W |
| South Corinth | 210 | 43.12 N | 73.51 W |
| South Corning | 210 | 42.07 N | 77.02 W |
| South Cotabato □[4] | 116 | 6.15 N | 125.00 E |
| South Creek ≃ | 170 | 33.36 S | 150.50 E |
| South Crest | 273d | 26.15 S | 28.07 E |
| South Dakota □[3], U.S. | 178 | 44.15 N | 100.00 W |
| South Dakota □[3], U.S. | 198 | 44.15 N | 100.00 W |
| South Dandalup ≃ | 168a | 32.35 S | 115.53 E |
| South Dandalup Dam ◆[6] | 168a | 32.38 S | 116.04 E |
| South Darenth | 260 | 51.24 N | 0.15 E |
| South Dartmouth | 207 | 41.35 N | 70.56 W |
| South Dayton | 210 | 42.21 N | 79.03 W |
| South Deerfield | 207 | 42.28 N | 72.36 W |
| South Dennis, Ma., U.S. | 207 | 41.41 N | 70.09 W |
| South Dennis, N.J., U.S. | 208 | 39.10 N | 74.49 W |
| South Dorset | 210 | 43.13 N | 73.04 W |
| South Dorset Downs ⋏[1] | 42 | 50.40 N | 2.25 W |
| South Dos Palos | 226 | 36.57 N | 120.39 W |
| South Downs ⋏[1] | 42 | 50.55 N | 0.25 W |
| South Dum Dum | 126 | 22.37 N | 88.25 E |
| South Duxbury | 207 | 42.01 N | 70.41 W |
| South East □[5] | 156 | 25.00 S | 25.45 E |
| Southeast Asia Treaty Organization Headquarters ʋ | 269a | 13.45 N | 100.31 E |
| South East Cape ›, Austl. | 166 | 43.39 S | 146.50 E |
| Southeast Cape ›, Ak., U.S. | 180 | 62.55 N | 169.42 W |
| Southeast Indian Ridge ✧[3] | 6 | 50.00 S | 110.00 E |
| South Easton | 207 | 42.02 N | 71.04 W |
| Southeast Pacific Basin ✧[1] | 6 | 60.00 S | 115.00 W |
| South East Point ›, Austl. | 166 | 39.00 S | 146.20 E |
| South East Point ›, Kiribati | 174o | 1.40 N | 157.10 W |
| South Egg Harbor | 208 | 39.31 N | 74.39 W |
| South Egremont | 207 | 42.09 N | 73.25 W |
| South Elkhorn Creek ≃ | 218 | 38.13 N | 84.48 W |
| South El Monte | 280 | 34.03 N | 118.02 W |
| Southend | 46 | 55.20 N | 5.38 W |
| Southend Municipal Airport ⊠ | 42 | 51.34 N | 0.41 E |
| Southend-on-Sea | 42 | 51.33 N | 0.43 E |
| Southend-on-Sea □[8] | 260 | 51.33 N | 0.41 E |
| Southend Pier ◆[5] | 260 | 51.31 N | 0.44 E |
| South English ≃ | 190 | 41.30 N | 91.56 W |
| Southern □[4], Malaŵi | 154 | 15.30 S | 35.00 E |
| Southern □[4], S.L. | 150 | 8.00 N | 12.15 W |
| Southern □[4], Zam. | 154 | 16.30 S | 27.00 E |
| Southern □[5], Bots. | 156 | 24.45 S | 24.00 E |
| Southern □[5], Ug. | 154 | 0.30 S | 30.30 E |
| Southern Alps ⋏ | 172 | 43.30 S | 170.30 E |
| Southern California, University of ʋ[2] | 280 | 34.02 N | 118.17 W |
| Southern Cook Islands II | 14 | 20.00 S | 159.00 W |
| Southern Cross | 162 | 31.13 S | 119.19 E |
| Southern Ghāts ⋏ | 122 | 9.30 N | 77.00 E |
| Southern Highlands □[5] | 164 | 6.00 S | 143.30 E |
| Southern Indian Lake ⊜ | 176 | 57.10 N | 98.40 W |
| Southern Leyte □[4] | 116 | 10.50 N | 124.55 E |
| Southern Lueti ≃ | 152 | 16.14 S | 23.13 E |
| Southern Pines | 192 | 35.10 N | 79.23 W |
| Southern Ute Indian Reservation ◆[4] | 200 | 37.05 N | 107.45 W |
| Southern View | 219 | 39.46 N | 89.39 W |
| Southern Yemen → Yemen □[1] | 144 | 15.00 N | 47.00 E |
| Southery | 42 | 52.32 N | 0.23 E |
| South Esk ≃, Austl. | 166 | 41.25 S | 147.08 E |
| South Esk ≃, Scot., U.K. | 46 | 56.42 N | 2.32 W |
| South Esk ≃, Scot., U.K. | 46 | 55.53 N | 3.04 W |
| Southesk Tablelands ⋏[1] | 162 | 20.50 S | 126.40 E |
| South Essex | 207 | 42.38 N | 70.46 W |
| South Euclid | 214 | 41.31 N | 81.31 W |
| Southey | 184 | 50.56 N | 104.30 W |
| South Fabius ≃ | 219 | 39.54 N | 91.30 W |
| South Fallsburg | 210 | 41.42 N | 74.37 W |
| South Farmbridge | 260 | 51.38 N | 0.41 E |
| South Farmingdale | 276 | 40.43 N | 73.26 W |
| Southfield, Ma., U.S. | 207 | 42.06 N | 73.14 W |
| Southfield, Mi., U.S. | 216 | 42.28 N | 83.13 W |
| Southfields | 210 | 41.15 N | 74.11 W |
| South Fiji Basin ✧[1] | 14 | 26.00 S | 175.00 E |
| Southfleet | 260 | 51.25 N | 0.19 E |
| South Floral Park | 276 | 40.43 N | 73.42 W |
| South Foreland › | 42 | 51.09 N | 1.23 E |
| South Fork, Co., U.S. | 200 | 37.40 N | 106.38 W |
| South Fork, Pa., U.S. | 214 | 40.22 N | 78.47 W |
| South Fort George | 182 | 53.54 N | 122.45 W |
| South Forty Foot Drain ≍ | 42 | 52.56 N | 0.15 W |
| South Fox Island I | 190 | 45.25 N | 85.50 W |
| South Fulton | 194 | 36.30 N | 88.52 W |
| South Gate, Ca., U.S. | 228 | 33.57 N | 118.12 W |
| Southgate, Fl., U.S. | 220 | 27.18 N | 82.32 W |
| Southgate, Mi., U.S. | 216 | 42.12 N | 83.11 W |
| Southgate ◆[8] | 260 | 51.38 N | 0.08 W |
| Southgate U.S.A. ◆[9] | 279a | 41.25 N | 81.32 W |
| South Georgia I | 244 | 54.15 S | 36.45 W |
| South Georgia and the South Sandwich Islands □[2] | 18 | 54.00 S | 38.00 W |
| South Gibson | 210 | 41.44 N | 75.38 W |
| South Glamorgan □[6] | 42 | 51.30 N | 3.25 W |
| South Glastonbury | 207 | 41.40 N | 72.35 W |
| South Glens Falls | 210 | 43.17 N | 73.38 W |
| South Grafton | 207 | 42.11 N | 71.42 W |
| South Grand ≃ | 194 | 38.18 N | 93.28 W |
| South Grand Island Bridge ◆[5] | 284a | 43.00 N | 78.56 W |
| South Green | 260 | 51.37 N | 0.26 E |
| South Greensburg | 214 | 40.17 N | 79.33 W |
| South Hackensack | 276 | 40.51 N | 74.02 W |
| South Hadley, Ma., U.S. | 188 | 42.15 N | 72.34 W |
| South Hadley, Ma., U.S. | 207 | 42.15 N | 72.34 W |
| South Hadley Falls | 207 | 42.13 N | 72.36 W |
| South Hamilton | 207 | 42.36 N | 70.52 W |
| South Hams ≚ | 42 | 50.22 N | 3.50 W |
| South Hanningfield | 260 | 51.39 N | 0.31 E |
| South Hanover | 283 | 42.05 N | 70.51 W |
| South Harbor c | 269f | 14.33 N | 120.58 E |
| South Hartford | 210 | 43.21 N | 73.25 W |
| South Harwich | 207 | 41.40 N | 70.02 W |
| South Hātia Island I | 124 | 22.19 N | 91.07 E |
| South Haven, In., U.S. | 216 | 41.32 N | 87.08 W |
| South Haven, Ks., U.S. | 198 | 37.03 N | 97.24 W |
| South Haven, Mi., U.S. | 216 | 42.24 N | 86.16 W |
| South Hayling | 42 | 50.47 N | 0.59 W |
| South Head ›, Austl. | 274a | 33.50 S | 151.17 E |
| South Head ›, N.Z. | 172 | 36.26 S | 174.14 E |
| South Heart ≃ | 182 | 55.34 N | 116.11 W |
| South Heights | 279b | 40.35 N | 80.14 W |
| South Hempstead | 276 | 40.41 N | 73.37 W |
| South Henderson | 192 | 36.17 N | 78.25 W |
| South Henik Lake ⊜ | 176 | 61.30 N | 97.30 W |
| South Hero | 188 | 44.38 N | 73.18 W |
| South Hetton | 44 | 54.48 N | 1.24 W |
| South Hill, N.Y., U.S. | 210 | 42.25 N | 76.33 W |
| South Hill, Va., U.S. | 192 | 36.43 N | 78.07 W |
| South Hills ◆[8] | 273d | 26.15 S | 28.05 E |
| South Hills Village ◆[9] | 279b | 40.21 N | 80.03 W |
| South Hingham | 207 | 42.11 N | 70.52 W |
| South Hogan Creek ≃ | 218 | 39.03 N | 84.54 W |
| South Holland | 216 | 41.36 N | 87.36 W |
| South Holston Lake ⊜[1] | 192 | 36.35 N | 82.00 W |
| South Honcut Creek ≃ | 226 | 39.19 N | 121.35 W |
| South Honshu Ridge ✧[3] | 14 | 24.00 N | 142.00 E |
| South Hopkinton | 207 | 41.24 N | 71.45 W |
| South Horr | 154 | 2.06 N | 36.55 E |
| South Houston | 222 | 29.39 N | 95.14 W |
| South Huntington | 276 | 40.49 N | 73.23 W |
| South Indian Basin ✧[1] | 6 | 60.00 S | 120.00 E |
| South Indian Lake | 184 | 56.46 N | 98.57 W |
| Southington, Ct., U.S. | 207 | 41.35 N | 72.52 W |
| Southington, Oh., U.S. | 214 | 41.19 N | 80.57 W |
| South International Falls | 190 | 48.35 N | 93.23 W |
| South Ionia | 216 | 42.57 N | 85.04 W |
| South Island I, India | 122 | 10.03 N | 72.17 E |
| South Island I, Kenya | 154 | 2.38 N | 36.36 E |
| South Island I, N.Z. | 172 | 43.00 S | 171.00 E |
| South Islet I | 116 | 8.44 N | 119.49 E |
| South Jacksonville | 219 | 39.42 N | 90.13 W |
| South Kemptville Creek ≃ | 212 | 44.54 N | 75.41 W |
| South Kenosha | 216 | 42.32 N | 87.50 W |
| South Kent | 207 | 41.40 N | 73.28 W |
| South Kirkby | 44 | 53.34 N | 1.20 W |
| South Konkan Hills ⋏[2] | 122 | 17.00 N | 73.30 E |
| South Korea → Korea, South □[1] | 98 | 36.30 N | 128.00 E |
| South Ladder Creek ≃ | 198 | 38.41 N | 101.34 W |
| Southlake | 222 | 32.57 N | 97.09 W |
| South Lake ⊜, On., Can. | 212 | 44.26 N | 76.13 W |
| South Lake ⊜, Fl., U.S. | 220 | 28.37 N | 80.52 W |
| South Lake Tahoe | 226 | 38.56 N | 119.58 W |
| South Lancaster | 207 | 42.26 N | 71.41 W |
| Southland, Ky., U.S. | 218 | 38.01 N | 84.31 W |
| Southland, Mi., U.S. | 216 | 42.13 N | 84.24 W |
| Southland, Tx., U.S. | 196 | 33.22 N | 101.33 W |
| Southland ◆[9] | 282 | 37.39 N | 122.06 W |
| South Laurel | 284c | 39.05 N | 76.52 W |
| Southlawn, Il., U.S. | 219 | 39.45 N | 89.37 W |
| Southlawn, Md., U.S. | 284c | 38.48 N | 76.59 W |
| South Layhill | 284c | 39.04 N | 77.03 W |
| South Lebanon | 218 | 39.22 N | 84.12 W |
| South Lee | 207 | 42.16 N | 73.16 W |
| South Lima | 210 | 42.51 N | 77.41 W |
| South Line Island I | 276 | 40.37 N | 73.30 W |
| South Llano ≃ | 196 | 30.30 N | 99.46 W |
| South Lockport | 284a | 43.09 N | 78.42 W |
| South Lorain | 279a | 41.27 N | 82.08 W |
| South Loup ≃ | 198 | 41.04 N | 98.40 W |
| South Luangwa National Park ♦ | 154 | 12.50 S | 31.45 E |
| South Luconia Shoals ✧[2] | 112 | 5.00 N | 112.42 E |
| South Lynnfield | 283 | 42.31 N | 71.00 W |
| South Lyon | 216 | 42.27 N | 83.39 W |
| South Macmillan ≃ | 180 | 63.03 N | 133.18 W |
| South Magnetic Pole ◆ | 9 | 65.18 S | 139.30 E |
| South Malosmadulu Atoll I[1] | 122 | 5.10 N | 72.58 E |
| South Manitou Island I | 190 | 45.01 N | 86.07 W |
| South Marsh Island I | 208 | 38.06 N | 76.02 W |
| South Medford | 202 | 42.18 N | 122.50 W |
| South Media | 285 | 39.54 N | 75.23 W |
| South Melbourne | 274b | 37.50 S | 144.57 E |
| South Merrimack | 207 | 42.48 N | 71.33 W |
| South Miami | 220 | 25.42 N | 80.17 W |
| South Miami Heights | 220 | 25.35 N | 80.22 W |
| South Middleboro | 207 | 41.49 N | 70.49 W |
| South Milford | 216 | 41.31 N | 85.16 W |
| South Mills | 192 | 36.26 N | 76.19 W |
| South Milwaukee | 216 | 42.54 N | 87.51 W |
| South Mimms | 260 | 51.42 N | 0.14 W |
| Southminster | 42 | 51.40 N | 0.50 E |
| South Mokelumne ≃ | 226 | 38.08 N | 121.35 W |
| South Molton | 42 | 51.01 N | 3.50 W |
| South Monroe | 216 | 41.54 N | 83.25 W |
| Southmont | 214 | 40.18 N | 78.56 W |
| South Montrose | 210 | 41.48 N | 75.53 W |
| South Moose Lake ⊜ | 184 | 53.46 N | 100.08 W |
| South Mountain | 208 | 39.51 N | 77.29 W |
| South Mountain ∧, U.S. | 208 | 39.40 N | 77.30 W |
| South Mountain ∧, Id., U.S. | 202 | 42.44 N | 116.54 W |
| South Mountain Reservation ♦ | 276 | 40.45 N | 74.18 W |
| South Mount Vernon | 214 | 40.23 N | 82.23 W |
| South Nahanni ≃ | 176 | 61.03 N | 123.20 W |
| South Naknek | 180 | 58.43 N | 157.00 W |
| South Nation ≃ | 188 | 45.34 N | 75.06 W |
| South Negril Point › | 241q | 18.15 N | 78.22 W |
| South New Berlin | 210 | 42.31 N | 75.23 W |
| South New Castle | 214 | 40.58 N | 80.21 W |
| South New River Canal ≍ | 220 | 26.04 N | 80.12 W |
| South Norfolk → Chesapeake | 208 | 36.43 N | 76.15 W |
| South Normanton | 44 | 53.06 N | 1.20 W |
| South Norwalk Reservoir ⊜[1] | 276 | 41.11 N | 73.27 W |
| South Norwood ◆[8] | 260 | 51.24 N | 0.04 W |
| South Nutfield | 260 | 51.14 N | 0.08 W |
| South Nyack | 276 | 41.04 N | 73.55 W |
| South Ockendon | 42 | 51.32 N | 0.18 E |
| South Ogden | 200 | 41.11 N | 111.58 W |
| Southold | 207 | 41.03 N | 72.25 W |


**Symbols** in the index entries represent the broad categories identified in the key at the right. Symbols with superior numbers (⋏[1]) identify subcategories (see complete key on page *I · 1).*

**Symbole** im Register stellen die rechts im Schlüssel erklärten Kategorien dar. Symbole mit hochgestellten Ziffern (⋏[1]) bezeichnen Unterabteilungen einer Kategorie (vgl. vollständiger Schlüssel auf Seite *I · 1).*

**Los símbolos** incluídos en el texto del índice representan las grandes categorías identificadas con la clave a la derecha. Los símbolos con numeros en su parte superior (⋏[1]) identifican las subcategorías (véase la clave completa en la página *I · 1).*

**Les symboles** de l'index représentent les catégories indiquées dans la légende à droite. Les symboles suivis d'un indice (⋏[1]) représentent des sous-catégories (voir légende complète à la page *I · 1).*

**Os símbolos** incluídos no texto do índice representam as grandes categorias identificadas com a chave à direita. Os símbolos com números em sua parte superior (⋏[1]) identificam as subcategorias (veja-se a chave completa à página *I · 1).*

| | | | | |
|---|---|---|---|---|
| ∧ Mountain | Berg | Montaña | Montagne | Montanha |
| ⋏ Mountains | Gebirge | Montañas | Montagnes | Montanhas |
| )( Pass | Paß | Paso | Col | Passo |
| V Valley, Canyon | Tal, Cañon | Valle, Cañón | Vallée, Canyon | Vale, Canhão |
| ≚ Plain | Ebene | Llano | Plaine | Planície |
| › Cape | Kap | Cabo | Cap | Cabo |
| I Island | Insel | Isla | Île | Ilha |
| II Islands | Inseln | Islas | Îles | Ilhas |
| ⚲ Other Topographic Features | Andere Topographische Objekte | Otros Elementos Topográficos | Autres données topographiques | Outros acidentes topográficos |

ESPAÑOL · FRANÇAIS · PORTUGUÊS


| Nombre / Nom / Nome | Página / Page | Lat.°′ | Long.°′ W = Oeste / W = Ouest |
|---|---|---|---|
| South Onondaga | 210 | 42.56 N | 76.13 W |
| South Orange | 276 | 40.47 N | 74.15 W |
| South Orkney Islands II | 9 | 60.35 S | 45.30 W |
| South Oroville | 226 | 39.30 N | 121.33 W |
| South Ossetia → Jugo Osetija □[9] | 84 | 42.20 N | 44.00 E |
| South Otselic | 210 | 42.38 N | 75.46 W |
| Southowram | 262 | 53.43 N | 1.50 W |
| South Oxhey | 260 | 51.38 N | 0.23 W |
| South Oyster Bay ᴄ | 276 | 40.38 N | 73.28 W |
| South Palo Duro Creek ≃ | 196 | 36.06 N | 101.29 W |
| South Para ≃ | 168b | 34.36 S | 138.45 E |
| South Para Reservoir ⊜[1] | 168b | 34.42 S | 138.52 E |
| South Paris | 188 | 44.13 N | 70.30 W |
| South Park | 216 | 41.44 N | 88.18 W |
| South Park ♠, N.Y., U.S. | 284a | 42.50 N | 78.50 W |
| South Park ♠, Pa., U.S. | 279b | 40.19 N | 80.01 W |
| South Pasadena, Ca., U.S. | 280 | 34.06 N | 118.08 W |
| South Pasadena, Fl., U.S. | 220 | 27.46 N | 82.43 W |
| South Pass )( | 200 | 42.22 N | 108.55 W |
| South Pass ⋓ | 175c | 7.14 N | 151.48 E |
| South Passage ⋓, Austl. | 171a | 27.22 S | 153.26 E |
| South Passage ⋓, Oh., U.S. | 214 | 41.35 N | 82.45 W |
| South Patrick Shores | 220 | 28.12 N | 80.35 W |
| South Pekin | 190 | 40.29 N | 89.39 W |
| South Pender | 224 | 48.45 N | 123.14 W |
| South Pender Island I | 224 | 48.45 N | 123.10 W |
| South Perth | 168a | 31.59 S | 115.52 E |
| South Petherton | 42 | 50.58 N | 2.49 W |
| South Philadelphia ◆[8] | 285 | 39.56 N | 75.10 W |
| South Philipsburg | 214 | 40.53 N | 78.13 W |
| South Pittsburg | 194 | 35.00 N | 85.42 W |
| South Plainfield | 210 | 40.34 N | 74.24 W |
| South Platte ≃ | 178 | 41.07 N | 100.42 W |
| South Platte, North Fork ≃ | 200 | 39.25 N | 105.10 W |
| South Point ›, Barb. | 241g | 13.02 N | 59.31 W |
| South Point ›, Pil. | 116 | 10.24 N | 122.30 E |
| South Pole ◆ | 9 | 90.00 S | 0.00 |
| South Porcupine | 190 | 48.28 N | 81.13 W |
| Southport, Austl. | 166 | 43.25 S | 146.59 E |
| Southport, Austl. | 171a | 27.58 S | 153.25 E |
| Southport, Eng., U.K. | 44 | 53.39 N | 3.01 W |
| Southport, Ct., U.S. | 207 | 41.08 N | 73.17 W |
| Southport, Fl., U.S. | 194 | 30.17 N | 85.38 W |
| Southport, In., U.S. | 218 | 39.39 N | 86.07 W |
| Southport, N.Y., U.S. | 210 | 42.03 N | 76.49 W |
| Southport, N.C., U.S. | 192 | 33.55 N | 78.01 W |
| South Portland | 188 | 43.38 N | 70.14 W |
| South Portsmouth | 218 | 38.43 N | 83.00 W |
| South Pottstown | 208 | 40.14 N | 75.39 W |
| South Prairie Creek ≃ | 224 | 47.08 N | 122.10 W |
| South Raisin ≃ | 206 | 45.08 N | 74.35 W |
| South Range | 190 | 47.04 N | 88.38 W |
| South Renovo | 214 | 41.19 N | 77.44 W |
| South Reservoir ⊜[1] | 283 | 42.27 N | 71.07 W |
| South Ribble □[8] | 262 | 53.45 N | 2.42 W |
| South River, On., Can. | 190 | 45.50 N | 79.23 W |
| South River, N.J., U.S. | 208 | 40.26 N | 74.23 W |
| South River ᴄ | 208 | 38.57 N | 76.29 W |
| South Rockwood | 216 | 42.04 N | 83.16 W |
| South Ronaldsay I | 46 | 58.46 N | 2.58 W |
| South Roxana | 219 | 38.50 N | 90.04 W |
| South Royalston | 207 | 42.37 N | 72.08 W |
| South Rukuru ≃ | 154 | 10.46 S | 34.14 E |
| South Russell | 214 | 41.25 N | 81.21 W |
| South Salmara | 124 | 25.55 N | 90.01 E |
| South Sand Bluff › | 158 | 31.19 S | 30.01 E |
| South Sandwich Islands II | 18 | 57.45 S | 26.30 W |
| South Sandwich Trench ✣[1] | 18 | 56.30 S | 25.00 W |
| South Sandy Creek ≃ | 212 | 43.43 N | 76.12 W |
| South San Francisco | 226 | 37.39 N | 122.24 W |
| South San Gabriel | 280 | 34.03 N | 118.05 W |
| South San Jose Hills | 280 | 34.01 N | 117.55 W |
| South San Ramon Creek ≃ | 282 | 37.42 N | 121.55 W |
| South Santiam ≃ | 202 | 44.41 N | 123.00 W |
| South Saskatchewan ≃ | 184 | 53.15 N | 105.05 W |
| South Saugeen ≃ | 212 | 44.08 N | 81.02 W |
| South Seaville | 208 | 39.10 N | 74.45 W |
| South Setauket | 210 | 40.54 N | 73.06 W |
| South Shafter | 226 | 35.28 N | 119.17 W |
| South Shetland Islands II | 9 | 62.00 S | 58.00 W |
| South Shields | 44 | 55.00 N | 1.25 W |
| South Shore | 218 | 38.43 N | 82.59 W |
| South Shore ◆[8] | 278 | 41.46 N | 87.35 W |
| South Shore Mall ◆[9] | 276 | 40.44 N | 73.15 W |
| South Shore Plaza ◆[9] | 283 | 42.13 N | 71.01 W |
| Southside | 174h | 2.49 S | 171.43 W |
| South Side ◆[8] | 279b | 40.26 N | 79.58 W |
| Southside Place | 222 | 29.42 N | 95.26 W |
| South Sioux City | 198 | 42.28 N | 96.24 W |
| South Skunk ≃ | 190 | 41.15 N | 92.02 W |
| South Slocan | 182 | 49.28 N | 117.32 W |
| South Solon | 218 | 39.44 N | 83.36 W |
| South Sound ⋓ | 48 | 53.02 N | 9.28 W |
| South Spicer Island I | 176 | 68.06 N | 79.13 W |
| South Standard | 219 | 39.21 N | 89.47 W |
| South Station ◆[5] | 283 | 42.21 N | 71.04 W |
| South Sterling | 210 | 41.17 N | 75.21 W |
| South Stony Brook | 276 | 40.53 N | 73.07 W |
| South Stradbroke Island I | 171a | 27.51 S | 153.25 E |
| South Streator | 216 | 40.39 N | 88.23 W |
| South Suburban → Behāla | 126 | 22.31 N | 88.19 E |
| South Sulphur ≃ | 196 | 33.23 N | 95.18 W |
| South Sunday Creek ≃ | 202 | 46.27 N | 105.54 W |
| South Superior | 200 | 41.45 N | 108.57 W |
| South Swansea | 207 | 41.43 N | 71.12 W |
| South Taranaki Bight ᴄ[3] | 172 | 39.40 S | 174.10 E |
| South Tasman Rise ✣[3] | 6 | 49.00 S | 148.00 E |
| South Temple | 208 | 40.24 N | 75.55 W |
| South Thompson ≃ | 182 | 50.41 N | 120.21 W |
| South Toms River | 208 | 39.56 N | 74.12 W |
| South Torrington | 198 | 42.02 N | 104.10 W |
| South Towanda | 210 | 41.45 N | 76.27 W |
| South Tucson | 200 | 32.11 N | 110.58 W |
| South Turkeyfoot Creek ≃ | 216 | 41.25 N | 83.58 W |
| South Twillingate Island I | 186 | 49.37 N | 54.47 W |
| South Tyne ≃ | 44 | 54.59 N | 2.08 W |
| South Ubian | 116 | 5.11 N | 120.30 E |
| South Uist I | 46 | 57.15 N | 7.21 W |
| South Umpqua ≃ | 202 | 43.20 N | 123.25 W |
| South Valley | 210 | 42.42 N | 74.43 W |
| South Valley Hills ⋏[2] | 285 | 40.00 N | 75.40 W |
| South Valley Stream | 276 | 40.38 N | 73.44 W |
| South Venice | 220 | 27.03 N | 82.25 W |
| South Ventana Cone ʌ | 204 | 36.17 N | 121.38 W |
| South Vestal | 210 | 42.01 N | 76.00 W |
| South Vietnam → Vietnam □[1] | 108 | 16.00 N | 108.00 E |
| Southview | 214 | 40.20 N | 80.16 W |
| Southview Apartments | 284c | 38.50 N | 77.00 W |
| South Wabasca Lake ⊜ | 182 | 55.54 N | 113.45 W |
| South Wales | 210 | 42.43 N | 78.35 W |
| South Walpole | 283 | 42.06 N | 71.15 W |
| Southwark ◆[8] | 260 | 51.30 N | 0.06 W |
| South Warren Reservoir ⊜[1] | 168b | 34.43 S | 138.55 E |
| Southwater | 42 | 51.01 N | 0.21 W |
| South Waverly | 210 | 41.59 N | 76.32 W |
| South Weald | 260 | 51.37 N | 0.16 E |
| Southwell | 44 | 53.05 N | 0.58 W |
| South Wellfleet | 207 | 41.55 N | 69.59 W |
| South Wellington | 224 | 49.06 N | 123.53 W |
| Southwest | 214 | 40.12 N | 79.32 W |
| South West Bay ᴄ | 240b | 25.00 N | 77.32 W |
| Southwest Branch ≃ | 284c | 38.53 N | 76.48 W |
| South Westbury | 276 | 40.45 N | 73.35 W |
| South West Cape ›, Austl. | 166 | 43.34 S | 146.02 E |
| South West Cape ›, N.Z. | 172 | 47.17 S | 167.28 E |
| Southwest Cape ›, Ak., U.S. | 180 | 63.18 N | 171.27 W |
| Southwest Cape ›, Vir. Is., U.S. | 241n | 17.41 N | 64.54 W |
| Southwest Channel ⋓ | 220 | 27.34 N | 82.45 W |
| South West City | 194 | 36.30 N | 94.36 W |
| South Westerlo | 210 | 42.27 N | 74.02 W |
| Southwest Greensburg | 214 | 40.17 N | 79.33 W |
| Southwest Harbor | 188 | 44.16 N | 68.19 W |
| Southwest Indian Ridge ✣[3] | 6 | 30.00 S | 60.00 E |
| Southwest Miramichi ≃ | 186 | 46.58 N | 65.35 W |
| Southwest Museum ᵿ | 280 | 34.06 N | 118.13 W |
| Southwest National Park ♠ | 166 | 43.15 S | 146.15 E |
| Southwest Pacific Basin ✣[1] | 6 | 40.00 S | 150.00 W |
| Southwest Point ›, Ba. | 238 | 25.51 N | 77.13 W |
| South West Point ›, Kiribati | 174o | 1.52 N | 157.33 W |
| Southwest Point ›, Pap. N. Gui. | 164 | 2.14 S | 146.34 E |
| South Weymouth | 283 | 42.10 N | 70.57 W |
| South Weymouth Naval Air Station ■ | 207 | 42.09 N | 70.57 W |
| South Whitley | 216 | 41.05 N | 85.37 W |
| South Whittier | 280 | 33.57 N | 118.02 W |
| South Wichita ≃ | 196 | 33.43 N | 99.29 W |
| Southwick, Eng., U.K. | 42 | 50.50 N | 0.13 W |
| Southwick, Ma., U.S. | 207 | 42.03 N | 72.46 W |
| South Williamson | 192 | 37.40 N | 82.17 W |
| South Williamsport | 210 | 41.13 N | 76.59 W |
| South Wilmington | 216 | 41.10 N | 88.16 W |
| South Windham | 188 | 43.44 N | 70.25 W |
| South Windsor | 207 | 41.49 N | 72.37 W |
| Southwold | 42 | 52.20 N | 1.40 E |
| Southwood | 210 | 42.59 N | 76.08 W |
| Southwood Acres | 207 | 41.59 N | 72.32 W |
| South Woodham Ferrers | 42 | 51.39 N | 0.37 E |
| South Woodslee | 214 | 42.14 N | 82.43 W |
| South Woodstock | 207 | 41.56 N | 71.57 W |
| Southworth | 224 | 47.31 N | 122.30 W |
| South Yadkin ≃ | 192 | 35.45 N | 80.27 W |
| South Yamhill ≃ | 224 | 45.13 N | 123.08 W |
| South Yarmouth | 207 | 41.40 N | 70.11 W |
| South Yarra | 274b | 37.51 S | 145.00 E |
| South Yorkshire □[6] | 44 | 53.30 N | 1.15 W |
| South Yuba ≃ | 226 | 39.17 N | 121.12 W |
| South Zeal | 42 | 50.44 N | 3.54 W |
| Soutpan | 158 | 28.43 S | 26.04 E |
| Soutpansberg ⋏ | 156 | 22.55 S | 29.30 E |
| Souttouf, Adrar ⋏ | 148 | 22.15 N | 15.40 W |
| Souvigny | 32 | 46.32 N | 3.11 E |
| Souzy-la-Briche | 261 | 48.32 N | 2.09 E |
| Sovata | 38 | 46.35 N | 25.04 E |
| Soverato | 68 | 38.41 N | 16.33 E |
| Sovere | 64 | 45.49 N | 10.01 E |
| Sovereign Hill Historical Park ⊥ | 169 | 37.37 S | 143.51 E |
| Sovereign Mountain ʌ | 180 | 62.08 N | 148.36 W |
| Soveria Mannelli | 68 | 39.05 N | 16.22 E |
| Sövestad | 41 | 55.30 N | 13.47 E |
| Sovetašen | 84 | 40.06 N | 44.33 E |
| Sovetka | 83 | 47.30 N | 39.15 E |
| Sovetsk, Ross. | 76 | 53.56 N | 37.39 E |
| Sovetsk, Ross. | 76 | 55.05 N | 21.53 E |
| Sovetsk, Ross. | 80 | 57.37 N | 48.58 E |
| Sovetskaja, Ross. | 80 | 49.00 N | 42.07 E |
| Sovetskaja, Ross. | 84 | 44.46 N | 41.11 E |
| Sovetskaja, Ross. | 84 | 44.02 N | 44.03 E |
| Sovetskaja Gavan' | 89 | 48.58 N | 140.18 E |
| Sovetskich Oficerov, pik ʌ | 85 | 38.26 N | 73.18 E |
| Sovetskij, Ross. | 76 | 60.32 N | 28.41 E |
| Sovetskij, Ross. | 80 | 56.46 N | 48.32 E |
| Sovetskij, Ross. | 86 | 51.04 N | 56.29 E |
| Sovetskij, Taj. | 85 | 38.02 N | 69.35 E |
| Sovetskij, Taj. | 85 | 40.11 N | 71.19 E |
| Sovetskoje, Kaz. | 85 | 42.17 N | 70.15 E |
| Sovetskoje, Ross. | 78 | 50.21 N | 39.01 E |
| Sovetskoje, Ross. | 80 | 51.27 N | 46.44 E |
| Sovetskoje, Ross. | 84 | 43.19 N | 43.36 E |
| Sovetskoje, Ross. | 84 | 42.52 N | 45.41 E |
| Šovgenovskij | 78 | 45.02 N | 40.14 E |
| Sovicille | 66 | 43.17 N | 11.13 E |
| Sovico | 266b | 45.39 N | 9.16 E |
| Søvik | 26 | 62.33 N | 6.18 E |
| Søvind | 41 | 55.54 N | 10.01 E |
| Sovpolje | 24 | 65.18 N | 43.55 E |
| Sovyets'kyy | 78 | 45.20 N | 34.56 E |
| Sow ≃ | 42 | 52.48 N | 2.00 W |
| Sowa Pan ≡ | 156 | 20.45 S | 26.00 E |
| Sowek | 164 | 0.49 S | 135.30 E |
| Sowerby, Eng., U.K. | 44 | 54.13 N | 1.21 W |
| Sowerby, Eng., U.K. | 262 | 53.42 N | 1.56 W |
| Sowerby Bridge | 44 | 53.43 N | 1.54 W |
| Soweto | 158 | 26.14 S | 27.54 E |
| Sowjetisches Ehrenmal ⊥ | 264a | 52.29 N | 13.28 E |
| Soy | 56 | 50.17 N | 5.31 E |
| Sōya-kaikyō → La Perouse Strait ⋓ | 89 | 45.45 N | 142.00 E |
| Sōya-misaki › | 92a | 45.31 N | 141.56 E |
| Soyang-chŏsuji ⊜[1] | 98 | 37.56 N | 127.53 E |
| Soyapango | 236 | 13.42 N | 89.09 W |
| Soyen | 64 | 48.07 N | 12.13 E |
| Soyers Lake ⊜ | 212 | 45.02 N | 78.37 W |
| Soyet | 124 | 24.12 N | 76.10 E |
| Soyland Moor ◆[3] | 262 | 53.40 N | 2.02 W |
| Soyo | 152 | 6.07 S | 12.18 E |
| Soyons | 62 | 44.53 N | 4.51 E |
| Sož (Sozh) ≃, Europe | 78 | 51.57 N | 30.48 E |
| Soz' ≃, Ross. | 82 | 56.48 N | 36.44 E |
| Sozh (Sož) ≃ | 78 | 51.57 N | 30.48 E |
| Šozimskij | 24 | 59.44 N | 52.16 E |
| Šožma | 24 | 61.56 N | 40.15 E |
| Sozopol | 38 | 42.25 N | 27.42 E |
| Sozzago | 266b | 45.24 N | 8.43 E |
| Spa | 56 | 50.30 N | 5.52 E |
| Spaatz Island I | 9 | 73.12 S | 75.00 W |
| Space Needle ᵿ | 224 | 47.38 N | 122.23 W |
| Space Obelisk ⊥ | 265b | 55.49 N | 37.38 E |
| Spadafora | 70 | 38.13 N | 15.22 E |
| Spada Lake ⊜[1] | 224 | 47.57 N | 121.40 W |
| Spaden | 52 | 53.34 N | 8.38 E |
| Spahl | 56 | 50.39 N | 9.55 E |
| Spaichingen | 58 | 48.04 N | 8.44 E |
| Spain (España) □[1], Europe | 22 | 40.00 N | 4.00 W |
| Spain (España) □[1], Europe | 34 | 40.00 N | 4.00 W |
| Spakenburg | 52 | 52.15 N | 5.23 E |
| Spalato → Split | 36 | 43.31 N | 16.27 E |
| Spalding, Austl. | 166 | 33.30 S | 138.37 E |
| Spalding, Sk., Can. | 184 | 52.20 N | 104.30 W |
| Spalding, Eng., U.K. | 42 | 52.47 N | 0.10 W |
| Spalding, Mo., U.S. | 219 | 39.38 N | 91.32 W |
| Spalding, Ne., U.S. | 198 | 41.41 N | 98.21 W |
| Spalt | 56 | 49.10 N | 10.55 E |
| Spam Island I | 174h | 2.48 S | 171.43 W |
| Spandau ◆[8] | 54 | 52.33 N | 13.12 E |
| Spandau, Berliner Forst ◆[3] | 264a | 52.35 N | 13.11 E |
| Spang | 41 | 54.56 N | 9.50 E |
| Spangenberg | 56 | 51.07 N | 9.40 E |
| Spangler | 214 | 40.38 N | 78.46 W |
| Spaniard's Bay | 186 | 47.37 N | 53.17 W |
| Spanien → Spain □[1] | 34 | 40.00 N | 4.00 W |
| Spanish | 190 | 46.12 N | 82.21 W |
| Spanish ≃ | 190 | 46.11 N | 82.19 W |
| Spanish Camp | 222 | 29.23 N | 96.10 W |
| Spanish Fork | 200 | 40.06 N | 111.39 W |
| Spanish Lake | 219 | 38.47 N | 90.12 W |
| Spanish North Africa □[2], Afr. | 34 | 35.53 N | 5.19 W |
| Spanish North Africa □[2], Afr. | 134 | 35.53 N | 5.19 W |
| Spanish Peak ʌ | 202 | 44.24 N | 119.46 W |
| Spanish Point › | 240a | 32.18 N | 64.48 W |
| Spanish Sahara → Western Sahara □[2] | 134 | 24.30 N | 13.00 W |
| Spanish Town, Br. Vir. Is. | 240m | 18.27 N | 64.26 W |
| Spanish Town, Jam. | 241q | 17.59 N | 76.57 W |
| Spannberg | 61 | 48.27 N | 16.44 E |
| Spantekow | 54 | 53.47 N | 13.32 E |
| Sparagio, Monte ʌ | 70 | 38.03 N | 12.46 E |
| Sparbach | 264b | 48.04 N | 16.11 E |
| Spargi, Isola I | 71 | 41.14 N | 9.21 E |
| Sparkford | 42 | 51.02 N | 2.34 W |
| Sparkill | 276 | 41.02 N | 73.56 W |
| Sparkle Lake | 210 | 41.18 N | 73.47 W |
| Sparkman | 194 | 33.55 N | 92.50 W |
| Sparks, Ga., U.S. | 192 | 31.10 N | 83.26 W |
| Sparks, Nv., U.S. | 226 | 39.32 N | 119.45 W |
| Sparland | 190 | 41.02 N | 89.26 W |
| Sparlingville | 214 | 42.58 N | 82.30 W |
| Sparneck | 54 | 50.09 N | 11.50 E |
| Sparreholm | 40 | 59.04 N | 16.49 E |
| Sparrow Bush | 210 | 41.23 N | 74.43 W |
| Sparrow Lake ⊜ | 212 | 44.49 N | 79.24 W |
| Sparrowpit | 262 | 53.19 N | 1.52 W |
| Sparrows Point | 208 | 39.13 N | 76.28 W |
| Sparrows Point › | 284b | 39.12 N | 76.30 W |
| Sparta, On., Can. | 212 | 42.42 N | 81.05 W |
| Sparta → Spárti, Ellás | 38 | 37.05 N | 22.27 E |
| Sparta, Ga., U.S. | 192 | 33.16 N | 82.58 W |
| Sparta, Il., U.S. | 194 | 38.07 N | 89.42 W |
| Sparta, Ky., U.S. | 218 | 38.40 N | 84.54 W |
| Sparta, Mi., U.S. | 190 | 43.09 N | 85.42 W |
| Sparta, N.J., U.S. | 210 | 41.02 N | 74.38 W |
| Sparta, N.C., U.S. | 192 | 36.30 N | 81.07 W |
| Sparta, Oh., U.S. | 214 | 40.24 N | 82.42 W |
| Sparta, Tn., U.S. | 194 | 35.55 N | 85.27 W |
| Sparta, Wi., U.S. | 190 | 43.56 N | 90.48 W |
| Sparta Brook ≃ | 276 | 41.08 N | 73.52 W |
| Spartak Garden ♠ | 265a | 59.51 N | 30.30 E |
| Sparta Lake | 210 | 41.03 N | 74.34 W |
| Spartanburg, In., U.S. | 218 | 40.03 N | 84.51 W |
| Spartanburg, S.C., U.S. | 192 | 34.56 N | 81.55 W |
| Spartansburg | 214 | 41.49 N | 79.41 W |
| Spartel, Cap › | 34 | 35.48 N | 5.56 W |
| Spárti (Sparta) | 38 | 37.05 N | 22.27 E |
| Spartivento, Capo ›, It. | 68 | 37.55 N | 16.04 E |
| Spartivento, Capo ›, It. | 71 | 38.53 N | 8.50 E |
| Spas-Demensk | 76 | 54.25 N | 34.01 E |
| Spas-Klepiki | 80 | 55.08 N | 40.13 E |
| Spass | 82 | 55.55 N | 35.55 E |
| Spassk | 86 | 49.32 N | 73.17 E |
| Spassk-Dal'nij | 89 | 44.37 N | 132.48 E |
| Spasskij | 86 | 53.42 N | 59.12 E |
| Spasskoje, Ross. | 76 | 53.06 N | 36.24 E |
| Spasskoje, Ross. | 80 | 55.52 N | 45.42 E |
| Spasskoje, Ross. | 82 | 54.05 N | 38.28 E |
| Spassk-R'azanskij | 80 | 54.24 N | 40.23 E |
| Spas-Zaulok | 82 | 56.29 N | 36.34 E |
| Spáta | 267c | 37.48 N | 23.55 E |
| Spátha, Ákra › | 38 | 35.42 N | 23.44 E |
| Spaulding | 219 | 39.52 N | 89.32 W |
| Spaulding, Lake ⊜[1] | 226 | 39.20 N | 120.37 W |
| Speaks | 222 | 29.15 N | 96.42 W |
| Spean, Glen V | 46 | 56.53 N | 4.45 W |
| Spean Bridge | 46 | 56.53 N | 4.54 W |
| Spear, Cape › | 186 | 47.32 N | 52.32 W |
| Spearfish | 198 | 44.29 N | 103.51 W |
| Spearman | 196 | 36.11 N | 101.11 W |
| Spearsville | 218 | 39.21 N | 86.11 W |
| Spearville | 198 | 37.51 N | 99.45 W |
| Spearwood | 168a | 32.07 S | 115.47 E |
| Speas Artemidos (Rock Tombs) ⊥ | 142 | 27.54 N | 30.52 E |
| Specchia | 68 | 39.57 N | 18.18 E |
| Spechtsbrunn | 54 | 50.30 N | 11.14 E |
| Spectacle Island I | 283 | 42.19 N | 70.59 W |
| Spectrum ♠ | 285 | 39.54 N | 75.10 W |
| Spectrum Range ⋏ | 180 | 57.30 N | 130.40 W |
| Spednic Lake ⊜ | 186 | 45.36 N | 67.35 W |
| Speed | 218 | 38.24 N | 85.45 W |
| Speed ≃ | 212 | 43.23 N | 80.22 W |
| Speedway | 218 | 39.48 N | 86.16 W |
| Speicher, Dtsch. | 56 | 49.56 N | 6.38 E |
| Speicher, Schw. | 58 | 47.24 N | 9.27 E |
| Speichersdorf | 60 | 49.52 N | 11.46 E |
| Speichersee ⊜ | 60 | 48.13 N | 11.45 E |
| Speightstown | 241g | 13.15 N | 59.39 W |
| Speigletown | 210 | 42.48 N | 73.38 W |
| Speikkogel ʌ | 61 | 47.14 N | 15.03 E |
| Speising ◆[8] | 264b | 48.10 N | 16.17 E |
| Speke ◆[8] | 262 | 53.21 N | 2.51 W |
| Speke Gulf ᴄ | 154 | 2.20 S | 33.15 E |
| Speke Hall ⊥ | 262 | 53.20 N | 2.52 W |
| Speldorf ◆[8] | 263 | 51.25 N | 6.52 E |
| Spelle | 52 | 52.22 N | 7.28 E |
| Spellen | 263 | 51.37 N | 6.37 E |
| Spello | 66 | 42.59 N | 12.40 E |
| Spelthorne □[8] | 260 | 51.25 N | 0.28 W |
| Spelve, Loch ᴄ | 46 | 56.22 N | 5.46 W |
| Spenard | 180 | 61.11 N | 149.55 W |
| Spence Bay | 176 | 69.32 N | 93.31 W |
| Spencer, In., U.S. | 194 | 39.17 N | 86.45 W |
| Spencer, Ia., U.S. | 198 | 43.08 N | 95.08 W |
| Spencer, Ma., U.S. | 207 | 42.14 N | 71.59 W |
| Spencer, Ne., U.S. | 198 | 42.52 N | 98.42 W |
| Spencer, N.Y., U.S. | 210 | 42.12 N | 76.29 W |
| Spencer, N.C., U.S. | 192 | 35.41 N | 80.26 W |
| Spencer, Oh., U.S. | 214 | 41.06 N | 82.07 W |
| Spencer, S.D., U.S. | 198 | 43.43 N | 97.35 W |
| Spencer, Tn., U.S. | 194 | 35.44 N | 85.28 W |
| Spencer, W.V., U.S. | 188 | 38.48 N | 81.21 W |
| Spencer, Wi., U.S. | 190 | 44.45 N | 90.17 W |
| Spencer, Cape ›, Austl. | 166 | 35.18 S | 136.53 E |
| Spencer, Cape ›, N.B., Can. | 186 | 45.12 N | 65.55 W |
| Spencer, Cape ›, Ak., U.S. | 180 | 58.14 N | 136.40 W |
| Spencer, Mount ʌ | 224 | 49.03 N | 124.38 W |
| Spencer, Point › | 180 | 65.18 N | 166.50 W |
| Spencer Brook ≃ | 283 | 42.28 N | 71.22 W |
| Spencer Creek ≃, On., Can. | 212 | 43.17 N | 79.54 W |
| Spencer Creek ≃, Mo., U.S. | 219 | 39.33 N | 91.20 W |
| Spencer Field ⊠ | 281 | 42.31 N | 83.33 W |
| Spencer Gulf ᴄ | 166 | 34.00 S | 137.00 E |
| Spencer Lake ⊜ | 224 | 47.16 N | 122.57 W |
| Spencerport | 210 | 43.11 N | 77.48 W |
| Spencertown | 210 | 42.20 N | 73.33 W |
| Spencerville, On., Can. | 212 | 44.51 N | 75.33 W |
| Spencerville, In., U.S. | 216 | 41.16 N | 84.55 W |
| Spencerville, Md., U.S. | 208 | 39.06 N | 76.58 W |
| Spencerville, Oh., U.S. | 216 | 40.42 N | 84.21 W |
| Spences Bridge | 182 | 50.25 N | 121.21 W |
| Spenge | 52 | 52.08 N | 8.28 E |
| Spennymoor | 44 | 54.42 N | 1.35 W |
| Spenser Mountains ⋏ | 172 | 42.15 S | 172.30 E |
| Sperenberg | 54 | 52.08 N | 13.22 E |
| Sperillen ⊜ | 26 | 60.28 N | 10.03 E |
| Sperling | 224 | 49.08 N | 122.33 W |
| Sperlinga | 70 | 37.46 N | 14.21 E |
| Sperlonga | 66 | 41.15 N | 13.26 E |
| Spermaceti Cove ᴄ | 276 | 40.26 N | 73.59 W |
| Sperone, Capo › | 71 | 38.57 N | 8.25 E |
| Sperrin Mountains ⋏ | 48 | 54.50 N | 7.05 W |
| Sperry Creek ≃ | 279a | 41.29 N | 81.53 W |
| Sperry Rand Corporation ᵿ[3] | 276 | 40.45 N | 73.42 W |
| Sperryville | 188 | 38.39 N | 78.13 W |
| Spessart ◆[1] | 56 | 50.10 N | 9.20 E |
| Spesutie Island I | 208 | 39.27 N | 76.05 W |
| Spétsai I | 38 | 37.16 N | 23.08 E |
| Spexard | 52 | 51.52 N | 8.24 E |
| Spey ≃ | 46 | 57.40 N | 3.06 W |
| Spey Bay ᴄ | 46 | 57.41 N | 3.00 W |
| Speyer | 56 | 49.19 N | 8.26 E |
| Speyerbach ≃ | 56 | 49.19 N | 8.27 E |
| Speyside | 241r | 11.18 N | 60.32 W |
| Spezia → La Spezia | 62 | 44.07 N | 9.50 E |
| Spezzano Albanese | 68 | 39.40 N | 16.19 E |
| Spezzano della Sila | 68 | 39.18 N | 16.20 E |
| Sphinx → Abū al-Hawl ⊥ | 142 | 29.59 N | 31.08 E |
| Spiazzo | 64 | 46.07 N | 10.40 E |
| Spiceland | 218 | 39.50 N | 85.26 W |
| Spicer | 198 | 45.13 N | 94.56 W |
| Spicer Creek ≃ | 284a | 43.02 N | 78.53 W |
| Spicer Meadow Reservoir ⊜[1] | 226 | 38.23 N | 119.59 W |
| Spicheren | 56 | 49.12 N | 6.58 E |
| Spickard | 194 | 40.14 N | 93.35 W |
| Spicket ≃ | 283 | 42.42 N | 71.09 W |
| Spieka | 52 | 53.45 N | 8.35 E |
| Spiekeroog I | 52 | 53.46 N | 7.42 E |
| Spiess Seamount ✣[3] | 8 | 54.40 S | 0.15 E |
| Spiez | 58 | 46.41 N | 7.39 E |
| Spijkenisse | 52 | 51.51 N | 4.20 E |
| Spilamberto | 64 | 44.32 N | 11.01 E |
| Spilimbergo | 64 | 46.07 N | 12.54 E |
| Spilinga | 68 | 38.37 N | 15.54 E |
| Spillersboda | 40 | 59.42 N | 18.51 E |
| Spillimacheen ≃ | 182 | 50.55 N | 116.20 W |
| Spillville | 190 | 43.12 N | 91.57 W |
| Spilsby | 44 | 53.11 N | 0.06 E |
| Spinazzola | 68 | 40.58 N | 16.06 E |
| Spīn Būldak | 120 | 31.01 N | 66.24 E |
| Spincourt | 56 | 49.20 N | 5.40 E |
| Spindale | 192 | 35.21 N | 81.55 W |
| Spindoli | 66 | 43.12 N | 12.54 E |
| Spinea-Orgnano | 64 | 45.29 N | 12.10 E |
| Spinetta Marengo | 62 | 44.53 N | 8.41 E |
| Spinnerstown | 208 | 40.26 N | 75.26 W |
| Spinoso | 68 | 40.16 N | 15.58 E |
| Spires → Speyer | 56 | 49.19 N | 8.26 E |
| Spirit Lake, Id., U.S. | 202 | 47.57 N | 116.52 W |
| Spirit Lake, Ia., U.S. | 198 | 43.25 N | 95.06 W |
| Spirit Lake ⊜ | 224 | 46.16 N | 122.08 W |
| Spirit River | 182 | 55.47 N | 118.50 W |
| Spiritwood | 184 | 53.22 N | 107.31 W |
| Spiro | 194 | 35.14 N | 94.37 W |
| Spirovo | 76 | 57.26 N | 34.59 E |
| Spišská Nová Ves | 30 | 48.57 N | 20.34 E |
| Spitak | 84 | 40.51 N | 44.16 E |
| Spital am Pyhrn | 61 | 47.39 N | 14.20 E |
| Spithead ⋓ | 42 | 50.45 N | 1.05 W |
| Spit Point › | 162 | 20.02 S | 119.00 E |
| Spitsbergen I | 12 | 78.45 N | 16.00 E |
| Spitsbergen Bank ✣[4] | 12 | 76.00 N | 23.00 E |
| Spittal an der Drau | 64 | 46.48 N | 13.30 E |
| Spittal of Glenshee | 46 | 56.48 N | 3.28 W |
| Spitz | 61 | 48.22 N | 15.25 E |
| Spitzer Berg ʌ[2] | 264a | 52.38 N | 13.35 E |
| Spivakivka | 83 | 49.03 N | 38.54 E |
| Spixworth | 42 | 52.40 N | 1.20 E |
| Spjelkavik | 26 | 62.28 N | 6.23 E |
| Splavnucha | 80 | 51.05 N | 45.22 E |
| Splendora | 222 | 30.14 N | 95.10 W |
| Split | 36 | 43.31 N | 16.27 E |
| Split, Cape › | 186 | 45.20 N | 64.30 W |
| Split Lake ⊜ | 184 | 56.08 N | 96.15 W |
| Splitrock Reservoir ⊜[1] | 276 | 40.58 N | 74.27 W |
| Spluga, Passo della (Splügenpass) )( | 58 | 46.30 N | 9.20 E |
| Splügen | 58 | 46.33 N | 9.20 E |
| Splügenpass (Passo della Spluga) )( | 58 | 46.30 N | 9.20 E |
| Spodsbjerg | 41 | 54.56 N | 10.50 E |
| Spofford | 196 | 29.11 N | 100.25 W |
| Špogi | 76 | 56.05 N | 26.44 E |
| Spokane | 202 | 47.39 N | 117.25 W |
| Spokane ≃ | 202 | 47.54 N | 118.20 W |
| Spokane, Mount ʌ | 202 | 47.55 N | 117.07 W |
| Spokane Indian Reservation ◆[4] | 202 | 47.55 N | 118.00 W |
| Spokojnaja | 84 | 44.15 N | 41.25 E |
| Spoleto | 66 | 42.44 N | 12.44 E |
| Spoltore | 66 | 42.27 N | 14.08 E |
| Spondigna | 64 | 46.38 N | 10.37 E |
| Spondon | 42 | 52.54 N | 1.25 W |
| Sponds Hill ʌ[2] | 262 | 53.19 N | 2.03 W |
| Spóng | 110 | 13.27 N | 105.34 E |
| Spoon ≃ | 194 | 40.18 N | 90.04 W |
| Spooner | 190 | 45.49 N | 91.53 W |
| Sporava | 76 | 52.25 N | 25.20 E |
| Spořice | 54 | 50.26 N | 13.25 E |
| Spornitz | 54 | 53.24 N | 11.43 E |
| Spornoje | 74 | 62.20 N | 151.03 E |
| Spørring | 41 | 56.18 N | 10.09 E |
| Sportforum ♠ | 264a | 52.33 N | 13.29 E |
| Sport Hill | 207 | 41.14 N | 73.16 W |
| Sporting Hill | 208 | 40.09 N | 76.26 W |
| Sportsman's Park Race Track ♠ | 278 | 41.50 N | 87.46 W |
| Spotorno | 62 | 44.14 N | 8.25 E |
| Spot Pond ⊜ | 283 | 42.27 N | 71.06 W |
| Spotswood, Austl. | 274b | 37.50 S | 144.53 E |
| Spotswood, N.J., U.S. | 208 | 40.23 N | 74.23 W |
| Spotsylvania | 208 | 38.12 N | 77.35 W |
| Spotsylvania □[6] | 208 | 38.15 N | 77.30 W |
| Spotsylvania Court House Battlefield ⊥ | 208 | 38.15 N | 77.35 W |
| Sprague, Mb., Can. | 184 | 49.02 N | 95.38 W |
| Sprague, Wa., U.S. | 202 | 47.18 N | 117.58 W |
| Sprague ≃ | 202 | 42.34 N | 121.51 W |
| Sprague, North Fork ≃ | 202 | 42.26 N | 121.07 W |
| Sprague, South Fork ≃ | 202 | 42.26 N | 121.07 W |
| Spragueville | 207 | 41.53 N | 71.32 W |
| Sprain Ridge Park ♠ | 276 | 40.59 N | 73.51 W |
| Sprankle Mills | 214 | 41.00 N | 79.07 W |
| Spratly Islands II | 108 | 10.00 N | 114.00 E |
| Spratt Point › | 212 | 44.36 N | 80.01 W |
| Spray | 202 | 44.50 N | 119.47 W |
| Spray Lakes Reservoir ⊜[1] | 182 | 50.55 N | 115.20 W |
| Spreča ≃ | 38 | 44.45 N | 18.06 E |
| Spreckels | 226 | 36.36 N | 121.34 W |
| Spreckelsville | 229a | 20.53 N | 156.24 W |
| Spree ≃ | 54 | 52.32 N | 13.13 E |
| Spreenhagen | 54 | 52.20 N | 13.52 E |
| Spreeufontein | 158 | 33.22 S | 20.45 E |
| Spreewald ◆[1] | 54 | 51.50 N | 14.05 E |
| Spremberg | 54 | 51.34 N | 14.22 E |
| Sprendlingen | 56 | 49.51 N | 7.59 E |
| Spresiano | 64 | 45.46 N | 12.16 E |
| Spring | 222 | 30.04 N | 95.25 W |
| Spring ≃, U.S. | 194 | 36.52 N | 94.44 W |
| Spring ≃, Ar., U.S. | 194 | 36.08 N | 91.05 W |
| Spring, North Fork ≃ | 194 | 37.18 N | 94.21 W |
| Spring, South Fork ≃ | 194 | 36.19 N | 91.30 W |
| Spring Arbor | 216 | 42.12 N | 84.33 W |
| Spring Bay ᴄ | 200 | 41.40 N | 112.50 W |
| Springbok | 156 | 29.43 S | 17.55 E |
| Springboro, Oh., U.S. | 218 | 39.33 N | 84.14 W |
| Springboro, Pa., U.S. | 214 | 41.48 N | 80.22 W |
| Spring Branch ≃ | 284b | 39.26 N | 76.35 W |
| Springbrook, On., Can. | 275b | 43.39 N | 79.47 W |
| Springbrook, Md., U.S. | 284c | 39.03 N | 77.00 W |
| Spring Brook, N.Y., U.S. | 210 | 42.49 N | 78.40 W |
| Spring Brook ≃ | 278 | 41.58 N | 87.59 W |
| Springbrook Forest | 284c | 39.03 N | 77.01 W |
| Springburn | 172 | 43.40 S | 171.28 E |
| Spring City, Pa., U.S. | 208 | 40.10 N | 75.32 W |
| Spring City, Tn., U.S. | 192 | 35.41 N | 84.51 W |
| Spring City, Ut,. U.S. | 200 | 39.28 N | 111.29 W |
| Spring Coulee V | 198 | 48.31 N | 100.54 W |
| Spring Creek, N.Z. | 172 | 41.28 S | 173.58 E |
| Spring Creek, Pa., U.S. | 214 | 41.53 N | 79.32 W |
| Spring Creek ≃, Austl. | 166 | 24.12 S | 140.58 E |
| Spring Creek ≃, U.S. | 198 | 40.30 N | 101.21 W |
| Spring Creek ≃, Ga., U.S. | 192 | 30.54 N | 84.45 W |
| Spring Creek ≃, Il., U.S. | 216 | 40.49 N | 87.50 W |
| Spring Creek ≃, Il., U.S. | 219 | 39.52 N | 89.37 W |
| Spring Creek ≃, Il., U.S. | 278 | 41.32 N | 88.04 W |
| Spring Creek ≃, Mo., U.S. | 219 | 38.21 N | 91.10 W |
| Spring Creek ≃, Nv., U.S. | 204 | 39.55 N | 117.50 W |
| Spring Creek ≃, N.D., U.S. | 198 | 47.15 N | 101.48 W |
| Spring Creek ≃, Pa., U.S. | 214 | 40.56 N | 77.47 W |
| Spring Creek ≃, Pa., U.S. | 214 | 41.24 N | 78.57 W |
| Spring Creek ≃, S.D., U.S. | 198 | 45.54 N | 100.18 W |
| Spring Creek ≃, S.D., U.S. | 198 | 43.52 N | 102.42 W |
| Spring Creek ≃, Tx., U.S. | 222 | 30.02 N | 95.16 W |
| Springdale, Nf., Can. | 186 | 49.30 N | 56.04 W |
| Springdale, Ar., U.S. | 194 | 36.11 N | 94.07 W |
| Springdale, Oh., U.S. | 218 | 39.17 N | 84.28 W |
| Springdale, Pa., U.S. | 214 | 40.32 N | 79.47 W |
| Springdale, S.C., U.S. | 192 | 33.57 N | 81.06 W |
| Springdale, Ut,. U.S. | 200 | 37.11 N | 112.59 W |
| Springdale, Wa., U.S. | 202 | 48.03 N | 117.44 W |
| Spring Dale, W.V., U.S. | 192 | 37.52 N | 80.48 W |
| Springe | 52 | 52.12 N | 9.32 E |
| Springer | 196 | 36.21 N | 104.35 W |
| Springers Brook ≃ | 285 | 39.44 N | 74.41 W |
| Springerville | 200 | 34.08 N | 109.17 W |
| Springfield, N.S., Can. | 186 | 44.38 N | 64.52 W |
| Springfield, On., Can. | 212 | 42.50 N | 80.56 W |
| Springfield, N.Z. | 172 | 43.20 S | 171.55 E |
| Springfield, S. Afr. | 158 | 29.02 S | 22.53 E |
| Springfield, Co., U.S. | 198 | 37.24 N | 102.36 W |
| Springfield, Fl., U.S. | 194 | 30.09 N | 85.36 W |
| Springfield, Ga., U.S. | 192 | 32.22 N | 81.18 W |
| Springfield, Il., U.S. | 219 | 39.48 N | 89.38 W |
| Springfield, Ky., U.S. | 194 | 37.41 N | 85.13 W |
| Springfield, Ma., U.S. | 207 | 42.06 N | 72.35 W |
| Springfield, Mi., U.S. | 216 | 42.19 N | 85.14 W |
| Springfield, Mn., U.S. | 198 | 44.14 N | 94.58 W |
| Springfield, Mo., U.S. | 194 | 37.12 N | 93.17 W |
| Springfield, N.J., U.S. | 276 | 40.43 N | 74.18 W |
| Springfield, Oh., U.S. | 218 | 39.55 N | 83.48 W |
| Springfield, Or., U.S. | 202 | 44.02 N | 123.01 W |
| Springfield, Pa., U.S. | 285 | 39.55 N | 75.19 W |
| Springfield, S.C., U.S. | 192 | 33.29 N | 81.16 W |
| Springfield, S.D., U.S. | 198 | 42.51 N | 97.53 W |
| Springfield, Tn., U.S. | 194 | 36.30 N | 86.53 W |
| Springfield, Vt., U.S. | 188 | 43.17 N | 72.28 W |
| Springfield, Va., U.S. | 284c | 38.45 N | 77.13 W |
| Springfield, Lake ⊜[1] | 219 | 39.44 N | 89.36 W |
| Springfield Center | 210 | 42.50 N | 74.53 W |
| Springfield Estates | 284c | 38.47 N | 77.11 W |
| Springfield Lake ⊜ | 285 | 40.11 N | 75.00 W |
| Springfield Lake ⊜[1] | 222 | 31.36 N | 96.33 W |
| Springfield Mall ◆[9] | 284c | 38.46 N | 77.11 W |
| Springfield Plateau ⋏[1] | 194 | 37.10 N | 93.30 W |
| Springfontein | 158 | 30.19 S | 25.36 E |
| Spring Garden | 246 | 6.59 N | 58.31 W |
| Spring Garden Brook ≃ | 276 | 40.46 N | 74.23 W |
| Spring Garden Township | 208 | 39.57 N | 76.44 W |
| Spring Glen, N.Y., U.S. | 210 | 41.40 N | 74.26 W |
| Spring Glen, Pa., U.S. | 208 | 40.38 N | 76.37 W |
| Spring Glen, Ut,. U.S. | 200 | 39.39 N | 110.51 W |
| Spring Green | 190 | 43.10 N | 90.04 W |
| Spring Grove, Il., U.S. | 216 | 42.26 N | 88.13 W |
| Spring Grove, Mn., U.S. | 190 | 43.33 N | 91.38 W |
| Spring Grove, Pa., U.S. | 208 | 39.52 N | 76.51 W |
| Springhill, N.S., Can. | 186 | 45.39 N | 64.03 W |
| Spring Hill, Ca., U.S. | 226 | 39.15 N | 121.03 W |
| Spring Hill, Fl., U.S. | 220 | 28.33 N | 82.27 W |
| Springhill, La., U.S. | 194 | 33.00 N | 93.28 W |
| Spring Hill, Pa., U.S. | 214 | 40.23 N | 78.40 W |
| Spring Hill, Tn., U.S. | 194 | 35.45 N | 86.55 W |
| Spring Hill, Tx., U.S. | 222 | 32.34 N | 94.48 W |
| Springhills | 216 | 40.16 N | 83.22 W |
| Spring Hope | 192 | 35.56 N | 78.06 W |
| Springhouse, B.C., Can. | 182 | 51.55 N | 122.07 W |
| Spring House, Pa., U.S. | 285 | 40.11 N | 75.14 W |
| Spring Lake, Mi., U.S. | 216 | 43.04 N | 86.11 W |
| Spring Lake, N.J., U.S. | 208 | 40.09 N | 74.01 W |
| Spring Lake, N.C., U.S. | 192 | 35.10 N | 78.58 W |
| Spring Lake ⊜, Mi., U.S. | 216 | 43.06 N | 86.11 W |
| Spring Lake ⊜, N.J., U.S. | 276 | 40.35 N | 74.25 W |
| Spring Lake Heights | 208 | 40.09 N | 74.01 W |
| Spring Mill, Oh., U.S. | 214 | 40.54 N | 82.36 W |
| Spring Mill, Pa., U.S. | 285 | 40.04 N | 75.17 W |
| Spring Mill Reservoir ⊜[1] | 262 | 53.39 N | 2.13 W |
| Spring Mills | 210 | 40.51 N | 77.34 W |
| Spring Mill State Park ♠ | 218 | 38.43 N | [illegible]6.25 W |
| Spring Mount | 208 | 40.17 N | [illegible]5.28 W |
| Spring Mountains ⋏ | 204 | 36.10 N | 1[illegible]5.40 W |
| Spring Pond ⊜ | 283 | 42.30 N | [illegible]0.57 W |
| Springport, In., U.S. | 218 | 40.03 N | [illegible]5.24 W |
| Springport, Mi., U.S. | 216 | 42.22 N | [illegible]4.41 W |
| Spring Run | 214 | 40.09 N | [illegible]3.47 W |
| Springs | 158 | 26.13 S | [illegible].25 E |
| Springs □[5] | 273d | 26.14 S | [illegible].30 E |
| Springs Aerodrome ⊠ | 273d | 26.15 S | 2[illegible].24 E |
| Springside | 285 | 40.04 N | 7[illegible].51 W |
| Springs Junction | 172 | 42.19 S | 17[illegible].11 E |
| Springsure | 166 | 24.07 S | 14[illegible].05 E |
| Springton | 168b | 34.43 S | 13[illegible].05 E |
| Springtown | 222 | 32.58 N | 97[illegible]41 W |
| Springvale, Austl. | 162 | 17.48 S | 127[illegible]41 E |
| Springvale, Austl. | 166 | 23.33 S | 140[illegible]2 E |
| Springvale, Austl. | 169 | 37.57 S | 145[illegible]9 E |
| Springvale, Me., U.S. | 188 | 43.28 N | 70[illegible]7 W |
| Springvale South | 274b | 37.58 S | 145.[illegible]9 E |
| Spring Valley, Ca., U.S. | 228 | 32.44 N | 116.[illegible] W |
| Spring Valley, Il., U.S. | 190 | 41.19 N | 89.[illegible] W |
| Spring Valley, Mn., U.S. | 190 | 43.41 N | 92.[illegible] W |
| Spring Valley, N.Y., U.S. | 210 | 41.06 N | 74.0[illegible] W |
| Spring Valley, Oh., U.S. | 218 | 39.36 N | 84.0[illegible] W |
| Spring Valley, Tx., U.S. | 222 | 29.47 N | 95.3[illegible] W |
| Spring Valley, Wi., U.S. | 190 | 44.50 N | 92.14 W |
| Spring Valley V | 204 | 39.15 N | 114.25 W |
| Spring Valley Creek ≃ | 204 | 39.20 N | 114.25 W |
| Springview | 198 | 42.49 N | 99.44 W |
| Springville, Al., U.S. | 194 | 33.46 N | 86.28 W |
| Springville, Ca., U.S. | 204 | 36.08 N | 118.49 W |
| Springville, Ia., U.S. | 190 | 42.03 N | 91.26 W |
| Springville, N.J., U.S. | 285 | 39.56 N | 74.52 W |
| Springville, N.Y., U.S. | 210 | 42.30 N | 78.40 W |
| Springville, Pa., U.S. | 210 | 41.42 N | 75.55 W |
| Springville, Ut,. U.S. | 200 | 40.09 N | 111.36 W |
| Springwater | 210 | 42.38 N | 77.35 W |
| Springwood | 170 | 33.42 S | 150.33 E |
| Sprint ≃ | 44 | 54.22 N | 2.45 W |
| Sprite Creek ≃ | 210 | 43.08 N | 74.44 W |
| Sproat Lake ⊜ | 182 | 49.16 N | 125.03 W |
| Sprockhövel | 56 | 51.22 N | 7.15 E |
| Sprogels Run ≃ | 285 | 40.14 N | 75.37 W |
| Sprogø I | 41 | 55.20 N | 10.58 E |
| Sprötze | 52 | 53.18 N | 9.49 E |
| Sproul | 214 | 40.16 N | 78.28 W |
| Sprout Brook ≃ | 276 | 40.54 N | 74.05 W |
| Spruce ≃ | 184 | 53.15 N | 105.43 W |
| Spruce Brook | 186 | 48.45 N | 58.11 W |
| Spruce Creek | 214 | 40.37 N | 78.08 W |
| Spruce Creek ≃ | 210 | 43.07 N | 74.46 W |
| Spruce Grove | 182 | 53.32 N | 113.55 W |
| Spruce Knob ʌ | 188 | 38.42 N | 79.32 W |
| Spruce Knob-Seneca Rocks National Recreation Area ♠ | 188 | 38.50 N | 79.20 W |
| Spruce Lake | 184 | 53.32 N | 109.05 W |
| Spruce Mountain ʌ, Az., U.S. | 200 | 34.28 N | 112.24 W |
| Spruce Mountain ʌ, Nv., U.S. | 204 | 40.33 N | 114.49 W |
| Spruce Pine, Al., U.S. | 194 | 34.23 N | 87.43 W |
| Spruce Pine, N.C., U.S. | 192 | 35.54 N | 82.03 W |
| Spruce Run Reservoir ⊜[1] | 210 | 40.40 N | 74.57 W |
| Spruce Run State Park ♠ | 210 | 40.40 N | 74.56 W |
| Spruce Woods Provincial Park ♠ | 184 | 49.42 N | 99.05 W |
| Spry | 208 | 39.55 N | 76.41 W |
| Spry Lake ⊜ | 212 | 44.44 N | 81.15 W |
| Spulico, Capo › | 68 | 39.58 N | 16.39 E |
| Spur | 196 | 33.28 N | 100.51 W |
| Spurfield | 182 | 55.13 N | 114.16 W |
| Spurger | 194 | 30.42 N | 94.11 W |
| Spurn Head › | 44 | 53.34 N | 0.07 E |
| Spurr, Mount ʌ | 180 | 61.18 N | 152.15 W |
| Sputendorf | 264a | 52.20 N | 13.13 E |
| Spuzzum | 182 | 49.41 N | 121.25 W |
| Spy Hill | 184 | 50.36 N | 101.41 W |
| Spy Pond ⊜ | 283 | 42.24 N | 71.09 W |
| Squally Channel ⋓ | 182 | 53.10 N | 129.15 W |
| Squamish | 182 | 49.42 N | 123.09 W |
| Squamish ≃ | 182 | 49.45 N | 123.09 W |
| Squam Lake ⊜ | 188 | 43.45 N | 71.32 W |
| Square Butte Creek ≃ | 198 | 46.55 N | 100.55 W |
| Square Lake ⊜ | 186 | 47.03 N | 68.20 W |
| Squatec | 186 | 47.53 N | 68.43 W |
| Squaw Cap Mountain ʌ | 186 | 47.53 N | 66.53 W |
| Squaw Creek ≃, Id., U.S. | 202 | 43.51 N | 116.22 W |
| Squaw Creek ≃, Il., U.S. | 278 | 42.21 N | 88.07 W |
| Squaw Creek ≃, Or., U.S. | 202 | 44.27 N | 121.20 W |
| Squaw Creek Lake ⊜[1] | 222 | 32.19 N | 97.47 W |
| Squaw Harbor | 180 | 55.11 N | 160.30 W |
| Squaw Hill ʌ | 200 | 41.48 N | 105.02 W |
| Squaw Island I | 284a | 42.56 N | 78.54 W |
| Squaw Peak ʌ, Ca., U.S. | 226 | 39.11 N | 120.16 W |
| Squaw Peak ʌ, Mt., U.S. | 202 | 47.10 N | 114.21 W |
| Squaw Rapids | 184 | 53.41 N | 103.20 W |
| Squaw Rapids Dam ◆[6] | 184 | 53.40 N | 103.25 W |
| Squaw Run ≃ | 279b | 40.29 N | 79.52 W |
| Squaw Valley State Recreation Area ♠ | 226 | 39.12 N | 120.15 W |
| Squibnocket Point › | 207 | 41.18 N | 70.47 W |
| Squilax | 182 | 50.52 N | 119.35 W |
| Squillace | 68 | 38.47 N | 16.31 E |
| Squillace, Golfo di ᴄ | 68 | 38.50 N | 16.50 E |
| Squinzano | 68 | 40.26 N | 18.03 E |
| Squire | 192 | 37.14 N | 81.36 W |
| Squires, Mount ʌ | 162 | 26.12 S | 127.28 E |
| Squirrel ≃ | 180 | 66.57 N | 160.27 W |
| Squirrel Hill ◆[8] | 279b | 40.26 N | 79.55 W |
| Squirrel Hill Tunnel ◆[5] | 279b | 40.26 N | 79.55 W |
| Squirrel's Heath ◆[8] | 260 | 51.35 N | 0.13 E |
| Sragen | 115a | 7.26 S | 111.02 E |
| Srbija (Serbia) □[3] | 38 | 44.00 N | 21.00 E |
| Srbobran | 38 | 45.33 N | 19.48 E |
| Srê Âmbĕl | 110 | 11.07 N | 103.46 E |
| Sredec | 38 | 42.21 N | 27.10 E |
| Sredinnyj chrebet ⋏ | 74 | 56.00 N | 158.00 E |
| Sredna Gora ⋏ | 38 | 42.30 N | 25.00 E |
| Sredn'aja Achtuba | 80 | 48.43 N | 44.52 E |
| Sredn'aja Mokla ≃ | 88 | 55.01 N | 119.37 E |
| Sredn'aja Nanaki, gora ʌ | 89 | 52.26 N | 132.50 E |
| Sredn'aja Ol'okma | 88 | 55.26 N | 120.33 E |
| Srednegorje | 76 | 60.34 N | 29.25 E |
| Sredneje Kujto, ozero ⊜ | 24 | 65.08 N | 31.15 E |
| Srednekolymsk | 74 | 67.27 N | 153.41 E |
| Srednerusskaja vozvyšennost' ⋏[1] | 72 | 52.00 N | 38.00 E |
| Srednesibirskoje ploskogorje ⋏[1] | 74 | 65.00 N | 105.00 E |
| Srednij Ikorec | 78 | 51.05 N | 39.45 E |
| Srednij Kalar | 88 | 55.51 N | 117.24 E |
| Srednij Ural ⋏ | 86 | 58.00 N | 59.00 E |
| Srednij Urgal | 89 | 51.09 N | 132.59 E |
| Srednij Vas'ugan | 86 | 59.16 N | 78.15 E |
| Srê Khtŭm | 110 | 12.10 N | 106.52 E |


| | English | Deutsch | Español | Français | Português |
|---|---|---|---|---|---|
| ≃ | River | Fluß | Río | Rivière | Rio |
| ≊ | Canal | Kanal | Canal | Canal | Canal |
| ʟ | Waterfall, Rapids | Wasserfall, Stromschnellen | Cascada, Rápidos | Chute d'eau, Rapides | Cascata, Rápidos |
| ⋓ | Strait | Meeresstraße | Estrecho | Détroit | Estreito |
| ᴄ | Bay, Gulf | Bucht, Golf | Bahía, Golfo | Baie, Golfe | Baía, Golfo |
| ⊜ | Lake, Lakes | See, Seen | Lago, Lagos | Lac, Lacs | Lago, Lagos |
| ≡ | Swamp | Sumpf | Pantano | Marais | Pântano |
| ⊓ | Ice Features, Glacier | Eis- und Gletscherformen | Accidentes Glaciales | Formes glaciaires | Acidentes glaciares |
| ⊤ | Other Hydrographic Features | Andere Hydrographische Objekte | Otros Elementos Hidrográficos | Autres données hydrographiques | Outros acidentes hidrográficos |
| ✣ | Submarine Features | Untermeerische Objekte | Accidentes Submarinos | Formes de relief sous-marin | Acidentes submarinos |
| □ | Political Unit | Politische Einheit | Unidad Politica | Entité politique | Unidade política |
| ᵿ | Cultural Institution | Kulturelle Institution | Institución Cultural | Institution culturelle | Institução cultural |
| ⊥ | Historical Site | Historische Stätte | Sitio Histórico | Site historique | Sitio histórico |
| ♠ | Recreational Site | Erholungs- und Ferienort | Sitio de Recreo | Centre de loisirs | Area de Lazer |
| ⊠ | Airport | Flughafen | Aeropuerto | Aéroport | Aeroporto |
| ■ | Military Installation | Militäranlage | Instalación Militar | Installation militaire | Instalação militar |
| ◆ | Miscellaneous | Verschiedenes | Misceláneo | Divers | Diversos |

ENGLISH: Name | Page | Lat.°′ | Long.°′ — DEUTSCH: Name | Seite | Breite°′ | Länge°′ E = Ost


| Name | Page | Lat.°′ | Long.°′ |
|---|---|---|---|
| Śrem | 30 | 52.08 N | 17.01 E |
| Srê Moăt | 110 | 13.18 N | 107.10 E |
| Sremska Mitrovica | 38 | 44.58 N | 19.37 E |
| Sremski Karlovci | 38 | 45.12 N | 19.57 E |
| Srêng ≃ | 110 | 13.21 N | 103.27 E |
| Srêpŏk ≃ | 110 | 13.33 N | 106.16 E |
| Sretensk | 88 | 52.15 N | 117.43 E |
| Sretenskoje | 88 | 56.28 N | 96.25 E |
| Srīdharpur | 126 | 23.04 N | 89.25 E |
| Sri Hargobindpur | 123 | 31.41 N | 75.39 E |
| Sri Jayawardenepura (Kotte) | 122 | 6.54 N | 79.54 E |
| Srīkākulam | 122 | 18.18 N | 83.54 E |
| Sri Kālahasti | 122 | 13.45 N | 79.43 E |
| Sri Lanka □[1], Asia | 118 | 7.00 N | 81.00 E |
| Sri Lanka □[1], Asia | 122 | 7.00 N | 81.00 E |
| Srīnagar, Bngl. | 126 | 23.32 N | 90.18 E |
| Srīnagar, India | 123 | 34.05 N | 74.49 E |
| Srīnagar, India | 124 | 30.13 N | 78.47 E |
| Srīnagar Airport ⊠ | 123 | 34.00 N | 74.52 E |
| Srīpur, Bngl. | 126 | 24.12 N | 90.29 E |
| Srīpur, Bngl. | 126 | 23.36 N | 89.24 E |
| Srīrampur, India | 122 | 19.34 N | 74.34 E |
| Srirāmpur, India | 272b | 22.49 N | 88.29 E |
| Srīrangam | 122 | 10.52 N | 78.41 E |
| Srīvardhan | 122 | 18.02 N | 73.01 E |
| Srīvilliputtūr | 122 | 9.31 N | 77.38 E |
| Środa Śląska | 30 | 51.10 N | 16.36 E |
| Środa Wielkopolski | 30 | 52.14 N | 17.17 E |
| Srpska Crnja | 38 | 45.43 N | 20.42 E |
| Ssangmun-ni ◆[8] | 271b | 37.39 N | 127.02 E |
| Ssuchunghsi | 100 | 22.06 N | 120.44 E |
| Ssup'ing → Siping | 89 | 43.12 N | 124.20 E |
| Staaken ◆[8] | 54 | 52.32 N | 13.08 E |
| Staaten ≃ | 164 | 16.24 S | 141.17 E |
| Staaten River National Park ♦ | 164 | 16.40 S | 143.00 E |
| Staatsburg | 210 | 41.50 N | 73.55 W |
| Staatz | 61 | 48.40 N | 16.29 E |
| Stabbursdalen Nasjonaipark ♦ | 24 | 70.06 N | 24.30 E |
| Staberhuk > | 54 | 54.24 N | 11.19 E |
| Stabroek | 50 | 51.20 N | 4.22 E |
| Stachy | 60 | 49.06 N | 13.40 E |
| Stack, Loch ⊜ | 46 | 58.20 N | 4.55 W |
| Stack Skerry I[2] | 46 | 59.01 N | 4.31 W |
| Stacksteads | 262 | 53.41 N | 2.13 W |
| Stacyville | 190 | 43.26 N | 92.46 W |
| Stad-Deiden | 52 | 52.16 N | 6.42 E |
| Stade | 52 | 53.36 N | 9.28 E |
| Staden, Bel. | 50 | 50.59 N | 3.01 E |
| Staden, Dtsch. | 56 | 50.20 N | 8.54 E |
| Stadion am Zoo ♦ | 263 | 51.14 N | 7.07 E |
| Städjan ∧ | 26 | 61.55 N | 12.52 E |
| Stadl an der Mur | 61 | 47.05 N | 13.58 E |
| Stadlandet >[1] | 26 | 62.07 N | 5.18 E |
| Stadlau ◆[8] | 264b | 48.14 N | 16.28 E |
| Stadl-Paura | 64 | 48.05 N | 13.53 E |
| Stadoličy | 78 | 51.44 N | 28.30 E |
| Stadskanaal | 52 | 53.00 N | 6.55 E |
| Stadtallendorf | 56 | 50.50 N | 9.01 E |
| Stadthagen | 52 | 52.19 N | 9.13 E |
| Stadtilm | 54 | 50.47 N | 11.05 E |
| Städtische Rahmede | 263 | 51.17 N | 7.40 E |
| Stadtkyll | 56 | 50.21 N | 6.32 E |
| Stadtlauringen | 56 | 50.11 N | 10.22 E |
| Stadtlengsfeld | 56 | 50.47 N | 10.07 E |
| Stadtlohn | 52 | 51.59 N | 6.55 E |
| Stadtoldendorf | 52 | 51.53 N | 9.37 E |
| Stadtprozelten | 56 | 49.47 N | 9.25 E |
| Stadtroda | 54 | 50.51 N | 11.44 E |
| Stadtsteinach | 54 | 50.09 N | 11.30 E |
| Stadt Wehlen | 54 | 50.58 N | 14.02 E |
| Stadum | 41 | 54.44 N | 9.03 E |
| Stäfa | 58 | 47.15 N | 8.44 E |
| Staffa I | 46 | 56.25 N | 6.20 W |
| Staffanstorp | 41 | 55.38 N | 13.13 E |
| Staffelberg ∧ | 56 | 50.06 N | 11.02 E |
| Staffelde | 264a | 52.44 N | 13.00 E |
| Staffelsee ⊜ | 64 | 47.42 N | 11.10 E |
| Staffelstein | 56 | 50.06 N | 11.00 E |
| Staffin | 46 | 57.37 N | 6.12 W |
| Staffora ≃ | 62 | 45.04 N | 9.01 E |
| Stafford, Eng., U.K. | 42 | 52.48 N | 2.07 W |
| Stafford, Ct., U.S. | 207 | 41.59 N | 72.17 W |
| Stafford, Ks., U.S. | 198 | 37.57 N | 98.36 W |
| Stafford, N.Y., U.S. | 210 | 42.59 N | 78.04 W |
| Stafford, Tx., U.S. | 222 | 29.37 N | 95.34 W |
| Stafford, Va., U.S. | 208 | 38.25 N | 77.24 W |
| Stafford □[6] | 208 | 38.25 N | 77.30 W |
| Staffordshire □[6] | 28 | 52.50 N | 2.00 W |
| Stafford Springs | 207 | 41.57 N | 72.18 W |
| Staffordsville | 188 | 37.49 N | 82.50 W |
| Staffordville | 207 | 41.59 N | 72.15 W |
| Stagen | 112 | 3.18 S | 116.10 E |
| Stag Pond ⊜ | 276 | 40.59 N | 74.42 W |
| Stahl-Berg ∧[2] | 264a | 52.21 N | 13.46 E |
| Stahlbrode | 54 | 54.14 N | 13.17 E |
| Stahle | 52 | 51.50 N | 9.25 E |
| Stahnsdorf | 54 | 52.23 N | 13.13 E |
| Stahringen | 58 | 47.47 N | 8.58 E |
| Staicele | 76 | 57.50 N | 24.45 E |
| Staines | 42 | 51.26 N | 0.31 W |
| Staines Reservoirs ⊜[1] | 260 | 51.27 N | 0.30 W |
| Stainforth | 44 | 53.36 N | 1.01 W |
| Staining | 44 | 53.49 N | 2.59 W |
| Stainland | 262 | 53.40 N | 1.53 W |
| Stainmore Forest ◆[3] | 44 | 54.30 N | 2.10 W |
| Stains | 261 | 48.57 N | 2.23 E |
| Stainz | 61 | 46.54 N | 15.16 E |
| Stairtown | 222 | 29.43 N | 97.44 W |
| Staked Plain → Estacado, Llano ≚ | 196 | 33.30 N | 102.40 W |
| Stäket | 40 | 59.28 N | 17.48 E |
| Stakhanov | 83 | 48.34 N | 38.40 E |
| Stakroge | 41 | 55.53 N | 8.51 E |
| Stalać | 38 | 43.40 N | 21.25 E |
| Stalbridge | 42 | 50.58 N | 2.23 W |
| Stalden | 58 | 46.14 N | 7.52 E |
| Staletti | 68 | 38.46 N | 16.32 E |
| Stalham | 42 | 52.47 N | 1.31 E |
| Stalheim | 26 | 60.50 N | 6.40 E |
| Stalhofen | 61 | 47.05 N | 15.16 E |
| Stalin → Varna, Blg. | 38 | 43.13 N | 27.55 E |
| Stalin → Brașov, Rom. | 38 | 45.39 N | 25.37 E |
| Stalin → Kuçovë, Shq. | 38 | 40.48 N | 19.54 E |
| Stalinabad → Dušanbe | 85 | 38.35 N | 68.48 E |
| Stalingrad → Volgograd | 80 | 48.44 N | 44.25 E |
| Stalino → Donets'k | 83 | 48.00 N | 37.48 E |
| Stalinogorsk → Novomoskovsk | 82 | 54.05 N | 38.13 E |
| Stalinsk → Novokuzneck | 86 | 53.45 N | 87.06 E |
| Stallarholmen | 40 | 59.22 N | 17.12 E |
| Ställberg | 40 | 59.59 N | 14.55 E |
| Ställdalen | 40 | 59.56 N | 14.56 E |
| Stallwang | 60 | 49.03 N | 12.40 E |
| Stalowa Wola | 30 | 50.35 N | 22.02 E |
| Stalybridge | 44 | 53.29 N | 2.03 W |
| Stambaugh | 190 | 46.04 N | 88.37 W |
| Stamford, Austl. | 166 | 21.16 S | 143.49 E |
| Stamford, Eng., U.K. | 42 | 52.39 N | 0.29 W |
| Stamford, Ct., U.S. | 207 | 41.03 N | 73.32 W |
| Stamford, N.Y., U.S. | 210 | 42.24 N | 74.36 W |
| Stamford, Tx., U.S. | 196 | 32.56 N | 99.48 W |
| Stamford, Vt., U.S. | 207 | 42.45 N | 73.04 W |
| Stamford, Lake ⊜[1] | 196 | 33.05 N | 99.35 W |
| Stamford Bridge | 44 | 53.59 N | 0.55 W |
| Stamford Brige Stadium ♦ | 260 | 51.29 N | 0.11 W |
| Stamford Harbor ⊂ | 276 | 41.02 N | 73.32 W |
| Stamford Museum ʋ | 276 | 41.07 N | 73.33 W |
| Stammbach | 54 | 50.09 N | 11.41 E |
| Stammersdorf ◆[8] | 264b | 48.18 N | 16.25 E |
| Stammham, Dtsch. | 60 | 48.15 N | 12.53 E |
| Stammham, Dtsch. | 60 | 48.52 N | 11.28 E |
| Stammheim, Dtsch. | 56 | 48.41 N | 8.46 E |
| Stammheim, Schw. | 58 | 47.38 N | 8.47 E |
| Stampede Reservoir ⊜[1] | 226 | 39.29 N | 120.07 W |
| Stamping Ground | 218 | 38.16 N | 84.41 W |
| Stampriet | 156 | 24.20 S | 18.28 E |
| Stamps | 194 | 33.21 N | 93.29 W |
| Stams | 64 | 47.16 N | 10.59 E |
| Stamsried | 60 | 49.16 N | 12.32 E |
| Stanaford | 188 | 37.48 N | 81.09 W |
| Stanardsville | 188 | 38.17 N | 78.26 W |
| Stanberry | 194 | 40.13 N | 94.32 W |
| Stanborough | 260 | 51.47 N | 0.13 W |
| Stancija-Gorčakovo | 85 | 40.25 N | 71.45 E |
| Stancionno-Ojašinskij | 86 | 55.28 N | 83.53 E |
| Standard, Ab., Can. | 182 | 51.07 N | 112.59 W |
| Standard, Ak., U.S. | 180 | 64.47 N | 148.32 W |
| Standard, Ca., U.S. | 226 | 37.59 N | 120.20 W |
| Standard, Pa., U.S. | 214 | 40.10 N | 79.32 W |
| Standard Oil Company Refinery ʋ[3] | 282 | 37.57 N | 122.24 W |
| Standard Shaft | 279b | 40.10 N | 79.32 W |
| Standedge Canal Tunnel ◆[5] | 262 | 53.34 N | 2.00 W |
| Standedge Railway Tunnel ◆[5] | 262 | 53.34 N | 2.00 W |
| Standerton | 158 | 26.58 S | 29.07 E |
| Standiford Field ⊠ | 218 | 38.11 N | 85.44 W |
| Standing Rock Indian Reservation ◆[4] | 198 | 45.50 N | 101.10 W |
| Standing Stone Creek ≃ | 214 | 40.30 N | 78.00 W |
| Standing Stones ⊥ | 46 | 58.12 N | 6.48 W |
| Standish, Eng., U.K. | 44 | 53.36 N | 2.41 W |
| Standish, Mi., U.S. | 190 | 43.58 N | 83.57 W |
| Standish Monument ⊥ | 283 | 42.01 N | 70.41 W |
| Standon | 42 | 51.53 N | 0.02 E |
| Stanfield, Az., U.S. | 200 | 32.52 N | 111.57 W |
| Stanfield, Or., U.S. | 202 | 45.46 N | 119.12 W |
| Stanford, S. Afr. | 158 | 34.26 S | 19.29 E |
| Stanford, Ca., U.S. | 226 | 37.25 N | 122.08 W |
| Stanford, Ky., U.S. | 192 | 37.31 N | 84.39 W |
| Stanford, Mt., U.S. | 202 | 47.09 N | 110.13 W |
| Stanford Center ◆[9] | 282 | 37.27 N | 122.10 W |
| Stanford Heights | 210 | 42.46 N | 73.53 W |
| Stanford le Hope | 42 | 51.31 N | 0.26 E |
| Stanford Linear Accelerator ʋ[3] | 282 | 37.25 N | 122.12 W |
| Stanford Rivers | 260 | 51.41 N | 0.13 E |
| Stanford University ʋ[2] | 282 | 37.26 N | 122.10 W |
| Stanfordville | 210 | 41.52 N | 73.43 W |
| Stånga | 26 | 57.17 N | 18.28 E |
| Stångån ≃ | 26 | 58.27 N | 15.37 E |
| Stångby | 41 | 55.46 N | 13.10 E |
| Stange | 26 | 60.43 N | 11.11 E |
| Stanger | 158 | 29.27 S | 31.14 E |
| Stanghella | 64 | 45.08 N | 11.45 E |
| Stanhope, Eng., U.K. | 44 | 54.45 N | 2.01 W |
| Stanhope, Ia., U.S. | 190 | 42.17 N | 93.47 W |
| Stanhope, N.J., U.S. | 210 | 40.54 N | 74.42 W |
| Stanislaus □[6] | 226 | 37.39 N | 121.00 W |
| Stanislaus ≃ | 226 | 37.40 N | 121.14 W |
| Stanislaus, Clark Fork ≃ | 226 | 38.22 N | 119.52 W |
| Stanislaus, Middle Fork ≃ | 226 | 38.09 N | 120.21 W |
| Stanislaus, North Fork ≃ | 226 | 38.09 N | 120.21 W |
| Stanislaus, South Fork ≃ | 226 | 38.04 N | 120.25 W |
| Stanislav → Ivano-Frankivs'k, Ukr. | 78 | 48.55 N | 24.43 E |
| Stanislav, Ukr. | 78 | 46.34 N | 32.09 E |
| Stanislavchyk | 78 | 48.58 N | 28.07 E |
| Stanisławów → Ivano-Frankivs'k | 78 | 48.55 N | 24.43 E |
| Stânișoara, Munții ⋀ | 38 | 47.10 N | 26.00 E |
| Staňkov | 60 | 49.34 N | 13.04 E |
| Stanley, Austl. | 166 | 40.46 S | 145.18 E |
| Stanley, N.B., Can. | 186 | 46.17 N | 66.44 W |
| Stanley, Falk. Is. | 254 | 51.42 S | 57.51 W |
| Stanley, H.K. | 271d | 22.13 N | 114.12 E |
| Stanley, Eng., U.K. | 44 | 54.52 N | 1.42 W |
| Stanley, Scot., U.K. | 46 | 56.28 N | 3.27 W |
| Stanley, N.Y., U.S. | 210 | 42.49 N | 77.06 W |
| Stanley, N.C., U.S. | 192 | 35.21 N | 81.05 W |
| Stanley, N.D., U.S. | 198 | 48.19 N | 102.23 W |
| Stanley, Va., U.S. | 188 | 38.34 N | 78.30 W |
| Stanley, Wi., U.S. | 190 | 44.57 N | 90.56 W |
| Stanley ≃ | 171a | 27.09 S | 152.32 E |
| Stanley, Mont ∧[2] | 273b | 4.19 S | 15.15 E |
| Stanley Bay ⊂ | 271d | 22.12 N | 114.12 E |
| Stanley Falls ʟ | 154 | 0.30 N | 25.12 E |
| Stanley Mills | 275b | 43.46 N | 79.44 W |
| Stanley Mound ∧ | 271d | 22.14 N | 114.12 E |
| Stanley Park ♦, B.C., Can. | 224 | 49.19 N | 123.09 W |
| Stanley Park ♦, Eng., U.K. | 262 | 53.26 N | 2.57 W |
| Stanley Park ♦, Eng., U.K. | 262 | 53.49 N | 3.02 W |
| Stanley Reservoir ⊜[1] | 122 | 11.54 N | 77.50 E |
| Stanleyville → Kisangani | 154 | 0.30 N | 25.12 E |
| Stanlow | 44 | 53.17 N | 2.52 W |
| Stanmore ◆[8] | 260 | 51.37 N | 0.19 W |
| Stannards | 210 | 42.05 N | 77.55 W |
| Stannington | 44 | 55.06 N | 1.40 W |
| Stanovoj chrebet ⋀ | 74 | 56.20 N | 126.00 E |
| Stanovoje nagorje (Stanovoy Mountains) ⋀ | 88 | 56.00 N | 114.00 E |
| Stanovoj Kolodez' | 76 | 52.51 N | 36.16 E |
| Stanovoy Mountains → Stanovoje nagorje ⋀ | 88 | 56.00 N | 114.00 E |
| Stans | 58 | 46.57 N | 8.22 E |
| Stansbury | 168b | 34.55 S | 137.47 E |
| Stansmore Range ⋀ | 162 | 21.23 S | 128.33 E |
| Stansstad | 58 | 46.59 N | 8.20 E |
| Stanstead | 206 | 45.01 N | 72.05 W |
| Stanstead □[6] | 206 | 45.10 N | 72.00 W |
| Stanstead Abbots | 42 | 51.47 N | 0.01 E |
| Stansted | 260 | 51.20 N | 0.18 E |
| Stansted Mountfitchet | 42 | 51.54 N | 0.12 E |
| Stanthorpe | 166 | 28.39 S | 151.57 E |
| Stanton, Eng., U.K. | 42 | 52.19 N | 0.53 E |
| Stanton, Ca., U.S. | 228 | 33.48 N | 117.59 W |
| Stanton, De., U.S. | 208 | 39.43 N | 75.37 W |
| Stanton, Ia., U.S. | 198 | 41.05 N | 95.11 W |
| Stanton, Ky., U.S. | 192 | 37.50 N | 83.51 W |
| Stanton, Mi., U.S. | 190 | 43.17 N | 85.04 W |
| Stanton, Mo., U.S. | 219 | 38.16 N | 91.06 W |
| Stanton, Ne., U.S. | 198 | 41.57 N | 97.13 W |
| Stanton, N.D., U.S. | 198 | 47.19 N | 101.22 W |
| Stanton, Tn., U.S. | 194 | 35.27 N | 89.24 W |
| Stanton, Tx., U.S. | 196 | 32.07 N | 101.47 W |
| Stantonsburg | 192 | 35.36 N | 77.49 W |
| Stanwell | 260 | 51.27 N | 0.29 W |
| Stanwell Moor | 260 | 51.28 N | 0.30 W |
| Stanwood | 224 | 48.14 N | 122.22 W |
| Stanwyck Estates | 285 | 39.42 N | 75.33 W |
| Stanychno-Luhans'ke | 83 | 48.39 N | 39.30 E |
| Stanzach | 58 | 47.23 N | 10.34 E |
| Stanz im Mürztal | 61 | 47.28 N | 15.30 E |
| Stapelburg | 54 | 51.53 N | 10.40 E |
| Stapelfeld | 52 | 53.36 N | 10.13 E |
| Staphorst | 52 | 52.37 N | 6.12 E |
| Stapleford | 42 | 52.56 N | 1.16 W |
| Stapleford Abbotts | 260 | 51.38 N | 0.10 E |
| Stapleford Aerodrome ⊠ | 260 | 51.39 N | 0.08 E |
| Stapleford Tawney | 260 | 51.40 N | 0.11 E |
| Staplehurst | 42 | 51.10 N | 0.33 E |
| Staples | 198 | 46.21 N | 94.47 W |
| Stapleton, Al., U.S. | 194 | 30.44 N | 87.47 W |
| Stapleton, Ne., U.S. | 198 | 41.28 N | 100.30 W |
| Stąporków | 30 | 51.09 N | 20.34 E |
| Star', Ross. | 76 | 53.37 N | 34.09 E |
| Star, Ms., U.S. | 194 | 32.05 N | 90.02 W |
| Star, N.C., U.S. | 192 | 35.24 N | 79.47 W |
| Stará Boleslav | 54 | 50.12 N | 14.42 E |
| Starachowice | 30 | 51.03 N | 21.04 E |
| Stara Fužina | 64 | 46.17 N | 13.54 E |
| Staraja | 265a | 59.55 N | 30.38 E |
| Staraja Belica, Bela. | 76 | 54.42 N | 29.38 E |
| Staraja Belica, Ross. | 78 | 51.59 N | 35.13 E |
| Staraja Belogorka | 80 | 52.05 N | 53.17 E |
| Staraja Derevn'a ◆[8] | 265a | 59.59 N | 30.15 E |
| Staraja Duginka | 82 | 54.20 N | 38.45 E |
| Staraja Kriuša | 78 | 50.12 N | 41.09 E |
| Staraja Kulatka | 80 | 52.43 N | 47.37 E |
| Staraja Kupavna | 82 | 55.48 N | 38.10 E |
| Staraja Majna | 80 | 54.36 N | 48.57 E |
| Staraja Poltavka | 80 | 50.28 N | 46.28 E |
| Staraja Porubežka | 80 | 52.03 N | 49.11 E |
| Staraja Račejka | 80 | 53.22 N | 48.03 E |
| Staraja Rudnja | 76 | 52.50 N | 30.17 E |
| Staraja Russa | 76 | 58.00 N | 31.23 E |
| Staraja Ruza | 82 | 55.39 N | 36.20 E |
| Staraja Sachča | 80 | 54.25 N | 49.58 E |
| Staraja Sitn'a | 82 | 54.56 N | 38.09 E |
| Staraja Terizmorga | 80 | 54.16 N | 44.32 E |
| Staraja Toropa | 76 | 56.17 N | 31.40 E |
| Staraja Veduga | 78 | 51.48 N | 38.31 E |
| Staraja Vičuga | 80 | 57.16 N | 41.53 E |
| Stara Mayachka | 78 | 46.30 N | 33.11 E |
| Staranzano | 64 | 45.49 N | 13.30 E |
| Stara Pazova | 38 | 44.59 N | 20.10 E |
| Stara Planina (Balkan Mountains) ⋀ | 38 | 42.45 N | 25.00 E |
| Stará Role | 54 | 50.14 N | 12.47 E |
| Stara Synyava | 78 | 49.36 N | 27.37 E |
| Stara Ushytsya | 78 | 48.35 N | 27.07 E |
| Starav, Ben ∧ | 46 | 56.32 N | 5.03 W |
| Stará Voda | 60 | 50.00 N | 12.36 E |
| Stara Vyzhivka | 78 | 51.27 N | 24.24 E |
| Stara Zagora | 38 | 42.25 N | 25.38 E |
| Starbejevo | 265b | 55.55 N | 37.28 E |
| Starbrick | 214 | 41.50 N | 79.12 W |
| Starbuck, Mb., Can. | 184 | 49.46 N | 97.36 W |
| Starbuck, Mn., U.S. | 198 | 45.36 N | 95.31 W |
| Starbuck, Wa., U.S. | 202 | 46.31 N | 118.07 W |
| Starbuck I | 14 | 5.37 S | 155.53 W |
| Starchenkove | 78 | 47.17 N | 36.59 E |
| Star City, Sk., Can. | 184 | 52.53 N | 104.21 W |
| Star City, Ar., U.S. | 194 | 33.56 N | 91.50 W |
| Star City, In., U.S. | 216 | 40.58 N | 86.33 W |
| Starcross | 42 | 50.38 N | 3.27 W |
| Stare Czarnowo | 54 | 53.16 N | 14.45 E |
| Staré Sedliště | 60 | 49.45 N | 12.42 E |
| Starford | 214 | 40.42 N | 78.58 W |
| Stargard Szczeciński (Stargard in Pommern) | 30 | 53.20 N | 15.02 E |
| Stargo | 200 | 33.04 N | 109.21 W |
| Star Harbour ⊂ | 175e | 10.47 S | 162.18 E |
| Stari Bar | 38 | 42.06 N | 19.08 E |
| Starica, Ross. | 76 | 56.30 N | 34.56 E |
| Starica, Ross. | 76 | 59.04 N | 29.30 E |
| Starica, Ross. | 80 | 48.13 N | 45.56 E |
| Stari Grad | 36 | 43.11 N | 16.36 E |
| Starij R'ad | 76 | 58.05 N | 34.54 E |
| Starina | 76 | 59.37 N | 44.42 E |
| Stari Popylyukhy | 78 | 48.18 N | 28.55 E |
| Stari Sanzhary | 78 | 49.25 N | 34.27 E |
| Stari Vlah ◆[1] | 38 | 43.35 N | 20.15 E |
| Star Junction | 214 | 40.04 N | 79.46 W |
| Stark □[6] | 214 | 40.48 N | 81.22 W |
| Starke | 192 | 29.56 N | 82.06 W |
| Starke □[6] | 216 | 41.18 N | 86.37 W |
| Starkey | 210 | 42.32 N | 76.56 W |
| Starkville | 194 | 33.27 N | 88.49 W |
| Star Lake | 224 | 47.22 N | 122.18 W |
| Star Mountains ⋀ | 164 | 5.05 S | 141.05 E |
| Starnberg | 60 | 48.00 N | 11.20 E |
| Starnberger See ⊜ | 64 | 47.55 N | 11.18 E |
| Starnikovo | 82 | 55.22 N | 38.24 E |
| Staroalejskoje | 86 | 51.00 N | 82.01 E |
| Starobačaty | 86 | 54.14 N | 86.07 E |
| Starobaltačevo | 86 | 56.01 N | 55.56 E |
| Starobesheve | 83 | 47.44 N | 38.03 E |
| Starobil's'k | 83 | 49.16 N | 38.56 E |
| Starobin | 76 | 52.44 N | 27.28 E |
| Staročerkasskaja | 83 | 47.15 N | 40.03 E |
| Starocuruchajtuj | 88 | 50.12 N | 119.15 E |
| Staroderev'ankov-Skaja | 78 | 46.08 N | 38.58 E |
| Starodub | 76 | 52.35 N | 32.46 E |
| Starod'umejevo | 80 | 55.16 N | 54.22 E |
| Starogan'kino | 80 | 53.55 N | 52.15 E |
| Starogard Gdański | 30 | 53.59 N | 18.33 E |
| Staroihnativka | 83 | 47.32 N | 37.47 E |
| Staroje | 76 | 59.16 N | 40.40 E |
| Staroje Bajsarovo | 80 | 55.31 N | 53.54 E |
| Staroje Drožžanoje | 80 | 54.44 N | 47.34 E |
| Staroje Ibrajkino | 80 | 54.52 N | 51.02 E |
| Staroje Jaškino | 80 | 52.49 N | 52.57 E |
| Staroje Jermakovo | 80 | 54.04 N | 51.59 E |
| Staroje Oleničevo | 80 | 45.34 N | 47.11 E |
| Staroje Rachino | 76 | 58.08 N | 32.39 E |
| Staroje Šajgovo | 80 | 54.18 N | 44.26 E |
| Staroje Šajmurzino | 80 | 54.45 N | 47.58 E |
| Staroje Sindrovo | 80 | 54.25 N | 44.06 E |
| Staroje Sjalo | 76 | 55.14 N | 29.54 E |
| Staroje Slavkino | 80 | 52.34 N | 45.08 E |
| Staroje Ustje | 80 | 53.28 N | 41.51 E |
| Starojurjevo | 80 | 53.21 N | 40.42 E |
| Starokostyantyniv | 78 | 49.46 N | 27.13 E |
| Starokozache | 78 | 46.21 N | 29.59 E |
| Starokuručevo | 80 | 55.09 N | 54.04 E |
| Starolaspa | 83 | 47.34 N | 37.59 E |
| Staroleuškovskaja | 78 | 45.59 N | 39.44 E |
| Starominskaja | 78 | 46.31 N | 39.04 E |
| Staromlynivka | 78 | 47.42 N | 36.49 E |
| Staromušta | 80 | 55.49 N | 54.14 E |
| Staromykhaylivka | 83 | 47.58 N | 37.36 E |
| Staronikolajevo | 82 | 55.37 N | 36.16 E |
| Staro-Podgorodneje | 82 | 54.46 N | 38.57 E |
| Staropokrovka | 85 | 42.50 N | 75.18 E |
| Staroščerbinovskaja | 78 | 46.37 N | 38.40 E |
| Staroseslavino | 80 | 53.12 N | 40.25 E |
| Starošešminsk | 80 | 55.22 N | 51.15 E |
| Starosiedle | 54 | 51.50 N | 14.50 E |
| Starosoldatskoje | 86 | 56.12 N | 72.37 E |
| Starosubchangulovo | 86 | 53.06 N | 57.26 E |
| Starotimoškino | 24 | 53.43 N | 47.32 E |
| Starotitarovskaja | 78 | 45.14 N | 37.09 E |
| Staroutkinsk | 86 | 57.14 N | 59.20 E |
| Starovirivka | 78 | 49.33 N | 35.42 E |
| Starožilovo | 80 | 54.14 N | 39.55 E |
| Starožil'sk | 80 | 56.34 N | 47.17 E |
| Star Peak ∧ | 204 | 40.32 N | 118.10 W |
| Starr | 214 | 41.32 N | 79.22 W |
| Starrucca | 210 | 41.54 N | 75.28 W |
| Start Bay ⊂ | 42 | 50.17 N | 3.36 W |
| Start Point > | 42 | 50.13 N | 3.38 W |
| Startup | 224 | 47.52 N | 121.44 W |
| Starvation Reservoir ⊜[1] | 200 | 40.15 N | 110.30 W |
| Starved Rock State Park ♦ | 216 | 41.19 N | 88.58 W |
| Starvja Darohi | 76 | 53.02 N | 28.16 E |
| Staryj Ajbesi | 80 | 54.57 N | 47.03 E |
| Staryj Bagr'až | 80 | 54.54 N | 51.39 E |
| Staryj Bir'uz'ak | 84 | 44.47 N | 46.54 E |
| Staryj Bol'ševik | 265b | 55.57 N | 37.47 E |
| Staryj Chop'or | 80 | 51.30 N | 42.58 E |
| Staryj Čindant | 88 | 50.33 N | 115.33 E |
| Staryje Burasy | 80 | 52.16 N | 46.09 E |
| Staryje Maty | 80 | 55.14 N | 53.55 E |
| Staryje Turdaki | 80 | 53.55 N | 45.29 E |
| Staryje Z'atcy | 80 | 57.21 N | 52.39 E |
| Staryj Kazangal | 80 | 50.15 N | 47.39 E |
| Staryj Kistruss | 80 | 54.28 N | 40.34 E |
| Staryj Lesken | 84 | 43.20 N | 43.55 E |
| Staryj Medved' | 76 | 58.18 N | 30.30 E |
| Staryj Oskol | 78 | 51.19 N | 37.51 E |
| Staryj Terek ≃ | 84 | 44.00 N | 47.24 E |
| Staryj Tukšum | 80 | 53.42 N | 48.33 E |
| Starý Plzenec | 60 | 49.42 N | 13.28 E |
| Stary Sącz | 30 | 49.34 N | 20.38 E |
| Staryy Chortoryys'k | 78 | 51.15 N | 25.54 E |
| Staryy Krym, Ukr. | 78 | 45.03 N | 35.05 E |
| Staryy Krym, Ukr. | 83 | 47.10 N | 37.30 E |
| Staryy Merchyk | 78 | 49.58 N | 35.46 E |
| Staryy Sambir | 78 | 49.27 N | 22.59 E |
| Stassfurt | 54 | 51.51 N | 11.34 E |
| Staszów | 30 | 50.34 N | 21.20 E |
| State Center | 190 | 42.01 N | 93.09 W |
| State College | 214 | 40.47 N | 77.51 W |
| State Fair Grounds ♦ | 284b | 39.27 N | 76.38 W |
| Stateline, Ca., U.S. | 226 | 38.57 N | 119.57 W |
| State Line, Ms., U.S. | 194 | 31.26 N | 88.28 W |
| Stateline, Nv., U.S. | 204 | 38.58 N | 119.56 W |
| Staten Island I | 276 | 40.35 N | 74.09 W |
| Staten Island Mall ◆[9] | 276 | 40.35 N | 74.10 W |
| Statenville | 192 | 30.42 N | 83.01 W |
| State Park Place | 219 | 38.40 N | 90.03 W |
| State Road | 192 | 36.19 N | 80.52 W |
| Statesboro | 192 | 32.26 N | 81.47 W |
| Statesville | 192 | 35.46 N | 80.53 W |
| Stateville Correctional Center ʋ | 278 | 41.35 N | 88.06 W |
| Station Peak | 162 | 21.10 S | 118.11 E |
| Statte | 68 | 40.34 N | 17.12 E |
| Statue of Liberty National Monument ♦ | 210 | 40.41 N | 74.03 W |
| Staubbachfall ʟ | 58 | 46.35 N | 7.55 E |
| Staubun | 76 | 52.48 N | 31.25 E |
| Staufen | 58 | 47.53 N | 7.44 E |
| Staufenberg | 56 | 50.40 N | 8.43 E |
| Staughton Vale | 169 | 37.51 S | 144.17 E |
| Staunton, Il., U.S. | 219 | 39.00 N | 89.47 W |
| Staunton, Va., U.S. | 188 | 38.08 N | 79.04 W |
| Staunton → Roanoke ≃ | 192 | 35.56 N | 76.43 W |
| Stavanger | 26 | 58.58 N | 5.45 E |
| Stave ≃ | 224 | 49.10 N | 122.26 W |
| Stave Lake ⊜ | 182 | 49.15 N | 122.21 W |
| Staveley | 44 | 53.16 N | 1.20 W |
| Stavelot | 56 | 50.23 N | 5.56 E |
| Stavely, Ab., Can. | 182 | 50.10 N | 113.38 W |
| Stavely, Eng., U.K. | 44 | 54.22 N | 2.49 W |
| Staveren | 52 | 52.53 N | 5.22 E |
| Stavern | 26 | 59.00 N | 10.02 E |
| Stavne | 78 | 48.59 N | 22.40 E |
| Stavropol', Ross. | 72 | 45.02 N | 41.59 E |
| Stavropol → Toljatti, Ross. | 80 | 53.31 N | 49.26 E |
| Stavropol' Kraj □[8] | 84 | 44.38 N | 43.30 E |
| Stavrovo | 80 | 56.08 N | 40.00 E |
| Stavsnäs | 40 | 59.17 N | 18.41 E |
| Stavyshche | 78 | 49.23 N | 30.12 E |
| Stawell | 166 | 37.04 S | 142.46 E |
| Stawell ≃ | 166 | 20.38 S | 142.55 E |
| Stawiski | 30 | 53.23 N | 22.09 E |
| Stawiszyn | 30 | 51.55 N | 18.07 E |
| Staxigoe | 46 | 58.28 N | 3.04 W |
| Stayky | 78 | 50.05 N | 30.54 E |
| Stayner | 212 | 44.25 N | 80.05 W |
| Stayton | 202 | 44.48 N | 122.47 W |
| Stazzema | 64 | 43.59 N | 10.19 E |
| Steamboat | 226 | 39.22 N | 119.44 W |
| Steamboat Creek ≃ | 226 | 39.31 N | 119.42 W |
| Steamboat Mountain ∧ | 200 | 41.58 N | 108.58 W |
| Steamboat Slough ≃ | 226 | 38.11 N | 121.40 W |
| Steamboat Springs | 200 | 40.29 N | 106.49 W |
| Steamburg | 210 | 42.07 N | 78.54 W |
| Stearns | 192 | 36.41 N | 84.28 W |
| Stearns Pond ⊜ | 283 | 42.37 N | 71.04 W |
| Stębark | 30 | 53.30 N | 20.08 E |
| Stebbins | 180 | 63.32 N | 162.18 W |
| Stebliv | 78 | 49.24 N | 31.06 E |
| Stechow | 54 | 52.38 N | 12.28 E |
| Steckborn | 58 | 47.40 N | 8.55 E |
| Stederdorf | 52 | 52.21 N | 10.15 E |
| Stedum | 52 | 53.18 N | 6.41 E |
| Steeg | 58 | 47.14 N | 10.17 E |
| Steel ≃ | 190 | 48.46 N | 86.54 W |
| Steel City | 210 | 40.38 N | 75.20 W |
| Steele, Mo., U.S. | 194 | 36.05 N | 89.49 W |
| Steele, N.D., U.S. | 198 | 46.51 N | 99.54 W |
| Steele ◆[8] | 263 | 51.27 N | 7.05 E |
| Steele, Mount ∧ | 200 | 41.50 N | 107.00 W |
| Steele Creek ≃, Tx., U.S. | 222 | 32.01 N | 97.28 W |
| Steele Creek ≃, Tx., U.S. | 222 | 31.13 N | 96.19 W |
| Steeles Corners | 275b | 43.48 N | 79.25 W |
| Steeleville | 194 | 38.00 N | 89.39 W |
| Steelhead | 224 | 49.13 N | 122.19 W |
| Steel's Drift | 158 | 27.21 S | 29.30 E |
| Steels Point > | 174c | 29.02 S | 168.00 E |
| Steels Run ≃ | 279b | 40.25 N | 79.38 W |
| Steelton, N.Y., U.S. | 284a | 42.47 N | 78.49 W |
| Steelton, Pa., U.S. | 208 | 40.14 N | 76.50 W |
| Steelville | 194 | 37.58 N | 91.21 W |
| Steenbergen | 52 | 51.35 N | 4.19 E |
| Steenburg Lake ⊜ | 212 | 44.50 N | 77.41 W |
| Steenderen | 52 | 52.04 N | 6.11 E |
| Steens Mountain ⋀ | 202 | 42.35 N | 118.40 W |
| Steenvoorde | 50 | 50.48 N | 2.35 E |
| Steenwijk | 52 | 52.47 N | 6.08 E |
| Steepbank ≃ | 184 | 57.01 N | 111.28 W |
| Steephill Lake ⊜ | 184 | 55.58 N | 103.08 W |
| Steep Holm I | 42 | 51.21 N | 3.07 W |
| Steeping ≃ | 44 | 53.06 N | 0.18 E |
| Steeple Claydon | 42 | 51.56 N | 0.59 W |
| Steep Point > | 162 | 26.08 S | 113.08 E |
| Steep Rock | 184 | 51.26 N | 98.48 W |
| Stefanie, Lake → Chew Bahir ⊜, Afr. | 144 | 4.40 N | 36.50 E |
| Stefanie, Lake (Chew Bahir) ⊜, Afr. | 144 | 4.40 N | 36.50 E |
| Stefansson Island I | 176 | 73.20 N | 105.45 W |
| Ștefan Vodă | 38 | 44.19 N | 27.19 E |
| Steffisburg | 58 | 46.47 N | 7.39 E |
| Steg | 58 | 47.21 N | 8.56 E |
| Stegalovka | 76 | 52.24 N | 38.19 E |
| Stege | 41 | 54.59 N | 12.18 E |
| Stegeborg | 26 | 58.26 N | 16.35 E |
| Stege Bugt ⊂ | 41 | 55.01 N | 12.05 E |
| Stegelitz | 54 | 53.08 N | 13.51 E |
| Steger | 216 | 41.28 N | 87.38 W |
| Stegersbach | 61 | 47.10 N | 16.10 E |
| Steglitz ◆[8] | 264a | 52.28 N | 13.19 E |
| Stehag | 41 | 55.54 N | 13.23 E |
| Stehekin | 224 | 48.18 N | 120.39 W |
| Stehekin ≃ | 224 | 48.21 N | 120.40 W |
| Ștei | 38 | 46.32 N | 22.28 E |
| Steiermark □[3] | 30 | 47.10 N | 15.10 E |
| Steigerwald ⋀ | 56 | 49.40 N | 10.20 E |
| Steigra | 54 | 51.18 N | 11.39 E |
| Steilacoom | 224 | 47.10 N | 122.36 W |
| Steimbke | 52 | 52.40 N | 9.22 E |
| Stein, Dtsch. | 56 | 49.25 N | 11.01 E |
| Stein, Dtsch. | 60 | 49.25 N | 11.01 E |
| Stein, Ned. | 56 | 50.57 N | 5.46 E |
| Stein, Schw. | 58 | 47.33 N | 7.58 E |
| Steina | 54 | 51.12 N | 14.01 E |
| Steinach, Dtsch. | 54 | 50.25 N | 11.10 E |
| Steinach, Dtsch. | 58 | 48.18 N | 8.04 E |
| Steinach, Öst. | 64 | 47.05 N | 11.28 E |
| Steinach ≃ | 54 | 50.11 N | 11.12 E |
| Steinamanger → Szombathely | 30 | 47.14 N | 16.38 E |
| Stein am Rhein | 58 | 47.40 N | 8.51 E |
| Steinau | 56 | 50.23 N | 9.27 E |
| Steinbach, Mb., Can. | 184 | 49.32 N | 96.41 W |
| Steinbach, Dtsch. | 56 | 48.43 N | 8.10 E |
| Steinberg ∧[2] | 263 | 51.05 N | 7.27 E |
| Steinberger Slough ≃ | 282 | 37.33 N | 122.13 W |
| Steinbourg | 56 | 48.46 N | 7.25 E |
| Steindorf | 61 | 46.42 N | 14.01 E |
| Steinen | 58 | 47.38 N | 7.44 E |
| Steinernes Meer ⋀ | 64 | 47.30 N | 12.58 E |
| Steinfeld, Dtsch. | 52 | 52.35 N | 8.12 E |
| Steinfeld, Dtsch. | 54 | 50.22 N | 10.44 E |
| Steinfeld, Öst. | 64 | 46.45 N | 13.15 E |
| Steinfort | 56 | 49.40 N | 5.55 E |
| Steinforth | 263 | 51.09 N | 6.32 E |
| Steinfurt | 52 | 52.09 N | 7.21 E |
| Steingaden | 58 | 47.42 N | 10.51 E |
| Steinhagen, Dtsch. | 52 | 52.00 N | 8.24 E |
| Steinhagen, Dtsch. | 54 | 54.13 N | 12.59 E |
| Steinhatchee ≃ | 192 | 29.40 N | 83.24 W |
| Steinhausen | 156 | 21.49 S | 18.20 E |
| Steinhausen ʋ[1] | 58 | 48.01 N | 9.41 E |
| Steinheid | 54 | 50.28 N | 11.04 E |
| Steinheim, Dtsch. | 52 | 51.52 N | 9.05 E |
| Steinheim, Dtsch. | 56 | 48.58 N | 9.16 E |
| Steinhöfel | 54 | 52.24 N | 14.10 E |
| Steinhöring | 60 | 48.05 N | 12.02 E |
| Steinhude | 52 | 52.27 N | 9.21 E |
| Steinhuder Meer ⊜ | 52 | 52.28 N | 9.19 E |
| Steinkjer | 26 | 64.01 N | 11.30 E |
| Steinkopf | 156 | 29.18 S | 17.43 E |
| Steinloge | 52 | 52.54 N | 8.19 E |
| Stein-Neukirch | 56 | 50.41 N | 8.03 E |
| Steinpass )( | 64 | 47.39 N | 12.45 E |
| Steinsdorf | 54 | 52.02 N | 14.40 E |
| Steinshamn | 26 | 62.47 N | 6.29 E |
| Steinstücken ◆[8] | 264a | 52.23 N | 13.08 E |
| Steinwiesen | 54 | 50.17 N | 11.28 E |
| Stekene | 50 | 51.12 N | 4.02 E |
| Stekl'anka | 76 | 59.08 N | 41.37 E |
| Steklino | 76 | 56.51 N | 32.10 E |
| Steksovo | 80 | 55.17 N | 43.25 E |
| Stella, It. | 62 | 44.24 N | 8.30 E |
| Stella, S. Afr. | 158 | 26.38 S | 24.48 E |
| Stella, Ne., U.S. | 198 | 40.13 N | 95.46 W |
| Stella Niagara | 210 | 43.12 N | 79.02 W |
| Stella-Plage | 50 | 50.29 N | 1.35 E |
| Stellaquo Indian Reserve ◆[4] | 182 | 54.03 N | 124.55 W |
| Stellarton | 186 | 45.34 N | 62.40 W |
| Stelle | 52 | 53.23 N | 10.06 E |
| Stellenbosch | 158 | 33.58 S | 18.50 E |
| Steller, Mount ∧ | 180 | 60.30 N | 143.02 W |
| Stelvio, Parco Nazionale dello ♦ | 64 | 46.30 N | 10.40 E |
| Stelvio, Passo dello )( | 64 | 46.32 N | 10.27 E |
| Stemwede | 52 | 52.25 N | 8.27 E |
| Stenay | 56 | 49.29 N | 5.11 E |
| Stendal | 54 | 52.36 N | 11.51 E |
| Stende | 76 | 57.09 N | 22.33 E |
| Stenden | 263 | 51.25 N | 6.27 E |
| Stenhammar slott ⊥ | 40 | 59.03 N | 16.31 E |
| Stenhouse Bay | 166 | 35.17 S | 136.56 E |
| Stenhousemuir | 46 | 56.02 N | 3.48 W |
| Stenico | 64 | 46.03 N | 10.51 E |
| Stenlille | 41 | 55.32 N | 11.36 E |
| Stenløse | 41 | 55.46 N | 12.12 E |
| Stenness, Loch of ⊜ | 46 | 59.00 N | 3.15 W |
| Stenón | 267c | 37.58 N | 23.25 E |
| Stenón Návstathmou ʮ | 267c | 37.58 N | 23.33 E |
| Stensätra | 40 | 60.36 N | 16.44 E |
| Stensele | 24 | 65.05 N | 17.09 E |
| Stenstorp | 26 | 58.16 N | 13.43 E |
| Stenstrup | 41 | 55.07 N | 10.31 E |
| Stentrop | 263 | 51.30 N | 7.49 E |
| Stenungsund | 26 | 58.05 N | 11.49 E |
| Stepan' | 78 | 51.10 N | 26.18 E |
| Stepanakert → Xankändi | 84 | 39.49 N | 46.44 E |
| Stepanavan | 84 | 41.00 N | 44.23 E |
| Stepancevo, Ross. | 80 | 56.08 N | 41.42 E |
| Stepancevo, Ross. | 82 | 56.22 N | 36.10 E |
| Stepancy | 78 | 49.42 N | 31.18 E |
| Stepanivka | 78 | 50.58 N | 34.37 E |
| Stepano-Krynka | 83 | 47.55 N | 38.21 E |
| Stepanovka, Ross. | 80 | 52.04 N | 53.02 E |
| Stepanovka, Ross. | 86 | 57.13 N | 67.26 E |
| Stepanovo | 82 | 55.43 N | 38.28 E |
| Stepanovskoje | 265b | 55.47 N | 37.10 E |
| Stepanščino | 82 | 55.15 N | 38.30 E |
| Stepenitz ≃ | 54 | 53.48 N | 11.10 E |
| Stephans-Dom ʋ[1] | 264b | 48.12 N | 16.23 E |
| Stephanskirchen | 64 | 47.51 N | 12.11 E |
| Stephen | 198 | 48.27 N | 96.52 W |
| Stephen A. Forbes State Park ♦ | 219 | 38.44 N | 88.46 W |
| Stephen F. Austin State Historic Park ♦ | 222 | 29.48 N | 96.05 W |
| Stephens | 194 | 33.24 N | 93.04 W |
| Stephens, Cape > | 172 | 40.42 S | 173.57 E |
| Stephens, Port ⊂ | 166 | 32.45 S | 152.05 E |
| Stephens City | 188 | 39.05 N | 78.13 W |
| Stephens Creek | 166 | 31.50 S | 141.30 E |
| Stephens Island I | 182 | 54.10 N | 130.45 W |
| Stephens Knob ∧[2] | 192 | 36.37 N | 84.20 W |
| Stephens Lake ⊜[1] | 184 | 56.26 N | 95.07 W |
| Stephens Mills | 210 | 42.23 N | 77.38 W |
| Stephenson | 190 | 45.24 N | 87.36 W |
| Stephenson, Lake ⊜ | 222 | 29.35 N | 94.40 W |
| Stephenson, Mount ∧ | 9 | 69.49 S | 69.43 W |
| Stephens Passage ʮ | 180 | 57.50 N | 133.50 W |
| Stephentown | 210 | 42.33 N | 73.23 W |
| Stephentown Center | 210 | 42.34 N | 73.25 W |
| Stephenville, Nf., Can. | 186 | 48.33 N | 58.35 W |
| Stephenville, Tx., U.S. | 196 | 32.13 N | 98.12 W |
| Stephenville Crossing | 186 | 48.30 N | 58.26 W |
| Stepn'ak | 86 | 52.50 N | 70.50 E |
| Stepney ◆[8] | 260 | 51.31 N | 0.02 W |
| Stepnica | 54 | 53.40 N | 14.36 E |
| Stepnoj | 80 | 48.56 N | 45.36 E |
| Stepnoje, Ross. | 80 | 51.24 N | 46.52 E |
| Stepnoje, Ross. | 84 | 44.17 N | 44.36 E |
| Step Pyramid → Ṣaqqārah ⊥ | 142 | 29.52 N | 31.14 E |
| Steps Point > | 174u | 14.22 S | 170.45 W |
| Steptoe Valley V | 204 | 39.25 N | 114.45 W |
| Stepurino | 76 | 56.24 N | 35.16 E |
| Sterdyń | 30 | 52.35 N | 22.18 E |
| Stereá Ellás □[4] | 38 | 38.30 N | 23.00 E |
| Sterkaar | 158 | 31.05 S | 23.42 E |
| Sterkrade ◆[8] | 263 | 51.31 N | 6.51 E |
| Sterkspruit | 158 | 30.32 S | 27.22 E |
| Sterkstroom | 158 | 31.32 S | 26.32 E |
| Sterlibaševo | 86 | 53.28 N | 55.15 E |
| Sterling, S. Afr. | 158 | 31.16 S | 21.28 E |
| Sterling, Ak., U.S. | 180 | 60.32 N | 150.48 W |
| Sterling, Co., U.S. | 198 | 40.37 N | 103.12 W |
| Sterling, Ct., U.S. | 207 | 41.42 N | 71.49 W |
| Sterling, Il., U.S. | 190 | 41.47 N | 89.41 W |
| Sterling, Ks., U.S. | 198 | 38.12 N | 98.12 W |
| Sterling, Ma., U.S. | 207 | 42.26 N | 71.45 W |
| Sterling, Mi., U.S. | 190 | 44.02 N | 84.01 W |
| Sterling, Ne., U.S. | 198 | 40.27 N | 96.22 W |
| Sterling, N.Y., U.S. | 210 | 43.20 N | 76.39 W |
| Sterling, Oh., U.S. | 214 | 40.58 N | 81.51 W |
| Sterling, Ok., U.S. | 196 | 34.45 N | 98.10 W |
| Sterling, Va., U.S. | 208 | 39.00 N | 77.25 W |
| Sterling City | 196 | 31.50 N | 100.59 W |
| Sterling Creek ≃ | 210 | 43.20 N | 76.42 W |
| Sterling Forest Lake ⊜ | 276 | 41.10 N | 74.16 W |
| Sterling Heights | 214 | 42.34 N | 83.01 W |
| Sterling Junction | 207 | 42.24 N | 71.46 W |
| Sterling Park | 282 | 37.41 N | 122.26 W |
| Sterling Run | 214 | 41.25 N | 78.12 W |
| Sterlington | 194 | 32.41 N | 92.05 W |
| Sterlitamak | 86 | 53.37 N | 55.58 E |
| Šternberg | 54 | 53.43 N | 11.49 E |
| Šternberk | 30 | 49.44 N | 17.18 E |
| Sternstein ∧ | 61 | 48.34 N | 14.16 E |
| Sterup | 41 | 54.44 N | 9.44 E |
| Sterzing → Vipiteno | 64 | 46.54 N | 11.26 E |
| Stęszew | 30 | 52.18 N | 16.42 E |
| Štětí | 54 | 50.25 N | 14.23 E |
| Stetson Pond ⊜ | 283 | 42.02 N | 70.50 W |
| Stetten am kalten Markt | 58 | 48.07 N | 9.04 E |
| Stettin → Szczecin | 30 | 53.24 N | 14.32 E |
| Stettiner Haff (Zalew Szczeciński) ⊂ | 54 | 53.46 N | 14.14 E |
| Stettler | 182 | 52.19 N | 112.43 W |
| Steuben □[6], In., U.S. | 216 | 41.38 N | 85.00 W |
| Steuben □[6], N.Y., U.S. | 210 | 42.20 N | 77.19 W |
| Steubenville | 214 | 40.22 N | 80.38 W |
| Steutz | 54 | 51.53 N | 12.05 E |
| Stevenage | 42 | 51.55 N | 0.14 W |
| Stevens, N.J., U.S. | 285 | 40.05 N | 74.49 W |
| Stevens, Pa., U.S. | 208 | 40.13 N | 76.09 W |
| Stevens, Lake ⊜ | 224 | 48.01 N | 122.05 W |
| Stevens, Mount ∧ | 172 | 40.48 S | 172.27 E |
| Stevens Creek ≃, Ca., U.S. | 282 | 37.26 N | 122.05 W |
| Stevens Creek ≃, S.C., U.S. | 192 | 33.34 N | 82.03 W |
| Stevens Creek Park ♦ | 282 | 37.17 N | 122.04 W |
| Stevens Creek Reservoir ⊜[1] | 282 | 37.17 N | 122.05 W |
| Stevens Institute of Technology ʋ[2] | 276 | 40.44 N | 74.02 W |
| Stevenson, Al., U.S. | 194 | 34.52 N | 85.50 W |
| Stevenson, Md., U.S. | 284b | 39.25 N | 76.43 W |
| Stevenson, Wa., U.S. | 224 | 45.42 N | 121.53 W |
| Stevenson Creek ≃ | 162 | 27.06 S | 135.33 E |
| Stevenson Entrance ʮ | 180 | 58.45 N | 152.20 W |
| Stevenson Lake ⊜ | 184 | 53.56 N | 96.09 W |
| Stevens Pass )( | 224 | 47.45 N | 121.04 W |
| Stevens Peak ∧ | 202 | 47.27 N | 115.46 W |
| Stevens Point | 190 | 44.31 N | 89.34 W |
| Stevenston | 46 | 55.39 N | 4.45 W |
| Stevens Village | 180 | 66.00 N | 149.05 W |
| Stevensville, On., Can. | 284a | 42.57 N | 79.04 W |
| Stevensville, Md., U.S. | 208 | 38.58 N | 76.18 W |
| Stevensville, Mi., U.S. | 216 | 42.00 N | 86.31 W |
| Stevensville, Mt., U.S. | 202 | 46.30 N | 114.05 W |
| Stevensville, Pa., U.S. | 210 | 41.46 N | 76.11 W |
| Stevinson | 226 | 37.20 N | 120.51 W |
| Stevns Klint ⊥[4] | 41 | 55.18 N | 12.27 E |
| Steward | 216 | 41.51 N | 89.01 W |
| Stewardson | 219 | 39.15 N | 88.37 W |
| Stewart, B.C., Can. | 182 | 55.56 N | 129.59 W |
| Stewart, Mn., U.S. | 190 | 44.43 N | 94.29 W |
| Stewart ≃ | 180 | 63.18 N | 139.25 W |
| Stewart, Cape > | 164 | 11.57 S | 134.45 E |
| Stewart, Isla I | 254 | 54.52 S | 71.12 W |
| Stewart, Mount ∧ | 166 | 20.12 S | 145.29 E |
| Stewart Island I | 172 | 47.00 S | 167.50 E |
| Stewart Islands II | 175e | 8.25 S | 162.52 E |
| Stewart Lake ⊜ | 219 | 40.09 N | 90.16 W |
| Stewart Manor | 276 | 40.43 N | 73.41 W |
| Stewarton | 46 | 55.41 N | 4.31 W |
| Stewartstown, N. Ire., U.K. | 48 | 54.35 N | 6.41 W |
| Stewartstown, Pa., U.S. | 208 | 39.45 N | 76.35 W |
| Stewartsville, Mo., U.S. | 194 | 39.45 N | 94.29 W |
| Stewartsville, N.J., U.S. | 208 | 40.41 N | 75.06 W |
| Stewartsville, Pa., U.S. | 279b | 40.21 N | 79.46 W |
| Stewart Valley | 184 | 50.36 N | 107.50 W |
| Stewartville | 190 | 43.51 N | 92.29 W |
| Stewiacke | 186 | 45.08 N | 63.21 W |
| Steyerberg | 52 | 52.34 N | 9.01 E |
| Steyning | 42 | 50.53 N | 0.20 W |
| Steynsburg | 158 | 31.15 S | 25.49 E |
| Steynsrus | 158 | 27.58 S | 27.33 E |
| Steyr | 61 | 48.03 N | 14.25 E |
| Steyr ≃ | 61 | 48.02 N | 14.25 E |
| Steyregg | 61 | 48.17 N | 14.22 E |
| Steytlerville | 158 | 33.21 S | 24.21 E |
| Stežki | 80 | 53.06 N | 41.13 E |
| Stezzano | 62 | 45.38 N | 9.39 E |
| Sthal | 126 | 24.12 N | 89.44 E |
| Stia | 66 | 43.48 N | 11.42 E |
| Štiavnické vrchy ⋀ | 30 | 48.40 N | 18.45 E |
| Stickle Pond ⊜ | 276 | 40.59 N | 74.25 W |
| Stickney, Eng., U.K. | 44 | 53.05 N | 0.01 E |
| Stickney, Il., U.S. | 216 | 41.49 N | 87.46 W |
| Stickney, S.D., U.S. | 198 | 43.35 N | 98.26 W |
| Stidsvig | 41 | 56.12 N | 13.08 E |
| Stiefing ≃ | 61 | 46.47 N | 15.35 E |
| Stiege | 54 | 51.40 N | 10.53 E |
| Stiene | 76 | 57.26 N | 24.34 E |
| Stienitzfliess ≃ | 264a | 52.33 N | 13.43 E |
| Stienitz-See ⊜ | 264a | 52.30 N | 13.49 E |
| Stiens | 52 | 53.15 N | 5.45 E |
| Stiepel ◆[8] | 263 | 51.25 N | 7.15 E |
| Stif | 148 | 36.09 N | 5.26 E |
| Stiftskirche ʋ[1] | 263 | 51.23 N | 7.00 E |
| Stige | 41 | 55.26 N | 10.25 E |
| Stigler | 196 | 35.15 N | 95.07 W |
| Stigliano | 68 | 40.24 N | 16.14 E |
| Stigtomta | 40 | 58.48 N | 16.47 E |
| Stih, hora ∧ | 78 | 48.37 N | 23.11 E |
| Stikine ≃ | 180 | 56.40 N | 132.30 W |
| Stikine Ranges ⋀ | 180 | 58.45 N | 130.00 W |
| Stiklestad | 26 | 63.48 N | 11.33 E |
| Stilbaai | 158 | 34.24 S | 21.26 E |
| Stiles | 210 | 40.40 N | 75.30 W |
| Stiles Pond ⊜ | 283 | 42.41 N | 71.02 W |
| Stilesville | 210 | 42.05 N | 75.24 W |
| Stilfontein | 158 | 26.50 S | 26.50 E |
| Stilís | 38 | 38.55 N | 22.36 E |
| Still | 148 | 34.20 N | 5.51 E |
| Stillaguamish ≃ | 224 | 48.11 N | 122.22 W |
| Stillaguamish, North Fork ≃ | 224 | 48.11 N | 122.07 W |
| Stillaguamish, South Fork ≃ | 224 | 48.11 N | 122.07 W |
| Stillhouse Hollow Lake ⊜[1] | 222 | 31.00 N | 97.35 W |
| Stilling | 41 | 56.04 N | 10.00 E |
| Stillman Valley | 216 | 42.07 N | 89.11 W |
| Stillmore | 192 | 32.26 N | 82.12 W |
| Still Pond | 208 | 39.19 N | 76.02 W |
| Still Run ≃ | 285 | 39.49 N | 75.18 W |
| Stillwater, B.C., Can. | 182 | 49.46 N | 124.18 W |
| Stillwater, Mn., U.S. | 190 | 45.03 N | 92.48 W |
| Stillwater, N.J., U.S. | 210 | 41.02 N | 74.52 W |
| Stillwater, N.Y., U.S. | 210 | 42.56 N | 73.39 W |
| Stillwater, Oh., U.S. | 214 | 40.20 N | 81.18 W |
| Stillwater, Ok., U.S. | 196 | 36.06 N | 97.03 W |
| Stillwater, Pa., U.S. | 210 | 41.09 N | 76.22 W |
| Stillwater ≃, Mt., U.S. | 202 | 45.38 N | 109.17 W |
| Stillwater ≃, Oh., U.S. | 218 | 39.47 N | 84.12 W |
| Stillwater Creek ≃ | 214 | 40.25 N | 81.22 W |
| Stillwater Range ⋀ | 204 | 39.50 N | 118.15 W |
| Stillwell, Il., U.S. | 219 | 40.13 N | 91.11 W |
| Stillwell, Ok., U.S. | 194 | 35.49 N | 94.38 W |
| Stilo | 68 | 38.29 N | 16.28 E |
| Stilo, Punta > | 68 | 38.28 N | 16.36 E |
| Stimberg ∧[2] | 263 | 51.40 N | 7.15 E |
| Stimigliano | 66 | 42.18 N | 12.34 E |
| Stimson, Mount ∧ | 202 | 48.31 N | 113.36 W |
| Stînca-Costești, Lacul ⊜[1] | 38 | 47.55 N | 27.10 E |
| Stinchar ≃ | 44 | 55.06 N | 5.00 W |
| Stinear Nunataks ⋀ | 9 | 69.42 S | 64.40 E |
| Stine Canal ≊ | 226 | 35.15 N | 119.08 W |


**Symbols** in the index entries represent the broad categories identified in the key at the right. Symbols with superior numbers (⋀[1]) identify subcategories (see complete key on page *I · 1).*

**Symbole** im Register stellen die rechts im Schlüssel erklärten Kategorien dar. Symbole mit hochgestellten Ziffern (⋀[1]) bezeichnen Unterabteilungen einer Kategorie (vgl. vollständiger Schlüssel auf Seite *I · 1).*

**Los símbolos** incluídos en el texto del índice representan las grandes categorías identificadas con la clave a la derecha. Los símbolos con numeros en su parte superior (⋀[1]) identifican las subcategorías (véase la clave completa en la página *I · 1).*

**Les symboles** de l'index représentent les catégories indiquées dans la légende à droite. Les symboles suivis d'un indice (⋀[1]) représentent des sous-catégories (voir légende complète à la page *I · 1).*

**Os símbolos** incluídos no texto do índice representam as grandes categorias identificadas com a chave à direita. Os símbolos com números em sua parte superior (⋀[1]) identificam as subcategorias (veja-se a chave completa à página *I · 1).*

| | | | | | |
|---|---|---|---|---|---|
| ∧ | Mountain | Berg | Montaña | Montagne | Montanha |
| ⋀ | Mountains | Gebirge | Montañas | Montagnes | Montanhas |
| )( | Pass | Paß | Paso | Col | Passo |
| V | Valley, Canyon | Tal, Cañon | Valle, Cañón | Vallée, Canyon | Vale, Canhão |
| ≚ | Plain | Ebene | Llano | Plaine | Planície |
| > | Cape | Kap | Cabo | Cap | Cabo |
| I | Island | Insel | Isla | Île | Ilha |
| II | Islands | Inseln | Islas | Îles | Ilhas |
| ⊥ | Other Topographic Features | Andere Topographische Objekte | Otros Elementos Topográficos | Autres données topographiques | Outros acidentes topográficos |

ESPAÑOL · FRANÇAIS · PORTUGUÊS


| Nombre / Nom / Nome | Página / Page / Página | Lat.°' | Long.°' W = Oeste / W = Ouest / W = Oeste |
|---|---|---|---|
| Stine Mountain ∧ | 202 | 45.44 N | 113.07 W |
| Stingray Point › | 208 | 37.33 N | 76.18 W |
| Stinking Water Creek ≃ | 198 | 40.22 N | 101.07 W |
| Stinnett | 196 | 35.49 N | 101.26 W |
| Stintino | 71 | 40.56 N | 8.13 E |
| Stintonville | 273d | 26.14 S | 28.13 E |
| Štip | 38 | 41.44 N | 22.12 E |
| Stiperstones ∧ | 42 | 52.35 N | 2.56 W |
| Stiring-Wendel | 56 | 49.12 N | 6.56 E |
| Stírka ∧ | 60 | 49.24 N | 13.34 E |
| Stirling, Austl. | 162 | 21.44 S | 133.45 E |
| Stirling, Austl. | 168a | 31.54 S | 115.47 E |
| Stirling, Austl. | 168b | 35.00 S | 138.43 E |
| Stirling, Ab., Can. | 182 | 49.30 N | 112.31 W |
| Stirling, On., Can. | 212 | 44.18 N | 77.33 W |
| Stirling, Scot., U.K. | 46 | 56.07 N | 3.57 W |
| Stirling, N.J., U.S. | 210 | 40.40 N | 74.29 W |
| Stirling, Mount ∧ | 162 | 31.50 S | 117.38 E |
| Stirling Castle ⊥ | 46 | 56.07 N | 3.57 W |
| Stirling City | 204 | 39.54 N | 121.31 W |
| Stirling Range ⋀ | 162 | 34.23 S | 117.50 E |
| Stirling Range National Park ♠ | 162 | 34.22 S | 118.00 E |
| Stirling Reservoir ⊜[1] | 168a | 33.08 S | 116.03 E |
| Stirrat | 192 | 37.43 N | 82.00 W |
| Stissing Mountain ∧ | 210 | 41.57 N | 73.42 W |
| Štitary | 61 | 48.56 N | 15.51 E |
| Stittsville | 212 | 45.15 N | 75.55 W |
| Stittville | 210 | 43.13 N | 75.17 W |
| Stjärnhov | 40 | 59.05 N | 17.00 E |
| Stjärnsund, Sve. | 40 | 60.26 N | 16.12 E |
| Stjärnsund, Sve. | 40 | 58.51 N | 14.55 E |
| Stjernøya I | 24 | 70.18 N | 22.45 E |
| Stjørdalshalsen | 26 | 63.28 N | 10.56 E |
| Stöberhai ∧ | 54 | 51.39 N | 10.34 E |
| Stobi ⊥ | 38 | 41.33 N | 21.59 E |
| Stock | 260 | 51.40 N | 0.27 E |
| Stock, Étang du ⊜ | 56 | 48.45 N | 6.55 E |
| Stockach | 58 | 47.51 N | 9.00 E |
| Stöckalp | 58 | 46.48 N | 8.17 E |
| Stockamöllan | 41 | 55.57 N | 13.22 E |
| Stockbridge, Eng., U.K. | 42 | 51.07 N | 1.29 W |
| Stockbridge, Ga., U.S. | 192 | 33.32 N | 84.14 W |
| Stockbridge, Ma., U.S. | 207 | 42.17 N | 73.19 W |
| Stockbridge, Mi., U.S. | 216 | 42.27 N | 84.10 W |
| Stockbridge Bowl ⊜ | 207 | 42.20 N | 73.19 W |
| Stockbridge Indian Reservation ◆[4] | 190 | 44.52 N | 88.53 W |
| Stockbury | 260 | 51.20 N | 0.39 E |
| Stockby | 40 | 59.20 N | 17.41 E |
| Stockdale, Oh., U.S. | 218 | 38.57 N | 82.51 W |
| Stockdale, Tx., U.S. | 196 | 29.14 N | 97.57 W |
| Stockelsdorf | 54 | 53.54 N | 10.38 E |
| Stöcken | 54 | 53.00 N | 10.40 E |
| Stockerau | 61 | 48.23 N | 16.13 E |
| Stockertown | 208 | 40.45 N | 75.15 W |
| Stockett | 202 | 47.21 N | 111.09 W |
| Stockheim | 56 | 50.19 N | 9.01 E |
| Stockholm, Sve. | 40 | 59.20 N | 18.03 E |
| Stockholm, Me., U.S. | 186 | 47.02 N | 68.08 W |
| Stockholm, N.J., U.S. | 210 | 41.05 N | 74.31 W |
| Stockholm, Lake ⊜ | 276 | 41.04 N | 74.32 W |
| Stockholms Län □[6] | 40 | 59.30 N | 18.20 E |
| Stock Island | 220 | 24.34 N | 81.45 W |
| Stockland | 216 | 40.37 N | 87.36 W |
| Stockport, Eng., U.K. | 44 | 53.25 N | 2.10 W |
| Stockport, N.Y., U.S. | 210 | 42.19 N | 73.45 W |
| Stockport □[8] | 262 | 53.23 N | 2.08 W |
| Stocksbridge | 44 | 53.27 N | 1.34 W |
| Stockstadt | 56 | 49.59 N | 9.04 E |
| Stocksund | 40 | 59.23 N | 18.04 E |
| Stockton, Austl. | 170 | 32.55 S | 151.47 E |
| Stockton, Al., U.S. | 194 | 30.59 N | 87.51 W |
| Stockton, Ca., U.S. | 226 | 37.57 N | 121.17 W |
| Stockton, Il., U.S. | 190 | 42.20 N | 90.00 W |
| Stockton, Ks., U.S. | 198 | 39.26 N | 99.15 W |
| Stockton, Md., U.S. | 208 | 38.03 N | 75.24 W |
| Stockton, Mo., U.S. | 194 | 37.41 N | 93.47 W |
| Stockton, N.J., U.S. | 208 | 40.24 N | 74.58 W |
| Stockton, N.Y., U.S. | 214 | 42.19 N | 79.22 W |
| Stockton, Ut,. U.S. | 200 | 40.27 N | 112.21 W |
| Stockton Heath, Eng., U.K. | 44 | 53.22 N | 2.34 W |
| Stockton Heath, Eng., U.K. | 262 | 53.22 N | 2.34 W |
| Stockton Metropolitan Airport ⊠ | 226 | 37.54 N | 121.15 W |
| Stockton-on-Tees | 44 | 54.34 N | 1.19 W |
| Stockton Plateau ⋀[1] | 196 | 30.30 N | 102.30 W |
| Stockton Reservoir ⊜[1] | 194 | 37.40 N | 93.45 W |
| Stockton Springs | 188 | 44.29 N | 68.51 W |
| Stockum, Dtsch. | 52 | 51.40 N | 7.42 E |
| Stockum, Dtsch. | 263 | 51.32 N | 7.47 E |
| Stockum, Dtsch. | 263 | 51.36 N | 6.39 E |
| Stockum, Dtsch. | 263 | 51.28 N | 7.22 E |
| Stockum ◆[8] | 263 | 51.16 N | 6.44 E |
| Stockville | 198 | 40.31 N | 100.22 W |
| Stockwell | 216 | 40.17 N | 86.46 W |
| Stockwell, Lake ⊜ | 285 | 39.51 N | 74.47 W |
| Stoco Lake ⊜ | 212 | 44.28 N | 77.18 W |
| Stoczek Łukowski | 30 | 51.58 N | 21.58 E |
| Stod | 60 | 49.39 N | 13.10 E |
| Stoddard Mountain ∧ | 228 | 34.42 N | 117.07 W |
| Stöde | 26 | 62.25 N | 16.35 E |
| Stodoliščе | 76 | 54.11 N | 32.39 E |
| Stœng Tréng | 110 | 13.31 N | 105.58 E |
| Stoer | 46 | 58.12 N | 5.20 W |
| Stoer, Point of › | 46 | 58.15 N | 5.21 W |
| Stoffberg | 156 | 25.29 S | 29.49 E |
| Stojba | 89 | 52.49 N | 131.43 E |
| Stoke | 260 | 51.27 N | 0.37 E |
| Stoke ≃ | 206 | 45.35 N | 71.58 W |
| Stoke, Monts ⋀ | 206 | 45.33 N | 71.42 W |
| Stoke D'Abernon | 260 | 51.19 N | 0.23 W |
| Stokenchurch | 42 | 51.40 N | 0.55 W |
| Stoke Newington ◆[8] | 260 | 51.34 N | 0.05 W |
| Stoke-on-Trent | 42 | 53.00 N | 2.10 W |
| Stoke Poges | 260 | 51.33 N | 0.35 W |
| Stokes, Mount ∧ | 172 | 41.06 S | 174.06 E |
| Stokes Inlet ⊂ | 162 | 33.50 S | 121.08 E |
| Stokesley | 44 | 54.28 N | 1.11 W |
| Stokes Point › | 166 | 40.10 S | 143.56 E |
| Stokes Range ⋀[2] | 164 | 15.46 S | 130.57 E |
| Stokhid ≃ | 78 | 51.52 N | 25.38 E |
| Stokkemarke | 41 | 54.50 N | 11.23 E |
| Stokksnes › | 24a | 64.17 N | 14.54 W |
| Stol ∧ | 38 | 44.13 N | 22.14 E |
| Stolac | 36 | 43.05 N | 17.58 E |
| Stolberg | 56 | 50.46 N | 6.13 E |
| Stolbišči | 80 | 55.39 N | 49.14 E |
| Stolboucha | 86 | 49.59 N | 84.30 E |
| Stolbovo | 76 | 52.38 N | 34.47 E |
| Stolbovoj, ostrov I | 74 | 74.05 N | 136.00 E |
| Stolby, zapovednik ♠ | 88 | 55.45 N | 92.45 E |
| Stolin | 78 | 51.53 N | 26.51 E |
| Stollberg | 54 | 50.42 N | 12.47 E |
| Stöllet | 26 | 60.24 N | 13.16 E |
| Stol'ne | 78 | 51.31 N | 31.55 E |
| Stolp → Słupsk | 30 | 54.28 N | 17.01 E |
| Stolpe | 264a | 52.40 N | 13.16 E |
| Stolpen | 54 | 51.05 N | 14.04 E |
| Stolper Heide ◆[3] | 264a | 52.39 N | 13.14 E |
| Stolpino | 80 | 57.24 N | 42.55 E |
| Stolzenau | 52 | 52.31 N | 9.04 E |
| Ston | 36 | 42.50 N | 17.42 E |
| Stondon Massey | 260 | 51.41 N | 0.18 E |
| Stone, Eng., U.K. | 42 | 52.54 N | 2.10 W |
| Stone, Eng., U.K. | 260 | 51.27 N | 0.16 E |
| Stoneboro | 214 | 41.20 N | 80.06 W |
| Stone Canyon Reservoir ⊜[1] | 280 | 34.07 N | 118.28 W |
| Stone Corral Creek ≃ | 226 | 39.16 N | 122.06 W |
| Stone Creek | 214 | 40.24 N | 81.34 W |
| Stonecutters Island I | 271d | 22.19 N | 114.08 E |
| Stonefort | 194 | 37.37 N | 88.42 W |
| Stoneham, Ma., U.S. | 283 | 42.28 N | 71.06 W |
| Stoneham, Pa., U.S. | 214 | 41.49 N | 79.07 W |
| Stone Harbor | 208 | 39.03 N | 74.45 W |
| Stonehaven | 46 | 56.57 N | 2.12 W |
| Stonehenge | 166 | 24.22 S | 143.17 E |
| Stonehenge ⊥ | 42 | 51.11 N | 1.49 W |
| Stonehill College ʊ[2] | 283 | 42.03 N | 71.05 W |
| Stonehouse, Eng., U.K. | 42 | 51.45 N | 2.17 W |
| Stonehouse, Scot., U.K. | 46 | 55.43 N | 4.00 W |
| Stone Indian Reserve ◆[4] | 182 | 51.54 N | 123.12 W |
| Stoneleigh | 42 | 52.21 N | 1.31 W |
| Stonelick Creek ≃ | 218 | 39.07 N | 84.13 W |
| Stonelick State Park ♠ | 218 | 39.13 N | 84.04 W |
| Stone Mountain | 192 | 33.48 N | 84.10 W |
| Stone Mountain ∧, Pa., U.S. | 210 | 40.37 N | 77.48 W |
| Stone Mountain ∧, Vt., U.S. | 188 | 44.34 N | 71.40 W |
| Stone Mountain Memorial State Park ♠ | 192 | 33.49 N | 84.06 W |
| Stone Park | 278 | 41.54 N | 87.53 W |
| Stoner | 182 | 53.36 N | 122.40 W |
| Stoner Creek ≃ | 218 | 38.18 N | 84.14 W |
| Stone Ridge | 210 | 41.51 N | 74.09 W |
| Stonerstown | 214 | 40.13 N | 78.16 W |
| Stones, East Fork ≃ | 194 | 35.59 N | 86.27 W |
| Stones, West Fork ≃ | 194 | 35.59 N | 86.27 W |
| Stones River National Battlefield ⊥ | 194 | 35.52 N | 86.26 W |
| Stonestown ◆[9] | 282 | 37.44 N | 122.28 W |
| Stonevilla | 279b | 40.18 N | 79.31 W |
| Stoneville | 192 | 36.27 N | 79.54 W |
| Stonewall, Mb., Can. | 184 | 50.09 N | 97.21 W |
| Stonewall, La., U.S. | 194 | 32.16 N | 93.49 W |
| Stonewall, Ms., U.S. | 194 | 32.07 N | 88.47 W |
| Stonewall, Ok., U.S. | 196 | 34.39 N | 96.31 W |
| Stonewall Manor | 284c | 38.53 N | 77.14 W |
| Stoney Creek | 212 | 43.13 N | 79.46 W |
| Stoney Point › | 214 | 42.18 N | 82.34 W |
| Stonington, Ct., U.S. | 207 | 41.20 N | 71.54 W |
| Stonington, Il., U.S. | 219 | 39.38 N | 89.11 W |
| Stonington, Me., U.S. | 188 | 44.09 N | 68.40 W |
| Stony ≃, Ak., U.S. | 180 | 61.45 N | 156.35 W |
| Stony ≃, Mn., U.S. | 190 | 47.44 N | 91.47 W |
| Stony Brook | 210 | 40.55 N | 73.08 W |
| Stony Brook ≃, Ct., U.S. | 276 | 41.04 N | 73.28 W |
| Stony Brook ≃, Ct., U.S. | 276 | 41.08 N | 73.22 W |
| Stony Brook ≃, Ma., U.S. | 283 | 42.38 N | 71.22 W |
| Stony Brook ≃, Ma., U.S. | 283 | 42.22 N | 71.16 W |
| Stony Brook ≃, N.J., U.S. | 276 | 40.19 N | 74.41 W |
| Stony Brook ≃, N.J., U.S. | 276 | 40.56 N | 74.26 W |
| Stony Brook Harbor ⊂ | 276 | 40.54 N | 73.10 W |
| Stony Brook Reservation ♠ | 283 | 42.16 N | 71.09 W |
| Stony Creek, Ct., U.S. | 207 | 41.15 N | 72.44 W |
| Stony Creek, Va., U.S. | 208 | 36.56 N | 77.24 W |
| Stony Creek ≃, Ca., U.S. | 204 | 39.41 N | 121.58 W |
| Stony Creek ≃, Il., U.S. | 278 | 41.41 N | 87.51 W |
| Stony Creek ≃, Mi., U.S. | 216 | 41.57 N | 83.18 W |
| Stony Creek ≃, Mi., U.S. | 216 | 43.00 N | 84.55 W |
| Stony Creek ≃, N.Y., U.S. | 212 | 43.49 N | 76.14 W |
| Stony Creek ≃, Pa., U.S. | 285 | 40.07 N | 75.21 W |
| Stony Creek ≃, Va., U.S. | 208 | 36.56 N | 77.23 W |
| Stony Creek, Middle Fork ≃ | 226 | 39.25 N | 122.31 W |
| Stony Creek, North Fork ≃ | 226 | 39.22 N | 122.37 W |
| Stony Creek, South Fork ≃ | 226 | 39.22 N | 122.39 W |
| Stony Creek Indian Reserve ◆[4] | 182 | 53.57 N | 124.07 W |
| Stony Creek Mills | 208 | 40.21 N | 75.52 W |
| Stonyford | 226 | 39.22 N | 122.32 W |
| Stony Gorge Reservoir ⊜[1] | 226 | 39.34 N | 122.31 W |
| Stony Indian Reserve ◆[4] | 182 | 51.10 N | 114.55 W |
| Stony Island I, Mi., U.S. | 281 | 42.07 N | 83.08 W |
| Stony Island I, N.Y., U.S. | 212 | 43.53 N | 76.25 W |
| Stony Kill ≃ | 210 | 42.24 N | 73.38 W |
| Stony Lake ⊜, Mb., Can. | 176 | 58.51 N | 98.35 W |
| Stony Lake ⊜, On., Can. | 212 | 44.33 N | 78.05 W |
| Stony Plain | 182 | 53.32 N | 114.00 W |
| Stony Plain Indian Reserve ◆[4] | 182 | 53.30 N | 113.45 W |
| Stony Point, Austl. | 169 | 38.22 S | 145.13 E |
| Stony Point, Mi., U.S. | 216 | 41.57 N | 83.16 W |
| Stony Point, N.Y., U.S. | 210 | 41.13 N | 73.59 W |
| Stony Point, N.C., U.S. | 192 | 35.51 N | 81.02 W |
| Stony Point › | 284a | 42.50 N | 78.52 W |
| Stony Point ›[1] | 212 | 43.52 N | 76.15 W |
| Stony Prairie | 214 | 41.21 N | 83.10 W |
| Stony Rapids | 176 | 59.16 N | 105.50 W |
| Stony Ridge | 214 | 41.30 N | 83.30 W |
| Stony River | 180 | 61.47 N | 156.41 W |
| Stony Run | 284b | 39.11 N | 76.42 W |
| Stony Run ≃ | 285 | 40.09 N | 75.32 W |
| Stony Stratford | 42 | 52.04 N | 0.52 W |
| Stoober Bach ≃ | 61 | 47.27 N | 16.35 E |
| Stop ≃ | 283 | 42.10 N | 71.19 W |
| Stopnica | 30 | 50.27 N | 20.57 E |
| Stoppenberg ◆[8] | 263 | 51.29 N | 7.02 E |
| Stör ≃ | 54 | 53.50 N | 11.29 E |
| Storå | 40 | 59.43 N | 15.08 E |
| Storå ≃ | 26 | 56.19 N | 8.19 E |
| Stora Alvaret ≡ | 26 | 56.30 N | 16.30 E |
| Stora Gla ⊜ | 26 | 59.30 N | 12.30 E |
| Stora Kloten ⊜ | 40 | 59.52 N | 15.16 E |
| Stora Le ⊜ | 26 | 59.05 N | 11.53 E |
| Stora Lulevatten ⊜ | 24 | 67.10 N | 19.16 E |
| Stora Mellösa | 40 | 59.13 N | 15.30 E |
| Stora Möja I, Sve. | 26 | 59.26 N | 18.55 E |
| Stora Möja I, Sve. | 40 | 59.26 N | 18.55 E |
| Stora Norn ⊜ | 40 | 60.14 N | 15.42 E |
| Stora Sjöfallets Nationalpark ♠ | 24 | 67.44 N | 18.16 E |
| Stora Skedvi | 40 | 60.24 N | 15.48 E |
| Stora Sundby | 40 | 59.16 N | 16.07 E |
| Storavan ⊜ | 24 | 65.40 N | 18.15 E |
| Stora Vika | 40 | 58.56 N | 17.48 E |
| Storby | 26 | 60.13 N | 19.34 E |
| Stord I | 26 | 59.53 N | 5.25 E |
| Store Andst | 41 | 55.29 N | 9.14 E |
| Storebælt ʉ | 41 | 55.30 N | 11.00 E |
| Store Heddinge | 41 | 55.19 N | 12.25 E |
| Store Magleby | 41 | 55.36 N | 12.38 E |
| Store Merløse | 41 | 55.33 N | 11.40 E |
| Støren | 26 | 63.02 N | 10.18 E |
| Store Sotra I | 26 | 60.18 N | 5.05 E |
| Storeton | 262 | 53.21 N | 3.03 W |
| Storey □[6] | 226 | 39.28 N | 119.30 W |
| Storfjärden ⊜ | 40 | 60.30 N | 17.23 E |
| Storfjorden ⊂[2] | 26 | 62.25 N | 6.30 E |
| Storfors | 40 | 59.32 N | 14.16 E |
| Störitzsee ⊜ | 264a | 52.23 N | 13.51 E |
| Störkanal ≊ | 54 | 53.36 N | 11.30 E |
| Storkerson Bay ⊂ | 176 | 73.00 N | 124.50 W |
| Storkerson Peninsula ›[1] | 176 | 72.30 N | 106.30 W |
| Storkow, Dtsch. | 54 | 53.19 N | 14.17 E |
| Storkow, Dtsch. | 54 | 52.15 N | 13.56 E |
| Storlien | 26 | 63.19 N | 12.06 E |
| Stormarn ◆[1] | 52 | 53.45 N | 10.20 E |
| Storm Bay ⊂ | 166 | 43.10 S | 147.32 E |
| Stormberg ∧ | 158 | 30.57 S | 26.41 E |
| Stormberge ⋀ | 158 | 31.27 S | 26.55 E |
| Storm King Mountain ∧ | 224 | 46.39 N | 122.10 W |
| Storm Lake | 198 | 42.38 N | 95.12 W |
| Storm Mountain ∧ | 180 | 59.37 N | 150.35 W |
| Stormont-Dundas and Glengarry □[6] | 206 | 45.10 N | 75.00 W |
| Stormsrivier | 158 | 33.59 S | 23.52 E |
| Stormsvlei | 158 | 34.05 S | 20.06 E |
| Stormville | 210 | 41.34 N | 73.45 W |
| Stornara | 68 | 41.17 N | 15.46 E |
| Stornarella | 68 | 41.15 N | 15.44 E |
| Stornorrforsen | 26 | 63.52 N | 20.03 E |
| Stornoway | 46 | 58.12 N | 6.23 W |
| Storo | 64 | 45.51 N | 10.35 E |
| Storoževaja | 84 | 43.53 N | 41.27 E |
| Storoževsk | 24 | 61.57 N | 52.16 E |
| Storozhynets' | 78 | 48.10 N | 25.43 E |
| Storrensjön ⊜ | 26 | 63.38 N | 12.34 E |
| Storrington | 42 | 50.55 N | 0.28 W |
| Storrs | 207 | 41.48 N | 72.15 W |
| Storsjøen ⊜, Nor. | 26 | 60.23 N | 11.40 E |
| Storsjøen ⊜, Nor. | 26 | 61.35 N | 11.12 E |
| Storsjön ⊜, Sve. | 26 | 62.48 N | 13.07 E |
| Storsjön ⊜, Sve. | 26 | 63.12 N | 14.18 E |
| Storsjön ⊜, Sve. | 40 | 60.34 N | 16.44 E |
| Storsjön ⊜, Sve. | 40 | 59.04 N | 17.12 E |
| Storsteinsfjellet ∧ | 24 | 68.14 N | 17.52 E |
| Storstrøm □[6] | 41 | 55.00 N | 11.55 E |
| Storstrømmen ʉ | 41 | 54.58 N | 11.55 E |
| Storstrømsbroen ◆[5] | 41 | 54.58 N | 11.50 E |
| Stort ≃ | 260 | 51.46 N | 0.01 E |
| Storthoaks | 184 | 49.22 N | 101.38 W |
| Storuman | 24 | 65.06 N | 17.06 E |
| Storuman ⊜[1] | 24 | 65.14 N | 16.54 E |
| Storuman-See → Storavan ⊜ | 24 | 65.40 N | 18.15 E |
| Storvarts gruve | 26 | 62.38 N | 11.31 E |
| Storvätteshågna ∧ | 26 | 62.07 N | 12.27 E |
| Storvik | 40 | 60.35 N | 16.32 E |
| Storvindeln ⊜ | 24 | 65.43 N | 17.05 E |
| Storvreta | 40 | 59.58 N | 17.42 E |
| Story | 202 | 44.34 N | 106.53 W |
| Story City | 190 | 42.11 N | 93.35 W |
| Stosch, Isla I | 254 | 49.09 S | 75.26 W |
| Stössen | 54 | 51.06 N | 11.55 E |
| Stotfold | 42 | 52.01 N | 0.14 W |
| Stötten, Dtsch. | 58 | 47.44 N | 10.42 E |
| Stötten, Dtsch. | 64 | 47.44 N | 10.42 E |
| Stotternheim | 54 | 51.03 N | 11.02 E |
| Stottville | 210 | 42.17 N | 73.44 W |
| Stoubcy | 76 | 53.29 N | 26.44 E |
| Stouchsburg | 208 | 40.23 N | 76.14 W |
| Stough Park ♠ | 280 | 34.12 N | 118.18 W |
| Stoughton, Sk., Can. | 184 | 49.41 N | 103.03 W |
| Stoughton, Eng., U.K. | 260 | 51.15 N | 0.35 W |
| Stoughton, Ma., U.S. | 207 | 42.07 N | 71.06 W |
| Stoughton, Wi., U.S. | 216 | 42.55 N | 89.13 W |
| Stoumont | 56 | 50.25 N | 5.48 E |
| Stoŭng ≃ | 110 | 12.50 N | 104.19 E |
| Stour ≃, Eng., U.K. | 42 | 51.52 N | 1.16 E |
| Stour ≃, Eng., U.K. | 42 | 50.43 N | 1.46 W |
| Stour ≃, Eng., U.K. | 42 | 51.18 N | 1.22 E |
| Stour ≃, Eng., U.K. | 42 | 52.20 N | 2.15 W |
| Stourbridge | 42 | 52.27 N | 2.09 W |
| Stourport-on-Severn | 42 | 52.21 N | 2.16 W |
| Stout Lake ⊜ | 184 | 52.08 N | 94.33 W |
| Stoutsville | 219 | 39.33 N | 91.51 W |
| Stover | 194 | 38.26 N | 92.59 W |
| Stow, Ma., U.S. | 207 | 42.26 N | 71.30 W |
| Stow, N.Y., U.S. | 214 | 42.09 N | 79.25 W |
| Stow, Oh., U.S. | 214 | 41.10 N | 81.27 W |
| Stowe, Pa., U.S. | 208 | 40.15 N | 75.40 W |
| Stowe, Vt., U.S. | 188 | 44.27 N | 72.41 W |
| Stowell | 194 | 29.47 N | 94.23 W |
| Stowe Township | 279b | 40.29 N | 80.04 W |
| Stow Maries | 260 | 51.40 N | 0.39 E |
| Stowmarket | 42 | 52.11 N | 1.00 E |
| Stow-on-the-Wold | 42 | 51.56 N | 1.44 W |
| Stowupland | 42 | 52.12 N | 1.01 E |
| Stoyoma Mountain ∧ | 182 | 49.59 N | 121.13 W |
| Stoystown | 214 | 40.06 N | 78.57 W |
| Stožec | 60 | 48.51 N | 13.50 E |
| Stra | 64 | 45.25 N | 12.00 E |
| Straach | 54 | 51.57 N | 12.35 E |
| Strabane, N. Ire., U.K. | 48 | 54.49 N | 7.27 W |
| Strabane, Pa., U.S. | 214 | 40.15 N | 80.11 W |
| Straberg | 263 | 51.05 N | 6.45 E |
| Strachan | 46 | 57.01 N | 2.32 W |
| Strachan Island I | 164 | 9.00 S | 142.10 E |
| Strachur | 46 | 56.10 N | 5.04 W |
| Stradbally | 48 | 53.00 N | 7.08 W |
| Stradbroke | 42 | 52.19 N | 1.16 E |
| Stradella | 62 | 45.05 N | 9.18 E |
| Stradone | 48 | 53.58 N | 7.14 W |
| Stradovn'a, ozero ⊜ | 82 | 56.53 N | 36.18 E |
| Stradzečy | 76 | 51.56 N | 23.40 E |
| Straelen | 56 | 51.27 N | 6.16 E |
| Strafford | 285 | 40.03 N | 75.25 W |
| Straffordville | 212 | 42.45 N | 80.47 W |
| Strahan | 166 | 42.09 S | 145.19 E |
| Straight Creek ≃ | 218 | 38.46 N | 83.55 W |
| Strakonice | 60 | 49.16 N | 13.55 E |
| Stralsund | 54 | 54.19 N | 13.05 E |
| Strambino | 62 | 45.23 N | 7.53 E |
| Strand | 158 | 34.06 S | 18.50 E |
| Stranda | 26 | 62.19 N | 6.54 E |
| Strande | 54 | 54.26 N | 10.12 E |
| Strandhill | 48 | 54.17 N | 8.36 W |
| Stranger Creek ≃ | 198 | 39.00 N | 95.01 W |
| Strangford | 48 | 54.22 N | 5.34 W |
| Strangford Lough ⊜ | 48 | 54.28 N | 5.35 W |
| Strängnäs | 40 | 59.23 N | 17.02 E |
| Strångsjö | 40 | 58.54 N | 16.12 E |
| Strangways ≃ | 164 | 14.52 S | 133.50 E |
| Strangways, Mount ∧ | 162 | 23.02 S | 133.51 E |
| Stranorlar | 48 | 54.48 N | 7.46 W |
| Stranraer | 44 | 54.55 N | 5.02 W |
| Strasbourg, Sk., Can. | 184 | 51.04 N | 104.57 W |
| Strasbourg, Fr. | 58 | 48.35 N | 7.45 E |
| Strasbourg, Aéroport ⊠ | 58 | 48.32 N | 7.38 E |
| Strasburg, Dtsch. | 54 | 53.30 N | 13.44 E |
| Strasburg, Co., U.S. | 198 | 39.44 N | 104.20 W |
| Strasburg, N.D., U.S. | 198 | 46.08 N | 100.09 W |
| Strasburg, Oh., U.S. | 214 | 40.35 N | 81.31 W |
| Strasburg, Pa., U.S. | 208 | 39.58 N | 76.11 W |
| Strasburg, Va., U.S. | 188 | 38.59 N | 78.21 W |
| Străşeni | 38 | 47.08 N | 28.36 E |
| Straševiči | 76 | 56.49 N | 34.36 E |
| Strašín | 60 | 49.08 N | 13.38 E |
| Stråssa | 40 | 59.45 N | 15.13 E |
| Strassburg → Strasbourg | 58 | 48.35 N | 7.45 E |
| Strasshof an der Nordbahn | 61 | 48.19 N | 16.39 E |
| Strasskirchen | 60 | 48.50 N | 12.43 E |
| Strata Florida Abbey ʊ[1] | 42 | 52.16 N | 3.51 W |
| Stratford, On., Can. | 212 | 43.22 N | 80.57 W |
| Stratford, N.Z. | 172 | 39.20 S | 174.17 E |
| Stratford, Ct., U.S. | 207 | 41.11 N | 73.08 W |
| Stratford, De., U.S. | 285 | 39.40 N | 75.38 W |
| Stratford, Ia., U.S. | 190 | 42.16 N | 93.55 W |
| Stratford, N.J., U.S. | 208 | 39.49 N | 75.00 W |
| Stratford, N.Y., U.S. | 210 | 43.11 N | 74.42 W |
| Stratford, Ok., U.S. | 196 | 34.47 N | 96.57 W |
| Stratford, Tx., U.S. | 196 | 36.20 N | 102.04 W |
| Stratford, Wi., U.S. | 190 | 44.48 N | 90.04 W |
| Stratford Centre | 206 | 45.47 N | 71.16 W |
| Stratford Point › | 276 | 41.09 N | 73.06 W |
| Stratford Square ◆[9] | 278 | 41.57 N | 88.07 W |
| Stratford-upon-Avon | 42 | 52.12 N | 1.41 W |
| Strathalbyn | 168b | 35.16 S | 138.54 E |
| Strathaven | 46 | 55.40 N | 4.04 W |
| Strathbogie Ranges ⋀ | 169 | 36.55 S | 145.45 E |
| Strathclair | 184 | 50.24 N | 100.24 W |
| Strathclyde □[4] | 46 | 56.00 N | 5.15 W |
| Strathcona Provincial Park ♠ | 182 | 49.40 N | 125.50 W |
| Strathdearn V | 46 | 57.15 N | 4.05 W |
| Strathdon | 46 | 57.11 N | 3.02 W |
| Strathearn V | 46 | 56.18 N | 3.45 W |
| Strathfield | 170 | 33.52 S | 151.06 E |
| Strathgordon | 166 | 42.46 S | 146.03 E |
| Strath Kanaird | 46 | 57.59 N | 5.11 W |
| Strathlorne | 186 | 46.11 N | 61.17 W |
| Strathmiglo | 46 | 56.16 N | 3.16 W |
| Strathmoor ◆[8] | 281 | 42.23 N | 83.11 W |
| Strathmore, Ab., Can. | 182 | 51.03 N | 113.23 W |
| Strathmore, Ca., U.S. | 204 | 36.08 N | 119.03 W |
| Strathmore, N.J., U.S. | 276 | 40.24 N | 74.13 W |
| Strathmore V | 46 | 56.39 N | 3.00 W |
| Strathpeffer | 46 | 57.35 N | 4.33 W |
| Strathpine | 171a | 27.19 S | 152.59 E |
| Strathroy | 214 | 42.57 N | 81.38 W |
| Strathy ≃ | 46 | 58.34 N | 4.00 W |
| Strathy Point › | 46 | 58.35 N | 4.02 W |
| Strattanville | 214 | 41.12 N | 79.19 W |
| Stratton, Eng., U.K. | 42 | 50.50 N | 4.31 W |
| Stratton, Eng., U.K. | 42 | 51.44 N | 1.59 W |
| Stratton, Co., U.S. | 198 | 39.18 N | 102.36 W |
| Stratton, Me., U.S. | 188 | 45.08 N | 70.26 W |
| Stratton, Ne., U.S. | 198 | 40.08 N | 101.13 W |
| Stratton, Oh., U.S. | 214 | 40.32 N | 80.38 W |
| Stratton Mountain ∧ | 188 | 43.05 N | 72.56 W |
| Stratton Saint Margaret | 42 | 51.35 N | 1.45 W |
| Straubenhardt | 56 | 48.51 N | 8.32 E |
| Straubing | 60 | 48.53 N | 12.34 E |
| Strauch | 263 | 51.09 N | 6.56 E |
| Straumen | 26 | 63.52 N | 11.18 E |
| Straupitz | 54 | 51.54 N | 14.07 E |
| Strausberg | 54 | 52.35 N | 13.53 E |
| Straus-Berger Stadtforst ♠ | 264a | 52.34 N | 13.52 E |
| Strausberg-Vorstadt | 264a | 52.32 N | 13.51 E |
| Straussberg | 54 | 51.23 N | 10.44 E |
| Straussee ⊜ | 264a | 52.35 N | 13.53 E |
| Straussfurt | 54 | 51.09 N | 10.59 E |
| Strausstown | 208 | 40.30 N | 76.11 W |
| Stravignano | 66 | 43.05 N | 12.49 E |
| Strawberry | 226 | 38.13 N | 118.35 W |
| Strawberry ≃, Ar., U.S. | 194 | 35.53 N | 91.13 W |
| Strawberry ≃, Ut,. U.S. | 200 | 40.10 N | 110.24 W |
| Strawberry Island I | 284a | 42.57 N | 78.55 W |
| Strawberry Mountain ∧ | 202 | 44.19 N | 118.43 W |
| Strawberry Point, Ca., U.S. | 282 | 37.54 N | 122.31 W |
| Strawberry Point, Ia., U.S. | 190 | 42.41 N | 91.32 W |
| Strawberry Point › | 283 | 42.15 N | 70.46 W |
| Strawberry Reservoir ⊜[1] | 200 | 40.11 N | 111.08 W |
| Strawberry Valley | 226 | 39.34 N | 121.06 W |
| Strawbridge Lake ⊜ | 285 | 39.57 N | 74.57 W |
| Strawn | 196 | 32.33 N | 98.29 W |
| Straw Pump | 279b | 40.19 N | 79.40 W |
| Stráž | 61 | 49.04 N | 14.54 E |
| Strážnice | 30 | 48.54 N | 17.18 E |
| Strážov | 60 | 49.18 N | 13.15 E |
| Strážske | 30 | 48.53 N | 21.50 E |
| Streaky Bay | 162 | 32.48 S | 134.13 E |
| Streaky Bay ⊂ | 162 | 32.36 S | 134.08 E |
| Streamwood | 216 | 42.01 N | 88.10 W |
| Streatham, Austl. | 169 | 37.41 S | 143.04 E |
| Streatham, B.C., Can. | 182 | 53.52 N | 126.12 W |
| Streatham ◆[8] | 260 | 51.26 N | 0.08 W |
| Streator | 216 | 41.07 N | 88.50 W |
| Strebersdorf ◆[8] | 264b | 48.18 N | 16.23 E |
| Středočeský Kraj □[4] | 30 | 49.55 N | 14.30 E |
| Stredoslovenský Kraj □[4] | 30 | 48.50 N | 19.10 E |
| Street | 42 | 51.07 N | 2.42 W |
| Streeter | 198 | 46.39 N | 99.21 W |
| Streetman | 222 | 31.53 N | 96.19 W |
| Streetsboro | 214 | 41.14 N | 81.20 W |
| Streets Run ≃ | 279b | 40.23 N | 79.56 W |
| Streetsville | 212 | 43.35 N | 79.42 W |
| Strehaia | 38 | 44.37 N | 23.12 E |
| Strehla | 54 | 51.21 N | 13.13 E |
| Střela ≃ | 60 | 49.55 N | 13.33 E |
| Strelasund ʉ | 54 | 54.20 N | 13.05 E |
| Streleckije Vyselki | 82 | 54.12 N | 38.57 E |
| Strelica | 78 | 51.37 N | 38.55 E |
| Střelice | 61 | 49.09 N | 16.30 E |
| Strelitzalt | 54 | 53.20 N | 13.05 E |
| Strelka | 86 | 58.05 N | 93.01 E |
| Strelka ≃ | 265a | 59.52 N | 30.03 E |
| Strelka-Čun'a | 74 | 61.45 N | 102.48 E |
| Strelkovo | 82 | 55.28 N | 37.37 E |
| Strel'na, Ross. | 24 | 66.06 N | 38.40 E |
| Strel'na, Ross. | 76 | 59.51 N | 30.02 E |
| Strel'na ≃ | 24 | 66.04 N | 38.39 E |
| Strel'skaja | 24 | 59.28 N | 47.47 E |
| Střelské Hoštice | 60 | 49.18 N | 13.46 E |
| Strem ≃ | 61 | 47.00 N | 16.31 E |
| Strembo | 64 | 46.09 N | 10.44 E |
| Stremilovo | 82 | 55.09 N | 37.09 E |
| Strenči | 76 | 57.37 N | 25.41 E |
| Strengen | 58 | 47.08 N | 10.27 E |
| Strensall | 44 | 54.03 N | 1.02 W |
| Stresa | 62 | 45.53 N | 8.32 E |
| Strèšyn | 76 | 52.43 N | 30.05 E |
| Stretford | 44 | 53.27 N | 2.19 W |
| Stretton, Austl. | 162 | 32.32 S | 117.41 E |
| Stretton, Eng., U.K. | 42 | 52.44 N | 0.35 W |
| Stretton, Eng., U.K. | 44 | 53.21 N | 2.35 W |
| Streu ≃ | 56 | 50.21 N | 10.16 E |
| Streufdorf | 54 | 50.21 N | 10.41 E |
| Strib | 41 | 55.32 N | 9.47 E |
| Striberg | 40 | 59.33 N | 14.56 E |
| Stříbro | 60 | 49.46 N | 13.00 E |
| Strichen | 46 | 57.34 N | 2.05 W |
| Strickherdicke | 263 | 51.29 N | 7.43 E |
| Strickland ≃ | 164 | 6.00 S | 142.05 E |
| Strigno | 64 | 46.04 N | 11.31 E |
| Strijen | 52 | 51.45 N | 4.33 E |
| Striker, Lake ⊜[1] | 222 | 31.57 N | 94.59 W |
| Strilkove | 78 | 45.54 N | 34.53 E |
| Stril'tsivka | 83 | 49.18 N | 39.52 E |
| Strimón (Struma) ≃ | 38 | 40.47 N | 23.51 E |
| Stringtown | 218 | 40.05 N | 86.29 W |
| Striven, Loch ⊂ | 46 | 55.58 N | 5.09 W |
| Strižament, gora ∧ | 84 | 44.46 N | 42.01 E |
| Striži | 80 | 58.30 N | 49.13 E |
| Strjama ≃ | 38 | 42.10 N | 24.56 E |
| Strobel | 252 | 32.03 S | 60.37 W |
| Strobel, Lago ⊜ | 254 | 48.22 S | 71.12 W |
| Strobl | 64 | 47.43 N | 13.29 E |
| Strobleton | 214 | 41.22 N | 79.25 W |
| Strøby | 41 | 55.23 N | 12.18 E |
| Stroeder | 254 | 40.11 S | 62.37 W |
| Strofádhes, Nísoi II | 38 | 37.15 N | 21.00 E |
| Strogino ◆[8] | 265b | 55.49 N | 37.25 E |
| Strogonof Point › | 180 | 56.53 N | 158.49 W |
| Stroh | 216 | 41.34 N | 85.11 W |
| Ströhen | 52 | 52.32 N | 8.41 E |
| Stroitel' | 78 | 50.47 N | 36.26 E |
| Strokestown | 48 | 53.47 N | 8.08 W |
| Strom ≃ | 54 | 53.15 N | 13.50 E |
| Stroma I | 46 | 58.41 N | 3.08 W |
| Stromberg, Dtsch. | 52 | 51.48 N | 8.12 E |
| Stromberg, Dtsch. | 56 | 49.57 N | 7.46 E |
| Stromboli, Isola I | 70 | 38.47 N | 15.13 E |
| Strome | 182 | 52.48 N | 112.04 W |
| Stromeferry | 46 | 57.21 N | 5.34 W |
| Strömkendorf | 54 | 53.58 N | 11.29 E |
| Stromness | 46 | 58.57 N | 3.18 W |
| Strömsberg | 40 | 60.24 N | 17.35 E |
| Strömsbro | 40 | 60.42 N | 17.10 E |
| Strömsbruk | 26 | 61.53 N | 17.19 E |
| Stromsburg | 198 | 41.06 N | 97.35 W |
| Strömsholm | 40 | 59.32 N | 16.15 E |
| Strömsnäsbruk | 26 | 56.33 N | 13.43 E |
| Strömstad | 26 | 58.56 N | 11.10 E |
| Strömsund | 26 | 63.51 N | 15.35 E |
| Strömsvattudal ⊜ | 26 | 63.56 N | 15.28 E |
| Stromyn' | 82 | 56.03 N | 38.29 E |
| Strong | 194 | 33.06 N | 92.20 W |
| Strong ≃ | 194 | 31.51 N | 90.08 W |
| Strong City | 198 | 38.23 N | 96.32 W |
| Stronghurst | 190 | 40.44 N | 90.54 W |
| Strongoli | 68 | 39.15 N | 17.03 E |
| Strongs Creek ≃ | 276 | 40.40 N | 73.22 W |
| Strongs Neck ›[1] | 276 | 40.58 N | 73.07 W |
| Strongstown | 214 | 40.33 N | 78.55 W |
| Strongsville | 214 | 41.18 N | 81.50 W |
| Strongsville Airport ⊠ | 279a | 41.19 N | 81.52 W |
| Stronsay I | 46 | 59.07 N | 2.37 W |
| Stronsay Firth ʉ | 46 | 59.02 N | 2.41 W |
| Stronsdorf | 61 | 48.39 N | 16.18 E |
| Strontian | 46 | 56.41 N | 5.34 W |
| Strood | 42 | 51.24 N | 0.28 E |
| Stropkov | 30 | 49.12 N | 21.40 E |
| Stropnice ≃ | 61 | 48.52 N | 14.30 E |
| Stroppiana | 62 | 45.14 N | 8.27 E |
| Stroud, Austl. | 166 | 32.20 S | 151.56 E |
| Stroud, Eng., U.K. | 42 | 51.45 N | 2.12 W |
| Stroud, Ok., U.S. | 196 | 35.44 N | 96.39 W |
| Stroudsburg | 210 | 40.59 N | 75.11 W |
| Strövelstorp | 41 | 56.09 N | 12.49 E |
| Strubenvale | 273d | 26.16 S | 28.28 E |
| Strücklingen | 52 | 53.07 N | 7.40 E |
| Struer | 26 | 56.29 N | 8.37 E |
| Struga | 38 | 41.11 N | 20.40 E |
| Strugi-Krasnyje | 76 | 58.17 N | 29.06 E |
| Struisbaai | 158 | 34.49 S | 20.04 E |
| Struisbult | 273d | 26.19 S | 28.29 E |
| Strule ≃ | 48 | 54.43 N | 7.25 W |
| Strullendorf | 56 | 49.51 N | 10.58 E |
| Strum | 190 | 44.32 N | 91.23 W |
| Struma (Strimón) ≃ | 38 | 40.47 N | 23.51 E |
| Strumble Head › | 42 | 52.02 N | 5.04 W |
| Strumica | 38 | 41.26 N | 22.38 E |
| Strümp | 263 | 51.17 N | 6.40 E |
| Strunino | 82 | 56.23 N | 38.34 E |
| Strupna | 82 | 54.43 N | 38.48 E |
| Struthers | 214 | 41.03 N | 80.36 W |
| Struy | 46 | 57.24 N | 4.39 W |
| Strydenburg | 158 | 29.58 S | 23.40 E |
| Strydomsvlei | 158 | 33.10 S | 23.03 E |
| Strydpoort | 158 | 27.00 S | 25.58 E |
| Stryker, Mt., U.S. | 182 | 48.40 N | 114.46 W |
| Stryker, Oh., U.S. | 216 | 41.30 N | 84.24 W |
| Strykersville | 210 | 42.42 N | 78.27 W |
| Stryków | 30 | 51.55 N | 19.37 E |
| Stryn | 26 | 61.55 N | 6.47 E |
| Strynø I | 41 | 54.54 N | 10.37 E |
| Strypa ≃ | 78 | 48.52 N | 25.26 E |
| Stryy | 78 | 49.15 N | 23.51 E |
| Stryy ≃ | 78 | 49.24 N | 24.13 E |
| Stryzhavka | 78 | 49.19 N | 28.28 E |
| Strzegom | 30 | 50.57 N | 16.21 E |
| Strzegowo-Osada | 30 | 52.55 N | 20.18 E |
| Strzelce Krajeńskie | 30 | 52.53 N | 15.32 E |
| Strzelce Opolskie | 30 | 50.31 N | 18.19 E |
| Strzelecki Creek ≃ | 166 | 29.37 S | 139.59 E |
| Strzelecki Desert ◆[2] | 166 | 28.00 S | 140.10 E |
| Strzeleckie, Mount ∧ | 162 | 21.10 S | 133.53 E |
| Strzelecki National Park ♠ | 166 | 40.14 S | 148.06 E |
| Strzelin | 30 | 50.47 N | 17.03 E |
| Strzelno | 30 | 52.38 N | 18.11 E |
| Strzyżów | 30 | 49.52 N | 21.47 E |
| Stuart, Fl., U.S. | 220 | 27.11 N | 80.15 W |
| Stuart, Ia., U.S. | 198 | 41.30 N | 94.19 W |
| Stuart, Ne., U.S. | 198 | 42.35 N | 99.08 W |
| Stuart, Va., U.S. | 192 | 36.38 N | 80.15 W |
| Stuart ≃ | 182 | 54.00 N | 123.32 W |
| Stuart, Central Mount ∧ | 162 | 21.54 S | 133.27 E |
| Stuart, Mount ∧ | 224 | 47.29 N | 120.54 W |
| Stuart Channel ʉ | 224 | 48.55 N | 123.45 W |
| Stuart Island I, Ak., U.S. | 180 | 63.35 N | 162.30 W |
| Stuart Island I, Wa., U.S. | 224 | 48.42 N | 123.12 W |
| Stuart Lake ⊜ | 182 | 54.32 N | 124.35 W |
| Stuart Mountains ⋀ | 172 | 45.00 S | 167.37 E |
| Stuart Range ⋀ | 162 | 29.10 S | 134.56 E |
| Stuarts Draft | 192 | 38.01 N | 79.02 W |
| Stubai V | 64 | 47.06 N | 11.19 E |
| Stubaier Alpen ⋀ | 64 | 47.10 N | 11.05 E |
| Stubalpe ⋀ | 61 | 47.06 N | 14.54 E |
| Stübbecken | 263 | 51.23 N | 7.36 E |
| Stubbekøbing | 41 | 54.53 N | 12.03 E |
| Stubbenfelde | 54 | 54.02 N | 14.01 E |
| Stubbington | 42 | 50.50 N | 1.13 W |
| Stubbins | 262 | 53.39 N | 2.19 W |
| Stubenberg | 61 | 47.14 N | 15.48 E |
| Stubla ≃ | 78 | 50.50 N | 26.04 E |
| Stubner Kogel ∧ | 64 | 47.07 N | 13.06 E |
| Studená | 61 | 49.11 N | 15.17 E |
| Studenec | 80 | 54.52 N | 48.16 E |
| Studenica, Manastir ʊ[1] | 38 | 43.21 N | 20.35 E |
| Studen Kladenec, Jazovir ⊜[1] | 38 | 41.37 N | 25.30 E |
| Studenok | 78 | 51.42 N | 34.07 E |
| Studholme Junction | 172 | 44.44 S | 171.08 E |
| Studi, Università degli ʊ[2] | 266b | 45.28 N | 9.14 E |
| Studland | 42 | 50.39 N | 1.58 W |
| Studley | 42 | 52.16 N | 1.52 W |
| Stud'onoje, Ross. | 80 | 51.36 N | 53.10 E |
| Stud'onoje, Ross. | 86 | 53.37 N | 77.31 E |
| Studsvik | 40 | 58.46 N | 17.23 E |
| Stugudal | 26 | 62.54 N | 11.52 E |
| Stugun | 26 | 63.10 N | 15.36 E |
| Stuhleck ∧ | 61 | 47.34 N | 15.47 E |
| Stühlingen | 58 | 47.44 N | 8.26 E |
| Stuhlweissenburg → Székesfehérvár | 30 | 47.12 N | 18.25 E |
| Stuhr | 52 | 53.01 N | 8.45 E |
| Stuie | 182 | 52.22 N | 126.02 W |
| Stukely, Lac ⊜ | 206 | 45.22 N | 72.15 W |
| Stull ≃ | 184 | 55.10 N | 92.39 W |
| Stull Lake ⊜ | 184 | 54.23 N | 92.34 W |
| Stülpe | 54 | 52.02 N | 13.19 E |
| Stumm | 64 | 47.17 N | 11.53 E |
| Stump Creek | 214 | 41.01 N | 78.50 W |
| Stump Creek ≃ | 276 | 40.28 N | 74.16 W |
| Stumpf | 263 | 51.06 N | 7.13 E |
| Stump Lake ⊜ | 198 | 47.54 N | 98.24 W |
| Stumsdorf | 54 | 51.37 N | 12.03 E |
| Stuorre Tjöure ∧ | 26 | 63.56 N | 13.30 E |
| Stupart ≃ | 184 | 56.00 N | 93.22 W |
| Stupava | 61 | 48.17 N | 17.02 E |
| Stupino | 82 | 54.53 N | 38.05 E |
| Stuppach | 56 | 49.27 N | 9.44 E |
| Stura ≃ | 62 | 45.09 N | 8.21 E |
| Stura di Ala ≃ | 62 | 45.18 N | 7.24 E |
| Stura di Demonte ≃ | 62 | 44.40 N | 7.53 E |
| Stura di Lanzo ≃ | 62 | 45.06 N | 7.44 E |
| Stura di Val Grande ≃ | 62 | 45.18 N | 7.24 E |
| Stura di Viù ≃ | 62 | 45.16 N | 7.26 E |
| Sturbridge | 207 | 42.06 N | 72.04 W |
| Sturdee | 162 | 31.52 S | 132.23 E |
| Sturge Island I | 9 | 67.27 S | 164.18 E |
| Sturgeon, Mo., U.S. | 219 | 39.14 N | 92.16 W |
| Sturgeon, Pa., U.S. | 279b | 40.23 N | 80.13 W |
| Sturgeon ≃, On., Can. | 190 | 46.19 N | 79.58 W |
| Sturgeon ≃, Sk., Can. | 184 | 53.12 N | 105.53 W |
| Sturgeon ≃, Mi., U.S. | 190 | 45.24 N | 84.38 W |
| Sturgeon ≃, Mi., U.S. | 190 | 45.50 N | 86.41 W |
| Sturgeon ≃, Mi., U.S. | 190 | 47.02 N | 88.30 W |
| Sturgeon Bay | 190 | 44.50 N | 87.22 W |
| Sturgeon Bay ⊂ | 184 | 52.00 N | 97.50 W |
| Sturgeon Falls | 190 | 46.22 N | 79.55 W |
| Sturgeon Lake ⊜, Ab., Can. | 182 | 55.06 N | [illegible]17.30 W |
| Sturgeon Lake ⊜, On., Can. | 184 | 55.25 N | [illegible]0.55 W |
| Sturgeon Lake ⊜, On., Can. | 212 | 44.28 N | [illegible]8.42 W |
| Sturgeon Lake ⊜, Wa., U.S. | 224 | 45.44 N | 1[illegible]2.48 W |
| Sturgeon Lake Indian Reserve ◆[4], Ab., Can. | 182 | 55.04 N | 1[illegible]7.29 W |
| Sturgeon Lake Indian Reserve ◆[4], Sk., Can. | 184 | 53.25 N | 1[illegible]3.05 W |
| Sturgeon Landing | 184 | 54.16 N | 1[illegible].49 W |
| Sturgeon Point › | 212 | 42.42 N | 7[illegible].03 W |
| Sturgis, Sk., Can. | 184 | 51.58 N | 10[illegible].32 W |
| Sturgis, Ky., U.S. | 194 | 37.32 N | 8[illegible].59 W |
| Sturgis, Mi., U.S. | 216 | 41.47 N | 8[illegible].25 W |
| Sturgis, Ms., U.S. | 194 | 33.20 N | 8[illegible].02 W |
| Sturgis, S.D., U.S. | 198 | 44.24 N | 10[illegible].30 W |
| Sturla | 62 | 44.24 N | [illegible].59 E |
| Sturminster Newton | 42 | 50.50 N | [illegible].19 W |
| Štúrovo | 30 | 47.48 N | 1[illegible].49 E |
| Sturry | 42 | 51.18 N | 1.[illegible]7 E |
| Sturt, Mount ∧ | 166 | 29.33 S | 141.[illegible]2 E |
| Sturt Creek | 162 | 19.10 S | 128.[illegible]0 E |
| Sturt Creek ≃ | 162 | 20.08 S | 127.[illegible]4 E |
| Sturtevant | 216 | 42.41 N | 87.[illegible]3 W |
| Sturt National Park ♠ | 166 | 29.00 S | 141.[illegible]0 E |
| Sturt Stony Desert ◆[2] | 166 | 28.30 S | 141.[illegible]0 E |
| Sturup flygplats ⊠ | 41 | 55.34 N | 13.[illegible] E |
| Stürzelberg | 263 | 51.08 N | 6.[illegible] E |
| Stutensee | 56 | 49.05 N | 8.[illegible] E |
| Stutterheim | 158 | 32.33 S | 27.[illegible] E |
| Stuttgart, Dtsch. | 56 | 48.46 N | 9.[illegible] E |
| Stuttgart, Ar., U.S. | 194 | 34.30 N | 91.[illegible] W |
| Stuttgart □[5] | 56 | 49.00 N | 9.[illegible] E |
| Stuttgart, Flughafen ⊠ | 56 | 48.41 N | 9.1[illegible] E |
| Stützengrün | 54 | 50.32 N | 12.3[illegible] E |
| Stützerbach | 54 | 50.38 N | 10.5[illegible] E |
| Stuyvesant | 210 | 42.24 N | 73.4[illegible] W |
| Stuyvesant Falls | 210 | 42.21 N | 73.4[illegible] W |
| Styal | 262 | 53.21 N | 2.1[illegible] W |
| Stykkishólmur | 24a | 65.06 N | 22.4[illegible] W |
| Styr ≃ | 78 | 52.07 N | 26.3[illegible] E |
| Styrum ◆[8] | 263 | 51.27 N | 6.51 E |
| Styx ≃, On., Can. | 212 | 44.11 N | 80.57 W |
| Styx ≃, Al., U.S. | 194 | 30.31 N | 87.27 W |
| Šu | 85 | 43.36 N | 73.45 E |
| Suaçuí Grande ≃ | 255 | 18.50 S | 41.46 W |
| Suai | 112 | 3.48 N | 113.38 E |
| Suain | 164 | 3.20 S | 142.55 E |
| Suaita | 246 | 6.07 N | 73.27 W |
| Suakin Archipelago II | 140 | 18.42 N | 38.30 E |
| Sual | 116 | 16.04 N | 120.05 E |
| Suan | 98 | 38.42 N | 126.22 [illegible] |
| Suao, T'aiwan | 100 | 24.36 N | 121.51 [illegible] |
| Su'ao, Zhg. | 100 | 25.38 N | 119.42 [illegible] |
| Suapure ≃ | 246 | 6.25 N | 66.23 W |
| Suaqui Grande | 232 | 28.24 N | 109.54 W |
| Suār | 124 | 29.02 N | 79.03 E |
| Suātala | 124 | 23.09 N | 79.02 E |
| Şuatima | 114 | 4.13 N | 96.04 E |
| Šubač | 76 | 60.22 N | 38.14 E |
| Subačius | 76 | 55.46 N | 24.47 E |
| Subah | 115a | 6.58 S | 109.52 E |
| Subaio | 256 | 22.30 S | 42.50 W |
| Subang | 115a | 6.34 S | 107.45 E |
| Şubansiri ≃ | 120 | 26.48 N | 93.50 E |
| Šubarkuduk | 86 | 49.13 N | 56.34 E |
| Subar Laut, Pulau I | 271c | 1.13 N | 103.50 E |
| Subarnapur | 272b | 22.58 N | 88.34 E |
| Şubarnarekha ≃ | 120 | 21.34 N | 87.24 E |
| Šubarši | 86 | 48.35 N | 57.12 E |
| Subashi | 85 | 38.22 N | 74.57 E |
| Subasio, Monte ∧ | 66 | 43.03 N | 12.40 E |
| Subate | 76 | 56.01 N | 25.56 E |
| Subay', 'Urūq as- ◆[2] | 144 | 22.15 N | 43.05 E |
| Subbiano | 66 | 43.34 N | 11.52 E |
| Subbotino | 86 | 53.04 N | 91.55 E |
| Subchankulovo | 80 | 54.34 N | 53.49 E |
| Subei | 102 | 39.27 N | 95.03 E |
| Subeita → Shivta, Ḥorvot ⊥ | 132 | 30.53 N | 34.38 E |
| Suben | 60 | 48.25 N | 13.26 E |
| Subhepur | 272a | 28.45 N | 77.16 E |
| Subi, Pulau I | 112 | 2.55 N | 108.50 E |
| Subiaco | 66 | 41.55 N | 13.06 E |
| Subic | 116 | 14.53 N | 120.14 E |
| Subic Bay ⊂ | 116 | 14.45 N | 120.13 E |
| Subic Bay Naval Base (U.S.) ■ | 116 | 14.47 N | 120.16 E |
| Subipur | 272b | 22.54 N | 88.08 E |
| Subk al-Ahad | 142 | 30.18 N | 31.02 E |
| Sublette | 198 | 37.28 N | 100.50 W |
| Sublett Range ⋀ | 202 | 42.20 N | 112.50 W |
| Sublime | 222 | 29.29 N | 96.48 W |
| Subotica | 38 | 46.06 N | 19.39 E |
| Suburban Airport ⊠ | 284c | 39.05 N | 76.50 W |
| Suburban Village | 285 | 39.58 N | 75.34 W |
| Suca | 144 | 6.31 N | 39.14 E |
| Sucarnoochee ≃ | 194 | 32.25 N | 88.02 W |
| Succasunna | 210 | 40.52 N | 74.38 W |
| Succor Creek ≃ | 202 | 43.38 N | 116.56 W |
| Suceava | 38 | 47.39 N | 26.19 E |
| Suceava □[6] | 38 | 47.30 N | 25.45 E |
| Suceava ≃ | 38 | 47.32 N | 26.32 E |
| Sucha [Beskidzka] | 30 | 49.44 N | 19.36 E |
| Suchaja | 88 | 52.32 N | 107.06 E |
| Suchań, Pol. | 30 | 53.17 N | 15.19 E |
| Suchan → Partizansk, Ross. | 89 | 43.08 N | 133.09 E |
| Suchana | 74 | 68.45 N | 118.00 E |
| Suchang | 107 | 30.34 N | 103.34 E |
| Süchbaatar | 88 | 50.15 N | 106.12 E |
| Süchbaatar □[4] | 102 | 45.30 N | 114.00 E |
| Suchdol ◆[8] | 54 | 50.08 N | 14.21 E |
| Suchdol nad Lužnicí | 61 | 48.54 N | 14.53 E |
| Suchedniów | 30 | 51.03 N | 20.51 E |
| Suchetgarh | 123 | 32.34 N | 74.40 E |
| Suchiapa | 234 | 16.37 N | 93.05 W |
| Suchiapa ≃ | 234 | 16.36 N | 93.01 W |
| Súchil | 234 | 23.38 N | 103.55 W |
| Suchiniči | 76 | 54.06 N | 35.20 E |
| Suchitepéquez □[5] | 236 | 14.25 N | 91.20 W |
| Suchitlán | 234 | 19.22 N | 103.43 W |
| Suchitoto | 236 | 13.56 N | 89.02 W |
| Suchobezvodnoje | 80 | 57.03 N | 44.50 E |
| Suchoborka | 24 | 59.06 N | 49.58 E |
| Suchodol, Ross. | 80 | 53.55 N | 51.14 E |
| Suchodol, Ross. | 82 | 54.27 N | 37.22 E |
| Suchodol'skij | 76 | 53.43 N | 38.17 E |
| Suchodrev ≃ | 82 | 54.44 N | 35.59 E |
| Suchoj | 80 | 47.06 N | 41.21 E |
| Suchoj Jelančik ≃ | 83 | 47.16 N | 38.25 E |
| Suchoj Log | 86 | 56.55 N | 62.01 E |
| Suchoj Pit | 86 | 58.48 N | 92.49 E |


| Symbol | English | Deutsch | Español | Français | Português |
|---|---|---|---|---|---|
| ≃ | River | Fluß | Río | Rivière | Rio |
| ≊ | Canal | Kanal | Canal | Canal | Canal |
| ʟ | Waterfall, Rapids | Wasserfall, Stromschnellen | Cascada, Rápidos | Chute d'eau, Rapides | Cascata, Rápidos |
| ʉ | Strait | Meeresstraße | Estrecho | Détroit | Estreito |
| ⊂ | Bay, Gulf | Bucht, Golf | Bahía, Golfo | Baie, Golfe | Baía, Golfo |
| ⊜ | Lake, Lakes | See, Seen | Lago, Lagos | Lac, Lacs | Lago, Lagos |
| ≡ | Swamp | Sumpf | Pantano | Marais | Pântano |
| ⊓ | Ice Features, Glacier | Eis- und Gletscherformen | Accidentes Glaciales | Formes glaciaires | Acidentes glaciares |
| ⊤ | Other Hydrographic Features | Andere Hydrographische Objekte | Otros Elementos Hidrográficos | Autres données hydrographiques | Outros acidentes hidrográficos |
| ✣ | Submarine Features | Untermeerische Objekte | Accidentes Submarinos | Formes de relief sous-marin | Acidentes submarinos |
| □ | Political Unit | Politische Einheit | Unidad Politica | Entité politique | Unidade política |
| ʊ | Cultural Institution | Kulturelle Institution | Institución Cultural | Institution culturelle | Institução cultural |
| ⊥ | Historical Site | Historische Stätte | Sitio Histórico | Site historique | Sitio histórico |
| ♠ | Recreational Site | Erholungs- und Ferienort | Sitio de Recreo | Centre de loisirs | Area de Lazer |
| ⊠ | Airport | Flughafen | Aeropuerto | Aéroport | Aeroporto |
| ■ | Military Installation | Militäranlage | Instalación Militar | Installation militaire | Instalação militar |
| ◆ | Miscellaneous | Verschiedenes | Misceláneo | Divers | Diversos |

ENGLISH / DEUTSCH


| Name | Page | Lat.°′ | Long.°′ |
|---|---|---|---|
| Suchoj Sambek ≃ | 83 | 47.23 N | 39.07 E |
| Suchona ≃ | 24 | 60.46 N | 46.24 E |
| Suchorečka | 80 | 52.49 N | 52.27 E |
| Suchotinka | 80 | 52.31 N | 41.35 E |
| Suchou → Suzhou | 106 | 31.18 N | 120.37 E |
| Suchoverkovo | 76 | 56.37 N | 35.35 E |
| Suchov Pervyj | 80 | 49.59 N | 43.28 E |
| Süchow → Xuzhou | 98 | 34.16 N | 117.11 E |
| Süchteln | 56 | 51.17 N | 6.22 E |
| Suchumi | 84 | 43.01 N | 41.02 E |
| Sucio ≃ | 246 | 7.27 N | 77.07 W |
| Suck ≃ | 48 | 53.16 N | 8.03 W |
| Sucker Creek ≃ | 212 | 44.09 N | 77.08 W |
| Sucker Creek Indian Reserve ◆ [4] | 182 | 55.28 N | 116.10 W |
| Sucker Lake ⊜ | 212 | 44.46 N | 78.16 W |
| Suckling, Mount ʌ | 164 | 9.45 S | 148.55 E |
| Sucre, Arg. | 258 | 34.30 S | 59.07 W |
| Sucre, Bol. | 248 | 19.02 S | 65.17 W |
| Sucre, Col. | 246 | 8.49 N | 74.44 W |
| Sucre, Ec. | 246 | 1.16 S | 80.26 W |
| Sucre □ [3] | 246 | 10.25 N | 63.30 W |
| Sucre □ [5], Col. | 246 | 9.00 N | 75.00 W |
| Sucre □ [5], Ven. | 286c | 10.25 N | 66.50 W |
| Sucúa | 246 | 2.28 S | 78.10 W |
| Sucuaro | 246 | 4.34 N | 68.50 W |
| Sucumbíos □ [4] | 246 | 0.06 N | 76.52 W |
| Sucunduri ≃ | 248 | 5.50 S | 59.32 W |
| Sucuriju | 250 | 1.39 N | 49.57 W |
| Sucuriú ≃ | 255 | 20.47 S | 51.38 W |
| Sucy-en-Brie | 50 | 48.46 N | 2.32 E |
| Sud □ [4] | 175f | 22.00 S | 166.30 E |
| Sud, Canal du ʯ | 238 | 18.40 N | 73.05 W |
| Sud, Grand Récif ⊹ [2] | 175f | 23.00 S | 167.02 E |
| Sud, Pointe › | 157a | 11.53 S | 43.49 E |
| Sud, Rivière du ≃ | 206 | 45.08 N | 73.15 W |
| Suda | 76 | 59.09 N | 37.33 E |
| Suda ≃ | 76 | 59.11 N | 37.30 E |
| Südafrika → South Africa □ [1] | 156 | 30.00 S | 26.00 E |
| Sudaj | 76 | 58.58 N | 43.08 E |
| Sudak | 78 | 44.52 N | 34.59 E |
| Südamerika → South America ⏏ [1] | 18 | 15.00 S | 60.00 W |
| Sudan | 196 | 34.04 N | 102.31 W |
| Sudan (As-Sūdān) □ [1], Afr. | 136 | 15.00 N | 30.00 E |
| Sudan (As-Sūdān) □ [1], Afr. | 140 | 15.00 N | 30.00 E |
| Sudan ◆ [1] | 10 | 10.00 N | 20.00 E |
| Sudañez | 248 | 19.06 S | 64.44 W |
| Sudarsan | 272b | 22.59 N | 88.17 E |
| Südbahnhof ◆ [5] | 264b | 48.11 N | 16.23 E |
| Sudberg ◆ [8] | 263 | 51.11 N | 7.08 E |
| Sudbišči | 76 | 52.57 N | 37.39 E |
| Sud'bodarovka | 80 | 52.19 N | 54.07 E |
| Südbrookmerland | 52 | 53.29 N | 7.24 E |
| Sudbury, On., Can. | 190 | 46.30 N | 81.00 W |
| Sudbury, Eng., U.K. | 42 | 52.02 N | 0.44 E |
| Sudbury, Ma., U.S. | 207 | 42.23 N | 71.25 W |
| Sudbury ≃ | 283 | 42.28 N | 71.22 W |
| Sudbury Center | 283 | 42.23 N | 71.25 W |
| Sudbury Reservoir ⊜ [1] | 207 | 42.19 N | 71.31 W |
| Südchinesisches Meer → South China Sea ⩪ [2] | 108 | 10.00 N | 113.00 E |
| Sudd → As-Sudd ◆ [1] | 140 | 8.00 N | 31.00 E |
| Sud Dakota → South Dakota □ [3] | 198 | 44.15 N | 100.00 W |
| Sudd an-Na'ām, Jabal ʌ | 142 | 29.49 N | 31.43 E |
| Suddie | 246 | 7.07 N | 58.29 W |
| Sude ≃ | 54 | 53.22 N | 10.45 E |
| Süderbrarup | 41 | 54.38 N | 9.46 E |
| Suderburg | 52 | 52.54 N | 10.27 E |
| Süderlügum | 41 | 54.52 N | 8.55 E |
| Suderwich | 263 | 51.37 N | 7.15 E |
| Sudeten → Sudety ⩘ | 30 | 50.30 N | 16.00 E |
| Sudety ⩘ | 30 | 50.30 N | 16.00 E |
| Süd-Georgien → South Georgia I | 244 | 54.15 S | 36.45 W |
| Sudi | 154 | 10.06 S | 39.57 E |
| Sudislavl' | 80 | 57.53 N | 41.43 E |
| Südkamen | 263 | 51.35 N | 7.39 E |
| Sud-Kivu □ [4] | 154 | 3.00 S | 28.30 E |
| Süd-Korea → Korea, South □ [1] | 98 | 36.30 N | 128.00 E |
| Sudlersville | 208 | 39.11 N | 75.51 W |
| Südlicher Bug → Pivdennyy Buh ≃ | 78 | 46.59 N | 31.58 E |
| Südlicher Indianer-See → Southern Indian Lake ⊜ | 176 | 57.10 N | 98.40 W |
| Südlohn | 52 | 51.57 N | 6.52 E |
| Sudnikovo | 82 | 55.53 N | 36.02 E |
| Sudogda | 80 | 55.57 N | 40.50 E |
| Sudomskaja vozvyšennost' ⩘ [1] | 76 | 57.25 N | 29.25 E |
| Sudong, Pulau I | 271c | 1.13 N | 103.44 E |
| Süd-Orkney-Inseln → South Orkney Islands II | 9 | 60.35 S | 45.30 W |
| Sudost' ≃ | 76 | 52.19 N | 33.24 E |
| Sud-Ouest □ [4] | 152 | 5.10 N | 9.00 E |
| Sud-Ouest, Pointe du › | 186 | 49.23 N | 63.36 W |
| Sudova Vyshnya | 78 | 49.49 N | 23.22 E |
| Südradde ≃ | 52 | 52.41 N | 7.34 E |
| Süd-Sandwich-Inseln → South Sandwich Islands II | 18 | 57.45 S | 26.30 W |
| Süd-Shetland-Inseln → South Shetland Islands II | 9 | 62.00 S | 58.00 W |
| Sudūd | 142 | 30.25 N | 30.54 E |
| Südwest-Kap → South West Cape › | 166 | 43.34 S | 146.02 E |
| Sudweyhe | 52 | 52.59 N | 8.53 E |
| Sudža | 78 | 51.12 N | 35.16 E |
| Sue | 96 | 33.35 N | 130.30 E |
| Sue ≃ | 140 | 7.41 N | 28.03 E |
| Sueca | 34 | 39.12 N | 0.19 W |
| Suecia → Sweden □ [1] | 24 | 62.00 N | 15.00 E |
| Sue Creek ⊂ | 284b | 39.17 N | 76.24 W |
| Suedberg | 208 | 40.32 N | 76.28 W |
| Suède → Sweden □ [1] | 24 | 62.00 N | 15.00 E |
| Suemez Island I | 182 | 55.17 N | 133.21 W |
| Suèvres | 50 | 47.40 N | 1.28 E |
| Suez → As-Suways | 142 | 29.58 N | 32.33 E |
| Suez, Gulf of → Suways, Khalīj as- ⊂ | 140 | 29.00 N | 32.50 E |
| Suez Canal → Suways, Qanāt as- ≖ | 142 | 29.55 N | 32.33 E |
| Sūf | 132 | 32.19 N | 35.50 E |
| Şufaynah | 128 | 23.09 N | 40.32 E |
| Suffern | 210 | 41.06 N | 74.09 W |
| Suffern Park | 276 | 41.07 N | 74.07 W |
| Suffield, Ab., Can. | 184 | 50.12 N | 111.10 W |
| Suffield, Ct., U.S. | 207 | 41.58 N | 72.39 W |
| Suffield, Oh., U.S. | 214 | 41.01 N | 81.21 W |
| Suffield, Canadian Forces Base ■ | 184 | 50.15 N | 111.10 W |
| Suffolk | 208 | 36.43 N | 76.35 W |
| Suffolk □ [6], Eng., U.K. | 42 | 52.10 N | 1.00 E |
| Suffolk □ [6], Ma., U.S. | 207 | 42.21 N | 71.04 W |
| Suffolk □ [6], N.Y., U.S. | 210 | 40.55 N | 72.40 W |
| Suffolk, Ruisseau ≃ | 206 | 45.48 N | 74.59 W |
| Şūfīān | 128 | 38.17 N | 45.59 E |
| Sufi-Kurgan | 85 | 40.02 N | 73.30 E |
| Sufu → Kashi | 85 | 39.29 N | 75.59 E |
| Suga-jima I | 94 | 34.29 N | 136.53 E |
| Sugana, Val V | 64 | 46.00 N | 11.40 E |
| Sugandha | 272b | 22.54 N | 88.20 E |
| Sugano | 268 | 35.44 N | 139.56 E |
| Sugar ≃, U.S. | 190 | 42.26 N | 89.12 W |
| Sugar ≃, N.H., U.S. | 188 | 43.24 N | 72.24 W |
| Sugar ≃, N.Y., U.S. | 212 | 43.31 N | 75.19 W |
| Sugar City | 202 | 43.52 N | 111.44 W |
| Sugarcreek, Oh., U.S. | 214 | 40.30 N | 81.39 W |
| Sugarcreek, Pa., U.S. | 214 | 41.25 N | 79.52 W |
| Sugar Creek ≃, U.S. | 216 | 40.47 N | 87.45 W |
| Sugar Creek ≃, Il., U.S. | 194 | 40.09 N | 89.38 W |
| Sugar Creek ≃, Il., U.S. | 219 | 38.28 N | 89.37 W |
| Sugar Creek ≃, Il., U.S. | 219 | 39.48 N | 89.32 W |
| Sugar Creek ≃, In., U.S. | 194 | 39.51 N | 87.21 W |
| Sugar Creek ≃, In., U.S. | 218 | 39.21 N | 86.00 W |
| Sugar Creek ≃, Mi., U.S. | 281 | 42.06 N | 83.36 W |
| Sugar Creek ≃, N.Y., U.S. | 210 | 42.38 N | 77.09 W |
| Sugar Creek ≃, Oh., U.S. | 214 | 40.31 N | 81.28 W |
| Sugar Creek ≃, Oh., U.S. | 216 | 40.57 N | 84.11 W |
| Sugar Creek ≃, Oh., U.S. | 218 | 39.27 N | 83.25 W |
| Sugar Creek ≃, Ok., U.S. | 196 | 35.05 N | 98.10 W |
| Sugar Creek ≃, Pa., U.S. | 210 | 41.47 N | 76.27 W |
| Sugar Creek ≃, Wi., U.S. | 216 | 42.43 N | 88.19 W |
| Sugar Grove, Il., U.S. | 216 | 41.45 N | 88.27 W |
| Sugargrove, Pa., U.S. | 214 | 41.59 N | 79.21 W |
| Sugar Grove, Va., U.S. | 192 | 36.46 N | 81.24 W |
| Sugar Hill | 192 | 34.06 N | 84.02 W |
| Sugar Island I, On., Can. | 212 | 44.26 N | 77.17 W |
| Sugar Island I, Mi., U.S. | 190 | 46.25 N | 84.12 W |
| Sugar Land | 222 | 29.37 N | 95.38 W |
| Sugar Loaf | 210 | 41.19 N | 74.17 W |
| Sugar Loaf → Pão de Açúcar ʌ | 287a | 22.57 S | 43.09 W |
| Sugarloaf ʌ [2] | 214 | 41.24 N | 81.06 W |
| Sugarloaf Hill ʌ [2] | 274b | 37.58 S | 145.19 E |
| Sugarloaf Key I | 220 | 24.40 N | 81.32 W |
| Sugarloaf Mountain ʌ, Ky., U.S. | 218 | 38.13 N | 83.32 W |
| Sugarloaf Mountain ʌ, Me., U.S. | 188 | 45.01 N | 70.22 W |
| Sugar Loaf Mountain ʌ, Md., U.S. | 208 | 39.16 N | 77.23 W |
| Sugar Loaf Mountain ʌ, Ok., U.S. | 194 | 35.02 N | 94.28 W |
| Sugarloaf Mountain ʌ [2] | 220 | 28.39 N | 81.44 W |
| Sugarloaf Peak ʌ | 280 | 34.14 N | 117.38 W |
| Sugarloaf Point ›, Austl. | 166 | 32.26 S | 152.33 E |
| Sugar Loaf Point ›, On., Can. | 284a | 42.52 N | 79.17 W |
| Sugarloaf Reservoir ⊜ [1] | 169 | 37.41 S | 145.18 E |
| Sugarloaf Ridge State Park ♠ | 226 | 38.26 N | 122.29 W |
| Sugar Notch | 210 | 41.11 N | 75.55 W |
| Sugar Pine Point State Park ♠ | 226 | 39.03 N | 120.07 W |
| Sugartown | 285 | 40.00 N | 75.31 W |
| Sugauli | 124 | 26.46 N | 84.44 E |
| Sugbai Passage ʯ | 116 | 5.22 N | 120.33 E |
| Sugbay | 116 | 7.31 N | 123.19 E |
| Sugbuhan Point › | 116 | 10.04 N | 126.04 E |
| Sugenheim | 56 | 49.36 N | 10.26 E |
| Suggi Lake ⊜ | 184 | 54.22 N | 102.47 W |
| Suginami ◆ [8] | 268 | 35.42 N | 139.38 E |
| Sugita ◆ [8] | 268 | 35.23 N | 139.38 E |
| Sugito | 94 | 36.02 N | 139.44 E |
| Şuğla Gölü ⊜ | 130 | 37.20 N | 32.02 E |
| Šugnou | 85 | 38.35 N | 70.20 E |
| Sugod | 116 | 12.03 N | 124.09 E |
| Sugoj ≃ | 74 | 64.15 N | 154.29 E |
| Şugonovo | 82 | 54.41 N | 36.41 E |
| Šugozero | 76 | 59.55 N | 34.12 E |
| Šugurovo, Ross. | 80 | 53.25 N | 46.29 E |
| Šugurovo, Ross. | 80 | 54.31 N | 52.06 E |
| Sugut ≃ | 112 | 6.26 N | 117.43 E |
| Suguta ≃ | 154 | 2.03 N | 36.33 E |
| Suguti | 154 | 1.44 S | 33.39 E |
| Suhai Hu ⊜ | 102 | 38.50 N | 94.00 E |
| Suhaitu | 102 | 44.50 N | 93.39 E |
| Şuḥār | 128 | 24.22 N | 56.45 E |
| Suheli Island I [1] | 122 | 10.03 N | 72.17 E |
| Suhl | 54 | 50.37 N | 10.41 E |
| Suhlendorf | 54 | 52.55 N | 10.46 E |
| Suhopolje | 36 | 45.48 N | 17.30 E |
| Suhr | 58 | 47.22 N | 8.05 E |
| Suhr ≃ | 58 | 47.25 N | 8.04 E |
| Suhum | 150 | 6.05 N | 0.27 W |
| Şuhut | 130 | 38.32 N | 30.33 E |
| Sūi | 120 | 28.37 N | 69.19 E |
| Suiá-Miçu ≃ | 250 | 11.13 S | 53.15 W |
| Suianzhan | 89 | 53.07 N | 125.20 E |
| Suiattle ≃ | 224 | 48.20 N | 121.33 W |
| Suichang | 100 | 28.34 N | 119.14 E |
| Suichuan | 100 | 26.26 N | 114.32 E |
| Suichuan ≃ | 100 | 26.30 N | 114.45 E |
| Suid Afrika → South Africa □ [1] | 156 | 30.00 S | 26.00 E |
| Suide | 102 | 37.32 N | 110.12 E |
| Suiding | 86 | 44.03 N | 80.49 E |
| Suido-suigenchi ⊜ [1] | 270 | 34.54 N | 135.17 E |
| Suidvaal | 158 | 26.52 S | 29.47 E |
| Suifenhe | 89 | 44.24 N | 131.10 E |
| Suifu, Nihon | 94 | 36.37 N | 140.29 E |
| Suifu → Yibin, Zhg. | 107 | 28.47 N | 104.38 E |
| Suigō-kokutei-kōen ♠ | 94 | 36.05 N | 140.20 E |
| Suigō-Tsukuba-kokutei-kōen ♠ | 94 | 36.00 N | 140.20 E |
| Suihua | 89 | 46.37 N | 127.00 E |
| Suijiang | 102 | 28.31 N | 104.07 E |
| Suileng | 89 | 47.18 N | 127.10 E |
| Suining, Zhg. | 100 | 33.54 N | 117.56 E |
| Suining, Zhg. | 102 | 26.21 N | 110.00 E |
| Suining, Zhg. | 107 | 30.31 N | 105.34 E |
| Suipacha | 252 | 34.45 S | 59.41 W |
| Suiping | 100 | 33.10 N | 113.57 E |
| Suippe ≃ | 50 | 49.25 N | 3.57 E |
| Suippes | 56 | 49.08 N | 4.32 E |
| Suir ≃ | 48 | 52.15 N | 7.00 W |
| Suisse → Switzerland □ [1] | 58 | 47.00 N | 8.00 E |
| Suisun Bay ⊂ | 226 | 38.06 N | 122.00 W |
| Suisun City | 226 | 38.14 N | 122.02 W |
| Suisun Creek ≃ | 226 | 38.12 N | 122.06 W |
| Suita | 96 | 34.45 N | 135.32 E |
| Suiti burnu › | 84 | 40.12 N | 50.22 E |
| Suitland | 284c | 38.50 N | 76.55 W |
| Suixi, Zhg. | 100 | 33.56 N | 116.46 E |
| Suixi, Zhg. | 102 | 21.25 N | 110.15 E |
| Suixian, Zhg. | 98 | 34.26 N | 115.05 E |
| Suixian, Zhg. | 100 | 31.42 N | 113.20 E |
| Suiyang, Zhg. | 89 | 44.26 N | 130.53 E |
| Suiyang, Zhg. | 102 | 27.56 N | 107.18 E |
| Suiyangdian | 100 | 32.04 N | 112.55 E |
| Suiza → Switzerland □ [1] | 58 | 47.00 N | 8.00 E |
| Suize ≃ | 58 | 48.08 N | 5.08 E |
| Şuizhong | 98 | 40.20 N | 120.19 E |
| Šuja, Ross. | 24 | 61.55 N | 34.12 E |
| Šuja, Ross. | 80 | 56.50 N | 41.23 E |
| Šuja ≃, Ross. | 24 | 61.54 N | 34.15 E |
| Šuja ≃, Ross. | 80 | 57.56 N | 43.15 E |
| Sujānagar | 126 | 23.57 N | 89.25 E |
| Sujāngarh | 120 | 27.42 N | 74.28 E |
| Sujāwal | 120 | 24.36 N | 68.05 E |
| Suji | 107 | 29.35 N | 103.37 E |
| Sujiabu | 100 | 31.38 N | 116.22 E |
| Sujiaqiao | 105 | 39.24 N | 116.10 E |
| Sujiatun | 104 | 41.40 N | 123.22 E |
| Sujiawan | 107 | 29.48 N | 104.57 E |
| Sujiawu | 105 | 39.17 N | 115.55 E |
| Şujiazui | 100 | 33.40 N | 119.29 E |
| Šujskoje | 76 | 59.22 N | 40.59 E |
| Sujutkina Kosa, mys › | 84 | 44.13 N | 47.15 E |
| Sukabihanawa | 112 | 9.30 S | 124.57 E |
| Sukabumi | 115a | 6.55 S | 106.56 E |
| Sukadana, Indon. | 112 | 1.15 S | 109.57 E |
| Sukadana, Indon. | 115a | 5.05 S | 105.33 E |
| Sukadana, Teluk ⊂ | 112 | 1.24 S | 109.50 E |
| Sukagawa | 92 | 37.17 N | 140.23 E |
| Sukamandi | 115a | 6.20 S | 107.39 E |
| Sukamara | 112 | 2.43 S | 111.11 E |
| Sukanegara | 115a | 7.06 S | 107.07 E |
| Sukapura | 115a | 7.52 S | 113.03 E |
| Sukaraja, Indon. | 112 | 2.21 S | 110.37 E |
| Sukaraja, Indon. | 115a | 7.27 S | 108.12 E |
| Sukaraja, Indon. | 115a | 7.27 S | 109.17 E |
| Sukarno, Pegunungan → Jaya, Puncak ʌ | 164 | 4.05 S | 137.11 E |
| Sukau | 112 | 5.32 N | 118.17 E |
| Sukchar | 272b | 22.42 N | 88.22 E |
| Sukch'ŏn | 98 | 39.24 N | 125.38 E |
| Sukematsu | 270 | 34.31 N | 135.26 E |
| Sukeva | 26 | 63.52 N | 27.26 E |
| Sukha Volnovakha ≃ | 83 | 47.37 N | 38.01 E |
| Sukhnah, 'Ayn ⩪ [4] | 142 | 29.35 N | 32.15 E |
| Sukhothai | 110 | 17.01 N | 99.49 E |
| Sukhumi → Suchumi | 84 | 43.01 N | 41.02 E |
| Sukhyy Torets' ≃ | 83 | 48.49 N | 37.36 E |
| Sukkertoppen (Maniitsoq) | 176 | 65.25 N | 52.53 W |
| Sukkozero | 24 | 63.11 N | 32.18 E |
| Sukkur | 120 | 27.42 N | 68.52 E |
| Sukkwan Island I | 182 | 55.05 N | 132.45 W |
| Suklāra | 126 | 23.11 N | 86.21 E |
| Sukmanovka | 78 | 51.47 N | 41.34 E |
| Sukodadi | 115a | 7.06 S | 112.19 E |
| Sukoharjo | 115a | 7.41 S | 110.50 E |
| Sukovo | 82 | 54.54 N | 38.19 E |
| Sukroml'a | 76 | 56.53 N | 34.44 E |
| Sukses | 156 | 21.01 S | 16.52 E |
| Suksun | 86 | 57.07 N | 57.24 E |
| Sukumo | 92 | 32.56 N | 132.44 E |
| Sukun, Pulau I | 115b | 8.07 S | 122.08 E |
| Sukunka ≃ | 182 | 55.37 N | 121.37 W |
| Sul, Baía ⊂ | 252 | 27.40 S | 48.35 W |
| Sul, Canal do ʯ | 250 | 0.10 S | 49.30 W |
| Sula I | 26 | 61.08 N | 4.55 E |
| Sula ≃, Ross. | 24 | 67.16 N | 52.07 E |
| Sula ≃, Ukr. | 78 | 49.40 N | 32.41 E |
| Sula, Kepulauan II | 112 | 1.52 S | 125.22 E |
| Sulaco ≃ | 236 | 15.01 N | 87.44 W |
| Sulaimān Khel | 123 | 33.41 N | 71.01 E |
| Sulaimān Range ⩘ | 120 | 30.30 N | 70.10 E |
| Sulak, Ross. | 80 | 51.52 N | 48.21 E |
| Sulak, Ross. | 84 | 43.16 N | 47.32 E |
| Sulak ≃ | 84 | 43.20 N | 47.34 E |
| Sulakyurt | 130 | 40.10 N | 33.44 E |
| Sulang | 115a | 6.48 S | 111.23 E |
| Sulat | 116 | 11.49 N | 125.27 E |
| Sulauan Point › | 116 | 8.37 N | 124.29 E |
| Sulawesi (Celebes) I | 112 | 2.00 S | 121.00 E |
| Sulawesi Selatan □ [4] | 112 | 3.30 S | 120.00 E |
| Sulawesi Tengah □ [4] | 112 | 1.00 N | 123.00 E |
| Sulawesi Tenggara □ [4] | 112 | 4.00 S | 122.00 E |
| Sulawesi Utara □ [4] | 112 | 0.30 N | 124.00 E |
| Sulaymān, Birak (Solomon's Pools) ⊥ | 132 | 31.41 N | 35.10 E |
| Sulby | 44 | 54.18 N | 4.29 W |
| Sulcis ◆ [1] | 71 | 39.04 N | 8.41 E |
| Suldalsvatnet ⊜ | 26 | 59.35 N | 6.45 E |
| Sūldeh | 128 | 36.34 N | 52.01 E |
| Sulechów | 30 | 52.06 N | 15.37 E |
| Sulęcin | 30 | 52.26 N | 15.08 E |
| Suleja | 86 | 55.09 N | 58.50 E |
| Sulejów | 30 | 51.22 N | 19.53 E |
| Sulejówek | 30 | 52.14 N | 21.17 E |
| Sulen, Mount ʌ | 164 | 3.25 S | 142.15 E |
| Sule Skerry I [2] | 46 | 59.05 N | 4.26 W |
| Suleymaniye Mosque ʋ [1] | 267b | 41.00 N | 28.57 E |
| Süleymanlı | 130 | 37.54 N | 36.50 E |
| Sülfeld | 52 | 53.48 N | 10.14 E |
| Šul'gino, Ross. | 82 | 54.33 N | 37.35 E |
| Sulğino, Ross. | 82 | 55.50 N | 35.55 E |
| Sulia | 154 | 1.32 S | 26.33 E |
| Suliki | 112 | 0.06 S | 100.27 E |
| Sulima | 150 | 6.58 N | 11.35 W |
| Sulin | 83 | 48.54 N | 40.07 E |
| Sulina | 38 | 45.09 N | 29.40 E |
| Sulina, Braţul ≃ [1] | 38 | 45.09 N | 29.41 E |
| Sulincheer | 102 | 42.41 N | 109.20 E |
| Sulingen | 52 | 52.41 N | 8.47 E |
| Sulinskij | 83 | 47.52 N | 40.06 E |
| Sulitelma ʌ | 24 | 67.08 N | 16.24 E |
| Sulkava | 26 | 61.47 N | 28.23 E |
| Sullana | 248 | 4.53 S | 80.41 W |
| Sullane ≃ | 48 | 51.53 N | 8.56 W |
| Sulligent | 194 | 33.54 N | 88.08 W |
| Sullivan, Il., U.S. | 194 | 39.35 N | 88.36 W |
| Sullivan, In., U.S. | 194 | 39.06 N | 87.24 W |
| Sullivan, Mo., U.S. | 219 | 38.12 N | 91.09 W |
| Sullivan, Oh., U.S. | 214 | 41.02 N | 82.13 W |
| Sullivan, Wi., U.S. | 216 | 43.00 N | 88.35 W |
| Sullivan □ [6], N.Y., U.S. | 210 | 41.39 N | 74.42 W |
| Sullivan □ [6], Pa., U.S. | 210 | 41.25 N | 76.29 W |
| Sullivan Canyon V | 280 | 34.03 N | 118.30 W |
| Sullivan Creek ≃ | 226 | 37.53 N | 120.25 W |
| Sullivan Lake ⊜ | 182 | 52.00 N | 112.00 W |
| Sullivanville | 210 | 42.14 N | 76.46 W |
| Sully-sur-Loire | 50 | 47.46 N | 2.22 E |
| Sulm ≃ | 61 | 46.45 N | 15.34 E |
| Sulmona | 66 | 42.03 N | 13.55 E |
| Sulot' ≃ | 82 | 56.41 N | 38.01 E |
| Sulphur, Yk., Can. | 180 | 63.47 N | 138.53 W |
| Sulphur, In., U.S. | 218 | 38.14 N | 86.28 W |
| Sulphur, Ky., U.S. | 218 | 38.29 N | 85.16 W |
| Sulphur, La., U.S. | 194 | 30.14 N | 93.22 W |
| Sulphur, Ok., U.S. | 196 | 34.30 N | 96.58 W |
| Sulphur ≃, Ab., Can. | 182 | 53.50 N | 119.10 W |
| Sulphur ≃, U.S. | 194 | 33.07 N | 93.52 W |
| Sulphur Creek ≃ | 198 | 44.46 N | 102.25 W |
| Sulphur Draw V | 196 | 33.12 N | 102.17 W |
| Sulphur Springs, In., U.S. | 218 | 40.00 N | 85.26 W |
| Sulphur Springs, Oh., U.S. | 214 | 40.52 N | 82.52 W |
| Sulphur Springs, Tx., U.S. | 222 | 33.08 N | 95.36 W |
| Sulphur Springs Draw V | 196 | 32.12 N | 101.36 W |
| Sulphur Springs Valley V | 200 | 31.50 N | 109.50 W |
| Sulsul | 144 | 5.06 N | 44.55 E |
| Sultan | 224 | 47.51 N | 121.48 W |
| Sultan ≃ | 224 | 47.52 N | 121.49 W |
| Sultana | 226 | 36.33 N | 119.20 W |
| Sultanahmet Mosque ʋ [1] | 267b | 41.00 N | 28.58 E |
| Sultan Alonto, Lake ⊜ | 116 | 7.53 N | 124.15 E |
| Sultana Point › | 168b | 35.08 S | 137.45 E |
| Sulṭanatābād ◆ [8] | 267d | 35.46 N | 51.28 E |
| Sultançiftligi ◆ [8] | 267b | 41.02 N | 29.13 E |
| Sultandağı | 130 | 38.32 N | 31.14 E |
| Sultan Dağı ʌ | 130 | 38.58 N | 27.26 E |
| Sultanhanı | 130 | 38.15 N | 33.33 E |
| Sultanhisar | 130 | 37.53 N | 28.10 E |
| Sultan Kudarat | 116 | 7.17 N | 124.16 E |
| Sultan Kudarat □ [4] | 116 | 6.20 N | 124.20 E |
| Sultan Mosque ʋ [1] | 271c | 1.18 N | 103.52 E |
| Sultānpur, India | 123 | 31.13 N | 75.11 E |
| Sultānpur, India | 124 | 26.16 N | 82.04 E |
| Sultānpur Dabās ◆ [8] | 272a | 28.46 N | 77.03 E |
| Sultan sa Barongis | 116 | 6.46 N | 124.38 E |
| Sultan-Saly | 83 | 47.21 N | 39.35 E |
| Sulu | 164 | 5.25 S | 151.00 E |
| Sulu □ [4] | 116 | 6.00 N | 121.00 E |
| Suluan Island I | 116 | 10.46 N | 125.57 E |
| Sulu Archipelago II | 116 | 6.00 N | 121.00 E |
| Sulu Basin ⊹ [1] | 12 | 8.00 N | 121.30 E |
| Sulu Chi ⊜ | 124 | 30.12 N | 86.20 E |
| Sülüklü | 130 | 39.05 N | 30.58 E |
| Sul'ukta | 85 | 39.56 N | 69.34 E |
| Sululta | 144 | 9.10 N | 38.48 E |
| Sulunṭah | 146 | 32.36 N | 21.43 E |
| Suluova (Suluca) | 130 | 40.47 N | 35.42 E |
| Sulūq | 146 | 31.39 N | 20.15 E |
| Sulusaj | 85 | 38.50 N | 67.05 E |
| Sulusaray | 130 | 40.00 N | 36.06 E |
| Sulu Sea ⩪ [2] | 116 | 8.00 N | 120.00 E |
| Sulutobe | 86 | 44.38 N | 66.05 E |
| Sulz | 58 | 48.18 N | 7.51 E |
| Sulz am Neckar | 58 | 48.21 N | 8.37 E |
| Sulzano | 64 | 45.41 N | 10.05 E |
| Sulzbach, Dtsch. | 56 | 49.18 N | 7.07 E |
| Sulzbach, Dtsch. | 56 | 49.00 N | 9.30 E |
| Sulzbach ≃ | 60 | 48.36 N | 13.02 E |
| Sulzbach am Kocher | 56 | 48.58 N | 9.50 E |
| Sulzbach-Rosenberg | 60 | 49.30 N | 11.45 E |
| Sulzberg, Dtsch. | 58 | 47.40 N | 10.21 E |
| Sulzberg, Dtsch. | 64 | 47.40 N | 10.21 E |
| Sulzberger Bay ⊂ | 9 | 77.00 S | 152.00 W |
| Sulzburg | 58 | 47.50 N | 7.42 E |
| Şülze | 52 | 52.46 N | 10.02 E |
| Šum, Ross. | 76 | 59.52 N | 31.46 E |
| Šum, Ross. | 88 | 54.51 N | 95.18 E |
| Şuma ◆ [8] | 270 | 34.39 N | 135.08 E |
| Šum'ači | 76 | 53.52 N | 32.25 E |
| Šumadija ◆ [1] | 38 | 44.10 N | 20.50 E |
| Sumalata | 112 | 0.59 N | 122.30 E |
| Sumallo ≃ | 224 | 49.14 N | 121.05 W |
| Şumampa | 252 | 29.22 S | 63.28 W |
| Šumanaj | 86 | 42.37 N | 59.08 E |
| Sumangat, Tanjong › | 116 | 6.35 N | 117.33 E |
| Sumano-ura ♠ | 96 | 34.38 N | 135.08 E |
| Sūmār | 128 | 33.52 N | 45.39 E |
| Sumarokovo | 82 | 55.46 N | 35.55 E |
| Sumas | 202 | 49.00 N | 122.15 W |
| Sumas ≃ | 224 | 49.09 N | 122.12 W |
| Sumatera (Sumatra) I | 108 | 0.05 S | 102.00 E |
| Sumatera Barat □ [4] | 112 | 0.30 S | 100.30 E |
| Sumatera Selatan □ [4] | 112 | 3.00 S | 104.00 E |
| Sumatera Utara □ [4] | 114 | 2.20 N | 99.00 E |
| Sum'atino | 82 | 55.00 N | 36.21 E |
| Sumatou | 107 | 30.28 N | 104.03 E |
| Sumatra → Sumatera I | 108 | 0.05 S | 102.00 E |
| Sumava Resorts | 216 | 41.10 N | 87.26 W |
| Sumayḥ | 140 | 12.43 N | 30.50 E |
| Sumba I | 115b | 10.00 S | 120.00 E |
| Sumba, Île I | 152 | 1.44 N | 19.32 E |
| Sumba, Selat ʯ | 115b | 9.05 S | 120.00 E |
| Sumbar ≃ | 128 | 38.00 N | 55.17 E |
| Sumbawa I | 115b | 8.40 S | 118.00 E |
| Sumbawa Besar | 115b | 8.30 S | 117.26 E |
| Sumbawanga | 154 | 7.58 S | 31.37 E |
| Sumbay | 248 | 15.58 S | 71.23 W |
| Sumbe | 152 | 11.13 S | 13.50 E |
| Sümber | 90 | 46.21 N | 108.20 E |
| Sumbilla | 34 | 43.10 N | 1.40 W |
| Sumbing, Gunung ʌ | 115a | 7.23 S | 110.04 E |
| Sumbu National Park ♠ | 154 | 8.50 S | 30.25 E |
| Sumburgh Head › | 46a | 59.53 N | 1.20 W |
| Sumburgh Roost ʯ | 46a | 59.49 N | 1.19 W |
| Şumbut | 80 | 55.33 N | 50.41 E |
| Sumbuya | 150 | 7.39 N | 11.58 W |
| Sumdo | 120 | 35.01 N | 78.41 E |
| Sumé | 250 | 7.39 S | 36.55 W |
| Sumedang | 115a | 6.52 S | 107.55 E |
| Sümeg | 30 | 46.59 N | 17.17 E |
| Šumek | 86 | 48.42 N | 85.32 E |
| Šumen | 38 | 43.16 N | 26.55 E |
| Sumène | 62 | 43.59 N | 3.43 E |
| Şumenep | 115a | 7.01 S | 113.52 E |
| Šumerl'a | 80 | 55.30 N | 46.26 E |
| Sumgait → Sumqayıt | 84 | 40.36 N | 49.38 E |
| Šumicha | 86 | 55.14 N | 63.19 E |
| Sumida ◆ [8] | 268 | 35.42 N | 139.48 E |
| Sumida ≃ | 268 | 35.40 N | 139.47 E |
| Sumidouro | 256 | 22.03 S | 42.41 W |
| Sumilao | 116 | 8.18 N | 124.57 E |
| Šumilina | 76 | 55.18 N | 29.37 E |
| Šumilinskaja | 80 | 49.58 N | 41.26 E |
| Suminoe ◆ [8] | 270 | 34.36 N | 135.28 E |
| Sumisu-jima I | 90 | 31.27 N | 140.03 E |
| Sumiswald | 58 | 47.02 N | 7.45 E |
| Sumiyoshi ◆ [8] | 270 | 34.36 N | 135.31 E |
| Sumki | 86 | 55.03 N | 65.44 E |
| Sumkino | 86 | 58.09 N | 68.21 E |
| Sumlog ≃ | 116 | 6.53 N | 126.02 E |
| Summer Bridge | 44 | 54.03 N | 1.41 W |
| Summerdale | 208 | 40.18 N | 76.56 W |
| Summerfield, Fl., U.S. | 220 | 29.00 N | 82.02 W |
| Summerfield, Mo., U.S. | 219 | 38.17 N | 91.49 W |
| Summerfield, N.C., U.S. | 192 | 36.12 N | 79.54 W |
| Summerford, Nf., Can. | 186 | 49.29 N | 54.47 W |
| Summerford, Oh., U.S. | 218 | 39.55 N | 83.29 W |
| Summerhill, Ire. | 48 | 53.29 N | 6.44 W |
| Summerhill, Pa., U.S. | 214 | 40.22 N | 78.46 W |
| Summer Island I | 190 | 45.34 N | 86.39 W |
| Summer Isles II | 46 | 58.02 N | 5.28 W |
| Summer Lake ⊜ | 202 | 42.50 N | 120.45 W |
| Summerland | 182 | 49.36 N | 119.41 W |
| Summerland Reserve ◆ [4] | 169 | 38.31 S | 145.10 E |
| Sümmern | 56 | 51.25 N | 7.43 E |
| Summer Palace ʋ | 265a | 59.53 N | 29.55 E |
| Summerseat | 262 | 53.38 N | 2.19 W |
| Summerside | 186 | 46.24 N | 63.47 W |
| Summersville, Mo., U.S. | 194 | 37.10 N | 91.39 W |
| Summersville, W.V., U.S. | 188 | 38.16 N | 80.51 W |
| Summerton | 192 | 33.36 N | 80.21 W |
| Summertown | 194 | 35.26 N | 87.18 W |
| Summerville, On., Can. | 275b | 43.37 N | 79.34 W |
| Summerville, Ga., U.S. | 192 | 34.28 N | 85.20 W |
| Summerville, Pa., U.S. | 214 | 41.06 N | 79.11 W |
| Summerville, S.C., U.S. | 192 | 33.00 N | 80.11 W |
| Summit, Eng., U.K. | 262 | 53.40 N | 2.05 W |
| Summit, Ak., U.S. | 180 | 63.20 N | 149.08 W |
| Summit, Il., U.S. | 216 | 41.47 N | 87.48 W |
| Summit, Ms., U.S. | 194 | 31.17 N | 90.28 W |
| Summit, N.J., U.S. | 210 | 40.44 N | 74.21 W |
| Summit, N.Y., U.S. | 210 | 42.35 N | 74.35 W |
| Summit, S.D., U.S. | 198 | 45.18 N | 97.02 W |
| Summit, Wa., U.S. | 224 | 47.10 N | 122.21 W |
| Summit □ [6] | 214 | 41.05 N | 81.31 W |
| Summit Creek ≃ | 224 | 46.00 N | 121.10 W |
| Summit Farms | 284b | 39.19 N | 76.32 W |
| Summit Hill | 210 | 40.49 N | 75.52 W |
| Summit Lake | 182 | 54.17 N | 122.38 W |
| Summit Lake ⊜ | 224 | 47.04 N | 123.07 W |
| Summit Mountain ʌ | 204 | 39.23 N | 116.28 W |
| Summit Park | 276 | 41.09 N | 74.03 W |
| Summit Park Mall ◆ [9] | 284a | 43.05 N | 78.56 W |
| Summit Peak ʌ | 200 | 37.21 N | 106.42 W |
| Summit Rock ʌ | 172 | 45.25 S | 170.04 E |
| Summit Station | 208 | 40.34 N | 76.12 W |
| Summitville, In., U.S. | 216 | 40.20 N | 85.38 W |
| Summitville, N.Y., U.S. | 210 | 41.37 N | 74.27 W |
| Summitville, Oh., U.S. | 214 | 40.41 N | 80.53 W |
| Summt | 264a | 52.41 N | 13.22 E |
| Şummter See ⊜ | 264a | 52.42 N | 13.23 E |
| Šumná | 61 | 48.56 N | 15.52 E |
| Sumnal | 120 | 35.45 N | 78.40 E |
| Sumner, Ia., U.S. | 190 | 42.50 N | 92.05 W |
| Sumner, Ms., U.S. | 194 | 33.58 N | 90.22 W |
| Sumner, Wa., U.S. | 224 | 47.12 N | 122.14 W |
| Sumner, Lake ⊜ | 172 | 42.42 S | 172.13 E |
| Sumner, Lake ⊜ [1] | 196 | 34.38 N | 104.25 W |
| Sumner Lake State Park ♠ | 196 | 34.38 N | 104.24 W |
| Sumner Strait ʯ | 180 | 56.15 N | 133.45 W |
| Sumoto | 96 | 34.21 N | 134.54 E |
| Şumpangbinangae | 112 | 4.24 S | 119.36 E |
| Šumperk | 30 | 49.58 N | 16.58 E |
| Sumpiuh | 115a | 7.37 S | 109.21 E |
| Sumprabum | 110 | 26.33 N | 97.34 E |
| Sumpter | 281 | 42.10 N | 83.29 W |
| Sumqayıt | 84 | 40.36 N | 49.38 E |
| Sumqayıt ≃ | 84 | 40.37 N | 49.37 E |
| Sumrall | 194 | 31.25 N | 89.32 W |
| Sumsar | 85 | 41.18 N | 71.19 E |
| Ş'umsi | 80 | 57.07 N | 51.37 E |
| Šumskij | 88 | 54.48 N | 99.09 E |
| Şumskij Posad | 24 | 64.15 N | 35.25 E |
| Šumšu, ostrov I | 74 | 50.45 N | 156.20 E |
| Sumter | 192 | 33.55 N | 80.20 W |
| Sumter □ [6] | 220 | 28.38 N | 82.08 W |
| Sumusṭā al-Waqf | 142 | 28.55 N | 30.51 E |
| Sumy | 78 | 50.55 N | 34.45 E |
| Sumy □ [4] | 78 | 51.00 N | 34.00 E |
| Sumzom | 102 | 29.45 N | 96.10 E |
| S'un' ≃, Ross. | 80 | 55.44 N | 54.16 E |
| Sun ≃, Mt., U.S. | 202 | 47.30 N | 111.19 W |
| Sun ≃, Zhg. | 107 | 29.13 N | 106.21 E |
| Suna, Kenya | 154 | 1.05 S | 34.26 E |
| Suna, Ross. | 80 | 57.51 N | 50.05 E |
| Suna ≃ | 24 | 62.08 N | 34.12 E |
| Sunagawa | 92a | 43.29 N | 141.55 E |
| Sun al-Heteimi ⩪ [4] | 132 | 31.05 N | 34.00 E |
| Sun' al-Menī'i ⩪ [4] | 132 | 31.07 N | 34.12 E |
| Sunām | 123 | 30.08 N | 75.48 E |
| Sunāmganj | 120 | 25.04 N | 91.24 E |
| Sunami | 94 | 35.25 N | 136.40 E |
| Sunan | 98 | 39.13 N | 125.41 E |
| Sunapee Lake ⊜ | 188 | 43.23 N | 72.03 W |
| Sunart, Loch ⊂ | 46 | 56.41 N | 5.43 W |
| Sunashinden | 268 | 35.53 N | 139.30 E |
| Sunbāṭ | 142 | 30.48 N | 31.12 E |
| Sunbright | 192 | 36.14 N | 84.40 W |
| Sunburst | 202 | 48.52 N | 111.54 W |
| Sunbury, Austl. | 169 | 37.35 S | 144.44 E |
| Sunbury, Eng., U.K. | 260 | 51.25 N | 0.26 W |
| Sunbury, N.C., U.S. | 192 | 36.26 N | 76.36 W |
| Sunbury, Oh., U.S. | 214 | 40.14 N | 82.51 W |
| Sunbury, Pa., U.S. | 210 | 40.51 N | 76.47 W |
| Sunchales | 252 | 30.56 S | 61.34 W |
| Sunch'ang | 98 | 35.23 N | 127.07 E |
| Sunchild Indian Reserve ◆ [4] | 182 | 52.43 N | 115.24 W |
| Sünching | 60 | 48.53 N | 12.21 E |
| Suncho Corral | 252 | 27.56 S | 63.27 W |
| Sunch'ŏn, C.M.I.K. | 98 | 39.26 N | 125.54 E |
| Sunch'ŏn, Taehan | 98 | 34.57 N | 127.28 E |
| Sun City, Az., U.S. | 200 | 33.35 N | 112.16 W |
| Sun City, Ca., U.S. | 228 | 33.42 N | 117.11 W |
| Sun City, Fl., U.S. | 220 | 27.40 N | 82.28 W |
| Sun City Center | 220 | 27.43 N | 82.21 W |
| Suncook | 188 | 43.07 N | 71.27 W |
| Suncook ≃ | 188 | 43.08 N | 71.28 W |
| Sunda, Selat (Sunda Strait) ʯ | 112 | 6.00 S | 105.45 E |
| Sundance | 198 | 44.24 N | 104.22 W |
| Sundar | 112 | 4.54 N | 115.12 E |
| Sundar ʌ | 124 | 28.26 N | 84.20 E |
| Sundarbans ◆ [1] | 126 | 22.00 N | 89.00 E |
| Sundargarh | 124 | 22.07 N | 84.02 E |
| Sundarnagar | 123 | 31.32 N | 76.53 E |
| Sunda Shelf ⊹ [4] | 14 | 5.00 N | 107.00 E |
| Sunda Strait → Sunda, Selat ʯ | 112 | 6.00 S | 105.45 E |
| Sunday Creek ≃ | 169 | 37.02 S | 145.05 E |
| Sundby, Dan. | 41 | 54.42 N | 11.48 E |
| Sundby, Sve. | 40 | 59.23 N | 17.03 E |
| Sundbyberg | 40 | 59.22 N | 17.58 E |
| Sundbyholm | 40 | 59.27 N | 16.37 E |
| Sundbyholm slott ⊥ | 40 | 59.27 N | 16.37 E |
| Sunde | 26 | 59.50 N | 5.43 E |
| Sunderland, On., Can. | 212 | 44.16 N | 79.04 W |
| Sunderland, Eng., U.K. | 44 | 54.55 N | 1.23 W |
| Sunderland, Ma., U.S. | 207 | 42.28 N | 72.34 W |
| Sunderland, Vt., U.S. | 210 | 43.06 N | 73.06 W |
| Sundern | 56 | 51.20 N | 8.00 E |
| Sünderup | 41 | 54.46 N | 9.27 E |
| Sundgau ◆ [1] | 58 | 47.40 N | 7.15 E |
| Sundhouse | 58 | 48.15 N | 7.36 E |
| Sundi-Lutete | 152 | 4.34 S | 14.14 E |
| Sundown, Austl. | 162 | 26.14 S | 133.12 E |
| Sundown, N.Y., U.S. | 210 | 41.53 N | 74.28 W |
| Sundown, Tx., U.S. | 196 | 33.27 N | 102.29 W |
| Sundra | 273d | 26.11 S | 28.33 E |
| Sundre | 182 | 51.48 N | 114.38 W |
| Sundridge, On., Can. | 190 | 45.46 N | 79.24 W |
| Sundridge, Eng., U.K. | 260 | 51.17 N | 0.08 E |
| Sunds | 41 | 56.12 N | 9.01 E |
| Sundsbruk | 26 | 62.27 N | 17.22 E |
| Sundsvall | 26 | 62.23 N | 17.18 E |
| Sundwig | 263 | 51.23 N | 7.47 E |
| Suneori | 268 | 35.56 N | 139.24 E |
| Sunfield | 216 | 42.45 N | 84.59 W |
| Sunfish Creek ≃ | 218 | 39.01 N | 83.03 W |
| Sunflower | 194 | 33.32 N | 90.32 W |
| Sunflower, Mount ʌ | 198 | 39.04 N | 102.01 W |
| Sungaianyar | 112 | 2.55 S | 116.18 E |
| Sungaiapit | 114 | 1.09 N | 102.10 E |
| Sungaibamban | 114 | 3.26 N | 99.09 E |
| Sungaibatu | 112 | 0.48 N | 110.45 E |
| Sungai Bayor | 114 | 5.15 N | 100.47 E |
| Sungaibuntu | 115a | 6.03 S | 107.24 E |
| Sungaidareh | 112 | 0.58 S | 101.30 E |
| Sungaigerong | 112 | 2.59 S | 104.52 E |
| Sungaiguntung | 112 | 0.18 N | 103.37 E |
| Sungaikakap | 112 | 0.04 S | 109.10 E |
| Sungai Kolok | 114 | 6.02 N | 101.58 E |
| Sungailangsat | 112 | 0.52 S | 101.18 E |
| Sungai Lembing | 114 | 3.55 N | 103.02 E |
| Sungailiat | 112 | 1.51 S | 106.08 E |
| Sungailimau | 112 | 0.31 S | 100.03 E |
| Sungaimanasip | 114 | 1.49 N | 100.54 E |
| Sungainipah | 114 | 0.57 N | 98.57 E |
| Sungaipakning | 114 | 1.20 N | 102.09 E |
| Sungaipenuh | 112 | 2.05 S | 101.23 E |
| Sungaipenyu | 112 | 0.16 N | 109.04 E |
| Sungai Petani | 114 | 5.39 N | 100.30 E |
| Sungaipinang | 112 | 0.48 S | 114.04 E |
| Sungairampah | 114 | 3.29 N | 99.09 E |
| Sungairotan, Indon. | 112 | 1.39 S | 102.51 E |
| Sungairotan, Indon. | 112 | 3.06 S | 104.18 E |
| Sungaisalak | 112 | 0.27 S | 102.59 E |
| Sungaiselan | 112 | 2.24 S | 105.59 E |
| Sungai Siput | 114 | 4.49 N | 101.04 E |
| Sungaitampang | 114 | 2.20 N | 100.07 E |
| Sungaitiram | 112 | 0.47 S | 117.12 E |
| Šungaj | 80 | 48.32 N | 46.46 E |
| Sungari → Songhua ≃ | 89 | 47.44 N | 132.32 E |
| Sungchiang → Songjiang | 106 | 31.01 N | 121.14 E |
| Sungezhuang | 105 | 40.15 N | 116.39 E |
| Sungguminasa | 112 | 5.12 S | 119.27 E |
| Sungi ≃ | 115b | 8.38 S | 115.06 E |
| Sungi Point › | 116 | 10.55 N | 125.50 E |
| Sungkai | 114 | 4.00 N | 101.19 E |
| Sung Kong I | 271d | 22.11 N | 114.17 E |
| Sung Noen | 110 | 14.54 N | 101.50 E |
| Sungsang | 112 | 2.22 S | 104.56 E |
| Sungshan Domestic Airport ⊠ | 269d | 25.04 N | 121.33 E |
| Sungurlu | 130 | 40.10 N | 34.23 E |
| Sunhezhen | 105 | 40.03 N | 116.31 E |
| Suni | 71 | 40.17 N | 8.33 E |
| Suning | 98 | 38.25 N | 115.50 E |
| Sunjiabu | 106 | 30.55 N | 118.54 E |
| Sunjiadizi | 104 | 42.09 N | 124.09 E |
| Sunjiagou | 104 | 40.45 N | 120.39 E |
| Sunjiajiang | 105 | 40.10 N | 115.32 E |
| Sunjiakanzi | 104 | 40.42 N | 123.02 E |
| Sunjiawan | 104 | 41.59 N | 121.42 E |
| Sunjiazhai | 106 | 30.55 N | 121.52 E |
| Sunjikāy | 140 | 12.20 N | 29.46 E |
| Sunkar, gora ʌ | 86 | 44.15 N | 73.50 E |
| Sunken Meadow State Park ♠ | 207 | 40.54 N | 73.16 W |
| Sunkośī ≃ | 124 | 26.55 N | 87.09 E |
| Sunland ◆ [8] | 280 | 34.16 N | 118.19 W |
| Sunland Park | 200 | 32.15 N | 106.45 W |
| Sunlight Creek ≃ | 202 | 44.47 N | 109.23 W |
| Sunlongwan | 104 | 41.19 N | 122.57 E |
| Sunman | 218 | 39.14 N | 85.05 W |
| Sunnansjö | 40 | 60.13 N | 14.57 E |
| Sunndalsøra | 26 | 62.40 N | 8.33 E |
| Sunne | 26 | 59.50 N | 13.09 E |
| Sunnemo | 40 | 59.53 N | 13.43 E |
| Sunnersta | 40 | 59.48 N | 17.39 E |
| Sunnī, Khawr V | 140 | 7.09 N | 28.41 E |
| Sunningdale | 260 | 51.24 N | 0.38 W |
| Sunninghill | 42 | 51.25 N | 0.40 W |
| Sunnybrae | 186 | 45.24 N | 62.30 W |
| Sunny Corner | 170 | 33.23 S | 149.53 E |
| Sunny Crest | 278 | 41.33 N | 87.42 W |
| Sunnydale | 224 | 47.28 N | 122.20 W |
| Sunnyland | 220 | 27.17 N | 82.29 W |
| Sunnylvsfjorden ⊂ [2] | 26 | 62.17 N | 7.01 E |
| Sunnynook | 182 | 51.17 N | 111.40 W |
| Sunnyridge | 273d | 26.10 S | 28.11 E |
| Sunnyside, Nf., Can. | 186 | 47.51 N | 53.55 W |
| Sunnyside, Ca., U.S. | 226 | 32.40 N | 117.01 W |
| Sunny Side, Tx., U.S. | 222 | 29.54 N | 96.04 W |
| Sunnyside, Ut,. U.S. | 200 | 39.33 N | 110.23 W |
| Sunnyside, Wa., U.S. | 202 | 46.19 N | 120.00 W |
| Sunnyside ⊥ | 276 | 41.03 N | 73.52 W |
| Sunnyslope, Ab., Can. | 182 | 51.40 N | 113.32 W |
| Sunnyslope, Wa., U.S. | 224 | 47.30 N | 122.44 W |
| Sunnyvale, Ca., U.S. | 226 | 37.22 N | 122.02 W |
| Sunnyvale, Tx., U.S. | 222 | 32.48 N | 96.33 W |
| Sunol | 282 | 37.36 N | 121.53 W |
| Sunol Ridge ʌ | 282 | 37.38 N | 121.56 W |
| Sun Prairie | 216 | 43.11 N | 89.12 W |
| Sunray | 196 | 36.01 N | 101.49 W |
| Sunrise, Ky., U.S. | 218 | 38.33 N | 84.14 W |
| Sunrise, Tx., U.S. | 222 | 31.17 N | 96.53 W |
| Sunrise, Wy., U.S. | 200 | 42.19 N | 104.42 W |
| Sunrise Heights | 216 | 42.18 N | 85.09 W |
| Sunrise Mall ◆ [9] | 276 | 40.41 N | 73.26 W |
| Sunrise Manor | 204 | 36.08 N | 115.04 W |
| Sunrise Peak ʌ | 224 | 46.20 N | 121.46 W |
| Sun River Terrace | 216 | 41.06 N | 87.45 W |
| Sunset, La., U.S. | 194 | 30.24 N | 92.04 W |
| Sunset, Tx., U.S. | 196 | 33.27 N | 97.46 W |
| Sunset ◆ [8] | 282 | 37.45 N | 122.30 W |
| Sunset Bay | 214 | 42.11 N | 79.24 W |
| Sunset Beach, Ca., U.S. | 280 | 33.43 N | 118.04 W |
| Sunset Beach, Hi., U.S. | 229c | 21.40 N | 158.02 W |
| Sunset Country ◆ [1] | 166 | 35.00 S | 141.30 E |
| Sunset Crater National Monument ♠ | 200 | 35.18 N | 111.21 W |
| Sunset Heights | 196 | 31.53 N | 102.22 W |
| Sunset Hill | 276 | 40.26 N | 74.35 W |
| Sunset Hills | 279b | 40.35 N | 80.15 W |
| Sunset Peak ʌ | 280 | 34.13 N | 117.42 W |
| Sunset Prairie | 182 | 55.50 N | 120.48 W |
| Sunset Valley | 214 | 40.18 N | 79.44 W |
| Sunshine, Austl. | 166 | 37.47 S | 144.50 E |
| Sunshine, Austl. | 169 | 37.47 S | 144.50 E |
| Sunshine, Ak., U.S. | 180 | 62.10 N | 150.04 W |
| Sunshine Island I | 271d | 22.16 N | 114.03 E |
| Sunshine Point › | 281 | 42.36 N | 82.47 W |
| Sunshine Skyway Bridge ◆ [5] | 220 | 27.37 N | 82.39 W |
| Suntai ≃ | 146 | 8.05 N | 10.04 E |
| Suntar | 74 | 62.10 N | 117.40 E |
| Suntar-Chajata, chrebet ⩘ | 74 | 62.00 N | 143.00 E |
| Suntaug Lake ⊜ | 283 | 42.32 N | 71.00 W |
| Süntel ⩘ | 52 | 52.12 N | 9.25 E |
| Sun Temple ʋ [1] | 273c | 29.55 N | 31.11 E |
| Sunter ◆ [8] | 269e | 6.09 S | 106.50 E |
| Sunter, Kali ≖ | 269e | 6.07 S | 106.50 E |
| Sunti ≃ | 272b | 22.37 N | 88.34 E |
| Suntrana | 180 | 63.51 N | 148.51 W |
| Suntsar | 128 | 25.31 N | 62.00 E |
| Suntu | 144 | 8.06 N | 36.57 E |
| Sun Valley, Id., U.S. | 202 | 43.41 N | 114.21 W |
| Sun Valley, Nv., U.S. | 226 | 39.34 N | 119.47 W |
| Sun Valley ◆ [8] | 280 | 34.14 N | 118.21 W |
| SunValley Center ◆ [9] | 282 | 37.58 N | 122.03 W |
| Sunwapta ≃ | 182 | 52.32 N | 117.41 W |
| Sunwi-do I | 98 | 37.44 N | 125.15 E |
| Sunwu | 89 | 49.27 N | 127.20 E |
| Sunwui → Jiangmen | 100 | 22.35 N | 113.05 E |
| Sunyani | 150 | 7.20 N | 2.20 W |
| Sunying | 98 | 34.30 N | 114.21 E |
| Sunža ≃ | 84 | 43.26 N | 46.08 E |
| Sunženskij chrebet ⩘ | 84 | 43.21 N | 45.00 E |
| Sun Zhong Shan Ling (Tomb of Sun Yat Sen) ⊥ | 106 | 32.10 N | 118.56 E |
| Suojarvi | 24 | 62.05 N | 32.21 E |
| Suolahti | 26 | 62.34 N | 25.52 E |
| Suomenlahti → Finland, Gulf of ⊂ | 26 | 60.00 N | 27.00 E |
| Suomenselkä ʌ | 26 | 63.59 N | 27.00 E |
| Suomi → Finland □ [1] | 24 | 64.00 N | 26.00 E |
| Suomussalmi | 26 | 64.53 N | 29.05 E |
| Suō-nada ⩪ [2] | 96 | 33.50 N | 131.30 E |
| Suonenjoki | 26 | 62.37 N | 27.08 E |
| Suontee ⊜ | 26 | 61.40 N | 26.30 E |
| Suordach | 74 | 66.43 N | 132.04 E |
| Suoshu | 106 | 31.57 N | 119.00 E |
| Supachuy | 248 | 19.29 S | 64.31 W |
| Supamo ≃ | 246 | 6.48 N | 61.50 W |
| Supaul | 124 | 26.07 N | 86.36 E |
| Supe | 144 | 8.37 N | 35.38 E |
| Superbe ≃ | 50 | 48.35 N | 3.53 E |
| Superga, Basilica di ʋ [1] | 62 | 45.05 N | 7.46 E |
| Superior, Az., U.S. | 200 | 33.17 N | 111.05 W |
| Superior, Mt., U.S. | 202 | 47.11 N | 114.53 W |
| Superior, Ne., U.S. | 198 | 40.01 N | 98.04 W |
| Superior, Wi., U.S. | 190 | 46.43 N | 92.06 W |
| Superior, Laguna ⊂ | 234 | 16.20 N | 94.55 W |
| Superior, Lake ⊜ | 190 | 48.00 N | 88.00 W |
| Superior Lake ⊜ | 228 | 35.15 N | 117.02 W |
| Superior Valley V | 228 | 35.16 N | 117.00 W |
| Supersano | 68 | 40.01 N | 18.14 E |


**Symbols** in the index entries represent the broad categories identified in the key at the right. Symbols with superior numbers (⩘ [1]) identify subcategories (see complete key on page *I · 1).*

**Symbole** im Register stellen die rechts im Schlüssel erklärten Kategorien dar. Symbole mit hochgestellten Ziffern (⩘ [1]) bezeichnen Unterabteilungen einer Kategorie (vgl. vollständiger Schlüssel auf Seite *I · 1).*

**Los símbolos** incluídos en el texto del índice representan las grandes categorías identificadas con la clave a la derecha. Los símbolos con numeros en su parte superior (⩘ [1]) identifican las subcategorías (véase la clave completa en la página *I · 1).*

**Les symboles** de l'index représentent les catégories indiquées dans la légende à droite. Les symboles suivis d'un indice (⩘ [1]) représentent des sous-catégories (voir légende complète à la page *I · 1).*

**Os símbolos** incluídos no texto do índice representam as grandes categorias identificadas com a chave à direita. Os símbolos com números em sua parte superior (⩘ [1]) identificam as subcategorias (veja-se a chave completa à página *I · 1).*

| | | | | | |
|---|---|---|---|---|---|
| ʌ | Mountain | Berg | Montaña | Montagne | Montanha |
| ⩘ | Mountains | Gebirge | Montañas | Montagnes | Montanhas |
| )( | Pass | Paß | Paso | Col | Passo |
| V | Valley, Canyon | Tal, Cañon | Valle, Cañón | Vallée, Canyon | Vale, Canhão |
| ≚ | Plain | Ebene | Llano | Plaine | Planície |
| › | Cape | Kap | Cabo | Cap | Cabo |
| I | Island | Insel | Isla | Île | Ilha |
| II | Islands | Inseln | Islas | Îles | Ilhas |
| ⏏ | Other Topographic Features | Andere Topographische Objekte | Otros Elementos Topográficos | Autres données topographiques | Outros acidentes topográficos |

**ESPAÑOL**

| Nombre | Página | Lat.°′ | Long.°′ W = Oeste |
|---|---|---|---|
| Supetar | 36 | 43.23 N | 16.33 E |
| Suphan Buri | 110 | 14.28 N | 100.07 E |
| Suphan Buri ≃ | 110 | 13.29 N | 100.17 E |
| Süphan Dağı ∧ | 84 | 38.56 N | 42.50 E |
| Supino | 66 | 41.37 N | 13.14 E |
| Supiori I | 164 | 0.45 S | 135.30 E |
| Supiy ≃ | 78 | 49.38 N | 31.48 E |
| Sūpkhār | 124 | 22.12 N | 80.56 E |
| Suponevo | 76 | 53.12 N | 34.18 E |
| Supoqiao | 107 | 30.40 N | 103.59 E |
| Süpplingen | 54 | 52.14 N | 10.54 E |
| Supraśl | 30 | 53.13 N | 23.20 E |
| Supraśl ≃ | 30 | 53.04 N | 22.56 E |
| Sup'ung | 98 | 40.27 N | 124.57 E |
| Sup'ung-chŏsuji ⊜ [1] | 98 | 40.30 N | 125.05 E |
| Supur | 126 | 23.01 N | 86.52 E |
| Suputinskij zapovednik ♠ | 89 | 43.40 N | 132.20 E |
| Sūq-'Abs | 144 | 15.59 N | 43.04 E |
| Sūq ash-Shuyūkh | 128 | 30.53 N | 46.28 E |
| Suq'at al-Jamal | 140 | 12.48 N | 27.42 E |
| Suqian | 100 | 33.59 N | 118.18 E |
| Suqiao, Zhg. | 100 | 34.08 N | 113.47 E |
| Suqiao, Zhg. | 105 | 39.03 N | 116.29 E |
| Sūq Suwayq | 128 | 24.23 N | 38.27 E |
| Suquamish | 224 | 47.43 N | 122.33 W |
| Suquṭrā (Socotra) I | 118 | 12.30 N | 54.00 E |
| Ṣūr (Tyre), Lubnān | 132 | 33.16 N | 35.11 E |
| Ṣūr, 'Umān | 118 | 22.35 N | 59.31 E |
| Sur, Cabo ≻ | 174z | 27.12 S | 109.26 W |
| Sur, Campos de Hielo ⍓ | 254 | 49.10 S | 73.30 W |
| Sur, Canal ʮ | 288 | 34.37 S | 58.15 W |
| Sur, Point ≻ | 226 | 36.18 N | 121.54 W |
| Sura | 80 | 53.53 N | 45.45 E |
| Sura ◆ [8] | 272b | 22.33 N | 88.25 E |
| Sura ≃ | 80 | 56.06 N | 46.00 E |
| Sura, Cape ≻ | 144 | 11.10 N | 47.30 E |
| Ṣūrāb, Pāk. | 120 | 28.29 N | 66.16 E |
| Šurab, Taj. | 85 | 40.03 N | 70.33 E |
| Surabaya | 115a | 7.15 S | 112.45 E |
| S'urachi, Nuraghe ⊥ | 71 | 40.01 N | 8.33 E |
| Ṣurad | 142 | 30.59 N | 30.54 E |
| Surag-san ∧ | 271b | 37.42 N | 127.04 E |
| Surahammar | 40 | 59.43 N | 16.13 E |
| Sūrak | 128 | 25.43 N | 58.48 E |
| Surakarta | 115a | 7.35 S | 110.50 E |
| Suramana | 112 | 0.50 S | 119.33 E |
| Surami | 84 | 42.01 N | 43.34 E |
| Ṣūrān, Īrān | 128 | 27.18 N | 62.04 E |
| Šuran, Ross. | 80 | 55.22 N | 49.50 E |
| Ṣūrān, Sūrīy. | 130 | 36.34 N | 37.13 E |
| Ṣūrān, Sūrīy. | 130 | 35.17 N | 36.45 E |
| Ṣuran ≃ | 58 | 46.02 N | 5.19 E |
| Šurany | 30 | 48.06 N | 18.14 E |
| Surar | 144 | 7.27 N | 40.57 E |
| Surat, Austl. | 166 | 27.09 S | 149.04 E |
| Sūrat, India | 120 | 21.10 N | 72.50 E |
| Sūratgarh | 123 | 29.19 N | 73.54 E |
| Surat Thani (Ban Don) | 110 | 9.08 N | 99.19 E |
| Surava | 80 | 52.57 N | 41.18 E |
| Suraž, Bela. | 76 | 55.25 N | 30.44 E |
| Suraż, Pol. | 30 | 52.58 N | 22.58 E |
| Suraž, Ross. | 76 | 53.01 N | 32.24 E |
| Surbiton ◆ [8] | 260 | 51.24 N | 0.18 W |
| Surbo | 68 | 40.24 N | 18.08 E |
| Surbourg | 56 | 48.55 N | 7.51 E |
| Surchan | 80 | 46.39 N | 49.38 E |
| Surchandarja □ [4] | 85 | 38.00 N | 67.30 E |
| Surchandarja ≃ | 85 | 37.58 N | 67.50 E |
| Surchdara | 85 | 38.37 N | 69.55 E |
| Ṣurchob ≃ | 85 | 38.53 N | 70.03 E |
| Šurči | 85 | 37.59 N | 67.47 E |
| Surco ≃ | 286d | 12.13 S | 77.03 W |
| Surdulica | 38 | 42.41 N | 22.10 E |
| Sûre (Sauer) ≃ | 56 | 49.44 N | 6.31 E |
| Şureanu, Munţii ⩕ | 38 | 45.38 N | 23.27 E |
| Šureksor, ozero ⊜ | 86 | 52.16 N | 75.50 E |
| Surendorf | 41 | 54.28 N | 10.04 E |
| Surendranagar | 120 | 22.42 N | 71.41 E |
| Suresnes | 261 | 48.52 N | 2.14 E |
| Suretka | 236 | 9.34 N | 82.56 W |
| Surf City | 208 | 39.39 N | 74.09 W |
| Surfers Paradise | 171a | 28.00 S | 153.26 E |
| Surfside, Fl., U.S. | 220 | 25.52 N | 80.07 W |
| Surfside, Tx., U.S. | 222 | 28.57 N | 95.17 W |
| Surgères | 32 | 46.07 N | 0.45 W |
| Surgidero | 240p | 22.41 N | 82.18 W |
| Surgijn ≃ | 88 | 47.20 N | 95.50 E |
| Surgoinsville | 192 | 36.28 N | 82.51 W |
| Sürgü | 130 | 38.01 N | 37.59 E |
| Sürgücü | 130 | 37.35 N | 40.44 E |
| Surgut | 74 | 61.14 N | 73.20 E |
| Surhuisterveen | 52 | 53.10 N | 6.10 E |
| Suri | 164 | 7.10 S | 143.55 E |
| Suria | 272b | 22.51 N | 88.33 E |
| Suriāpet | 122 | 17.09 N | 79.37 E |
| Suribachi-yama ∧ [2] | 174f | 24.45 N | 141.17 E |
| Suribao ≃ | 116 | 11.33 N | 125.28 E |
| Surigao | 116 | 9.45 N | 125.30 E |
| Surigao del Norte □ [4] | 116 | 9.35 N | 125.36 E |
| Surigao del Sur □ [4] | 116 | 9.00 N | 126.00 E |
| Surigao Strait ʮ | 116 | 10.15 N | 125.23 E |
| Surikova | 86 | 56.59 N | 91.31 E |
| Surin | 110 | 14.53 N | 103.29 E |
| Surinam → Suriname □ [1] | 250 | 4.00 N | 56.00 W |
| Suriname □ [1], S.A. | 242 | 4.00 N | 56.00 W |
| Suriname □ [1], S.A. | 250 | 4.00 N | 56.00 W |
| Šurinda | 88 | 55.13 N | 113.23 E |
| Suring | 190 | 44.59 N | 88.22 W |
| Sūrīyah → Syria □ [1] | 128 | 35.00 N | 38.00 E |
| S'urkum | 89 | 50.08 N | 140.31 E |
| S'urkum, mys ≻ | 89 | 50.05 N | 140.41 E |
| Šurma | 80 | 56.58 N | 50.21 E |
| Sūrmaq | 128 | 31.03 N | 52.48 E |
| Surmelin ≃ | 50 | 49.04 N | 3.31 E |
| Surnadalsøra | 26 | 62.59 N | 8.39 E |
| Surodadi | 115a | 6.53 S | 109.15 E |
| Surovaticha | 80 | 55.45 N | 43.56 E |
| Surovikino | 80 | 48.36 N | 42.51 E |
| Surovo | 88 | 55.37 N | 105.36 E |
| Surprise | 200 | 33.37 N | 112.19 W |
| Surprise, Lake ⊜ | 222 | 29.33 N | 94.41 W |
| Surprise Valley V | 204 | 41.35 N | 120.05 W |
| Surquillo | 286d | 12.07 S | 77.02 W |
| Surrency | 192 | 31.43 N | 82.11 W |
| Surrey, B.C., Can. | 224 | 49.12 N | 122.53 W |
| Surrey, N.D., U.S. | 198 | 48.14 N | 101.07 W |
| Surrey □ [6] | 42 | 51.10 N | 0.20 W |
| Surrey, University of ʊ [2] | 260 | 51.14 N | 0.36 W |
| Surrey Heath □ [8] | 260 | 51.23 N | 0.35 W |
| Surry | 208 | 37.08 N | 76.50 W |
| Surry □ [6] | 208 | 37.10 N | 76.50 W |
| Sursee | 58 | 47.10 N | 8.06 E |
| Sursés V | 58 | 46.34 N | 9.38 E |
| Sursk | 80 | 53.04 N | 45.42 E |
| Surskij Majdan | 80 | 55.01 N | 46.32 E |
| Surskoje | 80 | 54.30 N | 46.44 E |
| Surt | 146 | 31.12 N | 16.35 E |
| Surt, Khalīj (Gulf of Sidra) c | 146 | 31.30 N | 18.00 E |
| Surtainville | 28 | 49.25 N | 1.50 W |
| Surtanāhu | 120 | 26.22 N | 70.00 E |
| Surte | 26 | 57.49 N | 12.01 E |
| Surtsey I | 24a | 63.16 N | 20.32 W |
| Suru | 164 | 6.50 S | 144.45 E |
| Suru ≃ | 123 | 34.45 N | 76.12 E |
| Surubiú ≃ | 250 | 3.58 S | 48.52 W |
| Sürüç | 130 | 36.58 N | 38.24 E |
| Suruga-wan c | 94 | 34.51 N | 138.33 E |
| Suruí | 256 | 22.40 S | 43.07 W |
| Suruí ≃ | 287a | 22.42 S | 43.07 W |
| Surulangun | 112 | 2.37 S | 102.45 E |
| Suru-Lere ◆ [8] | 273a | 6.31 N | 3.22 E |
| Surumu ≃ | 246 | 3.22 N | 60.19 W |
| Surveyor Creek ≃ | 198 | 40.20 N | 102.38 W |

**FRANÇAIS**

| Nom | Page | Lat.°′ | Long.°′ W = Ouest |
|---|---|---|---|
| Surveyor Point ≻ | 168b | 34.47 S | 137.51 E |
| Survilliers | 261 | 49.06 N | 2.33 E |
| Surwold | 52 | 53.00 N | 7.30 E |
| Şury-le-Comtal | 62 | 45.32 N | 4.10 E |
| Šuryškary | 74 | 65.54 N | 65.22 E |
| Şuşa, Azer. | 84 | 39.45 N | 46.44 E |
| Susa, It. | 62 | 45.08 N | 7.03 E |
| Susa, Nihon | 96 | 34.37 N | 131.36 E |
| Suså ≃ | 41 | 55.11 N | 11.46 E |
| Susa, Valle di V | 62 | 45.09 N | 7.10 E |
| Sūsah | 146 | 32.54 N | 21.58 E |
| Susak, Otok I | 36 | 44.31 N | 14.18 E |
| Susaki | 96 | 33.22 N | 133.17 E |
| Susami | 96 | 33.33 N | 135.30 E |
| Susamyr | 85 | 42.09 N | 73.58 E |
| Susamyr ≃ | 85 | 42.08 N | 74.03 E |
| Susamyrtau, chrebet ⩕ | 85 | 42.08 N | 73.15 E |
| Susan | 208 | 37.22 N | 76.19 W |
| Susan ≃ | 204 | 40.19 N | 120.17 W |
| Susan, Port c | 224 | 48.10 N | 122.25 W |
| Sūsangerd | 128 | 31.34 N | 48.11 E |
| Susanino, Ross. | 76 | 59.30 N | 30.22 E |
| Susanino, Ross. | 80 | 58.09 N | 41.36 E |
| Susanino, Ross. | 89 | 52.47 N | 140.06 E |
| Susano | 256 | 23.32 S | 46.20 W |
| Susano □ [7] | 287b | 23.35 S | 46.18 W |
| Susanville | 204 | 40.24 N | 120.39 W |
| Šušary, Ross. | 265a | 59.46 N | 30.21 E |
| Šušary, Ross. | 265a | 59.48 N | 30.23 E |
| Susch | 58 | 46.46 N | 10.04 E |
| Susegana | 64 | 45.51 N | 12.15 E |
| Suşehri | 130 | 40.11 N | 38.06 E |
| Süsel | 54 | 54.04 N | 10.43 E |
| Šušenskoje | 86 | 53.19 N | 91.58 E |
| Sušice | 60 | 49.14 N | 13.32 E |
| Susitna | 180 | 61.33 N | 150.31 W |
| Susitna ≃ | 180 | 61.16 N | 150.30 W |
| Susleni | 38 | 47.25 N | 28.59 E |
| Suslonger | 80 | 56.18 N | 48.13 E |
| Sušn'aki Pervoje | 86 | 57.53 N | 88.47 E |
| Susobana ≃ | 94 | 36.37 N | 138.11 E |
| Susoh | 114 | 3.43 N | 96.50 E |
| Susong | 100 | 30.09 N | 116.06 E |
| Susono | 94 | 35.09 N | 138.54 E |
| Suspiro del Moro, Puerto )( | 34 | 37.04 N | 3.39 W |
| Susquehanna | 210 | 41.56 N | 75.36 W |
| Susquehanna □ [6] | 210 | 41.50 N | 75.50 W |
| Susquehanna ≃ | 188 | 39.33 N | 76.05 W |
| Susquehanna, West Branch ≃ | 210 | 40.53 N | 76.47 W |
| Susquehanna State Park ♠ | 208 | 39.36 N | 76.09 W |
| Susques | 252 | 23.25 S | 66.29 W |
| Sussa ≃ | 152 | 7.22 S | 17.05 E |
| Süssen | 56 | 48.41 N | 9.45 E |
| Süssenbrunn ◆ [8] | 264b | 48.17 N | 16.30 E |
| Süsser See ⊜ | 54 | 51.30 N | 11.40 E |
| Sussex, N.B., Can. | 186 | 45.43 N | 65.31 W |
| Sussex, N.J., U.S. | 210 | 41.12 N | 74.36 W |
| Sussex, Va., U.S. | 208 | 36.54 N | 77.16 W |
| Sussex, Wi., U.S. | 216 | 43.08 N | 88.13 W |
| Sussex □ [6], De., U.S. | 208 | 38.42 N | 75.23 W |
| Sussex □ [6], N.J., U.S. | 210 | 41.08 N | 74.41 W |
| Sussex □ [6], Va., U.S. | 208 | 36.50 N | 77.15 W |
| Sussex, Vale of V | 42 | 50.57 N | 0.17 W |
| Sussex Inlet | 170 | 35.11 S | 150.36 E |
| Sussey | 50 | 47.13 N | 4.22 E |
| Sustenhorn ∧ | 58 | 46.42 N | 8.28 E |
| Susten Pass )( | 58 | 46.44 N | 8.27 E |
| Şusteren | 52 | 51.04 N | 5.51 E |
| Šustikovo | 82 | 55.17 N | 35.59 E |
| Susu | 174m | 26.47 N | 128.19 E |
| Susubona | 175e | 8.18 S | 159.27 E |
| Susui | 112 | 4.56 N | 116.41 E |
| Susuman | 74 | 62.47 N | 148.10 E |
| Susurluk | 130 | 39.54 N | 28.10 E |
| Şusuzmüsellim | 130 | 41.06 N | 27.03 E |
| Šušvė ≃ | 76 | 55.10 N | 23.49 E |
| Susz | 30 | 53.44 N | 19.20 E |
| Sutāhāta | 126 | 22.08 N | 88.07 E |
| Sutak | 123 | 33.12 N | 77.28 E |
| Sutama | 94 | 35.47 N | 138.25 E |
| Sut-Chol' | 86 | 51.24 N | 91.17 E |
| Sütçüler | 130 | 37.30 N | 30.59 E |
| Sutera | 70 | 37.31 N | 13.44 E |
| Sutersville | 214 | 40.14 N | 79.48 W |
| Suthat, Wat ʊ [1] | 269a | 13.45 N | 100.30 E |
| Sutherland, Austl. | 170 | 34.02 S | 151.04 E |
| Sutherland, S. Afr. | 158 | 32.24 S | 20.40 E |
| Sutherland, Ia., U.S. | 198 | 42.58 N | 95.29 W |
| Sutherland, Ne., U.S. | 198 | 41.09 N | 101.07 W |
| Sutherland ≃ | 182 | 54.29 N | 125.05 W |
| Sutherland, Lake ⊜ | 224 | 48.05 N | 123.42 W |
| Sutherland Falls ∟ | 172 | 44.48 S | 167.44 E |
| Sutherlands | 168b | 34.10 S | 139.13 E |
| Sutherlin | 202 | 43.23 N | 123.18 W |
| Suthiāna | 272a | 28.31 N | 77.26 E |
| Sutjeska Nacionalni Park ♠ | 38 | 43.22 N | 18.45 E |
| Sutlej (Satluj) (Langqên) ≃ | 120 | 29.23 N | 71.02 E |
| Sutri | 66 | 42.14 N | 12.13 E |
| Sutrio | 64 | 46.31 N | 12.59 E |
| Sütschou → Xuzhou, Zhg. | 98 | 34.16 N | 117.11 E |
| Sutschou → Suzhou, Zhg. | 106 | 31.18 N | 120.37 E |
| Sutter | 226 | 39.10 N | 121.45 W |
| Sutter □ [6] | 226 | 39.08 N | 121.37 W |
| Sutter Buttes ∧ | 226 | 39.12 N | 121.50 W |
| Sutter Bypass ≃ | 226 | 38.47 N | 121.38 W |
| Sutter Creek | 226 | 38.23 N | 120.48 W |
| Sutter Creek ≃ | 226 | 38.22 N | 120.59 W |
| Sutton, Austl. | 171b | 35.10 S | 149.15 E |
| Sutton, P.Q., Can. | 206 | 45.06 N | 72.37 W |
| Sutton, Eng., U.K. | 42 | 52.23 N | 0.07 E |
| Sutton, Eng., U.K. | 260 | 51.12 N | 0.26 W |
| Sutton, Ak., U.S. | 180 | 61.43 N | 148.53 W |
| Sutton, Ma., U.S. | 207 | 42.09 N | 71.45 W |
| Sutton, Ne., U.S. | 198 | 40.36 N | 97.51 W |
| Sutton, W.V., U.S. | 188 | 38.39 N | 80.42 W |
| Sutton ◆ [8] | 42 | 51.22 N | 0.12 W |
| Sutton, Monts ⩕ | 206 | 45.05 N | 72.30 W |
| Sutton-at-Home | 260 | 51.25 N | 0.14 E |
| Sutton Bridge | 42 | 52.46 N | 0.12 E |
| Sutton Coldfield | 42 | 52.34 N | 1.48 W |
| Sutton Courtenay | 42 | 51.39 N | 1.17 W |
| Sutton Forest | 170 | 34.35 S | 150.19 E |
| Sutton in Ashfield | 44 | 53.08 N | 1.15 W |
| Sutton Lake ⊜ [1] | 188 | 38.40 N | 80.40 W |
| Sutton Lane Ends | 262 | 53.14 N | 2.06 W |
| Sutton Leach | 262 | 53.26 N | 2.42 W |
| Sutton on Sea | 44 | 53.19 N | 0.17 E |
| Sutton on Trent | 44 | 53.10 N | 0.49 W |
| Sutton Park | 276 | 40.49 N | 74.42 W |
| Sutton Place ⊥ | 260 | 51.16 N | 0.33 W |
| Suttons Bay | 190 | 44.58 N | 85.39 W |
| Sutton Scotney | 42 | 51.10 N | 1.21 W |
| Sutton Valence | 42 | 51.12 N | 0.36 E |
| Sutton Veny | 42 | 51.11 N | 2.08 W |
| Sutton Weaver | 262 | 53.18 N | 2.41 W |
| Sutton West | 212 | 44.18 N | 79.22 W |
| Suttor ≃ | 166 | 21.25 S | 147.45 E |
| Suttrop | 56 | 51.27 N | 8.22 E |
| Suttsu | 92a | 42.48 N | 140.14 E |
| Sutwik Island I | 180 | 56.34 N | 157.05 W |
| Suunduk ≃ | 86 | 51.46 N | 58.46 E |
| Suurberge ⩕ | 158 | 33.18 S | 25.32 E |
| Suurbraak | 158 | 34.00 S | 20.39 E |
| Suure-Jaani | 76 | 58.33 N | 25.28 E |
| Suur Munamägi ∧ [2] | 76 | 57.43 N | 27.04 E |
| Suur Pakri I | 76 | 59.20 N | 23.55 E |
| Suur väin ʮ | 76 | 58.35 N | 23.25 E |
| Suva | 175g | 18.08 S | 178.25 E |
| Suvainiškis | 76 | 56.10 N | 25.17 E |
| Şuvälan | 84 | 40.30 N | 50.09 E |
| Šuvalovo Oz'orki ◆ [8] | 265a | 60.02 N | 30.18 E |
| Suva Planina ⩕ | 38 | 43.10 N | 22.10 E |

**PORTUGUÊS**

| Nome | Página | Lat.°′ | Long.°′ W = Oeste |
|---|---|---|---|
| Suvarlı | 130 | 37.32 N | 37.38 E |
| Suvasvesi ⊜ | 26 | 62.39 N | 28.12 E |
| Suvereto | 66 | 43.05 N | 10.40 E |
| Suvo | 88 | 53.39 N | 110.00 E |
| Suvorka | 88 | 56.33 N | 103.24 E |
| Suvorov | 82 | 54.07 N | 36.30 E |
| Suvorove | 78 | 45.34 N | 28.59 E |
| Suvorovo | 82 | 56.07 N | 35.54 E |
| Suwa, Erit. | 144 | 14.17 N | 41.06 E |
| Suwa, Nihon | 94 | 36.02 N | 138.08 E |
| Suwa-ko ⊜ | 94 | 36.05 N | 138.05 E |
| Suwałki | 30 | 54.07 N | 22.56 E |
| Suwałki □ [4] | 30 | 54.10 N | 22.15 E |
| Suwannaphum | 110 | 15.33 N | 103.47 E |
| Suwannee ≃ | 192 | 29.18 N | 83.09 W |
| Suwannee Lake ⊜ | 184 | 56.08 N | 100.10 W |
| Suwanose-jima I | 93b | 29.38 N | 129.43 E |
| Suwanose-suidō ʮ | 93b | 29.32 N | 129.40 E |
| Suwarrow I [1] | 14 | 13.15 S | 163.05 W |
| Suwaydah | 130 | 35.46 N | 39.38 E |
| Şuwaylih | 132 | 32.02 N | 35.50 E |
| Suways, Khalīj as- (Gulf of Suez) c | 140 | 29.00 N | 32.50 E |
| Suways, Qanāt as- (Suez Canal) ≅ | 142 | 29.55 N | 32.33 E |
| Suwŏn | 98 | 37.17 N | 127.01 E |
| Suwon-dong | 98 | 41.54 N | 129.43 E |
| Suxi | 100 | 29.25 N | 120.07 E |
| Suxian | 100 | 33.38 N | 116.58 E |
| Suya | 150 | 9.28 N | 3.11 E |
| Suykbulak | 86 | 49.48 N | 80.50 E |
| Suyo | 246 | 4.30 S | 80.00 W |
| Suzak | 86 | 44.07 N | 68.28 E |
| Suzaka | 94 | 36.39 N | 138.19 E |
| Suzdal' | 80 | 56.25 N | 40.26 E |
| Suze ≃ | 58 | 47.08 N | 7.14 E |
| Suze-la-Rousse | 62 | 44.17 N | 4.51 E |
| Suzhi | 98 | 42.17 N | 113.42 E |
| Suzhou (Soochow) | 106 | 31.18 N | 120.37 E |
| Suzhuang | 105 | 40.04 N | 116.44 E |
| Suzi ≃ | 98 | 41.55 N | 124.17 E |
| Suzigou | 98 | 40.25 N | 123.25 E |
| S'uzikozero | 24 | 61.48 N | 37.20 E |
| Suz'omka | 76 | 52.19 N | 34.05 E |
| Suzu | 92 | 37.25 N | 137.17 E |
| Suzuka | 94 | 34.51 N | 136.35 E |
| Suzuka ≃ | 94 | 34.54 N | 136.39 E |
| Suzuka-kokutei-kōen ♠ | 94 | 35.00 N | 136.25 E |
| Suzuka-sammyaku ⩕ | 94 | 35.00 N | 136.25 E |
| Suzuki | 268 | 35.43 N | 139.31 E |
| S'uz'um | 80 | 58.02 N | 47.32 E |
| Suzu-misaki ≻ | 92 | 37.31 N | 137.21 E |
| Suzun | 86 | 53.47 N | 82.19 E |
| Suzzara | 64 | 45.00 N | 10.45 E |
| Sværdborg | 41 | 55.05 N | 11.54 E |
| Svalbard II | 12 | 78.00 N | 20.00 E |
| Svalöv | 41 | 55.55 N | 13.06 E |
| Svalyava | 78 | 48.33 N | 22.59 E |
| Svaneholm | 41 | 55.30 N | 13.28 E |
| Svaneke | 26 | 55.08 N | 15.09 E |
| Svanetskij chrebet ⩕ | 84 | 42.55 N | 42.42 E |
| Svängsta | 26 | 56.16 N | 14.46 E |
| Svanninge | 41 | 55.07 N | 10.15 E |
| Svanskog | 26 | 59.11 N | 12.33 E |
| Svapa ≃ | 78 | 51.44 N | 34.56 E |
| Şvappavaara | 24 | 67.39 N | 21.04 E |
| Švarcevskij | 82 | 54.06 N | 37.59 E |
| Şvärdsjö | 26 | 60.45 N | 15.55 E |
| Švaricha | 80 | 57.33 N | 49.37 E |
| Svartå | 40 | 59.08 N | 14.31 E |
| Svartälven ≃ | 40 | 59.19 N | 14.35 E |
| Svartån ≃ | 40 | 59.37 N | 16.33 E |
| Svarte | 41 | 55.25 N | 13.43 E |
| Svartenhuk ≻ [1] | 176 | 71.55 N | 55.00 W |
| Svärtinge | 40 | 58.39 N | 16.00 E |
| Svartisen ⍓ | 24 | 66.38 N | 14.00 E |
| Svartlöga I | 40 | 59.34 N | 19.03 E |
| Svartsjölandet I | 40 | 59.22 N | 17.41 E |
| Svataj | 74 | 67.57 N | 151.54 E |
| Svatava | 54 | 50.11 N | 12.35 E |
| Svatava ≃ | 54 | 50.11 N | 12.38 E |
| Sv'atica ≃ | 80 | 58.22 N | 51.43 E |
| Sv'atoj Nos, mys ≻, Ross. | 24 | 68.10 N | 39.45 E |
| Sv'atoj Nos, mys ≻, Ross. | 74 | 72.52 N | 140.42 E |
| Sv'atoj Nos, poluostrov ≻ [1] | 88 | 53.40 N | 108.50 E |
| Sv'atoslavka | 80 | 51.20 N | 43.26 E |
| Svatove | 83 | 49.23 N | 38.13 E |
| Svay Chék | 110 | 13.48 N | 102.58 E |
| Svay Riěng | 110 | 11.05 N | 105.48 E |
| Sveafallen ∟ | 40 | 59.10 N | 14.22 E |
| Svebølle | 41 | 55.38 N | 11.20 E |
| Sveča | 80 | 58.16 N | 47.32 E |
| Svedala | 41 | 55.30 N | 13.14 E |
| Svėdasai | 76 | 55.41 N | 25.22 E |
| Sveg | 26 | 62.02 N | 14.21 E |
| Şvegssjön ⊜ [1] | 26 | 62.03 N | 14.10 E |
| Švėkšna | 76 | 55.31 N | 21.37 E |
| Svelgen | 26 | 61.47 N | 5.15 E |
| Svelvik | 26 | 59.37 N | 10.24 E |
| Şven' | 76 | 53.09 N | 34.21 E |
| Švenčionėliai | 76 | 55.10 N | 26.00 E |
| Švenčionys | 76 | 55.07 N | 26.10 E |
| Svendborg | 41 | 55.03 N | 10.37 E |
| Svenljunga | 26 | 57.30 N | 13.07 E |
| Svennevad | 40 | 59.01 N | 15.22 E |
| Svensen | 224 | 46.10 N | 123.39 W |
| Svenstorp | 41 | 55.46 N | 13.15 E |
| Şvenstrup | 26 | 56.59 N | 9.52 E |
| Šventoji | 76 | 56.02 N | 21.05 E |
| Šventoji ≃ | 76 | 55.06 N | 24.22 E |
| Sverbejevo | 89 | 53.36 N | 123.15 E |
| Sverdlovo, Ross. | 80 | 51.16 N | 44.34 E |
| Sverdlovo, Ross. | 82 | 56.38 N | 36.37 E |
| Sverdlovsk → Jekaterinburg, Ross. | 86 | 56.51 N | 60.36 E |
| Sverdlovs'k, Ukr. | 83 | 48.05 N | 39.40 E |
| Sverdrup, ostrov I | 74 | 74.35 N | 79.30 E |
| Sverige → Sweden □ [1] | 24 | 62.00 N | 15.00 E |
| Şverkestaån ≃ | 40 | 59.28 N | 15.28 E |
| Švermov | 54 | 50.09 N | 14.05 E |
| Svesa | 78 | 51.57 N | 33.54 E |
| Sveti Arhandjel Mihajlo ʊ [1] | 38 | 42.07 N | 21.28 E |
| Sveti Jovan Bigorski ʊ [1] | 38 | 41.38 N | 20.37 E |
| Sveti Nikole | 38 | 41.52 N | 21.58 E |
| Sveti Petar u Šumi | 64 | 45.11 N | 13.52 E |
| Svetlahorsk | 76 | 52.38 N | 29.42 E |
| Svetlaja | 89 | 46.33 N | 138.18 E |
| Světlá nad Sázavou | 30 | 49.40 N | 15.25 E |
| Svetlogorsk | 76 | 54.57 N | 20.10 E |
| Svetlograd | 72 | 45.20 N | 42.40 E |
| Svetloje | 80 | 57.03 N | 53.38 E |
| Svetlyj, Ross. | 76 | 54.41 N | 20.08 E |
| Svetlyj, Ross. | 86 | 50.47 N | 60.53 E |
| Svetlyj, Ross. | 88 | 58.26 N | 115.55 E |
| Svetlyj Jar | 80 | 48.29 N | 44.46 E |
| Svetogorsk | 24 | 61.07 N | 28.51 E |
| Svetozarevo | 38 | 43.58 N | 21.16 E |
| Svežen'kaja | 80 | 54.01 N | 42.26 E |
| Şvidník | 30 | 49.18 N | 21.35 E |
| Švihov | 60 | 49.29 N | 13.17 E |
| Svijaga ≃ | 80 | 55.47 N | 48.40 E |
| Svilajnac | 38 | 44.14 N | 21.13 E |
| Svilengrad | 38 | 41.46 N | 26.12 E |
| Svindal | 26 | 58.30 N | 7.28 E |
| Svinecea Mare, Vârful ∧ | 38 | 44.48 N | 22.09 E |
| Svinesund | 26 | 59.06 N | 11.16 E |
| Svinninge | 41 | 55.43 N | 11.28 E |
| Svir | 76 | 54.51 N | 26.24 E |
| Svir' ≃ | 76 | 60.30 N | 32.48 E |
| Svirica | 76 | 60.29 N | 32.51 E |
| Svirsk | 88 | 53.04 N | 103.21 E |
| Svir'stroj | 76 | 60.48 N | 33.43 E |
| Sviščovka | 80 | 52.51 N | 43.44 E |
| Svislač, Bela. | 76 | 53.02 N | 24.06 E |
| Svislač, Bela. | 76 | 53.26 N | 28.59 E |
| Svislač ≃ | 76 | 53.26 N | 28.59 E |
| Svištov | 38 | 43.37 N | 25.20 E |
| Svit | 30 | 49.03 N | 20.12 E |
| Svitava ≃ | 30 | 49.09 N | 16.38 E |
| Svitávka | 30 | 49.30 N | 16.37 E |
| Svitavy | 30 | 49.45 N | 16.27 E |
| Svitino | 82 | 54.54 N | 35.49 E |
| Svitlovods'k | 78 | 49.04 N | 33.15 E |
| Svjacilavičy | 76 | 52.48 N | 31.19 E |
| Svobidnyy port | 78 | 46.20 N | 31.51 E |
| Svoboda, Ross. | 78 | 47.12 N | 40.39 E |
| Svoboda, Ross. | 78 | 51.58 N | 36.17 E |
| Svobodnaja | 89 | 46.48 N | 143.23 E |
| Svobodne | 83 | 47.32 N | 37.34 E |
| Svobodnyj, Ross. | 80 | 52.20 N | 46.22 E |
| Svobodnyj, Ross. | 89 | 51.24 N | 128.08 E |
| Svoge | 38 | 42.58 N | 23.21 E |
| Svojna | 82 | 54.09 N | 36.39 E |
| Svol'na ≃ | 76 | 55.43 N | 28.02 E |
| Svolvær | 24 | 68.14 N | 14.34 E |
| Svor | 54 | 50.47 N | 14.36 E |
| Svorkmo | 26 | 63.10 N | 9.45 E |
| Svratka ≃ | 61 | 49.11 N | 16.38 E |
| Svržno | 60 | 49.35 N | 12.46 E |
| Svullrya | 26 | 60.25 N | 12.24 E |
| Svystunivka | 83 | 49.29 N | 38.20 E |
| Swābi | 123 | 34.07 N | 72.28 E |
| Swadlincote | 42 | 52.47 N | 1.33 W |
| Swaffham | 42 | 52.39 N | 0.41 E |
| Swain | 210 | 42.29 N | 77.51 W |
| Swain Reefs ✦ [2] | 166 | 21.40 S | 152.15 E |
| Swainsboro | 192 | 32.35 N | 82.20 W |
| Swains Island I [1] | 14 | 11.03 S | 171.05 W |
| Swakop ≃ | 156 | 22.38 S | 14.36 E |
| Swakopmund | 156 | 22.41 S | 14.34 E |
| Swale □ [8] | 260 | 51.21 N | 0.41 E |
| Swale ≃ | 44 | 54.06 N | 1.20 W |
| Swale Canyon V | 224 | 45.49 N | 121.05 W |
| Swale Creek ≃ | 224 | 45.49 N | 121.05 W |
| Swaledale V | 44 | 54.25 N | 1.47 W |
| Swallowfield | 218 | 38.21 N | 84.51 W |
| Swalmen | 52 | 51.15 N | 6.02 E |
| Swamp City | 222 | 32.29 N | 94.56 W |
| Swampscott | 207 | 42.28 N | 70.55 W |
| Swan | 222 | 32.26 N | 95.22 W |
| Swan ≃, Austl. | 168a | 32.03 S | 115.45 E |
| Swan ≃, Can | 184 | 52.30 N | 100.47 W |
| Swan ≃, Ab., Can. | 182 | 55.31 N | 115.17 W |
| Swan ≃, Mn., U.S. | 190 | 47.01 N | 93.16 W |
| Swan ≃, Mt., U.S. | 202 | 48.04 N | 114.05 W |
| Swan Acres | 279b | 40.33 N | 80.02 W |
| Swanage | 42 | 50.37 N | 1.58 W |
| Swan Bay c | 169 | 38.14 S | 144.40 E |
| Swan Creek ≃, Austl. | 171a | 28.08 S | 152.13 E |
| Swan Creek ≃, Mi., U.S. | 216 | 41.58 N | 85.19 W |
| Swan Creek ≃, Mi., U.S. | 216 | 41.58 N | 83.17 W |
| Swan Creek ≃, Oh., U.S. | 216 | 41.39 N | 83.32 W |
| Swan Creek ≃, S.D., U.S. | 198 | 45.19 N | 100.15 W |
| Swan Creek, North Branch ≃ | 281 | 42.06 N | 83.23 W |
| Swan Creek Point ≻ | 281 | 42.40 N | 82.39 W |
| Swanee → Suwannee ≃ | 192 | 29.18 N | 83.09 W |
| Swan Hill | 166 | 35.21 S | 143.34 E |
| Swan Hills | 182 | 54.43 N | 115.24 W |
| Swan Hills ⩕ [2] | 182 | 54.48 N | 115.52 W |
| Swanington | 216 | 40.35 N | 87.17 W |
| Swan Island I | 169 | 38.15 S | 144.41 E |
| Swan Islands → Santanilla, Islas II | 238 | 17.25 N | 83.55 W |
| Swank Creek ≃ | 224 | 47.07 N | 120.45 W |
| Swan Lake, Mb., Can. | 184 | 49.24 N | 98.46 W |
| Swan Lake, Mt., U.S. | 202 | 47.55 N | 113.50 W |
| Swan Lake, N.Y., U.S. | 210 | 41.45 N | 74.47 W |
| Swan Lake ⊜, Mb., Can. | 184 | 52.30 N | 100.45 W |
| Swan Lake ⊜, On., Can. | 184 | 54.17 N | 91.12 W |
| Swan Lake ⊜, Il., U.S. | 219 | 38.57 N | 90.33 W |
| Swan Lake ⊜, Mn., U.S. | 190 | 44.19 N | 94.15 W |
| Swanland | 44 | 53.44 N | 0.29 W |
| Swanley | 42 | 51.24 N | 0.12 E |
| Swanlinbar | 48 | 54.10 N | 7.42 W |
| Swannanoa | 192 | 35.36 N | 82.23 W |
| Swannanoa, Lake ⊜ | 276 | 41.01 N | 74.31 W |
| Swan Peak ∧ | 202 | 47.43 N | 113.38 W |
| Swanquarter | 192 | 35.24 N | 76.20 W |
| Swan Range ⩕ | 202 | 47.50 N | 113.40 W |
| Swan Reach | 166 | 34.34 S | 139.36 E |
| Swan River | 184 | 52.06 N | 101.16 W |
| Swansboro | 192 | 34.41 N | 77.07 W |
| Swanscombe | 260 | 51.26 N | 0.18 E |
| Swansea, Austl. | 166 | 42.08 S | 148.04 E |
| Swansea, Austl. | 170 | 33.05 S | 151.38 E |
| Swansea, Wales, U.K. | 42 | 51.38 N | 3.57 W |
| Swansea, Il., U.S. | 219 | 38.32 N | 89.59 W |
| Swansea, Ma., U.S. | 207 | 41.44 N | 71.11 W |
| Swansea, S.C., U.S. | 192 | 33.44 N | 81.05 W |
| Swansea ◆ [8] | 275b | 43.38 N | 79.28 W |
| Swansea Bay c | 42 | 51.35 N | 3.52 W |
| Swans Island I | 188 | 44.10 N | 68.25 W |
| Swanson Lake ⊜ [1] | 198 | 40.09 N | 101.06 W |
| Swanton, Oh., U.S. | 216 | 41.35 N | 83.53 W |
| Swanton, Vt., U.S. | 206 | 44.55 N | 73.07 W |
| Swanville | 190 | 45.54 N | 94.38 W |
| Swanzey Center | 207 | 42.49 N | 72.10 W |
| Swarbacks Minn ʮ | 46a | 60.20 N | 1.36 W |
| Swartberg | 158 | 30.15 S | 29.23 E |
| Swarthmore | 208 | 39.54 N | 75.21 W |
| Swarthmore College ʊ [2] | 285 | 39.54 N | 75.21 W |
| Swart-Kei ≃ | 158 | 32.09 S | 27.24 E |
| Swart-Mfolozi ≃ | 158 | 28.22 S | 31.58 E |
| Swartplaas | 158 | 26.08 S | 26.57 E |
| Swartruggens | 156 | 25.40 S | 26.42 E |
| Swartruggens ⩕ | 158 | 33.02 S | 19.35 E |
| Swartswood Lake | 210 | 41.04 N | 74.51 W |
| Swartswood State Park ♠ | 210 | 41.05 N | 74.50 W |
| Swartz Creek | 216 | 42.57 N | 83.49 W |
| Swarupkāti | 126 | 22.45 N | 90.06 E |
| Swarupnagar | 126 | 22.49 N | 88.52 E |
| Swarzędz | 30 | 52.26 N | 17.05 E |
| Swasey Peak ∧ | 200 | 39.23 N | 113.19 W |
| Swasey Wash V | 200 | 39.15 N | 112.53 W |
| Swasiland → Swaziland □ [1] | 158 | 26.30 S | 31.30 E |
| Swāt ≃ | 123 | 34.20 N | 71.34 E |
| Swatara Creek ≃ | 208 | 40.11 N | 76.44 W |
| Swa-Tenda | 152 | 7.09 S | 17.07 E |
| Swatow → Shantou | 100 | 23.23 N | 116.41 E |
| Swauger Creek ≃ | 226 | 38.16 N | 119.16 W |
| Swauk Pass )( | 224 | 47.21 N | 120.40 W |
| Sway | 42 | 50.47 N | 1.37 W |
| Swayzee | 216 | 40.30 N | 85.49 W |
| Swaziland □ [1], Afr. | 138 | 26.30 S | 31.30 E |
| Swaziland □ [1], Afr. | 158 | 26.30 S | 31.30 E |
| Swea City | 190 | 43.23 N | 94.19 W |
| Swede Hill | 279b | 40.17 N | 79.34 W |
| Swedeland | 285 | 40.05 N | 75.20 W |
| Sweden (Sverige) □ [1], Europe | 22 | 62.00 N | 15.00 E |
| Sweden (Sverige) □ [1], Europe | 24 | 62.00 N | 15.00 E |
| Sweden Valley | 214 | 41.45 N | 77.56 W |
| Swede Run ≃ | 285 | 40.02 N | 74.58 W |
| Swedesboro | 208 | 39.44 N | 75.18 W |
| Swedesburg | 285 | 40.06 N | 75.20 W |
| Swedish Knoll ∧ | 200 | 39.16 N | 111.26 W |
| Swedru | 150 | 5.32 N | 0.43 W |
| Sween, Loch c | 46 | 55.59 N | 5.39 W |
| Sweeney Plan | 279b | 40.11 N | 79.48 W |
| Sweeny | 222 | 29.02 N | 95.41 W |
| Sweeny Park ♠ | 284a | 43.02 N | 78.52 W |
| Sweet Briar | 192 | 37.33 N | 79.04 W |
| Sweetgrass | 182 | 49.00 N | 111.57 W |
| Sweet Grass Creek ≃ | 202 | 45.47 N | 109.47 W |
| Sweetgrass Hills ⩕ [2] | 202 | 48.55 N | 111.30 W |
| Sweet Grass Indian Reserve ◆ [4] | 184 | 52.44 N | 108.45 W |
| Sweetheart Abbey ʊ [1] | 44 | 54.59 N | 3.38 W |
| Sweet Home, Or., U.S. | 202 | 44.23 N | 122.44 W |
| Sweet Home, Tx., U.S. | 222 | 29.21 N | 97.04 W |
| Sweetsers | 216 | 40.34 N | 85.46 W |
| Sweet Springs | 194 | 38.57 N | 93.24 W |
| Sweet Valley | 210 | 41.17 N | 76.09 W |
| Sweetwater, Fl., U.S. | 220 | 25.46 N | 80.21 W |
| Sweet Water, Il., U.S. | 219 | 40.03 N | 89.42 W |
| Sweetwater, Tn., U.S. | 192 | 35.36 N | 84.27 W |
| Sweetwater, Tx., U.S. | 196 | 32.28 N | 100.24 W |
| Sweetwater ≃ | 200 | 42.31 N | 107.02 W |
| Sweetwater Creek | 220 | 27.59 N | 82.33 W |
| Sweetwater Creek ≃, U.S. | 196 | 35.18 N | 99.57 W |
| Sweetwater Creek ≃, Tx., U.S. | 196 | 32.40 N | 100.06 W |
| Sweetwater Mountains ⩕ | 226 | 38.30 N | 119.17 W |
| Swellendam | 158 | 34.02 S | 20.26 E |
| Swepsonville | 192 | 36.01 N | 79.21 W |
| Swerdlovsk → Jekaterinburg | 86 | 56.51 N | 60.36 E |
| Świdnica (Schweidnitz) | 30 | 50.51 N | 16.29 E |
| Świdnik | 30 | 51.14 N | 22.41 E |
| Świdwin | 30 | 53.47 N | 15.47 E |
| Świebodzice | 30 | 50.52 N | 16.19 E |
| Świebodzin | 30 | 52.15 N | 15.32 E |
| Świecie | 30 | 53.25 N | 18.28 E |
| Świerzawa | 30 | 51.01 N | 15.54 E |
| Świerzno | 54 | 53.57 N | 14.59 E |
| Święta | 54 | 53.35 N | 14.36 E |
| Świętokrzyskie, Góry ⩕ | 30 | 50.55 N | 21.00 E |
| Świętokrzyski Park Narodowy ♠ | 30 | 50.55 N | 21.00 E |
| Swift ≃, Eng., U.K. | 42 | 52.23 N | 1.16 W |
| Swift ≃, Ak., U.S. | 180 | 61.53 N | 156.18 W |
| Swift ≃, Ma., U.S. | 207 | 42.12 N | 72.22 W |
| Swift Creek ≃, Al., U.S. | 194 | 32.25 N | 86.38 W |
| Swift Creek ≃, N.C., U.S. | 192 | 35.12 N | 77.05 W |
| Swift Creek ≃, N.C., U.S. | 192 | 35.57 N | 77.35 W |
| Swift Creek ≃, Va., U.S. | 208 | 37.17 N | 77.15 W |
| Swift Current | 184 | 50.17 N | 107.50 W |
| Swift Current Creek ≃ | 184 | 50.40 N | 107.44 W |
| Swifton | 194 | 35.49 N | 91.07 W |
| Swift Reservoir ⊜ [1] | 224 | 46.04 N | 122.05 W |
| Swiftwater | 210 | 41.06 N | 75.20 W |
| Swilly ≃ | 48 | 54.57 N | 7.42 W |
| Swilly, Lough c | 48 | 55.10 N | 7.38 W |
| Swimming ≃ | 276 | 40.21 N | 74.05 W |
| Swimming River Reservoir ⊜ [1] | 276 | 40.19 N | 74.07 W |
| Świna ≃ [1] | 54 | 53.55 N | 14.17 E |
| Swinburne, Cape ≻ | 176 | 71.14 N | 98.34 W |
| Swinden Reservoirs ⊜ [1] | 262 | 53.48 N | 2.10 W |
| Swindle Island I | 182 | 52.32 N | 128.35 W |
| Swindon | 42 | 51.34 N | 1.47 W |
| Swinemünde → Świnoujście | 30 | 53.53 N | 14.14 E |
| Swineshead | 42 | 52.56 N | 0.09 W |
| Swinford | 48 | 53.57 N | 8.57 W |
| Swinging Bridge Reservoir ⊜ [1] | 210 | 41.37 N | 74.48 W |
| Swinomish Indian Reservation ◆ [4] | 224 | 48.25 N | 122.33 W |
| Świnoujście (Swinemünde) | 30 | 53.53 N | 14.14 E |
| Swinton, Eng., U.K. | 44 | 53.28 N | 1.20 W |
| Swinton, Eng., U.K. | 262 | 53.31 N | 2.20 W |
| Swinton, Scot., U.K. | 46 | 55.43 N | 2.15 W |
| Swissvale | 279b | 40.25 N | 79.52 W |
| Swisttal | 56 | 50.40 N | 6.54 E |
| Switzerland □ [6] | 218 | 38.45 N | 85.04 W |
| Switzerland □ [1], Europe | 22 | 47.00 N | 8.00 E |
| Switzerland □ [1], Europe | 58 | 47.00 N | 8.00 E |
| Swona I | 46 | 58.45 N | 3.03 W |
| Swordfish Seamount ✦ [3] | 14 | 18.25 N | 158.25 W |
| Swords | 48 | 53.28 N | 6.13 W |
| Swords Range ⩕ | 166 | 21.57 S | 141.32 E |
| Swormville | 284a | 43.02 N | 78.42 W |
| Sworton Heath | 262 | 53.21 N | 2.28 W |
| Swoyerville | 210 | 41.18 N | 75.52 W |
| Syalach | 74 | 66.12 N | 124.00 E |
| Syam | 58 | 46.42 N | 5.57 E |
| Syāmnagar | 126 | 22.21 N | 89.07 E |
| Syāmpur, India | 126 | 22.18 N | 88.02 E |
| Syampur, India | 272b | 22.29 N | 88.13 E |
| Sybille Creek ≃ | 198 | 42.07 N | 105.02 W |
| Syburg ◆ [8] | 263 | 51.25 N | 7.29 E |
| Sycamore, Ga., U.S. | 192 | 31.40 N | 83.38 W |
| Sycamore, Il., U.S. | 216 | 41.59 N | 88.41 W |
| Sycamore, Oh., U.S. | 214 | 40.56 N | 83.10 W |
| Sycamore Creek ≃, Az., U.S. | 200 | 33.38 N | 111.40 W |
| Sycamore Creek ≃, Mi., U.S. | 216 | 42.43 N | 84.32 W |
| Sycamore Creek ≃, Oh., U.S. | 214 | 40.59 N | 83.12 W |
| Sycamore Creek ≃, Tx., U.S. | 196 | 29.14 N | 100.48 W |
| Sycamore Gardens | 285 | 39.42 N | 75.42 W |
| Sycamore Island I | 279b | 40.29 N | 79.52 W |
| Sycamore Slough ≃ | 226 | 38.48 N | 121.44 W |
| Sycan ≃ | 202 | 42.27 N | 121.15 W |
| Sycaway | 210 | 42.44 N | 73.39 W |
| Syčova | 86 | 57.35 N | 69.20 E |
| Syčovka | 76 | 55.50 N | 34.17 E |
| Syców | 30 | 51.19 N | 17.43 E |
| Sydenham, Austl. | 274b | 37.42 S | 144.46 E |
| Sydenham, On., Can. | 212 | 44.25 N | 76.36 W |
| Sydenham ◆ [8], S. Afr. | 273d | 26.09 S | 28.06 E |
| Sydenham ◆ [8], Eng., U.K. | 260 | 51.26 N | 0.03 W |
| Sydenham ≃, On., Can. | 190 | 42.33 N | 82.25 W |
| Sydenham ≃, On., Can. | 212 | 44.35 N | 80.57 W |
| Sydenham Lake ⊜ | 212 | 44.25 N | 76.35 W |
| Sydenham West | 274b | 37.41 S | 144.39 E |
| Sydney, Austl. | 170 | 33.52 S | 151.13 E |
| Sydney, Austl. | 274a | 33.52 S | 151.13 E |
| Sydney, N.S., Can. | 186 | 46.09 N | 60.11 W |
| Sydney, Fl., U.S. | 220 | 27.58 N | 82.12 W |
| Sydney, University of ʊ [2] | 274a | 33.53 S | 151.11 E |
| Sydney Bay c, On., Can. | 212 | 44.54 N | 81.05 W |
| Sydney Bay c, Norf. I. | 174c | 29.04 S | 167.57 E |
| Sydney Bay Bluff ⊥ [4] | 212 | 44.54 N | 81.07 W |
| Sydney Harbour Bridge ◆ [5] | 170 | 33.52 S | 151.12 E |
| Sydney Lake ⊜ | 184 | 50.40 N | 94.24 W |
| Sydney Mines | 186 | 46.14 N | 60.14 W |
| Sydney Point ≻ | 174d | 0.53 S | 169.36 E |
| Syedove | 83 | 47.03 N | 38.10 E |
| Syevernyy | 83 | 48.22 N | 39.56 E |
| Syeverodonets'k | 83 | 48.58 N | 38.27 E |
| Syevero-Hundorivs'kyy | 83 | 48.23 N | 39.54 E |
| Syferbult | 158 | 26.00 S | 27.20 E |
| Şygan | 279b | 40.21 N | 80.08 W |
| Šyičy | 76 | 52.15 N | 29.14 E |
| Syke | 52 | 52.54 N | 8.49 E |
| Sykesville, Md., U.S. | 208 | 39.22 N | 76.58 W |
| Sykesville, Pa., U.S. | 214 | 41.03 N | 78.49 W |
| Sykkylven | 26 | 62.24 N | 6.35 E |
| Syktyvkar | 24 | 61.40 N | 50.46 E |
| Sylacauga | 194 | 33.10 N | 86.15 W |
| Sylarna ∧ | 26 | 63.02 N | 12.13 E |
| Sylhet | 120 | 24.54 N | 91.52 E |
| Syloga | 24 | 63.50 N | [illegible]3.39 E |
| Sylt I | 30 | 54.54 N | 8.20 E |
| Sylva | 192 | 35.22 N | [illegible]3.13 W |
| Sylva ≃ | 86 | 57.39 N | [illegible]6.54 E |
| Sylvan Beach | 210 | 43.11 N | [illegible]5.43 W |
| Sylvan Glen | 285 | 40.11 N | [illegible]5.42 W |
| Sylvan Grove | 198 | 39.00 N | [illegible]8.23 W |
| Sylvan Hills | 194 | 34.50 N | [illegible]2.13 W |
| Sylvania, Austl. | 274a | 34.01 S | 1[illegible].07 E |
| Sylvania, Ga., U.S. | 192 | 32.45 N | [illegible].38 W |
| Sylvania, Oh., U.S. | 214 | 41.43 N | [illegible].42 W |
| Sylvania, Pa., U.S. | 210 | 41.48 N | 7[illegible].51 W |
| Sylvania Heights | 274a | 34.02 S | 15[illegible].06 E |
| Sylvan Lake, Ab., Can. | 182 | 52.19 N | 11[illegible].05 W |
| Sylvan Lake, Il., U.S. | 278 | 42.15 N | 8[illegible].03 W |
| Sylvan Lake, Mi., U.S. | 281 | 42.37 N | 8[illegible].20 W |
| Sylvan Lake ⊜, Ab., Can. | 182 | 52.21 N | 114.10 W |
| Sylvan Lake ⊜, In., U.S. | 216 | 41.29 N | 85.20 W |
| Sylvan Lake ⊜, Mi., U.S. | 281 | 42.37 N | 83.20 W |
| Sylvan Pass )( | 202 | 44.28 N | 110.[illegible]8 W |
| Sylvan Shores | 220 | 28.49 N | 81.[illegible]1 W |
| Sylvensteinsee ⊜ [1] | 64 | 47.34 N | 11.[illegible]2 E |
| Sylvester, Ga., U.S. | 192 | 31.31 N | 83.[illegible]0 W |
| Sylvester, Tx., U.S. | 196 | 32.43 N | 100.[illegible]5 W |
| Sylvester, Mount ∧ [2] | 186 | 48.11 N | 55.[illegible] W |
| Sylvia | 198 | 37.57 N | 98.[illegible] W |
| Şym | 74 | 60.20 N | 88.[illegible] E |
| Šymkent | 85 | 42.18 N | 69.[illegible] E |
| Symmes Creek ≃ | 188 | 38.26 N | 82.2[illegible] W |
| Syn'a | 24 | 65.22 N | 57.4[illegible] E |
| Syndal | 274b | 37.53 S | 145.0[illegible] E |
| Synel'nykove | 78 | 48.20 N | 35.3[illegible] E |
| Şynevir | 78 | 48.30 N | 23.3[illegible] E |
| Šyngystaj | 86 | 49.13 N | 85.5[illegible] E |
| Synivka | 78 | 50.33 N | 34.06 E |
| Synkovo | 82 | 55.21 N | 37.38 E |
| Synnyr, chrebet ⩕ | 88 | 56.50 N | 111.10 E |
| Syntul | 80 | 55.00 N | 41.18 E |
| Synyukha ≃ | 78 | 48.03 N | 30.51 E |
| Syon House ⊥ | 260 | 51.29 N | 0.19 W |
| Syosset | 210 | 40.49 N | 73.30 W |
| Syowa ʊ [3] | 9 | 69.00 S | 39.35 E |
| Syracuse → Siracusa, It. | 70 | 37.04 N | 15.18 E |
| Syracuse, In., U.S. | 216 | 41.25 N | 85.45 W |
| Syracuse, Ks., U.S. | 198 | 37.58 N | 101.45 W |
| Syracuse, Ne., U.S. | 198 | 40.39 N | 96.11 W |
| Syracuse, N.Y., U.S. | 210 | 43.02 N | 76.08 W |
| Syracuse Hancock International Airport ⊠, N.Y., U.S. | 210 | 43.07 N | 76.07 W |
| Syracuse Hancock International Airport ⊠, N.Y., U.S. | 212 | 43.07 N | 76.07 W |
| Syrau | 54 | 50.32 N | 12.05 E |
| Syrčan | 80 | 57.22 N | 50.15 E |
| Syrdarja | 85 | 40.52 N | 68.38 E |
| Syrdarja □ [4] | 85 | 40.30 N | 68.40 E |
| Syr Darya (Syrdar'ja) ≃ | 72 | 46.03 N | 61.00 E |
| Syre | 46 | 58.22 N | 4.14 W |
| Syre ≃ | 56 | 49.42 N | 6.29 E |
| Syria (Sūrīyah) □ [1], Asia | 118 | 35.00 N | 38.00 E |
| Syria (Sūrīyah) □ [1], Asia | 128 | 35.00 N | 38.00 E |
| Syriam | 110 | 16.46 N | 96.15 E |
| Syrian Desert → Shām, Bādiyat ash- ◆ [2] | 128 | 32.00 N | 40.00 E |
| Syrie → Syria □ [1] | 128 | 35.00 N | 38.00 E |
| Syrien → Syria □ [1] | 128 | 35.00 N | 38.00 E |
| Syrotyne | 83 | 48.55 N | 38.31 E |
| Şyrskij | 76 | 52.34 N | 39.29 E |
| Šyščycy | 76 | 53.13 N | 27.32 E |
| Sysert' | 86 | 56.29 N | 60.49 E |
| Sysmä | 26 | 61.30 N | 25.41 E |
| Sysola ≃ | 24 | 61.42 N | 50.53 E |
| Syssleböck | 26 | 60.44 N | 12.52 E |
| Syston | 42 | 52.42 N | 1.04 W |
| Systyg-Chem | 88 | 52.40 N | 95.30 E |
| Sytkivtsi | 78 | 48.54 N | 29.12 E |
| Syt'kovo | 76 | 56.31 N | 34.01 E |
| Sytykanskij, porog ∟ | 88 | 57.49 N | 118.33 E |
| Syukunoshō | 270 | 34.50 N | 135.32 E |
| Syväri ⊜ | 26 | 63.16 N | 28.06 E |
| Syvash, zatoka ʮ | 78 | 46.00 N | 34.30 E |
| Syvas'ke | 78 | 46.23 N | 34.34 E |
| Syzran' | 80 | 53.09 N | 48.27 E |
| Syzran' ≃ | 80 | 53.04 N | 48.26 E |
| Szabadka → Subotica | 38 | 46.06 N | 19.39 E |
| Szabolcs-Szatmár-Bereg □ [6] | 30 | 48.00 N | 22.10 E |
| Szada | 264c | 47.38 N | 19.19 E |
| Szamocin | 30 | 53.02 N | 17.08 E |
| Szamos (Someș) ≃ | 38 | 48.07 N | 22.20 E |
| Szamotuły | 30 | 52.37 N | 16.35 E |
| Szarvas | 30 | 46.52 N | 20.34 E |
| Szatmárnémeti → Satu Mare | 38 | 47.48 N | 22.53 E |
| Százhalombatta | 264c | 47.20 N | 18.56 E |
| Szczawnica | 30 | 49.26 N | 20.30 E |
| Szczecin (Stettin) | 30 | 53.24 N | 14.32 E |
| Szczecin □ [4] | 30 | 53.45 N | 15.00 E |
| Szczecinek (Neustettin) | 30 | 53.43 N | 16.42 E |
| Szczeciński, Zalew (Stettiner Haff) c | 54 | 53.46 N | 14.14 E |
| Szczekociny | 30 | 50.38 N | 19.50 E |
| Szczuczyn | 30 | 53.34 N | 22.18 E |
| Szczytno | 30 | 53.34 N | 21.00 E |
| Szechwan → Sichuan □ [4] | 102 | 31.00 N | 105.00 E |
| Szechwan Basin → Sichuan Pendi ≚ [1] | 102 | 30.00 N | 105.00 E |
| Szécsény | 30 | 48.06 N | 19.31 E |
| Szeged | 30 | 46.15 N | 20.09 E |
| Szeghalom | 30 | 47.01 N | 21.11 E |
| Székesfehérvár | 30 | 47.12 N | 18.25 E |
| Szekszárd | 30 | 46.21 N | 18.42 E |
| Szemenyecsörnye | 61 | 46.30 N | 16.37 E |
| Szentendre | 30 | 47.40 N | 19.05 E |
| Szentendrei-Duna ≃ [1] | 264c | 47.36 N | 19.05 E |
| Szentendrei-sziget I | 264c | 47.39 N | 19.07 E |
| Szentes | 30 | 46.39 N | 20.16 E |


| Symbol | English | Deutsch | Español | Français | Português |
|---|---|---|---|---|---|
| ≃ | River | Fluß | Río | Rivière | Rio |
| ≅ | Canal | Kanal | Canal | Canal | Canal |
| ∟ | Waterfall, Rapids | Wasserfall, Stromschnellen | Cascada, Rápidos | Chute d'eau, Rapides | Cascata, Rápidos |
| ʮ | Strait | Meeresstraße | Estrecho | Détroit | Estreito |
| c | Bay, Gulf | Bucht, Golf | Bahía, Golfo | Baie, Golfe | Baía, Golfo |
| ⊜ | Lake, Lakes | See, Seen | Lago, Lagos | Lac, Lacs | Lago, Lagos |
| ≡ | Swamp | Sumpf | Pantano | Marais | Pântano |
| ⍓ | Ice Features, Glacier | Eis- und Gletscherformen | Accidentes Glaciales | Formes glaciaires | Acidentes glaciares |
| ≚ | Other Hydrographic Features | Andere Hydrographische Objekte | Otros Elementos Hidrográficos | Autres données hydrographiques | Outros acidentes hidrográficos |

| Symbol | English | Deutsch | Español | Français | Português |
|---|---|---|---|---|---|
| ✦ | Submarine Features | Untermeerische Objekte | Accidentes Submarinos | Formes de relief sous-marin | Acidentes submarinos |
| □ | Political Unit | Politische Einheit | Unidad Politica | Entité politique | Unidade política |
| ʊ | Cultural Institution | Kulturelle Institution | Institución Cultural | Institution culturelle | Instituição cultural |
| ⊥ | Historical Site | Historische Stätte | Sitio Histórico | Site historique | Sitio histórico |
| ♠ | Recreational Site | Erholungs- und Ferienort | Sitio de Recreo | Centre de loisirs | Area de Lazer |
| ⊠ | Airport | Flughafen | Aeropuerto | Aéroport | Aeroporto |
| ■ | Military Installation | Militäranlage | Instalación Militar | Installation militaire | Instalação militar |
| ◆ | Miscellaneous | Verschiedenes | Misceláneo | Divers | Diversos |

| | | | |
|---|---|---|---|
| Szentgotthárd | **30** | 46.57 N | 16.17 E |
| Szentpéterfa | **61** | 47.06 N | 16.29 E |
| Szeping → Siping | **89** | 43.12 N | 124.20 E |
| Szépművészeti Museum ʊ | **264c** | 47.31 N | 19.05 E |
| Szerencs | **30** | 48.09 N | 21.13 E |
| Szigethalom | **264c** | 47.20 N | 19.00 E |
| Szigetszentmiklós | **264c** | 47.21 N | 19.03 E |
| Szilas-patak ≃ | **264c** | 47.36 N | 19.06 E |
| Szlichtyngowa | **30** | 51.43 N | 16.15 E |
| Szob | **30** | 47.50 N | 18.52 E |
| Szolnok | **30** | 47.10 N | 20.12 E |
| Szombathely | **30** | 47.14 N | 16.38 E |
| Szprotawa | **30** | 51.34 N | 15.33 E |
| Sztum | **30** | 53.56 N | 19.01 E |
| Szubin | **30** | 53.00 N | 17.44 E |
| Szydłowiec | **30** | 51.14 N | 20.51 E |
| Szypliszki | **30** | 54.15 N | 23.05 E |

T

| | | | |
|---|---|---|---|
| Ta ≃ | **94** | 36.17 N | 139.54 E |
| Taacyn ≃ | **102** | 45.09 N | 101.27 E |
| Taal | **116** | 13.53 N | 120.55 E |
| Taal, Lake ⊜ | **116** | 13.55 N | 121.00 E |
| Taalintehdas → Dalsbruk | **26** | 60.02 N | 22.31 E |
| Taan ≃ | **100** | 24.24 N | 120.36 E |
| Taancan Point › | **116** | 10.00 N | 125.01 E |
| Taavetti | **26** | 60.55 N | 27.34 E |
| Tabacal | **252** | 23.16 S | 64.15 W |
| Tabacal, Quebrada ≃ | **286c** | 10.31 N | 67.02 W |
| Tabaco | **116** | 13.23 N | 123.44 E |
| Tabacundo | **246** | 0.03 N | 78.12 W |
| Tabai ≃ | **164** | 3.01 S | 135.52 E |
| Tabalosos | **248** | 6.21 S | 76.41 W |
| Tabanan | **115b** | 8.32 S | 115.08 E |
| Tabango | **116** | 11.19 N | 124.22 E |
| Tabankulu | **158** | 30.58 S | 29.19 E |
| Tábara | **34** | 41.49 N | 5.57 W |
| Tabar Island I | **164** | 2.55 S | 152.05 E |
| Tabar Islands II | **164** | 2.50 S | 152.00 E |
| Tabarka | **148** | 36.57 N | 8.45 E |
| Tabarz | **54** | 50.52 N | 10.31 E |
| Ṭabas | **128** | 33.36 N | 56.54 E |
| Tabasará ≃ | **236** | 8.00 N | 81.39 W |
| Tabasco □[3] | **232** | 18.15 N | 93.00 W |
| Ṭabas Masīnā | **128** | 32.48 N | 60.14 E |
| Tabat | **86** | 52.57 N | 90.43 E |
| Tabatinga ≃ | **255** | 17.24 S | 43.18 W |
| Tabayama | **94** | 35.47 N | 138.55 E |
| Tabayin | **110** | 22.42 N | 95.19 E |
| Tabb | **208** | 37.08 N | 76.29 W |
| Tabei | **98** | 39.44 N | 122.29 E |
| Tabelbala | **148** | 29.23 N | 3.15 W |
| Tabelbala, Kahal ±[8] | **148** | 28.30 N | 2.00 W |
| Taber | **182** | 49.47 N | 112.08 W |
| Taberg, Sve. | **26** | 57.41 N | 14.05 E |
| Taberg, Sve. | **40** | 59.50 N | 14.08 E |
| Taberg, N.Y., U.S. | **210** | 43.18 N | 75.37 W |
| Tabernacle | **285** | 39.50 N | 74.42 W |
| Tabi | **152** | 8.10 S | 13.18 E |
| Tabiang | **174d** | 0.52 S | 169.35 E |
| Tabiano Terme | **64** | 44.48 N | 10.02 E |
| Tabira | **250** | 7.35 S | 37.33 W |
| Tabiteuea | **174t** | 1.25 N | 173.07 E |
| Tabiteuea I[1] | **14** | 1.20 S | 174.50 E |
| Tabla | **150** | 13.46 N | 3.01 E |
| Tabla, Cerro de la ∧ | **240m** | 18.03 N | 66.08 W |
| Tablada | **288** | 34.42 S | 58.32 W |
| Tablas, Cabo › | **252** | 31.51 S | 71.34 W |
| Tablas Island I | **116** | 12.24 N | 122.02 E |
| Tablas Plateau ⋏[1] | **116** | 9.43 N | 122.43 E |
| Tablas Strait ⋃ | **116** | 12.40 N | 121.48 E |
| Tablat | **34** | 36.24 N | 3.19 E |
| Table Bay ⊂ | **158** | 33.53 S | 18.27 E |
| Table Cape › | **172** | 39.06 S | 178.00 E |
| Tableland | **162** | 17.17 S | 127.00 E |
| Table Mountain ∧, Nf., Can. | **186** | 47.43 N | 59.13 W |
| Table Mountain ∧, S. Afr. | **158** | 33.57 S | 18.25 E |
| Table Mountain ∧, Az., U.S. | **200** | 32.49 N | 110.31 W |
| Table Rock | **198** | 40.10 N | 96.05 W |
| Table Rock Lake ⊜[1] | **194** | 36.35 N | 93.30 W |
| Tabletop ∧, Austl. | **162** | 22.32 S | 123.55 E |
| Table Top ∧, Az., U.S. | **200** | 32.46 N | 112.07 W |
| Tabletop Mountain ∧ | **171b** | 35.58 S | 148.30 E |
| Tabley Mere ⊜ | **262** | 53.17 N | 2.25 W |
| Tabligbo | **150** | 6.35 N | 1.30 E |
| Tablones | **240m** | 18.15 N | 65.45 W |
| Taboan ≃ | **116** | 17.57 N | 122.11 E |
| Taboão, Ribeirão do ≃ | **287b** | 23.40 S | 46.28 W |
| Taboão da Serra | **256** | 23.38 S | 46.46 W |
| Taboco ≃ | **248** | 19.53 S | 55.58 W |
| Taboga | **236** | 8.48 N | 79.33 W |
| Tabogon | **116** | 10.57 N | 124.02 E |
| Tábor, Česká Rep. | **30** | 49.25 N | 14.41 E |
| Tabor, Ross. | **74** | 71.16 N | 150.12 E |
| Tabor, Ia., U.S. | **198** | 40.53 N | 95.40 W |
| Tabor, N.J., U.S. | **276** | 40.52 N | 74.29 W |
| Tabor, S.D., U.S. | **198** | 42.56 N | 97.39 W |
| Tabor, Mount → Tavor, Har ∧ | **132** | 32.41 N | 35.23 E |
| Tabora | **154** | 5.01 S | 32.48 E |
| Tabora □[4] | **154** | 5.15 S | 32.45 E |
| Tabor City | **192** | 34.08 N | 78.52 W |
| Tabory | **86** | 58.31 N | 64.33 E |
| Tabou | **150** | 4.25 N | 7.21 W |
| Tabrīz | **128** | 38.05 N | 46.18 E |
| Tábua, Riacho da ≃ | **250** | 9.12 S | 44.25 W |
| Tabuaço | **34** | 41.07 N | 7.34 W |
| Tabuaeran I[1] | **14** | 3.52 N | 159.20 W |
| Tabuão | **256** | 21.59 S | 44.02 W |
| Tábuas | **256** | 22.12 S | 43.37 W |
| Tabu-dong | **98** | 36.03 N | 128.31 E |
| Tabuelan | **116** | 10.49 N | 123.52 E |
| Tabūk, Ar. Su. | **128** | 28.23 N | 36.35 E |
| Tabuk, Pil. | **116** | 17.24 N | 121.25 E |
| Tabuleiro | **256** | 21.22 S | 43.15 W |
| Tabuleiro do Norte | **250** | 5.15 S | 38.07 W |
| Tabuny | **86** | 52.46 N | 78.45 E |
| Tabuse | **96** | 33.57 N | 132.03 E |
| Tabuyung | **114** | 0.51 N | 99.00 E |
| Tabwémasana, Mont ∧ | **175f** | 15.20 S | 166.44 E |
| Täby | **40** | 59.30 N | 18.03 E |
| Tacagua, Quebrada ≃ | **286c** | 10.37 N | 67.02 W |
| Tacámbaro de Codallos | **234** | 19.14 N | 101.28 W |
| Tacaná | **236** | 15.14 N | 92.05 W |
| Tacaná, Volcán ∧[1] | **236** | 15.08 N | 92.06 W |
| Tacañitas | **252** | 28.38 S | 62.36 W |
| Tacaratu | **250** | 9.06 S | 38.10 W |
| Taceno | **58** | 46.02 N | 9.21 E |
| Taché, Lac ⊜ | **176** | 64.00 N | 120.00 W |
| Tacheng (Qoqek) | **86** | 46.45 N | 82.57 E |
| Tacherting | **60** | 48.05 N | 12.34 E |
| Tachia | **100** | 24.21 N | 120.37 E |
| Tachia ≃ | **100** | 24.20 N | 120.33 E |
| Tachiaochang Airport ⊠ | **107** | 32.01 N | 118.47 E |
| Tachiataš | **72** | 42.22 N | 59.35 E |
| Tachibana, Nihon | **96** | 33.11 N | 130.36 E |
| Tachibana, Nihon | **96** | 33.54 N | 132.17 E |
| Tachie ≃ | **182** | 54.40 N | 124.50 W |
| Tachikawa | **94** | 35.42 N | 139.25 E |
| Tachikawa Air Base ■ | **268** | 35.43 N | 139.25 E |
| Tachinger See ⊜ | **60** | 47.58 N | 12.45 E |
| Táchira □[3] | **246** | 7.50 N | 72.05 W |
| Tachoshui | **100** | 24.20 N | 121.44 E |
| Tachov | **60** | 49.48 N | 12.38 E |
| Tachta, Ross. | **80** | 45.54 N | 42.07 E |
| Tachta, Ross. | **89** | 53.08 N | 139.53 E |
| Tachta-Bazar | **128** | 35.57 N | 62.50 E |
| Tachtabrod | **86** | 52.38 N | 67.34 E |
| Tachtakupyr | **86** | 43.02 N | 60.17 E |
| Tachtamygda | **89** | 54.06 N | 123.34 E |
| Tacima | **250** | 6.30 S | 35.39 W |
| Tacina ≃ | **68** | 38.56 N | 16.53 E |
| Tacinskij | **80** | 48.13 N | 41.17 E |
| Taciuã, Lago ≃ | **246** | 4.29 S | 60.35 W |
| Tacloban | **116** | 11.15 N | 125.00 E |
| Taclobo | **116** | 12.20 N | 122.34 E |
| Tacna, Perú | **248** | 18.01 S | 70.15 W |
| Tacna, Az., U.S. | **200** | 32.41 N | 113.57 W |
| Tacna □[5] | **248** | 17.40 S | 70.20 W |
| Tacoignières | **261** | 48.50 N | 1.40 E |
| Tacoma | **224** | 47.15 N | 122.26 W |
| Tacoma Narrows Bridge ⊸[5] | **224** | 47.16 N | 122.33 W |
| Taconic | **207** | 42.02 N | 73.24 W |
| Taconic Range ⋏ | **210** | 42.30 N | 73.20 W |
| Taconic State Park ♠ | **210** | 42.05 N | 73.34 W |
| Tacony ⊸[8] | **285** | 40.02 N | 75.03 W |
| Tacony Creek ≃ | **285** | 40.01 N | 75.06 W |
| Tacony Creek Park ♠ | **285** | 40.02 N | 75.07 W |
| Tacony Palmyra Bridge ⊸[5] | **285** | 40.01 N | 75.02 W |
| Taco Pozo | **252** | 25.37 S | 63.17 W |
| Tacotalpa | **234** | 17.36 N | 92.49 W |
| Tacotalpa ≃ | **234** | 17.50 N | 92.52 W |
| Tacuarembó | **252** | 31.44 S | 55.59 W |
| Tacuarembó ≃ | **252** | 32.25 S | 55.29 W |
| Tacuarí ≃ | **252** | 32.46 S | 53.18 W |
| Tacuatí | **252** | 23.27 S | 56.35 W |
| Tacuba ⊸[8] | **286a** | 19.28 N | 99.12 W |
| Tacubaya ⊸[8] | **286a** | 19.25 N | 99.12 W |
| Tacuparé, Cachoeira ∟ | **250** | 5.20 S | 55.50 W |
| Tacurong | **116** | 6.42 N | 124.42 E |
| Tacuru, Bra. | **252** | 23.38 N | 55.01 W |
| Tacuru, Bra. | **255** | 23.38 S | 55.01 W |
| Tacurú, Laguna ⊜ | **258** | 34.58 S | 58.25 W |
| Tacutu (Takutu) ≃ | **246** | 3.01 N | 60.29 W |
| Tadain | **270** | 34.52 N | 135.24 E |
| Tadami | **92** | 37.21 N | 139.19 E |
| Tadaoka | **270** | 34.29 N | 135.24 E |
| Tadasuni | **71** | 40.06 N | 8.53 E |
| Tadcaster | **44** | 53.53 N | 1.16 W |
| Tademaït, Plateau du ⋏[1] | **148** | 28.30 N | 2.00 E |
| Tadenac Lake ⊜ | **212** | 45.03 N | 79.56 W |
| Tādepallegūdem | **122** | 16.50 N | 81.30 E |
| Tadía, Ciénaga de ⊜ | **246** | 6.48 N | 76.49 W |
| Tadine | **175f** | 21.33 S | 167.52 E |
| Tadio, Lagune ⊂ | **150** | 5.11 N | 5.15 W |
| Tadjemout | **148** | 25.37 N | 3.48 E |
| Tadjenanet | **34** | 36.08 N | 5.59 E |
| Tadjeraout, Oued V | **148** | 21.17 N | 1.19 E |
| Tadjoura | **144** | 11.47 N | 42.54 E |
| Tadjoura, Golfe de ⊂ | **144** | 11.42 N | 43.00 E |
| Tadley | **42** | 51.21 N | 1.08 W |
| Tado | **94** | 35.08 N | 136.38 E |
| Tadok | **114** | 3.58 N | 96.19 E |
| Tadotsu | **96** | 34.16 N | 133.45 E |
| Tadoule Lake ⊜ | **176** | 58.36 N | 98.20 W |
| Tadoussac | **186** | 48.09 N | 69.43 W |
| Tādpatri | **122** | 14.55 N | 78.01 E |
| Taduno | **112** | 1.55 S | 123.05 E |
| Tadworth | **42** | 51.17 N | 0.14 W |
| Tadzhikistan → Tajikistan □[1] | **72** | 39.00 N | 71.00 E |
| Tadžikabad | **85** | 39.07 N | 70.50 E |
| T'aean | **98** | 36.46 N | 126.16 E |
| T'aebaek-san ∧ | **98** | 37.06 N | 128.55 E |
| T'aebaek-sanmaek ⋏ | **98** | 37.40 N | 128.50 E |
| Taebu-do I | **98** | 37.15 N | 126.35 E |
| Taech'ŏn | **98** | 36.22 N | 126.34 E |
| Taech'ŏng-do I | **98** | 37.49 N | 124.43 E |
| Taedong | **98** | 39.05 N | 125.31 E |
| Taedong-gang ≃ | **98** | 38.42 N | 125.15 E |
| Taegu | **98** | 35.52 N | 128.35 E |
| Taegu □[4] | **98** | 35.50 N | 128.35 E |
| Taegwan | **98** | 40.13 N | 125.12 E |
| Taehan-Min'guk → Korea, South □[1] | **98** | 36.30 N | 128.00 E |
| Taehŭksan-do I | **98** | 34.40 N | 125.25 E |
| Taehŭng | **98** | 40.06 N | 126.56 E |
| Taehwajŏn | **271b** | 37.36 N | 126.52 E |
| T'aein | **98** | 35.40 N | 126.55 E |
| Taejin | **98** | 36.34 N | 129.24 E |
| Taejŏn | **98** | 36.20 N | 127.26 E |
| Taejujŏm | **98** | 38.24 N | 127.58 E |
| T'aemo-san ∧ | **271b** | 37.27 N | 127.04 E |
| Taeng ≃ | **110** | 19.06 N | 98.57 E |
| Taer | **102** | 34.09 N | 98.50 E |
| Ta'erwan | **100** | 31.49 N | 113.25 E |
| Taeryanghwa | **98** | 41.14 N | 129.42 E |
| Taf ≃ | **42** | 51.47 N | 4.26 W |
| Tafahi I | **14** | 15.51 S | 173.43 W |
| Tafahnā al-ʻAzab | **142** | 30.36 N | 31.15 E |
| Tafalla | **34** | 42.31 N | 1.40 W |
| Tafanlieh | **100** | 21.58 N | 120.46 E |
| Ṭafas | **132** | 32.44 N | 36.04 E |
| Tafāsīkh, Ghurd at- ±[8] | **142** | 29.43 N | 29.45 E |
| Tafassasset, Oued (Oued Tafassâsset) V | **148** | 20.56 N | 10.12 E |
| Tafassâsset, Ténéré du ⊸[2] | **146** | 21.00 N | 11.00 E |
| Tafea □[8] | **175f** | 19.30 S | 169.00 E |
| Tafelbaai → Table Bay ⊂ | **158** | 33.53 S | 18.27 E |
| Tafelberg ∧ | **250** | 3.55 N | 56.10 W |
| Tafermaar | **164** | 6.51 S | 134.06 E |
| Taff ≃ | **42** | 51.27 N | 3.09 W |
| Tafiré | **150** | 9.04 N | 5.10 W |
| Tafí Viejo | **252** | 26.44 S | 65.16 W |
| Taflan | **130** | 41.25 N | 36.09 E |
| Tafna, Oued ≃ | **34** | 35.17 N | 1.30 W |
| Tafo | **150** | 6.13 N | 0.22 W |
| Tafraoute | **148** | 29.40 N | 8.58 W |
| Taft, Īrān | **128** | 31.45 N | 54.14 E |
| Taft, Pil. | **116** | 11.54 N | 125.25 E |
| Taft, Ca., U.S. | **204** | 35.08 N | 119.27 W |
| Taft, Fl., U.S. | **220** | 28.23 N | 81.24 W |
| Taft, Ok., U.S. | **196** | 35.45 N | 95.32 W |
| Taft, Tx., U.S. | **196** | 27.58 N | 97.23 W |
| Taftān, Kūh-e ∧ | **128** | 28.36 N | 61.08 E |
| Tafton | **210** | 41.25 N | 75.11 W |
| Taga, Nihon | **94** | 35.13 N | 136.17 E |
| Taga, Nihon | **270** | 34.49 N | 135.49 E |
| Taga, W. Sam. | **175a** | 13.46 S | 172.28 W |
| Tagabukid | **116** | 7.00 N | 126.21 E |
| Taga Dzong | **124** | 27.04 N | 89.53 E |
| Tagagawik ≃ | **180** | 66.30 N | 159.00 W |
| Tagaj | **80** | 54.18 N | 47.39 E |
| Tagajō | **92** | 38.20 N | 141.00 E |
| Tagan | **86** | 54.57 N | 77.18 E |
| Tagana-an | **116** | 9.42 N | 125.35 E |
| Taganrog | **83** | 47.12 N | 38.56 E |
| Taganrogskij zaliv ⊂ | **78** | 47.00 N | 38.23 E |
| Tagant □[4] | **150** | 18.20 N | 11.30 W |
| Tagânt ⊸[1] | **150** | 18.00 N | 12.00 W |
| Tagapula Island I | **116** | 12.04 N | 124.12 E |
| Tågarp | **41** | 55.56 N | 12.57 E |
| Tagauayan Island I | **116** | 10.58 N | 121.13 E |
| Tagawa | **96** | 33.38 N | 130.49 E |
| Tagaytay | **116** | 14.06 N | 120.56 E |
| Tagbara | **152** | 5.56 N | 21.09 E |
| Tagbilaran | **116** | 9.39 N | 123.51 E |
| Tagdempt → Tihert | **148** | 35.28 N | 1.21 E |
| Tage | **164** | 6.20 S | 143.20 E |
| Tageren Canal ≡ | **174q** | 9.33 N | 138.09 E |
| Taggia | **62** | 43.52 N | 7.51 E |
| Taghit | **148** | 30.55 N | 2.02 W |
| Taghkanic Creek ≃ | **210** | 42.13 N | 73.45 W |
| Taghmon | **48** | 52.18 N | 6.39 W |
| Tagig | **269f** | 14.32 N | 121.04 E |
| Tagig ≃ | **269f** | 14.31 N | 121.05 E |
| Tagish Lake ⊜ | **180** | 59.45 N | 134.15 W |
| Tagliacozzo | **66** | 42.04 N | 13.14 E |
| Tagliamento ≃ | **64** | 45.38 N | 13.06 E |
| Tagliata, Monte della ∧ | **64** | 44.34 N | 9.48 E |
| Taglio di Po | **64** | 45.00 N | 12.12 E |
| Tagna | **88** | 53.36 N | 101.54 E |
| Tagna ≃ | **88** | 53.38 N | 101.53 E |
| Tago | **116** | 9.02 N | 126.13 E |
| Tago ≃ | **116** | 9.01 N | 126.14 E |
| Tagoloan | **116** | 8.32 N | 124.45 E |
| Tagolo Point › | **116** | 8.44 N | 123.23 E |
| Tagon Harbour ⊂ | **162** | 33.53 S | 123.00 E |
| Tagounit | **148** | 29.58 N | 5.36 W |
| Tagourâret ⊤[4] | **150** | 17.45 N | 7.43 W |
| Tagow Bāy | **120** | 35.42 N | 66.03 E |
| Tagrina, Oued V | **148** | 21.00 N | 6.16 E |
| Taguatinga | **255** | 12.25 S | 46.26 W |
| Tagubanhan Island I | **116** | 11.08 N | 123.07 E |
| Tagudin | **116** | 16.56 N | 120.27 E |
| Taguedoufat V | **150** | 14.50 N | 7.42 E |
| Taguke | **120** | 32.07 N | 84.35 E |
| Tagul ≃ | **88** | 55.35 N | 97.45 E |
| Tagula Island I | **160** | 11.30 S | 153.30 E |
| Tagum | **116** | 7.28 N | 125.48 E |
| T'agun | **86** | 53.56 N | 85.38 E |
| Tagun Bay ⊂ | **116** | 13.55 N | 123.46 E |
| Tagus (Tejo) (Tajo) ≃ | **34** | 38.40 N | 9.24 W |
| T'agyŏng-ni | **98** | 38.04 N | 126.03 E |
| Tah, Sebkha ⊜ | **148** | 27.45 N | 12.42 W |
| Taha | **89** | 47.33 N | 124.14 E |
| Tahaa I | **14** | 16.38 S | 151.30 W |
| Tahakopa | **172** | 46.31 S | 169.23 E |
| Tahala | **148** | 34.04 N | 4.20 W |
| Tahan, Gunong ∧ | **114** | 4.38 N | 102.14 E |
| Tahanaoute | **148** | 31.24 N | 7.54 W |
| Tahāneh-ye Ney Basteh | **128** | 32.59 N | 60.53 E |
| Tahara | **94** | 34.40 N | 137.16 E |
| Tahart | **148** | 22.51 N | 5.12 E |
| Tahat ∧ | **148** | 23.18 N | 5.47 E |
| Taheke | **172** | 35.27 S | 173.39 E |
| Ṭāherī | **128** | 27.42 N | 52.21 E |
| Tahgong, Puntan › | **174n** | 15.06 N | 145.39 E |
| Tahifet | **148** | 22.58 N | 5.55 E |
| Tahiryuak Lake ⊜ | **176** | 70.56 N | 112.20 W |
| Tahiti I | **174s** | 17.37 S | 149.27 W |
| Tahkuna nina › | **76** | 59.07 N | 22.36 E |
| Tāhlāb (Ṭālāb) ≃ | **128** | 28.09 N | 62.45 E |
| Tahlequah | **196** | 35.54 N | 94.58 W |
| Ṭahmā wa Minshāt ʻAbd as-Sayyid | **142** | 29.38 N | 31.14 E |
| Tahmoor | **170** | 34.13 S | 150.36 E |
| Tahneta Pass )( | **180** | 61.53 N | 147.20 W |
| Tahoe, Lake ⊜ | **226** | 39.07 N | 120.03 W |
| Tahoe City | **226** | 39.10 N | 120.08 W |
| Tahoe Lake ⊜ | **176** | 70.15 N | 108.45 W |
| Tahoe Valley | **204** | 38.55 N | 120.00 W |
| Tahoka | **196** | 33.10 N | 101.47 W |
| Taholah | **224** | 47.20 N | 124.17 W |
| Tahoua | **150** | 14.54 N | 5.16 E |
| Tahoua □[5] | **150** | 16.00 N | 5.00 E |
| Tahquamenon ≃ | **190** | 46.34 N | 85.02 W |
| Tahquamenon Falls State Park ♠ | **190** | 46.29 N | 85.05 W |
| Tahsi | **100** | 24.57 N | 121.53 E |
| Tahsis | **182** | 49.55 N | 126.39 W |
| Ṭahṭā | **140** | 26.46 N | 31.30 E |
| Tahtaköprü | **130** | 39.57 N | 29.39 E |
| Tahtsa Lake ⊜ | **182** | 53.42 N | 127.26 W |
| Tahtsa Peak ∧ | **182** | 53.33 N | 127.47 W |
| Tahu | **100** | 24.26 N | 120.52 E |
| Tahuamanu ≃ | **248** | 11.06 S | 67.36 W |
| Tahuata I | **174x** | 9.57 S | 139.05 W |
| Tahulandang, Pulau I | **112** | 2.20 N | 125.25 E |
| Tahuna | **112** | 3.37 N | 125.29 E |
| Tahuofang ⊜[1] | **104** | 41.55 N | 124.07 E |
| Tahuya ≃ | **224** | 47.23 N | 123.03 W |
| Ṭahwāy | **142** | 30.22 N | 30.52 E |
| Taï, C. Iv. | **150** | 5.52 N | 7.27 W |
| Tai, It. | **64** | 46.25 N | 12.20 E |
| Tai, Nihon | **270** | 34.31 N | 135.26 E |
| Tai ⊸[8] | **270** | 34.45 N | 135.00 E |
| Taiaçupeba | **256** | 23.40 S | 46.11 W |
| Tai'an, Zhg. | **98** | 36.12 N | 117.07 E |
| Tai'an, Zhg. | **104** | 41.23 N | 122.27 E |
| Tai'an, Zhg. | **107** | 30.05 N | 105.47 E |
| Tai'angang | **106** | 31.43 N | 121.40 E |
| Taiarapu, Presqu'île de ›[1] | **174s** | 17.47 S | 149.14 W |
| Taibai | **102** | 34.00 N | 107.18 E |
| Taibai Shan ∧, Zhg. | **98** | 39.19 N | 114.11 E |
| Taibai Shan ∧, Zhg. | **102** | 33.54 N | 107.46 E |
| Taibon Agordino | **64** | 46.18 N | 12.00 E |
| Taibus Qi (Baochang) | **98** | 41.56 N | 115.22 E |
| Taicang | **106** | 31.26 N | 121.07 E |
| T'aichou → Taizhou | **100** | 32.30 N | 119.58 E |
| Taichu → T'aichung | **100** | 24.09 N | 120.41 E |
| T'aichung | **100** | 24.09 N | 120.41 E |
| Taicunzhen | **106** | 31.27 N | 119.03 E |
| Taiden → Taejŏn | **98** | 36.20 N | 127.26 E |
| Taiei | **94** | 35.49 N | 140.25 E |
| Taieri ≃ | **172** | 46.03 S | 170.11 E |
| Taif → Aṭ-Ṭā'if | **144** | 21.16 N | 40.24 E |
| Taigu | **102** | 37.28 N | 112.30 E |
| Tai Hang | **271d** | 22.17 N | 114.11 E |
| Taihang Shan ⋏ | **102** | 38.00 N | 114.00 E |
| Taihape | **172** | 39.40 S | 175.48 E |
| Taihe, Zhg. | **100** | 33.11 N | 115.36 E |
| Taihe, Zhg. | **100** | 26.49 N | 114.55 E |
| Taihe, Zhg. | **107** | 30.10 N | 105.56 E |
| Taihezhen, Zhg. | **89** | 44.47 N | 123.29 E |
| Taihezhen, Zhg. | **107** | 30.07 N | 103.50 E |
| Taihezhen, Zhg. | **107** | 30.06 N | 106.03 E |
| Taiho | **174m** | 26.39 N | 128.07 E |
| Taihoku → T'aipei | **100** | 25.03 N | 121.30 E |
| T'aihsi | **100** | 23.42 N | 120.11 E |
| T'aihsien → Taizhou | **100** | 32.30 N | 119.58 E |
| Taihu | **100** | 30.26 N | 116.16 E |
| Tai Hu ⊜ | **106** | 31.15 N | 120.10 E |
| Taijiang | **102** | 26.32 N | 108.22 E |
| Taijimiao | **98** | 40.55 N | 113.46 E |
| Taijüan → Taiyuan | **102** | 37.55 N | 112.30 E |
| Taikang | **98** | 34.04 N | 114.50 E |
| Taikkyi | **110** | 17.19 N | 95.58 E |
| Taikou | **102** | 31.53 N | 111.07 E |
| Taiko-yama ∧ | **96** | 35.46 N | 135.12 E |
| Taikyu → Taegu | **98** | 35.52 N | 128.35 E |
| Tailai | **89** | 46.23 N | 123.27 E |
| Tai Lam Chung | **271d** | 22.22 N | 114.01 E |
| Tai Lam Chung Reservoir ⊜[1] | **271d** | 22.23 N | 114.01 E |
| Tailem Bend | **166** | 35.16 S | 139.27 E |
| Tailfingen | **58** | 48.15 N | 9.01 E |
| Tai Long, H.K. | **271d** | 22.25 N | 114.22 E |
| Tai Long, H.K. | **271d** | 22.13 N | 113.59 E |
| Tai Long Bay ⊂ | **271d** | 22.24 N | 114.24 E |
| Taima, Nihon | **96** | 34.30 N | 135.42 E |
| T'aima, T'aiwan | **100** | 22.37 N | 120.59 E |
| Taimba | **74** | 60.18 N | 98.58 E |
| Taimei | **100** | 23.19 N | 114.29 E |
| Tai Mong Tsai | **271d** | 22.24 N | 114.18 E |
| Tai Mo Shan ∧ | **271d** | 22.25 N | 114.07 E |
| Taimyr-Halbinsel → Tajmyr, poluostrov ›[1] | **74** | 76.00 N | 104.00 E |
| Tain | **46** | 57.48 N | 4.04 W |
| Tainaka | **270** | 34.36 N | 135.37 E |
| T'ainan | **100** | 23.00 N | 120.12 E |
| Taínaron, Ákra › | **38** | 36.22 N | 22.30 E |
| Taining | **100** | 26.54 N | 117.09 E |
| Tain-l'Hermitage | **62** | 45.04 N | 4.51 E |
| Tai O, H.K. | **100** | 22.15 N | 113.51 E |
| Taio, It. | **64** | 46.20 N | 11.04 E |
| Taiobeiras | **255** | 15.49 S | 42.14 W |
| Tai Pang Wan ⊂ | **100** | 22.30 N | 114.24 E |
| T'aipei, T'aiwan | **100** | 25.03 N | 121.30 E |
| T'aipei, T'aiwan | **269d** | 25.03 N | 121.30 E |
| T'aipei □[6] | **269d** | 25.00 N | 121.40 E |
| Taipei Bridge ⊸[5] | **269d** | 25.04 N | 121.30 E |
| T'aipeihsien | **100** | 25.00 N | 121.27 E |
| Taipei Institute of Technology ʊ[2] | **269d** | 25.02 N | 121.32 E |
| Taipei New Park ♠ | **269d** | 25.03 N | 121.31 E |
| T'aipei Shih □[7] | **269d** | 25.05 N | 121.33 E |
| Taiping, Malay. | **114** | 4.51 N | 100.44 E |
| Taiping, Zhg. | **100** | 22.49 N | 113.41 E |
| Taiping, Zhg. | **100** | 30.18 N | 118.12 E |
| Taiping, Zhg. | **102** | 22.40 N | 107.05 E |
| Taiping, Zhg. | **107** | 30.24 N | 103.37 E |
| Taipingchang, Zhg. | **102** | 27.25 N | 103.04 E |
| Taipingchang, Zhg. | **107** | 29.53 N | 106.04 E |
| Taipingchang, Zhg. | **107** | 29.55 N | 103.49 E |
| Taipingchang, Zhg. | **107** | 30.10 N | 106.21 E |
| Taipingchang, Zhg. | **107** | 30.39 N | 105.54 E |
| Taipingchang, Zhg. | **107** | 30.25 N | 103.46 E |
| Taipingchang, Zhg. | **107** | 29.33 N | 103.33 E |
| Taipingchuan, Zhg. | **89** | 44.23 N | 123.11 E |
| Taipingchuan, Zhg. | **98** | 42.36 N | 127.20 E |
| Taipingdian | **102** | 32.08 N | 111.45 E |
| Taipingkou | **100** | 29.50 N | 113.35 E |
| Taipingling | **89** | 43.26 N | 128.09 E |
| Taipingshan, Zhg. | **98** | 40.34 N | 122.25 E |
| Taipingshan, Zhg. | **104** | 41.36 N | 123.41 E |
| Taipingshao | **98** | 40.54 N | 125.08 E |
| Taipingsi | **107** | 29.24 N | 103.34 E |
| Taipingxigou | **104** | 42.36 N | 121.13 E |
| Taipingzhai | **104** | 42.14 N | 124.07 E |
| Taipingzhen, Zhg. | **89** | 46.44 N | 130.44 E |
| Taipingzhen, Zhg. | **102** | 35.42 N | 107.37 E |
| Taipingzhen, Zhg. | **107** | 29.24 N | 105.47 E |
| Taipingzhen, Zhg. | **107** | 30.26 N | 104.12 E |
| Taipingzhuang, Zhg. | **104** | 42.38 N | 123.45 E |
| Taipingzhuang, Zhg. | **105** | 40.03 N | 116.24 E |
| Taipingzhuang, Zhg. | **105** | 40.08 N | 117.36 E |
| Tai Po Hoi ⊂ | **271d** | 22.26 N | 114.12 E |
| Tai Po Tsai | **271d** | 22.21 N | 114.15 E |
| Taipu | **250** | 5.37 S | 35.36 W |
| Taira, Nihon | **94** | 36.26 N | 136.57 E |
| Taira → Iwaki, Nihon | **94** | 37.03 N | 140.55 E |
| Tairetá | **256** | 22.36 S | 43.42 W |
| Tairiqiao | **106** | 30.59 N | 121.33 E |
| Tais | **112** | 4.06 S | 102.34 E |
| Taisen-zan ∧ | **96** | 33.06 N | 131.17 E |
| Taisha → Izumo, Nihon | **96** | 35.22 N | 132.46 E |
| Taisha, Nihon | **96** | 35.24 N | 132.40 E |
| Taishaku-kyō ♠ | **96** | 34.53 N | 133.13 E |
| Taishaku-zan ∧, Nihon | **94** | 36.58 N | 139.28 E |
| Taishaku-zan ∧, Nihon | **270** | 34.47 N | 135.07 E |
| Taishan, Zhg. | **98** | 39.01 N | 113.36 E |
| Taishan, Zhg. | **102** | 22.16 N | 112.44 E |
| Taishanchang | **107** | 30.32 N | 106.42 E |
| Taishi, Nihon | **96** | 34.50 N | 134.33 E |
| Taishi, Nihon | **270** | 34.31 N | 135.39 E |
| Taishō | **96** | 33.12 N | 132.58 E |
| Taishō ⊸[8] | **270** | 34.38 N | 135.27 E |
| Tai Shui Hang | **271d** | 22.25 N | 14.13 E |
| Taishun | **100** | 27.33 N | 119.43 E |
| Tai Tam Bay ⊂ | **271d** | 22.13 N | 114.13 E |
| Taitao, Península de ›[1] | **254** | 46.30 S | 74.25 W |
| Taitapu | **172** | 43.40 S | 172.33 E |
| Taitō ⊸[8] | **268** | 35.43 N | 139.47 E |
| Tai Tong | **271d** | 22.25 N | 114.01 E |
| Taitouying | **98** | 40.02 N | 119.12 E |
| Taitō-zaki › | **94** | 35.18 N | 140.25 E |
| T'aitung | **100** | 22.45 N | 121.09 E |
| Taivalkoski | **26** | 65.34 N | 28.15 E |
| Tai Wan | **271d** | 22.10 N | 114.15 E |
| Taiwan (T'aiwan) □[1], Asia | **90** | 23.30 N | 121.00 E |
| Taiwan (T'aiwan) □[1], Asia | **100** | 23.30 N | 121.00 E |
| T'aiwan I | **100** | 23.30 N | 121.00 E |
| Taiwan Strait ⋃ | **100** | 24.00 N | 119.00 E |
| Tai Wan Tau | **271d** | 22.18 N | 114.17 E |
| Taixi | **100** | 24.42 N | 116.56 E |
| Taixian | **100** | 32.31 N | 120.09 E |
| Taixing | **106** | 32.11 N | 120.01 E |
| Taixizhen | **106** | 31.03 N | 119.49 E |
| Taiyang | **100** | 30.12 N | 119.19 E |
| Taiyanggong | **271a** | 39.58 N | 116.25 E |
| Taíyetos Óros ⋏ | **38** | 37.00 N | 22.20 E |
| Ṭaiyiba | **132** | 32.16 N | 35.01 E |
| Taiyuan | **102** | 37.55 N | 112.30 E |
| Taizhao | **120** | 30.01 N | 93.08 E |
| Taizhou | **100** | 32.30 N | 119.58 E |
| Taizhou Liedao II | **100** | 28.30 N | 121.53 E |
| Taizi ≃ | **98** | 41.00 N | 122.26 E |
| Ta'izz | **144** | 13.38 N | 44.04 E |
| Tāj al-ʻIzz | **142** | 30.57 N | 31.35 E |
| Tajarḥī | **146** | 24.21 N | 14.28 E |
| Tajbola | **24** | 68.26 N | 33.19 E |
| Tajdakovo | **82** | 54.29 N | 37.32 E |
| Tajerouine | **36** | 35.54 N | 8.34 E |
| Tajetteret, Oued V | **148** | 21.20 N | 7.22 E |
| Tajga | **86** | 56.04 N | 85.37 E |
| Tajgonos, mys › | **74** | 60.35 N | 160.08 E |
| Tajgonos, poluostrov ›[1] | **74** | 61.20 N | 161.00 E |
| Tajikistan □[1], Asia | **72** | 39.00 N | 71.00 E |
| Tajikistan □[1], Asia | **85** | 39.00 N | 71.00 E |
| Tajikstan → Tajikistan □[1] | **72** | 39.00 N | 71.00 E |
| Tajima | **94** | 37.12 N | 139.46 E |
| Tajimi | **94** | 35.19 N | 137.08 E |
| Tajique | **200** | 34.45 N | 106.17 W |
| Tajiri | **270** | 34.24 N | 135.18 E |
| Tajitos | **232** | 30.58 N | 112.18 W |
| Tajlakdžegen | **86** | 43.54 N | 60.29 E |
| Tajlakovy | **86** | 59.20 N | 74.04 E |
| Tāj Mahal ⊥ | **124** | 27.10 N | 78.03 E |
| Tajmura ≃ | **72** | 63.46 N | 98.01 E |
| Tajmyr, ozero ⊜ | **74** | 74.30 N | 102.30 E |
| Tajmyr, poluostrov ›[1] | **74** | 76.00 N | 104.00 E |
| Tajna | **88** | 56.27 N | 95.30 E |
| Tajninka | **265b** | 55.54 N | 37.45 E |
| Tajo → Tagus ≃ | **34** | 38.40 N | 9.24 W |
| Tajožnyj, Ross. | **86** | 56.09 N | 94.29 E |
| Tajožnyj, Ross. | **88** | 56.13 N | 94.55 E |
| Tajpur, India | **124** | 25.51 N | 85.41 E |
| Tajpur, India | **124** | 29.10 N | 78.29 E |
| Tājpur, India | **272b** | 22.44 N | 88.16 E |
| Tajpur Khurd ⊸[8] | **272a** | 28.35 N | 77.03 E |
| Tajšet | **88** | 55.57 N | 98.00 E |
| Tajsojgan | **80** | 48.19 N | 53.29 E |
| Tajturka | **88** | 52.51 N | 103.28 E |
| Tajumulco, Volcán ∧[1] | **236** | 15.02 N | 91.55 W |
| Tajuña ≃ | **34** | 40.07 N | 3.35 W |
| Tājūrā', Lībiyā | **146** | 32.53 N | 13.21 E |
| Tajura, Ross. | **88** | 57.00 N | 106.35 E |
| Tajura ≃ | **88** | 57.00 N | 106.35 E |
| Tajžina | **86** | 53.38 N | 87.28 E |
| Tak | **110** | 16.52 N | 99.08 E |
| Takāb | **128** | 36.24 N | 47.07 E |
| Takabanare-jima I | **174m** | 26.22 N | 127.59 E |
| Takabara | **150** | 11.50 N | 11.30 W |
| Takachiho | **92** | 32.42 N | 131.18 E |
| Takachu | **156** | 22.37 S | 21.58 E |
| Takada → Bungo-takada, Nihon | **96** | 33.33 N | 131.27 E |
| Takada → Yamato-takada, Nihon | **96** | 34.31 N | 135.45 E |
| Takagi | **268** | 35.56 N | 139.35 E |
| Takahagi | **94** | 36.43 N | 140.43 E |
| Takahama, Nihon | **94** | 34.55 N | 136.59 E |
| Takahama, Nihon | **94** | 37.00 N | 136.46 E |
| Takahama, Nihon | **96** | 35.29 N | 135.33 E |

ENGLISH

| Name | Page | Lat.°′ | Long.°′ |
|---|---|---|---|
| Takahara ≃ | **94** | 36.28 N | 137.15 E |
| Takahashi | **96** | 34.47 N | 133.37 E |
| Takahashi ≃ | **96** | 34.31 N | 133.42 E |
| Takahe, Mount ∧ | **9** | 76.16 S | 112.14 W |
| Takaido ⊸[8] | **268** | 35.40 N | 139.37 E |
| Takaishi | **96** | 34.32 N | 135.26 E |
| Takaka | **172** | 40.51 S | 172.48 E |
| Takakkaw Falls ∟ | **182** | 51.30 N | 116.28 W |
| Takalaou | **146** | 10.07 N | 19.48 E |
| Takalar | **112** | 5.28 S | 119.24 E |
| Takamatsu, Nihon | **94** | 36.46 N | 136.43 E |
| Takamatsu, Nihon | **96** | 34.20 N | 134.03 E |
| Takami-shima I | **96** | 34.19 N | 133.41 E |
| Takamiya | **96** | 34.47 N | 132.44 E |
| Takami-yama ∧ | **94** | 34.25 N | 136.05 E |
| Takamori | **94** | 35.33 N | 137.53 E |
| Takanabe | **92** | 32.08 N | 131.30 E |
| Takanawa-hantō ›[1] | **96** | 33.58 N | 132.56 E |
| Takanawa-san ∧ | **96** | 33.56 N | 132.51 E |
| Takane, Nihon | **94** | 36.02 N | 137.29 E |
| Takane, Nihon | **94** | 35.50 N | 138.25 E |
| Takanezawa | **94** | 36.37 N | 139.59 E |
| Takano | **96** | 35.02 N | 132.55 E |
| Takanosu | **92** | 40.13 N | 140.22 E |
| Takao → Kaohsiung | **100** | 22.38 N | 120.17 E |
| Takaoka | **94** | 36.45 N | 137.01 E |
| Takao-kokutei-kōen ♠ | **94** | 35.38 N | 139.15 E |
| Takao-san ∧, Nihon | **94** | 35.38 N | 139.15 E |
| Takao-san ∧, Nihon | **270** | 34.49 N | 135.51 E |
| Takapau | **172** | 40.02 S | 176.21 E |
| Takapuna | **172** | 36.47 S | 174.47 E |
| Takara-jima I | **93b** | 29.09 N | 129.13 E |
| Takarazuka | **270** | 34.49 N | 135.21 E |
| Takasago | **96** | 34.45 N | 134.48 E |
| Takasaki | **94** | 36.20 N | 139.01 E |
| Takase | **96** | 34.10 N | 133.45 E |
| Takase ≃ | **94** | 36.28 N | 137.52 E |
| Takashima, Nihon | **92** | 32.39 N | 129.45 E |
| Takashima, Nihon | **94** | 35.18 N | 136.01 E |
| Taka-shima I | **96** | 34.50 N | 131.50 E |
| Takashippu | **174m** | 26.24 N | 127.44 E |
| Takasu | **94** | 35.57 N | 136.53 E |
| Takata → Rikuzen-takata, Nihon | **92** | 39.01 N | 141.38 E |
| Takata → Joetsu, Nihon | **94** | 37.06 N | 138.15 E |
| Takata, Nihon | **96** | 33.06 N | 130.28 E |
| Takatō | **94** | 35.50 N | 138.04 E |
| Takatomi | **94** | 35.29 N | 136.47 E |
| Takatori | **96** | 34.27 N | 135.48 E |
| Takatori-yama ∧ | **96** | 33.18 N | 130.43 E |
| Takatori-yama ∧[2] | **268** | 35.18 N | 139.37 E |
| Takatsu ≃ | **96** | 34.42 N | 131.49 E |
| Takatsuki, Nihon | **94** | 35.28 N | 136.14 E |
| Takatsuki, Nihon | **96** | 34.51 N | 135.37 E |
| Takaungu | **154** | 3.41 S | 39.51 E |
| Ta-kaw | **110** | 21.36 N | 98.56 E |
| Takayama, Nihon | **94** | 36.08 N | 137.15 E |
| Takayama, Nihon | **94** | 36.37 N | 138.57 E |
| Takayama, Nihon | **94** | 36.40 N | 138.21 E |
| Takayama, Nihon | **270** | 34.45 N | 135.44 E |
| Takayanagi, Nihon | **94** | 37.13 N | 138.38 E |
| Takayanagi, Nihon | **268** | 35.25 N | 139.57 E |
| Tak Bai | **114** | 6.16 N | 102.03 E |
| Takčijan | **85** | 38.32 N | 68.03 E |
| Takebe | **96** | 34.52 N | 133.54 E |
| Takefu | **94** | 35.54 N | 136.10 E |
| Takehara | **96** | 34.21 N | 132.55 E |
| Takeli | **85** | 40.30 N | 69.25 E |
| Takenake | **120** | 34.11 N | 81.20 E |
| Takengon | **114** | 4.38 N | 96.50 E |
| Takeno ≃ | **96** | 35.45 N | 135.06 E |
| Takenotsuka ⊸[8] | **268** | 35.48 N | 139.48 E |
| Takeo | **92** | 33.12 N | 130.01 E |
| Takeoka | **268** | 35.12 N | 139.51 E |
| Tåkern ⊜ | **26** | 58.21 N | 14.48 E |
| Takeshi | **94** | 36.17 N | 138.14 E |
| Take-shima I | **93b** | 30.49 N | 130.26 E |
| Take-shima (Tok-to) II | **92** | 37.17 N | 131.53 E |
| Tākestān | **128** | 36.04 N | 49.43 E |
| Taketa | **96** | 32.58 N | 131.24 E |
| Taketoyo | **94** | 34.51 N | 136.55 E |
| Takêv | **110** | 10.59 N | 104.47 E |
| Take-yama ∧[2] | **268** | 35.13 N | 139.39 E |
| Takhādīd ⊤[4] | **128** | 29.59 N | 44.30 E |
| Takhār □[4] | **120** | 36.30 N | 69.30 E |
| Takhatpur | **124** | 22.09 N | 81.52 E |
| Takhli | **110** | 15.15 N | 100.21 E |
| Ta Khoa | **110** | 21.13 N | 104.18 E |
| Takht-e Jamshīd ⊥ | **128** | 29.57 N | 52.52 E |
| Takht-i-Bhāi | **123** | 34.17 N | 71.56 E |
| Tāki, India | **126** | 22.36 N | 88.55 E |
| Taki, Nihon | **94** | 34.30 N | 136.33 E |
| Taki, Nihon | **96** | 35.16 N | 132.38 E |
| Taki, Pap. N. Gui. | **175e** | 6.29 S | 155.50 E |
| Takijuk Lake ⊜ | **176** | 66.15 N | 113.05 W |
| Takikawa | **92a** | 43.33 N | 141.54 E |
| Takino | **96** | 34.56 N | 134.58 E |
| Takipur | **126** | 24.19 N | 87.58 E |
| Takitimu Mountains ⋏ | **172** | 45.41 S | 167.53 E |
| Takla Lake ⊜ | **182** | 55.25 N | 125.53 W |
| Takla Landing | **182** | 55.29 N | 125.58 W |
| Takla Makan → Taklimakan Shamo ⊸[2] | **90** | 39.00 N | 83.00 E |
| Taklimakan Shamo ⊸[2] | **90** | 39.00 N | 83.00 E |
| Tako | **94** | 35.44 N | 140.28 E |
| Takob | **85** | 38.50 N | 68.57 E |
| Tako-bana › | **96** | 35.36 N | 133.06 E |
| Takolekaju, Pegunungan ⋏ | **112** | 2.00 S | 121.00 E |
| Takoma Park | **284c** | 38.58 N | 77.00 W |
| Takoradi → Sekondi-Takoradi | **150** | 4.59 N | 1.43 W |
| Takotna | **180** | 62.56 N | 156.04 W |
| Takow → Kaohsiung | **100** | 22.38 N | 120.17 E |
| Takpochao, Okso ∧ | **174n** | 15.11 N | 145.45 E |
| Takrouna | **36** | 36.09 N | 10.20 E |
| Taksimo | **88** | 51.03 N | 107.50 E |
| Taksino | **82** | 56.19 N | 36.10 E |
| Takslesluk Lake ⊜ | **180** | 61.04 N | 162.55 W |
| Taksony | **264c** | 47.20 N | 19.04 E |
| Taku | **92** | 33.17 N | 130.08 E |
| Taku ≃ | **180** | 58.26 N | 133.59 W |
| Takuan, Mount ∧ | **175e** | 6.27 S | 155.36 E |
| Takua Pa | **110** | 8.53 N | 98.21 E |
| Taku Glacier ⊓ | **180** | 58.35 N | 134.10 W |
| Takum | **150** | 7.17 N | 9.59 E |
| Takuma | **96** | 34.13 N | 133.40 E |
| Takundi | **152** | 4.45 S | 16.34 E |
| Takutea I | **14** | 19.49 S | 158.18 W |
| Takut Tangub Bay ⊂ | **116** | 6.33 N | 122.15 E |
| Takutu (Tacutu) ≃ | **246** | 3.01 N | 60.29 W |
| Takuu Islands II | **14** | 4.45 S | 157.00 E |
| Takysie Lake | **182** | 53.54 N | 125.53 W |
| Tāl | **123** | 34.55 N | 72.13 E |
| Tala, Bngl. | **126** | 22.46 N | 89.16 E |
| Tāla, India | **124** | 23.43 N | 81.02 E |
| Tala, Méx. | **234** | 20.40 N | 103.42 W |
| Talā, Miṣr | **142** | 30.41 N | 30.56 E |
| Tala, Ur. | **252** | 34.21 S | 55.46 W |
| Tala, Arroyo del ≃ | **258** | 33.37 S | 56.34 W |
| Ṭālāb (Tāhlāb) ≃ | **128** | 28.09 N | 62.45 E |
| Talacogon | **116** | 8.28 N | 125.46 E |
| Talačyn | **76** | 54.25 N | 29.42 E |
| Talaga | **112** | 2.11 S | 125.53 E |
| Talagang | **123** | 32.55 N | 72.25 E |
| Talagante | **252** | 33.40 S | 70.56 W |
| Talagou | **104** | 41.37 N | 120.32 E |
| Ta Lai | **110** | 11.24 N | 107.23 E |
| Talaimannar | **122** | 9.05 N | 79.44 E |
| Talāja | **120** | 21.21 N | 72.03 E |
| Talak ⊸[1] | **150** | 18.20 N | 6.00 E |
| Talakag | **116** | 8.16 N | 124.37 E |
| Talakan | **89** | 49.38 N | 133.18 E |
| Talakivka | **83** | 47.10 N | 37.43 E |

DEUTSCH

| Name | Seite | Breite°′ | Länge°′ E = Ost |
|---|---|---|---|
| Tālāla | **120** | 21.02 N | 70.32 E |
| Talalayivka | **78** | 50.51 N | 33.08 E |
| Talamanca, Cordillera de ⋏ | **236** | 9.30 N | 83.40 W |
| Talamba | **123** | 30.32 N | 72.14 E |
| Talamone | **66** | 42.33 N | 11.08 E |
| Talana, It. | **71** | 40.02 N | 9.30 E |
| Talana, S. Afr. | **158** | 28.10 S | 30.15 E |
| Talandža | **89** | 49.27 N | 131.35 E |
| Talang, Gunung ∧ | **112** | 0.58 S | 100.39 E |
| Talangbatu | **112** | 4.06 S | 105.29 E |
| Talangbetutu | **112** | 2.53 S | 104.41 E |
| Talangpadang | **112** | 5.21 S | 104.11 E |
| Talangrimbo | **112** | 3.29 S | 105.25 E |
| Talant | **58** | 47.19 N | 5.00 E |
| Talap | **80** | 48.26 N | 48.03 E |
| Talara | **246** | 4.34 S | 81.17 W |
| Talarrubias | **34** | 39.02 N | 5.14 W |
| Talas | **85** | 42.32 N | 72.14 E |
| Talas □[4] | **85** | 42.30 N | 72.00 E |
| Talas ≃ | **85** | 44.02 N | 69.37 E |
| Talasea | **164** | 5.20 S | 150.05 E |
| Talasskij-Alatau, chrebet ⋏ | **85** | 42.10 N | 72.00 E |
| Talatakoh, Pulau I | **112** | 0.22 S | 122.05 E |
| Tal'at al-Jamā'ah, Rujm ∧ | **132** | 30.23 N | 35.30 E |
| Talata Mafara | **150** | 12.35 N | 6.04 E |
| Talaud, Kepulauan II | **108** | 4.20 N | 126.50 E |
| Talavera | **116** | 15.35 N | 120.55 E |
| Talavera de la Reina | **34** | 39.57 N | 4.50 W |
| Talawdī | **140** | 10.38 N | 30.23 E |
| Talayan | **116** | 6.55 N | 124.24 E |
| Tālbāndh | **126** | 22.03 N | 86.20 E |
| Talbingo | **171b** | 35.34 S | 148.18 E |
| Talbingo Reservoir ⊜[1] | **171b** | 35.43 S | 148.20 E |
| Talbot | **169** | 37.11 S | 143.43 E |
| Talbot ≃ | **212** | 44.28 N | 79.10 W |
| Talbot, Cape › | **164** | 13.48 S | 126.43 E |
| Talbot Brook | **168a** | 32.01 S | 116.40 E |
| Talbot Brook ≃ | **168a** | 32.10 S | 116.49 E |
| Talbot Islands II | **164** | 9.15 S | 142.08 E |
| Talbot Lake ⊜, Mb., Can. | **184** | 54.00 N | 99.55 W |
| Talbot Lake ⊜, On., Can. | **212** | 44.42 N | 78.51 W |
| Talbotton | **192** | 32.40 N | 84.32 W |
| Talbotville Royal | **214** | 42.48 N | 81.15 W |
| Talbragar ≃ | **166** | 32.12 S | 148.37 E |
| Talca | **252** | 35.26 S | 71.40 W |
| Talcahuano | **252** | 36.43 S | 73.07 W |
| Tālcher | **120** | 20.57 N | 85.13 E |
| Talchichitle, Isla I | **232** | 24.59 N | 108.04 W |
| Talco | **196** | 33.21 N | 95.06 W |
| Talcottville | **207** | 41.49 N | 72.30 W |
| Talcy, Château de ⊥ | **50** | 47.46 N | 1.27 E |
| Taldan | **89** | 53.40 N | 124.48 E |
| Tāldāngra | **126** | 23.02 N | 87.06 E |
| Taldom | **82** | 56.44 N | 37.32 E |
| Taldyapan, Kaz. | **80** | 48.07 N | 47.08 E |
| Taldyapan, Kaz. | **80** | 49.46 N | 50.14 E |
| Taldyk, pereval )( | **85** | 39.47 N | 73.11 E |
| Taldykorgan | **86** | 45.00 N | 78.23 E |
| Taldykorgan □[8] | **86** | 45.30 N | 78.30 E |
| Taldykuduk | **80** | 50.09 N | 49.33 E |
| Tale | **150** | 9.26 N | 1.07 W |
| Taleex | **144** | 9.09 N | 48.26 E |
| Talence | **32** | 44.49 N | 0.35 W |
| Talent | **202** | 42.14 N | 122.47 W |
| Tālesh | **128** | 37.48 N | 48.55 E |
| Taley | **152** | 6.40 N | 16.23 E |
| Talgar | **85** | 43.18 N | 77.18 E |
| Talgar, pik ∧ | **85** | 43.05 N | 77.20 E |
| Talgarreg | **42** | 52.08 N | 4.18 W |
| Talgarth | **42** | 52.00 N | 3.15 W |
| Ṭalḥ, 'Ilw aṭ- ∧[2] | **142** | 28.30 N | 29.38 E |
| Talhār | **120** | 24.53 N | 68.49 E |
| Tali, Pointe de › | **241o** | 15.56 N | 61.12 W |
| Talia, Austl. | **162** | 33.19 S | 134.54 E |
| Talia, Méx. | **196** | 25.44 N | 102.26 W |
| Taliabu, Pulau I | **112** | 1.48 S | 124.48 E |
| Talian Dao I | **98** | 39.03 N | 122.52 E |
| Talibon | **116** | 10.09 N | 124.19 E |
| Talibong, Ko I | **110** | 7.15 N | 99.23 E |
| Talica, Ross. | **76** | 58.44 N | 41.34 E |
| Talica, Ross. | **80** | 58.01 N | 51.30 E |
| Talica, Ross. | **86** | 57.00 N | 63.43 E |
| Talickij Čamlyk | **80** | 52.02 N | 40.32 E |
| Talien → Dalian | **98** | 38.53 N | 121.35 E |
| Talihina | **196** | 34.45 N | 95.02 W |
| Tālīkota | **122** | 16.29 N | 76.19 E |
| Talikud Island I | **116** | 6.56 N | 125.42 E |
| Talim Island I | **116** | 14.21 N | 121.14 E |
| Talimuashili | **85** | 39.08 N | 77.03 E |
| Taling Chan | **269a** | 13.46 N | 100.27 E |
| Taliouine | **148** | 30.36 N | 7.49 W |
| Taliparamba | **122** | 12.03 N | 75.21 E |
| Tali Post | **140** | 5.54 N | 30.47 E |
| Talisay, Pil. | **116** | 10.15 N | 123.51 E |
| Talisay, Pil. | **116** | 14.08 N | 122.55 E |
| Talisay, Pil. | **116** | 10.44 N | 122.58 E |
| Talisayan | **116** | 9.00 N | 124.55 E |
| Talisei, Pulau I | **112** | 1.51 N | 125.05 E |
| Talish-Mikeyli | **84** | 39.23 N | 48.22 E |
| Talish Mountains (Kūhhā-ye Ṭavālesh) ⋏ | **128** | 38.42 N | 48.18 E |
| Talisker | **46** | 57.17 N | 6.27 W |
| Taliwang | **115b** | 8.44 S | 116.52 E |
| Tal'ka | **76** | 53.22 N | 28.21 E |
| Talkeetna | **180** | 62.20 N | 150.07 W |
| Talkeetna Mountains ⋏ | **180** | 62.10 N | 148.15 W |
| Ṭalkhā | **142** | 31.03 N | 31.22 E |
| Talkheh ≃ | **128** | 37.52 N | 45.53 E |
| Talladale | **46** | 57.42 N | 5.29 W |
| Talladega | **194** | 33.26 N | 86.06 W |
| Tall 'Afar | **128** | 36.22 N | 42.27 E |
| Tallaght | **48** | 53.17 N | 6.21 W |
| Tal Lah, India | **126** | 22.19 N | 87.18 E |
| Tallah, Miṣr | **142** | 28.05 N | 30.44 E |
| Tallahaga Creek ≃ | **194** | 32.55 N | 88.58 W |
| Tallahala Creek ≃ | **194** | 31.12 N | 89.05 W |
| Tallahassee | **192** | 30.26 N | 84.16 W |
| Tallahatchie ≃ | **194** | 33.33 N | 90.10 W |
| Tall al-Abyaḍ | **130** | 36.41 N | 38.57 E |
| Tall al-ʻAmārnah (Akhetatem) ⊥ | **142** | 27.38 N | 30.54 E |
| Tall al-Maskhūtah (Succotah) ⊥ | **142** | 30.33 N | 32.07 E |
| Tall al-Muqayyar (Ur) ⊥ | **128** | 30.57 N | 46.09 E |
| Tallanalla | **168a** | 33.06 S | 116.07 E |
| Tallangatta | **166** | 36.13 S | 147.15 E |
| Tallangatta Creek ≃ | **171b** | 36.15 S | 147.13 E |
| Tallapoosa | **194** | 33.44 N | 85.17 W |
| Tallapoosa ≃ | **194** | 32.30 N | 86.16 W |
| Tallard | **62** | 44.28 N | 6.03 E |
| Talla Reservoir ⊜[1] | **46** | 55.29 N | 3.24 W |
| Tall ar-Ratābah (Pithom) ⊥ | **142** | 30.32 N | 32.06 E |
| Tall ar-Rubʻ (Mendes) ⊥ | **142** | 30.58 N | 31.31 E |
| Tallassee | **194** | 32.32 N | 85.53 W |
| Tall as-Sulṭān ⊥ | **132** | 31.52 N | 35.27 E |
| Tall Banī ʻUmrān | **142** | 27.40 N | 30.54 E |
| Tall Basṭah (Bubastis) ⊥ | **142** | 30.34 N | 31.31 E |
| Tällberg | **26** | 60.49 N | 15.00 E |
| Tall Bīsah | **130** | 34.50 N | 36.44 E |
| Tall-e Khosrow-ye Soflá | **128** | 30.37 N | 51.35 E |
| Talleyville | **208** | 39.48 N | 75.32 W |
| Tallinn | **76** | 59.25 N | 24.45 E |
| Tall Kalakh | **130** | 34.40 N | 36.15 E |
| Tall Kayf | **128** | 36.29 N | 43.08 E |
| Tall Kūjik | **130** | 36.48 N | 42.04 E |
| Tallmadge | **214** | 41.06 N | 81.27 W |
| Tallman | **276** | 41.07 N | 74.06 W |


**Symbols** in the index entries represent the broad categories identified in the key at the right. Symbols with superior numbers (⋏[1]) identify subcategories (see complete key on page *I · 1).*

**Symbole** im Register stellen die rechts im Schlüssel erklärten Kategorien dar. Symbole mit hochgestellten Ziffern (⋏[1]) bezeichnen Unterabteilungen einer Kategorie (vgl. vollständiger Schlüssel auf Seite *I · 1).*

**Los símbolos** incluídos en el texto del índice representan las grandes categorías identificadas con la clave a la derecha. Los símbolos con numeros en su parte superior (⋏[1]) identifican las subcategorías (véase la clave completa en la página *I · 1).*

**Les symboles** de l'index représentent les catégories indiquées dans la légende à droite. Les symboles suivis d'un indice (⋏[1]) représentent des sous-catégories (voir légende complète à la page *I · 1).*

**Os símbolos** incluídos no texto do índice representam as grandes categorias identificadas com a chave à direita. Os símbolos com números em sua parte superior (⋏[1]) identificam as subcategorias (veja-se a chave completa à página *I · 1).*

| | | | | |
|---|---|---|---|---|
| ∧ Mountain | Berg | Montaña | Montagne | Montanha |
| ⋏ Mountains | Gebirge | Montañas | Montagnes | Montanhas |
| )( Pass | Paß | Paso | Col | Passo |
| V Valley, Canyon | Tal, Cañon | Valle, Cañón | Vallée, Canyon | Vale, Canhão |
| ≃ Plain | Ebene | Llano | Plaine | Planície |
| › Cape | Kap | Cabo | Cap | Cabo |
| I Island | Insel | Isla | Île | Ilha |
| II Islands | Inseln | Islas | Îles | Ilhas |
| ± Other Topographic Features | Andere Topographische Objekte | Otros Elementos Topográficos | Autres données topographiques | Outros acidentes topográficos |

ESPAÑOL · FRANÇAIS · PORTUGUÊS


| Nombre / Nom / Nome | Página / Page | Lat.°′ | Long.°′ W = Oeste / Ouest |
|---|---|---|---|
| Tallman Mountain State Park ♦ | 276 | 41.01 N | 73.54 W |
| Talloires | 62 | 45.51 N | 6.13 E |
| Tallong | 170 | 34.44 S | 150.05 E |
| Tallow | 48 | 52.05 N | 8.00 W |
| Tallowa Dam ◆[6] | 170 | 34.47 S | 150.18 E |
| Tall Rāk | 142 | 30.54 N | 31.43 E |
| Tall Rif'at | 130 | 36.28 N | 37.06 E |
| Tall Salḥab | 130 | 35.15 N | 36.22 E |
| Tall Tamir | 130 | 36.39 N | 40.22 E |
| Tallula | 219 | 39.56 N | 89.56 W |
| Tallulah | 194 | 32.24 N | 91.11 W |
| Tally | 80 | 53.08 N | 53.04 E |
| Tally Ho | 274b | 37.52 S | 145.09 E |
| Tālma | 126 | 23.29 N | 89.54 E |
| Talmage, Ca., U.S. | 204 | 39.08 N | 123.10 W |
| Talmage, Ne., U.S. | 198 | 40.31 N | 96.01 W |
| Talmage, Pa., U.S. | 208 | 40.07 N | 76.13 W |
| Talmalmo | 171b | 35.56 S | 147.30 E |
| Talmas | 50 | 50.02 N | 2.20 E |
| Talmaz | 38 | 46.38 N | 29.40 E |
| Tal'menka | 86 | 53.51 N | 83.35 E |
| Talmine | 46 | 58.31 N | 4.26 W |
| Talmont | 32 | 46.28 N | 1.37 W |
| Tal'ne | 78 | 48.53 N | 30.42 E |
| Tal'niki | 88 | 52.47 N | 102.24 E |
| Talo ∧ | 144 | 10.44 N | 37.55 E |
| Taloda | 120 | 21.34 N | 74.13 E |
| Talofofo | 174p | 13.21 N | 144.45 E |
| Talofofo Bay ⊂ | 174p | 13.20 N | 144.46 E |
| Taloga | 196 | 36.02 N | 98.57 W |
| Taloje | 88 | 55.24 N | 95.40 E |
| Taloje Budrukh | 272c | 19.05 N | 73.05 E |
| Talok | 112 | 1.03 N | 118.48 E |
| Talon, Lake ⊜ | 190 | 46.18 N | 79.05 W |
| Talonan, Tano › | 115b | 9.07 S | 117.02 E |
| Tāloqān | 120 | 36.44 N | 69.33 E |
| Taloro ≏ | 71 | 40.08 N | 8.58 E |
| Talovaja | 78 | 51.06 N | 40.44 E |
| Talovka, Kaz. | 80 | 50.25 N | 47.35 E |
| Talovka, Ross. | 80 | 49.58 N | 45.01 E |
| Talovka, Ross. | 84 | 44.14 N | 46.36 E |
| Talovka, Ross. | 86 | 51.27 N | 81.54 E |
| Talovka, Ross. | 86 | 57.10 N | 93.09 E |
| Talpa | 196 | 31.47 N | 99.43 W |
| Talpa de Allende | 234 | 20.23 N | 104.51 W |
| Talquin, Lake ⊜[1] | 192 | 30.26 N | 84.33 W |
| Tālsa | 272b | 22.49 N | 88.33 E |
| Talsarnau | 42 | 52.54 N | 4.03 W |
| Talsi | 76 | 57.15 N | 22.36 E |
| Talšik | 86 | 53.42 N | 71.53 E |
| Taltal | 252 | 25.24 S | 70.29 W |
| Taltapin Lake ⊜ | 182 | 54.19 N | 125.20 W |
| Taltson ≏ | 176 | 61.23 N | 112.45 W |
| Talu | 112 | 0.14 N | 99.59 E |
| Taludaa | 112 | 0.20 N | 123.28 E |
| Taluk | 112 | 0.32 S | 101.35 E |
| Talumphuk, Laem › | 110 | 8.30 N | 100.10 E |
| Taluti, Teluk ⊂ | 164 | 3.21 S | 129.45 E |
| Talvik'ul'a | 24 | 68.45 N | 29.19 E |
| Talwandi Bhāi | 123 | 30.51 N | 74.56 E |
| Talwood | 166 | 28.30 S | 149.30 E |
| Taly | 78 | 49.51 N | 40.04 E |
| Ṭalyā | 142 | 30.16 N | 31.00 E |
| Tal-y-bont | 42 | 52.29 N | 3.59 W |
| Tama, Arg. | 252 | 30.31 S | 66.32 W |
| Tama, Nihon | 94 | 35.37 N | 139.27 E |
| Tama, Ia., U.S. | 190 | 41.58 N | 92.34 W |
| Tama ≏ | 94 | 35.32 N | 139.47 E |
| Tama Cemetery ◆ | 268 | 35.41 N | 139.31 E |
| Tamacuarí, Pico ∧ | 246 | 1.15 N | 64.45 W |
| Tamadjert | 148 | 25.36 N | 7.20 E |
| Tamagawa, Nihon | 94 | 37.12 N | 140.24 E |
| Tamagawa, Nihon | 96 | 34.01 N | 132.56 E |
| Tamagawa ◆[8] | 268 | 35.37 N | 139.39 E |
| Tamagawa-josui ≏ | 268 | 35.42 N | 139.35 E |
| Tamakautonga | 174v | 19.05 S | 169.55 W |
| Tamaki | 94 | 34.29 N | 136.38 E |
| Tāmākośī ≏ | 124 | 27.22 N | 85.59 E |
| Tama-kyūryō ⋏[2] | 268 | 35.35 N | 139.30 E |
| Tamala, Austl. | 162 | 26.42 S | 113.45 E |
| Tamala, Ross. | 80 | 52.33 N | 43.16 E |
| Tamalameque | 246 | 8.52 N | 73.49 W |
| Tamalave, Sierra ⋏ | 234 | 22.45 N | 99.15 W |
| Ṭamalāy | 142 | 30.30 N | 30.51 E |
| Tamale | 150 | 9.25 N | 0.50 W |
| Tamalea | 112 | 2.29 S | 119.19 E |
| Tamalpais, Mount ∧ | 226 | 37.56 N | 122.35 W |
| Tamalpais Valley | 226 | 37.53 N | 122.32 W |
| Tamamura | 94 | 36.18 N | 139.07 E |
| Taman, Indon. | 115a | 7.25 S | 112.41 E |
| Taman', Ross. | 78 | 45.13 N | 36.43 E |
| Tamana | 92 | 32.55 N | 130.33 E |
| Tamana I | 14 | 2.29 S | 175.59 E |
| Tamaná, Cerro ∧ | 246 | 5.02 N | 76.17 W |
| Tamana, Mount ∧[2] | 241r | 10.28 N | 61.12 W |
| Tamanaco ≏ | 246 | 9.25 N | 65.23 W |
| Tamanan | 115a | 8.01 S | 113.49 E |
| Tamanar | 148 | 31.00 N | 9.35 W |
| Tamandourirt, Oued V | 150 | 19.39 N | 2.04 W |
| Tamanduateí ≏ | 287b | 23.36 S | 46.35 W |
| Tamanhint | 146 | 27.13 N | 14.36 E |
| Tamani | 150 | 13.20 N | 6.50 W |
| Tamaniquá | 246 | 2.38 S | 65.44 W |
| Taman Negara ♦ | 114 | 4.43 N | 102.23 E |
| Tamano | 96 | 34.30 N | 133.56 E |
| Tamanquaré, Ilha I | 246 | 0.28 S | 64.55 W |
| Tamanskij zaliv ⊂ | 78 | 45.18 N | 36.45 E |
| Tamanthi | 110 | 25.19 N | 95.18 E |
| Tamanusi | 112 | 1.48 S | 121.18 E |
| Tamapatz | 234 | 21.35 N | 99.09 W |
| Tamaqua | 208 | 40.47 N | 75.58 W |
| Tamar ≏, Austl. | 166 | 41.04 S | 146.47 E |
| Tamar ≏, Nepāl | 124 | 26.55 N | 87.10 E |
| Tamar ≏, Eng., U.K. | 42 | 50.22 N | 4.10 W |
| Támara | 246 | 5.50 N | 72.10 W |
| Tamarac ≏ | 198 | 48.29 N | 97.07 W |
| Tamarack Lake ⊜[1] | 214 | 41.35 N | 80.05 W |
| Tamarite de Litera | 34 | 41.52 N | 0.26 E |
| Tamaroa | 194 | 38.08 N | 89.14 W |
| Tamarome | 164 | 2.54 S | 133.38 E |
| Tamarugal, Pampa del ≡ | 248 | 21.00 S | 69.25 W |
| Tamashima | 96 | 34.32 N | 133.40 E |
| Tamási | 30 | 46.38 N | 18.18 E |
| Tamaské | 150 | 14.49 N | 5.39 E |
| Tamatsukuri | 94 | 36.06 N | 140.25 E |
| Tamaulipas □[3] | 232 | 24.00 N | 98.45 W |
| Tamaya ≏ | 248 | 8.31 S | 74.13 W |
| Tamayu | 96 | 35.25 N | 133.01 E |
| Tama Zoological Park ♦ | 268 | 35.39 N | 139.24 E |
| Tamazula | 232 | 24.57 N | 106.57 W |
| Tamazula de Gordiano | 234 | 19.38 N | 103.15 W |
| Tamazulapan del Progreso | 234 | 17.41 N | 97.34 W |
| Tamazunchale | 234 | 21.16 N | 98.47 W |
| Tamba | 96 | 35.09 N | 135.25 E |
| Tambach-Dietharz | 54 | 50.48 N | 10.36 E |
| Tambacounda | 150 | 13.47 N | 13.40 W |
| Tambacounda □[4] | 150 | 14.00 N | 13.00 W |
| Tamba Dabatou | 150 | 11.48 N | 10.40 W |
| Tambak | 115a | 5.45 S | 112.37 E |
| Tambakboyo | 115a | 6.48 S | 111.50 E |
| Tamba-kōchi ⋏[1] | 92 | 35.20 N | 135.30 E |
| Tambakrejo | 115a | 7.16 S | 111.36 E |
| Tambalan | 112 | 3.08 N | 115.34 E |
| Tambangsawah | 112 | 3.02 S | 102.11 E |
| Tambara, Moç. | 154 | 16.45 S | 34.15 E |
| Tambara, Nihon | 96 | 33.54 N | 133.04 E |
| Tāmbaram | 122 | 12.55 N | 80.07 E |
| Tambaú ≏ | 256 | 21.34 S | 47.05 W |
| Tambault, Île à I | 275a | 45.29 N | 75.50 W |
| Tambea | 112 | 4.12 S | 121.36 E |
| Tambej | 74 | 71.30 N | 71.50 E |
| Tambelan, Kepulauan II | 112 | 1.00 N | 107.30 E |
| Tambelan Besar, Pulau I | 112 | 0.58 N | 107.34 E |
| Tambellup | 162 | 34.02 S | 117.39 E |
| Tamberías | 252 | 31.28 S | 69.25 W |
| Tambisan, Pulau I | 116 | 5.27 N | 119.10 E |
| Tambler | 116 | 6.03 N | 125.09 E |
| Tambo, Austl. | 166 | 24.53 S | 146.15 E |
| Tambo, Perú | 248 | 12.56 S | 74.01 W |
| Tambo ≏, Austl. | 166 | 37.51 S | 147.48 E |
| Tambo ≏, Perú | 248 | 17.10 S | 71.51 W |
| Tambo ≏, Perú | 248 | 10.43 S | 73.45 W |
| Tamboara | 255 | 23.09 S | 52.33 W |
| Tambo Grande | 248 | 4.56 S | 80.21 W |
| Tambohorano | 157b | 17.30 S | 43.58 E |
| Tamboli | 112 | 3.57 S | 121.20 E |
| Tambolongang, Pulau I | 112 | 6.36 S | 120.24 E |
| Tambopata ≏ | 248 | 12.36 S | 69.11 W |
| Tambor | 236 | 9.43 N | 85.01 W |
| Tambora, Gunung ∧ | 115b | 8.14 S | 117.55 E |
| Tamboril | 250 | 4.50 S | 40.20 W |
| Tamborine | 171a | 27.53 S | 153.08 E |
| Tamborine Mountain ∧[2] | 171a | 27.55 S | 153.10 E |
| Tamboritha, Mount ∧ | 166 | 37.28 S | 146.41 E |
| Tamboryacu ≏ | 246 | 2.31 S | 73.40 W |
| Tambov | 80 | 52.43 N | 41.25 E |
| Tambovka, Ross. | 80 | 47.18 N | 47.23 E |
| Tambovka, Ross. | 89 | 50.06 N | 128.04 E |
| Tambov Oblast' □[4] | 80 | 52.45 N | 41.30 E |
| Tambre ≏ | 34 | 42.49 N | 8.53 W |
| Tambu | 112 | 0.02 S | 119.52 E |
| Tambu, Teluk ⊂ | 112 | 0.02 N | 119.45 E |
| Tambulian Point › | 116 | 7.22 N | 123.27 E |
| Tambunan | 112 | 5.40 N | 116.22 E |
| Tambura | 140 | 5.36 N | 27.28 E |
| Tamchaket | 150 | 17.15 N | 10.40 W |
| Tam Chuak, Laem › | 110 | 8.33 N | 98.12 E |
| Tamdhas | 124 | 28.04 N | 83.14 E |
| Tame | 246 | 6.28 N | 71.44 W |
| Tame ≏ | 262 | 53.25 N | 2.09 W |
| Tameapa | 232 | 25.39 N | 107.22 W |
| Tamedda, Djebel ∧ | 148 | 32.48 N | 0.05 E |
| Tâmega ≏ | 34 | 41.05 N | 8.21 W |
| Tameghza | 148 | 34.23 N | 7.57 E |
| Tamel Aike | 254 | 48.19 S | 70.58 W |
| Tamelelt | 148 | 31.50 N | 7.29 W |
| Tamenghest | 148 | 22.56 N | 5.30 E |
| Tamenghest, Oued V | 148 | 22.10 N | 0.10 E |
| Tamenuen | 164 | 6.27 S | 139.48 E |
| Tamerton Foliot | 42 | 50.26 N | 4.08 W |
| Tamesí ≏ | 234 | 22.13 N | 97.52 W |
| Tameside □[8] | 262 | 53.29 N | 2.03 W |
| Tamga, Kyrg. | 85 | 42.09 N | 77.32 E |
| Tamga, Ross. | 89 | 45.34 N | 133.36 E |
| Tamgak, Monts ⋏ | 150 | 19.11 N | 8.42 E |
| Tamgué, Massif du ⋏ | 150 | 12.00 N | 12.18 W |
| Tamiahua | 234 | 21.16 N | 97.27 W |
| Tamiahua, Laguna de ⊂ | 234 | 21.35 N | 97.35 W |
| Tamiami Canal ≌ | 220 | 25.47 N | 80.15 W |
| Tamiang ≏ | 114 | 4.25 N | 98.16 E |
| Tamica | 24 | 64.10 N | 38.05 E |
| Tamil Harbor ⊂ | 174q | 9.30 N | 138.09 E |
| Tamil Nādu □[3] | 122 | 11.00 N | 78.15 E |
| Tamiment | 210 | 41.09 N | 75.02 W |
| Tamina | 222 | 30.11 N | 96.26 W |
| Tamir | 88 | 50.24 N | 107.25 E |
| Tamiryn ≏ | 88 | 47.48 N | 102.36 E |
| Tamiš (Timiș) ≏ | 38 | 44.51 N | 20.39 E |
| Tamitatoala ≏ | 255 | 11.56 S | 53.36 W |
| Ṭāmīyah | 142 | 29.29 N | 30.58 E |
| Tamkūhi | 124 | 26.41 N | 84.11 E |
| Tam Ky | 110 | 15.34 N | 108.29 E |
| Tamlūk | 126 | 22.18 N | 87.55 E |
| Tāmma | 120 | 25.11 N | 93.42 E |
| Tammaro ≏ | 68 | 41.09 N | 14.50 E |
| Tammerfors → Tampere | 26 | 61.30 N | 23.45 E |
| Tammisaari → Ekenäs | 26 | 59.58 N | 23.26 E |
| Tamms | 194 | 37.14 N | 89.16 W |
| Ṭammūh | 273c | 29.56 N | 31.16 E |
| Tāmna | 126 | 23.15 N | 86.21 E |
| Tämnarån ≏ | 40 | 60.31 N | 17.39 E |
| Tämnaren ⊜ | 40 | 60.10 N | 17.20 E |
| Tamnum | 144 | 15.07 N | 50.49 E |
| Tamon ◆[8] | 270 | 34.39 N | 135.04 E |
| Tampa, Ang. | 152 | 15.30 S | 13.27 E |
| Tampa, Fl., U.S. | 220 | 27.56 N | 82.27 W |
| Tampa Bay ⊂ | 220 | 27.45 N | 82.35 W |
| Tampa International Airport ⊠ | 220 | 27.59 N | 82.32 W |
| Tampamachoco, Laguna ⊂ | 234 | 21.00 N | 97.21 W |
| Tampang | 112 | 5.54 S | 104.43 E |
| Tampaón ≏ | 234 | 21.59 N | 98.36 W |
| Tamparan | 116 | 8.27 N | 117.13 E |
| Tampere | 26 | 61.30 N | 23.45 E |
| Tampico, Méx. | 234 | 22.13 N | 97.51 W |
| Tampico, Il., U.S. | 190 | 41.37 N | 89.47 W |
| Tampico, In., U.S. | 218 | 38.48 N | 85.58 W |
| Tampin | 114 | 2.28 N | 102.14 E |
| Tampiquito | 234 | 23.52 N | 98.14 W |
| Tampulonanjing, Gunung ∧ | 114 | 1.46 N | 99.24 E |
| Tam Quan | 110 | 14.35 N | 109.03 E |
| Tamra | 132 | 32.51 N | 35.12 E |
| Tamrau, Pegunungan ⋏ | 164 | 0.30 S | 132.27 E |
| Tamri | 148 | 30.43 N | 9.43 W |
| Tamsagbulag | 88 | 47.14 N | 117.21 E |
| Tamsalu | 76 | 59.10 N | 26.06 E |
| Tamshiyacu | 246 | 4.05 S | 72.58 W |
| Tamsweg | 64 | 47.08 N | 13.48 E |
| Tamu | 110 | 24.13 N | 94.18 E |
| Tamuín | 234 | 21.59 N | 98.45 W |
| Tamuk Island I | 116 | 6.27 N | 121.49 E |
| Tamuning | 174p | 13.29 N | 144.46 E |
| Tamura | 268 | 35.22 N | 139.22 E |
| Tamusuke | 85 | 38.03 N | 76.53 E |
| Tamworth, Austl. | 166 | 31.05 S | 150.55 E |
| Tamworth, On., Can. | 212 | 44.29 N | 77.00 W |
| Tamworth, Eng., U.K. | 42 | 52.39 N | 1.40 W |
| Tamyang | 98 | 35.21 N | 126.58 E |
| Tan ≏ | 100 | 23.57 N | 115.47 E |
| Tana, Chile | 248 | 19.27 S | 69.57 W |
| Tana, Nor. | 24 | 70.28 N | 28.18 E |
| Tana ≏, Cuba | 240p | 20.42 N | 77.25 W |
| Tana ≏, Kenya | 154 | 2.32 S | 40.31 E |
| T'an'a ≏, Ross. | 88 | 58.40 N | 120.30 E |
| Tana, Lake ⊜ | 144 | 12.00 N | 37.20 E |
| Tanabe, Nihon | 96 | 34.49 N | 135.46 E |
| Tanabe, Nihon | 96 | 33.44 N | 135.22 E |
| Tanabi | 255 | 20.37 S | 49.37 W |
| Tanacross | 180 | 63.23 N | 143.21 W |
| Tanafjorden ⊂[2] | 24 | 70.54 N | 28.40 E |
| Tanaga Island I | 180 | 51.50 N | 178.00 W |
| Tanaga Volcano ∧[1] | 180 | 51.53 N | 178.09 W |
| Tanagro ≏ | 68 | 40.38 N | 15.14 E |
| Tanaguarena | 286c | 10.37 N | 66.49 W |
| Tanagura | 94 | 37.02 N | 140.23 E |
| Tanah, Tanjung › | 115a | 6.29 S | 108.32 E |
| Tanahbala, Pulau I | 110 | 0.25 S | 98.25 E |
| Tanahgrogot | 112 | 1.55 S | 116.12 E |
| Tanahjampea, Pulau I | 112 | 7.05 S | 120.42 E |
| Tanahmasa, Pulau I | 110 | 0.12 S | 98.27 E |
| Tanahmerah, Indon. | 112 | 3.41 N | 117.31 E |
| Tanahmerah, Indon. | 164 | 6.05 S | 140.17 E |
| Tanah Merah, Malay. | 114 | 5.48 N | 102.09 E |
| Tanah Merah, Malay. | 114 | 2.36 N | 101.48 E |
| Tanahputih | 114 | 1.41 N | 101.03 E |
| Tanaka ◆[8] | 270 | 34.42 N | 134.59 E |
| Tanakeke, Pulau I | 112 | 5.30 S | 119.16 E |
| Tanakpur | 124 | 29.05 N | 80.07 E |
| Tan'am | 128 | 23.09 N | 56.29 E |
| Tanami | 162 | 19.59 S | 129.43 E |
| Tanami Desert ◆[2] | 162 | 20.00 S | 129.30 E |
| Tanan, Miṣr | 142 | 30.15 N | 31.14 E |
| Tan An, Viet | 110 | 8.46 N | 105.11 E |
| Tan An, Viet | 110 | 10.32 N | 106.25 E |
| Tanana | 180 | 65.10 N | 152.05 W |
| Tanana ≏ | 180 | 65.09 N | 151.55 W |
| Tananarive → Antananarivo | 157b | 18.55 S | 47.31 E |
| Tanapag | 174n | 15.14 N | 145.45 E |
| Tanapag, Lagunan ⊂ | 174n | 15.14 N | 145.44 E |
| Tanaro ≏ | 62 | 45.01 N | 8.47 E |
| Tanārūt, Wādī V | 146 | 30.08 N | 9.59 E |
| Tanashi | 94 | 35.44 N | 139.33 E |
| Tanat ≏ | 42 | 52.46 N | 3.07 W |
| Tanauan | 116 | 11.07 N | 125.01 E |
| Tanbar | 166 | 25.50 S | 141.55 E |
| Ṭanbidī | 142 | 28.38 N | 30.47 E |
| Tan Binh | 269c | 10.48 N | 106.40 E |
| Tanbu, Zhg. | 98 | 35.51 N | 118.17 E |
| Tanbu, Zhg. | 100 | 28.08 N | 114.12 E |
| Tancarville | 50 | 49.29 N | 0.28 E |
| Tancarville, Canal de ≌ | 50 | 49.28 N | 0.28 E |
| Tancha | 174m | 26.28 N | 127.50 E |
| Tan Chau | 110 | 10.48 N | 105.15 E |
| Tancheng | 98 | 34.37 N | 118.23 E |
| Tanchoj | 88 | 51.33 N | 105.07 E |
| Tanch'ŏn | 98 | 40.27 N | 128.54 E |
| Tancítaro | 234 | 19.20 N | 102.22 W |
| Tancítaro, Pico de ∧ | 234 | 19.23 N | 102.13 W |
| Tancochapa ≏ | 234 | 17.59 N | 94.04 W |
| Tanda, C. Iv. | 150 | 7.48 N | 3.10 W |
| Tānda, India | 123 | 31.42 N | 75.38 E |
| Tānda, India | 124 | 28.59 N | 78.56 E |
| Tānda, India | 124 | 26.33 N | 82.39 E |
| Tānda, Pāk. | 123 | 32.42 N | 74.22 E |
| Tandag | 116 | 9.04 N | 126.12 E |
| Tandah | 142 | 27.41 N | 30.46 E |
| Tandai | 154 | 19.36 S | 32.48 E |
| Tandaj | 80 | 47.33 N | 51.30 E |
| Tandala | 154 | 9.23 S | 34.14 E |
| Tandaltī | 140 | 13.01 N | 31.52 E |
| Ţăndărei | 38 | 44.38 N | 27.40 E |
| Tandaué | 152 | 17.00 S | 18.06 E |
| Tandian | 98 | 40.39 N | 124.46 E |
| Tandil | 252 | 37.19 S | 59.09 W |
| Tandjilé □[5] | 146 | 9.45 N | 16.30 E |
| Tandjilé ≏ | 146 | 9.45 N | 15.50 E |
| Tāndliānwāla | 123 | 31.02 N | 73.08 E |
| Tando Ādam | 120 | 25.46 N | 68.40 E |
| Tando Allāhyār | 120 | 25.28 N | 68.43 E |
| Tando Bāgo | 120 | 24.47 N | 68.58 E |
| Tando Muhammad Khān | 120 | 25.08 N | 68.32 E |
| Tandou Bougou | 152 | 3.32 S | 10.53 E |
| Tandou Lake ⊜ | 166 | 32.38 S | 142.05 E |
| Tandovo, ozero ⊜ | 86 | 55.07 N | 78.02 E |
| Tando Zinze | 152 | 5.22 S | 12.26 E |
| Tandragee | 48 | 54.20 N | 6.25 W |
| Tandridge | 260 | 51.14 N | 0.02 W |
| Tandridge □[8] | 260 | 51.17 N | 0.05 W |
| Tandslet | 41 | 54.55 N | 9.59 E |
| Tandubas | 116 | 5.10 N | 120.20 E |
| Tandubatu Island I | 116 | 5.13 N | 120.17 E |
| Tandula Tank ⊜[1] | 122 | 20.40 N | 81.12 E |
| Tandun | 112 | 0.36 N | 100.38 E |
| Tāndūr | 122 | 17.14 N | 77.35 E |
| Tanduy ≏ | 115a | 7.41 S | 108.47 E |
| Taneatua | 172 | 38.04 S | 177.01 E |
| Tanega-shima I | 93b | 30.40 N | 131.00 E |
| Taneichi | 92 | 40.26 N | 141.43 E |
| Tan Emellel | 148 | 27.30 N | 9.45 E |
| Tanete | 112 | 4.32 S | 119.36 E |
| Taneum Creek ≏ | 224 | 47.10 N | 120.40 W |
| Tanew ≏ | 30 | 50.31 N | 22.16 E |
| Taneytown | 208 | 39.39 N | 77.10 W |
| Tanezrouft ◆[2] | 148 | 24.00 N | 0.45 W |
| Tanezzuft, Wādī V | 146 | 25.51 N | 10.19 E |
| Tanforan Park ◆[9] | 282 | 37.38 N | 122.25 W |
| Tang ≏, Zhg. | 98 | 38.45 N | 115.35 E |
| Tang ≏, Zhg. | 100 | 32.09 N | 112.25 E |
| Tang ≏, Zhg. | 100 | 33.18 N | 117.46 E |
| Tang ≏, Zhg. | 104 | 41.15 N | 123.21 E |
| Tang ≏, Zhg. | 105 | 40.43 N | 116.38 E |
| Tanga, Ross. | 88 | 51.02 N | 111.33 E |
| Tånga, Sve. | 41 | 56.12 N | 12.46 E |
| Tanga, Tan. | 154 | 5.04 S | 39.06 E |
| Tanga □[4] | 154 | 5.00 S | 38.15 E |
| Tangail | 124 | 24.15 N | 89.55 E |
| Tangainony | 157b | 22.42 S | 47.45 E |
| Tanga Islands II | 14 | 3.30 S | 153.15 E |
| Tanga Langua › | 241k | 12.14 N | 61.39 W |
| Tangalla | 122 | 6.01 N | 80.48 E |
| Tangamong Lake ⊜ | 212 | 44.43 N | 77.51 W |
| Tangancícuaro [de Arista] | 234 | 19.54 N | 102.08 W |
| Tanganika, Lago → Tanganyika, Lake ⊜ | 154 | 6.00 S | 29.30 E |
| Tanganjika-See → Tanganyika, Lake ⊜ | 154 | 6.00 S | 29.30 E |
| Tanganyika, Lake ⊜ | 154 | 6.00 S | 29.30 E |
| Tangarana ≏ | 246 | 3.02 S | 75.08 W |
| Tangarare | 175e | 9.35 S | 159.39 E |
| Tanga-shima I | 96 | 34.40 N | 134.35 E |
| Tangba | 107 | 30.00 N | 105.46 E |
| Tangchi | 89 | 47.00 N | 123.46 E |
| Tangchigou | 104 | 41.04 N | 124.11 E |
| Tangcun, Zhg. | 100 | 29.50 N | 118.54 E |
| Tangcun, Zhg. | 100 | 25.26 N | 113.10 E |
| Tangdaohe | 98 | 40.38 N | 118.58 E |
| Tanger (Tangier) | 148 | 35.48 N | 5.45 W |
| Tanger □[4] | 148 | 35.35 N | 5.50 W |
| Tanger ≏ | 54 | 52.33 N | 11.59 E |
| Tangerang | 115a | 6.11 S | 106.37 E |
| Tangerhütte | 54 | 52.26 N | 11.48 E |
| Tangerine | 220 | 28.47 N | 81.38 W |
| Tang'erli | 105 | 39.09 N | 116.43 E |
| Tangermünde | 54 | 52.32 N | 11.58 E |
| Tangfang, Zhg. | 102 | 27.00 N | 101.08 E |
| Tangfang, Zhg. | 104 | 41.20 N | 120.34 E |
| Tangfang, Zhg. | 105 | 39.29 N | 118.01 E |
| Tangfangqiao | 106 | 31.45 N | 120.50 E |
| Tangfeng | 98 | 38.07 N | 115.30 E |
| Tanggangzi | 104 | 41.01 N | 122.54 E |
| Tanggeasinua, Pegunungan ⋏ | 112 | 3.24 S | 121.42 E |
| Tanggengtou | 106 | 30.55 N | 119.03 E |
| Tanggou | 100 | 33.59 N | 118.57 E |
| Tanggu | 105 | 39.01 N | 117.40 E |
| Tangguantun | 98 | 38.43 N | 116.55 E |
| Tanggul | 115a | 8.10 S | 113.26 E |
| Tanggulashan (Tuotuoheyan) | 120 | 34.05 N | 92.45 E |
| Tanggula Shan ⋏ | 120 | 33.00 N | 92.00 E |
| Tanggula Shankou )( | 120 | 32.59 N | 91.45 E |
| Tanggushiluke | 120 | 38.45 N | 80.55 E |
| Tanghe | 100 | 32.43 N | 112.48 E |
| Tanghekou | 105 | 40.44 N | 116.38 E |
| Tanghu | 105 | 39.11 N | 115.24 E |
| Tanghuang | 106 | 31.41 N | 119.25 E |
| Tangi | 123 | 34.18 N | 71.40 E |
| Tangier, N.S., Can. | 186 | 44.48 N | 62.42 W |
| Tangier → Tanger, Magreb | 148 | 35.48 N | 5.45 W |
| Tangier, Va., U.S. | 208 | 37.49 N | 75.59 W |
| Tangier Island I | 208 | 37.50 N | 76.00 W |
| Tangier Sound ⋈ | 208 | 38.02 N | 75.58 W |
| Tangijatuo | 107 | 29.36 N | 106.39 E |
| Tangipahoa ≏ | 194 | 30.20 N | 90.18 W |
| Tangjia | 100 | 22.23 N | 113.36 E |
| Tangjiagou | 100 | 30.48 N | 117.28 E |
| Tangjiang | 100 | 25.51 N | 114.44 E |
| Tangjiapao | 104 | 41.59 N | 122.14 E |
| Tangjiaqiao | 106 | 31.24 N | 119.12 E |
| Tangjiazhen | 106 | 31.13 N | 121.31 E |
| Tangjin | 98 | 36.54 N | 126.37 E |
| Tangkahan | 112 | 1.36 S | 113.52 E |
| Tangkak | 114 | 2.16 N | 102.33 E |
| Tangkou | 100 | 30.06 N | 118.11 E |
| Tanglad | 115b | 8.47 S | 115.35 E |
| Tanglewood, Fl., U.S. | 220 | 26.37 N | 81.53 W |
| Tanglewood, Tx., U.S. | 222 | 30.30 N | 96.59 W |
| Tanglewood ♦ | 207 | 42.21 N | 73.20 W |
| Tangling | 100 | 26.14 N | 119.24 E |
| Tanglitun | 104 | 41.45 N | 123.57 E |
| Tangmai | 102 | 30.08 N | 95.08 E |
| Tangmarg | 123 | 34.02 N | 74.26 E |
| Tangmazhai | 104 | 41.10 N | 122.44 E |
| Tang Nhon Phu | 269c | 10.50 N | 106.47 E |
| Tang-ni | 98 | 34.12 N | 126.52 E |
| Tango | 96 | 35.44 N | 135.06 E |
| Tango-hantō ›[1] | 96 | 35.40 N | 135.10 E |
| Tangowahine | 172 | 35.52 S | 173.56 E |
| Tangpu, Zhg. | 100 | 29.51 N | 120.47 E |
| Tangpu, Zhg. | 100 | 28.28 N | 114.58 E |
| Tangqi | 106 | 30.29 N | 120.11 E |
| Tangqiao | 106 | 31.13 N | 119.15 E |
| Tangra Yumco ⊜ | 120 | 31.00 N | 86.20 E |
| Tangsanying | 98 | 41.38 N | 117.40 E |
| Tangschan → Tangshan | 105 | 39.38 N | 118.11 E |
| Tangse | 114 | 5.01 N | 95.55 E |
| Tangshan, Zhg. | 105 | 40.10 N | 116.22 E |
| Tangshan, Zhg. | 105 | 39.38 N | 118.11 E |
| Tangshan, Zhg. | 106 | 32.05 N | 119.03 E |
| Tang Shan ∧ | 106 | 32.03 N | 119.02 E |
| Tangshi | 106 | 31.33 N | 120.51 E |
| Tangtou, Zhg. | 98 | 35.16 N | 118.35 E |
| Tangtou, Zhg. | 102 | 27.42 N | 108.17 E |
| Tangtou, Zhg. | 106 | 31.38 N | 120.19 E |
| Tangtouxia | 100 | 22.50 N | 114.06 E |
| Tangtse | 120 | 34.02 N | 78.11 E |
| Tanguá | 256 | 22.44 S | 42.43 W |
| Tangub | 116 | 8.03 N | 123.44 E |
| Tanguiéta | 150 | 10.37 N | 1.16 E |
| Tanguip Point › | 116 | 7.43 N | 126.32 E |
| Tanguj | 88 | 55.23 N | 100.58 E |
| Tangulbei | 154 | 0.48 N | 36.17 E |
| Tangusu, Telukan ⊂ | 116 | 5.27 N | 119.03 E |
| Tangwang ≏ | 89 | 46.40 N | 129.54 E |
| Tangxi | 100 | 29.04 N | 119.23 E |
| Tangxian | 98 | 38.45 N | 114.58 E |
| Tangxianzhen | 100 | 31.59 N | 113.07 E |
| Tangyan | 110 | 22.29 N | 98.24 E |
| Tangyi | 98 | 36.32 N | 115.47 E |
| Tangyin, Zhg. | 98 | 35.55 N | 114.21 E |
| Tangyin, Zhg. | 100 | 27.32 N | 116.16 E |
| Tangyuan | 89 | 46.42 N | 129.55 E |
| Tangzha | 106 | 32.05 N | 120.49 E |
| Tanhuato | 234 | 20.17 N | 102.20 W |
| Taniantaweng Shan ⋏ | 102 | 30.00 N | 98.00 E |
| Tanigami ◆[8] | 270 | 34.46 N | 135.10 E |
| Tanigawa-dake ∧ | 94 | 36.50 N | 138.56 E |
| Tanigumi | 94 | 35.31 N | 136.36 E |
| Tanimbar, Kepulauan II | 164 | 7.30 S | 131.30 E |
| Taninges | 58 | 46.07 N | 6.36 E |
| Tanintharyi □[8] | 110 | 12.00 N | 99.00 E |
| Tanır | 130 | 38.26 N | 36.55 E |
| Tanis (Zoan) ⊥ | 142 | 30.57 N | 31.53 E |
| Tanishpa ∧ | 120 | 31.10 N | 68.24 E |
| Tanjay | 116 | 9.31 N | 123.09 E |
| Tanjiafang | 98 | 36.41 N | 118.36 E |
| Tanjiahe | 100 | 31.58 N | 113.56 E |
| Tanjiang | 100 | 24.07 N | 116.32 E |
| Tanjiaqiao | 100 | 30.11 N | 118.15 E |
| Tanjil ≏ | 169 | 38.08 S | 146.17 E |
| Tanjong Dawai | 114 | 5.41 N | 100.22 E |
| Tanjong Malim | 114 | 3.41 N | 101.31 E |
| Tanjore → Thanjāvūr | 122 | 10.48 N | 79.09 E |
| Tanjung, Indon. | 112 | 2.11 S | 115.23 E |
| Tanjung, Indon. | 115a | 6.52 S | 108.52 E |
| Tanjung, Indon. | 115b | 8.21 S | 116.09 E |
| Tanjungbalai | 114 | 2.58 N | 99.48 E |
| Tanjungbatu, Indon. | 112 | 0.45 N | 117.26 E |
| Tanjungbatu, Indon. | 112 | 2.17 N | 118.05 E |
| Tanjungbatu, Indon. | 112 | 0.38 N | 103.26 E |
| Tanjungenim | 112 | 3.45 S | 103.48 E |
| Tanjungkarang-Telukbetung | 115a | 5.27 S | 105.16 E |
| Tanjunglabu | 112 | 2.57 S | 106.54 E |
| Tanjungmedan, Indon. | 114 | 1.26 N | 100.34 E |
| Tanjungmedan, Indon. | 114 | 2.06 N | 100.14 E |
| Tanjungmengedar | 114 | 2.39 N | 100.01 E |
| Tanjungpandan | 112 | 2.45 S | 107.39 E |
| Tanjungpinang | 112 | 0.55 N | 104.27 E |
| Tanjungpriok ◆[8] | 269e | 6.06 S | 106.53 E |
| Tanjungpura | 114 | 3.54 N | 98.26 E |
| Tanjungpusu | 112 | 0.01 S | 113.30 E |
| Tanjungraja | 112 | 3.21 S | 104.40 E |
| Tanjungredep | 112 | 2.09 N | 117.29 E |
| Tanjungsamak | 114 | 0.52 N | 103.03 E |
| Tanjungselor | 112 | 2.51 N | 117.22 E |
| Tanjungslamat | 114 | 3.49 N | 98.20 E |
| Tanjunguban | 112 | 1.03 N | 104.14 E |
| Tānk | 120 | 32.13 N | 70.23 E |
| Tan Kena | 148 | 26.33 N | 9.35 E |
| Tan Kien | 269c | 10.42 N | 106.35 E |
| Tankou | 100 | 25.48 N | 114.50 E |
| Tankwa ≏ | 158 | 32.20 S | 19.33 E |
| Tanlay | 50 | 47.50 N | 4.05 E |
| Tann, Dtsch. | 56 | 50.38 N | 10.01 E |
| Tann, Dtsch. | 60 | 48.19 N | 12.54 E |
| Tanna | 54 | 50.30 N | 11.51 E |
| Tanna I | 175f | 19.30 S | 169.20 E |
| Tannan | 96 | 35.05 N | 135.10 E |
| Tännäs | 26 | 62.27 N | 12.40 E |
| Tanna-tunnel ◆[5] | 94 | 35.06 N | 139.00 E |
| Tannay | 50 | 47.21 N | 3.36 E |
| Tanne | 54 | 51.41 N | 10.42 E |
| Tannenberg → Stębark | 30 | 53.30 N | 20.08 E |
| Tannenbergsthal | 54 | 50.26 N | 12.27 E |
| Tanner | 194 | 34.43 N | 86.58 W |
| Tanner, Mount ∧ | 182 | 49.40 N | 118.34 W |
| Tannersville, N.Y., U.S. | 210 | 42.12 N | 74.08 W |
| Tannersville, Pa., U.S. | 210 | 41.03 N | 75.18 W |
| Tännesberg | 60 | 49.32 N | 12.20 E |
| Tännforsen ⌊ | 26 | 63.27 N | 12.44 E |
| Tannhausen | 56 | 48.59 N | 10.21 E |
| Tannheim | 58 | 47.30 N | 10.31 E |
| Tannila | 26 | 65.29 N | 25.59 E |
| Tannis Bugt ⊂ | 26 | 57.40 N | 10.15 E |
| Tannroda | 54 | 50.52 N | 11.15 E |
| Tannu-Ola, chrebet ⋏ | 74 | 51.00 N | 94.00 E |
| Tannūrah, Ra's › | 128 | 26.40 N | 50.30 E |
| Tano, Nihon | 96 | 33.26 N | 134.00 E |
| Tano, Nihon | 270 | 34.57 N | 135.36 E |
| Tano ≏ | 150 | 5.07 N | 2.56 W |
| Tanon Strait ⋈ | 116 | 10.20 N | 123.30 E |
| Tânout | 150 | 14.58 N | 8.53 E |
| Tanpok ≏ | 250 | 3.27 N | 54.00 W |
| Tanque de Dolores | 234 | 23.40 N | 101.10 W |
| Tanque Grande, Ribeirão ≏ | 287b | 23.25 S | 46.28 W |
| Tan Qui Dong | 269c | 10.44 N | 106.42 E |
| Tanquinho | 255 | 11.58 S | 39.06 W |
| T'an' Šan' → Tien Shan ⋏ | 90 | 42.00 N | 80.00 E |
| Tansania → Tanzania □[1] | 154 | 6.00 S | 35.00 E |
| Tansboro | 285 | 39.46 N | 74.55 W |
| Tānsen | 124 | 27.52 N | 83.33 E |
| Tanshui | 100 | 25.10 N | 121.26 E |
| Tanshui ≏ | 100 | 25.11 N | 121.25 E |
| Tansilla | 150 | 12.26 N | 4.23 W |
| Tánsin, Isla de I | 236 | 15.17 N | 83.54 W |
| Tánsin, Laguna de ⊂ | 236 | 15.19 N | 83.58 W |
| Tan Son Nhut Airport ⊠ | 269c | 10.49 N | 106.40 E |
| Tansyk | 86 | 47.20 N | 79.52 E |
| Ṭanṭā | 142 | 30.47 N | 31.00 E |
| Tantabogue Creek ≏ | 222 | 31.00 N | 95.21 W |
| Tan-Tan | 148 | 28.26 N | 11.06 W |
| Tan-Tan □[4] | 148 | 28.05 N | 11.00 W |
| Tantangara Reservoir ⊜[1] | 171b | 35.45 S | 148.39 E |
| Tan Thoi Nhut | 269c | 10.50 N | 106.36 E |
| Tan Thuan Dong | 269c | 10.45 N | 106.44 E |
| Tāntipāra | 126 | 23.54 N | 87.22 E |
| Tantō | 96 | 35.29 N | 135.00 E |
| Tantonville | 58 | 48.28 N | 6.08 E |
| Tantou, Zhg. | 100 | 29.07 N | 121.09 E |
| Tantou, Zhg. | 100 | 26.03 N | 119.35 E |
| Tantou, Zhg. | 100 | 26.53 N | 115.26 E |
| Tantou Shan I | 100 | 29.11 N | 122.01 E |
| Tantoyuca | 234 | 21.21 N | 98.14 W |
| Tanuku | 122 | 16.45 N | 81.42 E |
| Tanuma | 94 | 36.22 N | 139.35 E |
| Tanumshede | 26 | 58.44 N | 11.19 E |
| Tanunda | 168b | 34.32 S | 138.57 E |
| Tan'urer ≏ | 180 | 64.44 N | 174.15 E |
| Tanushimaru | 96 | 33.21 N | 130.41 E |
| Tanvald | 30 | 50.45 N | 15.19 E |
| Tanwax Creek ≏ | 224 | 46.52 N | 122.27 W |
| Tanworth-in-Arden | 42 | 52.20 N | 1.50 W |
| Tanxi | 100 | 28.58 N | 115.38 E |
| Tanxia | 100 | 23.58 N | 115.34 E |
| Tanxu Shan I | 106 | 30.37 N | 121.37 E |
| Tanyang | 98 | 36.57 N | 128.21 E |
| Tanyeri | 130 | 39.37 N | 39.50 E |
| Tanyi | 98 | 35.14 N | 118.09 E |
| Tanymas ≏ | 85 | 38.25 N | 72.39 E |
| Tanzania □[1], Afr. | 138 | 6.00 S | 35.00 E |
| Tanzania □[1], Afr. | 154 | 6.00 S | 35.00 E |
| Tanzanie → Tanzania □[1] | 154 | 6.00 S | 35.00 E |
| Tanzawa-Ōyama-kokutei-kōen ♦ | 94 | 35.30 N | 139.10 E |
| Tanzawa-san ∧ | 94 | 35.28 N | 139.10 E |
| Tao ≏, Zhg. | 100 | 25.56 N | 115.06 E |
| Tao ≏, Zhg. | 102 | 35.52 N | 103.16 E |
| Tao, Ko I | 110 | 10.05 N | 99.52 E |
| Tao'an | 89 | 45.22 N | 122.47 E |
| Taochong | 100 | 31.04 N | 118.06 E |
| Taochuan | 102 | 25.07 N | 111.06 E |
| Taocun | 98 | 37.10 N | 121.05 E |
| Taodigou | 105 | 40.52 N | 116.14 E |
| Tao'er ≏ | 89 | 45.42 N | 124.05 E |
| Taoerdeng | 98 | 40.44 N | 119.02 E |
| Taohe | 105 | 39.12 N | 116.50 E |
| Taohua | 106 | 31.23 N | 120.04 E |
| Taohuachiyingzi | 104 | 42.18 N | 121.06 E |
| Taohua Dao I | 100 | 29.48 N | 122.17 E |
| Taohuanbuligai | 104 | 42.13 N | 122.14 E |
| Taohuatu | 104 | 41.40 N | 120.40 E |
| Taohuayuan | 106 | 30.34 N | 118.42 E |
| Taohuazhen | 105 | 40.04 N | 114.59 E |
| Taojiagou | 107 | 29.48 N | 104.48 E |
| Taojiahe | 100 | 30.55 N | 115.56 E |
| Taojialiang | 104 | 42.36 N | 121.25 E |
| Taolahusu | 98 | 42.34 N | 116.48 E |
| Taolaizhao | 89 | 44.51 N | 125.57 E |
| Taolakepa | 120 | 32.05 N | 85.22 E |
| Taole | 102 | 38.46 N | 106.40 E |
| Taolin | 98 | 34.30 N | 118.30 E |
| Taoling | 100 | 30.21 N | 118.16 E |
| Taoluo | 98 | 35.17 N | 119.24 E |
| T'aonan → Tao'an | 89 | 45.22 N | 122.47 E |
| Taongi I[1] | 14 | 14.37 N | 168.58 E |
| Taormina | 70 | 37.51 N | 15.17 E |
| Taos, Mo., U.S. | 219 | 38.30 N | 92.04 W |
| Taos, N.M., U.S. | 200 | 36.24 N | 105.34 W |
| Taos Pueblo | 200 | 36.26 N | 105.32 W |
| Taoudenni | 148 | 22.40 N | 4.00 W |
| Taougrite | 34 | 36.15 N | 0.55 E |
| Taounate | 148 | 34.25 N | 4.39 W |
| Taounate □[4] | 148 | 34.30 N | 4.40 W |
| Taoura | 36 | 36.09 N | 8.03 E |
| Taourirt | 148 | 34.25 N | 2.53 W |
| Taourirt ∧ | 148 | 24.03 N | 5.02 E |
| Taoussa | 150 | 16.55 N | 0.35 W |
| Taowu | 106 | 31.47 N | 118.46 E |
| Taoxi, Zhg. | 100 | 31.33 N | 117.00 E |
| Taoxi, Zhg. | 100 | 25.18 N | 116.05 E |
| Taoxi, Zhg. | 100 | 28.44 N | 119.36 E |
| Taoxiantun | 104 | 41.39 N | 123.27 E |
| Taoyuan, Zhg. | 100 | 25.48 N | 117.32 E |
| Taoyuan, Zhg. | 102 | 28.46 N | 111.20 E |
| Taozhu | 100 | 28.50 N | 121.31 E |
| Taozhuang | 106 | 30.58 N | 120.48 E |
| Tapa, Eesti | 76 | 59.16 N | 25.58 E |
| Tapa, India | 123 | 30.19 N | 75.21 E |
| Tapaan Island I | 116 | 5.28 N | 120.44 E |
| Tapacari | 248 | 17.31 S | 66.36 W |
| Tapachula | 232 | 14.54 N | 92.17 W |
| Tapaga, Cape › | 175a | 14.01 S | 171.23 W |
| Tapah | 114 | 4.11 N | 101.16 E |
| Tapah Road | 114 | 4.10 N | 101.12 E |
| Tapaje ≏ | 246 | 2.44 N | 78.07 W |
| Tapajós ≏ | 250 | 2.24 S | 54.41 W |
| Tapaktuan | 114 | 3.16 N | 97.11 E |
| Tapalpa | 234 | 19.57 N | 103.46 W |
| Tapalqué | 252 | 36.21 S | 60.01 W |
| Tapan | 112 | 2.10 S | 101.04 E |
| Tapanahony ≏ | 250 | 4.22 N | 54.27 W |
| Tapanui | 172 | 45.57 S | 169.16 E |
| Tapanuli, Teluk ⊂ | 114 | 1.38 N | 98.45 E |
| Tapasi | 126 | 23.40 N | 87.08 E |
| Tapauá | 248 | 5.45 S | 63.04 W |
| Tapauá ≏ | 248 | 5.40 S | 64.21 W |
| Tapawera | 172 | 41.24 S | 172.49 E |
| Tapaz | 116 | 11.16 N | 122.32 E |
| Tapejara | 252 | 28.04 S | 52.00 W |
| Tapera | 252 | 28.38 S | 52.52 W |
| Taperas | 248 | 17.54 S | 60.23 W |
| Taperoá, Bra. | 250 | 7.12 S | 36.49 W |
| Taperoá, Bra. | 255 | 13.31 S | 39.06 W |
| Tapes | 252 | 30.40 S | 51.23 W |
| Tapeta | 150 | 6.29 N | 8.51 W |
| Taphan Hin | 110 | 16.13 N | 100.26 E |
| Taphoen ≏ | 110 | 14.07 N | 99.25 E |
| Tāpi ≏, India | 120 | 21.06 N | 72.41 E |
| Ta Pi ≏, Thai | 110 | 9.05 N | 99.12 E |
| Tapiales | 288 | 34.42 S | 58.31 W |
| Tapiantana Channel ⋈ | 116 | 6.23 N | 122.00 E |
| Tapiantana Group II | 116 | 6.20 N | 122.00 E |
| Tapiantana Island I | 116 | 6.18 N | 121.59 E |
| Tapiche ≏ | 248 | 4.59 S | 73.51 W |
| Tapili | 154 | 3.25 N | 27.40 E |
| Tapilula | 234 | 17.14 N | 93.02 W |
| Taping (Daying) ≏ | 102 | 24.17 N | 97.14 E |
| Tapini | 164 | 8.20 S | 147.00 E |
| Tapiraí | 255 | 19.52 S | 46.01 W |
| Tapirapé ≏ | 250 | 10.41 S | 50.38 W |
| Tapiratiba | 256 | 21.28 S | 46.45 W |
| Tapis, Gunong ∧ | 114 | 4.03 N | 102.54 E |
| Tapiutan Island I | 116 | 11.12 N | 119.16 E |
| Tapiwa | 174d | 0.52 S | 169.35 E |
| Taplan National Park ♦ | 110 | 14.20 N | 102.20 E |
| Tāplejungg | 124 | 27.21 N | 87.40 E |
| Tapoa ≏ | 150 | 12.36 N | 2.29 E |
| Tapol | 146 | 8.31 N | 15.35 E |
| Tapolca | 30 | 46.53 N | 17.27 E |
| Tappahannock | 208 | 37.55 N | 76.51 W |
| Tappal | 124 | 28.03 N | 77.35 E |
| Tappan | 210 | 41.01 N | 73.56 W |
| Tappan, Lake ⊜[1] | 276 | 41.01 N | 73.59 W |
| Tappan Lake ⊜[1] | 214 | 40.21 N | 81.11 W |
| Tappan Zee ⊂ | 276 | 41.06 N | 73.53 W |
| Tappan Zee Bridge ◆[5] | 276 | 41.04 N | 73.54 W |
| Tappen | 198 | 46.52 N | 99.38 W |
| Tappernøje | 41 | 55.10 N | 11.59 E |
| Tappi-zaki › | 92 | 41.15 N | 140.21 E |
| Tappo | 150 | 10.12 N | 2.38 W |
| Tapps, Lake ⊜ | 224 | 47.13 N | 122.09 W |
| Tapsiā ◆[8] | 272b | 22.32 N | 88.22 E |
| Tapuaenuku ∧ | 172 | 42.00 S | 173.40 E |
| Tapuio ≏ | 250 | 3.41 S | 44.16 W |
| Tapul Group II | 116 | 5.30 N | 121.00 E |
| Tapul Island I | 116 | 5.4[illegible] N | 120.55 E |
| Tapun | 110 | 18.22 N | 95.27 E |
| Tapurucuara | 246 | 0.24 S | 65.02 W |
| Taputapu, Cape › | 174u | 14.1[illegible] S | 170.50 W |
| Taqāṭu' Hayyā | 140 | 18.20 N | 36.22 E |
| Taqian | 100 | 29.03 N | 117.03 E |
| Taqiao, Zhg. | 100 | 31.28 N | 118.25 E |
| Taqiao, Zhg. | 100 | 28.24 N | 117.02 E |
| Taqtaq | 128 | 35.53 N | 44.35 E |
| Taquara | 252 | 29.39 [illegible] | 50.47 W |
| Taquara ◆[8] | 287a | 22.55 [illegible] | 43.21 W |
| Taquara, Serra da ∧ | 256 | 22.12 S | 43.53 W |
| Taquaras, Ponta das › | 252 | 27.01 S | 48.34 W |
| Taquari, Bra. | 252 | 29.48 S | 51.51 W |
| Taquari, Bra. | 255 | 17.50 S | 53.17 W |
| Taquari ≏, Bra. | 248 | 19.15 S | 57.17 W |
| Taquari ≏, Bra. | 252 | 29.56 S | 51.44 W |
| Taquari, Pantanal do ≡ | 248 | 18.20 S | 56.30 W |
| Taquaritinga | 255 | 21.24 S | 48.30 W |
| Taquaruçu ≏, Bra. | 248 | 20.30 S | 55.49 W |
| Taquaruçu ≏, Bra. | 255 | 21.35 S | 52.07 W |
| Tar ≏, Kyrg. | 85 | 40.38 N | 73.26 E |
| Tar ≏, N.C., U.S. | 192 | 35.33 N | 77.05 W |
| Tara, Austl. | 166 | 27.17 S | [illegible]50.28 E |
| Tara, On., Can. | 212 | 44.28 N | [illegible]1.09 W |
| Tara, Ross. | 86 | 56.54 N | [illegible]4.22 E |
| Tara, Zam. | 154 | 16.56 S | [illegible]6.47 E |
| Tara ⋏ | 38 | 43.55 N | 9.25 E |
| Tara ≏, Europe | 38 | 43.21 N | 8.51 E |
| Tara ≏, Ross. | 86 | 56.42 N | [illegible]4.36 E |
| Taraba ≏ | 146 | 8.30 N | [illegible]0.15 E |
| Tarabine, Oued ti-n- V | 148 | 20.50 N | [illegible]7.25 E |
| Tarabuco | 248 | 19.10 S | [illegible].57 W |
| Ṭarābulus (Tripoli), Lībiyā | 146 | 32.54 N | 1[illegible].11 E |
| Ṭarābulus (Tripoli), Lubnān | 130 | 34.26 N | 3[illegible].51 E |
| Ṭarābulus (Tripolitania) □[9] | 146 | 31.00 N | 1[illegible].00 E |
| Tarabusi Creek ≏ | 281 | 42.24 N | 8[illegible].19 W |
| Tarabya ◆[8] | 267b | 41.08 N | 2[illegible].03 E |
| Tarach ≏ | 154 | 4.09 N | 3[illegible].56 E |
| Taraclia, Mol. | 38 | 46.34 N | 2[illegible].06 E |
| Taraclia, Mol. | 38 | 45.54 N | 28.38 E |
| Taradale | 172 | 39.32 S | 176[illegible]51 E |
| Taragaj ≏ | 85 | 41.35 N | 77[illegible]2 E |
| Tarāghin | 146 | 25.59 N | 14[illegible]6 E |
| Tarago | 170 | 35.04 S | 149[illegible]9 E |
| Tara Hills | 282 | 38.00 N | 122[illegible]9 W |
| Tarai ≡ | 124 | 26.35 N | 86.[illegible]0 E |
| Taraia | 124 | 26.05 N | 84.[illegible]3 E |
| Taraira (Traíra) ≏ | 246 | 1.04 S | 69.[illegible] W |
| Tara Island I | 116 | 12.17 N | 120.[illegible] E |
| Taraju | 115a | 7.27 S | 107.[illegible] E |
| Tarakan | 112 | 3.18 N | 117.[illegible] E |
| Tarakan, Pulau I | 112 | 3.21 N | 117.[illegible] E |
| Tarakanovka | 82 | 55.07 N | 35.4[illegible] E |
| Tārakeshwar | 126 | 22.54 N | 88.0[illegible] E |
| Taraklı | 130 | 40.24 N | 30.2[illegible] E |
| Taralga | 170 | 34.24 S | 149.4[illegible] E |
| Tarama | 175d | 24.40 N | 124.4[illegible] E |
| Taramakau ≏ | 172 | 42.34 S | 171.0[illegible] E |
| Taramana | 112 | 8.10 S | 124.5[illegible] E |
| Tarama-shima I | 175d | 24.39 N | 124.4[illegible] E |
| Tarana | 170 | 33.32 S | 149.5[illegible] E |
| Tārānagar | 123 | 28.41 N | 75.0[illegible] E |
| Taranaki, Mount ∧ | 172 | 39.18 S | 174.04 E |
| Tarancón | 34 | 40.01 N | 3.00 W |
| Tarandacuao | 234 | 19.59 N | 100.32 W |
| Taranga Island I | 172 | 35.58 S | 174.43 E |
| Tarangire National Park ♦ | 154 | 4.00 S | 36.00 E |
| Tarangnan | 116 | 11.54 N | 124.45 E |
| Tarango, Presa ⊜[1] | 286a | 19.22 N | 99.13 W |
| Taranivka | 78 | 49.37 N | 36.08 |
| Taransay I | 46 | 57.54 N | 7.01 W |
| Taranta Peligna | 66 | 42.01 N | 14.10 E |
| Tarantine, Murge ◆[1] | 68 | 40.22 N | 17.40 E |
| Taranto | 68 | 40.28 N | 17.15 E |
| Taranto □[4] | 68 | 40.37 N | 17.15 E |
| Taranto, Golfo di ⊂ | 68 | 40.10 N | 17.20 E |
| Tarapacá | 246 | 2.52 S | 69.44 W |
| Tarapoto | 248 | 6.30 S | 76.25 W |
| Ṭaraq al-Hbâri ◆[1] | 130 | 34.17 N | 39.16 E |
| Ṭaraq an-Na'jah ◆[1] | 130 | 34.16 N | 39.53 E |
| Ṭaraq Sidâoui ◆[1] | 130 | 34.33 N | 39.54 E |
| Taraquá | 246 | 0.06 N | 68.28 W |
| Tarare | 58 | 45.54 N | 4.26 E |
| Tarariras | 258 | 34.17 S | 57.37 W |
| Tararua Range ⋏ | 172 | 40.46 S | 175.23 E |
| Tarāsa Dwīp I | 110 | 8.15 N | 93.10 E |
| Tarascon, Fr. | 32 | 42.51 N | 1.36 E |
| Tarascon, Fr. | 62 | 43.48 N | 4.40 E |
| Tarashcha | 78 | 49.34 N | 30.29 E |
| Tarasht ◆[8] | 267d | 35.42 N | 51.21 E |
| Tarasivka | 83 | 49.40 N | 38.23 E |
| Tarasovka, Ross. | 83 | 49.28 N | 40.05 E |
| Tarasovka, Ross. | 265b | 55.58 N | 37.50 E |
| Tarasovo, Ross. | 24 | 66.13 N | 46.39 E |
| Tarasovo, Ross. | 24 | 62.49 N | 41.10 E |
| Tarasovo, Ross. | 80 | 58.18 N | 48.45 E |
| Tarasovo, Ross. | 88 | 55.52 N | 107.48 E |
| Tarasovskij | 78 | 48.43 N | 40.22 E |
| Tarasp | 58 | 46.38 N | 10.25 E |
| Tarat | 148 | 26.13 N | 9.18 E |
| Tarat, Oued V | 148 | 26.09 N | 9.20 E |
| Tarata, Bol. | 248 | 17.37 S | 66.01 W |
| Tarata, Perú | 248 | 17.28 S | 70.02 W |
| Taratai | 174t | 1.32 N | 173.00 E |
| Taratakbuluh | 112 | 0.23 N | 101.27 E |
| Tāratanr | 126 | 23.58 N | 86.29 E |
| Tarauacá | 248 | 8.10 S | 70.46 W |
| Tarauacá ≏ | 248 | 7.19 S | 70.15 W |
| Taravao, Baie de ⊂ | 174s | 17.43 S | 149.17 W |
| Taravao, Isthme de ±[3] | 174s | 17.43 S | 149.19 W |
| Taravo ≏ | 36 | 41.42 N | 8.49 E |
| Tarawa I[1] | 174t | 1.25 N | 173.00 E |
| Tarawera | 172 | 39.02 S | 176.35 E |
| Tarawera, Lake ⊜ | 172 | 38.12 S | 176.27 E |
| Tarawera, Mount ∧[1] | 172 | 38.14 S | 176.30 E |
| Tarazona | 34 | 41.54 N | 1.44 W |
| Tarazona de la Mancha | 34 | 39.15 N | 1.55 W |
| Tarba | 144 | 0.48 N | 42.39 E |
| Tårbæk | 41 | 55.47 N | 12.36 E |
| Tarbagataj, Ross. | 88 | 51.30 N | 107.22 E |
| Tarbagataj, Ross. | 88 | 52.07 N | 109.12 E |
| Tarbagataj, Ross. | 88 | 51.12 N | 109.05 E |
| Tarbagataj, chrebet ⋏ | 86 | 47.12 N | 83.00 E |
| Tarbat Ness › | 46 | 57.51 N | 3.47 W |
| Tarbela | 123 | 34.08 N | 72.49 E |
| Tarbela Reservoir ⊜[1] | 123 | 34.10 N | 72.50 E |
| Tarbert, Ire. | 48 | 52.32 N | 9.23 W |
| Tarbert, Scot., U.K. | 46 | 55.52 N | 5.26 W |
| Tarbert, Scot., U.K. | 46 | 57.54 N | 6.49 W |
| Tarbert, East Loch ⊂ | 46 | 57.52 N | 6.45 W |
| Tarbert, Loch ⊂ | 46 | 55.57 N | 6.00 W |
| Tarbert, West Loch ⊂, Scot., U.K. | 46 | 55.48 N | 5.32 W |
| Tarbert, West Loch ⊂, Scot., U.K. | 46 | 57.55 N | 6.54 W |
| Tarbes | 32 | 43.14 N | 0.05 E |
| Tarbet | 46 | 56.12 N | 4.43 W |
| Tarbock Green | 262 | 53.23 N | 2.49 W |
| Tarbolton | 46 | 55.31 N | 4.29 W |
| Tarboro | 192 | 35.53 N | 77.32 W |
| Tarbū | 146 | 26.02 N | 15.10 E |
| Tarcăului, Munții ⋏ | 38 | 46.45 N | 26.20 E |
| Tarcento | 64 | 46.13 N | 13.13 E |
| Tarchov Cholm, gora ∧[2] | 76 | 57.11 N | 38.25 E |
| Tarchovka | 265a | 60.04 N | 29.58 E |
| Tarcoola | 162 | 30.41 S | 134.33 E |
| Tarcoon | 166 | 30.18 S | 146.43 E |
| Tarcutta | 171b | 35.17 S | 147.44 E |
| Tarcutta Creek ≏ | 171b | 35.08 S | 147.36 E |


| Symbol | English | Deutsch | Español | Français | Português |
|---|---|---|---|---|---|
| ≏ | River | Fluß | Río | Rivière | Rio |
| ≌ | Canal | Kanal | Canal | Canal | Canal |
| ⌊ | Waterfall, Rapids | Wasserfall, Stromschnellen | Cascada, Rápidos | Chute d'eau, Rapides | Cascata, Rápidos |
| ⋈ | Strait | Meeresstraße | Estrecho | Détroit | Estreito |
| ⊂ | Bay, Gulf | Bucht, Golf | Bahía, Golfo | Baie, Golfe | Baía, Golfo |
| ⊜ | Lake, Lakes | See, Seen | Lago, Lagos | Lac, Lacs | Lago, Lagos |
| ≡ | Swamp | Sumpf | Pantano | Marais | Pântano |
| ✻ | Ice Features, Glacier | Eis- und Gletscherformen | Accidentes Glaciales | Formes glaciaires | Acidentes glaciares |
| ⊤ | Other Hydrographic Features | Andere Hydrographische Objekte | Otros Elementos Hidrográficos | Autres données hydrographiques | Outros acidentes hidrográficos |
| ◆ | Submarine Features | Untermeerische Objekte | Accidentes Submarinos | Formes de relief sous-marin | Acidentes submarinos |
| □ | Political Unit | Politische Einheit | Unidad Política | Entité politique | Unidade política |
| ◎ | Cultural Institution | Kulturelle Institution | Institución Cultural | Institution culturelle | Instituição cultural |
| ⊥ | Historical Site | Historische Stätte | Sitio Histórico | Site historique | Sitio histórico |
| ♦ | Recreational Site | Erholungs- und Ferienort | Sitio de Recreo | Centre de loisirs | Area de Lazer |
| ⊠ | Airport | Flughafen | Aeropuerto | Aéroport | Aeroporto |
| ■ | Military Installation | Militäranlage | Instalación Militar | Installation militaire | Instalação militar |
| ◆ | Miscellaneous | Verschiedenes | Misceláneo | Divers | Diversos |

Tārdah 272b 22.27 N 88.31 E
Tardajos 34 42.21 N 3.49 W
Tardoki-Jani, gora ∧ 89 48.55 N 138.04 E
Tardun 162 28.48 S 115.45 E
Taredo ◆[8] 272c 19.58 N 72.49 E
Taree 166 31.54 S 152.28 E
Tareja 74 73.20 N 90.37 E
Taremert-n-Akli, Oued V 148 25.49 N 5.17 E
Tärendö 24 67.10 N 22.38 E
Tarent, Golf von → Taranto, Golfo di ⊂ 68 40.10 N 17.20 E
Tarentaise V 62 45.30 N 6.30 E
Tarento, Golfo de → Taranto, Golfo di ⊂ 68 40.10 N 17.20 E
Tarentum 214 40.36 N 79.45 W
Tarf, Garaet et ⊜ 148 35.40 N 7.10 E
Ṭarfā', Baṭn aṭ- ≡ 128 23.50 N 51.27 E
Ṭarfā', Ra's aṭ- › 144 17.05 N 42.24 E
Ṭarfā', Wādī aṭ- V 142 28.25 N 30.50 E
Ṭarfāwī, Bi'r ▼[4], Miṣr 140 22.55 N 28.53 E
Tarfawi, Bi'r ▼[4], Sūd. 140 21.04 N 34.08 E
Tarfaya 148 27.58 N 12.55 W
Tarfside 46 56.54 N 2.50 W
Tarf Water ≃ 44 54.55 N 4.35 W
Targa 124 22.27 N 84.40 E
Targan ≃ 85 43.38 N 75.58 E
Target Rock National Wildlife Refuge ◆[4] 276 40.56 N 73.26 W
Targhee Pass )( 202 44.41 N 111.17 W
Targon 32 44.44 N 0.16 W
Tărgovište, Blg. 38 43.15 N 26.34 E
Târgoviște, Rom. 38 44.56 N 25.27 E
Târgu Bujor 38 45.52 N 27.54 E
Târgu Cărbunești 38 44.58 N 23.31 E
Târgu Frumos 38 47.13 N 27.00 E
Targuist 148 34.57 N 4.18 W
Târgu Jiu 38 45.02 N 23.17 E
Târgu Lăpuș 38 47.27 N 23.52 E
Târgu Mureș 38 46.33 N 24.33 E
Târgu-Neamț 38 47.12 N 26.22 E
Târgu Ocna 38 46.15 N 26.37 E
Târgu Secuiesc 38 46.00 N 26.08 E
Târgușor 38 44.28 N 28.25 E
Tarhjijt 148 29.05 N 9.24 W
Tarhu 102 41.09 N 107.58 E
Tarhūnah 146 32.26 N 13.38 E
Tari 164 5.50 S 143.00 E
Tarialan 86 49.47 N 91.55 E
Tariat 88 48.06 N 99.32 E
Táriba 246 7.49 N 72.13 W
Tarifa 34 36.01 N 5.36 W
Tarifa, Punta de › 34 36.00 N 5.37 W
Tariffville 207 41.54 N 72.45 W
Tarija 248 21.31 S 64.45 W
Tarija □[5] 248 21.30 S 64.00 W
Tarikere 122 13.43 N 75.49 E
Tariki 172 39.14 S 174.15 E
Tariku ≃ 164 3.04 S 138.09 E
Tarīm 144 16.03 N 48.59 E
Tarim ≃ 90 41.05 N 86.40 E
Tarimoro 234 20.17 N 100.45 W
Tarim Pendi ≚[1] 90 39.00 N 83.00 E
Taring 114 3.50 N 97.33 E
Tarīn Kowt 120 32.52 N 65.38 E
Taritatu ≃ 164 2.54 S 138.27 E
Tarituba 256 23.02 S 44.36 W
Tarjannevesi ⊜ 26 62.07 N 24.03 E
Tarka 150 14.37 N 7.55 E
Tarka ≃ 158 32.18 S 25.44 E
Tarka, Vallée de V 150 14.00 N 6.00 E
Tarkastad 158 32.00 S 26.16 E
Tarkazy 80 53.52 N 53.39 E
Tarkhankut, mys › 78 45.21 N 32.30 E
Tarkhūrān 128 34.41 N 50.00 E
Tarki 84 42.56 N 47.30 E
Tarkiln 207 41.57 N 71.36 W
Tarkington Bayou ≃ 222 30.10 N 94.59 W
Tarkio 194 40.26 N 95.22 W
Tarkio ≃ 198 40.10 N 95.26 W
Tarko-Sale 74 64.55 N 77.49 E
Tarkwa 150 5.19 N 1.59 W
Tarlac 116 15.29 N 120.35 E
Tarlac □[4] 116 15.30 N 120.25 E
Tarlac ≃ 116 15.45 N 120.27 E
Tarland 46 57.08 N 2.52 W
Tarlee 168b 34.16 S 138.46 E
Tarleton 44 53.41 N 2.50 W
T'arlevo 265a 59.42 N 30.27 E
Tarlo ≃ 170 34.28 S 150.04 E
Tarlo River National Park ♠ 170 34.31 S 149.55 E
Tarlscough 262 53.37 N 2.52 W
Tarm 26 55.55 N 8.32 E
Tarma 248 11.25 S 75.42 W
Tarmstedt 52 53.13 N 9.04 E
Tarn □[5] 32 43.50 N 2.00 E
Tarn ≃ 32 44.05 N 1.06 E
Tarna ≃ 30 47.31 N 19.59 E
Tärnaby 24 65.43 N 15.16 E
Tarnak ≃ 120 31.26 N 65.31 E
Tarna Mare 38 48.04 N 23.12 E
Târnava Mare ≃ 38 46.09 N 23.42 E
Târnava Mică ≃ 38 46.11 N 23.55 E
Târnăveni 38 46.20 N 24.17 E
Tårnby 41 55.38 N 12.36 E
Tarneit 274b 37.52 S 144.41 E
Tarn-et-Garonne □[5] 32 44.05 N 1.20 E
Tarnewitz 54 53.58 N 11.14 E
Tarnobrzeg 30 50.35 N 21.41 E
Tarnobrzeg □[4] 30 50.45 N 21.50 E
Tarnogród 30 50.23 N 22.45 E
Tarnogskij Gorodok 24 60.29 N 43.33 E
Tarnopol → Ternopil' 78 49.34 N 25.36 E
Târnova 38 48.10 N 27.40 E
Tarnów, Pol. 30 50.01 N 21.00 E
Tarnów, Pol. 54 52.47 N 14.58 E
Tarnów □[4] 30 50.00 N 21.00 E
Tarnowskie Góry 30 50.27 N 18.52 E
Tärnsjö 40 60.09 N 16.56 E
Tarn Tāran 123 31.27 N 74.55 E
Taro 175e 6.46 S 156.28 E
Taro ≃ 36 45.00 N 10.15 E
Taron 164 4.25 S 153.05 E
Tarong 166 26.46 S 151.51 E
Taronga Zoo ♠ 274a 33.51 S 151.15 E
Taroom 166 25.39 S 149.49 E
Tarouca 34 41.00 N 7.40 W
Taroudant 148 30.31 N 8.55 W
Ta Roun, Co ∧ 110 17.17 N 106.18 E
Tarp 41 54.40 N 9.23 E
Tarpey 226 36.47 N 119.41 W
Tarpon, Lake ⊜ 220 28.07 N 82.44 W
Tarpon Springs 220 28.08 N 82.45 W
Tarporley 44 53.09 N 2.40 W
Tarqui 246 1.35 S 75.15 W
Tarquinia 66 42.15 N 11.45 E
Tarqūmiyah 132 31.35 N 35.01 E
Tarra ≃ 246 9.05 N 72.30 W
Tarrabool Lake ⊜ 162 18.15 S 135.04 E
Tarrafal, C.V. 150a 16.58 N 25.19 W
Tarrafal, C.V. 150a 15.17 N 23.46 W
Tarragona 34 41.07 N 1.15 E
Tarragona □[4] 34 41.00 N 0.45 E
Tarraleah 166 42.18 S 146.27 E
Tarrant □[6] 222 32.47 N 97.18 W
Tarrant City 194 33.34 N 86.46 W
Tarrant Hinton 42 50.53 N 2.05 W
Tarrara Creek ≃ 208 36.33 N 77.10 W
Tarras 172 44.50 S 169.25 E
Tàrrega 34 41.39 N 1.09 E
Tarri 144 0.42 N 41.38 E
Tarrs 214 40.10 N 79.35 W
Tarrtown 214 40.51 N 79.31 W
Tarryall Creek ≃ 200 39.05 N 105.19 W
Tarrytown 210 41.04 N 73.51 W
Tarrytown Reservoir ⊜[1] 276 41.05 N 73.51 W
Tarsus 130 36.55 N 34.53 E
Tarta 128 40.02 N 52.46 E
Tartagal, Arg. 252 22.32 S 63.49 W
Tartagal, Arg. 252 28.40 S 59.52 W
Tärtär 84 40.20 N 46.55 E
Tärtär ≃ 84 40.35 N 47.22 E
Tartaro ≃ 64 45.02 N 11.30 E
Tartas ≃ 86 55.37 N 76.44 E
Tartu 76 58.23 N 26.43 E
Ṭarṭūs 130 34.53 N 35.53 E
Ṭarṭūs □[8] 130 35.00 N 36.00 E
Taruaçu 256 21.37 S 42.56 W
Tarui 94 35.22 N 136.32 E
Tarum ≃ 115a 5.59 S 107.03 E
Tarumi ◆[8] 270 34.38 N 135.03 E
Tarumirim 255 19.16 S 41.59 W
Tarumizu 92 31.29 N 130.42 E
Tarumovka 84 44.03 N 46.33 E
Tarusa 82 54.43 N 37.11 E
Tarusa ≃ 82 54.44 N 37.11 E
Ṭārūṭ 142 30.32 N 31.28 E
Tarutao, Ko I 114 6.35 N 99.40 E
Tarutino 82 55.07 N 36.56 E
Tarutung 114 2.01 N 98.58 E
Tarutyne 78 46.12 N 29.09 E
Tarvagatajn nuruu ⋀ 88 48.20 N 99.00 E
Tarves 46 57.22 N 2.13 W
Tarvisio 64 46.30 N 13.35 E
Tarvo ≃ 248 14.47 S 61.03 W
Tarwin ≃ 169 38.42 S 145.50 E
Tarwin, East Branch ≃ 169 38.34 S 146.00 E
Tarwin, West Branch ≃ 169 38.34 S 146.00 E
Tarza 24 62.30 N 40.25 E
Tarzan 196 32.18 N 101.58 W
Tarzana ◆[8] 280 34.10 N 118.32 W
Tarzo 64 45.58 N 12.14 E
Tas 80 48.27 N 51.02 E
Tas ≃ 42 52.36 N 1.18 E
Taşağıl 130 36.55 N 31.14 E
Tašanta 86 49.43 N 89.11 E
Tasaral 86 46.20 N 73.58 E
Tašauz 72 41.50 N 59.58 E
Tasāwah 146 25.58 N 13.30 E
Tasbuget 86 44.48 N 65.33 E
Taschkent → Taškent 85 41.20 N 69.18 E
Taşçı 130 38.13 N 35.48 E
Taşdelen 130 38.51 N 38.31 E
Tasejeva ≃ 86 58.06 N 94.01 E
Tasejevo 86 57.12 N 94.54 E
Taseko ≃ 182 52.00 N 123.40 W
Taseko Lakes ⊜ 182 51.15 N 123.35 W
Taseko Mountain ∧ 182 51.14 N 123.28 W
Tašelan 88 51.45 N 108.55 E
Tasendjanet, Oued V 148 24.36 N 1.07 E
Tāsgaon 122 17.02 N 74.36 E
Tashan, Zhg. 104 40.48 N 122.39 E
Tashan, Zhg. 104 40.51 N 120.56 E
Tashi Gang Dzong 120 27.19 N 91.34 E
Tashimalike 85 39.06 N 75.41 E
Tashiyi 100 29.43 N 112.48 E
Ṭashk, Daryācheh-ye ⊜ 128 29.45 N 53.30 E
Tashkent → Taškent 85 41.20 N 69.18 E
Tāshkurghān → Kholm 120 36.42 N 67.41 E
Tashuik'u 269d 25.13 N 121.30 E
Tasikmalaya 115a 7.20 S 108.12 E
Tasīl 132 32.50 N 35.58 E
Tåsinge I 41 55.00 N 10.36 E
Tašir 84 41.07 N 44.17 E
Taširovo 82 55.25 N 36.39 E
Tasitan 85 39.17 N 76.07 E
Tåsjö 26 64.13 N 15.54 E
Tåsjön ⊜ 26 64.15 N 15.47 E
Taskajevo 86 55.06 N 78.36 E
Taşkent, Tür. 130 36.55 N 32.31 E
Taškent (Tashkent), Uzb. 85 41.20 N 69.18 E
Taškent □[4] 85 41.00 N 69.30 E
Taškepri 128 36.18 N 62.38 E
Taşkesen 130 39.43 N 41.29 E
Taskesken 86 47.15 N 80.44 E
Taşköprü 130 41.30 N 34.14 E
Taskul 164 2.35 S 150.25 E
Taš-Kumyr 85 41.21 N 72.14 E
Taškyja 85 40.16 N 74.19 E
Tašla 80 51.47 N 52.46 E
Taşlı ≃ 267b 41.03 N 28.56 E
Tasman, Mount ∧ 172 43.34 S 170.09 E
Tasman Basin ✣[1] 6 43.00 S 158.00 E
Tasman Bay ⊂ 172 41.00 S 173.20 E
Tasmania □[3] 166 43.00 S 147.00 E
Tasmania I 166 42.00 S 147.00 E
Tasmanien → Tasmania I 166 42.00 S 147.00 E
Tasman Mountains ⋀ 172 41.07 S 172.33 E
Tasman Peninsula ›[1] 166 43.05 S 147.50 E
Tasman Sea ▼[2] 14 40.00 S 163.00 E
Tăşnad 38 47.29 N 22.35 E
Tasoba 80 49.47 N 49.52 E
Tasotkel'skoje vodochranilišče ⊜[1] 85 43.22 N 74.00 E
Taşova 130 40.46 N 36.20 E
Tasrār Sharīf 123 33.52 N 74.46 E
Taşrumi 84 38.48 N 44.04 E
Tassajara Creek ≃ 282 37.41 N 121.53 W
Tassara 150 16.48 N 5.39 E
Tassdorf 264a 52.30 N 13.47 E
Tassialouc, Lac ⊜ 176 59.03 N 74.00 W
Tassin-la-Demi-Lune 62 45.46 N 4.47 E
Tasso Lake ⊜ 212 45.27 N 78.56 W
Tassu, Serra di lu ∧ 71 41.01 N 9.08 E
Taštagol 86 52.47 N 87.53 E
Tastiota 232 28.22 N 111.23 W
Tåstrup 41 55.39 N 12.19 E
Taštyp 86 52.48 N 89.54 E
Taşucu 130 36.19 N 33.53 E
Tata, Magreb 148 29.44 N 7.56 W
Tata, Magy. 30 47.39 N 18.18 E
Tata □[4] 148 29.40 N 7.45 W
T'at'a, vulkan ∧[1] 92a 44.21 N 146.15 E
Tataa, Pointe › 174s 17.34 S 149.37 W
Tatabánya 30 47.34 N 18.26 E
Tatahuicapan 234 18.14 N 94.45 W
Tatal 80 47.17 N 46.16 E
Tatalin ≃ 102 37.30 N 95.28 E
Tata Mailau ∧ 112 8.55 S 125.30 E
Tatamy 208 40.44 N 75.15 W
Tataouine 148 32.56 N 10.27 E
Tata Raphael, Camp ■ 273b 4.18 S 15.17 E
Tatarbunary 78 45.49 N 29.36 E
Tatarija □[3], Ross. 72 55.00 N 51.00 E
Tatarija □[3], Ross. 80 55.00 N 51.00 E
Tatarinka 76 55.58 N 33.54 E
Tatarino 78 50.36 N 39.07 E
Tatarinovo, Ross. 82 55.13 N 37.56 E
Tatarinovo, Ross. 82 56.34 N 38.25 E
Tatarischer Sund → Tatarskij proliv ʯ 89 50.00 N 141.15 E
Tatarka, Bela. 76 53.16 N 28.48 E
Tatarka, Ross. 86 53.58 N 75.05 E
Tatarlar 130 41.46 N 26.55 E
Tatarovo ◆[8] 265b 55.46 N 37.26 E
Tātārpur ◆[8] 272a 28.39 N 77.07 E
Tatarsk 86 55.13 N 75.58 E
Tatarskij Kandyz 80 54.07 N 53.07 E
Tatarskij proliv (Tatar Strait) ʯ 89 50.00 N 141.15 E
Tatarskij Sajman 80 53.18 N 47.07 E
Tatarskoje-Maklakovo 80 55.48 N 45.34 E
Tatarstan → Tatarija □[3] 80 55.00 N 51.00 E
Tatar Strait → Tatarskij proliv ʯ 89 50.00 N 141.15 E
Tatau ≃ 112 3.07 N 112.49 E
Tatau Island I 164 2.50 S 152.00 E
Tataurovo, Ross. 76 58.44 N 43.20 E
Tataurovo, Ross. 80 57.48 N 49.34 E
Tataurovo, Ross. 88 51.37 N 112.56 E
Tate 192 34.25 N 84.22 W
Tate ≃ 166 17.22 S 143.44 E
Tatebayashi 94 36.15 N 139.32 E
Tate Gallery ʊ 260 51.29 N 0.08 W
Tateishi-misaki › 94 35.46 N 136.01 E
Tateiwa 94 37.05 N 139.32 E
Tateiwa-chosuichi ⊜[1] 96 34.33 N 132.10 E
Tateshina 94 36.16 N 138.19 E
Tateyama, Nihon 94 34.59 N 139.52 E
Tateyama, Nihon 94 36.40 N 137.19 E
Tate-yama ∧ 94 36.35 N 137.37 E
Tathlina Lake ⊜ 176 60.32 N 117.32 W
Tathlīth, Wādī V 144 20.44 N 44.17 E
Tathong Point › 271d 22.14 N 114.17 E
Tathra 166 36.44 S 149.59 E
Tatikawa → Tachikawa 94 35.42 N 139.25 E
Tatiščevo, Ross. 80 51.40 N 45.35 E
Tatiščevo, Ross. 82 56.24 N 37.31 E
Tatitlek 180 60.52 N 146.41 W
Tatla Lake 182 51.55 N 124.36 W
Tatla Lake ⊜ 182 52.00 N 124.25 W
Tatlayoko Lake 182 51.39 N 124.24 W
Tatlayoko Lake ⊜ 182 51.30 N 124.25 W
Tatlow, Mount ∧ 182 51.23 N 123.52 W
Tatnam, Cape › 176 57.16 N 91.00 W
Tatomi 94 35.36 N 138.31 E
Tatoosh Island I 224 48.24 N 124.44 W
Tatrang 120 38.28 N 85.35 E
Tatranský národní park ♠ 30 49.10 N 20.05 E
Tatrzański Park Narodowy ♠ 30 49.15 N 20.00 E
Tatsfield 260 51.18 N 0.02 E
Tatsuno, Nihon 94 35.59 N 137.59 E
Tatsuno, Nihon 96 34.52 N 134.33 E
Tatsunokuchi 94 36.27 N 136.35 E
Tatsuruhama 94 37.04 N 136.53 E
Tatsuyama 94 34.58 N 137.49 E
Tatta 120 24.45 N 67.55 E
Tattenhall 44 53.06 N 2.46 W
Tatti 85 43.12 N 73.19 E
Tatton Hall ⊥ 262 53.20 N 2.23 W
Tatton Mere ⊜ 262 53.19 N 2.22 W
Tatton Park ♠ 262 53.20 N 2.22 W
Tatu ≃ 100 24.12 N 120.29 E
Tatuapé ◆[8] 287b 23.32 S 46.34 W
Tatuk Lake ⊜ 182 53.32 N 124.15 W
Tatum, N.M., U.S. 196 33.15 N 103.19 W
Tatum, Tx., U.S. 222 32.19 N 94.31 W
Tat'ung → Datong 102 40.05 N 113.18 E
Tat'un Shan ∧ 269d 25.11 N 121.31 E
Tatvan 130 38.30 N 42.16 E
Tatzuli ≃ 100 24.08 N 121.39 E
Tau, Am. Sam. 174y 14.14 S 169.32 W
Tau, Kaz. 80 49.40 N 47.17 E
Tau, Nor. 26 59.04 N 5.54 E
Tau I 174y 14.15 S 169.30 W
Tauá 250 6.01 S 40.26 W
Tauanap, Mochun ʯ 175c 7.28 N 151.36 E
Taubaté 256 23.02 S 45.33 W
Tauber ≃ 56 49.46 N 9.31 E
Tauberbischofsheim 56 49.37 N 9.40 E
Taucha 54 51.23 N 12.30 E
Taučik 72 44.21 N 51.19 E
Tauer 54 51.50 N 14.28 E
Tauern-Tunnel ◆[5] 64 47.05 N 13.05 E
Täuffelen 58 47.04 N 7.12 E
Taufkirchen, Dtsch. 60 48.21 N 12.08 E
Taufkirchen, Dtsch. 64 48.03 N 11.37 E
Taufstein ∧ 56 50.31 N 9.14 E
Taughannock Creek ≃ 210 42.33 N 76.36 W
Taughannock Falls State Park ♠ 210 42.32 N 76.35 W
Tauini ≃ 246 0.30 N 58.22 W
Taujskaja guba ⊂ 74 59.20 N 150.20 E
Taukum, peski ◆[2] 86 44.50 N 75.30 E
Taulabé 236 14.38 N 87.59 W
Taulihawā 124 27.32 N 83.03 E
Taulov 41 55.33 N 9.37 E
Taumarunui 172 38.52 S 175.17 E
Taum Sauk Mountain ∧ 194 37.34 N 90.44 W
Taunay 248 20.18 S 56.05 W
Taunay, Cascatinha ᒐ 287a 22.57 S 43.17 W
Taung 158 27.33 S 24.47 E
Taungbon 110 15.25 N 97.50 E
Taungdwingyi 110 20.01 N 95.33 E
Taunggon 110 23.38 N 96.32 E
Taunggyi 110 20.47 N 97.02 E
Taungnyo Range ⋀ 110 15.38 N 97.56 E
Taungup 110 18.51 N 94.14 E
Taungup Pass )( 110 18.40 N 94.45 E
Taunsa 123 30.42 N 70.39 E
Taunsa Barrage ◆[6] 123 30.31 N 70.51 E
Taunton, Eng., U.K. 42 51.01 N 3.06 W
Taunton, Ma., U.S. 207 41.54 N 71.05 W
Taunton, N.Y., U.S. 210 43.01 N 76.13 W
Taunton ≃ 207 41.42 N 71.10 W
Taunton, Vale of V 42 51.02 N 3.08 W
Taunton Lake ⊜ 285 39.51 N 74.51 W
Taunton Lakes 285 39.51 N 74.51 W
Taunus ⋀ 56 50.10 N 8.15 E
Taunusstein 56 50.08 N 8.08 E
Taupiri 172 37.37 S 175.11 E
Tauplitz 61 47.33 N 14.00 E
Taupo 172 38.41 S 176.05 E
Taupo, Lake ⊜ 172 38.49 S 175.55 E
Tauragė 76 55.15 N 22.17 E
Taurak 86 51.35 N 85.01 E
Tauranga 172 37.42 S 176.10 E
Taurasi 68 41.00 N 14.57 E
Taureau, Réservoir ⊜[1] 206 46.46 N 73.50 W
Tauri ≃ 164 8.08 S 146.06 E
Taurianova 68 38.21 N 16.01 E
Tauripampa 248 12.35 S 76.07 W
Taurisano 68 39.57 N 18.13 E
Taurisma 248 15.10 S 72.51 W
Tauroa Point › 172 35.10 S 173.04 E
Taurovo 86 59.36 N 73.18 E
Taurus Mountains → Toros Dağları ⋀ 130 37.00 N 33.00 E
Tauste 34 41.55 N 1.15 W
Tautira 174s 17.44 S 149.09 W
Tauxigny 50 47.13 N 0.50 E
Tavaí 252 26.07 S 55.32 W
Tavajvaam ≃ 180 64.56 N 177.30 E
Tavajza 89 45.12 N 136.44 E
Ṭavālesh, Kūhhā-ye → Talish Mountains ⋀ 128 38.42 N 48.18 E
Tavanasa 58 46.45 N 9.04 E
Tavannes 58 47.13 N 7.12 E
Tavant 50 47.07 N 0.23 E
Tavares, Bra. 250 7.38 S 37.54 W
Tavares, Fl., U.S. 220 28.48 N 81.43 W
Tavares, Ilha dos I 287a 22.49 S 43.06 W
Tavarnelle Val di Pesa 66 43.33 N 11.10 E
Tavas 130 37.34 N 29.04 E
Tavastehus → Hämeenlinna 26 61.00 N 24.27 E
Tavaux 58 47.02 N 5.24 E
Tavda 86 58.03 N 65.15 E
Tavda ≃ 72 57.47 N 67.16 E
Tave ≃ 62 44.07 N 4.42 E
Tavera ≃ 64 46.29 N 11.21 E
Taverham 42 52.41 N 1.12 E
Taverna 68 39.01 N 16.35 E
Tavern Creek ≃ 194 38.19 N 92.18 W
Tavernelle, It. 64 44.18 N 10.04 E
Tavernelle, It. 66 43.00 N 12.09 E
Tavernes 62 43.36 N 6.01 E
Tavernes de la Valldigna 34 39.04 N 0.16 W
Tavernier 220 25.00 N 80.30 W
Tavernole sul Mella 64 45.45 N 10.14 E
Taverny 50 49.02 N 2.13 E
Taveta, Kenya 154 3.24 S 37.41 E
Taveta, Tan. 154 9.01 S 35.37 E
Taveuni I 175g 16.51 S 179.58 W
Taviano 68 39.59 N 18.05 E
Tavil'dara 85 38.43 N 70.28 E
Tavira 34 37.07 N 7.39 W
Tavistock, On., Can. 212 43.19 N 80.50 W
Tavistock, Eng., U.K. 42 50.33 N 4.08 W
Tavn-Gašun 80 46.01 N 45.55 E
Tavolara, Isola I 71 40.54 N 9.42 E
Tavoliere ◆[1] 68 41.35 N 15.25 E
Tavolžan 86 52.44 N 77.27 E
Tavor, Har (Mount Tabor) ∧ 132 32.41 N 35.23 E
Távora ≃ 34 41.09 N 7.35 W
Tavoy → Dawei 110 14.05 N 98.12 E
Tavoy Point › 110 13.32 N 98.10 E
Tavričanka 89 43.22 N 131.52 E
Tavričeskoje 86 54.35 N 73.38 E
Tavry 265a 59.55 N 30.42 E
Tavsalayihüseynan 130 38.38 N 40.32 E
Tavşanlı 130 39.33 N 29.30 E
Tavua 175g 17.27 S 177.51 E
Tavy ≃ 42 50.16 N 4.10 W
Taw ≃ 42 51.04 N 4.11 W
Tawa 172 41.10 S 174.51 E
Tawa ≃ 124 22.48 N 77.48 E
Tawaeli 112 0.43 S 119.51 E
Tawakoni, Lake ⊜[1] 222 32.55 N 96.00 W
Tawara 270 34.27 N 135.57 E
Tawarada 268 35.19 N 140.04 E
Tawaramoto 96 34.33 N 135.48 E
Tawas City 190 44.16 N 83.30 W
Tawau 112 4.15 N 117.54 E
Tawd ≃ 262 53.36 N 2.48 W
Tāwi ≃ 123 32.40 N 74.41 E
Ṭawīlah, Juzur II 140 27.35 N 33.46 E
Tawi-Tawi □[4] 116 5.20 N 120.00 E
Tawi-Tawi Group II 116 5.10 N 120.15 E
Tawi-Tawi Island I 116 5.10 N 120.00 E
Ṭawkar 140 18.26 N 37.44 E
Tawu 100 22.22 N 120.54 E
Ṭāwūq 128 35.08 N 44.27 E
Tāwurghā' 146 32.02 N 15.09 E
Tawwah Banī Ibrāhīm 142 28.05 N 30.41 E
Taxco de Alarcón 234 18.33 N 99.36 W
Taxenbach 64 47.17 N 12.58 E
Taxi 89 49.26 N 126.08 E
Taxila 123 33.44 N 72.49 E
Taxisco 236 14.04 N 90.28 W
Taxkorgan Tajik Zizhixian 120 37.49 N 75.14 E
Taxusi 102 32.58 N 98.10 E
Tay ≃, On., Can. 212 44.53 N 76.07 W
Tay ≃, Yk., Can. 180 62.34 N 134.22 W
Tay ≃, Scot., U.K. 46 56.22 N 3.21 W
Tay, Firth of ⊂[1] 46 56.26 N 3.00 W
Tay, Lake ⊜ 162 32.55 S 120.48 E
Tay, Loch ⊜ 46 56.31 N 4.10 W
Tayabamba 248 8.17 S 77.18 W
Tayabas 116 14.01 N 121.35 E
Tayabas Bay ⊂ 116 13.45 N 121.45 E
Tayan 112 0.02 S 110.07 E
Tayandu, Kepulauan II 164 5.30 S 132.15 E
Tayayi 105 39.25 N 115.03 E
Tayeegle 144 4.02 N 44.31 E
Taylor, B.C., Can. 182 56.10 N 120.41 W
Taylor, Az., U.S. 200 34.27 N 110.05 W
Taylor, Ar., U.S. 194 33.06 N 93.27 W
Taylor, Mi., U.S. 216 42.14 N 83.16 W
Taylor, Mo., U.S. 219 39.56 N 91.32 W
Taylor, Ne., U.S. 198 41.46 N 99.22 W
Taylor, Pa., U.S. 210 41.23 N 75.42 W
Taylor, Tx., U.S. 222 30.34 N 97.24 W
Taylor ≃ 200 38.40 N 106.51 W
Taylor, Mount ∧, N.Z. 172 43.30 S 171.19 E
Taylor, Mount ∧, N.M., U.S. 200 35.14 N 107.37 W
Taylor Creek ≃, On., Can. 275b 43.42 N 79.20 W
Taylor Creek ≃, Il., U.S. 219 39.13 N 90.18 W
Taylor Lake Village 222 29.36 N 95.03 W
Taylor Mountain ∧ 202 44.53 N 114.13 W
Taylor Mountains ⋀ 180 60.50 N 157.20 W
Taylor Run ≃ 285 39.57 N 75.39 W
Taylors 192 34.55 N 82.17 W
Taylors Bush Park ♠ 275b 43.42 N 79.19 W
Taylors Island 208 38.28 N 76.17 W
Taylor Springs 219 39.08 N 89.30 W
Taylors Run ≃ 279b 40.11 N 79.57 W
Taylorstown 214 40.10 N 80.23 W
Taylorsville, In., U.S. 218 39.17 N 85.57 W
Taylorsville, Ky., U.S. 194 38.01 N 85.20 W
Taylorsville, Ms., U.S. 194 31.49 N 89.25 W
Taylorsville, N.C., U.S. 192 35.55 N 81.10 W
Taylorsville Dam ◆[6] 218 39.53 N 84.10 W
Taylortown, N.J., U.S. 276 40.56 N 74.24 W
Taylortown, Oh., U.S. 214 40.28 N 80.40 W
Taylortown Reservoir ⊜[1] 276 40.58 N 74.22 W
Taylorville 219 39.32 N 89.17 W
Taylorville, Lake ⊜[1] 219 39.30 N 89.15 W
Taymā' 128 27.38 N 38.29 E
Taymouth 186 46.11 N 66.37 W
Taymyr Peninsula → Tajmyr, poluostrov ›[1] 74 76.00 N 104.00 E
Tay Ninh 110 11.18 N 106.06 E
Taynuilt 46 56.25 N 5.14 W
Tayoltita 232 24.05 N 105.56 W
Tayport 46 56.27 N 2.53 W
Táyros 267c 37.58 N 23.42 E
Tayside □[4] 46 56.30 N 3.30 W
Taytay, Pil. 116 10.49 N 119.31 E
Taytay, Pil. 116 14.34 N 121.08 E
Taytay Bay ⊂ 116 10.55 N 119.35 E
Tayu 115a 6.32 S 111.02 E
Tayüan, T'aiwan 100 25.04 N 121.11 E
Tayuan, Zhg. 89 51.27 N 124.16 E
Tayyārah 140 13.12 N 30.47 E
Tayyebāt 128 34.44 N 60.45 E
Taz ≃ 72 67.32 N 78.40 E
Taza 148 34.16 N 4.01 W
Taza □[4] 148 34.05 N 3.45 W
Tazawa-ko ⊜ 92 39.43 N 140.40 E
Tazenakht 148 30.35 N 7.12 W
Tazewell, Tn., U.S. 192 36.27 N 83.34 W
Tazewell, Va., U.S. 192 37.06 N 81.31 W
Tazhuang 105 39.55 N 117.13 E
Tazicheng 89 46.35 N 123.06 E
Tazigou ≃ 104 41.44 N 121.30 E
Tazin ≃ 176 60.26 N 110.45 W
Tazin Lake ⊜ 176 59.47 N 109.03 W
T'ažinskij 86 56.07 N 88.31 E
Tāzirbū ▼[4] 146 25.45 N 21.00 E
Tazishan 107 29.28 N 104.14 E
Tazlina 180 62.04 N 145.25 W
Tazlina Lake ⊜ 180 61.50 N 146.30 W
Tazoult-Lambese 34 35.29 N 6.15 E
Tazovskaja guba ⊂ 74 69.05 N 76.00 E
Tazovskij 74 67.28 N 78.42 E
Tazovskij poluostrov ›[1] 72 68.35 N 76.00 E
Tazrouk 148 23.25 N 6.16 E
Tazumal ⊥ 236 13.59 N 89.41 W
Tāzumuddin 126 22.29 N 90.53 E
Tazungdām 102 28.02 N 97.35 E
Tbessa 148 35.28 N 8.09 E
Tbilisi 84 41.43 N 44.49 E
Tbilisskaja 78 45.23 N 40.12 E
Tchad → Chad □[1] 146 15.00 N 19.00 E
Tchad, Lac (Lake Chad) ⊜ 146 13.20 N 14.00 E
Tchaguine Golo 146 10.03 N 16.19 E
Tchamba 150 9.02 N 1.25 E
Tch'ang-Cha → Changsha 100 28.12 N 112.58 E
Tchaourou 150 8.53 N 2.36 E
Tchefuncta ≃ 194 30.22 N 90.10 W
Tchékapika 152 1.17 S 16.11 E
Tcheliabinsk → Čel'abinsk 86 55.10 N 61.24 E
Tcheng-Tcheou → Zhengzhou 102 34.48 N 113.39 E
Tchentlo Lake ⊜ 182 55.11 N 125.00 W
Tchériba 150 12.16 N 3.05 W
Tchesinkut Lake ⊜ 182 54.05 N 125.40 W
Tchetti 150 7.50 N 1.40 E
Tchibanga 152 2.51 S 11.02 E
Tchigaï, Plateau du ⋀[1] 146 21.30 N 14.50 E
Tchikala-Tcholohanga 152 12.38 S 16.03 E
Tchin-Tabáradene 150 15.58 N 5.50 E
Tchitondi 152 4.33 S 12.08 E
Tcholliré 146 8.24 N 14.10 E
Tchong-K'ing → Chongqing 107 29.34 N 106.35 E
Tchořovice 60 49.27 N 13.48 E
Tchula 194 33.10 N 90.13 W
T.C. Steele State Memorial ⊥ 218 39.08 N 86.20 W
Tczew 30 54.06 N 18.47 E
Té ≃ 110 12.27 N 106.02 E
Te, Kinh ≡ 269c 10.45 N 106.42 E
Teá ≃ 246 0.30 S 65.09 W
Teaca 38 46.55 N 24.31 E
Teacapan 234 22.33 N 105.45 W
Tea Creek ≃ 284a 43.02 N 79.06 W
Teaehoa, Pointe › 174x 9.51 S 139.01 W
Teague 222 31.37 N 96.17 W
Teahupoo 174s 17.51 S 149.13 W
Te Anau 172 45.25 S 167.43 E
Te Anau, Lake ⊜ 172 45.12 S 167.48 E
Teanaway ≃ 224 47.10 N 120.50 W
Teanaway, Middle Fork ≃ 224 47.15 N 120.53 W
Teanaway, North Fork ≃ 224 47.22 N 120.53 W
Teaneck 210 40.53 N 74.00 W
Teangue 46 57.07 N 5.50 W
Teano 68 41.15 N 14.04 E
Teapa 234 17.33 N 92.57 W
Teapa ≃ 234 17.58 N 92.54 W
Te Araroa 172 37.38 S 178.22 E
Tearinibai 174t 1.35 N 172.58 E
Te Aroha 172 37.33 S 175.43 E
Teaticket 207 41.33 N 70.35 W
Tea Tree 162 22.11 S 133.17 E
Tea Tree Gully 168b 34.49 S 138.44 E
Te Atukura ∧ 174k 21.14 S 159.45 W
Te Awamutu 172 38.01 S 175.19 E
Teba, Esp. 34 36.58 N 4.56 W
Teba, Indon. 164 1.29 S 137.54 E
Tebakang 112 1.06 N 110.30 E
Tebas 256 21.35 S 42.44 W
Tebay 44 54.26 N 2.35 W
Tebbetts 219 38.37 N 91.57 W
Teberda 84 43.28 N 41.45 E
Teberdinskij zapovednik ♠ 84 43.20 N 41.45 E
Tebicuary ≃ 252 26.36 S 58.16 W
Tebicuary-Mí ≃ 252 26.26 S 56.51 W
Tebingbulan 112 3.03 S 103.44 E
Tebingtinggi, Indon. 112 0.36 N 101.36 E
Tebingtinggi, Indon. 112 3.36 S 103.05 E
Tebingtinggi, Indon. 114 3.20 N 99.09 E
Tebingtinggi, Pulau I 114 0.54 N 102.45 E
Tébourba 36 36.49 N 9.51 E
Téboursouk 148 36.28 N 9.15 E
Téboursouk, Monts de ⋀ 36 36.30 N 9.10 E
Tebra ≃ 76 56.51 N 21.12 E
Tebstrup 41 55.59 N 9.53 E
Tebulosmta, gora ∧ 84 42.33 N 45.19 E
Tebza ≃ 80 58.23 N 41.19 E
Teča ≃ 86 56.13 N 62.58 E
Tecalitlán 234 19.26 N 103.15 W
Tecamachalco 234 18.53 N 97.44 W
Tecate 232 32.34 N 116.38 W
Tech ≃ 32 42.36 N 3.03 E
Teche, Bayou ≃ 194 29.43 N 91.13 W
Techendorf 64 46.43 N 13.17 E
Techiman 150 7.35 N 1.56 W
Techimentia 150 7.11 N 2.02 W
Techirghiol 38 44.03 N 28.36 E
Techlé 148 21.35 N 14.58 W
Techou → Dezhou 98 37.27 N 116.18 E
Tecka 254 43.29 S 70.48 W
Tecka ≃ 254 42.37 S 70.25 W
Tecklenburg 52 52.13 N 7.48 E
Teckomatorp 41 55.52 N 13.05 E
Tecolote Creek ≃ 200 35.22 N 105.15 W
Tecolotlán 234 20.13 N 104.03 W
Tecolutla ≃ 234 20.29 N 97.00 W
Tecomán 234 18.55 N 103.53 W
Tecomate, Laguna ⊂ 234 16.35 N 99.25 W
Tecominoacán 234 17.53 N 93.37 W
Tecopa 204 35.50 N 116.13 W
Tecozautla 234 20.32 N 99.38 W
Tecpan ≃ 234 17.25 N 100.40 W
Tecpan de Galeana 234 17.15 N 100.41 W
Tecpán Guatemala 236 14.46 N 91.00 W
Tecpatan 234 17.08 N 93.18 W
Tecuala 234 22.23 N 105.27 W
Tecuamburro, Volcán ∧[1] 236 14.09 N 90.24 W
Tecuautzi, Cerro ∧ 286a 19.19 N 99.00 W
Tecuci 38 45.50 N 27.26 E
Tecumseh, On., Can. 214 42.19 N 82.54 W
Tecumseh, Mi., U.S. 216 42.00 N 83.56 W
Tecumseh, Ne., U.S. 198 40.22 N 96.11 W
Tecumseh, Ok., U.S. 196 35.15 N 96.56 W
Ted Ceidaar Dabole 144 4.24 N 43.55 E
Teddington ◆[8] 260 51.25 N 0.20 W
Tédji 146 11.46 N 21.19 E
Tedori ≃ 94 36.29 N 136.28 E
Tedrow 216 41.37 N 84.13 W
Tedžen 128 37.23 N 60.31 E
Tedžen (Harīrūd) ≃ 128 37.24 N 60.38 E
Tedženstroj 128 36.55 N 60.53 E
Teec Nos Pos 200 36.56 N 109.42 W
Teeli 86 51.07 N 90.14 E
Teels Marsh ≡ 204 38.12 N 118.21 W
Teen ⊜ 40 59.07 N 14.40 E
Teerijärvi → Terjärv 26 63.32 N 23.30 E
Tees ≃ 44 54.34 N 1.16 W
Tees Bay ⊂ 44 54.39 N 1.07 W
Teesdale V 44 54.38 N 2.07 W
Teesside → Middlesbrough 44 54.35 N 1.14 W
Tees-Side Airport ⊠ 44 54.31 N 1.25 W
Teeswater 212 44.00 N 81.17 W
Teeswater ≃ 212 44.18 N 81.17 W
Tefé 246 3.22 S 64.42 W
Tefé ≃ 242 3.35 S 64.47 W
Tefé, Lago ⊜ 246 3.27 S 64.47 W
Tefenni 130 37.18 N 29.47 E
Tefft 216 41.12 N 86.58 W
Tefle 150 5.59 N 0.35 E
Tegal 115a 6.52 S 109.08 E
Tegalombo 115a 8.04 S 111.17 E
Tégama ◆[1] 150 15.50 N 8.12 E
Tega-numa ⊜ 268 35.51 N 140.04 E
Tegel ◆[8] 54 52.35 N 13.17 E
Tegel, Berliner Forst ◆[3] 264a 52.37 N 13.16 E
Tegelen 52 51.21 N 6.09 E
Tegeler See ⊜ 264a 52.35 N 13.15 E
Tegernsee 64 47.43 N 11.45 E
Tegernsee ⊜ 64 47.42 N 11.45 E
Teggiano 68 40.23 N 15.32 E
Teghra 124 25.29 N 85.57 E
Tegid, Llyn ⊜ 42 52.53 N 3.36 W
Tegina 150 10.05 N 6.14 E
Tegineneng 112 5.12 S 105.10 E
Tegistyk 85 44.02 N 68.22 E
Teglio 64 46.10 N 10.04 E
Tégua I 175f 13.15 S 166.37 E
Tegualda 254 41.02 S 73.26 W
Tegucigalpa 236 14.06 N 87.13 W
Tegul'det 86 57.19 N 88.10 E
Tehachapi 228 35.07 N 118.26 W
Tehachapi Creek ≃ 228 35.17 N 118.38 W
Tehachapi Mountains ⋀ 228 35.00 N 118.40 W
Tehachapi Pass )( 228 35.06 N 118.18 W
Tehamiyam 140 18.20 N 36.32 E
Te Hapua 172 34.31 S 172.54 E
Tehar ◆[8] 272a 28.38 N 77.07 E
Te Haroto 172 39.08 S 176.36 E
Tehata 126 23.43 N 88.32 E
Tehek Lake ⊜ 176 64.55 N 95.38 W
Teheran → Tehrān 128 35.40 N 51.26 E
Téhini 150 9.36 N 3.40 W
Tehoohaivei, Cap › 174x 9.49 S 138.54 W
Te Hope O Te Keho, Cap › 174x 10.02 S 139.06 W
Tehoru 164 3.23 S 129.30 E
Tehrān, Īrān 128 35.40 N 51.26 E
Tehrān, Īrān 267d 35.40 N 51.26 E
Tehrān □[4] 128 35.30 N 51.30 E
Tehrān, University of ʊ[2] 267d 35.42 N 51.24 E
Tehran International Airport ⊠ 267d 35.41 N 51.19 E
Tehrān Pārs ◆[8] 267d 35.44 N 51.32 E
Tehrathum 124 27.07 N 87.32 E
Tehri 124 30.23 N 78.29 E
Tehuacán 234 18.27 N 97.23 W
Tehuacana 222 31.44 N 96.33 W
Tehuacana Creek ≃, Tx., U.S. 222 31.31 N 97.02 W
Tehuacana Creek ≃, Tx., U.S. 222 31.50 N 95.59 W
Tehuantepec 234 18.41 N 103.17 W
Tehuantepec ≃ 234 16.10 N 95.07 W
Tehuantepec, Golfo de ⊂ 234 16.00 N 94.50 W
Tehuantepec, Istmo de ⊥[3] 234 17.00 N 95.00 W
Tehuantepec Ridge ✣[3] 16 13.30 N 98.00 W
Tehuelches 254 46.56 S 67.27 W
Tehuipango 234 18.31 N 97.04 W
Tehuitzingo 234 18.21 N 98.17 W
Teià 266d 41.30 N 2.19 E
Teichl ≃ 61 47.46 N 14.10 E
Teichröda 54 50.45 N 11.18 E
Teichwolframsdorf 54 50.43 N 12.14 E
Teide, Parque Nacional del ♠ 148 28.15 N 16.30 W
Teide, Pico de ∧ 148 28.16 N 16.38 W
Teifi ≃ 42 52.07 N 4.42 W
Teifiside ◆[1] 42 52.02 N 4.22 W
Teiga Plateau ⋀[1] 140 15.38 N 25.40 E
Teign ≃ 42 50.33 N 3.29 W
Teignmouth 42 50.33 N 3.30 W
Teise ≃ 260 51.13 N 0.25 E
Teisendorf 64 47.51 N 12.49 E
Teisnach 60 49.02 N 13.00 E
Teith ≃ 46 56.08 N 3.59 W
Teixeira 250 7.13 S 37.15 W
Teixeira Pinto 150 12.10 N 13.55 W
Teixeira Soares 252 25.22 S 50.27 W
Teixeiro 34 43.07 N 8.03 W
Tejakula 115b 8.08 S 115.20 E
Tejamén 232 24.48 N 105.07 W
Tejkovo 80 56.52 N 40.34 E
Tejo → Tagus ≃ 34 38.40 N 9.24 W
Tejon Creek ≃ 228 35.08 N 118.53 W
Tejon Pass )( 228 34.48 N 118.52 W
Tejupan, Punta › 234 18.20 N 103.32 W
Tejupilco de Hidalgo 234 18.54 N 100.09 W
Te Kaha 172 37.44 S 177.41 E
Tekai ≃ 114 4.14 N 102.23 E
Tékakwitha, Île I 275a 45.25 N 73.42 W
Tekam ≃ 114 3.52 N 102.27 E
Tekamah 198 41.46 N 96.13 W
Te Kao 172 34.39 S 172.57 E
Tekapo, Lake ⊜ 172 43.53 S 170.31 E
Te Karaka 172 38.28 S 177.52 E
Tekāri 124 24.56 N 84.50 E
Te Kauwhata 172 37.24 S 175.09 E
Tekax 232 20.12 N 89.17 W
Teke 130 41.04 N 29.39 E
Teke, ozero ⊜ 86 53.48 N 73.00 E
Teke Burnu › 130 38.05 N 26.36 E
Tekeli 86 44.48 N 78.57 E
Tekeli Dağı ∧ 130 40.09 N 37.28 E
Tekes 86 43.10 N 81.43 E
Tekes ≃ 86 43.36 N 82.32 E
Tekeze (Satīt) ≃ 140 14.20 N 35.50 E
Tekirdağ 130 40.59 N 27.31 E
Tekirdağ □[4] 130 41.00 N 27.30 E
Tekkali 122 18.37 N 84.14 E
Tekke 130 40.43 N 36.12 E
Tekke Burnu › 130 40.02 N 26.10 E
Tekkiraz 130 40.59 N 37.08 E
Tekman 130 39.38 N 41.31 E
Tekoa 202 47.13 N 117.04 W
Tekong, Pulau I 271c 1.24 N 104.03 E
Tekong Kechil, Pulau I 271c 1.25 N 104.01 E
Tekonsha 216 42.05 N 84.59 W
Te Kopuru 172 36.02 S 173.56 E
Tekouiat, Oued V 148 22.25 N 2.35 E
Tékro ▼[4] 146 19.30 N 20.58 E
Tekstil'ščiki 82 55.57 N 37.49 E
Tekstil'ščiki ◆[8] 265b 55.42 N 37.44 E
Teku 112 0.46 S 123.26 E
Te Kuiti 172 38.20 S 175.10 E
Tekukor, Pulau I 271c 1.14 N 103.50 E
Tel ≃ 122 20.50 N 83.54 E
Tela, Hond. 236 15.44 N 87.27 W
Tela, India 272a 28.44 N 77.20 E
Tela, Bahía de ⊂ 236 15.48 N 87.30 W
Telaga 116 6.51 N 117.03 E
Telaga, Teluk ⊂ 114 2.10 N 98.00 E
Telaga-kulon 115a 6.58 S 108.18 E
Télagh 148 34.47 N 0.34 W
Telaopengsha Shan ∧ 120 30.33 N 86.25 E
Tel Ashqelon ⊥ 132 31.39 N 34.32 E
Telavåg 26 60.16 N 4.49 E
Telavi 84 41.55 N 45.28 E
Tel Aviv □[5] 132 32.05 N 34.48 E
Tel Aviv-Yafo 132 32.03 N 34.46 E
Telč 30 49.11 N 15.27 E
Tel'čje 76 53.21 N 36.20 E
Telde 148 28.00 N 15.25 W
Tele ≃, Afr. 158 30.26 S 27.33 E
Tele ≃, Zaïre 152 2.48 N 23.54 E
Teleckoje, ozero ⊜ 86 51.35 N 87.40 E
Telefomin 164 5.10 S 141.35 E
Telegapulang 112 2.55 S 112.25 E
Telegino 80 52.55 N 44.34 E
Telegrafo, Pizzo ∧ 70 37.37 N 13.10 E
Telegraph Canyon V 280 33.55 N 117.45 W
Telegraph Cove 182 50.33 N 126.50 W
Telegraph Creek 180 57.55 N 131.10 W
Telêmaco Borba 252 24.20 S 50.40 W
Telemark □[6] 26 59.30 N 8.40 E
Telemba 88 52.43 N 113.16 E


**Symbols** in the index entries represent the broad categories identified in the key at the right. Symbols with superior numbers (⋀[1]) identify subcategories (see complete key on page *I · 1).*

**Symbole** im Register stellen die rechts im Schlüssel erklärten Kategorien dar. Symbole mit hochgestellten Ziffern (⋀[1]) bezeichnen Unterabteilungen einer Kategorie (vgl. vollständiger Schlüssel auf Seite *I · 1).*

**Los símbolos** incluídos en el texto del índice representan las grandes categorías identificadas con la clave a la derecha. Los símbolos con numeros en su parte superior (⋀[1]) identifican las subcategorías (véase la clave completa en la página *I · 1).*

**Les symboles** de l'index représentent les catégories indiquées dans la légende à droite. Les symboles suivis d'un indice (⋀[1]) représentent des sous-catégories (voir légende complète à la page *I · 1).*

**Os símbolos** incluídos no texto do índice representam as grandes categorias identificadas com a chave à direita. Os símbolos com números em sua parte superior (⋀[1]) identificam as subcategorias (veja-se a chave completa à página *I · 1).*

| | English | Deutsch | Español | Français | Português |
|---|---|---|---|---|---|
| ∧ | Mountain | Berg | Montaña | Montagne | Montanha |
| ⋀ | Mountains | Gebirge | Montañas | Montagnes | Montanhas |
| )( | Pass | Paß | Paso | Col | Passo |
| V | Valley, Canyon | Tal, Cañon | Valle, Cañón | Vallée, Canyon | Vale, Canhão |
| ≚ | Plain | Ebene | Llano | Plaine | Planície |
| › | Cape | Kap | Cabo | Cap | Cabo |
| I | Island | Insel | Isla | Île | Ilha |
| II | Islands | Inseln | Islas | Îles | Ilhas |
| ⊥ | Other Topographic Features | Andere Topographische Objekte | Otros Elementos Topográficos | Autres données topographiques | Outros acidentes topográficos |

ESPAÑOL / FRANÇAIS / PORTUGUÊS

| Nombre / Nom / Nome | Página / Page | Lat. °′ | Long. °′ W = Oeste / Ouest |
|---|---|---|---|
| Telembí ≃ | 246 | 1.50 N | 78.16 W |
| Telén | 252 | 36.16 S | 65.30 W |
| Telen ≃ | 112 | 0.26 S | 116.42 E |
| Teleneşti | 38 | 47.30 N | 28.22 E |
| Teleno ʌ | 34 | 42.21 N | 6.23 W |
| Teleorman □[6] | 38 | 44.00 N | 25.15 E |
| Teleorman ≃ | 38 | 43.52 N | 25.26 E |
| Téléphone, Île du I | 273b | 4.20 S | 15.12 E |
| Telerig | 38 | 43.51 N | 27.40 E |
| Telertheba, Djebel ʌ | 148 | 24.10 N | 6.51 E |
| Telescope Peak ʌ | 204 | 36.10 N | 117.05 W |
| Telescope Point › | 241k | 12.08 N | 61.36 W |
| Telese | 68 | 41.13 N | 14.32 E |
| Telesterion ⊥ | 267c | 38.02 N | 23.32 E |
| Telferner | 222 | 28.51 N | 96.53 W |
| Telfes | 64 | 47.10 N | 11.22 E |
| Telford, Eng., U.K. | 42 | 52.40 N | 2.28 W |
| Telford, Pa., U.S. | 208 | 40.19 N | 75.19 W |
| Telfs | 64 | 47.18 N | 11.04 E |
| Telgte | 52 | 51.59 N | 7.47 E |
| Telica ≃ | 236 | 14.43 N | 86.08 W |
| Telica, Volcán ʌ[1] | 236 | 12.36 N | 86.50 W |
| Telida | 180 | 63.23 N | 153.16 W |
| Telikovka | 80 | 52.35 N | 48.17 E |
| Télimélé | 150 | 10.54 N | 13.02 W |
| Telixtlahuaca | 234 | 17.18 N | 96.54 W |
| Telizi | 265a | 59.42 N | 29.59 E |
| Teljo, Jabal ʌ | 140 | 14.42 N | 25.56 E |
| Telkwa | 182 | 54.42 N | 127.03 W |
| Telkwa ≃ | 182 | 54.41 N | 127.02 W |
| Tel Lakhish ⊥ | 132 | 31.34 N | 34.51 E |
| Tellaro ≃ | 70 | 36.50 N | 15.06 E |
| Tell City | 194 | 37.57 N | 86.46 W |
| Teller | 180 | 65.16 N | 166.22 W |
| Tellicherry | 122 | 11.45 N | 75.32 E |
| Tellico ≃ | 192 | 35.36 N | 84.13 W |
| Tellico Plains | 192 | 35.21 N | 84.17 W |
| Tellier | 254 | 47.39 S | 66.03 W |
| Tellier, Lac ⊜ | 206 | 46.23 N | 74.00 W |
| Tello | 246 | 3.04 N | 75.08 W |
| Telluride | 200 | 37.56 N | 107.48 W |
| Tel'ma | 88 | 52.43 N | 103.41 E |
| Tel'manove | 83 | 47.24 N | 38.02 E |
| Tel Megiddo (Armageddon) ⊥ | 132 | 32.35 N | 35.11 E |
| Telmen | 88 | 48.38 N | 97.37 E |
| Telmen nuur ⊜ | 88 | 48.50 N | 97.18 E |
| Tel Mond | 132 | 32.15 N | 34.56 E |
| Tel'novskij | 89 | 49.22 N | 142.05 E |
| Telo | 110 | 0.03 N | 98.16 E |
| Teloekbetoeng → Tanjungkarang-Telukbetung | 115a | 5.27 S | 105.16 E |
| Telogia Creek ≃ | 192 | 30.16 N | 84.44 W |
| Telok Anson | 114 | 4.02 N | 101.01 E |
| Telok Datok | 114 | 2.49 N | 101.31 E |
| Teloloapan | 234 | 18.21 N | 99.51 W |
| Telpaneca | 236 | 13.32 N | 86.17 W |
| Telsen | 254 | 42.24 S | 66.57 W |
| Telsen, Arroyo ≃ | 254 | 42.51 S | 66.48 W |
| Telšiai | 76 | 55.59 N | 22.15 E |
| Telti | 71 | 40.52 N | 9.21 E |
| Teltow | 54 | 52.23 N | 13.16 E |
| Teltow ◆[1] | 264a | 52.18 N | 13.25 E |
| Teltower Hochfläche ⩘[1] | 264a | 52.22 N | 13.20 E |
| Teltowkanal ≍ | 264a | 52.26 N | 13.35 E |
| Telukbatang | 112 | 1.00 S | 109.46 E |
| Telukbayur, Indon. | 112 | 2.09 N | 117.24 E |
| Telukbayur, Indon. | 112 | 1.00 S | 100.22 E |
| Telukbrombang | 114 | 2.03 N | 100.52 E |
| Telukbutun | 112 | 4.13 N | 108.12 E |
| Telukdalem | 114 | 0.34 N | 97.49 E |
| Teluklanjut | 112 | 0.09 N | 103.29 E |
| Teluklecak | 114 | 1.51 N | 101.44 E |
| Telukmerbau | 114 | 2.04 N | 100.38 E |
| Telukpambang | 114 | 1.28 N | 102.28 E |
| Teluk Punggur, Ujung › | 112 | 3.53 S | 102.17 E |
| Telumengtang Shan ʌ | 120 | 30.33 N | 86.27 E |
| Tem' | 88 | 55.21 N | 100.44 E |
| Tema | 150 | 5.38 N | 0.01 E |
| Temae | 174s | 17.29 S | 149.46 W |
| Temagami, Lake ⊜ | 190 | 47.00 N | 80.05 W |
| Temaju, Pulau I | 112 | 0.29 N | 108.52 E |
| Temalacacingo | 234 | 17.52 N | 98.41 W |
| Temalı Bendi ◆[6] | 267b | 41.04 N | 29.06 E |
| Te Manga ʌ | 174k | 21.13 S | 159.45 W |
| Temangan Baharu | 114 | 5.42 N | 102.09 E |
| Temangga | 112 | 0.27 N | 111.21 E |
| Temanggung | 115a | 7.18 S | 110.10 E |
| Temascal, Méx. | 234 | 23.24 N | 104.14 W |
| Temascal, Méx. | 234 | 18.15 N | 96.20 W |
| Tem'asovo | 86 | 52.59 N | 58.06 E |
| Temastián | 234 | 21.53 N | 103.28 W |
| Tematangi I[1] | 14 | 21.41 S | 140.40 W |
| Temax | 232 | 21.09 N | 88.56 W |
| Tembakul, Pulau I | 271c | 1.14 N | 103.52 E |
| Tembe | 154 | 0.16 S | 28.14 E |
| Tembe ≃ | 158 | 26.03 S | 32.26 E |
| Tembeling | 114 | 4.04 N | 102.19 E |
| Tembeling ≃ | 114 | 4.04 N | 102.20 E |
| Tembenči ≃ | 74 | 64.36 N | 99.58 E |
| Tembesi ≃ | 112 | 1.43 S | 103.06 E |
| Tembilahan | 112 | 0.19 S | 103.09 E |
| Tembisa | 158 | 25.58 S | 28.14 E |
| Temblador | 246 | 8.59 N | 62.44 W |
| Tembleque | 34 | 39.42 N | 3.30 W |
| Temblor Range ⩘ | 226 | 35.20 N | 119.55 W |
| Tembo Aluma | 152 | 7.42 S | 17.17 E |
| Tembuè | 154 | 14.52 S | 32.58 E |
| Tembuland □[9] | 158 | 31.30 S | 27.40 E |
| Teme ≃ | 42 | 52.09 N | 2.18 W |
| Temecula | 228 | 33.29 N | 117.08 W |
| Temecula Creek ≃ | 228 | 33.28 N | 117.08 W |
| Temelli | 130 | 39.44 N | 32.22 E |
| Temengor | 114 | 5.19 N | 101.22 E |
| Temengor, Tasek ⊜[1] | 114 | 5.30 N | 101.20 E |
| Temerin | 38 | 45.24 N | 19.53 E |
| Temerloh | 114 | 3.27 N | 102.25 E |
| Temescal Canyon V | 280 | 34.04 N | 118.32 W |
| Temescal Wash V | 228 | 33.40 N | 117.20 W |
| Temesvár → Timişoara | 38 | 45.45 N | 21.13 E |
| Temiang, Pulau I | 112 | 0.19 N | 104.23 E |
| Teminaabuan | 164 | 1.26 S | 132.01 E |
| Temir | 86 | 49.08 N | 57.06 E |
| Temir ≃ | 86 | 48.31 N | 57.27 E |
| Temirgojevskaja | 78 | 45.07 N | 40.16 E |
| Temirlanovka | 85 | 42.36 N | 69.17 E |
| Temirtau, Kaz. | 86 | 50.05 N | 72.56 E |
| Temirtau, Ross. | 86 | 53.08 N | 87.28 E |
| Témiscamie, Lac ⊜ | 186 | 51.11 N | 72.12 W |
| Témiscaming | 190 | 46.43 N | 79.06 W |
| Témiscouata, Lac ⊜ | 186 | 47.41 N | 68.47 W |
| Temixco | 234 | 18.50 N | 99.14 W |
| Temnik ≃ | 88 | 51.00 N | 106.18 E |
| Temnikov | 80 | 54.38 N | 43.12 E |
| Temnikovo | 265b | 55.43 N | 38.01 E |
| Temo ≃ | 71 | 40.17 N | 8.28 E |
| Temoaya | 234 | 19.28 N | 99.35 W |
| Temora | 166 | 34.26 S | 147.32 E |
| Temosachic | 232 | 28.57 N | 107.51 W |
| Tempe | 200 | 33.24 N | 111.54 W |
| Tempe, Danau ⊜ | 112 | 4.06 S | 119.57 E |
| Tempelfelde | 264a | 52.43 N | 13.43 E |
| Tempelhof ◆[8] | 264a | 52.28 N | 13.23 E |
| Temperance | 216 | 41.46 N | 83.34 W |
| Temperanceville | 208 | 37.53 N | 75.32 W |
| Temperley ◆[8] | 258 | 34.47 S | 58.24 W |
| Tempest, Mount ʌ[2] | 171a | 27.10 S | 153.26 E |
| Tempilang | 112 | 2.07 S | 105.40 E |
| Tempino | 112 | 1.44 S | 103.29 E |
| Tempio di Clitunno ⊥ | 66 | 42.48 N | 12.45 E |
| Tempio Pausania | 71 | 40.54 N | 9.06 E |
| Tempisque ≃ | 236 | 10.12 N | 85.14 W |
| Temple, Ok., U.S. | 196 | 34.16 N | 98.14 W |
| Temple, Pa., U.S. | 208 | 40.24 N | 75.55 W |
| Temple, Tx., U.S. | 222 | 31.05 N | 97.20 W |
| Temple City | 228 | 34.06 N | 118.03 W |
| Templecombe | 42 | 51.00 N | 2.25 W |
| Temple Ewell | 42 | 51.09 N | 1.16 E |
| Temple Hills Park | 284c | 38.48 N | 76.57 W |
| Templemore | 48 | 52.48 N | 7.50 W |
| Templers | 168b | 34.28 S | 138.45 E |
| Temple Sowerby | 44 | 54.39 N | 2.35 W |
| Templestowe | 169 | 37.45 S | 145.07 E |
| Temple Terrace | 220 | 28.02 N | 82.23 W |
| Templeton, P.Q., Can. | 212 | 45.29 N | 75.36 W |
| Templeton, Ca., U.S. | 226 | 35.33 N | 120.42 W |
| Templeton, In., U.S. | 216 | 40.31 N | 87.12 W |
| Templeton, Ma., U.S. | 207 | 42.33 N | 72.04 W |
| Templeton, Pa., U.S. | 214 | 40.55 N | 79.27 W |
| Templeton ≃ | 166 | 21.14 S | 138.13 E |
| Temple University ʊ[2] | 285 | 39.59 N | 75.09 W |
| Templeuve | 50 | 50.32 N | 3.10 E |
| Templi, Valle dei ⊥ | 70 | 37.17 N | 13.35 E |
| Templin | 54 | 53.07 N | 13.30 E |
| Templiner See ⊜ | 264a | 52.22 N | 13.01 E |
| Templo Island I | 116 | 13.09 N | 122.52 E |
| Tempoal ≃ | 234 | 21.47 N | 98.27 W |
| Tempoal de Sánchez | 234 | 21.31 N | 98.23 W |
| Tempy | 82 | 56.38 N | 37.18 E |
| Temr'uk | 78 | 45.17 N | 37.23 E |
| Temr'ukskij zaliv c | 78 | 45.24 N | 37.20 E |
| Temse | 50 | 51.08 N | 4.13 E |
| Temù | 64 | 46.15 N | 10.28 E |
| Temuco | 252 | 38.44 S | 72.36 W |
| Temuka | 172 | 44.15 S | 171.17 E |
| Temwen I | 174r | 6.52 N | 158.19 E |
| Tena | 246 | 0.59 S | 77.49 W |
| Tenabo | 232 | 20.03 N | 90.14 W |
| Tenafly | 210 | 40.55 N | 73.57 W |
| Tenaha | 194 | 31.57 N | 94.15 W |
| Tenakee Springs | 180 | 57.47 N | 135.13 W |
| Tenakill Brook ≃ | 276 | 40.59 N | 73.58 W |
| Tena Kourou ʌ[2] | 150 | 10.45 N | 5.25 W |
| Tenāli | 122 | 16.15 N | 80.35 E |
| Tenamaxtlán | 234 | 20.13 N | 104.10 W |
| Tenancingo [de Degollado] | 234 | 18.58 N | 99.36 W |
| Tenango de Arista | 234 | 19.07 N | 99.33 W |
| Tenantongo, Presa ⊜[1] | 286a | 19.28 N | 99.16 W |
| Tenasillahe Island I | 224 | 46.14 N | 123.27 W |
| Tenasserim | 110 | 12.05 N | 99.01 E |
| Tenay | 58 | 45.55 N | 5.30 E |
| Tenaya Creek ≃ | 226 | 37.44 N | 119.35 W |
| Tenbury Wells | 42 | 52.19 N | 2.35 W |
| Tenby | 42 | 51.41 N | 4.43 W |
| Tence | 62 | 45.07 N | 4.17 E |
| Tench Island I | 164 | 1.40 S | 150.40 E |
| Tencin | 62 | 45.19 N | 5.58 E |
| Tenda, Colle di (Col de Tende) )( | 62 | 44.09 N | 7.34 E |
| Tendaho | 144 | 11.48 N | 40.52 E |
| Tendai-san ʌ | 270 | 34.55 N | 135.28 E |
| Tende | 62 | 44.05 N | 7.36 E |
| Tende, Col de (Colle di Tenda) )( | 62 | 44.09 N | 7.34 E |
| Tende, Tunnel de ◆[5] | 62 | 44.09 N | 7.34 E |
| Ten Degree Channel )( | 110 | 10.00 N | 93.00 E |
| Tendeka | 158 | 27.44 S | 30.54 E |
| Tendō | 92 | 38.21 N | 140.22 E |
| Tendrara | 148 | 33.04 N | 1.59 W |
| Tendrivs'ka Kosa, ostriv ›[2] | 78 | 46.12 N | 31.50 E |
| Tendrivs'ka zatoka c | 78 | 46.15 N | 31.55 E |
| Tendürek Dağı ʌ | 84 | 39.22 N | 43.52 E |
| Ténenkou | 150 | 14.28 N | 4.55 W |
| Tenente Marques ≃ | 248 | 11.10 S | 59.56 W |
| Tenente Portela | 252 | 27.22 S | 53.45 W |
| Ténéré ◆[2] | 146 | 19.00 N | 10.30 E |
| Ténéré, Erg du ⫫[8] | 146 | 17.35 N | 10.55 E |
| Tenerife I | 148 | 28.19 N | 16.34 W |
| Ténès | 148 | 36.31 N | 1.14 E |
| Ténès, Cap › | 34 | 36.33 N | 1.21 E |
| Tenexpa | 234 | 17.11 N | 100.43 W |
| Tenextepango | 234 | 18.43 N | 98.57 W |
| Teng ≃ | 110 | 19.52 N | 97.45 E |
| Tengah, Kepulauan II | 112 | 7.30 S | 117.30 E |
| Teng'aopu | 104 | 41.05 N | 122.49 E |
| Tengchong | 102 | 25.04 N | 98.29 E |
| Tengeh Reservoir ⊜[1] | 271c | 1.21 N | 103.39 E |
| Tengen | 58 | 47.49 N | 8.40 E |
| Tenggara, Nusa (Lesser Sunda Islands) II | 108 | 9.00 S | 120.00 E |
| Tenggarong | 112 | 0.24 S | 116.58 E |
| Tengger Shamo ◆[2] | 102 | 38.00 N | 104.40 E |
| Tenggol, Pulau I | 114 | 4.48 N | 103.38 E |
| Tenghilan | 112 | 6.14 N | 116.19 E |
| Tengi ≃ | 114 | 3.24 N | 101.10 E |
| Tengiz, ozero ⊜ | 86 | 50.24 N | 68.57 E |
| Tengjiabao | 100 | 31.10 N | 115.29 E |
| Tengqiao | 110 | 18.22 N | 109.46 E |
| Tengra | 272b | 22.48 N | 88.32 E |
| Tengréla | 150 | 10.29 N | 6.24 W |
| Tengtian | 100 | 27.04 N | 115.40 E |
| Tengtiao (Na) ≃ | 110 | 22.05 N | 103.09 E |
| Ten'guševo | 80 | 54.46 N | 42.44 E |
| Tengxian, Zhg. | 98 | 35.08 N | 117.10 E |
| Tengxian, Zhg. | 102 | 23.21 N | 110.53 E |
| Teniente Rodolfo Marsh ʊ[3] | 9 | 62.12 S | 58.54 W |
| Tenigerbad | 58 | 46.42 N | 8.57 E |
| Teningen | 58 | 48.08 N | 7.49 E |
| Tenino | 224 | 46.51 N | 122.51 W |
| Tenis, ozero ⊜ | 86 | 56.09 N | 71.56 E |
| Teniya-zaki › | 174m | 26.33 N | 128.09 E |
| Teniz, ozero ⊜ | 86 | 54.08 N | 64.34 E |
| Tenjin ≃ | 96 | 35.30 N | 133.53 E |
| Tenjo, Mount ʌ[2] | 174p | 13.25 N | 144.42 E |
| Tenkāsi | 122 | 8.58 N | 77.18 E |
| Tenke, Zaïre | 154 | 10.35 S | 26.07 E |
| Tenke, Zaïre | 154 | 11.26 S | 26.45 E |
| Tenkeli | 74 | 70.01 N | 140.58 E |
| Tenkergynpil'gyn, laguna c | 180 | 68.30 N | 178.00 W |
| Ten'ki | 80 | 55.26 N | 49.00 E |
| Tenkiller Ferry Lake ⊜[1] | 196 | 35.43 N | 95.00 W |
| Tenkodogo | 150 | 11.47 N | 0.22 W |
| Tenmile ≃, Ma., U.S. | 283 | 41.58 N | 71.20 W |
| Tenmile ≃, N.Y., U.S. | 210 | 41.40 N | 73.31 W |
| Ten Mile Creek ≃, On., Can. | 284a | 43.07 N | 79.11 W |
| Ten Mile Creek ≃, Ky., U.S. | 218 | 38.43 N | 84.46 W |
| Tenmile Creek ≃, Oh., U.S. | 216 | 41.42 N | 83.33 W |
| Tenmile Creek ≃, Pa., U.S. | 188 | 40.08 N | 80.22 W |
| Tenmile Creek ≃, Tx., U.S. | 222 | 32.34 N | 96.34 W |
| Ten Mile Lake ⊜ | 186 | 51.06 N | 56.41 W |
| Tenmile Run ≃ | 276 | 40.27 N | 74.35 W |
| Tenmile Wash V | 200 | 32.52 N | 113.28 W |
| Tenmoku-san ʌ | 94 | 35.52 N | 139.03 E |
| Tenna ≃ | 66 | 43.14 N | 13.47 E |
| Tennant Creek | 162 | 19.40 S | 134.10 E |
| Tennenbronn | 58 | 48.11 N | 8.20 E |
| Tennengau ◆[1] | 64 | 47.40 N | 13.15 E |
| Tennengebirge ⩘ | 64 | 47.30 N | 13.15 E |
| Tennent | 208 | 40.16 N | 74.20 W |
| Tennent Pond ⊜ | 276 | 40.26 N | 74.20 W |
| Tennessee □[3] | 178 | 35.50 N | 85.30 W |
| Tennessee ≃ | 178 | 37.04 N | 88.33 W |
| Tennessee Colony | 222 | 31.50 N | 95.50 W |
| Tenneville | 56 | 50.06 N | 5.32 E |
| Tennille | 192 | 32.56 N | 82.48 W |
| Tenno | 64 | 45.55 N | 10.49 E |
| Tennōji ◆[8] | 270 | 34.39 N | 135.31 E |
| Teno | 252 | 34.52 S | 71.11 W |
| Tenom | 112 | 5.08 N | 115.57 E |
| Ténos, Pointe › | 240e | 14.48 N | 61.00 W |
| Tenosique | 232 | 17.29 N | 91.26 W |
| Tenri | 96 | 34.36 N | 135.51 E |
| Tenryū, Nihon | 94 | 35.16 N | 137.51 E |
| Tenryū, Nihon | 94 | 34.52 N | 137.49 E |
| Tenryū ≃ | 94 | 34.39 N | 137.47 E |
| Tensas ≃ | 194 | 31.38 N | 91.49 W |
| Tensed | 202 | 47.09 N | 116.55 W |
| Tensift, Oued ≃ | 148 | 32.02 N | 9.22 W |
| Ten Sleep | 202 | 44.02 N | 107.27 W |
| Tensta | 40 | 60.02 N | 17.40 E |
| Tente ◆[8] | 263 | 51.18 N | 7.14 E |
| Tenteksor ≡ | 80 | 47.18 N | 53.24 E |
| Tentena | 112 | 1.47 S | 120.39 E |
| Tenterden | 42 | 51.05 N | 0.42 E |
| Tenterfield | 166 | 29.03 S | 152.01 E |
| Tent Hill | 171a | 27.36 S | 152.14 E |
| Tenthill Creek ≃ | 171a | 27.34 S | 152.14 E |
| Ten Thousand Islands II | 220 | 25.50 N | 81.33 W |
| Tentolomatinan, Gunung ʌ | 112 | 0.56 N | 121.48 E |
| Tentugal | 250 | 1.19 S | 46.59 W |
| Tentulia | 272b | 22.50 N | 88.28 E |
| Teocaltiche | 234 | 21.26 N | 102.35 W |
| Teocelo | 234 | 19.23 N | 96.58 W |
| Teocuitatlán de Corona | 234 | 20.07 N | 103.24 W |
| Teodelina | 252 | 34.11 S | 61.32 W |
| Teófilo Cunha | 287a | 22.39 S | 43.34 W |
| Teófilo Otoni | 255 | 17.51 S | 41.30 W |
| Teofipol' | 78 | 49.50 N | 26.25 E |
| Teohotepapa, Pointe › | 174x | 9.46 S | 138.48 W |
| Teohotupa, Pointe › | 174x | 9.46 S | 138.50 W |
| Teo Lakes ⊜ | 184 | 51.30 N | 109.21 W |
| Teolo | 64 | 45.21 N | 11.40 E |
| Teomabal Island I | 116 | 6.20 N | 120.51 E |
| Teor | 64 | 45.51 N | 13.03 E |
| Teora | 68 | 40.51 N | 15.15 E |
| Teotihuacán ⊥ | 234 | 19.44 N | 98.50 W |
| Teotitlán de Flores Magón | 234 | 18.08 N | 97.05 W |
| Teotitlán del Valle | 234 | 17.02 N | 96.30 W |
| Tepa, Ghana | 150 | 7.00 N | 2.10 W |
| Tepa, Indon. | 164 | 7.52 S | 129.31 E |
| Tepalcatepec | 234 | 19.11 N | 102.51 W |
| Tepalcingo | 234 | 18.36 N | 98.51 W |
| Tepa Point › | 174v | 19.07 S | 169.56 W |
| Tepatitlán de Morelos | 234 | 20.49 N | 102.44 W |
| Tepatlaxco [de Hidalgo] | 234 | 19.04 N | 97.58 W |
| Tepe | 130 | 37.48 N | 40.47 E |
| Tepeaca | 234 | 18.58 N | 97.54 W |
| Tepeapulco | 234 | 19.47 N | 98.33 W |
| Tepebaşı | 130 | 36.40 N | 32.45 E |
| Tepechitlán | 234 | 21.40 N | 103.20 W |
| Tepeguaje | 196 | 25.40 N | 99.50 W |
| Tepeguajes | 234 | 23.30 N | 97.50 W |
| Tepehan | 130 | 38.06 N | 38.45 E |
| Tepehuanes | 232 | 25.21 N | 105.44 W |
| Tepehuanes ≃ | 232 | 25.10 N | 105.25 W |
| Tepeji de Ocampo | 234 | 19.54 N | 99.21 W |
| Tepelenë | 38 | 40.18 N | 20.01 E |
| Tepelmeme de Morelos | 234 | 17.51 N | 97.21 W |
| Tepelská vrchovina ⩘[1] | 60 | 50.00 N | 13.00 E |
| Tepeören | 130 | 41.04 N | 35.30 E |
| Tepepan ◆[8] | 286a | 19.16 N | 99.08 W |
| Tepe Saif | 267d | 35.36 N | 51.18 E |
| Tepetiltic, Volcán ʌ[1] | 234 | 21.15 N | 104.43 W |
| Tepetixtla | 234 | 17.13 N | 100.08 W |
| Tepetlixpa | 234 | 19.02 N | 98.49 W |
| Tepi | 144 | 7.10 N | 35.23 E |
| Tepic | 234 | 21.30 N | 104.54 W |
| Tepko | 168b | 34.58 S | 139.11 E |
| Teplá | 60 | 49.59 N | 12.52 E |
| Teplá ≃ | 54 | 50.14 N | 12.52 E |
| Teple ≃ | 83 | 48.47 N | 39.19 E |
| Teplice | 54 | 50.39 N | 13.48 E |
| Teplitz → Teplice | 54 | 50.39 N | 13.48 E |
| Teplooz'orsk | 89 | 49.00 N | 131.48 E |
| Teplovka | 80 | 51.33 N | 51.33 E |
| Teplovo | 80 | 55.25 N | 42.56 E |
| Teplyk | 78 | 48.40 N | 29.44 E |
| Tepoca, Bahía c | 232 | 30.15 N | 112.50 W |
| Tepoca, Punta › | 232 | 29.55 N | 112.46 W |
| Te Pohue | 172 | 39.15 S | 176.41 E |
| Tepopa, Cabo › | 232 | 29.22 N | 112.27 W |
| Te Puia | 172 | 38.04 S | 178.18 E |
| Te Puke | 172 | 37.47 S | 176.20 E |
| Tepuxtepec, Presa ⊜[1] | 234 | 20.02 N | 100.13 W |
| Tepuzhuacán | 234 | 20.53 N | 104.33 W |
| Tequila | 234 | 20.54 N | 103.47 W |
| Tequisquita Slough ≃ | 226 | 36.58 N | 121.27 W |
| Tequixquitla | 234 | 19.19 N | 97.40 W |
| Tequma | 132 | 31.27 N | 34.35 E |
| Ter ≃, Esp. | 34 | 42.01 N | 3.12 E |
| Ter ≃, Ityo. | 144 | 7.20 N | 42.11 E |
| Ter ≃, Eng., U.K. | 42 | 51.50 N | 0.36 E |
| Téra | 150 | 14.01 N | 0.45 E |
| Tera ≃ | 34 | 41.54 N | 5.44 W |
| Teradomari | 92 | 37.38 N | 138.46 E |
| Terai | 94 | 36.26 N | 136.30 E |
| Teraina I | 14 | 4.43 N | 160.24 W |
| Ter'ajevo | 82 | 56.11 N | 36.07 E |
| Terakhāda | 126 | 22.56 N | 89.40 E |
| Teralba | 170 | 32.58 S | 151.37 E |
| Teramo | 66 | 42.39 N | 13.42 E |
| Teramo □[4] | 66 | 42.39 N | 13.41 E |
| Terán | 234 | 16.45 N | 93.10 W |
| Terang | 169 | 38.14 S | 142.55 E |
| Teranum | 114 | 3.44 N | 101.49 E |
| Ter Apel | 52 | 52.53 N | 7.04 E |
| Teraruma | 164 | 8.00 S | 141.50 E |
| Teras | 114 | 3.45 N | 101.49 E |
| Teratak | 112 | 0.46 S | 110.32 E |
| Terborg | 52 | 51.55 N | 6.21 E |
| Terbuny | 76 | 52.08 N | 38.17 E |
| Tercan | 130 | 39.47 N | 40.24 E |
| Terceira I | 148a | 38.43 N | 24.13 W |
| Tercero ≃ | 252 | 32.55 S | 62.19 W |
| Tercero de Febrero, Parque ♠ | 288 | 34.34 S | 58.25 W |
| Terdal | 122 | 16.30 N | 75.03 E |
| Terdoppio, Torrente ≃ | 266b | 45.23 N | 8.50 E |
| Terebovlya | 78 | 49.18 N | 25.43 E |
| Terebuš | 82 | 54.16 N | 38.09 E |
| Terebutinec | 76 | 59.01 N | 33.39 E |
| Terechovo | 82 | 55.50 N | 35.45 E |
| Te Rehunga | 172 | 40.13 S | 176.01 E |
| Tereida | 140 | 10.35 N | 31.17 E |
| Terek, Kyrg. | 85 | 40.01 N | 73.33 E |
| Terek, Ross. | 84 | 43.29 N | 44.08 E |
| Terek ≃ | 84 | 43.44 N | 46.33 E |
| Terekli-Mekteb | 84 | 44.10 N | 45.53 E |
| Terek-Saj | 85 | 41.32 N | 71.09 E |
| Terektinskij chrebet ⩘ | 86 | 50.30 N | 86.00 E |
| Terekty | 80 | 48.34 N | 49.02 E |
| Terempa | 112 | 3.14 N | 106.14 E |
| Terence Bay | 186 | 44.28 N | 63.43 W |
| Teren'ga | 80 | 53.42 N | 48.24 E |
| Terengganu □[3] | 114 | 5.00 N | 103.00 E |
| Terengganu ≃ | 114 | 5.17 N | 103.05 E |
| Terenino | 76 | 54.31 N | 33.35 E |
| Terenkuduk | 80 | 48.24 N | 47.11 E |
| Terenni ⊥ | 150 | 16.30 N | 9.35 W |
| Terenos | 255 | 20.26 S | 54.50 W |
| Terenozek | 86 | 45.05 N | 64.59 E |
| Terensaj | 86 | 51.36 N | 59.31 E |
| Teresina | 250 | 5.05 S | 42.49 W |
| Tereška ≃ | 80 | 51.48 N | 46.26 E |
| Teresópolis | 256 | 22.26 S | 42.59 W |
| Terespol | 30 | 52.05 N | 23.36 E |
| Teresva | 78 | 48.01 N | 23.42 E |
| Terevaka, Cerro ʌ | 174z | 27.05 S | 109.23 W |
| Terezín | 54 | 50.31 N | 14.08 E |
| Tergauči | 85 | 41.11 N | 71.30 E |
| Tergnier | 50 | 49.39 N | 3.18 E |
| Tergun Daba Shan ⩘ | 102 | 38.25 N | 95.55 E |
| Terhorne | 52 | 53.02 N | 5.46 E |
| Teriang | 114 | 3.14 N | 102.25 E |
| Teriang ≃ | 114 | 3.19 N | 102.31 E |
| Teribe ≃ | 236 | 9.22 N | 82.32 W |
| Terib'orka | 24 | 69.08 N | 35.08 E |
| Terihi I | 174x | 10.02 S | 138.49 W |
| Terio | 164 | 8.25 S | 143.00 E |
| Terisakkan ≃ | 86 | 51.15 N | 67.10 E |
| Terjärv (Teerijärvi) | 26 | 63.32 N | 23.30 E |
| Terlago | 64 | 46.06 N | 11.02 E |
| Terlano | 64 | 46.32 N | 11.15 E |
| Terlingua | 196 | 29.19 N | 103.37 W |
| Terlingua Creek ≃ | 196 | 29.10 N | 103.36 W |
| Terlizzi | 68 | 41.08 N | 16.32 E |
| Termas de Río Hondo | 252 | 27.29 S | 64.52 W |
| Terme | 130 | 41.12 N | 36.59 E |
| Terme del Brennero (Brennerbad) | 64 | 46.58 N | 11.29 E |
| Terme di Stigliano | 66 | 42.09 N | 12.01 E |
| Terme di Suio | 68 | 41.18 N | 13.51 E |
| Terme di Valdieri | 62 | 44.12 N | 7.16 E |
| Termeno (Tramin) | 64 | 46.20 N | 11.14 E |
| Termez | 72 | 37.14 N | 67.16 E |
| Termignon | 62 | 45.17 N | 6.49 E |
| Terminal | 258 | 34.09 S | 57.31 W |
| Terminal Island I | 280 | 33.45 N | 118.15 W |
| Terminal Island Coast Guard Base ■ | 280 | 33.43 N | 118.17 W |
| Termini Imerese | 70 | 37.59 N | 13.42 E |
| Termini Imerese, Golfo di c | 70 | 38.01 N | 13.45 E |
| Terminillo, Monte ʌ | 66 | 42.28 N | 13.00 E |
| Términos, Laguna de c | 232 | 18.37 N | 91.33 W |
| Termit, Massif de ⩘ | 146 | 16.15 N | 11.17 E |
| Termoli | 66 | 42.00 N | 15.00 E |
| Termonde → Dendermonde | 50 | 51.02 N | 4.07 E |
| Termsdorf | 264a | 52.16 N | 13.07 E |
| Tern ≃ | 42 | 52.47 N | 2.32 W |
| Ternate, Indon. | 108 | 0.48 N | 127.24 E |
| Ternate, Pil | 116 | 14.17 N | 120.43 E |
| Ternberg | 61 | 47.58 N | 14.22 E |
| Ternej | 89 | 45.03 N | 136.37 E |
| Terneuzen | 52 | 51.20 N | 3.50 E |
| Terni | 66 | 42.34 N | 12.37 E |
| Terni □[4] | 66 | 42.41 N | 12.19 E |
| Ternitz | 61 | 47.44 N | 16.03 E |
| Ternivka, Ukr. | 78 | 47.02 N | 32.01 E |
| Ternivka, Ukr. | 78 | 48.32 N | 29.58 E |
| Ternoise ≃ | 50 | 50.23 N | 2.01 E |
| Ternopil' | 78 | 49.34 N | 25.36 E |
| Ternopil' □[4] | 78 | 49.30 N | 25.30 E |
| Ternovka, Ross. | 78 | 51.40 N | 41.37 E |
| Ternovka, Ross. | 80 | 53.09 N | 45.02 E |
| Ternovka, Ross. | 80 | 51.19 N | 42.56 E |
| Ternovoje | 80 | 51.03 N | 43.43 E |
| Ternovskaja | 78 | 45.53 N | 40.24 E |
| Ternuvate | 78 | 47.50 N | 36.09 E |
| Terny, Ukr. | 78 | 48.09 N | 33.33 E |
| Terny, Ukr. | 78 | 50.59 N | 33.59 E |
| Terny, Ukr. | 83 | 49.05 N | 37.57 E |
| Terolak | 114 | 3.53 N | 101.23 E |
| Terong | 114 | 4.43 N | 100.44 E |
| Terontola | 66 | 43.13 N | 12.02 E |
| Terpe | 54 | 51.32 N | 14.19 E |
| Terpenija, mys › | 89 | 48.39 N | 144.44 E |
| Terpenija, zaliv c | 89 | 49.00 N | 143.30 E |
| Terra Alta | 188 | 39.26 N | 79.32 W |
| Terra Bella | 204 | 35.58 N | 119.03 W |
| Terrace | 182 | 54.31 N | 128.35 W |
| Terrace Bay | 190 | 48.47 N | 87.06 W |
| Terracina | 66 | 41.17 N | 13.15 E |
| Terra del Sole | 66 | 44.11 N | 11.57 E |
| Terral | 196 | 33.53 N | 97.56 W |
| Terralba | 71 | 39.43 N | 8.39 E |
| Terra Linda | 282 | 38.01 N | 122.32 W |
| Terranova → Newfoundland □[4] | 176 | 52.00 N | 56.00 W |
| Terra Nova Bay c | 9 | 74.45 S | 164.30 E |
| Terranova da Sibari | 68 | 39.39 N | 16.20 E |
| Terranova di Pollino | 68 | 39.59 N | 16.18 E |
| Terranova di Sicilia → Gela | 70 | 37.04 N | 14.15 E |
| Terra Nova Lake ⊜ | 186 | 48.30 N | 54.20 W |
| Terra Nova National Park ♠ | 186 | 48.37 N | 53.56 W |
| Terranuova Bracciolini | 66 | 43.33 N | 11.35 E |
| Terra Rica | 255 | 22.43 S | 52.38 W |
| Terrarossa, Foce di )( | 64 | 44.12 N | 10.26 E |
| Terra Roxa | 252 | 24.08 S | 53.59 W |
| Terras, Pinhal do ◆[3] | 266c | 38.39 N | 9.02 W |
| Terra Santa | 250 | 2.06 S | 56.29 W |
| Terrasini | 70 | 38.09 N | 13.05 E |
| Terrassa | 34 | 41.34 N | 2.01 E |
| Terrasse-Vaudreuil | 206 | 45.24 N | 73.59 W |
| Terrasson-la-Villedieu | 32 | 45.08 N | 1.18 E |
| Terravecchia | 68 | 39.29 N | 16.58 E |
| Terrebonne | 206 | 45.42 N | 73.38 W |
| Terrebonne □[6] | 206 | 46.00 N | 74.10 W |
| Terrebonne Bay c | 194 | 29.09 N | 90.35 W |
| Terre Ceia | 220 | 27.35 N | 82.35 W |
| Terre-de-Bas | 241o | 15.51 N | 61.39 W |
| Terre-de-Bas I | 241o | 15.52 N | 61.38 W |
| Terre de Feu → Tierra del Fuego, Isla Grande de I | 254 | 54.00 S | 69.00 W |
| Terre-de-Haut | 241o | 15.58 N | 61.35 W |
| Terre-de-Haut I | 241o | 15.52 N | 61.35 W |
| Terre des Hommes ♠ | 275a | 45.31 N | 73.32 W |
| Terre Haute | 194 | 39.28 N | 87.24 W |
| Terre Hill | 208 | 40.09 N | 76.03 W |
| Terrell | 222 | 32.44 N | 96.16 W |
| Terrell, Lake ⊜ | 224 | 48.52 N | 122.41 W |
| Terrell Hills | 196 | 29.28 N | 98.27 W |
| Terrenceville | 186 | 47.40 N | 54.44 W |
| Terre-Neuve → Newfoundland □[4] | 176 | 52.00 N | 56.00 W |
| Terre Noire Creek ≃ | 194 | 33.49 N | 92.55 W |
| Terre Rouge Creek ≃ | 194 | 33.49 N | 93.11 W |
| Terrey Hills | 170 | 33.41 S | 151.14 E |
| Terrigal | 170 | 33.27 S | 151.27 E |
| Terrington Saint Clement | 42 | 52.45 N | 0.18 E |
| Territoires du Nord-Ouest → Northwest Territories □[4] | 176 | 70.00 N | 100.00 W |
| Territorio Británico del Océano Índico → British Indian Ocean Territory □[2] | 12 | 7.00 S | 72.00 E |
| Territorios del Noroeste → Northwest Territories □[4] | 176 | 70.00 N | 100.00 W |
| Terror Point › | 182 | 53.10 N | 129.56 W |
| Terrugem | 266c | 38.51 N | 9.20 W |
| Terry, Ms., U.S. | 194 | 32.05 N | 90.17 W |
| Terry, Mt., U.S. | 198 | 46.47 N | 105.18 W |
| Terry Peak ʌ | 198 | 44.19 N | 103.50 W |
| Terryville, Ct., U.S. | 207 | 41.40 N | 73.00 W |
| Terryville, N.Y., U.S. | 210 | 40.54 N | 73.03 W |
| Tersa, Ross. | 80 | 52.05 N | 47.32 E |
| Tersa, Ross. | 80 | 50.53 N | 43.48 E |
| Tersa ≃ | 80 | 50.46 N | 44.40 E |
| Tersakan Gölü ⊜ | 130 | 38.35 N | 33.06 E |
| Terschelling I | 52 | 53.24 N | 5.20 E |
| Tersiva, Punta ʌ | 62 | 45.37 N | 7.28 E |
| Terskej-Alatau, chrebet ⩘ | 85 | 41.55 N | 77.00 E |
| Terskij chrebet ⩘ | 84 | 43.32 N | 45.00 E |
| Terslev | 41 | 55.22 N | 11.59 E |
| Tersløse | 41 | 55.31 N | 11.30 E |
| Tertenia | 71 | 39.42 N | 9.34 E |
| Teru | 123 | 36.11 N | 72.45 E |
| Teruel, Col. | 246 | 2.44 N | 75.33 W |
| Teruel, Esp. | 34 | 40.21 N | 1.06 W |
| Teruel □[4] | 34 | 40.35 N | 0.45 W |
| Terujak | 114 | 4.23 N | 97.31 E |
| Tervakoski | 26 | 60.48 N | 24.37 E |
| Tervel | 38 | 43.45 N | 27.24 E |
| Tervola | 26 | 66.05 N | 24.48 E |
| Tervuren | 56 | 50.49 N | 4.31 E |
| Terwagne | 56 | 50.27 N | 5.20 E |
| Terwolde | 52 | 52.16 N | 6.06 E |
| Terzaghi Dam ◆[6] | 182 | 50.49 N | 122.12 W |
| Terzigno | 68 | 40.48 N | 14.29 E |
| Teržola | 84 | 42.12 N | 42.59 E |
| Tes | 88 | 50.27 N | 93.30 E |
| Teša | 80 | 55.30 N | 42.50 E |
| Tesalia | 246 | 2.29 N | 75.44 W |
| Tešanj | 38 | 44.37 N | 18.00 E |
| Tes-Chem (Tesijn) ≃ | 88 | 50.28 N | 93.04 E |
| Teschendorf | 54 | 52.51 N | 13.10 E |
| Tescott | 198 | 39.00 N | 97.52 W |
| Tesechoacán ≃ | 234 | 18.31 N | 95.42 W |
| Teseney | 144 | 15.07 N | 36.41 E |
| Tesero | 64 | 46.17 N | 11.31 E |
| Teshekpuk Lake ⊜ | 180 | 70.35 N | 153.30 W |
| Teshikaga | 92a | 43.29 N | 144.28 E |
| Te-shima I, Nihon | 96 | 34.29 N | 134.05 E |
| Te-shima I, Nihon | 96 | 34.24 N | 133.40 E |
| Teshio | 92a | 44.53 N | 141.44 E |
| Teshio ≃ | 92a | 44.53 N | 141.44 E |
| Teshio-sanchi ⩘ | 92a | 44.15 N | 142.05 E |
| Tešig | 88 | 49.56 N | 102.34 E |
| Tesijn (Tes-Chem) ≃ | 88 | 50.28 N | 93.04 E |
| Tesimo (Tisens) | 64 | 46.34 N | 11.10 E |
| Teslić | 38 | 44.37 N | 17.51 E |
| Teslin | 180 | 60.09 N | 132.45 W |
| Teslin ≃ | 180 | 61.34 N | 134.54 W |
| Teslin Lake ⊜ | 180 | 60.15 N | 132.57 W |
| Tesouras ≃ | 255 | 14.36 S | 50.51 W |
| Tesouro | 255 | 16.04 S | 53.34 W |
| Tesovo | 82 | 55.34 N | 36.05 E |
| Tesperhude | 52 | 53.24 N | 10.26 E |
| Tessa, Oued ≃ | 36 | 36.34 N | 8.54 E |
| Tessa-Araral, Oued V | 148 | 26.18 N | 1.58 E |
| Tessala, Djebel ʌ | 34 | 35.17 N | 0.48 W |
| Tessala, Monts du ⩘ | 34 | 35.25 N | 0.45 W |
| Tessalit | 150 | 20.12 N | 1.00 E |
| Tessancourt-sur-Aubette | 261 | 49.02 N | 1.55 E |
| Tessaoua | 150 | 13.45 N | 7.59 E |
| Tessei | 96 | 34.56 N | 133.20 E |
| Tessenderlo | 56 | 51.04 N | 5.05 E |
| Tesserete | 58 | 46.04 N | 8.58 E |
| Tessin | 54 | 54.01 N | 12.28 E |
| Tessin → Ticino □[3] | 58 | 46.20 N | 8.45 E |
| Tessy-sur-Vire | 32 | 48.58 N | 1.04 W |
| Test ≃ | 42 | 50.55 N | 1.29 W |
| Testa, Capo › | 71 | 41.14 N | 9.08 E |
| Teston, On., Can. | 275b | 43.52 N | 79.32 W |
| Teston, Eng., U.K. | 260 | 51.15 N | 0.26 E |
| Testour | 36 | 36.33 N | 9.27 E |
| Tesuque | 200 | 35.45 N | 105.55 W |
| Têt ≃ | 32 | 42.44 N | 3.02 E |
| Tetachuck Lake ⊜ | 182 | 53.20 N | 125.50 W |
| Tetagouche ≃ | 186 | 47.38 N | 65.41 W |
| Tetas, Punta › | 252 | 23.31 S | 70.38 W |
| Tetbury | 42 | 51.39 N | 2.10 W |
| Tete | 154 | 16.13 S | 33.35 E |
| Tete □[5] | 154 | 15.15 S | 32.40 E |
| Tété ≃ | 146 | 9.12 N | 20.29 E |
| Tête-à-la-Baleine | 186 | 50.41 N | 59.20 W |
| Tête du Parmelan ʌ | 58 | 45.57 N | 6.14 E |
| Tête-Jaune-Cache | 182 | 52.57 N | 119.26 W |
| Te Teko | 172 | 38.02 S | 176.48 E |
| Tetepare Island I | 175e | 8.43 S | 157.33 E |
| Tétépisca, Lac ⊜ | 186 | 51.00 N | 69.25 W |
| Teterboro | 276 | 40.52 N | 74.03 W |
| Teterboro Airport ⊠ | 276 | 40.51 N | 74.04 W |
| Téterchen | 56 | 49.14 N | 6.34 E |
| Tetere ≃ | 88 | 59.30 N | 105.00 E |
| Teteriv ≃ | 78 | 51.01 N | 30.05 E |
| Teterow | 54 | 53.46 N | 12.34 E |
| Teteven | 38 | 42.55 N | 24.16 E |
| Tetiaroa I[1] | 14 | 17.05 S | 149.32 W |
| Tetiyiv | 78 | 49.23 N | 29.41 E |
| Tetla | 234 | 19.26 N | 98.06 W |
| Tetlin | 180 | 63.08 N | 142.31 W |
| Tetlin Lake ⊜ | 180 | 63.05 N | 142.45 W |
| Teton | 202 | 43.53 N | 111.40 W |
| Teton ≃, Id., U.S. | 202 | 43.54 N | 111.51 W |
| Teton ≃, Mt., U.S. | 202 | 47.56 N | 110.31 W |
| Tetonia | 202 | 43.49 N | 111.09 W |
| Teton Range ⩘ | 202 | 43.45 N | 110.50 W |
| Tétouan | 148 | 35.34 N | 5.23 W |
| Tétouan □[4] | 148 | 35.30 N | 5.30 W |
| Tetovo | 38 | 42.01 N | 20.58 E |
| Tétreauville ◆[8] | 275a | 45.36 N | 73.32 W |
| Tetri-Ckaro | 84 | 41.34 N | 44.28 E |
| Tetschen → Děčín | 54 | 50.48 N | 14.13 E |
| Tetsuta | 96 | 34.56 N | 133.28 E |
| Tettau | 54 | 50.28 N | 11.15 E |
| Tettens | 52 | 53.38 N | 7.53 E |
| Tettnang | 58 | 47.40 N | 9.35 E |
| Tetuán → Tétouan | 148 | 35.34 N | 5.23 W |
| Tetufera, Mont ʌ | 174s | 17.40 S | 149.26 W |
| Tetulbāria | 126 | 21.58 N | 90.03 E |
| Tetulia ≃[1] | 126 | 22.15 N | 90.37 E |
| Teturi | 154 | 1.04 N | 29.08 E |
| Tet'uši | 80 | 54.57 N | 48.50 E |
| Tet'ušškoje | 80 | 54.18 N | 48.03 E |
| Teublitz | 60 | 49.13 N | 12.05 E |
| Teuchern | 54 | 51.07 N | 12.01 E |
| Teuco ≃ | 252 | 25.38 S | 60.12 W |
| Teufelshöhle ⫫[5] | 60 | 49.45 N | 11.25 E |
| Teufels-Insel → Diable, Île du I | 250 | 5.17 N | 52.35 W |
| Teufelsmoor ◆[3] | 52 | 53.15 N | 8.50 E |
| Teufen | 58 | 47.23 N | 9.23 E |
| Teufenbach | 61 | 47.08 N | 14.21 E |
| Teuhtli, Volcán ʌ[1] | 286a | 19.14 N | 99.01 W |
| Teulada | 71 | 38.58 N | 8.46 E |
| Teulada, Capo › | 71 | 38.52 N | 8.38 E |
| Teúl de González Ortega | 234 | 21.28 N | 103.29 W |
| Tèųli | 76 | 52.20 N | 24.15 E |
| Teulon | 184 | 50.23 N | 97.16 W |
| Teun, Pulau I | 164 | 6.59 S | 129.08 E |
| Teunom ≃ | 114 | 4.26 N | 95.48 E |
| Teunz | 60 | 49.29 N | 12.23 E |
| Teupitz | 54 | 52.08 N | 13.36 E |
| Teureubangan-cut | 114 | 3.12 N | 97.18 E |
| Teuri-tō I | 92a | 44.25 N | 141.19 E |
| Teuschnitz | 54 | 50.24 N | 11.23 E |
| Teutleben | 54 | 50.57 N | 10.33 E |
| Teutoburger Wald ◆[3] | 52 | 52.10 N | 8.15 E |
| Teutopolis | 194 | 39.07 N | 88.28 W |
| Teutschenthal | 54 | 51.27 N | 11.46 E |
| Teuva | 26 | 62.29 N | 21.44 E |
| Tevere (Tiber) ≃ | 66 | 41.44 N | 12.14 E |
| Teverya (Tiberias) | 132 | 32.47 N | 35.32 E |
| Teviot ≃ | 44 | 55.36 N | 2.26 W |
| Teviot Brook ≃ | 171a | 27.51 S | 152.57 E |
| Teviotdale V | 44 | 55.25 N | 2.50 W |
| Teviothead | 44 | 55.21 N | 2.56 W |
| Tevriz | 86 | 57.34 N | 72.24 E |
| Te Waewae Bay c | 172 | 46.15 S | 167.30 E |
| Tewah | 112 | 1.05 S | 113.42 E |
| Te Whaiti | 172 | 38.35 S | 176.47 E |
| Tewkesbury | 42 | 51.59 N | 2.09 W |
| Tewksbury | 207 | 42.36 N | 71.14 W |
| Tew-Mac Airport ⊠ | 283 | 42.36 N | 71.12 W |
| Têwo | 102 | 34.02 N | 103.05 E |
| Texada Island I | 182 | 49.40 N | 124.24 W |
| Texana, Lake ⊜[1] | 222 | 28.58 N | 96.32 W |
| Texarkana, Ar., U.S. | 194 | 33.26 N | 94.02 W |
| Texarkana, Tx., U.S. | 194 | 33.25 N | 94.02 W |
| Texas, Austl. | 166 | 28.51 S | 151.11 E |
| Texas, Oh., U.S. | 216 | 41.26 N | 83.57 W |
| Texas □[3], U.S. | 178 | 31.30 N | 99.00 W |
| Texas □[3], U.S. | 196 | 31.30 N | 99.00 W |
| Texas City | 222 | 29.23 N | 94.54 W |
| Texcaltitlán | 234 | 18.54 N | 99.55 W |
| Texcoco, Lago de ⊜ | 234 | 19.30 N | 99.00 W |
| Texel I | 52 | 53.05 N | 4.45 E |
| Texhoma | 196 | 36.30 N | 101.46 W |
| Texico | 196 | 34.23 N | 103.03 W |
| Texline | 196 | 36.23 N | 103.01 W |
| Texoma, Lake ⊜[1] | 196 | 33.55 N | 96.37 W |
| Teyateyaneng | 158 | 29.07 S | 27.34 E |
| Teyéa ⊥ | 38 | 37.29 N | 22.24 E |
| Teylān | 120 | 35.32 N | 64.47 E |
| Teynham | 42 | 51.20 N | 0.50 E |
| Teywarah | 120 | 33.21 N | 64.25 E |
| Teza ≃ | 80 | 56.32 N | 41.53 E |
| Teziutlán | 234 | 19.49 N | 97.21 W |
| Težler, gora ʌ | 84 | 40.42 N | 44.37 E |
| Tezoatlán de Segura y Luna | 234 | 17.42 N | 97.49 W |
| Tezpur | 120 | 26.37 N | 92.48 E |
| Tezu | 120 | 27.53 N | 96.11 E |
| Tezzeron Lake ⊜ | 182 | 54.41 N | 124.25 W |
| Tha ≃ | 110 | 20.07 N | 100.36 E |
| Tha-anne ≃ | 176 | 60.31 N | 94.37 W |
| Thabana-Ntlenyana ʌ | 158 | 29.28 S | 29.16 E |
| Thaba Nchu | 158 | 29.17 S | 26.52 E |
| Thabankulu ʌ | 158 | 27.30 S | 30.20 E |
| Thaba-Putsoa Range ⩘ | 158 | 29.45 S | 27.55 E |
| Thabaung | 110 | 17.02 N | 94.48 E |
| Thabawleikkyi | 110 | 12.01 N | 99.12 E |
| Thabazimbi | 156 | 24.41 S | 27.21 E |
| Thabor, Mont ʌ | 62 | 45.07 N | 6.34 E |
| Thabyu | 110 | 15.36 N | 98.29 E |
| Thacher Island I | 207 | 42.38 N | 70.35 W |
| Thādiq | 128 | 25.18 N | 45.52 E |
| Thagyettaw | 110 | 13.45 N | 98.09 E |
| Thai Binh | 110 | 20.27 N | 106.20 E |
| Thailand (Prathet Thai) □[1], Asia | 108 | 15.00 N | 100.00 E |
| Thailand (Prathet Thai) □[1], Asia | 110 | 15.00 N | 100.00 E |
| Thailand, Gulf of c | 110 | 10.00 N | 101.00 E |
| Thaïlande → Thailand □[1] | 110 | 15.00 N | 100.00 E |
| Thailandia → Thailand □[1] | 110 | 15.00 N | 100.00 E |
| Thai Muang | 110 | 8.24 N | 98.16 E |
| Thai Nguyen | 110 | 21.36 N | 105.50 E |
| Thak | 120 | 30.32 N | 70.13 E |
| Thakhek → Muang Khammouan | 110 | 17.24 N | 104.48 E |
| Thākurdwāra | 124 | 29.12 N | 78.51 E |
| Thākurdwāri | 272b | 22.34 N | 88.28 E |
| Thākurgaon | 124 | 26.02 N | 88.28 E |
| Thākurpukur | 272b | 22.28 N | 88.19 E |
| Thākurvādi | 272c | 18.54 N | 73.14 E |
| Thal, Dtsch. | 54 | 50.55 N | 10.23 E |
| Thal, Pāk. | 123 | 33.22 N | 70.33 E |
| Tha'l, Jabal ʌ | 140 | 14.13 N | 24.14 E |
| Thala | 36 | 35.35 N | 8.40 E |
| Thalang | 110 | 8.01 N | 98.19 E |
| Thal-Assling | 64 | 46.47 N | 12.38 E |
| Thalāthah | 142 | 30.35 N | 32.23 E |
| Thal Desert ◆[2] | 123 | 31.30 N | 71.40 E |
| Thale | 54 | 51.45 N | 11.03 E |
| Thalfang | 56 | 49.45 N | 6.59 E |
| Thalgau | 64 | 47.50 N | 13.15 E |
| Thalheim | 54 | 50.42 N | 12.53 E |
| Thalheim bei Wels | 61 | 48.09 N | 14.03 E |
| Tha Li | 110 | 17.37 N | 101.25 E |
| Thalia | 196 | 33.59 N | 99.32 W |
| Thālith, Ash-Shallāl ath- (Third Cataract) ∟ | 140 | 19.49 N | 30.19 E |
| Thalitter | 56 | 51.13 N | 8.53 E |
| Thalkirch | 58 | 46.38 N | 9.16 E |
| Thallon | 166 | 28.38 S | 148.52 E |
| Thallwitz | 54 | 51.26 N | 12.40 E |
| Thalmah, Marsā c | 142 | 29.03 N | 32.38 E |
| Thalmässing | 60 | 49.05 N | 11.13 E |
| Thalwil | 58 | 47.17 N | 8.34 E |
| Thamar, Jabal ʌ | 144 | 13.53 N | 45.12 E |
| Thame | 42 | 51.45 N | 0.59 W |
| Thames | 172 | 37.08 S | 175.33 E |
| Thames ≃, On., Can. | 190 | 42.19 N | 82.27 W |
| Thames ≃, Eng., U.K. | 42 | 51.28 N | 0.43 E |
| Thames ≃, Ct., U.S. | 207 | 41.18 N | 72.05 W |
| Thames, Firth of c | 172 | 37.00 S | 175.25 E |
| Thames Barrier ◆[6] | 260 | 51.29 N | 0.03 E |
| Thames Ditton | 260 | 51.23 N | 0.21 W |
| Thames Estuary c[1] | 260 | 51.30 N | 0.40 W |
| Thamesford | 212 | 43.04 N | 81.00 W |
| Thames Haven | 260 | 51.30 N | 0.31 E |
| Thamesville | 214 | 42.33 N | 81.59 W |
| Thāmit, Wādī V | 146 | 31.15 N | 16.06 E |
| Thammasat University ʊ[2] | 269a | 13.45 N | 100.30 E |
| Thamūd, Bi'r ∓[4] | 144 | 17.17 N | 49.56 E |
| Thāna, India | 122 | 19.12 N | 72.58 E |
| Thāna, Pāk. | 128 | 28.55 N | 63.45 E |
| Thāna Creek c | 272c | 19.00 N | 72.57 E |
| Thāna Gāzi | 124 | 27.25 N | 76.19 E |
| Thāna Kasba | 124 | 25.13 N | 77.20 E |
| Thanbyuzayat | 110 | 15.58 N | 97.44 E |
| Thandaung | 110 | 19.04 N | 96.41 E |
| Thānedārwāla | 123 | 32.36 N | 71.07 E |
| Thānesar | 124 | 29.59 N | 76.49 E |
| Thanet, Isle of I | 42 | 51.22 N | 1.20 E |
| Thanet Lake ⊜ | 212 | 44.47 N | 77.46 W |
| Thang Binh | 110 | 15.44 N | 108.22 E |
| Thangoo | 162 | 18.10 S | 122.22 E |
| Thangool | 166 | 24.29 S | 150.35 E |
| Thanh Hoa | 110 | 19.48 N | 105.46 E |
| Thanh My Tay | 269c | 10.49 N | 106.46 E |
| Thanh Pho Ho Chi Minh (Saigon), Viet | 110 | 10.45 N | 106.40 E |
| Thanh Pho Ho Chi Minh (Saigon), Viet | 269c | 10.45 N | 106.40 E |
| Thanjāvūr | 122 | 10.48 N | 79.09 E |
| Thann | 58 | 47.49 N | 7.05 E |
| Thannhausen | 58 | 48.17 N | 10.28 E |
| Thāno Bula Khān | 120 | 25.22 N | 67.50 E |
| Than Uyen | 110 | 22.00 N | 103.54 E |
| Thaoge ≃ | 156 | 20.27 S | 22.36 E |
| Thaon-les-Vosges | 58 | 48.15 N | 6.25 E |
| Tha Pla | 110 | 17.48 N | 100.32 E |
| Thap Than ≃ | 110 | 15.21 N | 104.06 E |
| Tharabwin West | 110 | 12.17 N | 99.03 E |
| Tharād | 120 | 24.24 N | 71.38 E |
| Tharandt | 54 | 50.59 N | 13.35 E |
| 't Harde | 52 | 52.25 N | 5.53 E |
| Thar Desert (Great Indian Desert) ◆[2] | 120 | 27.00 N | 71.00 E |
| Thargomindah | 166 | 28.00 S | 143.49 E |
| Thāri Pātan ʌ | 124 | 28.58 N | 82.04 E |
| Thar Nhom | 140 | 7.26 N | 30.29 E |
| Tharptown | 210 | 40.48 N | 76.34 W |
| Tharr, Wüste → Thar Desert ◆[2] | 120 | 27.00 N | 71.00 E |
| Tharrawaddy | 110 | 17.39 N | 95.48 E |
| Tharrawaw | 110 | 17.41 N | 95.28 E |
| Tharros ⊥ | 71 | 39.52 N | 8.26 E |
| Tharsuinn, Beinn ʌ | 46 | 57.47 N | 4.21 W |
| Tharthār, Buḩayrat ath- ⊜ | 128 | 34.00 N | 43.05 E |
| Tharthār, Wādī ath- V | 128 | 33.59 N | 43.12 E |
| Tharwa | 171b | 35.31 S | 149.04 E |
| Tha Sala | 110 | 8.40 N | 99.56 E |
| Thásos | 38 | 40.47 N | 24.42 E |


| Symbol | English | Deutsch | Español | Français | Português |
|---|---|---|---|---|---|
| ≃ | River | Fluß | Río | Rivière | Rio |
| ≍ | Canal | Kanal | Canal | Canal | Canal |
| ∟ | Waterfall, Rapids | Wasserfall, Stromschnellen | Cascada, Rápidos | Chute d'eau, Rapides | Cascata, Rápidos |
| )( | Strait | Meeresstraße | Estrecho | Détroit | Estreito |
| c | Bay, Gulf | Bucht, Golf | Bahía, Golfo | Baie, Golfe | Baía, Golfo |
| ⊜ | Lake, Lakes | See, Seen | Lago, Lagos | Lac, Lacs | Lago, Lagos |
| ≛ | Swamp | Sumpf | Pantano | Marais | Pântano |
| ⊓ | Ice Features, Glacier | Eis- und Gletscherformen | Accidentes Glaciales | Formes glaciaires | Acidentes glaciares |
| ≡ | Other Hydrographic Features | Andere Hydrographische Objekte | Otros Elementos Hidrográficos | Autres données hydrographiques | Outros acidentes hidrográficos |
| ✢ | Submarine Features | Untermeerische Objekte | Accidentes Submarinos | Formes de relief sous-marin | Acidentes submarinos |
| □ | Political Unit | Politische Einheit | Unidad Política | Entité politique | Unidade política |
| ʊ | Cultural Institution | Kulturelle Institution | Institución Cultural | Institution culturelle | Instituição cultural |
| ⊥ | Historical Site | Historische Stätte | Sitio Histórico | Site historique | Sitio histórico |
| ♠ | Recreational Site | Erholungs- und Ferienort | Sitio de Recreo | Centre de loisirs | Área de Lazer |
| ⊠ | Airport | Flughafen | Aeropuerto | Aéroport | Aeroporto |
| ■ | Military Installation | Militäranlage | Instalación Militar | Installation militaire | Instalação militar |
| ◆ | Miscellaneous | Verschiedenes | Misceláneo | Divers | Diversos |

| Name | Page | Lat.°′ | Long.°′ |
|---|---|---|---|
| Thásos I | 38 | 40.41 N | 24.47 E |
| Thásos ⊥ | 38 | 40.46 N | 24.33 E |
| Tha Tako | 110 | 15.38 N | 100.29 E |
| Thatcham | 42 | 51.25 N | 1.15 W |
| Thatch Cay I | 240m | 18.22 N | 64.52 W |
| Thatcher | 200 | 32.50 N | 109.45 W |
| Thatch Island I | 276 | 40.38 N | 73.23 W |
| That Khe | 110 | 22.16 N | 106.28 E |
| Thaton | 110 | 16.55 N | 97.22 E |
| That Phanom | 110 | 16.57 N | 104.44 E |
| Thatto Heath | 262 | 53.26 N | 2.45 W |
| Tha Tum | 110 | 15.19 N | 103.41 E |
| Thau, Bassin de c | 32 | 43.23 N | 3.36 E |
| Thaungdut | 110 | 24.26 N | 94.42 E |
| Thaungyin ≃ | 110 | 17.50 N | 97.42 E |
| Tha Uthen | 110 | 17.34 N | 104.36 E |
| Thawville | 216 | 40.41 N | 88.07 W |
| Thaxted | 42 | 51.57 N | 0.20 E |
| Thaya (Dyje) ≃ | 61 | 48.37 N | 16.56 E |
| Thayawthadangyi Kyun I | 110 | 12.20 N | 98.00 E |
| Thayer, Il., U.S. | 219 | 39.32 N | 89.46 W |
| Thayer, In., U.S. | 216 | 41.10 N | 87.20 W |
| Thayer, Ks., U.S. | 198 | 37.29 N | 95.28 W |
| Thayer, Mo., U.S. | 194 | 36.31 N | 91.32 W |
| Thayetchaung | 110 | 13.52 N | 98.16 E |
| Thayetmyo | 110 | 19.19 N | 95.11 E |
| Thayngen | 58 | 47.45 N | 8.42 E |
| Thazi | 110 | 20.51 N | 96.05 E |
| The Aldermen Islands II | 172 | 36.58 S | 176.05 E |
| Theale | 42 | 51.27 N | 1.04 W |
| Thealka | 192 | 37.49 N | 82.47 W |
| The Basin | 274b | 37.51 S | 145.19 E |
| Thebes → Thívai, Ellás | 38 | 38.21 N | 23.19 E |
| Thebes, Il., U.S. | 194 | 37.13 N | 89.28 W |
| Thebes ⊥ | 140 | 25.42 N | 32.37 E |
| The Birket ≃ | 262 | 53.24 N | 3.01 W |
| The Bluffs ✦[4] | 210 | 43.22 N | 76.40 W |
| The Bourne ≃ | 260 | 51.22 N | 0.29 W |
| The Calvados Chain II | 164 | 11.10 S | 152.40 E |
| The Camels Hump ∧ | 169 | 37.23 S | 144.35 E |
| The Capital ⊍ | 284c | 38.53 N | 77.00 W |
| The Cheviot ∧ | 44 | 55.28 N | 2.09 W |
| The Citadel ⊥, Magy. | 264c | 47.29 N | 19.03 E |
| The Citadel ⊥, Mișr | 273c | 30.02 N | 31.15 E |
| The Cloisters ⊍ | 276 | 40.52 N | 73.56 W |
| The Colony | 222 | 33.05 N | 96.52 W |
| The Coorong c | 168b | 35.40 S | 139.15 E |
| The Coteau ∧∧[2] | 184 | 51.10 N | 107.30 W |
| The Curragh ♠ | 48 | 53.10 N | 6.52 W |
| The Dalles | 224 | 45.35 N | 121.10 W |
| The Dalles Dam •[6] | 224 | 45.37 N | 121.08 W |
| The Deeps c | 46a | 60.09 N | 1.23 W |
| Thedford | 198 | 41.58 N | 100.34 W |
| Thedinghausen | 52 | 52.58 N | 9.01 E |
| The Downs ⊼[3] | 42 | 51.13 N | 1.27 E |
| Theebine | 166 | 25.57 S | 152.33 E |
| The English Companys Islands II | 164 | 11.50 S | 136.32 E |
| The Entrance | 170 | 33.21 S | 151.30 E |
| Theessen | 54 | 52.14 N | 12.02 E |
| The Fens •[1] | 42 | 52.38 N | 0.02 E |
| The Fishing Lakes ⊜ | 184 | 50.45 N | 103.51 W |
| The Flash ⊜ | 262 | 53.29 N | 2.33 W |
| The Flat Tops ∧∧ | 200 | 40.00 N | 107.10 W |
| The Forest of Nisene Marks State Park ♠ | 226 | 37.03 N | 121.53 W |
| The Glenkens •[1] | 44 | 55.10 N | 4.15 W |
| Thègon | 110 | 18.39 N | 95.25 E |
| The Granites | 162 | 20.35 S | 130.21 E |
| The Granites ∧ | 162 | 20.35 S | 130.20 E |
| The Graves II | 283 | 42.22 N | 70.52 W |
| The Grove | 222 | 31.16 N | 97.32 W |
| The Hague → 's-Gravenhage | 52 | 52.06 N | 4.18 E |
| The Heads > | 202 | 42.44 N | 124.31 W |
| The Hermitage ⊍ | 265a | 59.56 N | 30.20 E |
| The Home Park ♠ | 260 | 51.28 N | 0.36 W |
| The Hunters Hills ∧∧[2] | 172 | 44.30 S | 170.50 E |
| Theinkun | 110 | 11.53 N | 99.09 E |
| The Isles Lagoon c | 174o | 1.50 N | 157.23 W |
| Theiss → Tisa ≃ | 38 | 45.15 N | 20.17 E |
| Theissen | 54 | 51.05 N | 12.06 E |
| The Key Indian Reserve •[4] | 184 | 51.45 N | 102.08 W |
| The Lake Fleet Islands II | 212 | 44.18 N | 76.07 W |
| The Lakes National Park ♠ | 166 | 38.05 S | 147.40 E |
| The Little Minch ʉ | 46 | 57.35 N | 6.55 W |
| Thelon ≃ | 176 | 64.16 N | 96.05 W |
| The Long Mynd ∧ | 42 | 52.35 N | 2.48 W |
| The Lower Hope ≃[1] | 260 | 51.28 N | 0.28 E |
| Thelwall | 262 | 53.23 N | 2.32 W |
| The Lynd | 166 | 18.56 S | 144.30 E |
| Them | 41 | 56.06 N | 9.33 E |
| The Machars •[1] | 44 | 54.50 N | 4.33 W |
| The Mall in Columbia •[9] | 284b | 39.13 N | 76.52 W |
| Themar | 54 | 50.30 N | 10.37 E |
| The Meadows Race Track ♠ | 279b | 40.13 N | 80.12 W |
| The Mere ⊜ | 262 | 53.20 N | 2.24 W |
| Théméricourt | 261 | 49.05 N | 1.54 E |
| The Minch ʉ | 46 | 58.10 N | 5.50 W |
| The Mumbles | 42 | 51.34 N | 4.00 W |
| Then | 123 | 32.26 N | 75.44 E |
| The Narrows ʉ | 276 | 40.37 N | 74.03 W |
| The Navy Islands II | 212 | 44.21 N | 76.03 W |
| The Naze > | 42 | 51.53 N | 1.16 E |
| The Needles > | 42 | 50.39 N | 1.34 W |
| Thénezay | 32 | 46.43 N | 0.02 W |
| Thenia | 148 | 36.43 N | 3.34 E |
| Theniet el Hadd | 148 | 35.47 N | 2.01 E |
| The Oa >[1] | 46 | 55.37 N | 6.16 W |
| The Oaks, Austl. | 170 | 34.04 S | 150.34 E |
| The Oaks, Ca., U.S. | 226 | 39.13 N | 121.05 W |
| Theodore, Austl. | 166 | 24.57 S | 150.05 E |
| Theodore, Sk., Can. | 184 | 51.25 N | 102.54 W |
| Theodore, Al., U.S. | 194 | 30.32 N | 88.10 W |
| Theodore Francis Green Airport ⊠ | 207 | 41.44 N | 71.26 W |
| Theodore Roosevelt Inaugural National Historic Site ⊥ | 284a | 42.54 N | 78.52 W |
| Theodore Roosevelt Island I | 284c | 38.54 N | 77.03 W |
| Theodore Roosevelt Lake ⊜[1] | 200 | 33.42 N | 111.07 W |
| Theodore Roosevelt National Park (South Unit) ♠, N.D., U.S. | 198 | 46.55 N | 103.26 W |
| Theodore Roosevelt National Park (North Unit) ♠, N.D., U.S. | 198 | 47.34 N | 103.24 W |
| Theodor-Heuss-Brücke •[5] | 263 | 51.15 N | 6.45 E |
| Theog | 123 | 31.07 N | 77.21 E |
| Theólogos | 38 | 40.39 N | 24.41 E |
| The Orchards | 284b | 39.18 N | 76.50 W |
| Théoule-sur-Mer | 62 | 43.31 N | 6.57 E |
| The Oval ⊥ | 260 | 51.29 N | 0.07 W |
| The Pages II | 168b | 35.47 S | 138.17 E |
| The Paps ∧ | 48 | 52.00 N | 9.17 W |
| The Pas | 184 | 53.50 N | 101.15 W |
| The Peak ∧ | 192 | 36.24 N | 81.39 W |
| Thepha | 110 | 6.52 N | 100.58 E |
| The Pinnacle ∧[2] | 219 | 39.22 N | 90.55 W |
| Thérain ≃ | 50 | 49.15 N | 2.27 E |
| The Rajah ∧ | 182 | 53.15 N | 118.31 W |
| The Rand → Witwatersrant •[1] | 158 | 26.00 S | 27.00 E |
| The Range | 154 | 19.00 S | 31.04 E |
| Theresa | 212 | 44.12 N | 75.47 W |
| Theresa Creek ≃ | 166 | 23.26 S | 148.09 E |
| Theresa Park | 274a | 34.01 S | 150.39 E |
| Theresienstadt → Terezín | 54 | 50.31 N | 14.08 E |
| The Rhins >[1] | 44 | 54.50 N | 5.00 W |
| The Rip c | 169 | 38.17 S | 144.37 E |
| Thermaïkós Kólpos c | 38 | 40.23 N | 22.47 E |
| Thermalito | 226 | 39.31 N | 121.36 W |
| Thermopílai (Thermopylae) ⊥ | 38 | 38.48 N | 22.33 E |
| Thermopolis | 200 | 43.38 N | 108.12 W |
| Thermopylae → Thermopílai ⊥ | 38 | 38.48 N | 22.33 E |
| The Road c | 42a | 49.56 N | 6.20 W |
| The Rock | 166 | 35.16 S | 147.07 E |
| The Rockies ∧ | 224 | 46.39 N | 122.22 W |
| Theron Mountains ∧∧ | 9 | 79.05 S | 28.15 W |
| The Rope ✦[4] | 174e | 25.04 S | 130.05 W |
| Thérouanne | 50 | 50.38 N | 2.15 E |
| The Savannahs ⊜ | 220 | 27.19 N | 80.17 W |
| Theseion ⊥ | 267c | 37.58 N | 23.43 E |
| Thesiger Bay c | 176 | 71.30 N | 124.05 W |
| The Sisters ∧[2] | 162 | 26.17 S | 126.40 E |
| The Slot → New Georgia Sound ʉ | 175e | 8.00 S | 158.10 E |
| The Sluice ≚ | 262 | 53.41 N | 2.57 W |
| The Sny ≃ | 219 | 39.16 N | 90.44 W |
| The Solent ʉ | 42 | 50.46 N | 1.20 W |
| The Sound (Øresund) ʉ | 41 | 55.50 N | 12.40 E |
| The Springs | 207 | 40.52 N | 72.32 W |
| Thesprotikón | 38 | 39.15 N | 20.47 E |
| Thessalía □[4] | 38 | 39.30 N | 22.30 E |
| Thessalía □[9] | 38 | 39.30 N | 22.15 E |
| Thessalon | 190 | 46.15 N | 83.34 W |
| Thessaloníki (Salonika) | 38 | 40.38 N | 22.56 E |
| Thessalonique → Thessaloníki | 38 | 40.38 N | 22.56 E |
| The Storr ∧ | 46 | 57.31 N | 6.12 W |
| The Swale ʉ | 42 | 51.22 N | 0.56 E |
| Thet ≃ | 42 | 52.24 N | 0.45 E |
| The Tauride Palace ⊍ | 265a | 59.57 N | 30.23 E |
| The Terraces ✦[4] | 162 | 28.40 S | 121.30 E |
| Thetford | 42 | 52.25 N | 0.45 E |
| Thetford-Mines | 206 | 46.05 N | 71.18 W |
| The Thorofare ʉ | 208 | 37.15 N | 75.54 W |
| The Thumbs ∧ | 172 | 43.36 S | 170.44 E |
| Thetis Island | 224 | 49.59 N | 123.40 W |
| Thetis Island I | 224 | 49.00 N | 123.41 W |
| The Twelve Pins ∧ | 48 | 53.31 N | 9.50 W |
| The Twins ∧ | 172 | 41.14 S | 172.39 E |
| Theunissen | 158 | 28.30 S | 26.41 E |
| Theux | 56 | 50.32 N | 5.49 E |
| The Valley | 238 | 18.13 N | 63.04 W |
| Thevenard | 162 | 32.09 S | 133.38 E |
| Thevenard Island I | 162 | 21.27 S | 115.00 E |
| The Wash c | 42 | 52.55 N | 0.15 E |
| The Weald •[1] | 42 | 51.05 N | 0.05 E |
| The Whirlpool ≃ | 284a | 43.07 N | 79.04 W |
| The Winehead ∧ | 210 | 40.58 N | 77.28 W |
| The Wolds ∧∧[2] | 44 | 53.20 N | 0.10 W |
| The Woodlands | 222 | 30.09 N | 95.27 W |
| The Wrekin ∧[2] | 42 | 52.41 N | 2.34 W |
| Theydon Bois | 260 | 51.40 N | 0.06 E |
| Theys | 62 | 45.18 N | 6.00 E |
| Thiais | 261 | 48.46 N | 2.23 E |
| Thiant | 50 | 50.18 N | 3.27 E |
| Thiaucourt-Regniéville | 56 | 48.57 N | 5.52 E |
| Thibaudeau | 184 | 57.05 N | 94.08 W |
| Thiberville | 50 | 49.08 N | 0.27 E |
| Thibodaux | 194 | 29.47 N | 90.49 W |
| Thicket | 222 | 30.24 N | 94.38 W |
| Thicket Portage | 184 | 55.19 N | 97.42 W |
| Thiéblemont-Farémont | 58 | 48.41 N | 4.44 E |
| Thief ≃ | 198 | 48.08 N | 96.10 W |
| Thief Lake ⊜ | 198 | 48.30 N | 95.55 W |
| Thief River Falls | 198 | 48.07 N | 96.10 W |
| Thiéle (Zihl) ≃ | 58 | 47.03 N | 7.05 E |
| Thiel Mountains ∧∧ | 9 | 85.15 S | 91.00 W |
| Thielsen, Mount ∧ | 202 | 43.09 N | 122.04 W |
| Thiendorf | 54 | 51.17 N | 13.44 E |
| Thiene | 64 | 45.42 N | 11.29 E |
| Thiensville | 216 | 43.14 N | 87.58 W |
| Thiérache, Collines de la ∧∧[2] | 50 | 49.50 N | 3.50 E |
| Thierhaupten | 56 | 48.34 N | 10.54 E |
| Thiers | 62 | 45.51 N | 3.34 E |
| Thiersheim | 54 | 50.04 N | 12.07 E |
| Thierville-sur-Meuse | 56 | 49.10 N | 5.21 E |
| Thiès | 150 | 14.48 N | 16.56 W |
| Thiès □[4] | 150 | 14.45 N | 16.50 W |
| Thiesi | 71 | 40.31 N | 8.43 E |
| Thiessow | 54 | 54.16 N | 13.43 E |
| Thieux | 261 | 49.01 N | 2.40 E |
| Thieveley Pike ∧[2] | 262 | 53.45 N | 2.12 W |
| Thika | 154 | 1.03 S | 37.05 E |
| Thikombia Island I | 175g | 15.44 S | 179.55 W |
| Thilay | 56 | 49.52 N | 4.49 E |
| Thilenius, Cape > | 164 | 1.35 S | 149.57 E |
| Thimphu | 124 | 27.28 N | 89.39 E |
| Thines | 62 | 44.29 N | 4.03 E |
| Thingvallavatn ⊜ | 24a | 64.12 N | 21.10 W |
| Thingvellir | 24a | 64.17 N | 21.07 W |
| Thingvellir National Park ♠ | 24a | 64.17 N | 21.06 W |
| Thio | 175f | 21.37 S | 166.14 E |
| Thionville | 56 | 49.22 N | 6.10 E |
| Thiou | 150 | 13.48 N | 2.40 W |
| Thíra | 38 | 36.25 N | 25.26 E |
| Thíra (Santorini) I | 38 | 36.24 N | 25.29 E |
| Third ≃ | 276 | 40.49 N | 74.08 W |
| Third Cataract → Thālith, Ash-Shallāl ath- ⊾ | 140 | 19.49 N | 30.19 E |
| Third Cliff ✦[4] | 283 | 42.11 N | 70.43 W |
| Third Creek ≃, Mo., U.S. | 219 | 38.26 N | 91.40 W |
| Third Creek ≃, N.C., U.S. | 192 | 35.47 N | 80.31 W |
| Third Han-gang Bridge •[5] | 271b | 37.32 N | 127.00 E |
| Third Herring Brook ≃ | 283 | 42.07 N | 70.48 W |
| Third Lake ⊜ | 206 | 45.14 N | 71.12 W |
| Third Street Station •[5] | 282 | 37.46 N | 122.23 W |
| Thirlmere | 170 | 34.12 S | 150.34 E |
| Thirlmere ⊜ | 44 | 54.33 N | 3.04 W |
| Thirlmere Lakes National Park ♠ | 170 | 34.14 S | 150.32 E |
| Thiron | 50 | 48.19 N | 0.59 E |
| Thironne ≃ | 50 | 48.17 N | 1.15 E |
| Thirroul | 170 | 34.19 S | 150.56 E |
| Thirsk | 44 | 54.14 N | 1.20 W |
| Thirtieth Street Station •[5] | 285 | 39.57 N | 75.11 W |
| Thirtymile Creek ≃ | 198 | 46.22 N | 102.03 W |
| Thirtymile Point > | 210 | 43.22 N | 78.29 W |
| Thiruvārūr | 122 | 10.46 N | 79.39 E |
| Thisted | 26 | 56.57 N | 8.42 E |
| Thistilfjörður c | 24a | 66.20 N | 15.25 W |
| Thistledown Race Track ♠ | 279a | 41.26 N | 81.32 W |
| Thistle Island I | 166 | 35.00 S | 136.09 E |
| Thistletown •[8] | 275b | 43.44 N | 79.33 W |
| Thithia Island I | 175g | 17.45 S | 179.18 W |
| Thívai (Thebes) | 38 | 38.21 N | 23.19 E |
| Thiverval-Grignon | 261 | 48.51 N | 1.55 E |
| Thiviers | 32 | 45.25 N | 0.56 E |
| Thizy | 32 | 46.02 N | 4.19 E |
| Thjórsá ≃ | 24a | 63.47 N | 20.48 W |
| Thlewiaza ≃ | 176 | 60.28 N | 94.45 W |
| Thoa ≃ | 176 | 60.30 N | 109.47 W |
| Tho Chu, Dao II | 110 | 9.20 N | 103.28 E |
| Thoen | 110 | 17.36 N | 99.12 E |
| Thohoyandou | 156 | 23.00 S | 30.29 E |
| Thoi Binh | 110 | 9.21 N | 105.05 E |
| Thoirette | 58 | 46.16 N | 5.32 E |
| Thoiry | 261 | 48.52 N | 1.48 E |
| Thoissey | 58 | 46.10 N | 4.48 E |
| Tholen | 52 | 51.32 N | 4.12 E |
| Tholen I | 52 | 51.35 N | 4.05 E |
| Tholey | 56 | 49.29 N | 7.02 E |
| Thollon | 58 | 46.23 N | 6.43 E |
| Thomas, Ok., U.S. | 196 | 35.44 N | 98.44 W |
| Thomas, Pa., U.S. | 279b | 40.15 N | 80.06 W |
| Thomas, Wa., U.S. | 224 | 47.21 N | 122.13 W |
| Thomas, W.V., U.S. | 188 | 39.08 N | 79.29 W |
| Thomasboro | 216 | 40.15 N | 88.11 W |
| Thomas Creek ≃ | 202 | 44.40 N | 122.56 W |
| Thomas Hill Reservoir ⊜[1] | 194 | 39.40 N | 92.40 W |
| Thomas J. O'Brien Lock and Dam •[5] | 278 | 41.39 N | 87.35 W |
| Thomas Lake ⊜ | 184 | 57.00 N | 96.43 W |
| Thomas Mountains ∧∧ | 9 | 75.32 S | 70.57 W |
| Thomas Point > | 208 | 38.54 N | 76.28 W |
| Thomaston, Al., U.S. | 194 | 32.15 N | 87.37 W |
| Thomaston, Ct., U.S. | 207 | 41.40 N | 73.04 W |
| Thomaston, Ga., U.S. | 192 | 32.53 N | 84.19 W |
| Thomaston, Me., U.S. | 188 | 44.04 N | 69.10 W |
| Thomaston, N.Y., U.S. | 276 | 40.47 N | 73.43 W |
| Thomaston, Tx., U.S. | 222 | 29.00 N | 97.09 W |
| Thomastown, Austl. | 274b | 37.41 S | 145.01 E |
| Thomastown, Ire. | 48 | 52.31 N | 7.08 W |
| Thomasville, Al., U.S. | 194 | 31.54 N | 87.44 W |
| Thomasville, Ga., U.S. | 192 | 30.50 N | 83.58 W |
| Thomasville, N.C., U.S. | 192 | 35.52 N | 80.04 W |
| Thomasville, Pa., U.S. | 208 | 39.56 N | 76.51 W |
| Thomes Creek ≃ | 204 | 39.59 N | 122.06 W |
| Thom Lake ⊜ | 184 | 55.24 N | 96.08 W |
| Thomlinson, Mount ∧ | 182 | 55.33 N | 127.29 W |
| Thompson, Mb., Can. | 184 | 55.45 N | 97.45 W |
| Thompson, Ct., U.S. | 207 | 41.57 N | 71.51 W |
| Thompson, Ia., U.S. | 190 | 43.22 N | 93.46 W |
| Thompson, Mo., U.S. | 219 | 39.11 N | 91.59 W |
| Thompson, N.D., U.S. | 198 | 47.46 N | 97.06 W |
| Thompson, Oh., U.S. | 214 | 41.41 N | 81.03 W |
| Thompson, Pa., U.S. | 210 | 41.52 N | 75.31 W |
| Thompson ≃, B.C., Can. | 182 | 50.15 N | 121.33 W |
| Thompson ≃, U.S. | 194 | 39.45 N | 93.36 W |
| Thompson Creek ≃, U.S. | 198 | 45.04 N | 104.25 W |
| Thompson Creek ≃, Ms., U.S. | 194 | 31.10 N | 88.54 W |
| Thompson Falls | 202 | 47.35 N | 115.20 W |
| Thompson Island I | 283 | 42.23 N | 71.01 W |
| Thompson Pass )( | 180 | 61.08 N | 145.45 W |
| Thompson Peak ∧ | 204 | 41.00 N | 123.03 W |
| Thompson Place | 224 | 47.03 N | 122.45 W |
| Thompson Ridge | 210 | 41.34 N | 74.20 W |
| Thompson Run ≃ | 279b | 40.24 N | 79.50 W |
| Thompsons | 222 | 29.30 N | 95.36 W |
| Thompsons Creek ≃ | 284a | 43.03 N | 79.08 W |
| Thompson Sound ʉ | 172 | 45.09 S | 166.57 E |
| Thompsontown | 208 | 40.33 N | 77.14 W |
| Thompsonville | 190 | 44.31 N | 85.56 W |
| Thomsen ≃ | 176 | 74.08 N | 119.35 W |
| Thomson, Ga., U.S. | 192 | 33.28 N | 82.30 W |
| Thomson, Il., U.S. | 190 | 41.58 N | 90.06 W |
| Thomson, N.Y., U.S. | 210 | 43.07 N | 73.35 W |
| Thomson ≃, Austl. | 166 | 25.11 S | 142.53 E |
| Thomson ≃, Austl. | 169 | 37.58 S | 146.32 E |
| Thomson, Lake ⊜[1] | 169 | 37.45 S | 146.22 E |
| Thomson Lake ⊜[1] | 184 | 49.45 N | 106.35 W |
| Thon ≃ | 50 | 49.53 N | 3.55 E |
| Thon Buri | 110 | 13.43 N | 100.29 E |
| Thônes | 62 | 45.53 N | 6.20 E |
| Thong | 260 | 51.24 N | 0.24 E |
| Thong Hoe | 271c | 1.25 N | 103.42 E |
| Thong Tay Hoi | 269c | 10.50 N | 106.39 E |
| Thongwa | 110 | 16.46 N | 96.32 E |
| Thon Lac Nghiep | 110 | 11.20 N | 108.54 E |
| Thonnance-lès-Joinville | 58 | 48.27 N | 5.10 E |
| Thonon-les-Bains | 58 | 46.22 N | 6.29 E |
| Thonotosassa | 220 | 28.03 N | 82.18 W |
| Thonze | 110 | 17.38 N | 95.47 E |
| Thorah Island I | 212 | 44.27 N | 79.14 W |
| Thorame-Haute | 62 | 44.06 N | 6.33 E |
| Thorburn | 186 | 45.34 N | 62.33 W |
| Thoreau | 200 | 35.24 N | 108.13 W |
| Thorembais-les-Béguines | 56 | 50.40 N | 4.49 E |
| Thorenc | 62 | 43.48 N | 6.49 E |
| Thorens-Glières | 58 | 45.59 N | 6.15 E |
| Thorhild | 182 | 54.10 N | 113.07 W |
| Thorial | 140 | 8.40 N | 29.56 E |
| Thorigny-sur-Marne | 261 | 48.53 N | 2.42 E |
| Thorigny-sur-Oreuse | 50 | 48.17 N | 3.24 E |
| Thórisvatn ⊜ | 24a | 64.16 N | 18.54 W |
| Thörl | 61 | 47.31 N | 15.13 E |
| Thorlákshöfn | 24a | 63.53 N | 21.18 W |
| Thormanby | 44 | 54.10 N | 1.14 W |
| Thorn, Ned. | 52 | 51.10 N | 5.50 E |
| Thorn → Toruń, Pol. | 30 | 53.02 N | 18.35 E |
| Thornaby-on-Tees | 44 | 54.34 N | 1.18 W |
| Thornapple ≃, Mi., U.S. | 216 | 42.56 N | 85.28 W |
| Thornapple ≃, Wi., U.S. | 190 | 45.28 N | 91.16 W |
| Thornapple Lake ⊜ | 216 | 42.37 N | 85.11 W |
| Thornburg | 279b | 40.26 N | 80.05 W |
| Thornbury, Austl. | 274b | 37.45 S | 145.00 E |
| Thornbury, On., Can. | 212 | 44.34 N | 80.26 W |
| Thornbury, N.Z. | 172 | 46.17 S | 168.06 E |
| Thornbury, Eng., U.K. | 42 | 51.37 N | 2.32 W |
| Thorn Creek ≃ | 278 | 41.36 N | 87.35 W |
| Thorndale, On., Can. | 212 | 43.06 N | 81.08 W |
| Thorndale, Tx., U.S. | 222 | 30.36 N | 97.12 W |
| Thorndike | 207 | 42.11 N | 72.20 W |
| Thorndon | 42 | 52.17 N | 1.08 E |
| Thorne | 44 | 53.37 N | 0.58 W |
| Thorne ≃ | 184 | 54.56 N | 90.35 W |
| Thorne Bay | 182 | 55.44 N | 132.32 W |
| Thorney | 42 | 52.37 N | 0.07 W |
| Thorngumbald | 44 | 53.43 N | 0.10 W |
| Thornhill, On., Can. | 275b | 43.48 N | 79.25 W |
| Thornhill, S. Afr. | 273d | 26.07 S | 28.09 E |
| Thornhill, Scot., U.K. | 44 | 55.15 N | 3.46 W |
| Thornhurst | 210 | 41.11 N | 75.35 W |
| Thornleigh | 274a | 33.44 S | 151.05 E |
| Thornton, Austl. | 171a | 27.49 S | 152.23 E |
| Thornton, Eng., U.K. | 44 | 53.53 N | 3.02 W |
| Thornton, Eng., U.K. | 262 | 53.30 N | 3.00 W |
| Thornton, Eng., U.K. | 262 | 53.47 N | 1.51 W |
| Thornton, Scot., U.K. | 46 | 56.10 N | 3.09 W |
| Thornton, Ar., U.S. | 194 | 33.46 N | 92.29 W |
| Thornton, Ca., U.S. | 226 | 38.14 N | 121.25 W |
| Thornton, Co., U.S. | 200 | 39.52 N | 104.58 W |
| Thornton, Il., U.S. | 278 | 41.35 N | 87.37 W |
| Thornton, Pa., U.S. | 285 | 39.54 N | 75.32 W |
| Thornton, Tx., U.S. | 222 | 31.24 N | 96.34 W |
| Thornton Beach ♠ | 282 | 37.42 N | 122.30 W |
| Thornton Dale | 44 | 54.14 N | 0.43 W |
| Thornton Hough | 262 | 53.19 N | 3.03 W |
| Thornton-le-Moors | 262 | 53.16 N | 2.50 W |
| Thornton Moor Reservoir ⊜[1] | 262 | 53.47 N | 1.55 W |
| Thorntonville | 196 | 31.34 N | 102.55 W |
| Thornwood | 210 | 41.07 N | 73.46 W |
| Thornwood Common | 260 | 51.43 N | 0.08 E |
| Thorny Mountain ∧[2] | 194 | 37.06 N | 91.10 W |
| Thorofare | 285 | 39.50 N | 75.11 W |
| Thorold | 212 | 43.07 N | 79.12 W |
| Thorold South | 284a | 43.06 N | 79.12 W |
| Thoronet, Abbaye du ⊍[1] | 62 | 43.28 N | 6.16 E |
| Thorp, Wa., U.S. | 224 | 47.04 N | 120.40 W |
| Thorp, Wi., U.S. | 190 | 44.57 N | 90.47 W |
| Thorpe | 260 | 51.24 N | 0.32 W |
| Thorpe-le-Soken | 42 | 51.52 N | 1.10 E |
| Thorp Spring | 222 | 32.28 N | 97.49 W |
| Thorsby, Ab., Can. | 182 | 53.14 N | 114.03 W |
| Thorsby, Al., U.S. | 194 | 32.54 N | 86.42 W |
| Thorshavn → Tórshavn | 22 | 62.01 N | 6.46 W |
| Thórshöfn | 24a | 66.13 N | 15.17 W |
| Thorsø | 41 | 56.18 N | 9.48 E |
| Thorsteinson Lake ⊜ | 184 | 57.15 N | 97.30 W |
| Thot Not | 110 | 10.16 N | 105.32 E |
| Thouars | 32 | 46.59 N | 0.13 W |
| Thouin, Cape > | 162 | 20.20 S | 118.12 E |
| Thoune → Thun | 58 | 46.45 N | 7.37 E |
| Thourotte | 50 | 49.29 N | 2.53 E |
| Thousand Islands II | 212 | 44.15 N | 76.12 W |
| Thousand Islands International Bridge •[5] | 212 | 44.20 N | 75.58 W |
| Thousand Lake Mountain ∧ | 200 | 38.25 N | 111.29 W |
| Thousand Oaks | 228 | 34.10 N | 118.50 W |
| Thousand Ships Bay c | 175e | 8.25 S | 159.40 E |
| Thousand Springs Creek ≃ | 200 | 41.17 N | 113.51 W |
| Thowa ≃ | 154 | 1.33 S | 40.03 E |
| Thowgla Creek ≃ | 171b | 36.10 S | 147.57 E |
| Thrace □[9] | 38 | 41.20 N | 26.45 E |
| Thrakikón Pélagos ⊼[2] | 38 | 40.15 N | 24.28 E |
| Thrall | 222 | 30.35 N | 97.18 W |
| Thrapston | 42 | 52.24 N | 0.32 W |
| Thrasher Lake ⊜ | 212 | 44.55 N | 78.58 W |
| Thread Creek ≃ | 216 | 43.01 N | 83.42 W |
| Thredbo Village | 171b | 36.29 S | 148.19 E |
| Three Bridges | 208 | 40.31 N | 74.47 W |
| Three Brothers ∧ | 224 | 47.23 N | 120.45 W |
| Three Brothers Mountain ∧ | 224 | 49.10 N | 120.46 W |
| Three Creek ≃ | 208 | 36.47 N | 77.10 W |
| Three Fathoms Cove c | 271d | 22.26 N | 114.17 E |
| Three Fingered Jack ∧ | 202 | 44.29 N | 121.50 W |
| Three Fingers ∧ | 224 | 48.10 N | 121.41 W |
| Three Fools Creek ≃ | 224 | 48.53 N | 120.57 W |
| Three Forks | 202 | 45.53 N | 111.33 W |
| Three Hills | 182 | 51.42 N | 113.16 W |
| Three Hummock Island I | 166 | 40.26 S | 144.55 E |
| Three Kings Islands II | 172 | 34.10 S | 172.05 E |
| Three Lakes | 190 | 45.47 N | 89.09 W |
| Three M Airport ⊠ | 285 | 40.08 N | 74.51 W |
| Three Mile Bay | 212 | 44.04 N | 76.11 W |
| Three Mile Plains | 186 | 44.58 N | 64.07 W |
| Three Oaks | 216 | 41.47 N | 86.36 W |
| Three Pagodas Pass )( | 110 | 15.18 N | 98.23 E |
| Threepoint Lake ⊜ | 184 | 55.41 N | 98.56 W |
| Three Points, Cape > | 150 | 4.45 N | 2.06 W |
| Three Rivers, Austl. | 162 | 25.07 S | 119.09 E |
| Three Rivers → Trois-Rivières, P.Q., Can. | 206 | 46.21 N | 72.33 W |
| Three Rivers, Ma., U.S. | 207 | 42.10 N | 72.21 W |
| Three Rivers, Mi., U.S. | 216 | 41.56 N | 85.37 W |
| Three Rivers, Tx., U.S. | 196 | 28.27 N | 98.10 W |
| Three Rivers □[8] | 260 | 51.40 N | 0.27 W |
| Three Sisters | 158 | 31.54 S | 23.06 E |
| Three Sisters ∧ | 202 | 44.10 N | 121.46 W |
| Three Sisters Islands II | 175e | 10.10 S | 161.57 E |
| Three Springs, Austl. | 162 | 29.32 S | 115.45 E |
| Three Springs, Pa., U.S. | 214 | 40.12 N | 77.59 W |
| Threlkeld | 44 | 54.38 N | 3.03 W |
| Throat ≃ | 184 | 51.48 N | 93.30 W |
| Throckmorton | 196 | 33.10 N | 99.10 W |
| Throgs Neck •[8] | 276 | 40.49 N | 73.49 W |
| Throgs Neck Bridge •[5] | 276 | 40.48 N | 73.48 W |
| Throgs Point > | 276 | 40.48 N | 73.48 W |
| Throop | 210 | 41.27 N | 75.36 W |
| Throssel, Lake ⊜ | 162 | 27.27 S | 124.16 E |
| Throssell Range ∧∧ | 162 | 22.03 S | 121.43 E |
| Thrushel ≃ | 42 | 50.39 N | 4.15 W |
| Thruway Mall •[9] | 284a | 42.55 N | 78.46 W |
| Thu, Cu Lao I | 110 | 10.33 N | 108.57 E |
| Thuan Chau | 110 | 21.26 N | 103.41 E |
| Thu Dau Mot | 110 | 10.58 N | 106.39 E |
| Thu Duc | 269c | 10.51 N | 106.45 E |
| Thueyts | 62 | 44.41 N | 4.13 E |
| Thuilley-aux-Groseilles | 58 | 48.34 N | 5.58 E |
| Thuin | 50 | 50.20 N | 4.17 E |
| Thul | 120 | 28.14 N | 68.46 E |
| Thulaythiwāt, Tilāl ath- ∧ | 132 | 30.58 N | 36.40 E |
| Thulba ≃ | 56 | 50.11 N | 9.52 E |
| Thule | 16 | 76.34 N | 68.47 W |
| Thulī Bherī ≃ | 124 | 28.42 N | 82.16 E |
| Thum | 54 | 50.40 N | 12.57 E |
| Thumb Peak ∧ | 116 | 9.48 N | 118.36 E |
| Thumby | 41 | 54.35 N | 9.54 E |
| Thun | 58 | 46.45 N | 7.37 E |
| Thun Chang | 110 | 19.25 N | 100.53 E |
| Thunder Bay | 190 | 48.23 N | 89.15 W |
| Thunder Bay c, On., Can. | 190 | 48.24 N | 89.00 W |
| Thunder Bay c, On., Can. | 212 | 44.48 N | 80.03 W |
| Thunder Bay c, Mi., U.S. | 190 | 45.00 N | 83.22 W |
| Thunder Bay ≃ | 190 | 45.04 N | 83.25 W |
| Thunder Bay, North Branch ≃ | 190 | 45.08 N | 83.35 W |
| Thunderbird, Lake ⊜[1] | 196 | 35.15 N | 97.20 W |
| Thunderbolt | 192 | 32.02 N | 81.03 W |
| Thunder Butte ∧ | 198 | 45.19 N | 101.53 W |
| Thunder Butte Creek ≃ | 198 | 45.13 N | 101.42 W |
| Thunder Creek ≃, Sk., Can. | 184 | 50.23 N | 105.32 W |
| Thunder Creek ≃, Wa., U.S. | 224 | 48.40 N | 121.05 W |
| Thunder Hills ∧∧[2] | 184 | 54.30 N | 106.00 W |
| Thunder Mountain ∧[2] | 216 | 42.16 N | 86.20 W |
| Thundersley | 260 | 51.34 N | 0.35 E |
| Thunersee ⊜ | 58 | 46.40 N | 7.45 E |
| Thüngen | 56 | 49.56 N | 9.51 E |
| Thung Song | 110 | 8.09 N | 99.41 E |
| Thung Wa | 110 | 7.06 N | 99.46 E |
| Thur ≃, Fr. | 58 | 48.05 N | 7.23 E |
| Thur ≃, Schw. | 58 | 47.36 N | 8.35 E |
| Thurcroft | 44 | 53.24 N | 1.16 W |
| Thurgau □[3] | 58 | 47.35 N | 9.00 E |
| Thurgovie → Thurgau □[3] | 58 | 47.35 N | 9.00 E |
| Thüringen | 58 | 47.12 N | 9.45 E |
| Thüringen □[3] | 30 | 51.00 N | 11.00 E |
| Thüringer Wald ∧∧ | 30 | 50.40 N | 10.50 E |
| Thürkow | 54 | 53.50 N | 12.33 E |
| Thurles | 48 | 52.41 N | 7.49 W |
| Thurmont | 208 | 39.37 N | 77.24 W |
| Thurm | 54 | 50.46 N | 12.33 E |
| Thurn, Pass )( | 64 | 47.19 N | 12.24 E |
| Thurnau | 60 | 50.01 N | 11.23 E |
| Thurnham | 260 | 51.17 N | 0.36 E |
| Thurnscoe | 44 | 53.31 N | 1.19 W |
| Thurnwald Range ∧∧ | 164 | 4.45 S | 141.15 E |
| Thurø | 41 | 55.03 N | 10.40 E |
| Thurrock □[8] | 260 | 51.30 N | 0.21 E |
| Thursby | 44 | 54.51 N | 3.03 W |
| Thursday Island | 164 | 10.35 S | 142.13 E |
| Thurso, P.Q., Can. | 206 | 45.36 N | 75.15 W |
| Thurso, Scot., U.K. | 46 | 58.35 N | 3.32 W |
| Thurso ≃ | 46 | 58.36 N | 3.30 W |
| Thurstaston | 262 | 53.21 N | 3.08 W |
| Thurston | 42 | 52.15 N | 0.49 E |
| Thurston □[6] | 224 | 46.59 N | 122.42 W |
| Thurston Island I | 9 | 72.20 S | 99.00 W |
| Thusis | 58 | 46.42 N | 9.26 E |
| Thwaites Iceberg Tongue ⊓ | 9 | 74.45 S | 106.30 W |
| Thy •[1] | 26 | 57.00 N | 8.30 E |
| Thyborøn | 26 | 56.42 N | 8.13 E |
| Thylungra | 166 | 26.04 S | 143.28 E |
| Thyolo | 154 | 16.10 S | 35.10 E |
| Thyregod | 41 | 55.54 N | 9.16 E |
| Thysville → Mbanza-Ngungu | 152 | 5.15 S | 14.52 E |
| Tiadiaye | 150 | 14.25 N | 16.42 W |
| Tía Juana | 246 | 10.16 N | 71.22 W |
| Tian ≃ | 105 | 40.42 N | 116.33 E |
| Tiana, Esp. | 266d | 44.29 N | 2.16 E |
| Tiana, It. | 71 | 40.04 N | 9.08 E |
| Tian'anmen Square ⊥ | 271a | 39.55 N | 116.23 E |
| Tianbao | 100 | 24.36 N | 117.35 E |
| Tianchang | 100 | 32.41 N | 119.01 E |
| Tiancunpu | 105 | 39.06 N | 115.41 E |
| Tiandeng | 102 | 23.09 N | 107.10 E |
| Tiandong | 102 | 23.36 N | 107.08 E |
| Tian'e | 102 | 25.01 N | 107.20 E |
| Tianeti | 84 | 42.07 N | 44.59 E |
| Tianfanjie | 100 | 29.20 N | 116.50 E |
| Tiangang, Zhg. | 89 | 43.24 N | 125.54 E |
| Tiangang, Zhg. | 89 | 43.55 N | 127.00 E |
| Tiangongsi | 105 | 39.14 N | 115.53 E |
| Tianguá | 250 | 3.44 S | 40.59 W |
| Tianhe | 100 | 27.01 N | 114.30 E |
| Tianhekou | 100 | 32.08 N | 113.25 E |
| Tianhelong | 89 | 43.56 N | 120.39 E |
| Tianhuang | 98 | 35.29 N | 117.18 E |
| Tianjara, Mount ∧ | 170 | 35.11 S | 150.18 E |
| Tianjia, Zhg. | 104 | 41.07 N | 122.03 E |
| Tianjia, Zhg. | 107 | 29.40 N | 105.08 E |
| Tianjiaba | 102 | 32.08 N | 110.03 E |
| Tianjiatun | 104 | 41.39 N | 123.44 E |
| Tianjiawopu | 104 | 42.28 N | 122.38 E |
| Tianjiazhen | 100 | 29.56 N | 115.26 E |
| Tianjin (Tientsin) | 105 | 39.08 N | 117.12 E |
| Tianjing | 106 | 31.27 N | 120.46 E |
| Tianjin Shi (Tientsin Shih) □[7] | 98 | 39.30 N | 117.15 E |
| Tianjun | 102 | 37.25 N | 98.58 E |
| Tiankai | 105 | 39.38 N | 115.51 E |
| Tiankoura | 150 | 10.46 N | 3.16 W |
| Tiankoye | 150 | 12.35 N | 12.40 W |
| Tianlin, Zhg. | 102 | 24.14 N | 106.03 E |
| Tianlin, Zhg. | 107 | 29.49 N | 105.19 E |
| Tian Ling ∧ | 89 | 44.22 N | 129.52 E |
| Tianmashan | 106 | 31.04 N | 121.08 E |
| Tianmen | 100 | 30.39 N | 113.06 E |
| Tianmu Shan ∧∧ | 100 | 30.25 N | 119.30 E |
| Tianpu | 106 | 31.56 N | 121.07 E |
| Tianqiaochang | 104 | 40.52 N | 121.02 E |
| Tianqiaoling | 89 | 43.26 N | 129.38 E |
| Tianquan | 102 | 30.10 N | 102.48 E |
| Tian Shan → Tien Shan ∧∧ | 90 | 42.00 N | 80.00 E |
| Tianshenggang | 106 | 32.03 N | 120.45 E |
| Tianshifu | 98 | 41.17 N | 124.21 E |
| Tianshui | 102 | 34.30 N | 105.58 E |
| Tianshuijing, Zhg. | 102 | 40.17 N | 95.21 E |
| Tianshuijing, Zhg. | 104 | 41.19 N | 121.48 E |
| Tianshuituo | 105 | 39.20 N | 118.12 E |
| Tianshuizhan | 104 | 41.00 N | 123.34 E |
| Tiantai | 100 | 29.09 N | 121.02 E |
| Tiantang | 102 | 22.32 N | 111.55 E |
| Tiantou, Zhg. | 100 | 28.48 N | 120.39 E |
| Tiantou, Zhg. | 100 | 26.19 N | 115.57 E |
| Tianwangsi | 106 | 31.45 N | 119.12 E |
| Tianxin, Zhg. | 100 | 27.53 N | 113.06 E |
| Tianxin, Zhg. | 100 | 28.11 N | 114.35 E |
| Tianxin, Zhg. | 102 | 27.21 N | 111.00 E |
| Tianxingqiao | 106 | 32.05 N | 119.57 E |
| Tianxiyang | 100 | 26.31 N | 118.33 E |
| Tianyang | 102 | 23.51 N | 106.34 E |
| Tianyangping | 107 | 29.11 N | 105.16 E |
| Tianyar | 115b | 8.12 S | 115.30 E |
| Tianzhen | 98 | 40.28 N | 114.06 E |
| Tianzhongying | 100 | 33.13 N | 115.22 E |
| Tianzhu, Zhg. | 102 | 37.14 N | 102.59 E |
| Tianzhu, Zhg. | 102 | 26.50 N | 109.00 E |
| Tianzhuang, Zhg. | 100 | 25.43 N | 113.40 E |
| Tianzhuang, Zhg. | 105 | 39.25 N | 117.54 E |
| Tianzhuangtai | 104 | 40.50 N | 122.08 E |
| Tiao ≃ | 106 | 30.56 N | 120.11 E |
| Tiaodengchang | 107 | 30.47 N | 106.22 E |
| Tiarel | 174s | 17.32 S | 149.20 W |
| Tiarno | 64 | 45.53 N | 10.40 E |
| Tiaro | 166 | 25.44 S | 152.35 E |
| Tiassalé | 150 | 5.54 N | 4.50 W |
| Tiati ∧ | 154 | 1.19 N | 35.56 E |
| Ti'avea | 175a | 13.57 S | 171.24 W |
| Tiawichi Creek ≃ | 222 | 32.19 N | 94.44 W |
| Tiba → Chiba | 94 | 35.36 N | 140.07 E |
| Tibaji | 252 | 24.30 S | 50.24 W |
| Tibaji ≃ | 252 | 22.47 S | 51.01 W |
| Tibari | 154 | 5.01 N | 31.43 E |
| Tibasti, Sarīr •[2] | 146 | 24.00 N | 17.00 E |
| Tibati | 152 | 6.27 N | 12.38 E |
| Tibbermore | 46 | 56.22 N | 3.32 W |
| Tibbie | 194 | 31.21 N | 88.14 W |
| Tibe | 144 | 9.03 N | 37.08 E |
| Tibel'ti | 88 | 51.46 N | 103.11 E |
| Tiber → Tevere ≃ | 66 | 41.44 N | 12.14 E |
| Tiberias → Teverya | 132 | 32.47 N | 35.32 E |
| Tiberias, Lake → Kinneret, Yam ⊜ | 132 | 32.48 N | 35.35 E |
| Tiberina, Val V | 66 | 43.31 N | 12.10 E |
| Tibesti ∧∧ | 146 | 21.30 N | 17.30 E |
| Tibet → Xizang Zizhiqu □[4] | 90 | 32.00 N | 88.00 E |
| Tibet, Lake ⊜ | 220 | 28.27 N | 81.31 W |
| Tibet, Plateau of → Qing Zang Gaoyuan ∧∧[1] | 12 | 33.00 N | 92.00 E |
| Tibiao | 116 | 11.17 N | 122.02 E |
| Tibiao Point > | 116 | 11.18 N | 122.02 E |
| Tibidabo ∧ | 266d | 41.25 N | 2.07 E |
| Tibiri, Niger | 150 | 13.06 N | 4.00 E |
| Tibiri, Niger | 150 | 13.34 N | 7.04 E |
| Tibirke | 41 | 56.03 N | 12.07 E |
| Tiblawan | 116 | 6.29 N | 126.06 E |
| Tiblemont, Lac ⊜ | 190 | 48.14 N | 77.18 W |
| Tibnah | 132 | 32.59 N | 36.13 E |
| Tibnīn | 132 | 33.12 N | 35.25 E |
| Tibooburra | 166 | 29.26 S | 142.01 E |
| Tibro | 26 | 58.26 N | 14.10 E |
| Tiburon | 226 | 37.52 N | 122.27 W |
| Tiburón, Cabo > | 246 | 8.42 N | 77.24 W |
| Tiburón, Isla I | 232 | 29.00 N | 112.23 W |
| Tiburon Peninsula >[1] | 282 | 37.53 N | 122.28 W |
| Tiča, Jazovir ⊜[1] | 38 | 43.05 N | 26.45 E |
| Ticao Island I | 116 | 12.31 N | 123.42 E |
| Ticao Pass ʉ | 116 | 12.38 N | 123.47 E |
| Tice | 220 | 26.40 N | 81.48 W |
| Tice Creek ≃ | 282 | 37.53 N | 122.03 W |
| Ticehurst | 42 | 51.03 N | 0.25 E |
| Tichigan | 216 | 42.50 N | 88.12 W |
| Tichigan Lake ⊜ | 216 | 42.49 N | 88.13 W |
| Tîchît | 150 | 18.28 N | 9.30 W |
| Tîchît, Ḍahr ✦[4] | 150 | 18.30 N | 9.25 W |
| Tichmenevo, Ross. | 76 | 58.00 N | 38.36 E |
| Tichmenevo, Ross. | 89 | 49.12 N | 142.54 E |
| Ticho | 144 | 7.50 N | 39.32 E |
| Tichon | 24 | 59.23 N | 46.38 E |
| Tichonova Pustyn' | 82 | 54.38 N | 36.09 E |
| Tichonovka | 88 | 53.13 N | 104.13 E |
| Tichookeanskij | 89 | 43.00 N | 132.24 E |
| Tichoreck | 78 | 45.51 N | 40.09 E |
| Tichtozero | 24 | 65.35 N | 30.27 E |
| Tichvin | 76 | 59.39 N | 33.31 E |
| Tichvinskaja gr'ada ∧ | 76 | 59.30 N | 34.30 E |
| Ticino □[3] | 58 | 46.20 N | 8.45 E |
| Ticino ≃ | 36 | 45.09 N | 9.14 E |
| Tickfaw | 194 | 30.34 N | 90.28 W |
| Tickfaw ≃ | 194 | 30.20 N | 90.28 W |
| Tickhill | 44 | 53.26 N | 1.06 W |
| Ticomán •[8] | 286a | 19.31 N | 99.08 W |
| Ticonderoga | 188 | 43.50 N | 73.25 W |
| Ticul | 232 | 20.24 N | 89.32 W |
| Tīdah | 142 | 31.15 N | 30.50 E |
| Tidaholm | 26 | 58.11 N | 13.57 E |
| Tidan ≃ | 40 | 58.42 N | 13.58 E |
| Tiddim | 110 | 23.23 N | 93.39 E |
| Tide Lake ⊜ | 184 | 50.33 N | 111.20 W |
| Tideswell | 44 | 53.16 N | 1.46 W |
| Tidewater | 208 | 37.51 N | 76.42 W |
| Tidewater •[1] | 208 | 37.45 N | 77.00 W |
| Tidikelt ⊻ | 148 | 26.54 N | 1.20 E |
| Tidioute | 214 | 41.41 N | 79.24 W |
| Tidirhine, Jebel ∧ | 148 | 34.50 N | 4.30 W |
| Tidjikja | 150 | 18.33 N | 11.25 W |
| Tidö | 40 | 59.30 N | 16.28 E |
| Tidone ≃ | 62 | 45.04 N | 9.32 E |
| Tidore | 108 | 0.40 N | 127.26 E |
| Tiébissou | 150 | 7.10 N | 5.13 W |
| Tiechang, Zhg. | 98 | 41.44 N | 126.11 E |
| Tiechang, Zhg. | 100 | 24.10 N | 115.30 E |
| Tiechang, Zhg. | 102 | 26.34 N | 103.58 E |
| Tiechang, Zhg. | 105 | 40.04 N | 118.12 E |
| Tiechangpu | 107 | 29.29 N | 104.20 E |
| Tiefenbach, Dtsch. | 60 | 48.37 N | 13.24 E |
| Tiefenbach, Dtsch. | 60 | 49.26 N | 12.35 E |
| Tiefenbroich | 263 | 51.18 N | 6.49 E |
| Tiefencastel | 58 | 46.40 N | 9.35 E |
| Tiefensee | 54 | 52.41 N | 13.50 E |
| Tiefo | 107 | 29.45 N | 104.33 E |
| T'iehling → Tieling | 104 | 42.18 N | 123.49 E |
| Tiekou | 98 | 37.16 N | 121.13 E |
| Tiel | 52 | 51.54 N | 5.25 E |
| Tieli | 89 | 46.59 N | 128.02 E |
| Tieling | 104 | 42.18 N | 123.49 E |
| Tielt | 50 | 51.00 N | 3.19 E |
| Tielutou | 100 | 27.49 N | 115.48 E |
| Tiémé | 150 | 9.33 N | 7.19 W |
| T'ienching → Tianjin | 105 | 39.08 N | 117.12 E |
| T'ienchung | 100 | 23.52 N | 120.35 E |
| Tienen | 56 | 50.48 N | 4.57 E |
| Tiénigboué | 150 | 8.11 N | 5.43 W |
| Tienko | 150 | 10.14 N | 7.29 W |
| Tien Shan ∧∧ | 90 | 42.00 N | 80.00 E |
| T'ienshui → Tianshui | 102 | 34.30 N | 105.58 E |
| Tientsin → Tianjin | 105 | 39.08 N | 117.12 E |
| Tien Yen | 110 | 21.20 N | 107.24 E |
| Tiepido ≃ | 64 | 44.37 N | 10.59 E |
| Tie Plant | 194 | 33.44 N | 89.47 W |
| Tierga | 34 | 41.37 N | 1.36 W |
| Tiergarten •[8] | 264a | 52.31 N | 13.21 E |
| Tiergarten ♠ | 264a | 52.31 N | 13.21 E |
| Tieroko, Tarso ∧ | 146 | 20.45 N | 17.52 E |
| Tierp | 40 | 60.20 N | 17.30 E |
| Tierpark ♠ | 264a | 52.30 N | 13.32 E |
| Tierra Amarilla, Chile | 252 | 27.29 S | 70.17 W |
| Tierra Amarilla, N.M., U.S. | 200 | 36.42 N | 106.32 W |
| Tierra Blanca, Méx. | 196 | 27.12 N | 104.53 W |
| Tierra Blanca, Méx. | 234 | 18.25 N | 96.20 W |
| Tierra Blanca Creek ≃ | 196 | 35.00 N | 101.54 W |
| Tierra Buena | 226 | 39.09 N | 121.40 W |
| Tierra Colorada, Méx. | 234 | 17.10 N | 99.35 W |
| Tierra Colorada, Méx. | 234 | 17.56 N | 92.39 W |
| Tierra Colorada, Bajo de la ⊻[1] | 254 | 42.52 S | 66.48 W |
| Tierra de Campos •[1] | 34 | 42.10 N | 4.50 W |
| Tierra del Fuego □[8] | 254 | 54.00 S | 67.00 W |
| Tierra del Fuego, Isla Grande de I | 254 | 54.00 S | 69.00 W |
| Tierra del Fuego, Parque Nacional ♠ | 254 | 54.39 S | 68.30 W |
| Tierra del Norte → Severnaja Zeml'a II | 74 | 79.30 N | 98.00 E |
| Tierralta | 246 | 8.11 N | 76.04 W |
| Tierra Redonda Mountain ∧ | 226 | 35.47 N | 120.59 W |
| Tieshan | 100 | 30.14 N | 114.52 E |
| Tieshanguan | 100 | 23.30 N | 113.54 E |
| Tiétar ≃ | 34 | 39.50 N | 6.01 W |
| Tietê | 255 | 23.07 S | 47.43 W |
| Tietê ≃ | 255 | 20.40 S | 51.35 W |
| Tiéti | 175f | 20.57 S | 165.19 E |
| Tieton | 224 | 46.42 N | 120.45 W |
| Tieton ≃ | 224 | 46.45 N | 120.45 W |
| Tieton, South Fork ≃ | 224 | 46.38 N | 121.08 W |
| Tietzow | 264a | 52.43 N | 12.56 E |
| Tif | 148 | 27.00 N | 1.37 E |
| Tiffany Mountain ∧ | 202 | 48.40 N | 119.56 W |
| Tiffin | 214 | 41.07 N | 83.11 W |
| Tiffin ≃ | 216 | 41.17 N | 84.23 W |
| Tiflis → Tbilisi | 84 | 41.43 N | 44.49 E |
| Tifton | 192 | 31.27 N | 83.30 W |
| Tiftona | 192 | 35.05 N | 85.10 W |
| Tiga, Île I | 175f | 21.07 S | 167.49 E |
| Tiga, Pulau I | 112 | 5.43 N | 115.39 E |
| Tigalda Island I | 180 | 54.05 N | 165.05 W |
| Tigapuluh, Pegunungan ∧∧ | 112 | 1.05 S | 102.30 E |
| Tigard | 224 | 45.25 N | 122.46 W |
| Tigasaki → Chigasaki | 94 | 35.19 N | 139.24 E |
| Tigbauan | 116 | 10.41 N | 122.22 E |
| Tigeaux | 261 | 48.50 N | 2.54 E |
| Tiger Lake ⊜ | 220 | 27.53 N | 81.22 W |
| Tiger Stadium ♠ | 281 | 42.20 N | 83.04 W |
| Tigery | 261 | 48.38 N | 2.31 E |
| Tighennif | 148 | 35.20 N | 0.21 E |
| Tighina (Bender) | 38 | 46.48 N | 29.29 E |
| Tighvein ∧[2] | 46 | 55.30 N | 5.10 W |
| Tigil' | 74 | 57.48 N | 158.40 E |
| Tiglid | 148 | 28.31 N | 10.15 W |
| Tiglione ≃ | 62 | 44.48 N | 8.27 E |
| Tignale | 64 | 45.44 N | 10.44 E |
| Tignall | 192 | 33.52 N | 82.44 W |
| Tignère | 152 | 7.22 N | 12.39 E |
| Tignes | 62 | 45.30 N | 6.55 E |
| Tignish | 186 | 46.57 N | 64.02 W |
| Tignousti, Jebel ∧ | 148 | 31.31 N | 6.44 W |
| Tigoda ≃ | 76 | 59.22 N | 31.54 E |
| Tigray □[4] | 144 | 13.40 N | 40.00 E |
| Tigre, Arg. | 258 | 34.25 S | 58.34 W |
| Tigre, Col. | 246 | 2.28 N | 68.15 W |
| Tigre □[5] | 288 | 34.24 S | 58.37 W |
| Tigre ≃, Arg. | 288 | 34.25 S | 58.35 W |
| Tigre → Tigris ≃, Asia | 128 | 31.00 N | 47.25 E |
| Tigre ≃, Méx. | 234 | 22.43 N | 97.51 W |
| Tigre ≃, Perú | 246 | 4.26 S | 74.05 W |
| Tigre ≃, Ven. | 246 | 9.20 N | 62.30 W |
| Tigre, Cerro ∧ | 236 | 8.31 N | 83.28 W |
| Tigre, Isla del I | 258 | 34.47 S | 56.23 W |
| Tigre, Punta del > | 258 | 34.46 S | 56.33 W |
| Tigres, Baía dos c | 152 | 16.38 S | 11.46 E |
| Tigris (Dicle) (Dijlah) ≃ | 128 | 31.00 N | 47.25 E |
| Tiguabos | 240p | 20.14 N | 75.21 W |
| Tiguentourine | 148 | 27.50 N | 9.18 E |
| Tiguesmat ∧∧[2] | 148 | 24.54 N | 8.14 W |
| Tigy | 50 | 47.48 N | 2.12 E |
| Tigyaing | 110 | 23.46 N | 96.08 E |
| Tigzert, Oued V | 148 | 28.20 N | 9.35 W |
| Tigzirt | 34 | 36.54 N | 4.08 E |
| Tīh, Jabal at- ∧∧[1] | 140 | 29.30 N | 34.00 E |
| Tihāmah ⊻ | 128 | 26.00 N | 36.30 E |
| Tihany ⊥ | 30 | 46.54 N | 17.53 E |


**Symbols** in the index entries represent the broad categories identified in the key at the right. Symbols with superior numbers (∧∧[1]) identify subcategories (see complete key on page *I · 1)*.

**Symbole** im Register stellen die rechts im Schlüssel erklärten Kategorien dar. Symbole mit hochgestellten Ziffern (∧∧[1]) bezeichnen Unterabteilungen einer Kategorie (vgl. vollständiger Schlüssel auf Seite *I · 1)*.

**Los símbolos** incluídos en el texto del índice representan las grandes categorías identificadas con la clave a la derecha. Los símbolos con numeros en su parte superior (∧∧[1]) identifican las subcategorías (véase la clave completa en la página *I · 1)*.

**Les symboles** de l'index représentent les catégories indiquées dans la légende à droite. Les symboles suivis d'un indice (∧∧[1]) représentent des sous-catégories (voir légende complète à la page *I · 1)*.

**Os símbolos** incluídos no texto do índice representam as grandes categorias identificadas com a chave à direita. Os símbolos com números em sua parte superior (∧∧[1]) identificam as subcategorias (veja-se a chave completa à página *I · 1)*.

| | English | Deutsch | Español | Français | Português |
|---|---|---|---|---|---|
| ∧ | Mountain | Berg | Montaña | Montagne | Montanha |
| ∧∧ | Mountains | Gebirge | Montañas | Montagnes | Montanhas |
| )( | Pass | Paß | Paso | Col | Passo |
| V | Valley, Canyon | Tal, Cañon | Valle, Cañón | Vallée, Canyon | Vale, Canhão |
| ⊻ | Plain | Ebene | Llano | Plaine | Planície |
| > | Cape | Kap | Cabo | Cap | Cabo |
| I | Island | Insel | Isla | Île | Ilha |
| II | Islands | Inseln | Islas | Îles | Ilhas |
| ✦ | Other Topographic Features | Andere Topographische Objekte | Otros Elementos Topográficos | Autres données topographiques | Outros acidentes topográficos |

| ESPAÑOL Nombre / FRANÇAIS Nom / PORTUGUÊS Nome | Página / Page / Página | Lat.°' | Long.°' W = Oeste / W = Ouest / W = Oeste |
|---|---|---|---|
| Tihert | 148 | 35.28 N | 1.21 E |
| Tihnāwī, Wādī at- V | 142 | 28.11 N | 30.46 E |
| Tihua | | | |
| → Ürümqi | 86 | 43.48 N | 87.35 E |
| Tihuatlán | 234 | 20.43 N | 97.32 W |
| Tiilikkajärven | | | |
| kansallispuisto ♦ | 26 | 63.38 N | 28.20 E |
| Tijamuchi ≃ | 248 | 14.10 S | 64.58 W |
| Tijesno | 36 | 43.48 N | 15.39 E |
| Tijī | 146 | 32.01 N | 11.22 E |
| Tijuana | 232 | 32.32 N | 117.01 W |
| Tijuana ≃ | 204 | 32.33 N | 117.07 W |
| Tijuca ◆ 8 | 287a | 22.56 S | 43.14 W |
| Tijuca, Barra da ɥ | 287a | 23.01 S | 43.18 W |
| Tijuca, Lagoa da c | 287a | 22.59 S | 43.20 W |
| Tijuca, Parque | | | |
| Nacional da ♦ | 287a | 22.58 S | 43.15 W |
| Tijuca, Pico da ʌ | 287a | 22.56 S | 43.17 W |
| Tijucas | 252 | 27.14 S | 48.38 W |
| Tijucas do Sul | 252 | 25.55 S | 49.12 W |
| Tijuco ≃ | 255 | 18.40 S | 50.05 W |
| Tikal ⊥ | 232 | 17.20 N | 89.39 W |
| Tīkamgarh | 124 | 24.44 N | 78.50 E |
| Tikaré | 150 | 13.17 N | 1.43 W |
| Tikchik Lakes ⊜ | 180 | 60.07 N | 158.35 W |
| Tikei, Île I | 14 | 14.58 S | 144.32 W |
| Tikhand ◆ 8 | 272a | 28.31 N | 77.17 E |
| Tikhoretsk | | | |
| → Tichoreck | 78 | 45.51 N | 40.09 E |
| Tikitiki | 172 | 37.48 S | 178.24 E |
| Tiko | 152 | 4.05 N | 9.22 E |
| Tikokino | 172 | 39.49 S | 176.27 E |
| Tikrīt | 128 | 34.36 N | 43.42 E |
| Tikša | 24 | 64.07 N | 32.27 E |
| Tikšeozero, ozero ⊜ | 24 | 66.16 N | 31.53 E |
| Tiksi | 74 | 71.36 N | 128.48 E |
| Tiku | 112 | 0.24 S | 99.56 E |
| Til | 130 | 38.44 N | 41.49 E |
| Tiladummati Atoll I 1 | 122 | 6.50 N | 73.05 E |
| Tilamuta | 112 | 0.30 N | 122.20 E |
| Tilarán | 236 | 10.28 N | 84.59 W |
| Tilbalakan, Laguna c | 236 | 15.30 N | 84.17 W |
| Tilbānah | 142 | 30.59 N | 31.27 E |
| Tilburg | 52 | 51.34 N | 5.05 E |
| Tilbury, On., Can. | 214 | 42.16 N | 82.26 W |
| Tilbury, Eng., U.K. | 42 | 51.28 N | 0.23 E |
| Tilcara | 252 | 23.34 S | 65.22 W |
| Tilcha | 166 | 29.36 S | 140.54 E |
| Til-Châtel | 58 | 47.31 N | 5.10 E |
| Tilden, Il., U.S. | 219 | 38.12 N | 89.40 W |
| Tilden, Ne., U.S. | 198 | 42.02 N | 97.50 W |
| Tilden, Tx., U.S. | 196 | 28.28 N | 98.33 W |
| Tilden Lake ⊜ | 226 | 38.07 N | 119.36 W |
| Tilden Woods | 284c | 39.03 N | 77.09 W |
| Tilemsès | 150 | 15.37 N | 4.44 E |
| Tilemsi, Vallée du V | 150 | 16.15 N | 0.02 E |
| Tilff | 56 | 50.34 N | 5.35 E |
| Tilghman Island I | 208 | 38.42 N | 76.20 W |
| Tilhar | 124 | 27.59 N | 79.44 E |
| Tilia, Oued V | 148 | 27.27 N | 0.01 W |
| Tiliktino | 82 | 56.06 N | 36.36 E |
| Tilimsen | 148 | 34.52 N | 1.15 W |
| Tilin | 110 | 21.42 N | 94.04 E |
| Tilisarao | 252 | 32.44 S | 65.18 W |
| Till ≃, Eng., U.K. | 44 | 53.16 N | 0.37 W |
| Till ≃, Eng., U.K. | 44 | 55.41 N | 2.12 W |
| Tillaberi | 150 | 14.13 N | 1.27 E |
| Tillamook | 202 | 45.27 N | 123.50 W |
| Tillamook □ 6 | 224 | 45.25 N | 123.39 W |
| Tillamook ≃ | 224 | 45.28 N | 123.53 W |
| Tillamook Bay c | 224 | 45.30 N | 123.53 W |
| Tillamook Head > | 224 | 45.57 N | 124.00 W |
| Tillanchāng Dwīp I | 110 | 8.30 N | 93.37 E |
| Tillberga | 40 | 59.41 N | 16.37 E |
| Tille ≃ | 58 | 47.07 N | 5.21 E |
| Tillery, Lake ⊜ 1 | 192 | 35.17 N | 80.05 W |
| Tilley | 182 | 50.27 N | 111.39 W |
| Tilli | 126 | 23.57 N | 89.57 E |
| Tillia | 150 | 16.08 N | 4.47 E |
| Tillicoultry | 46 | 56.09 N | 3.45 W |
| Tillières-sur-Avre | 50 | 48.46 N | 1.04 E |
| Tilling Bourne ≃ | 260 | 51.13 N | 0.34 W |
| Tillmans Corner | 194 | 30.43 N | 88.05 W |
| Tillson | 210 | 41.49 N | 74.04 W |
| Tillsonburg | 212 | 42.51 N | 80.44 W |
| Tillyfourie | 46 | 57.11 N | 2.35 W |
| Tilogne | 150 | 15.58 N | 13.36 W |
| Tilomar | 112 | 9.21 S | 125.08 E |
| Tílos I | 38 | 36.25 N | 27.25 E |
| Tilpa | 166 | 30.57 S | 144.24 E |
| Tilrhemt | 148 | 33.10 N | 3.21 E |
| Tilsit | | | |
| → Sovetsk | 76 | 55.05 N | 21.53 E |
| Tilt ≃ | 46 | 56.46 N | 3.50 W |
| Tilton, Il., U.S. | 194 | 40.05 N | 87.38 W |
| Tilton, Ky., U.S. | 218 | 38.22 N | 83.45 W |
| Tilton, N.H., U.S. | 188 | 43.26 N | 71.35 W |
| Tilton ≃ | 224 | 46.33 N | 122.33 W |
| Tiltonsville | 214 | 40.10 N | 80.41 W |
| Tilzapotla | 234 | 18.29 N | 99.16 W |
| Tim | 78 | 51.37 N | 37.07 E |
| Tim ≃ | 76 | 52.15 N | 37.22 E |
| Ṭimā | 140 | 26.54 N | 31.26 E |
| Timah, Bukit ʌ 2 | 271c | 1.21 N | 103.47 E |
| Timahoe | 48 | 53.20 N | 6.49 W |
| Timaná | 246 | 1.58 N | 75.56 W |
| Timane ≃ | 248 | 20.34 S | 59.15 W |
| Timanskij kr'až ʌ | 24 | 65.00 N | 51.00 E |
| Timar | 84 | 38.49 N | 43.27 E |
| Timaricha | 80 | 57.33 N | 44.47 E |
| Timaru | 172 | 44.24 S | 171.15 E |
| Timaševo, Ross. | 80 | 53.21 N | 51.12 E |
| Timaševo, Ross. | 82 | 55.08 N | 36.29 E |
| Timaševsk | 78 | 45.37 N | 38.57 E |
| Timau, It. | 64 | 46.35 N | 13.00 E |
| Timau, Kenya | 154 | 0.05 N | 37.14 E |
| Timavo San Giovanni | 64 | 45.48 N | 13.37 E |
| Timay al-Amdīd | 142 | 30.57 N | 31.32 E |
| Timbákion | 38 | 35.04 N | 24.46 E |
| Timbalier Bay c | 194 | 29.10 N | 90.20 W |
| Timbaúba | 250 | 7.31 S | 35.19 W |
| Timbavati Game | | | |
| Reserve ◆ 4 | 156 | 24.27 S | 31.27 E |
| Timbedgha | 150 | 16.15 N | 8.10 W |
| Timber | 224 | 45.43 N | 123.17 W |
| Timber Creek | 164 | 15.39 S | 130.29 E |
| Timber Creek ≃ | 198 | 44.49 N | 98.17 W |
| Timber Lake, Il., U.S. | 278 | 42.14 N | 88.07 W |
| Timberlake, Oh., U.S. | 214 | 41.41 N | 81.25 W |
| Timber Lake, S.D., | | | |
| U.S. | 198 | 45.26 N | 101.04 W |
| Timber Run ≃ | 284b | 39.27 N | 76.52 W |
| Timber Trails | 278 | 41.52 N | 87.57 W |
| Timberview | 284b | 39.13 N | 76.45 W |
| Timbío | 246 | 2.20 N | 76.40 W |
| Timbiras | 250 | 4.15 S | 43.57 W |
| Timblin | 214 | 40.58 N | 79.12 W |
| Timbó, Bra. | 252 | 26.50 S | 49.18 W |
| Timbo, Guinée | 150 | 10.38 N | 11.50 W |
| Timbo, Liber. | 150 | 5.37 N | 9.43 W |
| Timbó ≃ | 287a | 22.52 S | 43.16 W |
| Timboon | 169 | 38.29 S | 142.59 E |
| Timbuctoo | 285 | 40.00 N | 74.49 W |
| Timbuktu | | | |
| → Tombouctou | 150 | 16.46 N | 3.01 W |
| Timbun Mata, Pulau I | 112 | 4.39 N | 118.28 E |
| Timel'ga | 86 | 58.53 N | 76.42 E |
| Timelkam | 60 | 48.00 N | 13.36 E |
| Times Square ⊥ | 276 | 40.45 N | 74.00 W |
| Timétrine | 150 | 19.27 N | 0.26 W |
| Timétrine ⩘ | 150 | 19.20 N | 0.42 W |
| Timeu Creek ≃ | 182 | 54.28 N | 114.27 W |
| Timewell | 219 | 40.00 N | 90.52 W |
| Timgad ⊥ | 148 | 35.29 N | 6.28 E |
| Timimoun | 148 | 29.14 N | 0.16 E |
| Timimoun, Sebkha de | | | |
| ⊜ | 148 | 29.00 N | 0.05 E |
| Timinar | 140 | 19.02 N | 30.29 E |
| Timi Ouli, Ehi ʌ | 146 | 21.08 N | 16.31 E |
| Timir'azevka | 86 | 53.39 N | 65.31 E |
| Timir'azevo | 76 | 55.05 N | 21.37 E |
| Timir'azevskij | 86 | 56.29 N | 84.54 E |
| Timirevo | 82 | 55.08 N | 39.10 E |
| Timirist, Râs > | 150 | 19.23 N | 16.32 W |
| Timirjazevo | 86 | 53.45 N | 66.30 E |
| Timiş □ 6 | 38 | 45.40 N | 21.20 E |
| Timiş (Tamiš) ≃ | 38 | 44.51 N | 20.39 E |
| Timiskaming, Lake ⊜ | 190 | 47.10 N | 79.25 W |
| Timişoara | 38 | 45.45 N | 21.13 E |
| Timkovo | 82 | 55.56 N | 38.37 E |
| Timmendorfer Strand | 54 | 54.00 N | 10.46 E |
| Timmernabben | 26 | 56.58 N | 16.26 E |
| Timmins | 190 | 48.28 N | 81.20 W |
| Timmonsville | 192 | 34.08 N | 79.56 W |
| Timms Hill ʌ 2 | 190 | 45.27 N | 90.11 W |
| Timok ≃ | 38 | 44.13 N | 22.40 E |
| Timon | 250 | 5.06 S | 42.49 W |
| Timonovo | 82 | 56.13 N | 37.02 E |
| Timor I | 112 | 9.00 S | 125.00 E |
| Timor Sea ⍑ 2 | 14 | 11.00 S | 128.00 E |
| Timor Timur □ 4 | 112 | 8.35 S | 126.00 E |
| Timor Trough ✣ 1 | 14 | 9.50 S | 126.00 E |
| Timošino, Ross. | 76 | 60.05 N | 36.10 E |
| Timošino, Ross. | 80 | 57.50 N | 44.25 E |
| Timotes | 246 | 8.59 N | 70.44 W |
| Timothy Lake ⊜ 1 | 224 | 45.07 N | 121.47 W |
| Timoudi | 148 | 29.19 N | 1.09 W |
| Timousserarène ≃ | 150 | 16.21 N | 8.07 E |
| Timpanogos Cave | | | |
| National Monument | | | |
| ♦ | 200 | 40.18 N | 111.52 W |
| Timpas Creek ≃ | 198 | 38.02 N | 103.38 W |
| Timpaus, Pulau I | 112 | 1.51 S | 124.01 E |
| Timperley | 262 | 53.24 N | 2.19 W |
| Timpson | 194 | 31.54 N | 94.23 W |
| Timpton ≃ | 74 | 58.43 N | 127.12 E |
| Timra | 26 | 62.31 N | 17.22 E |
| Timsāh, Buḥayrat at- | | | |
| (Lake Timsah) ⊜ | 142 | 30.34 N | 32.17 E |
| Timsah, Lake | | | |
| → Timsāh, | | | |
| Buḥayrat at- ⊜ | 142 | 30.34 N | 32.17 E |
| Timšer | 24 | 62.06 N | 54.40 E |
| Tims Ford Lake ⊜ 1 | 194 | 35.15 N | 86.10 W |
| Timun | 114 | 0.50 N | 103.22 E |
| Timur | 85 | 42.50 N | 68.26 E |
| Timur, Banjaran ⩘ | 114 | 5.00 N | 102.30 E |
| Timurni | 124 | 22.22 N | 77.22 E |
| Tīn, Ra's at- > | 146 | 32.37 N | 23.08 E |
| Tina ≃ | 158 | 31.18 S | 29.14 E |
| Tinaca Point > | 116 | 5.33 N | 125.20 E |
| Tinaco | 246 | 9.42 N | 68.26 W |
| Tinaga Island I | 116 | 14.28 N | 122.56 E |
| Ṭīnah, Khalīj aṭ- c | 140 | 31.08 N | 32.40 E |
| Tinahely | 48 | 52.48 N | 6.28 W |
| Tinaja, Punta > | 248 | 16.14 S | 73.39 W |
| Tinalmud | 116 | 13.36 N | 122.53 E |
| Tinambac | 116 | 13.49 N | 123.19 E |
| Tinambung | 112 | 3.31 S | 119.01 E |
| Ti-n-Amzi V | 150 | 18.20 N | 4.32 E |
| Tinapagee | 166 | 29.28 S | 144.23 E |
| Tinaquillo | 246 | 9.55 N | 68.18 W |
| Tindari, Capo > | 70 | 38.10 N | 15.03 E |
| Tinderry Peak ʌ | 171b | 35.42 S | 149.16 E |
| Tindila | 150 | 10.16 N | 8.15 W |
| Tindis | 126 | 21.35 N | 86.44 E |
| Tindivanam | 122 | 12.15 N | 79.39 E |
| Tindouf | 148 | 27.50 N | 8.04 W |
| Tindouf, Hamada de | | | |
| ◆ 1 | 148 | 27.30 N | 9.00 W |
| Tindouf, Sebkha de | | | |
| ≚ | 148 | 27.45 N | 7.15 W |
| Tineba, Pegunungan | | | |
| ⩘ | 112 | 1.40 S | 120.25 E |
| Tinée ≃ | 62 | 43.55 N | 7.11 E |
| Tineg ≃ | 116 | 17.38 N | 120.37 E |
| Tineo | 34 | 43.20 N | 6.25 W |
| Ting ≃ | 100 | 24.24 N | 116.35 E |
| Tinga ʌ | 146 | 9.21 N | 23.38 E |
| Tingambato | 234 | 19.30 N | 101.52 W |
| Tinggi, Pulau I | 114 | 2.18 N | 104.07 E |
| Tingha | 166 | 29.57 S | 151.13 E |
| Tinghert, Ḥamādat | | | |
| (Plateau du | | | |
| Tinghert) ⩘ 1 | 148 | 29.00 N | 9.00 E |
| Tinghert, Plateau du | | | |
| (Ḥamādat Tinghert) | | | |
| ⩘ 1 | 148 | 29.00 N | 9.00 E |
| Tinghsien | | | |
| → Dingxian | 98 | 38.32 N | 114.59 E |
| Tingkar ʌ | 116 | 5.20 N | 117.06 E |
| Ting Kau | 271d | 22.22 N | 114.05 E |
| Tingkawk Sakan | 110 | 26.04 N | 96.44 E |
| Tingkou | 98 | 36.34 N | 119.46 E |
| Tinglev | 41 | 54.56 N | 9.15 E |
| Tinglin | 106 | 30.53 N | 121.17 E |
| Tingliuhe | 98 | 39.34 N | 118.49 E |
| Tingloy | 116 | 13.40 N | 120.52 E |
| Tingmerkpuk | | | |
| Mountain ʌ | 180 | 68.34 N | 162.28 W |
| Tingo de Saposoa | 248 | 7.07 S | 76.38 W |
| Tingo María | 248 | 9.09 S | 75.56 W |
| Tingo María, Parque | | | |
| Nacional ♦ | 248 | 9.15 S | 76.05 W |
| Tingqian | 100 | 30.10 N | 115.54 E |
| Tingri, Zhg. | 120 | 28.35 N | 86.38 E |
| Tingri, Zhg. | 120 | 28.38 N | 87.04 E |
| Tingsiqiao | 100 | 29.50 N | 114.12 E |
| Tingsryd | 26 | 56.32 N | 14.59 E |
| Tingstäde | 26 | 57.44 N | 18.36 E |
| Tingsted | 41 | 54.49 N | 11.56 E |
| Tinguá | 256 | 22.36 S | 43.26 W |
| Tingüindín | 234 | 19.45 N | 102.29 W |
| Tinguiririca, Volcán | | | |
| ʌ 1 | 252 | 34.49 S | 70.21 W |
| Tingvoll | 26 | 62.54 N | 8.12 E |
| Tingvollfjorden c 2 | 26 | 62.50 N | 8.11 E |
| Tingwick | 206 | 45.50 N | 71.58 W |
| Tingwon Group II | 164 | 2.35 S | 149.45 E |
| Tingzitou | 106 | 30.12 N | 119.46 E |
| Tinharé, Ilha de I | 255 | 13.30 S | 38.58 W |
| Tinh Bien | 110 | 10.36 N | 104.57 E |
| Tinian | 174n | 14.58 N | 145.38 E |
| Tinian I | 174n | 15.00 N | 145.38 E |
| Tinian Harbor c | 174n | 14.57 N | 145.36 E |
| Tinié | 150 | 14.20 N | 1.28 W |
| Tiniguiban | 116 | 11.22 N | 119.30 E |
| Tinitian | 116 | 10.04 N | 119.12 E |
| Tinjar ≃ | 112 | 4.04 N | 114.18 E |
| Tinjil, Pulau I | 115a | 6.58 S | 105.47 E |
| Tinker Air Force | | | |
| Base ■ | 196 | 35.25 N | 97.24 W |
| Tinkers Creek ≃, | | | |
| Md., U.S. | 284c | 38.46 N | 76.57 W |
| Tinkers Creek ≃, | | | |
| Oh., U.S. | 214 | 41.22 N | 81.37 W |
| Tinkertown | 283 | 42.01 N | 70.44 W |
| Tinkisso ≃ | 150 | 11.21 N | 9.10 W |
| Tinley Creek ≃ | 278 | 41.39 N | 87.45 W |
| Tinley Creek Woods | | | |
| ♦ | 278 | 41.39 N | 87.47 W |
| Tinley Park | 216 | 41.34 N | 87.47 W |
| Tinniswood, Mount ʌ | 182 | 50.19 N | 123.50 W |
| Tinnoset | 26 | 59.43 N | 9.02 E |
| Tinnsjø ⊜ | 26 | 59.54 N | 8.55 E |
| Tinogasta | 252 | 28.04 S | 67.34 W |
| Tinompo | 112 | 2.09 S | 121.17 E |
| Tínos | 38 | 37.32 N | 25.10 E |
| Tínos I | 38 | 37.38 N | 25.10 E |
| Tinquipaya | 248 | 19.11 S | 65.51 W |
| Tin Rerhoh, Tassili ⩘ | 150 | 19.40 N | 4.00 E |
| Tinrhir | 148 | 31.28 N | 5.30 W |
| Tin Sam | 271d | 22.22 N | 114.11 E |
| Tinskoj | 88 | 56.10 N | 96.55 E |
| Tinsley | 194 | 32.43 N | 90.27 W |
| Tinsukia | 120 | 27.30 N | 95.22 E |
| Tintagel, B.C., Can. | 182 | 54.12 N | 125.35 W |
| Tintagel, Eng., U.K. | 42 | 50.40 N | 4.45 W |
| Tintagel Head > | 42 | 50.41 N | 4.46 W |
| Tintaldra | 171b | 36.03 S | 147.56 E |
| Tintas, Rio das ≃ | 287a | 22.52 S | 43.28 W |
| Tinte, Cerro ʌ | 248 | 22.40 S | 67.02 W |
| Tintern Abbey ʋ 1 | 42 | 51.41 N | 2.40 W |
| Tintern Parva | 42 | 51.42 N | 2.40 W |
| Tintigny | 56 | 49.41 N | 5.31 E |
| Tintina | 252 | 27.02 S | 62.43 W |
| Tintinara | 166 | 35.54 S | 140.03 E |
| Tintioulé | 150 | 10.13 N | 9.12 W |
| Tinto ʌ | 46 | 55.36 N | 3.39 W |
| Tinto ≃ | 34 | 37.12 N | 6.55 W |
| Tinton Falls | 276 | 40.19 N | 74.04 W |
| Ti-n-Toumma ◆ 1 | 146 | 16.04 N | 12.40 E |
| Tintwistle | 262 | 53.28 N | 1.58 W |
| Tinui | 172 | 40.53 S | 176.04 E |
| Tinwald | 172 | 43.55 S | 171.43 E |
| Ti-n-Zaouatene | 150 | 19.55 N | 2.52 E |
| Tinzap ≃ | 120 | 38.23 N | 77.24 E |
| Tio | 144 | 14.42 N | 40.58 E |
| Tioga, Il., U.S. | 219 | 40.13 N | 91.21 W |
| Tioga, N.D., U.S. | 198 | 48.23 N | 102.56 W |
| Tioga, Pa., U.S. | 210 | 41.55 N | 77.08 W |
| Tioga □ 6, N.Y., U.S. | 210 | 42.06 N | 76.16 W |
| Tioga □ 6, Pa., U.S. | 210 | 41.45 N | 77.17 W |
| Tioga ◆ 8 | 285 | 40.00 N | 75.10 W |
| Tioga ≃ | 210 | 42.09 N | 77.05 W |
| Tioga Center | 210 | 42.04 N | 76.21 W |
| Tioga Pass )( | 226 | 37.54 N | 119.16 W |
| Tioga Terrace | 210 | 42.03 N | 76.07 W |
| Tiojala | 24 | 61.10 N | 23.52 E |
| Tioman, Pulau I | 114 | 2.48 N | 104.10 E |
| Tiona | 214 | 41.45 N | 79.03 W |
| Tione di Trento | 64 | 46.02 N | 10.43 E |
| Tionesta | 214 | 41.30 N | 79.27 W |
| Tionesta Creek ≃ | 214 | 41.28 N | 79.22 W |
| Tionesta Lake ⊜ 1 | 214 | 41.28 N | 79.28 W |
| Tioor, Pulau I | 164 | 4.45 S | 131.45 E |
| Tior | 140 | 6.23 N | 31.11 E |
| Tioro | 112 | 4.41 S | 122.36 E |
| Tioro, Selat ɥ | 112 | 4.40 S | 122.20 E |
| Tioroniaradougou | 150 | 9.21 N | 5.38 W |
| Tioughnioga ≃ | 210 | 42.14 N | 75.51 W |
| Tioughnioga, East | | | |
| Branch ≃ | 210 | 42.36 N | 76.10 W |
| Tipasa | 34 | 36.35 N | 2.27 E |
| Tipitapa | 236 | 12.12 N | 86.06 W |
| Tipoca, Monte ʌ 2 | 250 | 3.34 N | 51.20 W |
| Tipp City | 218 | 39.57 N | 84.10 W |
| Tippecanoe, In., U.S. | 216 | 41.12 N | 86.06 W |
| Tippecanoe, Oh., | | | |
| U.S. | 214 | 40.16 N | 81.17 W |
| Tippecanoe □ 6 | 216 | 40.25 N | 86.53 W |
| Tippecanoe ≃ | 216 | 40.31 N | 86.47 W |
| Tippecanoe, Lake ⊜ | 216 | 41.20 N | 85.46 W |
| Tippecanoe | | | |
| Battlefield State | | | |
| Memorial ⊥ | 216 | 40.31 N | 86.52 W |
| Tippecanoe River | | | |
| State Park ♦ | 216 | 41.07 N | 86.36 W |
| Tipperary, Austl. | 164 | 13.44 S | 131.02 E |
| Tipperary, Ire. | 48 | 52.29 N | 8.10 W |
| Tipperary □ 6 | 48 | 52.40 N | 8.20 W |
| Tipton, Eng., U.K. | 42 | 52.32 N | 2.05 W |
| Tipton, Ca., U.S. | 226 | 36.03 N | 119.18 W |
| Tipton, In., U.S. | 216 | 40.16 N | 86.02 W |
| Tipton, Ia., U.S. | 190 | 41.46 N | 91.07 W |
| Tipton, Mi., U.S. | 216 | 42.01 N | 84.04 W |
| Tipton, Mo., U.S. | 194 | 38.39 N | 92.46 W |
| Tipton, Ok., U.S. | 196 | 34.30 N | 99.08 W |
| Tipton, Pa., U.S. | 214 | 40.38 N | 78.18 W |
| Tipton □ 6 | 216 | 40.17 N | 86.02 W |
| Tipton, Mount ʌ | 200 | 35.32 N | 114.12 W |
| Tiptonville | 194 | 36.22 N | 89.28 W |
| Tip Top Mountain ʌ | 190 | 48.16 N | 85.59 W |
| Tiptree | 42 | 51.49 N | 0.45 E |
| Tiptūr | 122 | 13.16 N | 76.29 E |
| Tiputini ≃ | 246 | 0.47 S | 75.32 W |
| Tiquicheo | 234 | 18.53 N | 100.44 W |
| Tīra | 132 | 32.14 N | 34.57 E |
| Tira Chapéu, Morro ʌ | 256 | 22.45 S | 44.39 W |
| Tiradentes | 255 | 21.07 S | 44.11 W |
| Tīrah, Bahr ≊ | 142 | 31.03 N | 31.15 E |
| Tīrān I | 128 | 27.56 N | 34.34 E |
| Tīrān, Madīq ɥ | 140 | 27.58 N | 34.28 E |
| Tiran, Strait of | | | |
| → Tīrān, Madīq ɥ | 140 | 27.58 N | 34.28 E |
| Tirana | | | |
| → Tiranë | 38 | 41.20 N | 19.50 E |
| Tiranë | 38 | 41.20 N | 19.50 E |
| Tirano | 64 | 46.13 N | 10.10 E |
| Tiraque | 248 | 17.37 S | 65.04 W |
| Tirari Desert ◆ 2 | 162 | 28.00 S | 138.20 E |
| Tiraspol | 38 | 46.51 N | 29.38 E |
| Tirat Karmel | 132 | 32.46 N | 34.58 E |
| Tirat Zevi | 132 | 32.25 N | 35.32 E |
| Tirau | 172 | 37.59 S | 175.45 E |
| Tire | 130 | 38.04 N | 27.45 E |
| Tirebolu | 130 | 41.00 N | 38.48 E |
| Tiree I | 46 | 56.31 N | 6.49 W |
| Tire Hill | 214 | 40.16 N | 78.55 W |
| Tires (Tiers), It. | 64 | 46.28 N | 11.31 E |
| Tires, Port. | 266c | 38.43 N | 9.21 W |
| Tires ◆ 1 | 148 | 23.30 N | 13.10 W |
| Tirhahart, Oued V | 148 | 23.45 N | 3.10 E |
| Tiria, Monte ʌ | 71 | 40.23 N | 9.16 E |
| Tirich Mīr ʌ | 123 | 36.15 N | 71.50 E |
| Tiriro | 150 | 10.27 N | 8.39 W |
| Tiris Zemmour □ 4 | 148 | 24.10 N | 9.30 W |
| Tirl'anskij | 86 | 54.14 N | 58.35 E |
| Tirna ≃ | 122 | 18.04 N | 76.57 E |
| Tírnavos | 38 | 39.45 N | 22.17 E |
| Tirnovo | | | |
| → Veliko Târnovo | 38 | 43.04 N | 25.39 E |
| Tiro | 214 | 40.54 N | 82.46 W |
| Tirodi | 120 | 21.41 N | 79.42 E |
| Tirol □ 3 | 64 | 47.15 N | 11.20 E |
| Tiroler Ache | | | |
| (Grossache) ≃ | 60 | 47.51 N | 12.30 E |
| Tirolo (Tirol) | 64 | 46.42 N | 11.10 E |
| Tiros | 255 | 19.00 S | 45.58 W |
| Tiroungoulou | 146 | 9.34 N | 22.09 E |
| Tīr Pol | 128 | 34.36 N | 61.15 E |
| Tirrenia | 66 | 43.38 N | 10.17 E |
| Tirreno, Mare | | | |
| → Tyrrhenian Sea | | | |
| ⍑ 2 | 36 | 40.00 N | 12.00 E |
| Tirry ≃ | 46 | 58.02 N | 4.26 W |
| Tirsā, Miṣr | 142 | 29.25 N | 30.49 E |
| Tirsā, Miṣr | 273c | 29.58 N | 31.12 E |
| Tirschenreuth | 60 | 49.53 N | 12.21 E |
| Tirso ≃ | 71 | 39.53 N | 8.32 E |
| Tirsted | 41 | 54.44 N | 11.21 E |
| Tirstrup | 41 | 56.18 N | 10.42 E |
| Tīrthahalli | 122 | 13.42 N | 75.14 E |
| Tirua Point > | 172 | 38.23 S | 174.38 E |
| Tiruchchirāppalli | 122 | 10.49 N | 78.41 E |
| Tiruchengodu | 122 | 11.23 N | 77.56 E |
| Tirukkalukkunram | 122 | 12.37 N | 80.04 E |
| Tirukkovilūr | 122 | 11.57 N | 79.12 E |
| Tiruliai | 76 | 55.47 N | 23.22 E |
| Tirumangalam | 122 | 9.50 N | 77.59 E |
| Tirunelveli | 122 | 8.44 N | 77.42 E |
| Tirupati | 122 | 13.39 N | 79.25 E |
| Tiruppattūr, India | 122 | 12.30 N | 78.34 E |
| Tiruppattūr, India | 122 | 10.08 N | 78.37 E |
| Tiruppur | 122 | 11.06 N | 77.21 E |
| Tirūr | 122 | 10.54 N | 75.55 E |
| Tiruttani | 122 | 13.11 N | 79.38 E |
| Tirutturaippūndi | 122 | 10.32 N | 79.39 E |
| Tiruvalla | 122 | 9.23 N | 76.34 E |
| Tiruvallūr | 122 | 13.09 N | 79.55 E |
| Tiruvannāmalai | 122 | 12.13 N | 79.04 E |
| Tiruvettipuram | 122 | 12.40 N | 79.33 E |
| Tirūvottiyūr | 122 | 13.09 N | 80.18 E |
| Tiruvur | 122 | 17.06 N | 80.38 E |
| Tisa (Tisza) (Tysa) ≃ | 38 | 45.15 N | 20.17 E |
| Tis'ah | 142 | 30.02 N | 32.35 E |
| Tisaiyanvilai | 122 | 8.20 N | 77.53 E |
| Tisaren ⊜ | 40 | 59.00 N | 15.08 E |
| Tisbury | 42 | 51.04 N | 2.03 W |
| Tisdale | 184 | 52.51 N | 104.04 W |
| Tishomingo, Ms., | | | |
| U.S. | 194 | 34.38 N | 88.13 W |
| Tishomingo, Ok., | | | |
| U.S. | 196 | 34.14 N | 96.40 W |
| Tisisat Falls ʟ | 144 | 11.29 N | 37.35 E |
| Ṭīsīyah | 132 | 32.24 N | 36.27 E |
| Tisjön ⊜ | 26 | 60.55 N | 12.58 E |
| Tiskilwa | 190 | 41.17 N | 89.30 W |
| Tiskino | 86 | 58.05 N | 83.10 E |
| Tiškovo, Ross. | 80 | 46.02 N | 48.36 E |
| Tiškovo, Ross. | 82 | 56.05 N | 37.44 E |
| Tisma | 236 | 12.05 N | 86.01 W |
| Tisnaren ⊜ | 40 | 58.57 N | 15.57 E |
| Tišnevo | 82 | 55.10 N | 36.17 E |
| Tišnov | 30 | 49.21 N | 16.25 E |
| Tisovec | 30 | 48.43 N | 19.57 E |
| Tissa | 146 | 7.26 N | 10.16 E |
| Tissemsilt | 148 | 35.35 N | 1.50 E |
| Tissø ⊜ | 41 | 55.35 N | 11.18 E |
| Tīsta ≃ | 124 | 25.23 N | 89.43 E |
| Tisul' | 86 | 55.45 N | 88.19 E |
| Tisvildeleje | 41 | 56.03 N | 12.05 E |
| Tisza (Tisa) (Tysa) ≃ | 38 | 45.15 N | 20.17 E |
| Tiszaföldvár | 30 | 46.59 N | 20.15 E |
| Tiszafüred | 30 | 47.37 N | 20.46 E |
| Tiszavasvári | 30 | 47.58 N | 21.22 E |
| Tit | 148 | 23.00 N | 5.10 E |
| Titaf | 148 | 27.26 N | 0.13 W |
| Titāgarh | 126 | 22.45 N | 88.22 E |
| Titano, Monte ʌ | 66 | 43.55 N | 12.28 E |
| Titao | 150 | 13.46 N | 2.04 W |
| Tit-Ary | 74 | 71.58 N | 127.01 E |
| Titel | 38 | 45.12 N | 20.18 E |
| Tithwāl | 123 | 34.24 N | 73.47 E |
| Titicaca, Lago ⊜ | 248 | 15.50 S | 69.20 W |
| Titicus | 207 | 41.18 N | 73.30 W |
| Titi Karangan | 114 | 5.31 N | 100.37 E |
| Titikaveka | 174k | 21.15 S | 159.45 W |
| Titilāgarh | 122 | 20.18 N | 83.09 E |
| Titisee-Neustadt | 58 | 47.54 N | 8.13 E |
| Titiwangsa, Banjaran | | | |
| ⩘ | 114 | 4.30 N | 101.25 E |
| Titlis ʌ | 58 | 46.47 N | 8.25 E |
| Tito | 68 | 40.35 N | 15.40 E |
| Titonka | 190 | 43.14 N | 94.02 W |
| Titou | 100 | 29.52 N | 112.42 E |
| Titova Korenica | 36 | 44.45 N | 15.43 E |
| Titovka | 83 | 48.59 N | 39.44 E |
| Titovo, Ross. | 80 | 53.17 N | 43.41 E |
| Titovo, Ross. | 82 | 54.19 N | 36.56 E |
| Titovo, Ross. | 82 | 55.35 N | 39.07 E |
| Titovo Velenje | 61 | 46.22 N | 15.07 E |
| Titov Veles | 38 | 41.41 N | 21.48 E |
| Titov vrh ʌ | 38 | 42.00 N | 20.51 E |
| Titran | 26 | 63.40 N | 8.18 E |
| Tittabawassee ≃ | 190 | 43.23 N | 83.59 W |
| Titteri ⩘ | 34 | 36.00 N | 3.30 E |
| Titterstone Clee Hill | | | |
| ʌ 2 | 42 | 52.23 N | 2.35 W |
| Titting | 60 | 49.00 N | 11.13 E |
| Tittling | 60 | 48.44 N | 13.23 E |
| Tittmoning | 60 | 48.04 N | 12.46 E |
| Titu | 38 | 44.41 N | 25.32 E |
| Titule | 154 | 3.17 N | 25.32 E |
| Titus □ 6 | 222 | 33.05 N | 94.58 W |
| Titusville, Fl., U.S. | 220 | 28.36 N | 80.48 W |
| Titusville, N.J., U.S. | 208 | 40.18 N | 74.52 W |
| Titusville, Pa., U.S. | 214 | 41.37 N | 79.40 W |
| Titz | 56 | 51.01 N | 6.25 E |
| Tiu Chung Chau I | 271d | 22.20 N | 114.19 E |
| Tiumpan Head > | 46 | 58.16 N | 6.09 W |
| Tiuni | 120 | 30.57 N | 77.51 E |
| Tiva ≃ | 154 | 2.20 S | 38.48 E |
| Tivaouane | 150 | 14.57 N | 16.49 W |
| Tiveden ⩘ 2 | 40 | 58.45 N | 14.40 E |
| Tiverton, Eng., U.K. | 42 | 50.55 N | 3.29 W |
| Tiverton, R.I., U.S. | 207 | 41.37 N | 71.12 W |
| Tivoli, Gren. | 241k | 12.10 N | 61.37 W |
| Tivoli, It. | 66 | 41.58 N | 12.48 E |
| Tivoli, N.Y., U.S. | 210 | 42.03 N | 73.54 W |
| Tivoli, Tx., U.S. | 196 | 28.27 N | 96.53 W |
| Tivoli ♦ | 41 | 55.40 N | 12.34 E |
| Ṭiwāl, Wādī V | 146 | 10.22 N | 22.43 E |
| Ṭiwāl al-'Abā ʌ | 130 | 36.20 N | 39.22 E |
| Tiwi, Pil. | 116 | 13.27 N | 123.41 E |
| Ṭīwī, 'Umān | 128 | 22.49 N | 59.16 E |
| Tiwuronto | 115b | 8.48 S | 120.09 E |
| Tixtla de Guerrero | 234 | 17.35 N | 99.26 W |
| Tiyās | 130 | 34.33 N | 37.40 E |
| Tiyo, Pegunungan ⩘ | 164 | 4.00 S | 135.30 E |
| Tizapán ◆ 8 | 286a | 19.20 N | 99.13 W |
| Tizapán El Alto | 234 | 20.10 N | 103.04 W |
| Tizimín | 232 | 21.10 N | 88.10 W |
| Tizi-Ouzou | 148 | 36.48 N | 4.02 E |
| Tizmant ash- | | | |
| Sharqīyah | 142 | 29.03 N | 31.03 E |
| Tiznados ≃ | 246 | 8.16 N | 67.47 W |
| Tiznit | 148 | 29.43 N | 9.44 W |
| Tiznit □ 4 | 148 | 29.40 N | 9.45 W |
| Tizoc | 196 | 25.41 N | 101.59 W |
| Tjällmo | 40 | 58.43 N | 15.21 E |
| Tjeukemeer ⊜ | 52 | 52.54 N | 5.50 E |
| Tjilatjap | | | |
| → Cilacap | 115a | 7.44 S | 109.00 E |
| Tjirebon | | | |
| → Cirebon | 115a | 6.44 S | 108.34 E |
| Tjolotjo | 154 | 19.47 S | 27.46 E |
| Tjøme I | 26 | 59.07 N | 10.24 E |
| Tjörn I | 26 | 58.00 N | 11.38 E |
| Tjörnarp | 41 | 56.00 N | 13.37 E |
| Tkibuli | 84 | 42.21 N | 42.59 E |
| Tkvarčeli | 84 | 42.51 N | 41.41 E |
| Tlachichuca | 234 | 19.06 N | 97.25 W |
| Tlacoapa | 234 | 17.09 N | 98.52 W |
| Tlacotalpan | 234 | 18.37 N | 95.40 W |
| Tlacotepec | 234 | 17.46 N | 99.59 W |
| Tlacuitapan | 234 | 21.14 N | 102.12 W |
| Tláhuac ◆ 8 | 286a | 19.16 N | 99.00 W |
| Tlahualilo de | | | |
| Zaragoza | 232 | 26.07 N | 103.27 W |
| Tlahuelilpan | 234 | 20.08 N | 99.14 W |
| Tlahuitoltepec | 234 | 17.04 N | 95.59 W |
| Tlajomulco de Zúñiga | 234 | 20.28 N | 103.27 W |
| Tlalchapa | 234 | 18.24 N | 100.28 W |
| Tlalcozotitlán | 234 | 17.54 N | 99.15 W |
| Tlalixtac de Cabrera | 234 | 17.04 N | 96.39 W |
| Tlalixtaquilla | 234 | 17.21 N | 98.28 W |
| Tlalnepantla | 234 | 19.33 N | 99.12 W |
| Tlalnepantla ≃ | 286a | 19.31 N | 99.16 W |
| Tlalpan ◆ 8 | 286a | 19.17 N | 99.10 W |
| Tlalpujahua | 234 | 19.48 N | 100.10 W |
| Tlaltenango de | | | |
| Sánchez Román | 234 | 21.47 N | 103.19 W |
| Tl'ančetamak | 80 | 55.28 N | 52.37 E |
| Tlapacoyan | 234 | 19.58 N | 97.13 W |
| Tlapa de Comonfort | 234 | 17.33 N | 98.33 W |
| Tlapaneco ≃ | 234 | 18.05 N | 98.48 W |
| Tlapehuala | 234 | 18.13 N | 100.31 W |
| Tlapeng | 156 | 23.15 S | 21.49 E |
| Tlaquepaque | 234 | 20.39 N | 103.19 W |
| Tl'arata | 84 | 42.07 N | 46.22 E |
| Tlatlauquitepec | 234 | 19.51 N | 97.29 W |
| Tlaxcala □ 3 | 234 | 19.25 N | 98.10 W |
| Tlaxcala de | | | |
| Xicotencatl | 234 | 19.19 N | 98.14 W |
| Tlaxcoapan | 234 | 20.05 N | 99.13 W |
| Tlaxco [de Morelos] | 234 | 19.37 N | 98.07 W |
| Tlaxmalac | 234 | 18.21 N | 99.25 W |
| Tlazazalca | 234 | 19.58 N | 102.04 W |
| Tletat ed Douair | 34 | 35.59 N | 2.55 E |
| Tlētē Ouāte Gharbī, | | | |
| Jabal ʌ | 130 | 35.20 N | 39.13 E |
| Tlevak Strait ɥ | 182 | 55.03 N | 132.58 W |
| Tlhakgameng | 158 | 26.27 S | 24.21 E |
| Tloch | 84 | 42.38 N | 46.28 E |
| Tlučiná | 60 | 49.44 N | 13.14 E |
| Tlumach | 78 | 48.52 N | 25.01 E |
| Tłuszcz | 30 | 52.26 N | 21.26 E |
| Tmassah | 146 | 26.22 N | 15.47 E |
| Tmīsān | 146 | 27.32 N | 13.19 E |
| Tnâot ≃ | 110 | 11.29 N | 104.57 E |
| Tnekvejem ≃ | 180 | 65.50 N | 177.31 E |
| Toa ≃ | 240p | 20.23 N | 74.32 W |
| Toa Alta | 240m | 18.23 N | 66.15 W |
| Toab | 46a | 59.53 N | 1.19 W |
| Toa Baja | 240m | 18.27 N | 66.15 W |
| Toabré ≃ | 236 | 8.56 N | 80.33 W |
| Toachi ≃ | 246 | 0.08 N | 79.18 W |
| Toahayaná | 232 | 26.08 N | 107.44 W |
| Toamasina | 157b | 18.10 S | 49.23 E |
| Toamasina □ 4 | 157b | 18.00 S | 48.40 E |
| Toandonggu | 98 | 40.33 N | 127.35 E |
| Toandos Peninsula | | | |
| > 1 | 224 | 47.43 N | 122.47 W |
| Toano, It. | 64 | 44.23 N | 10.34 E |
| Toano, Va., U.S. | 208 | 37.22 N | 76.48 W |
| Toano Draw V | 204 | 41.27 N | 114.35 W |
| Toano Range ⩘ | 204 | 40.50 N | 114.20 W |
| Toast | 192 | 36.30 N | 80.37 W |
| Toa Vaca, Embalse | | | |
| ⊜ 1 | 240m | 18.06 N | 66.28 W |
| Toay | 252 | 36.40 S | 64.21 W |
| Toba, Mali | 150 | 11.52 N | 7.28 W |
| Toba, Nihon | 94 | 34.29 N | 136.51 E |
| Toba, Zhg. | 102 | 31.18 N | 97.40 E |
| Toba ≃ | 182 | 50.30 N | 124.15 W |
| Toba, Danau ⊜ | 114 | 2.35 N | 98.50 E |
| Tobacco ≃ | 190 | 43.49 N | 84.24 W |
| Tobacco Plains | | | |
| Indian Reserve ◆ 4 | 182 | 49.04 N | 115.06 W |
| Tobacco Root | | | |
| Mountains ⩘ | 202 | 45.35 N | 112.00 W |
| Tobago I | 241r | 11.15 N | 60.40 W |
| Toba Inlet c | 182 | 50.20 N | 124.50 W |
| Toba Kākar Range ⩘ | 120 | 31.15 N | 68.00 E |
| Tobalaba Eulogio | | | |
| Sánchez, | | | |
| Aeródromo ⊠ | 286e | 33.27 S | 70.33 W |
| Tobalai, Pulau I | 164 | 1.37 S | 128.20 E |
| Tobarra | 34 | 38.35 N | 1.41 W |
| Tobas | 252 | 28.08 S | 62.42 W |
| Tobašino | 80 | 56.56 N | 47.40 E |
| Toba Tek Singh | 123 | 30.58 N | 72.29 E |
| Tobe | 96 | 33.44 N | 132.47 E |
| Tobejuba, Isla I | 246 | 9.20 N | 60.52 W |
| Tobekuduk | 86 | 49.50 N | 54.15 E |
| Tobelo | 108 | 1.44 N | 128.01 E |
| Tobelombang | 112 | 0.57 S | 122.00 E |
| Tobercurry | 48 | 54.03 N | 8.43 W |
| Tobermorey | 166 | 22.15 S | 138.00 E |
| Tobermory, Austl. | 166 | 27.17 S | 143.41 E |
| Tobermory, On., Can. | 190 | 45.15 N | 81.40 W |
| Tobermory, Scot., | | | |
| U.K. | 46 | 56.37 N | 6.05 W |
| Toberonochy | 46 | 56.13 N | 5.38 W |
| Tōbetsu | 92a | 43.13 N | 141.31 E |
| Tobi I | 108 | 3.00 N | 131.10 E |
| Tobias | 198 | 40.25 N | 97.20 W |
| Tobias Barreto | 250 | 11.11 S | 38.01 W |
| Tobiishi-bana > | 174f | 24.45 N | 141.17 E |
| Tobin, Mount ʌ | 204 | 40.22 N | 117.32 W |
| Tobin Lake ⊜, Austl. | 162 | 21.45 S | 125.49 E |
| Tobin Lake ⊜, Sk., | | | |
| Can. | 184 | 53.40 N | 103.35 W |
| Tobique ≃ | 186 | 46.46 N | 67.42 W |
| Tobi-shima I | 92 | 39.12 N | 139.34 E |
| Toblach | | | |
| → Dobbiaco | 64 | 46.44 N | 12.14 E |
| Tobo, Indon. | 164 | 3.34 S | 130.11 E |
| Tobo, Sve. | 40 | 60.16 N | 17.39 E |
| Toboali | 112 | 3.00 S | 106.30 E |
| Tobol | 86 | 52.40 N | 62.39 E |
| Tobol ≃ | 86 | 58.10 N | 68.12 E |
| Toboli | 112 | 0.43 S | 120.05 E |
| Tobol'sk | 86 | 58.12 N | 68.16 E |
| Tobong-san ʌ | 271b | 37.42 N | 127.01 E |
| Tobor | 150 | 12.39 N | 16.16 W |
| Toboso | 116 | 10.43 N | 123.31 E |
| Tobré | 150 | 10.12 N | 2.08 E |
| Tobruk | | | |
| → Ṭubruq | 146 | 32.05 N | 23.59 E |
| Tobseda | 24 | 68.36 N | 52.14 E |
| Tōbu | 94 | 36.21 N | 138.20 E |
| Toburdanovo | 80 | 55.22 N | 47.38 E |
| Toby, Mount ʌ | 207 | 42.29 N | 72.32 W |
| Tobyhanna | 210 | 41.10 N | 75.25 W |
| Tobyhanna Creek ≃ | 210 | 41.07 N | 75.39 W |
| Tobyhanna State | | | |
| Park ♦ | 210 | 41.13 N | 75.25 W |
| Tobyš ≃ | 24 | 65.30 N | 51.00 E |
| Toca Grande, Morro | | | |
| da ʌ | 287a | 22.58 S | 43.31 W |
| Tocantínia | 250 | 9.33 S | 48.22 W |
| Tocantinópolis | 250 | 6.20 S | 47.25 W |
| Tocantins □ 3 | 250 | 10.00 S | 48.00 W |
| Tocantins ≃, Bra. | 242 | 1.45 S | 49.10 W |
| Tocantins ≃, Bra. | 250 | 5.21 S | 55.58 W |
| Tocantinzinho ≃ | 255 | 13.57 S | 48.20 W |
| Toccoa | 192 | 34.34 N | 83.19 W |
| Toccoa (Ocoee) ≃ | 192 | 35.12 N | 84.40 W |
| Toce ≃ | 58 | 45.56 N | 8.29 E |
| Tochapan | 234 | 18.54 N | 97.37 W |
| Tochcha Lake ⊜ | 182 | 54.56 N | 125.54 W |
| Tochigi | 94 | 36.23 N | 139.44 E |
| Tochigi □ 5 | 94 | 36.45 N | 139.45 E |
| Tochimilco | 234 | 18.54 N | 98.34 W |
| Tochio | 92 | 37.28 N | 139.00 E |
| Tochoj | 88 | 50.30 N | 105.00 E |
| Tochta | 24 | 62.14 N | 48.48 E |
| Tochtamyš | 120 | 37.50 N | 74.39 E |
| Tockholes | 262 | 53.42 N | 2.31 W |
| Tockoje | 80 | 52.32 N | 52.45 E |
| Töcksfors | 26 | 59.30 N | 11.50 E |
| Točnik | 60 | 49.27 N | 13.19 E |
| Toco, Chile | 252 | 22.05 S | 69.35 W |
| Toco, Trin. | 241r | 10.50 N | 60.57 W |
| Tocoa | 236 | 15.41 N | 86.03 W |
| Tócome ≃ | 286c | 10.29 N | 66.49 W |
| Toconao | 252 | 23.11 S | 68.01 W |
| Tocopilla | 252 | 22.05 S | 70.12 W |
| Tocos do Moji | 256 | 22.22 S | 46.06 W |
| Tocuco ≃ | 246 | 9.36 N | 72.15 W |
| Tocumwal | 166 | 35.49 S | 145.34 E |
| Tocuyo ≃ | 246 | 11.03 N | 68.23 W |
| Tocuyo de la Costa | 246 | 11.02 N | 68.23 W |
| Toda | 94 | 35.48 N | 139.41 E |
| Toda Bhīm | 124 | 26.55 N | 76.49 E |
| Todaiji Temple ʋ 1 | 270 | 34.42 N | 135.51 E |
| Todang-ni | 271b | 37.37 N | 126.50 E |
| Toda Rāisingh | 120 | 26.01 N | 75.29 E |
| Todd | 214 | 40.16 N | 78.04 W |
| Todd ≃ | 162 | 24.52 S | 135.48 E |
| Todd Estates | 285 | 39.40 N | 75.43 W |
| Todd Fork ≃ | 218 | 39.21 N | 84.08 W |
| Todd Fork, East Fork | | | |
| ≃ | 218 | 39.24 N | 84.00 W |
| Toddington | 42 | 51.57 N | 0.32 W |
| Todd Point > | 284b | 39.15 N | 76.27 W |
| Toddville, Md., U.S. | 208 | 38.17 N | 76.04 W |
| Toddville, N.Y., U.S. | 210 | 41.17 N | 73.53 W |
| Todeli | 112 | 1.40 S | 124.29 E |
| Todenyang | 154 | 4.32 N | 35.56 E |
| Todi | 66 | 42.47 N | 12.24 E |
| Tödi ʌ | 58 | 46.49 N | 8.56 E |
| Todmorden, Austl. | 162 | 27.08 S | 134.48 E |
| Todmorden, Eng., | | | |
| U.K. | 44 | 53.43 N | 2.05 W |
| Todoga-saki > | 92 | 39.33 N | 142.05 E |
| Todoromi | 270 | 34.53 N | 135.28 E |
| Todos Santos, Bol. | 248 | 16.48 S | 65.08 W |
| Todos Santos, Méx. | 232 | 23.27 N | 110.13 W |
| Todos Santos, Bahía | | | |
| c | 232 | 31.48 N | 116.42 W |
| Todro | 154 | 3.21 N | 30.14 E |
| Todtenhausen | 52 | 52.20 N | 8.56 E |
| Todtmoos | 58 | 47.44 N | 8.00 E |
| Todtmoos Au | 58 | 47.42 N | 7.58 E |
| Todtnau | 58 | 47.50 N | 7.56 E |
| Toe Head > | 46 | 57.50 N | 7.08 W |
| Tōei | 94 | 35.04 N | 137.41 E |
| T'oejo | 98 | 39.54 N | 27.46 E |
| Toéssé | 150 | 11.50 N | 1.16 W |
| Toetoes Bay c | 172 | 46.38 S | 168.43 E |
| Tofield | 182 | 53.22 N | 112.40 W |
| Tofino | 182 | 49.09 N | 125.54 W |
| Töfsingdalens | | | |
| Nationalpark ♦ | 26 | 62.09 N | 12.30 E |
| Tofte | 26 | 59.33 N | 10.34 E |
| Toften ⊜ | 40 | 59.03 N | 14.36 E |
| Tofterup | 41 | 55.39 N | 8.50 E |
| Toftlund | 41 | 55.11 N | 9.04 E |
| Toga | 94 | 36.27 N | 1[illegible]7.02 E |
| Toga I | 175f | 13.26 S | 1[illegible]6.42 E |
| Togakushi | 94 | 36.44 N | 1[illegible]8.05 E |
| Togakushi-yama ʌ | 94 | 36.46 N | 1[illegible]8.04 E |
| Toganas | 80 | 50.49 N | [illegible]2.02 E |
| Tōgane | 94 | 35.33 N | 1[illegible].22 E |
| Togano, Monte ʌ | 58 | 46.06 N | [illegible].25 E |
| Togauchi | 96 | 34.34 N | 1[illegible].13 E |
| Togdheer □ 4 | 144 | 9.00 N | [illegible].00 E |
| Toggenburg V | 58 | 47.15 N | [illegible].10 E |
| Togho | 152 | 6.01 N | 1[illegible].26 E |
| Togi | 94 | 37.08 N | 13[illegible].44 E |
| Togiak | 180 | 59.04 N | 16[illegible].24 W |
| Togiak Bay c | 180 | 59.00 N | 16[illegible].30 W |
| Togian, Kepulauan II | 112 | 0.20 S | 12[illegible].00 E |
| Togian, Pulau I | 112 | 0.22 S | 12[illegible].56 E |
| Töging am Inn | 60 | 48.15 N | 1[illegible].35 E |
| Togliatti | | | |
| → Toljatti | 80 | 53.31 N | 4[illegible].26 E |
| Togni | 140 | 18.04 N | 3[illegible].13 E |
| Tōgō, Nihon | 94 | 35.05 N | 13[illegible].03 E |
| Tōgō, Nihon | 96 | 35.28 N | 13[illegible].53 E |
| Togo □ 1, Afr. | 134 | 8.00 N | 1.[illegible]0 E |
| Togo □ 1, Afr. | 150 | 8.00 N | 1.[illegible]0 E |
| Togochale | 144 | 9.33 N | 43.[illegible]8 E |
| Tōgō-ike ⊜ | 96 | 35.28 N | 133.[illegible]4 E |
| Togoron | 116 | 12.35 N | 123.[illegible]7 E |
| Tögrög, Mong. | 102 | 45.46 N | 94.[illegible]8 E |
| Tögrög, Mong. | 102 | 45.32 N | 102.[illegible]9 E |
| Togtoh | 102 | 40.22 N | 111.[illegible]1 E |
| Togučin | 86 | 55.16 N | 84.[illegible]3 E |
| Togur | 86 | 58.24 N | 82.[illegible]9 E |
| Togura | 94 | 36.29 N | 138.[illegible] E |
| Toguzak ≃ | 86 | 54.06 N | 62.[illegible] E |
| Toguzbulak | 85 | 42.06 N | 76.[illegible] E |
| Togwotee Pass )( | 202 | 43.45 N | 110.[illegible] W |
| Tōgyu-san ʌ | 98 | 35.46 N | 127.[illegible] E |
| Tōgyu-san Kukrip | | | |
| Kongwŏn ♦ | 98 | 35.52 N | 127.[illegible] E |
| Togyz | 86 | 47.34 N | 60.[illegible] E |
| Tōhaku | 96 | 35.30 N | 133.4[illegible] E |
| Tohakum Peak ʌ | 204 | 40.11 N | 119.2[illegible] W |
| Tohāna | 124 | 29.42 N | 75.5[illegible] E |
| Tohiea, Mont ʌ | 174s | 17.33 S | 149.4[illegible] W |
| Tohma ≃ | 130 | 38.31 N | 38.2[illegible] E |
| Toholampi | 26 | 63.46 N | 24.1[illegible] E |
| Tohopekaliga, Lake ⊜ | 220 | 28.12 N | 81.2[illegible] W |
| Tohor, Tanjong > | 114 | 1.51 N | 102.4[illegible] E |
| T'ohyŏn-ni | 98 | 39.53 N | 124.5[illegible] E |
| Toi, Nihon | 94 | 34.54 N | 138.4[illegible] E |
| Toi, Niue | 174v | 18.57 S | 169.51 W |
| Toijala | 26 | 61.10 N | 23.52 E |
| Toili | 112 | 1.27 S | 122.24 E |
| Toi-misaki > | 92 | 31.20 N | 131.22 E |
| Tōin | 94 | 35.05 N | 136.35 E |
| Toinya | 140 | 6.17 N | 29.44 E |
| Toi Sar | 120 | 31.06 N | 69.54 E |
| Toiyabe Range ⩘ | 204 | 39.10 N | 117.10 W |
| Tojg | 128 | 32.04 N | 61.48 E |
| To-jima I | 96 | 33.12 N | 132.22 E |
| Tojo, Indon. | 112 | 1.17 S | 121.11 E |
| Tōjō, Nihon | 96 | 34.53 N | 133.16 E |
| Tōjō, Nihon | 270 | 34.55 N | 135.04 [illegible] |
| Tojtepa | 85 | 41.03 N | 69.22 [illegible] |
| Tōju-in ʋ 1 | 94 | 35.19 N | 136.04 [illegible] |
| Tok | 180 | 63.19 N | 142.59 [illegible] |
| Tok ≃ | 80 | 52.46 N | 52.22 E |
| Tokaanu | 172 | 38.58 S | 175.46 E |
| Tokachi ≃ | 92a | 42.44 N | 143.42 E |
| Tokachi-dake ʌ | 92a | 43.25 N | 142.41 E |
| Tokachi-heiya ≚ | 92a | 43.00 N | 143.30 E |
| Tōkagi | 268 | 35.42 N | 139.56 E |
| Tokai, Malay. | 114 | 6.01 N | 100.24 E |
| Tōkai, Nihon | 94 | 35.00 N | 136.53 E |
| Tōkai, Nihon | 94 | 36.27 N | 140.34 E |
| Tokaj ≃ | 78 | 51.18 N | 41.04 E |
| Tokala | 112 | 1.47 S | 121.43 E |
| Tōkamachi | 94 | 37.08 N | 138.46 E |
| Tokanui | 172 | 46.34 S | 168.56 E |
| Tokara-kaikyō ɥ | 93b | 30.10 N | 130.10 E |
| Tokara-rettō II | 93b | 29.36 N | 129.43 E |
| Tokarevka | 86 | 50.08 N | 73.12 E |
| Tokar Game Reserve | | | |
| ◆ 4 | 140 | 18.15 N | 37.45 E |
| Tokar'ovka | 80 | 51.59 N | 41.09 E |
| Tokar'ovo, Ross. | 76 | 55.17 N | 35.04 E |
| Tokar'ovo, Ross. | 265b | 55.38 N | 37.55 E |
| Tokashiki-jima I | 93b | 26.11 N | 127.21 E |
| Tokat | 130 | 40.19 N | 36.34 E |
| Tokat □ 4 | 130 | 40.25 N | 36.30 E |
| Tŏkchŏk-kundo II | 98 | 37.14 N | 126.07 E |
| Tŏkch'ŏn | 98 | 39.46 N | 126.19 E |
| Tokeland | 224 | 46.42 N | 123.58 W |
| Tokelau □ 2 | 14 | 9.00 S | 171.45 W |
| Tokelau-Inseln | | | |
| → Tokelau □ 2 | 14 | 9.00 S | 171.45 W |
| Tokeneke Brook ≃ | 276 | 41.03 N | 73.28 W |
| Tŏkhŭng-ni | 98 | 40.02 N | 127.08 E |
| Toki | 94 | 35.21 N | 137.11 E |
| Toki ≃ | 94 | 35.12 N | 136.52 E |
| Tokio | | | |
| → Tōkyō | 94 | 35.42 N | 139.46 E |
| Toki Point > | 174a | 19.19 N | 166.35 E |
| Tokiwadaira | 268 | 35.48 N | 139.57 E |
| Tokke ⊜ | 26 | 59.01 N | 9.15 E |
| Tokko | 74 | 59.59 N | 119.52 E |
| Tokko ≃ | 88 | 58.42 N | 119.50 E |
| Toklar | 130 | 38.26 N | 36.01 E |
| Toklat ≃ | 180 | 64.27 N | 150.17 W |
| Tokma | 88 | 58.13 N | 105.42 E |
| Tokmak, Kyrg. | 85 | 42.55 N | 75.18 E |
| Tokmak, Ukr. | 78 | 47.15 N | 35.43 E |
| Toko | 172 | 39.20 S | 174.24 E |
| Tököl | 264c | 47.19 N | 18.58 E |
| Tokolimbu | 112 | 2.48 S | 121.34 E |
| Tokomaru | 172 | 40.28 S | 175.30 E |
| Tokomaru Bay | 172 | 38.08 S | 178.18 E |
| Tokoname | 94 | 34.53 N | 136.51 E |
| Toko Range ⩘ | 166 | 23.05 S | 138.20 E |
| Tokoro ≃ | 92a | 44.07 N | 144.05 E |
| Tokoroa | 172 | 38.14 S | 175.52 E |
| Tokorozawa | 94 | 35.47 N | 139.28 E |
| Tokovs'ke | 78 | 47.38 N | 33.59 E |
| Toksook Bay | 180 | 60.32 N | 165.06 W |
| Toksovo | 76 | 60.09 N | 30.31 E |
| Tok-to (Take-shima) II | 92 | 37.17 N | 131.53 E |
| Toktogul | 85 | 41.50 N | 72.50 E |
| Toktogul'skoje | | | |
| vodochranilišče ⊜ 1 | 85 | 41.50 N | 72.55 E |
| Toku Island I | 14 | 18.10 S | 174.11 W |
| Tokuji | 96 | 34.11 N | 131.40 E |
| Tokul Creek ≃ | 224 | 47.35 N | 121.50 W |
| Tokung | 112 | 0.18 S | 114.28 E |
| Tokuno-shima I | 93b | 27.45 N | 128.58 E |
| Tokur | 89 | 53.10 N | 132.53 E |
| Tokura | 270 | 34.58 N | 135.18 E |
| Tokura-tōge )( | 96 | 35.17 N | 134.31 E |
| Tokusaga-mine ʌ | 96 | 34.26 N | 131.41 E |
| Tokushima | 96 | 34.04 N | 134.34 E |
| Tokushima □ 5 | 96 | 33.45 N | 134.00 E |
| Tokuyama, Nihon | 94 | 35.42 N | 136.29 E |
| Tokuyama, Nihon | 96 | 34.03 N | 131.49 E |
| Tokwe ≃ | 154 | 21.09 S | 31.30 E |
| Tōkyō, Nihon | 94 | 35.42 N | 139.46 E |
| Tōkyō, Nihon | 268 | 35.42 N | 139.46 E |
| Tōkyō □ 5 | 94 | 35.45 N | 139.30 E |
| Tokyo Bay | | | |
| → Tōkyō-wan c | 94 | 35.25 N | 139.47 E |


| | | | | |
|---|---|---|---|---|
| ≃ River | Fluß | Río | Rivière | Rio |
| ≊ Canal | Kanal | Canal | Canal | Canal |
| ʟ Waterfall, Rapids | Wasserfall, Stromschnellen | Cascada, Rápidos | Chute d'eau, Rapides | Cascata, Rápidos |
| ɥ Strait | Meeresstraße | Estrecho | Détroit | Estreito |
| c Bay, Gulf | Bucht, Golf | Bahía, Golfo | Baie, Golfe | Baía, Golfo |
| ⊜ Lake, Lakes | See, Seen | Lago, Lagos | Lac, Lacs | Lago, Lagos |
| ⩧ Swamp | Sumpf | Pantano | Marais | Pântano |
| ⊓ Ice Features, Glacier | Eis- und Gletscherformen | Accidentes Glaciales | Formes glaciaires | Acidentes glaciares |
| ⍑ Other Hydrographic Features | Andere Hydrographische Objekte | Otros Elementos Hidrográficos | Autres données hydrographiques | Outros acidentes hidrográficos |
| ✣ Submarine Features | Untermeerische Objekte | Accidentes Submarinos | Formes de relief sous-marin | Acidentes submarinos |
| □ Political Unit | Politische Einheit | Unidad Politica | Entité politique | Unidade política |
| ʋ Cultural Institution | Kulturelle Institution | Institución Cultural | Institution culturelle | Instituição cultural |
| ⊥ Historical Site | Historische Stätte | Sitio Histórico | Site historique | Sitio histórico |
| ♦ Recreational Site | Erholungs- und Ferienort | Sitio de Recreo | Centre de loisirs | Area de Lazer |
| ⊠ Airport | Flughafen | Aeropuerto | Aéroport | Aeroporto |
| ■ Military Installation | Militäranlage | Instalación Militar | Installation militaire | Instalação militar |
| ◆ Miscellaneous | Verschiedenes | Misceláneo | Divers | Diversos |

ENGLISH: Name, Page, Lat.°′, Long.°′ — DEUTSCH: Name, Seite, Breite°′, Länge°′ E = Ost


Tōkyō-daigaku-uchūkūkan-kenkyūsho ⊕³ 92 31.17 N 131.05 E
Tokyo Disneyland ♦ 268 35.37 N 139.53 E
Tōkyō-kō ⊂ 268 35.37 N 139.47 E
Tōkyō-kokusai-kūkō ⊗ 94 35.45 N 140.21 E
Tokyo Station ✦⁵ 268 35.41 N 139.46 E
Tokyo Tower ⊕ 268 35.39 N 139.45 E
Tokyo University ⊕² 268 35.42 N 139.46 E
Tokyo University of Education ⊕² 268 35.43 N 139.44 E
Tōkyō-wan (Tokyo Bay) ⊂ 94 35.25 N 139.47 E
Tokyrau ≐ 86 46.48 N 75.24 E
Tokzār 120 35.52 N 66.26 E
Tol I 175c 7.22 N 151.37 E
Tolaga Bay 172 38.22 S 178.18 E
Tolala 112 2.56 S 121.06 E
Tolang 114 1.56 N 99.26 E
Tolbert 52 53.10 N 6.21 E
Tolbo Nuur 86 48.25 N 90.17 E
Tolbuchino 80 57.51 N 40.03 E
Tolderol Point ≻ 168b 35.22 S 139.10 E
Toldo, Pico del ∧ 240p 20.30 N 74.54 W
Tole, Kaz. 85 42.40 N 70.08 E
Tolé, Pan. 236 8.14 N 81.41 W
Toledo, Bol. 248 18.10 S 67.25 W
Toledo, Bra. 252 24.44 S 53.45 W
Toledo, Bra. 256 22.44 S 46.23 W
Toledo, Col. 246 7.19 N 72.28 W
Toledo, Esp. 34 39.52 N 4.01 W
Toledo, Pil. 116 10.23 N 123.38 E
Toledo, Il., U.S. 194 39.16 N 88.14 W
Toledo, Ia., U.S. 190 41.59 N 92.34 W
Toledo, Oh., U.S. 214 41.39 N 83.33 W
Toledo, Or., U.S. 202 44.37 N 123.56 W
Toledo, Wa., U.S. 224 46.26 N 122.50 W
Toledo, Ur. 258 34.45 S 56.05 W
Toledo □⁴ 34 39.45 N 4.00 W
Toledo □⁵ 236 16.20 N 88.55 W
Toledo, Montes de ∧ 34 39.33 N 4.20 W
Toledo Bend Reservoir ⊜¹ 194 31.30 N 93.45 W
Toledo Express Airport ⊗ 216 41.35 N 83.49 W
Tolentino 66 43.12 N 13.17 E
Tolfa 66 42.09 N 11.56 E
Tolfa, Monti della ∧ 66 42.08 N 11.54 E
Tolga, Alg. 148 34.46 N 5.22 E
Tolga, Nor. 26 62.25 N 11.00 E
Toli 86 45.57 N 83.37 E
Toliara 157b 23.21 S 43.40 E
Toliara □⁴ 157b 24.00 S 45.00 E
Tolima □⁵ 246 3.45 N 75.15 W
Tolima, Nevado del ∧ 246 4.40 N 75.19 W
Tolimán, Méx. 234 20.55 N 99.56 W
Tolimán, Méx. 234 19.36 N 103.55 W
Tolitoli 112 1.02 N 120.49 E
Toljatti (Togliatti) 80 53.31 N 49.26 E
Tol'ka 74 64.02 N 81.55 E
Tolkmicko 30 54.20 N 19.31 E
Tolland 207 41.52 N 72.22 W
Tolland □⁶ 207 41.52 N 72.22 W
Tollarp 26 55.56 N 13.59 E
Tollensesee ≐ 54 53.54 N 13.02 E
Tollensesee ⊜ 54 53.30 N 13.11 E
Tollesboro 218 38.33 N 83.34 W
Tollesbury 42 51.46 N 0.50 E
Tolleson 200 33.27 N 112.15 W
Tollhouse 226 37.01 N 119.23 W
Tolloche 252 25.30 S 63.32 W
Tølløse 41 55.37 N 11.45 E
Tollygunge ✦⁸ 272b 22.30 N 88.21 E
Tolmači 76 57.26 N 35.41 E
Tolmačovo 76 58.52 N 29.55 E
Tolmezzo 64 46.24 N 13.01 E
Tolmin 36 46.11 N 13.44 E
Tolna 30 46.26 N 18.46 E
Tolna □⁶ 30 46.30 N 18.35 E
Tolo 152 2.56 S 18.34 E
Tolo, Teluk ⊂ 112 2.00 S 122.30 E
Toloa, Houma ≻ 174w 21.17 S 175.08 W
Tolokiwa Island I 164 5.20 S 147.40 E
Tolomo 89 50.03 N 137.45 E
Tolong Bay ⊂ 116 9.20 N 122.49 E
Tolongoina 157b 21.33 S 47.31 E
Tolono 194 39.59 N 88.15 W
Tolosa 34 43.08 N 2.04 W
Tolosa, Aeródromo ⊗ 288 34.53 S 57.58 W
Tolovana ≐ 180 64.51 N 149.45 W
Tolpuddle 42 50.45 N 2.18 W
Tolsan-do I 98 34.38 N 127.45 E
Tol'skij Majdan 80 54.57 N 44.39 E
Tolsta Head ≻ 46 58.20 N 6.10 W
Tolstoj, mys ≻ 74 59.10 N 155.12 E
Tolstopal'cevo 265b 55.38 N 37.13 E
Tolt, North Fork ≐ 224 47.42 N 121.49 W
Toltén 254 39.13 S 73.14 W
Toltén ≐ 254 39.15 S 73.14 W
Tolti 123 35.02 N 76.06 E
Tolt-Seattle Water Supply Reservoir ⊜¹ 224 47.42 N 121.39 W
Tolú 246 9.31 N 75.35 W
Toluca 216 41.00 N 89.08 W
Toluca, Nevado de ∧¹ 234 19.08 N 99.44 W
Toluca de Lerdo 234 19.17 N 99.40 W
Tolvajarvi 24 62.17 N 31.27 E
Tolvdalselva ≐ 26 58.10 N 8.00 E
Tolve 68 40.42 N 16.01 E
Tolwa 140 6.38 N 32.37 E
Tolworth ✦⁸ 260 51.23 N 0.17 W
Tolyatti → Toljatti 80 53.31 N 49.26 E
Tolybaj 86 50.31 N 62.19 E
Tom' ≐, Ross. 86 56.50 N 84.27 E
Tom' ≐, Ross. 88 51.00 N 127.54 E
Toma 150 12.46 N 2.53 W
Tomago 170 32.50 S 151.44 E
Tomah 190 43.58 N 90.30 W
Tomahawk 190 45.28 N 89.43 W
Tomakivka 78 47.48 N 34.44 E
Tomakomai 92a 42.38 N 141.36 E
Tomani 112 4.50 N 115.55 E
Tomanivi ∧ 175g 17.37 S 178.01 E
Tomar, Kaz. 86 46.24 N 75.03 E
Tomar, Port. 34 39.36 N 8.25 W
Tomari 89 47.47 N 142.03 E
Tomarovka 78 50.41 N 36.14 E
Tomarza 130 38.27 N 35.49 E
Tomás Barrón (Eucaliptus) 248 17.35 S 67.31 W
Tomaszów Lubelski / Tomasbódega ∧² 40 59.24 N 14.58 E
Tomás Gomensoro 252 30.26 S 57.26 W
Tomashorod 78 51.19 N 27.02 E
Tomashpil' 78 48.33 N 28.31 E
Tomasine ≐ 190 46.40 N 76.16 W
Tomás Jofré 258 34.43 S 59.19 W
Tomášov 61 48.09 N 17.16 E
Tomaszów Lubelski 30 50.28 N 23.25 E
Tomaszów Mazowiecki 30 51.32 N 20.01 E
Tomatin 46 57.20 N 3.59 W
Tomatlán 234 19.56 N 105.15 W
Tomatlán ≐ 234 19.50 N 105.23 W
Tomave 248 20.06 S 66.35 W
Tomazina 255 23.46 S 49.58 W
Tomba di Nerone ✦⁸ 267a 41.57 N 12.27 E
Tombadonkéa 150 11.00 N 14.23 W
Tombador, Serra do ∧¹ 248 12.00 S 57.40 W
Tomball 222 30.06 N 95.37 W
Tombe 140 5.49 N 31.41 E
Tombigbee ≐ 194 31.04 N 87.58 W
Tombo, Punta ≻ 254 44.03 S 65.11 W
Tombôco 152 6.48 S 13.18 E
Tombolo 64 45.38 N 11.50 E
Tombos 255 20.55 S 42.02 W
Tombouctou (Timbuktu) 150 16.46 N 3.01 W
Tombouctou □⁴ 150 18.20 N 3.50 W
Tombs of the Caliphs ⊥ 273c 30.03 N 31.17 E
Tombstone 200 31.42 N 110.04 W
Tombstone Mountain ∧ 180 64.25 N 138.30 W
Tombua 152 15.49 S 11.53 E
Tom Burke 156 23.05 S 28.00 E
Tomdoun 46 57.04 N 5.03 W
Tomé 252 36.37 S 72.57 W
Tomea, Pulau I 112 5.45 S 123.56 E
Tomé-Açu 250 2.25 S 48.09 W
Tõmek 130 38.02 N 32.41 E
Tomelilla 26 55.33 N 13.57 E
Tomelloso 34 39.10 N 3.01 W
Tomenaryk 86 44.02 N 67.01 E
Tomerong 170 35.04 S 150.35 E
Tomhannock Reservoir ⊜¹ 210 42.51 N 73.33 W
Tomi ≐ 152 5.07 N 19.19 E
Tomich 46 57.18 N 4.48 W
Tomichi Creek ≐ 200 38.31 N 106.58 W
Tomifobia ≐ 206 45.11 N 72.02 W
Tomiko Lake ⊜ 190 46.32 N 79.49 W
Tomilino 265b 55.39 N 37.57 E
Tomini 112 0.30 N 120.32 E
Tomini, Teluk ⊂ 112 0.20 S 121.00 E
Tominian 150 13.17 N 4.35 W
Tomintoul 46 57.14 N 3.22 W
Tomio ≐ 270 34.35 N 135.44 E
Tomioka 94 36.15 N 138.54 E
Tomisato 94 35.44 N 140.19 E
Tomiura 94 35.03 N 139.50 E
Tomiyama, Nihon 94 35.11 N 137.48 E
Tomiyama, Nihon 94 35.05 N 139.51 E
Tomizawa 94 35.14 N 138.29 E
T'omkino 76 55.05 N 35.01 E
Tomkins Cove 210 41.15 N 73.59 W
Tomkinson Ranges ∧ 162 26.11 S 129.05 E
Tomkinsville 208 38.19 N 76.53 W
Tomlinson Run State Park ♦ 214 40.33 N 80.34 W
Tommerup Stationsby 41 55.19 N 10.13 E
Tommot 74 58.58 N 126.19 E
Tomnavoulin 46 57.18 N 3.19 W
T'omnyj 88 53.24 N 118.31 E
Tomo ≐ 246 5.20 N 67.48 W
Tomobe 94 36.20 N 140.20 E
Tomogashima-suidō ⊔ 96 34.17 N 135.00 E
Tomohon 112 1.19 N 124.49 E
Tömör Bulag 88 49.16 N 100.15 E
Tomori 174m 26.08 N 127.44 E
Tomori, Teluk ⊂ 112 1.58 S 121.28 E
Tompa 88 55.08 N 109.47 E
Tompkins, Nf., Can. 186 47.48 N 59.13 W
Tompkins, Sk., Can. 184 50.04 N 108.47 W
Tompkins □⁶ 210 42.27 N 76.30 W
Tompkins County Airport ⊗ 210 42.29 N 76.57 W
Tompkinsville 194 36.42 N 85.41 W
Tompo 112 0.56 N 120.20 E
Tom Price 162 22.41 S 117.43 E
Tom Price, Mount ∧ 162 22.39 S 117.40 E
Tomptokan 74 57.06 N 133.59 E
Tomra 26 62.35 N 6.56 E
Toms ≐ 208 39.57 N 74.07 W
Toms, Ridgeway Branch ≐ 208 40.00 N 74.14 W
Toms Cove ⊂ 208 37.53 N 75.22 W
Toms Creek ≐ 208 39.38 N 77.17 W
Tomsk 86 56.30 N 84.58 E
Tomsk Oblast' □⁴ 86 58.00 N 82.00 E
Toms River 208 39.58 N 74.12 W
Tom Steed Reservoir ⊜¹ 196 34.45 N 99.00 W
Tomtabacken ∧² 26 57.30 N 14.28 E
Tömük 130 36.41 N 34.22 E
Tomuzlovka ≐ 84 44.46 N 44.10 E
Ton 64 46.15 N 11.04 E
Tonadico 64 46.11 N 11.50 E
Tonaki-shima I 93b 26.21 N 127.09 E
Tonalá, Méx. 234 16.04 N 93.45 W
Tonalá, Méx. 234 20.37 N 103.14 W
Tonalá ≐ 234 18.13 N 94.11 W
Tonale, Passo del )( 64 46.16 N 10.35 E
Tonami 94 36.38 N 136.54 E
Tonantins 246 2.47 S 67.47 W
Tonantins ≐ 246 2.45 S 67.48 W
Tonara 71 40.02 N 9.10 E
Tonasket 202 48.42 N 119.26 W
Tonate 250 5.00 N 52.26 W
Tonatico 234 18.47 N 99.41 W
Tonawanda, N.Y., U.S. 210 42.59 N 78.52 W
Tonawanda, N.Y., U.S. 210 43.01 N 78.52 W
Tonawanda Channel ≐¹ 284a 43.04 N 79.00 W
Tonawanda Creek ≐ 210 43.02 N 78.53 W
Tonawanda Indian Reservation ✦⁴ 210 43.05 N 78.27 W
Tonawanda Island I 284a 43.02 N 78.53 W
Tonbara 96 35.05 N 132.47 E
Tonbo 110 18.31 N 95.05 E
Tonbridge 42 51.12 N 0.16 E
Tonbridge and Malling □⁸ 260 51.16 N 0.20 E
Tonda 270 34.50 N 135.36 E
Tonda 96 33.38 N 135.24 E
Tondabayashi 96 34.30 N 135.36 E
Tondano 112 1.19 N 124.54 E
Tønder 41 54.56 N 8.54 E
Tondhre 272c 19.05 N 73.08 E
Tondi 122 9.44 N 79.01 E
Tondibi 150 16.39 N 0.14 W
Tondidji 150 13.06 N 10.20 W
Tondi Kiwindi 150 14.28 N 2.02 E
Tondoro 156 17.45 S 18.50 E
Tone, Nihon 94 36.42 N 139.13 E
Tone, Nihon 94 35.51 N 140.09 E
Tone ≐ 94 35.44 N 140.51 E
Tonekābon 128 36.49 N 50.53 E
Tone-unga ≡ 268 35.54 N 139.53 E
Tonež 78 51.49 N 28.51 E
Tonga, Cam. 152 4.58 N 10.42 E
Tonga, Süd. 140 9.28 N 31.03 E
Tonga □¹ 14 20.00 S 175.00 W
Tongaat 158 29.37 S 31.03 E
Tonga Islands II 14 20.00 S 175.00 W
Tong'an 100 24.46 N 118.08 E
Tonganoxie 198 39.06 N 95.05 W
Tong'anqiao 106 31.22 N 120.27 E
Tonga Ridge ✦³ 14 21.00 S 175.00 W
Tongariro, Mount ∧ 172 39.08 S 175.38 E
Tongariro National Park ♦ 172 39.15 S 175.30 E
Tongas 115a 7.44 S 113.06 E
Tongatapu □⁸ 174w 21.10 S 175.10 W
Tongatapu I 174w 21.10 S 175.10 W
Tongatapu Group II 14 21.10 S 175.10 W
Tonga Trench ✦¹ 14 20.00 S 173.00 W
Tongbai, Zhg. 100 32.22 N 113.24 E
Tongbai, Zhg. 105 39.35 N 116.44 E
Tongbai Shan ∧ 100 32.20 N 113.15 E
Tongbai Shan ∧ 100 32.20 N 113.15 E
Tongbei 89 47.45 N 126.45 E
Tongcheng, Zhg. 100 31.03 N 116.58 E
Tongcheng, Zhg. 100 32.53 N 118.58 E
Tongcheng, Zhg. 100 29.11 N 113.40 E
Tongchengzha 100 31.30 N 118.07 E
Tongchengzhuang 105 39.22 N 117.36 E
T'ongch'ŏn 98 38.54 N 127.54 E
Tongchuan 100 35.01 N 109.01 E
Tongdaohu 102 35.25 N 118.33 E
Tongde 102 35.17 N 100.42 E
Tongerbao 104 41.26 N 123.02 E
Tongeren 56 50.47 N 5.28 E
Tongerlo 56 51.07 N 4.54 E
Tonggou 98 41.53 N 125.46 E
Tonggu, Zhg. 100 28.33 N 114.21 E
Tonggu, Zhg. 100 21.53 N 112.55 E
Tongguan, Zhg. 100 28.29 N 112.48 E
Tongguan, Zhg. 102 34.38 N 110.20 E
Tongguan, Zhg. 102 23.18 N 101.23 E
Tongguanyi 107 29.20 N 106.23 E
Tonghai 102 24.07 N 102.49 E
Tonghaikou 100 30.14 N 113.08 E
Tonghe, Zhg. 89 45.59 N 128.45 E
Tonghe, Zhg. 100 32.56 N 112.45 E
Tongho-ri 98 35.49 N 127.54 E
Tonghua (Kuaidamao), Zhg. 98 41.40 N 125.44 E
Tonghua, Zhg. 98 41.41 N 125.55 E
Tonghui ≐ 271a 39.53 N 116.41 E
Tongi 126 23.53 N 90.24 E
Tong Island I 164 2.05 S 147.50 E
Tongjiang, Zhg. 89 47.40 N 132.30 E
Tongjiang, Zhg. 102 31.58 N 107.14 E
Tongjiangchang 107 29.37 N 103.43 E
Tongjiangkou 104 42.37 N 123.11 E
Tongjing 100 31.47 N 118.33 E
Tongjosŏn-man ⊂ 98 39.30 N 128.00 E
Tongjuzhen 98 38.36 N 117.11 E
Tongken ≐ 89 46.31 N 126.22 E
Tongli 106 31.10 N 120.43 E
Tongliang 107 29.51 N 106.03 E
Tongliao 89 43.39 N 122.14 E
Tongling, Zhg. 100 30.53 N 117.46 E
Tongling, Zhg. 102 23.28 N 109.40 E
Tonglu 100 29.48 N 119.40 E
Tonglü Yunhe ≡ 106 32.04 N 121.40 E
Tongmang-ni 98 37.37 N 126.26 E
Tongmu, Zhg. 100 27.57 N 113.55 E
Tongmu, Zhg. 102 24.09 N 110.04 E
Tongnae 98 35.12 N 129.05 E
Tongnan 107 30.11 N 105.48 E
Tongno-gang ≐ 98 40.58 N 126.04 E
Tongo 166 30.30 S 143.45 E
Tongoa I 175f 16.54 S 168.34 E
Tongobory 157b 23.32 S 44.20 E
Tongololo Creek ≐ 162 22.06 S 121.08 E
Tongoy 252 30.15 S 71.30 W
Tongqin 100 28.52 N 119.56 E
Tongquansi 107 30.23 N 104.50 E
Tongquil Island I 116 6.02 N 121.51 E
Tongren, Zhg. 102 27.38 N 109.03 E
Tongren, Zhg. 102 35.32 N 101.54 E
Tongrengchang 107 30.02 N 106.42 E
Tongsa ≐ 124 26.52 N 90.57 E
Tongsa Dzong 124 27.31 N 90.30 E
Tongsan-ni 271b 37.38 N 126.53 E
Tongshan 100 29.38 N 114.29 E
Tongshi 98 35.26 N 117.43 E
Tongshuping 100 27.17 N 114.54 E
Tongta 110 21.20 N 99.16 E
Tongtai 100 32.38 N 120.47 E
Tongtan 107 28.56 N 105.17 E
Tongtian ≐ 102 33.26 N 97.00 E
Tongue 46 58.28 N 4.25 W
Tongue ≐, U.S. 202 46.24 N 105.52 W
Tongue ≐, N.D., U.S. 198 48.56 N 97.18 W
Tongue ≐, Tx., U.S. 196 34.07 N 100.25 W
Tongue, Kyle of ⊂ 46 58.30 N 4.26 W
Tongue of the Ocean ✦¹ 238 24.30 N 77.30 W
Tongue River Reservoir ⊜¹ 202 45.06 N 106.47 W
Tongwei 102 35.07 N 105.27 E
Tongxi 107 29.59 N 106.08 E
Tongxian 105 39.55 N 116.39 E
Tongxianchang 107 30.14 N 105.24 E
Tongxiang 106 30.38 N 120.32 E
Tongxin 102 36.59 N 105.58 E
Tongxinchang 107 29.42 N 106.26 E
Tongxing 107 30.35 N 106.12 E
Tongxu 98 34.29 N 114.28 E
Tongyang-ni 98 39.08 N 126.52 E
Tongyang Yunhe ≡ 106 32.02 N 120.48 E
Tongyu 89 44.48 N 123.05 E
Tongyuan, Zhg. 100 28.04 N 116.08 E
Tongyuan, Zhg. 102 30.28 N 120.42 E
Tongyuanpu 104 40.49 N 123.54 E
Tongzhaipu 100 32.48 N 112.44 E
Tongzi 102 28.08 N 106.49 E
Tongzidixia 104 41.08 N 120.34 E
Tonica 216 41.12 N 89.04 W
Tonila 234 19.26 N 103.31 W
Tönisberg 263 51.25 N 6.30 E
Tönisheide 263 51.19 N 7.05 E
Tönisvorst 56 51.19 N 6.29 E
Tonj 140 7.17 N 28.45 E
Tonj ≐ 140 26.10 N 75.47 E
Tonk 120 26.10 N 75.47 E
Tonkawa 196 36.40 N 97.18 W
Tonkin — Bac Phan □⁹ 110 22.00 N 105.00 E
Tonkin, Gulf of ⊂ 110 20.00 N 108.00 E
Tonkino 80 57.23 N 46.28 E
Tonkou, Mont ∧ 150 7.27 N 7.39 W
Tonkawa 110 23.36 N 96.58 E
Tônlé Sab, Bœng ⊜ 110 13.00 N 104.00 E
Tonle Sap — Tônlé Sab, Bœng ⊜ 110 13.00 N 104.00 E
Tonnay-Boutonne 32 45.58 N 0.42 W
Tonneins 32 44.23 N 0.19 E
Tonner Canyon ∨ 280 33.58 N 117.48 W
Tonnerre 32 47.51 N 3.58 E
Tönnet 40 60.14 N 13.30 E
Tönning 41 54.19 N 8.56 E
Tōno 92 39.19 N 141.32 E
Tonogaya 268 35.46 N 139.22 E
Tonopah 204 38.04 N 117.13 W
Tōnoshō, Nihon 94 35.49 N 140.42 E
Tōnoshō, Nihon 96 34.29 N 134.11 E
Tonosí 236 7.24 N 80.27 W
Tonquin 156 21.29 S 27.29 E
Tonquish Creek ≐ 281 42.21 N 83.28 W
Tons ≐ 124 25.17 N 82.04 E
Tonšajevo 80 57.44 N 47.00 E
Tønsberg 26 59.17 N 10.25 E
Tönsholt 263 51.38 N 6.58 E
Tonstad 26 58.40 N 6.43 E
Tonto Creek ≐ 200 33.46 N 111.15 W
Tontogany 216 41.25 N 83.44 W
Tonto National Monument ♦ 200 33.34 N 111.02 W
Tonya 130 40.53 N 39.16 E
Tonypandy 42 51.38 N 3.27 W
Tonyrefail 42 51.36 N 3.25 W
Toobeah 166 28.25 S 149.52 E
Toobli 150 6.24 N 8.15 W
Tooele 200 40.31 N 112.17 W
Toogoolawah 171a 27.06 S 152.23 E
Tool 222 32.16 N 96.10 W
Toolik ≐ 180 69.55 N 149.30 W
Tooma 171b 35.58 S 148.03 E
Tooma ≐ 171b 36.04 S 148.00 E
Tooma Reservoir ⊜¹ 171b 36.04 S 148.16 E
Toombridge 48 54.45 N 6.27 W
Toompine 166 27.13 S 144.22 E
Toomsboro 192 32.49 N 83.04 W
Toomyvara 48 52.50 N 8.02 W
Toongabbie 274a 33.47 S 150.57 E
Toora 169 38.40 S 146.20 E
Toora-Chem 88 52.28 N 96.17 E
Toorak 274b 37.51 S 145.01 E
Toormakeady 48 53.39 N 9.24 W
Toosey Indian Reserve ✦⁴ 182 51.56 N 122.29 W
Toot Hill 260 51.42 N 0.12 E
Tootias 144 3.57 N 43.57 E
Tootie, Mount ∧ 170 33.28 S 150.32 E
Tootsi 76 58.34 N 24.47 E
Toowoomba 171a 27.33 S 151.57 E
Toowong 171a 27.29 S 152.59 E
Topanga Canyon ∨ 280 34.05 N 118.36 W
Topanga State Park ♦ 280 34.06 N 118.33 W
Topar 86 49.32 N 72.50 E
Topawa 200 31.48 N 111.49 W
Topaz Lake ⊜ 226 38.41 N 119.32 W
Topçam 130 40.38 N 37.48 E
Topchănchi 126 23.54 N 86.12 E
Töpchin 54 52.10 N 13.34 E
Topčiha 86 52.49 N 83.10 E
Topeka, In., U.S. 216 41.32 N 85.32 W
Topeka, Ks., U.S. 198 39.02 N 95.40 W
Töpen 54 50.23 N 11.52 E
Topia 232 25.13 N 106.34 W
Topilejo ✦⁸ 286a 19.12 N 99.09 W
Topino ≐ 66 43.02 N 12.30 E
Topkanovo 82 54.43 N 38.29 E
Topkapı ✦⁸ 267b 41.02 N 28.54 E
Topkapı Palace ⊥ 267b 41.00 N 28.59 E
Topki 86 55.16 N 85.36 E
Topko, gora ∧ 74 57.08 N 137.24 E
Topl'a ≐ 30 48.45 N 21.45 E
Topley 182 54.30 N 126.18 W
Toplica ≐ 38 43.13 N 21.49 E
Toplița 38 46.55 N 25.21 E
T'oploje, Ross. 76 53.13 N 38.53 E
T'oploje, Ross. 76 53.37 N 37.36 E
T'oplyj Stan 80 53.58 N 50.10 E
T'oplyj Stan ✦⁸ 265b 55.37 N 37.30 E
Topo ≐ 286c 10.33 N 67.00 W
Topocalma, Punta ≻ 252 34.08 S 72.01 W
Top of Hebers 262 53.34 N 2.12 W
Topo Infiernito ∧ 286c 10.31 N 66.56 W
Topol'čany 30 48.34 N 18.10 E
Topoli 80 47.59 N 51.36 E
Topolobampo 232 25.36 N 109.03 W
Topolog 38 44.53 N 28.22 E
Topolovåţu Mare 38 45.46 N 21.37 E
Topolovgrad 38 42.05 N 26.20 E
Toporok 76 58.33 N 33.28 E
Topozero, ozero ⊜ 24 65.40 N 32.00 E
Toppenish 202 46.22 N 120.18 W
Toppenish Creek ≐ 202 46.20 N 120.11 W
Toppenish Ridge ∧ 224 46.18 N 120.40 W
Toppings 262 53.37 N 2.25 W
Toprakkale 130 37.06 N 36.07 E
Tops, Mount ∧ 162 21.50 S 134.00 E
Topsa 24 62.39 N 43.34 E
Topsfield 207 42.38 N 70.57 W
Topsham, Eng., U.K. 42 50.41 N 3.27 W
Topsham, Me., U.S. 188 43.55 N 69.58 W
Top Springs 164 16.38 S 131.50 E
Topton 208 40.30 N 75.42 W
Toquima Range ∧ 204 38.45 N 116.55 W
Toquop Wash ∨ 204 36.45 N 114.11 W
Tor 144 7.51 N 33.35 E
Torahime 94 35.25 N 136.16 E
Torano Castello 68 39.30 N 16.08 E
Torawitan, Tanjung ≻ 112 1.46 N 124.58 E
Toraya 248 14.03 S 73.18 W
Torbalı 130 38.10 N 27.21 E
Torbat-e Heydarīyeh 128 35.16 N 59.13 E
Torbat-e Jām 128 35.14 N 60.36 E
Torbay 186 47.40 N 52.44 W
Torbay □⁹ 42 50.26 N 3.34 W
Tor Bay ⊂ 42 50.25 N 3.30 W
Torbejevo, Ross. 80 54.05 N 43.15 E
Torbejevo, Ross. 82 54.44 N 36.11 E
Torbert, Mount ∧ 180 61.25 N 152.24 W
Torbino 76 58.35 N 32.53 E
Torbole 64 45.52 N 10.52 E
Torbreck, Mount ∧ 169 37.21 S 145.57 E
Torbrook 186 44.55 N 64.59 W
Torch ≐ 184 53.50 N 103.05 W
Torchany 76 55.34 N 46.36 E
Torchiarolo 68 40.29 N 18.03 E
Torch Lake ⊜ 190 45.00 N 85.19 W
Torchyn 78 50.46 N 24.59 E
Torcy 261 48.51 N 2.39 E
— Turda 38 46.34 N 23.47 E
Tordera ≐ 34 41.39 N 2.47 E
Tordesillas 34 41.30 N 5.00 W
Tordino ≐ 66 42.44 N 13.59 E
Tor di Quinto ✦⁸ 267a 41.56 N 12.28 E
Töre 26 65.54 N 22.39 E
Töreboda 40 58.43 N 14.08 E
Torej 88 50.33 N 104.50 E
Torekov 26 56.26 N 12.37 E
Toreno 34 42.42 N 6.30 W
Torez 83 48.01 N 38.37 E
Torfou 261 48.32 N 2.14 E
Torgau 54 51.34 N 13.00 E
Torgelow 54 53.37 N 14.00 E
Torgelower See ⊜ 54 53.19 N 12.47 E
Torgo 88 58.28 N 119.50 E
Torgun ≐ 80 50.15 N 46.18 E
Torhamn 26 56.05 N 15.50 E
Torhout 50 51.04 N 3.06 E
Torbulu 112 0.19 S 120.02 E
Toride 94 35.53 N 140.04 E
Torigakubi-misaki ≻ 94 37.10 N 138.06 E
Torigoe 94 36.21 N 136.36 E
Toriido 270 34.25 N 135.43 E
Torii-tōge )( 94 36.29 N 138.24 E
Torink 265a 59.47 N 30.07 E
Torino (Turin) 62 45.03 N 7.40 E
Torino □⁴ 62 45.08 N 7.22 E
Torino di Sangro Marina 66 42.11 N 14.32 E
Torio ≐ 34 42.35 N 5.34 W
Toriparu 255 16.20 S 53.55 W
Torit 154 4.24 N 32.34 E
Toritto 68 41.00 N 16.41 E
Toriya 94 36.59 N 136.54 E
Torjun 115a 7.10 S 113.13 E
Torkestān, Selseleh-ye Band-e ∧ 128 35.25 N 64.15 E
Torkovići 76 58.52 N 30.20 E
Torlinc 88 58.53 N 63.46 E
Torment, Point ≻ 162 17.02 S 123.36 E
Tormentine, Cape ≻ 186 46.07 N 63.47 W
Tormes ≐ 34 41.18 N 6.29 W
Tormestorp 41 56.07 N 13.44 E
Tormey 282 38.03 N 122.15 W
Tormini 64 45.36 N 10.29 E
Tormosin 80 48.12 N 42.42 E
Torna 24 68.04 N 44.10 E
Torna ∧ 122 18.16 N 73.37 E
Tornado Mountain ∧ 182 49.58 N 114.39 W
Tornal'a 30 48.25 N 20.20 E
Tornareccio 66 42.02 N 14.24 E
Tornberget ∧² 40 59.08 N 18.01 E
Tornby 44 53.36 N 0.44 W
Torneälven (Tornionjoki) ≐ 24 65.48 N 24.08 E
Torne Brook ≐ 276 41.08 N 74.10 W
Tornesch 52 53.41 N 9.43 E
Torneträsk ⊜ 24 68.20 N 19.10 E
Torngat Mountains ∧ 176 59.00 N 64.00 W
Tornillo 200 31.27 N 106.05 W
Tornillo Creek ≐ 196 29.11 N 103.03 W
Tornimparte 66 42.17 N 13.18 E
Torning 41 56.17 N 9.20 E
Tornio 26 65.51 N 24.08 E
Tornionjoki (Torneälven) ≐ 24 65.48 N 24.08 E
Tornquist 252 38.06 S 62.14 W
Tornyiszentmiklós 61 46.31 N 16.34 E
Toro 34 41.31 N 5.24 W
Toro, Arroyo ≐ 288 34.27 S 58.52 W
Toro, Cañada del ≐ 258 35.16 S 59.05 W
Toro, Cerro ∧ 252 29.10 S 69.48 W
Toro, Lago del ⊜ 254 51.14 S 72.45 W
Toro, Punta ≻ 252 33.47 S 71.49 W
Torobuku 112 4.25 S 122.26 E
Torodi 150 13.18 N 1.40 E
Toro-iseki ⊥ 94 34.57 N 138.24 E
Török 146 10.03 N 14.33 E
Torokina 175e 6.14 S 155.03 E
Törökszentmiklós 30 47.11 N 20.25 E
Torola ≐ 236 13.52 N 88.30 W
Torom 89 54.32 N 135.50 E
Torom ≐ 89 54.36 N 135.46 E
Toroni, Nevado ∧ 248 19.43 S 68.41 W
Toronto, Austl. 170 33.01 S 151.36 E
Toronto, On., Can. 212 43.39 N 79.23 W
Toronto, On., Can. 275b 43.39 N 79.23 W
Toronto, Ks., U.S. 198 37.47 N 95.56 W
Toronto, Oh., U.S. 214 40.27 N 80.36 W
Toronto, S.D., U.S. 198 44.34 N 96.38 W
Toronto □⁶ 275b 43.44 N 79.24 W
Toronto, Canadian Forces Base ■ 212 43.45 N 79.28 W
Toronto, University of ⊕² 275b 43.40 N 79.24 W
Toronto Harbour ⊂ 275b 43.38 N 79.22 W
Toronto Island Airport ⊗ 275b 43.38 N 79.24 W
Toronto Lake ⊜¹ 198 37.46 N 95.57 W
Toronto Reservoir ⊜¹ 210 41.38 N 74.51 W
Toronto Zoo, Metro ♦ 275b 43.49 N 79.11 W
Toro Peak ∧ 204 33.32 N 116.25 W
Toropec 76 56.30 N 31.39 E
Toropovo 82 54.21 N 36.07 E
Tororo 154 0.42 N 34.11 E
Toros (Acho), Plaza de ♦ 286d 12.02 S 77.02 W
Toros Dağları (Taurus Mountains) ∧ 130 37.00 N 33.00 E
Torošino 76 57.56 N 28.36 E
Torosozero 24 62.30 N 38.10 E
Torotoro 248 18.07 S 65.46 W
Torourne ∧² 174k 21.15 S 159.45 W
Torpa I 26 57.39 N 13.16 E
Torpè 71 40.38 N 9.40 E
Torphins 46 57.06 N 2.37 W
Tor Pignatara ✦⁸ 267a 41.52 N 12.32 E
Torpo 26 60.40 N 8.43 E
Torpoint 42 50.22 N 4.11 W
Torpy ≐ 182 53.44 N 120.55 W
Torquay, Austl. 169 38.21 S 144.19 E
Torquay, Eng., U.K. 42 50.28 N 3.30 W
Torquay, Sk., Can. 184 49.08 N 103.31 W
Torquemada 34 42.02 N 4.19 W
Torraca 68 40.07 N 15.38 E
Torrance, Ca., U.S. 228 33.50 N 118.20 W
Torrance, Pa., U.S. 214 40.25 N 79.14 W
Torrance Lake ⊜ 184 57.04 N 98.12 W
Torrance Municipal Airport ⊗ 280 33.48 N 118.20 W
Torrão 34 38.18 N 8.13 W
Torre Annunziata 68 40.45 N 14.27 E
Torrebaja 34 40.07 N 1.15 W
Torrebelvicino 64 45.43 N 11.18 E
Torre Beretti 62 45.04 N 8.40 E
Torreblanca 34 40.13 N 0.12 E
Torrebruna 66 41.52 N 14.33 E
Torrecilla ∧ 34 36.41 N 5.00 W
Torrecilla en Cameros 34 42.16 N 2.37 W
Torre del Campo 34 37.46 N 3.53 W
Torre del Greco 68 40.47 N 14.22 E
Torre del Lago Puccini 66 43.50 N 10.17 E
Torre de Moncorvo 34 41.10 N 7.03 W
Torre de'Passeri 66 42.14 N 13.56 E
Torre di Mosto 64 45.41 N 12.43 E
Torre di Santa Maria 64 46.14 N 9.51 E
Torredonjimeno 34 37.46 N 3.57 W
Torre Faro ✦⁸ 70 38.16 N 15.39 E
Torre Gaia ✦⁸ 267a 41.51 N 12.39 E
Torregrotta 70 38.11 N 15.21 E
Torrejon Air Base ■ 266a 40.28 N 3.28 W
Torrejoncillo 34 39.54 N 6.28 W
Torrejón de Ardoz 34 40.27 N 3.29 W
Torrejón-Tiétar, Embalse de ⊜¹ 34 39.50 N 5.50 W
Torrelaguna 34 40.50 N 3.32 W
Torrelavega 34 43.21 N 4.03 W
Torrellas, Riera de ≐ 266d 41.23 N 2.01 E
Torrelles de Llobregat 266d 41.21 N 1.59 E
Torrelletes 266d 41.21 N 1.57 E
Torremaggiore 68 41.41 N 15.17 E
Torremolinos 34 36.37 N 4.30 W
Torrenieri 66 43.05 N 11.33 E
Torrens ≐ 168b 34.56 S 138.30 E
Torrens, Lake ⊜ 166 31.00 S 137.50 E
Torrens, Mount ∧ 168b 34.52 S 138.56 E
Torrens Creek 166 20.46 S 145.02 E
Torrens Creek ≐ 166 22.22 S 145.09 E
Torrens Island I 168b 34.48 S 138.32 E
Torrent, Arg. 252 28.50 S 56.28 W
Torrent, Esp. 34 39.26 N 0.28 W
Torreões 256 21.52 S 43.33 W
Torreón 232 25.33 N 103.26 W
Torre Orsaia 68 40.08 N 15.28 E
Torre Pedrera 66 44.06 N 12.31 E
Torre Pellice 62 44.49 N 7.13 E
Torreperojil 34 38.02 N 3.17 W
Torres, Arg. 258 34.26 S 59.08 W
Torres, Bra. 252 29.21 S 49.44 W
Torres, Arroyo ≐ 288 34.39 S 58.45 W
Torres, Îles II 175f 13.15 S 166.37 E
Torre Santa Susanna 68 40.28 N 17.44 E
Torresdale ✦⁸ 285 40.03 N 75.00 W
Torres de Alcalá 34 35.10 N 4.16 W
Torres Martinez Indian Reservation ✦⁴ 204 33.35 N 116.02 W
Torres Novas 34 39.29 N 8.32 W
Torres Strait ⊔ 164 10.25 S 142.10 E
Torres Vedras 34 39.06 N 9.16 W
Torretta 70 38.08 N 13.14 E
Torrette di Fano 66 43.47 N 13.07 E
Torrevella 34 37.59 N 0.41 W
Torricella 68 40.21 N 17.29 E
Torricella in Sabina 66 42.16 N 12.52 E
Torricella Peligna 66 42.01 N 14.15 E
Torricella Sicura 66 42.39 N 13.39 E
Torricelli Mountains ∧ 164 3.25 S 142.20 E
Torridge ≐ 42 51.03 N 4.11 W
Torridon 46 57.33 N 5.31 W
Torridon, Loch ⊂ 46 57.35 N 5.46 W
Torriglia 62 44.31 N 9.10 E
Torrijos, Esp. 34 39.59 N 4.17 W
Torrijos, Pil. 116 13.19 N 122.05 E
Torrild 41 55.59 N 10.04 E
Torrimpietra ✦⁸ 267a 41.56 N 12.13 E
Torrington, Ct., U.S. 207 41.48 N 73.07 W
Torrington, Wy., U.S. 198 42.03 N 104.10 W
Torrinha 255 22.26 S 48.09 W
Torrita di Siena 66 43.10 N 11.46 E
Torröjen ⊜ 26 63.55 N 12.56 E
Torrox 34 36.46 N 3.58 W
Torrvarpen ⊜ 40 59.42 N 14.30 E
Torsåker 40 60.31 N 16.29 E
Tor Sapienza ✦⁸ 267a 41.54 N 12.35 E
Torsås 26 56.24 N 16.00 E
Torsburgen ⊥ 26 57.25 N 18.43 E
Torsby 26 60.08 N 13.00 E
Tors Cove 186 47.13 N 52.51 W
Torshälla 40 59.25 N 16.28 E
Tórshavn 22 62.01 N 6.46 W
Torside Reservoir ⊜¹ 262 53.29 N 1.54 W
Torsö 40 58.48 N 13.48 E
Torsö I 40 58.48 N 13.50 E
Torteval 43b 49.27 N 2.40 W
Torto ≐ 70 37.58 N 13.46 E
Tórtola I 240m 18.27 N 64.36 W
Tórtolas, Cerro de las ∧ 252 29.56 S 69.54 W
Tortolì 71 39.55 N 9.39 E
Tortona 62 44.54 N 8.52 E
Tortora 68 39.56 N 15.48 E
Tortoreto 66 42.48 N 13.55 E
Tortorici 70 38.02 N 14.49 E
Tortosa 34 40.48 N 0.31 E
Tortosa, Cap de ≻ 34 40.43 N 0.55 E
Tortue ≐ 186 50.18 N 65.23 W
Tortue, Île de la I 238 20.04 N 72.49 W
Tortue, Rivière de la ≐ 206 45.24 N 73.32 W
Tortuguero ≐ 236 10.34 N 83.31 W
Tortuguero, Laguna ⊂ 240m 18.28 N 66.26 W
Tortuguero, Parque Nacional ♦ 236 10.25 N 83.55 W
Tortuguitas 288 34.28 S 58.46 W
Tortum 130 40.19 N 41.35 E
Toru ≐ 114 1.26 N 98.46 E
Torualjgyr 85 42.32 N 76.26 E
Torue 112 0.58 S 120.18 E
Torugart, pereval (Turugart Shankou) )( 85 40.33 N 75.20 E
Torul 130 40.35 N 39.18 E
Toruń 30 53.02 N 18.35 E
Toruń □⁴ 30 53.20 N 19.00 E
Torunos 246 8.30 N 70.04 W
Torup, Sve. 26 56.58 N 13.05 E
Torup, Sve. 41 55.34 N 13.12 E
Tõrva 76 58.00 N 25.56 E
Tory 88 51.47 N 103.00 E
Tory Island I 48 55.16 N 8.14 W
Torysa ≐ 30 48.39 N 21.21 E
Tory Sound ⊔ 48 55.14 N 8.14 W
Toržok 76 57.03 N 34.58 E
Torzym 30 52.20 N 15.04 E
Tosa, Nihon 96 33.44 N 133.32 E
Tosa, Nihon 96 33.29 N 133.25 E
T'oša ≐ 80 55.38 N 42.09 E
T'osan 98 38.18 N 126.43 E
Tosari 115a 7.53 S 112.54 E
Tosa-shimizu 92 32.46 N 132.57 E
Tosa-wan ⊂ 96 33.20 N 133.40 E
Tosayama 96 33.38 N 133.32 E
Tosa-yamada 96 33.36 N 133.41 E
Tosca 156 25.53 S 23.58 E
Toscaig 46 57.24 N 5.50 W
Toscana (Tuscany) □⁴ 36 43.25 N 11.00 E
Toscano ≐ 234 18.01 N 102.32 W
Toscolano 64 45.38 N 10.37 E
Tösens 58 47.01 N 10.36 E
Toses, Collada de )( 34 42.19 N 2.01 E
Tōshi-jima I 94 34.31 N 136.53 E
Toshima ✦⁸ 268 35.44 N 139.43 E
To-shima I 94 34.31 N 139.17 E
Toshkivka 83 48.46 N 38.34 E
Tōshō-gū ⊕¹ 94 36.46 N 139.36 E
Tosi, Indon. 115b 9.35 S 118.57 E
Tosi, It. 66 43.45 N 11.31 E
Tosilei 144 1.25 N 41.24 E
Toškalykaja, gora ∧ 86 50.38 N 89.30 E
Tosna ≐ 265a 59.46 N 30.46 E
Tosno 76 59.33 N 30.53 E
Toson Cengel 88 48.47 N 98.15 E
Toson Hu ⊜ 102 35.18 N 98.54 E
T'osovo 76 55.37 N 34.30 E
T'osovo-Netyl'skij 76 58.57 N 31.04 E
T'osovskij 76 58.48 N 30.52 E
Töss ≐ 58 47.33 N 8.33 E
Tossens 52 53.34 N 8.16 E
Tossicia 66 42.33 N 13.39 E
Tostado 252 29.14 S 61.46 W
Tōstamaa 76 58.20 N 24.00 E
Tostedt 52 53.17 N 9.42 E
Tosterön I 40 59.25 N 17.00 E
Tostu 85 41.34 N 71.34 E
Tost uul ∧ 102 43.15 N 100.30 E
Tosu 96 33.22 N 130.31 E
Tosya 130 41.01 N 34.02 E
Totagatic ≐ 190 46.05 N 92.11 W
Totak ⊜ 26 59.42 N 7.57 E
Totana 34 37.46 N 1.30 W
Totanāla 126 22.05 N 87.40 E
Totatiche 234 21.56 N 103.27 W
Totban 80 46.47 N 49.06 E
Toteng 156 20.22 S 22.58 E
Tôtes 50 49.41 N 1.03 E
Totes Gebirge ∧ 30 47.42 N 13.55 E
T'otkino 78 51.17 N 34.16 E
Tot'ma 76 59.57 N 42.45 E
Totnes 42 50.25 N 3.41 W
Totness 250 5.53 N 56.19 W
Toto 152 7.08 S 14.16 E
Totonicapán 236 14.55 N 91.22 W
Totonicapán □⁵ 236 15.00 N 91.20 W
Totopotomoy Creek ≐ 208 37.41 N 77.13 W
Totora, Bol. 248 17.42 S 65.09 W
Totora, Bol. 248 17.48 S 68.07 W
Totoral 252 32.35 S 61.11 W
Totos 248 13.31 S 74.30 W
Tototlán 234 20.33 N 102.48 W
Totowa 210 40.54 N 74.12 W
Totoya Island I 175g 18.57 S 179.50 W
Totson Mountain ∧ 180 64.26 N 157.15 W
Totsuka ✦⁸ 268 35.24 N 139.32 E
Tottenham, Austl. 166 32.14 S 147.21 E
Tottenham, On., Can. 212 44.01 N 79.49 W
Tottenham ✦⁸ 260 51.35 N 0.04 W
Tottenham Hotspur Football Ground ♦ 260 51.36 N 0.04 W
Totten Inlet ⊂ 224 47.07 N 123.02 W
Totteridge ✦⁸ 276 40.31 N 74.15 W
Totteridge ✦⁸ 260 51.38 N 0.12 W
Tottington 44 53.37 N 2.20 W
Totton 42 50.56 N 1.29 W
Tottori 96 35.30 N 134.14 E
Tottori □⁵ 96 35.30 N 134.00 E
Tottori-sakyū ∧² 96 35.31 N 134.15 E
Totuskey Creek ≐ 208 37.52 N 76.45 W
Tou, Motu I 174k 21.11 S 159.48 W
Touba, C. Iv. 150 8.17 N 7.41 W
Touba, Sén. 150 14.51 N 15.53 W
Toubei 100 26.44 N 116.05 E
Toubéré Bafal 150 14.23 N 13.42 W
Toubkal, Jebel ∧ 148 31.05 N 7.55 W
Toubkal, Parc National du ♦ 148 31.05 N 7.55 W
Touboro 146 13.59 N 12.18 E
Touboro 152 7.47 N 15.22 E
T'ouch'eng 100 24.52 N 121.49 E
Touchet ≐ 202 46.02 N 118.41 W
Touchwood Hills ∧² 184 51.35 N 104.17 W
Touchwood Lake ⊜, Ab., Can. 182 54.50 N 111.23 W
Touchwood Lake ⊜, Mb., Can. 184 54.29 N 95.00 W
Toucy 50 47.44 N 3.18 E
Toudao ≐ 89 42.36 N 127.11 E
Toudaogou, Zhg. 98 42.46 N 129.12 E
Toudaogou, Zhg. 104 41.37 N 121.40 E
Toudaogou, Zhg. 105 40.58 N 117.59 E
Touët-sur-Var 62 43.57 N 7.00 E
Touffailles 32 44.16 N 1.03 E
Touggourt 148 33.10 N 6.00 E
Toughkenamon 285 39.50 N 75.46 W
Tougouri 150 13.19 N 0.31 W
Tougué 150 11.27 N 11.41 W
Touho 175f 20.47 S 165.14 E
Touiel, Oued ∨ 148 31.30 N 1.46 E
Touil, Oued ∨ 148 35.30 N 2.33 E
Touisset 207 41.43 N 71.13 W
Toukoto 150 13.27 N 9.53 W
Toukou 100 29.22 N 119.52 E
Toukley 170 33.16 S 151.33 E
Toukoto 150 13.27 N 9.53 W
Toul 58 48.41 N 5.54 E
Touléplеu 150 6.35 N 8.25 W
Toulin 100 23.03 N 114.50 E
Toulnustouc ≐ 186 49.35 N 68.24 W
Toulnustouc Nord-Est ≐ 186 50.56 N 67.44 W
Toulon, Fr. 62 43.07 N 5.56 E
Toulon, Il., U.S. 190 41.05 N 89.51 W
Toulon Lake ⊜ 204 40.01 N 118.40 W
Toulon-sur-Arroux 32 46.42 N 4.08 E
Toulouber ≐ 62 43.33 N 5.02 E
Toulourenc ≐ 62 44.14 N 5.09 E
Toulouse 32 43.36 N 1.26 E


**Symbols** in the index entries represent the broad categories identified in the key at the right. Symbols with superior numbers (∧¹) identify subcategories (see complete key on page I · 1).

**Symbole** im Register stellen die rechts im Schlüssel erklärten Kategorien dar. Symbole mit hochgestellten Ziffern (∧¹) bezeichnen Unterabteilungen einer Kategorie (vgl. vollständiger Schlüssel auf Seite I · 1).

**Los símbolos** incluídos en el texto del índice representan las grandes categorías identificadas con la clave a la derecha. Los símbolos con numeros en su parte superior (∧¹) identifican las subcategorías (véase la clave completa en la página I · 1).

**Les symboles** de l'index représentent les catégories indiquées dans la légende à droite. Les symboles suivis d'un indice (∧¹) représentent des sous-catégories (voir légende complète à la page I · 1).

**Os símbolos** incluídos no texto do índice representam as grandes categorias identificadas com a chave à direita. Os símbolos com números em sua parte superior (∧¹) identificam as subcategorias (veja-se a chave completa à página I · 1).

| Symbol | English | Deutsch | Español | Français | Português |
|---|---|---|---|---|---|
| ∧ | Mountain | Berg | Montaña | Montagne | Montanha |
| ∧ | Mountains | Gebirge | Montañas | Montagnes | Montanhas |
| )( | Pass | Paß | Paso | Col | Passo |
| ∨ | Valley, Canyon | Tal, Cañon | Valle, Cañón | Vallée, Canyon | Vale, Canhão |
| ≐ | Plain | Ebene | Llano | Plaine | Planície |
| ≻ | Cape | Kap | Cabo | Cap | Cabo |
| I | Island | Insel | Isla | Île | Ilha |
| II | Islands | Inseln | Islas | Îles | Ilhas |
| ≐ | Other Topographic Features | Andere Topographische Objekte | Otros Elementos Topográficos | Autres données topographiques | Outros acidentes topográficos |

ESPAÑOL

| Nombre | Página | Lat.°′ | Long.°′ W = Oeste |
|---|---|---|---|
| Toumen Shan I | 100 | 28.41 N | 121.46 E |
| Toumfafi | 150 | 15.02 N | 5.38 E |
| Toumodi | 150 | 6.33 N | 5.01 W |
| Tounan | 100 | 23.41 N | 120.28 E |
| Tounassine, Hamada ◆[2] | 148 | 28.30 N | 5.00 W |
| Toungo | 146 | 8.07 N | 12.03 E |
| Toungoo | 110 | 18.56 N | 96.26 E |
| Toupeng | 106 | 30.19 N | 120.31 E |
| Touques | 50 | 49.22 N | 0.06 E |
| Touques ≃ | 50 | 49.22 N | 0.06 E |
| Tour, Étang de la ⊜ | 261 | 48.40 N | 1.53 E |
| Toura, Monts du ⋏ | 150 | 7.40 N | 7.25 W |
| Touraine | 188 | 45.34 N | 75.47 W |
| Touraine □[9] | 32 | 47.12 N | 0.40 E |
| Tourakom | 110 | 18.26 N | 102.32 E |
| Tourane → Da Nang | 108 | 16.04 N | 108.13 E |
| Tourassine ⏚[4] | 148 | 24.37 N | 11.23 W |
| Tourbe ≃ | 56 | 49.10 N | 4.52 E |
| Tourcoing | 50 | 50.43 N | 3.09 E |
| Touriñan, Cabo > | 34 | 43.03 N | 9.18 W |
| Tournai | 50 | 50.36 N | 3.23 E |
| Tournan-en-Brie | 50 | 48.44 N | 2.46 E |
| Tourndo, Oued V | 148 | 22.15 N | 10.28 E |
| Tournesac ≃ | 50 | 47.27 N | 4.01 E |
| Tournon | 62 | 45.04 N | 4.50 E |
| Tournus | 58 | 46.34 N | 4.54 E |
| Touros | 250 | 5.12 S | 35.28 W |
| Tou Rout | 110 | 16.24 N | 107.00 E |
| Tourouvre | 50 | 48.35 N | 0.40 E |
| Tourrette-Levens | 62 | 43.47 N | 7.16 E |
| Tours | 50 | 47.23 N | 0.41 E |
| Tours-sur-Marne | 50 | 49.03 N | 4.07 E |
| Tours-sur-Meymont | 62 | 45.40 N | 3.35 E |
| Tourteron | 56 | 49.32 N | 4.39 E |
| Tourves | 62 | 43.24 N | 5.56 E |
| Toury | 50 | 48.12 N | 1.56 E |
| Toussaint Creek ≃ | 214 | 41.35 N | 83.04 W |
| Tousside, Pic ∧ | 146 | 21.02 N | 16.25 E |
| Toussoro, Mont ∧ | 146 | 9.18 N | 23.28 E |
| Toussus-le-Noble | 261 | 48.45 N | 2.07 E |
| Toussus-le-Noble, Aéroport de ⊠ | 261 | 48.45 N | 2.06 E |
| Toustain | 36 | 36.40 N | 8.15 E |
| Toutai, Zhg. | 89 | 45.40 N | 124.50 E |
| Toutai, Zhg. | 104 | 41.41 N | 121.11 E |
| Toutaizi | 104 | 42.19 N | 122.49 E |
| Toutle | 224 | 46.20 N | 122.41 W |
| Toutle ≃ | 224 | 46.17 N | 122.55 W |
| Toutle, North Fork ≃ | 224 | 46.23 N | 122.34 W |
| Toutle, South Fork ≃ | 224 | 46.20 N | 122.44 W |
| Toutle Mountain Range ⋏ | 224 | 46.20 N | 122.30 W |
| Toutuohe | 100 | 31.06 N | 116.25 E |
| Touws ≃ | 158 | 33.45 S | 21.11 E |
| Touwsrivier | 158 | 33.20 S | 20.00 E |
| Touzhan | 89 | 49.27 N | 119.41 E |
| Toužim | 60 | 50.04 N | 13.00 E |
| Töv □[4] | 88 | 47.30 N | 106.30 E |
| Tova | 24 | 65.58 N | 40.45 E |
| Tovar | 246 | 8.20 N | 71.46 W |
| Tovarkovo | 82 | 54.42 N | 35.57 E |
| Tovarkovskij | 76 | 53.40 N | 38.14 E |
| Tove ≃ | 42 | 52.05 N | 0.38 W |
| Tovey | 219 | 39.35 N | 89.27 W |
| Tovste | 78 | 48.50 N | 25.44 E |
| Tovtry ⋏[1] | 78 | 49.00 N | 26.10 E |
| Tovuz | 84 | 41.00 N | 45.38 E |
| Tow | 196 | 30.53 N | 98.28 W |
| Tōwa | 96 | 33.13 N | 132.53 E |
| Towaco | 210 | 40.55 N | 74.20 W |
| Towada | 92 | 40.37 N | 141.13 E |
| Towada-Hachimantai-kokuritsu-kōen ♠ | 92 | 40.35 N | 140.53 E |
| Towada-ko ⊜ | 92 | 40.28 N | 140.55 E |
| Towai | 172 | 35.29 S | 174.08 E |
| Towamencin Creek ≃ | 285 | 40.13 N | 75.23 W |
| Towanda, Il., U.S. | 216 | 40.34 N | 88.54 W |
| Towanda, Ks., U.S. | 198 | 37.47 N | 96.59 W |
| Towanda, Pa., U.S. | 210 | 41.46 N | 76.26 W |
| Towanda Creek ≃ | 210 | 41.45 N | 76.26 W |
| Towan Head > | 42 | 50.25 N | 5.07 W |
| Towar Gardens | 216 | 42.45 N | 84.28 W |
| Towari | 112 | 4.36 S | 121.29 E |
| Towcester | 42 | 52.08 N | 1.00 W |
| Tower | 190 | 47.48 N | 92.16 W |
| Tower City, N.D., U.S. | 198 | 46.55 N | 97.40 W |
| Tower City, Pa., U.S. | 208 | 40.35 N | 76.33 W |
| Tower Hamlets ◆[8] | 260 | 51.32 N | 0.03 W |
| Tower Hill, Austl. | 166 | 22.03 S | 144.36 E |
| Tower Hill, Il., U.S. | 219 | 39.23 N | 88.57 W |
| Towerhill Creek ≃ | 166 | 22.29 S | 144.39 E |
| Tower of London ⊥ | 260 | 51.30 N | 0.05 W |
| Tower Peak ∧ | 226 | 38.09 N | 119.33 W |
| Towers of Silence ʊ[1] | 272c | 18.58 N | 72.48 E |
| Tower Soudan State Park ♠ | 190 | 47.50 N | 92.15 W |
| Towla, Mount ∧ | 154 | 21.22 S | 29.52 E |
| Tow Law | 44 | 54.44 N | 1.49 W |
| Towlī | 84 | 39.11 N | 47.32 E |
| Town ≃ | 283 | 42.00 N | 70.57 W |
| Town and Country | 202 | 47.42 N | 117.23 W |
| Town Bank | 208 | 39.00 N | 74.56 W |
| Town Creek ≃, Al., U.S. | 194 | 34.46 N | 87.25 W |
| Town Creek ≃, Al., U.S. | 194 | 34.24 N | 86.11 W |
| Town Creek ≃, Oh., U.S. | 216 | 41.05 N | 84.25 W |
| Town Creek Manor | 208 | 38.19 N | 76.27 W |
| Towneley Hall ⊥ | 262 | 53.46 N | 2.13 W |
| Towner | 198 | 48.20 N | 100.24 W |
| Town Estates | 285 | 40.04 N | 74.52 W |
| Town Hill ∧[2] | 240a | 32.19 N | 64.44 W |
| Townline Tunnel ◆[5] | 284a | 42.57 N | 79.15 W |
| Town of Niagara | 284a | 43.06 N | 78.59 W |
| Town of Pines | 216 | 41.41 N | 86.58 W |
| Townsend, On., Can. | 212 | 42.54 N | 80.07 W |
| Townsend, De., U.S. | 208 | 39.23 N | 75.41 W |
| Townsend, Ma., U.S. | 207 | 42.40 N | 71.42 W |
| Townsend, Mt., U.S. | 202 | 46.19 N | 111.31 W |
| Townsend, Va., U.S. | 208 | 37.11 N | 75.57 W |
| Townsend, Mount ∧ | 171b | 36.25 S | 148.15 E |
| Townsend Island I | 276 | 40.38 N | 73.26 W |
| Townsends Inlet c | 208 | 39.07 N | 74.43 W |
| Townshend Island I | 166 | 22.15 S | 150.30 E |
| Township Line Run ≃ | 279b | 40.13 N | 79.33 W |
| Townsville | 166 | 19.16 S | 146.48 E |
| Townville | 214 | 41.41 N | 79.53 W |
| Towrang | 170 | 34.42 S | 149.51 E |
| Towrang, Mount ∧ | 170 | 34.46 S | 149.51 E |
| Towra Point > | 274a | 34.00 S | 151.10 E |
| Towr Kham | 123 | 34.08 N | 71.05 E |
| Towrzī, Afg. | 120 | 30.11 N | 65.59 E |
| Towrzī, Afg. | 128 | 32.38 N | 65.53 E |
| Towson | 208 | 39.24 N | 76.36 W |
| Towson State College ʊ[2] | 284b | 39.24 N | 76.37 W |
| Towuti, Danau ⊜ | 112 | 2.45 S | 121.32 E |
| Toxkan (Aksaj) ≃, Asia | 85 | 40.55 N | 78.16 E |
| Toxkan ≃, Zhg. | 90 | 41.08 N | 80.11 E |
| Toyah | 196 | 31.19 N | 103.47 W |
| Toyah Creek ≃ | 196 | 31.18 N | 103.27 W |
| Tōya-ko ⊜ | 92a | 42.35 N | 140.51 E |
| Toyama | 94 | 36.41 N | 137.13 E |
| Toyama □[5] | 94 | 36.30 N | 137.30 E |
| Toyama-heiya ≚ | 94 | 36.40 N | 137.15 E |
| Toyama-wan c | 94 | 36.50 N | 137.10 E |
| Toyapakeh | 115b | 8.41 S | 115.29 E |
| Tōyo, Nihon | 96 | 33.55 N | 133.05 E |
| Tōyō, Nihon | 96 | 33.30 N | 134.16 E |
| Toyo ≃ | 94 | 34.47 N | 137.20 E |
| Toyoake | 94 | 35.03 N | 137.01 E |
| Toyoda, Nihon | 94 | 34.45 N | 137.49 E |
| Toyoda, Nihon | 268 | 35.39 N | 139.23 E |

FRANÇAIS

| Nom | Page | Lat.°′ | Long.°′ W = Ouest |
|---|---|---|---|
| Toyofuta | 268 | 35.53 N | 139.57 E |
| Toyohama | 96 | 34.04 N | 133.38 E |
| Toyohara | 175d | 24.15 N | 123.48 E |
| Toyohashi | 94 | 34.46 N | 137.23 E |
| Toyohira | 96 | 34.40 N | 132.24 E |
| Toyokawa | 94 | 34.49 N | 137.24 E |
| Toyo-kawa-yōsui ≊ | 94 | 34.35 N | 137.03 E |
| Toyonaka, Nihon | 96 | 34.09 N | 133.42 E |
| Toyonaka, Nihon | 96 | 34.47 N | 135.28 E |
| Toyone | 94 | 35.09 N | 137.43 E |
| Toyono | 94 | 36.43 N | 138.16 E |
| Toyooka, Nihon | 94 | 35.33 N | 137.54 E |
| Toyooka, Nihon | 94 | 34.50 N | 137.52 E |
| Toyooka, Nihon | 96 | 35.32 N | 134.50 E |
| Toyooka, Nihon | 268 | 35.11 N | 139.58 E |
| Toyosaka, Nihon | 92 | 37.56 N | 139.13 E |
| Toyosaka, Nihon | 96 | 34.34 N | 132.50 E |
| Toyosato | 94 | 36.06 N | 140.02 E |
| Toyoshina | 94 | 36.18 N | 137.54 E |
| Toyota, Nihon | 94 | 35.05 N | 137.09 E |
| Toyota, Nihon | 94 | 36.46 N | 138.19 E |
| Toyota, Nihon | 96 | 34.12 N | 131.04 E |
| Toyota-ko ⊜ | 96 | 34.14 N | 131.08 E |
| Toyotomi | 94 | 35.34 N | 138.33 E |
| Toyotsu | 96 | 33.40 N | 130.58 E |
| Toyoura | 96 | 34.08 N | 130.58 E |
| Toy's Hill | 260 | 51.14 N | 0.06 E |
| Tozer, Mount ∧ | 164 | 12.45 S | 143.13 E |
| Tozeur | 148 | 33.55 N | 8.08 E |
| Tozi, Mount ∧ | 180 | 65.41 N | 150.58 W |
| Tozitna ≃ | 180 | 65.08 N | 152.23 W |
| Tpig | 84 | 41.47 N | 47.36 E |
| Traar ◆[8] | 263 | 51.23 N | 6.36 E |
| Trabaria, Bocca )( | 66 | 43.36 N | 12.14 E |
| Traben-Trarbach | 56 | 49.57 N | 7.06 E |
| Trabia | 70 | 37.59 N | 13.39 E |
| Trabiju | 255 | 22.03 S | 48.18 W |
| Trabuco, Arroyo ≃ | 228 | 33.31 N | 117.40 W |
| Trabzon | 130 | 41.00 N | 39.43 E |
| Trabzon □[4] | 130 | 40.50 N | 39.50 E |
| Tracadie | 186 | 47.31 N | 64.54 W |
| Trachselwald | 58 | 47.01 N | 7.45 E |
| Tra Cu | 110 | 9.42 N | 106.16 E |
| Tracy, P.Q., Can. | 206 | 46.01 N | 73.09 W |
| Tracy, Ca., U.S. | 226 | 37.44 N | 121.25 W |
| Tracy, Mn., U.S. | 198 | 44.14 N | 95.37 W |
| Tracy City | 194 | 35.15 N | 85.44 W |
| Tracyton | 224 | 47.36 N | 122.39 W |
| Tradate | 62 | 45.43 N | 8.54 E |
| Trade Lake ⊜ | 184 | 55.22 N | 103.44 W |
| Tradewater ≃ | 194 | 37.31 N | 88.03 W |
| Trading Bay c | 212 | 45.15 N | 78.55 W |
| Tradinghouse Creek Reservoir ⊜[1] | 222 | 31.35 N | 96.55 W |
| Traditional Cultures, Museum of ʊ | 269f | 14.31 N | 121.00 E |
| Trælleborg ⊥ | 41 | 55.23 N | 11.17 E |
| Traer | 190 | 42.11 N | 92.27 W |
| Traessu, Monte ∧ | 71 | 40.28 N | 8.40 E |
| Trafalgar, Austl. | 169 | 38.12 S | 146.09 E |
| Trafalgar, On., Can. | 275b | 43.29 N | 79.43 W |
| Trafalgar, In., U.S. | 218 | 39.24 N | 86.09 W |
| Trafalgar, Cabo > | 34 | 36.11 N | 6.02 W |
| Trafaria | 266c | 38.40 N | 9.14 W |
| Trafford | 214 | 40.23 N | 79.45 W |
| Trafford □[8] | 262 | 53.24 N | 2.21 W |
| Trafford, Lake ⊜ | 220 | 26.25 N | 81.30 W |
| Trafford Park | 262 | 53.28 N | 2.20 W |
| Trafoi | 64 | 46.33 N | 10.31 E |
| Tragacete | 34 | 40.21 N | 1.51 W |
| Tragliata ◆[8] | 267a | 41.58 N | 12.15 E |
| Tragwein | 61 | 48.20 N | 14.37 E |
| Traição, Córrego ≃ | 287b | 23.36 S | 46.41 W |
| Traíd | 34 | 40.40 N | 1.49 W |
| Traiguén | 252 | 38.15 S | 72.41 W |
| Traiguén, Isla I | 254 | 45.35 S | 73.42 W |
| Trail | 182 | 49.06 N | 117.42 W |
| Trail Creek | 216 | 41.41 N | 86.51 W |
| Trailer Estates | 220 | 27.24 N | 82.34 W |
| Trail Ridge ∧ | 192 | 30.35 N | 82.05 W |
| Traînel | 50 | 48.25 N | 3.27 E |
| Trainer | 285 | 39.50 N | 75.25 W |
| Traipu | 250 | 9.58 S | 37.01 W |
| Traíra (Taraira) ≃ | 246 | 1.04 S | 69.26 W |
| Trairão ≃ | 250 | 7.20 S | 51.14 W |
| Traíras ≃ | 255 | 14.07 S | 48.31 W |
| Trairi | 250 | 3.17 S | 39.15 W |
| Traisen | 61 | 48.02 N | 15.37 E |
| Traisen ≃ | 61 | 48.22 N | 15.46 E |
| Traiskirchen | 61 | 48.01 N | 16.18 E |
| Traismauer | 61 | 48.21 N | 15.44 E |
| Traîtres, Baie des c | 174x | 9.50 S | 139.02 W |
| Traitsching | 60 | 49.10 N | 12.39 E |
| Trajouce | 266c | 38.44 N | 9.20 W |
| Trakai | 76 | 54.38 N | 24.56 E |
| Trakt | 24 | 62.44 N | 51.11 E |
| Träkvista | 40 | 59.16 N | 17.47 E |
| Tralee | 48 | 52.16 N | 9.42 W |
| Tralee Bay c | 48 | 52.15 N | 9.59 W |
| Trá Lí → Tralee | 48 | 52.16 N | 9.42 W |
| Tramatza | 71 | 40.00 N | 8.39 E |
| Tramayes | 58 | 46.18 N | 4.36 E |
| Tramelan | 58 | 47.13 N | 7.06 E |
| Tra Mi | 110 | 15.20 N | 108.13 E |
| Tramin → Termeno | 64 | 46.20 N | 11.14 E |
| Trammel | 192 | 37.00 N | 82.17 W |
| Trammel Creek ≃ | 194 | 36.52 N | 86.23 W |
| Tramonti di sopra | 64 | 46.18 N | 12.47 E |
| Tramore | 48 | 52.10 N | 7.10 W |
| Tramperos Creek (Punta de Agua Creek) ≃ | 196 | 35.32 N | 102.27 W |
| Tramping Lake ⊜ | 184 | 52.08 N | 108.49 W |
| Tramutola | 68 | 40.19 N | 15.47 E |
| Trăn | 38 | 42.50 N | 22.39 E |
| Tranås | 26 | 58.03 N | 14.59 E |
| Trancão ≃ | 266c | 38.48 N | 9.06 W |
| Trancas | 252 | 26.13 S | 65.17 W |
| Tranco de Beas, Embalse de ⊜[1] | 34 | 38.10 N | 2.45 W |
| Trancoso | 34 | 40.47 N | 7.21 W |
| Trand | 123 | 34.38 N | 72.59 E |
| Tranderup | 41 | 54.52 N | 10.22 E |
| Tranebjerg | 41 | 55.50 N | 10.36 E |
| Tranekær | 41 | 55.00 N | 10.51 E |
| Tranemo | 26 | 57.29 N | 13.21 E |
| Tranent | 46 | 55.57 N | 2.58 W |
| Tränental | 158 | 27.09 S | 19.33 E |
| Trang | 110 | 7.33 N | 99.36 E |
| Trangahy | 157b | 19.07 S | 44.43 E |
| Trangan, Pulau I | 164 | 6.35 S | 134.20 E |
| Trangie | 166 | 32.02 S | 147.59 E |
| Tran Grande ≃ | 116 | 6.43 N | 124.01 E |
| Trängslet | 26 | 61.25 N | 13.40 E |
| Trani | 68 | 41.17 N | 16.26 E |
| Tranmere | 262 | 53.23 N | 3.01 W |
| Trannon ≃ | 42 | 52.31 N | 3.25 W |
| Tranoroa | 157b | 24.42 S | 45.04 E |
| Tranquebar | 122 | 11.02 N | 79.51 E |
| Tranqueras | 252 | 31.12 S | 55.45 W |
| Tranquility | 218 | 38.58 N | 83.32 W |
| Tranquillity | 226 | 36.38 N | 120.15 W |
| Transantarctic Mountains ⋏ | 9 | 85.00 S | 175.00 W |
| Trans-en-Provence | 62 | 43.30 N | 6.29 E |
| Transfer | 214 | 41.20 N | 80.26 W |
| Transit Airpark ⊠ | 284a | 43.06 N | 78.44 W |
| Transkei □[9] | 158 | 31.20 S | 29.00 E |
| Transquaking ≃ | 208 | 38.22 N | 76.00 W |
| Transsylvanische Alpen → Carpații Meridionali ⋏ | 38 | 45.30 N | 24.15 E |
| Transtrand | 26 | 61.05 N | 13.19 E |
| Transtrandsfjällen ∧ | 26 | 61.17 N | 13.00 E |
| Transylvania □[9] | 38 | 46.30 N | 24.00 E |

PORTUGUÊS

| Nome | Página | Lat.°′ | Long.°′ W = Oeste |
|---|---|---|---|
| Transylvanian Alps → Carpații Meridionali ⋏ | 38 | 45.30 N | 24.15 E |
| Tranters Creek ≃ | 192 | 35.33 N | 77.05 W |
| Traona | 58 | 46.09 N | 9.31 E |
| Trapalcó, Salinas de ≚ | 254 | 39.45 S | 66.45 W |
| Trapani | 70 | 38.01 N | 12.31 E |
| Trapani □[4] | 70 | 37.50 N | 12.40 E |
| Traphole Brook ≃ | 283 | 42.10 N | 71.11 W |
| Trappe, Md., U.S. | 208 | 38.39 N | 76.03 W |
| Trappe, Pa., U.S. | 208 | 40.12 N | 75.29 W |
| Trappenkamp | 54 | 54.03 N | 10.16 E |
| Trapper Peak ∧ | 202 | 45.54 N | 114.18 W |
| Trappes | 50 | 48.47 N | 2.00 E |
| Trappeto | 70 | 38.04 N | 13.03 E |
| Trapuá ≃ | 287b | 23.36 S | 46.17 W |
| Traralgon | 169 | 38.12 S | 146.32 E |
| Traralgon Creek ≃ | 169 | 38.10 S | 146.31 E |
| Traras, Monts des ⋏ | 34 | 35.10 N | 1.40 W |
| Trarza □[4] | 150 | 17.45 N | 15.45 W |
| Trârza ◆[1] | 150 | 18.00 N | 15.00 W |
| Trasacco | 66 | 41.57 N | 13.32 E |
| Trasadingen | 58 | 47.40 N | 8.26 E |
| Trascău, Munții ⋏ | 38 | 46.23 N | 23.33 E |
| Trasimeno, Lago ⊜ | 66 | 43.08 N | 12.06 E |
| Trask ≃ | 224 | 45.28 N | 123.53 W |
| Träslövsläge | 26 | 57.04 N | 12.16 E |
| Trasna | 82 | 54.45 N | 38.42 E |
| Trás-os-Montes □[9] | 34 | 41.30 N | 7.15 W |
| Trassem | 56 | 49.34 N | 6.31 E |
| Trăstenik | 38 | 43.31 N | 24.28 E |
| Trat | 110 | 12.14 N | 102.30 E |
| Tratalias | 71 | 39.06 N | 8.34 E |
| Tratzberg, Schloss ⊥ | 64 | 47.23 N | 11.44 E |
| Traun | 61 | 48.13 N | 14.14 E |
| Traun ≃, Dtsch. | 60 | 48.00 N | 12.32 E |
| Traun ≃, Öst. | 30 | 48.16 N | 14.22 E |
| Traunkirchen | 64 | 47.50 N | 13.47 E |
| Traunreut | 64 | 47.56 N | 12.35 E |
| Traunsee ⊜ | 64 | 47.51 N | 13.48 E |
| Traunstein, Dtsch. | 64 | 47.52 N | 12.38 E |
| Traunstein, Öst. | 61 | 48.26 N | 15.07 E |
| Traunstein ∧ | 64 | 47.52 N | 13.50 E |
| Trautenstein | 54 | 51.41 N | 10.43 E |
| Travagliato | 64 | 45.31 N | 10.05 E |
| Trave ≃ | 54 | 53.54 N | 10.50 E |
| Travedona | 62 | 45.48 N | 8.40 E |
| Travellers Lake ⊜ | 166 | 33.18 S | 142.00 E |
| Travemünde ◆[8] | 54 | 53.57 N | 10.52 E |
| Traver | 226 | 36.27 N | 119.29 W |
| Travers, Mount ∧ | 172 | 42.01 S | 172.44 E |
| Travers, Val de V | 58 | 46.57 N | 6.38 E |
| Traverse, Lake ⊜ | 198 | 45.43 N | 96.40 W |
| Traverse Bay c | 184 | 50.40 N | 96.25 W |
| Traverse City | 190 | 44.45 N | 85.37 W |
| Traversella | 62 | 45.30 N | 7.45 E |
| Traverse Peak ∧ | 180 | 65.10 N | 159.12 W |
| Traversetolo | 64 | 44.38 N | 10.23 E |
| Travers Reservoir ⊜[1] | 182 | 50.14 N | 112.51 W |
| Tra Vinh | 110 | 9.56 N | 106.20 E |
| Travis | 222 | 31.08 N | 97.00 W |
| Travis □[6] | 222 | 30.18 N | 97.40 W |
| Travis, Lake ⊜[1] | 196 | 30.27 N | 98.00 W |
| Travis Air Force Base ■ | 226 | 38.16 N | 121.55 W |
| Travnik | 36 | 44.14 N | 17.40 E |
| Trawalla | 169 | 37.26 S | 143.29 E |
| Trawbreaga Bay c | 48 | 55.17 N | 7.18 W |
| Trawick | 222 | 31.46 N | 94.45 W |
| Trawsfynydd | 42 | 52.54 N | 3.55 W |
| Trayning | 162 | 31.07 S | 117.48 E |
| Trazegnies | 50 | 50.28 N | 4.19 E |
| Trbovlje | 36 | 46.10 N | 15.03 E |
| Treadwell | 210 | 42.21 N | 75.03 W |
| Treales | 262 | 53.47 N | 2.51 W |
| Treasure Island | 220 | 27.46 N | 82.46 W |
| Treasure Island I | 226 | 37.48 N | 122.22 W |
| Treasure Island Naval Station ■ | 282 | 37.49 N | 122.22 W |
| Trebatsch | 54 | 52.05 N | 14.09 E |
| Trebbia ≃ | 62 | 45.04 N | 9.41 E |
| Trebbin | 54 | 52.13 N | 13.13 E |
| Třebechovice pod Orebem | 30 | 50.12 N | 16.00 E |
| Trebel | 54 | 52.59 N | 11.20 E |
| Trebel ≃ | 54 | 53.55 N | 13.01 E |
| Trebelsee ⊜ | 54 | 52.28 N | 12.47 E |
| Třebenice | 54 | 50.29 N | 14.00 E |
| Trebgast | 60 | 50.04 N | 11.33 E |
| Třebíč | 30 | 49.13 N | 15.53 E |
| Trebinje | 38 | 42.43 N | 18.20 E |
| Trebisacce | 68 | 39.52 N | 16.32 E |
| Trebišov | 30 | 48.40 N | 21.47 E |
| Trebitz | 54 | 51.45 N | 12.44 E |
| Trebizond → Trabzon | 130 | 41.00 N | 39.43 E |
| Trebjerg ∧[2] | 41 | 55.10 N | 10.14 E |
| Třebkov | 60 | 49.22 N | 14.04 E |
| Treble Mountain ∧ | 182 | 55.50 N | 129.51 W |
| Treblinka | 30 | 52.39 N | 22.03 E |
| Třeboň | 61 | 49.00 N | 14.47 E |
| Třebouň ∧ | 60 | 50.01 N | 12.59 E |
| Trebsen | 54 | 51.17 N | 12.45 E |
| Trebur | 56 | 49.56 N | 8.25 E |
| Trecastagni | 70 | 37.37 N | 15.05 E |
| Trecate | 62 | 45.26 N | 8.44 E |
| Trecchina | 68 | 40.02 N | 15.46 E |
| Trece Martires | 116 | 14.16 N | 120.50 E |
| Trecenta | 64 | 45.02 N | 11.28 E |
| Tred Avon River c | 208 | 38.42 N | 76.08 W |
| Tredegar | 42 | 51.47 N | 3.16 W |
| Tredici Archi, Ponte ◆[5] | 66 | 41.32 N | 14.57 E |
| Treene ≃ | 41 | 54.22 N | 9.05 E |
| Trees Mills | 279b | 40.23 N | 80.13 W |
| Treffen | 64 | 46.40 N | 13.52 E |
| Treffort | 58 | 46.16 N | 5.22 E |
| Treffurt | 56 | 51.08 N | 10.14 E |
| Trèfle, Lac du ⊜ | 206 | 46.36 N | 73.55 W |
| Tregaron | 42 | 52.13 N | 3.55 W |
| Tregnago | 64 | 45.31 N | 11.10 E |
| Tregosse Islets II | 166 | 17.41 S | 150.43 E |
| Tregubovo | 76 | 58.59 N | 31.33 E |
| Tréguier | 32 | 48.47 N | 3.14 W |
| Treharris | 42 | 51.41 N | 3.16 W |
| Treherne | 184 | 49.38 N | 98.41 W |
| Trehörningsjö | 26 | 63.42 N | 18.48 E |
| Treia, Dtsch. | 41 | 54.30 N | 9.17 E |
| Treia, It. | 66 | 43.19 N | 13.19 E |
| Treig, Loch ⊜ | 46 | 56.50 N | 4.44 W |
| Treinta y Tres | 252 | 33.14 S | 54.23 W |
| Treis | 56 | 50.10 N | 7.17 E |
| Treis-Karden | 56 | 50.11 N | 7.17 E |
| Trekkopje | 156 | 22.18 S | 14.53 E |
| Trélazé | 32 | 47.27 N | 0.28 W |
| Trelde Næs > | 41 | 55.37 N | 9.52 E |
| Trelew | 254 | 43.15 S | 65.18 W |
| Trelleborg | 41 | 55.22 N | 13.10 E |
| Treloar | 219 | 38.39 N | 91.10 W |
| Tremadog | 42 | 52.56 N | 4.09 W |
| Tremblant, Lac ⊜ | 206 | 46.15 N | 74.38 W |
| Tremblant, Mont ∧ | 206 | 46.16 N | 74.35 W |
| Tremblay, Hippodrome du ♠ | 261 | 48.50 N | 2.29 E |
| Tremblay-lès-Gonesse | 261 | 48.59 N | 2.34 E |
| Trembleur Lake ⊜ | 182 | 54.51 N | 125.07 W |
| Tremedal | 255 | 14.58 S | 41.24 W |
| Tremembé | 256 | 22.58 S | 45.33 W |
| Tremezzo | 58 | 45.59 N | 9.15 E |
| Tremino | 88 | 56.42 N | 98.04 E |
| Tremiti, Isole II | 66 | 42.07 N | 15.30 E |
| Tremo La )( | 124 | 27.44 N | 89.12 E |
| Tremont, Il., U.S. | 190 | 40.31 N | 89.29 W |
| Tremont, In., U.S. | 216 | 41.39 N | 87.02 W |
| Tremont, Pa., U.S. | 208 | 40.37 N | 76.23 W |
| Tremont ◆[8] | 276 | 40.51 N | 73.55 W |
| Tremont City | 218 | 40.00 N | 83.50 W |
| Tremonton | 200 | 41.42 N | 112.09 W |

| | | | |
|---|---|---|---|
| Třemošna | 60 | 49.49 N | 13.20 E |
| Třemošná ≃ | 60 | 49.52 N | 13.32 E |
| Tremp | 34 | 42.10 N | 0.54 E |
| Trempealeau | 190 | 44.00 N | 91.26 W |
| Trempealeau ≃ | 190 | 44.02 N | 91.32 W |
| Tremsbüttel | 52 | 53.44 N | 10.18 E |
| Trena | 144 | 10.45 N | 40.38 E |
| Trenčín | 30 | 48.54 N | 18.04 E |
| Trendelburg | 52 | 51.34 N | 9.25 E |
| Trenel | 252 | 35.42 S | 64.08 W |
| Trêng | 110 | 12.49 N | 102.54 E |
| Trenggalek | 115a | 8.03 S | 111.43 E |
| Trenque Lauquen | 252 | 35.58 S | 62.42 W |
| Trent, Dtsch. | 54 | 54.31 N | 13.15 E |
| Trent → Trento, It. | 64 | 46.04 N | 11.08 E |
| Trent ≃, On., Can. | 212 | 44.06 N | 77.34 W |
| Trent ≃, Eng., U.K. | 28 | 53.42 N | 0.41 W |
| Trent ≃, N.C., U.S. | 192 | 35.05 N | 77.02 W |
| Trent, Vale of V | 42 | 52.44 N | 1.50 W |
| Trent and Mersey Canal ≊ | 262 | 53.19 N | 2.39 W |
| Trente et un Milles, Lac des ⊜ | 188 | 46.12 N | 75.49 W |
| Trentham | 169 | 37.23 S | 144.19 E |
| Trentino-Alto Adige □[4] | 64 | 46.30 N | 11.20 E |
| Trento | 64 | 46.04 N | 11.08 E |
| Trento □[4] | 64 | 46.08 N | 11.07 E |
| Trentola-Ducenta | 68 | 40.59 N | 14.10 E |
| Trenton, N.S., Can. | 186 | 45.37 N | 62.38 W |
| Trenton, On., Can. | 212 | 44.06 N | 77.35 W |
| Trenton, Fl., U.S. | 192 | 29.36 N | 82.49 W |
| Trenton, Ga., U.S. | 192 | 34.52 N | 85.30 W |
| Trenton, Il., U.S. | 219 | 38.36 N | 89.40 W |
| Trenton, Ky., U.S. | 194 | 36.43 N | 87.15 W |
| Trenton, Mi., U.S. | 216 | 42.08 N | 83.10 W |
| Trenton, Mo., U.S. | 194 | 40.04 N | 93.36 W |
| Trenton, Ne., U.S. | 198 | 40.10 N | 101.00 W |
| Trenton, N.J., U.S. | 208 | 40.13 N | 74.44 W |
| Trenton, N.C., U.S. | 192 | 35.04 N | 77.21 W |
| Trenton, Oh., U.S. | 218 | 39.29 N | 84.28 W |
| Trenton, Tn., U.S. | 194 | 35.58 N | 88.56 W |
| Trenton, Tx., U.S. | 196 | 33.26 N | 96.20 W |
| Trenton, Canadian Forces Base ■ | 190 | 44.07 N | 77.33 W |
| Trenton Channel ≃[1] | 281 | 42.06 N | 83.11 W |
| Trentwood | 202 | 47.42 N | 117.13 W |
| Trepalade | 64 | 45.34 N | 12.24 E |
| Trepassey | 186 | 46.44 N | 53.22 W |
| Trepassey Bay c | 186 | 46.37 N | 53.20 W |
| Treptow ◆[8] | 54 | 52.29 N | 13.29 E |
| Trepuzzi | 68 | 40.24 N | 18.05 E |
| Trequanda | 66 | 43.11 N | 11.40 E |
| Tresa ≃ | 58 | 46.00 N | 8.43 E |
| Tres Algarrobos | 252 | 35.12 S | 62.46 W |
| Tres Árboles | 252 | 32.24 S | 56.43 W |
| Tres Arroyos | 252 | 38.23 S | 60.17 W |
| Tres Cerros | 254 | 48.13 S | 67.33 W |
| Treščevo | 82 | 54.11 N | 37.55 E |
| Tresckow | 210 | 40.54 N | 75.58 W |
| Tresco I | 42a | 49.57 N | 6.19 W |
| Três Corações | 256 | 21.42 S | 45.16 W |
| Trescore Balneario | 62 | 45.41 N | 9.50 E |
| Três Coroas | 252 | 29.32 S | 50.48 W |
| Tres de Febrero → Caseros | 258 | 34.36 S | 58.33 W |
| Tres de Febrero □[5] | 288 | 34.36 S | 58.35 W |
| Três de Maio | 252 | 27.47 S | 54.14 W |
| Tresenda | 64 | 46.10 N | 10.05 E |
| Tres Esquinas | 246 | 0.43 N | 75.16 W |
| Três Fronteiras | 255 | 20.13 S | 50.55 W |
| Treshnish Isles II | 46 | 56.30 N | 6.24 W |
| Treshnish Point > | 46 | 56.33 N | 6.21 W |
| Três Ilhas | 256 | 22.04 S | 43.29 W |
| Tresinaro ≃ | 64 | 44.39 N | 10.47 E |
| Tres Isletas | 252 | 26.21 S | 60.26 W |
| Treskino | 80 | 52.40 N | 44.40 E |
| Três Lagoas | 255 | 20.48 S | 51.43 W |
| Tres Lagos | 254 | 49.37 S | 71.30 W |
| Tres Lomas | 252 | 36.27 S | 62.51 W |
| Três Marias | 255 | 18.12 S | 45.14 W |
| Três Marias, Represa de ⊜[1] | 255 | 18.12 S | 45.15 W |
| Tres Montes, Golfo c | 254 | 46.54 S | 75.00 W |
| Tres Montes, Península >[1] | 254 | 46.50 S | 75.30 W |
| Tres Montosas ∧ | 200 | 34.06 N | 107.28 W |
| Tres Morros, Alto de ∧ | 246 | 7.08 N | 76.11 W |
| Tresnuraghes | 71 | 40.15 N | 8.31 E |
| Tres Padres, Pico ∧ | 286a | 19.35 N | 99.08 W |
| Tres Palacios ≃ | 196 | 28.45 N | 96.09 W |
| Tres Palos, Laguna c | 234 | 16.46 N | 99.44 W |
| Três Passos | 252 | 27.27 S | 53.56 W |
| Tres Picos | 234 | 15.52 N | 93.32 W |
| Tres Picos, Cerro ∧, Arg. | 252 | 38.09 S | 61.57 W |
| Tres Picos, Cerro ∧, Méx. | 234 | 16.12 N | 93.37 W |
| Tres Pinos | 226 | 36.48 N | 121.19 W |
| Tres Pinos Creek ≃ | 226 | 36.47 N | 121.21 W |
| Três Pontas | 256 | 21.22 S | 45.31 W |
| Três Pontas, Cabo das > | 152 | 10.23 S | 13.32 E |
| Tres Puntas, Cabo >, Arg. | 254 | 47.06 S | 65.53 W |
| Tres Puntas, Cabo >, Guat. | 236 | 15.56 N | 88.37 W |
| Três Ranchos | 255 | 18.22 S | 47.47 W |
| Tres Reyes Islands II | 116 | 13.14 N | 121.51 E |
| Três Rios, Bra. | 256 | 22.07 S | 43.12 W |
| Tres Ríos, C.R. | 236 | 9.54 N | 83.58 W |
| Tressancourt | 261 | 48.55 N | 2.00 E |
| Třešť | 30 | 49.18 N | 15.30 E |
| Tresta | 46a | 60.14 N | 1.21 W |
| Tres Valles | 234 | 18.15 N | 96.08 W |
| Tres Vírgenes, Volcán de las ∧[1] | 232 | 27.27 N | 112.34 W |
| Tres Zapotes ⊥ | 234 | 18.28 N | 95.24 W |
| Tret'akovskaja Galereja ʊ | 265b | 55.45 N | 37.37 E |
| Tretet | 114 | 4.40 N | 96.51 E |
| Trets | 62 | 43.27 N | 5.41 E |
| Tretten | 26 | 61.19 N | 10.19 E |
| Treuchtlingen | 56 | 48.57 N | 10.54 E |
| Treuen | 54 | 50.32 N | 12.18 E |
| Treuenbrietzen | 54 | 52.06 N | 12.52 E |
| Trevelín | 254 | 43.04 S | 71.28 W |
| Trèves → Trier | 56 | 49.45 N | 6.38 E |
| Trevi | 66 | 42.52 N | 12.45 E |
| Treviglio | 62 | 45.31 N | 9.35 E |
| Trevignano Romano | 66 | 42.09 N | 12.15 E |
| Treviño | 34 | 42.44 N | 2.45 W |
| Treviso | 64 | 45.40 N | 12.15 E |
| Treviso □[4] | 64 | 45.50 N | 12.13 E |
| Trevor | 216 | 42.30 N | 88.07 W |
| Trevorton | 208 | 40.46 N | 76.40 W |
| Trevose | 208 | 40.08 N | 74.58 W |
| Trevose Head > | 42 | 50.33 N | 5.01 W |
| Trevose Heights | 285 | 40.09 N | 74.59 W |
| Trévoux | 58 | 45.56 N | 4.46 E |
| Trexlertown | 208 | 40.33 N | 75.36 W |
| Trezevant | 194 | 36.00 N | 88.37 W |
| Trezzano sul Naviglio | 266b | 45.25 N | 9.04 E |
| Trezzo sull'Adda | 62 | 45.36 N | 9.31 E |
| Trgovište | 38 | 42.21 N | 22.05 E |
| Trhomné | 60 | 49.55 N | 13.05 E |
| Trhové Sviny | 61 | 48.51 N | 14.39 E |
| Triabunna | 166 | 42.30 S | 147.55 E |
| Triadelphia Reservoir ⊜[1] | 208 | 39.13 N | 77.01 W |
| Trialeti | 84 | 41.33 N | 44.07 E |
| Trialetskij chrebet ⋏ | 84 | 41.45 N | 43.50 E |
| Triana | 66 | 42.47 N | 11.33 E |
| Triánda | 38 | 36.24 N | 28.10 E |
| Triangle, Eng., U.K. | 262 | 53.42 N | 1.56 W |
| Triangle, Va., U.S. | 208 | 38.32 N | 77.20 W |
| Triangle Lake | 210 | 42.32 N | 74.13 W |

| | | | |
|---|---|---|---|
| Triangul'atorov, pik ∧ | 88 | 53.45 N | 97.00 E |
| Triángulos, Arrecifes ⊹[2] | 232 | 20.57 N | 92.16 W |
| Triaucourt-en-Argonne | 56 | 48.59 N | 5.04 E |
| Tribeni | 126 | 22.59 N | 88.24 E |
| Triberg | 58 | 48.08 N | 8.13 E |
| Tribes Hill | 210 | 42.57 N | 74.17 W |
| Tribobó | 287a | 22.52 S | 43.01 W |
| Triborough Bridge ◆[5] | 276 | 40.47 N | 73.55 W |
| Tri Brata, porog ʟ | 86 | 57.25 N | 95.39 E |
| Tribsees | 54 | 54.05 N | 12.45 E |
| Tribugá, Ensenada de c | 246 | 5.45 N | 77.20 W |
| Tribune, Sk., Can. | 184 | 49.15 N | 103.50 W |
| Tribune, Ks., U.S. | 198 | 38.28 N | 101.45 W |
| Tribune Channel ʯ | 182 | 50.50 N | 126.16 W |
| Tribuswinkel | 264b | 48.00 N | 16.16 E |
| Tricarico | 68 | 40.37 N | 16.09 E |
| Tricase | 68 | 39.56 N | 18.22 E |
| Tricesimo | 64 | 46.10 N | 13.13 E |
| Trichardt | 158 | 26.28 S | 29.13 E |
| Trichiana | 64 | 46.05 N | 12.07 E |
| Trichinopoly → Tiruchchirāppalli | 122 | 10.49 N | 78.41 E |
| Trichūr | 122 | 10.31 N | 76.13 E |
| Tri Cities | 222 | 32.09 N | 95.56 W |
| Tricot | 50 | 49.34 N | 2.35 E |
| Tri County Supply Canal ≊ | 198 | 40.49 N | 100.06 W |
| Trida | 166 | 33.01 S | 145.01 E |
| Trident Peak ∧ | 204 | 41.54 N | 118.25 W |
| Triebel | 54 | 50.21 N | 12.08 E |
| Trieben | 61 | 47.29 N | 14.30 E |
| Triebes | 54 | 50.41 N | 12.01 E |
| Triel-sur-Seine | 261 | 48.59 N | 2.00 E |
| Trient → Trento | 64 | 46.04 N | 11.08 E |
| Triepkendorf | 54 | 53.17 N | 13.20 E |
| Trier | 56 | 49.45 N | 6.38 E |
| Trier □[5] | 56 | 50.00 N | 6.40 E |
| Triesen | 58 | 47.06 N | 9.31 E |
| Trieste (Triest) (Trst) | 64 | 45.40 N | 13.46 E |
| Trieste □[4] | 64 | 45.40 N | 13.50 E |
| Trieste, Gulf of c | 64 | 45.40 N | 13.35 E |
| Triesting ≃ | 61 | 48.05 N | 16.24 E |
| Trieux | 56 | 49.20 N | 5.56 E |
| Triftern | 60 | 48.24 N | 13.01 E |
| Trigal | 248 | 18.17 S | 64.08 W |
| Triggiano | 68 | 41.04 N | 16.55 E |
| Triglav ∧ | 64 | 46.23 N | 13.50 E |
| Triglitz | 54 | 53.12 N | 12.05 E |
| Trigna, Pizzo ∧ | 70 | 37.58 N | 13.34 E |
| Trigno ≃ | 66 | 42.04 N | 14.48 E |
| Trigueros | 34 | 37.23 N | 6.50 W |
| Tríkala | 38 | 39.34 N | 21.46 E |
| Trikhonís, Límni ⊜ | 38 | 38.34 N | 21.28 E |
| Trikora, Puncak (Wilhelmina Peak) ∧ | 164 | 4.15 S | 138.45 E |
| Tri-Lakes | 216 | 41.14 N | 85.26 W |
| Trilbardou | 261 | 48.57 N | 2.48 E |
| Trilby | 220 | 28.27 N | 82.11 W |
| Trillick | 48 | 54.27 N | 7.30 W |
| Trilport | 50 | 48.57 N | 2.57 E |
| Trim | 48 | 53.34 N | 6.47 W |
| Triman | 120 | 29.38 N | 69.05 E |
| Trimbach | 58 | 47.22 N | 7.54 E |
| Trimble □[6] | 218 | 38.37 N | 85.20 W |
| Trim Creek ≃ | 216 | 41.10 N | 87.38 W |
| Trimdon | 44 | 54.42 N | 1.25 W |
| Trimont | 198 | 43.45 N | 94.42 W |
| Trimonte | 256 | 21.43 S | 42.35 W |
| Trin | 58 | 46.50 N | 9.22 E |
| Trinchera Creek ≃ | 200 | 37.19 N | 105.45 W |
| Trincheras, Méx. | 196 | 25.37 N | 101.55 W |
| Trincheras, Méx. | 232 | 30.24 N | 111.32 W |
| Trincomalee | 122 | 8.34 N | 81.14 E |
| Trincomali Channel ʯ | 224 | 48.02 N | 123.30 W |
| Trindade | 255 | 16.40 S | 49.30 W |
| Trindade I | 244 | 20.31 S | 29.19 W |
| Třinec | 30 | 49.41 N | 18.40 E |
| Tring | 42 | 51.48 N | 0.40 W |
| Trinidad, Bol. | 248 | 14.47 S | 64.47 W |
| Trinidad, Col. | 246 | 5.25 N | 71.40 W |
| Trinidad, Cuba | 240p | 21.48 N | 79.59 W |
| Trinidad, Hond. | 236 | 14.57 N | 88.45 W |
| Trinidad, Co., U.S. | 198 | 37.10 N | 104.30 W |
| Trinidad, Tx., U.S. | 222 | 32.08 N | 96.05 W |
| Trinidad, Ur. | 252 | 33.32 S | 56.54 W |
| Trinidad I | 241r | 10.30 N | 61.15 W |
| Trinidad ≃ | 234 | 17.49 N | 95.09 W |
| Trinidad, Golfo c | 254 | 49.55 S | 75.25 W |
| Trinidad, Isla I | 252 | 39.08 S | 61.58 W |
| Trinidad and Tobago □[1], N.A. | 230 | 11.00 N | 61.00 W |
| Trinidad and Tobago □[1], N.A. | 241r | 11.00 N | 61.00 W |
| Trinità | 62 | 44.30 N | 7.45 E |
| Trinità, Lago della ⊜ | 70 | 37.43 N | 12.46 E |
| Trinità d'Agultu | 71 | 40.59 N | 8.54 E |
| Trinitapoli | 68 | 41.21 N | 16.05 E |
| Trinité, Havre de la c | 240e | 14.44 N | 60.58 W |
| Trinity, Nf., Can. | 186 | 48.59 N | 53.55 W |
| Trinity, Tx., U.S. | 222 | 30.56 N | 95.22 W |
| Trinity □[6] | 222 | 31.07 N | 95.10 W |
| Trinity ≃, Ca., U.S. | 204 | 41.11 N | 123.42 W |
| Trinity ≃, Tx., U.S. | 222 | 29.47 N | 94.42 W |
| Trinity, Clear Fork ≃ | 196 | 32.46 N | 97.21 W |
| Trinity, East Fork ≃ | 222 | 32.30 N | 96.30 W |
| Trinity, Elm Fork ≃ | 222 | 32.47 N | 96.54 W |
| Trinity, South Fork ≃ | 204 | 40.54 N | 123.35 W |
| Trinity, West Fork ≃ | 196 | 32.48 N | 96.51 W |
| Trinity Bay c, Nf., Can. | 186 | 48.00 N | 53.40 W |
| Trinity Bay c, Tx., U.S. | 222 | 29.40 N | 94.45 W |
| Trinity Islands II | 180 | 56.33 N | 154.25 W |
| Trinity Mountain ∧ | 202 | 43.36 N | 115.26 W |
| Trinity Mountains ⋏ | 204 | 41.00 N | 122.30 W |
| Trinity Park ♠ | 275b | 43.39 N | 79.25 W |
| Trinity Peak ∧ | 204 | 40.14 N | 118.45 W |
| Trinity Site ⊥ | 200 | 33.41 N | 106.28 W |
| Trinkat Island I | 110 | 8.05 N | 93.30 E |
| Trinkitat | 140 | 18.41 N | 37.43 E |
| Trino | 62 | 45.12 N | 8.18 E |
| Trins | 64 | 47.05 N | 11.25 E |
| Trinway | 214 | 40.08 N | 82.00 W |
| Triolet | 157c | 20.03 S | 57.32 E |
| Triolo ≃ | 66 | 41.40 N | 15.34 E |
| Trion | 192 | 34.32 N | 85.18 W |
| Trionto ≃ | 68 | 39.37 N | 16.45 E |
| Trionto, Capo > | 68 | 39.37 N | 16.45 E |
| Triora | 62 | 43.59 N | 7.46 E |
| Tripa ≃ | 114 | 3.53 N | 96.23 E |
| Tripi | 70 | 38.03 N | 15.06 E |
| Triplett Creek ≃ | 218 | 38.10 N | 83.27 W |
| Triplett Creek, North Fork ≃ | 218 | 38.10 N | 83.31 W |
| Tripoli → Ṭarābulus, Lībiyā | 146 | 32.54 N | 13.11 E |
| Tripoli → Ṭarābulus, Lubnān | 130 | 34.26 N | 35.51 E |
| Tripoli, Ia., U.S. | 190 | 42.48 N | 92.15 W |
| Trípolis, Ellás | 38 | 37.31 N | 22.21 E |
| Tripolis → Ṭarābulus, Lībiyā | 146 | 32.54 N | 13.11 E |
| Tripolis ⊥ | 130 | 37.58 N | 28.59 E |
| Tripolitania → Ṭarābulus □[9] | 146 | 31.00 N | 15.00 E |
| Triponzo | 66 | 42.50 N | 12.56 E |
| Tripp | 198 | 43.13 N | 97.57 W |
| Trippstadt | 56 | 49.22 N | 7.46 E |
| Trips Subdivision | 281 | 42.34 N | 83.25 W |
| Triptis | 54 | 50.44 N | 11.52 E |
| Tripura □[3] | 120 | 24.00 N | 92.00 E |

| | | | |
|---|---|---|---|
| Triquet, Lac ⊜ | 186 | 50.42 N | 59.47 W |
| Trisanna ≃ | 58 | 47.07 N | 10.30 E |
| Tristan da Cunha Group II | 10 | 37.15 S | 12.30 W |
| Tristan Island I | 10 | 37.05 S | 12.17 W |
| Tristán Suárez | 258 | 34.53 S | 58.34 W |
| Tristao, Îles II | 150 | 10.53 N | 14.58 W |
| Tristate Village | 278 | 41.44 N | 87.57 W |
| Triste, Golfo c | 246 | 10.40 N | 68.10 W |
| Triśuli Gaṅggā ≃ | 124 | 27.49 N | [illegible]4.47 E |
| Tri Ton | 110 | 10.25 N | 1[illegible]5.00 E |
| Tritriva | 157b | 22.46 S | [illegible]6.07 E |
| Trittau | 52 | 53.37 N | [illegible]0.25 E |
| Trittenheim | 56 | 49.49 N | 6.54 E |
| Triuggio | 266b | 45.40 N | 9.16 E |
| Triumph | 194 | 29.20 N | [illegible]9.28 W |
| Triunfo, Igarapé ≃ | 250 | 6.22 S | [illegible]2.25 W |
| Trivandrum | 122 | 8.29 N | [illegible].55 E |
| Trivento | 66 | 41.47 N | [illegible].33 E |
| Trivero | 62 | 45.40 N | [illegible].10 E |
| Trivigno | 68 | 40.35 N | [illegible].59 E |
| Trnava | 30 | 48.23 N | 1[illegible].35 E |
| Trnovo → Veliko Târnovo | 38 | 43.04 N | 2[illegible].39 E |
| Tr'ochgolovyj Golec, gora ∧ | 88 | 53.22 N | 10[illegible].03 E |
| Tr'ochsv'atskoje | 82 | 56.29 N | 3[illegible].03 E |
| Trochtelfingen | 58 | 48.18 N | [illegible].14 E |
| Trochu | 182 | 51.50 N | 11[illegible].13 W |
| Troense | 41 | 55.02 N | 1[illegible].39 E |
| Trofa, Arroyo de ≃ | 266a | 40.30 N | [illegible].45 W |
| Trofaiach | 61 | 47.25 N | 1[illegible].00 E |
| Trofarello | 62 | 44.59 N | [illegible].44 E |
| Trögd >[1] | 40 | 59.31 N | 1[illegible].15 E |
| Trogen | 58 | 47.24 N | [illegible].28 E |
| Trogir | 36 | 43.31 N | 1[illegible].15 E |
| Troglav ∧ | 36 | 43.57 N | 1[illegible].36 E |
| Tröglitz | 54 | 51.04 N | 12[illegible]1 E |
| Troia | 68 | 41.22 N | 15[illegible]8 E |
| Troica | 76 | 54.24 N | 40[illegible]4 E |
| Troice-Lykovo ◆[8] | 265b | 55.47 N | 37[illegible]4 E |
| Troick, Ross. | 86 | 54.06 N | 61[illegible]5 E |
| Troick, Ross. | 88 | 57.25 N | 94[illegible]0 E |
| Troickaja | 78 | 45.08 N | 38[illegible]7 E |
| Troickij, Ross. | 80 | 50.14 N | 43[illegible]3 E |
| Troickij, Ross. | 80 | 50.14 N | 43[illegible]5 E |
| Troickij, Ross. | 86 | 50.41 N | 54.[illegible]8 E |
| Troickij, Ross. | 86 | 57.03 N | 63.[illegible]3 E |
| Troickij, Ross. | 88 | 54.36 N | 113.[illegible]9 E |
| Troickije Rosl'ai | 80 | 53.21 N | 41.[illegible]4 E |
| Troickij Sungur | 80 | 53.17 N | 47.[illegible] E |
| Troickij Zavod | 88 | 53.27 N | 102.[illegible] E |
| Troickoje, Ross. | 78 | 51.17 N | 41.[illegible] E |
| Troickoje, Ross. | 80 | 46.26 N | 44.[illegible] E |
| Troickoje, Ross. | 80 | 53.22 N | 48.[illegible] E |
| Troickoje, Ross. | 80 | 53.06 N | 52.[illegible] E |
| Troickoje, Ross. | 80 | 53.23 N | 52.[illegible] E |
| Troickoje, Ross. | 82 | 55.23 N | 37.[illegible] E |
| Troickoje, Ross. | 82 | 54.52 N | 37.[illegible] E |
| Troickoje, Ross. | 83 | 47.22 N | 38.5[illegible] E |
| Troickoje, Ross. | 86 | 52.19 N | 56.2[illegible] E |
| Troickoje, Ross. | 86 | 59.07 N | 58.2[illegible] E |
| Troickoje, Ross. | 86 | 52.58 N | 84.4[illegible] E |
| Troickoje, Ross. | 89 | 49.27 N | 136.3[illegible] E |
| Troicko-Pečorsk | 24 | 62.44 N | 56.0[illegible] E |
| Troina | 70 | 37.47 N | 14.3[illegible] E |
| Troina ≃ | 70 | 37.49 N | 14.4[illegible] E |
| Troisdorf | 56 | 50.49 N | 7.0[illegible] E |
| Trois Fourches, Cap des > | 148 | 35.26 N | 2.5[illegible] W |
| Trois-Pistoles | 186 | 48.07 N | 69.1[illegible] W |
| Trois Pitons, Morne ∧ | 240d | 15.22 N | 61.2[illegible] W |
| Trois Ponts | 56 | 50.22 N | 5.52 E |
| Trois-Rivières, P.Q., Can. | 206 | 46.21 N | 72.33 W |
| Trois-Rivières, Guad. | 241o | 15.59 N | 61.39 W |
| Trois-Rivières-Ouest | 206 | 46.19 N | 72.35 W |
| Troisvierges | 56 | 50.08 N | 6.00 E |
| Trojan | 38 | 42.51 N | 24.43 E |
| Trojanova Tabla ⊥ | 38 | 44.37 N | 22.20 E |
| Trojebratskij | 86 | 54.28 N | 66.01 E |
| Trojekurovo, Ross. | 76 | 53.00 N | 38.58 E |
| Trojekurovo, Ross. | 76 | 53.25 N | 39.43 E |
| Tr'okhizdenka | 83 | 48.45 N | 38.58 E |
| Troldhede | 41 | 55.59 N | 8.45 E |
| Trolleholm | 41 | 55.54 N | 13.15 E |
| Trollhättan | 26 | 58.16 N | 12.18 [illegible] |
| Trollheimen ∧ | 26 | 62.51 N | 9.05 [illegible] |
| Trombay ◆[8] | 272c | 19.02 N | 72.57 [illegible] |
| Trombetas ≃ | 250 | 1.55 S | 55.35 W |
| Tromelin, Île I | 138 | 15.52 S | 54.25 [illegible] |
| Tromello | 62 | 45.12 N | 8.52 [illegible] |
| Tromper Wiek c | 54 | 54.37 N | 13.24 [illegible] |
| Trompia, Val V | 64 | 45.44 N | 10.12 E |
| Trompsburg | 158 | 30.01 S | 25.46 E |
| Troms □[6] | 24 | 69.15 N | 19.40 E |
| Tromsø | 24 | 69.40 N | 18.58 E |
| Trona | 204 | 35.45 N | 117.22 W |
| Tronador, Monte ∧ | 254 | 41.10 S | 71.54 W |
| Troncoso | 234 | 22.44 N | 102.22 W |
| Trondheim | 26 | 63.25 N | 10.25 E |
| Trondheimsfjorden c[2] | 26 | 63.39 N | 10.49 E |
| Trondheimsleia ʯ | 26 | 63.30 N | 9.00 E |
| Tronto ≃ | 66 | 42.54 N | 13.55 E |
| Tronville-en-Barrois | 56 | 48.43 N | 5.17 E |
| Tronzano Vercellese | 62 | 45.21 N | 8.10 E |
| Troo | 50 | 47.47 N | 0.47 E |
| Troödos | 130 | 34.55 N | 32.53 E |
| Trooilapspan | 158 | 28.40 S | 21.25 E |
| Troon, Eng., U.K. | 42 | 50.12 N | 5.16 W |
| Troon, Scot., U.K. | 46 | 55.32 N | 4.40 W |
| Trooper | 285 | 40.09 N | 75.24 W |
| Troparevo | 82 | 55.23 N | 35.54 E |
| Tropar'ovo ◆[8] | 265b | 55.39 N | 37.29 E |
| Tropas, Rio das ≃ | 250 | 6.07 S | 57.28 W |
| Tropea | 68 | 38.41 N | 15.54 E |
| Trophy Mountain ∧ | 182 | 51.47 N | 119.48 W |
| Tropic | 200 | 37.37 N | 112.04 W |
| Tropojë | 38 | 42.24 N | 20.10 E |
| Troppau → Opava | 30 | 49.56 N | 17.54 E |
| Trosa | 40 | 58.54 N | 17.33 E |
| Troškovo | 80 | 57.19 N | 46.05 E |
| Troškūnai | 76 | 55.36 N | 24.51 E |
| Trosna | 76 | 52.26 N | 35.46 E |
| Trossingen | 58 | 48.04 N | 8.38 E |
| Trostan ∧ | 48 | 55.03 N | 6.09 W |
| Tröstau | 60 | 50.01 N | 11.57 E |
| Trostberg | 60 | 48.01 N | 12.32 E |
| Trostenskoje, ozero ⊜ | 82 | 55.52 N | 36.29 E |
| Trostyanets', Ukr. | 78 | 50.28 N | 34.59 E |
| Trostyanets', Ukr. | 78 | 48.31 N | 29.12 E |
| Trottiscliffe | 260 | 51.19 N | 0.21 E |
| Trotuș ≃ | 38 | 46.03 N | 27.14 E |
| Trotwood | 218 | 39.47 N | 84.18 W |
| Troublesome Creek ≃ | 219 | 39.54 N | 91.37 W |
| Troubridge Point > | 168b | 35.11 S | 137.41 E |
| Trou-du-Nord | 238 | 19.38 N | 72.01 W |
| Troup | 222 | 32.08 N | 95.07 W |
| Troup Head > | 46 | 57.41 N | 2.18 W |
| Troupsburg | 210 | 42.03 N | 77.33 W |
| Trout | 194 | 31.41 N | 92.10 W |
| Trout ≃, N.T., Can. | 176 | 61.19 N | 119.51 W |
| Trout ≃, N.A. | 206 | 45.05 N | 74.10 W |
| Trout Brook ≃, Ma., U.S. | 283 | 42.16 N | 71.18 W |
| Trout Brook ≃, Ma., U.S. | 283 | 42.39 N | 71.16 W |
| Trout Creek, Mi., U.S. | 190 | 46.28 N | 89.00 W |
| Trout Creek, Mt., U.S. | 182 | 47.50 N | 115.35 W |
| Trout Creek, N.Y., U.S. | 210 | 42.12 N | 75.17 W |
| Trout Creek ≃, Az., U.S. | 200 | 34.56 N | 113.36 W |


| | | | | |
|---|---|---|---|---|
| ≃ River | Fluß | Río | Rivière | Rio |
| ≊ Canal | Kanal | Canal | Canal | Canal |
| ʟ Waterfall, Rapids | Wasserfall, Stromschnellen | Cascada, Rápidos | Chute d'eau, Rapides | Cascata, Rápidos |
| ʯ Strait | Meeresstraße | Estrecho | Détroit | Estreito |
| c Bay, Gulf | Bucht, Golf | Bahía, Golfo | Baie, Golfe | Baía, Golfo |
| ⊜ Lake, Lakes | See, Seen | Lago, Lagos | Lac, Lacs | Lago, Lagos |
| ⁑ Swamp | Sumpf | Pantano | Marais | Pântano |
| ⍓ Ice Features, Glacier | Eis- und Gletscherformen | Accidentes Glaciales | Formes glaciaires | Acidentes glaciares |
| ⏚ Other Hydrographic Features | Andere Hydrographische Objekte | Otros Elementos Hidrográficos | Autres données hydrographiques | Outros acidentes hidrográficos |

| | | | | |
|---|---|---|---|---|
| ⊹ Submarine Features | Untermeerische Objekte | Accidentes Submarinos | Formes de relief sous-marin | Acidentes submarinos |
| □ Political Unit | Politische Einheit | Unidad Politica | Entité politique | Unidade política |
| ʊ Cultural Institution | Kulturelle Institution | Institución Cultural | Institution culturelle | Instituição cultural |
| ⊥ Historical Site | Historische Stätte | Sitio Histórico | Site historique | Sitio histórico |
| ♠ Recreational Site | Erholungs- und Ferienort | Sitio de Recreo | Centre de loisirs | Area de Lazer |
| ⊠ Airport | Flughafen | Aeropuerto | Aéroport | Aeroporto |
| ■ Military Installation | Militäranlage | Instalación Militar | Installation militaire | Instalação militar |
| ◆ Miscellaneous | Verschiedenes | Misceláneo | Divers | Diversos |

ENGLISH — Name / Page / Lat.°′ / Long.°′

DEUTSCH — Name / Seite / Breite°′ / Länge°′ E = Ost


| Name | Page | Lat.°′ | Long.°′ |
|---|---|---|---|
| Trout Creek ≐, Or., U.S. | 202 | 44.48 N | 121.03 W |
| Trout Creek ≐, Or., U.S. | 202 | 42.23 N | 118.36 W |
| Trout Creek ≐, Pa., U.S. | 285 | 40.07 N | 75.24 W |
| Trout Creek ≐, Wa., U.S. | 224 | 46.02 N | 121.12 W |
| Trout Creek Pass )( | 200 | 38.54 N | 105.58 W |
| Troutdale | 224 | 45.32 N | 122.23 W |
| Trout Lake | 224 | 45.59 N | 121.31 W |
| Trout Lake ⊜, B.C., Can. | 182 | 50.35 N | 117.26 W |
| Trout Lake ⊜, N.T., Can. | 176 | 60.35 N | 121.10 W |
| Trout Lake ⊜, On., Can. | 184 | 51.13 N | 93.20 W |
| Trout Lake ⊜, On., Can. | 190 | 46.18 N | 79.20 W |
| Trout Lake ⊜, On., Can. | 190 | 46.13 N | 80.35 W |
| Trout Lake Creek ≐ | 224 | 46.00 N | 121.30 W |
| Trout Peak ∧ | 202 | 44.36 N | 109.32 W |
| Trout River | 186 | 49.29 N | 58.08 W |
| Trout Run | 210 | 41.23 N | 77.03 W |
| Troutville, Pa., U.S. | 214 | 41.02 N | 78.47 W |
| Troutville, Va., U.S. | 192 | 37.25 N | 79.52 W |
| Trouville-sur-Mer | 50 | 49.22 N | 0.05 E |
| Trowbridge | 42 | 51.20 N | 2.13 W |
| Troxelville | 210 | 40.48 N | 77.12 W |
| Troy, Al., U.S. | 194 | 31.48 N | 85.58 W |
| Troy, Id., U.S. | 202 | 46.44 N | 116.46 W |
| Troy, Il., U.S. | 219 | 38.43 N | 89.52 W |
| Troy, In., U.S. | 194 | 37.59 N | 86.47 W |
| Troy, Ks., U.S. | 198 | 39.46 N | 95.05 W |
| Troy, Mi., U.S. | 214 | 42.34 N | 83.09 W |
| Troy, Mo., U.S. | 219 | 38.58 N | 90.58 W |
| Troy, Mt., U.S. | 202 | 48.27 N | 115.53 W |
| Troy, N.H., U.S. | 207 | 42.49 N | 72.10 W |
| Troy, N.Y., U.S. | 210 | 42.43 N | 73.41 W |
| Troy, N.C., U.S. | 192 | 35.21 N | 79.53 W |
| Troy, Oh., U.S. | 218 | 40.02 N | 84.12 W |
| Troy, Pa., U.S. | 210 | 41.47 N | 76.47 W |
| Troy, Tn., U.S. | 194 | 36.20 N | 89.09 W |
| Troy, Tx., U.S. | 222 | 31.12 N | 97.18 W |
| Troy → Truva ⊥ | 130 | 39.57 N | 26.15 E |
| Troyaniv | 78 | 50.07 N | 28.31 E |
| Troyanivka | 78 | 51.20 N | 25.17 E |
| Troy Brook ≐ | 276 | 40.50 N | 74.22 W |
| Troyes | 50 | 48.18 N | 4.05 E |
| Troy Grove | 216 | 41.28 N | 89.05 W |
| Troy Hills | 210 | 40.51 N | 74.23 W |
| Troyits'ke, Ukr. | 78 | 49.55 N | 38.19 E |
| Troyits'ke, Ukr. | 78 | 47.38 N | 30.19 E |
| Troyits'ke, Ukr. | 83 | 48.32 N | 38.23 E |
| Troyits'ko-Khartsyz'k | 83 | 47.58 N | 38.16 E |
| Troy Lake ⊜ | 204 | 34.49 N | 116.33 W |
| Troy Meadows ≡ | 276 | 40.50 N | 74.22 W |
| Troy Peak ∧ | 204 | 38.19 N | 115.30 W |
| Trpanj | 36 | 43.00 N | 17.17 E |
| Trst → Trieste | 64 | 45.40 N | 13.46 E |
| Trstená | 30 | 49.22 N | 19.37 E |
| Trstenik | 38 | 43.37 N | 21.00 E |
| Truax | 184 | 49.55 N | 104.58 W |
| Trubč'ovsk | 76 | 52.37 N | 33.44 E |
| Trubetčino | 76 | 52.53 N | 39.33 E |
| Trubino, Ross. | 82 | 54.58 N | 36.42 E |
| Trubino, Ross. | 82 | 55.59 N | 38.08 E |
| Trub'ož ≐ | 82 | 56.44 N | 38.51 E |
| Truchas | 200 | 36.02 N | 105.48 W |
| Truchas Peak ∧ | 200 | 35.58 N | 105.39 W |
| Truchtersheim | 58 | 48.40 N | 7.36 E |
| Trucial States → United Arab Emirates □[1] | 128 | 24.00 N | 54.00 E |
| Truckee | 226 | 39.19 N | 120.10 W |
| Truckee ≐ | 204 | 39.51 N | 119.24 W |
| Trucksville | 210 | 41.18 N | 75.56 W |
| Trud | 76 | 57.37 N | 33.58 E |
| Trudfront | 80 | 45.56 N | 47.41 E |
| Trudnovo | 86 | 56.39 N | 91.30 E |
| Trudovoj | 80 | 51.42 N | 52.43 E |
| Trues Creek ≐ | 276 | 40.41 N | 73.17 W |
| Truganina | 274b | 37.49 S | 144.43 E |
| Truim ≐ | 46 | 57.02 N | 4.10 W |
| Truite, Lac à la ⊜ | 190 | 47.16 N | 78.17 W |
| Trujillo, Col. | 246 | 4.10 N | 76.19 W |
| Trujillo, Esp. | 34 | 39.28 N | 5.53 W |
| Trujillo, Hond. | 236 | 15.55 N | 86.00 W |
| Trujillo, Méx. | 234 | 23.10 N | 103.13 W |
| Trujillo, Perú | 248 | 8.07 S | 79.02 W |
| Trujillo, Ven. | 246 | 9.22 N | 70.26 W |
| Trujillo □[3] | 246 | 9.25 N | 70.30 W |
| Trujillo Alto | 240m | 18.22 N | 66.01 W |
| Trujillo Creek ≐ | 196 | 35.28 N | 102.52 W |
| Truk Islands → Chuuk II | 175c | 7.25 N | 151.47 E |
| Truk Lagoon ⊂ | 175c | 7.25 N | 151.45 E |
| Trull Brook ≐ | 283 | 42.39 N | 71.15 W |
| Truman | 198 | 43.49 N | 94.26 W |
| Trumann | 194 | 35.40 N | 90.30 W |
| Trumansburg | 210 | 42.32 N | 76.39 W |
| Trumbauersville | 208 | 40.25 N | 75.23 W |
| Trumbull | 207 | 41.14 N | 73.12 W |
| Trumbull □[6] | 214 | 41.14 N | 80.52 W |
| Trumbull, Mount ∧ | 200 | 36.25 N | 113.10 W |
| Trumon | 114 | 2.49 N | 97.38 E |
| Trun, Fr. | 50 | 48.51 N | 0.02 E |
| Trun, Schw. | 58 | 46.45 N | 8.58 E |
| Trundle | 166 | 32.55 S | 147.43 E |
| Trung Luong | 110 | 13.57 N | 109.15 E |
| Trung Phan □[9] | 110 | 15.00 N | 108.00 E |
| Trunovskoje | 80 | 45.29 N | 42.08 E |
| Truro, Austl. | 168b | 34.25 S | 139.07 E |
| Truro, N.S., Can. | 186 | 45.22 N | 63.16 W |
| Truro, Eng., U.K. | 42 | 50.16 N | 5.03 W |
| Truro, Ma., U.S. | 207 | 41.59 N | 70.03 W |
| Trusan ≐ | 112 | 4.58 N | 115.11 E |
| Truscott | 196 | 33.45 N | 99.49 W |
| Trușeni | 38 | 47.04 N | 28.41 E |
| Trușești | 38 | 47.46 N | 27.01 E |
| Trusetal | 54 | 50.47 N | 10.25 E |
| Truskavets' | 78 | 49.16 N | 23.33 E |
| Truslejka | 80 | 53.54 N | 46.24 E |
| Trus Madi, Gunong ∧ | 112 | 5.33 N | 116.31 E |
| Truth or Consequences (Hot Springs) | 200 | 33.07 N | 107.15 W |
| Trutnov | 30 | 50.34 N | 15.55 E |
| Truva (Troy) ⊥ | 130 | 39.57 N | 26.15 E |
| Truxall | 279b | 40.33 N | 79.33 W |
| Truxton, Mo., U.S. | 219 | 39.00 N | 91.14 W |
| Truxton, N.Y., U.S. | 210 | 42.43 N | 76.02 W |
| Truxton Wash V | 200 | 35.38 N | 114.04 W |
| Truyère ≐ | 32 | 44.39 N | 2.34 E |
| Trwyn Cilan ≻ | 42 | 52.46 N | 4.30 W |
| Tryduby | 78 | 48.06 N | 30.24 E |
| Trylisy | 78 | 49.59 N | 29.50 E |
| Tryon, Ne., U.S. | 198 | 41.33 N | 100.57 W |
| Tryon, N.C., U.S. | 192 | 35.12 N | 82.14 W |
| Tryonville | 214 | 41.42 N | 79.47 W |
| Trypillya | 78 | 50.07 N | 30.46 E |
| Trysil | 26 | 61.19 N | 12.16 E |
| Trysilelva (Klarälven) ≐ | 26 | 59.23 N | 13.32 E |
| Tryškiai | 76 | 56.04 N | 22.35 E |
| Tryweryn ≐ | 42 | 52.55 N | 3.35 W |
| Trzcianka | 30 | 53.03 N | 16.28 E |
| Trzciel | 30 | 52.23 N | 15.52 E |
| Trzcińsko-Zdrój | 30 | 52.58 N | 14.35 E |
| Trzebiatów | 30 | 54.04 N | 15.14 E |
| Trzebiel | 54 | 51.37 N | 14.50 E |
| Trzebież | 30 | 53.42 N | 14.31 E |
| Trzebinia | 30 | 50.10 N | 19.18 E |
| Trzebnica | 30 | 51.19 N | 17.03 E |
| Trzemeszno | 30 | 52.35 N | 17.50 E |
| Trzęsacz | 54 | 54.05 N | 14.58 E |
| Tržič | 36 | 46.22 N | 14.19 E |
| Tsacha Lake ⊜ | 182 | 53.05 N | 124.40 W |
| Tsala Apopka Lake ⊜ | 220 | 28.52 N | 82.20 W |
| Tsamkong → Zhanjiang | 102 | 21.16 N | 110.28 E |
| Tsandi | 156 | 17.42 S | 14.50 E |
| Tsangano | 154 | 15.08 S | 34.32 E |
| Ts'anghsien → Cangzhou | 98 | 38.19 N | 116.51 E |
| T'sangwu → Wuzhou | 102 | 23.30 N | 111.27 E |
| Ts'aot'un | 100 | 23.59 N | 120.41 E |
| Tsarabaria | 157b | 13.46 S | 49.58 E |
| Tsaramandroso | 157b | 16.22 S | 47.02 E |
| Tsaratanana | 157b | 16.47 S | 47.39 E |
| Tsaratanana, Massif du ⩘ | 157b | 14.00 S | 49.00 E |
| Tsaraxaibis | 158 | 27.25 S | 19.22 E |
| Tsaritsyn → Volgograd | 80 | 48.44 N | 44.25 E |
| Tsarychanka | 78 | 48.57 N | 34.29 E |
| Tsau | 156 | 20.12 S | 22.22 E |
| Tsaukaib | 156 | 26.37 S | 15.31 E |
| Tsavo | 154 | 2.59 S | 38.28 E |
| Tsavo East National Park ♠ | 154 | 2.11 S | 38.25 E |
| Tsavo West National Park ♠ | 154 | 2.55 S | 37.55 E |
| Tsawwassen | 224 | 49.01 N | 123.06 W |
| Tsaydaychuz Peak ∧ | 182 | 53.02 N | 126.35 W |
| Tsayta Lake ⊜ | 182 | 55.25 N | 125.30 W |
| Tschad → Chad □[1] | 146 | 15.00 N | 19.00 E |
| Tschad-See → Chad, Lake ⊜ | 146 | 13.20 N | 14.00 E |
| Tschagguns | 58 | 47.05 N | 9.54 E |
| Tschamut | 58 | 46.40 N | 8.42 E |
| Tschangscha → Changsha | 100 | 28.12 N | 112.58 E |
| Tschangtschun → Changchun | 89 | 43.53 N | 125.19 E |
| Tscheljuskin, Kap → Čel'uskin, mys ≻ | 74 | 77.45 N | 104.20 E |
| Tschengtu → Chengdu | 107 | 30.39 N | 104.04 E |
| Tschenstochau → Częstochowa | 30 | 50.49 N | 19.06 E |
| Tschernitz | 54 | 51.35 N | 14.37 E |
| Tscheschkaja-Bucht → Češskaja guba ⊂ | 24 | 67.30 N | 46.30 E |
| Tschida, Lake ⊜[1] | 198 | 46.36 N | 101.54 W |
| Tschingtau → Qingdao | 98 | 36.06 N | 120.19 E |
| Tschittagong → Chittagong | 120 | 22.20 N | 91.50 E |
| Tschuktschen-Meer → Chukchi Sea ⩒[2] | 16 | 69.00 N | 171.00 W |
| Tschungking → Chongqing | 107 | 29.34 N | 106.35 E |
| Tsebrykove | 78 | 47.09 N | 30.06 E |
| Tsekanyani | 156 | 19.52 S | 26.39 E |
| Tsembeyi | 158 | 31.36 S | 27.03 E |
| Ts'engwen ≐ | 100 | 23.03 N | 120.03 E |
| Tsenke ≐ | 273b | 4.24 S | 15.26 E |
| Tses | 156 | 25.58 S | 18.08 E |
| Tsévié | 150 | 6.25 N | 1.13 E |
| Tshabong | 156 | 26.03 S | 22.29 E |
| Tshabuta | 152 | 7.47 S | 23.16 E |
| Tshane | 156 | 24.05 S | 21.54 E |
| Tshaneni | 158 | 26.00 S | 31.47 E |
| Tshangalele, Lac ⊜[1] | 154 | 10.55 S | 27.03 E |
| Tshangu ≐ | 273b | 4.25 S | 15.23 E |
| Tshela | 152 | 4.59 S | 12.56 E |
| Tshesebe | 156 | 21.51 S | 27.35 E |
| Tshibeke | 154 | 2.44 S | 28.36 E |
| Tshibinda | 154 | 2.19 S | 28.45 E |
| Tshibomba | 152 | 9.02 S | 22.34 E |
| Tshidilamolomo | 156 | 25.50 S | 24.41 E |
| Tshikapa | 152 | 6.25 S | 20.48 E |
| Tshilenge | 152 | 6.15 S | 23.46 E |
| Tshimbulu | 152 | 6.29 S | 22.51 E |
| Tshindjamba | 152 | 10.54 S | 22.41 E |
| Tshinota | 152 | 7.01 S | 20.57 E |
| Tshinsenda | 154 | 12.18 S | 27.58 E |
| Tshisuku | 152 | 6.26 S | 19.55 E |
| Tshitadi | 152 | 6.45 S | 21.45 E |
| Tshoa | 152 | 5.34 S | 12.41 E |
| Tshofa | 154 | 5.14 S | 25.15 E |
| Tshopo ≐ | 154 | 0.33 N | 25.07 E |
| Tshuapa ≐ | 152 | 0.14 S | 20.42 E |
| Tshukudu | 156 | 22.30 S | 23.22 E |
| Tshumbiri | 152 | 2.39 S | 16.14 E |
| Tshwaane | 156 | 22.29 S | 22.03 E |
| Tsiafajavona ∧ | 157b | 19.21 S | 47.15 E |
| Tsianaloka | 157b | 18.08 S | 44.50 E |
| Tsiémé ≐ | 273b | 4.15 S | 15.18 E |
| Tsiga | 152 | 1.32 S | 10.11 E |
| Tsihombe | 157b | 25.18 S | 45.29 E |
| Tsilmamo | 144 | 6.01 N | 35.17 E |
| Tsimanampetsotsa, Lac ⊜ | 157b | 24.08 S | 43.46 E |
| Tsimilofo | 157b | 24.59 S | 45.10 E |
| Tsimpsean Indian Reserve ◆[4] | 182 | 54.30 N | 130.22 W |
| Tsinan → Jinan | 98 | 36.40 N | 116.57 E |
| Tsineng | 158 | 27.06 S | 23.04 E |
| Tsinghai → Qinghai □[4] | 90 | 36.00 N | 96.00 E |
| Tsingkiang → Qingjiang | 100 | 33.35 N | 119.02 E |
| Tsingtao → Qingdao | 98 | 36.06 N | 120.19 E |
| Tsing Yi I | 271d | 22.21 N | 114.05 E |
| Tsingyuan → Baoding | 105 | 38.52 N | 115.29 E |
| Tsining → Jining | 98 | 35.25 N | 116.36 E |
| Tsinjoarivo | 157b | 19.37 S | 47.40 E |
| Tsinjomitondraka | 157b | 15.36 S | 47.08 E |
| Tsinling Shan → Qin Ling ⩘ | 102 | 34.00 N | 108.00 E |
| Tsintsabis | 156 | 18.45 S | 17.51 E |
| Tsiribihina ≐ | 157b | 19.42 S | 44.31 E |
| Tsiroanomandidy | 157b | 18.46 S | 46.02 E |
| Tsitondroina | 157b | 21.19 S | 46.00 E |
| Tsitsihar → Qiqihar | 89 | 47.19 N | 123.55 E |
| Tsitsikama Forest and Coastal National Park ♠ | 158 | 33.57 S | 23.53 E |
| Tsitsutl Peak ∧ | 182 | 52.44 N | 125.47 W |
| Tsivory | 157b | 24.04 S | 46.05 E |
| Tskhinvali → Cchinvali | 84 | 42.13 N | 43.56 E |
| Tsna → Cna ≐ | 80 | 54.32 N | 42.05 E |
| Tsobis | 156 | 19.27 S | 17.30 E |
| Tsolo | 158 | 31.18 S | 28.37 E |
| Tsomo | 158 | 32.00 S | 27.42 E |
| Tsomo ≐ | 158 | 32.25 S | 27.50 E |
| Tsoying | 100 | 22.41 N | 120.17 E |
| Tsu | 94 | 34.43 N | 136.31 E |
| Tsubakuro-dake ∧ | 94 | 36.24 N | 137.42 E |
| Tsubame | 92 | 37.39 N | 138.56 E |
| Tsubata | 94 | 36.40 N | 136.44 E |
| Tsuboro-suigenchi ⊜[1] | 270 | 34.24 N | 135.54 E |
| Tsuchiura | 94 | 36.05 N | 140.12 E |
| Tsuchiyama | 94 | 34.56 N | 136.17 E |
| Tsuda, Nihon | 96 | 34.17 N | 134.15 E |
| Tsuda, Nihon | 270 | 34.49 N | 135.43 E |
| Tsuen Wan (Quanwan) | 271d | 22.22 N | 114.07 E |
| Tsugaru-hantō ≻[1] | 92 | 41.00 N | 140.30 E |
| Tsugaru-heiya ≚ | 92 | 40.49 N | 140.27 E |
| Tsugaru-kaikyō ʊ | 92a | 41.35 N | 141.00 E |
| Tsuge | 94 | 34.37 N | 135.57 E |
| Tsugu | 94 | 35.10 N | 137.37 E |
| Tsuha | 174m | 26.14 N | 127.47 E |
| Tsuiki | 96 | 33.40 N | 131.03 E |
| Tsujidō | 268 | 35.20 N | 139.27 E |
| Tsukahara | 268 | 35.18 N | 139.58 E |
| Tsukechi | 94 | 35.38 N | 137.26 E |
| Tsuken-jima I | 174m | 26.15 N | 127.57 E |
| Tsukigase | 94 | 34.42 N | 136.02 E |
| Tsukinowa-kofun ⊥ | 96 | 34.55 N | 134.11 E |
| Tsukiyono | 94 | 36.41 N | 138.59 E |
| Tsukuba | 94 | 36.13 N | 140.06 E |
| Tsukuba-san ∧ | 94 | 36.13 N | 140.06 E |
| Tsukude | 94 | 34.59 N | 137.25 E |
| Tsukui | 94 | 35.35 N | 139.16 E |
| Tsukumi | 96 | 33.04 N | 131.52 E |
| Tsukumono ◆[8] | 270 | 34.50 N | 135.11 E |
| Tsukuryne | 83 | 48.05 N | 37.18 E |
| Tsukushi-heiya ≚ | 96 | 33.20 N | 130.30 E |
| Tsukushi-sanchi ⩘ | 92 | 33.30 N | 130.30 E |
| Tsumagoi | 94 | 36.31 N | 138.32 E |
| Tsuman' | 78 | 50.49 N | 25.53 E |
| Tsumeb | 156 | 19.13 S | 17.42 E |
| Tsumeki-zaki ≻ | 94 | 34.39 N | 138.59 E |
| Tsumis Park | 156 | 23.43 S | 17.28 E |
| Tsumkwe | 156 | 19.41 S | 20.30 E |
| Tsuna | 96 | 34.26 N | 134.54 E |
| Tsunan | 94 | 37.01 N | 138.39 E |
| Tsunashima ◆[8] | 268 | 35.32 N | 139.38 E |
| Tsunekami-misaki ≻ | 94 | 35.38 N | 135.49 E |
| Tsuni → Zunyi | 102 | 27.39 N | 106.57 E |
| Tsuno-shima I | 96 | 34.21 N | 130.51 E |
| Tsuru | 94 | 35.33 N | 138.55 E |
| Tsuruga | 94 | 35.39 N | 136.04 E |
| Tsurugaoka-hachimangu Shrine ⚑[1] | 268 | 35.19 N | 139.33 E |
| Tsurugashima | 268 | 35.56 N | 139.24 E |
| Tsuruga-wan ⊂ | 94 | 35.45 N | 136.04 E |
| Tsurugi | 94 | 36.27 N | 136.38 E |
| Tsurugi-dake ∧ | 94 | 36.37 N | 137.37 E |
| Tsurugi-san ∧ | 96 | 33.51 N | 134.06 E |
| Tsurugi-san-kokutei-kōen ♠ | 96 | 33.50 N | 134.06 E |
| Tsuruhara | 270 | 34.26 N | 135.20 E |
| Tsuruma | 268 | 35.51 N | 139.33 E |
| Tsurumi ◆[8] | 268 | 35.30 N | 139.41 E |
| Tsurumi ≐ | 94 | 35.29 N | 139.41 E |
| Tsurumi-dake ∧ | 96 | 33.17 N | 131.26 E |
| Tsuruoka | 92 | 38.44 N | 139.50 E |
| Tsushima, Nihon | 94 | 35.10 N | 136.43 E |
| Tsushima, Nihon | 96 | 33.05 N | 132.30 E |
| Tsushima II | 92 | 34.30 N | 129.22 E |
| Tsushima-kaikyō (Eastern Channel) ʊ | 92 | 34.00 N | 129.00 E |
| Tsuwano | 96 | 34.28 N | 131.46 E |
| Tsuyama | 96 | 35.03 N | 134.00 E |
| Tsuyazaki | 96 | 33.47 N | 130.28 E |
| Tsvitkove | 78 | 49.11 N | 31.33 E |
| Tsvitne | 78 | 48.57 N | 32.29 E |
| Tsybuliv | 78 | 49.06 N | 29.50 E |
| Tsyurupyns'k | 78 | 46.37 N | 32.43 E |
| Ttruchchendūr | 122 | 8.29 N | 78.07 E |
| Tu → Tsu | 94 | 34.43 N | 136.31 E |
| Tua | 152 | 3.38 S | 16.36 E |
| Tua ≐ | 34 | 41.13 N | 7.26 W |
| Tua, Tanjung ≻ | 115a | 5.54 S | 105.44 E |
| Tua Chau | 110 | 21.55 N | 103.21 E |
| Tuakau | 172 | 37.16 S | 174.57 E |
| Tual | 164 | 5.40 S | 132.45 E |
| Tualatin | 224 | 45.23 N | 122.45 W |
| Tualatin ≐ | 224 | 45.20 N | 122.39 W |
| Tualatin Mountains ⩘ | 224 | 45.40 N | 122.50 W |
| Tuam | 48 | 53.31 N | 8.50 W |
| Tuamarina | 172 | 41.26 S | 173.57 E |
| Tuamotu, Îles (Tuamotu Archipelago) II | 14 | 19.00 S | 142.00 W |
| Tuamotu Ridge ✦[3] | 14 | 17.00 S | 145.00 W |
| Tuan, Tanjong ≻ | 114 | 2.23 N | 101.52 E |
| Tuanan | 112 | 2.07 S | 114.24 E |
| Tuanfeng | 100 | 30.38 N | 114.51 E |
| Tuan Giao | 110 | 21.35 N | 103.25 E |
| Tuangku, Pulau I | 114 | 2.10 N | 97.16 E |
| Tuanlin | 98 | 39.35 N | 119.15 E |
| Tuannian | 107 | 29.55 N | 106.03 E |
| Tuanpi | 100 | 30.44 N | 115.13 E |
| Tuanshan | 98 | 40.02 N | 123.34 E |
| Tuanwang | 98 | 36.45 N | 120.38 E |
| Tuanxi | 102 | 27.28 N | 107.08 E |
| Tuapa | 174v | 18.57 S | 169.54 W |
| Tuapeka Mouth | 172 | 46.01 S | 169.31 E |
| Tuapse | 84 | 44.07 N | 39.05 E |
| Tuaran | 112 | 6.11 N | 116.14 E |
| Tuas | 114 | 1.19 N | 103.38 E |
| Tuasivi | 175a | 13.40 S | 172.07 W |
| Tuasivi, Cape ≻ | 175a | 13.40 S | 172.07 W |
| Tuatapere | 172 | 46.08 S | 167.41 E |
| Tuath, Loch ʊ | 46 | 56.30 N | 6.12 W |
| Tuba | 88 | 57.24 N | 102.48 E |
| Tuba ≐ | 86 | 53.57 N | 91.31 E |
| Tubac | 200 | 31.36 N | 111.02 W |
| Tuba City | 200 | 36.08 N | 111.14 W |
| T'ub'ak-Čekurča | 80 | 56.05 N | 49.56 E |
| Tubalan Head ≻ | 116 | 6.30 N | 125.35 E |
| Tuban | 115a | 6.54 S | 112.03 E |
| Tubarão | 252 | 28.30 S | 49.01 W |
| Ṭūbās | 132 | 32.19 N | 35.22 E |
| Tubau | 112 | 3.08 N | 113.42 E |
| Tubbataha Reefs ✦[2] | 116 | 8.51 N | 119.56 E |
| Tubbergen | 52 | 52.25 N | 6.46 E |
| Tubbs Island I | 282 | 38.08 N | 122.26 W |
| Ṭubhār | 142 | 29.19 N | 30.42 E |
| Tubig ≐ | 116 | 11.54 N | 125.25 E |
| Tubigan Island I | 116 | 6.26 N | 120.47 E |
| Tubingantan Point ≻ | 116 | 5.54 N | 120.55 E |
| Tübingen | 58 | 48.31 N | 9.02 E |
| Tübingen □[5] | 58 | 48.10 N | 9.30 E |
| Tubinskij | 86 | 52.53 N | 58.13 E |
| Tubize | 50 | 50.41 N | 4.12 E |
| T'ub-Karagan, mys ≻ | 84 | 44.39 N | 50.18 E |
| T'ub-Karagan, poluostrov ≻[1] | 84 | 44.30 N | 50.30 E |
| Tubli | 116 | 13.56 N | 124.09 E |
| Tubod | 116 | 8.03 N | 123.48 E |
| Tubre | 64 | 46.39 N | 10.27 E |
| Ṭubruq (Tobruk) | 146 | 32.05 N | 23.59 E |
| Tubuai I | 14 | 23.18 S | 149.30 W |
| Tuburan, Pil. | 116 | 10.44 N | 123.49 W |
| Tuburan, Pil. | 116 | 6.39 N | 122.16 E |
| Tubusereia | 164 | 9.33 S | 147.18 E |
| Tubutama | 200 | 30.53 N | 111.29 W |
| Tucacas | 246 | 10.48 N | 68.19 W |
| Tucacas, Punta ≻ | 246 | 10.50 N | 68.14 W |
| Tucalota Creek ≐ | 228 | 33.32 N | 117.10 W |
| Tucannon ≐ | 202 | 46.33 N | 118.11 W |
| Tucano | 250 | 10.58 S | 38.48 W |
| Tucava ≐ | 248 | 18.37 S | 58.59 W |
| T'uch'ang | 100 | 24.35 N | 121.29 E |
| Tucheim | 54 | 52.17 N | 12.11 E |
| Tüchen | 54 | 53.04 N | 12.05 E |
| T'uch'eng, T'aiwan | 269d | 24.59 N | 121.26 E |
| Tucheng, Zhg. | 98 | 38.53 N | 121.15 E |
| Tucheng, Zhg. | 102 | 28.12 N | 105.58 E |
| Tuchengzi, Zhg. | 98 | 41.20 N | 116.29 E |
| Tuchengzi, Zhg. | 98 | 40.29 N | 124.24 E |
| Tuchengzi, Zhg. | 104 | 42.27 N | 122.44 E |
| Tuchengzicun | 104 | 41.52 N | 120.41 E |
| Tuchengziwuhao | 98 | 40.56 N | 113.58 E |
| Tuchlovice | 54 | 50.06 N | 14.00 E |
| Tuchola | 30 | 53.35 N | 17.50 E |
| Tuchów | 30 | 49.54 N | 21.03 E |
| T'uchtet | 86 | 56.32 N | 89.19 E |
| Tuckahoe, N.J., U.S. | 208 | 39.17 N | 74.45 W |
| Tuckahoe, N.Y., U.S. | 276 | 40.57 N | 73.49 W |
| Tuckahoe ≐ | 208 | 39.17 N | 74.39 W |
| Tuckahoe Creek ≐ | 208 | 38.49 N | 75.53 W |
| Tuckanarra | 162 | 27.07 S | 118.05 E |
| Tucker Heights | 210 | 42.55 N | 73.55 W |
| Tuckerman | 194 | 35.43 N | 91.11 W |
| Tuckernuck Island I | 207 | 41.18 N | 70.15 W |
| Tuckerton, N.J., U.S. | 208 | 39.36 N | 74.20 W |
| Tuckerton, Pa., U.S. | 208 | 40.25 N | 75.57 W |
| Tuckfield, Mount ∧ | 162 | 18.44 S | 124.54 E |
| Tučkovo | 82 | 55.36 N | 36.28 E |
| Tucson | 200 | 32.13 N | 110.55 W |
| Tucumã ≐[1] | 246 | 3.58 S | 66.26 W |
| Tucumán → San Miguel de Tucumán | 252 | 26.49 S | 65.13 W |
| Tucumán □[4] | 252 | 27.00 S | 65.30 W |
| Tucumcari | 196 | 35.10 N | 103.43 W |
| Tucumcari Mountain ∧ | 196 | 35.08 N | 103.42 W |
| Tucunuco | 252 | 30.36 S | 68.38 W |
| Tucupido | 246 | 9.17 N | 65.47 W |
| Tucupita | 246 | 9.04 N | 62.03 W |
| Tucuruí | 250 | 3.42 S | 49.27 W |
| Tucuruí, Represa de ⊜[1] | 250 | 4.40 S | 49.20 W |
| Tucuruvi ◆[8] | 287b | 23.28 S | 46.35 W |
| Tuczna | 30 | 51.54 N | 23.26 E |
| Tud ≐ | 42 | 52.38 N | 1.15 E |
| Tudameda | 112 | 10.52 S | 122.55 E |
| Tudcum | 252 | 30.14 S | 69.15 W |
| Tudeå ≐ | 41 | 55.23 N | 11.13 E |
| Tudela, Esp. | 34 | 42.05 N | 1.36 W |
| Tudela, Pil. | 116 | 8.15 N | 123.50 E |
| Tudela de Duero | 34 | 41.35 N | 4.35 W |
| Tudian | 106 | 30.35 N | 120.37 E |
| Tudichang | 107 | 30.06 N | 103.56 E |
| Tuditang | 100 | 30.12 N | 114.18 E |
| Tudmur (Palmyra) | 130 | 34.33 N | 38.17 E |
| Tudu | 76 | 59.11 N | 26.51 E |
| Tudweiliog | 42 | 52.54 N | 4.35 W |
| Tuela ≐ | 34 | 41.30 N | 7.12 W |
| Tuen Mun | 271d | 22.24 N | 113.58 E |
| Tuenno | 64 | 46.20 N | 11.01 E |
| Tueré ≐ | 250 | 2.48 S | 50.59 W |
| Tuergate | 85 | 40.28 N | 75.21 E |
| Tufanbeyli | 130 | 38.16 N | 36.13 E |
| Tufānganj | 124 | 26.19 N | 89.40 E |
| Tuffé | 50 | 48.07 N | 0.31 E |
| Tufi | 164 | 9.05 S | 149.20 E |
| Tufo | 68 | 41.00 N | 14.47 E |
| Tufts University ⚑[2] | 283 | 42.24 N | 71.07 W |
| Tufu Point ≻ | 174y | 14.13 S | 169.32 W |
| Tugaske | 184 | 50.53 N | 106.16 W |
| Tugela | 158 | 29.09 S | 31.29 E |
| Tugela ≐ | 158 | 29.14 S | 31.30 E |
| Tugela Falls ⌊ | 158 | 28.45 S | 28.58 E |
| Tugela Ferry | 158 | 28.44 S | 30.27 E |
| Tug Fork ≐ | 192 | 38.06 N | 82.36 W |
| Tuggerah Lake ⊂ | 170 | 33.18 S | 151.30 E |
| Tughlakābād ◆[8] | 272a | 28.31 N | 77.16 E |
| Tugidak Island I | 180 | 56.30 N | 154.36 W |
| Tuğköyü | 130 | 38.27 N | 42.16 E |
| Tuglie | 68 | 40.04 N | 18.05 E |
| Tugnug Point ≻ | 116 | 11.21 N | 125.38 E |
| Tugolesskij Bor | 80 | 55.33 N | 39.49 E |
| Tugolukovo | 80 | 51.56 N | 41.40 E |
| Tugubun Point ≻ | 116 | 7.00 N | 126.27 E |
| Tuguegarao | 116 | 17.37 N | 121.44 E |
| Tugulym | 86 | 57.04 N | 64.39 E |
| Tugun | 171a | 28.09 S | 153.30 E |
| Tugur | 89 | 53.48 N | 136.48 E |
| Tugur ≐ | 89 | 53.48 N | 136.44 E |
| Tugurskij poluostrov ≻[1] | 89 | 54.00 N | 137.24 E |
| Tuguša | 88 | 55.57 N | 96.26 E |
| Tugutuj | 88 | 52.40 N | 104.50 E |
| Tuhai ≐ | 98 | 37.55 N | 118.05 E |
| Tuhepu | 104 | 40.54 N | 122.49 E |
| Tuhuangba | 102 | 31.40 N | 108.21 E |
| Tui | 34 | 42.03 N | 8.38 W |
| Tuibo | 89 | 44.01 N | 127.47 E |
| Tuichi ≐ | 248 | 14.36 S | 67.35 W |
| Tuim | 86 | 54.20 N | 89.55 E |
| Tuineje | 148 | 28.19 N | 14.03 W |
| Tuira ≐ | 246 | 8.21 N | 78.03 W |
| Tuirc, Beinn an ∧[2] | 46 | 55.34 N | 5.34 W |
| Tuitán | 234 | 21.08 N | 103.48 W |
| Tuitui | 256 | 22.47 S | 46.42 W |
| Tuj ≐ | 86 | 57.33 N | 72.31 E |
| T'ujabuguz | 85 | 40.58 N | 69.15 E |
| Tujemojnak | 86 | 49.20 N | 62.55 E |
| Tuji-ri | 98 | 41.31 N | 127.12 E |
| Tujmazy | 80 | 54.36 N | 53.42 E |
| Tüjn Gol ≐ | 102 | 45.04 N | 100.46 E |
| Tujunga ◆[8] | 280 | 34.15 N | 118.17 W |
| Tujunga Valley V | 280 | 34.17 N | 118.20 W |
| Tujunga Wash V | 280 | 34.09 N | 118.24 W |
| Tukaj | 86 | 55.24 N | 90.49 E |
| T'ukalinsk | 86 | 55.52 N | 72.12 E |
| Tukan | 86 | 53.50 N | 57.26 E |
| Tukan ≐ | 86 | 60.02 N | 71.36 E |
| Tukangbesi, Kepulauan II | 112 | 5.40 S | 123.50 E |
| Tukayel | 144 | 8.08 N | 45.22 E |
| Ṭūkh, Miṣr | 142 | 30.21 N | 31.12 E |
| Ṭūkh, Miṣr | 142 | 27.41 N | 30.49 E |
| Ṭūkh al-Aqlām | 142 | 30.52 N | 31.26 E |
| Ṭūkh al-Khayl | 142 | 28.06 N | 30.40 E |
| Tukituki ≐ | 172 | 39.36 S | 176.57 E |
| Tuk Méas | 110 | 10.40 N | 104.34 E |
| Tukolon' | 88 | 55.24 N | 107.42 E |
| Tukosméra, Mont ∧ | 175f | 19.35 S | 169.22 E |
| Tukpo | 154 | 4.25 N | 25.52 E |
| Tūkrah | 146 | 32.32 N | 20.34 E |
| Tuktoyaktuk | 180 | 69.27 N | 133.02 W |
| Tuktoyaktuk Peninsula ≻[1] | 180 | 69.45 N | 131.20 W |
| Tukuj-Mekteb | 84 | 44.20 N | 45.11 E |
| Tukums | 76 | 57.00 N | 23.10 E |
| Tukuran | 116 | 7.51 N | 123.35 E |
| Tukuringra, chrebet ⩘ | 89 | 54.20 N | 126.20 E |
| Tukuyu | 154 | 9.15 S | 33.39 E |
| T'uk'u Yüeh ∧ | 269d | 25.02 N | 121.38 E |
| Tukwila | 224 | 47.28 N | 122.15 W |
| Tula, Am. Sam. | 174u | 14.15 S | 170.34 W |
| Tula, It. | 71 | 40.44 N | 8.59 E |
| Tula, Méx. | 234 | 23.00 N | 99.43 W |
| Tula, Nig. | 146 | 9.50 N | 11.28 E |
| Tula, Ross. | 82 | 54.12 N | 37.37 E |
| Tula ≐, Kenya | 154 | 0.50 S | 39.51 E |
| Tula ≐, Méx. | 234 | 20.40 N | 99.30 W |
| Tula ⊥ | 234 | 20.06 N | 99.19 W |
| Tula de Allende | 234 | 20.03 N | 99.21 W |
| Tulaghi | 175e | 9.06 S | 160.09 E |
| Tulagt Ar ≐ | 120 | 36.35 N | 92.20 E |
| Tulai Nanshan ⩘ | 102 | 38.44 N | 98.20 E |
| Tūlak | 128 | 33.58 N | 63.44 E |
| Tulalip Indian Reservation ◆[4] | 224 | 48.06 N | 122.15 W |
| Tulancingo | 234 | 20.05 N | 98.22 W |
| Tulangbawang ≐ | 112 | 4.24 S | 105.52 E |
| Tula Oblast' □[4] | 76 | 54.00 N | 37.30 E |
| Tulaodian | 104 | 41.13 N | 121.27 E |
| T'ul'apsy | 86 | 57.28 N | 89.38 E |
| Tulare, Ca., U.S. | 226 | 36.12 N | 119.20 W |
| Tulare, S.D., U.S. | 198 | 44.44 N | 98.30 W |
| Tulare □[6] | 226 | 36.20 N | 119.18 W |
| Tulare Canal ≊ | 226 | 36.08 N | 119.25 W |
| Tulare Lake Bed ⊜ | 226 | 36.03 N | 119.49 W |
| Tulare Lake Canal ≊ | 226 | 36.04 N | 119.39 W |
| Tularosa | 200 | 33.04 N | 106.01 W |
| Tularosa ≐ | 200 | 33.41 N | 108.46 W |
| Tularosa Valley ≚[1] | 200 | 32.45 N | 106.10 W |
| Tulbagh | 158 | 33.17 S | 19.09 E |
| Tulbing | 264b | 48.16 N | 16.09 E |
| Tulbinger Kogel ∧[2] | 264b | 48.17 N | 16.09 E |
| Tulcán | 246 | 0.48 N | 77.43 W |
| Tulcea | 38 | 45.11 N | 28.48 E |
| Tulcea □[6] | 38 | 45.00 N | 29.00 E |
| Tul'chyn | 78 | 48.39 N | 28.52 E |
| Tulcingo de Valle | 234 | 18.03 N | 98.26 W |
| Tule ≐, Nic. | 236 | 11.20 N | 84.52 W |
| Tule ≐, Ca., U.S. | 226 | 36.03 N | 119.50 W |
| Tule, North Branch ≐ | 226 | 36.06 N | 119.22 W |
| Tule, South Branch ≐ | 226 | 36.05 N | 119.29 W |
| Tule Canal ≊ | 226 | 38.37 N | 121.35 W |
| Tule Creek ≐ | 196 | 34.40 N | 101.14 W |
| T'ulek | 85 | 41.56 N | 75.41 E |
| Tulelake | 204 | 41.57 N | 121.29 W |
| Tule Lake Sump ⊜[1] | 204 | 41.54 N | 121.32 W |
| Tulemalu Lake ⊜ | 176 | 62.58 N | 99.25 W |
| T'ulenij, ostrov I | 84 | 44.28 N | 47.30 E |
| Tule River Indian Reservation ◆[4] | 204 | 36.02 N | 118.42 W |
| Tulette | 62 | 44.17 N | 4.56 E |
| Tule Valley V | 200 | 39.20 N | 113.25 W |
| T'ul'gan | 86 | 52.22 N | 56.12 E |
| Tul'havičy | 78 | 51.47 N | 29.38 E |
| Tuli | 154 | 21.59 S | 29.15 E |
| Tuli ≐ | 154 | 21.48 S | 29.04 E |
| Tulia | 196 | 34.32 N | 101.45 W |
| Tuliahan ≐ | 269f | 14.41 N | 120.58 E |
| Tulica ≐ | 82 | 54.12 N | 37.37 E |
| Tulik Volcano ∧[1] | 180 | 53.22 N | 168.03 W |
| Tuling | 100 | 25.11 N | 118.50 E |
| Tuliszków | 30 | 52.05 N | 18.17 E |
| Tūlkarm | 132 | 32.19 N | 35.02 E |
| T'ul'kino | 86 | 59.49 N | 56.30 E |
| T'ul'kubas | 85 | 42.28 N | 70.02 E |
| Tulla | 48 | 52.52 N | 8.45 W |
| Tullahoma | 194 | 35.21 N | 86.12 W |
| Tullamarine | 274b | 37.41 S | 144.52 E |
| Tullamarine International Airport ⊠, Austl. | 169 | 37.40 S | 144.50 E |
| Tullamarine International Airport ⊠, Austl. | 274b | 37.40 S | 144.50 E |
| Tullamore, Austl. | 166 | 32.38 S | 147.34 E |
| Tullamore, On., Can. | 275b | 43.47 N | 79.46 W |
| Tullamore, Ire. | 48 | 53.16 N | 7.30 W |
| Tullaroop Creek ≐ | 169 | 36.53 S | 143.53 E |
| Tullaroop Reservoir ⊜[1] | 169 | 37.07 S | 143.52 E |
| Tull Bay ⊂ | 208 | 36.30 N | 76.04 W |
| Tulle | 32 | 45.16 N | 1.46 E |
| Tullgarn | 40 | 58.57 N | 17.35 E |
| Tullibigeal | 166 | 33.25 S | 146.44 E |
| Tullinge | 40 | 59.12 N | 17.53 E |
| Tullins | 62 | 45.18 N | 5.29 E |
| Tulln | 61 | 48.20 N | 16.03 E |
| Tullner Feld ◆[1] | 264b | 48.19 N | 16.10 E |
| Tulloch Reservoir ⊜[1] | 226 | 37.53 N | 120.35 W |
| Tullock Creek ≐ | 202 | 46.08 N | 107.27 W |
| Tullos | 194 | 31.49 N | 92.19 W |
| Tullow | 48 | 52.48 N | 6.44 W |
| Tullus | 140 | 11.03 N | 24.33 E |
| Tully, Austl. | 166 | 17.56 S | 145.56 E |
| Tully, N.Y., U.S. | 210 | 42.47 N | 76.06 W |
| Tully Dam ◆[6] | 207 | 42.39 N | 72.11 W |
| Tullytown | 208 | 40.09 N | 74.49 W |
| Ṭulmaythah | 146 | 32.43 N | 20.57 E |
| Tuloma ≐ | 24 | 68.52 N | 32.49 E |
| Tulpfontein | 158 | 32.44 S | 19.43 E |
| Tulsa | 196 | 36.09 N | 95.59 W |
| Tulsequah | 176 | 58.35 N | 133.35 W |
| Tulsī Lake ⊜ | 272c | 19.11 N | 72.55 E |
| Tulsīpur | 124 | 28.07 N | 82.18 E |
| Tulsk | 48 | 53.47 N | 8.16 W |
| Tul'skij | 84 | 44.31 N | 40.10 E |
| Tulstrup | 41 | 56.07 N | 9.46 E |
| Tultepec | 234 | 19.41 N | 99.08 W |
| Tultitlán | 286a | 19.39 N | 99.09 W |
| Tuluá | 246 | 4.06 N | 76.11 W |
| Tuluksak | 180 | 61.06 N | 160.58 W |
| Tulum | 232 | 20.13 N | 87.28 W |
| Tulum ⊥ | 232 | 20.12 N | 87.26 W |
| Tulumayo ≐ | 248 | 11.10 S | 75.16 W |
| Tulun | 88 | 54.35 N | 100.33 E |
| Tulungagung | 115a | 8.04 S | 111.54 E |
| Tulungselapan | 112 | 3.15 S | 105.19 E |
| Tuluran Island I | 116 | 10.59 N | 119.17 E |
| Tulu Welel ∧ | 144 | 8.53 N | 34.47 E |
| Tulyehualco ◆[8] | 286a | 19.15 N | 99.01 W |
| Tum | 164 | 3.38 S | 130.23 E |
| Tuma | 80 | 55.09 N | 40.34 E |
| Tuma ≐ | 236 | 13.03 N | 84.44 W |
| Tumacacori National Monument ♠ | 200 | 31.25 N | 111.01 W |
| Tumaco | 246 | 1.49 N | 78.46 W |
| Tumaco, Rada de ⊂ | 246 | 1.55 N | 78.45 W |
| Tumak | 80 | 46.14 N | 48.31 E |
| Tumalykol' | 86 | 48.21 N | 60.03 E |
| Tuman'an | 84 | 41.00 N | 44.40 E |
| Tuman-gang (Tumen) ≐ | 98 | 42.18 N | 130.41 E |
| Tumannaja, gora ∧ | 180 | 66.33 N | 179.43 E |
| Tumanovo | 76 | 55.25 N | 34.39 E |
| Tumanšet ≐ | 88 | 55.53 N | 97.30 E |
| Tumanskij | 180 | 63.58 N | 178.12 E |
| Tumany | 74 | 60.56 N | 155.56 E |
| Tumarbong | 116 | 10.23 N | 119.27 E |
| T'um'ati → Sklad | 74 | 71.55 N | 123.33 E |
| Tumatumari | 246 | 5.22 N | 59.00 W |
| Tumauini | 116 | 17.17 N | 121.49 E |
| Tumba | 40 | 59.12 N | 17.49 E |
| Tumba, Lac ⊜ | 152 | 0.48 S | 18.03 E |
| Tumbarumba | 171b | 35.47 S | 148.01 E |
| Tumbarumba Creek ≐ | 171b | 35.58 S | 148.03 E |
| Tumbes | 246 | 3.34 S | 80.28 W |
| Tumbes □[5] | 246 | 3.50 S | 80.30 W |
| Tumbes (Puyango) ≐ | 246 | 3.30 S | 80.27 W |
| Tumbes, Punta ≻ | 252 | 36.37 S | 73.07 W |
| Tumbiscatio de Ruiz | 234 | 18.31 N | 102.21 W |
| Tumble Mountain ∧ | 202 | 45.19 N | 110.02 W |
| Tumbler Ridge | 182 | 55.07 N | 120.55 W |
| Tumblong | 171b | 35.09 S | 148.00 E |
| Tumbotino | 80 | 55.59 N | 43.02 E |
| Tumbur | 154 | 4.20 N | 31.34 E |
| Tumby Bay | 166 | 34.22 S | 136.06 E |
| Tumča ≐ | 24 | 66.36 N | 30.48 E |
| Tŭmch'on-ni ◆[8] | 271b | 37.34 N | 126.51 E |
| T'umen', Ross. | 86 | 57.09 N | 65.32 E |
| Tumen, Zhg. | 98 | 42.58 N | 129.49 E |
| Tumen (Tuman-gang) ≐ | 98 | 42.18 N | 130.41 E |
| T'umencevo | 86 | 53.20 N | 81.31 E |
| T'umenec, porog ⌊ | 88 | 56.38 N | 99.00 E |
| T'umen' Oblast' □[4] | 86 | 58.00 N | 69.00 E |
| Tumenpu | 107 | 29.49 N | 103.39 E |
| Tumenskoje | 82 | 55.00 N | 38.32 E |
| Tumenzi | 102 | 37.43 N | 103.09 E |
| Tumeremo | 246 | 7.18 N | 61.30 W |
| Tumiritinga | 255 | 18.58 S | 41.38 W |
| Tumkūr | 122 | 13.21 N | 77.05 E |
| Tummel ≐ | 46 | 56.38 N | 3.40 W |
| Tumnin ≐ | 89 | 49.18 N | 140.22 E |
| Tumon Bay ⊂ | 174p | 13.31 N | 144.48 E |
| Tumos ≐ | 156 | 22.55 S | 14.37 E |
| Tumoteqi | 102 | 40.52 N | 111.28 E |
| Tumpang | 115a | 8.00 S | 112.46 E |
| Tumpat | 114 | 6.12 N | 102.10 E |
| Tumsar | 120 | 21.23 N | 79.44 E |
| Tumtum | 182 | 47.53 N | 117.40 W |
| Tumu, Ghana | 150 | 10.52 N | 1.59 W |
| Tumu, Zhg. | 105 | 40.23 N | 115.36 E |
| Tumuc-Humac Mountains ⩘ | 250 | 2.20 N | 55.00 W |
| Tumut | 171b | 35.18 S | 148.13 E |
| Tumut ≐ | 171b | 35.07 S | 148.13 E |
| Tumut Pond Reservoir ⊜[1] | 171b | 35.59 S | 148.25 E |
| Tumutuk | 80 | 55.02 N | 53.19 E |
| Tumwater | 224 | 47.00 N | 122.54 W |
| Tun ≐ | 110 | 17.25 N | 98.42 E |
| Tuna Canyon V | 280 | 34.03 N | 118.36 W |
| Tunago Lake ⊜ | 180 | 66.18 N | 125.50 W |
| Tuna-Hästberg | 40 | 60.20 N | 15.11 E |
| Tunapuna | 241r | 10.38 N | 61.23 W |
| Tunari, Cerro ∧ | 248 | 17.18 S | 66.22 W |
| Tunas Creek ≐ | 196 | 31.01 N | 102.11 W |
| Tunas de Zaza | 240p | 21.38 N | 79.33 W |
| Tūnat al-Jabal, Miṣr | 142 | 27.46 N | 30.44 E |
| Tūnat al-Jabal, Miṣr | 142 | 28.13 N | 30.43 E |
| Tunaydah | 140 | 25.31 N | 29.21 E |
| Tunbridge Wells → Royal Tunbridge Wells | 42 | 51.08 N | 0.16 E |
| Tunçbilek | 130 | 39.37 N | 29.29 E |
| Tunceli | 130 | 39.07 N | 39.32 E |
| Tunceli □[4] | 130 | 39.10 N | 39.30 E |
| Tunchang | 110 | 19.28 N | 110.08 E |
| T'unch'i → Tunxi | 100 | 29.44 N | 118.18 E |
| Tunda, Pulau I | 115a | 5.49 S | 106.16 E |
| Tundazi ∧ | 154 | 17.33 S | 28.05 E |
| Tündern | 52 | 52.04 N | 9.22 E |
| Tundik ≐ | 86 | 51.04 N | 77.24 E |
| Tūndla | 124 | 27.12 N | 78.17 E |
| Tundubai ⩒[4] | 140 | 18.31 N | 28.33 E |
| Tunduru | 154 | 11.07 S | 37.21 E |
| Tundža ≐ | 38 | 41.40 N | 26.34 E |
| Tune | 41 | 55.36 N | 12.11 E |
| Tunesien → Tunisia □[1] | 148 | 34.00 N | 9.00 E |
| T'unež, Ross. | 82 | 54.37 N | 38.29 E |
| Túnez → Tunis, Tun. | 148 | 36.48 N | 10.11 E |
| Túnez → Tunisia □[1] | 148 | 34.00 N | 9.00 E |
| T'ung ≐ | 74 | 63.46 N | 121.35 E |
| Tunga | 150 | 8.00 N | 9.19 E |
| Tunga ≐ | 122 | 14.00 N | 75.41 E |
| Tungabhadra ≐ | 122 | 15.57 N | 78.15 E |
| Tungabhadra Reservoir ⊜[1] | 122 | 15.16 N | 76.21 E |
| Tungaru | 140 | 10.14 N | 30.42 E |
| Tungauan Bay ⊂ | 116 | 7.28 N | 122.21 E |
| Tungchi University ⚑[2] | 269b | 31.18 N | 121.29 E |
| Tungchi Yü I | 100 | 23.15 N | 119.40 E |
| T'ungchou → Tongxian | 105 | 39.55 N | 116.39 E |
| T'ungch'uan → Tongchuan | 102 | 35.01 N | 109.01 E |
| Tungch'üan Tao I | 100 | 25.58 N | 119.58 E |
| Tungelsta | 40 | 59.06 N | 18.02 E |
| Tung Hai → East China Sea ⩒[2] | 90 | 30.00 N | 126.00 E |
| Tungho | 100 | 22.58 N | 121.18 E |
| T'unghsien → Tongxian | 105 | 39.55 N | 116.39 E |
| T'unghua → Tonghua | 98 | 41.41 N | 125.55 E |
| Tunghwa → Tonghua | 98 | 41.41 N | 125.55 E |
| Tungir ≐ | 88 | 55.24 N | 120.32 E |
| Tungirskij chrebet ⩘ | 88 | 54.40 N | 119.40 E |
| Tungkal ≐ | 112 | 0.49 S | 103.29 E |
| Tungkang | 100 | 22.28 N | 120.26 E |
| Tungkillo | 168b | 34.49 S | 139.04 E |
| Tungku | 112 | 5.01 N | 118.53 E |
| Tungla | 236 | 13.18 N | 84.26 W |
| T'ungliao → Tongliao | 89 | 43.39 N | 122.14 E |
| Tung Lung Island I | 271d | 22.15 N | 114.17 E |
| Tung O | 271d | 22.12 N | 114.08 E |
| Tungokočen | 88 | 53.33 N | 115.36 E |
| Tungsha Tao (Pratas Island) I | 90 | 20.42 N | 116.43 E |
| Tungshih | 100 | 24.15 N | 120.49 E |
| Tungsten | 180 | 61.57 N | 128.16 W |
| Tungsunga, Jabal ∧ | 140 | 11.29 N | 23.21 E |
| Tungting Tao I | 100 | 24.10 N | 118.14 E |
| Tungurahua □[4] | 246 | 1.15 S | 78.35 W |
| Tungurahua ∧[1] | 246 | 1.27 S | 78.26 W |
| Tungyin Tao I | 100 | 26.22 N | 120.30 E |
| Tuni | 122 | 17.21 N | 82.33 E |
| Tunia ≐ | 246 | 1.13 N | 72.44 W |
| Tunica | 194 | 34.41 N | 90.22 W |
| Tunis | 148 | 36.48 N | 10.11 E |
| Tūnis → Tunisia □[1] | 148 | 34.00 N | 9.00 E |
| Tunis, Golfe de ⊂ | 36 | 37.00 N | 10.30 E |
| Tunisia (Tunisie) □[1], Afr. | 134 | 34.00 N | 9.00 E |
| Tunisia (Tunisie) □[1], Afr. | 148 | 34.00 N | 9.00 E |
| Tunisie → Tunisia □[1] | 148 | 34.00 N | 9.00 E |
| Tunitas Creek ≐ | 282 | 37.21 N | 122.24 W |
| Tunja | 246 | 5.31 N | 73.22 W |
| Tunjang | 114 | 6.16 N | 100.21 E |
| Tunka | 88 | 51.45 N | 102.32 E |
| Tunkás | 232 | 20.54 N | 88.45 W |
| Tunkhannock | 210 | 41.32 N | 75.56 W |
| Tunkhannock Creek ≐ | 210 | 41.32 N | 75.57 W |
| Tunkhannock Creek, East Branch ≐ | 210 | 41.38 N | 75.43 W |
| Tunliu | 102 | 36.19 N | 112.54 E |
| Tunnel | 210 | 42.13 N | 75.44 W |
| Tunnel Hill, Ga., U.S. | 192 | 34.50 N | 85.02 W |
| Tunnelhill, Pa., U.S. | 214 | 40.29 N | 78.33 W |
| Tunnelton, In., U.S. | 218 | 38.46 N | 86.21 W |
| Tunnelton, W.V., U.S. | 188 | 39.23 N | 79.44 W |
| Tunnsjøen ⊜ | 24 | 64.43 N | 13.24 E |
| Tunø I | 41 | 55.57 N | 10.26 E |
| Tuntenhausen | 64 | 47.56 N | 12.01 E |
| Tuntum | 250 | 5.14 S | 44.39 W |
| Tuntutuliak | 180 | 60.22 N | 162.38 W |
| Tununak | 180 | 60.35 N | 165.16 W |
| Tunungayualok Island I | 176 | 56.05 N | 61.05 W |
| Tunuyán | 252 | 33.34 S | 69.01 W |
| Tunuyán ≐ | 252 | 34.03 S | 66.45 W |
| Tunxi | 100 | 29.44 N | 118.18 E |
| Tuo ≐, Zhg. | 100 | 33.16 N | 117.45 E |
| Tuo ≐, Zhg. | 102 | 28.57 N | 105.27 E |
| Tuobalage | 120 | 31.37 N | 88.10 E |
| Tuobuja | 74 | 62.00 N | 122.02 E |
| Tuocheng | 100 | 24.05 N | 115.13 E |
| Tuoe Shan ∧ | 102 | 24.20 N | 103.32 E |
| Tuoheji | 100 | 33.26 N | 117.26 E |
| Tuoj-Chaja | 74 | 62.32 N | 111.18 E |
| Tuoji Dao I | 98 | 38.09 N | 120.14 E |
| Tuokedingling | 120 | 32.45 N | 84.55 E |
| Tuokusidawan Ling ∧ | 120 | 37.14 N | 85.47 E |
| Tuoli | 105 | 39.46 N | 116.01 E |
| Tuolumne | 226 | 37.57 N | 120.14 W |
| Tuolumne □[6] | 226 | 37.59 N | 120.23 W |
| Tuolumne ≐ | 226 | 37.36 N | 121.10 W |
| Tuolumne, Lyell Fork ≐ | 226 | 37.53 N | 119.23 W |
| Tuolumne, North Fork ≐ | 226 | 37.54 N | 120.15 W |
| Tuolumne, South Fork ≐ | 226 | 37.50 N | 120.03 W |
| Tuolunduo | 89 | 50.35 N | 120.05 E |
| Tuong Duong | 110 | 19.16 N | 104.27 E |
| Tuotuo ≐ | 120 | 34.15 N | 93.11 E |
| Tuowu | 102 | 28.58 N | 102.13 E |
| T'up | 85 | 42.44 N | 78.22 E |
| Tupã | 255 | 21.56 S | 50.30 W |
| Tupaciguara | 255 | 18.35 S | 48.42 W |
| Tupana ≐ | 246 | 4.25 S | 60.05 W |
| Tupanciretã | 252 | 29.05 S | 53.51 W |
| Tuparro ≐ | 246 | 5.13 N | 67.50 W |
| Tupelo, Ms., U.S. | 194 | 34.15 N | 88.42 W |
| Tupelo, Ok., U.S. | 196 | 34.36 N | 96.25 W |
| Tupelo National Battlefield ⊥ | 194 | 34.13 N | 88.44 W |
| Tupi | 116 | 6.19 N | 124.57 E |
| Tupik | 88 | 54.26 N | 119.57 E |
| Tupilac | 116 | 7.40 N | 122.30 E |
| Tupinambarana, Ilha I | 246 | 3.00 S | 58.00 W |
| Tupi Paulista | 255 | 21.24 S | 51.34 W |
| Tupiraçaba | 255 | 14.29 S | 48.34 W |
| Tupiza | 248 | 21.27 S | 65.43 W |
| Tuplice | 30 | 51.41 N | 14.50 E |
| Tupman | 226 | 35.17 N | 119.21 W |
| Tupper | 182 | 55.31 N | 120.02 W |
| Tupper Lake | 188 | 44.13 N | 74.29 W |
| Tupperville | 214 | 42.36 N | 82.16 W |
| Tupungato | 252 | 33.22 S | 69.08 W |
| Tupungato, Cerro ∧ | 252 | 33.22 S | 69.47 W |
| Tupychiv | 78 | 51.46 N | 31.26 E |
| Tuqiao, Zhg. | 106 | 31.39 N | 120.24 E |
| Tuqiao, Zhg. | 106 | 31.56 N | 119.03 E |


**Symbols** in the index entries represent the broad categories identified in the key at the right. Symbols with superior numbers (⩘[1]) identify subcategories (see complete key on page *I · 1).*

**Symbole** im Register stellen die rechts im Schlüssel erklärten Kategorien dar. Symbole mit hochgestellten Ziffern (⩘[1]) bezeichnen Unterabteilungen einer Kategorie (vgl. vollständiger Schlüssel auf Seite *I · 1).*

**Los símbolos** incluídos en el texto del índice representan las grandes categorías identificadas con la clave a la derecha. Los símbolos con numeros en su parte superior (⩘[1]) identifican las subcategorías (véase la clave completa en la página *I · 1).*

**Les symboles** de l'index représentent les catégories indiquées dans la légende à droite. Les symboles suivis d'un indice (⩘[1]) représentent des sous-catégories (voir légende complète à la page *I · 1).*

**Os símbolos** incluídos no texto do índice representam as grandes categorias identificadas com a chave à direita. Os símbolos com números em sua parte superior (⩘[1]) identificam as subcategorias (veja-se a chave completa à página *I · 1).*

| | | | | |
|---|---|---|---|---|
| ∧ Mountain | Berg | Montaña | Montagne | Montanha |
| ⩘ Mountains | Gebirge | Montañas | Montagnes | Montanhas |
| )( Pass | Paß | Paso | Col | Passo |
| V Valley, Canyon | Tal, Cañon | Valle, Cañón | Vallée, Canyon | Vale, Canhão |
| ≚ Plain | Ebene | Llano | Plaine | Planície |
| ≻ Cape | Kap | Cabo | Cap | Cabo |
| I Island | Insel | Isla | Île | Ilha |
| II Islands | Inseln | Islas | Îles | Ilhas |
| ≗ Other Topographic Features | Andere Topographische Objekte | Otros Elementos Topográficos | Autres données topographiques | Outros acidentes topográficos |

Tuqiao, Zhg. 107 30.24 N 105.28 E
Tuqiaozhen 107 30.32 N 104.50 E
Tuquan 89 45.26 N 121.50 E
Túquerres 246 1.05 N 77.37 W
Tuquiaochang 107 29.47 N 106.01 E
Tura, India 124 25.31 N 90.13 E
Ţurā, Mişr 142 29.56 N 31.16 E
Tura, Ross. 74 64.17 N 100.15 E
Tura ≃, Ross. 86 57.12 N 66.56 E
Tura ≃, Ross. 88 51.36 N 114.09 E
Turabah 144 21.13 N 41.39 E
Turabah ⊤[4] 128 28.15 N 42.55 E
Turābah, 'Ayn at- ⊤[4] 132 31.36 N 35.25 E
Turāg ≃ 126 23.45 N 90.21 E
Turaiyūr 122 11.10 N 78.37 E
Turakina 172 40.02 S 175.13 E
Turakina ≃ 172 40.04 S 175.08 E
Turama ≃ 164 6.50 S 143.05 E
Turambhe 272c 19.04 N 73.01 E
Turan, Ross. 88 51.38 N 101.40 E
Turan, Ross. 88 52.08 N 93.55 E
Turangi 172 39.00 S 175.49 E
Turano ≃ 66 42.26 N 12.47 E
Turanskaja nizmennost' ≚ 86 44.30 N 63.00 E
Ţurāq al-'Ilab ⋏[2] 130 33.55 N 38.18 E
Turate 266b 45.39 N 9.00 E
Tur'at Ghunaym 142 31.16 N 31.29 E
Turaŭ 76 52.04 N 27.44 E
Ţurayf 128 31.44 N 38.33 E
Turbaco 246 10.20 N 75.25 W
Turbacz ∧ 30 49.33 N 20.08 E
Turbat 128 25.59 N 63.04 E
Turbenthal 58 47.27 N 8.51 E
Turbigo 62 45.32 N 8.44 E
Turbio ≃ 234 20.19 N 101.37 W
Turbiv 78 49.21 N 28.44 E
Turbo 246 8.06 N 76.43 W
Turbotville 210 41.06 N 76.46 W
Turčasovo 24 63.06 N 39.12 E
Turchi, Balata dei > 70 36.43 N 12.02 E
Turčiansky Svätý Martin — Martin 30 49.05 N 18.55 E
Turckheim 58 48.05 N 7.17 E
Turda 38 46.34 N 23.47 E
Turdej 76 53.22 N 38.01 E
Turee Creek 162 23.37 S 118.39 E
Turee Creek ≃ 162 23.35 S 117.25 E
Turek 30 52.02 N 18.30 E
Turen 115a 8.10 S 112.41 E
Turenki 26 60.55 N 24.38 E
Turfan — Turpan 86 42.56 N 89.10 E
Turfan Depression — Turpan Pendi ⩡[7] 86 42.40 N 89.10 E
Turffontein ◆[8] 273d 26.15 S 28.02 E
Turffontein Race Course ♣ 273d 26.14 S 28.03 E
Turgaj, Kaz. 86 49.38 N 63.28 E
Turgaj, Kaz. 86 51.46 N 72.44 E
Turgaj □[8] 86 50.00 N 65.20 E
Turgaj ≃ 86 48.01 N 62.45 E
Turgajskaja ložbina ⋁ 86 51.00 N 64.30 E
Turgajskoje plato ⋏[1] 86 51.00 N 64.00 E
Turgen', Kaz. 85 43.24 N 77.36 E
Türgen, Mong. 86 50.04 N 91.36 E
Turgen' ≃ 85 43.50 N 77.38 E
Turgenevka 88 53.02 N 105.41 E
Turgenevo 80 54.50 N 46.19 E
Turginovo 82 56.30 N 36.00 E
Turgojak 86 55.10 N 60.07 E
Turgoš 76 59.18 N 35.10 E
Tŭrgovishte — Târgovište 38 43.15 N 26.34 E
Turgut, Tür. 130 37.22 N 28.02 E
Turgut, Tür. 130 38.37 N 31.49 E
Turgutlu 130 38.30 N 27.43 E
Turgwi ≃ 154 20.28 S 32.18 E
Turhal 130 40.24 N 36.06 E
Türi, Eesti 76 58.48 N 25.26 E
Turi, It. 68 40.55 N 17.01 E
Turia ≃ 34 39.27 N 0.19 W
Turiaçu 250 1.41 S 45.21 W
Turiaçu ≃ 250 1.36 S 45.19 W
Turij Rog 89 45.14 N 131.58 E
Turilovka 83 49.06 N 40.13 E
Turimetta Head > 274a 33.42 S 151.19 E
Turimiquire, Cerro ∧ 246 10.07 N 63.53 W
Turin, Ab., Can. 182 49.58 N 112.31 W
Turin — Torino, It. 62 45.03 N 7.40 E
Turin, N.Y., U.S. 212 43.38 N 75.25 W
Turinge 40 59.12 N 17.27 E
Turinsk 86 58.03 N 63.42 E
Turinskaja Sloboda 86 57.37 N 64.25 E
Turiya ≃ 78 51.48 N 24.52 E
Turiys'k 78 51.07 N 24.31 E
Turka, Ross. 88 52.57 N 108.13 E
Turka, Ukr. 78 49.10 N 23.02 E
Turka ≃ 88 52.56 N 108.13 E
Turkana, Lake — Rudolf, Lake ⊜ 144 3.30 N 36.05 E
Türkei — Turkey □[1] 22 39.00 N 35.00 E
Türkeli Adası I 130 40.30 N 27.30 E
Turkestan 85 43.18 N 68.15 E
Turkestanskij chrebet ⋏ 85 39.35 N 69.15 E
Túrkeve 30 47.06 N 20.45 E
Turkey 196 34.23 N 100.53 W
Turkey (Türkiye) □[1], Asia 22 39.00 N 35.00 E
Turkey (Türkiye) □[1], Asia 130 39.00 N 35.00 E
Turkey ≃ 190 42.43 N 91.01 W
Turkey Branch ≃ 284c 38.52 N 76.48 W
Turkey City 214 41.11 N 79.37 W
Turkey Creek 164 17.02 S 128.12 E
Turkey Creek ≃, On., Can. 281 42.14 N 83.06 W
Turkey Creek ≃, U.S. 198 39.58 N 96.02 W
Turkey Creek ≃, In., U.S. 278 41.31 N 87.18 W
Turkey Creek ≃, Ia., U.S. 198 41.20 N 95.05 W
Turkey Creek ≃, Ks., U.S. 198 38.53 N 97.11 W
Turkey Creek ≃, Ne., U.S. 198 40.23 N 96.53 W
Turkey Creek ≃, Ok., U.S. 196 35.58 N 97.56 W
Turkey Creek ≃, Tx., U.S. 222 30.39 N 97.05 W
Turkey Island I 284c 38.58 N 77.12 W
Turkey Point >, On., Can. 212 42.40 N 80.21 W
Turkey Point >, Fl., U.S. 220 25.26 N 80.19 W
Turkey Point Provincial Park ♣ 212 42.40 N 80.22 W
Turkey Run State Park ♣ 194 39.54 N 87.13 W
Turkeytown 279b 40.12 N 79.44 W
Türkheim 58 48.03 N 10.38 E
Turki 80 51.59 N 43.16 E
Turkish Republic of Northern Cyprus — Cyprus, North □[1] 130 35.15 N 33.40 E
Türkiye — Turkey □[1] 22 39.00 N 35.00 E
Turkmān Deh 267d 35.40 N 51.36 E
Turkmenia — Turkmenistan □[1] 72 40.00 N 60.00 E
Turkmenija — Turkmenistan □[1] 72 40.00 N 60.00 E
Turkmenistan □[1], Asia 72 40.00 N 60.00 E
Turkmenistan □[1], Asia 128 39.00 N 60.00 E
Turkmeniya — Turkmenistan □[1] 72 40.00 N 60.00 E
Turkmen-Kala 128 37.26 N 62.20 E
Turkmenskij zaliv ⊂ 128 38.54 N 53.48 E
Turk Mine 154 19.45 S 28.50 E
Türkoğlu 130 37.31 N 36.49 E
Turks and Caicos Islands □[2], N.A. 230 21.45 N 71.35 W
Turks and Caicos Islands □[2], N.A. 238 21.45 N 71.35 W
Turks Island Passage ⊔ 238 21.25 N 71.19 W
Turks Islands II 238 21.24 N 71.07 W
Turks-und Caicos-Inseln — Turks and Caicos Islands □[2] 238 21.45 N 71.35 W
Turku (Åbo) 26 60.27 N 22.17 E
Turkwel ≃ 154 3.06 N 36.06 E
Turlan 85 43.36 N 69.03 E
Turley 196 36.14 N 95.58 W
Turlock 226 37.29 N 120.50 W
Turlock Lake ⊜[1] 226 42.17 N 73.21 W
Turmalina 255 17.17 S 42.45 W
Turmantas 76 55.42 N 26.27 E
Turmerito, Quebrada ≃ 286c 10.26 N 66.55 W
Turnagain ≃ 180 59.06 N 127.35 W
Turnagain, Cape > 172 40.29 S 176.37 E
Turnagain Arm ⊂ 180 61.00 N 150.00 W
Turnagain Island I 164 9.34 S 142.18 E
Turnau 61 47.33 N 15.20 E
Turnbull, Mount ∧ 200 33.04 N 110.16 W
Turnbull, Mount ∧[2] 162 21.03 S 131.57 E
Turneffe Islands II 232 17.22 N 87.51 W
Turner, Austl. 162 17.50 S 128.17 E
Turner, Mt., U.S. 202 48.50 N 108.24 W
Turner, Or., U.S. 202 44.50 N 122.57 W
Turner ≃ 162 20.21 S 118.25 E
Turner Field ⊠ 285 40.13 N 75.13 W
Turners Falls 207 42.36 N 72.33 W
Turners Peninsula >[1] 150 7.22 N 12.22 W
Turnersville, N.J., U.S. 285 39.46 N 75.03 W
Turnersville, Tx., U.S. 222 31.37 N 97.44 W
Turner Valley 182 50.40 N 114.17 W
Turnhout 56 51.19 N 4.57 E
Türnitz 61 47.57 N 15.30 E
Turnor Lake ⊜ 184 56.32 N 108.38 W
Turnov 30 50.35 N 15.10 E
Tŭrnovo — Veliko Târnovo 38 43.04 N 25.39 E
Turnpike Lake ⊜ 283 42.01 N 71.19 W
Turnu Măgurele 38 43.45 N 24.53 E
Turnu Roşu, Pasul )( 38 45.33 N 24.16 E
Turnu-Severin — Drobeta-Turnu Severin 38 44.38 N 22.39 E
Turobin 30 50.50 N 22.45 E
Turočak 86 52.16 N 87.08 E
Turon 198 37.48 N 98.25 W
Turon ≃ 170 33.03 S 149.43 E
Turopolje ≚ 36 45.40 N 16.05 E
Turopyn 78 51.00 N 24.27 E
Tuross ≃ 171b 36.09 S 149.39 E
Turovo 82 54.52 N 37.49 E
Turpan 86 42.56 N 89.10 E
Turpan Pendi (Turfan Depression) ⩡[7] 86 42.40 N 89.10 E
Turques et Caicos, Îles — Turks and Caicos Islands □[2] 238 21.45 N 71.35 W
Turquía — Turkey □[1] 22 39.00 N 35.00 E
Turquie — Turkey □[1] 22 39.00 N 35.00 E
Turquino, Pico ∧ 240p 19.59 N 76.50 W
Turrach 64 46.57 N 13.52 E
Turramurra 274a 33.44 S 151.08 E
Turrell 194 35.22 N 90.15 W
Turret Peak ∧ 200 34.15 N 111.53 W
Turriaco 64 45.49 N 13.26 E
Turrialba 236 9.54 N 83.41 W
Turrialba, Volcán ∧[1] 236 10.02 N 83.46 W
Turriers 62 44.24 N 6.10 E
Turriff 46 57.32 N 2.28 W
Turritano ◆[1] 71 40.45 N 8.35 E
Turrubares, Cerro ∧ 236 9.47 N 84.28 W
Tursi 68 40.15 N 16.28 E
Tursunzade 85 38.32 N 68.13 E
Turtas ≃ 86 59.06 N 68.52 E
Turtipār 124 26.10 N 83.54 E
Turtle ≃, Mb., Can. 184 51.07 N 99.39 W
Turtle ≃, On., Can. 184 48.51 N 92.45 W
Turtle, North Branch ≃ 198 47.57 N 97.35 W
Turtle Creek, N.B., Can. 186 45.58 N 64.53 W
Turtle Creek, Pa., U.S. 214 40.24 N 79.49 W
Turtle Creek ≃, Pa., U.S. 279b 40.23 N 79.51 W
Turtle Creek ≃, S.D., U.S. 198 44.55 N 98.29 W
Turtle Creek ≃, Wi., U.S. 216 42.29 N 89.03 W
Turtle-Flambeau Flowage ⊜[1] 190 46.05 N 90.11 W
Turtleford 184 53.23 N 108.56 W
Turtle Harbor Channel ⊔ 220 25.15 N 80.18 W
Turtle Islands II 150 7.37 N 13.02 W
Turtle Lake, N.D., U.S. 198 47.31 N 100.53 W
Turtle Lake, Wi., U.S. 190 45.23 N 92.08 W
Turtle Lake ⊜ 184 53.35 N 108.40 W
Turtle Mountain ∧[2] 184 49.00 N 100.15 W
Turtle Mountain Indian Reservation ◆[4] 198 48.51 N 99.45 W
Turtle Mountain Provincial Park ♣ 184 49.03 N 100.15 W
Turtmann 58 46.18 N 7.41 E
Turton and Entwistle Reservoir ⊜[1] 262 53.39 N 2.25 W
Turton Bottoms 262 53.38 N 2.24 W
Turton Moor ◆[3] 262 53.40 N 2.29 W
Turton Tower ◙ 262 53.38 N 2.25 W
Turu ≃ 74 64.38 N 100.00 E
Turua 172 37.14 S 175.34 E
Turuchan ≃ 74 65.56 N 87.42 E
Turuchansk 74 65.49 N 87.59 E
Turugart Shankou (pereval Torugart) )( 85 40.33 N 75.20 E
Turun-Porin lääni □[4] 26 61.20 N 22.30 E
Turuntajevo, Ross. 86 56.38 N 85.59 E
Turuntajevo, Ross. 88 52.12 N 107.37 E
Turusele ∧ 71 40.09 N 9.34 E
Turvo 252 28.56 S 49.41 W
Turvo ≃, Bra. 255 17.46 S 50.12 W
Turvo ≃, Bra. 255 19.56 S 49.55 W
Turvo ≃, Bra. 256 22.04 S 45.42 W
Turvo ≃, Bra. 256 22.29 S 44.15 W
Turvo Grande ≃ 256 21.42 S 44.22 W
Turvolândia 256 21.47 S 45.47 W
Turvo Pequeno ≃ 256 21.42 S 44.22 W
Turyu-san ∧ 98 41.10 N 128.47 E
Turzovka 30 49.25 N 18.39 E
Tusa 70 37.59 N 14.14 E
Tusa ≃ 70 38.01 N 14.16 E
Tusas, Rio ≃ 200 36.23 N 106.03 W
Tuscaloosa 194 33.12 N 87.34 W
Tuscaloosa, Lake ⊜[1] 194 33.20 N 87.35 W
Tuscania 66 42.25 N 11.52 E
Tuscany — Toscana □[4] 36 43.25 N 11.00 E
Tuscarawas 214 40.24 N 81.25 W
Tuscarawas □[6] 214 40.30 N 81.27 W
Tuscarawas ≃ 214 40.17 N 81.52 W
Tuscarora, N.Y., U.S. 210 42.38 N 77.52 W
Tuscarora, Pa., U.S. 208 40.46 N 76.02 W
Tuscarora Creek ≃, N.Y., U.S. 210 42.07 N 77.14 W
Tuscarora Creek ≃, Pa., U.S. 208 40.32 N 77.23 W
Tuscarora Creek, North Branch ≃ 210 42.05 N 77.18 W
Tuscarora Indian Reservation ◆[4] 210 43.09 N 78.57 W
Tuscarora Mountain ∧ 188 40.10 N 77.45 W
Tuscarora Mountains ⋏ 204 41.00 N 116.20 W
Tuscarora State Park ♣ 208 40.48 N 76.01 W
Tuscarora Tunnel ◆[5] 214 40.05 N 77.50 W
Tuscola, Il., U.S. 194 39.47 N 88.16 W
Tuscola, Tx., U.S. 196 32.12 N 99.48 W
Tuscolo ⊥ 267a 41.48 N 12.42 E
Tuscumbia, Al., U.S. 194 34.43 N 87.42 W
Tuscumbia, Mo., U.S. 194 38.13 N 92.27 W
Tuse 41 55.43 N 11.37 E
Tushan 98 34.14 N 117.51 E
Tušino ◆[8] 265b 55.50 N 37.26 E
Tuskegee 194 32.25 N 85.41 W
Tusker Rock II[1] 42 51.27 N 3.40 W
Tussenhausen, Dtsch. 58 48.06 N 10.34 E
Tussenhausen, Dtsch. 64 48.06 N 10.34 E
Tussey Mountain ∧ 214 40.25 N 78.07 W
Tüssling 60 48.13 N 12.36 E
Tustin 228 33.44 N 117.49 W
Tustin Marine Corps Air Station (Helicopter) ■ 280 33.43 N 117.50 W
Tustumena Lake ⊜ 180 60.12 N 150.50 W
Tuszyn 30 51.37 N 19.34 E
Tut 130 37.48 N 37.55 E
Tuta 152 14.37 S 20.45 E
Tutaekuri ≃ 172 39.30 S 176.54 E
Tutaizi 104 41.01 N 122.38 E
Tutajev 80 57.53 N 39.32 E
Tutak 84 39.32 N 42.46 E
Tutang 100 29.21 N 116.24 E
Tutbury 42 52.51 N 1.41 W
Tuthills Creek ≃ 276 40.45 N 73.02 W
Tuticorin 122 8.47 N 78.08 E
Tutin 38 42.59 N 20.20 E
T'ut'kovo 82 54.37 N 38.32 E
Tutóia 250 2.45 S 42.16 W
Tutoko, Mount ∧ 172 44.36 S 168.00 E
Tutong 112 4.50 N 114.40 E
Tutova ≃ 38 46.06 N 27.32 E
Tutow 54 53.55 N 13.16 E
Tutrakan 38 44.03 N 26.37 E
Tuttle, N.D., U.S. 198 47.08 N 99.59 W
Tuttle, Ok., U.S. 196 35.17 N 97.48 W
Tuttle Creek Lake ⊜[1] 198 39.22 N 96.40 W
Tuttlingen 58 47.59 N 8.49 E
Tutuala 112 8.24 S 127.15 E
Tutuban Station ◆[5] 269f 14.37 N 120.58 E
Tutu Bay ⊂ 116 5.55 N 121.12 E
Tutubu 154 5.30 S 32.41 E
Tutuí ≃ 250 2.39 S 54.10 W
Tutuila I 174u 14.18 S 170.42 W
Tuţūn 142 29.09 N 30.46 E
Tütüncü 130 40.04 N 27.43 E
Tutupaca, Volcán ∧[1] 248 17.01 S 70.22 W
Tutura 88 54.46 N 105.15 E
Tututalak Mountain ∧ 180 67.46 N 161.10 W
Tutwiler 194 34.00 N 90.25 W
Tutzing 64 47.54 N 11.17 E
Tuul ≃ 90 48.57 N 104.48 E
Tuupovaara 26 62.29 N 30.36 E
Tuusniemi 26 62.49 N 28.30 E
Tuutapu, Cerro ∧ 174z 27.08 S 109.24 W
Tuva □[3] 72 52.00 N 95.00 E
T'uva-Guba 24 69.08 N 33.32 E
Tuvalu □[1] 14 8.00 S 178.00 E
Tuvutha Island I 175g 17.40 S 178.48 W
Tuwang 107 29.06 N 105.48 E
Ţuwayq, Jabal ⋏ 118 23.00 N 46.00 E
Ţuwayyil ash-Shihāq ∧[2] 132 30.36 N 36.08 E
Tuxedo Park, De., U.S. 285 39.43 N 75.37 W
Tuxedo Park, N.Y., U.S. 210 41.11 N 74.11 W
Tuxer Alpen ⋏ 64 47.10 N 11.45 E
Tuxford, Sk., Can. 184 50.35 N 105.35 W
Tuxford, Eng., U.K. 44 53.13 N 0.53 W
Tuxiaqiao 100 28.47 N 121.29 E
Tuxpan, Méx. 234 19.33 N 103.24 W
Tuxpan, Méx. 234 19.34 N 100.28 W
Tuxpan, Méx. 234 21.57 N 105.18 W
Tuxpan, Méx. 234 20.57 N 97.24 W
Tuxpan ≃ 234 20.59 N 97.18 W
Tuxsun 86 42.47 N 88.38 E
Tuxtepec 234 18.06 N 96.07 W
Tuxtla Gutiérrez 234 16.45 N 93.07 W
Tuy ≃ 246 10.24 N 65.59 W
Tuy An 110 13.17 N 109.16 E
Tuyen Hoa 110 17.50 N 106.10 E
Tuyen Quang 110 21.49 N 105.13 E
Tuy Hoa 110 13.05 N 109.18 E
Tūysarkān 128 34.33 N 48.27 E
Tuyün — Duyun 102 26.12 N 107.31 E
Ţuyūr, Burj aţ- ∧[2] 140 20.55 N 27.55 E
Tuža 80 57.37 N 47.57 E
T'uzašu, pereval )( 85 42.21 N 73.48 E
T'uzbel' 85 40.34 N 73.21 E
Tuzdykol', ozero ⊜ 80 49.36 N 52.20 E
Tuz Gölü ⊜ 130 38.45 N 33.25 E
Tuzigoot National Monument ♣ 200 34.49 N 112.01 W
Ţūz Khurmātū 128 34.53 N 44.38 E
Tuzla, Bos. 38 44.32 N 18.41 E
Tuzla, Tür. 130 36.42 N 35.05 E
Tuzla ≃ 130 39.43 N 40.16 E
Tuzla Gölü ⊜ 130 39.02 N 35.50 E
Tuzlagözü 130 38.11 N 41.34 E
Tuzlov ≃ 83 47.23 N 40.08 E
Tuzluca 84 40.03 N 43.40 E
Tuzlukçu 130 38.28 N 31.38 E
Tuzly 78 45.52 N 30.05 E
Tuzuntla ≃ 234 18.51 N 100.44 W
Tvărdica 38 42.42 N 25.52 E
Tvardiţa 38 46.09 N 28.58 E
Tvedestrand 26 58.37 N 8.55 E
Tveitsund 26 59.01 N 8.32 E
Tver' (Kalinin) 82 56.52 N 35.55 E
Tverca ≃ 76 56.52 N 35.55 E
Tver' Oblast' □[4] 76 57.00 N 34.00 E
Twain Harte 226 38.02 N 120.14 W
Twann 58 47.06 N 7.10 E
Twardogóra 30 51.22 N 17.28 E
Tweed 212 44.29 N 77.19 W
Tweed ≃ 44 55.46 N 2.00 W
Tweeddale ⋁ 46 55.40 N 3.10 W
Tweede Exloërmond 52 52.55 N 6.58 E
Tweed Heads 171a 28.10 S 153.31 E
Tweedmouth 44 55.45 N 2.01 W
Tweedsmuir Provincial Park ♣ 182 52.55 N 126.05 W
Tweedy Mountain ∧ 202 45.29 N 112.58 W
Tweeling 158 27.38 S 28.31 E
Twee Rivieren 158 26.27 S 20.37 E
Tweespruit 158 29.11 S 27.01 E
Twello 52 52.14 N 6.06 E
Twelve Mile 216 40.52 N 86.13 W
Twelve Mile Creek ≃, On., Can. 212 43.11 N 79.16 W
Twelvemile Creek ≃, N.Y., U.S. 210 43.18 N 78.51 W
Twelvemile Island I 279b 40.32 N 79.51 W
Twelve Mile Lake ⊜, On., Can. 212 45.02 N 78.43 W
Twelve Mile Lake ⊜, Sk., Can 184 49.29 N 106.14 W
Tweng 64 47.11 N 13.36 E
Twente ◆[1] 52 52.17 N 6.40 E
Twentekanaal ≊ 52 52.15 N 6.40 E
Twentieth Century Fox Studios ◙[3] 280 34.03 N 118.25 W
Twentyfive Mile Wash ⋁ 200 37.33 N 111.07 W
Twenty Mile Creek ≃ 212 43.10 N 79.22 W
Twentynine Palms 204 34.08 N 116.03 W
Twentynine Palms Marine Corps Center ■ 204 34.25 N 116.10 W
Tweya 152 0.54 S 19.05 E
Twickenham ◆[8] 260 51.27 N 0.20 W
Twilight Cove ⊂ 162 32.16 S 126.03 E
Twilight Park 210 42.11 N 74.05 W
Twillingate 186 49.39 N 54.46 W
Twimberg 61 46.55 N 14.50 E
Twin Beach 216 42.34 N 83.24 W
Twin Bridge Farm 285 39.57 N 75.33 W
Twin Bridges 202 45.32 N 112.19 W
Twin Butte Creek ≃ 198 38.46 N 100.56 W
Twin Buttes ∧ 202 44.20 N 122.15 W
Twin Buttes Reservoir ⊜[1] 196 31.20 N 100.35 W
Twin City 192 32.34 N 82.09 W
Twin Creek ≃ 218 39.33 N 84.21 W
Twin Falls 202 42.33 N 114.27 W
Twin Heads ⋏ 162 20.13 S 126.30 E
Twin Hills 180 59.23 N 159.58 W
Twin Lakes, Ca., U.S. 226 36.58 N 122.00 W
Twin Lakes, Ga., U.S. 192 30.42 N 83.12 W
Twin Lakes, In., U.S. 216 41.19 N 86.23 W
Twin Lakes, Mi., U.S. 216 42.02 N 86.04 W
Twin Lakes, Oh., U.S. 214 41.11 N 81.21 W
Twin Lakes, Pa., U.S. 210 41.24 N 74.54 W
Twin Lakes, Wi., U.S. 216 42.31 N 88.14 W
Twin Lakes ⊜, Ca., U.S. 226 38.09 N 119.21 W
Twin Lakes ⊜, Ct., U.S. 207 42.02 N 73.26 W
Twin Lakes ⊜, Wa., U.S. 224 47.55 N 120.51 W
Twin Oaks 208 39.51 N 75.26 W
Twin Peak Islands II 162 34.00 S 122.50 E
Twin Peaks 228 34.12 N 117.12 W
Twin Peaks ⋏, Ca., U.S. 282 37.45 N 122.27 W
Twin Peaks ⋏, Id., U.S. 202 44.35 N 114.29 W
Twin Rocks, Or., U.S. 224 45.36 N 123.57 W
Twin Rocks, Pa., U.S. 214 40.29 N 78.51 W
Twinsburg 214 41.18 N 81.26 W
Twin Valley 198 47.15 N 96.15 W
Twisp 202 48.21 N 120.07 W
Twiss Green 262 53.27 N 2.32 W
Twist 52 52.38 N 7.03 E
Twiste ≃ 52 51.29 N 9.09 E
Twistetal 56 51.20 N 8.58 E
Twistringen 52 52.48 N 8.38 E
Twitchell Reservoir ⊜[1] 204 35.00 N 120.19 W
Twitya ≃ 180 64.10 N 128.12 W
Two, Channel ⊔ 220 24.50 N 80.45 W
Two Butte Creek ≃ 198 38.02 N 102.08 W
Twofold Bay ⊂ 166 37.06 S 149.55 E
Two Harbors 190 47.01 N 91.40 W
Two Hills 182 53.43 N 111.45 W
Two Lakes ⊜ 224 46.22 N 121.27 W
Two Medicine ≃ 202 48.29 N 112.14 W
Two Mile Creek ≃, On., Can. 284a 43.16 N 79.06 W
Twomile Creek ≃, N.Y., U.S. 284a 43.01 N 78.55 W
Twong 140 8.18 N 28.20 E
Two Penny Run ≃ 285 39.41 N 75.26 W
Two River Lake ⊜ 184 53.52 N 91.27 W
Two Rivers 190 44.09 N 87.34 W
Two Rivers Reservoir ⊜[1] 196 33.17 N 104.45 W
Two Thumb Range ⋏ 172 43.45 S 170.43 E
Two Wells 168b 34.36 S 138.30 E
Twrch ≃, Wales, U.K. 42 52.42 N 3.29 W
Twrch ≃, Wales, U.K. 42 51.46 N 3.46 W
Twyford, Eng., U.K. 42 51.01 N 1.19 W
Twyford, Eng., U.K. 42 51.29 N 0.53 W
Twymyn ≃ 42 52.38 N 3.44 W
Tyabb 169 38.16 S 145.11 E
Tyachiv 78 48.02 N 23.34 E
Tyahynka 78 46.47 N 33.04 E
Tyasmyn ≃ 78 49.05 N 32.48 E
Tybee Island 192 32.01 N 80.51 W
Tybju 24 60.37 N 50.20 E
Tychy 30 50.09 N 18.59 E
Tyczyn 30 49.58 N 22.02 E
Tydal 26 63.04 N 11.34 E
Tye 196 32.27 N 99.52 W
Tyende Creek ≃ 200 36.50 N 109.43 W
Tyendinaga Indian Reserve ◆[4] 212 44.11 N 77.07 W
Tyers ≃ 169 38.10 S 146.26 E
Tyfors 40 60.09 N 14.12 E
Tygarts Creek ≃ 218 38.43 N 82.57 W
Tygda 89 53.07 N 126.20 E
Tygda ≃ 89 52.35 N 127.55 E
Tygelsjö 41 55.31 N 13.00 E
Tygh Valley 224 45.14 N 121.10 W
Tyin ⊜ 26 61.17 N 8.13 E
Tyja ≃ 88 55.36 N 109.20 E
Tykhonovychi 78 51.56 N 32.09 E
Tylden 158 32.07 S 27.05 E
Tyldesley 44 53.31 N 2.28 W
Tyler, Mn., U.S. 198 44.16 N 96.08 W
Tyler, Pa., U.S. 214 41.14 N 78.32 W
Tyler, Tx., U.S. 222 32.21 N 95.18 W
Tyler □[6] 222 30.47 N 94.32 W
Tyler, Lake ⊜[1] 222 32.13 N 95.10 W
Tyler East, Lake ⊜[1] 222 32.15 N 95.10 W
Tyler Park 284c 38.52 N 77.12 W
Tylersburg 214 41.23 N 79.19 W
Tyler State Park ♣, Pa., U.S. 208 40.14 N 74.59 W
Tyler State Park ♣, Tx., U.S. 222 32.29 N 95.14 W
Tylersville 210 41.00 N 77.25 W
Tylerton 208 37.58 N 76.01 W
Tylertown 194 31.06 N 90.08 W
Tylihul ≃ 78 47.04 N 30.57 E
Tylihul's'kyy lyman ⊜ 78 46.48 N 31.08 E
Tylla 40 60.28 N 15.33 E
Tylösand 26 56.39 N 12.44 E
Tylöskog ⋏[2] 40 58.45 N 15.20 E
Tylovaj 80 57.30 N 53.47 E
Tylyhulo-Berezhanka 78 46.52 N 31.24 E
Tym ≃, Ross. 74 59.25 N 80.04 E
Tym' ≃, Ross. 89 51.51 N 143.10 E
Tymna, laguna ⊂ 180 64.00 N 178.30 E
Tymochtee Creek ≃ 214 40.57 N 83.16 W
Tymovskoje 89 50.51 N 142.39 E
Tymsk 86 59.24 N 80.18 E
Tynagh 48 53.09 N 8.22 W
Tyndall 198 42.59 N 97.51 W
Tyndall Air Force Base ■ 194 30.04 N 85.35 W
Tyndaris ⊥ 70 38.09 N 15.03 E
Tyndinskij 74 55.10 N 124.43 E
Tyndrum 46 56.27 N 4.44 W
Tyne ≃, Eng., U.K. 44 55.01 N 1.26 W
Tyne ≃, Scot., U.K. 46 56.01 N 2.37 W
Tyne and Wear □[6] 44 54.55 N 1.35 W
Tynemouth 44 55.01 N 1.24 W
Tyner 216 41.24 N 86.24 W
Tyngsboro 283 42.40 N 71.25 W
Tyngsjö 40 60.18 N 13.53 E
Týn nad Vltavou 30 49.14 N 14.26 E
Tynnelsö 40 59.25 N 17.06 E
Tynset 26 62.17 N 10.47 E
Tynytsya 78 51.08 N 32.54 E
Tyonek 180 61.02 N 151.17 W
Typta 88 54.35 N 104.31 E
Tyr 89 52.57 N 139.48 E
Tyre — Şūr, Lubnān 132 33.16 N 35.11 E
Tyre, Pa., U.S. 214 40.26 N 80.16 W
Tyresö 40 59.14 N 18.18 E
Tyret' 88 53.41 N 102.19 E
Tyrgetuj 88 51.27 N 113.46 E
Tyrifjorden ⊜ 26 60.02 N 10.08 E
Tyringe 41 56.10 N 13.35 E
Tyringham 207 42.14 N 73.12 W
Tyrka 88 54.30 N 107.09 E
Tyrma 89 50.03 N 132.12 E
Tyrma ≃ 89 50.29 N 131.18 E
Tyrnyauz 84 43.23 N 42.56 E
Tyrone, Ky., U.S. 218 38.01 N 84.50 W
Tyrone, N.Y., U.S. 210 42.25 N 77.03 W
Tyrone, Ok., U.S. 196 36.57 N 101.03 W
Tyrone, Pa., U.S. 214 40.40 N 78.14 W
Tyrone Lake ⊜ 281 42.42 N 83.43 W
Tyrrell, Lake ⊜ 166 35.21 S 142.50 E
Tyrrellspass 48 53.23 N 7.22 W
Tyrrhenian Sea (Mare Tirreno) ⊤[2] 36 40.00 N 12.00 E
Tyrrhenisches Meer — Tyrrhenian Sea ⊤[2] 36 40.00 N 12.00 E
Tysa (Tisa) (Tisza) ≃ 38 45.15 N 20.17 E
Tyshkivka 78 48.29 N 30.56 E
Tysmenytsya 78 48.54 N 24.49 E
Tysnesøy I 26 60.00 N 5.35 E
Tysons Corner 284c 38.55 N 77.14 W
Tysons Corner Center ◆[9] 284c 38.55 N 77.13 W
Tysons Green 284c 38.55 N 77.15 W
Tysse 26 60.22 N 5.45 E
Tyssedal 26 60.07 N 6.34 E
Tysslingen ⊜ 40 59.19 N 15.02 E
Tystberga 40 58.52 N 17.15 E
Tystrup Sø ⊜ 41 55.22 N 11.35 E
Tytherington 262 53.17 N 2.08 W
Tytuvėnai 76 55.36 N 23.12 E
Ty Ty 192 31.28 N 83.38 W
Tyumen' — T'umen' 86 57.09 N 65.32 E
Tyvriv 78 49.01 N 28.30 E
Tywa ≃ 54 53.13 N 14.29 E
Tywardreath 42 50.22 N 4.41 W
Tywi ≃ 42 51.46 N 4.22 W
Tywyn 42 52.35 N 4.05 W
Tzaneen 156 23.50 S 30.09 E
Tzekung — Zigong 107 29.24 N 104.47 E
Tzeliutsing — Zigong 107 29.24 N 104.47 E
Tzucacab 232 20.04 N 89.03 W
Tzukung — Zigong 107 29.24 N 104.47 E
Tzupo — Boshan, Zhg. 98 36.29 N 117.50 E
Tzupo — Zibo, Zhg. 98 36.47 N 118.01 E

U

Uaboe 174b 0.31 S 166.55 E
Uac, Mount ∧ 116 12.12 N 123.40 E
Uaçá ≃ 250 4.13 N 51.32 W
Uagadugu — Ouagadougou 150 12.22 N 1.31 W
Uamba 152 7.12 S 16.25 E
Uamba (Wamba) ≃, Afr. 152 3.56 S 17.12 E
Uamba ≃, Ang. 152 7.58 S 17.09 E
Uampochane 158 26.23 S 32.41 E
Uaoa Bay ⊂ 229a 20.56 N 156.16 W
Uaran — Ouarâne ◆[1] 134 21.00 N 10.30 W
Uato-Lari 112 8.45 S 126.34 E
Uatumã ≃ 246 2.26 S 57.37 W
Uauá 250 9.50 S 39.28 W
Uaupés (Vaupés) ≃ 246 0.02 N 67.16 W
Uaxactún ⊥ 232 17.24 N 89.39 W
Ubá 255 21.07 S 42.56 W
Uba ≃ 86 50.15 N 81.41 E
Übach-Palenberg 56 50.55 N 6.07 E
Ubagan ≃ 86 54.24 N 64.45 E
Ubai 164 5.40 S 150.40 E
Ubaidullaganj 124 22.59 N 77.36 E
Ubaitaba 255 14.18 S 39.20 W
Ubajara 250 3.51 S 40.56 W
Ubajara, Parque Nacional de ♣ 250 3.47 S 40.56 W
Ubangi (Oubangui) ≃ 152 0.30 S 17.42 E
Ubatã 255 14.12 S 39.31 W
Ubaté 246 5.19 N 73.49 W
Ubatuba 256 23.26 S 45.04 W
Ubatuba, Baía de ⊂ 256 23.27 S 45.02 W
Ubauro 120 28.10 N 69.44 E
Ubay 116 10.03 N 124.28 E
Ubaye 62 44.28 N 6.22 E
Ubaye ≃ 62 44.28 N 6.18 E
Ubayyiḍ, Wādī al- ⋁ 128 32.34 N 43.48 E
Ubby 41 55.37 N 11.13 E
Ube 96 33.56 N 131.15 E
Úbeda 34 38.01 N 3.22 W
Uberaba 255 19.45 S 47.55 W
Uberaba ≃ 255 20.07 S 48.31 W
Uberaba, Lagoa ⊜ 248 17.30 S 57.45 W
Überackern 60 48.11 N 12.52 E
Über dem Wind, Inseln — Leeward Islands II 238 17.00 N 63.00 W
Uberlândia 255 18.56 S 48.18 W
Überlingen 58 47.46 N 9.10 E
Überlinger See ⊂ 58 47.45 N 9.09 E
Übersee 64 47.49 N 12.28 E
Ubiaja 150 6.38 N 6.21 E
Ubid' ≃ 78 51.27 N 32.29 E
Ubili 154 1.07 S 26.55 E
Ubin, Pulau I 271c 1.24 N 103.58 E
Ubina, Peña ∧ 34 43.01 N 5.57 W
Ubinskoje 86 55.19 N 79.41 E
Ubinskoje, ozero ⊜ 86 55.30 N 80.05 E
Ubl'a 30 48.55 N 22.23 E
Ubly 190 43.42 N 82.55 W
Uboldo 266b 45.37 N 9.00 E
Ubombo 158 27.33 S 32.00 E
Ubondo 154 0.52 S 25.37 E
Ubon Ratchathani 110 15.14 N 104.54 E
Úborsko 60 49.20 N 13.09 E
Ubort' (Ubarc') ≃ 78 52.06 N 28.28 E
Ubrique 34 36.41 N 5.27 W
Ubudiah, Masjid ◙[1] 114 4.46 N 100.56 E
Ubundu (Ponthierville) 154 0.21 S 25.29 E
Ubur-Tochtor 88 50.06 N 113.37 E
Uča ≃, Ross. 82 56.02 N 37.37 E
Uča ≃, Ross. 265b 55.56 N 37.57 E
Ucacha 252 33.02 S 63.31 W
Uč-Adži 128 38.05 N 62.48 E
Učaly 86 54.19 N 59.27 E
Učami 74 63.50 N 96.29 E
Ucar 84 40.31 N 47.39 E
Učaral 86 46.10 N [illegible]0.56 E
Ucayali □[5] 248 9.00 S 74.00 W
Ucayali ≃ 242 4.30 S 73.27 W
Uccellina, Monti dell' ⋏ 66 42.38 N 1.05 E
Uccle 50 50.48 N 4.19 E
Uch 123 29.14 N 1.03 E
Uchab 156 19.47 S 7.42 E
Uchāna 124 29.28 N [illegible]6.10 E
Uchaud 62 43.45 N 4.16 E
Uchee Creek ≃ 192 32.18 N [illegible]4.57 W
Uchihara 94 36.22 N 1[illegible].21 E
Uchihata 270 34.25 N 1[illegible].27 E
Uchiko 96 33.33 N 1[illegible].39 E
Uchi Lake 184 51.05 N [illegible].35 W
Uchinada 94 36.39 N 1[illegible].39 E
Uchinomi 96 34.30 N 1[illegible].20 E
Uchinoura 92 31.16 N 13[illegible].05 E
Uchiumi 96 33.01 N 13[illegible].30 E
Uchiura-wan ⊂ 92a 42.20 N 14[illegible].40 E
Uchiza 248 8.29 S 7[illegible].23 W
Uchoa 255 20.56 S 4[illegible].13 W
Ucholovo 80 53.47 N 4[illegible].29 E
Uchra ≃ 80 58.20 N 3[illegible].00 E
Uchta, Ross. 24 61.12 N 3[illegible].32 E
Uchta, Ross. 24 63.33 N 5[illegible].38 E
Uchte 52 52.30 N [illegible].54 E
Uchte ≃ 54 52.46 N 11.45 E
Uchtoma 76 60.10 N 38.[illegible]2 E
Uchtspringe 54 52.32 N 11.36 E
Učinskij Ryboučastok 86 60.02 N 65.[illegible]0 E
Učinskoje vodochranilišče ⊜[1] 82 56.02 N 37.[illegible]5 E
Uckange 56 49.18 N 6.[illegible]9 E
Ückendorf ◆[8] 263 51.30 N 7.[illegible]7 E
Uckermark ◆[1] 54 53.10 N 13.[illegible]5 E
Uckfield 42 50.58 N 0.[illegible]6 E
Üçköşe 130 40.13 N 41.[illegible]0 E
Uckro 54 51.51 N 13.[illegible]7 E
Učkupr'uk 85 40.33 N 71.[illegible]4 E
Učkurgan 85 41.07 N 72.[illegible]5 E
Ucluelet 182 48.57 N 125.[illegible]3 W
Ucon 202 43.35 N 111.[illegible]7 W
Üçpınar 130 37.08 N 32.[illegible] E
Ucria 70 38.03 N 14.[illegible] E
Üçtepeler ∧ 130 39.39 N 42.[illegible] E
Učterek 85 41.45 N 73.[illegible] E
Úcua ≃ 152 8.35 S 13.[illegible] E
Učujevskij Majdan 80 54.33 N 44.[illegible] E
Učur ≃ 74 58.48 N 130.3[illegible] E
Uda ≃, Ross. 88 56.05 N 99.3[illegible] E
Uda ≃, Ross. 88 51.47 N 107.3[illegible] E
Uda ≃, Ross. 89 54.42 N 135.1[illegible] E
Udagamandalam 122 11.24 N 76.4[illegible] E
Udaipur 120 24.35 N 73.4[illegible] E
Udala 126 21.35 N 86.3[illegible] E
Udalguri 120 26.46 N 92.0[illegible] E
Udall 198 37.23 N 97.0[illegible] W
Udamalpet 122 10.35 N 77.1[illegible] E
Udankudi 122 8.26 N 78.01 E
Udaquiola 252 36.34 S 58.31 W
Udarnyj 89 49.07 N 142.0[illegible] E
Uday ≃ 78 50.05 N 33.07 E
Udaypur 124 26.56 N 86.31 E
Udbina 36 44.32 N 15.46 E
Udby 41 55.05 N 11.57 E
Uddeholm 40 60.01 N 13.37 E
Uddel 52 52.15 N 5.46 E
Uddevalla 26 58.21 N 11.55 E
Uddingston 46 55.50 N 4.06 W
Uddjaure ⊜ 24 65.55 N 17.49 E
Udel'naja 82 55.38 N 38.03 E
Udel'naja ◆[8] 265a 60.01 N 30.19 E
Uden 52 51.40 N 5.36 E
Udenhout 52 51.37 N 5.08 E
Uder 56 51.22 N 10.05 E
Üdersdorf 56 50.09 N 6.49
Udgīr 122 18.23 N 77.07
Udhampur 123 32.56 N 75.08 E
Udhruḥ 132 30.20 N 35.36 E
Udi 150 6.19 N 7.25 E
Udimskij 24 61.09 N 45.52 E
Udine 64 46.03 N 13.14 E
Udine □[4] 64 46.10 N 13.00 E
Udmurtia — Udmurtija □[3] 80 57.00 N 53.00 E
Udmurtija □[3], Ross. 72 57.00 N 53.00 E
Udmurtija □[3], Ross. 80 57.00 N 53.00 E
Udokan, chrebet ⋏ 88 56.20 N 118.10 E
Udoml'a 76 57.52 N 35.01 E
Udone-jima I 94 34.28 N 139.18 E
Udono 92 33.44 N 136.01 E
Udon Thani 110 17.26 N 102.46 E
Udor, Mount ∧ 162 23.30 S 131.01 E
Udot I 175c 7.23 N 151.43 E
Udskaja guba ⊂ 89 54.50 N 135.45 E
Udskoje 89 54.32 N 134.26 E
Udubo 146 11.57 N 10.38 E
Udupi 122 13.21 N 74.45 E
Udy 78 50.24 N 36.03 E
Udyl', ozero ⊜ 89 52.06 N 139.48 E
Udža 74 71.14 N 117.10 E
Uebigau 54 51.35 N 13.18 E
Uebonti 112 0.55 S 121.38 E
Uebonti, Teluk ⊂ 112 0.50 S 121.45 E
Uecker ≃ 54 53.45 N 14.04 E
Ueckeritz 54 54.00 N 14.02 E
Ueckermünde 54 53.44 N 14.03 E
Ueckermünder Heide ◆[3] 54 53.40 N 14.10 E
Ueda 94 36.24 N 138.16 E
Uedem 52 51.40 N 6.16 E
Uedesheim 263 51.10 N 6.48 E
Uegō 268 35.13 N 139.56 E
Ueharu 175d 24.25 N 123.46 E
Uehlfeld 56 49.40 N 10.43 E
Uele ≃ 136 4.09 N 22.26 E
Uelen 180 66.10 N 169.48 W
Uel'kal' 180 65.32 N 179.17 W
Uelsen 52 52.30 N 6.53 E
Uelzen, Dtsch. 52 52.58 N 10.33 E
Uelzen, Dtsch. 263 51.33 N 7.44 E
Ueno, Nihon 94 36.05 N 138.47 E
Ueno, Nihon 94 34.45 N 136.08 E
Ueno, Nihon 270 34.53 N 135.14 E
Uenohara 94 35.37 N 139.07 E
Ueno Park ♣ 268 35.43 N 139.46 E
Uenoshiba 270 34.33 N 135.28 E
Uerdingen ◆[8] 263 51.21 N 6.39 E
Uere ≃ 154 3.42 N 25.24 E
Uetersen 52 53.41 N 9.39 E
Uettingen 56 49.48 N 9.43 E
Uetz 264a 52.28 N 12.56 E
Uetze 52 52.28 N 10.11 E
Ufa 86 54.44 N 55.56 E
Ufa ≃ 86 54.40 N 56.00 E
Ufala, Punta > 70 38.22 N 14.59 E
Uffculme 42 50.54 N 3.20 W
Uffenheim 56 49.32 N 10.14 E
Uffing 64 47.43 N 11.09 E
Ufita ≃ 68 41.09 N 14.56 E
Ufra 128 40.00 N 53.02 E
Uft'uga ≃ 76 59.46 N 39.21 E
Ugab ≃ 156 21.08 S 13.40 E
Ugak Bay ⊂ 180 57.25 N 152.45 W
Ugāle 76 57.16 N 22.02 E
Ugalla ≃ 154 5.08 S 30.42 E
Ugamskij chrebet ⋏ 85 42.00 N 70.20 E
Uganda □[1] 154 1.00 N 32.00 E
Uganik Island I 180 57.53 N 153.28 W
Ugărčin 38 43.06 N 24.25 E
Ugarit ⊥ 130 35.35 N 35.45 E
Ugashik 180 57.32 N 157.25 W
Ugashik Bay ⊂ 180 57.34 N 157.38 W
Ugatkyn ≃ 180 68.24 N 171.30 E
Ugento 68 39.56 N 18.10 E
Ugep 150 5.48 N 8.05 E


| | | | | |
|---|---|---|---|---|
| ≃ River | Fluß | Río | Rivière | Rio |
| ≊ Canal | Kanal | Canal | Canal | Canal |
| ⌊ Waterfall, Rapids | Wasserfall, Stromschnellen | Cascada, Rápidos | Chute d'eau, Rapides | Cascata, Rápidos |
| ⊔ Strait | Meeresstraße | Estrecho | Détroit | Estreito |
| ⊂ Bay, Gulf | Bucht, Golf | Bahía, Golfo | Baie, Golfe | Baía, Golfo |
| ⊜ Lake, Lakes | See, Seen | Lago, Lagos | Lac, Lacs | Lago, Lagos |
| ≡ Swamp | Sumpf | Pantano | Marais | Pântano |
| ⊡ Ice Features, Glacier | Eis- und Gletscherformen | Accidentes Glaciales | Formes glaciaires | Acidentes glaciares |
| ⊤ Other Hydrographic Features | Andere Hydrographische Objekte | Otros Elementos Hydrográficos | Autres données hydrographiques | Outros acidentes hidrográficos |

| | | | | |
|---|---|---|---|---|
| ✢ Submarine Features | Untermeerische Objekte | Accidentes Submarinos | Formes de relief sous-marin | Acidentes submarinos |
| □ Political Unit | Politische Einheit | Unidad Politica | Entité politique | Unidade política |
| ◙ Cultural Institution | Kulturelle Institution | Institución Cultural | Institution culturelle | Instituição cultural |
| ⊥ Historical Site | Historische Stätte | Sitio Histórico | Site historique | Sitio histórico |
| ♣ Recreational Site | Erholungs- und Ferienort | Sitio de Recreo | Centre de loisirs | Area de Lazer |
| ⊠ Airport | Flughafen | Aeropuerto | Aéroport | Aeroporto |
| ■ Military Installation | Militäranlage | Instalación Militar | Installation militaire | Instalação militar |
| ◆ Miscellaneous | Verschiedenes | Misceláneo | Divers | Diversos |

Ugerløse 41 55.35 N 11.40 E
Uggiano la Chiesa 68 40.06 N 18.27 E
Ughaybish 140 10.52 N 31.05 E
Ughelli 150 5.29 N 5.59 E
Ugie 158 31.10 S 28.13 E
Ugie ≃ 46 57.30 N 1.47 W
Ugíjar 34 36.57 N 3.03 W
Ugine 62 45.45 N 6.25 E
Uglegorsk 89 49.02 N 142.03 E
Uglekamensk 89 43.13 N 133.11 E
Uglezavodsk 89 47.21 N 142.38 E
Uglič 76 57.32 N 38.19 E
Ugljan, Otok I 36 44.05 N 15.10 E
Uglovaja 80 57.01 N 52.57 E
Uglovka 76 58.14 N 33.31 E
Uglovoje 89 43.20 N 132.06 E
Uglovskoje 86 51.23 N 80.12 E
Ugodiči 80 57.10 N 39.30 E
Ugodskij Zavod 82 55.02 N 36.45 E
Ugol'naja, buchta c 180 63.00 N 179.20 E
Ugolnyy 180 62.58 N 179.17 E
Ugoma ∧ 154 4.00 S 28.45 E
Ugovizza 64 46.31 N 13.29 E
Ugra 76 54.47 N 34.17 E
Ugra ≃ 82 54.30 N 36.07 E
Ugr'umovo 82 55.09 N 37.40 E
Ugtaal Cajdam 88 48.17 N 105.25 E
Uguj 86 56.02 N 76.03 E
Uğurludağ 130 40.27 N 34.28 E
Ug'ut 85 41.24 N 74.50 E
Ugyak, Cape › 180 58.17 N 154.04 W
Uh (Uzh) ≃ 30 48.34 N 22.00 E
Uha-dong 98 40.41 N 125.38 E
Uhayjibah, Jabal al- ∧ 132 30.11 N 34.33 E
Uherčice 61 48.55 N 15.38 E
Uherské Hradiště 30 49.05 N 17.28 E
Uherský Brod 30 49.02 N 17.39 E
Uhingen 56 48.42 N 9.35 E
Úhlava ≃ 60 49.43 N 13.23 E
Uhldingen-Mühlhofen 58 47.44 N 9.15 E
Uhlenhorst 156 23.45 S 17.55 E
Ühlingen 58 47.43 N 8.19 E
Uhlman Lake ◎ 184 56.40 N 98.23 W
Uhlstädt 54 50.44 N 11.28 E
Uhniv 78 50.23 N 23.44 E
Uhrichsville 214 40.23 N 81.20 W
Uhroyidi 78 50.52 N 35.17 E
Uhyst, Dtsch. 54 51.11 N 14.13 E
Uhyst, Dtsch. 54 51.24 N 14.30 E
Uiche 152 12.03 S 21.02 E
Ui-do I 98 34.37 N 125.51 E
Uig 46 57.35 N 6.22 W
Uíge 152 7.37 S 15.03 E
Uíge □[5] 152 7.00 S 15.30 E
Ŭijŏngbu 98 37.44 N 127.03 E
Ŭiju 98 40.12 N 124.32 E
Uil 86 49.05 N 54.40 E
Uil ≃ 80 48.36 N 52.30 E
Uilpata, gora ∧ 84 42.48 N 43.48 E
Uimaharju 26 62.55 N 30.15 E
Uinebona ≃ 246 5.04 S 63.01 W
Uinskoje 86 56.53 N 56.35 E
Uinta ≃ 200 40.14 N 109.51 W
Uintah and Ouray Indian Reservation ●[4] 200 40.20 N 110.20 W
Uinta Mountains ⋀ 200 40.45 N 110.05 W
Uiraúna 250 6.31 S 38.25 W
Uis 156 21.08 S 14.49 E
Ŭisŏng 98 36.22 N 128.41 E
Uitenhage 158 33.40 S 25.28 E
Uitgeest 52 52.32 N 4.43 E
Uithoorn 52 52.14 N 4.50 E
Uithuizen 52 53.24 N 6.40 E
Uithuizermeeden 52 53.24 N 6.42 E
Uitspanning 158 26.46 S 29.56 E
Uj ≃, Asia 86 54.17 N 64.58 E
Uj ≃, Ross. 86 57.06 N 74.12 E
Ujae I[1] 14 9.05 N 165.40 E
Ujaly 86 44.37 N 60.57 E
Ujandina ≃ 74 68.23 N 145.50 E
Ujar 86 55.48 N 94.20 E
Ujarrás ⊥ 236 9.51 N 83.50 W
Ujedinenija, ostrov I 72 77.28 N 82.28 E
Ujelang I[1] 14 9.49 N 160.55 E
Ujemskij 24 64.29 N 40.50 E
Újezd, Česká Rep. 54 50.03 N 14.44 E
Újezd, Česká Rep. 60 49.26 N 13.27 E
Újezd u Brna 61 49.06 N 16.45 E
Újfehértó 30 47.48 N 21.40 E
Ujgursaj 85 40.53 N 71.03 E
Ujhāni 124 28.01 N 79.01 E
Uji 96 34.53 N 135.48 E
Uji ≃ 96 34.53 N 135.42 E
Uji-guntō II 92 31.11 N 129.27 E
Ujiie 94 36.41 N 139.58 E
Ujiji 154 4.55 S 29.41 E
Uji-tawara 96 34.51 N 135.52 E
Uji-yamada → Ise 94 34.29 N 136.42 E
Ujjain 120 23.11 N 75.46 E
Újkér 61 47.28 N 16.49 E
'Ujmān 128 25.25 N 55.27 E
Újpest ●[8] 264c 47.34 N 19.06 E
Ujście 30 53.04 N 16.43 E
Ujskoje 86 54.22 N 60.00 E
Ujuk 85 43.46 N 70.58 E
Ujum 85 38.22 N 70.51 E
Ujung 112 7.04 S 120.46 E
Ujungbatu 114 0.43 N 100.31 E
Ujungbatu, Pulau I 114 2.20 N 97.24 E
Ujungberung 115a 6.55 S 107.42 E
Ujunggading 110 0.16 N 99.33 E
Ujunggenteng 115a 7.22 S 106.24 E
Ujungkulon, Semenanjung ›[1] 115a 6.45 S 105.20 E
Ujungkulon National Park ♠ 115a 6.40 S 105.20 E
Ujunglamuru 112 4.40 S 119.58 E
Ujungpandang (Makasar) 112 5.07 S 119.24 E
Újvidék → Novi Sad 38 45.15 N 19.50 E
Uk 88 55.04 N 98.52 E
Uka, Nihon 174m 26.48 N 128.14 E
Uka, Ross. 74 57.50 N 162.06 E
Ukamas 158 28.02 S 19.45 E
Ukara Island I 154 1.50 S 33.03 E
Ukerewe Island I 154 2.03 S 33.00 E
Ukhaydir, Wādī V 132 30.55 N 37.01 E
Ukhra 126 23.39 N 87.14 E
Ukhrul 120 25.07 N 94.22 E
Ukhta → Uchta 24 63.33 N 53.38 E
Ukiah, Ca., U.S. 204 39.09 N 123.12 W
Ukiah, Or., U.S. 202 45.08 N 118.55 W
Ukibaru-jima I 174m 26.18 N 128.00 E
Ukiha 96 33.19 N 130.47 E
Uki Ni Masi Island I 175e 10.15 S 161.45 E
Ukmergė 76 55.15 N 24.45 E
Ukolnoi Island I 180 55.14 N 161.34 W
Ukraina → Ukraine □[1] 22 49.00 N 32.00 E
Ukraine □[1], Europe 22 49.00 N 32.00 E
Ukraine (Ukrayina) □[1], Europe 78 49.00 N 32.00 E
Ukrainka 86 54.39 N 71.20 E
Ukrayins'k 83 48.06 N 37.18 E
Ukrina ≃ 36 45.05 N 17.56 E
Uks'anskoje 86 55.57 N 63.01 E
Uktuz 86 55.38 N 68.30 E
Uktym 24 62.38 N 48.52 E
Uku 152 11.24 S 14.15 E
Ukui 112 0.09 S 102.11 E
Ukurejskij 88 52.24 N 116.49 E
Ukuti 154 3.39 N 33.32 E
Ukyō ●[8] 270 35.03 N 135.42 E
Ukyr 88 49.28 N 108.52 E
Ula, Bela. 76 55.14 N 29.15 E
Ula, India 272b 22.43 N 88.33 E
Ula, Tür. 130 37.05 N 28.26 E
Ula ≃, Bela. 76 55.14 N 29.14 E
Ūla ≃, Europe 76 54.10 N 24.20 E
Ulaanbaatar 88 47.55 N 106.53 E
Ulaanbaatar □[8] 88 47.55 N 106.53 E
Ulaanbadrach 102 44.07 N 110.11 E
Ulaan Chus 86 49.02 N 89.23 E
Ulaangom 86 49.58 N 92.02 E
Ulaan nuur ◎ 102 44.30 N 103.35 E
Ulaan Tajga ⋀ 88 50.45 N 98.30 E
Ula-Chuduk 80 47.39 N 45.34 E
Ulak Island I 181a 51.22 N 179.00 W
Ulakmedan 114 2.43 N 99.38 E
Ulamba 152 9.07 S 23.40 E
Ulamona 164 5.00 S 151.15 E
Ulan, Austl. 166 32.17 S 149.44 E
Ulan, Zhg. 102 36.59 N 98.26 E
Ulan Bator → Ulaanbaatar 88 47.55 N 106.53 E
Ulanbel' 86 44.48 N 71.10 E
Ulan Buh Shamo ●[2] 102 40.00 N 106.30 E
Ulan-Burgasy, chrebet ⋀ 88 52.45 N 109.00 E
Ulan-Erge 80 46.19 N 44.53 E
Ulang ≃ 236 14.27 N 83.14 W
Ulanhot → Horqin Youyi Qianqi 89 46.05 N 122.05 E
Ulānia 126 22.12 N 90.29 E
Ulaniv 78 49.42 N 28.08 E
Ulanove 78 51.46 N 34.18 E
Ulanovskij 82 54.04 N 37.51 E
Ulanów 30 50.30 N 22.16 E
Ulansuhai Nur ◎ 102 40.56 N 108.49 E
Ulan-Ude 88 51.50 N 107.37 E
Ulan Ul Hu ◎ 120 34.45 N 90.25 E
Ulan-Ušotej 88 50.45 N 105.29 E
Ular, Pulau I 271c 1.14 N 103.45 E
Ulaş 130 39.27 N 37.03 E
Ul'ašovo 24 65.27 N 56.57 E
Ulatis Creek ≃ 226 38.18 N 121.00 W
Ul'atuj 88 51.09 N 116.14 E
Ulawa Island I 175e 9.46 S 161.57 E
Ulawun, Mount ∧ 164 5.03 S 151.20 E
Ulaya 154 7.04 S 36.54 E
Ułazów 30 50.17 N 23.00 E
Ul'ba 86 50.16 N 83.22 E
Ul'banskij zaliv c 89 53.45 N 137.50 E
Ulchin 98 36.59 N 129.23 E
Ul'chun-Partija 88 49.56 N 112.46 E
Ulcinj 38 41.55 N 19.11 E
Ulco 158 28.21 S 24.15 E
Ulcombe 260 51.12 N 0.39 E
Ulcumayo 248 11.01 S 75.55 W
Uldum 41 55.51 N 9.36 E
Uldz ≃ 88 49.56 N 115.31 E
Uleåborg → Oulu 26 65.01 N 25.28 E
Ulefoss 26 59.17 N 9.16 E
Ulen 198 47.04 N 96.15 W
Ulety 88 51.22 N 112.29 E
Ulfborg 26 56.16 N 8.20 E
Ulft 52 51.54 N 6.23 E
Ulgueira 266c 38.47 N 9.28 W
Ulhās ≃ 272c 19.13 N 73.01 E
Ulhāsnagar 122 19.13 N 73.07 E
Uliast 86 48.57 N 91.17 E
Uliastaj (Džavchlant) 88 47.45 N 96.49 E
Ulice 60 49.45 N 13.09 E
Ulindi ≃ 154 1.40 S 25.52 E
Ulingan 164 4.30 S 145.25 E
Ulithi I[1] 108 9.58 N 139.40 E
Ulja 74 58.51 N 141.50 E
Uljanino 82 55.21 N 38.26 E
Uljanovka 76 59.38 N 30.46 E
Uljanovo, Ross. 76 53.43 N 35.32 E
Uljanovo, Uzb. 85 40.07 N 68.30 E
Uljanovsk 80 54.20 N 48.24 E
Ul'janovskij 86 50.02 N 73.42 E
Uljanovsk Oblast' □[4] 80 53.30 N 47.30 E
Uljanovskoje 89 46.17 N 142.13 E
Uljuan tekojärvi ◎ 26 64.19 N 25.57 E
Ul'kajak ≃ 86 48.54 N 62.00 E
Ul'kan 88 57.14 N 107.19 E
Ul'kan ≃ 88 55.53 N 107.45 E
Ul'ken-Karoj, ozero ◎ 86 54.00 N 71.58 E
Ulla ≃ 34 42.39 N 8.44 W
Ulladulla 170 35.21 S 150.29 E
Ulladulla Head › 170 35.22 S 150.30 E
Ullāpāra 126 24.19 N 89.34 E
Ullapool 46 57.54 N 5.10 W
Ullastrell 266d 41.31 N 1.58 E
Üllendahl ●[8] 263 51.17 N 7.11 E
Ullerslev 41 55.22 N 10.40 E
Ullervad 40 58.40 N 13.52 E
Ullin 194 37.17 N 89.11 W
Üllő 264c 47.23 N 19.21 E
Ullswater ◎ 44 54.34 N 2.54 W
Ullučaj ≃ 84 42.18 N 48.08 E
Ullŭng-do I 92 37.29 N 130.52 E
Ullvettern ◎ 40 59.27 N 14.16 E
Ullvi 40 59.42 N 16.37 E
Ulm, Dtsch. 58 48.24 N 10.00 E
Ulm, Mt., U.S. 202 47.25 N 111.30 W
Ul'ma ≃ 89 51.54 N 129.18 E
Ulmarra 166 29.37 S 153.02 E
Ulmen 56 50.13 N 6.59 E
Ulmeni 38 45.04 N 26.39 E
Ulmer, Mount ∧ 9 77.35 S 86.09 W
Ulongué 154 14.37 S 34.19 E
Ulpur 126 23.04 N 89.50 E
Ulricehamn 26 57.47 N 13.25 E
Ulrichskirchen 61 48.24 N 16.29 E
Ulrichstein 56 50.34 N 9.11 E
Ulrum 52 53.22 N 6.20 E
Ulsan 98 35.34 N 129.19 E
Ulsta 46a 60.30 N 1.09 W
Ulsteinvik 26 62.20 N 5.53 E
Ulster 210 41.51 N 76.30 W
Ulster □[6] 210 41.56 N 74.00 W
Ulster □[9] 48 54.35 N 7.00 W
Ulster ≃ 56 50.51 N 9.59 E
Ulster Canal ≅ 48 54.08 N 7.22 W
Ultimo, Val d' V 64 46.35 N 11.00 E
Ultraoriental, Cordillera (Serra do Divisor) ⋀ 248 8.20 S 73.30 W
Ulu, Indon. 112 2.45 N 125.24 E
Ulu, Ross. 74 60.19 N 127.24 E
Ulu, Sūd. 140 10.43 N 33.29 E
Ulúa ≃ 236 15.53 N 87.44 W
Ulubāria 126 22.28 N 88.06 E
Ulubat Gölü ◎ 130 40.10 N 28.35 E
Ulubey, Tür. 130 38.25 N 29.18 E
Ulubey, Tür. 130 40.53 N 37.43 E
Uluborlu 130 38.05 N 30.28 E
Uluçınar 130 36.27 N 35.51 E
Uludağ ∧ 130 40.04 N 29.13 E
Uludāngar 272b 22.51 N 88.31 E
Uludere 128 37.27 N 42.51 E
Ulugan Bay c 116 10.07 N 118.47 E
Ulugqat 85 39.48 N 74.21 E
Uluinggalau ∧ 175g 16.54 S 179.59 E
Ulujul ≃ 86 57.46 N 85.30 E
Ulukışla, Kıbrıs 130 35.13 N 33.37 E
Ulukışla, Tür. 130 37.33 N 34.30 E
Ulul I 14 8.35 N 149.40 E
Ulu Laho, Bukit ∧ 114 5.43 N 101.27 E
Ulunchan 88 54.51 N 111.02 E
Ulundi 158 28.17 S 31.26 E
Ulunga 89 46.31 N 136.56 E
Ulungur ≃ 86 46.59 N 87.27 E
Ulungur Hu ◎ 86 47.15 N 87.20 E
Ulurijskij Golec, gora ∧ 88 50.12 N 111.45 E
Uluru National Park ♠ 162 25.20 S 131.00 E
Ulus 130 41.35 N 32.39 E
Ulusara 126 24.16 N 90.36 E
Ulut ≃ 116 12.00 N 125.27 E
Ulutau, gora ∧ 86 48.39 N 66.56 E
Ulutau, gory ⋀ 86 49.00 N 67.00 E
Ulu Tiram 114 1.36 N 103.49 E
Ulu Yam 114 3.27 N 101.38 E
Ulva 272c 18.59 N 73.02 E
Ulva I 46 56.29 N 6.14 W
Ulvenhout 52 51.34 N 4.48 E
Ulverston 44 54.12 N 3.06 W
Ulverstone 166 41.09 S 146.10 E
Ulvöarna II 26 63.01 N 18.40 E
Ulvshale ›[1] 41 55.02 N 12.16 E
Ulvshyttan 40 60.18 N 15.22 E
Ulvsund ʯ 41 54.59 N 12.11 E
Ulyanivka 78 50.58 N 34.18 E
Ul'yanovka 78 48.20 N 30.13 E
Ulyanovsk → Uljanovsk 80 54.20 N 48.24 E
Ulysses, Ks., U.S. 198 37.34 N 101.21 W
Ulysses, Ne., U.S. 198 41.04 N 97.12 W
Ulysses, Pa., U.S. 214 41.54 N 77.46 W
Ulytau 86 48.39 N 67.01 E
Uly-Žylanšyk ≃ 86 48.51 N 63.47 E
Ulzë 38 41.41 N 19.54 E
Uma 89 52.36 N 120.37 E
Umag 36 45.25 N 13.32 E
Umaji 96 33.33 N 134.03 E
Umal'tinskij 89 51.56 N 133.36 E
Umán, Méx. 232 20.53 N 89.45 W
Uman', Ukr. 78 48.44 N 30.14 E
'Umān → Oman □[1] 118 22.00 N 58.00 E
Uman I 175c 7.18 N 151.53 E
Umanak 176 70.40 N 52.07 W
Umanak Fjord c[2] 176 70.55 N 53.00 W
Umancevo 80 47.44 N 44.16 E
Umargāon 122 20.12 N 72.45 E
Umari 250 6.38 S 38.42 W
Umari ≃ 248 7.05 S 64.34 W
'Umarī, Qā' al- ◎ 132 31.42 N 36.57 E
Umaria 124 23.32 N 80.50 E
Umarizal 250 5.59 S 37.49 W
Umarkot 120 25.22 N 69.44 E
Umatac 174p 13.18 N 144.39 E
Umatilla, Fl., U.S. 220 28.55 N 81.39 W
Umatilla, Or., U.S. 202 45.55 N 119.20 W
Umatilla ≃ 202 45.55 N 119.20 W
Umatilla, Lake ◎[1] 202 45.44 N 120.35 W
Umatilla Indian Reservation ●[4] 202 45.41 N 118.31 W
Umayan ≃ 116 8.13 N 125.50 E
Umaze 270 34.57 N 135.03 E
Umba 24 66.41 N 34.15 E
Umbagog Lake ◎ 188 44.45 N 71.05 W
Umbai 114 2.10 N 102.20 E
Umbaúba 250 11.22 S 37.39 W
Umbelasha ≃ 140 9.51 N 24.50 E
Umbertide 66 43.18 N 12.20 E
Umbogintwini 158 30.00 S 30.58 E
Umboi Island I 164 5.36 S 148.00 E
Umbrail, Pass (Giogo di Santa Maria) )( 64 46.34 N 10.25 E
Umbria □[4] 66 43.00 N 12.30 E
Umbriatico 68 39.21 N 16.55 E
Umbroli 272c 19.11 N 73.06 E
Umbukul 164 2.30 S 150.00 E
Umbuzero, ozero ◎ 24 67.43 N 34.25 E
Ume ≃ 154 16.40 S 28.26 E
Umeå 26 63.50 N 20.15 E
Umeälven ≃ 24 63.47 N 20.16 E
Umedani 270 34.44 N 135.51 E
Umedpur 126 22.31 N 89.59 E
Umfolozi Game Reserve ●[4] 158 28.19 S 31.50 E
Umfors 24 65.56 N 15.00 E
Umfreville Lake ◎ 184 50.18 N 94.45 W
Umfuli ≃ 154 17.30 S 29.23 E
Umgungundhlovu ⊥ 158 28.27 S 31.28 E
Umguza 154 19.25 S 27.51 E
Umhausen 64 47.08 N 10.56 E
Umhlanga Rocks 158 29.43 S 31.06 E
Umi 96 33.34 N 130.30 E
Umingan 116 15.56 N 120.50 E
Umkomaas 158 30.15 S 30.42 E
Umm ad-Daraj, Jabal ∧ 132 32.19 N 35.48 E
Umm 'Ajārim ⊥[8] 142 30.50 N 32.49 E
Umm al-Abīd 146 27.31 N 15.02 E
Umm al-'Arā'is, Wādī V 146 26.26 N 13.55 E
Umm al-Arānib 146 26.08 N 14.45 E
Umm al-Birak 128 23.25 N 39.13 E
Umm al-Ḥawāyā, Jabal ∧ 142 28.41 N 31.06 E
Umm al-Jimāl, Khirbat ⊥ 132 32.20 N 36.22 E
Umm al-Khashab 144 17.21 N 42.32 E
Umm al-Qaywayn 128 25.35 N 55.34 E
Umm al-Qiṭṭayn 132 32.19 N 36.38 E
Umm al-Quṣūr 142 27.23 N 30.54 E
Ummanz 54 54.28 N 13.10 E
Umm Artah, Wādī V 142 28.41 N 32.37 E
Umm as-Sa'd ⊥ 132 33.16 N 36.47 E
Umm Badr 140 14.14 N 27.57 E
Umm Balad, Wādī V 142 27.40 N 32.39 E
Umm Bayyū'd 140 12.05 N 31.40 E
Umm Bel 140 13.32 N 28.04 E
Umm Boim 140 11.43 N 25.57 E
Umm Dabbī 140 14.37 N 30.23 E
Umm Dam 140 13.45 N 30.59 E
Umm Dhibbān, Sūd. 140 14.14 N 29.37 E
Umm Dhibbān, Sūd. 140 15.26 N 32.51 E
Umm Digulgulaya 140 10.29 N 24.57 E
Umm Dīnār 142 30.12 N 31.04 E
Umm Durmān (Omdurman) 140 15.38 N 32.30 E
Umm el Faḥm 132 32.31 N 35.09 E
Ummeln 52 51.58 N 8.27 E
Ummendorf 54 52.09 N 11.11 E
Ummerstadt 54 50.15 N 10.48 E
Umm Habwah, Jabal ∧[2] 142 27.23 N 31.29 E
Umm Ḥamāṭ 132 31.02 N 35.46 E
Umm Jamālah 140 11.27 N 28.12 E
Umm Kaddādah 140 13.36 N 26.42 E
Umm Khunān 273c 29.55 N 31.15 E
Umm Khushayb, Wādī V 142 30.24 N 32.43 E
Umm Kuwaykah 140 13.00 N 32.17 E
Umm Lajj 128 25.04 N 37.13 E
Umm Marahik, Jabal ∧[2] 140 13.40 N 26.53 E
Umm Mirdi 140 18.59 N 33.32 E
Umm Mitmān ⊥[8] 142 30.41 N 32.30 E
Umm Qantur 140 14.17 N 31.22 E
Umm Qaṣr 128 30.02 N 47.56 E
Umm Qurayn 140 9.58 N 28.55 E
Umm Quṣayr 132 31.40 N 35.53 E
Umm Raqm, Jabal ∧ 142 30.14 N 31.52 E
Umm Rīshah, Birkat ◎ 142 30.21 N 30.22 E
Umm Rumaylah ⍑[4] 140 16.55 N 31.40 E
Umm Ruwābah 140 12.54 N 31.13 E
Umm Saggāt, Wādī V 140 15.15 N 23.12 E
Umm Saysabān, Jabal ∧ 132 29.45 N 35.10 E
Umm Sayyālah 140 14.25 N 31.10 E
Umm Shalīl 140 10.51 N 23.42 E
Umm Shanqah 140 13.14 N 27.14 E
Umm Shuṭūr 140 7.17 N 33.14 E
Umm Sidr, Wādī V 142 27.54 N 32.33 E
Umm Sughra ⍑[4] 140 15.03 N 27.12 E
Umm 'Umayd, Ra's ∧ 142 27.50 N 32.19 E
Umm 'Umayyid, Bi'r ⍑[4] 142 27.53 N 32.30 E
Umm 'Umayyid, Wādī V 142 27.37 N 32.41 E
Umm Urūmah I 128 25.46 N 36.32 E
Umm Walad 132 32.39 N 36.26 E
Umm Zaytah, Jabal ∧[2] 142 29.49 N 32.16 E
Umnak 180 53.17 N 168.20 W
Umnak Island I 180 53.25 N 168.10 W
Umnak Pass ʯ 180 53.20 N 167.45 W
Umnäs 24 65.24 N 16.10 E
Umniati 154 18.39 S 29.49 E
Umniati ≃ 154 17.30 S 29.23 E
Um'ot, Ross. 80 54.08 N 42.42 E
Um'ot, Ross. 80 52.31 N 42.58 E
Umpferstedt 54 50.59 N 11.25 E
Umpqua ≃ 202 43.42 N 124.03 W
Umpulo 152 12.38 S 17.42 E
'Umrān 144 15.50 N 43.56 E
'Umrānī, Wādī al- V 142 27.37 N 30.53 E
Umraniye 130 39.10 N 31.15 E
Umraniye ●[8] 267b 41.01 N 29.05 E
Umred 122 20.51 N 79.20 E
Umreth 120 22.42 N 73.07 E
Umsini, Gunung ∧ 164 1.22 S 133.45 E
Ŭmsŏng 98 36.56 N 127.41 E
Umstead State Park ♠ 192 35.52 N 78.47 W
Umtanum Creek ≃ 224 46.52 N 120.35 W
Umtata 158 31.35 S 28.47 E
Umtentweni 158 30.42 S 30.28 E
Umuahia 150 5.33 N 7.29 E
Umuarama 255 23.45 S 53.20 W
Umurbey 130 40.14 N 26.36 E
Umurlu 130 37.50 N 27.58 E
Umzimkulu 158 30.16 S 29.56 E
Umzingwani ≃ 154 22.12 S 29.56 E
Umzinto 158 30.22 S 30.33 E
Una, Bra. 255 15.18 S 39.04 W
Una, India 120 20.49 N 71.02 E
Una, India 123 31.29 N 76.17 E
Una ≃ 36 45.16 N 16.55 E
Una, Mount ∧ 172 42.13 S 172.35 E
Una, Ribeirão ≃ 287b 23.31 S 46.18 W
Unac ≃ 36 44.30 N 16.09 E
Uña de Gato 196 25.58 N 99.41 W
Unadilla, Ga., U.S. 192 32.15 N 83.44 W
Unadilla, N.Y., U.S. 210 42.19 N 75.18 W
Unadilla ≃ 210 42.20 N 75.25 W
Unaí 255 16.23 S 46.53 W
Unakami 94 35.46 N 140.45 E
Unalakleet 180 63.53 N 160.47 W
Unalaska 180 53.52 N 166.32 W
Unalaska Island I 180 53.45 N 166.45 W
Unanderra 170 34.27 S 150.52 E
Unango 154 12.50 S 35.20 E
Únanov 61 48.54 N 16.04 E
Unao 124 25.35 N 78.36 E
Unare ≃ 246 10.03 N 65.14 W
Unauna, Pulau I 112 0.10 S 121.35 E
Unayyir, Ḥarrat al- ⊥[9] 128 25.20 N 37.45 E
'Unayzah, Ar. Su. 128 26.06 N 43.56 E
'Unayzah, Urd. 132 30.29 N 35.48 E
'Unayzah, Jabal ∧, Asia 128 32.12 N 39.18 E
'Unayzah, Jabal ∧, Urd. 132 30.30 N 35.47 E
Unazuki 94 36.49 N 137.35 E
Uncasville 207 41.26 N 72.06 W
Unchahra 124 24.23 N 80.47 E
Ŭnch'ŏn 98 38.34 N 125.26 E
Uncia 248 18.27 S 66.37 W
Uncompahgre ≃ 200 38.45 N 108.06 W
Uncompahgre Peak ∧ 200 38.04 N 107.28 W
Uncompahgre Plateau ⋀[1] 200 38.30 N 108.25 W
Uncukul' 84 42.42 N 46.48 E
Uncular 130 40.28 N 41.28 E
Unda 88 51.42 N 116.56 E
Unda ≃ 88 51.25 N 116.05 E
Unden ◎ 40 58.47 N 14.26 E
Undenäs 40 58.39 N 14.25 E
Underberg 158 29.50 S 29.22 E
Under River 260 51.15 N 0.14 E
Undersåker 26 63.20 N 13.23 E
Underwood, In., U.S. 218 38.36 N 85.46 W
Underwood, N.D., U.S. 198 47.27 N 101.08 W
Underwood, Wa., U.S. 224 45.43 N 121.31 W
Undløse 41 55.36 N 11.35 E
Undory 80 54.37 N 48.25 E
Undu, Tanjung › 115b 10.05 S 120.51 E
Undu Point › 175g 16.08 S 179.57 W
Undva nina › 76 58.32 N 21.55 E
Unea Island I 164 4.55 S 149.10 E
Uneča 76 52.50 N 32.40 E
Uneča ≃ 76 52.50 N 31.56 E
Uneiuxi ≃ 246 0.34 S 64.58 W
Úněšov 60 49.53 N 13.09 E
Unga Island I 180 55.15 N 160.45 W
Ungama Bay c 154 2.45 S 40.20 E
Ungaran 115a 7.07 S 110.24 E
Ungarie 166 33.38 S 146.58 E
Ungarn → Hungary □[1] 30 47.00 N 20.00 E
Ungava, Péninsule d' ›[1] 176 60.00 N 74.00 W
Ungava Bay c 176 59.30 N 67.30 W
Ungch'ŏn 98 35.07 N 128.44 E
Unggi 98 42.20 N 130.24 E
Ungheni 38 47.12 N 27.48 E
Ungurkuj 88 50.27 N 106.58 E
Ungvár → Uzhhorod 78 48.37 N 22.18 E
Unhos 266c 38.50 N 9.07 W
Unhošť 54 50.04 N 14.08 E
Uni 80 57.46 N 51.30 E
União 250 4.35 S 42.52 W
União da Vitória 252 26.13 S 51.05 W
União dos Palmares 250 9.10 S 36.02 W
Unica 24 62.38 N 34.38 E
Unicoi 192 36.11 N 82.20 W
Unicorn Branch ≃ 208 39.15 N 75.52 W
Unidad Santa Fe ●[8] 286a 19.23 N 99.15 W
Uniejów 30 51.58 N 18.49 E
Unieux 62 45.24 N 4.16 E
Unije, Otok I 36 44.38 N 14.15 E
Unimak Island I 180 54.50 N 164.00 W
Unimak Pass ʯ 180 54.35 N 164.43 W
Unini ≃ 246 1.41 S 61.31 W
Unión, Arg. 252 35.09 S 65.57 W
Union, On., Can. 212 42.42 N 81.12 W
Unión, C.R. 236 8.36 N 83.03 W
Unión, Para. 252 24.48 S 56.33 W
Union, Il., U.S. 216 42.14 N 88.33 W
Union, Ia., U.S. 190 42.14 N 93.03 W
Union, Ky., U.S. 218 38.56 N 84.40 W
Union, La., U.S. 194 30.06 N 90.54 W
Union, Ms., U.S. 194 32.34 N 89.07 W
Union, Mo., U.S. 219 38.26 N 91.00 W
Union, N.J., U.S. 210 40.41 N 74.15 W
Union, Oh., U.S. 218 39.53 N 84.18 W
Union, Or., U.S. 202 45.12 N 117.51 W
Union, S.C., U.S. 192 34.42 N 81.37 W
Union, Wa., U.S. 224 47.21 N 123.06 W
Union, W.V., U.S. 192 37.35 N 80.32 W
Union □[6], In., U.S. 218 39.38 N 84.56 W
Union □[6], N.J., U.S. 208 40.40 N 74.11 W
Union □[6], Oh., U.S. 214 40.18 N 83.19 W
Union □[6], Pa., U.S. 210 40.58 N 76.54 W
Unión ●[8] 258 34.53 S 56.08 W
Union Bay 182 49.35 N 124.53 W
Union Beach 208 40.26 N 74.10 W
Union Bridge 208 39.34 N 77.10 W
Union Center 210 42.09 N 76.04 W
Union City, Ca., U.S. 226 37.35 N 122.04 W
Union City, Ga., U.S. 192 33.35 N 84.32 W
Union City, In., U.S. 194 40.07 N 85.05 W
Union City, Mi., U.S. 216 42.04 N 85.09 W
Union City, N.J., U.S. 276 40.46 N 74.01 W
Union City, Oh., U.S. 216 40.11 N 84.48 W
Union City, Pa., U.S. 214 41.53 N 79.50 W
Union City, Tn., U.S. 194 36.25 N 89.03 W
Union City Dam ●[6] 214 41.55 N 79.54 W
Uniondale, S. Afr. 158 33.40 S 23.08 E
Uniondale, In., U.S. 216 40.50 N 85.15 W
Uniondale, N.Y., U.S. 276 40.42 N 73.35 W
Union Dale, Pa., U.S. 210 41.43 N 75.30 W
Unión de Reyes 240p 22.48 N 81.32 W
Unión de San Antonio 234 21.06 N 101.58 W
Union des Émirats Arabes → United Arab Emirates □[1] 128 24.00 N 54.00 E
Unión de Tula 234 19.58 N 104.16 W
Union Flat Creek ≃ 202 46.50 N 117.59 W
Union Gap 202 46.33 N 120.28 W
Union Grove, Tx., U.S. 222 32.34 N 94.55 W
Union Grove, Wi., U.S. 216 42.41 N 88.03 W
Unión Hidalgo 234 16.28 N 94.50 W
Union Hill 210 43.13 N 77.23 W
Union Lake 216 42.36 N 83.26 W
Union Lake ◎, Mi., U.S. 216 42.03 N 85.11 W
Union Lake ◎, Mi., U.S. 281 42.37 N 83.26 W
Union Lake ◎, N.J., U.S. 208 39.25 N 75.03 W
Union Mills 216 41.29 N 86.46 W
Union Park 220 28.30 N 81.15 W
Union Pier 216 41.49 N 86.41 W
Union Point 192 33.36 N 83.04 W
Unionport, In., U.S. 218 40.07 N 85.06 W
Unionport, Oh., U.S. 214 40.21 N 80.51 W
Union Seamount ✦[3] 16 49.35 N 132.45 W
Union Springs, Al., U.S. 194 32.08 N 85.42 W
Union Springs, N.Y., U.S. 210 42.50 N 76.41 W
Union Station ●[5], On., Can. 275b 43.39 N 79.23 W
Union Station ●[5], Ca., U.S. 280 34.04 N 118.14 W
Union Station ●[5], D.C., U.S. 284c 38.54 N 77.00 W
Union Station ●[5], Il., U.S. 278 41.53 N 87.38 W
Uniontown, Al., U.S. 194 32.26 N 87.30 W
Uniontown, Ky., U.S. 194 37.46 N 87.55 W
Uniontown, Md., U.S. 208 39.35 N 77.06 W
Uniontown, Oh., U.S. 214 40.58 N 81.24 W
Uniontown, Pa., U.S. 188 39.54 N 79.44 W
Union Valley Reservoir ◎[1] 226 38.50 N 120.26 W
Union Village 207 41.59 N 71.32 W
Unionville, On., Can. 275b 43.52 N 79.18 W
Unionville, Ct., U.S. 207 41.45 N 72.53 W
Unionville, In., U.S. 218 39.14 N 86.25 W
Unionville, Mi., U.S. 190 43.39 N 83.27 W
Unionville, Mo., U.S. 194 40.28 N 93.00 W
Unionville, N.J., U.S. 285 40.01 N 74.46 W
Unionville, N.Y., U.S. 210 41.18 N 74.34 W
Unionville, Oh., U.S. 214 41.47 N 81.00 W
Unionville, Pa., U.S. 285 39.54 N 75.44 W
Unionville Center 214 40.08 N 83.21 W
Uniopolis 216 40.36 N 84.05 W
Unipouheos Indian Reserve ●[4] 184 53.52 N 110.21 W
Unisan 116 13.51 N 121.59 E
United 214 40.13 N 79.29 W
United Arab Emirates (Al-Imārāt al-'Arabīyah al-Muttaḥidah) □[1], Asia 118 24.00 N 54.00 E
United Arab Emirates (Al-Imārāt al-'Arabīyah al-Muttaḥidah) □[1], Asia 128 24.00 N 54.00 E
United Arab Republic → Egypt □[1] 140 27.00 N 30.00 E
United Kingdom □[1], Europe 22 54.00 N 2.00 W
United Kingdom □[1], Europe 28 54.00 N 2.00 W
United Kingdom Sovereign Base Area ■ 130 35.00 N 33.45 E
United Nations Headquarters ✿ 276 40.45 N 73.58 W
United States □[1] 178 38.00 N 97.00 W
United States Air Force Academy ■ 200 39.00 N 104.55 W
United States Coast Guard Academy ■ 207 41.22 N 72.06 W
United States Merchant Marine Academy ✿[2] 276 40.48 N 73.46 W
United States Military Academy ■ 210 41.23 N 73.58 W
United States Naval Academy ■ 208 38.59 N 76.30 W
United States Steel Corporation (Lorain Plant) ✿[3], Oh., U.S. 279a 41.27 N 82.07 W
United States Steel Corporation ✿[3], Pa., U.S. 279b 40.20 N 79.54 W
United States Steel Corporation Fairless Works ✿[3] 285 40.09 N 74.45 W
Unity 184 52.27 N 109.10 W
Unity Reservoir ◎[1] 279b 40.17 N 79.30 W
Universal City 196 29.32 N 98.17 W
Universal City ✿[3] 280 34.09 N 118.21 W
Universal Mall ●[9] 281 42.30 N 83.05 W
Universitaria, Ciudad ✿[2] 266d 41.23 N 2.08 E
University 194 34.21 N 89.32 W
University City 219 38.39 N 90.19 W
University Gardens 276 40.46 N 73.43 W
University Heights, Ca., U.S. 282 37.26 N 122.12 W
University Heights, Oh., U.S. 279a 41.29 N 81.32 W
University Park, Il., U.S. 216 41.36 N 87.39 W
University Park, Md., U.S. 284c 38.58 N 76.57 W
University Park, N.M., U.S. 200 32.06 N 106.39 W
University Park, Tx., U.S. 222 32.52 N 96.47 W
University Place 224 47.14 N 122.32 W
University View 218 40.00 N 83.03 W
Unjha 120 23.48 N 72.24 E
Unkel 56 50.35 N 7.13 E
Unken 64 47.39 N 12.43 E
Unkurda 86 55.48 N 59.24 E
Unley 168b 34.57 S 138.35 E
Unna 52 51.32 N 7.41 E
'Unnāb, Jabal al- ∧ 132 29.57 N 36.55 E
'Unnāb, Wādī al- V 132 30.11 N 36.39 E
Unnão 124 26.32 N 80.30 E
Uno, Canal Numero ≅ 252 36.17 S 57.08 W
Uno, Ilha I 150 11.12 N 16.15 W
Unoke 94 36.43 N 136.42 E
Ŭnp'a 98 38.26 N 125.45 E
Unpenji-san ∧ 96 34.02 N 133.44 E
Unqua Point › 276 40.39 N 73.26 W
Unquillo 252 31.14 S 64.19 W
Ŭnsan 98 39.25 N 126.01 E
Unseburg 54 51.56 N 11.30 E
Unserfrau → Madonna 64 46.43 N 10.52 E
Unsleben 56 50.22 N 10.15 E
Unst I 46a 60.45 N 0.53 W
Unstrut ≃ 54 51.10 N 11.48 E
Un't 88 49.07 N 102.50 E
Unten 174m 26.41 N 128.00 E
Unterägeri 58 47.08 N 8.35 E
Unterbach, Dtsch. 263 51.12 N 6.54 E
Unterbäch, Schw. 58 46.17 N 7.48 E
Unter dem Wind, Inseln → Windward Islands II 238 13.00 N 61.00 W
Unterföhring 60 48.12 N 11.38 E
Unterfranken □[5] 56 50.10 N 10.00 E
Unterglottertal 58 48.03 N 7.56 E
Untergriesbach 60 48.35 N 13.40 E
Untergrüne 263 51.22 N 7.39 E
Unterhaching 60 48.04 N 11.38 E
Unterhausen 58 48.26 N 9.16 E
Unterinntal V 64 47.24 N 11.47 E
Unterlaa ●[8] 264b 48.08 N 16.25 E
Unterlüss 52 52.50 N 10.17 E
Untermauerbach 264b 48.14 N 16.12 E
Untermünkheim 56 49.09 N 9.44 E
Unteröwisheim 56 49.08 N 8.40 E
Unterrath ●[8] 263 51.16 N 6.47 E
Unterschächen 58 46.52 N 8.47 E
Unterschleissheim, Dtsch. 60 48.17 N 11.34 E
Unterschleissheim, Dtsch. 60 48.17 N 11.34 E
Unterschneidheim 56 48.56 N 10.22 E
Unterschwaningen 56 49.04 N 10.37 E
Unterseen 58 46.41 N 7.51 E
Untertauern 64 47.18 N 13.30 E
Unterterzen 58 47.07 N 9.15 E
Unterthingau 58 47.46 N 10.31 E
Unterueckersee ◎ 54 53.17 N 13.51 E
Unterwasser 58 47.12 N 9.19 E
Unterweissbach 54 50.37 N 11.10 E
Unterwellenborn 54 50.39 N 11.26 E
Unterwössen 64 47.44 N 12.27 E
Unterzeiring 61 47.15 N 14.31 E
Untraverket 40 60.25 N 17.18 E
Unuli Horog 120 35.06 N 91.51 E
Ünye 130 41.08 N 37.17 E
Unža 80 58.01 N 44.01 E
Unža ≃ 80 57.20 N 43.08 E
Unzen-Amakusa-kokuritsu-kōen ♠ 92 32.45 N 130.17 E
Unzen-dake ∧ 92 32.45 N 130.17 E
Unže-Pavinskaja 86 58.53 N 64.02 E
Uojan 88 56.07 N 111.38 E
Uono ≃ 94 37.15 N 138.53 E
Uo-shima I 96 34.11 N 133.19 E
Uozu 94 36.48 N 137.24 E
Upa ≃ 76 54.02 N 36.15 E
Upala 236 10.47 N 85.02 W
Upanema 250 5.38 S 37.15 W
Upano ≃ 246 2.45 S 78.12 W
Upata 246 8.01 N 62.24 W
Upatoi Creek ≃ 192 32.22 N 84.58 W
Upavon 42 51.18 N 1.49 W
Ŭpchŏ-ri 98 37.53 N 125.09 E
Upchurch 260 51.23 N 0.39 E
Upemba, Lac ◎ 154 8.36 S 26.26 E
Upemba, Parc National de l' ♠ 154 9.10 S 26.35 E
Upernavik 176 72.47 N 56.10 W
Upgant-Schott 52 53.30 N 7.16 E
Uphal 140 6.58 N 34.16 E
Upham 198 48.34 N 100.43 W
Up Holland 262 53.33 N 2.44 W
Uphusen 52 53.01 N 8.58 E
Upi 116 6.57 N 124.09 E
Upía ≃ 246 4.18 N 72.45 W
Upington 158 28.25 S 21.15 E
Upire ≃ 246 11.27 N 68.58 W
Upland, Ca., U.S. 228 34.05 N 117.38 W
Upland, In., U.S. 216 40.28 N 85.29 W
Upland, Ne., U.S. 198 40.19 N 98.54 W
Upland, Pa., U.S. 285 39.51 N 75.23 W
Upleta 120 21.44 N 70.17 E
Upnuk Lake ◎ 180 60.21 N 158.58 W
Upolu I 175a 13.55 S 171.45 W
Upolu Point › 229d 20.16 N 155.51 W
Uporovo 86 56.18 N 66.17 E
Upper □[4] 150 10.30 N 1.30 W
Upper Arlington 218 40.00 N 83.03 W
Upper Arrow Lake ◎ 182 50.30 N 117.55 W
Upper Artichoke Reservoir ◎[1] 283 42.48 N 70.57 W
Upper Bay c 276 40.41 N 74.03 W
Upper Beaconsfield 274b 38.01 S 145.25 E
Upper Berkshire Valley 276 40.56 N 74.35 W
Upper Beverley Lake ◎ 212 44.37 N 76.05 W
Upper Black Eddy 210 40.35 N 75.07 W
Upper Blackville 186 46.39 N 65.52 W
Upper Brookville 276 40.51 N 73.34 W
Upper Canada Village ⊥ 206 44.57 N 75.03 W
Upper Castlereagh 274a 33.43 S 150.40 E
Upperco 208 39.33 N 76.50 W
Upper Coliban Reservoir ◎[1] 169 37.18 S 144.23 E
Upper Crystal Springs Reservoir ◎[1] 282 37.30 N 122.20 W
Upper Darby 208 39.55 N 75.16 W
Upper Demerara-Berbice □[4] 246 5.30 N 58.20 W
Upper des Lacs Lake ◎[1] 198 48.50 N 102.07 W
Upper Egypt → Aṣ-Ṣa'īd □[9] 140 26.00 N 32.00 E
Upper End 262 53.17 N 1.52 W
Upper Erskine Lake ◎ 276 41.06 N 74.15 W
Upper Fairmount 208 38.06 N 75.47 W
Upper Falls 284b 39.26 N 76.24 W
Upper Ferntree Gully 274b 37.54 S 145.19 E
Upper Fraser 182 54.07 N 121.56 W
Upper Ganga Canal ≅ 124 29.57 N 78.12 E
Upper Gap ʯ 212 44.06 N 76.50 W
Upper Goose Lake ◎ 184 51.44 N 92.44 W
Upper Greenwood Lake 276 41.10 N 74.22 W
Upper Greenwood Lake ◎ 276 41.11 N 74.23 W
Upper Hat Creek 182 50.38 N 121.35 W
Upper Humber ≃ 186 49.10 N 57.28 W
Upper Hutt 172 41.08 S 175.04 E
Upper Iowa ≃ 190 43.29 N 91.14 W
Upper Island Cove 186 47.39 N 53.12 W
Upper Keechi Creek ≃ 222 31.23 N 95.42 W
Upper Klamath Lake ◎ 202 42.23 N 122.55 W
Upper Lake 204 39.10 N 122.54 W
Upper Lake ◎ 204 41.44 N 120.08 W
Upper Lehigh 210 41.02 N 75.55 W
Upper Liard 180 60.02 N 128.55 W
Upper Machodoc Creek ≃ 208 38.18 N 77.02 W
Upper Manitou Lake ◎ 184 49.24 N 92.48 W
Upper Marlboro 208 38.48 N 76.45 W
Upper Matecumbe Key I 220 24.55 N 80.39 W
Upper Moutere 172 41.16 S 173.00 E
Upper Musquodoboit 186 45.08 N 62.57 W
Upper Mystic Lake ◎ 283 42.27 N 71.09 W
Upper Nyack 210 41.07 N 73.55 W
Upper Peirce Reservoir ◎[1] 271c 1.22 N 103.48 E
Upper Red Lake ◎ 198 48.10 N 94.40 W
Upper Rideau Lake ◎ 212 44.41 N 76.20 W
Upper River Rouge ≃ 281 42.23 N 83.16 W
Upper Saddle River 276 41.03 N 74.05 W
Upper Saint Clair 279b 40.21 N 80.05 W
Upper Sandusky 214 40.49 N 83.16 W
Upper San Leandro Reservoir ◎[1] 226 37.47 N 122.07 W
Upper Sheila 186 47.28 N 64.56 W
Upper Straits Lake ◎ 281 42.35 N 83.24 W


**Symbols** in the index entries represent the broad categories identified in the key at the right. Symbols with superior numbers (⋀[1]) identify subcategories (see complete key on page *I · 1).*

**Symbole** im Register stellen die rechts im Schlüssel erklärten Kategorien dar. Symbole mit hochgestellten Ziffern (⋀[1]) bezeichnen Unterabteilungen einer Kategorie (vgl. vollständiger Schlüssel auf Seite *I · 1).*

**Los símbolos** incluídos en el texto del índice representan las grandes categorías identificadas con la clave a la derecha. Los símbolos con numeros en su parte superior (⋀[1]) identifican las subcategorías (véase la clave completa en la página *I · 1).*

**Les symboles** de l'index représentent les catégories indiquées dans la légende à droite. Les symboles suivis d'un indice (⋀[1]) représentent des sous-catégories (voir légende complète à la page *I · 1).*

**Os símbolos** incluídos no texto do índice representam as grandes categorias identificadas com a chave à direita. Os símbolos com números em sua parte superior (⋀[1]) identificam as subcategorias (veja-se a chave completa à página *I · 1).*

| | English | Deutsch | Español | Français | Português |
|---|---|---|---|---|---|
| ∧ | Mountain | Berg | Montaña | Montagne | Montanha |
| ⋀ | Mountains | Gebirge | Montañas | Montagnes | Montanhas |
| )( | Pass | Paß | Paso | Col | Passo |
| V | Valley, Canyon | Tal, Cañon | Valle, Cañón | Vallée, Canyon | Vale, Canhão |
| ≃ | Plain | Ebene | Llano | Plaine | Planície |
| › | Cape | Kap | Cabo | Cap | Cabo |
| I | Island | Insel | Isla | Île | Ilha |
| II | Islands | Inseln | Islas | Îles | Ilhas |
| ⊥ | Other Topographic Features | Andere Topographische Objekte | Otros Elementos Topográficos | Autres données topographiques | Outros acidentes topográficos |

## ESPAÑOL

| Nombre | Página | Lat.°′ | Long.°′ W = Oeste |
|---|---|---|---|
| Upper Sumas | 224 | 49.01 N | 122.12 W |
| Upper Swan | 168a | 31.46 S | 116.01 E |
| Upper Takaka | 172 | 41.02 S | 172.50 E |
| Upper Takutu-Upper Essequibo □[4] | 246 | 3.00 N | 59.00 W |
| Upper Tean | 42 | 52.57 N | 1.58 W |
| Upper Tooting ◆[8] | 260 | 51.26 N | 0.10 W |
| Upper Trajan's Wall ⊥ | 38 | 46.35 N | 29.00 E |
| Upper Ugashik Lake ⊜ | 180 | 57.40 N | 156.43 W |
| Upper Volta → Burkina Faso □[1] | 150 | 13.00 N | 1.30 W |
| Upper Windigo Lake ⊜ | 184 | 52.30 N | 91.35 W |
| Upper Yarra Reservoir ⊜[1] | 169 | 37.41 S | 145.56 E |
| Upper Yosemite Fall ∟ | 226 | 37.45 N | 119.36 W |
| Uppingham | 42 | 52.35 N | 0.43 W |
| Uppland □[9] | 40 | 59.59 N | 17.48 E |
| Upplanda | 40 | 60.14 N | 17.44 E |
| Upplands Väsby | 40 | 59.31 N | 17.54 E |
| Uppsala | 40 | 59.52 N | 17.38 E |
| Uppsala Län □[6] | 40 | 60.00 N | 17.45 E |
| Upright, Cape › | 180 | 60.17 N | 172.15 W |
| Upsala → Uppsala | 40 | 59.52 N | 17.38 E |
| Upshi | 120 | 33.50 N | 77.49 E |
| Upshur □[6] | 222 | 32.45 N | 94.55 W |
| Upstart, Cape › | 166 | 19.42 S | 147.45 E |
| Upton, P.Q., Can. | 206 | 45.39 N | 72.41 W |
| Upton, Eng., U.K. | 44 | 53.37 N | 1.17 W |
| Upton, Eng., U.K. | 44 | 53.13 N | 2.52 W |
| Upton, Eng., U.K. | 260 | 51.30 N | 0.35 W |
| Upton, Eng., U.K. | 262 | 53.23 N | 3.06 W |
| Upton, Ky., U.S. | 194 | 37.27 N | 85.53 W |
| Upton, Ma., U.S. | 207 | 42.10 N | 71.36 W |
| Upton, Wy., U.S. | 198 | 44.05 N | 104.37 W |
| Upton Hill ʌ[2] | 169 | 36.52 S | 145.27 E |
| Upton upon Severn | 42 | 52.04 N | 2.13 W |
| Uptown ◆[8] | 278 | 41.58 N | 87.40 W |
| Upwell | 42 | 52.36 N | 0.12 E |
| Upwey | 274b | 37.54 S | 145.20 E |
| Uquía, Cerro ʌ | 246 | 4.22 N | 63.46 W |
| Ur → Tall al-Muqayyar ⊥ | 128 | 30.57 N | 46.09 E |
| Urabá, Golfo de ⊂ | 246 | 8.25 N | 76.53 W |
| Urachi | 84 | 42.21 N | 47.36 E |
| Uracoa | 246 | 9.00 N | 62.21 W |
| Urad | 54 | 52.15 N | 14.45 E |
| Uradome-kaigan ♠ | 96 | 35.35 N | 134.21 E |
| Urad Zhonghou Lianheqi | 102 | 41.42 N | 108.49 E |
| Uraga | 268 | 35.15 N | 139.43 E |
| Uraga-kō ⊂ | 268 | 35.14 N | 139.44 E |
| Uraga-suidō ʯ | 94 | 35.13 N | 139.45 E |
| Uragawara | 94 | 37.09 N | 138.26 E |
| Urahoro | 92a | 42.48 N | 143.39 E |
| Uraj | 86 | 60.08 N | 64.48 E |
| Urakan | 88 | 58.38 N | 106.01 E |
| Urakawa | 92a | 42.09 N | 142.47 E |
| Ural ≃ | 72 | 47.00 N | 51.48 E |
| Uralla | 166 | 30.39 S | 151.30 E |
| Ural Mountains → Ural'skije gory ⛰ | 72 | 60.00 N | 60.00 E |
| Uralo-Kl'uči | 88 | 56.03 N | 97.28 E |
| Uralove | 78 | 52.11 N | 33.34 E |
| Ural'sk | 80 | 51.14 N | 51.22 E |
| Ural'skij | 80 | 51.36 N | 51.40 E |
| Ural'skije gory (Ural Mountains) ⛰ | 72 | 60.00 N | 60.00 E |
| Urambo | 154 | 5.04 S | 32.03 E |
| Uran | 272c | 18.52 N | 72.56 E |
| Urana | 166 | 35.20 S | 146.16 E |
| Urandangi | 166 | 21.36 S | 138.18 E |
| Urandi | 255 | 14.46 S | 42.38 W |
| Urangan | 166 | 25.18 S | 152.54 E |
| Urania, Austl. | 168b | 34.31 S | 137.36 E |
| Urania, La., U.S. | 194 | 31.51 N | 92.17 W |
| Uranium City | 176 | 59.34 N | 108.36 W |
| Uranquinty | 171b | 35.12 S | 147.15 E |
| Urarey | 162 | 27.26 S | 122.18 E |
| Urariá, Paraná ≃[1] | 246 | 3.03 S | 57.43 W |
| Uraricaá ≃ | 246 | 3.20 N | 61.56 W |
| Uraricoera | 246 | 3.27 N | 60.59 W |
| Uraricoera ≃ | 246 | 3.02 N | 60.30 W |
| Uras | 71 | 39.42 N | 8.42 E |
| Urasaki | 174m | 26.40 N | 127.53 E |
| Urasoe | 174m | 26.15 N | 127.43 E |
| Ura-T'ube | 85 | 39.55 N | 68.59 E |
| Uravakonda | 122 | 14.57 N | 77.16 E |
| Uravan | 200 | 38.22 N | 108.44 W |
| Urawa | 94 | 35.51 N | 139.39 E |
| Urayasu | 94 | 35.39 N | 139.54 E |
| 'Urayfan Nāqah, Jabal ʌ | 132 | 30.22 N | 34.27 E |
| 'Urayyiḍah, Bi'r ⊤[4] | 142 | 29.00 N | 31.58 E |
| Urazmetovo | 86 | 53.49 N | 55.25 E |
| Urazovka | 80 | 55.24 N | 45.38 E |
| Urazovo | 78 | 50.07 N | 38.04 E |
| Urbach | 56 | 50.53 N | 7.05 E |
| Urban | 224 | 48.38 N | 122.40 W |
| Urbana, Ar., U.S. | 194 | 33.09 N | 92.26 W |
| Urbana, Il., U.S. | 194 | 40.06 N | 88.12 W |
| Urbana, In., U.S. | 216 | 40.53 N | 85.47 W |
| Urbana, Mo., U.S. | 194 | 37.50 N | 93.10 W |
| Urbana, Oh., U.S. | 218 | 40.06 N | 83.45 W |
| Urbancrest | 218 | 39.53 N | 83.05 W |
| Urbandale, Ia., U.S. | 190 | 41.37 N | 93.42 W |
| Urbandale, Mi., U.S. | 216 | 44.09 N | 85.11 W |
| Urbania | 66 | 43.40 N | 12.31 E |
| Urbanna | 208 | 37.38 N | 76.34 W |
| Urbano Noris | 240p | 20.36 N | 76.08 W |
| Urbano Santos | 250 | 3.12 S | 43.23 W |
| Urbe | 62 | 44.29 N | 8.36 E |
| Urbe, Aeroporto dell' ⊠ | 267a | 41.57 N | 12.30 E |
| Urbino | 66 | 43.43 N | 12.38 E |
| Urbisaglia | 66 | 43.12 N | 13.23 E |
| Urcos | 248 | 13.42 S | 71.38 W |
| Urda | 80 | 48.47 N | 47.26 E |
| Urdaneta | 116 | 15.59 N | 120.34 E |
| Urdenbach ◆[8] | 263 | 51.09 N | 6.53 E |
| Urdinarrain | 252 | 32.41 S | 58.53 W |
| Urdoma | 24 | 61.47 N | 48.32 E |
| Urdžar | 86 | 47.05 N | 81.38 E |
| Uré | 246 | 7.46 N | 75.31 W |
| Ure ≃, Fr. | 50 | 48.45 N | 0.11 E |
| Ure ≃, Eng., U.K. | 44 | 54.05 N | 1.20 W |
| Urèčča | 76 | 52.57 N | 27.54 E |
| Ûrein | 142 | 30.58 N | 30.42 E |
| Ureki | 84 | 41.59 N | 41.46 E |
| Ureliki | 180 | 64.23 N | 173.15 W |
| Uren' | 80 | 57.28 N | 45.49 E |
| Uren ⊜ | 40 | 58.59 N | 16.44 E |
| Urén ≃ | 236 | 9.33 N | 82.55 W |
| Ureña | 246 | 7.55 N | 72.28 W |
| Urenui | 172 | 39.00 S | 174.23 E |
| Uréparapara I | 175f | 13.32 S | 167.20 E |
| Ures | 232 | 29.26 N | 110.24 W |
| Ureshino, Nihon | 92 | 33.06 N | 129.59 E |
| Ureshino, Nihon | 94 | 34.37 N | 136.29 E |
| Ureterp | 52 | 53.05 N | 6.10 E |
| Urewera National Park ♠ | 172 | 38.40 S | 177.00 E |
| Urft ≃ | 56 | 50.35 N | 6.30 E |
| Urga → Ulaanbaatar, Mong. | 88 | 47.55 N | 106.53 E |
| Urga, Uzb. | 86 | 43.35 N | 58.30 E |
| Urgamal | 88 | 48.29 N | 94.20 E |
| Urgenč | 72 | 41.33 N | 60.38 E |
| Urgnano | 62 | 45.35 N | 9.41 E |
| Urgučenskij Golec, gora ʌ | 88 | 53.30 N | 118.08 E |
| Ürgüp | 130 | 38.38 N | 34.56 E |
| Urgut | 85 | 39.23 N | 67.15 E |
| Urho | 86 | 46.48 N | 89.45 E |

## FRANÇAIS

| Nom | Page | Lat.°′ | Long.°′ W = Ouest |
|---|---|---|---|
| Urho Kekkosen kansallispuisto ♠ | 24 | 68.10 N | 28.30 E |
| Uri, India | 123 | 34.05 N | 74.02 E |
| Uri, It. | 71 | 40.38 N | 8.29 E |
| Uri □[3] | 58 | 46.50 N | 8.40 E |
| Uriah | 194 | 31.18 N | 87.30 W |
| Uriangato | 234 | 20.09 N | 101.11 W |
| Uribante ≃ | 246 | 7.18 N | 70.44 W |
| Uribe | 246 | 3.13 N | 74.24 W |
| Uribelarrea | 258 | 35.09 S | 58.54 W |
| Uribia | 246 | 11.43 N | 72.16 W |
| Urich | 194 | 38.27 N | 94.00 W |
| Urick ◆[8] | 265a | 59.50 N | 30.11 E |
| Urickij | 86 | 53.19 N | 65.34 E |
| Urickoje | 78 | 52.02 N | 38.11 E |
| Urie ≃ | 46 | 57.19 N | 2.30 W |
| Urimba | 152 | 10.56 S | 16.32 E |
| Urión ≃[1] | 288 | 34.24 S | 58.31 W |
| Urique | 232 | 27.13 N | 107.55 W |
| Urique ≃ | 232 | 26.29 N | 107.58 W |
| Uri-Rotstock ʌ | 58 | 46.52 N | 8.33 E |
| Urituyacu ≃ | 246 | 4.45 S | 75.28 W |
| Uriuaná ≃ | 250 | 2.47 S | 50.29 W |
| Urizura | 94 | 36.30 N | 140.27 E |
| Urjala | 26 | 61.05 N | 23.32 E |
| Urk | 52 | 52.39 N | 5.36 E |
| Urkan ≃ | 89 | 53.27 N | 126.56 E |
| Urkarach | 84 | 42.11 N | 47.38 E |
| Urla | 130 | 38.18 N | 26.46 E |
| Urlați | 38 | 44.59 N | 26.14 E |
| Urlingford | 48 | 52.42 N | 7.35 W |
| Urlings | 240c | 17.02 N | 61.52 W |
| Urluk | 88 | 50.03 N | 107.55 E |
| Urma | 126 | 23.10 N | 86.15 E |
| Urman, Ross. | 86 | 54.52 N | 56.52 E |
| 'Urmān, Sūrīy. | 132 | 32.30 N | 36.45 E |
| Urmary | 80 | 55.42 N | 47.57 E |
| Urmetan | 85 | 39.27 N | 68.17 E |
| Urmi ≃ | 89 | 48.44 N | 134.16 E |
| Urmia → Orūmīyeh | 128 | 37.33 N | 45.04 E |
| Urmia, Lake → Orūmīyeh, Daryācheh-ye ⊜ | 128 | 37.40 N | 45.30 E |
| Urmston | 44 | 53.27 N | 2.21 W |
| Urnäsch | 58 | 47.19 N | 9.17 E |
| Urnersee ⊜ | 58 | 46.55 N | 8.37 E |
| Uroindo | 248 | 21.41 S | 64.41 W |
| Üröm | 264c | 47.36 N | 19.01 E |
| Uromi | 150 | 6.44 N | 6.18 E |
| Uroševac | 38 | 42.22 N | 21.09 E |
| Uroyán, Montañas de ⛰ | 240m | 18.14 N | 67.02 W |
| Urožajnoje, Ross. | 84 | 43.42 N | 44.13 E |
| Urožajnoje, Ross. | 84 | 44.47 N | 44.55 E |
| Urquhart, Glen V | 46 | 57.20 N | 4.35 W |
| Urrao | 246 | 6.20 N | 76.11 W |
| Urr Water ≃ | 44 | 54.53 N | 3.49 W |
| Ursa | 219 | 40.04 N | 91.22 W |
| Ursberg | 58 | 48.16 N | 10.27 E |
| Uršel'skij | 80 | 55.41 N | 40.13 E |
| Ursensollen | 60 | 49.24 N | 11.46 E |
| Ursk | 86 | 54.27 N | 85.24 E |
| Urspring | 56 | 48.33 N | 9.53 E |
| Urtazym | 86 | 52.12 N | 58.50 E |
| Urtigueira | 252 | 24.12 S | 50.55 W |
| Urt Moron | 120 | 37.00 N | 93.18 E |
| Uru ≃ | 255 | 15.24 S | 49.36 W |
| Uruaçu | 255 | 14.30 S | 49.10 W |
| Uruana | 255 | 15.30 S | 49.41 W |
| Uruapan | 204 | 31.38 N | 116.15 W |
| Uruapan del Progreso | 234 | 19.25 N | 102.04 W |
| Urubamba | 248 | 13.18 S | 72.07 W |
| Urubamba ≃ | 248 | 10.44 S | 73.45 W |
| Urubaxi ≃ | 246 | 0.31 S | 64.50 W |
| Urubu ≃, Bra. | 246 | 2.55 S | 58.25 W |
| Urubu ≃, Bra. | 250 | 10.51 S | 49.47 W |
| Uruburetama | 250 | 3.38 S | 39.30 W |
| Urucará | 250 | 2.32 S | 57.45 W |
| Uruch ≃ | 84 | 43.28 N | 44.06 E |
| Urucu ≃ | 246 | 4.11 S | 63.36 W |
| Uruçuca | 255 | 14.35 S | 39.16 W |
| Uruçuí | 250 | 7.14 S | 44.33 W |
| Uruçuí, Serra da ⛰[2] | 250 | 9.00 S | 44.45 W |
| Urucuia ≃ | 255 | 16.08 S | 45.05 W |
| Uruçuí-preto ≃ | 250 | 7.20 S | 44.38 W |
| Urucurituba | 250 | 2.41 S | 57.40 W |
| Urugi | 94 | 35.16 N | 137.42 E |
| Uruguaiana | 252 | 29.45 S | 57.05 W |
| Uruguay □[1], S.A. | 244 | 33.00 S | 56.00 W |
| Uruguay □[1], S.A. | 252 | 33.00 S | 56.00 W |
| Uruguay (Uruguai) ≃ | 252 | 34.12 S | 58.18 W |
| Urugudejevskij Golec, gora ʌ | 88 | 51.25 N | 102.09 E |
| Urul'ga | 88 | 51.45 N | 114.47 E |
| Urul'unguj ≃ | 88 | 50.24 N | 119.08 E |
| Ur'um, ozero ⊜ | 86 | 54.33 N | 78.30 E |
| Urumchi → Ürümqi | 90 | 43.48 N | 87.35 E |
| Ur'umkan ≃ | 88 | 52.35 N | 120.08 E |
| Ürümqi | 90 | 43.48 N | 87.35 E |
| Urundel | 252 | 23.33 S | 64.25 W |
| Ur'ung-Chaja | 74 | 72.48 N | 113.23 E |
| Uruoca | 250 | 3.20 S | 40.32 W |
| Urup | 84 | 43.52 N | 41.09 E |
| Urup ≃ | 84 | 44.49 N | 41.10 E |
| Urup, gora ʌ | 84 | 43.38 N | 40.58 E |
| Urup, ostrov I | 74 | 46.00 N | 150.00 E |
| Urupá ≃ | 248 | 10.54 S | 61.57 W |
| Urupadi ≃ | 250 | 3.51 S | 57.21 W |
| Urupês | 255 | 21.13 S | 49.17 W |
| Ur'upino | 88 | 52.46 N | 120.00 E |
| Ur'upinsk | 80 | 50.47 N | 41.59 E |
| Ururicaia, Ilha I | 250 | 1.30 S | 52.05 W |
| Uruša | 89 | 54.03 N | 122.54 E |
| Urus-Martan | 84 | 43.08 N | 45.32 E |
| Urusovo | 82 | 54.15 N | 38.26 E |
| Urussanga | 252 | 28.31 S | 49.19 W |
| Urussu | 80 | 54.36 N | 53.24 E |
| Urutaí | 255 | 17.28 S | 48.12 W |
| Urutaí, Ilha I | 250 | 1.07 S | 51.17 W |
| Urutaú | 252 | 25.42 S | 63.04 W |
| Uruti | 172 | 38.57 S | 174.32 E |
| Uru Uru, Lago ⊜ | 248 | 18.10 S | 67.10 W |
| Uruwira | 154 | 6.27 S | 31.21 E |
| Uryl' | 86 | 49.15 N | 86.20 E |
| Uryū-yama ʌ | 270 | 35.03 N | 135.48 E |
| Uryv | 78 | 51.07 N | 39.10 E |
| Urzajbaš | 80 | 54.43 N | 54.23 E |
| Urziceni | 38 | 44.43 N | 26.38 E |
| Ürzig | 56 | 49.59 N | 7.01 E |
| Urzulei | 71 | 40.06 N | 9.30 E |
| Uržum | 80 | 57.08 N | 50.00 E |
| Us | 261 | 49.06 N | 1.58 E |
| Us ≃ | 86 | 52.07 N | 92.15 E |
| Usa, Nihon | 96 | 33.31 N | 131.22 E |
| Usa, Ross. | 86 | 54.03 N | 88.45 E |
| Uša ≃, Bela. | 76 | 54.00 N | 28.55 E |
| Usa ≃, Ross. | 24 | 65.57 N | 56.55 E |
| Ušača ≃ | 76 | 55.32 N | 28.30 E |
| Ušačy | 76 | 55.11 N | 28.37 E |
| Usada Island I | 116 | 6.08 N | 120.33 E |
| Usadel | 54 | 53.26 N | 13.11 E |
| Uşak | 130 | 38.41 N | 29.25 E |
| Uşak □[4] | 130 | 38.35 N | 29.20 E |
| Ušaki | 76 | 59.29 N | 30.59 E |
| Usakos | 156 | 22.01 S | 15.32 E |
| Ušakovka | 83 | 48.48 N | 39.48 E |
| Ušakovo, Ross. | 86 | 56.22 N | 75.41 E |
| Ušakovo, Ross. | 89 | 51.55 N | 126.34 E |
| Usambara Mountains ⛰ | 154 | 4.45 S | 38.30 E |
| Usangu Flats ≋ | 154 | 8.30 S | 34.15 E |
| Usanovy | 86 | 59.28 N | 73.24 E |
| Ušaral | 85 | 43.54 N | 70.42 E |
| Usarp Mountains ⛰ | 9 | 71.10 S | 160.00 E |
| Úšava | 60 | 49.46 N | 12.40 E |
| Usaymir, Wādī al- V | 273c | 30.04 N | 31.23 E |
| Ušba, gora ʌ | 84 | 43.08 N | 42 40 E |

## PORTUGUÊS

| Nome | Página | Lat.°′ | Long.°′ W = Oeste |
|---|---|---|---|
| Ušbas ≃ | 85 | 43.55 N | 69.39 E |
| Usborne, Mount ʌ | 254 | 51.41 S | 58.50 W |
| Ušće | 38 | 43.28 N | 20.37 E |
| Uščerpje | 76 | 52.43 N | 31.53 E |
| Uscio | 62 | 44.25 N | 9.10 E |
| Usedom | 54 | 53.52 N | 13.55 E |
| Usedom (Uznam) I | 54 | 54.00 N | 14.00 E |
| Useldange | 56 | 49.47 N | 5.59 E |
| Usellus | 71 | 39.48 N | 8.51 E |
| Usen' ≃ | 80 | 54.44 N | 53.38 E |
| 'Usfān | 144 | 21.55 N | 39.21 E |
| Ushaa | 152 | 14.55 S | 23.18 E |
| Ushant → Ouessant, Île d' I | 32 | 48.28 N | 5.05 W |
| Ushashi | 154 | 2.00 S | 33.57 E |
| 'Ushayrah | 144 | 21.46 N | 40.38 E |
| Ushetu | 154 | 4.10 S | 32.16 E |
| Ushibuka | 92 | 32.11 N | 130.01 E |
| Ushiku | 94 | 35.58 N | 140.08 E |
| Ushimado | 96 | 34.37 N | 134.10 E |
| Ushuaia | 254 | 54.48 S | 68.18 W |
| Ushytsya ≃ | 78 | 48.35 N | 27.08 E |
| Usibelli | 180 | 63.51 N | 148.47 W |
| Usingen | 56 | 50.20 N | 8.32 E |
| Usini | 71 | 40.40 N | 8.32 E |
| Usinsk | 24 | 65.58 N | 56.39 E |
| Usisya | 154 | 11.09 S | 34.11 E |
| Usk, B.C., Can. | 182 | 54.38 N | 128.25 W |
| Usk, Wales, U.K. | 42 | 51.43 N | 2.54 W |
| Usk, Wa., U.S. | 202 | 48.18 N | 117.16 W |
| Usk ≃ | 42 | 51.36 N | 2.58 W |
| Uškanij kr'až ʌ | 180 | 65.15 N | 178.35 E |
| Uskedal | 26 | 59.56 N | 5.52 E |
| Usken ⊜ | 40 | 59.39 N | 15.01 E |
| Uskovo | 265b | 55.56 N | 37.19 E |
| Üsküb → Skopje | 38 | 41.59 N | 21.26 E |
| Uskumru ◆[8] | 267b | 41.12 N | 29.01 E |
| Uslar | 52 | 51.39 N | 9.38 E |
| Úslava ≃ | 60 | 49.45 N | 13.24 E |
| Usmajac | 234 | 19.52 N | 103.34 W |
| Usman', Ross. | 76 | 52.02 N | 39.44 E |
| Usman', Ross. | 89 | 51.29 N | 134.00 E |
| Usmanka | 80 | 52.49 N | 51.42 E |
| Usmānpur ◆[8] | 272a | 28.41 N | 77.15 E |
| Usmas ezers ⊜ | 76 | 57.11 N | 22.10 E |
| Usmat | 85 | 39.44 N | 67.40 E |
| Usmate Velate | 62 | 45.39 N | 9.21 E |
| Ušmunskij Golec, gora ʌ | 89 | 51.40 N | 118.35 E |
| Usmyn' | 76 | 55.52 N | 31.09 E |
| Ušna ≃ | 80 | 55.43 N | 42.12 E |
| Usoke | 154 | 5.06 S | 32.20 E |
| Usolje, Ross. | 80 | 53.23 N | 49.05 E |
| Usolje, Ross. | 82 | 56.49 N | 38.40 E |
| Usolje, Ross. | 86 | 59.25 N | 56.41 E |
| Usolje-Sibirskoje | 88 | 52.47 N | 103.38 E |
| Usolka ≃ | 86 | 57.47 N | 94.35 E |
| Uson | 116 | 12.13 N | 123.47 E |
| Usoro | 150 | 5.34 N | 6.13 E |
| Usovo | 265b | 55.44 N | 37.13 E |
| Uspallata | 252 | 32.35 S | 69.20 W |
| Uspanapa ≃ | 234 | 17.58 N | 94.29 W |
| Uspenka, Kaz. | 86 | 52.54 N | 77.25 E |
| Uspenka, Ross. | 80 | 50.38 N | 41.28 E |
| Uspenka, Ukr. | 83 | 48.23 N | 39.10 E |
| Uspenka, Ukr. | 83 | 47.43 N | 38.42 E |
| Uspenovka | 80 | 51.16 N | 53.36 E |
| Uspenskij | 86 | 48.42 N | 72.40 E |
| Uspenskoje | 82 | 55.43 N | 37.04 E |
| Usri ≃ | 126 | 24.03 N | 86.23 E |
| Uššaj | 86 | 43.50 N | 58.53 E |
| Ussassai | 71 | 39.49 N | 9.23 E |
| Usseglio | 62 | 45.14 N | 7.13 E |
| Ussel | 32 | 45.33 N | 2.18 E |
| Ussel ≃ | 56 | 48.44 N | 11.04 E |
| Usshers Creek ≃ | 284a | 43.03 N | 79.02 W |
| Usson-en-Forez | 62 | 45.23 N | 3.56 E |
| Ussure | 154 | 4.39 S | 34.23 E |
| Ussuri (Wusuli) ≃ | 89 | 48.27 N | 135.04 E |
| Ussurijsk | 89 | 43.48 N | 131.59 E |
| Üst | 123 | 36.56 N | 72.53 E |
| Usta | 80 | 57.26 N | 45.40 E |
| Usta ≃ | 80 | 56.53 N | 45.28 E |
| Ust'-Ajsk | 86 | 56.07 N | 57.40 E |
| Ustaoset | 26 | 60.30 N | 8.04 E |
| Ustaritz | 32 | 43.24 N | 1.27 W |
| Ust'-Bagar'ak | 86 | 56.08 N | 61.52 E |
| Ust'-Barguzin | 88 | 53.27 N | 108.59 E |
| Ust'-Belaja | 74 | 65.30 N | 173.20 E |
| Ust'-Bol'šereck | 74 | 52.48 N | 156.14 E |
| Ust'-B'ur' | 86 | 53.49 N | 90.15 E |
| Ust'-Buzulukskaja | 80 | 50.12 N | 42.10 E |
| Ust'-Bystr'anskaja | 80 | 47.49 N | 41.03 E |
| Ust'-Čaja | 86 | 58.17 N | 82.38 E |
| Ust'-Čaryšskaja Pristan' | 86 | 52.24 N | 83.39 E |
| Ust'-Čaun | 74 | 68.47 N | 170.30 E |
| Ust'-Choperskaja | 80 | 49.36 N | 42.24 E |
| Ust'-Chorna | 78 | 48.18 N | 23.56 E |
| Ust'-Cil'ma | 24 | 65.27 N | 52.06 E |
| Ust'-Čižapka | 86 | 59.02 N | 79.37 E |
| Ust'-Čornaja | 88 | 52.57 N | 119.02 E |
| Ust'-Dolyssy | 76 | 56.09 N | 29.39 E |
| Ust'-Doneckij | 80 | 47.39 N | 40.52 E |
| Ust'-Džegutinskaja | 84 | 44.05 N | 41.58 E |
| Úštěk | 54 | 50.36 N | 14.20 E |
| Ust'-Elegest | 88 | 51.32 N | 94.05 E |
| Uster | 58 | 47.21 N | 8.43 E |
| Ust'-Gr'aznucha | 80 | 50.28 N | 45.26 E |
| Ustica | 70 | 38.42 N | 13.11 E |
| Ustica, Isola di I | 70 | 38.42 N | 13.11 E |
| Ust'-Il'a | 88 | 50.25 N | 113.41 E |
| Ust'-Ilga | 88 | 55.00 N | 105.02 E |
| Ust'-Ilimsk | 88 | 58.00 N | 102.39 E |
| Ust'-Ilimskoje vodochranilišče ⊜[1] | 88 | 57.00 N | 102.15 E |
| Ust'-Ilyč | 24 | 62.32 N | 56.41 E |
| Ústí nad Labem | 54 | 50.40 N | 14.02 E |
| Ústí nad Orlicí | 30 | 49.58 N | 16.24 E |
| Ust'-Išim | 86 | 57.44 N | 71.10 E |
| Ust'-Izes | 86 | 55.56 N | 76.56 E |
| Ust'-Ižora | 265a | 59.48 N | 30.36 E |
| Ustja ≃ | 24 | 61.30 N | 42.36 E |
| Ust'-Javron'ga | 24 | 63.25 N | 44.21 E |
| Ustje, Ross. | 76 | 60.49 N | 32.49 E |
| Ustje, Ross. | 76 | 59.38 N | 39.43 E |
| Ustje, Ross. | 80 | 57.47 N | 39.47 E |
| Ustje, Ross. | 82 | 55.16 N | 36.20 E |
| Ustje, Ross. | 86 | 57.46 N | 94.42 E |
| Ustje-Kirovskoje | 76 | 58.45 N | 35.55 E |
| Ustka | 30 | 54.35 N | 16.50 E |
| Ust'-K'achta | 88 | 50.32 N | 106.16 E |
| Ust'-Kajtym | 86 | 57.23 N | 95.28 E |
| Ust'-Kalmanka | 86 | 52.07 N | 83.19 E |
| Ust'-Kamčatsk | 74 | 56.15 N | 162.30 E |
| Ust'-Kamenogorsk | 86 | 49.58 N | 82.38 E |
| Ust'-Kan, Ross. | 86 | 50.57 N | 84.45 E |
| Ust'-Kan, Ross. | 86 | 56.31 N | 93.48 E |
| Ust'-Karenga | 88 | 54.26 N | 116.30 E |
| Ust'-Karsk | 88 | 52.43 N | 118.48 E |
| Ust'-Katav | 86 | 54.56 N | 58.10 E |
| Ust'-Kemčug | 86 | 57.13 N | 90.30 E |
| Ust'-Kil'mez' | 80 | 56.57 N | 50.30 E |
| Ust'-Kišert' | 86 | 57.22 N | 57.15 E |
| Ust'-Koksa | 86 | 50.18 N | 85.36 E |
| Ust'-Kujda | 74 | 70.01 N | 135.36 E |
| Ust'-Kulom | 24 | 61.42 N | 53.40 E |
| Ust'-Kurd'um | 80 | 51.39 N | 46.12 E |
| Ust'-Kurenga | 86 | 57.27 N | 75.34 E |
| Ust'-Kut | 88 | 56.46 N | 105.40 E |
| Ust'-Labinsk | 78 | 45.13 N | 39.42 E |
| Ust'-Lubija | 88 | 52.36 N | 120.16 E |
| Ust'-Luga | 76 | 59.40 N | 28.15 E |
| Ust'-Lyža | 24 | 65.44 N | 56.36 E |
| Ust'-Maja | 74 | 60.25 N | 134.32 E |
| Ust'-Manja | 72 | 62.11 N | 60.20 E |
| Ust'-Naryk | 86 | 54.20 N | 87.25 E |
| Ust'-Nemda | 80 | 57.03 N | 50.22 E |
| Ust'-Nera | 74 | 64.34 N | 143.12 E |
| Ust'-Niman | 89 | 51.23 N | 132.42 E |
| Ust'-N'ukža | 88 | 56.34 N | 121.37 E |
| Uštobe | 86 | 45.16 N | 78.00 E |
| Ust'-Omčug | 74 | 61.09 N | 149.38 E |
| Ust'-Ordynskij | 88 | 52.48 N | 104.45 E |
| Ust'-Ordynskij Burjatskij Avtonomnyj Okrug □[8] | 88 | 53.30 N | 104.00 E |
| Ust'-Oz'ornaja | 88 | 50.42 N | 117.06 E |
| Ust'-Oz'ornoje | 86 | 58.54 N | 87.48 E |
| Ust'-Paden'ga | 24 | 61.53 N | 42.36 E |
| Ust'-Pečengskoje | 76 | 59.47 N | 42.37 E |
| Ust'-Pinega | 24 | 64.11 N | 41.56 E |
| Ust'-Pit | 86 | 58.59 N | 91.44 E |
| Ust'-Pogožje | 80 | 49.28 N | 44.38 E |
| Ustreka | 76 | 58.38 N | 34.33 E |
| Ust'-Reki | 24 | 62.12 N | 46.45 E |
| Ustroń | 30 | 49.43 N | 18.49 E |
| Ustrzyki Dolne | 30 | 49.26 N | 22.37 E |
| Ust'-Šara | 76 | 60.13 N | 33.57 E |
| Ust'-Ščerbedino | 80 | 51.53 N | 42.52 E |
| Ust'-Slav'anka ◆[8] | 265a | 59.50 N | 30.32 E |
| Ust'-Šonoša | 24 | 61.10 N | 41.18 E |
| Ust'-Sumy | 86 | 54.48 N | 80.26 E |
| Ust'-Tara | 86 | 56.41 N | 74.39 E |
| Ust'-Tarka | 86 | 55.34 N | 75.42 E |
| Ust'-Tašino | 89 | 51.07 N | 129.35 E |
| Ust'-Tygda | 89 | 52.35 N | 127.53 E |
| Ust'-Tym | 86 | 59.26 N | 80.08 E |
| Ust'-Tyrma | 89 | 50.29 N | 131.18 E |
| Ust'uckoje | 76 | 58.32 N | 35.20 E |
| Ust'-Uda | 88 | 54.10 N | 103.03 E |
| Üstükran | 130 | 39.16 N | 41.17 E |
| Ust'-Ulagan | 86 | 50.38 N | 87.58 E |
| Ust'-Umal'ta | 89 | 51.39 N | 133.18 E |
| Ust'-Undurga | 89 | 53.07 N | 118.04 E |
| Ust'-Unja | 24 | 61.48 N | 57.48 E |
| Ust'-Urgal | 89 | 51.09 N | 132.33 E |
| Ust'urt, plato ⛰[1] | 72 | 43.00 N | 56.00 E |
| Ust'-Us | 86 | 52.07 N | 92.17 E |
| Ust'-Usa | 24 | 65.59 N | 56.54 E |
| Ust'-Uza | 80 | 52.58 N | 45.17 E |
| Ust'užna | 76 | 58.51 N | 36.26 E |
| Ust'-Vichoreva | 88 | 56.47 N | 101.24 E |
| Ust'-Voja | 24 | 64.27 N | 57.40 E |
| Ust'-Vyjskaja | 24 | 62.57 N | 46.41 E |
| Ust'-Vym' | 24 | 62.14 N | 50.24 E |
| Ustylyh | 78 | 50.51 N | 24.09 E |
| Ustynivka | 78 | 47.57 N | 32.32 E |
| Ust'-Zaza | 88 | 53.10 N | 111.40 E |
| Ust'-Žuja | 88 | 58.48 N | 118.12 E |
| Usu | 86 | 44.27 N | 84.37 E |
| Usuchčaj | 84 | 41.25 N | 47.53 E |
| Usuda | 94 | 36.12 N | 138.29 E |
| Usugli | 88 | 52.39 N | 115.16 E |
| Usui | 96 | 33.34 N | 130.42 E |
| Usuki | 96 | 33.08 N | 131.49 E |
| Usuki-wan ⊂ | 96 | 33.10 N | 131.52 E |
| Usulután | 236 | 13.21 N | 88.27 W |
| Usumacinta ≃ | 232 | 18.24 N | 92.38 W |
| Usumbura → Bujumbura | 154 | 3.23 S | 29.22 E |
| Ušumun | 89 | 52.49 N | 126.27 E |
| Ušur | 80 | 57.47 N | 52.58 E |
| Usuyŏng | 98 | 34.35 N | 126.18 E |
| Usu-zan ʌ | 92a | 42.32 N | 140.51 E |
| Usv'aty | 76 | 55.45 N | 30.45 E |
| Uta | 71 | 39.17 N | 8.57 E |
| Utah □[3], U.S. | 178 | 39.30 N | 111.30 W |
| Utah □[3], U.S. | 200 | 39.30 N | 111.30 W |
| Utah Lake ⊜ | 200 | 40.13 N | 111.49 W |
| Utajärvi | 26 | 64.45 N | 26.23 E |
| Utamba | 154 | 1.06 S | 26.50 E |
| Utamboni ≃ | 152 | 1.00 N | 9.48 E |
| Utan | 115b | 8.24 S | 117.07 E |
| Utano | 94 | 34.28 N | 135.59 E |
| Utapi | 156 | 17.31 S | 15.08 E |
| Utashinai | 92a | 43.31 N | 142.03 E |
| Utata | 88 | 50.51 N | 102.45 E |
| 'Utaybah, Buḥayrat al- ⊜ | 132 | 33.32 N | 36.37 E |
| Ute | 198 | 42.03 N | 95.42 W |
| Ute ≃ | 248 | 15.28 S | 65.05 W |
| Ute Creek ≃ | 196 | 35.21 N | 103.50 W |
| Utegi | 154 | 1.20 S | 34.35 E |
| Utelle | 62 | 43.55 N | 7.15 E |
| Utembo ≃ | 152 | 17.06 S | 22.01 E |
| Ute Mountain Indian Reservation ◆[4] | 200 | 37.10 N | 108.35 W |
| Utena | 76 | 55.30 N | 25.36 E |
| Utengule | 154 | 8.57 S | 35.50 E |
| Ute Reservoir ⊜[1] | 196 | 36.21 N | 103.31 W |
| Úterský potok ≃ | 60 | 49.48 N | 13.06 E |
| Utersum | 30 | 54.43 N | 8.24 E |
| Utete | 154 | 7.59 S | 38.47 E |
| Utevka | 80 | 52.57 N | 50.58 E |
| Utfort | 263 | 51.28 N | 6.38 E |
| Uthai Thani | 110 | 15.22 N | 100.03 E |
| Uthal | 120 | 25.48 N | 66.37 E |
| U Thong | 110 | 14.22 N | 99.54 E |
| Uthumphon Phisai | 110 | 15.05 N | 104.08 E |
| Utiariti | 248 | 13.02 S | 58.17 W |
| Utica, Il., U.S. | 216 | 41.20 N | 89.00 W |
| Utica, In., U.S. | 218 | 38.20 N | 85.39 W |
| Utica, Ks., U.S. | 198 | 38.38 N | 100.10 W |
| Utica, Mi., U.S. | 214 | 42.37 N | 83.02 W |
| Utica, Ms., U.S. | 194 | 32.06 N | 90.37 W |
| Utica, Ne., U.S. | 198 | 40.54 N | 97.21 W |
| Utica, N.Y., U.S. | 210 | 43.06 N | 75.13 W |
| Utica, Oh., U.S. | 214 | 40.14 N | 82.27 W |
| Utica, Pa., U.S. | 214 | 41.26 N | 79.58 W |
| Utica → Utique ⊥ | 36 | 37.03 N | 10.03 E |
| Utiel | 34 | 39.34 N | 1.12 W |
| Utikoomak Lake Indian Reserve ◆[4] | 182 | 55.57 N | 115.30 W |
| Utikuma Lake ⊜ | 182 | 55.50 N | 115.25 W |
| Utila | 236 | 16.06 N | 86.54 W |
| Utila, Isla de I | 236 | 16.06 N | 86.56 W |
| Utinga | 287b | 23.38 S | 46.32 W |
| Utinga ≃ | 255 | 12.34 S | 41.20 W |
| Utique | 36 | 37.03 N | 10.03 E |
| Utique ⊥ | 36 | 37.03 N | 10.03 E |
| Utirik I[1] | 14 | 11.15 N | 169.48 E |
| Utlängan I | 26 | 56.01 N | 15.47 E |
| Utlyuts'kyy lyman ⊂[1] | 78 | 46.15 N | 35.12 E |
| Ut'ma | 86 | 57.35 N | 71.45 E |
| Utmānzai | 123 | 34.11 N | 71.46 E |
| Uto | 92 | 32.41 N | 130.40 E |
| Utö I | 40 | 58.56 N | 18.16 E |
| Utokota | 156 | 17.50 S | 20.22 E |
| Utonde | 152 | 1.56 N | 9.49 E |
| Utopia, Austl. | 162 | 22.14 S | 134.33 E |
| Utopia, Tx., U.S. | 196 | 29.37 N | 99.32 W |
| Utorgoš | 76 | 58.17 N | 30.15 E |
| Utraula | 124 | 27.19 N | 82.25 E |
| Utrecht, Ned. | 52 | 52.05 N | 5.08 E |
| Utrecht, S. Afr. | 158 | 27.38 S | 30.20 E |
| Utrecht □[4] | 52 | 52.05 N | 5.08 E |
| Utrera | 34 | 37.11 N | 5.47 W |
| Utroja ≃ | 76 | 57.23 N | 28.09 E |
| Utsaladdy | 224 | 48.15 N | 122.30 W |
| Utsira | 26 | 59.18 N | 4.54 E |
| Utsjoki | 24 | 69.53 N | 27.00 E |
| Utsumi | 96 | 34.21 N | 133.17 E |
| Utsunomiya | 94 | 36.33 N | 139.52 E |
| Utta | 80 | 46.23 N | 46.01 E |
| Uttamapālaiyam | 122 | 9.48 N | 77.20 E |
| Uttaradit | 110 | 17.38 N | 100.06 E |
| Uttarkāshi | 120 | 30.44 N | 78.27 E |
| Uttarpara-Kotrung | 272b | 22.40 N | 88.21 E |
| Uttar Pradesh □[3] | 120 | 27.00 N | 80.00 E |
| Uttendorf, Öst. | 60 | 48.09 N | 13.07 E |
| Uttendorf, Öst. | 64 | 47.17 N | 12.34 E |
| Uttenreuth | 60 | 49.36 N | 11.05 E |
| Uttenweiler | 58 | 48.09 N | 9.36 E |
| Ütterlingsen | 263 | 51.15 N | 7.45 E |
| Utting | 60 | 48.02 N | 11.05 E |
| Uttlesford □[8] | 260 | 51.47 N | 0.19 E |
| Uttoxeter | 42 | 52.54 N | 1.51 W |
| Utu | 154 | 1.45 S | 27.54 E |
| Utuado | 240m | 18.16 N | 66.42 W |
| Utukok ≃ | 180 | 70.04 N | 162.18 W |
| Utulei | 174u | 14.17 S | 170.40 W |
| Utunomiya → Utsunomiya | 94 | 36.33 N | 139.52 E |
| Utupua I | 14 | 11.16 S | 166.29 E |
| Utva ≃ | 86 | 51.28 N | 52.40 E |
| Utzenstorf | 58 | 47.08 N | 7.33 E |
| Uudenmaan lääni □[4] | 26 | 60.30 N | 25.00 E |
| Uulu | 76 | 58.17 N | 24.35 E |
| Üür ≃ | 88 | 50.18 N | 101.54 E |
| Uurainen | 26 | 62.30 N | 25.27 E |
| Uusikaarlepyy (Nykarleby) | 26 | 63.32 N | 22.32 E |
| Uusikaupunki (Nystad) | 26 | 60.48 N | 21.25 E |
| Uusimaa ◆[1] | 26 | 60.30 N | 25.00 E |
| Uvá, Bra. | 255 | 15.53 S | 50.25 W |
| Uva, Ross. | 80 | 56.59 N | 52.13 E |
| Uvá ≃ | 246 | 3.57 N | 68.24 W |
| Uvalda | 192 | 33.41 N | 83.25 W |
| Uvalde | 196 | 29.12 N | 99.47 W |
| Úvaly | 54 | 50.03 N | 14.47 E |
| Uvån ≃ | 40 | 60.01 N | 13.37 E |
| Uvaravičy | 76 | 52.36 N | 30.44 E |
| Uvarovka | 76 | 55.32 N | 35.37 E |
| Uvarovo | 80 | 51.59 N | 42.15 E |
| Uvas Creek ≃ | 226 | 36.58 N | 121.33 W |
| Uvas Reservoir ⊜[1] | 226 | 37.05 N | 121.42 W |
| Uvat | 86 | 59.09 N | 68.54 E |
| 'Uvda, Biq'at V | 132 | 29.57 N | 34.57 E |
| Uvdal | 26 | 60.16 N | 8.44 E |
| Uvel'skij | 86 | 54.26 N | 61.22 E |
| Uvernet | 62 | 44.22 N | 6.38 E |
| Uvero, Punta › | 241s | 11.21 N | 68.41 W |
| Uvinza | 154 | 5.06 S | 30.22 E |
| Uvira | 154 | 3.24 S | 29.08 E |
| Uvod' ≃ | 80 | 56.26 N | 41.26 E |
| Uvongo Beach | 158 | 30.51 S | 30.23 E |
| Uvs □[4] | 86 | 50.00 N | 92.00 E |
| Uvs nuur ⊜ | 74 | 50.20 N | 92.45 E |
| Uvworé › | 175f | 18.47 S | 169.16 E |
| Uwa | 96 | 33.20 N | 132.30 E |
| Uwajima | 96 | 33.13 N | 132.34 E |
| Uwa-kai ⊤[2] | 96 | 33.15 N | 132.15 E |
| 'Uwaybid, Jabal ʌ | 142 | 30.06 N | 32.09 E |
| Uwayl | 140 | 8.46 N | 27.24 E |
| 'Uwaynāt | 130 | 35.43 N | 36.05 E |
| 'Uwaynāt, Jabal al- ʌ | 140 | 21.54 N | 24.58 E |
| 'Uwayriḍ, Ḥarrat al- ≗[9] | 128 | 27.00 N | 37.30 E |
| Uwchland | 285 | 40.05 N | 75.42 W |
| Uwi, Pulau I | 112 | 1.05 N | 107.24 E |
| Uxbridge, On., Can. | 212 | 44.06 N | 79.07 W |
| Uxbridge, Ma., U.S. | 207 | 42.04 N | 71.37 W |
| Uxbridge ◆[8] | 260 | 51.33 N | 0.29 W |
| Uxmal ⊥ | 232 | 20.22 N | 89.46 W |
| Uyak Bay ⊂ | 180 | 57.36 N | 153.57 W |
| Uyama | 270 | 34.50 N | 135.41 E |
| U-yin | 110 | 22.53 N | 95.13 E |
| Uyo | 150 | 5.03 N | 7.56 E |
| Uyu ≃ | 110 | 24.51 N | 94.57 E |
| Uyuni | 248 | 20.28 S | 66.50 W |
| Uyuni, Salar de ≋ | 248 | 20.20 S | 67.42 W |
| Uza ≃, Ross. | 76 | 57.48 N | 29.31 E |
| Uza ≃, Ross. | 80 | 53.02 N | 45.18 E |
| Užanicha | 86 | 54.41 N | 81.02 E |
| Uzas | 86 | 57.04 N | 76.55 E |
| Užava | 76 | 57.14 N | 21.27 E |
| 'Uẓaym, Nahr al- ≃ | 128 | 34.01 N | 44.19 E |
| Uzbekistan □[1] | 72 | 41.00 N | 64.00 E |
| Uzboj ≃ | 128 | 39.30 N | 55.00 E |
| Uzda | 76 | 53.27 N | 27.13 E |
| Uzdin | 38 | 45.12 N | 20.38 E |
| Uzerche | 32 | 45.26 N | 1.34 E |
| Uzès | 62 | 44.01 N | 4.25 E |
| Uzgen | 85 | 40.46 N | 73.18 E |
| Uzh (Uh) ≃, Europe | 30 | 48.34 N | 22.00 E |
| Uzh ≃, Ukr. | 78 | 51.15 N | 30.12 E |
| Uzhhorod | 78 | 48.37 N | 22.18 E |
| Užice | 38 | 43.51 N | 19.51 E |
| Uzkij Lug | 88 | 50.42 N | 108.01 E |
| Uzkoje ◆[8] | 265b | 55.37 N | 37.32 E |
| Uzlovaja | 76 | 53.59 N | 38.10 E |
| Uzmorje | 80 | 51.15 N | 45.55 E |
| Uznach | 58 | 47.14 N | 9.00 E |
| Uznam (Usedom) I | 54 | 54.00 N | 14.00 E |
| Uzola ≃ | 80 | 56.32 N | 43.38 E |
| Uz'ukovo | 80 | 53.38 N | 49.43 E |
| Üzümlü, Tür. | 130 | 37.32 N | 31.37 E |
| Üzümlü, Tür. | 130 | 36.44 N | 29.14 E |
| Uzun | 85 | 38.22 N | 68.03 E |
| Uzun Ada I | 130 | 38.28 N | 26.42 E |
| Uzunagač, Kaz. | 85 | 43.13 N | 76.20 E |
| Uzunagač, Kaz. | 85 | 43.36 N | 76.19 E |
| Uzunbulak | 86 | 45.23 N | 84.06 E |
| Uzunca ≃ | 267b | 40.58 N | 28.50 E |
| Uzunköprü | 130 | 41.16 N | 26.41 E |
| Uzunkuduk | 85 | 40.33 N | 67.11 E |
| Uzunkuyu | 130 | 38.17 N | 26.33 E |
| Uzunovo | 82 | 54.32 N | 38.37 E |
| Užur | 86 | 55.20 N | 89.50 E |
| Užventis | 76 | 55.47 N | 22.39 E |
| Uzyn | 78 | 49.50 N | 30.24 E |
| **V** | | | |
| Vä | 26 | 55.59 N | 14.05 E |
| Vaajakoski | 26 | 62.16 N | 25.54 E |
| Vääksy | 26 | 61.11 N | 25.33 E |
| Vaal ≃ | 158 | 29.04 S | 23.38 E |
| Vaala | 26 | 64.26 N | 26.48 E |
| Vaaldam ⊜[1] | 158 | 26.55 S | 28.12 E |
| Vaalhartsdam ⊜[1] | 158 | 28.06 S | 24.55 E |
| Vaalkop ʌ | 158 | 31.21 S | 26.31 E |
| Vaals | 56 | 50.46 N | 6.01 E |
| Vaalserberg ʌ[2] | 56 | 50.45 N | 6.01 E |
| Vaalwater | 156 | 24.20 S | 28.03 E |
| Vaasa (Vasa) | 26 | 63.06 N | 21.36 E |
| Vaasan lääni □[4] | 26 | 63.00 N | 23.00 E |
| Vaassen | 52 | 52.17 N | 5.57 E |
| Vabalninkas | 76 | 55.58 N | 24.45 E |
| Vabkent | 128 | 40.02 N | 64.30 E |
| Vác | 30 | 47.47 N | 19.08 E |
| Vaca, Bol. | 248 | 19.54 S | 63.48 W |
| Vača, Ross. | 80 | 55.48 N | 42.46 E |
| Vaca, Mount ʌ | 226 | 38.24 N | 122.06 W |
| Vacacaí ≃ | 252 | 29.55 S | 53.06 W |
| Vaca Key I | 220 | 24.43 N | 81.04 W |
| Vacaria | 252 | 28.30 S | 50.56 W |
| Vacaria ≃, Bra. | 255 | 16.39 S | 42.45 W |
| Vacaria ≃, Bra. | 255 | 21.55 S | 53.59 W |
| Vacas, Arroyo de las ≃ | 258 | 34.00 S | 58.18 W |
| Vacaville | 226 | 38.21 N | 121.59 W |
| Vacca, Kaap › | 158 | 34.21 S | 21.53 E |
| Vaccarès, Étang de ⊂ | 62 | 43.32 N | 4.34 E |
| Vach ≃ | 74 | 60.45 N | 76.45 E |
| Vacha | 56 | 50.50 N | 10.01 E |
| Vache, Île à I | 238 | 18.05 N | 73.38 W |
| Vaches, Île aux I | 275a | 45.41 N | 73.40 W |
| Vaches, Rivière aux ≃ | 206 | 46.02 N | 72.46 W |
| Vachrušev | 89 | 48.59 N | 142.58 E |
| Vachš ≃ | 72 | 37.06 N | 68.18 E |
| Vachšskij chrebet ⛰ | 85 | 38.35 N | 69.45 E |
| Vachtan | 80 | 57.58 N | 46.42 E |
| Vači | 84 | 42.05 N | 47.13 E |
| Vacía Talega, Punta › | 240m | 18.27 N | 65.54 W |
| Vacoas | 157c | 20.18 S | 57.29 E |
| Vad, Ross. | 80 | 55.32 N | 44.12 E |
| Vad, Sve. | 40 | 60.02 N | 15.39 E |
| Vad ≃ | 80 | 54.33 N | 42.37 E |
| Väddö I | 40 | 60.00 N | 18.50 E |
| Vădeni | 38 | 45.22 N | [illegible]7.56 E |
| Vader | 224 | 46.24 N | 1[illegible]2.57 W |
| Vadheim | 26 | 61.13 N | 5.49 E |
| Vādi | 272c | 18.56 N | [illegible]3.06 E |
| Vadino | 76 | 55.16 N | [illegible]3.16 E |
| Vadinsk | 80 | 53.43 N | [illegible]3.04 E |
| Vadnagar | 120 | 23.47 N | [illegible]2.38 E |
| Vadodara | 122 | 22.18 N | [illegible]3.12 E |
| Vado de Cedillos | 200 | 31.05 N | 1[illegible].50 W |
| Vado de Piedra | 196 | 29.50 N | 1[illegible]4.40 W |
| Vado Hondo | 200 | 31.09 N | 1[illegible].22 W |
| Vado Ligure | 62 | 44.17 N | [illegible].27 E |
| Vadret, Piz ʌ | 58 | 46.41 N | [illegible].57 E |
| Vadsbro | 40 | 58.58 N | [illegible].36 E |
| Vadsø | 24 | 70.05 N | [illegible].46 E |
| Vadstena | 26 | 58.27 N | 1[illegible].54 E |
| Vaduz | 58 | 47.09 N | [illegible].31 E |
| Vadvetjåkko Nationalpark ♠ | 24 | 68.35 N | 1[illegible].20 E |
| Væggerløse | 41 | 54.42 N | 1[illegible].56 E |
| Værøy I | 24 | 67.40 N | 1[illegible].39 E |
| Vaga ≃ | 24 | 62.48 N | 4[illegible].56 E |
| Vagaj | 86 | 57.56 N | 6[illegible].01 E |
| Vagaj ≃ | 86 | 57.59 N | 6[illegible].01 E |
| Vågåmo | 26 | 61.53 N | [illegible].06 E |
| Vaganski Vrh ʌ | 36 | 44.22 N | 1[illegible].31 E |
| Vaggeryd | 26 | 57.30 N | 1[illegible].07 E |
| Vaghena Island I | 175e | 7.26 S | 15[illegible].46 E |
| Vaglia | 66 | 43.54 N | 1[illegible].17 E |
| Vaglio Basilicata | 68 | 40.40 N | 1[illegible].55 E |
| Vagney | 58 | 48.01 N | [illegible].43 E |
| Vagnhärad | 40 | 58.55 N | 17.30 E |
| Vagues | 258 | 34.19 S | 5[illegible].26 W |
| Váh ≃ | 30 | 47.55 N | 18.00 E |
| Vahrn → Varna | 64 | 46.44 N | 11.38 E |
| Vaiano | 66 | 43.58 N | 11.07 E |
| Vaich, Loch ⊜ | 46 | 57.43 N | 4.46 W |
| Vaiden | 194 | 33.19 N | 89.44 W |
| Vaigai ≃ | 122 | 9.21 N | 79.00 E |
| Vaigat ʯ | 176 | 70.11 N | 53.00 W |
| Vaihingen an der Enz | 56 | 48.56 N | 8.58 E |
| Vaijāpur | 122 | 19.55 N | 74.44 E |
| Vaikam | 122 | 9.46 N | 76.24 E |
| Väike-Maarja | 76 | 59.08 N | 26.[illegible]5 E |
| Väike Pakri I | 76 | 59.20 N | 24.[illegible]0 E |
| Vail, Co., U.S. | 200 | 39.38 N | 106.[illegible]2 W |
| Vail, Ia., U.S. | 198 | 42.03 N | 95.[illegible]1 W |
| Vaila I | 46a | 60.12 N | 1.[illegible]7 W |
| Vailala ≃ | 164 | 7.25 S | 145.[illegible]5 E |
| Vaileka | 175g | 17.23 S | 178.[illegible]9 E |
| Vail Lake ⊜[1] | 228 | 33.29 N | 116.[illegible]8 W |
| Vailly-sur-Aisne | 50 | 49.25 N | 3.[illegible]1 E |
| Vailly-sur-Sauldre | 50 | 47.27 N | 2.[illegible]9 E |
| Vail Mills | 210 | 43.03 N | 74.[illegible]3 W |
| Vailoatai | 174u | 14.22 S | 170.[illegible]7 W |
| Vail Point › | 212 | 44.43 N | 80.[illegible]5 W |
| Vails Gate | 210 | 41.27 N | 74.[illegible]4 W |
| Vaimali | 175f | 16.34 S | 168.[illegible] E |
| Vaiņode | 76 | 56.26 N | 21.[illegible] E |
| Vaiont, Lago di ⊜ | 64 | 46.16 N | 12.[illegible] E |
| Vaippār ≃ | 122 | 9.01 N | 78.[illegible] E |
| Vair ≃ | 58 | 48.27 N | 5.[illegible] E |
| Vairano Scalo | 68 | 41.20 N | 14.[illegible] E |
| Vairao | 174s | 17.47 S | 149.[illegible] W |
| Vaires-sur-Marne | 261 | 48.52 N | 2.[illegible] E |
| Vaison-la-Romaine | 62 | 44.14 N | 5.[illegible] E |
| Vaitahu | 174x | 9.56 S | 139.[illegible] W |
| Vaîte | 58 | 47.35 N | 5.4[illegible] E |
| Vaitogi | 174u | 14.21 S | 170.4[illegible] W |
| Vaitown | 150 | 6.52 N | 10.5[illegible] W |
| Vaitupu I | 14 | 7.28 S | 178.4[illegible] E |
| Vaja ≃ | 80 | 57.27 N | 46.0[illegible] E |
| Vajgač | 72 | 70.25 N | 58.4[illegible] E |
| Vajgač, ostrov I | 72 | 70.00 N | 59.3[illegible] E |
| Vajk' | 84 | 39.40 N | 45.3[illegible] E |
| Vakaga □[5] | 146 | 10.00 N | 22.3[illegible] E |
| Vakaga ≃ | 146 | 9.48 N | 21.3[illegible] E |
| Vākhān ≃ | 120 | 37.00 N | 72.4[illegible] E |
| Vākhān ◆[1] | 120 | 37.00 N | 73.0[illegible] E |
| Vakhrusheve | 83 | 48.10 N | 38.4[illegible] E |
| Vaklan | 272c | 19.07 N | 73.0[illegible] E |
| Vaksdal | 26 | 60.29 N | 5.4[illegible] E |
| Vala ≃ | 80 | 56.59 N | 51.1[illegible] E |
| Valaam | 24 | 61.23 N | 30.5[illegible] E |
| Valaam, ostrov I | 26 | 61.22 N | 30.5[illegible] E |
| Vålådalen | 26 | 63.10 N | 12.5[illegible] E |
| Valadeces | 196 | 26.14 N | 98.4[illegible] W |
| Valadim | 154 | 12.22 S | 36.1[illegible] E |
| Valais (Wallis) □[3] | 58 | 46.10 N | 7.30 E |
| Val-Alain | 206 | 46.24 N | 71.45 W |
| Valamaz | 80 | 57.32 N | 52.05 E |
| Valandovo | 38 | 41.19 N | 22.34 E |
| Valangin | 58 | 47.01 N | 6.54 E |
| Valap | 272c | 19.03 N | 73.08 E |
| Valare, Baie ⊂ | 174s | 17.31 S | 149.46 W |
| Valašské Klobouky | 30 | 49.08 N | 18.01 E |
| Valašské Meziříčí | 30 | 49.28 N | 17.58 E |
| Valatie | 210 | 42.24 N | 73.40 W |
| Vala Ull | 272c | 19.02 N | 73.07 E |
| Val-Bélair | 206 | 46.51 N | 71.26 W |
| Valbella | 58 | 46.45 N | 9.33 E |
| Vålberg | 26 | 59.24 N | 13.12 E |
| Valbert | 56 | 51.07 N | 7.44 E |
| Valbo | 40 | 60.40 N | 17.04 E |
| Valbondione | 64 | 46.02 N | 10.00 E |
| Valbonnais | 62 | 44.54 N | 5.54 E |
| Valbrona | 58 | 45.53 N | 9.18 E |
| Valcanuta ◆[8] | 267a | 41.53 N | 12.25 E |
| Vâlcea □[6] | 38 | 45.19 N | 24.00 E |
| Vâlčedrăm | 38 | 43.42 N | 23.27 |
| Valcheta | 254 | 40.42 S | 66.09 W |
| Valchetta ≃ | 267a | 41.58 N | 12.30 |
| Valchiusella | 62 | 45.32 N | 7.42 |
| Valcivières | 62 | 45.35 N | 3.48 E |
| Valcourt | 206 | 45.29 N | 72.18 W |
| Valdagno | 64 | 45.39 N | 11.18 E |
| Valdahon | 58 | 47.09 N | 6.21 E |
| Valdai Hills → Valdajskaja vozvyšennost' ⛰[2] | 76 | 57.00 N | 33.30 E |
| Valdaj, Ross. | 24 | 63.26 N | 35.30 E |
| Valdaj, Ross. | 76 | 57.59 N | 33.14 E |
| Valdajskaja vozvyšennost' ⛰[2] | 24 | 57.00 N | 33.30 E |
| Valdarno V | 66 | 43.35 N | 11.30 E |
| Valdavia ≃ | 34 | 42.24 N | 4.16 W |
| Val-David | 206 | 46.01 N | 74.12 W |
| Valdebeba, Arroyo de ≃ | 266a | 41.23 N | 2.10 E |
| Valdeblore | 62 | 44.04 N | 7.12 E |
| Val-de-Cães | 250 | 1.23 S | 48.29 W |
| Valdecañas, Embalse de ⊜[1] | 34 | 39.45 N | 5.30 W |
| Valdelândia | 255 | 15.11 S | 50.02 W |
| Val-de-Marne □[5] | 261 | 48.47 N | 2.29 E |
| Valdemārpils | 76 | 57.22 N | 22.35 E |
| Valdemarsvik | 26 | 58.12 N | 16.36 E |
| Valdepeñas | 34 | 38.46 N | 3.23 W |
| Valderaduey ≃ | 34 | 41.31 N | 5.42 W |
| Valderas | 34 | 42.05 N | 5.27 W |
| Valderice | 70 | 38.03 N | 12.38 E |
| Valderrama | 116 | 11.00 N | 122.08 E |
| Valderrobres | 34 | 40.53 N | 0.09 E |
| Valders | 190 | 44.03 N | 87.53 W |
| Valdés, Península ›[1] | 254 | 42.30 S | 64.00 W |
| Val-des-Bois | 188 | 45.54 N | 75.35 W |
| Valdese | 192 | 35.44 N | 81.33 W |
| Valdes Island I | 224 | 49.04 N | 123.38 W |
| Valdéz, Ec. | 246 | 1.15 N | 79.00 W |
| Valdez, Ak., U.S. | 180 | 61.07 N | 146.16 W |
| Valdieri | 62 | 44.17 N | 7.24 E |
| Val-d'Isère | 62 | 45.27 N | 6.59 E |
| Valdivia, Chile | 254 | 39.48 S | 73.14 W |
| Valdivia, Col. | 246 | 7.11 N | 75.27 W |
| Valdobbiadene | 64 | 45.54 N | 12.00 E |
| Valdoie | 58 | 47.40 N | 6.51 E |
| Val-d'Oise □[5] | 50 | 49.10 N | 2.10 E |
| Val-d'Or | 190 | 48.07 N | 77.47 W |
| Valdorf | 52 | 52.09 N | 8.51 E |

| | | | | |
|---|---|---|---|---|
| ≃ River | Fluß | Río | Rivière | Rio |
| ≖ Canal | Kanal | Canal | Canal | Canal |
| ∟ Waterfall, Rapids | Wasserfall, Stromschnellen | Cascada, Rápidos | Chute d'eau, Rapides | Cascata, Rápidos |
| ʯ Strait | Meeresstraße | Estrecho | Détroit | Estreito |
| ⊂ Bay, Gulf | Bucht, Golf | Bahía, Golfo | Baie, Golfe | Baía, Golfo |
| ⊜ Lake, Lakes | See, Seen | Lago, Lagos | Lac, Lacs | Lago, Lagos |
| ≋ Swamp | Sumpf | Pantano | Marais | Pântano |
| ⌓ Ice Features, Glacier | Eis- und Gletscherformen | Accidentes Glaciales | Formes glaciaires | Acidentes glaciares |
| ⊤ Other Hydrographic Features | Andere Hydrographische Objekte | Otros Elementos Hidrográficos | Autres données hydrographiques | Outros acidentes hidrográficos |

| | | | | |
|---|---|---|---|---|
| ✣ Submarine Features | Untermeerische Objekte | Accidentes Submarinos | Formes de relief sous-marin | Acidentes submarinos |
| □ Political Unit | Politische Einheit | Unidad Politica | Entité politique | Unidade política |
| ◡ Cultural Institution | Kulturelle Institution | Institución Cultural | Institution culturelle | Instituição cultural |
| ⊥ Historical Site | Historische Stätte | Sitio Histórico | Site historique | Sitio histórico |
| ♠ Recreational Site | Erholungs- und Ferienort | Sitio de Recreo | Centre de loisirs | Area de Lazer |
| ⊠ Airport | Flughafen | Aeropuerto | Aéroport | Aeroporto |
| ■ Military Installation | Militäranlage | Instalación Militar | Installation militaire | Instalação militar |
| ◆ Miscellaneous | Verschiedenes | Misceláneo | Divers | Diversos |

Valdosta 192 30.49 N 83.16 W
Valdres V 26 60.55 N 9.10 E
Valdurna (Durnholz) 64 46.44 N 11.26 E
Vale, Guernsey 43b 49.29 N 2.31 W
Vale, Or., U.S. 202 43.58 N 117.14 W
Valea lui Mihai 38 47.31 N 22.09 E
Vale de Lobos 266c 38.49 N 9.17 W
Valeene 218 38.26 N 86.24 W
Valeggio sul Mincio 64 45.21 N 10.44 E
Valehouse Reservoir ⊜[1] 262 53.29 N 1.57 W
Valemount 182 52.50 N 119.15 W
Valença, Bra. 255 13.22 S 39.05 W
Valença, Bra. 256 22.15 S 43.43 W
Valença, Port. 34 42.02 N 8.38 W
Valença do Piauí 250 6.24 S 41.45 W
Valençay 50 47.09 N 1.34 E
Valence → València, Esp. 34 39.28 N 0.22 W
Valence, Fr. 62 44.56 N 4.54 E
València, Esp. 34 39.28 N 0.22 W
Valencia, Hond. 236 14.47 N 85.18 W
Valencia, Pil. 116 7.57 N 125.03 E
Valencia, Pa., U.S. 214 40.40 N 79.59 W
Valencia, Ven. 246 10.11 N 68.00 W
València □[4] 34 39.30 N 0.45 W
València, Golf de c 34 39.50 N 0.30 E
Valencia, Lago de ⊜ 246 10.15 N 67.45 W
Valencia, Quebrada ≐ 286c 10.30 N 66.46 W
Valencia de Alcántata 34 39.25 N 7.14 W
Valencia de Don Juan 34 42.18 N 5.31 W
Valencia Island I 48 51.52 N 10.20 W
Valenciennes 50 50.21 N 3.32 E
Vălenii de Munte 38 45.12 N 26.03 E
Valensole 62 43.50 N 5.59 E
Valentano 66 42.34 N 11.49 E
Valente 250 11.34 S 39.27 W
Valentigney 58 47.28 N 6.50 E
Valentin 89 43.08 N 134.17 E
Valentín Alsina -•-[8] 288 34.40 S 58.25 W
Valentine, Ne., U.S. 198 42.52 N 100.33 W
Valentine, Tx., U.S. 196 30.34 N 104.29 W
Valentine Mountain ∧ 224 48.32 N 123.56 W
Valentinovka 265b 55.55 N 37.56 E
Valenton 261 48.45 N 2.28 E
Valenza 62 45.01 N 8.38 E
Valenzano 68 41.02 N 16.53 E
Valenzuela 269f 14.42 N 120.58 E
Våler 26 60.40 N 11.50 E
Valera 246 9.19 N 70.37 W
Valérien, Mont ∧[2] 261 48.53 N 2.13 E
Vale Royal □[8] 262 53.17 N 2.37 W
Valets, Lac ⊜ 190 48.32 N 76.30 W
Valette, La → Valletta 36 35.54 N 14.31 E
Valfabbrica 66 43.09 N 12.36 E
Valflaunès 62 43.48 N 3.52 E
Valfurva 64 46.27 N 10.25 E
Valfurva V 64 46.26 N 10.26 E
Valga 76 57.47 N 26.02 E
Valge ≐ 76 59.35 N 25.42 E
Valgorge 62 44.35 N 4.07 E
Valgrisanche 62 45.38 N 7.04 E
Valguarnera Caropepe 70 37.30 N 14.23 E
Valhalla, S. Afr. 158 25.49 S 28.08 E
Valhalla, N.Y., U.S. 210 41.04 N 73.46 W
Valhalla, Lake ⊜ 276 40.56 N 74.22 W
Valiente, Península >[1] 236 9.05 N 81.51 W
Valiente, Punta > 236 9.11 N 81.55 W
Valier, Il., U.S. 194 38.01 N 89.03 W
Valier, Mt., U.S. 202 48.18 N 112.14 W
Valier, Pa., U.S. 214 40.55 N 79.03 W
Valili ∧ 175g 16.39 S 179.10 E
Valinda 280 34.02 N 117.56 W
Valinhos 256 22.57 S 47.01 W
Valjevo 38 44.16 N 19.53 E
Valka 76 57.46 N 26.00 E
Valkeakoski 26 61.16 N 24.02 E
Valkenburg 56 50.52 N 5.50 E
Valkenswaard 52 51.21 N 5.28 E
V'alki 82 55.39 N 38.05 E
Valkininkas 76 54.21 N 24.50 E
Valky 78 49.50 N 35.37 E
Valla 40 59.02 N 16.23 E
Valladares 196 26.53 N 100.37 W
Valladolid, Ec. 246 4.33 S 79.08 W
Valladolid, Esp. 34 41.39 N 4.43 W
Valladolid, Méx. 232 20.41 N 88.12 W
Valladolid □[4] 34 41.40 N 4.50 W
Vallage -•-[1] 58 48.24 N 5.00 E
Vallåkra 41 55.58 N 12.52 E
Vallarsa 64 45.47 N 11.07 E
Vallata 68 41.02 N 15.15 E
Vallauris 62 43.35 N 7.03 E
Vallco Fashion Park -•-[9] 282 37.19 N 122.01 W
Valldal 26 62.20 N 7.21 E
Valldoreix 266d 41.28 N 2.04 E
Valle, Esp. 34 43.14 N 4.18 W
Valle, Lat. 76 56.30 N 24.44 E
Valle □[5] 236 13.30 N 87.35 W
Valle, Arroyo ≐ 226 37.39 N 121.54 W
Vallecas -•-[8] 266a 40.23 N 3.37 W
Valle Castellana 66 42.44 N 13.29 E
Vallecillo 196 26.40 N 99.58 W
Vallecito 226 38.07 N 120.27 W
Vallecitos 200 36.05 N 106.20 W
Vallecitos Creek ≐ 282 37.36 N 121.53 W
Vallecorsa 66 41.27 N 13.24 E
Valle Crucis Abbey ⊍[1] 42 52.59 N 3.12 W
Valle d'Aosta □[4] 36 45.45 N 7.25 E
Valle de Bravo 234 19.11 N 100.08 W
Valle de Guadalupe 234 21.00 N 102.37 W
Valle de Guanape 246 9.54 N 65.41 W
Valle de Juárez 234 19.53 N 102.51 W
Valle de la Pascua 246 9.13 N 66.00 W
Valle del Cauca □[5] 246 3.45 N 76.30 W
Valle de Olivos 232 27.12 N 106.17 W
Valle de Santiago 234 20.23 N 101.12 W
Valle de Zaragoza 232 27.28 N 105.49 W
Valle di Cadore 64 46.24 N 12.20 E
Valle di Sotto 64 46.25 N 10.21 E
Valledolmo 70 37.45 N 13.49 E
Valledupar 246 10.29 N 73.15 W
Valle Edén 252 31.50 S 56.09 W
Vallefiorita 68 38.46 N 16.27 E
Vallegrande 248 18.29 S 64.06 W
Valle Hermoso, Arg. 252 31.07 S 64.29 W
Valle Hermoso, Méx. 196 25.39 N 97.52 W
Vallehermoso, Pil. 116 10.20 N 123.19 E
Vallejo 226 38.06 N 122.15 W
Valle Lomellina 62 45.09 N 8.40 E
Vallelunga Pratameno 70 37.41 N 13.50 E
Valle Mosso 62 45.38 N 8.09 E
Vällen ⊜ 40 60.03 N 18.20 E
Vallenar 252 28.35 S 70.46 W
Vallendar 56 50.24 N 7.37 E
Vallensbæk 41 55.38 N 12.22 E
Vallentuna 40 59.32 N 18.05 E
Vallepietra 66 41.55 N 13.14 E
Valleraugue 62 44.05 N 3.38 E
Valle Redondo 204 32.31 N 116.46 W
Vallermosa 71 39.22 N 8.48 E
Vallerotonda 66 41.33 N 13.55 E
Valleroy 56 49.12 N 5.55 E
Valles → Ciudad de Valles 234 21.59 N 99.01 W
Valles Caldera ≜[6] 200 35.52 N 106.33 W
Vallet 32 47.10 N 1.16 W
Valletta 36 35.54 N 14.31 E
Valley, Al., U.S. 194 32.49 N 85.10 W
Valley, Ne., U.S. 198 41.18 N 96.20 W
Valley, Wa., U.S. 182 48.10 N 117.43 W
Valley ≐ 184 51.21 N 99.55 W
Valley Bend 188 38.46 N 79.56 W
Valley Center, Ca., U.S. 228 33.13 N 117.02 W
Valley Center, Ks., U.S. 198 37.50 N 97.22 W
Valley City, N.D., U.S. 198 46.55 N 97.59 W
Valley City, Oh., U.S. 214 41.14 N 81.56 W
Valley Cottage 210 41.07 N 73.57 W
Valley Creek ≐, Pa., U.S. 285 40.06 N 75.28 W
Valley Creek ≐, Pa., U.S. 285 39.58 N 75.40 W
Valley Creek ≐, Tx., U.S. 196 31.43 N 100.02 W
Valleydale 280 34.06 N 117.56 W
Valley Falls, Ks., U.S. 198 39.20 N 95.27 W
Valley Falls, N.Y., U.S. 210 42.54 N 73.34 W
Valley Falls, R.I., U.S. 207 41.54 N 71.23 W
Valley Farms 200 32.59 N 111.26 W
Valleyfield 186 49.08 N 53.37 W
Valley Forge 208 40.05 N 75.28 W
Valley Forge Estates 285 40.05 N 75.26 W
Valley Forge National Historical Park ♦ 208 40.06 N 75.27 W
Valley Grove 214 40.05 N 80.34 W
Valley Head, Al., U.S. 194 34.34 N 85.36 W
Valley Head, W.V., U.S. 188 38.32 N 80.02 W
Valley Home 226 37.50 N 120.55 W
Valley Mede 284b 39.17 N 76.50 W
Valley Mills 222 31.39 N 97.28 W
Valley of Desolation National Monument ♦ 158 32.17 S 24.30 E
Valley of Fire State Park ♦ 204 36.26 N 114.30 W
Valley of the Kings ⊥ 140 25.45 N 32.37 E
Valley Park 219 38.32 N 90.29 W
Valley Plaza -•-[9] 280 34.11 N 118.24 W
Valley Springs, Ca., U.S. 226 38.12 N 120.50 W
Valley Springs, S.D., U.S. 198 43.34 N 96.28 W
Valley Station 194 38.06 N 85.52 W
Valley Stream 210 40.39 N 73.42 W
Valley Stream ≐ 276 40.39 N 73.45 W
Valley Stream State Park ♦ 276 40.41 N 73.42 W
Valleyview, Ab., Can. 182 55.04 N 117.17 W
Valley View, Il., U.S. 216 41.50 N 88.03 W
Valley View, Oh., U.S. 279a 41.23 N 81.37 W
Valley View, Pa., U.S. 210 40.38 N 76.32 W
Valley View, Tx., U.S. 196 33.29 N 97.10 W
Vallgrund I 26 63.12 N 21.14 E
Valliant 196 34.00 N 95.05 W
Valli del Pasubio 64 45.41 N 11.15 E
Vallières 58 45.54 N 5.56 E
Vallimanca, Arroyo ≐ 252 35.40 S 60.02 W
Vallio 64 45.38 N 10.23 E
Vallirana 266d 41.23 N 1.56 E
Vallø 41 55.24 N 12.15 E
Vallo della Lucania 68 40.14 N 15.17 E
Valloire 62 45.10 N 6.26 E
Vallombrosa 66 43.44 N 11.32 E
Vallonia 218 38.50 N 86.05 W
Vallon-Pont-d'Arc 62 44.24 N 4.24 E
Vallorbe 58 46.43 N 6.22 E
Vallorcine 58 46.02 N 6.56 E
Vallouise 62 44.51 N 6.29 E
Vallromanes 266d 41.32 N 2.18 E
Valls 34 41.17 N 1.15 E
Valluga ∧ 58 47.09 N 10.12 E
Vallvidrera -•-[8] 266d 41.25 N 2.07 E
Vallvidrera, Riera de ≐ 266d 41.25 N 2.01 E
Val-Marie 184 49.14 N 107.44 W
Valmaseda 34 43.12 N 3.12 W
Valmeyer 219 38.17 N 90.18 W
Valmiera 76 57.33 N 25.24 E
Valmondois 261 49.06 N 2.12 E
Valmont 50 49.44 N 0.31 E
Valmontone 66 41.46 N 12.57 E
Valmy 56 49.05 N 4.46 E
Valognes 32 49.31 N 1.28 W
Valois 210 42.32 N 76.53 W
Valois, Baie de c 275a 45.26 N 73.47 W
Valok 78 45.47 N 34.57 E
Valona → Vlorë 38 40.27 N 19.30 E
Valongo 34 41.11 N 8.30 W
Valoria la Buena 34 41.48 N 4.32 W
Valožyn 76 54.05 N 26.32 E
Vālpārai 122 10.22 N 76.58 E
Valparaíso, Bra. 255 21.13 S 50.51 W
Valparaíso, Chile 252 33.02 S 71.38 W
Valparaíso, Méx. 234 22.46 N 103.34 W
Valparaiso, Fl., U.S. 194 30.29 N 86.29 W
Valparaiso, In., U.S. 216 41.28 N 87.03 W
Valparaiso, Ne., U.S. 198 41.04 N 96.49 W
Valparaíso □[4] 252 32.45 S 71.20 W
Valparaíso ≐ 234 22.33 N 103.39 W
Valpelline V 62 45.50 N 7.25 E
Valpovo 38 45.39 N 18.26 E
Valprato Soana 62 45.31 N 7.33 E
Valréas 62 44.23 N 4.59 E
Valrico 220 27.57 N 82.16 W
Val Roveto V 66 41.52 N 13.30 E
Vals ≐ 158 27.23 S 26.30 E
Vals, Tanjung > 164 8.26 S 137.38 E
Val-Saint-Michel 206 46.52 N 71.27 W
Valsbaai c 158 34.12 S 18.40 E
Valserine ≐ 58 46.06 N 5.50 E
Valserrhein ≐ 58 46.42 N 9.10 E
Valsertal V 58 46.37 N 9.10 E
Valsetz 202 44.50 N 123.39 W
Valsinni 68 40.10 N 16.26 E
Valsjöbyn 26 64.04 N 14.08 E
Valskog 40 59.27 N 15.57 E
Vals-les-Bains 62 44.40 N 4.22 E
Vals Platz 58 46.37 N 9.11 E
Vals-Près-le-Puy 62 45.01 N 3.52 E
Valstagna 64 45.51 N 11.39 E
Val-Suzon 58 47.25 N 4.54 E
Valtellina V 58 46.10 N 10.10 E
Valthermond 52 52.53 N 6.59 E
Valtice 61 48.44 N 16.45 E
Valtierrilla 234 20.32 N 101.08 W
Valtimo 26 63.40 N 28.48 E
Valtorta 58 45.59 N 9.32 E
Valtournanche 62 45.53 N 7.37 E
Valujec 76 52.46 N 33.23 E
Valujevka 80 46.44 N 43.43 E
Valujevo 265b 55.35 N 37.21 E
Valujki 78 50.13 N 38.08 E
Valvasone 64 45.59 N 12.52 E
Valverde 148 27.48 N 17.55 W
Valverde del Camino 34 37.34 N 6.45 W
Val Verde Park 228 34.27 N 118.40 W
Valyermo 228 34.26 N 117.50 W
Valyncy 76 55.42 N 28.11 E
Vamba ≐ 152 7.27 S 14.17 E
Vamdrup 41 55.25 N 9.17 E
Våmhus 26 61.08 N 14.28 E
Vamizi, Ilha I 154 11.02 S 40.40 E
Vammala 26 61.20 N 22.54 E
Vamori Wash V 200 31.57 N 112.21 W
Van, Tür. 128 38.28 N 43.20 E
Van, Pa., U.S. 214 41.19 N 79.40 W
Van, Tx., U.S. 222 32.31 N 95.38 W
Van □[4] 128 39.00 N 43.45 E
Vanajavesi ⊜ 26 61.09 N 24.15 E
Vanak -•-[8] 267d 35.45 N 51.23 E
Van Alstyne 196 33.25 N 96.34 W
Vanån ≐ 40 60.31 N 14.14 E
Vananda 182 49.45 N 124.33 W
Vanapa ≐ 164 9.05 S 147.10 E
Vanault-les-Dames 56 48.51 N 4.46 E
Vanavana I[1] 14 20.47 S 139.09 W
Vanavara 74 60.22 N 102.16 E
Van Buren, Ar., U.S. 194 35.26 N 94.20 W
Van Buren, In., U.S. 216 40.37 N 85.30 W
Van Buren, Me., U.S. 186 47.09 N 67.56 W
Van Buren, Mo., U.S. 194 36.59 N 91.00 W
Van Buren, Oh., U.S. 216 41.08 N 83.38 W
Van Buren □[6] 216 42.14 N 86.04 W
Van Buren Point 214 42.27 N 79.25 W
Vanč 85 38.23 N 71.26 E
Vanč ≐ 85 38.18 N 71.19 E
Vance Air Force Base ■ 196 36.21 N 97.55 W
Vanceboro 188 45.33 N 67.25 W
Vanceburg 218 38.35 N 83.19 W
Vancleave 194 30.32 N 88.41 W
Van Cortlandt Park ♦ 276 40.54 N 73.53 W
Van Cortlandtville 210 41.19 N 73.54 W
Vancouver, B.C., Can. 224 49.16 N 123.07 W
Vancouver, Wa., U.S. 224 45.38 N 122.39 W
Vancouver, Cape >, Austl. 162 35.01 S 118.12 E
Vancouver, Cape >, Ak., U.S. 180 60.33 N 165.27 W
Vancouver, Mount ∧ 180 60.20 N 139.40 W
Vancouver International Airport ⊠ 224 48.39 N 123.26 W
Vancouver Island I 182 49.45 N 126.00 W
Vancouver Island Ranges ∧∧ 182 49.25 N 125.25 W
Vancouver Lake ⊜ 224 45.41 N 122.44 W
Van Daalen ≐ 164 3.05 S 138.09 E
Vandalia, Il., U.S. 219 38.57 N 89.05 W
Vandalia, Mi., U.S. 216 41.55 N 85.55 W
Vandalia, Mo., U.S. 219 39.18 N 91.29 W
Vandalia, Oh., U.S. 218 39.53 N 84.11 W
Vandalia Lake ⊜[1] 219 39.01 N 89.09 W
Vändam 84 40.57 N 47.57 E
Vandavāsi 122 12.30 N 79.37 E
Vandekerckhove Lake ⊜ 184 57.02 N 101.25 W
Vandel 41 55.42 N 9.13 E
Vandenberg Air Force Base ■ 204 34.43 N 120.33 W
Van den Bosch, Tanjung > 164 4.06 S 132.55 E
Vandenesse 58 47.13 N 4.37 E
Vanderbijlpark 158 26.42 S 27.54 E
Vanderbilt, Mi., U.S. 190 45.08 N 84.39 W
Vanderbilt, Tx., U.S. 196 28.49 N 96.37 W
Vanderbilt Mansion National Historic Site ⊥ 210 41.47 N 73.56 W
Vanderbilt Museum ⊍ 276 40.54 N 73.22 W
Vandercook Lake 216 42.11 N 84.23 W
Vandergrift 214 40.36 N 79.33 W
Vanderhoof 182 54.01 N 124.01 W
Vanderlin Island I 164 15.44 S 137.02 E
Vandervoort 194 34.22 N 94.21 W
Van Diemen, Cape >, Austl. 164 11.10 S 130.23 E
Van Diemen, Cape >, Austl. 164 16.31 S 139.41 E
Van Diemen Gulf c 164 11.50 S 132.00 E
Vandling 210 41.38 N 75.29 W
Vandoeuvre-lès-Nancy 58 48.39 N 6.11 E
Vandoies (Vintl) 64 46.49 N 11.43 E
Vändra 76 58.39 N 25.02 E
Van Duzen ≐ 204 40.33 N 124.08 W
Vandúzi ≐ 154 18.56 S 34.01 E
Vandykpark 273d 26.16 S 28.19 E
Vandžiogala 76 55.07 N 23.58 E
Vanegas 234 23.51 N 100.52 W
Vänern ⊜ 26 58.55 N 13.30 E
Vänersborg 26 58.22 N 12.19 E
Van Etten 210 42.11 N 76.33 W
Vang, Mount ∧ 9 73.56 S 68.39 W
Vanga 154 4.39 S 39.13 E
Vangaindrano 157b 23.21 S 47.36 E
Vängelälven ≐ 26 63.41 N 16.25 E
Van Gölü ⊜ 128 38.33 N 42.46 E
Vangsnes 26 61.11 N 6.38 E
Vanguard 184 49.55 N 107.20 W
Vangunu, Mount ∧ 175e 8.42 S 158.00 E
Vangunu Island I 175e 8.38 S 158.00 E
Van Hook Arm c 198 47.50 N 102.25 W
Van Horn 196 31.02 N 104.49 W
Van Horne 190 42.00 N 92.05 W
Van Hornesville 210 42.54 N 74.50 W
Vani 84 42.06 N 42.30 E
Vanier 212 45.26 N 75.40 W
Vanikolo I 14 11.39 S 166.54 E
Vaniköy -•-[8] 267b 41.04 N 29.04 E
Vanimo 164 2.40 S 141.20 E
Vanino 89 49.05 N 140.15 E
Vānīvilāsa Sāgara ⊜[1] 122 13.52 N 76.26 E
Vāniyambādi 122 12.41 N 78.37 E
Vânju Mare 38 44.26 N 22.52 E
Vankarem 180 67.51 N 175.50 W
Vankarem ≐ 180 67.42 N 176.17 W
Vankarem, laguna c 180 67.40 N 176.00 W
Vankaremskaja nizmennost' = 180 67.30 N 176.00 W
Van Kleef Aquarium ♦ 271c 1.18 N 103.51 E
Vankleek Hill 206 45.31 N 74.39 W
Vanlay 50 48.02 N 4.01 E
Van Lear 192 37.46 N 82.45 W
Vanlue 216 40.58 N 83.28 W
Vanna I 24 70.09 N 19.51 E
Vännäs 26 63.55 N 19.45 E
Vanndale 194 35.18 N 90.46 W
Vanne ≐ 50 48.12 N 3.16 E
Vanne et du Loing, Aqueduc de ≍[1] 261 48.36 N 2.26 E
Vannes 32 47.39 N 2.46 W
Vannes-sur-Cosson 50 47.43 N 2.13 E
Van Ninh 110 12.42 N 109.14 E
Van Norman Lakes ⊜[1] 228 34.18 N 118.28 W
Vannovka 85 42.32 N 70.21 E
Van Nuys -•-[8] 228 34.11 N 118.26 W
Van Nuys Airport ⊠ 280 34.12 N 118.29 W
Van Nuys-Sherman Oaks War Memorial Park ♦ 280 34.10 N 118.27 W
Vanoi ≐ 64 46.06 N 11.45 E
Vanoise, Massif de la ∧∧ 62 45.20 N 6.40 E
Vanoise, Parc National de la ♦ 62 45.20 N 6.45 E
Van Ormer 214 40.41 N 78.30 W
Van Phong, Vung c 110 12.33 N 109.18 E
Van Reenen 158 28.22 S 29.24 E
Van Reenen's Plaats 158 30.55 S 21.14 E
Van Rees, Pegunungan ∧∧ 164 2.35 S 138.15 E
Vanrhynsdorp 158 31.36 S 18.44 E
Vanrook 166 16.57 S 141.57 E
Vanryndam ⊜[1] 273d 26.09 S 28.21 E
Vansant 192 37.13 N 82.05 W
Van Saun Mill Brook ≐ 276 40.55 N 74.03 W
Vansbro 40 60.31 N 14.13 E
Van Sciver Lake ⊜ 285 40.09 N 74.48 W
Van Sickle Island I 282 38.04 N 121.53 W
Vansittart Island I 176 65.50 N 84.00 W
Vansjön ⊜ 40 59.59 N 16.57 E
Vanskoje 76 58.56 N 36.52 E
Vanstadensrus 158 29.59 S 27.02 E
Vantaa (Vanda) 26 60.16 N 25.03 E
Vantaa ≐ 26 60.13 N 24.59 E
Vanthali 120 21.29 N 70.20 E
Vanua Lava I 175f 13.48 S 167.28 E
Vanua Levu I 175g 16.33 S 179.15 E
Vanua Mbalavu Island I 175g 17.40 S 178.57 W
Vanuatu □[1], Oc. 14 16.00 S 167.00 E
Vanuatu □[1], Oc. 175f 16.00 S 167.00 E
Vanves 261 48.50 N 2.18 E
Van Vleck 222 29.01 N 95.53 W
Van Voorhis 279b 40.10 N 79.58 W
Van Wert 216 40.52 N 84.35 W
Van Wert □[6] 216 40.52 N 84.35 W
Vanwyksdorp 158 33.46 S 21.28 E
Vanwyksvlei 158 30.18 S 21.49 E
Vanzaghello 266b 45.35 N 8.47 E
Vanzago 266b 45.32 N 9.00 E
Van Zandt □[6] 222 32.35 N 95.50 W
Vanzylsrus 158 26.52 S 22.04 E
Vao 175f 22.39 S 167.32 E
Vapnyarka 78 48.32 N 28.44 E
Vaqueros Creek ≐ 226 36.16 N 121.20 W
Var □[5] 62 43.30 N 6.20 E
Var ≐ 62 43.39 N 7.12 E
Vara 26 58.16 N 12.57 E
Vara ≐ 64 44.09 N 9.53 E
Varada ≐ 122 14.55 N 75.40 E
Varadero 240p 23.09 N 81.16 W
Varades 32 47.23 N 1.02 W
Varages 62 43.36 N 5.58 E
Varaita ≐ 62 44.49 N 7.36 E
Varaita, Valle V 62 44.35 N 7.10 E
Varakļāni 76 56.37 N 26.44 E
Varallo, It. 62 45.49 N 8.15 E
Varallo, It. 266b 45.40 N 8.38 E
Varāmīn 128 35.20 N 51.39 E
Vārānasi (Benares) 124 25.20 N 83.00 E
Varandej 24 68.48 N 58.00 E
Varangerfjorden c[2] 24 70.00 N 30.00 E
Varangerhalvøya >[1] 24 70.25 N 29.30 E
Varangéville 56 48.38 N 6.19 E
Varano, Lago Di c 68 41.53 N 15.45 E
Varano de'Melegari 64 44.41 N 10.01 E
Varapaeva 76 55.09 N 27.13 E
Varapodio 68 38.19 N 15.59 E
Varaždin 36 46.19 N 16.20 E
Varazze 62 44.22 N 8.34 E
Varberg 26 57.06 N 12.15 E
Varces 62 45.05 N 5.41 E
Varciche 84 42.08 N 42.43 E
Vardak □[4] 120 34.15 N 68.00 E
Vardaman 194 33.52 N 89.10 W
Vardar (Axiós) ≐ 38 40.35 N 22.50 E
Varde 26 55.38 N 8.29 E
Vardenik 84 40.08 N 45.27 E
Vardenis 84 40.11 N 45.43 E
Vardenskij chrebet ∧∧ 84 39.58 N 45.25 E
Vardhoúsia Óri ∧∧ 38 38.44 N 22.07 E
Vardø 24 70.21 N 31.02 E
Vardūj ≐ 123 37.01 N 70.47 E
Varedo 266b 45.36 N 9.09 E
Varegovo 80 57.47 N 39.17 E
Varel 52 53.22 N 8.10 E
Varela 252 34.07 S 66.27 W
Varėna 76 54.13 N 24.34 E
Varengeville-sur-Mer 50 49.55 N 0.59 E
Varenikovskaja 78 45.07 N 37.37 E
Varenna 58 46.01 N 9.17 E
Varenne ≐ 50 49.53 N 1.08 E
Varennes 206 45.41 N 73.26 W
Varennes, Îles de II 275a 45.40 N 73.27 W
Varennes-en-Argonne 56 49.14 N 5.02 E
Varennes-Jarcy 261 48.41 N 2.34 E
Varennes-Saint-Sauveur 58 46.29 N 5.15 E
Varennes-sur-Allier 32 46.19 N 3.24 E
Varennes-sur-Amance 58 47.54 N 5.37 E
Varenovka 83 47.18 N 39.02 E
Vareš 38 44.09 N 18.19 E
Varese 62 45.48 N 8.48 E
Varese □[4] 62 45.48 N 8.40 E
Varese, Lago di ⊜ 62 45.49 N 8.45 E
Varese Ligure 62 44.22 N 9.37 E
Varèze ≐ 62 45.25 N 4.45 E
Varfolomejevka 80 50.01 N 48.12 E
Vârfurile 38 46.19 N 22.31 E
Vårgårda 26 58.02 N 12.48 E
Vargas □[5] 286c 10.34 N 66.52 W
Vargaši 86 55.23 N 65.48 E
Vargem 256 22.53 S 46.25 W
Vargem, Riacho da ≐ 250 8.42 S 39.09 W
Vargem Alegre 256 22.30 S 43.55 W
Vargem do Laje 256 22.08 S 44.49 W
Vargem Grande 250 3.33 S 43.56 W
Vargem Grande -•-[8] 287a 22.59 S 43.29 W
Vargem Grande, Ribeirão da ≐ 256 22.17 S 45.40 W
Vargem Grande do Sul 256 21.50 S 46.53 W
Vargem Grande Paulista 256 23.36 S 47.01 W
Varginha 256 21.33 S 45.26 W
Vargön 26 58.22 N 12.22 E
Varigotti 62 44.11 N 8.24 E
Väringen ⊜ 40 59.26 N 15.23 E
Varirata National Park ♦ 164 9.20 S 147.20 E
Varjão 255 17.03 S 49.37 W
Varkallai 122 8.40 N 76.50 E
Varkaus 26 62.19 N 27.55 E
Varkhān ≐ 128 32.55 N 65.30 E
Varlamovo 86 54.38 N 60.40 E
Värmdölandet I 40 59.20 N 18.33 E
Värmeln ⊜ 26 59.32 N 12.54 E
Värmland □[9] 26 59.48 N 13.03 E
Värmlands Län □[6] 26 59.45 N 13.15 E
Värmlandsnäs >[1] 26 59.00 N 13.10 E
Varna, Blg. 38 43.13 N 27.55 E
Varna (Vahrn), It. 64 46.44 N 11.38 E
Varna, Ross. 86 53.24 N 60.58 E
Varna, N.Y., U.S. 210 42.27 N 76.26 W
Varna □[4] 38 43.24 N 27.33 E
Värnamo 26 57.11 N 14.02 E
Varnavino 80 57.24 N 45.04 E
Varnenski Zaliv c 38 43.11 N 27.56 E
Varner-Hogg Plantation State Historic Park ♦ 222 29.09 N 95.37 W
Varnhem 26 58.23 N 13.39 E
Varniai 76 55.45 N 22.22 E
Varnjany 76 54.44 N 26.01 E
Varnsdorf 54 50.52 N 14.40 E
Varnville 192 32.51 N 81.04 W
Värö 26 57.16 N 12.11 E
Városliget ♦ 264c 47.31 N 19.06 E
Varpaisjärvi 26 63.22 N 27.45 E
Várpalota 30 47.12 N 18.09 E
Varpan ⊜ 40 60.38 N 15.36 E
Varresbeck -•-[8] 263 51.15 N 7.06 E
Vars, On., Can. 212 45.21 N 75.21 W
Vars, Fr. 62 44.37 N 6.41 E
Vars, Col de )( 62 44.32 N 6.42 E
Văršec 38 43.12 N 23.17 E
Varsi 62 44.40 N 9.51 E
Varsinais-Suomi -•-[1] 26 60.40 N 22.30 E
Värska 76 57.58 N 27.38 E
Varsovie → Warszawa 30 52.15 N 21.00 E
Varsseveld 52 51.57 N 6.28 E
Vårsta 40 59.10 N 17.48 E
Varto 130 39.10 N 41.28 E
Vârtopu 38 44.12 N 23.21 E
V'artsil'a 24 62.11 N 30.41 E
Varty Lake ⊜ 212 44.23 N 76.48 W
Varuna ≐ 124 25.21 N 83.03 E
Varva 78 50.31 N 32.41 E
Varvarin 38 43.43 N 21.19 E
Varvarivka, Ukr. 78 48.42 N 36.02 E
Varvarivka, Ukr. 78 49.33 N 35.12 E
Varvarivka, Ukr. 83 49.05 N 38.24 E
Varysburg 210 42.46 N 78.19 W
Várzea 256 22.30 S 44.46 W
Várzea, Rio da ≐ 252 27.13 S 53.19 W
Várzea Alegre 250 6.47 S 39.17 W
Várzea da Palma 255 17.36 S 44.44 W
Varzea de Sintra 266c 38.49 N 9.24 W
Várzea Grande 248 15.39 S 56.08 W
Varzeão 252 24.34 S 49.26 W
Várzea Paulista 256 23.12 S 46.50 W


| ENGLISH Name | Page | Lat.°′ | Long.°′ |
|---|---|---|---|


Varzi, It. 62 44.49 N 9.12 E
Varzi, Ross. 80 56.03 N 52.50 E
Varzino 24 68.19 N 38.19 E
Varzo 58 46.12 N 8.15 E
Varzob 85 38.46 N 68.49 E
Varzob ≐ 85 38.30 N 68.45 E
Varzuga 24 67.24 N 36.32 E
Varzy 50 47.22 N 3.23 E
Varzyk 85 41.07 N 71.14 E
Vas 64 45.56 N 11.56 E
Vas □[6] 30 47.05 N 16.45 E
Vasa → Vaasa 26 63.06 N 21.36 E
Vasai (Bassein) 122 19.21 N 72.48 E
Vasalemma 76 59.14 N 24.18 E
Vašana ≐ 82 54.36 N 37.10 E
Vasar 272c 19.11 N 73.09 E
Vascão, Ribeirão do ≐ 34 37.31 N 7.31 W
Vașcău 38 46.28 N 22.28 E
Väse 40 59.23 N 13.57 E
Vāshi 272c 19.04 N 72.59 E
Vashkivtsi, Ukr. 78 48.24 N 27.08 E
Vashkivtsi, Ukr. 78 48.23 N 25.30 E
Vashon 224 47.26 N 122.27 W
Vashon Heights 224 47.30 N 122.28 W
Vashon Island I 224 47.24 N 122.27 W
Vasil'euka 76 52.15 N 31.31 E
Vasilevičy 76 52.14 N 29.49 E
Vasilija, mys > 180 64.34 N 178.33 E
Vasiliká 38 40.28 N 23.08 E
Vasiliški 76 53.47 N 24.51 E
Vasiljevka 89 46.52 N 134.03 E
Vasiljevo, Ross. 24 60.46 N 38.59 E
Vasiljevo, Ross. 80 55.52 N 48.42 E
Vasiljevskij, ostrov I 265a 59.56 N 30.15 E
Vasiljevskij Moch 76 57.01 N 35.55 E
Vasiljevskoje, Ross. 80 56.56 N 41.40 E
Vasiljevskoje, Ross. 80 56.31 N 45.49 E
Vasiljevskoje, Ross. 82 55.00 N 37.25 E
Vasiljevskoje, Ross. 82 56.20 N 37.54 E
Vasil'sursk 80 56.08 N 46.01 E
Vasis 86 57.22 N 74.44 E
Vaška ≐ 24 64.53 N 45.47 E
Vaskelovo 76 60.22 N 30.22 E
Vaskess Bay c 174o 1.51 N 157.31 W
Vaslui 38 46.38 N 27.44 E
Vaslui □[6] 38 46.30 N 27.45 E
Väsman ⊜ 40 60.11 N 15.04 E
Vass 192 35.15 N 79.16 W
Vassako-Bolo, Réserve Naturelle Intégrale de la -•-[4] 146 8.10 N 19.45 E
Vassar 190 43.22 N 83.35 W
Vassdalseggi ∧ 26 59.46 N 7.10 E
Vassieux-en-Vercors 62 44.53 N 5.22 E
Vassouras 256 22.25 S 43.40 W
Vassy 50 47.34 N 4.10 E
Västanfors 40 59.59 N 15.49 E
Västerås 40 59.37 N 16.33 E
Västeråsfjärden c 40 59.34 N 16.34 E
Västerbotten □[9] 26 64.36 N 20.04 E
Västerbottens Län □[6] 24 64.00 N 17.30 E
Västerby 40 60.19 N 15.55 E
Västerdalälven ≐ 40 60.33 N 15.08 E
Västerfärnebo 40 59.57 N 16.17 E
Västergötland □[9] 26 58.01 N 13.03 E
Västerhaninge 40 59.07 N 18.06 E
Västernorrlands Län □[6] 26 63.00 N 17.30 E
Västervik 26 57.45 N 16.38 E
Västmanland □[9] 40 59.38 N 15.15 E
Västmanlands Län □[6] 40 59.45 N 16.20 E
Vasto 66 42.07 N 14.42 E
Västra Laxsjön ⊜ 40 58.54 N 14.38 E
Västra Ringsjön ⊜ 41 55.53 N 13.28 E
Västra Torup 41 56.09 N 13.29 E
Vastseliina 76 57.44 N 27.17 E
Vas'ugan ≐ 86 59.07 N 80.46 E
Vas'uganje ≡ 86 58.00 N 77.00 E
Vas'unino 82 55.15 N 37.01 E
Vašutino 265b 55.56 N 37.26 E
Vašutkiny ozera ⊜ 24 68.06 N 61.18 E
Vasvár 30 47.03 N 16.49 E
Vasylivka 78 47.26 N 35.16 E
Vasyl'kiv 78 50.12 N 30.19 E
Vasyl'kivka 78 48.13 N 36.02 E
Vát 61 47.17 N 16.47 E
Vața de Jos 38 46.10 N 22.35 E
Vatan 32 47.05 N 1.48 E
Vaternish Point > 46 57.36 N 6.38 W
Vatersay I 46 56.55 N 7.32 W
Vaterstetten 60 48.07 N 11.47 E
Vatican (Cité du) → Vatican City □[1] 267a 41.54 N 12.27 E
Vatican City (Città del Vaticano) □[1], Europe 66 41.54 N 12.27 E
Vatican City (Città del Vaticano) □[1], Europe 267a 41.54 N 12.27 E
Vaticano, Capo > 68 38.38 N 15.50 E
Vatikanstadt → Vatican City □[1] 66 41.54 N 12.27 E
V'atka → Kirov 80 58.38 N 49.42 E
V'atka ≐ 80 55.36 N 51.30 E
Vatlirchvin, gora ∧ 180 68.08 N 179.52 W
Vatnajökull ᗑ 24a 64.25 N 16.50 W
Vatneyri 24a 65.38 N 23.57 W
Vätö I 40 59.49 N 18.57 E
Vatoa Island I 175g 19.50 S 178.13 W
Vatoloha ∧ 157b 17.52 S 47.48 E
Vatomandry 157b 19.20 S 48.59 E
Vatra Dornei 38 47.21 N 25.21 E
V'atskije Pol'any 80 56.14 N 51.04 E
V'atskij uval ∧∧[2] 80 57.20 N 49.10 E
V'atskoje, Ross. 80 57.52 N 40.16 E
V'atskoje, Ross. 89 48.44 N 135.43 E
Vattalkundu 122 10.10 N 77.46 E
Vättern ⊜ 26 58.24 N 14.36 E
Vättersee → Vättern ⊜ 26 58.24 N 14.36 E
Vattholma 40 60.01 N 17.44 E
Vättis 58 46.55 N 9.27 E
Vatu Ira Channel ʯ 175g 17.17 S 178.31 E
Vatukoula 175g 17.31 S 177.51 E
Vatulele I 175g 18.33 S 177.37 E
Vatulino 82 55.39 N 36.09 E
Vatutine 78 49.02 N 31.04 E
Vaubecourt 56 48.56 N 5.07 E
Vauclaix 50 47.14 N 3.49 E
Vauclin, Montagne du ∧ 240e 14.33 N 60.53 W
Vaucluse 274a 33.51 S 151.17 E
Vaucluse □[5] 62 44.00 N 5.10 E
Vaucluse, Fontaine de ⊥ 62 43.55 N 5.08 E
Vaucluse, Plateau de ∧∧[1] 62 44.00 N 5.22 E
Vaucouleurs 58 48.36 N 5.40 E
Vaucouleurs ≐ 261 48.59 N 1.44 E
Vaud □[3] 58 46.40 N 6.30 E
Vaudherland 261 49.00 N 2.29 E
Vaudoy-en-Brie 50 48.41 N 3.05 E
Vaudreuil (Saint-Michel-de-Vaudreuil) 206 45.24 N 74.01 W
Vaudreuil □[6] 206 45.26 N 74.15 W
Vaudreuil, Baie de c 275a 45.24 N 74.00 W
Vaufrey 58 47.21 N 6.55 E
Vaughan 212 43.47 N 79.36 W
Vaughn, N.M., U.S. 200 34.36 N 105.12 W
Vaughn, Wa., U.S. 224 47.21 N 122.46 W
Vaughnsville 216 40.53 N 84.09 W
Vaugneray 62 45.44 N 4.39 E
Vaugrigneuse 261 48.36 N 2.07 E
Vauhallan 261 48.44 N 2.12 E
Vaujours 261 48.56 N 2.35 E
Vaukavysk 76 53.10 N 24.28 E
Vaulovo 82 56.09 N 39.17 E


| DEUTSCH Name | Seite | Breite°′ | Länge°′ E = Ost |
|---|---|---|---|


Vaulruz 58 46.37 N 6.59 E
Vaulx-en-Velin 62 45.47 N 4.56 E
Vaupés □[8] 246 0.45 N 70.30 W
Vaupés (Uaupés) ≐ 246 0.02 N 67.16 W
Vauréal 261 49.02 N 2.02 E
Vauréal, Chute ∟ 186 49.34 N 62.42 W
Vauvenargues 62 43.33 N 5.36 E
Vauvert 62 43.42 N 4.17 E
Vauvillers 58 47.55 N 6.06 E
Vauvise ≐ 50 47.18 N 2.57 E
Vaux ≐ 50 49.33 N 4.17 E
Vaux, Ru des ≐ 261 48.42 N 2.00 E
Vauxhall 182 50.04 N 112.07 W
Vaux-le-Compte, Château de ⊥ 50 48.36 N 2.43 E
Vaux-le-Pénil 261 48.32 N 2.41 E
Vaux-lès-Saint-Claude 58 46.22 N 5.44 E
Vaux-le-Vicomte, Château de ⊥ 50 48.36 N 2.43 E
Vaux-Sous-Aubigny 58 47.39 N 5.17 E
Vaux-sur-Seine 261 49.00 N 1.58 E
Vavatenina 157b 17.28 S 49.12 E
Vava'u I 14 18.36 S 174.00 W
Vava'u Group II 14 18.40 S 174.00 W
Vavincourt 56 48.49 N 5.13 E
Vavoua 150 7.23 N 6.29 W
Vavož 80 56.47 N 51.55 E
Vavuniya 122 8.45 N 80.30 E
Vaxholm 40 59.24 N 18.20 E
Växjö 26 56.52 N 14.49 E
V'aža 78 49.16 N 41.01 E
Vaza-barris ≐ 250 11.10 S 37.10 W
Vazante 255 18.00 S 46.54 W
Vazante Grande ≐ 248 19.21 S 56.53 W
V'azemskij 89 47.32 N 134.48 E
Važgort 24 64.01 N 47.02 E
V'az'ma 76 55.13 N 34.18 E
V'az'ma ≐, Ross. 76 55.28 N 33.34 E
V'az'ma ≐, Ross. 82 56.29 N 35.49 E
V'azniki 80 56.15 N 42.10 E
Vazobe ∧ 157b 18.25 S 47.18 E
V'azovaja 80 57.39 N 45.44 E
V'azovka, Ross. 80 48.19 N 45.36 E
V'azovka, Ross. 80 51.48 N 45.47 E
V'azovka, Ross. 80 52.52 N 48.24 E
V'azovka, Ross. 80 50.52 N 43.57 E
V'azovoje, Ross. 78 51.54 N 36.59 E
V'azovoje, Ross. 78 51.09 N 37.01 E
Vazuza ≐ 76 56.10 N 34.35 E
Vazuzskoje vodochranilišče ⊜[1] 76 56.00 N 34.28 E
Vazzola 64 45.50 N 12.23 E
Veachland 218 38.12 N 85.11 W
Veado, Ilha do I 287a 22.57 S 43.06 W
Veazie 188 44.50 N 68.42 W
Veberöd 41 55.38 N 13.29 E
Veblen 198 45.51 N 97.17 W
Vecchiano 66 43.47 N 10.23 E
Vechelde 52 52.16 N 10.22 E
Vecht (Vechte) ≐ 52 52.35 N 6.05 E
Vechta 52 52.43 N 8.16 E
Vechte (Vecht) ≐ 52 52.35 N 6.05 E
Veckerhagen 52 51.30 N 9.35 E
Vecpiebalga 76 57.08 N 25.50 E
Vecsés 30 47.25 N 19.16 E
Vecumnieki 76 56.36 N 24.31 E
Vedado -•-[8] 286b 23.08 N 82.24 W
Vedano al Lambro 266b 45.37 N 9.16 E
Vedano Olona 62 45.46 N 8.53 E
Vedāranniyam 122 10.22 N 79.51 E
Vedbæk 41 55.51 N 12.34 E
Vedder Crossing 224 49.06 N 121.57 W
Veddige 26 57.16 N 12.19 E
Vedea 38 44.47 N 24.37 E
Vedea ≐ 38 43.43 N 25.32 E
Vedelago 64 45.41 N 12.01 E
Vedène 62 43.59 N 4.54 E
Vedeno 84 42.58 N 46.05 E
Vedeseta 58 45.53 N 9.32 E
Vedevåg 40 59.32 N 15.17 E
Vedi 84 39.56 N 44.42 E
Vedia 252 34.30 S 61.32 W
Vednoje 76 57.08 N 36.10 E
Vedomša 82 56.44 N 38.21 E
Vedrovo 80 57.33 N 42.52 E
Veedersburg 194 40.06 N 87.15 W
Veen 263 51.37 N 6.27 E
Veendam 52 53.06 N 6.58 E
Veenendaal 52 52.02 N 5.34 E
Veenhuizen 52 53.03 N 6.24 E
Veenoord 52 52.43 N 6.50 E
Veere 52 51.34 N 3.40 E
Veert 52 51.33 N 6.17 E
Vefsna ≐ 24 65.50 N 13.12 E
Vega 196 35.15 N 102.26 W
Vega I 24 65.39 N 11.50 E
Vega, Arroyo de la ≐ 266a 40.31 N 3.33 W
Vega Alta 240m 18.25 N 66.20 W
Vega Baja 240m 18.27 N 66.23 W
Vega Point > 181a 51.49 N 177.16 E
Vegår ⊜ 26 58.48 N 8.47 E
Vegesack -•-[8] 52 53.10 N 8.37 E
Veghel 52 51.37 N 5.33 E
Veglie 68 40.20 N 17.58 E
Vegreville 182 53.30 N 112.03 W
Veguita 200 34.30 N 106.46 W
Vehār Lake ⊜ 272c 19.09 N 72.55 E
Vehlefanz 264a 52.43 N 13.06 E
Vehnemoor -•-[3] 52 53.05 N 8.00 E
Veigné 50 47.17 N 0.44 E
Veil, Loch ⊜ 46 56.20 N 4.25 W
Veilsdorf 54 50.24 N 10.48 E
Veinte de Noviembre 196 25.47 N 97.33 W
Veinticinco de Agosto 258 34.24 S 56.25 W
Veinticinco de Mayo, Arg. 252 35.26 S 60.10 W
Veinticinco de Mayo, Arg. 252 34.35 S 68.33 W
Veinticinco de Mayo, Ur. 258 34.12 S 56.22 W
Veintiocho de Mayo 246 3.50 S 78.52 W
Veintiocho de Noviembre 254 51.39 S 72.18 W
Veintisiete de Abril 236 10.15 N 85.45 W
Veio ⊥ 66 42.02 N 12.24 E
Veiros 250 2.05 S 52.10 W
Veisiejai 76 54.06 N 23.42 E
Veitsbronn 56 49.31 N 10.53 E
Veitsch 61 47.35 N 15.30 E
Veitschalpe ∧∧ 61 47.39 N 15.30 E
Veitshöchheim 56 49.50 N 9.52 E
Vejbystrand 41 56.19 N 12.45 E
Vejdelevka 78 50.09 N 38.27 E
Vejen 41 55.29 N 9.09 E
Vejer de la Frontera 34 36.15 N 5.58 W
Vejlby 41 56.12 N 10.13 E
Vejle 41 55.42 N 9.32 E
Vejle □[6] 41 55.45 N 9.30 E
Vejle Fjord c 41 55.40 N 9.50 E
Vejprty 54 50.30 N 13.02 E
Vejrhøj ∧[2] 41 55.47 N 11.24 E
Vejrø I 41 55.02 N 11.22 E
Vekšor 24 60.33 N 49.26 E
Vel'a ≐ 82 56.31 N 37.41 E
Vela Luka 36 42.58 N 16.43 E
Velapāda 272c 18.59 N 73.04 E
Velardeña 232 25.04 N 103.44 W
Velas 148a 38.41 N 28.13 W
Velas, Cabo > 236 10.22 N 85.53 W
Velázquez 252 34.02 S 54.17 W
Velbert 56 51.20 N 7.02 E
Velburg 60 49.14 N 11.41 E
Velddrif 158 32.47 S 18.11 E
Velden, Dtsch. 60 48.19 N 12.16 E
Velden, Dtsch. 60 49.37 N 11.31 E
Velden, Öst. 61 46.37 N 14.03 E
Veldhoven 52 51.24 N 5.24 E
Velebit ∧∧ 36 44.38 N 15.03 E
Velebitski Kanal ʯ 36 45.00 N 14.50 E
Velegož 82 54.42 N 37.16 E


**Symbols** in the index entries represent the broad categories identified in the key at the right. Symbols with superior numbers (∧∧[1]) identify subcategories (see complete key on page *I · 1).*

**Symbole** im Register stellen die rechts im Schlüssel erklärten Kategorien dar. Symbole mit hochgestellten Ziffern (∧∧[1]) bezeichnen Unterabteilungen einer Kategorie (vgl. vollständiger Schlüssel auf Seite *I · 1).*

**Los símbolos** incluídos en el texto del índice representan las grandes categorías identificadas con la clave a la derecha. Los símbolos con numeros en su parte superior (∧∧[1]) identifican las subcategorías (véase la clave completa en la página *I · 1).*

**Les symboles** de l'index représentent les catégories indiquées dans la légende à droite. Les symboles suivis d'un indice (∧∧[1]) représentent des sous-catégories (voir légende complète à la page *I · 1).*

**Os símbolos** incluídos no texto do índice representam as grandes categorias identificadas com a chave à direita. Os símbolos com números em sua parte superior (∧∧[1]) identificam as subcategorias (veja-se a chave completa à página *I · 1).*

| | | | | |
|---|---|---|---|---|
| ∧ Mountain | Berg | Montaña | Montagne | Montanha |
| ∧∧ Mountains | Gebirge | Montañas | Montagnes | Montanhas |
| )( Pass | Paß | Paso | Col | Passo |
| V Valley, Canyon | Tal, Cañon | Valle, Cañón | Vallée, Canyon | Vale, Canhão |
| = Plain | Ebene | Llano | Plaine | Planície |
| > Cape | Kap | Cabo | Cap | Cabo |
| I Island | Insel | Isla | Île | Ilha |
| II Islands | Inseln | Islas | Îles | Ilhas |
| ≜ Other Topographic Features | Andere Topographische Objekte | Otros Elementos Topográficos | Autres données topographiques | Outros acidentes topográficos |

ESPAÑOL

| Nombre | Página | Lat.°′ | Long.°′ W = Oeste |
|---|---|---|---|
| Veleka ≏ | 38 | 42.04 N | 27.58 E |
| Velemín | 54 | 50.33 N | 13.59 E |
| Velen | 52 | 51.53 N | 6.59 E |
| Velencei-tó ⊜ | 30 | 47.12 N | 18.35 E |
| Velesa ≏ | 76 | 56.03 N | 31.58 E |
| Velešín | 61 | 48.50 N | 14.28 E |
| Velestínon | 38 | 39.23 N | 22.45 E |
| Velet'ma | 80 | 55.20 N | 42.25 E |
| Veleųščyna | 76 | 54.44 N | 28.35 E |
| Vélez | 246 | 6.01 N | 73.41 W |
| Velez de la Gomera, Peñón de I | 34 | 35.11 N | 4.21 W |
| Vélez-Málaga | 34 | 36.47 N | 4.06 W |
| Vélez-Rubio | 34 | 37.39 N | 2.04 W |
| Velgast | 54 | 54.16 N | 12.48 E |
| Vel'gija | 76 | 58.23 N | 33.59 E |
| Velhas, Canal do ≅ | 287a | 22.42 S | 43.22 W |
| Velhas, Rio das ≏ | 255 | 17.13 S | 44.49 W |
| Veličkovo | 82 | 54.59 N | 36.46 E |
| Velika Gorica | 36 | 45.43 N | 16.05 E |
| Velikaja, Ross. | 24 | 59.13 N | 49.04 E |
| Velikaja, Ross. | 180 | 64.04 N | 176.12 E |
| Velikaja ≏, Ross. | 74 | 64.40 N | 176.20 E |
| Velikaja ≏, Ross. | 76 | 57.48 N | 28.20 E |
| Velikaja Kema | 89 | 45.30 N | 137.12 E |
| Velika Kapela ⋏ | 36 | 45.15 N | 15.00 E |
| Velika Morava ≏ | 38 | 44.43 N | 21.03 E |
| Velika Plana | 38 | 44.20 N | 21.04 E |
| Velike Lašče | 36 | 45.50 N | 14.38 E |
| Veliki Bečkerek → Zrenjanin | 38 | 45.23 N | 20.24 E |
| Velikij Dvor | 82 | 56.46 N | 37.25 E |
| Velikije Luki | 76 | 56.20 N | 30.32 E |
| Velikij Ust'ug | 24 | 60.48 N | 46.18 E |
| Veliki kanal ≅ | 38 | 45.45 N | 18.50 E |
| Veliki Stol (Hochstuhl) ʌ | 61 | 46.26 N | 14.10 E |
| Veliki Vitorog ʌ | 36 | 44.07 N | 17.03 E |
| Velikoarch-angel'skoje | 78 | 50.51 N | 40.46 E |
| Velikodvorskaja | 76 | 60.18 N | 41.58 E |
| Velikodvorskij | 80 | 55.15 N | 40.41 E |
| Veliko Gradište | 38 | 44.45 N | 21.32 E |
| Velikoje, Ross. | 76 | 59.32 N | 36.59 E |
| Velikoje, Ross. | 80 | 57.21 N | 39.47 E |
| Velikoje, ozero ⊜, Ross. | 76 | 57.02 N | 36.34 E |
| Velikoje, ozero ⊜, Ross. | 80 | 55.13 N | 40.10 E |
| Velikonda Hills ⋏[2] | 122 | 14.45 N | 79.10 E |
| Velikookt'abr'skij | 76 | 57.26 N | 33.49 E |
| Velikorusskoje | 86 | 54.39 N | 74.38 E |
| Veliko Tărnovo | 38 | 43.04 N | 25.39 E |
| Velikovisočnoje | 24 | 67.16 N | 52.01 E |
| Velikovo | 76 | 59.18 N | 42.08 E |
| Velilla de San Antonio | 266a | 40.22 N | 3.29 W |
| Veli Lošinj | 36 | 44.31 N | 14.30 E |
| Vélingara, Sén. | 150 | 15.00 N | 14.40 W |
| Vélingara, Sén. | 150 | 13.09 N | 14.07 W |
| Velingrad | 38 | 42.04 N | 24.00 E |
| Velino ≏ | 66 | 42.33 N | 12.43 E |
| Velino, Monte ʌ | 66 | 42.09 N | 13.23 E |
| Velіž | 76 | 55.38 N | 31.12 E |
| Velіžany | 86 | 57.34 N | 65.49 E |
| Vélizy-Villacoublay | 261 | 48.47 N | 2.10 E |
| Veljaminovo, Ross. | 82 | 55.12 N | 37.52 E |
| Veljaminovo, Ross. | 82 | 55.53 N | 36.52 E |
| Velká Bíteš | 30 | 49.17 N | 16.13 E |
| Vel'ké Kapušany | 30 | 48.33 N | 22.04 E |
| Velké Meziříčí | 30 | 49.21 N | 16.00 E |
| Velké Němčie | 61 | 48.59 N | 16.40 E |
| Velké Pavlovice | 61 | 48.54 N | 16.49 E |
| Velký Bor | 60 | 49.22 N | 13.42 E |
| Velký Šenov | 54 | 51.00 N | 14.25 E |
| Velký Zvon ʌ | 60 | 49.33 N | 12.39 E |
| Vellach ≏ | 61 | 46.35 N | 14.29 E |
| Vella Gulf ꓵ | 175e | 8.00 S | 156.50 E |
| Vella Lavella I | 175e | 7.45 S | 156.40 E |
| Vellano | 66 | 43.57 N | 10.43 E |
| Vellār ≏ | 122 | 11.29 N | 79.46 E |
| Vellberg | 56 | 49.05 N | 9.53 E |
| Vellechevreux-et-Courbenans | 58 | 47.33 N | 6.32 E |
| Velletri | 66 | 41.41 N | 12.47 E |
| Vellinge | 41 | 55.28 N | 13.01 E |
| Vellmar | 56 | 51.21 N | 9.28 E |
| Vellore, On., Can. | 275b | 43.50 N | 79.34 W |
| Vellore, India | 122 | 12.56 N | 79.08 E |
| Velm | 264b | 48.03 N | 16.27 E |
| Velma | 196 | 34.27 N | 97.40 W |
| Vel'maj ≏ | 180 | 67.26 N | 175.28 W |
| Velmede | 56 | 51.21 N | 8.22 E |
| Velo d'Astico | 64 | 45.43 N | 11.23 E |
| Velp | 52 | 52.00 N | 5.59 E |
| Velp ≏ | 56 | 50.58 N | 5.05 E |
| Velpke | 54 | 52.24 N | 10.56 E |
| Velsen | 52 | 52.27 N | 4.39 E |
| Vel'sk | 24 | 61.05 N | 42.05 E |
| Vel't | 24 | 68.03 N | 49.55 E |
| Velten | 54 | 52.41 N | 13.10 E |
| Veltheim | 52 | 52.11 N | 8.58 E |
| Veltrusy | 54 | 50.14 N | 14.18 E |
| Veluwe ◆[1] | 52 | 52.12 N | 5.45 E |
| Veluwemeer ⊜ | 52 | 52.22 N | 5.38 E |
| Velva, It. | 62 | 44.16 N | 9.33 E |
| Velva, N.D., U.S. | 198 | 48.03 N | 100.55 W |
| Velvary | 54 | 50.15 N | 14.15 E |
| Velyka Bahachka | 78 | 49.47 N | 33.43 E |
| Velyka Bilozerka | 78 | 47.16 N | 34.42 E |
| Velyka Blahovishchenka | 78 | 46.51 N | 34.03 E |
| Velyka Chernihivka | 83 | 48.57 N | 39.25 E |
| Velyka Danylivka | 78 | 50.04 N | 36.19 E |
| Velyka Dymerka | 78 | 50.36 N | 30.55 E |
| Velyka Hlusha | 78 | 51.49 N | 25.02 E |
| Velyka Korenykha | 78 | 46.57 N | 31.54 E |
| Velyka Koshnytsya | 78 | 48.09 N | 28.27 E |
| Velyka Lepetykha | 78 | 47.11 N | 33.56 E |
| Velyka Mykhaylivka | 78 | 47.04 N | 29.52 E |
| Velyka Novosilka | 78 | 47.50 N | 36.50 E |
| Velyka Oleksandrivka | 78 | 47.20 N | 33.18 E |
| Velyka Rublivka | 78 | 49.53 N | 34.49 E |
| Velyka Vradyyivka | 78 | 47.52 N | 30.35 E |
| Velyki Birky | 78 | 49.32 N | 25.46 E |
| Velyki Dederkaly | 78 | 50.02 N | 26.07 E |
| Velyki Kopani | 78 | 46.29 N | 32.59 E |
| Velyki Korovyntsi | 78 | 49.59 N | 28.17 E |
| Velyki Krynky | 78 | 49.27 N | 33.29 E |
| Velyki Luchky | 78 | 48.26 N | 22.35 E |
| Velyki Mosty | 78 | 50.14 N | 24.06 E |
| Velyki Sorochyntsi | 78 | 50.03 N | 33.56 E |
| Velykoanadol's'kyy lis ♦ | 83 | 47.42 N | 37.23 E |
| Velykodolyns'ke | 78 | 46.21 N | 30.35 E |
| Velykoplos'ke | 78 | 47.01 N | 29.40 E |
| Velykots'k | 78 | 49.21 N | 40.02 E |
| Velykyy Bereznyy | 78 | 48.53 N | 22.27 E |
| Velykyy Burluk | 78 | 50.05 N | 37.24 E |
| Velykyy Bychkiv | 78 | 47.58 N | 24.03 E |
| Velykyy Hlubochyk | 78 | 49.37 N | 25.32 E |
| Velykyy Khutir | 78 | 49.52 N | 32.06 E |
| Velykyy Kuyal'nyk ≏ | 78 | 46.46 N | 30.36 E |
| Velykyy Loh | 83 | 48.15 N | 39.33 E |
| Velykyy Sukhodil | 83 | 48.25 N | 39.53 E |
| Velykyy Vys' ≏ | 78 | 48.17 N | 31.52 E |
| Velykyy Zhvanchyk | 78 | 48.46 N | 26.59 E |
| Velymche | 78 | 51.36 N | 24.44 E |
| Vémars | 261 | 49.04 N | 2.34 E |
| Vemdalen | 26 | 62.27 N | 13.52 E |
| Vemmenæs | 41 | 54.59 N | 10.40 E |
| Ven I | 41 | 55.54 N | 12.41 E |
| Venachar, Loch ⊜ | 46 | 56.13 N | 4.19 W |
| Venaco | 36 | 42.14 N | 9.10 E |
| Venadillo | 246 | 4.43 N | 74.55 W |
| Venado | 234 | 22.56 N | 101.05 W |
| Venado, Isla I | 241r | 10.00 N | 85.00 W |
| Venado, Isla del I | 236 | 11.57 N | 83.44 W |
| Venado Tuerto | 252 | 33.45 S | 61.58 W |

FRANÇAIS

| Nom | Page | Lat.°′ | Long.°′ W = Ouest |
|---|---|---|---|
| Venafiorita, Aeroporto di ⊠ | 71 | 40.53 N | 9.30 E |
| Venafro | 66 | 41.29 N | 14.02 E |
| Venâncio Aires | 252 | 29.36 S | 52.11 W |
| Venango | 214 | 41.46 N | 80.07 W |
| Venango □[6] | 214 | 41.24 N | 79.50 W |
| Venanson | 62 | 44.03 N | 7.15 E |
| Venant | 261 | 48.30 N | 2.06 E |
| Venarey-les-Laumes | 58 | 47.32 N | 4.26 E |
| Venaria | 62 | 45.08 N | 7.38 E |
| Venasca | 62 | 44.33 N | 7.24 E |
| Venasque | 62 | 43.59 N | 5.09 E |
| Vence | 62 | 43.43 N | 7.07 E |
| Venceslau Brás | 256 | 22.31 S | 45.21 W |
| Venceslau Braz | 255 | 23.51 S | 49.48 W |
| Vencimont | 56 | 50.02 N | 4.55 E |
| Venda □[9] | 156 | 23.00 S | 30.30 E |
| Venda Nova | 34 | 41.40 N | 7.58 W |
| Vendargues | 62 | 43.39 N | 3.58 E |
| Vendas Novas | 34 | 38.41 N | 8.28 W |
| Vendée □[5] | 32 | 46.40 N | 1.20 W |
| Vendéen, Bocage ◆[1] | 32 | 46.40 N | 1.30 W |
| Vendel | 40 | 60.10 N | 17.36 E |
| Vendelsö | 40 | 59.12 N | 18.12 E |
| Vendeuvre-sur-Barse | 58 | 48.14 N | 4.28 E |
| Vendin-lès-Béthune | 50 | 50.32 N | 2.37 E |
| Vendin-le-Vieil | 50 | 50.28 N | 2.52 E |
| Vendôme | 50 | 47.48 N | 1.04 E |
| Vendsyssel ◆[1] | 26 | 57.20 N | 10.00 E |
| Vendychany | 78 | 48.37 N | 27.48 E |
| Venecia, C.R. | 236 | 10.22 N | 84.17 W |
| Venecia → Venezia, It. | 64 | 45.27 N | 12.21 E |
| Venedig → Venezia | 64 | 45.27 N | 12.21 E |
| Venedocia | 216 | 40.44 N | 84.25 W |
| Venedy | 219 | 38.24 N | 89.39 W |
| Veneta, Laguna c | 64 | 45.25 N | 12.19 E |
| Venetia | 214 | 40.15 N | 80.03 W |
| Venetian Village | 216 | 42.24 N | 88.02 W |
| Venetie | 180 | 67.01 N | 146.25 W |
| Veneto □[4] | 64 | 45.30 N | 11.45 E |
| Venev | 82 | 54.21 N | 38.16 E |
| Venezia (Venice) | 64 | 45.27 N | 12.21 E |
| Venezia □[4] | 64 | 45.35 N | 12.34 E |
| Venezuela □[1], S.A. | 242 | 8.00 N | 66.00 W |
| Venezuela □[1], S.A. | 246 | 8.00 N | 66.00 W |
| Venezuela, Golfo de c | 246 | 11.30 N | 71.00 W |
| Venezuelan Basin ⊹[1] | 16 | 15.00 N | 68.00 W |
| Veng | 41 | 56.07 N | 9.53 E |
| Vengerovo | 86 | 55.41 N | 76.45 E |
| Vengurla | 122 | 15.52 N | 73.38 E |
| Veniaminof, Mount ʌ | 180 | 56.13 N | 159.18 W |
| Venice → Venezia, It. | 64 | 45.27 N | 12.21 E |
| Venice, Fl., U.S. | 220 | 27.05 N | 82.27 W |
| Venice, Il., U.S. | 219 | 38.40 N | 90.10 W |
| Venice, La., U.S. | 194 | 29.16 N | 89.21 W |
| Venice, Oh., U.S. | 214 | 41.27 N | 82.46 W |
| Venice, Pa., U.S. | 279b | 40.19 N | 80.14 W |
| Venice ◆[8] | 228 | 34.00 N | 118.29 W |
| Venice, Gulf of c | 64 | 45.15 N | 13.00 E |
| Venice Gardens | 220 | 27.04 N | 82.26 W |
| Venise → Venezia | 64 | 45.27 N | 12.21 E |
| Vénissieux | 62 | 45.41 N | 4.53 E |
| Venjan | 26 | 60.57 N | 13.55 E |
| Venjansjön ⊜ | 26 | 60.54 N | 14.00 E |
| Venkatagiri | 122 | 13.58 N | 79.35 E |
| Venlo | 52 | 51.24 N | 6.10 E |
| Vennesla | 26 | 58.17 N | 7.59 E |
| Vennhausen ◆[8] | 263 | 51.13 N | 6.51 E |
| Venosa | 68 | 40.57 N | 15.49 E |
| Vénosc | 62 | 44.59 N | 6.07 E |
| Venosta, Val V | 64 | 46.40 N | 10.35 E |
| Venoste, Alpi (Ötztaler Alpen) ⋏ | 64 | 46.45 N | 10.55 E |
| Venray | 52 | 51.32 N | 5.59 E |
| Vent | 64 | 46.52 N | 10.56 E |
| Vent, Îles du → Windward Islands II | 238 | 13.00 N | 61.00 W |
| Venta ≏ | 76 | 57.24 N | 21.33 E |
| Ventanas | 246 | 1.23 S | 79.25 W |
| Ventasso, Monte ʌ | 64 | 44.23 N | 10.17 E |
| Ventersburg | 158 | 28.09 S | 27.08 E |
| Ventersdorp | 158 | 26.17 S | 26.48 E |
| Venterspos | 273d | 26.18 S | 27.39 E |
| Venterstad | 158 | 30.47 S | 25.48 E |
| Venticano | 68 | 41.05 N | 14.50 E |
| Ventimiglia | 62 | 43.47 N | 7.36 E |
| Ventimiglia di Sicilia | 70 | 37.55 N | 13.34 E |
| Ventnor | 42 | 50.36 N | 1.11 W |
| Ventnor City | 208 | 39.20 N | 74.28 W |
| Ventotene | 66 | 40.48 N | 13.26 E |
| Ventotene, Isola I | 66 | 40.47 N | 13.25 E |
| Ventoux, Mont ʌ | 62 | 44.10 N | 5.17 E |
| Ventry | 48 | 52.08 N | 10.22 W |
| Ventspils | 76 | 57.24 N | 21.36 E |
| Ventuari ≏ | 246 | 3.58 N | 67.02 W |
| Ventura (San Buenaventura) | 228 | 34.16 N | 119.17 W |
| Ventura □[6] | 228 | 34.30 N | 119.00 W |
| Ventura ≏ | 228 | 34.16 N | 119.18 W |
| Venturina | 66 | 43.02 N | 10.36 E |
| Venus, Fl., U.S. | 220 | 27.04 N | 81.21 W |
| Venus, Pa., U.S. | 214 | 41.22 N | 79.29 W |
| Venus, Tx., U.S. | 222 | 32.26 N | 97.06 W |
| Vénus, Pointe ⊁ | 174s | 17.29 S | 149.29 W |
| Venus Bay c | 169 | 38.40 S | 145.43 E |
| Venustiano Carranza, Méx. | 232 | 16.21 N | 92.33 W |
| Venustiano Carranza, Méx. | 234 | 20.31 N | 97.38 W |
| Venustiano Carranza, Méx. | 234 | 19.44 N | 103.47 W |
| Venustiano Carranza, Bahía c | 232 | 19.20 N | 87.35 W |
| Venustiano Carranza, Presa ⊜[1] | 232 | 27.30 N | 100.40 W |
| Venzone | 64 | 46.20 N | 13.09 E |
| Vêore ≏ | 62 | 44.49 N | 4.49 E |
| Vép | 61 | 47.14 N | 16.44 E |
| Vepryk | 78 | 50.23 N | 34.11 E |
| Vepsovskaja vozvyšennost' ⋏[1] | 76 | 60.20 N | 35.15 E |
| Ver ≏ | 42 | 51.42 N | 0.20 W |
| Vera, Arg. | 252 | 29.28 S | 60.13 W |
| Vera, Esp. | 34 | 37.15 N | 1.52 W |
| Vera, Il., U.S. | 219 | 39.02 N | 89.07 W |
| Veracruz, Méx. | 200 | 32.25 N | 115.05 W |
| Veracruz, Méx. | 234 | 19.12 N | 96.08 W |
| Vera Cruz, Pa., U.S. | 208 | 40.30 N | 75.30 W |
| Veracruz □[3] | 234 | 19.20 N | 96.40 W |
| Veraguas □[4] | 236 | 8.30 N | 81.00 W |
| [illegible] | 76 | 53.48 N | 31.15 E |
| Verano Brianza | 266b | 45.41 N | 9.14 E |
| Veranópolis | 252 | 28.57 S | 51.33 W |
| Verāval | 122 | 20.54 N | 70.22 E |
| Verba | 78 | 50.17 N | 25.37 E |
| Verbania | 58 | 45.56 N | 8.33 E |
| Verbank | 210 | 41.44 N | 73.43 W |
| Verbano-Cusio-Ossola □[4] | 58 | 46.05 N | 8.20 E |
| Verbeek, Pegunungan ⋏ | 112 | 2.35 S | 121.25 E |
| Verberg | 263 | 51.22 N | 6.36 E |
| Verbicaro | 68 | 39.45 N | 15.55 E |
| Verbier | 58 | 46.06 N | 7.14 E |
| Verbilki | 82 | 56.32 N | 37.36 E |
| Verbinskij | 83 | 47.53 N | 40.02 E |
| Verblyuzhka | 78 | 48.23 N | 32.54 E |
| Verbovskij | 80 | 55.27 N | 42.15 E |
| Vercelli | 62 | 45.19 N | 8.25 E |
| Vercelli □[4] | 62 | 45.37 N | 8.20 E |

PORTUGUÊS

| Nome | Página | Lat.°′ | Long.°′ W = Oeste |
|---|---|---|---|
| Vercel-Villedieu-le-Camp | 58 | 47.11 N | 6.24 E |
| Verch'aja Irmen' | 86 | 54.35 N | 82.14 E |
| Verchazovka | 80 | 50.56 N | 48.46 E |
| Vercheje Talyzino | 80 | 55.06 N | 45.49 E |
| Verchères | 206 | 45.47 N | 73.21 W |
| Verchères □[6] | 206 | 45.45 N | 73.20 W |
| Verchn'aja Amga | 74 | 59.30 N | 126.08 E |
| Verchn'aja Angara ≏ | 88 | 55.42 N | 109.54 E |
| Verchn'aja Balkarija | 84 | 43.06 N | 43.24 E |
| Verchn'aja Buzinovka | 80 | 49.04 N | 43.12 E |
| Verchn'aja Čebula | 86 | 56.02 N | 87.36 E |
| Verchn'aja Chava | 78 | 51.50 N | 39.56 E |
| Verchn'aja Chila | 88 | 52.06 N | 115.54 E |
| Verchn'aja Dobrinka | 80 | 50.46 N | 45.03 E |
| Verchn'aja Gniluša | 78 | 50.16 N | 40.23 E |
| Verchn'aja Grajvoronka | 78 | 51.41 N | 37.46 E |
| Verchn'aja Inta | 24 | 66.00 N | 60.20 E |
| Verchn'aja Maza | 80 | 52.58 N | 47.56 E |
| Verchn'aja Orl'anka | 80 | 53.44 N | 51.04 E |
| Verchn'aja Pyšma | 86 | 56.55 N | 60.37 E |
| Verchn'aja Salda | 86 | 58.02 N | 60.33 E |
| Verchn'aja Serebr'akovka | 80 | 47.21 N | 42.14 E |
| Verchn'aja Sin'ačicha | 86 | 57.59 N | 61.40 E |
| Verchn'aja Sysert' | 86 | 56.26 N | 60.46 E |
| Verchn'aja Tajmyra ≏ | 74 | 74.15 N | 99.48 E |
| Verchn'aja Tarka | 86 | 56.37 N | 77.30 E |
| Verchnaja Tereška | 80 | 52.54 N | 47.24 E |
| Verchn'aja Tišanka | 78 | 51.19 N | 40.32 E |
| Verchn'aja Tojma | 24 | 62.13 N | 45.00 E |
| Verchn'aja Troica | 76 | 57.15 N | 37.08 E |
| Verchn'aja Tura | 86 | 58.22 N | 59.49 E |
| Verchn'aja Zaimka | 88 | 55.51 N | 110.09 E |
| Verchn'aja Zima | 88 | 53.48 N | 101.47 E |
| Verchneaks'onovskij | 80 | 48.21 N | 42.38 E |
| Verchneangarskij chrebet ⋏ | 88 | 56.20 N | 111.30 E |
| Verchne-Anikin | 83 | 48.09 N | 39.59 E |
| Verchnebakanskij | 78 | 44.52 N | 37.39 E |
| Verchneber'ozovskij | 86 | 50.17 N | 82.13 E |
| Verchnebuzanskij | 80 | 46.38 N | 48.02 E |
| Verchnecaricynskij | 80 | 48.23 N | 43.57 E |
| Verchnedneprovskij | 76 | 54.59 N | 33.21 E |
| Verchneimbatskoje | 74 | 63.11 N | 87.58 E |
| Verchnejarkejevo | 80 | 55.27 N | 54.19 E |
| Verchneje Šachlovo | 82 | 55.02 N | 37.15 E |
| Verchnemakejevka | 78 | 49.10 N | 41.03 E |
| Verchnemulomskoje vodochranilišče ⊜[1] | 24 | 68.30 N | 31.05 E |
| Verchnesjezžeje | 80 | 52.44 N | 51.15 E |
| Verchnespasskoje | 80 | 52.39 N | 41.47 E |
| Verchnetulomskij | 24 | 68.38 N | 31.45 E |
| Verchneural'sk | 86 | 53.53 N | 59.13 E |
| Verchneusinskoje | 86 | 52.14 N | 93.01 E |
| Verchnevil'ujsk | 74 | 63.27 N | 120.18 E |
| Verchnevolynskoje | 85 | 40.43 N | 68.51 E |
| Verchnij Amyl | 88 | 53.08 N | 94.30 E |
| Verchnij Avz'an | 86 | 53.32 N | 57.33 E |
| Verchnij Balyklej | 80 | 49.34 N | 45.10 E |
| Verchnij Baskunčak | 80 | 48.14 N | 46.44 E |
| Verchnij Byk | 78 | 50.43 N | 41.14 E |
| Verchnije Dvoriki | 82 | 56.28 N | 38.22 E |
| Verchnije Kigi | 86 | 55.25 N | 58.37 E |
| Verchnije Korobki | 80 | 50.19 N | 44.38 E |
| Verchnije Lipki | 80 | 49.38 N | 43.51 E |
| Verchnije Tatyšly | 86 | 56.17 N | 55.52 E |
| Verchnij Ikorec | 78 | 51.11 N | 39.46 E |
| Verchnij Karačan | 80 | 51.24 N | 41.46 E |
| Verchnij Krasnyj Pereval | 89 | 46.33 N | 134.37 E |
| Verchnij Kužebar | 86 | 53.22 N | 93.15 E |
| Verchnij Landech | 80 | 56.51 N | 42.36 E |
| Verchnij Leb'ažinskij | 80 | 46.45 N | 47.50 E |
| Verchnij Lomov | 80 | 53.28 N | 43.34 E |
| Verchnij Lomovec | 76 | 52.13 N | 38.37 E |
| Verchnij Mamon | 78 | 50.10 N | 40.23 E |
| Verchnij Most | 76 | 57.31 N | 28.50 E |
| Verchnij Nejvinskij | 86 | 57.17 N | 60.09 E |
| Verchnij Petr'ak | 86 | 57.29 N | 77.30 E |
| Verchnij Šergol'džin | 88 | 50.12 N | 108.20 E |
| Verchnij Tagil | 86 | 57.22 N | 59.56 E |
| Verchnij Takermen' | 80 | 55.39 N | 52.43 E |
| Verchnij Ufalej | 86 | 56.04 N | 60.14 E |
| Verchnij Ul'chun | 88 | 49.34 N | 112.32 E |
| Verchnij Uslon | 80 | 55.47 N | 48.57 E |
| Verchnij Zub, gora ʌ | 86 | 53.45 N | 89.15 E |
| Verchnyje Nikul'asy | 76 | 60.25 N | 30.45 E |
| Verchnyj Jenisej (Ulug-Chem) ≏ | 88 | 51.47 N | 92.00 E |
| Verchojansk | 74 | 67.35 N | 133.27 E |
| Verchojanskij chrebet ⋏ | 74 | 67.00 N | 129.00 E |
| Vercholensk | 88 | 54.06 N | 105.35 E |
| Verchopuja | 24 | 61.34 N | 41.31 E |
| Verchošižemje | 80 | 58.01 N | 49.07 E |
| Verchososna | 78 | 50.44 N | 38.14 E |
| Verchoturje | 86 | 58.52 N | 60.48 E |
| Verchoturovo | 86 | 58.22 N | 95.21 E |
| Verchovažje | 24 | 60.45 N | 42.00 E |
| Verchovino | 76 | 59.33 N | 43.19 E |
| Verchovje | 76 | 52.49 N | 37.14 E |
| Verchovl'an' | 82 | 55.03 N | 38.21 E |
| Verchozim | 80 | 52.56 N | 46.23 E |
| Verchuba | 86 | 50.29 N | 82.26 E |
| Verclause | 62 | 44.23 N | 5.26 E |
| Vercors ◆[1] | 62 | 44.57 N | 5.25 E |
| Verdalsøra | 26 | 63.48 N | 11.29 E |
| Verde ≏, Bra. | 248 | 11.54 S | 55.48 W |
| Verde ≏, Bra. | 248 | 13.33 S | 58.01 W |
| Verde ≏, Bra. | 250 | 10.27 S | 42.16 W |
| Verde ≏, Bra. | 255 | 15.07 S | 48.40 W |
| Verde ≏, Bra. | 255 | 17.05 S | 46.05 W |
| Verde ≏, Bra. | 255 | 18.01 S | 50.14 W |
| Verde ≏, Bra. | 255 | 19.11 S | 50.44 W |
| Verde ≏, Bra. | 255 | 19.55 S | 49.45 W |
| Verde ≏, Bra. | 255 | 21.12 S | 51.53 W |
| Verde ≏, Bra. | 256 | 21.34 S | 45.31 W |
| Verde ≏, Bra. | 256 | 21.38 S | 47.03 W |
| Verde ≏, Méx. | 234 | 16.45 N | 98.07 W |
| Verde ≏, Méx. | 234 | 20.42 N | 103.14 W |
| Verde ≏, Méx. | 234 | 21.37 N | 98.15 W |
| Verde ≏, Para. | 252 | 23.09 S | 57.37 W |
| Verde ≏, S.A. | 248 | 13.59 S | 60.24 W |
| Verde ≏, Az., U.S. | 200 | 33.33 N | 111.40 W |
| Verde, Arroyo ≏, Arg. | 254 | 41.56 S | 65.03 W |
| Verde, Arroyo ≏, Bol. | 248 | 11.25 S | 66.20 W |
| Verde, Cape ⊁ | 238 | 22.50 N | 74.52 W |
| Verde, Cerro ʌ | 234 | 20.30 N | 104.36 W |
| Verde, Costa ◆[2] | 71 | 39.34 N | 8.28 E |
| Verde Grande ≏ | 255 | 14.35 S | 43.53 W |
| Verde Island I | 116 | 13.33 N | 121.05 E |
| Verde Island Passage ꓵ | 116 | 13.34 N | 120.51 E |
| Verdello | 62 | 45.36 N | 9.37 E |
| Verden, Dtsch. | 52 | 52.55 N | 9.13 E |
| Verden, Ok., U.S. | 196 | 35.05 N | 98.05 W |
| Verde Pequeno ≏ | 255 | 14.48 S | 43.31 W |
| Verdesela, Pinhal da ♦ | 266c | 38.37 N | 9.08 W |
| Verdi | 226 | 39.31 N | 119.59 W |
| Verdigre | 198 | 42.35 N | 98.02 W |
| Verdigre Creek ≏ | 198 | 42.42 N | 98.03 W |
| Verdigris ≏ | 194 | 35.48 N | 95.19 W |
| Verdinho ≏ | 255 | 17.29 S | 50.27 W |
| Verdon ≏ | 62 | 43.43 N | 5.46 E |
| Verdon, Canal du ≅ | 62 | 43.43 N | 5.57 E |
| Verdoy | 210 | 42.46 N | 73.48 W |
| Verduga | 78 | 58.46 N | 29.12 E |
| Verdugo Mountains ⋏ | 228 | 34.13 N | 118.18 W |
| Verdun, P.Q., Can. | 206 | 45.27 N | 73.34 W |
| Verdun-sur-le-Doubs | 58 | 46.54 N | 5.01 E |
| Verdun-sur-Meuse | 56 | 49.10 N | 5.23 E |
| Verdura ≏ | 70 | 37.28 N | 13.12 E |
| Vereb'jo | 76 | 58.41 N | 32.42 E |
| Vereeniging | 158 | 26.38 S | 27.57 E |
| Veregin | 184 | 51.35 N | 102.05 W |
| Vereinigte Arabische Emirate → United Arab Emirates □[1] | 128 | 24.00 N | 54.00 E |
| Vereinigte Königreich → United Kingdom □[1] | 28 | 54.00 N | 2.00 W |
| Vereinigte Staaten → United States □[1] | 178 | 38.00 N | 97.00 W |
| Vereja, Ross. | 82 | 55.46 N | 39.06 E |
| Vereja, Ross. | 82 | 55.21 N | 36.11 E |
| Vereja, Ross. | 265b | 55.37 N | 38.02 E |
| Vereščagino, Ross. | 74 | 64.14 N | 87.37 E |
| Vereščagino, Ross. | 80 | 58.05 N | 54.40 E |
| Veresegyház | 264c | 47.39 N | 19.17 E |
| Veresoch | 78 | 51.19 N | 31.46 E |
| Veretje | 82 | 54.08 N | 36.17 E |
| Véretz | 50 | 47.22 N | 0.48 E |
| Verga | 285 | 39.52 N | 75.10 W |
| Verga, Cap ⊁ | 150 | 10.12 N | 14.27 W |
| Vergara | 252 | 32.56 S | 53.57 W |
| Vergato | 64 | 44.17 N | 11.07 E |
| Vergel | 196 | 25.39 N | 103.32 W |
| Vergeletto | 58 | 46.14 N | 8.36 E |
| Vergemont Creek ≏ | 166 | 24.12 S | 143.17 E |
| Vergennes | 188 | 44.10 N | 73.15 W |
| Verghereto | 66 | 43.47 N | 12.00 E |
| Vergiate | 62 | 45.43 N | 8.42 E |
| Vergons | 62 | 43.55 N | 6.35 E |
| Vergt | 32 | 45.02 N | 0.43 E |
| Verhnjadzvinsk | 76 | 55.47 N | 27.56 E |
| Verigino | 82 | 56.42 N | 38.08 E |
| Verín | 34 | 41.56 N | 7.26 W |
| Veringenstadt | 58 | 48.11 N | 9.12 E |
| Verin Talin | 84 | 40.23 N | 43.53 E |
| Veriora | 76 | 58.00 N | 27.21 E |
| Veríssimo | 255 | 19.42 S | 48.18 W |
| Verkeerdevlei | 158 | 28.48 S | 26.48 E |
| Verkhivtseve | 78 | 48.29 N | 34.14 E |
| Verkhna Khortytsya | 78 | 47.51 N | 35.01 E |
| Verkhne Syn'ovydne | 78 | 49.06 N | 23.34 E |
| Verkhneudinsk → Ulan-Ude | 88 | 51.50 N | 107.37 E |
| Verkhniy Rohachyk | 78 | 47.14 N | 34.21 E |
| Verkhniy Ufaley → Verchnij Ufalej | 86 | 56.04 N | 60.14 E |
| Verkhn'odniprovs'k | 78 | 48.39 N | 34.21 E |
| Verkhn'osadove | 78 | 44.42 N | 33.42 E |
| Verkhnyachka | 78 | 48.49 N | 30.02 E |
| Verkhnyaya Salda → Verchn'aja Salda | 86 | 58.02 N | 60.33 E |
| Verkhnye | 78 | 48.53 N | 38.28 E |
| Verkhnye ◆[8] | 83 | 48.53 N | 38.28 E |
| Verkhnyeduvannyy | 78 | 48.20 N | 39.48 E |
| Verkhovyna | 78 | 48.09 N | 24.47 E |
| Verkhoyansk → Verchojansk | 74 | 67.35 N | 133.27 E |
| Verkykerskop | 158 | 27.54 S | 29.17 E |
| Verl (Senne I) | 52 | 51.53 N | 8.31 E |
| Vermaaklikheid | 158 | 34.19 S | 21.01 E |
| Vermaas | 158 | 26.30 S | 25.59 E |
| Vermand | 50 | 49.52 N | 3.09 E |
| Vermejo ≏ | 196 | 36.30 N | 104.33 W |
| Vermelho ≏, Bra. | 250 | 9.16 S | 47.23 W |
| Vermelho ≏, Bra. | 250 | 7.44 S | 47.17 W |
| Vermelho ≏, Bra. | 250 | 5.33 S | 49.14 W |
| Vermelho ≏, Bra. | 255 | 14.54 S | 51.06 W |
| Vermenton | 50 | 47.40 N | 3.44 E |
| Vermette Lake ⊜ | 184 | 55.40 N | 109.05 W |
| Vermezzo | 266b | 45.24 N | 8.59 E |
| Vermiglio | 64 | 46.18 N | 10.42 E |
| Vermilion, Ab., Can. | 182 | 53.22 N | 110.51 W |
| Vermilion, Oh., U.S. | 214 | 41.25 N | 82.21 W |
| Vermilion □[6] | 216 | 40.08 N | 87.37 W |
| Vermilion ≏, Ab., Can. | 184 | 53.44 N | 110.18 W |
| Vermilion ≏, On., Can. | 190 | 46.16 N | 81.41 W |
| Vermilion ≏, Il., U.S. | 216 | 41.19 N | 89.04 W |
| Vermilion ≏, La., U.S. | 194 | 29.46 N | 92.09 W |
| Vermilion ≏, Mn., U.S. | 190 | 48.16 N | 92.30 W |
| Vermilion ≏, Oh., U.S. | 214 | 41.26 N | 82.22 W |
| Vermilion, Middle Fork ≏ | 216 | 40.12 N | 87.45 W |
| Vermilion, North Fork ≏, Il., U.S. | 216 | 40.49 N | 88.30 W |
| Vermilion, North Fork ≏, Il., U.S. | 216 | 40.13 N | 87.39 W |
| Vermilion, South Fork ≏ | 216 | 40.49 N | 88.30 W |
| Vermilion Bay | 184 | 49.51 N | 93.24 W |
| Vermilion Bay c | 194 | 29.40 N | 92.00 W |
| Vermilion Lake ⊜, On., Can. | 184 | 50.03 N | 92.13 W |
| Vermilion Lake ⊜, Mn., U.S. | 190 | 47.53 N | 92.25 W |
| Vermilion Pass ⟩( | 182 | 51.14 N | 116.03 W |
| Vermillion | 198 | 42.46 N | 96.55 W |
| Vermillion ≏ | 198 | 42.44 N | 96.53 W |
| Vermillion, East Fork ≏ | 198 | 43.44 N | 97.03 W |
| Vermillion, West Fork ≏ | 198 | 43.44 N | 97.03 W |
| Vermillion Bluffs ≛[4] | 200 | 40.50 N | 108.30 W |
| Vermillion Creek ≏, U.S. | 200 | 40.46 N | 108.53 W |
| Vermillion Creek ≏, Ks., U.S. | 198 | 39.12 N | 96.13 W |
| Vermont, Austl. | 274b | 37.50 S | 145.12 E |
| Vermont, Il., U.S. | 194 | 40.17 N | 90.25 W |
| Vermont □[3], U.S. | 178 | 43.50 N | 72.45 W |
| Vermont □[3], U.S. | 188 | 43.50 N | 72.45 W |
| Vermontville | 216 | 42.37 N | 85.01 W |
| Vernà, Pizzo di ʌ | 70 | 38.01 N | 15.15 E |
| Vernaison | 62 | 45.39 N | 4.49 E |
| Vernal | 200 | 40.27 N | 109.31 W |
| Vernalis | 226 | 37.37 N | 121.17 W |
| Vernante | 62 | 44.15 N | 7.32 E |
| Vernayaz | 58 | 46.08 N | 7.02 E |
| Verndale | 198 | 46.24 N | 95.01 W |
| Verner | 190 | 46.25 N | 80.07 W |
| Verneuil-L'Étang | 261 | 48.39 N | 2.50 E |
| Verneuil-sur-Avre | 50 | 48.44 N | 0.56 E |
| Verneuil-sur-Seine | 261 | 48.59 N | 1.59 E |
| Verneukpan ≛ | 158 | 30.00 S | 21.00 E |
| Verneukpan ≏ | 158 | 30.00 S | 21.10 E |
| Vernier | 58 | 46.13 N | 6.06 E |
| Verninge | 41 | 55.18 N | 10.13 E |
| Vernio | 66 | 44.03 N | 11.09 E |
| Vernole | 68 | 40.17 N | 18.18 E |
| Vernon, B.C., Can. | 182 | 50.16 N | 119.16 W |
| Vernon, On., Can. | 212 | 45.10 N | 75.28 W |
| Vernon, Fr. | 50 | 49.05 N | 1.29 E |
| Vernon, Al., U.S. | 194 | 33.45 N | 88.06 W |
| Vernon, Ca., U.S. | 280 | 34.01 N | 118.13 W |
| Vernon, Ct., U.S. | 207 | 41.49 N | 72.28 W |
| Vernon, Fl., U.S. | 194 | 30.37 N | 85.42 W |
| Vernon, Il., U.S. | 219 | 38.48 N | 89.05 W |
| Vernon, In., U.S. | 218 | 38.59 N | 85.36 W |
| Vernon, Mi., U.S. | 216 | 42.56 N | 84.02 W |
| Vernon, N.J., U.S. | 210 | 41.11 N | 74.29 W |
| Vernon, N.Y., U.S. | 210 | 43.05 N | 75.32 W |
| Vernon, Oh., U.S. | 214 | 41.23 N | 80.34 W |
| Vernon, Tx., U.S. | 196 | 34.09 N | 99.15 W |
| Vernon, Ut., U.S. | 200 | 40.05 N | 112.25 W |
| Vernon, Lake ⊜ | 212 | 45.20 N | 79.17 W |
| Vernon Dam ◆[6] | 207 | 42.46 N | 72.31 W |
| Vernon Hills | 216 | 42.13 N | 87.58 W |
| Vernonia | 224 | 45.51 N | 123.11 W |
| Vernon Lake ⊜[1] | 194 | 31.15 N | 93.25 W |
| Vernon River | 186 | 46.12 N | 62.50 W |
| Vernouillet | 261 | 48.58 N | 1.59 E |
| Vernoux-en-Vivarais | 62 | 44.54 N | 4.39 E |
| Verny | 56 | 49.01 N | 6.12 E |
| Vero ≏ | 34 | 42.00 N | 0.10 E |
| Vero Beach | 220 | 27.38 N | 80.23 W |
| Véroia | 38 | 40.31 N | 22.12 E |
| Verolanuova | 64 | 45.19 N | 10.04 E |
| Verolavecchia | 64 | 45.19 N | 10.03 E |
| Veroli | 66 | 41.41 N | 13.25 E |
| Verona, On., Can. | 212 | 44.29 N | 76.42 W |
| Verona, It. | 64 | 45.27 N | 11.00 E |
| Verona, Ky., U.S. | 218 | 38.49 N | 84.39 W |
| Verona, Ms., U.S. | 194 | 34.11 N | 88.43 W |
| Verona, N.J., U.S. | 276 | 40.49 N | 74.14 W |
| Verona, N.Y., U.S. | 210 | 43.08 N | 75.34 W |
| Verona, Oh., U.S. | 218 | 39.54 N | 84.29 W |
| Verona, Pa., U.S. | 279b | 40.30 N | 79.50 W |
| Verona, Wi., U.S. | 216 | 42.59 N | 89.31 W |
| Verona □[4] | 64 | 45.25 N | 11.02 E |
| Verona Beach | 210 | 43.12 N | 75.44 W |
| Verona Beach State Park ♦ | 210 | 43.14 N | 75.44 W |
| Verona Park | 216 | 42.21 N | 85.09 W |
| Verónica | 258 | 35.22 S | 57.20 W |
| Verperluda, ostrov I | 265a | 59.59 N | 30.01 E |
| Verplanck | 210 | 41.15 N | 73.58 W |
| Verran | 166 | 33.51 S | 136.18 E |
| Verrazano-Narrows Bridge ◆[5] | 210 | 40.36 N | 74.03 W |
| Verrès | 62 | 45.40 N | 7.42 E |
| Verrettes | 238 | 19.03 N | 72.28 W |
| Verrey-sous-Salmaise | 58 | 47.26 N | 4.40 E |
| Verrières, Bois de ♦ | 261 | 48.45 N | 2.15 E |
| Verrières-le-Buisson | 261 | 48.45 N | 2.16 E |
| Versa ≏ | 62 | 44.54 N | 8.16 E |
| Versailles, Fr. | 50 | 48.48 N | 2.08 E |
| Versailles, Il., U.S. | 194 | 39.53 N | 90.39 W |
| Versailles, In., U.S. | 218 | 39.04 N | 85.15 W |
| Versailles, Ky., U.S. | 218 | 38.03 N | 84.43 W |
| Versailles, Mo., U.S. | 194 | 38.25 N | 92.50 W |
| Versailles, N.Y., U.S. | 210 | 42.31 N | 78.59 W |
| Versailles, Oh., U.S. | 216 | 40.13 N | 84.29 W |
| Versailles, Pa., U.S. | 279b | 40.21 N | 79.51 W |
| Versailles, Château de ⊥ | 261 | 48.48 N | 2.07 E |
| Versailles, Parc de ♦ | 261 | 48.49 N | 2.06 E |
| Versailles State Park ♦ | 218 | 39.04 N | 85.13 W |
| Verse ≏ | 263 | 51.15 N | 7.46 E |
| Versec → Vršac | 38 | 45.07 N | 21.18 E |
| Versestausee ⊜[1] | 263 | 51.11 N | 7.41 E |
| Versien | 158 | 27.05 S | 27.52 E |
| Veršina Tei | 86 | 53.20 N | 89.36 E |
| Veršino-Darasunskij | 88 | 52.20 N | 115.32 E |
| Veršino-Šachtaminskij | 88 | 51.21 N | 117.50 E |
| Versmold | 52 | 52.02 N | 8.09 E |
| Versoix | 58 | 46.16 N | 6.10 E |
| Ver-sur-Launette | 261 | 49.06 N | 2.41 E |
| Vert | 261 | 48.57 N | 1.41 E |
| Vert, Cap ⊁ | 150 | 14.43 N | 17.30 W |
| Vert'ačij | 80 | 48.57 N | 43.53 E |
| Verte, Île I, P.Q., Can. | 186 | 48.02 N | 69.26 W |
| Verte, Île I, P.Q., Can. | 275a | 45.34 N | 73.30 W |
| Vertedero | 240m | 18.05 N | 66.15 W |
| Verteillac | 32 | 45.21 N | 0.22 E |
| Vertientes | 240p | 21.16 N | 78.09 W |
| Vertiyivka | 78 | 51.10 N | 31.51 E |
| Vertkovo | 82 | 56.07 N | 36.25 E |
| Vert-le-Grand | 261 | 48.34 N | 2.22 E |
| Vert-le-Petit | 261 | 48.33 N | 2.22 E |
| Vertlinskoje | 82 | 56.14 N | 36.58 E |
| Vertou | 32 | 47.10 N | 1.29 W |
| Vertova | 62 | 45.48 N | 9.50 E |
| Vert-Saint-Denis | 261 | 48.34 N | 2.37 E |
| Vertus | 50 | 48.54 N | 4.00 E |
| Verucchio | 66 | 43.59 N | 12.25 E |
| Verulam | 158 | 29.45 S | 31.02 E |
| Verulamium ⊥ | 42 | 51.45 N | 0.22 W |
| Verviers | 56 | 50.35 N | 5.52 E |
| Vervins | 50 | 49.50 N | 3.54 E |
| Verwall Gruppe ⋏ | 58 | 47.02 N | 10.10 E |
| Verwood | 42 | 50.53 N | 1.52 W |
| Veryan | 42 | 50.13 N | 4.54 W |
| Verzasca ≏ | 58 | 46.09 N | 8.52 E |
| Verzegnis | 64 | 46.25 N | 12.59 E |
| Verzenay | 50 | 49.10 N | 4.09 E |
| Verzino | 68 | 39.19 N | 16.51 E |
| Verzuolo | 62 | 44.36 N | 7.29 E |
| Verzy | 50 | 49.09 N | 4.10 E |
| Vesanto | 26 | 62.56 N | 26.25 E |
| Vesava ◆[8] | 272c | 19.08 N | 72.48 E |
| Vescovato, Fr. | 36 | 42.30 N | 9.26 E |
| Vescovato, It. | 64 | 45.10 N | 10.10 E |
| Vescovo di Squillace, Roccelletta del ⊥ | 68 | 38.48 N | 16.35 E |
| Vesdre ≏ | 56 | 50.37 N | 5.37 E |
| Vesela Hora | 83 | 48.43 N | 39.16 E |
| Vesele | 78 | 47.01 N | 34.55 E |
| Veselí nad Lužnicí | 30 | 49.11 N | 14.43 E |
| Veselí nad Moravou | 30 | 48.58 N | 17.22 E |
| Veseli Terny | 78 | 48.07 N | 33.32 E |
| Veselovskoje | 86 | 54.00 N | 78.43 E |
| Veselovskoje vodochranilišče ⊜[1] | 80 | 47.00 N | 41.18 E |
| Veselynove | 78 | 47.21 N | 31.14 E |
| Veselyy Podil | 78 | 49.36 N | 33.16 E |
| Vésenaz | 58 | 46.14 N | 6.12 E |
| Vešenskaja | 80 | 49.38 N | 41.43 E |
| Vesgre ≏ | 50 | 48.48 N | 1.36 E |
| Vesijärvi ⊜ | 26 | 61.06 N | 25.32 E |
| Vesjegonsk | 76 | 58.40 N | 37.16 E |
| Veškajma, Ross. | 80 | 54.04 N | 47.02 E |
| Veškajma, Ross. | 80 | 54.03 N | 47.08 E |
| Veški | 265b | 55.56 N | 37.37 E |
| Vesle ≏ | 50 | 49.23 N | 3.38 E |
| Vešn'aki ◆[8] | 265b | 55.44 N | 37.49 E |
| Ves'olaja Rošča | 86 | 53.47 N | 76.22 E |
| Vesole, Monte ʌ | 68 | 40.24 N | 15.10 E |
| Ves'oloje, Kaz. | 85 | 43.19 N | 77.06 E |
| Ves'oloje, Ross. | 80 | 50.17 N | 45.15 E |
| Ves'oloje, Ross. | 83 | 47.10 N | 38.45 E |
| Ves'oloje, Ross. | 86 | 51.54 N | 82.17 E |
| Ves'olo-Voznesenka | 83 | 47.09 N | 38.20 E |
| Ves'olyj, Ross. | 83 | 46.59 N | 40.44 E |
| Ves'olyj, Ross. | 84 | 47.20 N | 39.18 E |
| Ves'olyj Jar, Ross. | 86 | 51.18 N | 81.07 E |
| Ves'olyj Jar, Ross. | 89 | 43.57 N | 135.28 E |
| Ves'olyj Podol | 80 | 53.31 N | 65.54 E |
| Ves'olyj Pos'olok ◆[8] | 265a | 59.54 N | 30.28 E |
| Vesoul | 58 | 47.38 N | 6.10 E |
| Vespasiano | 255 | 19.40 S | 43.55 W |
| Vespolate | 62 | 45.21 N | 8.40 E |
| Vesta | 236 | 9.43 N | 83.03 W |
| Vest-Agder □[6] | 26 | 58.30 N | 7.10 E |
| Vestal | 210 | 42.05 N | 76.03 W |
| Vestal Center | 210 | 42.02 N | 76.01 W |
| Vestavia Hills | 194 | 33.26 N | 86.46 W |
| Vestbygd | 26 | 58.06 N | 6.35 E |
| Vesterålen II | 24 | 68.45 N | 15.00 E |
| Vester Egede | 41 | 55.17 N | 11.50 E |
| Vesterø Havn | 26 | 57.18 N | 10.56 E |
| Vester Skerninge | 41 | 55.04 N | 10.27 E |
| Vester Sottrup | 41 | 54.57 N | 9.43 E |
| Vestfjorden c[2] | 24 | 68.08 N | 15.00 E |
| Vestfold □[6] | 26 | 59.15 N | 10.10 E |
| Vestmannaeyjar | 24a | 63.26 N | 20.12 W |
| Vestone | 62 | 45.42 N | 10.24 E |
| Vestreno | 58 | 46.06 N | 9.18 E |
| Vestsjælland □[6] | 41 | 55.30 N | 11.30 E |
| Vestvågøya I | 24 | 68.15 N | 13.50 E |
| Vésubie ≏ | 62 | 43.52 N | 7.12 E |
| Vesubio → Vesuvio ʌ[1] | 68 | 40.49 N | 14.26 E |
| Vesuv → Vesuvio ʌ[1] | 68 | 40.49 N | 14.26 E |
| Vesuvio (Vesuvius) ʌ[1] | 68 | 40.49 N | 14.26 E |
| Vesuvius → Vesuvio ʌ[1] | 68 | 40.49 N | 14.26 E |
| Vesuvius Bay | 224 | 48.53 N | 123.35 W |
| Veszprém | 30 | 47.06 N | 17.55 E |
| Veszprém □[6] | 30 | 47.10 N | 17.40 E |
| Vésztő | 30 | 46.55 N | 21.16 E |
| Vet ≏ | 158 | 27.40 S | 25.40 E |
| Vetapālem | 122 | 15.47 N | 80.19 E |
| Veterans Stadium ♦ | 285 | 39.54 N | 75.10 W |
| Vétheuil | 50 | 49.04 N | 1.42 E |
| Vetju | 24 | 62.57 N | 50.44 E |
| Vetka | 76 | 52.33 N | 31.10 E |
| Vetlanda | 26 | 57.26 N | 15.04 E |
| Vetl'anka | 80 | 52.52 N | 51.09 E |
| Vetluga | 80 | 57.51 N | 45.47 E |
| Vetluga ≏ | 80 | 56.18 N | 46.24 E |
| Vetlužskij, Ross. | 80 | 57.11 N | 45.07 E |
| Vetlužskij, Ross. | 80 | 58.23 N | 45.26 E |
| Vetoškino | 80 | 57.18 N | 49.44 E |
| Vetovo | 38 | 43.42 N | 26.16 E |
| Vetralla | 66 | 42.19 N | 12.03 E |
| Vetren | 38 | 42.16 N | 24.03 E |
| Vetriolo | 64 | 46.02 N | 11.18 E |
| Vetrișoaia | 38 | 46.26 N | 28.13 E |
| Větřní | 61 | 48.46 N | 14.17 E |
| Vetryna | 76 | 55.25 N | 28.28 E |
| Vetschau | 54 | 51.47 N | 14.04 E |
| Vettisfossen ᒐ | 26 | 61.22 N | 7.55 E |
| Vetto | 64 | 44.29 N | 10.20 E |
| Vettore, Monte ʌ | 66 | 42.49 N | 13.16 E |
| Vetulonia | 66 | 42.51 N | 10.58 E |
| Veules-les-Roses | 50 | 49.52 N | 0.48 E |
| Veulettes-sur-Mer | 50 | 49.51 N | 0.36 E |
| Veurne (Furnes) | 50 | 51.04 N | 2.40 E |
| Vevay | 218 | 38.44 N | 85.04 W |
| Vevelstad | 24 | 65.43 N | 12.30 E |
| Veveno, Khawr V | 140 | 6.40 N | 32.58 E |
| Vevey | 58 | 46.28 N | 6.51 E |
| Vex | 58 | 46.13 N | 7.24 E |
| Veyle ≏ | 58 | 46.18 N | 4.50 E |
| Veynes | 62 | 44.32 N | 5.49 E |
| Veyrier | 62 | 45.53 N | 6.10 E |
| Vézelay | 50 | 47.28 N | 3.44 E |
| Vézelise | 58 | 48.29 N | 6.05 E |
| Vézénobres | 62 | 44.03 N | 4.09 E |
| Vézère ≏ | 32 | 44.53 N | 0.53 E |
| Vezirköprü | 130 | 41.09 N | 35.28 E |
| Vezouze ≏ | 58 | 48.35 N | 6.29 E |
| Vezza d'Oglio | 64 | 46.14 N | 10.24 E |
| Vezzana, Cima della ʌ | 64 | 46.17 N | 11.50 E |
| Vezzano | 64 | 46.05 N | 11.00 E |
| Vezzano Ligure | 64 | 44.09 N | 9.52 E |
| Viacha | 248 | 16.39 S | 68.18 W |
| Viadana | 64 | 44.56 N | 10.31 E |
| Viadutos | 252 | 27.34 S | 52.01 W |
| Viale | 252 | 31.53 S | 60.01 W |
| Vialonga | 266c | 38.52 N | 9.05 W |
| Via Mala V | 58 | 46.40 N | 9.26 E |
| Viamão | 252 | 30.05 S | 51.02 W |
| Viamonte | 252 | 33.44 S | 63.06 W |
| Vian | 196 | 35.29 N | 94.58 W |
| Viana | 250 | 3.13 S | 45.00 W |
| Viana, Ilha do I | 287a | 22.52 S | 43.08 W |
| Viana do Alentejo | 34 | 38.20 N | 8.00 W |
| Viana do Bolo | 34 | 42.11 N | 7.06 W |
| Viana do Castelo | 34 | 41.42 N | 8.50 W |
| Vianden | 56 | 49.57 N | 6.11 E |
| Vianen | 52 | 52.00 N | 5.05 E |
| Viangchan (Vientiane) | 110 | 17.58 N | 02.36 E |
| Viangphoukha | 110 | 20.41 N | 01.04 E |
| Viar ≏ | 34 | 37.36 N | 5.50 W |
| Viareggio | 64 | 43.52 N | 10.14 E |
| Viarmes | 50 | 49.08 N | 2.22 E |
| Viatka → Kirov | 80 | 58.38 N | 49.42 E |
| Viaur ≏ | 32 | 44.08 N | 2.23 E |
| Vibank | 184 | 50.20 N | 103.55 W |
| Víboras, Arroyo de las ≏ | 258 | 33.57 S | 58.21 W |
| Viborg, Dan. | 26 | 56.26 N | 9.24 E |
| Viborg → Vyborg, Ross. | 76 | 60.42 N | 28.45 E |
| Viborg, S.D., U.S. | 198 | 43.10 N | 97.04 W |
| Viborg □[6] | 41 | 56.18 N | 9.27 E |
| Vibo Valentia | 68 | 38.40 N | 16.06 E |
| Vibo Valentia □[4] | 68 | 38.40 N | 16.10 E |
| Vibraye | 50 | 48.03 N | 0.44 E |
| Viburnum | 194 | 37.42 N | 91.08 W |
| Viby | 41 | 55.33 N | 12.02 E |
| Viby ◆[8] | 41 | 56.07 N | 10.10 E |
| Vic (Vich) | 34 | 41.56 N | 2.15 E |
| Vic, Étang de c | 62 | 43.29 N | 3.50 E |
| Vicálvaro ◆[8] | 266a | 40.24 N | 3.36 W |
| Vícam | 232 | 27.35 N | 110.20 W |
| Vicarello | 66 | 42.10 N | 12.12 E |
| Vicari | 70 | 37.49 N | 13.34 E |
| Vicchio | 66 | 43.56 N | 11.28 E |
| Vicco | 192 | 37.12 N | 83.03 W |
| Vicebsk | 76 | 55.12 N | 30.11 E |
| Vicebsk □[8] | 76 | 55.20 N | 29.00 E |
| Vic-en-Bigorre | 32 | 43.23 N | 0.03 E |
| Vicente, Point ⊁ | 280 | 33.44 N | 118.25 W |
| Vicente Casares | 258 | 34.57 S | 58.38 W |
| Vicente de Carvalho | 256 | 23.56 S | 46.19 W |
| Vicente Guerrero, Méx. | 234 | 18.24 N | 102.53 W |
| Vicente Guerrero, Méx. | 234 | 19.08 N | 98.10 W |
| Vicente Guerrero, Méx. | 234 | 23.45 N | 103.59 W |
| Vicente Guerrero, Presa ⊜[1] | 234 | 24.00 N | 98.45 W |
| Vicente López | 258 | 34.32 S | 58.28 W |
| Vicente López □[5] | 288 | 34.32 S | 58.30 W |
| Vicente Noble | 238 | 18.23 N | 71.11 W |
| Vicenza | 64 | 45.33 N | 11.33 E |
| Vicenza □[4] | 64 | 45.40 N | 11.27 E |
| Viceroy | 184 | 49.27 N | 105.22 W |
| Vichada □[5] | 246 | 5.00 N | 69.30 W |
| Vichada ≏ | 246 | 4.55 N | 67.50 W |
| Vichadero | 252 | 31.48 S | 54.43 W |
| Vichigasta | 252 | 29.29 S | 67.31 W |
| Vichoreva | 88 | 56.47 N | 101.22 E |
| Vichorevka | 88 | 56.12 N | 101.09 E |
| Vichra ≏ | 76 | 54.01 N | 31.36 E |
| Vichuga → Vičuga | 80 | 57.13 N | 41.56 E |
| Vichuquén | 252 | 34.53 S | 72.00 W |
| Vichy | 50 | 46.08 N | 3.26 E |
| Vici | 196 | 36.08 N | 99.17 W |
| Vickery | 214 | 41.23 N | 82.56 W |
| Vicksburg, Mi., U.S. | 216 | 42.07 N | 85.31 W |
| Vicksburg, Ms., U.S. | 194 | 32.21 N | 90.52 W |
| Vicksburg, Pa., U.S. | 210 | 40.56 N | 76.59 W |
| Vicksburg National Military Park ♦ | 194 | 32.24 N | 90.52 W |
| Vico | 36 | 42.10 N | 8.48 E |
| Vico, Lago di ⊜ | 66 | 42.19 N | 12.10 E |
| Vico Canavese | 62 | 45.30 N | 7.47 E |
| Vico del Gargano | 68 | 41.54 N | 15.58 E |
| Vico Equense | 68 | 40.40 N | 14.25 E |
| Vicoforte | 62 | 44.22 N | 7.52 E |
| Vicopisano | 66 | 43.42 N | 10.35 E |
| Viçosa, Bra. | 250 | 9.22 S | 36.14 W |
| Viçosa, Bra. | 255 | 20.45 S | 42.53 W |
| Viçosa do Ceará | 250 | 3.34 S | 41.05 W |
| Vicosoprano | 58 | 46.22 N | 9.37 E |
| Vicovaro | 66 | 42.01 N | 12.54 E |
| Vic-sur-Aisne | 50 | 49.24 N | 3.07 E |
| Vic-sur-Cère | 58 | 44.59 N | 2.37 E |
| Vic-sur-Seille | 56 | 48.47 N | 6.32 E |
| Victor, Ca., U.S. | 226 | 38.08 N | 121.12 W |
| Victor, Id., U.S. | 202 | 43.36 N | 111.06 W |
| Victor, Ia., U.S. | 190 | 41.43 N | 92.17 W |
| Victor, Mt., U.S. | 202 | 46.25 N | 114.08 W |
| Victor, N.Y., U.S. | 210 | 42.58 N | 77.24 W |

| | | | | |
|---|---|---|---|---|
| ≏ River | Fluß | Río | Rivière | Rio |
| ≅ Canal | Kanal | Canal | Canal | Canal |
| ᒐ Waterfall, Rapids | Wasserfall, Stromschnellen | Cascada, Rápidos | Chute d'eau, Rapides | Cascata, Rápidos |
| ꓵ Strait | Meeresstraße | Estrecho | Détroit | Estreito |
| c Bay, Gulf | Bucht, Golf | Bahía, Golfo | Baie, Golfe | Baía, Golfo |
| ⊜ Lake, Lakes | See, Seen | Lago, Lagos | Lac, Lacs | Lago, Lagos |
| ≛ Swamp | Sumpf | Pantano | Marais | Pântano |
| ⊓ Ice Features, Glacier | Eis- und Gletscherformen | Accidentes Glaciales | Formes glaciaires | Acidentes glaciares |
| ⍑ Other Hydrographic Features | Andere Hydrographische Objekte | Otros Elementos Hidrográficos | Autres données hydrographiques | Outros acidentes hidrográficos |

| | | | | |
|---|---|---|---|---|
| ⊹ Submarine Features | Untermeerische Objekte | Accidentes Submarinos | Formes de relief sous-marin | Acidentes submarinos |
| □ Political Unit | Politische Einheit | Unidad Política | Entité politique | Unidade política |
| ■ Cultural Institution | Kulturelle Institution | Institución Cultural | Institution culturelle | Instituição cultural |
| ⊥ Historical Site | Historische Stätte | Sitio Histórico | Site historique | Sitio histórico |
| ♦ Recreational Site | Erholungs- und Ferienort | Sitio de Recreo | Centre de loisirs | Área de Lazer |
| ⊠ Airport | Flughafen | Aeropuerto | Aéroport | Aeroporto |
| ▪ Military Installation | Militäranlage | Instalación Militar | Installation militaire | Instalação militar |
| ◆ Miscellaneous | Verschiedenes | Misceláneo | Divers | Diversos |

ENGLISH / DEUTSCH


| Name | Page | Lat.°′ | Long.°′ |
| --- | --- | --- | --- |
| Victor, Lac ⊜ | **186** | 50.35 N | 61.50 W |
| Victorbur | **52** | 53.29 N | 7.20 E |
| Victor Harbor | **168b** | 35.34 S | 138.37 E |
| Victoria, Arg. | **252** | 32.37 S | 60.10 W |
| Victoria → Vitória, Bra. | **255** | 20.19 S | 40.21 W |
| Victoria, B.C., Can. | **224** | 48.25 N | 123.22 W |
| Victoria, P.E., Can. | **186** | 46.13 N | 63.29 W |
| Victoria, Chile | **252** | 38.13 S | 72.20 W |
| Victoria, Gren. | **241k** | 12.12 N | 61.42 W |
| Victoria, Guinée | **150** | 10.50 N | 14.33 W |
| Victoria (Xianggang), H.K. | **271d** | 22.17 N | 114.09 E |
| Victoria, Malay. | **112** | 5.17 N | 115.15 E |
| Victoria → Ciudad Victoria, Méx. | **234** | 23.44 N | 99.08 W |
| Victoria, Pil. | **116** | 13.12 N | 121.15 E |
| Victoria, Pil. | **116** | 15.35 N | 120.41 E |
| Victoria, Rom. | **38** | 45.45 N | 24.41 E |
| Victoria, Sey. | **138** | 4.38 S | 55.27 E |
| Victoria, Ks., U.S. | **198** | 38.51 N | 99.08 W |
| Victoria, Tx., U.S. | **196** | 28.48 N | 97.00 W |
| Victoria, Va., U.S. | **192** | 36.59 N | 78.13 W |
| Victoria □3 | **166** | 38.00 S | 145.00 E |
| Victoria □4 | **154** | 20.54 S | 31.21 E |
| Victoria □6, On., Can. | **212** | 44.35 N | 78.50 W |
| Victoria □6, Tx., U.S. | **222** | 28.55 N | 97.00 W |
| Victoria ⬥8 | **288** | 34.28 S | 58.31 W |
| Victoria ≃, Austl. | **160** | 15.12 S | 129.43 E |
| Victoria ≃, Nf., Can. | **186** | 48.45 N | 56.40 W |
| Victoria ≃, Méx. | **234** | 21.02 N | 99.50 W |
| Victoria, Isla I | **254** | 45.18 S | 73.58 W |
| Victoria, Lake ⊜, Afr. | **154** | 1.00 S | 33.00 E |
| Victoria, Lake ⊜, Austl. | **166** | 34.00 S | 141.16 E |
| Victoria, Mount ∧, Mya. | **110** | 21.14 N | 93.55 E |
| Victoria, Mount ∧, Pap. N. Gui. | **164** | 8.55 S | 147.35 E |
| Victoria, Pont ⬥5 | **275a** | 45.29 N | 73.32 W |
| Victoria and Albert Museum ʊ | **272c** | 18.59 N | 72.50 E |
| Victoria Beach | **184** | 50.43 N | 96.33 W |
| Victoria Beach ⊥2 | **273a** | 6.25 N | 3.25 E |
| Victoria de Durango → Durango | **234** | 24.02 N | 104.40 W |
| Victoria Falls | **154** | 17.56 S | 25.50 E |
| Victoria Falls ∟ | **154** | 17.55 S | 25.51 E |
| Victoria Falls National Park ♦ | **154** | 17.55 S | 25.40 E |
| Victoria Gardens ♦ | **272c** | 18.59 N | 72.50 E |
| Victoria Harbour | **212** | 44.45 N | 79.46 W |
| Victoria International Airport ⊠ | **224** | 48.39 N | 123.26 W |
| Victoria Island I, N.T., Can. | **176** | 71.00 N | 110.00 W |
| Victoria Island I, Nig. | **273a** | 6.26 N | 3.26 E |
| Victoria Lake ⊜ | **273d** | 26.14 S | 28.09 E |
| Victoria Lake ⊜1 | **186** | 48.18 N | 57.30 W |
| Victoria Land ⬥1 | **9** | 75.00 S | 163.00 E |
| Victoria Lawn Tennis Association Courts ♦ | **274b** | 37.51 S | 145.02 E |
| Victoria Memorial Hall ʊ | **271c** | 1.17 N | 103.51 E |
| Victoria Memorial Museum ʊ | **272b** | 22.33 N | 88.21 E |
| Victoria Nile ≃ | **154** | 2.14 N | 31.26 E |
| Victoria Park | **168a** | 31.58 S | 115.55 E |
| Victoria Park ♦, H.K. | **271d** | 22.17 N | 114.11 E |
| Victoria Park ♦, Eng., U.K. | **262** | 53.23 N | 2.34 W |
| Victoria Peak ∧, Belize | **232** | 16.48 N | 88.37 W |
| Victoria Peak ∧, B.C., Can. | **182** | 50.03 N | 126.06 W |
| Victoria Peak ∧, H.K. | **271d** | 22.17 N | 114.08 E |
| Victoria Peaks ⋏ | **116** | 9.22 N | 118.20 E |
| Victoria Point | **171a** | 27.35 S | 153.18 E |
| Victoria Range ⋏, N.Z. | **172** | 42.09 S | 172.08 E |
| Victoria Range ⋏, Pil. | **116** | 9.32 N | 118.23 E |
| Victoria River | **164** | 15.37 S | 131.08 E |
| Victoria River Downs | **164** | 16.24 S | 131.00 E |
| Victorias | **116** | 10.54 N | 123.05 E |
| Victoria State Car Club Race Circuit ♦ | **274b** | 37.45 S | 145.11 E |
| Victoria Station ⬥5 | **262** | 53.29 N | 2.15 W |
| Victoria Strait ⊔ | **176** | 69.15 N | 100.30 W |
| Victoria Terminus ⬥5 | **272c** | 18.57 N | 72.50 E |
| Victoria University of Manchester ʊ2 | **262** | 53.28 N | 2.14 W |
| Victoriaville | **206** | 46.03 N | 71.57 W |
| Victoria West | **158** | 31.25 S | 23.04 E |
| Victorica | **252** | 36.13 S | 65.27 W |
| Victorino | **246** | 2.48 N | 67.50 W |
| Victorino de la Plaza | **252** | 36.36 S | 62.40 W |
| Víctor Rosales | **234** | 22.57 N | 102.42 W |
| Victorville | **228** | 34.32 N | 117.17 W |
| Victory, Mount ∧ | **164** | 9.10 S | 149.05 E |
| Victory Gardens | **276** | 40.52 N | 74.32 W |
| Victory Heights | **214** | 41.22 N | 79.46 W |
| Victory Hills | **279b** | 40.11 N | 79.53 W |
| Victory Mills | **210** | 43.05 N | 73.36 W |
| Victory Monument ⊥ | **269a** | 13.46 N | 100.33 E |
| Vičuga | **80** | 57.13 N | 41.56 E |
| Vicuña | **252** | 30.02 S | 70.44 W |
| Vicuña Mackenna | **252** | 33.54 S | 64.23 W |
| Vidal, Kaap ≻ | **158** | 28.09 S | 32.33 E |
| Vidal Gormaz, Isla I | **254** | 52.00 S | 74.45 W |
| Vidalia, Ga., U.S. | **192** | 32.13 N | 82.24 W |
| Vidalia, La., U.S. | **194** | 31.33 N | 91.25 W |
| Vidal Ramos | **252** | 27.23 S | 49.22 W |
| Vidauban | **62** | 43.26 N | 6.26 E |
| Videbæk | **26** | 56.05 N | 8.38 E |
| Videira | **252** | 27.00 S | 51.08 W |
| Videle | **38** | 44.16 N | 25.31 E |
| Vidigueira | **34** | 38.13 N | 7.48 W |
| Vidim, Česká Rep. | **54** | 50.28 N | 14.31 E |
| Vidim, Ross. | **88** | 56.29 N | 103.09 E |
| Vidin | **38** | 43.59 N | 22.52 E |
| Vidisha | **124** | 23.32 N | 77.49 E |
| Vidlica | **24** | 61.10 N | 32.21 E |
| Vidnoje | **82** | 55.34 N | 37.41 E |
| Vidogošči | **82** | 56.42 N | 36.23 E |
| Vidor | **194** | 30.07 N | 94.00 W |
| Vidos ≃ | **267b** | 40.58 N | 28.53 E |
| Vidöstern ⊜ | **26** | 57.04 N | 14.01 E |
| Vidourle ≃ | **62** | 43.32 N | 4.08 E |
| Vidra, Rom. | **38** | 44.16 N | 26.11 E |
| Vidra, Rom. | **38** | 45.55 N | 26.54 E |
| Vidsel | **24** | 65.51 N | 20.24 E |
| Vidzeme □9 | **76** | 57.10 N | 25.30 E |
| Vidzy | **76** | 55.24 N | 26.38 E |
| Vie ≃ | **50** | 49.05 N | 0.04 E |
| Viecht | **60** | 48.30 N | 12.04 E |
| Viechtach | **60** | 49.05 N | 12.53 E |
| Viechtwang, Öst. | **61** | 47.55 N | 13.57 E |
| Viechtwang, Öst. | **64** | 47.55 N | 13.57 E |
| Viedma | **254** | 40.48 S | 63.00 W |
| Viedma, Lago ⊜ | **254** | 49.35 S | 72.35 W |
| Viehberg ∧ | **61** | 48.33 N | 14.37 E |
| Vieil Armand ⊥ | **58** | 47.52 N | 7.10 E |
| Vieillard, Lac du ⊜ | **190** | 47.23 N | 78.02 W |
| Vieille Case | **240d** | 15.36 N | 61.24 W |
| Vieira do Minho | **34** | 41.39 N | 8.09 W |
| Viejo, Cerro ∧ | **248** | 4.49 S | 79.27 W |
| Viekšniai | **76** | 56.16 N | 22.31 E |
| Vielank | **54** | 53.15 N | 11.08 E |
| Vielha | **34** | 42.42 N | 0.48 E |
| Vielle-Eglise-en-Yvelines | **261** | 48.40 N | 1.53 E |
| Vielsalm | **56** | 50.17 N | 5.55 E |
| Viels-Maisons | **50** | 48.54 N | 3.24 E |
| Viena → Vienne ≃ | **32** | 47.13 N | 0.05 E |
| Vienenburg | **54** | 51.57 N | 10.34 E |
| Vienna, On., Can. | **212** | 42.41 N | 80.48 W |
| Vienna → Wien, Öst. | **61** | 48.13 N | 16.20 E |
| Vienna, Ga., U.S. | **192** | 32.05 N | 83.47 W |
| Vienna, Il., U.S. | **194** | 37.25 N | 88.54 W |
| Vienna, In., U.S. | **218** | 38.39 N | 85.46 W |
| Vienna, Md., U.S. | **208** | 38.29 N | 75.49 W |
| Vienna, Mo., U.S. | **194** | 38.11 N | 91.56 W |
| Vienna, N.J., U.S. | **210** | 40.52 N | 74.53 W |
| Vienna, Oh., U.S. | **214** | 41.14 N | 80.40 W |
| Vienna, S.D., U.S. | **198** | 44.42 N | 97.30 W |
| Vienna, Va., U.S. | **208** | 38.29 N | 75.49 W |
| Vienna, Va., U.S. | **208** | 38.54 N | 77.15 W |
| Vienna, W.V., U.S. | **188** | 39.19 N | 81.32 W |
| Vienne, Fr. | **62** | 45.31 N | 4.52 E |
| Vienne → Wien, Öst. | **61** | 48.13 N | 16.20 E |
| Vienne □5 | **32** | 46.35 N | 0.30 E |
| Vienne ≃ | **32** | 47.13 N | 0.05 E |
| Vienne-en-Arthies | **261** | 49.04 N | 1.44 E |
| Vienne-le-Château | **56** | 49.11 N | 4.53 E |
| Vientiane → Viangchan | **110** | 17.58 N | 102.36 E |
| Vientos, Paso de los → Windward Passage ⊔ | **238** | 20.00 N | 73.50 W |
| Vieques | **240m** | 18.09 N | 65.27 W |
| Vieques, Aeropuerto ⊠ | **240m** | 18.07 N | 65.30 W |
| Vieques, Isla de I | **240m** | 18.08 N | 65.25 W |
| Vieques, Pasaje de ⊔ | **240m** | 18.11 N | 65.37 W |
| Vieques, Sonda de ⊔ | **240m** | 18.15 N | 65.23 W |
| Vière ≃ | **56** | 48.46 N | 4.41 E |
| Viereck | **54** | 53.32 N | 14.02 E |
| Vieremä | **26** | 63.45 N | 27.01 E |
| Vierfontein | **158** | 27.03 S | 26.46 E |
| Vierhouten | **52** | 52.20 N | 5.50 E |
| Vieringhausen ⬥8 | **263** | 51.11 N | 7.10 E |
| Vierlande ⬥1 | **52** | 53.26 N | 10.14 E |
| Viernau | **54** | 50.40 N | 10.32 E |
| Viernheim | **56** | 49.32 N | 8.34 E |
| Vierraden | **54** | 53.06 N | 14.17 E |
| Viersen | **56** | 51.15 N | 6.23 E |
| Vierumäki | **26** | 61.06 N | 25.57 E |
| Vierwaldstättersee ⊜ | **58** | 47.00 N | 8.28 E |
| Vierzehnheiligen ʊ1 | **56** | 50.08 N | 11.02 E |
| Vierzon | **50** | 47.13 N | 2.05 E |
| Viesca | **232** | 25.21 N | 102.48 W |
| Viesecke | **54** | 53.01 N | 12.01 E |
| Vieselbach | **54** | 51.00 N | 11.08 E |
| Viesīte | **76** | 56.21 N | 25.33 E |
| Vieste | **68** | 41.53 N | 16.10 E |
| Vietgest | **54** | 53.45 N | 12.20 E |
| Vietnam □1, Asia | **108** | 16.00 N | 108.00 E |
| Vietnam □1, Asia | **110** | 16.00 N | 108.00 E |
| Vietnam Veterans Memorial ⊥ | **284c** | 38.53 N | 77.03 W |
| Vietri di Potenza | **68** | 40.36 N | 15.30 E |
| Vietri sul Mare | **68** | 40.40 N | 14.44 E |
| Viet Tri | **110** | 21.18 N | 105.26 E |
| Vieux-Condé | **50** | 50.27 N | 3.34 E |
| Vieux-Ferette | **58** | 47.30 N | 7.18 E |
| Vieux-Fort, P.Q., Can. | **186** | 51.26 N | 57.49 W |
| Vieux-Fort, Guad. | **241o** | 15.57 N | 61.43 W |
| Vieux Fort, St. Luc. | **241f** | 13.44 N | 60.57 W |
| Vieux-Fort, Pointe du ≻ | **241o** | 15.57 N | 61.43 W |
| Vieux Fort Bay ⊂ | **241f** | 13.44 N | 60.58 W |
| Vieux-Habitants | **241o** | 16.04 N | 61.46 W |
| Vieux-Thann | **58** | 47.48 N | 7.08 E |
| Vievis | **76** | 54.46 N | 24.48 E |
| View Park | **280** | 34.00 N | 118.20 W |
| Vieytes | **258** | 35.16 S | 57.35 W |
| Vif | **62** | 45.03 N | 5.40 E |
| Vig | **41** | 55.51 N | 11.36 E |
| Viga ≃ | **76** | 59.14 N | 43.41 E |
| Vigala | **76** | 58.43 N | 24.22 E |
| Vigan | **116** | 17.34 N | 120.23 E |
| Vigarano Mainarda | **64** | 44.50 N | 11.30 E |
| Vigatto | **64** | 44.43 N | 10.20 E |
| Vigeland | **26** | 58.05 N | 7.18 E |
| Vigentino ⬥8 | **266b** | 45.25 N | 9.11 E |
| Vigersted | **41** | 55.29 N | 11.54 E |
| Vigese, Monte ∧ | **64** | 44.12 N | 11.06 E |
| Vigésima Quinta de Abril, Ponte ⬥5 | **266c** | 38.41 N | 9.11 W |
| Vigevano | **62** | 45.19 N | 8.51 E |
| Viggianello | **68** | 39.58 N | 16.05 E |
| Viggiano | **68** | 40.20 N | 15.54 E |
| Viggiù | **62** | 45.52 N | 8.54 E |
| Vigia | **250** | 0.48 S | 48.08 W |
| Vigie Airport ⊠ | **241f** | 14.01 N | 60.59 W |
| Vignacourt | **50** | 50.01 N | 2.12 E |
| Vignale | **266b** | 45.29 N | 8.36 E |
| Vignanello | **66** | 42.23 N | 12.17 E |
| Vigneulles-lès-Hattonchâtel | **56** | 48.59 N | 5.43 E |
| Vigneux-sur-Seine | **261** | 48.42 N | 2.25 E |
| Vignola | **64** | 44.29 N | 11.00 E |
| Vignory | **58** | 48.17 N | 5.06 E |
| Vignot | **56** | 48.46 N | 5.36 E |
| Vigny | **261** | 49.05 N | 1.56 E |
| Vigo | **34** | 42.14 N | 8.43 W |
| Vigo, Ría de ⊂1 | **34** | 42.15 N | 8.45 W |
| Vigodarzere | **64** | 45.27 N | 11.53 E |
| Vigo di Fassa | **64** | 46.25 N | 11.40 E |
| Vigolzone | **62** | 44.55 N | 9.40 E |
| Vigone | **62** | 44.51 N | 7.30 E |
| Vigonovo | **64** | 45.23 N | 12.00 E |
| Vigo-Rendena | **64** | 46.05 N | 10.43 E |
| Vigrestad | **26** | 58.34 N | 5.42 E |
| Viguzzolo | **62** | 44.54 N | 8.55 E |
| Vigy | **56** | 49.12 N | 6.18 E |
| Vihanti | **26** | 64.29 N | 25.00 E |
| Vihāri | **123** | 30.02 N | 72.21 E |
| Vihiers | **32** | 47.09 N | 0.32 W |
| Vihowa | **123** | 31.08 N | 70.30 E |
| Vihren ∧ | **38** | 41.46 N | 23.24 E |
| Vihti | **26** | 60.25 N | 24.20 E |
| Viiala | **26** | 61.13 N | 23.47 E |
| Viinijärvi | **26** | 62.39 N | 29.14 E |
| Viinijärvi ⊜ | **26** | 62.44 N | 29.17 E |
| Viipuri → Vyborg | **76** | 60.42 N | 28.45 E |
| Viişoara | **38** | 46.20 N | 28.26 E |
| Viitasaari | **26** | 63.04 N | 25.52 E |
| Viivikonna | **76** | 59.19 N | 27.42 E |
| Vijāpur | **120** | 23.34 N | 72.45 E |
| Vijayawāda | **122** | 16.31 N | 80.37 E |
| Vijosë (Aóös) ≃ | **38** | 40.37 N | 19.20 E |
| Vik | **40** | 59.44 N | 17.28 E |
| Vik ⊥ | **40** | 59.44 N | 17.27 E |
| Vika | **40** | 60.31 N | 15.42 E |
| Vikajärvi | **24** | 66.37 N | 26.12 E |
| Vikārābād | **122** | 17.20 N | 77.54 E |
| Vikbolandet ≻1 | **40** | 58.32 N | 16.40 E |
| Vikeke | **112** | 8.52 S | 126.22 E |
| Viken | **41** | 56.09 N | 12.34 E |
| Viken ⊜ | **26** | 58.39 N | 14.20 E |
| Vikern ⊜ | **40** | 59.30 N | 14.55 E |
| Vikersund | **26** | 59.59 N | 10.02 E |
| Vikhroli ⬥8 | **272c** | 19.07 N | 72.56 E |
| Viking | **182** | 53.06 N | 111.46 W |
| Viking Village | **218** | 39.05 N | 84.18 W |
| Vikmanshyttan | **40** | 60.17 N | 15.49 E |
| Vikna | **24** | 64.57 N | 10.58 E |
| Vikna I | **24** | 64.57 N | 10.58 E |
| Vikno | **78** | 48.34 N | 25.58 E |
| Vikramasingapuram | **122** | 8.43 N | 77.24 E |
| Viksøyri | **26** | 61.05 N | 6.35 E |
| Viktor | **24** | 66.09 N | 58.07 E |
| Viktorovka | **86** | 52.51 N | 62.32 E |
| Viktring | **61** | 46.35 N | 14.16 E |
| Vikulovo | **86** | 56.49 N | 70.37 E |
| Vil'a | **80** | 55.15 N | 42.13 E |
| Vila Alferes Chamusca | **156** | 24.29 S | 33.00 E |
| Vila Augusta | **287b** | 23.28 S | 46.32 W |
| Vila Babi | **287a** | 22.42 S | 43.23 W |
| Vila Boacaya ⬥8 | **287b** | 23.29 S | 46.44 W |
| Vila Caldas Xavier | **154** | 15.59 S | 34.12 E |
| Vila da Maganja | **154** | 17.18 S | 37.30 E |
| Vila da Ribeira Brava | **150a** | 16.37 N | 24.18 W |
| Viladecans | **266d** | 41.19 N | 2.00 E |
| Viladecavalls del Vallès | **266d** | 41.33 N | 1.58 E |
| Vila de Manica | **156** | 18.56 S | 32.53 E |
| Vila de Rei | **34** | 39.40 N | 8.09 W |
| Vila Dirce | **287b** | 23.35 S | 46.48 W |
| Vila do Bispo | **34** | 37.05 N | 8.55 W |
| Vila do Conde | **34** | 41.21 N | 8.45 W |
| Vila do Porto | **148a** | 36.56 N | 25.09 W |
| Vila Embaú | **256** | 22.37 S | 45.02 W |
| Vila Flor | **34** | 41.18 N | 7.09 W |
| Vila Fontes | **156** | 17.50 S | 35.21 E |
| Vila Formosa ⬥8 | **287b** | 23.34 S | 46.33 W |
| Vilafranca del Penedès | **34** | 41.21 N | 1.42 E |
| Vila Franca de Xira | **34** | 38.57 N | 8.59 W |
| Vila Galvão | **287b** | 23.27 S | 46.33 W |
| Vila Gamito | **154** | 14.12 S | 33.00 E |
| Vila Gomes da Costa | **156** | 24.19 S | 33.38 E |
| Vila Gouveia | **156** | 18.03 S | 33.11 E |
| Vila Guilherme ⬥8 | **287b** | 23.30 S | 46.36 W |
| Vilaine ≃ | **32** | 47.30 N | 2.27 W |
| Vila Isabel ⬥8 | **287a** | 22.55 S | 43.15 W |
| Vila Jaguára ⬥8 | **287b** | 23.31 S | 46.45 W |
| Viļaka | **76** | 57.11 N | 27.41 E |
| Vilalba | **34** | 43.18 N | 7.41 W |
| Vila Luísa | **156** | 25.44 S | 32.40 E |
| Vilama, Laguna de ⊜ | **252** | 22.36 S | 66.55 W |
| Vila Machado | **156** | 19.18 S | 34.11 E |
| Vila Madalena ⬥8 | **287b** | 23.33 S | 46.42 W |
| Vila Maria ⬥8 | **287b** | 23.31 S | 46.34 W |
| Vila Mariana ⬥8 | **287b** | 23.35 S | 46.38 W |
| Vila Matilde ⬥8 | **287b** | 23.32 S | 46.31 W |
| Vilanculos | **156** | 22.01 S | 35.19 E |
| Viļāni | **76** | 56.33 N | 26.57 E |
| Vila Nova ≃ | **250** | 0.04 S | 51.13 W |
| Vila Nova de Famalicão | **34** | 41.25 N | 8.32 W |
| Vila Nova de Foz Côa | **34** | 41.05 N | 7.12 W |
| Vila Nova de Gaia | **34** | 41.08 N | 8.37 W |
| Vilanova de la Roca | **266d** | 41.33 N | 2.17 E |
| Vilanova i la Geltrú | **34** | 41.14 N | 1.44 E |
| Vila Novo de Ourém | **34** | 39.39 N | 8.35 W |
| Vila Paiva de Andrada | **156** | 18.44 S | 34.03 E |
| Vila Progresso | **287a** | 22.55 S | 43.03 W |
| Vila Prudente ⬥8 | **287b** | 23.35 S | 46.33 W |
| Vila-real, Esp. | **34** | 39.56 N | 0.06 W |
| Vila Real, Port. | **34** | 41.18 N | 7.45 W |
| Vila Real de Santo António | **34** | 37.12 N | 7.25 W |
| Vilar Formoso | **34** | 40.37 N | 6.50 W |
| Vilarinho do Monte | **250** | 1.37 S | 52.01 W |
| Vilassar de Dalt | **266d** | 41.31 N | 2.22 E |
| Vilassar de Mar | **266d** | 41.30 N | 2.24 E |
| Vila Vasco da Gama | **154** | 14.54 S | 32.14 E |
| Vila Velha, Bra. | **250** | 3.13 N | 51.13 W |
| Vila Velha, Bra. | **255** | 20.20 S | 40.17 W |
| Vila Velha de Ródão | **34** | 39.38 N | 7.40 W |
| Vila Verde, Port. | **34** | 41.39 N | 8.26 W |
| Vila Verde, Port. | **266c** | 38.50 N | 9.22 W |
| Vila Viçosa | **34** | 38.47 N | 8.13 W |
| Vilcabamba, Cordillera de ⋏ | **248** | 12.45 S | 73.20 W |
| Vil'cha | **78** | 51.22 N | 29.24 E |
| Vil'che | **78** | 49.14 N | 22.53 E |
| Vildbjerg | **41** | 56.12 N | 8.46 E |
| Vilejka | **76** | 54.30 N | 26.53 E |
| Vilelas | **252** | 27.57 S | 62.38 W |
| Vilenki | **82** | 54.16 N | 38.55 E |
| Vil'gort, Ross. | **24** | 61.35 N | 50.40 E |
| Vil'gort, Ross. | **24** | 60.34 N | 56.24 E |
| Vilhelmina | **26** | 64.37 N | 16.39 E |
| Vilhena | **248** | 12.43 S | 60.07 W |
| Vilija (Neris) ≃ | **76** | 54.54 N | 23.53 E |
| Viljandi | **76** | 58.22 N | 25.36 E |
| Viljoensdrif | **158** | 26.44 S | 27.55 E |
| Viljoenshof | **158** | 34.40 S | 19.42 E |
| Viljoenskroon | **158** | 27.12 S | 27.00 E |
| Viljoenspos | **158** | 27.35 S | 30.30 E |
| Vilkaviškis | **76** | 54.39 N | 23.02 E |
| Vil'khova ≃ | **83** | 48.35 N | 39.17 E |
| Vil'kickogo, ostrov I, Ross. | **72** | 73.29 N | 75.50 E |
| Vil'kickogo, ostrov I, Ross. | **74** | 75.44 N | 152.20 E |
| Vil'kickogo, proliv ⊔ | **74** | 77.55 N | 103.00 E |
| Vilkija | **76** | 55.03 N | 23.35 E |
| Villa Abecia | **248** | 21.00 S | 65.23 W |
| Villa Aberastain | **252** | 31.39 S | 68.35 W |
| Villa Acuña → Ciudad Acuña | **232** | 29.18 N | 100.55 W |
| Villa Adelina ⬥8 | **288** | 34.31 S | 58.32 W |
| Villa Adriana ⊥ | **66** | 41.56 N | 12.45 E |
| Villa Alejandrina | **258** | 33.46 S | 58.21 W |
| Villa Alemana | **252** | 33.03 S | 71.23 W |
| Villa Álvarez | **234** | 19.14 N | 103.43 W |
| Villa Ana | **252** | 28.29 S | 59.37 W |
| Villa Ángela | **252** | 27.35 S | 60.43 W |
| Villa Atamisqui | **252** | 28.29 S | 63.48 W |
| Villa Atuel | **252** | 34.50 S | 67.54 W |
| Villaba | **116** | 11.13 N | 124.23 E |
| Villa Ballester ⬥8 | **258** | 34.32 S | 58.33 W |
| Villabassa (Niederdorf) | **64** | 46.44 N | 12.10 E |
| Villabate | **70** | 38.04 N | 13.26 E |
| Villabé | **261** | 48.35 N | 2.27 E |
| Villa Bella | **248** | 10.23 S | 65.24 W |
| Villa Berthet | **252** | 27.17 S | 60.25 W |
| Villablino | **34** | 42.56 N | 6.19 W |
| Villa Borghese ʊ | **267a** | 41.55 N | 12.29 E |
| Villa Bosch ⬥8 | **288** | 34.35 S | 58.34 W |
| Villa Bruzual | **246** | 9.20 N | 69.06 W |
| Villa Cañás, Arg. | **252** | 34.00 S | 61.36 W |
| Villacañas, Esp. | **34** | 39.38 N | 3.20 W |
| Villa Carlos Paz | **252** | 31.24 S | 64.31 W |
| Villacarriedo | **34** | 43.14 N | 3.48 W |
| Villacarrillo | **34** | 38.07 N | 3.05 W |
| Villa Castelli, Arg. | **252** | 29.00 S | 68.11 W |
| Villa Castelli, It. | **68** | 40.35 N | 17.28 E |
| Villacastín | **34** | 40.47 N | 4.25 W |
| Villach | **64** | 46.36 N | 13.50 E |
| Villacidro | **71** | 39.27 N | 8.44 E |
| Villa Ciudadela ⬥8 | **258** | 34.38 S | 58.34 W |
| Villa Clara □4 | **240p** | 22.30 N | 80.00 W |
| Villa Comaltitlan | **236** | 15.13 N | 92.35 W |
| Villa Concepción del Tío | **252** | 31.19 S | 62.50 W |
| Villa Constitución | **252** | 33.14 S | 60.20 W |
| Villa Cortese | **266b** | 45.34 N | 8.53 E |
| Villa Corzo | **234** | 16.10 N | 93.15 W |
| Villacoublay, Aérodrome de ⊠ | **261** | 48.45 N | 2.10 E |
| Villa Creek ≃ | **226** | 35.27 N | 120.58 W |
| Villa Cuauhtémoc, Méx. | **234** | 19.24 N | 99.34 W |
| Villa Cuauhtémoc, Méx. | **234** | 22.11 N | 97.50 W |
| Villada | **34** | 42.15 N | 4.58 W |
| Villa de Apaseo El Alto | **234** | 20.27 N | 100.37 W |
| Villa de Arista | **234** | 22.39 N | 100.50 W |
| Villa de Arriaga | **234** | 21.54 N | 101.23 W |
| Villadeati | **62** | 45.04 N | 8.10 E |
| Villa de Cos | **234** | 23.17 N | 102.21 W |
| Villa de Cura | **246** | 10.02 N | 67.29 W |
| Villa de Guadalupe | **234** | 23.22 N | 100.46 W |
| Villa del Carmen | **252** | 32.57 S | 65.03 W |
| Villa del Pueblito | **234** | 20.32 N | 100.27 W |
| Villa del Río | **34** | 37.59 N | 4.17 W |
| Villa del Rosario, Arg. | **252** | 31.35 S | 63.32 W |
| Villa del Rosario, Arg. | **252** | 30.47 S | 57.55 W |
| Villa de María | **252** | 29.54 S | 63.43 W |
| Villa de Mayo | **258** | 34.30 S | 58.41 W |
| Villa de Nova Sintra | **150a** | 14.52 N | 24.43 W |
| Villa de Reyes | **234** | 21.48 N | 100.56 W |
| Villa de San Antonio | **236** | 14.16 N | 87.36 W |
| Villa de San Francisco | **236** | 14.10 N | 86.58 W |
| Villa de Soto | **252** | 30.51 S | 64.59 W |
| Villa d'Este ⊥ | **267a** | 41.57 N | 12.48 E |
| Villa Devoto ⬥8 | **288** | 34.36 S | 58.31 W |
| Villa Diamante ⬥8 | **288** | 34.41 S | 58.26 W |
| Villa di Chiavenna | **58** | 46.20 N | 9.29 E |
| Villadiego | **34** | 42.31 N | 4.00 W |
| Villa Dolores | **252** | 31.56 S | 65.12 W |
| Villa Domínico ⬥8 | **258** | 34.41 S | 58.19 W |
| Villadose | **64** | 45.04 N | 11.53 E |
| Villadossola | **58** | 46.04 N | 8.16 E |
| Villa Elisa | **252** | 32.10 S | 58.24 W |
| Villa Elisa ⬥8 | **258** | 34.50 S | 58.05 W |
| Villa Escalante | **234** | 19.24 N | 101.39 W |
| Villa Flores | **234** | 16.14 N | 93.14 W |
| Villa Florida | **252** | 26.23 S | 57.09 W |
| Villafranca d'Asti | **62** | 44.55 N | 8.02 E |
| Villafranca del Bierzo | **34** | 42.36 N | 6.48 W |
| Villafranca de los Barros | **34** | 38.34 N | 6.20 W |
| Villafranca di Verona | **64** | 45.21 N | 10.50 E |
| Villafranca in Lunigiana | **64** | 44.17 N | 9.57 E |
| Villafranca Piemonte | **62** | 44.47 N | 7.33 E |
| Villafranca Sicula | **70** | 37.35 N | 13.17 E |
| Villafranca Tirrena | **70** | 38.14 N | 15.26 E |
| Villafrati | **70** | 37.54 N | 13.29 E |
| Villagarcía, Esp. | **34** | 42.36 N | 8.45 W |
| Villa García, Méx. | **234** | 22.10 N | 101.57 W |
| Village | **196** | 35.33 N | 97.33 W |
| Village Creek ≃, Ar., U.S. | **194** | 35.28 N | 91.19 W |
| Village Creek ≃, Tx., U.S. | **222** | 32.46 N | 97.09 W |
| Village Green | **285** | 39.52 N | 75.26 W |
| Villa General Roca | **252** | 32.39 S | 66.28 W |
| Village of Drummond Hill | **285** | 39.43 N | 75.42 W |
| Village of the Branch | **276** | 40.51 N | 73.11 W |
| Villa Gesell | **252** | 37.15 S | 56.55 W |
| Villa Giambruno | **288** | 34.48 S | 58.13 W |
| Villa González Ortega | **234** | 22.30 N | 101.55 W |
| Villagrán, Méx. | **232** | 24.29 N | 99.29 W |
| Villagrán, Méx. | **234** | 20.31 N | 100.59 W |
| Villagrande Strisaili | **71** | 39.58 N | 9.30 E |
| Villa Grazia | **70** | 38.09 N | 13.10 E |
| Villa Grove | **194** | 39.51 N | 88.09 W |
| Villaguay | **252** | 31.51 S | 59.01 W |
| Villa Guerrero, Méx. | **234** | 21.59 N | 103.36 W |
| Villa Guerrero, Méx. | **234** | 18.52 N | 99.39 W |
| Villa Guillermina | **252** | 28.14 S | 59.28 W |
| Villa Hayes | **252** | 25.06 S | 57.34 W |
| Villahermosa | **234** | 17.59 N | 92.55 W |
| Villa Hernandarias | **252** | 31.13 S | 59.59 W |
| Villa Hidalgo, Méx. | **204** | 30.59 N | 116.10 W |
| Villa Hidalgo, Méx. | **234** | 21.40 N | 102.36 W |
| Villa Hidalgo, Méx. | **234** | 21.44 N | 105.15 W |
| Villa Hidalgo Yalalag | **234** | 17.11 N | 96.11 W |
| Villa Huidobro | **252** | 34.50 S | 64.35 W |
| Villaines-la-Juhel | **32** | 48.21 N | 0.17 W |
| Villa Insurgentes | **232** | 25.12 N | 111.44 W |
| Villa Iris | **252** | 38.10 S | 63.15 W |
| Villa Jiménez | **234** | 19.55 N | 101.35 W |
| Villa José L. Suárez ⬥8 | **288** | 34.32 S | 58.35 W |
| Villa Juanita | **234** | 17.47 N | 95.09 W |
| Villa Juárez, Méx. | **232** | 27.10 N | 109.50 W |
| Villa Juárez, Méx. | **234** | 22.20 N | 100.17 W |
| Villa Krause | **252** | 31.34 S | 68.32 W |
| Villa La Angostura | **254** | 40.47 S | 71.40 W |
| Villalago | **66** | 41.56 N | 13.50 E |
| Villa Larca | **252** | 32.37 S | 64.59 W |
| Villa La Venta | **234** | 18.10 N | 94.07 W |
| Villalba, It. | **70** | 37.39 N | 13.50 E |
| Villalba, P.R. | **240m** | 18.08 N | 66.30 W |
| Villaldama | **232** | 26.30 N | 100.26 W |
| Villa Lia | **258** | 34.07 S | 59.26 W |
| Villalon | **116** | 11.31 N | 124.22 E |
| Villalón de Campos | **34** | 42.06 N | 5.02 W |
| Villalonga | **254** | 39.53 S | 62.35 W |
| Villalpando | **34** | 41.52 N | 5.24 W |
| Villa Lugano ⬥8 | **288** | 34.41 S | 58.28 W |
| Villalvernia | **62** | 44.49 N | 8.51 E |
| Villa Lynch ⬥8 | **288** | 34.36 S | 58.31 W |
| Villa Madero, Arg. | **288** | 34.42 S | 58.30 W |
| Villa Madero, Méx. | **234** | 19.24 N | 101.16 W |
| Villa Mainero | **232** | 24.32 N | 99.38 W |
| Villamar | **71** | 39.37 N | 8.59 E |
| Villa María, Arg. | **252** | 32.25 S | 63.15 W |
| Villa Maria, Pa., U.S. | **214** | 41.05 N | 80.30 W |
| Villa Maria del Triunfo | **286d** | 12.10 S | 76.56 W |
| Villa María Grande | **252** | 31.39 S | 59.54 W |
| Villa Martín, Bol. | **248** | 20.46 S | 67.47 W |
| Villamartín, Esp. | **34** | 36.52 N | 5.38 W |
| Villamarzana | **64** | 45.01 N | 11.41 E |
| Villamassargia | **71** | 39.16 N | 8.38 E |
| Villa Matoque | **252** | 25.49 S | 63.49 W |
| Villa Mazán | **252** | 28.40 S | 66.34 W |
| Villa Media Agua | **252** | 31.59 S | 68.25 W |
| Villa Mercedes | **252** | 30.07 S | 68.42 W |
| Villa Minozzo | **64** | 44.22 N | 10.28 E |
| Villamontes | **248** | 21.15 S | 63.30 W |
| Villa Morelos | **234** | 20.00 N | 101.25 W |
| Villandraut | **32** | 44.28 N | 0.23 W |
| Villa Nova, Md., U.S. | **284b** | 39.21 N | 76.44 W |
| Villa Nova, Oh., U.S. | **216** | 40.33 N | 84.26 W |
| Villanova, Pa., U.S. | **208** | 40.02 N | 75.20 W |
| Villanova d'Asti | **62** | 44.57 N | 7.56 E |
| Villanova Mondovì | **62** | 44.21 N | 7.45 E |
| Villanova Monferrato | **62** | 45.11 N | 8.28 E |
| Villanova Monteleone | **71** | 40.30 N | 8.28 E |
| Villanova sull'Arda | **64** | 45.01 N | 10.00 E |
| Villanova Tulo | **71** | 39.47 N | 9.13 E |
| Villanova University ʊ2 | **285** | 40.02 N | 75.21 W |
| Villa Nueva, Arg. | **252** | 32.26 S | 63.15 W |
| Villa Nueva, Arg. | **252** | 32.54 S | 68.47 W |
| Villanueva, Col. | **246** | 10.37 N | 72.59 W |
| Villa Nueva, Guat. | **236** | 14.31 N | 90.35 W |
| Villanueva, Hond. | **236** | 15.17 N | 88.00 W |
| Villanueva, Méx. | **234** | 22.21 N | 102.53 W |
| Villa Nueva, Nic. | **236** | 12.58 N | 86.49 W |
| Villanueva, N.M., U.S. | **200** | 35.16 N | 105.21 W |
| Villanueva de Córdoba | **34** | 38.20 N | 4.37 W |
| Villanueva de la Serena | **34** | 38.58 N | 5.48 W |
| Villanueva de la Sierra | **34** | 40.12 N | 6.24 W |
| Villanueva de los Infantes | **34** | 38.44 N | 3.01 W |
| Villanueva del Río y Minas | **34** | 37.39 N | 5.42 W |
| Villa Numancia | **288** | 34.55 S | 58.24 W |
| Villa Obregón | **234** | 21.07 N | 102.42 W |
| Villa Ocampo | **252** | 28.28 S | 59.22 W |
| Villa Ojo de Agua | **252** | 29.31 S | 63.42 W |
| Villa Oliva | **252** | 26.01 S | 57.53 W |
| Villa Opicina | **64** | 45.40 N | 13.49 E |
| Villa Oropeza | **248** | 19.10 S | 65.17 W |
| Villa Ottone (Uttenheim) | **64** | 46.52 N | 11.57 E |
| Villa Papale ʊ | **267a** | 41.45 N | 12.39 E |
| Villa Park, Ca., U.S. | **228** | 33.48 N | 117.48 W |
| Villa Park, Il., U.S. | **278** | 41.53 N | 87.59 W |
| Villa Park Dam ⬥6 | **280** | 33.48 N | 117.46 W |
| Villa Pérez | **240m** | 18.12 N | 66.47 W |
| Villapiana | **68** | 39.51 N | 16.28 E |
| Villapiana Lido | **68** | 39.48 N | 16.29 E |
| Villapinzón | **246** | 5.13 N | 73.36 W |
| Villa Potenza | **66** | 43.19 N | 13.25 E |
| Villaputzu | **71** | 39.26 N | 9.34 E |
| Villa Quinteros | **252** | 27.14 S | 65.33 W |
| Villa Quintilio Varo ⊥ | **267a** | 41.58 N | 12.47 E |
| Villa Ramírez | **252** | 32.11 S | 60.12 W |
| Villarcayo | **34** | 42.56 N | 3.34 W |
| Villar-d'Arène | **62** | 45.02 N | 6.20 E |
| Villard-Bonnot | **62** | 45.14 N | 5.53 E |
| Villard-de-Lans | **62** | 45.04 N | 5.33 E |
| Villardefrades | **34** | 41.43 N | 5.15 W |
| Villar del Arzobispo | **34** | 39.44 N | 0.49 W |
| Villareal | **116** | 11.34 N | 124.56 E |
| Villa Real ⬥8 | **288** | 34.37 S | 58.31 W |
| Villa Regina | **252** | 39.06 S | 67.04 W |
| Villa Reynolds | **252** | 33.43 S | 65.23 W |
| Villa Rica | **192** | 33.43 N | 84.55 W |
| Villa Rivero | **248** | 17.37 S | 65.48 W |
| Villaroche | **261** | 48.37 N | 2.39 E |
| Villaroche ⊠ | **261** | 48.37 N | 2.40 E |
| Villa Romana del Casale ⊥ | **70** | 37.22 N | 14.20 E |
| Villa Rosa, Arg. | **258** | 34.25 S | 58.52 W |
| Villarosa, It. | **70** | 37.35 N | 14.10 E |
| Villar Pellice | **62** | 44.48 N | 7.09 E |
| Villar Perosa | **62** | 44.56 N | 7.15 E |
| Villarreales | **196** | 26.07 N | 100.20 W |
| Villarrica, Chile | **254** | 39.16 S | 72.13 W |
| Villarrica, Col. | **246** | 3.58 N | 74.37 W |
| Villarrica, Para. | **252** | 25.45 S | 56.26 W |
| Villarrica, Lago ⊜ | **254** | 39.15 S | 72.06 W |
| Villarrobledo | **34** | 39.16 N | 2.36 W |
| Villarrubia de los Ojos | **34** | 39.13 N | 3.36 W |
| Villars, Arg. | **258** | 34.50 S | 58.56 W |
| Villars, Schw. | **58** | 46.18 N | 7.04 E |
| Villars-Colmars | **62** | 44.10 N | 6.36 E |
| Villars-en-Azois | **58** | 48.04 N | 4.45 E |
| Villars-les-Dombes | **58** | 46.00 N | 5.01 E |
| Villars-sur-Var | **62** | 43.56 N | 7.06 E |
| Villa Ruiz | **258** | 34.25 S | 59.15 W |
| Villas | **208** | 39.01 N | 74.56 W |
| Villa Sáenz Peña ⬥8 | **288** | 34.36 S | 58.31 W |
| Villa San Andrés ⬥8 | **288** | 34.33 S | 58.32 W |
| Villa Sandino | **236** | 12.03 N | 84.59 W |
| Villa San Giovanni | **68** | 38.13 N | 15.38 E |
| Villa San José | **252** | 32.12 S | 58.13 W |
| Villa San Martín | **252** | 28.18 S | 64.12 W |
| Villasanta | **62** | 45.37 N | 9.18 E |
| Villa Santa, Montaña ∧ | **236** | 14.12 N | 86.27 W |
| Villa Santa Maria | **66** | 41.57 N | 14.21 E |
| Villa Santina | **64** | 46.24 N | 12.55 E |
| Villa Santo Domingo | **234** | 23.20 N | 101.44 W |
| Villa Santos Lugares ⬥8 | **288** | 34.36 S | 58.32 W |
| Villasayas | **34** | 41.21 N | 2.37 W |
| Villa Serrano | **248** | 19.06 S | 64.22 W |
| Villasimius | **71** | 39.08 N | 9.31 E |
| Villasis | **116** | 15.54 N | 120.35 E |
| Villasor | **71** | 39.23 N | 8.56 E |
| Villa Talavera | **248** | 19.49 S | 65.25 W |
| Villa Tunari | **248** | 16.55 S | 65.25 W |
| Villa Turdera ⬥8 | **288** | 34.48 S | 58.25 W |
| Villa Unión, Arg. | **252** | 29.18 S | 68.12 W |
| Villa Unión, Arg. | **252** | 29.24 S | 62.47 W |
| Villa Unión, Méx. | **232** | 28.15 N | 100.43 W |
| Villa Unión, Méx. | **234** | 23.58 N | 104.02 W |
| Villa Unión, Méx. | **234** | 23.12 N | 106.14 W |
| Villa Urquiza ⬥8 | **288** | 34.34 S | 58.29 W |
| Villa Valeria | **252** | 34.20 S | 64.55 W |
| Villa Vallelonga | **66** | 41.52 N | 13.37 E |
| Villaverde ⬥8 | **266a** | 40.21 N | 3.42 W |
| Villaverla | **64** | 45.39 N | 11.29 E |
| Villa Verona | **226** | 39.28 N | 121.33 W |
| Villavicencio | **246** | 4.09 N | 73.37 W |
| Villaviciosa | **34** | 43.29 N | 5.26 W |
| Villaviciosa de Córdoba | **34** | 38.05 N | 5.01 W |
| Villa Victoria | **234** | 18.47 N | 103.24 W |
| Villa Viscarra | **248** | 17.59 S | 65.36 W |
| Villa Vomano | **66** | 42.37 N | 13.46 E |
| Villazón | **248** | 22.06 S | 65.36 W |
| Villa Zorraquín | **252** | 31.19 S | 58.02 W |
| Villé | **58** | 48.20 N | 7.18 E |
| Villebon, Lac ⊜ | **190** | 47.58 N | 77.17 W |
| Villebon-sur-Yvette | **261** | 48.42 N | 2.15 E |
| Villeconin | **261** | 48.31 N | 2.08 E |
| Villecresnes | **261** | 48.43 N | 2.32 E |
| Villecroze | **62** | 43.35 N | 6.16 E |
| Ville-d'Avray | **261** | 48.50 N | 2.11 E |
| Ville-de-Laval → Laval | **206** | 45.35 N | 73.45 W |
| Villedieu | **32** | 48.50 N | 1.13 W |
| Ville-en-Tardenois | **50** | 49.11 N | 3.48 E |
| Villefort | **62** | 44.26 N | 3.56 E |
| Villefranche | **58** | 45.59 N | 4.43 E |
| Villefranche-de-Rouergue | **32** | 44.21 N | 2.02 E |
| Villefranche-sur-Cher | **50** | 47.18 N | 1.46 E |
| Villefranche-sur-Mer | **62** | 43.42 N | 7.19 E |
| Villejuif | **50** | 48.48 N | 2.22 E |
| Villejust | **261** | 48.41 N | 2.14 E |
| Ville-Marie | **190** | 47.19 N | 79.26 W |
| Villemaur-sur-Vanne | **50** | 48.15 N | 3.44 E |
| Villemeux-sur-Eure | **50** | 48.40 N | 1.28 E |
| Villemoisson-sur-Orge | **261** | 48.40 N | 2.19 E |
| Villemomble | **261** | 48.53 N | 2.31 E |
| Villena | **34** | 38.38 N | 0.51 W |
| Ville Nacíonal | **234** | 17.50 N | 96.14 W |
| Villenauxe-la-Grande | **50** | 48.35 N | 3.33 E |
| Villeneuve, It. | **62** | 45.42 N | 7.14 E |
| Villeneuve, Schw. | **58** | 46.24 N | 6.55 E |
| Villeneuve-d'Ascq | **50** | 50.37 N | 3.10 E |
| Villeneuve-d'Aveyron | **32** | 44.26 N | 2.02 E |
| Villeneuve-de-Berg | **62** | 44.33 N | 4.30 E |
| Villeneuve-la-Garenne | **261** | 48.56 N | 2.20 E |
| Villeneuve-la-Guyard | **50** | 48.20 N | 3.04 E |
| Villeneuve-l'Archevêque | **50** | 48.14 N | 3.33 E |
| Villeneuve-le-Comte | **261** | 48.49 N | 2.50 E |
| Villeneuve-le-Roi | **50** | 48.44 N | 2.25 E |
| Villeneuve-lès-Avignon | **62** | 43.58 N | 4.48 E |
| Villeneuve-lès-Maguelonne | **62** | 43.32 N | 3.52 E |
| Villeneuve-Saint-Denis | **261** | 48.49 N | 2.48 E |
| Villeneuve-Saint-Georges | **50** | 48.44 N | 2.27 E |
| Villeneuve-sous-Dammartin | **261** | 49.02 N | 2.39 E |
| Villeneuve-sur-Lot | **32** | 44.25 N | 0.42 E |
| Villeneuve-sur-Yonne | **50** | 48.05 N | 3.18 E |
| Villennes-sur-Seine | **261** | 48.56 N | 2.00 E |
| Villenoy | **50** | 48.57 N | 2.52 E |
| Villeny | **50** | 47.37 N | 1.45 E |
| Villeparisis | **50** | 48.56 N | 2.37 E |
| Villepinte | **261** | 48.58 N | 2.32 E |
| Ville Platte | **194** | 30.41 N | 92.16 W |
| Villepreux | **261** | 48.50 N | 2.01 E |
| Villequier | **50** | 49.31 N | 0.40 E |
| Villeron | **261** | 49.03 N | 2.33 E |
| Villeroy | **50** | 48.59 N | 2.47 E |
| Villers-Bocage, Fr. | **32** | 49.05 N | 0.39 W |
| Villers-Bocage, Fr. | **50** | 49.59 N | 2.20 E |
| Villers-Bretonneux | **50** | 49.52 N | 2.31 E |
| Villers-Carbonnel | **50** | 49.52 N | 2.54 E |
| Villers-Cotterêts | **50** | 49.15 N | 3.05 E |
| Villers-devant-Orval | **56** | 49.37 N | 5.19 E |
| Villers-en-Arthies | **261** | 49.05 N | 1.44 E |
| Villersexel | **58** | 47.33 N | 6.26 E |
| Villers-Farlay | **58** | 47.00 N | 5.45 E |
| Villers-la-Ville | **50** | 50.35 N | 4.32 E |
| Villers-le-Lac | **58** | 47.04 N | 6.40 E |
| Villers-lès-Nancy | **58** | 48.40 N | 6.09 E |
| Villers-lès-Pots | **58** | 47.13 N | 5.21 E |
| Villers-Outréaux | **50** | 50.02 N | 3.18 E |
| Villers-Saint-Paul | **50** | 49.17 N | 2.29 E |
| Villers-Semeuse | **56** | 49.44 N | 4.45 E |
| Villerupt | **56** | 49.28 N | 5.56 E |
| Villerville | **50** | 49.24 N | 0.08 E |
| Ville-Saint-Georges → Saint-Georges | **188** | 46.07 N | 70.40 W |
| Villes-sur-Auzon | **62** | 44.03 N | 5.14 E |
| Ville-sur-Tourbe | **56** | 49.11 N | 4.47 E |
| Villeta | **246** | 5.01 N | 74.28 W |
| Villetta Barrea | **66** | 41.47 N | 13.56 E |
| Villeurbanne | **62** | 45.46 N | 4.53 E |
| Villevaudé | **261** | 48.55 N | 2.39 E |
| Villeziers | **261** | 48.40 N | 2.10 E |
| Villiers | **158** | 27.03 S | 28.35 E |
| Villiers-Adam | **261** | 49.04 N | 2.14 E |
| Villiersdorp | **158** | 34.00 S | 19.19 E |
| Villiers-le-Bâcle | **261** | 48.44 N | 2.08 E |
| Villiers-le-Bel | **261** | 49.00 N | 2.23 E |
| Villiers-le-Sec | **261** | 49.04 N | 2.23 E |
| Villiers-Saint-Frédéric | **261** | 48.49 N | 1.54 E |
| Villiers-Saint-Georges | **50** | 48.39 N | 3.25 E |
| Villiers-sur-Marne | **261** | 48.50 N | 2.33 E |
| Villiers-sur-Morin | **261** | 48.52 N | 2.53 E |
| Villigst | **263** | 51.26 N | 7.35 E |
| Villingen-Schwenningen | **58** | 48.04 N | 8.28 E |
| Villisca | **198** | 40.55 N | 94.58 W |
| Villmanstrand → Lappeenranta | **26** | 61.04 N | 28.11 E |
| Villmergen | **58** | 47.21 N | 8.15 E |
| Villorba | **64** | 45.44 N | 12.14 E |
| Villoresi, Canale ≍ | **266b** | 45.33 N | 9.19 E |
| Villotta | **64** | 45.52 N | 12.45 E |
| Vilm I | **54** | 54.19 N | 13.32 E |
| Vilmnitz | **54** | 54.21 N | 13.31 E |
| Vilna, Ab., Can. | **182** | 54.07 N | 111.55 W |
| Vilna → Vilnius, Liet. | **76** | 54.41 N | 25.19 E |
| Vilnius | **76** | 54.41 N | 25.19 E |
| Vil'nohirs'k | **78** | 48.29 N | 34.01 E |
| Vilosnes-sur-Meuse | **56** | 49.20 N | 5.14 E |
| Vilppula | **26** | 62.01 N | 24.31 E |
| Vils | **58** | 47.33 N | 10.38 E |
| Vils ≃, Dtsch. | **60** | 49.09 N | 11.58 E |
| Vils ≃, Dtsch. | **60** | 48.37 N | 13.11 E |
| Vils ≃, Europe | **58** | 47.33 N | 10.40 E |
| Vilsandi saar I | **76** | 58.23 N | 21.52 E |
| Vilsbiburg | **60** | 48.27 N | 12.12 E |
| Vilseck | **60** | 49.37 N | 11.48 E |
| Vil'shana | **78** | 49.13 N | 31.13 E |
| Vil'shanka | **78** | 48.14 N | 30.52 E |
| Vil'shany, Ukr. | **78** | 50.03 N | 35.53 E |
| Vil'shany, Ukr. | **78** | 49.47 N | 37.46 E |
| Vilsheim | **60** | 48.27 N | 12.07 E |
| Vilshofen | **60** | 48.39 N | 13.12 E |
| Vil'uj ≃ | **74** | 64.24 N | 126.26 E |
| Vil'ujsk | **74** | 63.45 N | 121.35 E |
| Vil'ujskoje vodochranilišče ⊜1 | **74** | 62.30 N | 111.00 E |
| Viluppuram | **122** | 11.56 N | 79.29 E |
| Vil'va | **86** | 58.37 N | 56.52 E |
| Vilvoorde | **50** | 50.56 N | 4.26 E |
| Vimercate | **62** | 45.37 N | 9.22 E |
| Vimianzo | **34** | 43.07 N | 9.02 W |
| Vimmerby | **26** | 57.40 N | 15.51 E |
| Vimodrone | **266b** | 45.31 N | 9.17 E |
| Vimoutiers | **50** | 48.55 N | 0.12 E |
| Vimpeli | **26** | 63.09 N | 23.48 E |
| Vimperk | **60** | 49.03 N | 13.47 E |
| Vimy | **50** | 50.22 N | 2.49 E |
| Vina | **204** | 39.55 N | 122.03 W |
| Vina ≃ | **146** | 7.45 N | 15.36 E |
| Viñac | **248** | 12.56 S | 75.47 W |
| Viña del Mar | **252** | 33.02 S | 71.34 W |
| Vinadi | **58** | 46.55 N | 10.29 E |
| Vinadio | **62** | 44.18 N | 7.10 E |
| Viñales | **240p** | 22.37 N | 83.43 W |
| Vinalhaven | **188** | 44.02 N | 68.49 W |
| Vinalhaven Island I | **188** | 44.05 N | 68.52 W |
| Vinantes | **261** | 49.01 N | 2.44 E |
| Vina Roni, Mount ∧ | **175e** | 8.10 S | 157.28 E |
| Vinaròs | **34** | 40.28 N | 0.29 E |
| Vinay | **62** | 45.13 N | 5.24 E |
| Vinazco ≃ | **234** | 20.56 N | 97.44 W |
| Vincennes, Fr. | **50** | 48.51 N | 2.26 E |
| Vincennes, In., U.S. | **194** | 38.40 N | 87.31 W |
| Vincennes, Bois de ♦ | **261** | 48.50 N | 2.25 E |
| Vincennes, Château de ⊥ | **261** | 48.51 N | 2.26 E |
| Vincennes, Étang de ⊜ | **261** | 48.47 N | 2.45 E |
| Vincennes Bay ⊂ | **9** | 66.30 S | 109.30 E |
| Vincent | **194** | 33.22 N | 86.22 W |
| Vincent, Point ≻ | **174c** | 29.00 S | 167.55 E |
| Vincentown | **208** | 39.56 N | 74.44 W |
| Vinces | **246** | 1.32 S | 79.45 W |
| Vincey | **58** | 48.20 N | 6.20 E |
| Vinchiaturo | **66** | 41.29 N | 14.35 E |
| Vinchina | **252** | 28.46 S | 68.10 W |
| Vinchos | **248** | 13.16 S | 74.21 W |
| Vinci | **66** | 43.47 N | 10.55 E |
| Vinco | **214** | 40.25 N | 78.52 W |
| Vindeby | **41** | 55.03 N | 10.38 E |
| Vindelälven ≃ | **24** | 63.54 N | 19.52 E |
| Vindeln | **26** | 64.12 N | 19.44 E |
| Vinden, Mount ∧ | **162** | 27.01 S | 115.38 E |
| Vinderslev | **41** | 56.15 N | 9.26 E |
| Vinderup | **26** | 56.29 N | 8.47 E |
| Vindhya Range ⋏ | **120** | 23.00 N | 77.00 E |
| Vinding | **41** | 55.41 N | 9.35 E |
| Vindinge | **41** | 55.19 N | 10.45 E |
| Vine Brook ≃ | **283** | 42.27 N | 71.13 W |
| Vinegar Hill ∧ | **202** | 44.43 N | 118.34 W |
| Vine Grove | **194** | 37.48 N | 85.58 W |
| Vine Hill | **282** | 38.00 N | 122.06 W |
| Vineland, Mi., U.S. | **216** | 42.03 N | 86.30 W |
| Vineland, N.J., U.S. | **208** | 39.29 N | 75.01 W |
| Vinemont | **194** | 34.14 N | 86.51 W |
| Vine Valley | **210** | 42.43 N | 77.20 W |
| Vineyard Canyon V | **226** | 35.46 N | 120.41 W |
| Vineyard Haven | **207** | 41.27 N | 70.36 W |
| Vineyard Lake ⊜ | **216** | 42.05 N | 84.13 W |
| Vineyard Sound ⊔ | **207** | 41.25 N | 70.46 W |
| Vingåker | **40** | 59.02 N | 15.52 E |
| Vingeanne ≃ | **58** | 47.21 N | 5.29 E |
| Ving Ngün | **110** | 22.37 N | 99.16 E |
| Vinh | **110** | 18.40 N | 105.40 E |
| Vinhais | **34** | 41.50 N | 7.00 W |
| Vinhas, Ribeira das ≃ | **266c** | 38.42 N | 9.25 W |
| Vinh Chau | **110** | 9.19 N | 105.59 E |
| Vinhedo | **256** | 23.01 S | 46.59 W |
| Vinh Loc | **269c** | 10.49 N | 106.34 E |
| Vinh Long | **110** | 10.15 N | 105.58 E |
| Vinh Tuy, Viet | **110** | 9.37 N | 105.22 E |
| Vinh Tuy, Viet | **110** | 17.24 N | 106.36 E |
| Vinica | **36** | 45.28 N | 15.15 E |
| Vinita | **196** | 36.38 N | 95.09 W |
| Vinkekuil | **158** | 32.42 S | 20.27 E |
| Vinkeveen | **52** | 52.13 N | 4.54 E |
| Vin'kivtsi | **78** | 49.02 N | 27.14 E |
| Vinkovci | **38** | 45.17 N | 18.49 E |
| Vinnhorst | **52** | 52.25 N | 9.43 E |
| Vinnitsa → Vinnytsya | **78** | 49.14 N | 28.29 E |
| Vinnum | **263** | 51.41 N | 7.24 E |
| Vinnytsya | **78** | 49.14 N | 28.29 E |
| Vinnytsya □4 | **78** | 49.00 N | 28.45 E |
| Vinogradovo, Ross. | **82** | 55.25 N | 38.32 E |
| Vinogradovo, Ross. | **82** | 55.57 N | 37.32 E |
| Vinogrobol' | **78** | 51.51 N | 36.26 E |
| Vinön I | **40** | 59.12 N | 15.43 E |
| Vinon-sur-Verdon | **62** | 43.43 N | 5.48 E |
| Vinovo | **62** | 44.57 N | 7.38 E |
| Vinslöv | **26** | 56.06 N | 13.55 E |
| Vinson Massif ∧ | **9** | 78.35 S | 85.25 W |
| Vinstra | **26** | 61.36 N | 9.45 E |
| Vintilă Vodă | **38** | 45.28 N | 26.44 E |
| Vinto | **248** | 17.58 S | 67.04 W |
| Vinton, Ia., U.S. | **190** | 42.10 N | 92.01 W |
| Vinton, La., U.S. | **194** | 30.11 N | 93.34 W |
| Vinton, Va., U.S. | **192** | 37.16 N | 79.53 W |
| Vintondale | **214** | 40.28 N | 78.55 W |
| Vintrosa | **40** | 59.15 N | 14.57 E |
| Viñuelas, Arroyo de ≃ | **266a** | 40.33 N | 3.33 W |
| Viny | **76** | 58.22 N | 32.13 E |
| Vinzelberg | **54** | 52.33 N | 11.40 E |
| Vinzili | **86** | 56.58 N | 65.46 E |
| Viola, Il., U.S. | **190** | 41.12 N | 90.35 W |
| Viola, N.Y., U.S. | **276** | 41.08 N | 74.05 W |
| Viola, Wi., U.S. | **190** | 43.30 N | 90.40 W |
| Viola, Val V | **64** | 46.27 N | 10.15 E |
| Violín, Isla I | **236** | 8.51 N | 83.39 W |
| Viols-le-Fort | **62** | 43.45 N | 3.42 E |
| Viosne ≃ | **50** | 49.03 N | 2.06 E |
| Vipava | **36** | 45.51 N | 13.58 E |
| Vipava ≃ | **64** | 45.54 N | 13.33 E |


(DEUTSCH column heads: Name, Seite, Breite°′, Länge°′ E = Ost)

**Symbols** in the index entries represent the broad categories identified in the key at the right. Symbols with superior numbers (⋏1) identify subcategories (see complete key on page *I · 1)*.

**Symbole** im Register stellen die rechts im Schlüssel erklärten Kategorien dar. Symbole mit hochgestellten Ziffern (⋏1) bezeichnen Unterabteilungen einer Kategorie (vgl. vollständiger Schlüssel auf Seite *I · 1)*.

**Los símbolos** incluídos en el texto del índice representan las grandes categorías identificadas con la clave a la derecha. Los símbolos con numeros en su parte superior (⋏1) identifican las subcategorías (véase la clave completa en la página *I · 1)*.

**Les symboles** de l'index représentent les catégories indiquées dans la légende à droite. Les symboles suivis d'un indice (⋏1) représentent des sous-catégories (voir légende complète à la page *I · 1)*.

**Os símbolos** incluídos no texto do índice representam as grandes categorias identificadas com a chave à direita. Os símbolos com números em sua parte superior (⋏1) identificam as subcategorias (veja-se a chave completa à página *I · 1)*.

| Symbol | English | Deutsch | Español | Français | Português |
| --- | --- | --- | --- | --- | --- |
| ∧ | Mountain | Berg | Montaña | Montagne | Montanha |
| ⋏ | Mountains | Gebirge | Montañas | Montagnes | Montanhas |
| )( | Pass | Paß | Paso | Col | Passo |
| V | Valley, Canyon | Tal, Cañon | Valle, Cañón | Vallée, Canyon | Vale, Canhão |
| ≚ | Plain | Ebene | Llano | Plaine | Planície |
| ≻ | Cape | Kap | Cabo | Cap | Cabo |
| I | Island | Insel | Isla | Île | Ilha |
| II | Islands | Inseln | Islas | Îles | Ilhas |
| ⊥ | Other Topographic Features | Andere Topographische Objekte | Otros Elementos Topográficos | Autres données topographiques | Outros acidentes topográficos |

**ESPAÑOL**

| Nombre | Página | Lat.°′ | Long.°′ W = Oeste |
|---|---|---|---|
| Vipiteno (Sterzing) | 64 | 46.54 N | 11.26 E |
| Vipos | 252 | 26.29 S | 65.22 W |
| Vipperow | 54 | 53.19 N | 12.41 E |
| Vir, Otok I | 36 | 44.18 N | 15.04 E |
| Vira | 58 | 46.08 N | 8.51 E |
| Virac | 116 | 13.35 N | 124.15 E |
| Viracopos, Aeroporto de ⊠ | 256 | 23.00 S | 47.08 W |
| Virac Point › | 116 | 13.31 N | 124.13 E |
| Viradouro | 255 | 20.53 S | 48.18 W |
| Virago Sound ɰ | 182 | 54.00 N | 132.36 W |
| Viramgām | 120 | 23.07 N | 72.02 E |
| Virandozero | 24 | 64.05 N | 35.58 E |
| Viranşehir | 130 | 37.13 N | 39.45 E |
| Vīrarājendrapet | 122 | 12.12 N | 75.48 E |
| Virbalis | 76 | 54.38 N | 22.49 E |
| Virden, Mb., Can. | 184 | 49.51 N | 100.55 W |
| Virden, Il., U.S. | 219 | 39.30 N | 89.46 W |
| Virden, N.M., U.S. | 200 | 32.41 N | 109.00 W |
| Vire | 32 | 48.50 N | 0.53 W |
| Vire ≃ | 32 | 49.20 N | 1.07 W |
| Virelles | 50 | 50.04 N | 4.20 E |
| Virelles, Étang de ⊜ | 50 | 50.04 N | 4.21 E |
| Vireux-Molhain | 56 | 50.05 N | 4.43 E |
| Virgem da Lapa | 255 | 16.49 S | 42.21 W |
| Virgen | 64 | 47.00 N | 12.27 E |
| Vírgen del San Cristóbal ♁[1] | 286e | 33.26 S | 70.39 W |
| Vírgenes, Cabo › | 254 | 52.22 S | 68.20 W |
| Vírgenes, Islas → British Virgin Islands □[2], N.A. | 240m | 18.30 N | 64.30 W |
| Vírgenes, Islas → Virgin Islands □[2], N.A. | 240m | 18.20 N | 64.50 W |
| Virgen Tal V | 64 | 47.00 N | 12.25 E |
| Virgil, On., Can. | 284a | 43.13 N | 79.08 W |
| Virgil, Ks., U.S. | 198 | 37.58 N | 96.00 W |
| Virgil, N.Y., U.S. | 210 | 42.31 N | 76.12 W |
| Virgilina | 192 | 36.33 N | 78.52 W |
| Virgilio | 64 | 45.07 N | 10.47 E |
| Virgin ≃ | 200 | 36.31 N | 114.20 W |
| Virgin, North Fork ≃ | 200 | 37.10 N | 113.01 W |
| Virginal-Samme | 50 | 50.38 N | 4.12 E |
| Virgin Gorda I | 240m | 18.30 N | 64.24 W |
| Virgin Gorda Peak ∧ | 240m | 18.30 N | 64.24 W |
| Virginia, Austl. | 168b | 34.40 S | 138.34 E |
| Virgínia, Bra. | 256 | 22.20 S | 45.06 W |
| Virginia, Ire. | 48 | 53.49 N | 7.04 W |
| Virginia, S. Afr. | 158 | 28.12 S | 26.49 E |
| Virginia, Il., U.S. | 219 | 39.57 N | 90.12 W |
| Virginia, Mn., U.S. | 190 | 47.31 N | 92.32 W |
| Virginia □[3] | 178 | 37.30 N | 78.45 W |
| Virginia Beach | 208 | 36.51 N | 75.58 W |
| Virginia City, Mt., U.S. | 202 | 45.17 N | 111.56 W |
| Virginia City, Nv., U.S. | 226 | 39.18 N | 119.38 W |
| Virginia Creek ≃ | 226 | 38.13 N | 119.14 W |
| Virginia Falls ⌊ | 180 | 61.38 N | 125.42 W |
| Virginia Gardens | 220 | 25.49 N | 80.17 W |
| Virginia Hills | 208 | 38.47 N | 77.06 W |
| Virginia Key I | 220 | 25.44 N | 80.09 W |
| Virginia Peak ∧ | 204 | 39.45 N | 119.28 W |
| Virginia Ranch Reservoir ⊜[1] | 226 | 39.20 N | 121.19 W |
| Virginia Range ⋏ | 226 | 39.18 N | 119.30 W |
| Virginiatown | 190 | 48.08 N | 79.35 W |
| Virginia Water | 260 | 51.24 N | 0.34 W |
| Virginia Water ⊜[1] | 260 | 51.24 N | 0.37 W |
| Virginie occidentale → West Virginia □[3] | 188 | 38.45 N | 80.30 W |
| Virgin Islands □[2], N.A. | 230 | 18.20 N | 64.50 W |
| Virgin Islands □[2], N.A. | 240m | 18.20 N | 64.50 W |
| Virgin Islands II | 240m | 18.00 N | 64.40 W |
| Virgin Islands National Park ♠ | 240m | 18.20 N | 64.45 W |
| Virginópolis | 255 | 18.45 S | 42.45 W |
| Virgin Passage ɰ | 240m | 18.20 N | 65.10 W |
| Virginville | 208 | 40.31 N | 75.52 W |
| Virgolândia | 255 | 18.27 S | 42.18 W |
| Virieu | 62 | 45.29 N | 5.28 E |
| Virieu-le-Grand | 62 | 45.51 N | 5.39 E |
| Virihaure ⊜ | 24 | 67.20 N | 16.35 E |
| Virje | 36 | 46.04 N | 16.59 E |
| Virkkala | 26 | 60.12 N | 24.01 E |
| Virklund | 41 | 56.07 N | 9.34 E |
| Virneburg | 56 | 50.20 N | 7.04 E |
| Virôchey | 110 | 13.59 N | 106.49 E |
| Viroflay | 50 | 48.48 N | 2.10 E |
| Viroin ≃ | 56 | 50.05 N | 4.43 E |
| Virojoki | 26 | 60.35 N | 27.42 E |
| Víron | 267c | 37.57 N | 23.45 E |
| Vironvay | 50 | 49.12 N | 1.13 E |
| Viroqua | 190 | 43.33 N | 90.53 W |
| Virovitica | 36 | 45.50 N | 17.23 E |
| Virpazar | 38 | 42.15 N | 19.05 E |
| Virrat | 26 | 62.14 N | 23.47 E |
| Virsbo | 40 | 59.52 N | 16.02 E |
| Virserum | 26 | 57.19 N | 15.35 E |
| Virtaniemi | 24 | 68.53 N | 28.27 E |
| Virton | 56 | 49.34 N | 5.32 E |
| Virtsu | 76 | 58.34 N | 23.31 E |
| Virú | 248 | 8.25 S | 78.45 W |
| Virudunagar | 122 | 9.36 N | 77.58 E |
| Viru-Jaagupi | 76 | 59.15 N | 26.28 E |
| Virulento | 196 | 28.52 N | 104.21 W |
| Virunga, Parc National de ♠ | 154 | 1.00 S | 29.15 E |
| Virungu | 154 | 7.04 S | 29.46 E |
| Viru-Nigula | 76 | 59.27 N | 26.41 E |
| Virvytė ≃ | 76 | 56.13 N | 22.34 E |
| Viry-Châtillon | 50 | 48.40 N | 2.23 E |
| Vis | 36 | 43.03 N | 16.12 E |
| Vis ≃, Fr. | 62 | 43.56 N | 3.42 E |
| Vis (Fish) ≃, Namibia | 156 | 28.07 S | 17.45 E |
| Vis ≃, S. Afr. | 158 | 30.53 S | 20.23 E |
| Vis, Otok I | 36 | 43.02 N | 16.11 E |
| Visale | 175e | 9.15 S | 159.42 E |
| Visalia | 226 | 36.19 N | 119.17 W |
| Visalia Airport ⊠ | 226 | 36.19 N | 119.23 W |
| Visayan Islands II | 12 | 11.00 N | 123.30 E |
| Visayan Sea ⊤[2] | 116 | 11.35 N | 123.51 E |
| Visbek | 52 | 52.48 N | 8.19 E |
| Visby | 26 | 57.38 N | 18.18 E |
| Viscaya, Bahía de → Biscay, Bay of ⊂ | 32 | 44.00 N | 4.00 W |
| Viscount | 184 | 51.57 N | 105.39 W |
| Viscount Melville Sound ɰ | 176 | 74.10 N | 108.00 W |
| Visé | 56 | 50.44 N | 5.42 E |
| Višegrad | 38 | 43.47 N | 19.17 E |
| Vis-en-Artois | 50 | 50.15 N | 2.56 E |
| Višera ≃ | 76 | 58.34 N | 31.24 E |
| Viserba | 66 | 44.05 N | 12.32 E |
| Viseu, Bra. | 250 | 1.12 S | 46.07 W |
| Viseu, Port. | 34 | 40.39 N | 7.55 W |
| Vişeu ≃ | 38 | 47.55 N | 24.09 E |
| Vişeu de Sus | 38 | 47.44 N | 24.22 E |
| Vishākhapatnam | 122 | 17.42 N | 83.18 E |
| Vishoek | 158 | 34.08 S | 18.26 E |
| Visim | 86 | 57.39 N | 59.30 E |
| Visingsö I | 26 | 58.03 N | 14.20 E |
| Visitation, Île de la I | 275a | 45.35 N | 73.40 W |
| Viskafors | 26 | 57.38 N | 12.50 E |
| Viskan ≃ | 26 | 57.14 N | 12.12 E |
| Viškil' | 80 | 58.05 N | 48.19 E |
| Viskinge | 41 | 55.40 N | 11.16 E |
| Visl'ajevo | 82 | 54.25 N | 36.43 E |
| Vislanda | 26 | 56.47 N | 14.27 E |
| Vislinskij zaliv ⊂ | 30 | 54.27 N | 19.40 E |
| Vismen ⊜ | 40 | 59.17 N | 14.17 E |
| Visnagar | 120 | 23.42 N | 72.33 E |
| Višn'aki | 265b | 55.47 N | 37.54 E |
| Višn'akovo | 82 | 55.45 N | 38.10 E |
| Višneva | 76 | 54.08 N | 26.14 E |
| Višnevoje | 80 | 52.38 N | 43.26 E |

**FRANÇAIS**

| Nom | Page | Lat.°′ | Long.°′ W = Ouest |
|---|---|---|---|
| Višňové | 61 | 48.59 N | 16.09 E |
| Višn'ovka | 86 | 50.49 N | 72.12 E |
| Viso, Monte ∧ | 62 | 44.40 N | 7.07 E |
| Visoki Dečani, Manastir ♁[1] | 38 | 42.30 N | 20.31 E |
| Visoko | 38 | 43.59 N | 18.11 E |
| Visokoi Island I | 18 | 56.42 S | 27.12 W |
| Visp | 58 | 46.18 N | 7.53 E |
| Vispa ≃ | 58 | 46.18 N | 7.52 E |
| Visrivier | 158 | 31.55 S | 25.25 E |
| Vissefjärda | 26 | 56.32 N | 15.35 E |
| Visselhövede | 52 | 52.59 N | 9.35 E |
| Vissenbjerg | 41 | 55.23 N | 10.08 E |
| Visso | 66 | 42.56 N | 13.05 E |
| Vissoie | 58 | 46.13 N | 7.36 E |
| Vista, Ca., U.S. | 228 | 33.12 N | 117.14 W |
| Vista, N.Y., U.S. | 210 | 41.12 N | 73.31 W |
| Vista Alegre, Arg. | 252 | 38.45 S | 68.11 W |
| Vista Alegre, Bra. | 256 | 21.27 S | 42.35 W |
| Vista Alegre, Chile | 286e | 33.30 S | 70.43 W |
| Vista Alegre, Perú | 286d | 12.09 S | 77.00 W |
| Vista Flores | 252 | 33.38 S | 69.09 W |
| Vistahermosa de Negrete | 234 | 20.16 N | 102.29 W |
| Vista Park | 228 | 35.21 N | 118.55 W |
| Vistina | 76 | 59.47 N | 28.29 E |
| Vistre ≃ | 62 | 43.40 N | 4.15 E |
| Vistula → Wisła ≃ | 30 | 54.22 N | 18.55 E |
| Vit ≃ | 38 | 43.41 N | 24.45 E |
| Vita, Mb., Can. | 184 | 49.08 N | 96.34 W |
| Vita, It. | 70 | 37.52 N | 12.49 E |
| Vita ≃ | 246 | 6.11 N | 67.31 W |
| Vitacura | 286e | 33.24 S | 70.36 W |
| Vitali | 116 | 7.22 N | 122.18 E |
| Vitanje | 36 | 46.23 N | 15.18 E |
| Vitarte | 248 | 12.02 S | 76.56 W |
| Vite | 122 | 17.17 N | 74.33 E |
| Vitebsk → Vicebsk | 76 | 55.12 N | 30.11 E |
| Vitebsk Station ◆[5] | 265a | 59.55 N | 30.21 E |
| Vitel, Laguna ⊜ | 258 | 35.32 S | 58.07 W |
| Viterbo | 66 | 42.25 N | 12.06 E |
| Viterbo □[4] | 66 | 42.25 N | 12.05 E |
| Vitiaz Strait ɰ | 164 | 5.50 S | 147.20 E |
| Vitichi | 248 | 20.13 S | 65.29 W |
| Vitigudino | 34 | 41.01 N | 6.26 W |
| Viti Levu I | 175g | 18.00 S | 178.00 E |
| Vitim | 74 | 59.28 N | 112.34 E |
| Vitim ≃ | 74 | 59.26 N | 112.34 E |
| Vitimskij | 88 | 58.14 N | 113.18 E |
| Vitimskoje ploskogorje ⋏[1] | 88 | 54.00 N | 113.30 E |
| Vitinia ◆[8] | 267a | 41.47 N | 12.24 E |
| Vitinja )( | 38 | 42.47 N | 23.49 E |
| Vitis | 61 | 48.45 N | 15.10 E |
| Vítkov | 30 | 49.46 N | 17.45 E |
| Vito | 175e | 6.02 S | 155.24 E |
| Vítor | 248 | 16.26 S | 71.49 W |
| Vitor ≃ | 248 | 16.37 S | 72.19 W |
| Vitória, Bra. | 250 | 2.54 S | 52.01 W |
| Vitória, Bra. | 255 | 20.19 S | 40.21 W |
| Vitoria (Gasteiz), Esp. | 34 | 42.51 N | 2.40 W |
| Vitória, Ilha da I | 256 | 23.45 S | 45.01 W |
| Vitória da Conquista | 255 | 14.51 S | 40.51 W |
| Vitória de Santo Antão | 250 | 8.07 S | 35.18 W |
| Vitória do Mearim | 250 | 3.28 S | 44.53 W |
| Vitorino Freire | 250 | 4.04 S | 45.10 W |
| Vitravo ≃ | 68 | 39.11 N | 17.05 E |
| Vitré | 32 | 48.08 N | 1.12 W |
| Vitrey-sur-Mance | 58 | 47.49 N | 5.45 E |
| Vitry-aux-Loges | 50 | 47.56 N | 2.16 E |
| Vitry-en-Artois | 50 | 50.20 N | 2.59 E |
| Vitry-la-Ville | 50 | 48.50 N | 4.28 E |
| Vitry-le-François | 56 | 48.44 N | 4.35 E |
| Vitry [-sur-Seine] | 50 | 48.48 N | 2.24 E |
| Vitshumbi | 154 | 0.41 S | 29.23 E |
| Vittangi | 24 | 67.41 N | 21.36 E |
| Vitteaux | 58 | 47.24 N | 4.32 E |
| Vittel | 58 | 48.12 N | 5.57 E |
| Vittinge | 40 | 59.54 N | 17.04 E |
| Vittoria, On., Can. | 212 | 42.46 N | 80.19 W |
| Vittoria, It. | 70 | 36.57 N | 14.32 E |
| Vittorio Veneto | 64 | 45.59 N | 12.18 E |
| Vittsjö | 26 | 56.20 N | 13.40 E |
| Vitulano | 68 | 41.10 N | 14.38 E |
| Vitznau | 58 | 47.01 N | 8.29 E |
| Viù | 62 | 45.14 N | 7.22 E |
| Vivarais □[9] | 62 | 44.40 N | 4.30 E |
| Vivarais, Monts du ⋏ | 62 | 44.55 N | 4.15 E |
| Viveiro | 34 | 43.40 N | 7.35 W |
| Viver | 34 | 39.55 N | 0.36 W |
| Viverols | 62 | 45.26 N | 3.53 E |
| Viverone, Lago di ⊜ | 62 | 45.25 N | 8.02 E |
| Vivi ≃ | 74 | 63.52 N | 97.50 E |
| Vivian | 194 | 32.52 N | 93.59 W |
| Viviers | 62 | 44.29 N | 4.41 E |
| Viviers-du-Lac | 62 | 45.39 N | 5.54 E |
| Vivione, Passo del )( | 64 | 46.02 N | 10.12 E |
| Vivonne | 32 | 46.26 N | 0.16 E |
| Vivoratá | 252 | 37.40 S | 57.39 W |
| Vivorillo, Cayos II | 236 | 15.50 N | 83.18 W |
| Viwa I | 175g | 17.08 S | 176.54 E |
| Vizagapatam → Vishākhapatnam | 122 | 17.42 N | 83.18 E |
| Vizcaíno, Desierto de ◆[2] | 232 | 27.40 N | 113.40 W |
| Vizcaíno, Isla I | 258 | 33.47 S | 59.15 W |
| Vize | 130 | 41.34 N | 27.45 E |
| Vize, ostrov I | 72 | 79.30 N | 77.00 E |
| Vizianagaram | 122 | 18.07 N | 83.25 E |
| Vizille | 62 | 45.05 N | 5.46 E |
| Vižinada | 36 | 45.20 N | 13.46 E |
| Vizinga | 24 | 61.05 N | 50.04 E |
| Vizzini | 70 | 37.10 N | 14.53 E |
| Vizzola | 266b | 45.38 N | 8.42 E |
| Vjalikaja Berastavica | 76 | 53.11 N | 24.01 E |
| Vjalikaja Maščanica | 76 | 53.58 N | 29.37 E |
| Vjaliki Bor | 78 | 52.02 N | 29.56 E |
| Vjalikija Aucjuki | 78 | 52.04 N | 29.32 E |
| Vjalikija Radvaničy | 76 | 52.02 N | 24.02 E |
| Vjaseja | 76 | 53.04 N | 27.41 E |
| Vjatčyn | 76 | 52.27 N | 28.10 E |
| Vjazyn' | 76 | 54.25 N | 27.10 E |
| Vjulka ≃ | 82 | 56.53 N | 37.57 E |
| Vjunka ≃ | 265b | 55.42 N | 38.01 E |
| Vjuny | 86 | 55.31 N | 82.55 E |
| Vlaanderen → Flanders □[9] | 50 | 51.00 N | 3.00 E |
| Vlaardingen | 52 | 51.54 N | 4.21 E |
| Vlachovo Březí | 60 | 49.05 N | 13.57 E |
| Vladař ∧ | 54 | 50.05 N | 13.14 E |
| Vlădeasa, Vârful ∧ | 38 | 46.45 N | 22.48 E |
| Vlădeni | 38 | 47.25 N | 27.20 E |
| Vladičin Han | 38 | 42.42 N | 22.04 E |
| Vladikavkaz | 84 | 43.03 N | 44.40 E |
| Vladimir | 80 | 56.10 N | 40.25 E |
| Vladimir Oblast' □[4] | 76 | 56.00 N | 40.30 E |
| Vladimirovka, Kaz. | 80 | 50.51 N | 51.08 E |
| Vladimirovka, Kaz. | 86 | 53.28 N | 64.02 E |
| Vladimirskij Tupik | 76 | 55.42 N | 33.18 E |
| Vladimirskoje | 80 | 56.49 N | 45.07 E |
| Vladivostok | 89 | 43.10 N | 131.56 E |
| Vladyčnoje | 76 | 58.49 N | 39.29 E |
| Vladykino ◆[8] | 265b | 55.52 N | 37.36 E |
| Vlasenica | 38 | 44.11 N | 18.56 E |
| Vlašim | 30 | 49.42 N | 14.54 E |
| Vlaskovo | 82 | 56.11 N | 36.31 E |
| Vlasotince | 38 | 42.58 N | 22.08 E |
| Vlasovo, Ross. | 74 | 70.48 N | 135.00 E |
| Vlasovo, Ross. | 82 | 56.38 N | 38.14 E |
| Vlazoviči | 76 | 53.01 N | 32.18 E |
| Vledder | 52 | 52.52 N | 6.12 E |
| Vleesbaai ⊂ | 158 | 34.16 S | 21.57 E |
| Vleikolk | 158 | 29.43 S | 20.50 E |
| Vleuten | 52 | 52.05 N | 5.02 E |
| Vlieland I | 52 | 53.15 N | 5.00 E |
| Vlijmen | 52 | 51.42 N | 5.15 E |
| Vlissingen (Flushing) | 52 | 51.26 N | 3.35 E |

**PORTUGUÊS**

| Nome | Página | Lat.°′ | Long.°′ W = Oeste |
|---|---|---|---|
| Vlodrop | 52 | 51.08 N | 6.05 E |
| Vloesberg → Flobecq | 50 | 50.44 N | 3.44 E |
| Vlonë → Vlorë | 38 | 40.27 N | 19.30 E |
| Vlorë | 38 | 40.27 N | 19.30 E |
| Vlorës, Gji i ⊂ | 38 | 40.25 N | 19.25 E |
| Vlotho | 52 | 52.10 N | 8.51 E |
| Vltava ≃ | 30 | 50.21 N | 14.30 E |
| Vnukovo | 82 | 55.38 N | 37.16 E |
| Vnukovo Airport ⊠ | 265b | 55.37 N | 37.17 E |
| Voca | 196 | 31.01 N | 99.11 W |
| Vochrinka | 82 | 55.24 N | 38.18 E |
| Vochtoga | 76 | 58.47 N | 41.07 E |
| Vočin | 36 | 45.37 N | 17.32 E |
| Vockerode | 54 | 51.51 N | 12.21 E |
| Vöckla ≃ | 64 | 48.00 N | 13.36 E |
| Vöcklabruck | 60 | 48.01 N | 13.39 E |
| Vöcklamarkt | 60 | 48.00 N | 13.29 E |
| Vodla ≃ | 24 | 61.49 N | 36.00 E |
| Vodlozero, ozero ⊜ | 24 | 62.20 N | 36.55 E |
| Vodňany | 30 | 49.09 N | 14.11 E |
| Vodnjan | 36 | 44.57 N | 13.51 E |
| Vodnyj | 24 | 63.32 N | 53.18 E |
| Vodo | 64 | 46.25 N | 12.14 E |
| Vodosalma | 24 | 64.29 N | 30.44 E |
| Vodovatovo | 80 | 55.24 N | 43.34 E |
| Vodzimonje | 80 | 56.49 N | 51.38 E |
| Voël ≃ | 158 | 33.07 S | 25.07 E |
| Voerde, Dtsch. | 52 | 51.35 N | 6.41 E |
| Voerde, Dtsch. | 263 | 51.18 N | 7.24 E |
| Vogelenzang | 52 | 52.19 N | 4.35 E |
| Vogelheim ◆[8] | 263 | 51.29 N | 6.59 E |
| Vogelkop → Doberai, Jazirah ›[1] | 164 | 1.30 S | 132.30 E |
| Vogel Peak → Dimlang ∧ | 146 | 8.24 N | 11.47 E |
| Vogelsang, Dtsch. | 54 | 53.43 N | 14.09 E |
| Vogelsang, Dtsch. | 56 | 50.35 N | 6.27 E |
| Vogelsberg ⋏ | 56 | 50.30 N | 9.15 E |
| Vogesen → Vosges ⋏ | 58 | 48.30 N | 7.10 E |
| Voghera | 62 | 44.59 N | 9.01 E |
| Vognema | 76 | 59.59 N | 38.10 E |
| Vogogna | 58 | 46.01 N | 8.17 E |
| Vogt | 58 | 47.47 N | 9.46 E |
| Vogtland ◆[1] | 54 | 50.30 N | 12.05 E |
| Vogtsburg | 58 | 48.05 N | 7.38 E |
| Voh | 175f | 20.58 S | 164.42 E |
| Vohburg an der Donau | 60 | 48.46 N | 11.37 E |
| Vohenstrauss | 60 | 49.37 N | 12.21 E |
| Vohibinany | 157b | 18.49 S | 49.04 E |
| Vohilava | 157b | 21.04 S | 48.00 E |
| Vohimarina | 157b | 13.21 S | 50.02 E |
| Vohipeno | 157b | 22.22 S | 47.51 E |
| Vohitsora | 157b | 23.54 S | 44.17 E |
| Vöhl | 56 | 51.12 N | 8.57 E |
| Võhma | 76 | 58.38 N | 25.33 E |
| Vöhrenbach | 58 | 48.02 N | 8.18 E |
| Vöhringen, Dtsch. | 58 | 48.16 N | 10.04 E |
| Vöhringen, Dtsch. | 58 | 48.20 N | 8.40 E |
| Vöhrum | 52 | 52.20 N | 10.10 E |
| Vohwinkel ◆[8] | 263 | 51.14 N | 7.09 E |
| Voi | 154 | 3.23 S | 38.34 E |
| Void | 58 | 48.41 N | 5.37 E |
| Voight Creek ≃ | 224 | 47.06 N | 122.10 W |
| Voikkaa | 26 | 60.56 N | 26.37 E |
| Voineşti | 38 | 47.05 N | 27.26 E |
| Voinjama | 150 | 8.25 N | 9.45 W |
| Voire ≃ | 58 | 48.27 N | 4.25 E |
| Voiron | 62 | 45.22 N | 5.35 E |
| Voise | 50 | 48.24 N | 1.43 E |
| Voise ≃ | 50 | 48.35 N | 1.35 E |
| Voisenon | 261 | 48.34 N | 2.40 E |
| Voisins-le-Bretonneux | 50 | 48.45 N | 2.03 E |
| Voiteur | 58 | 46.45 N | 5.37 E |
| Voitsberg | 61 | 47.03 N | 15.10 E |
| Voja ≃ | 80 | 57.23 N | 49.55 E |
| Vojens | 41 | 55.15 N | 9.19 E |
| Vojevodskoje | 86 | 52.47 N | 85.35 E |
| Vojkovice | 54 | 50.15 N | 13.02 E |
| Vojmsjön ⊜ | 26 | 64.55 N | 16.40 E |
| Vojnić | 36 | 45.19 N | 15.42 E |
| Vojnica | 24 | 65.12 N | 30.15 E |
| Vojtanov | 54 | 50.06 N | 12.19 E |
| Vojvodina □[4] | 38 | 45.00 N | 20.00 E |
| Voj-Vož, Ross. | 24 | 64.20 N | 55.03 E |
| Voj-Vož, Ross. | 24 | 62.56 N | 54.56 E |
| Vokeo Island I | 164 | 3.10 S | 144.05 E |
| Volano | 66 | 44.48 N | 12.15 E |
| Volant | 214 | 41.07 N | 80.16 W |
| Volary | 60 | 48.55 N | 13.54 E |
| Volcán, Arg. | 252 | 23.54 S | 65.27 W |
| Volcán, Pan. | 236 | 8.46 N | 82.38 W |
| Volcán Isluga, Parque Nacional ♠ | 248 | 19.30 S | 68.30 W |
| Volčanka | 80 | 52.33 N | 49.59 E |
| Volcano, Ca., U.S. | 226 | 38.26 N | 120.37 W |
| Volcano, Hi., U.S. | 229d | 19.25 N | 155.14 W |
| Volcano Island I | 116 | 14.00 N | 121.00 E |
| Volcano Islands → Kazan-rettō II | 14 | 25.00 N | 141.00 E |
| Volcán Poás, Parque Nacional ♠ | 236 | 10.10 N | 84.15 W |
| Volčansk | 86 | 59.56 N | 60.04 E |
| Volčenskij | 83 | 48.14 N | 40.07 E |
| Volchonka-Zil ◆[8] | 265b | 55.40 N | 37.37 E |
| Volchov | 76 | 59.55 N | 32.20 E |
| Volchov ≃ | 76 | 60.08 N | 32.20 E |
| Volčicha | 86 | 52.02 N | 80.23 E |
| Volčij Nos, mys › | 76 | 60.31 N | 32.35 E |
| Volčki | 80 | 52.29 N | 40.42 E |
| Volda | 26 | 62.09 N | 6.06 E |
| Volders | 64 | 47.17 N | 11.34 E |
| Volendam | 52 | 52.30 N | 5.04 E |
| Volga, Ross. | 76 | 57.57 N | 38.24 E |
| Volga, Ia., U.S. | 190 | 42.48 N | 91.32 W |
| Volga, S.D., U.S. | 198 | 44.19 N | 96.55 W |
| Volga ≃, Ross. | 72 | 45.55 N | 47.52 E |
| Volga ≃, Ia., U.S. | 190 | 42.45 N | 91.17 W |
| Volga-Baltic Canal → Volgo-Baltijskij kanal ≊ | 24 | 59.00 N | 38.00 E |
| Volgino | 76 | 58.27 N | 33.52 E |
| Volgo, ozero ⊜ | 76 | 56.55 N | 33.10 E |
| Volgo-Baltijskij kanal ≊ | 24 | 59.00 N | 38.00 E |
| Volgodonsk | 80 | 47.33 N | 42.08 E |
| Volgo-Donskoj sudochodnyj kanal imeni V.I. Lenina ≊ | 80 | 48.40 N | 43.37 E |
| Volgograd (Stalingrad) | 80 | 48.44 N | 44.25 E |
| Volgograd Oblast' □[4] | 80 | 49.30 N | 44.00 E |
| Volgogradskoje vodochranilišče ⊜[1] | 80 | 49.20 N | 45.00 E |
| Volgorečensk | 76 | 57.30 N | 41.02 E |
| Volintiri | 38 | 46.26 N | 29.37 E |
| Volissós | 38 | 38.29 N | 25.58 E |
| Volkach | 56 | 49.52 N | 10.13 E |
| Volkel | 52 | 51.38 N | 5.40 E |
| Völkermarkt | 61 | 46.39 N | 14.38 E |
| Völkermarkter Stausee ⊜[1] | 61 | 46.39 N | 14.38 E |
| Völkerschlacht-Denkmal ⊥ | 54 | 51.18 N | 12.24 E |
| Völklingen | 56 | 49.15 N | 6.50 E |
| Volkmarsen | 56 | 51.24 N | 9.07 E |
| Volkovo, Ross. | 76 | 59.15 N | 41.27 E |
| Volkovo, Ross. | 82 | 55.46 N | 36.15 E |
| Volkovo Cemetery ◆ | 265a | 59.54 N | 30.22 E |
| Volkovskoje | 82 | 54.49 N | 37.13 E |
| Volksdorf ◆[8] | 52 | 53.39 N | 10.10 E |
| Völksen | 52 | 52.13 N | 9.37 E |
| Volksrust | 158 | 27.24 S | 29.53 E |
| Vollenhove | 52 | 52.41 N | 5.58 E |
| Vollersode | 52 | 53.18 N | 8.56 E |
| Vollme | 263 | 51.10 N | 7.36 E |

| | | | |
|---|---|---|---|
| Vollore-Montagne | 62 | 45.47 N | 3.41 E |
| Vollore-Ville | 62 | 45.47 N | 3.36 E |
| Vollsjö | 41 | 55.42 N | 13.46 E |
| Volma ≃ | 76 | 53.35 N | 28.19 E |
| Volmarstein | 56 | 51.22 N | 7.23 E |
| Volme ≃ | 263 | 51.24 N | 7.27 E |
| Volmerange-les-Mines | 56 | 49.27 N | 6.05 E |
| Volmerswerth ◆[8] | 263 | 51.11 N | 6.46 E |
| Volmunster | 56 | 49.07 N | 7.21 E |
| Vol'naja Gorka | 76 | 58.43 N | 30.51 E |
| Volnay | 58 | 47.00 N | 4.47 E |
| Vol'noje, Ross. | 80 | 47.09 N | 47.38 E |
| Vol'noje, Ross. | 86 | 54.17 N | 71.21 E |
| Volnovakha | 83 | 47.36 N | 37.31 E |
| Vol'nyj | 80 | 45.55 N | 45.14 E |
| Vol'nyj, ostrov I | 265a | 59.58 N | 30.14 E |
| Voločajevka Vtoraja | 89 | 48.34 N | 134.34 E |
| Voločanka | 74 | 71.00 N | 94.28 E |
| Volochys'k | 78 | 49.32 N | 26.11 E |
| Volockaja | 76 | 60.17 N | 42.59 E |
| Volodarka, Ross. | 86 | 52.43 N | 83.38 E |
| Volodarka, Ukr. | 78 | 49.31 N | 29.55 E |
| Volodarsk, Ross. | 76 | 56.13 N | 43.10 E |
| Volodars'k, Ukr. | 83 | 48.06 N | 39.35 E |
| Volodars'ke | 83 | 47.12 N | 37.20 E |
| Volodarskij, Ross. | 80 | 46.24 N | 48.32 E |
| Volodarskij, Ross. | 82 | 55.30 N | 37.57 E |
| Volodarskij ◆[8] | 265a | 59.49 N | 30.05 E |
| Volodarskoje | 86 | 53.18 N | 68.08 E |
| Volodars'k-Volyns'kyy | 78 | 50.37 N | 28.25 E |
| Volodino | 86 | 57.06 N | 83.54 E |
| Volodymyrets' | 78 | 51.25 N | 26.08 E |
| Volodymyrivka, Ukr. | 78 | 47.32 N | 32.55 E |
| Volodymyrivka, Ukr. | 83 | 47.44 N | 37.23 E |
| Volodymyr-Volyns'kyy | 78 | 50.51 N | 24.20 E |
| Vologda | 76 | 59.12 N | 39.55 E |
| Vologda ≃ | 76 | 59.17 N | 40.13 E |
| Vologda Oblast' □[4] | 24 | 60.00 N | 40.00 E |
| Voloje | 76 | 54.09 N | 34.35 E |
| Volokolamsk | 82 | 56.02 N | 35.57 E |
| Volokonovka | 78 | 50.29 N | 37.51 E |
| Volokovaja | 24 | 66.28 N | 48.10 E |
| Volonga | 24 | 67.07 N | 47.41 E |
| Volonne | 62 | 44.07 N | 6.01 E |
| Vólos | 38 | 39.21 N | 22.56 E |
| Vološino, Ross. | 83 | 48.55 N | 39.56 E |
| Vološino, Ross. | 83 | 47.31 N | 39.40 E |
| Vološka | 24 | 61.20 N | 40.06 E |
| Volos'ka Balakliya | 83 | 49.37 N | 37.20 E |
| Vološn'a ≃ | 82 | 55.51 N | 35.54 E |
| Vološno | 76 | 58.29 N | 28.29 E |
| Volosovo | 76 | 59.26 N | 29.29 E |
| Volot | 76 | 57.56 N | 30.42 E |
| Volovets' | 78 | 48.43 N | 23.11 E |
| Volovo, Ross. | 76 | 53.35 N | 38.02 E |
| Volovo, Ross. | 78 | 52.03 N | 37.53 E |
| Volpago del Montello | 64 | 45.47 N | 12.07 E |
| Volpedo | 62 | 44.53 N | 8.59 E |
| Volpiano | 62 | 45.12 N | 7.46 E |
| Völpke | 54 | 52.08 N | 11.09 E |
| Völs → Fiè | 64 | 46.31 N | 11.30 E |
| Volsini, Monti ⋏ | 66 | 42.40 N | 11.55 E |
| Vol'sk | 80 | 52.02 N | 47.23 E |
| Volstruisleegte | 158 | 33.05 S | 23.28 E |
| Volta □[4] | 150 | 7.00 N | 0.30 E |
| Volta ≃ | 150 | 5.46 N | 0.41 E |
| Volta, Lake ⊜[1] | 150 | 7.30 N | 0.15 E |
| Volta Blanche (White Volta) ≃ | 150 | 9.10 N | 1.15 W |
| Voltaggio | 62 | 44.37 N | 8.50 E |
| Voltago | 64 | 46.16 N | 12.00 E |
| Volta Grande | 256 | 21.46 S | 42.32 W |
| Voltaire, Cape › | 164 | 14.16 S | 125.35 E |
| Volta Mantovana | 64 | 45.19 N | 10.39 E |
| Volta Noire (Black Volta) ≃ | 150 | 8.41 N | 1.33 W |
| Volta Redonda | 256 | 22.32 S | 44.07 W |
| Volta Rouge ≃ | 150 | 10.34 N | 0.30 W |
| Volterra | 66 | 43.24 N | 10.51 E |
| Vol'teva | 24 | 64.30 N | 44.12 E |
| Voltri | 62 | 44.26 N | 8.45 E |
| Volturara Appula | 68 | 41.30 N | 15.03 E |
| Volturara Irpina | 68 | 40.53 N | 14.55 E |
| Volturino | 68 | 41.28 N | 15.07 E |
| Volturino, Monte ∧ | 68 | 40.25 N | 15.49 E |
| Volturno ≃ | 66 | 41.01 N | 13.55 E |
| Volubilis ⊥ | 148 | 34.00 N | 5.30 W |
| Voluntown | 207 | 41.34 N | 71.52 W |
| Volusia □[6] | 220 | 28.51 N | 81.05 W |
| Vólvi, Límni ⊜ | 38 | 40.41 N | 23.23 E |
| Volx | 62 | 43.53 N | 5.51 E |
| Volyn' □[4] | 78 | 51.00 N | 25.00 E |
| Volyn' □[9] | 78 | 50.50 N | 27.00 E |
| Volyncy | 80 | 57.48 N | 45.28 E |
| Volyně | 60 | 49.10 N | 13.53 E |
| Volynka | 78 | 51.37 N | 32.26 E |
| Volyňka ≃ | 60 | 49.16 N | 13.54 E |
| Volyns'ka vysochyna ⋏[1] | 78 | 50.30 N | 25.30 E |
| Volzhskiy → Volžskij | 80 | 48.50 N | 44.44 E |
| Volžsk | 80 | 55.53 N | 48.21 E |
| Volžskij, Ross. | 80 | 53.27 N | 50.07 E |
| Volžskij, Ross. | 80 | 48.50 N | 44.44 E |
| Vom | 150 | 9.41 N | 8.42 E |
| Vomano ≃ | 66 | 42.39 N | 14.02 E |
| Vombsjön ⊜ | 41 | 55.41 N | 13.36 E |
| Vomp | 64 | 47.20 N | 11.41 E |
| Vonavona Island I | 175e | 8.15 S | 157.05 E |
| Vonda | 184 | 52.19 N | 106.06 W |
| Vondanka | 24 | 59.07 N | 47.49 E |
| Vondrozo | 157b | 22.49 S | 47.20 E |
| Von Frank Mountain ∧ | 180 | 63.33 N | 154.20 W |
| Võnnu | 76 | 58.17 N | 27.05 E |
| Vonozero | 76 | 60.22 N | 34.26 E |
| Vonsild | 41 | 55.27 N | 9.29 E |
| Von Treuer Tableland ⋏[1] | 162 | 26.38 S | 122.53 E |
| Voorburg | 52 | 52.05 N | 4.23 E |
| Voordeelspan | 158 | 29.05 S | 21.32 E |
| Voorheesville | 210 | 42.39 N | 73.56 W |
| Voorne I | 52 | 51.54 N | 4.08 E |
| Voorschoten | 52 | 52.07 N | 4.27 E |
| Voorst | 52 | 52.10 N | 6.09 E |
| Voorthuizen | 52 | 52.12 N | 5.35 E |
| Vop' ≃ | 76 | 54.56 N | 32.44 E |
| Vopnafjörður | 24a | 65.47 N | 14.44 W |
| Vopnafjörður ⊂ | 24a | 65.52 N | 14.40 W |
| Vörå (Vöyri) | 26 | 63.09 N | 22.15 E |
| Vor'a ≃, Ross. | 76 | 54.54 N | 35.01 E |
| Vor'a ≃, Ross. | 82 | 55.52 N | 38.13 E |
| Voranava | 76 | 54.09 N | 25.19 E |
| Vorarlberg □[3] | 58 | 47.15 N | 9.55 E |
| Vorau | 61 | 47.25 N | 15.54 E |
| Vorbasse | 41 | 55.38 N | 9.05 E |
| Vorbjovo | 88 | 57.23 N | 102.18 E |
| Vorchdorf | 60 | 48.00 N | 13.55 E |
| Vörden, Dtsch. | 52 | 52.28 N | 8.05 E |
| Vorden, Ned. | 52 | 52.07 N | 6.18 E |
| Vorder-Grauspitz ∧ | 58 | 47.03 N | 9.36 E |
| Vorderkrimml | 64 | 47.14 N | 12.12 E |
| Vordernberg | 61 | 47.28 N | 15.00 E |
| Vorderrhein ≃ | 58 | 46.49 N | 9.25 E |
| Vorderriss | 64 | 47.33 N | 11.26 E |
| Vordingborg | 41 | 55.01 N | 11.55 E |
| Voreifel ⋏ | 56 | 50.15 N | 7.10 E |
| Vóreion Aiyaíon □[4] | 38 | 38.30 N | 26.00 E |
| Voreppe | 62 | 45.18 N | 5.38 E |
| Vorey | 62 | 45.11 N | 3.54 E |
| Vorga | 76 | 53.45 N | 32.45 E |
| Vorhalle ◆[8] | 263 | 51.23 N | 7.28 E |
| Vorhelm | 52 | 51.48 N | 7.56 E |
| Vøringsfossen ⌊ | 26 | 60.26 N | 7.15 E |
| Vórioi Sporádhes II | 38 | 39.15 N | 23.55 E |
| Vórios Evvoïkós Kólpos ⊂ | 38 | 38.40 N | 23.15 E |
| Vorkuta | 24 | 67.27 N | 63.58 E |
| Vorlich, Ben ∧, Scot., U.K. | 46 | 56.20 N | 4.14 W |
| Vorlich, Ben ∧, Scot., U.K. | 46 | 56.17 N | 4.46 W |
| Vorma ≃ | 26 | 60.09 N | 11.27 E |
| Vormholz | 263 | 51.24 N | 7.18 E |
| Vormsi I | 76 | 59.00 N | 23.20 E |
| Vorobjevo, Ross. | 82 | 56.11 N | 35.45 E |
| Vorobjevo, Ross. | 86 | 56.08 N | 76.32 E |
| Vorobji | 82 | 55.09 N | 36.48 E |
| Vorobjovka | 80 | 50.38 N | 40.56 E |
| Vorob'jovo | 76 | 59.38 N | 40.55 E |
| Vorobyove | 78 | 45.20 N | 33.15 E |
| Vorokhta | 78 | 48.18 N | 24.36 E |
| Voron, porog ⌊ | 88 | 57.05 N | 98.40 E |
| Vorona ≃ | 80 | 51.22 N | 42.03 E |
| Voroncov | 38 | 47.43 N | 29.08 E |
| Voroncovka, Kaz. | 86 | 48.49 N | 81.32 E |
| Voroncovka, Ross. | 78 | 50.37 N | 40.21 E |
| Voroncovka, Ross. | 86 | 59.39 N | 60.14 E |
| Voroncovka, Ross. | 88 | 58.51 N | 112.56 E |
| Voroncovo, Ross. | 76 | 57.18 N | 28.42 E |
| Voroncovo, Ross. | 80 | 55.16 N | 40.27 E |
| Voronej → Voronež | 78 | 51.40 N | 39.10 E |
| Voronež | 78 | 51.40 N | 39.10 E |
| Voronež ≃ | 76 | 51.56 N | 39.25 E |
| Voronezh → Voronež | 78 | 51.40 N | 39.10 E |
| Voronež Oblast' □[4] | 78 | 51.00 N | 40.00 E |
| Voronežskij zapovednik ◆[4] | 76 | 51.56 N | 39.37 E |
| Voronino | 82 | 56.24 N | 36.52 E |
| Voronizh | 78 | 51.46 N | 33.28 E |
| Voronja ≃ | 24 | 69.10 N | 35.50 E |
| Voronjo, Ross. | 24 | 68.27 N | 35.21 E |
| Voronjo, Ross. | 80 | 58.00 N | 42.01 E |
| Voronki | 82 | 55.48 N | 37.16 E |
| Voron'ky | 78 | 50.14 N | 33.02 E |
| Voronok | 76 | 52.23 N | 32.40 E |
| Voronov, mys › | 76 | 60.15 N | 32.05 E |
| Voronovkova Niva | 76 | 57.04 N | 29.16 E |
| Voronovo, Ross. | 82 | 55.19 N | 37.10 E |
| Voronovo, Ross. | 86 | 56.01 N | 83.52 E |
| Voronovytsya | 78 | 49.06 N | 28.41 E |
| Vorontsivka | 78 | 45.51 N | 33.47 E |
| Voroshilov → Ussurijsk | 89 | 43.48 N | 131.59 E |
| Voroshilovsk → Stavropol' | 72 | 45.02 N | 41.59 E |
| Vorošilovgrad → Luhans'k | 83 | 48.34 N | 39.20 E |
| Vorotajevka | 80 | 51.56 N | 47.16 E |
| Vorotynec | 80 | 56.04 N | 45.52 E |
| Vorotynsk | 82 | 54.25 N | 36.05 E |
| Vorovskolesskaja | 84 | 44.23 N | 42.25 E |
| Vorožejka | 86 | 58.12 N | 90.02 E |
| Vorozhba | 78 | 51.12 N | 34.14 E |
| Vorpommern □[9] | 54 | 53.40 N | 13.45 E |
| Vorra | 60 | 49.33 N | 11.30 E |
| Vorsfelde | 54 | 52.26 N | 10.49 E |
| Vorskla ≃ | 78 | 48.53 N | 34.06 E |
| Vorsma | 80 | 55.59 N | 43.16 E |
| Vorst, Bel. | 56 | 51.04 N | 5.01 E |
| Vorst, Dtsch. | 56 | 51.18 N | 6.25 E |
| Vørterkaka Nunatak ∧ | 9 | 72.20 S | 27.29 E |
| Võrtsjärv ⊜ | 76 | 58.16 N | 26.03 E |
| Võru | 76 | 57.50 N | 27.01 E |
| Voruch | 85 | 39.52 N | 70.35 E |
| Vorzel' | 78 | 50.33 N | 30.09 E |
| Vosburg | 158 | 30.33 S | 22.52 E |
| Voschod | 80 | 47.24 N | 41.50 E |
| Vösendorf | 61 | 48.07 N | 16.20 E |
| Vosges □[5] | 58 | 48.10 N | 6.20 E |
| Vosges ⋏ | 58 | 48.30 N | 7.10 E |
| Vosja | 76 | 59.01 N | 41.11 E |
| Voskresenka, Ross. | 80 | 51.01 N | 46.28 E |
| Voskresenka, Ross. | 88 | 53.15 N | 119.31 E |
| Voskresenki | 82 | 54.57 N | 38.04 E |
| Voskresenovskoje | 265a | 59.43 N | 30.47 E |
| Voskresensk | 82 | 55.19 N | 38.42 E |
| Voskresens'ke | 78 | 47.02 N | 32.09 E |
| Voskresenskoje, Ross. | 76 | 53.12 N | 38.43 E |
| Voskresenskoje, Ross. | 76 | 58.54 N | 38.36 E |
| Voskresenskoje, Ross. | 76 | 59.26 N | 37.56 E |
| Voskresenskoje, Ross. | 76 | 57.49 N | 37.40 E |
| Voskresenskoje, Ross. | 80 | 56.51 N | 45.26 E |
| Voskresenskoje, Ross. | 80 | 51.51 N | 46.56 E |
| Voskresenskoje, Ross. | 82 | 54.07 N | 37.07 E |
| Voskresenskoje, Ross. | 82 | 56.20 N | 38.29 E |
| Voskresenskoje, Ross. | 86 | 53.08 N | 56.10 E |
| Voslapp | 52 | 53.36 N | 8.05 E |
| Voss | 26 | 60.39 N | 6.26 E |
| Vosselaar | 56 | 51.19 N | 4.53 E |
| Vossman's Beacon | 158 | 26.11 S | 30.40 E |
| Vostočnaja Kambal'nica | 24 | 68.18 N | 46.00 E |
| Vostočno-Kazachstan □[8] | 86 | 49.00 N | 84.00 E |
| Vostočno-Kounradskij | 86 | 47.02 N | 75.07 E |
| Vostočno-Sibirskoje more (East Siberian Sea) ⊤[2] | 12 | 74.00 N | 166.00 E |
| Vostočnyj, Ross. | 82 | 55.47 N | 37.52 E |
| Vostočnyj, Ross. | 86 | 58.48 N | 61.52 E |
| Vostočnyj, Ross. | 89 | 53.29 N | 143.03 E |
| Vostočnyj, Ross. | 89 | 48.17 N | 142.34 E |
| Vostočnyj Sajan ⋏ | 88 | 53.00 N | 97.00 E |
| Vostok I | 14 | 10.06 S | 152.23 W |
| Vostr'akovo | 82 | 55.23 N | 37.49 E |
| Vostrecovo | 89 | 45.53 N | 134.58 E |
| Vostrovo | 86 | 52.09 N | 80.38 E |
| Vosves | 261 | 48.31 N | 2.36 E |
| Votaw | 222 | 30.26 N | 94.41 W |
| Votice | 30 | 49.38 N | 14.39 E |
| Votkinsk | 80 | 57.03 N | 53.59 E |
| Votkinskoje vodochranilišče ⊜[1] | 86 | 57.00 N | 54.30 E |
| Vot'pa | 86 | 60.13 N | 62.57 E |
| Votuporanga | 255 | 20.24 S | 49.59 W |
| Voué | 50 | 48.28 N | 4.07 E |
| Vouga ≃ | 34 | 40.41 N | 8.40 W |
| Vougba | 152 | 5.10 N | 23.06 E |
| Vougeot | 58 | 47.10 N | 4.58 E |
| Vouillé | 32 | 46.39 N | 0.10 E |
| Voujeaucourt | 58 | 47.28 N | 6.46 E |
| Voulangis | 261 | 48.51 N | 2.54 E |
| Voulou | 146 | 8.33 N | 22.36 E |
| Voulx | 50 | 48.17 N | 2.58 E |
| Voulzie ≃ | 50 | 48.25 N | 3.12 E |
| Voutenay-sur-Cure | 50 | 47.33 N | 3.47 E |
| Vouvray | 50 | 47.25 N | 0.48 E |
| Vouvry | 58 | 46.20 N | 6.53 E |
| Vouziers | 56 | 49.24 N | 4.42 E |
| Vovcha ≃ | 78 | 48.00 N | 36.08 E |
| Vovchans'k | 78 | 50.18 N | 36.57 E |
| Vovchoyarivka | 83 | 48.50 N | 38.22 E |
| Voves | 50 | 48.16 N | 1.38 E |
| Vovkovyntsi | 78 | 49.13 N | 27.39 E |
| Vovodo ≃ | 140 | 5.40 N | 24.21 E |
| Vowinckel | 214 | 41.25 N | 79.14 W |
| Voxnan ≃ | 26 | 61.17 N | 16.26 E |
| Voyageurs National Park ♠ | 190 | 48.30 N | 93.00 W |
| Voyinka | 78 | 45.52 N | 33.59 E |
| Voykove | 78 | 45.31 N | 33.52 E |
| Voykovs'kyy | 83 | 47.46 N | 38.20 E |
| Voynyliv | 78 | 49.06 N | 24.30 E |
| Vöyri → Vörå | 26 | 63.09 N | 22.15 E |
| Voža ≃ | 82 | 54.38 N | 39.10 E |
| Vožajol' | 24 | 62.50 N | 51.17 E |
| Vožd' Proletariata | 76 | 55.26 N | 39.19 E |
| Vozdviženka | 80 | 53.10 N | 54.14 E |
| Vozdviženskoje, Ross. | 80 | 56.58 N | 45.37 E |
| Vozdviženskoje, Ross. | 80 | 45.50 N | 43.40 E |
| Vozdviženskoje, Ross. | 82 | 56.12 N | 38.04 E |
| Vozdvyzhivka | 78 | 47.46 N | 36.05 E |
| Vože, ozero ⊜ | 24 | 60.30 N | 39.00 E |
| Vožega | 76 | 60.29 N | 40.12 E |
| Vožega ≃ | 76 | 60.33 N | 39.11 E |
| Vožgaly | 80 | 58.09 N | 50.11 E |
| Vožgora | 24 | 64.32 N | 48.25 E |
| Voznesenje | 24 | 61.01 N | 35.27 E |
| Voznesenka, Kaz. | 86 | 52.24 N | 70.12 E |
| Voznesenka, Ukr. | 78 | 46.51 N | 35.26 E |
| Voznesenovka | 80 | 46.16 N | 44.21 E |
| Voznesens'k | 78 | 47.34 N | 31.20 E |
| Voznesenskoje, Ross. | 80 | 54.54 N | 42.46 E |
| Voznesenskoje, Ross. | 80 | 45.49 N | 43.25 E |
| Vozroždenija, ostrov I | 86 | 45.03 N | 59.12 E |
| Vozroždenije | 80 | 52.42 N | 48.12 E |
| Vozsiyats'ke | 78 | 47.41 N | 32.07 E |
| Vozžajevka | 89 | 50.44 N | 128.41 E |
| Vrå | 26 | 57.21 N | 9.57 E |
| Vráble | 30 | 48.15 N | 18.19 E |
| Vraca | 38 | 43.12 N | 23.33 E |
| Vračevo | 82 | 54.53 N | 39.10 E |
| Vrådal | 26 | 59.20 N | 8.25 E |
| Vrancea □[6] | 38 | 45.45 N | 27.00 E |
| Vrancei, Munţii ⋏ | 38 | 46.00 N | 26.30 E |
| Vrangel'a, mys › | 89 | 54.17 N | 138.39 E |
| Vrangel'a, ostrov I | 74 | 71.00 N | 179.30 W |
| Vranje | 38 | 42.3[illegible] N | 21.54 E |
| Vranov | 61 | 48.5[illegible] N | 15.49 E |
| Vranov [nad Topl'ou] | 30 | 48.5[illegible] N | 21.41 E |
| Vrbas | 38 | 45.35 N | 19.39 E |
| Vrbas ≃ | 36 | 45.06 N | 17.31 E |
| Vrbovec | 36 | 45.53 N | 16.25 E |
| Vrbovsko | 36 | 45.2[illegible] N | 15.05 E |
| Vrchlabí | 30 | 50.38 N | 15.37 E |
| Vrede | 158 | 27.30 S | 29.06 E |
| Vredefort | 158 | 27.05 S | 27.16 E |
| Vreden | 52 | 52.02 N | 6.52 E |
| Vredenburg | 158 | 32.5[illegible] S | 17.59 E |
| Vredenburgh | 194 | 31.4[illegible] N | 87.19 W |
| Vredendal | 158 | 31.4[illegible] S | 18.35 E |
| Vreed en Hoop | 246 | 6.48 N | 58.11 W |
| Vreeswijk | 52 | 52.0[illegible] N | 5.05 E |
| Vrena | 40 | 58.5[illegible] N | 16.41 E |
| Vresse | 56 | 49.5[illegible] N | 4.56 E |
| Vreta kloster ♁[1] | 26 | 58.2[illegible] N | 15.29 E |
| Vretstorp | 40 | 59.0[illegible] N | 14.52 E |
| Vrginmost | 36 | 45.2[illegible] N | 15.52 E |
| Vrhnika | 36 | 45.5[illegible] N | 14.18 E |
| Vriddhāchalam | 122 | 11.3[illegible] N | 79.20 E |
| Vriendschaps ≃ | 164 | 5.2[illegible] S | 138.53 E |
| Vries | 52 | 53.0[illegible] N | 6.35 E |
| Vriezenveen | 52 | 52.2[illegible] N | 6.38 E |
| Vrigne-Meuse | 56 | 49.4[illegible] N | 4.51 E |
| Vrigstad | 26 | 57.2[illegible] N | 14.28 E |
| Vrilissia | 267c | 38.0[illegible] N | 23.50 E |
| Vrille ≃ | 50 | 47.3[illegible] N | 2.52 E |
| Vrin | 58 | 46.3[illegible] N | 9.06 E |
| Vrin ≃ | 50 | 48.0[illegible] N | 3.20 E |
| Vrindāvan | 124 | 27.3[illegible] N | 77.42 E |
| Vrlika | 36 | 43.5[illegible] N | 16.24 E |
| Vrnograč | 36 | 45.1[illegible] N | 15.57 E |
| Vroeggedeel | 158 | 28.0[illegible] S | 22.32 E |
| Vron | 50 | 50.1[illegible] N | 1.45 E |
| Vrondádhes | 38 | 38.2[illegible] N | 26.08 E |
| Vroomshoop | 52 | 52.2[illegible] N | 6.34 E |
| Vrouenspan | 158 | 27.5[illegible] S | 20.24 E |
| Vroutek | 54 | 50.0[illegible] N | 13.24 E |
| Vršac | 38 | 45.0[illegible] N | 21.18 E |
| Vrsar | 64 | 45.0[illegible] N | 13.37 E |
| Vršič )( | 64 | 46.2[illegible] N | 13.44 E |
| Vrubivs'kyy | 83 | 48.2[illegible] N | 39.07 E |
| Vrútky | 30 | 49.0[illegible] N | 18.55 E |
| Vryburg | 158 | 26.5[illegible] S | 24.45 E |
| Vryheid | 158 | 27.4[illegible] S | 30.48 E |
| Vschody | 76 | 54.4[illegible] N | 34.06 E |
| Vselug, ozero ⊜ | 76 | 57.0[illegible] N | 32.42 E |
| Všepadly | 60 | 49.2[illegible] N | 13.06 E |
| Všeruby | 60 | 49.5[illegible] N | 13.15 E |
| Vsetín | 30 | 49.2[illegible] N | 17.59 E |
| Vsevidof, Mount ∧ | 180 | 53.0[illegible] N | 168.43 W |
| Vsevoložsk | 265a | 60.0[illegible] N | 30.40 E |
| Vtoroje Potapovo | 265b | 55.5[illegible] N | 37.58 E |
| Vtoryje Levyje Lamki | 80 | 53.1[illegible] N | 41.04 E |
| Vuadil' | 85 | 40.1[illegible] N | 71.43 E |
| Vuanggava Island I | 175g | 18.5[illegible] S | 178.54 W |
| Vučitrn | 38 | 42.4[illegible] N | 20.58 E |
| Vudor, gora ∧ | 85 | 38.1[illegible] N | 71.49 E |
| Vue-des-Alpes )( | 58 | 47.0[illegible] N | 6.53 E |
| Vught | 52 | 51.4[illegible] N | 5.17 E |
| Vuhlehirs'k | 83 | 48.1[illegible] N | 38.17 E |
| Vuhle-Zavod | 78 | 52.1[illegible] N | 32.53 E |
| Vuillafans | 58 | 47.0[illegible] N | 6.13 E |
| Vuitebœuf | 58 | 46.[illegible] N | 6.34 E |
| Vukovar | 38 | 45.2[illegible] N | 19.00 E |
| Vulcan, Ab., Can. | 182 | 50.2[illegible] N | 113.15 W |
| Vulcan, Rom. | 38 | 45.2[illegible] N | 23.17 E |
| Vulcan, Mi., U.S. | 190 | 45.4[illegible] N | 87.51 W |
| Vulcăneşti | 38 | 45.4[illegible] N | 28.24 E |
| Vulcano, Bocche di ɰ | 70 | 38.2[illegible] N | 14.57 E |
| Vulcano, Isola I | 70 | 38.2[illegible] N | 14.58 E |
| Vulcano, Monte ∧[2] | 70a | 35.5[illegible] N | 12.52 E |
| Vulci ⊥ | 66 | 42.2[illegible] N | 11.35 E |
| Vulkanichnyy khrebet ⋏ | 78 | 48.[illegible] N | 23.00 E |
| Vulture, Monte ∧ | 68 | 40.5[illegible] N | 15.38 E |
| Vul'vyvejem ≃ | 180 | 66.5[illegible] N | 179.10 W |
| Vung Tau | 110 | 10.2[illegible] N | 107.04 E |
| Vunindawa | 175g | 17.4[illegible] S | 178.19 E |
| Vunisea Station | 175g | 19.[illegible] S | 178.09 E |
| Vuoggatjålme | 24 | 66.[illegible] N | 16.22 E |
| Vuohijärvi | 26 | 61.[illegible] N | 26.48 E |
| Vuohijärvi ⊜ | 26 | 61.[illegible] N | 26.42 E |
| Vuokatti ∧[2] | 26 | 64.[illegible] N | 28.14 E |
| Vuoksa ≃ | 26 | 61.[illegible] N | 30.11 E |
| Vuoksa, ozero ⊜ | 76 | 60.[illegible] N | 29.50 E |
| Vuoksenniska | 26 | 61.[illegible] N | 28.49 E |
| Vurnary | 80 | 55.[illegible] N | 46.58 E |
| Vuturu, Pizzo ∧ | 70 | 37.5[illegible] N | 14.13 E |
| Vuya | 154 | 5.[illegible] N | 29.40 E |
| Vuyyūru | 122 | 16.[illegible] N | 80.51 E |
| Vuzenica | 61 | 46.[illegible] N | 15.10 E |
| Vvedenka | 86 | 54.[illegible] N | 63.45 E |
| Vvedenovka | 89 | 51.[illegible] N | 128.12 E |
| Vvedenskoje | 82 | 55.[illegible] N | 36.54 E |
| Vyāra | 120 | 21.[illegible] N | 73.24 E |
| Vyatka → Kirov | 80 | 58.[illegible] N | 49.42 E |
| V'yazivok | 78 | 49.[illegible] N | 31.25 E |
| Vyaz'ma → V'az'ma | 76 | 55.[illegible] N | 34.18 E |
| Vyazniki → V'azniki | 80 | 56.[illegible] N | 42.10 E |
| Vyborg | 76 | 60.[illegible] N | 28.45 E |
| Vyborgskij zaliv ⊂ | 76 | 60.[illegible] N | 28.24 E |
| Výčapy | 61 | 49.[illegible] N | 15.53 E |
| Vyčegda ≃ | 24 | 61.[illegible] N | 46.36 E |
| Vyčegodskij | 24 | 61.[illegible] N | 46.48 E |
| Vychino ◆[8] | 265b | 55.[illegible] N | 37.48 E |
| Východočeský Kraj □[4] | 30 | 50.[illegible] N | 16.00 E |
| Východoslovenský Kraj □[4] | 30 | 49.[illegible] N | 21.15 E |
| Vydrino, Ross. | 88 | 51.[illegible] N | 104.39 E |
| Vydrino, Ross. | 88 | 56.[illegible] N | 99.02 E |
| Vygoniči | 76 | 53.[illegible] N | 34.05 E |


| | | | | |
|---|---|---|---|---|
| ≃ River | Fluß | Río | Rivière | Rio |
| ≊ Canal | Kanal | Canal | Canal | Canal |
| ⌊ Waterfall, Rapids | Wasserfall, Stromschnellen | Cascada, Rápidos | Chute d'eau, Rapides | Cascata, Rápidos |
| ɰ Strait | Meeresstraße | Estrecho | Détroit | Estreito |
| ⊂ Bay, Gulf | Bucht, Golf | Bahía, Golfo | Baie, Golfe | Baía, Golfo |
| ⊜ Lake, Lakes | See, Seen | Lago, Lagos | Lac, Lacs | Lago, Lagos |
| ≡ Swamp | Sumpf | Pantano | Marais | Pântano |
| ⊓ Ice Features, Glacier | Eis- und Gletscherformen | Accidentes Glaciales | Formes glaciaires | Acidentes glaciares |
| ⊤ Other Hydrographic Features | Andere Hydrographische Objekte | Otros Elementos Hidrográficos | Autres données hydrographiques | Outros acidentes hidrográficos |

| | | | | |
|---|---|---|---|---|
| ✧ Submarine Features | Untermeerische Objekte | Accidentes Submarinos | Formes de relief sous-marin | Acidentes submarinos |
| □ Political Unit | Politische Einheit | Unidad Politica | Entité politique | Unidade política |
| ♁ Cultural Institution | Kulturelle Institution | Institución Cultural | Institution culturelle | Instituição cultural |
| ⊥ Historical Site | Historische Stätte | Sitio Histórico | Site historique | Sitio histórico |
| ♠ Recreational Site | Erholungs- und Ferienort | Sitio de Recreo | Centre de loisirs | Area de Lazer |
| ⊠ Airport | Flughafen | Aeropuerto | Aéroport | Aeroporto |
| ■ Military Installation | Militäranlage | Instalación Militar | Installation militaire | Instalação militar |
| ◆ Miscellaneous | Verschiedenes | Misceláneo | Divers | Diversos |

| Name (ENGLISH) / Name (DEUTSCH) | Page / Seite | Lat.°′ / Breite°′ | Long.°′ / Länge°′ E = Ost |
|---|---|---|---|
| Vygozero, ozero ⊜ | **24** | 63.35 N | 34.42 E |
| Vyhanaščy | **76** | 52.37 N | 25.55 E |
| Vyhoda | **78** | 48.56 N | 23.55 E |
| Vyjezdnoje | **80** | 55.23 N | 43.47 E |
| Vyježžij Log | **86** | 54.58 N | 93.57 E |
| Vyksa | **80** | 55.18 N | 42.11 E |
| Vylkove | **78** | 45.25 N | 29.35 E |
| Vylkovo | **86** | 53.05 N | 81.26 E |
| Vym' ≃ | **24** | 62.13 N | 50.25 E |
| Vynnyky | **78** | 49.48 N | 24.08 E |
| Vynohradiv | **78** | 48.09 N | 23.02 E |
| Vyntja | **86** | 60.31 N | 67.18 E |
| Vypolzovo | **76** | 57.53 N | 33.42 E |
| Vyrica | **76** | 59.25 N | 30.21 E |
| Vyrnwy ≃ | **42** | 52.46 N | 3.00 W |
| Vyrnwy, Lake ⊜ | **42** | 52.47 N | 3.30 W |
| Vyša | **80** | 53.52 N | 42.24 E |
| Vyša ≃ | **80** | 54.02 N | 42.06 E |
| Vyšehrad ●[8] | **54** | 50.01 N | 14.27 E |
| Vyšelej | **80** | 53.26 N | 45.29 E |
| Vyselki | **78** | 45.35 N | 39.38 E |
| Vyšesteblijevskaja | **78** | 45.12 N | 37.00 E |
| Vyšgorodok | **76** | 57.02 N | 28.01 E |
| Vyshcha Dubechna | **78** | 50.44 N | 30.40 E |
| Vyshkivs'kyi, pereval )( | **78** | 48.42 N | 23.38 E |
| Vyshneve | **78** | 48.27 N | 33.56 E |
| Vyshnivchyk | **78** | 49.02 N | 26.28 E |
| Vyshnivets' | **78** | 49.54 N | 25.45 E |
| Vyška, Ross. | **76** | 57.31 N | 35.57 E |
| Vyška, Turk. | **128** | 39.20 N | 54.08 E |
| Vyskod' | **76** | 57.46 N | 30.04 E |
| Vyškov, Česká Rep. | **30** | 49.16 N | 17.00 E |
| Vyškov, Ross. | **76** | 52.29 N | 31.41 E |
| Vyšná Radvaň | **30** | 49.07 N | 21.56 E |
| Vyšneol'šanoje | **76** | 52.08 N | 37.39 E |
| Vyšnevolockoje vodochranilišče ⊜[1] | **76** | 57.35 N | 34.28 E |
| Vyšnij Voločok | **76** | 57.35 N | 34.34 E |
| Vysočany ●[8] | **54** | 50.05 N | 14.31 E |
| Vysock | **76** | 60.36 N | 28.34 E |
| Vysokae | **76** | 52.22 N | 23.22 E |
| Vysokaja, gora ∧ | **89** | 45.59 N | 136.35 E |
| Vysokaja Gora | **80** | 55.56 N | 49.19 E |
| Vysoké Mýto | **30** | 49.57 N | 16.10 E |
| Vysoké Tatry ⋀ | **30** | 49.12 N | 20.05 E |
| Vysokiniči | **82** | 54.54 N | 36.55 E |
| Vysokogornyj | **89** | 50.09 N | 139.09 E |
| Vysokogorsk | **89** | 44.23 N | 135.23 E |
| Vysokoje, Kaz. | **85** | 42.30 N | 70.32 E |
| Vysokoje, Ross. | **76** | 56.43 N | 34.55 E |
| Vysokoje, Ross. | **76** | 54.02 N | 33.44 E |
| Vysokoje, Ross. | **82** | 54.30 N | 37.03 E |
| Vysokoje, Ross. | **265b** | 55.59 N | 37.09 E |
| Vysokopillya | **78** | 47.29 N | 33.32 E |
| Vysokovsk | **82** | 56.19 N | 36.33 E |
| Vysoký kámen ∧ | **61** | 49.06 N | 15.13 E |
| Vysots'k | **78** | 51.43 N | 26.39 E |
| Vyšší Brod | **61** | 48.37 N | 14.19 E |
| Vystupovychi | **78** | 51.34 N | 29.04 E |
| Vysun' ≃ | **78** | 47.07 N | 32.53 E |
| Vytebet' ≃ | **76** | 53.53 N | 35.38 E |
| Vytegra | **24** | 61.00 N | 36.24 E |
| Vytyazivka | **78** | 48.01 N | 31.53 E |
| Vyzhivka ≃ | **78** | 51.41 N | 24.35 E |
| Vyzhnytsya | **78** | 48.15 N | 25.12 E |
| Vzmorje | **89** | 47.51 N | 142.31 E |
| Vzvad | **76** | 58.10 N | 31.29 E |
| **W** | | | |
| W, Parc National du ♦ | **150** | 12.50 N | 2.30 E |
| Wa | **150** | 10.04 N | 2.29 W |
| Waabs | **41** | 54.32 N | 9.58 E |
| Waackaack Creek ≃ | **276** | 40.27 N | 74.08 W |
| Waadt → Vaud □[3] | **58** | 46.40 N | 6.30 E |
| Waajid | **144** | 3.48 N | 43.15 E |
| Waakirchen | **64** | 47.46 N | 11.40 E |
| Waal | **58** | 48.00 N | 10.46 E |
| Waal ≃ | **52** | 51.49 N | 4.58 E |
| Waalre | **52** | 51.24 N | 5.26 E |
| Waalwijk | **52** | 51.42 N | 5.04 E |
| Waao | **102** | 24.20 N | 104.40 E |
| Waar, Meos I | **164** | 2.05 S | 134.23 E |
| Waarschoot | **50** | 51.09 N | 3.36 E |
| Waasmunster | **50** | 51.06 N | 4.05 E |
| Wabag | **164** | 5.30 S | 143.40 E |
| Wabamun | **182** | 53.33 N | 114.28 W |
| Wabamun Indian Reserve ●[4] | **182** | 53.30 N | 114.30 W |
| Wabamun Lake ⊜ | **182** | 53.33 N | 114.35 W |
| Waban | **283** | 42.20 N | 71.14 W |
| Waban, Lake ⊜ | **283** | 42.17 N | 71.17 W |
| Wabana | **186** | 47.38 N | 52.57 W |
| Wabasca | **182** | 56.00 N | 113.53 W |
| Wabasca ≃ | **176** | 58.22 N | 115.20 W |
| Wabasca Indian Reserve ●[4] | **182** | 55.53 N | 113.32 W |
| Wabash, In., U.S. | **216** | 40.47 N | 85.49 W |
| Wabash, Oh., U.S. | **216** | 40.33 N | 84.45 W |
| Wabash □[6] | **216** | 40.48 N | 85.49 W |
| Wabash ≃ | **194** | 37.46 N | 88.02 W |
| Wabasha | **190** | 44.23 N | 92.01 W |
| Wabasso, Fl., U.S. | **220** | 27.44 N | 80.26 W |
| Wabasso, Mn., U.S. | **198** | 44.24 N | 95.15 W |
| Wabatongushi Lake ⊜ | **190** | 48.26 N | 84.15 W |
| Wabe Gestro ≃ | **144** | 4.17 N | 42.02 E |
| Wabe Mena ≃ | **144** | 5.32 N | 41.11 E |
| Wabeno | **190** | 45.26 N | 88.39 W |
| Wabera | **144** | 6.26 N | 40.42 E |
| Wabern | **56** | 51.06 N | 9.20 E |
| Wabigoon Lake ⊜ | **184** | 49.44 N | 92.44 W |
| Wabowden | **184** | 54.55 N | 98.38 W |
| Wabrah ⊤[4] | **128** | 27.26 N | 47.22 E |
| Wąbrzeźno | **30** | 53.17 N | 18.57 E |
| Wabu | **100** | 32.17 N | 116.55 E |
| Wabu Hu ⊜ | **100** | 32.23 N | 116.54 E |
| Wabuska | **226** | 39.08 N | 119.10 W |
| W.A.C. Bennett Dam ●[6] | **182** | 56.01 N | 122.10 W |
| Waccamaw ≃ | **192** | 33.21 N | 79.16 W |
| Waccamaw, Lake ⊜ | **192** | 34.17 N | 78.30 W |
| Waccasassa Bay c | **192** | 29.06 N | 82.52 W |
| Wachapreague | **208** | 37.36 N | 75.41 W |
| Wachapreague Inlet c | **208** | 37.35 N | 75.36 W |
| Wachau ●[1] | **61** | 48.18 N | 15.24 E |
| Wachenheim | **56** | 49.26 N | 8.10 E |
| Wachi | **96** | 35.15 N | 135.24 E |
| Wąchock, Klasztory ⋓[1] | **30** | 51.05 N | 21.01 E |
| Wachtberg | **56** | 50.37 N | 7.11 E |
| Wachtendonk | **56** | 51.24 N | 6.20 E |
| Wächtersbach | **56** | 50.15 N | 9.17 E |
| Wachusett Mountain ∧ | **207** | 42.29 N | 71.53 W |
| Wachusett Reservoir ⊜[1] | **207** | 42.23 N | 71.43 W |
| Wacissa | **192** | 30.21 N | 83.59 W |
| Wackersdorf | **60** | 49.19 N | 12.11 E |
| Waco | **222** | 31.32 N | 97.08 W |
| Waco Lake ⊜[1] | **222** | 31.34 N | 97.13 W |
| Waconda Lake ⊜[1] | **198** | 39.30 N | 98.24 W |
| Waconia | **190** | 44.51 N | 93.47 W |
| Wacouno ≃ | **186** | 50.54 N | 65.57 W |
| Wacousta | **216** | 42.49 N | 84.42 W |
| Wad | **120** | 27.21 N | 66.22 E |
| Wada, Nihon | **94** | 35.02 N | 140.01 E |
| Wada, Nihon | **94** | 36.12 N | 138.13 E |
| Wada, Nihon | **268** | 35.12 N | 139.38 E |
| Wada, Nihon | **270** | 34.33 N | 135.55 E |
| Wadagou | **104** | 42.27 N | 120.58 E |
| Wad Al-Ḥaddād | **140** | 13.49 N | 33.32 E |
| Wadamago | **144** | 8.55 N | 46.17 E |
| Wada-misaki > | **96** | 34.39 N | 135.11 E |
| Wādat Ga | **120** | 26.57 N | 97.37 E |
| Wadayama | **96** | 35.19 N | 134.52 E |
| Wad Bandah | **140** | 13.06 N | 27.57 E |
| Wad Ban Naqa | **140** | 16.30 N | 33.08 E |
| Wadbilliga National Park ♦ | **166** | 36.20 S | 149.35 E |
| Waddān | **146** | 29.10 N | 16.08 E |
| Waddān, Jabal ⋀[2] | **146** | 29.20 N | 16.20 E |
| Waddeneilanden II | **52** | 53.26 N | 5.30 E |
| Waddenzee ⊤[2] | **52** | 53.15 N | 5.15 E |
| Wadderin | **162** | 32.00 S | 118.27 E |
| Waddesdon | **42** | 51.51 N | 0.56 W |
| Waddi, Chappal ∧ | **152** | 7.02 N | 11.43 E |
| Waddingham | **44** | 53.27 N | 0.31 W |
| Waddington, Eng., U.K. | **44** | 53.10 N | 0.32 W |
| Waddington, N.Y., U.S. | **212** | 44.51 N | 75.12 W |
| Waddington, Mount ∧ | **182** | 51.23 N | 125.15 W |
| Waddinxveen | **52** | 52.03 N | 4.40 E |
| Waddy | **218** | 38.08 N | 85.04 W |
| Wade, Mount ∧ | **9** | 84.51 S | 174.15 W |
| Wadebridge | **42** | 50.32 N | 4.50 W |
| Wadena, Sk., Can. | **184** | 51.57 N | 103.47 W |
| Wadena, In., U.S. | **216** | 40.43 N | 87.16 W |
| Wadena, Mn., U.S. | **198** | 46.26 N | 95.08 W |
| Wädenswil | **58** | 47.14 N | 8.40 E |
| Wadern | **56** | 49.32 N | 6.53 E |
| Wadersloh | **52** | 51.44 N | 8.15 E |
| Wadesboro | **192** | 34.58 N | 80.04 W |
| Wadeville | **273d** | 26.16 S | 28.11 E |
| Wadeye | **164** | 14.13 S | 129.32 E |
| Wadgassen | **56** | 49.16 N | 6.47 E |
| Wad Ḥāmid | **140** | 16.30 N | 32.48 E |
| Wadham Islands II | **186** | 49.34 N | 53.50 W |
| Wadhams | **182** | 51.30 N | 127.31 W |
| Wadhurst | **42** | 51.04 N | 0.21 E |
| Wadian | **100** | 32.48 N | 112.30 E |
| Wādī as-Sīr | **132** | 31.57 N | 35.49 E |
| Wādī Ḥalfā' | **140** | 21.56 N | 31.20 E |
| Wādī Jimāl, Jazīrat I | **140** | 24.40 N | 35.10 E |
| Wādī Mūsā | **132** | 30.19 N | 35.29 E |
| Wading ≃, Ma., U.S. | **283** | 41.56 N | 71.13 W |
| Wading ≃, N.J., U.S. | **208** | 39.33 N | 74.28 W |
| Wading, West Branch ≃ | **208** | 39.40 N | 74.32 W |
| Wading River | **207** | 40.57 N | 72.50 W |
| Wādī Rashrāsh, Bi'r ⊤[4] | **142** | 29.26 N | 31.31 E |
| Wadley, Al., U.S. | **194** | 33.07 N | 85.33 W |
| Wadley, Ga., U.S. | **192** | 32.52 N | 82.24 W |
| Wad Madanī | **140** | 14.25 N | 33.28 E |
| Wadowice | **30** | 49.53 N | 19.30 E |
| Wadsworth, Il., U.S. | **216** | 42.26 N | 87.56 W |
| Wadsworth, Nv., U.S. | **204** | 39.38 N | 119.17 W |
| Wadsworth, N.Y., U.S. | **210** | 42.49 N | 77.54 W |
| Wadsworth, Oh., U.S. | **214** | 41.01 N | 81.43 W |
| Wadsworth Moor ●[3] | **262** | 53.48 N | 2.02 W |
| Wadu I | **122** | 5.51 N | 72.58 E |
| Waegwan | **98** | 35.58 N | 128.24 E |
| Waelder | **222** | 29.42 N | 97.18 W |
| Waenhuiskrans | **158** | 34.41 S | 20.14 E |
| Wafang | **98** | 41.44 N | 118.54 E |
| Wafania | **152** | 1.21 S | 20.20 E |
| Wafrah | **128** | 28.33 N | 48.02 E |
| Wagadugu → Ouagadougou | **150** | 12.22 N | 1.31 W |
| Wāgah | **123** | 31.36 N | 74.33 E |
| Wagait Aboriginal Reserve ●[4] | **164** | 13.00 S | 130.20 E |
| Wagang | **102** | 28.04 N | 103.10 E |
| Wagenborgen | **52** | 53.15 N | 6.56 E |
| Wagenfeld-Hasslingen | **52** | 52.33 N | 8.34 E |
| Wageningen, Ned. | **52** | 51.58 N | 5.40 E |
| Wageningen, Sur. | **250** | 5.46 N | 56.41 W |
| Wager Bay c | **176** | 65.26 N | 88.40 W |
| Wagerup | **168a** | 32.55 S | 115.54 E |
| Waggaman Heights | **284c** | 38.49 N | 76.57 W |
| Wagga Wagga | **171b** | 35.07 S | 147.22 E |
| Waggoner | **219** | 39.23 N | 89.39 W |
| Waghäusel | **56** | 49.14 N | 8.31 E |
| Wagin | **162** | 33.18 S | 117.21 E |
| Waging am See | **64** | 47.56 N | 12.43 E |
| Waginger See ⊜ | **64** | 47.56 N | 12.47 E |
| Wägitaler See ⊜ | **58** | 47.06 N | 8.55 E |
| Waglan Island I | **271d** | 22.11 N | 114.18 E |
| Wagna | **61** | 46.46 N | 15.34 E |
| Wagner | **198** | 43.04 N | 98.17 W |
| Wagner College ⋓[2] | **276** | 40.37 N | 74.07 W |
| Wagoner | **196** | 35.57 N | 95.22 W |
| Wagon Mound | **196** | 36.00 N | 104.42 W |
| Wagontire Mountain ∧ | **202** | 43.21 N | 119.53 W |
| Wagontown | **208** | 40.01 N | 75.51 W |
| Wagrain | **64** | 47.20 N | 13.18 E |
| Wagram → Deutsch Wagram | **61** | 48.18 N | 16.34 E |
| Wagrien ●[1] | **54** | 54.15 N | 10.45 E |
| Wągrowiec | **30** | 52.49 N | 17.11 E |
| Waha | **146** | 28.16 N | 19.54 E |
| Wahādurgañj | **124** | 27.32 N | 82.50 E |
| Wahai | **164** | 2.48 S | 129.30 E |
| Waharoa | **172** | 37.46 S | 175.46 E |
| Wāh Cantonment | **123** | 33.48 N | 72.42 E |
| Wahiawa | **229c** | 21.30 N | 158.01 W |
| Wāḥid | **142** | 30.49 N | 32.20 E |
| Wahkiakum □[6] | **224** | 46.16 N | 123.28 W |
| Wahlen | **56** | 49.37 N | 8.51 E |
| Wahlstedt | **54** | 53.57 N | 10.12 E |
| Wahnbachstausee ⊜[1] | **56** | 50.48 N | 7.19 E |
| Wahneta | **220** | 27.57 N | 81.44 W |
| Wahoo | **198** | 41.12 N | 96.37 W |
| Wahpeton | **198** | 46.15 N | 96.36 W |
| Wahran (Oran) | **148** | 35.43 N | 0.43 W |
| Wahrenbrück | **54** | 51.33 N | 13.22 E |
| Wahrenholz | **54** | 52.36 N | 10.36 E |
| Währing ●[8] | **264b** | 48.14 N | 16.21 E |
| Wahroonga | **274a** | 33.43 S | 151.07 E |
| Wahweap Creek ≃ | **200** | 37.02 N | 111.35 W |
| Wai, India | **122** | 17.56 N | 73.54 E |
| Wai, Indon. | **164** | 1.42 S | 127.59 E |
| Waialeale ∧ | **229b** | 22.04 N | 159.30 W |
| Waialua | **229c** | 21.34 N | 158.07 W |
| Waialua Bay c | **229c** | 21.36 N | 158.07 W |
| Waianae | **229c** | 21.26 N | 158.11 W |
| Waianae Range ⋀ | **229c** | 21.30 N | 158.10 W |
| Waianapanapa State Park ♦ | **229a** | 20.47 N | 156.01 W |
| Waiapu ≃ | **172** | 37.47 S | 178.29 E |
| Waiatoto ≃ | **172** | 43.59 S | 168.47 E |
| Waiau | **172** | 42.39 S | 173.03 E |
| Waiau ≃, N.Z. | **172** | 42.47 S | 173.22 E |
| Waiau ≃, N.Z. | **172** | 46.12 S | 167.38 E |
| Waiau ≃, N.Z. | **172** | 38.58 S | 177.24 E |
| Waibakul | **115b** | 9.36 S | 119.35 E |
| Waibeem | **164** | 0.28 S | 132.58 E |
| Waiblingen | **56** | 48.50 N | 9.19 E |
| Waibstadt | **56** | 49.18 N | 8.54 E |
| Waichagoumen | **98** | 40.54 N | 125.45 E |
| Waidbruck → Ponte Gardena | **64** | 46.36 N | 11.32 E |
| Waidhān | **124** | 24.04 N | 82.20 E |
| Waidhofen an der Thaya | **61** | 48.49 N | 15.18 E |
| Waidhofen an der Ybbs | **61** | 47.58 N | 14.47 E |
| Waidmannslust ●[8] | **264a** | 52.36 N | 13.20 E |
| Waidring | **64** | 47.35 N | 12.34 E |
| Waiehu | **229a** | 20.55 N | 156.30 W |
| Waigang | **106** | 31.22 N | 121.11 E |
| Waigatsch → Vajgač, ostrov I | **72** | 70.00 N | 59.30 E |
| Waigeo, Pulau I | **164** | 0.14 S | 130.45 E |
| Waigoumen | **98** | 41.24 N | 116.13 E |
| Waihao Downs | **172** | 44.48 S | 170.55 E |
| Waihau Bay | **172** | 37.37 S | 177.55 E |
| Waihee | **229a** | 20.56 N | 156.30 W |
| Waihee Point > | **229a** | 20.57 N | 156.31 W |
| Waiheke Island I | **172** | 36.48 S | 175.06 E |
| Waihi | **172** | 37.24 S | 175.51 E |
| Waihola | **172** | 46.02 S | 170.06 E |
| Waihopai ≃ | **172** | 41.31 S | 173.44 E |
| Waihou ≃ | **172** | 37.10 S | 175.32 E |
| Waihuantan | **106** | 30.25 N | 118.40 E |
| Waika | **154** | 2.21 S | 25.43 E |
| Waikabubak | **115b** | 9.38 S | 119.25 E |
| Waikaia | **172** | 45.44 S | 168.51 E |
| Waikaia ≃ | **172** | 45.53 S | 168.48 E |
| Waikanae | **172** | 40.53 S | 175.04 E |
| Waikane | **229c** | 21.30 N | 157.51 W |
| Waikapu | **229a** | 20.51 N | 156.30 W |
| Waikare, Lake ⊜ | **172** | 37.26 S | 175.13 E |
| Waikaremoana, Lake ⊜ | **172** | 38.46 S | 177.07 E |
| Waikari | **172** | 42.58 S | 172.41 E |
| Waikato ≃ | **172** | 37.23 S | 174.43 E |
| Waikelo | **115b** | 9.24 S | 119.14 E |
| Waikerie | **166** | 34.11 S | 139.59 E |
| Waikiki Beach ♦ | **229c** | 21.17 N | 157.50 W |
| Waikino | **172** | 37.25 S | 175.46 E |
| Waikouaiti | **172** | 45.36 S | 170.41 E |
| Waikuatang | **106** | 31.20 N | 120.41 E |
| Wailo | **144** | 9.25 N | 48.55 E |
| Wailua | **229b** | 22.03 N | 159.20 W |
| Wailua River State Park ♦ | **229b** | 22.02 N | 159.21 W |
| Wailuku | **229a** | 20.53 N | 156.30 W |
| Waimahaka | **172** | 46.31 S | 168.49 E |
| Waimakariri ≃ | **172** | 43.24 S | 172.42 E |
| Waimamaku | **172** | 35.33 S | 173.29 E |
| Waimana | **172** | 38.09 S | 177.05 E |
| Waimana ≃ | **172** | 38.04 S | 177.00 E |
| Waimanalo | **229c** | 21.21 N | 157.43 W |
| Waimangaroa | **172** | 41.43 S | 171.46 E |
| Waimangura | **115b** | 9.30 S | 119.14 E |
| Waimarama | **172** | 39.48 S | 176.59 E |
| Waimate | **172** | 44.44 S | 171.02 E |
| Waimea, Hi., U.S. | **229c** | 21.38 N | 158.03 W |
| Waimea, Hi., U.S. | **229d** | 21.57 N | 159.40 W |
| Waimea Canyon V | **229b** | 22.04 N | 159.39 W |
| Waimea Canyon State Park ♦ | **229b** | 22.04 N | 159.40 W |
| Waimes | **56** | 50.25 N | 6.07 E |
| Wainfleet All Saints | **44** | 53.07 N | 0.14 E |
| Wainganga ≃ | **122** | 18.50 N | 79.55 E |
| Waingapu | **115b** | 9.39 S | 120.16 E |
| Waini ≃ | **246** | 8.24 N | 59.51 W |
| Wainscott | **260** | 51.25 N | 0.31 E |
| Wainstalls | **262** | 53.45 N | 1.56 W |
| Wainuiomata | **172** | 41.16 S | 174.57 E |
| Wainunu Bay c | **175g** | 16.55 S | 178.53 E |
| Wainwright, Ab., Can. | **182** | 52.49 N | 110.52 W |
| Wainwright, Ak., U.S. | **180** | 70.38 N | 160.01 W |
| Wainwright, Oh., U.S. | **214** | 40.25 N | 81.25 W |
| Waiohau | **172** | 38.14 S | 176.51 E |
| Waiotira | **172** | 35.56 S | 174.12 E |
| Waiouru | **172** | 39.29 S | 175.40 E |
| Waipa ≃ | **172** | 37.41 S | 175.09 E |
| Waipahi | **172** | 46.07 S | 169.15 E |
| Waipahu | **229c** | 21.23 N | 158.00 W |
| Waipaoa | **172** | 38.32 S | 177.54 E |
| Waipara | **172** | 43.04 S | 172.45 E |
| Waipara ≃ | **172** | 43.09 S | 172.48 E |
| Waipawa | **172** | 39.56 S | 176.36 E |
| Waipiata | **172** | 45.11 S | 170.10 E |
| Waipio Acres | **229c** | 21.28 N | 158.00 W |
| Waipio Bay c | **229a** | 20.55 N | 156.13 W |
| Waipiro | **172** | 38.01 S | 178.20 E |
| Waipu | **172** | 35.59 S | 174.27 E |
| Waipukurau | **172** | 40.00 S | 176.34 E |
| Wairakei | **172** | 38.38 S | 176.06 E |
| Wairarapa, Lake ⊜ | **172** | 41.13 S | 175.15 E |
| Wairau ≃ | **172** | 41.30 S | 174.04 E |
| Wairau Valley | **172** | 41.34 S | 173.32 E |
| Wairio | **172** | 46.00 S | 168.02 E |
| Wairoa | **172** | 39.02 S | 177.25 E |
| Wairoa ≃ | **172** | 39.04 S | 177.26 E |
| Waisanzao | **106** | 30.57 N | 121.52 E |
| Waischenfeld | **60** | 49.51 N | 11.21 E |
| Waïsisi | **175f** | 19.30 S | 169.22 E |
| Waitahanui | **172** | 38.47 S | 176.05 E |
| Waitahuna | **172** | 45.59 S | 169.46 E |
| Waitakaruru | **172** | 37.15 S | 175.23 E |
| Waitaki ≃ | **172** | 44.57 S | 171.09 E |
| Waitara, Austl. | **274a** | 33.43 S | 151.07 E |
| Waitara, N.Z. | **172** | 39.00 S | 174.13 E |
| Waitara ≃ | **172** | 38.59 S | 174.14 E |
| Waitarere | **172** | 40.33 S | 175.12 E |
| Waita Reservoir ⊜[1] | **229b** | 21.55 N | 159.27 W |
| Waitati | **172** | 45.45 S | 170.34 E |
| Waita-zan ∧ | **96** | 33.08 N | 131.10 E |
| Waite Hill | **214** | 41.37 N | 81.22 W |
| Waitemata | **172** | 36.56 S | 174.42 E |
| Waite Park | **190** | 45.33 N | 94.13 W |
| Waitoa | **172** | 37.37 S | 175.38 E |
| Waitotara | **172** | 39.48 S | 174.44 E |
| Waitotara ≃ | **172** | 39.51 S | 174.41 E |
| Waitpinga | **168b** | 35.37 S | 138.29 E |
| Waitsburg | **202** | 46.16 N | 118.09 W |
| Waitzen → Vác | **30** | 47.47 N | 19.08 E |
| Waiuku | **172** | 37.15 S | 174.45 E |
| Waiuta | **172** | 42.18 S | 171.49 E |
| Waiwera South | **172** | 46.13 S | 169.30 E |
| Waiwo | **164** | 0.56 S | 131.03 E |
| Waiya | **164** | 3.13 S | 128.55 E |
| Waizenkirchen | **60** | 48.20 N | 13.52 E |
| Wajiki | **96** | 33.51 N | 134.30 E |
| Wajima | **92** | 37.24 N | 136.54 E |
| Wajir | **154** | 1.45 N | 40.04 E |
| Waka, Ityo. | **144** | 7.07 N | 37.26 E |
| Waka, Tx., U.S. | **196** | 36.17 N | 101.03 W |
| Waka, Zaïre | **152** | 1.01 N | 20.13 E |
| Wakajabi | **164** | 5.38 S | 134.24 E |
| Wakakusa | **94** | 35.36 N | 138.29 E |
| Wakakusa-yama ∧[2] | **270** | 34.42 N | 135.52 E |
| Wakamatsu → Aizu-wakamatsu | **92** | 37.30 N | 139.56 E |
| Wakami ≃ | **190** | 47.43 N | 82.22 W |
| Wakami Lake ⊜ | **190** | 47.29 N | 82.51 W |
| Wakamiya | **96** | 33.44 N | 130.37 E |
| Wakano-ura ♦ | **96** | 34.11 N | 135.11 E |
| Wakarusa | **216** | 41.32 N | 86.03 W |
| Wakarusa ≃ | **198** | 38.57 N | 95.05 W |
| Wakasa | **96** | 35.20 N | 134.24 E |
| Wakasa-wan c | **92** | 35.45 N | 135.40 E |
| Wakasa-wan-kokutei-kōen ♦ | **96** | 35.35 N | 135.30 E |
| Wakatipu, Lake ⊜ | **172** | 45.05 S | 168.34 E |
| Wakatomika Creek ≃ | **214** | 40.07 N | 82.00 W |
| Wakato-ōhashi ●[5] | **96** | 33.54 N | 130.49 E |
| Wakaw | **184** | 52.39 N | 105.44 W |
| Wakaw Lake ⊜ | **184** | 52.40 N | 105.35 W |
| Wakayama | **96** | 34.13 N | 135.11 E |
| Wakayama □[5] | **96** | 34.00 N | 135.20 E |
| Wakayanagi | **92** | 38.46 N | 141.08 E |
| Wake, Nihon | **96** | 34.48 N | 134.08 E |
| Wake, Zaïre | **152** | 0.48 S | 20.10 E |
| WaKeeney | **198** | 39.01 N | 99.53 W |
| Wakefield, N.Z. | **172** | 41.24 S | 173.03 E |
| Wakefield, Eng., U.K. | **44** | 53.42 N | 1.29 W |
| Wakefield, Ks., U.S. | **198** | 39.12 N | 97.00 W |
| Wakefield, Ma., U.S. | **207** | 42.30 N | 71.04 W |
| Wakefield, Ne., U.S. | **198** | 42.16 N | 96.51 W |
| Wakefield, Oh., U.S. | **218** | 38.59 N | 83.01 W |
| Wakefield, R.I., U.S. | **207** | 41.26 N | 71.30 W |
| Wakefield, Va., U.S. | **192** | 36.58 N | 76.59 W |
| Wakefield ≃ | **168b** | 34.10 S | 138.10 E |
| Wakefield Forest | **284c** | 38.50 N | 77.14 W |
| Wake Forest | **192** | 35.58 N | 78.30 W |
| Wake Island □[2], Oc. | **14** | 19.17 N | 166.36 E |
| Wake Island □[2], Oc. | **174a** | 19.17 N | 166.36 E |
| Wake Island I[1] | **174a** | 19.18 N | 166.38 E |
| Wake Island Air Force Base ■ | **174a** | 19.17 N | 166.37 E |
| Wake Lagoon c | **174a** | 19.18 N | 166.36 E |
| Wakema | **110** | 16.36 N | 95.11 E |
| Wakeman | **214** | 41.15 N | 82.23 W |
| Wakeman ≃ | **182** | 51.00 N | 126.30 W |
| Wakenda Creek ≃ | **194** | 39.19 N | 93.16 W |
| Wake Village | **194** | 33.26 N | 94.07 W |
| Wakhān → Vākhān ●[1] | **120** | 37.00 N | 73.00 E |
| Waki | **96** | 34.04 N | 134.09 E |
| Wakis | **164** | 6.13 S | 150.17 E |
| Wakita | **196** | 36.53 N | 97.55 W |
| Wakkanai | **92a** | 45.25 N | 141.40 E |
| Wakkerstroom | **158** | 27.24 S | 30.10 E |
| Wakō, Nihon | **268** | 35.47 N | 139.37 E |
| Wako, Pap. N. Gui. | **164** | 6.05 S | 149.05 E |
| Wakomata Lake ⊜ | **190** | 46.34 N | 83.22 W |
| Wakonassin ≃ | **190** | 46.28 N | 81.51 W |
| Wakonda | **198** | 43.00 N | 97.06 W |
| Wakre | **164** | 0.19 S | 131.09 E |
| Waku Kundo | **152** | 11.25 S | 15.07 E |
| Wakunai | **175e** | 5.52 S | 155.13 E |
| Wakusimi ≃ | **190** | 49.08 N | 82.17 W |
| Wala ≃ | **154** | 5.46 S | 32.04 E |
| Walachia □[9] | **38** | 44.00 N | 25.00 E |
| Walamba | **154** | 13.29 S | 28.45 E |
| Walanae ≃ | **112** | 4.08 S | 119.58 E |
| Walang | **102** | 28.33 N | 100.54 E |
| Wal Athiang | **140** | 7.42 N | 29.40 E |
| Walawe ≃ | **122** | 6.06 N | 81.01 E |
| Walbeck | **52** | 51.30 N | 6.15 E |
| Walberswick | **42** | 52.19 N | 1.39 E |
| Walborn Reservoir ⊜[1] | **214** | 40.59 N | 81.11 E |
| Walbran Creek ≃ | **224** | 48.34 N | 124.40 W |
| Walbridge | **214** | 41.35 N | 83.29 W |
| Wałbrzych (Waldenburg) | **30** | 50.46 N | 16.17 E |
| Walburg | **222** | 30.44 N | 97.35 W |
| Walbury Hill ∧[2] | **42** | 51.21 N | 1.30 W |
| Walcha | **166** | 30.59 S | 151.36 E |
| Walchensee ⊜ | **64** | 47.36 N | 11.20 E |
| Walcheren I | **52** | 51.33 N | 3.35 E |
| Walchsee | **64** | 47.39 N | 12.19 E |
| Walcott, B.C., Can. | **182** | 54.31 N | 126.51 W |
| Walcott, Ia., U.S. | **190** | 41.35 N | 90.46 W |
| Walcott, N.D., U.S. | **198** | 46.32 N | 96.56 W |
| Walcott, Lake ⊜[1] | **202** | 42.40 N | 113.23 W |
| Walcourt | **50** | 50.15 N | 4.25 E |
| Wałcz | **30** | 53.17 N | 16.28 E |
| Wald, Dtsch. | **58** | 47.56 N | 9.11 E |
| Wald, Dtsch. | **60** | 49.09 N | 12.20 E |
| Wald, Schw. | **58** | 47.17 N | 8.55 E |
| Wald ●[8] | **263** | 51.11 N | 7.03 E |
| Waldai → Valdajskaja vozvyšennost' ⋀[2] | **24** | 57.00 N | 33.30 E |
| Waldaist ≃ | **61** | 48.19 N | 14.34 E |
| Wald am Schoberpass | **61** | 47.27 N | 14.40 E |
| Waldbauer ●[8] | **263** | 51.18 N | 7.28 E |
| Waldbillig | **56** | 49.47 N | 6.18 E |
| Waldböckelheim | **56** | 49.49 N | 7.43 E |
| Waldbreitbach | **56** | 50.33 N | 7.25 E |
| Waldbröl | **56** | 50.53 N | 7.37 E |
| Waldbronn | **56** | 48.56 N | 8.29 E |
| Waldburg | **58** | 47.45 N | 9.43 E |
| Walddrehna | **54** | 51.45 N | 13.35 E |
| Waldeck, Dtsch. | **56** | 51.12 N | 9.04 E |
| Waldeck, Dtsch. | **60** | 49.52 N | 11.57 E |
| Walden, Co., U.S. | **200** | 40.43 N | 106.16 W |
| Walden, N.Y., U.S. | **210** | 41.33 N | 74.11 W |
| Walden, Lake ⊜ | **281** | 42.39 N | 83.46 W |
| Waldenbuch | **56** | 48.38 N | 9.07 E |
| Waldenburg, Dtsch. | **54** | 50.52 N | 12.36 E |
| Waldenburg, Dtsch. | **56** | 49.11 N | 9.38 E |
| Waldenburg → Wałbrzych, Pol. | **30** | 50.46 N | 16.17 E |
| Waldenburg, Schw. | **58** | 47.23 N | 7.45 E |
| Walden Pond ⊜, Ma., U.S. | **283** | 42.26 N | 71.20 W |
| Walden Pond ⊜, Ma., U.S. | **283** | 42.28 N | 71.00 W |
| Walden Ridge ∧ | **194** | 35.30 N | 85.15 W |
| Waldershof | **60** | 49.59 N | 12.04 E |
| Walderslade | **260** | 51.21 N | 0.32 E |
| Waldheim, Sk., Can. | **184** | 52.37 N | 106.38 W |
| Waldheim, Dtsch. | **54** | 51.04 N | 13.01 E |
| Waldighoffen | **58** | 47.33 N | 7.19 E |
| Wald im Pinzgau | **64** | 47.15 N | 12.14 E |
| Waldkappel | **56** | 51.08 N | 9.52 E |
| Waldkirch | **58** | 48.05 N | 7.57 E |
| Waldkirchen | **60** | 48.44 N | 13.37 E |
| Waldkirchen am Wesen | **60** | 48.26 N | 13.49 E |
| Waldkraiburg | **60** | 48.12 N | 12.28 E |
| Waldmohr | **56** | 49.23 N | 7.20 E |
| Waldmünchen | **60** | 49.23 N | 12.43 E |
| Waldnaab ≃ | **60** | 49.36 N | 12.08 E |
| Waldo, B.C., Can. | **182** | 49.13 N | 115.13 W |
| Waldo, Ar., U.S. | **194** | 33.21 N | 93.17 W |
| Waldo, Oh., U.S. | **214** | 40.27 N | 83.04 W |
| Waldoboro | **188** | 44.05 N | 69.22 W |
| Waldo Lake ⊜ | **283** | 42.07 N | 71.03 W |
| Waldo Lake ⊜[1] | **202** | 43.44 N | 122.03 W |
| Waldon ≃ | **42** | 50.51 N | 4.15 W |
| Waldorf | **208** | 38.37 N | 76.56 W |
| Waldport | **202** | 44.25 N | 124.04 W |
| Waldron, Sk., Can. | **184** | 50.51 N | 102.30 W |
| Waldron, Ar., U.S. | **194** | 34.53 N | 94.05 W |
| Waldron, In., U.S. | **218** | 39.27 N | 85.40 W |
| Waldron, Mi., U.S. | **216** | 41.43 N | 84.25 W |
| Waldron Island I | **224** | 48.43 N | 123.02 W |
| Waldsassen | **60** | 50.00 N | 12.18 E |
| Waldshut-Tiengen | **58** | 47.37 N | 8.13 E |
| Waldstatt | **58** | 47.21 N | 9.17 E |
| Waldthurn | **60** | 49.40 N | 12.20 E |
| Waldviertel ●[1] | **61** | 48.40 N | 15.15 E |
| Waldwick | **276** | 41.00 N | 74.07 W |
| Walea, Selat ⊔ | **112** | 0.40 S | 122.00 E |
| Walembele | **150** | 10.30 N | 1.58 W |
| Walensee ⊜ | **58** | 47.07 N | 9.12 E |
| Walenstadt | **58** | 47.07 N | 9.19 E |
| Wales, Ak., U.S. | **180** | 65.36 N | 168.05 W |
| Wales, Ma., U.S. | **207** | 42.04 N | 72.13 W |
| Wales, Wi., U.S. | **216** | 43.00 N | 88.23 W |
| Wales □[8] | **28** | 52.30 N | 3.30 W |
| Wales Center | **210** | 42.46 N | 78.32 W |
| Wales Island I, B.C., Can. | **182** | 54.45 N | 130.30 W |
| Wales Island I, N.T., Can. | **176** | 68.00 N | 86.43 W |
| Walewale | **150** | 10.21 N | 0.48 W |
| Walgett | **166** | 30.01 S | 148.07 E |
| Walgreen Coast ±[2] | **9** | 75.15 S | 105.00 W |
| Walhachin | **182** | 50.45 N | 120.59 W |
| Walhalla, N.D., U.S. | **198** | 48.55 N | 97.55 W |
| Walhalla, S.C., U.S. | **192** | 34.45 N | 83.03 W |
| Walhalla ⊥ | **60** | 49.03 N | 12.14 E |
| Walheim | **56** | 50.42 N | 6.10 E |
| Walhonding | **214** | 40.22 N | 82.09 W |
| Walhonding ≃ | **214** | 40.18 N | 81.53 W |
| Wali | **105** | 39.42 N | 118.20 E |
| Walia | **164** | 3.47 S | 138.32 E |
| Walikale | **154** | 1.25 S | 28.03 E |
| Walincourt | **50** | 50.04 N | 3.20 E |
| Walis Island I | **164** | 3.15 S | 143.20 E |
| Walkaway | **162** | 28.57 S | 114.48 E |
| Walkden | **44** | 53.32 N | 2.24 W |
| Walkenried | **54** | 51.35 N | 10.37 E |
| Walker, Ia., U.S. | **190** | 42.17 N | 91.46 W |
| Walker, Mi., U.S. | **216** | 43.00 N | 85.46 W |
| Walker, Mn., U.S. | **190** | 47.06 N | 94.35 W |
| Walker, N.Y., U.S. | **210** | 43.18 N | 77.52 W |
| Walker □[6] | **222** | 30.42 N | 95.35 W |
| Walker ≃ | **204** | 38.54 N | 118.47 W |
| Walker, Lac ⊜ | **186** | 50.16 N | 67.09 W |
| Walker, Mount ∧[2] | **171a** | 27.48 S | 152.34 E |
| Walker Basin Creek ≃ | **228** | 35.20 N | 118.47 W |
| Walker Bay c | **158** | 34.30 S | 19.20 E |
| Walker Creek ≃, Az., U.S. | **200** | 36.58 N | 109.42 W |
| Walker Creek ≃, Ma., U.S. | **283** | 42.38 N | 70.44 W |
| Walker Creek ≃, Wy., U.S. | **198** | 43.09 N | 104.52 W |
| Walker Lake ⊜, Mb., Can. | **184** | 54.42 N | 96.57 W |
| Walker Lake ⊜, Ak., U.S. | **180** | 67.10 N | 154.26 W |
| Walker Lake ⊜, Nv., U.S. | **204** | 38.44 N | 118.43 W |
| Walker Lake ⊜[1] | **210** | 40.48 N | 77.11 W |
| Walker Point > | **158** | 34.05 S | 22.57 E |
| Walker River Indian Reservation ●[4] | **204** | 39.00 N | 118.40 W |
| Walkers Mill | **279b** | 40.24 N | 80.08 W |
| Walkersville | **208** | 39.29 N | 77.21 W |
| Walkerton, On., Can. | **212** | 44.07 N | 81.09 W |
| Walkerton, In., U.S. | **216** | 41.28 N | 86.28 W |
| Walkerton, Va., U.S. | **208** | 37.43 N | 77.01 W |
| Walkertown | **192** | 36.10 N | 80.09 W |
| Walker Valley | **210** | 41.38 N | 74.23 W |
| Walkerville | **202** | 46.02 N | 112.32 W |
| Walk Mill | **262** | 53.46 N | 2.12 W |
| Wall, Pa., U.S. | **279b** | 40.24 N | 79.47 W |
| Wall, S.D., U.S. | **198** | 43.59 N | 102.14 W |
| Wallace, Ca., U.S. | **226** | 38.12 N | 120.59 W |
| Wallace, Id., U.S. | **202** | 47.28 N | 115.55 W |
| Wallace, Ne., U.S. | **198** | 40.50 N | 101.09 W |
| Wallace, N.Y., U.S. | **210** | 42.26 N | 77.28 W |
| Wallace, N.C., U.S. | **192** | 34.44 N | 77.59 W |
| Wallaceburg | **214** | 42.36 N | 82.23 W |
| Wallace Lake ⊜ | **279a** | 41.22 N | 81.52 W |
| Wallaceton | **214** | 40.57 N | 78.17 W |
| Wallacetown | **214** | 42.38 N | 81.28 W |
| Wallach | **263** | 51.35 N | 6.34 E |
| Wallacia | **170** | 33.52 S | 150.39 E |
| Wallal Downs | **162** | 19.47 S | 120.40 E |
| Wallam Creek ≃ | **166** | 28.40 S | 147.20 E |
| Wallan | **169** | 37.25 S | 144.59 E |
| Wallangarra | **166** | 28.56 S | 151.56 E |
| Wallaroo | **168b** | 33.56 S | 137.38 E |
| Wallaroo Mines | **168b** | 33.57 S | 137.41 E |
| Wallasey | **44** | 53.26 N | 3.03 W |
| Wallau | **56** | 50.56 N | 8.28 E |
| Walla Walla | **202** | 46.03 N | 118.20 W |
| Walldorf, Dtsch. | **54** | 50.36 N | 10.23 E |
| Walldorf, Dtsch. | **56** | 49.18 N | 8.38 E |
| Walldürn | **56** | 49.35 N | 9.22 E |
| Walled Lake | **216** | 42.32 N | 83.28 W |
| Walled Lake ⊜ | **281** | 42.31 N | 83.29 W |
| Wallen | **216** | 41.09 N | 85.09 W |
| Wallend | **260** | 51.27 N | 0.42 E |
| Wallenfels | **54** | 50.16 N | 11.28 E |
| Wallenhorst | **52** | 52.21 N | 8.01 E |
| Wallenpaupack, Lake ⊜ | **210** | 41.25 N | 75.12 W |
| Waller | **222** | 30.04 N | 95.56 W |
| Waller □[6] | **222** | 30.00 N | 96.00 W |
| Wallerawang | **170** | 33.25 S | 150.04 E |
| Wallern im Burgenland | **61** | 47.43 N | 16.56 E |
| Wallers | **50** | 50.22 N | 3.24 E |
| Wallersdorf | **60** | 48.44 N | 12.45 E |
| Wallersee ⊜ | **64** | 47.55 N | 13.11 E |
| Wallerstein | **56** | 48.53 N | 10.28 E |
| Wallgau | **64** | 47.31 N | 11.16 E |
| Wallgrove | **274a** | 33.47 S | 150.51 E |
| Wallhausen | **54** | 51.28 N | 11.12 E |
| Wallhead Airport ⊠ | **279a** | 41.21 N | 82.09 W |
| Wallingford, Eng., U.K. | **42** | 51.37 N | 1.08 W |
| Wallingford, Ct., U.S. | **207** | 41.27 N | 72.49 W |
| Wallingford, Pa., U.S. | **285** | 39.54 N | 75.22 W |
| Wallingford, Vt., U.S. | **188** | 43.28 N | 72.58 W |
| Wallington | **276** | 40.51 N | 74.06 W |
| Wallington ●[8] | **260** | 51.21 N | 0.09 W |
| Wallis | **222** | 29.37 N | 96.03 W |
| Wallis → Valais □[3] | **58** | 46.10 N | 7.30 E |
| Wallis, Îles II | **14** | 13.18 S | 176.10 W |
| Wallis and Futuna □[2] | **14** | 14.00 S | 177.00 W |
| Wallisellen | **58** | 47.25 N | 8.36 E |
| Wallisville | **222** | 29.50 N | 94.44 W |
| Wallisville Lake ⊜[1] | **222** | 29.50 N | 94.45 W |
| Wallkill | **210** | 41.36 N | 74.11 W |
| Wallkill ≃, U.S. | **210** | 41.51 N | 74.03 W |
| Wallkill ≃, U.S. | **276** | 41.11 N | 74.35 W |
| Wallkill, Wildcat Branch ≃ | **276** | 41.07 N | 74.36 W |
| Wall Lake, Ia., U.S. | **198** | 42.16 N | 95.05 W |
| Wall Lake, Mi., U.S. | **216** | 42.31 N | 85.24 W |
| Wall Lake ⊜ | **216** | 42.31 N | 85.23 W |
| Wallmer Bridge | **262** | 53.43 N | 2.48 W |
| Wallmerod | **56** | 50.29 N | 7.56 E |
| Wallops Island I | **208** | 37.52 N | 75.27 W |
| Wallowa | **202** | 45.34 N | 117.31 W |
| Wallowa ≃ | **202** | 45.43 N | 117.47 W |
| Wallowa Mountains ⋀ | **202** | 45.10 N | 117.30 W |
| Walls, Scot., U.K. | **46a** | 60.14 N | 1.35 W |
| Walls, Ms., U.S. | **194** | 34.57 N | 90.09 W |
| Wallsbüll | **41** | 54.47 N | 9.14 E |
| Wallsend, Austl. | **170** | 32.55 S | 151.40 E |
| Wallsend, Eng., U.K. | **44** | 55.00 N | 1.31 W |
| Wallstawe | **54** | 52.47 N | 11.01 E |
| Wall Town Drainage Ditch ≅ | **216** | 40.26 N | 88.10 W |
| Wallula, Lake ⊜[1] | **202** | 46.00 N | 119.00 W |
| Walmer, S. Afr. | **158** | 33.59 S | 25.36 E |
| Walmer, Eng., U.K. | **42** | 51.13 N | 1.24 E |
| Walmersley | **262** | 53.37 N | 2.18 W |
| Walney, Isle of I | **44** | 54.07 N | 3.15 W |
| Walnut, Ca., U.S. | **228** | 34.01 N | 117.51 W |
| Walnut, Il., U.S. | **190** | 41.33 N | 89.35 W |
| Walnut, Ia., U.S. | **198** | 41.28 N | 95.13 W |
| Walnut, Ks., U.S. | **198** | 37.36 N | 95.04 W |
| Walnut, Ms., U.S. | **194** | 34.56 N | 88.53 W |
| Walnut, N.C., U.S. | **192** | 35.50 N | 82.44 W |
| Walnut ≃ | **198** | 37.03 N | 97.00 W |
| Walnut Canyon National Monument ♦ | **200** | 35.10 N | 111.31 W |
| Walnut Canyon Reservoir ⊜[1] | **280** | 33.50 N | 117.45 W |
| Walnut Cove | **192** | 36.17 N | 80.08 W |
| Walnut Creek, Ca., U.S. | **226** | 37.54 N | 122.03 W |
| Walnut Creek, Oh., U.S. | **214** | 40.33 N | 81.43 W |
| Walnut Creek ≃, Ca., U.S. | **280** | 34.03 N | 118.01 W |
| Walnut Creek ≃, Ca., U.S. | **282** | 37.54 N | 122.03 W |
| Walnut Creek ≃, Ks., U.S. | **198** | 38.21 N | 98.41 W |
| Walnut Creek ≃, Oh., U.S. | **188** | 39.41 N | 82.59 W |
| Walnut Creek ≃, Tx., U.S. | **222** | 32.38 N | 97.00 W |
| Walnut Creek, Middle Fork ≃ | **198** | 38.32 N | 100.08 W |
| Walnut Creek, South Fork ≃ | **198** | 38.25 N | 99.53 W |
| Walnut Grove, Ca., U.S. | **226** | 38.15 N | 121.31 W |
| Walnut Grove, Mn., U.S. | **198** | 44.13 N | 95.28 W |
| Walnut Grove, Ms., U.S. | **194** | 32.35 N | 89.27 W |
| Walnut Heights | **282** | 37.53 N | 122.08 W |
| Walnut Hill | **219** | 38.29 N | 89.03 W |
| Walnut Lake | **281** | 42.33 N | 83.19 W |
| Walnut Lake ⊜ | **281** | 42.33 N | 83.20 W |
| Walnut Park | **280** | 33.58 N | 118.13 W |
| Walnutport | **208** | 40.45 N | 75.35 W |
| Walnut Ridge | **194** | 36.04 N | 90.57 W |
| Walnut Springs | **222** | 32.03 N | 97.45 W |
| Walpert Ridge ∧ | **282** | 37.38 N | 122.00 W |
| Walpeup | **166** | 35.08 S | 142.02 E |
| Walpole, Austl. | **162** | 34.57 S | 116.44 E |
| Walpole, Ma., U.S. | **207** | 42.08 N | 71.15 W |
| Walpole, N.H., U.S. | **188** | 43.04 N | 72.25 W |
| Walpole Island I | **214** | 42.34 N | 82.30 W |
| Walpole Island Indian Reserve ●[4] | **214** | 42.32 N | 82.37 W |
| Walpole Saint Peter | **42** | 52.42 N | 0.15 E |
| Walsall | **42** | 52.35 N | 1.58 W |
| Walschleben | **54** | 51.04 N | 10.56 E |
| Walsden | **262** | 53.42 N | 2.06 W |
| Walsenburg | **200** | 37.37 N | 104.46 W |
| Walsh, Austl. | **164** | 16.39 S | 143.54 E |
| Walsh, Ab., Can. | **184** | 49.57 N | 110.03 W |
| Walsh, Co., U.S. | **198** | 37.23 N | 102.16 W |
| Walsh, Ky., U.S. | **218** | 38.41 N | 82.58 W |
| Walsh ≃ | **164** | 16.31 S | 143.42 E |
| Walshaw Dean Reservoirs ⊜[1] | **262** | 53.48 N | 2.03 W |
| Walshville | **219** | 39.04 N | 89.37 W |
| Walsingham | **212** | 42.41 N | 80.32 W |
| Walsleben | **54** | 52.56 N | 12.40 E |
| Walsoorden | **52** | 51.23 N | 4.02 E |
| Walsrode | **52** | 52.52 N | 9.35 E |
| Walston | **214** | 40.58 N | 79.01 W |
| Walsum | **52** | 51.32 N | 6.41 E |
| Walt Disney World ♦ | **220** | 28.26 N | 81.35 W |
| Waltenhofen | **64** | 47.40 N | 10.17 E |
| Walterboro | **192** | 32.54 N | 80.40 W |
| Walter E. Long Lake ⊜[1] | **222** | 30.18 N | 97.36 W |
| Walter F. George Lake ⊜[1] | **192** | 31.49 N | 85.08 W |
| Walter Reed Army Medical Center ⋓ | **284c** | 38.58 N | 77.02 W |
| Walters | **196** | 34.21 N | 98.18 W |
| Waltersdorf, Dtsch. | **54** | 50.52 N | 14.38 E |
| Waltersdorf, Dtsch. | **264a** | 52.22 N | 13.35 E |
| Waltershausen | **54** | 50.53 N | 10.33 E |
| Waltershofen | **58** | 47.46 N | 9.55 E |
| Waltersville | **194** | 32.22 N | 90.52 W |
| Walthall | **194** | 33.36 N | 89.16 W |
| Waltham, Eng., U.K. | **44** | 53.31 N | 0.06 W |
| Waltham, Ma., U.S. | **207** | 42.22 N | 71.14 W |
| Waltham Abbey | **42** | 51.42 N | 0.01 E |
| Waltham Forest ●[8] | **42** | 51.35 N | 0.01 W |
| Waltham on the Wolds | **42** | 52.49 N | 0.49 W |
| Walthamstow ●[8] | **260** | 51.35 N | 0.01 W |
| Walthill | **198** | 42.08 N | 96.29 W |
| Walton, N.S., Can. | **186** | 45.14 N | 64.00 W |
| Walton, Eng., U.K. | **42** | 51.24 N | 0.25 W |
| Walton, Eng., U.K. | **42** | 51.58 N | 1.21 E |
| Walton, Fl., U.S. | **220** | 27.17 N | 80.15 W |
| Walton, In., U.S. | **216** | 40.39 N | 86.14 W |
| Walton, Ky., U.S. | **218** | 38.52 N | 84.36 W |
| Walton, N.Y., U.S. | **210** | 42.10 N | 75.07 W |
| Walton Hills | **214** | 41.22 N | 81.32 W |
| Walton-le-Dale | **44** | 53.45 N | 2.39 W |
| Walton on the Hill | **260** | 51.17 N | 0.15 W |
| Walton-on-the-Naze | **42** | 51.51 N | 1.16 E |
| Walton Run ≃ | **285** | 40.05 N | 74.59 W |
| Waltonville | **219** | 38.13 N | 89.02 W |
| Waltrop | **52** | 51.37 N | 7.23 E |
| Walt Whitman Bridge ●[5] | **285** | 39.54 N | 75.08 W |
| Walt Whitman Homes | **285** | 39.52 N | 75.11 W |
| Walt Whitman House State Historic Site ⊥ | **276** | 40.49 N | 73.25 W |
| Walt Whitman Mall ●[9] | **276** | 40.50 N | 73.25 W |
| Waltz | **216** | 42.06 N | 83.23 W |
| Walupt Lake ⊜ | **224** | 46.25 N | 121.28 W |
| Walvis Bay | **156** | 22.59 S | 14.31 E |
| Walvis Bay □[5] | **156** | 22.59 S | 14.31 E |
| Walvis Bay c | **156** | 22.57 S | 14.30 E |
| Walvis Ridge ⊹[3] | **10** | 28.00 S | 3.00 E |
| Walwa | **171b** | 35.58 S | 147.45 E |
| Walwen | **262** | 53.14 N | 3.15 W |
| Walworth, N.Y., U.S. | **210** | 43.08 N | 77.17 W |
| Walworth, Wi., U.S. | **216** | 42.31 N | 88.35 W |
| Walworth □[6] | **216** | 42.41 N | 88.32 W |
| Walyunga National Park ♦ | **168a** | 31.44 S | 116.04 E |
| Walyungup, Lake ⊜ | **168a** | 32.21 S | 115.47 E |
| Walze | **263** | 51.16 N | 7.31 E |
| Walzin, Château de ⊥ | **56** | 50.13 N | 4.55 E |
| Wama | **152** | 12.14 S | 15.33 E |
| Wamac | **219** | 38.31 N | 89.08 W |
| Wamba, Kenya | **154** | 0.59 N | 37.19 E |
| Wamba, Nig. | **150** | 8.58 N | 8.36 E |
| Wamba, Zaïre | **154** | 2.09 N | 28.00 E |
| Wamba (Uamba) ≃ | **152** | 3.56 S | 17.12 E |
| Wambel ●[8] | **263** | 51.32 N | 7.32 E |
| Wamego | **198** | 39.12 N | 96.18 W |
| Wamel | **52** | 51.53 N | 5.28 E |
| Wamesit | **283** | 42.37 N | 71.15 W |
| Wami ≃ | **154** | 6.08 S | 38.49 E |
| Wamiao | **100** | 30.49 N | 113.02 E |
| Wamic | **224** | 45.13 N | 121.16 W |
| Wamma ≃ | **164** | 3.23 S | 135.13 E |
| Wamme ≃ | **56** | 50.10 N | 5.16 E |
| Wamplers Lake ⊜ | **216** | 42.05 N | 84.09 W |
| Wampool ≃ | **44** | 54.54 N | 3.14 W |
| Wampsville | **210** | 43.04 N | 75.42 W |
| Wampú | **236** | 15.01 N | 85.02 W |
| Wampú ≃ | **236** | 14.59 N | 85.03 W |
| Wampum | **214** | 40.53 N | 80.20 W |
| Wampus ≃ | **276** | 41.07 N | 73.43 W |
| Wampus Lake Reservoir ⊜[1] | **276** | 41.09 N | 73.43 W |
| Wamsasi | **112** | 3.33 S | 126.10 E |
| Wamsutter | **200** | 41.40 N | 107.58 W |
| Wamuran | **171a** | 27.02 S | 152.52 E |
| Wanaaring | **166** | 29.42 S | 144.09 E |
| Wanaka | **172** | 44.42 S | 169.09 E |
| Wanaka, Lake ⊜ | **172** | 44.30 S | 169.08 E |
| Wanakah | **210** | 42.45 N | 78.54 W |
| Wanamassa | **208** | 40.14 N | 74.02 W |
| Wanamie | **210** | 41.10 N | 76.02 W |
| Wanamingo | **190** | 44.18 N | 92.47 W |
| Wan'an, Zhg. | **100** | 26.56 N | 117.22 E |
| Wan'an, Zhg. | **100** | 26.30 N | 114.49 E |
| Wan'an ≃ | **100** | 25.20 N | 117.21 E |
| Wan'anchang | **107** | 30.39 N | 104.25 E |
| Wanapiri | **164** | 4.33 S | 135.59 E |
| Wanapitei ≃ | **190** | 46.02 N | 80.51 W |
| Wanapitei Lake ⊜ | **190** | 46.45 N | 80.45 W |
| Wanapum Lake ⊜[1] | **202** | 47.00 N | 120.00 W |
| Wanaque | **210** | 41.02 N | 74.17 W |
| Wanaque ≃ | **276** | 40.58 N | 74.17 W |
| Wanaque Reservoir ⊜[1] | **210** | 41.05 N | 74.17 W |
| Wanatah | **216** | 41.25 N | 86.53 W |
| Wanau | **164** | 1.22 S | 132.42 E |
| Wanbaoshan | **89** | 44.12 N | 125.11 E |
| Wanbi | **166** | 34.46 S | 140.19 E |
| Wanblee | **198** | 43.34 N | 101.40 W |
| Wanborough | **42** | 51.33 N | 1.42 W |
| Wanchangchang | **107** | 29.43 N | 104.19 E |
| Wanchese | **192** | 35.50 N | 75.38 W |
| Wanda | **158** | 29.36 S | 24.28 E |
| Wandai | **164** | 3.41 S | 136.41 E |
| Wandana | **162** | 32.04 S | 133.49 E |
| Wandawega | **216** | 42.45 N | 88.40 W |
| Wande | **98** | 36.21 N | 116.56 E |
| Wanderer | **154** | 19.37 S | 29.59 E |
| Wandering | **168a** | 32.40 S | 116.40 E |
| Wandering ≃ | **182** | 55.05 N | 112.30 W |
| Wanderup | **41** | 54.41 N | 9.20 E |
| Wandhofen | **263** | 51.26 N | 7.33 E |
| Wandingzhen | **102** | 24.05 N | 98.04 E |
| Wandlitz | **54** | 52.45 N | 13.26 E |
| Wandlitzer See ⊜ | **264a** | 52.46 N | 13.27 E |
| Wando | **98** | 34.18 N | 126.47 E |
| Wan-do I | **98** | 34.21 N | 126.42 E |
| Wandoan | **166** | 26.08 S | 149.57 E |
| Wandsworth ●[8] | **42** | 51.27 N | 0.11 W |
| Waneta Lake ⊜ | **210** | 42.27 N | 77.06 W |
| Wanette | **196** | 34.57 N | 97.01 W |
| Wanfang | **104** | 41.57 N | 122.52 E |
| Wanfoxia | **102** | 40.04 N | 95.55 E |


**Symbols** in the index entries represent the broad categories identified in the key at the right. Symbols with superior numbers (⋀[1]) identify subcategories (see complete key on page *I · 1).*

**Symbole** im Register stellen die rechts im Schlüssel erklärten Kategorien dar. Symbole mit hochgestellten Ziffern (⋀[1]) bezeichnen Unterabteilungen einer Kategorie (vgl. vollständiger Schlüssel auf Seite *I · 1).*

**Los símbolos** incluídos en el texto del índice representan las grandes categorías identificadas con la clave a la derecha. Los símbolos con numeros en su parte superior (⋀[1]) identifican las subcategorías (véase la clave completa en la página *I · 1).*

**Les symboles** de l'index représentent les catégories indiquées dans la légende à droite. Les symboles suivis d'un indice (⋀[1]) représentent des sous-catégories (voir légende complète à la page *I · 1).*

**Os símbolos** incluídos no texto do índice representam as grandes categorias identificadas com a chave à direita. Os símbolos com números em sua parte superior (⋀[1]) identificam as subcategorias (veja-se a chave completa à página *I · 1).*

| | English | Deutsch | Español | Français | Português |
|---|---|---|---|---|---|
| ∧ | Mountain | Berg | Montaña | Montagne | Montanha |
| ⋀ | Mountains | Gebirge | Montañas | Montagnes | Montanhas |
| )( | Pass | Paß | Paso | Col | Passo |
| V | Valley, Canyon | Tal, Cañon | Valle, Cañón | Vallée, Canyon | Vale, Canhão |
| ≚ | Plain | Ebene | Llano | Plaine | Planície |
| > | Cape | Kap | Cabo | Cap | Cabo |
| I | Island | Insel | Isla | Île | Ilha |
| II | Islands | Inseln | Islas | Îles | Ilhas |
| ± | Other Topographic Features | Andere Topographische Objekte | Otros Elementos Topográficos | Autres données topographiques | Outros acidentes topográficos |

**ESPAÑOL**

| Nombre | Página | Lat.°′ | Long.°′ W = Oeste |
|---|---|---|---|
| Wanfried | 56 | 51.10 N | 10.10 E |
| Wanfu ≃ | 98 | 35.10 N | 116.35 E |
| Wang ≃ | 110 | 17.08 N | 99.02 E |
| Wanga | 154 | 2.58 N | 29.13 E |
| Wangal | 164 | 6.10 S | 134.12 E |
| Wanganderry, Mount ∧ | 170 | 34.20 S | 150.15 E |
| Wanganui | 172 | 39.56 S | 175.03 E |
| Wanganui ≃ | 172 | 39.56 S | 175.00 E |
| Wang'anzhen | 105 | 39.19 N | 114.54 E |
| Wangaratta | 166 | 36.22 S | 146.20 E |
| Wangary | 166 | 34.33 S | 135.29 E |
| Wangbaotaicun | 104 | 41.10 N | 123.18 E |
| Wangbenying | 105 | 40.28 N | 116.06 E |
| Wangbintun | 104 | 41.58 N | 123.43 E |
| Wangchang, Zhg. | 107 | 28.52 N | 105.55 E |
| Wangchang, Zhg. | 107 | 29.05 N | 104.40 E |
| Wangchangtuizigou | 104 | 41.14 N | 120.32 E |
| Wangcheng | 100 | 28.23 N | 112.48 E |
| Wang Chin | 110 | 17.53 N | 99.37 E |
| Wangcun | 98 | 36.41 N | 117.41 E |
| Wangcunkou | 100 | 28.22 N | 118.59 E |
| Wangdain | 124 | 29.02 N | 89.15 E |
| Wangdalong | 102 | 29.25 N | 99.03 E |
| Wangdian | 106 | 30.37 N | 120.44 E |
| Wangdu | 98 | 38.43 N | 115.09 E |
| Wangdu Phodrang | 124 | 27.29 N | 89.54 E |
| Wange | 154 | 2.00 S | 40.55 E |
| Wangels | 54 | 54.16 N | 10.45 E |
| Wangen an der Aare | 58 | 47.14 N | 7.39 E |
| Wangenbourg | 58 | 48.37 N | 7.19 E |
| Wangen im Allgäu | 58 | 47.41 N | 9.50 E |
| Wangerooge | 52 | 53.48 N | 7.54 E |
| Wangerooge I | 52 | 53.46 N | 7.55 E |
| Wangersen | 52 | 53.22 N | 9.25 E |
| Wangfu | 104 | 42.05 N | 121.29 E |
| Wanggameti, Gunung ∧ | 115b | 10.07 S | 120.14 E |
| Wanggangpu | 104 | 41.38 N | 123.09 E |
| Wanggao | 102 | 24.38 N | 111.30 E |
| Wanggezhuang | 105 | 40.00 N | 117.52 E |
| Wanggil-li | 271b | 37.36 N | 126.39 E |
| Wanggoutun | 104 | 41.40 N | 121.53 E |
| Wanghai | 98 | 40.26 N | 120.30 E |
| Wanghai Shan ∧ | 104 | 41.37 N | 121.41 E |
| Wanghechenggou | 104 | 41.52 N | 121.13 E |
| Wang Hin, Khlong ≊ | 269a | 13.48 N | 100.35 E |
| Wanghu | 98 | 39.47 N | 113.54 E |
| Wanghuzhuang | 105 | 38.50 N | 117.05 E |
| Wāngi | 58 | 47.30 N | 8.57 E |
| Wangingsha | 100 | 22.44 N | 113.33 E |
| Wangi Wangi | 170 | 33.04 S | 151.35 E |
| Wangiwangi, Pulau I | 112 | 5.20 S | 123.35 E |
| Wangji, Zhg. | 100 | 33.52 N | 118.44 E |
| Wangji, Zhg. | 100 | 34.00 N | 117.46 E |
| Wangjia, Zhg. | 106 | 31.59 N | 121.13 E |
| Wangjia, Zhg. | 106 | 32.07 N | 120.59 E |
| Wangjiadian, Zhg. | 100 | 31.26 N | 113.58 E |
| Wangjiadian, Zhg. | 105 | 40.03 N | 117.29 E |
| Wangjiagou | 104 | 42.33 N | 123.16 E |
| Wangjiajing, Zhg. | 98 | 37.49 N | 115.23 E |
| Wangjiajing, Zhg. | 98 | 39.56 N | 122.11 E |
| Wangjiang | 100 | 30.09 N | 116.41 E |
| Wangjiangjing | 106 | 30.53 N | 120.43 E |
| Wang Jian Mu (Tomb of Wang Jian) ⊥ | 107 | 30.38 N | 104.04 E |
| Wangjiaputun | 104 | 40.39 N | 122.50 E |
| Wangjiapuzi, Zhg. | 104 | 40.41 N | 122.24 E |
| Wangjiapuzi, Zhg. | 104 | 41.05 N | 123.34 E |
| Wangjiaqiao | 106 | 30.50 N | 119.18 E |
| Wangjiashan | 105 | 40.19 N | 114.45 E |
| Wangjiashao | 102 | 23.57 N | 102.18 E |
| Wangjiatai | 105 | 39.17 N | 117.29 E |
| Wangjiaying, Zhg. | 105 | 40.36 N | 116.34 E |
| Wangjiaying, Zhg. | 105 | 39.06 N | 115.59 E |
| Wangjiazhai | 106 | 31.21 N | 121.37 E |
| Wangjiazui | 106 | 31.16 N | 120.18 E |
| Wangkantou | 100 | 29.12 N | 120.09 E |
| Wangkou | 105 | 38.56 N | 116.44 E |
| Wangkui | 89 | 46.50 N | 126.30 E |
| Wanglanzhuang | 105 | 39.26 N | 118.01 E |
| Wangling | 100 | 27.13 N | 113.26 E |
| Wangliu | 100 | 32.25 N | 115.40 E |
| Wangmiao | 100 | 26.50 N | 112.52 E |
| Wangmulazi | 104 | 41.42 N | 124.02 E |
| Wang Noi | 110 | 14.13 N | 100.44 E |
| Wangong | 89 | 49.10 N | 118.53 E |
| Wangpan Shan II | 106 | 30.30 N | 121.15 E |
| Wangpan Yang c | 100 | 30.30 N | 121.46 E |
| Wangpingchang | 107 | 29.17 N | 105.45 E |
| Wangqing | 89 | 43.20 N | 129.48 E |
| Wangqingmen | 98 | 41.42 N | 125.23 E |
| Wangqingtuo | 105 | 39.11 N | 116.53 E |
| Wangqinzhuang | 105 | 39.15 N | 117.05 E |
| Wangqucun | 106 | 31.22 N | 120.19 E |
| Wangs | 58 | 47.02 N | 9.26 E |
| Wang Saphung | 110 | 17.18 N | 101.46 E |
| Wangshanhutun | 104 | 42.03 N | 122.37 E |
| Wangshi | 100 | 33.11 N | 116.04 E |
| Wangsi | 98 | 38.00 N | 116.55 E |
| Wangsim-ni ◆[8] | 271b | 37.36 N | 127.03 E |
| Wangsiying | 107 | 30.34 N | 103.29 E |
| Wangtai, Zhg. | 98 | 36.05 N | 119.59 E |
| Wangtai, Zhg. | 100 | 26.39 N | 117.57 E |
| Wangtan | 100 | 29.45 N | 120.40 E |
| Wang Thong | 110 | 16.50 N | 100.26 E |
| Wangtian | 100 | 25.59 N | 116.04 E |
| Wangting | 106 | 31.26 N | 120.26 E |
| Wangtongshitai | 104 | 42.05 N | 123.11 E |
| Wangtuan, Zhg. | 98 | 37.32 N | 116.08 E |
| Wangtuan, Zhg. | 98 | 37.17 N | 122.04 E |
| Wangtuanji | 100 | 33.12 N | 116.21 E |
| Wangu | 107 | 30.19 N | 106.05 E |
| Wanguzhen | 107 | 29.41 N | 105.57 E |
| Wangwenzhuang | 105 | 38.53 N | 117.15 E |
| Wangxiangshang | 106 | 31.29 N | 120.15 E |
| Wangxiangtai | 105 | 40.02 N | 115.09 E |
| Wangxiuqiao | 106 | 31.38 N | 121.03 E |
| Wangyangzhen | 107 | 29.44 N | 104.14 E |
| Wangyedian | 98 | 41.36 N | 118.17 E |
| Wangyefu | 98 | 41.50 N | 118.23 E |
| Wangyehmiao → Horqin Youyi Qianqi | 89 | 46.05 N | 122.05 E |
| Wangyiguantun | 104 | 42.36 N | 123.19 E |
| Wangzhai | 98 | 34.09 N | 116.47 E |
| Wangzhimawo | 105 | 39.39 N | 117.40 E |
| Wangzhong | 98 | 35.08 N | 116.58 E |
| Wangzhuang | 100 | 33.07 N | 117.29 E |
| Wangzhuangbu | 98 | 39.27 N | 113.56 E |
| Wangzhuangji | 98 | 34.09 N | 118.23 E |
| Wangzhuangzi | 105 | 39.17 N | 118.14 E |
| Wanham | 182 | 55.44 N | 118.24 W |
| Wanhedian | 100 | 32.16 N | 113.16 E |
| Wanheimerort ◆[8] | 263 | 51.24 N | 6.46 E |
| Wanhsien → Wanxian | 102 | 30.52 N | 108.22 E |
| Wanhuyu | 102 | 38.24 N | 110.40 E |
| Wani | 122 | 20.04 N | 78.57 E |
| Wani, Gunung ∧ | 112 | 4.29 S | 123.01 E |
| Wanica □[5] | 250 | 5.50 N | 55.10 W |
| Wanie-Rukula | 154 | 0.15 N | 25.32 E |
| Wanigela | 164 | 9.22 S | 149.10 E |
| Wanipigow ≃ | 184 | 51.11 N | 96.18 W |
| Wanjiabu | 100 | 28.51 N | 115.39 E |
| Wanjiaqiao | 106 | 30.25 N | 119.07 E |
| Wanjiatun | 98 | 40.03 N | 119.51 E |
| Wanjindian | 100 | 32.50 N | 114.46 E |
| Wānkāner | 120 | 22.37 N | 70.56 E |
| Wankendorf | 54 | 54.07 N | 10.13 E |
| Wanle Weyne | 144 | 2.37 N | 44.54 E |
| Wanli, T'aiwan | 269d | 25.11 N | 121.41 E |
| Wanli, Zhg. | 106 | 31.06 N | 120.16 E |
| Wanna | 52 | 53.44 N | 8.46 E |
| Wanna Lakes ⊜ | 162 | 28.30 S | 128.27 E |
| Wān Namton | 110 | 22.03 N | 99.33 E |
| Wanne-Eickel | 52 | 51.32 N | 7.09 E |
| Wanneroo | 168a | 31.45 S | 115.48 E |
| Wannery Creek ≃ | 162 | 22.47 S | 115.43 E |
| Wannian | 100 | 28.42 N | 117.03 E |

**FRANÇAIS**

| Nom | Page | Lat.°′ | Long.°′ W = Ouest |
|---|---|---|---|
| Wanning | 110 | 18.53 N | 110.26 E |
| Wannsee ◆[8] | 54 | 52.25 N | 13.09 E |
| Wanon Niwat | 110 | 17.38 N | 103.46 E |
| Wanouchi | 94 | 35.17 N | 136.38 E |
| Wānow | 120 | 32.38 N | 65.54 E |
| Wanparti | 122 | 16.22 N | 78.04 E |
| Wanquan | 98 | 40.52 N | 114.45 E |
| Wansbeck ≃ | 44 | 55.10 N | 1.34 W |
| Wansdorf | 264a | 52.38 N | 13.05 E |
| Wan-See → Van Gölü ⊜ | 128 | 38.33 N | 42.46 E |
| Wanshan | 107 | 30.23 N | 106.06 E |
| Wanshouchang | 107 | 29.26 N | 105.55 E |
| Wanstead | 172 | 40.08 S | 176.32 E |
| Wanstead ◆[8] | 260 | 51.34 N | 0.02 E |
| Wantage | 42 | 51.36 N | 1.25 W |
| Wantagh | 210 | 40.41 N | 73.30 W |
| Wantan | 102 | 30.03 N | 110.18 E |
| Wantirna | 274b | 37.51 S | 145.14 E |
| Wantirna South | 274b | 37.52 S | 145.14 E |
| Wanxian, Zhg. | 102 | 30.52 N | 108.22 E |
| Wanxian, Zhg. | 105 | 38.50 N | 115.09 E |
| Wanyuan | 102 | 32.04 N | 108.02 E |
| Wanzai | 100 | 28.06 N | 114.27 E |
| Wanzarīk | 146 | 27.31 N | 13.29 E |
| Wanzhuang | 105 | 39.34 N | 116.36 E |
| Wanzleben | 54 | 52.03 N | 11.26 E |
| Wapack Range ʎ | 207 | 42.48 N | 71.52 W |
| Wapakoneta | 216 | 40.34 N | 84.11 W |
| Wapanucka | 196 | 34.22 N | 96.25 W |
| Wapato | 202 | 46.26 N | 120.25 W |
| Wapawekka Hills ʎ[2] | 184 | 54.45 N | 104.20 W |
| Wapawekka Lake ⊜ | 184 | 54.55 N | 104.40 W |
| Wapella, Sk., Can. | 184 | 50.15 N | 102.00 W |
| Wapella, Il., U.S. | 219 | 40.13 N | 88.58 W |
| Wapello | 190 | 41.10 N | 91.11 W |
| Wapenamanda | 164 | 5.35 S | 143.55 E |
| Wapesi Lake ⊜ | 184 | 50.34 N | 92.21 W |
| Wāpi | 122 | 20.22 N | 72.54 E |
| Wapinda | 152 | 3.41 N | 22.48 E |
| Wapinitia Pass )( | 224 | 45.14 N | 121.42 W |
| Wapisu Lake ⊜ | 184 | 55.47 N | 99.11 W |
| Wapiti ≃ | 182 | 55.08 N | 118.18 W |
| Wapizagonke, Lac ⊜ | 206 | 46.43 N | 73.02 W |
| Waples | 222 | 32.29 N | 97.43 W |
| Wapoga ≃ | 164 | 2.42 S | 136.06 E |
| Wappapello, Lake ⊜[1] | 194 | 36.58 N | 90.20 W |
| Wapping | 207 | 41.50 N | 72.33 W |
| Wappinger Creek ≃ | 210 | 41.35 N | 73.57 W |
| Wappingers Falls | 210 | 41.35 N | 73.54 W |
| Wapsipinicon ≃ | 190 | 41.44 N | 90.20 W |
| Waptus Lake ⊜ | 224 | 47.30 N | 121.10 W |
| Wapus ≃ | 190 | 47.11 N | 76.06 W |
| Wapus Lake ⊜ | 184 | 56.27 N | 102.12 W |
| Waqf aş-Şawwān, Jibāl ʎ | 132 | 30.53 N | 36.48 E |
| Wāqid | 142 | 30.42 N | 30.44 E |
| Waqqāş | 132 | 32.33 N | 35.36 E |
| War | 192 | 37.18 N | 81.41 W |
| Wara | 94 | 35.45 N | 137.05 E |
| Warabi | 94 | 35.49 N | 139.41 E |
| Wārāh | 120 | 27.27 N | 67.48 E |
| Warakaraket I | 164 | 2.15 S | 130.36 E |
| Waramaug, Lake ⊜ | 207 | 41.42 N | 73.22 W |
| Warangal | 122 | 18.00 N | 79.35 E |
| Wararisbari, Tanjung > | 164 | 1.05 S | 136.23 E |
| Wārāseoni | 120 | 21.45 N | 80.02 E |
| Waratah, Austl. | 166 | 41.27 S | 145.32 E |
| Waratah, Austl. | 170 | 32.54 S | 151.44 E |
| Waratah Bay c | 166 | 38.51 S | 146.04 E |
| Warboys | 42 | 52.24 N | 0.04 W |
| Warbreccan | 166 | 24.18 S | 142.51 E |
| Warburg | 52 | 51.29 N | 9.08 E |
| Warburton, Austl. | 162 | 26.07 S | 126.35 E |
| Warburton, Austl. | 169 | 37.46 S | 145.41 E |
| Warburton, Pāk. | 123 | 31.33 N | 73.50 E |
| Warburton, Eng., U.K. | 262 | 53.24 N | 2.27 W |
| Warburton Aboriginal Reserve ◆[4] | 162 | 24.00 S | 128.15 E |
| Warburton Bay c | 176 | 63.50 N | 111.30 W |
| Warburton Creek ≃ | 166 | 27.55 S | 137.28 E |
| Warchha | 123 | 32.25 N | 71.59 E |
| Ward, N.Z. | 172 | 41.50 S | 174.08 E |
| Ward, Pa., U.S. | 285 | 39.53 N | 75.31 W |
| Ward ≃ | 166 | 26.32 S | 146.06 E |
| Ward, Mount ∧ | 172 | 43.52 S | 169.50 E |
| Warda | 222 | 30.03 N | 96.55 W |
| Ward Cove | 182 | 55.24 N | 131.44 W |
| Warden, S. Afr. | 158 | 27.56 S | 29.00 E |
| Warden, Wa., U.S. | 202 | 46.58 N | 119.02 W |
| Wardenburg | 52 | 53.04 N | 8.11 E |
| Warder | 54 | 53.59 N | 10.22 E |
| Wardersee ⊜ | 54 | 53.58 N | 10.26 E |
| Wardha | 122 | 20.45 N | 78.37 E |
| Wardha ≃ | 122 | 19.38 N | 79.48 E |
| Ward Hill ∧[2], Scot., U.K. | 46 | 58.54 N | 3.20 W |
| Ward Hill ∧[2], Scot., U.K. | 46 | 58.57 N | 3.09 W |
| Ward Hunt, Cape > | 164 | 8.05 S | 149.55 E |
| Ward Hunt Strait ɥ | 164 | 9.25 S | 149.55 E |
| Wardle | 44 | 53.39 N | 2.08 W |
| Wardlow | 182 | 50.54 N | 111.33 W |
| Ward Mountain ∧ | 202 | 46.10 N | 114.17 W |
| Wardner | 182 | 49.25 N | 115.26 W |
| Wardour, Vale of V | 42 | 51.05 N | 2.00 W |
| Wards Chapel | 284b | 39.24 N | 76.52 W |
| Wards Island I | 276 | 40.47 N | 73.56 W |
| Ward's Stone ∧ | 44 | 54.02 N | 2.38 W |
| Wardsville, On., Can. | 214 | 42.39 N | 81.45 W |
| Wardsville, Mo., U.S. | 219 | 38.29 N | 92.10 W |
| Wardswell Draw V | 196 | 32.39 N | 102.35 W |
| Wardt | 52 | 51.41 N | 6.25 E |
| Ware, Eng., U.K. | 42 | 51.49 N | 0.02 W |
| Ware, Ma., U.S. | 207 | 42.15 N | 72.14 W |
| Ware ≃ | 207 | 42.11 N | 72.22 W |
| War Eagle Creek ≃ | 194 | 36.14 N | 94.00 W |
| Waregem | 50 | 50.53 N | 3.25 E |
| Wareham, Eng., U.K. | 42 | 50.41 N | 2.07 W |
| Wareham, Ma., U.S. | 207 | 41.45 N | 70.43 W |
| Warehouse Point | 207 | 41.55 N | 72.37 W |
| Waremme | 56 | 50.41 N | 5.15 E |
| Waren, Dtsch. | 54 | 53.31 N | 12.40 E |
| Waren, Indon. | 164 | 2.16 S | 136.20 E |
| Warenai ≃ | 164 | 2.52 S | 135.55 E |
| Warenda | 166 | 22.37 S | 140.32 E |
| Warendorf | 52 | 51.57 N | 7.59 E |
| Ware River c | 208 | 37.23 N | 76.27 W |
| Ware Shoals | 192 | 34.23 N | 82.14 W |
| Waretown | 208 | 39.47 N | 74.11 W |
| Warffum | 52 | 53.23 N | 6.34 E |
| Warfusée-Abancourt | 50 | 49.52 N | 2.35 E |
| Warga | 52 | 53.08 N | 5.51 E |
| Wargalo | 144 | 6.17 N | 47.31 E |
| Wargla | 148 | 31.59 N | 5.25 E |
| Warialda | 166 | 29.32 S | 150.34 E |
| Wariap | 164 | 1.34 S | 134.11 E |
| Warilau | 164 | 5.24 S | 134.30 E |
| Warilau, Pulau I | 164 | 5.23 S | 134.33 E |
| Warin | 54 | 53.48 N | 11.42 E |
| Warinanco Park ♠ | 276 | 40.39 N | 74.14 W |
| Warin Chamrap | 110 | 15.12 N | 104.53 E |
| Waring Mountains ʎ | 180 | 66.50 N | 159.00 W |
| Wāris Alīganj | 124 | 25.01 N | 85.38 E |
| Warka | 30 | 51.47 N | 21.10 E |
| Warkopi | 164 | 1.08 S | 134.07 E |
| Warks Burn ≃ | 44 | 55.03 N | 2.08 W |
| Warkworth, On., Can. | 212 | 44.12 N | 77.53 W |
| Warkworth, N.Z. | 172 | 36.24 S | 174.40 E |
| Warkworth, Eng., U.K. | 44 | 55.21 N | 1.36 W |
| Warland, Eng., U.K. | 262 | 53.41 N | 2.05 W |
| Warland, Mt., U.S. | 182 | 48.30 N | 115.17 W |
| Warland Reservoir ⊜[1] | 262 | 53.41 N | 2.04 W |
| Warley → Smethwick | 42 | 52.30 N | 1.58 W |

**PORTUGUÊS**

| Nome | Página | Lat.°′ | Long.°′ W = Oeste |
|---|---|---|---|
| Warley Moor Reservoir ⊜[1] | 262 | 53.47 N | 1.57 W |
| Warlingham | 42 | 51.19 N | 0.04 W |
| Warlington | 42 | 51.39 N | 1.01 W |
| Warman | 184 | 52.20 N | 106.34 W |
| Warmandi | 164 | 0.22 S | 132.39 E |
| Warmbad, Namibia | 156 | 28.29 S | 18.41 E |
| Warmbad, S. Afr. | 156 | 24.55 S | 28.15 E |
| Warm Baths → Warmbad | 156 | 24.55 S | 28.15 E |
| Warm Beach | 224 | 48.10 N | 122.21 W |
| War Memorial Cross ⊥ | 169 | 37.20 S | 144.36 E |
| Warmenhuizen | 52 | 52.43 N | 4.44 E |
| Warmensteinach | 60 | 49.59 N | 11.47 E |
| Warmeriville | 50 | 49.21 N | 4.13 E |
| Warmington | 42 | 52.08 N | 1.24 W |
| Warminster, Eng., U.K. | 42 | 51.13 N | 2.12 W |
| Warminster, Pa., U.S. | 208 | 40.12 N | 75.06 W |
| Warminster Naval Air Development Center ■ | 285 | 40.12 N | 75.09 W |
| Warm Springs, Ga., U.S. | 192 | 32.53 N | 84.40 W |
| Warm Springs, Mt., U.S. | 202 | 46.11 N | 112.48 W |
| Warm Springs, Or., U.S. | 202 | 44.45 N | 121.15 W |
| Warm Springs, Va., U.S. | 192 | 38.02 N | 79.47 W |
| Warm Springs ≃ | 202 | 44.52 N | 121.04 W |
| Warm Springs Indian Reservation ◆[4] | 224 | 45.00 N | 121.25 W |
| Warm Springs Reservoir ⊜[1] | 202 | 43.37 N | 118.14 W |
| Warnbro Sound ɥ | 168a | 32.20 S | 115.40 E |
| Warnemünde ◆[8] | 54 | 54.10 N | 12.04 E |
| Warner, Ab., Can. | 182 | 49.17 N | 112.12 W |
| Warner, N.H., U.S. | 188 | 43.16 N | 71.49 W |
| Warner, Ok., U.S. | 196 | 35.29 N | 95.18 W |
| Warner Lakes ⊜ | 202 | 42.25 N | 119.50 W |
| Warner Mountains ʎ | 204 | 41.40 N | 120.20 W |
| Warner Peak ∧ | 202 | 42.27 N | 119.44 W |
| Warner Robins | 192 | 32.37 N | 83.36 W |
| Warners | 210 | 43.05 N | 76.20 W |
| Warners Pond ⊜ | 283 | 42.28 N | 71.24 W |
| Warnerville | 210 | 42.34 N | 74.30 W |
| Warnes, Arg. | 252 | 34.55 S | 60.31 W |
| Warnes, Bol. | 248 | 17.30 S | 63.10 W |
| Warnes Brook ≃ | 276 | 40.25 N | 74.18 W |
| Warneton | 50 | 50.45 N | 2.57 E |
| Warngau | 64 | 47.50 N | 11.41 E |
| Warnicker → Primorje | 76 | 54.57 N | 20.02 E |
| Warnkenhagen | 54 | 54.00 N | 11.04 E |
| Warnow ≃ | 54 | 54.06 N | 12.09 E |
| Warns | 52 | 52.52 N | 5.25 E |
| Warnsveld | 52 | 52.08 N | 6.13 E |
| Waroona | 168a | 32.50 S | 115.55 E |
| Warpath ≃ | 184 | 52.21 N | 98.26 W |
| Warra | 166 | 26.56 S | 150.55 E |
| Warrabri Aboriginal Reserve ◆[4] | 162 | 21.00 S | 134.20 E |
| Warracknabeal | 166 | 36.15 S | 142.24 E |
| Warr Acres | 196 | 35.31 N | 97.37 W |
| Warragamba Dam ◆[6] | 170 | 33.54 S | 150.36 E |
| Warragul | 169 | 38.10 S | 145.56 E |
| Warrandyte | 274b | 37.45 S | 145.13 E |
| Warrandyte South | 274b | 37.46 S | 145.14 E |
| Warrāq al-'Arab | 273c | 30.06 N | 31.12 E |
| Warrāq al-Ḥaḍar, Jazīrat I | 273c | 30.07 N | 31.13 E |
| Warrāq al-Hadar wa Ambūtbah wa Mīt an-Naṣārā | 273c | 30.06 N | 31.13 E |
| Warrawagine | 162 | 20.51 S | 120.42 E |
| Warrawee | 274a | 33.44 S | 151.07 E |
| Warrawolong, Mount ∧ | 170 | 33.03 S | 151.15 E |
| Warrawong | 170 | 34.29 S | 150.53 E |
| Warrego ≃ | 166 | 30.24 S | 145.21 E |
| Warrego Range ʎ | 166 | 25.00 S | 146.30 E |
| Warren, Austl. | 166 | 31.42 S | 147.50 E |
| Warren, Eng., U.K. | 262 | 53.14 N | 2.10 W |
| Warren, Ar., U.S. | 194 | 33.36 N | 92.03 W |
| Warren, Il., U.S. | 190 | 42.29 N | 89.59 W |
| Warren, In., U.S. | 216 | 40.40 N | 85.25 W |
| Warren, Ma., U.S. | 207 | 42.12 N | 72.11 W |
| Warren, Mi., U.S. | 216 | 42.28 N | 83.01 W |
| Warren, Mn., U.S. | 198 | 48.11 N | 96.46 W |
| Warren, Mo., U.S. | 219 | 39.47 N | 91.45 W |
| Warren, N.J., U.S. | 276 | 40.37 N | 74.30 W |
| Warren, Oh., U.S. | 214 | 41.14 N | 80.49 W |
| Warren, Or., U.S. | 224 | 45.49 N | 122.50 W |
| Warren, Pa., U.S. | 214 | 41.50 N | 79.08 W |
| Warren, R.I., U.S. | 207 | 41.43 N | 71.16 W |
| Warren □[6], In., U.S. | 216 | 40.21 N | 87.17 W |
| Warren □[6], Mo., U.S. | 219 | 38.45 N | 91.09 W |
| Warren □[6], N.J., U.S. | 210 | 40.49 N | 75.05 W |
| Warren □[6], N.Y., U.S. | 210 | 43.26 N | 73.43 W |
| Warren □[6], Oh., U.S. | 218 | 39.26 N | 84.13 W |
| Warren □[6], Pa., U.S. | 214 | 41.51 N | 79.08 W |
| Warren ≃ | 162 | 34.35 S | 115.50 E |
| Warren City | 222 | 32.33 N | 94.54 W |
| Warrendale | 214 | 40.39 N | 80.04 W |
| Warren Dunes State Park ♠ | 216 | 41.56 N | 86.36 W |
| Warren H. Manning State Park ♠ | 283 | 42.34 N | 71.18 W |
| Warren Park | 218 | 39.46 N | 86.03 W |
| Warren Peaks ʎ | 198 | 44.29 N | 104.28 W |
| Warrenpoint | 48 | 54.06 N | 6.15 W |
| Warren Point > | 180 | 69.44 N | 132.30 W |
| Warrens | 190 | 44.07 N | 90.29 W |
| Warrensburg, Il., U.S. | 219 | 39.56 N | 89.04 W |
| Warrensburg, Mo., U.S. | 194 | 38.45 N | 93.44 W |
| Warrensburg, N.Y., U.S. | 188 | 43.29 N | 73.46 W |
| Warrensville | 210 | 41.19 N | 76.57 W |
| Warrensville Heights | 214 | 41.26 N | 81.32 W |
| Warrenton, S. Afr. | 158 | 28.09 S | 24.47 E |
| Warrenton, Ga., U.S. | 192 | 33.24 N | 82.39 W |
| Warrenton, Mo., U.S. | 219 | 38.48 N | 91.08 W |
| Warrenton, N.C., U.S. | 192 | 36.23 N | 78.09 W |
| Warrenton, Or., U.S. | 224 | 46.09 N | 123.55 W |
| Warrenton, Tx., U.S. | 222 | 30.01 N | 96.44 W |
| Warrenton, Va., U.S. | 188 | 38.42 N | 77.47 W |
| Warrenville | 216 | 41.49 N | 88.10 W |
| Warrenzin | 54 | 53.54 N | 12.57 E |
| Warri | 150 | 5.31 N | 5.45 E |
| Warriedar Hill ∧[2] | 162 | 29.06 S | 117.06 E |
| Warriewood | 274a | 33.42 S | 151.18 E |
| Warrill Creek ≃ | 171a | 27.39 S | 152.44 E |
| Warrington, N.Z. | 172 | 45.43 S | 170.35 E |
| Warrington, Eng., U.K. | 44 | 53.24 N | 2.37 W |
| Warrington, Fl., U.S. | 194 | 30.23 N | 87.16 W |
| Warrington, Pa., U.S. | 285 | 40.15 N | 75.08 W |
| Warrington □[8] | 262 | 53.24 N | 2.33 W |
| Warrington Airport ⊠ | 285 | 40.16 N | 75.09 W |
| Warrior | 194 | 33.48 N | 86.48 W |
| Warrior Creek ≃ | 192 | 31.15 N | 83.34 W |
| Warrior Reefs ✣[2] | 164 | 9.35 S | 143.10 E |
| Warriors Mark | 214 | 40.42 N | 78.08 W |
| Warrnambool | 166 | 38.23 S | 142.29 E |
| Warroad | 198 | 48.54 N | 95.18 W |
| Warrumbungle National Park ♠ | 166 | 31.20 S | 149.00 E |
| Warsak | 123 | 34.10 N | 71.25 E |
| Warsaw → Warszawa, Pol. | 30 | 52.15 N | 21.00 E |
| Warsaw, Il., U.S. | 190 | 40.21 N | 91.26 W |
| Warsaw, In., U.S. | 216 | 41.14 N | 85.51 W |
| Warsaw, Ky., U.S. | 218 | 38.47 N | 84.54 W |
| Warsaw, Mo., U.S. | 194 | 38.14 N | 93.22 W |
| Warsaw, N.Y., U.S. | 210 | 42.44 N | 78.07 W |
| Warsaw, N.C., U.S. | 192 | 34.59 N | 78.05 W |
| Warsaw, Oh., U.S. | 214 | 40.20 N | 82.00 W |
| Warsaw, Va., U.S. | 208 | 37.57 N | 76.45 W |
| Warsaw Station ◆[5] | 265a | 59.54 N | 30.19 E |
| Warschau → Warszawa | 30 | 52.15 N | 21.00 E |
| Warscheneck ∧ | 61 | 47.39 N | 14.14 E |
| Warshiikh | 144 | 2.18 N | 45.48 E |
| Warsop | 44 | 53.13 N | 1.09 W |
| Warspite | 182 | 54.06 N | 112.37 W |
| Warstein | 56 | 51.26 N | 8.21 E |
| Warszawa (Warsaw) | 30 | 52.15 N | 21.00 E |
| Warszawa □[4] | 30 | 52.15 N | 21.00 E |
| Warta | 30 | 51.42 N | 18.38 E |
| Warta ≃ | 30 | 52.35 N | 14.39 E |
| Wartburg, S. Afr. | 158 | 29.25 S | 30.35 E |
| Wartburg, Tn., U.S. | 192 | 36.06 N | 84.35 W |
| Wartburg ⊥ | 54 | 50.58 N | 10.18 E |
| Wartenberg | 60 | 48.24 N | 11.59 E |
| Wartenberg ◆[8] | 264a | 52.34 N | 13.31 E |
| Warth | 58 | 47.15 N | 10.11 E |
| Warthan Creek ≃ | 226 | 36.08 N | 120.20 W |
| Warthausen | 58 | 48.08 N | 9.48 E |
| Warthe → Warta ≃ | 30 | 52.35 N | 14.39 E |
| Wartin | 54 | 53.15 N | 14.09 E |
| Warton, Eng., U.K. | 44 | 54.09 N | 2.47 W |
| Warton, Eng., U.K. | 44 | 53.45 N | 2.54 W |
| Warton Aerodrome ⊠ | 262 | 53.45 N | 2.54 W |
| Wartrace | 194 | 35.31 N | 86.20 W |
| Wartsberg ∧[2] | 263 | 51.25 N | 6.29 E |
| Waru | 164 | 3.24 S | 130.40 E |
| Warud | 120 | 21.28 N | 78.16 E |
| Warunta, Laguna de ⊜ | 236 | 15.23 N | 84.05 W |
| Waruta ≃ | 164 | 3.18 S | 140.08 E |
| Warwick, Austl. | 171a | 28.13 S | 152.02 E |
| Warwick, P.Q., Can. | 206 | 45.56 N | 71.59 W |
| Warwick, Eng., U.K. | 42 | 52.17 N | 1.34 W |
| Warwick, Md., U.S. | 208 | 39.25 N | 75.46 W |
| Warwick, N.Y., U.S. | 210 | 41.15 N | 74.21 W |
| Warwick, R.I., U.S. | 207 | 41.41 N | 71.22 W |
| Warwick ≃ | 208 | 37.05 N | 76.33 W |
| Warwick Castle ⊥ | 42 | 52.17 N | 1.34 W |
| Warwick Channel ɥ | 164 | 13.51 S | 136.16 E |
| Warwick Farm Racecourse and Motor Race Track ♠ | 274a | 33.55 S | 150.57 E |
| Warwickshire □[6] | 42 | 52.13 N | 1.37 W |
| Warza | 54 | 51.00 N | 10.41 E |
| Wasaga Beach | 212 | 44.31 N | 80.01 W |
| Wasagu | 150 | 11.25 N | 5.49 E |
| Wasatch Mountain State Park ♠ | 200 | 40.33 N | 111.31 W |
| Wasatch Plateau ʎ[1] | 200 | 39.20 N | 111.30 W |
| Wasatch Range ʎ | 200 | 40.40 N | 111.35 W |
| Wasāwewāla | 123 | 30.28 N | 73.40 E |
| Wasbank | 158 | 28.24 S | 30.05 E |
| Wasbister | 46 | 59.10 N | 3.07 W |
| Wascana Creek ≃ | 184 | 50.39 N | 104.55 W |
| Wäschenbeuren | 56 | 48.46 N | 9.41 E |
| Wasco, Ca., U.S. | 226 | 35.35 N | 119.20 W |
| Wasco, Or., U.S. | 224 | 45.35 N | 120.41 W |
| Wasco □[6] | 224 | 45.10 N | 121.12 W |
| Wase | 150 | 9.06 N | 9.59 E |
| Wase ≃ | 146 | 8.27 N | 10.06 E |
| Waseca | 190 | 44.04 N | 93.30 W |
| Waseda University ʋ[2] | 268 | 35.42 N | 139.43 E |
| Wasekamio Lake ⊜ | 184 | 56.45 N | 108.45 W |
| Wasen | 58 | 47.03 N | 7.48 E |
| Wasgomuwa National Park ♠ | 122 | 7.40 N | 80.45 E |
| Washademoak Lake ⊜ | 186 | 45.48 N | 65.58 W |
| Washago | 212 | 44.45 N | 79.20 W |
| Washburn, Il., U.S. | 190 | 40.55 N | 89.17 W |
| Washburn, Me., U.S. | 186 | 46.47 N | 68.09 W |
| Washburn, N.D., U.S. | 198 | 47.17 N | 101.01 W |
| Washburn, Wi., U.S. | 190 | 46.40 N | 90.53 W |
| Washburn ≃ | 44 | 53.54 N | 1.39 W |
| Washburn, Mount ∧ | 202 | 44.48 N | 110.25 W |
| Washburn Lake ⊜ | 176 | 70.03 N | 106.50 W |
| Washdyke | 172 | 44.21 S | 171.14 E |
| Washicoutai | 186 | 50.17 N | 60.42 W |
| Washiga-take ∧ | 94 | 35.56 N | 136.58 E |
| Wāshīm | 122 | 20.06 N | 77.09 E |
| Washimiya | 94 | 36.06 N | 139.40 E |
| Washington, Eng., U.K. | 44 | 54.55 N | 1.30 W |
| Washington, Ca., U.S. | 226 | 39.22 N | 120.48 W |
| Washington, Ct., U.S. | 207 | 41.37 N | 73.18 W |
| Washington, D.C., U.S. | 208 | 38.53 N | 77.02 W |
| Washington, D.C., U.S. | 284c | 38.53 N | 77.02 W |
| Washington, Ga., U.S. | 192 | 33.44 N | 82.44 W |
| Washington, Il., U.S. | 190 | 40.42 N | 89.24 W |
| Washington, In., U.S. | 194 | 38.39 N | 87.10 W |
| Washington, Ia., U.S. | 190 | 41.17 N | 91.41 W |
| Washington, Ks., U.S. | 198 | 39.49 N | 97.03 W |
| Washington, Ky., U.S. | 218 | 38.36 N | 83.48 W |
| Washington, La., U.S. | 194 | 30.36 N | 92.03 W |
| Washington, Mi., U.S. | 214 | 42.44 N | 83.02 W |
| Washington, Mo., U.S. | 219 | 38.33 N | 91.01 W |
| Washington, N.J., U.S. | 210 | 40.45 N | 74.58 W |
| Washington, N.C., U.S. | 192 | 35.31 N | 77.01 W |
| Washington, Pa., U.S. | 214 | 40.10 N | 80.14 W |
| Washington, Tx., U.S. | 222 | 30.20 N | 96.10 W |
| Washington, Ut,. U.S. | 200 | 37.07 N | 113.30 W |
| Washington, Va., U.S. | 188 | 38.42 N | 78.09 W |
| Washington □[6], Il., U.S. | 219 | 38.21 N | 89.23 W |
| Washington □[6], In., U.S. | 218 | 38.36 N | 86.06 W |
| Washington □[6], N.Y., U.S. | 210 | 43.15 N | 73.27 W |
| Washington □[6], Or., U.S. | 224 | 45.33 N | 123.07 W |
| Washington □[6], Pa., U.S. | 214 | 40.10 N | 80.15 W |
| Washington □[6], R.I., U.S. | 207 | 41.28 N | 71.35 W |
| Washington □[6], Tx., U.S. | 222 | 30.15 N | 96.20 W |
| Washington □[6], Wi., U.S. | 216 | 43.14 N | 88.15 W |
| Washington □[3], U.S. | 178 | 47.30 N | 120.30 W |
| Washington □[3], U.S. | 202 | 47.30 N | 120.30 W |
| Washington, Lake ⊜, Fl., U.S. | 220 | 28.07 N | 80.45 W |
| Washington, Lake ⊜, Wa., U.S. | 224 | 47.37 N | 122.15 W |
| Washington, Mount ∧ | 188 | 44.15 N | 71.15 W |
| Washington Court House | 218 | 39.32 N | 83.26 W |
| Washington Crossing | 208 | 40.17 N | 74.52 W |
| Washington Crossing State Historic Site ⊥ | 208 | 40.17 N | 74.53 W |
| Washington Depot | 207 | 41.38 N | 73.18 W |
| Washington Heights ◆[8] | 276 | 40.52 N | 73.56 W |
| Washington Island | 190 | 45.23 N | 86.55 W |
| Washington Island I | 190 | 45.23 N | 86.55 W |
| Washington Memorial Chapel ʋ[1] | 285 | 40.06 N | 75.26 W |
| Washington Mills | 210 | 43.03 N | 75.16 W |
| Washington Monument ♠ | 284c | 38.53 N | 77.03 W |
| Washington Monument State Park ♠ | 208 | 39.30 N | 77.38 W |
| Washington National Airport ⊠ | 208 | 38.51 N | 77.02 W |
| Washington-on-the-Brazos State Historic Park ♠ | 222 | 30.20 N | 96.09 W |
| Washington Park | 219 | 38.38 N | 90.05 W |
| Washington Park ♠, Il., U.S. | 278 | 41.48 N | 87.37 W |
| Washington Park ♠, Oh., U.S. | 279a | 41.27 N | 81.40 W |
| Washington Pass )( | 224 | 48.32 N | 120.39 W |
| Washington Place | 218 | 39.47 N | 86.01 W |
| Washington Rock State Park ♠ | 276 | 40.37 N | 74.28 W |
| Washington's Headquarters ⊥ | 285 | 40.06 N | 75.28 W |
| Washington Terrace | 200 | 41.10 N | 111.58 W |
| Washington Township | 276 | 40.54 N | 74.00 W |
| Washington Valley | 276 | 40.48 N | 74.32 W |
| Washington Valley Reservoir ⊜[1] | 276 | 40.36 N | 74.34 W |
| Washingtonville, N.Y., U.S. | 210 | 41.26 N | 74.10 W |
| Washingtonville, Oh., U.S. | 214 | 40.54 N | 80.46 W |
| Washingtonville, Pa., U.S. | 210 | 41.03 N | 76.40 W |
| Washita ≃ | 196 | 34.12 N | 96.50 W |
| Washoe □[6] | 226 | 39.22 N | 119.43 W |
| Washoe Lake ⊜ | 226 | 39.16 N | 119.48 W |
| Washougal | 224 | 45.34 N | 122.21 W |
| Washougal ≃ | 224 | 45.35 N | 122.23 W |
| Washow Bay c | 184 | 51.22 N | 96.47 W |
| Washtenaw □[6] | 216 | 42.15 N | 83.50 W |
| Washtucna | 202 | 46.45 N | 118.18 W |
| Wāshuk | 128 | 27.44 N | 64.48 E |
| Wasian | 164 | 1.54 S | 133.17 E |
| Wasilków | 30 | 53.12 N | 23.12 E |
| Wasilla | 180 | 61.35 N | 149.26 W |
| Wasior | 164 | 2.43 S | 134.30 E |
| Wasiri | 112 | 7.35 S | 126.38 E |
| Wāsiṭ □[4] | 128 | 32.45 N | 45.25 E |
| Waskada | 184 | 49.06 N | 100.46 W |
| Waskaganish | 176 | 51.30 N | 78.45 W |
| Waskahigan ≃ | 182 | 54.45 N | 117.12 W |
| Waskaiowaka Lake ⊜ | 184 | 56.30 N | 96.20 W |
| Waskatenau | 182 | 54.07 N | 112.47 W |
| Waskesiu Lake ⊜ | 184 | 53.56 N | 106.10 W |
| Waskom | 194 | 32.29 N | 94.04 W |
| Wąsosz | 30 | 51.34 N | 16.42 E |
| Waspam | 236 | 14.44 N | 83.58 W |
| Waspuk ≃ | 236 | 14.38 N | 84.26 W |
| Wasquehal | 50 | 50.40 N | 3.09 E |
| Wassaic | 210 | 41.48 N | 73.35 W |
| Wasselonne | 58 | 48.38 N | 7.27 E |
| Wassen | 58 | 46.42 N | 8.36 E |
| Wassenaar | 52 | 52.07 N | 4.24 E |
| Wassenberg | 56 | 51.06 N | 6.08 E |
| Wasseralfingen | 56 | 48.52 N | 10.06 E |
| Wasserbillig | 56 | 49.44 N | 6.30 E |
| Wasserburg am Inn | 60 | 48.04 N | 12.13 E |
| Wasserkuppe ∧ | 56 | 50.30 N | 9.56 E |
| Wasserkurl | 263 | 51.33 N | 7.38 E |
| Wasserleben | 54 | 51.55 N | 10.44 E |
| Wassertrüdingen | 56 | 49.02 N | 10.35 E |
| Wassigny | 50 | 50.01 N | 3.36 E |
| Wass Lake ⊜ | 184 | 53.40 N | 95.25 W |
| Wassmannsdorf | 264a | 52.22 N | 13.28 E |
| Wassou | 150 | 10.02 N | 13.39 W |
| Wassy | 58 | 48.30 N | 4.57 E |
| Wast Water ⊜ | 44 | 54.26 N | 3.18 W |
| Wasu | 164 | 6.00 S | 147.15 E |
| Wasum | 164 | 6.05 S | 149.20 E |
| Wasungen | 54 | 50.40 N | 10.22 E |
| Watabeag Lake ⊜ | 190 | 48.14 N | 80.32 W |
| Watampone (Bone) | 112 | 4.32 S | 120.20 E |
| Watamu Marine National Park ♠ | 154 | 3.23 S | 40.00 E |
| Waṭan, Wādī al- V | 142 | 30.26 N | 31.49 E |
| Watansopeng | 112 | 4.21 S | 119.53 E |
| Watapi Lake ⊜ | 184 | 55.18 N | 109.35 W |
| Watarai | 94 | 34.26 N | 136.37 E |
| Watarase ≃ | 94 | 36.13 N | 139.42 E |
| Wataru I | 122 | 5.43 N | 73.23 E |
| Watatic, Mount ∧ | 207 | 42.42 N | 71.53 W |
| Watauga | 222 | 32.51 N | 97.15 W |
| Watchet | 42 | 51.12 N | 3.20 W |
| Watch Hill | 207 | 41.18 N | 71.51 W |
| Watchung | 276 | 40.38 N | 74.27 W |
| Watchung Reservation ♠ | 276 | 40.41 N | 74.23 W |
| Water | 262 | 53.44 N | 2.14 W |
| Waterbeach | 42 | 52.16 N | 0.11 E |
| Waterberg | 156 | 20.28 S | 17.13 E |
| Waterberge ʎ | 156 | 24.30 S | 28.00 E |
| Waterberg Plateau Park ♠ | 156 | 20.30 S | 17.00 E |
| Waterbury, Ct., U.S. | 207 | 41.33 N | 73.02 W |
| Waterbury, Vt., U.S. | 188 | 44.20 N | 72.45 W |
| Waterdale | 158 | 30.40 S | 24.02 E |
| Wateree ≃ | 192 | 33.45 N | 80.37 W |
| Wateree Lake ⊜[1] | 192 | 34.25 N | 80.50 W |
| Waterend, Eng., U.K. | 260 | 51.47 N | 0.30 W |
| Water End, Eng., U.K. | 262 | 53.41 N | 2.15 W |
| Waterfall, Austl. | 170 | 34.08 S | 151.00 E |
| Waterfall, Pa., U.S. | 214 | 40.08 N | 78.04 W |
| Waterford, On., Can. | 212 | 42.56 N | 80.17 W |
| Waterford (Port Láirge), Ire. | 48 | 52.15 N | 7.06 W |
| Waterford, S. Afr. | 158 | 33.05 S | 25.00 E |
| Waterford, Ca., U.S. | 226 | 37.38 N | 120.46 W |
| Waterford, Ct., U.S. | 207 | 41.20 N | 72.09 W |
| Waterford, In., U.S. | 216 | 41.40 N | 86.50 W |
| Waterford, Mi., U.S. | 216 | 42.42 N | 83.24 W |
| Waterford, N.Y., U.S. | 210 | 42.47 N | 73.40 W |
| Waterford, Pa., U.S. | 214 | 41.56 N | 79.59 W |
| Waterford, Wi., U.S. | 216 | 42.45 N | 88.12 W |
| Waterford □[6] | 48 | 52.10 N | 7.40 W |
| Waterford Harbour c | 48 | 52.10 N | 6.55 W |
| Waterford Mills | 216 | 41.33 N | 85.50 W |
| Waterford Works | 208 | 39.43 N | 74.50 W |
| Watergate Bay c | 42 | 50.27 N | 5.05 W |
| Watergrasshill | 48 | 52.01 N | 8.21 W |
| Watergrove Reservoir ⊜[1] | 262 | 53.39 N | 2.08 W |
| Waterhen ≃ | 184 | 54.38 N | 107.47 W |
| Waterhen Lake ⊜, Mb., Can. | 184 | 52.06 N | 99.34 W |
| Waterhen Lake ⊜, Sk., Can. | 184 | 54.28 N | 108.25 W |
| Waterhouse Range ʎ | 162 | 24.01 S | 133.25 E |
| Wateringbury | 260 | 51.15 N | 0.25 E |
| Wateringen | 52 | 52.02 N | 4.16 E |
| Water Island | 276 | 40.41 N | 73.02 W |
| Waterkloof | 158 | 30.19 S | 25.18 E |
| Waterloo, Austl. | 164 | 16.38 S | 129.18 E |
| Waterloo, Austl. | 168a | 33.20 S | 115.47 E |
| Waterloo, Austl. | 168b | 33.59 S | 138.53 E |
| Waterloo, Bel. | 50 | 50.43 N | 4.23 E |
| Waterloo, On., Can. | 212 | 43.28 N | 80.31 W |
| Waterloo, P.Q., Can. | 206 | 45.21 N | 72.31 W |
| Waterloo, S.L. | 150 | 8.20 N | 13.04 W |
| Waterloo, Eng., U.K. | 44 | 53.28 N | 3.02 W |
| Waterloo, Al., U.S. | 194 | 34.55 N | 88.03 W |
| Waterloo, Il., U.S. | 219 | 38.20 N | 90.08 W |
| Waterloo, In., U.S. | 216 | 41.25 N | 85.01 W |
| Waterloo, Ia., U.S. | 190 | 42.29 N | 92.20 W |
| Waterloo, N.Y., U.S. | 210 | 42.54 N | 76.51 W |
| Waterloo, Wi., U.S. | 216 | 43.11 N | 88.59 W |
| Waterloo □[6] | 212 | 43.30 N | 80.30 W |
| Waterloo Bay c | 168b | 35.08 S | 137.26 E |
| Waterloo State Recreation Area ♠ | 216 | 42.22 N | 84.20 W |
| Waterlooville | 42 | 50.5[illegible] N | 1.02 W |
| Waterman, Il., U.S. | 216 | 41.4[illegible] N | 88.46 W |
| Waterman, Wa., U.S. | 224 | 47.3[illegible] N | 122.35 W |
| Waterman Mountain ∧ | 228 | 34.2[illegible] N | 117.56 W |
| Waterman Wash V | 200 | 33.2[illegible] N | 112.31 W |
| Water Mill | 207 | 40.5[illegible] N | 72.21 W |
| Waterport | 210 | 43.2[illegible] N | 78.16 W |
| Waterport Pond ⊜[1] | 212 | 43.1[illegible] N | 78.16 W |
| Waterproof | 194 | 31.4[illegible] N | 91.23 W |
| Waterside | 214 | 40.1[illegible] N | 78.23 W |
| Waterside Park | 276 | 40.5[illegible] N | 73.20 W |
| Watersmeet | 190 | 46.1[illegible] N | 89.10 W |
| Waterton ≃ | 182 | 49.3[illegible] N | 113.16 W |
| Waterton-Glacier International Peace Park ♠ | 202 | 48.4[illegible] N | 113.45 W |
| Waterton Lakes National Park ♠ | 182 | 49.0[illegible] N | 113.50 W |
| Watertown, Ct., U.S. | 207 | 41.3[illegible] N | 73.07 W |
| Watertown, Ma., U.S. | 207 | 42.2[illegible] N | 71.11 W |
| Watertown, N.Y., U.S. | 212 | 43.5[illegible] N | 75.54 W |
| Watertown, S.D., U.S. | 198 | 44.5[illegible] N | 97.06 W |
| Watertown, Wi., U.S. | 216 | 43.1[illegible] N | 88.43 W |
| Waterval-Boven | 156 | 25.4[illegible] S | 30.20 E |
| Watervale | 168b | 33.5[illegible] S | 138.38 E |
| Water Valley, Ms., U.S. | 194 | 34.0[illegible] N | 89.37 W |
| Water Valley, N.Y., U.S. | 284a | 42.4[illegible] N | 78.51 W |
| Water View | 208 | 37.4[illegible] N | 76.36 W |
| Waterville, N.S., Can. | 186 | 45.0[illegible] N | 64.41 W |
| Waterville, P.Q., Can. | 206 | 45.1[illegible] N | 71.54 W |
| Waterville, Ire. | 48 | 51.4[illegible] N | 10.13 W |
| Waterville, Ks., U.S. | 198 | 39.4[illegible] N | 96.44 W |
| Waterville, Me., U.S. | 188 | 44.3[illegible] N | 69.37 W |
| Waterville, Ma., U.S. | 207 | 42.4[illegible] N | 72.04 W |
| Waterville, Mn., U.S. | 190 | 44.1[illegible] N | 93.34 W |
| Waterville, N.Y., U.S. | 210 | 42.5[illegible] N | 75.22 W |
| Waterville, Oh., U.S. | 216 | 41.3[illegible] N | 83.43 W |
| Waterville, Pa., U.S. | 210 | 41.1[illegible] N | 77.22 W |
| Waterville, Wa., U.S. | 202 | 47.3[illegible] N | 120.04 W |
| Watervliet, Mi., U.S. | 216 | 42.1[illegible] N | 86.15 W |
| Watervliet, N.Y., U.S. | 210 | 42.4[illegible] N | 73.42 W |
| Watervliet Reservoir ⊜[1] | 210 | 42.4[illegible] N | 73.58 W |
| Wates, Indon. | 114 | 1.0[illegible] N | 100.16 E |
| Wates, Indon. | 115a | 7.5[illegible] S | 112.07 E |
| Wates, Indon. | 115a | 7.5[illegible] S | 110.10 E |
| Watford, On., Can. | 214 | 42.5[illegible] N | 81.53 W |
| Watford, Eng., U.K. | 42 | 51.4[illegible] N | 0.25 W |
| Watford □[8] | 260 | 51.4[illegible] N | 0.25 W |
| Watford City | 198 | 47.4[illegible] N | 103.16 W |
| Wa'th | 140 | 8.1[illegible] N | 32.07 E |
| Wathaman ≃ | 184 | 57.1[illegible] N | 102.52 W |
| Wathaman Lake ⊜ | 184 | 56.5[illegible] N | 103.43 W |
| Wathena | 198 | 39.4[illegible] N | 94.56 W |
| Watheroo | 162 | 30.1[illegible] S | 116.04 E |
| Watheroo National Park ♠ | 162 | 30.1[illegible] S | 115.52 E |
| Wathlingen | 52 | 52.3[illegible] N | 10.09 E |
| Wath upon Dearne | 44 | 53.2[illegible] N | 1.20 W |
| Wati | 120 | 28.0[illegible] N | 96.59 E |
| Watino | 182 | 55.4[illegible] N | 117.37 W |
| Watkins Glen | 210 | 42.2[illegible] N | 76.52 W |
| Watkins Glen International Raceway ♠ | 210 | 42.2[illegible] N | 76.55 W |
| Watkins Glen State Park ♠ | 210 | 42.2[illegible] N | 76.55 W |
| Watkins Island I | 284c | 39.02 N | 77.17 W |
| Watkins Lake ⊜ | 281 | 42.4[illegible] N | 83.22 W |
| Watkinsville | 192 | 33.51 N | 83.24 W |
| Watlaar | 164 | 5.28 S | 133.07 E |
| Watling Island → San Salvador I | 238 | 24.02 N | 74.28 W |
| Watlington | 42 | 51.37 N | 1.00 W |
| Watoga State Park ♠ | 188 | 38.07 N | 80.05 W |
| Watonga | 196 | 35.50 N | 98.24 W |
| Watonwan ≃ | 198 | 44.04 N | 94.07 W |
| Watopeka ≃ | 206 | 45.34 N | 72.00 W |
| Watou | 50 | 50.51 N | 2.37 E |
| Wat Phai Tan, Khlong ≊ | 269a | 13.48 N | 100.33 E |
| Watrous, Sk., Can. | 184 | 51.40 N | 105.28 W |
| Watrous, N.M., U.S. | 200 | 35.47 N | 104.58 W |
| Watsa | 154 | 3.03 N | 29.32 E |
| Watseka | 216 | 40.46 N | 87.44 W |
| Watsi Kengo | 152 | 0.48 S | 20.33 E |
| Watson, Austl. | 162 | 30.29 S | 131.31 E |
| Watson, Sk., Can. | 184 | 52.07 N | 104.31 W |
| Watson, In., U.S. | 218 | 38.22 N | 85.41 W |
| Watsonia | 274b | 37.43 S | 145.05 E |
| Watson Lake | 180 | 60.07 N | 128.48 W |
| Watsons Bay | 274a | 33.51 S | 151.17 E |
| Watsons Creek | 274b | 37.40 S | 145.13 E |
| Watsons Creek ≃ | 274b | 37.43 S | 145.16 E |
| Watsontown | 210 | 41.05 N | 76.51 W |
| Watsonville | 226 | 36.54 N | 121.45 W |
| Watt | 222 | 31.39 N | 96.51 W |
| Watten | 50 | 50.50 N | 2.13 E |
| Watten, Loch ⊜ | 46 | 58.29 N | 3.19 W |
| Wattens | 64 | 47.17 N | 11.36 E |
| Wattenscheid | 56 | 51.29 N | 7.08 E |
| Wattenwil | 58 | 46.46 N | 7.30 E |
| Wattignies | 50 | 50.35 N | 3.03 E |
| Wattiwarriganna ≃ | 162 | 28.57 S | 136.10 E |
| Wattle Flat | 170 | 33.08 S | 149.41 E |
| Wattle Glen | 274b | 37.40 S | 145.11 E |
| Wattle Park ♠ | 274b | 37.50 S | 145.07 E |
| Watt Mountain ∧ | 240d | 15.19 N | 61.19 W |
| Watton | 42 | 52.35 N | 0.48 E |
| Wattrelos | 50 | 50.42 N | 3.13 E |
| Watts ◆[8] | 280 | 33.56 N | 118.15 W |
| Watts Bar Lake ⊜[1] | 192 | 35.48 N | 84.39 W |
| Watts Branch ≃ | 284c | 39.03 N | 77.15 W |
| Wattsburg | 214 | 42.00 N | 79.49 W |
| Watts Island I | 208 | 37.48 N | 75.53 W |
| Watts Mills | 192 | 34.31 N | 82.02 W |
| Wattville | 273d | 26.13 S | 28.18 E |
| Wattwil | 58 | 47.18 N | 9.06 E |
| Watu | 152 | 3.18 S | 20.03 E |
| Watubela, Kepulauan II | 164 | 4.35 S | 131.40 E |
| Wat Wat | 164 | 4.29 S | 152.21 E |
| Watzespitze ∧ | 58 | 46.59 N | 10.48 E |
| Watzmann ∧ | 64 | 47.33 N | 12.55 E |
| Wau | 164 | 7.20 S | 146.45 E |
| Waubach | 56 | 50.55 N | 6.03 E |
| Waubaushene | 212 | 44.45 N | 79.42 W |
| Waubaushene Channel ɥ | 212 | 44.46 N | 79.45 W |
| Waubay | 198 | 45.19 N | 97.18 W |
| Waubay Lake ⊜ | 198 | 45.25 N | 97.25 W |
| Waubesa, Lake ⊜ | 216 | 43.01 | 89.20 W |
| Waubra | 169 | 37.21 | 143.39 E |
| Waubuno Creek ≃ | 212 | 42.58 | 81.08 W |
| Wauchope, Austl. | 162 | 20.36 | 134.15 E |
| Wauchope, Austl. | 166 | 31.27 | 152.44 E |
| Wauchula | 220 | 27.32 | 81.48 W |
| Wauconda, Il., U.S. | 216 | 42.15 | 88.08 W |
| Wauconda, Wa., U.S. | 182 | 48.43 | 119.00 W |
| Wauconda, Wa., U.S. | 202 | 48.43 | 119.00 W |
| Waugh | 184 | 49.40 | 95.13 W |
| Waugh Mountain ∧ | 202 | 45.29 | 114.47 W |
| Waukara, Bukit ∧ | 112 | 1.15 S | 119.42 E |
| Waukaringa | 166 | 32.18 S | 139.26 E |
| Waukarlycarly, Lake ⊜ | 162 | 21.25 S | 121.50 E |
| Waukegan | 216 | 42.21 N | 87.50 W |
| Waukena | 226 | 36.08 N | 119.31 W |
| Waukesha | 216 | 43.00 N | 88.13 W |
| Waukesha □[6] | 216 | 43.02 N | 88.20 W |
| Waukomis | 196 | 36.16 N | 97.53 W |
| Waukon | 190 | 43.16 N | 91.28 W |
| Waulsort | 56 | 50.13 N | 4.52 E |
| Wauna | 224 | 47.22 N | 122.38 W |
| Waunakee | 216 | 43.11 N | 89.27 W |


| Symbol | English | Deutsch | Español | Français | Português |
|---|---|---|---|---|---|
| ≃ | River | Fluß | Río | Rivière | Rio |
| ≊ | Canal | Kanal | Canal | Canal | Canal |
| ʟ | Waterfall, Rapids | Wasserfall, Stromschnellen | Cascada, Rápidos | Chute d'eau, Rapides | Cascata, Rápidos |
| ɥ | Strait | Meeresstraße | Estrecho | Détroit | Estreito |
| c | Bay, Gulf | Bucht, Golf | Bahía, Golfo | Baie, Golfe | Baía, Golfo |
| ⊜ | Lake, Lakes | See, Seen | Lago, Lagos | Lac, Lacs | Lago, Lagos |
| ≡ | Swamp | Sumpf | Pantano | Marais | Pântano |
| ʀ | Ice Features, Glacier | Eis- und Gletscherformen | Accidentes Glaciales | Formes glaciaires | Acidentes glaciares |
| ʃ | Other Hydrographic Features | Andere Hydrographische Objekte | Otros Elementos Hidrográficos | Autres données hydrographiques | Outros acidentes hidrográficos |
| ✣ | Submarine Features | Untermeerische Objekte | Accidentes Submarinos | Formes de relief sous-marin | Acidentes submarinos |
| □ | Political Unit | Politische Einheit | Unidad Politica | Entité politique | Unidade política |
| ʋ | Cultural Institution | Kulturelle Institution | Institución Cultural | Institution culturelle | Instituição cultural |
| ⊥ | Historical Site | Historische Stätte | Sitio Histórico | Site historique | Sitio histórico |
| ♠ | Recreational Site | Erholungs- und Ferienort | Sitio de Recreo | Centre de loisirs | Area de Lazer |
| ⊠ | Airport | Flughafen | Aeropuerto | Aéroport | Aeroporto |
| ■ | Military Installation | Militäranlage | Instalación Militar | Installation militaire | Instalação militar |
| ◆ | Miscellaneous | Verschiedenes | Misceláneo | Divers | Diversos |

ENGLISH — DEUTSCH


| Name | Page / Seite | Lat.°′ / Breite°′ | Long.°′ / Länge°′ E = Ost |
|---|---|---|---|
| Wauneta | 198 | 40.25 N | 101.22 W |
| Waupaca | 190 | 44.21 N | 89.05 W |
| Waupecan Creek ≃ | 216 | 41.20 N | 88.28 W |
| Waupoos Island I | 212 | 43.59 N | 76.58 W |
| Waupun | 190 | 43.38 N | 88.43 W |
| Wauregan | 207 | 41.44 N | 71.54 W |
| Waurika | 196 | 34.10 N | 97.59 W |
| Waurika Lake ⊜[1] | 196 | 34.15 N | 98.05 W |
| Wausa | 198 | 42.29 N | 97.32 W |
| Wausau | 190 | 44.57 N | 89.37 W |
| Wausaukee | 190 | 45.22 N | 87.57 W |
| Wauseon | 216 | 41.32 N | 84.08 W |
| Waushakum Pond ⊜ | 283 | 42.16 N | 71.26 W |
| Wautoma | 190 | 44.04 N | 89.17 W |
| Wauwa | 154 | 3.27 N | 27.21 E |
| Wauwatosa | 216 | 43.02 N | 88.00 W |
| Wauzeka | 190 | 43.05 N | 90.52 W |
| Wave Hill | 162 | 17.29 S | 130.57 E |
| Waveland, Ma., U.S. | 283 | 42.17 N | 70.53 W |
| Waveland, Ms., U.S. | 194 | 30.17 N | 89.22 W |
| Waveney ≃ | 42 | 52.28 N | 1.45 E |
| Waver ≃ | 44 | 54.52 N | 3.17 W |
| Waverley, Austl. | 169 | 37.53 S | 145.10 E |
| Waverley, Austl. | 274a | 33.54 S | 151.16 E |
| Waverley, N.Z. | 172 | 39.46 S | 174.38 E |
| Waverley, S. Afr. | 158 | 31.58 S | 26.28 E |
| Waverley, Ma., U.S. | 283 | 42.23 N | 71.11 W |
| Waverley ◆[8] | 273d | 26.08 S | 28.04 E |
| Waverly, Al., U.S. | 194 | 32.44 N | 85.35 W |
| Waverly, Fl., U.S. | 220 | 27.59 N | 81.37 W |
| Waverly, Il., U.S. | 219 | 39.35 N | 89.57 W |
| Waverly, Ia., U.S. | 190 | 42.43 N | 92.28 W |
| Waverly, Ks., U.S. | 198 | 38.23 N | 95.36 W |
| Waverly, Mi., U.S. | 216 | 42.44 N | 84.33 W |
| Waverly, Mn., U.S. | 190 | 45.04 N | 93.57 W |
| Waverly, Mo., U.S. | 194 | 39.12 N | 93.31 W |
| Waverly, Ne., U.S. | 198 | 40.55 N | 96.31 W |
| Waverly, N.Y., U.S. | 210 | 42.00 N | 76.31 W |
| Waverly, Oh., U.S. | 218 | 39.07 N | 82.59 W |
| Waverly, Pa., U.S. | 210 | 41.32 N | 75.42 W |
| Waverly, Tn., U.S. | 194 | 36.05 N | 87.47 W |
| Waverly, Va., U.S. | 208 | 37.02 N | 77.05 W |
| Waverly Hall | 192 | 32.41 N | 84.44 W |
| Wavre | 56 | 50.43 N | 4.37 E |
| Wavrin | 50 | 50.34 N | 2.55 E |
| Wāw | 140 | 7.42 N | 28.00 E |
| Wāw ≃ | 140 | 7.03 N | 27.13 E |
| Wawa, On., Can. | 190 | 47.59 N | 84.47 W |
| Wawa, Nig. | 150 | 9.55 N | 4.25 E |
| Wawa, Sūd. | 140 | 20.26 N | 30.21 E |
| Wawa ≃ | 236 | 13.53 N | 83.28 W |
| Wawaka | 216 | 41.27 N | 85.28 W |
| Wāw al-Kabīr | 146 | 25.20 N | 16.43 E |
| Wawanesa | 184 | 49.36 N | 99.41 W |
| Wawarsing | 210 | 41.46 N | 74.21 W |
| Wawasee, Lake ⊜ | 216 | 41.24 N | 85.41 W |
| Wawayanda State Park ♦ | 276 | 41.11 N | 74.26 W |
| Wawiag ≃ | 190 | 48.25 N | 91.07 W |
| Wawoi ≃ | 164 | 8.01 S | 143.33 E |
| Waworada, Teluk c | 115b | 8.44 S | 118.51 E |
| Wawota | 184 | 49.55 N | 102.00 W |
| Waxahachie | 222 | 32.23 N | 96.50 W |
| Waxahachie, Lake ⊜[1] | 222 | 32.20 N | 96.49 W |
| Waxhaw | 192 | 34.55 N | 80.44 W |
| Waxuecun | 106 | 31.07 N | 121.38 E |
| Waxweiler | 56 | 50.05 N | 6.22 E |
| Way, Lake ⊜ | 162 | 26.48 S | 120.18 E |
| Waya I | 175g | 17.18 S | 177.08 E |
| Wayabula | 108 | 2.17 N | 128.12 E |
| Wayaopu | 106 | 30.33 N | 118.53 E |
| Waycross | 192 | 31.12 N | 82.21 W |
| Wayi | 154 | 5.11 N | 30.10 E |
| Wayland, Ia., U.S. | 190 | 41.08 N | 91.39 W |
| Wayland, Ky., U.S. | 192 | 37.26 N | 82.48 W |
| Wayland, Ma., U.S. | 283 | 42.21 N | 71.21 W |
| Wayland, Mi., U.S. | 216 | 42.40 N | 85.38 W |
| Wayland, N.Y., U.S. | 210 | 42.34 N | 77.35 W |
| Wayland, Oh., U.S. | 214 | 41.10 N | 81.04 W |
| Waylyn | 192 | 32.51 N | 79.59 W |
| Waymansville | 218 | 39.04 N | 86.03 W |
| Waymart | 210 | 41.34 N | 75.24 W |
| Wayne, Ab., Can. | 182 | 51.23 N | 112.39 W |
| Wayne, Mi., U.S. | 216 | 42.16 N | 83.23 W |
| Wayne, Ne., U.S. | 198 | 42.13 N | 97.01 W |
| Wayne, N.J., U.S. | 210 | 40.55 N | 74.16 W |
| Wayne, N.Y., U.S. | 210 | 42.28 N | 77.06 W |
| Wayne, Oh., U.S. | 214 | 41.18 N | 83.28 W |
| Wayne, Ok., U.S. | 196 | 34.55 N | 97.18 W |
| Wayne, Pa., U.S. | 208 | 40.02 N | 75.23 W |
| Wayne, W.V., U.S. | 188 | 38.13 N | 82.26 W |
| Wayne □[6], Il., U.S. | 219 | 38.25 N | 88.40 W |
| Wayne □[6], In., U.S. | 218 | 39.50 N | 84.54 W |
| Wayne □[6], Mi., U.S. | 216 | 42.14 N | 83.12 W |
| Wayne □[6], N.Y., U.S. | 210 | 43.04 N | 77.00 W |
| Wayne □[6], Oh., U.S. | 214 | 40.48 N | 81.56 W |
| Wayne □[6], Pa., U.S. | 210 | 41.34 N | 75.16 W |
| Wayne City | 194 | 38.20 N | 88.35 W |
| Wayne Lakes | 218 | 40.01 N | 84.39 W |
| Waynesboro, Ga., U.S. | 192 | 33.05 N | 82.00 W |
| Waynesboro, Ms., U.S. | 194 | 31.40 N | 88.38 W |
| Waynesboro, Pa., U.S. | 208 | 39.45 N | 77.34 W |
| Waynesboro, Tn., U.S. | 194 | 35.19 N | 87.45 W |
| Waynesboro, Va., U.S. | 192 | 38.04 N | 78.53 W |
| Waynesburg, Oh., U.S. | 214 | 40.40 N | 81.15 W |
| Waynesburg, Pa., U.S. | 188 | 39.53 N | 80.10 W |
| Waynesfield | 216 | 40.36 N | 83.59 W |
| Wayne State University ʊ[2] | 281 | 42.21 N | 83.04 W |
| Waynesville, Il., U.S. | 194 | 40.15 N | 89.08 W |
| Waynesville, Mo., U.S. | 194 | 37.49 N | 92.12 W |
| Waynesville, N.C., U.S. | 192 | 35.29 N | 82.59 W |
| Waynesville, Oh., U.S. | 218 | 39.32 N | 84.05 W |
| Waynoka | 196 | 36.34 N | 98.52 W |
| Waynoka, Lake ⊜[1] | 218 | 38.55 N | 83.47 W |
| Wayoh Reservoir ⊜[1] | 262 | 53.39 N | 2.24 W |
| Waza | 146 | 11.25 N | 14.34 E |
| Waza, Parc National de ♦ | 146 | 11.20 N | 13.40 E |
| Wazah | 120 | 33.22 N | 69.26 E |
| Wāzah Khwāh | 120 | 32.12 N | 68.21 E |
| Waziers | 50 | 50.23 N | 3.07 E |
| Wāzin | 146 | 31.57 N | 10.40 E |
| Wazīrābād | 123 | 32.27 N | 74.07 E |
| Wazīrābād ◆[8] | 272a | 28.43 N | 77.14 E |
| Wāzirpur ◆[8] | 272a | 28.41 N | 77.10 E |
| Wazuka | 96 | 34.47 N | 135.55 E |
| Wazuka ≃ | 270 | 34.45 N | 135.53 E |
| Wda ≃ | 30 | 53.25 N | 18.29 E |
| Wé | 175f | 20.54 S | 167.16 E |
| We, Pulau I | 114 | 5.51 N | 95.18 E |
| Wea Creek ≃ | 216 | 40.24 N | 86.57 W |
| Weagamow Lake ⊜ | 184 | 52.53 N | 91.22 W |
| Weald Park ♦ | 260 | 51.38 N | 0.14 E |
| Wealdstone ◆[8] | 260 | 51.36 N | 0.20 W |
| Weam | 164 | 8.40 S | 141.08 E |
| Wear ≃ | 44 | 54.55 N | 1.22 W |
| Wearhead | 44 | 54.45 N | 2.13 W |
| Wearyan ≃ | 164 | 15.57 S | 136.51 E |
| Weatherford, Ok., U.S. | 196 | 35.31 N | 98.42 W |
| Weatherford, Tx., U.S. | 222 | 32.45 N | 97.47 W |
| Weatherford, Lake ⊜[1] | 222 | 32.47 N | 97.41 W |
| Weatherly | 210 | 40.56 N | 75.50 W |
| Weatogue | 207 | 41.51 N | 72.49 W |
| Weaubleau | 194 | 37.53 N | 93.32 W |
| Weaver, Austl. | 168b | 34.56 S | 137.40 E |
| Weaver, Al., U.S. | 194 | 33.45 N | 85.48 W |
| Weaver, Tx., U.S. | 222 | 33.10 N | 95.25 W |
| Weaver ≃ | 44 | 53.18 N | 2.43 W |
| Weaverham | 44 | 53.16 N | 2.35 W |
| Weaver Lake ⊜ | 184 | 52.45 N | 96.35 W |
| Weavertown | 279b | 40.16 N | 80.11 W |
| Weaverville, Ca., U.S. | 204 | 40.43 N | 122.56 W |
| Weaverville, N.C., U.S. | 192 | 35.41 N | 82.33 W |
| Webau | 54 | 51.10 N | 12.04 E |
| Webb, Sk., Can. | 184 | 50.11 N | 108.12 W |
| Webb, Ms., U.S. | 194 | 33.56 N | 90.20 W |
| Webb Brook ≃ | 283 | 42.32 N | 71.14 W |
| Webb City | 194 | 37.08 N | 94.27 W |
| Webber Lake ⊜ | 184 | 54.28 N | 94.00 W |
| Webberville | 216 | 42.40 N | 84.10 W |
| Webbwood | 190 | 46.16 N | 81.53 W |
| Weber ≃ | 200 | 41.13 N | 112.16 W |
| Weber, Mount ∧ | 182 | 55.32 N | 128.31 W |
| Weber City | 192 | 36.37 N | 82.33 W |
| Weber Creek ≃ | 226 | 38.46 N | 121.00 W |
| Weber Hill | 219 | 38.27 N | 90.34 W |
| Weberi Bekera | 144 | 9.39 N | 39.03 E |
| Webster, Ab., Can. | 182 | 55.26 N | 118.42 W |
| Webster, Fl., U.S. | 220 | 28.36 N | 82.03 W |
| Webster, In., U.S. | 218 | 39.54 N | 84.57 W |
| Webster, Ma., U.S. | 207 | 42.03 N | 71.52 W |
| Webster, N.Y., U.S. | 210 | 43.12 N | 77.25 W |
| Webster, Pa., U.S. | 214 | 40.11 N | 79.50 W |
| Webster, S.D., U.S. | 198 | 45.19 N | 97.31 W |
| Webster, Wi., U.S. | 190 | 45.52 N | 92.22 W |
| Webster City | 190 | 42.28 N | 93.48 W |
| Webster Crossing | 210 | 42.40 N | 77.38 W |
| Webster Groves | 219 | 38.35 N | 90.21 W |
| Webster Lake ⊜ | 216 | 41.19 N | 85.41 W |
| Websters Corners | 284a | 41.47 N | 78.45 W |
| Webster Springs | 188 | 38.28 N | 80.24 W |
| Weches | 222 | 31.33 N | 95.14 W |
| Wechmar | 54 | 50.53 N | 10.47 E |
| Wechselburg | 54 | 51.00 N | 12.47 E |
| Weda | 108 | 0.21 N | 127.52 E |
| Wedau ◆[8] | 263 | 51.24 N | 6.48 E |
| Wedau, Sportpark ♦ | 263 | 51.25 N | 6.47 E |
| Weddell Island I | 254 | 51.55 S | 61.00 W |
| Weddell Sea ⊤[2] | 9 | 72.00 S | 45.00 W |
| Wedderburn | 166 | 36.25 S | 143.37 E |
| Wedding ◆[8] | 54 | 52.33 N | 13.22 E |
| Weddinghofen | 263 | 51.36 N | 7.37 E |
| Wedel | 52 | 53.35 N | 9.41 E |
| Wedemark | 52 | 52.33 N | 9.44 E |
| Wedge, Central Mount ∧ | 162 | 22.51 S | 131.50 E |
| Wedge Mountain ∧ | 182 | 50.10 N | 122.50 W |
| Wedgeport | 186 | 43.44 N | 65.59 W |
| Wedgewood | 219 | 38.47 N | 90.17 W |
| Wedmore | 42 | 51.14 N | 2.49 W |
| Wedowee | 194 | 33.18 N | 85.29 W |
| Wedron | 216 | 41.26 N | 88.46 W |
| Weduar, Tanjung > | 164 | 6.00 S | 132.50 E |
| Wedweil | 140 | 9.00 N | 27.12 E |
| Wedza | 154 | 18.35 S | 31.35 E |
| Weebo | 162 | 28.01 S | 121.03 E |
| Weed | 204 | 41.25 N | 122.23 W |
| Weed Heights | 226 | 38.59 N | 119.12 W |
| Weedon | 206 | 45.42 N | 71.28 W |
| Weedon Beck | 42 | 52.14 N | 1.05 W |
| Weedon Island I | 220 | 27.51 N | 82.36 W |
| Weed Patch | 228 | 35.19 N | 118.55 W |
| Weed Patch Hill ∧[2] | 218 | 39.10 N | 86.13 W |
| Weedsport | 210 | 43.02 N | 76.33 W |
| Weedville | 214 | 41.17 N | 78.30 W |
| Weehawken | 276 | 40.46 N | 74.01 W |
| Weeim, Pulau I | 164 | 1.29 S | 130.14 E |
| Wee Jasper | 171b | 35.09 S | 148.41 E |
| Weekapaug | 207 | 41.20 N | 71.45 W |
| Weeki Wachee Spring ♦ | 220 | 28.32 N | 82.35 W |
| Weeki Wachee Swamp ≡ | 220 | 28.31 N | 82.37 W |
| Weeks Point > | 276 | 40.53 N | 73.39 W |
| Weekstown | 208 | 39.35 N | 74.36 W |
| Weelde | 56 | 51.25 N | 5.00 E |
| Weeley | 42 | 51.51 N | 1.07 E |
| Weel Shimbirro | 144 | 2.23 N | 44.16 E |
| Weems | 208 | 37.39 N | 76.26 W |
| Weende | 52 | 51.33 N | 9.55 E |
| Weenen | 158 | 28.57 S | 30.03 E |
| Weener | 52 | 53.10 N | 7.21 E |
| Weeney Bay c | 274a | 34.01 S | 151.10 E |
| Weeping Water | 198 | 40.52 N | 96.08 W |
| Weequahic Lake ⊜ | 276 | 40.42 N | 74.12 W |
| Weert | 52 | 51.15 N | 5.43 E |
| Weesatche | 222 | 28.51 N | 97.27 W |
| Weesby | 41 | 54.50 N | 9.08 E |
| Weesow | 264a | 52.39 N | 13.43 E |
| Weesp | 52 | 52.17 N | 5.02 E |
| Weetfeld ◆[8] | 263 | 51.38 N | 7.49 E |
| Weethalle | 166 | 33.53 S | 146.38 E |
| Weeting | 42 | 52.27 N | 0.37 E |
| Weeton | 262 | 53.48 N | 2.56 W |
| Weetulta | 168b | 34.15 S | 137.38 E |
| Wee Waa | 166 | 30.14 S | 149.26 E |
| Weeze | 52 | 51.37 N | 6.12 E |
| Wefensleben | 54 | 52.11 N | 11.09 E |
| Weferlingen | 54 | 52.19 N | 11.02 E |
| Wegberg | 56 | 51.08 N | 6.16 E |
| Wegdraai | 158 | 28.50 S | 21.52 E |
| Wegeleben | 54 | 51.53 N | 11.10 E |
| Wegendorf | 264a | 52.36 N | 13.45 E |
| Wegenstedt | 54 | 52.23 N | 11.11 E |
| Wegeringhausen | 56 | 51.02 N | 7.45 E |
| Weggis | 58 | 47.02 N | 8.26 E |
| Węgliniec | 30 | 51.17 N | 15.13 E |
| Węgorzewo | 30 | 54.14 N | 21.44 E |
| Węgorzyno | 30 | 53.32 N | 15.33 E |
| Węgrów | 30 | 52.25 N | 22.01 E |
| Wegscheid | 60 | 48.36 N | 13.48 E |
| Wehdel | 52 | 53.30 N | 8.48 E |
| Wehebach Stausee ⊜[1] | 56 | 50.45 N | 6.20 E |
| Wehingen | 58 | 48.08 N | 8.47 E |
| Wehofen ◆[8] | 263 | 51.32 N | 6.46 E |
| Wehr | 58 | 47.37 N | 7.54 E |
| Wehringhausen ◆[8] | 263 | 51.21 N | 7.27 E |
| Wehrsdorf | 54 | 51.03 N | 14.22 E |
| Wei ≃, Zhg. | 98 | 36.51 N | 115.43 E |
| Wei ≃, Zhg. | 98 | 37.05 N | 119.28 E |
| Wei ≃, Zhg. | 102 | 34.30 N | 110.20 E |
| Weichang (Zhuizishan) | 98 | 42.00 N | 117.32 E |
| Weichsel → Wisła ≃ | 30 | 54.22 N | 18.55 E |
| Weichselboden | 61 | 47.40 N | 15.10 E |
| Weichuan | 98 | 34.17 N | 113.58 E |
| Weicun | 106 | 31.59 N | 119.55 E |
| Weida | 54 | 50.45 N | 12.04 E |
| Weida ≃ | 54 | 50.47 N | 12.06 E |
| Weiden am See | 61 | 47.55 N | 16.52 E |
| Weidenberg | 60 | 49.57 N | 11.43 E |
| Weiden in der Oberpfalz | 60 | 49.41 N | 12.10 E |
| Weidenstetten | 56 | 48.33 N | 9.59 E |
| Weidhausen | 54 | 50.12 N | 11.08 E |
| Weiding | 60 | 49.16 N | 12.46 E |
| Weidling | 264b | 48.17 N | 16.19 E |
| Weidlingau ◆[8] | 264b | 48.13 N | 16.13 E |
| Weidlingbach | 264b | 48.16 N | 16.15 E |
| Weidlingerbach ≃ | 264b | 48.18 N | 16.20 E |
| Weifang | 98 | 36.42 N | 119.04 E |
| Weigelstown | 208 | 39.59 N | 76.49 W |
| Weigersdorf | 54 | 51.16 N | 14.39 E |
| Weihai | 98 | 37.28 N | 122.07 E |
| Weihaiwei → Weihai | 98 | 37.28 N | 122.07 E |
| Weiherhammer | 60 | 49.38 N | 12.04 E |
| Weihmichl | 60 | 48.36 N | 12.03 E |
| Weihnachtsinsel → Christmas Island □[2] | 112 | 10.30 S | 105.40 E |
| Wei Island I | 164 | 3.20 S | 144.25 E |
| Weijiagou | 105 | 40.28 N | 115.08 E |
| Weijiatang | 106 | 31.25 N | 118.55 E |
| Weijiazhuang | 105 | 39.37 N | 116.22 E |
| Weijiazui | 100 | 30.29 N | 117.20 E |
| Weijingtang | 106 | 31.27 N | 120.39 E |
| Weikersheim | 56 | 49.29 N | 9.54 E |
| Weil ≃ | 56 | 50.28 N | 8.16 E |
| Weil am Rhein | 58 | 47.37 N | 7.38 E |
| Weilburg | 56 | 50.29 N | 8.15 E |
| Weil der Stadt | 56 | 48.45 N | 8.52 E |
| Weiler | 58 | 47.36 N | 9.55 E |
| Weilerbach | 56 | 49.29 N | 7.37 E |
| Weilerswist | 56 | 50.45 N | 6.50 E |
| Weilheim | 64 | 47.50 N | 11.08 E |
| Weilheim an der Teck | 56 | 48.37 N | 9.32 E |
| Weilmoringle | 166 | 29.15 S | 146.51 E |
| Weilmünster | 56 | 50.26 N | 8.22 E |
| Weimar, Dtsch. | 54 | 50.59 N | 11.19 E |
| Weimar, Ca., U.S. | 226 | 39.02 N | 120.58 W |
| Weimar, Tx., U.S. | 222 | 29.42 N | 96.46 W |
| Weinan | 102 | 34.29 N | 109.29 E |
| Weinbach | 56 | 50.26 N | 8.18 E |
| Weinböhla | 54 | 51.10 N | 13.34 E |
| Weinel Cross Roads | 279b | 40.37 N | 79.37 W |
| Weiner | 194 | 35.37 N | 90.53 W |
| Weinfelden | 58 | 47.34 N | 9.06 E |
| Weingarten, Dtsch. | 56 | 49.05 N | 8.31 E |
| Weingarten, Dtsch. | 58 | 47.48 N | 9.38 E |
| Weinheim | 56 | 49.33 N | 8.39 E |
| Weining, Zhg. | 102 | 26.43 N | 104.18 E |
| Weining, Zhg. | 104 | 41.21 N | 123.49 E |
| Weinsberg | 56 | 49.10 N | 9.17 E |
| Weinsberger Wald ◆[3] | 61 | 48.30 N | 14.50 E |
| Weinstadt | 56 | 48.49 N | 9.23 E |
| Weinviertel ◆[1] | 61 | 48.38 N | 16.25 E |
| Weipa | 164 | 12.41 S | 141.52 E |
| Weippe | 202 | 46.22 N | 115.56 W |
| Weir, India | 124 | 27.01 N | 77.11 E |
| Weir, Ks., U.S. | 198 | 37.18 N | 94.46 W |
| Weir, Ms., U.S. | 194 | 33.16 N | 89.17 W |
| Weir ≃, Austl. | 166 | 28.50 S | 149.06 E |
| Weir ≃, Mb., Can. | 184 | 56.54 N | 93.21 W |
| Weir ≃, Ma., U.S. | 283 | 42.16 N | 70.53 W |
| Weir, Lake ⊜ | 220 | 29.00 N | 81.57 W |
| Weir River | 184 | 56.49 N | 94.04 W |
| Weirsdale | 220 | 28.58 N | 81.55 W |
| Weirton | 214 | 40.25 N | 80.35 W |
| Weisburd | 252 | 27.18 S | 62.36 W |
| Weisburg | 218 | 39.13 N | 85.03 W |
| Weischlitz | 54 | 50.26 N | 12.02 E |
| Weisendorf | 56 | 49.37 N | 10.49 E |
| Weiser | 202 | 44.15 N | 116.58 W |
| Weiser ≃ | 202 | 44.15 N | 116.59 W |
| Weishan (Xiazhen), Zhg. | 98 | 34.52 N | 117.09 E |
| Weishan, Zhg. | 100 | 29.20 N | 120.25 E |
| Weishan, Zhg. | 100 | 29.41 N | 120.48 E |
| Weishan, Zhg. | 102 | 25.15 N | 100.20 E |
| Weishancheng | 100 | 32.34 N | 113.24 E |
| Weishanhe | 104 | 40.47 N | 123.31 E |
| Weishan Hu ⊜ | 98 | 34.40 N | 117.15 E |
| Weishanzhuang | 105 | 39.40 N | 116.25 E |
| Weishi | 98 | 34.25 N | 114.11 E |
| Weiskirchen | 56 | 49.33 N | 6.49 E |
| Weismain | 54 | 50.05 N | 11.14 E |
| Weisner Mountain ∧ | 194 | 34.02 N | 85.40 W |
| Weissbriach | 64 | 46.41 N | 13.15 E |
| Weisse Elster ≃ | 54 | 51.26 N | 11.57 E |
| Weissenbach | 264b | 48.05 N | 16.13 E |
| Weissenbach am Lech | 58 | 47.26 N | 10.39 E |
| Weissenberg | 54 | 51.11 N | 14.40 E |
| Weissenborn | 54 | 50.52 N | 13.25 E |
| Weissenbrunn | 54 | 50.12 N | 11.20 E |
| Weissenburg | 58 | 46.39 N | 7.28 E |
| Weissenburg in Bayern | 56 | 49.01 N | 10.58 E |
| Weissenfels | 54 | 51.12 N | 11.58 E |
| Weissenhorn | 58 | 48.18 N | 10.09 E |
| Weissensee | 54 | 51.11 N | 11.04 E |
| Weissensee ◆[8] | 264a | 52.33 N | 13.27 E |
| Weissensee ⊜ | 64 | 46.42 N | 13.22 E |
| Weissenstadt | 54 | 50.06 N | 11.53 E |
| Weissenstein | 64 | 46.41 N | 13.44 E |
| Weissenstein ∧ | 58 | 47.15 N | 7.31 E |
| Weissenstein Tunnel ◆[5] | 58 | 47.12 N | 7.23 E |
| Weissenthurm | 56 | 50.24 N | 7.27 E |
| Weisser Main ≃ | 60 | 50.04 N | 11.24 E |
| Weisser Nil → White Nile ≃ | 140 | 15.38 N | 32.31 E |
| Weisser See → Beloje, ozero ⊜ | 76 | 60.11 N | 37.37 E |
| Weisser Stein ∧ | 56 | 50.23 N | 6.20 E |
| Weisses Meer → Beloje more ⊤[2] | 24 | 65.30 N | 38.00 E |
| Weisse Spitze ∧ | 64 | 46.52 N | 12.21 E |
| Weissfluh ∧ | 58 | 46.50 N | 9.48 E |
| Weisshorn ∧ | 58 | 46.06 N | 7.42 E |
| Weissig | 54 | 51.05 N | 13.52 E |
| Weisskugel (Palla Bianca) ∧ | 64 | 46.48 N | 10.44 E |
| Weiss Lake ⊜[1] | 192 | 34.15 N | 85.35 W |
| Weissmeer-Ostsee Kanal → Belomorsko-Baltijskij kanal ≍ | 24 | 62.48 N | 34.48 E |
| Weissport | 210 | 40.50 N | 75.42 W |
| Weisstannen | 58 | 46.59 N | 9.21 E |
| Weisswasser | 54 | 51.30 N | 14.38 E |
| Weisweiler | 56 | 50.50 N | 6.19 E |
| Weitang | 105 | 40.24 N | 117.24 E |
| Weitang ≃ | 104 | 42.19 N | 122.18 E |
| Weitendorf | 54 | 53.54 N | 12.16 E |
| Weitensfeld | 61 | 46.51 N | 14.11 E |
| Weiterstadt | 56 | 49.54 N | 8.35 E |
| Weitian | 100 | 27.43 N | 118.46 E |
| Weitin | 54 | 53.34 N | 13.12 E |
| Weiting | 106 | 31.22 N | 120.47 E |
| Weitmar ◆[8] | 263 | 51.27 N | 7.12 E |
| Weitnau | 58 | 47.38 N | 10.07 E |
| Weitou | 100 | 24.34 N | 118.34 E |
| Weitra | 61 | 48.42 N | 14.54 E |
| Weituo | 107 | 30.03 N | 106.08 E |
| Weitzgrund | 54 | 52.11 N | 12.32 E |
| Weiwan | 98 | 36.43 N | 115.54 E |
| Weixdorf | 54 | 51.09 N | 13.48 E |
| Weixi, Zhg. | 102 | 27.14 N | 99.12 E |
| Weixi, Zhg. | 107 | 30.12 N | 106.39 E |
| Weixian, Zhg. | 98 | 36.57 N | 115.15 E |
| Weixian, Zhg. | 98 | 36.22 N | 114.56 E |
| Weixian (Hanting), Zhg. | 98 | 36.52 N | 119.07 E |
| Weixin | 102 | 27.48 N | 105.06 E |
| Weiyuan | 107 | 29.33 N | 104.39 E |
| Weiyuan ≃ | 102 | 22.50 N | 100.20 E |
| Weiyuankou | 100 | 30.09 N | 115.15 E |
| Weiyuanpu | 98 | 42.39 N | 124.16 E |
| Weiz | 61 | 47.13 N | 15.37 E |
| Weizhen | 98 | 37.17 N | 114.44 E |
| Weizhou Dao I | 102 | 21.03 N | 109.04 E |
| Weizhou Wan c | 100 | 24.34 N | 118.30 E |
| Weizhuang | 105 | 39.02 N | 115.20 E |
| Weizi | 98 | 40.04 N | 123.10 E |
| Weizigou, Zhg. | 104 | 42.25 N | 122.47 E |
| Weizigou, Zhg. | 104 | 41.05 N | 120.38 E |
| Weizigou, Zhg. | 104 | 42.05 N | 120.34 E |
| Weizigoumen | 98 | 41.58 N | 116.49 E |
| Weiziyu | 98 | 41.29 N | 124.31 E |
| Wejherowo | 30 | 54.37 N | 18.15 E |
| Wekiva ≃ | 220 | 28.52 N | 81.23 W |
| Wekiwa Springs State Park ♦ | 220 | 28.43 N | 81.27 W |
| Wekoewa Punt > | 241s | 12.14 N | 68.24 W |
| Wekusko Lake ⊜ | 184 | 54.45 N | 99.50 W |
| Welaka | 192 | 29.28 N | 81.40 W |
| Welbourn Hill | 162 | 27.21 S | 134.06 E |
| Welch, Ok., U.S. | 196 | 36.52 N | 95.05 W |
| Welch, Tx., U.S. | 196 | 32.56 N | 102.08 W |
| Welch, W.V., U.S. | 192 | 37.25 N | 81.35 W |
| Welch Creek ≃ | 282 | 37.32 N | 121.51 W |
| Welches | 224 | 45.19 N | 121.57 W |
| Welch Peak ∧ | 224 | 49.10 N | 121.36 W |
| Welcome, On., Can. | 212 | 43.58 N | 78.21 W |
| Welcome, Mn., U.S. | 198 | 43.40 N | 94.37 W |
| Welcome, S.C., U.S. | 192 | 34.49 N | 82.26 W |
| Welcome Lake ⊜ | 212 | 45.25 N | 78.25 W |
| Welcome Monument ⊥ | 269e | 6.11 S | 106.49 E |
| Welden | 58 | 48.27 N | 10.40 E |
| Weldiya | 144 | 11.50 N | 39.41 E |
| Weldon, Sk., Can. | 184 | 53.00 N | 105.08 W |
| Weldon, Il., U.S. | 219 | 40.07 N | 88.45 W |
| Weldon, N.C., U.S. | 192 | 36.25 N | 77.35 W |
| Weldon, Tx., U.S. | 222 | 31.01 N | 95.34 W |
| Weldon ≃ | 194 | 40.06 N | 93.38 W |
| Weldona | 198 | 40.20 N | 103.58 W |
| Weldon Brook ≃ | 276 | 40.58 N | 74.35 W |
| Weleetka | 196 | 35.20 N | 96.08 W |
| Welega □[4] | 144 | 9.40 N | 35.50 E |
| Weleri | 115a | 6.58 S | 110.04 E |
| Welfare Island I | 276 | 40.45 N | 73.57 W |
| Welgedag | 273d | 26.12 S | 28.30 E |
| Welhamgreen | 260 | 51.44 N | 0.13 W |
| Welheim ◆[8] | 263 | 51.32 N | 6.59 E |
| Weligama | 122 | 5.58 N | 80.25 E |
| Welikaja → Velikaja ≃ | 76 | 57.48 N | 28.20 E |
| Welkenraedt | 56 | 50.40 N | 5.59 E |
| Welker Seamount ✦[3] | 16 | 55.07 N | 140.20 W |
| Welkite | 144 | 8.15 N | 37.50 E |
| Welkom | 158 | 27.59 S | 26.45 E |
| Well | 52 | 51.34 N | 6.06 E |
| Welland | 212 | 42.59 N | 79.15 W |
| Welland ≃, On., Can. | 212 | 43.04 N | 79.03 W |
| Welland ≃, Eng., U.K. | 42 | 52.52 N | 0.03 W |
| Welland Canal ≍ | 212 | 43.03 N | 79.13 W |
| Welland Junction | 284a | 42.57 N | 79.14 W |
| Wellard | 168a | 32.19 S | 115.50 E |
| Wellaune | 54 | 51.34 N | 12.33 E |
| Wellborn, Fl., U.S. | 192 | 30.13 N | 82.49 W |
| Wellborn, Tx., U.S. | 222 | 30.32 N | 96.18 W |
| Wellerode | 56 | 51.14 N | 9.34 E |
| Wellers Bay c | 212 | 44.00 N | 77.34 W |
| Wellers Creek ≃ | 278 | 42.03 N | 87.53 W |
| Wellesbourne | 42 | 52.12 N | 1.35 W |
| Welles Harbor c | 174g | 28.12 N | 177.26 W |
| Wellesley, On., Can. | 212 | 43.28 N | 80.45 W |
| Wellesley, Ma., U.S. | 207 | 42.17 N | 71.17 W |
| Wellesley ≃ | 168a | 33.17 S | 115.44 E |
| Wellesley College ʊ[2] | 283 | 42.18 N | 71.19 W |
| Wellesley Hills | 283 | 42.19 N | 71.17 W |
| Wellesley Island I | 212 | 44.19 N | 75.58 W |
| Wellesley Islands II | 164 | 16.42 S | 139.30 E |
| Wellesley Island State Park ♦ | 212 | 44.19 N | 76.01 W |
| Wellesley Lake ⊜ | 180 | 62.30 N | 139.50 W |
| Wellfleet | 207 | 41.56 N | 70.02 W |
| Well Hill | 260 | 51.21 N | 0.09 E |
| Wellin | 56 | 50.05 N | 5.07 E |
| Welling ◆[8] | 260 | 51.28 N | 0.07 E |
| Wellingborough | 42 | 52.19 N | 0.42 W |
| Wellinghofen ◆[8] | 263 | 51.28 N | 7.29 E |
| Wellington, Austl. | 166 | 32.33 S | 148.57 E |
| Wellington, B.C., Can. | 224 | 49.13 N | 124.01 W |
| Wellington, On., Can. | 212 | 43.57 N | 77.21 W |
| Wellington, N.Z. | 172 | 41.18 S | 174.47 E |
| Wellington, S. Afr. | 158 | 33.38 S | 18.57 E |
| Wellington, Eng., U.K. | 42 | 52.43 N | 2.31 W |
| Wellington, Eng., U.K. | 42 | 50.59 N | 3.14 W |
| Wellington, Co., U.S. | 200 | 40.42 N | 105.00 W |
| Wellington, Il., U.S. | 216 | 40.32 N | 87.41 W |
| Wellington, Ks., U.S. | 198 | 37.15 N | 97.22 W |
| Wellington, Mo., U.S. | 194 | 39.08 N | 93.58 W |
| Wellington, Nv., U.S. | 226 | 38.45 N | 119.22 W |
| Wellington, Oh., U.S. | 214 | 41.10 N | 82.13 W |
| Wellington, Tx., U.S. | 196 | 34.51 N | 100.12 W |
| Wellington, Ut,. U.S. | 200 | 39.32 N | 110.44 W |
| Wellington □[6] | 212 | 43.50 N | 80.30 W |
| Wellington, Isla I | 254 | 49.20 S | 74.40 W |
| Wellington Bay c, N.T., Can. | 176 | 69.30 N | 106.30 W |
| Wellington Bay c, On., Can. | 212 | 43.56 N | 77.21 W |
| Wellington Channel ʯ | 176 | 75.00 N | 93.00 W |
| Wellington Point | 171a | 27.29 S | 153.15 E |
| Wellington Reservoir ⊜[1] | 168a | 33.24 S | 116.01 E |
| Wellington Station | 186 | 46.27 N | 64.00 W |
| Wellman, Ia., U.S. | 190 | 41.27 N | 91.50 W |
| Wellman, Tx., U.S. | 196 | 33.03 N | 102.26 W |
| Wells, B.C., Can. | 182 | 53.06 N | 121.34 W |
| Wells, Eng., U.K. | 42 | 51.13 N | 2.39 W |
| Wells, Mi., U.S. | 190 | 45.47 N | 87.04 W |
| Wells, Mn., U.S. | 190 | 43.44 N | 93.43 W |
| Wells, Nv., U.S. | 204 | 41.06 N | 114.57 W |
| Wells, N.Y., U.S. | 210 | 43.24 N | 74.17 W |
| Wells, Tx., U.S. | 222 | 31.29 N | 94.56 W |
| Wells □[6] | 216 | 40.44 N | 85.11 W |
| Wells, Lake ⊜ | 162 | 26.43 S | 123.10 E |
| Wells, Mount ∧ | 168a | 32.42 S | 116.20 E |
| Wells, Mount ∧[2] | 162 | 17.26 S | 127.14 E |
| Wellsboro | 210 | 41.44 N | 77.18 W |
| Wells Bridge | 210 | 42.22 N | 75.15 W |
| Wellsburg, Ia., U.S. | 190 | 42.27 N | 92.56 W |
| Wellsburg, N.Y., U.S. | 210 | 42.00 N | 76.43 W |
| Wellsburg, W.V., U.S. | 214 | 40.16 N | 80.36 W |
| Wells Cathedral ʊ[1] | 42 | 51.13 N | 2.39 W |
| Wellsford | 172 | 36.17 S | 174.31 E |
| Wells Gray Provincial Park ♦ | 182 | 52.20 N | 120.00 W |
| Wells Lake ⊜ | 184 | 57.15 N | 101.00 W |
| Wells-next-the-Sea | 42 | 52.58 N | 0.51 E |
| Wells Point > | 284b | 39.17 N | 76.23 W |
| Wells State Park ♦ | 207 | 42.09 N | 72.05 W |
| Wells Tannery | 214 | 40.05 N | 78.10 W |
| Wellston, Oh., U.S. | 188 | 39.07 N | 82.31 W |
| Wellston, Ok., U.S. | 196 | 35.41 N | 97.03 W |
| Wellsville, Ks., U.S. | 198 | 38.43 N | 95.04 W |
| Wellsville, Mo., U.S. | 219 | 39.04 N | 91.34 W |
| Wellsville, N.Y., U.S. | 210 | 42.07 N | 77.56 W |
| Wellsville, Oh., U.S. | 214 | 40.36 N | 80.38 W |
| Wellsville, Pa., U.S. | 208 | 40.03 N | 76.56 W |
| Wellsville, Ut,. U.S. | 200 | 41.38 N | 111.55 W |
| Wellton | 200 | 32.40 N | 114.08 W |
| Welmel ≃ | 144 | 5.38 N | 40.47 E |
| Welmen | 263 | 51.39 N | 6.41 E |
| Welney | 42 | 52.31 N | 0.15 E |
| Welo □[4] | 144 | 11.50 N | 40.20 E |
| Welper | 263 | 51.25 N | 7.12 E |
| Wels | 61 | 48.10 N | 14.02 E |
| Welsberg → Monguelfo | 64 | 46.45 N | 12.06 E |
| Welschbillig | 56 | 49.51 N | 6.34 E |
| Welse ≃ | 54 | 53.10 N | 14.18 E |
| Welsford | 186 | 45.27 N | 66.20 W |
| Welsh | 194 | 30.14 N | 92.49 W |
| Welshpool, Austl. | 169 | 38.39 S | 146.26 E |
| Welshpool, Wales, U.K. | 42 | 52.40 N | 3.09 W |
| Welsickendorf | 54 | 51.54 N | 13.08 E |
| Welsleben | 54 | 52.00 N | 11.38 E |
| Weltenburg | 60 | 48.54 N | 11.50 E |
| Welver | 52 | 51.38 N | 7.57 E |
| Welverdiend | 158 | 26.23 S | 27.16 E |
| Welwitschia | 156 | 20.21 S | 14.57 E |
| Welwyn Garden City | 42 | 51.50 N | 0.13 W |
| Welwyn Hatfield □[8] | 260 | 51.47 N | 0.12 W |
| Welzheim | 56 | 48.53 N | 9.38 E |
| Welzow | 54 | 51.34 N | 14.10 E |
| Wem | 42 | 52.51 N | 2.44 W |
| Wema | 152 | 0.26 S | 21.38 E |
| Wembere ≃ | 154 | 4.10 S | 34.11 E |
| Wembley | 182 | 55.09 N | 119.08 W |
| Wembley ◆[8] | 260 | 51.33 N | 0.18 W |
| Wembley Stadium ♦, S. Afr. | 273d | 26.14 S | 28.03 E |
| Wembley Stadium ♦, Eng., U.K. | 260 | 51.33 N | 0.17 W |
| Wembury | 42 | 50.19 N | 4.05 W |
| Wemding | 56 | 48.52 N | 10.43 E |
| Wemeldinge | 52 | 51.31 N | 4.00 E |
| Wemme | 224 | 45.20 N | 121.57 W |
| Wemperhardt | 56 | 50.09 N | 6.05 E |
| Wemyss Bay | 46 | 55.53 N | 4.54 W |
| Wen ≃, Zhg. | 98 | 36.38 N | 119.22 E |
| Wen ≃, Zhg. | 98 | 35.28 N | 118.32 E |
| Wen'an | 105 | 38.52 N | 116.28 E |
| Wen'an Wa ≡ | 105 | 38.54 N | 116.37 E |
| Wenas Creek ≃ | 224 | 46.42 N | 120.35 W |
| Wenatchee | 202 | 47.25 N | 120.18 W |
| Wenatchee ≃ | 202 | 47.27 N | 120.19 W |
| Wenatchee, Lake ⊜ | 224 | 47.49 N | 120.47 W |
| Wenatchee Mountains ∧∧ | 202 | 47.20 N | 120.45 W |
| Wenchang | 110 | 19.41 N | 110.48 E |
| Wencheng | 100 | 27.50 N | 120.05 E |
| Wenchi | 150 | 7.42 N | 2.07 W |
| Wenchow → Wenzhou | 100 | 28.01 N | 120.39 E |
| Wendaohezi | 104 | 41.46 N | 124.09 E |
| Wendel | 279b | 40.18 N | 79.41 W |
| Wendell, Id., U.S. | 202 | 42.46 N | 114.42 W |
| Wendell, N.C., U.S. | 192 | 35.46 N | 78.22 W |
| Wendelsheim | 56 | 49.46 N | 7.59 E |
| Wendelstein | 60 | 49.21 N | 11.08 E |
| Wendelstein ∧ | 64 | 47.42 N | 12.00 E |
| Wendelville | 284a | 43.04 N | 78.47 W |
| Wenden, Dtsch. | 52 | 52.19 N | 10.30 E |
| Wenden, Dtsch. | 56 | 50.57 N | 7.51 E |
| Wenden, Az., U.S. | 200 | 33.49 N | 113.32 W |
| Wendeng | 98 | 37.12 N | 122.04 E |
| Wendesi | 164 | 2.25 S | 134.13 E |
| Wendilou | 104 | 41.13 N | 121.08 E |
| Wendisch Rietz | 54 | 52.13 N | 14.01 E |
| Wendish Baggendorf | 54 | 54.04 N | 12.56 E |
| Wendji | 152 | 0.04 S | 18.10 E |
| Wendland ◆[1] | 54 | 53.00 N | 11.10 E |
| Wendlingen | 58 | 48.40 N | 9.23 E |
| Wendo | 144 | 6.38 N | 38.27 E |
| Wendover, Eng., U.K. | 42 | 51.46 N | 0.46 W |
| Wendover, Ut,. U.S. | 200 | 40.44 N | 114.02 W |
| Wenduine | 50 | 51.18 N | 3.05 E |
| Wenebegon ≃ | 190 | 46.53 N | 83.12 W |
| Wenebegon Lake ⊜ | 190 | 47.24 N | 83.08 W |
| Wenfang | 100 | 28.02 N | 117.19 E |
| Weng | 60 | 48.40 N | 12.23 E |
| Weng ≃ | 100 | 24.10 N | 113.24 E |
| Weng'an | 102 | 26.53 N | 107.22 E |
| Wengbo | 120 | 31.23 N | 86.40 E |
| Wengcheng | 100 | 24.23 N | 113.51 E |
| Wengdang | 124 | 28.50 N | 90.03 E |
| Wenge | 152 | 0.03 N | 24.01 E |
| Wengen, Dtsch. | 58 | 47.41 N | 10.09 E |
| Wengen, Schw. | 58 | 46.36 N | 7.56 E |
| Wengern | 263 | 51.24 N | 7.21 E |
| Wengjiabu | 106 | 30.23 N | 120.21 E |
| Wengong | 107 | 30.11 N | 104.09 E |
| Wenguantun | 104 | 41.53 N | 123.30 E |
| Wengyang | 100 | 28.03 N | 120.58 E |
| Wengyuan | 100 | 24.21 N | 114.08 E |
| Wenham | 207 | 42.36 N | 70.53 W |
| Wenham Lake ⊜ | 283 | 42.35 N | 70.53 W |
| Wenham Swamp ≡ | 283 | 42.37 N | 70.55 W |
| Wenheng | 100 | 25.42 N | 116.45 E |
| Wenī | 124 | 28.21 N | 83.34 E |
| Wenigzell | 61 | 47.26 N | 15.47 E |
| Wenjiachang | 107 | 30.41 N | 103.55 E |
| Wenjiang | 107 | 30.42 N | 103.49 E |
| Wenjiangban | 100 | 26.01 N | 117.51 E |
| Wenjiazhen | 100 | 28.20 N | 116.05 E |
| Wenling | 100 | 28.22 N | 121.20 E |
| Wenlock | 164 | 13.06 S | 142.58 E |
| Wenlock ≃ | 164 | 12.02 S | 141.55 E |
| Wenlock Edge ⊥[4] | 42 | 52.30 N | 2.40 W |
| Wenlong | 100 | 24.48 N | 114.54 E |
| Wenmingsi | 100 | 25.33 N | 113.20 E |
| Wennigsen | 52 | 52.16 N | 9.34 E |
| Wenning ≃ | 44 | 54.07 N | 2.39 W |
| Wennington ◆[8] | 260 | 51.30 N | 0.13 E |
| Wenniu | 102 | 24.18 N | 104.31 E |
| Wenns | 58 | 47.10 N | 10.44 E |
| Weno I | 175c | 7.26 N | 151.52 E |
| Wenona, Il., U.S. | 216 | 41.03 N | 89.03 W |
| Wenona, Md., U.S. | 208 | 38.08 N | 75.57 W |
| Wenonah | 208 | 39.47 N | 75.08 W |
| Wenquan, Zhg. | 86 | 44.59 N | 81.04 E |
| Wenquan, Zhg. | 100 | 23.37 N | 113.43 E |
| Wenquansi | 104 | 41.20 N | 124.04 E |
| Wenshan | 102 | 23.30 N | 104.20 E |
| Wenshang | 98 | 35.44 N | 116.29 E |
| Wenshui, Zhg. | 102 | 28.28 N | 106.30 E |
| Wenshui, Zhg. | 102 | 37.28 N | 112.01 E |
| Wensickendorf | 264a | 52.45 N | 13.23 E |
| Wensleydale V | 44 | 54.19 N | 2.00 W |
| Wensum ≃ | 42 | 52.37 N | 1.19 E |
| Went ≃ | 44 | 53.39 N | 0.59 W |
| Wentorf | 52 | 53.30 N | 10.15 E |
| Wentworth, Austl. | 166 | 34.07 S | 141.55 E |
| Wentworth, N.C., U.S. | 192 | 36.24 N | 79.46 W |
| Wentworth, S.D., U.S. | 198 | 43.59 N | 96.57 W |
| Wentworth Falls | 170 | 33.43 S | 150.22 E |
| Wentworth Park | 273d | 26.07 S | 27.48 E |
| Wentworthville | 274a | 33.48 S | 150.58 E |
| Wentzville | 219 | 38.48 N | 90.51 W |
| Wenxi | 102 | 35.26 N | 111.11 E |
| Wenxian | 102 | 32.58 N | 104.46 E |
| Wenxingchang | 107 | 29.52 N | 106.29 E |
| Wenyu ≃ | 105 | 39.56 N | 116.40 E |
| Wenzenbach | 60 | 49.05 N | 12.12 E |
| Wenzhou | 100 | 28.01 N | 120.39 E |
| Wenzhu | 100 | 27.01 N | 113.58 E |
| Wenzhuangzicun | 104 | 42.16 N | 123.51 E |
| Weobley | 42 | 52.09 N | 2.51 W |
| Weohyakapka, Lake ⊜ | 220 | 27.49 N | 81.25 W |
| Wepener | 158 | 29.46 S | 27.00 E |
| Wépion | 56 | 50.25 N | 4.52 E |
| Weppersdorf | 61 | 47.35 N | 16.26 E |
| Wequetequock | 207 | 41.21 N | 71.52 W |
| Wera ≃ | 115b | 8.20 S | 120.43 E |
| Werbellin | 54 | 52.53 N | 13.41 E |
| Werbellinsee ⊜ | 54 | 52.54 N | 13.40 E |
| Werben, Dtsch. | 54 | 52.52 N | 11.58 E |
| Werben, Dtsch. | 54 | 51.45 N | 14.10 E |
| Werbomont | 56 | 50.23 N | 5.41 E |
| Werchojansker Gebirge → Verchojanskij chrebet ∧∧ | 74 | 67.00 N | 129.00 E |
| Werda | 156 | 25.15 S | 23.16 E |
| Werdau | 54 | 50.44 N | 12.22 E |
| Werden ◆[8] | 263 | 51.23 N | 7.00 E |
| Werder, Dtsch. | 54 | 52.23 N | 12.56 E |
| Werder, Ityo. | 144 | 6.58 N | 45.20 E |
| Werder ◆[1] | 54 | 53.40 N | 13.25 E |
| Werdohl | 56 | 51.15 N | 7.45 E |
| Were Ilu | 144 | 10.37 N | 39.28 E |
| Werfen | 64 | 47.28 N | 13.11 E |
| Weri | 164 | 3.12 S | 132.38 E |
| Werkel | 56 | 51.09 N | 9.18 E |
| Werkendam | 52 | 51.49 N | 4.53 E |
| Werl | 52 | 51.33 N | 7.54 E |
| Werlaburgdorf | 54 | 52.04 N | 10.31 E |
| Werl-Aspe | 52 | 52.04 N | 8.43 E |
| Werleshausen | 56 | 51.19 N | 9.54 E |
| Werlte | 52 | 52.51 N | 7.41 E |
| Wermelskirchen | 56 | 51.08 N | 7.13 E |
| Wermsdorf | 54 | 51.17 N | 12.56 E |
| Wern ≃ | 56 | 50.02 N | 9.44 E |
| Wernadinga | 166 | 18.07 S | 139.58 E |
| Wernau | 58 | 48.42 N | 9.25 E |
| Wernberg | 64 | 46.37 N | 13.56 E |
| Wernberg-Köblitz | 60 | 49.32 N | 12.10 E |
| Werne | 52 | 51.40 N | 7.38 E |
| Werne ◆[8] | 263 | 51.29 N | 7.18 E |
| Werneck, Bra. | 256 | 22.13 S | 43.19 W |
| Werneck, Dtsch. | 56 | 49.59 N | 10.05 E |
| Werneuchen | 54 | 52.38 N | 13.44 E |
| Wernigerode | 54 | 51.50 N | 10.47 E |
| Wernitz | 264a | 52.34 N | 12.55 E |
| Wernsdorf | 264a | 52.22 N | 13.43 E |
| Wernsdorfer See ⊜ | 264a | 52.23 N | 13.42 E |
| Wernstein | 60 | 48.30 N | 13.28 E |
| Werra ≃ | 30 | 51.26 N | 9.39 E |
| Werribee | 169 | 37.54 S | 144.40 E |
| Werribee ≃ | 169 | 37.59 S | 144.41 E |
| Werribee Gorge State Park ♦ | 169 | 37.40 S | 144.21 E |
| Werribee South | 169 | 37.56 S | 144.42 E |
| Werries | 52 | 51.41 N | 7.53 E |
| Werrington | 274a | 33.45 S | 150.46 E |
| Werris Creek | 166 | 31.21 S | 150.39 E |
| Werschweiler | 56 | 49.27 N | 7.13 E |
| Wersten ◆[8] | 263 | 51.11 N | 6.49 E |
| Wertach | 58 | 47.36 N | 10.25 E |
| Wertach ≃ | 58 | 48.24 N | 10.53 E |
| Wertheim | 56 | 49.46 N | 9.31 E |
| Werther, Dtsch. | 52 | 52.04 N | 8.24 E |
| Werther, Dtsch. | 54 | 51.29 N | 10.46 E |
| Wertingen | 56 | 48.34 N | 10.41 E |
| Wervershoof | 52 | 52.44 N | 5.09 E |
| Wervik | 50 | 50.47 N | 3.02 E |
| Wervin | 262 | 53.15 N | 2.52 W |
| Werwaru | 164 | 8.13 S | 128.11 E |
| Weschnitz ≃ | 56 | 49.43 N | 8.24 E |
| Weseke | 52 | 51.54 N | 6.51 E |
| Wesel | 52 | 51.40 N | 6.38 E |
| Wesel-Datteln-Kanal ≍ | 263 | 51.38 N | 6.36 E |
| Wesenberg | 54 | 53.17 N | 12.58 E |
| Wesendahl | 264a | 52.36 N | 13.49 E |
| Wesendorf | 52 | 52.35 N | 10.31 E |
| Weser ≃ | 52 | 53.32 N | 8.34 E |
| Weser-Ems □[5] | 52 | 52.45 N | 8.00 E |
| Wesergebirge ∧∧ | 52 | 52.15 N | 9.10 E |
| Wesham | 262 | 53.48 N | 2.53 W |
| Wesickaman Creek ≃ | 285 | 39.44 N | 74.43 W |
| Wesī Śahar | 124 | 28.15 N | 84.23 E |
| Weskan | 198 | 38.52 N | 101.57 W |
| Weslaco | 196 | 26.09 N | 97.59 W |
| Weslemkoon Lake ⊜ | 212 | 45.02 N | 77.25 W |
| Wesley, Dom. | 240d | 15.34 N | 61.19 W |
| Wesley, Ia., U.S. | 190 | 43.05 N | 93.59 W |
| Wesleyville, Nf., Can. | 186 | 49.09 N | 53.34 W |
| Wesleyville, Pa., U.S. | 214 | 42.08 N | 80.00 W |
| Wessel, Cape > | 164 | 10.59 S | 136.46 E |
| Wesseling | 56 | 50.49 N | 6.58 E |
| Wessel Islands II | 164 | 11.30 S | 136.25 E |
| Wesselsbron | 158 | 27.50 S | 25.23 E |
| Wesselsvlei | 158 | 27.23 S | 23.47 E |
| Wessington | 198 | 44.27 N | 98.41 W |
| Wessington Springs | 198 | 44.04 N | 98.34 W |
| Wessobrunn | 64 | 47.52 N | 11.01 E |
| Wesson | 194 | 31.42 N | 90.23 W |
| Wessum | 52 | 52.05 N | 6.58 E |
| West, Ms., U.S. | 194 | 33.11 N | 89.46 W |
| West, Tx., U.S. | 222 | 31.48 N | 97.05 W |
| West ≃, N.Y., U.S. | 210 | 42.41 N | 77.22 W |
| West ≃, Vt., U.S. | 188 | 42.52 N | 72.33 W |
| West Abington | 207 | 42.05 N | 70.58 W |
| Westacres | 216 | 42.35 N | 83.26 W |
| West Acton | 207 | 42.28 N | 71.28 W |
| West Alexander | 214 | 40.06 N | 80.31 W |
| West Alexandria | 218 | 39.44 N | 84.31 W |
| Westall, Point > | 162 | 32.55 S | 134.04 E |
| West Allen ≃ | 44 | 54.55 N | 2.19 W |
| West Allis | 216 | 43.01 N | 88.00 W |
| Westalton | 219 | 38.51 N | 90.13 W |
| West Amityville | 276 | 40.41 N | 73.26 W |
| West Andover | 207 | 42.39 N | 71.09 W |
| West Athens | 280 | 33.55 N | 118.18 W |
| West Atlantic City | 208 | 39.23 N | 74.28 W |
| West Babylon | 210 | 40.43 N | 73.21 W |
| Westbahnhof ◆[5] | 264b | 48.11 N | 16.20 E |
| West Baines ≃ | 164 | 15.36 S | 129.58 E |
| West Bangor | 210 | 40.52 N | 75.14 W |
| Westbank | 182 | 49.50 N | 119.38 W |
| West Bank □[9] | 132 | 31.40 N | 35.15 E |
| West Barnstable | 207 | 41.42 N | 70.22 W |
| West Barrington | 207 | 41.44 N | 71.20 W |
| West Bay, N.S., Can. | 186 | 45.43 N | 61.10 W |
| Westbay, Fl., U.S. | 194 | 30.17 N | 85.52 W |
| West Bay c, Fl., U.S. | 194 | 30.16 N | 85.47 W |
| West Bay c, Tx., U.S. | 222 | 29.15 N | 94.57 W |
| West Bay Shore | 276 | 40.42 N | 73.16 W |
| West Belmar | 208 | 40.10 N | 74.02 W |
| West Bend, Ia., U.S. | 198 | 42.57 N | 94.26 W |
| West Bend, Wi., U.S. | 190 | 43.25 N | 88.11 W |
| West Bengal □[3] | 124 | 24.00 N | 88.00 E |
| West Bergholt | 42 | 51.55 N | 0.51 E |
| West Berlin | 208 | 39.48 N | 74.56 W |
| West Bernard Creek ≃ | 222 | 29.23 N | 95.58 W |
| Westbevern | 52 | 52.01 N | 7.47 E |
| West Bhāgīrath Plain ≚ | 126 | 23.30 N | 88.00 E |
| West Bijou Creek ≃ | 198 | 39.51 N | 104.08 W |
| West Billerica | 283 | 42.33 N | 71.19 W |
| West Blocton | 194 | 33.07 N | 87.07 W |
| West Bloomfield | 210 | 42.54 N | 77.32 W |
| West Bolivar | 214 | 40.23 N | 79.10 W |
| Westborough | 207 | 42.16 N | 71.37 W |
| Westbourne | 184 | 50.09 N | 98.35 W |
| West Bow Creek ≃ | 198 | 42.46 N | 97.08 W |
| West Boxford | 283 | 42.42 N | 71.04 W |
| West Boylston | 207 | 42.22 N | 71.47 W |
| West Bradenton | 220 | 27.30 N | 82.37 W |
| West Branch, Ia., U.S. | 190 | 41.40 N | 91.20 W |
| West Branch, Mi., U.S. | 190 | 44.16 N | 84.14 W |
| West Branch Reservoir ⊜[1] | 210 | 41.25 N | 73.42 W |
| West Branch State Park ♦ | 214 | 41.07 N | 81.05 W |
| Westbridge | 182 | 49.10 N | 118.59 W |
| West Bridgewater | 207 | 42.01 N | 71.00 W |
| West Bridgford | 42 | 52.56 N | 1.08 W |
| West Bristol | 285 | 40.06 N | 74.53 W |
| West Bromwich | 42 | 52.31 N | 1.56 W |
| Westbrook, Austl. | 171a | 27.36 S | 151.52 E |
| Westbrook, On., Can. | 212 | 44.16 N | 76.38 W |
| Westbrook, Ct., U.S. | 207 | 41.17 N | 72.26 W |
| Westbrook, Me., U.S. | 188 | 43.40 N | 70.22 W |
| Westbrook, Mn., U.S. | 198 | 44.02 N | 95.26 W |
| Westbrook, Tx., U.S. | 196 | 32.21 N | 101.01 W |
| West Brook ≃ | 276 | 41.04 N | 74.18 W |
| West Brookfield | 207 | 42.14 N | 72.08 W |
| Westbrookville | 210 | 41.30 N | 74.34 W |
| West Burlington, Ia., U.S. | 190 | 40.49 N | 91.09 W |
| West Burlington, N.Y., U.S. | 210 | 42.42 N | 75.11 W |
| West Burra I | 46a | 60.05 N | 1.21 W |
| Westbury, Eng., U.K. | 42 | 52.41 N | 2.57 W |
| Westbury, Eng., U.K. | 42 | 51.16 N | 2.11 W |
| Westbury, N.Y., U.S. | 276 | 40.45 N | 73.35 W |
| Westbury-on-Severn | 42 | 51.50 N | 2.24 W |
| West Butte ∧ | 202 | 48.57 N | 111.32 W |
| Westby, Austl. | 171b | 35.30 S | 147.25 E |
| Westby, Mt., U.S. | 198 | 48.52 N | 104.03 W |
| Westby, Wi., U.S. | 190 | 43.39 N | 90.51 W |
| West Cache Creek ≃ | 196 | 34.13 N | 98.23 W |
| West Caicos I | 238 | 21.39 N | 72.28 W |
| West Calder | 46 | 55.52 N | 3.35 W |
| West Caldwell | 276 | 40.50 N | 74.18 W |
| West Cameron | 208 | 40.45 N | 76.41 W |
| West Camp | 210 | 42.07 N | 73.56 W |
| West Canada Creek ≃ | 188 | 43.01 N | 74.58 W |
| West Cape > | 172 | 45.54 S | 166.26 E |
| West Cape Howe > | 162 | 35.08 S | 117.36 E |
| West Cape May | 208 | 38.56 N | 74.56 W |


**Symbols** in the index entries represent the broad categories identified in the key at the right. Symbols with superior numbers (∧∧[1]) identify subcategories (see complete key on page *I · 1).*

**Symbole** im Register stellen die rechts im Schlüssel erklärten Kategorien dar. Symbole mit hochgestellten Ziffern (∧∧[1]) bezeichnen Unterabteilungen einer Kategorie (vgl. vollständiger Schlüssel auf Seite *I · 1).*

**Los símbolos** incluídos en el texto del índice representan las grandes categorías identificadas con la clave a la derecha. Los símbolos con numeros en su parte superior (∧∧[1]) identifican las subcategorías (véase la clave completa en la página *I · 1).*

**Les symboles** de l'index représentent les catégories indiquées dans la légende à droite. Les symboles suivis d'un indice (∧∧[1]) représentent des sous-catégories (voir légende complète à la page *I · 1).*

**Os símbolos** incluídos no texto do índice representam as grandes categorias identificadas com a chave à direita. Os símbolos com números em sua parte superior (∧∧[1]) identificam as subcategorias (veja-se a chave completa à página *I · 1).*

| | | | | | |
|---|---|---|---|---|---|
| ∧ | Mountain | Berg | Montaña | Montagne | Montanha |
| ∧∧ | Mountains | Gebirge | Montañas | Montagnes | Montanhas |
| )( | Pass | Paß | Paso | Col | Passo |
| V | Valley, Canyon | Tal, Cañon | Valle, Cañón | Vallée, Canyon | Vale, Canhão |
| ≚ | Plain | Ebene | Llano | Plaine | Planície |
| > | Cape | Kap | Cabo | Cap | Cabo |
| I | Island | Insel | Isla | Île | Ilha |
| II | Islands | Inseln | Islas | Îles | Ilhas |
| ⊥ | Other Topographic Features | Andere Topographische Objekte | Otros Elementos Topográficos | Autres données topographiques | Outros acidentes topográficos |

ESPAÑOL — Nombre | Página | Lat.°′ | Long.°′ W = Oeste
FRANÇAIS — Nom | Page | Lat.°′ | Long.°′ W = Ouest
PORTUGUÊS — Nome | Página | Lat.°′ | Long.°′ W = Oeste


| Nombre / Nom / Nome | Página / Page | Lat.°′ | Long.°′ |
|---|---|---|---|
| West Carlisle | 196 | 33.35 N | 101.56 W |
| West Caroline Basin ✦[1] | 14 | 4.00 N | 138.00 E |
| West Carrollton | 218 | 39.40 N | 84.15 W |
| West Carson | 280 | 33.57 N | 118.23 W |
| West Carthage | 212 | 43.58 N | 75.36 W |
| West Catfish Creek ≃ | 212 | 42.46 N | 81.04 W |
| West Channel ≃[1] | 180 | 68.51 N | 136.10 W |
| West Chelmsford | 283 | 42.37 N | 71.23 W |
| Westchester, Il., U.S. | 216 | 41.51 N | 87.52 W |
| West Chester, Pa., U.S. | 208 | 39.57 N | 75.36 W |
| Westchester, Va., U.S. | 284c | 38.51 N | 77.16 W |
| Westchester □[6] | 210 | 41.02 N | 73.46 W |
| Westchester ◆[8], Ca., U.S. | 280 | 33.55 N | 118.25 W |
| Westchester ◆[8], N.Y., U.S. | 276 | 40.51 N | 73.52 W |
| West Chester Airport ⊠ | 285 | 39.59 N | 75.35 W |
| Westchester County Airport ⊠ | 207 | 41.04 N | 73.43 W |
| Westchester Creek ≃ | 276 | 40.48 N | 73.51 W |
| Westchester Estates | 284c | 38.47 N | 76.55 W |
| Westchester Station | 186 | 45.37 N | 63.40 W |
| West Chester University of Pennsylvania ʊ[2] | 285 | 39.57 N | 75.36 W |
| West Chicago | 216 | 41.53 N | 88.12 W |
| West Clandon | 260 | 51.15 N | 0.30 W |
| West Clarksville | 210 | 42.08 N | 78.15 W |
| West Clear Creek ≃ | 200 | 34.34 N | 111.51 W |
| West Cleddau ≃ | 42 | 51.46 N | 4.54 W |
| Westcliffe | 200 | 38.08 N | 105.27 W |
| Westcliffe ◆[8] | 273d | 26.11 S | 28.02 E |
| Westcliff-on-Sea | 260 | 51.32 N | 0.41 E |
| West College Corner | 218 | 39.34 N | 84.48 W |
| West Collingswood Heights | 285 | 39.59 N | 75.07 W |
| West Columbia, S.C., U.S. | 192 | 33.59 N | 81.04 W |
| West Columbia, Tx., U.S. | 222 | 29.08 N | 95.38 W |
| West Concord, Ma., U.S. | 207 | 42.27 N | 71.23 W |
| West Concord, Mn., U.S. | 190 | 44.09 N | 92.53 W |
| West Conshohocken | 285 | 40.04 N | 75.19 W |
| West Cote Blanche Bay c | 194 | 29.40 N | 91.45 W |
| Westcott | 260 | 51.13 N | 0.22 W |
| Westcott Cove c | 276 | 41.02 N | 73.30 W |
| West Covina | 228 | 34.04 N | 117.56 W |
| West Creek | 208 | 39.38 N | 74.18 W |
| West Creek ≃, In., U.S. | 216 | 41.12 N | 87.30 W |
| West Creek ≃, Pa., U.S. | 214 | 41.30 N | 78.15 W |
| Westdale, Ma., U.S. | 283 | 42.01 N | 70.59 W |
| Westdale, N.Y., U.S. | 210 | 43.23 N | 75.49 W |
| West Danby | 210 | 42.19 N | 76.32 W |
| West Davenport | 210 | 42.27 N | 74.58 W |
| West Deane Park ♠ | 275b | 43.40 N | 79.34 W |
| West Decatur | 214 | 40.56 N | 78.17 W |
| West Delaware Aqueduct ≊[1] | 210 | 41.52 N | 74.31 W |
| Westdene ◆[8] | 273d | 26.11 S | 27.59 E |
| West Dennis | 207 | 41.39 N | 70.10 W |
| West Derby ◆[8] | 262 | 53.26 N | 2.54 W |
| West Derry | 214 | 40.20 N | 79.20 W |
| West Des Moines | 190 | 41.34 N | 93.42 W |
| West Ditch ≊ | 276 | 40.56 N | 74.19 W |
| West Dolores ≃ | 200 | 37.35 N | 108.21 W |
| West Drayton ◆[8] | 260 | 51.30 N | 0.29 W |
| West Duffins Creek ≃ | 212 | 43.51 N | 79.04 W |
| West Duxbury | 283 | 42.03 N | 70.47 W |
| West Easton | 210 | 40.41 N | 75.14 W |
| West Eaton | 210 | 42.51 N | 75.39 W |
| Westecunk Creek ≃ | 208 | 39.37 N | 74.16 W |
| West Edmeston | 210 | 42.46 N | 75.17 W |
| West Edmondale | 284b | 39.18 N | 76.43 W |
| West Elizabeth | 279b | 40.17 N | 79.54 W |
| West Elk Mountains ⺈ | 200 | 38.40 N | 107.15 W |
| West Elk Peak ʌ | 200 | 38.43 N | 107.13 W |
| West Elkton | 218 | 39.35 N | 84.33 W |
| West Ellicott | 214 | 42.05 N | 79.16 W |
| West Elmira | 210 | 42.04 N | 76.50 W |
| West End, Ba. | 238 | 26.41 N | 78.58 W |
| West End, Eng., U.K. | 260 | 51.44 N | 0.04 W |
| West End, Eng., U.K. | 260 | 51.20 N | 0.38 W |
| West End, Ar., U.S. | 194 | 34.13 N | 92.03 W |
| West End, Il., U.S. | 216 | 42.17 N | 89.09 W |
| West End, N.Y., U.S. | 210 | 42.28 N | 75.05 W |
| West End, N.C., U.S. | 192 | 35.14 N | 79.34 W |
| West End ◆[8], Eng., U.K. | 260 | 51.32 N | 0.24 W |
| West End ◆[8], Pa., U.S. | 279b | 40.27 N | 80.02 W |
| Westende, Bel. | 50 | 51.10 N | 2.46 E |
| Westende, Dtsch. | 263 | 51.25 N | 7.24 E |
| Westendorf | 64 | 47.26 N | 12.13 E |
| Westenfeld ◆[8] | 263 | 51.28 N | 7.09 E |
| Westenholz | 52 | 51.45 N | 8.28 E |
| Westenschouwen | 52 | 51.41 N | 3.42 E |
| Westerbauer ◆[8] | 263 | 51.20 N | 7.23 E |
| Westerblokker | 52 | 52.39 N | 5.08 E |
| Westerbönen | 263 | 51.36 N | 7.46 E |
| Westerbork | 52 | 52.51 N | 6.37 E |
| Westerburg | 56 | 50.33 N | 7.58 E |
| Westercelle | 52 | 52.36 N | 10.05 E |
| Westerdale | 46 | 58.27 N | 3.30 W |
| Westeregeln | 54 | 51.57 N | 11.23 E |
| Westerham | 42 | 51.16 N | 0.05 E |
| Westerhausen | 54 | 51.48 N | 11.03 E |
| Westerholt | 52 | 51.36 N | 7.05 E |
| Westerholz ◆[3] | 263 | 51.32 N | 7.28 E |
| Westerkappeln | 52 | 52.18 N | 7.52 E |
| Westerland | 30 | 54.54 N | 8.18 E |
| Westerlo, Bel. | 56 | 51.05 N | 4.55 E |
| Westerlo, N.Y., U.S. | 210 | 42.31 N | 74.03 W |
| Westerly | 207 | 41.22 N | 71.49 W |
| Western | 198 | 40.23 N | 97.11 W |
| Western □[4], Ghana | 150 | 5.30 N | 2.30 W |
| Western □[4], Kenya | 154 | 0.30 N | 34.35 E |
| Western □[4], Sol.Is. | 175e | 8.00 S | 157.00 E |
| Western □[4], Zam. | 152 | 16.00 S | 24.00 E |
| Western □[5], Pap. N. Gui. | 164 | 7.00 S | 142.00 E |
| Western □[5], Ug. | 154 | 1.00 N | 31.00 E |
| Western ≃ | 166 | 22.22 S | 142.25 E |
| Western Area □[4] | 150 | 8.20 N | 13.00 W |
| Western Australia □[3] | 160 | 25.00 S | 122.00 E |
| Western Branch ≃ | 284c | 38.55 N | 76.48 W |
| Western Canal ≊ | 226 | 39.28 N | 121.35 W |
| Western Cape □[4] | 158 | 33.30 S | 20.00 E |
| Western Channel ʉ | 98 | 34.40 N | 129.00 E |
| Western Cove c | 168b | 35.43 S | 137.38 E |
| Western Desert → Gharbīyah, Aṣ-Ṣaḥrā' al- ◆[2] | 140 | 27.00 N | 27.00 E |
| Western Division □[5] | 175g | 18.00 S | 177.30 E |
| Western Ghāts ⺈ | 122 | 14.00 N | 75.00 E |
| Western Highlands □[5] | 164 | 5.45 S | 144.30 E |
| Western Isles □[4] | 46 | 57.40 N | 7.00 W |
| Westernport | 188 | 39.29 N | 79.02 W |
| Western Port c | 169 | 38.22 N | 145.20 E |
| Western Port Bay c | 169 | 38.15 S | 145.20 E |
| Western Sahara □[2], Afr. | 134 | 24.30 N | 13.00 W |
| Western Sahara □[2], Afr. | 148 | 24.30 N | 13.00 W |
| Western Samoa □[1], Oc. | 14 | 13.55 S | 172.00 W |
| Western Samoa □[1], Oc. | 175a | 13.55 S | 172.00 W |
| Western Sayans → Zapadnyj Sajan ⺈ | 74 | 53.00 N | 94.00 E |
| Western Shore | 186 | 44.32 N | 64.19 W |
| Western Springs | 278 | 41.48 N | 87.54 W |
| Westernville | 210 | 43.18 N | 75.23 W |
| Westerschelde c[1] | 52 | 51.25 N | 3.45 E |
| Westerstede | 52 | 53.15 N | 7.55 E |
| Westervelt | 219 | 39.29 N | 88.52 W |
| Westerville | 214 | 40.07 N | 82.55 W |
| Westerwald ⺈ | 56 | 50.40 N | 7.55 E |
| West European Basin ✦[1] | 10 | 47.00 N | 15.00 W |
| West Exeter | 210 | 42.48 N | 75.09 W |
| West Fairview | 208 | 40.16 N | 76.54 W |
| Westfalen □[9] | 52 | 51.50 N | 7.30 E |
| Westfalenhalle ʊ | 263 | 51.30 N | 7.27 E |
| West Falkland I | 254 | 51.50 S | 60.00 W |
| West Falls | 210 | 42.42 N | 78.41 W |
| West Falmouth | 207 | 41.36 N | 70.38 W |
| West Fargo | 198 | 46.52 N | 96.54 W |
| West Farleigh | 260 | 51.15 N | 0.27 E |
| West Farmington | 214 | 41.23 N | 80.58 W |
| Westfield, Eng., U.K. | 42 | 50.55 N | 0.35 E |
| Westfield, Il., U.S. | 194 | 39.27 N | 88.01 W |
| Westfield, In., U.S. | 218 | 40.02 N | 86.07 W |
| Westfield, Ma., U.S. | 207 | 42.07 N | 72.45 W |
| Westfield, N.J., U.S. | 210 | 40.39 N | 74.20 W |
| Westfield, N.Y., U.S. | 214 | 42.19 N | 79.34 W |
| Westfield, Pa., U.S. | 210 | 41.55 N | 77.32 W |
| Westfield, Tx., U.S. | 222 | 30.01 N | 95.24 W |
| Westfield, Wi., U.S. | 190 | 43.53 N | 89.29 W |
| Westfield ≃ | 207 | 42.05 N | 72.35 W |
| Westfield, Middle Branch ≃ | 207 | 42.16 N | 72.52 W |
| Westfield, West Branch ≃ | 207 | 42.13 N | 72.52 W |
| Westfield Center | 214 | 41.01 N | 81.55 W |
| West Fiord c[2] | 176 | 76.02 N | 90.00 W |
| Westford, Ma., U.S. | 283 | 42.34 N | 71.26 W |
| Westford, N.Y., U.S. | 210 | 42.39 N | 74.48 W |
| West Fork | 194 | 35.55 N | 94.11 W |
| West Foxboro | 283 | 42.05 N | 71.17 W |
| West Frankfort | 194 | 37.53 N | 88.55 W |
| West Friesland □[9] | 52 | 52.45 N | 4.50 E |
| West Frisian Islands → Waddeneilanden II | 52 | 53.26 N | 5.30 E |
| West Fulton | 210 | 42.34 N | 74.28 W |
| Westgate | 166 | 26.35 S | 146.12 E |
| Westgate on Sea | 42 | 51.23 N | 1.21 E |
| West Genesee Terrace | 210 | 43.03 N | 76.16 W |
| West-Ghats → Western Ghāts ⺈ | 122 | 14.00 N | 75.00 E |
| West Gilgo Beach | 276 | 40.37 N | 73.25 W |
| West Glacier | 202 | 48.29 N | 113.58 W |
| West Glamorgan □[6] | 42 | 51.35 N | 3.35 W |
| West Glens Falls | 210 | 43.18 N | 73.43 W |
| West Glenville | 210 | 42.56 N | 74.04 W |
| West Goshen | 207 | 41.49 N | 73.15 W |
| West Granby | 207 | 41.57 N | 72.50 W |
| West Grand Lake ⊜ | 188 | 45.15 N | 67.50 W |
| West Groton | 207 | 42.36 N | 71.37 W |
| West Grove | 208 | 39.49 N | 75.49 W |
| Westham | 208 | 37.35 N | 77.32 W |
| West Ham ◆[8] | 260 | 51.31 N | 0.01 E |
| West Hamburg | 208 | 40.33 N | 76.00 W |
| West Ham Football Club ♠ | 260 | 51.32 N | 0.02 E |
| Westham Island I | 224 | 49.05 N | 123.10 W |
| West Hamlin | 188 | 38.17 N | 82.11 W |
| Westhampton, N.Y., U.S. | 207 | 40.49 N | 72.39 W |
| Westhampton, Va., U.S. | 284c | 38.54 N | 77.11 W |
| West Hanningfield | 260 | 51.40 N | 0.30 E |
| West Hanover | 283 | 42.07 N | 70.53 W |
| West Harbor c | 276 | 40.54 N | 73.32 W |
| West Harrison | 218 | 39.15 N | 84.49 W |
| West Hartford | 207 | 41.45 N | 72.44 W |
| West Hartland | 207 | 42.00 N | 72.58 W |
| Westhausen | 56 | 48.53 N | 10.11 E |
| Westhaven, Ca., U.S. | 204 | 41.03 N | 124.06 W |
| West Haven, Ct., U.S. | 207 | 41.16 N | 72.57 W |
| Westhaven, Il., U.S. | 278 | 41.35 N | 87.51 W |
| West Haverstraw | 210 | 41.12 N | 73.59 W |
| West Hazleton | 210 | 40.57 N | 75.59 W |
| Westhead | 262 | 53.34 N | 2.51 W |
| West Hebron | 210 | 43.14 N | 73.22 W |
| West Heidelberg | 274b | 37.45 S | 145.02 E |
| Westheim | 56 | 49.03 N | 9.44 E |
| West Helena | 194 | 34.33 N | 90.38 W |
| Westhemmerde | 263 | 51.33 N | 7.47 E |
| West Hempstead | 276 | 40.42 N | 73.39 W |
| West Henrietta | 210 | 43.02 N | 77.40 W |
| West Hickory | 214 | 41.34 N | 79.25 W |
| Westhill | 46 | 57.09 N | 2.17 W |
| West Hill ◆[8] | 275b | 43.46 N | 79.11 W |
| Westhofen | 263 | 51.25 N | 7.31 E |
| Westhoff | 222 | 29.12 N | 97.28 W |
| Westhoffen | 58 | 48.36 N | 7.26 E |
| West Hollywood, Ca., U.S. | 228 | 34.05 N | 118.21 W |
| West Hollywood, Fl., U.S. | 220 | 26.01 N | 80.10 W |
| Westholme | 224 | 49.52 N | 123.42 W |
| West Homestead | 279b | 40.24 N | 79.55 W |
| Westhope, N.D., U.S. | 198 | 48.54 N | 101.01 W |
| Westhope, Oh., U.S. | 216 | 41.18 N | 83.57 W |
| West Horndon | 260 | 51.34 N | 0.21 E |
| West Horsley | 260 | 51.16 N | 0.27 W |
| Westhoughton | 262 | 53.33 N | 2.32 W |
| West Hoxton | 274a | 33.55 S | 150.49 E |
| West Humber ≃ | 212 | 43.44 N | 79.33 W |
| West Humble | 260 | 51.15 N | 0.20 W |
| West Huntington | 276 | 40.42 N | 73.18 W |
| West Hurley | 210 | 42.00 N | 74.06 W |
| Westhuyzen | 158 | 27.30 S | 25.27 E |
| West Hyde | 260 | 51.37 N | 0.30 W |
| West Ice Shelf ⊓ | 9 | 67.00 S | 85.00 E |
| Westick | 263 | 51.35 N | 7.38 E |
| Westig | 263 | 51.22 N | 7.45 E |
| West Indies II | 230 | 19.00 N | 70.00 W |
| Westindische Inseln → West Indies II | 230 | 19.00 N | 70.00 W |
| West Irian → Irian Jaya □[4] | 164 | 5.00 S | 138.00 E |
| West Island I, Austl. | 164 | 15.36 S | 136.34 E |
| West Island I, Ma., U.S. | 207 | 41.36 N | 70.50 W |
| West Islip | 210 | 40.42 N | 73.18 W |
| West Jan Mayen Ridge ✦[3] | 10 | 71.00 N | 13.00 W |
| West Jefferson, N.C., U.S. | 192 | 36.24 N | 81.29 W |
| West Jefferson, Oh., U.S. | 218 | 39.56 N | 83.16 W |
| West Jordan | 200 | 40.36 N | 111.56 W |
| Westkapelle, Bel. | 50 | 51.19 N | 3.18 E |
| Westkapelle, Ned. | 52 | 51.32 N | 3.27 E |
| West Keansburg | 276 | 40.27 N | 74.09 W |
| West Kettle ≃ | 182 | 49.07 N | 119.00 W |
| West Kilbride | 46 | 55.42 N | 4.51 W |
| West Kill | 210 | 42.13 N | 74.31 W |
| West Kingsdown | 42 | 51.21 N | 0.17 E |
| West Kingston | 207 | 41.28 N | 71.33 W |
| West Kirby | 44 | 53.22 N | 3.10 W |
| Westkirchen | 52 | 51.53 N | 8.02 E |
| West Kittanning | 214 | 40.49 N | 79.32 W |
| West Lafayette, In., U.S. | 216 | 40.25 N | 86.54 W |
| West Lafayette, Oh., U.S. | 214 | 40.16 N | 81.45 W |
| Westlake, La., U.S. | 194 | 30.15 N | 93.15 W |
| Westlake, Oh., U.S. | 214 | 41.27 N | 81.55 W |
| Westlake, Tx., U.S. | 222 | 32.59 N | 97.12 W |
| West Lake ⋹, On., Can. | 212 | 43.56 N | 77.17 W |
| West Lake ⋹, Fl., U.S. | 220 | 25.12 N | 80.49 W |
| West Lake ⋹, N.J., U.S. | 276 | 40.58 N | 74.22 W |
| West Lamma Channel ʉ | 271d | 22.13 N | 114.04 E |
| West Lancashire □[8] | 262 | 53.35 N | 2.50 W |
| Westland, Mi., U.S. | 216 | 42.19 N | 83.24 W |
| Westland, Pa., U.S. | 214 | 40.17 N | 80.16 W |
| Westland Center ◆[9] | 281 | 42.20 N | 83.23 W |
| Westland National Park ♠ | 172 | 43.30 S | 170.10 E |
| Westlands | 207 | 42.37 N | 71.20 W |
| West Lanham Hills | 284c | 38.57 N | 76.53 W |
| West Laramie | 200 | 41.18 N | 105.37 W |
| West Lawn | 284c | 38.52 N | 77.11 W |
| West Lebanon, In., U.S. | 216 | 40.16 N | 87.23 W |
| West Lebanon, Pa., U.S. | 214 | 40.35 N | 79.22 W |
| West Leechburg | 214 | 40.37 N | 79.37 W |
| Westleigh, S. Afr. | 158 | 27.31 S | 27.21 E |
| Westleigh, Eng., U.K. | 262 | 53.30 N | 2.31 W |
| West Leipsic | 216 | 41.07 N | 84.00 W |
| Westley | 226 | 37.33 N | 121.12 W |
| West Leyden | 212 | 43.28 N | 75.28 W |
| West Liberty, Ia., U.S. | 190 | 41.34 N | 91.15 W |
| West Liberty, Ky., U.S. | 192 | 37.55 N | 83.15 W |
| West Liberty, Oh., U.S. | 216 | 40.15 N | 83.45 W |
| West Liberty, Pa., U.S. | 214 | 41.00 N | 80.03 W |
| West Liberty, W.V., U.S. | 214 | 40.10 N | 80.35 W |
| West Liberty ◆[8] | 279b | 40.24 N | 80.01 W |
| Westliche Sahara → Western Sahara □[2] | 148 | 24.30 N | 13.00 W |
| Westliche Sierra Madre → Madre Occidental, Sierra ⺈ | 232 | 25.00 N | 105.00 W |
| Westline | 214 | 41.47 N | 78.46 W |
| West Linn | 224 | 45.21 N | 122.36 W |
| West Linton | 46 | 55.46 N | 3.22 W |
| West Little Owyhee ≃ | 202 | 42.28 N | 117.15 W |
| Westlock | 182 | 54.09 N | 113.52 W |
| West Lorne | 214 | 42.36 N | 81.36 W |
| West Los Angeles ◆[8] | 280 | 34.03 N | 118.28 W |
| West Lulworth | 42 | 50.38 N | 2.15 W |
| West Lunga ≃ | 154 | 13.06 S | 24.39 E |
| West Lunga National Park ♠ | 154 | 12.55 S | 25.10 E |
| Westmalle | 52 | 51.18 N | 4.41 E |
| West Malling | 42 | 51.18 N | 0.25 E |
| West Malling Aerodrome ⊠ | 260 | 51.16 N | 0.24 E |
| West Manayunk | 285 | 40.01 N | 75.14 W |
| West Manchester | 218 | 39.54 N | 84.37 W |
| West Mansfield, Ma., U.S. | 207 | 41.59 N | 71.14 W |
| West Mansfield, Oh., U.S. | 216 | 40.24 N | 83.32 W |
| West Mariana Basin ✦[1] | 14 | 15.00 N | 137.00 E |
| West Mayfield | 214 | 40.47 N | 80.20 W |
| West Meadowview | 216 | 41.08 N | 87.52 W |
| Westmeath □[6] | 48 | 53.30 N | 7.30 W |
| West Medway | 207 | 42.08 N | 71.25 W |
| West Melbourne | 220 | 28.04 N | 80.39 W |
| West Memphis | 194 | 35.08 N | 90.11 W |
| West Meon | 42 | 51.01 N | 1.05 W |
| Westmere | 210 | 42.41 N | 73.52 W |
| West Mersea | 42 | 51.47 N | 0.55 E |
| West Miami | 220 | 25.45 N | 80.17 W |
| West Middlesex | 214 | 41.10 N | 80.27 W |
| West Middletown | 214 | 40.15 N | 80.25 W |
| West Midlands □[6] | 42 | 52.30 N | 2.00 W |
| West Mifflin | 214 | 40.22 N | 79.52 W |
| West Milford | 210 | 41.07 N | 74.22 W |
| West Millbury | 207 | 42.11 N | 71.48 W |
| West Mill Creek ≃ | 222 | 29.55 N | 96.17 W |
| West Milton, Oh., U.S. | 218 | 39.57 N | 84.19 W |
| West Milton, Pa., U.S. | 210 | 41.01 N | 76.52 W |
| West Milwaukee | 216 | 43.00 N | 87.58 W |
| West Mineola | 222 | 32.41 N | 95.31 W |
| Westminster, Ca., U.S. | 228 | 33.45 N | 118.02 W |
| Westminster, Co., U.S. | 200 | 39.50 N | 105.02 W |
| Westminster, Md., U.S. | 208 | 39.34 N | 76.59 W |
| Westminster, Ma., U.S. | 207 | 42.32 N | 71.54 W |
| Westminster, Oh., U.S. | 216 | 40.42 N | 83.58 W |
| Westminster, S.C., U.S. | 192 | 34.39 N | 83.05 W |
| Westminster ◆[8] | 260 | 51.30 N | 0.09 W |
| Westminster Abbey ʊ[1] | 260 | 51.30 N | 0.07 W |
| Westminster Mall ◆[9] | 280 | 33.45 N | 118.01 W |
| West Modesto | 226 | 37.37 N | 121.02 W |
| West Monroe | 194 | 32.31 N | 92.08 W |
| Westmont, Ca., U.S. | 280 | 33.56 N | 118.18 W |
| Westmont, Il., U.S. | 278 | 41.47 N | 87.58 W |
| Westmont, N.J., U.S. | 285 | 39.54 N | 75.02 W |
| Westmont, Pa., U.S. | 214 | 40.18 N | 78.57 W |
| West Monterey | 214 | 41.03 N | 79.39 W |
| West Montreal ≃ | 190 | 47.56 N | 80.39 W |
| West Moors | 42 | 50.49 N | 1.55 W |
| Westmoreland, Ks., U.S. | 198 | 39.23 N | 96.24 W |
| Westmoreland, N.Y., U.S. | 210 | 43.07 N | 75.24 W |
| Westmoreland, Tn., U.S. | 194 | 36.33 N | 86.14 W |
| Westmoreland, Va., U.S. | 208 | 38.04 N | 76.34 W |
| Westmoreland □[6], Pa., U.S. | 214 | 40.18 N | 79.33 W |
| Westmoreland □[6], Va., U.S. | 208 | 38.10 N | 76.50 W |
| Westmoreland City | 214 | 40.20 N | 79.41 W |
| Westmoreland State Park ♠ | 208 | 38.09 N | 76.50 W |
| Westmorland | 204 | 33.02 N | 115.37 W |
| Westmount | 206 | 45.29 N | 73.36 W |
| West Mountain ʌ | 188 | 43.51 N | 74.43 W |
| West Mud Creek ≃ | 222 | 32.07 N | 95.10 W |
| West Mustang Creek ≃ | 222 | 29.04 N | 96.26 W |
| West Nab ʌ | 262 | 53.35 N | 1.53 W |
| West Nanticoke | 210 | 40.13 N | 76.01 W |
| West New Britain □[5] | 164 | 5.45 S | 149.30 E |
| West Newbury | 207 | 42.48 N | 70.59 W |
| West Newton, Ma., U.S. | 283 | 42.21 N | 71.14 W |
| West Newton, Pa., U.S. | 214 | 40.12 N | 79.46 W |
| West New York | 276 | 40.47 N | 74.00 W |
| West Nicholson | 154 | 21.06 S | 29.25 E |
| West Nishnabotna ≃ | 198 | 40.39 N | 95.37 W |
| West Nodaway ≃ | 194 | 40.38 N | 95.01 W |
| West Norriton | 208 | 40.08 N | 75.22 W |
| West Norwood ◆[8] | 260 | 51.26 N | 0.06 W |
| West Novaya Zemlya Trough ✦[1] | 10 | 73.30 N | 50.00 E |
| West Nueces ≃ | 196 | 29.16 N | 99.56 W |
| West Nyack | 210 | 41.06 N | 73.58 W |
| West Okaw ≃ | 219 | 39.32 N | 88.42 W |
| Weston, Austl. | 170 | 32.49 S | 151.28 E |
| Weston, Malay. | 112 | 5.13 N | 115.36 E |
| Weston, Eng., U.K. | 262 | 53.19 N | 2.44 W |
| Weston, Co., U.S. | 200 | 37.07 N | 104.50 W |
| Weston, Ct., U.S. | 207 | 41.12 N | 73.22 W |
| Weston, Id., U.S. | 202 | 42.02 N | 111.58 W |
| Weston, Ma., U.S. | 207 | 42.22 N | 71.18 W |
| Weston, Mi., U.S. | 216 | 41.46 N | 84.06 W |
| Weston, Mo., U.S. | 194 | 39.24 N | 94.54 W |
| Weston, Ne., U.S. | 198 | 41.11 N | 96.44 W |
| Weston, Oh., U.S. | 216 | 41.20 N | 83.47 W |
| Weston, Or., U.S. | 202 | 45.48 N | 118.25 W |
| Weston, Pa., U.S. | 210 | 40.57 N | 76.09 W |
| Weston, W.V., U.S. | 188 | 39.02 N | 80.28 W |
| Weston □[8] | 275b | 43.43 N | 79.31 W |
| Westonaria | 273d | 26.19 S | 27.39 E |
| West Oneonta | 210 | 42.28 N | 75.07 W |
| Westönnen | 52 | 51.33 N | 7.58 E |
| Weston Reservoir ⊜[1] | 283 | 42.21 N | 71.18 W |
| Westons Mill Pond ⊜ | 276 | 40.28 N | 74.25 W |
| Westons Mills | 210 | 42.04 N | 78.23 W |
| Weston-super-Mare | 42 | 51.21 N | 2.59 W |
| Weston upon Trent | 42 | 52.45 N | 2.02 W |
| West Orange, N.J., U.S. | 276 | 40.47 N | 74.14 W |
| West Orange, Tx., U.S. | 194 | 30.05 N | 93.46 W |
| Westover, Md., U.S. | 208 | 38.07 N | 75.42 W |
| Westover, Pa., U.S. | 214 | 40.45 N | 78.40 W |
| Westover, Tn., U.S. | 194 | 35.36 N | 88.52 W |
| Westover, W.V., U.S. | 188 | 39.38 N | 79.58 W |
| Westover Air Force Base ■ | 207 | 42.12 N | 72.33 W |
| Westoverledingen | 52 | 53.10 N | 7.28 E |
| Westowne | 284b | 39.17 N | 76.43 W |
| West Palm Beach | 220 | 26.42 N | 80.03 W |
| West Palm Beach Canal ≊ | 220 | 26.38 N | 80.03 W |
| West Paris | 188 | 44.19 N | 70.34 W |
| West Park | 210 | 41.48 N | 73.58 W |
| West Paterson | 276 | 40.53 N | 74.11 W |
| West Pawlet | 210 | 43.21 N | 73.15 W |
| West Peckham | 260 | 51.15 N | 0.22 E |
| West Pensacola | 194 | 30.25 N | 87.16 W |
| Westphalia, Ks., U.S. | 198 | 38.10 N | 95.29 W |
| Westphalia, Mi., U.S. | 216 | 42.55 N | 84.47 W |
| Westphalia, Mo., U.S. | 219 | 38.26 N | 91.59 W |
| West Pittsburg, Ca., U.S. | 226 | 38.01 N | 121.56 W |
| West Pittsburg, Pa., U.S. | 214 | 40.55 N | 80.21 W |
| West Pittston | 210 | 41.19 N | 75.47 W |
| West Plains | 194 | 36.43 N | 91.51 W |
| West Point, Ca., U.S. | 226 | 38.23 N | 120.31 W |
| West Point, Ga., U.S. | 192 | 32.52 N | 85.11 W |
| Westpoint, In., U.S. | 216 | 40.21 N | 87.03 W |
| West Point, Ia., U.S. | 190 | 40.43 N | 91.27 W |
| West Point, Ky., U.S. | 194 | 37.59 N | 85.56 W |
| West Point, Ms., U.S. | 194 | 33.36 N | 88.39 W |
| West Point, Ne., U.S. | 198 | 41.50 N | 96.42 W |
| West Point, N.Y., U.S. | 210 | 41.23 N | 73.57 W |
| West Point, Oh., U.S. | 214 | 40.43 N | 80.42 W |
| West Point, Pa., U.S. | 285 | 40.12 N | 75.18 W |
| West Point, Va., U.S. | 208 | 37.31 N | 76.47 W |
| West Point ʌ | 180 | 64.57 N | 144.40 W |
| West Point ≻, Austl. | 166 | 35.01 S | 135.57 E |
| West Point ≻, P.E., Can. | 186 | 46.37 N | 64.25 W |
| West Point Lake ⊜[1] | 192 | 33.00 N | 85.10 W |
| West Pond ⊜ | 276 | 40.53 N | 73.38 W |
| Westport, Nf., Can. | 186 | 49.47 N | 56.38 W |
| Westport, N.S., Can. | 186 | 44.16 N | 66.21 W |
| Westport, On., Can. | 212 | 44.41 N | 76.26 W |
| Westport, Ire. | 48 | 53.48 N | 9.32 W |
| Westport, N.Z. | 172 | 41.45 S | 171.36 E |
| Westport, Ct., U.S. | 207 | 41.08 N | 73.21 W |
| Westport, In., U.S. | 218 | 39.10 N | 85.34 W |
| Westport, Ky., U.S. | 218 | 38.28 N | 85.28 W |
| Westport, Ma., U.S. | 207 | 41.37 N | 71.04 W |
| Westport, Or., U.S. | 224 | 46.07 N | 123.22 W |
| Westport, Pa., U.S. | 214 | 41.18 N | 77.51 W |
| Westport, Wa., U.S. | 224 | 46.53 N | 124.06 W |
| Westport Point | 207 | 41.31 N | 71.04 W |
| West Portsmouth | 218 | 38.45 N | 83.01 W |
| West Prairie ≃ | 182 | 55.30 N | 116.31 W |
| West Puente Valley | 280 | 34.04 N | 117.59 W |
| West Pullman ◆[8] | 278 | 41.41 N | 87.39 W |
| Westpunt ≻ | 241s | 12.37 N | 70.03 W |
| West Pymble | 274a | 33.46 S | 151.08 E |
| West Quoddy Head ≻ | 188 | 44.49 N | 66.57 W |
| West Rand | 273d | 26.07 S | 27.45 E |
| Westray I | 46 | 59.18 N | 3.00 W |
| Westray Firth ʉ | 46 | 59.12 N | 2.55 W |
| West Redding | 207 | 41.19 N | 73.26 W |
| Westrem | 50 | 50.58 N | 3.52 E |
| Westrich ◆[1] | 56 | 49.15 N | 7.20 E |
| West Richfield | 214 | 41.14 N | 81.39 W |
| West Richland | 202 | 46.18 N | 119.20 W |
| West River ⊥ | 208 | 38.52 N | 76.31 W |
| West Road ≃ | 182 | 53.19 N | 122.52 W |
| West Rosebud Creek ≃ | 202 | 45.29 N | 109.27 W |
| West Roxbury ◆[8] | 283 | 42.17 N | 71.09 W |
| West Rupert | 210 | 43.14 N | 73.14 W |
| West Rutland | 188 | 43.35 N | 73.02 W |
| West Ryde | 274a | 33.48 S | 151.05 E |
| West Sacramento | 226 | 38.34 N | 121.31 W |
| West Saint Marys ≃ | 186 | 45.15 N | 62.04 W |
| West Saint Modeste | 186 | 51.36 N | 56.42 W |
| West Salem, Il., U.S. | 194 | 38.31 N | 88.00 W |
| West Salem, Oh., U.S. | 214 | 40.58 N | 82.06 W |
| West Salem, Wi., U.S. | 190 | 43.53 N | 91.04 W |
| West Salt Creek ≃ | 200 | 39.13 N | 108.54 W |
| Westsamoa → Western Samoa □[1] | 175a | 13.55 S | 172.00 W |
| West Sand Lake | 210 | 42.39 N | 73.37 W |
| West Saugerties | 210 | 42.07 N | 74.03 W |
| West Sayville | 276 | 40.43 N | 73.05 W |
| West Sayville County Park ♠ | 276 | 40.43 N | 73.06 W |
| West Scenic Park | 220 | 27.55 N | 81.39 W |
| West Scotia Basin ✦[1] | 18 | 57.00 S | 53.00 W |
| West Seneca | 210 | 42.50 N | 78.45 W |
| West Shoal Lake ⊜ | 184 | 50.20 N | 97.41 W |
| West Siberian Plain → Zapadno-Sibirskaja ravnina ≚ | 72 | 60.00 N | 75.00 E |
| Westsibirisches Flachland → Zapadno-Sibirskaja ravnina ≚ | 72 | 60.00 N | 75.00 E |
| West Side Canal ≊ | 226 | 35.19 N | 119.23 W |
| West Side Tennis Club ♠ | 276 | 40.43 N | 73.51 W |
| West Simsbury | 207 | 41.52 N | 72.51 W |
| West Sister Island I | 214 | 41.44 N | 83.07 W |
| West Slope | 224 | 45.29 N | 122.45 W |
| West Spanish Peak ʌ | 200 | 37.23 N | 104.59 W |
| West Springfield, Ma., U.S. | 207 | 42.06 N | 72.37 W |
| West Springfield, Pa., U.S. | 214 | 41.57 N | 80.29 W |
| West Springfield, Va., U.S. | 208 | 38.46 N | 77.13 W |
| West Stewartstown | 206 | 44.59 N | 71.31 W |
| West Stockbridge | 207 | 42.20 N | 73.22 W |
| West Stony Creek ≃ | 216 | 43.15 N | 74.13 W |
| West Suffield | 207 | 41.59 N | 72.42 W |
| West Sunbury | 214 | 41.00 N | 79.54 W |
| West Sussex □[6] | 42 | 50.55 N | 0.35 W |
| West Terre Haute | 194 | 39.27 N | 87.27 W |
| West-Terschelling | 52 | 53.21 N | 5.13 E |
| West Thompson Lake ⊜[1] | 207 | 41.57 N | 71.54 W |
| West Thurrock | 260 | 51.29 N | 0.16 E |
| West Tiana | 207 | 40.52 N | 72.33 W |
| West Tilbury | 260 | 51.29 N | 0.24 E |
| West Tisbury | 207 | 41.22 N | 70.40 W |
| West Toodyay | 168a | 31.33 S | 116.27 E |
| West Torrens | 168b | 34.56 S | 138.32 E |
| Westtown, N.Y., U.S. | 210 | 41.20 N | 74.32 W |
| Westtown, Pa., U.S. | 285 | 39.56 N | 75.33 W |
| West Townsend | 207 | 42.40 N | 71.44 W |
| West Turffontein ◆[8] | 273d | 26.16 S | 28.02 E |
| West Union, Ia., U.S. | 190 | 42.57 N | 91.48 W |
| West Union, Oh., U.S. | 218 | 38.47 N | 83.32 W |
| West Union, W.V., U.S. | 188 | 39.17 N | 80.46 W |
| West Union Creek ≃ | 282 | 37.25 N | 122.16 W |
| West Unity | 216 | 41.35 N | 84.26 W |
| West University Place | 222 | 29.43 N | 95.26 W |
| West Upton | 207 | 42.10 N | 71.37 W |
| Westvale | 210 | 43.02 N | 76.13 W |
| West Valley, Mt., U.S. | 202 | 46.08 N | 113.01 W |
| West Valley, N.Y., U.S. | 210 | 42.24 N | 78.37 W |
| West Valley City | 200 | 40.42 N | 111.57 W |
| West Vancouver | 182 | 49.22 N | 123.12 W |
| West View | 214 | 40.31 N | 80.02 W |
| West View Amusement Park ♠ | 279b | 40.31 N | 80.02 W |
| Westview Heights | 207 | 41.33 N | 73.05 W |
| Westville, N.S., Can. | 186 | 45.34 N | 62.43 W |
| Westville, In., U.S. | 216 | 41.32 N | 86.54 W |
| Westville, N.H., U.S. | 207 | 42.49 N | 71.07 W |
| Westville, N.J., U.S. | 285 | 39.52 N | 75.07 W |
| Westville, Oh., U.S. | 218 | 40.07 N | 83.51 W |
| Westville, Ok., U.S. | 194 | 35.59 N | 94.34 W |
| Westville, Pa., U.S. | 214 | 41.13 N | 78.50 W |
| Westville Center | 206 | 44.57 N | 74.24 W |
| Westville Grove | 285 | 39.51 N | 75.07 W |
| Westville Lake ⊜[1] | 207 | 42.05 N | 72.05 W |
| Westville Oaks | 285 | 39.51 N | 75.08 W |
| West Virginia □[3], U.S. | 178 | 38.45 N | 80.30 W |
| West Virginia □[3], U.S. | 188 | 38.45 N | 80.30 W |
| West-Vlaanderen □[4] | 50 | 51.00 N | 3.00 E |
| West Walker ≃ | 226 | 38.53 N | 119.10 W |
| West Wallsend | 170 | 32.54 S | 151.35 E |
| Westward Ho! | 42 | 51.02 N | 4.15 W |
| West Wareham | 207 | 41.47 N | 70.45 W |
| West Warren | 207 | 42.12 N | 72.14 W |
| West Warwick | 207 | 41.42 N | 71.31 W |
| West Water ≃ | 46 | 56.47 N | 2.38 W |
| West Webster | 210 | 43.12 N | 77.29 W |
| Westwego | 194 | 29.54 N | 90.08 W |
| West Wellow | 42 | 50.58 N | 1.35 W |
| West Whittier | 280 | 33.59 N | 118.03 W |
| West Wickham ◆[8] | 260 | 51.22 N | 0.01 W |
| West Willington | 207 | 41.52 N | 72.18 W |
| West Willow | 216 | 42.14 N | 83.34 W |
| West Windsor | 210 | 42.06 N | 74.46 W |
| West Winfield, N.Y., U.S. | 210 | 42.53 N | 75.11 W |
| West Winfield, Pa., U.S. | 214 | 40.48 N | 79.42 W |
| Westwold | 182 | 50.28 N | 119.45 W |
| Westwood, Ca., U.S. | 204 | 40.18 N | 121.00 W |
| Westwood, In., U.S. | 218 | 39.55 N | 85.25 W |
| Westwood, Ma., U.S. | 207 | 42.12 N | 71.14 W |
| Westwood, Mi., U.S. | 216 | 42.18 N | 85.38 W |
| Westwood, N.J., U.S. | 210 | 40.59 N | 74.01 W |
| Westwood, Pa., U.S. | 214 | 40.18 N | 78.56 W |
| Westwood ◆[8] | 280 | 34.04 N | 118.27 W |
| Westwood Lakes | 220 | 25.44 N | 80.22 W |
| Westworth Village | 222 | 32.45 N | 97.25 W |
| West Wyalong | 166 | 33.55 S | 147.13 E |
| West Wycombe | 42 | 51.39 N | 0.49 W |
| West Yarmouth | 207 | 41.39 N | 70.14 W |
| West Yegua Creek ≃ | 222 | 30.20 N | 96.52 W |
| West Yellow Creek ≃ | 194 | 39.38 N | 93.04 W |
| West Yellowstone | 202 | 44.39 N | 111.06 W |
| West York | 208 | 39.57 N | 76.45 W |
| West Yorkshire □[6] | 44 | 53.45 N | 1.40 W |
| Wetan, Pulau I | 164 | 7.54 S | 129.32 E |
| Wetar, Pulau I | 112 | 7.48 S | 126.18 E |
| Wetar, Selat ʉ | 112 | 8.20 S | 126.30 E |
| Wetaskiwin | 182 | 52.58 N | 113.22 W |
| Wete | 154 | 5.04 S | 39.43 E |
| Wethau | 54 | 51.08 N | 11.52 E |
| Wetherby | 44 | 53.56 N | 1.23 W |
| Wetherill Park | 274a | 33.51 S | 150.54 E |
| Wethersfield | 207 | 41.43 N | 72.40 W |
| Wethmar | 263 | 51.37 N | 7.33 E |
| Wetiko Hills ⺈[2] | 184 | 54.30 N | 92.20 W |
| Wetluga → Vetluga ≃ | 80 | 56.18 N | 46.24 E |
| Wetmore | 198 | 39.38 N | 95.48 W |
| Wet Mountains ⺈ | 200 | 38.00 N | 105.10 W |
| Weto | 152 | 7.57 N | 7.50 E |
| Wetten | 52 | 51.34 N | 6.17 E |
| Wettenberg | 56 | 50.38 N | 8.39 E |
| Wetter, Dtsch. | 56 | 50.54 N | 8.43 E |
| Wetter, Dtsch. | 56 | 51.23 N | 7.23 E |
| Wetter ≃ | 56 | 50.18 N | 8.49 E |
| Wetterau ◆[1] | 56 | 50.15 N | 8.50 E |
| Wetteren | 50 | 51.00 N | 3.53 E |
| Wetterhorn ʌ | 58 | 46.39 N | 8.08 E |
| Wetterstein Gebirge ⺈ | 64 | 47.25 N | 11.05 E |
| Wettigan | 110 | 18.57 N | 95.21 E |
| Wettin | 54 | 51.35 N | 11.48 E |
| Wettingen | 58 | 47.28 N | 8.19 E |
| Wettringen | 52 | 52.12 N | 7.19 E |
| Wettstetten | 60 | 48.50 N | 11.25 E |
| Wetumka | 196 | 35.14 N | 96.14 W |
| Wetumpka | 194 | 32.32 N | 86.12 W |
| Wetwang | 44 | 54.01 N | 0.34 W |
| Wetzikon | 58 | 47.19 N | 8.47 E |
| Wetzlar | 56 | 50.33 N | 8.29 E |
| Wetzstein ʌ[2] | 54 | 50.27 N | 11.27 E |
| Wevelgem | 50 | 50.48 N | 3.10 E |
| Wevelinghoven | 56 | 51.06 N | 6.37 E |
| Wewahitchka | 192 | 30.06 N | 85.12 W |
| Wewak | 164 | 3.35 S | 143.40 E |
| Wewelsfleth | 52 | 53.50 N | 9.24 E |
| Wewer | 52 | 51.41 N | 8.42 E |
| Wewoka | 196 | 35.09 N | 96.29 W |
| Wexford, Ire. | 48 | 52.20 N | 6.27 W |
| Wexford, Pa., U.S. | 214 | 40.38 N | 80.03 W |
| Wexford □[6] | 48 | 52.20 N | 6.40 W |
| Wexford ◆[8] | 275b | 43.45 N | 79.18 W |
| Wexford Harbour c | 48 | 52.20 N | 6.24 W |
| Wey ≃ | 42 | 51.23 N | 0.28 W |
| Weyakwin Lake ⊜ | 184 | 54.30 N | 106.00 W |
| Weyanoke | 284c | 38.48 N | 77.09 W |
| Weyarn | 64 | 47.51 N | 11.48 E |
| Weyauwega | 190 | 44.19 N | 88.56 W |
| Weybridge | 42 | 51.23 N | 0.28 W |
| Weyburn | 184 | 49.41 N | 103.52 W |
| Weyer ◆[8] | 263 | 51.10 N | 7.01 E |
| Weyer Markt | 61 | 47.52 N | 14.41 E |
| Weyersheim | 56 | 48.43 N | 7.48 E |
| Weyhausen | 52 | 52.47 N | 10.23 E |
| Weyhe | 52 | 52.59 N | 8.52 E |
| Weymouth, N.S., Can. | 186 | 44.25 N | 66.00 W |
| Weymouth, Eng., U.K. | 42 | 50.36 N | 2.28 W |
| Weymouth, Ma., U.S. | 207 | 42.13 N | 70.56 W |
| Weymouth, N.J., U.S. | 208 | 39.30 N | 74.46 W |
| Weymouth, Cape ≻ | 164 | 12.37 S | 143.27 E |
| Weymouth Back ≃ | 283 | 42.15 N | 70.55 W |
| Weymouth Fore ≃ | 283 | 42.16 N | 70.56 W |
| Weymouth Great Pond ⊜ | 283 | 42.12 N | 71.02 W |
| Wezemaal | 52 | 50.57 N | 4.46 E |
| Wezep | 52 | 52.27 N | 6.00 E |
| Whakatane | 172 | 37.58 S | 177.00 E |
| Whakatane ≃ | 172 | 37.[illegible] S | 177.00 E |
| Whalan | 274a | 33.[illegible] S | 150.49 E |
| Whale Creek ≃ | 276 | 40.[illegible] N | 74.13 W |
| Whaley Bridge | 44 | 53.[illegible] N | 1.59 W |
| Whaley Lake | 210 | 41.[illegible] N | 73.40 W |
| Whaleysville | 208 | 38.[illegible] N | 75.18 W |
| Whaleyville | 208 | 36.[illegible] N | 76.41 W |
| Whalley | 44 | 53.[illegible] N | 2.24 W |
| Whalom | 207 | 42.[illegible] N | 71.44 W |
| Whalsay I | 46a | 60.[illegible] N | 0.59 W |
| Whangaehu ≃ | 172 | 40.[illegible] S | 175.06 E |
| Whangamata | 172 | 37.[illegible] S | 175.52 E |
| Whangamomona | 172 | 39.[illegible] S | 174.44 E |
| Whanganui National Park ♠ | 172 | 39.[illegible] S | 175.00 E |
| Whangara | 172 | 38.[illegible] S | 178.13 E |
| Whangarei | 172 | 35.[illegible] S | 174.19 E |
| Whangaruru Harbour c | 172 | 35.[illegible] S | 174.21 E |
| Whaplode | 42 | 52.[illegible] N | 0.02 W |
| Wharfe ≃ | 44 | 53.[illegible] N | 1.07 W |
| Wharfedale V | 44 | 54.[illegible] N | 1.56 W |
| Wharles | 262 | 53.[illegible] N | 2.50 W |
| Wharton, N.J., U.S. | 210 | 40.[illegible] N | 74.34 W |
| Wharton, Oh., U.S. | 214 | 40.[illegible] N | 83.21 W |
| Wharton, Tx., U.S. | 222 | 29.[illegible] N | 96.06 W |
| Wharton, W.V., U.S. | 188 | 37.[illegible] N | 81.40 W |
| Wharton □[6] | 222 | 29.[illegible] N | 96.13 W |
| Wharton Basin ✦[1] | 12 | 21.[illegible] S | 100.00 E |
| Wharton Lake ⊜ | 176 | 64.[illegible] N | 99.55 W |
| Wharton State Forest ♠ | 285 | 39.[illegible] N | 74.40 W |
| Whataroa | 172 | 43.[illegible] S | 170.25 E |
| Whatatutu | 172 | 38.[illegible] S | 177.50 E |
| What Cheer | 190 | 41.[illegible] N | 92.21 W |
| Whatcom □[6] | 224 | 48.[illegible] N | 121.59 W |
| Whatcom, Lake ⊜ | 224 | 48.[illegible] N | 122.20 W |
| Whately | 207 | 42.[illegible] N | 72.38 W |
| Whatley | 194 | 31.[illegible] N | 87.42 W |
| Whatshan Lake ⊜ | 182 | 50.[illegible] N | 118.03 W |
| Whauphill | 44 | 54.[illegible] N | 4.29 W |
| Wheao ≃ | 172 | 38.[illegible] S | 176.39 E |
| Wheatfield | 216 | 40.[illegible] N | 87.06 W |
| Wheatland, Ca., U.S. | 226 | 39.[illegible] N | 121.25 W |
| Wheatland, Ia., U.S. | 190 | 41.[illegible] N | 90.50 W |
| Wheatland, Pa., U.S. | 214 | 41.[illegible] N | 80.28 W |
| Wheatland, Wy., U.S. | 200 | 42.[illegible] N | 104.57 W |
| Wheatland Hills | 208 | 40.[illegible] N | 76.21 W |
| Wheatland Reservoir ⊜[1] | 200 | 41.[illegible] N | 105.36 W |
| Wheatley, On., Can. | 214 | 42.[illegible] N | 82.27 W |
| Wheatley, Eng., U.K. | 42 | 51.[illegible] N | 1.08 W |
| Wheatley, Ar., U.S. | 194 | 34.[illegible] N | 91.06 W |
| Wheatley Hill | 44 | 54.[illegible] N | 1.23 W |
| Wheaton, Il., U.S. | 216 | 41.[illegible] N | 88.06 W |
| Wheaton, Md., U.S. | 208 | 39.[illegible] N | 77.03 W |
| Wheaton, Mn., U.S. | 198 | 45.[illegible] N | 96.29 W |
| Wheaton Plaza ◆[9] | 284c | 39.[illegible] N | 77.03 W |
| Wheaton Regional Park ♠ | 284c | 39.[illegible] N | 77.02 W |
| Wheat Ridge | 200 | 39.[illegible] N | 105.04 W |
| Wheelbarrow Peak ʌ | 204 | 37.[illegible] N | 116.05 W |
| Wheeler, In., U.S. | 216 | 41.[illegible] N | 87.10 W |
| Wheeler, Ms., U.S. | 194 | 34.[illegible] N | 88.36 W |
| Wheeler, Tx., U.S. | 196 | 35.[illegible] N | 100.16 W |
| Wheeler ≃, P.Q., Can. | 176 | 57.[illegible] N | 67.13 W |
| Wheeler ≃, Sk., Can. | 184 | 57.[illegible] N | 105.30 W |
| Wheeler Air Force Base ■ | 229c | 21.[illegible] N | 158.03 W |
| Wheeler Dam ◆[6] | 283 | 42.[illegible] N | 71.12 W |
| Wheeler Island I | 282 | 38.[illegible] N | 121.56 W |
| Wheeler Lake ⊜[1] | 194 | 34.[illegible] N | 87.05 W |
| Wheeler Peak ʌ, Ca., U.S. | 226 | 38.[illegible] N | 119.17 W |
| Wheeler Peak ʌ, Nv., U.S. | 204 | 38.[illegible] N | 114.19 W |
| Wheeler Peak ʌ, N.M., U.S. | 200 | 36.[illegible] N | 105.25 W |
| Wheelersburg | 218 | 38.[illegible] N | 82.51 W |
| Wheelers Hill | 274b | 37.[illegible] S | 145.11 E |
| Wheeling, Il., U.S. | 216 | 42.[illegible] N | 87.55 W |
| Wheeling, W.V., U.S. | 214 | 40.[illegible] N | 80.43 W |
| Wheeling Creek ≃ | 214 | 40.[illegible] N | 80.41 W |
| Wheelock | 222 | 30.[illegible] N | 96.24 W |
| Wheelock ≃ | 44 | 53.[illegible] N | 2.26 W |
| Whelton | 262 | 53.[illegible] N | 2.36 W |
| Wheelwright, Arg. | 252 | 33.[illegible] S | 61.13 W |
| Wheelwright, Ky., U.S. | 192 | 37.[illegible] N | 82.43 W |
| Wheelwright Park ♠ | 283 | 42.[illegible] N | 70.49 W |
| Wheeny Creek ≃ | 170 | 33.[illegible] S | 150.50 E |
| Whela Creek ≃ | 162 | 26.[illegible] S | 116.50 E |
| Whelan, Mount ʌ[2] | 166 | 23.[illegible] S | 138.54 E |
| Whelpleyhill | 260 | 51.[illegible] N | 0.33 W |
| Whernside ʌ | 44 | 54.[illegible] N | 2.23 W |
| Whetstone Creek ≃ | 214 | 40.[illegible] N | 83.03 W |
| Whetstone Gulf State Park ♠ | 212 | 43.[illegible] N | 75.27 W |
| Whickham | 44 | 54.[illegible] N | 1.41 W |
| Whidbey Island I | 224 | 48.[illegible] N | 122.40 W |
| Whidbey Island Naval Air Station ■ | 224 | 48.[illegible] N | 122.37 W |
| Whiddon Down | 42 | 50.[illegible] N | 3.51 W |
| Whigham | 192 | 30.[illegible] N | 84.19 W |
| Whigville | 207 | 41.[illegible] N | 72.56 W |
| Whim Creek | 162 | 20.[illegible] S | 117.50 E |
| Whinham, Mount ʌ | 162 | 26.[illegible] S | 130.15 E |
| Whippany | 210 | 40.[illegible] N | 74.25 W |
| Whippany ≃ | 276 | 40.[illegible] N | 74.21 W |
| Whirl Creek ≃ | 212 | 43.[illegible] N | 81.12 W |
| Whirlwind Reefs ✦[2] | 164 | 4.[illegible] S | 148.16 E |
| Whiskey Peak ʌ | 200 | 42.[illegible] N | 107.35 W |
| Whiskeytown-Shasta-Trinity National Recreation Area ♠ | 204 | 40.[illegible] N | 122.15 W |
| Whisky Chitto Creek ≃ | 194 | 30.[illegible] N | 92.55 W |
| Whiston | 262 | 53.[illegible] N | 2.50 W |
| Whitacres | 207 | 41.[illegible] N | 72.39 W |
| Whitaker | 279b | 40.[illegible] N | 79.53 W |
| Whitakers | 192 | 36.[illegible] N | 77.42 W |
| Whitbourne | 186 | 47.[illegible] N | 53.32 W |
| Whitburn, Eng., U.K. | 44 | 54.[illegible] N | 1.22 W |
| Whitburn, Scot., U.K. | 46 | 55.[illegible] N | 3.42 W |
| Whitby, On., Can. | 212 | 43.[illegible] N | 78.56 W |
| Whitby, Eng., U.K. | 44 | 54.[illegible] N | 0.37 W |
| Whitby, Eng., U.K. | 262 | 53.[illegible] N | 2.54 W |
| Whitby Abbey ʊ[1] | 44 | 54.[illegible] N | 0.38 W |
| Whitchurch, Eng., U.K. | 42 | 51.[illegible] N | 0.51 W |
| Whitchurch, Eng., U.K. | 42 | 52.[illegible] N | 2.41 W |
| Whitchurch, Eng., U.K. | 42 | 51.[illegible] N | 1.20 W |
| Whitchurch, Eng., U.K. | 42 | 51.[illegible] N | 2.39 W |
| Whitchurch-Stouffville | 212 | 43.[illegible] N | 79.15 W |
| Whitcombe, Mount ʌ | 172 | 43.[illegible] S | 170.55 E |
| White, Ga., U.S. | 192 | 34.[illegible] N | 84.44 W |
| White, S.D., U.S. | 198 | 44.[illegible] N | 96.38 W |
| White □[6] | 216 | 40.[illegible] N | 86.46 W |
| White ≃, B.C., Can. | 182 | 50.[illegible] N | 115.35 W |
| White ≃, On., Can. | 190 | 48.[illegible] N | 86.16 W |
| White ≃, N.A. | 180 | 63.[illegible] N | 139.36 W |
| White ≃, U.S. | 194 | 33.[illegible] N | 91.03 W |
| White ≃, U.S. | 198 | 43.[illegible] N | 99.30 W |
| White ≃, U.S. | 200 | 40.[illegible] N | 109.41 W |
| White ≃, Az., U.S. | 200 | 33.[illegible] N | 110.13 W |
| White ≃, In., U.S. | 194 | 38.[illegible] N | 87.44 W |
| White ≃, Mi., U.S. | 190 | 43.[illegible] N | 86.21 W |
| White ≃, Nv., U.S. | 204 | 37.[illegible] N | 115.10 W |
| White ≃, Tx., U.S. | 196 | 33.[illegible] N | 100.56 W |
| White ≃, Vt., U.S. | 188 | 43.[illegible] N | 72.20 W |
| White ≃, Wa., U.S. | 224 | 47.[illegible] N | 122.15 W |
| White ≃, Wi., U.S. | 216 | 42.[illegible] N | 88.17 W |


| Symbol | English | Deutsch | Español | Français | Português |
|---|---|---|---|---|---|
| ≃ | River | Fluß | Río | Rivière | Rio |
| ≊ | Canal | Kanal | Canal | Canal | Canal |
| ⌞ | Waterfall, Rapids | Wasserfall, Stromschnellen | Cascada, Rápidos | Chute d'eau, Rapides | Cascata, Rápidos |
| ʉ | Strait | Meeresstraße | Estrecho | Détroit | Estreito |
| c | Bay, Gulf | Bucht, Golf | Bahía, Golfo | Baie, Golfe | Baía, Golfo |
| ⊜ | Lake, Lakes | See, Seen | Lago, Lagos | Lac, Lacs | Lago, Lagos |
| ≚ | Swamp | Sumpf | Pantano | Marais | Pântano |
| ⊓ | Ice Features, Glacier | Eis- und Gletscherformen | Accidentes Glaciales | Formes glaciaires | Acidentes glaciares |
| ⊽ | Other Hydrographic Features | Andere Hydrographische Objekte | Otros Elementos Hidrográficos | Autres données hydrographiques | Outros acidentes hidrográficos |
| ✦ | Submarine Features | Untermeerische Objekte | Accidentes Submarinos | Formes de relief sous-marin | Acidentes submarinos |
| □ | Political Unit | Politische Einheit | Unidad Política | Entité politique | Unidade política |
| ʊ | Cultural Institution | Kulturelle Institution | Institución Cultural | Institution culturelle | Instituição cultural |
| ⊥ | Historical Site | Historische Stätte | Sitio Histórico | Site historique | Sitio histórico |
| ♠ | Recreational Site | Erholungs- und Ferienort | Sitio de Recreo | Centre de loisirs | Area de Lazer |
| ⊠ | Airport | Flughafen | Aeropuerto | Aéroport | Aeroporto |
| ■ | Military Installation | Militäranlage | Instalación Militar | Installation militaire | Instalação militar |
| ◆ | Miscellaneous | Verschiedenes | Misceláneo | Divers | Diversos |

ENGLISH: Name · Page · Lat.°′ · Long.°′ — DEUTSCH: Name · Seite · Breite°′ · Länge°′ E = Ost


| Name | Page | Lat.°′ | Long.°′ |
|---|---|---|---|
| White, East Fork ≃, Az., U.S. | 200 | 33.47 N | 110.00 W |
| White, East Fork ≃, In., U.S. | 194 | 38.33 N | 87.14 W |
| White, Lake ⊜ | 162 | 21.05 S | 129.00 E |
| White, Lake ⊜[1] | 218 | 39.07 N | 83.02 W |
| White, North Fork ≃, Az., U.S. | 200 | 33.47 N | 110.00 W |
| White, North Fork ≃, Co., U.S. | 200 | 39.58 N | 107.38 W |
| White, South Fork ≃ | 200 | 39.58 N | 107.38 W |
| White, West Fork ≃ | 224 | 47.07 N | 121.37 W |
| White Bay c | 186 | 50.00 N | 56.30 W |
| White Bear Indian Reserve ◆[4] | 184 | 49.45 N | 102.15 W |
| White Bear Lake | 190 | 45.03 N | 93.00 W |
| Whitebear Lake ⊜ | 184 | 51.05 N | 108.05 W |
| White Bluff | 194 | 36.06 N | 87.13 W |
| White Breast Creek ≃ | 190 | 41.24 N | 93.02 W |
| White Butte ∧ | 198 | 46.23 N | 103.19 W |
| Whitecap Lake ⊜ | 184 | 56.54 N | 95.14 W |
| White Cap Mountain ∧ | 188 | 45.35 N | 69.13 W |
| White Castle | 194 | 30.10 N | 91.08 W |
| White Center | 224 | 47.31 N | 122.21 W |
| White Chuck ≃ | 224 | 48.11 N | 121.27 W |
| White City, Fl., U.S. | 220 | 29.53 N | 85.13 W |
| White City, Ks., U.S. | 198 | 38.47 N | 96.44 W |
| White City Stadium ♠ | 260 | 51.31 N | 0.14 W |
| White Clay Creek ≃, U.S. | 198 | 43.12 N | 102.48 W |
| White Clay Creek ≃, U.S. | 285 | 39.42 N | 75.37 W |
| White Cliffs, Austl. | 162 | 28.26 S | 122.57 E |
| White Cliffs, Austl. | 166 | 30.51 S | 143.05 E |
| White Cloud | 190 | 43.33 N | 85.46 W |
| White Cloud Island I | 212 | 44.50 N | 80.58 W |
| Whitecoomb ∧, N.Z. | 172 | 45.36 S | 169.05 E |
| White Coomb ∧, Scot., U.K. | 44 | 55.26 N | 3.20 W |
| Whitecourt | 182 | 54.09 N | 115.41 W |
| White Creek | 210 | 42.58 N | 73.18 W |
| White Creek ≃, In., U.S. | 218 | 38.58 N | 86.01 W |
| White Creek ≃, Wa., U.S. | 224 | 46.01 N | 121.08 W |
| White Deer, Pa., U.S. | 210 | 41.05 N | 76.52 W |
| White Deer, Tx., U.S. | 196 | 35.26 N | 101.10 W |
| White Deer Creek ≃ | 210 | 41.05 N | 76.53 W |
| White Earth ≃ | 198 | 48.09 N | 102.42 W |
| White Earth Indian Reservation ◆[4] | 198 | 47.18 N | 95.50 W |
| White Esk ≃ | 44 | 55.12 N | 3.10 W |
| Whiteface | 196 | 33.36 N | 102.37 W |
| Whiteface ≃ | 190 | 46.58 N | 92.48 W |
| Whiteface Mountain ∧ | 188 | 44.22 N | 73.54 W |
| Whitefield, Eng., U.K. | 44 | 53.33 N | 2.18 W |
| Whitefield, N.H., U.S. | 188 | 44.22 N | 71.36 W |
| Whitefish | 202 | 48.24 N | 114.20 W |
| Whitefish ≃ | 190 | 45.55 N | 86.57 W |
| Whitefish Bay | 216 | 43.06 N | 87.54 W |
| Whitefish Bay c, On., Can. | 184 | 49.26 N | 94.14 W |
| Whitefish Bay c, N.A. | 190 | 46.40 N | 84.50 W |
| Whitefish Lake ⊜, Ab., Can. | 182 | 54.22 N | 111.55 W |
| Whitefish Lake ⊜, Mb., Can. | 184 | 55.34 N | 93.13 W |
| Whitefish Lake ⊜, N.T., Can. | 176 | 62.41 N | 106.48 W |
| Whitefish Lake ⊜, On., Can. | 190 | 48.03 N | 84.29 W |
| Whitefish Lake ⊜, On., Can. | 212 | 45.18 N | 79.47 W |
| Whitefish Lake ⊜, On., Can. | 212 | 44.31 N | 76.14 W |
| Whitefish Lake ⊜, Ak., U.S. | 180 | 61.21 N | 160.00 W |
| Whitefish Lake ⊜, Mt., U.S. | 202 | 48.27 N | 114.22 W |
| White Fish Lake Indian Reserve ◆[4] | 182 | 54.20 N | 111.45 W |
| Whitefish Point | 190 | 46.45 N | 84.59 W |
| Whitefish Point › | 190 | 46.45 N | 85.00 W |
| Whitefish Range ⋏ | 202 | 48.40 N | 114.26 W |
| Whiteford | 208 | 39.42 N | 76.20 W |
| Whiteford Point › | 42 | 51.38 N | 4.14 W |
| White Fox | 184 | 53.27 N | 104.05 W |
| White Fox ≃ | 184 | 53.32 N | 104.00 W |
| Whitegate | 48 | 51.50 N | 8.14 W |
| White Gull Creek ≃ | 184 | 53.44 N | 104.20 W |
| Whitehall (Paulstown), Ire. | 48 | 52.41 N | 7.01 W |
| Whitehall, Scot., U.K. | 46 | 59.07 N | 2.37 W |
| White Hall, Ar., U.S. | 194 | 34.16 N | 92.05 W |
| White Hall, Il., U.S. | 219 | 39.26 N | 90.24 W |
| White Hall, Md., U.S. | 208 | 39.37 N | 76.37 W |
| Whitehall, Mi., U.S. | 190 | 43.24 N | 86.20 W |
| Whitehall, Mt., U.S. | 202 | 45.52 N | 112.05 W |
| Whitehall, N.Y., U.S. | 188 | 43.33 N | 73.24 W |
| Whitehall, Oh., U.S. | 218 | 39.58 N | 82.53 W |
| Whitehall, Pa., U.S. | 214 | 40.21 N | 79.59 W |
| Whitehall, Wi., U.S. | 190 | 44.22 N | 91.18 W |
| Whitehaven, Eng., U.K. | 44 | 54.33 N | 3.35 W |
| White Haven, Pa., U.S. | 210 | 41.03 N | 75.46 W |
| Whitehead | 48 | 54.46 N | 5.43 W |
| White Holme Reservoir ⊜[1] | 262 | 53.41 N | 2.02 W |
| Whitehorse, Yk., Can. | 180 | 60.43 N | 135.03 W |
| White Horse, N.J., U.S. | 208 | 40.11 N | 74.42 W |
| White Horse, Vale of V | 42 | 51.37 N | 1.37 W |
| Whitehorse Hill ∧[2] | 42 | 51.34 N | 1.34 W |
| Whitehouse, Scot., U.K. | 46 | 57.13 N | 2.37 W |
| Whitehouse, N.J., U.S. | 210 | 40.37 N | 74.46 W |
| Whitehouse, Oh., U.S. | 216 | 41.31 N | 83.48 W |
| White House, Tn., U.S. | 194 | 36.35 N | 86.49 W |
| Whitehouse, Tx., U.S. | 222 | 32.13 N | 95.14 W |
| White House ʊ | 284c | 38.54 N | 77.02 W |
| White House Station | 210 | 40.36 N | 74.46 W |
| White Island I, Ant. | 9 | 66.44 S | 48.35 E |
| White Island I, N.T., Can. | 176 | 65.50 N | 84.50 W |
| White Island I, N.Z. | 172 | 37.31 S | 177.11 E |
| White Lake, Mi., U.S. | 281 | 42.41 N | 83.33 W |
| White Lake, N.Y., U.S. | 210 | 41.40 N | 74.50 W |
| White Lake, S.D., U.S. | 198 | 43.43 N | 98.42 W |
| White Lake, Wi., U.S. | 190 | 45.09 N | 88.45 W |
| White Lake ⊜, On., Can. | 190 | 48.48 N | 85.36 W |
| White Lake ⊜, On., Can. | 212 | 44.47 N | 76.45 W |
| White Lake ⊜, On., Can. | 212 | 44.27 N | 77.03 W |
| White Lake ⊜, On., Can. | 212 | 45.18 N | 76.31 W |
| White Lake ⊜, La., U.S. | 194 | 29.45 N | 92.30 W |
| White Lake ⊜, Mi., U.S. | 281 | 42.40 N | 83.34 W |
| Whiteland | 218 | 39.33 N | 86.05 W |
| Whitelaw | 182 | 56.07 N | 118.04 W |
| Whiteley Village | 260 | 51.21 N | 0.26 W |
| White Lick Creek ≃ | 218 | 39.30 N | 86.23 W |
| White Lick Creek, East Fork ≃ | 218 | 39.35 N | 86.22 W |
| White Lick Creek, West Fork ≃ | 218 | 39.38 N | 86.23 W |
| Whiteman Air Force Base ■ | 194 | 38.44 N | 93.34 W |
| Whiteman Airpark ⊠ | 280 | 34.15 N | 118.25 W |
| Whiteman Range ⋏ | 164 | 5.50 S | 149.55 E |
| Whitemans Creek ≃ | 212 | 43.10 N | 80.21 W |
| Whitemark | 166 | 40.07 S | 148.01 E |
| White Marsh | 284b | 39.23 N | 76.26 W |
| Whitemarsh Run ≃ | 284b | 39.22 N | 76.25 W |
| White Meadow Lake | 210 | 40.55 N | 74.31 W |
| White Meadow Lake ⊜ | 276 | 40.55 N | 74.31 W |
| White Mills | 210 | 41.32 N | 75.12 W |
| White Mountain | 180 | 64.41 N | 163.24 W |
| White Mountain Peak ∧ | 204 | 37.38 N | 118.15 W |
| White Mountains ⋏, U.S. | 204 | 37.30 N | 118.15 W |
| White Mountains ⋏, Az., U.S. | 200 | 33.45 N | 109.40 W |
| White Mountains ⋏, N.H., U.S. | 188 | 44.10 N | 71.35 W |
| Whitemouth | 184 | 49.57 N | 95.59 W |
| Whitemouth ≃ | 184 | 50.07 N | 96.02 W |
| Whitemouth Lake ⊜ | 184 | 49.14 N | 95.40 W |
| Whitemud ≃ | 184 | 50.15 N | 98.37 W |
| Whiten Head › | 46 | 58.34 N | 4.36 W |
| White Nile (Al-Baḥr al-Abyaḍ) ≃ | 140 | 15.38 N | 32.31 E |
| White Nile Dam → Jabal al-Awliyā', Khazzān ◆[6] | 140 | 15.14 N | 32.29 E |
| White Oak, Md., U.S. | 284c | 39.02 N | 77.00 W |
| White Oak, Pa., U.S. | 279b | 40.20 N | 79.48 W |
| White Oak, Tx., U.S. | 222 | 32.32 N | 94.52 W |
| White Oak ≃ | 192 | 34.40 N | 77.07 W |
| White Oak Creek ≃, Oh., U.S. | 218 | 38.47 N | 83.57 W |
| White Oak Creek ≃, Tx., U.S. | 194 | 33.16 N | 94.39 W |
| White Oak Creek, East Fork ≃ | 218 | 39.00 N | 83.53 W |
| White Oak Creek, North Fork ≃ | 218 | 39.00 N | 83.53 W |
| White Oak Lake ⊜[1] | 194 | 33.40 N | 93.10 W |
| White Oak Regional Park ♠ | 279a | 40.21 N | 79.47 W |
| White Pass )(, N.A. | 180 | 59.38 N | 135.05 W |
| White Pass )(, Wa., U.S. | 224 | 46.38 N | 121.24 W |
| White Pigeon | 216 | 41.47 N | 85.38 W |
| White Pine, Mi., U.S. | 190 | 46.45 N | 89.35 W |
| Whitepine, Mt., U.S. | 182 | 47.45 N | 115.29 W |
| White Pine, Tn., U.S. | 192 | 36.06 N | 83.17 W |
| White Pines, Ca., U.S. | 226 | 38.18 N | 120.21 W |
| White Pines, Il., U.S. | 278 | 41.57 N | 87.57 W |
| White Plains, Md., U.S. | 208 | 38.35 N | 76.56 W |
| White Plains, N.Y., U.S. | 210 | 41.02 N | 73.45 W |
| White Plains, N.C., U.S. | 192 | 36.26 N | 80.38 W |
| White Pond ⊜ | 283 | 42.26 N | 71.23 W |
| White River, On., Can. | 190 | 48.35 N | 85.15 W |
| Whiteriver, Az., U.S. | 200 | 33.50 N | 109.57 W |
| White River, S.D., U.S. | 198 | 43.34 N | 100.44 W |
| White River Junction | 188 | 43.38 N | 72.19 W |
| White Rock | 224 | 49.02 N | 122.49 W |
| White Rock Creek ≃, Ks., U.S. | 198 | 39.55 N | 97.51 W |
| White Rock Creek ≃, Tx., U.S. | 222 | 30.54 N | 95.16 W |
| White Rock Creek ≃, Tx., U.S. | 222 | 32.43 N | 96.44 W |
| White Rock Lake ⊜[1] | 222 | 32.50 N | 96.44 W |
| White Rocks ∧ | 192 | 36.40 N | 83.27 W |
| Whiterocks ≃ | 200 | 40.26 N | 109.55 W |
| White Roding | 260 | 51.48 N | 0.16 E |
| White Russia → Belarus □[1] | 22 | 53.50 N | 28.00 E |
| Whitesail Lake ⊜ | 182 | 53.30 N | 127.00 W |
| White Salmon | 224 | 45.43 N | 121.29 W |
| White Salmon ≃ | 224 | 45.43 N | 121.31 W |
| Whitesand ≃ | 184 | 51.34 N | 101.55 W |
| White Sands Beach | 207 | 41.18 N | 72.09 W |
| White Sands Missile Range ■ | 200 | 32.23 N | 106.28 W |
| White Sands National Monument ♠ | 200 | 32.46 N | 106.20 W |
| Whitesboro, N.J., U.S. | 208 | 39.02 N | 74.51 W |
| Whitesboro, N.Y., U.S. | 210 | 43.07 N | 75.17 W |
| Whitesboro, Tx., U.S. | 196 | 33.39 N | 96.54 W |
| Whitesburg | 192 | 37.07 N | 82.49 W |
| White Sea → Beloje more ⊤[2] | 24 | 65.30 N | 38.00 E |
| White Settlement | 222 | 32.45 N | 97.27 W |
| Whiteshell Provincial Park ♠ | 184 | 50.00 N | 95.25 W |
| Whiteside | 219 | 39.11 N | 91.01 W |
| Whiteside, Canal ʁ | 254 | 53.55 S | 70.15 W |
| White's Landing | 214 | 41.25 N | 82.54 W |
| White Springs | 192 | 30.19 N | 82.45 W |
| White Stone | 208 | 37.38 N | 76.23 W |
| Whitestone ◆[8] | 276 | 40.47 N | 73.49 W |
| White Stone Lake ⊜ | 184 | 56.25 N | 97.31 W |
| Whitestown | 218 | 39.59 N | 86.20 W |
| White Sulphur Springs, Mt., U.S. | 202 | 46.32 N | 110.54 W |
| White Sulphur Springs, N.Y., U.S. | 210 | 41.48 N | 74.50 W |
| White Sulphur Springs, W.V., U.S. | 192 | 37.47 N | 80.17 W |
| Whites Valley | 210 | 41.42 N | 75.22 W |
| Whitesville, Ky., U.S. | 194 | 37.40 N | 86.52 W |
| Whitesville, N.Y., U.S. | 210 | 42.02 N | 77.45 W |
| Whitesville, W.V., U.S. | 188 | 37.58 N | 81.31 W |
| White Swan | 224 | 46.22 N | 120.43 W |
| Whiteswan Lakes ⊜ | 184 | 54.05 N | 105.10 W |
| Whitevale | 212 | 43.53 N | 79.09 W |
| White Valley | 214 | 40.25 N | 79.36 W |
| Whiteville, N.C., U.S. | 192 | 34.20 N | 78.42 W |
| Whiteville, Tn., U.S. | 194 | 35.19 N | 89.08 W |
| White Volta (Volta Blanche) ≃ | 150 | 9.10 N | 1.15 W |
| Whitewater, Ks., U.S. | 198 | 37.57 N | 97.08 W |
| Whitewater, Mt., U.S. | 202 | 48.45 N | 107.37 W |
| Whitewater, Wi., U.S. | 216 | 42.50 N | 88.43 W |
| Whitewater ≃, U.S. | 218 | 39.10 N | 84.47 W |
| Whitewater ≃, Ca., U.S. | 204 | 33.30 N | 116.03 W |
| Whitewater ≃, Mo., U.S. | 194 | 37.01 N | 89.43 W |
| Whitewater, Dry Fork ≃ | 218 | 39.11 N | 84.47 W |
| Whitewater, East Fork ≃ | 218 | 39.24 N | 85.01 W |
| Whitewater Baldy ∧ | 200 | 33.20 N | 108.39 W |
| Whitewater Bay c | 220 | 25.16 N | 81.00 W |
| Whitewater Creek ≃, N.A. | 202 | 48.30 N | 107.11 W |
| Whitewater Creek ≃, Ga., U.S. | 192 | 32.21 N | 84.03 W |
| Whitewater Creek ≃, Wi., U.S. | 216 | 42.52 N | 88.45 W |
| Whitewater Lake ⊜, Mb., Can. | 184 | 49.15 N | 100.20 W |
| Whitewater Lake ⊜, Wi., U.S. | 216 | 42.47 N | 88.42 W |
| Whitewater State Park ♠ | 218 | 39.36 N | 84.58 W |
| White Woman Creek ≃ | 198 | 38.25 N | 100.54 W |
| Whitewood, Austl. | 166 | 21.28 S | 143.36 E |
| Whitewood, Sk., Can. | 184 | 50.20 N | 102.15 W |
| Whitewood, S.D., U.S. | 198 | 44.27 N | 103.38 W |
| Whitewood, Lake ⊜ | 198 | 44.20 N | 97.18 W |
| Whitewright | 196 | 33.30 N | 96.23 W |
| Whitfield | 42 | 51.09 N | 1.18 E |
| Whithorn, Jam. | 241q | 18.15 N | 78.02 W |
| Whithorn, Scot., U.K. | 44 | 54.44 N | 4.25 W |
| Whitianga | 172 | 36.50 S | 175.42 E |
| Whiting, In., U.S. | 216 | 41.40 N | 87.29 W |
| Whiting, Ia., U.S. | 198 | 42.07 N | 96.08 W |
| Whiting, Ks., U.S. | 198 | 39.35 N | 95.36 W |
| Whiting, N.J., U.S. | 208 | 39.57 N | 74.22 W |
| Whiting, Wi., U.S. | 190 | 44.29 N | 89.33 W |
| Whiting Bay | 46 | 55.29 N | 5.06 W |
| Whiting Field Naval Air Station ■ | 194 | 30.43 N | 87.02 W |
| Whitingham | 207 | 42.47 N | 72.53 W |
| Whitinsville | 207 | 42.06 N | 71.40 W |
| Whitland | 42 | 51.50 N | 4.37 W |
| Whitley □[6] | 216 | 41.10 N | 85.29 W |
| Whitley Bay | 44 | 55.03 N | 1.25 W |
| Whitley City | 192 | 36.43 N | 84.28 W |
| Whitley Row | 260 | 51.15 N | 0.09 E |
| Whitman | 207 | 42.04 N | 70.56 W |
| Whitman Mission National Historic Site ⊥ | 202 | 46.01 N | 118.30 W |
| Whitmans Pond ⊜ | 283 | 42.12 N | 70.57 W |
| Whitman Square | 208 | 39.45 N | 75.03 W |
| Whitmire | 192 | 34.30 N | 81.36 W |
| Whitmore Lake | 216 | 42.25 N | 83.46 W |
| Whitmore Lake ⊜ | 281 | 42.26 N | 83.45 W |
| Whitmore Mountains ⋏ | 9 | 82.35 S | 104.30 W |
| Whitmore Village | 229c | 21.30 N | 158.01 W |
| Whitney, On., Can. | 212 | 45.30 N | 78.14 W |
| Whitney, Pa., U.S. | 214 | 40.15 N | 79.24 W |
| Whitney, Tx., U.S. | 222 | 31.57 N | 97.19 W |
| Whitney, Lake ⊜[1] | 222 | 31.55 N | 97.23 W |
| Whitney, Mount ∧ | 204 | 36.35 N | 118.18 W |
| Whitney Point | 210 | 42.19 N | 75.58 W |
| Whitney Point Lake ⊜[1] | 210 | 42.25 N | 75.55 W |
| Whitney Woods Reservation ♠ | 283 | 42.13 N | 70.51 W |
| Whitstable | 42 | 51.22 N | 1.02 E |
| Whitsunday Island I | 166 | 20.17 S | 148.59 E |
| Whittaker | 216 | 42.08 N | 83.36 W |
| Whittemore, Ia., U.S. | 198 | 43.03 N | 94.25 W |
| Whittemore, Mi., U.S. | 190 | 44.14 N | 83.48 W |
| Whittier, Ak., U.S. | 180 | 60.47 N | 148.42 W |
| Whittier, Ca., U.S. | 228 | 33.58 N | 118.01 W |
| Whittier, N.C., U.S. | 192 | 35.26 N | 83.22 W |
| Whittier Narrows Dam ◆[6] | 280 | 34.01 N | 118.04 W |
| Whittier Narrows Flood Control Basin ⊜[1] | 280 | 34.02 N | 118.04 W |
| Whittingham | 44 | 55.24 N | 1.54 W |
| Whittington | 42 | 52.52 N | 3.00 W |
| Whittle, Cap › | 186 | 50.11 N | 60.08 W |
| Whittle Hill ∧[2] | 262 | 53.40 N | 2.16 W |
| Whittle-le-Woods | 262 | 53.41 N | 2.38 W |
| Whittlesea, Austl. | 169 | 37.31 S | 145.07 E |
| Whittlesea, S. Afr. | 158 | 32.10 S | 26.50 E |
| Whittlesey | 42 | 52.34 N | 0.08 W |
| Whittlesey, Mount ∧[2] | 190 | 46.18 N | 90.37 W |
| Whitwell | 194 | 35.12 N | 85.31 W |
| Whitwick | 42 | 52.44 N | 1.21 W |
| Whitworth | 44 | 53.40 N | 2.10 W |
| Whitworth Peak ∧ | 224 | 49.05 N | 121.13 W |
| Wholdaia Lake ⊜ | 176 | 60.43 N | 104.10 W |
| Whonock | 224 | 49.11 N | 122.28 W |
| W. Howard Frankland Bridge ◆[5] | 220 | 27.56 N | 82.35 W |
| Whyalla | 166 | 33.02 S | 137.35 E |
| Whycocomagh | 186 | 45.59 N | 61.07 W |
| Whymper, Mount ∧ | 224 | 48.57 N | 124.10 W |
| Wiang Pa Pao | 110 | 19.22 N | 99.30 E |
| Wiang Phan | 110 | 20.26 N | 99.53 E |
| Wiarton | 212 | 44.45 N | 81.09 W |
| Wiasi | 150 | 10.21 N | 1.20 W |
| Wiau Lake ⊜ | 182 | 55.23 N | 111.18 W |
| Wiawso | 150 | 6.12 N | 2.29 W |
| Wiay I | 46 | 57.23 N | 7.13 W |
| Wiązów | 30 | 50.49 N | 17.11 E |
| Wibaux | 198 | 46.59 N | 104.11 W |
| Wiblingwerde | 263 | 51.18 N | 7.37 E |
| Wichian Buri | 110 | 15.39 N | 101.07 E |
| Wichita | 198 | 37.41 N | 97.20 W |
| Wichita ≃ | 196 | 34.07 N | 98.10 W |
| Wichita Falls | 196 | 33.54 N | 98.29 W |
| Wichita Mountains ⋏ | 196 | 34.45 N | 98.40 W |
| Wichlinghofen ◆[8] | 263 | 51.27 N | 7.30 E |
| Wick | 46 | 58.26 N | 3.06 W |
| Wick ≃ | 46 | 58.27 N | 3.05 W |
| Wickatunk | 276 | 40.21 N | 74.14 W |
| Wickede | 52 | 51.29 N | 7.52 E |
| Wickede ◆[8] | 263 | 51.32 N | 7.37 E |
| Wickenburg | 200 | 33.58 N | 112.43 W |
| Wickepin | 162 | 32.46 S | 117.30 E |
| Wicker Memorial Park ♠ | 278 | 41.34 N | 87.28 W |
| Wickett | 196 | 31.34 N | 102.59 W |
| Wickford | 42 | 51.38 N | 0.31 E |
| Wickham, Austl. | 162 | 20.31 S | 117.08 E |
| Wickham, P.Q., Can. | 206 | 45.45 N | 72.30 W |
| Wickham, Eng., U.K. | 42 | 50.54 N | 1.10 W |
| Wickham ≃ | 164 | 16.22 S | 131.06 E |
| Wickham, Cape › | 166 | 39.36 S | 143.57 E |
| Wickham Bishops | 260 | 51.47 N | 0.40 E |
| Wickham Market | 42 | 52.09 N | 1.22 E |
| Wickiup Reservoir ⊜[1] | 202 | 43.40 N | 121.43 W |
| Wickliffe, Ky., U.S. | 194 | 36.58 N | 89.05 W |
| Wickliffe, Oh., U.S. | 214 | 41.06 N | 80.43 W |
| Wickliffe, Oh., U.S. | 214 | 41.36 N | 81.27 W |
| Wicklow | 48 | 52.59 N | 6.03 W |
| Wicklow □[6] | 48 | 53.00 N | 6.30 W |
| Wicklow Head › | 48 | 52.58 N | 6.00 W |
| Wicklow Mountains ⋏ | 48 | 53.02 N | 6.24 W |
| Wickrath | 56 | 51.07 N | 6.24 E |
| Wicksteed Lake ⊜ | 190 | 46.46 N | 79.40 W |
| Wicomico | 208 | 37.17 N | 76.31 W |
| Wicomico □[6] | 208 | 38.22 N | 75.36 W |
| Wicomico ≃ | 208 | 38.13 N | 75.55 W |
| Wicomico Church | 208 | 37.49 N | 76.23 W |
| Wiconisco | 208 | 40.34 N | 76.41 W |
| Wiconisco Creek ≃ | 208 | 40.32 N | 76.58 W |
| Wid ≃ | 260 | 51.45 N | 0.27 E |
| Widas ≃ | 115a | 7.30 S | 112.08 E |
| Widden Brook ≃ | 170 | 32.32 S | 150.22 E |
| Widdern | 56 | 49.19 N | 9.25 E |
| Widdert ◆[8] | 263 | 51.08 N | 7.04 E |
| Widdop Reservoir ⊜[1] | 262 | 53.48 N | 2.06 W |
| Widdrington Station | 44 | 55.15 N | 1.36 W |
| Wide Bay c, Pap. N. Gui. | 164 | 5.05 S | 152.05 E |
| Wide Bay c, Ak., U.S. | 180 | 57.20 N | 156.25 W |
| Widecombe in the Moor | 42 | 50.35 N | 3.48 W |
| Widemouth Bay | 42 | 50.47 N | 4.32 W |
| Widen | 188 | 38.27 N | 80.51 W |
| Widener College ʊ[2] | 285 | 39.52 N | 75.21 W |
| Wide Open | 44 | 55.03 N | 1.38 W |
| Widerøe, Mount ∧ | 9 | 72.08 S | 23.30 E |
| Wide Ruin Wash V | 200 | 35.13 N | 109.52 W |
| Widford | 260 | 51.43 N | 0.27 E |
| Widgeegoara Creek ≃ | 166 | 27.30 S | 145.55 E |
| Widgiemooltha | 162 | 31.30 S | 121.34 E |
| Widnes | 44 | 53.22 N | 2.44 W |
| Wi-do I | 98 | 35.36 N | 126.17 E |
| Widodaren | 115a | 7.25 S | 111.14 E |
| Widuchowa | 54 | 53.10 N | 14.25 E |
| Widur | 124 | 27.55 N | 85.10 E |
| Wiebelskirchen | 56 | 49.22 N | 7.11 E |
| Więcbork | 30 | 53.22 N | 17.30 E |
| Wieck | 54 | 54.06 N | 13.26 E |
| Wied ≃ | 56 | 50.26 N | 7.27 E |
| Wieda | 54 | 51.38 N | 10.34 E |
| Wiederitzsch | 54 | 51.24 N | 12.22 E |
| Wiedlisbach | 58 | 47.15 N | 7.39 E |
| Wiefelstede | 52 | 53.15 N | 8.07 E |
| Wiehe | 54 | 51.16 N | 11.25 E |
| Wiehengebirge ⋏ | 52 | 52.20 N | 8.40 E |
| Wiehl | 56 | 50.57 N | 7.31 E |
| Wiek | 54 | 54.37 N | 13.17 E |
| Wieleń | 30 | 52.54 N | 16.10 E |
| Wielichowo | 30 | 52.08 N | 16.21 E |
| Wieliczka | 30 | 49.59 N | 20.04 E |
| Wielkopolska ◆[1] | 30 | 51.50 N | 17.20 E |
| Wielkopolski Park Narodowy ♠ | 30 | 52.15 N | 16.50 E |
| Wieluń | 30 | 51.14 N | 18.34 E |
| Wiemelhausen ◆[8] | 263 | 51.28 N | 7.13 E |
| Wien (Vienna), Öst. | 61 | 48.13 N | 16.20 E |
| Wien (Vienna), Öst. | 264b | 48.13 N | 16.20 E |
| Wien □[3] | 61 | 48.12 N | 16.22 E |
| Wien ≃ | 264b | 48.13 N | 16.23 E |
| Wien, Universität ʊ[2] | 264b | 48.13 N | 16.22 E |
| Wiener Berg ⋏[2] | 264b | 48.10 N | 16.22 E |
| Wienerherberg | 264b | 48.03 N | 16.33 E |
| Wiener Neudorf | 61 | 48.05 N | 16.19 E |
| Wiener Neustadt | 61 | 47.49 N | 16.15 E |
| Wiener Neustädter Kanal ≅ | 61 | 48.05 N | 16.22 E |
| Wienerwald ⋏ | 61 | 48.10 N | 16.00 E |
| Wienhausen | 52 | 52.35 N | 10.11 E |
| Wien-Schwechat, Flughafen ⊠ | 61 | 48.07 N | 16.33 E |
| Wiepke | 54 | 52.36 N | 11.20 E |
| Wieprz ≃ | 30 | 51.34 N | 21.49 E |
| Wieprza ≃ | 30 | 54.26 N | 16.22 E |
| Wieprz-Krzna, Kanał ≅ | 30 | 51.56 N | 22.56 E |
| Wiera ≃ | 56 | 50.55 N | 9.10 E |
| Wierden | 52 | 52.22 N | 6.35 E |
| Wieren | 54 | 52.53 N | 10.39 E |
| Wiergate | 194 | 31.00 N | 93.42 W |
| Wieringermeer ◆[1] | 52 | 52.45 N | 5.00 E |
| Wieringerwerf | 52 | 52.51 N | 5.02 E |
| Wieruszów | 30 | 51.18 N | 18.08 E |
| Wierzyca ≃ | 30 | 53.51 N | 18.50 E |
| Wies | 61 | 46.43 N | 15.16 E |
| Wies ʊ[1] | 58 | 47.40 N | 10.53 E |
| Wiesa | 54 | 50.36 N | 13.01 E |
| Wiesau | 60 | 49.55 N | 12.11 E |
| Wiesbaden | 56 | 50.05 N | 8.14 E |
| Wiescheid ◆[8] | 263 | 51.08 N | 6.59 E |
| Wiescherhöfen ◆[8] | 263 | 51.39 N | 7.46 E |
| Wiese ≃ | 58 | 47.35 N | 7.35 E |
| Wiesede | 52 | 53.27 N | 7.46 E |
| Wieselburg | 61 | 48.08 N | 15.09 E |
| Wiesen | 58 | 46.43 N | 9.43 E |
| Wiesenburg | 54 | 52.07 N | 12.26 E |
| Wiesenfeld | 56 | 51.16 N | 10.06 E |
| Wiesenfelden | 60 | 49.03 N | 12.32 E |
| Wiesensteig | 56 | 48.34 N | 9.37 E |
| Wiesent ≃ | 60 | 49.42 N | 11.05 E |
| Wiesentheid | 56 | 49.47 N | 10.20 E |
| Wiesenttal | 60 | 49.48 N | 11.16 E |
| Wieseth ≃ | 56 | 49.10 N | 10.39 E |
| Wieslautern | 56 | 49.06 N | 7.48 E |
| Wiesloch | 56 | 49.17 N | 8.42 E |
| Wiesmoor | 52 | 53.25 N | 7.43 E |
| Wieting | 61 | 46.52 N | 14.32 E |
| Wietmarschen | 52 | 52.31 N | 7.07 E |
| Wietze | 52 | 52.39 N | 9.50 E |
| Wietzen | 52 | 52.43 N | 9.04 E |
| Wietzendorf | 52 | 52.55 N | 9.59 E |
| Wigan | 44 | 53.33 N | 2.38 W |
| Wigan □[8] | 262 | 53.32 N | 2.35 W |
| Wiggensbach | 58 | 47.44 N | 10.14 E |
| Wigger ≃ | 58 | 47.18 N | 7.53 E |
| Wiggington | 260 | 51.47 N | 0.38 W |
| Wiggins, Co., U.S. | 198 | 40.13 N | 104.04 W |
| Wiggins, Ms., U.S. | 194 | 30.51 N | 89.08 W |
| Wiggins Fork ≃ | 202 | 43.27 N | 109.28 W |
| Wigglesworth | 44 | 54.01 N | 2.17 W |
| Wight, Isle of I | 42 | 50.40 N | 1.20 W |
| Wigmore, Eng., U.K. | 42 | 52.19 N | 2.51 W |
| Wigmore, Eng., U.K. | 260 | 51.21 N | 0.35 E |
| Wignehies | 50 | 50.01 N | 4.00 E |
| Wigston | 42 | 52.36 N | 1.05 W |
| Wigton | 44 | 54.49 N | 3.09 W |
| Wigtown | 44 | 54.52 N | 4.26 W |
| Wigtown Bay c | 44 | 54.46 N | 4.15 W |
| Wijalpurā | 124 | 26.55 N | 85.51 E |
| Wijchen | 52 | 51.48 N | 5.43 E |
| Wijhe | 52 | 52.24 N | 6.07 E |
| Wijk aan Zee | 52 | 52.29 N | 4.35 E |
| Wijk bij Duurstede | 52 | 51.58 N | 5.20 E |
| Wil | 58 | 47.27 N | 9.03 E |
| Wilbarger Creek ≃ | 222 | 30.11 N | 97.23 W |
| Wilber | 198 | 40.28 N | 96.57 W |
| Wilberforce, Austl. | 170 | 33.33 S | 150.50 E |
| Wilberforce, Oh., U.S. | 218 | 39.42 N | 83.52 W |
| Wilberforce Falls ⅃ | 176 | 67.07 N | 108.47 W |
| Wilbraham | 207 | 42.07 N | 72.25 W |
| Wilbur | 202 | 47.45 N | 118.42 W |
| Wilburton | 196 | 34.55 N | 95.18 W |
| Wilcannia | 166 | 31.34 S | 143.23 E |
| Wilcock, Península ›[1] | 254 | 50.40 S | 74.00 W |
| Wilcox, Sk., Can. | 184 | 50.07 N | 104.44 W |
| Wilcox, Ne., U.S. | 198 | 40.21 N | 99.10 W |
| Wilcox, Pa., U.S. | 214 | 41.34 N | 78.41 W |
| Wilcox, Tx., U.S. | 222 | 30.27 N | 96.22 W |
| Wilcox, Mount ∧ | 207 | 42.13 N | 73.16 W |
| Wildalpen | 61 | 47.39 N | 14.59 E |
| Wildau | 54 | 52.19 N | 13.38 E |
| Wildberg, Dtsch. | 54 | 52.52 N | 12.37 E |
| Wildberg, Dtsch. | 56 | 48.37 N | 8.44 E |
| Wildboarclough | 262 | 53.13 N | 2.02 W |
| Wildcat Canyon Regional Park ♠ | 282 | 37.56 N | 122.17 W |
| Wildcat Creek ≃, Ca., U.S. | 282 | 37.57 N | 122.23 W |
| Wildcat Creek ≃, In., U.S. | 216 | 40.28 N | 86.52 W |
| Wildcat Creek, Middle Fork ≃ | 216 | 40.25 N | 86.46 W |
| Wildcat Creek, South Fork ≃ | 216 | 40.26 N | 86.48 W |
| Wildcat Hill ∧[2] | 184 | 53.17 N | 102.30 W |
| Wild Coast ⩡[2] | 158 | 32.30 S | 28.45 E |
| Wilde ◆[8] | 288 | 34.42 S | 58.20 W |
| Wildegg | 58 | 47.25 N | 8.11 E |
| Wildeman ≃ | 164 | 5.33 S | 139.13 E |
| Wildemann | 52 | 51.49 N | 10.17 E |
| Wildenbruch | 264a | 52.17 N | 13.04 E |
| Wildenfels | 54 | 50.40 N | 12.35 E |
| Wildenstein | 58 | 47.59 N | 6.58 E |
| Wildenthal | 54 | 50.27 N | 12.37 E |
| Wilder | 202 | 43.40 N | 116.54 W |
| Wilderness | 158 | 34.00 S | 22.36 E |
| Wilderness of Judaea (Midbar Yehuda) ◆[2] | 132 | 31.30 N | 35.18 E |
| Wilderness State Park ♠ | 190 | 45.42 N | 84.57 W |
| Wildersville | 194 | 35.46 N | 88.21 W |
| Wildervank | 52 | 53.04 N | 6.51 E |
| Wildeshausen | 52 | 52.54 N | 8.26 E |
| Wildfield | 212 | 43.49 N | 79.44 W |
| Wildflecken | 56 | 50.23 N | 9.54 E |
| Wildfontein | 158 | 31.04 S | 24.50 E |
| Wildhaus | 58 | 47.12 N | 9.22 E |
| Wildhay ≃ | 182 | 54.02 N | 117.20 W |
| Wildhorn ∧ | 58 | 46.21 N | 7.22 E |
| Wildhorse Creek ≃, U.S. | 198 | 40.36 N | 102.00 W |
| Wildhorse Creek ≃, Ok., U.S. | 196 | 34.32 N | 97.10 W |
| Wild Horse Creek ≃, Wy., U.S. | 198 | 44.39 N | 106.08 W |
| Wild Horse Draw V | 196 | 31.11 N | 104.50 W |
| Wild Horse Hill ∧[2] | 168a | 33.12 S | 116.40 E |
| Wild Horse Lake ⊜ | 202 | 48.58 N | 110.00 W |
| Wild Horse Plains | 168b | 34.22 S | 138.17 E |
| Wildnest Lake ⊜ | 184 | 55.00 N | 102.20 W |
| Wildon | 61 | 46.53 N | 15.31 E |
| Wild Rice ≃, Mn., U.S. | 198 | 47.20 N | 96.50 W |
| Wild Rice ≃, N.D., U.S. | 198 | 46.45 N | 96.47 W |
| Wild Rice, South Branch ≃ | 198 | 47.12 N | 96.38 W |
| Wildrose, N.D., U.S. | 198 | 48.37 N | 103.11 W |
| Wild Rose, Wi., U.S. | 190 | 44.10 N | 89.14 W |
| Wildseeloder ∧ | 64 | 47.26 N | 12.32 E |
| Wildspitze ∧ | 64 | 46.53 N | 10.52 E |
| Wildstrubel ∧ | 58 | 46.24 N | 7.32 E |
| Wildwood, Ab., Can. | 182 | 53.37 N | 115.14 W |
| Wildwood, Fl., U.S. | 220 | 28.51 N | 82.02 W |
| Wildwood, Il., U.S. | 216 | 42.21 N | 88.00 W |
| Wildwood, N.J., U.S. | 208 | 38.59 N | 74.48 W |
| Wildwood, Lake ⊜ | 276 | 41.09 N | 74.32 W |
| Wild Wood Beach | 284b | 39.15 N | 76.25 W |
| Wildwood Canyon Park ♠ | 280 | 34.13 N | 118.17 W |
| Wildwood Crest | 208 | 38.58 N | 74.50 W |
| Wiley | 224 | 46.33 N | 120.39 W |
| Wilfersdorf | 61 | 48.35 N | 16.38 E |
| Wilge ≃, S. Afr. | 158 | 25.34 S | 29.10 E |
| Wilge ≃, S. Afr. | 158 | 27.03 S | 28.20 E |
| Wilgena | 162 | 30.46 S | 134.44 E |
| Wilgespruit ≃ | 273d | 26.07 S | 27.52 E |
| Wilhelm, Lake ⊜[1] | 214 | 41.23 N | 80.08 W |
| Wilhelm, Mount ∧ | 164 | 5.45 S | 145.05 E |
| Wilhelmina Gebergte ⋏ | 250 | 3.45 N | 56.30 W |
| Wilhelminakanaal ≅ | 52 | 51.47 N | 4.51 E |
| Wilhelminaoord | 52 | 52.53 N | 6.10 E |
| Wilhelmina Peak → Trikora, Puncak ∧ | 164 | 4.15 S | 138.45 E |
| Wilhelmsburg | 61 | 48.06 N | 15.36 E |
| Wilhelmsburg ◆[8] | 52 | 53.30 N | 10.00 E |
| Wilhelmsdorf | 58 | 47.52 N | 9.25 E |
| Wilhelmshaven | 52 | 53.31 N | 8.08 E |
| Wilhelmshöhe, Schloss ⊥ | 56 | 51.21 N | 9.22 E |
| Wilhelmshorst | 54 | 52.19 N | 13.03 E |
| Wilhelmstadt ◆[8] | 264a | 52.31 N | 13.11 E |
| Wilhelmstal | 156 | 21.54 S | 16.19 E |
| Wilhelmstein, Schloss ⊥ | 52 | 52.28 N | 9.18 E |
| Wilis, Gunung ∧ | 115a | 7.52 S | 111.48 E |
| Wilkau-Hasslau | 54 | 50.40 N | 12.31 E |
| Wilkerson Pass )( | 200 | 39.02 N | 105.32 W |
| Wilkes-Barre | 210 | 41.14 N | 75.52 W |
| Wilkes-Barre Scranton Airport ⊠ | 210 | 41.20 N | 75.45 W |
| Wilkesboro | 192 | 36.08 N | 81.09 W |
| Wilkes Island I | 174a | 19.18 N | 166.34 E |
| Wilkes Land ◆[1] | 9 | 69.00 S | 120.00 E |
| Wilkeson | 224 | 47.06 N | 122.02 W |
| Wilket Creek ≃ | 275b | 43.43 N | 79.21 W |
| Wilket Creek Park ♠ | 275b | 43.43 N | 79.21 W |
| Wilkhaven | 46 | 57.52 N | 3.45 W |
| Wilkie | 184 | 52.25 N | 108.43 W |
| Wilkinsburg | 214 | 40.26 N | 79.51 W |
| Wilkinson | 218 | 39.53 N | 85.36 W |
| Wilkinson Lakes ⊜ | 162 | 29.40 S | 132.39 E |
| Wilkins Sound ʁ | 9 | 70.15 S | 73.00 W |
| Wilkins Township | 279b | 40.25 N | 79.50 W |
| Will □[6] | 216 | 41.32 N | 88.05 W |
| Will, Mount ∧ | 180 | 57.31 N | 128.46 W |
| Willacoochee | 192 | 31.20 N | 83.02 W |
| Willamette ≃ | 202 | 45.39 N | 122.46 W |
| Willamette, Middle Fork ≃ | 202 | 44.01 N | 123.01 W |
| Willamette, North Fork ≃ | 202 | 43.46 N | 122.32 W |
| Willamina | 224 | 45.04 N | 123.29 W |
| Willamina Creek ≃ | 224 | 45.05 N | 123.28 W |
| Willandra Billabong Creek ≃ | 166 | 33.08 S | 144.06 E |
| Willapa | 224 | 46.40 N | 123.39 W |
| Willapa ≃ | 224 | 46.42 N | 123.50 W |
| Willapa Bay c | 224 | 46.37 N | 124.00 W |
| Willard, Mo., U.S. | 194 | 37.18 N | 93.25 W |
| Willard, N.M., U.S. | 200 | 34.35 N | 106.01 W |
| Willard, N.Y., U.S. | 210 | 42.40 N | 76.52 W |
| Willard, Oh., U.S. | 214 | 41.03 N | 82.44 W |
| Willard, Ut,. U.S. | 200 | 41.24 N | 112.02 W |
| Willard, Wa., U.S. | 224 | 45.48 N | 121.38 W |
| Willard, Punta › | 232 | 28.50 N | 113.15 W |
| Willards | 208 | 38.23 N | 75.20 W |
| Willaston, Austl. | 168b | 34.36 S | 138.45 E |
| Willaston, Eng., U.K. | 262 | 53.18 N | 3.00 W |
| Willaumez Peninsula ›[1] | 164 | 5.05 S | 150.05 E |
| Willcox | 200 | 32.15 N | 109.49 W |
| Willcox Playa ⊜ | 200 | 32.08 N | 109.51 W |
| Willebadessen | 52 | 51.37 N | 9.02 E |
| Willebroek | 50 | 51.04 N | 4.22 E |
| Willem Pretorius Game Reserve ◆[4] | 158 | 28.16 S | 27.13 E |
| Willemsoord | 52 | 52.49 N | 6.05 E |
| Willemstad, Ned. | 52 | 51.42 N | 4.26 E |
| Willemstad, Ned. Ant. | 241s | 12.06 N | 68.56 W |
| Willerburn Acres | 284c | 39.03 N | 77.10 W |
| Willeroo | 164 | 15.17 S | 131.35 E |
| Willer-sur-Thur | 58 | 47.51 N | 7.05 E |
| Willerswalde | 54 | 54.07 N | 13.08 E |
| Willesden ◆[8] | 260 | 51.33 N | 0.14 W |
| Willet | 210 | 42.28 N | 75.55 W |
| Willett Pond ⊜ | 283 | 42.11 N | 71.14 W |
| Willey Creek ≃ | 279a | 41.25 N | 81.25 W |
| William, Lac ⊜ | 206 | 46.07 N | 71.34 W |
| William, Mount ∧, Austl. | 166 | 37.17 S | 142.36 E |
| William, Mount ∧, Austl. | 169 | 37.13 S | 144.47 E |
| William, Mount ∧[2] | 168a | 32.57 S | 116.07 E |
| William Bill Dannelly Reservoir ⊜[1] | 194 | 32.10 N | 87.10 W |
| William Boyce Regional Park ♠ | 279b | 40.28 N | 79.45 W |
| William Girling Reservoir ⊜[1] | 260 | 51.37 N | 0.02 W |
| William H. Harsha Lake ⊜[1] | 218 | 39.02 N | 84.07 W |
| William Lake ⊜ | 184 | 53.50 N | 99.25 W |
| Williamnagar | 124 | 25.30 N | 90.35 E |
| William Patterson College ʊ[2] | 276 | 40.56 N | 74.12 W |
| William P. Gleason Park ♠ | 278 | 41.33 N | 87.21 W |
| William Preston Lane Jr. Memorial Bridge ◆[5] | 208 | 39.00 N | 76.28 W |
| Williams, Austl. | 168a | 33.01 S | 116.52 E |
| Williams, Az., U.S. | 200 | 35.14 N | 112.11 W |
| Williams, Ca., U.S. | 226 | 39.09 N | 122.08 W |
| Williams, Ia., U.S. | 190 | 42.29 N | 93.32 W |
| Williams, Mn., U.S. | 198 | 48.46 N | 94.57 W |
| Williams □[6] | 216 | 41.35 N | 84.33 W |
| Williams ≃, Austl. | 166 | 20.04 S | 141.08 E |
| Williams ≃, Austl. | 168a | 32.59 S | 116.24 E |
| Williams ≃, Austl. | 170 | 32.45 S | 151.45 E |
| Williams, Cape › | 9 | 70.29 S | 164.05 E |
| Williams Air Force Base ■ | 200 | 33.18 N | 111.40 W |
| Williams Bay | 216 | 42.34 N | 88.32 W |
| Williamsburg, On., Can. | 212 | 44.58 N | 75.15 W |
| Williamsburg, In., U.S. | 218 | 39.57 N | 84.59 W |
| Williamsburg, Ia., U.S. | 190 | 41.39 N | 92.00 W |
| Williamsburg, Ky., U.S. | 192 | 36.44 N | 84.09 W |
| Williamsburg, Ma., U.S. | 207 | 42.23 N | 72.43 W |
| Williamsburg, Mo., U.S. | 219 | 38.55 N | 91.42 W |
| Williamsburg, Oh., U.S. | 218 | 39.03 N | 84.03 W |
| Williamsburg, Pa., U.S. | 214 | 40.27 N | 78.12 W |
| Williamsburg, Va., U.S. | 208 | 37.16 N | 76.42 W |
| Williamsburg ◆[8] | 276 | 40.42 N | 73.57 W |
| Williamsburg Bridge ◆[5] | 276 | 40.43 N | 73.58 W |
| Williams Center | 216 | 41.26 N | 84.36 W |
| Williams Creek ≃, Austl. | 274a | 33.57 S | 150.58 E |
| Williams Creek ≃, In., U.S. | 218 | 39.36 N | 85.09 W |
| Williamsdale | 171b | 35.35 S | 149.09 E |
| Williamsfield | 214 | 41.32 N | 80.32 W |
| Williams Fork ≃ | 200 | 40.26 N | 107.39 W |
| Williams Lake | 182 | 52.08 N | 122.09 W |
| Williams Lake Indian Reserve ◆[4] | 182 | 52.07 N | 122.00 W |
| Williams Mountain ∧[2] | 194 | 34.15 N | 94.33 W |
| Williamson, N.Y., U.S. | 210 | 43.13 N | 77.11 W |
| Williamson, W.V., U.S. | 192 | 37.40 N | 82.16 W |
| Williamson □[6] | 222 | 30.40 N | 97.32 W |
| Williamson ≃ | 202 | 42.28 N | 121.57 W |
| Williamson, Mount ∧ | 204 | 36.39 N | 118.18 W |
| Williamson Head › | 9 | 69.09 S | 157.49 E |
| Williamsport, Nf., Can. | 186 | 50.32 N | 56.19 W |
| Williamsport, In., U.S. | 216 | 40.17 N | 87.17 W |
| Williamsport, Oh., U.S. | 214 | 39.35 N | 83.07 W |
| Williamsport, Pa., U.S. | 210 | 41.14 N | 77.00 W |
| Williamston, Mi., U.S. | 216 | 42.41 N | 84.16 W |
| Williamston, N.C., U.S. | 192 | 35.51 N | 77.03 W |
| Williamston, S.C., U.S. | 192 | 34.37 N | 82.28 W |
| Williamstown, Austl. | 168b | 34.40 S | 138.53 E |
| Williamstown, Austl. | 169 | 37.52 S | 144.54 E |
| Williamstown, On., Can. | 206 | 45.08 N | 74.35 W |
| Williamstown, Ky., U.S. | 218 | 38.38 N | 84.33 W |
| Williamstown, Ma., U.S. | 207 | 42.42 N | 73.12 W |
| Williamstown, N.J., U.S. | 208 | 39.41 N | 74.59 W |
| Williamstown, N.Y., U.S. | 212 | 43.26 N | 75.54 W |
| Williamstown, Pa., U.S. | 208 | 40.34 N | 76.37 W |
| Williamstown, Vt., U.S. | 188 | 44.07 N | 72.32 W |
| Williamstown, W.V., U.S. | 188 | 39.24 N | 81.27 W |
| Williamstown Junction | 285 | 39.45 N | 74.56 W |
| Williamstown Lake ⊜[1] | 218 | 38.41 N | 84.32 W |
| Williamsville, Il., U.S. | 219 | 39.57 N | 89.32 W |
| Williamsville, N.Y., U.S. | 210 | 42.57 N | 78.44 W |
| Williamtown | 170 | 32.49 S | 151.50 E |
| Willich | 56 | 51.16 N | 6.33 E |
| Willikies | 240c | 17.05 N | 61.42 W |
| Willimantic | 207 | 41.42 N | 72.12 W |
| Willimantic ≃ | 207 | 41.43 N | 72.12 W |
| Willingale | 260 | 51.44 N | 0.19 E |
| Willingboro | 208 | 40.01 N | 74.52 W |
| Willingdon, Ab., Can. | 182 | 53.50 N | 112.08 W |
| Willingdon, Eng., U.K. | 42 | 50.47 N | 0.15 E |
| Willingdon, Mount ∧ | 182 | 51.45 N | 116.15 W |
| Willingen | 56 | 51.17 N | 8.37 E |
| Willingham | 42 | 52.19 N | 0.04 E |
| Willington, Eng., U.K. | 42 | 52.50 N | 1.33 W |
| Willington, Eng., U.K. | 44 | 54.43 N | 1.41 W |
| Willis, Mi., U.S. | 216 | 42.09 N | 83.33 W |
| Willis, Tx., U.S. | 222 | 30.25 N | 95.28 W |
| Willis ≃ | 192 | 37.41 N | 78.07 W |
| Willisau | 58 | 47.07 N | 8.00 E |
| Willis Group II | 164 | 16.18 S | 150.00 E |
| Willis Island I | 186 | 48.48 N | 53.42 W |
| Williston, S. Afr. | 158 | 31.20 S | 20.53 E |
| Williston, Fl., U.S. | 192 | 29.23 N | 82.26 W |
| Williston, N.D., U.S. | 198 | 48.08 N | 103.38 W |
| Williston, Oh., U.S. | 214 | 41.36 N | 83.20 W |
| Williston, S.C., U.S. | 192 | 33.24 N | 81.25 W |
| Williston Lake ⊜[1] | 176 | 55.40 N | 123.40 W |
| Williston Park | 276 | 40.45 N | 73.38 W |
| Willisville | 194 | 37.59 N | 89.35 W |
| Willis Wharf | 208 | 37.30 N | 75.48 W |
| Williton | 42 | 51.10 N | 3.20 W |
| Willits | 204 | 39.24 N | 123.21 W |
| Willmar | 198 | 45.07 N | 95.02 W |
| Willmersdorf | 264a | 52.40 N | 13.41 E |
| Willmore Wilderness Provincial Park ♠ | 182 | 53.45 N | 119.00 W |
| Willoughby, Austl. | 170 | 33.48 S | 151.12 E |
| Willoughby, Oh., U.S. | 214 | 41.38 N | 81.25 W |
| Willoughby, Cape › | 166 | 35.51 S | 138.07 E |
| Willoughby Bay c | 240c | 17.02 N | 61.44 W |
| Willoughby Hills | 214 | 41.35 N | 81.25 W |
| Willow, Ak., U.S. | 180 | 61.45 N | 150.03 W |
| Willow, Mi., U.S. | 216 | 42.07 N | 83.24 W |
| Willow, N.Y., U.S. | 210 | 42.05 N | 74.14 W |
| Willow ≃, Ab., Can. | 182 | 55.58 N | 113.55 W |
| Willow ≃, B.C., Can. | 182 | 54.03 N | 122.21 W |
| Willow ≃, Mn., U.S. | 190 | 46.40 N | 93.35 W |
| Willow ≃, Wi., U.S. | 190 | 44.59 N | 92.46 W |
| Willowbrook, Sk., Can. | 184 | 51.13 N | 102.47 W |
| Willow Brook, Ca., U.S. | 280 | 33.54 N | 118.13 W |
| Willowbrook, Il., U.S. | 278 | 41.46 N | 87.56 W |
| Willowbrook, Md., U.S. | 284c | 39.02 N | 77.11 W |
| Willow Brook ≃, On., Can. | 212 | 43.53 N | 80.16 W |
| Willow Brook ≃, Eng., U.K. | 42 | 52.32 N | 0.24 W |
| Willow Brook ≃, N.J., U.S. | 276 | 40.20 N | 74.10 W |
| Willowbrook Mall ◆[9] | 276 | 40.53 N | 74.15 W |
| Willowbrook Park ♠ | 276 | 40.36 N | 74.09 W |
| Willow Bunch | 184 | 49.24 N | 105.37 W |
| Willow Bunch Lake ⊜ | 184 | 49.27 N | 105.28 W |
| Willow City | 198 | 48.36 N | 100.17 W |
| Willow Creek, Ca., U.S. | 204 | 40.56 N | 123.38 W |
| Willow Creek, Mt., U.S. | 202 | 45.49 N | 111.38 W |
| Willow Creek ≃, Ab., Can. | 182 | 49.46 N | 113.21 W |
| Willow Creek ≃, On., Can. | 212 | 44.25 N | 79.53 W |
| Willow Creek ≃, Ca., U.S. | 226 | 39.22 N | 122.05 W |
| Willow Creek ≃, Ca., U.S. | 226 | 37.09 N | 119.27 W |
| Willow Creek ≃, Il., U.S. | 216 | 41.42 N | 89.10 W |
| Willow Creek ≃, In., U.S. | 216 | 41.15 N | 85.08 W |
| Willow Creek ≃, Mi., U.S. | 281 | 42.20 N | 83.25 W |
| Willow Creek ≃, Mt., U.S. | 202 | 48.10 N | 111.11 W |
| Willow Creek ≃, Mt., U.S. | 202 | 48.09 N | 106.38 W |
| Willow Creek ≃, Mt., U.S. | 202 | 46.28 N | 108.28 W |
| Willow Creek ≃, Nv., U.S. | 204 | 38.10 N | 116.35 W |
| Willow Creek ≃, N.D., U.S. | 198 | 48.34 N | 100.27 W |
| Willow Creek ≃, Oh., U.S. | 279a | 41.20 N | 82.03 W |
| Willow Creek ≃, Or., U.S. | 202 | 44.00 N | 117.13 W |


**Symbols** in the index entries represent the broad categories identified in the key at the right. Symbols with superior numbers (⋏[1]) identify subcategories (see complete key on page *I · 1)*.

**Symbole** im Register stellen die rechts im Schlüssel erklärten Kategorien dar. Symbole mit hochgestellten Ziffern (⋏[1]) bezeichnen Unterabteilungen einer Kategorie (vgl. vollständiger Schlüssel auf Seite *I · 1)*.

**Los símbolos** incluídos en el texto del índice representan las grandes categorías identificadas con la clave a la derecha. Los símbolos con numeros en su parte superior (⋏[1]) identifican las subcategorías (véase la clave completa en la página *I · 1)*.

**Les symboles** de l'index représentent les catégories indiquées dans la légende à droite. Les symboles suivis d'un indice (⋏[1]) représentent des sous-catégories (voir légende complète à la page *I · 1)*.

**Os símbolos** incluídos no texto do índice representam as grandes categorias identificadas com a chave à direita. Os símbolos com números em sua parte superior (⋏[1]) identificam as subcategorias (veja-se a chave completa à página *I · 1)*.

| | English | Deutsch | Español | Français | Português |
|---|---|---|---|---|---|
| ∧ | Mountain | Berg | Montaña | Montagne | Montanha |
| ⋏ | Mountains | Gebirge | Montañas | Montagnes | Montanhas |
| )( | Pass | Paß | Paso | Col | Passo |
| V | Valley, Canyon | Tal, Cañon | Valle, Cañón | Vallée, Canyon | Vale, Canhão |
| ≚ | Plain | Ebene | Llano | Plaine | Planície |
| › | Cape | Kap | Cabo | Cap | Cabo |
| I | Island | Insel | Isla | Île | Ilha |
| II | Islands | Inseln | Islas | Îles | Ilhas |
| ⩡ | Other Topographic Features | Andere Topographische Objekte | Otros Elementos Topográficos | Autres données topographiques | Outros acidentes topográficos |

| Nombre / Nom / Nome | Página / Page | Lat.°′ | Long.°′ W = Oeste / Ouest |
|---|---|---|---|
| Willow Creek ≃, Or., U.S. | 202 | 45.48 N | 120.01 W |
| Willow Creek ≃, Ut., U.S. | 200 | 40.02 N | 109.45 W |
| Willow Creek, North Fork ≃ | 226 | 37.13 N | 119.30 W |
| Willow Creek, South Fork ≃ | 226 | 39.32 N | 122.10 W |
| Willowdale ⬥[8] | 275b | 43.47 N | 79.26 W |
| Willowdale State Forest ♠ | 283 | 42.40 N | 70.54 W |
| Willowdene | 273d | 26.18 S | 27.56 E |
| Willowemac | 210 | 41.55 N | 74.41 W |
| Willowemoc Creek ≃ | 210 | 41.53 N | 74.48 W |
| Willow Glen ⬥[8] | 282 | 37.18 N | 121.53 W |
| Willow Grove | 208 | 40.08 N | 75.06 W |
| Willow Grove Naval Air Station ■ | 208 | 40.12 N | 75.08 W |
| Willow Grove Park ♠ | 285 | 40.08 N | 75.08 W |
| Willow Hill | 214 | 40.06 N | 77.48 W |
| Willowick | 214 | 41.37 N | 81.28 W |
| Willow Lake | 198 | 44.37 N | 97.38 W |
| Willow Lake ⊜, N.T., Can. | 176 | 62.11 N | 119.10 W |
| Willow Lake ⊜, N.Y., U.S. | 276 | 40.43 N | 73.50 W |
| Willowlake ≃ | 176 | 62.52 N | 123.08 W |
| Willow Metropolitan Park ♠ | 281 | 42.08 N | 83.22 W |
| Willowmore | 158 | 33.17 S | 23.29 E |
| Willow Park | 222 | 32.45 N | 97.39 W |
| Willowra | 162 | 21.15 S | 132.35 E |
| Willowra Aboriginal Reserve ⬥[4] | 162 | 21.15 S | 132.35 E |
| Willow Reservoir ⊜[1] | 190 | 45.45 N | 89.50 W |
| Willow Ridge Estates | 284a | 43.01 N | 78.49 W |
| Willow River | 182 | 54.04 N | 122.28 W |
| Willow Run, De., U.S. | 285 | 39.44 N | 75.37 W |
| Willow Run, Mi., U.S. | 216 | 42.14 N | 83.35 W |
| Willow Run, Va., U.S. | 284c | 38.49 N | 77.10 W |
| Willow Run Airport ⊠ | 281 | 42.14 N | 83.32 W |
| Willows | 226 | 39.31 N | 122.11 W |
| Willow Springs, Ca., U.S. | 228 | 34.53 N | 118.18 W |
| Willow Springs, Il., U.S. | 278 | 41.44 N | 87.51 W |
| Willow Springs, Mo., U.S. | 194 | 36.59 N | 91.58 W |
| Willow Springs, Pa., U.S. | 279b | 40.19 N | 79.44 W |
| Willow Street | 208 | 39.59 N | 76.17 W |
| Willowvale | 158 | 32.16 S | 28.30 E |
| Willow Woods | 284c | 38.50 N | 77.16 W |
| Will Rogers Beach State Park ♠ | 280 | 34.01 N | 118.30 W |
| Will Rogers State Park ♠ | 280 | 34.03 N | 118.31 W |
| Willroth | 56 | 50.34 N | 7.31 E |
| Wills, Lake ⊜ | 162 | 21.25 S | 128.51 E |
| Wills Creek ≃, Austl. | 166 | 22.43 S | 140.02 E |
| Wills Creek ≃, Oh., U.S. | 188 | 40.09 N | 81.55 W |
| Wills Creek Lake ⊜[1] | 214 | 40.08 N | 81.45 W |
| Willseyville | 210 | 42.17 N | 76.23 W |
| Willshire | 216 | 40.45 N | 84.48 W |
| Wills Point | 222 | 32.43 N | 96.01 W |
| Willston | 284c | 38.52 N | 77.09 W |
| Willunga | 168b | 35.17 S | 138.33 E |
| Wilmar | 194 | 33.37 N | 91.55 W |
| Wilmer, Al., U.S. | 194 | 30.49 N | 88.21 W |
| Wilmer, Pa., U.S. | 285 | 40.07 N | 75.32 W |
| Wilmer, Tx., U.S. | 222 | 32.35 N | 96.41 W |
| Wilmerding | 279b | 40.23 N | 79.48 W |
| Wilmersdorf ⬥[8] | 264a | 52.30 N | 13.19 E |
| Wilmette | 216 | 42.04 N | 87.43 W |
| Wilmington, Austl. | 166 | 32.39 S | 138.07 E |
| Wilmington, Eng., U.K. | 260 | 51.26 N | 0.12 E |
| Wilmington, De., U.S. | 208 | 39.44 N | 75.32 W |
| Wilmington, Il., U.S. | 216 | 41.18 N | 88.08 W |
| Wilmington, Ma., U.S. | 207 | 42.32 N | 71.10 W |
| Wilmington, N.C., U.S. | 192 | 34.13 N | 77.56 W |
| Wilmington, Oh., U.S. | 218 | 39.26 N | 83.49 W |
| Wilmington, Vt., U.S. | 188 | 42.52 N | 72.52 W |
| Wilmington ⬥[8] | 280 | 33.47 N | 118.16 W |
| Wilmington Manor | 285 | 39.41 N | 75.35 W |
| Wilmington Manor Gardens | 285 | 39.40 N | 75.34 W |
| Wilmore, Ky., U.S. | 192 | 37.51 N | 84.39 W |
| Wilmore, Pa., U.S. | 214 | 40.23 N | 78.43 W |
| Wilmot, Ar., U.S. | 194 | 33.03 N | 91.34 W |
| Wilmot, Oh., U.S. | 214 | 40.39 N | 81.38 W |
| Wilmot, S.D., U.S. | 198 | 45.24 N | 96.51 W |
| Wilmot, Wi., U.S. | 216 | 42.31 N | 88.11 W |
| Wilmot Woods ♠ | 278 | 42.18 N | 87.56 W |
| Wilmslow | 44 | 53.20 N | 2.15 W |
| Wilna → Vilnius | 76 | 54.41 N | 25.19 E |
| Wilnecote | 42 | 52.36 N | 1.40 W |
| Wilnsdorf | 56 | 50.49 N | 8.09 E |
| Wilpattu National Park ♠ | 122 | 8.20 N | 80.00 E |
| Wilpen | 214 | 40.17 N | 79.12 W |
| Wilpshire | 262 | 53.47 N | 2.28 W |
| Wilsall | 202 | 45.59 N | 110.39 W |
| Wilsdruff | 54 | 51.05 N | 13.32 E |
| Wilseder Berg ∧[2] | 52 | 53.10 N | 9.56 E |
| Wilseyville | 226 | 38.23 N | 120.31 W |
| Wilshamstead | 42 | 52.05 N | 0.27 W |
| Wilson, Austl. | 166 | 32.00 S | 138.22 E |
| Wilson, Ar., U.S. | 194 | 35.34 N | 90.02 W |
| Wilson, Ct., U.S. | 207 | 41.48 N | 72.38 W |
| Wilson, Il., U.S. | 278 | 42.21 N | 87.54 W |
| Wilson, Ks., U.S. | 198 | 38.49 N | 98.28 W |
| Wilson, La., U.S. | 194 | 30.55 N | 91.06 W |
| Wilson, N.Y., U.S. | 210 | 43.18 N | 78.49 W |
| Wilson, N.C., U.S. | 192 | 35.43 N | 77.54 W |
| Wilson, Ok., U.S. | 196 | 34.09 N | 97.25 W |
| Wilson, Pa., U.S. | 208 | 40.41 N | 75.14 W |
| Wilson, Tx., U.S. | 196 | 33.19 N | 101.44 W |
| Wilson ≃, Austl. | 164 | 16.47 S | 128.17 E |
| Wilson ≃, Austl. | 166 | 27.38 S | 141.24 E |
| Wilson ≃, Or., U.S. | 224 | 45.28 N | 123.53 W |
| Wilson, Cape › | 176 | 66.59 N | 81.28 W |
| Wilson, Mount ∧, Az., U.S. | 200 | 35.59 N | 114.37 W |
| Wilson, Mount ∧, Ca., U.S. | 280 | 34.13 N | 118.04 W |
| Wilson, Mount ∧, Co., U.S. | 200 | 37.51 N | 107.59 W |
| Wilson, Mount ∧, Nv., U.S. | 204 | 38.15 N | 114.23 W |
| Wilson, Mount ∧, Or., U.S. | 224 | 45.04 N | 121.39 W |
| Wilson, Mount ∧[2], Austl. | 162 | 20.14 S | 127.39 E |
| Wilson, Mount ∧[2], Austl. | 168b | 35.13 S | 138.38 E |
| Wilson, Point ›, Austl. | 169 | 38.05 S | 144.30 E |
| Wilson, Point ›, Wa., U.S. | 224 | 48.08 N | 122.45 W |
| Wilson Cliffs ⩞[4] | 162 | 22.03 S | 127.09 E |
| Wilson Creek ≃, Tx., U.S. | 222 | 33.07 N | 96.35 W |
| Wilson Creek ≃, Wa., U.S. | 202 | 47.25 N | 119.07 W |
| Wilson Lake ⊜[1], Al., U.S. | 194 | 34.49 N | 87.30 W |
| Wilson Lake ⊜[1], Ks., U.S. | 198 | 38.57 N | 98.40 W |
| Wilson Range ⋏ | 162 | 28.50 S | 124.25 E |
| Wilson Run ≃, De., U.S. | 285 | 39.48 N | 75.35 W |
| Wilson Run ≃, Pa., U.S. | 279b | 40.13 N | 79.37 W |
| Wilsons Beach | 186 | 44.56 N | 66.56 W |
| Wilson's Creek National Battlefield ♠ | 194 | 37.06 N | 93.27 W |
| Wilsons Promontory › | 166 | 38.55 S | 146.20 E |
| Wilsons Promontory National Park ♠ | 166 | 39.00 S | 146.25 E |
| Wilsonville, Il., U.S. | 219 | 39.04 N | 89.51 W |
| Wilsonville, Ne., U.S. | 198 | 40.06 N | 100.06 W |
| Wilsonville, Or., U.S. | 224 | 45.18 N | 122.46 W |
| Wilster | 52 | 53.55 N | 9.22 E |
| Wilthen | 54 | 51.06 N | 14.24 E |
| Wilton, Eng., U.K. | 42 | 51.05 N | 1.52 W |
| Wilton, Ct., U.S. | 207 | 41.11 N | 73.26 W |
| Wilton, Me., U.S. | 188 | 44.35 N | 70.13 W |
| Wilton, N.H., U.S. | 207 | 42.50 N | 71.44 W |
| Wilton, N.Y., U.S. | 210 | 43.11 N | 73.45 W |
| Wilton, N.D., U.S. | 198 | 47.09 N | 100.46 W |
| Wilton, Wi., U.S. | 190 | 43.48 N | 90.31 W |
| Wilton ≃ | 164 | 14.45 S | 134.33 E |
| Wilton Creek ≃ | 212 | 44.12 N | 76.56 W |
| Wilton Farm Acres | 284b | 39.18 N | 76.50 W |
| Wilton Manors | 220 | 26.09 N | 80.08 W |
| Wiltshire □[6] | 42 | 51.15 N | 1.50 W |
| Wiltz | 56 | 49.57 N | 5.55 E |
| Wiluna | 162 | 26.36 S | 120.13 E |
| Wimapedi ≃ | 184 | 55.27 N | 99.07 W |
| Wimauma | 220 | 27.42 N | 82.17 W |
| Wimberley | 196 | 30.00 N | 98.06 W |
| Wimbleball Reservoir ⊜[1] | 42 | 51.04 N | 3.28 W |
| Wimbledon | 198 | 47.10 N | 98.27 W |
| Wimbledon ⬥[8] | 260 | 51.25 N | 0.12 W |
| Wimbledon Common ♠ | 260 | 51.26 N | 0.14 W |
| Wimborne Minster | 42 | 50.48 N | 1.59 W |
| Wimereux | 50 | 50.46 N | 1.37 E |
| Wimmelburg | 54 | 51.31 N | 11.30 E |
| Wimmenau | 56 | 48.55 N | 7.25 E |
| Wimmera ≃ | 169 | 36.55 S | 142.56 E |
| Wimmis | 58 | 46.41 N | 7.38 E |
| Winagami Lake ⊜ | 182 | 55.38 N | 116.45 W |
| Winam c | 154 | 0.15 S | 34.35 E |
| Winamac | 216 | 41.03 N | 86.36 W |
| Winburg | 158 | 28.37 S | 27.00 E |
| Winburne | 214 | 40.57 N | 78.08 W |
| Wincanton | 42 | 51.04 N | 2.25 W |
| Wincham | 262 | 53.16 N | 2.29 W |
| Winchcombe | 42 | 51.57 N | 1.58 W |
| Winchelsea, Austl. | 169 | 38.15 S | 143.59 E |
| Winchelsea, Eng., U.K. | 42 | 50.55 N | 0.42 E |
| Winchendon | 207 | 42.41 N | 72.02 W |
| Winchester, On., Can. | 212 | 45.06 N | 75.21 W |
| Winchester, N.Z. | 172 | 44.12 S | 171.17 E |
| Winchester, Eng., U.K. | 42 | 51.04 N | 1.19 W |
| Winchester, Ca., U.S. | 228 | 33.42 N | 117.05 W |
| Winchester, Id., U.S. | 202 | 46.14 N | 116.37 W |
| Winchester, Il., U.S. | 219 | 39.37 N | 90.27 W |
| Winchester, In., U.S. | 218 | 40.10 N | 84.58 W |
| Winchester, Ky., U.S. | 192 | 37.59 N | 84.10 W |
| Winchester, Ma., U.S. | 283 | 42.27 N | 71.08 W |
| Winchester, N.H., U.S. | 207 | 42.46 N | 72.23 W |
| Winchester, Oh., U.S. | 218 | 38.56 N | 83.39 W |
| Winchester, Tn., U.S. | 194 | 35.11 N | 86.06 W |
| Winchester, Tx., U.S. | 222 | 30.01 N | 97.01 W |
| Winchester, Va., U.S. | 188 | 39.11 N | 78.10 W |
| Winchester Cathedral ʊ[1] | 42 | 51.04 N | 1.19 W |
| Winchmore Hill | 260 | 51.39 N | 0.39 W |
| Winchmore Hill ⬥[8] | 260 | 51.38 N | 0.06 W |
| Wind ≃, Yk., Can. | 180 | 65.49 N | 135.18 W |
| Wind ≃, Wa., U.S. | 224 | 45.43 N | 121.47 W |
| Wind ≃, Wy., U.S. | 202 | 43.35 N | 108.13 W |
| Windang | 170 | 34.32 S | 150.53 E |
| Windau → Ventspils | 76 | 57.24 N | 21.36 E |
| Windber | 214 | 40.14 N | 78.50 W |
| Wind Cave National Park ♠ | 198 | 43.32 N | 103.25 W |
| Windeck | 56 | 50.48 N | 7.37 E |
| Winder | 192 | 33.59 N | 83.43 W |
| Winder, Lake ⊜ | 220 | 28.15 N | 80.51 W |
| Windera | 166 | 26.03 S | 151.50 E |
| Windermere, B.C., Can. | 182 | 50.30 N | 115.58 W |
| Windermere, Eng., U.K. | 44 | 54.23 N | 2.54 W |
| Windermere, Fl., U.S. | 220 | 28.30 N | 81.32 W |
| Windermere ⊜ | 44 | 54.22 N | 2.56 W |
| Windermere Lake ⊜ | 190 | 47.56 N | 83.47 W |
| Winder Village | 285 | 40.06 N | 74.52 W |
| Windfall, Ab., Can. | 182 | 54.11 N | 116.15 W |
| Windfall, In., U.S. | 216 | 40.21 N | 85.57 W |
| Windgap | 210 | 40.51 N | 75.18 W |
| Windham, Ct., U.S. | 207 | 41.41 N | 72.09 W |
| Windham, N.H., U.S. | 283 | 42.48 N | 71.18 W |
| Windham, N.Y., U.S. | 210 | 42.19 N | 74.15 W |
| Windham, Oh., U.S. | 214 | 41.14 N | 81.02 W |
| Windham □[6], Ct., U.S. | 207 | 41.55 N | 71.55 W |
| Windham □[6], Vt., U.S. | 207 | 42.50 N | 72.43 W |
| Windham Manor | 284c | 39.04 N | 77.00 W |
| Windhoek | 156 | 22.34 S | 17.06 E |
| Windigo ≃ | 184 | 53.22 N | 91.48 W |
| Windigo Lake ⊜ | 184 | 52.35 N | 91.32 W |
| Windisch | 58 | 47.29 N | 8.13 E |
| Windischeschenbach | 60 | 49.48 N | 12.09 E |
| Windischgarsten | 61 | 47.44 N | 14.20 E |
| Wind Lake | 216 | 42.49 N | 88.09 W |
| Wind Lake ⊜ | 216 | 42.50 N | 88.09 W |
| Windlass Run ≃ | 284b | 39.24 N | 76.24 W |
| Windleite ∧ | 54 | 51.22 N | 10.56 E |
| Windlesham | 260 | 51.22 N | 0.40 W |
| Windley Key I | 220 | 24.57 N | 80.35 W |
| Windmill Point ›, On., Can. | 284a | 42.52 N | 79.01 W |
| Windmill Point ›, Mi., U.S. | 281 | 42.22 N | 82.55 W |
| Windmill Point ›, Va., U.S. | 208 | 37.37 N | 76.17 W |
| Windom, Mn., U.S. | 198 | 43.51 N | 95.07 W |
| Windom, N.Y., U.S. | 210 | 42.47 N | 78.48 W |
| Windom Peak ∧ | 200 | 37.37 N | 107.35 W |
| Windorah | 166 | 25.26 S | 142.39 E |
| Windorf, Dtsch. | 60 | 48.37 N | 13.13 E |
| Windorf, Öst. | 61 | 48.27 N | 14.02 E |
| Window Rock | 200 | 35.40 N | 109.03 W |
| Wind Point | 216 | 42.47 N | 87.45 W |
| Wind River Indian Reservation ⬥[4] | 202 | 43.26 N | 109.00 W |
| Wind River Peak ∧ | 200 | 42.42 N | 109.07 W |
| Wind River Range ⋏ | 200 | 43.05 N | 109.25 W |
| Windrush ≃ | 42 | 51.42 N | 1.25 W |
| Windsbach | 56 | 49.14 N | 10.50 E |
| Windsor, Austl. | 168b | 34.25 S | 138.20 E |
| Windsor, Austl. | 170 | 33.37 S | 150.49 E |
| Windsor, Nf., Can. | 186 | 48.57 N | 55.40 W |
| Windsor, N.S., Can. | 186 | 44.59 N | 64.08 W |
| Windsor, On., Can. | 214 | 42.18 N | 83.01 W |
| Windsor, On., Can. | 281 | 42.18 N | 83.01 W |
| Windsor, P.Q., Can. | 206 | 45.34 N | 72.00 W |
| Windsor, Eng., U.K. | 42 | 51.29 N | 0.38 W |
| Windsor, Ca., U.S. | 204 | 38.33 N | 122.49 W |
| Windsor, Co., U.S. | 200 | 40.28 N | 104.54 W |
| Windsor, Ct., U.S. | 207 | 41.51 N | 72.38 W |
| Windsor, Il., U.S. | 194 | 39.26 N | 88.35 W |
| Windsor, In., U.S. | 218 | 40.09 N | 85.12 W |
| Windsor, Mo., U.S. | 194 | 38.31 N | 93.31 W |
| Windsor, N.J., U.S. | 208 | 40.15 N | 74.35 W |
| Windsor, N.Y., U.S. | 210 | 42.05 N | 75.39 W |
| Windsor, N.C., U.S. | 192 | 35.59 N | 76.56 W |
| Windsor, Oh., U.S. | 214 | 41.32 N | 80.56 W |
| Windsor, Pa., U.S. | 208 | 39.54 N | 76.35 W |
| Windsor, Vt., U.S. | 188 | 43.29 N | 72.23 W |
| Windsor, Va., U.S. | 208 | 36.48 N | 76.44 W |
| Windsor, Wi., U.S. | 216 | 43.13 N | 89.20 W |
| Windsor, Gare ⬥[5] | 275a | 45.30 N | 73.34 W |
| Windsor, University of ʊ[2] | 281 | 42.18 N | 83.04 W |
| Windsor Airport ⊠ | 214 | 42.17 N | 82.58 W |
| Windsor and Maidenhead □[8] | 260 | 51.28 N | 0.37 W |
| Windsor Castle ⊥ | 42 | 51.29 N | 0.36 W |
| Windsor Forest | 192 | 31.58 N | 81.07 W |
| Windsor Forest ⬥[3] | 42 | 51.27 N | 0.43 W |
| Windsor Great Park ♠ | 260 | 51.27 N | 0.37 W |
| Windsor Heights | 214 | 40.12 N | 80.40 W |
| Windsor Hills | 280 | 33.59 N | 118.21 W |
| Windsor Locks | 207 | 41.55 N | 72.37 W |
| Windsor Race Course ♠ | 260 | 51.29 N | 0.39 W |
| Windsor Raceway ♠ | 281 | 42.15 N | 83.05 W |
| Windsor Terrace | 284b | 39.19 N | 76.43 W |
| Windsorton | 158 | 28.16 S | 24.44 E |
| Windsorville | 207 | 41.53 N | 72.32 W |
| Windthorst | 196 | 33.34 N | 98.26 W |
| Windward Islands II | 238 | 13.00 N | 61.00 W |
| Windward Passage ʮ | 238 | 20.00 N | 73.50 W |
| Windy Hills | 285 | 39.48 N | 75.35 W |
| Windy Lake ⊜ | 184 | 54.22 N | 102.35 W |
| Windy Peak ∧, Co., U.S. | 200 | 38.21 N | 106.16 W |
| Windy Peak ∧, Wa., U.S. | 202 | 48.56 N | 119.58 W |
| Windy Run ≃ | 284c | 38.54 N | 77.05 W |
| Winefred ≃ | 184 | 56.02 N | 110.36 W |
| Winefred Lake ⊜ | 182 | 55.30 N | 110.35 W |
| Winejok | 140 | 9.01 N | 27.34 E |
| Winesburg | 214 | 40.37 N | 81.42 W |
| Winfield, Ab., Can. | 182 | 52.58 N | 114.26 W |
| Winfield, Al., U.S. | 194 | 33.55 N | 87.49 W |
| Winfield, Il., U.S. | 216 | 41.52 N | 88.10 W |
| Winfield, Ia., U.S. | 190 | 41.07 N | 91.26 W |
| Winfield, Ks., U.S. | 198 | 37.14 N | 96.59 W |
| Winfield, Mo., U.S. | 219 | 38.59 N | 90.44 W |
| Winfield, N.J., U.S. | 276 | 40.38 N | 74.17 W |
| Winfield, Tx., U.S. | 222 | 33.10 N | 95.07 W |
| Winfield, W.V., U.S. | 188 | 38.31 N | 81.53 W |
| Wing | 198 | 47.08 N | 100.16 W |
| Wing ≃ | 198 | 46.29 N | 94.58 W |
| Wingate, Eng., U.K. | 44 | 54.44 N | 1.23 W |
| Wingate, Md., U.S. | 208 | 38.16 N | 76.04 W |
| Wingate, N.C., U.S. | 192 | 34.59 N | 80.26 W |
| Wingate Mountains ⋏ | 164 | 14.29 S | 130.42 E |
| Wingates | 262 | 53.34 N | 2.32 W |
| Wingdale | 210 | 41.39 N | 73.34 W |
| Wingecarribee ≃ | 170 | 34.23 S | 150.07 E |
| Wingecarribee Reservoir ⊜[1] | 170 | 34.34 S | 150.30 E |
| Wingello | 170 | 34.42 S | 150.09 E |
| Wingene | 50 | 51.04 N | 3.16 E |
| Wingen-sur-Moder | 56 | 48.55 N | 7.22 E |
| Wingerworth | 44 | 53.12 N | 1.26 W |
| Wingham, Austl. | 166 | 31.52 S | 152.22 E |
| Wingham, On., Can. | 212 | 43.53 N | 81.19 W |
| Wingham, Eng., U.K. | 42 | 51.17 N | 1.13 E |
| Wing Lake Shores | 281 | 42.33 N | 83.17 W |
| Wingles | 50 | 50.29 N | 2.51 E |
| Wingo | 194 | 36.38 N | 88.44 W |
| Wings Field ⊠ | 285 | 40.08 N | 75.16 W |
| Wingst | 52 | 53.43 N | 9.03 E |
| Winhole Channel ʮ | 276 | 43.37 N | 73.48 W |
| Winhöring | 60 | 48.16 N | 12.39 E |
| Winifred | 202 | 47.33 N | 109.22 W |
| Winifreda | 252 | 36.15 S | 64.14 W |
| Winisk | 176 | 55.15 N | 85.12 W |
| Winisk ≃ | 176 | 55.17 N | 85.05 W |
| Winisk Lake ⊜ | 176 | 52.55 N | 87.22 W |
| Wink | 196 | 31.45 N | 103.06 W |
| Winkana | 110 | 15.44 N | 98.01 E |
| Winkelman | 200 | 32.59 N | 110.46 W |
| Winkelpos | 158 | 27.35 S | 26.49 E |
| Winklarn | 60 | 49.26 N | 12.29 E |
| Winkler, Mb., Can. | 184 | 49.11 N | 97.56 W |
| Winkler, Tx., U.S. | 222 | 31.56 N | 96.13 W |
| Winklern | 64 | 46.52 N | 12.52 E |
| Winlaw | 182 | 49.37 N | 117.34 W |
| Winlock | 224 | 46.29 N | 122.56 W |
| Winneba | 150 | 5.25 N | 0.36 W |
| Winnebago, Il., U.S. | 190 | 42.15 N | 89.14 W |
| Winnebago, Mn., U.S. | 190 | 43.46 N | 94.09 W |
| Winnebago, Ne., U.S. | 198 | 42.14 N | 96.28 W |
| Winnebago □[6] | 216 | 42.17 N | 89.06 W |
| Winnebago ≃ | 190 | 43.03 N | 92.57 W |
| Winnebago, Lake ⊜ | 190 | 44.00 N | 88.25 W |
| Winnebago Indian Reservation ⬥[4], Ne., U.S. | 198 | 42.15 N | 96.31 W |
| Winnebago Indian Reservation ⬥[4], Wi., U.S. | 190 | 44.15 N | 90.38 W |
| Winnecke, Mount ∧[2] | 162 | 18.47 S | 130.20 E |
| Winnecke Creek ≃ | 162 | 18.35 S | 131.34 E |
| Winneconne | 190 | 44.06 N | 88.42 W |
| Winneconnet | 283 | 41.59 N | 71.08 W |
| Winneconnet Pond ⊜ | 283 | 41.58 N | 71.08 W |
| Winnekendonk | 52 | 51.36 N | 6.17 E |
| Winnekenni Park ♠ | 283 | 42.47 N | 71.04 W |
| Winnemucca | 204 | 40.58 N | 117.44 W |
| Winnemucca Lake ⊜ | 204 | 40.09 N | 119.20 W |
| Winnenden | 56 | 48.53 N | 9.24 E |
| Winner | 198 | 43.22 N | 99.51 W |
| Winnetka | 216 | 42.06 N | 87.44 W |
| Winnetka ⬥[8] | 280 | 34.13 N | 118.35 W |
| Winnett | 202 | 47.00 N | 108.21 W |
| Winnfield | 194 | 31.55 N | 92.38 W |
| Winnibigoshish, Lake ⊜ | 190 | 47.27 N | 94.12 W |
| Winnie | 194 | 29.49 N | 94.23 W |
| Winning | 162 | 23.09 S | 114.32 E |
| Winningen, Dtsch. | 54 | 51.49 N | 11.26 E |
| Winningen, Dtsch. | 56 | 50.18 N | 7.31 E |
| Winnipeg | 184 | 49.53 N | 97.09 W |
| Winnipeg ≃ | 184 | 50.38 N | 96.19 W |
| Winnipeg, Lake ⊜ | 184 | 52.00 N | 97.00 W |
| Winnipeg Beach | 184 | 50.31 N | 96.58 W |
| Winnipegosis | 184 | 51.39 N | 99.56 W |
| Winnipegosis, Lake ⊜ | 184 | 52.30 N | 100.00 W |
| Winnipesaukee, Lake ⊜ | 188 | 43.35 N | 71.20 W |
| Winnsboro, La., U.S. | 194 | 32.09 N | 91.43 W |
| Winnsboro, S.C., U.S. | 192 | 34.22 N | 81.05 W |
| Winnsboro, Tx., U.S. | 222 | 32.57 N | 95.17 W |
| Winnsboro, Lake ⊜[1] | 222 | 32.55 N | 95.21 W |
| Winnsboro Mills | 192 | 34.21 N | 81.05 W |
| Winnweiler | 56 | 49.34 N | 7.51 E |
| Winona, Ks., U.S. | 198 | 39.03 N | 101.14 W |
| Winona, Mi., U.S. | 190 | 46.52 N | 88.55 W |
| Winona, Mn., U.S. | 190 | 44.03 N | 91.38 W |
| Winona, Ms., U.S. | 194 | 33.28 N | 89.43 W |
| Winona, Mo., U.S. | 194 | 37.00 N | 91.19 W |
| Winona, Oh., U.S. | 214 | 40.50 N | 80.54 W |
| Winona, Tx., U.S. | 222 | 32.29 N | 95.10 W |
| Winona Lake, In., U.S. | 216 | 41.13 N | 85.49 W |
| Winona Lake, N.Y., U.S. | 210 | 41.31 N | 74.03 W |
| Winona Lake ⊜ | 216 | 41.13 N | 85.50 W |
| Winooski | 188 | 44.29 N | 73.11 W |
| Winooski ≃ | 188 | 44.30 N | 73.15 W |
| Winooski, North Branch ≃ | 188 | 44.15 N | 72.35 W |
| Winschoten | 52 | 53.08 N | 7.02 E |
| Winscombe | 42 | 51.18 N | 2.50 W |
| Winsen, Dtsch. | 52 | 52.41 N | 9.54 E |
| Winsen, Dtsch. | 52 | 53.22 N | 10.12 E |
| Winsford, Eng., U.K. | 42 | 51.06 N | 3.33 W |
| Winsford, Eng., U.K. | 44 | 53.12 N | 2.32 W |
| Winshill | 42 | 52.48 N | 1.36 W |
| Winside | 198 | 42.10 N | 97.10 W |
| Winslow, Eng., U.K. | 42 | 51.57 N | 0.54 W |
| Winslow, Az., U.S. | 200 | 35.01 N | 110.41 W |
| Winslow, Me., U.S. | 188 | 44.32 N | 69.37 W |
| Winslow, N.J., U.S. | 285 | 39.39 N | 74.52 W |
| Winslow Reef ✢[2] | 14 | 1.36 S | 174.57 W |
| Winsted, Ct., U.S. | 207 | 41.55 N | 73.03 W |
| Winsted, Mn., U.S. | 190 | 44.57 N | 94.02 W |
| Winston, Fl., U.S. | 220 | 28.01 N | 82.00 W |
| Winston, Or., U.S. | 202 | 43.07 N | 123.24 W |
| Winston Churchill Memorial ʊ | 219 | 38.52 N | 91.58 W |
| Winston Creek ≃ | 224 | 46.30 N | 122.40 W |
| Winston-Salem | 192 | 36.05 N | 80.14 W |
| Winsum | 52 | 53.19 N | 6.31 E |
| Wintego Lake ⊜ | 184 | 55.33 N | 102.52 W |
| Winter | 190 | 45.49 N | 91.00 W |
| Winter Beach | 220 | 27.43 N | 80.25 W |
| Winterberg, Dtsch. | 56 | 51.11 N | 8.32 E |
| Winterberg, Dtsch. | 263 | 51.17 N | 7.18 E |
| Winterberg ∧[2] | 263 | 51.20 N | 7.13 E |
| Winterberge ⋏ | 158 | 32.28 S | 26.15 E |
| Winterbourne Abbas | 42 | 50.43 N | 2.34 W |
| Winter Creek ≃ | 280 | 34.12 N | 118.02 W |
| Winterfeld | 54 | 52.44 N | 11.14 E |
| Winter Garden | 220 | 28.33 N | 81.35 W |
| Winter Harbor | 188 | 44.23 N | 68.05 W |
| Winter Harbour | 182 | 50.31 N | 128.02 W |
| Winterhaven, Ca., U.S. | 204 | 32.44 N | 114.38 W |
| Winter Haven, Fl., U.S. | 220 | 28.01 N | 81.43 W |
| Winter Hill ∧[2] | 262 | 53.38 N | 2.31 W |
| Wintering ≃ | 198 | 48.12 N | 100.34 W |
| Wintering Lake ⊜ | 184 | 55.24 N | 97.42 W |
| Winter Island I, N.T., Can. | 176 | 66.14 N | 83.04 W |
| Winter Island I, Ca., U.S. | 282 | 38.03 N | 121.51 W |
| Winter Island I, Ma., U.S. | 283 | 42.32 N | 70.52 W |
| Winterlingen | 58 | 48.11 N | 9.07 E |
| Winter Park, Fl., U.S. | 220 | 28.35 N | 81.20 W |
| Winter Park, N.C., U.S. | 192 | 34.12 N | 77.53 W |
| Winterport | 188 | 44.38 N | 68.51 W |
| Winters, Ca., U.S. | 226 | 38.31 N | 121.58 W |
| Winters, Tx., U.S. | 196 | 31.57 N | 99.57 W |
| Winters Bayou ≃ | 222 | 30.22 N | 95.06 W |
| Winters Canal ≊ | 226 | 38.32 N | 121.58 W |
| Wintersdorf | 54 | 51.03 N | 12.21 E |
| Winterset, Ia., U.S. | 190 | 41.19 N | 94.00 W |
| Winterset, Oh., U.S. | 214 | 40.06 N | 81.25 W |
| Winter Springs | 220 | 28.41 N | 81.18 W |
| Winters Run ≃ | 208 | 39.26 N | 76.18 W |
| Winterstown | 208 | 39.50 N | 76.37 W |
| Wintersville | 214 | 40.22 N | 80.42 W |
| Winterswijk | 52 | 51.58 N | 6.44 E |
| Winterthur, Schw. | 58 | 47.30 N | 8.43 E |
| Winterthur, De., U.S. | 285 | 39.48 N | 75.35 W |
| Winterthur Museum ʊ | 285 | 39.48 N | 75.36 W |
| Winterton, Nf., Can. | 186 | 47.58 N | 53.20 W |
| Winterton, S. Afr. | 158 | 28.46 S | 29.35 E |
| Winterton, Eng., U.K. | 44 | 53.39 N | 0.36 W |
| Winterton-on-Sea | 42 | 52.43 N | 1.42 E |
| Winterville, Ga., U.S. | 192 | 33.58 N | 83.16 W |
| Winterville, Ms., U.S. | 194 | 33.30 N | 91.03 W |
| Winterville, N.C., U.S. | 192 | 35.31 N | 77.24 W |
| Winthrop, Ct., U.S. | 207 | 41.21 N | 72.29 W |
| Winthrop, Ia., U.S. | 190 | 42.28 N | 91.44 W |
| Winthrop, Me., U.S. | 188 | 44.18 N | 69.58 W |
| Winthrop, Ma., U.S. | 283 | 42.22 N | 70.59 W |
| Winthrop, Mn., U.S. | 190 | 44.32 N | 94.21 W |
| Winthrop, Wa., U.S. | 182 | 48.28 N | 120.11 W |
| Winthrop, Lake ⊜ | 283 | 42.11 N | 71.25 W |
| Winthrop Harbor | 216 | 42.28 N | 87.49 W |
| Wintinna | 162 | 27.44 S | 134.07 E |
| Wintinna Creek ≃ | 162 | 27.47 S | 134.14 E |
| Winton, Austl. | 166 | 22.23 S | 143.02 E |
| Winton, N.Z. | 172 | 46.09 S | 168.20 E |
| Winton, S. Afr. | 158 | 27.29 S | 22.34 E |
| Winton, Ca., U.S. | 226 | 37.23 N | 120.37 W |
| Winton, N.C., U.S. | 192 | 36.23 N | 76.55 W |
| Winton, Wa., U.S. | 224 | 47.44 N | 120.44 W |
| Wintzenheim | 58 | 48.04 N | 7.17 E |
| Winwick | 262 | 53.26 N | 2.36 W |
| Winz | 263 | 51.23 N | 7.09 E |
| Winzenberg | 263 | 51.06 N | 7.38 E |
| Winzer | 60 | 48.44 N | 13.04 E |
| Winzermark | 263 | 51.23 N | 7.08 E |
| Wipper ≃, Dtsch. | 54 | 51.47 N | 11.42 E |
| Wipper ≃, Dtsch. | 54 | 51.17 N | 11.10 E |
| Wipper ≃, Dtsch. | 263 | 51.07 N | 7.24 E |
| Wipperdorf | 54 | 51.28 N | 10.42 E |
| Wipperfeld | 263 | 51.05 N | 7.19 E |
| Wipperfürth | 56 | 51.07 N | 7.23 E |
| Wirātnagar | 124 | 26.29 N | 87.17 E |
| Wirendranagar | 124 | 28.35 N | 81.38 E |
| Wireton, Il., U.S. | 278 | 41.40 N | 87.42 W |
| Wireton, Pa., U.S. | 279b | 40.34 N | 80.14 W |
| Wirgañj | 124 | 27.00 N | 84.52 E |
| Wirges | 56 | 50.28 N | 7.48 E |
| Wiriagar ≃ | 164 | 2.17 S | 132.52 E |
| Wirksworth | 44 | 53.05 N | 1.34 W |
| Wirosari | 115a | 7.05 S | 111.05 E |
| Wirral □[8] | 262 | 53.22 N | 3.05 W |
| Wirral ›[1] | 44 | 53.20 N | 3.03 W |
| Wirraminna | 166 | 31.12 S | 136.15 E |
| Wirrulla | 162 | 32.24 S | 134.31 E |
| Wisbech | 42 | 52.40 N | 0.10 E |
| Wisby → Visby | 26 | 57.38 N | 18.18 E |
| Wiscasset | 188 | 44.00 N | 69.39 W |
| Wischhafen | 52 | 53.46 N | 9.19 E |
| Wisconsin □[3], U.S. | 178 | 44.45 N | 89.30 W |
| Wisconsin □[3], U.S. | 190 | 44.45 N | 89.30 W |
| Wisconsin ≃ | 190 | 43.00 N | 91.10 W |
| Wisconsin, Lake ⊜[1] | 190 | 43.24 N | 89.43 W |
| Wisconsin Dells | 190 | 43.37 N | 89.46 W |
| Wisconsin Dells V | 190 | 43.41 N | 89.49 W |
| Wisconsin Rapids | 190 | 44.23 N | 89.49 W |
| Wiscoy | 210 | 42.30 N | 78.05 W |
| Wisdom | 202 | 45.37 N | 113.27 W |
| Wisdom, Lake ⊜ | 164 | 5.20 S | 147.05 E |
| Wise | 192 | 36.58 N | 82.34 W |
| Wise □[6] | 222 | 33.07 N | 97.40 W |
| Wise ≃ | 202 | 45.48 N | 112.57 W |
| Wiseman | 180 | 67.25 N | 150.06 W |
| Wisemans Ferry | 170 | 33.24 S | 150.59 E |
| Wises Landing | 218 | 38.35 N | 85.25 W |
| Wishart | 184 | 51.34 N | 104.00 W |
| Wishaw | 46 | 55.47 N | 3.56 W |
| Wishek | 198 | 46.16 N | 99.33 W |
| Wishkah ≃ | 224 | 46.58 N | 123.45 W |
| Wishram | 224 | 45.39 N | 120.57 W |
| Wiske ≃ | 44 | 54.15 N | 1.26 W |
| Wisła | 30 | 49.40 N | 18.52 E |
| Wisła ≃ | 30 | 54.22 N | 18.55 E |
| Wisley Aerodrome ⊠ | 260 | 51.18 N | 0.28 W |
| Wisley Gardens ♠ | 260 | 51.19 N | 0.29 W |
| Wisłok ≃ | 30 | 50.13 N | 22.32 E |
| Wisłoka ≃ | 30 | 50.27 N | 21.23 E |
| Wismar, Dtsch. | 54 | 53.53 N | 11.28 E |
| Wismar, Guy. | 246 | 6.00 N | 58.18 W |
| Wismarbucht c | 54 | 53.57 N | 11.25 E |
| Wisner, La., U.S. | 194 | 31.58 N | 91.39 W |
| Wisner, Ne., U.S. | 198 | 41.59 N | 96.54 W |
| Wissahickon Creek ≃ | 285 | 40.01 N | 75.12 W |
| Wissant | 50 | 50.53 N | 1.40 E |
| Wissembourg | 56 | 49.02 N | 7.57 E |
| Wissen | 56 | 50.47 N | 7.43 E |
| Wissenkerke | 52 | 51.35 N | 3.45 E |
| Wissey ≃ | 42 | 52.33 N | 0.21 E |
| Wissinoming ⬥[8] | 285 | 40.01 N | 75.04 W |
| Wissous | 261 | 48.44 N | 2.20 E |
| Wister | 194 | 34.58 N | 94.43 W |
| Wisznice | 30 | 51.48 N | 23.12 E |
| Witbank | 158 | 25.56 S | 29.07 E |
| Witberge ⋏ | 158 | 30.45 S | 27.32 E |
| Witbooisvlei | 156 | 25.04 S | 18.27 E |
| Witchekan Lake ⊜ | 184 | 53.25 N | 107.35 W |
| Witches Falls National Park ♠ | 171a | 27.56 S | 153.10 E |
| Witch Hazel | 224 | 45.30 N | 122.46 W |
| Witdraai | 158 | 26.58 S | 20.45 E |
| Witfield | 273d | 26.11 S | 28.12 E |
| Witham | 42 | 51.48 N | 0.38 E |
| Witham ≃ | 44 | 53.06 N | 0.13 W |
| Withamsville | 218 | 39.03 N | 84.16 W |
| Withens Clough Reservoir ⊜[1] | 262 | 53.42 N | 2.02 W |
| Witheridge | 42 | 50.55 N | 3.42 W |
| Withernsea | 44 | 53.44 N | 0.02 E |
| Witherspoon, Mount ∧ | 180 | 61.23 N | 147.12 W |
| Withington ⬥[8] | 262 | 53.26 N | 2.14 W |
| Withington Green | 262 | 53.14 N | 2.18 W |
| Withlacoochee ≃, U.S. | 192 | 30.24 N | 83.10 W |
| Withlacoochee ≃, Fl., U.S. | 192 | 29.00 N | 82.45 W |
| Withnell | 262 | 53.42 N | 2.34 W |
| Withokspruit ≃ | 273d | 26.19 S | 28.21 E |
| Witjira National Park ♠ | 162 | 26.25 S | 135.40 E |
| Wit-Kei ≃ | 158 | 32.09 S | 27.24 E |
| Witkoppies ∧ | 158 | 27.44 S | 29.20 E |
| Witkowo | 30 | 52.27 N | 17.47 E |
| Witless Bay | 186 | 47.16 N | 52.50 W |
| Witley | 42 | 51.09 N | 0.38 W |
| Wit-Mfolozi ≃ | 158 | 28.22 S | 31.58 E |
| Witney | 42 | 51.48 N | 1.29 W |
| Witnica | 30 | 52.40 N | 14.55 E |
| Wit Nossob ≃ | 156 | 23.05 S | 18.45 E |
| Witpoort | 158 | 27.10 S | 26.08 E |
| Witrivier | 156 | 24.40 S | 31.00 E |
| Witry-lès-Reims | 50 | 49.18 N | 4.07 E |
| Witsand | 158 | 34.24 S | 20.50 E |
| Witt | 219 | 39.15 N | 89.20 W |
| Wittabrenna Creek ≃ | 166 | 29.20 S | 142.43 E |
| Witteberg ⋏ | 158 | 28.40 S | 28.02 E |
| Witteberge ⋏ | 158 | 33.18 S | 20.36 E |
| Wittelsheim | 58 | 47.49 N | 7.15 E |
| Witten | 56 | 51.26 N | 7.20 E |
| Wittenau ⬥[8] | 264a | 52.35 N | 13.20 E |
| Wittenberg → Lutherstadt Wittenberg, Dtsch. | 54 | 51.52 N | 12.39 E |
| Wittenberg, Wi., U.S. | 190 | 44.49 N | 89.10 W |
| Wittenberge | 54 | 53.00 N | 11.44 E |
| Wittenburg | 54 | 53.31 N | 11.04 E |
| Wittenhagen | 54 | 54.11 N | 13.05 E |
| Wittenheim | 58 | 47.49 N | 7.20 E |
| Wittenoom | 162 | 22.17 S | 118.19 E |
| Wittensee ⊜ | 41 | 54.23 N | 9.45 E |
| Wittering | 42 | 52.37 N | 0.27 W |
| Wittgensdorf | 54 | 50.53 N | 12.52 E |
| Wittichenau | 54 | 51.23 N | 14.14 E |
| Wittingen | 54 | 52.43 N | 10.44 E |
| Wittislingen | 56 | 48.37 N | 10.25 E |
| Wittlaer | 56 | 51.19 N | 6.44 E |
| Wittlich | 56 | 49.59 N | 6.53 E |
| Wittman | 208 | 38.47 N | 76.17 W |
| Wittmar | 54 | 52.07 N | 10.38 E |
| Wittmund | 52 | 53.34 N | 7.47 E |
| Witton Park ♠ | 262 | 53.45 N | 2.31 W |
| Wittow ›[1] | 54 | 54.38 N | 13.19 E |
| Wittstock | 54 | 53.10 N | 12.29 E |
| Witu | 154 | 2.23 S | 40.26 E |
| Witu Islands II | 164 | 4.40 S | 149.25 E |
| Witvlai | 156 | 22.23 S | 18.32 E |
| Witwatersrand, University of the ʊ[2] | 273d | 26.12 S | 28.02 E |
| Witwatersrand Gold Mine ⬥[7] | 273d | 26.12 S | 28.11 E |
| Witwatersrant ⬥[1] | 158 | 26.00 S | 27.00 E |
| Witzenhausen | 56 | 51.20 N | 9.51 E |
| Witzhelden | 263 | 51.07 N | 7.06 E |
| Witzputz | 156 | 27.25 S | 17.43 E |
| Wiveliscombe | 42 | 51.03 N | 3.19 W |
| Wivenhoe | 42 | 51.52 N | 0.58 E |
| Wivenhoe Reservoir ⊜[1] | 171a | 27.20 S | 152.35 E |
| Wiwa Creek ≃ | 184 | 50.02 N | 106.31 W |
| Wixom | 216 | 42.31 N | 83.32 W |
| Wiżajny | 30 | 54.23 N | 22.51 E |
| Wizernes | 50 | 50.43 N | 2.14 E |
| Wjatka → V'atka ≃ | 80 | 55.36 N | 51.30 E |
| W. Kerr Scott Reservoir ⊜[1] | 192 | 36.07 N | 81.15 W |
| Wkra ≃ | 30 | 52.27 N | 20.44 E |
| Wladiwostok → Vladivostok | 89 | 43.10 N | 131.56 E |
| Władysławowo | 30 | 54.49 N | 18.25 E |
| Wleń | 30 | 51.01 N | 15.40 E |
| Wlingi | 115a | 8.05 S | 112.19 E |
| Włocławek | 30 | 52.39 N | 19.02 E |
| Włocławek □[4] | 30 | 52.30 N | 19.05 E |
| Włodawa | 30 | 51.34 N | 23.32 E |
| Włoszczowa | 30 | 50.52 N | 19.59 E |
| Wnion ≃ | 42 | 52.45 N | 3.54 W |
| Woady Yaloak ≃ | 169 | 38.06 S | 143.33 E |
| Wobaer | 85 | 39.19 N | 75.32 W |
| Wöbbelin | 54 | 53.24 N | 11.30 E |
| Woburn | 207 | 42.28 N | 71.09 W |
| Woburn ⬥[8] | 275b | 43.46 N | 79.13 W |
| Woburn Sands | 42 | 52.01 N | 0.39 W |
| Woden, Austl. | 171b | 35.22 S | 149.08 E |
| Woden, Tx., U.S. | 222 | 31.30 N | 94.32 W |
| Wodgina | 162 | 21.11 S | 118.40 E |
| Wodonga | 166 | 36.07 S | 146.54 E |
| Wodzisław Śląski | 30 | 50.00 N | 18.28 E |
| Woensdrecht | 52 | 51.26 N | 4.18 E |
| Woerdeke | 85 | 39.41 N | 77.53 E |
| Woerden | 52 | 52.05 N | 4.54 E |
| Woerth | 56 | 48.56 N | 7.45 E |
| Woëvre ⬥[1] | 56 | 49.05 N | 5.40 E |
| Wofosi | 105 | 40.09 N | 115.18 E |
| Wo Fo Si (Temple of the Sleeping Buddha) ʊ[1] | 105 | 40.01 N | 116.12 E |
| Wognum | 52 | 52.41 N | 5.01 E |
| Wohlde | 41 | 54.24 N | 9.17 E |
| Wohlen | 58 | 47.21 N | 8.17 E |
| Wohlensee ⊜ | 58 | 46.58 N | 7.20 E |
| Wohlford, Lake ⊜[1] | 228 | 33.10 N | 116.59 W |
| Wohlthat Mountains ⋏ | 9 | 71.35 S | 12.20 E |
| Wohra ≃ | 56 | 50.49 N | 8.55 E |
| Woi | 140 | 7.53 N | 31.10 E |
| Woincourt | 50 | 50.04 N | 1.32 E |
| Woippy, Dtsch. | 56 | 49.09 N | 6.09 E |
| Woippy, Fr. | 56 | 49.09 N | 6.09 E |
| Wojcieszów | 30 | 50.58 N | 15.56 E |
| Wokalup | 168a | 33.06 S | 115.53 E |
| Wokam, Pulau I | 164 | 5.37 S | 134.30 E |
| Wokha | 120 | 26.06 N | 94.16 E |
| Woking, Ab., Can. | 182 | 55.35 N | 118.46 W |
| Woking, Eng., U.K. | 42 | 51.20 N | 0.34 W |
| Woking □[8] | 260 | 51.19 N | 0.32 W |
| Wokingham | 42 | 51.25 N | 0.51 W |
| Wokingham Creek ≃ | 166 | 22.19 S | 142.30 E |
| Wolbach | 198 | 41.24 N | 98.24 W |
| Wolbeck | 52 | 51.55 N | 7.43 E |
| Wolbrom | 30 | 50.24 N | 19.46 E |
| Wolcott, Ct., U.S. | 207 | 41.36 N | 72.59 W |
| Wolcott, In., U.S. | 216 | 40.45 N | 87.02 W |
| Wolcott, N.Y., U.S. | 210 | 43.13 N | 76.48 W |
| Wolcott Creek ≃ | 210 | 43.17 N | 76.50 W |
| Wolcottsburg | 210 | 43.04 N | 78.38 W |
| Wolcottsville | 210 | 43.07 N | 78.31 W |
| Wolcottville | 216 | 41.32 N | 85.22 W |
| Wołcza ≃ | 54 | 53.58 N | 14.53 E |
| Wołczenica ≃ | 54 | 53.52 N | 14.44 E |
| Wołczyn | 30 | 51.01 N | 18.03 E |
| Woldberg ⋏[1] | 52 | 52.25 N | 5.55 E |
| Woldegk | 54 | 53.27 N | 13.35 E |
| Woldingham | 260 | 51.17 N | 0.02 W |
| Woleai I[1] | 108 | 7.21 N | 143.52 E |
| Woleu-Ntem □[4] | 152 | 1.30 N | 12.00 E |
| Wolf ≃, On., Can. | 190 | 48.49 N | 88.30 W |
| Wolf ≃, U.S. | 194 | 35.09 N | 90.04 W |
| Wolf ≃, Ks., U.S. | 198 | 39.54 N | [illegible]5.11 W |
| Wolf ≃, Ms., U.S. | 194 | 30.21 N | [illegible]9.18 W |
| Wolf ≃, Wi., U.S. | 190 | 44.11 N | [illegible]8.48 W |
| Wolf, Isla I | 246a | 1.23 N | [illegible]1.49 W |
| Wolf, Volcán ∧[1] | 246a | 0.02 N | [illegible]1.20 W |
| Wolfach | 58 | 48.17 N | 8.13 E |
| Wolf-Bay | 186 | 50.16 N | [illegible]0.08 W |
| Wolf Creek, Mt., U.S. | 202 | 47.00 N | [illegible]2.04 W |
| Wolf Creek, Or., U.S. | 202 | 42.41 N | [illegible]3.23 W |
| Wolf Creek ≃, U.S. | 196 | 36.35 N | 99.30 W |
| Wolf Creek ≃, Ca., U.S. | 226 | 39.02 N | [illegible]21.08 W |
| Wolf Creek ≃, Co., U.S. | 200 | 40.12 N | [illegible]08.29 W |
| Wolf Creek ≃, In., U.S. | 216 | 41.15 N | 87.07 W |
| Wolf Creek ≃, Ia., U.S. | 190 | 42.20 N | 92.09 W |
| Wolf Creek ≃, Mt., U.S. | 198 | 48.05 N | 105.40 W |
| Wolf Creek ≃, Mt., U.S. | 202 | 47.37 N | 109.38 W |
| Wolf Creek ≃, Oh., U.S. | 214 | 41.16 N | 83.11 W |
| Wolf Creek ≃, Pa., U.S. | 214 | 41.03 N | 80.07 W |
| Wolf Creek ≃, S.D., U.S. | 198 | 43.21 N | 97.37 W |
| Wolf Creek ≃, S.D., U.S. | 198 | 44.42 N | 98.40 W |
| Wolf Creek Lake ⊜[1] | 198 | 38.14 N | 95.41 W |
| Wolf Creek Pass ⟩⟨ | 200 | 37.29 N | 106.48 W |
| Wolf Creek State Park ♠ | 219 | 39.30 N | 88.41 W |
| Wolfdale | 214 | 40.12 N | 80.17 W |
| Wolfe □[6] | 206 | 45.45 N | 71.30 W |
| Wolfeboro | 188 | 43.35 N | 71.12 W |
| Wolfe City | 196 | 33.22 N | 96.04 W |
| Wolfegg | 58 | 47.49 N | 9.47 E |
| Wolfe Island | 212 | 44.12 N | 76.26 W |
| Wolfe Island I | 212 | 44.12 N | 76.20 W |
| Wolfe Lake ⊜ | 212 | 44.40 N | 76.30 W |
| Wolfen | 54 | 51.40 N | 12.16 E |
| Wolfenbüttel | 52 | 52.10 N | 10.32 E |
| Wolfenden, Mount ∧ | 182 | 50.26 N | 127.33 W |
| Wolfenschiessen | 58 | 46.55 N | 8.24 E |
| Wolfertschwenden | 58 | 47.53 N | 10.16 E |
| Wolfforth | 196 | 33.30 N | 102.01 W |
| Wolfgangsee ⊜ | 64 | 47.44 N | 13.26 E |
| Wolfhagen | 56 | 51.19 N | 9.10 E |
| Wölfis | 54 | 50.48 N | 10.46 E |
| Wolf Island I | 212 | 44.3[illegible] N | 78.15 W |
| Wolflake, In., U.S. | 216 | 41.2[illegible] N | 85.30 W |
| Wolf Lake, Mi., U.S. | 216 | 43.1[illegible] N | 86.06 W |
| Wolf Lake ⊜, Ab., Can. | 182 | 54.4[illegible] N | 110.59 W |
| Wolf Lake ⊜, On., Can. | 212 | 44.4[illegible] N | 78.11 W |
| Wolf Lake ⊜, Yk., Can. | 180 | 60.4[illegible] N | 131.40 W |
| Wolf Lake ⊜, U.S. | 278 | 41.4[illegible] N | 87.31 W |
| Wolf Lake ⊜, N.J., U.S. | 276 | 40.5[illegible] N | 74.42 W |
| Wolf Mountain ∧ | 180 | 65.1[illegible] N | 154.02 W |
| Wolfpassing | 264b | 48.[illegible] N | 16.11 E |
| Wolf Point | 202 | 48.[illegible] N | 105.38 W |
| Wolframs-Eschenbach | 56 | 49.[illegible] N | 10.43 E |
| Wolfratshausen | 64 | 47.[illegible] N | 11.25 E |
| Wolf Rock I[2] | 28 | 49.[illegible] N | 5.49 W |
| Wolf Run | 214 | 40.[illegible] N | 80.54 W |
| Wolfsberg | 61 | 46.[illegible] N | 14.51 E |
| Wolfsberg ∧[2] | 263 | 51.[illegible] N | 6.27 E |
| Wolfsburg | 54 | 52.[illegible] N | 10.47 E |
| Wolf's Castle | 42 | 51.[illegible] N | 4.58 W |
| Wolfsegg am Hausruck | 60 | 48.[illegible] N | 13.40 E |
| Wolfstein | 56 | 49.[illegible] N | 7.36 E |
| Wolftrap Creek ≃ | 284c | 38.[illegible] N | 77.17 W |
| Wolf Trap Farms for the Performing Arts ♠ | 284c | 38.[illegible] N | 77.16 W |
| Wolfurt | 58 | 47.[illegible] N | 9.45 E |
| Wolfville | 186 | 45.[illegible] N | 64.22 W |
| Wolga → Volga ≃ | 72 | 45.[illegible] N | 47.52 E |
| Wolgan ≃ | 170 | 33.[illegible] S | 150.28 E |
| Wolgast | 54 | 54.[illegible] N | 13.46 E |
| Wolgograd → Volgograd | 80 | 48.[illegible] N | 44.25 E |
| Wolgograder Stausee → Volgogradskoje vodochranilišče ⊜[1] | 80 | 4[illegible].20 N | 45.00 E |
| Wolhusen | 58 | 4[illegible].04 N | 8.04 E |
| Wolin | 30 | 5[illegible].50 N | 14.35 E |
| Wolin I | 54 | 5[illegible].55 N | 14.31 E |
| Woliński Park Narodowy ♠ | 30 | 5[illegible].55 N | 14.30 E |
| Wolkenstein | 54 | 5[illegible].39 N | 13.04 E |
| Wolkersdorf | 61 | 4[illegible].23 N | 16.31 E |
| Wölkisch | 54 | 5[illegible].13 N | 13.21 E |
| Wolkramshausen | 54 | 5[illegible].25 N | 10.44 E |
| Wollangambe ≃ | 170 | [illegible].21 S | 150.35 E |
| Wollaston | 42 | [illegible].15 N | 0.40 W |
| Wollaston, Islas II | 254 | [illegible].40 S | 67.30 W |
| Wollaston Beach ⩞[2] | 283 | [illegible].17 N | 71.01 W |
| Wollaston Lake ⊜, On., Can. | 212 | [illegible].50 N | 77.50 W |
| Wollaston Lake ⊜, Sk., Can. | 176 | [illegible].15 N | 103.20 W |
| Wollaston Peninsula ›[1] | 176 | [illegible].00 N | 115.00 W |
| Wollemi Creek ≃ | 170 | [illegible].13 S | 150.31 E |
| Wollemi National Park ♠ | 166 | [illegible].50 S | 150.30 E |
| Wollogorang | 166 | [illegible]7.13 S | 137.57 E |
| Wollombi | 170 | [illegible].56 S | 151.09 E |
| Wollombi Brook ≃ | 170 | [illegible].33 S | 151.04 E |
| Wollondilly ≃ | 170 | [illegible]3.57 S | 150.26 E |
| Wollongong | 170 | [illegible]4.25 S | 150.54 E |
| Wöllstein | 56 | [illegible]9.49 N | 7.58 E |
| Wolmaransstad | 158 | [illegible]7.12 S | 26.13 E |
| Wolmirsleben | 54 | [illegible]1.57 N | 11.29 E |
| Wolmirstedt | 54 | [illegible]2.15 N | 11.37 E |
| Wolnzach | 60 | [illegible]8.36 N | 11.37 E |
| Wołomin | 30 | 52.21 N | 21.14 E |
| Wołów | 30 | 51.21 N | 16.39 E |
| Wolowaru | 115b | 8.46 S | 121.54 E |
| Wolseley, Sk., Can. | 184 | 50.25 N | 103.19 W |
| Wolseley, S. Afr. | 158 | 33.26 S | 19.12 E |
| Wolsey | 198 | 44.24 N | 98.28 W |
| Wolsingham | 44 | 54.44 N | 1.52 W |
| Wolsztyn | 30 | 52.08 N | 16.06 E |
| Wolterdingen | 52 | 53.02 N | 9.50 E |
| Woltersdorf, Dtsch. | 54 | 52.07 N | 13.12 E |
| Woltersdorf, Dtsch. | 54 | 52.24 N | 12.22 E |
| Woltersdorf, Dtsch. | 54 | 52.26 N | 13.45 E |
| Woluogu | 105 | 39.40 N | 117.46 E |
| Woluwe-Saint-Lambert (Sint-Lambrechts-Woluwe) | 56 | 50.51 N | 4.24 E |
| Wolvega | 52 | 52.53 N | 6.00 E |
| Wolverhampton | 42 | 52.36 N | 2.08 W |
| Wolverine | 190 | 45.16 N | 84.36 W |
| Wolverine Lake | 281 | 42.33 N | 83.29 W |
| Wolverine Loon Lake ⊜ | 281 | 42.33 N | 83.30 W |
| Wolverine Mountain ∧ | 180 | 65.20 N | 149.51 W |
| Wolvertem | 50 | 50.57 N | 4.18 E |
| Wolverton | 42 | 52.04 N | 0.50 W |
| Wolwehoek | 158 | 26.55 S | 27.48 E |
| Wölzerbach ≃ | 61 | 47.08 N | 14.23 E |
| Wolziger See ⊜ | 54 | 52.16 N | 13.50 E |
| Woman ≃ | 190 | 47.57 N | 82.19 W |
| Wombarra | 170 | 34.16 S | 150.58 E |
| Wombat, Mount ∧ | 169 | 36.51 S | 145.40 E |
| Wombeyan Caves ⩞[5] | 170 | 34.18 S | 149.56 E |


| Symbol | Deutsch | Español | Français | Português |
|---|---|---|---|---|
| ≃ River | Fluß | Río | Rivière | Rio |
| ≊ Canal | Kanal | Canal | Canal | Canal |
| ⌊ Waterfall, Rapids | Wasserfall, Stromschnellen | Cascada, Rápidos | Chute d'eau, Rapides | Cascata, Rápidos |
| ʮ Strait | Meeresstraße | Estrecho | Détroit | Estreito |
| c Bay, Gulf | Bucht, Golf | Bahía, Golfo | Baie, Golfe | Baía, Golfo |
| ⊜ Lake, Lakes | See, Seen | Lago, Lagos | Lac, Lacs | Lago, Lagos |
| ☷ Swamp | Sumpf | Pantano | Marais | Pântano |
| ⍓ Ice Features, Glacier | Eis- und Gletscherformen | Accidentes Glaciales | Formes glaciaires | Acidentes glaciares |
| ⍑ Other Hydrographic Features | Andere Hydrographische Objekte | Otros Elementos Hidrográficos | Autres données hydrographiques | Outros acidentes hidrográficos |
| ✢ Submarine Features | Untermeerische Objekte | Accidentes Submarinos | Formes de relief sous-marin | Acidentes submarinos |
| □ Political Unit | Politische Einheit | Unidad Política | Entité politique | Unidade política |
| ʊ Cultural Institution | Kulturelle Institution | Institución Cultural | Institution culturelle | Instituição cultural |
| ⊥ Historical Site | Historische Stätte | Sitio Histórico | Site historique | Sitio histórico |
| ♠ Recreational Site | Erholungs- und Ferienort | Sitio de Recreo | Centre de loisirs | Area de Lazer |
| ⊠ Airport | Flughafen | Aeropuerto | Aéroport | Aeroporto |
| ■ Military Installation | Militäranlage | Instalación Militar | Installation militaire | Instalação militar |
| ⬥ Miscellaneous | Verschiedenes | Misceláneo | Divers | Diversos |

ENGLISH | DEUTSCH


| Name / Name | Page / Seite | Lat.°′ / Breite°′ | Long.°′ / Länge°′ E = Ost |
|---|---|---|---|
| Wombourne | 42 | 52.32 N | 2.11 W |
| Wombwell | 44 | 53.31 N | 1.24 W |
| Womelsdorf | 208 | 40.22 N | 76.11 W |
| Women's Rights National Historical Park ♦ | 210 | 42.54 N | 76.47 W |
| Wommels | 52 | 53.06 N | 5.36 E |
| Wompatuck State Park ♦ | 283 | 42.13 N | 70.51 W |
| Wonarah | 162 | 19.55 S | 136.20 E |
| Wondai | 166 | 26.19 S | 151.52 E |
| Wondelgem | 50 | 51.05 N | 3.43 E |
| Wonderfonteinspruit ≃ | 273d | 26.16 S | 27.42 E |
| Wonderkop | 158 | 27.50 S | 27.26 E |
| Wonder Lake | 216 | 42.25 N | 88.21 W |
| Wonderland | 204 | 40.24 N | 121.19 W |
| Wonderland Center -•-[9] | 281 | 42.22 N | 83.20 W |
| Wondinong | 162 | 27.52 S | 118.25 E |
| Wŏndong-ni | 98 | 34.23 N | 126.40 E |
| Wonersh | 260 | 51.12 N | 0.33 W |
| Wonewoc | 190 | 43.39 N | 90.13 W |
| Wong ≃ | 124 | 27.10 N | 89.30 E |
| Wongan Hills | 162 | 30.53 S | 116.42 E |
| Wonga Park | 274b | 37.44 S | 145.16 E |
| Wonga-Wongué, Parc National de ♦ | 152 | 0.30 S | 9.30 E |
| Wonggarasi | 112 | 0.33 N | 121.36 E |
| Wong Ka Wai | 271d | 22.24 N | 113.58 E |
| Woniushi | 104 | 42.31 N | 123.03 E |
| Wŏnjang-ni | 98 | 39.05 N | 125.32 E |
| Wŏnju | 98 | 37.22 N | 127.58 E |
| Wonogiri | 115a | 7.49 S | 110.55 E |
| Wonokromo | 115a | 7.18 S | 112.44 E |
| Wonosari | 115a | 7.58 S | 110.35 E |
| Wonosegoro | 115a | 7.18 S | 110.39 E |
| Wonosobo | 115a | 7.22 S | 109.54 E |
| Wonotobo Vallen ⌞ | 250 | 4.22 N | 57.58 W |
| Wonreli | 112 | 8.05 S | 127.09 E |
| Wŏnsan | 98 | 39.09 N | 127.25 E |
| Wonthaggi | 169 | 38.36 S | 145.35 E |
| Woocalla | 166 | 31.42 S | 137.13 E |
| Wood, Pa., U.S. | 214 | 40.10 N | 78.08 W |
| Wood, S.D., U.S. | 198 | 43.29 N | 100.28 W |
| Wood □[6], Oh., U.S. | 216 | 41.22 N | 83.39 W |
| Wood □[6], Tx., U.S. | 222 | 32.48 N | 95.20 W |
| Wood ≃, B.C., Can. | 182 | 52.10 N | 118.30 W |
| Wood ≃, Sk., Can. | 184 | 50.08 N | 106.10 W |
| Wood ≃, U.S. | 207 | 41.26 N | 71.43 W |
| Wood ≃, Ak., U.S. | 180 | 64.35 N | 148.41 W |
| Wood ≃, Ne., U.S. | 198 | 41.02 N | 98.05 W |
| Wood ≃, Wy., U.S. | 202 | 44.07 N | 108.58 W |
| Wood, Mount ∧, Yk., Can. | 180 | 61.14 N | 140.31 W |
| Wood, Mount ∧, Mt., U.S. | 202 | 45.17 N | 109.49 W |
| Woodacre | 226 | 38.05 N | 122.36 W |
| Woodall Mountain ∧[2] | 194 | 34.45 N | 88.11 W |
| Wood Bay c | 180 | 69.45 N | 129.00 W |
| Woodberry Forest | 284c | 38.48 N | 76.56 W |
| Woodbine, Ga., U.S. | 192 | 30.57 N | 81.43 W |
| Woodbine, Ia., U.S. | 198 | 41.44 N | 95.42 W |
| Woodbine, Md., U.S. | 208 | 39.21 N | 77.03 W |
| Woodbine, N.J., U.S. | 208 | 39.14 N | 74.48 W |
| Woodbourne, N.Y., U.S. | 210 | 41.45 N | 74.35 W |
| Woodbourne, Oh., U.S. | 218 | 39.38 N | 84.10 W |
| Woodbourne, Pa., U.S. | 285 | 40.12 N | 74.53 W |
| Woodbridge, Eng., U.K. | 42 | 52.06 N | 1.19 E |
| Woodbridge, Ca., U.S. | 226 | 38.09 N | 121.18 W |
| Woodbridge, Ct., U.S. | 207 | 41.21 N | 73.00 W |
| Woodbridge, N.J., U.S. | 210 | 40.33 N | 74.17 W |
| Woodbridge, Va., U.S. | 208 | 38.39 N | 77.15 W |
| Woodbridge Center -•-[9] | 276 | 40.33 N | 74.18 W |
| Woodbridge Creek ≃ | 276 | 40.32 N | 74.15 W |
| Woodbridge Island I | 283 | 42.48 N | 70.50 W |
| Woodburn, Il., U.S. | 219 | 39.03 N | 90.00 W |
| Woodburn, In., U.S. | 216 | 41.07 N | 84.51 W |
| Woodburn, Or., U.S. | 224 | 45.08 N | 122.51 W |
| Woodbury, Eng., U.K. | 42 | 50.41 N | 3.24 W |
| Woodbury, Ct., U.S. | 207 | 41.32 N | 73.12 W |
| Woodbury, Ga., U.S. | 192 | 32.59 N | 84.34 W |
| Woodbury, Mi., U.S. | 216 | 42.46 N | 85.05 W |
| Woodbury, N.J., U.S. | 208 | 39.50 N | 75.09 W |
| Woodbury, N.Y., U.S. | 276 | 40.49 N | 73.28 W |
| Woodbury, Pa., U.S. | 214 | 40.14 N | 78.22 W |
| Woodbury, Tn., U.S. | 194 | 35.49 N | 86.04 W |
| Woodbury Creek ≃ | 285 | 39.52 N | 75.11 W |
| Woodbury Heights | 285 | 39.49 N | 75.09 W |
| Woodchester | 168b | 35.13 S | 138.57 E |
| Woodchopper | 180 | 65.18 N | 143.25 W |
| Woodchurch | 42 | 51.05 N | 0.46 E |
| Woodcliff Lake | 276 | 41.01 N | 74.04 W |
| Woodcliff Lake ⊜ | 276 | 41.01 N | 74.03 W |
| Woodcock | 214 | 41.45 N | 80.05 W |
| Woodcock, Mount ∧ | 162 | 19.16 S | 134.02 E |
| Woodcrest, Ca., U.S. | 228 | 33.52 N | 117.21 W |
| Woodcrest, Pa., U.S. | 285 | 39.59 N | 75.35 W |
| Wood Dale | 278 | 41.57 N | 87.58 W |
| Woodenbong | 166 | 28.23 S | 152.37 E |
| Woodend | 169 | 37.22 S | 144.32 E |
| Woodfibre | 182 | 49.40 N | 123.15 W |
| Woodfield -•-[9] | 278 | 42.03 N | 88.03 W |
| Woodford, Austl. | 171a | 26.57 S | 152.47 E |
| Woodford, Ire. | 48 | 53.03 N | 8.23 W |
| Woodford, Eng., U.K. | 262 | 53.21 N | 2.10 W |
| Woodford □[6], Il., U.S. | 216 | 40.43 N | 89.16 W |
| Woodford □[6], Ky., U.S. | 218 | 38.06 N | 84.15 W |
| Woodford -•-[8] | 260 | 51.36 N | 0.02 E |
| Woodford Aerodrome ⊠ | 262 | 53.20 N | 2.09 W |
| Woodford Bridge -•-[8] | 260 | 51.36 N | 0.04 E |
| Woodford Halse | 42 | 52.10 N | 1.12 W |
| Wood Green -•-[8] | 260 | 51.36 N | 0.07 W |
| Woodhall Spa | 44 | 53.09 N | 0.13 W |
| Woodham | 260 | 51.21 N | 0.30 W |
| Woodham Ferrers | 260 | 51.40 N | 0.36 E |
| Woodham Mortimer | 260 | 51.43 N | 0.37 E |
| Woodham Walter | 260 | 51.44 N | 0.37 E |
| Woodhaven | 216 | 42.08 N | 83.14 W |
| Woodhaven -•-[8] | 276 | 40.41 N | 73.51 W |
| Woodhead Reservoir ⊜[1] | 262 | 53.30 N | 1.52 W |
| Woodhill | 275b | 43.45 N | 79.41 W |
| Wood Hill ∧[2] | 283 | 42.39 N | 71.13 W |
| Woodhull, Il., U.S. | 190 | 41.10 N | 90.18 W |
| Woodhull, N.Y., U.S. | 210 | 42.05 N | 77.25 W |
| Woodinville | 224 | 47.45 N | 122.09 W |
| Wood Islands | 186 | 45.58 N | 62.45 W |
| Woodlake, Ca., U.S. | 204 | 36.25 N | 119.06 W |
| Wood Lake, Ne., U.S. | 198 | 42.38 N | 100.14 W |
| Woodlake, Tx., U.S. | 222 | 31.01 N | 95.02 W |
| Wood Lake ⊜, On., Can. | 212 | 45.01 N | 79.05 W |
| Wood Lake ⊜, Sk., Can. | 184 | 55.17 N | 103.17 W |
| Woodland, Ca., U.S. | 226 | 38.40 N | 121.46 W |
| Woodland, Ga., U.S. | 192 | 32.47 N | 84.33 W |
| Woodland, Il., U.S. | 216 | 40.43 N | 87.44 W |
| Woodland, Me., U.S. | 188 | 45.09 N | 67.24 W |
| Woodland, Mi., U.S. | 216 | 42.43 N | 85.08 W |
| Woodland, N.C., U.S. | 192 | 36.19 N | 77.12 W |
| Woodland, Pa., U.S. | 214 | 40.59 N | 78.20 W |
| Woodland, Wa., U.S. | 224 | 45.54 N | 122.44 W |
| Woodland Beach | 216 | 41.57 N | 83.19 W |
| Woodland Heights | 214 | 41.25 N | 79.43 W |
| Woodland Hills -•-[8] | 280 | 34.11 N | 118.35 W |
| Woodland Hills Park ♦ | 279a | 41.28 N | 81.36 W |
| Woodland Park, Co., U.S. | 200 | 38.59 N | 105.03 W |
| Woodland Park, Pa., U.S. | 210 | 41.18 N | 77.03 W |
| Woodlands, N.Z. | 172 | 46.22 S | 168.33 E |
| Woodlands, Sing. | 271c | 1.27 N | 103.46 E |
| Woodlands, N.Y., U.S. | 276 | 41.01 N | 73.50 W |
| Woodlawn, Il., U.S. | 219 | 38.20 N | 89.02 W |
| Woodlawn, Ky., U.S. | 194 | 37.02 N | 88.34 W |
| Woodlawn, Md., U.S. | 284b | 39.19 N | 76.43 W |
| Woodlawn, Md., U.S. | 284c | 38.57 N | 76.53 W |
| Woodlawn, Wa., U.S. | 224 | 47.01 N | 123.48 W |
| Woodlawn -•-[8] | 278 | 41.47 N | 87.36 W |
| Woodlawn Beach | 210 | 42.48 N | 78.51 W |
| Woodlawn Heights | 284b | 39.11 N | 76.39 W |
| Woodley | 42 | 51.28 N | 0.54 W |
| Woodlyn | 285 | 39.52 N | 75.20 W |
| Woodlynne | 285 | 39.55 N | 75.05 W |
| Woodmansey | 44 | 53.50 N | 0.29 W |
| Woodmansterne | 260 | 51.19 N | 0.10 W |
| Woodmere, N.Y., U.S. | 210 | 40.37 N | 73.42 W |
| Woodmere, Oh., U.S. | 279a | 41.28 N | 81.29 W |
| Woodmoor | 284b | 39.20 N | 76.44 W |
| Wood Mountain ∧ | 184 | 49.14 N | 106.20 W |
| Wood Mountain Indian Reserve -•-[4] | 184 | 49.21 N | 106.24 W |
| Woodplumpton | 262 | 53.48 N | 2.47 W |
| Woodport | 276 | 40.59 N | 74.36 W |
| Woodrarung Range ⋏ | 162 | 27.10 S | 115.30 E |
| Woodridge, Austl. | 171a | 27.38 S | 153.06 E |
| Woodridge, Mb., Can. | 184 | 49.17 N | 96.09 W |
| Woodridge, Il., U.S. | 216 | 41.44 N | 88.03 W |
| Wood-Ridge, N.J., U.S. | 276 | 40.50 N | 74.05 W |
| Woodridge, N.Y., U.S. | 210 | 41.43 N | 74.34 W |
| Wood River, Ak., U.S. | 180 | 59.04 N | 158.26 W |
| Wood River, Il., U.S. | 219 | 38.51 N | 90.05 W |
| Wood River, Ne., U.S. | 198 | 40.49 N | 98.35 W |
| Wood River Lakes ⊜ | 180 | 59.30 N | 158.45 W |
| Wood River Mountains ⋏ | 180 | 59.32 N | 159.30 W |
| Woodroffe ≃ | 166 | 21.28 S | 137.58 E |
| Woodroffe, Mount ∧ | 162 | 26.20 S | 131.45 E |
| Woodrow | 192 | 35.08 N | 77.05 W |
| Woodrow Wilson Memorial Bridge -•-[5] | 284c | 38.48 N | 77.02 W |
| Woodruff, Az., U.S. | 200 | 34.46 N | 110.02 W |
| Woodruff, S.C., U.S. | 192 | 34.44 N | 82.02 W |
| Woodruff, Wi., U.S. | 190 | 45.53 N | 89.41 W |
| Woodruff Creek ≃ | 281 | 42.21 N | 83.43 W |
| Woods | 168b | 34.15 S | 138.31 E |
| Woods, Lake ⊜ | 162 | 17.50 S | 133.30 E |
| Woods, Lake of the ⊜ | 184 | 49.15 N | 94.45 W |
| Woods Bay c | 212 | 45.08 N | 80.00 W |
| Woodsboro, Md., U.S. | 208 | 39.31 N | 77.18 W |
| Woodsboro, Tx., U.S. | 196 | 28.14 N | 97.19 W |
| Woodsburgh | 276 | 40.37 N | 73.42 W |
| Woods Creek ≃, N.Y., U.S. | 276 | 40.39 N | 73.24 W |
| Woods Creek ≃, N.Y., U.S. | 284a | 43.04 N | 78.58 W |
| Woodsfield | 188 | 39.45 N | 81.06 W |
| Woods Hole | 207 | 41.31 N | 70.40 W |
| Woodside, Austl. | 166 | 38.31 S | 146.52 E |
| Woodside, Austl. | 168b | 34.57 S | 138.52 E |
| Woodside, Eng., U.K. | 260 | 51.45 N | 0.11 W |
| Woodside, Ca., U.S. | 226 | 37.25 N | 122.15 W |
| Woodside, De., U.S. | 208 | 39.04 N | 75.34 W |
| Woodside, Pa., U.S. | 285 | 40.13 N | 74.53 W |
| Woodside -•-[8] | 276 | 40.45 N | 73.55 W |
| Woodside National Historic Park ♦ | 212 | 43.26 N | 80.08 W |
| Woodson, Il., U.S. | 219 | 39.38 N | 90.13 W |
| Woodson, Tx., U.S. | 196 | 33.01 N | 99.03 W |
| Woods Point | 169 | 37.35 S | 146.15 E |
| Woods Reservoir ⊜[1] | 194 | 35.20 N | 86.00 W |
| Woodstock, Austl. | 166 | 22.15 S | 141.57 E |
| Woodstock, N.B., Can. | 186 | 46.09 N | 67.34 W |
| Woodstock, On., Can. | 212 | 43.08 N | 80.45 W |
| Woodstock, Eng., U.K. | 42 | 51.52 N | 1.21 W |
| Woodstock, Ct., U.S. | 207 | 41.56 N | 71.58 W |
| Woodstock, Il., U.S. | 216 | 42.18 N | 88.26 W |
| Woodstock, Md., U.S. | 284b | 39.19 N | 76.52 W |
| Woodstock, N.Y., U.S. | 210 | 42.02 N | 74.07 W |
| Woodstock, Oh., U.S. | 218 | 40.10 N | 83.32 W |
| Woodstock, Vt., U.S. | 188 | 43.37 N | 72.31 W |
| Woodstock, Va., U.S. | 188 | 38.52 N | 78.30 W |
| Woodstown | 208 | 39.39 N | 75.19 W |
| Wood Street | 260 | 51.15 N | 0.38 W |
| Woodsville | 188 | 44.09 N | 72.02 W |
| Woodvale Airfield ⊠ | 262 | 53.35 N | 3.03 W |
| Wood Village | 224 | 45.32 N | 122.19 W |
| Woodville, Austl. | 168b | 34.53 S | 138.32 E |
| Woodville, On., Can. | 212 | 44.24 N | 78.59 W |
| Woodville, N.Z. | 172 | 40.20 S | 175.52 E |
| Woodville, Al., U.S. | 194 | 34.38 N | 86.16 W |
| Woodville, Ca., U.S. | 226 | 36.06 N | 119.12 W |
| Woodville, Fl., U.S. | 192 | 30.20 N | 84.15 W |
| Woodville, Ga., U.S. | 192 | 33.40 N | 83.06 W |
| Woodville, Ma., U.S. | 207 | 42.14 N | 71.33 W |
| Woodville, Mi., U.S. | 216 | 43.39 N | 85.40 W |
| Woodville, Ms., U.S. | 194 | 31.06 N | 91.17 W |
| Woodville, N.Y., U.S. | 210 | 42.40 N | 77.22 W |
| Woodville, Oh., U.S. | 214 | 41.27 N | 83.21 W |
| Woodville, Tx., U.S. | 194 | 30.46 N | 94.24 W |
| Woodward, Ia., U.S. | 190 | 41.51 N | 93.55 W |
| Woodward, Ok., U.S. | 196 | 36.26 N | 99.23 W |
| Woodward, Pa., U.S. | 210 | 40.54 N | 77.21 W |
| Woodward Reservoir ⊜[1] | 226 | 37.51 N | 120.52 W |
| Woodway, Tx., U.S. | 222 | 31.30 N | 97.12 W |
| Woodway, Wa., U.S. | 224 | 47.47 N | 122.23 W |
| Woodworth, Oh., U.S. | 214 | 40.59 N | 80.40 W |
| Woodworth, Wi., U.S. | 216 | 42.34 N | 88.00 W |
| Woody ≃ | 184 | 52.30 N | 100.51 W |
| Woody Creek ≃ | 202 | 47.27 N | 106.21 W |
| Woody Head › | 166 | 29.22 S | 153.22 E |
| Woody Island | 180 | 57.47 N | 152.22 W |
| Wool | 42 | 50.41 N | 2.14 W |
| Woolacombe | 42 | 51.10 N | 4.13 W |
| Woolamai, Cape › | 169 | 38.34 S | 145.21 E |
| Wool Bay | 168b | 35.00 S | 137.45 E |
| Wooldridge | 158 | 33.13 S | 27.15 E |
| Wooler | 44 | 55.33 N | 2.01 W |
| Woolford | 208 | 38.30 N | 76.11 W |
| Woolgangie | 162 | 31.10 S | 120.32 E |
| Woolgoolga | 166 | 30.07 S | 153.12 E |
| Woollahra | 274a | 33.53 S | 151.15 E |
| Woolmarket | 194 | 30.28 N | 88.59 W |
| Woolooware Bay c | 274a | 34.02 S | 151.09 E |
| Woolpit | 42 | 52.13 N | 0.54 E |
| Woolrich | 210 | 41.12 N | 77.23 W |
| Woolsey Peak ∧ | 200 | 33.10 N | 112.53 W |
| Woolston | 262 | 53.24 N | 2.32 W |
| Woolton -•-[8] | 262 | 53.23 N | 2.52 W |
| Woolwich -•-[8] | 260 | 51.29 N | 0.04 E |
| Woomargama | 171b | 35.50 S | 147.15 E |
| Woomera | 166 | 31.31 S | 137.10 E |
| Woomera Prohibited Area -•-[4] | 162 | 29.45 S | 134.30 E |
| Woonona | 170 | 34.21 S | 150.55 E |
| Woonsocket, R.I., U.S. | 207 | 42.00 N | 71.30 W |
| Woonsocket, S.D., U.S. | 198 | 44.03 N | 98.16 W |
| Woorabinda | 166 | 24.08 S | 149.28 E |
| Wooramel | 162 | 25.44 S | 114.17 E |
| Wooramel ≃ | 162 | 25.47 S | 114.10 E |
| Woorim | 171a | 27.08 S | 153.12 E |
| Wooroloo | 168a | 31.48 S | 116.19 E |
| Wooster | 214 | 40.48 N | 81.56 W |
| Wootton | 42 | 52.11 N | 0.53 W |
| Wootton Bassett | 42 | 51.33 N | 1.54 W |
| Wootton Wawen | 42 | 52.16 N | 1.47 W |
| Woqooyi Galbeed □[4] | 144 | 10.00 N | 44.00 E |
| Worb | 58 | 46.56 N | 7.34 E |
| Worbis | 54 | 51.25 N | 10.21 E |
| Worcester, S. Afr. | 158 | 33.39 S | 19.27 E |
| Worcester, Eng., U.K. | 42 | 52.11 N | 2.13 W |
| Worcester, Ma., U.S. | 207 | 42.15 N | 71.48 W |
| Worcester, N.Y., U.S. | 210 | 42.35 N | 74.45 W |
| Worcester, Pa., U.S. | 285 | 40.12 N | 75.21 W |
| Worcester □[6], Md., U.S. | 208 | 38.11 N | 75.24 W |
| Worcester □[6], Ma., U.S. | 207 | 42.16 N | 71.48 W |
| Worcester Municipal Airport ⊠ | 207 | 42.16 N | 71.52 W |
| Worden, Il., U.S. | 219 | 38.55 N | 89.50 W |
| Worden, Mt., U.S. | 202 | 45.57 N | 108.09 W |
| Worden Pond ⊜ | 207 | 41.26 N | 71.35 W |
| Wördern | 61 | 48.20 N | 16.13 E |
| Wörgl | 64 | 47.29 N | 12.04 E |
| Workai, Pulau I | 164 | 6.40 S | 134.40 E |
| Work Channel ꓵ | 182 | 54.30 N | 130.15 W |
| Workers' Stadium ♦ | 271a | 39.55 N | 116.27 E |
| Workington | 44 | 54.39 N | 3.35 W |
| Worksop | 44 | 53.18 N | 1.07 W |
| Workum | 52 | 52.57 N | 5.26 E |
| Worland | 202 | 44.01 N | 107.57 W |
| World End Pond ⊜ | 283 | 42.45 N | 71.12 W |
| Worli -•-[8] | 272c | 19.01 N | 72.50 E |
| Wörlitz | 54 | 51.50 N | 12.25 E |
| Wormerveer | 52 | 52.28 N | 4.46 E |
| Wormhoudt | 50 | 50.53 N | 2.28 E |
| Wormit | 46 | 56.25 N | 2.59 W |
| Wormley | 260 | 51.44 N | 0.01 W |
| Worms | 56 | 49.38 N | 8.22 E |
| Worms Head › | 42 | 51.34 N | 4.20 W |
| Wormshill | 260 | 51.17 N | 0.42 E |
| Wörnitz ≃ | 56 | 48.42 N | 10.45 E |
| Woronesch → Voronež | 78 | 51.40 N | 39.10 E |
| Woronoco | 207 | 42.09 N | 72.49 W |
| Woronora | 274a | 34.01 S | 151.03 E |
| Woronora ≃ | 274a | 34.00 S | 151.04 E |
| Woronora Reservoir ⊜[1] | 170 | 34.08 S | 150.56 E |
| Worplesdon | 260 | 51.16 N | 0.37 W |
| Worpswede | 52 | 53.13 N | 8.56 E |
| Wörrstadt | 56 | 49.50 N | 8.07 E |
| Wörsbach ≃ | 56 | 50.22 N | 8.09 E |
| Worsbrough | 44 | 53.31 N | 1.29 W |
| Worsley | 262 | 53.30 N | 2.23 W |
| Worsthorne | 262 | 53.47 N | 2.11 W |
| Wörth, Dtsch. | 60 | 48.15 N | 11.54 E |
| Worth, Dtsch. | 263 | 51.13 N | 7.39 E |
| Worth, Il., U.S. | 216 | 41.41 N | 87.47 W |
| Worth, Lake ⊜[1] | 222 | 32.48 N | 97.28 W |
| Wortham | 222 | 31.47 N | 96.27 W |
| Wörth am Rhein | 56 | 49.03 N | 8.16 E |
| Wörth an der Donau | 60 | 49.00 N | 12.25 E |
| Wörth an der Isar | 60 | 48.37 N | 12.24 E |
| Worthen | 42 | 52.38 N | 3.00 W |
| Wörther See ⊜ | 61 | 46.37 N | 14.10 E |
| Worthing | 42 | 50.48 N | 0.23 W |
| Worthington, In., U.S. | 194 | 39.07 N | 86.58 W |
| Worthington, Md., U.S. | 284b | 39.14 N | 76.47 W |
| Worthington, Mn., U.S. | 198 | 43.37 N | 95.35 W |
| Worthington, N.Y., U.S. | 276 | 41.02 N | 73.50 W |
| Worthington, Oh., U.S. | 214 | 40.05 N | 83.01 W |
| Worthington, Pa., U.S. | 214 | 40.50 N | 79.37 W |
| Worthington Peak ∧ | 204 | 37.55 N | 115.37 W |
| Wörthsee ⊜ | 60 | 48.03 N | 11.10 E |
| Worthville, Ky., U.S. | 218 | 38.36 N | 85.04 W |
| Worthville, Pa., U.S. | 214 | 41.02 N | 79.08 W |
| Worton | 208 | 39.16 N | 76.05 W |
| Wŏrun-dong | 98 | 39.36 N | 125.20 E |
| Wosimi | 164 | 2.54 S | 134.31 E |
| Wostok → Vostok ᵿ[3] | 9 | 78.30 S | 106.50 E |
| Wosu | 112 | 2.21 S | 121.50 E |
| Wotap, Pulau I | 164 | 7.21 S | 131.16 E |
| Wotho I[1] | 14 | 10.06 N | 165.59 E |
| Wotje I[1] | 14 | 9.27 N | 170.02 E |
| Wotton, P.Q., Can. | 206 | 45.44 N | 71.48 W |
| Wotton, Eng., U.K. | 260 | 51.13 N | 0.23 W |
| Wotton-under-Edge | 42 | 51.39 N | 2.21 W |
| Wotu | 112 | 2.35 S | 120.48 E |
| Woudenberg | 52 | 52.05 N | 5.25 E |
| Woudrichem | 52 | 51.49 N | 5.00 E |
| Woudsend | 52 | 52.56 N | 5.36 E |
| Wouldham | 260 | 51.21 N | 0.28 E |
| Wounded Knee | 198 | 43.08 N | 102.21 W |
| Wounded Knee Creek ≃ | 198 | 43.26 N | 102.32 W |
| Wounta | 236 | 13.33 N | 83.32 W |
| Wounta, Laguna de c | 236 | 13.38 N | 83.34 W |
| Wour | 146 | 21.21 N | 15.57 E |
| Wouri ≃ | 152 | 4.06 N | 9.43 E |
| Woutchaba | 152 | 5.13 N | 13.05 E |
| Wouw | 52 | 51.32 N | 4.24 E |
| Wowan | 166 | 23.55 S | 150.12 E |
| Wowoni, Pulau I | 112 | 4.08 S | 123.06 E |
| Woyla ≃ | 114 | 4.18 N | 95.56 E |
| Woy Woy | 170 | 33.30 S | 151.20 E |
| Woźniki | 30 | 50.36 N | 19.03 E |
| Wragby | 44 | 53.18 N | 0.19 W |
| Wrangel Island → Vrangel'a, ostrov I | 74 | 71.00 N | 179.30 W |
| Wrangell | 180 | 56.28 N | 132.23 W |
| Wrangell, Cape › | 181a | 52.50 N | 172.26 E |
| Wrangell, Mount ∧ | 180 | 62.00 N | 144.06 W |
| Wrangell Island I | 180 | 56.15 N | 132.10 W |
| Wrangell Mountains ⋏ | 180 | 62.00 N | 143.00 W |
| Wrangell-Saint Elias National Park ♦ | 180 | 61.00 N | 142.00 W |
| Wrath, Cape › | 46 | 58.37 N | 5.01 W |
| Wray | 198 | 40.04 N | 102.13 W |
| Wraysbury | 260 | 51.27 N | 0.33 W |
| Wrea Green | 262 | 53.46 N | 2.55 W |
| Wreck Bay c | 170 | 35.11 S | 150.40 E |
| Wreck Island I | 208 | 37.16 N | 75.48 W |
| Wreck Reef ✣[2] | 166 | 22.13 S | 155.17 E |
| Wrecks, Bay of c | 174o | 1.52 N | 157.17 W |
| Wredenhagen | 54 | 53.17 N | 12.31 E |
| Wremen | 52 | 53.39 N | 8.30 E |
| Wren | 216 | 40.48 N | 84.46 W |
| Wrens | 192 | 33.12 N | 82.23 W |
| Wrentham, Ab., Can. | 182 | 49.32 N | 112.10 W |
| Wrentham, Eng., U.K. | 42 | 52.23 N | 1.40 E |
| Wrentham, Ma., U.S. | 207 | 42.04 N | 71.19 W |
| Wrentham State Forest ♦ | 283 | 42.02 N | 71.20 W |
| Wrexham | 44 | 53.03 N | 3.00 W |
| Wriedel | 52 | 53.02 N | 10.18 E |
| Wriezen | 54 | 52.43 N | 14.08 E |
| Wright, Mount ∧, Austl. | 166 | 31.12 S | 142.26 E |
| Wright, Mount ∧, Mt., U.S. | 202 | 47.58 N | 112.49 W |
| Wright Brothers National Memorial ⊥ | 192 | 35.55 N | 75.50 W |
| Wright City, Mo., U.S. | 219 | 38.49 N | 91.01 W |
| Wright City, Ok., U.S. | 194 | 34.03 N | 95.00 W |
| Wright City, Tx., U.S. | 222 | 32.12 N | 94.59 W |
| Wrightington Bar | 262 | 53.37 N | 2.42 W |
| Wright Patman Lake ⊜[1] | 194 | 33.16 N | 94.14 W |
| Wright-Patterson Air Force Base ■ | 218 | 39.49 N | 84.03 W |
| Wright Peak ∧ | 204 | 38.59 N | 122.46 W |
| Wrights | 219 | 39.23 N | 90.18 W |
| Wrightsboro | 222 | 29.22 N | 97.34 W |
| Wrights Corners | 210 | 43.13 N | 78.46 W |
| Wrightson, Mount ∧ | 200 | 31.42 N | 110.50 W |
| Wrightstown, N.J., U.S. | 208 | 40.02 N | 74.37 W |
| Wrightstown, Pa., U.S. | 208 | 40.17 N | 74.58 W |
| Wrightstown, Wi., U.S. | 190 | 44.19 N | 88.09 W |
| Wrightsville, Ga., U.S. | 192 | 32.43 N | 82.43 W |
| Wrightsville, Pa., U.S. | 214 | 40.01 N | 76.31 W |
| Wrightsville Beach | 192 | 34.12 N | 77.47 W |
| Wrightwood | 228 | 34.21 N | 117.37 W |
| Wrigley, N.T., Can. | 180 | 63.16 N | 123.37 W |
| Wrigley, Tn., U.S. | 194 | 35.54 N | 87.20 W |
| Wrigley Field ♦ | 278 | 41.57 N | 87.39 W |
| Wrigley Gulf c | 9 | 74.00 S | 129.00 W |
| Writtle | 42 | 51.44 N | 0.26 E |
| Wrocław (Breslau) | 30 | 51.06 N | 17.00 E |
| Wrocław □[4] | 30 | 51.15 N | 17.00 E |
| Wrong Lake ⊜ | 184 | 52.38 N | 96.10 W |
| Wronki | 30 | 52.43 N | 16.23 E |
| Wrotham | 42 | 51.19 N | 0.19 E |
| Wrotham Heath | 260 | 51.18 N | 0.21 E |
| Wrottesley, Cape › | 176 | 74.33 N | 121.32 W |
| Wroughton | 42 | 51.31 N | 1.46 W |
| Wroxham | 42 | 52.42 N | 1.24 E |
| Wroxton | 184 | 51.14 N | 101.53 W |
| Września | 30 | 52.20 N | 17.34 E |
| Wschowa | 30 | 51.48 N | 16.19 E |
| Wu ≃, Zhg. | 98 | 34.25 N | 117.55 E |
| Wu ≃, Zhg. | 100 | 28.57 N | 116.39 E |
| Wu ≃, Zhg. | 100 | 24.48 N | 113.35 E |
| Wu ≃, Zhg. | 102 | 27.12 N | 109.48 E |
| Wu ≃, Zhg. | 102 | 29.43 N | 107.24 E |
| Wu ≃, Zhg. | 102 | 27.03 N | 109.53 E |
| Wu'an | 98 | 36.40 N | 114.12 E |
| Wubaozhen | 107 | 29.14 N | 104.29 E |
| Wubin | 162 | 30.06 S | 116.38 E |
| Wubu | 102 | 37.33 N | 110.39 E |
| Wuchagou | 89 | 46.46 N | 120.16 E |
| Wuchang, Zhg. | 89 | 44.54 N | 127.08 E |
| Wuchang → Wuhan, Zhg. | 100 | 30.36 N | 114.17 E |
| Wuchang Hu ⊜ | 100 | 30.17 N | 116.47 E |
| Wucheng, Zhg. | 98 | 37.09 N | 115.53 E |
| Wucheng (Jiucheng), Zhg. | 98 | 37.13 N | 116.02 E |
| Wucheng, Zhg. | 100 | 29.36 N | 118.10 E |
| Wucheng, Zhg. | 100 | 33.28 N | 113.44 E |
| Wucheng, Zhg. | 100 | 29.10 N | 115.59 E |
| Wuch'i | 100 | 24.16 N | 120.31 E |
| Wuchin → Changzhou | 106 | 31.47 N | 119.57 E |
| Wuch'iu Yü I | 100 | 25.00 N | 119.27 E |
| Wuchow → Wuzhou | 102 | 23.30 N | 111.27 E |
| Wuchuan, Zhg. | 102 | 41.05 N | 111.23 E |
| Wuchuan, Zhg. | 102 | 21.25 N | 110.40 E |
| Wuchuan, Zhg. | 102 | 28.25 N | 107.56 E |
| Wuchung → Wuzhong | 102 | 37.57 N | 106.10 E |
| Wucun | 105 | 38.57 N | 115.19 E |
| Wuda | 102 | 39.30 N | 106.40 E |
| Wudao | 98 | 39.28 N | 121.28 E |
| Wudaogou, Zhg. | 98 | 41.43 N | 127.05 E |
| Wudaogou, Zhg. | 98 | 42.08 N | 125.51 E |
| Wudaoliang | 120 | 35.11 N | 93.35 E |
| Wudaolianggou | 104 | 40.59 N | 120.35 E |
| Wudi | 98 | 37.44 N | 117.35 E |
| Wudian, Zhg. | 100 | 32.42 N | 117.18 E |
| Wudian, Zhg. | 100 | 31.57 N | 112.46 E |
| Wuding | 102 | 25.32 N | 102.23 E |
| Wuding ≃ | 102 | 37.05 N | 110.20 E |
| Wudinna | 166 | 33.03 S | 135.28 E |
| Wudu, Zhg. | 100 | 28.23 N | 118.14 E |
| Wudu, Zhg. | 100 | 27.37 N | 119.00 E |
| Wudu, Zhg. | 102 | 33.24 N | 104.50 E |
| Wuduhe | 102 | 31.03 N | 111.03 E |
| Wuerqihan | 89 | 49.37 N | 121.45 E |
| Wufeng | 102 | 30.11 N | 110.33 E |
| Wufeng Shan I | 106 | 31.07 N | 120.16 E |
| Wufengxi | 107 | 30.37 N | 104.29 E |
| Wufu | 100 | 30.06 N | 120.58 E |
| Wugang | 102 | 26.44 N | 110.38 E |
| Wugong | 102 | 34.20 N | 108.04 E |
| Wugong Shan ∧ | 100 | 27.35 N | 114.18 E |
| Wugong Shan ⋏ | 100 | 27.21 N | 113.50 E |
| Wugouying | 100 | 33.28 N | 114.08 E |
| Wugunuoer | 89 | 49.10 N | 119.19 E |
| Wuhai | 102 | 39.39 N | 106.41 E |
| Wuhan | 100 | 30.36 N | 114.17 E |
| Wuhe, Zhg. | 100 | 33.10 N | 117.54 E |
| Wuhe, Zhg. | 100 | 24.26 N | 115.25 E |
| Wuhle ≃ | 264a | 52.29 N | 13.34 E |
| Wuhsi → Wuxi | 106 | 31.35 N | 120.18 E |
| Wuhsing → Huzhou | 106 | 30.52 N | 120.06 E |
| Wuhu, Zhg. | 100 | 31.21 N | 118.22 E |
| Wuhu, Zhg. | 100 | 31.11 N | 118.35 E |
| Wuhua | 100 | 23.57 N | 115.48 E |
| Wuhuanchi | 104 | 42.20 N | 121.51 E |
| Wuhuang | 107 | 29.58 N | 104.46 E |
| Wuhudongmiao | 102 | 38.19 N | 107.20 E |
| Wüjang | 120 | 33.38 N | 79.50 E |
| Wuji, Zhg. | 98 | 38.13 N | 114.57 E |
| Wuji, Zhg. | 98 | 34.12 N | 119.02 E |
| Wujia ≃ | 102 | 41.10 N | 108.45 E |
| Wujiabeigou | 104 | 40.57 N | 123.50 E |
| Wujiang, Zhg. | 100 | 31.52 N | 118.28 E |
| Wujiang, Zhg. | 100 | 27.14 N | 115.15 E |
| Wujiang, Zhg. | 106 | 31.10 N | 120.38 E |
| Wujiangdu | 102 | 27.16 N | 106.48 E |
| Wujianpu | 107 | 29.10 N | 105.50 E |
| Wujiapai | 105 | 39.32 N | 117.18 E |
| Wujiapu | 105 | 38.52 N | 117.07 E |
| Wujiazhen | 107 | 29.38 N | 105.24 E |
| Wujiazhuang, Zhg. | 105 | 40.35 N | 115.20 E |
| Wujiazhuang, Zhg. | 106 | 32.18 N | 120.10 E |
| Wujiazi, Zhg. | 89 | 46.27 N | 123.34 E |
| Wujiazi, Zhg. | 104 | 42.13 N | 122.08 E |
| Wujiazi, Zhg. | 104 | 42.30 N | 121.10 E |
| Wujing | 100 | 25.16 N | 114.36 E |
| Wukang | 106 | 30.33 N | 119.58 E |
| Wukari | 150 | 7.51 N | 9.47 E |
| Wukeshu, Zhg. | 89 | 46.02 N | 123.45 E |
| Wukeshu, Zhg. | 89 | 44.48 N | 126.08 E |
| Wulai | 100 | 24.52 N | 121.33 E |
| Wulajia | 89 | 48.23 N | 129.58 E |
| Wulanheduojia | 102 | 42.40 N | 113.20 E |
| Wulanhutong | 98 | 41.44 N | 114.49 E |
| Wulanmutou | 104 | 42.23 N | 121.21 E |
| Wulanwusu, Zhg. | 86 | 44.20 N | 85.50 E |
| Wulanwusu, Zhg. | 102 | 41.39 N | 107.48 E |
| Wular Lake ⊜ | 123 | 34.20 N | 74.33 E |
| Wulasitai, Zhg. | 89 | 43.15 N | 121.27 E |
| Wulasitai, Zhg. | 89 | 43.28 N | 122.44 E |
| Wulateqianqi | 102 | 40.39 N | 109.05 E |
| Wulaxi | 102 | 28.38 N | 101.40 E |
| Wuleidao Wan c | 98 | 36.55 N | 122.00 E |
| Wulfen | 52 | 51.43 N | 7.00 E |
| Wülfrath | 56 | 51.17 N | 7.02 E |
| Wulfsen | 52 | 53.18 N | 10.08 E |
| Wulfsode | 52 | 53.04 N | 10.13 E |
| Wulften | 52 | 51.40 N | 10.10 E |
| Wulian (Hongning) | 98 | 35.47 N | 119.15 E |
| Wulian Feng ⋏ | 102 | 28.03 N | 103.57 E |
| Wuliangdian | 104 | 41.52 N | 122.16 E |
| Wuliang Shan ⋏ | 102 | 24.30 N | 100.45 E |
| Wuliaru, Pulau I | 164 | 7.27 S | 131.04 E |
| Wulichuan | 102 | 33.49 N | 111.08 E |
| Wulie ≃ | 105 | 40.54 N | 117.55 E |
| Wuling | 98 | 35.53 N | 114.36 E |
| Wuling Shan ∧ | 105 | 40.36 N | 117.29 E |
| Wulitaizi | 104 | 41.28 N | 123.21 E |
| Wulizhuang | 100 | 33.49 N | 118.57 E |
| Wulka ≃ | 61 | 47.52 N | 16.40 E |
| Wüllen | 52 | 52.04 N | 6.58 E |
| Wullwye Creek ≃ | 171b | 36.30 S | 148.49 E |
| Wulong, Zhg. | 102 | 29.20 N | 107.43 E |
| Wulong, Zhg. | 104 | 41.39 N | 124.13 E |
| Wulong ≃ | 98 | 36.35 N | 120.56 E |
| Wulongbei | 98 | 40.21 N | 124.16 E |
| Wulsdorf -•-[8] | 52 | 53.30 N | 8.35 E |
| Wultschau | 61 | 48.42 N | 14.50 E |
| Wulu ≃ | 85 | 39.38 N | 74.38 E |
| Wuluhan | 115a | 8.21 S | 113.33 E |
| Wuluhayingzi | 104 | 42.20 N | 121.34 E |
| Wulumuch'i → Ürümqi | 90 | 43.48 N | 87.35 E |
| Wulumuqi → Ürümqi | 90 | 43.48 N | 87.35 E |
| Wuluo | 102 | 26.09 N | 108.15 E |
| Wulur | 164 | 7.09 S | 128.39 E |
| Wulu Station -•-[5] | 271a | 39.56 N | 116.16 E |
| Wum | 152 | 6.23 N | 10.04 E |
| Wumang Dao I | 98 | 39.14 N | 123.03 E |
| Wumiaoxiang | 107 | 30.23 N | 104.17 E |
| Wuming | 102 | 23.10 N | 108.18 E |
| Wümme ≃ | 52 | 53.10 N | 8.44 E |
| Wunamu | 86 | 46.06 N | 85.44 E |
| Wundowie | 168a | 31.46 S | 116.22 E |
| Wundwin | 110 | 21.05 N | 96.02 E |
| Wuneba | 154 | 4.50 N | 30.20 E |
| Wungong Brook ≃ | 168a | 32.06 S | 115.59 E |
| Wuning | 100 | 29.17 N | 115.06 E |
| Wünnenberg | 52 | 51.31 N | 8.42 E |
| Wunnummin Lake ⊜ | 176 | 52.55 N | 89.10 W |
| Wun Rog | 140 | 9.00 N | 28.21 E |
| Wünschendorf | 54 | 50.48 N | 12.05 E |
| Wünsdorf | 54 | 52.10 N | 13.28 E |
| Wunsiedel | 60 | 50.02 N | 12.01 E |
| Wunstorf | 52 | 52.25 N | 9.26 E |
| Wuntho | 110 | 23.54 N | 95.41 E |
| Wunuer | 89 | 48.53 N | 121.15 E |
| Wupaowan | 107 | 29.50 N | 103.59 E |
| Wupatki National Monument ♦ | 200 | 35.24 N | 111.14 W |
| Wuping | 100 | 25.08 N | 116.06 E |
| Wupper ≃ | 263 | 51.05 N | 7.00 E |
| Wuppertal, Dtsch. | 56 | 51.16 N | 7.11 E |
| Wuppertal, Dtsch. | 263 | 51.16 N | 7.11 E |
| Wuppertal, S. Afr. | 158 | 32.15 S | 19.15 E |
| Wuqi, Zhg. | 100 | 27.10 N | 120.23 E |
| Wuqi, Zhg. | 102 | 37.08 N | 108.10 E |
| Wuqia | 85 | 39.42 N | 75.13 E |
| Wuqiang (Xiaofan) | 98 | 38.03 N | 115.58 E |
| Wuqing (Yangcun) | 105 | 39.23 N | 117.04 E |
| Wuraming | 168a | 32.48 S | 116.16 E |
| Wurarga | 162 | 28.25 S | 116.17 E |
| Würenlingen | 58 | 47.32 N | 8.16 E |
| Wurm ≃, Dtsch. | 56 | 51.08 N | 6.10 E |
| Würm ≃, Dtsch. | 56 | 48.53 N | 8.42 E |
| Würm ≃, Dtsch. | 60 | 48.10 N | 11.28 E |
| Wurmannsquick | 60 | 48.21 N | 12.47 E |
| Wurmberg ∧ | 54 | 51.45 N | 10.37 E |
| Wurno | 150 | 13.17 N | 5.24 E |
| Wurong | 164 | 6.07 S | 140.47 E |
| Würselen | 56 | 50.49 N | 6.08 E |
| Wursten, Land -•-[1] | 52 | 53.40 N | 8.35 E |
| Wurtsboro | 210 | 41.35 N | 74.29 W |
| Wurtsboro Hills | 210 | 41.36 N | 74.30 W |
| Wurtsmith Air Force Base ■ | 190 | 44.27 N | 83.23 W |
| Wuruf | 164 | 6.43 S | 146.25 E |
| Wuryantoro | 115a | 7.54 S | 110.51 E |
| Wurzbach | 54 | 50.28 N | 11.32 E |
| Würzburg | 56 | 49.48 N | 9.56 E |
| Wurzen | 54 | 51.22 N | 12.44 E |
| Wusanga | 152 | 3.22 S | 22.50 E |
| Wusha | 100 | 30.39 N | 117.18 E |
| Wushan, Zhg. | 100 | 32.04 N | 117.03 E |
| Wushan, Zhg. | 102 | 34.38 N | 105.04 E |
| Wushan, Zhg. | 102 | 31.05 N | 109.48 E |
| Wushan, Zhg. | 106 | 31.44 N | 118.58 E |
| Wusheng, Zhg. | 100 | 29.56 N | 119.25 E |
| Wusheng, Zhg. | 107 | 30.21 N | 106.17 E |
| Wushengchang | 107 | 29.00 N | 103.43 E |
| Wushenqi | 102 | 38.58 N | 109.01 E |
| Wushi, Zhg. | 102 | 22.11 N | 110.11 E |
| Wushi, Zhg. | 106 | 31.44 N | 120.59 E |
| Wushishi | 150 | 9.46 N | 6.07 E |
| Wushu | 100 | 26.20 N | 114.56 E |
| Wusi | 175f | 15.22 S | 166.36 E |
| Wusih → Wuxi | 106 | 31.35 N | 120.18 E |
| Wuskwatim Lake ⊜ | 184 | 55.32 N | 98.32 W |
| Wusong | 106 | 31.23 N | 121.29 E |
| Wusong ≃ | 106 | 31.15 N | 121.29 E |
| Wust | 54 | 52.33 N | 12.07 E |
| Wüsten | 52 | 52.06 N | 8.47 E |
| Wüstensachsen | 56 | 50.30 N | 10.00 E |
| Wusterhausen | 54 | 52.54 N | 12.28 E |
| Wusterhusen | 54 | 54.07 N | 13.37 E |
| Wustermark | 54 | 52.33 N | 12.56 E |
| Wüstermarke | 54 | 51.49 N | 13.36 E |
| Wusterwitz | 54 | 52.22 N | 12.18 E |
| Wüsting | 52 | 53.07 N | 8.20 E |
| Wustrau-Altfriesack | 54 | 52.51 N | 12.52 E |
| Wustrow, Dtsch. | 54 | 52.55 N | 11.07 E |
| Wustrow, Dtsch. | 54 | 54.05 N | 11.34 E |
| Wustrow ›[1] | 54 | 54.05 N | 11.34 E |
| Wusuli (Ussuri) ≃ | 89 | 48.27 N | 135.04 E |
| Wusuo | 100 | 25.02 N | 116.02 E |
| Wuta | 106 | 31.31 N | 120.39 E |
| Wutach ≃ | 58 | 47.37 N | 8.15 E |
| Wutai, Zhg. | 85 | 39.28 N | 78.09 E |
| Wutai, Zhg. | 86 | 44.36 N | 82.06 E |
| Wutai, Zhg. | 98 | 41.18 N | 113.59 E |
| Wutai, Zhg. | 102 | 38.44 N | 113.17 E |
| Wutai Shan ∧ | 98 | 39.04 N | 113.35 E |
| Wutai Shan ⋏ | 98 | 39.13 N | 113.45 E |
| Wutaizi | 104 | 42.27 N | 123.17 E |
| Wutan | 102 | 28.29 N | 111.40 E |
| Wutanchang | 107 | 29.15 N | 106.04 E |
| Wutang | 106 | 31.31 N | 119.10 E |
| Wutangdun | 106 | 30.38 N | 120.08 E |
| Wutangjie | 100 | 29.59 N | 122.22 E |
| Wuteve, Mount ∧ | 150 | 8.09 N | 9.56 W |
| Wutha-Farnroda | 54 | 50.56 N | 10.23 E |
| Wutianzhen | 100 | 30.23 N | 117.12 E |
| Wutong | 102 | 25.18 N | 110.01 E |
| Wutonghaolai | 89 | 42.55 N | 120.15 E |
| Wutongqiao | 107 | 29.26 N | 103.51 E |
| Wutongwozi | 102 | 42.27 N | 95.17 E |
| Wutöschingen | 58 | 47.40 N | 8.22 E |
| Wutsin → Changzhou | 106 | 31.47 N | 119.57 E |
| Wutun | 100 | 27.51 N | 118.04 E |
| Wut'ungch'iao → Wutongqiao | 107 | 29.26 N | 103.51 E |
| Wutungkiao → Wutongqiao | 107 | 29.26 N | 103.51 E |
| Wutuohuo | 102 | 40.51 N | 101.48 E |
| Wuustwezel | 50 | 51.23 N | 4.36 E |
| Wuvulu Island I | 164 | 1.45 S | 142.50 E |
| Wuwei, Zhg. | 100 | 31.18 N | 117.54 E |
| Wuwei (Liangzhou), Zhg. | 102 | 37.58 N | 102.49 E |
| Wuxi, Zhg. | 102 | 31.25 N | 109.34 E |
| Wuxi, Zhg. | 106 | 31.20 N | 118.39 E |
| Wuxi (Wuhsi), Zhg. | 106 | 31.35 N | 120.18 E |
| Wuxi ≃ | 100 | 29.00 N | 118.56 E |
| Wuxiang | 102 | 36.51 N | 113.00 E |
| Wuxingchang | 106 | 31.13 N | 119.23 E |
| Wuxuan | 102 | 23.36 N | 109.42 E |
| Wuyang, Zhg. | 100 | 33.26 N | 113.34 E |
| Wuyang, Zhg. | 100 | 25.41 N | 115.55 E |
| Wuyang, Zhg. | 102 | 26.41 N | 110.20 E |
| Wuyi, Zhg. | 98 | 37.49 N | 115.54 E |
| Wuyi, Zhg. | 100 | 32.13 N | 118.26 E |
| Wuyi, Zhg. | 100 | 28.54 N | 119.48 E |
| Wuying | 89 | 48.05 N | 129.15 E |
| Wuyi Shan ⋏ | 90 | 27.52 N | 117.40 E |
| Wuyuan, Zhg. | 100 | 29.15 N | 117.49 E |
| Wuyuan, Zhg. | 102 | 41.06 N | 108.29 E |
| Wuyun | 89 | 49.16 N | 129.37 E |
| Wuyunqiao | 100 | 26.02 N | 114.52 E |
| Wuyur ≃ | 89 | 47.00 N | 124.10 E |
| Wuzaizi | 104 | 42.28 N | 123.57 E |
| Wuzhai | 102 | 38.58 N | 111.55 E |
| Wuzhan | 89 | 45.51 N | 126.17 E |
| Wuzhen | 106 | 30.46 N | 120.29 E |
| Wuzhi Shan ∧, Zhg. | 105 | 40.29 N | 118.00 E |
| Wuzhi Shan ∧, Zhg. | 110 | 18.57 N | 109.43 E |
| Wuzhong | 102 | 38.00 N | 106.10 E |
| Wuzhou (Wuchow) | 102 | 23.30 N | 111.27 E |
| Wuzong | 106 | 32.14 N | 121.03 E |
| Wyaaba Creek ≃ | 164 | 16.27 S | 141.35 E |
| Wyaconda | 194 | 40.23 N | 91.55 W |
| Wyaconda ≃ | 194 | 40.04 N | 91.30 W |
| Wyalkatchem | 162 | 31.10 S | 117.22 E |
| Wyalusing | 210 | 41.40 N | 76.15 W |
| Wyalusing Creek ≃ | 210 | 41.40 N | 76.16 W |
| Wyandanch | 276 | 40.45 N | 73.21 W |
| Wyandot | 214 | 40.44 N | 83.08 W |
| Wyandot □[6] | 214 | 40.50 N | 83.17 W |
| Wyandotte | 216 | 42.12 N | 83.09 W |
| Wyandotte Cave ⊥[5] | 218 | 38.14 N | 86.18 W |
| Wyandotte National Wildlife Refuge -•-[4] | 281 | 42.14 N | 83.08 W |
| Wyandra | 166 | 27.15 S | 145.59 E |
| Wyangala, Lake ⊜[1] | 166 | 33.58 S | 148.55 E |
| Wyano | 214 | 40.12 N | 79.42 W |
| Wyatt, In., U.S. | 216 | 41.31 N | 86.10 W |
| Wyatt, Mo., U.S. | 194 | 36.54 N | 89.13 W |
| Wycheproof | 166 | 36.05 S | 143.14 E |
| Wychwood | 273d | 26.12 S | 28.08 E |
| Wyckoff | 210 | 41.00 N | 74.10 W |
| Wydgee | 162 | 28.51 S | 117.49 E |
| Wydgelee | 158 | 34.23 S | 20.26 E |
| Wy-Dit-Joli-Village | 261 | 49.06 N | 1.50 E |
| Wye | 42 | 51.11 N | 0.56 E |
| Wye ≃, On., Can. | 212 | 44.44 N | 79.52 W |
| Wye ≃, U.K. | 42 | 51.37 N | 2.39 W |
| Wye ≃, Eng., U.K. | 44 | 53.12 N | 1.37 W |
| Wyee | 170 | 33.11 S | 151.29 E |
| Wye Lake ⊜ | 212 | 44.43 N | 79.52 W |
| Wyemandoo ∧ | 162 | 28.31 S | 118.32 E |
| Wyeville | 190 | 44.01 N | 90.23 W |
| Wyhl | 58 | 48.09 N | 7.39 E |
| Wyhra ≃ | 54 | 51.09 N | 12.27 E |
| Wyk | 30 | 54.42 N | 8.34 E |
| Wyke Regis | 42 | 50.36 N | 2.29 W |
| Wykoff | 190 | 43.42 N | 92.16 W |
| Wylandville | 279b | 40.12 N | 80.08 W |
| Wyleswood Lake ⊜ | 279a | 41.20 N | 81.55 W |
| Wylie, Pa., U.S. | 279b | 40.27 N | 79.59 W |
| Wylie, Tx., U.S. | 222 | 33.01 N | 96.32 W |
| Wylie, Lake ⊜[1] | 192 | 35.07 N | 81.02 W |
| Wylye ≃ | 42 | 51.04 N | 1.52 W |
| Wymah | 171b | 36.02 S | 147.17 E |
| Wymark | 184 | 50.07 N | 107.44 W |
| Wymeswold | 42 | 52.47 N | 1.06 W |
| Wymondham | 42 | 52.34 N | 1.07 E |
| Wymore | 198 | 40.07 N | 96.39 W |
| Wynantskill | 210 | 42.42 N | 73.39 W |
| Wynberg | 158 | 34.02 S | 18.28 E |
| Wynbring | 162 | 30.33 S | 133.32 E |
| Wyncote | 285 | 40.05 N | 75.08 W |
| Wyndham, Austl. | 164 | 15.28 S | 128.06 E |
| Wyndham, N.Z. | 172 | 46.20 S | 168.51 E |
| Wyndmere | 198 | 46.16 N | 97.07 W |
| Wyndmoor | 285 | 40.04 N | 75.11 W |
| Wynigen | 58 | 47.06 N | 7.40 E |
| Wynndel | 182 | 49.11 N | 116.33 W |
| Wynne | 194 | 35.13 N | 90.47 W |
| Wynnewood, Ok., U.S. | 196 | 34.38 N | 97.09 W |
| Wynnewood, Pa., U.S. | 285 | 40.00 N | 75.16 W |
| Wynniatt Bay c | 176 | 72.55 N | 110.30 W |
| Wynnum | 171a | 27.27 S | 153.10 E |
| Wynona | 196 | 36.32 N | 96.19 W |
| Wynoochee ≃ | 224 | 46.58 N | 123.35 W |
| Wynoochee Lake ⊜[1] | 224 | 47.25 N | 123.35 W |
| Wynot | 198 | 42.44 N | 97.10 W |
| Wynyard, Austl. | 166 | 40.59 S | 145.41 E |
| Wynyard, Sk., Can. | 184 | 51.47 N | 104.10 W |
| Wyocena | 190 | 43.29 N | 89.18 W |
| Wyodak | 198 | 44.17 N | 105.22 W |
| Wyola Lake ⊜ | 162 | 29.08 S | 130.17 E |
| Wyoming, On., Can. | 190 | 42.57 N | 82.07 W |
| Wyoming, De., U.S. | 208 | 39.07 N | 75.33 W |
| Wyoming, Il., U.S. | 190 | 41.03 N | 89.46 W |
| Wyoming, Ia., U.S. | 190 | 42.03 N | 91.00 W |
| Wyoming, Mi., U.S. | 216 | 42.54 N | 85.42 W |
| Wyoming, N.Y., U.S. | 210 | 42.49 N | 78.05 W |
| Wyoming, Oh., U.S. | 218 | 39.13 N | 84.27 W |
| Wyoming, Pa., U.S. | 210 | 41.18 N | 75.50 W |
| Wyoming, R.I., U.S. | 207 | 41.30 N | 71.42 W |
| Wyoming □[6], N.Y., U.S. | 210 | 42.44 N | 78.08 W |
| Wyoming □[6], Pa., U.S. | 210 | 41.32 N | 75.57 W |
| Wyoming □[3] | 178 | 43.00 N | 107.30 W |
| Wyoming Peak ∧ | 200 | 42.36 N | 110.37 W |
| Wyomissing | 208 | 40.19 N | 75.57 W |
| Wyong | 170 | 33.17 S | 151.25 E |
| Wyong ≃ | 170 | 33.18 S | 151.28 E |
| Wyperfield National Park ♦ | 166 | 35.30 S | 142.00 E |
| Wyre ≃ | 44 | 53.55 N | 3.00 W |
| Wyreema | 171a | 27.39 S | 151.52 E |
| Wyre Forest -•-[3] | 42 | 52.23 N | 2.23 W |
| Wyrzysk | 30 | 53.10 N | 17.15 E |
| Wyśmierzyce | 30 | 51.38 N | 20.49 E |
| Wysoka | 30 | 53.11 N | 17.05 E |
| Wysokie Mazowieckie | 30 | 52.56 N | 22.32 E |
| Wysox | 210 | 41.46 N | 76.24 W |
| Wyszków | 30 | 52.36 N | 21.28 E |
| Wyszogród | 30 | 52.23 N | 20.11 E |
| Wythenshawe -•-[8] | 262 | 53.24 N | 2.17 W |
| Wythenshawe Hall ⊥ | 262 | 53.24 N | 2.17 W |
| Wytheville | 192 | 36.56 N | 81.05 W |
| Wytschegda → Vyčegda ≃ | 24 | 61.18 N | 46.36 E |
| Wyvis, Ben ∧ | 46 | 57.42 N | 4.35 W |
| **X** | | | |
| Xaafuun | 144 | 10.25 N | 51.16 E |
| Xaafuun, Raas › | 144 | 10.27 N | 51.24 E |
| Xàbia | 34 | 38.47 N | 0.10 E |
| Xabregas -•-[8] | 266c | 38.44 N | 9.07 W |
| Xá-Cassau | 152 | 9.02 S | 20.14 E |
| Xaçinçay ≃ | 84 | 40.13 N | 47.18 E |
| Xaclbal ≃ | 236 | 16.06 N | 90.58 W |
| Xaçmaz | 84 | 41.28 N | 48.48 E |
| Xaidulla | 120 | 36.21 N | 78.02 E |
| Xainza | 120 | 30.57 N | 88.38 E |
| Xaitongmoin | 124 | 29.22 N | 88.15 E |
| Xai-Xai | 156 | 25.02 S | 33.34 E |
| Xalapa | 234 | 19.32 N | 96.55 W |
| Xaldan | 84 | 40.43 N | 47.15 E |
| Xalin | 144 | 9.06 N | 48.37 E |
| Xalisco | 234 | 21.27 N | 104.54 W |
| Xallas ≃ | 34 | 42.54 N | 9.08 W |
| Xalostoc | 234 | 19.24 N | 98.03 W |
| Xalpatlahuac | 234 | 17.01 N | 99.18 W |
| Xaltianguis | 234 | 17.04 N | 99.50 W |
| Xam (Chu) ≃ | 110 | 19.53 N | 105.45 E |
| Xambioá | 250 | 6.25 S | 48.40 W |
| Xambrê ≃ | 255 | 24.02 S | 53.59 W |
| Xam Nua | 110 | 20.25 N | 104.02 E |
| Xá-Muteba | 152 | 9.34 S | 17.50 E |
| Xan (San) ≃ | 110 | 13.32 N | 105.58 E |
| Xang ≃ | 124 | 29.22 N | 89.09 E |
| Xangongo | 152 | 16.43 S | 15.01 E |


**Symbols** in the index entries represent the broad categories identified in the key at the right. Symbols with superior numbers (⋏[1]) identify subcategories (see complete key on page *I · 1)*.

**Symbole** im Register stellen die rechts im Schlüssel erklärten Kategorien dar. Symbole mit hochgestellten Ziffern (⋏[1]) bezeichnen Unterabteilungen einer Kategorie (vgl. vollständiger Schlüssel auf Seite *I · 1)*.

**Los símbolos** incluídos en el texto del índice representan las grandes categorías identificadas con la clave a la derecha. Los símbolos con numeros en su parte superior (⋏[1]) identifican las subcategorías (véase la clave completa en la página *I · 1)*.

**Les symboles** de l'index représentent les catégories indiquées dans la légende à droite. Les symboles suivis d'un indice (⋏[1]) représentent des sous-catégories (voir légende complète à la page *I · 1)*.

**Os símbolos** incluídos no texto do índice representam as grandes categorias identificadas com a chave à direita. Os símbolos com números em sua parte superior (⋏[1]) identificam as subcategorias (veja-se a chave completa à página *I · 1)*.

| | | | | |
|---|---|---|---|---|
| ∧ Mountain | Berg | Montaña | Montagne | Montanha |
| ⋏ Mountains | Gebirge | Montañas | Montagnes | Montanhas |
| )( Pass | Paß | Paso | Col | Passo |
| V Valley, Canyon | Tal, Cañon | Valle, Cañón | Vallée, Canyon | Vale, Canhão |
| ≚ Plain | Ebene | Llano | Plaine | Planície |
| › Cape | Kap | Cabo | Cap | Cabo |
| I Island | Insel | Isla | Île | Ilha |
| II Islands | Inseln | Islas | Îles | Ilhas |
| ⊥ Other Topographic Features | Andere Topographische Objekte | Otros Elementos Topográficos | Autres données topographiques | Outros acidentes topográficos |

ESPAÑOL — Nombre | Página | Lat.°' | Long.°' W = Oeste


Xankändi
 (Stepanakert) 84 39.49 N 46.44 E
Xanlar 84 40.34 N 46.20 E
Xanten 52 51.39 N 6.26 E
Xánthi 38 41.08 N 24.53 E
Xanxerê 252 26.53 S 52.23 W
Xapecó ≃ 252 27.06 S 53.01 W
Xapuri 248 10.39 S 68.31 W
Xapuri ≃ 248 10.39 S 68.30 W
Xarardheere 144 4.39 N 47.51 E
Xar Moron ≃, Zhg. 90 43.25 N 121.41 E
Xar Moron ≃, Zhg. 102 43.02 N 111.20 E
Xarrama ≃ 34 38.14 N 8.20 W
Xàtiva (Játiva) 34 38.59 N 0.31 W
Xau, Lake ⊜ 156 21.15 S 24.38 E
Xauen
 → Chaouen 148 35.10 N 5.16 W
Xavante ≃ 250 11.23 S 49.41 W
Xavantes ≃ 250 10.40 S 50.41 W
Xavantina 255 21.15 S 52.48 W
Xa Vo Dat 110 11.09 N 107.31 E
Xaxim 252 26.56 S 52.31 W
Xcalak 232 18.16 N 87.50 W
X-Can 232 20.50 N 87.43 W
Xelva 34 39.45 N 0.59 W
Xenia, Il., U.S. 219 38.38 N 88.38 W
Xenia, Oh., U.S. 218 39.41 N 83.55 W
Xénô 110 16.35 N 104.50 E
Xercavins, Arroyo de
 ≃ 266d 41.30 N 2.02 E
Xerém 256 22.33 S 43.18 W
Xeres
 → Jerez de la
 Frontera 34 36.41 N 6.08 W
Xertigny 58 48.03 N 6.24 E
Xeruã ≃ 248 6.03 S 67.50 W
Xhumo 156 21.07 S 24.42 E
Xi ≃, Zhg. 100 24.34 N 117.30 E
Xi ≃, Zhg. 100 25.14 N 118.03 E
Xi ≃, Zhg. 100 30.21 N 115.06 E
Xi ≃, Zhg. 102 42.20 N 100.20 E
Xi ≃, Zhg. 102 22.25 N 113.23 E
Xi ≃, Zhg. 104 41.15 N 123.32 E
Xi ≃, Zhg. 104 41.30 N 121.26 E
Xi ≃, Zhg. 107 30.26 N 103.48 E
Xiaang 106 30.45 N 120.07 E
Xiaba 100 24.54 N 116.06 E
Xiabai, Zhg. 106 31.12 N 119.50 E
Xiabai, Zhg. 106 30.29 N 120.00 E
Xiabanghu 100 30.31 N 112.38 E
Xiabian 104 40.51 N 120.30 E
Xiabuji 100 28.19 N 116.20 E
Xiacang 105 39.47 N 117.24 E
Xiache 100 24.40 N 115.08 E
Xiachengzi 89 44.41 N 130.27 E
Xiachuan Dao I 102 21.40 N 112.37 E
Xiacun 105 40.21 N 116.14 E
Xiadao 100 26.34 N 118.16 E
Xiadian, Zhg. 98 37.06 N 120.19 E
Xiadian, Zhg. 100 31.26 N 114.17 E
Xiadian, Zhg. 105 39.57 N 116.55 E
Xiadianjie 100 25.13 N 118.27 E
Xiafeidi 98 42.18 N 124.21 E
Xiafu, Zhg. 100 25.01 N 113.41 E
Xiafu, Zhg. 100 23.52 N 115.45 E
Xiagaixin 102 22.36 N 99.59 E
Xiagang 106 31.55 N 120.13 E
Xiagezhuang 98 36.41 N 120.25 E
Xiaguan, Zhg. 98 39.07 N 114.09 E
Xiaguan, Zhg. 102 25.34 N 100.14 E
Xiaguan, Zhg. 106 32.06 N 118.44 E
Xiaguanjunchang 104 41.28 N 121.40 E
Xiaguanpi 100 24.04 N 117.06 E
Xiagucheng 102 36.47 N 102.53 E
Xiagucun 106 30.56 N 119.09 E
Xiahada 104 41.58 N 124.08 E
Xiahailangzhai 104 41.35 N 123.46 E
Xiahe 102 35.18 N 102.30 E
Xiahuangjintun 104 41.57 N 123.48 E
Xiahuayuan 105 40.29 N 115.17 E
Xiajiabaozi 98 42.16 N 124.37 E
Xiajialou 104 42.25 N 123.39 E
Xiajiang 100 27.32 N 115.08 E
Xiajiangdun 106 31.14 N 120.24 E
Xiajiangwu 106 30.29 N 119.00 E
Xiajiayuan 106 32.13 N 120.38 E
Xiajiezi 102 27.28 N 101.35 E
Xiajin 98 36.55 N 115.57 E
Xiakou 100 28.28 N 118.31 E
Xialianggang 105 39.14 N 115.07 E
Xialufang 102 31.11 N 103.38 E
Xiamaguan 102 37.14 N 106.28 E
Xiamen (Amoy) 100 24.28 N 118.07 E
Xiamen Gang c 100 24.19 N 118.10 E
Xiamianzhen 107 30.08 N 106.32 E
Xiamin'ansutai 104 41.54 N 120.17 E
Xiamocun 106 31.09 N 119.22 E
Xi'an (Sian) 102 34.15 N 108.52 E
Xian ≃ 107 29.22 N 104.44 E
Xianchenggu 98 36.53 N 115.17 E
Xiandu 100 25.04 N 117.44 E
Xianfeng, Zhg. 100 25.42 N 117.53 E
Xianfeng, Zhg. 102 29.41 N 109.02 E
Xiang ≃, Zhg. 100 25.35 N 115.49 E
Xiang ≃, Zhg. 102 29.00 N 112.56 E
Xiang'an 100 31.12 N 117.46 E
Xiangcheng, Zhg. 100 33.28 N 114.53 E
Xiangcheng, Zhg. 100 33.53 N 113.29 E
Xiangcheng, Zhg. 102 28.59 N 99.45 E
Xiangcheng, Zhg. 106 31.29 N 120.44 E
Xiangfan 102 32.03 N 112.01 E
Xiangfuguan 100 28.30 N 115.26 E
Xiangfusi 107 30.06 N 104.24 E
Xianggang
 → Victoria 271d 22.17 N 114.09 E
Xianggongshi 100 28.25 N 113.32 E
Xianggongzhuang 105 39.48 N 118.19 E
Xianghe 105 39.46 N 116.59 E
Xiangheguan 100 33.08 N 113.26 E
Xianghuazhen 106 31.31 N 121.43 E
Xiangjia, Zhg. 106 31.20 N 120.31 E
Xiangjia, Zhg. 106 31.19 N 120.23 E
Xiangjiachang 107 30.08 N 104.18 E
Xiangkhoang 110 19.20 N 103.22 E
Xiangkhoang, Plateau
 de ⋀1 110 19.30 N 103.10 E
Xiangning 102 36.01 N 110.45 E
Xiangride 102 36.02 N 98.08 E
Xiangshan, Zhg. 100 29.28 N 121.51 E
Xiangshan, Zhg. 105 39.59 N 116.12 E
Xiangshan Gang c 100 29.38 N 121.48 E
Xiangshizhen 107 29.17 N 105.09 E
Xiangshui, Zhg. 100 23.15 N 114.10 E
Xiangshui, Zhg. 100 34.12 N 119.34 E
Xiangtan 100 27.51 N 112.54 E
Xiangtang 100 28.26 N 115.58 E
Xiangxiang 102 27.43 N 112.27 E
Xiangyang 105 39.13 N 115.25 E
Xiangyangkou 105 40.06 N 115.47 E
Xiangyin 100 28.40 N 112.53 E
Xiangyuan 102 36.32 N 113.00 E
Xiangyun 102 25.30 N 100.30 E
Xiangzhenpu 100 30.52 N 117.21 E
Xiangzhou, Zhg. 98 36.12 N 119.24 E
Xiangzhou, Zhg. 102 23.55 N 109.49 E
Xiangzhu 100 29.02 N 120.04 E
Xianinggang 100 28.20 N 112.56 E
Xianjiang 100 27.48 N 120.30 E
Xianju 100 28.51 N 120.44 E
Xianning 100 29.53 N 114.13 E
Xiannongtan Stadium
 ♦ 271a 39.52 N 116.23 E
Xiannübu 100 25.36 N 114.40 E
Xianru 89 43.11 N 128.02 E
Xianshichang 107 28.43 N 105.44 E
Xianshui ≃ 102 30.10 N 100.59 E
Xianshuigu 105 38.59 N 117.23 E
Xiantan, Zhg. 107 29.21 N 104.53 E
Xiantan, Zhg. 107 28.50 N 106.12 E
Xiantang 100 23.48 N 114.46 E


FRANÇAIS — Nom | Page | Lat.°' | Long.°' W = Ouest


Xianxia Ling ⋀ 100 28.30 N 118.46 E
Xianxian 98 38.13 N 116.06 E
Xianyang, Zhg. 100 28.02 N 118.30 E
Xianyang, Zhg. 102 34.22 N 108.42 E
Xianyou 100 25.23 N 118.40 E
Xianzhong 100 28.36 N 113.48 E
Xiao ≃ 100 28.11 N 120.14 E
Xiao'an ≃ 107 29.59 N 106.13 E
Xiao'ao 100 26.14 N 119.39 E
Xiaoazhang 102 23.42 N 104.58 E
Xiaobangniulu 104 41.34 N 122.46 E
Xiaobeigou 104 41.55 N 120.46 E
Xiaobeihe, Zhg. 104 42.39 N 123.58 E
Xiaobeihe, Zhg. 104 41.22 N 122.50 E
Xiaocaohu 86 43.06 N 88.30 E
Xiaochangshan Dao I 98 39.12 N 122.41 E
Xiaocheng 100 26.20 N 119.47 E
Xiaochengdu 106 30.59 N 120.04 E
Xiaochengzi, Zhg. 89 46.33 N 122.54 E
Xiaochengzi, Zhg. 89 42.56 N 123.12 E
Xiaochi 100 30.33 N 116.23 E
Xiaochikou 100 29.46 N 115.59 E
Xiaodanyang 106 31.38 N 118.43 E
Xiaodong 102 22.14 N 108.39 E
Xiao'ergou 89 49.12 N 123.42 E
Xiaofangshen 104 42.13 N 123.54 E
Xiaofanshan 105 40.16 N 115.19 E
Xiaofen 106 31.45 N 119.39 E
Xiaofeng 106 30.36 N 119.32 E
Xiaogan 100 30.55 N 113.54 E
Xiaogangkou 100 28.14 N 115.50 E
Xiaogaojiatun 104 41.02 N 121.59 E
Xiaogencaigangzi 104 41.48 N 122.42 E
Xiaogu 107 29.08 N 104.01 E
Xiaoguai 86 45.13 N 85.02 E
Xiaogushan 98 39.49 N 123.12 E
Xiaohaizhen 106 31.58 N 120.59 E
Xiaohaladaokou 98 42.37 N 119.32 E
Xiaohan 98 35.48 N 114.52 E
Xiaohe 106 32.01 N 119.52 E
Xiaohei Shan ⋀ 102 24.42 N 98.55 E
Xiaohekou 102 33.19 N 107.25 E
Xiaoheyan 98 42.26 N 119.38 E
Xiaoheying 102 32.37 N 104.23 E
Xiao Hinggan Ling
 (Lesser Khingan
 Range) ⋀ 89 48.45 N 127.00 E
Xiaohongmen 271a 39.49 N 116.26 E
Xiaohu 100 27.20 N 118.14 E
Xiaohuying 98 41.09 N 117.13 E
Xiaoji, Zhg. 98 36.45 N 121.01 E
Xiaoji, Zhg. 100 27.08 N 113.15 E
Xiaoji, Zhg. 100 32.38 N 119.48 E
Xiaojiachang 107 30.18 N 106.28 E
Xiaojiagang 100 31.06 N 113.55 E
Xiaojialing 100 29.35 N 116.32 E
Xiaojiang 100 25.08 N 114.59 E
Xiaojianji 100 33.23 N 116.29 E
Xiaojiawu 105 39.36 N 116.36 E
Xiaojiayingzi 98 40.17 N 118.47 E
Xiaojieling 100 31.36 N 115.09 E
Xiaojin 102 31.00 N 102.21 E
Xiaojingfang 105 39.22 N 116.34 E
Xiaojiu 89 45.15 N 127.47 E
Xiaokaoshantun 104 42.10 N 123.53 E
Xiaokuli 89 50.18 N 120.20 E
Xiaokunshan 106 31.02 N 121.07 E
Xiaolan 100 22.41 N 113.14 E
Xiaoliangshan 104 42.05 N 122.32 E
Xiaoling, Zhg. 89 45.20 N 127.18 E
Xiaoling, Zhg. 104 42.18 N 123.23 E
Xiaoling ≃ 104 41.06 N 121.07 E
Xiaolingzi 104 41.07 N 123.19 E
Xiaolinzhuang 104 41.36 N 124.01 E
Xiaolipu 98 36.24 N 116.35 E
Xiaolongtan 102 23.51 N 103.10 E
Xiaoluan ≃ 98 41.36 N 117.05 E
Xiaolüzhuang 106 31.57 N 119.25 E
Xiaomei 100 27.50 N 118.58 E
Xiaomei Guan ✕ 100 25.17 N 114.17 E
Xiaomiaozi 98 41.24 N 114.25 E
Xiaonanhai 107 29.23 N 106.27 E
Xiaopikou 98 35.47 N 115.53 E
Xiaopingyang 102 23.22 N 109.13 E
Xiao Qaidam He ⊜ 102 37.30 N 95.12 E
Xiaoqiao 100 26.57 N 118.30 E
Xiaoqiaotou 106 30.43 N 119.27 E
Xiaoqing ≃ 98 37.17 N 118.52 E
Xiaoqingchuizi 104 42.30 N 123.39 E
Xiaoquandong 102 41.14 N 95.26 E
Xiaosanjiazi 104 42.34 N 123.23 E
Xiaosha ≃ 104 41.13 N 122.45 E
Xiaoshakou 100 29.58 N 113.16 E
Xiaoshan 106 30.10 N 120.15 E
Xiaoshangqiao 100 33.43 N 113.58 E
Xiaoshi 100 27.27 N 116.49 E
Xiaoshixiang 100 30.36 N 116.38 E
Xiaoshu 106 30.48 N 119.46 E
Xiaoshun 100 29.11 N 119.51 E
Xiaosigou 98 40.53 N 118.33 E
Xiaosijia 104 42.24 N 120.46 E
Xiaotang 98 41.38 N 119.33 E
Xiaotanghe 98 42.04 N 127.10 E
Xiaotao 100 25.46 N 117.08 E
Xiaotazi 104 42.17 N 123.08 E
Xiaotian 100 31.12 N 116.33 E
Xiaotianji 100 32.45 N 115.36 E
Xiaotun 104 42.24 N 123.44 E
Xiaotunzicun 104 41.14 N 123.20 E
Xiaowa 104 41.03 N 122.04 E
Xiaowan 100 26.53 N 116.36 E
Xiaowangmiao 100 29.41 N 121.21 E
Xiaowutai Shan ⋀ 105 39.51 N 115.09 E
Xiaowutai Shan ⋀ 105 39.50 N 115.00 E
Xiaoxi 100 25.48 N 115.21 E
Xiaoxi ≃ 106 32.15 N 120.24 E
Xiaoxian 98 34.11 N 116.56 E
Xiaoxincheng 105 39.24 N 115.11 E
Xiaoxintian 271a 39.58 N 116.22 E
Xiaoxizhen 106 30.51 N 119.50 E
Xiaoyangjiadian 104 42.23 N 122.24 E
Xiaoyangqi 89 50.48 N 124.12 E
Xiaoyantai 104 41.26 N 123.10 E
Xiaoyaozhen 100 33.46 N 114.16 E
Xiaoyi 102 37.10 N 111.46 E
Xiaoying, Zhg. 98 37.18 N 118.04 E
Xiaoying, Zhg. 105 40.12 N 116.33 E
Xiaoyingcun 105 39.28 N 116.41 E
Xiaoyuan 107 30.00 N 104.56 E
Xiaozhan 105 38.55 N 117.25 E
Xiaozhang ≃ 105 39.47 N 117.22 E
Xiaozhongdian 102 27.40 N 99.46 E
Xiaozhuang 104 41.30 N 121.27 E
Xiaozhujiawan 106 31.24 N 121.01 E
Xiapu, Zhg. 100 26.52 N 120.01 E
Xiapu, Zhg. 100 27.49 N 114.26 E
Xiaqialafangzi 104 41.48 N 121.44 E
Xiaqi Dao I 100 29.42 N 122.15 E
Xiaqiubao 98 37.01 N 119.54 E
Xiasantumen 105 38.50 N 114.48 E
Xiashe 106 30.33 N 120.11 E
Xiashesi 100 27.46 N 112.57 E
Xiashi
 → Haining 106 30.32 N 120.41 E
Xiashu 106 32.11 N 119.10 E
Xiashuerfowei 89 50.23 N 120.47 E
Xiashuiquan 104 41.52 N 123.38 E
Xiataizi 105 40.37 N 117.45 E
Xiatang, Zhg. 100 33.45 N 112.39 E
Xiatang, Zhg. 106 31.29 N 118.41 E
Xiatangtian 106 30.55 N 120.12 E
Xiataohuatu 104 41.42 N 120.36 E
Xiawa 98 42.39 N 120.35 E
Xiawajiang 106 30.59 N 121.51 E
Xiawaziyu 104 41.15 N 123.38 E
Xiaxi 106 31.43 N 119.45 E
Xiaxian 102 35.11 N 111.15 E
Xiaxiangcheng 102 28.42 N 99.59 E
Xiaxikou 100 26.15 N 118.59 E
Xiaxinhe 106 31.40 N 119.31 E


PORTUGUÊS — Nome | Página | Lat.°' | Long.°' W = Oeste


Xiayang, Zhg. 100 28.48 N 119.41 E
Xiayang, Zhg. 100 26.46 N 117.59 E
Xiayang, Zhg. 100 24.39 N 116.52 E
Xiayi 98 34.14 N 116.06 E
Xiaying, Zhg. 98 37.03 N 119.25 E
Xiaying, Zhg. 105 40.10 N 117.25 E
Xiayunling 105 39.43 N 115.44 E
Xiazhang 98 36.08 N 116.57 E
Xiazhen 100 28.39 N 118.21 E
Xiazhuang, Zhg. 98 35.28 N 118.43 E
Xiazhuang, Zhg. 100 27.22 N 119.01 E
Xiazhuang, Zhg. 105 39.54 N 117.01 E
Xiazhuang, Zhg. 105 39.38 N 115.26 E
Xiazikou 105 39.01 N 115.25 E
Xiban 107 30.32 N 106.12 E
Xibaqianmou 104 40.59 N 121.35 E
Xibeiyingzi 104 41.55 N 121.38 E
Xibo ≃ 98 42.17 N 118.57 E
Xibu 100 31.46 N 118.17 E
Xicang 106 31.34 N 120.29 E
Xichang, Zhg. 102 27.58 N 102.13 E
Xichang, Zhg. 104 42.15 N 124.12 E
Xicheng 89 48.10 N 125.29 E
Xichong 102 31.00 N 105.52 E
Xicicun 105 39.29 N 116.08 E
Xico 234 19.25 N 97.00 W
Xicoténcatl 234 23.00 N 98.56 W
Xicotepec de Juárez 234 20.17 N 97.57 W
Xictle, Volcán ⋀1 286a 19.14 N 99.14 W
Xicun 100 27.46 N 114.14 E
Xidachuan 98 41.46 N 127.34 E
Xidapo 89 43.12 N 130.02 E
Xidaying 105 39.41 N 116.14 E
Xidian 100 29.32 N 121.26 E
Xiditou 105 39.16 N 117.23 E
Xidongting Shan ⋀ 106 31.07 N 120.16 E
Xié ≃ 246 0.54 N 67.11 W
Xiecun 105 39.00 N 115.31 E
Xiedian 100 33.27 N 113.28 E
Xiefang 100 26.12 N 116.41 E
Xieji 98 34.32 N 115.29 E
Xiejia 98 42.24 N 125.42 E
Xiejiagangzi 104 41.55 N 122.20 E
Xiejiapu 106 31.15 N 119.09 E
Xiejunmiac 107 30.15 N 103.40 E
Xielipuke 120 31.30 N 82.45 E
Xiemachang 107 29.46 N 106.22 E
Xiemata Shan ⋀ 89 50.28 N 120.47 E
Xiepu 100 30.02 N 121.37 E
Xieqiao, Zhg. 106 32.03 N 120.22 E
Xieqiao, Zhg. 106 30.29 N 120.34 E
Xietang 106 31.18 N 120.44 E
Xiexi 106 31.54 N 118.54 E
Xiexinggou 104 41.51 N 121.05 E
Xifei ≃ 100 32.38 N 116.39 E
Xifeng, Zhg. 98 42.43 N 124.40 E
Xifeng, Zhg. 102 27.02 N 106.30 E
Xifengkou 105 40.24 N 118.19 E
Xifocun 104 41.26 N 122.33 E
Xigangzi 89 49.58 N 127.20 E
Xigaolizhuangzi 104 41.40 N 122.55 E
Xigaotan 98 38.18 N 116.13 E
Xigaotun 98 40.27 N 122.36 E
Xigazê 120 29.17 N 88.53 E
Xiguanjiatun 104 42.35 N 123.10 E
Xiguanyingzi 104 41.50 N 120.37 E
Xihaikou 104 40.50 N 121.05 E
Xihan ≃ 102 33.30 N 106.02 E
Xihe, Zhg. 100 31.01 N 118.28 E
Xihe, Zhg. 100 31.41 N 113.27 E
Xihe, Zhg. 102 34.01 N 105.17 E
Xiheying 105 39.53 N 114.42 E
Xihezhuang 105 39.20 N 118.02 E
Xi Hu ⊜ 106 30.15 N 120.08 E
Xihua 100 33.47 N 114.31 E
Xihuangcang 106 31.43 N 121.40 E
Xihuanzidong 104 41.31 N 122.28 E
Xihuashan, Zhg. 100 25.28 N 114.20 E
Xihuashan, Zhg. 105 40.07 N 116.54 E
Xihuishan 104 41.41 N 122.38 E
Xiis 144 10.53 N 46.54 E
Xiji, Zhg. 102 35.58 N 105.44 E
Xiji, Zhg. 105 39.49 N 116.52 E
Xijialong 102 23.31 N 103.51 E
Xijiang 100 25.50 N 115.49 E
Xijianshanzi 104 40.47 N 120.48 E
Xi Jiao Airfield ⊠ 271a 39.58 N 116.15 E
Xijiapuzitun 104 41.26 N 123.50 E
Xijir Ulan Hu ⊜ 120 35.12 N 90.18 E
Xikou, Zhg. 89 46.40 N 120.40 E
Xikou, Zhg. 100 28.52 N 119.11 E
Xikou, Zhg. 100 25.26 N 118.45 E
Xikou, Zhg. 100 29.14 N 114.24 E
Xikou, Zhg. 100 29.11 N 114.23 E
Xikou, Zhg. 100 29.44 N 118.02 E
Xikou, Zhg. 106 30.40 N 118.41 E
Xikouxu 100 25.24 N 117.03 E
Xikouzi 89 53.06 N 120.40 E
Xilai 107 30.20 N 103.29 E
Xilaiqiao 106 32.03 N 119.54 E
Xilaizhen 106 32.07 N 120.25 E
Xilin 120 28.33 N 87.48 E
Xi Ling (Western
 Tombs) ⊥ 105 39.24 N 115.18 E
Xilintuo 120 30.08 N 88.04 E
Xilitla 234 21.20 N 98.58 W
Xiliuhe 105 38.58 N 116.32 E
Xiliushuyingzi 104 42.25 N 121.54 E
Xıllı 84 39.25 N 49.05 E
Xilókastron 38 38.05 N 22.38 E
Xiluga ≃ 98 42.21 N 118.38 E
Xiluncun 89 47.08 N 126.26 E
Ximagou 105 40.16 N 117.50 E
Ximakou 100 30.33 N 113.47 E
Ximalatu 89 47.00 N 122.01 E
Ximalin 98 40.48 N 114.29 E
Ximiao 102 41.09 N 100.17 E
Ximucheng 104 40.42 N 122.54 E
Xin ≃ 100 28.37 N 116.40 E
Xin'an, Zhg. 89 43.46 N 125.40 E
Xinan, Zhg. 100 25.26 N 117.35 E
Xin'an, Zhg. 100 26.44 N 116.13 E
Xin'an, Zhg. 100 23.02 N 114.56 E
Xin'an, Zhg. 105 39.09 N 116.38 E
Xin'an, Zhg. 106 31.47 N 120.09 E
Xin'an, Zhg. 106 31.30 N 120.22 E
Xin'an ≃ 100 29.33 N 118.58 E
Xin'andian 100 32.37 N 114.03 E
Xin'andu 100 30.52 N 116.53 E
Xin'anji 100 33.22 N 115.13 E
Xin'anjiang Shuiku
 ⊜1 100 29.27 N 119.06 E
Xin'anpu 104 42.39 N 123.27 E
Xin'anqiao 106 32.16 N 121.07 E
Xin'ansuo 102 23.16 N 103.27 E
Xin'anzhen, Zhg. 89 44.06 N 123.46 E
Xin'anzhen, Zhg. 105 39.45 N 117.32 E
Xi'nanzhuang 105 40.48 N 118.23 E
Xinavane 156 25.02 S 32.47 E
Xinba, Zhg. 98 34.27 N 119.09 E
Xinba, Zhg. 100 30.24 N 116.52 E
Xinba, Zhg. 106 32.08 N 120.39 E
Xinba, Zhg. 106 32.16 N 119.45 E
Xinbao'an 105 40.27 N 115.24 E
Xin Barag Youqi
 (Altan Emel) 88 48.41 N 116.53 E
Xin Barag Zuoqi
 (Amgalang) 88 48.14 N 118.18 E
Xinbin, Zhg. 98 41.42 N 125.02 E
Xinbin, Zhg. 106 30.56 N 121.04 E
Xinbo 98 42.19 N 117.44 E
Xincai 100 32.44 N 114.59 E
Xincang, Zhg. 106 30.25 N 120.42 E
Xincang, Zhg. 106 30.44 N 121.11 E
Xinchang, Zhg. 100 29.30 N 120.53 E
Xinchang, Zhg. 102 28.03 N 103.46 E
Xinchang, Zhg. 102 25.10 N 104.18 E
Xinchang, Zhg. 106 31.42 N 121.46 E
Xinchang, Zhg. 106 31.02 N 121.38 E
Xinchang, Zhg. 107 29.20 N 104.15 E
Xinchang, Zhg. 107 29.38 N 104.33 E
Xinchang, Zhg. 107 30.29 N 106.21 E
Xinchang, Zhg. 107 30.16 N 104.29 E
Xinchangzi 107 29.40 N 103.46 E
Xincheng, Zhg. 100 25.34 N 114.36 E
Xincheng, Zhg. 102 24.09 N 108.46 E
Xincheng
 (Gaobeidian), Zhg. 105 39.20 N 115.51 E
Xincheng, Zhg. 105 38.59 N 117.33 E
Xincheng, Zhg. 106 32.17 N 119.14 E
Xincheng, Zhg. 106 30.48 N 120.36 E
Xinchengzi 104 42.03 N 123.30 E
Xinchepaizi 86 44.55 N 84.30 E
Xincunji 100 32.53 N 115.31 E
Xindai 106 30.49 N 121.05 E
Xindi 104 42.21 N 120.31 E
Xindian, Zhg. 89 45.55 N 127.50 E
Xindian, Zhg. 98 37.07 N 114.49 E
Xindian, Zhg. 98 37.29 N 118.28 E
Xindian, Zhg. 100 33.07 N 112.38 E
Xindian, Zhg. 100 31.33 N 115.16 E
Xindian, Zhg. 100 33.38 N 113.51 E
Xindian, Zhg. 100 29.40 N 113.40 E
Xindian, Zhg. 105 40.11 N 116.11 E
Xindian, Zhg. 105 40.47 N 116.49 E
Xindian, Zhg. 105 39.10 N 116.27 E
Xindian, Zhg. 107 29.19 N 105.40 E
Xindianbu 100 32.24 N 116.22 E
Xindianzi, Zhg. 105 40.04 N 118.01 E
Xindianzi, Zhg. 107 28.49 N 103.35 E
Xindianzi, Zhg. 107 29.03 N 103.46 E
Xindianzi, Zhg. 107 29.52 N 106.06 E
Xindianzi, Zhg. 107 29.46 N 105.11 E
Xindianzi, Zhg. 107 29.43 N 104.01 E
Xindu 102 23.59 N 111.46 E
Xinfatuncun 104 41.13 N 122.28 E
Xinfeng, Zhg. 100 25.24 N 114.56 E
Xinfeng, Zhg. 100 27.26 N 116.40 E
Xinfeng, Zhg. 100 33.19 N 120.30 E
Xinfeng, Zhg. 100 24.04 N 114.12 E
Xinfeng, Zhg. 100 24.05 N 116.53 E
Xinfeng, Zhg. 106 31.09 N 118.40 E
Xinfeng, Zhg. 106 32.05 N 119.34 E
Xinfeng, Zhg. 106 30.43 N 120.55 E
Xinfeng ≃ 100 23.42 N 114.42 E
Xinfeng Shuiku ⊜1 100 23.52 N 114.30 E
Xing'an, Zhg. 89 48.49 N 121.45 E
Xing'an, Zhg. 102 25.37 N 110.31 E
Xin'gang, Zhg. 106 31.56 N 120.57 E
Xingang, Zhg. 106 32.03 N 120.25 E
Xing'antun 89 51.31 N 120.08 E
Xingcheng 104 40.37 N 120.43 E
Xingguo 100 26.21 N 115.19 E
Xinghai 102 35.31 N 99.36 E
Xinghe 98 40.48 N 113.58 E
Xinghua 100 32.57 N 119.50 E
Xinghua Wan c 100 25.20 N 119.20 E
Xingjing 102 29.43 N 102.59 E
Xingkai Hu (ozero
 Chanka) ⊜ 89 45.00 N 132.24 E
Xingliu 100 33.04 N 115.41 E
Xinglong, Zhg. 100 32.05 N 112.51 E
Xinglong, Zhg. 102 35.38 N 106.08 E
Xinglong, Zhg. 105 40.26 N 117.34 E
Xinglong, Zhg. 107 30.36 N 106.20 E
Xinglong, Zhg. 107 30.20 N 106.07 E
Xinglongchang, Zhg. 107 30.25 N 104.06 E
Xinglongchang, Zhg. 107 29.34 N 106.09 E
Xinglongchang, Zhg. 107 29.54 N 105.26 E
Xinglongcun 89 49.50 N 125.12 E
Xinglongdian, Zhg. 104 42.16 N 124.00 E
Xinglongdian, Zhg. 104 41.59 N 123.03 E
Xinglonggou, Zhg. 104 41.46 N 120.38 E
Xinglonggou, Zhg. 104 40.45 N 123.08 E
Xinglongpao 89 46.27 N 125.47 E
Xinglongtai 104 42.30 N 123.48 E
Xingning 100 24.09 N 115.45 E
Xingou, Zhg. 100 30.41 N 113.57 E
Xingou, Zhg. 100 30.08 N 112.56 E
Xingren 102 25.27 N 105.13 E
Xingrenbu 102 37.06 N 105.12 E
Xingshanbao 89 45.30 N 125.45 E
Xingtai 98 37.04 N 114.29 E
Xingtan 100 22.46 N 113.07 E
Xingtang 98 38.26 N 114.33 E
Xingtian 100 27.30 N 118.02 E
Xingu ≃ 242 1.30 S 51.53 W
Xinguan 100 33.38 N 118.05 E
Xingwenping 102 29.24 N 103.23 E
Xingxian 102 38.36 N 111.15 E
Xingxing 106 30.39 N 121.09 E
Xingyi, Zhg. 98 38.18 N 115.01 E
Xingyi, Zhg. 102 25.06 N 104.58 E
Xingzhuangzi 105 40.34 N 115.00 E
Xingzi 100 29.28 N 116.01 E
Xinhe, Zhg. 98 37.32 N 115.14 E
Xinhe, Zhg. 100 28.30 N 121.27 E
Xinhe, Zhg. 105 39.03 N 117.37 E
Xinhe, Zhg. 106 31.59 N 121.21 E
Xinhekou 89 48.22 N 130.45 E
Xinheng 100 23.38 N 116.18 E
Xinhezhen 106 31.35 N 121.31 E
Xinhezhuang 106 31.10 N 118.46 E
Xinhua 102 27.37 N 111.02 E
Xinhuai ≃ 100 34.23 N 120.05 E
Xinhuang 106 30.37 N 120.55 E
Xinhui 100 22.32 N 113.02 E
Xining (Sining) 102 36.38 N 101.55 E
Xiniu, Zhg. 100 24.10 N 113.07 E
Xiniu, Zhg. 106 31.25 N 120.07 E
Xiniuguchengzi 104 41.01 N 122.24 E
Xinji, Zhg. 98 35.19 N 115.36 E
Xinji, Zhg. 100 33.24 N 114.44 E
Xinji, Zhg. 105 39.52 N 117.10 E
Xinji, Zhg. 105 40.04 N 118.21 E
Xinjiaji 98 36.56 N 116.59 E
Xinjian, Zhg. 100 28.46 N 120.02 E
Xinjian, Zhg. 100 28.34 N 115.47 E
Xinjian, Zhg. 106 31.33 N 119.39 E
Xinjiang, Zhg. 100 24.29 N 113.52 E
Xinjiang, Zhg. 102 35.40 N 111.11 E
Xinjiang, Zhg. 106 32.05 N 120.40 E
Xinjianglang 106 30.58 N 120.54 E
Xinjiang Uygur
 Zizhiqu (Sinkiang)
 ▫4 90 40.00 N 85.00 E
Xinjiapu 105 40.32 N 115.57 E
Xinjiazhuang 105 40.31 N 114.58 E
Xinjie 102 26.48 N 101.15 E
Xinjieji 89 52.08 N 126.24 E
Xinjin (Pulandian),
 Zhg. 98 39.24 N 121.58 E
Xinjin, Zhg. 107 30.25 N 103.49 E
Xinjingzi 86 42.13 N 87.36 E
Xinjuntun 105 39.39 N 117.57 E
Xinkai ≃ 89 43.37 N 123.36 E
Xinkaigang 106 31.55 N 120.56 E
Xinkengdong 100 26.09 N 113.46 E
Xinle
 (Dongchangshou) 98 38.24 N 114.47 E
Xinli 89 44.41 N 126.45 E
Xinlitun, Zhg. 89 43.34 N 125.18 E
Xinlitun, Zhg. 104 42.00 N 122.09 E
Xinlitun, Zhg. 104 42.15 N 122.51 E
Xinlizhuang 105 39.17 N 116.10 E
Xinmin 104 42.00 N 122.48 E
Xinmintun 104 41.39 N 123.02 E
Xinning 102 26.19 N 110.45 E
Xinping 102 24.06 N 101.58 E
Xinpu 100 24.31 N 116.08 E
Xinqianhu 98 37.59 N 118.15 E
Xinqiao, Zhg. 106 31.32 N 119.04 E
Xinqiao, Zhg. 106 31.04 N 121.18 E
Xinqiao, Zhg. 107 29.32 N 106.28 E
Xinqiao, Zhg. 107 30.10 N 103.50 E
Xinqiao, Zhg. 107 30.33 N 105.33 E
Xinqiaotou 106 31.00 N 119.24 E
Xinqiaozhen 107 29.36 N 103.39 E
Xinqiu 98 41.53 N 119.41 E
Xinqizhou 100 28.56 N 115.50 E
Xinqu 86 44.57 N 85.15 E
Xinquan 100 25.23 N 116.38 E
Xinsanyu 106 31.58 N 120.07 E
Xinshao 102 27.11 N 111.20 E
Xinshengzhen 107 29.29 N 104.39 E
Xinshi, Zhg. 106 30.37 N 120.19 E
Xinshi, Zhg. 106 32.04 N 120.02 E
Xinshizhen, Zhg. 102 28.39 N 104.02 E
Xinshizhen, Zhg. 107 30.20 N 104.35 E
Xinshu ≃ 98 34.41 N 119.12 E
Xintai 98 35.54 N 117.44 E
Xintaimen 98 40.50 N 120.23 E
Xintaizi, Zhg. 104 41.06 N 122.42 E
Xintaizi, Zhg. 104 42.07 N 123.36 E
Xintang, Zhg. 100 23.08 N 113.36 E
Xintang, Zhg. 102 30.13 N 109.30 E
Xintang, Zhg. 106 31.02 N 119.59 E
Xintangcun 106 31.53 N 119.31 E
Xintanpu 100 29.43 N 114.54 E
Xintian 102 25.53 N 112.05 E
Xintun 104 42.11 N 123.45 E
Xinvi 105 40.04 N 118.21 E
Xinwei 100 25.21 N 115.48 E
Xinwen (Suncun) 98 35.53 N 117.40 E
Xinxian, Zhg. 100 31.38 N 114.51 E
Xinxian, Zhg. 102 38.25 N 112.48 E
Xinxiang 98 35.20 N 113.51 E
Xinxim ≃ 250 7.57 S 53.20 W
Xinxing, Zhg. 89 43.16 N 129.48 E
Xinxing, Zhg. 100 22.40 N 112.52 E
Xinxing, Zhg. 102 19.57 N 109.32 E
Xinxu, Zhg. 100 22.52 N 114.20 E
Xinxu, Zhg. 100 24.57 N 117.34 E
Xinyang 100 32.08 N 114.04 E
Xinyao 100 27.39 N 118.52 E
Xinye 100 32.33 N 112.21 E
Xinyi (Xin'anzhen),
 Zhg. 98 34.22 N 118.21 E
Xinyi (Dongzhen),
 Zhg. 102 22.13 N 110.50 E
Xinyi ≃ 100 34.29 N 119.49 E
Xinying 102 36.03 N 105.35 E
Xinyu 100 27.49 N 114.57 E
Xinyuan 86 43.08 N 82.31 E
Xinzao 100 23.02 N 113.26 E
Xinzha 102 23.41 N 101.09 E
Xinzhai, Zhg. 98 39.24 N 118.46 E
Xinzhai, Zhg. 98 36.24 N 118.37 E
Xinzhai, Zhg. 102 24.33 N 99.08 E
Xinzhan 100 33.33 N 114.50 E
Xinzhang 105 39.05 N 116.46 E
Xinzhangzi 105 40.45 N 117.50 E
Xinzhao 102 39.32 N 107.52 E
Xinzhazhen 106 31.50 N 119.52 E
Xinzhen, Zhg. 98 35.37 N 114.03 E
Xinzhen, Zhg. 105 39.01 N 116.22 E
Xinzhen, Zhg. 106 31.24 N 121.24 E
Xinzheng 100 34.25 N 113.43 E
Xinzhou, Zhg. 100 30.50 N 114.47 E
Xinzhou, Zhg. 102 19.48 N 109.18 E
Xinzhuang, Zhg. 98 35.05 N 117.56 E
Xinzhuang, Zhg. 271a 39.56 N 116.31 E
Xinzhuangtou 105 39.25 N 115.45 E
Xinzhuangzi, Zhg. 104 41.05 N 121.23 E
Xinzhuangzi, Zhg. 105 40.14 N 116.59 E
Xinzhuangzi, Zhg. 105 40.32 N 115.10 E
Xinzhuangzi, Zhg. 105 38.52 N 117.21 E
Xinzhuangzi, Zhg. 105 39.20 N 118.25 E
Xinzo de Limia 34 42.03 N 7.43 W
Xiongdi Yu II 100 23.33 N 117.40 E
Xiongjiachang 102 26.31 N 105.39 E
Xiongxian 105 38.59 N 116.05 E
Xiongyuecheng 98 40.10 N 122.08 E
Xipamanu
 (Chipamanu) ≃ 248 10.43 S 67.50 W
Xiping, Zhg. 100 28.27 N 119.29 E
Xiping, Zhg. 100 33.23 N 114.02 E
Xiping'anhe 104 40.47 N 122.01 E
Xiqia 106 31.03 N 119.37 E
Xiqilichiquan 89 49.59 N 119.27 E
Xiqin 100 26.33 N 118.06 E
Xiqing Shan ⋀ 102 35.30 N 101.30 E
Xique-Xique 250 10.50 S 42.44 W
Xırdalan 84 40.26 N 49.51 E
Xisanshilipu 100 32.40 N 117.31 E
Xisantai 98 39.38 N 121.37 E
Xishan, Zhg. 100 28.34 N 115.37 E
Xishan, Zhg. 105 39.38 N 118.10 E
Xishanqiao 106 31.57 N 118.43 E
Xishanxicun 105 40.01 N 116.50 E
Xisha Qundao
 (Paracel Islands) II 108 16.30 N 112.15 E
Xishijiazi 104 41.46 N 120.55 E
Xishiqiao 106 31.53 N 120.06 E
Xishu 98 36.41 N 113.49 E
Xishui 100 30.27 N 115.13 E
Xishuiyu 105 40.25 N 116.16 E
Xisuhupu 104 41.41 N 123.14 E
Xitai 98 40.37 N 120.12 E
Xitan 100 23.47 N 117.08 E
Xitang 106 30.57 N 120.53 E
Xitangqiao, Zhg. 106 31.49 N 120.38 E
Xitangqiao, Zhg. 106 30.37 N 121.01 E
Xitaoyuan 104 40.57 N 122.11 E
Xiti 120 33.27 N 82.48 E
Xitianmu Shan ⋀ 106 30.21 N 119.25 E
Xitiao ≃ 106 30.57 N 120.10 E
Xiting 106 32.07 N 121.00 E
Xitole 150 11.43 N 14.50 W
Xituan 105 39.29 N 115.47 E
Xiu ≃ 100 29.13 N 115.56 E
Xiujiangpu 104 41.17 N 123.02 E
Xiuning 100 29.47 N 118.10 E
Xiushan 102 28.29 N 108.52 E
Xiushui 100 29.04 N 114.33 E
Xiushui ≃ 104 42.03 N 122.58 E
Xiushuihe 104 42.22 N 123.01 E
Xiuyan 98 40.17 N 123.18 E
Xiva 34 39.28 N 0.43 W
Xiwei 100 25.22 N 117.46 E
Xiweizigou 104 42.01 N 121.59 E
Xiwenquan 107 29.42 N 106.07 E
Xiwu 100 29.40 N 121.30 E
Xiwukou 106 30.24 N 118.54 E
Xixabangma Feng ⋀ 124 28.22 N 85.50 E
Xixi 100 26.45 N 118.42 E
Xixia 102 33.22 N 111.28 E
Xixian, Zhg. 100 32.21 N 114.44 E
Xixian, Zhg. 102 36.43 N 110.52 E
Xixiang 102 32.48 N 107.55 E
Xixiangyang 105 39.33 N 116.02 E
Xixiaojie 104 40.42 N 122.12 E
Xixiashu 106 31.57 N 119.49 E
Xixing 106 30.11 N 120.13 E
Xixona 34 38.32 N 0.30 W
Xiyang, Zhg. 98 37.37 N 113.42 E
Xiyang, Zhg. 100 25.50 N 117.25 E
Xiyang, Zhg. 106 31.49 N 120.43 E
Xiyang, Zhg. 106 31.52 N 119.23 E
Xiyang Dao I 100 26.32 N 120.04 E
Xiyangji 100 33.25 N 116.22 E
Xiyangjiao 106 31.43 N 120.23 E
Xiyangshugou 104 40.41 N 122.44 E
Xiyangzhuang 106 31.50 N 119.22 E
Xiyingzi 104 41.55 N 122.34 E
Xiyou 98 37.24 N 119.56 E
Xiyushi 106 30.36 N 119.26 E
Xizang Zizhiqu (Tibet)
 ▫4 90 32.00 N 88.00 E
Xizhi ≃ 100 23.04 N 114.31 E
Xizhimen Station ◆5 271a 39.56 N 116.21 E
Xizhong Dao I 98 39.26 N 121.17 E
Xizhou 100 29.29 N 121.39 E
Xizi 98 41.48 N 119.16 E
Xocavänd 84 39.48 N 47.06 E
Xochiapa 234 17.39 N 95.46 W
Xochicalco ⊥ 234 18.48 N 99.19 W
Xochimilco ◆8 286a 19.16 N 99.06 W
Xochimilco, Lago de
 ⊜ 286a 19.16 N 99.06 W
Xochipala 234 17.48 N 99.39 W
Xochistlahuaca 234 16.47 N 98.15 W
Xochitlán 234 19.59 N 97.36 W
Xoka 120 29.58 N 93.48 E
Xom Binh Phuoc 269c 10.40 N [illegible]06.47 E
Xom Xoai Minh 269c 10.42 N [illegible]06.50 E
Xu ≃ 100 28.17 N [illegible]16.05 E
Xuancheng 106 30.58 N [illegible]18.45 E
Xuan'en 102 30.00 N [illegible]09.20 E
Xuanfeng 100 27.42 N [illegible]14.08 E
Xuang ≃ 110 19.58 N [illegible]02.15 E
Xuanhan 102 31.24 N [illegible]07.43 E
Xuanhua 105 40.37 N [illegible]15.03 E
Xuanhuadian 100 31.42 N [illegible]14.29 E
Xuanhui ≃ 98 38.07 N [illegible]17.45 E
Xuanjiabao 106 32.17 N 120.01 E
Xuanjiangying 98 41.25 N 116.45 E
Xuan Loc 110 10.56 N 107.14 E
Xuantan 107 29.12 N 105.34 E
Xuan Thoi Thuong 269c 10.52 N 106.34 E
Xuanwei 102 26.07 N 104.05 E
Xuanzhuang 105 39.29 N 118.07 E
Xubu 98 40.02 N 113.43 E
Xuchang, Zhg. 100 34.03 N 113.49 E
Xuchang, Zhg. 107 29.06 N 104.31 E
Xucheng 98 35.56 N 116.27 E
Xuchilquitongo 234 17.15 N 96.53 W
Xucun 106 30.27 N 120.22 E
Xudat 84 41.38 N 48.42 E
Xudazhuang 100 33.44 N 117.53 E
Xuddun 144 9.09 N 47.28 E
Xuddur 144 4.07 [illegible] 43.54 E
Xueao 100 29.27 [illegible] 121.30 E
Xuebu 106 31.43 N 119.22 E
Xuecheng 98 34.50 N 117.16 E
Xuedian, Zhg. 100 34.04 N 113.04 E
Xuedian, Zhg. 100 34.30 N 113.44 E
Xuefanggou 104 41.57 N 121.01 E
Xuefeng 100 33.21 N 118.22 E
Xuehu 98 34.08 N 116.27 E
Xueshan Zhang ⋀ 100 24.24 N 113.37 E
Xueshuiwen 89 49.10 N 129.45 E
Xuetangpuzi 104 40.38 N 123.53 E
Xueyanqiao 106 31.30 N 120.06 E
Xuezhen 106 31.35 N 118.38 E
Xuguanzhen 106 31.23 N 120.30 E
Xuguichenxiaodian 106 32.07 N 121.20 E
Xuguit Qi (Yakeshi) 89 49.17 N 120.41 E
Xuji 100 31.5[illegible] N 116.22 E
Xujiabu 100 29.27 N 116.18 E
Xujiadong 100 25.5[illegible] N 113.02 E
Xujiadu 100 28.1[illegible] N 114.44 E
Xujiagou 104 42.1[illegible] N 124.04 E
Xujiapuzi 104 40.4[illegible] N 123.18 E
Xujiatou 106 31.1[illegible] N 119.25 E
Xujiazhai, Zhg. 106 31.1[illegible] N 121.46 E
Xujiazhai, Zhg. 269b 31.2[illegible] N 121.17 E
Xuliying 105 39.2[illegible] N 116.02 E
Xun ≃, Zhg. 89 49.2[illegible] N 128.55 E
Xun ≃, Zhg. 102 23.2[illegible] N 111.18 E
Xungru 120 29.1[illegible] N 84.49 E
Xunhe 89 49.1[illegible] N 128.04 E
Xunhua 102 35.4[illegible] N 102.26 E
Xunjiansi 105 40.5[illegible] N 116.04 E
Xunke 89 49.5[illegible] N 128.25 E
Xunle 102 25.1[illegible] N 108.12 E
Xunmukou 98 34.0[illegible] N 114.42 E
Xunshansuo 98 37.1[illegible] N 122.29 E
Xunwu 100 24.5[illegible] N 115.38 E
Xunwu ≃ 100 24.2[illegible] N 115.26 E
Xunxian 98 35.[illegible]3 N 114.31 E
Xupu, Zhg. 102 27.[illegible]4 N 110.24 E
Xupu, Zhg. 106 31.[illegible]5 N 120.54 E
Xushe 106 31.[illegible]4 N 119.39 E
Xushi 106 31.[illegible]0 N 120.57 E
Xushui 105 39.[illegible]2 N 115.39 E
Xutian 98 34.[illegible]0 N 114.03 E
Xuwan 100 27.[illegible]5 N 116.31 E
Xuwen 102 20.[illegible]1 N 110.11 E
Xuxiandai 106 30.[illegible]0 N 120.47 E
Xuxiang 106 31.[illegible]3 N 120.13 E
Xuyen Moc 110 10.[illegible]4 N 107.25 E
Xuyi 100 33.[illegible]1 N 118.29 E
Xuyong 102 28.[illegible]0 N 105.24 E
Xuzhou (Süchow) 98 34.[illegible]6 N 117.11 E
Xuzhuang 106 31.[illegible]9 N 120.32 E


## Y


Yaak 182 4[illegible].50 N 115.42 W
Yaan 102 3[illegible].03 N 103.02 E
Yaapeet 166 35.46 S 142.03 E
Yaaq-Baraawe 144 [illegible].57 N 43.11 E
Yaba ◆8 273a [illegible].30 N 3.23 E
Yaba College of
 Technology ♥2 273a [illegible].32 N 3.23 E
Ya'bad 132 3[illegible].27 N 35.10 E
Yabakei 96 3[illegible].27 N 131.07 E
Yabassi 152 [illegible].28 N 9.58 E
Yabe 96 3[illegible].09 N 130.49 E
Yabe ≃ 96 3[illegible].06 N 130.26 E
Yabelo 144 [illegible].54 N 38.05 E
Yablis 236 1[illegible].10 N 83.49 W
Yablonovy Range
 → Jablonovyj
 chrebet ⋀ 88 [illegible]3.30 N 115.00 E
Yabluniv 78 [illegible].24 N 24.57 E
Yablychne 78 [illegible].18 N 35.14 E
Yabrīn ⍓4 128 [illegible].17 N 48.58 E
Yabrūd 130 [illegible].58 N 36.40 E
Yabu, Nihon 96 [illegible].22 N 134.47 E
Yabu, Nihon 174m [illegible].36 N 127.57 E
Yabucoa 240m [illegible].03 N 65.53 W
Yabuki 94 [illegible]7.12 N 140.19 E
Yabuli 89 [illegible]4.55 N 128.35 E
Yacambu, Parque
 Nacional ♦ 246 [illegible]9.40 N 69.42 W
Yacaré Norte, Riacho
 ≃ 252 [illegible]2.43 S 58.14 W
Yacheng 110 [illegible]8.25 N 109.11 E
Yachi ≃ 102 [illegible]7.18 N 107.15 E
Yachimata 94 35.39 N 140.19 E
Yachiyo, Nihon 94 35.43 N 140.07 E
Yachiyo, Nihon 94 36.10 N 139.53 E
Yacimiento Río
 Turbio 254 51.32 S 72.18 W
Yaco 248 17.09 S 67.24 W
Yaco (Iaco) ≃ 248 9.03 S 68.34 W
Yacolt 224 45.51 N 122.24 W
Yacuiba 248 22.02 S 63.45 W
Yacuma ≃ 248 13.38 S 65.23 W
Yacyretá, Isla I 252 27.25 S 56.30 W
Yada ≃ 96 35.38 N 134.37 E
Yādgīr 122 16.46 N 77.08 E
Yadkin ≃ 192 35.23 N 80.03 W
Yadkinville 192 36.08 N 80.39 W
Yad Mordekhay 132 31.35 N 34.34 E
Yadong 124 27.29 N 88.55 E
Yādūdah 132 32.40 N 36.04 E
Yaduty 78 51.22 N 32.19 E
Yaenengu 152 2.28 N 23.15 E
Yaeyama-rettō II 175c 24.20 N 124.00 E
Yāfā 132 32.41 N 35.17 E
Yafran 146 32.04 N 12.31 E
Yaftābād 267c 35.39 N 51.19 E
Yafuquan 85 39.12 N 76.09 E
Yagachi-shima I 174m 26.40 N 128.01 E
Yağcılar 130 39.25 N 28.23 E
Yageg 144 3.16 N 44.00 E
Yagi 96 35.04 N 135.32 E
Yagishiri-tō I 92 44.26 N 141.25 E
Yağlıca Dağı ⋀ 84 40.18 N 43.18 E
Yago 234 21.50 N 105.04 W
Yagonde 152 0.02 N 22.41 E
Yagoona 274 33.55 S 151.02 E
Yagoua 146 10.20 N 15.14 E
Yagradagzê Shan ⋀ 120 35.12 N 95.20 E
Yaguachi Nuevo 246 2.07 S 79.41 W


| | | | | |
|---|---|---|---|---|
| ≃ River | Fluß | Río | Rivière | Rio |
| ≊ Canal | Kanal | Canal | Canal | Canal |
| ⌞ Waterfall, Rapids | Wasserfall, Stromschnellen | Cascada, Rápidos | Chute d'eau, Rapides | Cascata, Rápidos |
| ⋈ Strait | Meeresstraße | Estrecho | Détroit | Estreito |
| c Bay, Gulf | Bucht, Golf | Bahía, Golfo | Baie, Golfe | Baía, Golfo |
| ⊜ Lake, Lakes | See, Seen | Lago, Lagos | Lac, Lacs | Lago, Lagos |
| ⁂ Swamp | Sumpf | Pantano | Marais | Pântano |
| ⊓ Ice Features, Glacier | Eis- und Gletscherformen | Accidentes Glaciales | Formes glaciaires | Acidentes glaciares |
| ⍓ Other Hydrographic Features | Andere Hydrographische Objekte | Otros Elementos Hidrográficos | Autres données hydrographiques | Outros acidentes hidrográficos |

| | | | | |
|---|---|---|---|---|
| -◆- Submarine Features | Untermeerische Objekte | Accidentes Submarinos | Formes de relief sous-marin | Acidentes submarinos |
| ▫ Political Unit | Politische Einheit | Unidad Política | Entité politique | Unidade política |
| ♥ Cultural Institution | Kulturelle Institution | Institución Cultural | Institution culturelle | Instituição cultural |
| ⊥ Historical Site | Historische Stätte | Sitio Histórico | Site historique | Sitio histórico |
| ♦ Recreational Site | Erholungs- und Ferienort | Sitio de Recreo | Centre de loisirs | Area de Lazer |
| ⊠ Airport | Flughafen | Aeropuerto | Aéroport | Aeroporto |
| ■ Military Installation | Militäranlage | Instalación Militar | Installation militaire | Instalação militar |
| ◆ Miscellaneous | Verschiedenes | Misceláneo | Divers | Diversos |

| Name | Page | Lat.°′ | Long.°′ |
|---|---|---|---|
| Yaguajay | 240p | 22.19 N | 79.14 W |
| Yaguala ≃ | 236 | 15.25 N | 86.40 W |
| Yaguará | 246 | 2.40 N | 75.31 W |
| Yaguaraparo | 246 | 10.34 N | 62.49 W |
| Yaguarí | 252 | 31.31 S | 54.58 W |
| Yaguarón (Jaguarão) ≃ | 252 | 32.39 S | 53.12 W |
| Yaguas ≃ | 246 | 2.45 S | 70.04 W |
| Yagur | 132 | 32.44 N | 35.04 E |
| Yahagi ≃ | 94 | 34.50 N | 136.59 E |
| Yahagong | 102 | 28.24 N | 99.11 E |
| Yahara ≃ | 190 | 42.48 N | 89.07 W |
| Yahata → Kitakyūshū | 96 | 33.53 N | 130.50 E |
| Yahe, Zhg. | 89 | 45.24 N | 130.24 E |
| Yahe, Zhg. | 106 | 31.44 N | 119.52 E |
| Yahila | 152 | 0.13 N | 24.28 E |
| Yahk | 182 | 49.05 N | 116.05 W |
| Yahmūm al-Asmar, Jabal ∧ | 142 | 29.56 N | 31.38 E |
| Yaho | 268 | 35.41 N | 139.27 E |
| Yahōga-take ∧ | 96 | 33.04 N | 130.50 E |
| Yahongqiao | 105 | 39.45 N | 117.51 E |
| Yahorlyts'kyy lyman ⊂ | 78 | 46.24 N | 31.50 E |
| Yahotyn | 78 | 50.17 N | 31.46 E |
| Yahualica | 234 | 21.08 N | 102.51 W |
| Yahuma | 152 | 1.05 N | 23.13 E |
| Yahyalı | 130 | 38.07 N | 35.22 E |
| Yai ≃ | 114 | 5.02 N | 101.47 E |
| Yai, Khao ∧, Asia | 110 | 12.27 N | 99.26 E |
| Yai, Khao ∧, Thai | 110 | 15.25 N | 99.20 E |
| Yainax Butte ∧ | 202 | 42.20 N | 121.16 W |
| Yaita, Nihon | 94 | 36.48 N | 139.56 E |
| Yaita, Nihon | 268 | 35.57 N | 140.03 E |
| Yaitopya → Ethiopia □ 1 | 144 | 9.00 N | 39.00 E |
| Yaizu | 94 | 34.52 N | 138.20 E |
| Yajiang | 102 | 30.02 N | 101.05 E |
| Yaka | 130 | 41.15 N | 34.01 E |
| Yakacık | 130 | 36.47 N | 36.10 E |
| Yakacık ◆ 8 | 267b | 40.55 N | 29.13 E |
| Yakage | 96 | 34.37 N | 133.35 E |
| Yakak, Cape › | 180 | 51.38 N | 177.00 W |
| Yakapınar | 130 | 37.00 N | 35.36 E |
| Yakarta → Jakarta | 115a | 6.10 S | 106.48 E |
| Yake-dake ∧ | 94 | 36.14 N | 137.35 E |
| Yake-yama ∧ | 94 | 36.55 N | 138.03 E |
| Yakhchāl, Afg. | 120 | 31.47 N | 64.41 E |
| Yakhchāl, Afg. | 128 | 31.47 N | 64.41 E |
| Yakhnyky | 78 | 50.26 N | 33.10 E |
| Yakima | 202 | 46.36 N | 120.30 W |
| Yakima □ 6 | 224 | 46.34 N | 121.03 W |
| Yakima ≃ | 202 | 46.15 N | 119.02 W |
| Yakima Firing Center ■ | 202 | 46.44 N | 120.10 W |
| Yakima Indian Reservation ◆ 4 | 224 | 46.16 N | 121.03 W |
| Yakkan ≃ | 96 | 33.34 N | 131.22 E |
| Yakmach | 128 | 28.45 N | 63.51 E |
| Yako | 150 | 12.58 N | 2.16 W |
| Yakō ◆ 8 | 268 | 35.32 N | 139.41 E |
| Yakobi Island I | 180 | 58.00 N | 136.30 W |
| Yakoma | 152 | 4.05 N | 22.27 E |
| Yakou | 100 | 24.46 N | 118.46 E |
| Yakuendai | 268 | 35.43 N | 140.03 E |
| Yakuluku | 154 | 4.20 N | 28.48 E |
| Yakumo | 92a | 42.15 N | 140.16 E |
| Yakuno | 96 | 35.19 N | 135.00 E |
| Yakushi-dake ∧ | 94 | 36.28 N | 137.33 E |
| Yakushi-ji ⛩ 1 | 94 | 36.25 N | 139.53 E |
| Yaku-shima I | 93b | 30.20 N | 130.30 E |
| Yakutat | 180 | 59.33 N | 139.44 W |
| Yakutat Bay ⊂ | 180 | 59.40 N | 140.00 W |
| Yakutat Seamount ✦ 3 | 16 | 35.15 N | 48.00 W |
| Yakutia → Jakutija □ 3 | 74 | 67.00 N | 125.00 E |
| Yakutsk → Jakutsk | 74 | 62.00 N | 129.40 E |
| Yakymivka | 78 | 46.42 N | 35.09 E |
| Yala, Ghana | 150 | 10.07 N | 1.52 W |
| Yala, Thai | 110 | 6.33 N | 101.18 E |
| Yalaha | 220 | 28.44 N | 81.48 W |
| Yalahau, Laguna ⊂ | 232 | 21.30 N | 87.15 W |
| Yalakdere | 130 | 40.36 N | 29.33 E |
| Yalama | 84 | 41.44 N | 48.34 E |
| Yalata | 162 | 31.29 S | 131.52 E |
| Yalata Aboriginal Reserve ◆ 4 | 162 | 31.30 S | 131.45 E |
| Yalca, Laguna ⊜ | 258 | 35.34 S | 57.55 W |
| Yalding | 260 | 51.13 N | 0.26 E |
| Yale, B.C., Can. | 182 | 49.34 N | 121.26 W |
| Yale, Mi., U.S. | 190 | 43.07 N | 82.47 W |
| Yale, Ok., U.S. | 196 | 36.06 N | 96.41 W |
| Yale, Va., U.S. | 208 | 36.50 N | 77.17 W |
| Yale, Lake ⊜ | 220 | 28.54 N | 81.45 W |
| Yale, Mount ∧ | 200 | 38.51 N | 106.18 W |
| Yale Lake ⊜ 1 | 224 | 46.00 N | 122.12 W |
| Yalgar ≃ | 162 | 26.09 S | 117.57 E |
| Yalgoo | 162 | 28.20 S | 116.41 E |
| Yalgorup National Park ♠ | 168a | 32.55 S | 115.41 E |
| Yali | 152 | 0.04 N | 21.03 E |
| Yaliji | 98 | 36.06 N | 114.56 E |
| Yalikamba | 152 | 1.17 S | 22.30 E |
| Yalinga | 152 | 6.31 N | 23.15 E |
| Yalisere | 152 | 0.11 N | 22.33 E |
| Yalleroi | 166 | 24.04 S | 145.45 E |
| Yallourn | 169 | 38.11 S | 146.21 E |
| Yallourn North | 169 | 38.09 S | 146.22 E |
| Yalnızçam Dağları ⋀ | 84 | 41.10 N | 42.25 E |
| Yalobusha ≃ | 194 | 33.33 N | 90.10 W |
| Yaloká | 152 | 5.19 N | 17.05 E |
| Yalong ≃ | 102 | 26.37 N | 101.48 E |
| Yaloupi ≃ | 250 | 2.47 N | 52.28 W |
| Yalova | 130 | 40.39 N | 29.15 E |
| Yalpuh, ozero ⊜ | 78 | 45.25 N | 28.37 E |
| Yalta, Ukr. | 78 | 44.30 N | 34.10 E |
| Yalta, Ukr. | 83 | 46.58 N | 37.16 E |
| Yaltushkiv | 78 | 48.58 N | 27.30 E |
| Yalu | 89 | 48.34 N | 122.09 E |
| Yalu (Amnok-kang) ≃, Asia | 98 | 39.55 N | 124.22 E |
| Yalu ≃, Zhg. | 89 | 46.56 N | 123.30 E |
| Yalufi | 152 | 0.45 N | 24.26 E |
| Yalvaç | 130 | 38.17 N | 31.11 E |
| Yalwal Creek ≃ | 170 | 34.50 S | 150.23 E |
| Yamachiche | 206 | 46.16 N | 72.50 W |
| Yamachiche ≃ | 206 | 46.16 N | 72.48 W |
| Yamada, Nihon | 92 | 39.28 N | 141.57 E |
| Yamada, Nihon | 94 | 35.49 N | 140.36 E |
| Yamada, Nihon | 94 | 36.34 N | 137.05 E |
| Yamada, Nihon | 96 | 33.33 N | 130.47 E |
| Yamada → Tosa-yamada, Nihon | 96 | 33.36 N | 133.41 E |
| Yamada, Nihon | 174m | 26.26 N | 127.47 E |
| Yamada, Nihon | 270 | 34.31 N | 135.39 E |
| Yamada, Nihon | 270 | 34.48 N | 135.32 E |
| Yamada ≃ | 270 | 34.47 N | 135.04 E |
| Yamaga, Nihon | 96 | 33.01 N | 130.41 E |
| Yamaga, Nihon | 96 | 33.27 N | 131.30 E |
| Yamagata, Nihon | 92 | 38.15 N | 140.20 E |
| Yamagata, Nihon | 94 | 36.38 N | 140.24 E |
| Yamagata, Nihon | 94 | 36.10 N | 137.52 E |
| Yamagawa | 92 | 31.12 N | 130.39 E |
| Yamaguchi, Nihon | 94 | 35.33 N | 137.33 E |
| Yamaguchi, Nihon | 96 | 34.10 N | 131.29 E |
| Yamaguchi, Nihon | 270 | 34.50 N | 135.15 E |
| Yamaguchi □ 5 | 96 | 34.20 N | 131.30 E |
| Yamaguchi-chosuichi ⊜ 1 | 268 | 35.46 N | 139.25 E |
| Yama-Hita-Hiko-san-kokutei-kōen ♠ | 96 | 33.25 N | 131.02 E |
| Yamakawa | 96 | 34.04 N | 134.15 E |
| Yamakita | 94 | 35.21 N | 139.05 E |
| Yamakuni | 96 | 33.24 N | 131.02 E |
| Yamakuni ≃ | 96 | 33.37 N | 131.12 E |
| Yamām, Jabal al- ∧ | 132 | 30.02 N | 35.28 E |
| Yamamoto, Nihon | 96 | 34.07 N | 133.44 E |
| Yamamoto, Nihon | 270 | 34.38 N | 135.38 E |
| Yamanaka | 94 | 36.15 N | 136.22 E |
| Yamanakako | 94 | 35.24 N | 138.52 E |
| Yamanaka-ko ⊜ | 94 | 35.25 N | 138.52 E |
| Yamanashi | 94 | 35.40 N | 138.40 E |
| Yamanashi □ 5 | 94 | 35.30 N | 138.30 E |
| Yamanouchi | 94 | 36.44 N | 138.25 E |
| Yamasaki | 96 | 35.00 N | 134.33 E |
| Yamashina ◆ 8 | 270 | 34.58 N | 135.49 E |
| Yamashiro, Nihon | 94 | 34.45 N | 135.49 E |
| Yamashiro, Nihon | 96 | 33.57 N | 133.45 E |
| Yamaska (Saint-Michel) | 206 | 46.00 N | 72.55 W |
| Yamaska □ 6 | 206 | 46.00 N | 72.45 W |
| Yamaska ≃ | 206 | 46.06 N | 72.56 W |
| Yamaska, Mont ∧ 2 | 206 | 45.27 N | 72.52 W |
| Yamaska Nord ≃ | 206 | 45.17 N | 72.51 W |
| Yamaska Sud-Est ≃ | 206 | 45.17 N | 72.55 W |
| Yamate | 270 | 34.30 N | 135.27 E |
| Yamatengwumulu | 102 | 38.38 N | 97.05 E |
| Yamato, Nihon | 94 | 35.48 N | 136.54 E |
| Yamato, Nihon | 94 | 35.29 N | 139.29 E |
| Yamato, Nihon | 94 | 37.10 N | 138.56 E |
| Yamato, Nihon | 96 | 33.08 N | 130.26 E |
| Yamato ≃ | 96 | 34.36 N | 135.26 E |
| Yamato-Aogaki-kokutei-kōen ♠ | 94 | 34.40 N | 135.50 E |
| Yamato-kōriyama | 96 | 34.38 N | 135.47 E |
| Yamato-takada | 96 | 34.31 N | 135.45 E |
| Yamatsuri | 94 | 36.52 N | 140.25 E |
| Yamazaki | 268 | 35.56 N | 139.54 E |
| Yamba | 166 | 29.26 S | 153.22 E |
| Yambata | 152 | 2.26 N | 21.58 E |
| Yambéring | 150 | 11.49 N | 12.21 W |
| Yambio | 154 | 4.34 N | 28.23 E |
| Yambol → Jambol | 38 | 42.29 N | 26.30 E |
| Yamboyo | 152 | 0.40 N | 22.18 E |
| Yambrasbamba | 248 | 5.45 S | 77.54 W |
| Yambuya | 154 | 1.16 N | 24.33 E |
| Yamdena, Pulau I | 164 | 7.36 S | 131.25 E |
| Yame | 96 | 33.28 N | 130.34 E |
| Ya Men ⊂ | 100 | 22.09 N | 113.05 E |
| Yamenkou | 105 | 39.53 N | 116.12 E |
| Yamenying | 89 | 43.25 N | 122.19 E |
| Yamethin | 110 | 20.26 N | 96.09 E |
| Yamhill | 224 | 45.21 N | 123.11 W |
| Yamhill □ 6 | 224 | 45.15 N | 123.20 W |
| Yamhill ≃ | 224 | 45.14 N | 123.00 W |
| Yamia | 150 | 13.24 N | 10.18 E |
| Yamizo-san ∧ | 94 | 36.56 N | 140.17 E |
| Yamma Yamma, Lake ⊜ | 166 | 26.20 S | 141.25 E |
| Yamoussoukro | 150 | 6.49 N | 5.17 W |
| Yampa | 200 | 40.09 N | 106.54 W |
| Yampa ≃ | 200 | 40.32 N | 108.59 W |
| Yampa Plateau ⋀ 1 | 200 | 40.25 N | 109.00 W |
| Yamparaez | 248 | 19.10 S | 65.10 W |
| Yampil', Ukr. | 78 | 48.16 N | 28.17 E |
| Yampil', Ukr. | 78 | 49.58 N | 26.14 E |
| Yampil', Ukr. | 78 | 51.57 N | 33.46 E |
| Yampil', Ukr. | 83 | 48.56 N | 37.58 E |
| Yamsay Mountain ∧ | 202 | 42.56 N | 121.22 W |
| Yamu | 102 | 43.48 N | 94.48 E |
| Yamuna ≃ | 120 | 25.25 N | 81.50 E |
| Yamuna Bridge ◆ 5 | 272a | 28.40 N | 77.14 E |
| Yamunānagar | 124 | 30.07 N | 77.18 E |
| Yamzho Yumco ⊜ | 120 | 28.58 N | 90.44 E |
| Yan | 114 | 5.48 N | 100.22 E |
| Yan ≃, S. Lan. | 122 | 8.55 N | 81.01 E |
| Yan ≃, Zhg. | 102 | 36.24 N | 110.28 E |
| Yanac | 166 | 36.08 S | 141.26 E |
| Yanacachi | 248 | 16.23 S | 67.43 W |
| Yanachaga-Chemillen, Parque Nacional ♠ | 248 | 10.10 S | 75.20 W |
| Yanadani | 96 | 33.32 N | 133.01 E |
| Yanagawa | 96 | 33.10 N | 130.24 E |
| Yanagi | 270 | 34.25 N | 135.56 E |
| Yanagimoto | 270 | 34.34 N | 135.51 E |
| Yanahara | 96 | 34.55 N | 134.05 E |
| Yanaha-shima I | 174m | 26.54 N | 127.56 E |
| Yanahuara | 248 | 16.24 S | 71.33 W |
| Yanai | 96 | 33.58 N | 132.07 E |
| Yanaka | 268 | 35.24 N | 140.01 E |
| Yanam | 122 | 16.44 N | 82.13 E |
| Yan'an | 102 | 36.36 N | 109.28 E |
| Yanaoca | 248 | 14.13 S | 71.26 W |
| Yanarsu | 130 | 38.02 N | 41.33 E |
| Yanbian | 102 | 26.55 N | 101.30 E |
| Yanbu | 100 | 23.05 N | 113.10 E |
| Yanbu' al-Baḥr | 128 | 24.05 N | 38.03 E |
| Yanbutou | 100 | 29.52 N | 115.04 E |
| Yanceyville | 192 | 36.24 N | 79.20 W |
| Yanchang | 102 | 36.31 N | 110.08 E |
| Yancheng, Zhg. | 100 | 33.36 N | 113.57 E |
| Yancheng, Zhg. | 100 | 33.24 N | 120.09 E |
| Yanchep | 168a | 31.33 S | 115.41 E |
| Yanchep National Park ♠ | 168a | 31.32 S | 115.40 E |
| Yanchi, Zhg. | 102 | 37.52 N | 107.22 E |
| Yanchi, Zhg. | 105 | 40.02 N | 115.53 E |
| Yanchuan | 102 | 36.56 N | 110.05 E |
| Yanco | 166 | 34.36 S | 146.25 E |
| Yanco Creek ≃ | 166 | 35.16 S | 145.07 E |
| Yanda Creek ≃ | 166 | 30.28 S | 145.45 E |
| Yandal | 162 | 27.33 S | 121.07 E |
| Yandama Creek ≃ | 166 | 30.00 S | 140.10 E |
| Yandé, Île I | 175f | 20.03 S | 163.49 E |
| Yande Aboriginal Reserve ◆ 4 | 162 | 21.35 S | 118.45 E |
| Yandev | 150 | 7.20 N | 9.01 E |
| Yandina | 175e | 9.07 S | 159.13 E |
| Yandja | 152 | 1.41 S | 17.43 E |
| Yandongi | 152 | 2.51 N | 22.16 E |
| Yandoon | 110 | 17.02 N | 95.39 E |
| Yandua Island I | 175g | 16.49 S | 178.18 E |
| Yandun | 102 | 42.20 N | 94.09 E |
| Yanfeng | 102 | 25.53 N | 101.01 E |
| Yanfolila | 150 | 11.11 N | 8.09 W |
| Yang ≃, Thai | 110 | 15.44 N | 104.00 E |
| Yang ≃, Zhg. | 105 | 40.24 N | 115.20 E |
| Yangambi | 154 | 0.47 N | 24.28 E |
| Yangan, Austl. | 171a | 28.12 S | 152.13 E |
| Yang'an, Zhg. | 98 | 37.38 N | 117.09 E |
| Yan'gang | 100 | 26.02 N | 116.22 E |
| Yangarakata | 154 | 3.01 N | 30.28 E |
| Yangasa Levu I | 175g | 18.57 S | 178.26 W |
| Yangbajain | 120 | 30.06 N | 90.33 E |
| Yangce | 100 | 32.58 N | 113.14 E |
| Yangcha | 98 | 41.11 N | 126.15 E |
| Yangchang | 107 | 30.22 N | 103.42 E |
| Yangcheng, Zhg. | 102 | 35.29 N | 112.25 E |
| Yangcheng, Zhg. | 106 | 31.24 N | 120.47 E |
| Yangcheng Hu ⊜ | 106 | 31.26 N | 120.47 E |
| Yangchiang → Yangjiang | 102 | 21.51 N | 111.56 E |
| Yangch'ŏn ◆ 8 | 271b | 37.34 N | 126.51 E |
| Yangchow → Yangzhou | 100 | 32.24 N | 119.26 E |
| Yangchu | 98 | 37.11 N | 120.47 E |
| Yangch'üan → Yangquan | 98 | 37.52 N | 113.36 E |
| Yangchun | 102 | 22.10 N | 111.46 E |
| Yangcun, Zhg. | 100 | 28.07 N | 117.40 E |
| Yangcun, Zhg. | 100 | 23.26 N | 114.30 E |
| Yangcun, Zhg. | 105 | 39.09 N | 115.50 E |
| Yangcunqiao | 100 | 29.36 N | 119.28 E |
| Yangdachengzi | 89 | 43.59 N | 124.25 E |
| Yangdalinzi | 98 | 42.38 N | 125.07 E |
| Yangdang | 100 | 32.23 N | 112.39 E |
| Yangdian | 106 | 31.08 N | 119.45 E |
| Yang'erzhuang | 98 | 38.18 N | 117.30 E |
| Yangfang | 105 | 40.07 N | 116.07 E |
| Yangfangpu | 105 | 40.48 N | 115.01 E |
| Yangfengang | 105 | 39.07 N | 116.52 E |
| Yangfenzhen | 106 | 30.28 N | 120.03 E |
| Yanggang Do □ 4 | 98 | 41.15 N | 128.00 E |
| Yangganzhen | 106 | 31.00 N | 119.15 E |
| Yanggao | 98 | 40.25 N | 113.44 E |
| Yanggezhuang | 105 | 40.09 N | 116.48 E |
| Yanggong-ni | 271b | 37.39 N | 126.37 E |
| Yanggu, Taehan | 98 | 38.06 N | 127.59 E |
| Yanggu, Zhg. | 98 | 34.44 N | 114.48 E |
| Yanggu, Zhg. | 98 | 36.08 N | 115.48 E |
| Yangguanpu | 100 | 32.13 N | 115.31 E |
| Yanghang | 106 | 31.22 N | 121.26 E |
| Yanghe | 100 | 33.47 N | 118.23 E |
| Yanghexi | 102 | 29.39 N | 108.40 E |
| Yanghu | 100 | 32.34 N | 116.30 E |
| Yanghua | 107 | 30.11 N | 104.45 E |
| Yanghua ≃ | 107 | 30.09 N | 104.42 E |
| Yangi-Yul' → Jangijul' | 85 | 41.07 N | 69.03 E |
| Yangji, Zhg. | 98 | 36.44 N | 113.56 E |
| Yangji, Zhg. | 98 | 34.25 N | 116.06 E |
| Yangji, Zhg. | 100 | 34.19 N | 119.28 E |
| Yangjia, Zhg. | 98 | 34.19 N | 119.28 E |
| Yangjia, Zhg. | 106 | 30.41 N | 120.15 E |
| Yangjiachang, Zhg. | 107 | 29.23 N | 104.21 E |
| Yangjiachang, Zhg. | 107 | 29.45 N | 105.21 E |
| Yangjiafeng | 100 | 30.49 N | 112.47 E |
| Yangjiagou | 105 | 39.18 N | 117.54 E |
| Yangjiajie | 107 | 30.18 N | 104.39 E |
| Yangjian | 106 | 31.39 N | 120.33 E |
| Yangjiang | 102 | 21.51 N | 111.56 E |
| Yangjiaogou | 98 | 37.16 N | 118.50 E |
| Yangjiaqiao, Zhg. | 100 | 27.44 N | 112.46 E |
| Yangjiaqiao, Zhg. | 106 | 31.53 N | 121.42 E |
| Yangjiaqiao, Zhg. | 106 | 32.02 N | 121.26 E |
| Yangjiatao | 105 | 39.49 N | 117.51 E |
| Yangjiawopu | 104 | 42.21 N | 122.57 E |
| Yangjiazeng | 105 | 40.12 N | 117.04 E |
| Yangjiazhangzi | 104 | 40.48 N | 120.33 E |
| Yangjie | 102 | 24.49 N | 100.22 E |
| Yangjishi | 100 | 26.39 N | 113.14 E |
| Yangkou | 100 | 26.47 N | 117.51 E |
| Yangkoushi | 100 | 28.39 N | 118.53 E |
| Yanglinjie | 100 | 29.07 N | 113.27 E |
| Yangliupu, Zhg. | 100 | 30.52 N | 118.37 E |
| Yangliupu, Zhg. | 107 | 30.09 N | 104.03 E |
| Yangliuqing | 105 | 39.08 N | 117.01 E |
| Yangloudong | 100 | 29.31 N | 113.44 E |
| Yanglousi | 100 | 29.30 N | 113.38 E |
| Yangluo | 100 | 30.41 N | 114.34 E |
| Yangluomayu | 104 | 40.47 N | 122.54 E |
| Yangmachang | 107 | 30.39 N | 103.45 E |
| Yangma Dao I | 98 | 37.28 N | 121.37 E |
| Yangmahe | 107 | 30.29 N | 104.31 E |
| Yangmeisi | 100 | 25.42 N | 114.30 E |
| Yangmiao, Zhg. | 98 | 34.11 N | 114.53 E |
| Yangmiao, Zhg. | 106 | 30.51 N | 120.49 E |
| Yangmingshan ◆ 8 | 269d | 25.09 N | 121.33 E |
| Yangming Shan ∧ | 102 | 26.03 N | 111.56 E |
| Yangmugou, Zhg. | 98 | 40.36 N | 124.28 E |
| Yangmugou, Zhg. | 104 | 41.11 N | 123.50 E |
| Yangmulin | 105 | 40.06 N | 115.12 E |
| Yangon (Rangoon) | 110 | 16.47 N | 96.10 E |
| Yangon □ 8 | 110 | 16.50 N | 96.10 E |
| Yangor | 174b | 0.31 S | 166.54 E |
| Yangpingguan | 102 | 32.51 N | 106.09 E |
| Yangpu | 100 | 27.14 N | 119.08 E |
| Yangp'yŏng | 98 | 37.30 N | 127.29 E |
| Yangp'yŏng-ni | 98 | 40.53 N | 127.58 E |
| Yangqi | 106 | 31.23 N | 119.57 E |
| Yangquan | 98 | 37.52 N | 113.36 E |
| Yangriwan | 102 | 31.37 N | 110.49 E |
| Yangsan | 98 | 35.21 N | 129.03 E |
| Yangshan, Zhg. | 98 | 41.13 N | 120.24 E |
| Yangshan, Zhg. | 98 | 35.13 N | 116.13 E |
| Yangshan, Zhg. | 102 | 24.28 N | 112.38 E |
| Yangshigangzi | 104 | 41.42 N | 122.59 E |
| Yangshitun | 104 | 42.06 N | 123.44 E |
| Yangshu | 106 | 31.39 N | 120.08 E |
| Yangshugemen | 105 | 40.55 N | 118.18 E |
| Yangshugoudonggou | 104 | 41.43 N | 120.41 E |
| Yangshuling | 98 | 41.02 N | 118.47 E |
| Yangshuo | 102 | 24.45 N | 110.24 E |
| Yangtan | 106 | 30.42 N | 119.11 E |
| Yangtian Zhang ∧ | 100 | 24.37 N | 115.38 E |
| Yangting | 98 | 37.24 N | 122.07 E |
| Yangtou | 100 | 23.26 N | 115.24 E |
| Yangtze → Chang ≃ | 90 | 31.48 N | 121.10 E |
| Yanguan | 106 | 30.26 N | 120.32 E |
| Yangwan, Zhg. | 100 | 28.22 N | 116.46 E |
| Yangwan, Zhg. | 106 | 31.03 N | 120.22 E |
| Yangxi, Zhg. | 100 | 30.11 N | 118.39 E |
| Yangxi, Zhg. | 100 | 27.18 N | 114.10 E |
| Yangxian | 102 | 33.03 N | 107.47 E |
| Yangxiang, Zhg. | 106 | 31.29 N | 119.35 E |
| Yangxiang, Zhg. | 106 | 31.12 N | 121.01 E |
| Yangxiangtun | 104 | 40.58 N | 122.48 E |
| Yangxiaodian | 100 | 31.46 N | 116.45 E |
| Yangximu ≃ | 104 | 42.04 N | 123.00 E |
| Yangxin, Zhg. | 98 | 37.39 N | 117.34 E |
| Yangxin, Zhg. | 100 | 29.51 N | 115.12 E |
| Yangxiudian | 271a | 39.44 N | 116.32 E |
| Yangyang | 98 | 38.04 N | 128.36 E |
| Yangyuan (Xicheng) | 98 | 40.01 N | 114.10 E |
| Yangze | 100 | 26.57 N | 118.23 E |
| Yangzhong | 106 | 32.16 N | 119.49 E |
| Yangzhou | 100 | 32.24 N | 119.26 E |
| Yangzhuang | 100 | 33.36 N | 118.58 E |
| Yangzhujuanzi | 104 | 41.38 N | 122.46 E |
| Yangzi | 100 | 31.19 N | 112.36 E |
| Yangzishao | 98 | 42.28 N | 126.09 E |
| Yanhaiyingzi | 104 | 41.52 N | 123.05 E |
| Yanhe, Zhg. | 100 | 31.16 N | 115.07 E |
| Yanhe, Zhg. | 102 | 28.37 N | 108.35 E |
| Yanhecheng | 105 | 40.04 N | 115.43 E |
| Yanheying | 98 | 40.02 N | 119.03 E |
| Yanhui | 98 | 37.54 N | 113.51 E |
| Yanina → Ioánnina | 38 | 39.40 N | 20.50 E |
| Yanji, Zhg. | 98 | 34.41 N | 115.27 E |
| Yanji, Zhg. | 98 | 42.57 N | 129.32 E |
| Yanji (Longjing), Zhg. | 98 | 42.47 N | 129.26 E |
| Yanji, Zhg. | 98 | 34.17 N | 115.39 E |
| Yanjia | 104 | 40.57 N | 121.41 E |
| Yanjiabao | 106 | 32.19 N | 120.07 E |
| Yanjiadian | 98 | 39.48 N | 121.49 E |
| Yanjiahe | 100 | 31.48 N | 114.50 E |
| Yanjiajie | 104 | 41.02 N | 121.32 E |
| Yanjiao | 105 | 39.56 N | 116.48 E |
| Yanjiapu | 105 | 39.52 N | 118.00 E |
| Yanjiatuozi | 104 | 42.27 N | 123.47 E |
| Yanjiawopeng | 104 | 40.59 N | 121.17 E |
| Yanjin | 98 | 35.11 N | 114.11 E |
| Yanjing, Zhg. | 102 | 29.00 N | 98.34 E |
| Yanjing, Zhg. | 107 | 29.56 N | 106.21 E |
| Yankalilla | 168b | 35.28 S | 138.21 E |
| Yankalilla Bay ⊂ | 168b | 35.28 S | 138.15 E |
| Yankari Game Reserve ◆ 4 | 146 | 9.45 N | 10.30 E |
| Yankdŏk | 98 | 39.14 N | 126.41 E |
| Yankee Lake | 210 | 41.35 N | 74.33 W |
| Yankee Springs State Recreation Area ♠ | 216 | 42.38 N | 85.30 W |
| Yankee Stadium ♠ | 276 | 40.50 N | 73.56 W |
| Yankeetown | 220 | 29.01 N | 82.42 W |
| Yankton | 198 | 42.52 N | 97.23 W |
| Yankton Indian Reservation ◆ 4 | 198 | 43.10 N | 98.22 W |
| Yanling, Zhg. | 98 | 34.07 N | 114.11 E |
| Yanling, Zhg. | 106 | 31.54 N | 119.30 E |
| Yanliumiao | 100 | 32.01 N | 116.52 E |
| Yanmeimeizi | 105 | 39.42 N | 115.03 E |
| Yanna | 166 | 26.56 S | 146.03 E |
| Yannarie ≃ | 162 | 22.28 S | 114.48 E |
| Yanqi | 90 | 42.00 N | 86.15 E |
| Yanqian, Zhg. | 100 | 24.54 N | 116.14 E |
| Yanqian, Zhg. | 100 | 26.15 N | 117.28 E |
| Yanqianhu | 104 | 42.16 N | 123.12 E |
| Yanqiao | 106 | 31.41 N | 120.17 E |
| Yanqidoumen | 106 | 31.17 N | 118.42 E |
| Yanqing | 105 | 40.28 N | 115.58 E |
| Yanque | 248 | 15.39 S | 71.39 W |
| Yanrey | 162 | 22.31 S | 114.48 E |
| Yanshan, Zhg. | 98 | 38.05 N | 117.13 E |
| Yanshan, Zhg. | 100 | 28.18 N | 117.41 E |
| Yanshan, Zhg. | 102 | 23.41 N | 104.21 E |
| Yan Shan ⋀ | 105 | 40.20 N | 117.40 E |
| Yanshankou | 105 | 39.59 N | 117.42 E |
| Yanshi | 100 | 25.17 N | 117.10 E |
| Yanshi ≃ | 100 | 25.20 N | 117.17 E |
| Yanshou | 89 | 45.28 N | 128.20 E |
| Yansi | 100 | 29.48 N | 118.20 E |
| Yanṭā | 132 | 33.36 N | 35.57 E |
| Yantabulla | 166 | 29.21 S | 145.00 E |
| Yantai (Chefoo), Zhg. | 98 | 37.33 N | 121.20 E |
| Yantai, Zhg. | 105 | 39.47 N | 116.38 E |
| Yantan, Zhg. | 100 | 28.28 N | 120.44 E |
| Yantan, Zhg. | 100 | 28.55 N | 120.11 E |
| Yantan, Zhg. | 107 | 29.17 N | 104.52 E |
| Yantian, Zhg. | 100 | 26.53 N | 119.53 E |
| Yantian, Zhg. | 100 | 27.21 N | 114.22 E |
| Yantic ≃ | 207 | 41.31 N | 72.05 W |
| Yantietang ⩸ | 106 | 31.49 N | 120.46 E |
| Yanting | 102 | 31.19 N | 105.23 E |
| Yantis | 222 | 32.56 N | 95.35 W |
| Yantongshan, Zhg. | 89 | 43.17 N | 126.00 E |
| Yantongshan, Zhg. | 105 | 40.42 N | 115.06 E |
| Yanu | 164 | 9.57 S | 148.25 E |
| Yanwangshan | 104 | 41.36 N | 123.57 E |
| Yanweigang | 98 | 34.30 N | 119.48 E |
| Yanxi | 100 | 24.46 N | 117.47 E |
| Yanxia | 100 | 29.34 N | 114.50 E |
| Yanxidu | 100 | 26.51 N | 114.58 E |
| Yanxing | 102 | 25.23 N | 101.42 E |
| Yan Yean Reservoir ⊜ 1 | 169 | 37.33 S | 145.08 E |
| Yanyegongsi | 106 | 32.02 N | 121.41 E |
| Yanyuan | 102 | 27.29 N | 101.32 E |
| Yanzhou | 98 | 35.33 N | 116.50 E |
| Yanziji | 106 | 32.09 N | 118.49 E |
| Yanzijiao | 102 | 23.38 N | 100.12 E |
| Yanzikou | 102 | 27.31 N | 105.21 E |
| Yao, Centraf. | 152 | 5.19 N | 19.36 E |
| Yao, Nihon | 96 | 34.37 N | 135.36 E |
| Yao, Tchad | 146 | 12.51 N | 17.34 E |
| Yao Airport ⊠ | 270 | 34.36 N | 135.36 E |
| Yao'an | 102 | 25.32 N | 101.12 E |
| Yaoba | 107 | 28.45 N | 105.39 E |
| Yaocun, Zhg. | 98 | 36.12 N | 113.50 E |
| Yaocun, Zhg. | 98 | 35.41 N | 116.57 E |
| Yaocun, Zhg. | 105 | 39.09 N | 115.32 E |
| Yaodafangshen | 104 | 42.27 N | 122.59 E |
| Yaoerwan | 105 | 40.49 N | 115.27 E |
| Yaogongbu | 100 | 29.51 N | 120.18 E |
| Yaohongcaopao | 104 | 40.55 N | 122.26 E |
| Yaohuamen | 106 | 32.08 N | 118.52 E |
| Yaohuangdi | 104 | 41.32 N | 122.48 E |
| Yaojiaji | 100 | 31.14 N | 114.22 E |
| Yaojiaqiao | 106 | 32.10 N | 119.46 E |
| Yaojiatun | 104 | 41.18 N | 121.57 E |
| Yaojiawopeng | 104 | 41.47 N | 122.25 E |
| Yaojie | 102 | 36.26 N | 102.59 E |
| Yaoling | 100 | 24.49 N | 113.58 E |
| Yaolugou | 98 | 40.34 N | 119.24 E |
| Yaoluzi | 104 | 41.26 N | 121.34 E |
| Yaopi | 100 | 26.52 N | 113.38 E |
| Yaopu | 100 | 32.14 N | 118.20 E |
| Yaoqianhutun | 104 | 41.32 N | 123.36 E |
| Yaoshizhen | 107 | 30.11 N | 105.30 E |
| Yaotou | 100 | 26.38 N | 114.48 E |
| Yaotsu | 94 | 35.28 N | 137.09 E |
| Yaotun, Zhg. | 89 | 49.28 N | 127.30 E |
| Yaotun, Zhg. | 104 | 40.59 N | 122.18 E |
| Yaotutun | 104 | 42.06 N | 123.29 E |
| Yaoundé | 152 | 3.52 N | 11.31 E |
| Yaowan | 98 | 34.12 N | 118.03 E |
| Yaowangmiao | 98 | 40.47 N | 120.10 E |
| Yaoxian | 102 | 34.56 N | 108.53 E |
| Yaoya ≃ | 236 | 13.28 N | 84.14 W |
| Yao Yai, Ko I | 110 | 8.00 N | 98.35 E |
| Yaozhan | 89 | 52.53 N | 125.13 E |
| Yap I | 174q | 9.31 N | 138.06 E |
| Yapacaní | 248 | 16.45 S | 64.18 W |
| Yapacani ≃ | 248 | 16.00 S | 64.25 W |
| Yapakopra | 164 | 4.24 S | 135.05 E |
| Yapehe | 152 | 0.13 S | 24.27 E |
| Yapei (Tamale Port) | 150 | 9.10 N | 1.10 W |
| Yapen, Pulau I | 164 | 1.45 S | 136.15 E |
| Yapen, Selat ⊔ | 164 | 1.30 S | 136.10 E |
| Yapero | 164 | 4.59 S | 137.11 E |
| Yapeyú | 252 | 29.28 S | 56.49 W |
| Yaphank | 207 | 40.50 N | 72.56 W |
| Yappar ≃ | 166 | 18.22 S | 141.16 E |
| Yapraklı | 130 | 40.46 N | 33.47 E |
| Yap Trench ✦ 1 | 14 | 8.30 N | 138.00 E |
| Yaqian | 100 | 26.38 N | 114.30 E |
| Ya'qūb | 140 | 12.29 N | 25.11 E |
| Yaque del Norte ≃ | 238 | 19.51 N | 71.41 W |
| Yaqui ≃ | 232 | 27.37 N | 110.39 W |
| Yaquina ≃ | 202 | 44.37 N | 124.04 W |
| Yara | 240p | 20.16 N | 76.57 W |
| Yaracuy □ 3 | 246 | 10.20 N | 69.10 W |
| Yaraka | 166 | 24.53 S | 144.04 E |
| Yaratuar | 164 | 2.58 S | 134.40 E |
| Yarbasan | 130 | 38.59 N | 28.49 E |
| Yarcombe | 42 | 50.52 N | 3.05 W |
| Yardea | 166 | 32.23 S | 135.32 E |
| Yardımcı | 130 | 37.00 N | 38.59 E |
| Yardımcı Burnu › | 130 | 36.13 N | 30.25 E |
| Yardımlı | 84 | 38.55 N | 48.15 E |
| Yardley | 208 | 40.14 N | 74.50 W |
| Yardville | 208 | 40.10 N | 74.39 W |
| Yare ≃ | 42 | 52.35 N | 1.44 E |
| Yaremcha | 78 | 48.27 N | 24.33 E |
| Yarí ≃ | 246 | 0.23 S | 72.16 W |
| Yariga-take ∧ | 94 | 36.20 N | 137.39 E |
| Yārik | 123 | 32.06 N | 70.47 E |
| Yarīm | 144 | 14.29 N | 44.21 E |
| Yaring | 110 | 6.52 N | 101.22 E |
| Yaritagua | 246 | 10.05 N | 69.08 W |
| Yarkand → Shache | 120 | 38.25 N | 77.16 E |
| Yarkand → Yarkant ≃ | 90 | 40.28 N | 80.52 E |
| Yarkant (Yarkand) ≃ | 90 | 40.28 N | 80.52 E |
| Yarker | 212 | 44.23 N | 76.46 W |
| Yarkhūn ≃ | 123 | 36.17 N | 72.30 E |
| Yarlarweelor | 162 | 25.35 S | 117.59 E |
| Yarle Lakes ⊜ | 162 | 30.15 S | 131.27 E |
| Yarloop | 168a | 32.57 S | 115.54 E |
| Yarlung → Brahmaputra ≃ | 120 | 24.02 N | 90.59 E |
| Yarma | 130 | 37.49 N | 32.54 E |
| Yarmolyntsi | 78 | 49.12 N | 26.50 E |
| Yarmouth, N.S., Can. | 186 | 43.50 N | 66.07 W |
| Yarmouth, Eng., U.K. | 42 | 50.42 N | 1.29 W |
| Yarmouth → Great Yarmouth, Eng., U.K. | 42 | 52.37 N | 1.44 E |
| Yarmouth, Me., U.S. | 188 | 43.48 N | 70.11 W |
| Yarmouth, Ma., U.S. | 207 | 41.42 N | 70.13 W |
| Yarmu | 164 | 4.18 S | 142.17 E |
| Yarmūk, Nahr al- ≃ | 132 | 32.38 N | 35.34 E |
| Yaroslavets' | 78 | 51.33 N | 33.40 E |
| Yarova | 83 | 49.03 N | 37.37 E |
| Yarra ≃ | 169 | 37.51 S | 144.54 E |
| Yarra Bend Park ♠ | 274b | 37.48 S | 145.01 E |
| Yarra Glen | 169 | 37.40 S | 145.23 E |
| Yarragon | 169 | 38.12 S | 146.04 E |
| Yarra Junction | 169 | 37.47 S | 145.37 E |
| Yarraloola | 162 | 21.34 S | 115.52 E |
| Yarram | 166 | 38.33 S | 146.41 E |
| Yarraman | 171a | 26.50 S | 151.59 E |
| Yarrangobilly | 171b | 35.39 S | 148.28 E |
| Yarrangobilly ≃ | 171b | 35.48 N | 148.23 E |
| Yarrangobilly Caves ⩡ 5 | 171b | 35.44 S | 148.29 E |
| Yarraville | 274b | 37.49 S | 144.53 E |
| Yarrawonga | 166 | 36.01 S | 146.00 E |
| Yarra Yarra Lakes ⊜ | 162 | 29.40 S | 115.47 E |
| Yarrow, B.C., Can. | 224 | 49.05 N | 122.02 W |
| Yarrow, Scot., U.K. | 46 | 55.32 N | 3.01 W |
| Yarrow ≃ | 262 | 53.40 N | 2.49 W |
| Yarrowee ≃ | 169 | 37.48 S | 143.56 E |
| Yarrow Point | 224 | 47.39 N | 122.13 W |
| Yarrow Reservoir ⊜ 1 | 262 | 53.38 N | 2.34 W |
| Yarrow Water ≃ | 46 | 55.34 N | 2.51 W |
| Yarrunga, Lake ⊜ 1 | 170 | 34.45 S | 150.20 E |
| Yarty ≃ | 42 | 50.47 N | 3.01 W |
| Yarumal | 246 | 6.58 N | 75.24 W |
| Yasa | 152 | 3.42 S | 21.24 E |
| Yasaka, Nihon | 96 | 35.39 N | 135.07 E |
| Yasaka, Nihon | 96 | 34.46 N | 132.04 E |
| Yasa-Lokwa | 152 | 5.15 S | 19.24 E |
| Yasato | 94 | 36.14 N | 140.12 E |
| Yasawa I | 175g | 16.47 S | 177.31 E |
| Yasawa Group II | 175g | 17.00 S | 177.23 E |
| Yasendu | 152 | 0.27 N | 24.20 E |
| Yasenivs'kyy | 83 | 48.10 N | 39.10 E |
| Yashanjie | 106 | 30.51 N | 119.03 E |
| Yashbum | 144 | 14.19 N | 46.56 E |
| Yashi | 150 | 12.23 N | 7.54 E |
| Yashikera | 150 | 9.46 N | 3.28 E |
| Ya-shima I | 96 | 33.44 N | 132.09 E |
| Yashima ♠ | 96 | 34.23 N | 134.08 E |
| Yashio | 268 | 35.49 N | 139.51 E |
| Yashiro | 96 | 34.55 N | 134.58 E |
| Yashiro-jima I | 96 | 33.55 N | 132.15 E |
| Yāsīn | 123 | 36.21 N | 73.19 E |
| Yasinya | 78 | 48.16 N | 24.20 E |
| Yasku | 146 | 12.20 N | 12.30 E |
| Yasnohirka | 83 | 48.47 N | 37.33 E |
| Yasothon | 110 | 15.45 N | 104.08 E |
| Yass | 166 | 34.50 S | 148.55 E |
| Yassıada I | 267b | 40.51 N | 29.00 E |
| Yassy → Iaşi | 38 | 47.10 N | 27.35 E |
| Yasu, Nihon | 94 | 35.03 N | 136.01 E |
| Yasu, Nihon | 96 | 33.32 N | 133.45 E |
| Yasuda | 96 | 33.26 N | 133.59 E |
| Yasugi | 96 | 35.26 N | 133.15 E |
| Yāsūj | 128 | 30.40 N | 51.36 E |
| Yasun Burnu › | 130 | 41.08 N | 37.41 E |
| Yasuní ≃ | 246 | 0.56 S | 75.23 W |
| Yasuni, Parque Nacional ♠ | 246 | 0.50 S | 76.15 W |
| Yasuoka | 94 | 35.22 N | 137.50 E |
| Yasuura | 96 | 34.17 N | 132.45 E |
| Yasuzuka | 94 | 37.08 N | 138.28 E |
| Yasynivka | 83 | 48.08 N | 37.57 E |
| Yasynuvata | 83 | 48.08 N | 37.51 E |
| Yata | 248 | 13.20 S | 66.35 W |
| Yata ≃, Bol. | 248 | 10.29 S | 65.26 W |
| Yata ≃, Centraf. | 146 | 10.23 N | 22.45 E |
| Yatabe | 94 | 36.02 N | 140.04 E |
| Yatağan | 130 | 37.20 N | 28.09 E |
| Yatakala | 150 | 14.48 N | 0.22 E |
| Yata-Ngaya, Réserve de Faune de la ◆ 4 | 146 | 9.15 N | 23.30 W |
| Yāṭar | 132 | 33.09 N | 35.20 E |
| Yatate-yama ∧ | 92 | 34.10 N | 129.10 E |
| Yaté | 175f | 22.09 S | 166.57 E |
| Yates □ 6 | 210 | 42.40 N | 77.03 W |
| Yatesboro | 214 | 40.48 N | 79.20 W |
| Yates Center | 198 | 37.52 N | 95.43 W |
| Yates City | 190 | 40.46 N | 90.00 W |
| Yathata Island I | 175g | 17.15 S | 179.32 W |
| Yathkyed Lake ⊜ | 176 | 62.41 N | 98.00 W |
| Yating | 102 | 25.03 N | 106.05 E |
| Yatomi | 94 | 35.06 N | 136.43 E |
| Yatsuga-take ∧ | 94 | 35.59 N | 138.23 E |
| Yatsuga-take-chūshin-kōgen-kokutei-kōen ♠ | 94 | 36.03 N | 138.20 E |
| Yatsuka | 96 | 35.17 N | 133.42 E |
| Yatsuo | 94 | 36.34 N | 137.08 E |
| Yatsushiro | 92 | 32.30 N | 130.36 E |
| Yatsushiro-kai ⊂ | 92 | 32.20 N | 130.25 E |
| Yaṭṭah | 132 | 31.27 N | 35.05 E |
| Yatta Plateau ⋀ 1 | 154 | 2.00 S | 38.00 E |
| Yatton | 42 | 51.24 N | 2.49 W |
| Yatuá ≃ | 246 | 1.43 N | 66.30 W |
| Yatusiro → Yatsushiro | 92 | 32.30 N | 130.36 E |
| Yauca | 248 | 15.40 S | 74.32 W |
| Yauca ≃ | 248 | 15.41 S | 74.31 W |
| Yauco | 240m | 18.02 N | 66.51 W |
| Yauco ≃ | 240m | 17.59 N | 66.48 W |
| Yauco, Embalse de ⊜ 1 | 240m | 18.07 N | 66.50 W |
| Yauli | 248 | 11.41 S | 76.06 W |
| Yaundé → Yaoundé | 152 | 3.52 N | 11.31 E |
| Yaupi | 246 | 2.59 S | 77.50 W |
| Yauri | 248 | 14.47 S | 71.29 W |
| Yautepec | 234 | 18.53 N | 99.04 W |
| Yau Tong | 271d | 22.18 N | 114.13 E |
| Yauyos | 248 | 12.24 S | 75.57 W |
| Yāval | 120 | 21.10 N | 75.42 E |
| Yavarí (Javari) ≃ | 242 | 4.21 S | 70.02 W |
| Yavarí Mirim ≃ | 246 | 4.31 S | 71.44 W |
| Yavaros | 232 | 26.42 N | 109.31 W |
| Yavatmāl | 122 | 20.24 N | 78.08 E |
| Yaven Yaven Creek ≃ | 171b | 35.06 S | 147.46 E |
| Yavero ≃ | 248 | 12.06 S | 72.57 W |
| Yavi | 130 | 39.48 N | 36.13 E |
| Yaví, Cerro ∧ | 246 | 5.32 N | 65.59 W |
| Yavita | 246 | 2.55 N | 67.26 W |
| Yaviza | 246 | 8.11 N | 77.41 W |
| Yavkine | 78 | 47.16 N | 32.37 E |
| Yavne | 132 | 31.53 N | 34.45 E |
| Yavoriv | 78 | 49.56 N | 23.23 E |
| Yavuzeli | 130 | 37.20 N | 37.33 E |
| Yavuzkemal | 130 | 40.43 N | 38.21 E |
| Yaw ≃ | 110 | 20.55 N | 94.49 E |
| Yawahara | 268 | 35.59 N | 140.01 E |
| Yawata, Nihon | 96 | 34.52 N | 135.42 E |
| Yawata → Kitakyūshū, Nihon | 96 | 33.53 N | 130.50 E |
| Yawata, Nihon | 268 | 35.32 N | 140.08 E |
| Yawatahama | 96 | 33.27 N | 132.24 E |
| Yaxchilán ⊥ | 232 | 16.54 N | 90.58 W |
| Yaxi | 102 | 27.32 N | 106.45 E |
| Yaxian | 110 | 18.20 N | 109.30 E |
| Yaxigang | 106 | 31.23 N | 119.10 E |
| Yaxley | 42 | 52.31 N | 0.16 W |
| Yayama | 152 | 1.16 S | 23.07 E |
| Yayladağı | 130 | 35.56 N | 36.01 E |
| Yayladere | 130 | 39.14 N | 40.03 E |
| Yaylak | 130 | 37.23 N | 38.20 E |
| Yayouta | 150 | 8.11 N | 8.30 W |
| Yayuan | 98 | 41.47 N | 126.11 E |
| Yazd | 128 | 31.53 N | 54.25 E |
| Yazd □ 4 | 128 | 32.00 N | 54.30 E |
| Yazi | 98 | 37.04 N | 121.17 E |
| Yazichangcun | 104 | 41.16 N | 122.26 E |
| Yazıhan | 130 | 38.36 N | 38.11 E |
| Yazmān | 123 | 29.08 N | 71.45 E |
| Yazoo ≃ | 194 | 32.22 N | 91.00 W |
| Yazoo City | 194 | 32.51 N | 90.24 W |
| Ybbs ≃ | 61 | 48.10 N | 15.06 E |
| Ybbs an der Donau | 61 | 48.11 N | 15.05 E |
| Ybbsitz | 61 | 47.56 N | 14.53 E |
| Ybor City | 220 | 27.57 N | 82.27 W |
| Ybycuí | 252 | 26.01 S | 57.03 W |
| Yding Skovhøj ∧ 2 | 41 | 56.00 N | 9.48 E |
| Ydstebøhavn | 26 | 59.08 N | 5.15 E |
| Ydžid Parma ⋀ | 24 | 63.06 N | 58.15 E |
| Ye | 110 | 15.15 N | 97.51 E |
| Yea | 169 | 37.13 S | 145.26 E |
| Yea ≃ | 169 | 37.11 S | 145.23 E |
| Yeading ◆ 8 | 260 | 51.32 N | 0.24 W |
| Yeadon, Eng., U.K. | 44 | 53.52 N | 1.41 W |
| Yeadon, Pa., U.S. | 285 | 39.56 N | 75.15 W |
| Yeagertown | 208 | 40.38 N | 77.34 W |
| Yealm ≃ | 42 | 50.18 N | 4.03 W |
| Yealmpton | 42 | 50.21 N | 3.59 W |
| Yebawgyi | 110 | 18.40 N | 94.35 E |
| Yebbi-Bou | 146 | 20.58 N | 18.04 E |
| Yébigué, Enneri V | 146 | 22.04 N | 17.49 E |
| Yèbles | 261 | 48.38 N | 2.46 E |
| Yebyu | 110 | 14.15 N | 98.12 E |
| Yecapixtla | 234 | 18.53 N | 98.52 W |
| Yecheng | 120 | 37.54 N | 77.25 E |
| Yech'ŏn | 98 | 36.40 N | 128.26 E |
| Yecla | 34 | 38.37 N | 1.07 W |
| Yécora | 232 | 28.20 N | 108.58 W |
| Yedashe | 110 | 19.09 N | 96.21 E |
| Yedi Göller Milli Parkı ♠ | 130 | 40.50 N | 31.30 E |
| Yedikule ◆ 8 | 267b | 40.59 N | 28.55 E |
| Yedikule ⊥ | 267b | 40.59 N | 28.55 E |
| Yédinga, Ouadi V | 146 | 15.46 N | 20.05 E |
| Yedseram ≃ | 146 | 12.30 N | 14.05 E |
| Yeed | 144 | 4.33 N | 43.02 E |
| Yeeda | 162 | 17.36 S | 123.39 E |
| Yeelanna | 166 | 34.09 S | 135.45 E |
| Yeelirrie | 162 | 27.17 S | 120.06 E |
| Yeernuozha Hu ⊜ | 120 | 32.30 N | 89.30 E |
| Yegor'yevsk → Jegorjevsk | 82 | 55.23 N | 39.02 E |
| Yegros | 252 | 26.24 S | 56.25 W |
| Yegua Creek ≃ | 222 | 30.23 N | 96.18 W |
| Yeguas, Punta › | 258 | 34.55 S | 56.19 W |
| Yeguas, Río de las ≃ | 34 | 37.22 N | 4.45 W |
| Yehliu | 269d | 25.12 N | 121.41 E |
| Yehliu Chia › | 269d | 25.13 N | 121.42 E |
| Yehud | 132 | 32.02 N | 34.53 E |
| Yei | 154 | 4.05 N | 30.40 E |
| Yei ≃ | 140 | 6.15 N | 30.13 E |
| Yeji, Ghana | 150 | 8.13 N | 0.39 W |
| Yeji, Zhg. | 100 | 31.52 N | 115.55 E |
| Yekaterinburg → Jekaterinburg | 86 | 56.51 N | 60.36 E |
| Yekaterinodar → Krasnodar | 78 | 45.02 N | 39.00 E |
| Yekaterinoslav → Dnipropetrovs'k | 78 | 48.27 N | 34.59 E |
| Yekokora ≃ | 152 | 1.20 N | 20.21 E |
| Yekumbo | 152 | 1.02 S | 23.27 E |
| Ye Kyun I | 110 | 18.37 N | 93.47 E |
| Yela Island I | 160 | 11.21 S | 154.09 E |
| Yelanets' | 78 | 47.42 N | 31.51 E |
| Yelarbon | 166 | 28.34 S | 150.45 E |
| Yelcho, Lago ⊜ | 254 | 43.18 S | 72.18 W |
| Yele | 150 | 8.25 N | 11.50 W |
| Yelets → Jelec | 76 | 52.37 N | 38.30 E |
| Yélimané | 150 | 15.08 N | 10.34 W |
| Yelizarove | 78 | 48.12 N | 34.33 E |
| Yelizavethradka | 78 | 48.48 N | 32.24 E |
| Yell I | 46a | 60.36 N | 1.06 W |
| Yellandu | 122 | 17.36 N | 80.20 E |
| Yellow ≃, U.S. | 194 | 30.33 N | 87.00 W |
| Yellow ≃, In., U.S. | 216 | 41.16 N | 86.50 W |
| Yellow ≃, Ia., U.S. | 190 | 43.05 N | 91.11 W |
| Yellow ≃, Wi., U.S. | 190 | 44.58 N | 91.18 W |
| Yellow ≃, Wi., U.S. | 190 | 43.59 N | 90.03 W |
| Yellow ≃, Wi., U.S. | 190 | 46.01 N | 92.22 W |
| Yellow → Huang ≃, Zhg. | 90 | 37.32 N | 118.19 E |
| Yellow Breeches Creek ≃ | 208 | 40.13 N | 76.51 W |
| Yellow Creek ≃, U.S. | 194 | 33.34 N | 88.20 W |
| Yellow Creek ≃, Co., U.S. | 200 | 40.10 N | 108.24 W |
| Yellow Creek ≃, Oh., U.S. | 214 | 40.34 N | 80.40 W |
| Yellow Creek ≃, Tn., U.S. | 194 | 36.26 N | 87.34 W |
| Yellow Creek, North Fork ≃ | 214 | 40.33 N | 80.42 W |
| Yellow Creek State Park ♠ | 214 | 40.35 N | 79.02 W |
| Yellowdine | 162 | 31.18 S | 119.39 E |
| Yellow Grass | 184 | 49.49 N | 104.08 W |
| Yellowhead Pass )( | 182 | 52.53 N | 118.28 W |
| Yellow House Draw V | 196 | 33.35 N | 101.50 W |
| Yellowknife | 176 | 62.27 N | 114.21 W |
| Yellowknife ≃ | 176 | 62.31 N | 114.19 W |
| Yellow Lake ⊜ | 212 | 44.20 N | 75.36 W |
| Yellow Medicine ≃ | 198 | 44.44 N | 95.25 W |
| Yellow Mountain ∧ | 166 | 32.30 S | 146.51 E |
| Yellow Sea ⩶ 2 | 90 | 36.00 N | 123.00 E |
| Yellow Springs | 218 | 39.48 N | 83.53 W |
| Yellowstone ≃ | 178 | 47.58 N | 103.59 W |
| Yellowstone, Clarks Fork ≃ | 202 | 45.39 N | 108.43 W |
| Yellowstone Falls ⌊ | 202 | 44.43 N | 110.30 W |
| Yellowstone Lake ⊜ | 202 | 44.25 N | 110.22 W |
| Yellowstone National Park | 202 | 44.59 N | 110.42 W |
| Yellowstone National Park ♠ | 202 | 44.30 N | 110.35 W |
| Yellowtail Dam ◆ 6 | 202 | 45.12 N | 107.57 W |
| Yell Sound ⊔ | 46a | 60.32 N | 1.15 W |
| Yellville | 194 | 36.13 N | 92.41 W |
| Yelm | 224 | 46.56 N | 122.36 W |
| Yelma | 162 | 26.30 S | 121.40 E |
| Yelvertoft | 166 | 20.13 S | 138.53 E |
| Yelverton | 42 | 50.30 N | 4.05 W |
| Yelwa | 150 | 10.51 N | 4.46 E |
| Yelyseyivka | 78 | 47.02 N | 36.24 E |
| Yema ≃ | 102 | 41.25 N | 95.10 E |
| Yemadu | 86 | 43.36 N | 81.50 E |
| Yemagong | 124 | 29.28 N | 89.06 E |
| Yemaotai | 104 | 42.20 N | 122.53 E |
| Yemassee | 192 | 32.41 N | 80.51 W |
| Yematan | 102 | 34.40 N | 98.16 E |
| Yemen (Al-Yaman) □ 1, Asia | 118 | 15.00 N | 47.00 E |
| Yemen (Al-Yaman) □ 1, Asia | 144 | 15.00 N | 47.00 E |
| Yemen, People's Democratic Republic of → Yemen □ 1 | 144 | 15.00 N | 47.00 E |
| Yemen, República Popular Democrática del → Yemen □ 1 | 144 | 15.00 N | 47.00 E |
| Yémen, République démocratique populaire du → Yemen □ 1 | 144 | 15.00 N | 47.00 E |
| Yemil'chyne | 78 | 50.52 N | 27.48 E |
| Yen | 152 | 2.27 N | 12.41 E |
| Yenagoa | 150 | 4.55 N | 6.19 E |
| Yenakiyeve | 83 | 48.14 N | 38.13 E |
| Yenangyaung | 110 | 20.28 N | 94.52 E |
| Yenanma | 110 | 19.46 N | 94.48 E |
| Yen Bai | 110 | 21.42 N | 104.52 E |
| Yen Chau | 110 | 21.03 N | 104.18 E |
| Yench'eng → Yancheng | 100 | 33.24 N | 120.09 E |
| Yenchi → Yanji | 98 | 42.57 N | 129.32 E |
| Yenda | 166 | 34.15 S | 146.11 E |
| Yende Millimou | 150 | 8.53 N | 10.11 W |
| Yendéré | 150 | 10.12 N | 4.58 W |
| Yendi | 150 | 9.26 N | 0.01 W |
| Ye-ngan | 110 | 21.09 N | 96.27 E |
| Yenge ≃ | 152 | 0.55 S | 20.40 E |
| Yengema | 150 | 8.43 N | 11.10 W |
| Yengisar | 85 | 38.57 N | 76.03 E |
| Yengo | 152 | 0.22 N | 15.29 E |
| Yengo, Mount ∧ | 170 | 32.59 S | 150.51 E |
| Yéni | 150 | 13.26 N | 2.59 E |
| Yeniçağa | 130 | 40.46 N | 32.02 E |
| Yenice, Tür. | 130 | 39.45 N | 28.55 E |
| Yenice, Tür. | 130 | 39.55 N | 27.18 E |
| Yenice, Tür. | 130 | 36.59 N | 35.03 E |
| Yenice, Tür. | 130 | 41.11 N | 32.19 E |
| Yenice ≃ | 130 | 41.35 N | 32.03 E |
| Yenicekale | 130 | 37.37 N | 36.37 E |
| Yeniceoba | 130 | 38.53 N | 32.48 E |
| Yenierenköy | 130 | 35.32 N | 34.11 E |
| Yenifoça | 130 | 38.44 N | 26.51 E |
| Yenikapı ◆ 8 | 267b | 41.00 N | 28.57 E |
| Yeniköy | 130 | 39.46 N | 28.00 E |
| Yeniköy ◆ 8 | 267b | 40.59 N | 28.53 E |
| Yenimehmetli | 130 | 39.26 N | 32.10 E |
| Yenipazar, Tür. | 130 | 37.48 N | 28.12 E |
| Yenipazar, Tür. | 130 | 40.11 N | 30.31 E |


| ENGLISH | DEUTSCH | | | |
|---|---|---|---|---|
| Name / Page / Lat.°′ / Long.°′ | Name / Seite / Breite°′ / Länge°′ E = Ost | | | |

**Symbols** in the index entries represent the broad categories identified in the key at the right. Symbols with superior numbers (⋀ 1) identify subcategories (see complete key on page *I · 1)*.

**Symbole** im Register stellen die rechts im Schlüssel erklärten Kategorien dar. Symbole mit hochgestellten Ziffern (⋀ 1) bezeichnen Unterabteilungen einer Kategorie (vgl. vollständiger Schlüssel auf Seite *I · 1)*.

**Los símbolos** incluídos en el texto del índice representan las grandes categorías identificadas con la clave a la derecha. Los símbolos con numeros en su parte superior (⋀ 1) identifican las subcategorías (véase la clave completa en la página *I · 1)*.

**Les symboles** de l'index représentent les catégories indiquées dans la légende à droite. Les symboles suivis d'un indice (⋀ 1) représentent des sous-catégories (voir légende complète à la page *I · 1)*.

**Os símbolos** incluídos no texto do índice representam as grandes categorias identificadas com a chave à direita. Os símbolos com números em sua parte superior (⋀ 1) identificam as subcategorias (veja-se a chave completa à página *I · 1)*.

| English | Deutsch | Español | Français | Português |
|---|---|---|---|---|
| ∧ Mountain | Berg | Montaña | Montagne | Montanha |
| ⋀ Mountains | Gebirge | Montañas | Montagnes | Montanhas |
| )( Pass | Paß | Paso | Col | Passo |
| V Valley, Canyon | Tal, Cañon | Valle, Cañón | Vallée, Canyon | Vale, Canhão |
| ≚ Plain | Ebene | Llano | Plaine | Planície |
| › Cape | Kap | Cabo | Cap | Cabo |
| I Island | Insel | Isla | Île | Ilha |
| II Islands | Inseln | Islas | Îles | Ilhas |
| ⩡ Other Topographic Features | Andere Topographische Objekte | Otros Elementos Topográficos | Autres données topographiques | Outros acidentes topográficos |

ESPAÑOL

| Nombre | Página | Lat.°′ | Long.°′ W = Oeste |
|---|---|---|---|
| Yenişehir | 130 | 40.16 N | 29.39 E |
| Yenisey | | | |
| → Jenisej ≐ | 72 | 71.50 N | 82.40 E |
| Yennadon | 224 | 49.14 N | 122.34 W |
| Yenne | 62 | 45.42 N | 5.46 E |
| Yennora | 274a | 33.52 S | 150.58 E |
| Yenshuichen | 100 | 23.20 N | 120.16 E |
| Yentna ≐ | 180 | 61.34 N | 150.28 W |
| Yeo ≐, Eng., U.K. | 42 | 51.02 N | 2.49 W |
| Yeo ≐, Eng., U.K. | 42 | 51.01 N | 3.50 W |
| Yeo ≐, Eng., U.K. | 42 | 50.45 N | 3.36 W |
| Yeola | 122 | 20.02 N | 74.29 E |
| Yeo Lake ⊜ | 162 | 28.04 S | 124.23 E |
| Yeoman | 216 | 40.40 N | 86.43 W |
| Yeoval | 166 | 32.45 S | 148.40 E |
| Yeovil | 42 | 50.57 N | 2.39 W |
| Yeoville ◆[8] | 273d | 26.12 S | 28.04 E |
| Yepachic | 232 | 28.26 N | 108.23 W |
| Yeppoon | 166 | 23.08 S | 150.45 E |
| Yerba Buena, | | | |
| Montaña ∧ | 236 | 14.05 N | 87.26 W |
| Yerba Buena Island I | 282 | 37.48 N | 122.22 W |
| Yères ≐ | 50 | 50.02 N | 1.19 E |
| Yerevan | | | |
| → Jerevan | 84 | 40.11 N | 44.30 E |
| Yerilla | 162 | 29.28 S | 121.49 E |
| Yering | 274b | 37.41 S | 145.23 E |
| Yerington | 226 | 38.59 N | 119.09 W |
| Yerington Indian | | | |
| Reservation ◆[4] | 226 | 39.05 N | 119.12 W |
| Yerkes | 285 | 40.10 N | 75.27 W |
| Yerkes Astronomical | | | |
| Observatory ʊ[3] | 216 | 42.34 N | 88.34 W |
| Yerkesik | 130 | 37.07 N | 28.17 E |
| Yerköy | 130 | 39.38 N | 34.29 E |
| Yerky | 78 | 48.59 N | 31.00 E |
| Yerlisu | 130 | 40.46 N | 26.39 E |
| Yermasóyia | 130 | 34.43 N | 33.05 E |
| Yermenonville | 261 | 48.33 N | 1.37 E |
| Yermo | 204 | 34.54 N | 116.49 W |
| Yeroḥam | 132 | 31.00 N | 34.55 E |
| Yerolimín | 38 | 36.28 N | 22.24 E |
| Yèrre ≐ | 50 | 48.01 N | 1.16 E |
| Yerres | 50 | 48.43 N | 2.30 E |
| Yerres ≐ | 50 | 48.43 N | 2.27 E |
| Yerseke | 52 | 51.29 N | 4.02 E |
| Yerupaja, Nevado ∧ | 248 | 10.16 S | 76.54 W |
| Yerushalayim (Al- | | | |
| Quds) (Jerusalem) | 132 | 31.46 N | 35.14 E |
| Yerushalayim □[5] | 132 | 31.45 N | 35.00 E |
| Yerville | 50 | 49.40 N | 0.54 E |
| Yeryk ≐ | 83 | 48.59 N | 38.30 E |
| Yesa, Embalse de ⊜[1] | 34 | 42.36 N | 1.09 W |
| Yesan | 98 | 36.41 N | 126.50 E |
| Yeshenpu | 104 | 40.51 N | 122.32 E |
| Yeshiva University ʊ[2] | 276 | 40.51 N | 73.55 W |
| Yeshvi | 272c | 18.55 N | 73.03 E |
| Yeşil ≐ | 130 | 41.24 N | 36.35 E |
| Yeşilçonlu | 130 | 40.13 N | 28.06 E |
| Yeşildere | 130 | 37.09 N | 33.31 E |
| Yeşilhisar | 130 | 38.21 N | 35.06 E |
| Yeşilkent | 130 | 36.59 N | 36.10 E |
| Yeşilköy | 130 | 40.57 N | 28.49 E |
| Yeşilköy Burnu › | 267b | 40.57 N | 28.50 E |
| Yeşilova | 130 | 37.30 N | 29.46 E |
| Yeşiltepe | 130 | 37.12 N | 33.02 E |
| Yeşilyazı | 130 | 39.20 N | 39.05 E |
| Yeşilyurt | 130 | 38.18 N | 38.15 E |
| Yeso | 196 | 34.26 N | 104.36 W |
| Yeso Creek ≐ | 196 | 34.13 N | 104.15 W |
| Yesŏng-gang ≐ | 98 | 37.53 N | 126.24 E |
| Yessentuki | | | |
| → Jessentuki | 84 | 44.03 N | 42.51 E |
| Yeste | 34 | 38.22 N | 2.18 W |
| Yes Tor ∧ | 42 | 50.42 N | 4.00 W |
| Yesud HaMa'ala | 132 | 33.03 N | 35.36 E |
| Yetholme | 170 | 33.27 S | 149.49 E |
| Yetman | 166 | 28.54 S | 150.46 E |
| Yetminster | 42 | 50.53 N | 2.33 W |
| Yetsou I | 152 | 2.08 S | 10.42 E |
| Yettem | 226 | 36.29 N | 119.16 W |
| Yetti | 164 | 3.00 S | 140.53 E |
| Yetti ◆[1] | 148 | 26.10 N | 7.50 W |
| Ye-u | 110 | 22.46 N | 95.26 E |
| Yeu, Île d' I | 32 | 46.42 N | 2.20 W |
| Yevlax | 84 | 40.36 N | 47.09 E |
| Yevpatoriya | | | |
| → Yevpatoriya, | | | |
| Ukr. | 78 | 45.12 N | 33.22 E |
| Yevpatoriya, Ukr. | 78 | 45.12 N | 33.22 E |
| Yevsuh | 83 | 49.13 N | 39.18 E |
| Yevsuh ≐ | 83 | 48.47 N | 39.19 E |
| Yexian, Zhg. | 98 | 37.13 N | 119.54 E |
| Yexian, Zhg. | 100 | 33.37 N | 113.20 E |
| Yexie | 106 | 30.56 N | 121.19 E |
| Yextla ≐ | 234 | 18.00 N | 100.06 W |
| Yeysk | | | |
| → Jejsk | 78 | 46.42 N | 38.16 E |
| Yeyuan | 98 | 36.22 N | 118.27 E |
| Yeywa | 110 | 21.41 N | 96.24 E |
| Yezd | | | |
| → Yazd | 128 | 31.53 N | 54.25 E |
| Yeze Hu ⊜ | 106 | 31.08 N | 120.40 E |
| Yezhuang | 105 | 39.10 N | 116.18 E |
| Yezhuhe | 105 | 40.53 N | 118.13 E |
| Ygatimí | 252 | 24.05 S | 55.30 W |
| Ygnacio Canal ≊ | 282 | 37.55 N | 122.03 W |
| Yguazú ≐ | 252 | 25.20 S | 55.00 W |
| Yhú | 252 | 24.59 S | 55.59 W |
| Yi | 98 | 42.08 N | 118.48 E |
| Yi ≐, Ur. | 252 | 33.07 S | 57.08 W |
| Yi ≐, Zhg. | 98 | 34.07 N | 118.15 E |
| Yi ≐, Zhg. | 100 | 34.10 N | 112.10 E |
| Yi ≐, Zhg. | 105 | 39.14 N | 115.46 E |
| Yi'an | 89 | 47.55 N | 125.20 E |
| Yiannitsá | 38 | 40.48 N | 22.25 E |
| Yíaros I | 38 | 37.37 N | 24.43 E |
| Yibao | 106 | 30.25 N | 119.53 E |
| Yibin (Ipin) | 107 | 28.47 N | 104.38 E |
| Yibug Caka ⊜ | 120 | 33.00 N | 86.25 E |
| Yibutan | 107 | 28.54 N | 104.40 E |
| Yicanghe | 100 | 32.47 N | 120.43 E |
| Yichang (Ichang) | 102 | 30.42 N | 111.17 E |
| Yicheng, Zhg. | 98 | 36.48 N | 114.17 E |
| Yicheng, Zhg. | 98 | 34.46 N | 117.37 E |
| Yicheng, Zhg. | 102 | 31.43 N | 112.07 E |
| Yichexun | 102 | 26.50 N | 103.28 E |
| Yichuan, Zhg. | 100 | 34.26 N | 112.24 E |
| Yichuan, Zhg. | 102 | 36.04 N | 110.06 E |
| Yichun, Zhg. | 90 | 47.42 N | 128.55 E |
| Yichun, Zhg. | 100 | 27.50 N | 114.23 E |
| Yicun | 105 | 38.57 N | 115.37 E |
| Yidan | 89 | 43.24 N | 125.25 E |
| Yidie | 102 | 37.08 N | 110.30 E |
| Yidu, Zhg. | 98 | 36.41 N | 118.28 E |
| Yidu, Zhg. | 102 | 30.22 N | 111.22 E |
| Yidun | 102 | 29.56 N | 99.22 E |
| Yiewsley ◆[8] | 260 | 51.31 N | 0.28 W |
| Yifag | 144 | 12.02 N | 37.44 E |
| Yifeng, Zhg. | 100 | 33.19 N | 113.47 E |
| Yifeng, Zhg. | 100 | 28.26 N | 114.46 E |
| Yigaolou | 106 | 30.56 N | 120.20 E |
| Yığılca | 130 | 40.58 N | 31.27 E |
| Yiğitler | 130 | 39.52 N | 26.37 E |
| Yigou | 98 | 35.51 N | 114.20 E |
| Yihe | 100 | 23.50 N | 114.53 E |
| Yihechang | 107 | 30.23 N | 106.24 E |
| Yi He Yuan (Summer | | | |
| Palace) ʊ | 105 | 40.00 N | 116.16 E |
| Yihezhuang, Zhg. | 98 | 37.53 N | 118.23 E |
| Yihezhuang, Zhg. | 104 | 41.15 N | 122.57 E |
| Yihuang | 100 | 27.34 N | 116.10 E |
| Yihuang ≐ | 100 | 28.05 N | 116.18 E |
| Yijiangzhen | 100 | 30.55 N | 118.28 E |
| Yijiawan | 100 | 27.58 N | 113.01 E |
| Yijiazi | 104 | 42.29 N | 122.41 E |
| Yijingpu | 105 | 40.08 N | 117.47 E |
| Yijinqiao | 100 | 30.54 N | 117.12 E |
| Yijun | 102 | 35.24 N | 109.00 E |
| Yikengaolu | 102 | 42.17 N | 98.19 E |

FRANÇAIS

| Nom | Page | Lat.°′ | Long.°′ W = Ouest |
|---|---|---|---|
| Yikou | 100 | 26.45 N | 117.00 E |
| Yilaha | 89 | 48.50 N | 125.10 E |
| Yilan | 89 | 46.19 N | 129.34 E |
| Yilaxi | 89 | 43.47 N | 126.08 E |
| Yıldız Dağı ∧ | 130 | 40.08 N | 36.56 E |
| Yıldız Dağları ⩘ | 38 | 41.50 N | 27.30 E |
| Yıldızeli | 130 | 39.52 N | 36.38 E |
| Yilehuli Shan ⩘ | 89 | 51.20 N | 124.30 E |
| Yili | 107 | 30.45 N | 105.58 E |
| Yiliang, Zhg. | 102 | 24.58 N | 103.07 E |
| Yiliang, Zhg. | 102 | 27.35 N | 104.01 E |
| Yiliekede | 89 | 48.51 N | 121.37 E |
| Yilin | 100 | 33.36 N | 119.37 E |
| Yiling | 100 | 32.30 N | 119.46 E |
| Yiliping | 120 | 37.55 N | 93.30 E |
| Yilliminning | 162 | 32.54 S | 117.22 E |
| Yilong, Zhg. | 89 | 47.28 N | 125.23 E |
| Yilong, Zhg. | 102 | 31.34 N | 106.19 E |
| Yilong, Zhg. | 102 | 25.20 N | 103.14 E |
| Yimachi | 104 | 42.11 N | 122.15 E |
| Yimatu | 104 | 41.55 N | 121.25 E |
| Yimen, Zhg. | 100 | 33.39 N | 116.02 E |
| Yimen, Zhg. | 102 | 24.43 N | 102.10 E |
| Yimuhe | 89 | 52.45 N | 120.07 E |
| Yin ≐, Mya. | 110 | 20.04 N | 95.01 E |
| Yin ≐, Zhg. | 98 | 42.19 N | 118.37 E |
| Yinan (Jiehu) | 98 | 35.37 N | 118.30 E |
| Yinbaing | 110 | 17.25 N | 97.46 E |
| Yinchuan | 102 | 38.30 N | 106.18 E |
| Yindarlgooda, Lake ⊜ | 162 | 30.45 S | 121.55 E |
| Yindi | 154 | 1.35 N | 27.40 E |
| Yinfang | 105 | 39.07 N | 114.52 E |
| Ying ≐ | 100 | 32.30 N | 116.32 E |
| Yingcheng | 100 | 30.57 N | 113.32 E |
| Yingchengzi, Zhg. | 89 | 44.08 N | 125.56 E |
| Yingchengzi, Zhg. | 98 | 38.58 N | 121.23 E |
| Yingchengzi, Zhg. | 104 | 41.50 N | 124.04 E |
| Yingchengzi, Zhg. | 104 | 42.22 N | 124.14 E |
| Yingde | 100 | 24.12 N | 113.24 E |
| Yingen | 102 | 41.09 N | 104.45 E |
| Yingfang | 105 | 40.14 N | 116.17 E |
| Yinggehai | 110 | 18.31 N | 108.44 E |
| Yinghe | 100 | 32.16 N | 116.31 E |
| Yingjin ≐ | 98 | 42.20 N | 119.19 E |
| Yingkoshih ≐ | 269d | 25.06 N | 121.43 E |
| Yingkou, Zhg. | 104 | 40.40 N | 122.14 E |
| Yingkou (Dashiqiao), | | | |
| Zhg. | 104 | 40.38 N | 122.30 E |
| Yingpan, Zhg. | 102 | 25.48 N | 106.18 E |
| Yingpan, Zhg. | 102 | 24.44 N | 99.38 E |
| Yingpanjie | 102 | 25.27 N | 98.24 E |
| Yingqiao | 100 | 33.58 N | 113.39 E |
| Yingshan, Zhg. | 100 | 30.45 N | 115.39 E |
| Yingshan, Zhg. | 100 | 31.38 N | 113.50 E |
| Yingshan, Zhg. | 102 | 31.08 N | 106.31 E |
| Yingshang | 100 | 32.38 N | 116.15 E |
| Yingshouyingzi, Zhg. | 105 | 40.33 N | 117.38 E |
| Yingshouyingzi, Zhg. | 105 | 40.49 N | 117.55 E |
| Yingtan | 100 | 28.14 N | 117.00 E |
| Yingtaogou | 104 | 42.08 N | 121.57 E |
| Yingtaoyuan | 104 | 41.10 N | 123.05 E |
| Yingtian | 100 | 28.50 N | 112.56 E |
| Yingxiangjie | 107 | 29.24 N | 105.11 E |
| Yingxianpu | 104 | 41.20 N | 121.31 E |
| Yining (Kuldja) | 86 | 43.54 N | 81.21 E |
| Yinjiadai | 106 | 32.03 N | 120.07 E |
| Yinjiang | 102 | 28.02 N | 108.28 E |
| Yinjiawopeng | 104 | 42.34 N | 121.01 E |
| Yinkeng | 100 | 26.14 N | 115.34 E |
| Yinliu | 105 | 39.59 N | 117.23 E |
| Yinmabin | 110 | 22.05 N | 94.54 E |
| Yinmahe | 89 | 44.07 N | 125.44 E |
| Yinmatu ≐ | 98 | 40.57 N | 117.43 E |
| Yinnietharra | 162 | 24.39 S | 116.11 E |
| Yinnyein | 110 | 16.48 N | 97.23 E |
| Yinong | 102 | 30.19 N | 101.01 E |
| Yinping | 98 | 34.15 N | 118.39 E |
| Yinqiaotou | 106 | 31.52 N | 119.13 E |
| Yin Shan ⩘ | 102 | 41.48 N | 109.00 E |
| Yinshanzhen | 107 | 29.41 N | 104.58 E |
| Yinwogou | 98 | 41.55 N | 117.55 E |
| Yinxian | 100 | 29.50 N | 121.38 E |
| Yinxiang | 106 | 31.55 N | 118.49 E |
| Yinxianji | 100 | 32.07 N | 116.32 E |
| Yinyangjie | 104 | 42.16 N | 121.23 E |
| Yinyuan | 102 | 23.26 N | 101.54 E |
| Yinzhan'ao | 100 | 23.33 N | 113.07 E |
| Yio Chu Kang | 271c | 1.23 N | 103.51 E |
| Yi'ong | 102 | 30.17 N | 94.51 E |
| Yi'ong ≐ | 120 | 29.56 N | 95.10 E |
| Yi Pak | 271d | 22.19 N | 114.00 E |
| Yipinchang | 107 | 29.17 N | 106.34 E |
| Yipinglang | 102 | 25.11 N | 101.51 E |
| Yiqian | 100 | 26.34 N | 116.11 E |
| Yirba Muda | 144 | 6.12 N | 38.42 E |
| Yirga Alem | 144 | 6.52 N | 38.22 E |
| Yirkā | 132 | 32.57 N | 35.13 E |
| Yirol | 140 | 6.33 N | 30.30 E |
| Yirrkala | 164 | 12.14 S | 136.56 E |
| Yirshi | 89 | 47.20 N | 119.45 E |
| Yirwa | 140 | 7.47 N | 27.15 E |
| Yisaduo | 102 | 28.50 N | 96.44 E |
| Yishan, Zhg. | 100 | 27.32 N | 120.32 E |
| Yishan, Zhg. | 102 | 24.40 N | 108.35 E |
| Yishui | 98 | 35.50 N | 118.41 E |
| Yishun | 271c | 1.26 N | 103.50 E |
| Yisikan | 89 | 49.09 N | 124.47 E |
| Yisra'el | | | |
| → Israel □[1] | 132 | 31.30 N | 35.00 E |
| Yisuhe | 100 | 27.46 N | 112.54 E |
| Yitajing | 102 | 42.32 N | 94.12 E |
| Yitang, Zhg. | 98 | 35.10 N | 118.16 E |
| Yitang, Zhg. | 100 | 31.06 N | 113.42 E |
| Yíthion | 38 | 36.45 N | 22.34 E |
| Yiting | 100 | 29.15 N | 119.57 E |
| Yitm, Wādī al- V | 132 | 29.34 N | 35.01 E |
| Yitong | 89 | 43.20 N | 125.17 E |
| Yitong ≐ | 98 | 42.40 N | 125.58 E |
| Yitulihe | 89 | 50.38 N | 121.34 E |
| Yiwu, Zhg. | 100 | 29.18 N | 120.04 E |
| Yiwu, Zhg. | 102 | 43.15 N | 94.45 E |
| Yiwu, Zhg. | 102 | 22.00 N | 101.28 E |
| Yiwulü Shan ⩘ | 104 | 41.42 N | 121.42 E |
| Yixi | 100 | 23.45 N | 116.38 E |
| Yixian, Zhg. | 100 | 29.55 N | 117.56 E |
| Yixian, Zhg. | 104 | 41.32 N | 121.15 E |
| Yixian, Zhg. | 105 | 39.21 N | 115.29 E |
| Yixiken | 89 | 52.57 N | 125.40 E |
| Yixing | 106 | 31.22 N | 119.50 E |
| Yixingbu | 105 | 39.12 N | 117.12 E |
| Yixingchang | 107 | 30.37 N | 106.38 E |
| Yixu | 100 | 26.02 N | 119.16 E |
| Yixun ≐ | 98 | 41.16 N | 117.35 E |
| Yiyang, Zhg. | 100 | 28.23 N | 117.25 E |
| Yiyang, Zhg. | 102 | 28.36 N | 112.20 E |
| Yiyang, Zhg. | 102 | 34.30 N | 112.10 E |
| Yiyuan (Nanma) | 98 | 36.11 N | 118.08 E |
| Yiyuankou | 98 | 40.10 N | 119.35 E |
| Yizhang | 100 | 25.26 N | 112.56 E |
| Yizheng | 106 | 32.16 N | 119.12 E |
| Yizikong | 102 | 25.38 N | 104.28 E |
| Yizre'él | 132 | 32.33 N | 35.20 E |
| Yizre'el, 'Émeq V | 132 | 32.36 N | 35.14 E |
| Ylakiai | 76 | 56.17 N | 21.51 E |
| Yläne | 26 | 60.53 N | 22.55 E |
| Ylihärmä | 26 | 63.09 N | 22.47 E |
| Yli-Kitka ⊜ | 26 | 66.08 N | 28.30 E |
| Ylimarkku | | | |
| → Övermark | 26 | 62.38 N | 21.30 E |
| Ylistaro | 26 | 62.57 N | 22.31 E |
| Ylivieska | 26 | 64.05 N | 24.33 E |
| Ylöjärvi | 26 | 61.33 N | 23.36 E |
| Ymeray | 261 | 48.31 N | 1.42 E |
| Ymir | 182 | 49.17 N | 117.13 W |
| Yndin | 24 | 61.24 N | 55.10 E |
| Yngaren ⊜ | 40 | 58.52 N | 16.35 E |
| Yngen ⊜ | 40 | 59.44 N | 14.18 E |
| Yntaly | 86 | 48.58 N | 70.55 E |
| Ynykčanskij | 74 | 60.15 N | 137.43 E |
| Yoakum | 222 | 29.17 N | 97.09 W |

PORTUGUÊS

| Nome | Página | Lat.°′ | Long.°′ W = Oeste |
|---|---|---|---|
| Yobi, Indon. | 164 | 1.43 S | 138.04 E |
| Yobi, Indon. | 164 | 1.42 S | 136.27 E |
| Yockanookany ≐ | 194 | 32.40 N | 89.40 W |
| Yoco | 246 | 10.36 N | 62.24 W |
| Yocona ≐ | 194 | 34.11 N | 90.11 W |
| Yōda | 268 | 35.24 N | 139.25 E |
| Yoder | 216 | 40.55 N | 85.10 W |
| Yodo ≐ | 96 | 34.41 N | 135.25 E |
| Yodoe | 96 | 35.28 N | 133.26 E |
| Yodogawa ◆[8] | 270 | 34.42 N | 135.28 E |
| Yoe | 208 | 39.55 N | 76.39 W |
| Yōga ◆[8] | 268 | 35.38 N | 139.38 E |
| Yogo | 94 | 35.33 N | 136.12 E |
| Yog Point › | 116 | 14.06 N | 124.12 E |
| Yoğuntaş | 130 | 41.50 N | 27.04 E |
| Yogyakarta | 115a | 7.48 S | 110.22 E |
| Yogyakarta □[4] | 115a | 7.45 S | 110.30 E |
| Yoho National Park ♠ | 182 | 51.26 N | 116.30 W |
| Yoichi | 92a | 43.12 N | 140.41 E |
| Yojoa, Lago de ⊜ | 236 | 14.50 N | 88.00 W |
| Yōju | 98 | 37.18 N | 127.37 E |
| Yōka | 96 | 35.24 N | 134.46 E |
| Yokadouma | 152 | 3.31 N | 15.03 E |
| Yōkaichi | 94 | 35.06 N | 136.12 E |
| Yōkaichiba | 94 | 35.42 N | 140.33 E |
| Yokamba | 152 | 0.01 N | 22.17 E |
| Yokana | 152 | 0.45 N | 22.53 E |
| Yokawa | 96 | 34.52 N | 135.06 E |
| Yokchi-do I | 98 | 34.38 N | 128.15 E |
| Yokkaichi, Nihon | 94 | 34.58 N | 136.37 E |
| Yokkaichi, Nihon | 96 | 33.32 N | 131.20 E |
| Yoko | 152 | 2.36 S | 20.06 E |
| Yokoate-jima I | 93b | 28.48 N | 129.00 E |
| Yokohama, Nihon | 94 | 35.27 N | 139.39 E |
| Yokohama, Nihon | 268 | 35.27 N | 139.39 E |
| Yokohama-kō ⊂ | 268 | 35.27 N | 139.39 E |
| Yokohama National | | | |
| University ʊ[2] | 268 | 35.25 N | 139.36 E |
| Yokohama Park | | | |
| Baseball Ground ♠ | 268 | 35.26 N | 139.39 E |
| Yokolo | 152 | 0.36 S | 23.04 E |
| Yokonuma | 268 | 35.58 N | 139.27 E |
| Yokoshiba | 94 | 35.40 N | 140.28 E |
| Yokosuka | 94 | 35.18 N | 139.40 E |
| Yokosuka District | | | |
| Naval | | | |
| Headquarters ■ | 268 | 35.17 N | 139.39 E |
| Yokosuka-kō ⊂ | 268 | 35.18 N | 139.39 E |
| Yokosuka Naval | | | |
| Base ■ | 94 | 35.18 N | 139.41 E |
| Yokota, Nihon | 96 | 35.10 N | 133.06 E |
| Yokota, Nihon | 268 | 35.23 N | 140.01 E |
| Yokota, Nihon | 270 | 34.40 N | 135.55 E |
| Yokota Air Base ■ | 268 | 35.45 N | 139.21 E |
| Yokote | 92 | 39.18 N | 140.34 E |
| Yola | 146 | 9.12 N | 12.29 E |
| Yolaina, Serranías de | | | |
| ⩘ | 236 | 11.40 N | 84.20 W |
| Yolboyu | 130 | 37.55 N | 40.00 E |
| Yolo | 226 | 38.44 N | 121.48 W |
| Yolo □[6] | 226 | 38.41 N | 121.46 W |
| Yolo ≐ | 273b | 4.19 S | 15.20 E |
| Yolo Bypass ≐ | 226 | 38.25 N | 121.40 W |
| Yolombó, Col. | 246 | 6.36 N | 75.01 W |
| Yolombo, Zaïre | 152 | 1.32 S | 23.15 E |
| Yolonga | 152 | 1.36 S | 23.12 E |
| Yom ≐ | 110 | 15.52 N | 100.16 E |
| Yombi | 152 | 1.26 S | 10.37 E |
| Yomou | 150 | 7.34 N | 9.16 W |
| Yona | 174p | 13.25 N | 144.47 E |
| Yonabaru | 174m | 26.12 N | 127.45 E |
| Yonago | 96 | 35.26 N | 133.20 E |
| Yonaguni | 175d | 24.27 N | 122.57 E |
| Yonaguni-shima I | 175d | 24.27 N | 123.00 E |
| Yonaha-dake ∧[2] | 174m | 26.43 N | 128.13 E |
| Yŏnan | 98 | 37.55 N | 126.10 E |
| Yoncalı | 130 | 39.01 N | 38.15 E |
| Yoncalla | 202 | 43.35 N | 123.16 W |
| Yŏnch'on ◆[8] | 271b | 37.38 N | 127.04 E |
| Yoneshiro ≐ | 92 | 40.13 N | 140.01 E |
| Yonezawa | 92 | 37.55 N | 140.07 E |
| Yŏngam | 98 | 34.48 N | 126.40 E |
| Yongamp'o | 98 | 39.55 N | 124.24 E |
| Yŏngan, C.M.I.K. | 98 | 41.15 N | 129.30 E |
| Yong'an, Zhg. | 100 | 25.58 N | 117.22 E |
| Yongan, Zhg. | 107 | 30.44 N | 106.16 E |
| Yong'an, Zhg. | 107 | 29.13 N | 104.46 E |
| Yong'an ≐ | 100 | 28.52 N | 121.04 E |
| Yonganbao | 98 | 40.15 N | 119.52 E |
| Yong'anchang | 107 | 30.24 N | 103.58 E |
| Yong'anshi | 100 | 28.13 N | 113.19 E |
| Yŏngbyŏn | 98 | 39.49 N | 125.48 E |
| Yongchang, Zhg. | 100 | 29.13 N | 119.20 E |
| Yongchang, Zhg. | 102 | 38.17 N | 101.59 E |
| Yongchangzhen | 106 | 31.42 N | 121.44 E |
| Yongcheng | 100 | 33.58 N | 116.21 E |
| Yongch'ŏn, C.M.I.K. | 98 | 39.59 N | 124.28 E |
| Yŏngch'ŏn, Taehan | 98 | 38.07 N | 127.05 E |
| Yŏngch'ŏn, Taehan | 98 | 35.58 N | 128.56 E |
| Yongch'ŏn-dong | 98 | 41.18 N | 129.40 E |
| Yongchuan | 107 | 29.21 N | 105.54 E |
| Yongchun | 100 | 25.21 N | 118.21 E |
| Yongdeng | 102 | 36.48 N | 103.14 E |
| Yongdian | 98 | 40.34 N | 124.48 E |
| Yongding | 100 | 24.46 N | 116.43 E |
| Yongding ≐, Zhg. | 100 | 24.42 N | 116.34 E |
| Yongding ≐, Zhg. | 105 | 39.20 N | 117.04 E |
| Yongdingmen Station | | | |
| ◆[5] | 271a | 39.52 N | 116.23 E |
| Yŏngdŏk | 98 | 36.26 N | 129.23 E |
| Yŏngdong | 98 | 36.10 N | 127.48 E |
| Yŏngdŭngp'o ◆[8] | 271b | 37.32 N | 126.54 E |
| Yongfeng, Zhg. | 100 | 29.44 N | 116.49 E |
| Yongfeng, Zhg. | 100 | 27.19 N | 115.24 E |
| Yongfengchang | 107 | 30.33 N | 105.05 E |
| Yongfu | 100 | 25.05 N | 117.20 E |
| Yonggang | 98 | 38.52 N | 125.21 E |
| Yonggangonch'ŏn | 98 | 38.53 N | 125.14 E |
| Yonggi | 98 | 36.24 N | 128.24 E |
| Yongguzhai | 98 | 34.05 N | 116.50 E |
| Yonghe | 100 | 28.18 N | 113.51 E |
| Yongheshi | 100 | 28.18 N | 113.51 E |
| Yonghŭng | 98 | 39.32 N | 127.13 E |
| Yŏnghŭng-do I | 98 | 37.16 N | 126.28 E |
| Yŏnghŭng-man ⊂ | 98 | 39.15 N | 127.30 E |
| Yongi | 89 | 43.40 N | 126.30 E |
| Yŏngil-man ⊂ | 98 | 36.02 N | 129.26 E |
| Yongji | 102 | 34.51 N | 110.29 E |
| Yongjia, Zhg. | 100 | 28.11 N | 120.42 E |
| Yongjia, Zhg. | 107 | 29.34 N | 106.01 E |
| Yŏngjong-do I | 98 | 37.30 N | 126.31 E |
| Yŏngju | 98 | 36.50 N | 128.37 E |
| Yongkang, Zhg. | 100 | 32.32 N | 117.24 E |
| Yongkang, Zhg. | 100 | 28.53 N | 120.02 E |
| Yongkou | 100 | 26.16 N | 118.19 E |
| Yongle, Zhg. | 89 | 45.45 N | 125.12 E |
| Yongle, Zhg. | 105 | 39.32 N | 115.59 E |
| Yongle ≐ | 100 | 26.54 N | 113.12 E |
| Yongledian | 105 | 39.43 N | 116.46 E |
| Yonglong | 106 | 31.34 N | 121.48 E |
| Yonglonghe | 100 | 30.46 N | 112.48 E |
| Yŏngmi-dong | 98 | 39.40 N | 125.31 E |
| Yongnian | | | |
| (Linmingguan) | 98 | 36.47 N | 114.30 E |
| Yongnianchang | 107 | 29.08 N | 104.51 E |
| Yongning, Zhg. | 100 | 24.43 N | 118.42 E |
| Yongning, Zhg. | 102 | 38.20 N | 106.17 E |
| Yongning, Zhg. | 102 | 22.42 N | 108.50 E |
| Yongning, Zhg. | 102 | 27.47 N | 100.38 E |
| Yongningcheng | 105 | 40.34 N | 116.11 E |
| Yongningjian | 98 | 39.56 N | 121.48 E |
| Yong Peng | 114 | 2.01 N | 103.04 E |
| Yongping, Zhg. | 100 | 28.12 N | 117.45 E |
| Yongping, Zhg. | 102 | 25.28 N | 99.33 E |
| Yongqing, Zhg. | 105 | 39.19 N | 116.29 E |
| Yongqing, Zhg. | 107 | 30.00 N | 105.27 E |
| Yongquan | 100 | 28.46 N | 121.19 E |
| Yongren | 102 | 26.08 N | 101.40 E |
| Yŏngsan-gang ≐ | 98 | 34.54 N | 126.32 E |
| Yongsan-ni | 98 | 38.52 N | 125.56 E |

| | | | |
|---|---|---|---|
| Yŏngsanp'o | 98 | 34.58 N | 126.44 E |
| Yongshan | 102 | 28.15 N | 103.24 E |
| Yongshanqiao | 100 | 29.06 N | 117.17 E |
| Yongsheng | 102 | 26.42 N | 100.43 E |
| Yongshou | 102 | 34.43 N | 108.05 E |
| Yongshun | 102 | 28.57 N | 109.41 E |
| Yongshunchang | 107 | 30.06 N | 105.26 E |
| Yongtai | 100 | 25.54 N | 118.58 E |
| Yŏngwŏl | 98 | 37.12 N | 128.28 E |
| Yŏngwŏn | 98 | 39.49 N | 126.32 E |
| Yongwŏn-ni | 98 | 40.41 N | 128.42 E |
| Yongxin, Zhg. | 100 | 26.56 N | 114.18 E |
| Yongxin, Zhg. | 107 | 28.59 N | 106.32 E |
| Yongxing, Zhg. | 98 | 40.11 N | 123.52 E |
| Yongxing, Zhg. | 100 | 26.08 N | 113.06 E |
| Yongxing, Zhg. | 102 | 39.08 N | 110.31 E |
| Yongxing, Zhg. | 106 | 31.56 N | 120.55 E |
| Yongxing, Zhg. | 107 | 30.34 N | 105.35 E |
| Yongxing, Zhg. | 107 | 30.13 N | 105.06 E |
| Yongxingchang, Zhg. | 107 | 29.02 N | 104.34 E |
| Yongxingchang, Zhg. | 107 | 29.37 N | 106.23 E |
| Yongxingchang, Zhg. | 107 | 30.20 N | 103.44 E |
| Yongxiu | 100 | 29.04 N | 115.49 E |
| Yŏngyang, Taehan | 98 | 36.40 N | 129.07 E |
| Yongyang, Zhg. | 100 | 26.57 N | 114.46 E |
| Yŏngyn | 98 | 39.18 N | 125.34 E |
| Yongyŏn-ni | 98 | 40.44 N | 126.09 E |
| Yongzhai | 100 | 27.59 N | 115.26 E |
| Yŏnhŭi-ri | 271b | 37.33 N | 126.41 E |
| Yŏnhwa-san ∧ | 98 | 40.46 N | 127.23 E |
| Yonibana | 150 | 8.26 N | 12.14 W |
| Yonkers | 210 | 40.55 N | 73.53 W |
| Yonkers Raceway ♠ | 276 | 40.55 N | 73.52 W |
| Yonne □[5] | 50 | 47.55 N | 3.45 E |
| Yonne ≐ | 32 | 48.23 N | 2.58 E |
| Yono | 94 | 35.53 N | 139.38 E |
| Yŏnp'yŏng-yŏlto II | 98 | 37.38 N | 125.40 E |
| Yonsei University ʊ[2] | 271b | 37.34 N | 126.56 E |
| Yoo, Enneri V | 146 | 19.24 N | 16.38 E |
| Yoontow | 144 | 0.08 S | 42.34 E |
| Yopal | 246 | 5.21 N | 72.23 W |
| Yop'o-ri | 98 | 38.50 N | 125.33 E |
| Yopurga | 85 | 39.15 N | 76.45 E |
| Yoqne'am | 132 | 32.39 N | 35.07 E |
| Yorba Linda | 228 | 33.53 N | 117.48 W |
| Yorii | 94 | 36.07 N | 139.12 E |
| Yorishima | 96 | 34.29 N | 133.35 E |
| York, Austl. | 168a | 31.53 S | 116.46 E |
| York, On., Can. | 212 | 43.41 N | 79.29 W |
| York, S.L. | 150 | 8.17 N | 13.11 W |
| York, Eng., U.K. | 44 | 53.58 N | 1.05 W |
| York, Al., U.S. | 194 | 32.29 N | 88.17 W |
| York, In., U.S. | 216 | 41.41 N | 84.49 W |
| York, Ne., U.S. | 198 | 40.52 N | 97.35 W |
| York, N.Y., U.S. | 210 | 42.52 N | 77.53 W |
| York, N.D., U.S. | 198 | 48.18 N | 99.34 W |
| York, Pa., U.S. | 208 | 39.57 N | 76.43 W |
| York, S.C., U.S. | 192 | 34.59 N | 81.14 W |
| York □[6], On., Can. | 212 | 43.55 N | 79.25 W |
| York □[6], Pa., U.S. | 208 | 39.58 N | 76.44 W |
| York □[6], Va., U.S. | 208 | 37.15 N | 76.40 W |
| York ≐, On., Can. | 212 | 45.20 N | 77.35 W |
| York ≐, P.Q., Can. | 186 | 48.49 N | 64.34 W |
| York ≐, Va., U.S. | 208 | 37.15 N | 76.23 W |
| York, Cape › | 164 | 10.42 S | 142.31 E |
| York, Kap › | 16 | 75.53 N | 66.12 W |
| York, Vale of V | 44 | 54.10 N | 1.20 W |
| Yorkana | 208 | 39.59 N | 76.35 W |
| York Center, Il., U.S. | 278 | 41.52 N | 87.59 W |
| York Center, Oh., | | | |
| U.S. | 216 | 40.24 N | 83.27 W |
| Yorkdale Centre ◆[9] | 275b | 43.44 N | 79.27 W |
| Yorke Peninsula ›[1] | 166 | 35.00 S | 137.30 E |
| Yorketown | 168b | 35.02 S | 137.36 E |
| York Factory | 184 | 57.00 N | 92.18 W |
| Yorkfield | 278 | 41.52 N | 87.56 W |
| York Haven | 208 | 40.06 N | 76.42 W |
| Yorklyn | 285 | 39.48 N | 75.40 W |
| York Minster ʊ[1] | 44 | 53.57 N | 1.04 W |
| York New Salem | 208 | 39.54 N | 76.47 W |
| Yorkshire, N.Y., U.S. | 210 | 42.31 N | 78.28 W |
| Yorkshire, Pa., U.S. | 208 | 39.59 N | 76.41 W |
| Yorkshire, Va., U.S. | 208 | 38.47 N | 77.27 W |
| Yorkshire Dales | | | |
| National Park ♠ | 44 | 54.13 N | 2.10 W |
| Yorkshire Wolds ⩘[2] | 44 | 54.00 N | 0.40 W |
| York Sound ȣ | 160 | 14.50 S | 125.05 E |
| York Springs | 208 | 40.00 N | 77.07 W |
| Yorkton | 184 | 51.13 N | 102.28 W |
| Yorktown, In., U.S. | 218 | 40.10 N | 85.29 W |
| Yorktown, Tx., U.S. | 222 | 28.58 N | 97.30 W |
| Yorktown, Va., U.S. | 208 | 37.14 N | 76.30 W |
| Yorktown ◆[9] | 278 | 41.51 N | 88.01 W |
| Yorktown Battlefield | | | |
| ⊥ | 208 | 37.13 N | 76.31 W |
| Yorktown Heights | 210 | 41.16 N | 73.46 W |
| Yorktown Manor | 207 | 41.38 N | 71.26 W |
| York Township | | | |
| Airport ⊠ | 278 | 41.51 N | 88.02 W |
| York University ʊ[2] | 275b | 43.47 N | 79.30 W |
| Yorkville, Il., U.S. | 216 | 41.38 N | 88.26 W |
| Yorkville, Mi., U.S. | 216 | 42.23 N | 85.24 W |
| Yorkville, N.Y., U.S. | 210 | 43.06 N | 75.16 W |
| Yorkville, Oh., U.S. | 214 | 40.09 N | 80.43 W |
| Yorkville ◆[8] | 275b | 43.40 N | 79.24 W |
| Yoro, Hond. | 236 | 15.09 N | 87.07 W |
| Yoro, Mali | 150 | 14.17 N | 2.08 W |
| Yōrō, Nihon | 94 | 35.18 N | 136.33 E |
| Yoro □[5] | 236 | 15.15 N | 87.15 W |
| Yōrō ≐ | 94 | 35.32 N | 140.04 E |
| Yoroi-zaki › | 94 | 34.24 N | 136.55 E |
| Yoron-jima I | 93b | 27.02 N | 128.26 E |
| Yōrō-no-taki ⌞ | 94 | 35.17 N | 136.32 E |
| Yorosso | 150 | 12.22 N | 4.47 W |
| Yosemite Creek ≐ | 226 | 37.44 N | 119.36 W |
| Yosemite National | | | |
| Park | 226 | 37.45 N | 119.35 W |
| Yosemite National | | | |
| Park ♠ | 226 | 37.51 N | 119.33 W |
| Yoshida, Nihon | 94 | 36.02 N | 139.02 E |
| Yoshida, Nihon | 94 | 34.46 N | 138.15 E |
| Yoshida, Nihon | 96 | 33.16 N | 132.33 E |
| Yoshida, Nihon | 96 | 34.40 N | 132.42 E |
| Yoshida, Nihon | 96 | 35.10 N | 132.51 E |
| Yoshida ≐ | 96 | 34.03 N | 131.02 E |
| Yoshii, Nihon | 94 | 36.15 N | 138.59 E |
| Yoshii, Nihon | 96 | 33.20 N | 130.45 E |
| Yoshii, Nihon | 96 | 34.38 N | 133.26 E |
| Yoshii, Nihon | 96 | 34.55 N | 134.06 E |
| Yoshii, Nihon | 270 | 34.53 N | 135.03 E |
| Yoshii ≐ | 96 | 34.36 N | 134.03 E |
| Yoshikawa, Nihon | 94 | 37.13 N | 138.25 E |
| Yoshikawa, Nihon | 94 | 35.53 N | 139.51 E |
| Yoshikawa, Nihon | 270 | 34.55 N | 135.28 E |
| Yoshimi | 94 | 36.02 N | 139.27 E |
| Yoshino, Nihon | 96 | 34.21 N | 135.51 E |
| Yoshino, Nihon | 96 | 34.06 N | 134.23 E |
| Yoshino ≐, Nihon | 94 | 34.22 N | 135.40 E |
| Yoshino ≐, Nihon | 96 | 34.05 N | 134.36 E |
| Yoshinodani | 94 | 36.17 N | 136.39 E |
| Yoshino-Kumano- | | | |
| kokuritsu-kōen ♠ | 92 | 34.07 N | 135.55 E |
| Yoshioka | 94 | 36.27 N | 139.01 E |
| Yoshiumi | 96 | 34.09 N | 133.03 E |
| Yoshiwa | 96 | 34.29 N | 132.09 E |
| Yoshkar-Ola | | | |
| → Joškar-Ola | 80 | 56.38 N | 47.52 E |
| Yosowilangun | 115a | 8.15 S | 113.18 E |
| Yos Sudarso, Pulau | | | |
| (Frederik | | | |
| Hendrikeiland) I | 164 | 7.50 S | 138.30 E |
| Yŏsu | 98 | 34.46 N | 127.44 E |
| Yotausito | 248 | 16.03 S | 63.03 W |
| Yōtei-zan ∧ | 92a | 42.49 N | 140.49 E |
| Yotsukaidō | 94 | 35.39 N | 140.10 E |
| Yotvata | 132 | 29.53 N | 35.03 E |
| You ≐, Zhg. | 100 | 26.23 N | 118.27 E |
| You ≐, Zhg. | 102 | 22.50 N | 108.06 E |
| You ≐, Zhg. | 102 | 28.27 N | 110.24 E |
| Youanmi | 162 | 28.37 S | 118.49 E |

| | | | |
|---|---|---|---|
| Youbou | 224 | 48.53 N | 124.13 W |
| Youcheng | 100 | 29.14 N | 116.48 E |
| Youfang | 106 | 32.09 N | 119.50 E |
| Youghal | 48 | 51.57 N | 7.51 W |
| Youghal Bay ⊂ | 48 | 51.52 N | 7.50 W |
| Youghiogheny ≐ | 214 | 40.22 N | 79.52 W |
| Yougoslavie | | | |
| → Yugoslavia □[1] | 22 | 44.00 N | 21.00 E |
| Youhe | 100 | 32.19 N | 113.50 E |
| Youjidong | 104 | 42.12 N | 121.07 E |
| Youkounkoun | 150 | 12.32 N | 13.08 W |
| Youlan | 100 | 28.34 N | 116.10 E |
| Young, Austl. | 166 | 34.19 S | 148.18 E |
| Young, Sk., Can. | 184 | 51.47 N | 105.46 W |
| Young, Az., U.S. | 200 | 34.06 N | 110.57 W |
| Young, Ur. | 252 | 32.41 S | 57.38 W |
| Young America | 216 | 40.34 N | 86.20 W |
| Younghusband | | | |
| Peninsula ›[1] | 166 | 36.00 S | 139.30 E |
| Youngs ≐ | 224 | 46.10 N | 123.49 W |
| Youngs, Lake ⊜ | 224 | 47.25 N | 122.07 W |
| Youngs Creek | 218 | 38.29 N | 86.30 W |
| Youngs Creek ≐ | 219 | 39.21 N | 91.51 W |
| Youngs Rock I[2] | 174e | 25.03 S | 130.07 W |
| Youngstown, Ab., | | | |
| Can. | 182 | 51.32 N | 111.13 W |
| Youngstown, Fl., | | | |
| U.S. | 192 | 30.21 N | 85.26 W |
| Youngstown, N.Y., | | | |
| U.S. | 210 | 43.14 N | 79.03 W |
| Youngstown, Oh., | | | |
| U.S. | 214 | 41.05 N | 80.38 W |
| Youngstown | | | |
| Municipal Airport ⊠ | 214 | 41.15 N | 80.41 W |
| Youngsville, La., U.S. | 194 | 30.05 N | 91.59 W |
| Youngsville, N.Y., | | | |
| U.S. | 210 | 41.48 N | 74.54 W |
| Youngsville, N.C., | | | |
| U.S. | 192 | 36.01 N | 78.28 W |
| Youngsville, Pa., U.S. | 214 | 41.51 N | 79.19 W |
| Youngwood | 214 | 40.14 N | 79.34 W |
| Youngwood Park ♠ | 279b | 40.14 N | 79.36 W |
| Yountville | 226 | 38.24 N | 122.22 W |
| Youshashan | 120 | 38.08 N | 91.10 E |
| Youssoufia | 148 | 32.16 N | 8.33 W |
| Youtingpu | 107 | 29.26 N | 105.45 E |
| Youville ◆[8] | 275a | 45.33 N | 73.39 W |
| Youxi, Zhg. | 100 | 28.45 N | 121.06 E |
| Youxi, Zhg. | 100 | 26.11 N | 118.09 E |
| Youxi, Zhg. | 107 | 29.12 N | 106.09 E |
| Youxian | 100 | 27.00 N | 113.21 E |
| Youxizhen | 107 | 30.35 N | 106.18 E |
| Youyang | 102 | 28.58 N | 108.41 E |
| Youyi | 89 | 46.44 N | 131.44 E |
| Youyu | 102 | 40.09 N | 112.32 E |
| Youzhagou | 106 | 31.04 N | 118.46 E |
| Youzhou | 105 | 40.09 N | 115.42 E |
| Yoweragabbie | 162 | 28.13 S | 117.39 E |
| Yŏyang-ni | 98 | 37.30 N | 128.43 E |
| Yozgat | 130 | 39.50 N | 34.48 E |
| Yozgat □[4] | 130 | 39.40 N | 35.10 E |
| Ypacaraí | 252 | 25.23 S | 57.16 W |
| Ypané ≐ | 252 | 23.29 S | 57.19 W |
| Ypé Jhú | 252 | 23.54 S | 55.20 W |
| Yport | 50 | 49.44 N | 0.19 E |
| Ypres | | | |
| → Ieper | 50 | 50.51 N | 2.53 E |
| Ypsilanti | 216 | 42.14 N | 83.36 W |
| Ypsilanti East | 216 | 42.15 N | 83.35 W |
| Yreka | 204 | 41.44 N | 122.38 W |
| Yrgajty ≐ | 85 | 43.03 N | 74.43 E |
| Yron ≐ | 56 | 49.10 N | 5.52 E |
| Ysabel Channel ȣ | 164 | 2.00 S | 150.00 E |
| Ysbyty Ystwyth | 42 | 52.20 N | 3.48 W |
| Yser (IJzer) ≐ | 50 | 51.09 N | 2.43 E |
| Ysieux, Ruisseau l' ≐ | 261 | 49.09 N | 2.22 E |
| Yssel | | | |
| → IJssel ≐ | 52 | 52.35 N | 5.50 E |
| Ysselmeer | | | |
| → IJsselmeer ⫪[2] | 52 | 52.45 N | 5.25 E |
| Yssingeaux | 62 | 45.08 N | 4.07 E |
| Ystad | 41 | 55.25 N | 13.49 E |
| Ystalyfera | 42 | 51.47 N | 3.47 W |
| Ysterfonteinpunt › | 158 | 33.22 S | 18.09 E |
| Ystrad ≐ | 44 | 53.13 N | 3.20 W |
| Ystrad Aeron | 42 | 52.11 N | 4.11 W |
| Ystradfellte | 42 | 51.48 N | 3.34 W |
| Ystradgynlais | 42 | 51.47 N | 3.45 W |
| Ystwyth ≐ | 42 | 52.24 N | 4.05 W |
| Ytambey ≐ | 252 | 24.46 S | 54.24 W |
| Ythan ≐ | 46 | 57.18 N | 2.00 W |
| Ytre Arna | 26 | 60.26 N | 5.30 E |
| Ytterharnäs | 40 | 60.39 N | 17.21 E |
| Ytterhogdal | 26 | 62.12 N | 14.51 E |
| Yttermalung | 40 | 60.35 N | 13.50 E |
| Ytterselö | 40 | 59.23 N | 17.15 E |
| Yttre Hållsfjärden ⊂[2] | 40 | 59.08 N | 17.40 E |
| Yttygran, ostrov I | 180 | 64.36 N | 172.40 W |
| Yū | 96 | 34.02 N | 132.13 E |
| Yu ≐ | 102 | 23.24 N | 110.05 E |
| Yu, Pulau I | 164 | 0.03 S | 129.36 E |
| Yu'alliq, Jabal ∧ | 140 | 30.22 N | 33.31 E |
| Yuam ≐ | 110 | 17.47 N | 97.45 E |
| Yuan | | | |
| → Red ≐, Asia | 110 | 20.17 N | 106.34 E |
| Yuan ≐, Zhg. | 100 | 28.09 N | 115.34 E |
| Yuan ≐, Zhg. | 102 | 28.58 N | 111.49 E |
| Yuan'an | 102 | 31.04 N | 111.26 E |
| Yuanao | 100 | 26.29 N | 119.48 E |
| Yuanbachang | 107 | 29.44 N | 105.27 E |
| Yuanhua | 106 | 30.25 N | 120.46 E |
| Yuanjiang | 102 | 23.34 N | 102.03 E |
| Yuankeng | 100 | 26.48 N | 117.44 E |
| Yüanli | 100 | 24.27 N | 120.39 E |
| Yüanlin | 100 | 23.58 N | 120.34 E |
| Yuanling | 102 | 28.20 N | 110.16 E |
| Yuanmou | 102 | 25.38 N | 101.54 E |
| Yuanshancun | 106 | 31.08 N | 120.20 E |
| Yuanshi | 98 | 37.45 N | 114.32 E |
| Yuantan, Zhg. | 100 | 32.47 N | 112.53 E |
| Yuantan, Zhg. | 100 | 23.39 N | 113.12 E |
| Yuantongsi | 107 | 30.13 N | 104.15 E |
| Yuantouzhu | 106 | 31.32 N | 120.14 E |
| Yuanxiang | 98 | 34.14 N | 115.19 E |
| Yuanxiangzhen | 106 | 31.39 N | 119.15 E |
| Yuanxing | 107 | 30.36 N | 104.59 E |
| Yuanyang (Yangwu), | | | |
| Zhg. | 98 | 35.04 N | 113.57 E |
| Yuanyang, Zhg. | 102 | 23.12 N | 102.52 E |
| Yuanyangpu | 107 | 30.10 N | 105.15 E |
| Yuanyangqiao | 107 | 29.41 N | 106.33 E |
| Yuasa | 96 | 34.02 N | 135.11 E |
| Yuat ≐ | 164 | 4.25 S | 143.55 E |
| Yuba | 102 | 29.27 N | 97.42 E |
| Yuba □[6] | 226 | 39.16 N | 121.17 W |
| Yuba ≐ | 226 | 39.07 N | 121.36 W |
| Yuba City | 226 | 39.08 N | 121.36 W |
| Yubara | 96 | 35.12 N | 133.45 E |
| Yubara-chosuichi ⊜ | 96 | 35.13 N | 133.43 E |
| Yūbari | 92a | 43.04 N | 141.59 E |
| Yūbari-sanchi ⩘ | 92a | 43.15 N | 142.20 E |
| Yubdo | 144 | 9.00 N | 35.22 E |
| Yūbetsu | 92a | 44.14 N | 143.37 E |
| Yūbetsu ≐ | 92a | 44.14 N | 143.37 E |
| Yucaipa | 228 | 34.02 N | 117.02 W |
| Yucatán □[3] | 232 | 20.50 N | 89.00 W |
| Yucatán, Canal de ȣ | 238 | 21.45 N | 85.45 W |
| Yucatan Peninsula | | | |
| (Península de | | | |
| Yucatán) ›[1] | 232 | 19.30 N | 89.00 W |
| Yucca | 200 | 34.52 N | 114.08 W |
| Yucca Lake ⊜ | 204 | 36.59 N | 116.01 W |
| Yucca Mountain ∧ | 204 | 36.56 N | 116.29 W |
| Yucca Valley | 204 | 34.07 N | 116.35 W |
| Yuchaozhuang | 105 | 39.35 N | 117.50 E |
| Yucheng, Zhg. | 98 | 36.56 N | 116.39 E |
| Yucheng, Zhg. | 106 | 30.32 N | 120.51 E |
| Yuci | 102 | 37.45 N | 112.41 E |
| Yuda | 92 | 39.20 N | 140.50 E |
| Yudaokou | 98 | 42.14 N | 116.48 E |

| | | | |
|---|---|---|---|
| Yudi Shan ∧ | 89 | 52.17 N | [illegible]21.52 E |
| Yudong | 106 | 32.02 N | [illegible]21.22 E |
| Yudu | 100 | 25.59 N | [illegible]15.24 E |
| Yue ≐ | 107 | 28.50 N | [illegible]04.21 E |
| Yuebo | 107 | 29.03 N | [illegible]04.12 E |
| Yuecheng | 100 | 32.39 N | [illegible]14.49 E |
| Yuechi | 107 | 30.33 N | [illegible]06.26 E |
| Yuejiatun | 104 | 41.10 N | 120.43 E |
| Yuejiawopeng | 104 | 41.35 N | 122.20 E |
| Yuekou | 100 | 30.32 N | 113.03 E |
| Yuelai | 106 | 31.56 N | 121.27 E |
| Yuelaichang, Zhg. | 107 | 29.44 N | 106.32 E |
| Yuelaichang, Zhg. | 107 | 28.53 N | 106.22 E |
| Yuemenpu | 107 | 30.28 N | 106.34 E |
| Yuendumu | 162 | 22.16 S | 131.49 E |
| Yuendumu Aboriginal | | | |
| Reserve ◆[4] | 162 | 22.20 S | 131.47 E |
| Yuen Long | 271d | 22.26 N | 114.02 E |
| Yuepu | 106 | 31.25 N | 121.26 E |
| Yueqing | 100 | 28.08 N | 120.58 E |
| Yuewang | 106 | 31.33 N | 121.09 E |
| Yuexi, Zhg. | 100 | 30.50 [illegible] | 116.24 E |
| Yuexi, Zhg. | 102 | 28.42 [illegible] | 102.28 E |
| Yueyang | 100 | 29.23 [illegible] | 113.06 E |
| Yuezi | 100 | 24.54 [illegible] | 115.02 E |
| Yufa | 105 | 39.31 [illegible] | 116.19 E |
| Yufeng | 107 | 30.37 [illegible] | 105.11 E |
| Yufu-dake ∧ | 96 | 33.17 [illegible] | 131.24 E |
| Yufuin | 96 | 33.15 [illegible] | 131.20 E |
| Yugan | 100 | 28.41 [illegible] | 116.41 E |
| Yugawara | 94 | 35.09 [illegible] | 139.04 E |
| Yuge | 96 | 34.15 [illegible] | 133.12 E |
| Yugoslavia | | | |
| (Jugoslavija) □[1], | | | |
| Europe | 22 | 44.00 N | 21.00 E |
| Yugoslavia | | | |
| (Jugoslavija) □[1], | | | |
| Europe | 38 | 44.0[illegible] N | 21.00 E |
| Yugou | 100 | 33.4[illegible] N | 118.55 E |
| Yuguan | 98 | 39.5[illegible] N | 119.22 E |
| Yuguo | 104 | 41.5[illegible] N | 123.15 E |
| Yuhang (Linping) | 106 | 30.2[illegible] N | 120.18 E |
| Yuhebu | 102 | 38.0[illegible] N | 109.37 E |
| Yuhu | 100 | 27.5[illegible] N | 120.08 E |
| Yuhuaizhuang | 105 | 39.2[illegible] N | 117.40 E |
| Yuhuan | 100 | 28.1[illegible] N | 121.12 E |
| Yuhuan Dao I | 100 | 28.0[illegible] N | 121.12 E |
| Yuhuang Ding ∧ | 98 | 36.5[illegible] N | 121.21 E |
| Yui | 94 | 35.0[illegible] N | 138.34 E |
| Yuin | 162 | 27.5[illegible] S | 116.02 E |
| Yujiachang | 107 | 29.5[illegible] N | 104.04 E |
| Yujiacun | 106 | 31.4[illegible] N | 121.48 E |
| Yujiang | 100 | 28.1[illegible] N | 116.47 E |
| Yujiaqiao | 106 | 31.3[illegible] N | 119.25 E |
| Yujiawan | 86 | 44.3[illegible] N | 86.45 E |
| Yukarıbey | 130 | 39.1[illegible] N | 27.06 E |
| Yukarıdudullu ◆[8] | 267b | 41.[illegible] N | 29.09 E |
| Yuke | 98 | 37.5[illegible] N | 115.39 E |
| Yūki, Nihon | 94 | 36.[illegible] N | 139.53 E |
| Yuki, Nihon | 96 | 34.[illegible] N | 132.16 E |
| Yuki, Nihon | 96 | 34.[illegible] N | 133.17 E |
| Yuki, Nihon | 96 | 33.[illegible] N | 134.36 E |
| Yukon, Ok., U.S. | 196 | 35.[illegible] N | 97.45 W |
| Yukon, Pa., U.S. | 214 | 40.[illegible] N | 79.41 W |
| Yukon □[4], Can. | 176 | 64.[illegible] N | 135.00 W |
| Yukon □[4], Can. | 180 | 64.[illegible] N | 135.00 W |
| Yukon ≐ | 180 | 62.[illegible] N | 163.59 W |
| Yukon Flats ⩸ | 180 | 66.[illegible] N | 146.00 W |
| Yukou | 105 | 40.[illegible] N | 117.00 E |
| Yukuhashi | 96 | 33.[illegible] N | 130.59 E |
| Yulan | 210 | 41[illegible] N | 74.56 W |
| Yulao | 102 | 23[illegible] N | 111.46 E |
| Yulara | 162 | 25[illegible] S | 131.04 E |
| Yule ≐ | 162 | 20[illegible] S | 118.17 E |
| Yule Bay ⊂ | 9 | 70[illegible] S | 166.40 E |
| Yule Island I | 164 | 8[illegible] S | 146.30 E |
| Yuli, Nig. | 146 | 9[illegible] N | 10.17 E |
| Yüli, T'aiwan | 100 | 23[illegible] N | 121.18 E |
| Yuli, Zhg. | 98 | 37[illegible] N | 121.25 E |
| Yuliang | 100 | 29[illegible]52 N | 118.30 E |
| Yuliangpu | 89 | 4[illegible]26 N | 121.55 E |
| Yulin, Zhg. | 102 | 2[illegible]36 N | 110.07 E |
| Yulin, Zhg. | 102 | 3[illegible]20 N | 109.29 E |
| Yulin, Zhg. | 110 | 1[illegible]16 N | 109.32 E |
| Yulincun | 105 | 4[illegible]12 N | 116.42 E |
| Yul-li | 98 | 3[illegible]52 N | 126.13 E |
| Yulong | 107 | 2[illegible]58 N | 104.22 E |
| Yuma, Az., U.S. | 200 | 3[illegible]43 N | 114.37 W |
| Yuma, Co., U.S. | 198 | 4[illegible]08 N | 102.43 W |
| Yuma, Bahía de ⊂ | 238 | 1[illegible]21 N | 68.35 W |
| Yuma Marine Corps | | | |
| Air Station ■ | 200 | 3[illegible]40 N | 114.38 W |
| Yuma Proving | | | |
| Ground ■ | 204 | 3[illegible].05 N | 114.25 W |
| Yumare | 246 | 1[illegible].37 N | 68.41 W |
| Yumbel | 252 | 3[illegible].08 S | 72.32 W |
| Yumbi, Zaïre | 152 | [illegible].53 S | 16.32 E |
| Yumbi, Zaïre | 154 | [illegible].14 S | 26.14 E |
| Yumbo | 246 | [illegible].35 N | 76.28 W |
| Yumen (Laojunmiao) | 102 | [illegible].56 N | 97.51 E |
| Yumenzhen | 102 | [illegible].17 N | 97.07 E |
| Yumesaki | 96 | [illegible].58 N | 134.42 E |
| Yumezaki ≐ | 96 | [illegible].47 N | 134.39 E |
| Yumin | 86 | [illegible].02 N | 82.37 E |
| Yumurtalık | 130 | [illegible].49 N | 35.45 E |
| Yun ≐ | 100 | [illegible].43 N | 114.04 E |
| Yuna, Austl. | 162 | [illegible].20 S | 115.00 E |
| Yuna, Nihon | 174m | [illegible].46 N | 128.12 E |
| Yuna ≐ | 238 | [illegible].12 N | 69.37 W |
| Yunak | 130 | [illegible]8.49 N | 31.45 E |
| Yunan (Ducheng) | 102 | [illegible].11 N | 111.29 E |
| Yunaska Island I | 180 | [illegible]2.40 N | 170.50 W |
| Yuncao | 100 | [illegible]1.26 N | 118.04 E |
| Yuncheng, Zhg. | 98 | [illegible]5.35 N | 115.54 E |
| Yuncheng, Zhg. | 102 | [illegible]5.00 N | 110.59 E |
| Yundamindra | 162 | [illegible]9.07 S | 122.02 E |
| Yundanyingzi | 104 | [illegible]2.00 N | 121.34 E |
| Yunderup | 168a | [illegible]32.35 S | 115.46 E |
| Yunfeng Ding ∧ | 106 | [illegible]30.56 N | 120.02 E |
| Yungas ◆[1] | 248 | [illegible]16.00 S | 67.45 W |
| Yungay, Chile | 252 | [illegible]37.07 S | 72.01 W |
| Yungay, Perú | 248 | 9.09 S | 77.44 W |
| Yungchi | | | |
| → Jilin | 89 | [illegible]43.51 N | 126.33 E |
| Yungchia | | | |
| → Wenzhou | 100 | [illegible]28.01 N | 120.39 E |
| Yungho | 269d | [illegible]25.01 N | 121.31 E |
| Yungning | | | |
| → Nanning | 102 | 22.48 N | 108.20 E |
| Yung Shue Wan | 271d | 22.14 N | 114.06 E |
| Yunhe | | | |
| → Peixian, Zhg. | 98 | 34.21 N | 117.59 E |
| Yunhe, Zhg. | 100 | 28.06 N | 119.34 E |
| Yunjin | 107 | 29.06 N | 105.40 E |
| Yunkai Dashan ⩘ | 102 | 22.30 N | 111.00 E |
| Yun Ling ⩘ | 102 | 27.20 N | 99.20 E |
| Yunlong, Zhg. | 102 | 25.50 N | 99.17 E |
| Yunlong, Zhg. | 107 | 30.31 N | 104.46 E |
| Yunluchang | 107 | 29.45 N | 105.57 E |
| Yunmeng | 100 | 31.02 N | 113.41 E |
| Yunmenling | 100 | 25.15 N | 115.49 E |
| Yunmenzhen | 107 | 30.06 N | 106.20 E |
| Yunnan □[4] | 102 | 24.00 N | 101.00 E |
| Yunnanfu | | | |
| → Kunming | 102 | 25.05 N | 102.40 E |
| Yunotani | 94 | 37.14 N | 139.01 E |
| Yunotsu | 96 | 35.05 N | 132.21 E |
| Yunta | 166 | 32.35 S | 139.33 E |
| Yunting | 106 | 31.53 N | 120.19 E |
| Yunwu Shan ∧ | 98 | 41.07 N | 116.34 E |
| Yunxi, Zhg. | 100 | 29.28 N | 113.16 E |
| Yunxi, Zhg. | 102 | 32.49 N | 110.13 E |
| Yunxian, Zhg. | 102 | 24.30 N | 100.03 E |
| Yunxian (Yunyang), | | | |
| Zhg. | 102 | 32.49 N | 110.49 E |
| Yunxiao | 10[illegible] | 24.04 N | 117.20 E |
| Yunyan ≐ | 10[illegible] | 34.39 N | 119.18 E |
| Yunyang, Zhg. | 10[illegible] | 33.28 N | 112.42 E |
| Yunyang, Zhg. | 10[illegible] | 30.58 N | 109.05 E |
| Yunzalin ≐ | 11[illegible] | 17.23 N | 97.40 E |


| | | | | | |
|---|---|---|---|---|---|
| ≐ | River | Fluß | Río | Rivière | Rio |
| ≊ | Canal | Kanal | Canal | Canal | Canal |
| ⌞ | Waterfall, Rapids | Wasserfall, Stromschnellen | Cascada, Rápidos | Chute d'eau, Rapides | Cascata, Rápidos |
| ȣ | Strait | Meeresstraße | Estrecho | Détroit | Estreito |
| ⊂ | Bay, Gulf | Bucht, Golf | Bahía, Golfo | Baie, Golfe | Baía, Golfo |
| ⊜ | Lake, Lakes | See, Seen | Lago, Lagos | Lac, Lacs | Lago, Lagos |
| ⩸ | Swamp | Sumpf | Pantano | Marais | Pântano |
| ⊓ | Ice Features, Glacier | Eis- und Gletscherformen | Accidentes Glaciales | Formes glaciaires | Acidentes glaciares |
| ⫪ | Other Hydrographic Features | Andere Hydrographische Objekte | Otros Elementos Hidrográficos | Autres données hydrographiques | Outros acidentes hidrográficos |

| | | | | | |
|---|---|---|---|---|---|
| ✣ | Submarine Features | Untermeerische Objekte | Accidentes Submarinos | Formes de relief sous-marin | Acidentes submarinos |
| □ | Political Unit | Politische Einheit | Unidad Politica | Entité politique | Unidade política |
| ʊ | Cultural Institution | Kulturelle Institution | Institución Cultural | Institution culturelle | Instituição cultural |
| ⊥ | Historical Site | Historische Stätte | Sitio Histórico | Site historique | Sitio histórico |
| ♠ | Recreational Site | Erholungs- und Ferienort | Sitio de Recreo | Centre de loisirs | Area de Lazer |
| ⊠ | Airport | Flughafen | Aeropuerto | Aéroport | Aeroporto |
| ■ | Military Installation | Militäranlage | Instalación Militar | Installation militaire | Instalação militar |
| ◆ | Miscellaneous | Verschiedenes | Misceláneo | Divers | Diversos |

ENGLISH: Name | Page | Lat.°′ | Long.°′ — DEUTSCH: Name | Seite | Breite°′ | Länge°′ E = Ost


| Name | Page | Lat.°′ | Long.°′ |
|---|---|---|---|
| Yunzhong | 100 | 29.13 N | 117.40 E |
| Yunzhou | 98 | 41.01 N | 115.44 E |
| Yuping | 102 | 27.07 N | 108.47 E |
| Yuqi | 106 | 31.43 N | 120.11 E |
| Yuqia | 102 | 38.07 N | 94.35 E |
| Yuqian'gou | 104 | 41.41 N | 121.28 E |
| Yuqiao Shuiku ⊜[1] | 105 | 40.02 N | 117.33 E |
| Yuqing | 102 | 27.05 N | 107.44 E |
| Yura, Nihon | 96 | 33.57 N | 135.07 E |
| Yura, Perú | 248 | 16.11 S | 71.40 W |
| Yura ≃ | 96 | 35.31 N | 135.17 E |
| Yurano-hana › | 96 | 33.01 N | 132.23 E |
| Yurécuaro | 234 | 20.20 N | 102.18 W |
| Yurga → Jurga | 86 | 55.42 N | 84.51 E |
| Yuri-jima I | 96 | 33.51 N | 132.32 E |
| Yurimaguas | 248 | 5.54 S | 76.05 W |
| Yuriria | 234 | 20.12 N | 101.09 W |
| Yuriria, Laguna de ⊜ | 234 | 20.15 N | 101.06 W |
| Yur'iyivka | 83 | 48.30 N | 39.00 E |
| Yurove | 78 | 51.22 N | 27.50 E |
| Yuruarí ≃ | 246 | 6.44 N | 61.40 W |
| Yurubi, Parque Nacional ♦ | 246 | 10.25 N | 68.42 W |
| Yürük | 130 | 40.56 N | 27.04 E |
| Yurumanguí ≃ | 246 | 3.27 N | 77.21 W |
| Yurungkax ≃ | 120 | 37.00 N | 79.55 E |
| Yuryev → Tartu | 76 | 58.23 N | 26.43 E |
| Yuryivka | 78 | 48.44 N | 36.02 E |
| Yusala, Laguna ⊜ | 248 | 14.05 S | 67.12 W |
| Yuşa Tepesi ∧[2] | 267b | 41.09 N | 29.05 E |
| Yuscarán | 236 | 13.55 N | 86.51 W |
| Yushan, Zhg. | 100 | 26.54 N | 118.36 E |
| Yushan, Zhg. | 100 | 28.41 N | 118.15 E |
| Yushan, Zhg. | 100 | 33.19 N | 113.41 E |
| Yü Shan ∧, T'aiwan | 100 | 23.28 N | 120.57 E |
| Yu Shan ∧, Zhg. | 100 | 26.06 N | 115.20 E |
| Yushanzhen | 102 | 29.38 N | 108.19 E |
| Yushu, Zhg. | 89 | 44.46 N | 126.34 E |
| Yushu (Jiegu), Zhg. | 102 | 33.01 N | 97.00 E |
| Yushugou | 86 | 44.07 N | 87.05 E |
| Yushulinzi, Zhg. | 98 | 41.30 N | 119.07 E |
| Yushulinzi, Zhg. | 98 | 40.59 N | 125.57 E |
| Yushupu | 104 | 41.10 N | 122.08 E |
| Yushutai, Zhg. | 89 | 43.30 N | 124.17 E |
| Yushutai, Zhg. | 104 | 41.42 N | 123.26 E |
| Yushuwan | 105 | 40.04 N | 115.35 E |
| Yusichang | 107 | 29.14 N | 105.25 E |
| Yūsofābād ◆[8] | 267d | 35.44 N | 51.25 E |
| Yuste, Monasterio de ⊥[1] | 34 | 40.08 N | 5.45 W |
| Yūsuf, Baḥr ≍ | 142 | 29.18 N | 30.50 E |
| Yusufeli | 130 | 40.50 N | 41.33 E |
| Yusuhara | 96 | 33.23 N | 132.55 E |
| Yusuhara ≃ | 96 | 33.11 N | 132.58 E |
| Yutai (Guting) | 98 | 35.02 N | 116.40 E |
| Yutian, Zhg. | 100 | 26.27 N | 114.36 E |
| Yutian, Zhg. | 105 | 39.53 N | 117.45 E |
| Yutian, Zhg. | 120 | 36.51 N | 81.40 E |
| Yuting | 100 | 29.50 N | 117.57 E |
| Yūtō | 94 | 34.42 N | 137.38 E |
| Yutou | 100 | 28.36 N | 118.30 E |
| Yuty | 252 | 26.32 S | 56.18 W |
| Yutz | 56 | 49.21 N | 6.11 E |
| Yütz'u → Yuci | 102 | 37.45 N | 112.41 E |
| Yūwan-dake ∧ | 93b | 28.18 N | 129.21 E |
| Yuwangcheng | 100 | 31.31 N | 114.29 E |
| Yüweng Tao I | 100 | 23.36 N | 119.30 E |
| Yuwŏnjin | 98 | 40.18 N | 126.37 E |
| Yuxarı Garabağ kanalı ≍ | 84 | 39.44 N | 47.57 E |
| Yuxi, Zhg. | 100 | 25.36 N | 119.18 E |
| Yuxi, Zhg. | 102 | 24.23 N | 102.34 E |
| Yuxi, Zhg. | 106 | 32.03 N | 121.11 E |
| Yuxi, Zhg. | 107 | 30.19 N | 105.47 E |
| Yuxian, Zhg. | 98 | 39.48 N | 114.33 E |
| Yuxian, Zhg. | 100 | 34.10 N | 113.28 E |
| Yuxian, Zhg. | 102 | 38.09 N | 113.25 E |
| Yuxiangpu | 98 | 34.27 N | 114.57 E |
| Yuxiangtou | 106 | 31.14 N | 120.53 E |
| Yuxikou | 100 | 31.26 N | 118.17 E |
| Yuyao | 100 | 30.04 N | 121.10 E |
| Yuya-wan ⊂ | 96 | 34.23 N | 130.56 E |
| Yuyŏn-ni | 98 | 38.42 N | 127.10 E |
| Yuyuan Tan ⊜ | 271a | 39.55 N | 116.18 E |
| Yuza | 92 | 39.01 N | 139.54 E |
| Yuzawa, Nihon | 92 | 39.10 N | 140.30 E |
| Yuzawa, Nihon | 94 | 36.56 N | 138.49 E |
| Yuzhno-Sakhalinsk → Južno-Sachalinsk | 89 | 46.58 N | 142.42 E |
| Yuzovka → Donets'k | 83 | 48.00 N | 37.48 E |
| Yuzuruha-san ∧ | 96 | 34.14 N | 134.49 E |
| Yvelines □[5] | 50 | 48.50 N | 1.50 E |
| Yvelines, Forêt des ♦ | 261 | 48.40 N | 1.55 E |
| Yverdon | 58 | 46.47 N | 6.39 E |
| Yvetot | 50 | 49.37 N | 0.46 E |
| Yvette | 261 | 48.43 N | 1.55 E |
| Yvette ≃ | 50 | 48.40 N | 2.20 E |
| Yvoir | 56 | 50.20 N | 4.53 E |
| Yvoire | 58 | 46.22 N | 6.20 E |
| Yvonand | 58 | 46.48 N | 6.45 E |
| Yvron ≃ | 50 | 48.39 N | 2.56 E |
| Ywamun | 110 | 20.31 N | 95.25 E |
| Ywathagyi | 110 | 22.18 N | 95.42 E |
| Ywathit | 110 | 19.10 N | 97.30 E |
| Yxlan I | 40 | 59.38 N | 18.52 E |
| Yxsjöberg | 40 | 60.03 N | 14.46 E |
| Yzeron | 62 | 45.42 N | 4.35 E |
| Yzeure | 32 | 46.34 N | 3.21 E |


## Z


| Name | Page | Lat.°′ | Long.°′ |
|---|---|---|---|
| Za ≃ | 102 | 32.00 N | 96.55 E |
| Za, Oued ≃ | 148 | 34.34 N | 3.03 W |
| Zaachila | 234 | 16.57 N | 96.45 W |
| Zaaimansdal | 158 | 33.35 S | 23.22 E |
| Zaajatskij | 86 | 52.53 N | 61.35 E |
| Zaalajskij chrebet ⋏ | 85 | 39.20 N | 72.30 E |
| Zaamin | 85 | 39.58 N | 68.24 E |
| Zaanstad | 52 | 52.26 N | 4.49 E |
| Zaatzke | 54 | 53.11 N | 12.24 E |
| Žabaj ≃ | 86 | 51.42 N | 68.22 E |
| Zabajkal'sk | 88 | 49.38 N | 117.19 E |
| Zăbala ≃ | 38 | 45.51 N | 26.46 E |
| Zabalac' | 76 | 53.56 N | 24.46 E |
| Zabalocce | 76 | 52.40 N | 28.34 E |
| Zăbalţ | 38 | 46.01 N | 21.55 E |
| Žabari | 38 | 44.21 N | 21.13 E |
| Zabarjad, Jazīrat I | 140 | 23.37 N | 36.12 E |
| Žabasak | 86 | 50.21 N | 61.40 E |
| Zāb-e Kūchek → Little Zab ≃ | 128 | 35.12 N | 43.25 E |
| Zaberfeld | 56 | 49.03 N | 8.55 E |
| Zabīd | 144 | 14.10 N | 43.17 E |
| Zabīd, Wādī V | 144 | 14.07 N | 43.06 E |
| Žabinka | 76 | 52.12 N | 24.01 E |
| Zabituj | 88 | 53.16 N | 102.50 E |
| Ząbkowice Śląskie | 30 | 50.36 N | 16.53 E |
| Žabljak | 38 | 43.09 N | 19.07 E |
| Zabłudów | 30 | 53.01 N | 23.20 E |
| Żabno | 30 | 50.09 N | 20.53 E |
| Zābol | 128 | 31.02 N | 61.30 E |
| Zābol □[4] | 120 | 32.00 N | 67.15 E |
| Zābolī | 128 | 27.07 N | 61.40 E |
| Zabolotiv | 78 | 48.29 N | 25.16 E |
| Zabolotje, Ross. | 82 | 55.32 N | 38.12 E |
| Zabolotje, Ross. | 82 | 56.40 N | 38.06 E |
| Zabolotje, Ross. | 82 | 54.24 N | 38.54 E |
| Zabolottya | 78 | 51.38 N | 24.15 E |
| Zabor'e | 76 | 55.55 N | 29.19 E |
| Zaborje, Ross. | 76 | 53.06 N | 31.42 E |
| Zaborje, Ross. | 76 | 54.51 N | 32.41 E |
| Zaborje, Ross. | 76 | 55.24 N | 31.34 E |
| Zaborje, Ross. | 82 | 55.23 N | 37.47 E |
| Zabory | 76 | 55.58 N | 32.17 E |
| Zabré | 150 | 11.10 N | 0.38 W |
| Zábřeh | 30 | 49.53 N | 16.52 E |
| Zabrze (Hindenburg) | 30 | 50.18 N | 18.46 E |
| Zaburun'e | 80 | 46.44 N | 50.09 E |
| Zabyčanne | 76 | 53.25 N | 31.52 E |
| Zabzugu | 150 | 9.17 N | 0.22 E |
| Zacapa | 236 | 14.58 N | 89.32 W |
| Zacapa □[5] | 236 | 15.00 N | 89.30 W |
| Zacapoaxtla | 234 | 19.53 N | 97.35 W |
| Zacapu | 234 | 19.50 N | 101.43 W |
| Zacata | 208 | 38.07 N | 76.47 W |
| Zacatecas | 234 | 22.47 N | 102.35 W |
| Zacatecas □[3] | 232 | 23.00 N | 103.00 W |
| Zacatecoluca | 236 | 13.30 N | 88.52 W |
| Zacatepec | 234 | 18.39 N | 99.12 W |
| Zacatlán | 234 | 19.56 N | 97.58 W |
| Zacatongo | 234 | 20.49 N | 104.33 W |
| Zacharias Creek ≃ | 285 | 40.11 N | 75.23 W |
| Zacharkovo | 265b | 55.47 N | 37.19 E |
| Zacharovo, Ross. | 76 | 54.22 N | 39.17 E |
| Zacharovo, Ross. | 82 | 56.31 N | 36.44 E |
| Zacharvan' | 24 | 66.21 N | 55.48 E |
| Zachary | 194 | 30.38 N | 91.09 W |
| Zachepylivka | 78 | 49.12 N | 35.14 E |
| Zachmet | 128 | 37.43 N | 62.30 E |
| Zachožje | 265a | 59.44 N | 30.51 E |
| Zachrebetnoje | 24 | 69.00 N | 36.25 E |
| Zacks Bay ⊂ | 276 | 40.36 N | 73.29 W |
| Zacoalco de Torres | 234 | 20.14 N | 103.35 W |
| Zacualpa | 236 | 15.05 N | 90.50 W |
| Zacualpan, Méx. | 234 | 21.15 N | 105.10 W |
| Zacualpan, Méx. | 234 | 20.28 N | 98.22 W |
| Zacualtipan | 234 | 20.39 N | 98.36 W |
| Zaculeu ⊥ | 236 | 15.21 N | 91.29 W |
| Začysce | 76 | 54.24 N | 28.45 E |
| Zadar | 36 | 44.07 N | 15.14 E |
| Zadetkale Kyun I | 110 | 10.08 N | 98.12 E |
| Zadetkyi Kyun I | 110 | 9.58 N | 98.13 E |
| Zadi (Inkisi) ≃ | 152 | 4.46 S | 14.52 E |
| Zadní Chodov | 60 | 49.54 N | 12.44 E |
| Zadoi | 120 | 33.10 N | 95.05 E |
| Zadonsk | 76 | 52.23 N | 38.57 E |
| Zadorra ≃ | 34 | 42.40 N | 2.54 W |
| Zaerap | 76 | 59.18 N | 36.37 E |
| Zafarabad | 85 | 40.11 N | 68.51 E |
| Ẓafar al-Qadīmah | 142 | 30.58 N | 31.37 E |
| Za'farānah, Bi'r ⊤[4] | 142 | 29.07 N | 32.33 E |
| Za'farānah, Ra's › | 142 | 29.06 N | 32.40 E |
| Zafarwāl | 123 | 32.21 N | 74.54 E |
| Zafer Burnu › | 130 | 35.42 N | 34.35 E |
| Zafferana Etnea | 70 | 37.41 N | 15.06 E |
| Zafferano, Capo › | 70 | 38.06 N | 13.30 E |
| Zafirovo | 38 | 44.00 N | 26.50 E |
| Zafra | 34 | 38.25 N | 6.25 W |
| Žaga | 64 | 46.18 N | 13.29 E |
| Zagabria → Zagreb | 36 | 45.48 N | 15.58 E |
| Żagań | 30 | 51.37 N | 15.19 E |
| Žagare | 76 | 56.21 N | 23.15 E |
| Zagarise | 68 | 39.00 N | 16.39 E |
| Zagarolo | 66 | 41.50 N | 12.50 E |
| Zagazig → Az-Zaqāzīq | 142 | 30.35 N | 31.31 E |
| Zaghouan | 148 | 36.24 N | 10.09 E |
| Zaghouan, Jebel ∧ | 36 | 36.21 N | 10.08 E |
| Zagnanado | 150 | 7.16 N | 2.21 E |
| Zagora | 148 | 30.22 N | 5.50 W |
| Zagora ⋏ | 36 | 43.40 N | 16.15 E |
| Zagor'anskij | 265b | 55.55 N | 37.55 E |
| Zagórów | 30 | 52.11 N | 17.55 E |
| Zagorskij | 89 | 47.19 N | 142.28 E |
| Zagórz | 30 | 49.31 N | 22.17 E |
| Zagreb | 36 | 45.48 N | 15.58 E |
| Zāgros, Kūhhā-ye ⋏ | 128 | 33.40 N | 47.00 E |
| Zagros Mountains → Zāgros, Kūhhā-ye ⋏ | 128 | 33.40 N | 47.00 E |
| Žagubica | 38 | 44.13 N | 21.48 E |
| Zagustaj | 88 | 51.58 N | 110.45 E |
| Za'gya ≃ | 120 | 31.55 N | 88.58 E |
| Zagyva ≃ | 30 | 47.10 N | 20.13 E |
| Zahana | 34 | 35.32 N | 0.25 W |
| Zāhedān | 128 | 29.30 N | 60.52 E |
| Zahīrābād | 122 | 17.41 N | 77.37 E |
| Zaḥlah | 130 | 33.51 N | 35.53 E |
| Zahna | 54 | 51.54 N | 12.47 E |
| Zahnitkiv | 78 | 48.03 N | 28.54 E |
| Zahns Airport ⊠ | 276 | 40.42 N | 73.24 W |
| Zaḥodnjaja Dzvina (Daugava) ≃ | 76 | 57.04 N | 24.03 E |
| Záhony | 30 | 48.25 N | 22.11 E |
| Záhorská Ves | 61 | 48.23 N | 16.51 E |
| Ẓahrān | 144 | 17.40 N | 43.30 E |
| Zahrensdorf, Dtsch. | 54 | 53.45 N | 11.40 E |
| Zahrensdorf, Dtsch. | 54 | 53.24 N | 10.48 E |
| Zahryzove | 83 | 49.31 N | 37.43 E |
| Zăicani | 38 | 47.59 N | 27.22 E |
| Zaidpur | 124 | 26.50 N | 81.20 E |
| Zaigrajevo | 88 | 51.50 N | 108.16 E |
| Zaijiafangzi | 104 | 41.17 N | 122.39 E |
| Zailijskij Alatau, chrebet ⋏ | 85 | 43.00 N | 77.00 E |
| Žailma, Kaz. | 85 | 43.46 N | 69.47 E |
| Žailma, Kaz. | 86 | 51.32 N | 61.37 E |
| Zaimka | 88 | 58.41 N | 100.40 E |
| Zaimokuza | 268 | 35.18 N | 139.33 E |
| Zainsk | 80 | 55.18 N | 52.06 E |
| Zaire □[5] | 152 | 7.00 S | 13.30 E |
| Zaire (Zaïre) □[1] | 138 | 4.00 S | 25.00 E |
| Zaïre → Congo ≃ | 138 | 6.04 S | 12.24 E |
| Zaizhuangzi | 105 | 40.02 N | 117.43 E |
| Zaj ≃ | 80 | 55.36 N | 51.40 E |
| Zajarsk | 88 | 56.10 N | 102.52 E |
| Zajcevka | 83 | 49.41 N | 40.00 E |
| Zajcevo, Ross. | 82 | 54.08 N | 37.26 E |
| Zajcevo, Ross. | 265b | 55.39 N | 37.11 E |
| Zaječar | 38 | 43.54 N | 22.17 E |
| Zaj-Karataj | 80 | 54.42 N | 52.22 E |
| Zajmo-Obryv | 83 | 47.02 N | 39.19 E |
| Zajsan | 86 | 47.28 N | 84.55 E |
| Zajsan, ozero ⊜ | 86 | 48.00 N | 84.00 E |
| Žajsk | 80 | 55.54 N | 42.32 E |
| Zajukovo | 84 | 43.37 N | 43.19 E |
| Zaka | 154 | 20.20 S | 31.29 E |
| Zakamensk | 88 | 50.23 N | 103.17 E |
| Zakarpattya □[4] | 78 | 48.30 N | 23.00 E |
| Zákas | 38 | 40.02 N | 21.16 E |
| Zakatnyj | 80 | 46.32 N | 44.04 E |
| Zakfero | 140 | 12.10 N | 27.35 E |
| Zakhidne | 78 | 51.29 N | 31.15 E |
| Zākhū | 128 | 37.08 N | 42.41 E |
| Zákinthos | 38 | 37.47 N | 20.53 E |
| Zákinthos I | 38 | 37.52 N | 20.44 E |
| Zakínthou, Porthmós ⊔ | 38 | 37.50 N | 21.00 E |
| Zakitne | 83 | 48.54 N | 37.58 E |
| Zakīyah | 132 | 33.20 N | 36.08 E |
| Zakliczyn | 30 | 49.51 N | 20.48 E |
| Zaklików | 30 | 50.47 N | 22.06 E |
| Zákolany | 54 | 50.10 N | 14.14 E |
| Zakopane | 30 | 49.19 N | 19.57 E |
| Zakotne | 83 | 49.28 N | 38.58 E |
| Zakouma | 146 | 10.54 N | 19.49 E |
| Zakouma, Parc National de ♦ | 146 | 10.45 N | 19.30 E |
| Zakroczym | 30 | 52.26 N | 20.37 E |
| Žaksy | 86 | 51.55 N | 67.20 E |
| Žaksybaj ≃ | 80 | 49.24 N | 53.18 E |
| Zákupy | 54 | 50.42 N | 14.40 E |
| Zala | 144 | 6.28 N | 37.20 E |
| Zala □[6] | 30 | 46.45 N | 16.50 E |
| Zala ≃ | 30 | 46.43 N | 17.16 E |
| Zalaegerszeg | 30 | 46.51 N | 16.51 E |
| Zalai-dombság ⋏[2] | 61 | 46.37 N | 16.48 E |
| Zalalövő | 30 | 46.51 N | 16.35 E |
| Zalamea de la Serana | 34 | 38.39 N | 5.39 W |
| Žalanaš | 86 | 51.12 N | 65.02 E |
| Zalanga | 150 | 10.37 N | 10.10 E |
| Žalany | 54 | 50.35 N | 13.55 E |
| Zalari | 88 | 53.34 N | 102.32 E |
| Zalaszentgrót | 30 | 46.59 N | 17.02 E |
| Zalatárnok | 61 | 46.42 N | 16.46 E |
| Zalau, Nig. | 150 | 10.20 N | 9.00 E |
| Zalău, Rom. | 38 | 47.11 N | 23.03 E |
| Žalauly, ozero ⊜ | 86 | 52.53 N | 74.10 E |
| Zaldívar, Laguna ⊜ | 286b | 22.58 N | 82.27 W |
| Žalec | 36 | 46.15 N | 15.10 E |
| Zalegošč' | 76 | 52.56 N | 36.53 E |
| Zalesje, Ross. | 76 | 54.51 N | 21.32 E |
| Zalesje, Ross. | 76 | 58.42 N | 36.10 E |
| Zalesovo | 86 | 54.00 N | 84.47 E |
| Zalingei | 140 | 12.54 N | 23.29 E |
| Zalishchyky | 78 | 48.38 N | 25.44 E |
| Zaliznychne | 78 | 47.53 N | 33.29 E |
| Žalon' ≃ | 78 | 51.33 N | 29.51 E |
| Zalozhtsi | 78 | 49.48 N | 25.24 E |
| Zalṭan | 146 | 32.57 N | 11.52 E |
| Zaltbommel | 52 | 51.48 N | 5.15 E |
| Žaltyr | 86 | 51.40 N | 69.50 E |
| Žaltyr, ozero ⊜ | 80 | 47.24 N | 51.07 E |
| Zalučje | 76 | 57.40 N | 31.46 E |
| Zaludok | 76 | 53.36 N | 24.59 E |
| Zalukokoaže | 84 | 43.54 N | 43.13 E |
| Zalun | 110 | 17.29 N | 95.34 E |
| Zal'vjanka ≃ | 76 | 53.24 N | 24.32 E |
| Zama, Nihon | 268 | 35.29 N | 139.24 E |
| Zama, Ms., U.S. | 194 | 32.58 N | 89.22 W |
| Zama, Camp ■ | 268 | 35.30 N | 139.24 E |
| Zama-iriya | 268 | 35.29 N | 139.24 E |
| Zamakh | 144 | 16.30 N | 47.35 E |
| Zamālik, Jazīrat az- I | 273c | 30.03 N | 31.13 E |
| Žaman-Akkol', ozero ⊜ | 86 | 48.58 N | 63.30 E |
| Žamankak | 80 | 48.56 N | 48.45 E |
| Žamantau, gora ∧[2] | 80 | 48.20 N | 51.50 E |
| Zamantı ≃ | 130 | 37.36 N | 35.35 E |
| Zamarino | 82 | 54.18 N | 37.11 E |
| Žambaj | 80 | 47.11 N | 50.34 E |
| Zambales □[4] | 116 | 15.20 N | 120.05 E |
| Zambales Mountains ⋏ | 116 | 15.45 N | 120.05 E |
| Žamberk | 30 | 50.05 N | 16.28 E |
| Zambezi | 152 | 13.33 S | 23.06 E |
| Zambezi (Zambeze) ≃ | 138 | 18.55 S | 36.04 E |
| Zambézia □[5] | 154 | 16.15 S | 37.30 E |
| Zambezi Escarpment ⊥[4] | 154 | 16.10 S | 30.30 E |
| Zambia □[1], Afr. | 138 | 14.30 S | 27.30 E |
| Zambia □[1], Afr. | 154 | 14.30 S | 29.00 E |
| Zambie → Zambia □[1] | 154 | 14.30 S | 27.30 E |
| Zamboanga | 116 | 6.54 N | 122.04 E |
| Zamboanga del Norte □[4] | 116 | 8.15 N | 123.00 E |
| Zamboanga del Sur □[4] | 116 | 7.50 N | 123.00 E |
| Zamboanga Peninsula ›[1] | 116 | 7.32 N | 122.16 E |
| Zamboanguita | 116 | 9.06 N | 123.12 E |
| Zambrano | 246 | 9.45 N | 74.49 W |
| Zambrone | 68 | 38.42 N | 15.59 E |
| Zambrów | 30 | 53.00 N | 22.15 E |
| Zâmbuè | 154 | 15.10 S | 30.50 E |
| Zambujal | 266c | 38.52 N | 9.07 W |
| Žambyl, Kaz. | 85 | 42.54 N | 71.22 E |
| Žambyl, Kaz. | 86 | 47.12 N | 71.42 E |
| Žambyl □[4] | 85 | 43.30 N | 72.30 E |
| Zamch | 30 | 50.20 N | 23.00 E |
| Zamežnaja | 24 | 65.02 N | 51.50 E |
| Zamfara ≃ | 150 | 12.05 N | 4.02 E |
| Zamhlay | 78 | 51.49 N | 31.13 E |
| Zami ≃ | 110 | 16.09 N | 97.58 E |
| Zamjany | 80 | 46.50 N | 47.40 E |
| Zamkavaja, hara ∧[2] | 76 | 53.30 N | 25.43 E |
| Zamora, Ec. | 246 | 4.04 S | 78.58 W |
| Zamora, Esp. | 34 | 41.30 N | 5.45 W |
| Zamora, Ca., U.S. | 226 | 38.48 N | 121.53 W |
| Zamora □[4] | 34 | 41.45 N | 6.00 W |
| Zamora ≃ | 246 | 2.59 S | 78.13 W |
| Zamora-Chinchipe □[4] | 246 | 4.15 S | 78.50 W |
| Zamora de Hidalgo | 234 | 19.59 N | 102.16 W |
| Zamość | 30 | 50.44 N | 23.15 E |
| Zamość □[4] | 30 | 50.35 N | 23.20 E |
| Zamozhne | 83 | 47.19 N | 37.49 E |
| Zams | 58 | 47.09 N | 10.35 E |
| Zamševa | 86 | 59.07 N | 89.14 E |
| Zamuro, Punta › | 246 | 11.26 N | 68.50 W |
| Zamzam, Wādī V | 146 | 31.26 N | 15.27 E |
| Zamzor | 88 | 55.21 N | 98.35 E |
| Zana ⊥ | 34 | 35.45 N | 6.05 E |
| Žanadarja | 86 | 44.45 N | 64.40 E |
| Zanaga | 152 | 2.51 S | 13.50 E |
| Žanakorgan | 85 | 43.55 N | 67.15 E |
| Zanapa ≃ | 234 | 17.58 N | 94.06 W |
| Žanašu | 80 | 47.27 N | 48.31 E |
| Žanatalap, Kaz. | 86 | 47.11 N | 61.52 E |
| Žanatalap, Kaz. | 86 | 47.06 N | 84.13 E |
| Žanatarlyk | 86 | 44.16 N | 73.12 E |
| Žanatas, Kaz. | 85 | 43.22 N | 70.12 E |
| Žanatas, Kaz. | 85 | 43.34 N | 69.45 E |
| Záncara ≃ | 34 | 39.18 N | 3.18 W |
| Zanda | 120 | 31.30 N | 79.30 E |
| Žandov | 54 | 50.44 N | 14.24 E |
| Zandvoort | 52 | 52.22 N | 4.32 E |
| Zandvoort, Circuit Autorace ♦ | 52 | 52.24 N | 4.32 E |
| Zane Hills ⋏[2] | 180 | 66.10 N | 156.00 W |
| Zanesfield | 216 | 40.20 N | 83.41 W |
| Zanesville, In., U.S. | 216 | 41.02 N | 85.00 W |
| Zanesville, Oh., U.S. | 188 | 39.56 N | 82.00 W |
| Zanevka | 265a | 59.56 N | 30.31 E |
| Zangakatun | 84 | 39.50 N | 45.03 E |
| Zangasso | 150 | 12.09 N | 5.37 W |
| Zängäzur silsiläsi ⋏ | 84 | 39.30 N | 45.54 E |
| Zanggezhuang | 98 | 37.28 N | 120.57 E |
| Zangguy | 120 | 37.22 N | 78.48 E |
| Zängilan | 84 | 39.06 N | 46.39 E |
| Žangiztobe | 86 | 49.16 N | 81.18 E |
| Zangji | 100 | 33.01 N | 113.52 E |
| Zangmār ≃ | 84 | 39.17 N | 44.50 E |
| Zânguè ≃ | 154 | 17.52 S | 35.20 E |
| Zangwan | 100 | 29.27 N | 117.23 E |
| Zanhuang | 98 | 37.38 N | 114.26 E |
| Zanjān | 128 | 36.40 N | 48.29 E |
| Zanjān □[4] | 128 | 36.30 N | 49.00 E |
| Zanjān ≃ | 128 | 37.08 N | 47.47 E |
| Zanjón | 252 | 27.55 S | 64.15 W |
| Zanjón ≃ | 252 | 31.16 S | 67.41 W |
| Žankala ⊥ | 86 | 44.29 N | 64.05 E |
| Žannetty, ostrov I | 74 | 76.43 N | 158.00 E |
| Zannone, Isola I | 66 | 40.58 N | 13.03 E |
| Zanpa-misaki › | 174m | 26.26 N | 127.43 E |
| Zanri | 102 | 28.58 N | 100.50 E |
| Zante → Zákinthos I | 38 | 37.52 N | 20.44 E |
| Žanterek | 86 | 47.57 N | 54.21 E |
| Zanthus | 162 | 31.02 S | 123.34 E |
| Zantiébougou | 150 | 11.24 N | 7.15 W |
| Zanyang | 98 | 34.00 N | 116.13 E |
| Zanzibar | 154 | 6.10 S | 39.11 E |
| Zanzibar I | 154 | 6.10 S | 39.20 E |
| Zanzibar Channel ⊔ | 154 | 6.00 S | 39.00 E |
| Zaohe | 98 | 34.03 N | 118.07 E |
| Zaoheshi | 100 | 26.53 N | 114.41 E |
| Zaojiang | 98 | 37.30 N | 115.43 E |
| Zaojiaochang | 107 | 29.58 N | 106.11 E |
| Zaojiatuo | 105 | 39.23 N | 118.11 E |
| Zaokskij | 82 | 54.44 N | 37.24 E |
| Zaolin | 100 | 26.24 N | 114.24 E |
| Zaorosongou | 152 | 5.02 N | 16.13 E |
| Zaoshi, Zhg. | 100 | 26.22 N | 112.50 E |
| Zaoshi, Zhg. | 100 | 30.51 N | 113.20 E |
| Zaostrovje, Ross. | 24 | 60.50 N | 30.22 E |
| Zaostrovje, Ross. | 76 | 60.38 N | 33.16 E |
| Zaouiet Azmour | 36 | 36.55 N | 11.01 E |
| Zaouiet el Mgaïz | 36 | 36.56 N | 10.50 E |
| Zaoxi | 100 | 30.13 N | 119.30 E |
| Zaoyang | 100 | 32.10 N | 112.43 E |
| Zaō-zan ∧ | 92 | 38.08 N | 140.26 E |
| Zaozernyj | 86 | 53.18 N | 71.52 E |
| Zaozhuang | 98 | 34.53 N | 117.34 E |
| Zaoz'orje, Ross. | 76 | 57.12 N | 38.15 E |
| Zaoz'orje, Ross. | 265b | 55.34 N | 38.02 E |
| Zaoz'ornyj | 86 | 55.58 N | 94.42 E |
| Zap | 198 | 47.17 N | 101.55 W |
| Zapadnaja Dvina | 76 | 56.16 N | 32.04 E |
| Zapadna Morava ≃ | 38 | 43.42 N | 21.23 E |
| Zapadno-Kazachstan □[8] | 80 | 50.00 N | 51.00 E |
| Zapadno-Sibirskaja ravnina ≚ | 72 | 60.00 N | 75.00 E |
| Zapadnyj Alamedin, pik ∧ | 85 | 42.32 N | 74.34 E |
| Zapadnyj chrebet ⋏ | 89 | 50.00 N | 142.25 E |
| Zapadnyj Karakol ≃ | 85 | 42.08 N | 74.05 E |
| Zapadnyj Sajan ⋏ | 74 | 53.00 N | 94.00 E |
| Západočeský Kraj □[4] | 30 | 49.45 N | 13.00 E |
| Západoslovenský Kraj □[4] | 30 | 48.20 N | 18.00 E |
| Zapala | 252 | 38.54 S | 70.04 W |
| Zapaleri, Cerro ∧ | 252 | 22.49 S | 67.11 W |
| Zapardiel ≃ | 34 | 41.29 N | 5.02 W |
| Zapata | 196 | 26.54 N | 99.16 W |
| Zapata, Península de ›[1] | 240p | 22.20 N | 81.35 W |
| Zapatera, Isla I | 236 | 11.45 N | 85.50 W |
| Zapatoca | 246 | 6.49 N | 73.17 W |
| Zapato Chino Creek ≃ | 226 | 36.09 N | 120.11 W |
| Zapatosa, Ciénaga de ⊜ | 246 | 9.05 N | 73.50 W |
| Zapfendorf | 56 | 50.01 N | 10.56 E |
| Zapiola | 258 | 35.03 S | 59.03 W |
| Zaplavnoje, Ross. | 80 | 52.58 N | 51.44 E |
| Zaplavnoje, Ross. | 80 | 48.43 N | 45.01 E |
| Zapl'usje | 76 | 58.26 N | 29.43 E |
| Zapokrovskij | 88 | 50.50 N | 119.05 E |
| Zapol'arnyj, Ross. | 24 | 69.26 N | 30.48 E |
| Zapol'arnyj, Ross. | 24 | 67.30 N | 63.42 E |
| Zapolje | 76 | 58.23 N | 29.41 E |
| Zapopan | 234 | 20.43 N | 103.24 W |
| Zaporizhzhya, Ukr. | 78 | 47.50 N | 35.10 E |
| Zaporizhzhya, Ukr. | 83 | 48.14 N | 38.41 E |
| Zaporizhzhya □[4] | 78 | 47.30 N | 35.30 E |
| Zaporojie → Zaporizhzhya | 78 | 47.50 N | 35.10 E |
| Zaporozh'ye → Zaporizhzhya | 78 | 47.50 N | 35.10 E |
| Zaporožskaja | 76 | 45.23 N | 36.52 E |
| Zapotán | 234 | 18.41 N | 103.39 W |
| Zapotillo | 246 | 4.25 S | 80.31 W |
| Zapotiltic | 234 | 19.37 N | 103.26 W |
| Zapotitlán | 234 | 19.31 N | 103.44 W |
| Zapotlán, Laguna ⊜ | 234 | 19.45 N | 103.30 W |
| Zapotlanejo | 234 | 20.38 N | 103.04 W |
| Zapovednoje | 76 | 55.04 N | 21.24 E |
| Zapovednyj | 89 | 42.52 N | 133.45 E |
| Zaprudn'a | 82 | 56.34 N | 37.26 E |
| Zaqatala | 84 | 41.38 N | 46.39 E |
| Zaqqūṭ | 146 | 28.29 N | 19.37 E |
| Zara → Zadar, Hrv. | 36 | 44.07 N | 15.14 E |
| Zara, Tür. | 130 | 39.55 N | 37.46 E |
| Zarāf, Baḥr az- ≃ | 140 | 9.25 N | 31.10 E |
| Zaragoza, Col. | 246 | 7.30 N | 74.52 W |
| Zaragoza, Esp. | 34 | 41.38 N | 0.53 W |
| Zaragoza, Méx. | 232 | 31.39 N | 106.20 W |
| Zaragoza, Méx. | 232 | 28.29 N | 100.55 W |
| Zaragoza, Méx. | 234 | 23.58 N | 99.46 W |
| Zaragoza, Méx. | 234 | 19.46 N | 97.33 W |
| Zaragoza, Méx. | 234 | 22.02 N | 100.44 W |
| Zaragoza □[4] | 34 | 42.30 N | 1.00 W |
| Zarajsk | 82 | 54.46 N | 38.53 E |
| Zaramag | 84 | 42.43 N | 43.57 E |
| Zarand | 128 | 30.48 N | 56.35 E |
| Zarand, Munții ⋏ | 38 | 46.10 N | 22.15 E |
| Zaranda Hill ∧[2] | 150 | 10.15 N | 9.35 E |
| Zarand-e Kohneh | 128 | 35.17 N | 50.30 E |
| Zaranj | 128 | 31.06 N | 61.53 E |
| Zarasai | 76 | 55.44 N | 26.15 E |
| Zárate | 258 | 34.06 S | 59.02 W |
| Zarautz | 34 | 43.17 N | 2.10 W |
| Zaraza | 246 | 9.21 N | 65.19 W |
| Žarbulak | 86 | 46.05 N | 82.04 E |
| Zarcero | 236 | 10.11 N | 84.23 W |
| Zärdab | 84 | 40.13 N | 47.43 E |
| Zardaly | 85 | 39.38 N | 70.57 E |
| Zard Kūh ∧ | 128 | 32.22 N | 50.04 E |
| Zarečensk | 24 | 66.40 N | 31.23 E |
| Zarečje, Ross. | 24 | 63.08 N | 44.46 E |
| Zarečje, Ross. | 76 | 56.52 N | 33.50 E |
| Zarečje, Ross. | 76 | 58.56 N | 39.40 E |
| Zarečje, Ross. | 265b | 55.41 N | 37.23 E |
| Zarečnyj, Ross. | 76 | 53.45 N | 39.35 E |
| Zarečnyj, Ross. | 80 | 57.28 N | 42.18 E |
| Zarečnyj, Ross. | 80 | 53.13 N | 45.13 E |
| Zarembo Island I | 180 | 56.20 N | 132.50 W |
| Zarephath | 276 | 40.32 N | 74.35 W |
| Zargān | 128 | 29.46 N | 52.43 E |
| Zarghūn Shahr | 120 | 32.51 N | 68.25 E |
| Zari | 146 | 13.04 N | 12.43 E |
| Zaria | 150 | 11.07 N | 7.44 E |
| Zarichne | 78 | 51.48 N | 26.06 E |
| Zarinskaja | 86 | 53.43 N | 84.58 E |
| Žarkamys | 86 | 47.56 N | 56.26 E |
| Żarki | 30 | 50.38 N | 19.22 E |
| Žarkova | 86 | 58.00 N | 87.17 E |
| Žarkovskij | 76 | 55.52 N | 32.17 E |
| Žarma | 86 | 48.48 N | 80.50 E |
| žarman, ozero ⊜ | 86 | 51.36 N | 64.30 E |
| Zarnān | 267d | 35.41 N | 51.09 E |
| Zărnești | 38 | 45.34 N | 25.19 E |
| Zarow ≃ | 54 | 53.46 N | 14.02 E |
| Zarqā', Nahr az- ≃ | 132 | 32.07 N | 35.33 E |
| Zarqā', Raqabat az- V | 140 | 9.14 N | 29.44 E |
| Zarqā' Mā'īn, Wādī V | 132 | 31.37 N | 35.34 E |
| Zarqūn | 142 | 31.07 N | 30.28 E |
| Zarrentin | 54 | 53.35 N | 10.55 E |
| Zarrīneh ≃ | 128 | 37.05 N | 45.54 E |
| Zarrīn Shahr | 128 | 32.32 N | 51.23 E |
| Žarsuat | 86 | 46.27 N | 80.48 E |
| Zarubino, Ross. | 76 | 58.44 N | 33.28 E |
| Zarubino, Ross. | 89 | 42.40 N | 131.04 E |
| Zaruma | 246 | 3.41 S | 79.37 W |
| Zarumilla | 246 | 3.30 S | 80.16 W |
| Żary (Sorau) | 30 | 51.38 N | 15.09 E |
| Žaryk | 86 | 48.52 N | 72.51 E |
| Žaryn' | 76 | 53.47 N | 33.04 E |
| Zarzaïtine | 148 | 28.18 N | 9.48 E |
| Zarzal | 246 | 4.24 N | 76.04 W |
| Zarzis | 148 | 33.30 N | 11.07 E |
| Zarzuela, Arroyo de la ≃ | 266a | 40.29 N | 3.45 W |
| Zarzuela, Hipodromo de la ♦ | 266a | 40.28 N | 3.45 W |
| Zasa | 76 | 56.17 N | 25.58 E |
| Zašejek | 24 | 67.25 N | 32.28 E |
| Zasenbeck | 54 | 52.40 N | 10.51 E |
| Zasieki | 54 | 51.43 N | 14.43 E |
| Zāskār ≃ | 123 | 34.10 N | 77.20 E |
| Zāskār Mountains ⋏ | 120 | 33.00 N | 78.00 E |
| Zaslaụe | 76 | 54.01 N | 27.15 E |
| Zaslaụskae vadasḫovišča ⊜[1] | 76 | 53.58 N | 27.22 E |
| Zasosna | 78 | 50.37 N | 38.23 E |
| Žastalap | 80 | 49.11 N | 50.24 E |
| Zastava | 24 | 59.12 N | 46.46 E |
| Zastávka | 61 | 49.11 N | 16.23 E |
| Zastavna | 78 | 48.31 N | 25.50 E |
| Zastron | 158 | 30.18 S | 27.07 E |
| Zasulje | 24 | 64.41 N | 47.48 E |
| Zasulle | 76 | 53.34 N | 26.50 E |
| Za'tarī, Wādī az- V | 132 | 32.09 N | 36.15 E |
| Žatec | 54 | 50.18 N | 13.32 E |
| Zaterečnyj | 84 | 44.48 N | 45.11 E |
| Z'at'kovo | 86 | 53.36 N | 80.20 E |
| Zatobol'sk | 86 | 53.12 N | 63.43 E |
| Zaton | 86 | 53.18 N | 83.49 E |
| Zatyshshya, Ukr. | 38 | 47.19 N | 29.51 E |
| Zatyshshya, Ukr. | 78 | 47.19 N | 29.51 E |
| Zauche ◆[1] | 54 | 52.15 N | 12.35 E |
| Zauchwitz | 54 | 52.12 N | 13.02 E |
| Zauel | 144 | 3.33 N | 43.45 E |
| Zaural'skoje plato ⋏[1] | 86 | 53.00 N | 62.00 E |
| Zavalla | 194 | 31.09 N | 94.26 W |
| Zavallya | 78 | 48.13 N | 30.01 E |
| Zaval'noje | 76 | 52.02 N | 39.51 E |
| Zave | 154 | 17.13 S | 30.02 E |
| Zaventem | 50 | 50.53 N | 4.28 E |
| Zavet | 38 | 43.46 N | 26.40 E |
| Zavetnoje | 80 | 47.07 N | 43.52 E |
| Zavety Iljiča | 89 | 49.02 N | 140.17 E |
| Zavidovići | 38 | 44.27 N | 18.09 E |
| Zavidovka | 82 | 54.16 N | 38.49 E |
| Zavidovo | 82 | 56.32 N | 36.32 E |
| Zavitinsk | 89 | 50.07 N | 129.27 E |
| Zavjalovo, Ross. | 80 | 56.47 N | 53.23 E |
| Zavjalovo, Ross. | 86 | 54.30 N | 82.27 E |
| Zavlekov | 60 | 49.20 N | 13.30 E |
| Zavod Michajlovskij | 80 | 56.32 N | 54.17 E |
| Zavodo-Petrovskij | 86 | 56.50 N | 66.45 E |
| Zavodoukovsk | 86 | 56.33 N | 66.32 E |
| Zavodouspenskoje | 86 | 56.51 N | 65.00 E |
| Zavodovski Island I | 18 | 56.20 S | 27.35 W |
| Zavodskoj, Ross. | 78 | 48.24 N | 40.19 E |
| Zavodskoj, Ross. | 86 | 53.04 N | 84.25 E |
| Zavolžje | 80 | 56.37 N | 43.26 E |
| Zavolžsk | 80 | 57.30 N | 42.10 E |
| Zavolžskoje | 80 | 46.59 N | 47.37 E |
| Zavoronežskoje | 80 | 52.53 N | 40.33 E |
| Zavorovo | 82 | 55.20 N | 38.13 E |
| Zāwa | 120 | 28.04 N | 66.23 E |
| Zawadzkie | 30 | 50.37 N | 18.29 E |
| Zawichost | 30 | 50.49 N | 21.52 E |
| Zawiercie | 30 | 50.30 N | 19.25 E |
| Zawīlah | 146 | 26.10 N | 15.07 E |
| Zāwiyat 'Abd al-Qādir | 142 | 31.02 N | 29.49 E |
| Zāwiyat Abū Musallum | 273c | 29.56 N | 31.10 E |
| Zāwiyat al-Amwāt | 142 | 28.04 N | 30.50 E |
| Zawiyat al-Judhāmī | 142 | 28.42 N | 30.54 E |
| Zāwiyat al-Mukhaylā | 146 | 32.09 N | 22.17 E |
| Zāwiyat Masūs | 146 | 31.33 N | 21.03 E |
| Zāwiyat Nābit | 273c | 30.07 N | 31.09 E |
| Zāwiyat Razīn | 142 | 30.25 N | 30.51 E |
| Zāwiyat Saqr | 142 | 30.56 N | 30.12 E |
| Zawiyat Shammās | 140 | 31.31 N | 26.24 E |
| Zāwiyat Sīdī Ghāzī | 142 | 31.03 N | 30.05 E |
| Zāwiyet an-Najjār | 273c | 30.11 N | 31.17 E |
| Zawr, Ra's az- ›, Ar. Su. | 128 | 27.25 N | 49.20 E |
| Zawr, Ra's az- ›, Kuwayt | 128 | 28.44 N | 48.24 E |
| Zäyämçay ≃ | 84 | 41.00 N | 45.59 E |
| Zāyandeh ≃ | 128 | 32.16 N | 52.53 E |
| Zaydābād | 120 | 34.17 N | 69.07 E |
| Zaytseve, Ukr. | 83 | 48.24 N | 38.02 E |
| Zaytseve, Ukr. | 83 | 48.32 N | 38.04 E |
| Zayü | 102 | 28.48 N | 97.27 E |
| Zayü ≃ | 102 | 28.28 N | 97.03 E |
| Zaza ≃ | 240p | 21.37 N | 79.32 W |
| Zaza, Presa ⊜[1] | 240p | 21.50 N | 79.23 W |
| Zaza del Medio | 240p | 22.00 N | 79.23 W |
| Zazafotsy | 157b | 22.13 S | 46.26 E |
| Zāzamt, Wādī V | 146 | 30.58 N | 14.49 E |
| Zazir, Oued V | 148 | 20.25 N | 5.30 E |
| Zban | 86 | 48.53 N | 63.58 E |
| Zbarazh | 78 | 49.39 N | 25.47 E |
| Zbąszyń | 30 | 52.16 N | 15.55 E |
| Zbąszynek | 30 | 52.15 N | 15.50 E |
| Zbečno | 60 | 50.03 N | 13.56 E |
| Zbiroh | 60 | 49.52 N | 13.47 E |
| Zboriv | 78 | 49.39 N | 25.08 E |
| Zborovy | 60 | 49.23 N | 13.31 E |
| Zbraslav | 30 | 49.59 N | 14.24 E |
| Zbruch ≃ | 78 | 48.32 N | 26.26 E |
| Zbůch | 60 | 49.41 N | 13.14 E |
| Ždanov → Mariupol' | 83 | 47.06 N | 37.33 E |
| Ždanova | 86 | 58.37 N | 88.58 E |
| Žd'ár | 60 | 50.03 N | 13.28 E |
| Žd'ár nad Sazavou | 30 | 49.34 N | 15.57 E |
| Ždiar | 30 | 49.17 N | 20.16 E |
| Zdice | 60 | 49.55 N | 13.59 E |
| Zdíkovec | 60 | 49.05 N | 13.42 E |
| Zdolbuniv | 78 | 50.31 N | 26.15 E |
| Zdroje ◆[8] | 54 | 53.20 N | 14.40 E |
| Zduńska Wola | 30 | 51.36 N | 18.57 E |
| Zduny | 30 | 51.39 N | 17.24 E |
| Zdvyzh ≃ | 78 | 51.01 N | 30.02 E |
| Ze ≃ | 105 | 38.50 N | 115.13 E |
| Zealandia | 184 | 51.37 N | 107.45 W |
| Zearing | 190 | 42.09 N | 93.17 W |
| Zēbāk | 120 | 36.32 N | 71.21 E |
| Zeballos | 182 | 49.59 N | 126.51 W |
| Zeballos, Monte ∧ | 254 | 47.01 S | 71.42 W |
| Zebediela | 156 | 24.19 S | 29.21 E |
| Zebila | 150 | 10.56 N | 0.29 W |
| Zebl'aki | 80 | 58.23 N | 45.45 E |
| Žebrák | 60 | 49.52 N | 13.56 E |
| Zebulon, Ga., U.S. | 192 | 33.06 N | 84.20 W |
| Zebulon, N.C., U.S. | 192 | 35.49 N | 78.18 W |
| Zechlinerhütte | 54 | 53.09 N | 12.51 E |
| Zeda, Monte ∧ | 58 | 46.03 N | 8.32 E |
| Zedang | 120 | 29.16 N | 91.46 E |
| Zeddine, Oued ≃ | 34 | 36.15 N | 1.48 E |
| Zedelgem | 50 | 51.09 N | 3.08 E |
| Zederhaus | 64 | 47.09 N | 13.30 E |
| Zeebrugge | 50 | 51.20 N | 3.12 E |
| Zeehan | 166 | 41.53 S | 145.20 E |
| Zeeland, Ned. | 52 | 51.42 N | 5.40 E |
| Zeeland, Mi., U.S. | 216 | 42.48 N | 86.01 W |
| Zeeland, N.D., U.S. | 198 | 45.58 N | 99.49 W |
| Zeeland □[4] | 52 | 51.27 N | 3.45 E |
| Zeelandbrug ◆[5] | 52 | 51.37 N | 3.53 E |
| Zeerust | 156 | 25.33 S | 26.06 E |
| Zeesen | 54 | 52.16 N | 13.38 E |
| Zeestow | 264a | 52.34 N | 12.58 E |
| Zeeuws-Vlaanderen □[9] | 52 | 51.19 N | 3.45 E |
| Ẓefat (Safad) | 132 | 32.58 N | 35.30 E |
| Žegalovo, Ross. | 80 | 54.43 N | 43.25 E |
| Žegalovo, Ross. | 265b | 55.54 N | 37.59 E |
| Žegdoči | 89 | 53.20 N | 120.49 E |
| Zege | 144 | 11.42 N | 37.23 E |
| Zegher, Ḥamādat ≃ | 146 | 27.18 N | 11.30 E |
| Zégoua | 150 | 10.30 N | 5.40 W |
| Zegrir, Oued V | 148 | 32.43 N | 5.00 E |
| Zeguo | 100 | 28.32 N | 121.20 E |
| Zehdenick | 54 | 52.59 N | 13.20 E |
| Zehlendorf | 54 | 52.47 N | 13.23 E |
| Zehlendorf ◆[8] | 54 | 52.26 N | 13.15 E |
| Zeigler | 194 | 37.53 N | 89.03 W |
| Zeil | 56 | 50.01 N | 10.35 E |
| Zeil, Mount ∧ | 162 | 23.24 S | 132.23 E |
| Zeiselmauer | 264b | 48.20 N | 16.11 E |
| Zeist | 52 | 52.05 N | 5.15 E |
| Zeithain | 54 | 51.19 N | 13.19 E |
| Zeitlarn | 60 | 49.05 N | 12.06 E |
| Zeitz | 54 | 51.03 N | 12.08 E |
| Zeja | 89 | 53.45 N | 127.15 E |
| Zeja ≃ | 89 | 50.13 N | 127.35 E |
| Zejskoje vodochranilišče ⊜[1] | 89 | 54.28 N | 127.45 E |
| Zekeriyaköy ◆[8] | 267b | 41.11 N | 29.01 E |
| Zekiah Swamp Run ≃ | 208 | 38.25 N | 76.57 W |
| Žel'abino | 265b | 55.52 N | 37.11 E |
| Žel'abužskaja | 82 | 54.36 N | 36.32 E |
| Zelaya | 258 | 34.21 S | 58.52 W |
| Zelaya □[5] | 236 | 13.00 N | 84.00 W |
| Želča ≃ | 76 | 58.19 N | 27.40 E |
| Žel'dyadyr ◆[1] | 86 | 49.30 N | 68.30 E |
| Želdybino | 82 | 56.14 N | 39.02 E |
| Zele | 50 | 51.04 N | 4.02 E |
| Żelechów | 30 | 51.49 N | 21.54 E |
| Zelee, Cape › | 175e | 9.45 S | 161.34 E |
| Zelená Lhota | 60 | 49.14 N | 13.10 E |
| Zelencovo | 76 | 59.52 N | 44.59 E |
| Zelenčukskaja | 84 | 43.52 N | 41.36 E |
| Zelene | 78 | 47.43 N | 33.12 E |
| Zelenec | 24 | 62.29 N | 55.16 E |
| Zelenga | 80 | 46.11 N | 48.37 E |
| Zelengora ⋏ | 38 | 43.15 N | 18.45 E |
| Zelenivka | 78 | 46.59 N | 36.14 E |
| Zelenoborskij | 24 | 66.49 N | 32.18 E |
| Zelenogorsk | 76 | 60.12 N | 29.42 E |
| Zelenograd | 82 | 56.01 N | 37.11 E |
| Zelenogradsk | 76 | 54.58 N | 20.29 E |
| Zelenokumsk | 84 | 44.24 N | 43.53 E |
| Želetava | 61 | 49.09 N | 15.38 E |
| Zeletin ≃ | 38 | 46.03 N | 27.23 E |
| Železinka | 86 | 53.32 N | 75.18 E |
| Železn'a | 82 | 54.31 N | 37.28 E |
| Železná Ruda | 60 | 49.09 N | 13.14 E |
| Železnik | 38 | 44.43 N | 20.23 E |
| Železnodorožnyj, Ross. | 24 | 62.35 N | 50.55 E |
| Železnodorožnyj, Ross. | 76 | 54.22 N | 21.19 E |
| Železnodorožnyj, Ross. | 82 | 55.45 N | 38.01 E |
| Železnodorožnyj, Uzb. | 86 | 43.04 N | 58.50 E |
| Železnogorsk | 76 | 52.22 N | 35.23 E |
| Železnogorsk-Ilimskij | 88 | 56.37 N | 104.08 E |
| Železnovodsk | 84 | 44.08 N | 43.02 E |
| Zelienople | 214 | 40.47 N | 80.08 W |
| Zelina | 36 | 45.58 N | 16.15 E |
| Zell, Dtsch. | 56 | 50.01 N | 7.10 E |
| Zell, Dtsch. | 56 | 49.49 N | 9.52 E |
| Zell, Dtsch. | 58 | 47.42 N | 7.51 E |
| Zell, Schw. | 58 | 47.09 N | 7.55 E |
| Zella-Mehlis | 54 | 50.39 N | 10.39 E |
| Zell am Harmersbach | 58 | 48.21 N | 8.04 E |
| Zell am Moos | 64 | 47.54 N | 13.19 E |
| Zell am See | 64 | 47.19 N | 12.47 E |
| Zell am Ziller | 64 | 47.14 N | 11.53 E |
| Zellersee ⊂ | 58 | 47.42 N | 9.03 E |
| Zeller See ⊜ | 64 | 47.19 N | 12.48 E |
| Zellingen | 56 | 49.53 N | 9.43 E |
| Zellwood | 220 | 28.44 N | 81.36 W |
| Želnava | 61 | 48.50 N | 13.57 E |
| Zel'onaja Rošča, Ross. | 76 | 60.10 N | 29.08 E |
| Zel'onaja Rošča, Ross. | 80 | 54.29 N | 52.02 E |
| Zel'onaja Rošča, Ross. | 83 | 47.07 N | 40.13 E |
| Zel'onodol'sk | 80 | 55.51 N | 48.33 E |
| Zel'onoje | 80 | 48.07 N | 51.31 E |
| Zel'onoje Ozero | 88 | 53.40 N | 116.36 E |
| Zel'onyj | 80 | 51.10 N | 50.41 E |
| Zel'onyj, ostrov (Shibotsu-Tō) I | 92a | 43.30 N | 146.09 E |
| Zelo Surrigone | 266b | 45.23 N | 8.59 E |
| Zelów | 30 | 51.28 N | 19.13 E |
| Žel'tau Ajtau ⋏ | 86 | 44.30 N | 74.00 E |
| Zeltweg | 61 | 47.11 N | 14.45 E |
| Zèl'va, Bela. | 76 | 53.09 N | 24.49 E |
| Želva, Liet. | 76 | 55.13 N | 25.06 E |
| Zelzate | 50 | 51.12 N | 3.49 E |
| Žemaičių Naumiestis | 76 | 55.22 N | 21.42 E |
| Žemaitija □[9] | 76 | 55.45 N | 23.00 E |
| Žembejtinskij | 80 | 50.30 N | 52.39 E |
| Zembin | 76 | 54.22 N | 28.13 E |
| Zembla Septentrional → Severnaja Zeml'a II | 74 | 79.30 N | 98.00 E |
| Zembra, Île I | 36 | 37.08 N | 10.48 E |
| Žemčug | 88 | 51.41 N | 102.24 E |
| Zemcy | 76 | 56.15 N | 32.23 E |
| Zemetčino | 80 | 53.30 N | 42.38 E |
| Zemgale □[9] | 76 | 56.30 N | 25.00 E |
| Zémio | 154 | 5.02 N | 25.08 E |
| Zeml'ansk | 78 | 51.54 N | 38.44 E |
| Zemmer | 56 | 49.53 N | 6.41 E |
| Zemmora | 34 | 35.44 N | 0.45 E |
| Zemmour ◆[1] | 148 | 24.50 N | 12.15 W |
| Zemo-Kedi | 84 | 41.26 N | 46.24 E |
| Zémongo, Réserve de Faune de ◆[4] | 140 | 6.45 N | 25.15 E |
| Zemoul, Oued V | 148 | 29.12 N | 7.52 W |
| Žemovo | 82 | 54.45 N | 38.49 E |
| Zempin | 54 | 54.04 N | 13.57 E |
| Zempoala | 234 | 19.24 N | 96.24 W |
| Zempoala ≃ | 234 | 20.16 N | 97.27 W |
| Zempoala ⊥ | 234 | 19.27 N | 96.23 W |
| Zempoala, Punta › | 234 | 19.28 N | 96.19 W |
| Zemst | 50 | 50.59 N | 4.28 E |
| Zemun | 38 | 44.50 N | 20.24 E |
| Zenas | 218 | 39.07 N | 85.29 W |
| Zendeh Jān | 128 | 34.21 N | 61.45 E |
| Zeneta | 184 | 50.44 N | 102.02 W |
| Zeng ≃ | 100 | 23.09 N | 113.46 E |
| Zengcheng | 100 | 23.19 N | 113.49 E |
| Zengjiawan | 105 | 39.22 N | 118.24 E |
| Zengkou ≃ | 105 | 39.19 N | 117.37 E |
| Zenica | 38 | 44.12 N | 17.55 E |
| Ẓenifim, Har ∧[2] | 132 | 30.06 N | 34.51 E |
| Zenith | 224 | 47.23 N | 122.19 W |
| Zenn ≃ | 56 | 49.31 N | 10.58 E |
| Zenne (Senne) ≃ | 50 | 51.04 N | 4.26 E |
| Zenon Park | 184 | 53.04 N | 103.45 W |
| Zenon Videla Dorna | 258 | 35.33 S | 58.53 W |
| Zenson di Piave | 64 | 45.41 N | 12.29 E |
| Zentralafrikanische Republik → Central African Republic □[1] | 136 | 7.00 N | 21.00 E |
| Zentral-Friedhof ◆ | 264b | 48.09 N | 16.27 E |
| Zentral-Massiv → Central, Massif ⋏ | 32 | 45.00 N | 3.10 E |
| Zentsūji | 96 | 34.14 N | 133.47 E |
| Zenza do Itombe | 152 | 9.16 S | 14.13 E |
| Zenzeli | 80 | 45.56 N | 47.03 E |
| Zepernick | 54 | 52.39 N | 13.32 E |
| Zephyr | 196 | 31.41 N | 98.48 W |
| Zephyr Cove | 226 | 39.00 N | 119.57 W |
| Zephyrhills | 220 | 28.14 N | 82.10 W |
| Zepu | 120 | 38.13 N | 77.16 E |
| Zérab, Ouadi V | 146 | 11.03 N | 19.47 E |
| Zeralda | 34 | 36.41 N | 2.53 E |
| Zeravšan | 85 | 39.11 N | 68.40 E |
| Zeravšan ≃ | 72 | 39.22 N | 63.45 E |
| Zeravšanskij chrebet ⋏ | 85 | 39.15 N | 68.30 E |
| Zerbst | 54 | 51.58 N | 12.04 E |
| Žerdevka | 80 | 51.51 N | 41.28 E |
| Zereh, Gowd-e ⊥[7] | 128 | 29.45 N | 61.50 E |
| Zerenda | 86 | 52.55 N | 69.10 E |
| Zerf | 56 | 49.36 N | 6.41 E |
| Zerga, Merja ⊂ | 34 | 34.51 N | 6.17 W |
| Zergenta | 80 | 47.42 N | 45.12 E |
| Zeri | 62 | 44.21 N | 9.46 E |
| Zerind | 38 | 46.37 N | 21.31 E |
| Żerków | 30 | 52.05 N | 17.34 E |
| Zermatt | 58 | 46.02 N | 7.45 E |
| Zernez | 58 | 46.43 N | 10.05 E |
| Zernograd | 78 | 46.50 N | 40.19 E |
| Žernovka | 82 | 54.49 N | 37.46 E |
| Zernsdorf | 54 | 52.18 N | 13.41 E |
| Zero ≃ | 64 | 45.32 N | 12.22 E |
| Zeroud, Oued V | 36 | 35.50 N | 10.13 E |
| Zerqan | 38 | 41.30 N | 20.21 E |
| Žešart | 24 | 62.05 N | 49.34 E |
| Zestafoni | 84 | 42.07 N | 43.02 E |
| Žest'anka | 80 | 51.36 N | 49.24 E |
| Žestoki | 82 | 56.19 N | 36.22 E |
| Žestylevo | 82 | 56.24 N | 37.39 E |
| Zetel | 52 | 53.25 N | 7.58 E |
| Žetybaj | 80 | 48.51 N | 48.04 E |
| Žetykol', ozero ⊜ | 86 | 51.02 N | 60.54 E |
| Zeulenroda | 54 | 50.39 N | 11.58 E |
| Zeuthen | 54 | 52.20 N | 13.37 E |
| Zeuthener See ⊜ | 264a | 52.21 N | 13.39 E |
| Zeven | 52 | 53.18 N | 9.16 E |


**Symbols** in the index entries represent the broad categories identified in the key at the right. Symbols with superior numbers (⋏[1]) identify subcategories (see complete key on page *I · 1).*

**Symbole** im Register stellen die rechts im Schlüssel erklärten Kategorien dar. Symbole mit hochgestellten Ziffern (⋏[1]) bezeichnen Unterabteilungen einer Kategorie (vgl. vollständiger Schlüssel auf Seite *I · 1).*

**Los símbolos** incluídos en el texto del índice representan las grandes categorías identificadas con la clave a la derecha. Los símbolos con numeros en su parte superior (⋏[1]) identifican las subcategorías (véase la clave completa en la página *I · 1).*

**Les symboles** de l'index représentent les catégories indiquées dans la légende à droite. Les symboles suivis d'un indice (⋏[1]) représentent des sous-catégories (voir légende complète à la page *I · 1).*

**Os símbolos** incluídos no texto do índice representam as grandes categorias identificadas com a chave à direita. Os símbolos com números em sua parte superior (⋏[1]) identificam as subcategorias (veja-se a chave completa à página *I · 1).*

| | English | Deutsch | Español | Français | Português |
|---|---|---|---|---|---|
| ∧ | Mountain | Berg | Montaña | Montagne | Montanha |
| ⋏ | Mountains | Gebirge | Montañas | Montagnes | Montanhas |
| )( | Pass | Paß | Paso | Col | Passo |
| V | Valley, Canyon | Tal, Cañon | Valle, Cañón | Vallée, Canyon | Vale, Canhão |
| ≚ | Plain | Ebene | Llano | Plaine | Planície |
| › | Cape | Kap | Cabo | Cap | Cabo |
| I | Island | Insel | Isla | Île | Ilha |
| II | Islands | Inseln | Islas | Îles | Ilhas |
| ⊥ | Other Topographic Features | Andere Topographische Objekte | Otros Elementos Topográficos | Autres données topographiques | Outros acidentes topográficos |

| ESPAÑOL Nombre / FRANÇAIS Nom / PORTUGUÊS Nome | Página / Page / Página | Lat.°′ | Long.°′ W = Oeste / W = Ouest / W = Oeste |
|---|---|---|---|
| Zevenaar | 52 | 51.56 N | 6.05 E |
| Zevenbergen | 52 | 51.38 N | 4.36 E |
| Zevenbergschen Hoek | 52 | 51.41 N | 4.40 E |
| Zevenwouden ● [1] | 52 | 52.57 N | 6.00 E |
| Zevio | 64 | 45.22 N | 11.08 E |
| Zeyādah Kot | 272b | 22.27 N | 88.20 E |
| Zeyawadi | 110 | 18.33 N | 96.26 E |
| Zeytinbağı | 130 | 40.23 N | 28.47 E |
| Zeytinburnu ● [8] | 267b | 40.59 N | 28.54 E |
| Zeytindağ | 130 | 38.58 N | 27.04 E |
| Zeyveh | 84 | 39.07 N | 47.42 E |
| Žezdy | 86 | 48.04 N | 67.05 E |
| Zeze | 270 | 35.00 N | 135.54 E |
| Zêzere ≐ | 34 | 39.28 N | 8.20 W |
| Žezkazgan, Kaz. | 86 | 47.53 N | 67.27 E |
| Žezkazgan, Kaz. | 86 | 47.47 N | 67.46 E |
| Žezkazgan □ [8] | 86 | 47.30 N | 70.00 E |
| Zghartā | 130 | 34.24 N | 35.54 E |
| Zgierz | 30 | 51.52 N | 19.25 E |
| Zgornje Hoče | 61 | 46.29 N | 15.38 E |
| Zgorzelec | 30 | 51.12 N | 15.01 E |
| Zhabuchaka Hu ⊜ | 120 | 31.30 N | 84.00 E |
| Zhadove | 78 | 52.03 N | 32.39 E |
| Zhage | 102 | 26.20 N | 103.51 E |
| Zhagenasongduo | 102 | 33.12 N | 94.33 E |
| Zhag'yab | 102 | 30.32 N | 98.00 E |
| Zhahasutai | 86 | 42.58 N | 85.20 E |
| Zhai ≐ | 100 | 32.19 N | 115.02 E |
| Zhaihe | 100 | 32.08 N | 114.54 E |
| Zhaili | 100 | 27.42 N | 117.22 E |
| Zhailing | 98 | 41.00 N | 116.53 E |
| Zhaiqiao | 106 | 31.35 N | 119.55 E |
| Zhaitang | 105 | 39.57 N | 115.42 E |
| Zhaitun | 104 | 41.46 N | 122.06 E |
| Zhakou, Zhg. | 102 | 29.59 N | 112.10 E |
| Zhakou, Zhg. | 106 | 30.23 N | 120.47 E |
| Zhakou, Zhg. | 106 | 30.13 N | 120.08 E |
| Zhalantun → Butha Qi | 89 | 48.02 N | 122.43 E |
| Zhalanyingzi | 104 | 41.29 N | 120.37 E |
| Zhalun | 120 | 32.25 N | 81.35 E |
| Zhaluomude | 89 | 49.13 N | 120.22 E |
| Zhancheng | 98 | 37.41 N | 117.46 E |
| Zhang ≐, Zhg. | 100 | 31.05 N | 113.11 E |
| Zhang ≐, Zhg. | 100 | 25.51 N | 114.46 E |
| Zhang ≐, Zhg. | 102 | 36.10 N | 115.05 E |
| Zhangbei | 98 | 41.04 N | 114.48 E |
| Zhangcang | 98 | 35.54 N | 119.57 E |
| Zhangcun, Zhg. | 100 | 33.20 N | 115.59 E |
| Zhangcun, Zhg. | 100 | 28.50 N | 117.57 E |
| Zhangcun, Zhg. | 106 | 30.28 N | 119.22 E |
| Zhangcun, Zhg. | 106 | 30.40 N | 119.57 E |
| Zhangdang | 104 | 41.54 N | 124.05 E |
| Zhangde | 100 | 34.07 N | 113.27 E |
| Zhangdiyingzi | 89 | 50.30 N | 127.16 E |
| Zhangdu | 100 | 30.38 N | 118.13 E |
| Zhangdu Hu ⊜ | 100 | 30.40 N | 114.42 E |
| Zhangfang | 105 | 39.35 N | 115.41 E |
| Zhangfengji | 98 | 35.14 N | 116.01 E |
| Zhanggang | 100 | 30.34 N | 112.51 E |
| Zhanggezhuang, Zhg. | 98 | 36.47 N | 119.47 E |
| Zhanggezhuang, Zhg. | 105 | 40.08 N | 116.56 E |
| Zhanggou | 104 | 42.07 N | 124.06 E |
| Zhangguangcai Ling ⋏ | 89 | 45.25 N | 129.20 E |
| Zhangguizhuang | 105 | 39.07 N | 117.18 E |
| Zhanggutai | 98 | 42.40 N | 122.28 E |
| Zhanghezhuang | 105 | 38.56 N | 114.56 E |
| Zhanghuang | 102 | 22.01 N | 109.27 E |
| Zhanghuanggang | 106 | 32.07 N | 120.30 E |
| Zhanghuban | 100 | 26.23 N | 118.29 E |
| Zhangji | 98 | 34.08 N | 117.24 E |
| Zhangjiachang, Zhg. | 107 | 29.26 N | 104.34 E |
| Zhangjiachang, Zhg. | 107 | 29.33 N | 104.54 E |
| Zhangjiachang, Zhg. | 107 | 29.57 N | 103.48 E |
| Zhangjiadian | 105 | 39.44 N | 114.54 E |
| Zhangjiagou | 100 | 30.18 N | 113.22 E |
| Zhangjiaji | 100 | 32.09 N | 112.23 E |
| Zhangjiajie | 104 | 41.28 N | 124.08 E |
| Zhangjiakou (Kalgan) | 105 | 40.50 N | 114.53 E |
| Zhangjiapang | 100 | 30.25 N | 115.47 E |
| Zhangjiapu | 104 | 41.18 N | 122.02 E |
| Zhangjiaqiao, Zhg. | 106 | 31.36 N | 120.36 E |
| Zhangjiaqiao, Zhg. | 107 | 30.02 N | 104.15 E |
| Zhangjiatou | 106 | 31.38 N | 119.05 E |
| Zhangjiatun, Zhg. | 104 | 41.05 N | 121.44 E |
| Zhangjiatun, Zhg. | 105 | 40.37 N | 114.57 E |
| Zhangjiawa | 105 | 40.10 N | 117.52 E |
| Zhangjiawan | 105 | 39.51 N | 116.41 E |
| Zhangjiawopu | 104 | 41.10 N | 122.17 E |
| Zhangjiayingzi | 104 | 42.04 N | 120.57 E |
| Zhangjingqiao | 106 | 31.39 N | 120.27 E |
| Zhangjinhe | 100 | 30.14 N | 112.35 E |
| Zhangliangdian | 100 | 33.42 N | 113.02 E |
| Zhangliantang | 106 | 31.01 N | 121.02 E |
| Zhangling | 98 | 36.32 N | 119.29 E |
| Zhanglu | 98 | 36.16 N | 115.33 E |
| Zhangmang | 100 | 32.03 N | 114.32 E |
| Zhangming | 102 | 31.49 N | 104.51 E |
| Zhangmuqiao | 100 | 31.26 N | 116.44 E |
| Zhangmushi | 100 | 27.01 N | 112.38 E |
| Zhangmutou | 100 | 22.55 N | 114.05 E |
| Zhangping | 100 | 25.19 N | 117.25 E |
| Zhangpu, Zhg. | 100 | 24.09 N | 117.36 E |
| Zhangpu, Zhg. | 106 | 31.17 N | 120.57 E |
| Zhangqiangzhen | 98 | 42.39 N | 122.59 E |
| Zhangqiao | 100 | 32.21 N | 117.38 E |
| Zhangqiu (Mingshui) | 98 | 36.43 N | 117.30 E |
| Zhangsanta | 102 | 39.37 N | 110.14 E |
| Zhangsanying | 98 | 41.34 N | 117.39 E |
| Zhangshitai | 104 | 41.50 N | 122.51 E |
| Zhangshuping | 102 | 31.20 N | 111.02 E |
| Zhangshuxia | 100 | 25.54 N | 112.45 E |
| Zhangtaitai | 104 | 40.59 N | 121.05 E |
| Zhangtaizi | 104 | 41.22 N | 123.16 E |
| Zhangting | 100 | 30.02 N | 121.19 E |
| Zhangwan | 100 | 26.43 N | 119.36 E |
| Zhangwenpu | 105 | 40.26 N | 116.04 E |
| Zhangwu, Zhg. | 104 | 42.22 N | 122.31 E |
| Zhangwu, Zhg. | 106 | 30.47 N | 119.33 E |
| Zhangwutaimen | 104 | 42.16 N | 122.42 E |
| Zhangxinliuji | 100 | 33.43 N | 115.48 E |
| Zhangyan, Zhg. | 106 | 31.48 N | 119.44 E |
| Zhangyan, Zhg. | 106 | 30.48 N | 121.16 E |
| Zhangyangongtun | 104 | 40.58 N | 120.46 E |
| Zhangye | 102 | 38.56 N | 100.27 E |
| Zhangze | 106 | 30.55 N | 121.15 E |
| Zhangzhishan | 106 | 31.56 N | 121.01 E |
| Zhangzhou (Longxi) | 100 | 24.33 N | 117.39 E |
| Zhangzhu | 106 | 31.16 N | 119.37 E |
| Zhangzhuang, Zhg. | 98 | 37.03 N | 116.32 E |
| Zhangzhuang, Zhg. | 98 | 36.02 N | 118.01 E |
| Zhangzhuang, Zhg. | 106 | 31.57 N | 119.52 E |
| Zhangzi Dao I | 98 | 39.00 N | 122.44 E |
| Zhanhua (Fuguo) | 98 | 37.42 N | 118.08 E |
| Zhanji | 98 | 34.14 N | 115.52 E |
| Zhanjiajing | 107 | 29.15 N | 104.55 E |
| Zhanjiang | 102 | 21.16 N | 110.28 E |
| Zhanjiaqiao, Zhg. | 100 | 29.19 N | 113.34 E |
| Zhanjiaqiao, Zhg. | 106 | 30.25 N | 120.08 E |
| Zhanyang | 100 | 25.30 N | 119.28 E |
| Zhanyi | 102 | 25.38 N | 103.43 E |
| Zhanyu | 89 | 44.31 N | 122.37 E |
| Zhao'an | 100 | 23.43 N | 117.10 E |
| Zhao'an Wan c | 100 | 23.38 N | 117.19 E |
| Zhaobeikou | 105 | 38.55 N | 116.06 E |
| Zhaochuan | 105 | 40.41 N | 115.18 E |
| Zhaocun | 105 | 39.35 N | 116.14 E |
| Zhaodong | 89 | 46.05 N | 125.59 E |
| Zhaogezhuang, Zhg. | 98 | 37.27 N | 120.37 E |
| Zhaogezhuang, Zhg. | 105 | 39.45 N | 118.24 E |
| Zhaoguang | 89 | 48.07 N | 126.43 E |
| Zhaohe | 100 | 33.12 N | 112.49 E |
| Zhaohuazhen | 107 | 29.02 N | 105.08 E |
| Zhaojiagou | 104 | 40.47 N | 123.27 E |
| Zhaojiapuzi | 104 | 40.51 N | 123.49 E |
| Zhaojiaqiao | 106 | 30.44 N | 121.12 E |
| Zhaojiatangfang | 104 | 42.07 N | 122.57 E |
| Zhaojiatun | 104 | 41.24 N | 121.53 E |
| Zhaojiawopeng | 104 | 42.30 N | 123.06 E |
| Zhaojiaying | 105 | 38.58 N | 116.42 E |
| Zhaojue | 102 | 28.15 N | 102.50 E |
| Zhaomaozhuang | 105 | 39.28 N | 117.59 E |
| Zhaomutun | 104 | 41.10 N | 121.38 E |
| Zhaoping | 102 | 24.03 N | 110.52 E |
| Zhaoqiao | 100 | 28.42 N | 114.45 E |
| Zhaoqing (Gaoyao) | 102 | 23.03 N | 112.27 E |
| Zhaosu | 86 | 43.06 N | 81.08 E |
| Zhaotan | 100 | 29.42 N | 116.48 E |
| Zhaotong | 102 | 27.19 N | 103.48 E |
| Zhaotun | 104 | 41.54 N | 121.59 E |
| Zhaoxian, Zhg. | 98 | 37.45 N | 114.46 E |
| Zhaoxian, Zhg. | 98 | 35.44 N | 118.55 E |
| Zhaoxing | 89 | 47.43 N | 131.19 E |
| Zhaoya | 107 | 29.00 N | 105.35 E |
| Zhaoyi | 105 | 39.55 N | 116.43 E |
| Zhaoyuan, Zhg. | 89 | 45.31 N | 125.09 E |
| Zhaoyuan, Zhg. | 98 | 37.22 N | 120.24 E |
| Zhaozhou | 89 | 45.41 N | 125.21 E |
| Zhaozhuang, Zhg. | 98 | 34.45 N | 116.27 E |
| Zhaozhuang, Zhg. | 98 | 34.14 N | 116.38 E |
| Zhaozhuangzi | 105 | 39.10 N | 117.20 E |
| Zhapu | 106 | 30.36 N | 121.05 E |
| Zhari Namco ⊜ | 120 | 31.05 N | 85.35 E |
| Zhashkiv | 78 | 49.15 N | 30.06 E |
| Zhashui | 102 | 33.40 N | 109.01 E |
| Zhaxi Co ⊜ | 120 | 32.10 N | 85.05 E |
| Zhaxigang | 120 | 32.32 N | 79.41 E |
| Zhayi | 102 | 28.34 N | 99.09 E |
| Zhaze | 106 | 32.09 N | 119.29 E |
| Zhdanivka | 83 | 48.10 N | 38.15 E |
| Zhdanov — Mariupol' | 83 | 47.06 N | 37.33 E |
| Zhdany | 78 | 50.12 N | 33.13 E |
| Zhecheng | 98 | 34.06 N | 115.19 E |
| Zhegao | 100 | 31.46 N | 117.45 E |
| Zhegu | 120 | 28.43 N | 91.43 E |
| Zhêhor | 102 | 31.41 N | 100.24 E |
| Zhejiang (Chekiang) □ [4] | 100 | 29.00 N | 120.00 E |
| Zhelang | 100 | 22.43 N | 115.32 E |
| Zhelanne | 83 | 48.13 N | 37.25 E |
| Zhelin, Zhg. | 100 | 29.14 N | 115.30 E |
| Zhelin, Zhg. | 100 | 23.36 N | 117.06 E |
| Zhelin, Zhg. | 106 | 30.50 N | 121.29 E |
| Zhen ≐ | 100 | 24.55 N | 113.44 E |
| Zhen'an | 102 | 33.27 N | 109.01 E |
| Zhenbeikou | 102 | 39.15 N | 106.17 E |
| Zhenbiancheng | 105 | 40.10 N | 115.49 E |
| Zhenchang, Zhg. | 105 | 39.47 N | 115.24 E |
| Zhenchang, Zhg. | 106 | 32.04 N | 121.02 E |
| Zhenfeng | 102 | 25.23 N | 105.41 E |
| Zheng'an | 102 | 28.31 N | 107.29 E |
| Zheng'anpu | 104 | 41.43 N | 121.56 E |
| Zhengcun | 105 | 39.13 N | 115.40 E |
| Zhengding | 98 | 38.10 N | 114.34 E |
| Zhengdongyu | 106 | 31.59 N | 120.10 E |
| Zhengfang | 100 | 28.42 N | 117.53 E |
| Zhengguanchang | 107 | 29.54 N | 106.35 E |
| Zhengguo | 100 | 23.25 N | 113.53 E |
| Zhenghe | 100 | 27.22 N | 118.50 E |
| Zhengji | 98 | 34.26 N | 117.01 E |
| Zhengjiadiancun | 104 | 41.05 N | 122.20 E |
| Zhengjiawu | 100 | 29.29 N | 120.05 E |
| Zhenglan Qi (Dund Hot) | 98 | 42.16 N | 115.49 E |
| Zhengning | 102 | 35.22 N | 108.24 E |
| Zhengping | 100 | 25.22 N | 114.46 E |
| Zhen'guosi | 271a | 39.51 N | 116.21 E |
| Zhengxiangbai Qi (Qagan Nur) | 98 | 42.16 N | 114.52 E |
| Zhengyang | 100 | 32.37 N | 114.23 E |
| Zhengyangguan | 100 | 32.28 N | 116.32 E |
| Zhengyi | 106 | 31.23 N | 120.52 E |
| Zhengzhou (Chengchow) | 102 | 34.48 N | 113.39 E |
| Zhengzhuang | 100 | 28.11 N | 119.01 E |
| Zhengzi | 107 | 29.22 N | 104.16 E |
| Zhengzichang | 107 | 29.08 N | 106.38 E |
| Zhenhai, Zhg. | 100 | 29.57 N | 121.42 E |
| Zhenhai, Zhg. | 100 | 24.16 N | 118.06 E |
| Zhenhai, Zhg. | 102 | 21.53 N | 112.25 E |
| Zhenjiang, Zhg. | 98 | 40.44 N | 125.28 E |
| Zhenjiang, Zhg. | 106 | 32.13 N | 119.26 E |
| Zhenjiangguan | 102 | 32.25 N | 103.35 E |
| Zhenjiaqiao | 106 | 32.08 N | 120.49 E |
| Zhenjinqiao | 107 | 30.12 N | 104.22 E |
| Zhenkang | 102 | 24.06 N | 99.16 E |
| Zhenlai | 89 | 45.52 N | 123.14 E |
| Zhenning | 102 | 26.05 N | 105.46 E |
| Zhenping | 102 | 33.08 N | 112.19 E |
| Zhenru | 106 | 31.15 N | 121.24 E |
| Zhentou | 100 | 27.04 N | 114.56 E |
| Zhentou ≐ | 100 | 32.58 N | 114.24 E |
| Zhentoudian | 100 | 29.10 N | 117.29 E |
| Zhentoushi | 100 | 28.01 N | 113.20 E |
| Zhenxi | 107 | 29.29 N | 104.33 E |
| Zhenxiaguan | 100 | 27.12 N | 120.28 E |
| Zhenxing | 98 | 42.38 N | 124.53 E |
| Zhenxiong | 102 | 27.27 N | 104.50 E |
| Zhenyu | 100 | 27.08 N | 120.18 E |
| Zhenyuan, Zhg. | 102 | 35.46 N | 107.18 E |
| Zhenyuan, Zhg. | 102 | 26.53 N | 108.19 E |
| Zhenze | 106 | 30.55 N | 120.30 E |
| Zhenzhumen | 98 | 41.53 N | 126.45 E |
| Zhenzichang, Zhg. | 107 | 29.59 N | 105.11 E |
| Zhenzichang, Zhg. | 107 | 29.52 N | 104.12 E |
| Zhenzichang, Zhg. | 107 | 30.38 N | 104.20 E |
| Zhenzijie | 107 | 28.48 N | 106.40 E |
| Zhenziling | 104 | 42.10 N | 124.12 E |
| Zhenzizhen | 105 | 39.50 N | 118.20 E |
| Zheqiao | 100 | 26.27 N | 112.48 E |
| Zherebets' ≐ | 83 | 48.57 N | 38.03 E |
| Zheriv ≐ | 78 | 51.12 N | 29.04 E |
| Zherong | 100 | 27.16 N | 119.54 E |
| Zheshan | 106 | 30.15 N | 120.24 E |
| Zhetang | 106 | 31.45 N | 118.55 E |
| Zhidan | 102 | 37.00 N | 108.40 E |
| Zhidoi | 102 | 33.08 N | 94.50 E |
| Zhierling | 98 | 40.26 N | 114.16 E |
| Zhigou | 98 | 35.55 N | 119.13 E |
| Zhijiang | 102 | 27.27 N | 109.41 E |
| Zhijin | 102 | 26.41 N | 105.37 E |
| Zhili | 106 | 30.52 N | 120.16 E |
| Zhitan | 100 | 29.35 N | 117.16 E |
| Zhitang, Zhg. | 106 | 31.33 N | 121.01 E |
| Zhitang, Zhg. | 106 | 31.36 N | 120.58 E |
| Zhitomir → Zhytomyr | 78 | 50.16 N | 28.40 E |
| Zhitouji | 100 | 33.28 N | 118.18 E |
| Zhiwucun | 106 | 30.38 N | 119.47 E |
| Zhixi | 100 | 23.57 N | 114.33 E |
| Zhixia | 100 | 29.42 N | 119.36 E |
| Zhixiqiao | 106 | 31.49 N | 119.29 E |
| Zhiyang | 100 | 33.47 N | 113.07 E |
| Zhizushan | 104 | 41.50 N | 121.24 E |
| Zhmerynka | 78 | 49.02 N | 28.06 E |
| Zhob | 120 | 31.20 N | 69.27 E |
| Zhob ≐ | 120 | 32.04 N | 69.50 E |
| Zhonganpu | 104 | 41.37 N | 121.58 E |
| Zhong'aozhen | 107 | 29.46 N | 105.41 E |
| Zhongba, Zhg. | 100 | 23.43 N | 115.22 E |
| Zhongba, Zhg. | 102 | 29.38 N | 84.13 E |
| Zhongbu, Zhg. | 100 | 31.25 N | 117.45 E |
| Zhongbu, Zhg. | 100 | 31.24 N | 121.01 E |
| Zhongbu, Zhg. | 105 | 38.58 N | 117.17 E |
| Zhongbu, Zhg. | 106 | 30.50 N | 120.10 E |
| Zhongchuan | 100 | 26.58 N | 119.27 E |
| Zhongcun | 100 | 31.38 N | 118.29 E |
| Zhongdai | 106 | 30.46 N | 120.59 E |
| Zhongdian | 102 | 27.50 N | 99.40 E |
| Zhongdu, Zhg. | 100 | 24.56 N | 116.26 E |
| Zhongdu, Zhg. | 100 | 33.04 N | 116.46 E |
| Zhongdu, Zhg. | 107 | 28.46 N | 103.58 E |
| Zhongduan | 100 | 25.17 N | 116.41 E |
| Zhongerchong | 104 | 41.58 N | 123.58 E |
| Zhonggang | 100 | 32.38 N | 115.45 E |
| Zhonggong | 98 | 36.30 N | 117.01 E |
| Zhonggoumen | 98 | 41.00 N | 116.26 E |
| Zhonggu | 104 | 42.27 N | 124.00 E |
| Zhongguan | 106 | 30.39 N | 120.11 E |
| Zhongguo → China □ [1] | 90 | 35.00 N | 105.00 E |
| Zhonghe | 102 | 27.11 N | 103.52 E |
| Zhonghechang | 107 | 30.12 N | 104.49 E |
| Zhongheying | 102 | 23.48 N | 103.36 E |
| Zhonghezhen | 107 | 30.34 N | 104.06 E |
| Zhonghuamen | 106 | 32.01 N | 118.46 E |
| Zhonghuopu | 100 | 29.44 N | 113.59 E |
| Zhongjianchang | 107 | 28.46 N | 106.13 E |
| Zhongjiang | 102 | 31.00 N | 104.18 E |
| Zhongjiatai | 104 | 40.48 N | 122.46 E |
| Zhonglou | 98 | 35.24 N | 119.02 E |
| Zhongluotan | 100 | 23.23 N | 113.23 E |
| Zhongluyantai | 104 | 41.32 N | 123.17 E |
| Zhongmeihe | 100 | 31.19 N | 116.45 E |
| Zhongmou | 98 | 34.46 N | 114.01 E |
| Zhongning | 102 | 37.27 N | 105.38 E |
| Zhongpingchang | 102 | 31.15 N | 110.10 E |
| Zhongqiao | 106 | 31.11 N | 119.11 E |
| Zhongsha | 100 | 26.24 N | 116.36 E |
| Zhongshan, Zhg. | 100 | 26.12 N | 117.26 E |
| Zhongshan (Shiqizhen), Zhg. | 100 | 22.31 N | 113.22 E |
| Zhongshan ʋ [3], Ant. | 9 | 69.22 S | 76.23 E |
| Zhongshan ʋ [3], Ant. | 9 | 69.22 S | 76.23 E |
| Zhongshan Park ♦ | 269b | 31.13 N | 121.25 E |
| Zhongtiao Shan ⋏ | 102 | 35.12 N | 111.35 E |
| Zhongting ≐ | 105 | 39.03 N | 116.46 E |
| Zhongtou | 100 | 34.00 N | 113.21 E |
| Zhongwei | 102 | 37.33 N | 105.10 E |
| Zhongwopu | 102 | 38.30 N | 102.59 E |
| Zhongxian, Zhg. | 100 | 27.17 N | 116.47 E |
| Zhongxian, Zhg. | 102 | 30.29 N | 108.05 E |
| Zhongxiang | 100 | 31.11 N | 112.33 E |
| Zhongxiangzhen | 107 | 29.50 N | 104.08 E |
| Zhongxin, Zhg. | 100 | 23.16 N | 113.38 E |
| Zhongxin, Zhg. | 100 | 24.14 N | 114.44 E |
| Zhongxin, Zhg. | 104 | 40.47 N | 124.08 E |
| Zhongxing, Zhg. | 106 | 32.17 N | 119.34 E |
| Zhongxing, Zhg. | 107 | 30.12 N | 103.32 E |
| Zhongxingchang | 107 | 29.07 N | 105.18 E |
| Zhongxinzhen, Zhg. | 107 | 30.16 N | 106.15 E |
| Zhongxinzhen, Zhg. | 107 | 30.30 N | 104.03 E |
| Zhongyangqu | 104 | 40.47 N | 122.05 E |
| Zhongyaozhan | 89 | 50.46 N | 125.54 E |
| Zhongyi | 100 | 31.08 N | 114.52 E |
| Zhongying | 105 | 39.38 N | 117.06 E |
| Zhongzangcun | 105 | 38.52 N | 115.38 E |
| Zhongzhan | 100 | 25.16 N | 114.24 E |
| Zhongzhuang | 105 | 39.25 N | 114.47 E |
| Zhou ≐ | 105 | 39.47 N | 117.23 E |
| Zhouba | 107 | 29.06 N | 103.43 E |
| Zhoubachang | 107 | 28.59 N | 103.52 E |
| Zhoucun | 98 | 36.47 N | 117.48 E |
| Zhoudangfan | 100 | 31.54 N | 114.31 E |
| Zhoujiachang | 107 | 30.33 N | 104.25 E |
| Zhoujiadai | 106 | 32.12 N | 120.26 E |
| Zhoujiadu | 106 | 31.11 N | 121.29 E |
| Zhoujiagou | 107 | 30.08 N | 104.30 E |
| Zhoujiatun, Zhg. | 104 | 41.29 N | 121.50 E |
| Zhoujiatun, Zhg. | 104 | 41.04 N | 120.47 E |
| Zhoujiatun, Zhg. | 104 | 41.16 N | 120.58 E |
| Zhoujiatun, Zhg. | 104 | 41.34 N | 121.05 E |
| Zhoujiawopu | 104 | 42.31 N | 122.45 E |
| Zhoujiayao | 104 | 41.19 N | 122.48 E |
| Zhoujingxiang | 106 | 31.32 N | 120.23 E |
| Zhoukoudianzhen | 105 | 39.41 N | 115.56 E |
| Zhoulichang | 107 | 29.55 N | 105.09 E |
| Zhouning | 100 | 27.16 N | 119.12 E |
| Zhoupo | 107 | 29.48 N | 104.01 E |
| Zhoupu | 106 | 31.07 N | 121.34 E |
| Zhouqu | 102 | 33.43 N | 104.10 E |
| Zhouquan | 106 | 30.35 N | 120.21 E |
| Zhoushan Dao I | 100 | 30.05 N | 122.10 E |
| Zhoushan Qundao II | 100 | 30.00 N | 122.00 E |
| Zhoushu | 106 | 31.28 N | 120.59 E |
| Zhoushuizi | 98 | 38.57 N | 121.34 E |
| Zhoutieqiao | 106 | 31.26 N | 120.00 E |
| Zhouwangmiao | 106 | 30.28 N | 120.29 E |
| Zhouxi | 100 | 29.13 N | 116.20 E |
| Zhouxiang | 100 | 30.10 N | 121.08 E |
| Zhouxinzhen | 106 | 31.30 N | 120.18 E |
| Zhouzhai | 106 | 32.02 N | 121.31 E |
| Zhouzhi | 102 | 34.12 N | 108.10 E |
| Zhouzhuang, Zhg. | 105 | 39.09 N | 115.18 E |
| Zhouzhuang, Zhg. | 106 | 31.06 N | 120.51 E |
| Zhouzhuang, Zhg. | 106 | 32.15 N | 120.08 E |
| Zhovkva | 78 | 50.04 N | 23.58 E |
| Zhovnyne | 78 | 49.23 N | 32.41 E |
| Zhovte, Ukr. | 78 | 47.47 N | 33.50 E |
| Zhovte, Ukr. | 78 | 48.30 N | 33.31 E |
| Zhovten', Ukr. | 78 | 49.03 N | 24.45 E |
| Zhovten', Ukr. | 78 | 47.14 N | 30.20 E |
| Zhovti Vody | 78 | 48.21 N | 33.31 E |
| Zhovtneve, Ukr. | 78 | 46.52 N | 32.02 E |
| Zhovtneve, Ukr. | 78 | 49.39 N | 34.09 E |
| Zhovtneve, Ukr. | 78 | 50.57 N | 34.22 E |
| Zhovtneve, Ukr. | 78 | 51.15 N | 28.07 E |
| Zhovtneve, Ukr. | 78 | 48.38 N | 33.04 E |
| Zhuanghang | 106 | 30.54 N | 121.23 E |
| Zhuanghe | 98 | 39.43 N | 123.01 E |
| Zhuangji | 98 | 34.20 N | 115.15 E |
| Zhuanglang | 102 | 34.58 N | 106.07 E |
| Zhuangtou | 105 | 40.55 N | 117.57 E |
| Zhuangtouyingzi, Zhg. | 104 | 41.43 N | 120.32 E |
| Zhuangtouyingzi, Zhg. | 104 | 41.50 N | 120.43 E |
| Zhuangxi | 107 | 30.33 N | 104.31 E |
| Zhuangyuanqiao | 100 | 27.54 N | 120.48 E |
| Zhuanping Shan ∧ | 107 | 29.07 N | 103.37 E |
| Zhuanqiao | 106 | 31.04 N | 121.23 E |
| Zhuantouwan | 100 | 31.29 N | 112.24 E |
| Zhuanwantai | 104 | 41.20 N | 122.22 E |
| Zhuao | 100 | 29.05 N | 121.16 E |
| Zhucang | 102 | 27.18 N | 107.26 E |
| Zhucheng | 98 | 36.00 N | 119.24 E |
| Zhudi | 269b | 31.12 N | 121.18 E |
| Zhudian | 100 | 30.33 N | 115.12 E |
| Zhuergan | 89 | 52.04 N | 120.48 E |
| Zhufengzhen | 106 | 30.35 N | 118.56 E |
| Zhufuo | 107 | 29.02 N | 105.51 E |
| Zhugan ≐ | 100 | 32.18 N | 114.42 E |
| Zhuganpu | 100 | 32.13 N | 114.39 E |
| Zhugao | 107 | 30.37 N | 104.40 E |
| Zhuge, Zhg. | 98 | 36.00 N | 118.32 E |
| Zhuge, Zhg. | 100 | 29.15 N | 119.18 E |
| Zhugentan | 107 | 29.25 N | 103.50 E |
| Zhugou | 98 | 36.52 N | 120.15 E |
| Zhugouzhen | 100 | 32.47 N | 113.42 E |
| Zhugusi | 102 | 37.01 N | 102.27 E |
| Zhuhai | 100 | 22.16 N | 113.33 E |
| Zhuhe | 100 | 29.44 N | 113.06 E |
| Zhuhongyu | 104 | 40.48 N | 123.00 E |
| Zhuji | 100 | 29.43 N | 120.14 E |
| Zhujiabeng | 106 | 31.21 N | 120.41 E |
| Zhujiachang, Zhg. | 100 | 30.03 N | 116.28 E |
| Zhujiachang, Zhg. | 107 | 29.48 N | 104.20 E |
| Zhujiadian | 107 | 30.03 N | 104.13 E |
| Zhujiafang | 104 | 41.20 N | 122.40 E |
| Zhujiahang | 106 | 30.51 N | 121.19 E |
| Zhujiane | 106 | 31.08 N | 120.53 E |
| Zhujia Jian I | 106 | 29.55 N | 122.25 E |
| Zhujiajiao | 106 | 31.06 N | 121.02 E |
| Zhujiajiaotou | 106 | 31.24 N | 121.11 E |
| Zhujiang Kou c [1] | 100 | 22.20 N | 113.45 E |
| Zhujiangqing | 100 | 27.18 N | 114.44 E |
| Zhujiawan, Zhg. | 100 | 32.28 N | 117.29 E |
| Zhujiawan, Zhg. | 105 | 40.08 N | 114.56 E |
| Zhujiawan, Zhg. | 104 | 41.04 N | 123.54 E |
| Zhujiawopeng | 104 | 42.27 N | 123.18 E |
| Zhujiesi | 102 | 33.34 N | 97.21 E |
| Zhukeng | 100 | 23.49 N | 112.55 E |
| Zhukou, Zhg. | 98 | 34.07 N | 115.04 E |
| Zhukou, Zhg. | 100 | 27.41 N | 118.53 E |
| Zhukou, Zhg. | 100 | 26.58 N | 117.16 E |
| Zhukovskiy → Žukovskij | 82 | 55.35 N | 38.08 E |
| Zhulanbu | 100 | 25.36 N | 115.46 E |
| Zhulin, Zhg. | 100 | 32.20 N | 113.38 E |
| Zhulin, Zhg. | 106 | 31.45 N | 119.27 E |
| Zhulong ≐ | 98 | 38.47 N | 115.59 E |
| Zhulongqiao | 100 | 32.21 N | 118.09 E |
| Zhuluke | 98 | 41.36 N | 119.54 E |
| Zhumadian | 100 | 32.58 N | 114.03 E |
| Zhuolu | 105 | 40.22 N | 115.12 E |
| Zhuoni | 102 | 34.32 N | 103.24 E |
| Zhuotian | 100 | 25.38 N | 116.13 E |
| Zhuoxian | 105 | 39.30 N | 115.58 E |
| Zhuozi | 102 | 40.52 N | 112.33 E |
| Zhuqianzongpuzi | 104 | 42.17 N | 123.18 E |
| Zhuqiao, Zhg. | 98 | 37.22 N | 120.05 E |
| Zhuqiao, Zhg. | 106 | 30.26 N | 120.36 E |
| Zhuqiao, Zhg. | 106 | 31.07 N | 121.44 E |
| Zhuravychi | 78 | 50.59 N | 25.43 E |
| Zhurivka | 78 | 50.31 N | 31.46 E |
| Zhurushan | 100 | 30.26 N | 113.48 E |
| Zhushan | 102 | 32.10 N | 110.19 E |
| Zhusigang | 100 | 31.14 N | 118.23 E |
| Zhutan | 100 | 28.04 N | 114.10 E |
| Zhutang, Zhg. | 106 | 31.06 N | 118.39 E |
| Zhutang, Zhg. | 106 | 31.47 N | 120.24 E |
| Zhutian | 100 | 28.43 N | 117.01 E |
| Zhuting, Zhg. | 100 | 27.24 N | 113.04 E |
| Zhuting, Zhg. | 100 | 27.48 N | 114.02 E |
| Zhuwo | 105 | 40.02 N | 115.48 E |
| Zhuwotuo | 107 | 30.31 N | 104.34 E |
| Zhuwumiao | 100 | 30.54 N | 116.19 E |
| Zhuxi, Zhg. | 100 | 28.10 N | 118.53 E |
| Zhuxi, Zhg. | 102 | 32.09 N | 109.42 E |
| Zhuxi, Zhg. | 107 | 29.32 N | 105.40 E |
| Zhuxianzhen | 98 | 34.37 N | 114.16 E |
| Zhuxichang | 100 | 28.58 N | 114.06 E |
| Zhuya | 98 | 36.38 N | 118.12 E |
| Zhuyang | 98 | 36.16 N | 117.22 E |
| Zhuyangxi | 107 | 29.03 N | 105.57 E |
| Zhuyangzhen | 102 | 34.20 N | 110.44 E |
| Zhuyivka | 83 | 48.04 N | 38.15 E |
| Zhuyuan | 107 | 29.34 N | 104.08 E |
| Zhuzeqiao | 106 | 31.34 N | 119.20 E |
| Zhuzhenji | 100 | 32.31 N | 118.42 E |
| Zhuzhou (Chuchow) | 100 | 27.50 N | 113.09 E |
| Zhuzikou | 100 | 29.17 N | 112.41 E |
| Zhydachiv | 78 | 49.23 N | 24.08 E |
| Zhyhaylivka | 78 | 50.38 N | 35.07 E |
| Zhytomyr | 78 | 50.16 N | 28.40 E |
| Zhytomyr □ [4] | 78 | 50.30 N | 28.30 E |
| Zi ≐, Zhg. | 98 | 37.12 N | 118.34 E |
| Zi ≐, Zhg. | 102 | 28.41 N | 112.43 E |
| Zi ≐, Zhg. | 102 | 31.59 N | 96.53 E |
| Zia Indian Reservation ● [4] | 200 | 35.30 N | 106.43 W |
| Zia International Airport ⊠ | 126 | 23.46 N | 90.23 E |
| Ziama Mansouria | 34 | 36.40 N | 5.29 E |
| Ziano | 64 | 46.17 N | 11.34 E |
| Ziārat | 120 | 30.23 N | 67.43 E |
| Ziārat-e Shāh Maqṣūd | 120 | 31.59 N | 65.30 E |
| Ziārat Gali Chāh ⊤ [4] | 128 | 28.20 N | 63.38 E |
| Žiar nad Hronom | 30 | 48.36 N | 18.52 E |
| Zibdīn | 132 | 33.22 N | 35.28 E |
| Zibo (Zhangdian) | 98 | 36.47 N | 118.01 E |
| Zicapa | 234 | 17.57 N | 99.02 W |
| Zicavo | 36 | 41.54 N | 9.08 E |
| Zichang | 102 | 37.19 N | 109.33 E |
| Žichovice | 60 | 49.16 N | 13.37 E |
| Zichuan | 98 | 36.38 N | 117.55 E |
| Žičicy | 76 | 55.07 N | 31.17 E |
| Zickhusen | 54 | 53.45 N | 11.25 E |
| Ziddi | 85 | 39.03 N | 68.48 E |
| Žideli | 86 | 48.40 N | 70.29 E |
| Zid'ky | 78 | 49.42 N | 36.21 E |
| Židlochovice | 61 | 49.02 N | 16.37 E |
| Ziębice | 30 | 50.37 N | 17.00 E |
| Ziegelroda | 54 | 51.20 N | 11.28 E |
| Ziegendorf | 54 | 53.18 N | 11.49 E |
| Ziegenhain | 56 | 50.55 N | 9.15 E |
| Ziegenhals | 264a | 52.21 N | 13.40 E |
| Ziegenrück | 54 | 50.37 N | 11.38 E |
| Zielona Góra (Grünberg) | 30 | 51.56 N | 15.31 E |
| Zielona Góra □ [4] | 30 | 52.00 N | 15.20 E |
| Ziemetshausen | 58 | 48.18 N | 10.31 E |
| Zierenberg | 56 | 51.22 N | 9.18 E |
| Zierikzee | 52 | 51.38 N | 3.55 E |
| Ziersdorf | 61 | 48.31 N | 15.55 E |
| Ziesar | 54 | 52.16 N | 12.17 E |
| Ziesendorf | 54 | 54.00 N | 12.02 E |
| Ziethen | 54 | 53.53 N | 13.40 E |
| Žiežmariai | 76 | 54.48 N | 24.27 E |
| Ziftā | 142 | 30.43 N | 31.15 E |
| Žigalgan | 84 | 44.36 N | 50.46 E |
| Žigalovo | 88 | 54.48 N | 105.08 E |
| Žigansk | 74 | 66.45 N | 123.20 E |
| Zigazinskij | 86 | 53.50 N | 57.20 E |
| Zigong (Tzukung) | 107 | 29.24 N | 104.47 E |
| Ziguéy | 146 | 14.43 N | 15.47 E |
| Zigui | 102 | 31.00 N | 110.31 E |
| Ziguinchor | 150 | 12.35 N | 16.16 W |
| Ziguinchor □ [4] | 150 | 12.45 N | 16.20 W |
| Žigulevsk | 80 | 53.25 N | 49.27 E |
| Žiguli | 80 | 53.22 N | 49.19 E |
| Žiguli ⋏ | 80 | 53.20 N | 49.40 E |
| Zigutaicun | 104 | 42.01 N | 121.16 E |
| Zig Zag, Cerro ∧ [2] | 286d | 12.12 S | 76.59 W |
| Zihedian | 98 | 36.48 N | 118.22 E |
| Zihl (Thiéle) ≐ | 58 | 47.03 N | 7.05 E |
| Zihuatanejo | 234 | 17.38 N | 101.33 W |
| Zihukou, Zhg. | 100 | 28.44 N | 112.33 E |
| Zihukou, Zhg. | 100 | 28.55 N | 118.08 E |
| Ziiyang | 102 | 32.31 N | 108.48 E |
| Zijančurino | 86 | 51.33 N | 56.55 E |
| Žijenkum | 85 | 42.50 N | 69.00 E |
| Zijiao | 98 | 37.21 N | 117.25 E |
| Zijin | 100 | 23.40 N | 115.11 E |
| Zijingguan | 105 | 39.23 N | 115.12 E |
| Zijin Shan ∧ [2] | 106 | 32.04 N | 118.51 E |
| Zikejevo | 76 | 53.44 N | 34.52 E |
| Zikhron Ya'aqov | 132 | 32.34 N | 34.57 E |
| Zikoufang | 100 | 26.22 N | 117.24 E |
| Zilair | 86 | 52.14 N | 57.30 E |
| Žilaja Kosa | 80 | 46.49 N | 53.12 E |
| Žilaja Tambica | 24 | 62.32 N | 36.09 E |
| Zile | 130 | 40.18 N | 35.54 E |
| Žilga | 85 | 41.43 N | 69.01 E |
| Zili | 102 | 26.50 N | 100.27 E |
| Žilina | 30 | 49.14 N | 18.46 E |
| Žilino | 76 | 54.54 N | 21.56 E |
| Zillah, Lībiyā | 146 | 28.33 N | 17.35 E |
| Zillah, Wa., U.S. | 202 | 46.24 N | 120.15 W |
| Ziller ≐ | 64 | 47.24 N | 11.50 E |
| Zillertal V | 64 | 47.20 N | 11.50 E |
| Zillertaler Alpen (Alpi Aurine) ⋏ | 64 | 47.00 N | 11.55 E |
| Zillis | 58 | 46.38 N | 9.27 E |
| Zillisheim | 58 | 47.41 N | 7.16 E |
| Zilly | 54 | 51.56 N | 10.49 E |
| Zilme | 144 | 16.25 N | 43.49 E |
| Žiloj Bor | 76 | 59.06 N | 34.37 E |
| Žil'ovo | 82 | 54.59 N | 38.02 E |
| Ziltendorf | 54 | 52.12 N | 14.37 E |
| Zilupe | 76 | 56.23 N | 28.07 E |
| Zilwaukee | 190 | 43.28 N | 83.55 W |
| Zima | 88 | 53.55 N | 102.04 E |
| Zima ≐ | 88 | 55.20 N | 100.43 E |
| Žima, gora ∧ | 88 | 53.18 N | 107.38 E |
| Zimapán | 234 | 20.45 N | 99.21 W |
| Zimatlán | 234 | 16.52 N | 96.47 W |
| Zimba | 154 | 17.19 S | 26.13 E |
| Zimbabwe □ [1], Afr. | 138 | 20.00 S | 30.00 E |
| Zimbabwe □ [1], Afr. | 154 | 20.00 S | 30.00 E |
| Zimbor | 38 | 47.00 N | 23.16 E |
| Zimella | 64 | 45.20 N | 11.22 E |
| Zimi | 150 | 7.19 N | 11.18 W |
| Zimljansker-Stausee → Ciml'anskoje vodochranilišče ⊜ [1] | 80 | 48.00 N | 43.00 E |
| Zimmara, Monte ∧ | 70 | 37.45 N | 14.16 E |
| Zimmern | 58 | 48.10 N | 8.36 E |
| Zimn'ackij | 80 | 49.44 N | 42.53 E |
| Zimnicea | 38 | 43.39 N | 25.21 E |
| Zimonino | 76 | 53.47 N | 31.52 E |
| Zimovniki | 80 | 47.08 N | 42.28 E |
| Zimovskoje | 86 | 57.31 N | 86.52 E |
| Zin, Naḥal V | 132 | 30.57 N | 35.19 E |
| Zinal | 58 | 46.08 N | 7.38 E |
| Zinapécuaro [de Figueroa] | 234 | 19.52 N | 100.49 W |
| Zinave, Parque Nacional de ♦ | 156 | 21.35 S | 33.35 E |
| Zinder | 150 | 13.48 N | 8.59 E |
| Zinder □ [5] | 146 | 15.00 N | 10.30 E |
| Zinga | 152 | 3.43 N | 18.35 E |
| Zinga Mulike | 154 | 9.09 S | 38.44 E |
| Zingaro, Passo dello )( | 70 | 37.43 N | 14.50 E |
| Zingst | 54 | 54.26 N | 12.41 E |
| Zingst ≻ [1] | 54 | 54.25 N | 12.50 E |
| Zingwanda | 140 | 7.10 N | 27.56 E |
| Ziniaré | 150 | 12.35 N | 1.18 W |
| Žiniške ≐ | 85 | 43.14 N | 78.30 E |
| Zinkgruvan | 40 | 58.49 N | 15.05 E |
| Zin'kiv, Ukr. | 78 | 50.13 N | 34.22 E |
| Zin'kiv, Ukr. | 78 | 49.04 N | 27.04 E |
| Zinnik → Soignies | 50 | 50.35 N | 4.04 E |
| Zinnowitz | 54 | 54.04 N | 13.55 E |
| Zinswiller | 56 | 48.55 N | 7.35 E |
| Zion, Il., U.S. | 216 | 42.26 N | 87.49 W |
| Zion, Md., U.S. | 208 | 39.40 N | 75.57 W |
| Zionhill | 208 | 40.29 N | 75.24 W |
| Zion National Park ♦ | 200 | 37.10 N | 113.00 W |
| Zionsville | 218 | 39.57 N | 86.15 W |
| Zionz Lake ⊜ | 184 | 51.25 N | 91.52 W |
| Zipaquirá | 246 | 5.02 N | 74.00 W |
| Žipkovšino | 88 | 51.52 N | 112.59 E |
| Zippori | 132 | 32.45 N | 35.17 E |
| Ziqlāb, Wādī V | 132 | 32.30 N | 35.34 E |
| Zir | 130 | 39.59 N | 32.31 E |
| Zīra | 123 | 30.58 N | 74.59 E |
| Žir'akovo | 86 | 57.53 N | 65.37 E |
| Zirándaro | 234 | 18.27 N | 100.59 W |
| Zirāpur | 124 | 24.01 N | 76.22 E |
| Žir'atino | 76 | 53.15 N | 33.44 E |
| Zirbitzkogel ∧ | 61 | 47.04 N | 14.34 E |
| Zirchow | 54 | 53.53 N | 14.08 E |
| Zirgan | 86 | 53.14 N | 55.55 E |
| Žirje, Otok I | 36 | 43.40 N | 15.39 E |
| Zirl | 64 | 47.17 N | 11.14 E |
| Zirndorf | 56 | 49.26 N | 10.58 E |
| Žirnov | 80 | 48.13 N | 41.06 E |
| Žirnovsk | 80 | 51.00 N | 44.46 E |
| Ziro | 120 | 27.38 N | 93.42 E |
| Žiroškino | 82 | 55.22 N | 38.03 E |
| Žirovnice | 30 | 49.15 N | 15.11 E |
| Zishan | 100 | 25.57 N | 115.35 E |
| Zistersdorf | 61 | 48.32 N | 16.45 E |
| Zisterzienserabtei ʋ [1] | 56 | 49.01 N | 8.47 E |
| Zisuntang | 106 | 30.38 N | 118.42 E |
| Zitadelle ⊥ | 264a | 52.33 N | 13.13 E |
| Žiteli | 24 | 65.04 N | 47.26 E |
| Žitenice | 54 | 50.35 N | 14.08 E |
| Žitjevo | 76 | 59.54 N | 41.06 E |
| Žitkovo | 76 | 60.42 N | 29.20 E |
| Žitkur | 80 | 48.57 N | 46.17 E |
| Zitlala | 234 | 17.38 N | 99.05 W |
| Zitlaltepec | 234 | 19.12 N | 97.54 W |
| Žitnoje | 80 | 45.49 N | 47.41 E |
| Zitong | 102 | 31.43 N | 105.10 E |
| Zittau | 54 | 50.54 N | 14.47 E |
| Zitundo | 156 | 26.45 S | 32.50 E |
| Ziwa Magharibi □ [4] | 154 | 2.00 S | 31.30 E |
| Ziway, Lake ⊜ | 144 | 8.00 N | 38.50 E |
| Ziwuji | 100 | 32.55 N | 115.58 E |
| Zixi, Zhg. | 100 | 27.42 N | 117.02 E |
| Zixi, Zhg. | 100 | 28.01 N | 117.46 E |
| Zixing | 100 | 25.58 N | 113.24 E |
| Ziya ≐ | 105 | 39.09 N | 117.10 E |
| Ziyamet | 130 | 35.28 N | 34.08 E |
| Ziyang | 107 | 30.07 N | 104.39 E |
| Ziyuan | 102 | 26.01 N | 110.31 E |
| Ziyun | 102 | 25.43 N | 106.05 E |
| Ziz, Oued V | 148 | 30.39 N | 4.26 W |
| Žizdra | 76 | 53.45 N | 34.44 E |
| Žizdra ≐ | 82 | 54.14 N | 36.12 E |
| Zizers | 58 | 46.56 N | 9.34 E |
| Zizhong | 107 | 29.48 N | 104.50 E |
| Zizhou | 102 | 37.37 N | 109.41 E |
| Žižica | 76 | 56.17 N | 31.21 E |
| Žižickoje, ozero ⊜ | 76 | 56.14 N | 31.15 E |
| Zjalëleny Bor | 76 | 54.01 N | 28.28 E |
| Zlarin | 36 | 43.42 N | 15.50 E |
| Zlatá Koruna ʋ [1] | 61 | 48.52 N | 14.22 E |
| Zlatar | 36 | 46.06 N | 16.05 E |
| Zlaté Moravce | 30 | 48.25 N | 18.24 E |
| Zlatograd | 38 | 41.23 N | 25.06 E |
| Zlatoust | 86 | 55.10 N | 59.40 E |
| Zlatoustovsk | 89 | 52.58 N | 133.38 E |
| Zlín | 30 | 49.13 N | 17.41 E |
| Zlīṭan | 146 | 32.28 N | 14.34 E |
| Žlobin | 76 | 52.54 N | 30.03 E |
| Złocieniec | 30 | 53.33 N | 16.01 E |
| Złoczew | 30 | 51.25 N | 18.36 E |
| Zlonice | 54 | 50.15 N | 14.07 E |
| Złotoryja | 30 | 51.08 N | 15.55 E |
| Złotów | 30 | 53.22 N | 17.02 E |
| Žlutice | 54 | 50.03 N | 13.10 E |
| Zlydnev | 80 | 48.46 N | 45.48 E |
| Zlynka, Ross. | 76 | 52.25 N | 31.44 E |
| Zlynka, Ukr. | 78 | 48.28 N | 31.32 E |
| Zmeinogorsk | 86 | 51.10 N | 82.13 E |
| Żmigród | 30 | 51.29 N | 16.55 E |
| Žminj | 36 | 45.09 N | 13.55 E |
| Zmi'ovka | 76 | 52.40 N | 36.23 E |
| Zmiyinyy, ostriv I | 78 | 45.15 N | 30.12 E |
| Zmiyiv | 78 | 49.40 N | 36.19 E |
| Zna → Cna ≐ | 80 | 54.32 N | 42.05 E |
| Znaim → Znojmo | 61 | 48.52 N | 16.02 E |
| Znamenka, Kaz. | 86 | 50.05 N | 79.32 E |
| Znamenka, Ross. | 76 | 54.54 N | 34.34 E |
| Znamenka, Ross. | 80 | 52.24 N | 41.26 E |
| Znamenka, Ross. | 86 | 53.10 N | 79.30 E |
| Znamenka, Ross. | 86 | 53.32 N | 91.54 E |
| Znamenka, Ross. | 88 | 54.42 N | 104.50 E |
| Znamensk | 76 | 54.37 N | 21.13 E |
| Znamenskoje, Ross. | 76 | 53.17 N | 35.41 E |
| Znamenskoje, Ross. | 80 | 53.19 N | 42.57 E |
| Znamenskoje, Ross. | 86 | 57.08 N | 73.55 E |
| Znamenskoje, Ross. | 265b | 55.45 N | 37.09 E |
| Znam'yanka | 78 | 48.43 N | 32.40 E |
| Znam'yanka Druha | 78 | 48.43 N | 32.35 E |
| Żnin | 30 | 52.52 N | 17.43 E |
| Znob-Novhorods'ke | 78 | 52.16 N | 33.38 E |
| Znojmo | 61 | 48.52 N | 16.02 E |
| Zoagli | 62 | 44.20 N | 9.16 E |
| Zoar | 158 | 33.30 S | 21.28 E |
| Zoar Village State Memorial ⊥ | 214 | 40.36 N | 81.27 W |
| Zoarville | 214 | 40.35 N | 81.24 W |
| Zobia | 154 | 2.58 N | 25.56 E |
| Zöblitz | 54 | 50.39 N | 13.14 E |
| Zóbuè | 154 | 15.38 S | 34.26 E |
| Zocca | 64 | 44.21 N | 10.59 E |
| Žochova, ostrov I | 74 | 76.04 N | 152.40 E |
| Zod | 84 | 40.12 N | 45.52 E |
| Žodzina | 76 | 54.06 N | 28.21 E |
| Žodziški | 76 | 54.38 N | 26.26 E |
| Zoétélé | 152 | 3.15 N | 11.53 E |
| Zoetermeer | 52 | 52.03 N | 4.30 E |
| Zofingen | 58 | 47.18 N | 7.57 E |
| Zogang | 102 | 29.55 N | 97.44 E |
| Zogno | 62 | 45.48 N | 9.40 E |
| Zográfos | 267c | 37.59 N | 23.46 E |
| Zohar | 132 | 31.36 N | 34.42 E |
| Zohar, Mizpé ∧ [2] | 132 | 31.13 N | 35.14 E |
| Zohreh ≐ | 128 | 30.04 N | 49.31 E |
| Zola Predosa | 64 | 44.29 N | 11.12 E |
| Zolder | 56 | 51.01 N | 5.18 E |
| Zoldo Alto | 64 | 46.22 N | 12.06 E |
| Zolfo Springs | 220 | 27.29 N | 81.47 W |
| Zolka ≐ | 84 | 44.17 N | 43.51 E |
| Żółkiewka | 30 | 50.55 N | 22.51 E |
| Zollhaus | 56 | 50.17 N | 8.04 E |
| Zollikofen | 58 | 47.00 N | 7.28 E |
| Zollikon | 58 | 47.20 N | 8.35 E |
| Zolling | 60 | 48.27 N | 11.46 E |
| Zol'noje | 80 | 53.27 N | 49.48 E |
| Zolochiv, Ukr. | 78 | 50.17 N | 35.59 E |
| Zolochiv, Ukr. | 78 | 49.47 N | 24.52 E |
| Zolotaja Gora | 89 | 54.16 N | 126.36 E |
| Zolota Lypa ≐ | 78 | 48.59 N | 25.04 E |
| Zolotari | 80 | 49.46 N | 46.21 E |
| Zolotar'ovka | 80 | 53.04 N | 45.20 E |
| Zolote | 83 | 48.41 N | 38.31 E |
| Zolotkovo | 80 | 55.32 N | 41.06 E |
| Zolotnyky | 78 | 49.17 N | 25.23 E |
| Zolotoje | 80 | 50.51 N | 45.53 E |
| Zolotonosha | 78 | 49.40 N | 32.02 E |
| Zolotucha | 80 | 47.49 N | 46.44 E |
| Zolotuchino | 78 | 52.05 N | 36.23 E |
| Zolotyy Potik | 78 | 48.54 N | 25.20 E |
| Žolymbet | 86 | 51.45 N | 71.44 E |
| Zomba | 154 | 15.23 [illegible] | 35.18 E |
| Zomergem | 50 | 51.07 [illegible] | 3.33 E |
| Zone Point ≻ | 42 | 50.08 [illegible] | 5.00 W |
| Zongchang | 107 | 28.52 [illegible] | 104.36 E |
| Zongjiaxiang | 269b | 31.12 [illegible] | 121.22 E |
| Zongo | 152 | 4.21 [illegible] | 18.36 E |
| Zonguldak | 130 | 41.27 [illegible] | 31.49 E |
| Zonguldak □ [4] | 130 | 41.30 [illegible] | 32.15 E |
| Zongwe | 154 | 5.05 [illegible] | 27.55 E |
| Zongyang | 100 | 30.42 [illegible] | 117.12 E |
| Zonhoven | 56 | 50.59 [illegible] | 5.21 E |
| Zonnebeke | 50 | 50.52 [illegible] | 2.59 E |
| Zons | 56 | 51.07 [illegible] | 6.50 E |
| Zonza | 36 | 41.45 [illegible] | 9.10 E |
| Zoo, Bahnhof ● [5] | 264a | 52.30 [illegible] | 13.20 E |
| Zooafskolk | 158 | 29.56 [illegible] | 20.24 E |
| Zoom ≐ | 52 | 51.30 [illegible] | 4.14 E |
| Zoppot → Sopot | 30 | 54.28 [illegible] | 18.34 E |
| Zopui | 120 | 23.39 [illegible] | 92.14 E |
| Zörbig | 54 | 51.37 [illegible] | 12.07 E |
| Zorge | 54 | 51.38 [illegible] | 10.38 E |
| Zorge ≐ | 54 | 51.27 [illegible] | 10.54 E |
| Zorgo | 150 | 12.15 [illegible] | 0.36 W |
| Zorgongo | 150 | 12.16 [illegible] | 0.48 W |
| Zorita | 34 | 39.17 [illegible] | 5.42 W |
| Zorkul', ozero ⊜ | 120 | 37.27 [illegible] | 73.40 E |
| Zorn ≐ | 56 | 48.45 N | 7.55 E |
| Zorneding | 60 | 48.05 N | 11.49 E |
| Zornica | 38 | 42.2[illegible] N | 26.56 E |
| Zorra, Arroyo de la ≐ | 196 | 29.31 N | 101.13 W |
| Zorritos | 246 | 3.4[illegible] S | 80.40 W |
| Zorykivka | 83 | 49.24 N | 39.51 E |
| Zoryns'k | 83 | 48.25 N | 38.34 E |
| Zorzor | 150 | 7.46 N | 9.28 W |
| Zöschen | 54 | 51.2[illegible] N | 12.07 E |
| Zossen | 54 | 52.1[illegible] N | 13.27 E |
| Zoti | 84 | 41.5[illegible] N | 42.28 E |
| Zottegem | 50 | 50.5[illegible] N | 3.48 E |
| Zou □ [5] | 150 | 8.0[illegible] N | 2.15 E |
| Zou ≐ | 150 | 6.2[illegible] N | 2.25 E |
| Zouan-Hounien | 150 | 6.5[illegible] N | 8.13 W |
| Zouar | 146 | 20.2[illegible] N | 16.32 E |
| Zouérat | 148 | 22.4[illegible] N | 12.30 W |
| Zoug → Zug | 58 | 47.1[illegible] N | 8.31 E |
| Zoulabot | 152 | 3.1[illegible] N | 14.02 E |
| Zoumagang | 107 | 29.2[illegible] N | 106.18 E |
| Zoumayi | 98 | 39.0[illegible] N | 114.34 E |
| Zouping | 98 | 36.5[illegible] N | 117.42 E |
| Zourma | 150 | 11.2[illegible] N | 0.49 W |
| Zousfana, Oued V | 148 | 30.2[illegible] N | 2.17 W |
| Zoutelande | 52 | 51.3[illegible] N | 3.30 E |
| Zoutkamp | 52 | 53.2[illegible] N | 6.18 E |
| Zouxian | 98 | 35.2[illegible] N | 117.00 E |
| Zova | 132 | 31.4[illegible] N | 35.06 E |
| Zovka | 76 | 58.2[illegible] N | 28.52 E |
| Zoziv | 78 | 49.1[illegible] N | 29.01 E |
| Zrenjanin | 38 | 45.2[illegible] N | 20.24 E |
| Zriba | 36 | 36.2[illegible] N | 10.16 E |
| Zrmanja ≐ | 36 | 44.[illegible]5 N | 15.32 E |
| Zruč nad Sázavou | 30 | 49.[illegible]5 N | 15.07 E |
| Zscherndorf | 54 | 51.[illegible]3 N | 12.15 E |
| Zschopau | 54 | 50.[illegible]4 N | 13.04 E |
| Zschopau ≐ | 54 | 51.[illegible]3 N | 13.03 E |
| Zschorlau | 54 | 50.[illegible]4 N | 12.38 E |
| Zschornewitz | 54 | 51.[illegible]3 N | 12.25 E |
| Zschortau | 54 | 51.[illegible]8 N | 12.21 E |
| Žuanbalyk | 86 | 45.[illegible]4 N | 61.51 E |
| Žuantobe | 86 | 44.[illegible]5 N | 68.54 E |
| Zuarungu | 150 | 10.[illegible]7 N | 0.48 W |
| Zuata ≐ | 246 | 7.[illegible]2 N | 65.22 W |
| Zubaydīyah, Jabal az- ∧ | 132 | 33.[illegible]8 N | 37.02 E |
| Zubayr, Jazā'ir az- II | 144 | 15.[illegible]5 N | 42.08 E |
| Zubayr, Wādī V | 142 | 27.[illegible]7 N | 32.41 E |
| Zubcov | 76 | 56.[illegible]0 N | 34.34 E |
| Zubkovychi | 78 | 51.[illegible]2 N | 27.41 E |
| Zubova Pol'ana | 80 | 54.[illegible]4 N | 42.51 E |
| Zubovka | 80 | 54.[illegible]6 N | 51.06 E |
| Zubovo, Ross. | 76 | 54.[illegible]3 N | 35.29 E |
| Zubovo, Ross. | 76 | 60.[illegible]9 N | 36.57 E |
| Zubovo, Ross. | 80 | 56.[illegible]2 N | 44.08 E |
| Zuccarello | 62 | 44.[illegible]7 N | 8.07 E |
| Zuccone, Monte ∧ | 62 | 44.[illegible]6 N | 9.37 E |
| Zuchwil | 58 | 47.[illegible]2 N | 7.33 E |
| Zuckerhütl ∧ | 64 | 46.[illegible]8 N | 11.09 E |
| Zudar | 54 | 54.[illegible]5 N | 13.20 E |
| Z'udev, ostrov I | 80 | 45.[illegible]5 N | 47.58 E |
| Zuel | 64 | 4[illegible].31 N | 12.08 E |
| Zuénoula | 150 | 7.26 N | 6.03 W |
| Zuera | 34 | 41.52 N | 0.47 W |
| Zufār ● [1] | 118 | 17.00 N | 54.10 E |
| Zufaytat Mashtūl | 142 | 30.20 N | 31.21 E |
| Zug | 58 | 47.10 N | 8.31 E |
| Zug □ [3] | 58 | 47.00 N | 8.30 E |
| Zugdeli | 88 | 5[illegible].03 N | 111.10 E |
| Zugdidi | 84 | 4[illegible].30 N | 41.53 E |
| Zugersee ⊜ | 58 | 4[illegible].08 N | 8.30 E |
| Zug Island I | 281 | 4[illegible].17 N | 83.07 W |
| Zugló ● [8] | 264c | 4[illegible].31 N | 19.08 E |
| Zugspitze ∧ | 64 | 4[illegible].25 N | 10.59 E |
| Zugurma Game Reserve ● [4] | 150 | [illegible].55 N | 5.00 E |
| Zühlsdorf | 264a | 5[illegible].44 N | 13.24 E |
| Zuhres | 83 | 4[illegible].01 N | 38.15 E |
| Zui | 76 | 5[illegible].06 N | 31.37 E |
| Zuid-Beijerland | 52 | 5[illegible].45 N | 4.22 E |
| Zuid-Beveland | 52 | 5[illegible].25 N | 3.45 E |
| Zuidbroek | 52 | 5[illegible].10 N | 6.52 E |
| Zuidelijk Flevoland ● [1] | 52 | 5[illegible].22 N | 5.20 E |
| Zuiderzee → IJsselmeer ⊤ [2] | 52 | 5[illegible].45 N | 5.25 E |
| Zuid-Holland □ [4] | 52 | 5[illegible].00 N | 4.30 E |
| Zuidhorn | 52 | 5[illegible].14 N | 6.24 E |
| Zuidlaren | 52 | 5[illegible].05 N | 6.41 E |
| Zuid-Willemsvaart ⊤ | 52 | 5[illegible].12 N | 5.52 E |
| Zuidwolde | 52 | 5[illegible].15 N | 6.25 E |
| Žuja ≐ | 88 | 5[illegible].45 N | 118.11 E |
| Zújar ≐ | 34 | [illegible].01 N | 5.47 W |
| Zújar, Embalse del ⊜ [1] | 34 | [illegible].50 N | 5.20 W |
| Zujevka | 80 | [illegible].25 N | 51.10 E |
| Z'ukajka | 80 | [illegible].12 N | 54.43 E |
| Žukopa | 76 | [illegible].33 N | 32.42 E |
| Žukopa ≐ | 76 | [illegible].54 N | 32.46 E |
| Žukovka, Ross. | 76 | [illegible].32 N | 33.46 E |
| Žukovka, Ross. | 86 | [illegible].05 N | 91.42 E |
| Žukovka, Ross. | 265b | [illegible].44 N | 37.15 E |


| | English | Deutsch | Español | Français | Português |
|---|---|---|---|---|---|
| ≐ | River | Fluß | Río | Rivière | Rio |
| | Canal | Kanal | Canal | Canal | Canal |
| L | Waterfall, Rapids | Wasserfall, Stromschnellen | Cascada, Rápidos | Chute d'eau, Rapides | Cascata, Rápidos |
| )( | Strait | Meeresstraße | Estrecho | Détroit | Estreito |
| c | Bay, Gulf | Bucht, Golf | Bahía, Golfo | Baie, Golfe | Baía, Golfo |
| ⊜ | Lake, Lakes | See, Seen | Lago, Lagos | Lac, Lacs | Lago, Lagos |
| | Swamp | Sumpf | Pantano | Marais | Pântano |
| | Ice Features, Glacier | Eis- und Gletscherformen | Accidentes Glaciales | Formes glaciaires | Acidentes glaciares |
| ⊤ | Other Hydrographic Features | Andere Hydrographische Objekte | Otros Elementos Hidrográficos | Autres données hydrographiques | Outros acidentes hidrográficos |
| ✢ | Submarine Features | Untermeerische Objekte | Accidentes Submarinos | Formes de relief sous-marin | Acidentes submarinos |
| □ | Political Unit | Politische Einheit | Unidad Política | Entité politique | Unidade política |
| ʋ | Cultural Institution | Kulturelle Institution | Institución Cultural | Institution culturelle | Instituição cultural |
| ⊥ | Historical Site | Historische Stätte | Sitio Histórico | Site historique | Sitio histórico |
| ♦ | Recreational Site | Erholungs- und Ferienort | Sitio de Recreo | Centre de loisirs | Area de Lazer |
| ⊠ | Airport | Flughafen | Aeropuerto | Aéroport | Aeroporto |
| ■ | Military Installation | Militäranlage | Instalación Militar | Installation militaire | Instalação militar |
| ● | Miscellaneous | Verschiedenes | Misceláneo | Divers | Diversos |

ENGLISH

| Name | Page | Lat.°′ | Long.°′ |
|---|---|---|---|
| Žukovskaja | **80** | 47.37 N | 42.28 E |
| Žukovskij | **82** | 55.35 N | 38.08 E |
| Žukovskoje | **80** | 46.05 N | 41.21 E |
| Żukowo | **30** | 54.21 N | 18.22 E |
| Zula | **144** | 15.11 N | 39.41 E |
| Zula ≃ | **234** | 20.21 N | 102.46 W |
| Žulanka | **86** | 54.22 N | 80.36 E |
| Zulayl, Wādī az- V | **132** | 32.09 N | 36.03 E |
| Žuldyz | **80** | 49.16 N | 49.30 E |
| Žulebino | **265b** | 55.42 N | 37.51 E |
| Zuli ≃ | **102** | 36.35 N | 104.35 E |
| Zulia □ 3 | **246** | 10.00 N | 72.10 W |
| Zulia ∧ | **154** | 4.07 N | 33.58 E |
| Zulia ≃ | **246** | 9.04 N | 72.18 W |
| Zülpich | **56** | 50.41 N | 6.39 E |
| Zulueta | **240p** | 22.22 N | 79.34 W |
| Zululand □ 9 | **158** | 28.10 S | 32.00 E |
| Z'ul'z'a | **88** | 52.33 N | 116.13 E |
| Žumaly | **80** | 50.29 N | 49.47 E |
| Zumar, Tur'at az- ≍ | **273c** | 29.58 N | 31.15 E |
| Zumarraga | **116** | 11.38 N | 124.50 E |
| Zumba | **246** | 4.52 S | 79.09 W |
| Zumbo | **154** | 15.36 S | 30.25 E |
| Zumbro ≃ | **190** | 44.18 N | 91.56 W |
| Zumbro, North Fork ≃ | **190** | 44.15 N | 92.29 W |
| Zumbro, South Fork ≃ | **190** | 44.15 N | 92.29 W |
| Zumbrota | **190** | 44.17 N | 92.40 W |
| Zumpango del Río | **234** | 17.39 N | 99.30 W |
| Zumpango de Ocampo | **234** | 19.48 N | 99.06 W |
| Zundert | **52** | 51.28 N | 4.40 E |
| Zundi | **152** | 10.28 S | 16.48 E |
| Zune | **156** | 18.59 S | 35.18 E |
| Zungeru | **150** | 9.48 N | 6.09 E |
| Zungri | **68** | 38.39 N | 15.59 E |
| Zungur | **150** | 9.58 N | 9.47 E |
| Zungwini | **158** | 27.34 S | 30.53 E |
| Zunhua | **105** | 40.12 N | 117.58 E |
| Zuni, N.M., U.S. | **200** | 35.04 N | 108.51 W |
| Zuni, Va., U.S. | **208** | 36.51 N | 76.49 W |
| Zuni ≃ | **200** | 34.39 N | 109.40 W |
| Zuni Indian Reservation ◆ 4 | **200** | 35.15 N | 108.20 W |
| Zunsuzhi | **102** | 44.40 N | 112.50 E |
| Zunyi | **102** | 27.39 N | 106.57 E |
| Zuo ≃ | **102** | 22.50 N | 108.06 E |
| Zuo'an | **100** | 26.10 N | 114.16 E |
| Zuodeng | **102** | 23.27 N | 106.57 E |
| Zuogezhuang | **105** | 39.01 N | 116.37 E |
| Zuomaozigou | **104** | 42.12 N | 120.41 E |
| Zuomuchedong Hu ⊜ | **120** | 28.25 N | 88.15 E |
| Zuoquan | **102** | 37.03 N | 113.30 E |
| Zuosuo | **102** | 27.45 N | 100.54 E |
| Zuotema | **120** | 35.50 N | 80.45 E |
| Zuowei | **105** | 40.41 N | 114.43 E |
| Zuoxiunulemiao | **88** | 48.08 N | 115.38 E |
| Zuoyun | **102** | 40.02 N | 112.54 E |
| Zuoz | **58** | 46.36 N | 9.58 E |
| Županja | **38** | 45.04 N | 18.42 E |
| Zūq Muṣbīḥ | **132** | 33.58 N | 35.37 E |
| Zura | **80** | 57.37 N | 53.26 E |
| Zūrābād | **128** | 38.49 N | 44.35 E |
| Žuravičy | **76** | 53.15 N | 30.33 E |
| Žuravl'ovka | **86** | 51.57 N | 69.56 E |
| Zurayghiṭ | **128** | 26.29 N | 40.33 E |
| Žurban | **89** | 54.12 N | 127.56 E |
| Zurich, On., Can. | **190** | 43.26 N | 81.37 W |
| Zurich, Ned. | **52** | 53.06 N | 5.23 E |
| Zürich, Schw. | **58** | 47.23 N | 8.32 E |
| Zürich □ 3 | **58** | 47.25 N | 8.40 E |
| Zürich, Flughafen ⊠ | **58** | 47.27 N | 8.33 E |
| Zurich, Lake ⊜ | **278** | 42.12 N | 88.06 W |
| Zürichsee ⊜ | **58** | 47.13 N | 8.45 E |
| Zurigo → Zürich | **58** | 47.23 N | 8.32 E |
| Zurmi | **150** | 12.46 N | 6.48 E |
| Żuromin | **30** | 53.04 N | 19.55 E |
| Zurq, Al-Qārāt az- ∧ 2 | **142** | 29.00 N | 29.55 E |
| Zürs | **58** | 47.10 N | 10.10 E |
| Zuru | **150** | 11.27 N | 5.12 E |
| Žuryn | **86** | 49.15 N | 57.37 E |
| Zurzach | **58** | 47.35 N | 8.18 E |
| Zuša ≃ | **76** | 53.27 N | 36.23 E |
| Zusam ≃ | **56** | 48.42 N | 10.45 E |
| Žusandala ◆ 2 | **86** | 44.20 N | 75.00 E |
| Zushi | **94** | 35.18 N | 139.35 E |
| Zusmarshausen | **58** | 48.24 N | 10.35 E |
| Züssow | **54** | 53.59 N | 13.32 E |
| Žut, Otok I | **36** | 43.52 N | 15.19 E |
| Zutiua ≃ | **250** | 3.43 S | 45.29 W |
| Žutovo Vtoroje | **80** | 47.49 N | 43.51 E |
| Zutphen | **52** | 52.08 N | 6.12 E |
| Zützen | **54** | 51.57 N | 13.38 E |
| Zuwārah | **146** | 32.56 N | 12.06 E |
| Zuwayzā | **132** | 31.42 N | 35.55 E |
| Zuya | **78** | 45.03 N | 34.20 E |
| Z'uzel'skij | **86** | 56.29 N | 60.07 E |
| Žužemberk | **36** | 45.50 N | 14.56 E |
| Z'uzino | **265b** | 55.40 N | 38.07 E |
| Z'uzino ◆ 8 | **265b** | 55.39 N | 37.35 E |
| Žuzymdyk | **85** | 43.05 N | 69.08 E |
| Zv'agino | **265b** | 55.59 N | 37.48 E |
| Zvannoje | **78** | 51.23 N | 34.33 E |
| Zvenigorod | **82** | 55.44 N | 36.51 E |
| Zvenigovo | **80** | 55.58 N | 48.02 E |
| Zvenyhorodka | **78** | 49.04 N | 30.57 E |
| Zverevo | **83** | 48.01 N | 40.07 E |
| Zverinogolovskoje | **86** | 54.28 N | 64.50 E |
| Zvezdec | **38** | 42.07 N | 27.25 E |
| Zvezdnyj | **88** | 56.49 N | 106.27 E |
| Zvíkovec | **60** | 49.56 N | 13.42 E |
| Zvishavane | **154** | 20.20 S | 30.02 E |
| Zvolen | **30** | 48.35 N | 19.08 E |
| Zvornik | **38** | 44.23 N | 19.06 E |
| Zwaag | **52** | 52.40 N | 5.05 E |
| Zwaagwesteinde | **52** | 53.15 N | 6.04 E |
| Zwadība | **152** | 3.04 N | 14.02 E |
| Zwanenburg | **52** | 52.23 N | 4.45 E |
| Zwartemeer | **52** | 52.43 N | 7.03 E |
| Zwarte Meer ⊜ | **52** | 52.37 N | 5.57 E |
| Zwartsluis | **52** | 52.37 N | 6.04 E |
| Zweckel ◆ 8 | **263** | 51.36 N | 6.59 E |
| Zwedru | **150** | 6.04 N | 8.08 W |
| Zweibrücken | **56** | 49.15 N | 7.21 E |
| Zweifall | **56** | 50.43 N | 6.15 E |
| Zweisimmen | **58** | 46.33 N | 7.22 E |
| Zweite Wiener Hochquellenleitung ≍ 1 | **61** | 48.10 N | 16.14 E |
| Zwenkau | **54** | 51.13 N | 12.19 E |
| Zwentendorf | **61** | 48.21 N | 15.55 E |
| Zwettl | **61** | 48.37 N | 15.10 E |
| Zwevegem | **50** | 50.48 N | 3.20 E |
| Zwevezele | **50** | 51.02 N | 3.12 E |
| Zwickau | **54** | 50.44 N | 12.29 E |
| Zwickauer Mulde ≃ | **54** | 51.10 N | 12.48 E |
| Zwiefalten | **58** | 48.14 N | 9.28 E |
| Zwiefaltendorf | **58** | 48.13 N | 9.31 E |
| Zwierzyniec | **30** | 50.37 N | 22.58 E |
| Zwiesel | **60** | 49.01 N | 13.14 E |

DEUTSCH

| Name | Seite | Breite°′ | Länge°′ E = Ost |
|---|---|---|---|
| Zwieselstein | **64** | 46.56 N | 11.02 E |
| Zwijndrecht | **52** | 51.49 N | 4.39 E |
| Zwillbrock | **52** | 52.04 N | 6.42 E |
| Zwingenberg, Dtsch. | **56** | 49.25 N | 9.02 E |
| Zwingenberg, Dtsch. | **56** | 49.43 N | 8.37 E |
| Zwischenahner Meer ⊜ | **52** | 53.12 N | 8.01 E |
| Zwochau | **54** | 51.28 N | 12.16 E |
| Zwoleń | **30** | 51.22 N | 21.35 E |
| Zwölfaxing | **264b** | 48.06 N | 16.28 E |
| Zwolle, Ned. | **52** | 52.30 N | 6.05 E |
| Zwolle, La., U.S. | **194** | 31.37 N | 93.38 W |
| Zwönitz | **54** | 50.38 N | 12.49 E |
| Zwota | **54** | 50.21 N | 12.25 E |
| Żychlin | **30** | 52.15 N | 19.39 E |
| Zymoetz ≃ | **182** | 54.33 N | 128.26 W |
| Zymohir'ya | **83** | 48.35 N | 38.56 E |
| Zyr'anka | **74** | 65.45 N | 150.51 E |
| Zyr'anovsk | **86** | 49.43 N | 84.20 E |
| Zyr'anovskij | **86** | 57.46 N | 61.42 E |
| Zyr'anskoje | **86** | 56.50 N | 86.38 E |
| Żyrardów | **30** | 52.04 N | 20.25 E |
| Zyryanovsk → Zyr'anovsk | **86** | 49.43 N | 84.20 E |
| Żyrzyn | **30** | 51.30 N | 22.07 E |
| Žytkavičy | **76** | 52.14 N | 27.54 E |
| Żywiec | **30** | 49.41 N | 19.12 E |
| Žyžma ≃ | **76** | 53.54 N | 25.36 E |


**Symbols** in the index entries represent the broad categories identified in the key at the right. Symbols with superior numbers (ʌ 1) identify subcategories (see complete key on page *I · 1)*.

**Symbole** im Register stellen die rechts im Schlüssel erklärten Kategorien dar. Symbole mit hochgestellten Ziffern (ʌ 1) bezeichnen Unterabteilungen einer Kategorie (vgl. vollständiger Schlüssel auf Seite *I · 1)*.

**Los símbolos** incluídos en el texto del índice representan las grandes categorías identificadas con la clave a la derecha. Los símbolos con numeros en su parte superior (ʌ 1) identifican las subcategorías (véase la clave completa en la página *I · 1)*.

**Les symboles** de l'index représentent les catégories indiquées dans la légende à droite. Les symboles suivis d'un indice (ʌ 1) représentent des sous-catégories (voir légende complète à la page *I · 1)*.

**Os símbolos** incluídos no texto do índice representam as grandes categorias identificadas com a chave à direita. Os símbolos com números em sua parte superior (ʌ 1) identificam as subcategorias (veja-se a chave completa à página *I · 1)*.

| | | | | |
|---|---|---|---|---|
| ∧ Mountain | Berg | Montaña | Montagne | Montanha |
| ʌ Mountains | Gebirge | Montañas | Montagnes | Montanhas |
| )( Pass | Paß | Paso | Col | Passo |
| V Valley, Canyon | Tal, Cañon | Valle, Cañón | Vallée, Canyon | Vale, Canhão |
| ≚ Plain | Ebene | Llano | Plaine | Planície |
| › Cape | Kap | Cabo | Cap | Cabo |
| I Island | Insel | Isla | Île | Ilha |
| II Islands | Inseln | Islas | Îles | Ilhas |
| ± Other Topographic Features | Andere Topographische Objekte | Otros Elementos Topográficos | Autres données topographiques | Outros acidentes topográficos |

# Key map of regional atlas coverage

**For a complete depiction of *all* scales and map series, see the REGIONAL INDEX MAPS, pp. *xiii-xv*.**

Each rectangle shows the exact geographic coverage of a one- or two-page regional map of the Atlas; its number is the page at which the map can be found.

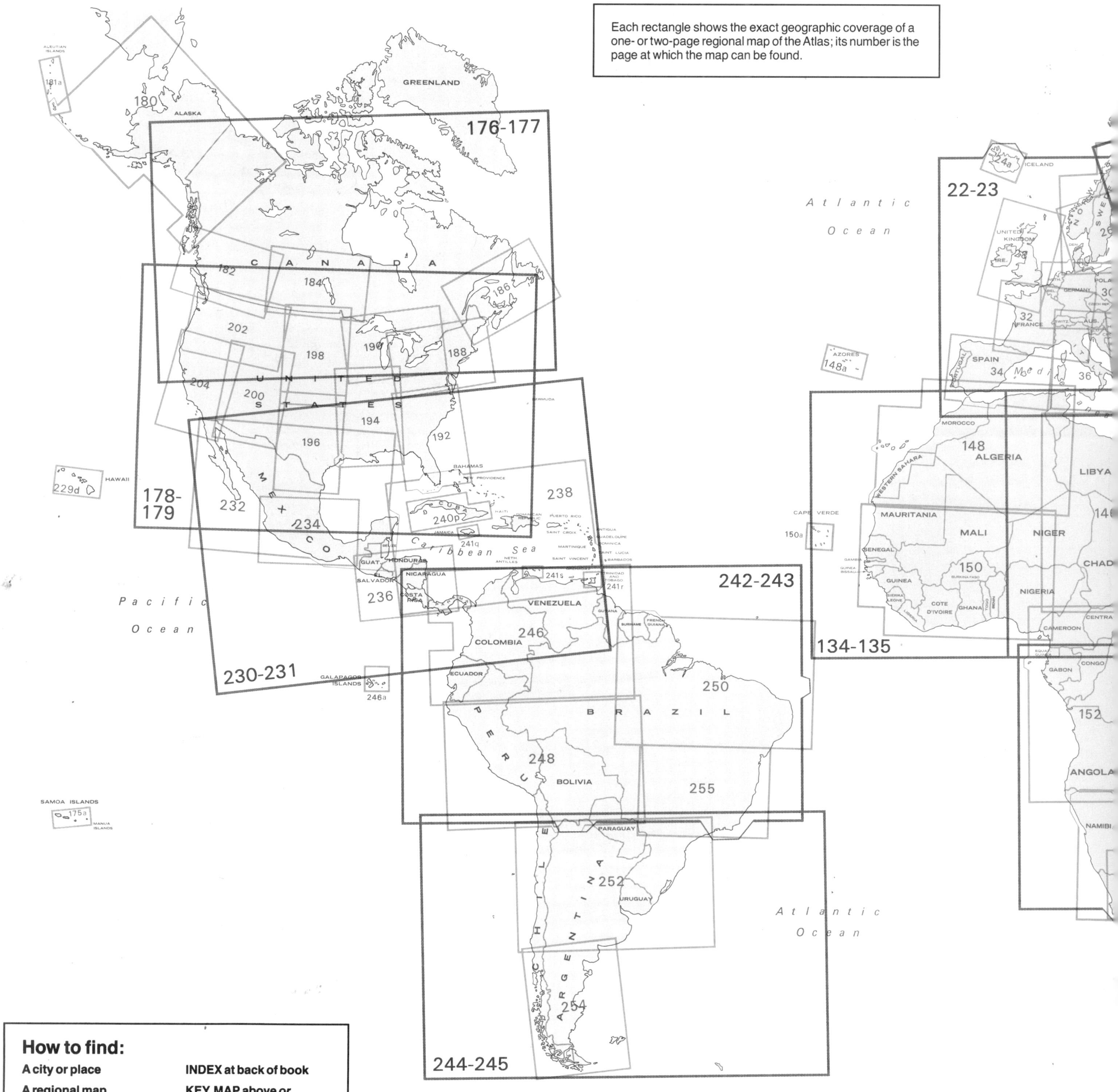

GREENLAND
ALASKA
ALEUTIAN ISLANDS
181a
180
176-177
178-179
C A N A D A
U N I T E D S T A T E S
182
184
186
188
190
192
194
196
198
200
202
204
HAWAII
229d
BERMUDA
BAHAMAS
238
240p
241q
241r
241s
M E X I C O
232
234
236
230-231
Caribbean Sea
GUAT.
HONDURAS
EL SALVADOR
NICARAGUA
COSTA RICA
Pacific Ocean
GALAPAGOS ISLANDS
246a
VENEZUELA
COLOMBIA
ECUADOR
246
242-243
250
B R A Z I L
P E R U
248
BOLIVIA
255
PARAGUAY
252
URUGUAY
C H I L E
A R G E N T I N A
254
244-245
SAMOA ISLANDS
175a
MANUA ISLANDS
Atlantic Ocean
AZORES
148a
CAPE VERDE
150a
ICELAND
24a
22-23
UNITED KINGDOM
IRE.
GERMANY
32
FRANCE
SPAIN
34
36
MOROCCO
148
ALGERIA
LIBYA
WESTERN SAHARA
MAURITANIA
MALI
NIGER
CHAD
150
SENEGAL
GAMBIA
GUINEA
GUINEA BISSAU
SIERRA LEONE
LIBERIA
COTE D'IVOIRE
GHANA
NIGERIA
CAMEROON
GABON
CONGO
134-135
152
ANGOLA
NAMIBI


## How to find:

| | |
|---|---|
| **A city or place** | **INDEX at back of book** |
| **A regional map** | **KEY MAP above *or* alphabetical LIST OF MAPS, pp. *vi-ix*** |
| **A country or state** | **KEY MAP above.** |
| **A physical feature (lake, mountain, river)** | **SELECTED MAP REFERENCES, p. *xvi*** |
| **Meaning of map symbols, typographic conventions, etc.** | **LEGEND TO MAPS, pp. *x-xii*** |
| **Population of a country, state, etc.** | **WORLD INFORMATION TABLE, pp. 296-299** |
| **Population of a city** | **POPULATION OF CITIES AND TOWNS, pp. 301-316** |
| **World patterns of economic and human geography** | **WORLD SCENE, pp. *xvii-xl* (*See* summary at right)** |

## Reference maps

**Regional maps of the world**


| | Pages |
|---|---|
| Africa | 134-159 |
| Asia: | |
| East (China, Japan) | 90-107 |
| South and Southwest (India, Middle East) | 118-133 |
| Southeast (Indochina, Indonesia) | 108-117 |
| Australia, New Zealand, and the Pacific Islands | 160-175 |
| Europe* | 22-71 |
| North America: | |
| U.S. and Canada | 176-229 |
| Middle America and Caribbean | 230-241 |
| South America | 242-258 |
| Commonwealth of Independent States and Baltic republics | 72-89 |


**Exact geographic coverage of each regional map**
*See* the KEY MAP above or the REGIONAL INDEX MAPS, pp. *xiii-xv*.

**Quick reference to the major places in the atlas**
*See* the alphabetical LIST OF PLACES opposite the Title Page.

**Symbols on the maps and what they mean**
*See* LEGEND TO MAPS, pp. *x-xii*.